THE EUROPA WORLD YEAR BOOK 2012

VOLUME 1

PART ONE: INTERNATIONAL ORGANIZATIONS
PART TWO: AFGHANISTAN–JORDAN

LONDON AND NEW YORK

53rd edition published 2012
by Routledge
2 Park Square, Milton Park, Abingdon, Oxon, OX14 4RN

Simultaneously published in the USA and Canada by Routledge
711 Third Avenue, New York, NY10017

Routledge is an imprint of the Taylor & Francis Group, an Informa business

First published 1926

ISBN: 978-1-85743-611-2 (The Set)
978-1-85743-612-9 (Vol. 1)
ISSN: 0956-2273

Senior Editor: Juliet Love

Senior Editor, Statistics: Philip McIntyre

Senior Editor, Directory: Iain Frame

Regional Editors: Imogen Gladman, Cathy Hartley, Dominic Heaney, Neil Higgins, Christopher Matthews, Jacqueline West

International Organizations Editor: Helen Canton

Contributing Editors: Catriona Holman, Katherine Murison, Jillian O'Brien

Statistics Researchers: Abhinav Srivastava *(Team Manager)*, Varun Wadhawan *(Lead Researcher)*, Mohd Khalid Ansari, Charu Arora *(Senior Researchers)*, Sasha Sadh, Nirbachita Sarkar, Akshay Sharma

Directory Editorial Researchers: Arijit Khasnobis *(Team Manager)*, Rima Kar, Surmeet Kaur, Birendra Pratap Nayak, Thoithoi Pukhrambam, C. Sandhya *(Senior Editorial Researchers)*, Shubha Banerjee, Saurav Goswami, Sakshi Mathur, Tessy Margaret Rajappan, K. Nungshithoibi Singha

Contributors: Christopher Bell, Katie Dawson, Lucy Dean, Kirstie Hughes, Catriona Marcham, Elizabeth Salzman, Anna Thomas, Edward Tyerman, Gareth Vaughan, Kristina Wischenkämper

Editorial Director: Paul Kelly

Typeset in New Century Schoolbook
by Data Standards Limited, Frome, Somerset

FOREWORD

THE EUROPA WORLD YEAR BOOK was first published in 1926. Since 1960 it has appeared in annual two-volume editions, and has become established as an authoritative reference work, providing a wealth of detailed information on the political, economic and commercial institutions of the world.

Volume 1 contains a comprehensive listing of more than 2,000 international organizations, commissions and specialized bodies, and the first part of the alphabetical survey of countries of the world, from Afghanistan to Jordan. Volume 2 contains countries from Kazakhstan to Zimbabwe. An Index of Territories covered in both volumes is to be found at the end of Volume 2.

The International Organizations section gives extensive coverage to the United Nations and its related agencies and bodies. There are also detailed articles concerning other major international and regional organizations; entries for many affiliated organizations appear within these articles. In addition, the section includes briefer details of some 1,300 other international organizations. A comprehensive Index of International Organizations is included at the end of Volume 1.

Each country is covered by an individual chapter, containing: an introductory survey including contemporary political history, economic affairs, constitution and government, regional and international co-operation, and public holidays; a statistical survey presenting the latest available figures on demographics, labour force, health and welfare, agriculture, forestry, fishing, mining, industry, currency and exchange rates, government finance, international reserves and the monetary sector, cost of living, national accounts, balance of payments, external trade, railways, roads, shipping, civil aviation, tourism, media and telecommunications, and education; and a directory section listing names, addresses and other useful facts about organizations in the fields of government, election commissions, political parties, diplomatic representation, judiciary, religions, the media, telecommunications, banking, insurance, trade and industry, development organizations, chambers of commerce, industrial and trade associations, utilities, trade unions, transport, tourism, defence, and education.

The entire content of the print edition of THE EUROPA WORLD YEAR BOOK is available online at www.europaworld.com. This prestigious resource incorporates sophisticated search and browse functions as well as specially commissioned visual and statistical content. An ongoing programme of updates of key areas of information ensures currency of content, and enhances the richness of the coverage for which THE EUROPA WORLD YEAR BOOK is renowned.

Readers are referred to the nine titles in the Europa Regional Surveys of the World series: AFRICA SOUTH OF THE SAHARA, CENTRAL AND SOUTH-EASTERN EUROPE, EASTERN EUROPE, RUSSIA AND CENTRAL ASIA, THE FAR EAST AND AUSTRALASIA, THE MIDDLE EAST AND NORTH AFRICA, SOUTH AMERICA, CENTRAL AMERICA AND THE CARIBBEAN, SOUTH ASIA, THE USA AND CANADA, and WESTERN EUROPE, available both in print and online, offer comprehensive analysis at regional, sub-regional and country level. More detailed coverage of international organizations is to be found in THE EUROPA DIRECTORY OF INTERNATIONAL ORGANIZATIONS.

The content of THE EUROPA WORLD YEAR BOOK is extensively revised and updated by a variety of methods, including direct mailing to all the institutions listed. Many other sources are used, such as national statistical offices, government departments and diplomatic missions. The editors thank the innumerable individuals and organizations world-wide whose generous co-operation in providing current information for this edition is invaluable in presenting the most accurate and up-to-date material available.

May 2012

ACKNOWLEDGEMENTS

The editors gratefully acknowledge particular indebtedness for permission to reproduce material from the following sources: the United Nations' statistical databases and *Demographic Yearbook*, *Statistical Yearbook*, *Monthly Bulletin of Statistics*, *Industrial Commodity Statistics Yearbook* and *International Trade Statistics Yearbook*; the United Nations Educational, Scientific and Cultural Organization's *Statistical Yearbook* and Institute for Statistics database; the *Human Development Report* of the United Nations Development Programme; the Food and Agriculture Organization of the United Nations' statistical database; the statistical databases of the World Health Organization; the statistical databases of the UNCTAD/WTO International Trade Centre; the International Labour Office's statistical database and *Yearbook of Labour Statistics*; the World Bank's *World Bank Atlas*, *Global Development Finance*, *World Development Report* and *World Development Indicators*; the International Monetary Fund's statistical database, *International Financial Statistics* and *Government Finance Statistics Yearbook*; the World Tourism Organization's *Compendium* and *Yearbook of Tourism Statistics*; the US Geological Survey; the International Telecommunication Union; the International Road Federation's *World Road Statistics* and *The Military Balance 2012*, a publication of the International Institute for Strategic Studies, Arundel House, 13–15 Arundel Street, London WC2R 3DX. Statistics Canada information is used with the permission of Statistics Canada. Users are forbidden to copy this material and/or redisseminate the data, in an original or modified form, for commercial purposes, without the expressed permission of Statistics Canada. Information on the availability of the wide range of data from Statistics Canada can be obtained from Statistics Canada's Regional Offices, its website at www.statcan.ca, and its toll-free access number 1-800-263-1136.

HEALTH AND WELFARE STATISTICS: SOURCES AND DEFINITIONS

Total fertility rate Source: WHO Statistical Information System (part of the Global Health Observatory). The number of children that would be born per woman, assuming no female mortality at child-bearing ages and the age-specific fertility rates of a specified country and reference period.

Under-5 mortality rate Source: WHO Statistical Information System. Defined by WHO as the probability of a child born in a specific year or period dying before reaching the age of five, if subject to the age-specific mortality rates of that year or period.

HIV/AIDS Source: UNAIDS. Estimated percentage of adults aged 15 to 49 years living with HIV/AIDS. < indicates 'fewer than'.

Health expenditure Source: WHO Statistical Information System.

US $ per head (PPP)

International dollar estimates, derived by dividing local currency units by an estimate of their purchasing-power parity (PPP) compared with the US dollar. PPPs are the rates of currency conversion that equalize the purchasing power of different currencies by eliminating the differences in price levels between countries.

% of GDP

GDP levels for OECD countries follow the most recent UN System of National Accounts. For non-OECD countries a value was estimated by utilizing existing UN, IMF and World Bank data.

Public expenditure

Government health-related outlays plus expenditure by social schemes compulsorily affiliated with a sizeable share of the population, and extrabudgetary funds allocated to health services. Figures include grants or loans provided by international agencies, other national authorities, and sometimes commercial banks.

Access to water and sanitation Source: WHO/UNICEF Joint Monitoring Programme on Water Supply and Sanitation (JMP) (Progress on Drinking Water and Sanitation, 2010 Update). Defined in terms of the percentage of the population using improved facilities in terms of the type of technology and levels of service afforded. For water, this includes house connections, public standpipes, boreholes with handpumps, protected dug wells, protected spring and rainwater collection; allowance is also made for other locally defined technologies. Sanitation is defined to include connection to a sewer or septic tank system, pour-flush latrine, simple pit or ventilated improved pit latrine, again with allowance for acceptable local technologies. Access to water and sanitation does not imply that the level of service or quality of water is 'adequate' or 'safe'.

Carbon dioxide emissions Source: World Bank, World Development Indicators database, citing the Carbon Dioxide Information Analysis Center (sponsored by the US Department of Energy). Emissions comprise those resulting from the burning of fossil fuels (including those produced during consumption of solid, liquid and gas fuels and from gas flaring) and from the manufacture of cement.

Human Development Index (HDI) Source: UNDP, *Human Development Report* (2011). A summary of human development measured by three basic dimensions: prospects for a long and healthy life, measured by life expectancy at birth; access to knowledge, measured by a combination of mean years of schooling and expected years of schooling; and standard of living, measured by GNI per head (PPP US $). The index value obtained lies between zero and one. A value above 0.8 indicates very high human development, between 0.7 and 0.8 high human development, between 0.5 and 0.7 medium human development and below 0.5 low human development. A centralized data source for all three dimensions was not available for all countries. In some cases other data sources were used to calculate a substitute value; however, this was excluded from the ranking. Other countries, including non-UNDP members, were excluded from the HDI altogether. In total, 187 countries were ranked for 2011.

CONTENTS

* A complete Index of International Organizations is to be found at the end of this volume.

PART TWO

Afghanistan–Jordan

An Index of Territories is to be found at the end of Volume 2.

ABBREVIATIONS

AB — Aktiebolag (Joint-Stock Company); Alberta
Abog. — Abogado (Lawyer)
Acad. — Academician; Academy
ACP — African, Caribbean and Pacific (countries)
ACT — Australian Capital Territory
AD — anno Domini
ADB — African Development Bank; Asian Development Bank
ADC — aide-de-camp
Adm. — Admiral
admin. — administration
AEC — African Economic Community; African Economic Conference
AfDB — African Development Bank
AG — Aktiengesellschaft (Joint-Stock Company)
AGOA — Africa Growth and Opportunity Act
AH — anno Hegirae
a.i. — ad interim
AID — (US) Agency for International Development
AIDS — acquired immunodeficiency syndrome
AK — Alaska
Al. — Aleja (Alley, Avenue)
AL — Alabama
ALADI — Asociación Latinoamericana de Integración
Alt. — Alternate
AM — Amplitude Modulation
a.m. — ante meridiem (before noon)
amalg. — amalgamated
Apdo — Apartado (Post Box)
APEC — Asia-Pacific Economic Cooperation
approx. — approximately
Apt — Apartment
AR — Arkansas
ARV — advanced retroviral
AŞ — Anonim Şirketi (Joint-Stock Company)
A/S — Aktieselskab (Joint-Stock Company)
ASEAN — Association of South East Asian Nations
asscn — association
assoc. — associate
ASSR — Autonomous Soviet Socialist Republic
asst — assistant
AU — African Union
Aug. — August
auth. — authorized
av., Ave — Avenija, Avenue
Av., Avda — Avenida (Avenue)
Avv. — Avvocato (Lawyer)
AZ — Arizona

b.b. — bez broja (without number)
BC — British Columbia
BC — before Christ
Bd — Board
Bd, Bld, Blv., Blvd — Boulevard
b/d — barrels per day
BFPO — British Forces' Post Office
Bhd — Berhad (Public Limited Company)
Bldg — Building
blk — block
Blvr — Bulevar
BP — Boîte postale (Post Box)
br.(s) — branch(es)
Brig. — Brigadier
BSE — bovine spongiform encephalopathy
BSEC — (Organization of the) Black Sea Economic Co-operation
bte — boîte (box)
Bul. — Bulvar (boulevard)
bulv. — bulvarīs (boulevard)

C — Centigrade
c. — circa; cuadra(s) (block(s))
CA — California
CACM — Central American Common Market
Cad. — Caddesi (Street)
CAP — Common Agricultural Policy
cap. — capital
Capt. — Captain
CAR — Central African Republic
CARICOM — Caribbean Community and Common Market
CBSS — Council of Baltic Sea States
CCL — Caribbean Congress of Labour
Cdre — Commodore
CEMAC — Communauté économique et monétaire de l'Afrique centrale
Cen. — Central
CEO — Chief Executive Officer
CET — common external tariff
CFA — Communauté Financière Africaine; Coopération Financière en Afrique centrale
CFE — Treaty on Conventional Armed Forces in Europe
CFP — Common Fisheries Policy; Communauté française du Pacifique; Comptoirs français du Pacifique
Chair. — Chairman/person/woman
Chih. — Chihuahua
CI — Channel Islands
Cia — Companhia
Cía — Compañía
Cie — Compagnie
c.i.f. — cost, insurance and freight
C-in-C — Commander-in-Chief
circ. — circulation
CIS — Commonwealth of Independent States
CJD — Creutzfeldt-Jakob disease
cm — centimetre(s)
cnr — corner
CO — Colorado
Co — Company; County
c/o — care of
Coah. — Coahuila
Col — Colonel
Col. — Colima; Colonia
COMESA — Common Market for Eastern and Southern Africa
Comm. — Commission; Commendatore
Commdr — Commander
Commdt — Commandant
Commr — Commissioner
Cond. — Condiminio
Conf — Confederation
confs — conferences
Cont. — Contador (Accountant)
COO — Chief Operating Officer
COP — Conference of (the) Parties
Corp. — Corporate
Corpn — Corporation
CP — Case Postale, Caixa Postal, Casella Postale (Post Box); Communist Party
C por A — Compañía por Acciones (Joint Stock Company)
CPOB — Central Post Office Box
CPSU — Communist Party of the Soviet Union
Cres. — Crescent
CSCE — Conference on Security and Cooperation in Europe
CSTAL — Confederación Sindical de los Trabajadores de América Latina
CT — Connecticut
CTCA — Confederación de Trabajadores Centro-americanos
Cttee — Committee
cu — cubic
cwt — hundredweight

DC — District of Columbia; Distrito Capital; Distrito Central
d.d. — delniška družba, dioničko društvo (joint stock company)
DE — Delaware; Departamento Estatal
Dec. — December
Del. — Delegación
Dem. — Democrat; Democratic
Dep. — Deputy
dep. — deposits
Dept — Department
devt — development
DF — Distrito Federal
Dgo — Durango
Diag. — Diagonal
Dir — Director
Div. — Division(al)
DM — Deutsche Mark
DMZ — demilitarized zone
DNA — deoxyribonucleic acid
DN — Distrito Nacional
Doc. — Docent
Dott. — Dottore/essa
DPRK — Democratic People's Republic of Korea
Dr — Doctor
Dr. — Drive
Dra — Doctora
Dr Hab. — Doktor Habilitowany (Assistant Professor)
DRC — Democratic Republic of the Congo
DR-CAFTA — Dominican Republic-Central American Free Trade Agreement
Drs — Doctorandus
DU — depleted uranium
dwt — dead weight tons

E — East; Eastern
EAC — East African Community
EBRD — European Bank for Reconstruction and Development
EC — European Community
ECA — (United Nations) Economic Commission for Africa
ECE — (United Nations) Economic Commission for Europe
ECF — Extended Credit Facility
ECLAC — (United Nations) Economic Commission for Latin America and the Caribbean
ECO — Economic Cooperation Organization
Econ. — Economics; Economist
ECOSOC — (United Nations) Economic and Social Council
ECOWAS — Economic Community of West African States
ECU — European Currency Unit

Edif. Edificio (Building)
edn edition
EEA European Economic Area
EFTA European Free Trade Association
e.g. exempli gratia (for example)
EIB European Investment Bank
EMS European Monetary System
EMU Economic and Monetary Union
eMv electron megavolt
Eng. Engineer; Engineering
EP Empresa Pública
ERM Exchange Rate Mechanism
ESACA Emisora de Capital Abierto Sociedad Anónima
Esc. Escuela; Escudos; Escritorio
ESCAP (United Nations) Economic and Social Commission for Asia and the Pacific
ESCWA (United Nations) Economic and Social Commission for Western Asia
esq. esquina (corner)
est. established; estimate; estimated
etc. et cetera
EU European Union
eV eingetragener Verein
excl. excluding
exec. executive
Ext. Extension

F Fahrenheit
f. founded
FAO Food and Agriculture Organization
f.a.s. free alongside ship
FDI foreign direct investment
Feb. February
Fed. Federal; Federation
feds federations
FL Florida
FM frequency modulation
fmr(ly) former(ly)
f.o.b. free on board
Fr Father
Fr. Franc
Fri. Friday
FRY Federal Republic of Yugoslavia
ft foot (feet)
FTA free trade agreement/area
FYRM former Yugoslav republic of Macedonia

g gram(s)
g. gatve (street)
GA Georgia
GATT General Agreement on Tariffs and Trade
GCC Gulf Cooperation Council
Gdns Gardens
GDP gross domestic product
GEF Gobal Environment Facility
Gen. General
GeV giga electron volts
GM genetically modified
GmbH Gesellschaft mit beschränkter Haftung (Limited Liability Company)
GMO(s) genetically modified organism(s)
GMT Greenwich Mean Time
GNI gross national income
GNP gross national product
Gov. Governor
Govt Government
GPOB General Post Office Box
Gro Guerrero
grt gross registered tons
GSM Global System for Mobile Communications
Gto Guanajuato
GWh gigawatt hour(s)

ha hectares
HD high-definition
HDI Human Development Index
HDTV high-definition television
HE His/Her Eminence; His/Her Excellency
hf hlutafelag (Limited Company)
HI Hawaii
HIPC heavily indebted poor country
HIV human immunodeficiency virus
hl hectolitre(s)
HLTF High Level Task Force
HM His/Her Majesty
Hon. Honorary, Honourable
HPAI highly pathogenic avian influenza
HQ Headquarters
HRH His/Her Royal Highness
HSC Harmonized System Classification
HSH His/Her Serene Highness
Hwy Highway

IA Iowa
IBRD International Bank for Reconstruction and Development
ICC International Chamber of Commerce; International Criminal Court
ICRC International Committee of the Red Cross
ICT information and communication technology
ICTR International Criminal Tribunal for Rwanda
ICTY International Criminal Tribunal for the former Yugoslavia
ID Idaho
IDA International Development Association
IDB Inter-American Development Bank
IDPs internally displaced persons
i.e. id est (that is to say)
IFC International Finance Corporation
IGAD Intergovernmental Authority on Development
IHL International Humanitarian Law
IL Illinois
ILO International Labour Organization/Office
IMF International Monetary Fund
IML International Migration Law
in (ins) inch (inches)
IN Indiana
Inc, Incorp. Incd Incorporated
incl. including
Ind. Independent
INF Intermediate-Range Nuclear Forces
Ing. Engineer
Insp. Inspector
Int. International
Inzå. Engineer
IP intellectual property
IPU Inter-Parliamentary Union
Ir Engineer
IRF International Road Federation
irreg. irregular
Is Islands
ISIC International Standard Industrial Classification
IT information technology
ITU International Telecommunication Union
ITUC International Trade Union Confederation
Iur. Lawyer
IUU illegal, unreported and unregulated

Jal. Jalisco
Jan. January
Jnr Junior
Jr Jonkheer (Esquire); Junior
Jt Joint

Kav. Kaveling (Plot)
kg kilogram(s)
KG Kommandit Gesellschaft (Limited Partnership)
kHz kilohertz
KK Kaien Kaisha (Limited Company)
km kilometre(s)
kom. komnata (room)
kor. korpus (block)
k'och. k'ochasi (street)
KS Kansas
küç küçasi (street)
kv. kvartal (apartment block); kvartira (apartment)
kW kilowatt(s)
kWh kilowatt hour(s)
KY Kentucky

LA Louisiana
lauk laukums (square)
lb pound(s)
LDCs Least Developed Countries
Lic. Licenciado
Licda Licenciada
LLC Limited Liability Company
LNG liquefied natural gas
LPG liquefied petroleum gas
Lt, Lieut Lieutenant
Ltd Limited

m metre(s)
m. million
MA Massachusetts
Maj. Major
Man. Manager; managing
MB Manitoba
mbH mit beschränkter Haftung (with limited liability)
MD Maryland
MDG Millennium Development Goal
MDRI multilateral debt relief initiative
ME Maine
Me Maître
mem.(s) member(s)
MEP Member of the European Parliament
Mercosul Mercado Comum do Sul (Southern Common Market)
Mercosur Mercado Común del Sur (Southern Common Market)
Méx. México
MFN most favoured nation
mfrs manufacturers
Mgr Monseigneur; Monsignor
MHz megahertz
MI Michigan
MIA missing in action
Mich. Michoacán
MIGA Multilateral Investment Guarantee Agency
Mil. Military
Mlle Mademoiselle
mm millimetre(s)
Mme Madame
MN Minnesota
mnt. mante (road)
MO Missouri
Mon. Monday
Mor. Morelos
MOU Memorandum of Understanding
movt movement
MP Member of Parliament
MS Mississippi
MSS Manuscripts
MT Montana
MW megawatt(s); medium wave
MWh megawatt hour(s)

N	North; Northern
n.a.	not available
nab.	naberezhnaya (embankment, quai)
NAFTA	North American Free Trade Agreement
nám.	náměstí (square)
Nat.	National
NATO	North Atlantic Treaty Organization
Nay.	Nayarit
NB	New Brunswick
NC	North Carolina
NCD	National Capital District
NCO	non-commissioned officer
ND	North Dakota
NE	Nebraska; North-East
NEPAD	New Partnership for Africa's Development
NGO	non-governmental organization
NH	New Hampshire
NJ	New Jersey
NL	Newfoundland and Labrador, Nuevo León
NM	New Mexico
NMP	net material product
no	numéro, número (number)
no.	number
Nov.	November
NPT	Non-Proliferation Treaty
nr	near
nrt	net registered tons
NS	Nova Scotia
NSW	New South Wales
NT	Northwest Territories
NU	Nunavut Territory
NV	Naamloze Vennootschap (Limited Company); Nevada
NW	North-West
NY	New York
NZ	New Zealand
OAPEC	Organization of Arab Petroleum Exporting Countries
OAS	Organization of American States
OAU	Organization of African Unity
Oax.	Oaxaca
Oct.	October
OECD	Organisation for Economic Cooperation and Development
OECS	Organisation of Eastern Caribbean States
Of.	Oficina (Office)
OH	Ohio
OIC	Organization of Islamic Cooperation
OK	Oklahoma
ON	Ontario
OPEC	Organization of the Petroleum Exporting Countries
opp.	opposite
OR	Oregon
ORB	OPEC Reference Basket
Org.	Organization
ORIT	Organización Regional Interamericana de Trabajadores
OSCE	Organization for Security and Cooperation in Europe
p.	page
p.a.	per annum
PA	Palestinian Authority; Pennsylvania
Parl.	Parliament(ary)
per.	pereulok (lane, alley)
PE	Prince Edward Island
Perm. Rep.	Permanent Representative
PF	Postfach (Post Box)
PICTs	Pacific Island countries and territories
PK	Posta Kutusu (Post Box)
Pl.	Plac, Plads (square)

pl.	platz; place; ploshchad (square)
PLC	Public Limited Company
PLO	Palestine Liberation Organization
p.m.	post meridiem (after noon)
PMB	Private Mail Bag
PNA	Palestinian National Authority
POB	Post Office Box
pp.	pages
PPP	purchasing-power parity
PQ	Québec
PR	Puerto Rico
pr.	prospekt, prospekti (avenue)
Pres.	President
PRGF	Poverty Reduction and Growth Facility
Prin.	Principal
Prof.	Professor
Propr	Proprietor
Prov.	Province; Provincial; Provinciale (Dutch)
prov.	provulok (lane)
PRSP	Poverty Reduction Strategy Paper
PSI	Policy Support Instrument, Poverty Strategies Initiative
pst.	puistotie (avenue)
PT	Perseroan Terbatas (Limited Company)
Pte	Private; Puente (Bridge)
Pty	Proprietary
p.u.	paid up
publ.	publication; published
Publr	Publisher
Pue.	Puebla
Pvt	Private
QC	Québec
QIP	Quick Impact Project
Qld	Queensland
Qro	Querétaro
Q. Roo	Quintana Roo
q.v.	quod vide (to which refer)
Rag.	Ragioniere (Accountant)
Rd	Road
R(s)	rand; rupee(s)
REC	regional economic communities
reg., regd	register; registered
reorg.	reorganized
Rep.	Republic; Republican; Representative
Repub.	Republic
res	reserve(s)
retd	retired
Rev.	Reverend
RI	Rhode Island
RJ	Rio de Janeiro
Rm	Room
RN	Royal Navy
ro-ro	roll-on roll-off
RP	Recette principale
Rp.(s)	rupiah(s)
Rpto	Reparto (Estate)
RSFSR	Russian Soviet Federative Socialist Republic
Rt	Right
S	South; Southern; San
SA	Société Anonyme, Sociedad Anónima (Limited Company); South Australia
SAARC	South Asian Association for Regional Cooperation
SACN	South American Community of Nations
SADC	Southern African Development Community
SA de CV	Sociedad Anónima de Capital Variable (Variable Capital Company)

SAECA	Sociedad Anónima Emisora de Capital Abierto
SAR	Special Administrative Region
SARL	Sociedade Anônima de Responsabilidade Limitada (Joint-Stock Company of Limited Liability)
SARS	Severe Acute Respiratory Syndrome
Sat.	Saturday
SC	South Carolina
SD	South Dakota
Sdn Bhd	Sendirian Berhad (Private Limited Company)
SDR(s)	Special Drawing Right(s)
SE	South-East
Sec.	Secretary
Secr.	Secretariat
Sen.	Senior; Senator
Sept.	September
SER	Sua Eccellenza Reverendissima (His Eminence)
SFRY	Socialist Federal Republic of Yugoslavia
SGP	Stability and Growth Pact
Sin.	Sinaloa
SIS	Small(er) Island States
SITC	Standard International Trade Classification
SJ	Society of Jesus
SK	Saskatchewan
Skt	Sankt (Saint)
SLP	San Luis Potosí
SMEs	small and medium-sized enterprises
s/n	sin número (without number)
Soc.	Society
Sok.	Sokak (Street)
Son.	Sonora
Şos.	Şosea (Road)
SP	São Paulo
SpA	Società per Azioni (Joint-Stock Company)
Sq.	Square
sq	square (in measurements)
Sr	Senior; Señor
Sra	Señora
Srl	Società a Responsabilità Limitata (Limited Company)
SRSG	Special Representative of the UN Secretary-General
SSR	Soviet Socialist Republic
St	Saint, Sint; Street
Sta	Santa
Ste	Sainte
STI(s)	sexually transmitted infection(s)
Str., str.	Strasse, strada, stradă, strasse (street)
str-la	stradelă (street)
subs.	subscribed; subscriptions
Sun.	Sunday
Supt	Superintendent
SUV	sports utility vehicle
sv.	Saint
SW	South-West
Tab.	Tabasco
Tamps	Tamaulipas
TAŞ	Turkiye Anonim Şirketi (Turkish Joint-Stock Company)
Tas	Tasmania
TD	Teachta Dàla (Member of Parliament)
tech., techn.	technical
tel.	telephone
TEU	20-ft equivalent unit
Thur.	Thursday
TN	Tennessee
tř	třída (avenue)
Treas.	Treasurer
Tue.	Tuesday
TV	television
TWh	terawatt hour(s)
TX	Texas

u.	utca (street)
u/a	unit of account
UAE	United Arab Emirates
UEE	Unidade Económica Estatal
UEMOA	Union économique et monetaire ouest-africaine
UK	United Kingdom
ul.	ulica, ulitsa (street)
UM	ouguiya
UN	United Nations
UNAIDS	United Nations Joint Programme on HIV/AIDS
UNCTAD	United Nations Conference on Trade and Development
UNDP	United Nations Development Programme
UNEP	United Nations Environment Programme
UNESCO	United Nations Educational, Scientific and Cultural Organization
UNHCHR	UN High Commissioner for Human Rights
UNHCR	United Nations High Commissioner for Refugees
UNICEF	United Nations Children's Fund
Univ.	University
UNODC	United Nations Office on Drugs and Crime
UNRWA	United Nations Relief and Works Agency for Palestine Refugees in the Near East
UNSMIS	United Nations Supervision Mission in Syria
UNWTO	World Tourism Organization
Urb.	Urbanización (District)
US	United States
USA	United States of America
USAID	United States Agency for International Development
USSR	Union of Soviet Socialist Republics
UT	Utah
VA	Virginia
VAT	value-added tax
VEB	Volkseigener Betrieb (Public Company)
v-CJD	new variant Creutzfeldt-Jakob disease
Ven.	Venerable
Ver.	Veracruz
VHF	Very High Frequency
VI	(US) Virgin Islands
Vic	Victoria
Vn	Veien (Street)
vol.(s)	volume(s)
VT	Vermont
vul.	vulitsa, vulytsa (street)
W	West; Western
WA	Washington (State); Western Australia
Wed.	Wednesday
WEU	Western European Union
WFP	World Food Programme
WFTU	World Federation of Trade Unions
WHO	World Health Organization
WI	Wisconsin
WSSD	World Summit on Sustainable Development
WTO	World Trade Organization
WV	West Virginia
WY	Wyoming
yr	year
YT	Yukon Territory
Yuc.	Yucatán

INTERNATIONAL TELEPHONE CODES

To make international calls to telephone and fax numbers listed in *The Europa World Year Book*, dial the international access code of the country from which you are calling, followed by the appropriate country code for the organization you wish to call (listed below), followed by the area code (if applicable) and telephone or fax number listed in the entry.

	Country code	+ or – GMT*
Abkhazia	7	+4
Afghanistan	93	+4½
Åland Islands	358	+2
Albania	355	+1
Algeria	213	+1
American Samoa	1 684	–11
Andorra	376	+1
Angola	244	+1
Anguilla	1 264	–4
Antigua and Barbuda	1 268	–4
Argentina	54	–3
Armenia	374	+4
Aruba	297	–4
Ascension Island	247	0
Australia	61	+8 to +10
Austria	43	+1
Azerbaijan	994	+5
Bahamas	1 242	–5
Bahrain	973	+3
Bangladesh	880	+6
Barbados	1 246	–4
Belarus	375	+2
Belgium	32	+1
Belize	501	–6
Benin	229	+1
Bermuda	1 441	–4
Bhutan	975	+6
Bolivia	591	–4
Bonaire	599	–4
Bosnia and Herzegovina	387	+1
Botswana	267	+2
Brazil	55	–3 to –4
British Indian Ocean Territory (Diego Garcia)	246	+5
British Virgin Islands	1 284	–4
Brunei	673	+8
Bulgaria	359	+2
Burkina Faso	226	0
Burundi	257	+2
Cambodia	855	+7
Cameroon	237	+1
Canada	1	–3 to –8
Cape Verde	238	–1
Cayman Islands	1 345	–5
Central African Republic	236	+1
Ceuta	34	+1
Chad	235	+1
Chile	56	–4
China, People's Republic	86	+8
Christmas Island	61	+7
Cocos (Keeling) Islands	61	+6½
Colombia	57	–5
Comoros	269	+3
Congo, Democratic Republic	243	+1
Congo, Republic	242	+1
Cook Islands	682	–10
Costa Rica	506	–6
Côte d'Ivoire	225	0
Croatia	385	+1
Cuba	53	–5
Curaçao	599	–4
Cyprus	357	+2
Czech Republic	420	+1
Denmark	45	+1

	Country code	+ or – GMT*
Djibouti	253	+3
Dominica	1 767	–4
Dominican Republic	1 809	–4
Ecuador	593	–5
Egypt	20	+2
El Salvador	503	–6
Equatorial Guinea	240	+1
Eritrea	291	+3
Estonia	372	+2
Ethiopia	251	+3
Falkland Islands	500	–4
Faroe Islands	298	0
Fiji	679	+12
Finland	358	+2
France	33	+1
French Guiana	594	–3
French Polynesia	689	–9 to –10
Gabon	241	+1
Gambia	220	0
Georgia	995	+4
Germany	49	+1
Ghana	233	0
Gibraltar	350	+1
Greece	30	+2
Greenland	299	–1 to –4
Grenada	1 473	–4
Guadeloupe	590	–4
Guam	1 671	+10
Guatemala	502	–6
Guernsey	44	0
Guinea	224	0
Guinea-Bissau	245	0
Guyana	592	–4
Haiti	509	–5
Honduras	504	–6
Hong Kong	852	+8
Hungary	36	+1
Iceland	354	0
India	91	+5½
Indonesia	62	+7 to +9
Iran	98	+3½
Iraq	964	+3
Ireland	353	0
Isle of Man	44	0
Israel	972	+2
Italy	39	+1
Jamaica	1 876	–5
Japan	81	+9
Jersey	44	0
Jordan	962	+2
Kazakhstan	7	+6
Kenya	254	+3
Kiribati	686	+12 to +13
Korea, Democratic People's Republic (North Korea)	850	+9
Korea, Republic (South Korea)	82	+9
Kosovo	381†	+3
Kuwait	965	+3
Kyrgyzstan	996	+5
Laos	856	+7
Latvia	371	+2
Lebanon	961	+2
Lesotho	266	+2
Liberia	231	0

	Country code	+ or – GMT*
Libya	218	+1
Liechtenstein	423	+1
Lithuania	370	+2
Luxembourg	352	+1
Macao	853	+8
Macedonia, former Yugoslav republic	389	+1
Madagascar	261	+3
Malawi	265	+2
Malaysia	60	+8
Maldives	960	+5
Mali	223	0
Malta	356	+1
Marshall Islands	692	+12
Martinique	596	–4
Mauritania	222	0
Mauritius	230	+4
Mayotte	262	+3
Melilla	34	+1
Mexico	52	–6 to –7
Micronesia, Federated States	691	+10 to +11
Moldova	373	+2
Monaco	377	+1
Mongolia	976	+7 to +9
Montenegro	382	+1
Montserrat	1 664	–4
Morocco	212	0
Mozambique	258	+2
Myanmar	95	+6½
Nagornyi Karabakh	374	+4
Namibia	264	+2
Nauru	674	+12
Nepal	977	+5¾
Netherlands	31	+1
New Caledonia	687	+11
New Zealand	64	+12
Nicaragua	505	–6
Niger	227	+1
Nigeria	234	+1
Niue	683	–11
Norfolk Island	672	+11½
Northern Mariana Islands	1 670	+10
Norway	47	+1
Oman	968	+4
Pakistan	92	+5
Palau	680	+9
Palestinian Autonomous Areas	970 or 972	+2
Panama	507	–5
Papua New Guinea	675	+10
Paraguay	595	–4
Peru	51	–5
Philippines	63	+8
Pitcairn Islands	872	–8
Poland	48	+1
Portugal	351	0
Puerto Rico	1 787	–4
Qatar	974	+3
Réunion	262	+4
Romania	40	+2
Russian Federation	7	+3 to +12
Rwanda	250	+2
Saba	599	–4
Saint-Barthélemy	590	–4
Saint Christopher and Nevis	1 869	–4
Saint Helena	290	0
Saint Lucia	1 758	–4
Saint-Martin	590	–4
Saint Pierre and Miquelon	508	–3
Saint Vincent and the Grenadines	1 784	–4
Samoa	685	+13
San Marino	378	+1
São Tomé and Príncipe	239	0
Saudi Arabia	966	+3
Senegal	221	0

	Country code	+ or – GMT*
Serbia	381	+1
Seychelles	248	+4
Sierra Leone	232	0
Singapore	65	+8
Sint Eustatius	1721	–4
Sint Maarten	599	–4
Slovakia	421	+1
Slovenia	386	+1
Solomon Islands	677	+11
Somalia	252	+3
South Africa	27	+2
South Ossetia	7	+4
South Sudan	211‡	+2
Spain	34	+1
Sri Lanka	94	+5½
Sudan	249	+2
Suriname	597	–3
Svalbard	47	+1
Swaziland	268	+2
Sweden	46	+1
Switzerland	41	+1
Syria	963	+2
Taiwan	886	+8
Tajikistan	992	+5
Tanzania	255	+3
Thailand	66	+7
Timor-Leste	670	+9
Togo	228	0
Tokelau	690	+15
Tonga	676	+13
Transnistria	373	+2
Trinidad and Tobago	1 868	–4
Tristan da Cunha	290	0
Tunisia	216	+1
Turkey	90	+2
'Turkish Republic of Northern Cyprus'	90 392	+2
Turkmenistan	993	+5
Turks and Caicos Islands	1 649	–5
Tuvalu	688	+12
Uganda	256	+3
Ukraine	380	+2
United Arab Emirates	971	+4
United Kingdom	44	0
United States of America	1	–5 to –10
United States Virgin Islands	1 340	–4
Uruguay	598	–3
Uzbekistan	998	+5
Vanuatu	678	+11
Vatican City	39	+1
Venezuela	58	–4½
Viet Nam	84	+7
Wallis and Futuna Islands	681	+12
Yemen	967	+3
Zambia	260	+2
Zimbabwe	263	+2

* The times listed compare the standard (winter) times in the various countries. Some countries adopt Summer (Daylight Saving) Time—i.e. +1 hour—for part of the year.

† Mobile telephone numbers for Kosovo use either the country code for Monaco (377) or the country code for Slovenia (386).

‡ Although South Sudan was assigned the international telephone code 211 by the International Telecommunication Union in July 2011, many mobile and fixed line telephone services continue to use either Sudanese (249) or Ugandan (256) networks. Therefore, all telephone numbers given for South Sudan include the full international dialling code.

Note: Telephone and fax numbers using the Inmarsat ocean region code 870 are listed in full. No country or area code is required, but it is necessary to precede the number with the international access code of the country from which the call is made.

PART ONE

International Organizations

UNITED NATIONS

Address: United Nations, New York, NY 10017, USA.

Telephone: (212) 963-1234; **fax:** (212) 963-4879; **internet:** www.un.org.

The United Nations (UN) was founded in 1945 to maintain international peace and security and to develop international co-operation in addressing economic, social, cultural and humanitarian problems.

The 'United Nations' was a name devised by President Franklin D. Roosevelt of the USA. It was first used in the Declaration by United Nations of 1 January 1942, when representatives of 26 nations pledged their governments to continue fighting together against the Axis powers.

The UN Charter was drawn up by the representatives of 50 countries at the UN Conference on International Organization, which met at San Francisco from 25 April to 26 June 1945. The representatives deliberated on the basis of proposals put forward by representatives of China, the USSR, the United Kingdom and the USA at Dumbarton Oaks in August–October 1944. The Charter was signed on 26 June 1945. Poland, not represented at the Conference, signed it later but nevertheless became one of the original 51 members.

The UN officially came into existence on 24 October 1945, when the Charter had been ratified by China, France, the USSR, the United Kingdom and the USA, and by a majority of other signatories. United Nations Day is celebrated annually on 24 October.

The UN's chief administrative officer is the Secretary-General, elected for a five-year term by the General Assembly on the recommendation of the Security Council. He acts in that capacity at all meetings of the General Assembly, the Security Council, the Economic and Social Council, and the Trusteeship Council, and performs such other functions as are entrusted to him by those organs. He is required to submit an annual report to the General Assembly and may bring to the attention of the Security Council any matter which, in his opinion, may threaten international peace.

Secretary-General: BAN KI-MOON (Republic of Korea) (2007–15).

Membership

MEMBERS OF THE UNITED NATIONS

(with assessments for percentage contributions to the UN budget for 2010–12, and year of admission)

Afghanistan	0.004	1946
Albania	0.010	1955
Algeria	0.128	1962
Andorra	0.008	1993
Angola	0.010	1976
Antigua and Barbuda	0.002	1981
Argentina	0.287	1945
Armenia	0.005	1992
Australia	1.933	1945
Austria	0.851	1955
Azerbaijan	0.015	1992
Bahamas	0.018	1973
Bahrain	0.039	1971
Bangladesh	0.010	1974
Barbados	0.008	1966
Belarus[1]	0.042	1945
Belgium	1.075	1945
Belize	0.001	1981
Benin	0.003	1960
Bhutan	0.001	1971
Bolivia	0.007	1945
Bosnia and Herzegovina	0.014	1992
Botswana	0.018	1966
Brazil	0.611	1945
Brunei	0.028	1984
Bulgaria	0.038	1955
Burkina Faso	0.003	1960
Burundi	0.001	1962
Cambodia	0.003	1955
Cameroon	0.011	1960
Canada	3.207	1945
Cape Verde	0.001	1975
Central African Republic	0.001	1960
Chad	0.002	1960
Chile	0.236	1945
China, People's Republic	3.189	1945
Colombia	0.105	1945
Comoros	0.001	1975
Congo, Democratic Republic	0.003	1960
Congo, Republic	0.003	1960
Costa Rica	0.034	1945
Côte d'Ivoire	0.010	1960
Croatia	0.097	1992
Cuba	0.071	1945
Cyprus	0.046	1960
Czech Republic[2]	0.349	1993
Denmark	0.736	1945
Djibouti	0.001	1977
Dominica	0.001	1978
Dominican Republic	0.042	1945
Ecuador	0.040	1945
Egypt	0.094	1945
El Salvador	0.019	1945
Equatorial Guinea	0.008	1968
Eritrea	0.001	1993
Estonia	0.040	1991
Ethiopia	0.008	1945
Fiji	0.004	1970
Finland	0.566	1955
France	6.123	1945
Gabon	0.014	1960
The Gambia	0.001	1965
Georgia	0.006	1992
Germany	8.018	1973
Ghana	0.006	1957
Greece	0.691	1945
Grenada	0.001	1974
Guatemala	0.028	1945
Guinea	0.002	1958
Guinea-Bissau	0.001	1974
Guyana	0.001	1966
Haiti	0.003	1945
Honduras	0.008	1945
Hungary	0.291	1955
Iceland	0.042	1946
India	0.534	1945
Indonesia	0.238	1950
Iran	0.233	1945
Iraq	0.020	1945
Ireland	0.498	1955
Israel	0.384	1949
Italy	4.999	1955
Jamaica	0.014	1962
Japan	12.530	1956
Jordan	0.014	1955
Kazakhstan	0.076	1992
Kenya	0.012	1963
Kiribati	0.001	1999
Korea, Democratic People's Republic	0.263	1991
Korea, Republic	2.260	1991
Kuwait	0.263	1963
Kyrgyzstan	0.001	1992
Laos	0.001	1955
Latvia	0.038	1991
Lebanon	0.033	1945
Lesotho	0.001	1966
Liberia	0.001	1945
Libya	0.129	1955
Liechtenstein	0.009	1990
Lithuania	0.065	1991
Luxembourg	0.090	1945
Macedonia, former Yugoslav republic	0.007	1993
Madagascar	0.003	1960
Malawi	0.001	1964
Malaysia	0.253	1957
Maldives	0.001	1965
Mali	0.003	1960
Malta	0.017	1964
Marshall Islands	0.001	1991
Mauritania	0.001	1961
Mauritius	0.011	1968
Mexico	2.356	1945
Micronesia, Federated States	0.001	1991
Moldova	0.002	1992
Monaco	0.003	1993
Mongolia	0.002	1961
Montenegro[3]	0.004	2006
Morocco	0.058	1956

Mozambique	0.003	1975
Myanmar	0.006	1948
Namibia	0.008	1990
Nauru	0.001	1999
Nepal	0.006	1955
Netherlands	1.873	1945
New Zealand	0.273	1945
Nicaragua	0.003	1945
Niger	0.002	1960
Nigeria	0.078	1960
Norway	0.871	1945
Oman	0.086	1971
Pakistan	0.082	1947
Palau	0.001	1994
Panama	0.022	1945
Papua New Guinea	0.002	1975
Paraguay	0.007	1945
Peru	0.090	1945
Philippines	0.090	1945
Poland	0.828	1945
Portugal	0.511	1955
Qatar	0.135	1971
Romania	0.177	1955
Russia[4]	1.602	1945
Rwanda	0.001	1962
Saint Christopher and Nevis	0.001	1983
Saint Lucia	0.001	1979
Saint Vincent and the Grenadines	0.001	1980
Samoa	0.001	1976
San Marino	0.003	1992
São Tomé and Príncipe	0.001	1975
Saudi Arabia	0.830	1945
Senegal	0.006	1960
Serbia[3]	0.037	2000
Seychelles	0.002	1976
Sierra Leone	0.001	1961
Singapore	0.335	1965
Slovakia[2]	0.142	1993
Slovenia	0.103	1992
Solomon Islands	0.001	1978
Somalia	0.001	1960
South Africa	0.385	1945
South Sudan[5]	—	2011
Spain	3.177	1955
Sri Lanka	0.019	1955
Sudan	0.010	1956
Suriname	0.003	1975
Swaziland	0.003	1968
Sweden	1.064	1946
Switzerland	1.130	2002
Syria	0.025	1945
Tajikistan	0.002	1992
Tanzania	0.008	1961
Thailand	0.209	1946
Timor-Leste	0.001	2002
Togo	0.001	1960
Tonga	0.001	1999
Trinidad and Tobago	0.044	1962
Tunisia	0.030	1956
Turkey	0.617	1945
Turkmenistan	0.026	1992
Tuvalu	0.001	2000
Uganda	0.006	1962
Ukraine[1]	0.087	1945
United Arab Emirates	0.391	1971
United Kingdom	6.604	1945
USA	22.000	1945
Uruguay	0.027	1945
Uzbekistan	0.010	1992
Vanuatu	0.001	1981
Venezuela	0.314	1945
Viet Nam	0.033	1977
Yemen[6]	0.010	1947/67
Zambia	0.004	1964
Zimbabwe	0.003	1980

Total Membership: 193 (April 2012)

[1] Until December 1991 both Belarus and Ukraine were integral parts of the USSR and not independent countries, but had separate UN membership.

[2] Czechoslovakia, which had been a member of the UN since 1945, ceased to exist as a single state on 31 December 1992. In January 1993, as Czechoslovakia's legal successors, the Czech Republic and Slovakia were granted UN membership, and seats on subsidiary bodies that had previously been held by Czechoslovakia were divided between the two successor states.

[3] Montenegro was admitted as a member of the UN on 28 June 2006, following its declaration of independence on 3 June; Serbia retained the seat formerly held by Serbia and Montenegro.

[4] Russia assumed the USSR's seat in the General Assembly and its permanent seat on the Security Council in December 1991, following the USSR's dissolution.

[5] South Sudan's percentage contribution to the UN budget was to be determined in June 2012.

[6] The Yemen Arab Republic (admitted to the UN as Yemen in 1947) and the People's Democratic Republic of Yemen (admitted as Southern Yemen in 1967) merged to form the Republic of Yemen in May 1990.

Note: In September 2011 the Executive President of the Palestinian Authority submitted a formal application for the admission to the UN of Palestine as an independent member state; this remained under consideration in early 2012.

SOVEREIGN STATES NOT IN THE UNITED NATIONS

(April 2012)

Taiwan (Republic of China) Vatican City (Holy See)

Diplomatic Representation

PERMANENT MISSIONS TO THE UNITED NATIONS

(April 2012)

Afghanistan: 360 Lexington Ave, 11th Floor, New York, NY 10017; tel. (212) 972-1212; fax (212) 972-1216; e-mail afgwatan@aol.com; Permanent Representative Dr ZAHIR TANIN.

Albania: 320 East 79th St, New York, NY 10075; tel. (212) 249-2059; fax (212) 535-2917; e-mail albania@un.int; Permanent Representative FERIT HOXHA.

Algeria: 326 East 48th St, New York, NY 10017; tel. (212) 750-1960; fax (212) 759-5274; e-mail algeria@un.int; internet www.algeria-un.org; Permanent Representative MOURAD BENMEHIDI.

Andorra: Two United Nations Plaza, 27th Floor, New York, NY 10017; tel. (212) 750-8064; fax (212) 750-6630; e-mail contact@andorraun.org; Permanent Representative NARCIS CASAL DE FONSDEVIELA.

Angola: 820 Second Ave, 12th Floor, New York, NY 10017; tel. (212) 861-5656; fax (212) 861-9295; e-mail themission@angolaun.org; internet www.angolamissionun.org; Permanent Representative ISMAEL ABRAÃO GASPAR MARTINS.

Antigua and Barbuda: 305 East 47th St, 6th Floor, New York, NY 10017; tel. (212) 541-4117; fax (212) 757-1607; e-mail unmission@abgov.org; internet www.abgov.org; Permanent Representative JOHN W. ASHE.

Argentina: One United Nations Plaza, 25th Floor, New York, NY 10017; tel. (212) 688-6300; fax (212) 980-8395; e-mail argentina@un.int; internet www.un.int/argentina; Permanent Representative JORGE ARGÜELLO.

Armenia: 119 East 36th St, New York, NY 10016; tel. (212) 686-9079; fax (212) 686-3934; e-mail armenia@un.int; internet www.un.int/armenia; Permanent Representative GAREN A. NAZARIAN.

Australia: 150 East 42nd St, 33rd Floor, New York, NY 10017; tel. (212) 351-6600; fax (212) 351-6610; e-mail australia@un.int; internet www.unny.mission.gov.au; Permanent Representative GARY QUINLAN.

Austria: 600 Third Ave, 31st Floor, New York, NY 10016; tel. (212) 542-8400; fax (212) 949-1840; e-mail new-york-ov@bmeia.gv.at; internet www.un.int/austria; Permanent Representative MARTIN SAJDIK.

Azerbaijan: 866 United Nations Plaza, Suite 560, New York, NY 10017; tel. (212) 371-2559; fax (212) 371-2784; e-mail azerbaijan@un.int; internet www.un.int/azerbaijan; Permanent Representative AGSHIN MEHDIYEV.

Bahamas: 231 East 46th St, New York, NY 10017; tel. (212) 421-6925; fax (212) 759-2135; e-mail mission@bahamasny.com; Permanent Representative PAULETTE A. BETHEL.

Bahrain: 866 Second Ave, 14th/15th Floor, New York, NY 10017; tel. (212) 223-6200; fax (212) 319-0687; e-mail newyork@bahrainun.org; internet www.un.int/bahrain; Permanent Representative JAMAL FARES ALROWAIEI.

Bangladesh: 227 East 45th St, 14th Floor, New York, NY 10017; tel. (212) 867-3434; fax (212) 972-4038; e-mail bangladesh@un.int; internet www.un.int/bangladesh; Permanent Representative ABULKALAM ABDUL MOMEN.

Barbados: 820 Second Ave, 9th Floor, New York, NY 10017; tel. (212) 551-4300; fax (212) 986-1030; e-mail prun@foreign.gov.bb; Permanent Representative JOSEPH E. GODDARD.

Belarus: 136 East 67th St, 4th Floor, New York, NY 10065; tel. (212) 535-3420; fax (212) 734-4810; e-mail belarus@un.int; internet www.un.int/belarus; Permanent Representative ANDREI DAPKIUNAS.

Belgium: One Dag Hammarskjöld Plaza, 885 Second Ave, 41st Floor, New York, NY 10017; tel. (212) 378-6300; fax (212) 681-7618; e-mail newyorkun@diplobel.fed.be; internet www.diplomatie.be/newyorkun; Permanent Representative JAN GRAULS.

Belize: 675 Third Ave, Suite 1911, New York, NY 10017; tel. (212) 986-1240; fax (212) 593-0932; e-mail blzun@aol.com; internet www.belizemission.com; Chargé d'affaires a. i. JANINE ELIZABETH COYE-FELSON.

Benin: 125 East 38th St, New York, NY 10016; tel. (212) 684-1339; fax (212) 684-2058; e-mail benun@undp.org; Permanent Representative JEAN-FRANCIS RÉGIS ZINSOU.

Bhutan: 343 43rd St, New York, NY 10017; tel. (212) 682-2268; fax (212) 661-0551; e-mail pmbnewyork@aol.com; Permanent Representative LHATU WANGCHUK.

Bolivia: 211 East 43rd St, 8th Floor, Rm 802, New York, NY 10017; tel. (212) 682-8132; fax (212) 682-8133; e-mail bolivia@un.int; internet www.bolivia-un.org; Permanent Representative PABLO SOLÓN.

Bosnia and Herzegovina: 420 Lexington Ave, Suites 607–608, New York, NY 10170; tel. (212) 751-9015; fax (212) 751-9019; e-mail bihnyun@aol.com; internet www.bhmisijaun.org; Permanent Representative IVAN BARBALIC.

Botswana: 154 East 46th St, New York, NY 10017; tel. (212) 889-2277; fax (212) 725-5061; e-mail botswana@un.int; Permanent Representative CHARLES THEMBANI NTWAAGAE.

Brazil: 747 Third Ave, 9th Floor, New York, NY 10017; tel. (212) 372-2600; fax (212) 371-5716; e-mail delbrasonu@delbrasonu.org; internet www.un.int/brazil; Permanent Representative MARIA LUIZA RIBEIRO VIOTTI.

Brunei: 771 United Nations Plaza, New York, NY 10017; tel. (212) 697-3465; fax (212) 697-9889; e-mail info@bruneimission-ny.org; Permanent Representative LATIF BIN TUAH.

Bulgaria: 11 East 84th St, New York, NY 10028; tel. (212) 737-4790; fax (212) 472-9865; e-mail bulgaria@un.int; internet www.un.int/bulgaria; Permanent Representative RAYKO STRAHILOV RAYTCHEV.

Burkina Faso: 866 United Nations Plaza, Suite 326, New York, NY 10017; tel. (212) 308-4720; fax (212) 308-4690; e-mail bfapm@un.int; internet www.burkina-onu.org; Permanent Representative DER KOGDA.

Burundi: 336 East 45th St, 12th Floor, New York, NY 10017; tel. (212) 499-0001; fax (212) 499-0006; e-mail ambabunewyork@yahoo.fr; Permanent Representative HERMÉNÉGILDE NIYONZIMA GAHUTU.

Cambodia: 327 East 58th St, New York, NY 10022; tel. (212) 336-0777; fax (212) 759-7672; e-mail cambodia@un.int; internet www.un.int/cambodia; Permanent Representative SEA KOSAL.

Cameroon: 22 East 73rd St, New York, NY 10021; tel. (212) 794-2296; fax (212) 249-0533; e-mail info@cameroonmission.org; internet www.cameroonmission.org; Permanent Representative TOMMO MONTHE.

Canada: One Dag Hammarskjöld Plaza, 885 Second Ave, 14th Floor, New York, NY 10017; tel. (212) 848-1100; fax (212) 848-1195; e-mail canada@un.int; internet www.un.int/canada; Permanent Representative GUILLERMO E. RISHCHYNSKI.

Cape Verde: 27 East 69th St, New York, NY 10021; tel. (212) 472-0333; fax (212) 794-1398; e-mail capeverde@un.int; Permanent Representative ANTONIO PEDRO MONTEIRO LIMA.

Central African Republic: 866 United Nations Plaza, Suite 444, New York, NY 10017; tel. (646) 415-9122; fax (646) 415-9149; e-mail repercaf.ny@gmail.com; Permanent Representative CHARLES-ARMEL DOUBANE.

Chad: 129 East 36th St, New York, NY 10017; tel. (212) 986-0980; fax (212) 986-0152; e-mail chadmission_un@hotmail.com; Permanent Representative AHMAD ALLAM-MI.

Chile: One Dag Hammarskjöld Plaza, 885 Second Ave, 40th Floor, New York, NY 10017; tel. (917) 322-6800; fax (917) 322-6890; e-mail chile@un.int; internet www.un.int/chile; Permanent Representative OCTAVIO ERRÁZURIZ GUILISASTI.

China, People's Republic: 350 East 35th St, New York, NY 10016; tel. (212) 655-6100; fax (212) 634-7626; e-mail chinamission_un@fmprc.gov.cn; internet www.china-un.org; Permanent Representative LI BAODONG.

Colombia: 140 East 57th St, 5th Floor, New York, NY 10022; tel. (212) 355-7776; fax (212) 371-2813; e-mail colombia@colombiaun.org; internet www.colombiaun.org; Permanent Representative NÉSTOR OSORIO.

Comoros: 866 United Nations Plaza, Suite 418, New York, NY 10017; tel. (212) 750-1637; fax (212) 750-1657; e-mail comoros@un.int; internet www.un.int/comoros; Permanent Representative MOHAMED TOIHIRI.

Congo, Democratic Republic: 866 United Nations Plaza, Suite 511, New York, NY 10017; tel. (212) 319-8061; fax (212) 319-8232; e-mail drcongo@un.int; internet www.un.int/drcongo; Permanent Representative CHRISTIAN ATOKI ILEKA.

Congo, Republic: 14 East 65th St, New York, NY 10065; tel. (212) 744-7840; fax (212) 744-7975; e-mail congo@un.int; Permanent Representative RAYMOND SERGE BALÉ.

Costa Rica: 211 East 43rd St, Rm 903, New York, NY 10017; tel. (212) 986-6373; fax (212) 986-6842; e-mail missioncostaricaun@yahoo.com; internet www.un.int/costarica; Permanent Representative EDUARDO ULIBARRI-BILBAO.

Côte d'Ivoire: 800 Second Ave, 5th Floor, New York, NY 10017; tel. (646) 649-5061; fax (646) 781-9974; e-mail cotedivoiremission@yahoo.com; internet www.un.int/cotedivoire; Permanent Representative YOUSSOUFOU BAMBA.

Croatia: 820 Second Ave, 19th Floor, New York, NY 10017; tel. (212) 986-1585; fax (212) 986-2011; e-mail cromiss.un@mvp.hr; internet www.un.mfa.hr; Permanent Representative RANKO VILOVIĆ.

Cuba: 315 Lexington Ave and 38th St, New York, NY 10016; tel. (212) 689-7215; fax (212) 779-1697; e-mail cuba@un.int; internet www.un.int/cuba; Permanent Representative PEDRO NÚNEZ MOSQUERA.

Cyprus: 13 East 40th St, New York, NY 10016; tel. (212) 481-6023; fax (212) 685-7316; e-mail mission@cyprusun.org; internet www.un.int/cyprus; Permanent Representative NICHOLAS EMILIOU.

Czech Republic: 1109–1111 Madison Ave, New York, NY 10028; tel. (646) 981-4000; fax (646) 981-4099; e-mail un.newyork@embassy.mzv.cz; internet www.mfa.cz/un.newyork; Permanent Representative EDITA HRDÁ.

Denmark: One Dag Hammarskjöld Plaza, 885 Second Ave, 18th Floor, New York, NY 10017; tel. (212) 308-7009; fax (212) 308-3384; e-mail nycmis@um.dk; internet www.missionfnnewyork.um.dk/en/; Permanent Representative CARSTEN STAUR.

Djibouti: 866 United Nations Plaza, Suite 4011, New York, NY 10017; tel. (212) 753-3163; fax (212) 223-1276; e-mail djibouti@nyct.net; Permanent Representative ROBLE OLHAYE.

Dominica: 800 Second Ave, Suite 400H, New York, NY 10017; tel. (212) 949-0853; fax (212) 808-4975; e-mail domun@onecommonwealth.org; Permanent Representative VINCE HENDERSON.

Dominican Republic: 144 East 44th St, 4th Floor, New York, NY 10017; tel. (212) 867-0833; fax (212) 297-2509; e-mail drun@un.int; internet www.un.int/dr; Permanent Representative HÉCTOR VIRGILIO ALCÁNTARA MEJIA.

Ecuador: 866 United Nations Plaza, Rm 516, New York, NY 10017; tel. (212) 935-1680; fax (212) 935-1835; e-mail missionecuador@nyct.net; internet www.ecuadoronu.com; Permanent Representative LUIS GALLEGOS.

Egypt: 304 East 44th St, New York, NY 10017; tel. (212) 503-0300; fax (212) 949-5999; e-mail egypt@un.int; Permanent Representative MAGED ABDELFATTAH ABDELAZIZ.

El Salvador: 46 Park Ave, New York, NY 10016; tel. (212) 679-1616; fax (212) 725-7831; e-mail elsalvador@un.int; Permanent Representative JOAQUÍN ALEXANDER MAZA MARTELLI.

Equatorial Guinea: 242 East 51st St, New York, NY 10022; tel. (212) 223-2324; fax (212) 223-2366; e-mail equatorialguineamission@yahoo.com; Permanent Representative ANATOLIO NDONG MBA.

Eritrea: 800 Second Ave, 18th Floor, New York, NY 10017; tel. (212) 687-3390; fax (212) 687-3138; e-mail mission@eritrea-un.org; internet www.un.int/eritrea; Permanent Representative ARAYA DESTA.

Estonia: 3 Dag Hammarskjöld Plaza, 305 East 47th St, Unit 6B, New York, NY 10017; tel. (212) 883-0640; fax (646) 514-0099; e-mail mission.newyork@mfa.ee; Permanent Representative MARGUS KOLGA.

Ethiopia: 866 Second Ave, 3rd Floor, New York, NY 10017; tel. (212) 421-1830; fax (212) 754-0360; e-mail ethiopia@un.int; internet www.un.int/ethiopia; Permanent Representative TEKEDA ALEMU.

Fiji: 630 Third Ave, 7th Floor, New York, NY 10017; tel. (212) 687-4130; fax (212) 687-3963; e-mail fiji@un.int; internet www.fijiprun.org; Permanent Representative PETER THOMSON.

Finland: 866 United Nations Plaza, Suite 222, New York, NY 10017; tel. (212) 355-2100; fax (212) 759-6156; e-mail sanomat.yke@formin.fi; internet www.un.int/finland; Permanent Representative JARMO VIINANEN.

France: One Dag Hammarskjöld Plaza, 245 East 47th St, 44th Floor, New York, NY 10017; tel. (212) 308-5700; fax (212) 421-6889; e-mail france@un.int; internet www.un.int/france; Permanent Representative GÉRARD ARAUD.

Gabon: 18 East 41st St, 9th Floor, New York, NY 10017; tel. (212) 686-9720; fax (212) 689-5769; e-mail gabon@un.int; Permanent Representative NELSON MESSONE.

The Gambia: 800 Second Ave, Suite 400F, New York, NY 10017; tel. (212) 949-6640; fax (212) 856-9820; e-mail gambia@un.int; internet gambia.un.int; Permanent Representative SUSAN WAFFA-OGOO.

Georgia: One United Nations Plaza, 26th Floor, New York, NY 10021; tel. (212) 759-1949; fax (212) 759-1832; e-mail georgia@un.int; internet www.un.int/georgia; Permanent Representative ALEXANDRE LOMAIA.

Germany: 871 United Nations Plaza, New York, NY 10017; tel. (212) 940-0400; fax (212) 940-0402; e-mail info@new-york-un.diplo.de; internet www.germany-info.org/un; Permanent Representative HANS PETER WITTIG.

Ghana: 19 East 47th St, New York, NY 10017; tel. (212) 832-1300; fax (212) 751-6743; e-mail ghanaperm@aol.com; Permanent Representative KEN KANDA.

Greece: 866 Second Ave, 13th Floor, New York, NY 10017; tel. (212) 888-6900; fax (212) 888-4440; e-mail mission@greeceun.org; internet www.greeceun.org; Permanent Representative ANASTASSIS MITSIALIS.

Grenada: 800 Second Ave, Suite 400K, New York, NY 10017; tel. (212) 599-0301; fax (212) 599-1540; e-mail grenada@un.int; Permanent Representative DESSIMA M. WILLIAMS.

Guatemala: 57 Park Ave, New York, NY 10016; tel. (212) 679-4760; fax (212) 685-8741; e-mail guatemala@un.int; internet www.un.int/guatemala; Permanent Representative GERT ROSENTHAL.

Guinea: 140 East 39th St, New York, NY 10016; tel. (212) 687-8115; fax (212) 687-8248; e-mail missionofguinea@aol.com; Permanent Representative MAMADOU TOURÉ.

Guinea-Bissau: 800 Second Ave, Suite 400F, New York, NY 10017; tel. (917) 770-5598; fax (212) 856-9820; e-mail gnbun@undp.org; Permanent Representative JOÃO SOARES DA GAMA.

Guyana: 801 Second Ave, 5th Floor, New York, NY 10017; tel. (212) 573-5828; fax (212) 573-6225; e-mail guyana@un.int; Permanent Representative GEORGE WILFRIED TALBOT.

Haiti: 801 Second Ave, Rm 600, New York, NY 10017; tel. (212) 370-4840; fax (212) 661-8698; e-mail haiti@un.int; Permanent Representative LÉO MÉRORÈS.

Honduras: 866 United Nations Plaza, Suite 417, New York, NY 10017; tel. (212) 752-3370; fax (212) 223-0498; e-mail honduras_un@hotmail.com; internet www.un.int/honduras; Permanent Representative MARY ELIZABETH FLORES FLAKE.

Hungary: 227 East 52nd St, New York, NY 10022; tel. (212) 752-0209; fax (212) 755-5395; e-mail hungary@un.int; internet www.un.int/hungary; Permanent Representative CSABA KÖRÖSI.

Iceland: 800 Third Ave, 36th Floor, New York, NY 10022; tel. (212) 593-2700; fax (212) 593-6269; e-mail unmission@mfa.is; internet www.iceland.org/un/nyc; Permanent Representative GRÉTA GUNNARSDÓTTIR.

India: 235 East 43rd St, New York, NY 10017; tel. (212) 490-9660; fax (212) 490-9656; e-mail india@un.int; internet www.un.int/india; Permanent Representative HARDEEP SINGH PURI.

Indonesia: 325 East 38th St, New York, NY 10016; tel. (212) 972-8333; fax (212) 972-9780; e-mail ptri@indonesiamission-ny.org; internet www.indonesiamission-ny.org; Permanent Representative DESRA PERCAYA.

Iran: 622 Third Ave, 34th Floor, New York, NY 10017; tel. (212) 687-2020; fax (212) 867-7086; e-mail iran@un.int; internet www.un.int/iran; Permanent Representative MOHAMMAD KHAZAEE.

Iraq: 14 East 79th St, New York, NY 10075; tel. (212) 737-4433; fax (212) 772-1794; e-mail iraqny@un.int; internet www.iraqunmission.org/; Permanent Representative HAMID AL-BAYATI.

Ireland: 885 Second Ave, 19th Floor, New York, NY 10017; tel. (212) 421-6934; fax (212) 752-4726; e-mail ireland@un.int; internet www.irelandunnewyork.org; Permanent Representative ANNE ANDERSON.

Israel: 800 Second Ave, New York, NY 10017; tel. (212) 499-5510; fax (212) 499-5516; e-mail un@israel.org; internet www.israel-un.org; Permanent Representative RON PROSOR.

Italy: Two United Nations Plaza, 24th Floor, New York, NY 10017; tel. (212) 486-9191; fax (212) 486-1036; e-mail info.italyun@esteri.it; internet www.italyun.esteri.it; Permanent Representative CESARE MARIA RAGAGLINI.

Jamaica: 767 Third Ave, 9th Floor, New York, NY 10017; tel. (212) 935-7509; fax (212) 935-7607; e-mail jamaica@un.int; internet www.un.int/jamaica; Permanent Representative RAYMOND OSBOURNE WOLFE.

Japan: 866 United Nations Plaza, 2nd Floor, New York, NY 10017; tel. (212) 223-4300; fax (212) 751-1966; e-mail japan.mission@un-japan.org; internet www.un.int/japan; Permanent Representative TSUNEO NISHIDA.

Jordan: 866 Second Ave, 4th Floor, New York, NY 10017; tel. (212) 832-9553; fax (212) 832-5346; e-mail missionun@jordanmissionun.com; Permanent Representative Prince ZEID RA'AD ZEID AL-HUSSEIN.

Kazakhstan: 3 Dag Hammarskjöld Plaza, 305 East 47th St, 3rd Floor, New York, NY 10017; tel. (212) 230-1900; fax (212) 230-1172; e-mail kazakhstan@un.int; internet www.kazakhstanun.org; Permanent Representative BYRGANYM AITIMOVA.

Kenya: 866 United Nations Plaza, Rm 486, New York, NY 10017; tel. (212) 421-4740; fax (212) 486-1985; e-mail kenya@un.int; internet www.un.int/kenya/; Permanent Representative MACHARIA KAMAU.

Korea, Democratic People's Republic: 820 Second Ave, 13th Floor, New York, NY 10017; tel. (212) 972-3105; fax (212) 972-3154; e-mail dpr.korea@verizon.net; Permanent Representative SIN SON HO.

Korea, Republic: 335 East 45th St, New York, NY 10017; tel. (212) 439-4000; fax (212) 986-1083; e-mail korea@un.int; internet www.un.int/korea; Permanent Representative KIM SOOK.

Kuwait: 321 East 44th St, New York, NY 10017; tel. (212) 973-4300; fax (212) 370-1733; e-mail kuwaitmission@msn.com; internet www.kuwaitmission.com; Permanent Representative MANSOUR AYYAD AL-OTAIBI.

Kyrgyzstan: 866 United Nations Plaza, Suite 477, New York, NY 10017; tel. (212) 486-4214; fax (212) 486-5259; e-mail kyrgyzstan@un.int; internet www.un.int/kyrgyzstan; Permanent Representative TALAIBEK KYDYROV.

Laos: 317 East 51st St, New York, NY 10022; tel. (212) 832-2734; fax (212) 750-0039; e-mail lao@un.int; internet www.un.int/lao; Permanent Representative SALEUMXAY KOMMASITH.

Latvia: 333 East 50th St, New York, NY 10022; tel. (212) 838-8877; fax (212) 838-8920; e-mail mission.un-ny@mfa.gov.lv; Permanent Representative NORMANS PENKE.

Lebanon: 866 United Nations Plaza, Rm 531–533, New York, NY 10017; tel. (212) 355-5460; fax (212) 838-2819; e-mail contact@lebanonun.org; internet www.un.int/lebanon; Permanent Representative NAWAF A. SALAM.

Lesotho: 204 East 39th St, New York, NY 10016; tel. (212) 661-1690; fax (212) 682-4388; e-mail lesotho@un.int; internet www.un.int/lesotho; Permanent Representative MOTLATSI RAMAFOLE.

Liberia: 866 United Nations Plaza, Suite 480, New York, NY 10017; tel. (212) 687-1033; fax (212) 687-1035; e-mail liberia@un.int; Permanent Representative MARJON V. KAMARA.

Libya: 309–315 East 48th St, New York, NY 10017; tel. (212) 752-5775; fax (212) 593-4787; e-mail libyanmis2011@yahoo.com; internet www.libyanmission-un.org; Permanent Representative ABDURRAHMAN MOHAMED SHALGHAM.

Liechtenstein: 633 Third Ave, 27th Floor, New York, NY 10017; tel. (212) 599-0220; fax (212) 599-0064; e-mail mission@nyc.llv.li; internet www.un.int/liechtenstein; Permanent Representative CHRISTIAN WENAWESER.

Lithuania: 708 Third Ave, 10th Floor, New York, NY 10018; tel. (212) 983-9474; fax (212) 983-9473; e-mail lithuania@un.int; internet www.un.int/lithuania; Permanent Representative DALIUS ČEKUOLIS.

Luxembourg: 17 Beekman Pl., New York, NY 10022; tel. (212) 935-3589; fax (212) 935-5896; e-mail newyork.rp@mae.etat.lu; internet www.un.int/luxembourg; Permanent Representative SYLVIE LUCAS.

Macedonia, former Yugoslav republic: 866 United Nations Plaza, Suite 517, New York, NY 10017; tel. (212) 308-8504; fax (212) 308-8724; e-mail macedonia@nyct.net; internet www.macedonia-un.org; Permanent Representative PAJO AVIROVIKJ.

Madagascar: 820 Second Ave, Suite 800, New York, NY 10017; tel. (212) 986-9491; fax (212) 986-6271; e-mail repermad@verizon.net; internet www.un.int/madagascar; Permanent Representative PAJO AVIROVIKJ.

Malawi: 866 United Nations Plaza, Suite 486, New York, NY 10017; tel. (212) 317-8738; fax (212) 317-8729; e-mail malawiun@aol.com; Permanent Representative BRIAN G. BOWLER.

Malaysia: 313 East 43rd St, New York, NY 10017; tel. (212) 986-6310; fax (212) 490-8576; e-mail malnyun@kln.gov.my; internet www.un.int/malaysia; Permanent Representative HANIFF HUSSEIN.

Maldives: 800 Second Ave, Suite 400E, New York, NY 10017; tel. (212) 599-6195; fax (212) 661-6405; e-mail maldives@un.int; internet www.un.int/maldives; Permanent Representative ABDUL GHAFOOR MOHAMED.

Mali: 111 East 69th St, New York, NY 10021; tel. (212) 737-4150; fax (212) 472-3778; e-mail malionu@aol.com; internet www.un.int/mali; Permanent Representative OUMAR DAOU.

Malta: 249 East 35th St, New York, NY 10016; tel. (212) 725-2345; fax (212) 779-7097; e-mail malta-un.newyork@gov.mt; Permanent Representative CHRISTOPHER GRIMA.

Marshall Islands: 800 Second Ave, 18th Floor, New York, NY 10017; tel. (212) 983-3040; fax (212) 983-3202; e-mail marshallislands@un.int; internet marshallislands.un.int; Permanent Representative PHILLIP H. MULLER.

Mauritania: 116 East 38th St, New York, NY 10016; tel. (212) 252-0113; fax (212) 252-0175; e-mail mauritania@un.int; internet www.un.int/wcm/content/site/mauritania; Permanent Representative AHMED OULD TEGUEDI.

Mauritius: 211 East 43rd St, 15th Floor, New York, NY 10017; tel. (212) 949-0190; fax (212) 697-3829; e-mail mauritius@un.int; internet www.un.int/mauritius; Permanent Representative MILAN JAYA NYAMRAJSINGH MEETARBHAN.

Mexico: Two United Nations Plaza, 28th Floor, New York, NY 10017; tel. (212) 752-0220; fax (212) 688-8862; e-mail mexico@un.int; internet www.sre.gob.mx/onu; Permanent Representative LUIS ALFONSO DE ALBA GÓNGORA.

Micronesia, Federated States: 820 Second Ave, Suite 17A, New York, NY 10017; tel. (212) 697-8370; fax (212) 697-8295; e-mail fsmun@fsmgov.org; internet www.fsmgov.org/fsmun; Permanent Representative JANE JIMMY CHIGIYAL.

Moldova: 35 East 29th St, New York, NY 10016; tel. (212) 447-1867; fax (212) 447-4067; e-mail unmoldova@aol.com; internet www.un.int/moldova; Permanent Representative VLADIMIR LUPAN.

Monaco: 866 United Nations Plaza, Suite 520, New York, NY 10017; tel. (212) 832-0721; fax (212) 832-5358; e-mail monaco@un.int; internet www.un.int/monaco; Permanent Representative ISABELLE PICCO.

Mongolia: 6 East 77th St, New York, NY 10075; tel. (212) 737-3874; fax (212) 861-9464; e-mail mongolia@un.int; internet www.un.int/mongolia; Permanent Representative OCHIR ENKHTSETSEG.

Montenegro: 801 Second Ave, 7th Floor, New York, NY 10017; tel. (212) 661-3700; fax (212) 661-3755; e-mail un.newyork@mfa.gov.me; Permanent Representative MILORAD ŠĆEPANOVIĆ.

Morocco: 866 Second Ave, 6th and 7th Floors, New York, NY 10017; tel. (212) 421-1580; fax (212) 980-1512; e-mail info@morocco-un.org; internet www.un.int/morocco; Permanent Representative MOHAMMED LOULICHKI.

Mozambique: 420 East 50th St, New York, NY 10022; tel. (212) 644-5965; fax (212) 644-5972; e-mail mozambique@un.int; internet www.un.int/mozambique; Permanent Representative ANTÓNIO GUMENDE.

Myanmar: 10 East 77th St, New York, NY 10075; tel. (212) 744-1271; fax (212) 744-1290; e-mail myanmar@un.int; Permanent Representative U THAN SWE.

Namibia: 360 Lexington Ave, Suite 1502, New York, NY 10017; tel. (212) 685-2003; fax (212) 685-1561; e-mail namibia@un.int; internet www.un.int/namibia; Permanent Representative WILFRIED INOTIRA EMVULA.

Nauru: 800 Second Ave, Suite 400A, New York, NY 10017; tel. (212) 937-0074; fax (212) 937-0079; e-mail nauru@un.int; internet www.un.int/nauru; Permanent Representative MARLENE INEMWIN MOSES.

Nepal: 820 Second Ave, Suite 17B, New York, NY 10017; tel. (212) 370-3988; fax (212) 953-2038; e-mail nepal@un.int; internet www.un.int/nepal; Permanent Representative GYAN CHANDRA ACHARYA.

Netherlands: 235 East 45th St, 16th Floor, New York, NY 10017; tel. (212) 519-9500; fax (212) 370-1954; e-mail netherlands@un.int; internet www.pvnewyork.org; Permanent Representative HERMAN SCHAPER.

New Zealand: 600 Third Ave, 14th Floor, New York, NY 10016; tel. (212) 826-1960; fax (212) 758-0827; e-mail nzmissionny@earthlink.net; internet www.nzmissionny.org; Permanent Representative JIM MCLAY.

Nicaragua: 820 Second Ave, 8th Floor, New York, NY 10017; tel. (212) 490-7997; fax (212) 286-0815; e-mail nicaragua@un.int; internet www.un.int/nicaragua; Permanent Representative MARIA RUBIALES DE CHAMORRO.

Niger: 417 East 50th St, New York, NY 10022; tel. (212) 421-3260; fax (212) 753-6931; e-mail niger@nigerun.org; internet www.un.int/niger; Permanent Representative BOUBACAR BOUREIMA.

Nigeria: 828 Second Ave, New York, NY 10017; tel. (212) 953-9130; fax (212) 697-1970; e-mail nigeria@un.int; Permanent Representative U. JOY OGWU.

Norway: 825 Third Ave, 39th Floor, New York, NY 10022; tel. (212) 421-0280; fax (212) 688-0554; e-mail delun@mfa.no; internet www.un.norway-un.org; Permanent Representative MORTEN WETLAND.

Oman: 3 Dag Hammarskjöld Plaza, 305 East 47th St, 12th Floor, New York, NY 10017; tel. (212) 355-3505; fax (212) 644-0070; e-mail oman@un.int; Permanent Representative LYUTHA S. AL-MUGHAIRY.

Pakistan: 8 East 65th St, New York, NY 10021; tel. (212) 879-8600; fax (212) 744-7348; e-mail pakistan@un.int; internet www.pakun.org; Permanent Representative Syeda ABIDA HUSSAIN.

Palau: 866 United Nations Plaza, Suite 575, New York, NY 10017; tel. (212) 813-0310; fax (212) 813-0317; e-mail mission@palauun.org; internet www.palauun.org; Permanent Representative STUART BECK.

Panama: 866 United Nations Plaza, Suite 4030, New York, NY 10017; tel. (212) 421-5420; fax (212) 421-2694; e-mail emb@panama-un.org; Permanent Representative PABLO ANTONIO THALASSINÓS.

Papua New Guinea: 201 East 42nd St, Suite 405, New York, NY 10017; tel. (212) 557-5001; fax (212) 557-5009; e-mail pngmission@pngun.org; Permanent Representative ROBERT GUBA AISI.

Paraguay: 211 East 43rd St, Suite 400, New York, NY 10017; tel. (212) 687-3490; fax (212) 818-1282; e-mail paraguay@un.int; Permanent Representative JOSÉ ANTONIO DOS SANTOS.

Peru: 820 Second Ave, Suite 1600, New York, NY 10017; tel. (212) 687-3336; fax (212) 972-6975; e-mail onuper@aol.com; internet www.un.int/peru; Permanent Representative ENRIQUE ROMÁN-MOREY.

Philippines: 556 Fifth Ave, 5th Floor, New York, NY 10036; tel. (212) 764-1300; fax (212) 840-8602; e-mail newyorkpm@gmail.com; internet www.un.int/philippines; Permanent Representative LIBRAN N. CABACTULAN.

Poland: 9 East 66th St, New York, NY 10021; tel. (212) 744-2506; fax (212) 517-6771; e-mail polandun@polandun.org; internet www.polandun.org; Permanent Representative WITOLD SOBKÓW.

Portugal: 866 Second Ave, 9th Floor, New York, NY 10017; tel. (212) 759-9444; fax (212) 355-1124; e-mail portugal@un.int; internet www.un.int/portugal; Permanent Representative JOSÉ FILIPE MENDES MORAES CABRAL.

Qatar: 809 United Nations Plaza, 4th Floor, New York, NY 10017; tel. (212) 486-9335; fax (212) 758-4952; e-mail qatar-e@qatarmission.org; Permanent Representative MESHAL HAMAD MOHAMED JABR AL-THANI.

Romania: 573–577 Third Ave, New York, NY 10016; tel. (212) 682-3273; fax (212) 682-9746; e-mail romania@un.org; internet mpnewyork.mae.ro; Permanent Representative SIMONA MIRELA MICULESCU.

Russia: 136 East 67th St, New York, NY 10065; tel. (212) 861-4900; fax (212) 628-0252; e-mail rusun@un.int; internet www.un.int/russia; Permanent Representative VITALII I. CHURKIN.

Rwanda: 124 East 39th St, New York, NY 10016; tel. (212) 679-9010; fax (212) 679-9133; e-mail rwaun@un.int; Permanent Representative EUGÈNE-RICHARD GASANA.

Saint Christopher and Nevis: 414 East 75th St, 5th Floor, New York, NY 10021; tel. (212) 535-1234; fax (212) 535-6854; e-mail sknmission@aol.com; internet www.stkittsnevis.org; Permanent Representative DELANO FRANK BART.

Saint Lucia: 800 Second Ave, 9th Floor, New York, NY 10017; tel. (212) 697-9360; fax (212) 697-4993; e-mail slumission@aol.com; internet www.un.int/stlucia; Permanent Representative DONATUS ST. AIMEE.

Saint Vincent and the Grenadines: 800 Second Ave, Suite 400G, New York, NY 10017; tel. (212) 599-0950; fax (212) 599-1020; e-mail svgun@aol.com; Permanent Representative CAMILLO M. GONSALVES.

Samoa: 800 Second Ave, Suite 400J, New York, NY 10017; tel. (212) 599-6196; fax (212) 599-0797; e-mail samoa@un.int; Permanent Representative ALI'IOAIGA FETURI ELISAIA.

San Marino: 327 East 50th St, New York, NY 10022; tel. (212) 751-1234; fax (212) 751-1436; e-mail sanmarinoun@hotmail.com; Permanent Representative DANIELE BODINI.

São Tomé and Príncipe: 460 Park Ave, 11th Floor, New York, NY 10022; tel. (212) 317-0533; fax (212) 317-0580; e-mail stp@un.int; Permanent Representative OVIDIO MANUEL BARBOSA PEQUENO.

Saudi Arabia: 809 United Nations Plaza, 10th and 11th Floors, New York, NY 10017; tel. (212) 557-1525; fax (212) 983-4895; e-mail saudi-mission@un.int; internet www.saudi-un-ny.org; Permanent Representative ABDULLAH YAHYA AL-MOUALLIMI.

Senegal: 238 East 68th St, New York, NY 10021; tel. (212) 517-9030; fax (212) 517-3032; e-mail senegal.mission@yahoo.fr; internet www.un.int/senegal; Permanent Representative ABDOU SALAM DIALLO.

Serbia: 854 Fifth Ave, New York, NY 10065; tel. (212) 879-8700; fax (212) 879-8705; e-mail info@serbiamissionun.org; internet www.un.int/serbia; Permanent Representative FEODOR STARČEVIĆ.

Seychelles: 800 Second Ave, Suite 400C, New York, NY 10017; tel. (212) 972-1785; fax (212) 972-1786; e-mail seychelles@un.int; Permanent Representative RONALD JEAN JUMEAU.

Sierra Leone: 245 East 49th St, New York, NY 10017; tel. (212) 688-1656; fax (212) 688-4924; e-mail sierraleone@un.int; Permanent Representative SHEKOU MOMODOU TOURAY.

Singapore: 231 East 51st St, New York, NY 10022; tel. (212) 826-0840; fax (212) 826-2964; e-mail singapore@un.int; internet www.mfa.gov.sg/newyork; Permanent Representative ALBERT CHUA.

Slovakia: 801 Second Ave, 12th Floor, New York, NY 10017; tel. (212) 286-8418; fax (212) 286-8419; e-mail un.newyork@mzv.sk; internet www.msv.sk/unnewyork; Permanent Representative MILOŠ KOTEREC.

Slovenia: 600 Third Ave, 24th Floor, New York, NY 10016; tel. (212) 370-3007; fax (212) 370-1824; e-mail slovenia@un.int; internet www.un.int/slovenia; Permanent Representative SANJA ŠTIGLIC.

Solomon Islands: 800 Second Ave, Suite 400L, New York, NY 10017; tel. (212) 599-6193; fax (212) 661-8925; e-mail simun@solomons.com; Permanent Representative COLLIN D. BECK.

Somalia: 425 East 61st St, Suite 702, New York, NY 10021; tel. (212) 688-9410; fax (212) 759-0651; e-mail somalia@un.int; internet www.iaed.org/somalia; Permanent Representative ELMI AHMED DUALE.

South Africa: 333 East 38th St, 9th Floor, New York, NY 10016; tel. (212) 213-5583; fax (212) 692-2498; e-mail pmun.newyork@foreign.gov.za; internet www.southafrica-newyork.net/pmun; Permanent Representative BASU SANGQU.

Spain: One Dag Hammarskjöld Plaza, 245 East 47th St, 36th Floor, New York, NY 10017; tel. (212) 661-1050; fax (212) 949-7247; e-mail spain@spainun.org; internet www.spainun.org; Permanent Representative FERNANDO ARIAS.

Sri Lanka: 630 Third Ave, 20th Floor, New York, NY 10017; tel. (212) 986-7040; fax (212) 986-1838; e-mail mail@slmission.com; internet www.slmission.com; Permanent Representative PALITHA T. B. KOHONA.

Sudan: 305 East 47th St, 3 Dag Hammarskjöld Plaza, 4th Floor, New York, NY 10017; tel. (212) 573-6033; fax (212) 573-6160; e-mail sudan@sudanmission.org; Permanent Representative DAFFA-ALLA ELHAG ALI OSMAN.

Suriname: 866 United Nations Plaza, Suite 320, New York, NY 10017; tel. (212) 826-0660; fax (212) 980-7029; e-mail suriname@un.int; internet www.un.int/suriname; Permanent Representative HENRY LEONARD MACDONALD.

Swaziland: 408 East 50th St, New York, NY 10022; tel. (212) 371-8910; fax (212) 754-2755; e-mail swazinymission@yahoo.com; Permanent Representative ZWELETHU MNISI.

Sweden: One Dag Hammarskjöld Plaza, 885 Second Ave, 46th Floor, New York, NY 10017; tel. (212) 583-2500; fax (212) 583-2549; e-mail sweden@un.int; internet www.un.int/sweden; Permanent Representative MÅRTEN GRUNDITZ.

Switzerland: 633 Third Ave, 29th Floor, New York, NY 10017; tel. (212) 286-1540; fax (212) 286-1555; e-mail vertretung-un@nyc.rep.admin.ch; internet www.switzerland/un.org; Permanent Representative PAUL R. SEGER.

Syria: 820 Second Ave, 15th Floor, New York, NY 10017; tel. (212) 661-1313; fax (212) 983-4439; e-mail exesec.syria@gmail.com; internet www.syria-un.org; Permanent Representative BASHAR JA'AFARI.

Tajikistan: 216 East 49th St, 4th Floor, New York, NY 10017; tel. (212) 207-3315; fax (212) 207-3855; e-mail tajikistan@un.int; internet www.un.int/wcm/content/site/tajikistan; Permanent Representative SIRODJIDIN MUKHRIDINOVICH ASLOV.

Tanzania: 201 East 42nd St, 17th Floor, New York, NY 10017; tel. (212) 972-9160; fax (212) 682-5232; e-mail tzrepny@aol.com; Permanent Representative OMBENI YOHANA SEFUE.

Thailand: 351 East 52nd St, New York, NY 10022; tel. (212) 754-2230; fax (212) 754-2535; e-mail thailand@un.int; Permanent Representative NORACHIT SINHASENI.

Timor-Leste: 866 Second Ave, Suite 441, New York, NY 10017; tel. (212) 759-3675; fax (212) 759-4196; e-mail timor-leste@un.int; internet www.un.int/timor-leste; Permanent Representative SOFIA MESQÍTA BORGES.

Togo: 112 East 40th St, New York, NY 10016; tel. (212) 490-3455; fax (212) 983-6684; e-mail togo@un.int; Permanent Representative KODJO MENAN.

Tonga: 250 East 51st St, New York, NY 10022; tel. (917) 369-1025; fax (917) 369-1024; e-mail tongaunmission@aol.com; Permanent Representative SONATANE TU'AKINAMOLAHI TAUMOEPEAU-TUPOU.

Trinidad and Tobago: 122 East 42nd St, 39th Floor, New York, NY 10017; tel. (212) 697-7620; fax (212) 682-3580; e-mail tto@un.int; internet www.un.int/trinidadandtobago; Permanent Representative RODNEY CHARLES.

Tunisia: 31 Beekman Pl., New York, NY 10022; tel. (212) 751-7503; fax (212) 751-0569; e-mail tunisnyc@nyc.rr.com; internet www.tunisiaonline.com/tunisia-un/index.html; Permanent Representative OTHMAN JERANDI.

Turkey: 821 United Nations Plaza, 10th Floor, New York, NY 10017; tel. (212) 949-0150; fax (212) 949-0086; e-mail turkey@un.int; internet www.un.int/turkey; Permanent Representative ERTUĞRUL APAKAN.

Turkmenistan: 866 United Nations Plaza, Suite 424, New York, NY 10017; tel. (212) 486-8908; fax (212) 486-2521; e-mail turkmenistan@un.int; internet www.un.int/wcm/content/site/turkmenistan; Permanent Representative Dr AKSOLTAN T. ATAYEVA.

Tuvalu: 800 Second Ave, Suite 400D, New York, NY 10017; tel. (212) 490-0534; fax (212) 808-4975; e-mail tuvalu@onecommonwealth.org; Permanent Representative AFELEE F. PITA.

Uganda: 336 East 45th St, New York, NY 10017; tel. (212) 949-0110; fax (212) 687-4517; e-mail ugandaunny@un.int; internet ugandamissionunny.net; Permanent Representative RUHAKANA RUGUNDA.

Ukraine: 220 East 51st St, New York, NY 10022; tel. (212) 759-7003; fax (212) 355-9455; e-mail uno_us@mfa.gov.ua; internet www.mfa.gov.ua/uno/en; Permanent Representative YURIY A. SERHEYEV.

United Arab Emirates: 3 Dag Hammarskjöld Plaza, 305 East 47th St, 7th Floor, New York, NY 10017; tel. (212) 371-0480; fax (212) 371-4923; e-mail uae@uaemission.com; Permanent Representative AHMED ABDULRAHMAN AL-JERMAN.

United Kingdom: One Dag Hammarskjöld Plaza, 885 Second Ave, New York, NY 10017; tel. (212) 745-9200; fax (212) 745-9316; e-mail uk@un.int; internet ukun.fco.gov.uk/en; Permanent Representative Sir MARK LYALL GRANT.

USA: 140 East 45th St, New York, NY 10017; tel. (212) 415-4000; fax (212) 415-4443; e-mail usa@un.int; internet www.usunnewyork.usmission.gov; Permanent Representative SUSAN RICE.

Uruguay: 866 United Nations Plaza, Suite 322, New York, NY 10017; tel. (212) 752-8240; fax (212) 593-0935; e-mail uruguay@un.int; internet www.un.int/uruguay; Permanent Representative JOSÉ LUIS CANCELA GÓMEZ.

Uzbekistan: 801 Second Ave, 20th Floor, New York, NY 10017; tel. (212) 486-4242; fax (212) 486-7998; e-mail uzbekistan@un.int; internet www.un.int/wcm/content/site/uzbekistan; Permanent Representative MURAD ASKAROV.

Vanuatu: 800 Second Ave, Suite 400B, New York, NY 10017; tel. (212) 661-4303; fax (212) 661-5544; e-mail vanunmis@aol.com; Permanent Representative (vacant).

Venezuela: 335 East 46th St, New York, NY 10017; tel. (212) 557-2055; fax (212) 557-3528; e-mail venezuela@un.int; internet www.un.int/venezuela; Permanent Representative JORGE VALERO BRICEÑO.

Viet Nam: 866 United Nations Plaza, Suite 435, New York, NY 10017; tel. (212) 644-0594; fax (212) 644-5732; e-mail info@vietnam-un.org; internet www.vietnam-un.org; Permanent Representative LE HOAI TRUNG.

Yemen: 413 East 51st St, New York, NY 10022; tel. (212) 355-1730; fax (212) 750-9613; e-mail yemen@un.int; internet www.un.int/yemen; Permanent Representative JAMAL ABDULLAH AL-SALLAL.

Zambia: 237 East 52nd St, New York, NY 10022; tel. (212) 888-5770; fax (212) 888-5213; e-mail zambia@un.int; internet www.un.int/zambia; Permanent Representative MWABA PATRICIA KASESE-BOTA.

Zimbabwe: 128 East 56th St, New York, NY 10022; tel. (212) 980-9511; fax (212) 308-6705; e-mail zimnewyork@gmail.com; Permanent Representative CHITSAKA CHIPAZIWA.

OBSERVERS

Intergovernmental organizations, etc., which have received an invitation to participate in the sessions and the work of the General Assembly as Observers, maintaining permanent offices at the UN:

African Union: 305 East 47th St, 5th Floor, 3 Dag Hammarskjöld Plaza, New York, NY 10017; tel. (212) 319-5490; fax (212) 319-7135; e-mail aumission_ny@yahoo.com; internet www.aumission-ny.org; Permanent Observer TÉTE ANTÓNIO.

Asian-African Legal Consultative Organization: 188 East 76th St, Apt 26B, New York, NY 10021; tel. (917) 623-2861; fax (206) 426-5442; e-mail aalco@un.int; Permanent Observer ROY LEE.

Caribbean Community (CARICOM): 88 Burnett Ave, Maplewood, NJ 07040; tel. (973) 378-9333; fax (973) 327-2671; e-mail caripoun@gmail.com; Permanent Observer NOEL SINCLAIR.

Central American Integration System: 320 West 75th St, Suite 1A, New York, NY 10023; tel. (212) 682-1550; fax (212) 682-2155; e-mail ccampos@sgsica-ny.org; Permanent Observer CARLOS CAMPOS.

Commonwealth Secretariat: 800 Second Ave, 4th Floor, New York, NY 10017; tel. (212) 599-6190; fax (212) 808-4975; e-mail comsec@thecommonwealth.org.

Cooperation Council for the Arab States of the Gulf: One Dag Hammarskjöld Plaza, 885 Second Ave, 40th Floor, New York, NY 10017; tel. (212) 319-3088; fax (212) 319-3434; Permanent Observer ADNAN AHMED ABDULLAH AL-ANSARI.

European Union: 222 East 41st St, 20th Floor, New York, NY 10017; tel. (212) 371-3804; fax (212) 758-2718; e-mail delegation-new-york@ec.europa.eu; internet www.europa-eu-un.org; the Observer is the Permanent Representative to the UN of the country currently exercising the Presidency of the Council of Ministers of the European Union; Head of Delegation THOMAS MAYR-HARTING.

Holy See: 25 East 39th St, New York, NY 10016; tel. (212) 370-7885; fax (212) 370-9622; e-mail office@holyseemission.org; internet www.holyseemission.org; Permanent Observer Most Rev. FRANCIS ASSISI CHULLIKATT (Titular Archbishop of Ostra).

International Committee of the Red Cross: 801 Second Ave, 18th Floor, New York, NY 10017; tel. (212) 599-6021; fax (212) 599-6009; e-mail newyork.nyc@icrc.org; Head of Delegation WALTER A. FÜLLEMANN.

International Criminal Court: 866 United Nations Plaza, Suite 476, New York, NY 10017; tel. (212) 486-1362; fax (212) 486-1361; e-mail liaisonofficeny@icc-cpi.int; Head of Liaison Office KAREN ODABA MOSOTI.

International Criminal Police Organization: One United Nations Plaza, Rm 2610, New York, NY 10017; tel. (917) 367-3463; fax (917) 367-3476; e-mail c.perrin@interpol.int; Special Representative WILLIAM J. S. ELLIOTT (Canada).

International Development Law Organization: 336 East 45th St, New York, NY 10017; tel. (212) 867-9707; fax (212) 867-9717; e-mail pcivili@idlo.int; Permanent Observer PATRIZIO M. CIVILI.

International Federation of Red Cross and Red Crescent Societies: 420 Lexington Ave, Suite 2811, New York, NY 10017; tel. (212) 338-0161; fax (212) 338-9832; e-mail ifrcny@un.int; Head of Delegation and Permanent Observer MARWAN JILANI.

International Institute for Democracy and Electoral Assistance: 336 East 45th St, 14th Floor, New York, NY 10017; tel. (212) 286-1084; fax (212) 286-0260; e-mail unobserver@idea.int; Permanent Observer MASSIMO TOMMASOLI.

International Olympic Committee: 708 Third Ave, 6th Floor, New York, NY 10017; tel. (212) 209-3952; fax (212) 209-7100; e-mail IOC-UNObserver@olympic.org; Permanent Observer MARIO PESCANTE.

International Organization for Migration: 122 East 42nd St, Suite 1610, New York, NY 10168; tel. (212) 681-7000; fax (212) 867-5887; e-mail unobserver@iom.int; Permanent Observer MICHELE KLEIN-SOLOMON.

International Organization of La Francophonie (Organisation Internationale de la Francophonie): 801 Second Ave, Suite 605, New York, NY 10017; tel. (212) 867-6771; fax (212) 867-3840; e-mail francophonie@un.int; Permanent Observer FILIPE SAVADOGO.

International Seabed Authority: One United Nations Plaza, Rm 1140, New York, NY 10017; tel. (212) 963-6470; fax (212) 963-0908; e-mail seaun@un.org; Permanent Observer NII ALLOTEY ODUNTON.

International Trade Union Confederation: 211 East 43rd St, Suite 710, New York, NY 10017, USA; tel. (212) 370-0180; fax (212) 370-0188; e-mail unoffice@ituc-csi.org; Perm. Rep. GEMMA ADABA.

International Tribunal for the Law of the Sea: Two United Nations Plaza, Rm 430, New York, NY 10017; tel. (212) 963-3963; fax (212) 963-5847; Permanent Observer SHUNJI YANAI (Pres. of the Tribunal).

Inter-Parliamentary Union: 220 East 42nd St, Suite 3002, New York, NY 10017; tel. (212) 557-5880; fax (212) 557-3954; e-mail ny-office@mail.ipu.org; Permanent Observer ANDA FILIP.

IUCN (International Union for Conservation of Nature): 801 Second Ave, 13th Floor, New York, NY 10017; tel. (212) 286-1076; fax (212) 286-1079; e-mail iucn@un.int; Permanent Observer NARINDER KAKAR (India).

League of Arab States: 866 United Nations Plaza, Suite 494, New York, NY 10017; tel. (212) 838-8700; fax (212) 355-3909; e-mail arableague@un.int; Permanent Observer (vacant).

Organization of Islamic Cooperation: 320 East 51st St, New York, NY 10022; tel. (212) 883-0140; fax (212) 883-0143; e-mail oicny@un.int; internet www.oicun.org; Permanent Observer UFUK GOKCEN.

Palestine: 115 East 65th St, New York, NY 10021; tel. (212) 288-8500; fax (212) 517-2377; e-mail palestine-observer-mission@un.int; internet www.un.int/palestine; Permanent Observer RIYAD H. MANSOUR.

Partners in Population and Development: 336 East 45th St, 14th Floor, New York, NY 10017; tel. (212) 286-1082; fax (212) 286-0260; e-mail srao@ppdsec.org; Permanent Observer SETHURAMIAH L.N. RAO.

Sovereign Military Order of Malta: 216 East 47th St, 8th Floor, New York, NY 10017; tel. (212) 355-6213; fax (212) 355-4014; e-mail orderofmalta@un.int; Permanent Observer ROBERT L. SHAFER.

University for Peace: 801 Second Ave, 13th Floor, New York, NY 10017; tel. (212) 286-1076; fax (212) 286-1079; e-mail nyinfo@upeace.org; Permanent Observer NARINDER KAKAR (India).

The following intergovernmental organizations have a standing invitation to participate as Observers, but do not maintain permanent offices at the United Nations: African, Caribbean and Pacific Group of States; African Development Bank; Agency for the Prohibition of Nuclear Weapons in Latin America and the Caribbean; Andean Community; Asian Development Bank; Association of Caribbean States; Association of Southeast Asian Nations; Collective Security Treaty Organization; Common Fund for Commodities; Commonwealth of Independent States; Communauté économique des états de l'Afrique centrale; Community of Sahel-Saharan States; Comunidade dos Países de Língua Portuguesa; Conference on Interaction and Confidence-building Measures in Asia; Council of Europe; East African Community; Economic Community of West African States; Economic Cooperation Organization; Energy Charter Conference; Eurasian Development Bank; Eurasian Economic Community; GUAM: Organization for Democracy and Economic Development; Hague Conference on Private International Law; Ibero-American General Secretariat; Global fund to Fight AIDS, Tuberculosis and Malaria; Indian Ocean Commission; Inter-American Development Bank; Intergovernmental Authority on Development; International Centre for Migration Policy Development; International Conference on the Great Lakes Region of Africa; International Fund for Saving the Aral Sea; International Humanitarian Fact-Finding Commission; International Hydrographic Organization; Islamic Development Bank; Italian-Latin American Institute; Latin American Economic System; Latin American Integration Association; Latin American Parliament; OPEC Fund for International Development; Organisation for Economic Co-operation and Development; Organisation of Eastern Caribbean States; Organization for Security and Co-operation in Europe; Organization of American States; Organization of the Black Sea Economic Cooperation; Pacific Islands Forum; Parliamentary Assembly of the Mediterranean; Permanent Court of Arbitration; Regional Centre on Small Arms and Light Weapons in the Great Lakes Region, the Horn of Africa and Bordering States; Shanghai Cooperation Organization; South Asian Association for Regional Cooperation; South Centre; Southern African Development Community; Union of South American Nations; World Customs Organization.

United Nations Information Centres/Services

Algeria: 9A rue Emile Payen, Hydre, Algiers; tel. and fax (21) 48 08 71; fax (21) 69 23 15; e-mail unic.dz@undp.org; internet algiers.unic.org.

Argentina: Junín 1940, 1°, 1113 Buenos Aires; tel. (11) 4803-7671; fax (11) 4804-7545; e-mail unic.buenosaires@unic.org; internet www.unic.org.ar; also covers Uruguay.

Armenia: 375010 Yerevan, 14 Petros Adamian St; tel. (10) 56-02-12; fax (10) 56-14-06; e-mail armineh.haladjian@unic.org; internet www.un.am.

Australia: Level 1, 7 National Circuit, Barton, ACT 2600; tel. (2) 6270-9200; fax (2) 6273-8206; e-mail unic.canberra@unic.org; internet www.un.org.au; also covers Fiji, Kiribati, Nauru, New Zealand, Samoa, Tonga, Tuvalu and Vanuatu.

Austria: POB 500, Vienna International Centre, 1400 Vienna; tel. (1) 26060-4666; fax (1) 26060-5899; e-mail unis@unvienna.org; internet www.unis.unvienna.org; also covers Hungary, Slovakia and Slovenia.

Azerbaijan: 1001 Baku, UN 50th Anniversary St 3; tel. (12) 498-98-88; fax (12) 498-32-35; e-mail dpi@un-az.org; internet azerbaijan.unic.org.

Bahrain: POB 26814, UN House, Bldg 69, Rd 1901, Manama 319; tel. 17311600; fax 17311500; e-mail registry.bh@undp.org; internet www.un.org.bh; also covers Qatar and the United Arab Emirates.

Bangladesh: IDB Bhahan, 8th Floor, Rokeya Sharani Sher-e-Bangla Nagar, Dhaka 1207; tel. (2) 8117868; fax (2) 8112343; e-mail info.unic@undp.org; internet www.unicdhaka.org.

Belarus: 220050 Minsk, vul. Kirova 17, 6th Floor; tel. (17) 227-48-76; fax (17) 226-03-40; e-mail dpi_unit.by@undp.org; internet www.un.by.

Belgium: Residence Palace, rue de la Loi, Quartier Rubens, Block C2, 1040 Brussels; tel. (2) 788-84-84; fax 788-84-85; e-mail info@unric.org; internet www.unric.org.

Bolivia: Calle 14 esq. Sánchez Bustamante, Ed. Metrobol II, Calacoto, La Paz; tel. (2) 2624512; fax (2) 2795820; e-mail unic.lapaz@unic.org; internet www.nu.org.bo.

Brazil: Palacio Itamaraty, Avda Marechal Floriano 196, 20080-002 Rio de Janeiro; tel. (21) 2253-2211; fax (21) 2233-5753; e-mail unic.brazil@unic.org; internet rio.unic.org.

Burkina Faso: BP 135, 14 ave de la Grande Chancellerie, Secteur 4, Ouagadougou; tel. 50-30-60-76; fax 50-31-13-22; e-mail cinu.oui@fasonet.bf; internet ouagadougou.unic.org; also covers Chad, Mali and Niger.

Burundi: BP 2160, ave de la Révolution 117, Bujumbura; tel. (2) 225018; fax (2) 241798; e-mail unicbuj@undp.org; internet bujumbura.unic.org.

Cameroon: PB 836, Immeuble Tchinda, rue 2044, Yaoundé; tel. 221-23-67; fax 221-23-68; e-mail unic.cm@unic.org; internet yaounde.unic.org; also covers the Central African Republic and Gabon.

Chile: Edif. Naciones Unidas, Avda Dag Hammarskjöld, Casilla 179-D, Santiago; tel. (2) 210-2000; fax (2) 228-1947; e-mail dpisantiago@eclac.cl.

Colombia: Calle 100, No. 8A-55, 10°, Edificio World Trade Center, Torre C, Bogotá 2; tel. (1) 257-6044; fax (1) 257-6244; e-mail unic.bogota@unic.org; internet www.nacionesunidas.org.co; also covers Ecuador and Venezuela.

Congo, Democratic Republic: PB 7248, blvd du 30 juin, Kinshasa; tel. 884-5537; fax 884-3675; e-mail unic.kinshasa@undp.org; internet www.undp.org.cd.

Congo, Republic: POB 13210, ave Foch, Case ORTF 15, Brazzaville; tel. 661-20-68; fax 281-27-44; e-mail unic.cg@undp.org; internet brazzaville.unic.org.

Czech Republic: nam. Kinských 6, 150 00 Prague 5; tel. 257199831; fax 257316761; e-mail info@osn.cz; internet www.osn.cz.

Egypt: 1 Osiris St, Garden City, Cairo; tel. (2) 7900022; fax (2) 7953705; e-mail info@unic-eg.org; internet www.unic-eg.org; also covers Saudi Arabia.

Eritrea: Ardinet St, Zone 4, Admin. 07, Asmara; tel. (1) 151166; fax (1) 151081; e-mail dpi.er@undp.org; internet asmara.unic.org.

Ethiopia: POB 3001, Africa Hall, Addis Ababa; tel. (11) 5515826; fax (11) 5510365; e-mail ecainfo@un.org.

Georgia: 0179 Tbilisi, Eristavi St 9; tel. (32) 99-85-58; fax (32) 25-02-71; e-mail uno.tbilisi@unic.org; internet georgia.unic.org.

Ghana: POB GP 2339, Gamel Abdul Nassar/Liberia Rds, Accra; tel. (21) 665511; fax (21) 665578; e-mail unic.ghana@unic.org; internet accra.unic.org; also covers Sierra Leone.

India: 55 Lodi Estate, New Delhi 110 003; tel. (11) 24628877; fax (11) 24620293; e-mail unicindia@unicindia.org; internet www.unic.org.in; also covers Bhutan.

Indonesia: Gedung Surya, 14th Floor, 9 Jalan M. H. Thamrin Kavling, Jakarta 10350; tel. (21) 3983-1011; fax (21) 3983-1014; e-mail unic-jakarta@unic-jakarta.org; internet www.unic-jakarta.org.

Iran: POB 15875-4557; 8 Shahrzad Blvd, Darrous, Tehran; tel. (21) 2287-3837; fax (21) 2287-3395; e-mail unic.tehran@unic.org; internet www.unic-ir.org.

Japan: UNU Bldg, 8th Floor, 53–70 Jingumae 5-chome, Shibuya-ku, Tokyo 150 0001; tel. (3) 5467-4451; fax (3) 5467-4455; e-mail unic@untokyo.jp; internet www.unic.or.jp.

Kazakhstan: 26 Bokei Khan St, 010000 Astana; tel. (717) 259-25-50; fax (717) 259-25-40; e-mail registry.astana.kz@undp.org; internet www.un.kz.

Kenya: POB 30552, United Nations Office, Gigiri, Nairobi; tel. (20) 7623677; fax (20) 7624349; e-mail nairobi.unic@unon.org; internet www.unicnairobi.org; also covers Seychelles and Uganda.

Lebanon: UN House, Riad es-Solh Sq., POB 11-8575, Beirut; tel. (1) 978533; fax (1) 970424; e-mail unic-beirut@un.org; internet www.unicbeirut.org; also covers Jordan, Kuwait and Syria.

Lesotho: POB 301, Maseru 100; tel. (22) 312496; fax (22) 310042; e-mail unic.maseru@unic.org; internet maseru.unic.org.

Liberia: Dubar Bldg, Virginia, Monrovia; tel. 2260195; fax 205407; e-mail registry.1r@undp.org.

Libya: POB 286, Khair Aldeen Baybers St, Hay al-Andalous, Tripoli; tel. (21) 4770251; fax (21) 4777343; e-mail tripoli@un.org; internet tripoli.unic.org.

Madagascar: 159 rue Damantsoa Ankorahotra, Antananarivo; tel. (20) 2233050; fax (20) 2233057; e-mail unic.ant@moov.mg; internet antananarivo.unic.org.

Mexico: Presidente Masaryk 29, 2°, Col. Chapultepec Morales, México 11 570, DF; tel. (55) 5263-9725; fax (55) 5203-8638; e-mail unicmex@un.org.mx; internet www.cinu.org.mx; also covers Cuba and the Dominican Republic.

Morocco: BP 601; rue Tarik ibn Zyad 6, Rabat; tel. (3) 7768633; fax (3) 7768377; e-mail unicmor@unicmor.ma; internet www.unicmor.ma.

Myanmar: 6 Natmauk Rd, Tamwe P.O., Yangon; tel. (1) 546933; fax (1) 542634; e-mail unic.myanmar@undp.org; internet yangon.unic.org.

Namibia: Private Bag 13351, Paratus Bldg, 372 Independence Ave, Windhoek; tel. (61) 233035; fax (61) 233036; e-mail unic@un.na; internet windhoek.unic.org.

Nepal: POB 107, UN House, Kathmandu; tel. (1) 524200; fax (1) 523991; e-mail registry.np@undp.org; internet kathmandu.unic.org.

Nigeria: 17 Alfred Rewane (formerly Kingsway) Rd, Ikoyi, Lagos; tel. (1) 4630915; fax (1) 4630916; e-mail lagos@unic.org; internet lagos.unic.org.

Pakistan: POB 1107, House No. 26, 88th St, G-6/3, Islamabad; tel. (51) 2270610; fax (51) 2271856; e-mail unic.islamabad@unic.org; internet www.unic.org.pk.

Panama: UN House Bldg 128, Ciudad del Saber, Clayton, Panama City; tel. (7) 301-0035; fax (7) 301-0037; e-mail unic.panama@unic.org; internet www.cinup.org.

Paraguay: Casilla de Correo 1107; Edif. Naciones Unidas, Avda Mariscal López, Asunción; tel. (21) 614443; fax (21) 611988; e-mail unic.py@undp.org; internet asuncion.unic.org.

Peru: POB 14-0199, Av. Perez Aranibar 750, Magdalena, Lima 17; tel. (1) 625-9000; e-mail unic.lima@unic.org; internet www.uniclima.org.pe.

Philippines: POB 7285 ADC (DAPO), 1300 Domestic Rd, Pasay City, Metro Manila; tel. (2) 338-5520; fax (2) 338-0177; e-mail unic.manila@unic.org; internet www.unicmanila.org; also covers Papua New Guinea and Solomon Islands.

Poland: Al. Niepodległości 186; 00-608 Warsaw; tel. (22) 8255784; fax (22) 8257706; e-mail unic.poland@unic.org; internet www.unic.un.org.pl.

Romania: 011975 Bucharest, Bd. Primaverii 48A; tel. (21) 201-78-77; fax (21) 201-78-80; e-mail unic.romania@unic.org; internet www.onuinfo.ro.

Russia: 119002 Moscow, per. Glazovskii 4/16; tel. (499) 241-28-94; fax (495) 695-21-38; e-mail dpi-moscow@unic.ru; internet www.unic.ru.

Senegal: Immeuble SOUMEX, 3rd Floor, Mamelles, Almadies, Dakar; tel. 869-99-11; fax 860-51-48; e-mail unicdakar@cinu-dakar.org; internet dakar.unic.org; also covers Cape Verde, Côte d'Ivoire, The Gambia, Guinea-Bissau and Mauritania.

South Africa: Metro Park Bldg, 351 Schoemann St, POB 12677, Pretoria 0126; tel. (12) 354-8506; fax (12) 354-8501; e-mail unic.pretoria@unic.org; internet pretoria.unic.org.

Sri Lanka: POB 1505, 202/204 Bauddhaloka Mawatha, Colombo 7; tel. (11) 2580691; fax (11) 2501396; e-mail unic.lk@undp.org; internet colombo.unic.org.

Sudan: POB 1992, UN Compound, House No. 7, Blk 5, Gamma'a Ave, Khartoum; tel. (183) 773121; fax (183) 773772; e-mail unic.sd@undp.org; internet khartoum.unic.org; also covers Somalia.

Switzerland: Palais des Nations, 1211 Geneva 10; tel. 229172302; fax 229170030; e-mail press_geneva@unog.ch; internet www.unog.ch.

Tanzania: POB 9224, Msimbazi Creek Housing Estate Ltd, King's Way, Mafinga St, Plot 134/140, Kinondoni, Dar es Salaam; tel. (22) 2199326; fax (22) 2667633; e-mail unic.daressalaam@unic.org; internet daressalaam.unic.org.

Thailand: ESCAP, United Nations Bldg, Rajadamnern Nok Ave, Bangkok 10200; tel. (2) 288-1234; fax (2) 288-1000; e-mail unisbkk.unescap@un.org; internet www.unescap.org/unis; also covers Cambodia, Laos, Malaysia, Singapore and Viet Nam.

Togo: 468 angle rue Atimé et ave de la Libération, Lomé; tel. and fax 221-23-06; e-mail cinutogo@cafe.tg; internet lome.unic.org; also covers Benin.

Trinidad and Tobago: 2nd Floor, Bretton Hall, 16 Victoria Ave, Port of Spain; tel. 623-4813; fax 623-4332; e-mail unic.portofspain@unic.org; internet www.unicpos.org.tt; also covers Antigua and Barbuda, Aruba, the Bahamas, Barbados, Belize, Dominica, Grenada, Guyana, Jamaica, the Netherlands Antilles, Saint Christopher and Nevis, Saint Lucia, Saint Vincent and the Grenadines, and Suriname.

Tunisia: BP 863, 41 ave Louis Braille, Tunis; tel. (71) 902-203; fax (71) 906-811; e-mail unic.tunis@unic.org; internet www.unictunis.org.tn.

Turkey: PK 407, Birlik Mahallesi, 2 Cad. No. 11, 06610 Cankaya, Ankara; tel. (312) 4541052; fax (312) 4961499; e-mail unic.ankara@unic.org; internet www.unicankara.org.tr.

Ukraine: 01021 Kyiv, Klovsky uzviz, 1; tel. (44) 253-93-63; fax (44) 253-26-07; e-mail registry@un.org.ua; internet www.un.org.ua.

USA: 1775 K St, NW, Suite 400, Washington, DC 20006; tel. (202) 331-8670; fax (202) 331-9191; e-mail unicdc@unicwash.org; internet www.unicwash.org.

Uzbekistan: 100029 Tashkent, Shevchenko ko'ch 4; tel. (71) 120-34-50; fax (71) 120-34-85; e-mail registry@undp.org; internet www.un.uz.

Western Europe: United Nations Regional Information Centre, Residence Palace, Bloc C, Level 7, 155 rue de la Loi/Wetstraat, 1040 Brussels, Belgium; tel. (2) 788-84-84; fax (2) 788-84-85; e-mail info@unric.org; internet www.unric.org; serves Belgium, Cyprus, Denmark, Finland, France, Germany, Greece, The Holy See, Iceland, Ireland, Italy, Luxembourg, Malta, Monaco, the Netherlands, Norway, Portugal, San Marino, Spain, Sweden, United Kingdom; also provides liaison with the institutions of the European Union.

Yemen: POB 237; St 5, off Al-Boniya St, Handhal Zone, San'a; tel. (1) 274000; fax (1) 274043; e-mail unicyem@y.net.ye; internet www.unicyem.org.

Zambia: POB 32905, Revenue House, Ground Floor, Cairo Rd (Northend), Lusaka; tel. (21) 1228478; fax (21) 1222958; e-mail unic.lusaka@unic.org; internet lusaka.unic.org; also covers Botswana, Malawi and Swaziland.

Zimbabwe: POB 4408, Sanders House, 2nd Floor, First St/Jason Moyo Ave, Harare; tel. (4) 777047; fax (4) 750476; e-mail unic.harare@unic.org; internet harare.unic.org.

Conferences

Global conferences are convened regularly by the United Nations. Special sessions of the General Assembly assess progress achieved in the implementation of conference action plans. The following global conferences were scheduled for 2012:

Conference on Disarmament (Jan.–March, May–June, July–Sept.: Geneva, Switzerland);

High-level Dialogue on Financing for Development (March: New York, USA);

UN Conference on Sustainable Development (UNCSD) (Rio+20) (June: Rio de Janeiro, Brazil);

UN Conference on the Arms Trade Treaty (July: New York, USA);

World Urban Forum-6 (Sept.: Naples, Italy);

ICAO high-level global aviation security conference (Sept.: Montreal, Canada);

UN Climate Change Conference (Nov.–Dec.: Qatar, with support from the Republic of Korea).

System-wide Coherence

The Senior Management Group, a committee of senior UN personnel established in 1997, acts as the Secretary-General's cabinet and as the central policy-planning body of the United Nations. The 28-member UN System Chief Executives Board for Co-ordination—CEB, convenes at least twice a year under the chairmanship of the Secretary-General to co-ordinate UN system-wide policies, activities and management issues. The UN Development Group (UNDG) unites, under the chairmanship of the Administrator of UNDP, the heads of some 32 UN funds, programmes and departments concerned with sustainable development, in order to promote coherent policy at country level. The UNDG is supported by the UN Development Operations Coordination Office (DOCO). Several inter-agency mechanisms, including UN-Energy, UN-Oceans and UN-Water, facilitate UN system-wide inter-agency co-operation and coherence. Project management services are provided throughout the UN system of entities and organizations, as well as to certain bilateral donors, international financial institutions and governments, by the United Nations Office for Project Services—UNOPS. UNOPS, founded in 1995 and a member of the UNDG, is self-financing, funded by fees earned from the services that it provides. The Inter-Agency Standing Committee—IASC, founded in 1992, comprises the executive heads of 17 leading UN and other agencies and NGO consortia, who convene at least twice a year under the leadership of the Emergency Relief Co-ordinator (see OCHA). It co-ordinates and administers the international response to complex and major humanitarian disasters, and the development of relevant policies.

In February 2005 the Secretary-General appointed a High-level Panel on United Nations System-wide Coherence in the Areas of Development, Humanitarian Assistance and the Environment, to study means of strengthening UN performance; in November the Panel published a report entitled *Ten ways for the UN to 'deliver as one'*, outlining the following 10 recommendations for future inter-agency co-operation: (i) the UN should 'deliver as one' at country level, with one leader, one programme, one budget and, where appropriate, one office; (ii) a UN Sustainable Development Board should be established to oversee the One UN Country Programme; (iii) a Global Leaders' Forum should be established within ECOSOC to upgrade its policy co-ordination role in economic, social and related issues; (iv) the UN Secretary-General, the President of the World Bank and the Executive Director of the IMF should initiate a process to review, update and conclude formal agreements on their respective roles and relations at the global and country levels; (v) a Millennium Development Goal (MDG) funding mechanism should be established to provide multi-year funding for the One UN Country Programme; (vi) the UN's leading role in humanitarian disasters and transition from relief to development should be enhanced; (vii) international environmental governance should be strengthened and made more coherent in order to improve effectiveness and targeted action of environmental activities in the UN system; (viii) a dynamic UN entity focused on gender equality and women's empowerment should be established; (ix) a UN common evaluation system should be established, while other business practices, such as human resource polices, planning and results-based management, should be upgraded and harmonized across the UN system to stimulate improved performance; and (x) the Secretary-General should establish an independent task force to eliminate further duplication within the UN system and, where necessary, to consolidate UN entities. In 2007 a *Delivering as One* pilot initiative was launched to test enhanced co-ordination in the provision of development assistance, based on the principles of one leader, one budget, one programme, and one office, in eight volunteer countries: Albania, Cape Verde, Mozambique, Pakistan, Rwanda, Tanzania, Uruguay, and Viet Nam. The CEB has established an action framework for co-ordinating system-wide activities to address climate change under the *Delivering as One* commitment. An Evaluation Management Group (EMG) was appointed by the Secretary-General in February 2011 to assess lessons learnt hitherto from the *Delivering as One* initiative. In January 2012 the Secretary-General announced a second generation of inter-agency *Delivering as One* co-operation, with a focus on enhanced monitoring of results and accountability.

In April 2009, having undertaken—under the chairmanship of the Director-General of the ILO—a comprehensive review of the challenges confronting the international community in view of the then developing global economic crisis, the CEB endorsed nine Joint Crisis Initiatives (JCIs), built upon the *Delivering as One* commitment and aimed at alleviating the impact of the economic situation and building a fair and inclusive globalization, allowing for sustainable economic, social and environmental development. The initiatives—led by one or more CEB participating agency, with the voluntary participation of others as co-operating organizations—were as follows: i) additional financing for the most vulnerable, to be implemented through the development of a joint World Bank-UN system mechanism, including through the Vulnerability Fund proposed in early 2009 by the World Bank; led by UNDP and the World Bank; ii) ensuring food security by strengthening feeding programmes and expanding support to farmers in developing countries; led by FAO, WFP and IFAD; iii) promoting trade, through combating protectionism, including through the conclusion of the Doha round, and through strengthening aid-for-trade financing-for-trade initiatives; led by UNCTAD and WTO; iv) a new Green Economy Initiative aimed at promoting investment in long-term environmental sustainability; led by UNEP; v) a new Global Jobs Pact; led by ILO; vi) a new Social Protection Floor, ensuring access to basic social services, shelter, and empowerment and protection of the most vulnerable; led by ILO and WHO; vii) emergency activities to meet humanitarian needs and promote security; led by WFP; viii) technology and innovation; led by ITU, UNIDO and WIPO; and ix) strengthening monitoring and analysis surveillance, and implementing an effective early warning system; led by IMF and the UN Department of Social and Economic Affairs.

CO-ORDINATING AND INTER-AGENCY BODIES

UN System Chief Executives Board for Co-ordination (CEB): CEB Secretariat (Geneva), Rm c551, UN Geneva Office, Palais des Nations, 1211 Geneva 10, Switzerland; tel. 2291071234; fax 229170123; CEB Secretariat (New York), United Nations, New York, NY 10017, USA; tel. (212) 963-1234; fax (212) 963-4879; internet www.unsceb.org; f. 1946 as the Administrative Committee on Co-ordination, present name adopted in 2001; meets at least twice a year under the chairmanship of the UN Sec.-Gen. to co-ordinate UN system-wide policies, management issues and activities; supported by the High-Level Committee on Programmes (HLCP), concerned with global policy and issues; by the High-Level Committee on Management (HLCM), concerned with co-ordinating activities across the UN system; and by the UN Development Group (UNDG) (see below); thematic areas of interest in 2012 include: Africa; business practices; climate change; conflict prevention;

gender mainstreaming; the global financial and economic crisis, and related Joint Crisis Initiatives; International Public Sector Accounting Standards (IPSAs), which are being adopted system-wide; knowledge-sharing; the MDGs; science and technology; security and safety of staff; and system-wide coherence; mems: heads of 27 UN agencies and of WTO; Sec. THOMAS STELZER (Austria).

UN Development Operations Co-ordination Office (DOCO): One United Nations Plaza, DC1-1600, New York, NY 10017, USA; tel. (212) 906-5500; fax (212) 906-3609; tel. www.undg.org; f. 1997, to support the UNDG, which unites, under the chairmanship of the Administrator of UNDP, the heads of some 32 UN funds, programmes and departments concerned with sustainable development, in order to promote coherent policy at country level; the DOCO supports UN orgs in delivering coherent, efficient support at country level; the Office supports and strengthens the Resident Co-ordinator system, through funding, policy guidance and training; administers the UN Country Co-ordination Fund, which provides resources to Resident Co-ordinators; assists the UNDG with developing simplified and harmonized policies in areas such as ICT, human resources, procurement, and financial affairs; targets tailored support to Resident Co-ordinator offices and UN country teams (UNCTs) operating in transition countries; sends specialist help teams to conduct post-conflict needs assessments; provides technical support for the work of the UNDG; Dir DEBBIE LANDEY (Canada).

UN-Energy: UN Energy Secretariat, c/o UN Department of Economic and Social Affairs, Two United Nations Plaza, New York, NY 10017, USA; internet www.un-energy.org; f. 2002; established following the 2002 World Summit on Sustainable Development (WSSD), held in Johannesburg, South Africa, as a mechanism to promote coherence among UN agencies in energy matters, and to develop increased collective engagement between UN agencies and key external stakeholders; it aims to increase information-sharing, to promote and facilitate joint programming, and to develop action-oriented approaches to co-ordination; focal areas of activity include energy access, renewable energy, and energy efficiency; the sub-programme UN-Energy Africa (UNEA) was established in May 2004, by a meeting of African ministers responsible for energy affairs; UNEA is the principal inter-agency mechanism in the field of energy within Africa; Chair. KANDEH K. YUMKELLA (Sierra Leone).

UN-Oceans: UN-Oceans Secretariat, c/o UNDP Water and Ocean Governance Programme, One United Nations Plaza, New York, NY 10017, USA; tel. (212) 906-5300; e-mail Andrew.Hudson@undp.org; internet www.unoceans.org; f. 2003; has task forces on Marine Biodiversity beyond National Jurisdiction; on Establishing a Regular Process for Global Assessment of the Marine Environment; on Global Partnership for Climate, Fisheries and Aquaculture; and on Marine Protected Areas and Other Area-Based Management Tools; inter-agency activities in 2012 include updating the *UN Atlas of the Oceans*, an internet-based information system for policy makers and scientists, accessible at www.oceansatlas.org/index.jsp; implementing the Programme of Action for the Protection of the Marine Environment; undertaking the 'Assessment of Assessments' (AoA), under the co-leadership of UNEP and UNESCO/IOC; the International Coral Reef Initiative (ICRI); the Joint Group of Experts on the Scientific Aspects of Marine Environmental Protection (GESAMP); the Global Ocean Observing System (led by UNESCO/IOC); the Global Climate Observing System (led by WMO); organizing World Oceans Day, held annually on 8 June; and developing the International Waters focal area under the Global Environment Facility; UN-Ocean's Secretariat rotates between hosts, 2010–12: UNDP; Co-ordinator Dr ANDREW HUDSON.

UN-Water: UN-Water Secretariat, Rm 2250, c/o UN Department of Economic and Social Affairs, Two United Nations Plaza, New York, NY 10017, USA; fax (212) 963-4340; e-mail unwater@un.org; internet www.unwater.org; f. 2003 as an inter-agency mechanism to foster greater co-operation and information-sharing among UN agencies and other partners on water-related issues; specific agencies host activities and programmes on behalf of UN-Water, which is not itself an implementing body; senior programme managers from UN-Water member agencies meet twice a year, and an elected Exec. Head (upgraded from Chairperson in Feb. 2012), who, with a deputy, is selected every two years on a rotating basis, oversee the larger work programme and represent UN-Water at international conferences and at other fora; a permanent Secretariat, hosted by the UN Department for Economic and Social Affairs in New York, provides administrative, technical and logistical support; UN-Water collaborates closely with the UN Sec.-Gen.'s Advisory Board on Water and Sanitation; through the provision of information, building a knowledge base, and providing a platform, UN-Water aims to strengthen co-ordination and coherence among UN entities concerned with all aspects of freshwater and sanitation, including surface and groundwater resources, the interface between freshwater and seawater, and water-related disasters; mandated to promote regional inter-agency networking arrangements (in 2012 UN-Water Africa was operational); appoints task forces with a focus on specific areas of interest, such as: indicators, monitoring and reporting; gender and water; sanitation; transboundary waters; climate change and water; and country-level co-ordination; conducts four specific programmes: the World Water Assessment Programme (WWAP), which is hosted and led by UNESCO, and synthesizes data and information, and issues triennial *World Water Development Reports*, comprehensively reviewing the state of the world's freshwater resources; the WHO / UNICEF Joint Monitoring Programme on Water Supply and Sanitation (JMP), established by WHO and UNICEF in 1990, and acting as the official mechanism of the UN mandated to monitor global progress towards achieving the MDG targets for drinking-water and sanitation, issuing regular *Joint Monitoring Programme on Water Supply and Sanitation* reports; and, in support of the International Decade for Action Water for Life 2005–15: the UN-Water Decade Programme on Capacity Development (UNW-DPC), launched in 2007, and hosted by the UN University, in Bonn, Germany; and the UN-Water Decade Programme on Advocacy and Communication (UNW-DPAC), based in Zaragoza, Spain, and also launched in 2007, which aims to develop communication campaigns on the benefits of sound water management for poverty reduction, and to advocate for actions to implement effective water policies; UN-Water monitors and reports on progress achieved towards reaching internationally agreed water and sanitation targets, with a particular focus on the targets set by the MDGs and by the 2002 World Summit on Sustainable Development; Exec. Head MICHEL JARRAUD (France) (Sec.-Gen. of WMO); Sec. KENZA KAOUAKIB-ROBINSON.

Finance

UN member states pay assessed contributions towards the regular budget, towards peace-keeping operations, to international tribunals, and to the Capital Master Plan (which manages renovation works at UN headquarters in New York, USA).

Since the late 1990s the UN has suffered financial difficulties, owing to an expansion of the organization's political and humanitarian activities and delay on the part of member states in paying their contributions. In 1993 the UN Secretary-General formulated a series of economy measures to be applied throughout the organization, in order to avert a financial crisis. However, the fragility of the UN's financial situation has persisted, partly owing to delays in the process between approval of a peace-keeping operation and receipt of contributions for that budget. In December 1997 a UN Development Account was established to channel administrative savings achieved as a result of reforms to the UN's administrative structure towards financing development projects. In December 2000 the General Assembly approved a restructuring of scale of assessment calculations, the methodology and accuracy of which had been contested in recent years, particularly by the USA. From 2001 the level of US contributions to the regular annual budget was reduced from 25% to 22%, while annual contributions were raised for several nations with rapidly developing economies. The USA contributes 27% of the UN peace-keeping budget. At 5 October 2011 134 member states had paid their regular budget assessments for 2011 in full, while some US $867m. remained outstanding in unpaid regular budget assessments. In addition, many member states owed outstanding assessment contributions to the peace-keeping and international tribunal budgets at that time. It was announced in early 2011 that the USA had reduced by one-third the level of its outstanding assessment contributions at end-2010.

In 1997 a US business executive, Ted Turner, announced a donation of US $1,000m. to finance UN humanitarian and environmental causes. The donation has been paid in instalments and administered through his 'UN Foundation', and a UN Fund for International Partnerships (UNFIP) was established by the UN Secretary-General in 1998 to facilitate relations between the UN system and the UN Foundation. The Foundation, which is also sustained by resources from other partners and by grassroots donors, supports the UN through advocacy, grant-making, and the implementation of public-private partnerships.

In December 2011 the UN Secretary-General approved a proposed regular budget of US $5,152.3m. for the two-year period 2012–13. Initiatives provided for under the 2012–13 budget, with the aim of reducing organizational costs, included the introduction of salary freezes for administrative staff; the initiation of reforms to the 'recosting' process (whereby, hitherto, additional funding had been sought after the announcement of budgeted expenditure, in order to offset variances caused by exchange rates and inflation); the development of advanced transparency efforts, including public coverage (via webcast) of all formal committee meetings; and the strengthening of oversight and accountability capabilities.

PROPOSED TWO-YEAR BUDGET OF THE UNITED NATIONS
(US $'000)

	2012–13
Overall policy-making, direction and co-ordination	721,788.3
Political affairs	1,333,849.3
International justice and law	93,155.1
International co-operation for development	436,635.7
Regional co-operation for development	532,892.3
Human rights and humanitarian affairs	326,574.2
Public information	176,092.1
Common support services	600,210.0
Internal oversight	38,254.2
Jointly financed activities and special expenses	131,219.1
Capital expenditures	64,886.9
Safety and security	213,412.4
Development Account	29,243.2
Staff Assessment	451,086.8
Total	5,152,299.6

United Nations Publications

Demographic Yearbook.
Index to Proceedings (of the General Assembly; the Security Council; the Economic and Social Council; the Trusteeship Council).
International Law Catalogue.
Monthly Bulletin of Statistics.
Population and Vital Statistics Report (quarterly).
Statement of Treaties and International Agreements (monthly).
Statistical Yearbook.
UN Chronicle (quarterly).
United Nations Disarmament Yearbook.
United Nations Juridical Yearbook.
World Economic and Social Survey.
World Situation and Prospects.
World Statistics Pocketbook.
Yearbook of the United Nations.

Other UN publications are listed in the chapters dealing with the agencies concerned.

Secretariat

According to the UN Charter the Secretary-General is the chief administrative officer of the organization, and he/she may appoint further Secretariat staff as required. The principal departments and officers of the Secretariat are listed below. The chief administrative staff of the UN Regional Commissions and of all the subsidiary organs of the UN are also members of the Secretariat staff and are listed in the appropriate chapters. The Secretariat staff also includes a number of special missions and special appointments, including some of senior rank.

The Secretary-General chairs the Senior Management Group (SMG), a committee of senior UN personnel that acts as a cabinet and as the central policy-planning body of the UN. Two subsidiary committees of the SMG, the Policy Committee and the Management Committee, were inaugurated in 2005 to enhance the efficiency of high-level decision-making.

The Secretariat comprises about 15,000 staff holding appointments continuing for a year or more, but excluding staff working for the UN specialized agencies and subsidiary organs.

In July 1997 the Secretary-General initiated a comprehensive reform of the administration of the UN and abolished some 1,000 Secretariat posts. The reforms aimed to restructure the Secretariat's substantive work programme around the UN's five core missions, i.e. peace and security, economic and social affairs, development co-operation, humanitarian affairs and human rights. During 1997 the Centre for Human Rights and the Office of the High Commissioner for Human Rights were consolidated into a single office under the reform process, while a new Office for Drug Control and Crime Prevention was established, within the framework of the UN Office in Vienna, to integrate efforts to combat crime, drug abuse and terrorism; this was subsequently renamed the UN Office on Drugs and Crime. In December a new post of Deputy Secretary-General was created to assist in the management of Secretariat operations, in particular the ongoing reform process, and represent the Secretary-General as required.

In July 2000 the UN Secretary-General launched the Global Compact, a voluntary initiative comprising leaders in the fields of business, labour and civil society who have undertaken to promote human rights, the fundamental principles of the ILO, and protection of the environment; the Global Compact is administered from the Global Compact Office, in the Executive Office of the Secretary-General. In December 2001, on the recommendation of the Secretary-General, the General Assembly established the Office of the High Representative for the Least Developed Countries, Landlocked Developing Countries and Small Island Developing States. In May 2002 the Secretary-General appointed the first United Nations Security Co-ordinator. A new Department for Safety and Security, headed by an Under-Secretary-General for Safety and Security and replacing the Office of the United Nations Security Co-ordinator, was established in February 2005, taking over responsibility for the safety of UN personnel.

In June 2004 a Panel of Eminent Persons on Civil Society and UN Relationships—appointed by the Secretary-General in February 2003, as part of the ongoing UN reform process, with a mandate to explore and make recommendations on the interaction between civil society, private sector enterprise, parliaments and the UN—issued its final report. A High-Level Panel on Threats, Challenges and Change was appointed by the Secretary-General in November 2003 (in the aftermath of the deaths in August of 21 UN staff members, including Sergio Vieira de Mello, UN High Commissioner for Human Rights, in a terrorist attack in Baghdad, Iraq): it was to evaluate the ability of the UN to address threats to the peace and security of the international community, and to recommend relevant policy and institutional changes, including reforms to the Security Council; the Panel published its findings in December 2004. The report of the Secretary-General entitled 'In Larger Freedom: Towards Development, Security and Human Rights for All', issued in March 2005 after consideration of the High-Level Panel's report, proposed a realignment of the Secretariat's structure, entailing the establishment of a peace-building support office and strengthening support within the body for mediation by the Secretary-General (his 'good offices'), democracy, and the rule of law. He also determined to establish a cabinet-style decision-making executive within the Secretariat, supported by a small subsidiary cabinet secretariat, and proposed a higher level of managerial authority for the role of Secretary-General. Further proposals included the appointment of a Scientific Adviser to the Secretary-General, mandated to supply strategic scientific advice on policy matters, and a comprehensive review of the functioning of the Office of Internal Oversight Services. The Secretary-General's reform proposals were reviewed by the World Summit of UN heads of state held in September (see General Assembly). In December an Ethics Office responsible for applying a uniform set of ethical standards was established within the Secretariat. From January 2008 the UN ethical code was extended to cover employees of all UN funds and programmes. In March 2006 the Secretary-General issued a report entitled 'Investing in the United Nations' in which he outlined proposals to strengthen the role of the Secretariat through a realignment of staff skills, involving relocating personnel and core practices away from headquarters; increasing management accountability and introducing a single comprehensive annual report of the Secretariat's activities; upgrading information technology capabilities; and streamlining the budget. In July 2007 a new Department of Field Support was established within the Secretariat to provide expert administrative and logistical support for UN peace-keeping operations in the field.

In February 2005 the Secretary-General appointed a High-level Panel on United Nations System-wide Coherence in the Areas of Development, Humanitarian Assistance and the Environment, to study means of strengthening UN performance, and, in November, the Panel published a report entitled *Ten ways for the UN to 'deliver as one'*, outlining 10 recommendations for future inter-agency co-operation. In February 2011 the Secretary-General appointed an Evaluation Management Group (EMG) to assess lessons learnt from the *Delivering as One* initiative.

In February 2006 the Secretary-General inaugurated an Internet Governance Forum, with a secretariat hosted by the UN Geneva Office, to pursue the objectives of the World Summit on the Information Society. The Forum incorporates a Multi-stakeholder Advisory Group which meets three times a year.

In 2007 the UN Secretary-General established a Millennium Development Goal Gap Task Force, which was to track, systematically and at both international and country level, existing international commitments in the areas of official development assistance, market access, debt relief, access to essential medicines and technology. The Task Force, led by the UN Department of Economic and Social Affairs and by UNDP, includes more than 20 UN agencies, and also OECD and WTO.

The UN Secretariat and the Iraqi Government jointly chair the International Compact for Iraq, a five-year framework for co-operation between Iraq and the international community that was launched in May 2007.

In April 2008 the Secretary-General announced that he was to chair a new High Level Task Force (HLTF) on the Global Food Security Crisis, comprising the heads of UN bodies and experts from the UN and the wider international community. The HLTF was to address the impact of soaring global levels of food and fuel prices and formulate a comprehensive framework for action, with a view to preventing the escalation of widespread hunger, malnutrition and related social unrest. The Department of Economic and Social Affairs, with the IMF, leads an initiative to strengthen monitoring and analysis surveillance, and to implement an effective warning system, one of nine Joint Crisis Initiatives that were endorsed in April 2009 by the UN System Chief Executives Board for Co-ordination (CEB), with the aim of alleviating the impact of the global economic and financial crisis on poor and vulnerable populations.

In May 2011 the UN Secretary-General appointed Atul Khare, hitherto Assistant Secretary-General for Peace-keeping Operations, as head of a new Change Management Team (CMT), which was to guide an agenda for further reform of the UN, commencing with the formulation of a comprehensive plan to streamline processes, increase accountability and improve the efficiency of the delivery of its mandates.

In September 2011, at the annual Private Sector Forum, organized by the UN Global Compact, with UNIDO and UN-Energy, at the UN General Assembly, in New York, the UN Secretary-General launched a new initiative, Sustainable Energy for All by 2030, and a high-level group responsible for its implementation. The initiative aimed to meet three interlinked global targets: universal access to modern energy services; doubling energy efficiency; and doubling the share of renewable energy in world's energy supply. The year 2012 was designated by the General Assembly as International Year of Sustainable Energy for All.

In January 2012, at the commencement of his second five-year term of office, covering the period 2012–16, Ban Ki-Moon announced a five-year agenda for action with the following priority areas of activity: sustainable development; prevention in the areas of natural disaster risk reduction, violent conflict, and human rights abuses; building a more secure world; supporting nations in transition; working with and for women and young people; enhancing system-wide partnership; and strengthening the UN. The agenda envisaged a second generation of inter-agency *Delivering as One* co-operation, focusing on enhanced monitoring of results and accountability.

Secretary-General: BAN KI-MOON (Republic of Korea).

Deputy Secretary-General: Dr ASHA-ROSE MTENGETI MIGIRO (Tanzania) (until 30 June 2012), JAN ELIASSON (Sweden) (designate).

OFFICES AND DEPARTMENTS OF THE SECRETARIAT

Executive Office of the Secretary-General

Under-Secretary-General, Chef de Cabinet: SUSANA MALCORRA (Argentina).

Deputy Chef de Cabinet, Assistant Secretary-General: (vacant).

Spokesperson for the Secretary-General: MARTIN NESIRKY (France).

Executive Director of the Global Compact: GEORG KELL (Germany).

Assistant Secretary-General for Planning and Policy Co-ordination: (vacant).

Assistant Secretary-General, Chief Information Technology Officer: CHOI SOON-HONG.

Department for Disarmament Affairs

Under-Secretary-General: ANGELA KANE (Germany).

Department for Safety and Security

Under-Secretary-General: GREGORY B. STARR (USA).

Assistant Under-Secretary-General: MBARANGA GASARABWE (Rwanda).

Department of Economic and Social Affairs

Under-Secretary-General: SHA ZUKANG (People's Republic of China).

Under-Secretary-General for Gender Equality and the Advancement of Women: MICHELLE BACHELET (Chile).

Assistant Secretary-General for Intergovernmental Support and Strategic Partnerships at UN Women: LAKSHMI PURI (India).

Assistant Secretary-General for Policy and Programmes at UN Women: JOHN HENDRA (Canada).

Assistant Secretary-General, Economic Development: KWAME SUNDARAM JOMO (Malaysia).

Assistant Secretary-General, Policy Co-ordination and Inter-Agency Affairs: THOMAS STELZER (Austria).

Department of Field Support

Under-Secretary-General: AMEERAH HAQ (Bangladesh) (designate).

Assistant Secretary-General: ANTHONY BANBURY (USA).

Department of General Assembly and Conference Management

Under-Secretary-General: MUHAMMAD SHAABAN (Egypt), YUKIO TAKASU (Japan) (designate).

Assistant Secretary-General for General Assembly Affairs and Conference Management: FRANZ BAUMANN (Germany).

Assistant Secretary-General for Programme Planning, Budget and Accounts: MARIA EUGENIA CASAR PEREZ (Mexico).

Department of Management

Under-Secretary-General: ANGELA KANE (Germany).

Assistant Secretary-General, Central Support Services: WARREN SACH (United Kingdom).

Assistance Secretary-General, Controller: MARÍA EUGENIA CASAR (Mexico).

Assistant Secretary-General, Human Resources Management: CATHERINE POLLARD (Guyana).

Department of Peace-keeping Operations

Under-Secretary-General: HERVÉ LADSOUS (France).

Assistant Secretary-General: EDMOND MULET (Guatemala).

Assistant Secretary-General, Military Adviser for Peace-keeping Operations: Lt-Gen. BABACAR GAYE (Senegal).

Assistant Secretary-General, Rule of Law and Security Institutions: DMITRY TITOV (Russia).

Department of Political Affairs

Under-Secretary-General: B. LYNN PASCOE (USA).

Assistant Secretary-General: TAYÉ-BROOK ZERIHOUN (Ethiopia).

Assistant Secretary-General: OSCAR FERNANDEZ-TARANCO (Argentina).

Department of Public Information

Under-Secretary-General: KIYOTAKA AKASAKA (Japan).

Office for the Co-ordination of Humanitarian Affairs

Under-Secretary-General for Humanitarian Affairs and Emergency Relief Co-ordinator: VALERIE AMOS (United Kingdom).

Deputy Emergency Relief Co-ordinator and Assistant Secretary-General for Humanitarian Affairs: CATHERINE BRAGG (Canada).

Office of Internal Oversight Services

Under-Secretary-General: CARMEN L. LAPOINTE (Canada).

Assistant Secretary-General: DAVID MUCHOKO KANJA (Kenya) (designate).

Office of Legal Affairs

Under-Secretary-General, The Legal Counsel: PATRICIA O'BRIEN (Ireland).

Assistant Secretary-General, Legal Affairs: D. STEPHEN MATHIAS (USA).

Office of the Capital Master Plan

Assistant Secretary-General, Executive Director of the Office of the Capital Master Plan: MICHAEL ADLERSTEIN (USA).

Assistant Secretary-General, Legal Affairs: D. STEPHEN MATHIAS (USA).

Office of the High Representative for the Least Developed Countries, Landlocked Developing Countries and Small Island Developing States

Under-Secretary-General and High Representative, and Special Adviser on Africa: CHEICK SIDI DIARRA (Mali).

Office of the Special Representative of the Secretary-General for Children and Armed Conflict

Under-Secretary-General and Special Representative: RADHIKA COOMARASWAMY (Sri Lanka).

Office of the United Nations High Commissioner for Human Rights

Palais des Nations, 1211 Geneva 10, Switzerland; tel. 229179000; fax 229179010; internet www.unhchr.ch.

High Commissioner: NAVANETHEM PILLAY (South Africa).

Deputy High Commissioner: KYUNG-WHA KANG (Republic of Korea).

Assistant Secretary-General: IVAN ŠIMONOVIC (Croatia).

Office on Drugs and Crime

Under-Secretary-General: YURI FEDOTOV (Russia).

Peace-building Support Office

Assistant Secretary-General: JUDY CHENG-HOPKINS (Malaysia).

UN Ombudsperson and Mediation Services

Assistant Secretary-General, UN Ombudsman: JOHNSTONE BARKAT (USA).

Geneva Office

Palais des Nations, 1211 Geneva 10, Switzerland; tel. 2291071234; fax 229170123; internet www.unog.ch.

Director-General: KASSYM-JOMART TOKAYEV (Kazakhstan).

Nairobi Office

POB 30552, Nairobi, Kenya; tel. (20) 7621234.

Director-General and Under-Secretary-General: SAHLE-WORK ZEWDE (Ethiopia).

Vienna Office

Vienna International Centre, POB 500, 1400 Vienna, Austria; tel. (1) 26060; fax (1) 263-3389; internet www.unvienna.org.

Director-General: YURI FEDOTOV (Russia).

SPECIAL HIGH LEVEL APPOINTMENTS OF THE UN SECRETARY-GENERAL

Special Advisers

Special Adviser: JOSEPH V. REED (USA).

Special Adviser: RIZA IQBAL (Pakistan).

Special Adviser: EDWARD LUCK (USA).

Special Adviser and Mediator in the Border Dispute between Equatorial Guinea and Gabon: NICOLAS MICHEL (Switzerland).

Special Adviser on Africa: MAGED ABDELAZIZ (Egypt).

Special Adviser on Cyprus: ALEXANDER DOWNER (Australia).

Special Adviser on Human Security: YUKIO TAKASU (Japan).

Special Adviser on Innovative Financing for Development: PHILIPPE DOUSTE-BLAZY (France).

Special Adviser on Internet Governance: NITIN DESAI (India).

Special Adviser on Myanmar: VIJAY NAMBIAR (India).

Special Adviser on the International Compact with Iraq and Other Political Issues: IBRAHIM GAMBARI (Nigeria).

Special Adviser on Sport for Development and Peace: WIFRIED LEMKE (Germany).

Special Adviser on the Global Compact: KLAUS M. LEISINGER (Germany).

Special Adviser on the Millennium Development Goals: JEFFREY D. SACHS (USA).

Special Adviser on the Prevention of Genocide: FRANCIS DENG (Sudan).

Special Adviser on Yemen: JAMAL BENOMAR (Morocco).

Special Envoys

Joint Special Envoy of the UN and the League of Arab States on the Syrian Crisis: KOFI ANNAN (Ghana).

Special Envoy for Assistance to Pakistan: RAUF ENGIN SOYSAL (Turkey).

Special Envoy for the Implementation of UN Security Council Resolution 1559 (on Lebanon): TERJE ROED-LARSEN (Norway).

Special Envoy for HIV/AIDS in Africa: ELIZABETH MATAKA (Botswana).

Special Envoy for HIV/AIDS in Asia and in the Pacific: NAFIS SADIK (Pakistan).

Special Envoy for HIV/AIDS in the Caribbean Region: Dr EDWARD GREENE (Guyana).

Special Envoy for HIV/AIDS in Eastern Europe: (vacant).

Special Envoy for Malaria: RAY CHAMBERS (USA).

Special Envoy for Sudan and South Sudan: HAILE MENKERIOS (South Africa).

Special Envoy on the Great Lakes Region: OLUSEGUN OBASANJO (Nigeria).

Special Envoy to Libya: ABDELILAH AL-KHATIB (Jordan).

Special Envoy to Stop Tuberculosis: JORGE SAMPAIO (Portugal).

Special Envoys on Climate Change: GRO HARLEM BRUNDTLAND (Norway), RICARDO LAGOS ESCOBAR (Chile), FESTUS MOGAE (Botswana), SRGJAN KERIM (FYRM).

Special Representatives

UN Representative to the Georgia Joint Incident Prevention and Response Mechanism and to the international discussions in Geneva on security and stability and the return of IDPs: ANTII TURUNEN (Finland).

Special Representative to the AU: ZACHARY MUBURI-MUITA (Kenya).

Special Representative for Migration: PETER SUTHERLAND (Ireland).

Special Representative for the Implementation of the International Strategy for Disaster Reduction: (vacant).

Special Representative for the United Nations International School: MICHAEL ADLERSTEIN (USA).

Special Representative on Food Security and Nutrition; and on Avian and Human Influenza: Dr DAVID NABARRO (United Kingdom).

Special Representative on the Issue of Human Rights and Transnational Corporations and other Business Enterprises: JOHN RUGGIE (USA).

Special Representative on Sexual Violence in Conflict: MARGOT WALLSTRÖM (Sweden) (until 31 May 2012).

Special Representative on Violence against Children: MARTA SANTOS PAIS (Portugal).

Other Special High Level Appointments

Head of the International Commission against Impunity in Guatemala: CARLOS CASTRESANA FERNÁNDEZ (Spain).

High-level Co-ordinator for Compliance by Iraq with its Obligations Regarding the Repatriation or Return of all Kuwaiti and Third Country Nationals or their Remains, as well as the Return of all Kuwaiti Property, including Archives seized by Iraq: GENNADY P. TARASOV (Russia).

High Representative for the Alliance of Civilizations: JORGE SAMPAIO (Portugal).

Joint UN-AU Chief Mediator for Darfur, a. i.: IBRAHIM GAMBARI (Nigeria).

Personal Envoy for Haiti: BILL (WILLIAM JEFFERSON) CLINTON (USA).

Personal Envoy for the Greece-FYRM Talks: MATTHEW NIMETZ (USA).

Personal Envoy for Western Sahara: CHRISTOPHER ROSS (USA).

Personal Representative on the Border Controversy between Guyana and Venezuela: NORMAN GIRVAN (Jamaica).

Representative for Human Rights of IDPs: WALTER KÄLIN (Switzerland).

Special Co-ordinator for Lebanon: MICHAEL C. WILLIAMS (United Kingdom).

Special Co-ordinator for the Middle East Peace Process, Personal Representative to the Palestine Liberation Organization and the Palestinian Authority, and the Secretary-General's Envoy to the Quartet: ROBERT H. SERRY (Netherlands).

Further Special Representatives and other high-level appointees of the UN Secretary-General are listed in entries on UN peace-keeping and peace-building missions and under Offices and Departments of the UN Secretariat. The Secretary-General also appoints distinguished figures in the worlds of arts and sports as Messengers of Peace, as a means of focusing global attention to the UN's activities.

General Assembly

The General Assembly was established as a principal organ of the United Nations under the UN Charter. It first met on 10 January 1946. It is the main deliberative organ of the United Nations, and the only one composed of representatives of all the UN member states. Each delegation consists of not more than five representatives and five alternates, with as many advisers as may be required. The Assembly meets regularly for three months each year, and special sessions may also be held. It has specific responsibility for electing the Secretary-General and members of other UN councils and organs, and for approving the UN budget and the assessments for financial contributions by member states. It is also empowered to make recommendations (but not binding decisions) on questions of international security and co-operation.

The regular session of the General Assembly commences in mid-September. After the election of its President and other officers, the Assembly opens its general debate, a two-week period during which the head of each delegation makes a formal statement of his or her government's views on major world issues. Since 1997 the Secretary-General has presented his report on the work of the UN at the start of the general debate. The Assembly then begins examination of the principal items on its agenda: it acts directly on some agenda items, but most business is handled by the six Main Committees (listed below), which study and debate each item and present draft resolutions to the Assembly. After a review of the report of each Main Committee, the Assembly formally approves or rejects the Committee's recommendations. On designated 'important questions', such as recommendations on international peace and security, the admission of new members to the United Nations, or budgetary questions, a two-thirds majority is needed for adoption of a resolution. Other questions may be decided by a simple majority. In the Assembly, each member has one vote. Voting in the Assembly is sometimes replaced by an effort to find consensus among member states, in order to strengthen support for the Assembly's decisions: the President consults delegations in private to find out whether they are willing to agree to adoption of a resolution without a vote; if they are, the President can declare that a resolution has been so adopted.

Special sessions of the Assembly may be held to discuss issues which require particular attention (e.g. illicit drugs) and 'emergency special sessions' may also be convened to discuss situations on which the UN Security Council has been unable to reach a decision. The Assembly's 10th emergency special session, concerning Illegal Israeli Actions in Occupied East Jerusalem and the rest of the Occupied Palestinian Territory, commenced in April 1997 and has been subsequently reconvened intermittently. The 23rd meeting of the session, called in December 2003 by Arab and non-aligned countries, requested that the International Court of Justice (ICJ) render an advisory opinion on the legal consequences arising from the construction of a wall by Israel in the Occupied Palestinian Territory including in and around East Jerusalem; this action was taken by the General Assembly following two failures by the Security Council to adopt resolutions on the matter. The 24th meeting of the session was convened in July 2004 to discuss the ICJ's ruling on this matter, which had been delivered earlier in that month. A special session on children, reviewing progress made since the World Summit for Children, held in 1990, and the adoption in 1989 of the Convention on the Rights of the Child, was convened in May 2002. In January 2005 a special session took place to commemorate the 60th anniversary of the liberation of the Nazi concentration camps.

The Assembly's 55th session (from September 2000) was designated as the Millennium Assembly. In early September a Millennium Summit of UN heads of state or government was convened to debate 'The Role of the United Nations in the 21st Century'. The Millennium Summit issued the UN Millennium Declaration, identifying the values and principles that should guide the organization in key areas including peace, development, environment, human rights, protection of the vulnerable, and the special needs of the African continent; and specified six fundamental values underlying international relations: freedom; equality; solidarity; tolerance; respect for nature; and a sense of shared responsibility for the global economy and social development. The summit adopted the following so-called Millennium Development Goals (MDGs), each incorporating specific targets to be attained by 2015: the eradication of extreme poverty and hunger; attainment of universal primary education; promotion of gender equality and empowerment of women; reduction of child mortality rates; improvement in maternal health rates; combating HIV/AIDS, malaria and other diseases; ensuring environmental sustainability; and the development of a global partnership for development. Reform of the Security Council and the need for increased UN co-operation with the private sector, non-governmental organizations and civil society in pursuing its goals were also addressed by the summit. Progress in attaining the MDGs was to be reviewed on a regular basis. A five-year review conference of the Millennium Declaration was convened in September 2005 at the level of heads of state and of government.

In October 2003 the President of the Assembly appointed six facilitators to oversee discussions on means of revitalizing the Assembly, and in mid-December the Assembly adopted a landmark resolution that, while reaffirming relevant provisions of the UN Charter and the UN Millennium Declaration, outlined a number of reforms to the Assembly's operations. The changes, aimed at enhancing the Assembly's authority, role, efficiency and impact, were to take effect following broad consultations over the next two years. The resolution provided for a regular meeting of the Presidents of the Assembly, Security Council and ECOSOC, with a view to strengthening co-operation and complementarity in the respective work programmes of the three bodies. In July 2004 the Assembly adopted a resolution on further revitalization of its work, with provisions for streamlining its agenda, sharpening the focus of the six Main Committees, and reducing paperwork.

In March 2005 the Secretary-General presented to the General Assembly a report entitled 'In Larger Freedom: Towards Development, Security and Human Rights for All'. Building on the September 2000 Millennium Declaration, the report focused on three main pillars, defined as: 'Freedom from Want', urging developing countries to improve governance and combat corruption, and industrialized nations to increase funds for development assistance and debt relief and to provide immediate free market access to all exports from least developed countries; 'Freedom from Fear', urging states to agree a new consensus on security matters and adopting a definition of an act of terrorism as one 'intended to cause death or serious bodily harm to civilians or non-combatants with the purpose of intimidating a population or compelling a government or an international organization to do or abstain from doing any act'; and 'Freedom to Live in Dignity', urging the international community to support the principle of 'responsibility to protect'. The report also detailed a number of recommendations for strengthening the UN, which were subsequently considered by the September 2005 World Summit of UN heads of state. These included: rationalizing the work of the Assembly (see above) and focusing its agenda on substantive topical issues, such as international migration and the conclusion of a new comprehensive international strategy against terrorism; restructuring the Secretariat; expanding the membership of the Security Council; and establishing a new UN Human Rights Council to replace the Commission on Human Rights. In December the General Assembly, acting concurrently with the Security Council, authorized the establishment of an intergovernmental advisory Peace-building Commission, which had been recommended in September by the World Summit. The Assembly and Council also authorized at that time the creation of a Peace-building Fund. In March 2006 the Assembly authorized the establishment of the new Human Rights Council. Both the Peace-building Commission and Human Rights Council were inaugurated in June. In February 2007 the Assembly appointed five ambassadors to host negotiations aimed at advancing the process of Security Council reform.

In early October 2008 the General Assembly voted to ask the ICJ for an Advisory Opinion on the legal status of the unilateral declaration of independence, in February of that year, of the Provincial Institutions of Self-Government of Kosovo. Later in October, in view of the ongoing international financial crisis, the President of the General Assembly announced that a body would be established to review the global financial system, including the role of the World Bank and the IMF. The first plenary meeting of the resulting Commission of Experts of the President of the UN General Assembly on Reforms of the International Monetary and Financial System was held in January 2009, and, in September, the Commission issued a report addressing the origins of, and outlining recommendations for the future global response to, the ongoing crisis; the latter included proposals to establish a new global reserve system, a new global credit facility to complement the IMF, a new global co-ordination council, and an International Debt Restructuring Court. In late June the General Assembly convened a UN Conference on the World Financial and Economic Crisis and its Impact on Development.

In September 2009 the General Assembly adopted, by consensus, its first resolution on the 'Responsibility to Protect', promoting efforts to protect the world's population from genocide, war crimes, ethnic cleansing and other crimes against humanity.

World leaders participating in the 65th session of the General Assembly, commencing in September 2010, adopted a document entitled 'Keeping the Promise: United to Achieve the MDGs'; the document called on the President of the Assembly's 68th session, in 2013, to organize a special event to follow up progress on attaining the MDGs. Meanwhile, the UN Secretary-General was requested to report annually on progress until 2015, and to recommend means of advancing the UN development agenda thereafter.

President of 66th Session: (from Sept. 2011) NASSIR ABDULAZIZ AL-NASSER (Qatar).

MAIN COMMITTEES

There are six Main Committees, on which all members have a right to be represented. Each Committee includes an elected Chairperson and two Vice-Chairs.

First Committee: Disarmament and International Security.

Second Committee: Economic and Financial.

Third Committee: Social, Humanitarian and Cultural.

Fourth Committee: Special Political and Decolonization.

Fifth Committee: Administrative and Budgetary.

Sixth Committee: Legal.

OTHER SESSIONAL COMMITTEES

General Committee: f. 1946; composed of 28 members, including the Assembly President, the 21 Vice-Presidents of the Assembly and the Chairs of the six Main Committees.

Credentials Committee: f. 1946; composed of nine members appointed at each Assembly session.

POLITICAL AND SECURITY MATTERS

Special Committee on Peace-keeping Operations: f. 1965; 34 appointed members.

Disarmament Commission: f. 1978 (replacing body f. 1952); 61 members.

UN Scientific Committee on the Effects of Atomic Radiation: f. 1955; 21 members.

Committee on the Peaceful Uses of Outer Space: f. 1959; 61 members; has a Legal Sub-Committee and a Scientific and Technical Sub-Committee.

Ad Hoc Committee on the Indian Ocean: f. 1972; 44 members.

Committee on the Exercise of the Inalienable Rights of the Palestinian People: f. 1975; 25 members.

Special Committee on the Implementation of the Declaration on Decolonization: f. 1961; 24 members.

Ad Hoc Committee on Terrorism: f. 1996.

DEVELOPMENT

Commission on Science and Technology for Development: f. 1992; 33 members.

Committee on Energy and Natural Resources Development: f. 1998; 24 members.

United Nations Environment Programme (UNEP) Governing Council: f. 1972; 58 members.

LEGAL QUESTIONS

International Law Commission: f. 1947; 34 members elected for a five-year term; originally established in 1946 as the Committee on the Progressive Development of International Law and its Codification.

Advisory Committee on the UN Programme of Assistance in Teaching, Study, Dissemination and Wider Appreciation of International Law: f. 1965; 25 members.

UN Commission on International Trade Law: f. 1966; 36 members.

Special Committee on the Charter of the United Nations and on the Strengthening of the Role of the Organization: f. 1975; composed of all UN members.

There is also a UN Administrative Tribunal and a Committee on Applications for Review of Administrative Tribunal Judgments.

ADMINISTRATIVE AND FINANCIAL QUESTIONS

Advisory Committee on Administrative and Budgetary Questions: f. 1946; 16 members appointed for three-year terms.

Committee on Contributions: f. 1946; 18 members appointed for three-year terms.

International Civil Service Commission: f. 1972; 15 members appointed for four-year terms.

Committee on Information: f. 1978, formerly the Committee to review UN Policies and Activities; 95 members.

There is also a Board of Auditors, Investments Committee, UN Joint Staff Pension Board, Joint Inspection Unit, UN Staff Pension Committee, Committee on Conferences, and Committee for Programme and Co-ordination.

SUBSIDIARY BODIES

Human Rights Council: f. 2006, replacing the fmr Commission on Human Rights (f. 1946); inaugural meeting held in June 2006; mandated to promote universal respect for the protection of all human rights and fundamental freedoms for all; addresses and makes recommendations on situations of violations of human rights; promotes the effective co-ordination and mainstreaming of human rights within the UN system; supports human rights education and learning and provides advisory services, technical assistance and capacity-building support; serves as a forum for dialogue on thematic issues connected with human rights; makes recommendations to the General Assembly for the advancement of international human rights law; promotes the full implementation of human rights obligations undertaken by states; aims to contribute, through dialogue and co-operation, towards the prevention of human rights violations, and to ensure prompt responses to human rights emergencies; the Human Rights Council Advisory Committee functions as a think-tank under the direction of the Council; in March 2011 the Council established an independent international commission of inquiry into the human rights situation in Syria; the commission's first report was published in November, and an update issued in March 2012; in Feb. 2012 the Advisory Committee adopted seven recommendations for approval by the Council, concerning: the rights of peasants; the right to food; human rights and international solidarity; the right of peoples to peace; human rights and issues related to terrorist hostage-taking; traditional values of humankind; and enhancement of international co-operation in the field of human rights; the agenda of the 19th session of the Council, undertaken during Feb.–March 2012, included the right to adequate housing; social and cultural rights; sexual orientation and gender identity; the right to food; juvenile justice; and alleged violations of human rights in countries including Côte d'Ivoire, Iran, Libya, Myanmar and Syria; the first cycle of the Universal Periodic Review (UPR), an assessment of the human rights situation in all mem. states that commenced in 2006, was to end at the 19th session; 47 mems; Pres. LAURA DUPUY LASSERRE (Uruguay).

Peace-building Commission: f. 2006; inaugural meeting held in June 2006; an intergovernmental advisory body, subsidiary simultaneously to both the General Assembly and the Security Council; mandated to focus international attention on reconstruction, institution-building and sustainable development in countries emerging from conflict and to advise on and propose integrated strategies for post-conflict recovery; in December 2009 the President of the General Assembly appointed three co-facilitators: the Permanent Representatives of Ireland, Mexico and South Africa, to undertake, during 2010, a review of the Peace-building Commission's activities; in July 2010 the co-facilitators published a report entitled 'Review of the United Nations Peacebuilding Architecture', based upon extensive consultations with UN member states and with other stakeholders; 31 mem. states; Chair. Dr A. K. ABDUL MOMEN (Bangladesh).

Peace-building Fund: f. 2006; finances (through two funding facilities, the Immediate Response Facility and the Peace-building Recovery Facility) projects in countries that are on the agenda of the Peace-building Commisson, or that have been declared eligible for assistance by the Secretary-General; initiatives in receipt of funding must fulfil at least one of the following criteria: they respond to imminent threats to a peace process, build or strengthen national capacities to promote coexistence and peaceful resolution of conflict, stimulate economic revitalization facilitating peace, or re-establish essential administrative services; the Fund is replenished by voluntary contributions; its guidelines were revised in 2009; during 2007–11 the Fund allocated US $327.8m. in 22 countries.

Security Council

The Security Council was established as a principal organ under the United Nations Charter; its first meeting was held on 17 January 1946. Its task is to promote international peace and security in all parts of the world.

MEMBERS

Permanent members: People's Republic of China, France, Russia, United Kingdom, USA, known as the P-5. The remaining 10 members are normally elected (five each year) by the General Assembly for two-year periods (five countries from Africa and Asia, two from Latin America, one from eastern Europe, and two from western Europe and others).

Non-permanent members in 2012: Colombia, Germany, India, Portugal and South Africa (term expires 31 December 2012); and Azerbaijan, Guatemala, Morocco, Pakistan and Togo (term expires 31 December 2013).

Rotation of the Presidency in 2012: South Africa (January); Togo (February); United Kingdom (March); USA (April); Azerbaijan (May); People's Republic of China (June); Colombia (July); France (August); Germany (September); Guatemala (October); India (November); Morocco (December).

Organization

The Security Council has the right to investigate any dispute or situation which might lead to friction between two or more countries, and such disputes or situations may be brought to the Council's attention either by one of its members, by any member state, by the General Assembly, by the Secretary-General or even, under certain conditions, by a state which is not a member of the UN.

The Council has the right to recommend ways and means of peaceful settlement and, in certain circumstances, the actual terms of settlement. In the event of a threat to or breach of international peace or an act of aggression, the Council has powers to take 'enforcement' measures in order to restore international peace and security. These include severance of communications and of economic and diplomatic relations and, if required, action by air, land and sea forces.

All members of the UN are pledged by the Charter to make available to the Security Council, on its call and in accordance with special agreements, the armed forces, assistance and facilities necessary to maintain international peace and security. These agreements, however, have not yet been concluded.

The Council is organized to be able to function continuously. The Presidency of the Council is held monthly in turn by the member states in English alphabetical order. Each member of the Council has one vote. On procedural matters decisions are made by the affirmative vote of any nine members. For decisions on other matters the required nine affirmative votes must include the votes of the five permanent members. This is the rule of 'great power unanimity' popularly known as the 'veto' privilege. In practice, an abstention by one of the permanent members is not regarded as a veto. Any member, whether permanent or non-permanent, must abstain from voting in any decision concerning the pacific settlement of a dispute to which it is a party. Any member of the UN that is party to a dispute under consideration by the Council may participate in the Council's discussions without a vote.

The allocation of the Security Council's permanent seats reflects the post-Second World War international situation. It is envisaged that reforms to the Council should be implemented aimed at establishing a more equitable regional representation and recognizing the current global balance of power. Consideration of such reform commenced in 1993 at the 48th Session of the General Assembly, which established a Working Group to assess the issue. Agreement on the size and composition of an expanded Security Council has been hindered by conflicting national and regional demands. Brazil, India, Japan and Germany (the 'Group of Four—G4') have requested the status of permanent members without veto rights; while Italy, Pakistan and other middle-ranking countries (known as 'Uniting for Consensus') have requested a 25-member Council with 10 new non-permanent seats; and the African Union (AU) has contended that African states should receive two permanent seats with veto power, and that there should be four further new permanent seats and five non-permanent seats. In September 2000 the UN Millennium Summit declared support for continued discussions on reform of the Council. The report of the High-Level Panel on Threats, Challenges and Change (see Secretariat), issued in December 2004, stated that the role of the developed countries that contribute most to the UN financially (in terms of contributions to assessed budgets), militarily (through participation in peace-keeping operations), and diplomatically should be reflected in the Council's decision-making processes, as well as the interests of the broader membership (particularly those of developing countries). The report proposed two models for the expansion of the Council. The first entailed the provision of six new permanent seats (broadening the current regional representation on the Council), with no veto, and of three non-permanent seats with a two-year term; while the second entailed the establishment of a new category of eight 'semi-permanent' seats to be occupied for periods of four years. In his report entitled 'In Larger Freedom: Towards Development, Security and Human Rights for All', issued in March 2005 (see General Assembly), the Secretary-General supported the High-Level Panel's proposals on Security Council reform. The proposals were reviewed by the World Summit of UN heads of state convened by the General Assembly in September. In February 2007 the General Assembly appointed five ambassadors to advance the process of Security Council reform by hosting negotiations on the following five key issues: categories of membership; veto power; regional representation; the size of an enlarged Council; and the working methods of the Council and its relationship with the General Assembly. In February 2009 a phase of intergovernmental negotiations on Security Council reform was launched, with three rounds of negotiations held during February–September. Prior to the commencement, in December, of the fourth round, some 138 member states jointly sent a letter to the chairperson of the negotiations requesting that a text should be prepared detailing the options under discussion. Consequently, the fifth round of intergovernmental negotiations, which opened in June 2010, were based on a prepared text. The first meeting of the eighth round of negotiations took place in November 2011.

Activities

As the UN organ primarily responsible for maintaining peace and security, the Security Council is empowered to deploy UN forces in the event that a dispute leads to fighting. It may also authorize the use of military force by a coalition of member states or a regional organization. A summit meeting of the Council convened during the Millennium Summit in September 2000 issued a declaration on ensuring an effective role for the Council in maintaining international peace and security, with particular reference to Africa. In June 2006 an intergovernmental advisory UN Peace-building Commission (see below) was inaugurated as a subsidiary advisory body of both the Security Council and the General Assembly, its establishment having been authorized by the Security Council and General Assembly, acting concurrently, in December 2005. The annual reports of the Commission were to be submitted to the Security Council for debate. During 2011 the Security Council continued to monitor closely all existing peace-keeping and political missions and the situations in countries where missions were being undertaken, and to authorize extensions of their mandates accordingly. The Council authorized the establishment of two new peace-keeping missions in that year: the UN Interim Security Force for Abyei (UNISFA)—concerning the disputed Abyei border area between Sudan and South Sudan—in June, and the UN Mission in South Sudan (UNMISS) in July.

In 2011 major priorities of the Council's formal agenda included consideration of African issues (such as ongoing crises in Côte d'Ivoire, Somalia and Sudan); of mass protests and political upheaval in several North African and Arab states (including Libya, Syria and Yemen); and of post-conflict situations (particularly Burundi, CAR, Guinea-Bissau and Sierra Leone). The Council focused also on the January 2011 referendum on independence for South Sudan, and the ensuing admission in July of the newly independent South Sudan as a UN member state (pursuant to the Council's recommendation to that effect made on 13 July to the General Assembly); and on the application by Palestine in September for membership of the organization. During 2011 the Security Council adopted 66 resolutions, 40 of which related to Africa; issued 22 presidential statements; and convened some 213 public meetings. Numerous meetings and debates were held to consider African matters, with a focus on peace and security, conflict prevention and resolution, peace-building, the humanitarian situation, return of refugees and IDPs, and development strategies. A Council special mission to Africa was undertaken in May 2011, covering Khartoum, Sudan; Juba, in the then soon-to-be independent South Sudan; Addis Ababa, Ethiopia; and Nairobi, Kenya.

On 12 September 2001 the Security Council expressed its unequivocal condemnation of the terrorist attacks against targets in the USA, which had occurred on the previous day. It expressed its readiness to combat terrorism and reiterated the right to individual or collective self-defence in accordance with the UN Charter. At the end of September the Council adopted Resolution 1373, establishing a Counter-Terrorism Committee (CTC) to monitor a range of measures to combat international terrorism, including greater international co-operation and information exchange and suppressing the financing of terrorist groups. A special session of the Council at ministerial level was convened on the issue of terrorism in November. The Council continued to review the work of the CTC and to urge all states to submit reports on efforts to implement Resolution 1373, as well as to ratify relevant international conventions and protocols. In January 2003 the Council met at ministerial level to discuss international terrorism, including the issue of particular states maintaining stocks of weapons of mass destruction. The meeting adopted a resolution urging intensified efforts to combat terrorism and full co-operation with the CTC. The CTC has made efforts to strengthen contacts with international, regional and sub-regional organizations, and in March 2003 it convened a meeting of 57 such groupings and agreed on a co-ordinated approach to the suppression of terrorism. A follow-up meeting was convened in March 2004. In that month the Council adopted a resolution to strengthen the CTC by classifying it as a special subsidiary body of the Council, headed by a Bureau and assisted by an Executive Directorate (the Counter-Terrorism Committee Executive Directorate—CTED). In December 2010 the Council extended the mandate of the CTED until 31 December 2013. In April 2004 the Council adopted Resolution 1540—which considered the threat posed by the possible acquisition and use by non-state actors, particularly terrorists, of weapons of mass destruction, and urged all states to establish controls to prevent the proliferation of such weapons—and established the '1540 Committee' to monitor its implementation. In April 2006 and August 2008 the 1540 Committee reported to the Security Council on the status of implementation of Resolution 1540. The December 2004 report of the High-Level Panel on Threats, Challenges and Change stated that, confronted by a terrorism 'nightmare scenario', the Council would need to take earlier, more pro-active and more decisive action than hitherto.

The imposition of sanctions by the Security Council as a means of targeting regimes and groupings that are deemed to threaten international peace and security has increased significantly in recent years and has been subjected to widespread scrutiny regarding enforceability and the potential adverse humanitarian consequences for general populations. In the latter respect the Council has, since 1999, incorporated clauses on humanitarian assessment in its resolutions; the sanctions that took effect against the Taliban regime in Afghanistan and al-Qa'ida in January 2001 were the first to entail mandatory monitoring of the humanitarian impact. In 2000 a proposal was submitted to the Council regarding the establishment of a permanent body to monitor sanctions violations. The UN Secretary-General established an informal working group in April 2000 to evaluate sanctions policy. During 2006 the group submitted a report to the Security Council recommending that resolutions enforcing sanctions should clearly specify intended goals and targets, include incentives to reward partial compliance, and focus in particular on the finances and movements of leaders (so-called 'smart sanctions'). In April 2000 the Council authorized the establishment of a temporary monitoring mechanism to investigate alleged violations of the sanctions imposed against the UNITA rebels in Angola, owing to their failure to implement earlier Council resolutions demanding compliance with the obligations of the peace process in that country. In July 2000 the Council voted to prohibit the exportation of all rough diamonds from Sierra Leone that had not been officially certified by that country's Government. (It had become evident that the ongoing conflicts in Sierra Leone and Angola were fuelled by rebel groups' illegal exploitation of diamond resources and use of the proceeds derived therefrom to purchase armaments.) In December a panel of experts appointed by the Council issued a report on the connections between the illicit exportation of diamonds from Sierra Leone and the international trade in armaments. In March 2001 the Council banned the purchase of diamonds exported from Liberia, and demanded that the Liberian authorities refrain from purchasing so-called 'conflict diamonds' from illegal sources and cease providing support to rebel organizations, with particular reference to the main rebel grouping active in Sierra Leone. The Council also re-imposed an embargo on the sale or supply of armaments to Liberia and imposed diplomatic restrictions on senior Liberian government officials, with effect from May. In January 2003 the Council endorsed a new diamond certification scheme, known as the *Kimberley Process*, which had entered into effect on 1 January following an agreement reached by some 30 governments to regulate the trade in rough diamonds and eliminate the illegal sale of diamonds to fund conflicts. In May the Council imposed, additionally, a ban on the sale of timber products originating in Liberia. In December the Council endorsed the imposition against Liberia of a revised sanctions regime, to complement developments in the peace process there. The sale or supply of arms and related materiels to Liberia (except for use by the UN Mission in Liberia—UNMIL) and the purchase of rough diamonds and timber products from that country remained prohibited, and restrictions remained in force on travel by designated Liberian individuals. In June 2006 the Council terminated the sanctions on the purchase of timber products from Liberia, and in April 2007 the sanctions on the purchase of rough diamonds from that country were withdrawn. In May 2002 the Council suspended the travel restrictions on senior officials of the UNITA movement in Angola, following the signing of a cease-fire agreement ending hostilities in that country. All sanctions against UNITA were removed in December and the relevant Sanctions Committee, established pursuant to a resolution adopted in 1993, was dissolved. In September 2003 the Council voted to end punitive measures imposed against Libya in 1992 and 1993 relating to the destruction of a commercial airline flight over Lockerbie, United Kingdom, in December 1988. In July 2003 the Council banned the sale or supply of armaments and other military assistance to militias in the Democratic Republic of the Congo (DRC), and in November an arms embargo, travel restrictions and an assets freeze were imposed on designated individuals and entities in Côte d'Ivoire.

In February 2011 the Security Council, in reaction to violent measures recently taken by the regime of the Libyan leader Col Muammar al-Qaddafi against opposition groupings, imposed a new arms embargo against the Libyan regime. In March the Security Council adopted Resolution 1973, which imposed a no-fly zone in Libya's airspace, strengthened the sanctions against the Qaddafi regime (including freezing financial assets), demanded an immediate cease-fire, and authorized member states to take 'all necessary measures to protect civilians and civilian populated areas under threat of attack' by forces loyal to Qaddafi, 'while excluding a foreign occupation force of any form on any part of Libyan territory'. Later in that month NATO members determined to enforce the UN sanctioned no-fly zone over Libya, alongside a military operation to prevent further attacks on civilians and civilian-populated areas, undertaken by a multinational coalition under British, French and US command; at the end of March NATO assumed full command of the operation to protect civilians in Libya. The NATO operation was terminated at the end of October, following the overthrow of the Qaddafi regime. At the beginning of November the Security Council urged the new authorities in Libya to ensure the security of the former Qaddafi regime's large weapons stockpile, expressing concern that the proliferation of such armaments might fuel terrorist activities, including those of al-Qaida. The Council also demanded that the Libyan authorities, in co-ordination with international bodies, destroy any stockpiled chemical weaponry. In December the Council removed financial sanctions against the Libyan banking sector.

In July 2004 the Security Council imposed an arms embargo against non-governmental entities and individuals—including the Janjaweed militias—in Darfur, Sudan, and demanded that the Sudanese Government disarm the militias. In July 2007 the Security Council authorized the deployment of the AU/UN Hybrid Operation in Darfur (UNAMID), and during 2011 the Council continued to consult closely on the Darfur situation with the UN Secretariat, the AU and the Sudanese Government. In April 2012 the Council, concerned at escalating tensions between Sudan and recently independent South Sudan, demanded that the two states redeploy their forces from Abyei (Sudan); that they withdraw forces from their joint border and immediately end mounting cross-border violence; that Sudanese rebels should vacate oilfields in Heglig (Sudan); that Sudan should cease aerial bombardments of South Sudan; and that a summit should be convened between the two states to resolve outstanding concerns.

In December 2009, adopting Resolution 1907, the Council imposed an arms embargo, travel restrictions and assets freeze against the Eritrean political and military leadership, who were found to have provided political, financial and logistical support to armed groups engaged in undermining the reconciliation process in Somalia, and to have acted aggressively towards Djibouti.

In February 2007 the UN Security Council endorsed the deployment of the AU Mission in Somalia (AMISOM), which had been established by the AU in January, with a mandate to contribute to the political stabilization of Somalia; the Security Council proposed that the mission should eventually be superseded by a UN operation focusing on the post-conflict restoration of Somalia. AMISOM became operational in May 2007. In December 2010 the UN Security Council, concerned at continuing unrest and terrorist attacks in Somalia, extended AMISOM's mandate until 30 September 2011 and requested the AU to increase the mission's numbers to 12,000. AMISOM's mandate was extended further, in September 2011, until 31 October 2012. In so doing, the UN Security Council requested the AU to 'urgently increase' the mission's strength to the then mandated level of 12,000. In late February 2012 the Security Council voted unanimously to strengthen the mission further, to comprise 17,700 troops, and to expand its areas of operation. The resolution also banned trade in charcoal with Somalia, having identified that commodity as a significant source of revenue for militants.

In June, October and December 2008, November 2009, April and November 2010, and April and November 2011, the Security Council adopted, respectively, Resolutions 1816, 1838, 1846, 1897, 1918, 1950, 1976, and 2015, on combating piracy being perpetrated against ships off the coast of Somalia and in the Gulf of Aden. A Contact Group on Piracy off the Coast of Somalia (CGPCS), established in January 2009 to facilitate discussion and the co-ordination of actions among states and organizations engaged in suppressing piracy off the coast of Somalia, reports periodically on its progress to the Security Council. In January 2011 the then Special Adviser to the UN Secretary-General on Legal Issues Related to Piracy off the Coast of Somalia, in a briefing to the Security Council, proposed 25 comprehensive measures to address the issue, including the establishment of specialized piracy courts in the region, and the promotion of regional economic development programmes, with a view to finding solutions on land, also, to the ongoing criminal activities at sea.

In April 2005 the Security Council authorized the establishment of an independent commission to assist the Lebanese authorities with their investigation into a terrorist attack perpetrated in February that had killed 23 people, including the former Prime Minister of that country, Rafik Hariri. In October the investigating commission reported that it suspected officials and other individuals from both Lebanon and Syria of involvement in the fatal attack. Consequently, in that month the Security Council adopted a resolution imposing travel and economic sanctions against such suspected individuals, and requiring the Syrian authorities to detain named Syrian suspects and to co-operate fully and unconditionally with the commission. In March 2006 the Council adopted a resolution requesting the UN Secretary-General to negotiate an agreement with the Lebanese Government on the establishment of an international tribunal to try those suspected of involvement in the February 2005 terrorist attack. The resulting agreement on the Special Tribunal for Lebanon was endorsed by the Security Council in May 2007. The Tribunal, based in The Hague, Netherlands, comprises both international and Lebanese judges and was to apply Lebanese (not international) law. In February 2012 the UN Secretary-General extended the mandate of the Special Tribunal for a further three years, with effect from 1 March. In August 2006, following eruption in the previous month of full-scale conflict in southern Lebanon between the Israeli armed forces and the militant Shi'a organization, Hezbollah, the Security Council adopted a resolution calling for a full cessation of hostilities and the immediate withdrawal of all Israeli forces.

In early February 2012 the People's Republic of China and Russia vetoed a Security Council resolution to endorse a proposed peace plan that had been agreed in late January by ministers of the League of Arab States to end the ongoing and escalating conflict in Syria. In mid-February League ministers proposed the creation of a joint Arab-UN peace-keeping mission to Syria. Towards the end of that month the Secretaries-General of the UN and of the League appointed Kofi Annan—formerly the UN Secretary-General—as their Joint Special Envoy on the Syrian Crisis. A six-point peace plan proposed in March by Annan was accepted, towards the end of that month, by the Syrian Government. In mid-April the Security Council adopted, unanimously, a resolution authorizing an advance team of up to 30 unarmed military observers to monitor a cease-fire by all parties to the Syrian violence, pending the deployment of a full cease-fire supervision mission. Soon afterwards the UN Secretary-General reported to the Security Council that, as violence had escalated since the attempt to impose a cease-fire, and Syrian forces had not withdrawn from urban areas, a full team of 300 unarmed observers should be promptly deployed. Consequently, on 21 April, the Security Council unanimously authorized the establishment of the UN Supervision Mission in Syria (UNSMIS), initially for a 90-day period.

In October 2006 the Security Council adopted a resolution demanding that the Democratic People's Republic of Korea (North Korea) abandon all programmes related to nuclear weapons, ballistic missiles and other weapons of mass destruction in a complete, verifiable and irreversible manner; an embargo was imposed by the Council on the supply of arms, military technology and luxury goods to that country, and the foreign assets of personnel connected to its weapons programme were frozen. In April 2009 the Council strongly condemned a long-range missile test conducted by North Korea, in violation of the October 2006 resolution. In June 2009 the Council adopted a resolution that deplored a further nuclear test conducted by North Korea, in late May, imposed a total embargo on arms exports from, and strengthened the prohibition on the importation of armaments into, that country.

In December 2006 the Security Council imposed sanctions against Iran, including an embargo related to that country's nuclear and ballistic missile programmes and punitive measures targeted at individuals and entities connected to the programmes. In March 2007 the Council adopted a further resolution imposing a ban on the export of arms from Iran, and, in March 2008, an additional resolution was adopted authorizing inspections of any cargo to and from Iran suspected of concealing prohibited equipment; strengthening the monitoring of Iranian financial institutions; and adding names to the existing list of individuals and companies subject to asset and travel restrictions. A resolution adopted in June 2010 strengthened the sanctions further.

In September 2002 the then US President, George W. Bush, expressed concern that Iraq was challenging international security owing to its non-compliance with previous UN resolutions relating to the elimination of weapons of mass destruction. Subsequently, diplomatic discussions intensified regarding the need for a new UN resolution on Iraq, amidst increasing pressure from the US administration to initiate military action. An open debate was held in the Security Council in October, at the request of the Non-aligned Movement. On 8 November the Council adopted Resolution 1441 providing for an enhanced inspection mission and a detailed timetable according to which Iraq would have a final opportunity to comply with its disarmament obligations. Following Iraq's acceptance of the resolution, inspectors from the UN Monitoring, Verification and Inspection Commission (UNMOVIC, established in 1999 by the Council) and the IAEA arrived in Iraq in late November 2002, with Council authorization to have unrestricted access to all areas and the right to interview Iraqi scientists and weapons experts. In early December Iraq submitted a declaration of all aspects of its weapons programmes, as required under Resolution 1441. In early January 2003 UNMOVIC's then Executive Chairman, Dr Hans Blix, briefed the Council on Iraq's declaration and the inspection activities. A full update was presented to the Council on 27 January, as required by Resolution 1441, 60 days after the resumption of inspections. The then Director-General of the IAEA, Dr Mohammad el-Baradei, called for an ongoing mandate for his inspectors to clarify the situation regarding nuclear weapons. However, Blix declared that Iraq had potentially misled the UN on aspects of its chemical and biological weapons programmes and urged more active and substantive co-operation on the part of the Iraqi authorities to determine the existence or otherwise of proscribed items and activities. On 14 February Blix reported to the Council that the Iraqi authorities had recently become more active in proposing and undertaking measures to co-operate with UNMOVIC, and on 7 March he noted that Iraq had started to destroy, under UNMOVIC supervision, its Al Samoud 2 missiles and associated items, having accepted the conclusion of an international panel that these exceeded the permissible range decreed by the Council. Blix declared that the destruction to date of 34 Al Samoud 2 missiles and other items represented a 'substantial measure of disarmament', and that a significant Iraqi effort was under way to clarify a major source of uncertainty regarding quantities of biological and chemical weapons that had been unilaterally destroyed in 1991. Blix stated that UNMOVIC inspectors would require a number of further months in which to verify sites and items, analyse documents, interview relevant persons and draw conclusions, with a view to verifying Iraq's compliance with Resolution 1441. Meanwhile, extensive debate was conducted in the Council regarding Iraq's acceptance of its disarmament obligations and appropriate consequent measures, including the need for a new Council resolution to enforce Resolution 1441. On 24 February 2003 the USA, the United Kingdom and Spain submitted a draft resolution to the Council stating that Iraq had failed to co-operate 'immediately, unconditionally and actively' with UNMOVIC, as required by Resolution 1441, and insisting upon immediate full co-operation, failing which military force should be used to remove the incumbent regime; France, Germany and Russia, however, demanded that UNMOVIC should be given more time to fulfil its mandate. On 18 March UNMOVIC personnel were withdrawn from Iraq in view of the abandonment by the USA, the United Kingdom and Spain of efforts to win the Council's support for their draft resolution and a consequent ultimatum by the USA that the Iraqi leadership should leave the country immediately or face a military invasion. Unilateral military action by US, British and allied forces commenced on 19 March. On that day, presenting to the Council UNMOVIC's draft work programme (required under Resolution 1284 to be formulated within a fixed period after the commencement of inspection activities), Blix stated that the Commission's experts had found that the Iraqi authorities had hitherto supplied only limited new information that would be of substantial assistance in resolving outstanding issues of concern. Upon the initiation of military action Iraq's petroleum exports under an existing oil-for-food programme were suspended immediately. On 28 March the Security Council adopted a resolution enabling technical adjustments to the oil-for-food programme and authorizing the UN Secretary-General to facilitate the delivery and receipt of goods contracted by the Iraqi Government for the humanitarian needs of its people.

On 22 May 2003, following the overthrow of Saddam Hussain in April, the Security Council adopted Resolution 1483, withdrawing economic sanctions against Iraq, and providing for the resumption of petroleum exports and the phasing-out, by November, of the oil-for-food programme. The resolution also supported the formation by the Iraqi people, assisted by the 'Coalition Provisional Authority' (the occupying powers under unified command) and a new Special Representative of the Secretary-General, of an Iraqi-run interim administration, pending the establishment by the Iraqi people of an internationally recognized, representative government that would assume the responsibilities of the Authority. On the same day an open meeting of the Council was briefed on the post-conflict situation in Iraq by several UN agencies conducting humanitarian operations there and also by the International Committee of the Red Cross. The

Council reaffirmed in Resolution 1483 that Iraq must meet its disarmament obligations and declared that the Council would revisit the mandates of UNMOVIC and the IAEA in this regard. Reporting on UNMOVIC's activities in June, shortly before retiring as the Commission's Executive Chairman, Blix stated that, although responsibility for weapons inspections in Iraq had been taken over by a US-led Iraq Survey Group, UNMOVIC remained available to continue its work in the field. Blix declared that while significant quantities of proscribed items remained unaccounted for in Iraq and might exist, it was not justifiable to assume that they must exist. In mid-August the Council authorized the establishment of the UN Assistance Mission for Iraq (UNAMI), which was mandated to support the Secretary-General in fulfilling his responsibilities under Resolution 1483. Shortly afterwards the newly appointed Special Representative of the Secretary-General for Iraq (and UN High Commissioner for Human Rights), Sergio Vieira de Mello, and 21 other UN staff were killed in a terrorist attack on the UNAMI headquarters in Baghdad. In response the Council adopted a resolution strongly condemning all forms of violence against participants in humanitarian operations and urging that perpetrators thereof should be brought to justice. Subsequently, until the formation of the Iraqi Interim Government at the end of June 2004 (see below), UNAMI operated primarily from outside Iraq. In mid-October 2003 the Council authorized a multinational peace-keeping force, under unified command, to help maintain security in Iraq and to support UNAMI and the institutions of the Iraqi interim administration. (The mandate of the multinational force was most recently extended to 31 July 2012.) In November 2003 the Council adopted a resolution that stressed the importance of continuing to enforce the ban on trade in armaments with Iraq and authorized the establishment of a sanctions committee to identify those individuals and entities holding the outstanding financial assets of the former Saddam Hussain regime. In April 2004 the Council adopted a resolution welcoming the decision of the Secretary-General in the previous month to appoint a high-level panel to investigate allegations of fraud and corruption in the administration of the oil-for-food programme. The panel's final report, released in October 2005, found that there had been serious manipulation of the humanitarian aims of the programme: the Saddam Hussain regime was accused of having diverted US $1,800m. in illicit surcharges and bribes from the scheme, and more than 2,000 companies were reported to have received illicit payments. Resolution 1546, adopted by the Council in June 2004, endorsed the newly formed Iraq Interim Government and outlined a timetable for Iraq's transition to democratic government. The resolution was approved after several weeks of discussions mainly concerned with the extent of Iraqi sovereignty and the continued presence of multinational forces in that country. The Council welcomed the elections held in January 2005 to the new Iraq Transitional National Assembly, while reaffirming the role of the Special Representative of the Secretary-General and UNAMI in support of Iraqi efforts to promote national dialogue, and urging the international community to continue to provide advisers and technical support towards UN activities in Iraq. The Council has reiterated demands for the repatriation of all Kuwaiti and third country nationals who had been missing since the 1990 Gulf War and for the return of their property. In June 2007 the Security Council voted to terminate UNMOVIC's mandate, noting testimonials that all of Iraq's known weapons of mass destruction had been deactivated and that the Iraqi Government had declared its support for international non-proliferation regimes. The Council also terminated the mandate of the IAEA weapons inspectors in Iraq.

The Council provides a forum for discussion of the situation in the Middle East and violence in the West Bank and Gaza and in Israel and to support a comprehensive and just settlement to the situation based on relevant Council resolutions, the outcome (including the principle of 'land for peace') of the Madrid Conference held in October–November 1991; agreements previously reached by the parties (including the 'statement of joint understanding' made in November 2007, see below); and the peace initiative of Saudi Crown Prince Abdullah that was endorsed by the Arab League summit in March 2002. In the latter month the Council adopted Resolution 1397, which envisaged two separate states of Israel and Palestine existing within secure and recognized borders. In November 2003 the Council endorsed the adoption in April by the so-called 'Quartet' comprising envoys from the UN, EU, Russia and USA of a 'performance-based roadmap to a permanent two-state solution to the Israeli-Palestinian conflict'. The Council welcomed the summit meeting held in February 2005, in Sharm el-Sheikh, Egypt, between the Palestinian and Israeli leaders, at which they reaffirmed commitment to the stalled roadmap initiative, and the Council also welcomed conciliatory actions subsequently taken by both sides. In July the Council convened an open debate on the situation in the Middle East, at the request of Arab member states of the UN. In December 2006 the Council endorsed a presidential statement expressing deep concern over the continuing insecurity in the Middle East and restating the key role of the Quartet. The UN Secretary-General attended a conference held in Annapolis, Maryland, USA, in November 2007, at which participants agreed to implement their respective obligations under the 2003 roadmap to achieving a two-state solution to the Israeli-Palestinian conflict, and a statement of 'joint understanding' was made by the Israeli and Palestinian leaders. Addressing an open debate on the Middle East situation in March 2008, the Secretary-General reaffirmed commitment to the ongoing framework for resolving the conflict and, noting that the Israeli and Palestinian leaders had in the previous month made a commitment to reaching a settlement promptly, urged that momentum towards a resolution of the conflict be maintained. In September, however, the Special Co-ordinator for the Middle East Peace Process reported to the Security Council that no agreement had yet been reached on core issues. In mid-December the Security Council adopted a resolution reaffirming its support for the agreements and negotiations resulting from the November 2007 Annapolis summit, and urging an intensification of efforts to achieve a peaceful two-state outcome. In January 2009, in response to the intensive bombardment of the Gaza Strip by Israeli forces that commenced in late December 2008 with the stated aim of ending rocket attacks launched by Hamas and other militant groups on Israeli targets, the Security Council adopted Resolution 1860, in which it expressed grave concern at the escalation of violence and stressed that Palestinian and Israeli civilian populations must be protected. In May 2009 the Council convened an open debate on the Middle East, at the level of ministers for foreign affairs, and expressed support for an initiative of the Quartet, and other interested parties, to hold a conference in Moscow; this was subsequently held in March 2010. An open debate on the Middle East situation, convened by the Council in July 2011, noted progress achieved in Palestinian state-building and urged the prompt resumption of negotiations on a two-state outcome. In September 2011 the Council met to consider Palestine's application in that month for full UN membership.

In February 2008 the Council met in emergency session in reaction to Kosovo's unilateral declaration of independence from Serbia. Pending new guidance from the Council, Resolution 1244 governing the UN Interim Administration in Kosovo and Metohija (UNMIK) was to remain in force; following the enactment of a new Kosovan Constitution in June, providing for the transfer of executive powers from the UN to the elected Kosovan authorities and for an EU police and justice mission to assume supervisory responsibilities from the UN, the Council met to discuss a proposal of the UN Secretary-General for the reconfiguration of UNMIK. Discussions on the future status of Kosovo remained a priority for the Security Council in 2011.

The Security Council monitored and considered the situation in Haiti during 2011, and stressed the importance of the activities of the UN Stabilization Mission in Haiti (MINUSTAH) in supporting the presidential elections held in March of that year, and in continuing to restore stability following the devastating earthquake of January 2010.

In February 2006 the Security Council endorsed the Afghanistan Compact, which had been adopted in the previous month as a framework for the partnership between Afghanistan and the international community. In June 2008 the Council adopted a resolution in which it expressed concern at the smuggling into Afghanistan of chemicals used for refining heroin. The Security Council addressed the situation in Afghanistan at regular intervals during 2011, and in March held a public meeting on Afghanistan at which it was briefed by the SSRG and Head of the UN Assistance Mission in Afghanistan (UNAMA, established in March 2002) on the situation in the country. The SSRG urged full international support for the transition to Afghan responsibility and ownership of its own governance, security and development efforts, and confirmed that the UN would continue to support Afghanistan after that transition. In March 2012 the Council extended UNAMA's mandate until March 2013. It has also successively extended the mandate of the International Security Assistance Force in Afghanistan (most recently to October 2012).

In recent years the Council has made statements, adopted resolutions and held open debates on a number of other ongoing themes, including the protection of children from the effects of armed conflict; the protection of civilians in armed conflict situations; curbing the proliferation of small arms and light weapons; women; the role of the UN in supporting justice and the rule of law; security sector reform; non-proliferation of weapons of mass destruction; the relationship between the Council and regional organizations; the role of the Council in addressing humanitarian crises; and the role of the UN in post-conflict national reconciliation.

SPECIAL SUBSIDIARY BODIES

Counter-Terrorism Committee (CTC): f. 2001, pursuant to Security Council Resolution 1373 (2001) and, in March 2004, in accordance with Resolution 1535 (2004), elevated to a special subsidiary body; comprises a Plenary (composed of the Council member states) and a Bureau; assisted by an Executive Directorate (the Counter-Terrorism Committee Executive Directorate—CTED, which became operational in December 2005); since Sept. 2005 the CTC has also been mandated to monitor member states' implementation of Resolution 1624 (2005), concerning incitement to commit acts of terrorism; Chair. HARDEEP SINGH PURI (India); Exec. Dir, Counter-Terrorism Exec. Directorate MICHAEL PETER FFLOYD SMITH (Australia).

The UN Peace-building Commission, which was inaugurated in June 2006, its establishment having been authorized by the Security Council and General Assembly in December 2005, is a subsidiary advisory body of both the Council and Assembly.

COMMITTEES

In April 2012 there were three **Standing Committees**, each composed of representatives of all Council member states:

Committee of Experts on Rules of Procedure (studies and advises on rules of procedure and other technical matters);

Committee on the Admission of New Members;

Committee on Council Meetings away from Headquarters.

Ad hoc Committees, which are established as needed, comprise all Council members and meet in closed session:

Governing Council of the UN Compensation Commission established by Security Council Resolution 692 (1991);

1540 Committee established pursuant to Security Council Resolution 1540 (2004).

Within this category are the Sanctions Committees, which may be established to oversee economic or political enforcement measures, imposed by the Security Council to maintain or restore international peace and security. At April 2012 the following committees were operational:

Security Council Committee established pursuant to Resolution 1988 (2011) concerning the Taliban in Afghanistan;

Security Council Committee established pursuant to Resolution 1970 (2011) concerning the Libyan Arab Jamahiriya;

Security Council Committee established pursuant to Resolution 1737 (2006) concerning Iran;

Security Council Committee established pursuant to Resolution 1718 (2006) concerning the Democratic People's Republic of Korea;

Security Council Committee established pursuant to Resolution 1636 (2005) concerning Syria;

Security Council Committee established pursuant to Resolution 1591 (2005) concerning Sudan;

Security Council Committee established pursuant to Resolution 1572 (2004) concerning Côte d'Ivoire;

Security Council Committee established pursuant to Resolution 1533 (2004) concerning the Democratic Republic of the Congo;

Security Council Committee established pursuant to Resolution 1521 (2003) concerning Liberia;

Security Council Committee established pursuant to Resolution 1518 (2003) concerning the financial assets of the former Iraqi regime;

Security Council Committee established pursuant to Resolutions 1267 (1999) and 1989 (2011) concerning al-Qa'ida and the Taliban and associated individuals and entities;

Security Council Committee established pursuant to Resolution 751 (1992) concerning Somalia and Resolution 1907 (2009) concerning Eritrea.

Office of the Ombudsperson of the 1267 Committee: Rm TB-08041D, UN Plaza, New York, NY 10017, USA; f. Dec. 2009; reviews requests from individuals, groups, undertakings or entities seeking to be removed from the Consolidated List maintained by the Security Council Committee established pursuant to Resolution 1267 (1999) concerning al-Qa'ida and the Taliban; Ombudsperson KIMBERLY PROST.

In June 1993 an Informal Working Group on Documentation and other procedural questions was established. An Informal Working Group on General Issues on Sanctions was established in 2000 to consider ways of improving the effectiveness of UN sanctions and a Working Group on Peace-keeping Operations was established in January 2001. In March 2002 an Ad Hoc Working Group on Conflict Prevention and Resolution in Africa was established. A Working Group established (in October 2004) pursuant to Resolution 1566 was mandated to consider practical measures to be imposed upon individuals, groups or entities involved in or associated with terrorist activities, other than those designated by the Committee on al-Qa'ida and the Taliban; and the possibility of establishing an international fund to compensate victims of terrorist acts and their families. A Working Group on Children and Armed Conflict was established in July 2005.

AD HOC INTERNATIONAL TRIBUNALS

INTERNATIONAL RESIDUAL MECHANISM FOR CRIMINAL TRIBUNALS

The Residual Mechanism was established by Security Council Resolution 1966 (December 2010) to undertake some essential functions of the International Tribunal for the Former Yugoslavia (ICTY) and of the International Criminal Tribunal for Rwanda (ICTR) upon their planned closure. The Residual Mechanism was to comprise two branches, based in Arusha, Tanzania (due to commence operations on 1 July 2012), and in The Hague, Netherlands (to be operational from 1 July 2013). In January 2012 the UN Secretary-General appointed John Hocking, the ICTY Registrar, to be concurrently Registrar of the Mechanism, and in February Theodor Meron, the ICTY President, and Hassan Bubacar Jallow, the ICTR Prosecutor, were appointed to be, respectively, President and Prosecutor of the Residual Mechanism. The Mechanism was to operate for an initial period of four years from the first commencement date (1 July 2012). It was to conduct any appeals against Tribunal judgements filed following its entry into operation.

President of the Residual Mechanism: THEODOR MERON (Poland).

Prosecutor of the Residual Mechanism: HASSAN BUBACAR JALLOW (The Gambia).

Registrar of the Residual Mechanism: JOHN HOCKING (Australia).

INTERNATIONAL CRIMINAL TRIBUNAL FOR THE FORMER YUGOSLAVIA—ICTY

Address: Registry: Public Information Unit, POB 13888, 2501 EW The Hague, Netherlands.

Telephone: (70) 512-5343; **fax:** (70) 512-5355; **internet:** www.icty.org.

In May 1993 the Security Council, acting under Article VII of the UN Charter, adopted Resolution 827, which established an ad hoc 'war crimes' tribunal. The so-called International Tribunal for the Prosecution of Persons Responsible for Serious Violations of International Humanitarian Law Committed in the Territory of the Former Yugoslavia (also referred to as the International Criminal Tribunal for the former Yugoslavia—ICTY) was inaugurated in The Hague, Netherlands, in November. The ICTY consists of a Chief Prosecutor's office, and 16 permanent judges, of whom 11 sit in three trial chambers and five sit in a seven-member appeals chamber (with the remaining two appeals chamber members representing the ICTR, see below). In addition, a maximum at any one time of nine *ad litem* judges, drawn from a pool of 27, serve as required. Public hearings were initiated in November 1994. The first trial proceedings commenced in May 1996, and the first sentence was imposed by the Tribunal in November. In July and November 1995 the Tribunal formally charged the Bosnian Serb political and military leaders Radovan Karadžić and Gen. Ratko Mladić, on two separate indictments, with genocide, crimes against humanity, violation of the laws and customs of war and serious breaches of the Geneva Conventions. In July 1996 the Tribunal issued international warrants for their arrest. Amended indictments, confirmed in May 2000, and announced in October and November, respectively, included the withdrawal of the fourth charge against Mladić. Karadžić was eventually detained in July 2008, and Mladić was captured in May 2011. In April 2000 Momčilo Krajišnik, a senior associate of Karadžić, was detained by the ICTY, charged with genocide, war crimes and crimes against humanity. Biljana Plavšić, another former Bosnian Serb political leader, surrendered to the Tribunal in January 2001, also indicted on charges of genocide, war crimes and crimes against humanity. In the following month three Bosnian Serb former soldiers were convicted by the ICTY of utilizing mass rape and the sexual enslavement of women as instruments of terror in wartime. In February 2003 Plavšić was sentenced to 11 years' imprisonment, having pleaded guilty in October 2002 to one of the charges against her (persecutions: a crime against humanity). (Under a plea agreement reached with the Tribunal the remaining charges had been withdrawn.) In mid-1998 the ICTY began investigating reported acts of violence against civilians committed by both sides in the conflict in the southern Serbian province of Kosovo and Metohija. In early 1999 there were reports of large-scale organized killings, rape and expulsion of the local Albanian population by Serbian forces. In April ICTY personnel visited refugee camps in neighbouring countries in order to compile evidence of the atrocities, and obtained intelligence information from NATO members regarding those responsible for the incidents. In May the then President of the then Federal Republic of Yugoslavia (FRY, which was renamed Serbia and Montenegro in February 2003, and divided into separate states of Montenegro and

Serbia in 2006), Slobodan Milošević, was indicted, along with three senior government ministers and the chief-of-staff of the army, charged with crimes against humanity and violations of the customs of war committed in Kosovo since 1 January 1999; international warrants were issued for their arrests. In June, following the establishment of an international force to secure peace in Kosovo, the ICTY established teams of experts to investigate alleged atrocities at 529 identified grave sites. The new FRY administration, which had assumed power following legislative and presidential elections in late 2000, contested the impartiality of the ICTY, proposing that Milošević and other members of the former regime should be tried before a national court. In April 2001 Milošević was arrested by the local authorities in Belgrade. Under increasing international pressure, the Federal Government approved his extradition in June, and he was immediately transferred to the ICTY, where he was formally charged with crimes against humanity committed in Kosovo in 1999. A further indictment of crimes against humanity committed in Croatia during 1991–92 was confirmed in October 2001, and a third indictment, which included charges of genocide committed in Bosnia and Herzegovina in 1991–95, was confirmed in November 2001. In February 2002 the Appeals Chamber ordered that the three indictments be considered in a single trial. The trial commenced later in that month. Milošević, however, continued to protest at the alleged illegality of his arrest and refused to recognize the jurisdiction of the Court. The case was delayed repeatedly owing to the ill health of the defendant, and in March 2006 he died in captivity. In August 2001 the ICTY passed its first sentence of genocide, convicting a former Bosnian Serb military commander, Gen. Radislav Kristić, for his role in the deaths of up to 8,000 Bosnian Muslim men and boys in Srebrenica in July 1995. In January 2003 Fatmir Limaj, an ethnic Albanian deputy in the Kosovo parliament and former commander of the Kosovo Liberation Army (KLA), was indicted by the ICTY on several counts of crimes against humanity and war crimes that were allegedly committed in mid-1998 against Serb and Albanian detainees at the KLA's Lapusnik prison camp. Limaj was arrested in Slovenia in February 2003 and transferred to ICTY custody in early March. In July 2011 Serbian authorities arrested Goran Hadžic, who had been the last remaining indictee at large. At March 2012 the ICTY had indicted a total of 161 people. Of those who had appeared in proceedings before the Tribunal, 13 had been acquitted, 64 had received a final guilty sentence, and 13 had been referred to national jurisdictions. Some 35 people had completed their sentences. At that time proceedings were ongoing against 35 people accused by the Tribunal, including some 16 who were on trial, and 17 at the appeals stage. The ICTY's completion strategy envisaged that the Tribunal's activities would be terminated on 30 June 2013, and that from 1 July 2013 outstanding essential functions of the Tribunal would be taken over by the International Residual Mechanism for Criminal Tribunals. Appeals procedures were expected to be finalized by the end of 2014, apart from any appeal in the Radovan Karadžić case, which was expected to be finalized subsequently, and any appeals relating to Gen. Ratko Mladić or Goran Hadžic. The ICTY was to complete all appellate proceedings for which the notice of appeal against the judgement or sentence was filed before the start date of the Mechanism. The ICTY assisted with the establishment of the War Crimes Chamber within the Bosnia and Herzegovina state court, which became operational in March 2005, and also helped Croatia to strengthen its national judicial capacity to enable war crimes to be prosecuted within that country

President of the ICTY: THEODOR MERON (Poland).

ICTY Prosecutor: SERGE BRAMMERTZ (Belgium).

ICTY Registrar: JOHN HOCKING (Australia).

INTERNATIONAL CRIMINAL TRIBUNAL FOR RWANDA—ICTR

Address: Registry: Arusha International Conference Centre, POB 6016, Arusha, Tanzania.

Telephone: (212) 963-2850; **fax:** (212) 963-2848; **e-mail:** ictr-press@un.org; **internet:** www.ictr.org.

In November 1994 the Security Council adopted Resolution 955, establishing the ICTR to prosecute persons responsible for genocide and other serious violations of humanitarian law that had been committed in Rwanda and by Rwandans in neighbouring states. Its temporal jurisdiction was limited to the period 1 January to 31 December 1994. UN Secretary Council Resolution 977, adopted in February 1995, determined that the seat of the Tribunal would be located in Arusha, Tanzania. The Tribunal consists of 11 permanent judges, of whom nine sit in four trial chambers and two sit in the seven-member appeals chamber that is shared with the ICTY and based at The Hague. A high security UN Detention Facility, the first of its kind, was constructed within the compound of the prison in Arusha and opened in 1996. In August 2002 the UN Security Council endorsed a proposal by the ICTR President to elect a pool of 18 *ad litem* judges to the Tribunal with a view to accelerating its activities. In October 2003 the Security Council increased the number of *ad litem* judges who may serve on the Tribunal at any one time from four to nine. The first plenary session of the Tribunal was held in The Hague in June 1995; formal proceedings at its permanent headquarters in Arusha were initiated in November. The first trial of persons charged by the Tribunal commenced in January 1997, and sentences were imposed in July. In September 1998 the former Rwandan Prime Minister, Jean Kambanda, and a former mayor of Taba, Jean-Paul Akayesu, both Hutu extremists, were found guilty of genocide and crimes against humanity; Kambanda subsequently became the first person ever to be sentenced under the 1948 Convention on the Prevention and Punishment of the Crime of Genocide. In October 2000 the Tribunal rejected an appeal by Kambanda. In November 1999 the Rwandan Government temporarily suspended co-operation with the Tribunal in protest at a decision of the appeals chamber to release an indicted former government official owing to procedural delays. (The appeals chamber subsequently reversed this decision.) In 2001 two ICTR investigators employed on defence teams were arrested and charged with genocide, having been found to be working at the Tribunal under assumed identities. Relations between the Rwandan Government and the ICTR deteriorated again in 2002, with the then Chief Prosecutor accusing the Rwandan authorities of failing to facilitate the travel of witnesses to the Tribunal and withholding access to documentary materials, and counter-accusations by the Rwandan Government that the Tribunal's progress was too slow, that further suspected perpetrators of genocide had been inadvertently employed by the Tribunal and that Rwandan witnesses attending the Tribunal had not received sufficient protection. Reporting to the UN Security Council in July, the then Chief Prosecutor alleged that the Rwandan refusal to co-operate ensued from her recent decision to indict former members of the Tutsi-dominated Rwanda Patriotic Army for human rights violations committed against Hutus in 1994. In January 2004 a former minister of culture and education, Jean de Dieu Kamuhanda, was found guilty on two counts of genocide and extermination as a crime against humanity. In the following month Samuel Imanishimwe, a former military commander, was convicted on seven counts of genocide, crimes against humanity and serious violations of the Geneva Conventions. In December 2008 Théoneste Bagosora, Aloys Ntabakuze and Anatole Nsengiyumva, former high-ranking military commanders, were found guilty of genocide, crimes against humanity and war crimes, and were each sentenced to life imprisonment. By March 2012 the Tribunal had delivered judgments against 69 accused, of whom 10 were acquitted, and 17 were appealing their convictions. Trial proceedings relating to five cases were ongoing at that time, while one indictee was awaiting trial; two cases were being tried in France under French national jurisdiction and a further case was referred in June for the first time to be tried in the Rwandan national court system. Eight fugitives wanted by the Tribunal remained at large. In late March the ICTR had ordered the case of a further suspect at large, Charles Sikubwabo, to be referred to the Rwandan High Court for trial. It was envisaged that from 1 July 2012 the International Residual Mechanism for Criminal Tribunals would take over outstanding essential functions of the Tribunal.

Both the ICTY and ICTR have been supported by teams of investigators and human rights experts working in the field to collect forensic and other evidence in order to uphold indictments. Evidence of mass graves resulting from large-scale unlawful killings has been uncovered in both regions.

President of the ICTR: VAGN JOENSEN (Denmark).

ICTR Prosecutor: HASSAN BUBACAR JALLOW (The Gambia).

ICTR Registrar: ADAMA DIENG (Senegal).

Trusteeship Council

The Trusteeship Council (comprising the People's Republic of China—a non-active member until May 1989, France, Russia, the United Kingdom and the USA) was established to supervise United Nations Trust Territories through their administering authorities and to promote the political, economic, social and educational advancement of their inhabitants towards self-government or independence (see Charter). On 1 October 1994 the last territory remaining under UN trusteeship, the Republic of Palau (part of the archipelago of the Caroline Islands), declared its independence under a compact of free association with the USA, its administering authority. The Security Council terminated the Trusteeship Agreement on 10 November, having determined that the objectives of the agreement had been fully attained. On 1 November the Trusteeship Council formally suspended its operations; thereafter it was to be convened on an extraordinary basis as required. The report of the UN Secretary-General entitled 'In Larger Freedom: Towards Development, Security and Human Rights for All', issued in March 2005, proposed that the Trusteeship Council should be terminated.

Economic and Social Council—ECOSOC

ECOSOC promotes world co-operation on economic, social, cultural and humanitarian problems. (See Charter of the United Nations.)

MEMBERS

Fifty-four members are elected by the General Assembly for three-year terms: 18 are elected each year. Membership is allotted by regions as follows: Africa 14 members, Western Europe and other developed countries 13, Asia 11, Latin America 10, Eastern Europe 6.

BUREAU

The Bureau, with responsibility for formulating the agenda and programme of work for the Council, is elected by the Council at its first meeting of the year. It comprises a President and four Vice-Presidents, each representing different regions.

President: MILOŠ KOTEREC (Slovakia) (2012).

ACTIVITIES

The Council, which meets annually for a four-week substantive session in July, alternately in New York and Geneva, is mainly a central policy-making and co-ordinating organ. It has a co-ordinating function between the UN and the specialized agencies, and also makes consultative arrangements with approved voluntary or non-governmental organizations which work within the sphere of its activities (some 3,337 organizations had consultative status in 2011). The Council has functional and regional commissions to carry out much of its detailed work. ECOSOC's purview extends to more than 70% of the human and financial resources of the UN system. The Council was given a leading role in following up the implementation of the Monterrey Consensus, adopted by the March 2002 International Conference on Financing for Development.

The report of the UN Secretary-General entitled 'In Larger Freedom: Towards Development, Security and Human Rights for All', issued in March 2005, outlined a number of proposed changes to ECOSOC aimed at improving its effectiveness. These included: the organization by the Council of annual ministerial-level progress reviews (AMRs) of agreed development goals, in particular the Millennium Development Goals (MDGs) pledged by UN heads of state and government in September 2000; the inauguration of a regular high-level Development Co-operation Forum (see below); the organization by the Council, whenever required, of meetings to assess and promote co-ordinated responses to threats to development, such as famines, epidemics and major natural disasters; and the development of a permanent structure within the Council for monitoring the economic and social dimensions of conflicts, with the aim of improving prospects for long-term recovery, reconstruction and reconciliation, and working in co-operation with the proposed new Peace-building Commission. The AMR process was initiated in 2007, comprising a series of global and regional preparatory meetings prior to the main review held during the annual session of the Council in July. As part of the review several countries each year prepare National Voluntary Presentations to demonstrate challenges, best practices and progress in implementing development goals. The theme of the 2012 AMR was 'promoting productive capacity, employment and decent work to eradicate poverty in the context of inclusive, sustainable and equitable economic growth at all levels for achieving the MDGs'.

Every year, normally in March or April, ECOSOC holds high-level consultations with the IMF, World Bank, WTO and UNCTAD. The 2012 consultations were held in March, in New York, USA, on the theme 'coherence, co-ordination and co-operation in the context of financing for development'.

DEVELOPMENT CO-OPERATION FORUM—DCF

The biennial high-level Development Co-operation Forum (DCF), held in New York, was inaugurated in July 2007. The Forum is mandated to advance the implementation of all internationally agreed development goals, including the MDGs, and to promote dialogue to find effective ways of supporting international development. The first Forum was convened in June–July 2008, with participation by UN bodies, bilateral development agencies, regional development banks, civil society and private sector representatives. The second DCF was held in June 2010. During 2011 two High-Level Symposia were held (in May, in Mali, and in October, in Luxembourg) in preparation for the third DCF, to be held in June-July 2012.

FUNCTIONAL COMMISSIONS

Commission on Crime Prevention and Criminal Justice: f. 1992; aims to formulate an international convention on crime prevention and criminal justice; 40 members.

Commission on Narcotic Drugs: f. 1946; mainly concerned in combating illicit traffic; 53 members; there is a Sub-Commission on Illicit Drug Traffic and Related Matters in the Near and Middle East.

Commission on Population and Development: f. 1946; advises the Council on population matters and their relation to socio-economic conditions; 47 members.

Commission on Science and Technology for Development: f. 1992; works on the restructuring of the UN in the economic, social and related fields; administration of the Commission undertaken by UNCTAD; 43 members.

Commission for Social Development: f. 1946 as the Social Commission; advises ECOSOC on issues of social and community development; 46 members.

Commission on the Status of Women: f. 1946; aims at equality of political, economic and social rights for women, and supports the right of women to live free of violence; 45 members.

Commission on Sustainable Development: f. 1993 to oversee integration into the UN's work of the objectives set out in 'Agenda 21', the programme of action agreed by the UN Conference on Environment and Development in June 1992; 53 members.

Statistical Commission: Standardizes terminology and procedure in statistics and promotes the development of national statistics; 24 members.

United Nations Forum on Forests: f. 2000; composed of all states members of the United Nations and its specialized agencies.

REGIONAL COMMISSIONS

(see United Nations Regional Commissions)

Economic Commission for Africa (ECA).

Economic Commission for Europe (ECE).

Economic Commission for Latin America and the Caribbean (ECLAC).

Economic and Social Commission for Asia and the Pacific (ESCAP).

Economic and Social Commission for Western Asia (ESCWA).

STANDING COMMITTEES

Committee on Negotiations with Intergovernmental Agencies: f. 1946.

Committee on Non-Governmental Organizations: f. 1946; 19 members.

Committee for Programme and Co-ordination: f. 1962; 34 members.

EXPERT BODIES

Committee for Development Policy: f. 1965 (as Cttee for Devt Planning), renamed in 1988; 24 members serving in a personal capacity for three-year terms.

Committee of Experts on International Co-operation in Tax Matters: f. 2004; 25 members serving in a personal capacity.

Committee of Experts on Public Administration: f. 1967 (as Group of Experts in Public Admin. and Finance), renamed 2002; 24 members serving in a personal capacity.

Committee of Experts on the Transport of Dangerous Goods and on the Globally Harmonized System of Classification and Labelling of Chemicals: 37 members serving as governmental experts.

Committee on Economic, Social and Cultural Rights: f. 1985; 18 members serving in a personal capacity.

Permanent Forum on Indigenous Issues: f. 2000; 16 members serving in a personal capacity.

United Nations Group of Experts on Geographical Names: f. 1972; 23 members serving as governmental experts.

In addition there are two ad hoc bodies: the open-ended working group on informatics and the open-ended intergovernmental group of experts on energy and sustainable development. Other ad hoc mechanisms in 2011 were advisory groups on African countries emerging from conflict, an ad hoc advisory group on Haiti, and the UN Public-Private Alliance for Rural Development.

RELATED BODIES

International Narcotics Control Board: f. 1964; 13 members.

Programme Co-ordination Board for the Joint UN Programme on HIV/AIDS (UNAIDS): f. 1995; 22 members.

UNDP/UNFPA Executive Board: 36 members, elected by ECOSOC.

UN-Habitat Governing Council: 58 members, elected by ECOSOC.

UNHCR Executive Committee: 53 members, elected by ECOSOC.

UNICEF Executive Board: 36 members, elected by ECOSOC.

WFP Executive Board: one-half of the 36 members are elected by ECOSOC, one-half by FAO; governing body of the World Food Programme.

International Court of Justice

Address: Peace Palace, Carnegieplein 2, 2517 KJ The Hague, Netherlands.

Telephone: (70) 302-23-23; **fax:** (70) 364-99-28; **e-mail:** information@icj-cij.org; **internet:** www.icj-cij.org.

Established in 1945, the Court (sometimes referred to as the World Court) is the principal judicial organ of the UN. All members of the UN are parties to the Statute of the Court. (See Charter.)

THE JUDGES

(April 2012; in order of precedence)

	Term Ends*
President: PETER TOMKA (Slovakia)	2021
Vice-President: BERNARDO SEPÚLVEDA -AMOR (Mexico)	2015
Judges:	
HISASHI OWADA (Japan)	2021
RONNY ABRAHAM (France)	2015
KENNETH KEITH (New Zealand)	2015
MOHAMED BENNOUNA (Morocco)	2015
LEONID SKOTNIKOV (Russia)	2015
ANTÔNIO AUGUSTO CANÇADO TRINDADE (Brazil)	2018
ABDULQAWI AHMED YUSUF (Somalia)	2018
CHRISTOPHER GREENWOOD (United Kingdom)	2018
XUE HANQIN (People's Republic of China)	2021
JOAN E. DONOGHUE (USA)	2015
GIORGIO GAJA (Italy)	2021
JULIA SEBUTINDE (Uganda)	2021
DALVEER BHANDARI (India)	2018

* Each term ends on 5 February of the year indicated.

Registrar: PHILIPPE COUVREUR (Belgium).

The Court is composed of 15 judges, each of a different nationality, elected with an absolute majority by both the General Assembly and the Security Council. Representation of the main forms of civilization and the different legal systems of the world are borne in mind in their election. Candidates are nominated by national panels of jurists.

The judges are elected for nine years and may be re-elected; elections for five seats are held every three years. The Court elects its President and Vice-President for each three-year period. Members may not have any political, administrative, or other professional occupation, and may not sit in any case with which they have been otherwise connected than as a judge of the Court. For the purposes of a case, each side—consisting of one or more states—may, unless the Bench already includes a judge with a corresponding nationality, choose a person from outside the Court to sit as a judge on terms of equality with the Members. Judicial decisions are taken by a majority of the judges present, subject to a quorum of nine Members. The President has a casting vote.

FUNCTIONS

The International Court of Justice operates in accordance with a Statute which is an integral part of the UN Charter. Only states may be parties in cases before the Court; those not parties to the Statute may have access in certain circumstances and under conditions laid down by the Security Council.

The Jurisdiction of the Court comprises:

1. All cases which the parties refer to it jointly by special agreement (indicated in the list below by a stroke between the names of the parties);

2. All matters concerning which a treaty or convention in force provides for reference to the Court through the inclusion of a jurisdictional clause. Some 300 agreements, both bilateral and multilateral, have been notified to the Court's Registry, for example: Treaty of Peace with Japan (1951); European Convention for Peaceful Settlement of Disputes (1957); Single Convention on Narcotic Drugs (1961); International Convention on the Elimination of All Forms of Racial Discrimination (1966); Protocol relating to the Status of Refugees (1967); Convention on the Suppression of the Unlawful Seizure of Aircraft (1970); Convention on the Elimination of All Forms of Discrimination against Women (1979); Convention against Torture and Other Cruel, Inhuman or Degrading Treatment or Punishment (1984); International Convention for the Suppression of the Financing of Terrorism (1999);

3. Legal disputes between states which have recognized the jurisdiction of the Court as compulsory for specified classes of dispute. Declarations by the following 66 states accepting the compulsory jurisdiction of the Court are in force (although many with reservations): Australia, Austria, Barbados, Belgium, Botswana, Bulgaria, Cambodia, Cameroon, Canada, the Democratic Republic of the Congo, Costa Rica, Côte d'Ivoire, Cyprus, Denmark, Djibouti, Dominica, the Dominican Republic, Egypt, Estonia, Finland, The Gambia, Germany, Georgia, Greece, Guinea, Guinea-Bissau, Haiti, Honduras, Hungary, India, Japan, Kenya, Lesotho, Liberia, Liechtenstein, Luxembourg, Madagascar, Malawi, Malta, Mauritius, Mexico, the Netherlands, New Zealand, Nicaragua, Nigeria, Norway, Pakistan, Panama, Paraguay, Peru, the Philippines, Poland, Portugal, Senegal, Slovakia, Somalia, Spain, Sudan, Suriname, Swaziland, Sweden, Switzerland, Togo, Uganda, the United Kingdom and Uruguay.

Disputes as to whether the Court has jurisdiction are settled by the Court.

Judgments are without appeal, but are binding only for the particular case and between the parties. States appearing before the Court undertake to comply with its Judgment. If a party to a case fails to do so, the other party may apply to the Security Council, which may make recommendations or decide upon measures to give effect to the Judgment.

Advisory opinions on legal questions may be requested by the General Assembly, the Security Council or, if so authorized by the Assembly, other United Nations organs or specialized agencies.

Rules of Court governing procedure are made by the Court under a power conferred by the Statute.

CASES

Judgments

Since 1946 some 152 cases have been referred to the Court relating to legal disputes or legal questions. Some were removed from the list as a result of settlement or discontinuance, or on the grounds of a lack of basis for jurisdiction. Cases which have been the subject of a Judgment by the Court include: Monetary Gold Removed from Rome in 1943 (Italy *v.* France, United Kingdom and USA); Sovereignty over

Certain Frontier Land (Belgium/Netherlands); Arbitral Award made by the King of Spain on 23 December 1906 (Honduras *v.* Nicaragua); Temple of Preah Vihear (Cambodia *v.* Thailand); South West Africa (Ethiopia and Liberia *v.* South Africa); Northern Cameroons (Cameroon *v.* United Kingdom); North Sea Continental Shelf (Federal Republic of Germany/Denmark and Netherlands); Appeal relating to the Jurisdiction of the ICAO Council (India *v.* Pakistan); Fisheries Jurisdiction (United Kingdom *v.* Iceland; Federal Republic of Germany *v.* Iceland); Nuclear Tests (Australia *v.* France; New Zealand *v.* France); Aegean Sea Continental Shelf (Greece *v.* Turkey); United States of America Diplomatic and Consular Staff in Tehran (USA *v.* Iran); Continental Shelf (Tunisia/Libya); Delimitation of the Maritime Boundary in the Gulf of Maine Area (Canada/USA); Continental Shelf (Libya/Malta); Application for revision and interpretation of the Judgment of 24 February 1982 in the case concerning the Continental Shelf (Tunisia *v.* Libya); Military and Paramilitary Activities in and against Nicaragua (Nicaragua *v.* USA); Frontier Dispute (Burkina Faso/Mali); Delimitation of Maritime Boundary (Denmark *v.* Norway); Maritime Boundaries (Guinea-Bissau *v.* Senegal); Elettronica Sicula SpA (USA *v.* Italy); Land, Island and Maritime Frontier Dispute (El Salvador/Honduras, in one aspect of which Nicaragua was permitted to intervene) (also, in 2003, Application for Revision of the 1992 Judgment in the Case concerning the Land, Island and Maritime Frontier Dispute, requested by El Salvador); Delimitation of Maritime Boundary in the area between Greenland and Jan Mayen island (Denmark *v.* Norway); Maritime Delimitation and Territorial Questions between Qatar and Bahrain (Qatar *v.* Bahrain); Territorial Dispute (Libya/Chad); East Timor (Portugal *v.* Australia); the Gabčíkovo–Nagymaros Hydroelectric Project (Hungary *v.* Slovakia); Fisheries Jurisdiction (Spain *v.* Canada); Delimitation of the Boundary around Kasikili Sedudu Island (Botswana *v.* Namibia); La Grand case (Germany *v.* USA); Arrest Warrant of 11 April 2000 (Democratic Republic of the Congo—DRC *v.* Belgium); Land and Maritime Boundary between Cameroon and Nigeria (Cameroon *v.* Nigeria, with Equatorial Guinea intervening); Sovereignty over Pulau Ligatan and Pulau Sipadan (Indonesia/Malaysia); Destruction of Oil Platforms (Iran *v.* USA); Avena and other Mexican Nationals (Mexico *v.* USA); Legality of Use of Force (Serbia and Montenegro *v.* Belgium; Canada; France; Germany; Italy; the Netherlands; Portugal; and the United Kingdom); Certain Property (Liechtenstein *v.* Germany); Frontier Dispute (Benin/Niger); Armed Activities on the Territory of the Congo (DRC *v.* Burundi; Rwanda; and Uganda); Application of the Convention on the Prevention and Punishment of the Crime of Genocide (Bosnia and Herzegovina *v.* Serbia and Montenegro); Territorial and Maritime Dispute in the Caribbean Sea (Nicaragua *v.* Honduras); a Case Concerning the Sovereignty of Pedra Branca/Pulau Batu Puteh, Middle Rocks and South Ledge (Malaysia/Singapore); Certain Questions of Mutual Assistance in Criminal Matters (Djibouti *v.* France); Request for Interpretation of the Judgment of 31 March 2004 in the Case concerning Avena and Other Mexican Nationals (Mexico *v.* USA); Maritime Delimitation in the Black Sea (Romania *v.* Ukraine); a Dispute regarding Navigational and Related Rights (Costa Rica *v.* Nicaragua); Pulp Mills on the River Uruguay (Argentina *v.* Uruguay); Ahmadou Sadio Diallo (Republic of Guinea *v.* Democratic Republic of the Congo); Application of the International Convention on the Elimination of All Forms of Racial Discrimination (Georgia *v.* Russia); Application of the Interim Accord of 13 September 1995 (former Yugoslav Republic of Macedonia *v.* Greece); and Jurisdictional Immunities of the State (Germany *v.* Italy: Greece intervening).

Pending Cases

In 2012 the following contentious cases were under consideration, or pending before the Court: a request by Slovakia for an additional judgment in the dispute with Hungary concerning the Gabčíkovo–Nagymaros Hydroelectric Project (initial Judgment having been delivered in Sept. 1997); further deliberation of the case brought by the DRC against Uganda concerning armed activities on its territory (initial Judgment having been delivered in Dec. 2005); a case brought by Croatia against Serbia concerning the application of the 1948 Convention on the Prevention and Punishment of the Crime of Genocide (Judgment on the preliminary objections regarding jurisdiction and admissibility having been delivered in Nov. 2008); a case brought by Peru against Chile on maritime delimitation in the Pacific ocean; a case brought by Ecuador concerning alleged aerial spraying by Colombia of toxic herbicides over Ecuadorian territory; a territorial and maritime dispute brought by Nicaragua against Colombia; proceedings brought by Belgium against Senegal concerning its obligation to prosecute, or extradite for prosecution, the former President of Chad; proceedings instituted by Australia against Japan for alleged breach of its obligations under the International Convention for the Regulation of Whaling; a joint application by Burkina Faso and Niger regarding a frontier dispute; a case brought by Costa Rica against Nicaragua for allegedly violating Costa Rica's territorial integrity during the construction of a canal and through interference in the San Juan River; a case brought by Nicaragua against Costa Rica concerning alleged violations of Nicaraguan sovereignty and major environmental damages to its territory through the construction of a road in Costa Rica alongside the San Juan River; and an application by Cambodia requesting interpretation of a 1962 Judgment in the case concerning the Temple of Preah Vihear (Cambodia *v.* Thailand).

Advisory Opinions

Matters on which the Court has delivered an Advisory Opinion at the request of the United Nations General Assembly include the following: Condition of Admission of a State to Membership in the United Nations; Competence of the General Assembly for the Admission of a State to the United Nations; Interpretation of the Peace Treaties with Bulgaria, Hungary and Romania; International Status of South West Africa; Reservations to the Convention on the Prevention and Punishment of the Crime of Genocide; Effect of Awards of Compensation Made by the United Nations Administrative Tribunal (UNAT); Western Sahara; Application for Review of UNAT Judgment No. 333; Applicability of the Obligation to Arbitrate under Section 21 of the United Nations Headquarters Agreement of 26 June 1947 (relating to the closure of the Observer Mission to the United Nations maintained by the Palestine Liberation Organization); Legality of the Use or Threat of Nuclear Weapons; and Legal Consequences of the Construction of a Wall by Israel in the Occupied Palestinian Territory (delivered in July 2004); and the legality of a unilateral declaration of independence by the Provisional Institutions of Self-Government of Kosovo (delivered in July 2010).

An Advisory Opinion has been given at the request of the Security Council: Legal Consequences for States of the continued presence of South Africa in Namibia (South West Africa) notwithstanding Security Council resolution 276 (1970).

In 1989 (at the request of the UN Economic and Social Council—ECOSOC) the Court gave an Advisory Opinion on the Applicability of Article 6, Section 22, of the Convention on the Privileges and Immunities of the United Nations. The Court has also, at the request of UNESCO, given an Advisory Opinion on Judgments of the Administrative Tribunal of the ILO upon Complaints made against UNESCO, and on the Constitution of the Maritime Safety Committee of the Inter-Governmental Maritime Consultative Organization (IMCO), at the request of IMCO. In July 1996 the Court delivered an Advisory Opinion on the Legality of the Use by a State of Nuclear Weapons in Armed Conflict, requested by WHO. In April 1999 the Court delivered an Advisory Opinion, requested by ECOSOC, on the Difference Relating to Immunity from Legal Process of a Special Rapporteur of the Commission on Human Rights. In February 2012 the Court delivered an Advisory Opinion, requested by the International Fund for Agricultural Development, relating to a judgment rendered by the Administrative Tribunal of the International Labour Organization.

Finance

The UN budget appropriation for the Court for the two-year period 2012–13 amounted to US $47.8m.

Publications

Acts and Documents, No. 6 (contains Statute and Rules of the Court, the Resolution concerning its internal judicial practice and other documents).

Bibliography (annually).

Pleadings (Written Pleadings and Statements, Oral Proceedings, Correspondence).

Reports (Judgments, Opinions and Orders).

Yearbook.

UNITED NATIONS FUNDAMENTAL TREATIES

Charter of the United Nations

(Signed 26 June 1945)

(Note: The report of the UN Secretary-General entitled 'In Larger Freedom: Towards Development, Security and Human Rights for All', issued in March 2005, proposed the following amendments to the Charter: the elimination of the 'enemy' clauses in Articles 53 and 107; the deletion from the Charter of Chapter XIII, 'The Trusteeship Council'; and the deletion of Article 47 on The Military Staff Committee and related references.)

WE THE PEOPLES OF THE UNITED NATIONS DETERMINED

to save succeeding generations from the scourge of war, which twice in our lifetime has brought untold sorrow to mankind, and to reaffirm faith in fundamental human rights, in the dignity and worth of the human person, in the equal rights of men and women and of nations large and small, and

to establish conditions under which justice and respect for the obligations arising from treaties and other sources of international law can be maintained, and

to promote social progress and better standards of life in larger freedom,

AND FOR THESE ENDS

to practise tolerance and live together in peace with one another as good neighbours, and

to unite our strength to maintain international peace and security, and

to ensure, by the acceptance of principles and the institution of methods, that armed force shall not be used, save in the common interest, and

to employ international machinery for the promotion of the economic and social advancement of all peoples,

HAVE RESOLVED TO COMBINE OUR EFFORTS TO ACCOMPLISH THESE AIMS.

Accordingly, our respective Governments, through representatives assembled in the city of San Francisco, who have exhibited their full powers found to be in good and due form, have agreed to the present Charter of the United Nations and do hereby establish an international organization to be known as the United Nations.

I. PURPOSES AND PRINCIPLES

Article 1

The Purposes of the United Nations are:
1. To maintain international peace and security, and to that end: to take effective collective measures for the prevention and removal of threats to the peace, and for the suppression of acts of aggression or other breaches of the peace, and to bring about by peaceful means, and in conformity with the principles of justice and international law, adjustment or settlement of international disputes or situations which might lead to a breach of the peace;
2. To develop friendly relations among nations based on respect for the principle of equal rights and self-determination of peoples, and to take other appropriate measures to strengthen universal peace;
3. To achieve international co-operation in solving international problems of an economic, social, cultural, or humanitarian character, and in promoting and encouraging respect for human rights and for fundamental freedoms for all without distinction as to race, sex, language, or religion; and
4. To be a centre for harmonizing the accusations of nations in the attainment of these common ends.

Article 2

The Organization and its Members, in pursuit of the Purposes stated in Article 1, shall act in accordance with the following Principles.
1. The Organization is based on the principle of the sovereign equality of all its Members;
2. All Members, in order to ensure to all of them the rights and benefits resulting from membership, shall fulfil in good faith the obligations assumed by them in accordance with the present Charter;
3. All Members shall settle their international disputes by peaceful means in such a manner that international peace and security, and justice, are not endangered;
4. All Members shall refrain in their international relations from the threat or use of force against the territorial integrity or political independence of any state, or in any manner inconsistent with the Purposes of the United Nations;
5. All Members shall give the United Nations every assistance in any action it takes in accordance with the present Charter, and shall refrain from giving assistance to any state against which the United Nations is taking preventive or enforcement action;
6. The Organization shall ensure that states which are not Members of the United Nations act in accordance with these Principles so far as may be necessary for the maintenance of international peace and security;
7. Nothing contained in the present Charter shall authorize the United Nations to intervene in matters which are essentially within the domestic jurisdiction of any state or shall require the Members to submit such matters to settlement under the present Charter; but this principle shall not prejudice the application of enforcement measures under Chapter VII.

II. MEMBERSHIP

Article 3

The original Members of the United Nations shall be the states which, having participated in the United Nations Conference on International Organization at San Francisco, or having previously signed the Declaration by United Nations of January 1, 1942, sign the present Charter and ratify it in accordance with Article 110.

Article 4

1. Membership in the United Nations is open to all other peace-loving states which accept the obligations contained in the present Charter and, in the judgement of the Organization, are able and willing to carry out these obligations.
2. The admission of any such state to membership in the United Nations will be effected by a decision of the General Assembly upon the recommendation of the Security Council.

Article 5

A member of the United Nations against which preventive or enforcement action has been taken by the Security Council may be suspended from the exercise of the rights and privileges of membership by the General Assembly upon the recommendation of the Security Council. The exercise of these rights and privileges may be restored by the Security Council.

Article 6

A Member of the United Nations which has persistently violated the Principles contained in the present Charter may be expelled from the Organization by the General Assembly upon the recommendation of the Security Council.

III. ORGANS

Article 7

1. There are established as the principal organs of the United Nations: a General Assembly, a Security Council, an Economic and Social Council, a Trusteeship Council, an International Court of Justice, and a Secretariat.
2. Such subsidiary organs as may be found necessary may be established in accordance with the present Charter.

Article 8

The United Nations shall place no restrictions on the eligibility of men and women to participate in any capacity and under conditions of equality in its principal and subsidiary organs.

IV. THE GENERAL ASSEMBLY

Composition

Article 9

1. The General Assembly shall consist of all the Members of the United Nations.

2. Each Member shall have not more than five representatives in the General Assembly.

Functions and Powers

Article 10

The General Assembly may discuss any questions or any matters within the scope of the present Charter or relating to the powers and functions of any organs provided for in the present Charter, and, except as provided in Article 12, may make recommendations to the Members of the United Nations or to the Security Council or to both on any such questions or matters.

Article 11

1. The General Assembly may consider the general principles of co-operation in the maintenance of international peace and security, including the principles governing disarmament and the regulation of armaments, and may make recommendations with regard to such principles to the Members or to the Security Council or to both.
2. The General Assembly may discuss any questions relating to the maintenance of international peace and security brought before it by any Member of the United Nations, or by the Security Council, or by a state which is not a Member of the United Nations in accordance with Article 35, paragraph 2, and, except as provided in Article 12, may make recommendations with regard to any such question to the state or states concerned or to the Security Council or both. Any such question on which action is necessary shall be referred to the Security Council by the General Assembly either before or after discussion.
3. The General Assembly may call the attention of the Security Council to situations which are likely to endanger international peace and security.
4. The powers of the General Assembly set forth in this Article shall not limit the general scope of Article 10.

Article 12

1. While the Security Council is exercising in respect of any dispute or situation the functions assigned to it in the present Charter, the General Assembly shall not make any recommendations with regard to that dispute or situation unless the Security Council so requests. 2.
2. The Secretary-General, with the consent of the Security Council, shall notify the General Assembly at each session of any matters relative to the maintenance of international peace and security which are being dealt with by the Security Council and shall similarly notify the General Assembly, or the Members of the United Nations if the General Assembly is not in session, immediately the Security Council ceases to deal with such matters.

Article 13

1. The General Assembly shall initiate studies and make recommendations for the purpose of:

(a) promoting international co-operation in the political field and encouraging the progressive development of international law and its codification;

(b) promoting international co-operation in the economic, social, cultural, educational, and health fields, and assisting in the realization of human rights and fundamental freedoms for all without distinction as to race, sex, language, or religion.

2. The further responsibilities, functions and powers of the General Assembly with respect to matters mentioned in paragraph 1(b) above are set forth in Chapters IX and X.

Article 14

Subject to the provision of Article 12, the General Assembly may recommend measures for the peaceful adjustment of any situation, regardless of origin, which it deems likely to impair the general welfare or friendly relations among nations, including situations resulting from a violation of the provisions of the present Charter setting forth the Purposes and Principles of the United Nations.

Article 15

1. The General Assembly shall receive and consider annual and special reports from the Security Council; these reports shall include an account of the measures that the Security Council has decided upon or taken to maintain international peace and security.
2. The General Assembly shall receive and consider reports from the other organs of the United Nations.

Article 16

The General Assembly shall perform such functions with respect to the international trusteeship system as are assigned to it under Chapters XII and XIII, including the approval of the trusteeship agreements for areas not designated as strategic.

Article 17

1. The General Assembly shall consider and approve the budget of the Organization.
2. The expenses of the Organization shall be borne by the Members as apportioned by the General Assembly
3. The General Assembly shall consider and approve any financial and budgetary arrangements with specialized agencies referred to in Article 57 and shall examine the administrative budgets of such specialized agencies with a view to making recommendations to the agencies concerned.

Voting

Article 18

1. Each Member of the General Assembly shall have one vote.
2. Decisions of the General Assembly on important questions shall be made by a two-thirds majority of the members present and voting. These questions shall include: recommendations with respect to the maintenance of international peace and security, the election of the non-permanent Members of the Security Council, the election of the Members of the Economic and Social Council, the election of Members of the Trusteeship Council in accordance with paragraph 1(c) of Article 86, the admission of new Members to the United Nations, the suspension of the rights and privileges of membership, the expulsion of Members, questions relating to the operation of the trusteeship system, and budgetary questions.
3. Decisions on other questions, including the determination of additional categories of questions to be decided by a two-thirds majority, shall be made by a majority of the members present and voting.

Article 19

A Member of the United Nations which is in arrears in the payment of its financial contributions to the Organization shall have no vote in the General Assembly if the amount of its arrears equals or exceeds the amount of the contributions due from it for the preceding two full years. The General Assembly may, nevertheless, permit such a Member to vote if it is satisfied that the failure to pay is due to conditions beyond the control of the Member.

Procedure

Article 20

The General Assembly shall meet in regular annual sessions and in such special sessions as occasion may require. Special sessions shall be convoked by the Secretary-General at the request of the Security Council or of a majority of the members of the United Nations.

Article 21

The General Assembly shall adopt its own rules of procedure. It shall elect its President for each session.

Article 22

The General Assembly may establish such subsidiary organs as it deems necessary for the performance of its functions.

V. THE SECURITY COUNCIL

Composition

Article 23

1. The Security Council shall consist of 11 Members of the United Nations. The Republic of China, France, the Union of Soviet Socialist Republics, the United Kingdom of Great Britain and Northern Ireland, and the United States of America shall be permanent members of the Security Council. The General Assembly shall elect six other Members of the United Nations to be non-permanent members of the Security Council, due regard being specially paid, in the first instance to the contribution of Members of the United Nations to the maintenance of international peace and security and to the other purposes of the Organization, and also to equitable geographical distribution.
2. The non-permanent members of the Security Council shall be elected for a term of two years. In the first election of the non-permanent members, however, three shall be chosen for a term of one year. A retiring member shall not be eligible for immediate re-election.
3. Each member of the Security Council shall have one representative.

Note: From 1971 the Chinese seat in the UN General Assembly and its permanent seat in the Security Council were occupied by the People's Republic of China. In December 1991 Russia assumed the former USSR's seat in the UN General Assembly and its permanent seat in the Security Council.

Functions and Powers

Article 24

1. In order to ensure prompt and effective action by the United Nations, its Members confer on the Security Council primary responsibility for the maintenance of international peace and security, and agree that in carrying out its duties under this responsibility the Security Council acts on their behalf.
2. In discharging these duties the Security Council shall act in accordance with the Purposes and Principles of the United Nations. The specific powers granted to the Security Council for the discharge of these duties are laid down in Chapters VI, VII, VIII and XII.
3. The Security Council shall submit annual and, when necessary, special reports to the General Assembly for its consideration.

Article 25

The Members of the United Nations agree to accept and carry out the decisions of the Security Council in accordance with the present Charter.

Article 26

In order to promote the establishment and maintenance of international peace and security with the least diversion for armaments of the world's human and economic resources, the Security Council shall be responsible for formulating, with the assistance of the Military Staff Committee referred to in Article 47, plans to be submitted to the Members of the United Nations for the establishment of a system for the regulation of armaments.

Voting

Article 27

1. Each member of the Security Council shall have one vote.
2. Decisions of the Security Council on procedural matters shall be made by an affirmative vote of seven members.
3. Decisions of the Security Council on all other matters shall be made by an affirmative vote of seven members including the concurring votes of the permanent members; provided that, in decisions under Chapter VI, and under paragraph 3 of Article 52, a party to a dispute shall abstain from voting.

Procedure

Article 28

1. The Security Council shall be so organized as to be able to function continuously. Each member of the Security Council shall for this purpose be represented at all times at the seat of the Organization.
2. The Security Council shall hold periodic meetings at which each of its members may, if it so desires, be represented by a member of the government or by some other specially designated representative.
3. The Security Council may hold meetings at such places other than the seat of the Organization as in its judgment will best facilitate its work.

Article 29

The Security Council may establish such subsidiary organs as it deems necessary for the performance of its functions.

Article 30

The Security Council shall adopt its own rules of procedure, including the method of selecting its President.

Article 31

Any Member of the United Nations which is not a member of the Security Council may participate, without vote, in the discussion of any question brought before the Security Council whenever the latter considers that the interests of that Member are specially affected.

Article 32

Any Member of the United Nations which is not a member of the Security Council or any state which is not a Member of the United Nations, if it is a party to a dispute under consideration by the Security Council, shall be invited to participate, without vote, in the discussion relating to the dispute. The Security Council shall lay down such conditions as it deems just for the participation of a state which is not a Member of the United Nations.

VI. PACIFIC SETTLEMENT OF DISPUTES

Article 33

1. The parties to any dispute, the continuance of which is likely to endanger the maintenance of international peace and security, shall, first of all, seek a solution by negotiation, enquiry, mediation, conciliation, arbitration, judicial settlement, resort to regional agencies or arrangements, or other peaceful means of their own choice.
2. The Security Council shall, when it deems necessary, call upon the parties to settle their disputes by such means.

Article 34

The Security Council may investigate any dispute, or any situation which might lead to international friction or give rise to a dispute, in order to determine whether the continuance of the dispute or situation is likely to endanger the maintenance of international peace and security.

Article 35

1. Any Member of the United Nations may bring any dispute, or any situation of the nature referred to in Article 34, to the attention of the Security Council or of the General Assembly.
2. A state which is not a Member of the United Nations may bring to the attention of the Security Council or of the General Assembly any dispute to which it is a party if it accepts in advance, for the purposes of the dispute, the obligations of pacific settlement provided in the present Charter.
3. The proceedings of the General Assembly in respect of matters brought to its attention under this Article will be subject to the provisions of Articles 11 and 12.

Article 36

1. The Security Council may, at any stage of a dispute of the nature referred to in Article 33 or of a situation of like nature, recommend appropriate procedures or methods of adjustment.
2. The Security Council should take into consideration any procedures for the settlement of the dispute which have already been adopted by the parties.
3. In making recommendations under this Article the Security Council should also take into consideration that legal disputes should as a general rule be referred by the parties to the International Court of Justice in accordance with the provisions of the statute of the Court.

Article 37

1. Should the parties to a dispute of the nature referred to in Article 33, fail to settle it by the means indicated in that Article, they shall refer it to the Security Council.
2. If the Security Council deems that the continuance of the dispute is in fact likely to endanger the maintenance of international peace and security, it shall decide whether to take action under Article 36 or to recommend such terms of settlement as it may consider appropriate.

Article 38

Without prejudice to the provisions of Articles 33 to 37, the Security Council may, if all the parties to any dispute so request, make recommendations to the parties with a view to a pacific settlement of the dispute.

VII. ACTION WITH RESPECT TO THREATS TO THE PEACE, BREACHES OF THE PEACE, AND ACTS OF AGGRESSION

Article 39

The Security Council shall determine the existence of any threat to the peace, breach of the peace, or act of aggression and shall make recommendations, or decide what measures shall be taken in accordance with Articles 41 and 42, to maintain or restore international peace and security.

Article 40

In order to prevent an aggravation of the situation, the Security Council may, before making the recommendations or deciding upon the measures provided for in Article 39, call upon the parties concerned to comply with such provisional measures as it deems necessary or desirable. Such provisional measures shall be without prejudice to the rights, claims, or position of the parties concerned.

The Security Council shall duly take account of failure to comply with such provisional measures.

Article 41

The Security Council may decide what measures not involving the use of armed force are to be employed to give effect to its decisions, and it may call upon the Members of the United Nations to apply such measures. These may include complete or partial interruption of economic relations and of rail, sea, air, postal, telegraphic, radio, and other means of communication, and the severance of diplomatic relations.

Article 42

Should the Security Council consider that measures provided for in Article 41 would be inadequate or have proved to be inadequate, it may take such action by air, sea, or land forces as may be necessary to maintain or restore international peace and security. Such action may include demonstrations, blockade, and other operations by air, sea, or land forces of Members of the United Nations.

Article 43

1. All Members of the United Nations, in order to contribute to the maintenance of international peace and security, undertake to make available to the Security Council, on its call and in accordance with a special agreement or agreements, armed forces, assistance, and facilities, including rights of passage, necessary for the purpose of maintaining international peace and security.
2. Such agreement or agreements shall govern the numbers and types of forces, their degree of readiness and general location, and the nature of the facilities and assistance to be provided.
3. The agreement or agreements shall be negotiated as soon as possible on the initiative of the Security Council. They shall be concluded between the Security Council and Members or between the Security Council and groups of Members and shall be subject to ratification by the signatory states in accordance with their respective constitutional processes.

Article 44

When the Security Council has decided to use force it shall, before calling upon a Member not represented on it to provide armed forces in fulfilment of the obligations assumed under Article 43, invite that Member, if the Member so desires, to participate in the decisions of the Security Council concerning the employment of contingents of that Member's armed forces.

Article 45

In order to enable the United Nations to take urgent military measures, Members shall hold immediately available national air-force contingents for combined international enforcement action. The strength and degree of readiness of these contingents and plans for their combined action shall be determined, within the limits laid down in the special agreement and agreements referred to in Article 43, by the Security Council with the assistance of the Military Staff Committee.

Article 46

Plans for the application of armed force shall be made by the Security Council with the assistance of the Military Staff Committee.

Article 47

1. There shall be established a Military Staff Committee to advise and assist the Security Council on all questions relating to the Security Council's military requirements for the maintenance of international peace and security, the employment and command of forces placed at its disposal, the regulation of armaments, and possible disarmament.
2. The Military Staff Committee shall consist of the Chiefs of Staff of the permanent members of the Security Council or their representatives. Any Member of the United Nations not permanently represented on the Committee shall be invited by the Committee to be associated with it when the efficient discharge of the Committee's responsibilities requires the participation of that Member in its work.
3. The Military Staff Committee shall be responsible under the Security Council for the strategic direction of any armed forces placed at the disposal of the Security Council. Questions relating to the command of such forces shall be worked out subsequently.
4. The Military Staff Committee, with the authorization of the Security Council and after consultation with appropriate regional agencies, may establish regional sub-committees.

Article 48

1. The action required to carry out the decisions of the Security Council for the maintenance of international peace and security shall be taken by all the Members of the United Nations or by some of them, as the Security Council may determine.
2. Such decisions shall be carried out by the Members of the United Nations directly and through their action in the appropriate international agencies of which they are members.

Article 49

The Members of the United Nations shall join in affording mutual assistance in carrying out the measures decided upon by the Security Council.

Article 50

If preventive or enforcement measures against any state are taken by the Security Council, any other state, whether a Member of the United Nations or not, which finds itself confronted with special economic problems arising from the carrying out of those measures shall have the right to consult the Security Council with regard to a solution of those problems.

Article 51

Nothing in the present Charter shall impair the inherent right of individual or collective self-defence if an armed attack occurs against a Member of the United Nations, until the Security Council has taken measures necessary to maintain international peace and security. Measures taken by Members in the exercise of this right of self-defence shall be immediately reported to the Security Council and shall not in any way affect the authority and responsibility of the Security Council under the present Charter to take at any time such action as it deems necessary in order to maintain or restore international peace and security.

VIII. REGIONAL ARRANGEMENTS

Article 52

1. Nothing in the present Charter precludes the existence of regional arrangements or agencies for dealing with such matters relating to the maintenance of international peace and security as are appropriate for regional action, provided that such arrangements or agencies and their activities are consistent with the Purposes and Principles of the United Nations.
2. The Members of the United Nations entering into such arrangements or constituting such agencies shall make every effort to achieve pacific settlement of local disputes through such regional agencies before referring them to the Security Council.
3. The Security Council shall encourage the development of pacific settlement of local disputes through such regional arrangements or by such regional agencies either on the initiative of the states concerned or by reference from the Security Council.
4. This Article in no way impairs the application of Articles 34 and 35.

Article 53

1. The Security Council shall, where appropriate, utilize such regional arrangements or agencies for enforcement action under its authority. But no enforcement action shall be taken under regional arrangements or by regional agencies without the authorization of the Security Council, with the exception of measures against any enemy state, as defined in paragraph 2 of this Article, provided for pursuant to Article 107 or in regional arrangements directed against renewal of aggressive policy on the part of any such state, until such time as the Organization may, on request of the Governments concerned, be charged with the responsibility for preventing further aggression by such a state.
2. The term enemy state as used in paragraph I of this Article applies to any state which during the Second World War has been an enemy of any signatory of the present Charter.

Article 54

The Security Council shall at all times be kept fully informed of activities undertaken or in contemplation under regional arrangements or by regional agencies for the maintenance of international peace and security.

IX. INTERNATIONAL ECONOMIC AND SOCIAL CO-OPERATION

Article 55

With a view to the creation of conditions of stability and well-being which are necessary for peaceful and friendly relations among nations based on respect for the principle of equal rights and self-determination of peoples, the United Nations shall promote:

(a) higher standards of living, full employment, and conditions of economic and social progress and development;
(b) solutions of international economic, social, health, and related problems; and international cultural and educational co-operation; and
(c) universal respect for, and observance of, human rights and fundamental freedoms for all without distinction as to race, sex, language, or religion.

Article 56

All Members pledge themselves to take joint and separate action in co-operation with the Organization for the achievement of the purposes set forth in Article 55.

Article 57

1. The various specialized agencies, established by intergovernmental agreement and having wide international responsibilities, as defined in their basic instruments, in economic, social, cultural, educational, health, and related fields, shall be brought into relationship with the United Nations in accordance with the provisions of Article 63.
2. Such agencies thus brought into relationship with the United Nations are hereinafter referred to as specialized agencies.

Article 58

The Organization shall make recommendations for the co-ordination of the policies and activities of the specialized agencies.

Article 59

The Organization shall, where appropriate, initiate negotiations among the states concerned for the creation of any new specialized agencies required for the accomplishment of the purposes set forth in Article 55.

Article 60

Responsibility for the discharge of the functions of the Organization set forth in this Chapter shall be vested in the General Assembly and, under the authority of the General Assembly, in the Economic and Social Council, which shall have for this purpose the powers set forth in Chapter X.

X. THE ECONOMIC AND SOCIAL COUNCIL

Composition

Article 61

1. The Economic and Social Council shall consist of 18 Members of the United Nations elected by the General Assembly.
2. Subject to the provisions of paragraph 3, six members of the Economic and Social Council shall be elected each year for a term of three years. A retiring member shall be eligible for immediate re-election.
3. At the first election, 18 members of the Economic and Social Council shall be chosen. The term of office of six members so chosen shall expire at the end of one year, and of six other members at the end of two years, in accordance with arrangements made by the General Assembly.
4. Each member of the Economic and Social Council shall have one representative.

Functions and Powers

Article 62

1. The Economic and Social Council may make or initiate studies and reports with respect to international economic, social, cultural, educational, health, and related matters and may make recommendations with respect to any such matters to the General Assembly, to the Members of the United Nations, and to the specialized agencies concerned.
2. It may make recommendations for the purpose of promoting respect for, and observance of, human rights and fundamental freedoms for all.
3. It may prepare draft conventions for submission to the General Assembly, with respect to matters falling within its competence.
4. It may call, in accordance with the rules prescribed by the United Nations, international conferences on matters falling within its competence.

Article 63

1. The Economic and Social Council may enter into agreements with any of the agencies referred to in Article 57, defining the terms on which the agency concerned shall be brought into relationship with the United Nations. Such agreements shall be subject to approval by the General Assembly.
2. It may co-ordinate the activities of the specialized agencies through consultation with and recommendations to such agencies and through recommendations to the General Assembly and to the Members of the United Nations.

Article 64

1. The Economic and Social Council may take appropriate steps to obtain regular reports from the specialized agencies. It may make arrangements with the Members of the United Nations and with specialized agencies to obtain reports on the steps taken to give effect to its own recommendations and to recommendations on matters falling within its competence made by the General Assembly.
2. It may communicate its observations on these reports to the General Assembly.

Article 65

The Economic and Social Council may furnish information to the Security Council and shall assist the Security Council upon its request.

Article 66

1. The Economic and Social Council shall perform such functions as fall within its competence in connection with the carrying out of the recommendations of the General Assembly.
2. It may, with the approval of the General Assembly, perform services at the request of Members of the United Nations and at the request of specialized agencies.
3. It shall perform such other functions as are specified elsewhere in the present Charter or as may be assigned to it by the General Assembly.

Voting

Article 67

1. Each member of the Economic and Social Council shall have one vote.
2. Decisions of the Economic and Social Council shall be made by a majority of the members present and voting.

Procedure

Article 68

The Economic and Social Council shall set up commissions in economic and social fields and for the promotion of human rights, and such other commissions as may be required for the performance of its functions.

Article 69

The Economic and Social Council shall invite any Member of the United Nations to participate, without vote, in its deliberations on any matter of particular concern to that Member.

Article 70

The Economic and Social Council may make arrangements for representatives of the specialized agencies to participate, without vote, in its deliberations and in those of the commissions established by it, and for its representatives to participate in the deliberations of the specialized agencies.

Article 71

The Economic and Social Council may make suitable arrangements for consultation with non-governmental organizations which are concerned with matters within its competence. Such arrangements may be made with international organizations and, where appropriate, with national organizations after consultation with the Member of the United Nations concerned.

Article 72

1. The Economic and Social Council shall adopt its own rules of procedure, including the method of selecting its President.
2. The Economic and Social Council shall meet as required in accordance with its rules, which shall include provision for the convening of meetings on the request of a majority of its members.

XI. NON-SELF-GOVERNING TERRITORIES

Article 73

Members of the United Nations which have or assume responsibilities for the administration of territories whose peoples have not yet attained a full measure of self-government recognize the principle that the interests of the inhabitants of these territories are paramount, and accept as a sacred trust the obligation to promote to the utmost, within the system of international peace and security established by the present Charter, the well-being of the inhabitants of these territories, and, to this end:

(a) to ensure, with due respect for the culture of the peoples concerned, their political, economic, social, and educational advancement, their just treatment, and their protection against abuses;
(b) to develop self-government, to take due account of the political aspirations of the peoples, and to assist them in the progressive development of their free political institutions, according to the particular circumstances of each territory and its peoples and their varying stages of advancement;
(c) to further international peace and security;
(d) to promote constructive measures of development, to encourage research, and to co-operate with one another and, when and where appropriate, with specialized international bodies with a view to the practical achievement of the social, economic, and scientific purposes set forth in this Article; and
(e) to transmit regularly to the Secretary-General for information purposes, subject to such limitations as security and constitutional considerations may require, statistical and other information, of a technical nature relating to economic, social, and educational conditions in the territories for which they are respectively responsible other than those territories to which Chapters XII and XIII apply.

Article 74

Members of the United Nations also agree that their policy in respect of the territories to which this Chapter applies, no less than in respect of their metropolitan areas, must be based on the general principles of good-neighbourliness, due account being taken of the interests and well-being of the rest of the world, in social, economic, and commercial matters.

XII. INTERNATIONAL TRUSTEESHIP SYSTEM

Article 75

The United Nations shall establish under its authority an international trusteeship system for the administration and supervision of such territories as may be placed thereunder by subsequent individual agreements. These territories are hereinafter referred to as trust territories.

Article 76

The basic objectives of the trusteeship system, in accordance with the Purposes of the United Nations laid down in Article 1 of the present Charter, shall be:

(a) to further international peace and security;
(b) to promote the political, economic, social, and educational advancement of the inhabitants of the trust territories, and their progressive development towards self-government or independence as may be appropriate to the particular circumstances of each territory and its peoples and the freely expressed wishes of the peoples concerned, and as may be provided by the terms of each trusteeship agreement;
(c) to encourage respect for human rights and for fundamental freedoms for all without distinction as to race, sex, language, or religion, and to encourage recognition of the interdependence of the peoples of the world; and
(d) to ensure equal treatment in social, economic, and commercial matters for all Members of the United Nations and their nationals, and also equal treatment for the latter in the administration of justice, without prejudice to the attainment of the foregoing objectives and subject to the provisions of Article 80.

Article 77

1. The trusteeship system shall apply to such territories in the following categories as may be placed thereunder by means of trusteeship agreements.
(a) territories now held under mandate;
(b) territories which may be detached from enemy states as a result of the Second World War; and
(c) territories voluntarily placed under the system by states responsible for their administration.

2. It will be a matter for subsequent agreement as to which territories in the foregoing categories will be brought under the trusteeship system and upon what terms.

Article 78

The trusteeship system shall not apply to territories which have become Members of the United Nations, relationship among which shall be based on respect for the principle of sovereign equality.

Article 79

The terms of trusteeship for each territory to be placed under the trusteeship system, including any alteration or amendment, shall be agreed upon by the states directly concerned, including the mandatory power in the case of territories held under mandate by a Member of the United Nations, and shall be approved as provided for in Articles 83 and 85.

Article 80

1. Except as may be agreed upon in individual trusteeship agreements, made under Articles 77, 79, and 81, placing each territory under the trusteeship system, and until such agreements have been concluded, nothing in this Chapter shall be construed in or of itself to alter in any manner the rights whatsoever of any states or any peoples or the terms of existing international instruments to which Members of the United Nations may respectively be parties.
2. Paragraph 1 of this Article shall not be interpreted as giving grounds for delay or postponement of the negotiation and conclusion of agreements for placing mandated and other territories under the trusteeship system as provided for in Article 77.

Article 81

The trusteeship agreement shall in each case include the terms under which the trust territory will be administered and designate the authority which will exercise the administration of the trust territory. Such authority, hereinafter called the administering authority, may be one or more states or the Organization itself.

Article 82

There may be designated, in any trusteeship agreement, a strategic area or areas which may include part or all of the trust territory to which the agreement applies, without prejudice to any special agreement or agreements made under Article 43.

Article 83

1. All functions of the United Nations relating to strategic areas, including the approval of the terms of the trusteeship agreements and of their alteration or amendment, shall be exercised by the Security Council.
2. The basic objectives set forth in Article 76 shall be applicable to the people of each strategic area.
3. The Security Council shall, subject to the provisions of the trusteeship agreements and without prejudice to security considerations, avail itself of the assistance of the Trusteeship Council to perform those functions of the United Nations under the trusteeship system relating to political, economic, social, and educational matters in the strategic areas.

Article 84

It shall be the duty of the administering authority to ensure that the trust territory shall play its part in the maintenance of international peace and security. To this end the administering authority may make use of volunteer forces, facilities, and assistance from the trust territory in carrying out the obligations towards the Security Council undertaken in this regard by the administering authority, as well as for local defence and the maintenance of law and order within the trust territory.

Article 85

1. The functions of the United Nations with regard to trusteeship agreements for all areas not designated as strategic, including the approval of the terms of the trusteeship agreements and of their alteration or amendment, shall be exercised by the General Assembly.
2. The Trusteeship Council, operating under the authority of the General Assembly, shall assist the General Assembly in carrying out these functions.

XIII. THE TRUSTEESHIP COUNCIL

Composition

Article 86

1. The Trusteeship Council shall consist of the following Members of the United Nations:
(a) those Members administering trust territories;

(b) such of those Members mentioned by name in Article 23 as are not administering trust territories; and
(c) as many other Members elected for three-year terms by the General Assembly as may be necessary to ensure that the total number of members of the Trusteeship Council is equally divided between those Members of the United Nations which administer trust territories and those which do not.

2. Each member of the Trusteeship Council shall designate one specially qualified person to represent it therein.

Note: On 1 October 1994 the Republic of Palau, the last remaining territory under UN trusteeship, became independent. The Trusteeship Council formally suspended operations on 1 November; subsequently it was to be convened, as required, on an extraordinary basis.

Functions and Powers

Article 87

The General Assembly and, under its authority, the Trusteeship Council, in carrying out their functions, may:
(a) consider reports submitted by the administering authority
(b) accept petitions and examine them in consultation with the administering authority
(c) provide for periodic visits to the respective trust territories at times agreed upon with the administering authority; and
(d) take these and other actions in conformity with the terms of the trusteeship agreements.

Article 88

The Trusteeship Council shall formulate a questionnaire on the political, economic, social, and educational advancement of the inhabitants of each trust territory, and the administering authority for each trust territory within the competence of the General Assembly shall make an annual report to the General Assembly upon the basis of such questionnaire.

Voting

Article 89

1. Each member of the Trusteeship Council shall have one vote.
2. Decisions of the Trusteeship Council shall be made by a majority of the members present and voting.

Procedure

Article 90

1. The Trusteeship Council shall adopt its own rules of procedure, including the method of selecting its President.
2. The Trusteeship Council shall meet as required in accordance with its rules, which shall include provision for the convening of meetings on the request of a majority of its members.

Article 91

The Trusteeship Council shall, when appropriate, avail itself of the assistance of the Economic and Social Council and of the specialized agencies in regard to matters with which they are respectively concerned.

XIV. THE INTERNATIONAL COURT OF JUSTICE

Article 92

The International Court of Justice shall be the principal judicial organ of the United Nations. It shall function in accordance with the annexed Statute, which is based upon the Statute of the Permanent Court of International Justice and forms an integral part of the present Charter.

Article 93

1. All Members of the United Nations are *ipso facto* parties to the Statute of the International Court of Justice.
2. A state which is not a Member of the United Nations may become a party to the Statute of the International Court of Justice on condition to be determined in each case by the General Assembly upon the recommendation of the Security Council.

Article 94

1. Each Member of the United Nations undertakes to comply with the decision of the International Court of Justice in any case to which it is a party.
2. If any party to a case fails to perform the obligations incumbent upon it under a judgment rendered by the Court, the other party may have recourse to the Security Council, which may, if it deems necessary, make recommendations or decide upon measures to be taken to give effect to the judgment.

Article 95

Nothing in the present Charter shall prevent Members of the United Nations from entrusting the solution of their differences to other tribunals by virtue of agreements already in existence or which may be concluded in the future.

Article 96

1. The General Assembly or the Security Council may request the International Court of Justice to give an advisory opinion on any legal question.
2. Other organs of the United Nations and specialized agencies, which may at any time be so authorized by the General Assembly, may also request advisory opinions of the Court on legal questions arising within the scope of their activities.

XV. THE SECRETARIAT

Article 97

The Secretariat shall comprise a Secretary-General and such staff as the Organization may require. The Secretary-General shall be appointed by the General Assembly upon the recommendation of the Security Council. He shall be the chief administrative officer of the Organization.

Article 98

The Secretary-General shall act in that capacity in all meetings of the General Assembly, of the Security Council, of the Economic and Social Council, and of the Trusteeship Council, and shall perform such other functions as are entrusted to him by these organs. The Secretary-General shall make an annual report to the General Assembly on the work of the Organization.

Article 99

The Secretary-General may bring to the attention of the Security Council any matter which in his opinion may threaten the maintenance of international peace and security.

Article 100

1. In the performance of their duties the Secretary-General and the staff shall not seek or receive instructions from any government or from any other authority external to the Organization. They shall refrain from any action which might reflect on their position as international officials responsible only to the Organization.
2. Each Member of the United Nations undertakes to respect the exclusively international character of the responsibilities of the Secretary-General and the staff and not to seek to influence them in the discharge of their responsibilities.

Article 101

1. The staff shall be appointed by the Secretary-General under regulations established by the General Assembly.
2. Appropriate staffs shall be permanently assigned to the Economic and Social Council, the Trusteeship Council, and, as required, to other organs of the United Nations. These staffs shall form a part of the Secretariat.
3. The paramount consideration in the employment of the staff and in the determination of the conditions of service shall be the necessity of securing the highest standards of efficiency, competence, and integrity. Due regard shall be paid to the importance of recruiting the staff on as wide a geographical basis as possible.

XVI. MISCELLANEOUS PROVISIONS

Article 102

1. Every treaty and every international agreement entered into by any Member of the United Nations after the present Charter comes into force shall as soon as possible be registered with the Secretariat and published by it.
2. No party to any such treaty or international agreement which has not been registered in accordance with the provisions of paragraph 1 of this Article may invoke that treaty or agreement before any organ of the United Nations.

Article 103

In the event of a conflict between the obligations of the Members of the United Nations under the present Charter and their obligations under any other international agreement, their obligations under the present Charter shall prevail.

Article 104

The Organization shall enjoy in the territory of each of its Members such legal capacity as may be necessary for the exercise of its functions and the fulfilment of its purposes.

Article 105

1. The Organization shall enjoy in the territory of each of its Members such privileges and immunities as are necessary for the fulfilment of its purposes.
2. Representatives of the Members of the United Nations and officials of the Organization shall similarly enjoy such privileges and immunities as are necessary for the independent exercise of their functions in connection with the Organization.
3. The General Assembly may make recommendations with a view to determining the details of the application of paragraphs 1 and 2 of this Article or may propose conventions to the Members of the United Nations for this purpose.

XVII. TRANSITIONAL SECURITY ARRANGEMENTS

Article 106

Pending the coming into force of such special agreements referred to in Article 43 as in the opinion of the Security Council enable it to begin the exercise of its responsibilities under Article 42, the parties to the Four-Nation Declaration signed at Moscow, October 30, 1943, and France, shall, in accordance with the provisions of paragraph 5 of that Declaration, consult with one another and as occasion requires with other Members of the United Nations with a view to such joint action on behalf of the Organization as may be necessary for the purpose of maintaining international peace and security.

Article 107

Nothing in the present Charter shall invalidate or preclude action, in relation to any state which during the Second World War has been an enemy of any signatory to the present Charter, taken or authorized as a result of that war by the Governments having responsibility for such action.

XVIII. AMENDMENTS

Article 108

Amendments to the present Charter shall come into force for all Members of the United Nations when they have been adopted by a vote of two-thirds of the members of the General Assembly and ratified in accordance with their respective constitutional processes by two-thirds of the Members of the United Nations, including all the permanent members of the Security Council.

Article 109

1. A General Conference of the Members of the United Nations for the purpose of reviewing the present Charter may be held at a date and place to be fixed by a two-thirds vote of the members of the General Assembly and by a vote of any seven members of the Security Council. Each Member of the United Nations shall have one vote in the conference.
2. Any alteration of the present Charter recommended by a two-thirds vote of the conference shall take effect when ratified in accordance with their respective constitutional processes by two-thirds of the Members of the United Nations including all the permanent members of the Security Council.
3. If such a conference has not been held before the tenth annual session of the General Assembly following the coming into force of the present Charter, the proposal to call such a conference shall be placed on the agenda of that session of the General Assembly, and the conference shall be held if so decided by a majority vote of the members of the General Assembly and by a vote of any seven members of the Security Council.

XIX. RATIFICATION AND SIGNATURE

Article 110

1. The present Charter shall be ratified by the signatory states in accordance with their respective constitutional processes.
2. The ratifications shall be deposited with the Government of the United States of America, which shall notify all the signatory states of each deposit as well as the Secretary-General of the Organization when he has been appointed.
3. The present Charter shall come into force upon the deposit of ratifications by the Republic of China, France, the Union of Soviet Socialist Republics, the United Kingdom of Great Britain and Northern Ireland, and the United States of America, and by a majority of the other signatory states. A protocol of the ratifications deposited shall thereupon be drawn up by the Government of the United States of America which shall communicate copies thereof to all the signatory states.
4. The states signatory to the present Charter which ratify it after it has come into force will become original Members of the United Nations on the date of the deposit of their respective ratifications.

Article 111

The present Charter, of which the Chinese, French, Russian, English, and Spanish texts are equally authentic, shall remain deposited in the archives of the Government of the United States of America. Duly certified copies thereof shall be transmitted by that Government to the Governments of the other signatory states.

In faith whereof the representatives of the Governments of the United Nations have signed the present Charter.

Done at the city of San Francisco the twenty-sixth day of June, one thousand nine hundred and forty-five.

AMENDMENTS

The following amendments to Articles 23 and 27 of the Charter came into force in August 1965.

Article 23

1. The Security Council shall consist of 15 Members of the United Nations. The Republic of China, France, the Union of Soviet Socialist Republics, the United Kingdom of Great Britain and Northern Ireland, and the United States of America shall be permanent members of the Security Council. The General Assembly shall elect 10 other Members of the United Nations to be non-permanent members of the Security Council, due regard being specially paid, in the first instance to the contribution of Members of the United Nations to the maintenance of international peace and security and to the other purposes of the Organization, and also to equitable geographical distribution.
2. The non-permanent members of the Security Council shall be elected for a term of two years. In the first election of the non-permanent members after the increase of the membership of the Security Council from 11 to 15, two of the four additional members shall be chosen for a term of one year. A retiring member shall not be eligible for immediate re-election.
3. Each member of the Security Council shall have one representative.

Article 27

1. Each member of the Security Council shall have one vote.
2. Decisions of the Security Council on procedural matters shall be made by an affirmative vote of nine members.
3. Decisions of the Security Council on all other matters shall be made by an affirmative vote of nine members including the concurring votes of the permanent members; provided that, in decisions under Chapter VI and under paragraph 3 of Article 52, a party to a dispute shall abstain from voting.

The following amendments to Article 61 of the Charter came into force in September 1973.

Article 61

1. The Economic and Social Council shall consist of 54 Members of the United Nations elected by the General Assembly.
2. Subject to the provisions of paragraph 3, 18 members of the Economic and Social Council shall be elected each year for a term of three years. A retiring member shall be eligible for immediate re-election.
3. At the first election after the increase in the membership of the Economic and Social Council from 27 to 54 members, in addition to the members elected in place of the nine members whose term of office expires at the end of that year, 27 additional members shall be elected. Of these 27 additional members, the term of office of nine members so elected shall expire at the end of one year, and of nine other members at the end of two years, in accordance with arrangements made by the General Assembly.
4. Each member of the Economic and Social Council shall have one representative.

The following amendment to Paragraph 1 of Article 109 of the Charter came into force in June 1968.

Article 109

1. A General Conference of the Members of the United Nations for the purpose of reviewing the present Charter may be held at a date and place to be fixed by a two-thirds vote of the members of the General Assembly and by a vote of any nine members of the Security Council. Each Member of the United Nations shall have one vote in the conference.

Universal Declaration of Human Rights

(Adopted 10 December 1948)

Whereas recognition of the inherent dignity and of the equal and inalienable rights of all members of the human family is the foundation of freedom, justice and peace in the world,

Whereas disregard and contempt for human rights have resulted in barbarous acts which have outraged the conscience of mankind, and the advent of a world in which human beings shall enjoy freedom of speech and belief and freedom from fear and want has been proclaimed as the highest aspiration of the common people,

Whereas it is essential, if man is not to be compelled to have recourse, as a last resort, to rebellion against tyranny and oppression, that human rights should be protected by the rule of law,

Whereas it is essential to promote the development of friendly relations between nations,

Whereas the peoples of the United Nations have in the Charter reaffirmed their faith in fundamental human rights, in the dignity and worth of the human person and in the equal rights of men and women and have determined to promote social progress and better standards of life in larger freedom,

Whereas Member States have pledged themselves to achieve, in co-operation with the United Nations, the promotion of universal respect for and observance of human rights and fundamental freedoms,

Whereas a common understanding of these rights and freedoms is of the greatest importance for the full realization of this pledge, Now, therefore,

The General Assembly

Proclaims this Universal Declaration of Human Rights as a common standard of achievement for all peoples and all nations, to the end that every individual and every organ of society, keeping this Declaration constantly in mind, shall strive by teaching and education to promote respect for these rights and freedoms and by progressive measures, national and international, to secure their universal and effective recognition and observance, both among the peoples of Member States themselves and among the peoples of territories under their jurisdiction.

Article 1

All human beings are born free and equal in dignity and rights. They are endowed with reason and conscience and should act towards one another in a spirit of brotherhood.

Article 2

Everyone is entitled to all the rights and freedoms set forth in this Declaration, without distinction of any kind, such as race, colour, sex, language, religion, political or other opinion, national or social origin, property, birth or other status.

Furthermore, no distinction shall be made on the basis of the political, jurisdictional or international status of the country or territory to which a person belongs, whether it be independent, trust, non-self-governing or under any other limitation of sovereignty.

Article 3

Everyone has the right to life, liberty and security of person.

Article 4

No one shall be held in slavery or servitude; slavery and the slave trade shall be prohibited in all their forms.

Article 5

No one shall be subjected to torture or to cruel, inhuman or degrading treatment or punishment.

Article 6

Everyone has the right to recognition everywhere as a person before the law.

Article 7

All are equal before the law and are entitled without any discrimination to equal protection of the law. All are entitled to equal protection against any discrimination in violation of this Declaration and against any incitement to such discrimination.

Article 8

Everyone has the right to an effective remedy by the competent national tribunals for acts violating the fundamental rights granted him by the constitution or by law.

Article 9

No one shall be subjected to arbitrary arrest, detention or exile.

Article 10

Everyone is entitled in full equality to a fair and public hearing by an independent and impartial tribunal, in a determination of his rights and obligations and of any criminal charge against him.

Article 11

1. Everyone charged with a penal offence has the right to be presumed innocent until proved guilty according to law in a public trial at which he has had all the guarantees necessary for his defence.
2. No one shall be held guilty of any penal offence on account of any act or omission which did not constitute a penal offence, under national or international law, at the time when it was committed. Nor shall a heavier penalty be imposed than the one that was applicable at the time the penal offence was committed.

Article 12

No one shall be subjected to arbitrary interference with his privacy, family, home or correspondence, nor to attacks upon his honour and reputation. Everyone has the right to the protection of the law against such interference or attacks.

Article 13

1. Everyone has the right to freedom of movement and residence within the borders of each state.
2. Everyone has the right to leave any country, including his own, and to return to his country.

Article 14

1. Everyone has the right to seek and to enjoy in other countries asylum from persecution.
2. This right may not be invoked in the case of prosecutions genuinely arising from non-political crimes or from acts contrary to the purposes and principles of the United Nations.

Article 15

1. Everyone has the right to a nationality.
2. No one shall be arbitrarily deprived of his nationality nor denied the right to change his nationality.

Article 16

1. Men and women of full age, without any limitation due to race, nationality or religion, have the right to marry and to found a family. They are entitled to equal rights as to marriage, during marriage and at its dissolution.
2. Marriage shall be entered into only with the free and full consent of the intending spouses.
3. The family is the natural and fundamental group unit of society and is entitled to protection by society and the State.

Article 17

1. Everyone has the right to own property alone as well as in association with others.
2. No one shall be arbitrarily deprived of his property.

Article 18

Everyone has the right to freedom of thought, conscience and religion; this right includes freedom to change his religion or belief, and freedom, either alone or in community with others and in public or private, to manifest his religion or belief in teaching, practice, worship and observance.

Article 19

Everyone has the right to freedom of opinion and expression; this right includes freedom to hold opinions without interference and to seek, receive and impart information and ideas through any media and regardless of frontiers.

Article 20

1. Everyone has the right to freedom of peaceful assembly and association.
2. No one may be compelled to belong to an association.

Article 21

1. Everyone has the right to take part in the government of his country, directly or through freely chosen representatives.
2. Everyone has the right of equal access to public service in his country.
3. The will of the people shall be the basis of the authority of government; this will shall be expressed in periodic and genuine elections which shall be by universal and equal suffrage and shall be held by secret vote or by equivalent free voting procedures.

Article 22

Everyone, as a member of society, has the right to social security and is entitled to realization, through national effort and international co-operation and in accordance with the organization and resources of each state, of the economic, social and cultural rights indispensable for his dignity and the free development of his personality.

Article 23

1. Everyone has the right to work, to free choice of employment, to just and favourable conditions of work and to protection against unemployment.
2. Everyone, without any discrimination, has the right to equal pay for equal work.
3. Everyone who works has the right to just and favourable remuneration ensuring for himself and his family an existence worthy of human dignity, and supplemented, if necessary, by other means of social protection.
4. Everyone has the right to form and to join trade unions for the protection of his interests.

Article 24

Everyone has the right to rest and leisure, including reasonable limitation of working hours and periodic holidays with pay.

Article 25

1. Everyone has the right to a standard of living adequate for the health and well-being of himself and of his family, including food, clothing, housing and medical care and necessary social services, and the right to security in the event of unemployment, sickness, disability, widowhood, old age or other lack of livelihood in circumstances beyond his control.
2. Motherhood and childhood are entitled to special care and assistance. All children, whether born in or out of wedlock, shall enjoy the same social protection.

Article 26

1. Everyone has the right to education. Education shall be free, at least in the elementary and fundamental stages. Elementary education shall be compulsory. Technical and professional education shall be made generally available and higher education shall be equally accessible to all on the basis of merit.
2. Education shall be directed to the full development of the human personality and to the strengthening of respect for human rights and fundamental freedoms. It shall promote understanding, tolerance and friendship among all nations, racial or religious groups, and shall further the activities of the United Nations for the maintenance of peace.
3. Parents have a prior right to choose the kind of education that shall be given to their children.

Article 27

1. Everyone has the right freely to participate in the cultural life of the community, to enjoy the arts and to share in scientific advancement and its benefits.
2. Everyone has the right to the protection of the moral and material interests resulting from any scientific, literary or artistic production of which he is the author.

Article 28

Everyone is entitled to a social and international order in which the rights and freedoms set forth in this Declaration can be fully realized.

Article 29

1. Everyone has duties to the community in which alone the free and full development of his personality is possible.
2. In the exercise of his rights and freedoms, everyone shall be subject only to such limitations as are determined by law solely for the purpose of securing due recognition and respect for the rights and freedoms of others and of meeting the just requirements of morality, public order and the general welfare in a democratic society.
3. These rights and freedoms may in no case be exercised contrary to the purposes and principles of the United Nations.

Article 30

Nothing in this Declaration may be interpreted as implying for any state, group or person any right to engage in any activity or to perform any act aimed at the destruction of any of the rights and freedoms set forth herein.

UNITED NATIONS REGIONAL COMMISSIONS

Economic Commission for Europe—ECE

Address: Palais des Nations, 1211 Geneva 10, Switzerland.

Telephone: 229174444; **fax:** 229170505; **e-mail:** info.ece@unece.org; **internet:** www.unece.org.

The UN Economic Commission for Europe (ECE) was established in 1947 and was, with ECAFE (now ESCAP), the earliest of the five regional economic commissions set up by the UN Economic and Social Council (ECOSOC). The Commission promotes pan-European and transatlantic economic integration. It provides a multilateral forum for dialogue and co-operation on economic and sectoral issues for governments from European countries, as well as central Asian republics, the USA, Canada and Israel. It provides analysis, policy advice and assistance to governments, gives focus to UN global mandates on economic issues, and establishes norms, standards and conventions to facilitate international co-operation within and outside the region.

MEMBERS

Albania
Andorra
Armenia
Austria
Azerbaijan
Belarus
Belgium
Bosnia and Herzegovina
Bulgaria
Canada
Croatia
Cyprus
Czech Republic
Denmark
Estonia
Finland
France
Georgia
Germany
Greece
Hungary
Iceland
Ireland
Israel
Italy
Kazakhstan
Kyrgyzstan
Latvia
Liechtenstein
Lithuania
Luxembourg
Macedonia, former Yugoslav republic
Malta
Moldova
Monaco
Montenegro
Netherlands
Norway
Poland
Portugal
Romania
Russia
San Marino
Serbia
Slovakia
Slovenia
Spain
Sweden
Switzerland
Tajikistan
Turkey
Turkmenistan
Ukraine
United Kingdom
USA
Uzbekistan

Organization

(April 2012)

COMMISSION

The Commission, the highest decision-making body of the organization, holds biennial formal sessions in Geneva to review the economic situation and decide on activities for the coming two years. The 64th session was held in March 2011. As well as taking strategic decisions the Commission provides a forum for senior-level dialogue on regional economic development policy.

EXECUTIVE COMMITTEE

The Executive Committee prepares the formal sessions of the Commission, implements the decisions of the Commission, and acts on behalf of the Commission between the sessions of that body. The Executive Committee also reviews and approves the programmes of work of the sectoral committees, which report at least once a year to the Executive Committee.

SECRETARIAT

The Secretariat services the meetings of the Commission and its sectoral committees and publishes periodic surveys and reviews, including a number of specialized statistical bulletins (see list of publications below). The Executive Secretary carries out secretarial functions for the executive bodies of several regional conventions and their protocols (see below).

Executive Secretary: SVEN ALKALAJ (Bosnia and Herzegovina).

SECTORAL COMMITTEES

Committee on Economic Co-operation and Integration;

Committee on Environmental Policy;

Committee on Housing and Land Management;

Committee on Inland Transport;

Committee on Sustainable Energy;

Committee on Timber;

Committee on Trade;

Conference of European Statisticians.

Activities

ECE's original purpose, when it was established by ECOSOC in 1947, was to give effective aid to the countries devastated by the Second World War. It was granted permanent status in 1951. During the 'cold war' period it served as the only major instrument of economic dialogue and co-operation linking the communist countries of central and eastern Europe with the countries of western Europe, and achieved the harmonization of a number of aspects of transport and trade, such as road signs, safety and anti-pollution standards for motor vehicles, standards for the transport of perishable or dangerous goods, and agreements on customs procedures. During the 1990s, when political changes in central and eastern Europe had allowed countries there to undergo transition from a centrally planned economy to a market economy, ECE adopted the role of assisting these countries, including the newly independent countries that had formerly been part of the USSR and Yugoslavia, and it extended its activities to the central Asian countries, which became members of both ECE and ESCAP.

The guiding principle of ECE activities is the promotion of sustainable economic growth among its member countries. To this end it provides a forum for communication among states; negotiates international legal instruments concerning trade, transport and the environment; and supplies statistics and economic and environmental analysis. The implications for ECE of the enlargement of the European Union (EU) and ongoing developments in member states with economies in transition, generated significant debate during the mid-2000s on the future direction of the Commission's work. The 59th session of ECE, convened in February 2004, commissioned a comprehensive, external evaluation of the state of ECE. The report, which was published in June 2005, included the following recommendations: more effective governance and management of the Commission, including restructuring work divisions and sub-programmes and identifying specialized areas of competence; raising the political profile of the Commission; co-ordinating the regional implementation of the UN Millennium Development Goals (MDGs); improving co-operation with other organizations, in particular a partnership with UNDP and with other regional commissions; and strengthening the participation of the private sector and non-governmental organizations in the Commission. Greater priority was to be given to the environment and transport, and to the specific problems affecting countries with economies in transition. The 61st session of ECE, convened in December 2005, adopted the resulting Work Plan on ECE Reform. The reform process was reviewed by the Commission in 2009. The 64th session of ECE, held in March 2011, focused on the Commission's role in promoting pan-European economic integration, addressing in particular the regional transport and trade infrastructure, and energy co-operation.

Economic Co-operation and Integration: The programme on Economic Co-operation and Integration, which is implemented by the Committee on Economic Co-operation and Integration, has the following thematic focuses: strengthening the competitiveness of member states' economies by promoting the knowledge-based economy and innovation; facilitating the development of entrepreneurship and the emergence of new enterprises; facilitating effective regulatory policies and corporate governance, including those in the financial sector; promoting public-private partnerships for domestic and foreign investment; maintaining intellectual property rights; and other relevant aspects of international economic co-operation and integration. At its inaugural session in September 2006 the Committee adopted a programme of work and established three teams of specialists, on innovation and competitiveness policies, on intellectual property, and on public-private partnerships (PPPs), which support programme implementation in these thematic areas. The third session of the Committee, held in December 2008, determined to enhance the practical dimension of its work, in particular the capacity-building activities in transition economies. In April 2011 it was announced that an International Centre of Excellence on PPPs was to be established in Geneva, under the aegis of ECE. Since 2006 ECE has hosted, jointly with the World Bank Institute and the Asian Development Bank, an annual global meeting, 'PPP Days', of PPP practitioners and experts. The theme of the 2012 meeting, held in February, in Geneva, was 'Strengthening institutions and frameworks for better PPP delivery'.

The UN Special Programme for the Economies of Central Asia (SPECA), begun in 1998, is implemented jointly by ECE and ESCAP: SPECA helps the participating countries to strengthen regional co-operation, particularly in the areas of water resources, energy and transport, and creates incentives for economic development and integration into the economies of Asia and Europe. The establishment of a joint UNECE-ESCAP SPECA Regional Office in Central Asia is under consideration. ECE also provides technical assistance to the Southeast European Co-operative Initiative.

Environment: ECE facilitates and promotes co-operation among member governments in developing and implementing policies for environmental protection, the rational use of natural resources, and sustainable development. It supports the integration of environmental policy into sectoral policies, seeks solutions to environmental problems, particularly those of a transboundary nature, and assists in strengthening environmental management capabilities, particularly in countries in transition. A programme of Environmental Performance Review helps individual countries to improve the effectiveness of environmental management and policies. The Committee on Environmental Policy brings governments together to formulate policy and provides a forum for the exchange of experience and good practices. It facilitates and prepares the Environment for Europe process, the focus of which is a ministerial-level conference normally held every four years (the 2011 meeting was held in September, in Astana, Kazakhstan, addressing two main themes: 'Sustainable Management of Water and Water-related Ecosystems' and 'Greening the Economy: Mainstreaming the Environment into Economic Development'). ECE also supports a Pan-European Programme (PEP) on transport, health and the environment, and sponsors a programme co-ordinating efforts to develop education for sustainable development in the ECE region. ECE has negotiated five environmental conventions, for which it serves as the secretariat: the Convention on Long-range Transboundary Air Pollution (which entered into force in 1983 and has been extended by eight protocols); the Convention on the Protection and Use of Transboundary Watercourses and International Lakes (also known as the Water Convention, 1996, two protocols); the Convention on Environmental Impact Assessment in a Transboundary Context (Espoo Convention, 1997, one protocol, which entered into force in July 2010); the Convention on the Transboundary Effects of Industrial Accidents (2000, one protocol) and the Convention on Access to Information, Public Participation in Decision-making and Access to Justice in Environmental Matters (Aarhus Convention, 2001). A Protocol (to the Aarhus Convention) on Pollutant Release and Transfer Registers (PRTRs), which was adopted in May 2003, entered into force in October 2009. All UN member states are encouraged to accede to the Protocol. In July 2011 the meeting of the parties to the Aarhus Convention determined to encourage accession to the Convention, also, by states outside the ECE region. An amendment to extend the Water Convention to extra-regional members, adopted in 2003, was reviewed by a strategic workshop in February 2012, at which time it had been ratified by 20 parties. Within the context of the amendment, in December 2011 ECE organized a high level conference to promote greater co-operation between European and Asian countries in the management and protection of transboundary waters. In February 2012 the legal board of the Water Convention agreed proposals to establish an implementation committee, which would be presented to the meeting of parties to the Convention, scheduled to convene in November.

In June 2011 parties to the Espoo Convention issued a caution against Ukraine—the first ever such caution—for non-compliance with its obligations under the Convention, in relation to alleged environmental damage caused to the ecosystem of the Danube delta (a UNESCO World Heritage Site) by the ongoing Bystroe (Bâstroe) channel project, which aims to provide a deep-water route linking the Danube and the Black Sea.

Forestry and Timber: ECE's Timber Committee works closely, through an integrated programme, with the European Forestry Commission of the FAO to promote sustainable forest management. It compiles data and analyses long-term trends and prospects for forestry and timber; keeps under review developments in the forest industries, including environmental and energy-related aspects; and publishes an annual market review of forest products. The Committee meets annually to review the programme, as well as to discuss policy and market trends and outlook. Assistance in the form of workshops and expert advice is provided to help countries that are undergoing economic transition to develop their forestry sectors. A strategic plan for the period 2008–13 was approved at a joint meeting of the Committee and the FAO Commission in October 2008, convened to coincide with events organized within the framework of European Forest Week. In March 2010 ECE and FAO launched a study of the state of forests and forestry management in Europe; the results were collated in the 2011 edition of the *State of Europe's Forests*, which was issued in June of that year.

Housing, Land Management and Population: The Committee organizes sub-regional workshops and seminars, and provides policy advice in the form of country profiles on the housing sector and land administration reviews, undertaken by experts. The Committee works to improve housing conditions as well as spatial planning and land administration policy. In particular, it promotes the provision of adequate housing, both in the Eastern European countries undergoing socio-economic transition and in deprived neighbourhoods in Western Europe. The Committee and its Working Party on Land Administration prepare guidance on urban renewal, condominium management, housing finance, land administration, social housing and energy efficiency in housing. The Committee organizes sub-regional workshops and seminars, and provides policy advice, through its country profiles on the housing sector and land administration reviews, which are prepared by teams of experts. In 2008 the Real Estate Market Advisory Group was established to support the Working Party on Land Administration's activities and to help structure a sustainable housing market. In April 2011 ECE published an Action Plan for Energy Efficient Housing in the UNECE Region, aimed at introducing institutional, technological and cultural changes needed to improve energy efficiency in the housing sector.

ECE tracks demographic and societal change through its Population Unit. The Generations and Gender Programme, initiated in 2000, works to improve the knowledge base for policy-making in ECE countries. In November 2007 ECE organized a Conference on Ageing to discuss the implications of regional fertility rates that had fallen below replacement level. A conference of experts and policy-makers, held in Geneva, in May 2008, examined the causes and consequences of demographic change. A new Working Group on Ageing was established, and convened for its inaugural meeting in December, to undertake a programme of action to counter the challenges of ageing societies. A Ministerial Conference on Ageing, on the theme of 'Ensuring a society for all ages' was scheduled to be held, in Vienna, Austria, in September 2012.

Statistics: The Conference of European Statisticians (CES) and ECE's Statistical Division have the task of co-ordinating international statistical activities in the region, by reviewing the most topical statistical areas, identifying gaps and duplication, and looking for issues not hitherto addressed. The CES plenary sessions and seminars offer a forum for senior statisticians, often leading to work in new areas and the preparation of new standards and recommendations. The CES and the Statistical Division work to develop methodology in compiling and disseminating economic, social and demographic statistics, for example in harmonizing methods of compiling gross domestic product, national accounts and other economic indicators; measuring the distorting effect of globalization on national statistical systems; and finding sound methods of measuring sustainable development. The Division helps countries, especially those undergoing economic transition, to improve their statistical systems in accordance with the UN Fundamental Principles of Official Statistics, by advising on legislation and institutions and on how to ensure the independence and impartiality of official statistics. It maintains an online statistical database, allowing comparison of major economic and social indicators, and publishes guidelines on the editing of statistical data.

Sustainable Energy: Through its Committee on Sustainable Energy, subsidiary bodies and projects, ECE's sub-programme on sustainable energy works to promote a sustainable energy development strategy for the region, with the following objectives: sustained access to high quality energy services for all individuals in the ECE region; security of energy supplies in the short, medium and long term; facilitating the transition to a more sustainable energy future and reducing health and environmental impacts resulting from the production, transport and use of energy; promoting well-balanced energy network systems across the region, tailored to optimize operating efficiencies and overall regional co-operation; ensuring sustained improvements in energy efficiency, in production and use, particularly in countries with economies in transition; and, in the context of post-EU enlargement, integrating energy restructuring, legal, regulatory and energy pricing reforms, as well as the social dimension, into energy policy making. Activities include labelling classification systems and related legal and policy frameworks; liberalization of energy markets, pricing policies and supply security; harmonization of energy policies and practices; rational use of energy, efficiency and conservation; energy infrastructure, including interconnection of gas networks; cleaner electricity production from coal and other fossil fuels; the Energy Efficiency 21 Project (GEE21, the first meeting of which was convened in July 2009); the promotion and development—through the UNECE Gas Centre programme—of a market-based gas industry in countries with economies in transition; and providing technical assistance and operational activities in energy to countries with economies in transition. In December 2011 ECE convened a regional preparatory meeting for the United Nations Conference on Sustainable Development (the so-called 'Rio + 20' conference), scheduled to be held in June 2012.

Trade: ECE's Committee on Trade aims to focus on the facilitation of international trade by means of simpler and better-integrated trade procedures, electronic business methods, common agricultural quality standards, and the harmonization of technical regulations. The Committee works closely with other organizations, and provides a forum for dialogue between the public and the private sector. The UN Centre for Trade Facilitation and Electronic Business (UN/CEFACT, established in 2002 as part of ECE) works to reduce delays and costs in international transactions by simplifying procedures. ECE's Working Party on Agricultural Quality Standards develops and updates commercial quality standards for fruit, vegetables and other agricultural products, in co-operation with OECD, and promotes the application of these standards through regional seminars and workshops. The Working Party on Regulatory Co-operation and Standardization Policies aims to harmonize product regulations and standards, the diversity of which can seriously impede trade. It has developed an international model for technical harmonization to assist countries wishing to standardize their rules on specific products or sectors. In December 2011 the ECE Executive Committee established a new group of experts, within the Working Party, to develop a set of recommendations on the application of risk management to regulatory work. ECE's Advisory Group on Market Surveillance aims to combat the proliferation of counterfeit and pirated goods.

In December 2011 ECE hosted a Global Trade Facilitation Conference, organized by the five UN regional commissions, which requested the commissions prepare a roadmap to develop and enhance 'Single Window' facilities and information exchange in global supply chains.

Transport: ECE aims to promote a coherent, efficient, safe and sustainable transport system through the development of international agreements, conventions, norms and standards relating to road, rail, inland water and combined transport. These international legal instruments, which are developed by specialized intergovernmental working parties with participation from, among others, transport equipment manufacturers, consumers and road users, include measures for improving vehicle safety and limiting vehicle emissions, simplifying border crossing procedures, improving road traffic safety, setting the conditions for developing coherent infrastructure networks, and providing for the safe transport of dangerous goods. One of the working groups, the World Forum for Harmonization of Vehicle Regulations, has global participation. In January 2012 ECE's Working Party on Pollution and Energy adopted proposals to amend regulations on the emissions requirements of heavy duty vehicles. The proposals were to be presented to the World Forum for Harmonization of Vehicle Regulations in June for final approval. ECE addresses transport trends and economics and compiles transport statistics, and provides a forum for the exchange of technical and legal expertise in the field of inland transport. In 2005, a Master Plan was elaborated for investment in the Trans-European Motorway (TEM) and the Trans-European Railway (TER) projects, with the aim of improving the road and rail networks in 21 central, eastern and south-eastern European countries. A revision of the Master Plan was adopted in 2007. In July 2009 ECE signed an agreement with Slovakia to host the central project office of the TER initiative. In April 2010 the national co-ordinators for the TEM and TER projects in 13 countries adopted a new Innsbruck Initiative for safe, secure, prosperous and environmentally friendly transport. Objectives of the Innsbruck Initiative, which were to be incorporated into the TEM and TER work plans for 2011–15, included: the development of transport infrastructure to improve safety, environmental performance and security; encouraging measures conducive to secure and safe transport, and promoting the proper design of transport infrastructure; supporting interoperability between transport modes, intermodal connections and combined transport systems; and promoting the introduction of Intelligent Transport Systems, with a particular focus on increasing transport safety and security, and minimizing traffic congestion and air pollution. Another project, undertaken jointly with ESCAP, aims to develop Euro-Asian transport links. In February 2008 ECE established a Group of Experts on Hinterland Connections of Seaports to study the effectiveness of existing container management and inland transport connections with seaports, and to compile a set of recommendations. In conjunction with the European Office of WHO ECE administers a Transport, Health and Environment Pan-European Programme, which aims to promote sustainable transport policies and systems. A Conference on Improving Road Safety in South-Eastern Europe, organized by ECE, was held in Halkida, Greece, in June 2009. ECE and the other UN regional commissions were to play a key role in implementing the UN Decade of Action for Road Safety, covering 2011–20, which aimed to reduce the rate of road fatalities.

Finance

The proposed appropriation for ECE's regular budget in 2012–13 was US $65.2m.

Publications

UNECE Report (annually).

UNECE Weekly.

UNECE Compendium of Legal Instruments, Norms and Standards.

UNECE Countries in Figures.

Report of the Conference of European Statisticians (annually).

Trade Promotion Directory (annually).

For its different areas of activity ECE produces statistical bulletins, reports, performance reviews, country profiles, standards, agreements, recommendations, discussion papers, guidelines and manuals.

Economic and Social Commission for Asia and the Pacific—ESCAP

Address: United Nations Bldg, Rajadamnern Nok Ave, Bangkok 10200, Thailand.

Telephone: (2) 288-1234; **fax:** (2) 288-1000; **e-mail:** unisbkk.unescap@un.org; **internet:** www.unescap.org.

The Commission was founded in 1947, at first to assist in post-war reconstruction, and subsequently to encourage the economic and social development of Asia and the Far East; it was originally known as the Economic Commission for Asia and the Far East (ECAFE). The title ESCAP, which replaced ECAFE, was adopted after a reorganization in 1974. ESCAP's main objectives are to promote inclusive and sustainable economic and social development in Asia and the Pacific, and to help member countries to achieve internationally agreed development goals.

MEMBERS

Afghanistan	Korea, Democratic People's Republic	Philippines
Armenia	Korea, Republic	Russia
Australia	Kyrgyzstan	Samoa
Azerbaijan	Laos	Singapore
Bangladesh	Malaysia	Solomon Islands
Bhutan	The Maldives	Sri Lanka
Brunei	Marshall Islands	Tajikistan
Cambodia	Micronesia, Federated States	Thailand
China, People's Republic	Mongolia	Timor-Leste
Fiji	Myanmar	Tonga
France	Nauru	Turkey
Georgia	Nepal	Turkmenistan
India	Netherlands	Tuvalu
Indonesia	New Zealand	United Kingdom
Iran	Pakistan	USA
Japan	Palau	Uzbekistan
Kazakhstan	Papua New Guinea	Vanuatu
Kiribati		Viet Nam

ASSOCIATE MEMBERS

American Samoa	Hong Kong	Northern Mariana Islands
Cook Islands	Macao	
French Polynesia	New Caledonia	
Guam	Niue	

Organization

(April 2012)

COMMISSION

The main legislative organ of ESCAP is the Commission, which meets annually at ministerial level to examine the region's problems, to review progress, to establish priorities and to decide upon the recommendations of the Executive Secretary or the subsidiary bodies of the Commission. It reports to the UN Economic and Social Council (ECOSOC). Ministerial and intergovernmental conferences on specific issues may be held on an ad hoc basis with the approval of the Commission, although no more than one ministerial conference and five intergovernmental conferences may be held during one year.

COMMITTEES AND SPECIAL BODIES

Specialized committees and special bodies have been established to advise the Commission and help to oversee the work of the Secretariat. They meet every two years, while any sub-committees meet in the intervening years. There are Committees on Macroeconomic Policy, Poverty Reduction and Inclusive Development; Trade and Investment; Transport; Environment and Development; Information and Communications Technology; Disaster Risk Reduction; Social Development; and Statistics. The two special bodies cover Least Developed and Landlocked Developing Countries; and Pacific Island Developing Countries.

In addition, an Advisory Committee of permanent representatives and other representatives designated by members of the Commission functions as an advisory body; it generally meets every month.

SECRETARIAT

The Secretariat operates under the guidance of the Commission and its subsidiary bodies. It consists of the Office of the Executive Secretary and two servicing divisions, covering administration and programme management, in addition to the following substantive divisions: Environment and Development; Information and Communications Technology and Disaster Risk Reduction; Macroeconomic Policy and Development; Social Development; Statistics; Trade and Investment; and Transport.

Executive Secretary: NOELEEN HEYZER (Singapore).

SUB-REGIONAL OFFICES

ESCAP Pacific Operations Centre (EPOC): Private Mail Bag, Suva, Fiji; tel. 3319669; fax 3319671; e-mail epoc@un.org; internet www.unescap.org/epoc; f. 1984, relocated to Fiji 2005; responsible for ESCAP's sub-programme on Development of Pacific Island Countries and Territories; assists Pacific island governments in forming and implementing national sustainable development strategies, particularly poverty reduction programmes that create access to services by socially vulnerable groups; conducts research, promotes regional co-operation and knowledge-sharing, and provides advisory services, training and pilot projects; Dir IOSEFA MAIAVA (Samoa).

Sub-Regional Office for East and North-East Asia: Meet-you-all Tower, 17th Floor, Techno Park, 7-50 Songdo-dong, Yeonsu-gu, Incheon, Republic of Korea; tel. (32) 458-6601; fax (32) 458-6699; e-mail vanlaere@un.org; f. 2010; covers activities in the People's Republic of China, Japan, the Democratic People's Republic of Korea, the Republic of Korea, Mongolia and Russia; Dir KILAPARTI RAMAKRISHNA.

Sub-regional Office for South and South-West Asia: Qutab Institutional Area, C-2, POB 4575, New Delhi 110 016, India; tel. (11) 309737100; f. 2011; serves Afghanistan, Bangladesh, Bhutan, India, Iran, Maldives, Nepal, Pakistan, Sri Lanka and Turkey; Dir Dr NAGESH KUMAR (Samoa).

In May 2011 an agreement was signed to establish a Sub-Regional Office for North and Central Asia, in Almatı, Kazakhstan.

Activities

ESCAP acts as a UN regional centre, providing the only intergovernmental forum that includes the whole of Asia and the Pacific, and executing a wide range of development programmes through technical assistance, advisory services to governments, research, training and information. In May 2002, having considered the recommendations of an intergovernmental review meeting held in March, ESCAP determined to implement a restructuring of its structures and thematic priorities. Three main thematic programmes were identified: poverty reduction; managing globalization; and emerging social issues. In May 2007 the Commission, meeting in Almatı, Kazakhstan, commemorated the 60th anniversary of ESCAP and reaffirmed its central role in fostering regional and sub-regional co-operation. In April 2008 the Commission approved a new conference structure and requested a reorganization of the Secretariat in order to reflect the new structure and programme of work for the two years 2010–11.

Social Development: ESCAP's Social Development Division, formerly the Emerging Social Issues Division, comprises three sections: Social Protection and Integration; Social Policy and Population; and Gender Equality. The Division's main objective is to assess and respond to regional trends and challenges in social development, and to help member countries to build more inclusive societies, through social and financial policies and measures promoting social protection, social inclusion, gender equality and development. The Social Protection and Integration Section aims to strengthen the capacity of public and non-government institutions to address the problems of marginalized social groups and to promote initiatives to provide income to the poor. The Gender Equality Section promotes the advancement of women by helping to improve their access to education, economic resources, information and communication technologies and decision-making; it is also committed to combating violence against women, including trafficking. The Social Policy and Population Section focuses on issues concerning ageing, youth, disability, migration and population. Activities include providing technical assistance to national population programmes, promoting the rights of people with disabilities, supporting improvement of access to social services by poor people, and helping governments to form policies that take into account the increasing proportion of older people in the population. ESCAP chairs the UN Interagency Group on Youth, which was established to promote implementation of the World Programme of Action on Youth, UN Millennium Development Goals (MDGs) relating to young people, and events concerning the International Year of Youth (2010–11).

The Division implements global and regional mandates, such as the Programme of Action of the World Summit for Social Development and the Jakarta Plan of Action on Human Resources Development. The Biwako Millennium Framework for Action towards an Inclusive, Barrier-free and Rights-based Society for Persons with Disabilities in Asia and the Pacific was adopted by ESCAP as a regional guideline underpinning the Asian and Pacific Decade of Disabled Persons (2003–12). In 1998 ESCAP initiated a programme of assistance in establishing a regional network of Social Development Management Information Systems (SOMIS). ESCAP collaborated with other agencies towards the adoption, in November 2001, of a Regional Platform on Sustainable Development for Asia and the Pacific. The Commission undertook regional preparations for the World Summit on Sustainable Development, which was held in Johannesburg, South Africa, in August–September 2002. In following up the summit ESCAP undertook to develop a biodiversity park, which was officially inaugurated in Rawalpindi, Pakistan, in January 2005. The Commission also prepares specific publications relating to population and implements the Programme of Action of the International Conference on Population and Development. The Secretariat co-ordinates the Asia-Pacific Population Information Network (POPIN). The fifth Asia and Pacific Population Conference, sponsored by ESCAP, was held in Bangkok, Thailand, in December 2002. Expert group meetings to assess implementation of the Plan of Action on Population and Poverty adopted at the Conference were held in November 2005 and in February 2009. In September 2004 ESCAP convened a senior-level intergovernmental meeting on the regional review and implementation of the Beijing Platform for Action (Beijing + 10), relating to gender equality. A further intergovernmental review meeting, Beijing + 15, was hosted by ESCAP in November 2009. In September 2011 ESCAP hosted the inaugural meeting of an Asia-Pacific Regional Advisory Group on Women, Peace and Security, which was established in the previous year to support the effective implementation throughout the region of UN Security Council Resolution 1325 relating to the impact of conflict on women and girls and their role in peace-building. The 67th Commission, meeting in Bangkok, in May 2011, pledged commitment to protecting the poor and vulnerable sectors of the region's population from the aftershocks of economic and natural crises. In February 2012 ESCAP hosted a high level intergovernmental meeting which endorsed an action plan towards greater regional co-operation in achieving global commitments to address and eliminate HIV/AIDS.

Environment and Development: ESCAP is concerned with strengthening national capabilities to achieve environmentally sound and sustainable development by integrating economic concerns, such as the sustainable management of natural resources, into economic planning and policies. The Environment and Development Division comprises sections on Energy Security, Environment and Development Policy, and Water Security. Activities include the promotion of integrated water resources development and management, including water quality and conservation and a reduction in water-related natural disasters; strengthening the formulation of policies in the sustainable development of land and mineral resources; and the consideration of energy resource options, such as rural energy supply, energy conservation and the planning of power networks. The Division administers a North-East Asia Subregional Programme for Environmental Co-operation (NEASPEC). Through the Division ESCAP prepares a report entitled *State of the Environment in Asia and the Pacific* which is published at five-yearly intervals. ESCAP helps to organize a ministerial conference on environment and development, also convened every five years. The Division received a mandate from the ministerial commission held in 2005 to work on issues related to climate change caused by global warming: it collates information, conducts regional seminars on adapting to climate change, and provides training in clean technology and guidance on reduction of harmful gas emissions. In March 2008 ESCAP organized an inaugural meeting of the Asia-Pacific Regional Platform on Climate Change and Development. In the following month ESCAP organized the first Asia-Pacific Mayors' Forum on Environmentally Sustainable Urban Infrastructure Development, convened in Ulsan, Republic of Korea. In June 2011 ESCAP hosted an Asia-Pacific Urban Forum, in Bangkok, which was convened on the theme 'Cities of opportunity: Partnerships for an inclusive and sustainable future'. In September an expert group meeting on sustainable energy development in Asia and the Pacific, organized by ESCAP, UNDP, UNIDO and FAO, focused on the need for developing national policies in the region aimed at ensuring universal access to clean and efficient energy services, as a means of advancing poverty reduction and improving health and well-being.

In May 2010 the 66th Commission, convened in Incheon, Republic of Korea, adopted a Declaration urging countries to strengthen and adopt 'green growth' strategies, in order to support recovery from the global economic and financial crisis and to achieve sustainable economic and social development. The sixth ministerial conference on environment and development, convened in Astana, Kazakhstan, in September–October, adopted a Ministerial Declaration on Green Growth, committing member countries to promoting environmentally sustainable economic growth and development. The conference also adopted a Regional Implementation Plan for Sustainable Development in Asia and the Pacific, covering the period 2011–15, and a Green Bridge Initiative to promote environmental partnerships and co-operation between Europe and Asia. In February 2012 ESCAP's Committee on Environment and Development endorsed the so-called 'Seoul Outcome', which was concluded in October 2011 by the Asia-Pacific Regional Preparatory Meeting for the UN Conference on Sustainable Development ('Rio + 20'), held in South Korea. The Committee also undertook to review regional priorities and commitments to sustainable growth in advance of the UN Conference, to be held in June 2012.

Information and Communications Technology and Disaster Risk Reduction: ESCAP's Information and Communications Technology (ICT) and Disaster Risk Reduction Division comprises the following sections: ICT and Development; Disaster Risk Reduction; and Space Technology Applications. The Division aims to strengthen capacity for access to and the application of ICT and space technology, in order to enhance socio-economic development and maximize the benefits of globalization. It supports the development of cross-sectoral policies and strategies, and also supports regional co-operation aimed at sharing knowledge between advanced and developing economies and in areas such as cyber-crime and information security. In May 2005 the Commission approved the establishment, in South Korea, of the Asian and Pacific Training Centre for ICT for Development (APCICT); APCICT was inaugurated in June 2006 (see below). In June 2005 the Division convened a senior-level meeting of experts to consider technical issues relating to disaster management and mitigation in Asia and the Pacific. The Division organized several conferences in preparation for the second phase of the World Summit on the Information Society (WSIS), which took place in November, and co-ordinates regional activities aimed at achieving WSIS targets for the widespread use of ICT by 2015. It helps members to include space technology in their development planning, for example the use of satellites in meteorology, disaster prevention, remote sensing and distance learning. In August 2007 the Division hosted an international meeting on the use of space technology to combat avian influenza and other infectious diseases. A meeting of national policy-makers on disaster management was convened in March 2008 to discuss access to satellite information as a means of predicting and managing natural disasters. In September 2010 an agreement was reached to establish a Regional Co-operative Mechanism on Disaster Monitoring and Early Warning, Particularly Drought. An expert group meeting to consider priority areas for the mechanism was convened in Beijing, People's Republic of China, in March 2011.

The Division's policy with relation to disaster risk reduction is guided by the Hyogo Framework for Action, covering the period 2005–15, which was adopted by the World Conference on Disaster Reduction, held in Kobe, Hyogo, Japan, in January 2005. The accompanying Declaration, adopted by the Conference, emphasized the need to develop and strengthen regional strategies and operational mechanisms in order to ensure rapid and effective disaster response. A new Committee on Disaster Risk Reduction convened for an inaugural session in March 2009; participants agreed to strengthen information and knowledge-sharing in relation to risk reduction. During 2010 ESCAP worked with the International Strategy for Disaster Reduction to produce an *Asia and Pacific Disaster Report*, which was published in October. Following the massive earthquake and consequent devastating sea movements (tsunami) that occurred in late December 2004 in the Indian Ocean, ESCAP assisted other UN and international agencies with an initial emergency response and undertook early reviews of the impact of the event. In January 2005 the Executive Secretary appointed a Task Force on Tsunami Disaster Management to assist countries to address issues relating to natural disaster management, and to raise those issues at a regional level. The chairman of the Task Force was also appointed co-chair of an Inter-Agency Regional Task Force on Tsunami Relief and Rehabilitation that was established at a heads of agency meeting, convened by ESCAP later in that month, with particular responsibility to exchange information relating to rehabilitation and reconstruction in the aftermath of the tsunami disaster and to more general capacity-building on disaster preparedness. At the end of January a ministerial meeting, in Phuket, Thailand, approved the establishment of a regional tsunami early-warning system. ESCAP administers the voluntary, multi-donor Tsunami Regional Trust Fund, which was inaugurated in late 2005 to support reconstruction and national and regional efforts to establish the early-warning system. In March 2011 ESCAP and the government of Thailand, the founding donor of the Fund, signed an agreement to expand the mandate of the Fund and rename it as the Multi-Donor Trust Fund for Tsunami, Disaster and Climate Preparedness in Indian Ocean and Southeast Asian Countries. In 2011, in May and December, ESCAP helped to organise expert meetings to consider the experiences of the tsunami and earthquake in Japan, in March of that year, and observe lessons for regional disaster preparedness. In February 2012 ESCAP hosted a forum to reflect on the experiences of the extensive flooding which caused large-scale economic and humanitarian devastation in parts of Southeast Asia in 2011.

Macroeconomic Policy and Development: The work of the Division, formerly the Poverty and Development Division, is undertaken by the following sections: Development Policy, and Macroeconomic Policy and Analysis. The Division aims to increase the understanding of the economic and social development situation in the region, with particular attention given to the attainment of the MDGs, sustainable economic growth, poverty alleviation, the integration of environmental concerns into macroeconomic decisions and policy-making processes, and enhancing the position of the region's disadvantaged economies, including those Central Asian countries undergoing transition from a centrally-planned economy to a market economy. The Division is responsible for the provision of technical assistance, and the production of relevant documents and publications. It publishes the *Economic and Social Survey of Asia and the Pacific*. The 63rd Commission, meeting in Almatı, Kazakhstan, in May 2007, endorsed a regional plan, developed by ESCAP, UNDP and the Asian Development Bank, to help poorer member countries to achieve the MDGs. Assistance was to be provided in the following areas: knowledge and capacity-building; expertise; resources; advocacy; and regional co-operation in delivering public goods (including infrastructure and energy security). The Commission also approved a resolution urging greater investment in health care in all member countries. In 2009 the Macroeconomic Policy and Development Division co-ordinated the preparation of a joint report of all five UN Regional Commissions, entitled *The Global Economic and Financial Crisis: Regional Impacts, Responses and Solutions*, which was published in May. In February 2010 a regional report on achieving the MDGs acknowledged the impact of the crisis and highlighted the need to strengthen social protection throughout the region. In December 2011 ESCAP hosted a meeting of senior officials to address the implementation of the Istanbul Programme of Action for the Least Developed Countries for the Decade 2011–20 in the Asia-Pacific region.

Statistics: ESCAP's Statistics Division provides training and advice in priority areas, including national accounts statistics, poverty indicators, gender statistics, population censuses and surveys, and the strengthening and management of statistical systems. It supports co-ordination throughout the region of the development, implementation and revision of selected international statistical standards, and, in particular, co-ordinates the International Comparison Programme (ICP) for Asia and the Pacific (part of a global ICP initiative). The Division disseminates comparable socio-economic statistics, with increased use of the electronic media, promotes the use of modern technology in the public sector and trains senior level officials in the effective management of ICT. Training is provided by the Statistical Institute for Asia and the Pacific (see below).

Trade and Investment: ESCAP aims to help members to benefit from globalization by increasing global and regional flows of trade and investment. Its Trade and Investment Division provides technical assistance and advisory services. It aims to enhance institutional capacity-building; gives special emphasis to the needs of least-developed, land-locked and island developing countries, and to Central Asian countries that are in transition to a market economy, in accelerating their industrial and technological advancement, promoting their exports, and furthering their integration into the region's economy; supports the development of electronic commerce and other information technologies in the region; and promotes the intra-regional and inter-subregional exchange of trade, investment and technology through the strengthening of institutional support services such as regional information networks.

The Division functions as the secretariat of the Asia-Pacific Trade Agreement (APTA), concluded in 1975 to promote regional trade through mutually agreed concessions by the participating states (in 2012 they comprised Bangladesh, China, India, South Korea, Laos and Sri Lanka; accession proceedings for Mongolia were ongoing). Since 2004 the Division has organized an annual Asia-Pacific Business Forum, involving representatives of governments, the private sector and civil society. It operates the Asia-Pacific Trade and Investment Agreements Database, the Trade and Transport Facilitation Online Database and an online *Directory of Trade and Investment-Related Organizations*, and publishes the *Asia-Pacific Trade and Investment Review* twice a year. The Division acts as the Secretariat of the Asia-Pacific Research and Training Network on Trade (ARTNeT), established in 2004, which aims to enhance the region's research capacity. ESCAP, with the World Trade Organization (WTO), implements a technical assistance programme, helping member states to implement WTO agreements and to participate in ongoing multilateral trade negotiations. In March 2009 ESCAP launched the UN Network of Experts for Paperless Trade in Asia and the Pacific (UN NExT).

Transport: ESCAP's Transport Division aims to improve the regional movement of goods and people, and to assist member states to manage and to benefit from globalization. The Division has three sections: Transport Infrastructure; Transport Facilitation and Logistics; and Transport Policy and Development (incorporating a sub-programme on Tourism). In April 2008 the ESCAP Commission determined to establish a Forum of Asian Ministers of Transport to provide strategic guidance for the development of efficient, reliable and cost-effective transport services throughout the region. The inaugural meeting of the Forum was held in December 2009, in Bangkok, Thailand. Principal infrastructure projects undertaken by the Transport Division have been the development of the Trans-Asian Railway and of the Asian Highway road network (see below). Other activities are aimed at improving the planning process in developing infrastructure facilities and services, in accordance with the Regional Action Programme of the New Delhi Action Plan on Infrastructure Development in Asia and the Pacific (which was adopted at a ministerial conference held in October 1996), and at enhancing private sector involvement in national infrastructure development through financing, management, operations and risk-sharing. The Division aims to reduce the adverse environmental impact of the provision of infrastructure facilities and to promote more equitable and easier access to social amenities. An Intergovernmental Agreement on the Asian Highway Network (adopted in 2003, identifying some 141,000 km of roads in 32 countries) came into effect in July 2005. By September 2011 the working group on the highway network estimated that more than 10,000 km of the highway network had been upgraded to meet the minimum standards set by the Agreement. In November 2005 ESCAP organized an intergovernmental meeting to conclude a draft agreement on the establishment of a Trans-Asian Railway Network. The intergovernmental accord was adopted in April 2006, and entered into force in June 2009, at which time it had received 22 signatures and been ratified by eight member states. The network was to comprise some 114,000 km of rail routes over 28 countries. The first meeting of a working group on the Trans-Asian Railway Network was held in December, in Bangkok, Thailand. ESCAP supports the development of dry ports along the Asian Highway and Trans-Asian Railway networks as part of an integrated regional transport and logistical system. In 2004 ESCAP and the UN Economic Commission for Europe (ECE) initiated a project for developing Euro-Asian transport linkages, aiming to identify and overcome the principal obstacles (physical and otherwise) along the main transport routes linking Asia and Europe. In November 2003 ESCAP approved a new initiative, the Asia-Pacific Network for Transport and Logistics Education and Research (ANTLER), to comprise education, training and research centres throughout the region. In November 2006 the Ministerial Conference on Transport, held in Busan, South Korea, adopted the Busan Declaration, which outlined a long-term development strategy for regional transport and identified investment priorities. The meeting also adopted a Ministerial Declaration on Road Safety which pledged to implement safety measures to save some 600,000 lives in the region in the period 2007–15.

ESCAP's tourism concerns include the development of human resources, improved policy planning for tourism development, greater investment in the industry, and minimizing the environmental impact of tourism. A Plan of Action for Sustainable Tourism in the Asia and Pacific Region (1999–2005) was adopted in April 1999; a second phase of the Plan, to cover the period 2006–12, was adopted at an intergovernmental meeting held in Bali, Indonesia, in December 2005. A Network of Asia-Pacific Education and Training Institutes in Tourism, established in 1997, comprised 261 institutes and organizations in 45 countries and states in 2012.

CO-OPERATION WITH OTHER ORGANIZATIONS

ESCAP works with other UN agencies and non-UN international organizations, non-governmental organizations, academic institutions and the private sector; such co-operation includes joint planning of programmes, preparation of studies and reports, participating in meetings, and sharing information and technical expertise. In July 1993 a memorandum of understanding (MOU) was signed by ESCAP and the Asian Development Bank, outlining priority areas of co-operation between the two organizations. These were: regional and sub-regional co-operation; issues concerning the least-developed, land-locked and island developing member countries; poverty alleviation; women in development; population; human resource development; the environment and natural resource management; statistics and data bases; economic analysis; transport and communications; and industrial restructuring and privatization. The two organizations were to co-operate in organizing workshops, seminars and conferences, in implementing joint projects, and in exchanging information and data on a regular basis. A new MOU between the two organizations was signed in May 2004 with an emphasis on achieving poverty reduction throughout the region. In 2001 ESCAP, with the Bank and UNDP, established a tripartite regional partnership to promote the MDGs (see above); a joint report on implementation of the goals was prepared by the partnership and published in June 2005 prior to a global review, conducted at the UN General Assembly in September. In May 2007

ESCAP endorsed a regional plan developed by the partnership with the aim of addressing regional challenges (in particular those faced by poorer countries) to the achievement of the MDGs. A High-level Subregional Forum on Accelerating Achievement of the Millennium Development Goals in South Asia was organized by the partnership in February 2012. The annual regional review on progress towards achieving the MDGs was released at the meeting. The UN Special Programme for the Economies of Central Asia (SPECA), begun in 1998, is implemented jointly by ESCAP and ECE (see below). In May 2007 ESCAP signed an MOU with ECE and the Eurasian Economic Community to strengthen co-operation in sustainable development, in support of the MDGs. In the following month ESCAP signed an MOU with the International Organization for Migration (IOM) to provide for greater co-operation and co-ordination on international migration issues. In September 2008 ESCAP and the IOM organized an Asia-Pacific high-level meeting on international migration and development.

Special Programme for the Economies of Central Asia (SPECA): launched in 1998 by the presidents of central Asian states, SPECA is supported jointly by ESCAP and ECE. It aims to strengthen sub-regional co-operation by enabling the discussion of regional issues and offering technical assistance. Six project working groups cover: transport and border crossing; water and energy resources; trade; knowledge-based development; statistics; and gender and economy. The SPECA Economic Forum meets annually in conjunction with the sessions of the SPECA Governing Council, composed of the national co-ordinators of member countries. The 2011 Forum was convened in Aşgabat, Turkmenistan, in November, on the theme '20 Years of Regional Economic Cooperation in Central Asia: Successes, Challenges and Prospects'. During 2009, in response to requests by SPECA member countries for the further strengthening of the Special Programme, ESCAP and ECE determined to establish a SPECA Regional Office in Central Asia, with the aim of improving liaison with governments, the business and academic communities, and of supporting project implementation. Participating countries: Afghanistan, Azerbaijan, Kazakhstan, Kyrgyzstan, Tajikistan, Turkmenistan and Uzbekistan.

REGIONAL INSTITUTIONS

Asian and Pacific Centre for Agricultural Engineering and Machinery (APCAEM): A-7/F, China International Science and Technology Convention Centre, 12 Yumin Rd, Chaoyang District, Beijing 100029, People's Republic of China; tel. (10) 8225-3581; fax (10) 8225-3584; e-mail info@unapcaem.org; internet www.unapcaem.org; f. 1977 as Regional Network for Agricultural Engineering and Machinery, elevated to regional centre in 2002; aims to reduce poverty by enhancing environmentally sustainable agriculture and food production, and applying 'green' and modern agro-technology for the well-being of producers and consumers; work programmes comprise agricultural engineering, food chain management, and agro-enterprise development and trade; undertakes research, training, technical assistance and the exchange of information. Active mems: Bangladesh, People's Republic of China, Fiji, India, Indonesia, Iran, Democratic People's Republic of Korea, Republic of Korea, Mongolia, Nepal, Pakistan, Philippines, Sri Lanka, Thailand, Viet Nam; Dir LeRoy Hollenbeck (USA); publ. *APCAEM Policy Brief* (quarterly).

Asian and Pacific Centre for Transfer of Technology: APCTT Bldg, POB 4575, C-2 Qutab Institutional Area, New Delhi 110 016, India; tel. (11) 26966509; fax (11) 26856274; e-mail postmaster@apctt.org; internet www.apctt.org; f. 1977 to assist countries of the ESCAP region by strengthening their capacity to develop, transfer and adopt technologies relevant to the region, and to identify and promote regional technology development and transfer; operates Business Asia Network (www.business-asia.net) to promote technology-based co-operation, particularly between small and medium-sized enterprises; Dir Dr Krishnamurthy Ramanathan; publs *Asia Pacific Tech Monitor*, *VATIS Updates on Biotechnology*, *Food Processing*, *Ozone Layer Protection*, *Non-Conventional Energy*, and *Waste Management* (each every 2 months).

Asian and Pacific Training Centre for ICT for Development (APCICT): Bonbudong, 3rd Floor Songdo Techno Park, 7-50 Songdo-dong, Yeonsu-gu, Incheon City, Republic of Korea; tel. 245-1700; fax 245-7712; e-mail info@unapcict.org; internet www.unapcict.org; f. 2006 to provide training to ICT policy-makers and professionals, advisory services and analytical studies, to promote best practices in the field of ICT, and to contribute to narrowing the digital divide in the region; developed an Academy of ICT Essentials for Government Leaders, a virtual Academy, and an e-Collaborative hub; Dir Hyuen-Suk Rhee.

Centre for Alleviation of Poverty through Sustainable Agriculture (CAPSA): Jalan Merdeka 145, Bogor 16111, Indonesia; tel. (251) 343277; fax (251) 336290; e-mail capsa@uncapsa.org; internet www.uncapsa.org; f. 1981 as CGPRT Centre, current name adopted 2010; initiates and promotes socio-economic and policy research, training, dissemination of information and advisory services to enhance food security in Asia and the Pacific; Dir Dr Katinka Weinberger (Germany).

Statistical Institute for Asia and the Pacific (SIAP): JETRO-IDE Building, 2–2 Wakaba 3-chome, Mihama-ku, Chiba-shi, Chiba 2618787, Japan; tel. (43) 2999782; fax (43) 2999780; e-mail staff@unsiap.or.jp; internet www.unsiap.or.jp; f. 1970 as Asian Statistical Institute, present name adopted 1977; became a subsidiary body of ESCAP in 1995; trains government statisticians at the Institute and in various co-operating countries in Asia and the Pacific; prepares teaching materials, assists in the development of training on official statistics in national and sub-regional centres; Dir Margarita Guerrero (Philippines).

ASSOCIATED BODIES

ESCAP/WMO Typhoon Committee: Av. de 5 de Outubro, Coloane, Macao, SAR, People's Republic of China; tel. 88010531; fax 88010530; e-mail info@typhooncommittee.org; internet www.typhooncommittee.org; f. 1968; an intergovernmental body affiliated to ESCAP and regional body of the Tropical Cyclone Programme of the World Meteorological Organization; promotes disaster preparedness, trains personnel on meteorology, hydrology and disaster risk reduction and co-ordinates research. The committee's programme is supported by national resources and also by other international and bilateral assistance; Mems: Cambodia, People's Republic of China, Democratic People's Republic of Korea, Republic of Korea, Hong Kong SAR, Japan, Laos, Macao SAR, Malaysia, Philippines, Singapore, Thailand, USA, Viet Nam; Sec. Olavo Rasquinho.

WMO/ESCAP Panel on Tropical Cyclones: PTC Secretariat, Meteorological Complex, Pitras Buk. Rd, Sector H-8/2, Islamabad 44000, Pakistan; tel. (51) 9250365; fax (51) 9250368; e-mail PTC.Sectt@ptc-wmoescap.org; internet www.ptc-wmoescap.org; f. 1972 to mitigate damage caused by tropical cyclones in the Bay of Bengal and the Arabian Sea; mems: Bangladesh, India, Maldives, Myanmar, Oman, Pakistan, Sri Lanka, Thailand; Sec. Dr Qamar-uz-Zaman Chaudhry.

Finance

For the two-year period 2012–13 ESCAP's programme budget, an appropriation from the UN budget, was US $98.6m. The regular budget is supplemented annually by funds from various sources for technical assistance.

Publications

Annual Report.

Asia-Pacific Development Journal (2 a year).

Asia-Pacific in Figures (annually).

Asia-Pacific Population Journal (3 a year).

Asia-Pacific Trade and Investment Report (annually).

Asia and Pacific Disaster Report.

Bulletin on Asia-Pacific Perspectives (annually).

Economic and Social Survey of Asia and the Pacific (annually).

Environment and Sustainable Development News (quarterly).

ESCAP Energy News (2 a year).

ESCAP Human Resources Development Newsletter (2 a year).

ESCAP Population Data Sheet (annually).

ESCAP Tourism Review (annually).

Foreign Trade Statistics of Asia and the Pacific (every 2 years).

Key Economic Developments and Prospects in the Asia-Pacific Region (annually).

Population Headliners (several a year).

Poverty Alleviation Initiatives (quarterly).

Socio-Economic Policy Brief (several a year).

State of the Environment in Asia and the Pacific (every 5 years).

Statistical Indicators for Asia and the Pacific (quarterly).

Statistical Newsletter (quarterly).

Statistical Yearbook for Asia and the Pacific.

Technical Co-operation Yearbook.

Transport and Communications Bulletin for Asia and the Pacific (annually).

Water Resources Journal (annually).

Manuals; country and trade profiles; commodity prices; statistics; Atlas of Mineral Resources of the ESCAP Region (country by country).

Economic Commission for Latin America and the Caribbean—ECLAC

Address: Edif. Naciones Unidas, Avda Dag Hammarskjöld 3477, Vitacura, Casilla 179-D, Santiago, Chile.

Telephone: (2) 2102000; **fax:** (2) 2080252; **e-mail:** dpisantiago@eclac.cl; **internet:** www.eclac.cl.

The UN Economic Commission for Latin America was founded by the UN Economic and Social Council (ECOSOC) in 1948 to co-ordinate policies for the promotion of economic development in the Latin American region. The current name of the Commission was adopted in 1984.

MEMBERS

Antigua and Barbuda	El Salvador	Paraguay
Argentina	France	Peru
Bahamas	Germany	Portugal
Barbados	Grenada	Saint Christopher and Nevis
Belize	Guatemala	Saint Lucia
Bolivia	Guyana	Saint Vincent and the Grenadines
Brazil	Haiti	Spain
Canada	Honduras	Suriname
Chile	Italy	Trinidad and Tobago
Colombia	Jamaica	United Kingdom
Costa Rica	Japan	USA
Cuba	Korea, Republic	Uruguay
Dominica	Mexico	Venezuela
Dominican Republic	Netherlands	
Ecuador	Nicaragua	
	Panama	

ASSOCIATE MEMBERS

Anguilla	Cayman Islands	Puerto Rico
Aruba	Montserrat	Turks and Caicos
British Virgin Islands	Netherlands Antilles	United States Virgin Islands

Organization

(April 2012)

COMMISSION

The Commission, comprising representatives of every member state, normally meets every two years at ministerial level. It considers matters relating to the economic and social development of the region, reviews activities of the organization, and adopts programmes of work. The 33rd session was held in Brasilía, Brazil, in May–June 2010; the 34th session was scheduled to be convened in El Salvador, in 2012. Member states may meet between Commission meetings in an ad hoc Committee of the Whole. The Commission has established the following ad hoc and permanent bodies:

Caribbean Development and Co-operation Committee;

Committee of High-level Government Experts;

Committee on Central American Economic Co-operation;

Committee on South-South Co-operation;

Regional Conference on Women;

Regional Council for Planning of ILPES;

Statistical Conference of the Americas.

SECRETARIAT

The Secretariat employs more than 500 staff and is headed by the Offices of the Executive Secretary and of the Secretary of the Commission. ECLAC's work programme is carried out by the following divisions: Economic Development (including a Development Studies Unit); Economic and Social Planning (ILPES, see below); International Trade and Integration; Natural Resources and Infrastructure (including a Transport Unit); Population (CELADE, see below); Production, Productivity and Management (including an Agricultural Development Unit, a joint ECLAC/UNIDO Industrial and Technological Development Unit and a Unit on Investment and Corporate Strategies); Social Development; Statistics; Programme Planning and Operations; Sustainable Development and Human Settlements; and Gender Affairs. There are also a Development Studies Unit and a Public Information and Web Services Section.

Executive Secretary: ALICIA BÁRCENA IBARRA (Mexico).

SUB-REGIONAL OFFICES

Caribbean: 1 Chancery Lane, POB 1113, Port of Spain, Trinidad and Tobago; tel. 224-8000; fax 623-8485; e-mail registry@eclacpos.org; internet www.eclacpos.org; f. 1956; covers non-Spanish-speaking Caribbean countries; functions as the secretariat for the Caribbean Development and Co-operation Committee; Dir DIANE QUARLESS.

Central America and Spanish-speaking Caribbean: Avda Presidente Masaryk 29, Colonia Chapultepec Morales, Postal 6-718, 11570 México, DF; tel. (55) 5263-9600; fax (55) 5531-1151; e-mail registromexico@cepal.org; internet www.cepal.org.mx; f. 1951; covers Central America and Spanish-speaking Caribbean countries; Dir HUGO E. BETETA.

There are also national offices, in Buenos Aires, Argentina; Brasilía, Brazil; Bogotá, Colombia; and Montevideo, Uruguay; and a liaison office in Washington, DC, USA.

Activities

ECLAC collaborates with regional governments in the investigation and analysis of regional and national economic problems, and provides guidance in the formulation of development plans. The activities of its different divisions include research, monitoring of trends and policies, and comparative studies; analysis; publication of information; provision of technical assistance; organizing and participating in workshops, seminars and conferences; training courses; and co-operation with national, regional and international organizations, including non-governmental organizations and the private sector. ECLAC's 29th session, held in Brasilía, Brazil, in May 2002, adopted the Brasilía Resolution, which outlined a strategic agenda to meet the challenges of globalization. Proposed action included the consolidation of democracy, strengthening social protection, the formulation of policies to reduce macroeconomic and financial vulnerability, and the development of sustainable and systemic competitiveness in order to build, gradually, an international social agenda based on rights.

The 32nd session of the Commission was convened in June 2008 in Santo Domingo, Dominican Republic. It considered a report, prepared by the Secretariat, entitled 'Structural Change and Productivity Growth—20 years later. Old problems, new opportunities'. The meeting endorsed its conclusions and voted to pursue further study of productive development and innovation policies and best practices. The Commission also requested that the Secretariat research challenges facing the region caused by escalating fuel and food costs at that time. The meeting approved a new programme of work for the period 2010–11, which aimed to promote policies to reduce vulnerability, to foster long-term production development strategies, to improve sustainable development policies, to improve the management of global issues at a regional level, and to strengthen social cohesion, reduce social risks and reinforce gender mainstreaming. In June 2009 ECLAC hosted a meeting of experts and officials from the region's ministries of finance to pursue discussions on structural reform and other measures to counter the impact of the global financial and economic crisis.

In June 2010 the 33rd session of the Commission, held in Brasilía, Brazil, adopted a new work programme for the two-year period 2012–13. The programme's main areas of activity aimed: to strengthen the region's access to financing for development; to contribute to improving the global, regional and national financial architecture; to heighten the productive potential of the region and reduce productivity gaps, with special emphasis on innovation and new technologies; to improve the region's position in the global economy through trade, co-operation and regional integration; to promote a social covenant through greater social equality, lower social risks and further inclusion of a gender perspective in public policies; to improve policies for sustainable development and energy efficiency and address the effects of climate change; and to improve the development of institutions that deal with the management of global and cross-border issues and the provision of public goods at a regional level. The focus of the Commission meeting was a report entitled 'Time for Equality: Closing gaps, opening trails', which identified economic, social and structural disparities throughout the region. Representatives of member states determined to pursue development efforts with a stronger equality agenda.

ECLAC works closely with other agencies within the UN system and with other regional and multinational organizations. In January 2010 ECLAC offered its total co-operation in the immediate humanitarian tasks resulting from the earthquake that caused extensive damage and loss of life in Haiti and in any future reconstruction process. In March, following a massive earthquake in Chile, ECLAC established a joint working group, with UNDP, OCHA and the Chilean authorities, to define priority areas for emergency funding. In February 2011 ECLAC hosted a meeting of representatives of UN agencies in order to initiate production of an inter-agency document in preparation for the UN Conference on Environment and Sustainable Development, scheduled to be convened in Rio de Janeiro, Brazil, in May 2012, 20 years after the first so-called Earth Summit; the resulting document was discussed at a meeting convened at ECLAC headquarters in September 2011.

ECLAC supports member countries in negotiations of bilateral or sub-regional free trade agreements, in particular with the USA. In January 2002 ECLAC hosted an Interregional Conference on Financing for Development, held in Mexico City, which it had organized as part of the negotiating process prior to the World Summit on Financing for Development, held in March. In June senior representatives of ECLAC, UNDP, the World Bank and the Inter-American Development Bank agreed to co-ordinate activities in pursuit of the development goals proclaimed by the Millennium Summit meeting of the UN General Assembly in September 2000. ECLAC was to adapt the objectives of the so-called Millennium Development Goals (MDGs) to the reality of countries in the region. In July 2004 the 30th session of the Commission approved the establishment of an intergovernmental forum to monitor the implementation of decisions emerging from the World Summit on Sustainable Development, held in Johannesburg, South Africa, in September 2002. In January 2006 ECLAC organized the first Regional Implementation Forum on Sustainable Development, as mandated by the UN Commission on Sustainable Development. In January 2003 a regional conference was convened, in the Dominican Republic, in preparation for the World Summit on the Information Society (WSIS), the first phase of which was held in December, in Geneva, Switzerland. In July 2004 delegates to the 30th session of the Commission requested that ECLAC co-ordinate a regional preparatory meeting to define objectives and proposals for the second phase of the Summit in 2005. The regional ministerial meeting was convened in Rio de Janeiro, Brazil, in June 2005, and a Regional Action Plan, eLAC 2007, was approved to support national and regional projects that incorporate information and communications technology for use in economic and social development in the region. A second plan, eLAC2010, was adopted by ministers in February 2008, to assist countries to attain the global targets identified by the WSIS. The first Follow-up Meeting of eLAC2010 was convened in April 2009. A third Ministerial Conference on the Information Society in Latin America and the Caribbean was convened in Lima, Peru, in November 2010, at which a new action plan, eLAC2015, was approved. ECLAC serves as the technical secretariat for a regional dialogue on the costs of international connections, broadband services and digital inclusion, which was inaugurated in August 2010. In May 2011 ECLAC launched a new Regional Broadband Observatory (ORBA), which was to facilitate public policy decision-making with regard to the provision of broadband services and in October ECLAC organized its first so-called 'School for broadband policymakers'. In that month, the fourth meeting of the regional dialogue on broadband endorsed ORBA proposals relating to minimum download speeds and connectivity.

In November 2003 a Regional Intergovernmental Conference on Ageing was convened, in Santiago, Chile, to further the objectives of a World Assembly on Ageing that had been held in Madrid, Spain, in April 2002. A second Regional Intergovernmental Conference on Ageing was held in Brasília, Brazil, in December 2007. In November 2003 ECLAC launched REDESA, a web-based network of institutions and experts in social and environmental statistics. The first phase of a Macroeconomic Dialogue Network (REDIMA I) was established in 2003, to assist communication on macroeconomic issues between economists from the region's central banks and ministries of finance: a second phase, REDIMA II, was initiated in 2005. In July 2007 ECLAC organized the fourth Statistical Conference of the Americas (SCA), which is convened every two years to promote the development and improvement of national statistics (in particular their comparability), and to encourage co-operation between national statistical offices and regional and international organizations. The fifth SCA was held in Bogotá, Colombia, in August 2009. ECLAC organizes an annual competition to encourage small-scale innovative social projects in local communities. In June 2008 ECLAC signed an agreement with the UN's International Research and Training Institute for the Advancement of Women (INSTRAW) to establish an observatory on gender equality in Latin America and the Caribbean. In July 2009 ECLAC signed a further agreement with the UN World Tourism Organization to strengthen co-operation in measuring and analysing tourism statistics and indicators. In January 2010 ECLAC initiated a joint project with the Inter-American Development Bank to conduct an economic analysis of the impact of climate change on the region. In January 2012 ECLAC and the Union of Universities of Latin America and the Caribbean signed a five-year co-operation agreement providing a frame work for collaboration between officials and consultants in the shared goal of improving research, debate and training of professionals.

In July 2006 Japan became the first Asian nation to be granted full membership of ECLAC. The membership of the Republic of Korea was formally approved in July 2007.

Latin American and Caribbean Institute for Economic and Social Planning (Instituto Latinoamericano y del Caribe de Planificacion Economica y Social—ILPES): Edif. Naciones Unidas, Avda Dag Hammarskjöld 3477, Vitacura, Casilla 179-D, Santiago, Chile; tel. (2) 2102507; fax (2) 2066104; e-mail ilpes@cepal.org; internet www.eclac.cl/ilpes/; f. 1962; supports regional governments through the provision of training, advisory services and research in the field of public planning policy and co-ordination; Dir JORGE MATTAR MÁRQUEZ (Mexico).

Latin American Demographic Centre (Centro Latinoamericano y Caribeno de Demografia—CELADE): Edif. Naciones Unidas, Avda Dag Hammarskjöld 3477, Casilla 179-D, Santiago, Chile; tel. (2) 2102021; fax (2) 2080196; e-mail celade@eclac.cl; internet www.eclac.cl/celade; f. 1957, became an autonomous entity within ECLAC in 1971 and was fully incorporated into ECLAC as its Population Division in 1997; provides technical assistance to governments, universities and research centres in demographic analysis, population policies, integration of population factors in development planning, and data processing; conducts courses on demographic analysis for development and various national and regional seminars; provides demographic estimates and projections, documentation, data processing, computer packages and training; Dir DIRK JASPERS-FAIJER.

Finance

For the two-year period 2012–13 ECLAC's proposed regular budget, an appropriation from the UN, amounted to US $110.3m. In addition, extra-budgetary activities are financed by governments, other organizations, and UN agencies.

Publications

(in English and Spanish)

CEPAL Review (3 a year).

Challenges/Desafios (2–3 a year, with UNICEF).

Demographic Observatory (2 a year).

ECLAC Notes (quarterly).

Economic Survey of Latin America and the Caribbean (annually).

FAL Bulletin (Trade Facilitation and Transport in Latin America) (monthly).

Foreign Investment in Latin America and the Caribbean (annually).

Latin America and the Caribbean in the World Economy (annually).

Latin American Economic Outlook (annually).

Notas de Población (2 a year).

Preliminary Overview of the Economies of Latin America and the Caribbean (annually).

Social Panorama of Latin America (annually).

Statistical Yearbook for Latin America and the Caribbean.

Water Resources Newsletter (2 a year).

Studies, reports, bibliographical bulletins.

Economic Commission for Africa—ECA

Address: Menelik II Ave, POB 3001, Addis Ababa, Ethiopia.

Telephone: (11) 5517200; **fax:** (11) 5514416; **e-mail:** ecainfo@uneca.org; **internet:** www.uneca.org.

The UN Economic Commission for Africa (ECA) was founded in 1958 by a resolution of the UN Economic and Social Council (ECOSOC) to initiate and take part in measures for facilitating Africa's economic development.

MEMBERS

Algeria	Eritrea	Niger
Angola	Ethiopia	Nigeria
Benin	Gabon	Rwanda
Botswana	The Gambia	São Tomé and Príncipe
Burkina Faso	Ghana	Senegal
Burundi	Guinea	Seychelles
Cameroon	Guinea-Bissau	Sierra Leone
Cape Verde	Kenya	Somalia
Central African Republic	Lesotho	South Africa
Chad	Liberia	Sudan
Comoros	Libya	Swaziland
Congo, Democratic Republic	Madagascar	Tanzania
Congo, Republic	Malawi	Togo
Côte d'Ivoire	Mali	Tunisia
Djibouti	Mauritania	Uganda
Egypt	Mauritius	Zambia
Equatorial Guinea	Morocco	Zimbabwe
	Mozambique	
	Namibia	

Organization

(April 2012)

COMMISSION

The Commission may only act with the agreement of the government of the country concerned. It is also empowered to make recommendations on any matter within its competence directly to the government of the member or associate member concerned, to governments admitted in a consultative capacity, and to the UN Specialized Agencies. The Commission is required to submit for prior consideration by ECOSOC any of its proposals for actions that would be likely to have important effects on the international economy.

CONFERENCE OF AFRICAN MINISTERS

The Conference, which meets every year, is attended by ministers responsible for finance, planning and economic development, representing the governments of member states, and is the main deliberative body of the Commission. The Commission's responsibility to promote concerted action for the economic and social development of Africa is vested primarily in the Conference, which considers matters of general policy and the priorities to be assigned to the Commission's programmes, considers inter-African and international economic policy, and makes recommendations to member states in connection with such matters.

OTHER POLICY-MAKING BODIES

Five intergovernmental committees of experts attached to the Sub-regional Offices (see below) meet annually and report to the Commission through a Technical Preparatory Committee of the Whole, which was established in 1979 to deal with matters submitted for the consideration of the Conference.

Seven other committees meet regularly to consider issues relating to the following policy areas: women and development; development information; sustainable development; human development and civil society; industry and private sector development; natural resources and science and technology; and regional co-operation, infrastructure and integration.

SECRETARIAT

The Secretariat provides the services necessary for the meeting of the Conference of Ministers and the meetings of the Commission's subsidiary bodies, carries out the resolutions and implements the programmes adopted there. It comprises the Office of the Executive Secretary and the following divisions: Food Security and Sustainable Development; Governance and Public Administration; ICT, Science and Technology; Economic Development and New Partnership for Africa's Development (NEPAD); Regional Integration and Trade; the African Centre for Gender and Social Development; and the African Centre for Statistics.

Executive Secretary: CARLOS LOPES (Guinea-Bissau).

SUB-REGIONAL OFFICES

The Sub-regional Offices (SROs) aim to enable member states to play a more effective role in the process of African integration and to facilitate the integration efforts of the other UN agencies active in the sub-regions. In addition, the SROs act as the operational arms of ECA at national and sub-regional levels with a view to: ensuring harmony between the objectives of sub-regional and regional programmes and those defined by the Commission; providing advisory services; facilitating sub-regional economic co-operation, integration and development; collecting and disseminating information; stimulating policy dialogue; and promoting gender issues. Under the radical restructuring of the ECA, completed in 2006, the SROs were given an enhanced role in shaping the Commission's agenda and programme implementation, and were also designated as privileged partners of the regional economic communities. (The following five of Africa's regional economic communities are regarded as the pillars of the envisaged African Economic Community: the Common Market for Eastern and Southern Africa—COMESA, the Communauté économique des états de l'Afrique centrale—CEEAC, the Economic Community of West African States—ECOWAS, the Southern African Development Community—SADC, and the Union of the Arab Maghreb.)

Central Africa: POB 14935, Yaoundé, Cameroon; tel. 2222-0861; fax 2223-3185; e-mail sroca@uneca.org; Dir EMILE AHOHE.

East Africa: POB 4654, Kigali, Rwanda; tel. 586549; fax 586546; e-mail APedro@uneca.org; Dir ANTONIO M. A. PEDRO.

North Africa: BP 2062 Rabat Ryad, Morocco; tel. (3) 771-78-29; fax (3) 771-27-02; e-mail srdc-na@uneca.org; Dir KARIMA BOUNEMRA BEN SOLTANE.

Southern Africa: POB 30647, Lusaka, Zambia; tel. (1) 228502; fax (1) 236949; e-mail srdcsa.uneca@uneca.org; Dir BEATRICE KIRASO (Uganda).

West Africa: POB 744, Niamey, Niger; tel. 72-29-61; fax 72-28-94; e-mail srdcwest@eca.ne; Dir FATOUMATA BA.

Activities

The Commission's activities are designed to encourage sustainable socio-economic development in Africa and to increase economic co-operation among African countries and between Africa and other parts of the world. The Secretariat has been guided in its efforts by major regional strategies, including the Abuja Treaty on the establishment of an African Economic Community, signed under the aegis of the Organization of African Unity (OAU, now African Union—AU) in 1991, the UN System-wide Support to the AU and NEPAD (approved in 2006, see below, replacing the UN System-wide Special Initiative on Africa that covered 1996–2005), and the UN New Agenda for the Development of Africa, which covered the period 1991–2000. In 2006 ECA initiated a major reform process in order to strengthen its capacity to promote regional integration and to help Africa to meet its particular needs. Greater emphasis to be placed on knowledge generation and networking, advocacy, advisory services and technical co-operation, as well as co-operation with other regional organizations. A high-level review of the reforms was undertaken in 2009, resulting in further restructuring of some programmes and divisions.

ICT, SCIENCE AND TECHNOLOGY

The ICT (Information and Communications Technology), Science and Technology Division has responsibility for co-ordinating the implementation of the Harnessing Information Technology for Africa project and for implementing the African Information Society Initiative (AISI), which was started in 1996 to support the creation of an African information and communications infrastructure. ECA is responsible for overseeing quality enhancement and dissemination of statistical databases; for improving access to information by means of enhanced library and documentation services and output; and for strengthening geo-information systems for sustainable development. In addition, ECA encourages member governments to liberalize the telecommunications sector and stimulate imports of computers in order to enable the expansion of information technology throughout Africa. ECA manages the Information Technology Centre for Africa (see below). The Commission administers the Partnership for Information and Communication Technologies in

Africa (PICTA), which was established in 1999 as an informal grouping of donors and agencies concerned with developing an information society in Africa. In 1999 ECA's Committee on Development Information established the African Virtual Library and Information Network (AVLIN) as a hub for the exchange of data among African researchers and policy-makers. In August 2000 ECA launched the Africa Knowledge Networks Forum (AKNF). The Forum, to be convened on an annual basis under ECA auspices, was to facilitate co-operation in information-sharing and research between professional research and development networks, and also between these and policy-makers, educators, civil society organizations and the private sector. It was to provide technical support to the African Development Forum (see below). In May 2003 ECA launched the e-Policy Resource Network for Africa, under the Global e-Policy Resource Network initiative aimed at expanding the use and benefits of information and communication technologies. ECA provided institutional and logistical support to an African Ministerial Committee which was established in April 2004 to consider proposals of the first phase of the World Summit on Information Society (WSIS), convened in December 2003. ECA co-ordinated preparations for the African Regional Preparatory Conference in February 2005 for the second phase of the WSIS, which was convened in Tunis, Tunisia, in November of the same year. ECA was awarded responsibility for the Task Force on e-Government, following the summit meeting. The ECA Science and Technology Network (ESTNET) provides an information service on science and technology for African policy-makers and others. In March 2008 ECA organized a conference entitled Science with Africa to link African science-based organizations and businesses with their global counterparts; the second Science with Africa conference, held in June 2010, adopted a set of recommendations on how African countries might leverage science and technology to carry forwards their development agenda. In February 2009 representatives of UN agencies, NEPAD, the AU, and media executives, convened the first Regional Media Dialogue, in The Vaal, South Africa, at the end of which they adopted a Consensus Declaration and series of recommendations relating to the increasing role of the media in Africa's development. In July the first International Conference on African Digital Libraries and Archives, held under ECA auspices, urged the establishment of an ECA African Digital Library and Archives Programme. In October 2011 ECA organized, with the AU, a regional conference which approved the establishment of an Africa Internet Governance Forum (IGF), in accordance with the recommendations of the WSIS. ECA was to provide the secretariat for new body.

GOVERNANCE AND PUBLIC ADMINISTRATION

The role of ECA's Governance and Public Administration Division is to improve member states' capacity for good governance and development management. The Division provides support for the African Peer Review Mechanism, a NEPAD initiative whereby participating member governments mutually assess compliance with a number of codes, standards and commitments that uphold good governance and sustainable development. The Division also helps civil society organizations to participate in governance; supports the development of private sector enterprises; and helps to improve public administration in member states. To achieve these aims the Division provides technical assistance and advisory services, conducts studies, and organizes training workshops, seminars and conferences at national, sub-regional and regional levels for ministers, public administrators and senior policy-makers, as well as for private and non-governmental organizations. In October 1999 the first African Development Forum (ADF)—initiated by ECA as a process to formulate an agenda for effective sustainable development in African countries—was held in Addis Ababa, Ethiopia. It was intended that regular ADF meetings would consider a specific development issue. ADF VII was convened in October 2010, on the theme 'Acting on Climate Change for Sustainable Development in Africa'. In March 2011 the ECA launched the Africa Platform for Development Effectiveness (APDEv, accessible at www.africa-platform.org), a multi-stakeholder platform and organizing mechanism for policy-makers in the continent. The first African Governance Forum (AGF) was hosted by ECA, in Addis Ababa, in July 1997. AGF VIII, addressing the theme 'Democracy, Elections, and the Management of Diversity in Africa', was to be held in Johannesburg, South Africa, in 2012. In 2005 the first *African Governance Report (AGR-1)* was published by ECA, monitoring progress towards good governance in 27 countries. A second Report, issued in August 2009, found improvements over the past few years in the observance of human rights and the rule of law, as well as in competitive electoral politics and the scope of political representation, although party and electoral systems were deemed to be weak and poorly structured. Advances were judged to have been made in economic governance, public sector management, private sector development and corporate governance, while weaknesses were highlighted in the management of the tax system and in service delivery, and corruption was cited as a major challenge to achieving sustainable economic progress and development in Africa. *AGR-3*, addressing elections and diversity management in Africa, was under development in 2011. A *Mutual Review of Development Effectiveness in Africa Report (MRDE)*, jointly compiled by the ECA's Governance and Public Administration Division and OECD, is issued annually; the Review considers progress achieved hitherto in delivering commitments made by African countries and their development partners, and outlines future key priorities. The interim (preliminary) issue of *MRDE 2011* was issued in May of that year.

AFRICAN CENTRE FOR GENDER AND SOCIAL DEVELOPMENT

ECA aims to improve the socio-economic prospects of women through the promotion of equal access to resources and opportunities, and equal participation in decision-making. An African Centre for Gender and Development (renamed as above in 2006) was established in 1975 to service all national, sub-regional and regional bodies involved in development issues relating to gender and the advancement of women. The Centre manages the African Women's Development Fund, which was established in June 2000. An African Women's Rights Observatory, launched in 1995, monitors gender equality and the advancement of women. The preliminary results of a new African Gender and Development Index were presented in January 2005, measuring how far member states had met their commitments towards international agreements on gender equality and women's advancement. The African Women's Decade, covering 2010–20, was launched in October 2010 under the theme 'Grassroots approach to gender equality and women's empowerment'. A Commission on HIV/AIDS and Governance in Africa, with its secretariat based at ECA headquarters, was launched in September 2003. The Commission, an initiative of the UN Secretary-General, was mandated to assess the impact of the HIV/AIDS pandemic on national structures and African economic development and to incorporate its findings in a Final Report; this was issued in October 2005.

FOOD SECURITY AND SUSTAINABLE DEVELOPMENT

ECA's Food Security and Sustainable Development Division aims to strengthen the capacity of member countries to design institutional structures and implement policies and programmes, in areas such as food production, population, environment and human settlements, to achieve sustainable development. It also promotes the use of science and technology in achieving sustainable development. ECA promotes food security in African countries through raising awareness of the relationship between population, food security, the environment and sustainable development; encouraging the advancement of science and technology in member states; and providing policy analysis support and technical advisory services aimed at strengthening national population policies. In March 2010 ECA issued a report urging member countries to build upon the outcomes of the Abuja Food Security Summit, organized by the AU in December 2006, by establishing a common market of strategic food and agricultural commodities. From 2005 ECA increased its work devoted to the changes in climate caused by global warming, and the resulting threat posed by drought, floods and other extreme events. In 2006, with the AU and the African Development Bank (AfDB), it established a 10-year Climate for Development in Africa Programme (Clim-Dev Africa) to improve the collection of climate-related data and assist in forecasting and risk management. ECA provides the technical secretariat for Clim-Dev Africa. In December 2007 ECA announced the establishment of an African Climate Policy Centre (ACPC), to help member states to incorporate climate-related concerns in their development policies so as to counter the impact of climate change. The first Climate Change and Development in Africa Conference (CCDA-I) was held in Addis Ababa, Ethiopia, in October 2011. Members were encouraged, inter alia, to incorporate climate change data and analysis in their policy-making decisions, to identify means of increasing agricultural productivity, including water management and soil enrichment, and to develop strategies for low carbon development.

ECA assists member states in the assessment and use of water resources and the development of river and lake basins common to more than one country. ECA encourages co-operation between countries with regard to water issues and collaborates with other UN agencies and regional organizations to promote technical and economic co-operation in this area. In 1992, on the initiative of ECA, the Interagency Group for Water in Africa (now UN-Water/Africa) was established to co-ordinate and harmonize the water-related activities of the UN and other organizations on the continent. ECA has been particularly active in efforts to promote the integrated development of the water resources of the Zambezi river basin and of Lake Victoria. In December 2003 ECA hosted the Pan-African Implementation and Partnership Conference on Water (PANAFCON).

STATISTICS

The African Centre for Statistics was established in 2006 as a new division of ECA, to encourage the use of statistics in national planning, to provide training and technical assistance for the compilation, analysis and dissemination of statistics, and to prepare members for the 2010 round of population censuses. An Advisory Board on Statistics in Africa, comprising 15 experts from national statistical offices, sub-regional bodies and training institutes, meets annually to advise ECA on statistical developments in Africa and guide its activities. The Statistical Commission for Africa (StatCom-Africa), comprising representatives of national statistical offices, regional and international institutions and development partners, meets every two years as the principal body overseeing statistical development in Africa, with annual working groups monitoring progress and deciding on activities. In January 2012 StatCom-Africa, meeting in Cape Town, South Africa, adopted the Robben Island Declaration on Statistical Development, which aimed to strengthen methods of data collection and analysis, of harmonizing statistics in Africa and upgrading the system of national accounts. ECA assists its member states in population data collection and data processing; analysis of demographic data obtained from censuses or surveys; training demographers; formulation of population policies and integrating population variables in development planning, through advisory missions and through the organization of national seminars on population and development; and in dissemination of demographic information.

REGIONAL INTEGRATION, INFRASTRUCTURE AND TRADE

ECA's Regional Integration, Infrastructure and Trade Division comprises sections concerning regional integration; infrastructure and natural resources development; and trade and international negotiations. ECA supports the implementation of the AU's regional integration agenda, through research; policy analysis; strengthening capacity and the provision of technical assistance to the regional economic communities; and working on transboundary initiatives and activities across a variety of sectors. In October 2008 ECA launched an Observatory on Regional Integration in Africa, an internet-based repository of knowledge and information aimed at supporting the activities of policy-makers, member states, regional economic communities, and other stakeholders. The Trade and International Negotiations Section conducts research and outreach activities aimed at ensuring best practice in trade policy development and undertakes research and dissemination activities on bilateral and international trade negotiations (such as the ongoing multilateral trade negotiations under the World Trade Organization) with a view to helping African countries to benefit from globalization through trade. In April 2003 ECA and the AfDB synchronized their annual meetings in an effort to find a common position on addressing the principal challenges confronting the continent. They concluded that development was constrained by national debt, a persistent decline in exports, and weak economic growth rates. They also urged a thorough review of development strategies to determine whether poor outcomes were the result of bad policy, poor implementation or external factors. The African Trade Policy Centre (ATPC), established in 2003, aims to strengthen the human, institutional and policy capacities of African governments to formulate and implement sound trade policies and participate more effectively in international trade negotiations. The Centre takes both a national and regional perspective, and provides a rapid response to technical needs arising from ongoing trade negotiations.

ECA and the World Bank jointly co-ordinate the sub-Saharan Africa Transport Programme (SSATP), established in 1987, which aims to facilitate policy development and related capacity-building in the continent's transport sector. A meeting of all participants in the programme is held annually. The regional Road Management Initiative (RMI) under the SSATP seeks to encourage a partnership between the public and private sectors to manage and maintain road infrastructure more efficiently and thus to improve country-wide communications and transportation activities. An Urban Mobility component of the SSATP aims to improve sub-Saharan African urban transport services, while a Trade and Transport component aims to enhance the international competitiveness of regional economies through the establishment of more cost-effective services for shippers. The Railway Restructuring element focuses on the provision of financially sustainable railway enterprises. In December 2003 the first Central African Forum on Transport Infrastructure and Regional Integration was convened by ECA. In November 2005 a meeting of sub-Saharan African ministers of transport, convened in Bamako, Mali, on the fringes of the SSATP Annual General Meeting, adopted a resolution aimed at developing Africa's transport infrastructure, focusing on the importance of incorporating transport issues into poverty reduction strategies, ensuring sustainable financing for Africa's road programmes, and prioritizing road safety issues. The African Road Safety Conference, convened in Accra, Ghana, in February 2007, by African ministers responsible for transport and health, reaffirmed road safety as a key development priority and pledged to set and achieve measurable national targets for road safety and the prevention of traffic injuries in all member states. A meeting of experts convened in September 2011 to review the development of interconnected Trans-African Highways (TAH) reported that by that time the TAH comprised some nine principal axes of roads across the continent, but that about one-quarter of an envisaged final network was yet to be constructed. The meeting recommended the adoption of an intergovernmental agreement on the TAH, and adopted a series of 10 recommendations aimed at accelerating the development of the highways interconnection initiative. In November 2011 the second African Road Safety Conference, convened by ECA within the framework of the SSATP, approved an Action Plan, which aimed to halve the number of road crash fatalities by 2020.

The Division supports efforts to advance the development of Africa's extensive mineral and energy resources, focusing on promoting co-operation, integration and public-private sector partnerships; facilitating policy decisions and dissemination of best practices; and supporting capacity building. The Southern and Eastern African Mineral Centre, established by ECA in Dar-es-Salaam, Tanzania, in 1977, opened its membership to all African states in 2007. The Centre provides data-processing, training, analytical services and research on mineral applications. An international study group to review African mining was convened by ECA for the first time in October 2007. ECA's Energy Programme provides assistance to member states in the development of indigenous energy resources and the formulation of energy policies to extricate member states from continued energy crises. In May 2004 ECA was appointed as the secretariat of a new UN-Energy/Africa initiative which aimed to facilitate the exchange of information, good practices and knowledge-sharing among UN organizations and with private sector companies, non-governmental organizations, power utilities and other research and academic institutions. In December 2011 ECA and the AU organized a second conference of African ministers responsible for mineral resources development.

ECONOMIC DEVELOPMENT AND NEPAD

ECA provides guidance to the policy-making organs of the UN and the AU on the formulation of policies supporting the achievement of Africa's development objectives. It contributes to the work of the General Assembly and of specialized agencies by providing an African perspective in the preparation of development strategies. The former UN System-wide Special Initiative on Africa, covering the decade 1995–2006, aimed to mobilize resources and to implement a series of political and economic development objectives; the Initiative was followed by the UN System-wide Support to the AU and NEPAD, launched in 2006. NEPAD was established by the AU in 2001, and ECA was assigned the task of co-ordinating UN support for NEPAD at the regional level. In February 2010 a new NEPAD Planning and Co-ordination Committee (NPCC) was established as a technical body of the AU, to replace the former NEPAD Secretariat, with the aim of improving the implementation of NEPAD projects at country level. In April 2010 ECA and the NPCC concluded a memorandum of understanding strengthening collaboration between the two bodies. In the following month ECA, the AU and the AfDB issued their fourth joint *Assessing Regional Integration in Africa* report (ARIA IV), urging enhanced action to lower business costs in order to help facilitate intra-African trade.

Within the Economic Development and NEPAD Division, a Finance, Industry and Investment Section supports members to analyse the challenges of mobilizing domestic and external resources for promoting investment and industrial development. Principal focus areas are foreign aid, debt, private capital flows, and savings and remittances. It also assists member states to implement effective policies and strategies to enhance their investment prospects and competitiveness in the global production system. A Macroeconomic Analysis Section assists member states to improve their capacity to formulate, implement and monitor sound macroeconomic policies and better institutional frameworks, with a view to achieving sustainable development. The Section also focuses on policy advocacy and collaboration with development organizations and institutions, produces publications and provides training, conferences and workshops. It undertakes macroeconomic research and policy analysis in the following areas: macroeconomic modelling and planning; growth strategies; fiscal and monetary policies; and debt management. The Section also prepares background documents for the annual Conference of African Ministers of Finance, Planning, and Economic Development. A separate Section serves to support members reviewing their progress towards and in implementing internationally agreed development objectives, including the Millennium Development Goals (MDGs) and those defined by the 2001 Brussels Programme of Action for least developed countries. The Section prepares annual reviews and supports capacity building and the sharing of knowledge among African countries.

In March 2009 the Coalition for Dialogue on Africa (CoDA) was launched, by ECA, the AU and the AfDB, as an independent African forum to serve as an umbrella for all existing forums on Africa. ECA hosts its secretariat. CoDA meetings, including a multi-stakeholder dialogue forum, were convened in Tunis, in November, to consider Africa's recovery from the global economic and financial crisis, and regional integration. In February 2010 CoDA met, again in Tunis, to discuss transforming the Coalition into a fully independent, non-governmental African initiative, with a chief executive; and to develop a work programme. A CoDA policy forum was held in Abidjan, Côte d'Ivoire, in May, on 'Financing Regional Integration in Africa'. Meeting in October 2010, on the sidelines of ADF VII, CoDA urged African leaders to continue to pursue participation multinational negotiations on climate change. A CoDA policy forum on foreign direct investments in land in Africa was convened in Lisbon, Portugal, in June 2011.

In June 2009 ECA and the AU hosted, in Cairo, Egypt, a joint meeting of African ministers of finance and economic affairs, which considered the impact on the region of the global crisis. During that month a joint report of all five UN Regional Commissions, entitled *The Global Economic and Financial Crisis: Regional Impacts, Responses and Solutions*, was launched. In October 2010 the ECA, AU and AfDB established a Joint Secretariat (based at ECA headquarters) to enhance coherence and collaboration in support of Africa's development agenda. In May 2011 ECA launched the *ECA LDC Monitor*, an internet-based tool aimed at assessing economic progress in member Least-Developed Countries. The theme of the 2011 *Economic Report on Africa*, released in September of that year, was 'Development in Africa: The Role of the State in Economic Transformation'. Since 2006 ECA and AfDB have organized an annual African Economic Conference (AEC), aimed at enabling an exchange of ideas among economists and policy-makers on development policy. The sixth AEC was held in Addis Ababa, Ethiopia, in October 2011, on the theme 'Green Economy and Structural Transformation in Africa'.

ASSOCIATED BODY

Information Technology Centre for Africa (ITCA): POB 3001, Addis Ababa, Ethiopia; tel. (11) 551-4534; fax (11) 551-0512; e-mail itca@uneca.org; internet www.uneca.org/itca; f. 1999 to strengthen the continent's communications infrastructure and promote the use of information and communications technologies in planning and policy-making; stages exhibitions and provides training facilities; Man MAKANE FAYE.

Finance

ECA's proposed regular budget for the two-year period 2012–13, an appropriation from the UN budget, was US $138.3m.

Publications

African Governance Report.

African Statistical Yearbook.

Africa's Sustainable Development Bulletin.

African Women's Report.

Africa Youth Report.

ATPC News.

The ECA Echo (2 a month).

Economic Report on Africa.

ESTNET Newsletter (annually).

GenderNet (2 a year).

Insight (quarterly Southern Africa Office newsletter).

One Africa.

PICTA Bulletin (monthly).

Sustainable Development Report on Africa (every 2 years).

Assessing Regional Integration in Africa (ARIA) report series, country reports, policy and discussion papers, reports of conferences and meetings, training series, working paper series.

Economic and Social Commission for Western Asia—ESCWA

Address: Riad el-Solh Sq., POB 11-8575, Beirut, Lebanon.

Telephone: (1) 981301; **fax:** (1) 981510; **e-mail:** webmaster-escwa@un.org; **internet:** www.escwa.un.org.

The UN Economic Commission for Western Asia was established in 1974 by a resolution of the UN Economic and Social Council (ECOSOC), to provide facilities of a wider scope for those countries previously served by the UN Economic and Social Office in Beirut (UNESOB). The name 'Economic and Social Commission for Western Asia' (ESCWA) was adopted in 1985.

MEMBERS

Bahrain	Palestine
Egypt	Qatar
Iraq	Saudi Arabia
Jordan	Sudan
Kuwait	Syria
Lebanon	United Arab Emirates
Oman	Yemen

Organization

(April 2012)

COMMISSION

The Commission meets every two years in ministerial session to determine policy and establish work directives. Representatives of UN bodies and specialized agencies, regional organizations, other UN member states, and non-governmental organizations having consultative status with ECOSOC may attend as observers. The 26th ministerial session of the Commission was convened in May 2010, and the 27th was scheduled to be convened in May 2012.

PREPARATORY COMMITTEE

The Committee has the task of reviewing programming issues and presenting recommendations in that regard to the sessions of the Commission. It is the principal subsidiary body of the Commission and functions as its policy-making structure. Seven specialized intergovernmental committees have been established (see below) to consider specific areas of activity, to report on these to the Preparatory Committee and to assist the Committee in formulating ESCWA's medium-term work programmes: they meet every two years, except for the Committee on Transport, which meets annually.

SUBSIDIARY COMMITTEES

Statistical Committee: established in 1992;

Committee on Social Development: established in 1994;

Committee on Energy: established in 1995;

Committee on Water Resources: established in 1995;

Committee on Transport: established in 1997;

Committee on Liberalization of Foreign Trade and Economic Globalization: established in 1997;

Committee on Women: established in 2003.

In addition, an Advisory Committee meets every four months at ESCWA headquarters: it comprises the heads of diplomatic missions in the host country, and a senior representative of the host country, and fulfils a consultative role, while providing a means of communication between member governments and the ESCWA Secretariat. A further Technical Committee, made up of senior officials from member countries, was established pursuant to a decision of the 24th ministerial session of the Commission held in May 2006. The Committee held its inaugural meeting in January 2008 and was to convene every six months, with a mandate to advise and assist the Secretariat in formulating strategy and future priorities and implementing programmes of work. The Consultative Committee on Scientific Technological Development and Technological Innovation was established in 2001 and meets every two years. It comprises experts from public institutions, the private sector, civil society and research centres.

SECRETARIAT

The Secretariat comprises an Executive Secretary, a Deputy Executive Secretary, and the following administrative and programme divisions: Administrative Services; Economic Development and Globalization; Information and Communications Technology; Programme Planning and Technical Co-operation; Social Development; Statistics; and Sustainable Development and Productivity. Each division is headed by a Chief, who is accountable to the Executive Secretary. In addition, there is an ESCWA Centre for Women (established in 2003, formerly part of the Social Development Division), and a Unit for Emerging and Conflict Related Issues, established in 2006.

Executive Secretary: RIMA KHALAF (Jordan).

Activities

ESCWA aims to support development and to further economic co-operation and integration in western Asia. ESCWA undertakes or sponsors studies of economic, social and development issues of the region, collects and disseminates information, and provides advisory services to member states in various fields of economic and social development. It also organizes conferences and intergovernmental and expert group meetings and sponsors training workshops and seminars. ESCWA adopts biennial strategic frameworks as the basis for its programme planning.

Much of ESCWA's work is carried out in co-operation with other UN bodies, as well as with other international and regional organizations, for example the League of Arab States, the Cooperation Council for the Arab States of the Gulf (GCC) and the Organization of Islamic Cooperation (OIC). In May 2009 ESCWA co-hosted, with the International Labour Organization and the Syrian Government, a Regional High-Level Consultative Forum on the Impacts of the International Financial Crisis on the ESCWA Member Countries. The meeting adopted the Damascus Declaration, comprising a set of proposals for member countries to respond more effectively to the crisis, including support for greater investment in the region by ESCWA's sovereign wealth funds, adopting fiscal stimulus policies, and strengthening the efficiency of their regulatory frameworks. The Forum identified ESCWA as being key to enhancing the participation of Arab and Islamic financial institutions in member countries' efforts to counter the effects of the crisis. ESCWA's 26th ministerial session was convened, in May 2010, on the theme 'The Role of Youth and their Empowerment'.

In June 2011 ESCWA hosted the 15th meeting of a Regional Co-ordination Mechanism for Arab States, at which regional directors and officials from more than 20 UN agencies and other international and regional organizations considered the recent political and social reforms in several Arab countries. The grouping reaffirmed its commitment to strengthening co-operation in order to support more inclusive and sustainable development in the region. It also resolved to establish a new thematic working group to achieve greater regional integration. In mid-2011 ESCWA undertook an internal review of its work programmes in order to enhance its capacity to address the emerging needs of societies in transition. In January 2012 the UN Secretary-General addressed a High-level Meeting on Reform and Transition to Democracy, organized by ESCWA. The meeting emphasized the need to incorporate human rights and principles of social justice as essential elements of future economic strategies in countries in the region in order to secure democracy, as well as to protect and promote the empowerment of women and to stimulate youth employment opportunities.

ECONOMIC DEVELOPMENT AND GLOBALIZATION

Through its Economic Development and Globalization Division ESCWA aims to assist member states to achieve sustainable economic development in the region and to integrate more fully into the world economy. A Financing for Development Team aims to assist member countries to implement the recommendations of the Monterrey Consensus, adopted at the International Conference on Financing for Development, held in Monterrey, Mexico, in March 2002. Other concerns are to encourage domestic, intra-regional and foreign investment, to facilitate transboundary flows of goods, services, people and capital, by integrating regional markets (for example through the Greater Arab Free Trade Area) and to support member countries with debt management. The Division's Trade Team works to advance regional trading integration, as well as greater participation of the region in the multilateral trading system. It acts as a forum for member countries in preparation for multilateral trade negotiations, such as those within the Doha Round of negotiations under the World Trade Organization. An Economic Analysis Team aims to increase the capacity of member countries to co-ordinate economic policies. It makes continuous assessments of the region's macroeconomic performances; conducts economic research, modelling and forecasting; monitors the region's progress towards the UN Millennium Development Goals (MDGs); and disseminates its findings to support dialogue at various regional meetings. The Division aims to help member countries to increase their exports and to encourage domestic and foreign investment. The work of the Division's Transport Team includes the development of an integrated transport system in the Arab Mashreq region; development of a regional transport information system; formation of national and regional transport and trade committees, representing both the private and public sectors; simplification of cross-border trading procedures; and the use of electronic data exchange for more efficient transport and trade. In May 2008 the 25th ministerial session of the Commission adopted a Convention on International Multi-modal Transport of Goods in the Arab Mashreq.

EMERGING AND CONFLICT-RELATED ISSUES

In January 2006 a Unit for Emerging and Conflict-related Issues (ECRI) was established to consolidate and develop ESCWA's activities in conflict and post-conflict countries and areas, including Iraq, the Palestinian territories and, initially, southern Lebanon. Following the Israeli military strikes that targeted the Lebanese bases of the militant Shi'a organization Hezbollah in July–August of that year, the mandate of ECRI was expanded to cover all of Lebanon. ECRI's priority areas include analysis and policy formulation for reducing the causes of conflict; capacity-building to improve the effectiveness of public administration and the rule of law; forging partnerships among civic entities at local and regional level; and working with other ESCWA divisions to meet the special needs of countries affected by conflicts. ESCWA administers an E-Caravan mobile computer school programme, to provide ICT training to communities in southern Lebanon. Other projects include: provision of regional and local 'networking academies' in Iraq, to give training in information technology; the Smart Communities Project, providing modern technology for villages in Iraq; improvement of statistics related to gender in Iraq; and support of the Coalition of Arab-Palestinian Civil Society Organizations. Regional expert group meetings organized by ECRI have included 'Strengthening Good Governance Practices in Conflict Affected Countries: Current Priorities and Future Interventions', and 'Policies for Peace-building and Conflict Prevention in Western Asia'. In September 2011 ESCWA hosted an expert group meeting, in part chaired by ECRI, to consider the impact of conflict on progress towards achieving the MDGs in countries in the region. In the following month ECRI contributed to a seminar on participatory governance in crisis-affected Arab countries.

ESCWA CENTRE FOR WOMEN

The ESCWA Centre for Women was established in October 2003. Its main focus of activities is the empowerment and advancement of women. It also aims to incorporate issues relating to gender in regional projects and programmes. The Centre monitors developments, compiles country profiles on the status of women, provides support for formulating relevant legislation, raises awareness by publishing reports and studies, and organizes conferences. In December 2003 ESCWA issued its first *Status of Arab Women* report; this was to assess the situation of Arab women at two-yearly intervals. The 2011 edition focused on equal participation in decision-making. In September 2008 the ESCWA Secretary-General launched a guide entitled *Gender in the Millennium Development Goals*, which summarized the key regional gender issues in the context of each MDG and provided a statistical framework for evaluating and following up adherence to international agreements relating to gender equality, in the context of reporting progress in achieving (by 2015) the Arab MDGs. During 2011 the Centre's activities included organizing training workshops relating to implementation of the Convention on the Elimination of All Forms of Discrimination against Women (CEDAW) and the protection of women in conflict situations.

INFORMATION AND COMMUNICATIONS TECHNOLOGY

The Information and Communications Technology Division works to increase the capabilities of ESCWA member countries in harnessing information and communications technology (ICT) in support of sustainable development and regional integration. It aims to narrow the so-called digital gap between Arab countries and other regions, and, consequently, to improve the competitiveness of local industries and the effectiveness of local services. It supports the formation of ICT policies and infrastructure, by providing technical assistance, pilot projects, studies and meetings of experts. ESCWA was responsible for advising member countries on the implementation of recommendations issued by the first phase of the World Summit on the

Information Society, held in December 2003, and on preparations for the second phase of the Summit, which was convened in Tunis, Tunisia, in November 2005. As a follow-up to the Summit, ESCWA undertook to collate a profile of the region's information society based on national profile reports. A Regional Follow-up to the Outcome of the World Summit on the Information Society was held in Damascus, Syria, in June 2009. In November ESCWA organized a regional workshop on Arabic domain names and internet governance, held in Sharm el-Sheikh, Egypt. In 2010 ESCWA continued to work with the League of Arab States to formulate an application for use of a '.arab' internet domain. In July 2011 ESCWA co-organized, with the Arab League and International Telecommunication Union, a Partnership Building Forum for the Implementation of the Arab Top Level Domains. Consultations to establish an Arab Internet Governance Forum (IGF) were formally initiated in February 2012. The 26th session of the Commission, held in May 2010, resolved to establish an ESCWA Technology Centre, in order to strengthen member states' ICT capabilities. An agreement was signed with the Government of Jordan, in December, to host the Centre in that country's capital, Amman.

SOCIAL DEVELOPMENT

ESCWA's Social Development Division encourages regional co-operation in promoting comprehensive and integrated social policies, so as to achieve greater social equality and well-being, and to alleviate poverty, social exclusion, gender imbalances and social tension. It advises governments on the importance of integrating social analysis into policy-making, identifies methods for the effective formulation, implementation and monitoring of social policy, and assists national and regional research on social development. ESCWA's objectives with regard to population are to increase awareness and understanding of links between population factors and poverty, human rights and the environment, and to strengthen the capacities of member states to analyse and assess demographic trends and migration. In the area of social participatory development ESCWA aims to further the alleviation of poverty and to generate a sustainable approach to development through greater involvement of community groups, institutions and users of public services in decision-making. The Division's work on social policy in the city analyses urban problems, such as poverty, unemployment, violence, and failure to integrate vulnerable and marginal groups, and aims to assist policy-makers in ensuring that all city-dwellers have equal access to public services. ESCWA provides a forum for preparatory and follow-up meetings to global conferences. In December 2011 ESCWA organized a second regional review meeting of the International Plan of Action on Ageing, which resulted from the World Assembly, held in Madrid, Spain in 2002. In May 2010 ESCWA's 26th ministerial session emphasized the need to secure employment opportunities for young people. Efforts to increase the involvement of young people, and of women, in development programmes were also promoted, in particular at a time when the region was attempting to recover from the effects of the global financial and economic crisis. At early 2010 an estimated 60% of the region's population were under 25 years of age. In November 2011 ESCWA organized an inter-regional seminar on 'Participatory Development and Conflict Resolution: Path of Democratic Transition and Social Justice', to address aspects of the political and social changes taking place in several countries in the region.

STATISTICS

ESCWA helps to develop the statistical systems of member states in accordance with the UN Fundamental Principles of Official Statistics, in order to improve the accuracy and comparability of economic and social data, and to make the information more accessible to planners and researchers. It aims to improve human and institutional capacities, in particular in the use of statistical tools for data analysis, to expand the adoption and implementation of international statistical methods, and to promote co-operation to further the regional harmonization of statistics. ESCWA assists members in preparing for population and housing censuses, in accordance with the UN 2010 World Population and Housing Census Programme. In December 2011 ESCWA hosted a workshop on Population Census Preparedness. A Trade and Transport Statistics Team compiles, processes and disseminates statistics on international trade and transport within the region, and assists member countries to develop their statistical capacity in this sector.

SUSTAINABLE DEVELOPMENT AND PRODUCTIVITY

The work of ESCWA's Sustainable Development and Productivity Division is undertaken by four teams, covering: energy for sustainable development; water and environment; technology and enterprise development; and sustainable agriculture and rural development. ESCWA aims to counter the problem of an increasing shortage of freshwater resources and deterioration in water quality resulting from population growth, agricultural land use and socio-economic development, by supporting measures for more rational use and conservation of water resources, and by promoting public awareness of and community participation in water and environmental protection projects. The Division assists governments in the formulation and implementation of capacity-building programmes and the development of surface and groundwater resources. ESCWA promotes greater co-operation among member and non-member countries in the management and use of shared water resources, and supports the Arab Integrated Water Resources Management Network (AWARENET, comprising some 120 research and training institutes). ESCWA supports co-operation in the establishment of electricity distribution and supply networks throughout the region and promotes the use of alternative sources of energy and the development of new and renewable energy technologies. It places a special emphasis on increasing the access of poor people to cheap energy and water, and on the creation of new jobs. The Division promotes the application of environmentally sound technologies in order to achieve sustainable development, as well as measures to recycle resources, minimize waste and reduce the environmental impact of transport operations and energy use. ESCWA collaborates with national, regional and international organizations in monitoring and reporting on emerging environmental issues and to pursue implementation of Agenda 21, which was adopted at the June 1992 UN Conference on Environment and Development, with particular regard to land and water resource management and conservation. In July 2011 ESCWA hosted a regional meeting concerned with 'Economic Policies Supporting the Transition to a Green Economy in the Arab Region'. In September ESCWA hosted a conference on 'The Role of Green Industries in Promoting Socio-Economic Development in the Arab Countries'. ESCWA organized a series of preparatory meetings to formulate a regional strategy for the UN Conference on Sustainable Development ('Rio + 20'), scheduled to be held in Rio de Janeiro, Brazil, in June 2012. In February ESCWA organized, jointly with the International Food Policy Research Institute, an international conference on food security in the Arab region.

Finance

ESCWA's proposed regular budget allocation from the UN budget for the two years 2012–13 was US $62.6m.

Publications

ESCWA Annual Report.

UN-ESCWA Weekly News.

Analysis of Performance and Assessment of Growth and Productivity in the ESCWA Region.

Annual Review of Developments in Globalization and Regional Integration.

Compendium of Environment Statistics.

Compendium of Social Statistics and Indicators.

Country and Regional Profiles for Sustainable Development Indicators.

ESCWA Centre for Women Newsletter (monthly).

Estimates and Forecasts for GDP Growth in the ESCWA Region.

External Trade Bulletin of the ESCWA Region (annually).

International Comparison Program Newsletter.

Review of Industry in ESCWA Member Countries.

Review of Information and Communications Technology and Development.

Status of Arab Women Report (every 2 years).

Survey of Economic and Social Developments in the ESCWA Region.

Transport Bulletin.

Weekly News.

ESCWA publishes reports, case studies, assessments, guides and manuals on the subjects covered by its various Divisions.

OTHER UNITED NATIONS BODIES

Office for the Co-ordination of Humanitarian Affairs—OCHA

Address: United Nations Plaza, New York, NY 10017, USA.

Telephone: (212) 963-1234; **fax:** (212) 963-1312; **e-mail:** ochany@un.org; **internet:** ochaonline.un.org.

OCHA was established in January 1998 as part of the UN Secretariat, and has a mandate to mobilize and co-ordinate international humanitarian assistance and to provide policy and other advice on humanitarian issues. It replaced the Department of Humanitarian Affairs, established in 1992.

Organization

(April 2012)

OCHA has headquarters in New York, and in Geneva, Switzerland. It maintains regional support offices in Dakar, Senegal (for west Africa), Johannesburg, South Africa (southern Africa) and Nairobi, Kenya (central and east Africa); and deploys regional disaster response advisers in Panama (for Latin America and the Caribbean), Kobe, Japan (Asia), and Suva, Fiji (the Pacific). OCHA also maintains field presences in Africa, Europe, Asia and Latin America. In 2012 there were 2,005 staff posts, of which one-third were based at the headquarters.

Under-Secretary-General for Humanitarian Affairs and Emergency Relief Co-ordinator: VALERIE AMOS (United Kingdom).

Activities

OCHA's mandate is to work with UN agencies, governments, inter-governmental humanitarian organizations and non-governmental organizations to ensure that a prompt, co-ordinated and effective response is provided to complex emergencies and natural disasters. OCHA monitors developments throughout the world and undertakes contingency planning. It liaises with UN Resident Co-ordinators, Humanitarian Co-ordinators and country teams, and reaches agreement with other UN bodies regarding the division of responsibilities, which may include field missions to assess requirements, organizing inter-agency Consolidated Appeals for financial assistance (see below), and mobilizing other resources. The Emergency Relief Co-ordinator is the principal adviser to the UN Secretary-General on humanitarian issues. He chairs the Inter-Agency Standing Committee (IASC), which co-ordinates and administers the international response to humanitarian disasters and the development of relevant policies. The Co-ordinator also acts as Convener of the Executive Committee for Humanitarian Affairs, which provides a forum for humanitarian agencies, as well as the political and peace-keeping departments of the UN Secretariat, to exchange information on emergency situations and humanitarian issues. In view of the serious challenges posed by the increasing frequency and intensity of extreme natural hazard events, combined with other developing 'mega-trends', such as the ongoing global crisis in food price levels, OCHA aims (in co-operation with governments and development agencies) to place a stronger focus on disaster risk reduction and preparedness and on increasing national disaster management capacities; and also on enabling the international emergency response system to respond successfully to these greater requirements. OCHA's strategic framework for 2010–13 aimed (through the Office's functions of co-ordination, advocacy, policy, information management and humanitarian financing) to promote an effective international response to humanitarian requirements; and to support, when emergencies arise, national efforts to co-ordinate the system-wide response. The framework incorporated the three principal goals of providing a more enabling environment for humanitarian action; establishing a more effective humanitarian co-ordination system; and strengthening OCHA management and administration.

OCHA participates in the High Level Task Force (HLTF) on the Global Food Crisis, which was established in April 2008 by the UN Secretary-General to promote a unified response to soaring food and fuel prices and other factors adversely affecting the supply and accessibility of food, and to formulate a Comprehensive Framework for Action.

OCHA's Early Warning Unit identifies and monitors potentially emerging humanitarian crises, as well as humanitarian emergencies at risk of deterioration and potentially resurgent humanitarian emergencies. Analysis by the Unit determines the at-risk areas to which inter-agency contingency planning missions should be directed.

OCHA maintains internet-based Integrated Regional Information Networks (IRINs). The first IRIN was created in 1995 in Nairobi, Kenya, to disseminate information on the humanitarian situation in central and east Africa. Additional IRINs have since been established in Abidjan, Côte d'Ivoire (covering west Africa), Johannesburg, South Africa (for southern Africa) and Islamabad, Pakistan (for central Asia). The IRINs provide new coverage of a total of 46 countries in sub-Saharan Africa and eight countries in central Asia. A complementary service, ReliefWeb, launched in 1996, monitors crises and publishes information on the internet.

OCHA's Humanitarian Emergency and Response Co-ordination branches (based, respectively, at the New York and Geneva headquarters) co-operate in mobilizing and co-ordinating international emergency assistance. The Response Co-ordination branch facilitates and participates in situation assessment missions; prepares briefings and issues Situation Reports to inform the international community on ongoing humanitarian crises, the type and level of assistance required and action being undertaken; and provides administrative support to OCHA field offices. The Emergency Services branch, based at the Geneva headquarters, undertakes disaster-preparedness activities and manages international rapid response missions in the field. UN Disaster Assessment and Co-ordination (UNDAC) teams, established by OCHA with the aid of donor governments, are available for immediate deployment to help to determine requirements and to co-ordinate assistance in those countries affected by disasters, for example by establishing reliable telecommunications and securing other logistical support. OCHA maintains a Central Register of Disaster Management Capacities, which may be available for international assistance. In addition, a stockpile of emergency equipment and supplies is maintained at the UN Humanitarian Response Depot in Brindisi, Italy, ready for immediate dispatch. The Field Co-ordination Support Section of the Emergency Services Branch acts as the secretariat of INSARAG, an inter-governmental network dealing with urban search and rescue (USAR) issues. INSARAG facilitates information exchange, defines standards for international USAR assistance, and develops methodology for international co-ordination in earthquake response. A joint OCHA/UNEP Environment Unit mobilizes and co-ordinates international assistance in environmental emergency situations. In 2007 a new UN inter-agency Displacement and Protection Support Section (DPSS), reporting to the Emergency Relief Co-ordinator, was established, with the aim of strengthening and co-ordinating the inter-agency collaborative response to the plight of people displaced from their homes by civil conflict and natural disasters.

The focal point within the UN system for co-ordinating disaster reduction activities in the socio-economic, humanitarian and development fields is the International Strategy for Disaster Reduction (ISDR), which has an Inter-Agency Secretariat (UN/ISDR) based in Geneva (see below). In January 2005 the UN/ISDR organized a World Conference on Disaster Reduction, held in Kobe, Japan, which launched the International Early Warning Programme (IEWP), comprising UN bodies and agencies including the ISDR, UNEP, WFP and WMO. The IEWP was to improve global resilience to natural disasters (such as droughts, wildland fires, volcanic eruptions, earthquakes, tsunamis—tidal waves, floods and hurricanes) by improving the exchange of observational data, promoting education on disaster preparedness, and ensuring an effective response mechanism to be activated on the issue of warnings. The Kobe Conference also adopted the Hyogo Declaration and the Hyogo Framework of Action (HFA) covering the period 2005–15, which had the following strategic goals: integrating disaster risk reduction into sustainable development policies and planning; development and strengthening of institutions, mechanisms and capacities to build resilience to hazards; and the systematic incorporation of risk reduction approaches into the implementation of emergency preparedness, response and recovery programmes. In July 2008 OCHA, in collaboration with UN/ISDR, issued guidelines for governments, local authorities and other stakeholders on the implementation of Priority Five of the HFA: 'Disaster Preparedness for Effective Response at all Levels'. OCHA has joint responsibility, with UNICEF and WFP, for managing emergency telecommunications assistance under the co-ordinated Cluster Approach to providing humanitarian assistance to IDPs developed by the IASC in 2005 (see below). In 2010 the ISDR recorded 373 natural disasters, which resulted in the deaths of some 297,000 people.

OCHA facilitates the inter-agency Consolidated Appeals Process (CAP), which aims to organize a co-ordinated response to resource mobilization following humanitarian crises. Participants in the process include UN bodies and agencics and other international governmental and non-governmental organizations (including the International Red Cross and Red Crescent Movement). Under guidelines adopted by the IASC in 1994, the CAP was clearly defined as a programming mechanism rather than simply an appeal process. Technical guidelines adopted in 1999 established a framework for developing a Common Humanitarian Action Plan (CHAP) to address a crisis, co-ordinating the relevant inter-agency appeal (on the basis of the CHAP), and preparing strategic monitoring reports. CAP appeals for 2012, seeking an estimated US $7,700m., were issued in December 2011; they contained action plans relating to complex humanitarian crises affecting some 51m. people in 16 countries and involving most globally active humanitarian organizations. The largest appeals were for Somalia ($1,522m.), Sudan (1,066m.), Kenya (764m.), South Sudan ($763m.) and Democratic Republic of the Congo ($719m.).

In December 2005 the UN General Assembly adopted a resolution establishing a new Central Emergency Response Fund (CERF), expanding the former Central Emergency Revolving Fund (founded in 1991) to comprise a US $450m. grant facility, in addition to the existing $50m. revolving element, with a view to ensuring a more predictable and timely response to humanitarian crises. Both the grant and revolving facilities are financed by voluntary contributions from member states. Up to two-thirds of the grant facility can be allocated to life-saving rapid response initiatives. The upgraded Fund, administered on behalf of the UN Secretary-General by the Emergency Relief Co-ordinator in consultation with humanitarian agencies and relevant humanitarian co-ordinators, had three principle objectives: promotion of early action and response to save lives in the case of newly emerging crises or deterioration of existing complex crises, through an initial injection of funds before further donor contributions become available; enhanced response to time-crucial requirements based on demonstrable needs; and strengthening core elements of humanitarian response in underfunded crises. UN agencies and their implementing partners were to be able to access the Fund within 72 hours of the onset of a crisis. The new CERF became operational in March 2006, and by January 2012 had raised more than $2,400m. from 124 donor states. OCHA organizes Emergency Response Funds (ERFs) to respond to unforeseen humanitarian planning requirements; and Common Humanitarian Funds (CRFs) to provide a predictable pool of funding for critical humanitarian situations.

In December 2012, in response to severe food insecurity and malnutrition in the Sahel region of West Africa—caused by drought, poor harvests, rising food prices, and eroded resilience to repeated adverse conditions—OCHA and other UN agencies, chaired by the IASC, launched a 'Response Plan for a Food Security and Nutrition Crisis in the Sahel'; a revised version of the Plan was issued in February 2012. Some US $724m. was requested in funding for the Plan, including $480m. to address food security requirements, and $243m. in support of nutrition interventions. Under the CAP appeal for 2012 some US $447m. was requested to alleviate worsening food insecurity and to support conflict-affected communities in Yemen; by late April 2012 only 20% of the required donor funding for Yemen had been achieved.

GLOBAL CLUSTER LEADS

IASC co-ordinates agency assistance to IDPs through a 'Cluster Approach' (initiated in 2005); this currently comprises 11 core areas of humanitarian activity, with designated global cluster lead agencies, as follows:

Camp Co-ordination/Management: UNHCR (conflict situations), IOM (natural disasters).

Early Recovery: UNDP.

Education: UNICEF, Save The Children.

Emergency Shelter: UNHCR (conflict situations), International Federation of Red Cross and Red Crescent Societies (natural disasters).

Emergency Telecommunications: OCHA, WFP.

Food Security: FAO, WFP.

Health: WHO.

Logistics: WFP.

Nutrition: UNICEF.

Protection: UNHCR.

Water, Sanitation and Hygiene: UNICEF.

Finance

OCHA's budgetary requirements for 2012 were estimated at US $285.4m.

Publications

Annual Report.

OCHA in 2012–2013.

OCHA News (weekly).

Associated Body

Inter-Agency Secretariat of the International Strategy for Disaster Reduction—UN/ISDR: International Environment House II, 7–9 Chemin de Balexert, 1219 Châtelaine, Geneva 10, Switzerland; tel. 229178908; fax 229178964; e-mail isdr@un.org; internet www.unisdr.org; operates as secretariat of the International Strategy for Disaster Reduction (ISDR), adopted by UN member states in 2000 as a strategic framework aimed at guiding and co-ordinating the efforts of humanitarian organizations, states, intergovernmental and non-governmental organizations, financial institutions, technical bodies and civil society representatives towards achieving substantive reduction in disaster losses, and building resilient communities and nations as the foundation for sustainable development activities; UN/ISDR promotes information sharing to reduce disaster risk, and serves as the focal point providing guidance for the implementation of the Hyogo Framework for Action (HFA), adopted in 2005 as a 10-year plan of action for protecting lives and livelihoods against disasters; Head, Special Representative of the UN Secretary-General for Disaster Risk Reduction MARGARETA WAHLSTRÖM.

Office of the United Nations High Commissioner for Human Rights—OHCHR

Address: Palais des Nations, 1211 Geneva 10, Switzerland.

Telephone: 229179000; **fax:** 229179022; **e-mail:** infodesk@ohchr.org; **internet:** www.ohchr.org.

The Office is a body of the UN Secretariat and is the focal point for UN human rights activities. Since 1997 it has incorporated the Centre for Human Rights. OHCHR is guided by relevant resolutions of the General Assembly, the Charter of the United Nations, the Universal Declaration of Human Rights and subsequent human rights instruments, the Vienna Declaration and programme of action adopted by the 1993 World Conference on Human Rights (see below), and the outcome document of the 2005 World Summit of the General Assembly.

Organization

(April 2012)

HIGH COMMISSIONER

In December 1993 the UN General Assembly decided to establish the position of a United Nations High Commissioner for Human Rights (UNHCHR) following a recommendation of the World Conference on Human Rights, held in Vienna, Austria, in June of that year. The High Commissioner, who is the UN official with principal responsibility for UN human rights activities, is appointed by the UN Secretary-General, with the approval of the General Assembly, for a four-year term in office, renewable for one term. The High Commissioner is assisted by a Deputy High Commissioner for Human Rights.

High Commissioner: NAVANETHEM PILLAY (South Africa).

Deputy High Commissioner: KYUNG-WHA KHANG (Republic of Korea).

ADMINISTRATION

OHCHR's Executive Direction and Management comprises the following units: the Executive Office of the High Commissioner; the Policy, Planning, Monitoring, and Evaluation Section; the Communications Section; the Civil Society Unit; the Field Safety and Security Section; and the Donor and External Relations Section. OHCHR's headquarters contains the following four substantive Divisions: Field Operations and Technical Co-operation; Research and Right to Development; Special Procedures; and the Human Rights Council and Treaties Division. There is also a Programme Support and Management Services unit, and a branch office in New York, USA, that aims to ensure that human rights issues are fully integrated into the broader UN development and security agenda.

FIELD PRESENCES

As the Office's involvement in field work has expanded, in support of UN peace-making, peace-keeping and peace-building activities, a substantial structure of field presences has developed. In 2012 there were OHCHR regional offices in Addis Ababa, Ethiopia (covering East Africa); Bangkok, Thailand (South-east Asia); Beirut, Lebanon (the Middle East); Bishkek, Kyrgyzstan (Central Asia); Panama City, Panama (Central America); Santiago, Chile (South America); Pretoria, South Africa (Southern Africa); and Suva, Fiji (the Pacific); as well as an OHCHR Regional Centre for Human Rights and Democracy for Central Africa, based in Yaoundé, Cameroon. OHCHR country offices with human rights promotion and protection mandates were being maintained in Angola, Bolivia, Cambodia, Colombia, Guatemala, Mexico, Nepal, the Palestinian territories, Serbia (including Kosovo), Togo and Uganda. At 30 September 2011 some 532 OHCHR staff members (48%) were based in the field. At that time the Office was supporting 884 human rights officers serving in the human rights components of 15 peace missions, as well as 18 human rights officers who were participating in UN country teams. The Office was also undertaking a number of technical co-operation projects.

Activities

The mandate of OHCHR incorporates the following functions and responsibilities: the promotion and protection of human rights throughout the world; the reinforcement of international co-operation in the field of human rights; the promotion of universal ratification and implementation of international standards; the establishment of a dialogue with governments to ensure respect for human rights; and co-ordination of efforts by other UN programmes and organs to promote respect for human rights. Upon request OHCHR undertakes assessments of national human rights needs, in consultation with governments. Through the provision of guidance and training it supports the establishment of independent national human rights institutions. The Office may also study and react to cases of serious violations of human rights, and may undertake diplomatic efforts to prevent violations. It also produces educational and other information material to enhance understanding of human rights. OHCHR co-operates with academic bodies and non-governmental organizations working in the area of human rights.

The Office offers support and expertise to the UN system's human rights monitoring mechanisms, including the Human Rights Council (established in 2006) and the Universal Periodic Review (UPR, also established in 2006, to assess, cyclically, the human rights situation in all UN member states). OHCHR supports the committees that observe implementation of the following core international human rights treaties: the International Covenant on Civil and Political Rights, which entered into force in 1976; the International Covenant on Economic, Social and Cultural Rights (1976); the Convention against Torture and Other Cruel, Inhuman or Degrading Treatment or Punishment (1987); the Optional Protocol of the Convention against Torture (2006); the Convention on the Rights of the Child (1990) and its optional Protocols on Involvement of Children in Armed Conflict, on Sale of Children, Child Prostitution and Child Pornography, and on a Communications Procedure—allowing individual children to submit complaints about specific violations of their human rights under the Convention; the International Convention on the Protection of the Rights of All Migrant Workers and Members of Their Families (1990); the Convention on the Rights of Persons with Disabilities (2008); and the International Convention for the Protection of All Persons from Enforced Disappearance (2010).

In 2005 the High Commissioner published a Plan of Action for the future development of the Office and the development of the UN's human rights agenda. The Plan proposed greater involvement of the Office in both setting and ensuring—through improved monitoring and public reporting of violations and the provision of sustained technical assistance and advice at country level—the implementation of human rights norms. The World Summit of heads of state and government convened by the General Assembly in December 2005 noted the Plan of Action and made a commitment to the expansion of the UN human rights programme and to increasing the Office's funding. The High Commissioner subsequently issued consecutive biennial strategic management plans for the Office. The most recent plan, covering 2012–13, focused on the following six thematic priorities and strategies: countering discrimination, in particular racial discrimination, discrimination on the grounds of sex, religion, and discrimination against others who are marginalized; combating impunity and strengthening accountability, the rule of law and democratic society; pursuing economic, social and cultural rights, and combating inequalities and poverty, including in the context of the economic, food and climate crises; protecting human rights in the context of migration; protecting human rights in situations of armed conflict, violence and insecurity; and strengthening human rights mechanisms and the progressive development of international human rights law.

OHCHR was the lead agency in undertaking preparations for the World Conference against Racism, Racial Discrimination, Xenophobia and Related Intolerance, convened in Durban, South Africa, in August–September 2001, and attended by representatives of 168 governments. The following five core themes were addressed at Durban: sources, causes, forms and contemporary manifestations of racism; victims; prevention, education and protection measures; provision of remedies and redress (i.e. compensation); and future strategies to achieve full and effective equality. The Conference adopted the 'Durban Declaration' and a Programme of Action, in accordance with which national plans of action were to be implemented by participating states: universal ratification of the International Convention on the Elimination of all Forms of Racism (ICERD) was to be prioritized, with the broadest possible ratification of other human rights instruments, and national legislation was to be improved in line with the ICERD. On the recommendation of the Conference an interim Anti-discrimination Unit was established within OHCHR to enable the Office to play a leading role in following up the implementation of the Programme of Action. OHCHR also participated in preparations for the follow-up Durban Review Conference, which was convened in Geneva, Switzerland, in April 2009, to evaluate progress towards the achievement of the objectives set by the 2001 World Conference, and to address current major issues. The latter included the concept of defamation of religions within the existing framework of international human rights law, as a matter of incitement to religious hatred; improving understanding of different legislative patterns and judicial practices world-wide; ongoing challenges impeding the implementation of the Durban Programme of Action, such as slow progress towards eradicating extreme poverty and hunger and the effects of the global financial and food crises and of climate change, all deemed to have disproportionately severe effects on already vulnerable population groups; growing diversification of societies—resulting from globalization—exacerbated by competition for scarce resources, placing migrants at increased risk of racism; and attitudes engendered by increasing implementation of counter-terrorism measures (particularly in view of the international terrorist attacks that occurred on 11 September 2001, shortly after the end of the Durban World Conference). The 2009 Review Conference issued an Outcome Document which identified further measures and initiatives aimed at combating and eliminating, with OHCHR involvement, manifestations of racism, racial discrimination, xenophobia and related intolerance.

OHCHR assisted with the preparation of the International Convention for the Protection of All Persons from Enforced Disappearance, which was opened for signature in February 2007 and entered into force in December 2010; by February 2012 the Convention had been ratified by 31 states.

The Office promotes adherence to the Second Optional Protocol to the International Covenant on Civil and Political Rights, Aiming at the Abolition of the Death Penalty, which had been ratified by 73 states by February 2012; states where the Protocol is binding are obliged not to conduct executions or extradite individuals to a country where the death penalty is enforced, to take all necessary steps towards definitively abolishing the death penalty, and to report on their efforts in this respect.

The Office acts as the secretariat for three grant-making humanitarian funds: the UN Voluntary Fund for Victims of Torture, which was established in 1981; the Voluntary Fund for Indigenous Populations (established in 1985); and the Voluntary Fund on Contemporary Forms of Slavery (established in 1991).

OHCHR field offices and operations ('field presences'—see above) undertake a variety of activities, such as training and other technical assistance, support for Special Rapporteurs (usually appointed by the Commission on Human Rights to investigate human rights emergencies), monitoring and fact-finding. Increasingly they provide support to conflict prevention, peace-making, peace-keeping and peace-building activities. OHCHR co-operates with the UN Department of Peace-keeping Operations and Department of Political Affairs in developing the human rights component of peace-keeping and peace-building missions. In 2012 OHCHR was concerned with 35 thematic mandates, and with the following 10 country mandates (serviced by the Field Operations and Technical Co-operation Division): Burundi (mandate established in 2004; and most recently extended in 2008), Cambodia (1993; 2011), Côte d'Ivoire (2011), Democratic Republic of Korea (2004; 2011), Haiti (1995; 2011), Iran (2011), Myanmar (1992; 2011), Palestinian Territories (1993), Somalia (1993; 2011), Syria (2011), and Sudan (2009; 2011).

The OHCHR quick response desk co-ordinates urgent appeals for assistance in addressing human rights emergencies. The High Commissioner issues reports on human rights emergencies to the Commission on Human Rights.

TECHNICAL CO-OPERATION PROGRAMME

The UN Technical Co-operation Programme in the Field of Human Rights was established in 1955 to assist states, at their request, to strengthen their capacities in the observance of democracy, human rights, and the rule of law. Examples of work undertaken within the framework of the programme include training courses and workshops on good governance and the observance of human rights, expert advisory services on the incorporation of international human rights standards into national legislation and policies and on the formulation of national plans of action for the promotion and protection of human rights, fellowships, the provision of information and documentation, and consideration of promoting a human rights culture. In recent years the Programme, one of the key components of OHCHR's activities, has expanded to undertake UN system-wide human rights support activities, for example in the area of peace-keeping (see above).

Finance

OHCHR's activities are financed from the regular budget of the UN, as well as by voluntary contributions (which are channelled through the Trust Fund for the Support of the Activities of the UNHCHR and the Voluntary Fund for Technical Co-operation in the Field of Human Rights), and the three humanitarian trust funds administered by the Office. For the two years 2012–13 the projected regular budget appropriation for OHCHR amounted to US $156.5m. In addition, to cover expenditure over that period, the Office was to appeal to the international community for voluntary contributions of $291.6m. Voluntary contributions in support of OHCHR's activities are channelled through two main humanitarian funds: the Trust Fund for the Support of the Activities of the High Commissioner for Human Rights, and the Voluntary Fund for Technical Co-operation in the Field of Human Rights; there is also a small special fund supporting human rights education activities in Cambodia.

Publications

A Handbook for Civil Society.

Annual Report.

Fact sheet series.

Human Rights Quarterly.

Human rights study series.

Professional training series.

Other reference material, reports, proceedings of conferences, workshops, etc.

UN Women —United Nations Entity for Gender Equality and the Empowerment of Women

Address: 304 East 45th St, 15th Floor, New York, NY 10017, USA.
Telephone: (212) 906-6400; **fax:** (212) 906-6705; **internet:** www.unwomen.org.

The UN Entity for Gender Equality and the Empowerment of Women, referred to most commonly as UN Women, was established by the UN General Assembly in July 2010 in order to strengthen the UN's capacity to promote gender equality, the empowerment of women, and the elimination of discrimination against women and girls. It commenced operations on 1 January 2011. It has a universal mandate covering all countries.

Organization

(April 2012)

EXECUTIVE BOARD

The Executive Board comprises representatives from 41 countries around the world who serve on a rotating basis. The first Board was elected, by ECOSOC, in November 2010 for an initial three-year term. A five-member Bureau was elected by the Board in December.

SECRETARIAT

Executive Director and Under-Secretary-General: MICHELLE BACHELET (Chile).

Activities

UN Women was established in order to consolidate the resources and mandates of existing UN bodies working to promote gender equality. It incorporated the functions of the Office of the Special Adviser on Gender Issues and Advancement of Women, the Division for the Advancement of Women of the Secretariat, the United Nations Development Fund for Women (UNIFEM) and the International Research and Training Institute for the Advancement of Women (INSTRAW).

UN Women supports deliberations on international policy, standards and norms by UN member states in intergovernmental bodies such as the Commission on the Status of Women. It also co-ordinates UN system-wide efforts to achieve gender equality; and assists countries with putting international standards into practice.

The core areas of activity of UN Women are identified as: Violence against Women; Peace and Security; Leadership and Participation; Economic Empowerment; Making National Plans and Budgets Gender-Responsive; Human Rights; and the Millennium Development Goals. The organization aims to work with national partners, regional organizations and UN country teams to extend the necessary expert technical, practical and advocacy assistance to further gender equality efforts. Civil society organizations are actively encouraged to collaborate with UN Women. By February 2012 UN Women was active in 52 countries.

In all areas of activity UN Women aims to promote implementation of internationally agreed standards as incorporated, for example, in the Convention on the Elimination of All Forms of Discrimination against Women (1979); the Beijing Declaration and Platform for Action (approved at the Fourth World Conference on Women, held in 1995); the Millennium Declaration (2000); and UN Security Council commitments such as Resolution 1325 (2000) on women, peace and security.

UN Women's first Strategic Plan, covering the period 2011–13, envisaged combating gender-based discrimination, to create equal opportunities and to ensure the comprehensive development of women and girls to enable them to be active agents of change; and upholding the rights of women in all efforts to further development, human rights, peace and security.

VIOLENCE AGAINST WOMEN

By the end of 2011 the UN Women's Trust Fund to End Violence Against Women, established in 1997, maintained a portfolio of 96 active grants covering 86 countries. Under its 14th grant-making cycle, covering 2009–10, the Fund allocated US $20.5m. to 26 initiatives in 33 countries and territories.

In November 2010 UNIFEM, operating as part of UN Women, inaugurated a new initiative, the Global Safe Cities Free of Violence Against Women and Girls Programme. Pilot projects were to be implemented in the poorest areas of five cities: Quito (Ecuador), Cairo (Egypt), New Delhi (India), Port Moresby (Papua New Guinea) and Kigali (Rwanda).

UN Women supports a public campaign ('Say NO—UNiTE'), which was launched in 1998 by the UN Secretary-General's initiative to end violence against women. The UN Entity maintains the Virtual Knowledge Centre to End Violence against Women and Girls (accessible at www.endvawnow.org), envisaged as a global one-stop resource for formulating and implementing anti-violence programmes.

PEACE AND SECURITY

UN Women has played a leading role in the development of an inter-agency framework for implementing and monitoring UN Security Council Resolution 1325 (adopted in October 2000), which urged the full and equal participation of women in peace-building efforts, and consideration of the protection needs of women and girls during conflict, and in post-conflict rehabilitation and recovery initiatives. In 2011 UN Women reported that fewer than 6% of national reconstruction budgets made specific provision for the particular needs of women and girls, and that, since 1992, fewer than 10% of peace negotiators had been female.

LEADERSHIP AND PARTICIPATION

With the Inter-Parliamentary Union, UN Women reported in the 2012 *Women in Politics* situation summary that, at 1 January of that year, only 27 countries world-wide had achieved female parliamentary representation of 30% or more, and that there were at that time only 17 female elected heads of state or government. UN Women supports national efforts to advance women's political leadership, including through constitutional reforms and through special temporary measures to raise the number of women in political positions. It supports women in acquiring the skills needed to be effective politicians, and by ensuring that election management bodies respond to women's concerns. In March 2012 the Executive Director of UN Women urged the broader use of quotas to expand participation by women in parliaments.

In 2011 UN Women deployed experts to Tunisia to support that country's newly formed electoral subcommission in its work to ensure gender parity, and also to assist with transitional justice and reconciliation processes. During that year UN Women helped Tunisian women's groups with refreshing advocacy skills. In 2011 UN Women also provided support to a coalition of 500 women's groups in Egypt.

ECONOMIC EMPOWERMENT

UN Women advocates for economic empowerment as a women's right, promoting it as a significant benefit for societies and economies. The Entity supports countries with enacting legislation and implementing policies aimed at increasing women's access to economic resources, and at establishing services that support sustainable livelihoods.

UN Women's multi-donor Fund for Gender Equality (established in 2009) aims to support women in attaining political and economic empowerment. The Fund's first cycle, covering 2009–10, allocated US $37.5m. in grants to 40 programmes in 35 countries. The Fund focuses its support on women's organizations, civil society groups, and governments, and distributes two types of grant: catalytic grants, aimed at accelerating progress in advancing gender equality; and implementation grants, aimed at consolidating existing gender equality infrastructures.

In October 2011 a Social Protection Floor Advisory Group, launched in August 2010 by ILO and WHO, and chaired by UN-Women's Executive Director, issued a report entitled *Social Protection Floor for a Fair and Inclusive Globalization*.

In September 2011 UN Women and WFP announced a joint initiative to provide income generating opportunities for women in rural areas.

NATIONAL PLANNING AND BUDGETING

UN Women advocates for provisions on gender equality to be integrated into national and local policies, plans, budgets and statistical data, and for gender equality to be a priority in channelling development assistance. UN Women provides support to national institutions that aim to make advancements for women.

MILLENNIUM DEVELOPMENT GOALS

UN Women supports the 'Global Strategy for Women's and Children's Health', launched by heads of state and government participating in the September 2010 UN Summit on the MDGs; some US $40,000m. has been pledged towards women's and child's health and achieving goals (iv) Reducing Child Mortality and (v) Improving Maternal Health.

Finance

The General Assembly estimated that the organization required a minimum annual budget of US $500m., which was to be financed by voluntary contributions and from the regular UN budget. Donor contributions to UN Women in 2011 totalled $235m, and were forecast to increase to $400m. in 2012 and to $500m. in 2013. UN Women was allocated an appropriation of $14.5m. from the UN regular budget for 2012–13.

Publications

Annual Report.

Progress of the World's Women (every 2 years).

Words to Action (quarterly).

World Survey on the Role of Women in Development (every 5 years).

Women in Parliament (with the IPU, annually).

United Nations Children's Fund—UNICEF

Address: 3 United Nations Plaza, New York, NY 10017, USA.

Telephone: (212) 326-7000; **fax:** (212) 887-7465; **e-mail:** info@unicef.org; **internet:** www.unicef.org.

UNICEF was established in 1946 by the UN General Assembly as the UN International Children's Emergency Fund, to meet the emergency needs of children in post-war Europe. In 1950 its mandate was expanded to respond to the needs of children in developing countries. In 1953 the General Assembly decided that UNICEF should become a permanent branch of the UN system, with an emphasis on programmes giving long-term benefits to children everywhere, particularly those in developing countries. In 1965 UNICEF was awarded the Nobel Peace Prize.

Organization

(April 2012)

EXECUTIVE BOARD

The Executive Board, as the governing body of UNICEF, comprises 36 member governments from all regions, elected in rotation for a three-year term by ECOSOC. The Board establishes policy, reviews programmes and approves expenditure. It reports to the General Assembly through ECOSOC.

SECRETARIAT

The Executive Director of UNICEF is appointed by the UN Secretary-General in consultation with the Executive Board. The administration of UNICEF and the appointment and direction of staff are the responsibility of the Executive Director, under policy directives laid down by the Executive Board, and under a broad authority delegated to the Executive Director by the Secretary-General. Around 85% of UNICEF staff positions are based in field offices.

Executive Director: Anthony Lake (USA).

UNICEF OFFICES

UNICEF has a network of eight regional and 127 field offices serving 155 countries and territories. Its offices in Tokyo, Japan, and Brussels, Belgium, support fund-raising activities; UNICEF's supply division is administered from the office in Copenhagen, Denmark. A research centre concerned with advocacy for child rights and development is based in Florence, Italy.

Belgium: rue Montoyer 14, 1000 Brussels; tel. (2) 513-22-51; fax (2) 513-22-90; e-mail brussels@unicef.org; internet unicef.be.

Japan: UNU Headquarters Bldg, 8th Floor, 53–70, Jingumae 5-chome, Shibuya-ku, Tokyo 150-0001, Japan; tel. (3) 5467-4431; fax (3) 5467-4437; e-mail tokyo@unicef.org; internet www.unicef.or.jp.

Regional Office for the Americas and the Caribbean: Apdo 0843-03045, Panamá, Panama; tel. (507) 301-7400; e-mail thahn@unicef.org; internet www.uniceflac.org.

Regional Office for Central and Eastern Europe and the Commonwealth of Independent States: Palais des Nations, 1211 Geneva 10, Switzerland; tel. 229095433; fax 229095909; e-mail ceecis@unicef.org; internet www.unicef.org/ceecis.

Regional Office for East Asia and the Pacific: POB 2-154, Bangkok 10200, Thailand; tel. (2) 2805931; fax (2) 2803563; e-mail eapro@unicef.org; internet www.unicef.org/eapro/.

Regional Office for Eastern and Southern Africa: POB 44145, Nairobi, Kenya 00100; tel. (20) 7621234; fax (20) 7622678; e-mail unicefesaro@unicef.org.

Regional Office for the Middle East and North Africa: POB 1551, 11821 Amman, Jordan; tel. (6) 5539977; fax (6) 5538880; e-mail menaro@unicef.org.jo.

Regional Office for South Asia: POB 5815, Leknath Marg, Kathmandu, Nepal; tel. (1) 4419082; fax (1) 4419479; e-mail rosa@unicef.org.

Regional Office for West and Central Africa: POB 29720, Dakar-Yoff, Senegal; tel. 33-869-58-58; fax 33-820-89-65; e-mail wcaro@unicef.org; internet www.unicef.org/wcaro/index.html.

UNICEF Innocenti Research Centre: Piazza SS. Annunziata 12, 50122 Florence, Italy; tel. (055) 20330; fax (055) 2033220; e-mail info@unicef-irc.org; internet www.unicef-irc.org; f. 1988; undertakes research in two thematic areas: Social and economic policies and children; and Child protection and implementation of international standards for children; Dir GORDON ALEXANDER.

UNICEF Supply Division: UNICEF Plads, Freeport 2100, Copenhagen, Denmark; tel. 35-27-35-27; fax 35-26-94-21; e-mail supply@unicef.org; internet www.unicef.org/supply; responsible for overseeing UNICEF's global procurement and logistics operations.

NATIONAL COMMITTEES

UNICEF is supported by 36 National Committees, mostly in industrialized countries, whose volunteer members raise money through various specific campaigns and activities, including the sale of greetings cards and collection of foreign coins. The Committees also undertake advocacy and awareness campaigns on a number of issues and provide an important link with the general public.

Activities

UNICEF is dedicated to the well-being of children, adolescents and women and works for the realization and protection of their rights within the frameworks of the Convention on the Rights of the Child, which was adopted by the UN General Assembly in 1989, and by 2012 was almost universally ratified, and of the Convention on the Elimination of All Forms of Discrimination Against Women, adopted by the UN General Assembly in 1979. Promoting the full implementation of the Conventions, UNICEF aims to ensure that children worldwide are given the best possible start in life and attain a good level of basic education, and that adolescents are given every opportunity to develop their capabilities and participate successfully in society. The Fund also continues to provide relief and rehabilitation assistance in emergencies. Through its extensive field network in more than 150 developing countries and territories, UNICEF undertakes, in co-ordination with governments, local communities and other aid organizations, programmes in health, nutrition, education, water and sanitation, the environment, gender issues and development, and other fields of importance to children. Emphasis is placed on low-cost, community-based programmes. UNICEF programmes are increasingly focused on supporting children and women during critical periods of their life, when intervention can make a lasting difference. Since the 1950s UNICEF has engaged the services of prominent individuals as Goodwill Ambassadors and Advocates, who can use their status to attract attention to particular causes and support UNICEF's objectives.

The principal themes of UNICEF's medium-term strategic plan for the period 2006–13 are: young child survival and development; basic education and gender equality (including the Fund's continued leadership of the UN Girls' Education Initiative, see below); HIV/AIDS and children (including participation in the Joint UN Programme on HIV/AIDS—UNAIDS—see below); child protection from violence, exploitation and abuse; and policy advocacy and partnerships for children's rights. These priority areas are guided by the relevant UN Millennium Development Goals (MDGs) adopted by world leaders in 2000, and by the 'A World Fit for Children' declaration and plan of action endorsed by the UN General Assembly Special Session on Children in 2002. The 'A World Fit for Children' declaration reaffirmed commitment to the agenda of the 1990 World Summit for Children. The plan of action resolved to work towards the attainment by 2015 of 21 new goals and targets supporting the MDGs in the areas of education, health and the protection of children; these included: a reduction of mortality rates for infants and children under five by two-thirds; a reduction of maternal mortality rates by three-quarters; a reduction by one-third in the rate of severe malnutrition among children under the age of five; and enrolment in primary education by 90% of children. UNICEF issues regular reports that monitor progress in achieving the MDGs. The ninth in the series, entitled *Progress for Children: Achieving the MDGs with Equity (No. 9)*, was published in September 2010. UNICEF supports the 'Global Strategy for Women's and Children's Health', launched by heads of state and government participating in the September 2010 UN Summit on the MDGs; some US $40,000m. has been pledged towards women's and child's health and achieving goals (iv) Reducing Child Mortality and (v) Improving Maternal Health. In 2012 a roadmap was being developed towards the Fund's next medium-term strategic plan, which was to cover the period 2014–17; the new plan was to be passed to the Executive Board for approval in late 2013.

UNICEF estimates that more than 500,000 women die every year during pregnancy or childbirth, largely because of inadequate maternal healthcare, and nearly 4m. newborns die within 28 days of birth. For every maternal death, approximately 30 further women suffer permanent injuries or chronic disabilities as a result of complications during pregnancy or childbirth. Under the Global Partnership for Maternal, Newborn and Child Health, UNICEF works with WHO, UNFPA and other partners in countries with high maternal mortality to improve maternal health and prevent maternal and newborn death through the integration of a continuum of home, community, outreach and facility-based care, embracing every stage of maternal, newborn and child health. UNICEF and partners work with governments and policy-makers to ensure that ante-natal and obstetric care is a priority in national health plans. UNICEF's recent activities in this area have included support for obstetric facilities and training in, and advocacy of, women's health issues, such as ending child marriage, eliminating female genital mutilation/cutting (FGM/C), preventing malaria and promoting the uptake of tetanus toxoid vaccinations and iron and folic acid supplements among pregnant women.

YOUNG CHILD SURVIVAL AND DEVELOPMENT

In 2010 UNICEF allocated some 50% of total programme assistance to young child survival and development. In 2009 UNICEF estimated that around 8.1m. children under five years of age died (compared with some 20m. child mortalities in 1960 and some 13m. in 1990)—mainly in developing countries (three-quarters occurring in the People's Republic of China, the Democratic Republic of the Congo, India, Nigeria, and Pakistan), and the majority from largely preventable causes. UNICEF has worked with WHO and other partners to increase global immunization coverage against the following six diseases: measles, poliomyelitis, tuberculosis, diphtheria, whooping cough and tetanus. In 2003 UNICEF, WHO, the World Bank and other partners established a new Child Survival Partnership, which acts as a forum for the promotion of co-ordinated action in support of efforts to save children's lives in 68 targeted developing countries. UNICEF, WHO, the World Bank and the UN Population Division established an Inter-agency Group for Child Mortality Estimation (IGME) in 2004, to advance work on monitoring progress towards meeting the MDG on reducing child mortality. In September 2005 UNICEF, WHO and other partners launched the Partnership for Maternal, Newborn and Child Health, which aimed to accelerate progress towards the attainment of the MDGs to reduce child and maternal mortality. In 2000 UNICEF, WHO, the World Bank and a number of public- and private-sector partners launched the Global Alliance for Vaccines and Immunization (GAVI), subsequently renamed the GAVI Alliance, which aims to protect children of all nationalities and socio-economic groups against vaccine-preventable diseases. GAVI's strategy includes improving access to sustainable immunization services, expanding the use of existing vaccines, accelerating the development and introduction of new vaccines and technologies and promoting immunization coverage as a focus of international development efforts. In 2006 UNICEF, WHO and other partners launched the Global Immunization Vision and Strategy (GIVS), a global 10-year framework, covering 2006–15, aimed at reducing deaths due to vaccine-preventable diseases by at least two-thirds compared to 2000 levels, by 2015; and increasing national vaccination coverage levels to at least 90%. (In 2009 the global child vaccination coverage rate was estimated at 82%.) From 2006 a Global Immunization Meeting was convened annually by UNICEF, WHO and GAVI Alliance partners; the fifth Meeting, held in February 2010, addressed issues including means of improving routine vaccination and supporting accelerated disease control initiatives; the introduction of new vaccines; and vaccine supply, including the status of pandemic influenza vaccines.

UNICEF works to improve safe water supply, sanitation and hygiene, and thereby reduce the risk of diarrhoea and other water-borne diseases. In partnership with other organizations the Fund supports initiatives to make schools in more than 90 developing countries safer through school-based water, sanitation and hygiene programmes. UNICEF places great emphasis on increasing the testing and protection of drinking water at its source as well as in the home. UNICEF, the World Bank and other partners participate in the Global Public-Private Partnership for Handwashing with Soap, which was established in 2001 with the aim of empowering communities in developing countries to prevent diarrhoea and respiratory infections through the promotion of the practice of thorough hand-washing with soap. In 2006 UNICEF and partners established the Global Task Force on Water and Sanitation with the aim of providing all children with access to safe water, and accelerating progress towards MDG targets on safe drinking water and basic sanitation.

UNICEF-assisted programmes for the control of diarrhoeal diseases promote the low-cost manufacture and distribution of pre-packaged salts or home-made solutions. The use of 'oral rehydration therapy' has risen significantly in recent years, and is believed to prevent more than 1m. child deaths annually. During 1990–2000 diarrhoea-related deaths were reduced by one-half. UNICEF also promotes the need to improve sanitation and access to safe water supplies in developing nations in order to reduce the risk of diarrhoea and other water-borne diseases (see 20/20 initiative, below). To control acute respiratory infections, another leading cause of death in children under five in developing countries, UNICEF works with WHO in training health workers to diagnose and treat the associated diseases. At the UN General Assembly Special Session on Children, in 2002, goals were set to reduce measles deaths by 50%. Expanded efforts by UNICEF, WHO and other partners led to a reduction in world-wide measles deaths by 78% between 2000 and 2008. Around 1m. children die from malaria every year, mainly in sub-Saharan Africa. In October 1998 UNICEF, together with WHO, UNDP and the World Bank, inaugurated a new global campaign, Roll Back Malaria, to fight the disease. UNICEF is actively engaged in developing innovative and effective ways to distribute highly-subsidized insecticide-treated mosquito nets at local level, thereby increasing the proportion of children and pregnant women who use them.

According to UNICEF estimates, around 25% of children under five years of age are underweight, while each year malnutrition contributes to more than one-third of the child deaths in that age group and leaves millions of others with physical and mental disabilities. UNICEF supports national efforts to reduce malnutrition, for example, fortifying staple foods with micronutrients, widening women's access to education, improving the nutritional status of pregnant women, strengthening household food security and basic health services, providing food supplies in emergencies, and promoting sound childcare and feeding practices. Since 1991 more than 19,000 hospitals in about 130 countries have been designated 'baby-friendly', having implemented a set of UNICEF and WHO recommendations entitled '10 steps to successful breast-feeding'. The Executive Director of UNICEF chairs the Lead Group of the Scaling Up Nutrition (SUN) initiative, which convened its first meeting in April 2012, and comprises 27 national leaders and agencies jointly providing strategic guidance with a view to improving child and maternal nutrition. SUN, initiated in 2009, and co-ordinated by the UN Secretary-General's Special Representative for Food Security and Nutrition, aims to increase the coverage of interventions that improve nutrition during the first 1,000 days of a child's life (such as exclusive breastfeeding, optimal complementary feeding practices, and provision of essential vitamins and minerals); and to ensure that national nutrition plans are implemented and that government programmes take nutrition into account. The activities of SUN are guided by the Framework for Scaling up Nutrition, which was published in April 2010 and subsequently endorsed by more than 100 partners, including UN agencies, governments, research institutions, and representatives of civil society and of the private sector; and by the SUN Roadmap, finalized in September 2010.

The results of integrated approaches to child health, such as the Accelerated Child Survival and Development (ACSD) strategy and community-based Integrated Management of Childhood Illnesses (IMCI) programme, have demonstrated new potential to reduce child mortality. The ACSD strategy, implemented by UNICEF since 2002, is an intensive combination of life-saving interventions including the promotion of antenatal care, vaccination and breast-feeding, volunteer health-worker follow-up of newborns, and the distribution of insecticide-treated mosquito nets. Focused in 97 high-mortality districts in 11 mainly West African countries, ACSD has reached around 16m. people, including 2.8m. children under the age of five.

BASIC EDUCATION AND GENDER EQUALITY

In 2010 UNICEF allocated some 20% of total programme assistance to basic education and gender equality. UNICEF considers education to be a fundamental human right, and works to ensure all children receive equal access to quality education. UNICEF participated in and fully supports the objectives and framework for action adopted by the World Education Forum in Dakar, Senegal, in April 2000, including the Education for All initiative. UNICEF was assigned formal responsibility within the initiative for education in emergencies, early childhood care and technical and policy support. UNICEF leads and acts as the secretariat of the United Nations Girls' Education Initiative (UNGEI), which aims to increase the enrolment of girls in primary schools in more than 100 countries. It is estimated that more than 100m. school-age children world-wide, of whom more than one-half are girls, remain deprived of basic education. In May 2010 UNGEI convened the first ever international conference on 'Engendering Empowerment: Education and Equality' ('E4'), in Dakar, Senegal. The E4 conference unanimously adopted the Dakar Declaration on Accelerating Girls' Education and Gender Equality, in which it urged that increased focus should be placed on accelerating access to education for the most socially deprived girls, deemed to be the most disadvantaged group in education.

UNICEF advocates the implementation of the Child Friendly School model, designed to facilitate the delivery of safe, quality education. UNICEF, in partnership with UNESCO, has developed an Essential Learning Package to support countries to reduce disparities in the provision of basic education. The initiative was implemented for the first time by Burkina Faso in 2003, and has since been adopted by a further 11 countries in West and Central Africa.

It was reported in 2011 that the literacy rate for young women aged between 15–24 in Afghanistan was 18%, compared with 50% for young men. In 2005 approximately 500,000 girls in Afghanistan were enrolled in schools for the first time, and in March 2007 an UNGEI project (the Afghanistan Girls' Education Initiative—AGEI) was launched in that country.

Major 'back-to-school' campaigns and enrolment drives were launched in countries struck by the December 2004 Indian Ocean tsunamis; within three months of the disaster 90% of affected children had returned to school. Similar campaigns have been undertaken in countries emerging from civil conflict, for example Kyrgyzstan, Somalia and South Sudan, and include advocacy efforts as well as the distribution of essential educational supplies, often in the form of specially designed 'school-in-a-box' kits.

HIV/AIDS AND CHILDREN

In 2010 UNICEF allocated some 5% of total programme assistance to combating HIV/AIDS. UNICEF is concerned at the danger posed by HIV/AIDS to the realization of children's rights and aims to provide expertise, support, logistical co-ordination and innovation towards ending the epidemic and limiting its impact on children and their mothers. At the end of 2009 it was estimated that 2.5m. children under the age of 15 were living with HIV/AIDS world-wide. During that year some 370,000 children under the age of 15 were estimated to have been newly infected with HIV, while 260,000 died as a result of AIDS and AIDS-related illnesses. Some 16.6m. children world-wide have lost one or both parents to AIDS since the start of the pandemic, and as a result of HIV/AIDS many children have suffered poverty, homelessness, discrimination, and loss of education and other life opportunities. UNICEF's priorities in this area include prevention of infection among young people (through, for example, support for education programmes and dissemination of information through the media), reduction in mother-to-child transmission, care and protection of orphans and other vulnerable children, and care and support for children, young people and parents living with HIV/AIDS. UNICEF works closely in this field with governments and co-operates with other UN agencies in the Joint UN Programme on HIV/AIDS (UNAIDS), which became operational on 1 January 1996. Young people aged 15–24 are reported to account for around 45% of new HIV infections world-wide. In July 2002 UNICEF, UNAIDS and WHO jointly produced a study entitled *Young People and HIV/AIDS: Opportunity in Crisis*, examining young people's sexual behaviour patterns and knowledge of HIV/AIDS. UNICEF advocates Life Skills-Based Education as a means of empowering young people to cope with challenging situations and of encouraging them to adopt healthy patterns of behaviour. In July 2004 UNICEF and other partners produced a *Framework for the Protection, Care and Support of Orphans and Vulnerable Children Living in a World with HIV and AIDS*. In October 2005 UNICEF launched Unite for Children, Unite against AIDS, a campaign that was to provide a platform for child-focused advocacy aimed at reversing the spread of HIV/AIDS amongst children, adolescents and young people; and to provide a child-focused framework for national programmes based on the following four pillars (known as the 'Four Ps'): the prevention of mother-to-child HIV transmission, improved provision of paediatric treatment, prevention of infection among adolescents and young people, and protection and support of children affected by HIV/AIDS. In December 2009 UNICEF issued its fourth *Children and AIDS: A Stocktaking Report*, detailing ongoing progress and challenges. In October 2010 UNICEF issued its first Mother-Baby Pack, containing drugs to prevent mother-to-child transmission of HIV in the poorest households. In June 2011 a high-level meeting on HIV/AIDs convened at UN headquarters launched a global plan towards eliminating new HIV infections among children by 2015.

At December 2009 it was estimated that of the total cases of children aged 0–14 living with HIV/AIDS 2.3m. were in sub-Saharan Africa, 150,000 in South and South-East Asia, 53,000 in Latin America and the Caribbean, 21,000 in the Middle East and North Africa, 19,400 in Europe and Central Asia, 8,000 in East Asia, 4,500 in North America and 3,100 in the Pacific region.

CHILD PROTECTION FROM VIOLENCE, EXPLOITATION AND ABUSE

UNICEF is actively involved in global-level partnerships for child protection, including the Inter-Agency Co-ordination Panel on Juvenile Justice; the Inter-Agency Working Group on Unaccompanied and Separated Children; the Donors' Working Group on Female FGM/C (see above); the Better Care Network; the Study on Violence Against Children; the Inter-Agency Standing Committee (IASC) Task Force on Protection from Sexual Exploitation and Abuse in Humanitarian Crises; and the IASC Task Force on Mental Health and Psychological Support in Emergency Settings.

UNICEF estimates that the births of around 48m. children annually (about 36% of all births) are not registered, and that some 63% of births occuring in South Asia, and 55% of births in sub-Saharan Africa, are unregistered. UNICEF promotes universal registration in order to prevent the abuse of children without proof of age and nationality, for example through trafficking, forced labour, early marriage and military recruitment.

UNICEF estimates that some 158m. children aged from five–14 are engaged in child labour, while around 1.2m. children world-wide are trafficked each year. The Fund, which vigorously opposes the exploitation of children as a violation of their basic human rights, works with the ILO and other partners to promote an end to exploitative and hazardous child labour, and supports special projects to provide education, counselling and care in developing countries. UNICEF co-sponsored and actively participated in the Third Congress Against Commercial Sexual Exploitation of Children, held in Rio de Janeiro, Brazil, in November 2008.

More than 250,000 children are involved in armed conflicts as soldiers, porters and forced labourers. UNICEF encourages ratification of the Optional Protocol to the Convention on the Rights of the Child on the involvement of children in armed conflict, which was adopted by the General Assembly in May 2000 and entered into force in February 2002, and bans the compulsory recruitment of combatants below the age of 18. The Fund also urges states to make unequivocal statements endorsing 18 as the minimum age of voluntary recruitment to the armed forces. UNICEF, with Save the Children, co-chairs the Steering Group of the Paris Principles, which aims to support the implementation of a series of 'Commitments', first endorsed in 2007, to end the recruitment of children, support the release of children from the armed forces and facilitate their reintegration into civilian life. By the end of 2010 95 countries had voluntarily signed up to the Paris Commitments. It is estimated that landmines kill and maim between 8,000 and 10,000 children every year. UNICEF supports mine awareness campaigns, and promotes the full ratification of the Convention on the Prohibition of the Use, Stockpiling, Production and Transfer of Anti-Personnel Mines and on their Destruction, which was adopted in December 1997 and entered into force in March 1999. By February 2012 the Convention had been ratified by 159 countries.

POLICY AND ADVOCACY AND PARTNERSHIPS FOR CHILDREN'S RIGHTS

In 2010 UNICEF allocated some 11% of total programme assistance to policy and advocacy and partnerships for children's rights. UNICEF's annual publication *The State of the World's Children* includes social and economic data relevant to the well-being of children. In 1995 UNICEF developed its Multiple Indicator Cluster Survey (MICS) method of data collection, which is used as a main tool in measuring progress towards the achievement of the UN MDGs.

The UNICEF Regional Monitoring Project (MONEE) was undertaken during 1992–2001 to monitor the effects of economic and social transition on children in Central and South-Eastern Europe and the former USSR. Since 2003 the UNICEF Innocenti Research Centre has published an annual social monitoring report, addressing the state of child wellbeing in Eastern European and Central Asian states with economies in transition. The *Innocenti Social Monitor 2009* reviewed the effects of the global economic crisis on children in the region.

Since 2005 young people from the Group of Eight (G8) nations (Canada, France, Germany, Italy, Japan, Russia, the United Kingdom and the USA) and selected emerging countries (Brazil, People's Republic of China, Egypt, India, Mexico and South Africa in 2009) have participated in a Junior 8 (J8) summit, which is organized with support from UNICEF on the fringes of the annual G8 summit. The J8 summits address issues including education, energy, climate change, HIV/AIDS, the global financial crisis, and tolerance. The fifth J8 summit meeting took place in L'Aquila, Italy, in July 2009. In June 2010 the first ever G(irls)20 summit was convened in Toronto, Canada, immediately prior to a summit of G20 leaders; the participants represented the G20 countries, and, in addition, a young female representative of the African Union was invited to attend.

UNICEF aims to break the cycle of poverty by advocating for the provision of increased development aid to developing countries, and aims to help poor countries obtain debt relief and to ensure access to basic social services. UNICEF was the leading agency in promoting the 20/20 initiative, which was endorsed at the World Summit for Social Development, held in Copenhagen, Denmark, in March 1995. The initiative encouraged the governments of developing and donor countries to allocate at least 20% of their domestic budgets and official development aid to healthcare, primary education, and low-cost safe water and sanitation.

Through this focus area, UNICEF seeks to work with partners to strengthen capacities to design and implement cross-sectoral social and economic policies, child-focused legislative measures and budgetary allocations that enable countries to meet their obligations under the Convention on the Rights of the Child and the Convention on the Elimination of All Forms of Discrimination against Women. UNICEF has identified the following priority areas of support to 'upstream' policy work: child poverty and disparities; social budgeting; decentralization; social security and social protection; holistic legislative reform for the two Conventions; and the impact of migration on children.

HUMANITARIAN RESPONSE

UNICEF provides emergency relief assistance to children and young people affected by conflict, natural disasters and food crises. In situations of violence and social disintegration the Fund provides support in the areas of education, health, mine-awareness and psychosocial assistance, and helps to demobilize and rehabilitate child soldiers. In 2010 funding requirements for humanitarian activities amounted to US $1,153.7m., of which the largest allocation, $172.0m., was for Sudan, and $122.5m. for the Democratic Republic of the Congo.

In 1999 UNICEF adopted a Peace and Security Agenda to help guide international efforts in this field. Emergency education assistance includes the provision of 'Edukits' in refugee camps and the reconstruction of school buildings. In the area of health the Fund co-operates with WHO to arrange 'days of tranquillity' in order to facilitate the immunization of children in conflict zones. Psychosocial assistance activities include special programmes to support traumatized children and help unaccompanied children to be reunited with parents or extended families.

In July 2011 UNICEF estimated that more than 2m. malnourished young children required urgent assistance owing to severe and prolonged drought conditions, compounded by high food prices, in Somalia (where famine was formally declared in two regions), Djibouti, Ethiopia and Kenya; around 500,000 of affected children in the Horn of Africa were deemed to be acutely undernourished and in a life-threatening situation. UNICEF undertook immunization campaigns, airlifted supplies—including therapeutic food and medicine, and equipment to supply clean water to IDPs—into Somalia (which was also destabilized by violent unrest), and, with other humanitarian agencies, established emergency feeding centres in countries neighbouring Somalia. During that month UNICEF requested some US $31.8m. in donor funding to provide support to children and their mothers in the region at that time. Families in Somalia were provided with food vouchers that could be exchanged for essential items at local markets.

In the mid-2000s UNICEF country offices prepared contingency plans for a possible future avian influenza pandemic among humans, with a particular focus on children, as part of the inter-agency response to the threat.

Since 1998 UNICEF's humanitarian response has been structured within a framework of identified Core Commitments for Children in Humanitarian Action (CCCs). Revised CCCs were issued in April 2010 to reflect new humanitarian structures and best practices. The revised CCCs incorporated UNICEF's commitment to working in partnership with international organizations, national authorities and civil society in order to strengthen risk reduction, disaster preparedness and response, and early recovery. During 2005 the UN's Inter-Agency Standing Committee (IASC), concerned with co-ordinating the international response to humanitarian disasters, developed a concept of organizing agency assistance to IDPs through the institutionalization of a 'Cluster Approach', comprising 11 core areas of activity. UNICEF is the lead agency for the clusters on Education (jointly with Save The Children); Nutrition; and Water, Sanitation and Hygiene. In addition, it leads the Gender-based Violence Area of Responsibility sub-cluster (jointly with UNFPA) and the Child Protection Area of Responsibility sub-cluster within the Protection Cluster.

Finance

UNICEF is funded by voluntary contributions from governments and non-governmental and private sector sources. UNICEF's income is divided into contributions for 'regular resources' (used for country programmes of co-operation approved by the Executive Board, programme support, and management and administration costs) and contributions for 'other resources' (for special purposes, including expanding the outreach of country programmes of co-operation, and ensuring capacity to deliver critical assistance to women and children, for example during humanitarian crises). UNICEF's total income in 2010 was US $3,682m., of which $2,083m. (57%) was from governments, $1,188m. (32%) from the private sector and non-governmental organizations, and $356m. (10%) from inter-organizational arrangements.

UNICEF's total expenditure in 2010 was $3,653m. Some 53% of the Fund's total programme expenditure in that year was allocated to activities in Africa south of the Sahara, 26% to activities in Asia, 9% to Latin America and the Caribbean, 4% to the Middle East and North Africa, 3% to Central and Eastern Europe and the CIS, and 5% to interregional projects.

UNICEF, UNDP and UNFPA are committed to integrating their budgets from 2014.

Publications

Progress for Children (in English, French and Spanish).

The State of the World's Children (annually, in Arabic, English, French, Russian and Spanish and about 30 other national languages).

UNICEF Annual Report (in English, French and Spanish).

UNICEF at a Glance (in English, French and Spanish).

UNICEF Humanitarian Action Report (annually).

Reports and studies; series on children and women; nutrition; education; children's rights; children in wars and disasters; working children; water, sanitation and the environment; analyses of the situation of children and women in individual developing countries.

United Nations Conference on Trade and Development—UNCTAD

Address: Palais des Nations, 1211 Geneva 10, Switzerland.

Telephone: 229171234; **fax:** 229170057; **e-mail:** info@unctad.org; **internet:** www.unctad.org.

UNCTAD was established in December 1964. It is the principal instrument of the UN General Assembly concerned with trade and development, and is the focal point within the UN system for integrated treatment of trade and development and interrelated issues of finance, technology, investment, and sustainable development. It aims to help developing countries—particularly the Least Developed Countries, Small Island Developing States, Landlocked Developing Countries, economies in transition, and the so-called structurally weak, vulnerable and small economies—to maximize their trade and development opportunities, especially in view of the increasing globalization and liberalization of the world economy.

Organization

(April 2012)

CONFERENCE

The Conference is the organization's highest policy-making body and normally meets every four years at ministerial level to formulate major policy guidelines and to decide on UNCTAD's mandate and work priorities. The 13th session took place in Doha, Qatar, in April 2012. As well as its 194 members, many intergovernmental and non-governmental organizations (NGOs) participate in UNCTAD's work as observers.

TRADE AND DEVELOPMENT BOARD

The Trade and Development Board oversees the activities of UNCTAD in between the organization's quadrennial conferences. The Board comprises elected representatives from 153 UNCTAD member states and is responsible for ensuring the overall consistency of UNCTAD's activities, as well as those of its subsidiary bodies. The Board meets in a regular annual session lasting about 10 days, at which it examines global economic issues. It may also meet a further three times a year to deal with urgent policy issues and to address institutional matters.

COMMISSIONS

The Trade and Development Board has two Commissions: the Trade and Development Commission; and the Investment, Enterprise and Development Commission. The role of the commissions is to conduct policy dialogues, to consider the reports of expert meetings, to manage and recommend for approval the work programmes of expert meetings within their purview, and to promote and strengthen synergies among UNCTAD's three pillars of work: research and analysis; technical co-operation; and intergovernmental consensus-building. Each Commission holds one session per year. In addition to the Intergovernmental Group of Experts on Competition Law and Policy and the Intergovernmental Working Group of Experts on International Standards of Accounting and Reporting, the Commissions may convene up to eight expert meetings a year on specific issues. Of the eight, six have now been established as multi-year expert meetings and cover issues such as commodities, transport and trade facilitation, investment, enterprises and science, technology and innovation (STI), services, and South-South co-operation.

SECRETARIAT

The secretariat comprises the following divisions: Globalization and Development Strategies; Investment and Enterprise; International Trade in Goods and Services, and Commodities; Technology and Logistics; Africa, Least Developed Countries and Special Programmes; and Management.

The UNCTAD secretariat, comprising some 400 staff, undertakes policy analysis; monitoring, implementation and follow-up of decisions of intergovernmental bodies; technical co-operation in support of UNCTAD's policy objectives; and information exchanges and consultations of various types.

Secretary-General: Dr SUPACHAI PANITCHPAKDI (Thailand).

Deputy Secretary-General: PETKO DRAGANOV (Bulgaria).

Activities

UNCTAD's activities are underpinned by its three 'pillars': consensus-building; research, policy analysis and data collection; and technical assistance.

In April 2008 the 12th session of the Conference, convened in Accra, Ghana, on the theme 'Addressing the opportunities and challenges of globalization for development', adopted the Accra Accord, which built upon the São Paulo Consensus adopted by the 11th session, held in São Paulo, Brazil, in June 2004, while providing updated policy analysis, policy responses, and guidelines to strengthen UNCTAD and to enhance its development role, its impact, and its institutional effectiveness. The Accord served as a strategic framework for the work of the organization and established specific policy direction for the next four years. It requested UNCTAD to foster a better understanding of the feasible ways and means of ensuring that the positive impact of globalization and trade on development is maximized; to enhance its work on the special needs of the African continent and of Least Developed Countries; to enhance its work on the special needs and problems of Small Island Developing States, Landlocked Developing Countries, and other structurally weak, vulnerable and small economies; to assist transit developing countries with their special challenges in relation to infrastructure and transport; to make a contribution to the implementation and follow-up to the outcomes of relevant global conferences; and to continue to contribute to the achievement of internationally agreed development goals, including the UN Millennium Development Goals (MDGs).

UNCTAD has a clear mandate to assist with the implementation of: (i) the Programme of Action for LDCs, which resulted from the third UN Conference on the LDCs, held in May 2001; (ii) the Mauritius Strategy on the Programme of Action for the Sustainable Development of Small Island Developing States, adopted by the UN Conference on Small Islands held in Port Louis, Mauritius, in January 2005; and (iii) the Almatı Programme of Action, that was adopted in August 2003 by the International Ministerial Conference of Landlocked and Transit Developing Countries and Donor Countries and International Financial and Development Institutions on Transit Transport Co-operation. (See below.) As part of a concerted response to the ongoing global economic and food crises, G20 leaders agreed in November 2008 to help developing countries gain access to finance despite the challenging global financial conditions. UNCTAD continues to emphasise the importance of providing financial access to developing countries.

UNCTAD, with WTO, leads an initiative on promoting trade—through combating protectionism, including through the conclusion of the Doha round, and by strengthening aid-for-trade financing-for-trade initiatives—the third of nine activities that were launched in April 2009 by the UN System Chief Executives Board for Co-ordination (CEB), with the aim of alleviating the impact on poor and vulnerable populations of the developing global economic crisis.

In February 2012 the UNCTAD Secretary-General issued a report entitled *Development-led Globalization: Towards Sustainable and Inclusive Development Paths*, in which he urged a change of direction in the global economic system—a 'global new deal'—to enable more stable and inclusive economic progress. 'Development-centred globalization' was the theme of the 13th session of the UNCTAD conference held in Doha, Qatar, in April.

The March 2012 conference of heads of state or government of the BRICS informal grouping of large emerging economies, comprising Brazil, Russia, India, People's Republic of China, and South Africa (together accounting for some 20% of global GDP), expressed commitment to advancing UNCTAD's work.

INTERNATIONAL TRADE IN GOODS AND SERVICES, AND COMMODITIES

In working to secure development gains from participation in international trade and globalization, the Division on International Trade in Goods and Services monitors and assesses trends in the international trading system from a development perspective. Among other activities, each year UNCTAD prepares an assessment of key developments in the international trading system for consideration and deliberation by the Trade and Development Board and the UN General Assembly. The Division quantifies the positive interaction between trade and development, and has developed the Trade and Development Index (TDI), covering 125 countries, as a diagnostic tool for policy-makers and researchers. It supports international trade and trade negotiations, and provides assistance to developing countries in clarifying and exploring the development dimension of the international trading system, particularly the WTO Doha Round negotiations, and in strengthening regional economic integration. It promotes South-South trade, including through trade finance and through the Global System of Trade Preferences among Developing Countries (GSTP); UNCTAD supports the second round of negotiations among GSTP participants, and services the 1989 GSTP Agreement. UNCTAD aims to increase the participation of developing countries in global services trade. Support is given to developing countries to enhance their knowledge of issues of particular concern to them relating to services, to assess the contribution of services to development, and to reform and formulate regulatory and institutional frameworks focused on building supply capacity. UNCTAD works to increase developing countries' participation in new and dynamic sectors of global trade, including creative products and industries, and serves as a global centre of excellence in managing trade data, statistics and related analytical software. It maintains a Trade Analysis and Information System (TRAINS) database, covering some 160 countries, and an Agricultural Trade Policy Simulation Model (ATPSM); and helps countries to set up competition policies and laws, and to develop voluntary norms to combat anti-competitive practices in national and global markets and to promote consumer welfare. UNCTAD is the focal point of work on competition policy and related consumer welfare within the UN system and hosts an annual meeting of an Intergovernmental Group of Experts on Competition Law and Policy. In 2005 UNCTAD established ad hoc voluntary peer reviews (VPR) on competition law and policy. Developing countries are also helped to design policies and strategies to strengthen their competitive productive capacities and trade-related infrastructures. The Conference aims to promote the achievement through trade of the UN MDGs, and to promote UN system-wide coherence on trade matters. It services a number of UN task forces and co-ordination mechanisms to facilitate greater synergy and co-operation in the UN's development work. A joint UNEP/UNCTAD Capacity Building Task Force on Trade, Environment and Development aims to strengthen the capacities of countries to address issues relating to trade, the environment and development. UNCTAD also supports research and technical assistance in a range of subjects linking trade and the environment, including organic agriculture, the use of renewable energy technologies and the protection of traditional knowledge. The 2009/10 edition of the triennial *Trade and Environment Review* focused on 'Promoting poles of clean growth to foster the transition to a more sustainable economy'.

UNCTAD and the WTO jointly manage the International Trade Centre (ITC), based in Geneva, which helps developing countries and countries with economies in transition to achieve sustainable human development through the export of goods and services.

INVESTMENT AND ENTERPRISE

As the focal point of the UN system on matters related to investment UNCTAD promotes the understanding of key issues, particularly matters related to foreign direct investment (FDI) and enterprise development. The Division on Investment and Enterprise (DIAE) also assists developing countries, in particular LDCs and countries with special needs, in formulating and implementing active policies aimed at boosting productive capacities and international competitiveness and in participating more fully in international investment agreements (IIAs). In order to accomplish this objective, the DIAE carries out research and policy analysis on the development impact of FDI in the areas of IIAs, national FDI policies, intellectual property, and enterprise development and business facilitation. An *IIA Monitor* is published four times a year. Technical assistance includes organizing seminars for policy-makers and the training of trade negotiators, some of it through a distance-learning programme. The annual *World Investment Report (WIR)* is a main point of reference for policy-makers and practitioners in this area, providing data on issues pertaining to FDI and transnational corporations (TNCs), as well as analysing trends and developments in FDI, examining the implications of activities by TNCs in relation to these trends, and assessing consequent international and national policy issues of relevance to developing countries. The 2011 edition of *WIR* had a special focus on the strategic use of non-equity modes by TNCs in their management of global value chains and international operations. The DIAE also assists developing countries in establishing an enabling policy framework for attracting and benefiting from FDI. In this respect, UNCTAD supports these nations in undertaking Investment Policy Reviews (IPRs), objective analyses of how national policy, regulatory and institutional systems attract or inhibit FDI; by 2012 some 32 IPRs had been implemented. UNCTAD also assists developing countries in implementing the recommendations of IPRs. Other capacity-building programmes include assistance to developing countries in collecting, improving, and harmonizing statistics on FDI; in negotiating international investment agreements; in investment promotion and facilitation; and in linking foreign affiliates and domestic enterprises. UNCTAD is also mandated to provide a platform for international dialogue on best practices in investment policies, and supports developing countries in promoting their enterprise development, through upgrading entrepreneurship, harmonizing international accounting and reporting standards, developing competitive insurance markets, and through an e-tourism initiative. UNCTAD's Empretec programme, initiated in 32 developing countries world-wide, trains and encourages entrepreneurs. The DIAE also services the Intergovernmental Group of Experts on International Standards on Accounting and Reporting (ISAR), which aims to assist developing countries and economies in transition with the implementation of best practices in corporate transparency and accounting. Since 2008 UNCTAD has organized a World Investment Forum, held every two years, to promote dialogue among government ministers, corporate executives, investors and heads of investment promotion agencies on investment-related issues and challenges. The third Forum was convened in Doha, Qatar, in April 2012.

GLOBALIZATION AND DEVELOPMENT STRATEGIES

UNCTAD works to promote policies and strategies at national and international levels, and analyses issues related to globalization, international trade and finance, in support of economic management for sustainable development. Every September UNCTAD publishes its flagship *Trade and Development Report (TDR)*. The 2012 *TDR* was to focus on income inequality. Through its Debt Management and Financial Analysis System (DMFAS), a joint programme with the World Bank, UNCTAD provides assistance to developing countries on debt management, helping debtor countries to analyse data, make projections, and plan strategies for debt repayment and reorganization with the help of modern information technology. By 2012 the programme had supported 69 countries. UNCTAD provides training for operators and senior officials to raise awareness of institutional reforms that might be necessary for effective debt management. UNCTAD also supports developing countries in their negotiations on debt owed to developed countries' governments, in the context of the Paris Club, and every year it provides a report on the external debt of developing countries to the UN General Assembly. Since 1995 UNCTAD has also provided technical assistance and economic analyses to support the Palestinian people and the development of the Palestinian economy. In 2008 the Accra Accord (see above) determined to intensify support to Palestine in order to alleviate economic and social hardships and to strengthen its state-building efforts.

TECHNOLOGY AND LOGISTICS

Within the UN system UNCTAD provides intellectual leadership and serves as a source of expertise in the areas of science, technology, innovation and information and communication technologies. Substantive and technical servicing is provided to the Commission on Science and Technology for Development (CSTD), and work is undertaken in the areas of science, technology and innovation policy, as well as technology transfer. In the area of information and communication technologies (ICTs), relevant mandates are implemented through policy research, and providing support to enable the participation of developing countries and transition economies in international discussions and policy debates. Furthermore, technical assistance projects are undertaken with a view to helping build the capacity of developing countries in the areas of science, technology, innovation and ICTs. UNCTAD's annual *Information Economy Report* tracks recent ICT trends and assesses strategies to enhance the development impact of these technologies in developing countries. The 2011 edition of the *Report* focused the use of ICTs to accelerate progress in private sector development. In 2004 UNCTAD established its Virtual Institute on Trade and Development, a special programme that aims to strengthen capacities at universities in developing and transition countries for the teaching and researching of trade issues. In June of that year UNCTAD launched an e-tourism initiative to help small economies and island developing countries reach their full tourism development potential using ICTs. In 2001 UNCTAD established its regular three-week flagship course on trade and development, 'Key Issues on the International Economic Agenda'. UNCTAD's work on trade logistics focuses on research and analysis, technical assistance and consensus building. Analytical studies and reports are prepared in the field of transport, and advice is provided to advance developing country policy makers' and traders' understanding of international trade mechanisms and frameworks. The ASYCUDA programme software, adopted by more than 90 countries world-wide, helps automate customs procedures and further facilitate trade transactions.

AFRICA AND SPECIAL PROGRAMMES

Development of Africa: UNCTAD undertakes analysis of African socio-economic issues and uses its findings to advance global understanding of that continent's development challenges, and to promote action at national, regional and international levels with a view to accelerating both regional development and greater participation by African countries in the global economy; UNCTAD co-operates closely with the New Partnership for Africa's development (NEPAD), with a particular focus on its agriculture, market access and diversification areas of activity; UNCTAD also participates in the annual regional consultations of UN agencies active in Africa. In July 2005, meeting in Gleneagles, Scotland, the annual summit of G8 leaders determined to double assistance to Africa by 2010, as first recommended by UNCTAD in 2000. Since 2000 UNCTAD has published an annual *Economic Development in Africa Report*, which analyses development issues specific to Africa and makes policy recommendations for African countries and the international community. The 2011 edition focused on 'Fostering industrial development in Africa in the new global environment'.

Landlocked Developing Countries (LLDCs): in 2012 there were 31 LLDCs, of which 15 were located in Africa, 12 were in Asia, two (Bolivia and Paraguay) were in Latin America, and two (Armenia and Moldova) were in Eastern Europe; LLDCs experience strong challenges to growth and development owing to factors including poor physical infrastructure, weak institutional and productive capacities, small domestic markets, remoteness from maritime ports and therefore world markets, and high vulnerability to external shocks; the need to transport goods through neighbouring territory tends to incur high transaction costs resulting in reduced competitiveness; UNCTAD's multidimensional approach to land-locked states includes developing adequate national transport networks and efficient transit systems, promoting regional or sub-regional economic integration, and encouraging FDI in economic activities that are not distance-sensitive. In 1995 the Global Framework for Transit Transport Co-operation between Land-locked and Transit Developing Countries and the Donor Community was endorsed by the UN General Assembly, with a view to enhancing transit systems and enabling LLDCs to reduce their marginalization from world markets. In 2003 the UN convened an international ministerial conference, in Almatı, Kazakhstan, which aimed to enhance transit transport co-operation between land-locked and transit developing countries. The resulting Almatı Declaration and Almatı Programme of Action addressed infrastructure development and maintenance, transit policy issues, and trade facilitation measures. UNCTAD participates in the implementation of the Almatı Programme of Action through analytical work on the transit transport and related development problems confronting LLDCs, and also through the provision of technical assistance to these countries in areas such as trade facilitation and electronic commerce. In 2005 the first meeting of LLDC Ministers responsible for trade, convened in Asunción, Paraguay, adopted the Asunción Platform for the Doha Development Round, which aimed to harmonize the positions of LLDCs in multilateral trade negotiations.

Least Developed Countries (LDCs): UNCTAD aims to give particular attention to the needs of the world's 48 LDCs, the large majority of which (34) are in Africa; the UN has since 1971 (using established criteria based on gross national income per capita, weak human assets—as measured through a composite Human Assets Index, and economic vulnerability—as measured through a composite Economic Vulnerability Index) classified as LDCs states that are deemed highly disadvantaged in their development processes; in view of the UN's recognition of the particular challenges confronting LDCs, the development partners of these countries, including UN agencies and programmes, have adopted certain special support measures aimed at: reducing LDCs' competitive disadvantages in the global economy; supporting the development of LDCs' physical infrastructure and human resources; and enhancing their institutional capacities; LDC-specific treatment is focused on three main areas of international co-operation: the multilateral trading system (where special concessions, such as non-reciprocal market access preferences, are granted to LDCs); development financing (where donors are expected to give especially favourable consideration to LDCs when making decisions on concessionary financing); and technical assistance (with priority being given to LDCs under all UN development programming); UNCTAD's eighth session, held in February 1992, requested that detailed analyses of the socio-economic situations and domestic policies of the LDCs, of their resource needs, and of external factors affecting their economies, be undertaken as part of UNCTAD's work programme. The ninth session, held in April–May 1996, determined that particular attention be given to the problems of the LDCs in all areas of UNCTAD's work. The 10th session, convened in February 2000, focused on the impact of globalization on developing economies and on means of improving trade opportunities for LDCs. In June 2004 the 11th session noted the increasing marginalization of the LDCs in the global economy and urged UNCTAD to consider solutions to this marginalization. In April 2008 the 12th session emphasized the urgent need to take global action to protect the world's poor from the ongoing global financial and food crises and ensuing global recession. Three UN Conferences on the Least Developed Countries have been convened under UNCTAD auspices, in 1981, 1990, and 2001. LDC III, held in Brussels, in May 2001, adopted a Programme of Action for the Least Developed Countries for the Decade 2001–10, which was reviewed annually by UNCTAD. UNCTAD contributed to LDC IV, which took place in Istanbul, Turkey, in May 2011. LDC IV approved the Istanbul Programme of Action, which included a provision that national parliaments should be engaged in debating development strategies as well as in overseeing their implementation, and had the ultimate objective of enabling at least one-half of current LDCs to graduate from LDC status by 2020. UNCTAD publishes an annual *Least Developed Countries Report*, which in 2011 focused on the theme 'The Potential Role of South-South Co-operation for Inclusive and Sustainable Development'.

Small Island Developing States (SIDS): since 1974 the UN has recognized the particular problems of SIDS, which are deemed to be at greater risk of marginalization from the global economy than many other developing countries, owing to adverse consequences arising from their small size; remoteness from large markets (resulting in high transport costs); high economic vulnerability to economic and natural shocks beyond domestic control; fragile ecosystems and high exposure to globally induced phenomena such as rises in sea levels; and frequently unstable agricultural production, owing to increased exposure to natural disasters; there is no formal listing of SIDS, but, for analytical purposes, UNCTAD uses an unofficial list comprising 29 SIDS; the Global Conference on the Sustainable Development of SIDS (held in Barbados, in April–May 1994) adopted a Programme of Action for the Sustainable Development of SIDS; an International Meeting to Review the Implementation of the Programme of Action (convened in Mauritius, in January 2005) approved the Mauritius Strategy for the Further Implementation of the Programme of Action for the Sustainable Development of SIDS, which addressed the serious disadvantages suffered by many SIDS in the global economy; a High-level Review Meeting on the implementation of the Mauritius Strategy, convened in September 2010, adopted an Outcome Document reaffirming commitment to supporting SIDS' development efforts, noting with concern uneven progress made by SIDS towards achieving the MDGs, acknowledging the significant threat posed to SIDS by climate change and sea level rises, and recognizing the need to advance internationally a preventive approach towards alleviating the effects of natural disasters on SIDS, including reducing risks and properly integrating risk management into development policies.

SPECIAL UNIT ON COMMODITIES

UNCTAD, through its Special Unit on Commodities, provides analysis and technical co-operation and builds international consensus among member States on deepening understanding of the relationship between commodity production and trade and poverty reduction. Major areas of activity include focusing on making the commodity sector an instrument of poverty reduction by facilitating the access of small and poor commodity producers to markets; supporting diversification towards higher-value products and encouraging the stronger parts of the value chain to support the weaker parts; promoting the use of market-based instruments for generating finance, particularly for the disadvantaged parts of the value chain; focusing on the role of exchanges as facilitators for commodity-based development; publishing statistics; finding ways to enable producers to meet both official and private sector standards; developing ways of promoting broad-based economic development and diversification in mining-dependent areas; enhancing activities dealing with energy, particularly oil and gas, and organizing annual conferences on oil and gas trade and finance in Africa; and convening and servicing UN conferences relating to international commodity bodies. UNCTAD convenes annually a Global Commodities Forum, most recently in January 2012.

CHIEF EXECUTIVES BOARD (CEB) INTER-AGENCY CLUSTER ON TRADE AND PRODUCTIVE CAPACITY

UNCTAD leads the UN's CEB Inter-agency Cluster on Trade and Productive Capacity, which was established in April 2007 to co-ordinate trade and development operations at national and regional levels within the UN system. Other partner organizations in the Cluster are: UNIDO, UNDP, FAO, the International Trade Centre, WTO, the five UN Regional Commissions, UNEP, UNOPS, and (since December 2010) the UN Commission on International Trade Law. The Cluster has participated in pilot activities under the 'Delivering as One' process.

Finance

The operational expenses of UNCTAD are borne by the regular budget of the UN, and amount to approximately US $50m. annually. Technical co-operation activities, financed from extra-budgetary resources, amount to some $25m. annually.

Publications

Development and Globalization: Facts and Figures.

Economic Development in Africa Report.

Information Economy Report.

Least Developed Countries Report (annually).

Review of Maritime Transport (annually).

Trade and Development Report (annually).

Trade and Environment Review.

UNCTAD Handbook of Statistics (annually, also available on DVD-Rom and online).

World Commodity Survey.

World Investment Report (annually).

Policy briefs, other abstracts, reviews and reports.

United Nations Development Programme—UNDP

Address: One United Nations Plaza, New York, NY 10017, USA.

Telephone: (212) 906-5300; **fax:** (212) 906-5364; **e-mail:** hq@undp.org; **internet:** www.undp.org.

The Programme was established in 1965 by the UN General Assembly. Its central mission is to help countries to eradicate poverty and achieve a sustainable level of human development, an approach to economic growth that encompasses individual well-being and choice, equitable distribution of the benefits of development, and conservation of the environment. UNDP advocates for a more inclusive global economy. UNDP co-ordinates global and national efforts to achieve the UN Millennium Development Goals.

Organization

(April 2012)

UNDP is responsible to the UN General Assembly, to which it reports through ECOSOC.

EXECUTIVE BOARD

The Executive Board is responsible for providing intergovernmental support to, and supervision of, the activities of UNDP and the UN Population Fund (UNFPA). It comprises 36 members: eight from Africa, seven from Asia and the Pacific, four from eastern Europe, five from Latin America and the Caribbean and 12 from western Europe and other countries. Members serve a three-year term.

SECRETARIAT

Offices and divisions at the Secretariat include: an Operations Support Group; Offices of the United Nations Development Group, the Human Development Report, Development Studies, Audit and Performance Review, Evaluation, and Communications; and Bureaux for Crisis Prevention and Recovery; Partnerships; Development Policy; and Management. Five regional bureaux, all headed by an assistant administrator, cover: Africa; Asia and the Pacific; the Arab states; Latin America and the Caribbean; and Europe and the Commonwealth of Independent States. UNDP's Administrator (the third most senior UN official, after the Secretary-General and the Deputy Secretary-General) is in charge of strategic policy and overall co-ordination of UN development activities (including the chairing of the UN Development Group), while the Associate Administrator supervises the operations and management of UNDP programmes.

Administrator: HELEN CLARK (New Zealand).

Associate Administrator: REBECA GRYNSPAN (Costa Rica).

Assistant Administrator and Director of the Bureau for Crisis Prevention and Recovery: JORDAN RYAN (USA).

Assistant Administrator and Director of the Bureau for Development Policy: OLAV KJØRVEN (Norway).

Assistant Administrator and Director of the Bureau of Management: JENS WANDEL (Denmark).

Assistant Administrator and Director of the Partnerships Bureau: SIGRID KAAG (Netherlands).

COUNTRY OFFICES

In almost every country receiving UNDP assistance there is an office, headed by the UNDP Resident Representative, who usually also serves as the UN Resident Co-ordinator, responsible for the co-ordination of all UN technical assistance and development activities in that country, so as to ensure the most effective use of UN and international aid resources.

Activities

UNDP describes itself as the UN's global development network, advocating for change and connecting countries to knowledge, experience and resources to help people build a better life. In 2012 UNDP was active in 177 countries. It provides advisory and support services to governments and UN teams with the aim of advancing sustainable human development and building national development capabilities. Assistance is mostly non-monetary, comprising the provision of experts' services, consultancies, equipment and training for local workers. Developing countries themselves contribute significantly to the total project costs in terms of personnel, facilities, equipment and supplies. UNDP also supports programme countries in attracting aid and utilizing it efficiently.

From the mid-1990s UNDP assumed a more active co-ordinating role within the UN system. In 1997 the UNDP Administrator was appointed to chair the UN Development Group (UNDG), which was established as part of a series of structural reform measures initiated by the UN Secretary-General, with the aim of preventing duplication and strengthening collaboration between all UN agencies, programmes and funds concerned with development. The UNDG promotes coherent policy at country level through the system of UN Resident Co-ordinators (see above), the Common Country Assessment mechanism (CCA, a process for evaluating national development needs), and the UN Development Assistance Framework (UNDAF, for planning and co-ordination development operations at country level, based on the CCA).

During the late 1990s UNDP undertook an extensive internal process of reform, which placed increased emphasis on its activities in the field and on performance and accountability. In 2001 UNDP established a series of Thematic Trust Funds to enable increased support of priority programme activities. In accordance with the more results-oriented approach developed under the reform process UNDP introduced a new Multi-Year Funding Framework (MYFF), which outlined the country-driven goals around which funding was to be mobilized, integrating programme objectives, resources, budget and outcomes. The MYFF was to provide the basis for the Administrator's Business Plans for the same duration and enables policy coherence in the implementation of programmes at country, regional and global levels. A Results-Oriented Annual Report (ROAR) was produced for the first time in 2000 from data compiled by country offices and regional programmes. New measures were introduced in 2006 to improve UNDP's management accountability, internal auditing, evaluation and procurement procedures.

The 2008–13 Strategic Plan emphasized UNDP's 'overarching' contribution to achieving sustainable human development through capacity development strategies, to be integrated into all areas of activity. (The UNDP Capacity Development Group, established in 2002 within the Bureau for Development Policy, organizes UNDP capacity development support at local and national level.) Other objectives identified by the 2008–13 Plan included strengthening national ownership of development projects and promoting and facilitating South-South co-operation.

In 2012 UNDP was working to advance the UN's development agenda through engagement with the MDGs Acceleration Framework (see below); with the UN Conference on Sustainable Development (UNCSD), scheduled to be held in Rio de Janeiro, Brazil, in June; and with the formulation of a post-2015 system-wide development framework. A new strategic plan was being developed for 2014–17, which aimed to strengthen UNDP's capacity to deliver results.

UNDP, jointly with the World Bank, leads an initiative on 'additional financing for the most vulnerable', the first of nine activities that were launched in April 2009 by the UN System Chief Executives Board for Co-ordination (CEB), with the aim of alleviating the impact on poor and vulnerable populations of the developing global economic crisis.

MILLENNIUM DEVELOPMENT GOALS

UNDP, through its leadership of the UNDG and management of the Resident Co-ordinator system, has a co-ordinating function as the focus of UN system-wide efforts to achieve the so-called Millennium Development Goals (MDGs), pledged by UN member governments attending a summit meeting of the UN General Assembly in September 2000. The objectives were to establish a defined agenda to reduce poverty and improve the quality of lives of millions of people and to serve as a framework for measuring development. There are eight MDGs, as follows, for which one or more specific targets have been identified:

i) to eradicate extreme poverty and hunger, with the aim of reducing by 50% (compared with the 1990 figure) the number of people with an income of less than US $1 a day and those suffering from hunger by 2015, and to achieve full and productive employment and decent work for all, including women and young people;

ii) to achieve universal primary education by 2015;

iii) to promote gender equality and empower women, in particular to eliminate gender disparities in primary and secondary education by 2005 and at all levels by 2015;

iv) to reduce child mortality, with a target reduction of two-thirds in the mortality rate among children under five by 2015 (compared with the 1990 level);

v) to improve maternal health, specifically to reduce by 75% the numbers of women dying in childbirth and to achieve universal access to reproductive health by 2015 (compared with the 1990 level);

vi) to combat HIV/AIDS, malaria and other diseases, with targets to have halted and begun to reverse the incidence of HIV/AIDS, malaria and other major diseases by 2015 and to achieve universal access to treatment for HIV/AIDS for all those who need it by 2010;

vii) to ensure environmental sustainability, including targets to integrate the principles of sustainable development into country policies and programmes, to reduce by 50% (compared with the 1990 level) the number of people without access to safe drinking water by 2015, and to achieve significant improvement in the lives of at least 100m. slum dwellers by 2020;

viii) to develop a global partnership for development, including an open, rule-based, non-discriminatory trading and financial system, and efforts to deal with international debt, to address the needs of least developed countries and landlocked and small island developing states, to provide access to affordable, essential drugs in developing countries, and to make available the benefits of new technologies.

UNDP plays a leading role in efforts to integrate the MDGs into all aspects of UN activities at country level and to ensure that the MDGs are incorporated into national development strategies. The Programme supports efforts by countries, as well as regions and sub-regions, to report on progress towards achievement of the goals, and on specific social, economic and environmental indicators, through the formulation of MDG reports. These form the basis of a global report, issued annually by the UN Secretary-General since mid-2002. UNDP also works to raise awareness of the MDGs and to support advocacy efforts at all levels, for example through regional publicity campaigns, target-specific publications and the Millennium Campaign to generate support for the goals in developing and developed countries. UNDP provides administrative and technical support to the Millennium Project, an independent advisory body established by the UN Secretary-General in 2002 to develop a practical action plan to achieve the MDGs. Financial support of the Project is channelled through a Millennium Trust Fund, administered by UNDP. In January 2005 the Millennium Project presented its report, based on extensive research conducted by teams of experts, which included recommendations for the international system to support country level development efforts and identified a series of 'Quick Wins' to bring conclusive benefit to millions of people in the short-term. International commitment to achieve the MDGs by 2015 was reiterated at a World Summit, convened in September 2005. In December 2006 UNDP and the Spanish Government concluded an agreement on the establishment of the MDG Achievement Fund (MDG-F), which aims to support the acceleration of progress towards the achievement of the MDGs and to enhance co-operation at country level between UN development partners. UNDP and the UN Department of Economic and Social Affairs are lead agencies in co-ordinating the work of the Millennium Development Goals Gap Task Force, which was established by the UN Secretary-General in May 2007 to track, systematically and at both international and country level, existing international commitments in the areas of official development assistance, market access, debt relief, access to essential medicines and technology. In November the UN, in partnership with two major US companies, launched an online MDG Monitor (www.mdgmonitor.org) to track progress and to support organizations working to achieve the goals. In September 2010 UNDP launched the MDGs Acceleration Framework, which aimed to support countries in identifying and overcoming barriers to eradicating extreme poverty and achieving sustainable development.

DEMOCRATIC GOVERNANCE

UNDP supports national efforts to ensure efficient and accountable governance, to improve the quality of democratic processes, and to build effective relations between the state, the private sector and civil society, which are essential to achieving sustainable development. As in other practice areas, UNDP assistance includes policy advice and technical support, capacity-building of institutions and individuals, advocacy and public information and communication, the promotion and brokering of dialogue, and knowledge networking and sharing of good practices.

UNDP works to strengthen parliaments and other legislative bodies as institutions of democratic participation. It assists with constitutional reviews and reform, training of parliamentary staff, and capacity-building of political parties and civil organizations as part of this objective. UNDP undertakes missions to help prepare for and ensure the conduct of free and fair elections. It helps to build the long-term capacity of electoral institutions and practices within a country, for example by assisting with voter registration, the establishment of electoral commissions, providing observers to verify that elections are free and fair, projects to educate voters, and training journalists to provide impartial election coverage.

Within its justice sector programme UNDP undertakes a variety of projects to improve access to justice, in particular for the poor and disadvantaged, and to promote judicial independence, legal reform and understanding of the legal system. UNDP also works to promote access to information, the integration of human rights issues into activities concerned with sustainable human development, and support for the international human rights system.

UNDP is mandated to assist developing countries to fight corruption and improve accountability, transparency and integrity (ATI). It has worked to establish national and international partnerships in support of its anti-corruption efforts and used its role as a broker of knowledge and experience to uphold ATI principles at all levels of public financial management and governance. UNDP publishes case studies of its anti-corruption efforts and assists governments to conduct self-assessments of their public financial management systems.

In March 2002 a UNDP Governance Centre was inaugurated in Oslo, Norway, to enhance the role of UNDP in support of democratic governance and to assist countries to implement democratic reforms in order to achieve the MDGs. In 2012 the Centre's areas of focus were: access to information and e-governance; access to justice and rule of law; anti-corruption; civic engagement; electoral systems and processes; human rights; local governance; parliamentary development; public administration; and women's empowerment. The Democratic Governance Network (DGP-Net) allows discussion and the sharing of information. An iKnow Politics Network, supported by UNDP, aims to help women become involved in politics.

Within the democratic governance practice area UNDP supports more than 300 projects at international, country and city levels designed to improve conditions for the urban poor, in particular through improvement in urban governance. The Local Initiative Facility for Urban Environment (LIFE) undertakes small-scale projects in low-income communities, in collaboration with local authorities, the private sector and community-based groups, and promotes a participatory approach to local governance. UNDP also works closely with the UN Capital Development Fund to implement projects in support of decentralized governance, which it has recognized as a key element to achieving sustainable development goals.

UNDP aims to ensure that, rather than creating an ever-widening 'digital divide', ongoing rapid advancements in information and communications technology (ICT) are harnessed by poorer countries to accelerate progress in achieving sustainable human development. UNDP advises governments on ICT policy, promotes digital entrepreneurship in programme countries and works with private sector partners to provide reliable and affordable communications networks. The Bureau for Development Policy operates the Information and Communication Technologies for Development Programme, which aims to establish technology access centres in developing countries. A Sustainable Development Networking Programme focuses on expanding internet connectivity in poorer countries through building national capacities and supporting local internet sites. UNDP has used mobile internet units to train people even in isolated rural areas. In 1999 UNDP, in collaboration with an international communications company, Cisco Systems, and other partners, launched NetAid, an internet-based forum (accessible at www.netaid.org) for mobilizing and co-ordinating fundraising and other activities aimed at alleviating poverty and promoting sustainable human development in the developing world. With Cisco Systems and other partners, UNDP has worked to establish academies of information technology to support training and capacity-building in developing countries. UNDP and the World Bank jointly host the secretariat of the Digital Opportunity Task Force, a partnership between industrialized and developing countries, business and non-governmental organizations (NGOs) that was established in 2000. UNDP is a partner in the Global Digital Technology Initiative, launched in 2002 to strengthen the role of ICT in achieving the development goals of developing countries. In January 2004 UNDP and Microsoft Corporation announced an agreement to develop jointly ICT projects aimed at assisting developing countries to achieve the MDGs.

POVERTY REDUCTION

UNDP's activities to facilitate poverty eradication include support for capacity-building programmes and initiatives to generate sustainable livelihoods, for example by improving access to credit, land and technologies, and the promotion of strategies to improve education and health provision for the poorest elements of populations (especially women and girls). UNDP aims to help governments to reassess their development priorities and to design initiatives for sustainable human development. In 1996, following the World Summit for Social Development, which was held in Copenhagen, Denmark, in March 1995, UNDP launched the Poverty Strategies Initiative (PSI) to strengthen national capacities to assess and monitor the extent of poverty and to combat the problem. All PSI projects were to involve representatives of governments, the private sector, social organizations and research institutions in policy debate and formulation. Following the introduction, in 1999, by the World Bank and IMF of Poverty Reduction Strategy Papers (PRSPs), UNDP has helped governments to draft these documents, and, since 2001, has linked the papers to efforts to achieve and monitor progress towards the MDGs. In early 2004 UNDP inaugurated the International Poverty Centre, in Brasília, Brazil, which fosters the capacity of countries to formulate and implement poverty reduction strategies and encourages South-South co-operation in all relevant areas of research and decision-making. In particular, the Centre aims to assist countries to meet MDGs through research into and implementation of pro-poor policies that encourage social protection and human development, and through the monitoring of poverty and inequality. UNDP's Secretariat hosts the Special Unit for South-South Co-operation (SU/SSC), which was established by the United Nations General Assembly in 1978.

UNDP country offices support the formulation of national human development reports (NHDRs), which aim to facilitate activities such as policy-making, the allocation of resources, and monitoring progress towards poverty eradication and sustainable development. In addition, the preparation of Advisory Notes and Country Co-operation Frameworks by UNDP officials helps to highlight country-specific aspects of poverty eradication and national strategic priorities. In January 1998 the Executive Board adopted eight guiding principles relating to sustainable human development that were to be implemented by all country offices, in order to ensure a focus to UNDP activities. Since 1990 UNDP has published an annual *Human Development Report*, incorporating a Human Development Index, which ranks countries in terms of human development, using three key indicators: life expectancy, adult literacy and basic income required for a decent standard of living. UNDP's 2011 *Human Development Report*, published in November, was to focus on the need to address in tandem the urgent global challenges of achieving sustainability and equity, and identified policies at global and national level to advance progress. The Report includes a Human Poverty Index and a Gender-related Development Index, which assesses gender equality on the basis of life expectancy, education and income. Jointly with the International Labour Organization (ILO) UNDP operates a Programme on Employment for Poverty Reduction, which undertakes analysis and studies, and supports countries in improving their employment strategies.

UNDP is committed to ensuring that the process of economic and financial globalization, including national and global trade, debt and capital flow policies, incorporates human development concerns. It aimed to ensure that the Doha Development Round of World Trade Organization (WTO) negotiations should achieve an expansion of trade opportunities and economic growth to less developed countries. With the UN Conference on Trade and Development (UNCTAD), UNDP manages a Global Programme on Globalization, Liberalization and Sustainable Human Development, which aims to support greater integration of developing countries into the global economy. UNDP manages a Trust Fund for the Integrated Framework for Trade-related Technical Assistance to Least Developed Countries, which was inaugurated in 1997 by UNDP, the IMF, the International Trade Centre, UNCTAD, the World Bank and the WTO.

Jointly with the UN Economic Commission for Africa and other agencies, UNDP operates a project on Trade Capacity Development for Sub-Saharan Africa, to help African countries take a greater share of global markets, reinforce African negotiating capacities, and strengthen regional co-operation. In May 2008 UNDP launched a regional initiative to assist African countries in negotiating, managing and regulating large-scale investment contracts, particularly in the exploitation of natural resources, so as to ensure that the host country (and especially its poorest people) receives the maximum benefit.

In 1996 UNDP initiated a process of collaboration between city authorities world-wide to promote implementation of the commitments made at the 1995 Copenhagen summit for social development and to help to combat aspects of poverty and other urban problems, such as poor housing, transport, the management of waste disposal, water supply and sanitation. The World Alliance of Cities Against Poverty was formally launched in 1997, in the context of the International Decade for the Eradication of Poverty. The seventh global Forum of the Alliance took place in February 2010.

UNDP sponsors the International Day for the Eradication of Poverty, held annually on 17 October.

ENVIRONMENT AND ENERGY

UNDP plays a role in developing the agenda for international co-operation on environmental and energy issues, focusing on the relationship between energy policies, environmental protection, poverty and development. UNDP promotes development practices that are environmentally sustainable, for example through the formulation and implementation of Poverty Reduction Strategies and National Strategies for Sustainable Development. Together with the UN Environment Programme (UNEP) and the World Bank, UNDP is an implementing agency of the Global Environment Facility (GEF), which was established in 1991 to finance international co-operation in projects to benefit the environment.

UNDP recognizes that desertification and land degradation are major causes of rural poverty and promotes sustainable land management, drought preparedness and reform of land tenure as means of addressing the problem. It also aims to reduce poverty caused by land degradation through implementation of environmental conventions at a national and international level. In 2002 UNDP inaugurated an Integrated Drylands Development Programme which aimed to ensure that the needs of people living in arid regions are met and considered at a local and national level. The Drylands Development Centre implements the programme in 19 African, Arab and West Asian countries. UNDP is also concerned with sustainable management of forestries, fisheries and agriculture. Its Biodiversity Global Programme assists developing countries and communities to integrate issues relating to sustainable practices and biodiversity into national and global practices. Since 1992 UNDP has administered a Small Grants Programme, funded by the GEF, to support community-based initiatives concerned with biodiversity conservation, prevention of land degradation and the elimination of persistent organic pollutants. The Equator Initiative was inaugurated in 2002 as a partnership between UNDP, representatives of governments, civil society and businesses, with the aim of reducing poverty in communities along the equatorial belt by fostering local partnerships, harnessing local knowledge and promoting conservation and sustainable practices.

In 2006 UNDP inaugurated a new multi-partner initiative, Mangroves for the Future (MFF), to promote investment in coastal ecosystem conservation, in particular in those countries affected by the December 2004 tsunami, in order to support sustainable development. The project was to focus on mangrove swamps, which formerly provided a natural protection against flooding, but which have been cleared in order to provide land for rice-growing, fish-farming or shrimp-farming. In April 2008 a regional technical review forum of the initiative was convened, in Ahungalla, Sri Lanka, to assess programmes of work and national strategies. MFF was expanded to include Pakistan and Viet Nam, and to undertake regional coastal management projects.

In December 2005 UNDP (in collaboration with Fortis, a private sector provider of financial services) launched the MDG Carbon Facility, whereby developing countries that undertake projects to reduce emissions of carbon dioxide, methane and other gases responsible for global warming may sell their 'carbon credits' to finance further MDG projects. The first projects under the MDG Carbon Facility were inaugurated in February 2008, in Uzbekistan, the former Yugoslav republic of Macedonia, Yemen and Rwanda.

UNDP supports efforts to promote international co-operation in the management of chemicals. It was actively involved in the development of a Strategic Approach to International Chemicals Management which was adopted by representatives of 100 governments at an international conference convened in Dubai, UAE, in February 2006.

UNDP works to ensure the effective governance of freshwater and aquatic resources, and promotes co-operation in transboundary water management. It works closely with other agencies to promote safe sanitation, ocean and coastal management, and community water supplies. In 1996 UNDP, with the World Bank and the Swedish International Development Agency, established a Global Water Partnership to promote and implement water resources management. UNDP, with the GEF, supports a range of projects which incorporate development and ecological requirements in the sustainable management of international waters. including the Global Mercury Project, a project for improved municipal waste-water management in coastal cities of the African, Caribbean and Pacific states, a Global Ballast Water Management Programme and an International Waters Learning Exchange and Resources Network.

CRISIS PREVENTION AND RECOVERY

UNDP is not primarily a relief organization, but collaborates with other UN agencies in countries in crisis and with special circumstances to promote relief and development efforts, in order to secure the foundations for sustainable human development and thereby increase national capabilities to prevent or mitigate future crises. In particular, UNDP is concerned to achieve reconciliation, reintegration and reconstruction in affected countries, as well as to support emergency interventions and management and delivery of programme aid. It aims to facilitate the transition from relief to longer-term recovery and rehabilitation. Special development initiatives in post-conflict countries include the demobilization of former combatants and destruction of illicit small armaments, rehabilitation of communities for the sustainable reintegration of returning populations and the restoration and strengthening of democratic institutions. UNDP is seeking to incorporate conflict prevention into its development strategies. It has established a mine action unit within its Bureau for Crisis Prevention and Recovery in order to strengthen national and local de-mining capabilities including surveying, mapping and clearance of anti-personnel landmines. It also works to increase awareness of the harm done to civilians by cluster munitions, and participated in the negotiations that culminated in May 2008 with the adoption of an international Convention on Cluster Munitions, which in February 2010 received its 30th ratification, enabling its entry into force on 1 August. UNDP also works closely with UNICEF to raise awareness and implement risk reduction education programmes, and manages global partnership projects concerned with training, legislation and the socio-economic impact of anti-personnel devices. In 2005 UNDP adopted an '8-Point Agenda' aimed at improving the security of women and girls in conflict situations and promoting their participation in post-crisis recovery processes. In late 2006 UNDP began to administer the newly established Peacebuilding Fund, the purpose of which is to strengthen essential services to maintain peace in countries that have undergone conflict. During 2008 UNDP developed a new global programme aimed at strengthening the rule of law in conflict and post-conflict countries; the programme placed particular focus on women's access to justice, institution-building and transitional justice.

In 2006 UNDP launched an Immediate Crisis Response programme (known as 'SURGE') aimed at strengthening its capacity to respond quickly and effectively in the recovery phase following a conflict or natural disaster. Under the programme Immediate Crisis Response Advisors—UNDP staff with special expertise in at least one of 12 identified areas, including early recovery, operational support and resource mobilization—are swiftly deployed, in a 'SURGETeam', to UNDP country offices dealing with crises. In 2008 Immediate Crisis Response Advisors were deployed to northern Cameroon (in February) in response to a sudden influx of Chadian refugees; to Chad (also in February) to review the destruction of the local UNDP office in a period of violent unrest; to Myanmar (May) to assess the aftermath of Cyclone Nargis; and to Haiti (September) following a series of hurricanes there. In January 2009 a SURGETeam was deployed to assess the situation in Gaza, in view of the onset in December 2008 of an intense period of conflict. Following the earthquake that devastated Haiti in January 2010 a SURGETeam, comprising four experts on operations, recovery and security, was deployed immediately to assess the operational requirements of UNDP's office there; subsequently 24 SURGE advisers developed a SURGE work plan for the country.

UNDP is the focal point within the UN system for strengthening national capacities for natural disaster reduction (prevention, preparedness and mitigation relating to natural, environmental and technological hazards). UNDP's Bureau of Crisis Prevention and Recovery, in conjunction with the Office for the Co-ordination of Humanitarian Affairs and the secretariat of the International Strategy for Disaster Reduction, oversees the system-wide Capacity for Disaster Reduction Initiative (CADRI), which was inaugurated in 2007, superseding the former United Nations Disaster Management Training Programme. In February 2004 UNDP introduced a Disaster Risk Index that enabled vulnerability and risk to be measured and compared between countries and demonstrated the correspondence between human development and death rates following natural disasters. UNDP was actively involved in preparations for the second World Conference on Disaster Reduction, which was held in Kobe, Japan, in January 2005. Following the Kobe Conference UNDP initiated a new Global Risk Identification Programme. During 2005 the Inter-Agency Standing Committee, concerned with co-ordinating the international response to humanitarian disasters, developed a concept of providing assistance through a 'cluster' approach, comprising core areas of activity (see OCHA). UNDP was designated the lead agency for the Early Recovery cluster, linking the immediate needs following a disaster with medium- and long-term recovery efforts.

HIV/AIDS

UNDP regards the HIV/AIDS pandemic as a major challenge to development, and advocates making HIV/AIDS a focus of national planning and national poverty reduction strategies; supports decentralized action against HIV/AIDS at community level; helps to strengthen national capacities at all levels to combat the disease; and aims to link support for prevention activities, education and treatment with broader development planning and responses. UNDP places a particular focus on combating the spread of HIV/AIDS through the promotion of women's rights. UNDP is a co-sponsor, jointly with the World Health Organization (WHO) and other UN bodies, of the Joint UN Programme on HIV/AIDS (UNAIDS), which became operational on 1 January 1996. UNAIDS co-ordinates UNDP's HIV and Development Programme. UNDP works in partnership with the Global Fund to Fight HIV/AIDS, Tuberculosis and Malaria, in particular to support the local principal recipient of grant financing and to help to manage fund projects.

UNDP administers a global programme concerned with intellectual property and access to HIV/AIDS drugs, to promote wider and cheaper access to antiretroviral drugs, in accordance with the agreement on Trade-Related Aspects of Intellectual Property Rights (TRIPS), amended by the WTO in 2005 to allow countries without a pharmaceutical manufacturing capability to import generic copies of patented medicines.

Finance

UNDP and its various funds and programmes are financed by the voluntary contributions of members of the UN and the Programme's participating agencies, cost-sharing by recipient governments and third-party donors. In 2008 UNDP's gross regular (core) income was US $1,100m., and total non-core contributions amounted to $3,700m. Of total provisional programme expenditure of $4,096m. in 2008, some 34.9% was allocated to fostering democratic governance; 30.6% to achieving the MDGs and reducing human poverty; 16.0% to supporting crisis prevention and recovery; and 9.9% to managing energy and the environment for sustainable development. Some 28% of provisional total programme expenditure was allocated to Latin America and the Caribbean; 22% to Asia and the Pacific; 21% to Africa; 12% to the Arab states; and 8% to Europe and the CIS. For the period 2008–11 total voluntary contributions were projected at $20,600m., of which $5,300m. constituted regular (core) resources, $5,000m. bilateral donor contributions, $5,500m. contributions from multilateral partners, and $4,800m. cost-sharing by recipient governments.

UNDP, UNFPA and UNICEF are committed to integrating their budgets from 2014.

Publications

Annual Report of the Administrator.
Choices (quarterly).

Human Development Report (annually).
Poverty Report (annually).
Results-Oriented Annual Report.

Associated Funds and Programmes

UNDP is the central funding, planning and co-ordinating body for technical co-operation within the UN system. A number of associated funds and programmes, financed separately by means of voluntary contributions, provide specific services through the UNDP network. UNDP manages a trust fund to promote economic and technical co-operation among developing countries.

GLOBAL ENVIRONMENT FACILITY (GEF)

The GEF, which is managed jointly by UNDP, the World Bank (which hosts its secretariat) and UNEP, began operations in 1991 and was restructured in 1994. Its aim is to support projects in the six thematic areas of: climate change, the conservation of biological diversity, the protection of international waters, reducing the depletion of the ozone layer in the atmosphere, arresting land degradation and addressing the issue of persistent organic pollutants. Capacity-building to allow countries to meet their obligations under international environmental agreements, and adaptation to climate change, are priority cross-cutting components of these projects. The GEF acts as the financial mechanism for the Convention on Biological Diversity and the UN Framework Convention on Climate Change. UNDP is responsible for capacity-building, targeted research, pre-investment activities and technical assistance. UNDP also administers the Small Grants Programme of the GEF, which supports community-based activities by local NGOs, and the Country Dialogue Workshop Programme, which promotes dialogue on national priorities with regard to the GEF. In October 2010 donor countries pledged US $4,350m. for the fifth periodic replenishment of GEF funds (GEF-5), covering the period 2011–14.

Chair. and CEO: MONIQUE BARBUT (France).

Executive Co-ordinator of UNDP-GEF Unit: YANNICK GLEMAREC; 304 East 45th St, 9th Floor, New York, NY 10017, USA; fax (212) 906-6998; e-mail gefinfo@undp.org; internet www.undp.org/gef/.

MDG ACHIEVEMENT FUND (MDG-F)

The Fund, established in accordance with an agreement concluded in December 2006 between UNDP and the Spanish Government, aims to support the acceleration of progress towards the achievement of the MDGs and to advance country-level co-operation between UN development partners. The Fund operates through the UN development system and focuses mainly on financing collaborative UN activities addressing multi-dimensional development challenges. The Spanish Government provided initial financing to the Fund of nearly €528m., adding $98m. in September 2008. By 2012 some 128 programmes were under way in 49 countries, in the thematic areas of children and nutrition; climate change; conflict prevention; culture and development; economic governance; gender equality and women's empowerment; and youth employment.

Director of MDG-F Secretariat: SOPHIE DE CAEN (Canada); MDG-F Secretariat, c/o UNDP, One United Nations Plaza, New York, NY 10017, USA; tel. (212) 906-6180; fax (212) 906-5364; e-mail pb.mdgf.secretariat@undp.org; internet www.mdgfund.org.

MONTREAL PROTOCOL

Through its Montreal Protocol/Chemicals Unit UNDP collaborates with public and private partners in developing countries to assist them in eliminating the use of ozone-depleting substances (ODS), in accordance with the Montreal Protocol to the Vienna Convention for the Protection of the Ozone Layer, through the design, monitoring and evaluation of ODS phase-out projects and programmes. In particular, UNDP provides technical assistance and training, national capacity-building and demonstration projects and technology transfer investment projects.

PROGRAMME OF ASSISTANCE TO THE PALESTINIAN PEOPLE (PAPP)

PAPP, established in 1978, is committed to strengthening institutions in the Israeli-occupied Territories and emerging Palestinian autonomous areas, to creating employment opportunities and to stimulating private and public investment in the area to enhance trade and export potential. Examples of PAPP activities include the following: construction of sewage collection networks and systems in the northern Gaza Strip; provision of water to 500,000 people in rural and urban areas of the West Bank and Gaza; construction of schools, youth and health centres; support to vegetable and fish traders through the construction of cold storage and packing facilities; and provision of loans to strengthen industry and commerce. In January 2009, in response to the intensive bombardment of the Gaza Strip by Israeli forces during December 2008–January 2009, with the stated aim of ending rocket attacks launched by Hamas and other militant groups on Israeli targets ('Operation Cast Lead'), PAPP distributed food packages to more than 30,000 Palestinians in the territory who were not served by UNRWA. In September 2011 PAPP launched a Consolidated Plan of Assistance, covering the period 2012–14, which aimed to support the Palestinian people in the following areas: energy resources; transport and management systems; affordable and adequate housing; education; public health services and systems; and heritage conservation.

UNDP Special Representative in the Occupied Palestinian Territories: FRODE MAURING; POB 51359, Jerusalem; tel. (2) 6268200; fax (2) 6268222; e-mail registry.papp@undp.org; internet www.undp.ps.

UNDP DRYLANDS DEVELOPMENT CENTRE (DDC)

The Centre, based in Nairobi, Kenya, was established in February 2002, superseding the former UN Office to Combat Desertification and Drought (UNSO). (UNSO had been established following the conclusion, in October 1994, of the UN Convention to Combat Desertification in Those Countries Experiencing Serious Drought and/or Desertification, Particularly in Africa; in turn, UNSO had replaced the former UN Sudano-Sahelian Office.) The DDC was to focus on the following areas: ensuring that national development planning takes account of the needs of dryland communities, particularly in poverty reduction strategies; helping countries to cope with the effects of climate variability, especially drought, and to prepare for future climate change; and addressing local issues affecting the utilization of resources.

Officer-in-Charge: ELIE KODSIE; UN Gigiri Compound, United Nations Ave, POB 30552, 00100 Nairobi, Kenya; tel. (20) 7624640; fax (20) 7624648; e-mail ddc@undp.org; internet www.undp.org/drylands.

UNDP-UNEP POVERTY-ENVIRONMENT INITIATIVE (UNPEI)

UNPEI, inaugurated in February 2007, supports countries in developing their capacity to launch and maintain programmes that mainstream poverty-environment linkages into national development planning processes, such as MDG achievement strategies and PRSPs. In May 2007 UNDP and UNEP launched the Poverty-Environment Facility (UNPEF) to co-ordinate, and raise funds in support of, UNPEI.

Officer-in-Charge: DAVID SMITH; UN Gigiri Compound, United Nations Avenue, POB 30552, 00100 Nairobi, Kenya; e-mail facility.unpei@unpei.org; internet www.unpei.org.

UNITED NATIONS CAPITAL DEVELOPMENT FUND (UNCDF)

The Fund was established in 1966 and became fully operational in 1974. It invests in poor communities in least developed countries (LDCs) through local governance projects and microfinance operations, with the aim of increasing such communities' access to essential local infrastructure and services and thereby improving their productive capacities and self-reliance. UNCDF encourages participation by local people and local governments in the planning, implementation and monitoring of projects. The Fund aims to promote the interests of women in community projects and to enhance their earning capacities. A Special Unit for Microfinance (SUM), established in 1997 as a joint UNDP/UNCDF operation, was fully integrated into UNCDF in 1999. UNCDF/SUM helps to develop financial services for poor communities and supports UNDP's MicroStart initiative, which supports private sector and community-based initiatives in generating employment opportunities. UNCDF hosts the UN high-level Advisors Group on Inclusive Financial Sectors, established in respect of recommendations made during the 2005 International Year of Microcredit. In November 2008 UNCDF launched MicroLead, a US $26m. fund that was to provide loans to leading microfinance institutions and other financial service providers (MFIs/FSPs) in developing countries; MicroLead was also to focus on the provision of early support to countries in post-conflict situations. In 2010 UNCDF had a programme portfolio with a value of around $200m., in support of initiatives ongoing in 38 LDCs.

Executive Secretary: DAVID MORRISON (Canada); Two United Nations Plaza, 26th Floor, New York, NY 10017, USA; fax (212) 906-6479; e-mail info@uncdf.org; internet www.uncdf.org.

UNITED NATIONS VOLUNTEERS (UNV)

The United Nations Volunteers is an important source of middle-level skills for the UN development system supplied at modest cost, particularly in the least developed countries (LDCs). Volunteers expand the scope of UNDP project activities by supplementing the work of international and host-country experts and by extending the influence of projects to local community levels. UNV also supports technical co-operation within and among the developing countries by encouraging volunteers from the countries themselves and by forming regional exchange teams comprising such volunteers. UNV is involved in areas such as peace-building, elections, human rights, humanitarian relief and community-based environmental programmes, in addition to development activities.

The UN International Short-term Advisory Resources (UNISTAR) Programme, which is the private sector development arm of UNV, has increasingly focused its attention on countries in the process of economic transition. Since 1994 UNV has administered UNDP's Transfer of Knowledge Through Expatriate Nationals (TOKTEN) programme, which was initiated in 1977 to enable specialists and professionals from developing countries to contribute to development efforts in their countries of origin through short-term technical assignments. In March 2000 UNV established an Online Volunteering Service to connect development organizations and volunteers using the internet; in 2010, 127 online volunteers made their skills available through the Online Volunteering Service.

In December 2011 UNV issued the first *State of the World's Volunteerism Report*, on the theme 'Universal Values for Global Well-being'.

By 2012 the total number of people who had served as UNVs amounted to around 40,000, deployed to more than 140 countries. During 2010 some 7,765 national and international UNVs were deployed in 132 countries, on 7,960 assignments.

Executive Co-ordinator: FLAVIA PANSIERI (Italy); POB 260111, 53153 Bonn, Germany; tel. (228) 8152000; fax (228) 8152001; e-mail information@unvolunteers.org; internet www.unv.org.

United Nations Environment Programme—UNEP

Address: POB 30552, Nairobi 00100, Kenya.

Telephone: (20) 621234; **fax:** (20) 623927; **e-mail:** unepinfo@unep.org; **internet:** www.unep.org.

The United Nations Environment Programme was established in 1972 by the UN General Assembly, following recommendations of the 1972 UN Conference on the Human Environment, in Stockholm, Sweden, to encourage international co-operation in matters relating to the human environment.

Organization

(April 2012)

GOVERNING COUNCIL

The main functions of the Governing Council (which meets every two years in ordinary sessions, with special sessions taking place in the alternate years) are to promote international co-operation in the field of the environment and to provide general policy guidance for the direction and co-ordination of environmental programmes within the UN system. It comprises representatives of 58 states, elected by the UN General Assembly, for four-year terms, on a regional basis. The Global Ministerial Environment Forum (first convened in 2000) meets annually as part of the Governing Council's regular and special sessions. The Governing Council is assisted in its work by a Committee of Permanent Representatives.

SECRETARIAT

Offices and divisions at UNEP headquarters include the Offices of the Executive Director and Deputy Executive Director; the Secretariat for Governing Bodies; Offices for Evaluation and Oversight, Programme Co-ordination and Management, and Resource Mobilization; and Divisions of Communications and Public Information, Early Warning and Assessment, Environmental Policy Implementation, Technology, Industry and Economics, Regional Co-operation, Environmental Law and Conventions, and Global Environment Facility Co-ordination.

Executive Director: ACHIM STEINER (Germany).

Deputy Executive Director: AMINA MOHAMED (Kenya).

REGIONAL OFFICES

UNEP maintains six regional offices. These work to initiate and promote UNEP objectives and to ensure that all programme formulation and delivery meets the specific needs of countries and regions. They also provide a focal point for building national, sub-regional and regional partnership and enhancing local participation in UNEP initiatives. A co-ordination office has been established at headquarters to promote regional policy integration, to co-ordinate programme planning, and to provide necessary services to the regional offices.

Africa: POB 30552, Nairobi, Kenya; tel. (20) 7624292; e-mail roainfo@unep.org; internet www.unep.org/roa.

Asia and the Pacific: United Nations Bldg, 2nd Floor, Rajadamnern Nok Ave, Bangkok 10200, Thailand; tel. (2) 288-1870; fax (2) 280-3829; e-mail uneproap@un.org; internet www.unep.org/roap.

Europe: 11–13 chemin des Anémones, 1219 Châtelaine, Geneva, Switzerland; tel. 229178279; fax 229178024; e-mail roe@unep.ch; internet www.unep.ch/roe.

Latin America and the Caribbean: Ciudad del Saber, Edif. 103, Avda Morse, Corregimiento de Ancón, Ciudad de Panamá, Panama; tel. 305-3100; fax 305-3105; e-mail enlace@pnuma.org; internet www.pnuma.org.

North America: 900 17th St NW, Suite 506, Washington, DC 20006, USA; tel. (202) 785-0465; fax (202) 785-2096; e-mail uneprona@un.org; internet www.rona.unep.org.

UNEP New York Office: DC-2 Bldg, Room 0803, Two United Nations Plaza, New York, NY 10017, USA; tel. (212) 963-8210; fax (212) 963-7341; e-mail unepnyo@un.org; internet www.unep.org/newyork.

West Asia: POB 10880, Manama, Bahrain; tel. 17812777; fax 17825110; e-mail uneprowa@unep.org.bh; internet www.unep.org.bh.

OTHER OFFICES

Convention on International Trade in Endangered Species of Wild Fauna and Flora (CITES): 15 chemin des Anémones, 1219 Châtelaine, Geneva, Switzerland; tel. 229178139; fax 227973417; e-mail info@cites.org; internet www.cites.org; Sec.-Gen. JOHN SCANLON (Australia).

Global Programme of Action for the Protection of the Marine Environment from Land-based Activities: GPA Co-ordination Unit, UNEP, POB 30552, 00100 Nairobi, Kenya; tel. (20) 7621206; fax (20) 7624249; internet www.gpa.unep.org.

Regional Co-ordinating Unit for East Asian Seas: UN Bldg, 2nd Floor, Rajadamnern Nok Ave, Bangkok 10200, Thailand; tel. (2) 288-1860; fax (2) 281-2428; e-mail kleesuwan.unescap@un.org; internet www.cobsea.org; Co-ordinator Dr ELLIK ADLER.

Regional Co-ordinating Unit for the Caribbean Environment Programme: 14–20 Port Royal St, Kingston, Jamaica; tel. 922-9267; fax 922-9292; e-mail rcu@cep.unep.org; internet www.cep.unep.org; Co-ordinator NELSON ANDRADE COLMENARES.

Secretariat of the Basel Convention: CP 356, 13–15 chemin des Anémones, 1219 Châtelaine, Geneva, Switzerland; tel. 229178218; fax 227973454; e-mail sbc@unep.ch; internet www.basel.int; Exec. Sec. KATHERINA KUMMER PEIRY.

Secretariat of the Mediterranean Action Plan on the Implementation of the Barcelona Convention: Leoforos Vassileos Konstantinou 48, POB 18019, 11610 Athens, Greece; tel. (210) 7273100; fax (210) 7253196; e-mail unepmedu@unepmap.gr; internet www.unepmap.org.

Secretariat of the Multilateral Fund for the Implementation of the Montreal Protocol: 1800 McGill College Ave, 27th Floor, Montréal, QC, Canada H3A 3J6; tel. (514) 282-1122; fax (514) 282-0068; e-mail secretariat@unmfs.org; internet www.multilateralfund.org; Chief Officer MARIA NOLAN.

UNEP/CMS (Convention on the Conservation of Migratory Species of Wild Animals) Secretariat: Hermann-Ehlers-Str. 10, 53113 Bonn, Germany; tel. (228) 8152402; fax (228) 8152449; e-mail secretariat@cms.int; internet www.cms.int; Exec. Sec. ELIZABETH MARUMA MREMA.

UNEP Division of Technology, Industry and Economics: 15 rue de Milan, 75441 Paris, Cedex 09, France; tel. 1-44-37-14-50; fax 1-44-37-14-74; e-mail unep.tie@unep.fr; internet www.unep.org/dtie; Dir SYLVIE LEMMET (France).

UNEP International Environmental Technology Centre (IETC): 2–110 Ryokuchi koen, Tsurumi-ku, Osaka 538-0036, Japan;

tel. (6) 6915-4581; fax (6) 6915-0304; e-mail ietc@unep.or.jp; internet www.unep.or.jp; Dir PER BAKKEN.

UNEP Ozone Secretariat: POB 30552, Nairobi, Kenya; tel. (20) 762-3851; fax (20) 762-4691; e-mail ozoneinfo@unep.org; internet ozone.unep.org; Exec. Sec. MARCO GONZÁLEZ (Costa Rica).

UNEP-SCBD (Convention on Biological Diversity—Secretariat): 413 St Jacques St, Suite 800, Montréal, QC, Canada H2Y 1N9; tel. (514) 288-2220; fax (514) 288-6588; e-mail secretariat@cbd.int; internet www.cbd.int; Exec. Sec. BRAULIO FERREIRA DE SOUZA DIAS (Brazil).

UNEP Secretariat for the UN Scientific Committee on the Effects of Atomic Radiation: Vienna International Centre, Wagramerstrasse 5, POB 500, 1400 Vienna, Austria; tel. (1) 26060-4330; fax (1) 26060-5902; e-mail malcolm.crick@unscear.org; internet www.unscear.org; Sec. Dr MALCOLM CRICK.

Activities

UNEP represents a voice for the environment within the UN system. It is an advocate, educator, catalyst and facilitator, promoting the wise use of the planet's natural assets for sustainable development. It aims to maintain a constant watch on the changing state of the environment; to analyse the trends; to assess the problems using a wide range of data and techniques; and to undertake or support projects leading to environmentally sound development. It plays a catalytic and co-ordinating role within and beyond the UN system. Many UNEP projects are implemented in co-operation with other UN agencies, particularly UNDP, the World Bank group, FAO, UNESCO and WHO. About 45 intergovernmental organizations outside the UN system and 60 international non-governmental organizations (NGOs) have official observer status on UNEP's Governing Council, and, through the Environment Liaison Centre in Nairobi, UNEP is linked to more than 6,000 non-governmental bodies concerned with the environment. UNEP also sponsors international conferences, programmes, plans and agreements regarding all aspects of the environment.

In February 1997 the Governing Council, at its 19th session, adopted a ministerial declaration (the Nairobi Declaration) on UNEP's future role and mandate, which recognized the organization as the principal UN body working in the field of the environment and as the leading global environmental authority, setting and overseeing the international environmental agenda. In June a special session of the UN General Assembly, referred to as 'Rio + 5', was convened to review the state of the environment and progress achieved in implementing the objectives of the UN Conference on Environment and Development (UNCED—known as the Earth Summit), that had been held in Rio de Janeiro, Brazil, in June 1992. UNCED had adopted Agenda 21 (a programme of activities to promote sustainable development in the 21st century) and the 'Rio + 5' meeting adopted a Programme for Further Implementation of Agenda 21 in order to intensify efforts in areas such as energy, freshwater resources and technology transfer. The meeting confirmed UNEP's essential role in advancing the Programme and as a global authority promoting a coherent legal and political approach to the environmental challenges of sustainable development. An extensive process of restructuring and realignment of functions was subsequently initiated by UNEP, and a new organizational structure reflecting the decisions of the Nairobi Declaration was implemented during 1999. UNEP played a leading role in preparing for the World Summit on Sustainable Development (WSSD), held in August–September 2002 in Johannesburg, South Africa, to assess strategies for strengthening the implementation of Agenda 21. Governments participating in the conference adopted the Johannesburg Declaration and WSSD Plan of Implementation, in which they strongly reaffirmed commitment to the principles underlying Agenda 21 and also pledged support to all internationally agreed development goals, including the UN Millennium Development Goals adopted by governments attending a summit meeting of the UN General Assembly in September 2000. Participating governments made concrete commitments to attaining several specific objectives in the areas of water, energy, health, agriculture and fisheries, and biodiversity. These included a reduction by one-half in the proportion of people world-wide lacking access to clean water or good sanitation by 2015, the restocking of depleted fisheries by 2015, a reduction in the ongoing loss in biodiversity by 2010, and the production and utilization of chemicals without causing harm to human beings and the environment by 2020. Participants determined to increase usage of renewable energy sources and to develop integrated water resources management and water efficiency plans. A large number of partnerships between governments, private sector interests and civil society groups were announced at the conference. The UN Conference on Sustainable Development (UNCSD) (also known as Earth Summit 2012 and as 'Rio + 20') was scheduled to be convened in June 2012, again in Rio de Janeiro.

In May 2000 UNEP's first annual Global Ministerial Environment Forum (GMEF), was held in Malmö, Sweden, attended by environment ministers and other government delegates from more than 130 countries. Participants reviewed policy issues in the field of the environment and addressed issues such as the impact on the environment of population growth, the depletion of earth's natural resources, climate change and the need for fresh water supplies. The Forum issued the Malmö Declaration, which identified the effective implementation of international agreements on environmental matters at national level as the most pressing challenge for policy-makers. The Declaration emphasized the importance of mobilizing domestic and international resources and urged increased co-operation from civil society and the private sector in achieving sustainable development. The GMEF was subsequently convened annually.

EARLY WARNING AND ASSESSMENT

The Nairobi Declaration resolved that the strengthening of UNEP's information, monitoring and assessment capabilities was a crucial element of the organization's restructuring, in order to help establish priorities for international, national and regional action, and to ensure the efficient and accurate dissemination of information on emerging environmental trends and emergencies.

UNEP's Division of Early Warning and Assessment analyses the world environment, provides early warning information and assesses global and regional trends. It provides governments with data and helps them to use environmental information for decision-making and planning.

UNEP's Global Environment Outlook (GEO) process of environmental analysis and assessment, launched in 1995, is supported by an extensive network of collaborating centres. The fourth 'umbrella' report on the GEO process (*GEO-4*) was issued in October 2007, identifying climate change, land degradation and loss of biodiversity as the world's greatest environmental challenges. *GEO-5* was to be available online from May 2012. In recent years regional and national GEO reports have been issued focusing on Africa, the Andean region, the Atlantic and Indian oceans, Brazil, the Caucasus, Latin America and the Caribbean, North America, and the Pacific; and the following thematic GEO reports have been produced: *The Global Deserts Outlook* (2006) and *The Global Outlook for Ice and Snow* (2007). Various GEO technical reports have also been published.

In 1998 UNEP and the World Meteorological Organization (WMO) established the Intergovernmental Panel on Climate Change (IPCC, see below), as an objective source of scientific information about the warming of the earth's atmosphere. UNEP's Global International Waters Assessment (GIWA) considers all aspects of the world's water-related issues, in particular problems of shared transboundary waters, and of future sustainable management of water resources. UNEP is also a sponsoring agency of the Joint Group of Experts on the Scientific Aspects of Marine Environmental Pollution and contributes to the preparation of reports on the state of the marine environment and on the impact of land-based activities on that environment. In November 1995 UNEP published a Global Biodiversity Assessment, which was the first comprehensive study of biological resources throughout the world. The UNEP-World Conservation Monitoring Centre (UNEP-WCMC), established in June 2000 in Cambridge, United Kingdom, manages and interprets data concerning biodiversity and ecosystems, and makes the results available to governments and businesses. In October 2008 UNEP-WCMC, in partnership with the IUCN, launched a new online database of the world's national parks and protected areas; detailed images of more than 100,000 sites could be viewed on the site. In 2007 the Centre undertook the 2010 Biodiversity Indicators Programme, with the aim of supporting decision-making by governments so as to reduce the threat of extinction facing vulnerable species. UNEP is a partner in the International Coral Reef Action Network—ICRAN, which was established in 2000 to monitor, manage and protect coral reefs world-wide. In June 2001 UNEP launched the Millennium Ecosystem Assessment, which was completed in March 2005. Other major assessments undertaken include the International Assessment of Agricultural Science and Technology for Development; the Solar and Wind Energy Resource Assessment; the Regionally Based Assessment of Persistent Toxic Substances; the Land Degradation Assessment in Drylands; and the Global Methodology for Mapping Human Impacts on the Biosphere (GLOBIO) project.

In June 2010 delegates from 85 countries, meeting in Busan, Republic of Korea, at the third conference addressing the creation of a new Intergovernmental Science-Policy Platform on Biodiversity and Ecosystem Services (IPBES), adopted the Busan Outcome Document finalizing details of the establishment of the IPBES. The Platform, inaugurated in December 2010, following approval of the Outcome Document by the UN General Assembly, was to undertake, periodically, assessments, based on current scientific literature, of biodiversity and ecosystem outputs beneficial to humans, including timber, fresh water, fish and climatic stability. The first plenary session of IPBES was convened in October 2011.

UNEP's environmental information network includes the UNEP-INFOTERRA programme, which facilitates the exchange of environmental information through an extensive network of national 'focal points' (national environmental information centres, usually located in the relevant government ministry or agency). By February 2012 177 countries were participating in the network, whereby UNEP promotes public access to environmental information, as well as participation in environmental concerns. UNEP's information, monitoring and assessment structures also serve to enhance early-warning capabilities and to provide accurate information during an environmental emergency.

In September 2008 the UN Reduced Emissions from Deforestation and Forest Degradation (UN-REDD) Programme, a collaboration between UNEP, UNDP and FAO, was launched. Through a trust fund, established in July 2008, UN-REDD aimed to enable donors to pool resources to promote a transformation of forest resource use patterns. In August 2011 UN-REDD endorsed a Global Programme Framework covering 2011–15. Leaders from countries in the Amazon, Congo and Borneo-Mekong forest basins participated, in June 2011, in the Summit of Heads of State and Government on Tropical Forest Ecosystems, held in Brazzaville, Republic of the Congo; the meeting issued a declaration recognising the need to protect forests in order to combat climate change, and to conduct future mutual dialogue. In that month UNEP issued a report focusing on the economic benefits of expanding funding for forests.

ENVIRONMENTAL LAW AND CONVENTIONS

UNEP promotes international environmental legislation and the development of policy tools and guidelines in order to achieve the sustainable management of the world environment. It helps governments to implement multilateral environmental agreements, and to report on their results. At a national level it assists governments to develop and implement appropriate environmental instruments and aims to co-ordinate policy initiatives. Training in various aspects of environmental law and its applications is provided. The ninth Global Training Programme on Environmental Law and Policy was conducted by UNEP in November 2009; regional training programmes are also offered. UNEP supports the development of new legal, economic and other policy instruments to improve the effectiveness of existing environmental agreements. It updates a register of international environmental treaties, and publishes handbooks on negotiating and enforcing environmental law. It acts as the secretariat for a number of regional and global environmental conventions (see list above). In June 2011 UNEP launched the Multilateral Environmental Agreements Information and Knowledge Management Initiative, which aimed to expand the sharing of information on more than 12 international agreements relating to the protection of the environment.

UNEP worked in collaboration with WMO to formulate the 1992 UN Framework Convention on Climate Change (UNFCCC), with the aim of reducing the emission of gases that have a warming effect on the atmosphere (known as greenhouse gases). (See Secretariat of the UN Framework Convention on Climate Change, below.)

In late June 2009 the first meeting was convened, in Belgrade, Serbia, of a new Consultative Group of Ministers and High-level Representatives on International Environment Governance; the meeting reviewed UNEP's role and stressed the linkages between sustainable environmental policies and development. From end-June–early July five successive UNEP Executive Directors and other prominent environmentalists met, in Glion, Switzerland, to discuss means of bringing about change in the functioning of the world economy to prioritize a sustainable approach to using and preserving the environment for the benefit of long-term human welfare.

UNEP was instrumental in the drafting of a Convention on Biological Diversity (CBD) to preserve the immense variety of plant and animal species, in particular those threatened with extinction. The Convention entered into force at the end of 1993; by February 2012 192 states and the European Union (EU) were parties to the CBD. The CBD's Cartagena Protocol on Biosafety (so called as it had been addressed at an extraordinary session of parties to the CBD convened in Cartagena, Colombia, in February 1999) was adopted at a meeting of parties to the CBD in January 2000, and entered into force in September 2003; by February 2012 the Protocol had been ratified by 160 states parties and the EU. The Protocol regulates the transboundary movement and use of living modified organisms resulting from biotechnology, in order to reduce any potential adverse effects on biodiversity and human health. It establishes an Advanced Informed Agreement procedure to govern the import of such organisms. In January 2002 UNEP launched a major project aimed at supporting developing countries with assessing the potential health and environmental risks and benefits of genetically modified (GM) crops, in preparation for the Protocol's entry into force. In February the parties to the CBD and other partners convened a conference on ways in which the traditional knowledge and practices of local communities could be preserved and used to conserve highly threatened species and ecosystems. The sixth conference of parties to the CBD, held in April 2002, adopted detailed voluntary guidelines concerning access to genetic resources and sharing the benefits attained from such resources with the countries and local communities where they originate; a global work programme on forests; and a set of guiding principles for combating alien invasive species. In October 2010 the 10th conference of the parties to the CBD, meeting in Nagoya, Japan, approved the Nagoya-Kuala Lumpur Supplementary Protocol to the CBD, with a view to establishing an international regime on access and benefit sharing (ABS) of genetic resources, alongside a strategic 10-year plan with targets and timetables to combat loss of the planet's nature-based resources. The Supplementary Protocol was opened for signature in March 2011, and by February 2012 had been signed by 92 states. The UN Decade on Biodiversity was being celebrated during 2011–20. UNEP supports co-operation for biodiversity assessment and management in selected developing regions and for the development of strategies for the conservation and sustainable exploitation of individual threatened species (e.g. the Global Tiger Action Plan). It also provides assistance for the preparation of individual country studies and strategies to strengthen national biodiversity management and research. UNEP administers the Convention on International Trade in Endangered Species of Wild Flora and Fauna (CITES), which entered into force in 1975 and comprised 175 states parties at February 2012. CITES has special programmes on the protection of elephants, falcons, great apes, hawksbill turtles, sturgeons, tropical timber (jointly with the International Tropical Timber Organization), and big leaf mahogany. Meeting in St Petersburg, Russia, in November 2010, at the International Tiger Forum, the heads of UNODC, the Convention on International Trade in Endangered Species of Wild Fauna and Flora (CITES), the World Customs Organization, INTERPOL and the World Bank jointly approved the establishment of a new International Consortium on Combating Wildlife Crime (ICCWC), with the aim of combating the poaching of wild animals and illegal trade in wild animals and wild animal products.

In December 1996 the Lusaka Agreement on Co-operative Enforcement Operations Directed at Illegal Trade in Wild Flora and Fauna entered into force, having been concluded under UNEP auspices in order to strengthen the implementation of the CBD and CITES in Eastern and Central Africa. UNEP and UNESCO jointly co-sponsor the Great Apes Survival Project (GRASP), which was launched in May 2001. GRASP supports, in 23 'great ape range states' (of which 21 are in Africa and two—Indonesia and Malaysia—in South-East Asia), the conservation of gorillas, chimpanzees, orang-utans and bonobos. GRASP's first intergovernmental meeting, held in Kinshasa, Democratic Republic of the Congo in September 2005, was attended by representatives of governments of great ape habitat states, donor and other interested states, international organizations, NGOs, and private-sector and academic interests. The meeting adopted a Global Strategy for the Survival of Great Apes, and the Kinshasa Declaration pledging commitment and action towards achieving this goal. GRASP, CITES and the World Association of Zoos and Aquariums jointly declared 2009 the Year of the Gorilla. In June 2009 160 government representatives participating in a conference to mark the Year of the Gorilla, convened in Frankfurt, Germany, issued the Frankfurt Declaration to Call for Better Protection of Gorillas.

The Convention on the Conservation of Migratory Species of Wild Animals (CMS, also referred to as the Bonn Convention), concluded under UNEP auspices in 1979, aims to conserve migratory avian, marine and terrestrial species throughout the range of their migration. The secretariat of the CMS is hosted by UNEP. At February 2012 there were 116 states parties to the Convention. A number of agreements and memoranda of understanding (MOU) concerning conservation have been concluded under the CMS. Agreements cover the conservation of African-Eurasian Migratory Waterbirds (1999), Populations of European Bats (1994), Small Cetaceans of the Baltic, North East Atlantic, Irish and North Seas (1994), Cetaceans of the Black Seas, Mediterranean and Contiguous Atlantic Area (2001), Seals in the Wadden Sea (1991), Albatrosses and Petrels (2004), and Gorillas and their Habitats (2008). MOU cover the conservation of the Siberian Crane (1993), the Slender-billed Curlew (1994), Marine Turtles of the Atlantic Coast of Africa (1999), Marine Turtles of the Indian Ocean and South-east Asia (2001), the Great Bustard (2001), the Bukhara Deer (2002), the Aquatic Warbler (2003), the West African Elephant (2005), the Saiga Antelope (2005), Pacific Island Cetaceans (2006), the Ruddy-headed Goose (2006), Grassland Birds (2007), Atlantic Populations of the Mediterranean Monk Seal (2007), Dugongs (2007), the Manatee and Small Cetaceans of Western Africa and Macaronesia (2008), Migratory Birds of Prey in Africa and Eurasia (2008), High Andean Flamingos and their Habitats (2008), Migratory Sharks (2010), and the Southern Huemul (2010).

In October 1994 87 countries, meeting under UN auspices, signed a Convention to Combat Desertification (see UNDP Drylands Development Centre), which aimed to provide a legal framework to counter the degradation of arid regions. An estimated 75% of all drylands have suffered some land degradation, affecting approximately 1,000m. people in 110 countries. UNEP continues to support the implementation of the Convention, as part of its efforts to protect land resources. UNEP also aims to improve the assessment of dryland degradation and desertification in co-operation with governments and other international bodies, as well as identifying the causes of degradation and measures to overcome these.

UNEP is the principal UN agency for promoting environmentally sustainable water management. It regards the unsustainable use of water as one of the most urgent environmental issues, and estimates that two-thirds of the world's population will suffer chronic water shortages by 2025, owing to rising demand for drinking water as a result of growing populations, decreasing quality of water because of pollution, and increasing requirements of industries and agriculture. In 2000 UNEP adopted a new water policy and strategy, comprising assessment, management and co-ordination components. The Global International Waters Assessment (see above) is the primary framework for the assessment component. The management component includes the Global Programme of Action (GPA) for the Protection of the Marine Environment from Land-based Activities (adopted in November 1995), which focuses on the effects of pollution on freshwater resources, marine biodiversity and the coastal ecosystems of small island developing states. UNEP promotes international co-operation in the management of river basins and coastal areas and for the development of tools and guidelines to achieve the sustainable management of freshwater and coastal resources. In 2007 UNEP initiated a South-South Co-operation programme on technology and capacity-building for the management of water resources. UNEP provides scientific, technical and administrative support to facilitate the implementation and co-ordination of 14 regional seas conventions and 13 regional plans of action. UNEP's Regional Seas Programme aims to protect marine and coastal ecosystems, particularly by helping governments to put relevant legislation into practice.

UNEP administers the Basel Convention on the Control of Transboundary Movements of Hazardous Wastes and their Disposal, which entered into force in 1992 with the aim of preventing the uncontrolled movement and disposal of toxic and other hazardous wastes, particularly the illegal dumping of waste in developing countries by companies from industrialized countries. At February 2012 177 countries and the EU were parties to the Convention.

In 1996 UNEP, in collaboration with FAO, began to work towards promoting and formulating a legally binding international convention on prior informed consent (PIC) for hazardous chemicals and pesticides in international trade, extending a voluntary PIC procedure of information exchange undertaken by more than 100 governments since 1991. The Convention was adopted at a conference held in Rotterdam, Netherlands, in September 1998, and entered into force in February 2004. It aims to reduce risks to human health and the environment by restricting the production, export and use of hazardous substances and enhancing information exchange procedures. UNEP played a leading role in formulating a multilateral agreement to reduce and ultimately eliminate the manufacture and use of Persistent Organic Pollutants (POPs), which are considered to be a major global environmental hazard. The Stockholm Convention on POPs, targeting 12 particularly hazardous pollutants, was adopted by 127 countries in May 2001 and entered into force in May 2004. In May 2009 the fourth conference of parties to the Stockholm Convention agreed on a list of nine further POPs; these were incorporated into the Convention in an amendment that entered into force in August 2010.

In February 2009 140 governments agreed, under the auspices of UNEP, to launch negotiations on the development of an international treaty to combat toxic mercury emissions world-wide. The first session of the intergovernmental negotiating committee on preparing the proposed treaty was convened in June 2010, in Stockholm, Sweden. The second session was held January 2011, in Chiba, Japan, and a third took place in October–November, in Nairobi. Pending the adoption of the planned treaty (envisaged for 2013) it was agreed that a voluntary Global Mercury Partnership would address mercury pollution.

UNEP was the principal agency in formulating the 1987 Montreal Protocol to the Vienna Convention for the Protection of the Ozone Layer (1985), which provided for a 50% reduction in the production of chlorofluorocarbons (CFCs) by 2000. An amendment to the Protocol was adopted in 1990, which required complete cessation of the production of CFCs by 2000 in industrialized countries and by 2010 in developing countries. The Copenhagen Amendment, adopted in 1992, stipulated the phasing out of production of hydrochlorofluorocarbons (HCFCs) by 2030 in developed countries and by 2040 in developing nations. Subsequent amendments aimed to introduce a licensing system for all controlled substances, and imposed stricter controls on the import and export of HCFCs, and on the production and consumption of bromochloromethane (Halon-1011, an industrial solvent and fire extinguisher). In September 2007 the states parties to the Vienna Convention agreed to advance the deadline for the elimination of HCFCs: production and consumption were to be frozen by 2013, and were to be phased out in developed countries by 2020 and in developing countries by 2030. A Multilateral Fund for the Implementation of the Montreal Protocol was established in June 1990 to promote the use of suitable technologies and the transfer of technologies to developing countries, and support compliance by developing countries with relevant control measures. UNEP, UNDP, the World Bank and UNIDO are the sponsors of the Fund, which by February 2012 had approved financing for more than 6,875 projects and activities in 145 developing countries at a cost of more than US $2,800m. The eighth replenishment of the Fund, covering the period 2012–14, raised $400m. in new contributions from donors. In September 2009, following ratification by Timor-Leste, the Montreal Protocol, with 196 states parties, became the first agreement on the global environment to attain universal ratification.

GLOBAL ENVIRONMENT FACILITY

UNEP, together with UNDP and the World Bank, is an implementing agency of the Global Environment Facility (GEF), established in 1991 to help developing countries, and those undergoing economic transition, to meet the costs of projects that benefit the environment in six specific areas: biological diversity, climate change, international waters, depletion of the ozone layer, land degradation and persistent organic pollutants. Important cross-cutting components of these projects include capacity-building to allow countries to meet their obligations under international environmental agreements (described above), and adaptation to climate change. During 1991–2011 some 522 projects were approved by the GEF to be implemented by UNEP, with a total value amounting to US $1,646m. UNEP services the Scientific and Technical Advisory Panel, which provides expert advice on GEF programmes and operational strategies.

TECHNOLOGY, INDUSTRY AND ECONOMICS

UNEP's Division of Technology, Industry and Economics encourages governments and the private sector to develop and adopt policies and practices that are cleaner and safer, make efficient use of natural resources, incorporate environmental costs, ensure the environmentally sound management of chemicals, and reduce pollution and risks to human health and the environment. In collaboration with other organizations UNEP works to formulate international guidelines and agreements to address these issues. UNEP also promotes the transfer of appropriate technologies and organizes conferences and training workshops to provide sustainable production practices. Relevant information is disseminated through the International Cleaner Production Information Clearing House. By February 2012 UNEP, together with UNIDO, had established 47 National Cleaner Production Centres in developing and transition countries to promote a preventive approach to industrial pollution control. In October 1998 UNEP adopted an International Declaration on Cleaner Production, with a commitment to implement cleaner and more sustainable production methods and to monitor results. In 1997 UNEP and the Coalition for Environmentally Responsible Economies initiated the Global Reporting Initiative, which, with participation by corporations, business associations and other organizations, develops guidelines for voluntary reporting by companies on their economic, environmental and social performance. In April 2002 UNEP launched the 'Life Cycle Initiative', which evaluates the impact of products over their entire life cycle (from manufacture to disposal) and aims to assist governments, businesses and other consumers with adopting environmentally sound policies and practice, in view of the upward trend in global consumption patterns. UNEP Finance Initiatives (FI) is a programme encouraging banks, insurance companies and other financial institutions to invest in an environmentally responsible way: an annual FI Global Roundtable meeting is held, together with regional meetings. In April 2007 UNEP hosted the first annual Business for Environment (B4E) meeting, on corporate environmental responsibility, in Singapore; the 2012 meeting was to be held in April, in Berlin, Germany. During 2007 UNEP's Programme on Sustainable Consumption and Production established an International Panel for Sustainable Resource Management (comprising experts whose initial subjects of study were to be the environmental risks of biofuels and of metal recycling), and initiated forums for businesses and NGOs in this field. In May 2011 the International Panel issued a *Decoupling Report* that urged the separation of the global economic growth rate from the rate of natural resource consumption. The report warned that, by 2050, without a change of direction, humanity's consumption of minerals, ores, fossil fuels and biomass were on course to increase threefold. Later in May 2011 the Panel released a report focusing on the need to increase the recycling of metals world-wide.

In October 2008, in response to the global economic, fuel and food crises that escalated during that year, UNEP launched the *Green Economy Initiative (GEI)*, also known as the 'Global Green New Deal', which aimed to mobilize and refocus the global economy towards investments in clean technologies and the natural infrastructure (for example the infrastructures of forests and soils), with a view to, simultaneously, combating climate change and promoting employment. The UNEP Executive Director stated that the global crises were in part related to a broad market failure that promoted speculation while precipitating escalating losses of natural capital and nature-based assets, compounded by an over-reliance on finite, often subsidized fossil fuels. The GEI, which was initially to be operational for a two-year period, was to have three key dimensions: the compilation of the *Green Economy* report, to provide an analysis of how public policy might support markets in accelerating the transition towards a low-carbon green economy; the Green Jobs Initiative, a partnership launched by UNEP, the ILO and the International Trade Union Confederation in 2007 (and joined in 2008 by the International Organisation of Employers); and the Economics of Ecosystems and Biodiversity (TEEB) partnership project, focusing on valuation issues. In February 2009 UNEP issued a report, entitled *The Environmental Food Crisis: Environment's Role in Averting Future Food Crises*, that urged a transformation in the way that food is produced, handled and disposed of, in order to feed the world's growing population and protect the environment; at that time the UNEP Executive Director emphasized the need for a 'Green revolution in a Green Economy'. In April 2009 the UN System Chief Executives Board for Co-ordination (CEB) endorsed the UNEP-led GEI as the fourth of nine UN initiatives aimed at alleviating the impact of the global economic crisis on poor and vulnerable populations.

In 1994 UNEP inaugurated the International Environmental Technology Centre (IETC), based in Osaka, Japan. The Centre promotes and implements environmentally sound technologies for disaster prevention and post-disaster reconstruction; sustainable production and consumption; and water and sanitation (in particular waste-water management and more efficient use of rainwater).

The Division's Chemicals branch was established to promote the sound management of hazardous substances, central to which has been the International Register of Potentially Toxic Chemicals (IRPTC). UNEP aims to facilitate access to data on chemicals and hazardous wastes, in order to assess and control health and environmental risks, by using the IRPTC as a clearing house facility of relevant information and by publishing information and technical reports on the impact of the use of chemicals. UNEP provides technical support for implementing the Convention on Persistent Organic Pollutants (see above), encouraging the use of alternative pesticides, and monitoring the emission of pollutants through the burning of waste. UNEP administers the Strategic Approach to International Chemicals Management, adopted by the International Conference on Chemicals in 2006. With UNDP, UNEP helps governments to integrate sound management of chemicals into their development planning.

The Division's OzonAction branch promotes information exchange, training and technological awareness, helping governments and industry in developing countries to undertake measures towards the cost-effective phasing-out of ozone-depleting substances (see under Environmental Law and Conventions, above).

UNEP also encourages the development of alternative and renewable sources of energy, as part of its efforts to mitigate climate change. To achieve this, UNEP has created the Global Network on Energy for Sustainable Development, linking 20 centres of excellence in industrialized and developing countries to conduct research and exchange information on environmentally sound energy technology resources. UNEP's Rural Energy Enterprise Development (REED) initiative helps the private sector to develop affordable 'clean' energy technologies, such as solar crop-drying and water-heating, wind-powered water pumps and efficient cooking stoves. UNEP is a member of the Global Bioenergy Partnership initiated by the G8 group of industrialized countries to support the sustainable use of biofuels. Through its Sustainable Transport Programme UNEP promotes the use of renewable fuels and the integration of environmental factors into transport planning, while the Sustainable Buildings and Construction Initiative promotes energy efficiency in the construction industry. In conjunction with UN-Habitat, UNDP, the World Bank and other organizations and institutions, UNEP promotes environmental concerns in urban planning and management through the Sustainable Cities Programme, and projects concerned with waste management, urban pollution and the impact of transportation systems.

During 2007 UNEP (with WMO and WTO) convened a second International Conference on Climate Change and Tourism, together with two meetings on sustainable tourism development and a conference on global eco-tourism.

In January 2011 UNEP and the World Tourism Organization launched the Global Partnership for Sustainable Tourism, also comprising other UN agencies, OECD, 18 governments, and other partners, with the aim of guiding policy and developing projects in the area of sustainable tourism, providing a global platform for discussion, and facilitating progress towards a green economy.

In June 2009 UNEP and WTO jointly issued a report entitled *Trade and Climate Change*, reviewing the intersections between trade and climate change from the perspectives of: the science of climate change; economics; multilateral efforts to combat climate change; and the effects on trade of national climate change policies. During that month UNEP welcomed OECD's 'Green Growth' declaration, which urged the adoption of targeted policy instruments to promote green investment, and emphasized commitment to the realization of an ambitious and comprehensive post-2012 global climate agreement. In January 2012 UNEP, OECD, the World Bank, and the Global Green Growth Institute (established in June 2010 in Seoul, Republic of Korea) launched the Green Growth Knowledge Platform. The Platform, accessible at www.greengrowthknowledge.org, aims to advance efforts to identify and address major knowledge gaps in green growth theory and practice, and to support countries in formulating and implementing policies aimed at developing a green economy.

REGIONAL CO-OPERATION AND REPRESENTATION

UNEP maintains six regional offices. These work to initiate and promote UNEP objectives and to ensure that all programme formulation and delivery meets the specific needs of countries and regions. They also provide a focal point for building national, sub-regional and regional partnerships and enhancing local participation in UNEP initiatives. UNEP's Division of Regional Co-operation promotes regional policy integration, co-ordinates programme planning, and provides necessary services to the regional offices. UNEP provides administrative support to several regional conventions, and organizes regional conferences and training programmes.

COMMUNICATIONS AND PUBLIC INFORMATION

UNEP's public education campaigns and outreach programmes promote community involvement in environmental issues. Further communication of environmental concerns is undertaken through coverage in the press, broadcasting and electronic media, publications (see below), an information centre service and special promotional events, including World Environment Day (celebrated on 5 June; slogan in 2012: 'Green Economy: Does It Include You'), the Focus on Your World photography competition, and the awarding of the annual Sasakawa Prize (to recognize distinguished service to the environment by individuals and groups) and of the Champions of the Earth awards (for outstanding environmental leaders from each of UNEP's six regions). An annual Global Civil Society Forum (preceded by regional consultative meetings) is held in association with UNEP's Governing Council meetings. From April 2007 UNEP undertook a two-year programme on strengthening trade unions' participation in environmental processes. UNEP's Tunza programme for children and young people includes conferences, online discussions and publications. UNEP co-operates with the International Olympic Committee, the Commonwealth Games organizing body and international federations for football, athletics and other sports to encourage 'carbon neutral' sporting events and to use sport as a means of outreach. UNEP's Billion Tree Campaign, initiated in February 2007, initially encouraged governments, community organizations and individuals to plant 1,000m. trees before the end of the year, and exceeded that target; by February 2012 some 12,598m. trees had been planted under the continuing campaign.

Finance

Project budgetary resources approved by the Governing Council for UNEP's activities during 2012–13 totalled US $474m. UNEP is allocated a contribution from the regular budget of the United Nations, and derives most of its finances from voluntary contributions to the Environment Fund and to trust funds.

Publications

Annual Report.

CBTF (Capacity Building Task Force on Trade, Environment and Development) Newsletter.

DEWA/GRID Europe Quarterly Bulletin. E+ (Energy, Climate and Sustainable Development).

The Environment and Poverty Times.

Global 500.

Great Apes Survival Project Newsletter.

IETC (International Environmental Technology Centre) Insight.

Life Cycle Initiatives Newsletter.

Our Planet (quarterly).

Planet in Peril: Atlas of Current Threats to People and the Environment.

ROA (Regional Office for Africa) News (2 a year).

Tourism Focus (2 a year).

RRC.AP (Regional Resource Centre for Asia and the Pacific) Newsletter.

Sustainable Consumption Newsletter.

Tunza (quarterly magazine for children and young people).

UNEP Chemicals Newsletter.

UNEP Year Book.

World Atlas of Biodiversity.

World Atlas of Coral Reefs.

World Atlas of Desertification.

Studies, reports (including the *Global Environment Outlook* series), legal texts, technical guidelines, etc.

Associated Bodies

UN Conference on Sustainable Development (UNCSD): UNCSD (also known as Rio+20 and as the Earth Summit+20) is scheduled to be convened in Rio de Janeiro, Brazil, on 20–22 June 2012, with participation at the level of heads of state or government. Rio+20 commemorates the 20th anniversary of the 1992 UN Conference on Environment and Development (UNCED), also held in Rio de Janeiro, and the 10th anniversary of the World Summit on Sustainable Development (WSSD), held in 2002, in Johannesburg, South Africa. In May 2010 the UN Secretary-General appointed the Under-Secretary-General for Economic and Social Affairs as the Secretary-General of Rio+20. A Conference Secretariat was established within the UN Department of Economic and Social Affairs. Rio+20 aims to assess progress towards, and secure renewed political commitment for sustainable development, with a focus on the following themes: (i) a green economy in the context of sustainable development and poverty eradication, and (ii) the Institutional Framework for Sustainable Development (IFSD). It is envisaged that Rio+20 will produce a focused political document on future sustainable development. An inclusive preparatory process, involving stakeholders in the Conference, was implemented during 2010–early 2012. The UNCSD Secretariat, with other partners, prepared a series of briefs on Rio+20 issues—such as trade and the green economy; options for strengthening the IFSD; oceans; sustainable cities; green jobs and social inclusion; reducing disaster risk and building resilience; food security and sustainable agriculture; and water—to be made available to policy makers and other interested stakeholders as a basis for discussion.

UNCSD Secretariat: Two UN Plaza, Rm DC2-2220 New York, NY 10017, USAe-mail uncsd2012@un.org; internet www.uncsd2012.org/rio20/index.html.

Sec.-Gen.: SHA ZUKANG (People's Republic of China).

Exec. Co-ordinators: H. ELIZABETH THOMPSON (Barbados), BRICE LALONDE (France).

Intergovernmental Panel on Climate Change (IPCC): established in 1988 by WMO and UNEP; comprises some 3,000 scientists as well as other experts and representatives of all UN member governments. Approximately every five years the IPCC assesses all available scientific, technical and socio-economic information on anthropogenic climate change. The IPCC provides, on request, scientific, technical and socio-economic advice to the Conference of the Parties to the UN Framework Convention on Climate Change (UNFCCC) and to its subsidiary bodies, and compiles reports on specialized topics, such as *Aviation and the Global Atmosphere*, *Regional Impacts of Climate Change*, and (issued in March 2012) *Managing the Risks of Extreme Events and Disasters to Advance Climate Change Adaptation*. The IPCC informs and guides, but does not prescribe, policy. In December 1995 the IPCC presented evidence to 120 governments, demonstrating 'a discernible human influence on global climate'. In 2001 the Panel issued its *Third Assessment Report,* in which it confirmed this finding and presented new and strengthened evidence attributing most global climate warming over the past 50 years to human activities. The IPCC's *Fourth Assessment Report*, the final instalment of which was issued in November 2007, concluded that increases in global average air and ocean temperatures, widespread melting of snow and ice, and the rising global average sea level, demonstrate that the warming of the climate system is unequivocal; that observational evidence from all continents and most oceans indicates that many natural systems are being affected by regional climate changes; that a global assessment of data since 1970 has shown that it is likely that anthropogenic warming has had a discernable influence on many physical and biological systems; and that other effects of regional climate changes are emerging. The *Fourth Assessment Report* was awarded a share of the Nobel Peace Prize for 2007. In January 2010 the IPCC accepted criticism that an assertion in the 2007 *Report*, concerning the rate at which Himalayan glaciers were melting, was exaggerated, and in February 2010 the Panel agreed that the *Report* had overstated the proportion of the Netherlands below sea level. In late February it was announced that an independent board of scientists would be appointed to review the work of the IPCC. The *Fifth Assessment Report* of the IPCC was to be published in 2014. In May 2011 a meeting of delegates from IPCC member states determined that a 13-member executive committee, under the leadership of the IPCC Chairman, should be established to supervise the day-to-day operations of the Panel and to consider matters requiring urgent action.

Chair.: RAJENDRA K. PACHAURI (India).

Secretariat of the UN Framework Convention on Climate Change (UNFCCC): Haus Carstanjen, Martin-Luther-King-Strasse 8, 53175 Bonn, Germany; tel. (228) 815-1000; fax (228) 815-1999; e-mail secretariat@unfccc.int; internet unfccc.int; WMO and UNEP worked together to formulate the Convention, in response to the first report of the IPCC, issued in August 1990, which predicted an increase in the concentration of 'greenhouse' gases (i.e. carbon dioxide and other gases that have a warming effect on the atmosphere) owing to human activity. The UNFCCC was signed in May 1992 and formally adopted at the UN Conference on Environment and Development, held in June. It entered into force in March 1994. It committed countries to submitting reports on measures being taken to reduce the emission of greenhouse gases and recommended stabilizing these emissions at 1990 levels by 2000; however, this was not legally binding. Following the second session of the Conference of the Parties (COP) of the Convention, held in July 1996, multilateral negotiations ensued to formulate legally binding objectives for emission limitations. At the third COP, held in Kyoto, Japan, in December 1997, 38 industrial nations endorsed mandatory reductions of combined emissions of the six major gases by an average of 5.2% during the five-year period 2008–12, to pre-1990 levels. The so-called Kyoto Protocol was to enter into force on being ratified by at least 55 countries party to the UNFCCC, including industrialized countries with combined emissions of carbon dioxide in 1990 accounting for at least 55% of the total global greenhouse gas emissions by developed nations. The fourth COP, convened in Buenos Aires, Argentina, in November 1998, adopted a plan of action to promote implementation of the UNFCCC and to finalize the operational details of the Kyoto Protocol. These included the Clean Development Mechanism, by which industrialized countries may obtain credits towards achieving their reduction targets by assisting developing countries to implement emission-reducing measures, and a system of trading emission quotas. The fifth COP, held in Bonn, Germany, in October–November 1999, and the first session of the sixth COP, convened in The Hague, Netherlands, in November 2000, failed to reach agreement on the implementation of the Buenos Aires plan of action, owing to a lack of consensus on several technical matters, including the formulation of an effective mechanism for ascertaining compliance under the Kyoto Protocol, and adequately defining a provision of the Protocol under which industrialized countries may obtain credits towards achieving their reduction targets in respect of the absorption of emissions resulting from activities in the so-called land-use, land-use change and forestry (LULUCF) sector. Further, informal, talks were held in Ottawa, Canada, in early December. Agreement on implementing the Buenos Aires action plan was finally achieved at the second session of the sixth COP, held in Bonn in July 2001. The seventh COP, convened in Marrakech, Morocco, in October–November, formally adopted the decisions reached in July, and elected 15 members to the Executive Board of the Clean Development Mechanism. In March 2002 the USA (the most prolific national producer of harmful gas emissions) announced that it would not ratify the Kyoto Protocol. The Kyoto Protocol eventually entered into force on 16 February 2005, 90 days after its ratification by Russia. Negotiations commenced in May 2007 on establishing a new international arrangement eventually to succeed the Kyoto Protocol. Participants in COP 13, convened in Bali, Indonesia, in December 2007, adopted the Bali Roadmap, detailing a two-year process leading to the planned conclusion of the schedule of negotiations in December 2009. Further rounds of talks were held during 2008 in Bangkok, Thailand (March–April); Bonn (June); and Accra, Ghana (August). The UN Climate Change Conference (COP 14), convened in Poznań, Poland, in December 2008, finalized the Kyoto Protocol's Adaptation Fund, which was to finance projects and programmes in developing signatory states that were particularly vulnerable to the adverse effects of climate change. Addressing the Conference, the UN Secretary-General urged the advancement of a 'Green New Deal', to address simultaneously the ongoing global climate and economic crises. COP 15 was held, concurrently with the fifth meeting of parties to the Kyoto Protocol, in Copenhagen, Denmark, in December 2009. Heads of state and government and other delegates attending the Conference approved the Copenhagen Accord, which determined that international co-operative action should be taken, in the context of sustainable development, to reduce global greenhouse gas emissions so as to hold the ongoing increase in global temperature below 2°C. It was agreed that enhanced efforts should be undertaken to reduce vulnerability to climate change in developing countries, with special reference to least developed countries, small island states and Africa. Developed countries agreed to pursue the achievement by 2020 of strengthened carbon emissions targets, while developing nations were to implement actions to slow down growth in emissions. A new Copenhagen Green Climate Fund was to be established to support climate change mitigation actions in developing countries, and a Technology Mechanism was also to be established, with the aim of accelerating technology development and transfer in support of climate change adaptation and mitigation activities. COP 16, convened, concurrently with the sixth meeting of parties to the Kyoto Protocol, in Cancun, Mexico, in November–December 2010, adopted several decisions (the 'Cancun Agreements'), which included mandating the establishment of a Cancun Adaptation Framework and associated Adaptation Committee, and approving a work programme which was to consider approaches to environmental damage linked to unavoidable impacts of climate change in vulnerable countries, as well as addressing forms of adaptation action, such as: strengthening the resilience of ecological systems; undertaking impact, vulnerability and adaptation assessments; engaging the participation of vulnerable communities in ongoing processes; and valuing traditional indigenous knowledge alongside the best available science. UN system-wide activities to address climate change are co-ordinated by an action framework established by the UN Chief Executives Board for Co-ordination under the UN *Delivering as One* commitment. By April 2012 the Kyoto Protocol had been ratified by 192 states and the European Community, including ratifications by industrialized nations with combined responsibility for 63.7% of greenhouse gas emissions by developed nations in 1990 (although excluding participation by the USA; in December Canada announced its intention to withdraw from the Protocol). COP 17, held in Durban, South Africa, in November–December 2011 concluded with an agreement on a 'Durban Platform for Enhanced Action'. The Platform incorporated agreements to extend the Kyoto provisions regarding emissions reductions by industrialized nations for a second phase (the commitment period, of either five or eight years, to be determined during 2012), to follow on from the expiry at end-2012 of the first commitment phase, and to initiate negotiations on a new, inclusive global emissions arrangement, to be concluded in 2015, that would come into effect in 2020 with 'legal force'. During the conference sufficient funds were committed to enable the Green Climate Fund to be inaugurated and a commitment was concluded to establish the Adaptation Committee.

Executive Secretary: CHRISTIANA FIGUERES (Costa Rica).

United Nations High Commissioner for Refugees—UNHCR

Address: CP 2500, 1211 Geneva 2 dépôt, Switzerland.

Telephone: 227398111; **fax:** 227397312; **e-mail:** unhcr@unhcr.org; **internet:** www.unhcr.org.

The Office of the High Commissioner was established in 1951 to provide international protection for refugees and to seek durable solutions to their problems. In 1981 UNHCR was awarded the Nobel Peace Prize.

All UNHCR personnel are required to sign, and all interns, contracted staff and staff from partner organizations are required to acknowledge, a Code of Conduct, to which is appended the UN Secretary-General's bulletin on special measures for protection from sexual exploitation and sexual abuse. The post of Senior Adviser to the High Commissioner on Gender Issues, within the Executive Office, was established in 2004.

Organization

(April 2012)

HIGH COMMISSIONER

The High Commissioner is elected by the United Nations General Assembly on the nomination of the Secretary-General, and is responsible to the General Assembly and to the UN Economic and Social Council (ECOSOC).

High Commissioner: ANTÓNIO MANUEL DE OLIVEIRA GUTERRES (Portugal).

Deputy High Commissioner: THOMAS ALEXANDER ALEINIKOFF (USA).

EXECUTIVE COMMITTEE

The Executive Committee of the High Commissioner's Programme (ExCom), established by ECOSOC, gives the High Commissioner policy directives in respect of material assistance programmes and advice in the field of international protection. In addition, it oversees UNHCR's general policies and use of funds. ExCom, which comprises representatives of 66 states, both members and non-members of the UN, meets once a year.

ADMINISTRATION

Headquarters, based in Geneva, Switzerland, include the Executive Office, comprising the offices of the High Commissioner, the Deputy High Commissioner and the two Assistant High Commissioners (for Operations and Protection). The Inspector General, the Director of the UNHCR liaison office in New York, and the Director of the Ethics Office (established in 2008) report directly to the High Commissioner. The principal administrative Divisions cover: International Protection; Programme and Support Management; Emergency Security and Supply; Financial and Administrative Management; Human Resources Management; External Relations; and Information Systems and Telecommunications. A UNHCR Global Service Centre, based in Budapest, Hungary, was inaugurated in 2008 to provide administrative support to the Headquarters. There are five regional bureaux covering Africa, Asia and the Pacific, Europe, the Americas, and North Africa and the Middle East. In 2012 UNHCR employed around 7,190 regular staff, of whom about 85% were working in the field. At that time there were 396 UNHCR offices in 123 countries.

Activities

The competence of the High Commissioner extends to any person who, owing to well-founded fear of being persecuted for reasons of race, religion, nationality or political opinion, is outside the country of his or her nationality and is unable or, owing to such fear or for reasons other than personal convenience, remains unwilling to accept the protection of that country; or who, not having a nationality and being outside the country of his or her former habitual residence, is unable or, owing to such fear or for reasons other than personal convenience, is unwilling to return to it. This competence may be extended, by resolutions of the UN General Assembly and decisions of ExCom, to cover certain other 'persons of concern', in addition to refugees meeting these criteria. Refugees who are assisted by other UN agencies, or who have the same rights or obligations as nationals of their country of residence, are outside the mandate of UNHCR.

In recent years there has been a significant shift in UNHCR's focus of activities. Increasingly UNHCR has been called upon to support people who have been displaced within their own country (i.e. with similar needs to those of refugees but who have not crossed an international border) or those threatened with displacement as a result of armed conflict. In addition, greater support has been given to refugees who have returned to their country of origin, to assist their reintegration, and UNHCR is working to enable local communities to support the returnees, frequently through the implementation of Quick Impact Projects (QIPs). In 2004 UNHCR led the formulation of a UN system-wide Strategic Plan for internally displaced persons (IDPs). During 2005 the UN's Inter-Agency Standing Committee (IASC), concerned with co-ordinating the international response to humanitarian disasters, developed a concept of organizing agency assistance to IDPs through the institutionalization of a 'Cluster Approach', currently comprising 11 core areas of activity (see OCHA). UNHCR is the lead agency for the clusters on Camp Co-ordination and Management (in conflict situations; the International Organization for Migration leads that cluster in natural disaster situations), Emergency Shelter, and (jointly with OHCHR and UNICEF) Protection.

From the mid-2000s the scope of UNHCR's mandate was widened from the protection of people fleeing persecution and violence to encompass, also, humanitarian needs arising from natural disasters.

In July 2006 UNHCR issued a '10 Point Plan of Action on Refugee Protection and Mixed Migration' (*10 Point Plan*), a framework document detailing 10 principal areas in which UNHCR might make an impact in supporting member states with the development of comprehensive migration strategies. The 10 areas covered by the Plan were as follows: co-operation among key players; data collection and analysis; protection-sensitive entry systems; reception arrangements; mechanisms for profiling and referral; differentiated processes and procedures; solutions for refugees; addressing secondary movements; return of non-refugees and alternative migration options; and information strategy. A revised version of the *10 Point Plan* was published in January 2007. Addressing the annual meeting of ExCom in October 2007 the High Commissioner, while emphasizing that UNHCR was not mandated to manage migration, urged a concerted international effort to raise awareness and comprehension of the broad patterns (including the scale, complexity, and causes—such as poverty and the pursuit of improved living standards) of global displacement and migration. In order to fulfil UNHCR's mandate to support refugees and others in need of protection within ongoing mass movements of people, he urged better recognition of the mixed nature of many 21st century population flows, often comprising both economic migrants and refugees, asylum seekers and victims of trafficking who required detection and support. It was also acknowledged that conflict and persecution—the traditional reasons for flight—were being increasingly compounded by factors such as environmental degradation and the detrimental effects of climate change. A Dialogue on Protection Challenges, convened by the High Commissioner in December 2007, agreed that the *10 Point Plan* should be elaborated further. Regional activities based on the Plan have been focused on Central America, Western Africa, Eastern Africa and Southern Asia; and on countries along the Eastern and South-Eastern borders of European Union member states.

In 2009 UNHCR launched the first annual Global Needs Assessment (GNA), with the aim of mapping comprehensively the situation and needs of populations of concern falling under the mandate of the Office. The GNA was to represent a blueprint for planning and decision-making for UNHCR, populations of concern, governments and other partners. In 2008 a pilot GNA, undertaken in eight countries, revealed significant unmet protection needs including in education, food security and nutrition, distribution of non-food items, health, access to clean water and sanitation, shelter, and prevention of sexual violence.

UNHCR's global strategic priorities for 2012–13 were: to promote a favourable protection environment; to promote fair protection processes and increase levels of documentation; to ensure security from violence and exploitation; to provide basic needs and services; and to pursue durable solutions.

At December 2010 the total global population of concern to UNHCR, based on provisional figures, amounted to 33.9m. At that time the refugee population world-wide totalled 10.5m., of whom 8.5m. were being hosted by developing countries. UNHCR was also concerned with some 197,626 recently returned refugees, 14.7m. IDPs, 2.9m. returned IDPs, 3.5m. stateless persons, and 837,478 asylum seekers. UNHCR maintains an online statistical population database.

UNHCR is one of the 10 co-sponsors of UNAIDS.

World Refugee Day, sponsored by UNHCR, is held annually on 20 June.

INTERNATIONAL PROTECTION

As laid down in the Statute of the Office, UNHCR's primary function is to extend international protection to refugees and its second function is to seek durable solutions to their problems. In the exercise of its mandate UNHCR seeks to ensure that refugees and asylum seekers are protected against *refoulement* (forcible return), that they receive asylum, and that they are treated according to internationally recognized standards. UNHCR pursues these objectives by a variety of means that include promoting the conclusion and ratification by states of international conventions for the protection of refugees. UNHCR promotes the adoption of liberal practices of asylum by states, so that refugees and asylum seekers are granted admission, at least on a temporary basis.

The most comprehensive instrument concerning refugees that has been elaborated at the international level is the 1951 United Nations Convention relating to the Status of Refugees. This Convention, the scope of which was extended by a Protocol adopted in 1967, defines the rights and duties of refugees and contains provisions dealing with a variety of matters which affect the day-to-day lives of refugees. The application of the Convention and its Protocol is supervised by UNHCR. The Office has actively encouraged states to accede to the Convention (which had 145 parties at March 2012) and the Protocol (146 parties at March 2012). Important provisions for the treatment of refugees are also contained in a number of instruments adopted at the regional level. These include the 1969 Convention Governing the Specific Aspects of Refugee Problems adopted by the Organization of African Unity (now the African Union—AU) member states in 1969, the European Agreement on the Abolition of Visas for Refugees, and the 1969 American Convention on Human Rights. In October 2009 AU member states adopted the AU Convention for the Protection and Assistance of IDPs in Africa, the first legally binding international treaty providing legal protection and support to internally displaced populations. An increasing number of states have also adopted domestic legislation and/or administrative measures to implement the international instruments, particularly in the field of procedures for the determination of refugee status. UNHCR has sought to address the specific needs of refugee women and children, and has also attempted to deal with the problem of military attacks on refugee camps, by adopting and encouraging the acceptance of a set of principles to ensure the safety of refugees. In recent years it has formulated a strategy designed to address the fundamental causes of refugee flows.

UNHCR has been increasingly concerned with the problem of statelessness, where people have no legal nationality, and promotes new accessions to the 1954 Convention Relating to the Status of Stateless Persons and the 1961 Convention on the Reduction of Statelessness. UNHCR maintains that a significant proportion of the global stateless population has not hitherto been systematically identified. In December 2011 UNHCR organized a ministerial meeting, in Geneva, to commemorate the 60th anniversary of the 1951 Refugee Convention and the 50th anniversary of the 1961 Convention on the Reduction of Statelessness, and to reaffirm commitment to the central role played by these instruments. A number of participants at the meeting made pledges to address statelessness, including improving procedures for identifying stateless people on their territories, enhancing civil registration systems, and raising awareness on the options available to stateless people.

ASSISTANCE ACTIVITIES

The first phase of an assistance operation uses UNHCR's capacity of emergency response. This enables UNHCR to address the immediate needs of refugees at short notice, for example, by employing specially trained emergency teams and maintaining stockpiles of basic equipment, medical aid and materials. A significant proportion of UNHCR expenditure is allocated to the next phase of an operation, providing 'care and maintenance' in stable refugee circumstances. This assistance can take various forms, including the provision of food, shelter, medical care and essential supplies. Also covered in many instances are basic services, including education and counselling.

As far as possible, assistance is geared towards the identification and implementation of durable solutions to refugee problems—this being the second statutory responsibility of UNHCR. Such solutions generally take one of three forms: voluntary repatriation, local integration or resettlement in another country. Where voluntary repatriation, increasingly the preferred solution, is feasible, the Office assists refugees to overcome obstacles preventing their return to their country of origin. This may be done through negotiations with governments involved, or by providing funds either for the physical movement of refugees or for the rehabilitation of returnees once back in their own country. Some 197,000 refugees repatriated voluntarily to their home countries in 2010. UNHCR supports the implementation of the Guidance Note on Durable Solutions for Displaced Persons, adopted in 2004 by the UN Development Group.

When voluntary repatriation is not an option, efforts are made to assist refugees to integrate locally and to become self-supporting in their countries of asylum. This may be done either by granting loans to refugees, or by assisting them, through vocational training or in other ways, to learn a skill and to establish themselves in gainful occupations. One major form of assistance to help refugees re-establish themselves outside camps is the provision of housing. In cases where resettlement through emigration is the only viable solution to a refugee problem, UNHCR negotiates with governments in an endeavour to obtain suitable resettlement opportunities, to encourage liberalization of admission criteria and to draw up special immigration schemes. During 2010 an estimated 73,000 refugees were resettled under UNHCR auspices.

UNHCR aims to integrate certain priorities into its programme planning and implementation, as a standard discipline in all phases of assistance. The considerations include awareness of specific problems confronting refugee women, the needs of refugee children, the environmental impact of refugee programmes and long-term development objectives. A Policy Development and Evaluation Service reviews systematically UNHCR's operational effectiveness.

EAST ASIA AND THE PACIFIC

In 1998 the Hong Kong authorities formally terminated the policy of granting a port of first asylum to Vietnamese 'boat people'. In February 2000 UNHCR welcomed a decision by the Hong Kong authorities to offer permanent residency status to the occupants of the last remaining Vietnamese detention camp (totalling 973 refugees and 435 'non-refugees'). By the end of May, when the camp was closed, more than 200 Vietnamese had failed to apply for residency. In 1995, in accordance with an agreement concluded with the People's Republic of China Government, UNHCR initiated a programme to redirect its local assistance to promote long-term self-sufficiency in the poorest settlements, including support for revolving-fund rural credit schemes. UNHCR favours the local integration of the majority of the Vietnamese refugee population in China as a durable solution to the situation. At 31 December 2010 there were an estimated 300,897 Vietnamese refugees in mainland China.

During 2012 UNHCR was advocating for the accession of the Hong Kong Special Administrative Region—which attracts mixed inflows of refugees, asylum seekers and economic migrants—to the 1951 United Nations Convention relating to the Status of Refugees (of which China is a signatory).

A large-scale process to resettle Myanma refugees from Thailand to third countries commenced in 2004. From 2009 UNHCR aimed to upgrade its activities in the Rakhine region of northern Myanmar, covering health, education, water and sanitation, agriculture and infrastructure improvement, in order to assist the reintegration of Muslim returnees to the area, as well as stateless residents (numbering around 750,000 in 2010). From late 2008 there were significant outflows of Muslims from Rakhine towards Malaysia, as well as to Indonesia and Thailand; UNHCR has worked with regional governments for the adoption of a collective approach to addressing the situation. UNHCR assisted 10,823 Myanma refugees with resettlement in 2010, reducing the numbers still sheltering in (nine) border camps to 95,718 at the end of that year. At 31 December 2010 there were some 76,120 Myanma refugees in Malaysia (all UNHCR-assisted), of whom 21,104 arrived during that year. In addition, an estimated 29,226 Myanma refugees (Rohingya Muslims) were receiving basic care from UNHCR in two camps in Bangladesh, having fled persecution in the 1990s. In 2012 UNHCR also aimed to improve the conditions of an estimated 200,000 unregistered Myanma refugees living outside its camps in Bangladesh.

UNHCR has sought access, so far unsuccessfully, to Laotian Hmong would-be asylum seekers sheltering since 2005 in temporary shelters in Thailand, whom the Thai authorities classify as illegal migrants. During 2005–10 some 7,500 Lao-Hmong were forcibly returned from Thailand to Laos, including some 4,000 who were returned en masse in December 2009.

In 2008 Thailand was the focus of a pilot project for UNHCR's Global Needs Assessment (formally inaugurated in 2009, see above). In view of the project's findings, UNHCR aimed to enhance its efforts to improve protection and to facilitate durable solutions for refugees in that country.

Renewed violent unrest in Timor-Leste that erupted in April 2006 resulted in significant new population displacement within the country, and, at the end of that year, more than 155,200 Timorese IDPs were of concern to UNHCR. During May–August 2006 the Office provided immediate relief to the newly uprooted IDPs, in the form of non-food items such as tents, and was subsequently involved in IDP protection and reconciliation activities. In January 2012 UNHCR formally ended its operations in Timor-Leste with the closure of its office in the capital, Dili.

UNHCR endeavours to facilitate safe passage to the Republic of Korea for people who have fled from the Democratic People's Republic of Korea to China and other countries in the region.

In February 2002 an Asia-Pacific regional ministerial conference on people smuggling, trafficking in persons and related transnational crime, held in Bali, Indonesia, launched the Bali Process, a series of regional capacity-building workshops, and other initiatives, with participation by UNHCR. The Process aimed, inter alia, to improve intelligence sharing; to enhance co-operation among law enforcement agencies, and between border agencies; to promote the enactment of national legislation relating to people smuggling; to encourage a focus on addressing the root causes of illegal migration; and to support states in adopting best practices in asylum management. Further regional ministerial conferences were convened to review the Bali Process in April 2003, April 2009, and March 2011. The March 2011 conference adopted a regional co-operation framework for combating people smuggling.

SOUTH ASIA

From the late 1970s civil strife in Afghanistan resulted in massive population displacements, including movements of refugees from that country into Pakistan and Iran which created a massive refugee population, reaching a peak of almost 6.3m. people in 1990. In September 2001, prompted by the threat of impending military action directed by a US-led global coalition against targets in the Taliban-administered areas of Afghanistan, UNHCR launched an emergency relief operation to cope with the potentially large further movement of Afghan refugees and IDPs. UNHCR urged the adoption of more liberal border policies by surrounding countries and began substantially to reinforce its presence in Iran and Pakistan. Emergency contingency plans were also formulated for a relief initiative to assist a projected increase in IDP numbers (in addition to the large numbers of people already displaced) inside Afghanistan. Large population movements out of cities were reported from the start of the international political crisis. An estimated 6m. Afghans (about one-quarter of the total population) were believed to be extremely vulnerable, requiring urgent food aid and other relief supplies. In mid-September all foreign UN field staff were withdrawn from Afghanistan for security reasons; meanwhile, in order to address the humanitarian situation, a Crisis Group was established by several UN agencies, including UNHCR, and a crisis management structure came into operation at UNHCR headquarters. In October (when air-strikes were initiated against Afghanistan) UNHCR opened a staging camp at a major crossing point on the Afghanistan-Pakistan border, and put in place a system for monitoring new refugee arrivals (implemented by local people rather than by UNHCR personnel). It was estimated that from October 2001–January 2002 about 50,000 Afghan refugees entered Pakistan officially, while about 150,000 crossed into the country at unofficial border points; many reportedly sought refuge with friends and relatives. Much smaller movements into Iran were reported. Spontaneous repatriations also occurred during that period (reportedly partly owing to the poor conditions at many camps in Pakistan), and UNHCR-assisted IDP returns were also undertaken. UNHCR resumed operations within Afghanistan in mid-November 2001, distributing supplies and implementing QIPs, for example the provision of warm winter clothing. From that month some 130,000 Afghan refugees in Pakistan were relocated from inadequate accommodation to new camps. In March 2002 tripartite accords on repatriation were concluded by UNHCR with the Afghan authorities and with Iran and Pakistan. During 2002–end-2010 more than 5m. refugees returned to Afghanistan from Pakistan and Iran; of these, 117,870 returned voluntarily, with UNHCR assistance, during 2010. The operational environment within Afghanistan, however, was highly challenging during the 2000s, with the security situation remaining extremely unstable in 2012. Where possible the Agency provides returning refugees with transport and an initial reintegration package, including a cash grant and food and basic household items, and monitors their situation. Particular focus is placed upon the situation of returnee women and prevention of gender-based violence, and on encouraging the return of professional workers, especially doctors and teachers. The Office also works to improve local infrastructure and water supply facilities, and has completed the construction of more than 200,000 shelter units. UNHCR aims to strengthen the capacity of the Afghan Government to manage the return and sustainable reintegration of refugees and IDPs. During 2012 UNHCR's access to IDPs in conflict zones in Afghanistan remained insecure and unreliable. At 31 December 2010 Pakistan was hosting some 1.9m. Afghan refugees. Meanwhile, some 1.0m. UNHCR-assisted Afghan refugees remained in Iran (in addition to about 1m. unregistered Afghan migrants), and 9,094 Afghan refugees remained in India (all UNHCR-assisted). In March 2009 UNHCR and the Pakistani authorities signed an accord extending the stay of Afghan refugees in Pakistan until the end of 2012.

In 1991–92 thousands of people of Nepalese ethnic origin living in Bhutan sought refuge from alleged persecution by fleeing to eastern Nepal. In December 2000 Bhutan and Nepal reached agreement on a joint verification mechanism for the repatriation of the refugees, which had been hitherto the principal issue precluding a resolution of the situation. The first verification of Bhutanese refugees was undertaken in March 2001. In March 2008 UNHCR launched an operation, in co-operation with the International Organization for Migration and the governments of Nepal and the resettlement countries, to resettle more than 10,000 Nepalese refugees from Bhutan, mainly to the USA. At end-December 2010 some 74,536 Bhutanese refugees remained in Nepal (compared with 107,000 at March 2008), of whom some 56,000 had expressed an interest in resettlement. In 2012 UNHCR was to facilitate the resettlement of up to 16,000 Bhutanese refugees from Nepal. During 2007 the Nepalese Government extended citizenship to some 2.6m. of the 3.5m. stateless people hitherto resident in Nepal.

During 1983–2001 hostilities between the Sri Lankan Government and Tamil separatists resulted in the displacement of more than 1m. Sri Lankan Tamil refugees (who sought shelter in India) and IDPs. Ongoing efforts by UNHCR to repatriate the Sri Lankan refugees were disrupted in late 1995 by an offensive by Sri Lankan government troops against the northern Jaffna peninsula, which caused a massive displacement of the local Tamil population. Increasing insecurity from late 1999 prompted further population movements. However, following the conclusion of a cease-fire agreement between the Sri Lankan Government and Tamil separatists in February 2002, the number of spontaneous returns accelerated. From April 2006 conflict between Tamil separatists and the Sri Lankan Government escalated once again, prompting a new wave of internal displacement and refugee movements to India during 2006–08, and in January 2008 the 2002 cease-fire agreement was abrogated, further intensifying the situation. Some 303,471 people were newly displaced during April 2006–October 2008, and a further 31,809 Sri Lankans were newly displaced during November 2008–February 2009. In May 2009 the Sri Lankan Government declared an end to military operations against the Tamil separatists. From 2006 UNHCR screened, registered and provided emergency accommodation for civilians displaced from the conflict zone, monitored the human rights situation, and advised the Sri Lankan authorities about the treatment of the displaced population. At 31 December 2010 there remained 273,772 Sri Lankan IDPs of concern to UNHCR and 161,128 recently returned IDPs, as well as an estimated 178,308 Sri Lankan refugees remaining in camps in southern India. By August 2011 some 395,000 IDPs had returned to their homes, with the IDP returns process expected to be completed in 2012. UNHCR's priorities for 2012 were to continue providing material assistance to, and monitoring the protection needs of, IDPs and returnees; to help build the capacity of national institutions and local agencies involved in reintegration activities; and to implement community-based QIPs. At end-December 2010 India's total refugee population of some 184,821 also included 100,003 refugees from China (mainly Tibetans).

CENTRAL ASIA

In the early 2000s UNHCR implemented an initiative to integrate locally up to 10,000 Tajik refugees of Kyrgyz ethnic origin in Kyrgyzstan and 12,500 Tajik refugees of Turkmen origin in Turkmenistan; this process was facilitated by the conclusion in mid-2003 of a Kyrgyz-Tajik agreement on a simplified procedure for citizenship acquisition. From 1 July 2006 UNHCR terminated refugee status for exiled Tajiks, although the Office continued to support their voluntary repatriation. By the end of that year most of the former Tajik refugees in Kyrgyzstan and Turkmenistan had become naturalized citizens of those countries, as planned; in 2008 all remaining Tajik refugees in Kyrgyzstan were granted Kyrgyz citizenship. UNHCR has helped the Kyrgyz authorities to integrate the former Tajiks. UNHCR ascertained that there were 21,157 stateless people residing in Kyrgyzstan at end-2010, either without documentation or holding expired USSR passports; the Office and the Kyrgyz authorities have aimed to work together to support applications by the stateless individuals for Kyrgyz citizenship.

During mid-2010 UNHCR distributed relief items (including tents, blankets and plastic sheeting) to some of an estimated 75,000 Kyrgyz refugees who had sought shelter in temporary camps and accommodation centres in Uzbekistan following the eruption of violent conflict in southern Kyrgyzstan in June. At that time UNHCR—which estimated that some 375,000 people had become displaced inside Kyrgyzstan, including some 40,000 with urgent shelter requirements—also established an emergency office in Jalal-Abad, southern Kyrgyzstan; worked to verify the number of displaced, to visit the areas where they were focused, and to assess their needs; and sent air deliveries of relief items to Osh, southern Kyrgyzstan. Furthermore some 75,000 Kyrgyz fled the violence to Uzbekistan. UNHCR co-ordinated the relief efforts in Uzbekistan, and also the protection and emergency shelter humanitarian clusters and non-food relief cluster within Kyrgyzstan.

From late 2001 about 9,000 Afghan refugees repatriated from Tajikistan under the auspices of UNHCR and the International Organization for Migration. UNHCR expressed concern following the adoption by the Tajikistan authorities in May 2002 of refugee legislation that reportedly contravened the 1951 Convention relating to the Status of Refugees and its 1967 Protocol. During 2006 nearly 1,500 Afghan refugees were resettled from Tajikistan to third countries, leaving a remaining Afghan refugee population in that country of about 1,000; UNHCR has pursued durable solutions for their local integration. Increasing numbers of Afghan asylum-seekers fled to Tajikistan in 2010.

In 2003 UNHCR agreed to participate in a European Union/UNDP Border Management Programme in Central Asia (BOMCA). At the request of the Uzbekistan Government UNHCR closed its Uzbekistan office in April 2006. A regional office for Central Asia was inaugurated in Almatı, Kazakhstan, in 2008. UNHCR assisted the Kazakh authorities with the preparation of draft national refugee legislation during that year.

UNHCR reported in 2010 that compliance with the Convention relating to the Status of Refugees was problematic in the Central Asia region. The Office's priorities in Central Asia in 2012 included registering and profiling people of concern using modern data collection tools; improving the regional capacity for refugee status determination; seeking to improve self-reliance among refugees and asylum seekers, with a particular focus on urban situations; and preventing and reducing statelessness.

NORTH AFRICA AND THE MIDDLE EAST

Given the lack of progress in achieving a settlement agreement for Western Sahara, UNHCR co-ordinates humanitarian assistance for the estimated 165,000 Sahrawis registered as refugees in five camps in the Tindouf area of Algeria. In September 2009 UNHCR resolved to expand its confidence-building programme, which was launched in 2004 mainly to facilitate family visits; by 2012 around 12,000 people had participated in family visits under the programme.

As a result of serious instability in Libya from mid-February 2011, nearly 100,000 people soon became displaced from the eastern coastal city of Benghazi and surrounding areas; furthermore large numbers (estimated at 656,000 by August) of Libyans and former foreign residents in Libya fled to nearby countries, including 57,221 Libyan nationals who were seeking shelter in Tunisia, and 63,747 Libyans in Egypt. UNHCR dispatched teams to Egypt and Libya to provide support. In response to the crisis within Libya, UNHCR—which maintained a small international staff in the Libyan capital, Tripoli, and organized presences in Benghazi and Tobruk in the east of the country—transported supplies into Libya and provided material assistance to refugees and other vulnerable groups there. During the initial months of the crisis UNHCR airlifted tents, and items such as blankets, sleeping mats, jerry cans, and kitchen sets, to several thousand people gathered in border areas. At the request of the Tunisian Government, UNHCR and other agencies established a number of camps at the Libya-Tunisia border. Furthermore, thousands of Libyans (mainly Berbers) fled Libya's Western Mountain region into Tunisia, the majority being accommodated there by local families. By late August UNHCR had registered nearly 60,000 Libyan refugees sheltering in southern Tunisia. UNHCR distributed ration cards to Libyan refugees in urban areas of Tunisia. UNHCR expressed reiterated concern in September 2011 for the safety of foreign nationals (mainly migrant workers) remaining in Libya. Sub-Saharan Africans were reported to be at particular risk of persecution. Meanwhile, in early 2011, UNHCR and IOM jointly conducted the humanitarian evacuation of more than 100,000 third country nationals from Egypt and Tunisia, which had also experienced serious civil unrest.

Yemen has historically hosted refugees from the Horn of Africa. Of an estimated 74,000 people who made the crossing in 2009, Ethiopians (numbering about 42,000) represented for the first time a larger group than Somalis; about 309 people were presumed to have drowned during the crossing in that year. UNHCR operates two reception centres to process incomers, and four other offices, in Yemen. At 31 December 2010 Yemen was hosting an estimated 190,092, mostly Somali (179,845), refugees; the majority of these were residing in urban areas, while some 11,000 were accommodated in the al-Kharaz camp. Ongoing violent conflict in northern Yemen has also generated internal displacement, and at the end of 2010 there were an estimated 220,994 IDPs in Yemen. In 2008 Yemen participated in a pilot project for UNHCR's Global Needs Assessment (formally inaugurated in 2009, see above). The Assessment recommended interventions to improve provision in the areas of food security and nutrition, non-food items, water and education. UNHCR's priorities in Yemen in 2011 included organizing joint screening teams with the Yemen Government to identify, protect and assist people of concern; improving the access of urban refugees to education, microcredit, vocational training, employment and business opportunities; and supporting the Government in identifying, registering and monitoring conflict-affected IDPs.

In view of an increase in irregular migrant and asylum seeker flows—mainly from Eritrea, Ethiopia, Iraq and Sudan—to and through Egypt (with many migrants and asylum seekers seeking to enter Israel illegally) in recent years, UNHCR has made efforts to identify asylum seekers and to assess their claims, as well as undertaking outreach activities focused on increased community participation in protection and assistance programmes and, through the provision of training, enhancing the capacity of the Egyptian authorities to provide refugee protection. The populations of concern to UNHCR, and also the poorest sectors of local communities, were made particularly vulnerable at that time by the high cost of living and the adverse global economic situation.

In March 2003, in view of the initiation of US-led military action against the Saddam Hussain regime in Iraq, UNHCR and the International Federation of Red Cross and Red Crescent Societies signed an agreement on co-operation in providing humanitarian relief in Iraq and neighbouring countries. From mid-2003, following the overthrow of the Saddam Hussain Government, UNHCR developed plans for the eventual phased repatriation of more than 500,000 of the large population of Iraqis exiled world-wide, and for the return to their homes of some 800,000 IDPs, contingent, however, upon the stabilization of the political and security situation in the country. The Office assumed responsibility for assisting about 50,000 refugees from other countries (including some 34,000 Palestinians—of whom an estimated 10,798 remained at end-2010) who had been supported by the previous Iraqi administration but were now suffering harassment; many had abandoned their homes in Iraq owing to insufficient security and inadequate supplies. Negotiations with Iran were initiated in mid-2003 to enable Iranian refugees to repatriate across the Iraq–Iran border. From March–May 2003, and following the bomb attack in August on the UN headquarters in Baghdad, all international UN humanitarian personnel were withdrawn from Iraq, leaving national staff to conduct operations on the ground. During 2003–05 some 315,000 spontaneous returns by Iraqi refugees and asylum seekers and 496,000 returns by IDPs were reported. However, owing to the ongoing unstable security situation, UNHCR and the Iraqi Interim Government (inaugurated in June 2004) discouraged Iraqi refugees from returning home, and UNHCR warned governments hosting Iraqi refugees against repatriation, as well as advising continued protection of Iraqi asylum seekers. During 2006–07, owing to escalating violent sectarian unrest, it was reported that more than 1.5m. Iraqis had become newly displaced and that many people—including skilled and professional workers—had left Iraq, further inhibiting the national recovery process. In April 2007 an International Conference on Addressing the Humanitarian Needs of Refugees and Internally Displaced Persons inside Iraq and in Neighbouring Countries was convened in Geneva by the UN High Commissioner for Refugees. UNHCR remains highly concerned for foreign refugees remaining in Iraq (totalling 34,655 at end-2010). UNHCR has a small international presence (re-established in March 2008) in Baghdad, Basrah, Erbil, Kirkuk and Mosul, and 15 Protection and Assistance Centres, as well as 40 mobile teams. Through its network of offices UNHCR monitors population movements and the well-being of refugees, IDPs and returnees throughout Iraq. At 31 December 2010, the total Iraqi IDP population amounted to 1.3m., around 200,000 IDPs having returned to their homes during that year. The Office provides returnees (who numbered 28,896 in 2010), in accordance with a case-by-case approach, with counselling, limited transportation and livelihood grants. UNHCR's priorities in Iraq in 2012 were to continue to provide for basic needs and essential services, including maintaining supplies of potable water, and building, maintaining and improving shelter structures; to promote security from violence and exploitation; to improve the quality of the Government's registration and profiling activities; to facilitate access to legal assistance for people of concern; and to pursue durable solutions for populations of concern.

At the end of 2010 it was estimated that there were 1m. Iraqis sheltering in Syria (135,200 UNHCR-assisted) and 450,000 (30,100 UNHCR-protected) in Jordan, as well as smaller groups of Iraqis in other neighbouring countries, placing considerable strain on local infrastructure and services. UNHCR significantly strengthened its outreach capacity in countries bordering Iraq from 2008, when the Iraqi refugee population became particularly vulnerable owing to sharp increases in food and commodity prices. In 2010 UNHCR and the Syrian Government concluded a Co-operation Agreement providing the legal basis for the Office's activities in that country. UNHCR registered some 23,000 newly arrived Iraqi refugees in Syria during 2010. In 2010 UNHCR's activities in support of Iraqi populations of concern included the provision of remedial classes; outreach to parents by education volunteers; distribution of education grants; and support with access to health care. UNHCR has particularly focused assistance on vulnerable refugees with specific needs, such as female-headed households, children and the elderly. During 2007–end-2010 114,300 Iraqi refugees were referred for resettlement, and more than 60,700 left for third countries. At end-2010 some 29,956 asylum applications by Iraqis (5,141 UNHCR-assisted) in other countries were pending, globally. UNHCR has pursued accelerated departures and additional resettlement opportunities for the most vulnerable Iraqi refugees. The violent unrest that emerged in Syria in 2011, and was ongoing in early 2012, was expected to disrupt resettlement activities relating to Iraqi refugees there. During 2010 expenditure on the Iraq situation amounted to US $508m.

At the end of 2010 Kuwait was hosting 96,459 people of concern to UNHCR, mainly *bidoun* (stateless people, totalling 93,000), Iraqis and Palestinians.

In March 2002 UNHCR signed a new agreement with the Iranian Government to grant access to the large Afghan refugee population in detention centres throughout that country and to undertake a screening programme for asylum seekers, in order to deal with the problem of undocumented refugees. During 2008 the Iranian authorities implemented an on-line refugee registration process, referred to as Amayesh III, under which the details of more than 900,000 people were registered; identity cards were issued to refugees registered under Amayesh III, and, subsequently, temporary work-permits began to be issued to Amayesh III card holders with a view to finding temporary solutions in Iran for the Afghan refugees. UNHCR envisaged utilizing the data collated under Amayesh III in its planning processes. During 2002–11 more than 5.7m. refugees returned to Afghanistan from Iran and Pakistan; of these, 117,870 returned voluntarily, with UNHCR assistance, during 2010. At 31 December 2010 some 1.0m. UNHCR-assisted Afghan refugees remained in Iran (in addition to about 1m. unregistered Afghan migrants).

SUB-SAHARAN AFRICA

UNHCR has provided assistance to refugees and internally displaced populations in many parts of the continent where civil conflict, violations of human rights, drought, famine or environmental degradation have forced people to flee their home regions. The majority of African refugees and returnees are located in countries that are themselves suffering major economic problems and are thus unable to provide the basic requirements of the uprooted people. In March 2004 a UNHCR-sponsored Dialogue on Voluntary Repatriation and Sustainable Reintegration in Africa endorsed the creation of an international working group—comprising African Governments, UN agencies, the AU and other partners—to support the return and sustainable reintegration of refugees in several African countries, including Angola, Burundi, the Democratic Republic of the Congo (DRC), Eritrea, Liberia, Rwanda, Sierra Leone, Somalia and Sudan. At 31 December 2010 there were an estimated 10.2m. people of concern to UNHCR in sub-Saharan Africa.

The Horn of Africa, afflicted by famine and long-term internal conflict, has suffered large-scale population movements in recent decades. During 1992–mid-2006 more than 1m. Somalis (of whom about 485,000 received UNHCR assistance) returned to their country, having sought sanctuary in neighbouring states following the January 1991 overthrow of the former Somali president Siad Barre. The humanitarian situation in Somalia has remained highly insecure, and deteriorated significantly during 2007–12. In 2010 more than 200,000 people were newly displaced within Somalia, and a further 70,000 fled as new refugees to neighbouring countries. At 31 December 2010 the Somalian IDP population totalled an estimated 1.5m. Severe food insecurity in southern areas of Somalia that escalated in 2011—with a state of famine officially declared in two areas from July 2011–early February 2012—exacerbated further the ongoing humanitarian crisis in that country. At September 2011 an estimated 3.7m. Somalis were estimated to be food-insecure, and many Somali rural households were reported to have migrated in search of food and support towards the conflict-affected Somali capital, Mogadishu, and into neighbouring countries. At that time most of Somalia was designated by the UN at security level 5 ('high'), with Mogadishu and other south-central areas at level 6 ('extreme insecurity'): therefore there was very limited access for humanitarian workers. Following the July 2011 famine declaration UNHCR distributed more than 27,000 emergency assistance packages to 174,000 IDPs in southern Somalia and Mogadishu, and supported nearly 270,000 IDPs throughout the country through the provision of emergency relief items such as blankets, mattresses, kitchen sets, and plastic sheeting. UNHCR maintains a presence in Puntland and in Somaliland, but directs its Somalia programme from Nairobi, Kenya. UNHCR is responsible for co-ordinating the UN's emergency shelter and protection clusters in Somalia, and, with OCHA, co-leads the Puntland IDP Task Force, established in late 2010 with the aim of devising a comprehensive strategy aimed at improving the situation of local IDPs. The Office's priorities within Somalia for 2012 were to protect people of concern within larger mixed migratory flows; to prioritize the most vulnerable asylum seekers in need of resettlement; to provide subsistence allowances to people of concern with urgent needs; to support initiatives aimed at promoting self-reliance and livelihood opportunities; to facilitate access to schools and health facilities; and to reduce xenophobia in host communities towards refugees and asylum seekers.

There was at 31 December 2010 an estimated total Somali refugee population of 770,148, of whom 351,773 were in Kenya (all assisted by UNHCR) and 179,845 in Yemen (98,855 UNHCR-assisted). During 2007 Kenya enacted a Refugee Act, in accordance with which it was to assume a more active role in managing the registration and status determination of refugees. In November 2010 UNHCR appealed to the Kenyan authorities to cease the ongoing forcible return to Somalia of up to 8,000 Somali refugees accommodated hitherto in the Mandera camp in northeast Kenya. By February 2012 some 443,530 Somali refugees were accommodated at Kenya's Dadaab complex of camps, comprising the Hagadera, Dagahaley, Ifo, Ifo East, Ifo West and Kambioos camps; Hagadera (with 134,586 Somali residents) was at that time the largest refugee camp in the world. UNHCR was to continue to protect and assist Somalian refugees during 2012, while considering possibilities for voluntary repatriation, local integration and resettlement. There were an estimated 300,000 Kenyan IDPs at 31 December 2010.

At 31 December 2010 an estimated 387,288 Sudanese were exiled as refugees, mainly in Chad, Uganda, Kenya, and Ethiopia, owing to a history of civil unrest in southern Sudan and the emergence in early 2003 of a new conflict zone in the western Sudanese province of Darfur (see below). The Ugandan Government, hosting an estimated 19,382 Sudanese refugees at end-2010 (all UNHCR-assisted), has provided new resettlement sites and, jointly with UNHCR and other partners, has developed a Self-Reliance Strategy, which envisages achieving self-sufficiency for the long-term refugee population through integrating services for refugees into existing local structures. In 2006 the Ugandan Government adopted a new Refugee Act that included gender-based persecution as grounds for granting refugee status. At end-2010 there were some 125,598 IDPs in Uganda, and some 302,991 returned Ugandan IDPs. In February 2006 UNHCR and Sudan signed tripartite agreements with Ethiopia, the DRC and the Central African Republic to provide a legal framework for the repatriation of Sudanese refugees remaining in those countries. From 2008 violent attacks committed by Ugandan Lord's Resistance Army rebels on communities in the southern Sudan-DRC-Central African Republic (CAR) border region displaced numerous southern Sudanese people, and forced thousands of displaced DRC villagers northwards into Sudan. At 31 December 2010 some 103,798 Eritreans were sheltering in Sudan, of whom 66,278 were receiving UNHCR assistance.

In August 2011, following the independence in July of South Sudan, the Sudanese Government amended legislation to deprive individuals who acquired South Sudan nationality of Sudanese citizenship. UNHCR expressed concern over the implications of this for significant numbers of people of mixed Sudanese/South Sudanese origin living in border areas. UNHCR's activities in South Sudan in 2012 were to focus on strengthening relevant institutional and legal frameworks; combating sexual and gender-based violence; protecting people at risk of statelessness; and supporting refugees, returnees, IDPs and host communities by targeting assistance at vulnerable families such as female-headed households, and implementing livelihoods programmes and QIPs.

From April 2003 more than 200,000 refugees from Sudan's western Darfur region sought shelter across the Sudan-Chad border, having fled an alleged campaign of killing, rapes and destruction of property conducted by pro-government militias against the indigenous population. In addition, 2m.–3m. people became displaced within Darfur itself. The Office organized airlifts of basic household items to the camps, aimed to improve and expand refugees' access to sanitation, healthcare and education, to manage supplementary and therapeutic feeding facilities in order to combat widespread malnutrition, to provide psychosocial support to traumatized refugees, and to promote training and livelihood programmes. The Chad-Darfur operation has been hampered by severe water shortages resulting from the arid environment of the encampment areas, necessitating costly UNHCR deliveries of stored water, and by intense insecurity. A significant deterioration from 2006 in the security situation in the eastern areas of Chad bordering Darfur (where resources were already stretched to the limit), as well as in Darfur itself, led to further population displacement in the region, including the displacement of significant numbers of Chadians. At January 2012 some 39,500 Chadian refugees and Chadians in refugee-like situations were sheltering inside Darfur (of whom just under one-half were UNHCR-assisted), and there were also around 130,000 Chadian IDPs who had fled inwards from the Chad-Sudan border region. At end-December 2010 Chad was hosting 285,500 refugees from Darfur, accommodated in 12 UNHCR camps. UNHCR established a presence within western Darfur in June 2004, and in early 2012 the Office was providing protection assistance to around 2.7m. displaced and returned Darfurians, as well as Chadian refugees, in the region. Following the establishment of the AU/UN Hybrid Operation in Darfur (UNAMID) in December 2007, UNHCR opened a liaison office near the UNAMID base in northern Darfur. UNHCR teams have undertaken efforts to train Sudanese managers of camps in Darfur in the areas of protection and human rights. The Office has also established in the area a number of women's centres providing support to survivors of sexual violence, and several centres for IDP youths, as well as rehabilitating conflict-damaged schools. In 2012 a gradual shift in programming from a primarily protection-oriented, camp-based approach to pursuing durable solutions was under way. A continuing volatile security situation in the CAR from 2003 resulted in significant population displacement into southern border areas of Chad; by early 2012 more than 70,000 CAR refugees were accommodated by UNHCR in camps there, and at 31 December 2010 there were an estimated 192,529 IDPs inside the CAR.

UNHCR's activities in assisting refugees in West Africa have included a focus on the prevention of sexual and gender-based violence in refugee camps—a regional action plan to combat such violence was initiated in 2002—and collaboration with other agencies to ensure continuity between initial humanitarian assistance and long-term development support. UNHCR provided assistance to 120,000 people displaced by the extreme insecurity that developed in Côte d'Ivoire from September 2002. About 25,000 Côte d'Ivoire refugees fled to southern Liberia, and others sought shelter in Ghana, Guinea and Mali. In addition, between November and January 2003 an estimated 40,000 Liberian refugees in Côte d'Ivoire repatriated, in both spontaneous and partly UNHCR-assisted movements, having suffered harassment since the onset of the conflict. UNHCR initiated a number of QIPs aimed at rehabilitating the infrastructure of communities that were to receive returned Côte d'Ivoire refugees. At 31 December 2010 there were 514,515 IDPs in that country. As a consequence of unrest that erupted in Côte d'Ivoire following a disputed presidential election held in October–November 2010, an estimated 200,000 people became displaced from their homes in western Côte d'Ivoire, and some 150,000 Ivorian nationals fled to Liberia, during December 2010–April 2011. In response to the influx of Côte d'Ivoire refugees into Liberia, UNHCR facilitated the registration of the new refugees and mobilized the delivery of food aid and non-food relief items, as well as material for constructing a campsite. UNHCR planned to support some 55,000 Ivorian refugee returns, and 72,000 IDP returns in Côte d'Ivoire, during 2012.

Since 1993 the Great Lakes region of central Africa has experienced massive population displacement, causing immense operational challenges and demands on the resources of international humanitarian and relief agencies. During the late 1990s UNHCR resolved to work, in co-operation with UNDP and WFP, to rehabilitate areas previously inhabited by refugees in central African countries of asylum and undertook to repair roads, bridges and other essential transport infrastructure, improve water and sanitation facilities, and strengthen the education sector. However, the political stability of the Great Lakes region remained extremely uncertain, and, from August 1998, DRC government forces and rebels became involved in a civil war in which the militaries of several regional governments were also implicated. From late 1998 substantial numbers of DRC nationals fled to neighbouring countries (mainly Tanzania and Zambia) or were displaced within the DRC. Meanwhile, the DRC, in turn, was hosting a significant refugee population. In view of the conclusion, in December 2002, of a peace agreement providing for the staging of elections in the DRC after a transition period of 24 months, UNHCR planned for eventual mass refugee returns. The Office, in co-operation with other UN agencies, was to assist efforts to demobilize, disarm and repatriate former combatants. Owing to incessant rebel activity, insecurity continued to prevail, however, during 2003–early 2012, in north-eastern areas of the DRC, resulting in further population displacements. In September 2005 UNHCR and the DRC and Tanzanian Governments signed a tripartite agreement on facilitating refugee returns of DRC refugees from Tanzania, and, during 2005–early 2012 UNHCR assisted 60,000 such returns. The status of Tanzania's Nyaragusu camp, sheltering mainly refugees from the DRC, was under review in 2012. A tripartite agreement on assistance was concluded by the Burundian and Tanzanian Governments and UNHCR in August 2003. In April 2010 the UN High Commissioner for Refugees expressed gratitude to the Tanzanian authorities for offering citizenship to 162,000 long-standing Burundian refugees. In February 2012 the Burundi-Tanzania-UNHCR tripartite commission confirmed that Tanzania's Mtabila camp, hosting 38,378 Burundian refugees, would close at the end of 2012, and that its residents would be repatriated to Burundi during April–November. UNHCR concluded similar tripartite accords in 2003 with the Rwandan Government and other states hosting Rwandan refugees, paving the way subsequently for significant voluntary refugee returns to Rwanda. In 2010 UNHCR assisted a total of 10,900 refugee returns to that country. The major populations of concern to UNHCR in the Great Lakes region at 31 December 2010 were, provisionally, as follows: 1.7m. IDPs, 460,740 returned IDPs and 166,366 refugees in the DRC; 157,167 IDPs in Burundi; 55,398 refugees in Rwanda; and a refugee population of 109,286 in Tanzania, very significantly reduced from 602,088 at end-2004. At the end of 2010 some 124,244 DRC refugees (all of whom were UNHCR-assisted) were sheltering in the Republic of the Congo. Long-standing DRC refugees in the Republic of the Congo are largely self-sufficient, with many refugees working as farmers and fishermen; the Office has aimed to promote the local integration of those unwilling to return to the DRC.

In September 2010 a regional conference on refugee protection and international migration, convened in Dar es Salaam, Tanzania, adopted an action plan to address mixed movements and irregular migration from eastern Africa, the Horn of Africa and the Great Lakes region to southern Africa; this was being implemented during 2011–12.

It was estimated that in all more than 4.3m. Angolans were displaced from their homes during the 1980s and 1990s, owing to long-term civil conflict. Following the signing of the Luanda Peace Agreement in April 2002 between the Angolan Government and rebels of the União National para a Independência Total de Angola, UNHCR made preparations for the voluntary repatriation of a projected 400,000 Angolan refugees sheltering elsewhere in southern Africa. By the end of 2004 the Office had rehabilitated the nine main repatriation corridors into Angola, and by the end of 2005 a total of nearly 4.4m. IDPs, refugees and demobilized fighters had reportedly returned home. UNHCR has assisted the Angolan Government with the development of a Sustainable Reintegration Initiative for returned refugees. From May 2009–early 2011 Angola forcibly returned home some 160,000 DRC refugees. In response to the initial forced repatriations, some 51,000 Angolan refugees were expelled from the DRC to Angola during 2009. An Angola-DRC agreement to suspend the mutual expulsions and enter into consultations, concluded in October 2009, was subsequently not adhered to by the Angolan authorities. At 31 December 2010 an estimated 134,858 Angolans were still sheltering in neighbouring countries, including 79,817 in the DRC and 25,265 in Zambia. HIV/AIDS- and mine-awareness training have been made available by UNHCR at refugee reception centres.

Zimbabwe was the country of origin of the largest number of asylum-seekers world-wide in 2010, with 149,400 new applications made by Zimbabwean nationals in that year.

THE AMERICAS AND THE CARIBBEAN

UNHCR's activities in Central and South America are currently guided by the Mexico Plan of Action (MPA), adopted in November 2004. The MPA aims to address ongoing population displacement problems in Latin America, with a particular focus on the humanitarian crisis in Colombia and the border areas of its neighbouring countries (see below), and the increasing numbers of refugees concentrated in urban centres in the region. The Cities of Solidarity pillar of the MPA assists UNHCR with facilitating the local integration and self-sufficiency of people in urban areas who require international protection; the Borders of Solidarity pillar addresses protection at international borders; and the Resettlement in Solidarity pillar promotes co-operation in resettling refugees. In November 2010 regional leaders adopted the Brasília Declaration on the Protection of Refugees and Stateless Persons in the Americas, in which they committed to revitalizing the MPA pillars.

UNHCR supports the Regional Conference on Migration (RCM, also know as the 'Puebla Process'), which was launched in March 1996 to promote regional co-operation on migration, and comprises the governments of Belize, Canada, Costa Rica, the Dominican Republic, El Salvador, Guatemala, Honduras, Mexico, Nicaragua, Panama and the USA. A Regional Conference on Refugee Protection and International Migration in the Americas, held in San José, Costa Rica, in November 2009, addressed key protection challenges in the context of an environment characterized by complex mixed migratory population movements.

In 1999 the Colombian Government approved an operational plan proposed by UNHCR to address a massive population displacement that had arisen in that country (escalating significantly from 1997), as a consequence of ongoing long-term internal conflict and alleged human rights abuses committed by paramilitary groups. In recent years the military capacity of the security forces has advanced, and demobilization of militants was undertaken during 2003–06. None the less, insecurity and population displacement have persisted within Colombia, exacerbated by a rise in organized crime and by the emergence of new illegal armed groups; some 100,000 Colombians were newly displaced in 2010. Indigenous and Afro-Colombian peoples in remote, rural districts, particularly along the Pacific Coast, in central areas, in Antioquia, and in border areas neighbouring Ecuador and Venezuela, have been particularly vulnerable. Intra-urban displacement among 1.7m. Colombian urban IDPs has also caused concern, with gang conflict contributing to an environment where sexual and gender-based violence, forced recruitment, and extortion have become commonplace. Measures, including the Government's Victims and Land Restitution Bill, signed in June 2011, have been introduced to enable the victims of forced displacement to claim reparations for and restitution of their holdings. Within Colombia UNHCR's protection activities have included ensuring an adequate, functioning legal framework for the protection of IDPs and enabling domestic institutions to supervise compliance with national legislation regarding the rights of IDPs; strengthening representation for IDPs and other vulnerable people; and developing local protection networks. UNHCR has also advised on public policy formulation in the areas of emergency response, IDP registration, health, education, housing, income-generation and protection of policy rights; and has endeavoured to promote durable solutions for IDPs, in particular local integration. The Office has also co-operated with UNICEF to improve the provision of education to displaced children. UNHCR works to provide legal protection and educational and medical support to around 500,000 Colombians who have fled to but not sought asylum in neighbouring countries. The Office's strategy for supporting countries receiving displaced Colombians (of whom the majority were not registered as refugees) has included border-monitoring activities, entailing the early warning of potential refugee movements, and provision of detailed country-of-origin data. UNHCR has offered technical assistance in relation to the Colombia-Ecuador Neighborhood Commission, established in 1989 and reactivated, following a period of inactivity, in November 2010. At the end of 2010 around 3.7m. IDPs within Colombia remained of concern to UNHCR. By that time an estimated 120,403 Colombians (52,059 UNHCR-assisted) were living as refugees in Ecuador, while 204,467 (21,067 UNHCR-assisted) Colombians were sheltering in Venezuela; the majority of these (in both countries) had not sought official protection but were living in 'refugee-like' situations. In 2012 UNHCR's presence in Colombia included 10 field offices and a branch office in Bogotá.

Following the devastating earthquake that struck Haiti in January 2010, UNHCR provided assistance to the international humanitarian response operation in the areas of camp registration and profiling matters; shelter co-ordination; and supporting OHCHR in its efforts to assist the displaced population outside Port-au-Prince and earthquake survivors living outside registered camps. UNHCR also implemented a number of QIPs, and provided material support to Haitian evacuees in the neighbouring Dominican Republic. In June 2010 UNHCR opened an office in Santo Domingo, Dominican Republic. In July 2011 UNHCR and OHCHR urged governments to suspend all involuntary returns to Haiti, owing to the ongoing fragile protection environment in that country and continuing displacement of some 680,000 people; the IDPs remained in more than 1,000 tented camps in earthquake-affected areas. During 2012 UNHCR was to support the authorities in reforming systems for recording civil documentation, including the registration of births, and in improving the legal framework relating to nationality. UNHCR's activities in the Dominican Republic in 2012 were to include assisting the authorities with addressing a backlog of asylum claims, helping to provide birth certificates and civil documentation to undocumented Haitian migrants and people of Haitian descent, to enable their access to legal protection and also to basic services. The Office was also to implement QIPs aimed at income generation and local infrastructure improvement in support of the most vulnerable undocumented Haitians in the Dominican Republic.

Canada and the USA are major countries of resettlement for refugees. UNHCR provides counselling and legal services for asylum seekers in these countries. At 31 December 2010 the estimated refugee populations totalled 165,549 in Canada and 264,574 in the USA, while asylum seekers numbered 51,025 and 6,285, respectively.

CENTRAL AND SOUTH-EASTERN EUROPE

The political changes in Central and Eastern Europe during the early 1990s resulted in a dramatic increase in the number of asylum seekers and displaced people in the region. UNHCR was the agency designated by the UN Secretary-General to lead the UN relief operation to assist those affected by the conflict in the former Yugoslavia. It was responsible for the supply of food and other humanitarian aid to the besieged capital of Bosnia and Herzegovina, Sarajevo, and to Muslim and Croatian enclaves in the country, under the armed escort of the UN Protection Force. Assistance was provided not only to Bosnian refugees in Croatia and displaced people within Bosnia and Herzegovina's borders, but also, in order to forestall further movements of people, to civilians whose survival was threatened. The operation was often seriously hampered by armed attacks (resulting, in some cases, in fatalities), distribution difficulties and underfunding from international donors. The Dayton peace agreement, which was signed in December 1995, bringing an end to the conflict, secured the right for all refugees and displaced persons freely to choose their place of residence within the new territorial arrangements of Bosnia and Herzegovina. Thus, the immediate effect of the peace accord was further population displacement, including a mass exodus of almost the entire Serb population of Sarajevo. Under the peace accord, UNHCR was responsible for planning and implementing the repatriation of all Bosnian refugees and displaced persons, then estimated at 2m.; however, there were still immense obstacles to freedom of movement, in particular for minorities wishing to return to an area dominated by a different politico-ethnic faction. Returns by refugees and IDPs (including significant numbers of refugees returning to areas where they represented minority ethnic communities) accelerated from 2000, owing to an improvement in security conditions. In July 2002 the heads of state of Bosnia and Herzogovina, Croatia and the Federal Republic of Yugoslavia (FRY, which was renamed Serbia and Montenegro in 2003, and was divided into separate sovereign states of Montenegro and Serbia in June 2006) met in Sarajevo with a view to resolving a number of outstanding issues, including the return of remaining refugees. In January 2005 the concerned parties adopted the Sarajevo Declaration, committing to resolve remaining population displacement issues through the 'Sarajevo Process' (also referred to as the '3x3 Initiative'). In March 2010 the foreign affairs ministers of Bosnia and Herzegovina, Croatia, Montenegro and Serbia convened in Belgrade, Serbia, at the International Conference: Durable Solutions for Refugees and IDPs: Co-operation Among Countries of the Region, to address continuing obstacles to durable solutions for those persons in the region who were continuing to live in a protracted refugee situation. The repossession by their rightful owners and reconstruction of illegally appropriated properties have been key issues for returned refugees to the region. In January 2011 the UN High Commissioner for Refugees appointed a personal envoy to assist the governments of Bosnia and Herzegovina, Croatia, Montenegro and Serbia in developing a binding common commitment and regional programme to address the protracted population displacement in the region. By December 2010 there was still an estimated total Bosnian refugee population of 63,004, of whom some 25,614 were receiving assistance from UNHCR. The majority of the Bosnian refugee population were in Germany and Serbia. At end-2010 there were also 113,365 IDPs of concern to UNHCR in Bosnia and Herzegovina. In 2012 the Office aimed to improve access to documentation (civil status documentation and late birth registration) for apparently stateless people in the region, with a particular focus on the Roma minority.

In the late 1990s attacks by Serbian forces against members of a separatist movement in the southern Serbian province of Kosovo and Metohija resulted in an estimated 1.3m. Kosovar Albanians being displaced. In June 1999, following a cease-fire accord and an agreement by the FRY to withdraw all forces and paramilitary units, UNHCR initiated a large-scale registration operation of Kosovar refugees and emergency operation to assist the displaced population within Kosovo. In mid-2000 UNHCR scaled down its emergency humanitarian activities in Kosovo and provided a UN Humanitarian Co-ordinator to oversee the transition to long-term reconstruction and development, in co-operation with the UN Interim Administration Mission in Kosovo (UNMIK). UNHCR and OSCE have periodically jointly assessed the situation of minority communities in Kosovo; minority returns (numbering during 2000–11 around 13,250 from Serbia to Kosovo, and 3,857 returning to places of origin within Kosovo) and integration have reportedly been impeded by discrimination against and intimidation of minorities in the province. Throughout the region UNHCR is concerned to reduce and prevent statelessness. The Office has undertaken a civil registration programme for undocumented IDPs in Kosovo and Serbia, particularly members of Roma, Ashkali and Egyptian communities in Kosovo, deemed to be at risk of statelessness. At the end of 2010 there were still 228,442 IDPs in Serbia. In addition, Serbia was hosting 73,608 refugees, of whom 21,047 were from Bosnia and Herzegovina and 52,483 from Croatia. UNHCR has expanded its durable solution programmes for IDPs in Serbia, by assisting with the construction of social housing, by providing cash grants to help people to move to the new accommodation, and by organizing self-reliance projects. At the end of 2010 more than 18,000 people remained displaced within Kosovo, of whom the majority were in the Mitrovica area. From 2010 forced returns from western European countries outnumbered voluntary returns to Kosovo, challenging Kosovo's capacity for absorption, reintegration, and its protection capabilities. Some 2,500 minority returns were envisaged in 2012.

EASTERN EUROPE

In June 2007, following the publication in June 2006 of its *10 Point Plan* for assisting member states with the management of refugee protection and mixed migration, UNHCR issued a '10 Point Plan of Action on Refugee Protection and Mixed Migration for Countries along the Eastern and South-Eastern Borders of European Union Member States', providing a framework for discussion between UNHCR and the governments of Belarus, Moldova and Ukraine, and also clarifying UNHCR's operational relationship in that sub-region with the International Organization for Migration and non-governmental organizations. During 2007 UNHCR undertook a study on the local integration of refugees in Belarus, Moldova and Ukraine, at the request of those countries' governments.

In the early 1990s UNHCR co-ordinated international humanitarian efforts to assist some 500,000 people displaced by the conflict between Armenia and Azerbaijan. Of the 12 emergency camps established, the last were closed in December 2007. At 31 December 2010 Azerbaijan was still supporting an IDP population totalling 592,860. During 2011 UNHCR prioritized strengthening the national asylum system; promoting refugee self-sufficiency, particularly among those living in urban environments; giving advocacy for the rights of IDPs; and working for durable solutions fo IDPs, including local integration.

In Georgia, where almost 300,000 people left their homes as a result of civil conflict from 1991, UNHCR has attempted to encourage income-generating activities among the displaced population, to increase the Georgian Government's capacity to support those people and to assist the rehabilitation of people returning to their areas of origin. In July 2008 the Georgian authorities adopted a National IDP Action Plan, drafted with support from UNHCR, which was expected to provide a basis for future durable solutions. During August of that year UNHCR provided humanitarian assistance, including the distribution of blankets, jerry-cans and kitchen sets, to people affected by a period of violent insecurity that escalated in July between Georgian and South Ossetian separatist forces, further intensifying in early August when Georgia launched a military offensive on the South Ossetian capital Tskhinvali, a stronghold of the separatists, and Russian forces responded by supporting the South Ossetian counter-attack and by crossing into Georgian territory. The heightened insecurity resulted in the temporary displacement of some 134,000 people within Georgia and of nearly 35,000 from South to North Ossetia (Russian Federation). In the following month, once the conflict had abated, UNHCR teams began regular visits to assess the humanitarian situation in villages in the Georgia–South Ossetia buffer zone area north of the Georgian town of Gori. More than 32,000 of those who had fled from South to North Ossetia returned to their homes swiftly. There were 359,716 Georgian IDPs at 31 December 2010, including about 22,000 people who remained displaced by the August 2008 conflict. In 2008 Georgia was the focus of a pilot project for UNHCR's Global Needs Assessment (formally inaugurated in 2009, see above).

In recent years UNHCR has conducted regular missions into the Russian separatist republic of Chechnya (the Chechen Republic of Ichkeriya) to monitor and support the reintegration of more than 200,000 IDPs who had fled civil unrest since the mid-1990s. UNHCR has also conducted interviews of returnees to Chechnya from neighbouring Ingushetiya in order to ensure that returns have been voluntary rather than enforced. It was estimated at end-2010 that around 6,500 Chechen refugees remained in Ingushetiya. At the end of 2010 there were reportedly still around 30,000 displaced people within Chechnya. There were also an estimated 3,500 Chechen IDPs in Dagestan. During 2003–10 some 255,000 IDPs were reported to have returned to Chechnya from elsewhere in the Russian Federation.

CO-OPERATION WITH OTHER ORGANIZATIONS

UNHCR works closely with other UN agencies, intergovernmental organizations and non-governmental organizations (NGOs) to increase the scope and effectiveness of its operations. Within the UN system UNHCR co-operates, principally, with the WFP in the distribution of food aid, UNICEF and WHO in the provision of family welfare and child immunization programmes, OCHA in the delivery of emergency humanitarian relief, UNDP in development-related activities and the preparation of guidelines for the continuum of emergency assistance to development programmes, and the Office of the UN High Commissioner for Human Rights. UNHCR also has close working relationships with the International Committee of the Red Cross and the International Organization for Migration. UNHCR planned to engage with nearly 700 NGOs in 2012–13. In recent years UNHCR has pursued a strategy to engage private sector businesses in supporting its activities through the provision of donations (cash contributions and 'in kind'), of loaned expertise, and of marketing related to designated causes.

TRAINING

UNHCR organizes training programmes and workshops to enhance the capabilities of field workers and non-UNHCR staff, in the following areas: the identification and registration of refugees; people-orientated planning; resettlement procedures and policies; emergency response and management; security awareness; stress management; and the dissemination of information through the electronic media.

Finance

The United Nations' regular budget finances a proportion of UNHCR's administrative expenditure. The majority of UNHCR's programme expenditure (about 98%) is funded by voluntary contributions, mainly from governments. The Private Sector and Public Affairs Service aims to increase funding from non-governmental donor sources, for example by developing partnerships with foundations and corporations. Following approval of the Unified Annual Programme Budget any subsequently identified requirements are managed in the form of Supplementary Programmes, financed by separate appeals. UNHCR's projected funding requirements for 2011 totalled US $3,320.0m.

Publications

Global Trends (annually).

Refugees (quarterly, in English, French, German, Italian, Japanese and Spanish).

Refugee Resettlement: An International Handbook to Guide Reception and Integration.

Refugee Survey Quarterly.

Refworld (annually).

Sexual and Gender-based Violence Against Refugees, Returnees and Displaced Persons: Guidelines for Prevention and Response.

The State of the World's Refugees (every 2 years).

Statistical Yearbook (annually).

UNHCR Handbook for Emergencies.

Press releases, reports.

Statistics

POPULATIONS OF CONCERN TO UNHCR BY REGION
('000 persons, at 31 December 2010, provisional figures)

	Refugees*	Asylum seekers	Returned refugees†	Others of concern‡
Africa	2,409	330	43	7,395
Asia	5,475	72	152	10,172
Europe	1,587	303	2	1,101
Latin America/ Caribbean	374	99	71	3,672
North America	430	57	—	—
Oceania	34	3	—	—
Total	10,550	837	198	22,340

* Includes persons recognized as refugees under international law, and also people receiving temporary protection and assistance outside their country but who have not been formally recognized as refugees.

† Refugees who returned to their place of origin during 2010.

‡ Mainly internally displaced persons (IDPs), former IDPs who returned to their place of origin during 2010, and stateless persons.

POPULATIONS OF CONCERN TO UNHCR BY COUNTRY*
('000 persons, at 31 December 2010, provisional figures)

	Refugees†	Asylum seekers	Returned refugees†	Others of concern†
Africa				
Burundi	29.4	12.1	4.8	158.2
Cameroon	104.3	2.4	—	—
CAR	21.6	1.2	0.0	192.5
Chad	347.9	0.1	0.0	181.0
DRC	161.3	0.9	16.6	2,182.1
Congo, Rep.	133.1	5.5	0.1	—
Côte d'Ivoire	26.2	0.3	0.0	537.1
Ethiopia	154.3	1.0	0.0	—
Kenya	402.9	28.0	0.3	320.0
Somalia	1.9	24.1	0.0	1,464.0
South Africa	57.9	171.7	—	—
Sudan	178.3	6.0	7.0	1,767.1
Tanzania	109.3	1.2	—	162.3
Uganda	135.8	20.8	0.1	428.6
Asia				
Afghanistan	6.4	0.0	118.0	1,193.5
Bangladesh	229.3	—	—	—
China, People's Republic‡	301.0	0.1	0.0	—
Egypt	95.1	25.1	14.3	0.1
India	184.8	3.7	—	—
Iran	1,073.4	1.8	0.0	—
Iraq	34.6	3.1	28.9	1,758.3
Jordan	450.9	2.2	—	—
Malaysia	81.5	11.3	—	120.0
Myanmar	—	—	—	859.4
Nepal	89.8	0.9	0.0	800.6
Pakistan	1,900.6	2.1	0.0	2,138.9
Sri Lanka	0.2	0.1	5.1	440.0
Syria	1,005.5	2.4	—	300.0
Thailand	96.7	10.3	—	542.5
Yemen	190.1	2.6	—	315.7
Europe				
Azerbaijan	1.9	0.0	—	594.9
Bosnia and Herzegovina	7.0	0.2	0.9	171.4
Estonia	0.0	0.0	—	101.0
France	200.7	48.6	—	1.1
Georgia	0.6	0.0	0.0	361.5
Germany	594.3	52.0	—	24.2
Latvia	0.1	0.1	—	326.9
Russian Federation	4.9	1.5	0.0	126.1
Serbia	73.6	0.2	0.4	238.7
Sweden	82.6	18.6	—	9.3
United Kingdom	238.2	14.9	—	0.2
Latin America/ Caribbean				
Colombia	0.2	0.2	0.0	3,672.1
Ecuador	121.2	49.9	—	—
Venezuela	201.5	15.9	—	—
North America				
Canada	165.5	51.0	—	—
USA	264.6	6.3	—	—

* The list includes only those countries having 100,000 or more persons of concern to UNHCR.

† See table above for definitions.

‡ Excluding Hong Kong Special Administrative Region.

ORIGIN OF MAJOR POPULATIONS OF CONCERN TO UNHCR*
('000 persons, 31 December 2010, provisional figures)

Origin	Population of concern to UNHCR
Afghanistan	4,404.5
Colombia	4,128.0
Iraq	3,387.5
DRC	2,718.6
Somalia	2,256.8
Pakistan	2,198.9
Sudan	2,185.2

* Data exclude (some 4,966,664 at 31 December 2010) Palestinian refugees who come under the mandate of UNRWA, although (at 31 December 2010) 96,545 Palestinians who are outside the UNRWA area of operation, for example those in Iraq and Libya, are considered to be of concern to UNHCR.

United Nations Human Settlements Programme— UN-Habitat

Address: POB 30030, 00100 Nairobi, Kenya.

Telephone: (20) 7623120; **fax:** (20) 7623477; **e-mail:** infohabitat@unhabitat.org; **internet:** www.unhabitat.org.

UN-Habitat was established as the United Nations Centre for Human Settlements, UNCHS-Habitat, in October 1978 to service the intergovernmental Commission on Human Settlements. It became a full UN programme in January 2002, serving as a focus for human settlements and sustainable urban development activities in the UN system. UN-Habitat was mandated by the Second UN Conference on Human Settlements, Habitat II, which was held in Istanbul, Turkey, in June 1996, to pursue the Habitat Agenda, focusing on the objectives of adequate shelter for all and sustainable human settlements in an urbanizing world; further mandates are derived from the September 2000 UN Millennium Forum Declaration and Agenda for Action, and from the June 2001 Habitat II review conference's Declaration on Cities and other Human Settlements in the New Millennium.

Organization

(April 2012)

GOVERNING COUNCIL

The Governing Council (formerly the Commission on Human Settlements) meets once every two years and has 58 members, serving for four years. Sixteen members are from Africa, 13 from Asia, 10 from Latin America and the Caribbean, six from eastern European countries, and 13 from western European and other countries. The Committee of Permanent Representatives to UN-Habitat, which meets at least four times a year, functions as an inter-sessional subsidiary body of the Governing Council. The Governing Council reports to the UN General Assembly through ECOSOC.

SECRETARIAT

The Secretariat services the Governing Council, implements its resolutions and ensures the integration and co-ordination of technical co-operation, research and policy advice. It comprises the Office of the Executive Director; the Regional and Technical Co-operation Division; the Monitoring and Research Division; the Shelter and Sustainable Human Settlements Development Division; and the Financing Human Settlements Division.

Executive Director: JOAN CLOS (Spain).

REGIONAL OFFICES

Regional Office for Africa and the Arab States: POB 30030, Nairobi, Kenya 00100; tel. (20) 623221; fax (20) 623904; e-mail roaas@unhabitat.org; internet www.unhabitat.org/roaas.

Regional Office for Asia and the Pacific: ACROS Fukuoka Building, 8th Floor 1-1-1 Tenjin, Chuo-ku Fukuoka 810, Japan; tel. (92) 724-7121; fax (92) 724-7124; e-mail habitat.fukuoka@unhabitat.org; internet www.fukuoka.unhabitat.org.

Regional Office for Latin America and the Caribbean: Rua Rumânia 20, Cosme Velho 22240-140, Rio de Janeiro, Brazil; tel. (21) 3235-8550; fax (21) 3235-8566; e-mail rolac@habitat-lac.org; internet www.onuhabitat.org.

In addition, there are Liaison and Information Offices in Geneva, Switzerland; Brussels, Belgium; Budapest, Hungary; New York, USA; Beijing, the People's Republic of China; Moscow, Russia; and Chennai, India. A Best Practices Offices for City-to-City Co-operation is located in Barcelona, Spain. Habitat Programme Managers are located in almost 40 UNDP country offices.

Activities

Since 2008 at least one-half of the world's population has been resident in towns and cities (compared with about one-third in 1950; and forecast to rise to 70% by 2050). Of the world's urban population, about one-third (about 1,000m. people) lives in slums without access to basic sanitation. Many local authorities do not have adequate mechanisms to monitor either formal or informal urban growth in a systematic manner. UN-Habitat supports and conducts capacity-building and operational research, provides technical co-operation and policy advice, and disseminates information with the aim of strengthening the development and management of human settlements. It is mandated to support the UN Millennium Development Goals (MDGs) of halving, by 2015, the proportion of people without sustainable access to safe drinking water and improving significantly the lives of at least 100m. slum dwellers by 2020.

In June 1996 representatives of 171 national governments and of more than 500 municipal authorities attending Habitat II adopted a Global Plan of Action (the 'Habitat Agenda'), which incorporated detailed programmes of action to realize economic and social development and environmental sustainability, and endorsed the conference's objectives of ensuring 'adequate shelter for all' and 'sustainable human settlements development in an urbanizing world'. UN-Habitat provides the leadership and serves as a focal point for the implementation of the Agenda. It collaborates with national governments, private sector and non-governmental institutions and UN bodies to achieve the objectives of Agenda 21 (see below). A special session of the UN General Assembly, entitled 'Istanbul + 5', was held in June 2001 to report on the implementation of the recommendations of the Habitat II conference. The special session adopted a Declaration on Cities and Other Human Settlements in the New Millennium that reaffirmed commitment to the objectives of the Habitat Agenda and urged an intensification of efforts towards eradicating widespread poverty, which was identified as the main impediment to achieving these, and towards promoting good governance. The special session also resolved to increase international co-operation in several other areas, including addressing HIV/AIDS, urban crime and violence, environmental issues, and the problems posed by conflicts and refugees; and recommended the enhancement of the status and role of UNCHS (Habitat). Consequently, in December 2001 the General Assembly authorized the elevation of the body to a full UN programme with a strengthened mandate to address and implement the Habitat Agenda and, in January 2002, UN-Habitat was inaugurated.

UN-Habitat's activities over the six-year period 2008–13 are governed by a medium-term strategic and institutional plan, adopted in April 2007, that aims by 2013 to help establish the necessary conditions for arresting the growth of slums and to set the stage for the subsequent reduction in and reversal of the number of slum dwellers world-wide. The plan focuses on: advocacy and monitoring; affordable land and housing; environmentally sound basic infrastructure and services; participatory urban planning, management and governance; and innovative human settlements finance, with each focus area accompanied by a set of strategic objectives and achievement indicators. In addition, a peer review mechanism comprising several Habitat Agenda partners was to be established during the period of the plan as a means of monitoring progress and achievement. UN-Habitat's work programme for 2012–13 was being implemented through the following four sub-programmes: Shelter and sustainable human development; Monitoring the Habitat Agenda; Regional and technical co-operation; and Human settlements financing.

In February 2009 UN-Habitat and the International Olympic Committee signed a Memorandum of Understanding aimed at encouraging the empowerment through sport of young people living in vulnerable and disadvantaged communities world-wide. It was envisaged that the agreement would support development through sport and would promote the MDGs to alleviate poverty and to improve the living conditions of slum dwellers everywhere. (More than one-half of slum dwellers are young people.) A follow-up committee was to meet annually to develop further a programme of international co-operation between the two organizations. In October 2010 UN-Habitat signed a partnership agreement with the University for Peace to support a Masters degree in Sustainable Urban Governance and Peace.

In June 2011 a UN-HABITAT Charter of Values was launched; this was to provide a framework underpinning joint activities with private sector partners.

UN-Habitat has participated in the preparatory process for the UN Conference on Sustainable Development (Rio+20), scheduled to be held in June 2012, in Rio de Janeiro, Brazil. In April 2011 the Governing Council adopted a resolution on 'Sustainable urban development through expanding equitable access to land, housing, basic services and infrastructure', underpinning UN-Habitat's contribution to Rio+20.

SHELTER AND SUSTAINABLE HUMAN SETTLEMENT DEVELOPMENT

The UN Housing Rights Programme (UNHRP), launched jointly by UN-Habitat and OHCHR in April 2002, supports states and other stakeholders with the implementation of their Habitat Agenda commitments to realizing the universal right to adequate housing. In 2004 UN-Habitat established an Advisory Group on Forced Evictions, with a mandate to monitor forced evictions of people with no or inadequate legal security of tenure, and to identify and promote alternatives including in situ upgrading of accommodation and negotiated resettlement. UN-Habitat's programme on Rapid Urban Sector Profiling for Sustainability (RUSPS) involves an accelerated action-oriented assessment of urban conditions in particular cities in seven thematic areas (governance; slums; gender and HIV/AIDS; urban environment; local economic development; basic urban services; and cultural heritage), with a view to developing and implementing tailor-made urban poverty reduction policies. Through its Strengthening Training Institutions programme UN-Habitat supports regional and national training institutions by organizing regional workshops to develop capacity-building strategies and to analyse training need assessments; by designing new training manuals and other tools; by developing, jointly with partners, generic training manuals and handbooks; by educating trainers; and by supporting institutions with the design and implementation of national training programmes. In addition, UN-Habitat supports training and other activities designed to strengthen management development (in particular in the provision and maintenance of services and facilities) at local and community level.

UN-Habitat implements a programme entitled 'Localizing Agenda 21' (LA21), to assist local authorities in developing countries to achieve more sustainable development and to address local environmental and infrastructure-related problems. The Programme targets secondary cities and supports city-to-city co-operation initiatives. A Sustainable Cities Programme, operated jointly with UNEP, is concerned with incorporating environmental issues into urban planning and management, in order to ensure sustainable and equitable development. The Programme is active in some 30 cities world-wide, although a prepared series of policy guidelines is used in many others. Some 95% of the Programme's resources are spent at city level to strengthen the capacities of municipal authorities and their public-, private- and community-sector partners in the field of environmental planning and management, with the objective that the concepts and approaches of the Programme are replicated throughout the region.

An Urban Management Programme aims to strengthen the contribution of cities and towns in developing countries towards human development, including economic growth, social advancements, the reduction of poverty and the improvement of the environment. The Programme (active in 140 cities in 58 countries) is an international technical co-operation project, of which UN-Habitat is the executing agency, the World Bank is an associated agency, while UNDP provides core funding and monitoring. The Programme is operated through regional offices, in collaboration with bilateral and multilateral support agencies, and brings together national and local authorities, community leaders and representatives of the private sector to consider specific issues and solutions to urban problems. The related Safer Cities Programme was initiated in 1996 to prevent and address urban violence through capacity-building at local government and city level. In November 2010 UN-Habitat, working with UNIFEM, now part of UN Women, inaugurated a Global Safe Cities for Women and Girls Programme. Pilot projects were to be implemented in the poorest areas of five cities: Quito (Ecuador), Cairo (Egypt), New Delhi (India), Port Moresby (Papua New Guinea) and Kigali (Rwanda). UN-Habitat's Global Campaign for Secure Tenure and Global Campaign on Urban Governance both emphasize urban poverty reduction.

UN-Habitat is supporting the development of a Sustainable Urban Development Network (SUD-Net) which aims to mobilize local, regional and global partners to achieve a multilateral and interdisciplinary approach to sustainable urban development. SUD-Net envisaged strengthening capacity building at local level, involving the local community in decision-making, and promoting knowledge sharing and the exchange of good practices. A Cities in Climate Change Initiative was established in 2008 as a component of SUD-Net. It aimed to work with local governments and other bodies involved in the environmental planning and management process in order to address problems relating to climate change and to reduce greenhouse gas emissions. UN-Habitat was actively involved in the 15th Conference of the Parties (COP) of the UN Framework Convention on Climate Change (UNFCCC), which was held in Copenhagen, Denmark, in December 2009. In particular, it urged greater support to cities working to reduce the emission of harmful gases and to counter the impact of climate change. In September 2010 UN-Habitat, with UNEP and the World Bank, launched an International Standard for Determining Greenhouse Gas Emissions for Cities. In December, prior to the 16th COP of the UNFCCC, held in Cancun, Mexico, UN-Habitat joined with five other UN agencies in declaring their commitment to work to counter climate change.

UN-Habitat contributes to relief, rehabilitation and development activities undertaken by the UN in areas affected by regional and civil conflict. In December 2003 UN-Habitat signed a Memorandum of Understanding with UNHCR that covered several areas of co-operation including sheltering refugees and returnees, settlement and infrastructure planning, and property rights. Within the inter-agency emergency response system UN-Habitat provides shelter, water and sanitation under the Emergency Shelter and Early Recovery 'clusters'. UN-Habitat also provides assessment and technical support in the aftermath of natural disasters and is concerned with sustainable reconstruction, capacity-building, risk reduction and emergency preparedness activities and flood vulnerability reduction. Reconstruction and recovery activities are co-ordinated by the Risk and Disaster Management Unit. In November 2010 UN-Habitat concluded a technical assessment of the damage and housing needs resulting from extensive flooding in Pakistan in July–August.

In September 2011 the first annual 'Shelter Academy', a gathering of mayors and senior local government officials from Africa, Asia and Latin America, met in Rotterdam, Netherlands, to discuss the challenges that climate change presents to port cities.

FINANCING HUMAN SETTLEMENTS

UN-Habitat participates in implementing the human settlements component of Agenda 21, which was adopted at the UN Conference on Environment and Development in June 1992, and is also responsible for the chapter of Agenda 21 that refers to solid waste management and sewage-related issues. The Settlement Infrastructure and Environment Programme was initiated in 1992 to support developing countries in improving the environment of human settlements through policy advice and planning, infrastructure management and enhancing awareness of environmental and health concerns in areas such as water, sanitation, waste management and transport. In October 2002 UN-Habitat launched a Water and Sanitation Trust Fund, with the aim of supporting the goal of halving the proportion of the world's population lacking access to basic sanitation or clean water by 2015, that was set by the World Summit on Sustainable Development (WSSD), held in Johannesburg, South Africa, during August–September 2002 to assess strategies for strengthening the implementation of Agenda 21. The Water and Sanitation Programme promotes policy dialogue, information exchange, water education and awareness-raising; monitors progress towards achieving the MDG targets on improving access to safe water and sanitation; and designs replicable model-setting initiatives, i.e. the Lake Victoria Region Water and Sanitation Initiative and the Mekong Regional Water and Sanitation Initiative. The Water and Sanitation Programme incorporates two regional sub-programmes. The Managing Water for African Cities Programme, jointly co-ordinated by UN-Habitat and UNEP, promotes efficient water demand management, capacity-building to alleviate the environmental impact of urbanization on freshwater resources, information exchange on water management and conservation issues, and the exchange of best practices in urban water management. In March 2003 UN-Habitat and the Asian Development Bank (ADB) signed an agreement on the establishment of a parallel Water for Asian Cities Programme.

In 2009 UN-Habitat concluded preparations to establish a Global Water Operators' Partnership Alliance (GWOPA) secretariat, in accordance with decisions adopted at the fourth World Water Forum, held in Mexico, in March 2006. The first international conference of the GWOPA was convened in Zaragoza, Spain, in December 2009. The Alliance supports the establishment and development of regional Water Operators' Partnerships, and supports training and capacity building activities. The Alliance, in collaboration with Google and an international benchmarking network, has developed a Geo-Referenced Utility Benchmarking System (GRUBS) as a means of presenting utility performance (benchmarking) data in a searchable format online. The benchmarking of service providers was a key component of a separate h2.O Monitoring Services to Inform and Empower Initiative which aimed to improve methodologies for monitoring the urban environment and acquiring data and to enhance the effectiveness of investment planning. The project also envisaged the development and application of Urban Inequity Surveys and Citizen Report Cards.

UN-Habitat administers a Global Energy Network for Urban Settlements (GENUS) which aims to support and encourage partnerships between the public and private sector, governmental and non-governmental organizations, and other international, national and civil society agencies concerned with improving energy access for the urban poor, in order to advance best practices, technologies and capacity-building. The first GENUS workshop was convened in Yogyakara, Indonesia, in May 2009, with a focus on transport for the urban poor in Asia. A second was held in Nairobi, Kenya, in October, on slum electrification in Africa. In October 2010, at a meeting on 'Energy from Waste', held in San José, Costa Rica, GENUS in Latin America was inaugurated, with a focus on elaborating solutions for waste management.

In October 2003 UN-Habitat predicted that, owing to unprecedented urban growth, accompanied by poverty and social inequalities, the number of slum dwellers world-wide would double to about 2,000m. by 2030. The September 2005 World Summit of UN heads of state approved the development of a Slum Upgrading Facility (SUF) to improve access to credit and other resources for slum dwellers, in order to improve their homes and living conditions. Pilot projects were subsequently established in Ghana, Indonesia, Sri Lanka and Tanzania. Within each project Local Finance Facilities have been established, both at city and national level, to help communities access credit from local commercial banks.

In April 2007 the UN-Habitat Governing Council approved the establishment of a trust fund—the Experimental Reimbursable Seeding Operations and Other Innovative Mechanism (ERSO)—within the Habitat and Human Settlements Foundation, to support the financing of loans and credits for low-income housing, infrastructure and settlements upgrading. In November 2008 a new Opportunities Fund for Urban Youth-Led Development was inaugurated.

MONITORING AND RESEARCH

UN-Habitat maintains a Global Urban Observatory (GUO) to monitor implementation of the Habitat Agenda and to report on and support local and national plans of action and ongoing research and development. The Observatory operates through GUONet, a global network of regional, national and local urban observatories, and through partner institutions that provide training and other capacity-building expertise. The Observatory also maintains the GUO databases of urban indicators, statistics and city profiles. The Observatory works closely with the Best Practices and Local Leadership Programme, which was established in 1997 to support the implementation of the Habitat Agenda through the use of information and networking. In May 2008 the GUO helped to organize an expert meeting on slum identification, mapping and monitoring, held in Enschede, Netherlands; issues under discussion included methodologies for identifying slums, for example geo-information technologies such as Geographic Information Systems and Remote Sensing. In April 2011 UN-HABITAT launched www.urbangateway.org, a forum for knowledge-sharing among urban policy makers and managers globally.

In November 2004 UN-Habitat hosted the first meeting of the Global Research Network on Human Settlements (HS-Net). HS-Net was to act as a forum for human settlements researchers, research institutions and networks, and was to advise the UN-Habitat Secretariat on the preparation of its two 'flagship reports', the *Global Report on Human Settlements* and *State of the World's Cities*. For the two-year period 2010–11 UN-Habitat prepared, additionally, four editions of *State of the Region's Cities*, for Africa, Asia and the Pacific, Eastern Europe, and Latin America.

WORLD URBAN FORUM

UN-Habitat provides the secretariat of the World Urban Forum (WUF), the first of which was held in April–May 2002, in Nairobi, Kenya, with participation by national governments and Habitat Agenda partners. The Forum represented a merger of the former Urban Environment Forum and International Forum on Urban Poverty. It aims to promote international co-operation in shelter and urban development issues. The second WUF was held in Barcelona, Spain, in September 2004; the third in Vancouver, Canada, in June 2006; and the fourth in Nanjing, PRC, in November 2008. WUF 5 was held in Rio de Janeiro, Brazil, in March 2010. The sixth WUF was scheduled to be convened in Naples, Italy, in September 2012, on the theme 'The Urban Future'. Since 2006 a youth forum has been convened prior to the main Forum. In 2010 this was restructured as the World Urban Youth Assembly further to promote youth-led development.

ASSOCIATED BODY

Cities Alliance: 1818 H St, NW, Washington, DC, 20433 USA; tel. (202) 473-9233; fax (202) 522-3224; e-mail info@citiesalliance.org; internet www.citiesalliance.org; f. 1999, jointly by UNCHS (Habitat) and the World Bank, as a coalition of local authorities, governments and development organizations; aims to reduce urban poverty and improve the effectiveness of urban development co-operation and urban investment; in Sept. 2000 the UN Millennium Summit endorsed the Alliance's new Cities without Slums action plan as a target within its Millennium Development Goals i.e. 'by 2020, to have achieved a significant improvement in the lives of at least 100m. slum dwellers'; facilitates collaboration between govts and authorities to achieve best practices in slum upgrading initiatives; supports the formulation of city development strategies (CDS) in order to promote equitable and sustainable urban growth; in 2009 established a new CDS sub-group to develop a CDS conceptual framework; mems: UNEP, UN-Habitat, the World Bank, European Union, Shack/Slumdwellers International, United Cities and Local Government, World Association of the Major Metropolises (Metropolis), 16 national govts; assoc. mems: ILO, UNDP; Man. WILLIAM COBBETT.

Finance

UN-Habitat's work programme is financed from the UN regular budget, and from voluntary contributions to the UN Habitat and Human Settlements Foundation and to the Programme's technical co-operation activities. The approved budget for the two-year period 2012–13 amounted to US $393.2m. comprising a regular budget allocation of $22.4m., $180.7m. from the Habitat and Human Settlements Foundation (of which $110.5m. was for special purposes), and $190.0m. from the Technical Co-operation Fund.

Publications

Global Report on Human Settlements (annually).

State of the World's Cities (every 2 years).

State of the Region's Cities.

UMP e-Newsletter (quarterly).

Urban World (quarterly).

Technical reports and studies, occasional papers, bibliographies, directories.

United Nations Office on Drugs and Crime—UNODC

Address: Vienna International Centre, POB 500, 1400 Vienna, Austria.

Telephone: (1) 26060-0; **fax:** (1) 26060-5866; **e-mail:** unodc@unodc.org; **internet:** www.unodc.org.

The UN Office on Drugs and Crime (UNODC) was established in November 1997 (as the Office for Drug Control and Crime Prevention—ODCCP) to strengthen the UN's integrated approach to issues relating to drug control, crime prevention and international terrorism. A reform programme was launched in 2002 aimed at integrating further the Office's areas of activity. The Office was renamed in October of that year. It comprises two principal components: the United Nations Drug Programme and the United Nations Crime Programme.

Organization

(April 2012)

UNODC comprises the following four divisions: Operations; Treaty Affairs; Research and Public Affairs; and Management. There is a UNODC liaison office in New York and there are 54 field offices world-wide.

Executive Director: YURI FEDOTOV (Russia).

Activities

UNITED NATIONS DRUG PROGRAMME

The UN Drug Programme was established in 1991 as the UN International Drug Control Programme (UNDCP) and was renamed in 2002. It is responsible for co-ordinating the activities of all UN specialized agencies and programmes in matters of international drug control. The structures of the former Division of Narcotic Drugs, the UN Fund for Drug Abuse Control and the secretariat of the International Narcotics Control Board (see below) were integrated into the Programme. Accordingly, it became the focal point for promoting the UN Decade Against Drug Abuse (1991–2000) and for assisting member states to implement the Global Programme of Action that was adopted by the UN General Assembly in 1990 with the objective of achieving an international society free of illicit drugs and drug abuse. At a special session of the General Assembly, held in June 1998, heads of state and representatives of some 150 countries adopted a global strategy, formulated on the basis of UNDCP proposals, to reduce significantly the production of and demand for illicit substances over the next decade. UNDCP subsequently launched the Global Assessment Programme on Drug Abuse (GAP), which aimed to establish one global and nine regional drug abuse data systems to collect and evaluate data on the extent of and patterns of illegal substance abuse. In March 2009 UNODC reviewed progress since the 1998 General Assembly special session and adopted a Draft Political Declaration and Plan of Action on the future of drug control. The Declaration recognized that countries have a shared responsibility for solving the global drugs problem, and recommended a 'balanced and comprehensive approach', an emphasis on human rights, and a focus on health as a basis for international drugs policy. The Action Plan proposed some 30 solutions to problems in the following six areas of concern: reducing drug abuse and dependence; reducing the illicit supply of drugs; control of precursors and of amphetamine-type stimulants; international co-operation to eradicate the illicit cultivation of crops and to provide alternative development; countering money-laundering; and judicial co-operation. UNODC supports national monitoring systems that assess the extent and evolution of illicit crops in the world's principal drug-growing countries: Bolivia, Colombia and Peru (coca); Afghanistan, Laos and Myanmar (opium; Afghanistan accounted for around 90% of global opium supply in 2011); and Morocco (cannabis). Crop surveys are facilitated by a combination of satellite sensing (with the assistance of the European Space Agency), aerial surveillance and ground-level surveys, which provide a reliable collection and analysis mechanism for data on the production of illicit substances. UNODC's Alternative Development Programme supports projects to create alternative sources of income for farmers economically dependent on the production of illicit narcotic crops. In March 2012 UNODC and the UN Industrial Development Organization signed a memorandum of understanding on establishing a strategic partnership aimed at promoting grass-roots development and alternative livelihoods in poor rural communities hitherto dependent on the cultivation of illegal drugs crops. The UN Drug Programme aims to suppress trafficking in illegal substances and supports efforts to enhance regional and cross-border co-operation in implementing law enforcement initiatives. It serves as an international centre of expertise and information on drug abuse control, with the capacity to provide legal and technical assistance in relevant areas of concern. It supports governments in efforts to strengthen their institutional capacities for drug control (for example, drug identification and drug law enforcement training) and to prepare and implement national drug control 'action plans'.

The Programme's approach to reducing demand for illicit drugs combines strategies in the areas of prevention, treatment and rehabilitation. It sponsors activities to generate public awareness of the harmful effects of drug abuse, for example through its Global Youth Network project, which aims to involve young people in prevention activities, and through the system of goodwill ambassadors associated with its 'Sports Against Drugs' campaign. The Programme works with governments, as well as non-governmental and private organizations and local community partners, in the detection, treatment, rehabilitation and social reintegration of drug addicts. It also undertakes research to monitor the drugs problem: for example, assessing the characteristics of drug-takers and the substances being used in order to help identify people at risk of becoming drug-takers and to enhance the effectiveness of national programmes to address the issue (see also GAP, above).

Through the joint UNODC-World Customs Organization Container Control Programme, which has been operational since 2004 and consists of port control units that comprise both analysts and search teams of customs and police officers, maritime containers are systematically targeted and inspected with a view to ensuring that they have not been commandeered for criminal purposes; the Programme has intercepted containers that were in the process of carrying illicit drugs, as well as precursor chemicals, endangered species, hazardous materials and goods misleadingly labelled for fraudulent purposes. During 2010 UNODC launched the Airport Communication Project (AIRCOP), initially focusing on 10 international airports, located in West Africa, Brazil and Morocco. Under the Project, Joint Airport Interdiction Task Forces (JAITFs) were to be established with connections to international law enforcement databases and communication networks, to enable information sharing, including the instantaneous transmission between international airports of operational information on passengers and cargo, in order to facilitate the interception of illicit cargo.

The Programme promotes implementation of the following major treaties which govern the international drug control system: the Single Convention on Narcotic Drugs (1961) and a Protocol amending the Convention (1972); the Convention on Psychotropic Substances (1971); and the UN Convention against Illicit Traffic in Narcotic Drugs and Psychotropic Substances (1988). Among other important provisions, these treaties aim to restrict severely the production of narcotic drugs, while ensuring an adequate supply for medical and scientific purposes, to prevent profits obtained from the illegal sale of drugs being diverted into legal usage and to secure the extradition of drugs-traffickers and the transfer of proceedings for criminal prosecution. The Programme assists countries to adapt their national legislation and drug policies to facilitate their compliance with these conventions and to enhance co-ordinated inter-governmental efforts to control the movement of narcotic drugs. It services meetings of the International Narcotics Control Board (INCB), an independent body responsible for promoting and monitoring government compliance with the provisions of the drug control treaties, and of the Commission on Narcotic Drugs, which, as a functional committee of ECOSOC, is the main policy-making organ within the UN system on issues relating to international drug abuse control. The 52nd session of the Commission on Narcotic Drugs, held at UNODC headquarters in March 2009, adopted a Political Declaration and Plan of Action on International Co-operation towards an Integrated and Balanced Strategy to Counter the World Drug Problem. The INCB is promoting co-ordinated global action to prevent illicit internet sales of internationally controlled prescription drugs by so-called 'online pharmacies'. The increasing occurrence globally of abuse of prescription drugs was reported on by the INCB in February 2010.

UNODC co-operates closely with other international, regional and non-governmental organizations and maintains dialogue with agencies advocating drug abuse control. It is a co-sponsor of the Joint Programme on HIV/AIDS (UNAIDS), which was established on 1 January 1996. UNODC's participation is in recognition of the importance of international drug control efforts in preventing the spread of HIV/AIDS. In October 2004 UNODC and the World Customs Organization launched a joint Container Control Programme aimed at improving port control measures in developing countries.

Some 80% of opiates produced in Afghanistan are smuggled out of that country by transnational organized criminal groups via Iran and Pakistan, with the remainder being routed through central Asian countries; illegal trafficking threatens regional security and development and enriches criminal networks. In May 2003, at a Ministerial Conference on Drug Routes from Central Asia to Europe, convened in Paris, France, UNODC played a leading role in launching the Paris Pact, a partnership of more than 50 countries and international organizations aimed at combating the traffic in and consumption of Afghan opiates and related problems in affected countries along the Afghan opiates-trafficking routes. In June 2006 a further Ministerial Conference, on Drug Trafficking Routes from Afghanistan, held in Moscow, Russia, demonstrated support for the Paris Pact. In October 2007, within the frame of the Paris Pact, UNODC organized a meeting of senior international counter-narcotics officials, in Kabul, Afghanistan, aimed at strengthening efforts to restrict the supply of illicit drugs from Afghanistan. UNODC supports the Central Asia Regional Information and Co-ordination Centre (CARICC), which was established in Almatı, Kazakhstan, in February 2006, to combat illicit drugs-trafficking in that region. In April UNODC and the Collective Security Treaty Organization (then comprising Armenia, Belarus, Kazakhstan, Kyrgyzstan, Russia and Tajikistan; Uzbekistan joined in June) signed a protocol on developing joint projects and sharing information with the aim of addressing drugs-trafficking, terrorism and transborder crime in Central Asia. In December 2008 UNODC launched the Rainbow Strategy, a regional initiative comprising seven operational plans (covering areas such as precursor chemicals, border management, financial flows, and drug abuse prevention and treatment), aimed at facilitating the implementation of the Paris Pact. The Triangular Initiative, organized by UNODC and launched in June 2007, promotes drugs control co-operation between Afghanistan, Iran and Paksistan. In December 2011 UNODC launched a new regional programme for Afghanistan and neighbouring countries. Meeting in February 2012 partners in the Paris Pact adopted the Vienna Declaration on committing to act in a 'balanced and comprehensive manner' against the illicit Afghan opium trade.

In October 2008—during a High-level Conference on Drugs Trafficking as a Security Threat to West Africa, convened jointly by UNODC, ECOWAS and the Cape Verde Government, in Praia, Cape Verde—UNODC published a report identifying the expanding use in recent years of points in West Africa (particularly Guinea-Bissau and Ghana) as a transit route for narcotics being traded illegally between Latin America and Europe. The Executive Director of UNODC warned that West Africa was at risk of becoming an epicentre for drugs-trafficking, representing a serious threat to public health and security in the region. He proposed the establishment of a West African intelligence-sharing centre, and urged the promotion of development and the strengthening of the rule of law as a means of reducing regional vulnerability to drugs and crime. At the Conference ECOWAS adopted a Political Declaration on Drugs Trafficking and Organized Crime in West Africa, and approved an ECOWAS Regional Response Plan. In March 2009 UNODC and the African Union (AU) launched a joint project in support of a Plan of Action on Drug Control and Crime Prevention (2007–12) that had been adopted by the AU in December 2007. The UNODC-AU co-operation aimed to strengthen the policy-making, norm-setting and capacity-building capabilities of the AU Commission and sub-regional organizations (notably ECOWAS). In July 2009 UNODC released a report entitled *Transnational Trafficking and the Rule of Law in West Africa: A Threat Assessment*, which addressed the regional impact of trafficking in human beings, illicit drugs, petroleum, cigarettes, toxic waste and electronic waste ('e-waste'). The report also addressed the prevalence in West Africa of trafficking in counterfeit medications, including antibiotics, antiretroviral drugs and medicines to combat malaria and TB, many of which contained few active ingredients. In that month UNODC, other UN agencies, ECOWAS and INTERPOL launched the *West Africa Coast Initiative (WACI)*, which aimed to build national and regional capacities to combat drugs-trafficking and organized crime in, initially, four pilot post-conflict countries: Côte d'Ivoire, Guinea-Bissau, Liberia and Sierra Leone. In February 2010 the pilot countries signed the 'WACI- Freetown Commitment', endorsing the implementation of the initiative, and agreeing to establish specialized transnational crime units on their territories. WACI activities were to be expanded to Guinea during 2012.

UNITED NATIONS CRIME PROGRAMME

Through the United Nations Crime Programme, which is implemented by the Centre for International Crime Prevention (CICP), established in 1997, UNODC is responsible for crime prevention, criminal justice and criminal law reform. The Programme oversees the application of international standards and norms relating to these areas, for example the Minimum Rules for the Treatment of Prisoners, Conventions against Torture, and Other Cruel, Inhuman or Degrading Treatment or Punishment, and Safeguards Guaranteeing the Protection of the Rights of Those Facing the Death Penalty. The Programme provides member states with technical assistance to strengthen national capacities to establish appropriate legal and criminal justice systems and to combat transnational organized crime (see below). It supports the Commission on Crime Prevention and Criminal Justice, a functional committee of ECOSOC, which provides guidance in developing global anti-crime policies. The Programme manages the Global Programme against Corruption, a Global Programme on Organized Crime, which aims to analyse emerging transnational criminal organizations and assist countries to formulate strategies to combat the problem, and a Global Programme against Trafficking in Human Beings (trafficking in human beings for sexual exploitation or forced labour is regarded as the fastest-growing area of international organized crime). In March 2007 UNODC and partners initiated the UN Global Initiative to

Fight Human Trafficking (UN.GIFT), with the aim of raising awareness world-wide of the phenomenon, promoting effective preventative measures, and improving law enforcement methods. In February 2008 UN.GIFT organized the Vienna Forum to Fight Human Trafficking, with participation by UN member states and agencies, other international organizations, academics, and representatives of the private sector and civil society. In February 2009 UNODC issued the *Global Report on Trafficking in Persons*, which used data drawn from 155 countries to compile an assessment of the world-wide scope of human trafficking and ongoing means of combating it. The Report included an overview of trafficking patterns, of legal steps taken in response, and also country-specific information on reported trafficking and prosecutions. The Report found sexual exploitation to be the most common purpose of human trafficking (representing 79% of incidences), followed by forced labour (18%), although it was stated that the prevalence of trafficking for forced labour may be under-represented. About one-fifth of known trafficking victims were reported to be children. Intra-regional and domestic trafficking were found to be more common than long-distance trafficking in persons. In March 2009 UNODC launched the Blue Heart Campaign against Human Trafficking, which aimed to use the media and the social networking arena to raise awareness of global trafficking. UNODC administers a UN Voluntary Trust Fund for Victims of Trafficking in Persons, which was established in November 2010 to support the objectives of a new UN Global Plan of Action to Combat Trafficking in Persons, adopted by the UN General Assembly in July of that year.

The CICP supported member states in the preparation of the UN Convention against Transnational Organized Crime (UNTOC, also known as the Palermo Convention), which was opened for signature in December 2000 at a UN conference on combating organized crime held in Sicily, Italy, and entered into force in September 2003. UNTOC has three additional Protocols: the Protocol to Prevent, Suppress and Punish Trafficking in Persons, especially Women and Children (entered into force December 2003, sometimes referred to as the 'Trafficking Protocol'); the Protocol against the Smuggling of Migrants by Land, Air and Sea (entered into force January 2004); and the Protocol against the Illicit Manufacturing and Trafficking in Firearms, Their Parts and Components and Ammunition (entered into force July 2005). The Programme assisted with the formulation of the UN Convention against Corruption (UNCAC), which was opened for signature in December 2003 in Merida, Mexico, and entered into force in December 2005; the implementation of UNCAC in signatory states was to be monitored systematically under a mechanism established in November 2009.

The UN Crime Programme promotes research and undertakes studies of new forms of crime prevention, in collaboration with the UN Interregional Crime and Justice Research Institute (UNICRI). It also maintains a UN Crime and Justice Information Network database (UNCJIN), which provides information on national crime statistics, publications and links to other relevant intergovernmental agencies and research and academic institutes. In October 2008 UNODC and INTERPOL signed a joint agreement establishing the first International Anti-Corruption Academy; the Academy, to be based in Laxenburg, Austria, was to provide training to police personnel, government officials, academics and representatives of NGOs and private sector entities. An online UNODC/INTERPOL training course, aimed at people engaged in international co-operation against terrorism, was launched in October 2009.

UNODC provides assistance to states in the area of penal reform, placing particular emphasis on training prison staff and responding to the needs of women and vulnerable prisoners. The 18th session of the Commission on Crime Prevention and Criminal Justice, hosted at UNODC headquarters in April 2009, promoted a shift from a punitive to a more rehabilitative approach to addressing crime, and urged a reduction in prison overcrowding and the advancement of the provision of legal aid in criminal justice systems. The meeting also discussed means of addressing the emergence of a 'global crime wave': the agenda covered issues including economic fraud (often conducted over the internet), identity-related crime, mafia penetration of the international financial system, and cyber-terrorism.

The UNODC's Terrorism Prevention Branch, established in 1999, researches trends in terrorist activity and assists countries to improve their capabilities to investigate and prevent acts of terrorism. The Branch promotes international co-operation in combating the problem, and has initiated a study into the connections between terrorist activity and other forms of crime. A comprehensive global database on global terrorism, including counter-terrorism conventions, national criminal laws and relevant case laws, was launched by UNODC in June 2009.

The UN Global Programme against Money Laundering (GPML), established in March 1999, assists governments with formulating legislation against money laundering and establishing and maintaining appropriate frameworks to counter the problem. GPML activities include the provision of technical assistance, training, and the collection, research and analysis of crime data. The Programme, in collaboration with other governmental organizations, law enforcement agencies and academic institutions, co-ordinates the International Money Laundering Information Network (IMoLIN), an internet-based information resource (accessible at www.imolin.org). IMoLIN incorporates the Anti-Money Laundering International Database (a comprehensive database on money-laundering legislation throughout the world that constituted a key element in the Office's activities in support of the elaboration of UNTOC—see above). At the first GPML Forum, held in the Cayman Islands in March 2000, the governments of 31 participating 'offshore' financial centres agreed in principle to adopt internationally accepted standards of financial regulation and measures against money laundering.

UNODC organized several regional preparatory meetings prior to the 11th UN Congress on Crime Prevention and Criminal Justice, which was held in Bangkok, Thailand, in April 2005.

In December 2008 the Executive Director of UNODC made a number of recommendations aimed at deterring, arresting and prosecuting individuals engaging in maritime piracy in waters off the Horn of Africa, including a proposal that so-called 'ship-riders' should be deployed on warships operating in that area, with responsibility for arresting pirates and bringing them to justice in neighbouring countries. UNODC supports states in the region with the implementation of the UNTOC and other relevant international instruments. During 2009 UNODC launched a counter-piracy programme (CPP), with an initial focus on Kenya, where, by early 2012, some 50 people had been convicted of piracy. The programme supports efforts to detain and prosecute piracy suspects, and supports financial intelligence units and law enforcement agencies in East Africa and the Horn of Africa. The CPP's mandate has been widened to cover six countries in the region. In February 2012 UNODC's Executive Director reported that, in 2011, pirates made US $170m. in ransom money from hijacking vessels, that the laundering of the proceeds of piracy was causing consumer prices to rise steeply in the Horn of Africa, and that illicit money flows linked to piracy were also being reinvested into other criminal activities, involving drugs, weaponry, alcohol smuggling, and human trafficking. In late 2012 UNODC, the World Bank and INTERPOL were jointly to issue a report on illicit financial flows linked to piracy. During November 2011 the UN Secretary-General sent an assessment mission—co-led by UNODC and the UN Department of Political Affairs—to several Gulf of Guinea states (Benin, Nigeria, Gabon and Angola) to determine the scope of the threat of piracy in the Gulf of Guinea region. Some 28 pirate attacks were reported in the Gulf of Guinea in 2011, a sharp increase over 11 attacks reported in 2010.

Meeting in St Petersburg, Russia, in November 2010, at the International Tiger Forum, the heads of UNODC, the Convention on International Trade in Endangered Species of Wild Fauna and Flora (CITES), the World Customs Organization, INTERPOL and the World Bank jointly approved the establishment of a new International Consortium on Combating Wildlife Crime (ICCWC), with the aim of combating the poaching of wild animals and illegal trade in wild animals and wild animal products.

In 2007 UNODC and the World Bank jointly launched the Stolen Asset Recovery (StAR) initiative, which aimed to address the theft of public assets from developing countries, and to promote direct government-to-government assistance. Activities to be implemented under StAR included developing and strengthening partnerships, and implementing pilot programmes aimed at recovering stolen assets through the provision of technical support, including the promotion of mutual legal assistance. In April 2009 the G20 recommended that StAR review and propose mechanisms to strengthen international co-operation relating to asset recovery.

A UNODC regional programme for Eastern Africa, covering 2009–12, was adopted in November 2009 by a regional ministerial conference on 'Promoting the Rule of Human Security in Eastern Africa', held in Nairobi, Kenya. The programme was based on the following three pillars: countering trafficking, organized crime and terrorism; combating corruption and promoting justice and integrity; and improving health and human development. In December 2010 UNODC and the League of Arab States jointly launched a five-year Regional Programme on Drug Control, Crime Prevention and Criminal Justice Reform for the Arab States, covering the period 2011–15, and based, similarly, on the following pillars: countering illicit trafficking, organized crime and terrorism; promoting justice and integrity; and drug prevention and improving health.

Finance

UNODC receives an allocation from the regular budget of the UN (US $40.9m. in 2012–13), although voluntary contributions from member states and private organizations represent the majority (about 90%) of its resources. UNODC's total projected resources for the two-year period 2012–13 amounted to some $417.8 m.

Publications

Afghanistan Opium Survey (annual).
Bulletin on Narcotics.
Forum on Crime and Society.
eNews@UNODC (electronic newsletter).
Global Report on Crime and Justice.
Global Report on Trafficking in Persons.
Multilingual Dictionary of Narcotic Drugs and Psychotropic Substances Under International Control.
Technical Series.
The United Nations and Juvenile Justice: A Guide to International Standards and Best Practices.
UNODC Update (quarterly).
World Drug Report.

United Nations Peace-keeping

Address: Department of Peace-keeping Operations, Room S-3727-B, United Nations, New York, NY 10017, USA.

Telephone: (212) 963-8077; **fax:** (212) 963-9222; **internet:** www.un.org/Depts/dpko/.

United Nations peace-keeping operations have been conceived as instruments of conflict control. The UN has used these operations in various conflicts, with the consent of the parties involved, to maintain international peace and security, without prejudice to the positions or claims of parties, in order to facilitate the search for political settlements through peaceful means such as mediation and the good offices of the UN Secretary-General. Each operation is established with a specific mandate, which requires periodic review by the UN Security Council. In 1988 the United Nations Peace-keeping Forces were awarded the Nobel Peace Prize.

United Nations peace-keeping operations fall into two categories: peace-keeping forces and observer missions. Peace-keeping forces are composed of contingents of military and civilian personnel, made available by member states. These forces assist in preventing the recurrence of fighting, restoring and maintaining peace, and promoting a return to normal conditions. To this end, peace-keeping forces are authorized as necessary to undertake negotiations, persuasion, observation and fact-finding. They conduct patrols and interpose physically between the opposing parties. Peace-keeping forces are permitted to use their weapons only in self-defence.

Military observer missions are composed of officers (usually unarmed), who are made available, on the Secretary-General's request, by member states. A mission's function is to observe and report to the Secretary-General (who, in turn, informs the Security Council) on the maintenance of a cease-fire, to investigate violations and to do what it can to improve the situation. Peace-keeping forces and observer missions must at all times maintain complete impartiality and avoid any action that might affect the claims or positions of the parties.

A UN Stand-by Arrangements System (UNSAS) became operational in 1994; participating countries make available specialized civilian and military personnel as well as other services and equipment. In January 1995 the UN Secretary-General presented a report to the Security Council, reassessing the UN's role in peace-keeping. The document stipulated that UN forces in conflict areas should not be responsible for peace-enforcement duties, and included a proposal for the establishment of a 'rapid reaction' force, which would be ready for deployment within a month of being authorized by the Security Council. During 2000–08 the multinational UN Stand-by Forces High Readiness Brigade (SHIRBRIG), based in Denmark, was available to the UN, deploying troops to the UN Mission in Ethiopia and Eritrea (in 2000) and the UN Mission in Liberia (2003), and assisting (during 2004–05) with preparations for the deployment of the UN Mission in Sudan. In March 2003 a SHIRBRIG team supported ECOWAS in planning the deployment of a peace-keeping mission to Côte d'Ivoire. In 2007 it was asked to assist the African Union (AU) in planning its mission in Sudan (AMISOM), and, during 2008, it assisted the AU with the development of an African Standby Force. SHIRBRIG was fully disbanded in June 2009.

In August 2000 a report on UN peace-keeping activities prepared by a team of experts appointed by the Secretary-General assessed the aims and requirements of peace-keeping operations and recommended several measures to improve the performance of the Department of Peace-keeping Operations (DPKO), focusing on its planning and management capacity from the inception of an operation through to post-conflict peace-building activities, and on its rapid response capability. Proposed reforms included the establishment of a body to improve co-ordination of information and strategic analysis requirements; the promotion of partnership arrangements between member states (within the context of UNSAS) enabling the formation of several coherent multinational brigades, and improved monitoring of the preparedness of potential troop contributor nations, with a view to facilitating the effective deployment of most operations within 30 days of their authorization in a Security Council resolution; the adoption of 'on-call' reserve lists to ensure the prompt deployment of civilian police and specialists; the preparation of a global logistics support strategy; and a restructuring of the DPKO to improve administrative efficiency. The study also urged an increase in resources for funding peace-keeping operations and the adoption of a more flexible financing mechanism, and emphasized the importance of the UN's conflict prevention activities. In November the Security Council, having welcomed the report, adopted guidelines aimed at improving its management of peace-keeping operations, including providing missions with clear and achievable mandates. In June 2001 the Council adopted a resolution incorporating a Statement of principles on co-operation with troop-contributing countries, which aimed to strengthen the relationship between those countries and the UN and to enhance the effectiveness of peace-keeping operations. A new Rapid Deployment Level within UNSAS was inaugurated in July 2002. In 2004 the Department established a Special Investigation Team, at the request of the UN Secretary-General, which, in November, visited the Democratic Republic of the Congo to examine allegations of sexual exploitation and abuse committed by peace-keeping personnel. In July 2007 a new Department of Field Operations was established within the UN Secretariat to provide expert support and resources to enhance personnel, budget, information and communication technology, and other logistical aspects of UN peace-keeping operations in the field. At the same time a restructuring of the DPKO was initiated. A new Office for the Rule of Law and Security Institutions was established, and the Military Division was reconstituted as the Office of Military Affairs.

The UN's peace-keeping forces and observer missions are financed in most cases by assessed contributions from member states of the organization. In recent years a significant expansion in the UN's peace-keeping activities has been accompanied by a perpetual financial crisis within the organization, as a result of the increased financial burden and some member states' delaying payment. At 31 March 2012 outstanding assessed contributions to the peace-keeping budget amounted to some US $2,180m.

By April 2012 the UN had deployed a total of 67 peace-keeping operations, of which 13 were authorized in the period 1948–88 and 54 since 1988. At 31 March 2012 117 countries were contributing some 98,607 uniformed personnel to the then 15 ongoing operations, of whom 82,153 were peace-keeping troops, 14,421 police and 2,033 military observers.

In 2012 the DPKO was also directly supporting the UN Assistance Mission in Afghanistan, a political and peace-building mission that was established in March 2002.

African Union (AU)/UN Hybrid Operation in Darfur—UNAMID

Address: El Fasher, Sudan.

Joint AU-UN Special Representative: IBRAHIM GAMBARI (Nigeria).

Force Commander: Lt-Gen. PATRICK NYAMVUMBA (Rwanda).

Police Commissioner: JAMES OPPONG-BOANUH (Ghana).

Establishment and Mandate: UNAMID was established by a resolution of the UN Security Council in July 2007, authorized to take necessary action to support the implementation and verification of the Darfur Peace Agreement signed in May 2006 by the Sudanese Government and a rebel faction in Darfur, southern Sudan. UNAMID was also mandated to protect civilians, to provide security for humanitarian assistance, to support an inclusive political process, to contribute to the promotion of human rights and rule of law, and to monitor and report on the situation along the borders with Chad and the Central African Republic. An AU-UN Joint Mediation Support Team for Darfur (JMST) and a Tripartite Committee on UNAMID (including representatives of the UN, AU and Government of Sudan) meet periodically.

Activities: UNAMID assumed command of the AU Mission in Sudan (AMIS), comprising 10 battalions, in December 2007. In February 2008 UNAMID's Joint Special Representative signed a status of forces agreement with the minister of foreign affairs of Sudan, covering logistical aspects of the mission. In March UNAMID police units conducted their first confidence-building patrols in areas under rebel control in northern Darfur. In May UNAMID's Force Commander condemned aerial attacks against villages in northern Darfur, allegedly by Sudanese forces. Throughout 2008 an estimated 317,000 civilians were newly displaced from their homes in Darfur. A delegation of the UN Security Council visited the region in June and expressed concern at the mission's lack of adequate equipment and troop levels. In July 2008 the UN designated Darfur a 'security phase four' area (a designation that permits the UN to relocate staff temporarily pending an improvement in the security situation). At the end of June 2008 a new joint AU-UN Chief Mediator was appointed, based at UNAMID headquarters in El Fasher. A Joint Support Co-ordination Mechanism (JSCM) Office in Addis Ababa, Ethiopia, comprising liaison officers and communications equipment, was established in November to ensure effective consultation between the UN and AU headquarters. In October 2008 the UN Secretary-General reported that little progress had been achieved in the implementation of the 2006 Darfur Peace Agreement, that violent unrest continued to prevail, and that the conditions in Darfur were not conducive to undertaking a successful peace-keeping operation. From late 2008 activities were undertaken to bring the 10 former AMIS battalions up to full strength in terms of military personnel and equipment. Nevertheless, the Secretary-General reported in February 2009 (at which time the designated security level in Darfur remained at phase four) that UNAMID's operational capabilities continued to be limited by lack of critical and key military enabling equipment, logistical constraints, and the reluctance of many troop- and police-contributing countries to deploy to it well-trained personnel and efficient contingent-owned equipment. In addition, there was concern at restrictions on the movement of troops and on the issuing of visa and vehicle licence applications that were being imposed by the Sudanese authorities. In January 2009 UNAMID, jointly with OHCHR, issued a public report on a law enforcement operation by the Sudan Government in August 2008 against targets in Kalma camp for internally displaced persons (IDPs) in southern Darfur, that had resulted in 33 civilian fatalities and 108 civilian injuries; the report found that the use of force had been indiscriminate and disproportionate, in violation of international law. UNAMID has provided a security presence around Kalma camp. In early 2009 an escalation of violence in the Mahajeriya region of southern Darfur resulted in the displacement of some 46,000 people, the majority of whom moved to the Zam Zam refugee camp near El Fasher. UNAMID undertook to deliver daily water supplies, as well as to conduct protection patrols in and around the camp. The mission also began construction of a community policy centre in the camp. UNAMID provided security and other logistical support to help to ensure the continued distribution of humanitarian assistance following the expulsion from the country, in March, of 13 international non-governmental organizations (NGOs) and the dissolution of three national NGOs by the Sudanese authorities (who claimed that they had collaborated with investigations being conducted by the International Criminal Court). From late 2009 UNAMID provided logistical support to the Government's disarmament, demobilization and rehabilitation programme. In January 2010 the UN Secretary-General reported that the capability of UNAMID batallions in Darfur continued to be a cause of concern, with a number of units not having sufficient major equipment. At that time UNAMID undertook geophysical investigations to locate new water sources around mission camps. UNAMID assisted the former UN Mission in Sudan and the Sudanese authorities with transporting electoral materials to remote locations and with training more than 10,000 local police officers in preparation for the municipal, legislative and presidential elections that were held in April.

In November 2009 an inaugural conference of Darfurian civil society organizations was convened, in Doha, Qatar, in order to strengthen and to further political negotiations to achieve a peace settlement. A second conference was held in July 2010. In February and March 2010, respectively, two rebel groupings that had been operating in Darfur signed framework agreements with the Sudanese Government aimed at resolving the conflict; however, consequent negotiations with the largest rebel group, aimed at securing a cease-fire, stalled in May. During that month violent unrest in Darfur caused nearly 600 fatalities, the highest number since the deployment of the mission. UNAMID strengthened security measures and provided additional medical care in some of the larger IDP camps where inter-tribal conflict was becoming a major security concern. In late July 7,000 people in Kalma camp sought refuge at the UNAMID Community Policing Centre. In the following month UNAMID and the Sudanese Government agreed to establish a joint committee to resolve problems in Kalma, which hosted some 82,000 IDPs. In late August a consultative meeting of representatives of UNAMID, the AU, the USA and the Sudanese President agreed that UNAMID and the Sudanese Government would work closely together to improve the security situation in Darfur and to support stabilization and development of the region. The UN Secretary-General welcomed efforts by the Sudanese authorities to investigate, and restore order in the aftermath of, an attack launched in early September by armed assailants targeting local men attending the market in the Northern Darfur village of Tabarat, causing some 37 fatalities and precipitating the displacement of around 3,000 villagers.

In early April 2011 the Sudanese National Electoral Commission initiated preparations for a referendum to be held on the future status of Darfur, and requested material and technical assistance from UNAMID. Towards the end of April the JMST presented a draft peace agreement to the Sudan Government and rebel groupings. The draft agreement was considered by an All-Darfur Stakeholders' Conference, convened, with support from UNAMID, in Doha, Qatar, in late May; participants in the Conference endorsed a communiqué providing for the draft document (the Doha Document for Peace in Darfur—DDPD) to form the basis for achieving a permanent cease-fire and comprehensive Darfurian peace settlement. The DDPD addressed issues including power sharing, wealth sharing, human rights, justice and reconciliation, compensation, returns, and internal dialogue, and provided for the establishment of a Cease-fire Commission, a Darfur Regional Authority, and for a Darfuri to be appointed as the second Vice-President of Sudan. In June the UN Secretary-General welcomed the DDPD as the basis for resolving the Darfur conflict. In mid-July the Sudanese Government and the 'Liberation and Justice Movement', an alliance of rebel groupings, signed an accord on the adoption of the DDPD. Shortly afterwards the two sides also signed a Protocol on the Political Participation of the Liberation and Justice Movement and Integration of its Forces. Meanwhile, UNAMID, a participant in the DDPD Implementation Follow-on Commission, prepared, with civil society representatives, a plan for the dissemination throughout Darfur of information on the Document. In August UNAMID chaired the first meeting of the Cease-Fire Commission established under the provisions of the DDPD.

During late May–early June 2011 UNAMID intervened to assist 11 IDPs at Hassa Hissa camp who had been detained by a gang of youths also sheltering there; although the detainees were eventually released, it was reported in June that 11 IDPs in the area had been killed. At the beginning of May UNAMID and humanitarian agencies active in Darfur launched Operation Spring Basket, aimed at enhancing access to remote parts of Darfur and thereby providing humanitarian aid to around 400,000 beneficiaries. UNAMID continued to implement Quick Impact Projects in Darfur, in support of the education sector, infrastructure and local facilities. UNAMID, where requested, provides logistical and security support to humanitarian agencies assisting returnees to West Darfur. In response to reported cases of crop destruction by nomads in West Darfur, and complaints that returnees from Chad were also contributing to crop destruction, UNAMID liaised in the second half of 2011 with local crop protection committees. The formation in 2011 of a subcommittee comprising UNAMID and Sudanese government security entities led to a significant decrease in restrictions on the movements of UNAMID security patrols in the latter part of the year. There were continued reports of criminal attacks on UN personnel, including the theft of UNAMID vehicles, during 2008–12. The number of reported carjackings reportedly decreased from 2011, however, following the implementation by UNAMID of new preventative measures.

Operational Strength: UNAMID has an authorized strength of up to 19,555 military personnel and 6,432 police. The mission's operational strength at 31 March 2012 comprised 17,768 troops, 313 military observers and 5,366 police officers; the mission was supported by 479 UN Volunteers and (at 31 December 2011) by 1,104 international civilian personnel and 2,918 local civilian staff.

Finance: The budget for UNAMID amounted to US $1,689m. for the period 1 July 2011–30 June 2012, funded from a Special Account comprising assessed contributions from UN member states.

United Nations Disengagement Observer Force—UNDOF

Address: Camp Faouar, Syria.

Force Commander: Maj.-Gen. NATALIO C. ECARMA (Philippines).

Establishment and Mandate: UNDOF was established for an initial period of six months by a UN Security Council resolution in May 1974, following the signature in Geneva, Switzerland, of a disengagement agreement between Syrian and Israeli forces. The mandate has since been extended by successive resolutions. The initial task of the mission was to take over territory evacuated in stages by the Israeli troops, in accordance with the disengagement agreement, to hand over territory to Syrian troops, and to establish an area of separation on the Golan Heights.

Activities: UNDOF continues to monitor the area of separation; it carries out inspections of the areas of limited armaments and forces; uses its best efforts to maintain the cease-fire; carries out demining activities; and undertakes activities of a humanitarian nature, such as arranging the transfer of prisoners and war-dead between Syria and Israel. The Force operates exclusively on Syrian territory.

During 2011 demonstrations by anti-Government protesters in Syria extended to the area of UNDOF's operations; the Force continued to supervise the area of separation using fixed positions and patrols, and undertook fortnightly inspections of equipment and force levels in the areas of limited armaments and forces. In mid-May and early June groups of Palestinian protesters gathered at a site known as the 'family shouting place', opposite the village of Majdal Chams in the area of limitation on the Israeli-occupied Golan side; on the second occasion the protesters attempted to breach the cease-fire line. UNDOF monitored the proceedings using armoured patrols, engaged with the Syrian and Israeli militaries, and attempted to diffuse tensions. Subsequently UNDOF strengthened its force protection measures, including the fortification of its positions.

Operational Strength: At 31 March 2012 the mission comprised 1,043 troops, and supported by 144 international and local civilian personnel (as at 31 December 2011). Military observers of UNTSO's Observer Group Golan help UNDOF in the performance of its tasks, as required.

Finance: The General Assembly appropriation for the operation over the period 1 July 2011–30 June 2012 amounted to US $50.5m.

United Nations Integrated Mission in Timor-Leste—UNMIT

Address: Dili, Timor-Leste.

Telephone: 3301400; **fax:** 3304410; **internet:** www.unmit.org.

Special Representative of the UN Secretary-General and Head of Office: Ameerah Haq (Bangladesh) (until 9 June 2012).

Police Commissioner: Luis Miguel Carrilho (Portugal).

Establishment and Mandate: In succession to the UN Mission in Support of East Timor (UNMISET), the UN Transitional Administration in East Timor (UNTAET) and the UN Office in Timor-Leste (UNOTIL), UNMIT was established by UN Security Council Resolution 1704 in August 2006 to support the Timor-Leste authorities with consolidating stability, promoting democratic governance and facilitating the process of national reconciliation. The mission was to co-operate with the Australian-led International Stabilization Force (ISF, also comprising troops from Malaysia, New Zealand and Portugal), which had been deployed to Timor-Leste in late May 2006 to secure key installations following an eruption of violent unrest in the previous month. The mission was authorized to assist with all aspects of the staging of the 2007 presidential and legislative elections, with restoring and maintaining public security, and with the promotion of human rights and justice.

Activities: In January 2007 UNMIT signed a trilateral agreement with the Timorese authorities and Australian Government to enhance co-ordination of all security-related activities. During the first half of 2007 the UNMIT police presence was expanded to provide full support to the Timorese national police and ISF in facilitating public security during the electoral process. In May UNMIT reported that the presidential election, conducted in April–May, had been 'free and fair'. Parliamentary elections were conducted in late June, and in early August the Special Representative of the UN Secretary-General (SRSG) welcomed the establishment of a new coalition Government. The inauguration of the new Government, however, prompted renewed violent unrest in several districts of the country. Consequently, during August, UNMIT convened a meeting of representatives of national political groupings to address means of calming the unrest, and also offered practical assistance to the Timorese authorities towards restoring security and delivering humanitarian aid to those affected by the violence. In November a delegation of the UN Security Council visited the country. In February 2008 the UN condemned violent attacks against the Prime Minister and President in Timor-Leste. In that month, in extending UNMIT's mandate by one year, the Security Council requested that UNMIT continue to assist the Government to enhance the effectiveness of the judiciary, to review and reform the security sector, to co-ordinate donor co-operation for institutional capacity-building, and to assist in the formulation of poverty reduction and economic growth strategies. In June UNMIT confirmed that it was to assist the Timor-Leste authorities to undertake a comprehensive review of its security sector. In August the mission published a second report on the human rights situation in Timor-Leste, focusing on access to justice and the security sector. The mission's mandate was extended by a further 12-month period in February 2009. In March the Prime Minister and the SRSG announced that there was to be a gradual resumption of responsibilities for police operations by the national police force, the Policia Nacional de Timor-Leste (PNTL), contingent on the outcome of a joint assessment process. The first transfer of primary responsibility for policing from UNMIT to the PNTL was officially conducted in Lautém district in May 2009, and in September the PNTL assumed responsibility for the national police training centre, in Dili. In February 2010 the UN Security Council endorsed a recommendation of the Secretary-General to reconfigure the UNMIT police component, including its drawdown, in accordance with the phased transfer of policing responsibilities to the PNTL. In January a technical assessment mission was sent to Timor-Leste to make recommendations to the UN Secretary-General concerning UNMIT's role during 2010–12. By that time UNMIT had transferred responsibility to the PNTL for policing in 10 districts and six units, and an Immigration Department, Border Patrol Unit and INTERPOL office were operational. In February 2011 the UN Security Council, extending the mission's mandate by a further 12-month period, acknowledged the need for a continued UN police presence in the country in order to support further constitutional development, PNTL capacity building and preparations for presidential and parliamentary elections, scheduled to be conducted, respectively, in March and June 2012. In late February 2011 a PNTL-UNMIT Police Joint Development Plan—with five priority areas for UNMIT police capacity-building support: legislation, training, administration, discipline and operations—was signed, and UNMIT police have subsequently focused on its implementation. By January 2012 UNMIT police had completed some 175 of the 576 activities provided for under the Plan. UNMIT supported the organization of local democratic governance forums during October–November 2011, and, in December, of a national forum on food security.

In September 2011 the SSRG and the Timor-Leste Government signed a Joint Transition Plan, to guide the transfer of UNMIT's responsibilities during the mission's withdrawal from the country, which was to be completed by December 2012.

Operational Strength: At 31 March 2012 UNMIT comprised 1,242 police officers and 33 military liaison officers; it was assisted by 274 UN Volunteers and (at 31 December 2011) by a team of 398 international and 879 local civilian staff.

Finance: The General Assembly apportioned US $196.1m. to finance the operation during the period 1 July 2011–30 June 2012.

United Nations Interim Administration Mission in Kosovo—UNMIK

Address: Priština, Kosovo.

Special Representative of the UN Secretary-General and Head of Office: Farid Zarif (Afghanistan).

Establishment and Mandate: In June 1999 NATO suspended a 10-week aerial offensive against the then Federal Republic of Yugoslavia (which was renamed 'Serbia and Montenegro' in 2003 and divided into separate sovereign states of Montenegro and Serbia in June 2006), following an agreement by the Serbian authorities to withdraw all security and paramilitary forces from the southern province of Kosovo and Metohija, where Serbian repression of a separatist movement had prompted a humanitarian crisis and co-ordinated international action to resolve the conflict. The UN Security Council adopted Resolution 1244, which outlined the terms of a political settlement for Kosovo and provided for the deployment of international civilian and security personnel. The security presence, termed the Kosovo Peace Implementation Force (KFOR), was to be led by NATO, while the UN was to oversee all civilian operations. UNMIK was established under the terms of Resolution 1244 as the supreme legal and executive authority in Kosovo, with responsibility for all civil administration and for facilitating the reconstruction and rehabilitation of the province as an autonomous region. For the first time in a UN operation other organizations were mandated to co-ordinate aspects of the mission in Kosovo, under the UN's overall jurisdiction. The four key elements, or Pillars, of UNMIK were (I) humanitarian affairs (led by UNHCR); (II) civil administration; (III) democratization and institution-building (OSCE); and (IV) economic reconstruction (EU). At the end of the first year of UNMIK's presence the element of humanitarian assistance was phased out. A new Pillar (I), concerned with police and justice, was established in May 2001, under the direct leadership of the UN.

Activities, 1999–2002: On arriving in Kosovo at the end of June 1999, UNMIK and KFOR established a Joint Implementation Commission to co-ordinate and supervise the demilitarization of the Kosovo Liberation Army. UNMIK initiated a mass information campaign (and later administered new radio stations in Kosovo) to urge co-operation with the international personnel in the province and tolerance for all ethnic communities. A Mine Co-ordinating Centre supervised efforts to deactivate anti-personnel devices and to ensure the safety of the returning ethnic Albanian population. In July the UN Secretary-General's Special Representative (SRSG) took office, and chaired the first meeting of the Kosovo Transitional Council (KTC), which had been established by the UN as a multi-ethnic consultative organ, the highest political body under UNMIK, to help to restore law and order in the province and to reintegrate the local administrative infrastructure. In August a Joint Advisory Council on Legislative Matters was constituted, with representatives of UNMIK and the local judiciary, in order to consider measures to eliminate discrimination from the province's legal framework. At the end of July UNMIK personnel began to supervise customs controls at Kosovo's international borders. Other developments in the first few months of UNMIK's deployment included the inauguration of joint commissions on energy and public utilities, education, and health, a Technical Advisory Commission on establishing a judiciary and prosecution service, and, in October, the establishment of a Fuel Supervisory Board to administer the import, sale and distribution of petroleum. Central financial institutions for the province were inaugurated in November. In the same month UNMIK established a Housing and Property Directorate and a Claims Commission in order to resolve residential property disputes. In September the KTC agreed to establish a Joint Security Committee, in response to concerns at the escalation of violence in the province, in particular attacks on remaining Serbian civilians. In mid-December the leaders of the three main political groupings in Kosovo agreed on provisional power-sharing arrangements with UNMIK. The so-called Kosovo-UNMIK Joint Interim Administrative Structure established an eight-member executive Interim Administrative Council and a framework of administrative departments. In January 2000 UNMIK oversaw the inauguration of the Kosovo Protection Corps, a civilian agency comprising mainly former members of the newly demilitarized Kosovo Liberation Army, which was to provide an emergency response service and a humanitarian assistance capacity, to assist in de-mining operations and contribute to rebuilding local infrastructure. In August UNMIK, in view of its mandate to assist with the regeneration of the local economy, concluded an agreement with a multinational consortium to rehabilitate the Trepca non-ferrous mining complex. During mid-2000 UNMIK organized the voter registration process for municipal elections, which were held in late October. In mid-December the Supreme Court of Kosovo was inaugurated, comprising 16 judges appointed by the SRSG. During 2000 UNMIK police and KFOR co-operated in conducting joint security operations; the establishment of a special security task force to combat ethnically motivated political violence, comprising senior UNMIK police and KFOR members, was agreed in June. From January 2001 UNMIK international travel documents were distributed to Kosovars without Yugoslav passports. From June, in response to ongoing concern at violence between ethnic Albanians and security forces in the former Yugoslav republic of Macedonia (FYRM), UNMIK designated 19 authorized crossing points at Kosovo's international borders with Albania and the FYRM, and its boundaries with Montenegro and Serbia. In mid-May the SRSG signed the Constitutional Framework on Interim Self-Government, providing for the establishment of a Constitutional Assembly. UNMIK undertook efforts to register voters, in particular those from minority ethnic groups, and to continue to facilitate the return of displaced persons to their home communities. The last session of the KTC was held in October, and a general election was conducted, as scheduled, in mid-November. In December the SRSG inaugurated the new 120-member Assembly. However, disagreements ensued among the three main political parties represented in the Assembly concerning the appointment of the positions of President and Prime Minister. In February 2002 the SRSG negotiated an agreement with the leaders of the main political parties that resolved the deadlock in establishing the Interim Government. Accordingly, in March, the new President, Prime Minister and Interim Government were inaugurated, enabling the commencement of the process of developing self-governing institutions. In November the mission established the UNMIK Administration—Mitrovica, superseding parallel institutions that had operated hitherto in Serb-dominated northern Mitrovica, and thereby extending UNMIK's authority over all Kosovo. During that month a second series of municipal elections took place.

2003–05: In March 2003 a Transfer Council was established with responsibility for transferring competencies from UNMIK to the provisional institutions of self-government (PISG). In June UNMIK, with UNDP, launched a Rapid Response Returns Facility (RRRF) to assist returnees from inside and outside Kosovo through the provision of housing and socio-economic support. In October the SRSG invited Kosovan and Serb leaders, as well as representatives of the international Contact Group on the Balkans, to participate in direct talks. The outcome of the meeting, held in Vienna, Austria, was an agreement to pursue a process of direct dialogue. In March 2004 two working groups, concerned with energy and with missing persons, were established within the framework of direct dialogue; however, the process was suspended following serious ethnic violence that occurred during that month (see below). Also in October 2003 UNMIK established a task force to combat corruption, and concluded with Montenegro a Memorandum of Understanding (MOU) on Police Co-operation, with the aim of jointly targeting organized crime. In the following month a MOU was signed with the International Commission on Missing Persons, formalizing co-operation in using DNA technology to identify missing persons.

In December 2003 the SRSG and the Kosovan Prime Minister jointly launched *Standards for Kosovo*, drafted by the UN and partners and detailing eight fundamental democratic standards to be applied in the territory. Leaders of the Serb community declined to participate in the process. At the end of March 2004 the SRSG and Prime Minister Rexhapi launched the Kosovo Standards Implementation Plan, outlining 109 standards and goals, as a mechanism for reviewing the standards and assessing the progress of the PISG. In mid-March rioting erupted in Kosovska Mitrovica and violent clashes between Serb and Albanian communities occurred throughout the province. After two days of serious incidents 19 civilians were reported to have been killed, some 1,000 injured and an estimated 4,100 people from the Kosovan Serb, Roma and Ashkali communities had been displaced. In addition, 730 houses and 36 sites of cultural or religious importance had been damaged or destroyed. UNMIK undertook to restore the confidence of the affected communities, to assist with the reconstruction of damaged infrastructure, and to investigate the organizers and main perpetrators of the violence. It also initiated a review of its own operational procedures, as well as the conduct of local politicians. The priority areas for the mission were identified as providing a secure environment, including the protection of minorities, and ensuring the success of the Standards Implementation Plan. In August a newly appointed SRSG also re-emphasized the need to stimulate the local economy. In that month UNMIK, with UNDP and the local authorities, launched a youth employment creation project. In September UNMIK established a Financial Information Centre to help to deter money-laundering and other related offences. UNMIK assisted in preparations for legislative elections, to be held in October, and supported efforts to ensure a large and representative voter turn-out. In November the SRSG met the newly elected political leaders and agreed on the establishment of new ministries for energy and mining, local government, and returns and communities. The inaugural session of the new Assembly was convened in December. In that month the SRSG and the new Prime Minister, Ramush Haradinaj, concluded an agreement on making the Standards a priority for the Kosovan Government and on action for their implementation. In January 2005 a new UNMIK Senior Adviser on Minority Issues was appointed in order to assist the Government's efforts to integrate fully minorities into Kosovan society. In March Haradinaj resigned following notification of his indictment by the International Criminal Tribunal for the former Yugoslavia. UNMIK supported the establishment of a coalition administration, and announced the establishment of a new body to promote political consensus within the province. The first meeting of the so-called Kosovo Forum, to which all political leaders were invited, was convened in June. During March–May meetings of the working groups, convened within the framework of direct dialogue between Serbia and Kosovo, were held, concerned with missing persons, energy and return of displaced persons. In October the UN Secretary-General recommended that political negotiations on the future status of the province commence. A Special Envoy for the Future Status Process, Martii Ahtisaari, was appointed in the following month. In December new UNMIK regulations provided for the establishment of Ministries of Justice and of Internal Affairs.

2006–12: In March 2006 the Housing and Property Directorate was superseded by the Kosovo Property Agency. In August UNMIK and the Kosovan Ministry of Transport signed a memorandum governing the transfer of responsibility for the humanitarian transportation of minority communities in Kosovo from UNMIK to the Ministry. During that month the Interim Government approved the European Partnership Action Plan, which replaced the Kosovo Standards Implementation Plan during late 2006 as the basic reference document concerning standards. The 109 standards goals enshrined in the Standards Implementation Plan were incorporated into the Action Plan. Negotiations on the future status of Kosovo were organized by the Special Envoy for the Future Status Process during 2006, and in February 2007 he presented a Settlement Proposal to the relevant parties. The provisional Proposal, which provided for a Kosovan constitution, flag and national anthem and for Kosovo to apply for independent membership of international organizations, while remaining under close international supervision, was rejected by many Kosovan Serbs on the grounds that it appeared to advance the advent of a fully independent Kosovo, and also by extremist Kosovan Albanian elements since it did not guarantee immediate full independence. During violent protests against the proposals organized by radical Kosovo Albanians two protesters were killed by Kosovan and UNMIK police, leading to the resignations of the UNMIK Police Commissioner and the Kosovan Minister of Internal Affairs. The Special Envoy pursued further discussions with all parties; however, in March he declared an end to the negotiation process. A few days later he presented revisions to the Settlement Proposal. In April a delegation of the UN Security Council visited the region to consider the final settlement plans. In July the UN Secretary-General issued a technical assessment of the progress achieved in Kosovo towards implementing the Standards. He also noted ongoing ethnic tensions in the province that were threatening further progress and a low rate of minority returns. A troika of the Contact Group on Kosovo, comprising representatives of the EU, Russia and USA, was established to undertake intensive negotiations to determine a final status for the province. In December, however, the troika reported that no agreement had been reached.

UNMIK monitored the preparation for and conduct of a general election in Kosovo, held in November 2007. In February 2008 the mission appealed for restraint following a declaration of independence from Serbia, announced by the newly inaugurated Kosovan Assembly. In the following month the mission condemned a violent attack, by Serbian protesters, against a Court in northern Mitrovica, and subsequent clashes with UNMIK and KFOR personnel who regained control of the building. In early April the UN Secretary-General confirmed that UNMIK and the provisions of Security Council Resolution 1244 remained in effect and should be adhered to by the Kosovan and Serbian authorities. In mid-June a new Kosovan Constitution entered in force, providing for the transfer of executive powers from the UN to the elected authorities and for an EU police and justice mission to assume supervisory responsibilities from the UN. The UN Secretary-General confirmed that UNMIK was to be reconfigured; however, Serbian opposition to the Constitution and political divisions within the UN Security Council regarding the governance of the territory had prevented a new resolution being agreed. The EU 'Pillar' of the mission was terminated on 30 June. UNMIK worked closely with the EU to establish and deploy the EU Rule of Law Mission in Kosovo (EULEX), under the overall authority of the UN. In June the issuance of UNMIK travel documents was terminated as a result of a decision by the Kosovan authorities to produce national passports. UNMIK continued to monitor the implementation of the Standards for Kosovo programme and worked to strengthen co-operation between international agencies working in Kosovo. EULEX assumed responsibility for police and judicial functions in December, and reached full operational capacity in April 2009. Meanwhile, during 2009–10 UNMIK pursued practical co-operation with local authorities and reoriented its field presence to focus on areas occupied by ethnic non-Albanians. In July 2010 the International Court of Justice ruled that Kosovo had legitimately seceded from Serbia in February 2008. In mid-2010 UNMIK, jointly with the UN Kosovo Team, developed a new UN Strategic Framework for Kosovo, which was endorsed in September. During 2010–12 UNMIK continued its efforts to facilitate the participation of Kosovo in international and regional arrangements and conferences. By 31 December 2011 the UNMIK Human Rights Advisory Panel had completed 166 of a total of 525 cases under its consideration.

In 2012 UNMIK was continuing to facilitate dialogue among all communities in Kosovo. With a view to diffusing local tensions in northern areas, UNMIK has facilitated a new security co-ordination forum, comprising KFOR, EULEX, the OSCE and northern Kosovo Serb leaders. The mission monitors security arrangements provided to principal Serbian Orthodox religious sites, and facilitates UNESCO's cultural protection activities in Kosovo.

Operational Strength: At 31 March 2012 UNMIK comprised nine military officers and seven civilian police officers, in addition to (at 31 December 2011) 148 international and 215 local civilian staff, and 25 UN Volunteers.

Finance: The General Assembly apportioned US $44.9m. to the Special Account for UNMIK to finance the operation during the period 1 July 2011–30 June 2012.

United Nations Interim Force in Lebanon—UNIFIL

Address: Naqoura, Lebanon.

Force Commander and Chief of Mission: Maj.-Gen. PAOLO SERRA (Italy).

Establishment and Mandate: UNIFIL was established by UN Security Council Resolution 425 in March 1978, following an invasion of Lebanon by Israeli forces. The force was mandated to confirm the withdrawal of Israeli forces, to restore international peace and security, and to assist the Government of Lebanon in ensuring the return of its effective authority in southern Lebanon. UNIFIL also extended humanitarian assistance, including the provision of food, water, and medical and dental services, to the population of the area, particularly following the second Israeli invasion of Lebanon in 1982. In April 1992, in accordance with its mandate, UNIFIL completed the transfer of part of its zone of operations to the control of the Lebanese army.

Activities, 1998–2005: In March 1998 the Israeli Government announced that it recognized Security Council Resolution 425, requiring the unconditional withdrawal of its forces from southern Lebanon. It stipulated, however, that any withdrawal of its troops must be conditional on receiving security guarantees from the Lebanese authorities. In April 2000 the Israeli Government formally notified the UN Secretary-General of its intention to comply with Security Council Resolution 425. The Security Council endorsed an operational plan to enable UNIFIL to verify the withdrawal. In mid-June the UN Secretary-General confirmed that Israeli forces had fully evacuated from southern Lebanon. Soon afterwards UNIFIL reported several Israeli violations of the line of withdrawal, the so-called Blue Line. The Israeli Government agreed to rectify these by the end of July, and on 24 July the UN Secretary-General confirmed that no serious violations remained. UNIFIL, reinforced with additional troops, patrolled the area vacated by the Israeli forces, monitored the line of withdrawal, undertook de-mining activities, and continued to provide humanitarian assistance. From August the Lebanese Government deployed a Joint Security Force to the area and began re-establishing local administrative structures and reintegrating basic services into the rest of the country. However, the authorities declined to deploy military personnel along the border zone, on the grounds that a comprehensive peace agreement with Israel would first need to be achieved. In November, following two serious violations of the Blue Line in the previous month by both Israeli troops and Hezbollah militia, the Security Council urged the Lebanese Government to take effective control of the whole area vacated by Israel and to assume international responsibilities. In January 2001 the UN Secretary-General reported that UNIFIL no longer exercised control over the area of operation, which remained relatively stable. The Security Council endorsed his proposals to reconfigure the Force in order to focus on its remaining mandate of maintaining and observing the cease-fire along the line of withdrawal; this was completed by the end of 2002. Violations of the Blue Line were reported throughout 2002 and 2003 and, despite restrictions on its movements, UNIFIL increased its patrols. UNIFIL also helped to clear areas of land of anti-personnel devices and to assist the integration of the formerly occupied zone into the rest of the country. In July 2004 UNIFIL representatives, with other UN officials, worked to defuse tensions following an alleged Hezbollah sniper attack against Israeli forces and subsequent Israeli violations of Lebanese airspace. At the end of that year the UN expressed concern at further repeated violations of the Blue Line from both sides. A serious breach of the cease-fire occurred in May 2005. In June UNIFIL reported attacks on Israeli troop positions by Hezbollah militia and a forceful response by the Israeli Defence Force. In November UNIFIL brokered a cease-fire following further hostilities across the Blue Line, initiated by Hezbollah; however, there were reports of a missile attack on Israeli positions in the following month. The Security Council subsequently urged all parties to end violations of the Blue Line and for the Lebanese Government to maintain order and exert greater authority throughout its territory.

2006–12: In mid-July 2006 a full-scale conflict erupted between the Israeli armed forces and Hezbollah, following the capture by Hezbollah of two Israeli soldiers, and the killing of three others. An estimated 1,000 Lebanese civilians were killed and 900,000 displaced from their homes during the unrest. A cease-fire between Hezbollah and Israel entered into effect in mid-August, following the adoption by the UN Security Council of Resolution 1701. The provisions of the resolution also demanded 'the immediate cessation by Hezbollah of all attacks and the immediate cessation by Israel of all offensive military operations' in Lebanon; welcomed a recent decision of the Lebanese Government to deploy 15,000 armed troops in southern Lebanon; increased the Force's authorized troop strength to a maximum of 15,000; and expanded its mandate to include monitoring the cease-fire, supporting the Lebanese troop deployment in southern Lebanon, facilitating humanitarian access to civilian communities, and assisting voluntary and safe returns of people displaced by the conflict.

In September 2006 a new Strategic Military Cell, reporting to the Under-Secretary-General for Peace-keeping Operations, was established to provide military guidance to UNIFIL. In the following month a Maritime Task Force was established, the first in a UN peace-keeping operation, to patrol the waters off the Lebanese coast in order to counter illegal trade in arms. A UN Mine Action Co-ordination Centre of South Lebanon was also established to co-ordinate efforts to locate and destroy unexploded munitions. In June 2007 six soldiers serving under UNIFIL were killed in a car bomb attack in south-eastern Lebanon. In January 2008 the Security Council condemned an attack on a UNIFIL patrol. In August the Security Council, while authorizing a 12-month extension to the mission's mandate, recognized UNIFIL's contribution to achieving a stable security environment since the 2006 conflict and welcomed an increase in co-ordinated activities between UNIFIL and Lebanese forces. In January 2009 UNIFIL initiated an investigation into evidence that rockets had been fired from Lebanon towards Israel, and others had been discovered ready to fire, and strengthened border patrols. A review of UNIFIL's operational effectiveness was conducted in late 2009; in February 2010 recommendations were issued, on the basis of the review, on means of making the Force in future more task-oriented and flexible. The review also emphasized the need to formalize a mechanism for regular strategic dialogue between UNIFIL and the Lebanese armed forces. In August the Force Commander convened an extraordinary tripartite meeting with senior representatives of the Lebanese Armed Forces and the Israeli Defense Forces, following a violent encounter along the Blue Line.

In February 2011 UNIFIL conducted a large-scale disaster preparedness exercise with the Lebanese Armed Forces in the Tyre area. The UN Security Council strongly condemned a terrorist attack perpetrated against a UNIFIL convoy near Saida in late July, injuring six peace-keepers. At the beginning of August Lebanese and Israeli forces briefly exchanged fire across the Blue Line in the Wazzani River area; UNIFIL subsequently investigated the incident, and made a number of recommendations aimed at preventing a recurrence. The UN Secretary-General reported in November 2011 that Israeli violations of Lebanese airspace—mainly by unmanned vehicles, but occasionally by fighter aircraft—were continuing to occur almost daily, mainly by unmanned aerial vehicles, but also on occasion by fighter jets. At that time UNIFIL was undertaking up to 10,000 patrols each month.

Operational Strength: At 31 March 2012 the Force comprised 11,984 military personnel; it was supported (at 31 December 2011) by 348 international and 660 local civilian staff. UNIFIL is assisted in its tasks by military observers of the United Nations Truce Supervision Organization (see below).

Finance: The General Assembly appropriation for the operation for the period 1 July 2011–30 June 2012 amounted to US $545.5m.

United Nations Interim Security Force for Abyei—UNISFA

Address: Abyei Town, Sudan.

Head of Mission and Force Commander: Lt-Gen. TADESSE WEREDE TESFAY (Ethiopia).

Establishment and Mandate: Following the final conclusion in January 2005 of a Comprehensive Peace Agreement (CPA)—including a Protocol on the Resolution of the Conflict in Abyei Area (the 'Abyei Protocol'), signed in May 2004—between the Sudan Government and opposition Sudan People's Liberation Movement (SPLM), ongoing contention over the competing claims to land ownership in, and the future status of, Abyei presented an impediment to the implementation of the Agreement and to the advancement of stability in the region. From early January 2011, prior to the referendum held in that month on self-determination for South Sudan, heightened tensions and outbreaks of violence were reported in the Abyei region (located at Sudan's border with South Sudan—which eventually gained independence on 9 July 2011). In mid-January and early March the parties to the Comprehensive Peace Agreement agreed on temporary security arrangements for the Abyei region; the ongoing insecurity, however, deteriorated further. Immediately prior to the establishment of UNISFA unrest in Abyei had escalated significantly, displacing around 113,000 people, including most of the civilian inhabitants of the town of Abyei. The 'Temporary Arrangements for the Administration and Security of the Abyei Area'—an accord adopted in mid-June 2011 by the Sudanese Government and rebels, governing the withdrawal of their respective forces from Abyei—facilitated the deployment of the peace-keeping operation. The Temporary Arrangements provided for the establishment of an Abyei Area Administration, to be administered jointly by an SPLM-nominated Chief Administrator and a Government-nominated Deputy, which was mainly to exercise powers determined in the Abyei Protocol to the CPA; responsibility for supervising security and stability, however, was transferred by the Temporary Arrangements to a newly-established Abyei Joint Oversight Committee, comprising members from each party to the conflict, as well as to an AU facilitator.

UNISFA was established by UN Security Resolution 1990 on 27 June 2011, with an initial mandated term of six months. The Force is mandated to protect civilians and humanitarian personnel in Abyei; to facilitate the free movement of humanitarian aid; to monitor and verify the redeployment of government and rebel forces from the Abyei Area; to participate in relevant Abyei Area bodies; to provide demining assistance and advice on technical matters; to strengthen the capacity of the Abyei Police Service; and, as necessary, to provide—in co-operation with the Abyei Police Service—security for the regional oil infrastructure.

Activities: Under the auspices of the 'Friends of Abyei', chaired by the Resident Co-ordinator in Sudan, a planning team, comprising representatives of UN agencies, donor and INGOs, developed during 2011 a humanitarian joint recovery programming strategy for Abyei; it was envisaged that people displaced by the violence in Abyei would only be returned there following the planned withdrawal of forces and the full deployment of UNISFA. At the end of June 2011 the parties to the conflict in Abyei signed an Agreement on Border Security, in which they reaffirmed commitment to a Joint Political and Security Mechanism, established under an agreement concluded in December 2010; and created a safe demilitarized border zone, pending the resolution of the status of disputed areas; UNISFA was requested to provide force protection for a planned international border monitoring verification mission. Since its inauguration UNISFA has conducted regular air and ground patrols, and has established permanent operating bases in Abyei Town, Agok, and Diffra. In March 2012 the UN Secretary-General reported that the security situation in Abyei remained tense, owing to the continued presence—in violation of the June 2011 Agreement on Border Security—of unauthorized Sudanese armed forces, South Sudanese police, and rebels in the area; as well as owing to ongoing large-scale nomadic migration, and IDP returns. In April 2012 the UN Security Council demanded that Sudan and South Sudan redeploy their forces from Abyei; that the two sides withdraw forces from their joint border and cease escalating cross-border violence with immediate effect, with the support of UNIFSA and through the establishment of a demilitarized border zone; that Sudanese rebels should vacate oilfields in Heglig (Sudan); that Sudan should cease aerial bombardments of South Sudan; and that a summit should be convened between the two states to resolve outstanding concerns.

Operational Strength: UNISFA has a maximum authorized strength of 4,200 military personnel and 50 police. At 31 March 2012 UNISFA comprised 3,716 troops and 83 military observers; it was supported (as at 31 December 2011) by 32 international civilian staff members.

United Nations Military Observer Group in India and Pakistan—UNMOGIP

Address: Rawalpindi, Pakistan (November–April); Srinagar, India (May–October).

Head of Mission and Chief Military Observer: Maj.-Gen. RAUL GLOODTDOFSKY FERNANDEZ (Uruguay).

Establishment and Mandate: The Group was established in 1948 by UN Security Council resolutions aiming to restore peace in the region of Jammu and Kashmir, the status of which had become a matter of dispute between the Governments of India and Pakistan. Following a cease-fire that came into effect in January 1949 the military observers of UNMOGIP were deployed to assist in its observance. There is no periodic review of UNMOGIP's mandate.

Activities: In 1971, following the signature of a new cease-fire agreement, India claimed that UNMOGIP's mandate had lapsed, since it was originally intended to monitor the agreement reached in 1949. Pakistan, however, regarded UNMOGIP's mission as unchanged, and the Group's activities have continued, although they have been somewhat restricted on the Indian side of the 'line of control', which was agreed by India and Pakistan in 1972.

Operational Strength: At 31 March 2012 there were 38 military observers deployed on both sides of the 'line of control'; the mission was supported by 76 international and local civilian personnel (as at 31 December 2011).

Finance: The approved budget for the operation for the period 2012–13 was US $21.1m.

United Nations Mission for the Referendum in Western Sahara—MINURSO

Address: el-Aaiún, Western Sahara.

Special Representative of the UN Secretary-General and Chief of Mission: HANY ABDEL-AZIZ (Egypt).

Force Commander: Maj.-Gen. ABDUL HAFIZ (Bangladesh).

Establishment and Mandate: In April 1991 the UN Security Council endorsed the establishment of MINURSO to verify a cease-fire in the disputed territory of Western Sahara, which came into effect in September 1991, and to implement a settlement plan, involving the repatriation of Western Saharan refugees (in co-ordination with UNHCR), the release of all Sahrawi political prisoners, and the organization of a referendum on the future of the territory. Western Sahara is claimed by Morocco, the administering power since 1975, and by the Algerian-supported Frente Popular para la Liberación de Saguia el Hamra y Río de Oro—Frente Polisario. Although originally envisaged for January 1992, the referendum was postponed indefinitely. In 1992 and 1993 the UN Secretary-General's Special Representative (SRSG) organized negotiations between the Frente Polisario and the Moroccan Government, which were in serious disagreement regarding criteria for eligibility to vote in the plebiscite. In March 1993 the Security Council advocated that further efforts should be made to compile a satisfactory electoral list and to resolve the outstanding differences on procedural issues. The identification and registration operation was formally initiated in August 1994. In December 1995 the UN Secretary-General reported that the identification of voters had stalled, owing to persistent obstruction of the process on the part of the Moroccan and Frente Polisario authorities. In May 1996 the Security Council endorsed a recommendation of the Secretary-General to suspend the identification process until all sides demonstrate their willingness to co-operate with the mission. The Council decided that MINURSO's operational capacity should be reduced by 20%, with sufficient troops retained to monitor and verify the cease-fire.

Activities, 1997–2000: In 1997 the Secretary-General of the UN appointed James Baker, a former US Secretary of State, as his Personal Envoy to the region to revive efforts to negotiate a resolution to the dispute. Baker obtained the support of Morocco and the Frente Polisario to conduct direct talks; these were initiated in June, in Lisbon, Portugal, under the auspices of the UN, and attended by Algeria and Mauritania in an observer capacity. In September the two sides concluded an agreement which aimed to resolve the outstanding issues of contention, including a commitment by both parties to identify eligible Sahrawi voters on an individual basis, in accordance with the results of the last official census in 1974, and a code of conduct to ensure the impartiality of the poll. In October 1997 the Security Council increased the strength of the mission, to enable it to supervise nine identification centres. The process of voter identification resumed in December, and by September 1998 the initial identification process had been completed. However, the controversial issue of the eligibility of 65,000 members of three Saharan tribal groups remained unresolved. In October the Security Council endorsed a series of measures to advance the referendum, including a strengthened Identification Commission to consider requests from any applicant from the three disputed tribal groups on an individual basis. In November, following a visit to the region by the Secretary-General, the Frente Polisario accepted the proposals, and in March 1999 the Moroccan Government signed an agreement with the UN to secure the legal basis of the MINURSO operation. In May the Moroccan Government and the Frente Polisario agreed in principle to a draft plan of action for cross-border confidence measures. In July 1999 the UN published the first part of a provisional list of qualified voters. An appeals process then commenced, in accordance with the settlement plan. In late November almost 200 Moroccan prisoners of war were released by the Frente Polisario, following a series of negotiations led by the SRSG. The identification of applicants from the three disputed Saharan tribal groups was completed at the end of December. In January 2000 the second, final part of the provisional list of qualified voters was issued, and a six-week appeals process ensued.

2001–12: In June 2001 the Personal Envoy of the UN Secretary-General elaborated a draft Framework Agreement on the Status of Western Sahara as an alternative to the settlement plan. The draft Agreement envisaged the disputed area remaining part of Morocco, but with substantial devolution of authority. Any referendum would be postponed. The Security Council authorized Baker to discuss the proposals with all concerned parties. However, the Frente Polisario and Algeria rejected the draft Agreement. In November the Security Council, at the insistence of the Frente Polisario, requested the opinion of the UN Legal Counsel regarding the legality of two short-term reconnaissance licences granted by Morocco to international petroleum companies for operation in Western Sahara. In January 2002 the Secretary-General's Personal Envoy visited the region and met with leaders of both sides. He welcomed the release by the Frente Polisario of a further 115 Moroccan prisoners, but urged both sides to release all long-term detainees. In July the Frente Polisario released a further 101 Moroccan prisoners, leaving a total of 1,260 long-term detainees, of whom 816 had been held for more than 20 years. During February–November 2003 the Frente Polisario released 643 more prisoners. Morocco continued to detain 150 Sahrawi prisoners. In January the Secretary-General's Personal Envoy presented to both sides and to the Governments of neighbouring states a new arrangement for a political settlement, providing for self-determination, that had been requested by Resolution 1429 of the Security Council. In July the Frente Polisario accepted the so-called Peace Plan for Self-Determination of the People of Western Sahara. In April 2004, however, it was rejected by the Moroccan Government.

In March 2004 MINURSO co-operated with UNHCR to implement a family visits programme, providing for exchange of contacts of relatives divided by the dispute. MINURSO provided transport and other logistical support for the scheme, which was intended to be part of a series of humanitarian confidence-building measures. James Baker resigned as Personal Envoy of the Secretary-General in June. In September the SRSG, who had assumed responsibility for pursuing a political solution, held his first series of formal meetings with all parties to the dispute. In April 2005 the Secretary-General advised that MINURSO's force strength be maintained given the lack of progress in negotiating a political settlement. In July the Secretary-General appointed a new Personal Envoy for the Western Sahara, Peter van Walsum, who undertook his first visit to heads of state in the region in October in an attempt to review the 2003 Peace Plan. The Frente Polisario released all remaining Moroccan prisoners in August 2005.

In early 2006 Morocco established a Royal Advisory Council for Saharan Affairs that comprised Moroccan political parties and Sahrawi leaders, but not the Frente Polisario. In February a ministerial delegation of the Moroccan Government presented the member states of the Group of Friends of Western Sahara (France, Russia, Spain, the United Kingdom and the USA), as well as Germany and the UN Secretary-General, with the basics of a possible future plan for granting extended autonomy to Western Sahara. In April 2007 the UN Security Council reiterated a strong request that both parties enter into discussions without preconditions. In June direct talks between representatives of the Moroccan Government and the Frente Polisario, attended by representatives of Algeria and Mauritania, were held under the auspices of the Personal Envoy of the UN Secretary-General in Manhasset, NY, USA. Further negotiations were conducted in August. Both sides were reported to have agreed that the process should continue and that the current status quo in Western Sahara was unacceptable. The third and fourth rounds of discussions between the two sides, held in January and March 2008, respectively, secured further commitment by both sides to continue the process of negotiations. In February 2009 the newly appointed Personal Envoy, Christopher Ross, visited the region for the first time to meet with representatives of the Moroccan Government, Frente Polisario authorities and the Group of Friends. Ross visited the region for a second time in June to prepare for an informal meeting of the main parties. The talks, which were held in Dürnstein, Austria, in August, secured a commitment by the Moroccan Government and the Frente Polisario to continue negotiations as soon as possible. At a second informal meeting, held in Westchester County, NY, USA, in February 2010, both parties agreed once again to continue with negotiations; however, an *impasse* remained, concerning the issue of self-determination, with the Frente Polisario requesting a referendum for Western Sahara that would present multiple options, including independence, and the Moroccan Government favouring a negotiated autonomy for the area. At the third, fourth and fifth rounds of talks, held, respectively, in November and December 2010, and in January 2011, no significant progress was achieved. In early February 2011 the parties met with UNHCR to review the humanitarian confidence-building measures initiated during 2004. A sixth and seventh round of negotiations were convened in March and June 2011. The eighth, round took place in Manhasset, New York, in late July, and again ended in *impasse*, with each party continuing to reject the other's proposal as the sole basis of future negotiations. Negotiations were renewed in March 2012, in Greentree, NY.

The mission has headquarters in the north and south of the disputed territory. There is a liaison office in Tindouf, Algeria, which was established in order to maintain contact with the Frente Polisario (which is based in Algeria) and the Algerian Government.

Operational Strength: At 31 March 2012 MINURSO comprised 203 military observers, 27 troops and five police officers; it was supported by 19 UN Volunteers, and (at 31 December 2011) by 164 international and 101 local civilian personnel.

Finance: The General Assembly appropriation to cover the cost of the mission for the period 1 July 2011–30 June 2012 amounted to US $63.2m.

United Nations Mission in Liberia—UNMIL

Address: Monrovia, Liberia.

Special Representative of the UN Secretary-General and Head of Mission: KARIN LANDGREN (Sweden).

Force Commander: Lt-Gen. MUHAMMAD KHALID (Pakistan).

Police Commissioner: GAUTAM SAWANG (India).

Establishment and Mandate: UNMIL was authorized by the UN Security Council in September 2003 to support the implementation of the cease-fire accord agreed in June and the Comprehensive Peace Agreement concluded in August by the parties to the conflict in Liberia. UNMIL was mandated to assist with the development of an action plan for the disarmament, demobilization, reintegration and, where appropriate, repatriation of all armed groups and to undertake a programme of voluntary disarmament; to protect civilians and UN personnel, equipment and facilities; to support humanitarian and human rights activities; to support the implementation of national security reforms; and, in co-operation with ECOWAS and other partners, to assist the National Transitional Government (inaugurated in mid-October) with the training of a national police force and the restructuring of the military. Troops were also to assist with the rehabilitation of damaged physical infrastructure, in particular the road network. On 1 October UNMIL assumed authority from an ECOWAS-led multinational force in Liberia (the ECOWAS Mission in Liberia—ECOMIL), which had been endorsed by the Security Council in August; ECOMIL's 3,600 troops were reassigned to UNMIL, which then had an authorized maximum strength of 15,000 military personnel.

Activities, 2003–05: In 2004 UNMIL's civil affairs component assessed the functional capacities of public administration structures, including government ministries, in order to assist the National Transitional Government in re-establishing authority throughout Liberia. UNMIL was to support the National Transitional Government in preparing the country for national elections, which were expected to be held in October 2005. In December 2003 the programme for disarmament, demobilization, rehabilitation and reintegration (DDRR) officially commenced when the first cantonment site was opened. However, the process was disrupted by an unexpectedly large influx of former combatants and a few days later the process was temporarily suspended. In mid-January 2004 an agreement was concluded by all parties on necessary prerequisites to proceeding with the programme, including the launch of an information campaign, which was to be co-ordinated and organized by UNMIL, and the construction of new reception centres and cantonment sites. The DDRR process resumed, under UNMIL command, in mid-April. A training programme for the country's new police service was inaugurated in July and the first UN-trained police officers were deployed at the end of the year. By July 2007 some 3,500 officers had graduated from the UN training programme. In August 2004 UNMIL launched a further vocational training scheme for some 640 former combatants to learn building skills. By the end of October, when the disarmament phase of the DDRR programme was officially terminated, more than 96,000 former combatants, including 10,000 child soldiers, had handed over their weapons. Some 7,200 commenced formal education. At the same time, however, UNMIL troops were deployed throughout the country to restore order, after an outbreak of sectarian hostilities prompted widespread looting and destruction of property and businesses. In early December the Special Representative of the UN Secretary-General (SRSG) hosted a meeting of the heads of all West African peace-keeping and political missions, in order to initiate a more integrated approach to achieving stability and peace throughout the region.

During 2005 UNMIL continued to work to integrate ex-combatants into society through vocational training schemes, and to support community rehabilitation efforts, in particular through the funding of Quick Impact Projects. By August an estimated 78,000 former combatants had participated in rehabilitation and reintegration schemes, funded bilaterally and by a Trust Fund administered by the UN Development Programme. A programme to enrol 20,000 disarmed combatants in formal education was initiated in November. UNMIL provided technical assistance to the National Elections Commission, which, in April, initiated a process of voter registration in preparation for presidential and legislative elections. UNMIL was also concerned with maintaining a peaceful and secure environment for the electoral campaigns and polling days and undertook a large-scale civic education campaign in support of the democratic election process. In October UNMIL, with the Transitional Government, established a Joint National Security Operations Centre. The elections were held, as scheduled, in October, with a second-round presidential poll in November.

2006–12: In 2006 UNMIL determined to strengthen its focus on the rule of law, economic recovery and good governance. It also pledged to support the new Government in efforts to remove UN sanctions against sales of rough diamonds and to become a member of the Kimberley Process Certification Scheme by providing air support for surveillance and mapping activities in mining areas. Throughout 2006 and 2007 UNMIL personnel undertook projects to rehabilitate and construct roads and bridges, police stations, courtrooms and educational facilities. The mission also initiated, with the support of other UN agencies, a scheme to create employment throughout the country. In March 2007 UNMIL initiated a Sports for Peace programme to promote national reconciliation. In late April the UN Security Council removed the embargo against sales of diamonds from Liberia, and in the following month UNMIL transferred control of the regional diamond certification office to the national authorities.

In September 2006 the UN Security Council endorsed a recommendation by the Secretary-General that a consolidation, drawdown and withdrawal plan for UNMIL should be developed and implemented; the consolidation phase was completed in December 2007. In August 2007 the UN Secretary-General recognized the efforts of the new Government in consolidating peace and promoting economic recovery in the country. In the following month the Security Council endorsed a plan to reduce UNMIL's military component by 2,450 troops between October and September 2008, and to reduce the number of police officers by 498 in the period April 2008–December 2010. In April 2008 the SRSG reported that greater progress was needed in the training and restructuring of Liberia's security forces to enable the proposed drawdown of UNMIL personnel and transfer of responsibility to proceed. In September 2008 the Security Council approved an increase of 240 in the authorized number of personnel deployed as part of UNMIL's police component, to provide strategic advice and expertise in specialized files and operational support to regular policing activities. UNMIL continued to monitor and control security incidents, local demonstrations, cross-border activities and drugs-trafficking. In June 2009 the UN Secretary-General issued a special report recommending a further reduction of UNMIL's military component, of some 2,029 troops, in the period October 2009–May 2010, and that UNMIL's mandate be revised to enable the mission to support the authorities in preparing for presidential and legislative elections to be held in late 2011. In accordance with a UN Security Council resolution adopted in September 2009, UNMIL, the UN country team in Liberia, the Liberian National Electoral Commission, and other stakeholders subsequently developed a multi-sector electoral assistance project, with a view to supporting the planned election. In July 2009 an UNMIL training programme for the new Armed Forces of Liberia was initiated. The Liberian Government officially assumed responsibilities for the development of the Armed Forces of Liberia in January 2010. In February UNMIL troops intervened to restore order in Lofa County, in north-western Liberia, following widespread inter-ethnic violence, during which four people died and several churches and mosques were set on fire. In September the SRSG reported that the security situation in the country was stable, but remained fragile. She observed that the country required greater national reconciliation and more progress towards resolving issues concerning access to land, strengthening public confidence in the justice system and developing an independent security sector. The third stage of UNMIL's drawdown was completed, as planned, in May. In February 2011 formal responsibility for guarding the Special Court for Sierra Leone was transferred from UNMIL to the Sierra Leone police force. In September 2010 the UN Security Council authorized UNMIL to assist the Liberian Government with staging the 2011 elections, through the provision of logistical support, co-ordination of international electoral assistance, and support for Liberian institutions and political parties in creating an atmosphere conducive to the conduct of peaceful elections. Following the successful staging of legislative and presidential elections in October–November 2011, a reduction in the mission's authorized strength was anticipated. A technical assessment mission, scheduled to arrive in Liberia in February 2012, was to assess progress made in achieving the mission's strategic objectives, and was to evaluate the capacity of national security institutions and their ability to operate independently of UNMIL.

The impact on Liberia of violent unrest in neighbouring Côte d'Ivoire during late 2010–early 2011, including an influx into Liberia of Ivorian combatants, represented a major security threat to Liberia in 2011, which the Liberian authorities and UNMIL worked to address. In July 2011 UNMIL destroyed a cache of weaponry and ammunition believed to have been hidden by Côte d'Ivoire combatants. From May that year the Liberian military, supported by UNMIL, increased its presence along the Liberia-Côte d'Ivoire border, and UNMIL and UNOCI intensified inter-mission co-operation, including undertaking joint border patrols under the so-called 'Operation Mayo'. In June UNMIL and UNOCI conducted a joint assessment mission in western Côte d'Ivoire. In 2011 UNMIL also conducted operations along Liberia's borders with Guinea and Sierra Leone, with the Liberian Government and the Guinean and Sierra Leone authorities. UNMIL strengthened its monitoring in 2011 of electoral, legal, political, public information, security and human rights matters prior to the elections conducted in October–November. Equal airtime was given by UNMIL Radio to all participating parties. The mission also co-ordinated international assistance to the electoral process through a Donor Co-ordination Group.

Operational Strength: At 31 March 2012 UNMIL comprised 7,781 troops, 135 military observers, and 1,279 police officers, supported by 227 UN Volunteers, and (as at 31 December 2011) by 479 international civilian personnel and 995 local civilian staff.

Finance: The General Assembly appropriation to the Special Account for UNMIL amounted to US $525.6m. for the period 1 July 2011–30 June 2012.

United Nations Mission in South Sudan—UNMISS

Address: Juba, Sudan.

Special Representative of the Secretary-General: HILDE JOHNSON (Norway).

Establishment and Mandate: UNMISS was established in July 2011 upon the independence of South Sudan. The mission succeeded the former UN Mission in the Sudan (UNMIS). UNMISS is mandated to support the consolidation of peace, thereby fostering longer-term state-building and economic development; to support the South Sudan authorities with regard to conflict prevention, mitigation, and the protection of civilians; and to develop the new Government's capacity to provide security, to establish the rule of law, and to strengthen the security and justice sectors.

Activities: From July 2011 UNMISS liaised with the South Sudan Government and provided good offices to facilitate inclusive consultative processes involving all the stakeholders invested in nation-building. The mission responded to a request by the South Sudan authorities to support the development of a national security strategy; assisted, with UNDP, the South Sudan Disarmament, Demobilization and Reintegration Commission in preparing a disarmament, demobilization and reintegration policy; and cleared and opened (by November) some 121 km of road, through its Mine Action Service. During August–September the UNMISS Human Rights Unit undertook a fact-finding operation. UNMISS also supported the new Government's ratification of principal international human rights treaties, and monitored the harmonization of the national legislative framework with international human rights standards. In early August UNMISS and the Government of South Sudan signed a status-of-forces agreement guaranteeing the mission's freedom of movement throughout the new country; during the second half of 2011, however, UNMISS reported several restrictions on its movements. Planned deployments under UNMISS to LRA-affected areas were doubled, in comparison with deployments mandated under UNMIS. From the inception of UNMISS its forces were deployed mainly in response to violent unrest in Jonglei State, which persisted into 2012. Further UNMISS deployments in the second half of 2011 included deterrence operations in Western Equatoria, and a mission to support the integration of rebel forces in Pibor. UNMISS police activities focused on training and advising the new South Sudan Police Service.

From January 2012 relations between South Sudan and Sudan deteriorated significantly, owing to factors including the disputed delineation of the two countries' joint border, mutual accusations of support for anti-government rebel militia groups, control of the Sudanese territory of Abyei (Sudan, see UNMISS), and the dependence at that time of landlocked South Sudan on the use of Sudanese infrastructure (a pipeline and Port Sudan) for the export of petroleum. In February South Sudan and Sudan signed a memorandum of understanding on non-aggression and co-operation, committing each state to respecting the other's sovereignty and territorial integrity. In early April an AU High Level Implementation Panel, facilitating discussions between the two sides, presented to both parties a draft Joint Decision for Reduction of Tension, providing for the immediate cessation of hostilities between the two states, and the withdrawal of armed forces of each state from the territory of the other. Shortly afterwards the UN Security Council made several demands of both parties, including that they redeploy their forces from forward positions and end cross-border violence with immediate effect; that Sudan should cease aerial bombardments of South Sudan; that South Sudan and Sudan should redeploy forces from Abyei; and that a summit should be convened between the two states to resolve outstanding concerns. In mid-April an UNMISS support base was among buildings damaged by an aerial bombardment by Sudanese forces of Mayom, in Unity State, South Sudan, which resulted in several fatalities in that settlement.

Operational Strength: UNMISS has an authorized strength comprising up to 7,000 military personnel and up to 900 civilian police personnel. At 31 March 2012 UNMISS comprised 4,913 troops, 132 military observers and 488 police officers; it was supported by 270 UN Volunteers and (as at 31 December 2011) by 734 international and 1,824 local civilian personnel.

United Nations Operation in Côte d'Ivoire—UNOCI

Address: Abidjan, Côte d'Ivoire.

Special Representative of the Secretary-General and Head of Mission: ALBERT (BERT) GERARD KOENDERS (Netherlands).

Force Commander: Maj.-Gen. GNAKOUDÈ BÉRÉNA (Togo).

Police Commissioner: Maj.-Gen. JEAN MARIE BOURRY (France).

Establishment and Mandate: UNOCI was authorized by the UN Security Council in February 2004 and began operations in early April. It was mandated to observe and monitor the implementation of the Linas-Marcoussis Accord, signed by the parties to the conflict in Côte d'Ivoire in January 2003, and hitherto supported by the UN Mission in Côte d'Ivoire (MINUCI), forces of the Economic Community of West African States—ECOWAS and French peace-keeping troops. UNOCI was authorized also to assist with the disarmament, demobilization and reintegration of rebel groups, to protect civilians and UN personnel, institutions and equipment, and to support ongoing humanitarian and human rights activities. With a contingent of the French *'Licorne'* peace-keeping force, UNOCI was to monitor a so-called Zone of Confidence separating the two areas of the country under government and rebel control.

Activities, 2003–04: In July 2003 all parties, attending a meeting of West African heads of state that had been convened by the UN Secretary-General and the President of Ghana, endorsed the Accra III Agreement identifying means of implementing the Linas-Marcoussis Accord. UNOCI was to participate in a tripartite monitoring group, together with ECOWAS and the African Union, to oversee progress in implementing the agreement. In mid-August UNOCI launched a radio station, in accordance with its mandate, to assist the process of national reunification, and in the following month established some secure transit routes between the areas under government and rebel control in order to facilitate travel and enable family reunions. None the less, by October UNOCI officials expressed concern at ongoing violations of human rights and a deterioration in security, as well as a lack of progress in implementing provisions of the peace accords.

In early November 2004 government troops violated the cease-fire and the Zone of Confidence by launching attacks against rebel Forces Nouvelles in the north of the country. An emergency session of the UN Security Council, convened following an escalation of the hostilities and a fatal air strike on a French peace-keeping unit, urged both sides to refrain from further violence. Security further deteriorated in the south of the country when French troops destroyed the government air force, prompting rioting in the capital, Abidjan, and violence directed towards foreign nationals. UNOCI assisted with the evacuation of foreign workers and their families and provided secure refuge for other personnel. In mid-November the Security Council imposed an immediate embargo on the sale or supply of armaments to Côte d'Ivoire and demanded a cessation of hostilities and of the use of media broadcasts to incite hatred and violence against foreigners. UNOCI was to monitor the terms of the resolution and to broadcast its own messages of support for the peace process. By the end of that month reports indicated that the security situation had improved and that some of the estimated 19,000 who fled the country to Liberia had started to return. In addition, conditions in the northern city of Bouaké were improving as water and electricity supplies were restored. In December UNOCI funded three Quick Impact Projects, in order to highlight the humanitarian aspect of the mission, and commenced joint patrols with government forces to uphold security in Abidjan.

2005–12: In February 2005 the UN Security Council demanded that all parties co-operate with UNOCI in compiling a comprehensive list of armaments under their control as preparation for implementing a programme of disarmament, demobilization and reintegration. In March UNOCI increased its presence in western regions of the country owing to an increase in reported violent incidents. In the following month UNOCI troops were deployed to the border regions with Liberia and Ghana in order to support implementation of the UN-imposed arms embargo. UNOCI troops also monitored the withdrawal of heavy weaponry by both government forces and the Forces Nouvelles. In June UN representatives condemned the massacre of almost 60 civilians in Duékoué, in the west of the country, and urged that an inquiry be held into the incident. UNOCI reinforcements were sent to restore stability in the area and undertook joint patrols with local forces. Later in that month the UN Security Council authorized an increase in UNOCI's military and civilian police components, as well as the redeployment of troops from other missions in the region in order to restore security in the country. In July UN troops, investigating reports of violent attacks by rebel groups, were prevented from entering two towns north of Abidjan. UNOCI later complained at further reported obstruction of human rights and civilian police teams. In spite of persisting concerns regarding the political and human rights situation in the country, UNOCI continued to provide logistical and technical assistance to the independent national electoral commission in preparing for elections, scheduled to be held in October; however, these were later postponed. A Transitional Government of National Unity was formed in December. In early 2006 UN property and personnel were subjected to hostile attacks during a period of unrest by groups protesting against a report of an International Working Group, co-chaired by the SRSG, that had recommended the dissolution of the national assembly (the mandate of which had already expired). Several hundred humanitarian personnel were evacuated from the country. At the end of February UNOCI initiated a large-scale operation to provide security for school examinations, to be held in the north of the country for the first time in three years. In June the Security Council authorized an increase in the mission's force strength by 1,025 military personnel and 475 police officers needed to strengthen security throughout the country and undertake disarmament operations. In October UNOCI conducted joint border patrols with UN forces in Liberia to monitor movements of combatants and weapons. In January 2007 the Security Council formally enlarged UNOCI's mandate to co-ordinate with UNMIL to monitor the arms embargo and to conduct a voluntary repatriation and resettlement programme for foreign ex-combatants. The Council's resolution also defined UNOCI's mandate as being to monitor the cessation of hostilities and movements of armed groups; to assist programmes for the disarmament, demobilization and reintegration of all combatants; to disarm and dismantle militias; to support population identification and voter registration programmes; to assist the reform of the security sector and other activities to uphold law and order; to support humanitarian assistance and the promotion of human rights; and to provide technical support for the conduct of free and fair elections no later than 31 October. A new political agreement to work towards national reconciliation was signed by leaders of the opposing parties in Ouagadougou, Burkina Faso, in March. According to the Ouagadougou Agreement the Zone of Confidence was to be dismantled and replaced by a UN-monitored 'green line'. UNOCI organized a series of meetings to ensure the support of traditional leaders for the peace process. In June UNOCI condemned a rocket attack on a plane carrying the country's Prime Minister. The process of disarmament was officially launched at the end of July; it was, however, hindered by underfunding of the arrangements for the reintegration of former militia members. In August 2008 UNOCI, in collaboration with UNDP, initiated a scheme of 'micro projects' to help to reduce poverty and youth unemployment and facilitate the reintegration of ex-combatants.

The redeployment of UNOCI troops from the former Zone of Confidence was completed by late July 2008, when the last observation post was officially closed. In April UNOCI announced that the presidential election was scheduled to be held later in that year on 30 November. UNOCI personnel were assisting in the rehabilitation of polling stations and in supporting the independent electoral commission. In July the SRSG met with the country's President to confirm UN support for the electoral process and plans to implement security arrangements. The process of voter identification and registration was formally inaugurated in mid-September, with UNOCI to provide transport and other logistical assistance in support of the electoral and registration processes. The electoral preparations, however, were disrupted by severe logistical problems, and in November the election was officially postponed. A new timetable, providing for the election to be held in November 2009 and for voter identification and registration processes to be concluded by 30 June, was announced in May; the election was, however, subsequently postponed once again, until 2010, owing to delays in preparing and publishing the provisional electoral list. The list was eventually issued in November 2009. In January 2010, however, a parallel list was found to be in existence, prompting the Côte d'Ivoire President in February to dissolve both the electoral commission and the national Government, in order to maintain the credibility of the process; a new electoral commission and Government were appointed at the end of that month. None the less, the consequent national tension and outbreak of violence caused the electoral process to remain stalled.

In view of a deterioration in the security situation in Guinea in late 2009 UNOCI forces intensified at that time air and ground patrols of the Côte d'Ivoire–Guinea border area.

During 2010 UNOCI developed, jointly with the Côte d'Ivoire military and French *'Licorne'* force, a co-ordinated plan for helping ensure the security of the planned election. In September an agreement on a final voters list was concluded by the leaders of the three main political parties, and this list was officially certified by the SRSG on 24 September. At the end of September the UN Security Council approved a temporary increase of UNOCI's authorized military and police personnel from 8,650 to 9,150, to be deployed with immediate effect. The first round of the long planned presidential election was held on 31 October, and, following certification of the results of the first round by the SRSG on 12 November, a second electoral round was contested by the two first round forerunners on 28 November. (The incumbent President, Laurent Gbagbo, had received the most votes at the first round, but by a margin that did not constitute an outright victory.) At the beginning of December the electoral commission, supported by the UN, confirmed that Gbagbo's opponent, Alassane Ouattara, had won the presidential election; on the following day, however, the national constitutional council rejected the final results, declaring Gbagbo to be the winner. International opinion, including the UN, African Union and ECOWAS, continued to endorse Ouattara as the rightfully elected new Ivorian President, and the UN Secretary-General and French Government rejected demands by Gbagbo, who refused to concede defeat to Ouattara, that UNOCI and *Licorne* troops should leave Côte d'Ivoire. From mid-December serious violent unrest erupted, with numerous fatalities, as well as obstructions to the movement and activities of UNOCI peace-keepers, and attacks on UN personnel and on the UNOCI headquarters, reported during late 2010–early 2011. In mid-January 2011 the Security Council authorized the deployment of an additional 2,000 military personnel to UNOCI, until end-June 2011; and extended, until end-June 2011, the temporary additional military and police capabilities authorized in September 2010.

On 30 March 2011 the UN Security Council adopted Resolution 1975, urging all Ivorian parties to respect the will of the electorate and therefore to acknowledge the election of Ouattara as Côte d'Ivoire President. Resolution 1975 emphasized that UNOCI might use 'all necessary measures' in executing its mandate to protect civilians under threat of attack. On the following day forces loyal to Ouattara advanced on Abidjan, while UNOCI peacekeepers took control of the capital's airport. In early April UNOCI and *Licorne* forces directed fire at pro-Gbagbo heavy artillery and armoured vehicles. On 9 April UNOCI troops fired on pro-Gbagbo forces, in response to a reported Gbagbo-sanctioned attack on Ouattara at an Abidjan hotel. UNOCI and *Licorne* air strikes were undertaken on the following day against pro-Gbagbo heavy weaponry, reportedly inflicting significant damage on the presidential palace. On 11 April forces loyal to Ouattara arrested Gbagbo, with assistance from *Licorne*; Gbagbo and his entourage were then placed under UNOCI guard. Ouattara was eventually inaugurated as President in May.

During the first half of May 2011 the UN Secretary-General dispatched an assessment mission to examine, and make a number of recommendations on, the situation in Côte d'Ivoire. The Secretary-General subsequently recommended that UNOCI play a greater role in helping the national authorities to stabilize the security situation, with a particular focus on Abidjan and western (including border) areas. Accordingly, UNOCI was to increase joint patrols with the Côte d'Ivoire military and police; and was to facilitate the resumption of law enforcement responsibilities by the police and gendarmerie; to deter the activities of militias; and to assist in the protection of civilians. UNOCI was also to continue to collect, secure and dispose of weaponry; and to assist in demining activities. It was recommended that UNOCI, in close co-operation with UNMIL, should enhance its support to the Côte d'Ivoire and Liberian authorities to monitor and address cross-border security challenges, and should increase patrols of the Côte d'Ivoire-Liberia border area (under the so-called 'Operation Mayo'); in June UNOCI and UNMIL conducted a joint assessment mission in western Côte d'Ivoire. It was recommended following the May assessment that UNOCI should provide assistance for the development of a UN justice support programme; support the capacity development for the police, gendarmerie and corrections officers; deploy an expert to work with the authorities on security sector reform; assist the Government in developing a new national programme for demobilization, disarmament and reintegration of combatants, and dismantling of militias, that would be tailored to the post April 2011 context; continue to support the registration and profiling of former combatants; support the organization and conduct of the legislative elections; and strengthen its human rights monitoring activities. UNOCI provided logistical and security support to facilitate the conduct of legislative elections that were held in Côte d'Ivoire in December 2011; in February 2012 the SSRG determined that the electoral process had been 'free, fair, just and transparent' in 193 of the 204 parliamentary constituencies that had been polled; results in the remaining constituencies had, however, been found by the Constitutional Court to be irregular, and had consequently been annulled.

Operational Strength: At 31 March 2012 UNOCI had an operational strength of 9,402 troops, 203 military observers and 1,352 police officers; it was supported by 292 UN Volunteers, and (at 31 December 2011) by 399 international and 754 local civilian personnel.

Finance: The General Assembly appropriated US $486.7m. to finance the mission during the period 1 July 2011–30 June 2012.

United Nations Organization Stabilization Mission in the Democratic Republic of the Congo—MONUSCO

Address: Kinshasa, Democratic Republic of the Congo.

Liaison offices are situated in Kigali (Rwanda) and Pretoria (South Africa). A logistics base is located in Entebbe, Uganda.

Special Representative of the UN Secretary-General and Chief of Mission: ROGER MEECE (USA).

Force Commander: Lt-Gen. CHANDER PRAKASH (India).

Police Commissioner: ABDALLAH WAFY (Niger).

Establishment and Mandate: On 1 July 2010 MONUSCO succeeded the former United Nations Mission in the Democratic Republic of the Congo (MONUC), which had been established by the UN Security Council in August 1999 and had been operational until the end of June 2010. MONUSCO was inaugurated—to reflect a new phase in the ongoing peace process in the Democratic Republic of the Congo (DRC)—as a consequence of the adoption, in late May 2010, of Security Council Resolution 1925. Resolution 1925 emphasized that the DRC regime (which had reportedly requested the full withdrawal of the UN peace-keeping presence) should bear primary responsibility for maintaining security and promoting peace-building and development in the country, and authorized MONUSCO's deployment until, initially, 30 June 2011 (the mandate was subsequently extended until 30 June 2012). MONUSCO was to comprise, initially, a maximum of 19,815 military personnel, 760 military observers, 391 police personnel and 1,050 members of formed police units, with future reconfigurations to be determined as the situation evolved on the ground. The mission was to use all necessary means to carry out its mandate, which focused on protecting civilians and humanitarian personnel, as well as protecting UN staff, facilities, installations and equipment; supporting the DRC regime in efforts towards stabilizing the country and consolidating peace, including helping with strengthening the capacity of the military and with police reforms, developing and implementing a multi-year joint UN justice support programme, consolidating state authority in areas freed from the control of armed militia, providing technical and logistics support for local and national elections at the request of the Government, and monitoring the arms embargo against rebel militia active in the DRC; providing human rights training to DRC government officials, security service personnel, journalists, and civil society organizations; and advancing child protection, combating sexual violence, and promoting the representation of women in decision-making roles. MONUSCO was to focus its military forces in eastern areas of the DRC, while maintaining a reserve force that could be deployed elsewhere at short notice. MONUSCO screens DRC battalion commanders for human rights violations prior to the provision of logistical and other support.

Activities: From mid-2010 MONUSCO implemented several Quick Impact Projects, including the establishment of new press and vocational training centres and the rehabilitation of play areas and schools. The mission continued to support the Government's disarmament, demobilization and rehabilitation initiative, and through its regional radio network the mission aimed to encourage defections from the LRA. In late July MONUSCO established a mobile base in Beni, North Kivu province, in order to enhance security for humanitarian personnel working to provide essential medical and food assistance to an estimated 90,000 people who had been temporarily displaced by an escalation of fighting in that area between the national armed forces and the Ugandan rebel group, the Allied Democratic Forces. In the following month three peace-keepers were killed in an attack on their base in Kirumba, North Kivu. In September MONUSCO initiated special patrols in North Kivu to enhance civilian protection following a series of violent attacks, including mass rapes, by illegal armed groups. During 2010–11 MONUSCO worked to launch community alert networks aimed at enhancing the protection of civilians; under the community alert system, settlements in isolated areas were enabled to request, through mission community liaison assistants, intervention to deter threatened attacks. MONUSCO also provided technical advice, logistical support, and police electoral security training, during the preparation for legislative and presidential elections that were held in November–December 2011, and the mission also provided security patrols before, during and after the electoral process. (The outcome of the presidential election was disputed.) During 2011 MONUSCO documented several hundred reported violations of human rights linked to the electoral process, affecting, in particular, political opposition supporters, journalists and human rights defenders.

During 2011 MONUSCO conducted 46 joint protection team missions with DRC armed forces, in North and South Kivu, Equateur, Ituri and Haut Uélé and Katanga. In late April MONUSCO implemented Operation Easter Shield, aimed an enhancing civilian protection and facilitating the delivery of humanitarian assistance in the northeastern Doruma area (bordering South Sudan), following reports of LRA attacks there. MONUSCO also undertook road rehabilitation activities in north-eastern DRC in 2011.

During late 2011 MONUSCO, with the UN DRC country team, finalized the 2011–13 UN Transitional Framework for the DRC, defining areas of collaboration between MONUSCO and other UN agencies.

Operational Strength: At 31 March 2012 MONUSCO comprised 17,129 troops, 733 military observers and 1,367 police officers (including formed police units), supported by 612 UN Volunteers and (at 31 December 2011) by 963 international and 2,857 local civilian personnel.

Finance: The budget for the mission amounted to US $1,419.9m. for the period 1 July 2011–30 June 2012, funded from a Special Account comprising assessed contributions from UN member states.

United Nations Peace-keeping Force in Cyprus—UNFICYP

Address: Nicosia, Cyprus.

Special Representative of the UN Secretary-General and Chief of Mission: Lisa M. Buttenheim (USA).

Force Commander: Maj.-Gen. Chao Liu (People's Republic of China).

Establishment and Mandate: UNFICYP was established in March 1964 by a UN Security Council resolution (initially for a three-month duration) to prevent a recurrence of fighting between the Greek and Turkish Cypriot communities, and to contribute to the maintenance of law and order and a return to normal conditions. The Force controls a 180-km buffer zone, established (following the Turkish intervention in 1974) between the cease-fire lines of the Turkish forces and the Cyprus National Guard. It is mandated to investigate and act upon all violations of the cease-fire and buffer zone. The Force also performs humanitarian functions, such as facilitating the supply of electricity and water across the cease-fire lines, and offering emergency medical services.

In October 2004 the Security Council endorsed the recommendations of the Secretary-General's review team, which included a reduction in the mission's authorized strength from 1,230 to 860 military personnel, to include 40 military observers and liaison officers, and an increase in the deployment of civilian police officers from 44 to 69.

Activities, 1996–2005: In August 1996 serious hostilities between elements of the two communities in the UN-controlled buffer zone resulted in the deaths of two people and injuries to many others, including 12 UN personnel. Following further intercommunal violence, UNFICYP advocated the prohibition of all weapons and military posts along the length of the buffer zone. The Force also proposed additional humanitarian measures to improve the conditions of minority groups living in the two parts of the island. In July 1997 a series of direct negotiations between the leaders of the two communities was initiated, in the presence of the UN Secretary-General's Special Adviser; however, the talks were suspended at the end of that year. In November 1999 the Greek Cypriot and Turkish Cypriot leaders agreed to participate in proximity negotiations, to be mediated by the UN. Consequently, five rounds of these took place during the period December 1999–November 2000. In January 2002 a new series of direct talks between the leaders of the two communities commenced, under the auspices of the Secretary-General's Special Adviser. In May the Secretary-General visited Cyprus and met the two leaders. Further meetings between the Secretary-General and the two leaders took place in September (in Paris, France) and October (New York, USA). In November he submitted to them for consideration a document providing the basis for a comprehensive settlement agreement; a revised version of the document was released in the following month. A further revised version of the draft settlement plan document was presented to the leaders of the two communities during a visit by the Secretary-General to Cyprus in late February 2003. He urged that both sides put this to separate simultaneous referendums at the end of March, in the hope that, were the settlement plan approved, Cyprus would be able to accede to the European Union (EU) in a reunited state on 1 May 2004. Progress stalled, however, at a meeting between the two sides held in early March 2003 in The Hague, Netherlands. In April the Security Council adopted a resolution calling upon both parties to continue to work towards a settlement using the Secretary-General's plan as the unique basis for future negotiations. In reports to the Security Council the UN Secretary-General has consistently recognized UNFICYP as being indispensable to maintaining calm on the island and to creating the best conditions for his good offices. In November 2003 he noted that a number of restrictions placed on UNFICYP's activities during 2000 by the Turkish Cypriot authorities and Turkish forces remained in place. In February 2004 the Greek Cypriot and Turkish Cypriot leaders committed themselves to the Secretary-General's settlement plan. Negotiations on settling outstanding differences were chaired by the Secretary-General's Special Adviser for Cyprus throughout March. Despite a lack of agreement when the two sides met with the Secretary-General in late March, a finalized text was presented at the end of that month. The proposed Foundation Agreement was subsequently put to referendums in both sectors in April when it was approved by two-thirds of Turkish Cypriot voters, but rejected by some 75% of Greek Cypriot voters. In June the Secretary-General determined to undertake a comprehensive review of UNFICYP's mandate and force levels, in view of the political developments on the island, and announced his decision not to resume his good offices. In November 2004 UNFICYP troops initiated an EU-funded project to remove anti-personnel landmines from the buffer zone separating the two communities. A second phase of the project was launched in August 2005 (and completed in November 2006); it terminated in February 2011, by which time an estimated 27,000 landmines had been removed.

2006–12: In July 2006 the Turkish Cypriot leader and the Greek Cypriot President met, under the auspices of the UN Secretary-General. The leaders agreed on a set of principles and decisions aimed at reinstating the negotiating process. In September 2007 UNFICYP hosted a second meeting of the leaders of the two communities. They agreed on a need to initiate a settlement process and confirmed that they would continue a bi-communal dialogue under UN auspices. A new Greek Cypriot President was elected in February 2008. In the following month the Special Representative of the UN Secretary-General (SRSG) convened a meeting of the two leaders, who agreed to the establishment of technical committees and working groups in preparation for detailed political negotiations. The leaders also agreed to reopen a crossing between the two communities at Ledra Street, Nicosia. A ceremony to mark the event was held in early April. A second round of discussions was held, at the residence of the SRSG, in May. In July the two leaders agreed in principle on the issue of a single sovereignty and citizenship and initiated a review of the technical committees and working groups. Full negotiations on a political settlement for the island were inaugurated in early September, supported by the newly appointed Special Adviser of the UN Secretary-General, Alexander Downer. By August 2009 the two leaders had met 40 times in the preceding 12-month period, discussing issues concerning governance and power sharing, the EU, security and guarantees, territory, property, and economic matters. The second round of full negotiations commenced in September, and by September 2010 a further 44 meetings had been conducted. UNFICYP personnel during that year focused efforts on the maintenance of the military status quo, de-mining, and the facilitation of civilian activities in the buffer zone. In October the Limnitis/Yesilirmak crossing point was reopened. In November the UN Secretary-General met directly with the two leaders in order to reinvigorate the settlement discussions. A further meeting between the Secretary-General and the leaders of the two communities was convened in January 2011, at which both sides agreed to intensify efforts to reach substantive agreement. In June the UN Security Council strongly urged the leaders to advance the momentum of the negotiations. A meeting held in the following month between the Secretary-General and the Greek Cypriot and Turkish Cypriot leaders agreed on an intensified schedule of regular negotiations during late July–late October, with enhanced engagement by the UN. Two meetings covering contentious property ownership issues were convened in September between the two leaders, with the participation of UN property experts. In October 2011 and January 2012 further meetings were held between the UN Secretary-General and the two leaders, in Greentree, NY, USA, aimed at assessing progress made in the ongoing negotiations, and at addressing unresolved core issues, especially related to power-sharing, property, territory and citizenship. In November 2011 the Security Council further extended UNFICYP's mandate, to 15 June 2012.

Operational Strength: At 31 March 2012 UNFICYP had an operational strength of 864 troops and 68 police officers; it was supported by 148 international and local civilian staff (as at 31 December 2011).

Finance: The General Assembly appropriated US $58.2m. to the Special Account for UNFICYP to finance the period 1 July 2011–30 June 2012.

United Nations Stabilization Mission in Haiti—MINUSTAH

Address: Port-au-Prince, Haiti.

Special Representative of the UN Secretary-General and Head of Mission: MARIANO FERNÁNDEZ (Chile).

Force Commander: Maj.-Gen. FERNANDO RODRIGUES GOULART (Brazil).

Police Commissioner: MARC TARDIF (Canada).

Establishment and Mandate: In early 2004 political tensions within Haiti escalated as opposition groups demanded political reforms and the resignation of President Jean-Bertrand Aristide. Increasingly violent public demonstrations took place throughout the country, in spite of diplomatic efforts by regional organizations to resolve the crisis, and in February armed opposition forces seized control of several northern cities. At the end of that month, with opposition troops poised to march on the capital and growing pressure from the international community, President Aristide tendered his resignation and fled the country. On that same day the UN Security Council, acting upon a request by the interim President, authorized the establishment of a Multinational Interim Force (MIF) to help to secure law and order in Haiti. The Council also declared its readiness to establish a follow-on UN mission. In April the Security Council agreed to establish MINUSTAH, which was to assume authority from the MIF with effect from 1 June. MINUSTAH was mandated to create a stable and secure environment, to support the transitional government in institutional development and organizing and monitoring elections, and to monitor the human rights situation. Among its declared objectives was the improvement of living conditions of the population through security measures, humanitarian actions and economic development.

Activities, 2004–09: In September 2004 MINUSTAH worked closely with other UN agencies and non-governmental organizations to distribute food and other essential services to thousands of people affected by a tropical storm, although at the end of that year MINUSTAH's priority continued to be the security situation in the country. By that time the following civil units had become fully operational: electoral assistance; child protection; gender; civil affairs; human rights; and HIV/AIDS. In January 2005 MINUSTAH, with the UN Development Programme, the Haitian Government and the Provisional Electoral Council, signed an agreement on the organization of local, parliamentary and presidential elections, to be held later in that year. In May the UN Secretary-General expressed concern at the security environment with respect to achieving political transition. In the following month the Security Council approved a temporary reinforcement of MINUSTAH to provide increased security in advance of the elections. The military component was to comprise up to 7,500 troops (an additional strength of 750 troops) and the civilian police force up to 1,897 officers. From mid-2005 MINUSTAH forces worked to improve security in the country, in particular to reduce the criminal activities of armed groups in poorer urban areas. In November MINUSTAH deployed experts to train electoral agents and supervisors; however, the electoral timetable was delayed. Presidential and legislative elections were conducted in early February 2006. MINUSTAH officers provided security during the voting and maintained order as the results were being clarified. The mission subsequently pledged to support a post-election process of national dialogue and reconciliation and measures to strengthen the country's police force in order to re-establish law and order in areas of the capital, Port-au-Prince. A second round of voting in the legislative election was conducted in April. In August the UN Security Council determined that the mission should strengthen its role in preventing crime and reducing community violence, in particular kidnappings and other activities by local armed groups. In February 2007 MINUSTAH launched a large-scale operation in the Cité Soleil quarter of Port-au-Prince in order to extend its security presence in the most vulnerable locations and to counter the activities of criminal gangs. At the same time UN personnel helped to rehabilitate education, youth and medical facilities in those areas. In April MINUSTAH provided security and logistical support during the conduct of local municipal and mayoral elections. By November an estimated 9,000 local police officers had graduated from MINUSTAH training institutes. Efforts to control gang violence and uphold security in the poorest urban areas were ongoing in 2007–09. In February 2008 MINUSTAH announced that it was to fund six local infrastructure improvement projects to generate temporary employment for 7,000 people in the Cité Soleil and Martissant districts of Port-au-Prince. In April there were violent local demonstrations concerning the rising cost of living, during which several MINUSTAH personnel were attacked and property was damaged. A contingent of the mission subsequently distributed food aid to some 3,000 families in the poorest quarters of the capital. In August–September MINUSTAH personnel undertook emergency relief and rehabilitation activities, including evacuation of local residents and the distribution of humanitarian aid, to assist some of the 800,000 people affected by tropical storms which struck the country consecutively during a period of three weeks. From mid-2008 MINUSTAH strengthened its presence along the country's border with the Dominican Republic to counter illegal drugs-trafficking and improve security in the region. In December the mission undertook its first joint operation with the local police authorities to seize illegal drugs. Later in that month it was announced that the first and second rounds of planned partial senatorial elections would be held, respectively, in April and June 2009; during December 2008–February 2009 MINUSTAH and the police authorities jointly conducted a security assessment of new voting centres. Also during December 2008 MINUSTAH, international donors and representatives of the Haitian Government participated in a workshop that resulted in the adoption of a legislative agenda for 2009. During 2009 MINUSTAH, as well as implementing projects aimed at reducing violence in the community, provided technical security capacity-building support to the national police.

2010–12: In January 2010 a major earthquake struck Haiti, and destroyed the MINUSTAH headquarters in Port-au-Prince. Subsequently it was confirmed that more than 60 mission staff had been killed, among them Hédi Annabi, the then Special Representative of the Secretary-General (SRSG), his deputy, and the acting police commissioner for the mission; almost 180 further UN personnel were unaccounted for. Later in January, following the natural disaster, the UN Security Council adopted a resolution increasing the strength of the mission, to enable it to support the immediate recovery, reconstruction and stability efforts in Haiti. The temporary deployment of an additional 680 police officers was authorized by the Security Council in June, in order to strengthen the capacity of the Haitian national police force. MINUSTAH extended technical, logistical and administrative assistance to the country's authorities in preparation for presidential and legislative elections, which were conducted in November. The Head of Mission maintained regular dialogue with all presidential candidates throughout the electoral process. MINUSTAH contributed to efforts to restore order and to maintain stability following violent reactions to preliminary election results in December. The mission developed a revised security strategy to ensure a stable environment for the second round of voting in the presidential election, held in March 2011. From October 2010 MINUSTAH provided logistical support to counter a severe outbreak of cholera, including the construction of temporary treatment centres, public education efforts, transportation of personnel, emergency medicines and supplies, and the distribution of potable water in affected areas. In January 2011 the UN Secretary-General appointed a panel of independent experts to assess the outbreak amid widespread speculation within the country that a contingent of MINUSTAH troops was the source. In May, following the publication of the report, the UN Secretary-General announced his intention to establish a task force to consider its findings and recommendations. During January 2011 MINUSTAH launched a major initiative, with the national police force, to seize known criminals, as well as to undertake youth training schemes in some of the poorest urban areas. In October the UN Security Council extended MINUSTAH's mandate until 15 October 2012, and authorized a reduction in the mission's authorized strength by 1,600 personnel, to be completed by June 2012, in order to redress the mission's post-earthquake expansion. In January 2012 MINUSTAH reported that the post-earthquake population of IDPs in camps had reduced by two-thirds.

Operational Strength: At 31 March 2012 MINUSTAH comprised 7,526 troops and 3,247 police officers; there was also a support team of 558 international civilian staff and 1,362 local civilian staff (as at 31 December 2011), and 224 UN Volunteers.

Finance: The mission is financed by assessments in respect of a Special Account. The budget for the period 1 July 2011–30 June 2012 amounted to US $793.5m.

United Nations Supervision Mission in Syria—UNSMIS

Address: Damascus, Syria.

Chief Military Observer: Maj.-Gen. ROBERT MOOD (Norway).

Joint Special Envoy of the UN and the League of Arab States on the Syrian Crisis: KOFI ANNAN (Ghana).

Establishment and Mandate: UNSMIS was established by the UN Security Council in April 2012, for an initial period of 90 days, with a mandate to monitor a cease-fire between Syrian government forces and pro-democracy protesters, and to observe and support the full implementation of a six-point peace plan that had been proposed in March by the Joint Special Envoy of the UN and the League of Arab States on the Syrian Crisis, and accepted during that month by the Syrian authorities. UNSMIS was to be deployed 'expeditiously', subject to an assessment by the UN Secretary-General of relevant developments in Syria, including the consolidation of the—fragile—cease-fire. The UN Secretary-General demanded that the Syrian regime ensure UNSMIS's 'full, unimpeded, and immediate' freedom of movement and access, unobstructed communications, and safety. During March 2011–April 2012 more than 9,000 people were reported to have been killed, and many more displaced, by the unrest in Syria.

The six-point Syrian peace plan, the implementation of which was to supported by UNSMIS, envisaged: (i) a commitment to working with the Joint Envoy in an inclusive Syrian-led political process aimed at addressing the legitimate aspirations and concerns of the Syrian people; (ii) a UN-monitored cease-fire by all parties, including a commitment by the Syrian regime to withdraw troops and heavy weaponry from population centres; (iii) a commitment to enabling the timely provision of humanitarian assistance to all areas affected by the fighting, and the immediate implementation of a daily two-hour humanitarian pause; (iv) the expedited release of arbitrarily arrested detainees; (v) free access and movement for journalists; and (vi) freedom of association and the right to demonstrate peacefully for all.

Military Strength: UNSMIS was to comprise an initial deployment of up to 300 unarmed military observers, supported by an appropriate civilian component.

United Nations Truce Supervision Organization—UNTSO

Address: Government House, Jerusalem.

Head of Mission and Chief-of-Staff: Maj.-Gen. JUHA KILPIA (Finland).

Establishment and Mandate: UNTSO was established initially to supervise the truce called by the UN Security Council in Palestine in May 1948 and has assisted in the application of the 1949 Armistice Agreements. Its activities have evolved over the years, in response to developments in the Middle East and in accordance with the relevant resolutions of the Security Council. There is no periodic renewal procedure for UNTSO's mandate.

Activities: UNTSO observers assist UN peace-keeping forces in the Middle East, at present UNIFIL and UNDOF. The mission maintains offices in Beirut, Lebanon and Damascus, Syria. In addition, UNTSO operates a number of outposts in the Sinai region of Egypt to maintain a UN presence there. UNTSO observers have been available at short notice to form the nucleus of new peace-keeping operations.

In July 2006 the UN Secretary-General strongly condemned the killing by Israeli fire of four members of UNTSO who had been supporting UNIFIL during the full-scale conflict that erupted in that month between the Israeli armed forces and Hezbollah.

Military Strength: The operational strength of UNTSO at 31 March 2012 was 151 military observers. The mission is supported by 232 international and local civilian staff (as at 31 December 2011).

Finance: UNTSO expenditures are covered by the regular budget of the United Nations. The appropriation for the two-year period 2012–13 was US $70.3m.

United Nations Peace-building

Address: Department of Political Affairs, United Nations, New York, NY 10017, USA.

Telephone: (212) 963-1234; **fax:** (212) 963-4879; **internet:** www.un.org/Depts/dpa/.

The Department of Political Affairs provides support and guidance to UN peace-building operations and political missions working in the field to prevent and resolve conflicts or to promote enduring peace in post-conflict societies.

The World Summit of UN heads of state held in September 2005 approved recommendations made by the UN Secretary-General in his March 2005 report entitled 'In Larger Freedom: Towards Development, Security and Human Rights for All' for the creation of an intergovernmental advisory Peace-building Commission. In December the UN Security Council and General Assembly authorized the establishment of the Commission; it was inaugurated, as a special subsidiary body of both the Council and Assembly, in June 2006. A multi-year standing peace-building fund, financed by voluntary contributions from member states and mandated to support post-conflict peace-building activities, was established in October 2006. A Peace-building Support Office was established within the UN Secretariat to administer the fund, as well as to support the Commission. In 2012 the Peace-building Commission was actively concerned with the situation in six African countries: Burundi, Central African Republic, Guinea, Guinea-Bissau, Liberia and Sierra Leone.

The UN Assistance Mission in Afghanistan is directed by the Department of Peace-keeping Operations.

Office of the Special Representative of the UN Secretary-General for West Africa—UNOWA

Address: BP 23851 Dakar-Ponty, 5 ave Carde, Immeuble Caisse de sécurité sociale, Dakar, Senegal.

Telephone: (221) 849-07-29; **fax:** (221) 842-50-95; **internet:** www.un.org/unowa.

Special Representative of the UN Secretary-General: SAID DJINNIT (Algeria).

Establishment and Mandate: UNOWA was established, with an initial three-year mandate, from January 2002, to elaborate an integrated approach by the United Nations to the prevention and management of conflict in West Africa; and to promote peace, security and development in the sub-region. (UNOWA's mandate has subsequently been renewed, most recently for a further three years until December 2013.) In pursuit of these objectives, the Special Representative of the Secretary-General (SRSG) meets regularly with the leaders of UN regional and political offices in West Africa.

Activities: UNOWA supports the development of a regional harmonized approach to disarmament, demobilization and reintegration in West Africa, and its projects have included an initiative to address cross-border challenges, such as mercenaries, child-soldiers and small arms proliferation. UNOWA also aims to support and facilitate a sub-regional approach to issues that impact stability in West Africa, in particular electoral processes and the transfer of power. UNOWA works with the Economic Community of West African

States (ECOWAS), whose projects embrace security sector reform (identified as a key priority for the sub-region), small arms, trans-border co-operation, etc. A trilateral partnership between UNOWA, the European Union and ECOWAS has also been established. In July 2009 UNOWA, with the UN Office on Drugs and Crime, the UN Department of Peace-keeping Operations and INTERPOL, inaugurated a West Africa Coast Initiative (WACI) to support the ECOWAS Regional Action Plan, which aimed to counter the problem of illicit drugs trafficking, organized crime, and drug abuse in West Africa. WACI provides advice, equipment, technical assistance and specialized training, and supports the establishment of Transnational Crime Units in each country. UNOWA, with the UN Office for the Co-ordination of Humanitarian Affairs (OCHA), has worked to address economic, political, security and humanitarian problems that confront the populations of certain border areas in West Africa through the development of integrated, multi-agency strategies in respect of four border clusters: Guinea/Côte d'Ivoire/Liberia/Sierra Leone (Guinea Forestière); Mali/Burkina Faso/Côte d'Ivoire/Ghana; Mauritania/Mali/Niger; and Senegal/The Gambia/Guinea-Bissau. UNOWA works closely with OCHA in strengthening the UN's regional humanitarian response. It is also concerned to promote respect for human rights and to support the full consideration of gender issues in conflict management and peace-building activities.

In May 2011 UNOWA organized a Regional Conference on Elections and Stability in West Africa, in Praia, Cape Verde; the Conference adopted the Praia Declaration on Elections and Stability in West Africa, identifying practical recommendations for improving electoral processes in the region. A round table meeting was convened in September, in New York, USA, by UNOWA and the International Peace Institute, further to discuss issues raised by the Conference. In the following month UNOWA supported the organization by the West African Human Rights Defenders Network of a panel discussion on the role of civil society organizations in elections; as a consequence of the panel discussion, civil society organizations in the subregion adopted a roadmap for the implementation of the Praia Declaration.

In early December 2011 UNOWA, jointly with OHCHR, ECOWAS, the African Union, the Mano River Union and the Organisation Internationale de la Francophonie, convened a Regional Conference on Impunity, Justice and Human Rights in West Africa, in Bamako, Mali; the Conference adopted the Bamako Declaration and a strategic framework, outlining recommendations aimed at strengthening good governance and the rule of law, in order to promote stability and development in West Africa.

The SRSG serves as chairman of the Cameroon-Nigeria Mixed Commission, which has met regularly since December 2002, and hosts high level meetings of the heads of UN peace missions in West Africa. UNOWA conducts regional good offices missions.

Operational Strength: At 29 February 2012 UNOWA comprised three military advisers, and (as at 31 December 2011) 19 international civilian and 16 local civilian personnel.

Office of the United Nations Special Co-ordinator for Lebanon—UNSCOL

Address: UN House, Riad el-Solh Sq., POB 11, 8577 Beirut, Lebanon.

E-mail: unscol-website@un.org; **internet:** unscol.unmissions.org.

Special Co-ordinator for Lebanon: Derek Plumbly (United Kingdom).

Establishment and Mandate: The Office of the United Nations Special Co-ordinator for Lebanon was established in February 2007, replacing the Office of the Personal Representative of the UN Secretary-General for southern Lebanon (established in August 2000). The Office co-ordinates the UN presence in Lebanon and is the focal point for the core group of donor countries supporting Lebanon. The Office works closely with the expanded UN peace-keeping mission in Lebanon, UNIFIL. The Special Co-ordinator is responsible for supervising implementation of Security Council Resolution 1701, which was adopted in August 2006, and called for a cessation of hostilities in Lebanon.

Operational Strength: At 31 December 2011 UNSCOL comprised 19 international civilian and 55 local civilian personnel.

Office of the United Nations Special Co-ordinator for the Middle East Peace Process—UNSCO

Address: Gaza; Jerusalem; Ramallah.

Special Co-ordinator for the Middle East Peace Process: Robert R. Serry (Netherlands).

Establishment and Mandate: The Office of the United Nations Special Co-ordinator for the Middle East (UNSCO) was established in June 1994 after the conclusion of the Declaration of Principles on Interim (Palestinian) Self-Government Arrangements—the 'Oslo Accord'. UNSCO was to seek, during the transition process envisaged by the Declaration, to ensure 'an adequate response to the needs of the Palestinian people and to mobilise financial, technical, economic and other assistance'. In 1995 UNSCO's mandate was reconfigured as the Office of the Special Co-ordinator for the Middle East Peace Process and Personal Representative of the Secretary-General to the Palestine Liberation Organization and the Palestine (National) Authority (PA).

Activities: The Office has been mandated to assist in all issues related to the humanitarian situation confronting the Palestinian people, and supports negotiations and the implementation of political agreements. The Regional Affairs Unit (RAU) of the Office assists in the fulfilment of that part of the Office's mandate that requires it to co-ordinate its work and to co-operate closely with all of the parties to the Middle East peace process, including the Governments of Israel, Lebanon, Syria, Jordan and Egypt, the PA, Palestinian civil society, the Arab League, and individual Arab states that have assumed a key role in facilitating the peace process. The Special Co-ordinator also collaborates closely with key international actors, in particular those that, together with the UN, constitute the Middle East Quartet, i.e. the European Union, Russia and the USA, and serves as the Envoy of the UN Secretary-General to the Quartet. In addition to the RAU, UNSCO maintains a Media Office and a Research Unit.

Operational Strength: At 31 December 2011 UNSCO comprised 30 international civilian and 29 local civilian personnel.

United Nations Assistance Mission in Afghanistan—UNAMA

Address: POB 5858, Grand Central Station, New York, NY 10163-5858, USA.

Telephone: (813) 246000; **fax:** (831) 246069; **e-mail:** spokesperson-unama@un.org; **internet:** www.unama-afg.org.

Special Representative of the UN Secretary-General: Ján Kubiš (Slovakia).

Deputy Special Representative of the UN Secretary-General, Political Affairs: Nicholas Haysom (South Africa).

Deputy Special Representative of the UN Secretary-General, Relief, Recovery and Reconstruction: Michael Keating (United Kingdom).

Establishment and Mandate: The United Nations Assistance Mission in Afghanistan (UNAMA) was established by the UN Security Council in March 2002. UNAMA's mandate has subsequently been renewed annually, most recently to March 2013. The Mission was initially authorized to fulfil tasks assigned to the UN under the December 2001 Bonn Agreement on provisional arrangements for Afghanistan. The process determined by the Bonn Agreement terminated in September 2005. Subsequently UNAMA assumed responsibility for assisting the Afghan Government with the implementation of an Afghanistan Compact, which was adopted by the London Conference on Afghanistan, co-chaired by the UN and Afghanistan from 31 January–1 February 2006, as a framework for co-operation between the Afghan authorities, the UN and the international community. The Compact identifies three key and interdependent pillars of activity for its term: security; governance, rule of law and human rights; and economic and social development. In addition, the Compact aims to promote the elimination of Afghanistan's narcotics industry. UNAMA was mandated to provide political and strategic advice for the peace process; to provide good offices; to promote human rights; to provide technical assistance; and, in co-operation with the Afghan authorities, to manage all UN humanitarian relief, recovery, reconstruction and development activities. Peace-building tasks that fall under UNAMA's political mandate include the prevention and resolution of conflicts; building confidence and the promotion of national reconciliation; monitoring the political and human rights situation; and investigating human rights violations. As appropriate, UNAMA is charged with recommending corrective actions; maintaining dialogue with Afghan leaders, political parties, civil society groups, institutions and representatives of the central authorities; and undertaking good offices to foster the peace process.

Activities: UNAMA co-ordinates all of the activities of the UN system, whose programme of work is determined by Afghan needs and priorities. Nineteen UN agencies work together with their Afghan government counterparts and with national and international NGO partners. The Paris International Conference in Support of Afghanistan, convened in June 2008, agreed that UNAMA should expand its efforts to co-ordinate international activities in Afghanistan and endorsed a new Afghanistan National Development

Strategy. In early 2009 UNAMA established a new political unit to co-ordinate efforts, in collaboration with local political parties, observers and civil society organizations, to promote a free and fair environment for the presidential and provincial council elections that were held in August. During that year UNAMA expanded its presence in the country to eight regional and 15 provincial offices. The London International Conference in Support of Afghanistan, convened in January 2010, renewed the commitment of the international community and Afghan authorities to the implementation of a reform-oriented nation-building agenda. In July an International Conference on Afghanistan, co-chaired by the UN, was convened for the first time in Kabul. The meeting endorsed a new Afghanistan National Development Strategy: Prioritization and Implementation Plan, for the period to mid-2013, which aimed to facilitate the transition to full Afghan governance. UNAMA was to support the so-called Kabul process by providing electoral assistance to the independent Afghan electoral commissions; fostering national political dialogue and regional engagement; promoting regional co-operation, though confidence-building measures and a Kabul Silk Road initiative (inaugurated in early 2010 by the SRSG to promote informal dialogue between the Government, the UN and Ambassadors of neighbouring countries); and co-ordinating UN and international aid in support of the Government's national development and governance priorities. In October the SRSG met members of a new High Peace Council, and concluded an agreement to provide technical and practical assistance to the Council in support of the process of national peace and reconciliation. In April 2011 three UNAMA international staff members were killed during violent protests near the UN compound in Mazar-e-Sharif. An international conference on Afghanistan held in Bonn, Germany, in December, confirmed long-term commitment to supporting Afghanistan through a newly designated Transformation Decade, to cover 2015–24, and noted the importance of the UN role, and that the mandate of UNAMA was under review as the Afghan authorities assumed increased leadership responsibilities. In late February 2012 a UNAMA compound in Kunduz, north-eastern Afghanistan, was attacked during violent protests that erupted following reports that US troops based in Afghanistan had unintentionally burned copies of the Koran.

During October 2010–August 2011 UNAMA conducted interviews with 379 inmates detained at 47 Afghan detention facilities operated either by the National Directorate of Security or by the national police, and, in October 2011, the mission released a report concluding that allegations by prisoners of mistreatment and torture at several of the facilities were credible. The report detailed a number of key recommendations aimed at preventing the recurrence of ill treatment of detainees.

UNAMA, jointly with OHCHR, issues an annual report on *Protection of Civilians in Armed Conflict*. The 2011 report, released in February 2012, found that civilian casualties arising from the Afghan conflict had, in 2011, risen for the fifth consecutive year, numbering 3,021, compared with 2,790 in 2010.

In November 2010 the UN signed an agreement with the Kuwaiti Government to establish a UNAMA Support Office in that country.

Operational Strength: At 29 February 2012 UNAMA comprised 13 military observers, two police personnel and 76 UN Volunteers; there were, in addition, 417 international civilian and 1,746 local civilian personnel (as at 31 December 2011).

United Nations Assistance Mission for Iraq—UNAMI

Address: Amman, Jordan.

Telephone: (6) 5504700; **fax:** (6) 5504705; **e-mail:** achouri@un.org; **internet:** www.uniraq.org.

Special Representative of the UN Secretary-General for Iraq: MARTIN KOBLER (Germany).

Deputy Special Representative of the UN Secretary-General for Political, Electoral and Constitutional Support: GYÖRGY BUSZTIN (Hungary).

Deputy Special Representative of the UN Secretary-General for Development and Humanitarian Support: CHRISTINE MCNAB (Sweden).

Establishment and Mandate: The United Nations Assistance Mission for Iraq (UNAMI) was initially established by UN Security Council Resolution 1500 (14 August 2003) as a one-year mission to co-ordinate and support humanitarian efforts in post-conflict Iraq. Later in August, however, terrorist attacks on the UNAMI headquarters in Baghdad killed the newly appointed Special Representative of the UN Secretary-General for Iraq (and UN High Commissioner for Human Rights), Sergio Vieira de Mello, and 21 other UN personnel. UN international staff were subsequently withdrawn from Iraq, and, until the formation of the Iraqi Interim Government at the end of June 2004, UNAMI operated primarily from outside Iraq (from Cyprus, Jordan and Kuwait). Meanwhile, political and security concerns were urgently reviewed by the UN Secretary-General. UNAMI consists of two pillars—political and reconstruction and development—and a Human Rights Office (HRO), which maintains links with the Office of the Higher Commissioner for Human Rights. Generally, the work of the political pillar is carried out in support of the good offices and facilitation role of the Special Representative of the Secretary-General (SRSG). The political office also supports, as necessary, the HRO and the reconstruction and development pillar. In April–May 2004 the UN helped to establish an Independent Electoral Commission of Iraq (IECI). In accordance with the mandate afforded it under UN Security Council Resolution 1546 (June 2004), UNAMI assisted in the convening of an Iraqi national conference in August, including in the selection of a Consultative Council.

UNAMI is mandated, under Resolution 1546, 'to promote the protection of human rights, national reconciliation, and judicial and legal reform in order to strengthen the rule of law in Iraq'. Through two units, the HRO monitors and reports on the human rights situation and addresses the reconstruction of Iraqi national human rights institutions. HRO activities include providing technical support and training to the ministries of justice, defence and human rights; the establishment of a national centre for missing and disappeared persons in Iraq; and the establishment of a national human rights institution. UNAMI is also mandated to promote dialogue and effective procedures to resolve disputed international boundaries.

Activities: In January 2005 elections were held in Iraq to choose a Transitional National Assembly that would be charged with drafting a permanent constitution. These elections also formed the basis for the establishment of a Transitional Government and presidency. UNAMI's electoral unit assisted and advised the IECI, which was responsible for the organization and conduct of these elections. From May until October 2005, in response to requests for assistance from the Transitional Government, UNAMI provided support and advice to the constitution-making process. In early 2007 UNAMI facilitated and observed the process of reconfiguring the IECI as the Independent High Electoral Commission (IHEC). UNAMI continued to assist the IHEC in capacity- and institution-building and provided technical support during provincial and national legislative elections conducted in 2009–10. In December 2011 the Iraqi authorities requested that UNAMI serve in an impartial advisory capacity in the then ongoing process to select IHEC commissioners.

With regard to reconstruction and development, UNAMI aims are: to address the long-term challenge of achieving sustainable food security; to strengthen the overall quality of education and service delivery at all levels; to support policy development, and preserve and conserve the tangible and intangible Iraqi cultural heritage; to improve the human development situation in Iraq and promote good governance by strengthening institutional capacity, contributing to the creation of employment opportunities and providing policy advice; to support the national health strategy of the Iraqi Ministry of Health in meeting basic health needs; to formulate and implement programmes on institutional/policy reform, capacity-building, and service provision necessary to rehabilitate and develop the infrastructure of human settlements; and to support the Iraqi authorities in providing adequate assistance and effective protection to uprooted populations in Iraq, and to assist them in preventing new displacement as well as in achieving durable solutions. UNAMI works closely with some 16 other UN agencies, funds and programmes to co-ordinate assistance activities through the UN Country Team for Iraq.

In April 2009 the Special Representative of the UN Secretary-General presented a report on the disputed internal boundaries of northern Iraq, concluding a year-long process of analysis and consultation. In June the Special Representative launched a Task Force on Dialogue, with senior representatives of the Iraqi Prime Minister and Kurdistan Regional Government. The Task Force convened, under UN auspices, regularly during late 2009 and the first half of 2010, to consider the UNAMI report and facilitate further political dialogue.

UNAMI endorsed the International Compact for Iraq, a five-year framework for co-operation between Iraq and the international community jointly chaired by the Iraqi Government and the UN Secretariat, that was launched in May 2007. In August the UN Security Council approved Resolution 1770, which expanded UNAMI's mandate to incorporate a responsibility to promote, support and facilitate the implementation of the International Compact, as well as the co-ordination and delivery of humanitarian assistance, and to support and advise on national reconciliation efforts. In August 2008 UNAMI and the Iraqi Government signed a UN Assistance Strategy for Iraq 2008–10, which focused on greater collaboration and co-financing of projects. In May 2010 a new UN Development Assistance Framework was signed by the UN and the Iraqi Government, covering the period 2011–14. It identified the priority areas for UN support being to contribute to: inclusive economic growth;

environmental management; promoting good governance and protection of human rights; ensuring access to improved basic services for all; and investment in the capacities of women, youth and children to enable their full participation in all aspects of life in Iraq.

Operational Strength: At 29 February 2012 UNAMI personnel (based in Iraq, Jordan and Kuwait) comprised 353 troops, eight military advisers, and four police; they were assisted by 393 international civilian staff and 500 local civilian staff (as at 31 December 2011).

United Nations Office in Burundi—BNUB

Address: BP 6899, Gatumba Rd, Bujumbura, Burundi.

Telephone: 22205165; **internet:** binub.unmissions.org.

Special Representative of the UN Secretary-General and Head of Office: (vacant).

Establishment and Mandate: The United Nations Office in Burundi (Bureau des Nations Unies au Burundi—BNUB) was established on 1 January 2011, as a successor to the UN Integrated Office in Burundi (BINUB), which had operated in the country since 2007. BNUB represented a commitment by the UN to maintaining a scaled-down presence in the country, for an initial 12-month period, in order to support the country's progress towards peace consolidation and long-term development. BNUB mandate was to support the efforts of the Burundi Government to strengthen the independence, capacities and legal frameworks of key national institutions, in accordance with international standards and principles; to facilitate political dialogue and broad-based participation in political life; to support efforts to fight impunity, in particular through the establishment of transitional justice mechanisms to strengthen national unity, and to promote justice and reconciliation within Burundi's society, and to provide operational support to the functioning of these bodies; to promote and protect human rights, and strengthen national capacities in that area; to ensure that all strategies and policies with respect to public finance and the economic sector, in particular the next Poverty Reduction Strategy Paper (PRSP), have a focus on peace-building, equitable growth, and addressing the needs of the most vulnerable population; and to provide support to Burundi's 2011 chairmanship of the East African Community, as well as providing advice, as requested, on regional integration issues. The Office was to work to ensure effective co-ordination among UN agencies in Burundi.

In December 2011 the UN Security Council extended the mandate of BNUB until 15 February 2013, emphasizing, in so doing, that significant challenges remained in areas including human rights, democratic governance, civilian protection, combating corruption, security sector reform, and promoting economic development.

Operational Strength: At 29 February 2012 BNUB comprised one military adviser, one police officer, and six UN Volunteers, as well as 52 international civilian staff and 63 local civilian staff (as at 31 December 2011).

United Nations Integrated Peace-building Office in Sierra Leone—UNIPSIL

Address: Cabenda Hotel, 14 Signal Hill Rd, POB 5, Freetown, Sierra Leone.

Telephone: (76) 692810; **internet:** unipsil.unmissions.org.

Executive Representative of the UN Secretary-General: Jens Anders Toyberg-Frandzen (Denmark).

Establishment and Mandate: The Office was established on 1 October 2008, in accordance with UN Security Council Resolution 1829 (4 August 2008), as a successor to the United Nations Integrated Office in Sierra Leone (UNIOSIL). UNIOSIL had been established in January 2006 following the expiry of the mandate of the large UN peace-keeping operation in Sierra Leone, UNAMSIL, and assisted the Government of Sierra Leone to consolidate peace and to build the capacity of national institutions to support democracy and economic and social development. The key elements of UNIPSIL's mandate were to support the Government of Sierra Leone: to identify and resolve tensions and areas of potential conflict; to monitor and promote human rights, democratic institutions and the rule of law, including efforts to counter transnational organized crime and drugs-trafficking; to consolidate good governance reforms, in particular anti-corruption bodies; to support decentralization; and to co-ordinate with and support the work of the Peace-building Commission, as well as the implementation of a Peace-building Co-operation Framework. UNIPSIL was to work closely with the Economic Community of West African States (ECOWAS), the Mano River Union, other international partners and other UN missions in the region. The head of UNIPSIL, the Executive Representative of the UN Secretary-General, also serves as the Resident Representative of the UN Development Programme and as the UN Resident and Humanitarian Co-ordinator. In December 2008 UNIPSIL, with all other UN agencies and programmes working in Sierra Leone, as well as the African Development Bank, adopted a Joint Vision to co-ordinate facilities and services in order to help to consolidate a sustainable peace in the country.

Operational Strength: At 29 February 2012 UNIPSIL comprised seven police personnel and eight UN Volunteers; it was supported by 38 international civilian and 31 local civilian personnel (as at 31 December 2011).

United Nations Integrated Peace-building Office in the Central African Republic—BINUCA

Address: BP 3338, PK 4 ave Boganda, Bangui, Central African Republic.

Telephone: 21-61-70-98; **internet:** binuca.unmissions.org.

Special Representative of the UN Secretary-General and Head of Office: Margaret Vogt (Nigeria).

Establishment and Mandate: The United Nations Integrated Peace-building Office in the CAR (BINUCA) was inaugurated on 1 January 2010, replacing the UN Peace-building Office in the CAR (BONUCA), which was established in February 2000, following the withdrawal of the UN Peace-keeping Mission in the Central African Republic (MINURCA). BINUCA is mandated to support national and local efforts to develop governance reforms and electoral processes; to support the completion of disarmament, demobilization and reintegration programme activities; to help to restore state authority in the provinces; to promote respect for human rights and the rule of law; to support the UN Mission in the CAR and Chad (MINURCAT); and to ensure that child protection measures are observed. Successive extensions of BINUCA's mandate were approved by the Security Council in December 2010 and December 2011 (the former by one year, and the latter until 31 January 2013).

Operational Strength: At 29 February 2012 BINUCA comprised two military observers, two police and five UN Volunteers; in addition, it was supported by 67 international civilian and 75 local civilian personnel (as at 31 December 2011).

United Nations Integrated Peace-building Office in Guinea-Bissau—UNIOGBIS

Address: UN Bldg, CP 179, Rua Rui Djassi, Bissau, Guinea-Bissau.

Telephone: 20-36-18; **fax:** 20-36-13; **internet:** uniogbis.unmissions.org.

Special Representative of the UN Secretary-General and Head of Office: Joseph Mutaboba (Rwanda).

Establishment and Mandate: Established to assist the Peace-building Commission in its multi-dimensional engagement with Guinea-Bissau, the United Nations Integrated Peace-building Office in Guinea-Bissau (UNIOGBIS) first became operational in January 2010, succeeding the UN Peace-building Office in Guinea-Bissau (UNOGBIS). Unlike other UN peace-building missions, UNOGBIS had not been preceded by a UN peace-keeping mission.

Activities: From 2003 the work of UNOGBIS, which preceded UNIOGBIS, focused on transition to civilian rule in the aftermath of a military coup that took place in that year. UNOGBIS was mandated by the UN Security Council to promote national reconciliation, respect for human rights and the rule of law; to support national capacity for conflict prevention; to encourage reform of the security sector and stable civil-military relations; to encourage government efforts to suppress trafficking in small arms; and to collaborate with a 'comprehensive peace-building strategy' to strengthen state institutions and mobilize international resources. In December 2007 the UN Security Council authorized a revised mandate for UNOGBIS to support efforts by the Guinea-Bissau authorities to counter illegal drugs-trafficking. UNOGBIS undertook training of electoral agents and journalists in preparation for legislative elections, conducted in November 2008, and co-ordinated the activities of international observers monitoring the voting. In June 2009 the UN Security Council endorsed the establishment of UNIOGBIS, which succeeded UNOGBIS from 1 January 2010. From mid-2010 UNIOGBIS facilitated the preparation of meetings of security and defence forces, as part of a National Reconciliation Conference process. It also worked to enhance the co-ordination and effectiveness of international assistance to further defence and security sector reform, co-operated with the UN Mine Action Service to assess the country's weapons and ammunition stockpiles, and supported the national authorities to combat human trafficking, drugs trafficking and other areas of organized crime. During 2011 UNIOGBIS, with UNDP, provided support to the organizing committee of the National

Reconciliation Conference process. The Office also supported the ongoing constitutional review process, and provided technical and financial assistance to the National Technical Independent Mixed Commission, responsible for the selection of police officers. In September a model police station, established with support from UNIOGBIS, was inaugurated in Bissau; 12 further model police stations were planned.

Operational Strength: At 29 February 2012 UNIOGBIS comprised 14 police officers, two military advisers and seven UN Volunteers; in addition, there were 55 international civilian and 48 local civilian personnel (as at 31 December 2011).

United Nations Political Office for Somalia—UNPOS

Address: POB 48246-00100, Nairobi, Kenya.

Telephone: (20) 7622131; **fax:** (20) 7622697; **e-mail:** unpos_pio@un.org; **internet:** unpos.unmissions.org.

Special Representative of the UN Secretary-General and Head of Office: AUGUSTINE P. MAHIGA (Tanzania).

Establishment and Mandate: The United Nations Political Office for Somalia (UNPOS) was established in 1995 with the objective of assisting the Secretary-General to advance peace and reconciliation in the country by utilizing its contacts with Somali leaders and civic organizations. Owing to the security situation in that country, UNPOS was administered from offices in Nairobi, Kenya. UNPOS provides good offices, co-ordinates international political support and financial assistance to peace and reconciliation initiatives, and monitors and reports on developments in the country. In 2002–04 UNPOS supported the Somali National Reconciliation Conference that was organized in Nairobi under the auspices of the Intergovernmental Authority on Development, and worked with international partners to facilitate agreement among Somali leaders on a transitional administration. By early 2005 the Conference had established a broad-based Transitional Federal Government, which was able to relocate to Somalia from its temporary base in Kenya. The UN Security Council consequently authorized UNPOS to promote reconciliation through dialogue between Somali parties; to assist efforts to address the 'Somaliland' issue; to co-ordinate the support of Somalia's neighbours and other international partners for the country's peace process; and to assume a leading political role in peace-building initiatives. In January 2012 the Special Representative of the Secretary-General (SRSG), with several core UNPOS staff members, relocated from Nairobi to the Somali capital, Mogadishu; the last SRSG to be based in Mogadishu had departed there in 1995.

Activities: In spite of an outbreak of hostilities in May 2006, the Transitional Federal Institutions continued to function during that year and to co-operate with the UN's Special Representative to pursue peace negotiations. In May 2008 the Special Representative chaired inter-Somali peace negotiations, held in Djibouti. An agreement was reached in June, and formally signed in August, on the cessation of hostilities and the establishment of a Joint Security Committee and a High Level Committee on political issues. In March 2009 UNPOS organized a meeting, in Djibouti, with representatives of the Somali business community. A committee was established to develop and implement a strategy to support entrepreneurs. From mid-2009 UNPOS, with AMISOM and key members of the transitional Government and the international community acting in Somalia, met as a revised Joint Security Committee. In April 2010 UNPOS signed a Memorandum of Understanding with IGAD and AMISOM, in order to strengthen co-ordination of activities between the organizations in support of the peace process. In early 2011 UNPOS supported a consensus-building process to enable the transitional period of government to conclude, as determined under the Djibouti Peace Agreement, in August. In June the Special Representative facilitated the signing of the so-called Kampala Accord by the President and Speaker of the Transitional Federal Parliament providing for the establishment of a new interim administration to undertake the tasks necessary to end the transitional phase; a presidential election and election for a new Speaker were to take place no later than August 2012. In September 2011 the Special Representative helped to organize, in the Somali capital Mogadishu, a High Level Consultative Meeting on Ending Transition, attended by high level representatives of the Transitional Federal Institutions, the regional administrations serving Galmudug and Puntland, and other international partners. The meeting endorsed a roadmap for the forthcoming 12-month period. UNPOS was to establish a new dedicated unit to administer the implementation mechanisms identified in the roadmap.

Operational Strength: At 29 February 2012 UNPOS was composed of three military advisers and three police officers; there were, in addition, 55 international civilian and 28 local civilian personnel (as at 31 December 2011).

United Nations Regional Centre for Preventive Diplomacy for Central Asia—UNRCCA

Address: Aşgabat, Archabil Shaeli 43, Turkmenistan.

Special Representative of the UN Secretary-General and Head of Office: MIROSLAV JENČA (Slovakia).

Establishment and Mandate: The Centre was inaugurated in December 2007, with the objective of assisting and supporting the governments of Kazakhstan, Kyrgyzstan, Tajikistan, Turkmenistan and Uzbekistan to enhance their conflict prevention capacities through dialogue, confidence-building measures and partnerships, in order to respond to existing threats and emerging challenges in the Central Asian region. The Centre is administered by the UN Department of Political Affairs.

Activities: The Centre monitors and analyses the situation in Central Asia, including maintaining close contact with the UN Assistance Mission in Afghanistan, to attain early warning of potential conflict, co-ordinates the efforts of international agencies to promote sustainable development and conflict prevention, facilitates the implementation of regional and international agreements and frameworks of action, and organizes training, workshops and seminars. For the period 2012–14 the Centre identified the following as priority areas of activity: liaising with the governments of the region and, with their concurrence, with other parties concerned on issues relevant to preventive diplomacy; monitoring and analyzing the situation on the ground and providing the UN Secretary-General with current information related to conflict prevention efforts; maintaining contacts with relevant regional organizations, encouraging their peace-making efforts and initiatives, and facilitating co-ordination and information exchange with due regard to their specific mandates; providing a political framework and leadership for the preventive activities of the UN country teams in the region, and supporting the efforts of the Resident Co-ordinators; maintaining close contact with UNAMA to ensure a comprehensive and integrated analysis of the situation in the region. In December 2010 UNRCCA, with the UN Counter-Terrorism Implementation Task Force and the EU, convened the first of a series of expert meetings on measures to combat terrorism in Central Asia. In May 2011 the Centre hosted the third annual meeting of deputy ministers of foreign affairs of Central Asian countries, at which measures to enhance co-operation and strengthen stability in the region were discussed.

Operational Strength: At 31 December 2011 the Centre was served by eight international civilian and 22 local civilian personnel.

United Nations Regional Office for Central Africa—UNOCA

Address: BP 23773, Cité de la Démocratie, Villas 55–57, Libreville, Gabon.

Telephone: (241) 741-401; **fax:** (241) 741-402.

Special Representative of the UN Secretary-General: ABOU MOUSSA (Chad).

Establishment and Mandate: UNOCA—covering the 10 member states of the Communauté économique des états de l'Afrique centrale (CEEAC): Angola, Burundi, Cameroon, Central African Republic, Chad, Democratic Republic of the Congo, Republic of the Congo, Equatorial Guinea, Gabon, and São Tomé and Príncipe—was inaugurated in March 2011, having been established through an exchange of letters, finalized in August 2010, between the UN Secretary-General and the UN Security Council. UNOCA is mandated, initially for a period of two years, to extend the UN's good offices and other assistance to regional states and organizations in support of preventive diplomacy and the consolidation of peace. The Office is also mandated to work closely with UN and other entities to address cross-border challenges, such as organized crime, trafficking in arms, and the activities of armed groups (including the Lord's Resistance Army).

Activities: UNOCA's priority areas of activity include: supporting conflict mediation, and, where requested, assisting with the peaceful conduct of elections in the region; facilitating cohesion in the general work of the UN in the region, including in partnership with other agencies, such as UNDP, UNODC, UN Women and OHCHR; promoting activities in partnership with the private sector and civil society networks; co-ordinating UN efforts in the region against armed groups; undertaking studies on regional challenges and threats; providing technical assistance aimed at advancing early warning and mediation capabilities; helping to build the capacity of CEEAC; promoting the formulation of a regional integrated approach to addressing cross-border insecurity; and combating maritime insecurity in the Gulf of Guinea.

Operational Strength: At 29 February 2012 the Office comprised one military adviser, supported (as at 31 December 2011) by 15 international civilian and six local civilian personnel.

United Nations Support Mission in Libya—UNSMIL

Address: Tripoli, Libya.

Special Representative of the UN Secretary-General: Ian Martin (United Kingdom).

Establishment and Mandate: Following the outbreak of conflict in Libya in February 2011, UNSMIL was established in September, for an initial period of three months, with a mandate to support Libya's transitional authorities in restoring public security and the rule of law; promoting inclusive political dialogue and national reconciliation; embarking upon the process of drafting a new constitution and preparing for democratic elections. UNSMIL is also mandated to support the Libyan authorities in extending state authority, through the strengthening of emerging accountable institutions; restoring public services; promoting and protecting human rights (particularly for vulnerable groups); supporting transitional justice; taking the immediate steps required to initiate economic recovery; and co-ordinating support that may be requested from other multilateral and bilateral actors. In December the UN Security Council extended the mission for a further three month period and expanded its mandate to include assisting and supporting the transitional authorities to address the threats of proliferation of all arms, missiles and related materiel.

Operational Strength: At 31 December 2011 the Office was served by 34 international civilian personnel and one local civilian staff member.

United Nations Population Fund—UNFPA

Address: 605 Third Ave, New York, NY 10158, USA.

Telephone: (212) 297-5000; **fax:** (212) 370-0201; **e-mail:** hq@unfpa.org; **internet:** www.unfpa.org.

Created in 1967 as the Trust Fund for Population Activities, the UN Fund for Population Activities (UNFPA) was established as a Fund of the UN General Assembly in 1972 and was made a subsidiary organ of the UN General Assembly in 1979, with the UNDP Governing Council (now the Executive Board) designated as its governing body. In 1987 UNFPA's name was changed to the United Nations Population Fund (retaining the same acronym).

Organization

(April 2012)

EXECUTIVE DIRECTOR

The Executive Director, who has the rank of Under-Secretary-General of the UN, is responsible for the overall direction of the Fund, working closely with governments, other United Nations bodies and agencies, and non-governmental and international organizations to ensure the most effective programming and use of resources in population activities.

Executive Director: Babatunde Osotimehin (Nigeria).

Deputy Executive Director: Kate Gilmore (Australia).

EXECUTING AGENCIES

UNFPA provides financial and technical assistance to developing countries and countries with economies in transition, at their request. In many projects assistance is extended through member organizations of the UN system (in particular, FAO, the ILO, UNESCO and WHO), although projects are executed increasingly by national governments themselves. The Fund may also call on the services of international, regional and national non-governmental and training organizations, as well as research institutions. In addition, UNFPA's nine country technical services teams, composed of experts from the UN, its specialized agencies and non-governmental organizations, assist countries at all stages of project/programme development and implementation.

FIELD ORGANIZATION

UNFPA operates field offices, each headed by an UNFPA Representative, in some 112 countries. In other countries UNFPA uses UNDP's field structure of Resident Representatives as the main mechanism for performing its work. The field offices assist governments in formulating requests for aid and co-ordinate the work of the executing agencies in any given country or area. UNFPA has nine regional technical services teams (see above). UNFPA's strategic plan for the period 2008–11 provided for the establishment of five regional offices (located in Bangkok, Thailand; Bratislava, Slovakia; Cairo, Egypt; Johannesburg, South Africa; and Panama City, Panama) and six sub-regional offices.

Activities

UNFPA aims to promote health, in particular reproductive health, and gender equality as essential elements of long-term sustainable development. It aims to assist countries, at their request, to formulate policies and strategies to reduce poverty and support development and to collect and analyse population data to support better understanding of their needs. UNFPA's activities are broadly defined by the Programme of Action adopted by the International Conference on Population and Development (ICPD), which was held in Cairo, Egypt, in September 1994; UNFPA was designated the lead agency in following up the objectives of Programme of Action, which envisaged universal access to reproductive health care services and family planning services, a reduction in infant, child and maternal mortality, a reduction in the rate of HIV infection, improving life expectancy at birth, and universal access to primary education for all children by 2015. The Programme also emphasized the necessity of empowering and educating women, in order to achieve successful sustainable human development. A special session of the UN General Assembly (entitled ICPD + 5, and attended by delegates from 177 countries) was held in June–July 1999 to assess progress in achieving the objectives of the Cairo Conference and to identify priorities for future action. ICPD + 5 adopted several key actions for further implementation of the Programme of Action. These included advancing understanding of the connections between poverty, gender inequalities, health, education, the environment, financial and human resources, and development; focusing on the economic and social implications of demographic change; greater incorporation of gender issues into social and development policies and greater involvement of women in decision-making processes; greater support for HIV/AIDS prevention activities; and strengthened political commitment to the reproductive health of adolescents. Several new objectives were adopted by the special session, including the achievement of 60% availability of contraceptives and reproductive health care services by 2005, 80% by 2010, with universal availability by 2015. The ICPD objectives were incorporated into the Millennium Development Goals (MDGs), agreed in September 2000 by a summit of UN heads of state or government, and have been included in national development frameworks and poverty reduction strategies. The 10th and 15th anniversaries of the ICPD were commemorated by meetings of the General Assembly convened in, respectively, October 2004 and October 2009. In February 2012 UNFPA launched a new website, icpdbeyond2014.org, providing formal updates on progress made under the IPCD Programme of Action. The overall objective for UNFPA's strategic plan for the period 2011–13, adopted by the Executive Board in October 2011, was to advance the right to sexual and reproductive health by accelerating progress towards the MDG of improving maternal health, with priority focus given to the goals of: reducing maternal deaths; and achieving universal access to reproductive health, including family planning (see below).

REPRODUCTIVE HEALTH AND RIGHTS

UNFPA recognizes that improving reproductive health is an essential requirement for improving the general welfare of the population and the basis for empowering women and achieving sustainable social and economic development. The ICPD succeeded in raising the political prominence of reproductive health issues and stimulating consideration by governments of measures to strengthen and restructure their health services and policies. In October 2007 the UN General Assembly officially incorporated the aim of achieving, by 2015, universal access to reproductive health into the target for Goal 5 of the MDGs. UNFPA encourages the integration of family planning into all maternal, child and other reproductive health care. Its efforts to improve the quality of these services include support for the training of healthcare personnel and promoting greater accessibility to education and services. Many reproductive health projects focus on the reduction of maternal mortality (i.e. deaths related to pregnancy), which was included as a central objective of the ICPD Programme, and recognized as a legitimate element of international human rights instruments concerning the right to life/survival. Projects to reduce maternal deaths, which amount to about 500,000 each year, have focused on improving accessibility to essential obstetric care and ensuring the provision of skilled attendance to women in labour. The ICPD reported that a major cause of maternal deaths was unsafe abortions, and urged governments to confront the issue as a major public health concern. UNFPA is concerned with reducing the use of abortion (i.e. its use as a means of family planning). UNFPA was an active member of a core planning group of international organizations and partnerships that organized the first Women Deliver conference, held in London, United Kingdom, in October 2007. Participants, including government ministers and representatives of organizations, private sector foundations and non-government bodies, endorsed a final commitment to increase investment in women's health and to make improving maternal health a development priority. In February 2008 UNFPA appealed for donations to its new Maternal Health Thematic Fund, which aimed to support efforts in 75 developing countries to improve maternal health care; by end-2010 some US $60 million in donations by the Thematic Fund. In addition to maternal deaths, an estimated 10m.–15m. women suffer serious or long-lasting illnesses or disabilities as a result of inadequate care in pregnancy and childbirth. In 2003 UNFPA launched a Global Campaign to End Fistula, which aims to improve the prevention and treatment of this obstetric condition in 30 countries in Africa and Asia and to achieve its elimination by 2015. UNFPA supports research into contraceptives and training in contraceptive technology. UNFPA organizes indepth studies on national contraceptive requirements and aims to ensure an adequate supply of contraceptives and reproductive health supplies to developing countries. In the early 2000s the Fund and other partners developed a Reproductive Health Commodity Strategy (RHCS), which aimed to improve developing countries' self-sufficiency in the management and provision of reproductive health commodities. UNFPA encourages partnerships between private sector interests and the governments of developing nations, with a view to making affordable commercial contraceptive products more easily available to consumers and thereby enabling governments to direct subsidies at the poorest sectors of society.

UNFPA is a co-sponsor of the Joint UN Programme on HIV/AIDS (UNAIDS), and is the UNAIDS convening agency with responsibility for young people and for condom programming, as well as taking a leading role in the UNAIDS inter-agency task team on gender and HIV/AIDS. The Fund, in co-operation with the other participants in UNAIDS, aims to strengthen the global response to the HIV/AIDS epidemic, and is also concerned to reduce levels of other sexually transmitted infections (STIs) and reproductive tract infections (RTIs), and of infertility. UNFPA gives special attention to the specific needs of adolescents, for example through education and counselling initiatives, and to women in emergency situations. The Fund maintains that meeting the reproductive health needs of adolescents is an urgent priority in combating poverty and HIV/AIDS. Through the joint Adolescent Girls Initiative, UNFPA, UNICEF and WHO promote policy dialogues in 10 countries.

UNFPA takes a lead role in an emergency situation, following natural disaster or conflict, in providing basic supplies and services to protect reproductive health, in particular in the most vulnerable groups, i.e. young girls and pregnant women. It also helps to conduct rapid health assessments and censuses, supports counselling, education and training activities, and the construction of clinics and other health facilities, following humanitarian crises. UNFPA works with local authorities to prevent an escalation of sexual violence and to ensure that rapid and appropriate treatment and care is given to survivors of sexual violence. At the end of 2010 UNFPA appealed for US $53.3m. through the UN Consolidated Appeals Process (CAP) for 2011; of this, $27.9m. (52%) was to be allocated to humanitarian activities in Haiti.

POPULATION AND DEVELOPMENT

UNFPA promotes work on population as a central component of the goals of the international community to eradicate poverty and achieve sustainable development. UNFPA helps countries to formulate and implement comprehensive population policies as a part of any sustainable development strategies, and aims to ensure that the needs and concerns of women are incorporated into development and population policies. Research, educational and advocacy activities are undertaken to focus on specific aspects of development and population concern, for example migration, ageing and environmental sustainability. UNFPA provides assistance and training for national statistical offices in undertaking basic data collection, for example censuses and demographic surveys. UNFPA also provides assistance for analysis of demographic and socio-economic data, for research on population trends and for the formulation of government policies. A *State of World Population* report is published annually. The 2011 edition was issued in October of that year, the month when the global population was formally deemed to have reached 7,000m., and was subtitled 'People and possibilities in a world of 7 billion'; the 2011 report placed a strong emphasis on investment in young people. UNFPA supports a programme of fellowships in demographic analysis, data processing and cartography.

GENDER EQUALITY

A fundamental aspect of UNFPA's mission is to achieve gender equality, in order to promote the basic human rights of women and, through the empowerment of women, to support the elimination of poverty. Incorporated into all UNFPA activities are efforts to improve the welfare of women, in particular by providing reproductive choice, to eradicate gender discrimination, and to protect women from sexual and domestic violence and coercion. UNFPA's Strategic Framework on Gender Mainstreaming and Women's Empowerment for 2008–11 focused on the following six priority areas: setting policy for the ICPD Programme of Action and the MDGs; reproductive health; ending gender-based violence; adolescents and youth; emergency and post-emergency situations; and men and boys: partners for equality. The Fund aims to encourage the participation of women at all levels of decision- and policy-making and supports programmes that improve the access of all girls and women to education and grant women equal access to land, credit and employment opportunities. UNFPA aims to eradicate traditional practices that harm women, and works jointly with UNICEF to advance the eradication of female genital mutilation. UNFPA actively participates in efforts to raise awareness of and implement Resolution 1325 of the UN Security Council, adopted in October 2000, which addresses the impact of armed conflict on women and girls, the role of women in peace-building, and gender dimensions in peace processes and conflict resolution. Other activities are directed at particular issues concerning girls and adolescents and projects to involve men in reproductive health care initiatives.

Finance

UNFPA is supported entirely by voluntary contributions from governments and private donors. The Fund's total income for 2010–11 was projected at US $1,400m. Programme expenditure in that biennium was projected at $1,190.9m. Following the election of President Obama of the USA in January 2009, US funding, which had been suspended in 2002, was restored to UNFPA.

UNFPA, UNDP and UNICEF are committed to integrating their budgets from 2014.

Publications

Annual Report.

Campaign to End Fistula: The Year In Review (annually).

State of World Population (annually, in Arabic, English, French, Russian and Spanish).

Reports, technical publications, guidelines and manuals.

United Nations Relief and Works Agency for Palestine Refugees in the Near East—UNRWA

Address: Gamal Abd al-Nasser St, Gaza City.

Telephone: (8) 2887333; **fax:** (8) 2887555.

Address: Bayader Wadi Seer, POB 140157, Amman 11814, Jordan.

Telephone: (6) 5808100; **fax:** (6) 5808335; **e-mail:** unrwa-pio@unrwa.org; **internet:** www.un.org/unrwa.

UNRWA was established by the UN General Assembly to provide relief, health, education and welfare services for Palestine refugees in the Near East, initially on a short-term basis. UNRWA began operations in May 1950 and, in the absence of a solution to the refugee problem, its mandate has subsequently been extended by the General Assembly.

Organization

(April 2012)

UNRWA employs an international staff of about 120 and more than 24,200 local staff, mainly Palestine refugees. The Commissioner-General is the head of all UNRWA operations and reports directly to the UN General Assembly. UNRWA has no governing body, but its activities are reviewed annually by an Advisory Commission. In November 2005 the UN General Assembly approved an expansion of the Commission from 10 members to 21, reflecting the funding commitments in recent years of the governments concerned. It also authorized the Palestinian authorities, the European Community and the League of Arab States to attend as observers.

During 2007–10 UNRWA underwent a formal period of organizational development, aimed at strengthening its management capacity; thereafter the reform process continued, informally.

Commissioner-General: FILIPPO GRANDI (Italy).

Deputy Commissioner-General: MARGOT B. ELLIS (USA).

FIELD OFFICES

Each field office is headed by a director and has departments responsible for education, health and relief and social services programmes, finance, administration, supply and transport, legal affairs and public information. Operational support officers work in Gaza and the West Bank to monitor and report on the humanitarian situation and facilitate UNRWA field activities.

Gaza: POB 61; Al Azhar Rd, Rimal Quarter, Gaza City; tel. (8) 6777333; fax (8) 6777390.

Jordan: POB 143464, 11814 Amman; Al Zubeidi Bldg No. 16, Mustafa Bin Abdullah St, Barakeh, Tla'a Al-Ali, Amman; tel. (6) 5809100; fax (6) 5809134.

Lebanon: POB 11-0947, Beirut 1107 2060; Bir Hassan, Beirut; tel. (1) 840490; fax (1) 840466; e-mail lebanon@unrwa.org.

Syria: POB 4313; UN Compound, Mezzah Highway/Beirut Rd, Damascus; tel. (11) 6133035; fax (11) 6133047.

West Bank: POB 19149, Jerusalem; Sheik Jarrah Qtr, East Jerusalem; tel. (2) 5890400; fax (2) 5322714.

LIAISON OFFICES

Belgium: Centre d'Affaires ATEAC 11, rond point Schumann, 1040 Brussels; tel. (2) 256-75-85; fax (2) 256-75-03.

Egypt: 2 Dar-el-Shifa St, Garden City, POB 227, Cairo; tel. (2) 794-8502; fax (2) 794-8504.

Switzerland: Rms 92–94, Annex 1, Le Bocage, Palais des Nations, ave de la Paix, 1211 Geneva; tel. 229172057; fax 229170656.

USA: One United Nations Plaza, Room DC1–1265, New York, NY 10017; tel. (212) 963-2255; fax (212) 935-7899.

Activities

ASSISTANCE ACTIVITIES

Since 1950 UNRWA has been the main provider of relief, health, education and social services for Palestine refugees in Lebanon, Syria, Jordan, the West Bank and the Gaza Strip. For UNRWA's purposes, a Palestine refugee is one whose normal residence was in Palestine for a minimum of two years before the 1948 conflict and who, as a result of the Arab–Israeli hostilities, lost his or her home and means of livelihood. To be eligible for assistance, a refugee must reside in one of the five areas in which UNRWA operates and be in need. A refugee's descendants who fulfil certain criteria are also eligible for UNRWA assistance. After the renewal of Arab–Israeli hostilities in the Middle East in June 1967, hundreds of thousands of people fled from the fighting and from Israeli-occupied areas to east Jordan, Syria and Egypt. UNRWA provided emergency relief for displaced refugees and was additionally empowered by a UN General Assembly resolution to provide 'humanitarian assistance, as far as practicable, on an emergency basis and as a temporary measure' for those persons other than Palestine refugees who were newly displaced and in urgent need. In practice, UNRWA lacked the funds to aid the other displaced persons and the main burden of supporting them devolved on the Arab governments concerned. The Agency, as requested by the Government of Jordan in 1967 and on that Government's behalf, distributes rations to displaced persons in Jordan who are not registered refugees of 1948. UNRWA's emergency humanitarian support activities for Palestinian refugees include the provision of basic food and medical supplies; the implementation of a programme of emergency workdays, which aims to provide employment and income for labourers with dependants, while improving the local infrastructure; the provision of extra schooling days to make up for those missed because of the conflict, trauma counselling for children, and post-injury rehabilitation; and the reconstruction of shelters. UNRWA undertook a US $52m. emergency relief programme to support Palestinian refugees during 1982–85, following the Israeli invasion of southern Lebanon in June 1982. An expanded programme of assistance was implemented in the West Bank and Gaza during 1987–92 in response to the social and economic consequences of the so-called first Palestinian *intifada* (uprising) against Israel, and Israeli countermeasures. In June 2004 UNRWA and the Swiss Government hosted an international conference, convened in Geneva, with participation by representatives of 67 countries and 34 international organizations, aimed at addressing the humanitarian needs of Palestinian refugees; further to a decision of the conference a Department of Infrastructure and Camp Improvement was established at UNRWA headquarters, to address the deteriorating living conditions in many camps. In recent years diminishing funding has necessitated a retrenchment of the Agency's assistance activities, with the average annual spending per refugee falling by about one-half since 1975.

At 1 January 2012 UNRWA was providing essential services to 5m. registered refugees. Of these, an estimated 1.5m. (29%) were living in 58 camps serviced by the Agency (of which: 19 were in the West Bank; 12 were in Lebanon; 10 were in Jordan; nine were in Syria; and eight were in Gaza), while the remaining refugees had settled in local towns and villages of the host countries. UNRWA's three principal areas of activity are 'Acquired knowledge and skills', 'A long and healthy life', and 'A decent standard of living'. Some 85% of the Agency's 2012 regular budget was devoted to these three operational programmes.

'Acquired knowledge and skills' accounted for 53% of UNRWA's 2012 regular budget. In the 2011/12 school year there were 485,754 pupils enrolled in 699 UNRWA schools, and 19,217 educational staff. UNRWA also operated 10 vocational and teacher-training centres, which provided a total of 6,652 training places, and three other educational sciences faculties. Technical co-operation for the Agency's education programme is provided by UNESCO. During the 2010/11 school year UNRWA was prevented from enrolling some 40,000 eligible children in schools in Gaza as building materials required for the construction of necessary new schools had not been supplied to the territory since 2007.

'Long and healthy lives' accounted for 19% of UNRWA's 2012 regular budget. At 1 January 2012 there were 138 primary health care units providing outpatient medical care, disease prevention and control, maternal and child health care and family planning services, of which 117 also offered dental care and a further 123 had laboratory services. At that time the number of health staff totalled 3,595. UNRWA also operates a hospital in the West Bank and offers assistance towards emergency and other secondary treatment, mainly through contractual agreements with non-governmental and private hospitals. Technical assistance for the health programme is provided by WHO. UNRWA offers mental health care to refugees, in particular children, experiencing psychological stress. The Agency aims to provide essential environmental health services. Nearly all camp shelters are connected to water networks, and by January 2012 87% were connected to sewerage networks.

'Decent standard of living' accounted for 13.5% of UNRWA's regular budget for 2012. These services comprise the distribution of food rations, the provision of emergency shelter and the organization of welfare programmes for the poorest refugees (at 1 January 2012 293,718 refugees, or nearly 6% of the total registered refugee population, were eligible to receive special hardship assistance). In 2012 UNRWA was providing technical and financial support to 49 women's programme centres and 35 community-based rehabilitation centres.

In order to encourage Palestinian self-reliance the Agency issues grants to ailing businesses and loans to families who qualify as special hardship cases. In 1991 UNRWA launched an income generation programme, which provides capital loans to small businesses and micro-enterprises with the objective of creating sustainable employment and eliminating poverty, particularly in the Occupied Territories. The programme was extended to Palestinian refugees in the West Bank in 1996 and in Jordan and Syria in 2003. By January 2012 265,571 loans, with a total estimated value of US $302m., had been awarded under the programme.

RECENT EMERGENCIES

From the commencement, in the second half of 2000, of the so-called second Palestinian al Aqsa *intifada* (uprising), and Israel's restriction from that time on the issuing of permits to enter or leave Gaza to only medical humanitarian cases, UNRWA became the lead agency with responsibility for the co-ordination and delivery of emergency assistance, as well as for monitoring the immediate needs of the local populations, and launched successive emergency appeals for assistance to Palestinian refugees in Gaza and the West Bank. The UNRWA Commissioner-General repeatedly expressed deep concern at the worsening humanitarian situation in the Palestinian territories, at the demolition of homes in Gaza and the West Bank by Israeli military forces, at the entry restrictions imposed by Israel against the Gaza Strip, which were causing extreme food shortages, and at restrictions on the movements of UN international staff within Gaza, which were severely impeding the Agency's activities. UNRWA repeatedly expressed concern at the construction by Israel, from 2002, of the West Bank 'security fence', or 'barrier', which was estimated to affect some 200,000 people through loss of land, water, agricultural resources and education, and hindered UNRWA's ability to provide and distribute humanitarian assistance. UNRWA has continued to monitor closely the construction and impact of the barrier.

Following the victory by the militant Islamic Resistance Movement (Hamas, opposed to any accommodation with Israel) at legislative elections held in the Palestinian Autonomous Territories in January 2006 and the installation of a Hamas-led administration there in March, the EU and USA announced that they would withhold direct aid to the Palestinian National Authority (PA), but would increase their contributions to humanitarian organizations engaged in the region. During 2006 UNRWA protested repeatedly that its activities in Gaza were being severely disrupted owing to the constant closure of the Karni crossing between Gaza and Israel. In late August the Agency reported that its operations in Gaza were nearly stalled and that the difficulties with access to the area had resulted in acute shortages of food, fuel and construction supplies. In July of that year UNRWA appealed for US $7.2m. to fund emergency humanitarian assistance for Palestinian refugees based in Lebanon and Syria who had been affected as a consequence of the conflict that erupted in that month between the Israeli armed forces and the militant Shi'a organization Hezbollah. The Agency was also assisting Lebanese civilians displaced by the conflict who had sought shelter in UNRWA schools. By the end of 2006 UNRWA reported its extreme concern at the socio-economic crisis affecting the Palestinian people, caused partly by the withholding of official donor assistance and ongoing restrictions on access and movement of people and goods. It launched an appeal for $246.2m. in emergency funding, mostly to meet basic humanitarian requirements, in 2007. In July 2007 UNRWA announced that it had suspended all public works rehabilitation and construction projects in Gaza owing to a lack of basic supplies resulting from a land, sea and air blockade imposed since June of that year on the Gaza Strip by Israel and Egypt (strengthening the existing border restrictions).

In May 2007 an outbreak of sectarian violence in northern Lebanon disrupted UNRWA's supply of humanitarian assistance and forced an estimated 27,000 people to leave their homes. In June UNRWA issued a flash appeal for US $12.7m. to meet the immediate needs of the displaced refugees and to improve the conditions at Beddawi camp, which was providing temporary shelter to the majority of those fleeing the fighting. In September UNRWA issued an emergency appeal for northern Lebanon, amounting to $54.8m. for the period 1 September 2007–31 August 2008, to meet the needs of the affected population and to support the rehabilitation of the Nahr el-Bared camp, which had been extensively damaged by the fighting. By the end of September 2011 some 7,439 people remained displaced from Nahr el-Bared.

In December 2008 UNRWA issued an appeal for more than US $275m. in international donations for 2009 under the UN Consolidated Appeals Process (CAP), in view of the deepening vulnerability of Palestinian refugees affected by the continuing blockade imposed by Israel, entrenched poverty and unprecedented high levels of unemployment. The Agency stated that the dependency of Gaza and the West Bank on external aid had deepened during 2008. In late December, in response to the intensive bombardment of the Gaza Strip by Israeli forces that commenced at that time with the stated aim of ending rocket attacks launched by Hamas and other militant groups on Israeli targets, the UNRWA Commissioner-General expressed horror at the extensive destruction and loss of life caused by the Israeli action and, while recognizing Israel's legitimate security concerns, urged the Israeli military to cease the bombardment and to respect all international conventions regarding the protection of non-combatants in times of conflict to which Israel is a signatory. At the end of December UNRWA launched a flash appeal for $34m. to meet Gaza's urgent humanitarian requirements (including the provision of essential health supplies, food, cash assistance, materials for housing repairs, fuel, and shelter requirements for displaced Palestinian civilians) over a period of four months. Israeli air strikes were reported by UNRWA at that time to have inflicted significant damage to Gaza's fragile infrastructure and to have destroyed its public service capacity. The Agency, which had suspended its food assistance during the second half of December owing to insufficient supplies, demanded that border crossings should be reopened permanently. At the beginning of January 2009 Israeli forces initiated a ground invasion of Gaza.

In early January 2009 the UN Secretary-General urged an immediate cease-fire in Gaza and denounced as unacceptable recent Israeli attacks on three UNRWA-run schools that had resulted in a substantial number of civilian fatalities and injuries. At that time around 25 UNRWA schools were serving as temporary shelters to Palestinians who had been displaced by the ongoing violence. Soon afterwards UNRWA suspended its movements through Gaza (including, once again, food distribution) owing to Israeli air strikes on humanitarian convoys that had caused several fatalities. On 8 January the UN Security Council adopted Resolution 1860 demanding an immediate cease-fire in Gaza, culminating in the full withdrawal of Israeli forces; the unimpeded provision throughout Gaza of food, fuel and medical treatment; improved international arrangements to prevent arms and ammunition smuggling; intra-Palestinian reconciliation; and renewed efforts to achieve a comprehensive long-term peace between Israel and Palestine. In mid-January UNRWA's field headquarters in Gaza was struck and set alight by Israeli shells that reportedly contained incendiary white phosphorus; the UN Secretary-General protested strongly against the attack. On 18 January Israel, while maintaining its positions in Gaza, ceased hostilities; Hamas responded by announcing a week-long cessation of hostilities against Israeli targets, in order to permit Israel to withdraw its armed forces fully from the territory. The Israeli withdrawal was completed on 21 January. By the time of the cease-fire the Israeli offensive had reportedly killed 1,340 people in Gaza (including 460 children and 106 women), and had wounded some 5,320 people (including 1,855 children and 795 women). At the height of the crisis UNRWA provided refuge for 50,896 Palestinians in 50 shelters.

In late January 2009 the UN launched a flash appeal for US $615m. (in addition to its CAP appeal for 2009) to cover the emergency requirements of UNRWA and other aid agencies over a period of six–nine months in supporting civilians in Gaza through the provision of food, water, sanitation, health care and shelter, other basic services, education, psychological care, emergency repairs and rehabilitation, and clearing unexploded ordnance. At that time UNRWA was serving some 900,000 refugees in Gaza, while other civilians were being supported by the WFP. For several days in early February UNRWA suspended the importation of humanitarian supplies into Gaza following the confiscation by the Hamas authorities of deliveries of foodstuffs and blankets. At that time UNRWA's activities in Gaza were also being restricted by the refusal of the Israeli authorities to permit entry into the territory of nylon pellets for making plastic food distribution bags, and paper and exercise books for educational use. In early March the UN Secretary-General appealed to international donors participating in the International Conference on the Palestinian Economy and Gaza Reconstruction, convened in Sharm esh-Sheikh, Egypt, for contributions to support and rebuild Gaza. The Secretary-General emphasized at that meeting the importance of maintaining a durable cease-fire, open border crossings into Gaza, and Palestinian reconciliation. In August UNRWA issued a Gaza Ramadan Appeal, requesting an additional $181m. in donations to fund food assistance, shelter improvements, job creation and the rehabilitation of education and health facilities for the poorest and most vulnerable groups of refugees living in Gaza.

In January 2010 UNRWA launched its emergency appeal for that year, amounting to US $323.3m. At the end of May the UNRWA Commissioner-General and the UN Special Co-ordinator for the Middle East Peace Process issued a joint statement strongly condemning an attack perpetrated at that time by Israeli security forces against a flotilla of vessels that was travelling through international waters with the aim of carrying humanitarian aid to Gaza; the Israeli action resulted in the deaths of nine civilians and wounded more than 40 further passengers. The joint statement stressed that such fatalities would be avoidable if Israel were to terminate its blockade of Gaza. It was reported at the end of 2011 that UNRWA's funding appeal for that year (of US $379.7m.) was only 40% funded. In December 2011 UNRWA appealed for $318.2m. in support of its activities in 2012, of which $103.3m. was for Gaza and $214.9m. for the West Bank. Of the total amount nearly 80% was for the provision of emergency food and livelihood support for food-insecure families. A report issued by UNRWA in December 2011 found that, despite a recent expansion of economic activity in Gaza, the rate of unemployment amongst refugees there stood at 33.8% in the first half of 2011, one of the highest in the world. In January 2012 the UN General Assembly adopted a resolution that urged donor nations to increase contributions to the Agency, in order to address its funding shortfall.

Statistics

REFUGEES REGISTERED WITH UNRWA
(1 January 2012)

Country	Number	% of total
Jordan	1,979,580	41
Gaza Strip	1,167,572	24
West Bank	727,471	15
Syria	486,946	10
Lebanon	436,154	9
Total	4,797,723	100

Finance

UNRWA is financed almost entirely by voluntary contributions from governments and the European Union, the remainder being provided by UN bodies, non-governmental organizations, business corporations and private sources, which also contribute to extra-budgetary activities. UNRWA's regular budget for 2012–13, covering recurrent expenditure on sectoral activities, totalled US $1,251m.

Publication

Annual Report of the Commissioner-General of UNRWA.

United Nations Training and Research Institutes

United Nations Institute for Disarmament Research—UNIDIR

Address: Palais des Nations, 1211 Geneva 10, Switzerland.

Telephone: 229173186; **fax:** 229170176; **e-mail:** unidir@unog.ch; **internet:** www.unidir.org.

UNIDIR is an autonomous institution within the United Nations. It was established by the General Assembly in 1980 for the purpose of undertaking independent research on disarmament and related problems, particularly international security issues. UNIDIR's statute became effective on 1 January 1985. The Director of UNIDIR reports annually to the General Assembly on the activities of the Institute. The UN Secretary-General's Advisory Board on Disarmament Studies functions as UNIDIR's Board of Trustees.

The work of the Institute is based on the following objectives: to provide the international community with more diversified and complete data on problems relating to international security, the armaments race and disarmament in all fields, so as to facilitate progress towards greater global security and towards economic and social development for all peoples; to promote informed participation by all states in disarmament efforts; to assist ongoing negotiations on disarmament, and continuing efforts to ensure greater international security at a progressively lower level of armaments, in particular nuclear weapons, by means of objective studies and analyses; and to conduct long-term research on disarmament in order to provide a general insight into the problems involved and to stimulate new initiatives for negotiations. UNIDIR's activities are grouped into the following five areas: weapons of mass destruction; weapons of societal disruption; security and society; emerging threats; and improving processes and creating synergies.

The work programme of UNIDIR is reviewed annually and is subject to approval by its Board of Trustees. During 2011 UNIDIR organized conferences, workshops and seminars on a range of issues, including: multilateral approaches to the nuclear fuel cycle; implementation of the 2010 NPT Review Conference Action Plan; global cybersecurity challenges, and 'international law and war in cyberspace'; developing an effective arms trade treaty; and space security. Examples of ongoing research projects in 2012 include: Supporting the Arms Trade Treaty Negotiations through Regional Discussions and Expertise Sharing (see below); Understanding Disarmament; Research and Development for an Evidence-based Reintegration Programming Tool; Emerging Security Threats; Weapons of Mass Destruction; International Co-operation Mechanisms on Nuclear Security; Norms on Explosive Weapons; Perspectives on Cyber War: Legal Frameworks and Transparency and Confidence Building; and Promoting Implementation of the NPT Action Plan 2012. Research projects are conducted within the Institute, or commissioned to individual experts or research organizations. For some major studies, multinational groups of experts are established. The Institute offers a research fellowship programme focusing on topics relating to regional security. UNIDIR maintains a database on research institutes (DATARIs) in the field of international security.

The Institute organizes (jointly with the Quaker United Nations Office and the Centre on Conflict, Development and Peacebuilding of the Graduate Institute of International and Development Studies) the Geneva Forum, which aims to serve as a focal point for discussion of disarmament and arms control issues, engaging government and non-governmental officials, UN personnel, media representatives and academics. The Geneva Forum publishes the *Media Guide to Disarmament and Arms Control*.

In early 2012 UNIDIR was supporting the preparatory process leading to the UN Conference on the Arms Trade Treaty, which was scheduled to be held in July of that year, in New York, with the aim of establishing a legally binding instrument to set the highest possible international standards of control and transparency to guide the import, export and transfer of conventional weapons.

The Institute is financed mainly by voluntary contributions from governments and public or private organizations. A contribution to the costs of the Director and staff may be provided from the UN regular budget.

Director: THERESA A. HITCHENS (USA).

Publications: *Annual Report*, *Disarmament Forum* (quarterly), *UNIDIR Highlights*, research reports (6 a year), research papers (irregular).

United Nations Institute for Training and Research—UNITAR

Address: Palais des Nations, 1211 Geneva 10, Switzerland.

Telephone: 229178455; **fax:** 229178047; **e-mail:** info@unitar.org; **internet:** www.unitar.org.

UNITAR was established in 1963, as an autonomous body within the United Nations, in order to provide training for diplomats and other officials and to enhance the effectiveness of the UN. UNITAR's training activities, including seminars, workshops, distance and online training, and fellowships, are now open to any professional working in the relevant field. UNITAR established offices in New York, USA, (in 1996), in Hiroshima, Japan (in 2003), and in Brasília, Brazil (in 2010), to provide specialist or regional training activities.

UNITAR's Training Department is focused on three main areas of activity: peace, security and diplomacy; environment; and governance. The Peace, Security and Diplomacy Unit incorporates programmes on multilateral diplomacy, international law, peacemaking and conflict prevention, and peace-keeping training. The Environment Unit manages programmes concerning environmental governance and law, chemicals and waste management, climate change, and biodiversity. Within the Governance Unit are programmes on public finance and trade, and on e-governance. The Unit also administers the Local Development and Decentralization Programme, which operates partly through a network of International Training Centres for Local Actors (CIFAL) to train local authorities in issues relating to sustainable development, the efficient management of local services, and urbanization.

UNITAR's Research Department is concerned with the application of new technologies to training and knowledge systems innovation. It administers the UNITAR Operational Satellite Applications Programme (UNOSAT) which aims to ensure that information from satellite earth observation is available and used effectively by relief and development organizations, as well as to help to monitor human rights and security and to support territorial planning. In 2003 UNOSAT developed a humanitarian rapid mapping service, providing rapid acquisition and processing of satellite imagery for use by agencies co-ordinating emergency relief, as well as recovery and rehabilitation efforts.

UNITAR is responsible for organizing annual retreats of the UN Secretary-General, and of the Departments of Peace-keeping Operations and of Political Affairs. The Institute also organizes an annual seminar of the Special Representatives of the UN Secretary-General. In April 2008 UNITAR inaugurated a Geneva Lecture Series which aimed to generate public awareness and engage leading personalities in a consideration of global challenges.

In November 2011, as part of a series of activities related to reform of the UN, UNITAR organized a workshop on 'System-wide Coherence in UN Development Activities', focusing on ongoing initiatives to improve co-ordination of the organization and its coherence mechanisms.

UNITAR is financed by voluntary contributions from UN member states, by donations from foundations and other non-governmental sources, and by income generated by its Reserve Fund.

Executive Director: (vacant).

United Nations Interregional Crime and Justice Research Institute—UNICRI

Address: Viale Maestri del Lavoro 10, 10127 Turin, Italy.

Telephone: (011) 6537111; **fax:** (011) 6313368; **e-mail:** information@unicri.it; **internet:** www.unicri.it.

The Institute was established in 1968 as the United Nations Social Defence Research Institute. Its present name was adopted by a resolution of ECOSOC in 1989. The Institute undertakes research, training and information activities in the fields of crime prevention and criminal justice, at international, regional and national levels.

In collaboration with national governments, UNICRI aims to establish a reliable base of knowledge and information on organized crime; to identify strategies for the prevention and control of crime, within the framework of contributing to socio-economic development and protecting human rights; and to design systems to support policy formulation, implementation and evaluation. UNICRI organizes workshops and conferences, and promotes the exchange of information through its international documentation centre on criminology. The Programme incorporates the following operational units: a department on Justice, Protection and Ethics, focusing on country projects, as well as victim surveys and biomedical research; a Security Governance/Counter Terrorism Laboratory, which provides support to the International Permanent Observatory (IPO) on Security during Major Events, as well as other regional security efforts (i.e. an IPO Americas network and the second phase of a European Union project on major events security, EU-SEC II), participates in the UN Counter-Terrorism Implementation Task Force, administers a 'programme of excellence' for policy-makers concerning security governance, and supports efforts to combat illicit trafficking in chemical, biological, radiological and nuclear weapons; an Emerging Crimes and Anti-Human Trafficking unit, incorporating projects concerned with trafficking in human beings, in particular women and children, and other emerging crimes, such as counterfeiting, environmental crime and 'cyber' crime; and a Training and Advanced Education Department, which administers educational courses, a summer school on migration, and a Masters of Law in International Organizations, International Criminal Law and Crime Prevention. During 2010–11 UNICRI, the ICTY and the OSCE Office for Democratic Institutions and Human Rights (ODIHR) implemented the EU-funded War Crimes Justice Project, aimed at strengthening the capacity of national judiciaries in the Balkans to address war crimes cases. In 2009 UNICRI inaugurated three regional offices of the Security Governance/Counter Terrorism Laboratory: in Lucca, Italy, to specialize in dialogue and innovation; in Lisbon, Portugal, to promote technical projects on public/private partnerships; and in Boston, USA, to focus on security in the urban environment. UNICRI maintains a Liaison Office in Rome, Italy, to strengthen collaboration with local institutions and civil bodies and with UN agencies. In June 2009 UNICRI opened a new office at the University of Pomezia, Italy, to conduct postgraduate, Masters and other specialized training courses.

UNICRI is funded by the United Nations Crime Prevention and Criminal Justice Fund, which is financed by voluntary contributions from UN member states, non-governmental organizations, academic institutions and other concerned bodies.

Officer-in-Charge: Dr Jonathan Lucas (Seychelles).

Publications: *Brochure*, *F3–Freedom from Fear* (online journal, in collaboration with the Max Planck Institute for Foreign and International Criminal Law), training materials, reports, research studies.

United Nations Research Institute for Social Development—UNRISD

Address: Palais des Nations, 1211 Geneva 10, Switzerland.

Telephone: 229173020; **fax:** 229170650; **e-mail:** info@unrisd.org; **internet:** www.unrisd.org.

UNRISD was established in 1963 as an autonomous body within the United Nations, to conduct multi-disciplinary research into the social dimensions of contemporary problems affecting development.

The Institute aims to provide governments, development agencies, grass-roots organizations and scholars with a better understanding of how development policies and processes of economic, social and environmental change affect different social groups.

UNRISD research is undertaken in collaboration with a network of national research teams drawn from local universities and research institutions. UNRISD aims to promote and strengthen research capacities in developing countries. Its main focus areas are the eradication of poverty; the promotion of democracy and human rights; environmental sustainability; gender equality; and the effects of globalization. During 2010–14 UNRISD's research agenda 'Social Development in an Uncertain World' covered two main themes: social policies for inclusive and sustainable development' and 'political and institutional dynamics of social development'. In November 2009 UNRISD sponsored an international conference, convened in Geneva, Switzerland, addressing the Social and Political Dimensions of the Global Crisis: Implications for Developing Countries. In September 2010 UNRISD published a Flagship Report entitled *Combating Poverty and Inequality: Structural Change, Social Policy and Politics*, which resulted from major research initiatives, including on poverty reduction and poverty regimes, and on social policy in a development context.

The Institute is supported by voluntary grants from governments, and also receives financing from other UN organizations, and from various other national and international agencies.

Director: Dr Sarah Cook (United Kingdom).

Publications: *Conference News*, *e-Bulletin* (quarterly), *UNRISD News* (2 a year), discussion papers and monographs, special reports, programme and occasional papers.

United Nations System Staff College

Address: Viale Maestri del Lavoro 10, 10127 Turin, Italy.

Telephone: (011) 6535911; **fax:** (011) 6535902; **e-mail:** info@unssc.org; **internet:** www.unssc.org.

In July 2001 the UN General Assembly approved a statute for the UN System Staff College (UNSSC), which, it envisaged, would provide knowledge management, training and continuous learning opportunities for all UN personnel, with a view to developing UN system-wide co-operation and operational effectiveness. The inaugural meeting of the Board of Governors was held in November, and the College formally began operations on 1 January 2002. It aims to promote the exchange of knowledge and shared learning, to administer learning and training workshops, to provide support and expert advice, and to act as a clearing house for learning activities. It provides an online orientation course for new UN staff members and provides extensive learning support to the Resident Co-ordinators. A UN Leaders Programme, focusing on strategic leadership theory, practice and skills, was inaugurated in May 2009. In 2012 the College's activities were organized under the following programmes: the UN Leaders Programme; UN Coherence (including support of the 'Delivering as One' agenda); Knowledge and Management; Peace and Security; and Development and Human Rights.

The UNSSC is financed by a combination of course fees, voluntary grants from governments and contributions in kind from various UN organizations in the form of staff secondments.

Director: (vacant).

United Nations University—UNU

Address: 53–70, Jingumae 5-chome, Shibuya-ku, Tokyo 150-8925, Japan.

Telephone: (3) 5467-1212; **fax:** (3) 3499-2828; **e-mail:** mbox@unu.edu; **internet:** www.unu.edu.

The University is sponsored jointly by the UN and UNESCO. It is an autonomous institution within the UN, guaranteed academic freedom by a charter approved by the General Assembly in 1973. It is governed by a 28-member University Council of scholars and scientists, of whom 24 are appointed by the Secretary-General of the UN and the Director-General of UNESCO (who, together with the Executive Director of UNITAR, are *ex officio* members of the Council; the Rector is also on the Council). The University works through networks of collaborating institutions and individuals. These include Associated Institutions (universities and research institutes linked with UNU under general agreements of co-operation). UNU undertakes multi-disciplinary research on problems that are the concern of the UN and its agencies, and works to strengthen research and training capabilities in developing countries. It administers joint graduate and international post-graduate courses and organizes an advanced seminar series and a global seminar series, which aims to generate awareness about contemporary global issues and the role of the UN in addressing them. In December 2008 the UNU Council endorsed the process of accreditation required for UNU to award its own degrees. In January 2009 UNU established a new Institute for Sustainability and Peace, which integrated the academic activities of two main programme areas: peace and governance, and environment and sustainable development. The Institute aimed to promote a transdisciplinary approach to issues affecting human security and sustainability.

The University oversees a network of research and training centres and programmes world-wide, comprising: the UNU Institute for Environment and Human Security (UNU-EHS), based in Bonn, Germany; the World Institute for Development Economics Research (UNU-WIDER) in Helsinki, Finland; the Economic and Social Research and Training Centre on Innovation and Technology (UNU-MERIT) in Maastricht, Netherlands; the International Institute for Software Technology (UNU-IIST) in Macao; the UNU Institute for Natural Resources in Africa (UNU-INRA) in Accra, Ghana (with a mineral resources unit in Lusaka, Zambia); the UNU Programme for Biotechnology in Latin America and the Caribbean (UNU-BIOLAC), based in Caracas, Venezuela; the International Leadership Institute (UNU-ILI) in Amman, Jordan; the Institute of Advanced Studies (UNU-IAS), based in Yokohama, Japan; the UNU International Network on Water, Environment and Health (UNU-INWEH) in Hamilton, Canada; the UNU Programme on Comparative Regional Integration Studies (UNU-CRIS), in Bruges, Belgium; the UNU Food and Nutrition Programme for Human and Social Development (UNU-FNP), based at Cornell University, USA; the UNU International Institute for Global Health (UNU-IIGH), based in Kuala Lumpur, Malaysia; the UNU Geothermal Training Programme (UNU-GTP) and UNU Fisheries Training Programme (UNU-FTP), both in Reykjavík, Iceland; and the UN-Water Decade Programme on Capacity Development, based in Bonn, Germany. In 1993 the UNU established a research centre focusing on international conflict (INCORE), as a joint project with the University of Ulster, United Kingdom.

The UNU Centre in Tokyo, Japan, co-ordinates much of the activities of the UNU and ensures close co-operation with the UN system. It is also supported by a Vice-Rectorate in Europe, based in Bonn, Germany, which is also responsible for promoting UNU's presence in Africa. In December 2008 the UNU Council approved an initiative to 'twin' institutes, in order to promote greater collaboration between centres in developed and less developed regions. The first twinning arrangement was to link the new Institute for Sustainability and Peace with UNU-INRA, in Ghana, and initiate a joint research project concerning education for sustainable development. A Memorandum of Understanding on the establishment of a new body, the UNU Institute for Integrated Management of Material Fluxes and Resources (UNU-FLORES) was signed in November 2010. The Institute was to be based in Dresden, Germany, with a twin institute in Maputo, Mozambique.

UNU is financed by voluntary contributions from UN member states.

Rector: Prof. Dr KONRAD OSTERWALDER (Switzerland).

Publications: *Our World 2.0* (online magazine), *UNU Update* (regular online newsletter), *UNU Press Newsletter* (quarterly), journals, abstracts, research papers.

University for Peace

Address: POB 138-6100, San José, Costa Rica.

Telephone: 2205-9000; **fax:** 2249-1929; **e-mail:** info@upeace.org; **internet:** www.upeace.org.

The University for Peace (UPEACE) was established in 1980 to conduct research on, *inter alia*, disarmament, mediation, the resolution of conflicts, the preservation of the environment, international relations, peace education and human rights. The Council of the University (the governing body, comprising 17 members) was reconstituted in March 1999, meeting for the first time since 1994, and initiated a programme of extensive reforms and expansion. A programme of short courses for advanced international training was reintroduced in 2001. In 2000 a Centre and Policy Institute was established in Geneva, Switzerland, and an Institute for Media, Peace and Security was inaugurated, with administrative headquarters in Paris, France. In 2001 the World Centre for Research and Training in Conflict Resolution was established in Bogotá, Colombia. In December 2006 UPEACE inaugurated a Human Rights Centre, which aimed to conduct research, education and training in theory and practice of human rights issues. A UPEACE Centre for Executive Education offers seminars and workshops to business executives and other professionals in fields concerning leadership, conflict resolution and peace education. In 2012 regular Masters degrees were available in Environmental Security and Peace (also with a specialization in Climate Change and Security); Gender and Peacebuilding; International Law and Human Rights; International Law and the Settlement of Disputes; International Peace Studies; Media, Peace and Conflict Studies; Natural Resources and Peace; Peace Education; Responsible Management and Sustainable Economic Development; and Sustainable Urban Governance and Peace.

UPEACE aims to develop a global network of partner institutions. A Central Asia Programme, concerned with education in peacebuilding and conflict prevention in the former Soviet Central Asia, was initiated in 2000. In January 2002 the University launched an Africa Programme, which aims to build African capacity for education, training and research on matters related to peace and security. A UPEACE Academic Advisory Council, mandated to improve the organization of the University's academic programme and build partnerships and networks with other academic institutions for collaboration in the areas of both teaching and research, was inaugurated in May 2003. Under an Asia Leaders Programme UPEACE offers a Master of Arts (MA) in International Peace Studies as a dual degree with the Ateneo de Manila University, the Philippines. A further dual MA for Asian students is offered in collaboration with the Hankuk University of Foreign Studies, Republic of Korea. An MA dual degree in Natural Resources and Sustainable Development is conducted with the American University in Washington, DC, USA. UPEACE aims to strengthen education capacities in developing countries. In September 2007 UPEACE, in collaboration with the Government of the Netherlands, initiated a programme to promote the teaching of peace and conflict studies in the Horn of Africa, the Middle East and South Asia. In November 2009 UPEACE signed a partnership agreement with the Peace and Sport international forum, based in Monaco, under which both organizations determined to establish a joint training programme.

Rector: JOHN J. MARESCA (USA).

Publications: *Peace and Conflict Review* (2 a year), *African Peace and Conflict Journal* (quarterly).

World Food Programme—WFP

Address: Via Cesare Giulio Viola 68, Parco dei Medici, 00148 Rome, Italy.

Telephone: (06) 65131; **fax:** (06) 6513-2840; **e-mail:** wfpinfo@wfp.org; **internet:** www.wfp.org.

WFP, the principal food assistance organization of the United Nations, became operational in 1963. It aims to alleviate acute hunger by providing emergency relief following natural or man-made humanitarian disasters, and supplies food assistance to people in developing countries to eradicate chronic undernourishment, to support social development and to promote self-reliant communities.

Organization

(April 2012)

EXECUTIVE BOARD

The governing body of WFP is the Executive Board, comprising 36 members, 18 of whom are elected by the UN Economic and Social Council (ECOSOC) and 18 by the Council of the Food and Agriculture Organization (FAO). The Board meets four times each year at WFP headquarters.

SECRETARIAT

WFP's Executive Director is appointed jointly by the UN Secretary-General and the Director-General of FAO and is responsible for the management and administration of the Programme. Around 90% of WFP staff members work in the field. WFP administers some 87 country offices, in order to provide operational, financial and management support at a more local level, and maintains six regional bureaux, located in Bangkok, Thailand (for Asia), Cairo, Egypt (for the Middle East, Central Asia and Eastern Europe), Panama City, Panama (for Latin America and the Caribbean), Johannesburg, South Africa (for Southern Africa), Kampala, Uganda (for Central and Eastern Africa), and Dakar, Senegal (for West Africa).

Executive Director: ERTHARIN COUSIN (USA) (from May 2012).

Activities

WFP is the only multilateral organization with a mandate to use food assistance as a resource. It is the second largest source of assistance in the UN, after the World Bank Group, in terms of actual transfers of resources, and the largest source of grant aid in the UN system. WFP handles more than one-third of the world's food assistance. WFP is also the largest contributor to South–South trade within the UN system, through the purchase of food and services from developing countries (at least three-quarters of the food purchased by the Programme originates in developing countries). WFP's mission is to provide food assistance to save lives in refugee and other emergency situations, to improve the nutrition and quality of life of vulnerable groups and to help to develop assets and promote the self-reliance of poor families and communities. WFP aims to focus its efforts on the world's poorest countries and to provide at least 90% of its total assistance to those designated as 'low-income food-deficit'. At the World Food Summit, held in November 1996, WFP endorsed the commitment to reduce by 50% the number of undernourished people, no later than 2015. During 2010 WFP food assistance, distributed through development projects, emergency operations (EMOPs) and protracted relief and recovery operations (PRROs), benefited some 109.2m. people, including 89m. women and children, and 15.4m. IDPs, in 75 countries. Total food deliveries in 2010 amounted to 4.6m. metric tons.

WFP rations comprise basic food items (staple foods such as wheat flour or rice; pulses such as lentils and chickpeas; vegetable oil fortified with vitamins A and D; sugar; and iodized salt). Where possible basic rations are complemented with special products designed to improve the nutritional intake of beneficiaries. These include fortified blended foods, principally 'Corn Soya Blend', containing important micronutrients; ready-to-use foods, principally peanut-based pastes enriched with vitamins and minerals trademarked as 'Plumpy Doz' and 'Supplementary Plumpy', which are better suited to meeting the nutritional needs of young and moderately malnourished children; high energy biscuits, distributed in the first phases of emergencies when cooking facilities may be scarce; micronutrient powder ('sprinkles'), which can be used to fortify home cooking; and compressed food bars, given out during disaster relief operations when the distribution and preparation of local food is not possible. The Programme's food donations must meet internationally agreed standards applicable to trade in food products. In May 2003 WFP's Executive Board approved a policy on donations of genetically modified (GM) foods and other foods derived from biotechnology, determining that the Programme would continue to accept donations of GM/biotech food and that, when distributing it, relevant national standards would be respected. It is WFP policy to buy food as near to where it is needed as possible, with a view to saving on transport costs and helping to sustain local economies. From 2008 targeted cash and voucher schemes started to be implemented, as a possible alternative to food rations (see below). During 2011 WFP and several corporate partners started to implement pilot schemes in targeted areas in Bangladesh and Indonesia under a new Project Laser Beam (PLB) initiative, aimed at addressing child malnutrition. With other UN agencies, governments, research institutions, and representatives of civil society and of the private sector, WFP supports the Scaling up Nutrition (SUN) initiative, which was initiated in 2009, under the co-ordination of the UN Secretary-General's Special Representative for Food Security and Nutrition, with the aim of increasing the coverage of interventions that improve nutrition during the first 1,000 days of a child's life (such as exclusive breastfeeding, optimal complementary feeding practices, and provision of essential vitamins and minerals); and ensuring that nutrition plans are implemented at national level, and that government programmes take nutrition into account.

WFP aims to address the causes of chronic malnourishment, which it identifies as poverty and lack of opportunity. It emphasizes the role played by women (who are most likely to sow, reap, harvest and cook household food) in combating hunger, and endeavours to address the specific nutritional needs of women, to increase their access to food and development resources, and to promote girls' education. WFP estimates that females represent four-fifths of people engaged in farming in Africa and three-fifths of people engaged in farming in Asia, and that globally women are the sole breadwinners in one-third of households. Increasingly WFP distributes food assistance through women, believing that vulnerable children are more likely to be reached in this way. In September 2011 WFP and UN Women announced an agreement to provide income generating opportunities for women in rural areas. The Programme also focuses resources on supporting the nutrition and food security of households and communities affected by HIV/AIDS, and on promoting food security as a means of mitigating extreme poverty and vulnerability and thereby combating the spread and impact of HIV/AIDS. In February 2003 WFP and the Joint UN Programme on HIV/AIDS (UNAIDS) concluded an agreement to address jointly the relationship between HIV/AIDS, regional food shortages and chronic hunger, with a particular focus on Africa, Southeast Asia and the Caribbean. In October of that year WFP became a co-sponsor of UNAIDS. WFP also urges the development of new food assistance strategies as a means of redressing global inequalities and thereby combating the threat of conflict and international terrorism.

WFP is a participant in the High Level Task Force (HLTF) on the Global Food Security Crisis, which was established by the UN Secretary-General in April 2008 with the aim of addressing the global impact of soaring levels of food and commodity prices, and of formulating a comprehensive framework for action. WFP participated in the High-Level Conference on World Food Security and the Challenges of Climate Change and Bioenergy that was convened by FAO in June. At that time WFP determined to allocate some US $1,200m. in extra-budgetary funds to alleviate hunger in the worst-affected countries. In January 2009 the HLTF participated in a follow-up high-level meeting convened in Madrid, Spain, and attended also by 62 government ministers and representatives from 126 countries. The meeting agreed to initiate a consultation process with regard to the establishment of a Global Partnership for Agriculture, Food Security and Nutrition. WFP participated in a World Summit on Food Security, organized by FAO, in Rome, in November 2009, which aimed to secure greater coherence in the global governance of food security and set a 'new world food order'.

WFP, with FAO and IFAD, leads an initiative on ensuring food security by strengthening feeding programmes and expanding support to farmers in developing countries, the second of nine activities that were launched in April 2009 by the UN System Chief Executives Board for Co-ordination (CEB), with the aim of alleviating the impact on poor and vulnerable populations of the developing global economic crisis. WFP also solely leads an initiative on emergency activities to meet humanitarian needs and promote security, the seventh of the CEB activities launched in April 2009.

In June 2008 WFP's Executive Board approved a strategic plan, covering the period 2008–13, that shifted the focus of WFP's activities from the supply of food to the supply of food assistance, and provided a new institutional framework to support vulnerable populations affected by the ongoing global food crisis and by possible future effects of global climate change. The five principal objectives of the 2008–13 plan were: saving lives and protecting livelihoods in emergencies; preparing for emergencies; restoring and rebuilding lives after emergencies; reducing chronic hunger and undernutrition everywhere; and strengthening the capacity of countries to reduce hunger. The plan emphasized prevention of hunger through early warning systems and analysis; local purchase of food; the maintenance of efficient and effective emergency response systems; and the use of focused cash and voucher programmes (including electronic vouchers) to ensure the accessibility to vulnerable people in urban environments of food that was locally available but, owing to the high level of market prices and increasing unemployment, beyond their financial means. It was envisaged that the cash and voucher approach would reduce the cost to WFP of transporting and storing food supplies, and would also benefit local economies (both being long-term WFP policy objectives). Some 2.9m. people were assisted through cash and voucher programmes during 2010.

WFP has developed a range of mechanisms to enhance its preparedness for emergency situations (such as conflict, drought and other natural disasters) and to improve its capacity for responding effectively to crises as they arise. Through its Vulnerability Analysis and Mapping (VAM) project, WFP aims to identify potentially vulnerable groups by providing information on food security and the capacity of different groups for coping with shortages, and to enhance emergency contingency-planning and long-term assistance objectives. VAM produces food security analysis reports, guidelines, reference documents and maps. In 2009 VAM field units were operational in 43 countries world-wide. The key elements of WFP's emergency response capacity are its strategic stores of food and logistics equipment (drawn from 'stocks afloat': ships loaded with WFP food supplies that can be re-routed to assist in crisis situations; development project stocks redesignated as emergency project contingency reserves; and in-country borrowing from national food reserves enabled by bilateral agreements); stand-by arrangements to enable the rapid deployment of personnel, communications and other essential equipment; and the Augmented Logistics Intervention Team for Emergencies (ALITE), which undertakes capacity assessments and contingency-planning. When engaging in a crisis WFP dispatches an emergency preparedness team to quantify the amount and type of food assistance required, and to identify the beneficiaries of and the timescale and logistics (e.g. means of transportation; location of humanitarian corridors, if necessary; and designated food distribution sites, such as refugee camps, other emergency shelters and therapeutic feeding centres) underpinning the ensuing EMOP. Once the EMOP has been drafted, WFP launches an appeal to the international donor community for funds and assistance to enable its implementation. WFP special operations are short-term logistics and infrastructure projects that are undertaken to facilitate the movement of food aid, regardless of whether the food is provided by the Agency itself. Special operations typically complement EMOPs or longer rehabilitation projects.

During 2000 WFP led efforts, undertaken with other UN humanitarian agencies, for the design and application of local UN Joint Logistics Centre facilities, which aimed to co-ordinate resources in an emergency situation. In 2001 a UN Humanitarian Response Depot was opened in Brindisi, Italy, under the direction of WFP experts, for the storage of essential rapid response equipment. In that year the Programme published a set of guidelines on contingency planning. Since 2003 WFP has been mandated to provide aviation transport services to the wider humanitarian community. During 2005 the UN's Inter-Agency Standing Committee (IASC), concerned with co-ordinating the international response to humanitarian disasters, developed a concept of organizing agency assistance to IDPs through the institutionalization of a 'Cluster Approach', currently comprising

11 core areas of activity. WFP was designated the lead agency for the clusters on Emergency Telecommunications (jointly with OCHA and UNICEF) and Logistics. During January 2008–June 2009 WFP implemented a special operation to improve country-specific communications services in order to enhance country-level cluster capacities. A review of the humanitarian cluster approach, undertaken during 2010, concluded that a new cluster on Food Security should be established. The new cluster, established accordingly in 2011, is led jointly by WFP and FAO, and aims to combine expertise in food aid and agricultural assistance in order to boost food security and to improve the resilience of food-insecure disaster-affected communities.

WFP aims to link its relief and development activities to provide a continuum between short-term relief and longer-term rehabilitation and development. In order to achieve this objective, WFP aims to promote capacity-building elements within relief operations, e.g. training, income-generating activities and environmental protection measures; and to integrate elements that strengthen disaster mitigation into development projects, including soil conservation, reafforestation, irrigation infrastructure, and transport construction and rehabilitation. In all its projects WFP aims to assist the most vulnerable groups (such as nursing mothers and children) and to ensure that beneficiaries have an adequate and balanced diet. Through its development activities, WFP aims to alleviate poverty in developing countries by promoting self-reliant families and communities. No individual country is permitted to receive more than 10% of the Programme's available development resources. WFP's Food-for-Assets development operations pay workers living in poverty with food in return for participation in self-help schemes and labour-intensive projects, with the aim of enabling vulnerable households and communities to focus time and resources on investing in lasting assets with which to raise themselves out of poverty (rather than on day-to-day survival). Food-for-Assets projects provide training in new techniques for achieving improved food security (such as training in new agricultural skills or in the establishment of home gardening businesses); and include, for example, building new irrigation or terracing infrastructures; soil and water conservation activities; and allocating food rations to villagers to enable them to devote time to building schools and clinics. In areas undermined by conflict WFP offers food assistance as an incentive for former combatants to put down their weapons and learn new skills. WFP focuses on providing good nutrition for the *first 1,000 days of life*, from the womb to two years of age, in order to lay the foundations for a healthy childhood and adulthood. WFP's *1,000 days plus* approach supports children over the age of two through school feeding activities, which aim to expand educational opportunities for poor children (given that it is difficult for children to concentrate on studies without adequate food and nutrition, and that food-insecure households frequently have to choose between educating their children or making them work to help the family to survive), and to improve the quality of the teaching environment. During 2010 school feeding projects benefited 21.1m. children. As an incentive to promote the education of vulnerable children, including orphans and children with HIV/AIDS, and to encourage families to send their daughters to school, WFP also implements 'take-home ration' projects, under which it provides basic food items to certain households, usually including sacks of rice and cans of cooking oil. WFP's Purchase for Progress (P4P) programme, launched in September 2008, expands the Programme's long-term 'local procurement' policy, enabling smallholder and low-income farmers in developing countries to supply food to WFP's global assistance operations. Under P4P farmers are taught techniques and provided with tools to enable them to compete competitively in the market-place. P4P also aims to identify and test specific successful local practices that could be replicated to benefit small-scale farmers on a wider scale. During 2008–13 P4P initiatives were being piloted in 21 countries, in Africa, Latin America and Asia. By 2012 WFP had established links under P4P with more than 1,000 farmers' organizations representing more than 1.1m. farmers worldwide. In September 2009 WFP, the Global Alliance for Improved Nutrition and other partners launched Project Laser Beam (PLB), a five-year public-private partnership aimed at eradicating eradicating child malnutrition; PLB initially undertook pilot projects in Bangladesh and India.

Since 1999 WFP has been implementing PRROs, where the emphasis is on fostering stability, rehabilitation and long-term development for victims of natural disasters, displaced persons and refugees. PRROs are introduced no later than 18 months after the initial EMOP and last no more than three years. When undertaken in collaboration with UNHCR and other international agencies, WFP has responsibility for mobilizing basic food commodities and for related transport, handling and storage costs.

In 2009 WFP operational expenditure in Europe and the CIS amounted to US $50.4m. (1.3% of total operational expenditure in that year).

During July 2009–December 2011 WFP implemented a PRRO in Georgia—costing US $22.2m. and guided by an inter-agency needs assessment that was conducted in October 2008—to enable a smooth transition from emergency relief to livelihood creation and restoration for some 130,000 beneficiaries whose circumstances had been adversely affected by the military conflict over South Ossetia that erupted between Georgia and Russia in August 2008 (causing massive population displacement, loss of agricultural assets and disruption to livelihoods), as well as by the impact of the ongoing global financial crisis. WFP was also to continue to support highly vulnerable Georgians who had been displaced in 1992 through conflict, and to provide food assistance to Georgians affected by HIV/AIDS and TB. During August 2010–July 2015 WFP was undertaking a development programme aimed at improving access to education for some 370,000 vulnerable children in Tajikistan, and over the period 1 January 2011–31 December 2013 it was implementing a project aimed at assisting TB patients and their families in that country. In November 2008 WFP approved an EMOP to provide emergency winter assistance in early 2009 to food-insecure people in Kyrgyzstan; the EMOP was subsequently extended through the 2009–10 and 2010–11 winter seasons. A development programme to support sustainable school feeding was being undertaken in Armenia during mid-2010–mid-2013.

In 2009 WFP operational expenditure in Latin America and the Caribbean amounted to US $243.0m. Of the total regional expenditure $113.9m. was for emergency relief operations, $22.4m. for agricultural, rural and human resource development projects, and $4.2m. for special operations. During July 2011–June 2014 WFP was implementing a $13.6m. PRRO aimed at supporting 120,100 Colombian refugees sheltering in Ecuador. A PRRO implemented within Colombia over the period 2008–end-2011 provided food assistance to 530,000 IDPs and individuals in food-insecure communities affected by violent unrest. A country programme being undertaken in Nicaragua over the period 2008–12, at a cost of $18.6m. and with 225,000 planned beneficiaries, focused on improving mother-and-child health, and on the implementation of food for education and food for training projects. A country programme (costing $10m. and aimed at 125,000 beneficiaries) was being undertaken in Bolivia during 2008–12, with a focus on providing food-based interventions for children aged from two to five years; giving food assistance to primary school children and street children; and offering technical assistance in emergency preparedness and response to government institutions. During 2008–13 WFP's new P4P programme (see above) was being piloted in El Salvador, Honduras, Guatemala and Nicaragua.

WFP estimated in late 2009, immediately prior to the severe earthquake that struck Haiti in January 2010, that around one-third of the Haitian population was food-insecure. The agency has provided long-term support in the areas of nutrition and health, education, and disaster mitigation activities, to vulnerable people in that country who have been affected by political and civil unrest, successive natural disasters (including hurricanes), escalating food prices, and poor infrastructure. In January 2010 WFP appealed for US $475.3m. to fund a complex emergency humanitarian operation in response to the earthquake that caused devastation in Haiti in that month. WFP's relief activities aimed to target food assistance towards the most vulnerable survivors of the disaster, and were focused on the provision of school meals (aiming initially to reach 72,000 children in 148 schools in the Port-au-Prince area); a scheme to distribute nutritious food products (such as Supplementary Plumpy) to 53,000 children aged under five years, and to 16,000 pregnant and breast-feeding mothers; and the carefully targeted distribution to around 300,000 vulnerable families (comprising an estimated 1.5m. beneficiaries) of full food baskets including rice, beans, corn soya blend, oil and salt. In February WFP hosted a high-level meeting in Rome to launch a global partnership aimed at developing a future food security plan for Haiti.

In 2010 the five sub-regions of sub-Saharan Africa represented the main regional focus of WFP relief activities; during that year operational expenditure there amounted to US $2,340.8m. (59% of WFP's total annual operational expenditure), including $1,978.5m. for relief operations and $169.8m. for development projects. During 2008–13 WFP's new P4P programme (see above) was being piloted in Burkina Faso, the Democratic Republic of the Congo, Ethiopia, Ghana, Kenya, Liberia, Malawi, Mali, Mozambique, Rwanda, Sierra Leone, Sudan, Tanzania, Uganda and Zambia.

Drought-affected communities in the Horn of Africa are a particular focus of WFP's sub-Saharan Africa activities. By mid-2011, as a result of crop failure and livestock loss following two consecutive seasons of poor rainfall, a severe drought prevailed in the Horn of Africa, with southern Somalia, in particular, a focus of humanitarian emergency. The situation in Somalia was exacerbated by the long-term lack of effective government there, the inaccessibility of extensive rebel-controlled areas, and high food prices which had further limited access to adequate nutrition. An estimated 3.7m. southern Somalis were estimated to be suffering food insecurity at that time—with the rate of acute malnutrition reaching 30% in some areas—and, over the period July 2011–early February 2012, the UN declared a state of famine in two southern Somali regions. It was reported in July 2011 that many Somali rural households were migrating in search of food and support to the conflict-affected Somali capital, Mogadishu, as well as into neighbouring countries. During July 2011–December 2012 an EMOP was being undertaken which aimed to provide 239,820 metric tons of food assistance to 3.9m. beneficiaries in Somalia. Over the period January 2009–December 2011 some 130,271 Eritrean, Somali and Sudanese refugees sheltering in Ethiopia benefited from an $83.9m. PRRO. A $174.6m. PRRO to provide food assistance to 474,000 Somali and Sudanese refugees in Kenya, and 54,000 beneficiaries in the host population, was undertaken during the period 1 October 2009–30 September 2011. From 2009–13 WFP was implementing a country development programme, costing $106.3m., that was to support annually about 650,000 Kenyan primary school children in food-insecure areas and to assist annually around 78,000 food-insecure Kenyans affected by HIV/AIDS to graduate from food support. A one-year emergency operation in Sudan for 2010 aimed to provide 665,550 metric tons of food aid to 6.4m. beneficiaries at a cost of $873.7m. In April 2009 WFP approved a PRRO targeting an annual maximum of 881,000 beneficiaries in Uganda over April 2009–March 2012; the total cost of the PRRO amounted to $177.1m., including an allocation of $3m. to finance a pilot cash transfer scheme.

In 2010 and, again, from early 2012, the Sahel region of West Africa (including parts of Niger, Mali, Mauritania, Burkina Faso, Chad, Gambia, northern Nigeria and Senegal) was affected by severe drought, causing acute food insecurity. In early 2012, in response, WFP aimed to provide emergency food assistance to some 3.3m. beneficiaries in Niger, 750,000 in Mali, and 400,000 Mauritanians. A $46.4m. country development programme being implemented in Niger during 2009–13, and targeting 1.3m. beneficiaries, was to increase access to basic education, especially for girls; to strengthen the prevention and mitigation of food insecurity during lean periods; and to contribute to improving the health and nutritional status of patients living with HIV/AIDS and TB. In February 2009 WFP launched a cash transfer and voucher programme in urban areas of Ouagadougou, Burkina Faso (the first such programme to be implemented in Africa), targeting 120,000 people adversely affected by high food prices. Under the new programme family representatives were to be given over a six-month period up to six vouchers, valued at $3 each month, and exchangeable in participating shops for maize, cooking oil, sugar, salt and soap. Vulnerable families with young children were to receive rations of 'Plumpy Doz' (see above). In the following month a similar food voucher scheme was initiated in Bobo-Dioulasso, Burkina Faso, targeting 60,000 people. During September 2009–August 2011 WFP undertook a PRRO in Liberia, at a cost of US $39.8m., to assist the ongoing post-conflict recovery process there through livelihood asset rehabilitation; school feeding; nutrition interventions; and capacity-building, including the implementation of P4P schemes. At the beginning of January 2011 WFP commenced the distribution of high energy biscuits to the most vulnerable of more than 20,000 Côte d'Ivoire refugees who, owing to serious violent unrest, had fled to Liberia from late 2010. From February–July 2011 an EMOP to provide food aid to the Côte d'Ivoire refugees was undertaken; by April an estimated 150,000 Ivorian refugees had sought shelter in Liberia. During March–September 2011 WFP implemented an EMOP to provide food aid to 125,000 vulnerable Ivorian IDPs.

In 2009 WFP operational expenditure in the Middle East and North Africa amounted to US $175.2m. (4.4% of total operational expenditure in that year), including $161.7m. for emergency relief operations and $10.4m. for development operations. WFP has been engaged in preventing hunger in Iraq, undertaking activities including surveying food security, strengthening national capacity, assisting a newly established distribution system, and supporting a government-administered school feeding programme. In January 2008 WFP initiated a programme to provide emergency food assistance to some 750,000 IDPs in Iraq, as well as to 362,000 Iraqis sheltering in Syria. A mobile telephone-based system has been used to send food voucher codes to Iraqi beneficiaries of WFP assistance in Syria; the codes can be used to purchase items in local stores. WFP subsequently extended the term and scope of that operation, which was to have been terminated in June 2009, to support an additional 577,000 Iraqis until the end of March 2010; from 1 April 2010–31 March 2012 a PRRO succeeded the emergency programme, benefiting nearly 1.8m. Iraqis through the provision of 189,504 metric tons of food assistance. According to a comprehensive food security and vulnerability analysis of Iraq published in November 2008, communities in 41 out of 115 districts of the country remained at that time vulnerable to food insecurity. In December 2007 WFP undertook a Rapid Food Security Needs Assessment of the situation in the Palestinian territories. In January 2009 WFP provided *meals-ready-to-eat* (MREs, which do not require conventional heating facilities) to people affected by the sustained Israeli military offensive against targets in Gaza that commenced in late December 2008, including to 16,000 Palestinians in UNRWA shelters and 7,000 Palestinians in hospitals. A global appeal, Operation Lifeline Gaza, was launched in January 2009 to fund the provision of WFP emergency assistance, initially for a 12-month period; Operation Lifeline Gaza was subsequently extended to 31 December 2011. In total some $4.8m. was allocated under the programme in the form of cash vouchers, and some $105.2m. in the form of food rations. From 1 January 2011–31 December 2012 WFP was implementing a project targeting food assistance in support of destitute and marginalized groups in the West Bank; the scheme was to help some 454,500 beneficiaries annually, focusing on meeting immediate food needs, enhancing food consumption, and improving dietery diversity, and aimed to promote long-term resilience by supporting the re-establishment of agricultural livelihoods in conflict-affected areas. An electronic food voucher system implemented by WFP in the Palestinian territories during 2010 assisted 32,000 people in the West Bank and more than 15,000 in Gaza; the vouchers could be spent in selected shops, thereby also benefiting local shop-owners and food producers. During 2009 a food safety net programme was introduced in Yemen to support vulnerable populations adversely affected by high food prices and conflict. A PRRO was being undertaken in Yemen during 1 January 2010–31 December 2012 aimed at alleviating acute food insecurity and very high incidence of malnutrition there. In mid-March 2012 a survey produced by WFP—in conjunction with UNICEF and the Yemen authorities—on the food situation in that country, reported that hunger had doubled since 2009, stating that nearly 5m. Yemenis were unable to produce or to buy sufficient food.

In response to the outbreak of conflict in Libya from mid-February 2011, WFP launched a US $4m. operation to augment and co-ordinate logistics and emergency telecommunications in that country. In mid-April WFP announced that it had opened a humanitarian corridor for the transportation of food and other assistance to communities in western areas of the country, which had hitherto been isolated by heavy fighting. A $121.6m. emergency operation aimed at supplying food aid to vulnerable populations affected by the conflict in Libya, and in Egypt and Tunisia (which had also been affected by violent unrest in early 2011), was implemented during March 2011–February 2012.

During October 2011–June 2012 WFP was undertaking an EMOP to assist some 100,000 people affected by violent unrest in Syria.

In 2009 WFP operational expenditure in Asia amounted to US $763.4m. (19.2% of total operational expenditure in that year), including $650.8m. for emergency relief operations, $27.0m. for special operations, and $77.3m. for agricultural, rural and human resource development projects. During 2008–13 WFP's new P4P programme (see above) was being piloted in Afghanistan and Laos.

WFP has been active in Afghanistan, where violent conflict and natural disasters (mainly severe drought) have caused massive and protracted population displacement and food insecurity; the latter has been aggravated in recent years by volatile food prices. Restricted humanitarian access, limited institutional capacities, devastated infrastructure, and the country's landlocked geography have contributed to a crisis in which, by 2010, 31% of the population were estimated by WFP to be food-insecure, with a further 23% at risk of food insecurity. In April 2010 WFP launched a three-year PRRO throughout Afghanistan (to terminate in March 2013) which was to target a maximum of 7.6m. beneficiaries annually, at a total cost to the Programme of $1,204m. The PRRO aimed to provide food assistance to conflict- and disaster-affected people, IDPs and other vulnerable groups (such as malnourished children and pregnant and nursing women); to support—through the provision of basic education and basic skills training for women and girls—the re-establishment of the livelihoods of adversely-affected communities and families; and to advance the availability of TB treatment. A PRRO, costing $117.8m., was implemented during January–December 2011 to assist, through nutrition interventions and school-feeding, some 371,000 IDPs, returnees and host communities in northern Sri Lanka. An EMOP was undertaken from 1 August 2011–31 January 2012 with the aim of providing food assistance and early recovery support to an estimated 500,000 people displaced by flooding that occurred in eastern Sri Lanka during November 2010–January 2011. In 2009 a food safety net programme was introduced in Pakistan, to support vulnerable populations adversely affected by high food prices. In August 2010 WFP responded to severe flooding that devastated northern and central areas of Pakistan, seriously adversely affecting at least 15m. people and leaving an estimated 8m. survivors in need of urgent food assistance, by mobilizing its long-term local humanitarian presence to distribute food supplies throughout the affected areas. WFP appealed to the international community at that time for some $164m. to extend massively the scope of ongoing operations in Pakistan. A PRRO providing food assistance to 9.5m. beneficiaries in Pakistan, over the period 1 January 2011–31 December 2012, was targeted at flood-affected communities in Balochistan, Khyber Pakhtunkhwa, and the Federally Administered Tribal Areas of Pakistan.

The food situation in the Democratic People's Republic of Korea (North Korea) has required substantial levels of emergency food supplies in recent years, owing to natural disasters and consistently poor harvests. During 1995–99 an estimated 1.5m.–3.5m. people died of starvation in North Korea. In August 2005 the North Korean

Government requested WFP to shift its focus from emergency relief to development activities and consequently, in February 2006, WFP approved a US $102.2m. PRRO for North Korea, covering the period 1 April 2006–31 March 2008, which followed on from 10 successive emergency operations that had hitherto achieved some progress in reducing rates of malnutrition in that country. The two-year PRRO aimed to provide 150,000 metric tons of food aid to 1.9m. people, and to support the Government's strategy to achieve long-term food security. The operation provided for the distribution to young children and women of child-bearing age of vitamin- and mineral-enriched domestically produced foods, and for the allocation of cereal rations to underemployed communities with a view to enabling them to build and rehabilitate agricultural and other community assets. A short-term emergency operation to assist 215,000 people affected by floods that struck North Korea in August 2007 was implemented during August–November of that year. In June 2008 a WFP/FAO Rapid Food Security Assessment of that country found that access to food had deteriorated significantly since 2007, particularly for urban households in areas of low industrial activity, who had been severely affected by rising food and fuel prices, reductions in food rationing and decreasing rates of employment. WFP subsequently approved a $503.6m. EMOP covering the period 1 September 2008–30 November 2009 (later extended to June 2010), which aimed to target assistance at food-insecure populations through mother and child nutrition activities; food assistance to schools, elderly people and other vulnerable groups; and food for community development activities. WFP stated that comprehensive interventions were required to improve agricultural production in North Korea, and that, conditions permitting, humanitarian assistance would be reduced following the expiry of the emergency operation and the long-term development approach pursued under the 2006–08 PRRO would be resumed. Accordingly, in June 2010, a new PRRO was approved, covering the two-year period until June 2012, which was to target 157,047 metric tons of nutrition support at women and children, at a total cost to WFP of $96m. In view of worsening food insecurity caused by high rainfall in 2010 and a harsh winter over 2010–11, the North Korean Government made a formal appeal to WFP in January 2011 requesting emergency food assistance. WFP, FAO and UNICEF conducted an inter-agency rapid food security assessment of the country during February–March. WFP initiated an EMOP covering 1 April 2011–31 March 2012, which aimed to support some 3.5m. vulnerable people (mainly women and children), incorporating and expanding activities launched under the PRRO initiated in June 2010. The PRRO was suspended, to be renewed following the completion of the EMOP.

A PRRO to improve the food security, nutrition status and livelihoods of vulnerable populations in Myanmar (targeting 2.0m. individuals), at a cost of US $121.8m., was being implemented during the three-year period 1 January 2010–31 December 2012. In late September 2007 WFP urged the Myanmar authorities to ease restrictions on the movement of food supplies that had been imposed owing to unrest in that country, as these were inhibiting WFP's implementation of its relief activities; assurances were reportedly received from the Myanmar regime at the end of that month that WFP would be permitted to undertake its scheduled food deliveries. In October WFP urged the Myanmar authorities to pursue critical social and economic reforms aimed at reducing poverty and hunger in that country, stating that international humanitarian assistance could not meet all the requirements of the Myanma population. An EMOP was undertaken during May–November 2008 to provide food assistance to 750,000 people in Myanmar, in response to the devastation caused by Cyclone Nargis in early May to domestic food stocks, livestock, crops, shrimp farms, fishing ponds, fish hatcheries, fishing boats and other food production assets.

An EMOP to provide food assistance to 1.6m. people whose livelihoods had been affected by long-term conflict in Mindanao, Philippines, was implemented over the period 1 June 2008–31 May 2009. From late September 2009 a series of typhoons resulted in extensive flooding in the Philippines, causing serious damage in the capital city, Manila, and in Luzon, the country's main rice-producing region. In response, WFP launched a US $57m. relief operation, which targeted assistance at more than 1m. people. Owing to further heavy rains, flooding and landslides in 2010–11 the operation was extended. In October 2011 WFP provided immediate food assistance (including High Energy Biscuits) to communities in northern Luzon whose lands were flooded by Typhoon Nesat. During 1 July 2010–31 December 2011 WFP implemented a development programme in Laos aimed at addressing malnutrition in mothers and children. In June 2011 WFP approved a country programme for Cambodia covering the period 2011–16, aimed at improving food security. In September 2008 a PRRO was approved to assist on average 255,600 vulnerable people in Timor-Leste per year over the two-year period 1 September 2008–31 August 2010; this was subsequently extended until August 2011.

Finance

The Programme is funded by voluntary contributions from donor countries, intergovernmental bodies such as the European Commission, and the private sector. Contributions are made in the form of commodities, finance and services (particularly shipping). Commitments to the International Emergency Food Reserve (IEFR), from which WFP provides the majority of its food supplies, and to the Immediate Response Account of the IEFR (IRA), are also made on a voluntary basis by donors. WFP's projected budget for 2012 amounted to some US $5,484.4m. Contributions by donors were forecast at $3,750m.

Publications

Annual Report.

Food and Nutrition Handbook.

School Feeding Handbook.

World Hunger Series.

Statistics

OPERATIONAL EXPENDITURE IN 2009 BY REGION AND TYPE*

(US $ '000)

Region	Development	Relief	Special operations
Sub-Saharan Africa	187,950	2,171,822	28,958
Asia	77,256	650,793	27,036
Latin America and the Caribbean	22,353	113,970	4,232
North Africa and the Middle East	10,440	161,727	1,576
Europe and the CIS	—	499,992	413
Total†	275,906	3,239,887	176,364

* Excludes programme support and administrative costs.

† Includes operational expenditures such as trust fund expenditures that cannot be apportioned by project/operation.

Food and Agriculture Organization of the United Nations—FAO

Address: Viale delle Terme di Caracalla, 00100 Rome, Italy.

Telephone: (06) 5705-1; **fax:** (06) 5705-3152; **e-mail:** fao-hq@fao.org; **internet:** www.fao.org.

FAO, the first specialized agency of the UN to be founded after the Second World War, aims to alleviate malnutrition and hunger, and serves as a co-ordinating agency for development programmes in the whole range of food and agriculture, including forestry and fisheries. It helps developing countries to promote educational and training facilities and to create appropriate institutions.

MEMBERS

FAO has 191 member nations; the European Union is a member organization. The Faroe Islands and Tokelau are associate members.

Organization

(April 2012)

CONFERENCE

The governing body is the FAO Conference of member nations. It meets every two years, formulates policy, determines the organization's programme and budget on a biennial basis, and elects new members. It also elects the Director-General of the Secretariat and the Independent Chairman of the Council. Regional conferences are also held each year.

COUNCIL

The FAO Council is composed of representatives of 49 member nations, elected by the Conference for rotating three-year terms. It is the interim governing body of FAO between sessions of the Conference. There are eight main Governing Committees of the Council: the Finance and Programme Committees, and the Committees on Commodity Problems, Fisheries, Agriculture, Forestry, World Food Security, and Constitutional and Legal Matters.

SECRETARIAT

There are some 3,600 FAO staff, of whom about one-half are based at headquarters. FAO maintains five regional offices (see below), nine sub-regional offices, five liaison offices (in Yokohama, Japan; Washington, DC, USA, liaison with North America; Geneva, Switzerland and New York, USA, with the UN; and Brussels, Belgium, with the European Union), and some 74 country offices. Work is undertaken by the following departments: Agriculture and Consumer Protection; Economic and Social Development; Fisheries and Aquaculture; Forestry; Human, Financial and Physical Resources; Knowledge and Communication; Natural Resource Management and Environment; and Technical Co-operation.

Director-General: Dr José Graziano da Silva (Brazil).

REGIONAL OFFICES

Africa: POB 1628, Accra, Ghana; tel. (21) 675000; fax (21) 668427; e-mail fao-raf@fao.org; internet www.fao.org/world/regional/raf/index_en.asp; Regional Rep. Maria Helena de Morais Semedo; Sub-Regional Rep. for West Africa Musa Saihou Mbenga.

Asia and the Pacific: Maliwan Mansion, 39 Phra Atit Rd, Bangkok 10200, Thailand; tel. (2) 697-4000; fax (2) 697-4445; e-mail fao-rap@fao.org; internet www.fao.org/world/regional/rap; Regional Rep. Hiroyuki Konuma.

Europe and Central Asia: 1068 Budapest, Benczur u. 34, Hungary; tel. (1) 461-2000; fax (1) 351-7029; e-mail fao-seur@fao.org; internet www.fao.org/world/regional/reu; Regional Rep. Fernanda Guerrieri (Italy).

Latin America and the Caribbean: Avda Dag Hammarskjöld 3241, Casilla 10095, Vitacura, Santiago, Chile; tel. (2) 923-2100; fax (2) 923-2101; e-mail fao-rlc@field.fao.org; internet www.rlc.fao.org; Regional Rep. (vacant).

Near East: 11 El-Eslah el-Zerai St, Dokki, POB 2223, Cairo, Egypt; tel. (2) 3316000; fax (2) 7495981; e-mail fao-rne@fao.org; internet www.fao.org/world/Regional/RNE/index_en.htm; Regional Rep. Saad Aied al-Otaibi.

Activities

FAO aims to raise levels of nutrition and standards of living by improving the production and distribution of food and other commodities derived from farms, fisheries and forests. FAO's ultimate objective is the achievement of world food security, 'Food for All'. The organization provides technical information, advice and assistance by disseminating information; acting as a neutral forum for discussion of food and agricultural issues; advising governments on policy and planning; and developing capacity directly in the field.

In November 1996 FAO hosted the World Food Summit, which was held in Rome and was attended by heads of state and senior government representatives of 186 countries. Participants approved the Rome Declaration on World Food Security and the World Food Summit Plan of Action, with the aim of halving the number of people afflicted by undernutrition, then estimated to total 828m. worldwide, by no later than 2015. A review conference to assess progress in achieving the goals of the summit, entitled World Food Summit: Five Years Later, held in June 2002, reaffirmed commitment to this objective, which is also incorporated into the UN Millennium Development Goals (MDGs). During that month FAO announced the formulation of a global 'Anti-Hunger Programme', which aimed to promote investment in the agricultural sector and rural development, with a particular focus on small-scale farmers, and to enhance food access for those most in need, for example through the provision of school meals, schemes to feed pregnant and nursing mothers and food-for-work programmes. FAO hosts the UN System Network on Rural Development and Food Security, comprising some 20 UN bodies, which was established in 1997 as an inter-agency mechanism to follow-up the World Food Summits.

In November 1999 the FAO Conference approved a long-term Strategic Framework for the period 2000–15, which emphasized national and international co-operation in pursuing the goals of the 1996 World Food Summit. The Framework promoted interdisciplinarity and partnership, and defined three main global objectives: constant access by all people to sufficient, nutritionally adequate and safe food to ensure that levels of undernourishment were reduced by 50% by 2015 (see above); the continued contribution of sustainable agriculture and rural development to economic and social progress and well-being; and the conservation, improvement and sustainable use of natural resources. It identified five corporate strategies (each supported by several strategic objectives), covering the following areas: reducing food insecurity and rural poverty; ensuring enabling policy and regulatory frameworks for food, agriculture, fisheries and forestry; creating sustainable increases in the supply and availability of agricultural, fisheries and forestry products; conserving and enhancing sustainable use of the natural resource base; and generating knowledge. In October 2007 the report of an Independent External Evaluation (IEE) into the role and functions of FAO recommended that the organization elaborate a plan for reform to ensure its continued efficiency and effectiveness. In November 2008 a Special Conference of member countries approved a three-year Immediate Plan of Action to reform the governance and management of the organization based on the recommendations of the IEE.

In December 2007 FAO inaugurated an Initiative on Soaring Food Prices (ISFP) to help to boost food production in low-income developing countries and improve access to food and agricultural supplies in the short term, with a view to countering an escalation since 2006 in commodity prices. (During 2006–08 the Food Price Index maintained by FAO recorded that international prices for many basic food commodities had increased by around 60%, and the FAO Cereal Price Index, covering the prices of principal food staples such as wheat, rice and maize, recorded a doubling in the international price of grains over that period.) In April 2008 the UN Secretary-General appointed FAO's Director-General as Vice-Chairman of a High Level Task Force (HLTF) on the Global Food Security Crisis, which aimed to address the impact of the ongoing soaring levels of food and fuel prices and formulate a comprehensive framework for action. In June FAO hosted a High Level Conference on World Food Security and the Challenges of Climate Change and Bioenergy. The meeting adopted a Declaration on Food Security, urging the international donor community to increase its support to developing countries and countries with economies in transition. The Declaration also noted an urgent need to develop the agricultural sectors and expand food production in such countries and for increased investment in rural development, agriculture and agribusiness. In January 2009 a follow-up high level meeting was convened in Madrid, Spain, and attended by 62 government ministers and representatives from 126 countries. The meeting agreed to initiate a consultation process with regard to the establishment of a Global Partnership for Agriculture, Food Security and Nutrition to strengthen international co-ordination and governance for food security. FAO's long-standing Committee on World Food Security (CFS) underwent reform in 2009; henceforth the Committee was to be a central component of the new Global Partnership, and was to influence hunger elimination programmes at global, regional and national level, taking into account that food security relates not just to agriculture but also to economic access to food, adequate nutrition, social safety nets and human rights.

In May 2009 the European Union donated €106m. to FAO, to support farmers and improve food security in 10 developing countries in Africa, Asia and the Caribbean that were particularly badly affected by the recently emerged global food crisis. Addressing the World Grain Forum, convened in St Petersburg, Russia, in June 2009, the FAO Director-General demanded a more effective and coherent global governance system to ensure future world food security, and urged that a larger proportion of development aid should be allocated to agriculture, to enable developing countries to invest in rural infrastructures. During June it was estimated that, in 2009, the number of people world-wide suffering chronic, daily hunger had risen to an unprecedented 1,020m., of whom an estimated 642m. were in Asia and the Pacific; 265m. in sub-Saharan Africa; 53m. in Latin America and the Caribbean; and 42m. in the Middle East and North Africa. Around 15m. people resident in developed countries were estimated at that time to be afflicted by chronic hunger. The *OECD-FAO Agricultural Outlook 2009–18*, issued in June 2009, found the global agriculture sector to be showing more resilience to the ongoing world-wide economic crisis than other sectors, owing to the status of food as a basic human necessity. However, the report warned that the state of the agriculture sector could become more fragile if the ongoing global downturn were to worsen. In July the FAO Director-General welcomed the L'Aquila Joint Statement on Global Food Security (promoting sustainable agricultural development), and the Food Security Initiative with commitments of US $20,000m., that were approved in that month by G8 leaders.

In mid-October 2009 a high-level forum of experts was convened by FAO to discuss policy on the theme 'How to Feed the World in 2050'. In November 2009 FAO organized a World Summit on Food Security, in Rome, with the aim of achieving greater coherence in the global governance of food security and setting a 'new world food order'. Leaders attending the Summit issued a declaration in which they adopted a number of strategic objectives, including: ensuring urgent action towards achieving World Food Summit objectives/the UN MDG relating to reducing undernutrition; promoting the new Global Partnership for Agriculture, Food Security and Nutrition and fully committing to reform of the CFS; reversing the decline in national and international funding for agriculture, food security and rural development in developing countries, and encouraging new investment to increase sustainable agricultural production; reducing poverty and working towards achieving food security and access to 'Food for All'; and confronting proactively the challenges posed by climate change to food security. The Summit determined to base its pursuit of these strategic objectives on the following *Five Rome Principles for Sustainable Global Food Security*: (i) investment in country-owned plans aimed at channelling resources to efficient results-based programmes and partnerships; (ii) fostering strategic co-ordination at national, regional and global level to improve governance, promote better allocation of resources, avoid duplication of efforts and identify response gaps; (iii) striving for a comprehensive twin-track approach to food security comprising direct action to combat hunger in the most vulnerable, and also medium- and long-term sustainable agricultural, food security, nutrition and rural development programmes to eliminate the root causes of hunger and poverty, including through the progressive realization of the right to adequate food; (iv) ensuring a strong role for the multilateral system by sustained improvements in efficiency, responsiveness, co-ordination and effectiveness of multilateral institutions; and (v) ensuring sustained and substantial commitment by all partners to investment in agriculture and food security and nutrition, with provision of necessary resources in a timely and reliable fashion, aimed at multi-year plans and programmes.

FAO, with WFP and IFAD, leads an initiative to strengthen feeding programmes and expand support to farmers in developing countries, the second of nine activities that were launched in April 2009 by the UN System Chief Executives Board for Co-ordination (CEB), with the aim of alleviating the impact on poor and vulnerable populations of the developing global economic crisis.

With other UN agencies, FAO attended the Summit of the World's Regions on Food Insecurity, held in Dakar, Senegal, in January 2010. The summit urged that global governance of food security should integrate players on every level, and expressed support for the developing Global Partnership for Agriculture, Food Security and Nutrition.

In February 2011 the FAO Food Price Index, at 238 points, recorded the highest levels of global food prices since 1990, with prices having risen in each consecutive month during July 2010–February 2011 (and having, in December 2010, exceeded the previous peak reached during mid-2008). The Cereal Price Index also recorded in February 2011 the highest price levels since mid-2008. FAO maintains, additionally, a Dairy Price Index, an Oils/Fats Price Index, a Meat Price Index and a Sugar Price Index. In March 2012 the Food Price Index averaged 216 points.

In June 2011 agriculture ministers from G20 countries adopted an action plan aimed at stabilizing food price volatility and agriculture, with a focus on improving international policy co-ordination and agricultural production; promoting targeted emergency humanitarian food reserves; and developing, under FAO auspices, an Agricultural Market Information System (AMIS) to improve market transparency.

FAO's annual *State of Food Insecurity in the World* report (see below), compiled in 2011 with help from IFAD and WFP, maintained that volatile and high food prices were likely to continue, rendering poorer consumers, farmers and nations more vulnerable to poverty and hunger.

World Food Day, commemorating the foundation of FAO, is held annually on 16 October. In May 2010 FAO launched an online petition entitled the *1billionhungry project*, with the aim of raising awareness of the plight of people world-wide suffering from chronic hunger.

AGRICULTURE AND CONSUMER PROTECTION

FAO's overall objective is to lead international efforts to counter hunger and to improve levels of nutrition. Within this context FAO is concerned to improve crop and grassland productivity and to develop sustainable agricultural systems to provide for enhanced food security and economic development. It provides member countries with technical advice for plant improvement, the application of plant biotechnology, the development of integrated production systems and rational grassland management. There are groups concerned with the main field cereal crops, i.e. rice, maize and wheat, which *inter alia* identify means of enhancing production, collect and analyse relevant data and promote collaboration between research institutions, government bodies and other farm management organizations. In 1985 and 1990 FAO's International Rice Commission endorsed the use of hybrid rice, which had been developed in the People's Republic of China, as a means of meeting growing demand for the crop, in particular in the Far East, and has subsequently assisted member countries to acquire the necessary technology and training to develop hybrid rice production. In Africa FAO has collaborated with the West African Rice Development Association to promote and facilitate the use of new rice varieties and crop management practices. FAO actively promotes the concept of Conservation Agriculture, which aims to minimize the need for mechanical soil tillage or additional farming resources and to reduce soil degradation and erosion.

FAO is also concerned with the development and diversification of horticultural and industrial crops, for example oil seeds, fibres and medicinal plants. FAO collects and disseminates data regarding crop trials and new technologies. It has developed an information processing site, Ecocrop, to help farmers identify appropriate crops and environmental requirements. FAO works to protect and support the sustainable development of grasslands and pasture, which contribute to the livelihoods of an estimated 800m. people world-wide.

FAO's plant protection service incorporates a range of programmes concerned with the control of pests and the use of pesticides. In February 2001 FAO warned that some 30% of pesticides sold in developing countries did not meet internationally accepted quality standards. In November 2002 FAO adopted a revised International Code of Conduct on the Distribution and Use of Pesticides (first adopted in 1985) to reduce the inappropriate distribution and use of pesticides and other toxic compounds, particularly in developing countries. In September 1998 a new legally binding treaty on trade in hazardous chemicals and pesticides was adopted at an international conference held in Rotterdam, Netherlands. The so-called Rotterdam Convention required that hazardous chemicals and pesticides banned or severely restricted in at least two countries should not be exported unless explicitly agreed by the importing country. It also identified certain pesticide formulations as too dangerous to be used by farmers in developing countries, and incorporated an obligation that countries halt national production of those hazardous compounds. The treaty entered into force in February 2004. FAO co-operates with UNEP to provide secretariat services for the Convention. FAO has promoted the use of Integrated Pest Management (IPM) initiatives to encourage the use, at local level, of safer and more effective methods of pest control, such as biological control methods and natural predators.

FAO hosts the secretariat of the International Plant Protection Convention (first adopted in 1951, revised in 1997) which aims to prevent the spread of plant pests and to promote effective control measures. The secretariat helps to define phytosanitary standards, promote the exchange of information and extend technical assistance to contracting parties (177 at March 2012).

FAO is concerned with the conservation and sustainable use of plant and animal genetic resources. It works with regional and international associations to develop seed networks, to encourage the use of improved seed production systems, to elaborate quality control and certification mechanisms and to co-ordinate seed security activities, in particular in areas prone to natural or man-made disasters. FAO has developed a World Information and Early Warning System (WIEWS) to gather and disseminate information concerning plant genetic resources for food and agriculture and to undertake periodic assessments of the state of those resources. FAO is also developing, as part of the WIEWS, a Seed Information Service to extend information to member states on seeds, planting and new technologies. In June 1996 representatives of more than 150 governments convened in Leipzig, Germany, at an International Technical Conference organized by FAO to consider the use and conservation of plant genetic resources as an essential means of enhancing food security. The meeting adopted a Global Plan of Action, which included measures to strengthen the development of plant varieties and to promote the use and availability of local varieties and locally adapted crops to farmers, in particular following a natural disaster, war or civil conflict. In November 2001 the FAO Conference adopted the International Treaty on Plant Genetic Resources for Food and Agriculture (also referred to as the Seed Treaty), with the aim of providing a framework to ensure access to plant genetic resources and to related knowledge, technologies, and—through the Treaty's Benefit-sharing Fund (BSF)—funding. The Seed Treaty entered into force in June 2004, having received the required number of ratifications, and, by March 2012, had 127 states parties. The BSF assists poor farmers in developing countries with conserving, and also adapting to climate change, their most important food crops; in 2011 the Fund supported 11 high-impact projects for small-scale farmers in four regions. It was hoped that international donors would raise US $116m. for the BSF by 2014. By end-2010 some 1,750 gene banks had been established world-wide, storing more than 7m. plant samples.

FAO's Animal Production and Health Division is concerned with the control and management of major animal diseases, and, in recent years, with safeguarding humans from livestock diseases. Other programmes are concerned with the contribution of livestock to poverty alleviation, the efficient use of natural resources in livestock production, the management of animal genetic resources, promoting the exchange of information and mapping the distribution of livestock around the world. In 2001 FAO established a Pro-Poor Livestock Policy Initiative to support the formulation and implementation of livestock-related policies to improve the livelihood and nutrition of the world's rural poor, with an initial focus on the Andean region, the Horn of Africa, West Africa, South Asia and the Mekong.

The Emergency Prevention System for Transboundary Animal and Plant Pests and Diseases (EMPRES) was established in 1994 to strengthen FAO's activities in the prevention, early warning, control and, where possible, eradication of pests and highly contagious livestock diseases (which the system categorizes as epidemic diseases of strategic importance, such as rinderpest or foot-and-mouth; diseases requiring tactical attention at international or regional level, e.g. Rift Valley fever; and emerging diseases, e.g. bovine spongiform encephalopathy—BSE). EMPRES has a desert locust component, and has published guidelines on all aspects of desert locust monitoring. FAO assumed responsibility for technical leadership and co-ordination of the Global Rinderpest Eradication Programme (GREP), which had the objective of eliminating that disease by 2011; in June 2011 the FAO Conference adopted a resolution declaring global freedom from rinderpest. In November 1997 FAO initiated a Programme Against African Trypanosomiasis, which aimed to counter the disease affecting cattle in almost one-third of Africa. In November 2004 FAO established a specialized Emergency Centre for Transboundary Animal Disease Operations (ECTAD) to enhance FAO's role in assisting member states to combat animal disease outbreaks and in co-ordinating international efforts to research, monitor and control transboundary disease crises. In May 2004 FAO and the World Organisation for Animal Health (OIE) signed an agreement to clarify their respective areas of competence and improve co-operation, in response to an increase in contagious transboundary animal diseases (such as foot-and-mouth disease and avian influenza, see below). The two bodies agreed to establish a global framework on the control of transboundary animal diseases, entailing improved international collaboration and circulation of information. In early 2006 FAO, OIE and the World Health Organization (WHO) agreed on the establishment of a Global Early Warning and Response System for Major Animal Diseases, including Zoonoses (GLEWS), in order to strengthen their joint capacity to detect, monitor and respond to animal disease threats. In October 2006 FAO inaugurated a new Crisis Management Centre (CMC) to co-ordinate (in close co-operation with OIE) the organization's response to outbreaks of H5N1 and other major emergencies related to animal or food health.

In September 2004 FAO and WHO declared an ongoing epidemic in certain east Asian countries of the H5N1 strain of highly pathogenic avian influenza (HPAI) to be a 'crisis of global importance': the disease was spreading rapidly through bird populations and was also transmitting to human populations through contact with diseased birds (mainly poultry). In that month FAO published *Recommendations for the Prevention, Control and Eradication of Highly Pathogenic Avian Influenza in Asia*. In April 2005 FAO and OIE established an international network of laboratories and scientists (OFFLU) to exchange data and provide expert technical advice on avian influenza. In the following month FAO, with WHO and OIE, launched a global strategy for the progressive control of the disease. In November a conference on Avian Influenza and Human Pandemic Influenza, jointly organized by FAO, WHO and OIE and the World Bank, issued a plan of action identifying a number of responses, including: supporting the development of integrated national plans for H5N1 containment and human pandemic influenza preparedness and response; assisting countries with the aggressive control of H5N1 and with establishing a more detailed understanding of the role of wild birds in virus transmission; nominating rapid response teams of experts to support epidemiological field investigations; expanding national and regional capacity in surveillance, diagnosis, and alert and response systems; expanding the network of influenza laboratories; establishing multi-country networks for the control or prevention of animal transboundary diseases; expanding the global antiviral stockpile; strengthening veterinary infrastructures; and mapping a global strategy and work plan for co-ordinating antiviral and influenza vaccine research and development. In June 2006 FAO and OIE convened a scientific conference on the spread and management of H5N1 that advocated early detection of the disease in wild birds, improved biosecurity and hygiene in the poultry trade, rapid response to disease outbreaks, and the establishment of a global tracking and monitoring facility involving participation by all relevant organizations, as well as by scientific centres, farmers' groupings, bird-watchers and hunters, and wildlife and wild bird habitat conservation bodies. The conference also urged investment in telemetry/satellite technology to improve tracking capabilities. International conference and pledging meetings on the disease were convened in Washington, DC, USA, in October 2005, Beijing, People's Republic of China, in January 2006, Bamako, Mali, in December and in New Delhi, India, in December 2007. In August 2008 a new strain of HPAI not previously recorded in sub-Saharan Africa was detected in Nigeria. In October the sixth international ministerial conference on avian influenza was convened in Sharm el-Sheikh, Egypt. FAO, with WHO, UNICEF, OIE, the World Bank and the UN System Influenza Co-ordinator, presented a new strategic framework, within the concept of 'One World, One Health', to improve understanding and co-operation with respect to emerging infectious diseases, to strengthen animal and public health surveillance and to enhance response mechanisms. During 2003–end-2011 outbreaks of H5N1 were recorded in 63 countries and territories, and some 250m. domestic and wild birds consequently died or were culled.

In December 2011 the conference of parties to the CMS officially ratified the establishment of a Scientific Task Force on Wildlife and Ecosystem Health, with FAO participation, reflecting a shift in focus from the isolated targeting avian influenza towards a 'One Health' policy of caring for the health of animals, humans, and the ecosystems that support them; a Task Force on Avian Influenza and Wild Birds, established under the CMS in August 2005, was to continue as a core focus area within the larger Scientific Task Force.

In April 2009, in response to a major outbreak in humans of the swine influenza variant pandemic (H1N1) 2009, the FAO Crisis Management Centre mobilized a team of experts to increase animal disease surveillance and maintain response readiness to protect the global pig sector from infection with the emerging virus. In early May FAO, OIE, WHO and WTO together issued a statement stressing that pork products handled in accordance with hygienic practices could not be deemed a source of infection.

In December 1992 FAO, with WHO, organized an International Conference on Nutrition, which approved a World Declaration on Nutrition and a Plan of Action, aimed at promoting efforts to combat malnutrition as a development priority. Since the conference, more than 100 countries have formulated national plans of action for nutrition, many of which were based on existing development plans such as comprehensive food security initiatives, national poverty alleviation programmes and action plans to attain the targets set by the World Summit for Children in September 1990. FAO promotes other efforts, at household and community level, to improve nutrition and food security, for example a programme to support home gardens. It aims to assist the identification of food-insecure and vulnerable populations, both through its *State of Food Insecurity in the World* reports and taking a lead role in the development of Food

Insecurity and Vulnerability Information and Mapping Systems (FIVIMS), a recommendation of the World Food Summit. In 1999 FAO signed a Memorandum of Understanding with UNAIDS on strengthening co-operation to combat the threat posed by the HIV/AIDS epidemic to food security, nutrition and rural livelihoods. FAO is committed to incorporating HIV/AIDS into food security and livelihood projects, to strengthening community care and to highlighting the importance of nutrition in the care of those living with HIV/AIDS.

FAO is committed to promoting food quality and safety in all different stages of food production and processing. It supports the development of integrated food control systems by member states, which incorporate aspects of food control management, inspection, risk analysis and quality assurance. The joint FAO/WHO Codex Alimentarius Commission, established in 1962, aims to protect the health of consumers, ensure fair trade practices and promote the co-ordination of food standards activities at an international level. In January 2001 a joint team of FAO and WHO experts issued a report concerning the allergenicity of foods derived from biotechnology (i.e. genetically modified—GM—foods). In July the Codex Alimentarius Commission agreed the first global principles for assessing the safety of GM foods, and approved a series of maximum levels of environmental contaminants in food. In June 2004 FAO published guidelines for assessing possible risks posed to plants by living modified organisms. In July 2001 the Codex Alimentarius Commission adopted guidelines on organic livestock production, covering organic breeding methods, the elimination of growth hormones and certain chemicals in veterinary medicines, and the use of good quality organic feed with no meat or bone meal content. In January 2003 FAO organized a technical consultation on biological risk management in food and agriculture which recognized the need for a more integrated approach to so-called biosecurity, i.e. the prevention, control and management of risks to animal, human and plant life and health. FAO has subsequently developed a *Toolkit*, published in 2007, to help countries to develop and implement national biosecurity systems and to enhance biosecurity capacity.

FAO aims to assist member states to enhance the efficiency, competitiveness and profitability of their agricultural and food enterprises. FAO extends assistance in training, capacity-building and the formulation of agribusiness development strategies. It promotes the development of effective 'value chains', connecting primary producers with consumers, and supports other linkages within the agribusiness industry. Similarly, FAO aims to strengthen marketing systems, links between producers and retailers and training in agricultural marketing, and works to improve the regulatory framework for agricultural marketing. FAO promotes the use of new technologies to increase agricultural production and extends a range of services to support mechanization, including training, maintenance, testing and the promotion of labour saving technologies. Other programmes are focused on farm management, post-harvest management, food and non-food processing, rural finance, and rural infrastructure. FAO helps reduce immediate post-harvest losses, with the introduction of improved processing methods and storage systems. FAO participates in PhAction, a forum of 12 agencies that was established in 1999 to promote post-harvest research and the development of effective post-harvest services and infrastructure.

FAO's Joint Division with the International Atomic Energy Agency (IAEA) is concerned with the use of nuclear techniques in food and agriculture. It co-ordinates research projects, provides scientific and technical support to technical co-operation projects and administers training courses. A joint laboratory in Seibersdorf, Austria, is concerned with testing biotechnologies and in developing non-toxic fertilizers (especially those that are locally available) and improved strains of food crops (especially from indigenous varieties). In the area of animal production and health, the Joint Division has developed progesterone-measuring and disease diagnostic kits. Other sub-programmes of the Joint Division are concerned with soil and water, plant breeding and nutrition, insect pest control and food and environmental protection.

In March 2011, in view of the severe damage suffered by the Fukushima Daiichi nuclear plant in Japan, following an earthquake and tsunami, FAO, the IAEA and WHO issued a joint statement on food safety issues in the aftermath of the emergency, emphasizing their commitment to mobilizing knowledge and expertise in support of the Japanese authorities.

NATURAL RESOURCES MANAGEMENT AND ENVIRONMENT

FAO is committed to promoting the responsible and sustainable management of natural resources and other activities to protect the environment. FAO assists member states to mitigate the impact of climate change on agriculture, to adapt and enhance the resilience of agricultural systems to climate change, and to promote practices to reduce the emission of greenhouse gases from the agricultural sector. In recent years FAO has strengthened its work in the area of using natural biomass resources as fuel, both at grassroots level and industrial processing of cash crops. In 2006 FAO established the International Bioenergy Platform to serve as a focal point for research, data collection, capacity-building and strategy formulation by local, regional and international bodies concerned with bioenergy. FAO also serves as the secretariat for the Global Bioenergy Partnership, which was inaugurated in May 2006 to facilitate the collaboration between governments, international agencies and representatives of the private sector and civil society in the sustainable development of bioenergy.

FAO aims to enhance the sustainability of land and water systems, and as a result to secure agricultural productivity, through the improved tenure, management, development and conservation of those natural resources. The organization promotes equitable access to land and water resources and supports integrated land and water management, including river basin management and improved irrigation systems. FAO has developed AQUASTAT as a global information system concerned with water and agricultural issues, comprising databases, country and regional profiles, surveys and maps. AquaCrop, CropWat and ClimWat are further productivity models and databases which have been developed to help to assess crop requirements and potential yields. Since 2003 FAO has participated in UN Water, an inter-agency initiative to co-ordinate existing approaches to water-related issues. In December 2008 FAO organized a Ministerial Conference on Water for Agriculture and Energy in Africa: 'the Challenges of Climate Change', in Sirte, Libya, which was attended by representatives of 48 African member countries and other representatives of international, regional and civil organizations.

Within the FAO's Natural Resources Management and Environment Department is a Research and Extension Division, which provides advisory and technical services to support national capacity-building, research, communication and education activities. It maintains several databases which support and facilitate the dissemination of information, for example relating to proven transferable technologies and biotechnologies in use in developing countries. The Division advises countries on communication strategies to strengthen agricultural and rural development, and has supported the use of rural radio. FAO is the UN lead agency of an initiative, 'Education for Rural People', which aims to improve the quality of and access to basic education for people living in rural areas and to raise awareness of the issue as an essential element of achieving the MDGs. The Research and Extension Division hosts the secretariat of the Global Forum on Agricultural Research, which was established in October 1996 as a collaboration of research centres, non-governmental and private sector organizations and development agencies. The Forum aims to strengthen research and promote knowledge partnerships concerned with the alleviation of poverty, the increase in food security and the sustainable use of natural resources. The Division also hosts the secretariat of the Science Council of the Consultative Group on International Agricultural Research (CGIAR), which, specifically, aims to enhance and promote the quality, relevance and impact of science within the network of CGIAR research centres and to mobilize global scientific expertise.

In September 2009 FAO published, jointly with the Centre for Indigenous People's Nutrition and Environment (CINE—based in McGill University, Montreal, Canada) a report entitled *Indigenous People's Food Systems: The Many Dimensions of Culture, Diversity and Environment for Nutrition and Health*, which aimed to demonstrate the wealth of knowledge on nutrition retained within indigenous communities world-wide.

FISHERIES AND AQUACULTURE

FAO aims to facilitate and secure the long-term sustainable development of fisheries and aquaculture, in both inland and marine waters, and to promote its contribution to world food security. In March 1995 a ministerial meeting of fisheries adopted the Rome Consensus on World Fisheries, which identified a need for immediate action to eliminate overfishing and to rebuild and enhance depleting fish stocks. In November the FAO Conference adopted a Code of Conduct for Responsible Fishing, which incorporated many global fisheries and aquaculture issues (including fisheries resource conservation and development, fish catches, seafood and fish processing, commercialization, trade and research) to promote the sustainable development of the sector. In February 1999 the FAO Committee on Fisheries adopted new international measures, within the framework of the Code of Conduct, in order to reduce over-exploitation of the world's fish resources, as well as plans of action for the conservation and management of sharks and the reduction in the incidental catch of seabirds in longline fisheries. The voluntary measures were endorsed at a ministerial meeting, held in March and attended by representatives of some 126 countries, which issued a declaration to promote the implementation of the Code of Conduct and to achieve sustainable management of fisheries and aquaculture. In March 2001 FAO adopted an international plan of action to address the continuing problem of so-called illegal, unreported and unregulated fishing (IUU). In that year FAO estimated that about one-half of major marine fish stocks were fully exploited, one-quarter under-exploited, at least 15% over-exploited, and 10% depleted or recovering from depletion. IUU was estimated to account for up to 30% of total catches in certain fisheries. In October FAO and the Icelandic Government jointly organized the Reykjavík Conference on Responsible Fisheries in the Marine Ecosystem, which adopted a declaration on pursuing responsible and sustainable fishing activities in the context of ecosystem-based fisheries management (EBFM). EBFM involves determining the boundaries of individual marine ecosystems, and maintaining or rebuilding the habitats and biodiversity of each of these so that all species will be supported at levels of maximum production. In March 2005 FAO's Committee of Fisheries adopted voluntary guidelines for the so-called eco-labelling and certification of fish and fish products, i.e. based on information regarding capture management and the sustainable use of resources. In March 2007 the Committee agreed to initiate a process of negotiating an internationally-binding agreement to deny port access to fishing vessels involved in IUU activities; the eventual 'Agreement on Port State Measures to Prevent, Deter and Eliminate Illegal, Unreported and Unregulated Fishing' was endorsed by the Conference in November 2009.

FAO undertakes extensive monitoring, publishing every two years *The State of World Fisheries and Aquaculture*, and collates and maintains relevant databases. It formulates country and regional profiles and has developed a specific information network for the fisheries sector, GLOBEFISH, which gathers and disseminates information regarding market trends, tariffs and other industry issues. FAO aims to extend technical support to member states with regard to the management and conservation of aquatic resources, and other measures to improve the utilization and trade of products, including the reduction of post-harvest losses, preservation marketing and quality assurance. FAO promotes aquaculture (which contributes almost one-third of annual global fish landings) as a valuable source of animal protein and income-generating activity for rural communities. It has undertaken to develop an ecosystem approach to aquaculture (EAA) and works to integrate aquaculture with agricultural and irrigation systems. In February 2000 FAO and the Network of Aquaculture Centres in Asia and the Pacific (NACA) jointly convened a Conference on Aquaculture in the Third Millennium, which was held in Bangkok, Thailand, and attended by participants representing more than 200 governmental and non-governmental organizations. The Conference debated global trends in aquaculture and future policy measures to ensure the sustainable development of the sector. It adopted the Bangkok Declaration and Strategy for Aquaculture Beyond 2000.

FORESTRY

FAO is committed to the sustainable management of trees, forests and forestry resources. It aims to address the critical balance of ensuring the conservation of forests and forestry resources while maximising their potential to contribute to food security and social and economic development. In March 2009 the Committee on Forestry approved a new 10-year FAO Strategic Plan for Forestry, replacing a previous strategic plan initiated in 1999. The new plan, which was 'dynamic' and was to be updated regularly, covered the social, economic and environmental aspects of forestry. The first World Forest Week was held in March 2009 and the second in October 2010. 2011 was declared the International Year of Forests by the UN General Assembly.

FAO assists member countries to formulate, implement and monitor national forestry programmes, and encourages the participation of all stakeholders in developing plans for the sustainable management of tree and forest resources. FAO also helps to implement national assessments of those programmes and of other forestry activities. At a global level FAO undertakes surveillance of the state of the world's forests and publishes a report every two years. A separate *Forest Resources Assessment* is published every five years; the latest (for 2010) was initiated in March 2008. FAO is committed to collecting and disseminating accurate information and data on forests. It maintains the Forestry Information System (FORIS) to make relevant information and forest-related databases widely accessible.

FAO is a member of the Collaborative Partnership on Forests, which was established in April 2004 on the recommendation of the UN's Economic and Social Council. FAO organizes a World Forestry Congress, generally held every six years; the 13th Congress was convened in Buenos Aires, Argentina, in October 2009.

ECONOMIC AND SOCIAL DEVELOPMENT

FAO provides a focal point for economic research and policy analysis relating to food security and sustainable development. It produces studies and reports on agricultural development, the impact of development programmes and projects, and the world food situation, as well as on commodity prices, trade and medium-term projections. It supports the development of methodologies and guidelines to improve research into food and agriculture and the integration of wider concepts, such as social welfare, environmental factors and nutrition, into research projects. In November 2004 the FAO Council adopted a set of voluntary Right to Food Guidelines, and established a dedicated administrative unit, that aimed to 'support the progressive realization of the right to adequate food in the context of national food security' by providing practical guidance to countries in support of their efforts to achieve the 1996 World Food Summit commitment and UN MDG relating to hunger reduction. FAO's Statistical Division assembles, analyses and disseminates statistical data on world food and agriculture and aims to ensure the consistency, broad coverage and quality of available data. The Division advises member countries on enhancing their statistical capabilities. It maintains FAOSTAT as a core database of statistical information relating to nutrition, fisheries, forestry, food production, land use, population, etc. In 2004 FAO developed a new statistical framework, CountrySTAT, to provide for the organization and integration of statistical data and metadata from sources within a particular country. By 2012 CountrySTAT systems had been developed in 25 developing countries. FAO's internet-based interactive World Agricultural Information Centre (WAICENT) offers access to agricultural publications, technical documentation, codes of conduct, data, statistics and multimedia resources. FAO compiles and co-ordinates an extensive range of international databases on agriculture, fisheries, forestry, food and statistics, the most important of these being AGRIS (the International Information System for the Agricultural Sciences and Technology) and CARIS (the Current Agricultural Research Information System). In June 2000 FAO organized a high-level Consultation on Agricultural Information Management (COAIM), which aimed to increase access to and use of agricultural information by policy-makers and others. The second COAIM was held in September 2002 and the third meeting was convened in June 2007.

FAO's Global Information and Early Warning System (GIEWS), which become operational in 1975, maintains a database on and monitors the crop and food outlook at global, regional, national and sub-national levels in order to detect emerging food supply difficulties and disasters and to ensure rapid intervention in countries experiencing food supply shortages. It publishes regular reports on the weather conditions and crop prospects in sub-Saharan Africa and in the Sahel region, issues special alerts which describe the situation in countries or sub-regions experiencing food difficulties, and recommends an appropriate international response. FAO has also supported the development and implementation of Food Insecurity and Vulnerability Information and Mapping Systems (FIVIMS) and hosts the secretariat of the inter-agency working group on development of the FIVIMS. In October 2007 FAO inaugurated an online Global Forum on Food Security and Nutrition, to contribute to the compilation and dissemination of information relating to food security and nutrition throughout the world. In December 2008 a regular report issued by GIEWS identified 33 countries as being in crisis and requiring external assistance, of which 20 were in Africa, 10 in Asia and the Near East and three in Latin America and the Caribbean. All countries were identified as lacking the resources to deal with critical problems of food insecurity, including many severely affected by the high cost of food and fuel. The publication *Crop Prospects and Food Situation* reviews the global situation, and provides regional updates and a special focus on countries experiencing food crises and requiring external assistance, on a quarterly basis. *Food Outlook*, issued in June and November, analyses developments in global food and animal feed markets.

TECHNICAL CO-OPERATION

The Technical Co-operation Department has responsibility for FAO's operational activities, including policy development assistance to member countries; the mobilization of resources; investment support; field operations; emergency operations and rehabilitation; and the Technical Co-operation Programme.

FAO provides policy advice to support the formulation, implementation and evaluation of agriculture, rural development and food security strategies in member countries. It administers a project to assist developing countries to strengthen their technical negotiating skills, in respect to agricultural trade issues. FAO also aims to co-ordinate and facilitate the mobilization of extrabudgetary funds from donors and governments for particular projects. It administers a range of trust funds, including a Trust Fund for Food Security and Food Safety, established in 2002 to generate resources for projects to combat hunger, and the Government Co-operative Programme. FAO's Investment Centre, established in 1964, aims to promote greater external investment in agriculture and rural development by assisting member countries to formulate effective and sustainable projects and programmes. The Centre collaborates with international financing institutions and bilateral donors in the preparation of projects, and administers cost-sharing arrangements, with, typically, FAO funding 40% of a project. The Centre is a co-chair (with the German Government) of the Global Donor Platform for Rural Development, which was established in 2004, comprising multilateral, donor and international agencies, development banks and research institutions, to improve the co-ordination and effectiveness of rural development assistance.

FAO's Technical Co-operation Programme, which was inaugurated in 1976, provides technical expertise and funding for small-scale projects to address specific issues within a country's agriculture, fisheries or forestry sectors. An Associate Professional Officers programme co-ordinates the sponsorship and placement of young professionals to gain experience working in an aspect of rural or agricultural development.

FAO's Special Programme for Food Security (SPFS), initiated in 1994, assists low-income countries with a food deficit to increase food production and productivity as rapidly as possible, primarily through the widespread adoption by farmers of improved production technologies, with emphasis on areas of high potential. Within the SPFS framework are national and regional food security initiatives, all of which aim towards the MDG objective of reducing the incidence of hunger by 50% by 2015. The SPFS is operational in more than 100 countries. The Programme promotes South-South co-operation to improve food security and the exchange of knowledge and experience. Some 40 bilateral co-operation agreements are in force, for example, between Gabon and the People's Republic of China, Egypt and Cameroon, and Viet Nam and Benin. In 2012 some 66 countries were categorized formally as 'low-income food-deficit'.

FAO organizes an annual series of fund-raising events, 'TeleFood', some of which are broadcast on television and the internet, in order to raise public awareness of the problems of hunger and malnutrition. Since its inception in 1997 public donations to TeleFood have exceeded some US $29m. (2012), financing more than 3,200 'grassroots' projects in 130 countries. The projects have provided tools, seeds and other essential supplies directly to small-scale farmers, and have been especially aimed at helping women.

The Technical Co-operation Division co-ordinates FAO's emergency operations, concerned with all aspects of disaster and risk prevention, mitigation, reduction and emergency relief and rehabilitation, with a particular emphasis on food security and rural populations. FAO works with governments to develop and implement disaster prevention policies and practices. It aims to strengthen the capacity of local institutions to manage and mitigate risk and provides technical assistance to improve access to land for displaced populations in countries following conflict or a natural disaster. Other disaster prevention and reduction efforts include dissemination of information from the various early-warning systems and support for adaptation to climate variability and change, for example by the use of drought-resistant crops or the adoption of conservation agriculture techniques. Following an emergency FAO works with governments and other development and humanitarian partners to assess the immediate and longer-term agriculture and food security needs of the affected population. It has developed an Integrated Food Security and Humanitarian Phase Classification Scheme to determine the appropriate response to a disaster situation. Emergency co-ordination units may be established to manage the local response to an emergency and to facilitate and co-ordinate the delivery of inter-agency assistance. In order to rehabilitate agricultural production following a natural or man-made disaster FAO provides emergency seed, tools, other materials and technical and training assistance. During 2005 the UN's Inter-Agency Standing Committee, concerned with co-ordinating the international response to humanitarian disasters, developed a concept of providing assistance through a 'cluster' approach, comprising core areas of activity. FAO was designated the lead agency for the then Agriculture cluster. A review of the humanitarian cluster approach, undertaken during 2010, concluded that a new cluster on Food Security should be established, replacing the Agriculture cluster. The new cluster, established accordingly in 2011, is led jointly by FAO and WFP, and aims to combine expertise in agricultural assistance and food aid in order to boost food security and to improve the resilience of food-insecure disaster-affected communities. FAO also contributes the agricultural relief and rehabilitation component of the UN's Consolidated Appeals Process (CAP), which aims to co-ordinate and enhance the effectiveness of the international community's response to an emergency; by end-November 2011 FAO had received US $200m. in funding in response to its appeals under the 2011 CAP process. In April 2004 FAO established a Special Fund for Emergency and Rehabilitation Activities to enable it to respond promptly to a humanitarian crisis before making an emergency appeal for additional resources.

During 2008–early 2012 projects (providing fertilizers, seeds and other support necessary to ensure the success of harvests) were undertaken in more than 90 countries under the framework of the Initiative on Soaring Food Prices (see above); some US $314m. in project funding was provided by the EU Food Facility, while other projects (to the value of $37m.) were implemented through FAO's Technical Co-operation Programme.

FAO Statutory Bodies

(based at the Rome headquarters, unless otherwise indicated)

African Commission on Agricultural Statistics: c/o FAO Regional Office for Africa, POB 1628, Accra, Ghana; e-mail vincent.ngendakumana@fao.org; f. 1961 to advise member countries on the development and standardization of food and agricultural statistics; 37 member states.

African Forestry and Wildlife Commission: f. 1959 to advise on the formulation of forest policy and to review and co-ordinate its implementation on a regional level; to exchange information and advise on technical problems; 42 member states.

Agriculture, Land and Water Use Commission: c/o FAO Regional Office, POB 2223, Cairo, Egypt; f. 2000 by merger of the Near East Regional Commission on Agriculture and the Regional Commission on Land and Water Use in the Near East; 23 member states.

Animal Production and Health Commission for Asia and the Pacific: c/o FAO Regional Office, Maliwan Mansion, 39 Phra Atit Rd, Bangkok 10200, Thailand; f. 1975 to support national and regional livestock production and research; 17 member states.

Asia and Pacific Commission on Agricultural Statistics: c/o FAO Regional Office, Maliwan Mansion, 39 Phra Atit Rd, Bangkok 10200, Thailand; e-mail rap-statistics.fao.org; internet www.faorap-apcas.org; f. 1963; reviews recent developments in agricultural statistical systems, provides a platform for the exchange of ideas relating to the state of food and agricultural statistics in the region; senior officials responsible for the development of agricultural statistics from 25 member states.

Asia and Pacific Plant Protection Commission: c/o FAO Regional Office, Maliwan Mansion, Phra Atit Rd, Bangkok 10200, Thailand; f. 1956 (new title 1983) to strengthen international co-operation in plant protection to prevent the introduction and spread of destructive plant diseases and pests; 25 member states.

Asia-Pacific Fishery Commission: c/o FAO Regional Office, Maliwan Mansion, 39 Phra Atit Rd, Bangkok 10200, Thailand; f. 1948 to develop fisheries, encourage and co-ordinate research, disseminate information, recommend projects to governments, propose standards in technique and management measures; 20 member states.

Asia-Pacific Forestry Commission: internet www.apfcweb.org; f. 1949 to advise on the formulation of forest policy, and review and co-ordinate its implementation throughout the region; to exchange information and advise on technical problems; 29 member states.

Caribbean Plant Protection Commission: c/o FAO Sub-Regional Office for the Caribbean, POB 631-C, Bridgetown, Barbados; tel. 426-7110; fax 427-6075; e-mail fao-slac@fao.org; internet www.fao.org/world/subregional/slac; f. 1967 to preserve the existing plant resources of the area; 13 member states.

Codex Alimentarius Commission (Joint FAO/WHO Food Standards Programme): e-mail codex@fao.org; internet www.codexalimentarius.net; f. 1962 to make proposals for the co-ordination of all international food standards work and to publish a code of international food standards; Trust Fund to support participation by least-developed countries was inaugurated in 2003; there are numerous specialized Codex committees, e.g. for food labelling, hygiene, additives and contaminants, pesticide and veterinary residues, milk and milk products, and processed fruits and vegetables; and an intergovernmental task force on antimicrobial resistance; 184 member states and the European Union (at March 2012).

Commission for Controlling the Desert Locust in Northwest Africa: f. 1971 to promote research on control of the desert locust in NW Africa.

Commission for Controlling the Desert Locust in Southwest Asia: f. 1964 to carry out all possible measures to control plagues of the desert locust in Afghanistan, India, Iran and Pakistan.

Commission for Controlling the Desert Locust in the Central Region: c/o FAO Regional Office for the Near East, POB 2223, Cairo, Egypt; 16 member states.

Commission for Inland Fisheries of Latin America: Avda Dag Hammarskjöld 3241, Casilla 10095, Vitacura, Santiago, Chile; f. 1976 to promote, co-ordinate and assist national and regional fishery and limnological surveys and programmes of research and development leading to the rational utilization of inland fishery resources; 21 member states.

Commission on Genetic Resources for Food and Agriculture: internet www.fao.org/ag/cgrfa/default.htm; f. 1983 as the Commission on Plant Genetic Resources, renamed in 1995; provides a forum for negotiation on the conservation and sustainable utilization of genetic resources for food and agriculture, and the equitable sharing of benefits derived from their use; 164 member states.

Commission on Livestock Development for Latin America and the Caribbean: Avda Dag Hammarskjöld 3241, Casilla 10095, Vitacura, Santiago, Chile; f. 1986; 24 member states.

Commission on Phytosanitary Measures: f. 1997 as the governing body of the revised International Plant Protection Commission.

Committee for Inland Fisheries of Africa: f. 1971 to promote improvements in inland fisheries and aquaculture in Africa.

European Commission on Agriculture: f. 1949 to encourage and facilitate action and co-operation in technological agricultural problems among member states and between international organizations concerned with agricultural technology in Europe.

European Commission for the Control of Foot-and-Mouth Disease: internet www.fao.org/ag/againfo/commissions/en/eufmd/eufmd.html; f. 1953 to promote national and international action for the control of the disease in Europe and its final eradication.

European Forestry Commission: f. 1947 to advise on the formulation of forest policy and to review and co-ordinate its implementation on a regional level; to exchange information and to make recommendations; 27 member states.

European Inland Fisheries Advisory Commission: internet www.fao.org/fi/body/eifac/eifac.asp; f. 1957 to promote improvements in inland fisheries and to advise member governments and FAO on inland fishery matters; 34 member states.

Fishery Committee for the Eastern Central Atlantic: f. 1967.

General Fisheries Council for the Mediterranean—GFCM: internet www.fao.org/fi/body/rfb/index.htm; f. 1952 to develop aquatic resources, to encourage and co-ordinate research in the fishing and allied industries, to assemble and publish information, and to recommend the standardization of equipment, techniques and nomenclature.

Indian Ocean Fishery Commission: f. 1967 to promote national programmes, research and development activities, and to examine management problems; 41 member states.

International Poplar Commission: f. 1947 to study scientific, technical, social and economic aspects of poplar and willow cultivation; to promote the exchange of ideas and material between research workers, producers and users; to arrange joint research programmes, congresses, study tours; to make recommendations to the FAO Conference and to National Poplar Commissions.

International Rice Commission: internet www.fao.org/ag/AGP/AGPC/doc/field/commrice/welcome.htm; f. 1949 to promote national and international action on production, conservation, distribution and consumption of rice, except matters relating to international trade; supports the International Task Force on Hybrid Rice, the Working Group on Advanced Rice Breeding in Latin America and the Caribbean, the Inter-regional Collaborative Research Network on Rice in the Mediterranean Climate Areas, and the Technical Co-operation Network on Wetland Development and Management/Inland Valley Swamps; 60 member states.

Latin American and Caribbean Forestry Commission: f. 1948 to advise on formulation of forest policy and review and co-ordinate its implementation throughout the region; to exchange information and advise on technical problems; meets every two years; 31 member states.

Near East Forestry Commission: f. 1953 to advise on formulation of forest policy and review and co-ordinate its implementation throughout the region; to exchange information and advise on technical problems; 20 member states.

North American Forestry Commission: f. 1959 to advise on the formulation and co-ordination of national forest policies in Canada, Mexico and the USA; to exchange information and to advise on technical problems; three member states.

South West Indian Ocean Fisheries Commission: f. 2005 to promote the sustainable development and utilization of coastal fishery resources of East Africa and island states in that sub-region; 14 member states.

Western Central Atlantic Fishery Commission: f. 1973 to assist international co-operation for the conservation, development and utilization of the living resources, especially shrimps, of the Western Central Atlantic.

Finance

FAO's Regular Programme, which is financed by contributions from member governments, covers the cost of FAO's Secretariat, its Technical Co-operation Programme (TCP) and part of the cost of several special action programmes. The regular budget for the two-year period 2010–11 totalled US $1,000m. Much of FAO's technical assistance programme and emergency (including rehabilitation) support activities are funded from extra-budgetary sources, predominantly by trust funds that come mainly from donor countries and international financing institutions; voluntary donor contributions to FAO were projected at around $1,200m. in 2010–11.

Publications

Commodity Review and Outlook (annually).

Crop Prospects and Food Situation (5/6 a year).

Ethical Issues in Food and Agriculture.

FAO Statistical Yearbook (annually).

FAOSTAT Statistical Database (online).

Food Outlook (2 a year).

Food Safety and Quality Update (monthly; electronic bulletin).

Forest Resources Assessment.

The State of Agricultural Commodity Markets (every 2 years).

The State of Food and Agriculture (annually).

The State of Food Insecurity in the World (annually).

The State of World Fisheries and Aquaculture (every 2 years).

The State of the World's Forests (every 2 years).

Unasylva (quarterly).

Yearbook of Fishery Statistics.

Yearbook of Forest Products.

Commodity reviews, studies, manuals. A complete catalogue of publications is available at www.fao.org/icatalog/inter-e.htm.

International Atomic Energy Agency—IAEA

Address: POB 100, Wagramerstrasse 5, 1400 Vienna, Austria.

Telephone: (1) 26000; **fax:** (1) 26007; **e-mail:** official.mail@iaea.org; **internet:** www.iaea.org.

The International Atomic Energy Agency (IAEA) is an intergovernmental organization, established in 1957 in accordance with a decision of the General Assembly of the United Nations. Although it is autonomous, the IAEA is administratively a member of the United Nations, and reports on its activities once a year to the UN General Assembly. Its main objectives are to enlarge the contribution of atomic energy to peace, health and prosperity throughout the world and to ensure, so far as it is able, that assistance provided by it or at its request or under its supervision or control is not used in such a way as to further any military purpose. The 2005 Nobel Peace Prize was awarded, in two equal parts, to the IAEA and to the Agency's Director-General.

MEMBERS

The IAEA has 154 members. Some 72 intergovernmental and non-governmental organizations have formal agreements with the IAEA.

Organization

(April 2012)

GENERAL CONFERENCE

The Conference, comprising representatives of all member states, convenes each year for general debate on the Agency's policy, budget and programme. It elects members to the Board of Governors, and approves the appointment of the Director-General; it admits new member states.

BOARD OF GOVERNORS

The Board of Governors consists of 35 member states elected by the General Conference. It is the principal policy-making body of the Agency and is responsible to the General Conference. Under its own authority, the Board approves all safeguards agreements, important projects and safety standards.

SECRETARIAT

The Secretariat, comprising 2,338 staff at 31 December 2010, is headed by the Director-General, who is assisted by six Deputy

Directors-General. The Secretariat is divided into six departments: Technical Co-operation; Nuclear Energy; Nuclear Safety and Security; Nuclear Sciences and Applications; Safeguards; and Management. A Standing Advisory Group on Safeguards Implementation advises the Director-General on technical aspects of safeguards.

Director-General: YUKIYA AMANO (Japan).

Activities

In recent years the IAEA has implemented several reforms of its management structure and operations. The three pillars supporting the Agency's activities are: technology (assisting research on and practical application of atomic energy for peaceful uses), safety, and verification (ensuring that special fissionable and other materials, services, equipment and information made available by the Agency or at its request or under its supervision are not used for any non-peaceful purpose).

TECHNICAL CO-OPERATION AND TRAINING

The IAEA provides assistance in the form of experts, training and equipment to technical co-operation projects and applications world-wide, with an emphasis on radiation protection and safety-related activities. Training is provided to scientists, and experts and lecturers are assigned to provide specialized help on specific nuclear applications. The IAEA supported the foundation in September 2003 of the World Nuclear University, comprising a world-wide network of institutions that aim to strengthen international co-operation in promoting the safe use of nuclear power in energy production, and in the application of nuclear science and technology in areas including sustainable agriculture and nutrition, medicine, fresh water resources management and environmental protection.

FOOD AND AGRICULTURE

In co-operation with FAO, the Agency conducts programmes of applied research on the use of radiation and isotopes in fields including: efficiency in the use of water and fertilizers; improvement of food crops by induced mutations; eradication or control of destructive insects by the introduction of sterilized insects (radiation-based Sterile Insect Technique); improvement of livestock nutrition and health; studies on improving efficacy and reducing residues of pesticides, and increasing utilization of agricultural wastes; and food preservation by irradiation. The programmes are implemented by the Joint FAO/IAEA Division of Nuclear Techniques in Food and Agriculture and by the FAO/IAEA Agriculture and Biotechnology Laboratory, based at the IAEA's laboratory complex in Seibersdorf, Austria. A Training and Reference Centre for Food and Pesticide Control, based at Seibersdorf, supports the implementation of national legislation and trade agreements ensuring the quality and safety of food products in international trade. The Agency's Marine Environment Laboratory (IAEA-MEL), in Monaco, studies radionuclides and other ocean pollutants.

LIFE SCIENCES

In co-operation with the World Health Organization (WHO), the IAEA promotes the use of nuclear techniques in medicine, biology and health-related environmental research, provides training, and conducts research on techniques for improving the accuracy of radiation dosimetry.

The IAEA/WHO Network of Secondary Standard Dosimetry Laboratories (SSDLs) comprises 81 laboratories in 62 member states. The Agency's Dosimetry Laboratory in Seibersdorf performs dose inter-comparisons for both SSDLs and radiotherapy centres. The IAEA undertakes maintenance plans for nuclear laboratories; national programmes of quality control for nuclear medicine instruments; quality control of radioimmunoassay techniques; radiation sterilization of medical supplies; and improvement of cancer therapy through the IAEA Programme of Action for Cancer Therapy (PACT), inaugurated in 2004, and through which Agency works with WHO and other partners. In May 2009 the IAEA and WHO launched a new Joint Programme on Cancer Control, aimed at enhancing efforts to fight cancer in the developing world.

PHYSICAL AND CHEMICAL SCIENCES

The Agency's programme in physical sciences includes industrial applications of isotopes and radiation technology; application of nuclear techniques to mineral exploration and exploitation; radiopharmaceuticals; and hydrology, involving the use of isotope techniques for assessment of water resources. Nuclear data services are provided, and training is given for nuclear scientists from developing countries. The Physics, Chemistry and Instrumentation Laboratory at Seibersdorf supports the Agency's research in human health, industry, water resources and environment. The Abdus Salam International Centre for Theoretical Physics, based in Trieste, Italy, operates in accordance with a tripartite agreement in force between the IAEA, UNESCO and the Italian Government.

NUCLEAR POWER

In 2012 there were 435 nuclear power plants in operation and 63 reactors under construction world-wide. Nuclear power accounts for about 13% of total electrical energy generated globally. The IAEA helps developing member states to introduce nuclear-powered electricity-generating plants through assistance with planning, feasibility studies, surveys of manpower and infrastructure, and safety measures. The Agency also assesses life extension and decommissioning strategies for ageing nuclear power plants. It publishes books on numerous aspects of nuclear power, and provides training courses on safety in nuclear power plants and other topics. An energy data bank collects and disseminates information on nuclear technology, and a power-reactor information system monitors the technical performance of nuclear power plants. There is increasing interest in the use of nuclear reactors for seawater desalination and radiation hydrology techniques to provide potable water. In July 1992 the EC, Japan, Russia and the USA signed an agreement to co-operate in the engineering design of an International Thermonuclear Experimental Reactor (ITER); the People's Republic of China, Republic of Korea (South Korea) and India subsequently also joined the process. The project aims to demonstrate the scientific and technological feasibility of fusion energy, with the aim of providing a source of clean, abundant energy in the 21st century. In June 2005 the states participating in ITER agreed that the installation should be constructed in Cadarache, France, and in November 2006 an ITER Agreement was concluded, establishing, upon its entry into force in October 2007, a formal ITER organization, with responsibility for constructing, operating and decommissioning ITER. It was envisaged that ITER would enter fully into operation by 2026. In May 2001 the International Project on Innovative Nuclear Reactors and Fuel Cycles (INPRO) was inaugurated. INPRO, which has 28 members, aims to promote nuclear energy as a means of meeting future sustainable energy requirements and to facilitate the exchange of information by member states to advance innovations in nuclear technology. The IAEA is a permanent observer at the Generation IV International Forum (GIF), which was inaugurated in 2000 and aims to establish a number of international collaborative nuclear research and development agreements. In 2010 the IAEA established an Integrated Nuclear Infrastructure Group (ING), which aimed to integrate information from disparate databases to enable more effective planning; to offer training in the use of planning tools; to provide legislative assistance; to provide guidance on ensuring self-assessment capabilities among governmental and operating organizations; and to organize education and training materials. An advisory Technical Working Group on Nuclear Power Infrastructure was also initiated during 2010.

RADIOACTIVE WASTE MANAGEMENT

The Agency provides practical help to member states in the management of radioactive waste. The Waste Management Advisory Programme (WAMAP) was established in 1987, and undertakes advisory missions in member states. A code of practice to prevent the illegal dumping of radioactive waste was drafted in 1989, and another on the international transboundary movement of waste was drafted in 1990. A ban on the dumping of radioactive waste at sea came into effect in 1994, under the Convention on the Prevention of Marine Pollution by Dumping of Wastes and Other Matters. The IAEA was to determine radioactive levels, for purposes of the Convention, and provide assistance to countries for the safe disposal of radioactive wastes. A new category of radioactive waste—very low level waste (VLLW)—was introduced in the early 2000s. A VLLW repository, at Morvilliers, France, became fully operational in 2004. The Agency has issued modal regulations for the air, sea and land transportation of all radioactive materials.

In September 1997 the IAEA adopted a Joint Convention on the Safety of Spent Fuel Management and on the Safety of Radioactive Waste Management. The first internationally binding legal device to address such issues, the Convention was to ensure the safe storage and disposal of nuclear and radioactive waste, during both the construction and operation of a nuclear power plant, as well as following its closure. The Convention entered into force in June 2001, and had been ratified by 63 parties at February 2012.

NUCLEAR SAFETY

The IAEA's nuclear safety programme encourages international co-operation in the exchange of information, promoting implementation of its safety standards and providing advisory safety services. It includes the IAEA International Nuclear Event Scale (INES), which measures the severity of nuclear events, incidents and accidents; the Incident Reporting System; an emergency preparedness programme (which maintains an Emergency Response Centre, located in Vienna,

Austria); operational safety review teams; the International Nuclear Safety Group (INSAG); the Radiation Protection Advisory Team; and a safety research co-ordination programme. The safety review teams provide member states with advice on achieving and maintaining a high level of safety in the operation of nuclear power plants, while research programmes establish risk criteria for the nuclear fuel cycle and identify cost-effective means to reduce risks in energy systems. A new version of the INES, issued in July 2008, incorporated revisions aimed at providing more detailed ratings of activities including human exposure to sources of radiation and the transportation of radioactive materials.

The nuclear safety programme promotes a global safety regime, which aims to ensure the protection of people and the environment from the effects of ionizing radiation and the minimization of the likelihood of potential nuclear accidents, etc. Through the Commission on Safety Standards (which has sub-committees on nuclear safety standards, radiation safety standards, transport safety standards and waste safety standards) the programme establishes IAEA safety standards and provides for their application. In September 2006 the IAEA published a new primary safety standard, the Fundamental Safety Principles, representing a unified philosophy of nuclear safety and protection that was to provide the conceptual basis for the Agency's entire safety standards agenda. The IAEA's *Safety Glossary Terminology Used in Nuclear Safety and Radiation Protection* is updated regularly. In 2010 IAEA established a Global Safety Assessment (G-SAN), facilitating collaboration between experts world-wide with the aim of harmonizing nuclear safety.

The Convention on the Physical Protection of Nuclear Material was signed in 1980, and committed contracting states to ensuring the protection of nuclear material during transportation within their territory or on board their ships or aircraft. In July 2005 delegates from 89 states party adopted a number of amendments aimed at strengthening the Convention.

Following a serious accident at the Chernobyl nuclear power plant in Ukraine (then part of the USSR) in April 1986, two conventions were formulated by the IAEA and entered into force in October. The first, the Convention on Early Notification of a Nuclear Accident, commits parties to provide information about nuclear accidents with possible transboundary effects at the earliest opportunity (it had 113 parties by February 2012); and the second, the Convention on Assistance in the Case of a Nuclear Accident or Radiological Emergency, commits parties to endeavour to provide assistance in the event of a nuclear accident or radiological emergency (this had 108 parties by February 2012). During 1990 the IAEA organized an assessment of the consequences of the Chernobyl accident, undertaken by an international team of experts, who reported to an international conference on the effects of the accident, convened at the IAEA headquarters in Vienna in May 1991. In February 1993 INSAG published an updated report on the Chernobyl incident, which emphasized the role of design factors in the accident, and the need to implement safety measures in the RBMK-type reactor. In March 1994 an IAEA expert mission visited Chernobyl and reported continuing serious deficiencies in safety at the defunct reactor and the units remaining in operation. An international conference reviewing the radiological consequences of the accident, 10 years after the event, was held in April 1996, co-sponsored by the IAEA, WHO and the European Commission. The last of the Chernobyl plant's three operating units was officially closed in December 2000. During the 2000s the IAEA was offering a wide range of assistance with the decommissioning of Chernobyl. In April 2009 the IAEA, UNDP, UNICEF and WHO launched the International Chernobyl Research and Information Network (ICRIN), a three-year initiative, costing US $2.5m., which aimed to provide up-to-date scientific information and sound practical advice to communities in areas of Ukraine, Belarus and Russia that remained affected by the Chernobyl accident. In November 2008 the IAEA and other UN agencies approved a UN Action Plan on Chernobyl to 2016, which had been developed by UNDP, and was envisaged as a framework for the regeneration of these areas.

An International Convention on Nuclear Safety was adopted at an IAEA conference in June 1994. The Convention applies to land-based civil nuclear power plants: adherents commit themselves to fundamental principles of safety, and maintain legislative frameworks governing nuclear safety. The Convention entered into force in October 1996 and had been ratified by 74 states by February 2012.

In September 1997 more than 80 member states adopted a protocol to revise the 1963 Vienna Convention on Civil Liability for Nuclear Damage, fixing the minimum limit of liability for the operator of a nuclear reactor at 300m. Special Drawing Rights (SDRs, the accounting units of the IMF) in the event of an accident. The amended protocol also extended the length of time during which claims may be brought for loss of life or injury. It entered into force in October 2003. The International Expert Group on Nuclear Liability (INLEX) was established in the same year. A Convention on Supplementary Compensation for Nuclear Damage established a further compensatory fund to provide for the payment of damages following an accident; contributions to the Fund were to be calculated on the basis of the nuclear capacity of each member state. The Convention had four contracting states by February 2012.

In July 1996 the IAEA co-ordinated a study on the radiological situation at the Mururoa and Fangatauta atolls, following the French nuclear test programmes in the South Pacific. Results published in May 1998 concluded that there was no radiological health risk and that neither remedial action nor continued environmental monitoring was necessary.

The IAEA is developing a training course on measurement methods and risk analysis relating to the presence of depleted uranium (which can be used in ammunition) in post-conflict areas. In November 2000 IAEA specialists participated in a fact-finding mission organized by UNEP in Kosovo and Metohija, which aimed to assess the environmental and health consequences of the use of depleted uranium in ammunition by NATO during its 1999 aerial offensive against the then Federal Republic of Yugoslavia. (A report on the situation was published by UNEP in March 2001.) In June 2003 the Agency published the results of an assessment undertaken in 2002 of the possible long-term radiological impact of depleted uranium residues, derived from the 1991 Gulf War, at several locations in Kuwait; it determined that the residues did not pose a health threat to local populations.

In May 2001 the IAEA convened an international conference to address the protection of nuclear material and radioactive sources from illegal trafficking. In September, in view of the perpetration of major terrorist attacks against targets in the USA during that month, the IAEA General Conference addressed the potential for nuclear-related terrorism. It adopted a resolution that emphasized the importance of the physical protection of nuclear material in preventing its illicit use or the sabotage of nuclear facilities and nuclear materials. Three main potential threats were identified: the acquisition by a terrorist group of a nuclear weapon; acquisition of nuclear material to construct a nuclear weapon or cause a radiological hazard; and violent acts against nuclear facilities to cause a radiological hazard. In March 2002 the Board of Governors approved in principle an action plan to improve global protection against acts of terrorism involving nuclear and other radioactive materials. The plan addressed the physical protection of nuclear materials and facilities; the detection of malicious activities involving radioactive materials; strengthening national control systems; the security of radioactive sources; evaluation of security and safety at nuclear facilities; emergency response to malicious acts or threats involving radioactive materials; ensuring adherence to international guidelines and agreements; and improvement of programme co-ordination and information management. It was estimated that the Agency's upgraded nuclear security activities would require significant additional annual funding. In March 2003 the IAEA organized an International Conference on Security of Radioactive Sources, held in Vienna. In April 2005 the UN General Assembly adopted the International Convention for the Suppression of Acts of Nuclear Terrorism. The Convention, which opened for signature in September of that year and entered into force in July 2007, established a definition of acts of nuclear terrorism and urged signatory states to co-operate in the prevention of terrorist attacks by sharing information and providing mutual assistance with criminal investigations and extradition proceedings. Under the provisions of the Convention it was required that any seized nuclear or radiological material should be held in accordance with IAEA safeguards. By the end of 2010 a total of 1,980 incidents had been reported to the Illicit Trafficking Database (ITDB) since its creation in 1995; of the 147 incidents that were reported to have occurred during 2010, 13 involved illegal possession of and attempts to sell nuclear material or radioactive sources; 22 involved reported theft or loss; and 111 concerned discoveries of uncontrolled material, unauthorized disposals, and inadvertent unauthorized shipments and storage. The ITDB had 107 participant states in that year.

In June 2004 the Board of Governors approved an international action plan on the decommissioning of nuclear facilities; the plan was revised in 2007. In September 2007 the IAEA launched a Network of Centres of Excellence for Decommissioning. In 2012 the Agency was managing four ongoing international projects related to safe decommissioning.

In October 2008 the IAEA inaugurated the International Seismic Safety Centre (ISSC) within the Agency's Department of Safety and Security. The ISSC was to serve as a focal point for avoiding and mitigating the consequences of extreme seismic events on nuclear installations world-wide, and was to be supported by a committee of high-level experts in the following areas: geology and tectonics; seismology; seismic hazard; geotechnical engineering; structural engineering; equipment; and seismic risk. In August 2007, and January–February and December 2008, the IAEA sent missions to visit the Kashiwazaki-Kariwa nuclear power plant in Japan, in order to learn about the effects on that facility of an earthquake that struck it in July 2007, and to identify and recommend future precautions. In March 2011, in the aftermath of the severe earthquake and tsunami flooding that had struck and severely damaged Fukushima Daiichi nuclear power plant, the Japanese authorities requested IAEA support in monitoring the effects of the ensuing release of radiation on the environment and on human health. Accordingly, the IAEA dispatched radiation monitoring teams to Japan to provide assistance to local experts, with a particular focus on: worker radiation protection, food safety, marine and soil science, and Boiling Water Reactor (BWR) technology. In partnership with WMO, the IAEA also provided weather forecast updates as part of its immediate emergency response. In late March the IAEA, FAO and WHO issued a joint statement on food safety issues following the Fukushima nuclear emergency, emphasizing their commitment to mobilizing knowledge and expertise in support of the Japanese authorities. During late May–early June 2011 an IAEA team comprising 20 international experts visited Japan to assess the ongoing state of nuclear safety in that country. In 2011–12 the IAEA issued regular status reports on the situation at Fukushima Daiichi, covering environmental radiation monitoring; workers' exposure to radiation; and ongoing conditions at the plant.

In June 2011, in view of the Fukushima Daiichi accident, the IAEA Ministerial Conference on Nuclear Safety adopted a Ministerial Declaration which formed the basis of the first IAEA Action Plan for Nuclear Safety. The Plan, which was unanimously endorsed in September 2011 by the 55th General Conference, emphasized greater transparency in nuclear safety matters and the improvement of safety regimes, including the strengthening of peer reviews, emergency and response mechanisms, and national regulatory bodies. Safety standards were to be reviewed and an assessment of the vulnerabilities of nuclear power plants was to be undertaken.

DISSEMINATION OF INFORMATION

The International Nuclear Information System (INIS), which was established in 1970, provides a computerized indexing and abstracting service. Information on the peaceful uses of atomic energy is collected by member states and international organizations and sent to the IAEA for processing and dissemination (see list of publications below). The IAEA also co-operates with FAO in an information system for agriculture (AGRIS) and with the World Federation of Nuclear Medicine and Biology, and the non-profit Cochrane Collaboration, in maintaining an electronic database of best practice in nuclear medicine. The IAEA Nuclear Data Section provides cost-free data centre services and co-operates with other national and regional nuclear and atomic data centres in the systematic world-wide collection, compilation, dissemination and exchange of nuclear reaction data, nuclear structure and decay data, and atomic and molecular data for fusion.

SAFEGUARDS

The Treaty on the Non-Proliferation of Nuclear Weapons (known also as the Non-Proliferation Treaty or NPT), which entered into force in 1970, requires each 'non-nuclear-weapon state' (one which had not manufactured and exploded a nuclear weapon or other nuclear explosive device prior to 1 January 1967) which is a party to the Treaty to conclude a safeguards agreement with the IAEA. Under such an agreement, the state undertakes to accept IAEA safeguards on all nuclear material in all its peaceful nuclear activities for the purpose of verifying that such material is not diverted to nuclear weapons or other nuclear explosive devices. In May 1995 the Review and Extension Conference of parties to the NPT agreed to extend the NPT indefinitely, and reaffirmed support for the IAEA's role in verification and the transfer of peaceful nuclear technologies. At the next review conference, held in April–May 2000, the five 'nuclear-weapon states'—China, France, Russia, the United Kingdom and the USA—issued a joint statement pledging their commitment to the ultimate goal of complete nuclear disarmament under effective international controls. A further review conference was convened in May 2005. The 2010 review conference, held in May of that year, unanimously adopted an outcome document containing a 22-point action plan aimed at advancing nuclear disarmament, non-proliferation and the peaceful uses of nuclear energy over the following five years. The Conference also proposed that a regional conference should be convened to address means of eliminating nuclear and other weapons of mass destruction in the Middle East; resolved that the nuclear-weapon states should commit to further efforts to reduce and ultimately eliminate all types of nuclear weapons, including through unilateral, bilateral, regional and multilateral measures, with specific emphasis on the early entry into force and full implementation of the Treaty on Measures for the Further Reduction and Limitation of Strategic Offensive Arms (known as the New START Treaty), signed by the Presidents of Russia and the USA in April 2010; and determined that the Conference on Disarmament should immediately establish a subsidiary body to address nuclear disarmament within the context of an agreed and comprehensive programme of work. The Conference noted a five-point proposal of the UN Secretary-General for nuclear disarmament, including consideration of negotiations on a convention on nuclear weapons, and recognized the interests of non-nuclear-weapon states in constraining nuclear-weapon states' development of nuclear weapons. At February 2012 185 non-nuclear-weapon states and the five nuclear-weapon states were parties to the NPT. A number of non-nuclear-weapon states, however, had not complied, within the prescribed time-limit, with their obligations under the Treaty regarding the conclusion of the relevant safeguards agreement with the Agency.

The five nuclear-weapon states have concluded safeguards agreements with the Agency that permit the application of IAEA safeguards to all their nuclear activities, excluding those with 'direct national significance'. A Comprehensive Nuclear Test Ban Treaty (CTBT) was opened for signature in September 1996, having been adopted by the UN General Assembly. The Treaty was to enter into international law upon ratification by all 44 nations with known nuclear capabilities. A separate verification organization was to be established, based in Vienna. A Preparatory Commission for the treaty organization became operational in 1997. By April 2012 183 countries had signed the CTBT and 157 had ratified it, including 36 of the 44 states with known nuclear capabilities (known as the 'Annex II states', of which the remaining eight were: China, Egypt, Iran, Israel, and the USA, which were at that time signatories to the CTBT; and the Democratic People's Republic of Korea—North Korea, India, and Pakistan, which had not signed the Treaty). In October 1999 ratification of the CTBT was rejected by the US Senate. President Obama of the USA indicated in April 2009 that ratification of the Treaty would be pursued by his regime. The May 2010 NPT review conference determined that all nuclear-weapon states should undertake to ratify the CTBT, and emphasized that, pending the entry into force of the CTBT, all states should refrain from conducting test explosions of nuclear weapons.

Several regional nuclear weapons treaties require their member states to conclude comprehensive safeguards agreements with the IAEA, including the Treaty for the Prohibition of Nuclear Weapons in Latin America (Tlatelolco Treaty, with 33 states party at February 2012); the South Pacific Nuclear-Free Zone Treaty (Rarotonga Treaty, 13 states party at February 2012); the Treaty in the South-East Asia Nuclear-Weapon Free Zone (Treaty of Bangkok, adopted in 1995, 10 states party at February 2012); and the African Nuclear-Weapon Free Zone Treaty (Pelindaba Treaty, adopted in 1996, with 30 states party at February 2012). In September 2006 experts from Kazakhstan, Kyrgyzstan, Tajikistan, Turkmenistan and Uzbekistan adopted a treaty on establishing a Central Asian Nuclear Weapon Free Zone (CANWFZ); all five states subsequently ratified the treaty. At the end of 2010 IAEA safeguards agreements were in force with 175 states, covering 674 nuclear facilities. During that year the Agency conducted 1,983 inspections. Expenditure on the Safeguards Regular Budget for 2010 was €116.1m., and extra-budgetary programme expenditure amounted to €18.2m. The IAEA maintains an imagery database of nuclear sites, and is installing digital surveillance systems (including unattended and remote monitoring capabilities) to replace obsolete analogue systems.

In June 1995 the Board of Governors approved measures to strengthen the safeguards system, including allowing inspection teams greater access to suspected nuclear sites and to information on nuclear activities in member states, reducing the notice time for inspections by removing visa requirements for inspectors and using environmental monitoring (i.e. soil, water and air samples) to test for signs of radioactivity. In April 1996 the IAEA initiated a programme to prevent and combat illicit trafficking of nuclear weapons, and in May 1998 the IAEA and the World Customs Organization signed a Memorandum of Understanding to enhance co-operation in the prevention of illicit nuclear trafficking. In May 1997 the Board of Governors adopted a model additional protocol approving measures to strengthen safeguards further, in order to ensure the compliance of non-nuclear-weapon states with IAEA commitments. The new protocol compelled member states to provide inspection teams with improved access to information concerning existing and planned nuclear activities, and to allow access to locations other than known nuclear sites within that country's territory. By December 2010 104 states had ratified additional protocols to their safeguards agreements.

The IAEA's Safeguards Analytical Laboratory (at the Seibersdorf complex) analyses nuclear fuel-cycle samples collected by IAEA safeguards inspectors.

In April 1992 North Korea ratified a safeguards agreement with the IAEA. Subequently, however, that country refused to permit full access to all its facilities for IAEA inspectors to ascertain whether material capable of being used for the manufacture of nuclear weapons was being generated and stored. In March 1993 North Korea announced its intention to withdraw from the NPT, although, in June, it suspended this decision. In June 1994 the IAEA Board of Governors halted IAEA technical assistance to North Korea because of continuous violation of the NPT safeguards agreements. In the same month North Korea withdrew from the IAEA (though not from the NPT); however, it allowed IAEA inspectors to conduct safeguards activities at its Yongbyon nuclear site. In October the Governments of North Korea and the USA concluded an agreement whereby the former agreed to halt construction of two new nuclear reactors, on condition that it received international aid for the construction of two 'light water' reactors (which could not produce materials for the manufacture of nuclear weapons). North Korea also agreed to allow IAEA inspections of all its nuclear sites, but only after the installation of one of the light water reactors had been completed (entailing a significant time lapse). From 1995 the IAEA pursued technical discussions with the North Korean authorities as part of the Agency's efforts to achieve the full compliance with the IAEA safeguards agreement; however, little overall progress was achieved, owing to the obstruction of inspectors by the authorities in that country, including their refusal to provide samples for analysis. In accordance with a decision of the General Conference in September 2001, IAEA inspectors subsequently resumed a continuous presence in North Korea. The authorities in that country permitted low-level inspections of the Yongbyon site by an IAEA technical team in January and May 2002. However, in December, following repeated requests by the IAEA that North Korea verify the accuracy of reports that it was implementing an undeclared uranium enrichment programme, the authorities disabled IAEA safeguards surveillance equipment placed at three facilities in Yongbyon and took measures to restart reprocessing capabilities at the site, requesting the immediate withdrawal of the Agency's inspectors. In early January 2003 the IAEA Board of Governors adopted a resolution deploring North Korea's non-co-operation and urging its immediate and full compliance with the Agency. Shortly afterwards, however, North Korea announced its withdrawal from the NPT, while stating that it would limit its nuclear activities to peaceful purposes. In February the IAEA found North Korea to be in further non-compliance with its safeguards agreement, and condemned the reported successful reactivation of the Yongbyon reactor. In August a series of six-party talks on the situation was launched, involving North Korea, China, Japan, the Republic of Korea (South Korea), Russia and the USA, under the auspices of the Chinese Government. In September 2004 the General Conference adopted a resolution that urged North Korea to dismantle promptly and completely any nuclear weapons programme and to recognize the verification role of the Agency, while strongly encouraging the ongoing diplomatic efforts to achieve a peaceful outcome. In February 2005 North Korea suspended its participation in the six-party talks, and asserted that it had developed nuclear weapons as a measure of self-defence. The talks resumed during July–September, when the six parties signed a joint statement, in which North Korea determined to resume its adherence to the NPT and Agency safeguards, and consequently to halt its development of nuclear weapons; the USA and South Korea affirmed that no US nuclear weapons were deployed on the Korean Peninsula; the five other parties recognized North Korea's right to use nuclear energy for peaceful purposes, and agreed to consider at a later date the provision of a light water reactor to that country; and all parties undertook to promote co-operation in security and economic affairs. A timetable for future progress was to be established at the next phase of the six-party talks, the first session of which convened briefly in early November; North Korea, however, subsequently announced that it would only resume the talks pending the release by the USA of recently-frozen financial assets. In July 2006 the UN Security Council condemned a recent ballistic missile test by North Korea, noting the potential of such missiles to be used for delivering nuclear, chemical or biological payloads, and urged that country to return immediately to the six-party talks without precondition and work towards the implementation of the September 2005 joint statement. In early 2006 October the IAEA Director-General expressed serious concern in response to an announcement by North Korea that it had conducted a nuclear test. In mid-October the Security Council adopted Resolution 1718, demanding that North Korea suspend all activities related to its ballistic missile programme, abandon all nuclear weapons and existing nuclear programmes, abandon all other existing weapons of mass destruction and ballistic missile programmes in a complete, verifiable and irreversible manner, and return to the six-party talks. The Council also imposed sanctions against North Korea.

The six-party talks were resumed in February 2007, and resulted in an ad hoc agreement by all the participants that North Korea would shut down and seal—for the purpose of eventual abandonment—the Yongbyon facility, and would invite back IAEA personnel to conduct all necessary monitoring and verifications; that North Korea would discuss with the other parties a list of all its nuclear programmes; that it would would enter into negotiations with the USA aimed at resolving pending bilateral issues and moving toward full diplomatic relations; that the USA would initiate the process of removing the designation of North Korea as a state-sponsor of terrorism; that North Korea and Japan would start negotiations aimed at normalizing their relations; and that the parties would agree to co-operate in security and economic affairs (as detailed under the September 2005 joint statement). In the latter regard, the parties agreed to the provision of emergency energy assistance to North Korea. In July 2007 an IAEA team visited the country and verified the shutdown of the Yongbyon facility. Upon the resumption of the six-party talks in late September, the participants adopted an agreement wherein North Korea resolved to disable permanently its nuclear facilities.

In mid-April 2009 a long-range rocket test conducted by North Korea, in violation of UN Security Council Resolution 1718 (see above), was unanimously condemned by the Council. North Korea responded by announcing its withdrawal from the six-party talks; withdrawing from the ad hoc agreement concerning the Yongbyon facility reached in February 2007; stating its intention to restart the Yongbyon facility; and ceasing, with immediate effect, all co-operation with the IAEA. Accordingly, IAEA inspectors removed all seals and surveillance equipment from the Yongbyon complex and departed the country. A further nuclear test conducted by North Korea in late May 2009 was deplored by the Security Council, which strengthened the sanctions regime against that country, in June, and demanded that it rejoin the NPT. Reporting to the Board of Governors in June and September the IAEA Director-General urged all concerned parties to continue to work through diplomatic channels for a comprehensive solution that would bring North Korea back to the NPT and address that country's security concerns and humanitarian, economic and political requirements. In September 2011 the 55th IAEA Conference expressed concern at reports of the construction of a new uranium enrichment facility and light water reactor in North Korea. At the end of October discussions were held between North Korean and US government representatives concerning restarting the suspended six-party talks. It was announced at the end of February 2012 that North Korea, under new leadership since December 2011, had agreed to suspend uranium enrichment and nuclear testing, and to permit the return of IAEA inspectors, in return for significant provision of food aid from the USA. In April, however, the USA suspended the agreement following a failed long-range missile launch, which North Korea declared to be an attempt to send a satellite into orbit. The UN Security Council condemned the launch as a violation of UN resolutions.

In September 2003 the IAEA adopted a resolution demanding that the Iranian Government sign, ratify and fully implement an additional protocol to its safeguards agreement promptly and unconditionally. The Agency also urged Iran to suspend its uranium enrichment and reprocessing activities, pending satisfactory application of the provisions of the additional protocol. Iran issued a declaration of its nuclear activities in October, and, in December, signed an additional protocol and agreed to suspend uranium enrichment processing. The Agency dispatched inspectors to Iran from October to conduct an intensive verification process. In April 2004 the IAEA Director-General visited Iran and concluded an agreement on a joint action plan to address the outstanding issues of the verification process. Iran provided an initial declaration under the (as yet unratified) additional protocol in May. In June, however, the Director-General expressed his continued concern at the extent of Iranian co-operation with IAEA inspectors. In September the Board of Governors adopted a resolution in which it strongly regretted continuing enrichment-related and reprocessing activities by Iran and requested their immediate suspension. The Director-General announced in late November that the suspension had been verified. In August 2005 the Agency adopted a resolution condemning Iran for resuming uranium conversion. In the following month a further resolution was adopted by the Board of Governors, in support of a motion by the European Union, citing Iran's non-compliance with the NPT and demanding that Iran accelerate its co-operation with the Agency regarding the outstanding issues. In February 2006 the Board of Governors adopted a resolution that recalled repeated failures by Iran to comply with its obligations under its NPT safeguards agreement, expressed serious concern at the nature of Iran's nuclear programme, and urged that, with a view to building confidence in the exclusively peaceful nature of the programme, Iran should suspend fully all activities related to uranium enrichment (reportedly resumed in January) and reprocessing; ratify and fully implement the additional protocol agreed in 2003; and implement transparency measures extending beyond its formal arrangements with the Agency. The resolution requested the IAEA Director-General to report the steps required of Iran to the UN Security Council and to inform the Security Council of all related IAEA documents and resolutions. In response, the Iranian authorities declared that they would suspend all legally non-binding measures imposed by the IAEA, including containment and surveillance measures provided for under the additional protocol, and that consequently all IAEA seals and cameras should be removed from Iranian sites by mid-February 2006. At the end of July the UN Security Council, having reviewed the relevant information provided by the IAEA Director-General, issued Resolution 1696, in which it demanded that Iran suspend all enrichment-related and reprocessing activities, including research and development, within a period of one month, and stipulated that non-compliance might result in the imposition on Iran of economic and diplomatic sanctions. The resolution requested that the IAEA Director-General submit to the Council at the end of August a report on Iran's response. The report, which was made public in mid-September, found that Iran had not suspended its enrichment-related activities and was still not in compliance with the provisions of the additional protocol. In December the Security Council imposed sanctions against Iran, and in March 2007 the Council imposed a ban on the export of arms from that country.

In June 2007 the IAEA Director-General and the Iranian authorities agreed to develop within 60 days a plan on the modalities for resolving outstanding safeguards implementation issues; accordingly, in August, a workplan on this area (also detailing procedures and timelines) was finalized. At that time the IAEA declared that previous Agency concerns about plutonium reprocessing activities in Iran were now resolved, as its findings had verified earlier statements made by the Iranian authorities. At the end of that month the IAEA Director-General reported that Iran had not yet suspended its uranium enrichment activities. The IAEA Director-General visited Iran in January 2008 to discuss with the Iranian administration means of accelerating the implementation of safeguards and confidence-building measures. It was agreed that remaining verification issues that had been specified in the August 2007 workplan should be resolved by mid-February 2008. In February 2008 the IAEA Board of Governors reported that Iran was still pursuing its uranium enrichment activities, and that the Iranian Government needed to continue to build confidence about the scope and purported peaceful nature of its nuclear programme. Consequently, in the following month, the UN Security Council adopted a new resolution on Iran in which it professed concern for the proliferation risk presented by the Iranian nuclear programme and authorized inspections of any cargo to and from Iran suspected of transporting prohibited equipment; strengthened the monitoring of Iranian financial institutions; and added names to the existing list of individuals and companies subject to asset and travel restrictions.

In May 2008 the IAEA Director-General, at the request of the UN Security Council, circulated a report to both the Security Council and the IAEA Board of Governors on the *Implementation of the NPT Safeguards Agreement and Relevant Provisions of Security Council Resolutions 1737 (2006), 1747 (2007), and 1803 (2008) in the Islamic Republic of Iran*, which concluded that there remained several areas of serious concern, including an ongoing 'green salt' project; high explosives testing; a missile re-entry vehicle project; some procurement activities of military-related institutions; outstanding substantive explanations regarding information with a possible military dimension; and Iran's continuing enrichment-related activities. In September the UN Security Council adopted a new resolution that reiterated demands that Iran cease enriching uranium. Reporting on the situation in February 2009, the IAEA Director-General stated that Iran continued to enrich uranium. Iran was urged once again to implement its additional protocol and other transparency measures.

In September 2009 the IAEA was informed by Iran that a second uranium enrichment facility was under construction in its territory; the Iranian authorities stated that the facility was to be used for peaceful purposes. The IAEA determined to send safeguards inspectors to examine the plant, located at an underground site near Qom, southwest of Tehran. In November the IAEA Board of Governors adopted a resolution urging Iran to suspend immediately construction at Qom; to engage with the IAEA on resolving all outstanding issues concerning its nuclear programme; to comply fully and without qualification with its safeguards obligations, specifically to provide requested clarifications regarding the purpose of the Qom enrichment plant and the chronology of its design and construction; and to confirm that no other undeclared facilities were planned or under construction. A report by the IAEA Secretary-General issued in February 2010 stated that, while the IAEA continued to verify the non-diversion of declared nuclear material in Iran, the Iranian authorities had not provided the necessary degree of co-operation to enable the Agency to confirm that all nuclear material in Iran was not being diverted for military purposes. In June the UN Security Council adopted Resolution 1929 strengthening the UN sanction regime against Iran. Resolution 1929 also established a panel of experts to assist with monitoring and enforcing the implementation of the Iran sanctions. In November 2011 the IAEA Board of Governors adopted a resolution expressing 'deep and increasing concern' over the unresolved issues regarding the Iranian nuclear programme and calling upon Iran to engage seriously and without preconditions in discussions aimed at restoring international confidence in the exclusively peaceful nature of its nuclear activities. With a view to intensifying dialogue, senior IAEA experts visited Iran in late January–February 2012, and again in late February. On both occasions the IAEA team requested, but was denied, access to the military complex at Parchin, southeast of Tehran, which was suspected to be the site of an explosives containment vessel; clarification of unresolved issues relating to possible military dimensions of Iran's nuclear programme was not achieved. An IAEA report on the Iran situation, issued in late February, found that uranium enrichment had increased threefold since late 2011, in particular at the underground site near Qom; it was maintained by the Iranian authorities, however, that this material was required for a medical research reactor. The report also claimed that the installation of centrifuges at the Natanz uranium enrichment plant, in central Iran, had accelerated.

The IAEA Conference adopted a resolution in September 2009 that expressed concern about Israel's nuclear capabilities and called upon Israel to accede to the NPT and to place all its nuclear facilities under comprehensive IAEA safeguards.

In June 2011 the IAEA Board of Governors adopted a resolution noting with serious concern the conclusion of the Agency that a building destroyed at Dair Alzour, Syria, in September 2007, was very likely an undeclared nuclear reactor; the resolution requested Syria to remedy urgently non-compliance with its Safeguards Agreement and called upon that country promptly to bring into force and implement an Additional Protocol to its Safeguards Agreement. IAEA officials visited Syria in October 2011 to pursue the matter, but were not granted sufficient access to locations believed to be functionally related to the Dair Alzour site. In November the IAEA Director-General demanded that Syria co-operate fully with the Agency in connection with unresolved issues relating to Dair Alzour and other locations.

In November 2011 the IAEA convened, in Vienna, a Forum on the Experience of Possible Relevance to the Creation of a Nuclear-Weapon-Free-Zone in the Middle East.

NUCLEAR FUEL CYCLE

The Agency promotes the exchange of information between member states on technical, safety, environmental, and economic aspects of nuclear fuel cycle technology, including uranium prospecting and the treatment and disposal of radioactive waste; it provides assistance to member states in the planning, implementation and operation of nuclear fuel cycle facilities and assists in the development of advanced nuclear fuel cycle technology. The Agency operates a number of databases and a simulation system related to the nuclear fuel cycle through its Integrated Nuclear Fuel Cycle Information System (iNFCIS). Every two years, in collaboration with OECD, the Agency prepares estimates of world uranium resources, demand and production.

Finance

The Agency is financed by regular and voluntary contributions from member states. Expenditure approved under the regular budget for 2012 amounted to some €333m., while the target for voluntary contributions to finance the IAEA technical co-operation programme in that year was €88m.

Publications

Annual Report.

Atoms for Peace.

Fundamental Safety Principles.

IAEA Bulletin (quarterly).

IAEA Newsbriefs (every 2 months).

IAEA Safety Glossary Terminology Used in Nuclear Safety and Radiation Protection.

IAEA Yearbook.

INIS Atomindex (bibliography, 2 a month).

INIS Reference Series.

INSAG Series.

Legal Series.

Meetings on Atomic Energy (quarterly).

The Nuclear Fuel Cycle Information System: A Directory of Nuclear Fuel Cycle Facilities.

Nuclear Fusion (monthly).

Nuclear Safety Review (annually).

Nuclear Technology Review (annually).

Panel Proceedings Series.

Publications Catalogue (annually).

Safety Series.

Technical Directories.

Technical Reports Series.

International Bank for Reconstruction and Development—IBRD (World Bank)

Address: 1818 H St, NW, Washington, DC 20433, USA.

Telephone: (202) 473-1000; **fax:** (202) 477-6391; **e-mail:** pic@worldbank.org; **internet:** www.worldbank.org.

The IBRD was established in December 1945. Initially it was concerned with post-war reconstruction in Europe; since then its aim has been to assist the economic development of member nations by making loans where private capital is not available on reasonable terms to finance productive investments. Loans are made either directly to governments, or to private enterprises with the guarantee of their governments. The World Bank, as it is commonly known, comprises the IBRD and the International Development Association (IDA). The affiliated group of institutions, comprising the IBRD, IDA, the International Finance Corporation (IFC), the Multilateral Investment Guarantee Agency (MIGA) and the International Centre for Settlement of Investment Disputes (ICSID, see below), is referred to as the World Bank Group.

MEMBERS

There are 188 members. Only members of the International Monetary Fund (IMF) may be considered for membership in the World Bank. Subscriptions to the capital stock of the Bank are based on each member's quota in the IMF, which is designed to reflect the country's relative economic strength. Voting rights are related to shareholdings.

Organization

(April 2012)

Officers and staff of the IBRD serve concurrently as officers and staff in IDA. The World Bank has offices in New York, Brussels, Paris (for Europe), Frankfurt, London, Geneva and Tokyo, as well as in more than 100 countries of operation. Country Directors are located in some 30 country offices.

BOARD OF GOVERNORS

The Board of Governors consists of one Governor appointed by each member nation. Typically, a Governor is the country's finance minister, central bank governor, or a minister or an official of comparable rank. The Board normally meets once a year.

EXECUTIVE DIRECTORS

With the exception of certain powers specifically reserved to them by the Articles of Agreement, the Governors of the Bank have delegated their powers for the conduct of the general operations of the World Bank to a Board of Executive Directors which performs its duties on a full-time basis at the Bank's headquarters. There are 25 Executive Directors (see table below); each Director selects an Alternate. Five Directors are appointed by the five members having the largest number of shares of capital stock, and the rest are elected by the Governors representing the other members. The President of the Bank is Chairman of the Board.

The Executive Directors fulfil dual responsibilities. First, they represent the interests of their country or groups of countries. Second, they exercise their authority as delegated by the Governors in overseeing the policies of the Bank and evaluating completed projects. Since the Bank operates on the basis of consensus (formal votes are rare), this dual role involves frequent communication and consultations with governments so as to reflect accurately their views in Board discussions.

The Directors consider and decide on Bank policy and on all loan and credit proposals. They are also responsible for presentation to the Board of Governors at its Annual Meetings of an audit of accounts, an administrative budget, the *Annual Report* on the operations and policies of the World Bank, and any other matter that, in their judgement, requires submission to the Board of Governors. Matters may be submitted to the Governors at the Annual Meetings or at any time between Annual Meetings.

PRINCIPAL OFFICERS

The principal officers of the Bank are the President of the Bank, three Managing Directors, two Senior Vice-Presidents and 25 Vice-Presidents.

President and Chairman of Executive Directors: ROBERT B. ZOELLICK (USA) (until 30 June 2012), Dr JIM YONG KIM (USA) (from 1 July 2012).

Managing Directors: Sri MULYANI INDRAWATI (Indonesia), MAHMOUD MOHIELDIN (Egypt), CAROLINE ANSTEY (United Kingdom).

Activities

The World Bank's primary objectives are the achievement of sustainable economic growth and the reduction of poverty in developing countries. In the context of stimulating economic growth the Bank promotes both private sector development and human resource development and has attempted to respond to the growing demands by developing countries for assistance in these areas. In September 2001 the Bank announced that it was to become a full partner in implementing the UN Millennium Development Goals (MDGs), and was to make them central to its development agenda. The objectives, which were approved by governments attending a special session of the UN General Assembly in September 2000, represented a new international consensus to achieve determined poverty reduction targets. The Bank was closely involved in preparations for the International Conference on Financing for Development, which was held in Monterrey, Mexico, in March 2002. The meeting adopted the Monterrey Consensus, which outlined measures to support national development efforts and to achieve the MDGs. During 2002/03 the Bank, with the IMF, undertook to develop a monitoring framework to review progress in the MDG agenda. The first *Global Monitoring Report* was issued by the Bank and the IMF in April 2004.

In October 2007 the Bank's President defined the following six strategic themes as priorities for Bank development activities: the poorest countries; fragile and post-conflict states; middle-income countries; global public goods; the Arab world; and knowledge and learning. In May 2008 the Bank established a Global Food Crisis Response Programme (GFRP, see below) to assist developing countries affected by the escalating cost of food production. In December the Bank resolved to establish a new facility to accelerate the provision of funds, through IDA, for developing countries affected by the global decline in economic and financial market conditions. The Bank participated in the meeting of heads of state and government of the Group of 20 (G20) leading economies, that was held in Washington, DC, USA, in November 2008 to address the global economic situation, and pursued close collaboration with other multinational organizations, in particular the IMF and OECD, to analyse the impact of the ongoing economic instability. In January 2009 the Bank's President proposed the establishment of a Vulnerability Fund to support essential investment projects in developing countries, to be financed by developed economies appropriating 0.7% of their economic stimulus measures to the Fund. During early 2009 the Bank elaborated its operational response to the global economic crisis. Three operational platforms were devised to address the areas identified as priority themes, i.e. protecting the most vulnerable against the effects of the crisis; maintaining long-term infrastructure investment programmes; and sustaining the potential for private sector-led economic growth and employment creation. Consequently, a new Vulnerability Financing Facility was established, incorporating the GFRP and a new Rapid Social Response Programme, to extend immediate assistance to the poorest groups in affected low- and middle-income countries. Infrastructure investment was to be supported through a new Infrastructure Recovery and Assets Platform, which was mandated to release funds to secure existing infrastructure projects and to finance new initiatives in support of longer-term economic development. Private sector support for infrastructure projects, bank recapitalization, microfinance, and trade financing was to be led by IFC.

In February 2009 the Bank, with the European Bank for Reconstruction and Development (EBRD) and the European Investment Bank, inaugurated a Joint International Financial Institutions (IFI) Action Plan to support the banking systems in central and eastern Europe and to finance lending to businesses in the region affected by the global economic crisis. Under the Plan the Banks initially committed €24,500m. over a two-year period. The Plan also identified the need to conduct joint assessments of the financing needs of the largest bank groups and to accelerate the delivery of co-ordinated assistance. The Action Plan concluded in March 2011, by which time more than €33,000m. had been provided under the initiative, including €9,600m. from the World Bank Group. A separate plan, the European Banking Co-ordination Initiative (the 'Vienna Initiative') was established in early 2009 in order to support banking operations in emerging European economies. The World Bank facilitated the establishment, in 2010, of two committees within the framework of the Initiative concerned with local currency finance development and with enhancing absorption of EU structural funds in emerging Europe. In 2011 two new committees were established (and co-chaired by the Bank) to consider non-performing loans in the region and the challenges of implementing the Basel III capital framework programme.

The Bank's efforts to reduce poverty include the compilation of country-specific assessments and the formulation of country assistance strategies (CASs) to review and guide the Bank's country programmes. In 1998/99 the Bank's Executive Directors endorsed a Comprehensive Development Framework (CDF) to effect a new approach to development assistance based on partnerships and country responsibility, with an emphasis on the interdependence of the social, structural, human, governmental, economic and environmental elements of development. The CDF, which aimed to enhance the overall effectiveness of development assistance, was formulated after a series of consultative meetings organized by the Bank and attended by representatives of governments, donor agencies, financial institutions, non-governmental organizations, the private sector and academics. In December 1999 the Bank introduced a new approach to implement the principles of the CDF, as part of its strategy to enhance the debt relief scheme for heavily indebted poor countries (HIPCs, see below). Applicant countries were requested to formulate, in consultation with external partners and other stakeholders, a results-oriented national strategy to reduce poverty, to be presented in the form of a Poverty Reduction Strategy Paper (PRSP). In cases where there might be some delay in issuing a full PRSP, it was permissible for a country to submit a less detailed 'interim' PRSP (I-PRSP) in order to secure the preliminary qualification for debt relief. The approach also requires the publication of annual progress reports. In 2001 the Bank introduced a new Poverty Reduction Support Credit to help low-income countries to implement the policy and institutional reforms outlined in their PRSP. Increasingly, PRSPs have been considered by the international community to be the appropriate country-level framework to assess progress towards achieving the MDGs.

FINANCIAL OPERATIONS

IBRD capital is derived from members' subscriptions to capital shares, the calculation of which is based on their quotas in the IMF. At 30 June 2011 the total subscribed capital of the IBRD was US $193,732m., of which the paid-in portion was $11,720m. (6.1%); the remainder is subject to call if required. Most of the IBRD's lendable funds come from its borrowing, on commercial terms, in world capital markets, and also from its retained earnings and the flow of repayments on its loans. IBRD loans carry a variable interest rate, rather than a rate fixed at the time of borrowing.

IBRD loans usually have a 'grace period' of five years and are repayable over 15 years or fewer. Loans are made to governments, or must be guaranteed by the government concerned, and are normally made for projects likely to offer a commercially viable rate of return. In 1980 the World Bank introduced structural adjustment lending, which (instead of financing specific projects) supports programmes and changes necessary to modify the structure of an economy so that it can restore or maintain its growth and viability in its balance of payments over the medium term.

The IBRD and IDA together made 362 new lending and investment commitments totalling US $43,005.6m. during the year ending 30 June 2011, compared with 354 (amounting to $58,747.1m.) in the previous year. During 2010/11 the IBRD alone approved commitments totalling $26,737.2m. (compared with $44,197.4m. in the previous year), of which $9,169.4m. (34%) was allocated to Latin America and the Caribbean, $6,369.6m. (24%) to projects in East Asia and the Pacific, and $5,470.0 (20%) to Europe and Central Asia. Disbursements by the IBRD in the year ending 30 June 2011 amounted to $21,879m. (For details of IDA operations, see separate chapter on IDA.)

IBRD operations are supported by medium- and long-term borrowings in international capital markets. During the year ending 30 June 2011 the IBRD's net income amounted to US $930m.

In September 1996 the World Bank/IMF Development Committee endorsed a joint initiative to assist HIPCs to reduce their debt burden to a sustainable level, in order to make more resources available for poverty reduction and economic growth. A new Trust Fund was established by the World Bank in November to finance the initiative. The Fund, consisting of an initial allocation of US $500m. from the IBRD surplus and other contributions from multilateral creditors, was to be administered by IDA. In early 1999 the World Bank and IMF initiated a comprehensive review of the HIPC initiative. By April meetings of the Group of Seven industrialized nations (G7) and of the governing bodies of the Bank and IMF indicated a consensus that the scheme needed to be amended and strengthened, in order to allow more countries to benefit from the initiative, to accelerate the process by which a country may qualify for assistance, and to enhance the effectiveness of debt relief. In June the G7 and Russia (known as the G8), meeting in Cologne, Germany, agreed to increase contributions to the HIPC Trust Fund and to cancel substantial amounts of outstanding debt, and proposed more flexible terms for eligibility. In September the Bank and IMF reached an agreement on an enhanced HIPC scheme. During the initial phase of the process to ensure suitability for debt relief, each applicant country should formulate a PRSP, and should demonstrate prudent financial management in the implementation of the strategy for at least one year, with support from the IMF and IDA. At the pivotal 'decision point' of the process, having thus developed and successfully applied the poverty reduction strategy, applicant countries still deemed to have an unsustainable level of debt were to qualify for interim debt relief from the IMF and IDA, as well as relief on highly concessional terms from other official bilateral creditors and multilateral institutions. During the ensuing 'interim period' countries were required successfully to implement further economic and social development reforms, as a final demonstration of suitability for securing full debt relief at the 'completion point' of the scheme. Data produced at the decision point was to form the base for calculating the final debt relief (in contrast to the original initiative, which based its calculations on projections of a country's debt stock at the completion point). In the majority of cases a sustainable level of debt was targeted at 150% of the net present value (NPV) of the debt in relation to total annual exports (compared with 200%–250% under the original initiative). Other countries with a lower debt-to-export ratio were to be eligible for assistance under the scheme, providing that their export earnings were at least 30% of GDP (lowered from 40% under the original initiative) and government revenue at least 15% of GDP (reduced from 20%). In March 2005 the Bank and the IMF implemented a new Debt Sustainability Framework in Low-income Countries to provide guidance on lending to low-income countries and to improve monitoring and prevention of the accumulation of unsustainable debt. In June finance ministers of the G8 proposed providing additional resources to achieve the full cancellation of debts owed by eligible HIPCs to assist those countries to meet their MDG targets. Countries that had reached their completion point were to qualify for immediate assistance. In July the heads of state and government of G8 countries requested that the Bank ensure the effective delivery of the additional funds and provide a framework for performance measurement. In September the Bank's Development Committee and the International Monetary and Financial Committee of the IMF endorsed the proposal, subsequently referred to as the Multilateral Debt Relief Initiative (MDRI). The Committees agreed to protect the financial capability of IDA, as one of the institutions (with the IMF and the African Development Bank) which was to meet the additional cancellation commitments, and to develop a monitoring programme. At July 2011 assistance committed under the HIPC initiative amounted to an estimated $76,000m. (in 2010 NPV terms), of which the World Bank Group had committed $14,900m. At that time the estimated costs of the MDRI amounted to $52,500m. in nominal value terms, of which the Bank's share amounted to an estimated $35,300m. By the end of 2011 32 countries (Afghanistan, Benin, Bolivia, Burkina Faso, Burundi, Cameroon, Central African Republic, Democratic Republic of the Congo, Republic of Congo, Ethiopia, The Gambia, Ghana, Guinea-Bissau, Guyana, Haiti, Honduras, Liberia, Madagascar, Malawi, Mali, Mauritania, Mozambique, Nicaragua, Niger, Rwanda, São Tomé and Príncipe, Senegal, Sierra Leone, Tanzania, Togo, Uganda and Zambia) had reached completion point under the enhanced HIPC initiative, while four countries had reached decision point. A further four countries were deemed eligible, or potentially eligible, for the initiative.

During 2000/01 the World Bank strengthened its efforts to counter the problem of HIV and AIDS in developing countries. In November 2001 the Bank appointed its first Global HIV/AIDS Adviser. In September 2000 a new Multi-Country HIV/AIDS Programme for Africa (MAP) was launched, initially with $500m., in collaboration with UNAIDS and other major donor agencies and non-governmental organizations. In February 2002 the Bank approved an additional $500m. for a second phase of MAP. A MAP initiative for the Caribbean, with a budget of $155m., was launched in 2001. The Bank has undertaken research into the long-term effects of HIV/AIDS, and hosts the Global HIV/AIDS Monitoring and Evaluation Support Team of UNAIDS. In November 2004 the Bank launched an AIDS Media Center to improve access to information regarding HIV/AIDS, in particular to journalists in developing countries. It has also established a resource library to strengthen HIV/AIDS monitoring and evaluation systems. In July 2009 the Bank published a report, with UNAIDS, concerned with the impact of the global economic crisis on HIV prevention and treatment programmes. A new regional report on HIV/AIDS in the Middle East and North Africa, entitled 'Time for Strategic Action', was published in June 2010.

In March 2007 the Board of Executive Directors approved an action plan to develop further its Clean Energy for Development Investment Framework, which had been formulated in response to a request by the G8 heads of state, meeting in Gleneagles, United Kingdom, in July 2005. The action plan focused on efforts to improve access to clean energy, in particular in sub-Saharan Africa; to accelerate the transition to low carbon-emission development; and to support adaptation to climate change. In October 2008 the Bank

Group endorsed a new Strategic Framework on Development and Climate Change, which aimed to guide the Bank in supporting the efforts of developing countries to achieving growth and reducing poverty, while recognizing the operational challenges of climate change. In June 2010 the Bank appointed a Special Envoy to lead the Bank's representation in international discussions on climate change. In February 2012 the Bank supported the establishment of a Global Partnership for Oceans.

In February 2012 the Bank opened a new Global Centre on Conflict, Security and Development in Nairobi, Kenya, in order to enhance its support for the poorest people living in some 30 countries considered 'fragile' or affected by conflict. The Centre was to help co-ordinate development efforts in those countries, to improve the efficiency of financial support, and to serve as a focus for experts and practitioners to share knowledge and experience.

TECHNICAL ASSISTANCE AND ADVISORY SERVICES

In addition to providing financial services, the Bank also undertakes analytical and advisory services, and supports learning and capacity-building, in particular through the World Bank Institute, the Staff Exchange Programme and knowledge-sharing initiatives. The Bank has supported efforts, such as the Global Development Gateway, to disseminate information on development issues and programmes, and, since 1988, has organized the Annual Bank Conference on Development Economics (ABCDE) to provide a forum for the exchange and discussion of development-related ideas and research. In September 1995 the Bank initiated the Information for Development Programme (InfoDev) with the aim of fostering partnerships between governments, multilateral institutions and private-sector experts in order to promote reform and investment in developing countries through improved access to information technology.

The provision of technical assistance to member countries has become a major component of World Bank activities. The economic and sector work (ESW) undertaken by the Bank is the vehicle for considerable technical assistance and often forms the basis of CASs and other strategic or advisory reports. In addition, project loans and credits may include funds earmarked specifically for feasibility studies, resource surveys, management or planning advice, and training. The World Bank Institute has become one of the most important of the Bank's activities in technical assistance. It provides training in national economic management and project analysis for government officials at the middle and upper levels of responsibility. It also runs overseas courses aiming to build up local training capability, and administers a graduate scholarship programme. Technical assistance (usually reimbursable) is also extended to countries that do not need Bank financial support, e.g. for training and transfer of technology. The Bank encourages the use of local consultants to assist with projects and stimulate institutional capability.

The Project Preparation Facility (PPF) was established in 1975 to provide cash advances to prepare projects that may be financed by the Bank. In 1992 the Bank established an Institutional Development Fund (IDF), which became operational on 1 July; the purpose of the Fund was to provide rapid, small-scale financial assistance, to a maximum value of US $500,000, for capacity-building proposals. In 2002 the IDF was reoriented to focus on good governance, in particular financial accountability and system reforms.

ECONOMIC RESEARCH AND STUDIES

In the 1990s the World Bank's research, conducted by its own research staff, was increasingly concerned with providing information to reinforce the Bank's expanding advisory role to developing countries and to improve policy in the Bank's borrowing countries. The principal areas of current research focus on issues such as maintaining sustainable growth while protecting the environment and the poorest sectors of society, encouraging the development of the private sector, and reducing and decentralizing government activities.

Consultative Group on International Agricultural Research (CGIAR): founded in 1971 under the sponsorship of the World Bank (which provides its secretariat), FAO and UNDP. IFAD is also a co-sponsor. The Group was established to raise funds for international agricultural research work for improving crops and animal production in developing countries, and works in partnership with governments, international and regional organizations, private businesses and foundations to support 15 research centres; during 2010 CGIAR implemented a major reorganization: a CGIAR Fund, of which the Bank was nominated as trustee, was established as a multi-trust fund to administer donations to the various programmes, while a Consortium, governed by a 10-member board, was established to unite the strategic and funding supervision of the research centres; a new Independent Science Partnership Council was also established to promote the quality, relevance and impact of science in the CGIAR and to advise on strategic scientific issues; Chair. CGIAR Fund Council INGER ANDERSEN (Denmark); Chair. CGIAR Consortium Bd CARLOS PÉREZ DEL CASTILLO (Uruguay).

CO-OPERATION WITH OTHER ORGANIZATIONS

The World Bank co-operates with other international partners with the aim of improving the impact of development efforts. It collaborates with the IMF in implementing the HIPC scheme and the two agencies work closely to achieve a common approach to development initiatives. The Bank has established strong working relationships with many other UN bodies, in particular through a mutual commitment to poverty reduction objectives. In May 2000 the Bank signed a joint statement of co-operation with OECD. The Bank holds regular consultations with other multilateral development banks and with the European Union with respect to development issues. The Bank-NGO Committee provides an annual forum for discussion with non-governmental organizations (NGOs). Strengthening co-operation with external partners was a fundamental element of the Comprehensive Development Framework, which was adopted in 1998/99 (see above). In 2001/02 a Partnership Approval and Tracking System was implemented to provide information on the Bank's regional and global partnerships. In June 2007 the World Bank and the UN Office on Drugs and Crime launched a joint Stolen Asset Recovery (StAR) initiative, as part of the Bank's new Governance and Anti-Corruption (GAC) strategy. In April 2009 the G20 recommended that StAR review and propose mechanisms to strengthen international co-operation relating to asset recovery. The first global forum on stolen asset recovery and development was convened by StAR in June 2010.

In 1997 the Bank, in partnership with the IMF, UNCTAD, UNDP, the World Trade Organization (WTO) and the International Trade Commission, established an Integrated Framework for Trade-related Assistance to Least Developed Countries, at the request of the WTO, to assist those countries to integrate into the global trading system and improve basic trading capabilities. Also in 1997 a Partnerships Group was established to strengthen the Bank's work with development institutions, representatives of civil society and the private sector. The Group established a new Development Grant Facility, which became operational in October, to support partnership initiatives and to co-ordinate all of the Bank's grant-making activities. The Bank establishes and administers trust funds, open to contributions from member countries and multilateral organizations, NGOs, and private sector institutions, in order to support development partnerships. By 30 June 2011 the Bank had a portfolio of 1,038 active trust funds, with assets of some US $29,100m.

In June 1995 the World Bank joined other international donors (including regional development banks, other UN bodies, Canada, France, the Netherlands and the USA) in establishing a Consultative Group to Assist the Poorest (CGAP), which was to channel funds to the most needy through grass-roots agencies. An initial credit of approximately US $200m. was committed by the donors. The Bank manages the CGAP Secretariat, which is responsible for the administration of external funding and for the evaluation and approval of project financing. The CGAP provides technical assistance, training and strategic advice to microfinance institutions and other relevant bodies. As an implementing agency of the Global Environment Facility (GEF) the Bank assists countries to prepare and supervise GEF projects relating to biological diversity, climate change and other environmental protection measures. It is an example of a partnership in action which addresses a global agenda, complementing Bank country assistance activities. Other funds administered by the Bank include the Global Program to Eradicate Poliomyelitis, launched during the financial year 2002/03, the Least Developed Countries Fund for Climate Change, established in September 2002, an Education for All Fast-Track Initiative Catalytic Trust Fund, established in 2003/04, and a Carbon Finance Assistance Trust Fund, established in 2004/05. In 2006/07 the Bank established a Global Facility for Disaster Reduction and Recovery. In September 2007 the Bank's Executive Directors approved a Carbon Partnership Facility and a Forest Carbon Partnership Facility to support its climate change activities. In May 2008 the Bank inaugurated the Global Food Crisis Response Programme (GFRP) to provide financial support, with resources of some $1,200m., to help meet the immediate needs of countries affected by the escalating cost of food production and by food shortages. Grants and loans were to be allocated on the basis of rapid needs assessments, conducted by the Bank with FAO, WFP and IFAD. As part of the facility a Multi-Donor Trust Fund was established to facilitate co-ordination among donors and to leverage financial support for the rapid delivery of seeds and fertilizer to small-scale farmers. In April 2009 the Bank increased the resources available under the GFRP to $2,000m. By mid-2011 $1,500m. had been approved under the GFRP for initiatives in 40 countries, of which $1,155m. had been disbursed. In that month a new trust fund was established to support a Global Agriculture and Food Security Programme (GAFSP), with total donations amounting to $900m. from the Governments of Canada, Republic of Korea, Spain and the USA and the Bill and Melinda

Gates Foundation. The first funds under the GAFSP were issued in June, amounting to $224m. to finance projects to improve agricultural productivity in Bangladesh, Haiti, Rwanda, Sierra Leone and Togo. In early November 2011 the Bank's President urged the forthcoming summit meeting of the G20 to address issues relating to food shortages and food price volatility.

The Bank is a lead organization in providing reconstruction assistance following natural disasters or conflicts, usually in collaboration with other UN agencies or international organizations, and through special trust funds. In May 2011 the Bank co-hosted, with the Global Facility for Disaster Reduction and Recovery and the UN International Strategy for Disaster Reduction, the first World Reconstruction Conference, which concluded an agreement to develop a framework for international co-operation in post disaster recovery and reconstruction. In November 2001 the Bank worked with UNDP and the Asian Development Bank to assess the needs of Afghanistan following the removal of the Taliban authorities in that country. At an International Conference on Reconstruction Assistance to Afghanistan, held in Tokyo, Japan, in January 2002, the Bank's President proposed extending US $500m. in assistance over a 30-month period, and providing an immediate amount of $50m.–$70m. in grants. In May an Afghanistan Reconstruction Trust Fund was established to provide a co-ordinated financing mechanism to support the interim administration in that country. The Bank is the Administrator of the Trust, which is managed jointly by the Bank, the Asian Development Bank, the Islamic Development Bank and UNDP. By May 2010 contributions to the Trust Fund amounted to $4,361.2m., pledged by 30 countries, of which $3,715.4m. was paid-in. Disbursements under the Fund amounted to $3,112.0m. at that time. In May 2003 a Bank representative participated in an international advisory and monitoring board to assess reconstruction and development needs following international conflict in Iraq and removal of its governing regime. In October the Bank, with the UN Development Group, published a report identifying 14 priority areas for reconstruction, with funding requirements of $36,000m. over the period 2004–07, which was presented to an international donor conference held later in that month. The conference, held in Madrid, Spain, approved the establishment of an International Reconstruction Fund Facility for Iraq to channel international donations and to co-ordinate reconstruction activities. In January 2004 the Bank's Board of Executive Directors authorized the Bank to administer an integral part of the facility, the Iraq Trust Fund (ITF), to finance a programme of emergency projects and technical assistance. By January 2009 the ITF was financing 18 project grants, amounting to $481.6m. The Bank was a partner, with the Iraqi Government, the UN Secretariat, the IMF and other financial institutions, in the International Compact with Iraq, a five-year framework for co-operation that was launched in May 2007. At the end of 2004 the Bank responded immediately to assist countries affected by a massive earthquake and subsequent tsunami which devastated many coastal areas of some 14 countries in the Indian Ocean. Bank staff undertook assessments and other efforts to accelerate recovery planning, mobilize financial support and help to co-ordinate relief and recovery efforts. Some $672m. was allocated by the Bank, mainly in grants to be directed to Indonesia, Sri Lanka and the Maldives, for the first phase of reconstruction efforts. By June 2005 the Bank had committed more than $835m. to countries affected by the tsunami, in particular to repair damaged services, to assist the reconstruction of housing and to restore livelihoods. The Bank administers a Multi-Donor Trust Fund for Aceh and North Sumatra that was established by the Indonesian Government to manage some $500m. in pledged aid. By 30 September 2009 $685.2m. had been pledged for the Multi-Donor Trust Fund, of which some $399m. had been disbursed. In October 2005 the Bank, with the Asian Development Bank, undertook a preliminary damage and needs assessment following a massive earthquake in north-west Pakistan. The cost of the disaster was estimated at $5,200m., with initial reconstruction funding requirements of $3,500m. An international donors' conference was convened in November. In February 2007 the Bank approved a new framework policy to accelerate the response to a disaster or emergency situation in order to fund essential recovery and rehabilitation activities. In January 2010 the Bank issued $100m. in immediate emergency funding to support recovery efforts in Haiti following an earthquake which caused extensive damage and loss of life. By June the Bank had extended some $479m. in grants to support Haiti reconstruction and rehabilitation; at the end of May it cancelled the remaining $36m. outstanding debt owed by Haiti. The Bank acts as trustee of a multi-donor Haiti Reconstruction Fund, which was established in March at an international donors' conference.

The Bank has worked with FAO, WHO and the World Organisation of Animal Health (OIE) to develop strategies to monitor, contain and eradicate the spread of highly pathogenic avian influenza. In September 2005 the Bank organized a meeting of leading experts on the issue and in November it co-sponsored, with FAO, WHO and OIE, an international partners' conference, focusing on control of the disease and preparedness planning for any future related influenza pandemic in humans. In January 2006 the Bank's Board of Directors approved the establishment of a funding programme (the Global Program for Avian Influenza Control and Human Pandemic Preparedness and Response—GPAI), with resources of up to US $500m., to assist countries to combat the disease. Later in that month the Bank co-sponsored, with the European Commission and the People's Republic of China, an International Ministerial Pledging Conference on Avian and Human Pandemic Influenza (AHI), convened in Beijing. Participants pledged some $1,900m. to fund disease control and pandemic preparedness activities at global, regional and country levels. Commitments to the AHI facility amounted to $126m. at January 2009. In June the Bank approved an additional $500m. to expand the GPAI in order to fund emergency operations required to prevent and control outbreaks of the new swine influenza variant pandemic (H1N1).

EVALUATION

The Independent Evaluation Group is an independent unit within the World Bank. It conducts Country Assistance Evaluations to assess the development effectiveness of a Bank country programme, and studies and publishes the results of projects after a loan has been fully disbursed, so as to identify problems and possible improvements in future activities. In addition, the department reviews the Bank's global programmes and produces the *Annual Review of Development Effectiveness*. In 1996 a Quality Assurance Group was established to monitor the effectiveness of the Bank's operations and performance. In March 2009 the Bank published an Action Plan on Aid Effectiveness, based on the Accra Agenda for Action that had been adopted in September 2008 during the Third High Level Forum on Aid Effectiveness, held in Ghana.

In September 1993 the Bank established an independent Inspection Panel, consistent with the Bank's objective of improving project implementation and accountability. The Panel, which became operational in September 1994, was to conduct independent investigations and report on complaints from local people concerning the design, appraisal and implementation of development projects supported by the Bank. By the end of 2011 the Panel had received 77 formal requests for inspection.

IBRD INSTITUTIONS

World Bank Institute (WBI): founded in March 1999 by merger of the Bank's Learning and Leadership Centre, previously responsible for internal staff training, and the Economic Development Institute (EDI), which had been established in 1955 to train government officials concerned with development programmes and policies. The new Institute aimed to emphasize the Bank's priority areas through the provision of training courses and seminars relating to poverty, crisis response, good governance and anti-corruption strategies. The Institute supports a Global Knowledge Partnership, which was established in 1997 to promote alliances between governments, companies, other agencies and organizations committed to applying information and communication technologies for development purposes. Under the EDI a World Links for Development programme was also initiated to connect schools in developing countries with partner establishments in industrialized nations via the internet. In 1999 the WBI expanded its programmes through distance learning, a Global Development Network, and use of new technologies. A new initiative, Global Development Learning Network (GDLN), aimed to expand access to information and learning opportunities through the internet, video conferences and organized exchanges. The WBI had also established 60 formal partnership arrangements with learning centres and public, private and non-governmental organizations to support joint capacity building programmes; many other informal partnerships were also in place. During 2009/10 new South-South Learning Middle-income country (MIC)–OECD Knowledge Exchange facilities were established. At 2012 the WBI was focusing its work on the following areas: fragile and conflict-affected states; governance; growth and competitiveness; climate change; health systems; public-private partnerships in infrastructure; and urban development; Vice-Pres. SANJAY PRADHAN (India); publs *Annual Report*, *Development Outreach* (quarterly), other books, working papers, case studies.

International Centre for Settlement of Investment Disputes (ICSID): founded in 1966 under the Convention of the Settlement of Investment Disputes between States and Nationals of Other States. The Convention was designed to encourage the growth of private foreign investment for economic development, by creating the possibility, always subject to the consent of both parties, for a Contracting State and a foreign investor who is a national of another Contracting State to settle any legal dispute that might arise out of such an investment by conciliation and/or arbitration before an impartial, international forum. The governing body of the Centre is its Administrative Council, composed of one representative of each Contracting State, all of whom have equal voting power. The President of the World Bank is (*ex officio*) the non-voting Chairman of the Administrative Council. At April 2012 381 cases had been registered with the Centre, of which 233 had been concluded and 148 were pending consideration. At that time 148 countries had signed and ratified the Convention to become ICSID Contracting States; Sec.-Gen. MEG KINNEAR (Canada).

Publications

Abstracts of Current Studies: The World Bank Research Program (annually).
African Development Indicators (annually).
Annual Report on Operations Evaluation.
Annual Report on Portfolio Performance.
Annual Review of Development Effectiveness.
Doing Business (annually).
Global Commodity Markets (quarterly).
Global Development Finance (annually).
Global Economic Prospects (annually).
ICSID Annual Report.
ICSID Review—Foreign Investment Law Journal (2 a year).
Joint BIS-IMF-OECD-World Bank Statistics on External Debt (quarterly).
News from ICSID (2 a year).
Poverty Reduction and the World Bank (annually).
Poverty Reduction Strategies Newsletter (quarterly).
Research News (quarterly).
Staff Working Papers.
The World Bank and the Environment (annually).
World Bank Annual Report.
World Bank Atlas (annually).
World Bank Economic Review (3 a year).
World Bank Research Observer.
World Development Indicators (annually).
World Development Report (annually).

Statistics

LENDING OPERATIONS, BY SECTOR
(projects approved, year ending 30 June; US $ million)

	2010	2011
Agriculture, fishing and forestry	2,618.2	2,128.8
Education	4,944.6	1,733.1
Energy and mining	9,925.1	5,807.4
Finance	9,136.5	897.5
Health and other social services	6,792.0	6,707.7
Industry and trade	1,251.3	2,167.9
Information and communication	146.3	640.3
Public administration, law and justice	10,828.1	9,673.5
Transportation	9,002.0	8,638.9
Water, sanitation and flood protection.	4,102.8	4,617.7
Total	58,747.1	43,005.6

IBRD INCOME AND EXPENDITURE
(year ending 30 June; US $ million)

Revenue	2009	2010	2011
Income from loans	3,835	2,493	2,472
Income from investments and securities	603	367	367
Other income	599	1,248	1,431
Total income	5,037	4,108	4,270

Expenditure	2009	2010	2011
Borrowing expenses	2,739	1,750	1,687
Administrative expenses	1,244	1,421	1,457
Contributions to special programmes	197	168	147
Provision for loan losses	284	–32	–45
Other financial expenses	1	1	1
Total	4,465	3,308	3,247
Operating income	572	800	1,023
Effects of adjustment and accounting charge	2,542	–1,877	–93
Net income	3,114	–1,077	930

IBRD LOANS AND IDA CREDITS APPROVED, BY SECTOR AND REGION
(1 July 2010–30 June 2011; US $ million)

Sector	Africa	East Asia and Pacific	South Asia	Europe and Central Asia	Latin America and the Caribbean	Middle East and North Africa	Total
Agriculture, fishing and forestry	843.1	324.5	374.6	121.3	212.8	251.5	2,127.8
Education	497.6	163.7	463.8	220.4	347.6	40.0	1,733.1
Energy and mining	890.1	1,695.2	760.1	1,870.3	591.7	0.0	5,807.4
Finance	106.8	31.7	46.0	380.1	281.9	50.0	896.5
Health and other social services	591.4	289.8	1,298.6	1,203.7	3,088.9	234.3	6,706.7
Industry and trade	432.8	245.6	375.6	253.1	750.5	109.3	2,166.9
Information and communications	259.0	27.9	166.4	27.9	108.7	50.4	640.3
Public administration, law and justice	1,855.6	2,221.0	1,566.6	1,663.1	2,039.1	327.1	9,672.5
Transportation	937.9	1,941.9	3,913.5	242.5	1,119.6	482.5	8,637.9
Water, sanitation and flood protection	645.7	1,055.6	1,164.9	142.4	1,088.4	519.7	4,616.7
Total	7,060.0	7,997.0	10,130.0	6,124.7	9,629.2	2,064.7	43,005.6
of which: IBRD	55.9	6,369.6	3,730.4	5,470.0	9,169.4	1,941.9	26,737.2
IDA	7,004.1	1,627.4	6,399.6	654.7	459.8	122.8	16,268.4

IBRD OPERATIONS AND RESOURCES, 2006–11
(years ending 30 June; US $ million)

	2006/07	2007/08	2008/09	2009/10	2010/11
Loans approved	12,829	13,468	32,911	44,197	26,737
Gross disbursements	11,055	10,490	18,565	28,855	21,879
New medium- to long-term borrowings	10,209	15,526	39,092	31,696	29,722
Net income	–140	1,491	3,114	–1,077	930
Subscribed capital	189,801	189,801	189,918	189,943	193,732
Loans outstanding	97,805	99,050	105,698	120,103	132,459

Source: World Bank, *Annual Report 2011*.

EXECUTIVE DIRECTORS AND THEIR VOTING POWER
(February 2012)

Executive Director	Casting votes of	IBRD Total votes	IBRD % of total	IDA* Total votes	IDA* % of total
Appointed:					
IAN SOLOMON	USA	265,219	15.78	2,270,761	10.53
NOBUMITSU HIYASHI	Japan	158,654	9.44	1,873,292	8.68
INGRID G. HOVEN	Germany	82,700	4.92	1,214,226	5.63
AMBROISE FAYOLLE	France	73,945	4.40	831,465	3.85
SUSANNA MOOREHEAD	United Kingdom	73,945	4.40	1,215,716	5.64
Elected:					
KONSTANTIN HUBER (Austria)	Austria, Belarus†, Belgium, Czech Republic, Hungary, Kosovo, Luxembourg, Slovakia, Slovenia, Turkey	79,445	4.73	981,539	4.55
MARTA GARCIA (Spain)	Costa Rica, El Salvador, Guatemala, Honduras, Mexico, Nicaragua, Spain, Venezuela†	76,362	4.54	550,758	2.55
RUUD TREFFERS (Netherlands)	Armenia, Bosnia and Herzegovina, Bulgaria†, Croatia, Cyprus, Georgia, Israel, the former Yugoslav republic of Macedonia, Moldova, Montenegro, Netherlands, Romania†, Ukraine	73,269	4.36	926,568	4.29
MARIE-LUCIE MORIN (Canada)	Antigua and Barbuda†, The Bahamas, Barbados Belize, Canada, Dominica, Grenada, Guyana, Ireland, Jamaica†, Saint Christopher and Nevis, Saint Lucia, Saint Vincent and the Grenadines	62,217	3.70	935,564	4.34
ROGERIO STUDART (Brazil)	Brazil, Colombia, Dominican Republic, Ecuador, Haiti, Panama, Philippines, Suriname†, Trinidad and Tobago	59,938	3.57	725,951	3.37
JOHN WHITEHEAD (Australia)	Australia, Cambodia, Kiribati, Republic of Korea, Marshall Islands, Federated States of Micronesia, Mongolia, New Zealand, Palau, Papua New Guinea, Samoa, Solomon Islands, Tuvalu, Vanuatu	58,060	3.46	859,404	3.98
PIERO CIPOLLONE (Italy)	Albania, Greece, Italy, Malta†, Portugal, San Marino†, Timor-Leste	56,705	3.37	689,151	3.19
ANNA BRANDT (Sweden)	Denmark, Estonia, Finland, Iceland, Latvia, Lithuania, Norway, Sweden	55,352	3.29	1,148,520	5.32
MUKESH N. PRASAD (India)	Bangladesh, Bhutan, India, Sri Lanka	54,945	3.27	920,094	4.26
JORG FFRIEDEN (Switzerland)	Azerbaijan, Kazakhstan, Kyrgyzstan, Poland, Serbia, Switzerland, Tajikistan, Turkmenistan†, Uzbekistan	52,427	3.12	969,013	4.49
JAVED TALAT (Pakistan)	Afghanistan, Algeria, Ghana, Iran, Morocco, Pakistan, Tunisia	51,823	3.08	494,576	2.29
MERZA H. HASAN (Kuwait)	Bahrain†, Egypt, Iraq, Jordan, Kuwait, Lebanon, Libya, Maldives, Oman, Qatar†, Syria, United Arab Emirates, Yemen	47,335	2.82	516,225	2.39
SHAOLIN YANG	People's Republic of China	45,049	2.68	449,652	2.08
VADIM GRISHIN	Russia	45,045	2.68	68,902	0.32
ABDULRAHMAN M. ALMOFADHI	Saudi Arabia	45,045	2.68	694,140	3.22
HEKINUS MANAO (Indonesia)	Brunei†, Fiji, Indonesia, Laos, Malaysia, Myanmar, Nepal, Singapore, Thailand, Tonga, Viet Nam	41,096	2.45	658,051	3.05
FELIX ALBERTO CAMARASA (Argentina)	Argentina, Bolivia, Chile, Paraguay, Peru, Uruguay†	37,499	2.23	316,125	1.47
RENOSI MOKATE (South Africa)	Angola, Nigeria, South Africa	29,543	1.76	224,365	1.04
AGAPITO MENDES DIAS (São Tomé and Príncipe)	Benin, Burkina Faso, Cameroon, Cape Verde, Central African Republic, Chad, Comoros, Democratic Republic of the Congo, Republic of the Congo, Côte d'Ivoire, Djibouti, Equatorial Guinea, Gabon, Guinea-Bissau, Mali, Mauritania, Mauritius, Niger, São Tomé and Príncipe, Senegal, Togo	27,742	1.65	1,024,528	4.75
HASSAN AHMED TAHA (Sudan)	Botswana, Burundi, Eritrea, Ethiopia, The Gambia, Kenya, Lesotho, Liberia, Malawi, Mozambique, Namibia†, Rwanda, Seychelles†, Sierra Leone, Sudan, Swaziland Tanzania, Uganda, Zambia, Zimbabwe	26,943	1.60	1,014,891	4.70

Note: Guinea (1,542 votes in IBRD and 33,987 in IDA), Madagascar (1,672 votes in IBRD and 54,982 in IDA), and Somalia (802 votes in IBRD and 10,506 in IDA) did not participate in the 2010 regular election of Executive Directors; South Sudan became a member in April 2012.
* IDA as at 31 December 2011.
† Member of the IBRD only (not IDA).

International Development Association—IDA

Address: 1818 H Street, NW, Washington, DC 20433, USA.

Telephone: (202) 473-1000; **fax:** (202) 477-6391; **internet:** www.worldbank.org/ida.

The International Development Association began operations in November 1960. Affiliated to the IBRD, IDA advances capital to the poorer developing member countries on more flexible terms than those offered by the IBRD.

MEMBERS

IDA has 172 members.

Organization

(April 2012)

Officers and staff of the IBRD serve concurrently as officers and staff of IDA.

President and Chairman of Executive Directors: ROBERT B. ZOELLICK (USA) (until 30 June 2012), Dr JIM YONG KIM (USA) (from 1 July 2012).

Activities

IDA assistance is aimed at the poorer developing countries (i.e. those with an annual GNP per capita of less than US $1,175 were to qualify for assistance in 2011/12) in order to support their poverty reduction strategies. Under IDA lending conditions, credits can be extended to countries whose balance of payments could not sustain the burden of repayment required for IBRD loans. Terms are more favourable than those provided by the IBRD; credits are for a period of 35 or 40 years, with a 'grace period' of 10 years, and carry no, or very low, interest and service charges. From 1 July 2011 the maturity of credits was to be 25 or 40 years, with a grace period of five or 10 years. In 2012 81 countries were eligible for IDA assistance, including 10 small-island economies with a GNP per head greater than $1,175, but which would otherwise have little or no access to Bank funds, and 16 so-called 'blend borrowers' which are entitled to borrow from both IDA and the IBRD.

IDA's total development resources, consisting of members' subscriptions and supplementary resources (additional subscriptions and contributions), are replenished periodically by contributions from the more affluent member countries. In December 2007 an agreement was concluded to replenish IDA resources by some US $41,600m., for the period 1 July 2008–30 June 2011, of which $25,100m. was pledged by 45 donor countries. In March 2010 negotiations on the 16th replenishment of IDA funds (IDA16) commenced, in Paris, France. Participants determined that the overarching theme of IDA16 should be achieving development results, and the following areas of focus be 'special themes': gender; climate change; fragile and conflicted affected states; and crisis response. Replenishment meetings were subsequently held in Bamako, Mali, in June, and in Washington, DC, USA, in October. An agreement was concluded in December, at a meeting convened in Brussels, Belgium. The IDA16 replenishment amounted to $49,300m., to cover the period 1 July 2011–30 June 2014, of which $26,400m. was committed by 51 donor countries.

During the year ending 30 June 2011 new IDA commitments amounted to US $16,269m. for 230 projects, compared with $14,550m. for 190 projects in the previous year. Of total IDA assistance during 2010/11 $7,004m. (43%) was for Africa and $6,340m. (39%) for South Asia. In that financial year some 42% of lending was for infrastructure projects (including energy and mining, transportation, water sanitation and flood protection, and information and communications and technologies sectors), 23% for law, justice and public administration and 20% for social sector projects. In August 2010 the World Bank determined to reallocate some $900m. of IDA funding of planned and ongoing projects in order to support emergency relief and reconstruction activities in areas of Pakistan damaged by extensive flooding.

In December 2008 the Bank's Board of Executive Directors approved a new IDA facility, the Financial Crisis Response Fast Track Facility, to accelerate the provision of up to US $2,000m. of IDA15 resources to help the poorest countries to counter the impact of the global economic and financial crisis. The first operations approved under the Facility, in February 2009, were for Armenia (amounting to $35m.) and the Democratic Republic of Congo ($100m.) in support of employment creation and infrastructure development initiatives and meeting the costs of essential services. In December the Board of Executive Directors approved a pilot Crisis Response Window to deploy an additional $1,300m. of IDA funds to support the poorest countries affected by the economic crisis until the end of the IDA15 period (30 June 2011). The new facility was proposed during a mid-term review of IDA15, held in November, with the aim of assisting those countries to maintain spending on sectors critical to achieving the Millennium Development Goals. Permanent funding for the Crisis Response Window, which additionally was to assist low-income countries manage the impact of natural disasters, was agreed as part of the IDA16 replenishment accord in December 2010. In mid-2011 $250m. was allocated from the Crisis Response Window to provide relief and longer-term rehabilitation assistance to areas of the Horn of Africa affected by a severe drought. In September the World Bank announced that $30m. of those funds were to be disbursed through UNHCR in order to improve basic facilities in settlements occupied by persons displaced as a result of the drought. In December the World Bank's Board of Executive Directors approved the establishment of an Immediate Response Mechanism in order to accelerate the provision of assistance to IDA-eligible countries following a natural disaster or economic crisis.

IDA administers a Trust Fund, which was established in November 1996 as part of a World Bank/IMF initiative to assist heavily indebted poor countries (HIPCs). In September 2005 the World Bank's Development Committee and the International Monetary and Financial Committee of the IMF endorsed a proposal of the Group of Eight (G8) industrialized countries to cancel the remaining multilateral debt owed by HIPCs that had reached their completion point under the scheme (see IBRD). In December IDA convened a meeting of donor countries to discuss funding to uphold its financial capability upon its contribution to the so-called Multilateral Debt Relief Initiative (MDRI). IDA's participation in the scheme was approved by the Board of Executive Directors in March 2006 and entered into effect on 1 July. During IDA15 US $6,300m. was allocated to the provision of debt relief under the MDRI, $1,700m. under the HIPC initiative and a further $1,100m. to finance arrears clearance operations. At July 2011 the estimated cost of the HIPC initiative was $76,000m., of which IDA commitments totalled $14,900m.; IDA's contribution to the MDRI was estimated at $35,300m. in nominal value terms (or some 67% of the total cost of the MDRI). By the end of December 2011 32 countries had reached completion point to receive assistance under the initiative.

Publication

Annual Report.

Statistics

IDA OPERATIONS AND RESOURCES, 2007–11
(years ending 30 June; US $ million)

	2006/07	2007/08	2008/09	2009/10	2010/11
Commitments	11,867	11,235	14,041*	14,550	16,269
Disbursements	8,579	9,160	9,219	11,460	10,282
Number of projects	188	199	176	190	230

* Includes an HIPC grant of US $45.5m.
Source: World Bank, *Annual Report 2011*.

International Finance Corporation—IFC

Address: 2121 Pennsylvania Ave, NW, Washington, DC 20433, USA.

Telephone: (202) 473-3800; **fax:** (202) 974-4384; **e-mail:** information@ifc.org; **internet:** www.ifc.org.

IFC was founded in 1956 as a member of the World Bank Group to stimulate economic growth in developing countries by financing private sector investments, mobilizing capital in international financial markets, and providing technical assistance and advice to governments and businesses.

MEMBERS

IFC has 184 members.

Organization

(April 2012)

IFC is a separate legal entity in the World Bank Group. Executive Directors of the World Bank also serve as Directors of IFC. The President of the World Bank is *ex officio* Chairman of the IFC Board of Directors, which has appointed him President of IFC. Subject to his overall supervision, the day-to-day operations of IFC are conducted by its staff under the direction of the Executive Vice-President. The senior management team includes 10 Vice-Presidents responsible for regional and thematic groupings. At the end of June 2011 IFC had 3,354 staff members, of whom 54% were based in field offices in 86 countries.

PRINCIPAL OFFICERS

President: Robert B. Zoellick (USA), Dr Jim Yong Kim (USA) (from 1 July 2012).

Executive Vice-President: Lars Thunell (Sweden).

REGIONAL AND INDUSTRY DEPARTMENTS

IFC's regional departments cover: sub-Saharan Africa; East Asia and the Pacific; South Asia; Central and Eastern Europe; Southern Europe and Central Asia; Latin America and the Caribbean; and the Middle East and North Africa. They aim to develop strategies for member countries, promote businesses, and strengthen relations with governments and the private sector. The Industry Departments include Agribusiness; Environment and Social Development; Global Capital Markets Development; Global Financial Markets; Global Information and Communications Technologies (jointly managed with the World Bank); Global Manufacturing and Services; Health and Education; Infrastructure; Oil, Gas, Mining and Chemicals (jointly managed with the World Bank); Private Equity and Investment Funds; and Syndication and Resource Mobilization.

REGIONAL AND RESIDENT MISSIONS

There are Regional and Resident Missions in Australia, Bangladesh, Brazil, Cambodia, People's Republic of China, Dominican Republic, Egypt, Guyana, Haiti, India, Kazakhstan, Laos, Liberia, Mongolia, Russia, Serbia, South Africa, Sri Lanka, Trinidad and Tobago, Turkey, United Arab Emirates and Viet Nam. There are also Special Representatives in France, Germany and the United Kingdom (for Europe), an office in Tokyo, Japan, and other programme co-ordinators, managers and investment officers in more than 50 additional countries.

Activities

IFC aims to promote economic development in developing member countries by assisting the growth of private enterprise and effective capital markets. It finances private sector projects, through loans, the purchase of equity, quasi-equity products, and risk management services, and assists governments to create conditions that stimulate the flow of domestic and foreign private savings and investment. IFC may provide finance for a project that is partly state-owned, provided that there is participation by the private sector and that the project is operated on a commercial basis. IFC also mobilizes additional resources from other financial institutions, in particular through syndicated loans, thus providing access to international capital markets. IFC provides a range of advisory services to help to improve the investment climate in developing countries and offers technical assistance to private enterprises and governments. In 2008 IFC formulated a policy document to help to increase its impact in the three-year period 2009–11. The IFC Road Map identified five strategic 'pillars' as priority areas of activity: strengthening the focus on frontier markets (i.e. the lowest-income countries or regions of middle-income countries, those affected by conflict, or underdeveloped industrial sectors); building long-term partnerships with emerging 'players' in developing countries; addressing climate change and securing environmental and social sustainability; promoting private sector growth in infrastructure, health and education; and developing local financial markets. From late 2008 IFC's overriding concern was to respond effectively to the difficulties facing member countries affected by the global economic and financial crisis and to maintain a sustainable level of development. In particular it aimed to preserve and create employment opportunities, to support supply chains for local businesses, and to provide credit.

To be eligible for financing projects must be profitable for investors, as well as financially and economically viable; must benefit the economy of the country concerned; and must comply with IFC's environmental and social guidelines. IFC aims to promote best corporate governance and management methods and sustainable business practices, and encourages partnerships between governments, non-governmental organizations and community groups. In 2001/02 IFC developed a Sustainability Framework to help to assess the longer-term economic, environmental and social impact of projects. The first Sustainability Review was published in mid-2002. In 2002/03 IFC assisted 10 international banks to draft a voluntary set of guidelines (the Equator Principles), based on IFC's environmental, social and safeguard monitoring policies, to be applied to their global project finance activities. In September 2009 IFC initiated a Performance Standards Review Process to define new standards to be applied within the Equator Principles framework. At January 2012 73 financial institutions had signed up to the Equator Principles.

In November 2004 IFC announced the establishment of a Global Trade Finance Programme (GTFP), with initial funding of some US $500m., which aimed to support small-scale importers and exporters in emerging markets, and to facilitate South–South trade in goods and services, by providing guarantees for trade transactions, as well as extending technical assistance and training to local financial institutions. Additional funding of $500m. was approved in January 2007, and in October 2008, by which time there were 147 confirming banks from 70 countries participating in the initiative and 126 issuing banks in 66 countries. In December, as part of a set of measures to support the global economy, the Board of Directors approved an expansion of the GTFP, doubling its funding to $3,000m. Other initiatives included the establishment of an Infrastructure Crisis Facility to provide investment for existing projects affected by a lack of private funding, and a new Bank Capitalization Fund (to be financed, up to $3,000m., with the Japan Bank for International Co-operation) to provide investment and advisory services to banks in emerging markets. In May 2009 IFC established an Asset Management Company, as a wholly owned subsidiary, to administer the Capitalization Fund. In February of that year IFC inaugurated a Microfinance Enhancement Facility, with a German development bank, to extend credit to microfinancing institutions and to support lending to low-income borrowers, with funds of up to $500m. IFC committed $1,000m. in funds to a new Global Trade Liquidity Program (GTLP), which was inaugurated by the World Bank Group in April, with the aim of mobilizing support of up to $50,000m. in trade transactions through financing extended by governments, other development banks and the private sector. In October IFC established a Debt and Asset Recovery Program to help to restore stability and growth by facilitating loan restructuring for businesses and by investing in funds targeting distressed assets and companies. IFC pledged to contribute $1,550m. to the Program over a three-year period, and aimed to mobilize resources through partnerships with other international financial institutions and private sector companies.

IFC's authorized capital is US $2,450m. At 30 June 2011 paid-in capital was $2,369m. The World Bank was originally the principal source of borrowed funds, but IFC also borrows from private capital markets. IFC's net income amounted to $1,579m. (after a $600m. grant transfer to IDA), compared with $1,746m. in 2009/10 (after a $600m. transfer to IDA). In December 2008 the Board of Directors approved a Sovereign Funds Initiative to enable IFC to raise and manage commercial capital from sovereign funds. In July 2010 the Board of Directors recommended a special capital increase of $130m., to raise authorized capital to $2,580m. The increase required the approval of the Board of Governors.

In the year ending 30 June 2011 project financing approved by IFC amounted to US $18,660m. for 518 projects in 102 countries (compared with $18,041 for 528 projects in the previous year). Of the total approved in 2010/11, $12,186m. was for IFC's own account, while $6,474m. was in the form of loan syndications and parallel loans, underwriting of securities issues and investment funds and funds mobilized by the IFC Asset Management Company. Generally, IFC limits its financing to less than 25% of the total cost of a project, but may take up to a 35% stake in a venture (although never as a majority shareholder). Disbursements for IFC's account amounted to $6,715m. in 2010/11.

In 2010/11 the largest proportion of investment commitments, for IFC's account, was allocated to Europe and Central Asia (26%); Latin America and the Caribbean received 24%, sub-Saharan Africa and East Asia and the Pacific each received 14%, the Middle East and North Africa received 11%, and South Asia 10%. In that year 33% of total financing committed was for global financial markets. Other commitments included infrastructure (17%) and manufacturing (12%).

IFC's Advisory Services are a major part of the organization's involvement with member countries to support the development of private enterprises and efforts to generate funding, as well as to enhance private sector participation in developing infrastructure. Advisory services cover the following five main areas of expertise: the business enabling environment (i.e improving the investment climate in a country); access to financing (including developing financing institutions, improving financial infrastructure and strengthening regulatory frameworks); infrastructure (mainly encouraging private sector participation); environment and social sustainability; and corporate advice (in particular in support of small and medium-sized enterprises—SMEs). In December 2008 the Board of Directors determined to provide additional funding to IFC advisory services in order to strengthen the capacity of financial institutions and governments to respond to the crisis in the global financial markets. At 30 June 2011 there were 642 active Advisory Service projects with a value of US $820m. Total expenditure on Advisory Services during that year amounted to $206.7m. IFC manages, jointly financed with the World Bank and MIGA, the Foreign Investment Advisory Service (FIAS), which provides technical assistance and advice on promoting foreign investment and strengthening the country's investment framework at the request of governments. Under the Technical Assistance Trust Funds Program (TATF), established in 1988, IFC manages resources contributed by various governments and agencies to provide finance for feasibility studies, project identification studies and other types of technical assistance relating to project preparation. In 2004 a Grassroots Business Initiative was established, with external donor funding, to support businesses that provide economic opportunities for disadvantaged communities in Africa, Latin America, and South and Southeast Asia. Since 2002 IFC has administered an online SME Toolkit to enhance the accessibility of business training and advice. By 2011 the service was available in 16 languages.

Since 2004 IFC has presented an annual Client Leadership Award to a chosen corporate client who most represents IFC values in innovation, operational excellence and corporate governance.

Publications

Annual Report.
Doing Business (annually).
Emerging Stock Markets Factbook (annually).
Lessons of Experience (series).
Outcomes (quarterly).
Results on the Ground (series).
Review of Small Businesses (annually).
Sustainability Report (annually).
Other handbooks, discussion papers, technical documents, policy toolkits, public policy journals.

Statistics

IFC OPERATIONS AND RESOURCES, 2009–11
(fiscal years ending 30 June; US $ million, unless otherwise stated)

	2009	2010	2011
Approved investments			
Number of new projects	447	528	518
Total investment programme*	14,509	18,042	18,660
Commitments for IFC's own account	10,547	12,664	12,186
Disbursements			
Total financing disbursed	7,598	9,648	8,744
For IFC's own account	5,640	6,793	6,715
Resources and income			
Borrowings	25,711	31,106	38,211
Paid-in capital	2,369	2,369	2,369
Retained earnings	13,042	14,788	16,367
Net income	–151	1,746	1,579

* Including parallel loans, structured finance, other mobilization and IFC initiatives, and IFC Asset Management Company.

Source: IFC, *Annual Report 2011.*

Multilateral Investment Guarantee Agency—MIGA

Address: 1818 H Street, NW, Washington, DC 20433, USA.

Telephone: (202) 473-6163; **fax:** (202) 522-2630; **internet:** www.miga.org.

MIGA was founded in 1988 as an affiliate of the World Bank. Its mandate is to encourage the flow of foreign direct investment to, and among, developing member countries, through the provision of political risk insurance and investment marketing services to foreign investors and host governments, respectively.

MEMBERS

MIGA has 176 member countries. Membership is open to all countries that are members of the World Bank.

Organization

(April 2012)

MIGA is legally and financially separate from the World Bank. It is supervised by a Council of Governors (comprising one Governor and one Alternate of each member country) and an elected Board of Directors (of no less than 12 members).

President: ROBERT B. ZOELLICK (USA) (until 30 June 2012), Dr JIM YONG KIM (USA) (from 1 July 2012).

Executive Vice-President: IZUMI KOBAYASHI (Japan).

Activities

The convention establishing MIGA took effect in April 1988. Authorized capital was US $1,082m., although the convention provided for an increase of capital stock upon the admission of new members. In April 1998 the Board of Directors approved an increase in MIGA's capital base. A grant of $150m. was transferred from the IBRD as part of the package, while the capital increase (totalling $700m. callable capital and $150m. paid-in capital) was approved by MIGA's Council of Governors in April 1999. A three-year subscription period then commenced, covering the period April 1999–March 2002 (later extended to March 2003). At 30 June 2011 110 countries had subscribed $749.9m. of the general capital increase. At that time total subscriptions to the capital stock amounted to $1,912.8m., of which $364.9m. was paid-in.

MIGA guarantees eligible investments against losses resulting from non-commercial risks, under the following main categories:

(i) transfer risk resulting from host government restrictions on currency conversion and transfer;

(ii) risk of loss resulting from legislative or administrative actions of the host government;

(iii) repudiation by the host government of contracts with investors in cases in which the investor has no access to a competent forum;

(iv) the risk of armed conflict and civil unrest;

(v) risk of a sovereign not honouring a financial obligation or guarantee.

Before guaranteeing any investment, MIGA must ensure that it is commercially viable, contributes to the development process and is not harmful to the environment. During the fiscal year 1998/99 MIGA and IFC appointed the first Compliance Advisor and Ombudsman to consider the concerns of local communities directly affected by MIGA- or IFC-sponsored projects. In February 1999 the Board of Directors approved an increase in the amount of political risk insurance available for each project, from US $75m. to $200m.

During 2003/04 MIGA established a new fund, the Invest-in-Development Facility, to enhance the role of foreign investment in attaining the Millennium Development Goals. In 2005/06 MIGA supported for the first time a project aimed at selling carbon credits gained by reducing greenhouse gas emissions; it provided US $2m. in guarantee coverage to the El Salvador-based initiative. In April 2009 the Board of Directors approved modifications to MIGA's policies and operational regulations in order to enhance operational flexibility and efficiency, in particular in the poorest countries and those affected by conflict. In November 2010 the Council of Governors approved amendments to MIGA's convention (the first since 1988) to broaden the eligibility for investment projects and to enhance the effectiveness of MIGA's development impact.

During the year ending 30 June 2011 MIGA issued 50 investment insurance contracts for 38 projects with a value of US $2,100m. (compared with 28 contracts amounting to $1,500m. in 2009/10). Since 1990 the total investment guarantees issued amounted to some $24,500m., through 1,030 contracts in support of 651 projects.

MIGA works with local insurers, export credit agencies, development finance institutions and other organizations to promote insurance in a country, to ensure a level of consistency among insurers and to support capacity-building within the insurance industry. MIGA also offers investment marketing services to help to promote foreign direct investment in developing countries and in transitional economies, and to disseminate information on investment opportunities. MIGA maintains an internet service (www.pri-center.com), providing access to political risk management and insurance resources, in order to support those objectives. In early 2007 MIGA's technical assistance services were amalgamated into the Foreign Advisory Investment Service (FIAS, see IFC), of which MIGA became a lead partner, along with IFC and the World Bank. During 2000/01 an office was established in Paris, France, to promote and co-ordinate European investment in developing countries, in particular in Africa and Eastern Europe. In March 2002 MIGA opened a regional office, based in Johannesburg, South Africa. In September a new regional office was inaugurated in Singapore, in order to facilitate foreign investment in Asia. A Regional Director for Asia and the Pacific was appointed, for the first time, in August 2010 to head a new Asian Hub, operating from offices in Singapore, Hong Kong SAR and the People's Republic of China.

In July 2004 an Afghanistan Investment Guarantee Facility, to be administered by MIGA, became operational to provide political risk guarantees for foreign investors in that country.

In November 2008 a West Bank and Gaza Investment Guarantee Trust Fund was inaugurated to encourage greater private sector investment in those territories. The new fund, co-sponsored by the European Investment Bank, the Japanese Government and the Palestinian (National) Authority, was to be administered by MIGA.

In April 2009 MIGA announced a new initiative to support financial institutions affected by the global economic crisis through broadened political risk guarantees for liquidity support or recapitalization of their banking subsidiaries. Some €3,000m. was allocated to finance investments in Europe and Central Asia.

Publications

Annual Report.

MIGA News (online newsletter; every 2 months).

World Investment and Political Risk (annually).

Other guides, brochures and regional briefs.

International Civil Aviation Organization—ICAO

Address: 999 University St, Montréal, QC H3C 5H7, Canada.

Telephone: (514) 954-8219; **fax:** (514) 954-6077; **e-mail:** icaohq@icao.int; **internet:** www.icao.int.

The Convention on International Civil Aviation was signed in Chicago in 1944. As a result, ICAO was founded in 1947 to develop the techniques of international air navigation and to help in the planning and improvement of international air transport.

MEMBERS

ICAO has 191 contracting states.

Organization

(April 2012)

ASSEMBLY

Composed of representatives of all member states, the Assembly is the organization's legislative body and meets at least once every three years. It reviews the work of the organization, sets out the work programme for the next three years, approves the budget and determines members' contributions. The 37th Assembly took place in September–October 2010.

COUNCIL

Composed of representatives of 36 member states, elected by the Assembly. It is the executive body, and establishes and supervises subsidiary technical committees and makes recommendations to member governments; meets in virtually continuous session; elects the President, appoints the Secretary-General, and administers the finances of the organization. The Council is assisted by the Air Navigation Commission, the Air Transport Committee, the Committee on Joint Support of Air Navigation Services, the Finance Committee, the Committee on Unlawful Interference and the Technical Co-operation Committee. The functions of the Council are:

(i) to adopt international standards and recommended practices and incorporate them as annexes to the Chicago Convention on International Civil Aviation;

(ii) to arbitrate between member states on matters concerning aviation and implementation of the Convention;

(iii) to investigate any situation which presents avoidable obstacles to development of international air navigation;

(iv) to take whatever steps are necessary to maintain safety and regularity of operation of international air transport;

(v) to provide technical assistance to the developing countries under the UN Development Programme and other assistance programmes.

President of the Council: ROBERTO KOBEH GONZÁLEZ (Mexico).

SECRETARIAT

The Secretariat, headed by a Secretary-General, is divided into five main divisions: the Air Navigation Bureau, the Air Transport Bureau, the Technical Co-operation Bureau, the Legal Bureau, and the Bureau of Administration and Services.

Secretary-General: RAYMOND BENJAMIN (France).

REGIONAL OFFICES

Asia and Pacific: 252/1 Vibhavadi-Rangsit Rd, Ladyao, Chatuchak, Bangkok 10900, Thailand; tel. (2) 537-8189; fax (2) 537-8199; e-mail icao_apac@bangkok.icao.int; internet www.bangkok.icao.int; Regional Dir MOKHTAR AHMED AWAN.

Eastern and Southern Africa: Limuru Rd, Gigiri, POB 46294, Nairobi, Kenya; tel. (20) 7622395; fax (20) 7623028; e-mail icao@icao.unon.org; internet www.icao.int/esaf; Regional Dir MESHESHA BELAYNEH.

European and North Atlantic: 3 bis Villa Émile-Bergerat, 92522 Neuilly-sur-Seine Cédex, France; tel. 1-46-41-85-85; fax 1-46-41-85-00; e-mail icaoeurnat@paris.icao.int; internet www.paris.icao.int; f. 1944; Regional Dir LUIS FONSECA DE ALMEIDA.

Middle East: POB 85, Cairo Airport Post Office Terminal One, Cairo 11776, Egypt; tel. (2) 267-4840; fax (2) 267-4843; e-mail icaomid@cairo.icao.int; internet www.icao.int/mid; Regional Dir MOHAMED R. M. KHONJI.

North America, Central America and the Caribbean: Apdo Postal 5-377, CP 06500, México, DF, Mexico; tel. (55) 5250-3211; fax (55) 5203-2757; e-mail icao_nacc@mexico.icao.int; internet www.mexico.icao.int; Regional Dir L. J. MARTIN.

South America: ave Víctor Andrés Belaúnde 147, San Isidro, Lima, Peru; tel. (1) 611-8686; fax (1) 611-8689; e-mail mail@lima.icao.int; internet www.lima.icao.int; Regional Dir JOSÉ MIGUEL CEPPI.

Western and Central Africa: 15 blvd de la République, BP 2356, Dakar, Senegal; tel. 839-9393; fax 823-6926; e-mail icaowacaf@dakar.icao.int; internet www.icao.int/wacaf; Regional Dir MAM SAIT JALLOW.

Activities

ICAO aims to ensure the safe and orderly growth of civil aviation; to encourage skills in aircraft design and operation; to improve airways, airports and air navigation; to prevent the waste of resources in unreasonable competition; to safeguard the rights of each contracting party to operate international air transport; and to prevent discriminatory practices. ICAO collects and publishes statistics relating to civil aviation. In October 2010 the Council adopted an ICAO Framework, detailing the following as strategic objectives for the period 2011–13: to enhance global civil aviation safety; to enhance global civil aviation security; and to foster the harmonized and economically viable development of international civil aviation in a manner that does not impact unduly on the environment. ICAO's first, second and third business plans, covering 2005–07, 2008–10, and 2011–13, respectively, placed a growing emphasis on performance planning and results-based management.

SAFETY

ICAO aims to ensure and enhance all aspects of air safety and security. A Global Aviation Safety Plan (GASP) was initiated in 1998 to promote safety measures. ICAO assists member countries to develop appropriate educational and training activities. It also supports programmes to assist the victims of aircraft accidents. A Universal Safety Oversight Audit Programme (USOAP) became operational on 1 January 1999, providing for mandatory, systematic and harmonized safety audits regularly to be undertaken in member states in fields including the airworthiness of aircraft, flight operations and personnel licensing, with results to be compiled in an Audit Findings and Differences Database. In October 2001 the Assembly approved the concept of an International Financial Facility for Aviation Safety (IFFAS) to provide funds to states to adhere to ICAO safety-related standards. The Facility became effective in 2003. In October 2004 the Assembly recognized the USOAP as having significantly contributed to raising the level of safety oversight world-wide and endorsed its expansion, from 1 January 2005, to incorporate, in a new comprehensive systems approach (CSA), all safety-related provisions of the annexes to the Chicago Convention; by the end of 2011 ICAO had completed 180 CSA audits, and four further audits were to be undertaken during 2012. The October 2004 Assembly also requested ICAO to accelerate the development of standards and guidance under its programme for the prevention of Controlled Flight Into Terrain accidents; urged contracting states strictly to control the movement and storage of man-portable defence systems; and resolved to review standards relating to the health of passengers and crews, as an integral element of safe air travel. In late 2005, following a series of aircraft accidents, ICAO determined to convene a meeting of Directors-General of Civil Aviation in order to assess the status of aviation safety, to identify ways to achieve improvements in safety standards, and to develop a new framework of safety measures. The conference, convened in March 2006, endorsed a Global Strategy for Aviation Safety. The declaration issued at the meeting stipulated that, *inter alia,* provisions should be implemented for safety-related information, including results of audits within the USOAP, to be shared among states, the public and other interested parties. Also at the March 2006 conference, the Directors-General endorsed Part I of a Global Aviation Safety Roadmap, delivered to ICAO in December of 2005 by the Industry Safety Strategy Group. The Roadmap identified mid- and long-term goals related to air-safety oversight and regulation matters. In December 2006 Part II of the Roadmap was finalized, outlining strategies for achieving these objectives. An updated GASP, based on the Roadmap, was published in June 2007, and in 2011 the GASP was enhanced further. In September 2007 the Assembly endorsed a new Comprehensive Regional Implementation Plan for Aviation Safety in Africa, which had been formulated by African governments, with representatives of the local civil aviation authorities and air industry. In September 2010 ICAO, the EU, the US Department of Transportation, and the International Air Transport Association, formally approved the establishment of a new Global Safety Information Exchange (GSIE), with the aim of improving the overall level of international aviation safety.

In December 2011 ICAO released the first *State of Global Aviation Safety* report, addressing global aviation safety performance. The report envisaged that the volume of scheduled aviation traffic worldwide, which had reached a record 30.5m. departures in 2010, would rise to 52m. annually by 2030.

ICAO maintains a Flight Safety Information Exchange (FSIX) website at www.icao.int/fsix/safety.cfm, to help to disseminate safety-related information, including safety and security audits, within the aviation community. The main subject areas cover safety oversight information, resolving safety deficiencies, regional regulations and safety management. It was announced in July 2008 that all states audited under the USOAP had given consent for ICAO to publish the audit findings on the FSIX website, in accordance with the outcome of the March 2006 conference of Directors-General of Civil Aviation.

In April 2010, in view of the eruption of the Eyjafjallajökull volcano, in Iceland, ICAO established the ICAO European and North Atlantic Volcanic Ash Task Force (EUR/NAT VATF), to establish a co-ordinated region-wide operational approach to volcanic ash emergencies. In the following month the Task Force agreed a common working agenda to improve contingency plans for preventing accidents in the wake of any future eruption, as well as minimizing disruptions of service and severe economic impact on the airline industry. In March 2012 ICAO issued a manual entitled *Flight Safety and Volcanic Ash*, which was based on the work of the Task Force, and aimed to provide air transport operators with a scientific basis for future post-volcanic eruption decision making.

SECURITY

In October 1998 a protocol to the Chicago Convention, prohibiting the use of weapons against civil aircraft in flight, entered into effect, having been adopted in 1984 following an attack on a Korean Airlines passenger flight. In 2000 ICAO developed model legislation to cover offences committed on board aircraft by unruly passengers (other than hijacking, sabotage etc., which are already governed by international legislation). Following the terrorist attacks perpetrated against targets in the USA in September 2001, involving the use of hijacked aircraft as weapons, the 33rd Assembly—held in September–October—adopted a Declaration on the Misuse of Civil Aircraft as Weapons of Destruction and Other Terrorist Acts involving Civil Aviation. The Declaration urged a review of ICAO's aviation security programme and consideration of the initiation of a programme to audit airport security arrangements and member states' civil aviation security programmes. In October the Council established a Special Group on Aviation War Risk Insurance to make recommendations on the development of a co-ordinated and long-term approach in this area. A proposal by the Special Group concerning the establishment of a Global Scheme on Aviation War Risk Insurance (Globaltime), to be provided by a non-profit entity with initial multilateral government support, was approved in principle by the Council in May 2002. A high-level ministerial conference, convened under ICAO auspices in February of that year to discuss preventing, combating and eradicating acts of terrorism involving civil aviation, and strengthening the organization's role in overseeing the adoption and national implementation of security-related standards and procedures, endorsed a global Aviation Security Plan of Action and reaffirmed the responsibility of states to ensure aviation security on their territories. The Plan provided for development of an effective global response to emerging threats; strengthened security-related provisions of the Convention on International Civil Aviation; and enhanced co-ordination of regional and sub-regional audit programmes. In June a Universal Security Audit Programme was launched, as part of the Aviation Security Plan of Action, to help to identify and correct deficiencies in the implementation of security-related standards. The first round of security audits of all contracting states was completed by the end of 2007, and a second cycle of audits was being implemented during 2008–13. A new Implementation Support and Development Branch was established in June 2007 to support member states with significant safety oversight or security deficiencies and to help to implement correction action plans. In September 2010 the Diplomatic Conference on Aviation Security, convened under ICAO auspices in Beijing, People's Republic of China, adopted two new international legal instruments: the Convention on the Suppression of Unlawful Acts Relating to International Civil Aviation, and the Protocol Supplementary to the Convention for the Suppression of Unlawful Seizure of Aircraft. In October 2010 the Assembly adopted the ICAO Declaration on Aviation Security, which included a roadmap aimed at further protecting global air transport from terrorist and other security threats, through the development of security screening procedures and increased capacity-building assistance. In the following month the Chicago Convention annex on security was amended to enhance air cargo security standards.

ICAO convened regional security conferences in New Delhi, India in September 2011; Dakar, Senegal, in October 2011; Moscow, Russia, in November 2011; Kuala Lumpur, Malaysia, in January 2012; Caracas, Venezuela, in February 2012; and Manama, Bahrain, in April 2012 under a process that was to culminate in a high-level global security conference, to be held in Montréal in September.

ICAO is developing a globally inter-operable system of Machine Readable Travel Documents (MRTDs), incorporating biometric identification data, in order to enhance airport and international security, and has provided technical assistance to support the efforts of contracting states to develop MRTDs. ICAO's objective that all states issue machine readable passports by 1 April 2010 was not universally met. The Organization has specified 24 November 2015 as the obligatory deadline for universal machine readable compliance, by which time non machine readable documents are to be phased out.

NAVIGATION

ICAO's Air Navigation Bureau develops technical studies for the Air Navigation Commission, as well as recommendations for standards and recommended practices relating to the safety, regularity and efficiency of international air navigation. Areas of activity include meteorology, automated data interchange systems, accident investigation and prevention, aviation medicine and air traffic management. In March 1998 the ICAO Council adopted a Global Air Navigation Plan for Communications, Navigation, Surveillance, and Air Traffic Management (CNS/ATM) Systems. In May an international conference was held in Rio de Janeiro, Brazil, to consider implementation of the CNS/ATM systems. The conference urged greater financing and co-operation between states to ensure that the CNS/ATM becomes the basis of a global ATM system. An Air Traffic Management Operational Concept Panel, which was to develop standards and recommend procedures for the development of an integrated ATM system, was convened for the first time in March–April 1999. In October 1998 the Assembly adopted a Charter on the Rights and Obligations of States relating to Global Navigation Satellite Systems (GNSS) to serve as an interim framework on the GNSS. A long-term legal framework on principles governing the GNSS, including a new international convention, remains under consideration. The 11th Air Navigation Conference, convened by ICAO in September–October 2003, in Montréal, endorsed an operational concept for a globally harmonized air navigation system that aimed to enhance safety and reduce airspace and airport congestion. In 2005 ICAO assisted countries and international organizations to develop preparedness strategies with regard to the threat of a pandemic of highly pathogenic avian influenza. In 2010 some 171 bilateral 'open skies' air services agreements, involving 103 states, were in force, as well as at least 15 liberalized agreements or arrangements at regional level. In April 2009 ICAO and major global aviation stakeholders adopted a declaration calling for the rapid implementation of Performance-based Navigation (PBN), a new air navigation concept setting clear performance targets for specific flight operations, and emphasizing the use of accurate satellite-based navigation aids, with the aim of contributing further to improving the safety, efficiency and sustainability of the global air transport system; all of the ICAO Regional Offices have established PBN task forces, which, with a global PBN Task Force, support countries' implementation of PBN.

ENVIRONMENTAL PROTECTION

ICAO activities with respect to the environment are primarily focused on areas that require a co-ordinated international approach, i.e. aircraft noise and engine emissions. International standards and guidelines for noise certification of aircraft and international provisions for the regulation of aircraft engine emissions have been adopted and published in Annex 16 to the Chicago Convention. ICAO provides briefings and written submissions to meetings of the parties to the United Nations Framework Convention on Climate Change (UNFCCC), having been recognized in the 1997 Kyoto Protocol to the UNFCCC as the global body through which industrialized nations were to pursue the limitation or reduction of so-called greenhouse gas emissions from international aviation. In 1998 ICAO's Committee on Aviation Environmental Protection (CAEP) recommended a reduction of 16% in the permissible levels of nitrogen oxides emitted by aircraft engines. The new limits, to be applicable to new engine designs from 2003, were adopted by the ICAO Council in early 1999. Further reduced limits were approved in 2004. In June 2001 the Council adopted a stricter noise standard (applicable from 1 January 2006) for jet and large propeller-driven aircraft, as well as new noise limits for helicopters and new provisions concerning re-certification. In October the Assembly approved a series of measures developed by the Committee concerning a balanced approach to aircraft noise and based on the following elements: quieter aircraft; land-use planning and management in the vicinity of airports; operational procedures for noise abatement; and operating restrictions. In 2008 the CAEP launched a series of Independent Expert (IE) reviews to establish technology and operational mid-term (i.e. 10-year) and long-term (20-year) objectives for progress in the reduction of noise, fuel burn and the emission of nitrogen oxides.

In September 2007 the ICAO Council determined to establish a new Group on International Aviation and Climate Change (GIACC), comprising senior government officials, in order to formulate an 'aggressive' programme of action on aviation and climate change, with a framework to help to achieve emissions reductions, for example through fuel efficiency targets and other voluntary measures. The GIACC held its inaugural meeting in February 2008. ICAO's first Environmental Report was published in September 2007, covering technical and policy aspects of aviation's impact on the environment. In October 2010 the 37th session of the ICAO Assembly adopted a resolution aimed at reducing the impact of aviation emissions on climate change, and providing a roadmap for action until 2050.

In June 2008 an online ICAO Carbon Emissions Calculator was launched, a methodology for estimating the carbon dioxide emissions from air travel for use in devising carbon footprint offset programmes.

ICAO SPECIFICATIONS

These are contained in annexes to the Chicago Convention, and in three sets of Procedures for Air Navigation Services (PANS Documents). The specifications are periodically revised in keeping with developments in technology and changing requirements. The 18 annexes to the Convention include personnel licensing, rules relating to the conduct of flights, meteorological services, aeronautical charts, air–ground communications, safety specifications, identification, air traffic control, rescue services, environmental protection, security and the transporting of dangerous goods. Technical Manuals and Circulars are issued to facilitate implementation.

TECHNICAL CO-OPERATION

ICAO's Technical Co-operation Bureau promotes the implementation of ICAO Standards and Recommended Practices, including the CNS/ATM (see above) and safety oversight measures, and assists developing countries in the execution of various projects, financed by UNDP and other sources. The TRAINAIR programme helps relevant institutions to develop a standard aviation training package, and promotes international co-operation in training and course development.

ICAO works in close co-operation with other UN bodies, such as the World Meteorological Organization, the UNFCCC, the International Telecommunication Union, the Universal Postal Union, the World Health Organization (WHO) and the International Maritime Organization. Non-governmental organizations which also participate in ICAO's work include the International Air Transport Association, the Airports Council International, the International Federation of Air Line Pilots' Associations, and the International Council of Aircraft Owner and Pilot Associations. In June 2003 ICAO published measures for preventing the spread by air travel of Severe Acute Respiratory Syndrome (SARS) and other contagious diseases, based on guidelines issued by WHO, and in 2009 ICAO supported member states in developing effective, globally harmonized national aviation contingency plans aimed at controlling the spread of pandemic (H1N1) 2009 (swine flu).

Finance

ICAO is financed mainly by contributions from member states. The authorized budget for the triennium 2011–13 totalled US 273.1m. (allocated as follows: $87.6m. in 2011, $90.2m. in 2012, and $95.3m. in 2013).

Publications

Annual Report of the Council.

Aviation Training Directory.

Directory of National Civil Aviation Administrations (online database).

ICAO Environmental Report.

ICAO Journal (6 a year, in English, French and Spanish).

State of Global Aviation Safety.

World of Civil Aviation.

Conventions, agreements, rules of procedures, regulations, technical publications and manuals.

International Fund for Agricultural Development—IFAD

Address: Via Paolo di Dono 44, 00142 Rome, Italy.

Telephone: (06) 54591; **fax:** (06) 5043463; **e-mail:** ifad@ifad.org; **internet:** www.ifad.org.

IFAD was established in 1977, following a decision by the 1974 UN World Food Conference, with a mandate to combat hunger and eradicate poverty on a sustainable basis in the low-income, food-deficit regions of the world. Funding operations began in January 1978.

MEMBERS

IFAD has 168 members.

Organization

(April 2012)

GOVERNING COUNCIL

Each member state is represented in the Governing Council (the Fund's highest authority) by a Governor and an Alternate. Sessions are held annually with special sessions as required. The Governing Council elects the President of the Fund (who also chairs the Executive Board) by a two-thirds majority for a four-year term. The President is eligible for re-election.

EXECUTIVE BOARD

Consists of 18 members and 18 alternates, elected by the Governing Council, who serve for three years. The Executive Board is responsible for the conduct and general operation of IFAD and approves loans and grants for projects; it holds three regular sessions each year. An independent Office of Evaluation reports directly to the Board.

The governance structure of the Fund is based on the classification of members. Membership of the Executive Board is distributed as follows: eight List A countries (i.e. industrialized donor countries), four List B (petroleum-exporting developing donor countries), and six List C (recipient developing countries), divided equally among the three Sub-List C categories (i.e. for Africa, Europe, Asia and the Pacific, and Latin America and the Caribbean).

President and Chairman of Executive Board: KANAYO F. NWANZE (Nigeria).

Vice-President: YUKIKO OMURA (Japan).

DEPARTMENTS

IFAD has three main administrative departments, each headed by an Assistant President: Finance and Administration; Programme Management (with five regional Divisions and a Technical Advisory Division); and External Affairs (including a Policy Division, Communication Division and a Resource Mobilization Unit). Offices of the General Counsel and of Internal Audit report to the Office of the President and Vice-President.

Activities

IFAD provides financing primarily for projects designed to improve food production systems in developing member states and to strengthen related policies, services and institutions. In allocating resources IFAD is guided by: the need to increase food production in the poorest food-deficit countries; the potential for increasing food production in other developing countries; and the importance of improving the nutrition, health and education of the poorest people in developing countries, i.e. small-scale farmers, artisanal fishermen, nomadic pastoralists, indigenous populations, rural women, and the rural landless. All projects emphasize the participation of beneficiaries in development initiatives, both at the local and national level. Issues relating to gender and household food security are incorporated into all aspects of its activities. IFAD is committed to achieving the Millennium Development Goals (MDGs), pledged by governments attending a special session of the UN General Assembly in September 2000, and, in particular, the objective to reduce by 50% the proportion of people living in extreme poverty by 2015. In 2001 the Fund introduced new measures to improve monitoring and impact evaluation, in particular to assess its contribution to achieving the MDGs.

In May 2011 the Executive Board adopted IFAD's Strategic Framework for 2011–15, in which it reiterated its commitment to improving rural food security and nutrition, and enabling the rural poor to overcome their poverty. The 2011–15 Strategic Framework was underpinned by five strategic objectives: developing a natural resource and economic asset base for poor rural communities, with improved resilience to climate change, environmental degradation and market transformation; facilitating access for the rural poor to services aimed at reducing poverty, improving nutrition, raising incomes and building resilience in a changing environment; supporting the rural poor in managing profitable, sustainable and resilient farm and non-farm enterprises and benefiting from decent employment opportunities; enabling the rural poor to influence policies and institutions that affect their livelihoods; and enabling institutional and policy environments that support agricultural production and the related non-farm activities.

IFAD is a participant in the High Level Task Force (HLTF) on the Global Food Security Crisis, which was established by the UN Secretary-General in April 2008 and aims to address the impact of soaring global levels of food and fuel prices and to formulate a comprehensive framework for action. In June IFAD participated in the High-Level Conference on World Food Security and the Challenges of Climate Change and Bioenergy, convened by FAO in Rome, Italy. The meeting adopted a Declaration on Food Security, which noted an urgent need to develop the agricultural sectors and expand food production in developing countries and countries with economies in transition, and for increased investment in rural development, agriculture and agribusiness. In January 2009 the HLTF participated in a follow-up high level meeting convened in Madrid, Spain, which agreed to initiate a consultation process with regard to the establishment of a Global Partnership for Agriculture, Food Security and Nutrition. IFAD was to contribute to a new Agricultural Market Information System (AMIS), aimed at increasing market transparency, which was agreed by a meeting of agriculture ministers from G20 countries, held in June 2011 to address the stabilization of food price volatility. In October 2011 IFAD and WFP helped FAO to compile its annual *State of Food Insecurity in the World* report, which maintained that volatile and high food prices were likely to continue, rendering poorer consumers, farmers and states more vulnerable to poverty and hunger.

IFAD, with FAO and WFP, leads an initiative on ensuring food security by strengthening feeding programmes and expanding support to farmers in developing countries, the second of nine activities that were launched in April 2009 by the UN System Chief Executives Board for Co-ordination (CEB), with the aim of alleviating the impact on poor and vulnerable populations of the developing global economic crisis.

IFAD is a leading repository of knowledge, resources and expertise in the field of rural hunger and poverty alleviation. In 2001 it renewed its commitment to becoming a global knowledge institution for rural poverty-related issues. Through its technical assistance grants, IFAD aims to promote research and capacity-building in the agricultural sector, as well as the development of technologies to increase production and alleviate rural poverty. In recent years IFAD has been increasingly involved in promoting the use of communication technology to facilitate the exchange of information and experience among rural communities, specialized institutions and organizations, and IFAD-sponsored projects. Within the strategic context of knowledge management, IFAD has supported initiatives to establish regional electronic networks, such as Electronic Networking for Rural Asia/Pacific (ENRAP, conducted over three phases during the period 1998–2010), and FIDAMERICA in Latin America and the Caribbean (conducted over four phases during 1995–2009), as well as to develop other lines of communication between organizations, local agents and the rural poor.

IFAD is empowered to make both loans and grants. Loans are available on highly concessionary, hardened, intermediate and ordinary terms. Highly concessionary loans carry no interest but have an annual service charge of 0.75% and a repayment period of 40 years; loans approved on hardened terms carry no interest charge, have an annual service charge of 0.75%, and are repaid over 20 years; intermediate loans are subject to a variable interest charge, equivalent to 50% of the interest rate charged on World Bank loans, and are repaid over 20 years; and ordinary loans carry a variable interest charge equal to that levied by the World Bank, and are repaid over 15–18 years. New Debt Sustainability Framework (DSF) grant financing was introduced in 2007 in place of highly concessional loans for heavily indebted poor countries (HIPCs). In 2010 highly concessionary loans represented some 66.3% of total lending in that year, DSF grants 18.8%, intermediate loans 3.4%, and ordinary loans 9.7%. Research and technical assistance grants are awarded to projects focusing on research and training, and for project preparation and development. In order to increase the impact of its lending resources on food production, the Fund seeks as much as possible to attract other external donors and beneficiary governments as co-financiers of its projects. In 2010 external cofinancing accounted for some 28.5% of all project funding, while domestic contributions, i.e. from recipient governments and other local sources, accounted for 38.2%.

The IFAD Indigenous Peoples Assistance Facility was created in 2007 to fund microprojects that aim to build upon the knowledge and natural resources of indigenous communities and organizations. In September 2010, the Executive Board approved the establishment of a new Spanish Food Security Cofinancing Facility Trust Fund (the 'Spanish Trust Fund'), which was to be used to provide loans to IFAD borrower nations. On 31 December 2010 the Spanish Government provided, on a loan basis, €285.5m. to the Spanish Trust Fund.

In November 2006 IFAD was granted access to the core resources of the HIPC Trust Fund, administered by the World Bank, to assist in financing the outstanding debt relief on post-completion point countries participating in the HIPC debt relief initiative (see under IBRD). By December 2011 36 of 39 eligible countries had passed their decision points, thereby qualifying for HIPC debt relief assistance from IFAD, and 32 countries had reached completion point, thereby qualifying for full and irrevocable debt reduction.

At the end of 2010 total IFAD loans approved since 1978 amounted to US $11,926.6m. for 859 projects. During the same period the Fund approved 2,315 research and technical assistance grants, at a cost of $745.5m. In 2010 IFAD approved 30 loans and 14 DSF grants, amounting in total to $807.4m., for a total of 33 projects, as follows: $266.4m. for eight projects in Eastern and Southern Africa (or 33.0% of the total committed in that year), $194.2m. for seven operations in Asia and the Pacific (24.1%), $152.4m. for five projects in Western and Central Africa (18.9%), $125.4m. for seven projects in the Near East, North Africa and Europe (15.5%) and $69.0m. for six projects in Latin America and the Caribbean (8.5%). Research and technical assistance grants amounting to $51.2m. were awarded, bringing the total financial assistance approved in 2010 to $845.4m., compared with $717.5m. in the previous year.

IFAD's development projects usually include a number of components, such as infrastructure (e.g. improvement of water supplies, small-scale irrigation and road construction); input supply (e.g. improved seeds, fertilizers and pesticides); institutional support (e.g. research, training and extension services); and producer incentives (e.g. pricing and marketing improvements). IFAD also attempts to enable the landless to acquire income-generating assets: by increasing the provision of credit for the rural poor, it seeks to free them from dependence on the capital market and to generate productive activities.

In addition to its regular efforts to identify projects and programmes, IFAD organizes special programming missions to selected countries to undertake a comprehensive review of the constraints affecting the rural poor, and to help countries to design strategies for the removal of these constraints. In general, projects based on the recommendations of these missions tend to focus on institutional improvements at the national and local level to direct inputs and services to small farmers and the landless rural poor. Monitoring and evaluation missions are also sent to check the progress of projects and to assess the impact of poverty reduction efforts.

The Fund supports projects that are concerned with environmental conservation, in an effort to alleviate poverty that results from the deterioration of natural resources. In addition, it extends environmental assessment grants to review the environmental consequences of projects under preparation. IFAD administers the Global Mechanism of the 1996 Convention to Combat Desertification in those Countries Experiencing Drought and Desertification, particularly in Africa. The Mechanism mobilizes and channels resources for the implementation of the Convention (having supported, by September 2011, action programmes in 29 countries) and IFAD is its largest financial contributor. IFAD is an executing agency of the Global Environmental Facility, specializing in the area of combating rural poverty and environmental degradation.

During 1998 the Executive Board endorsed a policy framework for the Fund's provision of assistance in post-conflict situations, with the aim of achieving a continuum from emergency relief to a secure basis from which to pursue sustainable development. In July 2001 IFAD and UNAIDS signed a memorandum of understanding on developing a co-operation agreement.

During the late 1990s IFAD established several partnerships within the agribusiness sector, with a view to improving performance at project level, broadening access to capital markets, and encouraging the advancement of new technologies. Since 1996 it has chaired the Support Group of the Global Forum on Agricultural Research (GFAR), which facilitates dialogue between research centres and institutions, farmers' organizations, non-governmental bodies, the private sector and donors. In October 2001 IFAD became a co-sponsor of the Consultative Group on International Agricultural Research (CGIAR). In 2006 IFAD reviewed the work of the International Alliance against Hunger, which was established in 2004 to enhance co-ordination among international agencies and non-governmental organizations concerned with agriculture and rural development, and national alliances against hunger. In November 2009 IFAD and the Islamic Development Bank concluded a US $1,500m. framework cofinancing agreement for jointly financing priority projects during 2010–12 in many of the 52 countries that had membership of both organizations.

Finance

In accordance with the Articles of Agreement establishing IFAD, the Governing Council periodically undertakes a review of the adequacy of resources available to the Fund and may request members to make additional contributions. A target of US $1,500m. was set for the ninth replenishment of IFAD funds, covering the period 2013–15. The provisional budget for administrative expenses for 2012 amounted to $144.1m., while some $12m. was budgeted in that year to the Fund's capital budget.

Publications

Annual Report.
IFAD Update (2 a year).
Rural Poverty Report.
Staff Working Papers (series).

International Labour Organization—ILO

Address: 4 route des Morillons, 1211 Geneva 22, Switzerland.
Telephone: 227996111; **fax:** 227988685; **e-mail:** ilo@ilo.org; **internet:** www.ilo.org.

The ILO was founded in 1919 to work for social justice as a basis for lasting peace. It carries out this mandate by promoting decent living standards, satisfactory conditions of work and pay and adequate employment opportunities. Methods of action include the creation of international labour standards; the provision of technical co-operation services; and research and publications on social and labour matters. In 1946 the ILO became a specialized agency associated with the UN. It was awarded the Nobel Peace Prize in 1969. The ILO's tripartite structure gives representation to employers' and workers' organizations alongside governments.

MEMBERS

The ILO has 183 members.

Organization

(April 2012)

INTERNATIONAL LABOUR CONFERENCE

The supreme deliberative body of the ILO, the Conference meets annually in Geneva, with a session devoted to maritime questions when necessary; it is attended by about 2,000 delegates, advisers and observers. National delegations are composed of two government delegates, one employers' delegate and one workers' delegate. Non-governmental delegates can speak and vote independently of the views of their national government. The Conference elects the Governing Body and adopts International Labour Conventions and Recommendations. Every two years the Conference adopts the ILO Budget. The 100th Conference was held in June 2011.

The President and Vice-Presidents hold office for the term of the Conference only.

GOVERNING BODY

The ILO's executive council meets three times a year in Geneva to decide policy and programmes. It is composed of 28 government members, 14 employers' members and 14 workers' members. Ten of the titular government seats are held permanently by 'states of chief industrial importance': Brazil, the People's Republic of China, France, Germany, India, Italy, Japan, Russia, the United Kingdom and the USA. The remaining 18 are elected from other countries every three years. Employers' and workers' members are elected as individuals, not as national candidates.

Among the Committees formed by the Governing Body are: the Programme, Financial and Administrative Committee; the Building Sub-Committee; the Committee on Freedom of Association; the Committee on Legal Issues and International Labour Standards; the Sub-Committee on Multinational Enterprises; the Committee on Employment and Social Policy; the Committee on Sectoral and Technical Meetings and Related Issues; the Committee on Technical Co-operation; the Working Party on the Social Dimension of Globalization; and the Working Party on the Functioning of the Governing Body and the International Labour Conference.

Chairperson: (2011–12) GREG VINES (Australia).

Employers' Vice-Chairperson: DANIEL FUNES DE RIOJA (Argentina).

Workers' Vice-Chairperson: LUC CORTEBEECK (Belgium).

INTERNATIONAL LABOUR OFFICE

The International Labour Office is the ILO's secretariat, operational headquarters and publishing house. It is staffed in Geneva and in the field by about 2,500 people of some 110 nationalities. Operations are decentralized to regional, area and branch offices in nearly 40 countries.

Director-General: JUAN O. SOMAVÍA (Chile) (until 30 September 2012).

REGIONAL OFFICES

Africa: Africa Hall, 6th Floor, Menelik II Ave, Addis Ababa, Ethiopia; tel. (11) 544-4480; fax (11) 544-5573; e-mail addisababa@ilo.org.

Arab States: POB 11-4088, Beirut, Lebanon; tel. (1) 752400; fax (1) 752405; e-mail beirut@ilo.org.

Asia and the Pacific: POB 2-349, Bangkok 10200, Thailand; tel. (2) 881234; fax (2) 881735; e-mail bangkok@ilo.org.

Europe and Central Asia: 4 route des Morillons, 1211 Geneva 22, Switzerland; tel. 227996666; fax 227996061; e-mail europe@ilo.org.

Latin America and the Caribbean: Apdo Postal 14–124, Lima, Peru; tel. (1) 6150300; fax (1) 6150400; e-mail oit@oit.org.pe.

Activities

The ILO pursues the goal of 'Decent Work for All' and, in 1999, adopted a Decent Work Agenda, which has four basic pillars: employment, as the principal route out of poverty; rights, which empower men and women to escape from poverty; social protection, which safeguards against poverty; and tripartism and social dialogue, regarding the participation of employers' and workers' organizations as of key importance in shaping government policy for poverty reduction. Through the Decent Work Agenda the ILO supports the UN's Millennium Development Goals, adopted by UN heads of state participating in the Millennium Summit convened in September 2000.

STANDARDS AND FUNDAMENTAL PRINCIPLES AND RIGHTS AT WORK

One of the ILO's primary functions is the adoption by the International Labour Conference of conventions and recommendations setting minimum labour standards. Through ratification by member states, conventions create binding obligations to put their provisions into effect. Recommendations provide guidance as to policy and practice. By February 2012 a total of 189 conventions and 201 recommendations had been adopted, ranging over a wide field of social and labour matters. Together they form the International Labour Code. The Committee of Experts on the Application of Conventions and Recommendations and the Conference Committee on the Application of Standards monitor the adoption of international labour standards. In June 1998 the Conference adopted a Declaration on Fundamental Principles and Rights at Work, establishing four fundamental (core) labour standards: freedom of association, the abolition of forced labour, the abolition of child labour, and the elimination of discrimination in employment promotion, training and the protection of workers. All member states are obliged to observe these standards, whether or not they have ratified the corresponding international conventions. The following eight ILO core conventions have been identified by the Governing Body as fundamental to the rights of people at work, irrespective of the levels of development of individual member states: (relating to the core labour standard of freedom of association) Freedom of Association and Protection of the Right to Organise Convention (No. 87), Right to Organise and Collective Bargaining Convention (No. 98); (abolition of forced labour) Forced Labour Convention (No. 29), Abolition of Forced Labour Convention (No. 105); (equality) Equal Remuneration Convention (No. 100), Discrimination (Employment and Occupation) Convention (No. 111); (elimination of child labour) Minimum Age Convention (No. 138), Worst Forms of Child Labour Convention (No. 182). By February 2012 some 135 countries had ratified all of the core conventions; three member states: the Maldives, Marshall Islands, and Tuvalu, had ratified none of them.

In May 2003 the ILO issued the first global report on discrimination at work, *Time for Equality at Work*, compiled as a follow-up to the 1998 Declaration on Fundamental Principles and Rights at Work.

From 1996 the ILO resolved to strengthen its efforts, working closely with UNICEF, to encourage member states to ratify and to implement relevant international standards on child labour. In June 1999 the International Labour Conference adopted the Worst Forms of Child Labour Convention (No. 182); the convention entered into force in November 2000. By February 2012 it had been ratified by 174 states. The Organization helped to organize an International Conference on Child Labour, convened in The Hague, Netherlands, in February 2002. A further Global Conference on Child Labour was held in The Hague, in May 2010, organized by the Government of the Netherlands in collaboration with the ILO; the meeting adopted a 'Roadmap' to strengthen the global effort to eliminate the worst forms of child labour. In November 2010 the Governing Body endorsed a new Global Plan of Action for achieving the elimination of the worst forms of child labour by 2016. By February 2012 the ILO's International Programme for the Elimination of Child Labour (IPEC, established in 1992) was operational in 88 countries. Under IPEC emphasis was placed on the elimination of the most severe forms of labour such as hazardous working conditions and occupations, child prostitution and trafficking of children. In addition, IPEC gives special attention to children who are particularly vulnerable, for example those under 12 years of age. IPEC launched a resource guide on child trafficking and sexual exploitation to coincide with the third World Congress against Sexual Exploitation of Children and Adolescents, convened in Rio de Janeiro, Brazil, in November 2008. The ILO-sponsored World Day against Child Labour is held annually on 12 June.

In June 2011 the International Labour Conference adopted the Convention on Decent Work for Domestic Workers, establishing global standards for up to 100m. domestic labourers world-wide.

EMPLOYMENT

The ILO aims to monitor, examine and report on the situation and trends in employment throughout the world, and considers the effects on employment and social justice of economic trade, investment and related phenomena. In October 2008 the ILO expressed concern that, without prompt and co-ordinated actions by governments, the numbers of unemployed and working poor world-wide were likely to rise severely as a result of the developing global financial crisis; it was predicted that the construction, automotive, tourism, finance, services and real estate sectors would be worst affected. ILO leads an initiative on promoting a 'Global Jobs Pact', the fifth of nine activities that were launched in April 2009 by the UN System Chief Executives Board for Co-ordination (CEB), with the aim of alleviating the impact on poor and vulnerable populations of the developing global economic crisis. The Global Jobs Pact is a co-ordinated labour recovery strategy, based on promoting sustainable enterprises. The International Labour Conference endorsed the new Pact in June 2009. In September, addressing a summit meeting of G20 leaders held in Pittsburgh, USA, which had welcomed the Pact, the ILO Director-General applauded the G20 leaders' stated commitment to implementing economic recovery plans that emphasized decent work and prioritized employment growth. In October the ILO reported that workers employed by and through temporary labour agencies were particularly badly affected by the continuing financial and economic crisis. The June 2010 session of the International Labour Conference urged governments to place employment and social protection at the centre of economic recovery policies. In June 2011 the ILO published a study entitled *The Global Crisis: Causes, responses and challenges*, focusing on the role that well-designed employment and social policies should play in promoting job creation and equitable economic growth. In December 2011 the ILO and the MasterCard Foundation launched Work4Youth, a partnership aimed at promoting decent work among young people. In January 2012 the ILO Director-General—addressing a panel on 'Averting a Lost Generation' at the 2012 annual meeting of the World Economic Forum, convened in Davos-Klosters, Switzerland—strongly urged the development of a new policy paradigm to promote inclusive employment opportunities for unemployed youth. In April 2012 the ILO and World Bank released a joint report entitled *Inventory of Policy Responses to the Financial and Economic Crisis*, and a companion web-based data tool that provided a detailed record of policies that had been implemented by governments during 2008–10 with a view to limiting the economic and social impacts of the global crisis and to boosting employment. It was envisaged that stocktaking and reviewing past crisis response measures would facilitate the design of efficient and effective policies to address future economic downturns.

In January 2012 the ILO estimated that 200m. workers worldwide (6% of the global labour force) were unemployed in 2011 (an increase of 27m. over 2007, prior to the impact of the continuing global economic and jobs crisis) and reported that around 1,520m. members of the global labour force were in vulnerable employment. In addition, it was estimated that around 456m. workers globally were living on or less than US $1.25 a day (categorized as 'working poor'). The ILO predicted at that time that some 400m. new jobs would need to be created over the next 10 years to avert a further increase in the level of unemployment, and estimated the rate of global youth unemployment in 2011 at 12.7%.

In February 2002 the ILO established a World Commission on the Social Dimension of Globalization to consider means of utilizing economic globalization to stimulate economic growth and reduce poverty. The Commission issued its final report, entitled *A Fair Globalization*, in February 2004; this was endorsed by the 92nd International Labour Conference, held in June. In March 2003 the ILO adopted the Global Employment Agenda, a comprehensive framework for managing changes to employment derived from the developing global economy, through investment in knowledge and skills, maintaining a healthy labour market and ensuring adequate social safety nets. In November 2007 the ILO convened a Forum on Decent Work for a Fair Globalization, in Lisbon, Portugal, comprising some 300 representatives of the ILO tripartite social partners, and other interested parties, to address the possibility of establishing a new Decent Work Movement to overcome growing global inequality. In June 2008, as the outcome of tripartite consultations based on the work of the World Commission on the Social Dimension of Globalization and its final report, the landmark *ILO Declaration on Social Justice for a Fair Globalization*, building on the Philadelphia Declaration (1944) and the Declaration on Fundamental Principles and Rights at Work (1998), was adopted by the International Labour Conference. The Declaration placed the Decent Work Agenda at the core of ILO activities.

The ILO's programme sector on skills, knowledge and employability supports governments in structuring policies for improved investment in learning and training for enhanced employability, productivity and social inclusion. The programme focuses on promoting access to training and decent work for specific groups, such as youths, the disabled, and workers in the informal economy, and on protecting the rights of the elderly. The Job Creation and Enterprise Development Programme aims to assist governments, employers, workers and other related groups with fostering a successful business environment, for example through the identification and implementation of appropriate policies, legal frameworks and management strategies, the promotion of access to business development and training services, and the promotion of local economic development programmes. It also incorporates a specific programme to promote the development of micro- and small enterprises, in co-operation with governments, communities and other social partners. The ILO's Gender Promotion Programme aims to promote effective gender mainstreaming and is responsible for a global programme for the creation of more and better jobs for women and men. The programme assists countries to develop and implement National Action Plans to achieve this objective. A programme on crisis response and reconstruction addresses the effect on employment of armed conflicts, natural disasters, social movements or political transitions, and financial and economic disruptions. The impact of current global financial and economic trends on employment creation, poverty alleviation and social exclusion are addressed by the ILO's Social Finance Programme. The programme works to reduce vulnerability, to create jobs through enterprise development, and to make financial policies more employment-sensitive, for example by providing information on microfinance and promoting microfinance institutions, and by conducting research on the impact of financial sector liberalization on the poor.

The Multinational Enterprise Programme is responsible for the promotion of and follow-up to the Tripartite Declaration of Principles concerning Multinational Enterprises and Social Policy, which was adopted in 1977 and amended in 2000. The Declaration provides international guidelines, agreed by governments and employers' and workers' organizations, on investment policy and practice. The programme is also responsible for co-ordinating work on corporate social responsibility, as well as for the ILO's participation in the Global Compact, an initiative of the UN Secretary-General, which was inaugurated in 2000, comprising leaders in the fields of business, labour and civil society who undertook to promote human rights, the fundamental principles of the ILO, and protection of the environment.

The ILO maintains technical relations with the IMF, the World Bank, OECD, the WTO and other international organizations on global economic issues, international and national strategies for employment, structural adjustment, and labour market and training policies. In May 2011 the ILO and OECD signed a memorandum of understanding on strengthening mutual co-operation. In September of that year the ILO and WTO jointly issued a publication entitled *Making Globalization Socially Sustainable*.

In 2007 the ILO, UNEP and the International Trade Union Confederation launched in partnership the Green Jobs Initiative (the International Organisation of Employers joined in 2008). The Initiative aims to promote the creation of decent jobs as a consequence of new environmental policies required to transform ongoing global environmental challenges. In September 2008 it released a report entitled *Green Jobs: Towards Decent Work in a Sustainable, Low-Carbon World*, the first comprehensive study on the impact of the emergent 'green economy' on the labour market.

SOCIAL PROTECTION

Access to an adequate level of social protection is recognized in the ILO's 1944 Declaration of Philadelphia, as well as in a number of international labour standards, as a basic right of all individuals. The ILO aims to enable countries to extend social protection to all groups in society and to improve working conditions and safety at work. The fundamental premise of the ILO's programme sector on socio-economic security is that basic security for all is essential for productive work and human dignity in the future global economy. The achievement of basic security is deemed to entail the attainment of basic humanitarian needs, including universal access to health services and a decent level of education. The programme aims to address the following concerns: what constitutes socio-economic security and insecurity in member countries; identifying the sources of such insecurity; and identifying economic, labour and social policies that could improve socio-economic security while promoting sustainable economic growth. The programme focuses on the following dimensions of work-based security: the labour market (the provision of adequate employment opportunities); employment (for example, protection against dismissal); occupational security (the opportunity to develop a career); work (protection against accidents, illness and stress at work); skills; income; and representation (the right to collective representation in the labour market, through independent trade unions and employers' associations, etc.). The ILO's Social Security Policy and Development Branch assists member states and constituents in the design, reform and implementation of social security policies based on the principles embodied in international labour standards, with a special focus on developing strategies to extend social security coverage. The Branch provides general research and analysis of social security issues; extends technical assistance to member states for designing, reforming and expanding social security schemes; provides services to enable community-based organizations to develop their own social security systems; promotes and oversees the implementation of ILO standards on social security; develops training programmes and materials; and disseminates information. The Financial, Actuarial and Statistical Services Branch aims to improve the financial planning, management and governance of national social security schemes and social protection systems. In June 2003 the ILO inaugurated a Global Campaign on Social Security and Coverage for All, with a particular focus on the informal economy. The ILO estimates that only one-fifth of the world's population has sufficient social security coverage. The key operational tool of the Campaign is the ILO's STEP (Strategies and Tools against Social Exclusion and Poverty) Programme which undertakes field work, research, training and the dissemination of knowledge to help to extend social protection and combat social exclusion. The International Social Security Association (ISSA), based at ILO headquarters, unites social security agencies and organizations, with the aim of supporting excellence in social security administration as a means of promoting the social dimension in the era of rapid economic globalization.

The ILO's Programme on Safety and Health at Work and the Environment aims to protect workers in hazardous occupations; to provide protection to vulnerable groups of workers outside the scope of normal protection measures; to improve the capacity of governments and employers' and workers' organizations to address workers' well-being, extend the scope of occupational health care etc.; and to ensure that policy-makers recognize and document the social and economic impact of implementing measures that enhance workers' protection. The ILO Guidelines on Occupational Safety and Health Management Systems (ILO-OSH 2001) provides a framework of action at an international, national and organizational level. The ILO's Conditions of Work Branch conducts research and provides advocacy, training and technical co-operation to governments and employers' and workers' organizations in areas such as wages, working time, maternity protection and life outside of work. The International Migration Branch focuses on protecting the rights, and promoting the integration, of migrant workers, forging international consensus on the management of migration, and furthering knowledge of international migration. In June 2004 the 92nd International Labour Conference adopted a plan of action providing for the development of a multilateral framework to extend labour protection standards to migrant workers. In December 2010 ILO and the OSCE jointly published a study entitled *Strengthening Migration Governance*. The ILO's Global Programme on HIV/AIDS and the World of Work, formally established in November 2000, issued a code of practice in May 2001, focusing on prevention, management and mitigation of the impact of HIV/AIDS on the world of work, support for HIV/AIDS-affected workers, and eliminating discrimination on the basis of perceived HIV status. The ILO is a co-sponsor of the Joint UN Programme on HIV/AIDS (UNAIDS), which was established on 1 January 1996 to co-ordinate and strengthen world-wide action against HIV/AIDS. In July 2004 an ILO report assessed the financial cost of HIV/AIDS in terms of loss of output and estimated the impact of the epidemic on the global labour force. The ILO adopted a Code of Practice on HIV/AIDS and the World of Work in October 2005. In June 2010 the International Labour Conference adopted a new international labour standard on HIV/AIDS and the world of work, representing the first international human rights instrument related to HIV/AIDS and employment. A new ILO list of occupational diseases was adopted by the Governing Body in March 2010; this aimed to assist member countries with the prevention, recording, notification and, where applicable, compensation of illnesses caused by work.

ILO, with WHO, leads the Social Protection Floor initiative, the sixth activity launched in April 2009 by CEB, to alleviate the effects of the global economic crisis. In October 2011 a Social Protection Floor Advisory Group, launched in August 2010 under the initiative, issued a report entitled *Social Protection Floor for a Fair and Inclusive Globalization*, which urged that basic income and services should be guaranteed for all, stating that this would promote both stability and economic growth globally.

In December 2011 the ILO launched the ILO Global Business and Disability Network, a new global knowledge-sharing platform (accessible at www.businessanddisability.org), which was aimed at promoting the inclusion of people with disabilities in the workplace.

The ILO sponsors the World Day for Safety and Health at Work, held annually on 28 April.

SOCIAL DIALOGUE

This area was identified as one of the four strategic objectives in order to concentrate and reinforce the ILO's support for strengthening the process of tripartism, the role and activities of its tripartite constituents (i.e. governments, employers and workers' organizations), and, in particular, their capacity to engage in and to promote the use of social dialogue. The ILO recognizes that the enactment of labour laws, and ensuring their effective enforcement, collective bargaining and other forms of co-operation are important means of promoting social justice. It aims to assist governments and employers' and workers' organizations to establish sound labour relations, to adapt labour laws to meet changing economic and social needs, and to improve labour administration. In August 2006 ILO inaugurated a joint programme with the International Finance Corporation, 'Better Work', to improve labour standards within a competitive global market. In May 2009 both organizations signed a co-operation agreement to initiate a second phase of the programme in order to extend and expand its impact.

The Social Dialogue, Labour Law and Labour Administration Department maintains an International Observatory of Labour Law which provides information concerning national labour legislation and facilitates the dissemination of information regarding development in labour law throughout the world. The Department also supports the training and professional development of labour court judges and publishes the proceedings of meetings of European labour court judges.

Successive International Labour Conferences have focused special attention on reports of ongoing infringements of, and continued failure over several years to implement, the Freedom of Association and Protection of the Right to Organize Convention, 1948 (No. 87) in Belarus and Myanmar. A commission to examine alleged abuses of trade union rights in Myanmar was established in November 2003. A Committee on Freedom of Association examines allegations of abuses committed against trade union organizations and reports to the Governing Body.

INSTITUTES

International Institute for Labour Studies (IILS): 4 route des Morillons, 1211 Geneva 22, Switzerland; tel. 227996128; fax 227998542; e-mail inst@ilo.org; established in 1960 and based at the ILO's Geneva headquarters, the Institute promotes the study and discussion of policy issues of concern to the ILO and its constituents, i.e. governments, employers and workers. The core theme of the Institute's activities is the interaction between labour institutions, development and civil society in a global economy. It identifies emerging social and labour issues by developing new areas for research and action, and encourages dialogue on social policy between the tripartite constituency of the ILO and the international academic community and other experts. The Institute maintains research networks, conducts courses, seminars and social policy forums, and supports internships and visiting scholar and internship programmes. The ILO Director-General is Chairman of the Board of the Institute.

International Training Centre of the ILO (ITC-ILO): Viale Maestri del Lavoro 10, 10127 Turin, Italy; tel. (011) 693-6111; fax (011) 663-8842; e-mail communications@itcilo.org; internet www .itcilo.org; f. 1964 by the ILO to offer advanced training facilities for managers, trainers and social partners, and technical specialists from ILO mem. states; became operational in 1965; the Centre has been increasingly used by its partners to provide training for improving the management of development and for building national capacities to sustain development programmes; through training and learning the ITC-ILO develops human resources and institutional capacity in pursuit of the ILO's goal of decent work for men and women; Exec. Dir PATRICIA O'DONOVAN.

Finance

The proposed regular budget for the two years 2012–13 was US $861.6.

Publications

(in English, French and Spanish unless otherwise indicated)

Bulletin of Labour Statistics (quarterly).

Global Employment Trends.

Global Employment Trends for Youth.

Global Wage Report.

International Labour Review (quarterly).

International studies, surveys, works of practical guidance or reference (on questions of social policy, manpower, industrial relations, working conditions, social security, training, management development, etc).

Key Indicators of the Labour Market (2 a year).

Labour Law Documents (selected labour and social security laws and regulations; 3 a year).

Official Bulletin (3 a year).

Reports (for the annual sessions of the International Labour Conference, etc.; also in Arabic, Chinese and Russian).

World Employment Report (every 2–3 years).

World Labour Report (every 2 years).

World of Work (magazine issued in several languages; 5 a year).

Yearbook of Labour Statistics.

Also maintains a database on international labour standards, ILOLEX, and a database on national labour law, NATLEX, in electronic form.

International Maritime Organization—IMO

Address: 4 Albert Embankment, London, SE1 7SR, United Kingdom.

Telephone: (20) 7735-7611; **fax:** (20) 7587-3210; **e-mail:** info@imo.org; **internet:** www.imo.org.

The Inter-Governmental Maritime Consultative Organization (IMCO) began operations in 1959, as a specialized agency of the UN to facilitate co-operation among governments on technical matters affecting international shipping. Its main functions are the achievement of safe, secure and efficient navigation, and the control of pollution caused by ships and craft operating in the marine environment. IMCO became IMO in 1982.

MEMBERS

IMO has 170 members and three associate members.

Organization

(April 2012)

ASSEMBLY

The Assembly consists of delegates from all member countries, who each have one vote. Associate members and observers from other governments and the international agencies are also present. Regular sessions are held every two years. The 27th session was convened in London, United Kingdom, in November 2011.

The Assembly is responsible for the election of members to the Council and approves the appointment of the Secretary-General of the Secretariat. It considers reports from all subsidiary bodies and decides the action to be taken on them; it votes the agency's budget and determines the work programme and financial policy. The Assembly also recommends to members measures to promote maritime safety and security, and to prevent and control maritime pollution from ships.

COUNCIL

The Council is the governing body of the Organization between the biennial sessions of the Assembly. Its members, representatives of 40 states, are elected by the Assembly for a term of two years. The Council appoints the Secretary-General; transmits reports by the subsidiary bodies, including the Maritime Safety Committee, to the Assembly, and reports on the work of the Organization generally; submits budget estimates and financial statements with comments and recommendations to the Assembly. The Council normally meets twice a year.

Facilitation Committee: The Facilitation Committee deals with measures to facilitate maritime travel and transport and matters arising from the 1965 Facilitation Convention. Membership is open to all IMO member states.

MARITIME SAFETY COMMITTEE

The Maritime Safety Committee is open to all IMO members. The Committee meets at least once a year and submits proposals to the Assembly on technical matters affecting the safety of shipping. In December 2002 a conference of contracting states to the 1974 International Convention for the Safety of Life at Sea (see below) adopted a series of security measures relating to the international maritime and port industries that had been formulated by the Safety Committee in view of the major terrorist attacks perpetrated against targets in the USA in September 2001. In January 2012 a Department for Member State Audit and Implementation Support was established within the Committee.

SUB-COMMITTEES:

Bulk Liquids and Gases*
Carriage of Dangerous Goods, Solid Cargoes, Containers
Fire Protection
Flag State Implementation*
Radiocommunications and Search and Rescue
Safety of Navigation
Ship Design and Equipment
Stability and Load Lines and Fishing Vessel Safety
Standards of Training and Watchkeeping

* Also sub-committees of the Marine Environment Protection Committee.

LEGAL COMMITTEE

Established by the Council in June 1967 to deal initially with legal issues connected with the loss of the tanker *Torrey Canyon,* and subsequently with any legal problems laid before IMO. Membership is open to all IMO member states.

MARINE ENVIRONMENT PROTECTION COMMITTEE

Established by the eighth Assembly (1973) to co-ordinate IMO's work on the prevention and control of marine pollution from ships, and to assist IMO in its consultations with other UN bodies, and with international organizations and expert bodies in the field of marine pollution. Membership is open to all IMO members.

TECHNICAL CO-OPERATION COMMITTEE

Evaluates the implementation of projects for which IMO is the executing agency, and generally reviews IMO's technical assistance programmes. Established in 1965 as a subsidiary body of the Council, and formally institutionalized by means of an amendment to the IMO constitution in 1984. Membership is open to all IMO member states.

SECRETARIAT

The Secretariat consists of the Secretary-General (who serves a four-year term of office), and a staff appointed by the Secretary-General and recruited on as wide a geographical basis as possible. The Secretariat comprises the following divisions: Administrative; Conference; Legal Affairs and External Relations; Marine Environment; Maritime Safety; and Technical Co-operation.

Secretary-General: KOJI SEKIMIZU (Japan).

Activities

The 27th regular session of the Assembly, held in London in November 2011, adopted a high-level action plan for 2012–13, and approved a new Strategic Plan for the Organization. The Strategic Plan—covering the period 2012–17—focused on areas including the environmental impact of global shipping activities; the elimination of substandard shipping; piracy; and the implementation of effective measures to alleviate the humanitarian impact of piracy, and to address seaborne migration and stowaways. The Assembly also endorsed the appointment of a new Secretary-General, elected a new Council, approved the Organization's budget for 2012–13, and adopted a wide range of technical and other resolutions, including a resolution on combating piracy (see below).

From 2005 IMO brought to the attention of the UN Security Council serious concerns over acts of piracy and armed robbery being perpetrated against ships off the coast of Somalia and in the Gulf of Aden. In June, October and December 2008, November 2009, April and November 2010, and April and November 2011, the Security Council adopted successive resolutions on combating piracy. The issue was also one of the focal areas of a UN General Assembly resolution on 'Oceans and the law of the sea', adopted in February 2009. A high-level sub-regional meeting of states from the Western Indian Ocean, the Gulf of Aden and Red Sea areas, held under IMO auspices in Djibouti, in late January 2009, adopted the Djibouti Code of Conduct concerning the Repression of Piracy and Armed Robbery. The Code, which by February 2012 had been signed by 18 of the 21 countries eligible as signatories, promotes the implementation of those aspects of relevant UN Security Council resolutions, and of the February 2009 General Assembly resolution on Oceans and the law of the sea, which fall within IMO's area of competence. Signatories to the Code have agreed to co-operate lawfully in the apprehension, investigation and prosecution of people suspected of committing or facilitating acts of piracy; in the seizure of suspect vessels; in the rescue of ships, persons and property subject to acts of armed robbery; and to collaborate in the conduct of security operations. The Code also provides for sharing related information on matters related to maritime security. Meeting in May–June 2009 the Maritime Safety Committee approved revised guidance to governments, and also to shipowners, ship operators, ship masters and crews, on suppressing piracy. In December 2009 the IMO Assembly adopted a resolution supporting UN Security Council efforts to combat piracy, and also adopted a revised code of practice for investigating crimes of piracy and armed robbery against ships. The November 2011 IMO Assembly adopted a further resolution on 'combating piracy and armed robbery against ships in waters off the coast of Somalia', urging universal compliance with guidance promulgated by the Organization on preventive, evasive and defensive measures; encouraging governments to decide, as a matter of national policy, whether ships entitled to fly their flag should be authorized to carry privately contracted armed security personnel; strongly encouraging port and coastal states to promulgate their national policies on the embarkation, disembarkation and carriage of privately contracted armed security personnel and security-related equipment; and urging governments to ensure that owners and operators of ships entitled to fly their flag take fully into account the welfare of seafarers affected by piracy.

In December 2009 the 26th session of the Assembly determined that from 2015 the Organization's Member State Audit Scheme, aimed at comprehensively assessing national implementation of IMO instruments, should become mandatory.

In May 2010 the Maritime Safety Committee adopted a set of 'goal-based standards' (GBS)—structural standards conforming to functional requirements that had been developed by the Committee—with which, henceforth, newly constructed oil tankers and bulk carriers were to comply. The GBS were the first ever standards set by IMO for ship construction. At that time the Committee also adopted guidelines giving IMO a role in verifying compliance with the provisions of the International Convention for the Safety of Life at Sea (SOLAS) (see below). In July 2011 states parties to the MARPOL Convention adopted amendments to Annex VI (relating to prevention of air pollution from ships) to make mandatory the Energy Efficiency Design Index (EEDI), for new ships, of 400 gross tonnage and above, and the Ship Energy Efficiency Management Plan (SEEMP) for all ships. The revised regulations were expected to enter into force on 1 January 2013.

In June 2010 five new navigational areas (NAVAREAs) and meteorological areas (METAREAs), delineated by IMO and WMO respectively, were established in Arctic waters, expanding the World-Wide Navigational Warning System (WWNWS) into the region and thereby enabling ships operating there to receive necessary information about navigational and meteorological hazards. In 2012 the Sub-Committee on Ship Design and Equipment was developing a new mandatory Polar Code, which was to supplement relevant instruments, including MARPOL and SOLAS, to take into account risks specific to ships operating in remote and environmentally extreme polar waters.

In September 2010 IMO launched a new Seafarers' Rights International Centre, located at the London headquarters of the International Transport Workers' Federation.

In November 2011 IOM, jointly with the Intergovernmental Oceanographic Commission, UNDP, and FAO, released a *The Blueprint for Ocean and Coastal Sustainability*, aimed at improving the management of oceans and coastal areas.

IMO sponsors an annual Day of the Seafarer, held on 25 June. World Maritime Day is celebrated annually on 23 September; the theme for 2012 was to be 'IMO: One hundred years after the Titanic', and the role of the IMO in promoting safety at sea.

CONVENTIONS

(of which IMO is the depository)

Convention on Facilitation of International Maritime Traffic, 1965: came into force in March 1967.

International Convention on Load Lines, 1966: came into force in July 1968; Protocol, adopted in 1988, came into force in February 2000; numerous other amendments.

International Convention on Tonnage Measurement of Ships, 1969: Convention embodies a universal system for measuring ships' tonnage. Came into force in 1982.

International Convention relating to Intervention on the High Seas in Cases of Oil Pollution Casualties, 1969: came into force in May 1975; a Protocol adopted in 1973 came into force in 1983.

International Convention on Civil Liability for Oil Pollution Damage, 1969: came into force in June 1975; amended by Protocols of 1976, 1984 and 1992 (which was to replace the original Convention); further amendments to the 1992 Protocol, adopted in 2000, came into force in November 2003.

International Convention on the Establishment of an International Fund for Compensation for Oil Pollution Damage, 1971: came into force in October 1978; amended by Protocols of 1976, 1984 and 1992 (which replaced the original Convention); further amendments to the 1992 Protocol, adopted in 2000, came into force in November 2003; a Protocol to establish a Supplementary Fund was adopted in 2003 and came into force in March 2005.

Convention relating to Civil Liability in the Field of Maritime Carriage of Nuclear Material, 1971: came into force in 1975.

Special Trade Passenger Ships Agreement, 1971: came into force in 1974.

Convention on the International Regulations for Preventing Collisions at Sea, 1972: came into force in July 1977; numerous amendments.

Convention on the Prevention of Marine Pollution by Dumping of Wastes and Other Matter ('London Convention'), 1972: came into force in August 1975; numerous amendments, including, 1993, to incorporate a ban on low-level nuclear waste, which came into force in February 1994; Protocol, which was to replace the original Convention, adopted in 1996.

Hong Kong International Convention for the Safe and Environmentally Sound Recycling of Ships, 2009: adopted in May 2009, and opened for signature during September 2009–August 2010; was to enter into force 24 months after ratification by 15 states representing 40% of global merchant shipping by gross tonnage.

International Convention for Safe Containers, 1972: came into force in September 1977.

International Convention for the Prevention of Pollution from Ships, 1973: (as modified by the Protocol of 1978, known as MARPOL 73/78); came into force in October 1983; extended to include regulations to prevent air pollution in September 1997; came into force in May 2005; a revised MARPOL Annex VI: Prevention of Air Pollution from Ships was adopted in October 2008 and entered into force in July 2010; further amendments to Annex VI were adopted in July 2011 establishing a North American Emission Control Area; a revised MARPOL Annex III: Prevention of Pollution from Packaged Goods, and a revised MARPOL Annex V: Regulations for the Prevention of Pollution by Garbage from Ships, were approved in October 2010; in July 2011 a revision to Annex I, banning heavy fuel oil from the Antarctic region, was adopted.

International Convention for the Safety of Life at Sea (SOLAS), 1974: came into force in May 1980; a Protocol drawn up in 1978 came into force in May 1981; a second Protocol, of 1988, came into force in February 2000; amendments including special measures to enhance maritime safety came into force in July 2004, and further amendments strengthening international passenger ship safety regulations entered into force in July 2010.

Athens Convention relating to the Carriage of Passengers and their Luggage by Sea, 1974: came into force in April 1987.

Convention on the International Maritime Satellite Organization, 1976: came into force in July 1979.

Convention on Limitation of Liability for Maritime Claims, 1976: came into force in December 1986; a Protocol came into force in May 2004.

International Convention for the Safety of Fishing Vessels, Torremolinos, 1977: replaced by a Protocol adopted in 1993; to come into force 12 months after 15 countries with an aggregate fleet of at least 14,000 vessels of 24 metres in length and over have become parties thereto.

International Convention on Standards of Training, Certification and Watchkeeping (STCW) for Seafarers, 1978: came into force in April 1984; restructured by amendments that entered into force in February 1997, and further amendments adopted in June 2010; countries deemed to be implementing the Convention fully are recorded on a so-called 'white list'.

International Convention on Maritime Search and Rescue, 1979: came into force in June 1985.

Convention for the Suppression of Unlawful Acts against the Safety of Maritime Navigation, 1988: came into force in March 1992. Further Protocol adopted in October 2005.

Protocol for the Suppression of Unlawful Acts against the Safety of Fixed Platforms located on the Continental Shelf, 1988: came into force in March 1992; further Protocol adopted in October 2005.

International Convention on Salvage, 1989: came into force in July 1996.

International Convention on Oil Pollution, Preparedness, Response and Co-operation, 1990: came into force in May 1995.

International Convention on Maritime Liens and Mortgages, 1992: came into force in September 2004.

International Convention on Standards on Training, Certification and Watchkeeping for Fishing Vessel Personnel (STCW-F), 1995: will enter into force on 29 September 2012, 12 months after receiving the required 15 ratifications.

International Convention on Liability and Compensation for Damage in Connection with the Carriage of Hazardous and Noxious Substances by Sea, 1996: will come into force 18 months after 12 states of which four have not less than 2m. units of gross tonnage have become parties thereto.

International Convention on Civil Liability for Bunker Oil Pollution Damage, 2001: entered into force November 2008.

International Convention on the Control of Harmful Anti-fouling Systems on Ships, 2001: entered into force September 2008.

International Convention for the Control and Management of Ships' Ballast Water and Sediments, 2004: will come into force 12 months after 30 states representing not less than 35% of the world's merchant shipping tonnage have become parties thereto.

Nairobi International Convention on the Removal of Wrecks, 2007: will enter into force 12 months after 10 states have become parties thereto.

Port State Control Agreements: Paris Memorandum of Understanding (MOU) on Port State Control, 1982; Viña del Mar Agreement, 1992; Tokyo MOU, 1993; Caribbean MOU, 1996; Mediterranean MOU, 1997; Indian Ocean MOU, 1998; Abuja MOU, 1999; Black Sea, MOU, 2000. An International Ship and Port Facility Security Code was adopted under IMO auspices in December 2002 and entered into force in July 2004.

TRAINING INSTITUTES

IMO International Maritime Law Institute (IMLI): POB 31, Msida, MSD 1000, Malta; tel. 21319343; fax 21343092; e-mail info@imli.org; internet www.imli.org; f. 1988; provides degree courses, other training courses, study and research facilities for specialists in maritime law; promotes the development and dissemination of knowledge and expertise in the international legal regime of merchant shipping and related areas; Dir Prof. DAVID ATTARD; publs *IMLI News*, *IMLI e-News*, *IMLI Global Directory*.

World Maritime University (WMU): POB 500, Citadellsvägen 29, 201 24 Malmö, Sweden; tel. (40) 356300; fax (40) 128442; e-mail info@wmu.se; internet www.wmu.se; f. 1983; offers postgraduate courses in maritime disciplines, a master's and doctoral programme and professional development courses; undertakes various research projects; Pres. Prof. BJÖRN KJERFVE (USA/Sweden); publs *WMU News*, *WMU Handbook*, *WMU Journal of Maritime Affairs* (2 a year), several books on maritime issues.

OTHER AFFILIATED BODIES

Partnership in Environmental Management for the Seas of East Asia (PEMSEA): POB 2502, Quezon City, 1165 Philippines; tel. (2) 9292992; fax (2) 9269712; e-mail info@pemsea.org; internet www.pemsea.org; administered by UNOPS in conjunction with UNDP and the Global Environment Facility; aims to build interagency, intersectoral and intergovernmental partnerships for the implementation of the Sustainable Development Strategy for the Seas of East Asia (SDS-SEA).

Regional Marine Pollution Emergency Response Centre for the Mediterranean Sea (REMPEC): Maritime House, Lascaris Wharf, Valletta VLT 1921, Malta; tel. 21337296; fax 21339951; e-mail rempec@rempec.org; internet www.rempec.org; f. 1976 as the Regional Oil Combating Centre for the Mediterranean Sea; administered by IMO in conjunction with the Regional Seas Programme of the UN Environment Programme; aims to develop measures to prevent and combat pollution from ships in the Mediterranean; responsible for implementing a new EU-funded regional project, initiated in November 2005, for Euro-Mediterranean co-operation on maritime safety and prevention of pollution from ships; Dir FRÉDÉRIC HÉBERT (France).

Regional Marine Pollution Emergency, Information and Training Center for the Wider Caribbean Region: Fokkerweg 26, Willemstad Curaçao, Netherlands Antilles; tel. 461-4012; fax 461-1996; e-mail rempeitc@cep.unep.org; internet cep.unep.org/racrempeitc; f. 1995; aims to help prevent and respond to major pollution incidents in the region's marine environment; administered by IMO in conjunction with UNEP's Regional Seas Programme.

Finance

Contributions are received from the member states, with the amount paid calculated according to the tonnage of a member state's merchant fleet. The 10 top contributors in 2010 were: Panama, Liberia, Bahamas, Marshall Islands, the United Kingdom, Greece, Singapore, Malta, Japan and the People's Republic of China. The budget appropriation for the two years 2012–13, approved by the Assembly in November 2011, amounted to £62.2m., comprising £30.5m. for 2012 and £31.7m. for 2013.

Publications

IMO News (quarterly).

Ships' Routeing.

Numerous specialized publications, including international conventions of which IMO is the depository.

International Monetary Fund—IMF

Address: 700 19th St, NW, Washington, DC 20431, USA.

Telephone: (202) 623-7000; **fax:** (202) 623-4661; **e-mail:** publicaffairs@imf.org; **internet:** www.imf.org.

The IMF was established at the same time as the World Bank in December 1945, to promote international monetary co-operation, to facilitate the expansion and balanced growth of international trade and to promote stability in foreign exchange.

MEMBERS

The IMF has 188 members.

Organization

(April 2012)

Managing Director: CHRISTINE LAGARDE (France).

First Deputy Managing Director: DAVID LIPTON (USA).

Deputy Managing Directors: NAOYUKI SHINOHARA (Japan), NEMAT SHAFIK (Egypt/United Kingdom/USA), MIN ZHU (People's Republic of China).

BOARD OF GOVERNORS

The highest authority of the Fund is exercised by the Board of Governors, on which each member country is represented by a Governor and an Alternate Governor. The Board normally meets once a year. The Board of Governors has delegated many of its powers to the Executive Directors. However, the conditions governing the admission of new members, adjustment of quotas and the election of Executive Directors, as well as certain other important powers, remain the sole responsibility of the Board of Governors. The voting power of each member on the Board of Governors is related to its quota in the Fund (see table below).

In September 1999 the Board of Governors adopted a resolution to transform the Interim Committee of the Board of Governors (established in 1974) into the International Monetary and Financial Committee (IMFC). The IMFC, which held its inaugural meeting in April 2000, comprises 24 members, representing the same countries or groups of countries as those on the Board of Executive Directors (see below). It advises and reports to the Board on matters relating to the management and adaptation of the international monetary and financial system, sudden disturbances that might threaten the system and proposals to amend the Articles of Agreement, but has no decision-making authority.

The Development Committee (the Joint Ministerial Committee of the Boards of Governors of the World Bank and the IMF on the Transfer of Real Resources to Developing Countries, created in 1974, with a structure similar to that of the IMFC) reviews development policy issues and financing requirements.

BOARD OF EXECUTIVE DIRECTORS

The 24-member Board of Executive Directors, responsible for the day-to-day operations of the Fund, is in continuous session in Washington, under the chairmanship of the Fund's Managing Director or Deputy Managing Directors. The USA, United Kingdom, Germany, France and Japan each appoint one Executive Director. There is also one Executive Director each from the People's Republic of China, Russia and Saudi Arabia, while the remainder are elected by groups of all other member countries. As in the Board of Governors, the voting power of each member is related to its quota in the Fund, but in practice the Executive Directors normally operate by consensus. In December 2010 the Board of Governors endorsed a proposal to amend the composition of the Board of Executive Directors in order to increase the representation of emerging dynamic economies and developing countries. The proposal, which required ratification of an Amendment to the Articles of Agreement by members holding 85% of the total voting power, also provided for Board to be fully elected.

The Managing Director of the Fund serves as head of its staff, which is organized into departments by function and area. In 2012 the Fund employed some 2,400 staff members from 144 countries.

REGIONAL REPRESENTATION

There is a network of regional offices and Resident Representatives in more than 90 member countries. In addition, special information and liaison offices are located in Tokyo, Japan (for Asia and the Pacific), in New York, USA (for the United Nations), and in Europe (Paris, France; Geneva, Switzerland; Belgium, Brussels; and Warsaw, Poland, for Central Europe and the Baltic states).

Principal Office in Europe: 64–66 ave d'Iéna, 75116 Paris, France; tel. 1-40-69-30-70; fax 1-47-23-40-89; Dir EMMANUEL VAN DER MENSBRUGGHE (Belgium).

Regional Office for Asia and the Pacific: 21F Fukoku Seimei Bldg, 2-2-2, Uchisaiwai-cho, Chiyodu-ku, Tokyo 100, Japan; tel. (3) 3597-6700; fax (3) 3597-6705; f. 1997; Dir SHOGO ISHII (Japan).

Regional Office for Central Europe and the Baltics: 00-108 Warsaw, 37C Zielna, Poland; tel. (22) 3386700; fax (22) 3386500; e-mail cee-office@imf.org; f. 2005; Senior Regional Rep. MARK ALLEN.

Activities

The purposes of the IMF, as defined in the Articles of Agreement, are:

(i) To promote international monetary co-operation through a permanent institution which provides the machinery for consultation and collaboration on monetary problems;

(ii) To facilitate the expansion and balanced growth of international trade, and to contribute thereby to the promotion and maintenance of high levels of employment and real income and to the development of members' productive resources;

(iii) To promote exchange stability, to maintain orderly exchange arrangements among members, and to avoid competitive exchange depreciation;

(iv) To assist in the establishment of a multilateral system of payments in respect of current transactions between members and in the elimination of foreign exchange restrictions which hamper the growth of trade;

(v) To give confidence to members by making the general resources of the Fund temporarily available to them, under adequate safeguards, thus providing them with the opportunity to correct maladjustments in their balance of payments, without resorting to measures destructive of national or international prosperity;

(vi) In accordance with the above, to shorten the duration of and lessen the degree of disequilibrium in the international balances of payments of members.

In joining the Fund, each country agrees to co-operate with the above objectives. In accordance with its objective of facilitating the expansion of international trade, the IMF encourages its members to accept the obligations of Article VIII, Sections two, three and four, of the Articles of Agreement. Members that accept Article VIII undertake to refrain from imposing restrictions on the making of payments and transfers for current international transactions and from engaging in discriminatory currency arrangements or multiple currency practices without IMF approval. At the end of 2011 some 90% of members had accepted Article VIII status.

In 2000/01 the Fund established an International Capital Markets Department to improve its understanding of financial markets and a separate Consultative Group on capital markets to serve as a forum for regular dialogue between the Fund and representatives of the private sector. In mid-2006 the International Capital Markets Department was merged with the Monetary and Financial Systems Department to create the Monetary and Capital Markets Department, with the intention of strengthening surveillance of global financial transactions and monetary arrangements. In June 2008 the Managing Director presented a new Work Programme, comprising the following four immediate priorities for the Fund: to enable member countries to deal with the current crises of reduced economic growth and escalating food and fuel prices, including efforts by the Fund to strengthen surveillance activities; to review the Fund's lending instruments; to implement new organizational tools and working practices; and to advance further the Fund's governance agenda.

The deceleration of economic growth in the world's major economies in 2007 and 2008 and the sharp decline in global financial market conditions, in particular in the second half of 2008, focused international attention on the adequacy of the governance of the international financial system and of regulatory and supervisory frameworks. The IMF aimed to provide appropriate and rapid financial and technical assistance to low-income and emerging economies most affected by the crisis and to support a co-ordinated, multinational recovery effort. The Fund worked closely with the Group of 20 (G20) leading economies to produce an Action Plan, in November 2008, concerned with strengthening regulation, transparency and integrity in financial markets and reform of the international financial system. In March 2009 the IMF released a study on the 'Impact of the Financial Crisis on Low-income Countries', and in that month convened, with the Government of Tanzania, a high-level conference, held in Dar es Salaam, to consider the effects of the global financial situation on African countries, as well as areas for future partnership and growth. Later in that month the Executive Board approved a series of reforms to enhance the effectiveness of the Fund's lending framework, including new conditionality criteria, a new flexible credit facility and increased access limits (see below).

In April 2009 a meeting of G20 heads of state and government, convened in London, United Kingdom, determined to make available substantial additional resources through the IMF and other multinational development institutions in order to strengthen global financial liquidity and support economic recovery. There was a commitment to extend US $250,000m. to the IMF in immediate bilateral financial contributions (which would be incorporated into an expanded New Arrangements to Borrow facility) and to support a general allocation of special drawing rights (SDRs), amounting to a further $250,000m. It was agreed that additional resources from sales of IMF gold were to be used to provide $6,000m. in concessional financing for the poorest countries over the next two to three years. The G20 meeting also resolved to implement several major reforms to strengthen the regulation and supervision of the international financial system, which envisaged the IMF collaborating closely with a new Financial Stability Board. In September G20 heads of state and government endorsed a Mutual Assessment Programme, which aimed to achieve sustainable and balanced growth, with the IMF providing analysis and technical assistance. In January 2010 the IMF initiated a process to review its mandate and role in the 'post-crisis' global economy. Short-term priorities included advising countries on moving beyond the policies they implemented during the crisis; reviewing the Fund's mandate in surveillance and lending, and investigating ways of improving the stability of the international monetary system; strengthening macro-financial and cross-country analyses, including early warning exercises; and studying ways to make policy frameworks more resilient to crises. In November 2011 G20 heads of state and government, meeting in Cannes, France, agreed to initiate an immediate review of the Fund's resources, with a view to securing global financial stability which had been undermined by high levels of debt in several euro zone countries. In December European Union heads of state and government agreed to allocate to the IMF additional resources of up to $270,000m. in the form of bilateral loans.

A joint meeting of the IMFC, G20 finance ministers and governors of central banks, convened in April 2012, in Washington, DC, USA, welcomed a decision in March by euro zone member states to strengthen European firewalls through broader reform efforts and the availability of central bank swap lines, and determined to enhance IMF resources for crisis prevention and resolution, announcing commitments from G20 member states to increasing, by more than US $430,000m., resources to be made available to the IMF as part of a protective firewall to serve the entire IMF membership.

In September 2011 the IMF joined other international financial institutions active in the Middle East and North Africa region to endorse the so-called Deauville Partnership, established by the G8 in May to support political and economic reforms being undertaken by several countries, notably Egypt, Jordan, Morocco and Tunisia. The Fund was committed to supporting those countries to maintain economic and financial stability, and to promote inclusive growth.

SPECIAL DRAWING RIGHTS

The SDR was introduced in 1970 as a substitute for gold in international payments, and was intended eventually to become the principal reserve asset in the international monetary system. SDRs are allocated to members in proportion to their quotas. In October 1996 the Executive Board agreed to a new allocation of SDRs in order to achieve their equitable distribution among member states (i.e. all members would have an equal number of SDRs relative to the size of their quotas). In particular, this was deemed necessary since 38 countries that had joined the Fund since the last allocation of SDRs in 1981 had not yet received any of the units of account. In September 1997, at the annual meeting of the Executive Board, a resolution approving a special allocation of SDR 21,400m. was passed, in order to ensure an SDR to quota ratio of 29.32%, for all member countries. The proposed Fourth Amendment to the Articles of Agreement was to come into effect following its acceptance by 60% of member countries, having 85% of the total voting power. The final communiqué of the G20 summit meeting, held in April, endorsed the urgent ratification of the Fourth Amendment. In August the Amendment entered into force, having received approval by the USA. The special allocation, equivalent to some US $33,000m., was implemented on 9 September.

In August 2009 the Board of Governors approved a third general allocation of SDRs, amounting to SDR 161,200m., which become available to all members, in proportion to their existing quotas, effective from 28 August.

From 1974 to 1980 the SDR was valued on the basis of the market exchange rate for a basket of 16 currencies, belonging to the members with the largest exports of goods and services; since 1981 it has been based on the currencies of the five largest exporters (France, Germany, Japan, the United Kingdom and the USA), although the list of currencies and the weight of each in the SDR valuation basket is revised every five years. In January 1999 the IMF incorporated the new currency of the European Economic and Monetary Union, the euro, into the valuation basket; it replaced the French and German currencies, on the basis of their conversion rates with the euro as agreed by the EU. From 1 January 2006 the relative weights assigned to the currencies in the valuation basket were redistributed. The value of the SDR averaged US $1.57868 in 2011, and at 20 April 2012 stood at $1.54481.

The Second Amendment to the Articles of Agreement (1978) altered and expanded the possible uses of the SDR in transactions with other participants. These 'prescribed holders' of the SDRs have the same degree of freedom as Fund members to buy and sell SDRs and to receive or use them in loans, pledges, swaps, donations or settlement of financial obligations.

QUOTAS

Each member is assigned a quota related to its national income, monetary reserves, trade balance and other economic indicators. A member's subscription is equal to its quota and is payable partly in SDRs and partly in its own currency. The quota determines a member's voting power, which is based on one vote for each SDR 100,000 of its quota *plus* the 250 votes to which each member is entitled. A member's quota also determines its access to the financial resources of the IMF, and its allocation of SDRs.

Quotas are reviewed at intervals of not more than five years, to take into account the state of the world economy and members' different rates of development. Special increases, separate from the general review, may be made in exceptional circumstances. In June 1990 the Board of Governors authorized proposals for a Ninth General Review of quotas. At the same time the Board stipulated that the quota increase, of almost 50%, could occur only after the Third Amendment of the IMF's Articles of Agreement had come into effect. The amendment provides for the suspension of voting and other related rights of members that do not fulfil their obligations under the Articles. By September 1992 the necessary proportion of IMF members had accepted the amendment, and it entered into force in November. The 10th General Review of quotas was concluded in December 1994, with the Board recommending no further increase in quotas. In October 1996 the Fund's Managing Director advocated an increase in quotas under the latest review of at least two-thirds in the light of the IMF's reduced liquidity position. (The IMF had extended unprecedentedly large amounts in stand-by arrangements during the period 1995–96, notably to Mexico and Russia.) In January 1998 the Board of Governors adopted a resolution in support of an increase in quotas of 45%. The required consent of member states constituting 85% of total quotas had been granted by January 1999 to enable the 11th General Review of Quotas to enter into effect. The 12th General Review was initiated in December 2001, and was concluded at the end of January 2003 without an increase in quotas. The 13th General Review was concluded, without an increase in quotas, in January 2008. In September 2006 the Board of Governors adopted a resolution on Quota and Voice Reform in the IMF, representing a two-year reform package aimed at improving the alignment of the quota shares of member states to represent more accurately their relative positions in the global economy and also to enhance the participation and influence of emerging market and low-income countries. An immediate ad hoc quota increase was approved for the People's Republic of China, the Republic of Korea, Mexico and Turkey. In March 2008 the Executive Board approved a second round of ad hoc quota increases as part of the proposed extensive reform of the governance and quota structure, which also committed the Fund to regular, five-yearly realignments of quotas. The proposals were to come into effect upon being accepted by member states representing 85% of total votes. In April 2009 G20 heads of state and government further endorsed the quota and voice reform measures and urged the IMF to complete a general review of quotas by January 2011. The 2008 Quota and Voice Reform agreement entered into effect in March 2011, providing for quota increases for 54 member countries with emerging or dynamic economies and an increase in basic votes for low-income countries, in order to strengthen their participation mechanism. In November 2010 the Executive Board responded to a request by the G20 for a further realignment of quotas, and in December the Board of Governors endorsed an agreement concluding the 14th General Review of Quotas to provide for a 100% increase in quotas, to some SDR 476,800m. and adjustment of quota shares to ensure appropriate representation for emerging economies and developing countries. The agreement included a commitment to undertake a comprehensive review of the quota formula by January 2013 and to conclude a 15th General Review by January 2014. The reforms required acceptance of three-fifths of members representing 85% of voting power in order to enter into effect. At April 2012 total quotas in the Fund amounted to SDR 238,116.4m.

RESOURCES

Members' subscriptions form the basic resource of the IMF. They are supplemented by borrowing. Under the General Arrangements to Borrow (GAB), established in 1962, the Group of Ten industrialized nations (G10—Belgium, Canada, France, Germany, Italy, Japan, the Netherlands, Sweden, the United Kingdom and the USA) and Switzerland (which became a member of the IMF in May 1992 but which had been a full participant in the GAB from April 1984) undertake to lend the Fund as much as SDR 17,000m. in their own currencies to assist in fulfilling the balance of payments requirements of any member of the group, or in response to requests to the Fund from countries with balance of payments problems that could threaten the stability of the international monetary system. In 1983 the Fund entered into an agreement with Saudi Arabia, in association with the GAB, making available SDR 1,500m., and other borrowing arrangements were completed in 1984 with the Bank for International Settlements, the Saudi Arabian Monetary Agency, Belgium and Japan, making available a further SDR 6,000m. In 1986 another borrowing arrangement with Japan made available SDR 3,000m. In May 1996 GAB participants concluded an agreement in principle to expand the resources available for borrowing to SDR 34,000m., by securing the support of 25 countries with the financial capacity to support the international monetary system. The so-called New Arrangements to Borrow (NAB) was approved by the Executive Board in January 1997. It was to enter into force, for an initial five-year period, as soon as the five largest potential creditors participating in NAB had approved the initiative and the total credit arrangement of participants endorsing the scheme had reached at least SDR 28,900m. While the GAB credit arrangement was to remain in effect, the NAB was expected to be the first facility to be activated in the event of the Fund's requiring supplementary resources. In July 1998 the GAB was activated for the first time in more than 20 years in order to provide funds of up to US $6,300m. in support of an IMF emergency assistance package for Russia (the first time the GAB had been used for a non-participant). The NAB became effective in November, and was used for the first time as part of an extensive programme of support for Brazil, which was adopted by the IMF in early December. (In March 1999, however, the activation was cancelled.) In November 2008 the Executive Board initiated an assessment of IMF resource requirements and options for supplementing resources in view of an exceptional increase in demand for IMF assistance. In February 2009 the Board approved the terms of a borrowing agreement with the Government of Japan to extend some SDR 67,000m. (some $100,000m.) in supplemental funding, for an initial one-year period. In April G20 heads of state and government resolved to expand the NAB facility, to incorporate all G20 economies, in order to increase its resources by up to SDR 367,500m. ($500,000m.). The G20 summit meeting held in September confirmed that it had contributed the additional resources to the NAB. In April 2010 the IMF's Executive Board approved the expansion and enlargement of NAB borrowing arrangements; these came into effect in March 2011, having completed the ratification process. By December 37 members or state institutions were participating in the NAB, and had committed SDR 366,116m. in supplementary resources.

FINANCIAL ASSISTANCE

The Fund makes resources available to eligible members on an essentially short-term and revolving basis to provide members with temporary assistance to contribute to the solution of their payments problems. Before making a purchase, a member must show that its balance of payments or reserve position makes the purchase necessary. Apart from this requirement, reserve tranche purchases (i.e. purchases that do not bring the Fund's holdings of the member's currency to a level above its quota) are permitted unconditionally. Exchange transactions within the Fund take the form of members' purchases (i.e. drawings) from the Fund of the currencies of other members for the equivalent amounts of their own currencies.

With further purchases, however, the Fund's policy of conditionality means that a recipient country must agree to adjust its economic policies, as stipulated by the IMF. All requests other than for use of the reserve tranche are examined by the Executive Board to determine whether the proposed use would be consistent with the Fund's policies, and a member must discuss its proposed adjustment programme (including fiscal, monetary, exchange and trade policies) with IMF staff. New guidelines on conditionality, which, *inter alia*, aimed to promote national ownership of policy reforms and to introduce specific criteria for the implementation of conditions given different states' circumstances, were approved by the Executive Board in September 2002. In March 2009 the Executive Board approved reforms to modernize the Fund's conditionality policy, including greater use of pre-set qualification criteria and monitoring structural policy implementation by programme review (rather than by structural performance criteria).

Purchases outside the reserve tranche are made in four credit tranches, each equivalent to 25% of the member's quota; a member must reverse the transaction by repurchasing its own currency (with SDRs or currencies specified by the Fund) within a specified time. A credit tranche purchase is usually made under a 'Stand-by Arrangement' with the Fund, or under the Extended Fund Facility. A Stand-by Arrangement is normally of one or two years' duration, and the amount is made available in instalments, subject to the member's observance of 'performance criteria'; repurchases must be made within three-and-a-quarter to five years. An Extended Arrangement is normally of three years' duration, and the member must submit detailed economic programmes and progress reports for each year; repurchases must be made within four-and-a-half to 10 years. In October 1994 the Executive Board approved an increase in members' access to IMF resources, on the basis of a recommendation by the then Interim Committee. The annual access limit under IMF regular tranche drawings, Stand-by Arrangements and Extended Fund Facility credits was increased from 68% to 100% of a member's quota, with the cumulative access limit set at 300%. In March 2009 the Executive Board agreed to double access limits for non-concessional loans to 200% and 600% of a member's quota for annual and cumulative access respectively. In 2009/10 regular funding arrangements approved (and augmented) amounted to SDR 74,175m. (compared with SDR 66,736m. in the previous financial year and SDR 1,333m. in 2007/08).

In October 1995 the Interim Committee of the Board of Governors endorsed recent decisions of the Executive Board to strengthen IMF financial support to members requiring exceptional assistance. An Emergency Financing Mechanism was established to enable the IMF to respond swiftly to potential or actual financial crises, while additional funds were made available for short-term currency stabilization. The Mechanism was activated for the first time in July 1997, in response to a request by the Philippines Government to reinforce the country's international reserves, and was subsequently used during that year to assist Thailand, Indonesia and the Republic of Korea. It was used in 2001 to accelerate lending to Turkey. In September 2008 the Mechanism was activated to facilitate approval of a Stand-by Arrangement amounting to SDR 477.1m. for Georgia, which urgently needed to contain its fiscal deficit and undertake rehabilitation measures following a conflict with Russia in the previous month. In November the Board approved a Stand-by Arrangement of SDR 5,169m., under the Emergency Financing Mechanism procedures, to support an economic stabilization programme in Pakistan, one for Ukraine, amounting to SDR 11,000m., and another of SDR 10,538m. for Hungary, which constituted 1,015% of its quota, to counter exceptional pressures on that country's banking sector and the Government's economic programme. An arrangement for Latvia, amounting to SDR 1,522m., was approved in the following month. In May 2010 the Board endorsed a three-year Stand-by Arrangement for Greece amounting to SDR 26,400m., accounting for some 2,400% of that country's new quota (under the 2008 quota reform). The Arrangement was approved under the Emergency Financing Mechanism, as part of a joint financial assistance package with the euro area countries, which aimed to alleviate Greece's sovereign debt crisis and to support an economic recovery and reform programme. In July 2011 the Fund completed a fourth review of the country's economic performance under the Stand-by Arrangement, enabling a further disbursement of SDR 2,900m. At that time total Fund disbursements under the Arrangement amounted to SDR 15,600m.

In October 2008 the Executive Board approved a new Short-Term Liquidity Facility (SLF) to extend exceptional funds (up to 500% of quotas) to emerging economies affected by the turmoil in international financial markets and economic deceleration in advanced economies. Eligibility for lending under the new Facility was to be based on a country's record of strong macroeconomic policies and having a sustainable level of debt. In March 2009 the Executive Board decided to replace the SLF with a Flexible Credit Line (FCL) facility, which, similarly, was to provide credit to countries with strong economic foundations, but was also to be primarily considered as precautionary. In addition, it was to have a longer repayment period (of up to five years) and have no access 'cap'. The first arrangement under the FCL was approved in April for Mexico, making available funds of up to SDR 31,528m. for a one-year period. Three FCL arrangements, amounting to SDR 52,184m., were approved in 2009/10, accounting for more than 70% of Fund lending commitments in that year.

In January 2006 a new Exogenous Shocks Facility (ESF) was established to provide concessional assistance to economies adversely affected by events deemed to be beyond government control, for example commodity price changes, natural disasters, or conflicts in neighbouring countries that disrupt trade. Loans under the ESF were to be offered on the same terms as those of the Poverty Reduction and Growth Facility (PRGF) for low-income countries without a PRGF in place. In September 2008 modifications to the ESF were approved, including a new rapid-access component (to provide up to 25% of a country's quota) and a high-access component (to provide up to 75% of quota). These came into effect in late November.

In January 2010 the Fund introduced new concessional facilities for low-income countries as part of broader reforms to enhance flexibility of lending and to focus support closer to specific national requirements. The three new facilities aimed to support country-owned programmes to achieve macroeconomic positions consistent with sustainable poverty reduction and economic growth. They carried zero interest rate, although this was to be reviewed every two years. An Extended Credit Facility (ECF) succeeded the existing PRGF to provide medium-term balance of payments assistance to low-income members. ECF loans were to be repayable over 10 years, with a five-and-a-half-year grace period. A Standby Credit Facility (SCF) replaced the high-access component of the Exogenous Shocks Facility (see above) in order to provide short-term balance of payments financial assistance, including on a precautionary basis. SCF loans were to be repayable over eight years, with a grace period of four years. A new Rapid Credit Facility was to provide rapid financial assistance to members requiring urgent balance of payments assistance, under a range of circumstances. Loans were repayable over 10 years, with a five-and-a-half-year grace period.

In May 2001 the Executive Board decided to provide a subsidized loan rate for emergency post-conflict assistance for PRGF-eligible countries, in order to facilitate the rehabilitation of their economies and to improve their eligibility for further IMF concessionary arrangements. In January 2005 the Executive Board decided to extend the subsidized rate for natural disasters.

During 2009/10 the IMF approved nine new Stand-by Arrangements amounting to SDR 19,825m. (compared with 14 Arrangements totalling some SDR 34,249m. in the previous year). In 2009/10 two new EFF arrangements, amounting to SDR 205m., and 11 ECF/ESF arrangements, amounting to SDR 1,961m., were approved. During 2009/10 members' purchases from the general resources account amounted to SDR 21,087m., compared with SDR 16,363m. in the previous year. Outstanding IMF credit at 30 April 2010 totalled SDR 46,349m., compared with SDR 24,625m. in the previous year.

IMF participates in the initiative to provide exceptional assistance to heavily indebted poor countries (HIPCs), in order to help them to achieve a sustainable level of debt management. The initiative was formally approved at the September 1996 meeting of the Interim Committee, having received the support of the 'Paris Club' of official creditors, which agreed to increase the relief on official debt from 67% to 80%. In all 41 HIPCs were identified, of which 33 were in sub-Saharan Africa. Resources for the HIPC initiative were channelled through the PRGF Trust. In early 1999 the IMF and the World Bank initiated a comprehensive review of the HIPC scheme, in order to consider modifications of the initiative and to strengthen the link between debt relief and poverty reduction. A consensus emerged among the financial institutions and leading industrialized nations to enhance the scheme, in order to make it available to more countries, and to accelerate the process of providing debt relief. In September the IMF Board of Governors expressed its commitment to undertaking an off-market transaction of a percentage of the Fund's gold reserves (i.e. a sale, at market prices, to central banks of member countries with repayment obligations to the Fund, which were then to be made in gold), as part of the funding arrangements of the enhanced HIPC scheme; this was undertaken during the period December 1999–April 2000. Under the enhanced initiative it was agreed that countries seeking debt relief should first formulate, and successfully implement for at least one year, a national poverty reduction strategy (see above). In May 2000 Uganda became the first country to qualify for full debt relief under the enhanced scheme. In September 2005 the IMF and the World Bank endorsed a proposal of the Group of Eight (G8) nations to achieve the cancellation by the IMF, IDA and the African Development Bank of 100% of debt claims on countries that had reached completion point under the HIPC initiative, in order to help them to achieve their Millennium Development Goals. The debt cancellation was to be undertaken within the framework of a Multilateral Debt Relief Initiative (MDRI). The IMF's Executive Board determined, additionally, to extend MDRI debt relief to all countries with an annual per caput GDP of US $380, to be financed by IMF's own resources. Other financing was to be made from existing bilateral contributions to the PRGF Trust Subsidy Account. In December the Executive Board gave final approval to the first group of countries assessed as eligible for 100% debt relief under the MDRI, including 17 countries that had reached completion point at that time, as well as Cambodia and Tajikistan. The initiative became effective in January 2006 once the final consent of the 43 contributors to the PRGF Trust Subsidy Account had been received. By the end of 2011 a further 15 countries had qualified for MDRI relief. As at July the IMF had committed some $6,500m. in debt relief under the HIPC initiative, of a total of $76,000m. pledged for the initiative (in 2010 net present value terms); at that time the cost to the IMF of the MDRI amounted to some $3,900m. (in nominal value terms). In June 2010 the Executive Board approved the establishment of a Post-Catastrophe Debt Relief Trust (PCDR Trust) to provide balance of payments assistance to low-income members following an exceptional natural disaster.

SURVEILLANCE

Under its Articles of Agreement, the Fund is mandated to oversee the effective functioning of the international monetary system. Accordingly, the Fund aims to exercise firm surveillance over the exchange rate policies of member states and to assess whether a country's economic situation and policies are consistent with the objectives of sustainable development and domestic and external stability. The Fund's main tools of surveillance are regular, bilateral consultations with member countries conducted in accordance with Article IV of the Articles of Agreement, which cover fiscal and monetary policies, balance of payments and external debt developments, as well as policies that affect the economic performance of a country, such as the labour market, social and environmental issues and good governance, and aspects of the country's capital accounts, and finance and banking sectors. In April 1997 the Executive Board agreed to the voluntary issue of Press Information Notices (PINs) following each member's Article IV consultation, to those member countries wishing to make public the Fund's views. Other background papers providing information on and analysis of economic developments in individual countries continued to be made available. The Executive Board monitors global economic developments and discusses policy implications from a multilateral perspective, based partly on World Economic Outlook reports and Global Financial Stability Reports. In addition, the IMF studies the regional implications of global developments and policies pursued under regional fiscal arrangements. The Fund's medium-term strategy, initiated in 2006, determined to strengthen its surveillance policies to reflect new challenges of globalization for international financial and macroeconomic stability. In June 2007 the Executive Board approved a Decision on Bilateral Surveillance to update and clarify principles for a member's exchange rate policies and to define best practice for the Fund's bilateral surveillance activities. In October 2008 the Board adopted a Statement of Surveillance Priorities, based on a series of economic and operational policy objectives, for the period 2008–11. The need to enhance surveillance and economic transparency was a priority throughout 2009 as the Fund assessed the global economic and financial crisis and its own role in future crisis prevention. The IMF, with the UN Department for Economic and Social Affairs, leads an initiative to strengthen monitoring and analysis surveillance, and to implement an effective warning system, one of nine initiatives that were endorsed in April 2009 by the UN System Chief Executives Board for Co-ordination (CEB), with the aim of alleviating the impact of the global crisis on poor and vulnerable populations. In September 2010 the Executive Board decided that regular financial stability assessments, within the Financial Sector Assessment Programme framework (see below), were to be a mandatory exercise for 25 jurisdictions considered to have systemically important financial sectors.

In April 1996 the IMF established the Special Data Dissemination Standard (SDDS), which was intended to improve access to reliable economic statistical information for member countries that have, or are seeking, access to international capital markets. In March 1999 the IMF undertook to strengthen the Standard by the introduction of a new reserves data template. By December 2011 69 countries had subscribed to the Standard. The financial crisis in Asia, which became apparent in mid-1997, focused attention on the importance of IMF surveillance of the economies and financial policies of member states and prompted the Fund further to enhance the effectiveness of its surveillance through the development of international standards in order to maintain fiscal transparency. In December 1997 the Executive Board approved a new General Data Dissemination System (GDDS), to encourage all member countries to improve the production and dissemination of core economic data. The operational phase of the GDDS commenced in May 2000. By December 2011 102 countries were participating in the GDDS. The Fund maintains a Dissemination Standards Bulletin Board, which aims to ensure that information on SDDS subscribing countries is widely available.

In April 1998 the then Interim Committee adopted a voluntary Code of Good Practices on Fiscal Transparency: Declaration of Principles, which aimed to increase the quality and promptness of official reports on economic indicators, and in September 1999 it adopted a Code of Good Practices on Transparency in Monetary and Financial Policies: Declaration of Principles. The IMF and World Bank jointly established a Financial Sector Assessment Programme (FSAP) in May 1999, initially as a pilot project, which aimed to promote greater global financial security through the preparation of confidential detailed evaluations of the financial sectors of individual countries. In September 2009 the IMF and World Bank determined to enhance the FSAP's surveillance effectiveness with new features, for example introducing a risk assessment matrix, targeting it more closely to country needs, and improving its cross-country analysis and perspective. As part of the FSAP Fund staff may conclude a Financial System Stability Assessment (FSSA), addressing issues relating to macroeconomic stability and the strength of a country's financial system. A separate component of the FSAP are Reports on the Observance of Standards and Codes (ROSCs), which are compiled after an assessment of a country's implementation and observance of internationally recognized financial standards.

In March 2000 the IMF Executive Board adopted a strengthened framework to safeguard the use of IMF resources. All member countries making use of Fund resources were to be required to publish annual central bank statements audited in accordance with internationally accepted standards. It was also agreed that any instance of intentional misreporting of information by a member country should be madc public. In the following month the Executive Board approved the establishment of an Independent Evaluation Office (IEO) to conduct objective evaluations of IMF policy and operations. The Office commenced activities in July 2001. In 2008/09 the Office concluded an evaluation report on IMF Involvement in International Trade Policy Issues for consideration by the Board. In January 2010 the Office published a report on IMF Interactions with Member Countries. At that time two further projects were under development: the IMF's Research Agenda, and the IMF's Role in the Run-up to the Current Financial and Economic Crisis.

In April 2001 the Executive Board agreed on measures to enhance international efforts to counter money-laundering, in particular through the Fund's ongoing financial supervision activities and its programme of assessment of offshore financial centres (OFCs). In November the IMFC, in response to the terrorist attacks against targets in the USA, which had occurred in September, resolved, *inter alia*, to strengthen the Fund's focus on surveillance, and, in particular, to extend measures to counter money-laundering to include the funds of terrorist organizations. It determined to accelerate efforts to assess offshore centres and to provide technical support to enable poorer countries to meet international financial standards. In March 2004 the Board of Directors resolved that an anti-money laundering and countering the financing of terrorism (AML/CFT) component be introduced into regular OFC and FSAP assessments conducted by the Fund and the World Bank, following a pilot programme undertaken from November 2002 with the World Bank, the Financial Action Task Force and other regional supervisory bodies. The first phase of the OFC assessment programme was concluded in February 2005, at which time 41 of 44 contacted jurisdictions had been assessed and the reports published. In May 2008 the IMF's Executive Board agreed to integrate the OFC programme into the FSAP.

TECHNICAL ASSISTANCE

Technical assistance is provided by special missions or resident representatives who advise members on every aspect of economic management, while more specialized assistance is provided by the IMF's various departments. In 2000/01 the IMFC determined that technical assistance should be central to the IMF's work in crisis prevention and management, in capacity-building for low-income countries, and in restoring macroeconomic stability in countries following a financial crisis. Technical assistance activities subsequently underwent a process of review and reorganization to align them more closely with IMF policy priorities and other initiatives.

Since 1993 the IMF has delivered some technical assistance, aimed at strengthening local capacity in economic and financial management, through regional centres. The first, established in that year, was a Pacific Financial Technical Assistance Center, located in Fiji. A Caribbean Regional Technical Assistance Centre (CARTAC), located in Barbados, began operations in November 2001. In October 2002 an East African Regional Technical Assistance Centre (East AFRITAC), based in Dar es Salaam, Tanzania, was inaugurated and a second AFRITAC was opened in Bamako, Mali, in May 2003, to cover the West African region. In October 2004 a new technical assistance centre for the Middle East (METAC) was inaugurated, based in Beirut, Lebanon. A regional technical assistance centre for Central Africa, located in Libreville, Gabon, was inaugurated in 2006/07. The fourth AFRITAC, located in Port Louis, Mauritius, serving Southern Africa and the Indian Ocean, was inaugurated in October 2011. A Regional Technical Assistance Centre for Central America, Panama and the Dominican Republic (CAPTAC-DR), was inaugurated in June 2009, in Guatemala City, Guatemala. In September 2002 the IMF signed a memorandum of understanding with the African Capacity Building Foundation to strengthen collaboration, in particular within the context of a new IMF Africa Capacity-Building Initiative.

The IMF Institute, which was established in 1964, trains officials from member countries in macroeconomic management, financial analysis and policy, balance of payments methodology and public finance. The IMF Institute also co-operates with other established regional training centres and institutes in order to refine its delivery of technical assistance and training services. The IMF is a co-sponsor, with the Austrian authorities, the EBRD, OECD and WTO, of the Joint Vienna Institute, which was opened in the Austrian capital in October 1992 and which trains officials from former centrally-planned economies in various aspects of economic management and public administration. In May 1998 an IMF-Singapore Regional Training Institute (an affiliate of the IMF Institute) was inaugurated, in collaboration with the Singaporean Government, in order to provide training for officials from the Asia-Pacific region. In 1999 a Joint Regional Training Programme, administered with the Arab Monetary Fund, was established in the United Arab Emirates. During 2000/01 the Institute established a new joint training programme for government officials of the People's Republic of China, based in Dalian, Liaoning Province. A Joint Regional Training Centre for Latin America became operational in Brasília, Brazil, in 2001. In July 2006 a Joint India-IMF Training Programme was inaugurated in Pune, India.

Publications

Annual Report.

Balance of Payments Statistics Yearbook.

Civil Society Newsletter (quarterly).

Direction of Trade Statistics (quarterly and annually).

Emerging Markets Financing (quarterly).

F & D—Finance and Development (quarterly).

Financial Statements of the IMF (quarterly).

Global Financial Stability Report (2 a year).

Global Monitoring Report (annually, with the World Bank).

Government Finance Statistics Yearbook.

Handbook on Securities Statistics (published jointly by IMF, BIS and the European Central Bank).

IMF Commodity Prices (monthly).

IMF Financial Activities (weekly, online).

IMF in Focus (annually).

IMF Research Bulletin (quarterly).

IMF Survey (monthly, and online).

International Financial Statistics (monthly and annually).

Joint BIS-IMF-OECD-World Bank Statistics on External Debt (quarterly).

Quarterly Report on the Assessments of Standards and Codes.

Staff Papers (quarterly).

World Economic Outlook (2 a year).

Other country reports, regional outlooks, economic and financial surveys, occasional papers, pamphlets, books.

Statistics

QUOTAS
(SDR million)

	April 2012
Afghanistan	161.9
Albania	60.0
Algeria	1,254.7
Angola	286.3
Antigua and Barbuda	13.5
Argentina	2,117.1
Armenia	92.0
Australia	3,236.4
Austria	2,113.9
Azerbaijan	160.9
Bahamas	130.3
Bahrain	135.0
Bangladesh	533.3
Barbados	67.5
Belarus	386.4
Belgium	4,605.2
Belize	18.8
Benin	61.9
Bhutan	6.3
Bolivia	171.5
Bosnia and Herzegovina	169.1
Botswana	87.8
Brazil	4,250.5
Brunei	215.2
Bulgaria	640.2
Burkina Faso	60.2
Burundi	77.0
Cambodia	87.5

—continued	April 2012
Cameroon	185.7
Canada	6,369.2
Cape Verde	9.6
Central African Republic	55.7
Chad	66.6
Chile	856.1
China, People's Republic	9,525.9
Colombia	774.0
Comoros	8.9
Congo, Democratic Republic	533.0
Congo, Republic	84.6
Costa Rica	164.1
Côte d'Ivoire	325.2
Croatia	365.1
Cyprus	158.2
Czech Republic	1,002.2
Denmark	1,891.4
Djibouti	15.9
Dominica	8.2
Dominican Republic	218.9
Ecuador	347.8
Egypt	943.7
El Salvador	171.3
Equatorial Guinea	52.3
Eritrea	15.9
Estonia	93.9
Ethiopia	133.7
Fiji	70.3
Finland	1,263.8
France	10,738.5
Gabon	154.3
The Gambia	31.1
Georgia	150.3
Germany	14,565.5
Ghana	369.0
Greece	1,101.8
Grenada	11.7
Guatemala	210.2
Guinea	107.1
Guinea-Bissau	14.2
Guyana	90.9
Haiti	81.9
Honduras	129.5
Hungary	1,038.4
Iceland	117.6
India	5,821.5
Indonesia	2,079.3
Iran	1,497.2
Iraq	1,188.4
Ireland	1,257.6
Israel	1,061.1
Italy	7,882.3
Jamaica	273.5
Japan	15,628.5
Jordan	170.5
Kazakhstan	365.7
Kenya	271.4
Kiribati	5.6
Korea, Republic	3,366.4
Kosovo	59.0
Kuwait	1,381.1
Kyrgyzstan	88.8
Laos	52.9
Latvia	142.1
Lebanon	266.4
Lesotho	34.9
Liberia	129.2
Libya	1,123.7
Lithuania	183.9
Luxembourg	418.7
Macedonia, former Yugoslav republic	68.9
Madagascar	122.2
Malawi	69.4
Malaysia	1,773.9
Maldives	10.0
Mali	93.3
Malta	102.0
Marshall Islands	3.5
Mauritania	64.4
Mauritius	101.6
Mexico	3,625.7
Micronesia, Federated States	5.1
Moldova	123.2
Mongolia	51.1

—continued	April 2012
Montenegro	27.5
Morocco	588.2
Mozambique	113.6
Myanmar	258.4
Namibia	136.5
Nepal	71.3
Netherlands	5,162.4
New Zealand	894.6
Nicaragua	130.0
Niger	65.8
Nigeria	1,753.2
Norway	1,883.7
Oman	237.0
Pakistan	1,033.7
Palau	3.1
Panama	206.6
Papua New Guinea	131.6
Paraguay	99.9
Peru	638.4
Philippines	1,019.3
Poland	1,688.4
Portugal	1,029.7
Qatar	302.6
Romania	1,030.2
Russia	5,945.4
Rwanda	80.1
Saint Christopher and Nevis	8.9
Saint Lucia	15.3
Saint Vincent and the Grenadines	8.3
Samoa	11.6
San Marino	22.4
São Tomé and Príncipe	7.4
Saudi Arabia	6,985.5
Senegal	161.8
Serbia	467.7
Seychelles	10.9
Sierra Leone	103.7
Singapore	1,408.0
Slovakia	427.5

—continued	April 2012
Slovenia	275.0
Solomon Islands	10.4
Somalia	44.2
South Africa	1,868.5
South Sudan	123.0
Spain	4,023.4
Sri Lanka	413.4
Sudan	169.7
Suriname	92.1
Swaziland	50.7
Sweden	2,395.5
Switzerland	3,458.5
Syria	293.6
Tajikistan	87.0
Tanzania	198.9
Thailand	1,440.5
Timor-Leste	8.2
Togo	73.4
Tonga	6.9
Trinidad and Tobago	335.6
Tunisia	286.5
Turkey	1,455.8
Turkmenistan	75.2
Tuvalu	1.8
Uganda	180.5
Ukraine	1,372.0
United Arab Emirates	752.5
United Kingdom	10,738.5
USA	42,122.4
Uruguay	306.5
Uzbekistan	275.6
Vanuatu	17.0
Venezuela	2,659.1
Viet Nam	460.7
Yemen	243.5
Zambia	489.1
Zimbabwe	353.4

FINANCIAL ACTIVITIES
(SDR million, year ending 30 April)

Type of Transaction	2006	2007	2008	2009	2010	2011
Total disbursements	2,559	2,806	1,952	17,082	22,488	27,527
Purchases by facility (General Resources Account)*	2,156	2,329	1,468	16,363	21,087	26,616
Loans under PRGF/ECF/ESF arrangements	403	477	484	719	1,402	914
Repurchases and repayments	35,991	14,678	3,324	2,301	764	3,412
Repurchases	32,783	14,166	2,905	1,833	275	2,268
SAF/PRGF/ECF/ESF loan repayments	3,208	512	419	468	489	1,144
Total outstanding credit provided by Fund (end of year)	23,144	11,216	9,844	24,625	46,350	70,421
Of which:						
General Resources Account	19,227	7,334	5,896	20,426	41,238	65,539
SAF Arrangements	9	9	9	9	9	9
PRGF/ ECF/ESF Arrangements†	3,819	3,785	3,873	4,124	5,037	4,807
Trust Fund	89	89	66	66	66	66

* Including reserve tranche purchases.
† Including Saudi Fund for Development associated loans.
Source: IMF, *Annual Report 2011*.

BOARD OF EXECUTIVE DIRECTORS
(April 2012)

Director	Casting Votes of	Total Votes	%
Appointed:			
MEG LUNDSAGER	USA	421,961	16.76
MITSUHIRO FURUSAWA	Japan	157,022	6.23
HUBERT TEMMEYER	Germany	146,392	5.81
AMBROISE FAYOLLE	France	108,122	4.29
ALEXANDER GIBBS	United Kingdom	108,122	4.29
Elected:			
WILLY KIEKENS (Belgium)	Austria, Belarus, Belgium, Czech Republic, Hungary, Kosovo, Luxembourg, Slovakia, Slovenia, Turkey	125,191	4.97
CARLOS PÉREZ-VERDÍA (Mexico)	Costa Rica, El Salvador, Guatemala, Honduras, Mexico, Nicaragua, Spain, Venezuela	117,029	4.64
MENNO SNEL (Netherlands)	Armenia, Bosnia and Herzegovina, Bulgaria, Croatia, Cyprus, Georgia, Israel, the former Yugoslav republic of Macedonia, Moldova, Montenegro, Netherlands, Romania, Ukraine	113,835	4.52
ARRIGO SADUN (Italy)	Albania, Greece, Italy, Malta, Portugal, San Marino, Timor-Leste	107,223	4.26
DER JIUN CHIA (Singapore)	Brunei, Cambodia, Fiji, Indonesia, Laos, Malaysia, Myanmar, Nepal, Philippines, Singapore, Thailand, Tonga, Viet Nam	99,023	3.81
TAO ZHANG	People's Republic of China	95,996	3.81
CHRISTOPHER LEGG (Australia)	Australia, Kiribati, Republic of Korea, Marshall Islands, Federated States of Micronesia, Mongolia, New Zealand, Palau, Papua New Guinea, Samoa, Seychelles, Solomon Islands, Tuvalu, Uzbekistan, Vanuatu	91,302	3.62
THOMAS HOCKIN (Canada)	Antigua and Barbuda, The Bahamas, Barbados, Belize, Canada, Dominica, Grenada, Ireland, Jamaica, Saint Christopher and Nevis, Saint Lucia, Saint Vincent and the Grenadines	90,672	3.60
BENNY ANDERSEN (Denmark)	Denmark, Estonia, Finland, Iceland, Latvia, Lithuania, Norway, Sweden	85,615	3.40
MOAKETSI MAJORO (Lesotho)	Angola, Botswana, Burundi, Eritrea, Ethiopia, The Gambia, Kenya, Lesotho, Liberia, Malawi, Mozambique, Namibia, Nigeria, Sierra Leone, South Africa, Sudan, Swaziland, Tanzania, Uganda, Zambia, Zimbabwe	81,022	3.22
A. SHAKOUR SHAALAN (Egypt)	Bahrain, Egypt, Iraq, Jordan, Kuwait, Lebanon, Libya, Maldives, Oman, Qatar, Syria, United Arab Emirates, Yemen	81,061	3.18
ARVIND VIRMANI (India)	Bangladesh, Bhutan, India, Sri Lanka	70,693	2.81
PAULO NOGUEIRA BATISTA, Jr (Brazil)	Brazil, Colombia, Dominican Republic, Ecuador, Guyana, Haiti, Panama, Suriname, Trinidad and Tobago	70,616	2.80
AHMED ABDULKARIM ALKHOLIFEY	Saudi Arabia	70,592	2.80
RÉNE WEBER (Switzerland)	Azerbaijan, Kazakhstan, Kyrgyzstan, Poland, Serbia, Switzerland, Tajikistan, Turkmenistan	69,818	2.77
ALEKSEI V. MOZHIN	Russia	60,191	2.39
JAFAR MOJARRAD (Iran)	Afghanistan, Algeria, Ghana, Iran, Morocco, Pakistan, Tunisia	57,071	2.26
ALFREDO MACLAUGHLIN (Argentina)	Argentina, Bolivia, Chile, Paraguay, Peru, Uruguay	46,317	1.84
KOSSI ASSIMAIDOU (Togo)	Benin, Burkina Faso, Cameroon, Cape Verde, Central African Republic, Chad, Comoros, Democratic Republic of the Congo, Republic of the Congo, Côte d'Ivoire, Djibouti, Equatorial Guinea, Gabon, Guinea-Bissau, Mali, Mauritius, Niger, Rwanda, São Tomé and Príncipe, Senegal, Togo	38,973	1.55

Note: The total number of votes does not include the votes of Guinea, Madagascar, Somalia and South Sudan (amounting to 0.27% of the total of votes in the General Department and the Special Drawing Rights Department), as these countries did not participate in the 2010 election of Executive Directors.

International Telecommunication Union—ITU

Address: Place des Nations, 1211 Geneva 20, Switzerland.

Telephone: 227305111; **fax:** 227337256; **e-mail:** itumail@itu.int; **internet:** www.itu.int.

Founded in 1865, ITU became a specialized agency of the UN in 1947. It acts *inter alia* to encourage world co-operation for the improvement and national use of telecommunications to promote technical development, to harmonize national policies in the field, and to promote the extension of telecommunications throughout the world.

MEMBERS

ITU has 193 member states. More than 700 scientific and technical companies, public and private operators, broadcasters and other organizations are also ITU members.

Organization

(April 2012)

PLENIPOTENTIARY CONFERENCE

The supreme organ of ITU; normally meets every four years. The main tasks of the Conference are to elect ITU's leadership, establish policies, revise the Constitution and Convention (see below) and approve limits on budgetary spending. The 2010 Conference was held in Guadalajara, Mexico, in October; the 2014 Conference was scheduled to be convened in Busan, Republic of Korea.

WORLD CONFERENCES ON INTERNATIONAL TELECOMMUNICATIONS

The World Conferences on International Telecommunications are held at the request of members and after approval by the Plenipotentiary Conference. The World Conferences are authorized to review and revise the regulations applying to the provision and operation of international telecommunications services. Separate Conferences are held by the Union's three sectors (see below): Radiocommunication Conferences (every two or three years); Telecommunication Standardization Assemblies (every four years or at the request of one-quarter of ITU members); and Telecommunication Development Conferences (every four years).

ITU COUNCIL

The Council meets annually in Geneva and is composed of 48 members elected by the Plenipotentiary Conference.

The Council ensures the efficient co-ordination and implementation of the work of the Union in all matters of policy, administration and finance, in the interval between Plenipotentiary Conferences, and approves the annual budget.

GENERAL SECRETARIAT

The Secretary-General is elected by the Plenipotentiary Conference and is assisted by a Co-ordination Committee that also comprises the Deputy Secretary-General and the Directors of the three sector Bureaux. The General Secretariat comprises departments for Administration and Finance; Conferences and Publications; Information Services; Internal Audit; ITU Telecom (conference organization); Legal Affairs; and Strategic Planning and Membership. The Secretariat's staff totals some 800, representing more than 80 nationalities; the official and working languages are Arabic, Chinese, English, French, Russian and Spanish.

Secretary-General: HAMADOUN I. TOURÉ (Mali).

Deputy Secretary-General: HOULIN ZHAO (People's Republic of China).

Constitution and Convention

Between 1865 and 1992 each Plenipotentiary Conference adopted a new Convention of ITU. At the Additional Plenipotentiary Conference held in December 1992, in Geneva, Switzerland, a new Constitution and Convention were signed. They were partially amended by the following two Plenipotentiary Conferences held in Kyoto, Japan, in 1994, and Minneapolis, USA, in 1998. The Constitution contains the fundamental provisions of ITU, whereas the Convention contains other provisions which complement those of the Constitution and which, by their nature, require periodic revision.

The Constitution establishes the purposes and structure of the Union, contains the general provisions relating to telecommunications and special provisions for radio, and deals with relations with the UN and other organizations. The Convention establishes the functioning of the Union and the three sectors, and contains the general provisions regarding conferences and assemblies. Both instruments are further complemented by the *Radio Regulations* and the *International Telecommunications Regulations* (see below).

Activities

In December 1992 an Additional Plenipotentiary Conference, convened in Geneva, Switzerland, determined that the ITU should be restructured into three sectors corresponding to its main functions: standardization; radiocommunication; and development. In October 1994 the ordinary Plenipotentiary Conference, held in Kyoto, Japan, adopted ITU's first strategic plan. In November 1998 the Conference, convened in Minneapolis, USA, adopted a second strategic plan, for the period 1999–2003, which recognized new trends and developments in the world telecommunication environment, such as globalization, liberalization, and greater competition, assessed their implications for ITU, and proposed new strategies and priorities to enable the Union to function effectively. The meeting approved the active involvement of ITU in governance issues relating to the internet, and recommended that a World Summit on the Information Society (WSIS, see below) be convened, given the rapid developments in that field. In October 2002 the Plenipotentiary Conference, convened in Marrakesh, Morocco, adopted a third strategic plan, for the period 2004–07 which emphasized ITU's role in facilitating universal access to the global information economy and society. ITU was to take a lead role in UN initiatives concerning information and communication technologies and support all efforts to overcome the digital divide. The 2006 Conference, held in November, in Antalya, Turkey, adopted a fourth strategic plan covering the period 2008–11, which outlined the future course of the Union, and endorsed ITU's essential role in 'Bridging the Digital Divide' and in leading the multi-stakeholder process for the follow-up and implementation of relevant WSIS objectives. Main thematic areas of focus include: the implementation of the ITU's Global Cybersecurity Agenda; pursuing the objective of 'connecting the unconnected' by 2015; developing emergency telecommunications as a critical pillar of disaster management; and implementing the Next Generation Network (NGN) Global Standards Initiative. In October 2010 the Plenipotentiary Conference, held in Guadalajara, Mexico, adopted new strategic and financial plans for the period 2012–15, as well as a series of resolutions concerning, *inter alia*, enhanced collaboration with relevant international organizations and regional registries in the development of Internet Protocol-based networks and internet governance, the implementation of a programme of work on confirmity and interoperability, bridging the standardization gap between developed and developing countries, supporting further NGN development and its deployment in developing countries, promoting collation of information relating to human exposure to electromagnetic fields, and the establishment of a new Council Working Group on internet-related public policy issues.

ITU's Telecom division organizes major global and regional conferences which bring together governments, non-governmental bodies and representatives of the telecommunications industry. The next major conference, ITU World Telecoms, was scheduled to be held in Dubai, in October 2012.

The Global Cybersecurity Agenda (GCA) was formulated as part of ITU's commitments to implement the WSIS 'Action Line' on building confidence and security in the use of information and communication technologies, and was inaugurated in May 2007. It aimed to provide a framework for international co-operation to enhance confidence in and the security of the information society, structured on the following five work areas: legal measures; technical and procedural measures; organizational structures; capacity building; and international co-operation. In September 2008 ITU signed a Memorandum of Understanding (MOU) with the International Multilateral Partnership against Cyber Threats (IMPACT) to collaborate in efforts to strengthen cybersecurity and to transfer the operations and administration of the GCA to IMPACT. In November ITU inaugurated a Child Online Protection (COP) initiative, to be incorporated into the GCA framework, in order to address the specific cybersecurity issues relating to young people. A new COP Global Initiative was launched in November 2010 to promote the implementation, through national action plans, industry codes of conduct, awareness training etc, of previously developed strategies and guidelines. In May 2011 ITU signed an MOU with the UN Office on Drugs and Crime to promote co-operation at a global level to counter cyber crime. At the same time a separate MOU was signed with Symantec, a private provider of security intelligence and systems management.

ITU, with UNIDO and WIPO, leads an initiative on promoting technology and innovation, the eighth of nine activities that were launched in April 2009 by the UN System Chief Executives Board for Co-ordination (CEB), with the aim of alleviating the impact on poor and vulnerable populations of the developing global economic crisis.

In May 2010 ITU, with UNESCO, established a Broadband Commission for Digital Development, to comprise high level representatives of governments, industry and international agencies concerned with the effective deployment of broadband networks as an essential element of economic and social development objectives. The Commission released its first report, with a series of recommendations for the rapid development of broadband world-wide, in September, prior to the UN Millennium Development Goal Review Summit. A second report, focusing on bringing high-speed connectivity to the poorest communities, was issued in June 2011.

The ITU publishes an annual report entitled *Measuring the Information Society*, which includes an ICT Development Index (IDI), measuring the state of ICT development world-wide (covering 152 countries in the 2011 edition, released in September of that year). The report also features an ICT Price Basket, reflecting the combined cost of mobile-cellular, fixed-telephone and fixed-broadband tariffs.

WORLD SUMMIT ON THE INFORMATION SOCIETY

ITU took a lead role in organizing the WSIS, which was held, under the auspices of the UN Secretary-General, in two phases: the first took place in Geneva in December 2003, and the second in Tunis, Tunisia in November 2005. The Geneva meeting, attended by representatives of 175 countries, recognized the central role of ITU in building an information society and approved a Declaration of Principles and Plan of Action, which urged co-operation by public and private sector stakeholders, civil society interests and UN agencies in encouraging new projects and partnerships aimed at bridging the so-called international digital divide. It entrusted ITU with addressing issues relating to cybersecurity. The second meeting adopted the Tunis Agenda for the Information Society, which called upon the UN Secretary-General to establish an Internet Governance Forum (IGF), with a view to establishing a more inclusive dialogue on global internet policy. In March 2006 the UN Secretary-General announced that a small secretariat would be formed to assist with convening the planned Forum, the first session of which was held in Athens, Greece, in October–November. IGFs have subsequently been held annually (September 2011: Nairobi, Kenya; September 2012: Baku, Azerbaijan). ITU hosts an annual WSIS Forum, in May, to address issues relating to follow-up and implementation by all stakeholders in the process. A UN Group on the Information Society was established in April 2006 to address UN implementation of the WSIS Plan of Action.

RADIOCOMMUNICATION SECTOR

The role of the sector (ITU-R) is globally to manage, and to ensure the equitable and efficient use of, the radio-frequency spectrum by all radiocommunication services, including those that use satellite orbits (the latter being in increasing demand from fixed, mobile, amateur, broadcasting, emergency telecommunications, environmental monitoring and communications services, global positioning systems, meteorology and space research services). The sector also conducts studies, and adopts recommendations on sector issues. The *Radio Regulations*, which first appeared in 1906, include general rules for the assignment and use of frequencies and the associated orbital positions for space stations. They include a Table of Frequency Allocations (governing the use of radio frequency bands between 9 kHz and 400 GHz) for the various radio services (*inter alia* radio broadcasting, television, radio astronomy, navigation aids, point-to-point service, maritime mobile, amateur). They are reviewed and revised by the World Radiocommunication Conferences: the most recent revision was issued in 2008. The technical work on issues to be considered by the conferences is conducted by Radiocommunication Assemblies, on the basis of recommendations made by Study Groups. These groups of experts study technical questions relating to radiocommunications, according to a study programme formulated by the Assemblies. The Assemblies may approve, modify or reject any recommendations of the Study Groups, and are authorized to establish new groups and to abolish others. The procedural rules used in the application of the Radio Regulations may be considered by a Radio Regulations Board, which may also perform duties relating to the allocation and use of frequencies and consider cases of interference. ITU-R is responsible for defining and recommending standards and frequency arrangements for international mobile telecommunications (IMT), in collaboration with governments, industry and the private sector. In October 2007 the Radiocommunication Assembly agreed to define as 'IMT-Advanced' new systems and capabilities that extend beyond the existing 'IMT 2000' systems. In January 2012 the Radiocommunication Assembly specified standards for IMT-Advanced technologies and agreed that 'LTE-Advanced' and WirelessMAN-Advanced' met the criteria for classification as IMT-Advanced.

The January 2012 Radiocommunication Assembly determined to conduct further studies on the development of a continuous time standard, aimed at replacing the current system of 'Coordinated Universal Time' (UTC), and repressing the use of 'leap seconds' that is standardized within UTC.

The administrative work of the sector is the responsibility of the Radiocommunication Bureau, which is headed by an elected Director, who is assisted by an Advisory Group. The Bureau co-ordinates the work of Study Groups, provides administrative support for the Radio Regulations Board, and works alongside the General Secretariat to prepare conferences and to provide relevant assistance to developing countries. The Bureau maintains the Maritime Mobile Access and Retrieval System (MARS), which provides access to operational information registered in the ITU maritime database.

Director: FRANÇOIS RANCY (France).

TELECOMMUNICATION STANDARDIZATION SECTOR

The Telecommunication Standardization sector (ITU-T) studies technical, operational and tariff issues in order to standardize telecommunications throughout the world. The sector's conferences adopt the *International Telecommunications Regulations*, which establish ITU guidelines to guarantee the effective provision of telecommunication services. Recommendations may be approved outside of the four-year interval between conferences if a sectoral Study Group (comprising private and public sector experts) concludes such action to be urgent. Study Groups are engaged in the following areas of interest: operational aspects of service provision, networks and performance; tariff and accounting principles; telecommunication management; protection against electromagnetic environmental effects; outside plant and related indoor installations; integrated broadband cable networks and television and sound transmission; signalling requirements and protocols; performance and quality of service; NGN; optical and other transport network infrastructures; multimedia terminals, systems and applications; security, languages and telecommunications softwares; and mobile telecommunications networks. The Telecommunication Standardization Advisory Group (TSAG) reviews sectoral priorities, programmes, operations and administrative matters, and establishes, organizes and provides guidelines to the Study Groups. The 2004 World Telecommunication Standardization Assembly (WTSA), convened in October, in Florianópolis, Brazil, adopted an action plan for addressing the global standardization gap. Consequently a Group on Bridging the Standardization Gap was established within the TSAG. The 2008 WTSA was held in Johannesburg, South Africa, in October; it was preceded for the first time by a Global Standards Symposium that addressed means of enabling increased participation by developing countries in the standards making process, as well as considering challenges to the standards agenda, such as accessibility and climate change. ITU Global Standards Initiatives cover: Identity Management; Internet Protocol; Television; and NGN. The 2008 WTSA *inter alia* resolved to reduce greenhouse gas emissions arising from the use of ICTs. The 2012 WTSA was scheduled to be convened in November, in Dubai, UAE.

Preparations for conferences and other meetings of the sector are made by the Telecommunication Standardization Bureau. It administers the application of conference decisions, as well as relevant provisions of the International Telecommunications Regulations. The Bureau is headed by an elected Director, who is assisted by an Advisory Group. The Director reports to conferences and to the ITU Council on the activities of the sector.

Director: MALCOLM JOHNSON (United Kingdom).

TELECOMMUNICATION DEVELOPMENT SECTOR

The sector's objectives are to facilitate and enhance telecommunications development by offering, organizing and co-ordinating technical co-operation and assistance activities, to promote the development of telecommunication infrastructure, networks and services in developing countries, to facilitate the transfer of appropriate technologies and the use of resources, and to provide advice on issues specific to telecommunications. The sector implements projects under the UN development system or other funding arrangements. In January 2005 ITU launched an initiative to establish a network of some 100 Multipurpose Community Telecentres in 20 African countries, with the aim of providing broader access to ICTs. A global development initiative entitled 'Connect the World' was introduced by ITU in June, with the aim of providing access to ICTs to 1,000m. people without connectivity. The initiative, involving 22 stakeholders, was developed within the context of the WSIS agenda to encourage new projects and partnerships to bridge the digital divide. The first in a series of regional summits was held in October 2007 in Kigali, Rwanda, with the aim of mobilizing the human, financial and technical resources required to close ICT gaps throughout Africa. The summit generated investment commitments in excess of US $5,500m., and agreed to accelerate ICT connectivity goals in the region to 2012 (from 2015). The second summit, 'Connect

CIS', was convened in Minsk, Belarus, in November 2009. Since 2001 ITU has supported the establishment of Internet Training Centres, by working in partnership with multinational and local private companies and training institutes. By December 2010 80 Centres had been established under the initiative.

The sector holds conferences regularly to encourage international co-operation in the development of telecommunications, and to determine strategies for development. Conferences consider the result of work undertaken by Study Groups on issues of benefit to developing countries, including development policy, finance, network planning and operation of services. The fourth World Telecommunication Development Conference (WTDC), convened in March 2006, in Doha, Qatar, addressed development priorities in the context of the Digital Divide, and the promotion of international co-operation to strengthen telecommunication infrastructure and institutions in developing countries. The fifth WTDC, held in Hyderabad, India, in May–June 2010, adopted the Hyderabad Action Plan, detailing strategies for fostering future global ICT and telecommunications development. Availability of NGN and extensive access to broadband services, wireless technologies and the internet were deemed to be catalysts for advancing a global information society and world-wide economic, social and cultural development.

ITU aims to support international humanitarian efforts in the event of an emergency by deploying temporary telecommunications and assessing the damage to the information infrastructure and its rehabilitation needs. ITU played a key role in drafting and promoting the Tampere Convention on the Provision of Telecommunication Resources for Disaster Mitigation and Relief Operations that was signed in 1998 and entered into force in January 2005. The Convention aimed to facilitate the deployment and use of telecommunications equipment in an emergency situation, in particular by removing regulatory barriers.

The administrative work of the sector is conducted by the Telecommunication Development Bureau, which may also study specific problems presented by a member state. The Director of the Bureau reports to conferences and the ITU Council, and is assisted by an Advisory Board.

Director: BRAHIMA SANOU (Burkina Faso).

Finance

The budget for the two-year period 2012–13 amounted to 319.1m. Swiss francs.

Publications

ITU Global Directory.

ITU News (10 a year, in English, French and Spanish).

ITU Yearbook of Statistics (annually).

Measuring the Information Society.

Operational Bulletin.

World Information Society Report.

Conventions, databases, statistics, regulations, technical documents and manuals, conference documents.

United Nations Educational, Scientific and Cultural Organization—UNESCO

Address: 7 place de Fontenoy, 75352 Paris 07 SP, France.

Telephone: 1-45-68-10-00; **fax:** 1-45-67-16-90; **e-mail:** bpi@unesco.org; **internet:** www.unesco.org.

UNESCO was established in 1946 'for the purpose of advancing, through the educational, scientific and cultural relations of the peoples of the world, the objectives of international peace and the common welfare of mankind'.

MEMBERS

UNESCO has 195 members (including Palestine, given full membership in October 2011) and six associate members.

Organization

(April 2012)

GENERAL CONFERENCE

The supreme governing body of the Organization, the Conference meets in ordinary session once in two years and is composed of representatives of the member states. It determines policies, approves work programmes and budgets and elects members of the Executive Board.

EXECUTIVE BOARD

The Board, comprising 58 members, prepares the programme to be submitted to the Conference and supervises its execution; it meets twice a year.

SECRETARIAT

The organization is headed by a Director-General, appointed for a four-year term. There are Assistant Directors-General for the main thematic sectors, i.e education, natural sciences, social and human sciences, culture, and communication and information, as well as for the support sectors of external relations and co-operation and of administration.

Director-General: IRINA BOKOVA (Bulgaria).

CO-OPERATING BODIES

In accordance with UNESCO's constitution, national Commissions have been set up in most member states. These help to integrate work within the member states and the work of UNESCO. Most member states also have their own permanent delegations to UNESCO. UNESCO aims to develop partnerships with cities and local authorities.

FIELD CO-ORDINATION

UNESCO maintains a network of offices to support a more decentralized approach to its activities and enhance their implementation at field level. Cluster offices provide the main structure of the field co-ordination network. These cover a group of countries and help to co-ordinate between member states and with other UN and partner agencies operating in the area. In 2010 there were 27 cluster offices covering 148 states. In addition 21 national offices serve a single country, including those in post-conflict situations or economic transition and the nine most highly populated countries. The regional bureaux (see below) provide specialized support at a national level.

REGIONAL BUREAUX

Regional Bureau for Education in Africa (BREDA): 12 ave L. S. Senghor, BP 3318, Dakar, Senegal; tel. 849-23-23; fax 823-86-23; e-mail dakar@unesco.org; internet www.dakar.unesco.org; Dir ANN THERESE NDONG-JATTA.

Regional Bureau for Science and Technology in Africa: POB 30592, Nairobi, Kenya; tel. (20) 7621-234; fax (20) 7622-750; e-mail nairobi@unesco.org; internet www.unesco-nairobi.org; f. 1965 to execute UNESCO's regional science programme, and to assist in the planning and execution of national programmes; Dir JOSEPH M. G. MASSAQUOI.

Regional Bureau for Education in the Arab States: POB 5244, Cité Sportive, Beirut, Lebanon; tel. (1) 850013; fax (1) 834854; e-mail beirut@unesco.org; internet www.unesco.org/en/beirut; Dir ABDEL MONEIM OSMAN.

Regional Bureau for Sciences in the Arab States: 8 Abdel Rahman Fahmy St, Garden City, Cairo 11511, Egypt; tel. (2) 7945599; fax (2) 7945296; e-mail cairo@unesco.org; also covers informatics; Dir Dr TAREK SHAWKI.

Regional Bureau for Science and Culture in Europe: Palazzo Zorzi, 4930 Castello, 30122 Venice, Italy; tel. (041) 260-1511; fax (041) 528-9995; e-mail veniceoffice@unesco.org; internet www.unesco.org/venice; Dir ENGELBERT RUOSS.

Regional Bureau for Culture in Latin America and the Caribbean (ORCALC): Calzada 551, esq. D, Vedado, Havana 4, Cuba; tel. (7) 833-3438; fax (7) 833-3144; e-mail habana@unesco.org.cu; internet www.unesco.org.cu; f. 1950; activities include research and programmes of cultural development and cultural tourism; maintains a documentation centre and a library of 14,500 vols; Dir HERMAN VAN HOOFF; publs *Oralidad* (annually), *Boletín Electrónico* (quarterly).

Regional Bureau for Education in Latin America and the Caribbean (OREALC): Calle Enrique Delpiano 2058, Providencia, Santiago, Chile; Casilla 127, Correo 29, Providencia, Santiago, Chile; tel. (2) 472-4600; fax (2) 655-1046; e-mail santiago@unesco.org; internet www.unesco.org/santiago; f. 1963; Dir JORGE SEQUEIRA.

Regional Bureau for Science for Latin America and the Caribbean: Calle Dr Luis Piera 1992, 2°, Casilla 859, 11000 Montevideo, Uruguay; tel. 2413 2075; fax 2413 2094; e-mail orcyt@unesco.org.uy; internet www.unesco.org.uy; also cluster office for Argentina, Brazil, Chile, Paraguay, Uruguay; Dir JORGE GRANDI.

Regional Bureau for Education in Asia and the Pacific: POB 967, Bangkok 10110, Thailand; tel. (2) 391-0577; fax (2) 391-0866; e-mail bangkok@unescobkk.org; internet www.unescobkk.org; Dir GWANG-JO KIM.

Regional Science Bureau for Asia and the Pacific: UNESCO Office, Jalan Galuh II 5, Kebayoran Baru, Jakarta 12110, Indonesia; tel. (21) 7399818; fax (21) 72796489; e-mail jakarta@unesco.org; internet www.unesco.or.id; Dir HUBERT J. GIJZEN.

Activities

In the implementation of all its activities UNESCO aims to contribute to achieving the UN Internationally Agreed Development Goals, and the UN Millennium Development Goal (MDG) of halving levels of extreme poverty by 2015, as well as other MDGs concerned with education and sustainable development. UNESCO was the lead agency for the International Decade for a Culture of Peace and Non-violence for the Children of the World (2001–10). In November 2007 the General Conference approved a medium-term strategy to guide UNESCO during the period 2008–13. UNESCO's central mission as defined under the strategy was to contribute to building peace, the alleviation of poverty, sustainable development and intercultural dialogue through its core programme sectors (Education; Natural Sciences; Social and Human Sciences; Culture; and Communication and Information). The strategy identified five 'overarching objectives' for UNESCO in 2008–13, within this programme framework: Attaining quality education for all; Mobilizing scientific knowledge and science policy for sustainable development; Addressing emerging ethical challenges; Promoting cultural diversity and intercultural dialogue; and Building inclusive knowledge societies through information and communication.

The 2008–13 medium-term strategy reaffirmed the organization's commitment to prioritizing Africa and its development efforts. In particular, it was to extend support to countries in post-conflict and disaster situations and strengthen efforts to achieve international targets and those identified through the New Partnership for Africa's Development (NEPAD, see under African Union). A further priority for UNESCO, to be implemented through all its areas of work, was gender equality. Specific activities were to be pursued in support of the welfare of youth, least developed countries and small island developing states.

EDUCATION

UNESCO recognizes education as an essential human right, and an overarching objective for 2008–13 was to attain quality education for all. Through its work programme UNESCO is committed to achieving the MDGs of eliminating gender disparity at all levels of education and attaining universal primary education in all countries by 2015. The focus of many of UNESCO's education initiatives are the nine most highly-populated developing countries (Bangladesh, Brazil, the People's Republic of China, Egypt, India, Indonesia, Mexico, Nigeria and Pakistan), known collectively as the E-9 ('Education-9') countries.

UNESCO leads and co-ordinates global efforts in support of 'Education for All' (EFA), which was adopted as a guiding principle of UNESCO's contribution to development following a world conference, convened in March 1990. In April 2000 several UN agencies, including UNESCO and UNICEF, and other partners sponsored the World Education Forum, held in Dakar, Senegal, to assess international progress in achieving the goal of Education for All and to adopt a strategy for further action (the 'Dakar Framework'), with the aim of ensuring universal basic education by 2015. The Dakar Framework, incorporating six specific goals, emphasized the role of improved access to education in the reduction of poverty and in diminishing inequalities within and between societies. UNESCO was appointed as the lead agency in the implementation of the Framework, focusing on co-ordination, advocacy, mobilization of resources, and information-sharing at international, regional and national levels. It was to oversee national policy reforms, with a particular focus on the integration of EFA objectives into national education plans. An EFA Global Action Plan was formulated in 2006 to reinvigorate efforts to achieve EFA objectives and, in particular, to provide a framework for international co-operation and better definition of the roles of international partners and of UNESCO in leading the initiative. UNESCO's medium-term strategy for 2008–13 committed the organization to strengthening its role in co-ordinating EFA efforts at global and national levels, promoting monitoring and capacity-building activities to support implementation of EFA objectives, and facilitating mobilization of increased resources for EFA programmes and strategies (for example through the EFA-Fast Track Initiative, launched in 2002 to accelerate technical and financial support to low-income countries).

UNESCO advocates 'Literacy for All' as a key component of Education for All, regarding literacy as essential to basic education and to social and human development. UNESCO is the lead agency of the UN Literacy Decade (2003–12), which aims to formulate an international plan of action to raise literacy standards throughout the world and to assist policy-makers to integrate literacy standards and goals into national education programmes. The Literacy Initiative for Empowerment (LIFE) was developed as an element of the Literacy Decade to accelerate efforts in some 35 countries where illiteracy is a critical challenge to development. UNESCO is also the co-ordinating agency for the UN Decade of Education for Sustainable Development (2005–14), through which it aims to establish a global framework for action and strengthen the capacity of education systems to incorporate the concepts of sustainable development into education programmes. The April 2000 World Education Forum recognized the global HIV/AIDS pandemic to be a significant challenge to the attainment of Education for All. UNESCO, as a co-sponsor of UNAIDS, takes an active role in promoting formal and non-formal preventive health education. Through a Global Initiative on HIV/AIDS and Education (EDUCAIDS) UNESCO aims to develop comprehensive responses to HIV/AIDS rooted in the education sector, with a particular focus on vulnerable children and young people. An initiative covering the 10-year period 2006–15, the Teacher Training Initiative in sub-Saharan Africa, aims to address the shortage of teachers in that region (owing to HIV/AIDS, armed conflict and other causes) and to improve the quality of teaching.

A key priority area of UNESCO's education programme is to foster quality education for all, through formal and non-formal educational opportunities. It assists members to improve the quality of education provision through curricula content, school management and teacher training. UNESCO aims to expand access to education at all levels and to work to achieve gender equality. In particular, UNESCO aims to strengthen capacity-building and education in natural, social and human sciences and promote the use of new technologies in teaching and learning processes. In May 2010 UNESCO, jointly with ITU, established a Broadband Commission for Digital Development, to comprise high level representatives of governments, industry and international agencies concerned with the effective deployment of broadband networks as an essential element of economic and social development objectives.

The Associated Schools Project (ASPnet—comprising more than 9,000 institutions in 180 countries in 2012) has, since 1953, promoted the principles of peace, human rights, democracy and international co-operation through education. It provides a forum for dialogue and for promoting best practices. At tertiary level UNESCO chairs a University Twinning and Networking (UNITWIN) initiative, which was established in 1992 to establish links between higher education institutions and to foster research, training and programme development. A complementary initiative, Academics Across Borders, was inaugurated in November 2005 to strengthen communication and the sharing of knowledge and expertise among higher education professionals. In October 2002 UNESCO organized the first Global Forum on International Quality Assurance, Accreditation and the Recognition of Qualifications to establish international standards and promote capacity-building for the sustainable development of higher education systems.

Within the UN system UNESCO is responsible for providing technical assistance and educational services in the context of emergency situations. This includes establishing temporary schools, providing education for refugees and displaced persons, as well as assistance for the rehabilitation of national education systems. In Palestine, UNESCO collaborates with UNRWA to assist with the training of teachers, educational planning and rehabilitation of schools. In February 2010 UNESCO agreed to form an International Co-ordination Committee in support of Haitian culture, in view of the devastation caused by an earthquake that had struck that country in January, causing 230,000 fatalities and the destruction of local infrastructure and architecture.

In February 2010 a high-level meeting on Education for All, comprising ministers of education and international co-operation, and representatives from international and regional organizations, civil society and the private sector, was held to assess the impact on education of the ongoing global economic crisis, and to consider related challenges connected to social marginalization.

NATURAL SCIENCES

The World Summit on Sustainable Development, held in August–September 2002, recognised the essential role of science (including mathematics, engineering and technology) as a foundation for achieving the MDGs of eradicating extreme poverty and ensuring environmental sustainability. UNESCO aims to promote this function within the UN system and to assist member states to utilize and foster the benefits of scientific and technical knowledge. A key objective for the medium-term strategy (2008–13) was to mobilize science knowledge and policy for sustainable development. Throughout the natural science programme priority was to be placed on Africa, least developed countries and small island developing states. The Local and Indigenous Knowledge System (LINKS) initiative aims to strengthen dialogue among traditional knowledge holders, natural and social scientists and decision-makers to enhance the conservation of biodiversity, in all disciplines, and to secure an active and equitable role for local communities in the governance of resources.

In November 1999 the General Conference endorsed a Declaration on Science and the Use of Scientific Knowledge and an agenda for action, which had been adopted at the World Conference on Science, held in June–July 1999, in Budapest, Hungary. By leveraging scientific knowledge, and global, regional and country level science networks, UNESCO aims to support sustainable development and the sound management of natural resources. It also advises governments on approaches to natural resource management, in particular the collection of scientific data, documenting and disseminating good practices and integrating social and cultural aspects into management structures and policies. UNESCO's Man and the Biosphere Programme supports a world-wide network of biosphere reserves (comprising 580 biosphere reserves in 114 countries in 2012), which aim to promote environmental conservation and research, education and training in biodiversity and problems of land use (including the fertility of tropical soils and the cultivation of sacred sites). The third World Congress of Biosphere Reserves, held in Madrid, Spain, in February 2008, adopted the Madrid Action Plan, which aimed to promote biosphere reserves as the main internationally-designated areas dedicated to sustainable development. UNESCO also supports a Global Network of National Geoparks (89 in 27 countries in 2012) which was inaugurated in 2004 to promote collaboration among managed areas of geological significance to exchange knowledge and expertise and raise awareness of the benefits of protecting those environments. UNESCO organizes regular International Geoparks Conferences; the fifth was to be held in May 2012, in Unzen Volcanic Area Global Geopark, Japan.

UNESCO promotes and supports international scientific partnerships to monitor, assess and report on the state of Earth systems. With the World Meteorological Organization and the International Council of Science, UNESCO sponsors the World Climate Research Programme, which was established in 1980 to determine the predictability of climate and the effect of human activity on climate. UNESCO hosts the secretariat of the World Water Assessment Programme (WWAP), which prepares the periodic *World Water Development Report*. UNESCO is actively involved in the 10-year project, agreed by more than 60 governments in February 2005, to develop a Global Earth Observation System of Systems (GEOSS). The project aims to link existing and planned observation systems in order to provide for greater understanding of the earth's processes and dissemination of detailed data, for example predicting health epidemics or weather phenomena or concerning the management of ecosystems and natural resources. UNESCO's Intergovernmental Oceanographic Commission serves as the Secretariat of the Global Ocean Observing System. The International Geoscience Programme, undertaken jointly with the International Union of Geological Sciences (IUGS), facilitates the exchange of knowledge and methodology among scientists concerned with geological processes and aims to raise awareness of the links between geoscience and sustainable socio-economic development. The IUGS and UNESCO jointly initiated the International Year of Planet Earth (2008).

UNESCO is committed to contributing to international efforts to enhance disaster preparedness and mitigation. Through education UNESCO aims to reduce the vulnerability of poorer communities to disasters and improve disaster management at local and national levels. It also co-ordinates efforts at an international level to establish monitoring networks and early-warning systems to mitigate natural disasters, in particular in developing tsunami early-warning systems in Africa, the Caribbean, the South Pacific, the Mediterranean Sea and the North East Atlantic similar to those already established for the Indian and Pacific oceans. Other regional partnerships and knowledge networks were to be developed to strengthen capacity-building and the dissemination of information and good practices relating to risk awareness and mitigation and disaster management. Disaster education and awareness were to be incorporated as key elements in the UN Decade of Education for Sustainable Development (see above). UNESCO is also the lead agency for the International Flood Initiative, which was inaugurated in January 2005 at the World Conference on Disaster Reduction, held in Kobe, Japan. The Initiative aims to promote an integrated approach to flood management in order to minimize the damage and loss of life caused by floods, mainly with a focus on research, training, promoting good governance and providing technical assistance. The fifth International Conference on Flood Management was convened in Tsukuba, Japan, in September 2011.

A priority of the natural science programme has been to promote policies and strengthen human and institutional capacities in science, technology and innovation. At all levels of education UNESCO aims to enhance teaching quality and content in areas of science and technology and, at regional and sub-regional level, to strengthen co-operation mechanisms and policy networks in training and research. With the International Council of Scientific Unions and the Third World Academy of Sciences, UNESCO operates a short-term fellowship programme in the basic sciences and an exchange programme of visiting lecturers.

UNESCO is the lead agency of the New Partnership for Africa's Development (NEPAD) Science and Technology Cluster and the NEPAD Action Plan for the Environment.

SOCIAL AND HUMAN SCIENCES

UNESCO is mandated to contribute to the world-wide development of the social and human sciences and philosophy, which it regards as of great importance in policy-making and maintaining ethical vigilance. The structure of UNESCO's Social and Human Sciences programme takes into account both an ethical and standard-setting dimension, and research, policy-making, action in the field and future-oriented activities. One of UNESCO's so-called overarching objectives in the period 2008–13 was to address emerging ethical challenges.

A priority area of UNESCO's work programme on Social and Human Sciences has been to promote principles, practices and ethical norms relevant for scientific and technological development. The programme fosters international co-operation and dialogue on emerging issues, as well as raising awareness and promoting the sharing of knowledge at regional and national levels. UNESCO supports the activities of the International Bioethics Committee (IBC—a group of 36 specialists who meet under UNESCO auspices) and the Intergovernmental Bioethics Committee, and hosts the secretariat of the 18-member World Commission on the Ethics of Scientific Knowledge and Technology (COMEST), established in 1999, which aims to serve as a forum for the exchange of information and ideas and to promote dialogue between scientific communities, decision-makers and the public.

The priority Ethics of science and technology element aims to promote intergovernmental discussion and co-operation; to conduct explorative studies on possible UNESCO action on environmental ethics and developing a code of conduct for scientists; to enhance public awareness; to make available teaching expertise and create regional networks of experts; to promote the development of international and national databases on ethical issues; to identify ethical issues related to emerging technologies; to follow up relevant declarations, including the Universal Declaration on the Human Genome and Human Rights (see below); and to support the Global Ethics Observatory, an online world-wide database of information on applied bioethics and other applied science- and technology-related areas (including environmental ethics) that was launched in December 2005 by the IBC.

UNESCO itself provides an interdisciplinary, multicultural and pluralistic forum for reflection on issues relating to the ethical dimension of scientific advances, and promotes the application of international guidelines. In May 1997 the IBC approved a draft version of a Universal Declaration on the Human Genome and Human Rights, in an attempt to provide ethical guidelines for developments in human genetics. The Declaration, which identified some 100,000 hereditary genes as 'common heritage', was adopted by the UNESCO General Conference in November and committed states to promoting the dissemination of relevant scientific knowledge and co-operating in genome research. In October 2003 the General Conference adopted an International Declaration on Human Genetic Data, establishing standards for scientists working in that field, and in October 2005 the General Conference adopted the Universal Declaration on Bioethics and Human Rights. At all levels UNESCO aims to raise awareness and foster debate about the ethical implications of scientific and technological developments and promote exchange of experiences and knowledge between governments and research bodies.

UNESCO recognizes that globalization has a broad and significant impact on societies. It is committed to countering negative trends of social transformation by strengthening the links between research and policy formulation by national and local authorities, in particular concerning poverty eradication. In that respect, UNESCO promotes the concept that freedom from poverty is a fundamental human right. In 1994 UNESCO initiated an international social science research programme, the Management of Social Transformations (MOST), to promote capacity-building in social planning at all levels of decision-making. In 2003 the Executive Board approved a continuation of the programme but with a revised strategic objective of strengthening links between research, policy and practice. In 2008–13 UNESCO aimed to promote new collaborative social science research programmes and to support capacity-building in developing countries.

UNESCO aims to monitor emerging social or ethical issues and, through its associated offices and institutes, formulate preventative action to ensure they have minimal impact on the attainment of UNESCO's objectives. As a specific challenge UNESCO is committed to promoting the International Convention against Doping in Sport, which entered into force in 2007. UNESCO also focuses on the educational and cultural dimensions of physical education and sport and their capacity to preserve and improve health.

Fundamental to UNESCO's mission is the rejection of all forms of discrimination. It disseminates information aimed at combating racial prejudice, works to improve the status of women and their access to education, promotes equality between men and women, and raises awareness of discrimination against people affected by HIV/AIDS, in particular among young people. In 2004 UNESCO inaugurated an initiative to enable city authorities to share experiences and collaborate in efforts to counter racism, discrimination, xenophobia and exclusion. As well as the International Coalition of Cities against Racism, regional coalitions were to be formed with more defined programmes of action. An International Youth Clearing House and Information Service (INFOYOUTH) aims to increase and consolidate the information available on the situation of young people in society, and to heighten awareness of their needs, aspirations and potential among public and private decision-makers. Supporting efforts to facilitate dialogue among different cultures and societies and promoting opportunities for reflection and consideration of philosophy and human rights, for example the celebration of World Philosophy Day, are also among UNESCO's fundamental aims.

CULTURE

In undertaking efforts to preserve the world's cultural and natural heritage UNESCO has attempted to emphasize the link between culture and development. In December 1992 UNESCO established the World Commission on Culture and Development, to strengthen links between culture and development and to prepare a report on the issue. The first World Conference on Culture and Development was held in June 1999, in Havana, Cuba. In November 2001 the General Conference adopted the UNESCO Universal Declaration on Cultural Diversity, which affirmed the importance of intercultural dialogue in establishing a climate of peace. UNESCO's medium-term strategy for 2008–13 recognized the need for a more integrated approach to cultural heritage as an area requiring conservation and development and one offering prospects for dialogue, social cohesion and shared knowledge.

UNESCO aims to promote cultural diversity through the safeguarding of heritage and enhancement of cultural expressions. In January 2002 UNESCO inaugurated the Global Alliance on Cultural Diversity, to promote partnerships between governments, non-governmental bodies and the private sector with a view to supporting cultural diversity through the strengthening of cultural industries and the prevention of cultural piracy. In October 2005 the General Conference approved an International Convention on the Protection of the Diversity of Cultural Expressions. It entered into force in March 2007 and the first session of the intergovernmental committee servicing the Convention was convened in Ottawa, Canada, in December.

UNESCO's World Heritage Programme, inaugurated in 1978, aims to protect historic sites and natural landmarks of outstanding universal significance, in accordance with the 1972 UNESCO Convention Concerning the Protection of the World Cultural and Natural Heritage, by providing financial aid for restoration, technical assistance, training and management planning. The medium-term strategy for 2008–13 acknowledged that new global threats may affect natural and cultural heritage. It also reinforced the concept that conservation of sites contributes to social cohesion. During mid-2011–mid-2012 the 'World Heritage List' comprised 936 sites globally, of which 725 had cultural significance, 183 were natural landmarks, and 28 were of 'mixed' importance. Examples include: the Great Barrier Reef (in Australia), the Galapagos Islands (Ecuador), Chartres Cathedral (France), the Taj Mahal at Agra (India), Auschwitz concentration camp (Poland), the historic sanctuary of Machu Picchu (Peru), Robben Island (South Africa), the Serengeti National Park (Tanzania), and the archaeological site of Troy (Turkey). UNESCO also maintains a 'List of World Heritage in Danger', comprising 35 sites during mid-2011–mid-2012, in order to attract international attention to sites particularly at risk from the environment or human activities.

UNESCO supports the safeguarding of humanity's non-material 'intangible' heritage, including oral traditions, music, dance and medicine. An Endangered Languages Programme was initiated in 1993. By 2012 the Programme estimated that, of some 6,700 languages spoken world-wide, about one-half were endangered. It works to raise awareness of the issue, for example through publication of the *Atlas of the World's Languages in Danger of Disappearing,* to strengthen local and national capacities to safeguard and document languages, and administers a Register of Good Practices in Language Preservation. In October 2003 the UNESCO General Conference adopted a Convention for the Safeguarding of Intangible Cultural Heritage, which provided for the establishment of an intergovernmental committee and for participating states to formulate national inventories of intangible heritage. The Convention entered into force in April 2006 and the intergovernmental committee convened its inaugural session in November. The second session was held in Tokyo, Japan, in September 2007. A Representative List of the Intangible Cultural Heritage of Humanity, inaugurated in November 2008, comprised, at February 2012, 232 elements ('masterpieces of the oral and intangible heritage of humanity') deemed to be of outstanding value; these included: Chinese calligraphy; falconry; several dances, such as the tango, which originated in Argentina and Uruguay, and the dances of the Ainu in Japan; the chant of the Sybil on Majorca, Spain; and the Ifa Divination System (Nigeria). The related List of Intangible Cultural Heritage in Need of Urgent Safeguarding comprised 27 elements in February 2012, such as the Naqqāli form of story-telling in Iran, the Saman dance in Sumatra, Indonesia, and the Qiang New Year Festival in Sichuan Province, the People's Republic of China. UNESCO's culture programme also aims to safeguard movable cultural heritage and to support and develop museums as a means of preserving heritage and making it accessible to society as a whole.

In November 2001 the General Conference authorized the formulation of a Declaration against the Intentional Destruction of Cultural Heritage. In addition, the Conference adopted the Convention on the Protection of the Underwater Cultural Heritage, covering the protection from commercial exploitation of shipwrecks, submerged historical sites, etc., situated in the territorial waters of signatory states. UNESCO also administers the 1954 Hague Convention on the Protection of Cultural Property in the Event of Armed Conflict and the 1970 Convention on the Means of Prohibiting and Preventing the Illicit Import, Export and Transfer of Ownership of Cultural Property. In 1992 a World Heritage Centre was established to enable rapid mobilization of international technical assistance for the preservation of cultural sites. Through the World Heritage Information Network (WHIN), a world-wide network of more than 800 information providers, UNESCO promotes global awareness and information exchange.

UNESCO aims to support the development of creative industries and or creative expression. Through a variety of projects UNESCO promotes art education, supports the rights of artists, and encourages crafts, design, digital art and performance arts. In October 2004 UNESCO launched a Creative Cities Network to facilitate public and private sector partnerships, international links, and recognition of a city's unique expertise. In 2012 the following cities were participating in the Network: Aswan (Egypt), Icheon (Republic of Korea), Kanazawa (Japan) and Santa Fe (Mexico) (UNESCO Cities of Craft and Folk Art); Berlin (Germany), Buenos Aires (Argentina), Graz (Austria), Montreal (Canada), Nagoya and Kobe (Japan), Seoul (Republic of Korea), Shanghai and Shenzhen (PRC), Saint-Etienne (France) (UNESCO Cities of Design); Chengdu (PRC), Östersund (Sweden), Popayan (Colombia) (UNESCO Cities of Gastronomy); Dublin (Republic of Ireland), Edinburgh (United Kingdom), Iowa City (USA), Melbourne (Australia), Reykjavik (Iceland) (UNESCO Cities of Literature); Bologna (Italy), Ghent (Belgium), Glasgow (United Kingdom), Seville (Spain) (UNESCO Cities of Music); Bradford (United Kingdom), Sydney (Australia) (UNESCO Cities of Film); and Lyon (France) (UNESCO City of Media Arts). UNESCO is active in preparing and encouraging the enforcement of international legislation on copyright, raising awareness on the need for copyright protection to uphold cultural diversity, and is contributing to the international debate on digital copyright issues and piracy.

Within its ambition of ensuring cultural diversity, UNESCO recognizes the role of culture as a means of promoting peace and dialogue. Several projects have been formulated within a broader concept of Roads of Dialogue. In Central Asia a project on intercultural dialogue follows on from an earlier multi-disciplinary study of the ancient Silk Roads trading routes linking Asia and Europe, which illustrated many examples of common heritage. Other projects include a study of the movement of peoples and cultures during the slave trade, a Mediterranean Programme, the Caucasus Project and the Arabia Plan, which aims to promote world-wide knowledge and understanding of Arab culture. UNESCO has overseen an extensive programme of work to formulate histories of humanity and regions, focused on ideas, civilizations and the evolution of societies and cultures. These have included the *General History of Africa, History of Civilizations of Central Asia,* and *History of Humanity*. UNESCO endeavoured to consider and implement the findings of the Alliance of Civilizations, a high-level group convened by the UN Secretary-

General that published a report in November 2006. UNESCO signed a Memorandum of Understanding with the Alliance during its first forum, convened in Madrid, Spain, in January 2008.

UNESCO was designated as the lead UN agency for organizing the International Year for the Rapprochement of Cultures (2010). In February 2010, at the time of the launch of the International Year, the UNESCO Director-General established a High Panel on Peace and Dialogue among Cultures, which was to provide guidance on means of advancing tolerance, reconciliation and balance within societies world-wide.

COMMUNICATION AND INFORMATION

UNESCO regards information, communication and knowledge as being at the core of human progress and well-being. The Organization advocates the concept of knowledge societies, based on the principles of freedom of expression, universal access to information and knowledge, promotion of cultural diversity, and equal access to quality education. In 2008–13 it determined to consolidate and implement this concept, in accordance with the Declaration of Principles and Plan of Action adopted by the World Summit on the Information Society (WSIS) in November 2005.

A key strategic objective of building inclusive knowledge societies was to be through enhancing universal access to communication and information. At national and global levels UNESCO promotes the rights of freedom of expression and of access to information. It promotes the free flow and broad diffusion of information, knowledge, data and best practices, through the development of communications infrastructures, the elimination of impediments to freedom of expression, and the development of independent and pluralistic media, including through the provision of advisory services on media legislation, particularly in post-conflict countries and in countries in transition. UNESCO recognizes that the so-called global 'digital divide', in addition to other developmental differences between countries, generates exclusion and marginalization, and that increased participation in the democratic process can be attained through strengthening national communication and information capacities. UNESCO promotes policies and mechanisms that enhance provision for marginalized and disadvantaged groups to benefit from information and community opportunities. Activities at local and national level include developing effective 'infostructures', such as libraries and archives and strengthening low-cost community media and information access points, for example through the establishment of Community Multimedia Centres (CMCs). Many of UNESCO's principles and objectives in this area are pursued through the Information for All Programme, which entered into force in 2001. It is administered by an intergovernmental council, the secretariat of which is provided by UNESCO. UNESCO also established, in 1982, the International Programme for the Development of Communication (IPDC), which aims to promote and develop independent and pluralistic media in developing countries, for example by the establishment or modernization of news agencies and newspapers and training media professionals, the promotion of the right to information, and through efforts to harness informatics for development purposes and strengthen member states' capacities in this field. In March 2011 the IPDC approved funding for 93 new media development projects in developing and emerging countries worldwide.

UNESCO supports cultural and linguistic diversity in information sources to reinforce the principle of universal access. It aims to raise awareness of the issue of equitable access and diversity, encourage good practices and develop policies to strengthen cultural diversity in all media. In 2002 UNESCO established Initiative B@bel as a multidisciplinary programme to promote linguistic diversity, with the aim of enhancing access of under-represented groups to information sources as well as protecting underused minority languages. In December 2009 UNESCO and the Internet Corporation for Assigned Names and Numbers (ICANN) signed a joint agreement which aimed to promote the use of multilingual domain names using non-Latin script, with a view to promoting linguistic diversity. UNESCO's Programme for Creative Content supports the development of and access to diverse content in both the electronic and audiovisual media. The Memory of the World project, established in 1992, aims to preserve in digital form, and thereby to promote wide access to, the world's documentary heritage. Documentary material includes stone tablets, celluloid, parchment and audio recordings. By February 2012 245 inscriptions had been included on the project's register; three inscriptions originated from international organizations: the Archives of the ICRC's former International Prisoners of War Agency, 1914–23, submitted by the ICRC, and inscribed in 2007; the League of Nations Archives, 1919–46, submitted by the UN Geneva Office, and inscribed in 2009; and the UNRWA Photo and Film Archives of Palestinian Refugees' Documentary Heritage, submitted by UNRWA, and also inscribed in 2009. In September 2012 UNESCO was to organize an International Conference on the 'Memory of the World in the Digital Age: Digitization and Preservation', in Vancouver, Canada. UNESCO also supports other efforts to preserve and disseminate digital archives and, in 2003, adopted a Charter for the Preservation of Digital Heritage. In April 2009 UNESCO launched the internet based World Digital Library, accessible at www.wdl.org, which aims to display primary documents (including texts, charts and illustrations), and authoritative explanations, relating to the accumulated knowledge of a broad spectrum of human cultures.

UNESCO promotes freedom of expression, of the press and independence of the media as fundamental human rights and the basis of democracy. It aims to assist member states to formulate policies and legal frameworks to uphold independent and pluralistic media and infostructures and to enhance the capacities of public service broadcasting institutions. In regions affected by conflict UNESCO supports efforts to establish and maintain an independent media service and to use it as a means of consolidating peace. UNESCO also aims to develop media and information systems to respond to and mitigate the impact of disaster situations, and to integrate these objectives into wider UN peace-building or reconstruction initiatives. UNESCO is the co-ordinating agency for 'World Press Freedom Day', which is held annually on 3 May. The theme for 2012 was to be 'New Voices: Media Freedom Helping to Transform Societies'. It also awards an annual World Press Freedom Prize. UNESCO maintains an Observatory on the Information Society, which provides up-to-date information on the development of new ICTs, analyses major trends, and aims to raise awareness of related ethical, legal and societal issues. UNESCO promotes the upholding of human rights in the use of cyberspace. In 1997 it organized the first International Congress on Ethical, Legal and Societal Aspects of Digital Information ('INFOethics').

UNESCO promotes the application of information and communication technology for sustainable development. In particular it supports efforts to improve teaching and learning processes through electronic media and to develop innovative literacy and education initiatives, such as the ICT-Enhanced Learning (ICTEL) project. UNESCO also aims to enhance understanding and use of new technologies and support training and ongoing learning opportunities for librarians, archivists and other information providers.

Finance

UNESCO's activities are funded through a regular budget provided by contributions from member states and extrabudgetary funds from other sources, particularly UNDP, the World Bank, regional banks and other bilateral Funds-in-Trust arrangements. UNESCO co-operates with many other UN agencies and international non-governmental organizations.

UNESCO's Regular Programme budget for the two years 2012–13 was US $685.7m.

In response to a decision, in late October 2011, by a majority of member states participating in the UNESCO General Conference to admit Palestine as a new member state, the USA decided to withhold from UNESCO significant annual funding. In early 2012 a formal application (submitted in October 2011 by the Executive President of the Palestinian Authority) for full UN membership for Palestine—and thereby formal recognition as an independent state—remained under consideration by the UN Security Council.

Publications

(mostly in English, French and Spanish editions; Arabic, Chinese and Russian versions are also available in many cases)

Atlas of the World's Languages in Danger of Disappearing (online).

Copyright Bulletin (quarterly).

Encyclopedia of Life Support Systems (online).

Education for All Global Monitoring Report.

International Review of Education (quarterly).

International Social Science Journal (quarterly).

Museum International (quarterly).

Nature and Resources (quarterly).

The New Courier (quarterly).

Prospects (quarterly review on education).

UNESCO Sources (monthly).

UNESCO Statistical Yearbook.

UNESCO World Atlas of Gender Equality in Education.

World Communication Report.

World Educational Report (every 2 years).

World Heritage Review (quarterly).

World Information Report.

World Science Report (every 2 years).

Books, databases, video and radio documentaries, statistics, scientific maps and atlases.

Specialized Institutes and Centres

Abdus Salam International Centre for Theoretical Physics: Strada Costiera 11, 34151 Trieste, Italy; tel. (040) 2240111; fax (040) 224163; e-mail sci_info@ictp.it; internet www.ictp.it; f. 1964; promotes and enables advanced study and research in physics and mathematical sciences; organizes and sponsors training opportunities, in particular for scientists from developing countries; aims to provide an international forum for the exchange of information and ideas; operates under a tripartite agreement between UNESCO, IAEA and the Italian Government; Dir FERNANDO QUEVEDO (Guatemala).

International Bureau of Education (IBE): POB 199, 1211 Geneva 20, Switzerland; tel. 229177800; fax 229177801; e-mail doc .centre@ibe.unesco.org; internet www.ibe.unesco.org; f. 1925, became an intergovernmental organization in 1929 and was incorporated into UNESCO in 1969; the Council of the IBE is composed of representatives of 28 member states of UNESCO, designated by the General Conference; the Bureau's fundamental mission is to deal with matters concerning educational content, methods, and teaching/learning strategies; an International Conference on Education is held periodically; Dir CLEMENTINA ACEDO (Venezuela); publs *Prospects* (quarterly review), *Educational Innovation* (newsletter), educational practices series, monographs, other reference works.

UNESCO European Centre for Higher Education (CEPES): Str. Stirbei Vodà 39, 010102 Bucharest, Romania; tel. (1) 313-0839; fax (1) 312-3567; e-mail info@cepes.ro; f. 1972; Head of Office a. i. PETER J. WELLS.

UNESCO Institute for Information Technologies in Education: 117292 Moscow, ul. Kedrova 8, Russia; tel. (495) 129-29-90; fax (495) 129-12-25; e-mail info@iite.ru; internet www.iite.ru; the Institute aims to formulate policies regarding the development of, and to support and monitor the use of, information and communication technologies in education; it conducts research and organizes training programmes; Chair BADARCH DENDEV (acting).

UNESCO Institute for Life-long Learning: Feldbrunnenstr. 58, 20148 Hamburg, Germany; tel. (40) 448-0410; fax (40) 410-7723; e-mail uil@unesco.org; internet www.unesco.org/uil/index.htm; f. 1951, as the Institute for Education; a research, training, information, documentation and publishing centre, with a particular focus on adult basic and further education and adult literacy; Dir ARNE CARLSEN.

UNESCO Institute for Statistics: CP 6128, Succursale Centre-Ville, Montréal, QC, H3C 3J7, Canada; tel. (514) 343-6880; fax (514) 343-6882; e-mail uis@unesco.org; internet www.uis.unesco.org; f. 2001; collects and analyses national statistics on education, science, technology, culture and communications; Dir HENDRIK VAN DER POL (Netherlands).

UNESCO Institute for Water Education: Westvest 7, 2611 AX Delft, Netherlands; tel. (15) 2151-715; fax (15) 2122-921; e-mail info@ unesco-ihe.org; internet www.unesco-ihe.org; f. 2003; activities include education, training and research; and co-ordination of a global network of water sector organizations; advisory and policy-making functions; setting international standards for postgraduate education programmes; and professional training in the water sector; Rector ANDRÁS SZÖLLÖSI-NAGY.

UNESCO International Centre for Technical and Vocational Education and Training: UN Campus, Hermann-Ehlers-Str. 10, 53113 Bonn, Germany; tel. (228) 8150-100; fax (228) 8150-199; e-mail info@unevoc.unesco.org; internet www.unevoc.unesco.org; f. 2002; promotes high-quality lifelong technical and vocational education in UNESCO's member states, with a particular focus on young people, girls and women, and the disadvantaged; Head SHYAMAL MAJUMDAR (India).

UNESCO International Institute for Capacity Building in Africa (UNESCO–IICBA): ECA Compound, Africa Ave, POB 2305, Addis Ababa, Ethiopia; tel. (11) 5445284; fax (11) 514936; e-mail info@unesco-iicba.org; internet www.unesco-iicba.org; f. 1999 to promote capacity building in the following areas: teacher education; curriculum development; educational policy, planning and management; and distance education; Dir ARNALDO NHAVOTO.

UNESCO International Institute for Educational Planning (IIEP): 7–9 rue Eugène Delacroix, 75116 Paris, France; tel. 1-45-03-77-00; fax 1-40-72-83-66; e-mail info@iiep.unesco.org; internet www .unesco.org/iiep; f. 1963; serves as a world centre for advanced training and research in educational planning; aims to help all member states of UNESCO in their social and economic development efforts, by enlarging the fund of knowledge about educational planning and the supply of competent experts in this field; legally and administratively a part of UNESCO, the Institute is autonomous, and its policies and programme are controlled by its own Governing Board, under special statutes voted by the General Conference of UNESCO; a satellite office of the IIEP is based in Buenos Aires, Argentina; Dir KHALIL MAHSHI (Jordan).

UNESCO International Institute for Higher Education in Latin America and the Caribbean: Avda Los Chorros con Calle Acueducto, Edif. Asovincar, Altos de Sebucán, Apdo 68394, Caracas 1062-A, Venezuela; tel. (212) 286-0555; fax (212) 286-0527; e-mail prensa@unesco.org.ve; internet www.iesalc.unesco.org.ve; Dir PEDRO HENRÍQUEZ GUAJARDO (acting).

United Nations Industrial Development Organization—UNIDO

Address: Vienna International Centre, Wagramerstr. 5, POB 300, 1400 Vienna, Austria.

Telephone: (1) 260260; **fax:** (1) 2692669; **e-mail:** unido@unido.org; **internet:** www.unido.org.

UNIDO began operations in 1967, as an autonomous organization within the UN Secretariat, and became a specialized agency of the UN in 1985. UNIDO's objective is to promote sustainable industrial development in developing nations and states with economies in transition. It aims to assist such countries to integrate fully into the global economic system by mobilizing knowledge, skills, information and technology to promote productive employment, competitive economies and sound environment.

MEMBERS

UNIDO has 174 members.

Organization

(April 2012)

GENERAL CONFERENCE

The General Conference, which consists of representatives of all member states, meets once every two years. It is the chief policy-making organ of the Organization, and reviews UNIDO's policy concepts, strategies on industrial development and budget. The 14th General Conference was convened, in Vienna, Austria, in November–December 2011, on the theme 'The new industrial revolution: making it sustainable'.

INDUSTRIAL DEVELOPMENT BOARD

The Board consists of 53 members elected by the General Conference for a four-year period. It reviews the implementation of the approved work programme, the regular and operational budgets and other General Conference decisions, and, every four years, recommends a candidate for the post of Director-General to the General Conference for appointment.

PROGRAMME AND BUDGET COMMITTEE

The Committee, consisting of 27 members elected by the General Conference for a two-year term, assists the Industrial Development Board in preparing work programmes and budgets.

SECRETARIAT

The Secretariat comprises the office of the Director-General and three divisions, each headed by a Managing Director: Programme Development and Technical Co-operation; Programme Co-ordination and Field Operations; and Administration. In 2012 UNIDO employed around 700 regular staff members at its headquarters and other established offices.

Director-General: KANDEH YUMKELLA (Sierra Leone).

FIELD REPRESENTATION

UNIDO has 17 country offices and 12 regional offices. UNIDO's field activities throughout the world are assisted annually by around 2,800 experts.

Activities

UNIDO bases its assistance on two core functions: serving as a global forum for generating and disseminating industry-related knowledge; and designing and implementing technical co-operation programmes in support of its clients' industrial development efforts. The two core functions are complementary and mutually supportive: policy-makers benefit from experience gained in technical co-operation projects, while, by helping to define priorities, the Organization's analytical work identifies where technical co-operation will have greatest impact. Its assistance is also underpinned by the following three thematic priorities: poverty reduction through productive activities; trade capacity-building; and environment and energy. The comprehensive services provided by UNIDO cover:

(i) Industrial governance and statistics;

(ii) Promotion of investment and technology;

(iii) Industrial competitiveness and trade;

(iv) Private sector development;

(v) Agro-industries;

(vi) Sustainable energy and climate change;

(vii) The Montreal Protocol;

(viii) Environment management.

UNIDO promotes the achievement by 2015 of all the Millennium Development Goals (MDGs) adopted by the September 2000 UN Millennium Summit, with a particular focus on using industrial development in support of: eradicating extreme poverty and hunger; promoting gender equality and empowering women; ensuring environmental protection; and developing a global partnership for development. In December 2005 the 11th session of the General Conference adopted a *Strategic Long-term Vision Statement* covering the period 2005–15, focused on promoting the Organization's three thematic priorities.

UNIDO participates in the UN System Chief Executives' Board for Co-ordination—CEB's Inter-Agency Cluster on Trade and Productive Capacity, chaired by UNCTAD and also comprising UNDP, FAO, the International Trade Centre (ITC), WTO and the UN regional commissions; the Cluster, in line with the UN's *Delivering as One* agenda, aims to co-ordinate trade and development operations at the national and regional levels within the UN system. In March 2008 UNIDO organized a high-level dialogue entitled UN System-wide Coherence: The Next Steps, with a view to mapping future UN inter-agency co-operation.

UNIDO, with ITU and WIPO, leads an initiative on promoting technology and innovation, the eighth of nine activities that were launched in April 2009 by the CEB, with the aim of alleviating the impact on poor and vulnerable populations of the developing global economic crisis.

UNIDO also supports collaborative efforts between countries with complementary experience or resources in specific sectors. The investment and technology promotion network publicizes investment opportunities, provides information to investors and promotes business contacts between industrialized and developing countries and economies in transition. UNIDO is increasingly working to achieve investment promotion and transfer of technology and knowledge among developing countries. The Organization has developed several databases, including the Biosafety Information Network Advisory Service (BINAS), the Business Environment Strategic Toolkit (BEST), Industrial Development Abstracts (IDA, providing information on technical co-operation), and the International Referral System on Sources of Information (IRS).

In November 2011 UNIDO published a new *Connectedness Index*, measuring and ranking national 'knowledge networks' to assist private sector policy makers; the report was subtitled 'Networks for prosperity: achieving development goals through knowledge sharing'.

UNIDO has helped to establish and operate the following International Technology Centres: the International Centre for Science and High Technology (based in Trieste, Italy); the International Centre for Advancement of Manufacturing Technology (Bangalore, India); the UNIDO Regional Centre for Small Hydro Power (Trivandum, India); the Centre for the Application of Solar Energy (Perth, Australia); the International Centre of Medicine Biotechnology (Obolensk, Russia); the International Materials Assessment and Application Centre (Rio de Janeiro, Brazil); the International Centre for Materials Technology Promotion (Beijing, People's Republic of China); and the Shenzhen International Technology Promotion Centre (also in China).

The Organization promotes South-South industrial co-operation. A UNIDO Centre for South-South Industrial Co-operation (UCSSIC) was established in India, and, in July 2008, a further UCSSIC was inaugurated in Beijing.

POVERTY REDUCTION THROUGH PRODUCTIVE ACTIVITIES

UNIDO provides support to policy-making bodies in developing countries to promote competitive industries and private sector development, with a particular focus on: the creation of competitiveness intelligence units in major public and private sector institutions; and the establishment of industrial observatories, with the role of monitoring global trade and industry trends, and benchmarking national and company performance. During 2007 UNIDO introduced an online private sector development toolkit, to provide support to policy-makers.

Encouraging foreign direct investment, and promoting technology transfer and technology diffusion projects aimed at strengthening developing countries' national innovation systems, are key elements of the Organization's poverty reduction strategy.

UNIDO implements a programme for small and medium-sized enterprise (SME) cluster development, which aims to enhance linkages between small businesses and support institutions, in order to assist them with realizing their full growth potential. A Rural and Women's Entrepreneurship Development Programme promotes businesses in developing countries with a particular focus on women and youth. UNIDO recognizes that agro-based industries play a major role in the transition from traditional rural to competitive manufacturing-based economies, and therefore supports the development of the skills and technologies required to advance those industries in developing countries. In the area of food-processing programmes have been initiated to upgrade agro-based value chains, and to open market channels for agro-products. Through its efforts to strengthen developing countries' food supplies and facilitate access to markets, technology and investment, UNIDO also contributes to UN system-wide efforts to address the ongoing global food security crisis. In April 2008 UNIDO, jointly with FAO, IFAD and the Indian Government, organized the Global Agro-Industries Forum: Improving Competitiveness and Development Impact, convened in New Delhi, India; and in November UNIDO helped to organize an International Conference on Sharing Innovative Agribusiness Solutions, held in Cairo, Egypt. The Organization also implements projects aimed at restoring agro-industries that have been adversely affected by violent conflict and natural disasters, and has undertaken studies and projects aimed at strengthening the textile and garment industries.

In March 2012 UNIDO and the UN Office on Drugs and Crime signed a Memorandum of Understanding on establishing a strategic partnership aimed at promoting grass-roots development and alternative livelihoods in poor rural communities hitherto dependent on the cultivation of illegal drugs crops.

UNIDO provides advice to governmental agencies and industrial institutions to improve the management of human resources. The Organization also undertakes training projects to develop human resources in specific industries, and aims to encourage the full participation of women in economic progress through gender awareness programmes and practical training to improve women's access to employment and business opportunities.

UNIDO participated in the Third United Nations Conference on the Least Developed Countries (LDC-III), held in Brussels, Belgium, in May 2001. The Organization launched a package of 'deliverables' (special initiatives) in support of the Programme of Action adopted by the Conference, which emphasized the importance of productive capacity in the international development agenda. These related to energy, market access (the enablement of LDCs to participate in international trade), and SME networking and cluster development (with a particular focus on agro-processing and metal-working). LDC-IV was convened in May–June 2011 in Istanbul, Turkey.

UNIDO places a major focus on industrialization in Africa, the advancement of which is regarded as essential to that continent's full integration into the global economy; challenges include the prevalence there of LDCs, limited industrial skills and technological capabilities, weak support from institutions, inadequate financing and underdeveloped domestic and regional markets. UNIDO welcomed the African Union Action Plan for the Accelerated Industrial Development of Africa, which was launched in January 2008, and promotes African regional integration as beneficial for the industrialization of the continent. UNIDO plays a leading role in co-ordinating Africa Industrialization Day, held annually on 20 November. UNIDO has developed national programmes for 24 African countries; these have emphasized capacity-building for the enhancement of industrial competitiveness and private sector development, which is regarded as a major priority for the transformation of African economies. The basic philosophy has been to identify, jointly with key stakeholders in major industrial sub-sectors, the basic tools required to determine their national industrial development needs and priorities. This process has facilitated the definition and establishment of comprehensive national medium- and long-term industrial development agendas. In March 2010 UNIDO convened a high-level conference, in Abuja, Nigeria, on means of developing agribusiness and agro-industries in Africa; the conference endorsed a new African Agribusiness and Agro-industries Development Initiative (known as '3ADI'), a programme framework and funding mechanism enabling public and private sector interests to mobilize resources for investment in development of the African agri-food sector.

TRADE CAPACITY-BUILDING

UNIDO implements programmes that build industrial capacities, in both public and private institutions, to formulate policies and strategies for developing trade competitiveness. The Organization has developed a comprehensive programme to improve deficiencies in standards, metrology, accreditation and conformity infrastructure, to help developing countries overcome technical barriers while improving product quality, to meet the standards required in the global trading arena. UNIDO also helps countries to comply with global sanitary and phyto-sanitary standards. Efforts in the area of post-conflict rebuilding of quality infrastructures have been undertaken. UNIDO's industrial business development services—such as business incubators, rural entrepreneurship development and SME cluster development—for SME support institutions are aimed at enabling SMEs to play a key role in economic growth. Aid-for-trade activities are undertaken, including programmes that link debt swaps to trade-related technical co-operation. The Organization assists with the establishment of export consortia, through which SMEs can pool knowledge, financial resources and contacts to improve their export potential while also reducing costs. Promotion of business partnership has been strengthened through the Organization's world-wide network of investment and technology promotion offices, investment promotion units, and subcontracting and partnership exchanges. UNIDO contributes to the UN Global Compact aimed at promoting corporate social responsibility (CSR). In 2008 the Organization prepared a paper entitled *CSR, SMEs and Public Policy in Middle and Low Income Countries: Issues and Options for UNIDO*, which explored the links between public policy interventions, SMEs and CSR.

UNIDO has pursued efforts to overcome the so-called 'digital divide' between and within countries. The Organization has helped to develop electronic and mobile business for SMEs in developing countries and economies in transition. It has also launched an internet-based electronic platform, UNIDO Exchange (accessible at exchange.unido.org) for sharing intelligence and fostering business partnerships. UNIDO's Technology Foresight initiative, launched in 1999, involves the systematic visualization of long-term developments in the areas of science, technology, industry, economy and society, with the aim of identifying technologies capable of providing future economic and social benefits. The initiative is being implemented in Asia, Latin America and the Caribbean, and in Central and Eastern Europe and the CIS.

In March 2002, while participating in the International Conference on Financing and Development, held in Monterrey, Mexico, UNIDO launched an initiative designed to facilitate access to international markets for developing countries and countries with transitional economies by assisting them in overcoming barriers to trade.

ENVIRONMENT AND ENERGY

UNIDO's Energy and Climate Change Branch supports patterns of energy use by industry that are environmentally sustainable and likely to mitigate climate change. UNIDO encourages energy efficiency and implements a programme to promote access to renewable sources of energy, essential for conducting modern productive activities. UNIDO has organized a number of conferences relating to renewable energy. In April 2009 a report was issued entitled *UNIDO and Renewable Energy: Greening the Industrial Agenda*, outlining the Organization's renewable energy promotion efforts. In August–September 2002 the Organization participated in the World Summit on Sustainable Development (WSSD), held in Johannesburg, South Africa, at which it launched an initiative seeking to promote rural energy for productive use. UNIDO's Lighting up Rural Africa programme develops small hydropower projects for rural electrification and industrial usage. The Global Mercury Project focuses on reducing mercury pollution caused by artisanal gold mining, and a Participatory Control of Desertification and Poverty Reduction in the Arid and Semi-Arid High Plateau Ecosystems of Eastern Morocco scheme, jointly developed with IFAD, promotes natural regeneration and efficient land use. UNIDO is engaged in capacity-building activities for developing biotechnology projects. In October 2010 UNIDO participated in the fourth global ministerial conference on renewable energy, which took place in New Delhi, India, on the theme 'Upscaling and Mainstreaming Renewables for Energy Security, Climate Change and Economic Development'; the first, second and third conferences had been held in Bonn, Germany, in June 2004; in Beijing, China, in November 2005; and Washington, USA, in March 2008.

In September 2009 UNIDO, with UNEP, ILO, ESCAP and the Philippines Government organized the International Conference on Green Industry in Asia, in Manila; the conference adopted the Manila Declaration and Framework for Action, detailing measures aimed at reducing the resource-intensity and carbon emissions of Asian industries. UNIDO subsequently focused on developing a series of activities aimed at assisting the implementation of the Framework in those Asian countries wishing to implement it, including the preparation of green industry policy guidelines and of country status reports on eco-efficiency. Green-industry pilot programmes were to be undertaken in Asia and elsewhere.

As one of the implementing agencies of the Multilateral Fund for the Implementation of the Montreal Protocol, UNIDO implements projects that help developing countries to reduce the use of ozone-depleting substances. From 2007 the Organization contributed to the formulation of national plans in support of the freezing by 2013 of the production of hydrochlorofluorocarbons (HCFCs). It is also involved in implementing the Kyoto Protocol of the Framework Convention on Climate Change (relating to greenhouse gas emissions) in old factories world-wide. UNIDO has helped to develop 10 national ozone units responsible for designing, monitoring and implementing programmes to phase out ozone-depleting substances. By December 2008 33 National Cleaner Production Centres (NCPCs), five National Cleaner Production Programmes, and, in Latin America, a regional network of cleaner production centres, had been established, under a joint UNIDO/UNEP programme that was launched in 1994 to promote the use and development of environmentally sustainable technologies and to build national capacities in cleaner production. In February 2010 UNIDO, in partnership with the Norwegian Government and the Global Carbon Capture and Storage Institute, launched a project aimed at developing a global technology roadmap for carbon capture and storage for industrial processes.

The Director-General of UNIDO serves as the chairperson of UN-Energy, the inter-agency mechanism that aims to promote system-wide co-operation in the UN's response to energy-related issues. UNIDO, on behalf on UN-Energy, identifies areas for collaboration between the UN and private sector in addressing challenges posed by climate change and the achievement of sustainable development.

In December 2007 the General Conference endorsed a Strategic Approach to International Chemicals Management. A programme promoting chemical leasing encourages improved co-operation between chemicals producers and users, and helps companies to comply with environmental regulations. UNIDO has supported countries with the preparation of national implementation plans for the effective removal of persistent organic pollutants. The Organization has undertaken a number of technical assistance projects and schemes aimed at helping countries to adopt energy management standards, and has also co-operated with the International Organization for Standardization on the development of an international energy management standard.

UNIDO and UN-Energy supported the UN Global Compact in organizing the annual Private Sector Forum, held in September 2011, in New York, USA, at which the UN Secretary-General launched a new initiative, Sustainable Energy for All by 2030, and a high-level group responsible for its implementation.

The 2011 edition of UNIDO's annual *Industrial Development Report*, issued in January 2012, highlighted the importance of prioritizing industrial energy efficiency in the pursuit of sustainable industrial development, with a particular focus on developing countries.

Finance

The provisional regular budget for the two years 2012–13 amounted to €153.2m., financed mainly by assessed contributions payable by member states. There was an operational budget of some €27.9m. for the same period, financed mainly by voluntary contributions. The Industrial Development Fund is used by UNIDO to finance development projects that fall outside the usual systems of multilateral funding.

Publications

Annual Report.

Connectedness Index.

Development of Clusters and Networks of SMEs.

Gearing up for a New Development Agenda.

Industrial Development Report.
Industry for Growth into the New Millennium.
International Yearbook of Industrial Statistics (annually).
Making It: Industry for Development (quarterly).
Manual for the Evaluation of Industrial Projects.
Manual for Small Industrial Businesses.
Reforming the UN System—UNIDO's Need-Driven Model.
UNIDOScope (monthly, electronic newsletter).
Using Statistics for Process Control and Improvement: An Introduction to Basic Concepts and Techniques.
World Information Directory of Industrial Technology and Investment Support Services.

Several other manuals, guidelines, numerous working papers and reports.

Universal Postal Union—UPU

Address: Case Postale 13, 3000 Bern 15, Switzerland.

Telephone: 313503111; **fax:** 313503110; **e-mail:** info@upu.int; **internet:** www.upu.int.

The General Postal Union was founded by the Treaty of Berne (1874), beginning operations in July 1875. Three years later its name was changed to the Universal Postal Union. In 1948 the UPU became a specialized agency of the UN. The UPU promotes the sustainable development of high-quality, universal, efficient and accessible postal services.

MEMBERS

The UPU has 192 members.

Organization

(April 2012)

CONGRESS

The supreme body of the Union is the Universal Postal Congress, which meets, in principle, every four years. Congress focuses on general principles and broad policy issues. It is responsible for the Constitution (the basic act of the Union), the General Regulations (which contain provisions relating to the application of the Constitution and the operation of the Union), changes in the provision of the Universal Postal Convention, approval of the strategic plan and budget parameters, formulation of overall policy on technical co-operation, and for elections and appointments. Amendments to the Constitution are recorded in Additional Protocols, of which there are currently seven. The 24th Congress was convened in Geneva, Switzerland, in July–August 2008, under the chairmanship of Kenya. The 25th Universal Postal Congress was scheduled to be held in Doha, Qatar, during September–October 2012.

COUNCIL OF ADMINISTRATION

The Council meets annually at Bern. It is composed of a Chairman and representatives of 41 member countries of the Union elected by the Universal Postal Congress on the basis of an equitable geographical distribution. It is responsible for supervising the affairs of the Union between Congresses. The Council also considers policies that may affect other sectors, such as standardization and quality of service, provides a forum for considering the implications of governmental policies with respect to competition, deregulation and trade-in-service issues for international postal services, and considers intergovernmental aspects of technical co-operation. The Council approves the Union's budget, supervises the activities of the International Bureau and takes decisions regarding UPU contacts with other international agencies and bodies. It is also responsible for promoting and co-ordinating all aspects of technical assistance among member countries. The Council has a subsidiary WTO Issues Project Group.

POSTAL OPERATIONS COUNCIL (POC)

As the technical organ of the UPU, the POC, which holds annual sessions and comprises 40 elected member countries, is responsible for the operational, economic and commercial aspects of international postal services. The POC has the authority to amend and enact the Detailed Regulations of the Universal Postal Convention, on the basis of decisions made at Congress. It promotes the studies undertaken by some postal services and the introduction of new postal products. It also prepares and issues recommendations for member countries concerning uniform standards of practice. On the recommendation of the 1999 Beijing Congress the POC established a Standards Board with responsibility for approving standards relating to telematics, postal technology and Electronic Data Interchange (EDI). The POC aims to assist national postal services to modernize postal products, including letter and parcel post, financial services and expedited mail services.

CONSULTATIVE COMMITTEE

The Consultative Committee, established in September 2004 by the 23rd (Bucharest) Congress, provides a platform for dialogue between postal industry stakeholders and represents the interests of the wider international postal sector. It has 27 members, comprising non-governmental organizations representing customers, delivery service providers, workers' organizations, suppliers of goods and services to the postal sector and other organizations. Membership of the Committee is open to non-government organizations with an interest in international postal services, representing customers, delivery service providers, suppliers of goods and services to the postal sector, and workers' organizations; and also to private companies with an interest in international postal services, such as private operators, direct marketers, international mailers, and printers. All members are extended full observer status in all organs of the Union. The Committee convenes twice a year, in Bern, to coincide with meetings of the Council of Administration and the Postal Operations Council.

INTERNATIONAL BUREAU

The day-to-day administrative work of the UPU is executed through the International Bureau, which provides secretariat and support facilities for the UPU's bodies. It serves as an instrument of liaison, information and consultation for the postal administration of the member countries and promotes technical co-operation among Union members. It also acts as a clearing house for the settlement of accounts between national postal administrations for inter-administration charges related to the exchange of postal items and international reply coupons. The Bureau supports the technical assistance programmes of the UPU, organizes regular conferences and workshops, and serves as an intermediary between the UPU, the UN, its agencies and other international organizations, customer organizations and private delivery services. Increasingly the Bureau has assumed a greater role in postal administration, through two co-operatives: the Telematics Co-operative and the Express Mail Service (EMS) Co-operative. The Telematics Co-operative, with voluntary participation by public, semi-public, and private postal operators, supports the use of new technologies in the improvement and expansion of postal services. Its operational arm is the Postal Technology Centre (PTC, supported by five Regional Support Centres world-wide), which manages three core activities: Post*Net, a global postal communication network, using EDI to provide monitoring services, a track-and-trace system, and postal remuneration and billing; the International Postal System (IPS), an integrated international mail management system, providing automated processing of dispatches and end-to-end tracking of items; and the International Financial System (IFS), a software application facilitating international money order services. The EMS Co-operative, comprising (at February 2012) 170 EMS designated operators covering 90% of global EMS traffic, regulates the provision of a high-quality, competitive global EMS service, and operates through an EMS Unit.

Director-General of the International Bureau: EDOUARD DAYAN (France).

Activities

The essential principles of the Union are the following:

(i) to develop social, cultural and commercial communication between people through the efficient operation of the postal services;

(ii) to guarantee freedom of transit and free circulation of postal items;

(iii) to ensure the organization, development and modernization of the postal services;

(iv) to promote and participate in postal technical assistance between member countries;

(v) to ensure the interoperability of postal networks by implementing a suitable policy of standardization;

(vi) to meet the changing needs of customers;

(vii) to improve the quality of service.

In addition to the Constitution and the General Regulations, the Universal Postal Convention is also a compulsory Act of the UPU (binding on all member countries), in view of its importance in the postal field and historical value. The Convention and its Detailed Regulations contain the common rules applicable to the international postal service and provisions concerning letter- and parcel-post. The Detailed Regulations are agreements concluded by the national postal administrations elected by Congress to the POC. The POC is empowered to revise and enact these, taking into account decisions made at Congress.

The 24th Congress, convened in Geneva, Switzerland (under the chairmanship of Kenya), in July–August 2008, adopted a new Postal Payment Services Agreement and its Regulations (the original version of which was adopted by the 1999 Beijing Congress to replace the former Money Orders, Giro and Cash-on-Delivery Agreements). The Agreement (adherence to which is optional for UPU member states) aims to enable postal operators to operate faster, more secure and more accessible electronic money transfer services to communities without access to banks in developing regions that have poor access to formal money transfer networks.

In recent years the UPU has reviewed its activities and has focused on the following factors underlying the modern postal environment: the growing role played by technology; the expanding reach of the effects of globalization; and the need to make the customer the focus of new competitive strategies. In October 2002 the UPU organized a Strategy Conference entitled 'Future Post', at which delegates representing governments and postal services addressed challenges confronting the postal industry. The 23rd Congress, held in September–October 2004, adopted the Bucharest World Postal Strategy, detailing a number of objectives to be pursued in the postal sector over the next four years; a new package of proposals for so-called terminal dues; a new quality of standards and targets for international mail services; a resolution relating to security, the combating of terrorism and prevention of money-laundering through use of the mail network; and a proposal to amend the UPU Convention to recognize legally the Electronic Postmark as an optional postal service. In July–August 2008 the 24th Congress adopted the Nairobi Postal Strategy to guide the Union's activities during 2009–12. The Strategy focused on modernizing global postal services at all levels, in terms of institutional reform, improvement in the quality of service, security of postal services, and promoting a universal postal service (UPS); and also in terms of raising awareness of the impact of postal services on the environment and climate change. The UPU Secretary-General stated during the 24th Congress that UPU's future agenda would focus on e-commerce, technological development, intelligent mail, facilitation of international trade and exchanges, electronic money transfers, sustainable development, international co-operation, postal infrastructure at the service of development policies, and improvements to the UPS. The 24th Congress determined to establish minimum security standards and processes for postal operators, and to invite postal administrations to co-operate more closely with customs authorities to identify counterfeit or pirated articles dispatched through the mail. In December 2009 UPU released the results of its first world-wide survey of greenhouse gas emissions generated by postal operations. At the UN Climate Change Conference, held in Copenhagen, Denmark, later in that month, UPU pledged to promote more environmentally-friendly methods of processing and delivering mail. In September 2010 UPU organized a Strategy Conference, in Nairobi, to initiate the process of defining a new global postal strategy prior to the 25th Congress. The meeting concluded that the adoption of new technologies and the diversification of postal services were critical elements of a future strategy. In January 2012 UPU released a study monitoring the development of postal e-services, which were divided into: e-post services (such as internet-access points in post offices, postal electronic mailboxes and online direct mail); e-finance services (electronic invoicing, electronic remittances, electronic bill payments); e-commerce services (online subscriptions to periodicals, secure web certificates); and e-government services (including electronic payment of retirement pensions, online passport applications, electronic customs documents).

In April 2011 a new UPU inter-committee security group, with participation by postal operators and international organizations, met for the first time to pursue the development and application of global postal security standards.

In January 2010 UPU established a task force of postal experts to co-ordinate efforts to support and rehabilitate postal services in Haiti, following a devastating earthquake in that country. In November 2011 a new UPU Emergency and Solidarity Fund (ESF) became operational; the ESF was to facilitate the recovery of basic postal services in countries affected by natural disaster and armed conflict, and was to be financed by voluntary contributions from governments and postal sector partners.

POSTAL ENVIRONMENT

The 2004 Bucharest Congress approved a UPU policy on extraterritorial offices of exchange (ETOEs), defined as offices of facilities operated by or in connection with a postal operator on the territory of another country for the commercial purpose of drawing business in markets outside its national territory. The Council of Administration's WTO Issues Project Group monitors developments on trade in services, keeps member states informed on trade developments, and promotes awareness of WTO issues of interest to the UPU. In recent years the UPU has been concerned with developing the role of the postal sector in the modern information society and in reducing the digital divide between industrialized and developing nations. The UPU pursues the following objectives in line with the Geneva Plan of Action adopted during the first phase of the World Summit on the Information Society convened in December 2003: facilitating, through the global postal infrastructure, unprecedented access to knowledge and ICTs; advancing the physical, electronic and financial dimensions of the global postal network; transferring postal administrations' expertise in physical communications management to the internet (particularly in the areas of identity management and SPAM control); and helping to build confidence and security in the use of ICTs. At the World Telecommunication Development Conference, convened in Hyderabad, India, in May–June 2010, the UPU, jointly with the International Telecommunications Union, launched a publication on innovation in the postal sector, entitled *ICTs, New Services and Transformation of the Post*. The UPU conducts market analysis to assist postal administrations in adapting to globalization and technological advances in world markets. A Postal Economics Programme implemented by the UPU conducts economic research aimed at analysing the uneven postal sector development of developing countries and providing growth models for the postal sectors of developing countries. In recent years the UPU has focused on the role of postal administrations in supporting the use of e-commerce activities by micro- and small enterprises in least developed and developing countries.

On 1 October 2003 a new UPU clearing system (UPU*Clearing) became operational to enable postal operators to exchange bills electronically. During 2004 the UPU sponsored an application to the Internet Corporation for Assigned Names and Numbers (ICANN) to obtain a top-level internet domain, .post, for use, *inter alia*, by national and other postal operators, postal-related organizations, regional associations, UPU-regulated services, and trademarks and brand names. Negotiations between ICANN and the UPU on contract terms for the .post domain were concluded in October 2009 and an agreement was signed in December.

In March 2007 the UPU and the International Air Transport Association signed a memorandum of understanding on developing and harmonizing standards and increasing the use of technologies (such as bar coding, radio frequency identification, and the processing of electronic data) to improve air mail flows.

UPU helps to organize a regular World Postal Business Forum, which addresses postal sector challenges and trends; the 2011 Forum was convened in September, in Stuttgart, Germany, concurrently with the 15th annual POST-EXPO, an exhibition displaying recent post-related technological innovations and systems. The 16th POST-EXPO was scheduled to be held in September 2012, in Brussels, Belgium.

POSTAL DEVELOPMENT

The UPU's International Bureau undertakes quality tests on postal products and services world-wide, monitoring some 900 international links through the use of test letters and parcels; the Bureau also publishes end-to-end delivery standards. The UPU sends consultants to selected countries to promote the implementation of improvements in quality of service. The first phase of testing a new performance-measuring facility, the Global Monitoring System (GMS), was initiated in August 2009 by postal operators in 21 countries. The GMS commenced operations in January 2010.

The UPU has conducted research into the effects of postal sector regulatory reforms. The UPU's Integrated Postal Reform and Development Plan (IPDP) aims to enhance co-operation in promoting postal sector reform; under IPDP guidelines the principal aim of the postal sector reform process is to ensure that the state obligation to provide the UPS is met, and that the conditions required to modernize the postal sector are established, with a view to benefiting both individual citizens and business. Through its programme on development co-operation the UPU provides postal technical assistance to developing member countries. The 2008 Congress and the Nairobi Postal Strategy promoted the regional implementation of global development strategies; UPU implements a Regional Development Plan (RDP) aimed at providing a coherent framework for regional development activities.

The UPU has undertaken projects to develop human resources in the postal sector. It has developed guides, training materials and training models through its Trainpost programme, and organizes capacity-building training workshops in developing countries and on a regional basis. The UPU promotes environmental sustainability in the postal sector, encouraging recycling programmes and the use of environment-friendly products and resources. The UPU has produced guidelines on cost accounting to be used as a management tool by postal administrations.

The 1999 Congress approved the establishment of a Quality of Service Fund, which was to be financed by industrialized member countries (by a 7.5% increase in dues) in order to support service improvement projects in developing member states. The Fund became operative in 2001 and had by the end of 2010 approved 570 projects, benefiting some 150 national postal services. The 2008 Congress determined to extend the Fund's period of operation (originally to have expired in that year) to 2016.

Finance

All of the UPU's regular budget expenses are financed by member countries, based on a contribution class system. The UPU's annual budget amounts to some 37m. Swiss francs.

Publications

Postal Statistics.

*POST*Info* (online newsletter of postal technology centre).

Union Postale (quarterly, in French, German, English, Arabic, Chinese, Spanish and Russian).

UPU EDI Messaging Standards.

UPU Technical Standards.

Other guides and industry reports.

World Health Organization—WHO

Address: 20 ave Appia, 1211 Geneva 27, Switzerland.

Telephone: 227912111; **fax:** 227913111; **e-mail:** info@who.int; **internet:** www.who.int.

WHO, established in 1948, is the lead agency within the UN system concerned with the protection and improvement of public health.

MEMBERS

WHO has 193 members.

Organization

(April 2012)

WORLD HEALTH ASSEMBLY

The Assembly meets in Geneva, once a year. It is responsible for policy-making and the biennial programme and budget; appoints the Director-General; admits new members; and reviews budget contributions.

EXECUTIVE BOARD

The Board is composed of 34 health experts designated by a member state that has been elected by the World Health Assembly to serve on the Board; each expert serves for three years. The Board meets at least twice a year to review the Director-General's programme, which it forwards to the Assembly with any recommendations that seem necessary. It advises on questions referred to it by the Assembly and is responsible for putting into effect the decisions and policies of the Assembly. It is also empowered to take emergency measures in case of epidemics or disasters.

Chairman: RAHHAL EL-MAKKAOUI (Morocco).

SECRETARIAT

Director-General: Dr MARGARET CHAN (People's Republic of China).

Deputy Director-General: Dr ANARFI ASAMOA-BAAH (Ghana).

Assistant Directors-General: Dr BRUCE AYLWARD (Canada) (Polio, Emergencies and Country Collaboration), FLAVIA BUSTREO (Italy) (Family, Women's and Children's Health), OLEG CHESTNOV (Italy) (Non-communicable Diseases and Mental Health), Dr CARISSA F. ETIENNE (Dominica) (Health Systems and Services), KEIJI FUKUDA (USA) (Health Security and Environment), MOHAMED ABDI JAMA (Somalia) (General Management), MARIE-PAULE KIENY (France) (Innovation, Information, Evidence and Research), HIROKI NAKATANI (Japan) (HIV/AIDS, TB, Malaria and Neglected Tropical Diseases).

PRINCIPAL OFFICES

Each of WHO's six geographical regions has its own organization, consisting of a regional committee representing relevant member states and associate members, and a regional office staffed by experts in various fields of health.

Africa Office: Cité du Djoue BP 06, Brazzaville, Republic of the Congo; tel. 83-91-00; fax 83-95-01; e-mail regafro@whoafro.org; internet www.afro.who.int; Dir Dr LUÍS GOMES SAMBO (Angola).

Americas Office: Pan-American Health Organization, 525 23rd St, NW, Washington, DC 20037, USA; tel. (202) 974-3000; fax (202) 974-3663; e-mail director@paho.org; internet www.paho.org; also administers The Caribbean Epidemiology Centre (CAREC); Dir Dr MIRTA ROSES PERIAGO (Argentina).

Eastern Mediterranean Office: POB 7608, Abdul Razzak al Sanhouri St, Cairo (Nasr City) 11371, Egypt; tel. (2) 2765000; fax (2) 6702492; e-mail postmaster@emro.who.int; internet www.emro.who.int; Dir Dr HUSSEIN ABDUL RAZZAQ GEZAIRY (Saudi Arabia).

Europe Office: 8 Scherfigsvej, 2100 Copenhagen Ø, Denmark; tel. 39-17-17-17; fax 39-17-18-18; e-mail postmaster@euro.who.int; internet www.euro.who.int; Dir ZSUZSANNA JAKAB (Hungary).

South-East Asia Office: World Health House, Indraprastha Estate, Mahatma Gandhi Rd, New Delhi 110002, India; tel. (11) 23370804; fax (11) 23379507; e-mail registry@searo.who.int; internet www.searo.who.int; Dir Dr SAMLEE PLIANBANGCHANG.

Western Pacific Office: POB 2932, Manila 1000, Philippines; tel. (2) 5288001; fax (2) 5211036; e-mail pio@wpro.who.int; internet www.wpro.who.int; Dir Dr SHIN YOUNG SOO (Republic of Korea).

WHO Centre for Health Development: I. H. D. Centre Bldg, 9th Floor, 5–1, 1-chome, Wakinohama-Kaigandori, Chuo-ku, Kobe, Japan; tel. (78) 230-3100; fax (78) 230-3178; e-mail wkc@wkc.who.int; internet www.who.or.jp; f. 1995 to address health development issues; Dir Dr JACOB KUMARESAN (India).

WHO European Office for Investment for Health and Development: Palazzo Franchetti, S. Marco 2847, 30124 Venice, Italy; tel. (041) 279-3865; fax (041) 279-3869; e-mail info@ihd.euro.who.int; f. 2003 to develop a systematic approach to the integration of social and economic factors into European countries' development strategies.

WHO Lyon Office for National Epidemic Preparedness and Response: 58 ave Debourg, 69007 Lyon, France; tel. 4-72-71-64-70; fax 4-72-71-64-71; e-mail oms@lyon.who.int; internet www.who.int/ihr/lyon/en/index.html; supports global capacity-building for detection of and response to epidemics of infectious diseases; provides bridging role between WHO headquarters, the regional offices and ongoing activities in the field; Dir Dr GUÉNAËL RODIER.

Activities

WHO's objective is stated in its constitution as 'the attainment by all peoples of the highest possible level of health'. 'Health' is defined as 'a state of complete physical, mental and social well-being and not merely the absence of disease and infirmity'.

WHO has developed a series of international classifications, including the *International Statistical Classification of Disease and Related Health Problems (ICD)*, providing an etiological framework of health conditions, and currently in its 10th edition; and the complementary *International Classification of Functioning, Disability and Health (ICF)*, which describes how people live with their conditions.

WHO acts as the central authority directing international health work, and establishes relations with professional groups and government health authorities on that basis.

It provides, on request from member states, technical and policy assistance in support of programmes to promote health, prevent and control health problems, control or eradicate disease, train health workers best suited to local needs and strengthen national health systems. Aid is provided in emergencies and natural disasters.

A global programme of collaborative research and exchange of scientific information is carried out in co-operation with about 1,200 national institutions. Particular stress is laid on the widespread communicable diseases of the tropics, and the countries directly concerned are assisted in developing their research capabilities.

It keeps diseases and other health problems under constant surveillance, promotes the exchange of prompt and accurate information and of notification of outbreaks of diseases, and administers the International Health Regulations (the most recently revised version of which entered into force in June 2007). It sets standards for the quality control of drugs, vaccines and other substances affecting health. It formulates health regulations for international travel.

It collects and disseminates health data and carries out statistical analyses and comparative studies in such diseases as cancer, heart disease and mental illness.

It receives reports on drugs observed to have shown adverse reactions in any country, and transmits the information to other member states.

It promotes improved environmental conditions, including housing, sanitation and working conditions. All available information on effects on human health of the pollutants in the environment is critically reviewed and published.

Co-operation among scientists and professional groups is encouraged. The organization negotiates and sustains national and global partnerships. It may propose international conventions and agreements, and develops and promotes international norms and standards. The organization promotes the development and testing of new technologies, tools and guidelines. It assists in developing an informed public opinion on matters of health.

WHO's first global strategy for pursuing 'Health for all' was adopted in May 1981 by the 34th World Health Assembly. The objective of 'Health for all' was identified as the attainment by all citizens of the world of a level of health that would permit them to lead a socially and economically productive life, requiring fair distribution of available resources, universal access to essential health care, and the promotion of preventive health care. In May 1998 the 51st World Health Assembly renewed the initiative, adopting a global strategy in support of 'Health for all in the 21st century', to be effected through regional and national health policies. The new framework was to build on the primary health care approach of the initial strategy, but aimed to strengthen the emphasis on quality of life, equity in health and access to health services. The following have been identified as minimum requirements of 'Health for all':

Safe water in the home or within 15 minutes' walking distance, and adequate sanitary facilities in the home or immediate vicinity;

Immunization against diphtheria, pertussis (whooping cough), tetanus, poliomyelitis, measles and tuberculosis;

Local health care, including availability of essential drugs, within one hour's travel;

Trained personnel to attend childbirth, and to care for pregnant mothers and children up to at least one year old.

In the implementation of all its activities WHO aims to contribute to achieving by 2015 the UN Millennium Development Goals (MDGs) that were agreed by the September 2000 UN Millennium Summit. WHO has particular responsibility for the MDGs of: reducing child mortality, with a target reduction of two-thirds in the mortality rate among children under five; improving maternal health, with a specific goal of reducing by 75% the numbers of women dying in childbirth; and combating HIV/AIDS, malaria and other diseases. In addition, it directly supports the following Millennium 'targets': halving the proportion of people suffering from malnutrition; halving the proportion of people without sustainable access to safe drinking water and basic sanitation; and providing access, in co-operation with pharmaceutical companies, to affordable, essential drugs in developing countries. Furthermore, WHO reports on 17 health-related MDG indicators; co-ordinates, jointly with the World Bank, the High-Level Forum on the Health MDGs, comprising government ministers, senior officials from developing countries, and representatives of bilateral and multilateral agencies, foundations, regional organizations and global partnerships; and undertakes technical and normative work in support of national and regional efforts to reach the MDGs.

The 11th General Programme of Work, for the period 2006–15, defined a policy framework for pursuing the principal objectives of building healthy populations and combating ill health. The Programme took into account: increasing understanding of the social, economic, political and cultural factors involved in achieving better health and the role played by better health in poverty reduction; the increasing complexity of health systems; the importance of safeguarding health as a component of humanitarian action; and the need for greater co-ordination among development organizations. It incorporated four interrelated strategic directions: lessening excess mortality, morbidity and disability, especially in poor and marginalized populations; promoting healthy lifestyles and reducing risk factors to human health arising from environmental, economic, social and behavioural causes; developing equitable and financially fair health systems; and establishing an enabling policy and an institutional environment for the health sector and promoting an effective health dimension to social, economic, environmental and development policy. WHO is the sponsoring agency for the Health Workforce Decade (2006–15).

In its work WHO adheres to a six-point agenda covering: promoting development; fostering health security; strengthening health systems; harnessing research, information and evidence; enhancing partnerships; and improving performance.

During 2005 the UN's Inter-Agency Standing Committee (IASC), concerned with co-ordinating the international response to humanitarian disasters, developed a concept of organizing agency assistance to IDPs through the institutionalization of a 'Cluster Approach', comprising 11 core areas of activity. WHO was designated the lead agency for the cluster on Health.

WHO, with ILO, leads the Social Protection Floor initiative, the sixth of nine activities that were launched in April 2009 by the UN System Chief Executives Board for Co-ordination (CEB), with the aim of alleviating the impact on poor and vulnerable populations of the developing global economic crisis. In October 2011 a Social Protection Floor Advisory Group, launched in August 2010 under the initiative, issued a report entitled *Social Protection Floor for a Fair and Inclusive Globalization*, which urged that basic income and services should be guaranteed for all, stating that this would promote both stability and economic growth globally.

COMMUNICABLE DISEASES

WHO identifies infectious and parasitic communicable diseases as a major obstacle to social and economic progress, particularly in developing countries, where, in addition to disabilities and loss of productivity and household earnings, they cause nearly one-half of all deaths. Emerging and re-emerging diseases, those likely to cause epidemics, increasing incidence of zoonoses (diseases or infections passed from vertebrate animals to humans by means of parasites, viruses, bacteria or unconventional agents), attributable to factors such as environmental changes and changes in farming practices, outbreaks of unknown etiology, and the undermining of some drug therapies by the spread of antimicrobial resistance, are main areas of concern. In recent years WHO has noted the global spread of communicable diseases through international travel, voluntary human migration and involuntary population displacement.

WHO's Communicable Diseases group works to reduce the impact of infectious diseases world-wide through surveillance and response; prevention, control and eradication strategies; and research and product development. The group seeks to identify new technologies and tools, and to foster national development through strengthening health services and the better use of existing tools. It aims to strengthen global monitoring of important communicable disease problems, and to create consensus and consolidate partnerships around targeted diseases and collaborates with other groups at all stages to provide an integrated response. In 2000 WHO and several partner institutions in epidemic surveillance established the Global Outbreak Alert and Response Network (GOARN). Through the Network WHO aims to maintain constant vigilance regarding outbreaks of disease and to link world-wide expertise to provide an immediate response capability. From March 2003 WHO, through the Network, was co-ordinating the international investigation into the global spread of Severe Acute Respiratory Syndrome (SARS), a previously unknown atypical pneumonia. From the end of that year WHO was monitoring the spread through several Asian countries of the virus H5N1 (a rapidly mutating strain of zoonotic highly pathogenic avian influenza—HPAI) that was transmitting to human populations through contact with diseased birds, mainly poultry. It was feared that H5N1 would mutate into a form transmissable from human to human. In March 2005 WHO issued a *Global Influenza Preparedness Plan*, and urged all countries to develop national influenza pandemic preparedness plans and to stockpile antiviral drugs. In May, in co-operation with FAO and the World Organisation for Animal Health (OIE), WHO launched a Global Strategy for the Progressive Control of Highly Pathogenic Avian Influenza. A conference on Avian Influenza and Human Pandemic Influenza that was jointly organized by WHO, FAO, OIE and the World Bank in November 2005 issued a plan of action identifying a number of responses, including: supporting the development of integrated national plans for H5N1 containment and human pandemic influenza preparedness and response; assisting countries with the aggressive control of H5N1 and with establishing a more detailed understanding of the role of wild birds in virus transmission;

nominating rapid response teams of experts to support epidemiological field investigations; expanding national and regional capacity in surveillance, diagnosis, and alert and response systems; expanding the network of influenza laboratories; establishing multi-country networks for the control or prevention of animal transboundary diseases; expanding the global antiviral stockpile; strengthening veterinary infrastructures; and mapping a global strategy and work plan for co-ordinating antiviral and influenza vaccine research and development. An International Pledging Conference on Avian and Human Influenza, convened in January 2006 in Beijing, People's Republic of China, and co-sponsored by the World Bank, European Commission and Chinese Government, in co-operation with WHO, FAO and OIE, requested a minimum of US $1,200m. in funding towards combating the spread of the virus. By 12 April 2012 a total of 602 human cases of H5N1 had been laboratory confirmed, in Azerbaijan, Bangladesh, Cambodia, China, Djibouti, Egypt, Indonesia, Iraq, Laos, Myanmar, Nigeria, Pakistan, Thailand, Turkey and Viet Nam, resulting in 355 deaths. Cases in poultry had become endemic in parts of Asia and Africa, and outbreaks in poultry had also occurred in some European and Middle Eastern countries.

In April 2009 GOARN sent experts to Mexico to work with health authorities there in response to an outbreak of confirmed human cases of a new variant of swine influenza A(H1N1) that had not previously been detected in animals or humans. In late April, by which time cases of the virus had been reported in the USA and Canada, the Director-General of WHO declared a 'public health emergency of international concern'. All countries were instructed to activate their national influenza pandemic preparedness plans (see above). At the end of April the level of pandemic alert was declared to be at phase five of a six-phase (phase six being the most severe) warning system that had been newly revised earlier in the year. Phase five is characterized by human-to-human transmission of a new virus into at least two countries in one WHO region. On 11 June WHO declared a global pandemic (phase six on the warning scale, characterized by human-to-human transmission in two or more WHO regions). The status and development of pandemic influenza vaccines was the focus of an advisory meeting of immunization experts held at the WHO headquarters in late October. In June 2010 the WHO Director-General refuted allegations, levelled by a British medical journal and by the Parliamentary Assembly of the Council of Europe, regarding the severity of pandemic (H1N1) 2009 and the possibility that the Organization had, in declaring the pandemic, used advisers with a vested commercial interest in promoting pharmaceutical industry profitability. In August 2010 the WHO Director-General declared that transmission of the new H1N1 virus had entered a post-pandemic phase.

A severe outbreak of infection with Enterohemorrhagic Escherichia Coli (EHEC), and the related Haemolytic Uraemic Syndrome (HUS), believed to have originated in raw bean and seed sprouts, occurred in Germany from late May–July 2011. By 21 July some 857 cases of HUS (including 32 fatalities), and 3,078 cases of infection with EHEC (16 fatalities), had been reported in that country. In addition, some 51 HUS cases (two fatalities) and 89 EHEC cases (no fatalities) had been reported in a further 15 countries, almost all in recent visitors to Germany. In early June WHO confirmed that the cases involved a rare strain of EHEC that had never before been reported in a mass outbreak.

One of WHO's major achievements was the eradication of smallpox. Following a massive international campaign of vaccination and surveillance (begun in 1958 and intensified in 1967), the last case was detected in 1977 and the eradication of the disease was declared in 1980. In May 1996 the World Health Assembly resolved that, pending a final endorsement, all remaining stocks of the variola virus (which causes smallpox) were to be destroyed on 30 June 1999, although 500,000 doses of smallpox vaccine were to remain, along with a supply of the smallpox vaccine seed virus, in order to ensure that a further supply of the vaccine could be made available if required. In May 1999, however, the Assembly authorized a temporary retention of stocks of the virus until 2002. In late 2001, in response to fears that illegally held virus stocks could be used in acts of biological terrorism (see below), WHO reassembled a team of technical experts on smallpox. In January 2002 the Executive Board determined that stocks of the virus should continue to be retained, to enable research into more effective treatments and vaccines. World Health Assemblies (most recently in May 2011) have affirmed that the remaining stock of variola virus should be destroyed following the completion of the ongoing research. The state of variola virus research was to be reviewed in 2014, by the 67th World Health Assembly, which was to discuss nominating a deadline for the destruction of the remaining virus stocks.

In 1988 the World Health Assembly launched the Global Polio Eradication Initiative (GPEI), which aimed, initially, to eradicate poliomyelitis by the end of 2000; this target was subsequently extended to 2013 (see below). Co-ordinated periods of Supplementary Immunization Activity (SIA, facilitated in conflict zones by the negotiation of so-called 'days of tranquility'), including National Immunization Days (NIDs), Sub-National Immunization Days (SNIDs), mop-up campaigns, VitA campaigns (Vitamin A is administered in order to reduce nutritional deficiencies in children and thereby boost their immunity), and Follow up/Catch up campaigns, have been employed in combating the disease, alongside the strengthening of routine immunization services. Since the inauguration of the GPEI WHO has declared the following regions 'polio-free': the Americas (1994); Western Pacific (2000); and Europe (2002). Furthermore, type 2 wild poliovirus has been eradicated globally (since 1999), although a type 2 circulating vaccine-derived poliovirus (cVDPV) was reported to be active in northern Nigeria during 2006–early 2010. In January 2004 ministers of health of affected countries, and global partners, meeting under the auspices of WHO and UNICEF, adopted the Geneva Declaration on the Eradication of Poliomyelitis, in which they made a commitment to accelerate the drive towards eradication of the disease, by improving the scope of vaccination programmes. Significant progress in eradication of the virus was reported in Asia during that year. In sub-Saharan Africa, however, an outbreak originating in northern Nigeria in mid-2003—caused by a temporary cessation of vaccination activities in response to local opposition to the vaccination programme—had spread, by mid-2004, to 10 previously polio-free countries. These included Côte d'Ivoire and Sudan, where ongoing civil unrest and population displacements impeded control efforts. During 2004–05 some 23 African governments, including those of the affected West and Central African countries, organized, with support from the African Union, a number of co-ordinated mass vaccination drives, which resulted in the vaccination of about 100m. children. By mid-2005 the sub-regional epidemic was declared over; it was estimated that since mid-2003 it had resulted in the paralysis of nearly 200 children. In Nigeria itself, however, the number of confirmed wild poliovirus cases had by 2006 escalated to 1,122 from 202 in 2002. In February 2007 the GPEI launched an intensified eradication effort aimed at identifying and addressing the outstanding operational, technical and financial barriers to eradication. The May 2008 World Health Assembly adopted a resolution urging all remaining polio-affected member states to ensure the vaccination of every child during each SIA. By the end of 2008, having received independent advice that the intensified eradication effort initiated in 2007 had demonstrated that the remaining challenges to eradication were surmountable, the GPEI endorsed a strategic plan covering the period 2009–13 (replacing a previous plan for 2004–08), with the aim of achieving the interruption of type 1 wild poliovirus transmission in India, and the cessation of all prolonged outbreaks in Africa by the end of 2009; the interruption of all poliovirus transmission in Afghanistan, India and Pakistan, of type 1 wild poliovirus transmission in Nigeria, and of all wild poliovirus transmission elsewhere in Africa, by end-2010; the interruption of type 3 wild poliovirus transmission in Nigeria by end-2011; and the eradication of new cVDPVs within six months of detection by end-2013. During 2009, however, polio outbreaks, which were subsequently eradicated, occurred in 10 of 15 previously polio-free countries in Africa. In June 2010 a new strategic plan, covering 2010–12, was launched, incorporating the following targets: cessation in mid-2010 of all polio outbreaks with onset in 2009; cessation by end-2010 of all re-established wild poliovirus transmission; cessation by end-2011 of all transmission in at least two of the four countries designated at that time as polio-endemic (i.e. Afghanistan, India, Nigeria, and Pakistan); and the cessation by end-2012 of all transmission. Some 650 polio cases were confirmed world-wide in 2011, of which 340 were in the then four polio-endemic countries (Pakistan, 198 cases; Afghanistan, 80 cases; Nigeria, 61 cases; and India one case), and 310 cases were recorded in non-endemic countries (including 132 cases in Chad and 93 cases in Democratic Republic of the Congo). (In 1988, in comparison, 35,000 cases had been confirmed in 125 countries, with the actual number of cases estimated at around 350,000.) India was declared to be no longer polio-endemic in February 2012.

WHO's Onchocerciasis Control Programme in West Africa (OCP), active during 1974–2002, succeeded in eliminating transmission in 10 countries in the region, excepting Sierra Leone, of onchocerciasis ('river blindness', spread by blackflies, and previously a major public health problem and impediment to socio-economic development in West Africa). It was estimated that under the OCP some 18m. people were protected from the disease, 600,000 cases of blindness prevented, and 25m. ha of land were rendered safe for cultivation and settlement. The former headquarters of the OCP, based in Ouagadougou, Burkina Faso, was transformed into a Multi-disease Surveillance Centre. In January 1996 another initiative, the African Programme for Onchocerciasis Control (APOC), covering 19 countries outside West Africa, became operational, with funding co-ordinated by the World Bank and with WHO as the executing agency.

The Onchocerciasis Elimination Programme in the Americas (OEPA), launched in 1992, co-ordinates work to control the disease in six Latin American countries where it is endemic. In January 1998 a new 20-year programme to eliminate lymphatic filariasis was initiated, with substantial funding and support from two major pharmaceutical companies, and in collaboration with the World Bank, the Arab Fund for Economic and Social Development and the governments of Japan, the United Kingdom and the USA. South American trypanosomiasis ('Chagas disease') is endemic in Central and South America, causing the deaths of some 45,000 people each year and infecting a further 16m.–18m. A regional intergovernmental commission is implementing a programme to eliminate Chagas from the Southern Cone region of Latin America. The countries of the Andean region of Latin America initiated a plan for the elimination of transmission of Chagas disease in February 1997, and a similar plan was launched by Central American governments in October. In July 2007, to combat the expansion of Chagas disease into some European countries, the Western Pacific, and the USA, as well as the re-emergence of the disease in areas such as the Chaco, in Argentina and Bolivia, where it was thought to have been eradicated, WHO established a Global Network for Chagas Disease Elimination.

WHO is committed to the elimination of leprosy (the reduction of the prevalence of leprosy to less than one case per 10,000 population). The use of a highly effective combination of three drugs (known as multi-drug therapy—MDT) resulted in a reduction in the number of leprosy cases world-wide from 10m.–12m. in 1988 to 213,036 registered cases in January 2010. In 2008 some 249,007 cases were detected in 121 countries. The number of countries having more than one case of leprosy per 10,000 had declined to four by January 2007 (Brazil, Democratic Republic of the Congo, Mozambique and Nepal), compared with 122 in 1985. The country with the highest prevalence of leprosy cases in 2007 was Brazil (3.21 per 10,000 population) and the country with the highest number of cases was India (139,252). The Global Alliance for the Elimination of Leprosy was launched in November 1999 by WHO, in collaboration with governments of affected countries and several private partners, including a major pharmaceutical company, to support the eradication of the disease through the provision of free MDT treatment; WHO has supplied free MDT treatment to leprosy patients in endemic countries since 1995. In June 2005 WHO adopted a Strategic Plan for Further Reducing the Leprosy Burden and Sustaining Leprosy Control Activities, covering the period 2006–10 and following on from a previous strategic plan for 2000–05. In 1998 WHO launched the Global Buruli Ulcer Initiative, which aimed to co-ordinate control of and research into Buruli ulcer, another mycobacterial disease. In July of that year the Director-General of WHO and representatives of more than 20 countries, meeting in Yamoussoukro, Côte d'Ivoire, signed a declaration on the control of Buruli ulcer. In May 2004 the World Health Assembly adopted a resolution urging improved research into, and detection and treatment of, Buruli ulcer.

The Special Programme for Research and Training in Tropical Diseases, established in 1975 and sponsored jointly by WHO, UNDP and the World Bank, as well as by contributions from donor countries, involves a world-wide network of some 5,000 scientists working on the development and application of vaccines, new drugs, diagnostic kits and preventive measures, and applied field research on practical community issues affecting the target diseases.

The objective of providing immunization for all children by 1990 was adopted by the World Health Assembly in 1977. Six diseases (measles, whooping cough, tetanus, poliomyelitis, tuberculosis and diphtheria) became the target of the Expanded Programme on Immunization (EPI), in which WHO, UNICEF and many other organizations collaborated. As a result of massive international and national efforts, the global immunization coverage increased from 20% in the early 1980s to the targeted rate of 80% by the end of 1990. In 2006 WHO, UNICEF and other partners launched the Global Immunization Vision and Strategy (GIVS), a global 10-year framework, covering 2006–15, aimed at reducing deaths due to vaccine-preventable diseases by at least two-thirds compared to 2000 levels, by 2015; and increasing national vaccination coverage levels to at least 90%. In 2009 the global child vaccination coverage rate was estimated at 82%.

In June 2000 WHO released a report entitled 'Overcoming Antimicrobial Resistance', in which it warned that the misuse of antibiotics could render some common infectious illnesses unresponsive to treatment. At that time WHO issued guidelines which aimed to mitigate the risks associated with the use of antimicrobials in livestock reared for human consumption.

HIV/AIDS, TB, MALARIA AND NEGLECTED DISEASES

Combating the human immunodeficiency virus/acquired immunodeficiency syndrome (HIV/AIDS), tuberculosis (TB) and malaria are organization-wide priorities and, as such, are supported not only by their own areas of work but also by activities undertaken in other areas. TB is the principal cause of death for people infected with the HIV virus and an estimated one-third of people living with HIV/AIDS globally are co-infected with TB. In July 2000 a meeting of the Group of Seven industrialized nations and Russia, convened in Genoa, Italy, announced the formation of a new Global Fund to Fight AIDS, TB and Malaria (as previously proposed by the UN Secretary-General and recommended by the World Health Assembly).

The HIV/AIDS epidemic represents a major threat to human well-being and socio-economic progress. Some 95% of those known to be infected with HIV/AIDS live in developing countries, and AIDS-related illnesses are the leading cause of death in sub-Saharan Africa. It is estimated that more than 25m. people world-wide died of AIDS during 1981–2008. WHO supports governments in developing effective health sector responses to the HIV/AIDS epidemic through enhancing their planning and managerial capabilities, implementation capacity, and health systems resources. The Joint UN Programme on HIV/AIDS (UNAIDS) became operational on 1 January 1996, sponsored by WHO and other UN agencies; the UNAIDS secretariat is based at WHO headquarters. Sufferers of HIV/AIDS in developing countries have often failed to receive advanced antiretroviral (ARV) treatments that are widely available in industrialized countries, owing to their high cost. In May 2000 the World Health Assembly adopted a resolution urging WHO member states to improve access to the prevention and treatment of HIV-related illnesses and to increase the availability and affordability of drugs. A WHO-UNAIDS HIV Vaccine Initiative was launched in that year. In June 2001 governments participating in a special session of the UN General Assembly on HIV/AIDS adopted a Declaration of Commitment on HIV/AIDS. WHO, with UNAIDS, UNICEF, UNFPA, the World Bank, and major pharmaceutical companies, participates in the 'Accelerating Access' initiative, which aims to expand access to care, support and ARVs for people with HIV/AIDS. In March 2002, under its 'Access to Quality HIV/AIDS Drugs and Diagnostics' programme, WHO published a comprehensive list of HIV-related medicines deemed to meet standards recommended by the Organization. In April WHO issued the first treatment guidelines for HIV/AIDS cases in poor communities, and endorsed the inclusion of HIV/AIDS drugs in its *Model List of Essential Medicines* (see below) in order to encourage their wider availability. The secretariat of the International HIV Treatment Access Coalition, founded in December of that year by governments, non-governmental organizations, donors and others to facilitate access to ARVs for people in low- and middle-income countries, is based at WHO headquarters. In September 2006, Brazil, Chile, France, Norway and the United Kingdom launched UNITAID, an international drug purchase facility aiming to provide sustained, strategic market intervention, with a view to reducing the cost of medicines for priority diseases and increasing the supply of drugs and diagnostics. In July 2008, UNITAID created the Medicines Patent Pool; the Pool, a separate entity, was to focus on increasing access to HIV medicines in developing countries. The Pool is funded by UNITAID, under a five-year arrangement. By the end of 2010 an estimated 6.6m. people in developing and middle-income countries were receiving appropriate HIV treatment, compared with 4m. at end-2008. In May 2011 the 64th World Health Assembly adopted a new Global Health Sector Strategy on HIV/AIDS, covering 2011–15, which aimed to promote greater innovation in HIV prevention, diagnosis, treatment, and the improvement of care services to facilitate universal access to care for HIV patients. WHO supports the following *Three Ones* principles, endorsed in April 2004 by a high-level meeting organized by UNAIDS, the United Kingdom and the USA, with the aim of strengthening national responses to the HIV/AIDS pandemic: for every country there should be one agreed national HIV/AIDS action framework; one national AIDS co-ordinating authority; and one agreed monitoring and evaluation system.

In December 2011 the UN General Assembly adopted a Political Declaration on HIV/AIDS, outlining 10 targets to be attained by 2015: reducing by 50% sexual transmission of HIV; reducing by 50% HIV transmission among people who inject drugs; eliminating new HIV infections among children, and reducing AIDS-related maternal deaths; ensuring that at least 15m. people living with HIV are receiving ARVs; reducing by 50% TB deaths in people living with HIV; reaching annual global investment of at least US $22,000m. in combating AIDS in low- and medium-resource countries; eliminating gender inequalities and increasing the capacity of women and girls to self-protect from HIV; promoting the adoption of legislation and policies aimed at eliminating stigma and discrimination against people living with HIV; eliminating HIV-related restrictions on travel; strengthening the integration of the AIDS response in global health and development efforts.

The total number of people world-wide living with HIV/AIDS at December 2010 was estimated at 34.0m., including some 2.7m. children under 15 years of age. It was reported that 2.6m. people were newly infected during that year. At December 2010 an estimated 22.9m. people in sub-Saharan Africa were estimated to have HIV/AIDS, of whom 1.9m. were newly affected during that year. More people were living with HIV/AIDS in South Africa than in any other country world-wide (an estimated 5.6m., with an estimated national adult prevalence rate of 17.8%, at end-2009), while the national adult prevalence rates at that time were 25.9% in Swaziland, 24.8% in Botswana, and 23.6% in Lesotho, and exceeded 10% in Malawi, Mozambique, Namibia, Zambia and Zimbabwe.

In 1995 WHO established a Global Tuberculosis Programme to address the challenges of the TB epidemic, which had been declared a global emergency by the Organization in 1993. According to WHO estimates, one-third of the world's population carries the TB bacillus. In 2009 this generated 9.4m. new active cases (1.1m. in people co-infected with HIV), and killed 1.7m. people (0.4m. of whom were also HIV-positive). Some 22 high-burden countries account for four-fifths of global TB cases. The largest concentration of TB cases is in South-East Asia. WHO provides technical support to all member countries, with special attention given to those with high TB prevalence, to establish effective national tuberculosis control programmes. WHO's strategy for TB control includes the use of the expanded DOTS (direct observation treatment, short-course) regime, involving the following five tenets: sustained political commitment to increase human and financial resources and to make TB control in endemic countries a nation-wide activity and an integral part of the national health system; access to quality-assured TB sputum microscopy; standardized short-course chemotherapy for all cases of TB under proper case-management conditions; uninterrupted supply of quality-assured drugs; and maintaining a recording and reporting system to enable outcome assessment. Simultaneously, WHO is encouraging research with the aim of further advancing DOTS, developing new tools for prevention, diagnosis and treatment, and containing new threats (such as the HIV/TB co-epidemic). Inadequate control of DOTS in some areas, leading to partial and inconsistent treatments, has resulted in the development of drug-resistant and, often, incurable strains of TB. The incidence of so-called Multidrug Resistant TB (MDR-TB) strains, that are unresponsive to at least two of the four most commonly used anti-TB drugs, has risen in recent years, and WHO estimates that about four-fifths are 'super strains', resistant to at least three of the main anti-TB drugs; an estimated 3.3% of new TB cases were reported to be MDR in 2009. MDR-TB cases occur most frequently in Eastern Europe, Central Asia, the People's Republic of China, and India; it was reported in 2010 that in certain areas of the former Soviet Union up to 28% of all new TB cases were MDR. WHO has developed DOTS-Plus, a specialized strategy for controlling the spread of MDR-TB in areas of high prevalence. By August 2010 59 countries had reported at least one case of Extensive Drug Resistant TB (XDR-TB), defined as MDR-TB plus resistance to additional drugs. XDR-TB is believed to be most prevalent in Eastern Europe and Asia. In 2007 WHO launched the Global MDR/XDR Response Plan, which aimed to expand diagnosis and treatment to cover, by 2015, some 85% of TB patients with MDR-TB.

The 'Stop TB' partnership, launched by WHO in 1999, in partnership with the World Bank, the US Government and a coalition of non-governmental organizations, co-ordinates the Global Plan to Stop TB, which represents a roadmap for TB control covering the period 2006–15. The Global Plan aims to facilitate the achievement of the MDG of halting and beginning to reverse by 2015 the incidence of TB by means of access to quality diagnosis and treatment for all; to supply ARVs to 3m. TB patients co-infected with HIV; to treat nearly 1m. people for MDR-TB (this target was subsequently altered by the 2007 Global MDR/XDR Response Plan, see above); to develop a new anti-TB drug and a new vaccine; and to develop rapid and inexpensive diagnostic tests at the point of care. A second phase of the Global Plan, launched in late 2010 and covering 2011–15, updated the Plan to take account of actual progress achieved since its instigation in 2006. The Global TB Drug Facility, launched by 'Stop TB' in 2001, aims to increase access to high-quality anti-TB drugs for sufferers in developing countries. In 2007 'Stop TB' endorsed the establishment of a new Global Laboratory Initiative with the aim of expanding laboratory capacity.

In December 2010 WHO endorsed a new rapid nucleic acid amplification test (NAAT) that provided an accurate diagnosis of TB in around 100 minutes; it was envisaged that NAAT, by eliminating the current wait of up to three months for a TB diagnosis, would greatly enhance management of the disease and patient care.

In October 1998 WHO, jointly with UNICEF, the World Bank and UNDP, formally launched the Roll Back Malaria (RBM) programme. The disease acutely affects at least 350m.–500m. people, and kills an estimated 1m. people, every year. Some 85% of all malaria cases occur in sub-Saharan Africa. It is estimated that the disease directly causes 18% of all child deaths in that region. The global RBM Partnership, linking governments, development agencies, and other parties, aims to mobilize resources and support for controlling malaria. The RBM Partnership Global Strategic Plan for the period 2005–15, adopted in November 2005, lists steps required to intensify malaria control interventions with a view to attaining targets set by the Partnership for 2010 and 2015 (the former targets include: ensuring the protection of 80% of people at risk from malaria and the diagnosis and treatment within one day of 80% of malaria patients, and reducing the global malaria burden by one-half compared with 2000 levels; and the latter: achieving a 75% reduction in malaria morbidity and mortality over levels at 2005). WHO recommends a number of guidelines for malaria control, focusing on the need for prompt, effective antimalarial treatment, and the issue of drug resistance; vector control, including the use of insecticide-treated bednets; malaria in pregnancy; malaria epidemics; and monitoring and evaluation activities. WHO, with several private and public sector partners, supports the development of more effective anti-malaria drugs and vaccines through the 'Medicines for Malaria' venture.

Joint UN Programme on HIV/AIDS (UNAIDS): 20 ave Appia, 1211 Geneva 27, Switzerland; tel. 227913666; fax 227914187; e-mail communications@unaids.org; internet www.unaids.org; established in 1996 to lead, strengthen and support an expanded response to the global HIV/AIDS pandemic; activities focus on prevention, care and support, reducing vulnerability to infection, and alleviating the socio-economic and human effects of HIV/AIDS; launched the Global Coalition on Women and AIDS in Feb. 2004; guided by UN Security Council Resolution 1308, focusing on the possible impact of AIDS on social instability and emergency situations, and the potential impact of HIV on the health of international peace-keeping personnel; by the UN Millennium Development Goals adopted in Sept. 2000; by the Declaration of Commitment on HIV/AIDS agreed in June 2001 by the first-ever Special Session of the UN General Assembly on HIV/AIDS, which acknowledged the AIDS epidemic as a 'global emergency'; and the Political Declaration on HIV/AIDS, adopted by the June 2006 UN General Assembly High Level Meeting on AIDS; launched the Global Coalition on Women and AIDS in Feb. 2004; co-sponsors: WHO, UNICEF, UNDP, UNFPA, UNODC, the ILO, UNESCO, the World Bank, WFP, UNHCR; Exec. Dir MICHEL SIDIBÉ (Mali).

NON-COMMUNICABLE DISEASES AND MENTAL HEALTH

The Non-communicable Diseases (NCDs) and Mental Health group comprises departments for the surveillance, prevention and management of uninfectious diseases, and departments for health promotion, disability, injury prevention and rehabilitation, substance abuse and mental health. Surveillance, prevention and management of NCDs, tobacco, and mental health are organization-wide priorities.

Addressing the social and environmental determinants of health is a main priority of WHO. Tobacco use, unhealthy diet and physical inactivity are regarded as common, preventable risk factors for the four most prominent NCDs: cardiovascular diseases, cancer, chronic respiratory disease and diabetes. It is estimated that the four main NCDs are collectively responsible for an estimated 35m. deaths—60% of all deaths—globally each year, and that up to 80% of cases of heart disease, stroke and type 2 diabetes, and more than one-third of cancers, could be prevented by eliminating shared risk factors, the main ones being: tobacco use, unhealthy diet, physical inactivity and harmful use of alcohol. WHO envisages that the disease burden and mortality from these diseases will continue to increase, most rapidly in Africa and the Eastern Mediterranean, and that the highest number of deaths will occur in the Western Pacific region and in South-East Asia. WHO aims to monitor the global epidemiological situation of NCDs, to co-ordinate multinational research activities concerned with prevention and care, and to analyse determining factors such as gender and poverty. The 53rd World Health Assembly, convened in May 2000, endorsed a Global Strategy for the Prevention and Control of NCDs. In May 2008 the 61st World Health Assembly endorsed a new Action Plan for 2008–13 for the Global Strategy for the Prevention and Control of NCDs, based on the vision of the 2000 Global Strategy. The Action Plan aimed to provide a roadmap establishing and strengthening initiatives on the surveillance, prevention and management of NCDs, and emphasized the need to invest in NCD prevention as part of sustainable socio-economic development planning.

The sixth Global Conference on Health Promotion, convened jointly by WHO and the Thai Government, in Bangkok, Thailand, in August 2005, adopted the Bangkok Charter for Health Promotion in a Globalized World, which identified ongoing key challenges, actions and commitments.

In May 2004 the World Health Assembly endorsed a Global Strategy on Diet, Physical Activity and Health; it is estimated that more than 1,000m. adults world-wide are overweight, and that, of these, some 300m. are clinically obese. WHO has studied obesity-related issues in co-operation with the International Association for the Study of Obesity (IASO). The International Task Force on Obesity, affiliated to the IASO, aims to encourage the development of new policies for managing obesity. WHO and FAO jointly commissioned an expert report on the relationship of diet, nutrition and physical activity to chronic diseases, which was published in March 2003.

WHO's programmes for diabetes mellitus, chronic rheumatic diseases and asthma assist with the development of national initiatives, based upon goals and targets for the improvement of early detection, care and reduction of long-term complications. WHO's cardiovascular diseases programme aims to prevent and control the major cardiovascular diseases, which are responsible for more than 14m. deaths each year. It is estimated that one-third of these deaths could have been prevented with existing scientific knowledge. The programme on cancer control is concerned with the prevention of cancer, improving its detection and cure, and ensuring care of all cancer patients in need. In May 2004 the World Health Assembly adopted a resolution on cancer prevention and control, recognizing an increase in global cancer cases, particularly in developing countries, and stressing that many cases and related deaths could be prevented. The resolution included a number of recommendations for the improvement of national cancer control programmes. In May 2009 WHO and the IAEA launched a Joint Programme on Cancer Control, aimed at enhancing efforts to fight cancer in the developing world. WHO is a co-sponsor of the Global Day Against Pain, which is held annually on 11 October. The Global Day highlights the need for improved pain management and palliative care for sufferers of diseases such as cancer and AIDS, with a particular focus on patients living in low-income countries with minimal access to opioid analgesics, and urges recognition of access to pain relief as a basic human right.

The WHO Human Genetics Programme manages genetic approaches for the prevention and control of common hereditary diseases and of those with a genetic predisposition representing a major health factor. The Programme also concentrates on the further development of genetic approaches suitable for incorporation into health care systems, as well as developing a network of international collaborating programmes.

WHO works to assess the impact of injuries, violence and sensory impairments on health, and formulates guidelines and protocols for the prevention and management of mental problems. The health promotion division promotes decentralized and community-based health programmes and is concerned with developing new approaches to population ageing and encouraging healthy lifestyles and self-care. It also seeks to relieve the negative impact of social changes such as urbanization, migration and changes in family structure upon health. WHO advocates a multi-sectoral approach—involving public health, legal and educational systems—to the prevention of injuries, which represent 16% of the global burden of disease. It aims to support governments in developing suitable strategies to prevent and mitigate the consequences of violence, unintentional injury and disability. Several health promotion projects have been undertaken, in collaboration between WHO regional and country offices and other relevant organizations, including: the Global School Health Initiative, to bridge the sectors of health and education and to promote the health of school-age children; the Global Strategy for Occupational Health, to promote the health of the working population and the control of occupational health risks; Community-based Rehabilitation, aimed at providing a more enabling environment for people with disabilities; and a communication strategy to provide training and support for health communications personnel and initiatives. In 2000 WHO, UNESCO, the World Bank and UNICEF adopted the joint Focusing Resources for Effective School Health (FRESH Start) approach to promoting life skills among adolescents.

WHO supports the UN Convention, and its Optional Protocol, on the Rights of Persons with Disabilities, which came into force in May 2008, and seeks to address challenges that prevent the full participation of people with disabilities in the social, economic and cultural lives of their communities and societies; at that time the WHO Director-General appointed a Taskforce on Disability to ensure that WHO was reflecting the provisions of the Convention overall as an organization and in its programme of work.

In February 1999 WHO initiated a new programme, 'Vision 2020: the Right to Sight', which aimed to eliminate avoidable blindness (estimated to be as much as 80% of all cases) by 2020. Blindness was otherwise predicted to increase by as much as twofold, owing to the increased longevity of the global population.

The Tobacco or Health Programme aims to reduce the use of tobacco, by educating tobacco-users and preventing young people from adopting the habit. In 1996 WHO published its first report on the tobacco situation world-wide. According to WHO, about one-third of the world's population aged over 15 years smoke tobacco, which causes approximately 3.5m. deaths each year (through lung cancer, heart disease, chronic bronchitis and other effects). In 1998 the 'Tobacco Free Initiative', a major global anti-smoking campaign, was established. In May 1999 the World Health Assembly endorsed the formulation of a Framework Convention on Tobacco Control (FCTC) to help to combat the increase in tobacco use (although a number of tobacco growers expressed concerns about the effect of the convention on their livelihoods). The FCTC entered into force in February 2005. The greatest increase in tobacco use is forecast to occur in developing countries. In 2008 WHO published a comprehensive analysis of global tobacco use and control, the *WHO Report on the Global Tobacco Epidemic*, which designated abuse of tobacco as one of the principal global threats to health, and predicted that during the latter part of the 21st century the vast majority of tobacco-related deaths would occur in developing countries. The Report identified and condemned a global tobacco industry strategy to target young people and adults in the developing world, and it detailed six key proven strategies, collectively known as the 'MPOWER package', that were aimed at combating global tobacco use: monitoring tobacco use and implementing prevention policies; protecting people from tobacco smoke; offering support to people to enable them to give up tobacco use; warning about the dangers of tobacco; enforcing bans on tobacco advertising, promotion and sponsorship; and raising taxes on tobacco. The MPOWER package provided a roadmap to support countries in building on their obligations under the FCTC. The FCTC obligates its states parties to require 'health warnings describing the harmful effects of tobacco use' to appear on packs of tobacco and their outside packaging, and recommends the use of warnings that contain pictures. WHO provides technical and other assistance to countries to support them in meeting this obligation through the Tobacco Free Initiative. WHO encourages governments to adopt tobacco health warnings meeting the agreed criteria for maximum effectiveness in convincing consumers not to smoke: these appear on both the front and back of a cigarette pack, should cover more than half of the pack, and should contain pictures.

WHO's Mental Health and Substance Abuse department was established in 2000 from the merger of formerly separate departments to reflect the many common approaches in managing mental health and substance use disorders.

WHO defines mental health as a 'state of well-being in which every individual realizes his or her own potential, can cope with the normal stresses of life, can work productively and fruitfully, and is able to make a contribution to her or his community'. WHO's Mental Health programme is concerned with mental health problems that include unipolar and bipolar affective disorders, psychosis, epilepsy, dementia, Parkinson's disease, multiple sclerosis, drug and alcohol dependency, and neuropsychiatric disorders such as post-traumatic stress disorder, obsessive compulsive disorder and panic disorder. Although, overall, physical health has improved, mental, behavioural and social health problems are increasing, owing to extended life expectancy and improved child mortality rates, and factors such as war and poverty. WHO aims to address mental problems by increasing awareness of mental health issues and promoting improved mental health services and primary care. In October 2008 WHO launched the so-called mental health Gap Action Programme (mhGAP), which aimed to improve services addressing mental, neurological and substance use disorders, with a special focus on low and middle income countries. It was envisaged that, with proper care, psychosocial assistance and medication, many millions of patients in developing countries could be treated for depression, schizophrenia, and epilepsy; prevented from attempting suicide; and encouraged to begin to lead normal lives. A main focus of mhGAP concerns forging strategic partnerships to enhance countries' capacity to combat stigma commonly associated with mental illness, reduce the burden of mental disorders, and promote mental health. WHO is a joint partner in the Global Campaign against Epilepsy: Out of the Shadows, which aims to advance understanding, treatment, services and prevention of epilepsy world-wide.

The Substance Abuse programme addresses the misuse of all psychoactive substances, irrespective of legal status and including alcohol. WHO provides technical support to assist countries in formulating policies with regard to the prevention and reduction of the health and social effects of psychoactive substance abuse, and undertakes epidemiological surveillance and risk assessment, advocacy and the dissemination of information, strengthening national and regional prevention and health promotion techniques and strategies, the development of cost-effective treatment and rehabilitation approaches, and also encompasses regulatory activities as required under the international drugs-control treaties in force. In May 2010 WHO endorsed a new global strategy to reduce the harmful use of alcohol; this promoted measures including taxation on alcohol, minimizing outlets selling alcohol, raising age limits for those buying alcohol, and the employment of effective measures to deter people from driving while under the influence of alcohol.

In June 2010 WHO launched the Global Network of Age-Friendly Cities, as part of a broader response to the ageing of populations world-wide. The Network was to support cities in creating urban environments that would enable older people to remain active and healthy.

FAMILY AND COMMUNITY HEALTH

WHO's Family and Community Health group addresses the following areas of work: child and adolescent health, research and programme development in reproductive health, making pregnancy safer and men's and women's health. Making pregnancy safer is an organization-wide priority. The group's aim is to improve access to sustainable health care for all by strengthening health systems and fostering individual, family and community development. Activities include newborn care; child health, including promoting and protecting the health and development of the child through such approaches as promotion of breast-feeding and use of the mother-baby package, as well as care of the sick child, including diarrhoeal and acute respiratory disease control, and support to women and children in difficult circumstances; the promotion of safe motherhood and maternal health; adolescent health, including the promotion and development of young people and the prevention of specific health problems; women, health and development, including addressing issues of gender, sexual violence, and harmful traditional practices; and human reproduction, including research related to contraceptive technologies and effective methods. In addition, WHO aims to provide technical leadership and co-ordination on reproductive health and to support countries in their efforts to ensure that people: experience healthy sexual development and maturation; have the capacity for healthy, equitable and responsible relationships; can achieve their reproductive intentions safely and healthily; avoid illnesses, diseases and injury related to sexuality and reproduction; and receive appropriate counselling, care and rehabilitation for diseases and conditions related to sexuality and reproduction.

WHO supports the 'Global Strategy for Women's and Children's Health', launched by heads of state and government participating in the September 2010 UN Summit on the MDGs; some US $40,000m. has been pledged towards women's and child's health and achieving goals (iv) Reducing Child Mortality and (v) Improving Maternal Health.

In September 1997 WHO, in collaboration with UNICEF, formally launched a programme advocating the Integrated Management of Childhood Illness (IMCI). IMCI recognizes that pneumonia, diarrhoea, measles, malaria and malnutrition cause some 70% of the approximately 11m. childhood deaths each year, and recommends screening sick children for all five conditions, to obtain a more accurate diagnosis than may be achieved from the results of a single assessment. WHO's Division of Diarrhoeal and Acute Respiratory Disease Control encourages national programmes aimed at reducing childhood deaths as a result of diarrhoea, particularly through the use of oral rehydration therapy and preventive measures. The Division is also seeking to reduce deaths from pneumonia in infants through the use of a simple case-management strategy involving the recognition of danger signs and treatment with an appropriate antibiotic.

In March 1996 WHO's Centre for Health Development opened at Kobe, Japan. The Centre researches health developments and other determinants to strengthen policy decision-making within the health sector.

SUSTAINABLE DEVELOPMENT AND HEALTHY ENVIRONMENTS

The Sustainable Development and Healthy Environments group focuses on the following areas of work: health in sustainable development; nutrition; health and environment; food safety; and emergency preparedness and response. Food safety is an organization-wide priority.

WHO promotes recognition of good health status as one of the most important assets of the poor. The Sustainable Development and Healthy Environment group seeks to monitor the advantages and disadvantages for health, nutrition, environment and development arising from the process of globalization (i.e. increased global flows of capital, goods and services, people, and knowledge); to integrate the issue of health into poverty reduction programmes; and to promote human rights and equality. Adequate and safe food and nutrition is a priority programme area. WHO collaborates with FAO, WFP, UNICEF and other UN agencies in pursuing its objectives relating to nutrition and food safety. It has been estimated that 780m. people world-wide cannot meet basic needs for energy and protein, more than 2,000m. people lack essential vitamins and minerals, and that 170m. children are malnourished. In December 1992 WHO and FAO hosted an international conference on nutrition, at which a World Declaration and Plan of Action on Nutrition was adopted to make the fight against malnutrition a development priority. Following the conference, WHO promoted the elaboration and implementation of national plans of action on nutrition. WHO aims to support the enhancement of member states' capabilities in dealing with their nutrition situations, and addressing scientific issues related to preventing, managing and monitoring protein-energy malnutrition; micronutrient malnutrition, including iodine deficiency disorders, vitamin A deficiency, and nutritional anaemia; and diet-related conditions and NCDs such as obesity (increasingly affecting children, adolescents and adults, mainly in industrialized countries), cancer and heart disease. In 1990 the World Health Assembly resolved to eliminate iodine deficiency (believed to cause mental retardation); a strategy of universal salt iodization was launched in 1993. In collaboration with other international agencies, WHO is implementing a comprehensive strategy for promoting appropriate infant, young child and maternal nutrition, and for dealing effectively with nutritional emergencies in large populations. Areas of emphasis include promoting healthcare practices that enhance successful breast-feeding; appropriate complementary feeding; refining the use and interpretation of body measurements for assessing nutritional status; relevant information, education and training; and action to give effect to the International Code of Marketing of Breast-milk Substitutes. The food safety programme aims to protect human health against risks associated with biological and chemical contaminants and additives in food. With FAO, WHO establishes food standards (through the work of the Codex Alimentarius Commission and its subsidiary committees) and evaluates food additives, pesticide residues and other contaminants and their implications for health. The programme provides expert advice on such issues as food-borne pathogens (e.g. listeria), production methods (e.g. aquaculture) and food biotechnology (e.g. genetic modification). In July 2001 the Codex Alimentarius Commission adopted the first global principles for assessing the safety of genetically modified (GM) foods. In March 2002 an intergovernmental task force established by the Commission finalized 'principles for the risk analysis of foods derived from biotechnology', which were to provide a framework for assessing the safety of GM foods and plants. In the following month WHO and FAO announced a joint review of their food standards operations. In February 2003 the FAO/WHO Project and Fund for Enhanced Participation in Codex was launched to support the participation of poorer countries in the Commission's activities. WHO supports, with other UN agencies, governments, research institutions, and representatives of civil society and of the private sector, the initiative on Scaling up Nutrition (SUN), which was initiated in 2009, under the co-ordination of the UN Secretary-General's Special Representative for Food Security and Nutrition, with the aim of increasing the coverage of interventions that improve nutrition during the first 1,000 days of a child's life (such as exclusive breastfeeding, optimal complementary feeding practices, and provision of essential vitamins and minerals); and ensuring that nutrition plans are implemented at national level, and that government programmes take nutrition into account. The activities of SUN are guided by the Framework for Scaling up Nutrition, which was published in April 2010; and by the SUN Roadmap, finalized in September 2010.

WHO's programme area on environmental health undertakes a wide range of initiatives to tackle the increasing threats to health and well-being from a changing environment, especially in relation to air pollution, water quality, sanitation, protection against radiation, management of hazardous waste, chemical safety and housing hygiene. In 2008 it was estimated that some 1,200m. people world-wide had no access to clean drinking water, while a further 2,600m. people are denied suitable sanitation systems. WHO helped launch the Water Supply and Sanitation Council in 1990 and regularly updates its *Guidelines for Drinking Water Quality*. In rural areas the emphasis continues to be on the provision and maintenance of safe and sufficient water supplies and adequate sanitation, the health aspects of rural housing, vector control in water resource management, and the safe use of agrochemicals. In urban areas assistance is provided to identify local environmental health priorities and to improve municipal governments' ability to deal with environmental conditions and health problems in an integrated manner; promotion of the 'Healthy City' approach is a major component of the programme. Other programme activities include environmental health information development and management, human resources development, environmental health planning methods, research and work on problems relating to global environment change, such as UV-radiation. The WHO Global Strategy for Health and Environment, developed in response to the WHO Commission on Health and Environment which reported to the UN Conference on Environment and Development in June 1992, provides the framework for programme activities. In May 2008 the 61st World Health Assembly adopted a resolution urging member states to take action to address the impact of climate change on human health.

Through its International EMF Project WHO is compiling a comprehensive assessment of the potential adverse effects on human health deriving from exposure to electromagnetic fields (EMF). In May 2011 the International Agency for Research on Cancer, an agency of WHO, classified radiofrequency EMF as possibly carcinogenic to humans, on the basis of an increased risk for glioma (malignant brain cancer) associated with the use of wireless phones.

WHO's work in the promotion of chemical safety is undertaken in collaboration with the ILO and UNEP through the International Programme on Chemical Safety (IPCS), the Central Unit for which is located in WHO. The Programme provides internationally evaluated scientific information on chemicals, promotes the use of such information in national programmes, assists member states in establishment of their own chemical safety measures and programmes, and helps them strengthen their capabilities in chemical emergency preparedness and response and in chemical risk reduction. In 1995 an Inter-organization Programme for the Social Management of Chemicals was established by UNEP, the ILO, FAO, WHO, UNIDO and OECD, in order to strengthen international co-operation in the field of chemical safety. In 1998 WHO led an international assessment of the health risk from bendocine disruptors (chemicals which disrupt hormonal activities).

In September 2005 a forum comprising representatives of WHO, IAEA, UNDP, UNEP, FAO, OCHA, the World Bank and the UN Scientific Committee on the effects of Atomic Radiation, and the governments of Belarus, Russia and Ukraine, issued an assessment of the long-term health, environmental and socio-economic effects of the 1986 Chornobyl (Chernobyl) nuclear reactor accident.

Since the major terrorist attacks perpetrated against targets in the USA in September 2001, WHO has focused renewed attention on the potential malevolent use of bacteria (such as bacillus anthracis, which causes anthrax), viruses (for example, the variola virus, causing smallpox) or toxins, or of chemical agents, in acts of biological or chemical terrorism. In September 2001 WHO issued draft guidelines entitled 'Health Aspects of Biological and Chemical Weapons'.

Within the UN system, WHO's Department of Emergency and Humanitarian Action co-ordinates the international response to emergencies and natural disasters in the health field, in close co-operation with other agencies and within the framework set out by the UN's Office for the Co-ordination of Humanitarian Affairs. In this context, WHO provides expert advice on epidemiological surveillance, control of communicable diseases, public health information and health emergency training. Its emergency preparedness activities include co-ordination, policy-making and planning, awareness-building, technical advice, training, publication of standards and guidelines, and research. Its emergency relief activities include organizational support, the provision of emergency drugs and supplies and conducting technical emergency assessment missions. The Division's objective is to strengthen the national capacity of member states to reduce the adverse health consequences of disasters. In responding to emergency situations, WHO always tries to develop projects and activities that will assist the national authorities concerned in rebuilding or strengthening their own capacity to handle the impact of such situations. Under the UN's inter-agency Consolidated Appeals Process (CAP) for 2011, launched in November 2010, WHO appealed for US $162.5m. to fund its emergency humanitarian operations.

WHO's emergency response to a severe earthquake in the Pacific Ocean, measuring 9.0 on the international Richter scale, and a tsunami, that in mid-March 2011 devastated northeastern coastal areas of Japan and destroyed part of the Fukushima Daiichi nuclear plant, included collating available technical guidelines on nuclear issues; developing plans to address potential nuclear-related human health needs that might arise from the incident; making available funds for initiating training and planning to address related psychosocial issues; and issuing information on food safety. In late March 2011 WHO, FAO and the IAEA issued a joint statement on food safety issues in the aftermath of the Fukushima nuclear emergency, emphasizing their commitment to mobilizing knowledge and expertise in support of the Japanese authorities.

HEALTH TECHNOLOGY AND PHARMACEUTICALS

WHO's Health Technology and Pharmaceuticals group, made up of the departments of essential drugs and other medicines, vaccines and other biologicals, and blood safety and clinical technology, covers the following areas of work: essential medicines—access, quality and rational use; immunization and vaccine development; and worldwide co-operation on blood safety and clinical technology. Blood safety and clinical technology are an organization-wide priority.

The Department of Essential Drugs and Other Medicines promotes public health through the development of national drugs policies and global guidelines and through collaboration with member countries to promote access to essential drugs, the rational use of medicines and compliance with international drug-control requirements. The department comprises four teams: Policy Access and Rational Use; the Drug Action Programme; Quality, Safety and the Regulation of Medicines; and Traditional Medicine.

The Department of Vaccines and Other Biologicals undertakes activities related to quality assurance and safety of biologicals; vaccine development; vaccine assessment and monitoring; access to technologies; and the development of policies and strategies aimed at maximizing the use of vaccines.

The Policy Access and Rational Use team and the Drug Action Programme assist in the development and implementation by member states of pharmaceutical policies, in ensuring a supply of essential drugs of good quality at low cost, and in the rational use of drugs. Other activities include global and national operational research in the pharmaceutical sector, and the development of technical tools for problem solving, management and evaluation. The Policy Access and Rational Use team also has a strong advocacy and information role, promulgated through a periodical, the *Essential Drugs Monitor*, an extensive range of technical publications, and an information dissemination programme targeting developing countries.

The Quality, Safety and Regulation of Medicines team supports national drug-regulatory authorities and drug-procurement agencies and facilitates international pharmaceutical trade through the exchange of technical information and the harmonization of internationally respected norms and standards. In particular, it publishes the *International Pharmacopoeia (Ph. Int.)*, the *Consultative List of International Nonproprietary Names for Pharmaceutical Substances*, and annual and biennial reports of Expert Committees responsible for determining relevant international standards for the manufacture and specification of pharmaceutical and biological products in international commerce. It provides information on the safety and efficacy of drugs, with particular regard to counterfeit and substandard projects, to health agencies and providers of health care, and it maintains the pharmaceuticals section of the UN *Consolidated List of Products whose Consumption and / or Sale have been Banned, Withdrawn, Severely Restricted or Not Approved by Governments*. The *WHO Model List of Essential Medicines* is updated about every two years and is complemented by corresponding model prescribing information; the 17th *Model List* was published in March 2011. The first *Model List of Medicines for Children* was produced in October 2007. The *WHO Model Formulary* (current edition: 2008) gives detailed information on the safe and effective use of all essential drugs. The first *WHO Model Formulary for Children*, listing more than 240 essential medicines, as well as recommended usage, dosage, adverse effects and contraindications, for treating children between the ages 0–12, was issued in June 2010.

The Traditional Medicine team encourages and supports member states in the integration of traditional medicine into national healthcare systems and in the appropriate use of traditional medicine, through the provision of technical guidelines, standards and methodologies. In May 2002 WHO adopted a strategy on the regulation of traditional medicine and complementary or alternative medicines (TM/CAM). A WHO Congress on Traditional Medicine was held in November 2008, in Beijing, People's Republic of China.

In January 1999 the Executive Board adopted a resolution on WHO's Revised Drug Strategy which placed emphasis on the inequalities of access to pharmaceuticals, and also covered specific aspects of drugs policy, quality assurance, drug promotion, drug donation, independent drug information and rational drug use. Plans of action involving co-operation with member states and other international organizations were to be developed to monitor and analyse the pharmaceutical and public health implications of international agreements, including trade agreements. In April 2001 experts from WHO and the World Trade Organization participated in a workshop to address ways of lowering the cost of medicines in less developed countries. In the following month the World Health Assembly adopted a resolution urging member states to promote equitable access to essential drugs, noting that this was denied to about one-third of the world's population. WHO participates with other partners in the 'Accelerating Access' initiative, which aims to expand access to antiretroviral drugs for people with HIV/AIDS.

WHO reports that 2m. children die each year of diseases for which common vaccines exist. In September 1991 the Children's Vaccine Initiative (CVI) was launched, jointly sponsored by the Rockefeller Foundation, UNDP, UNICEF, the World Bank and WHO, to facilitate the development and provision of children's vaccines. The CVI has as its ultimate goal the development of a single oral immunization shortly after birth that will protect against all major childhood diseases. An International Vaccine Institute was established in Seoul, Republic of Korea, as part of the CVI, to provide scientific and technical services for the production of vaccines for developing countries. A comprehensive survey, *State of the World's Vaccines and Immunization*, was published by WHO, jointly with UNICEF, in 1996; a revised edition of the survey was issued in 2003. In 1999 WHO, UNICEF, the World Bank and a number of public and private sector partners formed the Global Alliance for Vaccines and Immunization (GAVI), which aimed to expand the provision of existing vaccines and to accelerate the development and introduction of new vaccines and technologies, with the ultimate goal of protecting children of all nations and from all socio-economic backgrounds against vaccine-preventable diseases.

WHO supports states in ensuring access to safe blood, blood products, transfusions, injections, and healthcare technologies.

INFORMATION, EVIDENCE AND RESEARCH

The Information, Evidence and Research group addresses the following areas of work: evidence for health policy; health information management and dissemination; and research policy and promotion and organization of health systems. Through the generation and dissemination of evidence the Information, Evidence and Research group aims to assist policy-makers assess health needs, choose intervention strategies, design policy and monitor performance, and thereby improve the performance of national health systems.

The group also supports international and national dialogue on health policy.

WHO co-ordinates the Health InterNetwork Access to Research Initiative (HINARI), which was launched in July 2001 to enable relevant authorities in developing countries to access biomedical journals through the internet at no or greatly reduced cost, in order to improve the world-wide circulation of scientific information; by 2012 more than 8,500 journals and 7,000 e-books were being made available to health institutions in more than 100 countries.

In 2004 WHO developed the World Alliance on Patient Safety, further to a World Health Assembly resolution in 2002. Since renamed WHO Patient Safety, the programme was launched to facilitate the development of patient safety policy and practice across all WHO member states.

HEALTH DAYS

World Health Day is observed on 7 April every year, and is used to promote awareness of a particular health topic ('Aging and health: good health adds life to years', in 2012). World Leprosy Day is held every year on 30 January, World TB Day on 24 March, World No Tobacco Day on 31 May, World Heart Day on 24 September, World Mental Health Day on 10 October, World Diabetes Day, in association with the International Diabetes Federation, on 14 November, World AIDS Day on 1 December, and World Asthma Day on 11 December.

ASSOCIATED AGENCY

International Agency for Research on Cancer: 150 Cours Albert Thomas, 69372 Lyon Cedex 08, France; tel. 4-72-73-84-85; fax 4-72-73-85-75; e-mail www@iarc.fr; internet www.iarc.fr; established in 1965 as a self-governing body within the framework of WHO, the Agency organizes international research on cancer. It has its own laboratories and runs a programme of research on the environmental factors causing cancer. Mems: Australia, Belgium, Canada, Denmark, Finland, France, Germany, Italy, Japan, Netherlands, Norway, Spain, Sweden, Switzerland, United Kingdom, USA; Dir Dr CHRISTOPHER WILD (United Kingdom).

Finance

WHO's regular budget is provided by assessment of member states and associate members. An additional fund for specific projects is provided by voluntary contributions from members and other sources, including UNDP and UNFPA.

A total programme budget of US $4,804m. was proposed for the two years 2012–13; of the total some $3,419m. (71.2%) was allocated to WHO programmes; $922m. (19.2%) to special programmes and collaborative arrangements; and $462m. (9.6%) to outbreak and crisis response (governed by acute emergency events).

WHO PROPOSED BUDGET APPROPRIATIONS BY REGION, 2012–13

Region	Amount (US $ million)	% of total budget
Africa	1,409	29.3
Americas	257	5.3
South-East Asia	505	10.5
Europe	266	5.5
Eastern Mediterranean	725	15.1
Western Pacific	316	6.6
Headquarters	1,325	27.6
Total	4,804	100.0

Publications

Bulletin of WHO (monthly).

Eastern Mediterranean Health Journal (annually).

International Classification of Functioning, Disability and Health—ICF.

International Pharmacopoeia.

International Statistical Classification of Disease and Related Health Problems.

International Travel and Health.

Model List of Essential Medicines (every two years).

Pan-American Journal of Public Health (annually).

3 By 5 Progress Report.

Toxicological Evaluation of Certain Veterinary Drug Residues in Food (annually).

Weekly Epidemiological Record (in English and French, paper and electronic versions available).

WHO Drug Information (quarterly).

WHO Global Atlas of Traditional, Complementary and Alternative Medicine.

WHO Model Formulary.

WHO Report on the Global Tobacco Epidemic.

World Health Report (annually, in English, French and Spanish).

World Cancer Report.

World Malaria Report (with UNICEF).

Zoonoses and Communicable Diseases Common to Man and Animals.

Technical report series; catalogues of specific scientific, technical and medical fields available.

World Intellectual Property Organization—WIPO

Address: 34 chemin des Colombettes, BP 18, 1211 Geneva 20, Switzerland.

Telephone: 223389111; **fax:** 227335428; **e-mail:** wipo.mail@wipo.int; **internet:** www.wipo.int.

WIPO was established by a Convention signed in Stockholm in 1967, which came into force in 1970. It became a specialized agency of the UN in December 1974.

MEMBERS

WIPO has 184 members.

Organization

(April 2012)

GENERAL ASSEMBLY

The General Assembly is one of the three WIPO governing bodies, and is composed of all states that are party to the WIPO Convention and that are also members of any of the WIPO-administered Unions (see below). The Assembly meets in ordinary session once a year to agree on programmes and budgets. It elects the Director-General, who is the executive head of WIPO. Prior to the adoption of a new Treaty, the General Assembly may convene a Diplomatic Conference (a high-level meeting of member states) to finalize negotiations.

CONFERENCE

All member states are represented in the Conference, which meets in ordinary session once every two years.

CO-ORDINATION COMMITTEE

Countries belonging to the Committee are elected from among the member states of WIPO, the Executive Committee of the International Union for the Protection of Industrial Property (Paris Union, relating to the Paris Convention, see below), the Executive Committee of the International Union for the Protection of Literary and Artistic Works (Berne Union, relating to the Berne Convention, also see below), and, *ex officio,* Switzerland. It meets in ordinary session once a year.

ASSEMBLIES OF THE UNIONS

The Assemblies of member states of the Paris Union, the Berne Union, the other Unions of WIPO-administered international agreements (the Budapest Union, Hague Union, Lisbon Union, Locarno Union, Madrid Union—Marks, Nice Union, PCT (Patent Co-operation Treaty) Union, Strasbourg Agreement Concerning the International Patent Classification—IPC—Union, and Vienna Union), and the Assemblies of member states of the Rome Convention

Intergovernmental Committee, the Patent Law Treaty, WIPO Copyright Treaty, and of the WIPO Performances and Phonograms Treaty) also contribute to the WIPO decision-making process. In September 2009 meetings of the WIPO Assemblies were, for the first time, preceded by a two-day high-level ministerial gathering ('ministerial segment').

INTERNATIONAL BUREAU

The International Bureau, as WIPO's secretariat, prepares the meetings of the various bodies of WIPO and the Unions, mainly through the provision of reports and working documents. It organizes the meetings, and sees that the decisions are communicated to all concerned, and, as far as possible, that they are carried out.

The International Bureau implements projects and initiates new ones to promote international co-operation in the field of intellectual property. It acts as an information service and publishes reviews. It is also the depository of most of the treaties administered by WIPO.

Separate regional bureaux, under the co-ordination of the International Bureau, channel technical assistance to member states in the Middle East, Africa, the Far East and Australasia, and Latin America and the Caribbean.

Director-General: FRANCIS GURRY (Australia).

There are four ad hoc Standing Committees, comprising experts, on: Law of Patents; Law of Trademarks, Industrial Designs and Geographical Indications; Copyright and Related Rights; and Information Technologies. A Standing Committee may establish a working group to examine specific issues in detail. There is also a Committee on Development and Intellectual Property, and an Advisory Committee on Enforcement. Some 250 non-governmental organizations have observer status at WIPO. WIPO has co-ordination offices in Brussels, Belgium; Toyko, Japan; Singapore; and New York, USA.

Activities

WIPO works to ensure that the rights of creators and owners of intellectual property (IP), 'creations of the mind', are protected throughout the world, with a view to facilitating the advancement of science, technology and the arts and promoting international trade. IP comprises two principal branches: industrial property (patents and other rights in technological inventions, rights in trademarks, industrial designs, geographical indications—including appellations of origin, etc.) and copyright and related rights (covering literary, musical, artistic and photographic works; and also the rights of performing artists in their performances, of producers of phonograms in their recordings, and of broadcasters in their audiovisual media broadcasts). IP rights enable the owner of a copyright, patent or trademark (the 'creator') to benefit from their work. In December 2008 member states adopted a revised strategic framework for WIPO comprising the following nine strategic goals: promoting the balanced evolution of the international normative framework for IP; providing premier global IP services; facilitating the use of IP for development; co-ordinating and developing a global IP infrastructure; developing as a world reference source for IP information and analysis; promoting international co-operation on building respect for IP; addressing IP in relation to global policy issues; developing a responsive communications interface between WIPO, its member states and all stakeholders; and developing an efficient administrative and financial support structure to enable the Organization better to deliver its programmes.

In October 2008 a WIPO strategic realignment programme (SRP) was launched, which was to introduce a corporate culture and to review the Organization's strategic objectives, structures, programmes and resources, to enable it to fulfill its mandate more effectively. In September 2010 member states endorsed proposed reforms to the Organization and adopted a new medium-term strategic plan for 2011–15, based on the Organization's nine strategic goals.

WIPO administers and encourages member states to sign and enforce international treaties relating to the protection of IP, of which the most fundamental are the Paris Convention for the Protection of Industrial Property (1883), the Berne Convention for the Protection of Literary and Artistic Works (1886), and the Patent Co-operation Treaty (PCT).

WIPO's Advisory Committee on Enforcement (ACE, established in October 2002) co-ordinates with other organizations and the private sector to enforce IP rights by combating piracy and counterfeiting; promoting public education; implementing national and regional training programmes for relevant stakeholders; and facilitating, through its IPEIS Electronic Forum, the exchange of information on enforcement issues. WIPO helps to organize the periodic Global Congress on Combating Counterfeiting and Piracy, which was established in 2004 as an international forum of senior public sector representatives and business leaders who gather to develop strategies against counterfeiting and piracy.

GLOBAL IP INFRASTRUCTURE

The co-ordination and development of a global IP infrastructure, to enhance the world-wide promotion of science, new technologies and innovation, was one of the new strategic goals approved by WIPO member states in December 2008. In September 2009 a WIPO global symposium of IP authorities met to discuss means of establishing a more accessible, digital and borderless global IP infrastructure. In 2012 the global IP infrastructure comprised the following pillars: IP institutions and authorities; capacity-building and networking; electronic data interchange among IP offices; international classifications in the fields of trademarks and industrial design; standards and technical agreements; databases; services; and an information-sharing forum (the Global Symposium of IP Authorities, of which the third was convened in September 2011).

DEVELOPING LAWS AND STANDARDS

One of WIPO's major activities is the progressive development and harmonization of IP laws, standards, and practices among its member states, in the areas of industrial property law and copyright law. The organization prepares new treaties and undertakes the revision of the existing treaties that it administers. WIPO administers international classifications established by treaties and relating to inventions, marks and industrial designs: periodically it reviews these to ensure their improvement in terms of coverage and precision. WIPO also carries out studies on issues in the field of IP that could be the subject of model laws or guidelines for implementation at national or international levels. The organization seeks to simplify and harmonize national IP legislation and procedures (for example through implementation of the Trademark Law Treaty, 1994, and development of the Patent Law Treaty, 2000) in order to make the registration of IP more easily accessible.

WIPO implements two programmes that provide legal and technical assistance on the formulation of strong IP laws and systems specifically to, respectively, developing countries and countries with economies in transition.

WIPO DIGITAL AGENDA

WIPO promotes the development of the use of Information and Communication Technology (ICT) for storing, accessing and using valuable IP data, and to provide a forum for informed debate and for the exchange of expertise on IP. The rapid advancement of digital communications networks has posed challenges regarding the protection and enforcement of IP rights. WIPO has undertaken a range of initiatives to address the implications for copyright and industrial property law, and for electronic commerce transcending national jurisdictions. WIPO's Electronic Commerce Section co-ordinates programmes and activities relating to the IP aspects of electronic commerce. In September 1999 WIPO organized the first International Conference on Electronic Commerce and IP; the 'WIPO Digital Agenda', which establishes a series of guidelines and objectives, was launched by the Organization at the Conference. The second International Conference on Electronic Commerce and IP was held in September 2001. In January 2001, under its Digital Agenda, WIPO launched WIPOnet, a global digital network of IP information sources capable of transmitting confidential data. The Organization also manages WIPO Gold, launched in June 2010 as an online repository of searchable IP data, and maintains WIPO Lex, an online search facility for IP national laws and treaties.

IP FOR DEVELOPMENT

WIPO aims to support governments and organizations in establishing policies and structures to harness the potential of IP for development. In 2005 WIPO founded an Office for Strategic Use of IP for Development (OSUIPD), which comprises the following four divisions: the Creative Industries Division (CID); the IP and Economic Development Division (IPEDD); the IP and New Technologies Division (IPNT Division); and the Small and Medium-Sized Enterprises Division (SMEs Division). The OSUIPD supports member states—with a particular focus on developing countries and those with economies in transition—in successfully utilizing the IP system for cultural, economic and social development; assists SMEs; and aims to enhance capacity in the area of managing IP assets.

In May 2005 WIPO, jointly with UNCTAD, UNIDO, WHO and the WTO, organized an international seminar focusing on IP and Development and IP and Public Policy. Areas covered included biodiversity; competition policy; copyright and related rights in the digital environment; creating value from intellectual property (IP) assets; national best practices; public health; traditional knowledge; and technology transfer. WIPO has subsequently organized a number of international and national seminars on the strategic use of IP for economic and social development.

In September 2007 WIPO member states adopted the WIPO Development Agenda. The Agenda comprises a series of recommendations that incorporate 45 agreed proposals covering the following six clusters of activities: Technical Assistance and Capacity Building; Norm-setting, Flexibilities, Public Policy and Public Knowledge; Technology Transfer, ICT and Access to Knowledge; Assessments, Evaluation and Impact Studies; Institutional Matters including Mandate and Governance; and Other Issues (for example, ensuring that IP enforcement is viewed within the context of broader societal interests). A Committee on Development and IP (CDIP) was established in October 2007 to formulate a work programme for the implementation of these recommendations, and to monitor their implementation. The OSUIPD co-operates closely with all departments of WIPO involved in the implementation of the Development Agenda.

WIPO aims to modernize national IP systems. It offers technical assistance to increase the capabilities of developing countries to benefit from the international IP framework, with a view to promoting the optimal use of human and other resources and thereby contributing to national prosperity. WIPO supports governments with IP-related institution-building, human resources development, and preparation and implementation of legislation. The OSUIPD helps countries to formulate national IP strategies. The WIPO Worldwide Academy, established in March 1998, undertakes training, teaching and research on IP matters, focusing particularly on developing countries. The Academy maintains a Distance Learning Centre using online facilities, digital multimedia technology and video conferencing. WIPO's Information and Documentation Centre holds extensive reference materials. Under its Digital Agenda WIPO aims to assist the integration of developing countries into the internet environment, particularly through the use of WIPOnet (see above). In March 2007 WIPO helped to organize the first annual symposium for IP academies, in Rio de Janeiro, Brazil, which established the Global Network of IP Academies (GNIPA) as a framework for co-operation. The fifth GNIPA symposium was convened in August 2011, in Washington, DC, USA.

WIPO advises countries on obligations under the WTO's agreement on Trade-Related Aspects of IP Rights (TRIPS). The two organizations have jointly implemented a technical co-operation initiative to assist least developed countries with harmonizing their national legislative and administrative structures in compliance with the TRIPS accord; the original deadline for completion of the initiative, 1 January 2006, was extended in November 2005 to 1 July 2013.

WIPO presented a programme of action to the Third UN Conference on the Least Developed Countries (LDCs-III, held in Brussels, Belgium in May 2001), which was aimed at strengthening LDCs' IP systems. In May 2009 WIPO launched a Japan-funded programme aimed at promoting the use of IP in Africa and LDCs as a catalyst for economic and commercial development. Representatives of LDCs attending a WIPO high-level forum on the strategic use of intellectual property for prosperity and development, held in July 2009, reaffirmed commitment to integrating IP and innovation strategies into their national development planning. WIPO participated in the preparation of LDC-IV, which was held in May 2011, in Istanbul, Turkey.

WIPO, with ITU and UNIDO, leads an initiative on promoting technology and innovation, the eighth of nine activities that were launched in April 2009 by the UN System Chief Executives Board for Co-ordination (CEB), with the aim of alleviating the impact on poor and vulnerable populations of the developing global economic crisis.

In June 2011 WIPO launched a new project to establish a common digital platform across 11 countries in West Africa, with the aim of simplifying the identification of protected musical works in that region.

COPYRIGHT AND RELATED RIGHTS

Through its Copyright and Related Rights sector WIPO works on the development of international norms and standards in the area of copyright and related rights (these being legal concepts and instruments that both protect the rights of creators of works and aim to contribute to national development); and also actively promotes, through the organization of meetings and seminars, the so-called 'WIPO Internet Treaties' (the WIPO Copyright Treaty—WCT and WIPO Performances and Phonograms Treaty—WPPT), which were enacted as part of the WIPO Digital Agenda with the aim of updating copyright law in the light of new digital technologies. In July 2008 WIPO convened an international workshop on digital preservation and copyright.

In July 2007 the Organization published the *WIPO Guide on Managing Intellectual Property for Museums*, which acknowledged that institutions of the cultural heritage community in industrialized countries were increasingly regarded as owners of shared IP resources (for example, their own contextualized or interpretative authoritative content), rather than as merely users of IP, and aimed to assist museums and the broader cultural heritage community to use the international IP system to enhance the future management of their collections in the digital environment. In May 2011 WIPO and the International Council of Museums (ICOM) signed a memorandum of understanding on collaboration in the management of IP options, and in the mediation of disputes, in the area of cultural heritage and museums, with a particular focus on copyright issues, traditional knowledge and traditional cultural expressions, and the digitization of cultural artifacts.

SMALL AND MEDIUM-SIZED ENTERPRISES

A programme focusing on the IP concerns of small and medium-sized enterprises was approved by the WIPO General Assembly in September 2000. An International Forum on IP and SMEs, organized jointly by WIPO and the Italian Government in Milan, Italy in February 2001, adopted the Milan Plan of Action for helping SMEs to benefit fully from the IP system. WIPO publishes a number of guides and manuals aimed specifically at SMEs.

TRADITIONAL KNOWLEDGE, EXPRESSIONS OF FOLKLORE, GENETIC RESOURCES

In view of the advances in technology and economic globalization in recent years WIPO has focused increasingly on the relationship between IP and issues such as traditional knowledge (TK), biological diversity, environmental protection and human rights. In 1998–99 WIPO made fact-finding visits to 3,000 TK stakeholders in 60 locations world-wide, and in 2001, following an open review of the 1998–99 consultations, the Organization published the first ever report on the IP concerns of holders of TK. In April 2000 the organization convened its first Meeting on IP and Genetic Resources (GR). A WIPO Intergovernmental Committee on IP and GR, TK and Folklore (IGC) was established in September of that year. In January 2002 an international forum organized by WIPO adopted the Muscat Declaration on IP and TK, recognizing the contribution of TK to international co-operation. In October 2005 the WIPO Voluntary Fund for Accredited Indigenous and Local Communities was inaugurated with a view to supporting the participation of accredited indigenous and local communities in the work of the IGC. In December 2006 the 10th session of the IGC identified 10 key questions relating to the protection of traditional cultural expressions (TCE) and expressions of folklore (EoF), and to the protection of TK. A commentary process on the issues raised was subsequently undertaken. In December 2007 WIPO convened a roundtable on building the capacity of indigenous communities in the area of IP, TK, GR and TCE. The 12th session of the IGC, convened in February 2008, determined to prepare a working document that was to describe, and to illustrate any gaps in, the existing provisions at international level providing protection for TCE/EoF; and that was to consider means of addressing any gaps identified. The resulting 'gap analyses' were reviewed by the 13th IGC session, convened in October of that year. In July 2009 the 14th session of the IGC agreed on the future negotiation and adoption of an internationally legally binding instrument aimed at ensuring the effective protection of biodiversity, TK, GR and TCEs. Text-based negotiations on the proposed legal framework were initiated in May 2010, and, in February 2012, the 20th session of the IGC consolidated proposals arising from the negotiations into a single text, which was to be considered by the WIPO General Assembly in October 2012.

WIPO's Creative Heritage Project supports indigenous communities with the employment of new digital technologies to record and archive expressions of their cultural heritage. The Project manages the WIPO Creative Heritage Digital Gateway, an internet portal to collections of indigenous cultural heritage. A pilot project was launched in September 2008 under the auspices of the Creative Heritage Project to provide training to specific indigenous communities in documenting their cultural traditions, in archiving the documentation relating to their heritage, and in protecting their rights regarding the authorization of third party use of this material; the first focus of the initiative was the Kenyan Maasai.

In September 2007 WIPO launched a series of open-policy symposia to address issues related to the use and impact of IP in the life sciences; the fourth round of symposia, convened in April 2008, addressed using life sciences patent landscaping for public policy purposes. WIPO has commissioned expert analyses of the patent landscapes relating to priority areas of concern for public health policy-makers, including avian influenza and neglected diseases.

In November 2009 WIPO supported the Indian Government in convening an International Conference on TK, in New Delhi, India, with participation by international experts in TK, GR and TCEs.

ENFORCEMENT OF IP RIGHTS

WIPO's Advisory Committee on Enforcement (ACE) provides technical assistance and co-ordinates with other organizations and with the private sector to combat counterfeiting and piracy activities; provides public education; supports the implementation of national and regional training programmes; and promotes the exchange of information on enforcement issues.

ARBITRATION AND MEDIATION CENTRE

WIPO maintains the WIPO Arbitration and Mediation Centre, which became operational in October 1994, to facilitate the settlement of IP disputes between private parties. Since its inception the Centre has deliberated on more than 210 requests for arbitration (relating to, *inter alia*, patent infringements, patent licenses, software licenses, distribution agreements for pharmaceutical products, research and development agreements, trademark co-existence agreements, consultancy agreements, and joint venture agreements); and more than 70 requests for mediation (relating to, *inter alia*, patent disputes, software/ICT, copyright, trademark co-existence, employment issues in an IP context, and engineering disputes). The Centre organizes arbitrator and mediator workshops and assists in the development of WIPO model contract clauses and industry-specific resolution schemes. The Centre offers parties to disputes the option of using the WIPO Electronic Case Facility (WIPO ECAF), which provides for secure web-based filing, storing and retrieval of case-related submissions.

The Arbitration and Mediation Centre also offers a Domain Name Dispute Resolution service, which plays a leading role in reviewing cases of conflict between trademarks and internet domain names (such as com, .net, .org, and .info), and some 65 country code top-level domains (ccTLDs), in accordance with the Uniform Domain Name Dispute Resolution Policy (UDRP) that was, on WIPO's recommendation, adopted by the Internet Corporation for Assigned Names and Numbers—ICANN in October 1999. WIPO's first Internet Domain Name Process, a series of international consultations, undertaken in 1999, issued several recommendations for controlling the abuse of trademarks on the internet. A second Internet Domain Name Process, completed in 2001, addressed the improper registration of other identifiers ('cybersquatting'), including standard non-proprietary names for pharmaceutical substances, names and acronyms of intergovernmental organizations, geographical indications and terms, and trade names. By December 2010 some 20,047 cases concerning disputes over generic top-level domains had been filed with the Centre, covering around 35,000 separate domain names; the principal areas of complainant activity were biotechnology and pharmaceuticals, and banking and finance. In addition to UDRP cases, the Centre deals with cases relating to registrations in the start-up phase of new domains, in accordance with so-called 'Sunrise' policies. WIPO publishes an online Legal Index of WIPO UDRP Panel Decisions and also maintains an online database of cybersquatting cases: a record 2,696 complaints regarding alleged cybersquatting were filed with the Centre in 2010. From December 2009 the Centre offered a paperless UDRP process, which became mandatory in March 2010.

INTERNATIONAL REGISTRATION SERVICES

WIPO maintains the following international registration services:

International registration of trademarks: operating since 1893; during 2010 there were 37,533 registrations and 21,949 renewals of trademarks; publ. *WIPO Gazette of International Marks* (every two weeks).

International deposit of industrial designs: operating since 1928; during 2010 2,382 applications were made for deposits, renewals and prolongations of 11,238 industrial designs; publ. *International Designs Bulletin* (monthly).

International applications for patents: operating since 1978; provisionally, 181,900 record copies of international applications for patents under the PCT were received in 2011, with the fastest area of growth in the area of digital communications; publ. *World Intellectual Property Indicators* (annually), *PCT Review* (annually), *Weekly Published PCT Data* (monthly, on dvd, from www.wipo.int/patentscope/en/data/data_download.html). A series of Patent Colloquia were convened during October 2006–November 2007, aimed at enhancing the international patent system.

WIPO-ADMINISTERED TREATIES

INTELLECTUAL PROPERTY TREATIES

(status at April 2012)

The IP Treaties administered by WIPO define internationally agreed basic standards of IP protection in each member state.

Paris Convention for the Protection of Industrial Property: signed 20 March 1883, last revised in 1967; 174 states party.

Berne Convention for the Protection of Literary and Artistic Works: signed 9 Sept. 1886, last revised in 1971; 165 states party.

Madrid Agreement for the Repression of False or Deceptive Indications of Source on Goods: signed 14 April 1891; 35 states party.

Rome Convention for the Protection of Performers, Producers of Phonograms and Broadcasting Organizations: signed 26 October 1961; 91 states party.

Phonograms Convention for the Protection of Producers of Phonograms against Unauthorized Duplication of their Phonograms: signed 29 October 1971; 77 states party.

Brussels Convention Relating to the Distribution of Programme-carrying Signals Transmitted by Satellite: signed 21 May 1974; 35 states party.

Nairobi Treaty on the Protection of the Olympic Symbol: signed 26 September 1981; 50 states party.

Treaty on the International Registration of Audiovisual Works (Film Register Treaty): signed 20 April 1989; 13 states party.

Trademark Law Treaty: signed 27 October 1994; 50 states party.

WIPO Copyright Treaty (WCT): signed 20 December 1996; 89 states party.

WIPO Performances and Phonograms Treaty (WPPT): signed 20 December 1996; 89 states party.

Patent Law Treaty, 2000: entered into force 28 April 2005; 32 states party.

Singapore Treaty on the Law of Trademarks: entered into force 16 March 2009; 26 states party.

Washington Treaty on Intellectual Property in Respect of Integrated Circuits: signed 26 May 1989; three ratifications.

GLOBAL PROTECTION SYSTEM TREATIES

(status at April 2012)

WIPO administers a small number of treaties, listed below, that cover inventions (patents), trademarks and industrial designs, under which one international registration or filing has effect in any of the relevant signatory states. The services provided by WIPO under its so-called Global Protection System treaties simplify the registration process and reduce the cost of making individual applications or filings in each country in which protection for a given IP right is sought. The most widely used of these treaties is the PCT, under which a single international patent application is valid in all signatory countries selected by the applicant. The PCT system has expanded rapidly in recent years. The PCT-SAFE (Secure Applications Filed Electronically) system became operational in February 2004, safeguarding the electronic filing of patent applications. Patent applications can be accessed through WIPO's PatentScope search facility. The corresponding treaties concerning the international registration of trademarks and industrial designs are, respectively, the Madrid Agreement (and its Protocol), and the Hague Agreement. From 1 January 2010 the earliest of the three Acts of the Hague Agreement (the 1934 London Act, deemed to be obsolete) was suspended to streamline the administration of the Agreement.

Madrid Agreement Concerning the International Registration of Marks: signed 14 April 1891; 56 states party.

The Hague Agreement Concerning the International Registration of Industrial Designs: signed 16 November 1925; 60 states party.

Lisbon Agreement for the Protection of Appellations of Origin and their International Registration: signed 31 October 1958; 27 states party.

Patent Co-operation Treaty (PCT): signed 19 June 1970; 144 states party.

Budapest Treaty on the International Recognition of the Deposit of Micro-organisms for the Purposes of Patent Procedure: signed 28 April 1977; 75 states party.

Protocol Relating to the Madrid Agreement Concerning the International Registration of Marks: signed 28 June 1989; 84 contracting states.

INTERNATIONAL CLASSIFICATION TREATIES

(status at April 2012)

The International Classification Treaties administered by WIPO create classification systems that organize information concerning inventions, trademarks and industrial designs. The International Classification treaties have established permanent committees of experts mandated periodically to revise and update the classification systems.

Locarno Agreement Establishing an International Classification for Industrial Designs: signed 8 October 1968; 52 states party.

Nice Agreement Concerning the International Classification of Goods and Services for the Purposes of the Registration of Marks: signed 15 June 1957; 83 states party.

Strasbourg Agreement Concerning the International Patent Classification (IPC): signed 24 March 1971; 62 states party.

Vienna Agreement Establishing an International Classification of the Figurative Elements of Marks: signed 12 June 1973; 31 states party.

Finance

The approved budget for the two years 2012–13 amounted to 647.4m. Swiss francs. Around 85% of WIPO's revenue derives from the international registration systems maintained by the organization; the remainder derives mainly from contributions by member states.

Publications

Les appellations d'origine (annually, in French).

Essential Elements of Intellectual Property.

Industrial Property and Copyright (monthly, in English and French; every 2 months, in Spanish).

Intellectual Property for Small and Medium-sized Enterprises.

Industrial Property Statistics (CD-Rom).

Intellectual Property in Asia and the Pacific (quarterly, in English).

Intellectual Property Profile of the Least Developed Countries.

International Designs Bulletin (monthly, in English and French).

PCT Gazette (weekly, in English and French).

WIPO Academy Review.

WIPO Gazette of International Marks (every two weeks, in English and French).

World Intellectual Property Indicators.

WIPO Magazine (every 2 months, in English, French and Spanish).

WIPO Overview.

World Patent Report (annually).

A collection of industrial property and copyright laws and treaties; a selection of publications related to intellectual property.

World Meteorological Organization—WMO

Address: 7 bis, ave de la Paix, CP 2300, 1211 Geneva 2, Switzerland.

Telephone: 227308111; **fax:** 227308181; **e-mail:** wmo@wmo.int; **internet:** www.wmo.int.

WMO was established in 1950 and was recognized as a Specialized Agency of the UN in 1951, operating in the fields of meteorology, climatology, operational hydrology and related fields, as well as their applications.

MEMBERS

WMO has 189 members.

Organization

(April 2012)

WORLD METEOROLOGICAL CONGRESS

The supreme body of the Organization, the Congress, is convened every four years and represents all members; it adopts regulations, and determines policy, programme and budget. The 16th Congress was held in May–June 2011. An extraordinary session of the Congress was to be convened in October 2012.

EXECUTIVE COUNCIL

The Council has 37 members and meets at least once a year to prepare studies and recommendations for the Congress; it supervises the implementation of Congress resolutions and regulations, informs members on technical matters and offers advice.

SECRETARIAT

The Secretariat acts as an administrative, documentary and information centre; undertakes special technical studies; produces publications; organizes meetings of WMO constituent bodies; acts as a link between the meteorological and hydrometeorological services of the world, and provides information for the general public. The WMO Secretariat hosts the secretariat of the intergovernmental Group on Earth Observations (GEO), which was founded by participants at the Earth Observation Summit convened in Washington, DC, USA, in July 2003.

Secretary-General: Michel Jarraud (France).

REGIONAL ASSOCIATIONS

Members are grouped in six Regional Associations (Africa, Asia, Europe, North America, Central America and the Caribbean, South America and the South-West Pacific), whose task is to co-ordinate meteorological activity within their regions and to examine questions referred to them by the Executive Council. Sessions are held at least once every four years.

TECHNICAL COMMISSIONS

The Technical Commissions are composed of experts nominated by the members of the Organization. Sessions are held at least once every four years. The Commissions cover the following areas: Basic Systems; Climatology; Instruments and Methods of Observation; Atmospheric Sciences; Aeronautical Meteorology; Agricultural Meteorology; Hydrology; Oceanography and Marine Meteorology.

WORLD CLIMATE CONFERENCE

The First World Climate Conference was convened in 1979 and the Second World Climate Conference took place in 1990. WMO co-operated with other UN agencies to prepare for the third World Climate Conference, which was convened, in Geneva, in August–September 2009.

Activities

In June 2011 the 16th World Meteorological Congress determined that WMO's five priority areas of activity during 2011–15 would be: developing the newly-endorsed Global Framework for Climate Services; enhancing the agency's contribution to disaster risk reduction; improving observation and information systems; strengthening developing countries' capacity to share in scientific advances and their applications; and advancing the efficiency of meteorological services in the aviation sector. The 16th Congress also recommended that WMO should prepare a cross-cutting Capacity Development Strategy to co-ordinate and enhance existing capacity building activities.

GLOBAL FRAMEWORK FOR CLIMATE SERVICES

The third World Climate Conference, convened in August–September 2009, resolved to establish the Global Framework for Climate Services, to act as a platform for dialogue on climate change between providers of climate services (for example national meteorological and hydrometeorological services) and service users, such as policy-makers and farmers. The new Framework, developed by a High-level Task Force during 2010–early 2011, was endorsed by the 16th World Meteorological Congress in June 2011. An extraordinary session of the World Meteorological Congress was to be convened in October 2012 to review and adopt a draft implementation plan of the new Global Framework.

WORLD WEATHER WATCH (WWW) PROGRAMME

Combining facilities and services provided by the members, the Programme's primary purpose is to make available meteorological and related geophysical and environmental information enabling them to maintain efficient meteorological services. Facilities in regions outside any national territory (outer space, ocean areas and Antarctica) are maintained by members on a voluntary basis. In May 2007 the 15th WMO Congress made a number of decisions aimed at improving the WWW Programme, including instruments and observation methods and assisting developing countries to strengthen their operational capacities. WMO's World Weather Information Services website (worldweather.wmo.int) provides weather observations in nine languages.

Antarctic Activities: co-ordinates WMO activities related to the Antarctic, in particular the surface and upper-air observing programme, plans the regular exchange of observational data and products needed for operational and research purposes, studies problems related to instruments and methods of observation peculiar to the Antarctic, and develops appropriate regional coding practices. Contacts are maintained with scientific bodies dealing with Antarctic research and with other international organizations on aspects of Antarctic meteorology.

Data Management: monitors the integration of the different components of the WWW Programme, with the intention of increasing the efficiency of, in particular, the Global Observing System, the Global Data Processing System and the Global Telecommunication System. The Data Management component of the WWW Programme develops data handling procedures and standards for enhanced forms of data representation, in order to aid member countries to process large volumes of meteorological data.

Emergency Response Activities: assists national meteorological services to respond effectively to man-made environmental emergencies, particularly nuclear accidents, through the development, co-ordination and implementation of WMO/IAEA established procedures and response mechanisms for the provision and exchange of observational data and specialized transport model products. In the immediate aftermath of the devastating earthquake and tsunami flooding that struck Japan in March 2011, disabling the Fukushima Daiichi nuclear power plant, WMO, in partnership with the IAEA, undertook weather forecast monitoring

Global Data Processing and Forecasting System: consists of World Meteorological Centres (WMCs) in Melbourne (Australia), Moscow (Russia) and Washington, DC (USA); 40 Regional/Specialized Meteorological Centres (RSMCs); and 188 National Meteorological Centres. The WMCs and RSMCs provide analyses, forecasts and warnings for exchange on the Global Telecommunications System. Some centres concentrate on the monitoring and forecasting of environmental quality and special weather phenomena, such as tropical cyclones, monsoons, droughts, etc., which have a major impact on human safety and national economies. These analyses and forecasts are designed to assist the members in making local and specialized forecasts.

Global Observing System: makes simultaneous observations at around 11,000 land stations. Meteorological information is also received from 3,000 aircraft, 7,000 ships, 600 drifting buoys, and nine polar orbiting and six geostationary meteorological satellites. About 160 members operate some 1,300 ground stations equipped to receive picture transmissions from geostationary and polar-orbiting satellites.

WMO Integrated Global Observing Systems (WIGOS): approved by the 15th World Meteorological Congress (2007). The 16th World Meteorological Congress (2011) decided that priority should be given to developing WIGOS to enable it to become operational by 2016.

WMO Information System (WIS): became operational in January 2012 as a single co-ordinated global infrastructure responsible for telecommunications and data management, aimed at expanding the global exchange of weather, climate and water data. It was conceived of as a pillar of WMO's activities for managing and moving weather, climate and water information in the 21st century. The core infrastructure of the WIS consists of: Global Information System Centres (GISCs), Data Collection or Production Centres (DCPCs), and National Centres (NCs).

Global Telecommunication System: provides telecommunication services for the rapid collection and exchange of meteorological information and related data; consists of: the Main Telecommunication Network (MTN), six Regional Meteorological Telecommunication networks, and the national telecommunication networks. The system operates through 183 National Meteorological Centres, 29 Regional Telecommunications Hubs and the three WMCs.

Instruments and Methods of Observation Programme: promotes the world-wide standardization of meteorological and geophysical instruments and methods of observation and measurement to meet agreed accuracy requirements. It provides related guidance material and training assistance in the use and maintenance of the instruments.

System Support Activity: provides guidance and support to members in the planning, establishment and operation of the WWW Programme. It includes training, technical co-operation support, system and methodology support, operational WWW evaluations, advanced technology support, an operations information service, and the WWW Programme referral catalogue.

Tropical Cyclone Programme: established in response to UN General Assembly Resolution 2733 (XXV), aims to develop national and regionally co-ordinated systems to ensure that the loss of life and damage caused by tropical cyclones and associated floods, landslides and storm surges are reduced to a minimum. The Programme supports the transfer of technology, and includes five regional tropical cyclone bodies covering more than 60 countries, to improve warning systems and collaboration with other international organizations in activities related to disaster mitigation. The 16th World Meteorological Congress determined that the Programme should be strengthened to provide capacity-building support to Least Developed Countries and Small Island Developing States.

WORLD CLIMATE PROGRAMME

Adopted by the Eighth World Meteorological Congress (1979), the World Climate Programme (WCP) comprises the following components: World Climate Data and Monitoring Programme (WCDMP), World Climate Applications and Climate Information Services (CLIPS) Programme (WCASP), World Climate Impact Assessment and Response Strategies Programme (WCIRP), World Climate Research Programme (WCRP). The 16th World Meteorological Congress (2011) adopted a restructured and strengthened World Climate Programme and decided that it would be a key programme in the delivery of the newly-endorsed Global Framework for Climate Services. The WCP is supported by the Global Climate Observing System (GCOS), which provides comprehensive observation of the global climate system, involving a multi-disciplinary range of atmospheric, oceanic, hydrologic, cryospheric and biotic properties and processes. In 1997–98 the GCOS was particularly active in monitoring the impact of the El Niño weather phenomenon on the climate system. The objectives of the WCP are: to use existing climate information to improve economic and social planning; to improve the understanding of climate processes through research, so as to determine the predictability of climate and the extent of man's influence on it; and to detect and warn governments of impending climate variations or changes, either natural or man-made, which may significantly affect critical human activities.

Co-ordination of the overall Programme is the responsibility of WMO, together with direct management of the WCDMP and WCASP. The UN Environment Programme (UNEP) has accepted responsibility for the WCIRP, while the WCRP is jointly administered by WMO, the International Council for Science (ICSU) and UNESCO's Intergovernmental Oceanographic Commission. Other organizations involved in the Programme include FAO, WHO, and the Consultative Group on International Agricultural Research (CGIAR). In addition, the WCP supports the WMO/UNEP Intergovernmental Panel on Climate Change and the implementation of international agreements, such as the UN Framework Convention on Climate Change; and co-ordinates climate activities within WMO.

World Climate Applications and Climate Information and Services Programme (WCASP): promotes applications of climate knowledge in the areas of food production, water, energy (especially solar and wind energy), urban planning and building, human health, transport, tourism and recreation.

World Climate Data and Monitoring Programme (WCDMP): aims to make available reliable climate data for detecting and monitoring climate change for both practical applications and research purposes. The major projects are: the Climate Change Detection Project (CCDP); development of climate databases; computer systems for climate data management (CLICOM); the World Data and Information Referral Service (INFOCLIMA); the Climate Monitoring System; and the Data Rescue (DARE) project.

World Climate Impact Assessment and Response Strategies Programme (WCIRP): aims to make reliable estimates of the socio-economic impact of climate changes, and to assist in forming national policies accordingly. It concentrates on: study of the impact of climate variations on national food systems; assessment of the impact of man's activities on the climate, especially through increasing the amount of carbon dioxide and other radiatively active gases in the atmosphere; and developing the methodology of climate impact assessments.

World Climate Research Programme (WCRP): organized jointly with the Intergovernmental Oceanographic Commission of UNESCO and the ICSU, to determine to what extent climate can be predicted, and the extent of man's influence on climate. Its three specific objectives are: establishing the physical basis for weather predictions over time ranges of one to two months; understanding and predicting the variability of the global climate over periods of several years; and studying the long-term variations and the response of climate to natural or man-made influence over periods of several decades. Studies include: changes in the atmosphere caused by emissions of carbon dioxide, aerosols and other gases; the effect of cloudiness on the radiation balance; the effect of ground water storage and vegetation on evaporation; the Arctic and Antarctic climate process; and the effects of oceanic circulation changes on the global atmosphere.

Global Climate Observing System (GCOS): aims to ensure that data on climate are obtained and made available for: climate system monitoring and climate change detection and attribution; assessing impacts of, and vulnerability to, climate variability and change, e.g. extreme events, terrestrial ecosystems, etc., and analysing options for adaptation; research to improve understanding, modelling and prediction of the climate system; and application to sustainable economic development. The strategy of the GCOS has been to work with its international and regional partners and to engage countries both directly and through international fora such as WMO, other GCOS sponsors and the UN Framework Convention on Climate Change.

ATMOSPHERIC RESEARCH AND ENVIRONMENT PROGRAMME

This major Programme aims to help members to implement research projects; to disseminate relevant scientific information; to draw the attention of members to outstanding research problems of major importance, such as atmospheric composition and environment changes; and to encourage and help members to incorporate the results of research into operational forecasting or other appropriate techniques, particularly when such changes of procedure require international co-ordination and agreement.

Global Atmosphere Watch (GAW): a world-wide system that integrates most monitoring and research activities involving the long-term measurement of atmospheric composition, and is intended to serve as an early warning system to detect further changes in atmospheric concentrations of 'greenhouse' gases, changes in the ozone layer and associated ultraviolet radiation, and in long-range transport of pollutants, including acidity and toxicity of rain, as well as the atmospheric burden of aerosols. The instruments of these globally standardized observations and related research are a set of 22 global stations in remote areas and, in order to address regional effects, some 200 regional stations measuring specific atmospheric chemistry parameters, such as ozone and acid deposition. GAW is the main contributor of data on chemical composition and surface ultraviolet radiation to the GCOS. Through GAW, WMO has collaborated with the UN Economic Commission for Europe (ECE) and has been responsible for the meteorological part of the Monitoring and Evaluation of the Long-range Transmission of Air Pollutants in Europe. In this respect, WMO has arranged for the establishment of two Meteorological Synthesizing Centres (Oslo, Norway, and Moscow, Russia) which provide daily analysis of the transport of pollution over Europe. GAW also gives attention to atmospheric chemistry studies, prepares scientific assessments and encourages integrated environmental monitoring. Quality Assurance/Science Activity Centres have been established to ensure an overall level of quality in GAW. Atmospheric composition information is maintained by and available through a series of six GAW World Data Centres. GAW operates the GAW Urban Environment Meteorological Research Programme (GURME), which assists National Meteorological and Hydrological Services (NMHSs) in dealing with regional and urban pollution monitoring and forecasting, through the provision of guidelines and information on the requisite measuring and modelling infrastructures, and by bringing together NMHSs, regional and city administrations and health authorities. GURME is being developed in co-operation with the World Health Organization.

WMO and other agencies support UNESCO's International Oceanographic Commission with implementing tsunami warning systems for the Caribbean region, the north-eastern Atlantic, the Mediterranean and connected seas, and the Pacific. An Indian Ocean Tsunami Warning and Mitigation System became operational in June 2006. In May 2007 the 15th WMO Congress stressed the importance of developing and maintaining tsunami warning systems and ocean forecast/warning systems.

Physics of Clouds and Weather Modification Research Programme: encourages scientific research on cloud physics and chemistry, with special emphasis on interaction between clouds and atmospheric chemistry, as well as weather modification such as precipitation enhancement ('rain-making') and hail suppression. It provides information on world-wide weather modification projects, and guidance in the design and evaluation of experiments. It also studies the chemistry of clouds and their role in the transport, transformation and dispersion of pollution.

Tropical Meteorology Research Programme: aims to promote and co-ordinate members' research efforts into such important problems as monsoons, tropical cyclones, meteorological aspects of droughts in the arid zones of the tropics, rain-producing tropical weather systems, and the interaction between tropical and mid-latitude weather systems. This should lead to a better understanding of tropical systems and forecasting, and thus be of economic benefit to tropical countries.

World Weather Research Programme (WWRP): promotes the development and application of improved weather forecasting techniques. The Programme is primarily concerned with forecasting weather events that have the potential to cause considerable socio-economic dislocation. Advances in forecasting capability are pursued through a combination of improved scientific understanding (gained through field experiments and research), forecast technique development, the demonstration of new forecasting capabilities, and the transfer of these advances to all NMHSs in conjunction with related training through various Research Development Projects (RDPs) and Forecast Demonstration Projects (FDPs). In particular, THORPEX: a Global Atmospheric Research Programme, is being developed and implemented as part of the WWRP to accelerate improvements in the accuracy of 1–14-day weather forecasts in order to achieve social and economic benefits. The Programme builds upon ongoing advances within the basic research and operational forecasting communities. It aims to make progress by enhancing international collaboration between these communities and with users of forecast products.

APPLICATIONS OF METEOROLOGY PROGRAMME

Public Weather Services Programme: assists members in providing reliable and effective weather and related services for the benefit of the public. The main objectives of the Programme are: to strengthen members' capabilities to meet the needs of the community through the provision of comprehensive weather and related services, with particular emphasis on public safety and welfare; and to foster a better understanding by the public of the capabilities of national meteorological services and how best to use their services.

Agricultural Meteorology Programme: the study of weather and climate as they affect agriculture and forestry, the selection of crops and their protection from disease and deterioration in storage, soil conservation, phenology and physiology of crops and productivity and health of farm animals; the Commission for Agricultural Meteorology supervises the applications projects and also advises the Secretary-General in his efforts to co-ordinate activities in support of food production. There are also special activities in agrometeorology to monitor and combat drought and desertification, to apply climate and real-time weather information in agricultural planning and operations, and to help improve the efficiency of the use of human labour, land, water and energy in agriculture; close co-operation is maintained with FAO, centres of CGIAR and UNEP. The 16th World Meteorological Congress (2011) approved the use of a standardized meteorological drought index to enhance drought monitoring and early warning systems.

Aeronautical Meteorology Programme: provides operational meteorological information required for safe, regular and efficient air navigation, as well as meteorological assistance to non-real-time activities of the aviation industry. The objective is to ensure the world-wide provision of cost-effective and responsive aviation operations. The Programme is implemented at global, regional and national levels, the Commission for Aeronautical Meteorology (CAeM) playing a major role, taking into account relevant meteorological developments in science and technology, studying aeronautical requirements for meteorological services, promoting international standardization of methods, procedures and techniques, and considering requirements for basic and climatological data as well as aeronautical requirements for meteorological observations and specialized instruments and enhanced understanding and awareness of the impact of aviation on the environment. Activities under this Programme are carried out, where relevant, with the International Civil Aviation Organization (ICAO) and in collaboration with users of services provided to aviation.

Marine Meteorology and Oceanography Programme: undertakes operational monitoring of the oceans and the maritime atmosphere; collection, exchange, archival recording and management of marine data; processing of marine data, and the provision of marine meteorological and oceanographic services in support of the safety of life and property at sea and of the efficient and economic operation of all sea-based activities. The joint WMO/Intergovernmental Oceanographic Commission (IOC) Technical Commission for Oceanography and Marine Meteorology (JCOMM) has broad responsibilities in the overall management of the Programme. Many programme elements are undertaken jointly with the IOC, within the context of JCOMM, and also of the Global Ocean Observing System (GOOS). Close co-operation also occurs with the International Maritime Organization (IMO), as well as with other bodies both within and outside the UN system.

HYDROLOGY AND WATER RESOURCES PROGRAMME

The overall objective of this major Programme is to apply hydrology to meet the needs of sustainable development and use of water and related resources; for the mitigation of water-related disasters; and to ensure effective environment management at national and international levels. The 16th World Meteorological Congress (2011) determined that the Programme should be strengthened to meet a growing need for sustainable water resources management. The Programme consists of the following mutually supporting component programmes:

Programme on Basic Systems in Hydrology (BSH): provides the basis and framework for the majority of the scientific and technical aspects of WMO activities in hydrology and water resources. The BSH covers the collection, transmission and storage of data, the transfer of operationally proven technology through the Hydrological Operational Multipurpose System (HOMS), and the development of the World Hydrological Cycle Observing System

(WHYCOS), with the aim of improving countries' capacity to supply reliable water-related data, and manage and exchange accurate and timely water resources information.

Programme on Forecasting and Applications in Hydrology (FAH): covers aspects of the Hydrology and Water Resources Programme relating to hydrological modelling and forecasting, and to the application of hydrology in studies of global change. The FAH organizes activities in support of water resources development and management, and hazard mitigation, and promotes interdisciplinary co-operation to enhance flood forecasting at the national, regional and global level. The Programme is linked to the World Climate and Tropical Cyclone programmes.

Programme on Sustainable Development of Water Resources (SDW): encourages the full participation of hydrological services in national planning and in the implementation of actions consequent to the relevant recommendations of the United Nations Conference on Environment and Development (UNCED, held in Rio de Janeiro, Brazil, in 1992), and the World Summit on Sustainable Development (WSSD, held in Johannesburg, South Africa, in 2002).

Programme on Capacity Building in Hydrology and Water Resources (CBH): provides a framework under which National Hydrological Services (NHSs) are supported in their institutional development, through education and training activities, development of guidance material, assistance in the preparation of water legislation, reorganization of services and changes in administrative and legal frameworks.

Programme on Water-related Issues (WRI): maintains WMO's important role in international activities relating to water resource assessment and hydrological forecasting. A major aspect of this component programme is the organization's collaboration with other UN agencies.

Other WMO programmes contain hydrological elements, which are closely co-ordinated with the Hydrology and Water Resources Programme. These include the Tropical Cyclone Programme, the World Climate Programme, and the Global Energy and Water Budget Experiment of the World Climate Research Programme.

EDUCATION AND TRAINING PROGRAMME

The overall objective of this Programme is to assist members in developing adequately trained staff to meet their responsibilities for providing meteorological and hydrological information services.

Activities include surveys of the training requirements of member states, the development of appropriate training programmes, the monitoring and improvement of the network of 23 Regional Meteorological Training Centres, the organization of training courses, seminars and conferences and the preparation of training materials. The Programme also arranges individual training programmes and the provision of fellowships. The Panel of Experts on Education and Training was established by the Executive Council to serve as an advisory body on all aspects of technical and scientific education and of training in meteorology and operational hydrology.

TECHNICAL CO-OPERATION PROGRAMME

The objective of the WMO Technical Co-operation Programme is to assist developing countries in improving their meteorological and hydrological services so that they can serve the needs of their people more effectively. This is achieved through improving, *inter alia,* their early warning systems for severe weather; their agricultural-meteorological services, to facilitate more reliable and fruitful food production; and the assessment of climatological factors for economic planning. At a regional level the Programme concentrates on disaster prevention and mitigation. In 2006 a Severe Weather Forecasting Demonstration Project was launched in southeastern Africa; the 15th WMO Congress (2007) determined that this should be expanded and implemented throughout Africa and in the southwest Pacific region, and the 16th Congress decided that it should be expanded further.

Programme for the Least Developed Countries: has as its long-term objective enhancement of the capacities of the NMHSs of LDCs so that they can contribute efficiently and in a timely manner to socio-economic development efforts. Priority areas are poverty alleviation and natural disaster preparedness and mitigation. Specific projects will be developed for individual countries and at a sub-regional level for countries in Africa, Asia and the Pacific.

Voluntary Co-operation Programme (VCP): WMO assists members in implementing the WWW Programme to develop an integrated observing and forecasting system. Member governments contribute equipment, services and fellowships for training, in addition to cash donations.

WMO also carries out assistance projects under Trust Fund arrangements, financed by national authorities, either for activities in their own country or in a beneficiary country and managed by UNDP, the World Bank, regional development banks, the European Union and others. WMO provides assistance to UNDP in the development of national meteorological and hydrological services, in the application of meteorological and hydrological data to national economic development, and in the training of personnel.

REGIONAL PROGRAMME

WMO's Regional Programme cuts across the other major WMO programmes of relevance to the regions and addresses meteorological, hydrological and other geophysical issues which are unique to and of common concern to a region or group of regions. It provides a framework for the formulation of most of the global WMO Programmes and serves as a mechanism for their implementation at the national, subregional and regional levels. The Programme provides support to the WMO regional associations and contributes to the development of NMHSs through capacity-building and other priority activities identified by members or relevant economic groups and organizations within the respective regions.

NATURAL DISASTER PREVENTION AND MITIGATION PROGRAMME

The purpose of this cross-cutting Programme is to ensure the integration of relevant activities being carried out by the various WMO programmes in the area of disaster prevention and mitigation, and to provide for the effective co-ordination of pertinent WMO activities with the related activities of international, regional and national organizations, including civil defence organizations. The Programme should also provide scientific and technical support to WMO actions made in response to disaster situations, and its activities should emphasize pre-disaster preparedness and be based on activities within a number of WMO programmes, including the Public Weather Services and other components of the Applications of Meteorology Programme. The Programme will serve as a vehicle for enabling the delivery of increasingly accurate and reliable warnings of severe events, especially through co-ordinating WMO actions aimed at improving mechanisms and communications for the delivery, use and evaluation of warnings, provision of prompt advice and assistance to members; and at enhancing effective international co-operation and collaboration.

SPACE PROGRAMME

The 14th WMO Congress, held in 2003, initiated this new, cross-cutting programme to increase the effectiveness of, and contributions from, satellite systems for WMO programmes. Congress recognized the critical importance of data, products and services provided by the expanded space-based component of the GCOS. In recent years the use by WMO members of satellite data, products and services has grown tremendously, to the benefit of almost all WMO programmes and WMO-supported programmes. The 53rd session of the Executive Council adopted a landmark decision to expand the space-based component of the GCOS to include appropriate research and development ('R&D') and environmental satellite missions. The Congress agreed that the Commission for Basic Systems should continue to play a leading role, in full consultation with the other technical commissions for the Space Programme. Anticipated benefits from the Programme include an increasing contribution to the development of the GCOS, as well as to that of other WMO-supported programmes and associated observing systems, through the provision of continuously improved data, products and services, from both operational and R&D satellites. The Programme also aims to facilitate and promote the wider availability and meaningful utilization worldwide of such improved data. The 16th Congress agreed to pursue the development of an architecture for climate monitoring from space.

INTERNATIONAL POLAR DECADE AND GLOBAL CRYOSPHERE WATCH

WMO considers the polar regions (including the 'Third Pole'—the Himalayan and Tibetan Plateau) as extremely important in terms of their impact on global weather, water and climate. WMO, jointly with the International Council for Science, sponsored the International Polar Year (IPY), which was observed during March 2007–March 2008, although the full scientific programme associated with the IPY covered two annual cycles over the period March 2007–March 2009. The IPY focused on the Arctic and Antarctic polar regions and involved more than 200 projects addressing a wide range of physical, biological and social areas of research. The 16th World Meteorological Congress (2011) agreed to work with other international organizations to organize a future International Polar Decade. The 16th Congress also supported the need to establish an observational framework for polar regions, including an Antarctic Observing Network; determined to support a Global Integrated Polar Prediction System; and decided to develop, with international partners, the Global Cryosphere Watch. The Congress emphasized the significance, in terms of climate change prediction, of the cryosphere—i.e. water in its frozen state, including snow cover, sea, lake and river ice, glaciers, ice caps, ice sheets and permafrost, spanning all latitudes, in approximately 100 countries.

CO-OPERATION WITH OTHER BODIES

As a Specialized Agency of the UN, WMO actively participates in the UN system. Within the 'UN Delivering as One' process WMO and UNESCO were assigned the lead role in developing a Climate Knowledge Base. WMO, in addition, has concluded a number of formal agreements and working arrangements with international organizations both within and outside the UN system, at the intergovernmental and non-governmental level. As a result, WMO participates in major international conferences convened under the auspices of the UN or other organizations. In 1988 WMO, jointly with UNEP, established the Intergovernmental Panel on Climate Change as an advisory scientific body concerned with assessing and reporting the scientific, technical and socio-economic information relating to climate change. In response to the first report of the Panel, published in 1990, WMO and UNEP worked together to formulate the UN Framework Convention on Climate Change, which was signed in May 1992 and entered into force in March 1994. Other co-sponsored programmes are the World Climate Research Programme, the Global Climate Observing System, and the Global Ocean Observing System.

INTERNATIONAL DAY

World Meteorological Day is observed every year on 23 March. The theme in 2012 was 'Powering our future with weather, climate and water'.

Finance

WMO is financed by contributions from members on a proportional scale of assessment. For the 16th financial period, the four years 2012–15, a regular budget of 276m. Swiss francs was approved, and voluntary resources were projected at 175m. Swiss francs. Outside this budget, WMO implements a number of projects as executing agency for UNDP or else under trust fund.

Publications

Annual Report.

MeteoWorld.

WMO Bulletin (quarterly in English, French, Russian and Spanish).

World Climate News.

Reports, technical regulations, manuals and notes and training publications.

World Tourism Organization—UNWTO

Address: Capitán Haya 42, 28020 Madrid, Spain.

Telephone: (91) 5678100; **fax:** (91) 5713733; **e-mail:** omt@unwto.org; **internet:** www.world-tourism.org.

The World Tourism Organization (UNWTO) was formally established in 1975 following transformation of the International Union of Official Travel Organisations into an intergovernmental body, in accordance with a resolution of the UN General Assembly approved in 1969. The organization became a specialized agency of the UN in December 2003. It aims to promote and develop sustainable tourism, in particular in support of socio-economic growth in developing countries.

MEMBERS

155 member states, seven territories as associate members, 418 affiliate members.

Organization

(April 2012)

GENERAL ASSEMBLY

The General Assembly meets every two years to approve the budget and programme of work of the organization and to consider issues of concern for the tourism sector. It consists of representatives of all full and associate members; affiliate members and representatives of other international organizations participate as observers. The 19th General Assembly was convened in Gyeongju, Republic of Korea, in October 2011.

EXECUTIVE COUNCIL

The Council, comprising 29 members elected by the General Assembly, is the governing body responsible for supervising the activities of the organization. It meets twice a year. The following specialized committees are subsidiary organs of the Council and advise on management and programme content: Programme; Budget and Finance; Statistics and Macroeconomic Analysis of Tourism; Market Intelligence and Promotion; Sustainable Development of Tourism; and Quality Support and Trade. In addition, there is a World Committee on Tourism Ethics and a Sub-committee for the Review of Applications for Affiliate Membership.

REGIONAL COMMISSIONS

There are six regional commissions, comprising all members and associate members from that region, which meet at least once a year to determine the organization's priorities and future activities in the region. The commissions cover Africa, the Americas, East Asia and the Pacific, Europe, the Middle East, and South Asia.

SECRETARIAT

The Secretariat is responsible for implementing the organization's work programme. The Secretary-General is supported by three Executive Directors, all based at headquarters. A regional support office for Asia and the Pacific is based in Osaka, Japan. Six regional representatives, based at the Secretariat, support national tourism authorities, act as a liaison between those authorities and international sources of finance, and represent the body at national and regional events.

Secretary-General: TALEB RIFAI (Jordan).

AFFILIATE MEMBERS

UNWTO is unique as an intergovernmental body in extending membership to operational representatives of the industry and other related sectors, for example transport companies, educational institutions, insurance companies, publishing groups. A UNWTO Education Council aims to support UNWTO's education and human resource development activities. It undertakes research projects, grants awards for innovation and the application of knowledge in tourism, and co-ordinates a tourism labour market observatory project. The UNWTO Business Council groups together the affiliate members from the private sector and aims to promote and facilitate partnerships between the industry and governments. A third group of the affiliate membership is the UNWTO Destinations Council, which acts as an operational body supporting the UNWTO Destination Management programme with particular concern for issues relevant to tourist destinations, for example local tourism marketing, economic measurements and management of congestion.

Chair. of Board of UNWTO Affiliate Members: EULOGIO BORDAS (Spain).

Activities

The World Tourism Organization promotes the development of responsible, sustainable and universally accessible tourism within the broad context of contributing to economic development, international prosperity and peace and respect for human rights. As a UN specialized agency UNWTO aims to emphasize the role of tourism as a means of supporting socio-economic development and achieving the UN Millennium Development Goals (MDGs). Through its network of affiliated members UNWTO extends its activities and objectives to the private sector, tourism authorities and educational institutions. In October 2008 the Executive Council approved the establishment of a Tourism Resilience Committee, which was to consider the response of the tourist industry to the deterioration of the global economy and the role of tourism in economic stimulus programmes. The Committee convened for the first time in January 2009. In September WMO published a 'Roadmap for Recovery' which highlighted the role of tourism and travel in job creation and economic recovery, including its contribution to creating a 'green economy'. The Roadmap was endorsed by the General Assembly, meeting in October. At that time ministers of tourism of several industrialized and developing economies determined to form a grouping to promote the Roadmap at high-level international discussions. Meetings of the so-called T.20 were subsequently convened, with the full support of UNWTO, in Johannesburg, South Africa, in February 2010; in Buyeo, Republic of Korea, in October of that year; and in Paris, France, in October 2011; with the fourth to be held in Mérida, Mexico, in May 2012. In March 2011 UNWTO, with the Government of Andorra, organized an inaugural Global Tourism Forum, which brought together representatives of international agencies, private sector companies, and other partners, to promote the role of tourism in a sustainable global economic recovery and to harness collective support for the competitive and responsible development of the tourism sector.

DEVELOPMENT ASSISTANCE

UNWTO aims to support member states to develop and promote their tourist industry in order to contribute to socio-economic growth and poverty alleviation. Activities to transfer technical skills and knowledge to developing countries are fundamental tasks for the organization. It aims to assist member countries to develop tourism plans and strategies and helps to secure and manage specific development projects, for example the formulation of tourism legislation in Syria, hotel classification in Bolivia and statistics development in Botswana. Other aspects of developing tourism concern the involvement of local communities, fostering public-private partnerships and the preservation of cultural and natural heritage. UNWTO maintains a register of specialized consultants and firms to undertake appropriate missions.

In September 2002 at the World Summit on Sustainable Development, held in Johannesburg, South Africa, UNWTO, in collaboration with the UN Conference on Trade and Development (UNCTAD), launched the Sustainable Tourism-Eliminating Poverty (ST-EP) initiative. It aimed to encourage social, economic and ecologically sustainable tourism with the aim of alleviating poverty in the world's poorest countries. In September 2004 UNWTO signed an agreement with the Republic of Korea providing for the establishment of a ST-EP Foundation in the capital, Seoul. UNWTO has conducted a series of capacity-building seminars and other training activities concerning tourism and poverty alleviation, within the framework of the ST-EP initiative. It convenes an annual ST-EP forum, in Berlin, Germany, to involve a range of tourism agencies and companies in the scheme. Project identification missions have been conducted in some 30 developing countries with a focus on local level tourism development and small-scale entrepreneurial schemes. The first Pan-African Conference on Sustainable Tourism Management in African National Parks and Protected Areas was scheduled to be convened by UNWTO in Arusha, Tanzania, in October 2012.

MARKET, COMPETITIVENESS AND STATISTICS

UNWTO aims to ensure that quality standards and safety and security aspects are incorporated into all tourism products and services. It is also concerned with the social impact of tourism and the regulatory trading framework. UNWTO has formulated international standards for tourism measurement and reporting. It compiles comprehensive tourism statistics and forecasts. A Tourism Satellite Account (TSA) was developed to analyse the economic impact of tourism. It was endorsed by the UN Statistical Commission in 2000 and is recognized as a framework for providing internationally comparable data. (An updated Recommended Methodological Framework was introduced in 2008.) The TSA is also considered by UNWTO to be a strategic project within the broader objective of developing a system of tourism statistics. In October 2005 a world conference on TSAs, held in the Iguazu region of Argentina, Brazil and Paraguay, agreed on 10 defined objectives to extend and develop the use of TSAs. Further international conferences on tourism statistics have been held in Malaga, Spain, in October 2008, and in Bali, Indonesia, in March–April 2009.

UNWTO assists governments and tourist professionals to identify, analyse and forecast tourism trends and to assess the relative performance of each country's tourist industry. The organization also assists member states with tourism promotion through marketing tools and the formulation of tourism development strategies. A Market Intelligence and Promotion Committee was formally established in October 2002. Following the terrorism attacks against targets in the USA in September 2001 a Tourism Recovery Committee was established to monitor events affecting tourism, to help to restore confidence in the industry and to strengthen UNWTO activities concerned with safety and security.

In 1991 UNWTO's General Assembly approved a series of Recommended Measures for Tourism Safety which member states were encouraged to apply. UNWTO has established a Safety and Security in Tourism Network to consider aspects of the recommended measures and to facilitate collaboration between institutions and experts concerned with safety and security issues. The Network publishes national factsheets on safety and security in countries and tourist destinations, compiled by a designated national tourism administration focal point, for use by tourism professionals and the general public. Other essential quality standards promoted by the organization are hygiene and food safety, accessibility, product and pricing transparency and authenticity. UNWTO is also concerned with ensuring that tourist activities are in keeping with the surrounding environment.

In January 2005 the Executive Council convened its first ever emergency session in response to the devastation of many coastal areas in the Indian Ocean caused by a series of earthquakes and tsunamis at the end of 2004. The Council, meeting in Phuket, Thailand, along with other regional organizations, private sector representatives and tourism experts, adopted an action plan to support the recovery of the tourism sector in many of the affected areas, to help to restore tourist confidence in the region and to rehabilitate tourism infrastructure, in particular in Thailand, the Maldives, Indonesia and Sri Lanka. A co-ordinating unit to oversee the longer-term projects was established in February 2005 and its functions were integrated into UNWTO's broader emergency response framework in mid-2006. In 2005 UNWTO pledged its commitment to working with governments and the private sector to incorporate tourism concerns into preparedness programmes relating to the threat of highly pathogenic avian influenza. A Tourism Emergency Response Network (TERN) was established in April 2006 as a grouping of travel organizations committed to supporting UN efforts to respond to avian influenza and the threat of a potential human pandemic. UNWTO maintains a tourism emergency tracking system, which identifies recent outbreaks of the disease. In 2008 UNWTO developed a new online service, SOS.travel, to support crisis preparedness and management within the tourist industry and to enable individual travellers to enhance their own personal safety and security.

UNWTO participates as an observer at the World Trade Organization on issues relating to trade in tourism services, with particular concern to negotiations under the General Agreement on Trade in Services (GATS) for a separate annex on tourism. UNWTO hosts a voluntary working group on liberalization.

In order to generate awareness of tourism among the international community UNWTO sponsors a World Tourism Day, held each year on 27 September. In 2011 the official events were hosted by Egypt, focusing on 'Linking Cultures'. The theme of the 2012 events was to be 'Tourism and Sustainable Energy: Powering Sustainable Development'.

SUSTAINABLE TOURISM DEVELOPMENT

UNWTO aims to encourage and facilitate the application of sustainable practices within the tourism industry. It publishes guides on sustainable development and compilations for good practices for use by local authorities. UNWTO has also published manuals for tourism planning at regional, national and local level and has organized seminars on planning issues in developing countries. UNWTO actively promotes voluntary initiatives for sustainability including labelling schemes, certification systems and awards.

In 1999 UNWTO was mandated, together with the UN Environment Programme, to assume responsibility for the International Year of Ecotourism which was held in 2002, as well as all preparatory and follow-up activities. A World Ecotourism Summit, which was convened in Québec, Canada in May, was attended by delegates from 132 countries. It resulted in the Québec Declaration, containing guidelines for sustainable ecotourism development and management. UNWTO publishes a series of compilations of good practices for small and medium-sized businesses involved with ecotourism. UNWTO sponsored the first International Conference on Climate Change and Tourism, which was held in Djerba, Tunisia, in April 2003. A final declaration of the conference urged that UNWTO take the lead in focusing international attention on the issue and called upon all parties to continue research efforts, to encourage sustainability in tourism, to generate awareness and to implement defined actions. The second International Conference on Climate Change and Tourism, organized by UNWTO, UNEP and WMO, was convened in Davos, Switzerland, in October 2007. The meeting concluded the Davos Declaration, which urged greater action by the tourism sector to respond to the challenges of climate change, for example by employing new energy efficiency technologies, in order to support the objectives of the UN Millennium Development Goals. UNWTO supported the development of a new initiative to promote responsible and sustainable tourism, which was inaugurated as the 'Live the Deal' global campaign during the 15th Conference of the Parties to the UN Framework Convention on Climate Change, held in Copenhagen, Denmark, in December 2009.

In January 2011 UNWTO and UNEP launched the Global Partnership for Sustainable Tourism, also comprising other UN agencies, the OECD, 18 governments, and other partners, with the aim of guiding policy and developing projects in the area of sustainable tourism, providing a global platform for discussion, and facilitating progress towards a green economy.

In May 2011 UNWTO participated in a special event on Tourism for Sustainable Development and Poverty Reduction, which was organized at the fourth UN Conference on Least Developed Countries (LDC-IV), held in Istanbul, Turkey. Tourism is a major source of export earnings in more than one-half of LDCs.

In early 2012 UNWTO and the Ramsar Convention on Wetlands jointly supported the annual celebration, on 2 February, of World Wetlands Day, on the theme 'Wetlands and Tourism'; the two bodies collaborated at that time in producing information material on the topic of sustainable tourism and Wetland sites (such as the Great Barrier Reef, Australia, and the Okavango Delta in Botswana).

In 1997 a Task Force for the Protection of Children from Sexual Exploitation in Tourism was established by UNWTO as a forum for governments, industry associations and other organizations to work together with the aim of identifying, preventing and eradicating the sexual exploitation of children. In March 2007 the mandate of the Task Force was expanded to include protection of children and young people against all forms of exploitation in tourism, including child labour and trafficking. In November 2008 the Task Force, meeting during the World Travel Market in London, United Kingdom, inaugurated a new 'Protect Children Campaign' to generate awareness of the abuse of children and to harness global support for its protection efforts. In 1999 the General Assembly adopted a Global Code of Ethics for Tourism. The Code, which was endorsed by a special resolution of the UN General Assembly in 2001, aims to protect resources upon which tourism depends and to ensure that the economic benefits of tourism are distributed equitably. A World Committee on Tourism Ethics, established in 2003 to support the implementation of the Code, held its first meeting in Rome, Italy, in February 2004 and has subsequently been convened on an annual basis. A permanent secretariat for the Committee was inaugurated in November 2008. In March 2000 UNWTO, with UNESCO and UNEP, established a Tour Operators Initiative to encourage socially responsible tourism development within the industry.

In November 2007 the General Assembly resolved to appoint the organization's first Special Adviser on Women and Tourism.

In 1994 UNWTO, in co-operation with UNESCO, initiated a project to promote tourism, in support of economic development, along the traditional Silk Road trading routes linking Asia and Europe. In October 2004 a Silk Road Tourism Office was opened in Samarkand, Uzbekistan. In December 2008 UNWTO, in collaboration with UNDP, initiated a UN Silk Road City award scheme further to promote tourism and development along the trading route. In October 2009 the General Assembly adopted the Astana Declaration in support of a Silk Road Initiative, which aimed to promote the tourism potential of the countries along the Silk Road. The fifth international meeting of participants in the Silk Road project was convened in Samarkand, in October 2010. Representatives of 26 countries endorsed UNWTO's development of a Silk Road Action Plan. An updated Silk Road Action Plan was approved at a ministerial meeting held in March 2012, in Berlin, Germany. In 1995 UNWTO and UNESCO launched the Slave Route project to stimulate tourism and raise cultural awareness in several West African countries. In October 2007 UNWTO hosted an International Conference on Tourism, Religion and the Dialogue of Cultures, in Córdoba, Spain, to contribute to the discussion and promotion of the UN initiative for an Alliance of Civilizations.

EDUCATION AND KNOWLEDGE MANAGEMENT

UNWTO is committed to supporting education and training within the tourism industry and to developing a network of specialized research and training institutes. Most activities are undertaken by the UNWTO Education Council and the Themis Foundation. A specialized office concerned with human resource development was opened in September 2003, in Andorra. In September 2010 UNWTO inaugurated a Knowledge Network (UNWTO.Know) of institutes, universities, and public and private organizations, with the aim of facilitating a broad approach to the development of tourism policy, governance and practices. The inaugural meeting of UNWTO.Know took place in Madrid, Spain, in January 2011. In June of that year the Network, which by that time comprised more than 120 institutions from 40 countries, organized the UNWTO Algarve Forum, held in Vilamoura, Portugal, with participation by more than 300 representatives from the tourism sector, as well as academics. The Forum, conceived as a means of bridging theory and practice in tourism, adopted the Algarve Consensus, detailing guidelines and policy programmes aimed at directing the future development and good governance of the sector.

UNWTO Themis Foundation: Avinguda Dr Vilanova 9, Edif. Thaïs 4c, Andorra la Vella, Andorra; tel. 802600; fax 829955; e-mail wto.themis@andorra.ad; internet themis.unwto.org; aims to promote quality and efficiency in tourism education and training. Works closely with the human resource development programme of UNWTO and promotes UNWTO's specialized training products and services, in particular the TedQual certification and the Practicum programme for tourism officials; Exec. Dir Omar Valdez.

INFORMATION AND COMMUNICATIONS

In January 2004 UNWTO hosted the first World Conference on Tourism Communications. Regular regional conferences have since been organized, within the framework of a Special Programme for Capacity Sharing in International Tourism Communications (TOURCOM), to enhance the capacity of regional and national tourism authorities to apply international standards and best practices to the promotion and communication of tourism.

UNWTO aims to act as a clearing house of information for the tourist industry. A UNWTO Documentation Centre collates extensive information on tourism activities and promotes access to and exchange of information among member states and affiliated partners. The Centre offers access to tourism legislation and other regulatory procedures through its LEXTOUR database on the internet. The Centre also administers a tourism information database (INFODOCTOUR). A Thesaurus on Tourism and Leisure Activities was published in 2001.

Finance

The budget for the two-year period 2012–13 amounted to €25.2m.

Publications

Compendium of Tourism Statistics.

Tourism Market Trends (annually).

Yearbook of Tourism Statistics.

UNWTOBC Interactive (monthly).

UNWTO News (3 a year, in English, French and Spanish).

UNWTO World Tourism Barometer (3 a year).

Other research or statistical reports, studies, guidelines and factsheets.

AFRICAN DEVELOPMENT BANK—AfDB

Address: Statutory headquarters: rue Joseph Anoma, 01 BP 1387, Abidjan 01, Côte d'Ivoire.

Telephone: 20-20-44-44; **fax:** 20-20-49-59; **e-mail:** afdb@afdb.org; **internet:** www.afdb.org.

Address: Temporary relocation agency: 15 ave du Ghana, angle des rues Pierre de Coubertin et Hedi Nouira, BP 323, 1002 Tunis Belvédère, Tunisia.

Telephone: (71) 103-900; **fax:** (71) 351-933.

Established in 1964, the Bank began operations in July 1966, with the aim of financing economic and social development in African countries. The Bank's headquarters are officially based in Abidjan, Côte d'Ivoire. Since February 2003, however, in view of ongoing insecurity in Côte d'Ivoire, the Bank's operations have been conducted, on a long-term temporary basis, from Tunis, Tunisia.

AFRICAN MEMBERS*

Algeria	Equatorial Guinea	Namibia
Angola	Eritrea	Niger
Benin	Ethiopia	Nigeria
Botswana	Gabon	Rwanda
Burkina Faso	The Gambia	São Tomé and Príncipe
Burundi	Ghana	Senegal
Cameroon	Guinea	Seychelles
Cape Verde	Guinea-Bissau	Sierra Leone
Central African Republic	Kenya	Somalia
Chad	Lesotho	South Africa
Comoros	Liberia	Sudan
Congo, Democratic Republic	Libya	Swaziland
Congo, Republic	Madagascar	Tanzania
Côte d'Ivoire	Malawi	Togo
Djibouti	Mali	Tunisia
Egypt	Mauritania	Uganda
	Mauritius	Zambia
	Morocco	Zimbabwe
	Mozambique	

* An application for full membership of the Bank was submitted in May 2011 by the authorities of South Sudan (which, in July, became an independent state); this remained under review at April 2012. In September 2011 the Bank and the South Sudan Government signed an agreement on general co-operation, enabling the extension of financial and technical support to South Sudan pending that country's accession to full Bank membership.

There are also 24 non-African members.

Organization

(April 2012)

BOARD OF GOVERNORS

The highest policy-making body of the Bank, which also elects the Board of Directors and the President. Each member country nominates one Governor, usually its Minister of Finance and Economic Affairs, and an alternate Governor or the Governor of its Central Bank. The Board meets once a year. The 2012 meeting was scheduled to be convened in Arusha, Tanzania, in May–June.

BOARD OF DIRECTORS

The Board, elected by the Board of Governors for a term of three years, is responsible for the general operations of the Bank and meets on a weekly basis. The Board has 20 members.

OFFICERS

The President is responsible for the organization and the day-to-day operations of the Bank under guidance of the Board of Directors. The President is elected for a five-year term and serves as the Chairman of the Board of Directors. The President oversees the following senior management: Chief Economist; Vice-Presidents of Finance, Corporate Services, Country and Regional Programmes and Policy, Sector Operations, and Infrastructure, Private Sector and Regional Integration; Auditor General; General Counsel; Secretary-General; and Ombudsman. Bank field offices are located in some 27 member countries under a strategy of decentralization. The Bank plans to establish external representation offices in Tokyo, Japan; Brussels, Belgium; and in Washington, DC, USA.

Executive President and Chairman of Board of Directors: DONALD KABERUKA (Rwanda).

FINANCIAL STRUCTURE

The African Development Bank (AfDB) Group of development financing institutions comprises the African Development Fund (ADF) and the Nigeria Trust Fund (NTF), which provide concessionary loans, and the AfDB itself. The Group uses a unit of account (UA), which, at December 2010, was valued at US $1.54003.

The capital stock of the Bank was at first exclusively open for subscription by African countries, with each member's subscription consisting of an equal number of paid-up and callable shares. In 1978, however, the Governors agreed to open the capital stock of the Bank to subscription by non-regional states on the basis of nine principles aimed at maintaining the African character of the institution. The decision was finally ratified in May 1982, and the participation of non-regional countries became effective on 30 December. It was agreed that African members should still hold two-thirds of the share capital, that all loan operations should be restricted to African members, and that the Bank's President should always be an African national. In May 1998 the Board of Governors approved an increase in capital of 35%, and resolved that the non-African members' share of the capital be increased from 33.3% to 40%. In May 2010 the Board of Governors approved a general capital increase of 200%. At 31 December 2010 the Bank's authorized capital was UA 67,687.5m. (compared with UA 22,120.0m. at the end of 2009); subscribed capital at the end of 2010 was UA 23,924.6m. (of which the paid-up portion was UA 2,375.6m.).

Activities

At the end of 2010 the Bank Group had approved total lending of UA 62,228.7m. since the beginning of its operations in 1967. In 2010 the Group approved 139 lending operations amounting to UA 4,099.8m., compared with UA 8,064.5m. in the previous year when there was exceptional demand for short-term trade and credit facilities from member countries adversely affected by the global financial and economic crisis. Of the total amount approved in 2010 UA 3,674.5m. was for loans and grants, UA 203.0m. for heavily indebted poor countries (HIPC) debt relief, UA 189.9m. for equity participation and UA 32.4m. for special funds. Of the total loans and grants approved in 2010, UA 2,603.6m. (71%) was for infrastructure projects (of which UA 1,239.4m. was for transportation).

In 2006 the Bank established a High Level Panel of eminent personalities to advise on the Bank's future strategic vision. The Panel issued its report, 'Investing in Africa's future—The AfDB in the 21st Century', in February 2008. In May the Bank's President announced that the new medium-term strategy for 2008–12 was to focus on the achievement of the Millennium Development Goals (MDGs) and on shared and sustainable economic growth. It envisaged a significant increase in Bank operations and in its institutional capacity. In mid-2008 the Bank established an African Food Crisis Response initiative to extend accelerated support to members affected by the sharp increase in the cost of food and food production. The initiative aimed to reduce short-term food poverty and malnutrition, with funds of some UA 472.0m., and to support long-term sustainable food security, with funding of UA 1,400m. In February 2009 the Bank hosted a meeting of the heads of multilateral development banks and of the IMF to discuss recent economic developments, the responses of each institution and future courses of action. In March the Bank's Board of Directors endorsed four new initiatives to help to counter the effects of the crisis: the establishment of an Emergency Liquidity Facility, with funds of some US $1,500m., to assist members with short-term financing difficulties; a new Trade Finance Initiative, with funds of up to $1,000m., to provide credit for trade financing operations; a Framework for the Accelerated Resource Transfer of ADF Resources; and enhanced policy advisory support. The Bank also agreed to contribute $500m. to a multinational Global Trade Liquidity Program, which commenced operations in mid-2009. In September the Bank initiated a consultative process for a sixth general capital increase. An increase of 200% was endorsed by a committee of the governing body representing the Bank's shareholders, meeting in April 2010, in order to enable the Bank to sustain its increased level of lending. The capital increase was formally approved by the Board of Governors in May.

In November 2008 the Bank hosted a special conference of African ministers of finance and central bank governors to consider the impact on the region of the contraction of the world's major economies and the recent volatility of global financial markets. The meeting determined to establish a Committee of African Finance Ministers and Central Bank Governors, comprising 10 representatives from each Bank region, with a mandate to examine further the impact of the global financial crisis on Africa, to review the responses by member governments, and to develop policy options. The so-called Committee of Ten (C10) convened for its inaugural meeting in Cape Town, South Africa, in January 2009. In March the C10 adopted a paper outlining the major concerns of African countries in preparation for the meeting of heads of state of the Group of 20 (G20) leading economies, held in London, United Kingdom, in early April. The third meeting of the Committee, held in Abuja, Nigeria, in July, reviewed economic indicators and developments since the G20 meeting and appealed for all commitments to low-income countries pledged at the summit to be met. The Committee also issued a series of messages for the next G20 summit meeting, held in Pittsburgh, USA, in September, including a request for greater African participation in the G20 process and in international economic governance. The fourth meeting of the C10, convened in February 2010, determined that it should meet formally two times a year, with other informal meetings and meetings of deputies to be held in between; the Secretariat of the Committee was to be provided by the AfDB.

In May 2011 the Group of Eight (G8) industrialized nations, in collaboration with regional and international financial institutions and the governments of Egypt and Tunisia, established a Deauville Partnership to support political and economic reforms being undertaken by several countries in North Africa and the Middle East, notably Egypt, Jordan, Morocco and Tunisia. The AfDB supported the establishment of the Partnership and was to chair a Co-ordination Platform. In September Kuwait, Qatar, Saudi Arabia, Turkey and the UAE joined the Partnership.

Since 1996 the Bank has collaborated closely with international partners, in particular the World Bank, in efforts to address the problems of HIPCs (see IBRD). Of the 41 countries identified as potentially eligible for assistance under the scheme, 33 were in sub-Saharan Africa. Following the introduction of an enhanced framework for the initiative, the Bank has been actively involved in the preparation of Poverty Reduction Strategy Papers, that provide national frameworks for poverty reduction programmes. In April 2006 the Board of Directors endorsed a new Multilateral Debt Relief Initiative (MDRI), which provided for 100% cancellation of eligible debts from the ADF, the IMF and the International Development Association to secure additional resources for countries to help them attain their MDGs. ADF's participation in the MDRI, which became effective in September, was anticipated to provide some UA 5,570m. (US $8,540m.) in debt relief.

The Bank contributed funds for the establishment, in 1986, of the Africa Project Development Facility, which assists the private sector in Africa by providing advisory services and finance for entrepreneurs: it was managed by the International Finance Corporation (IFC), until replaced by the Private Enterprise Partnership for Africa in April 2005. In 1989 the Bank, in co-ordination with IFC and the UN Development Programme (UNDP), created the African Management Services Company (AMSCo), which provides management support and training to private companies in Africa. The Bank is one of three multilateral donors, with the World Bank and UNDP, supporting the African Capacity Building Foundation, which was established in 1991 to strengthen and develop institutional and human capacity in support of sustainable development activities. The Bank hosts the secretariat of an Africa Investment Consortium, which was inaugurated in October 2005 by several major African institutions and donor countries to accelerate efforts to develop the region's infrastructure. An Enhanced Private Sector Assistance Initiative was established, with support from the Japanese Government, in 2005 to support the Bank's strategy for the development of the private sector. The Initiative incorporated an Accelerated Cofinancing Facility for Africa and a Fund for African Private Sector Assistance. In October 2010 the Board of Directors agreed to convert the Fund into a multi-donor trust fund.

In November 2006 the Bank Group, with the UN Economic Commission for Africa (ECA), organized an African Economic Conference (AEC), which has since become an annual event. The sixth AEC was held in Addis Ababa, in October 2011, on the theme 'Green Economy and Structural Transformation in Africa'. In September 2011 the Bank organized a regional meeting on peace-building and state-building in Africa, in preparation for the Fourth High Level Forum on Aid Effectiveness, which was held in Busan, Republic of Korea, in November–December.

In March 2000 African ministers of water resources endorsed an African Water Vision and a Framework for Action to pursue the equitable and sustainable use and management of water resources in Africa in order to facilitate socio-economic development, poverty alleviation and environmental protection. An African Ministers' Council on Water (AMCOW) was established in April 2002 to provide the political leadership and focus for implementation of the Vision and the Framework for Action. AMCOW requested the Bank to establish and administer an African Water Facility Special Fund, in order to provide the financial requirements for achieving their objectives; this became operational in December. In March the Bank approved a Rural Water Supply and Sanitation Initiative to accelerate access in member countries to sustainable safe water and basic sanitation, in order to meet the requirements of several MDGs. In March 2008 the Bank hosted the first African Water Week, organized jointly with AMCOW, on the theme of 'Accelerating Water Security for the Socio-economic Development of Africa'. The Bank co-ordinated and led Africa's regional participation in the Sixth World Water Forum, which was held in Marseilles, France, in March 2012. The Bank was actively involved in preparing for the fourth Africa Carbon Forum, which was convened in Addis Ababa, Ethiopia, in April 2012 (previous fora having been held in September 2008, March 2010 and July 2011).

The Bank hosts the secretariat of the Congo Basin Forest Fund, which was established in June 2008, as a multi-donor facility, with initial funding from Norway and the United Kingdom, to protect and manage the forests in that region.

The Bank provides technical assistance to regional member countries in the form of experts' services, pre-investment feasibility studies, and staff training. Much of this assistance is financed through bilateral trust funds contributed by non-African member states. The Bank's African Development Institute provides training for officials of regional member countries in order to enhance the management of Bank-financed projects and, more broadly, to strengthen national capacities for promoting sustainable development. The Institute also manages an AfDB/Japan Fellowship programme that provides scholarships to African students to pursue further education. A Joint Africa Institute, established jointly by the Bank, the World Bank and the IMF, was operational from November 1999–end-2009, offering training opportunities and strengthening capacity building. In 1990 the Bank established the African Business Round Table (ABR), which is composed of the chief executives of Africa's leading corporations. The ABR aims to strengthen Africa's private sector, promote intra-African trade and investment, and attract foreign investment to Africa. The ABR is chaired by the Bank's Executive President. In 2008 the Bank endorsed a Governance Strategic Directions and Action Plan as a framework for countering corruption and enhancing democratic governance in Africa in the period 2008–12.

In 1990 a Memorandum of Understanding (MOU) for the Reinforcement of Co-operation between the Organization of African Unity, now African Union (AU), the UN Economic Commission for Africa and the AfDB was signed by the three organizations. A joint secretariat supports co-operation activities between the organizations. In March 2009 a new Coalition for Dialogue on Africa (CoDA) was inaugurated by the Bank, the ECA and the AU. In 1999 a Co-operation Agreement was formally concluded between the Bank and the Common Market for Eastern and Southern Africa (COMESA). In March 2000 the Bank signed an MOU on its strategic partnership with the World Bank. Other MOUs were signed during that year with the United Nations Industrial Development Organization, the World Food Programme, and the Arab Maghreb Union. In September 2008 the Bank supported the establishment of an African Financing Partnership, which aimed to mobilize private sector resources through partnerships with regional development finance institutions. The Bank hosts the secretariat of the Partnership. It also hosts the secretariat of the Making Finance Work for Africa Partnership, which was established, by the G8, in October 2007, in order to support the development of the financial sector in the sub-Saharan region. In December 2010 the Bank signed an MOU with the Islamic Development Bank to promote economic development in common member countries through co-financing and co-ordinating projects in priority areas. It signed an MOU with the European Bank for Reconstruction and Development (EBRD) in September 2011. The Bank is actively involved in the New Partnership for Africa's Development (NEPAD), established in 2001 to promote sustainable development and eradicate poverty throughout the region. Since 2004 it has been a strategic partner in NEPAD's African Peer Review Mechanism. In 2011 the Bank supported the development of a Program for Infrastructure Development in Africa (PIDA), as a joint initiative with NEPAD and the AU.

AFRICAN DEVELOPMENT BANK

The Bank makes loans at a variable rate of interest, which is adjusted twice a year, plus a commitment fee of 0.75%. Lending approved amounted to UA 2,581.1m. for 59 operations in 2010, including resources allocated under the HIPC debt relief initiative, the Post-conflict Country Facility (see below), and equity participations, compared with UA 5,604.1m. for 84 loans in the previous year. Lending for private sector projects amounted to UA 1,206m. in 2010. Since October 1997 new fixed and floating rate loans have been made available.

AFRICAN DEVELOPMENT FUND

The ADF commenced operations in 1974. It grants interest-free loans to low-income African countries for projects with repayment over 50 years (including a 10-year grace period) and with a service charge of 0.75% per annum. Grants for project feasibility studies are made to the poorest countries.

In May 1994 donor countries withheld any new funds owing to dissatisfaction with the Bank's governance. In May 1996, following the implementation of various institutional reforms to strengthen the Bank's financial management and decision-making capabilities and to reduce its administrative costs, an agreement was concluded on the seventh replenishment of ADF resources. Donor countries pledged some US $2,690m. for the period 1996–98. An additional allocation of $420m. was endorsed at a special donors' meeting held in Osaka, Japan, in June. The seventh replenishment provided for the establishment of an ADF Microfinance Initiative (AMINA), initially for a two-year period, to support small-scale capacity-building projects. In January 1999 negotiations on the eighth replenishment of the Fund were concluded with an agreement to provide additional resources amounting to $3,437m. The replenishment was approved by the Board of Governors in May, and came into effect in December. In September 2002 donor countries pledged $3,500m. for the ninth replenishment of the Fund, covering the period 2002–04. The so-called ADF-10 was concluded in December 2004, with an agreement to replenish the Fund by some $5,400m. It was agreed that poverty reduction and the promotion of sustainable growth were to remain the principal objectives of the Fund for the period 2005–07. In December 2007 donor countries committed $8,900m. to replenish the Fund for the three-year period 2008–10, during which there was to be a focus on infrastructure, governance and regional integration. The funding arrangements for ADF-11 allocated UA 408m. to a new Fragile States Facility to support the poorer regional member countries, in particular those in a post-conflict or transitional state. The Facility was to incorporate the Post-Conflict Country Facility, which was established in 2003 to help certain countries to clear their arrears and accelerate their progress within the HIPC process. An agreement was concluded by donors in October 2010 to increase contributions to the Fund by 10.6%, to some $9,350m., under ADF-12, covering the period 2011–13. ADF-12 was to support ongoing institutional reform and capacity building, as well as efforts to stimulate economic growth in Africa's lowest income countries. Operational priorities included climate change adaptation and mitigation measures, regional economic integration, and private sector development.

In 2010 lending under the ADF amounted to UA 1,456.7m. for 65 projects, compared with UA 2,427.0m. for 77 projects in the previous year.

NIGERIA TRUST FUND

The Agreement establishing the NTF was signed in February 1976 by the Bank and the Government of Nigeria. The Fund is administered by the Bank and its loans are granted for up to 25 years, including grace periods of up to five years, and carry 0.75% commission charges and 4% interest charges. The loans are intended to provide financing for projects in co-operation with other lending institutions. The Fund also aims to promote the private sector and trade between African countries by providing information on African and international financial institutions able to finance African trade.

Operations under the NTF were suspended in 2006, pending a detailed assessment and consideration of the Fund's activities which commenced in November. The evaluation exercise was concluded in July 2007 and an agreement was reached in November to authorize the Fund to continue activities for a further 10-year period. Two operations, amounting to UA 29.5m., were approved in 2010.

Publications

Annual Report.

Annual Development Effectiveness Review.

AfDB Business Bulletin (10 a year).

AfDB Statistics Pocketbook.

AfDB Today (every 2 months).

African Competitiveness Report.

African Development Report (annually).

African Development Review (3 a year).

African Economic Outlook (annually, with OECD).

African Statistical Journal (2 a year).

Annual Procurement Report.

Economic Research Papers.

Gender, Poverty and Environmental Indicators on African Countries (annually).

OPEV Sharing (quarterly newsletter).

Quarterly Operational Summary.

Selected Statistics on African Countries (annually).

Summaries of operations and projects, background documents, Board documents.

Statistics

SUMMARY OF BANK GROUP OPERATIONS
(millions of UA)

	2009	2010	Cumulative total*
AfDB approvals†			
Number	84	59	1,259
Amount	5,604.07	2,581.13	36,008.07
Disbursements	2,352.29	1,339.85	20,541.59
ADF approvals†			
Number	77	65	2,387
Amount	2,426.96	1,456.72	25,708.19
Disbursements	1,726.43	1,165.84	14,801.85
NTF approvals			
Number	3	2	82
Amount	5.70	29.53	371.33
Disbursements	4.87	5.02	227.07
Special Funds‡			
Number	17	13	73
Amount approved	27.76	32.38	141.12
Group total†			
Number	181	139	3,801
Amount approved	8,064.49	4,099.75	62,228.72
Disbursements	4,083.59	2,510.70	35,570.51

* Since the initial operations of the three institutions (1967 for AfDB, 1974 for ADF and 1976 for NTF).

† Approvals include loans and grant operations, private and public equity investments, emergency operations, HIPC debt relief, loan reallocations and guarantees, the Post-Conflict Country Facility and the Fragile States Facility.

‡ The African Water Fund, the Rural Water Supply and Sanitation Initiative and the Global Environment Facility.

GROUP LOAN AND GRANT OPERATIONS BY SUB-REGION AND COUNTRY
(millions of UA)

Sub-region/Country	2009	2010	Cumulative total*
Central Africa			
Cameroon	43.4	71.7	1,015.8
Central African Republic	19.5	—	178.2
Chad	32.2	0.7	440.6
Congo, Democratic Republic	65.0	158.3	1,617.7
Congo, Republic	12.8	3.4	320.6
Equatorial Guinea	—	—	130.7
Gabon	102.0	0.5	1,029.4
Sub-total	274.9	234.6	4,733.0
East Africa			
Burundi	10.7	34.1	391.2
Comoros	15.9	0.6	82.7
Djibouti	0.3	—	179.2
Eritrea	2.0	12.9	93.7
Ethiopia	—	224.4	2,062.3
Kenya	135.0	116.7	1,249.1
Rwanda	57.3	41.1	579.2
Seychelles	13.7	0.3	104.4
Somalia	—	—	151.4
Sudan	—	0.7	361.5
Tanzania	152.0	129.6	1,626.6
Uganda	128.7	—	1,495.5
Sub-total	515.6	560.3	8,376.7
North Africa			
Algeria	0.5	—	1,890.2
Egypt	77.9	651.4	3,760.9
Libya	—	0.6	0.6
Mauritania	112.4	3.6	500.8
Morocco	583.0	519.7	5,637.5
Tunisia	276.7	296.6	4,460.3
Sub-total	1,050.4	1,471.9	16,250.4
Southern Africa			
Angola	12.0	—	369.3
Botswana	1,111.0	2.1	1,513.9
Lesotho	17.4	—	333.7

Sub-region/Country—*continued*	2009	2010	Cumulative total*
Madagascar	1.1	—	802.2
Malawi	49.1	14.7	754.6
Mauritius	437.9	0.3	751.2
Mozambique	31.6	37.9	1,180.9
Namibia	0.6	0.6	169.0
South Africa	1,732.9	403.7	3,184.4
Swaziland	—	0.3	300.4
Zambia	0.3	32.6	813.7
Zimbabwe	1.3	0.7	728.8
Sub-total	3,395.2	492.8	10,902.2
West Africa			
Benin	22.0	43.0	594.8
Burkina Faso	62.6	35.2	776.4
Cape Verde	37.0	20.5	237.7
Côte d'Ivoire	324.8	23.0	1,511.6
Gambia	9.0	—	243.1
Ghana	117.4	111.0	1,498.0
Guinea	5.2	—	718.3
Guinea-Bissau	14.1	5.7	207.1
Liberia	13.8	31.2	229.2
Mali	49.5	66.5	845.5
Niger	2.0	54.2	457.6
Nigeria	365.0	67.8	2,989.8
São Tomé and Príncipe	1.0	5.0	109.6
Senegal	169.5	70.8	939.7
Sierra Leone	36.3	29.2	356.9
Togo	12.8	32.5	247.4
Sub-total	1,242.0	595.8	11,962.8
Multinational	1,027.0	319.1	3,706.8
Total	7,505.7	3,674.5	55,932.0

* Since the initial operations of the three institutions (1967 for AfDB, 1974 for ADF and 1976 for NTF).

Source: African Development Bank, *Annual Report 2010*.

AFRICAN UNION—AU

Address: Roosvelt St, Old Airport Area, POB 3243, Addis Ababa, Ethiopia.

Telephone: (11) 5517700; **fax:** (11) 5517844; **e-mail:** webmaster@africa-union.org; **internet:** au.int.

In May 2001 the Constitutive Act of the African Union entered into force. In July 2002 the African Union (AU) became fully operational, replacing the Organization of African Unity (OAU), which had been founded in 1963. The AU aims to support unity, solidarity and peace among African states; to promote and defend African common positions on issues of shared interest; to encourage human rights, democratic principles and good governance; to advance the development of member states by encouraging research and by working to eradicate preventable diseases; and to promote sustainable development and political and socio-economic integration, including co-ordinating and harmonizing policy between the continent's various 'regional economic communities' (see below).

MEMBERS*

Algeria	Eritrea	Nigeria
Angola	Ethiopia	Rwanda
Benin	Gabon	São Tomé and Príncipe
Botswana	The Gambia	Senegal
Burkina Faso	Ghana	Seychelles
Burundi	Guinea	Sierra Leone
Cameroon	Guinea-Bissau	Somalia
Cape Verde	Kenya	South Africa
Central African Republic	Lesotho	South Sudan‡
Chad	Liberia	Sudan
Comoros	Libya	Swaziland
Congo, Democratic Republic	Madagascar†	Tanazania
Congo, Republic	Malawi	Togo
Côte d'Ivoire	Mali†	Tunisia
Dijbouti	Mauritania†	Uganda
Egypt	Mauritius	Zambia
Equatorial Guinea	Mozambique	Zimbabwe
	Namibia	
	Niger	

* The Sahrawi Arab Democratic Republic (SADR–Western Sahara) was admitted to the OAU in February 1982, following recognition by more than one-half of the member states, but its membership was disputed by Morocco and other states which claimed that a two-thirds' majority was needed to admit a state whose existence was in question. Morocco withdrew from the OAU with effect from November 1985, and has not applied to join the AU. The SADR ratified the Constitutive Act in December 2000 and is a full member of the AU.

† Mauritania's participation in the activities of the AU was suspended in August 2008, following the overthrow of its constitutional Government in a military *coup d'état*. In March 2009 Madagascar's participation in the activities of the AU was suspended, following the forced resignation of its elected President and transfer of power to the military. Mali was suspended from AU participation follow the overthrow of that country's Government by a military coup in March 2012, and, in April, Guinea-Bissau was also suspended following a military coup, pending the restoration of constitutional order.

‡ South Sudan was admitted as a member of the AU in August 2011.

Note: The Constitutive Act stipulates that member states in which Governments accede to power by unconstitutional means are liable to suspension from participating in the Union's activities and to the imposition of sanctions by the Union.

Organization

(April 2012)

ASSEMBLY

The Assembly, comprising member countries' heads of state and government, is the supreme organ of the Union and meets at least once a year (with alternate sessions held in Addis Ababa, Ethiopia) to determine and monitor the Union's priorities and common policies and to adopt its annual work programme. Resolutions are passed by a two-thirds' majority, procedural matters by a simple majority. Extraordinary sessions may be convened at the request of a member state and on approval by a two-thirds' majority. A chairperson is elected at each meeting from among the members, to hold office for one year. The Assembly ensures compliance by member states with decisions of the Union, adopts the biennial budget, appoints judges of the African Court of Human and Peoples' Rights, and hears and settles disputes between member states. The first regular Assembly meeting was held in Durban, South Africa, in July 2002, and a first extraordinary summit meeting of the Assembly was convened in Addis Ababa in February 2003. The 18th ordinary session of the Assembly took place in Addis Ababa, in January 2012. The 19th ordinary session was scheduled to be held in Lilongwe, Malawi, in June–July 2012. The theme of both 2012 summits was 'Boosting Intra-African Trade'.

Chairperson: (2012/13) YAYI BONI (Pres. of Benin).

EXECUTIVE COUNCIL

Consists of ministers of foreign affairs and others and meets at least twice a year (in February and July), with provision for extraordinary sessions. The Council's Chairperson is the minister of foreign affairs (or another competent authority) of the country that has provided the Chairperson of the Assembly. Prepares meetings of, and is responsible to, the Assembly. Determines the issues to be submitted to the Assembly for decision, co-ordinates and harmonizes the policies, activities and initiatives of the Union in areas of common interest to member states, and monitors the implementation of policies and decisions of the Assembly.

PERMANENT REPRESENTATIVES COMMITTEE

The Committee, which comprises Ambassadors accredited to the AU and meets at least once a month. It is responsible to the Executive Council, which it advises, and whose meetings, including matters for the agenda and draft decisions, it prepares.

COMMISSION

The Commission is the permanent secretariat of the organization. It comprises a Chairperson (elected for a four-year term of office by the Assembly), Deputy Chairperson and eight Commissioners (responsible for: peace and security; political affairs; infrastructure and energy; social affairs; human resources, science and technology; trade and industry; rural economy and agriculture; and economic affairs) who are elected on the basis of equal geographical distribution. Members of the Commission serve a term of four years and may stand for re-election for one further term of office. Further support staff assist the smooth functioning of the Commission. The Commission represents the Union under the guidance of, and as mandated by, the Assembly and the Executive Council, and reports to the Executive Council. It deals with administrative issues, implements the decisions of the Union, and acts as the custodian of the Constitutive Act and Protocols, and other agreements. Its work covers the following domains: control of pandemics; disaster management; international crime and terrorism; environmental management; negotiations relating to external trade; negotiations relating to external debt; population, migration, refugees and displaced persons; food security; socio-economic integration; and all other areas where a common position has been established by Union member states. It has responsibility for the co-ordination of AU activities and meetings.

In 2012 plans were under way to transform the Commission into a new African Union Authority.

Chairperson: JEAN PING (Gabon).

SPECIALIZED TECHNICAL COMMITTEES

There are specialized committees for monetary and financial affairs; rural economy and agricultural matters; trade, customs and immigration matters; industry, science and technology, energy, natural resources and environment; transport, communications and tourism; health, labour and social affairs; and education, culture and human resources. These have responsibility for implementing the Union's programmes and projects.

PAN-AFRICAN PARLIAMENT

The Pan-African Parliament comprises five deputies (including at least one woman) from each AU member state, presided over by an elected President assisted by four Vice-Presidents. The President and Vice-Presidents must equitably represent the central, northern, eastern, southern and western African states. The Parliament convenes at least twice a year; an extraordinary session may be called by a two-thirds' majority of the members. The Parliament currently has only advisory and consultative powers. Its eventual evolution into an institution with full legislative authority is planned. The Parliament is headquartered at Midrand, South Africa.

President: Dr MOUSSA IDRISS NDÉLÉ (Chad).

AFRICAN COURT OF JUSTICE AND HUMAN RIGHTS

An African Court of Human and Peoples' Rights (ACHPR) was created following the entry into force in January 2004 of the Protocol to the African Charter on Human and Peoples' Rights Establishing the ACHPR (adopted in June 1998). In February 2009 a protocol (adopted in July 2003) establishing an African Court of Justice entered into force. The Protocol on the Statute of the African Court of Justice and Human Rights, aimed at merging the ACHPR and the African Court of Justice, was opened for signature in July 2008, and had, by March 2012, been ratified by three states.

PEACE AND SECURITY COUNCIL

The Protocol to the Constitutive Act of the African Union Relating to the Peace and Security Council of the African Union entered into force on 26 December 2003; the 15-member elected Council was formally inaugurated in May 2004. It acts as a decision-making body for the prevention, management and resolution of conflicts.

ECONOMIC, SOCIAL AND CULTURAL COUNCIL

The Economic, Social and Cultural Council (ECOSOCC), inaugurated in March 2005, was to have an advisory function and to comprise representatives of civic, professional and cultural bodies at national, regional and diaspora levels. Its main organs were to be: an elected General Assembly; Standing Committee; Credential Committee; and Sectoral Cluster Communities. It is envisaged that the Council will strengthen the partnership between member governments and African civil society. Following ECOSOCC's inauguration a consultation process was launched on the organization of elections to the planned General Assembly. Prior to the activation of the Assembly, in 2008, an interim elected Standing Committee held office for a two-year period. The Sectoral Cluster Communities were to be established to formulate opinions and influence AU decision-making in the following 10 areas: peace and security; political affairs; infrastructure and energy; social affairs and health; human resources, science and technology; trade and industry; rural economy and agriculture; economic affairs; women and gender; and cross-cutting programmes.

NEW PARTNERSHIP FOR AFRICA'S DEVELOPMENT (NEPAD)

NEPAD Planning and Co-ordination Agency (NPCA): POB 1234, Halfway House, Midrand, 1685 South Africa; tel. (11) 313-3716; fax (11) 313-3684; e-mail africam@nepad.org; internet www.nepad.org; f. Feb. 2010, as a technical body of the AU, to replace the former NEPAD Secretariat, with the aim of improving the country-level implementation of projects; NEPAD was launched in 2001 as a long-term strategy to promote socio-economic development in Africa; adopted Declaration on Democracy, Political, Economic and Corporate Governance and the African Peer Review Mechanism in June 2002; the July 2003 AU Maputo summit decided that NEPAD should be integrated into AU structures and processes; a special 'Brainstorming on NEPAD' summit, held in Algiers, Algeria in March 2007, issued a 13-point communiqué on the means of reforming the Partnership; a further Review Summit on NEPAD, convened in Dakar, Senegal, in April 2008, reaffirmed the centrality of NEPAD as the overarching developmental programme for Africa; the UN allocated US $12.6m. in support of NEPAD under its 2012–13 budget; CEO Dr IBRAHIM ASSANE MAYAKI.

PROPOSED INSTITUTIONS

In 2012 three financial institutions, for managing the financing of programmes and projects, remained to be established: an African Central Bank; an African Monetary Fund; and an African Investment Bank.

Activities

From the 1950s various attempts were made to establish an inter-African organization. In November 1958 Ghana and Guinea (later joined by Mali) drafted a Charter that was to form the basis of a Union of African States. In January 1961 a conference was held at Casablanca, Morocco, attended by the heads of state of Ghana, Guinea, Mali, Morocco, and representatives of Libya and of the provisional government of the Algerian Republic (GPRA). Tunisia, Nigeria, Liberia and Togo declined the invitation to attend. An African Charter was adopted and it was decided to institute an African Military Command and an African Common Market. Between October 1960 and March 1961 three conferences were held by French-speaking African countries: at Abidjan, Côte d'Ivoire; Brazzaville, Republic of the Congo (ex-French); and Yaoundé, Cameroon. None of the 12 countries that attended these meetings had been present at the Casablanca Conference. These conferences led to the signing, in September 1961, at Tananarive, Madagascar, of a charter establishing the Union africaine et malgache, later the Organisation commune africaine et mauricienne (OCAM). In May 1961 a conference was held at Monrovia, Liberia, attended by the heads of state or representatives of 19 countries: Cameroon, Central African Republic, Chad, Congo Republic (ex-French), Côte d'Ivoire, Dahomey, Ethiopia, Gabon, Liberia, Madagascar, Mauritania, Niger, Nigeria, Senegal, Sierra Leone, Somalia, Togo, Tunisia and Upper Volta. Meeting again (with the exception of Tunisia and with the addition of the ex-Belgian Congo Republic) in January 1962 at Lagos, Nigeria, they established a permanent secretariat and a standing committee of ministers of finance, and accepted a draft charter for an Organization of Inter-African and Malagasy States.

It was the Conference of Addis Ababa, convened in 1963, which finally brought together African states despite the regional, political and linguistic differences that divided them. The ministers of foreign affairs of 32 African states attended the Preparatory Meeting held in mid-May: Algeria, Burundi, Cameroon, Central African Republic, Chad, Congo (Brazzaville—now Republic of the Congo), Congo (Léopoldville—now Democratic Republic of the Congo), Côte d'Ivoire, Dahomey (now Benin), Ethiopia, Gabon, Ghana, Guinea, Liberia, Libya, Madagascar, Mali, Mauritania, Morocco, Niger, Nigeria, Rwanda, Senegal, Sierra Leone, Somalia, Sudan, Tanganyika (now Tanzania), Togo, Tunisia, Uganda, the United Arab Republic (Egypt) and Upper Volta (now Burkina Faso). The topics discussed by the meeting were: (i) the creation of an Organization of African States; (ii) co-operation among African states in the following fields: economic and social; education, culture and science; collective defence; (iii) decolonization; (iv) apartheid and racial discrimination; (v) the effects of economic grouping on the economic development of Africa; (vi) disarmament; (vii) the creation of a Permanent Conciliation Commission; and (viii) Africa and the United Nations. The Heads of State Conference that opened on 23 May 1963 drew up the Charter of the Organization of African Unity, which was then signed by the heads of 30 states on 25 May. The Charter was essentially functional and reflected a compromise between the concept of a loose association of states favoured by the Monrovia Group and the federal idea supported by the Casablanca Group, in particular by Ghana.

In May 1994 the Abuja Treaty Establishing the African Economic Community (AEC, signed in June 1991) entered into force. The formation of the Community was then expected to be a gradual process, to be completed by 2028, although the process has subsequently been accelerated. An extraordinary summit meeting, convened in September 1999, in Sirte, Libya, at the request of the then Libyan leader Col al-Qaddafi, determined to establish an African Union, based on the principles and objectives of the OAU and AEC, but furthering African co-operation, development and integration. Heads of state declared their commitment to accelerating the establishment of regional institutions, including a pan-African parliament, a court of human and peoples' rights and a central bank, as well as the implementation of economic and monetary union, as provided for by the Abuja Treaty Establishing the AEC. In July 2000 at the annual OAU summit meeting, held at Lomé, Togo, 27 heads of state and government signed the draft Constitutive Act of the African Union, which was to enter into force one month after ratification by two-thirds of member states' legislatures; this was achieved on 26 May 2001. The Union was inaugurated, replacing the OAU, on 9 July 2002, at a summit meeting of heads of state and government held in Durban, South Africa, after a transitional period of one year had elapsed since the endorsement of the Act in July 2001. During the transitional year, pending the transfer of all assets and liabilities to the Union, the OAU Charter remained in effect. A review of all OAU treaties was implemented, and those deemed relevant were retained by the AU. The four key organs of the AU were launched in July 2002. Morocco is the only African country that is not a member of the AU. The AU aims to strengthen and advance the process of African political and socio-economic integration initiated by the OAU. The Union operates on the basis of both the Constitutive Act and the Abuja Treaty.

The AU has the following areas of interest: peace and security; political affairs; infrastructure and energy; social affairs; human resources, science and technology; trade and industry; rural economy and agriculture; and economic affairs. In July 2001 the OAU adopted a New African Initiative, which was subsequently renamed the New Partnership for Africa's Development (NEPAD). NEPAD, which was officially launched in October, represents a long-term strategy for socio-economic recovery in Africa and aims to promote the strengthening of democracy and economic management in the region. The heads of state of Algeria, Egypt, Nigeria, Senegal and South Africa played leading roles in its preparation and management. In June 2002 NEPAD heads of state and government adopted a Declaration on Democracy, Political, Economic and Corporate Governance and announced the development of an African Peer Review Mechanism (APRM—whose secretariat was to be hosted by the UN Economic Commission for Africa). Meeting during that month the Group of Seven industrialized nations and Russia (the G8) welcomed the formation of NEPAD and adopted an Africa Action Plan in support of the initiative. NEPAD is ultimately answerable to the AU Assembly. The inaugural summit of the Assembly, held in Durban, South Africa, in July 2002, issued a Declaration on the Implementation of NEPAD, which urged all member states to adopt the Declaration on Democracy, Political, Economic and Corporate Governance and to participate in the peer review process. By March 2012 some 11 nations had completed the APRM process. NEPAD focuses on the following sectoral priorities: infrastructure (covering information and communication technologies, energy, transport, water and sanitation); human resources development; agriculture; culture; science and technology; mobilizing resources; market access; and the environment. It implements action plans concerned with capacity building, the environment, and infrastructure. The summit meeting of the AU Assembly convened in Maputo, Mozambique, in July 2003 determined that NEPAD should be integrated into AU structures and processes. In March 2007 a special NEPAD summit held in Algiers, Algeria, issued a 13-point communiqué on the best means of achieving this objective without delay. The centrality of NEPAD as the overarching developmental programme for Africa was reaffirmed by a further summit meeting, convened in Dakar, Senegal, in April 2008, which also published a number of further key decisions aimed at guiding the future orientation of the Partnership. In February 2010 African leaders approved the establishment of the NEPAD Planning and Co-ordination Agency (NPCA), a technical body of the AU, to replace the former NEPAD Secretariat, with the aim of improving the implementation of projects at country level. The Chairperson of the African Union Commission (AUC) exercises supervisory authority over the NPCA.

The eighth AU Assembly, held in January 2007 in Cairo, Egypt, adopted a decision on the need for a 'Grand Debate on the Union Government', concerned with the possibility of establishing an AU Government as a precursor to the eventual creation of a United States of Africa. The ninth Assembly, convened in July 2007 in Accra, Ghana, adopted the Accra Declaration, in which AU heads of state and government expressed commitment to the formation of a Union Government of Africa and ultimate aim of creating a United States of Africa, and pledged, as a means to this end, to accelerate the economic and political integration of the African continent; to rationalize, strengthen and harmonize the activities of the regional economic communities; to conduct an immediate audit of the organs of the AU ('Audit of the Union'); and to establish a ministerial committee to examine the concept of the Union Government. A panel of eminent persons was subsequently established to conduct the proposed institutional Audit of the Union; the panel became operational at the beginning of September, and presented its review to the 10th Assembly, which was held in January–February 2008 in Addis Ababa. A committee comprising 10 heads of state was appointed to consider the findings detailed in the review.

In March 2005 the UN Secretary-General issued a report on the functioning of the United Nations which included a clause urging donor nations to focus particularly on the need for a 10-year plan for capacity-building within the AU. The UN System-wide Support to the AU and NEPAD was launched in 2006, following on from the UN System-wide Special Initiative on Africa, which had been undertaken over the decade 1996–2005.

PEACE AND SECURITY

The Protocol to the Constitutive Act of the African Union Relating to the Establishment of the Peace and Security Council, adopted by the inaugural AU summit of heads of state and government in July 2002, entered into force in December 2003, superseding the 1993 Cairo Declaration on the OAU Mechanism for Conflict Prevention, Management and Resolution. The Protocol provides for the development of a collective peace and security framework (known as the African Peace and Security Architecture—APSA). This includes a 15-country Peace and Security Council, operational at the levels of heads of state and government, ministers of foreign affairs, and permanent representatives, to be supported by a five-member advisory Panel of the Wise, a Continental Early Warning System, an African Standby Force and a Peace Fund (superseding the OAU Peace Fund, which was established in June 1993). In March 2004 the Executive Council elected 15 member states to serve on the inaugural Peace and Security Council. The activities of the Peace and Security Council include the promotion of peace, security and stability; early warning and preventive diplomacy; peace-making mediation; peace support operations and intervention; peace-building activities and post-conflict reconstruction; and humanitarian action and disaster management. The Council was to implement the common defence policy of the Union, and to ensure the implementation of the 1999 OAU Convention on the Prevention and Combating of Terrorism (which provided for the exchange of information to help counter terrorism and for signatory states to refrain from granting asylum to terrorists). Member states were to set aside standby troop contingents for the planned African Standby Force, which was to be mandated to undertake observation, monitoring and other peace-support missions; to deploy in member states as required to prevent the resurgence or escalation of violence; to intervene in member states as required to restore stability; to conduct post-conflict disarmament and demobilization and other peace-building activities; and to provide emergency humanitarian assistance. The Council was to harmonize and co-ordinate the activities of other regional security mechanisms. An extraordinary AU summit meeting, convened in Sirte, Libya, in February 2004, adopted a declaration approving the establishment of the multinational African Standby Force, under which five regional brigades are being developed, to be deployed in African-led peace support operations. A Policy Framework Document on the establishment of the African Standby Force and the Military Staff Committee was approved by the third regular summit of AU heads of state, held in July 2004.

The extraordinary OAU summit meeting convened in Sirte, Libya, in September 1999 determined to hold a regular ministerial Conference on Security, Stability, Development and Co-operation in Africa (CSSDCA): the first CSSDCA took place in Abuja, Nigeria, in May 2000. The CSSDCA process provides a forum for the development of policies aimed at advancing the common values of the AU and AEC in the areas of peace, security and co-operation. In December 2000 OAU heads of state and government adopted the Bamako Declaration, concerned with arresting the circulation of small arms on the continent.

In May 2003 the AU, UNDP and UN Office for Project Services agreed a US $6.4m. project entitled 'Support for the Implementation of the Peace and Security Agenda of the African Union'. In June of that year a meeting of the G8 and NEPAD adopted a Joint Africa/G8 Plan to enhance African capabilities to undertake Peace Support Operations. Within the framework of the Plan, a consultation between the AU, the NEPAD Secretariat, the G8, the African regional economic communities, as well as the European Union (EU) and UN and other partners, was convened in Addis Ababa in April 2005. In September 2002 and October 2004 the AU organized high-level intergovernmental meetings on preventing and combating terrorism in Africa. An AU Special Representative on Protection of Civilians in Armed Conflict Situations in Africa was appointed in September 2004.

In January 2005 the African Union Non-Aggression and Common Defence Pact was adopted to promote co-operation in developing a common defence policy and to encourage member states to foster an attitude of non-aggression. The Pact, which entered into force in December 2009, establishes measures aimed at preventing inter- and intra-state conflicts and arriving at peaceful resolutions to conflicts. It also sets out a framework defining, *inter alia,* the terms 'aggression' and 'intervention' and determining those situations in which intervention may be considered an acceptable course of action. As such, the Pact stipulates that an act, or threat, of aggression against an individual member state is to be considered an act, or threat, of aggression against all members states.

In recent years the AU has been involved in peace-making and peace-building activities in several African countries and regions.

In April 2003 the AU authorized the establishment of a 3,500-member African Mission in Burundi (AMIB) to oversee the implementation of cease-fire accords in that country, support the disarmament and demobilization of former combatants, and ensure favourable conditions for the deployment of a future UN peace-keeping presence. In June 2004 AMIB was terminated and its troops 'rehatted' as participants in the then newly authorized UN Operation in Burundi (ONUB, which was terminated in 2006).

The July 2003 Maputo Assembly determined to establish a post-conflict reconstruction ministerial committee on Sudan. The first meeting of the committee, convened in March 2004, resolved to dispatch an AU team of experts to southern Sudan to compile a preliminary assessment of that region's post-conflict requirements; this was undertaken in late June. In early April, meeting in N'Djamena, Chad, the Sudan Government and other Sudanese parties signed, under AU auspices, a Humanitarian Cease-fire Agreement providing for the establishment of an AU-led Cease-fire Commission and for the deployment of an AU military observer mission (the AU Mission in the Sudan—AMIS) to the western Sudanese region of Darfur, where widespread violent unrest (including reportedly systematic attacks on the indigenous civilian population by pro-government militias), resulting in a grave humanitarian crisis, had prevailed since early 2003. Following the adoption in late May 2004 of an accord on the modalities for the implementation of the Humanitarian Cease-fire Agreement (also providing for the future deployment of an armed protection force as an additional component of AMIS, as requested by a recent meeting of the Peace and Security Council), the Cease-fire Commission was inaugurated at the end of that month and, at the beginning of June, the Commission's headquarters were opened in El Fasher, Sudan; some 60 AMIS military observers were dispatched to the headquarters during that month. In early July the AU Assembly agreed to increase the strength of AMIS to 80 observers. From mid-2004 the AU mediated negotiations between the parties to the conflict in Darfur on the achievement of a comprehensive peace agreement. AMIS's military component, agreed in May 2004, initially comprising 310 troops from Nigeria and Rwanda and mandated to monitor the cease-fire and protect the Mission, began to be deployed in mid-August. In October the Peace and Security Council decided to expand AMIS into a full peace-keeping operation, eventually to comprise 3,300 troops, police and civilian support staff. The mission's mandate was enhanced to include promoting increased compliance by all parties with the cease-fire agreement and helping with the process of confidence-building; responsibility for monitoring compliance with any subsequent agreements; assisting IDP and refugee returns; and contributing to the improvement of the security situation throughout Darfur. In April 2005 the Peace and Security Council authorized the further enhancement of AMIS to comprise, by the end of September, some 6,171 military personnel, including up to 1,560 civilian police personnel. A pledging conference for the mission, convened in April, resulted in commitments from AU partners and some member states totalling US $291.6m.; the promised funding included $77.4m. from the EU and $50m. from the USA. In March 2006 the Peace and Security Council agreed, in principle, to support the transformation of AMIS into a UN operation. In late March Arab League heads of state agreed to provide funding for the AU force to remain operational and voted to support Sudanese opposition to the deployment of non-African peace-keeping troops. In late April, following talks in Abuja, Nigeria, AU mediators submitted a proposed peace agreement to representatives of the Sudanese Government and rebel groups; the so-called Darfur Peace Agreement (DPA) was signed on 5 May by the Sudanese Government and the main rebel grouping (the Sudan Liberation Movement).

In August 2006 the UN Security Council expanded the mandate of UNMIS to provide for its deployment to Darfur, in order to enforce a cease-fire and support the implementation of DPA. The Council also requested the UN Secretary-General to devise jointly with the AU, in consultation with the parties to the DPA, a plan and schedule for a transition from AMIS to a sole UN operation in Darfur. The Sudanese Government, however, initially rejected the concept of an expanded UN peace-keeping mission, on the grounds that it would compromise national sovereignty. Eventually, in late December, the UN, AU and Sudanese Government established a tripartite mechanism which was to facilitate the implementation of a UN-formulated three-phase approach, endorsed by the AU Peace and Security Council in November, that would culminate in a hybrid AU/UN mission in Darfur. In January 2007 UNMIS provided AMIS with supplies and extra personnel under the first ('light') phase of the approach; the second ('heavy') phase, finalized in that month, was to involve the delivery of force enablers, police units, civilian personnel and mission support items. UNMIS continued to make efforts to engage the non-signatories of the DPA in the political process in Darfur. In June the AU and UN special representatives for Darfur defined a political road-map to lead eventually to full negotiations in support of a peaceful settlement to the sub-regional conflict. In August the first AU/UN-chaired 'pre-negotiation' discussions with those rebel groups in Darfur that were not party to the DPA approved an agreement on co-operation in attempting to secure a settlement.

In June 2007 the Sudanese Government agreed to support unconditionally the deployment of the Hybrid UN/AU Operation in Darfur (UNAMID); UNAMID was authorized by the UN Security Council in the following month, with a mandated force ceiling of up to 26,000 troops and police officers, supported by 5,000 international and local civilian staff, and a mandate to take necessary action to support the implementation and verification of the May 2006 Darfur Peace Agreement. UNAMID was also mandated to protect civilians, to provide security for humanitarian assistance, to support an inclusive political process, to contribute to the promotion of human rights and rule of law, and to monitor and report on the situation along the borders with Chad and the Central African Republic (CAR). An AU-UN Joint Mediation Support Team for Darfur (JMST) and a Tripartite Committee on UNAMID (including representatives of AU, the UN and Government of Sudan), meet periodically. UNAMID assumed command of AMIS (then comprising 10 battalions) in December 2007. In February 2008 UNAMID's Joint Special Representative signed a status of forces agreement with the minister of foreign affairs of Sudan, covering logistical aspects of the mission. In March UNAMID police units conducted their first confidence-building patrols in areas under rebel control in northern Darfur. In May UNAMID's Force Commander condemned aerial attacks against villages in northern Darfur, allegedly by Sudanese forces.

At the end of June 2008 a new joint AU-UN Chief Mediator was appointed, based at UNAMID headquarters in El Fasher. A Joint Support Co-ordination Mechanism (JSCM) Office in Addis Ababa, comprising liaison officers and communications equipment, was established in November to ensure effective consultation between AU headquarters and the UN. In October 2008 the UN Secretary-General reported that little progress had been achieved in the implementation of the 2006 Darfur Peace Agreement and that violent unrest continued to prevail, and that the conditions in Darfur were not conducive to undertaking a successful peace-keeping operation. From 2008 activities were under way to bring the 10 former AMIS battalions up to full strength in terms of military personnel and equipment. Nevertheless, the UN Secretary-General reported in February 2009 that UNAMID's operational capabilities continued to be limited by lack of critical and key military enabling equipment, logistical constraints, and the reluctance of many troop- and police-contributing countries to deploy to it well-trained personnel and efficient contingent-owned equipment. In January 2010 the UN Secretary-General reported that the capability of UNAMID battalions in Darfur continued to be a cause of concern, with a number of units not having sufficient major equipment. In November 2009 an inaugural conference of Darfurian civil society organizations was convened, in Doha, Qatar, in order to strengthen and to further political negotiations to achieve a peace settlement. A second conference was held in July 2010. In February and March 2010, respectively, two rebel groupings that had been operating in Darfur signed framework agreements with the Sudanese Government aimed at resolving the conflict; however, consequent negotiations with the largest rebel group, aimed at securing a cease-fire, stalled in May. During that month violent unrest in Darfur caused nearly 600 fatalities, the highest number since the deployment of the mission. UNAMID strengthened security measures and provided additional medical care in some of the larger IDP camps. In late August a consultative meeting of representatives of UNAMID, the AU, the USA and the Sudanese President agreed that UNAMID and the Sudanese Government would work closely together to improve the security situation in Darfur and to support stabilization and development of the region. There were continued reports of criminal attacks on UN personnel, including the carjacking of UNAMID vehicles, during 2008–12. The number of carjackings reportedly decreased from 2011, however, following the implementation by UNAMID of new preventative measures.

In April 2011 the Sudanese National Electoral Commission initiated preparations for a referendum to be held on the future status of Darfur, and requested material and technical assistance from UNA-

MID. Towards the end of April the JMST presented a draft peace agreement to the Sudan Government and rebel groupings. The agreement was considered by an All-Darfur Stakeholders' Conference, convened, with support from UNAMID, in Doha, Qatar, in late May; participants in the Conference endorsed a communiqué providing for the draft document (the Doha Document for Peace in Darfur—DDPD) to form the basis for achieving a permanent ceasefire and comprehensive Darfurian peace settlement. The DDPD addressed issues including power sharing, wealth sharing, human rights, justice and reconciliation, compensation, returns, and internal dialogue, and provided for the establishment of a Ceasefire Commission, a Darfur Regional Authority, and for a Darfuri to be appointed as the second Vice-President of Sudan. In June the UN Secretary-General welcomed the DDPD as the basis for resolving the Darfur conflict. In mid-July the Sudanese Government and the 'Liberation and Justice Movement', an alliance of rebel groupings, signed an accord on the adoption of the DDPD. Shortly afterwards the two sides also signed a Protocol on the Political Participation of the Liberation and Justice Movement and Integration of its Forces. Meanwhile, UNAMID, a participant in the DDPD Implementation Follow-on Commission, prepared, with civil society representatives, a plan for the dissemination throughout Darfur of information on the Document. In August UNAMID chaired the first meeting of the Cease-Fire Commission established under the provisions of the DDPD.

UNAMID's operational strength in March 2012 comprised 17,768 troops, 313 military observers and 5,366 police officers. At April 2012 UNAMID was being led by the Joint AU-UN Special Representative, Ibrahim Gambari.

Meeting in January 2006 the Peace and Security Council accepted in principle the future deployment of an AU Peace Support Mission in Somalia, with a mandate to support that member country's transitional federal institutions; meanwhile, it was envisaged that an IGAD peace support mission (IGASOM, approved by IGAD in January 2005 and endorsed by that month's AU summit) would be stationed in Somalia. In mid-March 2006 the IGAD Assembly reiterated its support for the deployment of IGASOM, and urged the UN Security Council to grant an exemption to the UN arms embargo applied to Somalia in order to facilitate the regional peace support initiative. At a consultative meeting on the removal of the arms embargo, convened in mid-April, in Nairobi, Kenya, representatives of the Somali transitional federal authorities presented for consideration by the AU and IGAD a draft national security and stabilization plan. It was agreed that a detailed mission plan should be formulated to underpin the proposed AU/IGAD peace missions. In January 2007 the Peace and Security Council authorized the deployment of the AU Mission in Somalia (AMISOM), in place of the proposed IGASOM. AMISOM was to be deployed for an initial period of six months, with a mandate to contribute to the political stabilization of Somalia. It was envisaged that AMISOM would evolve into a UN operation focusing on the post-conflict restoration of Somalia. In the following month the UN Security Council endorsed AMISOM and proposed that it should eventually be superseded by such a UN operation. AMISOM became operational in May 2007. In mid-September 2009 the AU strongly condemned terrorist attacks that were perpetrated against the AMISOM headquarters in Mogadishu, Somalia, killing more than 20 people, including the Deputy Force Commander of the Mission, and injuring a further 40. AMISOM reached its then mandated strength of 8,000 troops in November 2010. In the following month the UN Security Council, concerned at continuing unrest and terrorist attacks, extended AMISOM's mandate until 30 September 2011 and requested the AU to increase the mission's numbers to 12,000. AMISOM's mandate was extended further, in September 2011, until 31 October 2012. In so doing, the UN Security Council requested the AU urgently to increase the mission's strength to the then mandated level of 12,000. In late February 2012 the Security Council voted unanimously to enhance the mission further, to comprise 17,700 troops, and to expand its areas of operation. At that time the Council also banned trade in charcoal with Somalia, having identified that commodity as a significant source of revenue for militants.

In February 2008 the AU welcomed the efforts of African leaders, including the outgoing Chairman of the AU Assembly, President Kufuor of Ghana, and the former UN Secretary-General, Kofi Annan, to secure a peaceful outcome to the political crisis and violent unrest that had erupted in Kenya following the disputed outcome of a presidential election staged in December 2007. In March 2008 the Pan-African Parliament sent an observer mission to monitor the legislative and presidential elections that were held concurrently in Zimbabwe. In February 2009 the Assembly welcomed ongoing political progress in Zimbabwe and demanded the immediate suspension of international sanctions against that country.

In November 2008 the AU and International Conference on the Great Lakes Region jointly convened, in Nairobi, Kenya, with participation by the UN Secretary-General, a regional summit on ongoing heightened insecurity in eastern regions of the Democratic Republic of the Congo.

In August 2008, following the overthrow of its constitutional Government in a military *coup d'état*, Mauritania was suspended from participating in the activities of the AU. Guinea was suspended from the AU during December 2008–December 2010, also following a *coup d'état*; Guinea's membership suspension was lifted in view of presidential elections held in 2010. In March 2009 the AU suspended Madagascar from participation in its activities, following the forced resignation of the elected President, Mark Ravalomanana, and transfer of power to the military. In February 2010 Niger was suspended from participation in AU activities, following a *coup d'état*; Niger's membership suspension was lifted in March 2011, following the successful organization, in October 2010, of a referendum on a new constitution, and of legislative and presidential elections in early 2011.

In March 2011 a High-Level Ad Hoc Committee on Libya, comprising the leaders of Republic of the Congo, Mali, Mauritania, South Africa and Uganda, was formed to facilitate dialogue among the parties to the conflict that had emerged in Libya in early 2011. In mid-March the Committee urged an immediate halt to the military intervention in Libya that followed the adoption by the UN Security Council of Resolution 1973, which, *inter alia*, imposed a no-fly zone in Libya's airspace and authorized UN member states to take 'all necessary measures to protect civilians and civilian populated areas under threat of attack' by forces loyal to Col al-Qaddafi, 'while excluding a foreign occupation force of any form on any part of Libyan territory'. During March the Committee developed a Roadmap for the Peaceful Resolution of the Crisis in Libya, which urged an immediate cessation of hostilities; the facilitation by the Libyan authorities of the delivery of humanitarian assistance to vulnerable populations; the protection of all foreign nationals, including African migrant workers; the adoption and implementation of political reforms to eliminate the causes of the conflict; and better co-ordination of the international community's crisis resolution efforts. In early April it was reported that the Libyan regime had accepted the provisions of the AU Roadmap; the opposition forces active in Libya, however, refused to approve it, demanding that al-Qaddafi relinquish power. The 17th regular summit of AU heads of state and government, convened in late June–early July 2011, endorsed a set of Proposals on a Framework Agreement for a Political Solution to the Crisis in Libya, which had been developed by the High-Level Ad Hoc Committee in the context of the AU Roadmap. The summit also determined to disregard the arrest warrant for al-Qaddafi and members of his regime that had been issued in late June by the International Criminal Court. In early July the High-Level Ad Hoc Committee formally presented the Proposals for a Framework Agreement to the parties to the Libyan conflict; these were rejected by the rebel forces.

In mid-August 2011, following several months of civil conflict in Libya, and of Security Council Resolution 1973-mandated NATO action there, anti-government forces began to make significant advances against the al-Qaddafi régime, and, by 23 August, the rebels had taken control of the Libyan capital, Tripoli, and had conquered al-Qaddafi's fortified compound in the city. Meeting shortly afterwards, at the level of heads of state and government, the AU Peace and Security Council noted with deep appreciation the efforts undertaken by the High-Level Ad Hoc Committee on Libya in pursuit of a political solution to the ongoing conflict, within the context of the AU Roadmap and the Proposals on a Framework Agreement. The Council urged Libyan stakeholders to accelerate the process leading to the formation of an all-inclusive transitional government for that country, and emphasized the commitment of the AU to work with the UN, the Arab League, the Organization of Islamic Cooperation, NATO, and the EU, in support of the Libyan people. In late September the AU reiterated its concerns for the security of African migrant workers based in Libya. In September 2011 the AU recognized the National Transitional Council as the de facto government of Libya.

In early 2011 the Peace and Security Council held a series of meetings to consider ongoing unrest in Côte d'Ivoire, where the security situation had deteriorated following the refusal of the outgoing President Laurent Gbagbo to acknowledge the outcome of presidential elections held in 2010, and consequently to cede power. In late January 2011 the Council, meeting at the level of heads of state and government, determined to establish a High-level Panel on Côte d'Ivoire. The Panel, which was inaugurated at the end of that month, included five African leaders, the AU Chairperson, and the President of the ECOWAS Commission. Meeting in mid-March 2011 the Peace and Security Council decided that an AU High Representative should be appointed to pursue a peaceful resolution of the Côte d'Ivoire political crisis, through the implementation of peace proposals developed by the High-level Panel. The legitimately elected President, Alassane Ouattara, was eventually inaugurated in May 2011.

The EU assists the AU financially in the areas of: peace and security; institutional development; governance; and regional economic integration and trade. In June 2004 the European Commission activated for the first time its newly-established Africa Peace Facility

(APF), which aims to contribute to the African peace and security agenda, including, since 2007, conflict prevention and post-conflict stabilization. The APF was endowed with €300m. during 2008–mid-2011, allocated as follows: €65m. towards the operationalization of the African Peace and Security Architecture and Africa-EU dialogue; €200m. to peace support operations (the Fund's core area of activity); €15m. towards early response; and €20m. for evaluation and for unforeseen requirements. Since October 2007 APF and UN funding have jointly financed the deployment of UNAMID.

During 2004–10 the APF channelled more than €60m. towards peace support operations in the CAR, including support for the deployment, since July 2008, of the Mission for the Consolidation of Peace in the CAR—MICOPAX, which, under the auspices of the Communauté économique des états de l'Afrique centrale, superseded the Multinational Force in the Central African Republic (established in 2002). MICOPAX has a military strength of around 520 troops, and a civilian component that includes a police unit of 150 officers.

In March 2010 officials from the AU, IGAD, COMESA, the EAC, the Inter-regional Co-ordinating Committee and the UN Economic Commission for Africa attended an interactive dialogue hosted by the Indian Ocean Commission, at Quatre Bornes, Mauritius.

The AU was to host the first global summit on the African diaspora in May 2012, in Midrand, South Africa, to be followed in June by an AU summit focused on, and with participation by, representatives of the diaspora.

INFRASTRUCTURE, ENERGY AND THE ENVIRONMENT

Meeting in Lomé, Togo, in July 2001, OAU heads of state and government authorized the establishment of an African Energy Commission (AFREC), with the aim of increasing co-operation in energy matters between Africa and other regions. AFREC was launched in February 2008. It was envisaged at that time that an African Electrotechnical Standardization Commission (AFSEC) would also become operational, as a subsidiary body of AFREC.

In 1964 the OAU adopted a Declaration on the Denuclearization of Africa, and in April 1996 it adopted the African Nuclear Weapons Free Zone Treaty (also known as the 'Pelindaba Treaty'), which identifies Africa as a nuclear weapons-free zone and promotes co-operation in the peaceful uses of nuclear energy.

In 1968 OAU member states adopted the African Convention on the Conservation of Nature and Natural Resources. The Bamako Convention on the Ban of the Import into Africa and the Control of Transboundary Movement and Management of Hazardous Wastes within Africa was adopted by OAU member states in 1991 and entered into force in April 1998.

In June 2010 a consultative meeting was convened between the AU, COMESA, IGAD, and other regional partners, aimed at advancing co-ordination and harmonization of their activities governing the environment. It was envisaged that the AU should facilitate the development of a comprehensive African Environmental Framework, to guide pan-continental and REC environmental activities. At that time the AU was in the process of integrating two regional fora—the African Ministerial Conference on Water and the African Ministerial Conference on the Environment—into its structures, as specialized institutes.

In February 2007 the first Conference of African Ministers responsible for Maritime Transport was convened to discuss maritime transport policy in the region. A draft declaration was submitted at the Conference, held in Abuja, Nigeria, outlining the AU's vision for a common maritime transport policy aimed at 'linking Africa' and detailing programmes for co-operation on maritime safety and security and the development of an integrated transport infrastructure. The subsequently adopted Abuja Maritime Transport Declaration formally provided for an annual meeting of maritime transport ministers, to be hosted by each region in turn in a rotational basis. In July 2009 the AU Assembly decided to establish an African Agency for the Protection of Territorial and Economic Waters of African Countries.

In January 2012 the Executive Council endorsed a new African Civil Aviation Policy (AFCAP); and also endorsed the African Action Plan for the UN 2011–20 Decade of Action on Road Safety.

POLITICAL AND SOCIAL AFFAIRS

The African Charter on Human and People's Rights, which was adopted by the OAU in 1981 and entered into force in October 1986, provided for the establishment of an 11-member African Commission on Human and People's Rights, based in Banjul, The Gambia. A Protocol to the Charter, establishing an African Court of People's and Human Rights, was adopted by the OAU Assembly of Heads of State in June 1998 and entered into force in January 2004. In February 2009 a protocol (adopted in July 2003) establishing an African Court of Justice entered into force. The Protocol on the Statute of the African Court of Justice and Human Rights, aimed at merging the African Court of Human and Peoples' Rights and the African Court of Justice, was opened for signature in July 2008. A further Protocol, relating to the Rights of Women, was adopted by the July 2003 Maputo Assembly. The African Charter on the Rights and Welfare of the Child was opened for signature in July 1990 and entered into force in November 1999. A Protocol to the Abuja Treaty Establishing the AEC relating to the Pan-African Parliament, adopted by the OAU in March 2001, entered into force in December 2003. The Parliament was inaugurated in March 2004 and was, initially, to exercise advisory and consultative powers only, although its eventual evolution into an institution with full legislative powers is envisaged. In March 2005 the advisory Economic, Social and Cultural Council was inaugurated.

The July 2002 inaugural summit meeting of AU heads of state and government adopted a Declaration Governing Democratic Elections in Africa, providing guidelines for the conduct of national elections in member states and outlining the AU's electoral observation and monitoring role. In April 2003 the AU Commission and the South African Independent Electoral Commission jointly convened an African Conference on Elections, Democracy and Governance. In February 2012 a new African Charter on Democracy, Elections and Governance entered into force, having been at that time by 15 AU member states.

In recent years several large population displacements have occurred in Africa, mainly as a result of violent conflict. In 1969 OAU member states adopted the Convention Governing the Specific Aspects of Refugee Problems in Africa, which entered into force in June 1974 and had been ratified by 45 states at March 2011. The Convention promotes close co-operation with UNHCR. The AU maintains a Special Refugee Contingency Fund to provide relief assistance and to support repatriation activities, education projects, etc., for displaced people in Africa. In October 2009 AU member states participating in a regional Special Summit on Refugees, Returnees and IDPs in Africa, convened in Kampala, Uganda, adopted the AU Convention for the Protection and Assistance of IDPs in Africa, the first legally binding international treaty providing legal protection and support to people displaced within their own countries by violent conflict and natural disasters; the Convention had received four ratifications by March 2012. The AU aims to address pressing health issues affecting member states, including the eradication of endemic parasitic and infectious diseases and improving access to medicines. An African Summit on HIV/AIDS, TB and other related Infectious Diseases was convened, under OAU auspices, in Abuja in March 2001 and, in May 2006, an AU Special Summit on HIV/AIDS. TB and Malaria was convened, also in Abuja, to review the outcomes of the previous Summit. The 2006 Special Summit adopted the Abuja Call for Accelerated Action on HIV/AIDS, TB and Malaria, and, in September of that year AU ministers of health adopted the Maputo Plan of Action for the operationalisation of the Continental Policy Framework for Sexual and Reproductive Health, covering 2007–10, aimed at advancing the goal of achieving universal access to comprehensive sexual and reproductive health services in Africa; in July 2010 the Plan was extended over the period 2010–15. In January 2012 the 18th AU Assembly meeting decided to revitalize AIDS Watch Africa (AWA), an advocacy platform established in April 2001, and hitherto comprising several regional heads of states, to be an AU Heads of State and Government Advocacy and Accountability Platform with continent-wide representation. AWA's mandate was to be extended to cover, also, TB and malaria. In March 2012 NEPAD and UNAIDS signed an agreement on advancing sustainable responses to HIV/AIDS, health and development across Africa. An AU Scientific, Technical and Research Commission is based in Lagos, Nigeria, and a Centre for Linguistic and Historical Studies by Oral Tradition is based in Niamey, Niger.

In July 2004 the Assembly adopted the Solemn Declaration on Gender Equality in Africa (SDGEA), incorporating a commitment to reporting annually on progress made towards attaining gender equality. The first conference of ministers responsible for women's affairs and gender, convened in Dakar, Senegal, in October 2005, adopted the Implementation Framework for the SDGEA, and Guidelines for Monitoring and Reporting on the SDGEA, in support of member states' reporting responsibilities.

The seventh AU summit, convened in Banjul, The Gambia, in July 2006, adopted the African Youth Charter, providing for the implementation of youth policies and strategies across Africa, with the aim of encouraging young African people to participate in the development of the region and to take advantage of increasing opportunities in education and employment. The Charter outlined the basic rights and responsibilities of youths, which were divided into four main categories: youth participation; education and skills development; sustainable livelihoods; and health and well-being. The Charter, which entered into force in August 2010, also details the obligations of member states towards young people.

In December 2007 the AU adopted a Plan of Action on Drug Control and Crime Prevention covering the period 2007–12, and determined to establish a follow-up mechanism to monitor and evaluate its implementation. In March 2009 the AU and UNODC (which in October 2008 had published a report identifying the expanding use in recent years of West Africa as a transit route for narcotics being illegally traded between Latin America and Europe) launched a joint initiative to support the Plan. The AU-UNODC co-operation aimed to strengthen the policy-making, norm-setting and capacity-building capabilities of the AU Commission and sub-regional organizations (notably ECOWAS).

AU efforts to combat human trafficking are guided by the 2006 Ouagadougou Action Plan to Combat Trafficking in Human Beings. In June 2009 the AU launched AU COMMIT, a campaign aimed at raising the profile of human trafficking on the regional development agenda. It was estimated at that time that nearly 130,000 people in sub-Saharan Africa and 230,000 in North Africa and the Middle East had been recruited into forced labour, including sexual exploitation, as a result of trafficking; many had also been transported to Western Europe and other parts of the world.

TRADE, INDUSTRY AND ECONOMIC CO-OPERATION

In October 1999 a conference on Industrial Partnerships and Investment in Africa was held in Dakar, Senegal, jointly organized by the OAU with UNIDO, the ECA, the African Development Bank and the Alliance for Africa's Industrialization. In June 1997 the first meeting between ministers of the OAU and the EU was convened in New York, USA. In April 2000 the first EU-Africa summit of heads of state and government was held in Cairo, under the auspices of the EU and OAU. The summit adopted the Cairo Plan of Action, which addressed areas including economic integration, trade and investment, private-sector development in Africa, human rights and good governance, peace and security, and development issues such as education, health and food security. The second EU-Africa summit meeting was initially to have been held in April 2003 but was postponed, owing to disagreements concerning the participation of President Mugabe of Zimbabwe, against whom the EU had imposed sanctions. In February 2007 the EU and the AU began a period of consultation on a joint EU-Africa Strategy, aimed at outlining a long-term vision of the future partnership between the two parties. The Strategy was adopted by the second EU-Africa Summit, which was convened, finally, in December 2007, in Lisbon, Portugal (with participation by President Mugabe). The third EU-Africa Summit, held in November 2010, in Tripoli, Libya, confirmed commitment to the Strategy and adopted an action plan on co-operation, covering 2011–13. A fourth EU-Africa Business Forum was convened alongside the November 2010 summit. A Joint Africa-EU Task Force meets regularly, most recently in March 2012, to consider areas of co-operation.

Co-operation between African states and the People's Republic of China is undertaken within the framework of the Forum on China-Africa Co-operation (FOCAC). The first FOCAC ministerial conference was held in October 2000; the second in December 2003; the third (organized alongside a China-Africa leaders' summit) in November 2006; and the fourth in November 2009. The fifth FOCAC ministerial conference was scheduled to be held in July 2012. Africa–USA trade is underpinned by the US African Growth and Opportunity Act (AGOA), adopted in May 2000 to promote the development of free market economies in Africa. Regular Africa-EU and Africa-South America ('ASA') summits are convened. The most recent (third) Africa-EU summit was held in November 2010, in Libya. The most recent (second) ASA summit, convened by the AU and Union of South American Nations—UNASUR in Porlamar, Margarita Island, Venezuela, in September 2009, adopted the Margarita Declaration and Action Plan, covering issues of common concern, including combating climate change, and developing an alternative financial mechanism to address the global economic crisis. The third ASA summit was to take place in May 2012, in Malabo, Equatorial Guinea.

The AU aims to reduce obstacles to intra-African trade and to reverse the continuing disproportionate level of trade conducted by many African countries with their former colonial powers. In June 2005 an AU conference of Ministers of Trade was convened, in Cairo, to discuss issues relating to the development of Trade in Africa, particularly in the context of the World Trade Organization's (WTO) Doha Work Programme. The outcome of the meeting was the adoption of the Cairo Road Map on the Doha Work Programme, which addressed several important issues including the import, export and market access of agricultural and non-agricultural commodities, development issues and trade facilitation.

In June 1991 the OAU Assembly of Heads of State signed the Abuja Treaty Establishing the African Economic Community (AEC). The Treaty was to enter into force after ratification by two-thirds of member states. It was envisaged at that time that the Community was to be established by 2028, following a gradual six-phase process involving the co-ordination, harmonization and progressive integration of the activities of all existing and future sub-regional economic unions. (There are 14 so-called 'regional economic communities', or RECs, in Africa, including the following major RECs that are regarded as the five pillars, or building blocks, of the AEC: the Common Market for Eastern and Southern Africa—COMESA, the Communauté économique des états de l'Afrique centrale—CEEAC, the Economic Community of West African States—ECOWAS, the Southern African Development Community—SADC, and the Union of the Arab Maghreb. The subsidiary RECs are: the Communauté économique et monétaire de l'Afrique centrale—CEMAC, the Community of Sahel-Saharan States—CEN-SAD, the East African Community—EAC, the Economic Community of the Great Lakes Countries, the Intergovernmental Authority on Development—IGAD, the Indian Ocean Commission—IOC, the Mano River Union, the Southern African Customs Union, and the Union économique et monétaire ouest-africaine—UEMOA.) The Abuja Treaty entered into force on 12 May 1994, having been ratified by the requisite number of OAU member states. The inaugural meeting of the AEC took place in June 1997. In July 2007 the ninth AU Assembly adopted a Protocol on Relations between the African Union and the RECs, aimed at facilitating the harmonization of policies and ensuring compliance with the schedule of the Abuja Treaty.

In January 2012 the 18th summit of AU leaders endorsed a new Framework, Roadmap and Architecture for Fast Tracking the Establishment of a Continental Free Trade Area (CFTA), and an Action Plan for Boosting Intra-African Trade. The summit determined that the implementation of the CFTA process should follow these milestones: the finalization by 2014 of the EAC-COMESA-SADC Tripartite FTA initiative; the completion during 2012–14 of other REC FTAs; the consolidation of the Tripartite and other regional FTAs into the CFTA initiative during 2015–16; and the establishment of an operational CFTA by 2017. The January 2012 summit invited ECOWAS, CEEAC, CEN-SAD and the Union of the Arab Maghreb to draw inspiration from the EAC-COMESA-SADC Tripartite initiative and to establish promptly a second pole of regional integration, thereby accelerating continental economic integration. The summit welcomed the UN Conference on Sustainable Development (UNCSD), scheduled to be held in June of that year, and recognized the need to strengthen the AU's institutional framework for sustainable development, deeming that promoting the transition to 'green' and 'blue' economies would accelerate continental progress towards sustainable development.

In February 2008 the AU Assembly endorsed the AU Action Plan for the Accelerated Industrial Development of Africa (AIDA), which had been adopted in September 2007 by the first extraordinary session of the Conference of African Ministers of Industry. The Action Plan details a set of programme and activities aimed at stimulating a competitive and sustainable industrial development process.

A roadmap and plan of action for promoting microfinance in Africa was finalized in 2009, and is under consideration.

The AU leadership participated in the summit meeting of G8 heads of state and government that was convened in Huntsville, Canada, in June 2010; the summit also included an African Outreach meeting with the leaders of Algeria, Ethiopia, Malawi, Nigeria, Senegal and South Africa.

In October 2010 the AU, ECA and African Development Bank established a Joint Secretariat to enhance coherence and collaboration in support of Africa's development agenda.

RURAL ECONOMY AND AGRICULTURE

In July 2003 the second Assembly of heads of state and government adopted the Maputo Declaration on Agriculture and Food Security in Africa, focusing on the need to revitalize the agricultural sector and to combat hunger on the continent by developing food reserves based on African production. The leaders determined to deploy policies and budgetary resources to remove current constraints on agricultural production, trade and rural development; and to implement the Comprehensive Africa Agriculture Programme (CAADP). The CAADP, which is implemented through NEPAD, focuses on the four pillars of sustainable land and water management; market access; food supply and hunger; and agricultural research. CAADP heads of state have agreed the objective of allocating at least 10% of national budgets to investment in agricultural productivity. The CAADP aims by 2015 to achieve dynamic agricultural markets between African countries and regions; good participation in and access to markets by farmers; a more equitable distribution of wealth for rural populations; more equitable access to land, practical and financial resources, knowledge, information, and technology for sustainable development; development of Africa's role as a strategic player in the area of agricultural science and technology; and environmentally sound agricultural production and a culture of sustainable management of natural resources.

In December 2006 AU leaders convened at a Food Security Summit in Abuja adopted a declaration of commitment to increasing intra-African trade by promoting and protecting as strategic commodities at the continental level cotton, legumes, maize, oil palm, rice and beef, dairy, fisheries and poultry products; and promoting and protecting as strategic commodities at the sub-regional level cassava, sorghum and millet. The AU leaders also declared a commitment to initiating the implementation of the NEPAD Home-grown School Feeding Project, the African Regional Nutrition Strategy, the NEPAD African Nutrition Initiative, and the NEPAD 10-Year Strategy for Combating Vitamin and Mineral Deficiency.

In December 2006 the AU adopted the Great Green Wall of the Sahara and Sahel Initiative (GGWSSI), comprising a set of cross-sectoral actions and interventions (including tree planting) that were aimed at conserving and protecting natural resources, halting soil degradation, reducing poverty, and increasing land productivity in some 20 countries in the Sahara and Sahel areas.

The AU's Programme for the Control of Epizootics (PACE) has co-operated with FAO to combat the further spread of the Highly Pathogenic Avian Influenza (H5N1) virus, outbreaks of which were reported in poultry in several West African countries in the 2000s; joint activities have included establishing a regional network of laboratories and surveillance teams and organizing regional workshops on H5N1 control.

In April 2009 AU ministers responsible for agriculture met to address the challenges to the continent posed by high food prices, climate change and the ongoing global financial and economic crisis. In July 2009 the 13th regular session of the Assembly issued a Declaration on Land Issues and Challenges in Africa, and the Sirte Declaration on Investing in Agriculture for Economic Growth and Food Security. The Sirte Declaration urged member states to review their land sector policies, and determined to undertake studies on the establishment of an appropriate institutional framework, and to launch an African Fund for Land Policy, in support of these efforts. The meeting also urged the establishment of a 'South to South Forum for Agricultural Development in Africa', recommitted to the Maputo Declaration, and urged member states to expand efforts to accelerate the implementation of the CAADP.

In January 2011 the Executive Council endorsed the Accelerated African Agribusiness and Agro-Industries Development Initiative (3ADI), which had been launched at a high-level conference on the development of agribusiness and agro-industries in Africa, convened in Abuja, Nigeria, in March 2010. The framework for the implementation of the 3ADI is the Strategy for the Implementation of the AU Plan of Action for the Accelerated Industrial Development of Africa (AIDA), adopted by African ministers responsible for industry, in October 2008; the Ministerial Action Plan for the Least Developed Countries (LDCs), adopted in December 2009 by LDC ministers responsible for industry and trade; and the Abuja Declaration on Development of Agribusiness and Agro-industries in Africa, adopted by the March 2010 Abuja high-level conference. The initiative aims to mobilize private sector investment, from domestic, regional and international sources, in African agribusiness and agro-industrial development, with the long-term objective of achieving, by 2020, highly productive and profitable agricultural value chains.

The First Conference of African Ministers of Fisheries and Aquaculture (CAMFA) was convened in September 2010, in Banjul, The Gambia. In January 2011 the Executive Council urged member states to adopt and integrate ecosystem approaches in their national and regional fisheries management plans; to strengthen measures to address Illegal, Unreported and Unregulated (IUU) fishing; and to eliminate barriers to intra-regional trade in fish and fishery products.

HUMANITARIAN RESPONSE

In December 2005 a ministerial conference on disaster reduction in Africa, organized by the AU Commission, adopted a programme of action for the implementation of the Africa Regional Strategy for Disaster Risk Reduction (2006–15), formulated in the context of the Hyogo Framework of Action that had been agreed at the World Conference on Disaster Reduction held in Kobe, Japan, in January 2005. A second ministerial conference on disaster reduction, convened in April 2010, urged all member states, and the RECs, to take necessary measures to implement the programme of action. In August 2010 the AU and OCHA signed an agreement detailing key areas of future co-operation on humanitarian issues, with the aim of strengthening the AU's capacity in the areas of disaster preparedness and response, early warning, co-ordination, and protection of civilians affected by conflict or natural disaster.

In late August 2011 AU leaders convened at the first AU Pledging Conference promised to donate some US $350m. towards relief efforts to alleviate the impact of severe drought and famine in the Horn of Africa, which was reported at that time to be affecting up to 12.5m. people.

Finance

The 2012 budget, adopted by the Executive Council in December 2011, totalled US $274.9m., comprising an operational budget of $114.8m. and a programme budget $159.29m. Some 75% of the operational budget is financed by contributions from Algeria, Egypt, Libya, Nigeria and South Africa. Around 90% of programme budgetary funding derives from the AU's development partners.

Specialized Agencies

African Civil Aviation Commission (AFCAC): 1 route de l'Aéroport International LSS, BP 2356, Dakar, Senegal; tel. 859-88-00; fax 820-70-18; e-mail secretariat@afcac.org; internet www.afcac.org; f. 1969 to co-ordinate civil aviation matters in Africa and to co-operate with ICAO and other relevant civil aviation bodies; promotes the development of the civil aviation industry in Africa in accordance with provisions of the 1991 Abuja Treaty; fosters the application of ICAO Standards and Recommended Practices; examines specific problems that might hinder the development and operation of the African civil aviation industry; 53 mem states; promotes co-ordination and better utilization and development of African air transport systems and the standardization of aircraft, flight equipment and training programmes for pilots and mechanics; organizes working groups and seminars, and compiles statistics; Sec.-Gen. IYABO SOSINA.

African Telecommunications Union (ATU): ATU Secretariat, POB 35282 Nairobi, 00200 Kenya; tel. (20) 4453308; fax (20) 4453359; e-mail sg@atu-uat.org; internet www.atu-uat.org; f. 1999 as successor to Pan-African Telecommunications Union (f. 1977); promotes the rapid development of information communications in Africa, with the aim of making Africa an equal participant in the global information society; works towards universal service and access and full inter-country connectivity; promotes development and adoption of appropriate policies and regulatory frameworks; promotes financing of development; encourages co-operation between members and the exchange of information; advocates the harmonization of telecommunications policies; 46 national mems, 18 associate mems comprising fixed and mobile telecoms operators; Sec.-Gen. ABDOULKARIM SOUMAILA.

Pan-African Institution of Education for Development (PIED): 49 ave de la Justice, BP 1764, Kinshasa I, Democratic Republic of the Congo; tel. (81) 2686091; fax (81) 2616091; e-mail iped .educ@ipedorg.cd; internet www.ipedorg.cd; f. 1973, became specialized agency in 1986, present name adopted 2001; undertakes educational research and training, focuses on co-operation and problem-solving, acts as an observatory for education; publs *Bulletin d'Information* (quarterly), *Revue africaine des sciences de l'éducation* (2 a year), *Répertoire africain des institutions de recherche* (annually).

Pan-African News Agency (PANAPRESS): BP 4056, ave Bourguiba, Dakar, Senegal; tel. 869-12-34; fax 824-13-90; e-mail panapress@panapress.com; internet www.panapress.com; f. 1979 as PanAfrican News Agency, restructured under current name in 1997; regional headquarters in Khartoum, Sudan; Lusaka, Zambia; Kinshasa, Democratic Republic of the Congo; Lagos, Nigeria; Tripoli, Libya; began operations in May 1983; receives information from national news agencies and circulates news in Arabic, English, French and Portuguese; publs *Press Review*, *In-Focus*.

Pan-African Postal Union (PAPU): POB 6026, Arusha, Tanzania; tel. (27) 2543263; fax (27) 2543265; e-mail sg@papu.co.tz; internet www.upap-papu.org; f. 1980 to extend members' co-operation in the improvement of postal services; 43 mem. countries; Sec.-Gen. RODAH MASAVIRU; publ. *PAPU News*.

Supreme Council for Sport in Africa (SCSA): POB 1363, Yaoundé, Cameroon; tel. 223-95-80; fax 223-45-12; e-mail scsa_yaounde@yahoo.com; f. 1966; co-ordinating authority and forum for the development and promotion of sports in Africa; hosts All Africa Games, held every four years; mems: sports ministers from 53 countries; Sec.-Gen. SONSTONE KASHIBA; publ. *Newsletter* (monthly).

ANDEAN COMMUNITY OF NATIONS

(COMUNIDAD ANDINA DE NACIONES—CAN)

Address: Paseo de la República 3895, San Isidro, Lima 27; Apdo 18-1177, Lima 18, Peru.

Telephone: (1) 4111400; **fax:** (1) 2213329; **e-mail:** contacto@comunidadandina.org; **internet:** www.comunidadandina.org.

The organization was established in 1969 as the Acuerdo de Cartagena (the Cartagena Agreement), also referred to as the Grupo Andino (Andean Group) or the Pacto Andino (Andean Pact). In March 1996 member countries signed a Reform Protocol of the Cartagena Agreement, in accordance with which the Andean Group was superseded in August 1997 by the Andean Community of Nations (CAN). The Community was to promote greater economic, commercial and political integration within a new Andean Integration System (Sistema Andino de Integración), comprising the organization's bodies and institutions.

MEMBERS

Bolivia	Colombia	Ecuador	Peru

Note: Argentina, Brazil, Chile, Paraguay and Uruguay are associate members. Mexico, Panama and Spain have observer status. Venezuela withdrew from the Community in April 2006.

Organization

(April 2012)

ANDEAN PRESIDENTIAL COUNCIL

The presidential summits, which had been held annually since 1989, were formalized under the 1996 Reform Protocol of the Cartagena Agreement as the Andean Presidential Council. The Council is the highest-level body of the Andean Integration System, and provides the political leadership of the Community.

COMMISSION

The Commission consists of a plenipotentiary representative from each member country, with each country holding the presidency in turn. The Commission is the main policy-making organ of the Andean Community, and is responsible for co-ordinating Andean trade policy.

COUNCIL OF FOREIGN MINISTERS

The Council of Foreign Ministers meets annually or whenever it is considered necessary, to formulate common external policy and to co-ordinate the process of integration.

GENERAL SECRETARIAT

In August 1997 the General Secretariat assumed the functions of the Board of the Cartagena Agreement. The General Secretariat is the body charged with implementation of all guidelines and decisions issued by the bodies listed above. It submits proposals to the Commission for facilitating the fulfilment of the Community's objectives. Members are appointed for a three-year term. Under the reforms agreed in March 1996 the Secretary-General is elected by the Council of Foreign Ministers for a five-year term, and has enhanced powers to adjudicate in disputes arising between member states, as well as to manage the sub-regional integration process. There are three Directors-General.

Secretary-General a.i.: Dr ADALID CONTRERAS BASPINEIRO (Bolivia).

PARLIAMENT

Parlamento Andino: Avda 13, No. 70-61, Bogotá, Colombia; tel. (1) 217-3357; fax (1) 348-2805; e-mail correo@parlamentoandino.org; internet www.parlamentoandino.org; f. 1979; comprises five members from each country, and meets in each capital city in turn; makes recommendations on regional policy; in April 1997 a new protocol was adopted that provided for the election of members by direct and universal voting; Pres. REBECA DELGADO BURGOA (Bolivia).

COURT OF JUSTICE

Tribunal de Justicia de la Comunidad Andina: Juan de Dios Martínez Mera 34-380 y Portugal, Sector Iglesia de Fátima, Quito, Ecuador; tel. (2) 3331417; e-mail tjca@tribunalandino.org.ec; internet www.tribunalandino.org.ec; f. 1979, began operating in 1984; a protocol approved in May 1996 (which came into force in August 1999) modified the Court's functions; its main responsibilities are to resolve disputes among member countries and interpret community legislation; comprises one judge from each member country, appointed for a six-year renewable period; the Presidency is assumed annually by each judge in turn; Pres. (2012) JOSÉ VICENTE TROYA JARAMILLO (Ecuador).

Activities

In May 1979, at Cartagena, Colombia, the Presidents of the then five member countries signed the 'Mandate of Cartagena', which envisaged greater economic and political co-operation, including the establishment of more sub-regional development programmes (especially in industry). In May 1989 the Group undertook to revitalize the process of Andean integration, by withdrawing measures that obstructed the programme of trade liberalization, and by complying with tariff reductions that had already been agreed upon. In May 1991, in Caracas, Venezuela, a summit meeting of the Andean Group agreed the framework for the establishment of a free trade area on 1 January 1992 (achieved in February 1993) and for an eventual Andean common market.

In March 1996 heads of state, meeting in Trujillo, Peru, agreed to a substantial restructuring of the Andean Group. They signed the Reform Protocol of the Cartagena Agreement, providing for the establishment of the Andean Community of Nations, which was to have greater ambitious economic and political objectives. Consequently, in August 1997 the Andean Community was inaugurated, and the Group's Junta was replaced by a new General Secretariat, headed by a Secretary-General with enhanced executive and decision-making powers. The initiation of these reforms was designed to accelerate harmonization in economic matters.

In April 2006 the President of Venezuela announced his intention to withdraw that country from the Andean Community, with immediate effect, expressing opposition to the bilateral free trade agreements signed by Colombia and Peru with the USA, on the grounds that they would undermine efforts to achieve regional economic integration. The Community countered that Venezuela's commitment to Andean integration had been placed in doubt by its declared allegiance to other regional groupings, in particular the Mercado Común del Sur (Mercosur).

POLITICAL CO-OPERATION

In June 2002 Community ministers of defence and of foreign affairs approved an Andean Charter for Peace and Security, establishing principles and commitments for the formulation of a policy on sub-regional security, the establishment of a zone of peace, joint action in efforts to counter terrorism, and the limitation of external defence spending. Other provisions included commitments to eradicate illegal trafficking in firearms, ammunition and explosives, to expand and reinforce confidence-building measures, and to establish verification mechanisms to strengthen dialogue and efforts in those areas. In January 2003 the Community concluded a co-operation agreement with Interpol providing for collaboration in combating national and transnational crime, and in June the presidential summit adopted an Andean Plan for the Prevention, Combating and Eradication of Small, Light Weapons. The heads of state, convened in Quirama, Colombia, also endorsed a new strategic direction for the Andean integration process based on developing the Andean common market, common foreign policy and social agenda, the physical integration of South America, and sustainable development.

A sub-regional workshop to formulate an Andean Plan to Fight Corruption was held in April 2005, organized by the General Secretariat and the European Commission. Heads of state expressed their commitment to the Plan in mid-2007, and in September 2008 Offices of the Controller General and other supervisory bodies in Andean countries agreed to implement the Plan. In November a meeting was convened, at the request of heads of state, of a Community Council of treasury or finance ministers, heads of central banks and ministers responsible for economic planning, in order to analyse the effects on the region of the severe global economic and financial downturn. The Council met again in February 2009 to consider various technical studies that had been undertaken.

At the 13th presidential summit, held in Valencia, Venezuela, in June 2001, heads of state adopted an Andean Co-operation Plan for the Control of Illegal Drugs and Related Offences, designed to promote a united approach to combating these problems. In July 2005 the Council of Foreign Ministers approved an Andean Alternative Development Strategy, which aimed to support sustainable local development initiatives, including alternatives to the production of illegal drug crops. In August 2009 the Council approved a financing agreement with the European Union (EU) to implement an anti-illegal drug programme in the Andean Community.

In June 2003 ministers of foreign affairs and foreign trade adopted 16 legal provisions aimed at giving maximum priority to the social dimension of integration within the Community, including a measure providing for mobility of workers between member countries. A new Andean passport system, which had been approved in 2001, entered into effect in December 2005.

TRADE

A council for customs affairs met for the first time in January 1982, aiming to harmonize national legislation within the group. In December 1984 the member states launched a common currency, the Andean peso, aiming to reduce dependence on the US dollar and to increase regional trade. The new currency was to be supported by special contributions to the Fondo Andino de Reservas (now the Fondo Latinoamericano de Reservas) amounting to US $80m., and was to be 'pegged' to the US dollar, taking the form of financial drafts rather than notes and coins.

The 'Caracas Declaration' of May 1991 provided for the establishment of an Andean free trade area (AFTA), which entered into effect (excluding Peru—see below) in February 1993. Heads of state also agreed in May 1991 to create a common external tariff (CET), to standardize member countries' trade barriers in their dealings with the rest of the world, and envisaged the eventual creation of an Andean common market. In December heads of state defined four main levels of external tariffs (between 5% and 20%). In August 1992 the Group approved a request by Peru for the suspension of its rights and obligations under the Pact, thereby enabling the other members to proceed with hitherto stalled negotiations on the CET. Peru was readmitted as a full member of the Group in 1994, but participated only as an observer in the ongoing negotiations.

In November 1994 ministers of trade and integration, meeting in Quito, Ecuador, concluded a final agreement on a four-tier structure of external tariffs (although Bolivia was to retain a two-level system). The CET agreement came into effect on 1 February 1995, covering 90% of the region's imports which were to be subject to the following tariff bands: 5% for raw materials; 10%–15% for semi-manufactured goods; and 20% for finished products. In order to reach an agreement, special treatment and exemptions were granted, while Peru, initially, was to remain a 'non-active' member of the accord. In June 1997 an agreement was concluded to ensure Peru's continued membership of the Community, which provided for that country's integration into AFTA. The Peruvian Government determined to eliminate customs duties on some 2,500 products with immediate effect. The process of incorporating Peru into AFTA was completed by January 2006.

In May 1999 the 11th presidential summit agreed to establish the Andean Common Market by 2005; the Community adopted a policy on border integration and development to prepare the border regions of member countries for the envisaged free circulation of people, goods, capital and services, while consolidating sub-regional security. In June 2001 the Community agreed to recognize national identification documents issued by member states as sufficient for tourist travel in the sub-region. Community heads of state, meeting in January 2002 at a special Andean presidential summit, agreed to consolidate and improve the free trade zone by mid-2002 and apply a new CET (with four levels, i.e. 0%, 5%, 10% and 20%). To facilitate this process a common agricultural policy was to be adopted and macro-economic policies were to be harmonized. In October member governments determined the new tariff levels applicable to 62% of products and agreed the criteria for negotiating levels for the remainder. Although the new CET was to become effective on 1 January 2004, this date was subsequently postponed. In January 2006 ministers of trade approved a working programme to define the Community's common tariff policy, which was to incorporate a flexible CET. The value of intra-Community trade totalled some US $5,774m. in 2009, and increased to $7,810m. in 2010.

In May 2011 the Commission approved the establishment of an Andean Committee on Micro, Small and Medium-sized Enterprises (MSMEs), mandated to advise and support the Commission and General Secretariat in efforts to support MSMEs. At the same time the Commission endorsed the establishment of an Andean Observatory on MSMEs as a mechanism for monitoring the development and needs of MSMEs in the sub-region, as well as the impact of corporate policy instruments on their competitiveness.

EXTERNAL RELATIONS

In September 1995 heads of state of member countries identified the formulation of common positions on foreign relations as an important part of the process of relaunching the integration initiative. A Protocol Amending the Cartagena Agreement was signed in June 1997 to confirm the formulation of a common foreign policy. During 1998 the General Secretariat held consultations with government experts, academics, representatives of the private sector and other interested parties to help formulate a document on guidelines for a common foreign policy. The guidelines, establishing the principles, objectives and mechanisms of a common foreign policy, were approved by the Council of Foreign Ministers in 1999. In July 2004 Andean ministers of foreign affairs approved new guidelines for an Andean common policy on external security. The ministers, meeting in Quito, Ecuador, also adopted a Declaration on the Establishment of an Andean Peace Zone, free from nuclear, chemical or biological weapons. In April 2005 the Community Secretariat signed a memorandum of understanding with the Organization for the Prohibition of Chemical Weapons, which aimed to consolidate the Andean Peace Zone, assist countries to implement the Chemical Arms Convention and promote further collaboration between the two groupings.

A co-operation agreement with the EU was signed in April 1993, establishing a Mixed Commission to further deliberation and co-operation between the two organizations. A Euro-Andean Forum is held periodically to promote mutual co-operation, trade and investment. In February 1998 the Community signed a co-operation and technical assistance agreement with the EU in order to combat drugs trafficking. At the first summit meeting of Latin American and Caribbean (LAC) and EU leaders held in Rio de Janeiro, Brazil, in June 1999, Community-EU discussions were held on strengthening economic, trade and political co-operation and on the possibility of concluding an Association Agreement. In May 2002 the EU adopted a Regional Strategy for the Andean Community covering the period 2002–06. Following the second LAC and EU summit meeting, held in May 2002 in Madrid, Spain, a Political Dialogue and Co-operation Agreement was signed in December 2003. In May 2004 a meeting of the two sides held during the third LAC-EU summit, in Guadalajara, Mexico, confirmed that an EU-CAN Association Agreement was a common strategic objective. In January 2005 an ad hoc working group was established in order to undertake a joint appraisal exercise on regional economic integration. The fourth LAC and EU summit meeting, held in Vienna, Austria, in May 2006, approved the establishment of an EU-LAC Parliamentary Assembly; this was inaugurated in November. Negotiations on an Association Agreement were formally inaugurated at the meeting of Andean heads of state held in Tarifa, Bolivia, in June 2007, and the first round of negotiations was held in September. In May 2008 heads of state of the Andean Community confirmed that they would continue to negotiate the agreement as a single group; however, in December the EU announced that it was to commence negotiations for separate free trade agreements with Colombia and Peru. Bolivia criticized the decision as undermining the Andean integration process. In March 2010 the EU-CAN Mixed Commission agreed on a programme of co-operation in 2011–13, with funding commitments of €17.5m. for projects concerned with economic integration, countering illicit drugs production and trafficking, and environmental protection. An EU-CAN summit meeting was held in Madrid in May 2010.

Since December 1991 exports from Andean Community countries have benefited from preferential access to US markets under the Andean Trade Preference Act. In August 2002 the legislation was renewed and amended under a new Andean Trade Preference and Drug Eradication Act, which provided duty free access for more than 6,000 products with the objective of supporting legal trade transactions in order to help to counter the production and trafficking of illegal narcotic drugs. The Act was initially scheduled to expire in December 2006, but has been periodically extended by the US Congress. In December 2008 the US President suspended Bolivia's eligibility under the Act owing to its failure to meet its counter-narcotics requirements.

In August 1999 the Secretary-General of the Community visited Guyana in order to promote bilateral trading opportunities and to strengthen relations with the Caribbean Community. The Community held a meeting on trade relations with the Caribbean Community during 2000.

In March 2000 the Andean Community concluded an agreement to establish a political consultation and co-operation mechanism with the People's Republic of China. At the first ministerial meeting within this framework, which took place in October 2002, it was agreed that consultations would be held thereafter on a biennial basis. The first meeting of the Council of Foreign Ministers with the Chinese Vice-President took place in January 2005. A high-level meeting between senior officials from Community member states and Japan was organized in December 2002; further consultations were to be convened, aimed at cultivating closer relations.

In April 1998, at the 10th Andean presidential summit, an agreement was signed with Panama establishing a framework for negotiations providing for the conclusion of a free trade accord by the end of 1998 and for Panama's eventual associate membership of the Community. A political dialogue and co-operation agreement, a requirement for Panama's associate membership status, was signed by both sides in September 2007. Mexico was invited to assume observer status in September 2004. In November 2006 Mexico and the Andean Community signed an agreement to establish a mechanism for political dialogue and co-operation in areas of mutual interest. The first meeting of the mechanism was held in New York, USA, in September 2007. In November 2004 the Community signed a framework agreement with the Central American Integration System (SICA) to strengthen dialogue and co-operation between the two blocs of countries. In January 2011 the Secretaries-General of the two organizations, meeting in San Salvador, El Salvador, determined to reactivate the agreement and pursue greater collaboration.

The Community signed a framework agreement with Mercosur on the establishment of a free trade accord in April 1998. Although negotiations between the Community and Mercosur were subsequently delayed, bilateral agreements between the countries of the two groupings were extended. Preferential tariff agreements were concluded with Brazil and Argentina, entering into effect in July 1999 and August 1999 and August 2000, respectively. The Community commenced negotiations on drafting a preferential tariff agreement with (jointly) El Salvador, Guatemala and Honduras in March 2000. In September leaders of the Community and Mercosur, meeting at a summit of Latin American heads of state, determined to relaunch negotiations, with a view to establishing a free trade area. In July 2001 ministers of foreign affairs of the two groupings approved the establishment of a formal mechanism for political dialogue and co-ordination in order to facilitate negotiations and to enhance economic and social integration. In December 2003 Mercosur and the Andean Community signed an Economic Complementary Agreement providing for free trade provisions, according to which tariffs on 80% of trade between the two groupings were to be phased out by 2014 and tariffs to be removed from the remaining 20% of, initially protected, products by 2019. The accord did not enter into force in July 2004, as planned, owing to delays in drafting the tariff reduction schedule. Members of the Latin American Integration Association (Aladi) remaining outside Mercosur and the Andean Community—Cuba, Chile and Mexico—were to be permitted to apply to join the envisaged larger free trade zone. In July 2005 the Community granted Argentina, Brazil, Paraguay and Uruguay associate membership of the grouping, as part of efforts to achieve a reciprocal association agreement. Chile was granted observer status in December 2004, and in September 2006 was formally invited to join the Community as an associate member. In December the first meeting of the CAN-Chile Joint Commission was convened in Cochabamba, Bolivia. An agreement on Chile's full participation in all Community bodies and mechanisms was approved in July 2007. In February 2010 ministers of foreign affairs of the Community and Mercosur agreed to establish a CAN–Mercosur Mixed Commission to facilitate enhanced co-operation between the countries of the two organizations.

In December 2004 leaders from 12 Latin American countries attending a pan-South American summit, convened in Cusco, Peru, approved in principle the creation of a new South American Community of Nations (SACN). It was envisaged that negotiations on the formation of the new Community, which was to entail the merger of the Andean Community, Mercosur and Aladi (with the participation of Chile, Guyana and Suriname), would be completed within 15 years. A region-wide meeting of ministers of foreign affairs was held in April 2005, within the framework of establishing the SACN. The first South American Community meeting of heads of state convened in September, in Brasília, Brazil. The meeting issued mandates to the heads of sub-regional organizations to consider integration processes, the convergence of economic agreements and common plans of action.

In April 2007, at the first South American Energy Summit, held in Margarita Island, Venezuela, heads of state endorsed the establishment of a Union of South American Nations (UNASUR), to replace the SACN as the lead organization for regional integration. It was envisaged that UNASUR would have political decision-making functions, supported by a small permanent secretariat, to be located in Quito, and would co-ordinate on economic and trade matters with the Andean Community, Mercosur and Aladi. At a summit meeting convened in May 2008, in Brasília, a constitutional document formally establishing UNASUR was signed. In December Brazil hosted a Latin American and Caribbean Summit on Integration and Development, which aimed to strengthen the commitment by all countries in the region to work together in support of sustainable development. The meeting issued the Salvador Declaration, which pledged support to strengthen co-operation among the regional and sub-regional groupings, to pursue further consultation and joint efforts to counter regional effects of the global financial crisis, and to promote closer collaboration on issues including energy, food security, social development, physical infrastructure and natural disaster management. The first informal meeting of the General Secretariat of the Andean Community and UNASUR was held in January 2010, in Lima, Peru.

At a special meeting of the Andean Council of Presidents, held in Bogotá, Colombia, in November 2011, heads of state agreed to strengthen the CAN, and requested that the acting Secretary-General of the Community identify jointly, with the General Secretariats of both Mercosur and UNASUR, common and complementary elements and differences prior to the future convergence of the three processes.

Spain was awarded observer status in August 2011.

INDUSTRY AND ENERGY

In May 1987 member countries signed the Quito Protocol, modifying the Cartagena Agreement, to amend the strict rules that had formerly been imposed on foreign investors in the region. In March 1991 the Protocol was amended, with the aim of further liberalizing foreign investment and stimulating an inflow of foreign capital and technology. External and regional investors were to be permitted to repatriate their profits (in accordance with the laws of the country concerned) and there was no stipulation that a majority shareholding must eventually be transferred to local investors. A further directive, adopted in March, covered the formation of multinational enterprises to ensure that at least two member countries have a shareholding of 15% or more of the capital, including the country where the enterprise was to be based. These enterprises were entitled to participate in sectors otherwise reserved for national enterprises, subject to the same conditions as national enterprises in terms of taxation and export regulations, and to gain access to the markets of all member countries. In September 1999 Colombia, Ecuador and Venezuela signed an accord to facilitate the production and sale of vehicles within the region; the agreement became effective in January 2000.

In November 1988 member states established a bank, the Banco Intermunicipal Andino, which was to finance public works. In October 2004 a sub-regional committee on small and medium-sized enterprises (SMEs) endorsed efforts by the Community Secretariat to establish an Andean System of SME Guarantees to facilitate their access to credit.

In May 1995 the Group initiated a programme to promote the use of cheap and efficient energy sources and greater co-operation in the energy sector. The programme planned to develop a regional electricity grid. During 2003 efforts were undertaken to establish an Andean Energy Alliance, with the aim of fostering the development of integrated electricity and gas markets, as well as developing renewable energy sources, promoting 'energy clusters' and ensuring regional energy security. The first meeting of ministers of energy, electricity, hydrocarbons and mines, convened in Quito, Ecuador, in January 2004, endorsed the Alliance. In August 2011 representatives of Andean electricity regulatory bodies, including that of Chile, agreed upon transitional arrangements to provide for trade in surplus electricity and greater interconnectivity. Andean Community heads of state, meeeting in Bogotá, Colombia, in November, pledged to boost the integration of regional energy. In February 2012 the Community held the first meeting of representatives of mining and environment authorities to discuss issues relating to illegal mining activities, in order to promote co-ordinated efforts against those activities, and to initiate the development of a legal directive to counter illegal mining.

TRANSPORT AND COMMUNICATIONS

The Andean Community has pursued efforts to improve infrastructure throughout the region. In 1983 the Commission formulated a plan to assist land locked Bolivia, particularly through improving roads connecting it with neighbouring countries and the Pacific Ocean. An 'open skies' agreement, giving airlines of member states equal rights to airspace and airport facilities within the grouping, was signed in May 1991. In June 1998 the Commission approved the establishment of an Andean Commission of Land Transportation Authorities, to oversee the operation and development of land transportation services. Similarly, an Andean Committee of Water Transportation Authorities was established to ensure compliance with Community regulations regarding ocean transportation activities. The Community aims to facilitate the movement of goods throughout the region by the use of different modes of transport ('multimodal transport') and to guarantee operational standards. It also intends to harmonize Community transport regulations and standards with those of Mercosur countries. In September 2005 the first summit meeting of the proposed SACN issued a declaration to support and accelerate infrastructure, transport and communications integration throughout the region.

In August 1996 a regulatory framework was approved for the development of a commercial Andean satellite system. In December 1997 the General Secretariat approved regulations for granting authorization for the use of the system; the Commission subsequently granted the first Community authorization to an Andean multinational enterprise (Andesat), comprising 48 companies from all five member states. In 1994 the Community initiated efforts to establish digital technology infrastructure throughout the Community: the resulting Andean Digital Corridor comprises ground, underwater and satellite routes providing a series of cross-border interconnections between the member countries. In 2000 an Andean Internet System was operational in Colombia, Ecuador and Venezuela. In May 1999 the Andean Committee of Telecommunications

Authorities agreed to remove all restrictions to free trade in telecommunications services (excluding sound broadcasting and television) by 1 January 2002. The Committee also determined to formulate provisions on interconnection and the safeguarding of free competition and principles of transparency within the sector. In November 2006 the Andean Community approved a new regulatory framework for the commercial exploitation of the Andean satellite system belonging to member states.

Asociación de Empresas de Telecomunicaciones de la Comunidad Andina (ASETA): Calle La Pradera E7–41 y San Salvador, Casilla 17-1106042, Quito, Ecuador; tel. (2) 256-3812; fax (2) 256-2499; e-mail aseta@aseta.org; internet www.aseta.org; f. 1974; co-ordinates improvements in national telecommunications services, in order to contribute to the further integration of the countries of the Andean Community; Sec.-Gen. MARCELO LÓPEZ ARJONA.

RURAL DEVELOPMENT AND FOOD SECURITY

In 1984 the Andean Food Security System was created to develop the agrarian sector, replace imports progressively with local produce, and improve rural living conditions. In April 1998 the Presidential Council instructed the Commission, together with ministers of agriculture, to formulate an Andean Common Agricultural Policy, including measures to harmonize trade policy instruments and legislation on animal and plant health. The 12th Andean presidential summit, held in June 2000, authorized the adoption of the concluded Policy and the enforcement of a plan of action for its implementation. In January 2002, at the special Andean presidential summit, it was agreed that all countries in the bloc would adopt price stabilization mechanisms for agricultural products.

In July 2004 Andean ministers of agriculture approved a series of objectives and priority actions to form the framework of a Regional Food Security Policy. Also in July Andean heads of state endorsed the Andean Rural Development and Agricultural Competitiveness Programme to promote sub-regional efforts in areas such as rural development, food security, production competitiveness, animal health and technological innovation. In October 2005 ministers of trade and of agriculture approved the establishment of a special fund to finance the programme, the Fund for Rural Development and Agricultural Productivity. In late 2010 it was reported that the Fund was part-financing 14 production projects in rural and border areas where poverty was prevalent.

ENVIRONMENT

In March–April 2005 the first meeting of an Andean Community Council of Ministers of the Environment and Sustainable Development was convened, in Paracas, Peru. An Andean Environmental Agenda, covering the period 2006–10, aimed to strengthen the capacities of member countries with regard to environmental and sustainable development issues, in particular biodiversity, climate change and water resources. In accordance with the Agenda the Community was working to establish an Andean Institute for Biodiversity, and to establish and implement regional strategies on integrated water resource management and on climate change. In June 2007 the Secretariat signed an agreement with Finland to develop a regional biodiversity programme in the Amazon region of Andean member countries (BioCAN). The Council of Foreign Ministers, meeting in February 2010, approved implementation of BioCAN. In October 2007 the Secretariat organized Clima Latino, hosted by two city authorities in Ecuador, comprising conferences, workshops and cultural events at which climate change was addressed. The Community represented member countries at the conference of parties to the UN Framework Convention on Climate Change, held in Bali, Indonesia, in December, and demanded greater international political commitment and funding to combat the effects of climate change, in particular to monitor and protect the Amazon rainforest. In November 2011, at a special meeting of the Andean Council of Presidents in Bogotá, Colombia, heads of state asserted their intention to work together to reach a common position for the UN Conference on Sustainable Development ('Rio + 20'), scheduled to be held in 2012.

In July 2002 an Andean Committee for Disaster Prevention and Relief (CAPRADE) was established to help mitigate the risk and impact of natural disasters in the sub-region. CAPRADE was to be responsible for implementing the Andean Strategy for Disaster Prevention and Relief, which was approved by the Council of Foreign Ministers in July 2004. A new Strategy for Natural Disaster Prevention and Relief was approved in August 2009, which aimed to link activities for disaster prevention and relief to those related to the environmental agenda, climate change and integrated water management. An Andean University Network in Risk Management and Climate Change promotes information exchange between some 32 institutions.

SOCIAL INTEGRATION

Several formal agreements and institutions have been established within the framework of the Andean Integration System to enhance social development and welfare. In May 1999 the 11th Andean presidential summit adopted a 'multidimensional social agenda' focusing on job creation and on improvements in the fields of education, health and housing throughout the Community. In June 2000 the 12th presidential summit instructed the Andean institutions to prepare individual programmes aimed at consolidating implementation of the Community's integration programme and advancing the development of the social agenda, in order to promote greater involvement of representatives of civil society. In July 2004 Community heads of state declared support for a new Andean Council of Social Development Ministers. Other bodies established in 2003/04 included Councils of Ministers of Education and of Ministers responsible for Cultural Policies, and a Consultative Council of Municipal Authorities. During 2009 work was undertaken to develop and implement an Integral Plan for Social Development, first approved by the Council of Foreign Ministers in September 2004. In August 2009 the Council of Foreign Ministers endorsed the establishment of an Andean Council of Authorities of Women's Affairs as a forum for regional consideration of equal opportunities and gender issues. In March 2010 representatives of Andean cultural authorities determined to initiate an Andean Development Plan for Cultural Industries. In the previous month a Permanent Working Network on Andean Cinema was established. In December Andean ministers of foreign affairs endorsed 2011 as the Andean Year of Social Integration, which aimed to promote Community policies and initiatives regarding equality, cohesion and social and territorial integration. In July 2011 Andean ministers responsible for social development approved 11 Andean Social Development Objectives, which they pledged to achieve by 2019, and a new Andean Economic and Social Cohesion Strategy to support the accomplishment of those targets.

In June 2007 Community heads of state approved the establishment of a Working Committee on Indigenous People's Rights. In July the Community convened the first forum of intellectuals and researchers to strengthen the debate on indigenous issues and their incorporation into the integration process. A Consultative Council of Indigenous Peoples of the Andean Community was founded in September to promote the participation of representatives of indigenous communities in the Andean integration process.

INSTITUTIONS

Consejo Consultivo de Pueblos Indígenos de la Comunidad Andina (Consultative Council of Indigenous Peoples of the Andean Community): Paseo de la República 3895, Lima, Peru; tel. (1) 4111400; fax (1) 2213329; f. 2007; first meeting held in September 2008; aims to strengthen the participation of indigenous peoples in the sub-regional integration process.

Consejo Consultivo Empresarial Andino (Andean Business Advisory Council): Asociación Nacional de Industriales, Calle 73, No. 8–13, Bogotá, Colombia; tel. (1) 3268500; fax (1) 3473198; e-mail jnarino@andi.com.co; first meeting held in Nov. 1998; an advisory institution within the framework of the Sistema Andino de Integración; comprises elected representatives of business organizations; advises Community ministers and officials on integration activities affecting the business sector; Chair. JUAN CAMILO NARIÑO ALCOCER (Colombia).

Consejo Consultivo Laboral Andino (Andean Labour Advisory Council): Paseo de la República 3832, Of. 502, San Isidro, Lima 27, Peru; tel. (1) 6181701; fax (1) 6100139; e-mail cutperujcb@gmail.com; internet www.ccla.org.pe; f. 1998; an advisory institution within the framework of the Sistema Andino de Integración; comprises elected representatives of labour organizations; advises Community ministers and officers on related labour issues; Chair. VÍCTOR JOSÉ PARDO RODRÍGUEZ (Colombia).

Convenio Andrés Bello (Andrés Bello Agreement): Avda Carrera 20 85-60, Bogotá, Colombia; tel. (1) 644-9292; fax (1) 610-0139; e-mail ecobello@col1.telecom.com.co; internet www.convenioandresbello .org; f. 1970, modified in 1990; aims to promote integration in the educational, technical and cultural sectors; a new Inter-institutional Co-operation Agreement was signed with the Secretariat of the CAN in Aug. 2003; mems: Bolivia, Chile, Colombia, Cuba, Dominican Republic, Ecuador, Mexico, Panama, Paraguay, Peru, Spain, Venezuela; Exec. Sec. Dr FRANCISCO HUERTA MONTALVO (Ecuador).

Convenio Hipólito Unanue (Hipólito Unanue Agreement): Edif. Cartagena, Paseo de la República 3832, 3°, San Isidro, Lima, Peru; tel. (1) 2210074; fax (1) 2222663; e-mail postmaster@conhu.org.pe; internet www.orasconhu.org; f. 1971 on the occasion of the first meeting of Andean ministers of health; became part of the institutional structure of the Community in 1998; aims to enhance the development of health services, and to promote regional co-ordination in areas such as environmental health, disaster preparedness and the prevention and control of drug abuse; Exec. Sec. Dr CAROLINE CHANG CAMPOS (Ecuador).

Convenio Simón Rodríguez (Simón Rodríguez Agreement): Paseo de la República 3895, esq. Aramburú, San Isidro, Lima 27, Peru; tel. (1) 4111400; fax (1) 2213329; promotes a convergence of social and labour conditions throughout the Community, for example, working hours and conditions, employment and social security policies, and to promote the participation of workers and employers in the sub-regional integration process; Protocol of Modification signed in June 2001; ratification process ongoing.

Corporación Andina de Fomento (CAF) (Andean Development Corporation): Torre CAF, Avda Luis Roche, Altamira, Apdo 5086, Caracas, Venezuela; tel. (212) 2092111; fax (212) 2092444; e-mail infocaf@caf.com; internet www.caf.com; f. 1968, began operations in 1970; aims to encourage the integration of the Andean countries by specialization and an equitable distribution of investments; conducts research to identify investment opportunities, and prepares the resulting investment projects; gives technical and financial assistance; and attracts internal and external credit; auth. cap. US $10,000m.; subscribed or underwritten by the governments of member countries, or by public, semi-public and private sector institutions authorized by those governments; the Board of Directors comprises representatives of each country at ministerial level; mems: the Andean Community, Argentina, Brazil, Chile, Costa Rica, Jamaica, Mexico, Panama, Paraguay, Spain, Trinidad and Tobago, Uruguay, Venezuela, and 15 private banks in the Andean region; Exec. Pres. Enrique García Rodríguez (Bolivia).

Fondo Latinoamericano de Reservas (FLAR) (Latin American Reserve Fund): Avda 82 12–18, 7°, POB 241523, Bogotá, Colombia; tel. (1) 634-4360; fax (1) 634-4384; e-mail flar@flar.net; internet www.flar.net; f. 1978 as the Fondo Andino de Reservas to support the balance of payments of member countries, provide credit, guarantee loans, and contribute to the harmonization of monetary and financial policies; adopted present name in 1991, in order to allow the admission of other Latin American countries; in 1992 the Fund began extending credit lines to commercial cos for export financing; it is administered by an Assembly of the ministers of finance and economy of the member countries, and a Board of Directors comprising the Presidents of the central banks of the member states; mems: Bolivia, Colombia, Costa Rica, Ecuador, Peru, Uruguay, Venezuela; subscribed cap. US $2,343.8m. cap. p.u. $1,864.5m. (31 Aug. 2010); Exec. Pres. Ana María Carrasquilla.

Universidad Andina Simón Bolívar (Simón Bolívar Andean University): Real Audiencia 73, Casilla 545, Sucre, Bolivia; tel. (4) 6460265; fax (4) 6460833; e-mail uasb@uasb.edu.bo; internet www.uasb.edu.bo; f. 1985; institution for postgraduate study and research; promotes co-operation between other universities in the Andean region; branches in Quito (Ecuador), La Paz (Bolivia), Caracas (Venezuela) and Cali (Colombia); Pres. (Sucre Office) José Luis Guitiérrez Sardán.

Publications

Reports, working papers, sector documents, council proceedings.

ARAB FUND FOR ECONOMIC AND SOCIAL DEVELOPMENT—AFESD

Address: POB 21923, Safat, 13080 Kuwait.

Telephone: 24959000; **fax:** 24815760; **e-mail:** hq@arabfund.org; **internet:** www.arabfund.org.

Established in 1968 by the Economic Council of the Arab League, the Fund began its operations in 1974. It participates in the financing of economic and social development projects in the Arab states.

MEMBERS

All member countries of the League of Arab States.

Organization

(April 2012)

BOARD OF GOVERNORS

The Board of Governors consists of a Governor and an Alternate Governor appointed by each member of the Fund. The Board of Governors is considered as the General Assembly of the Fund, and has all powers.

BOARD OF DIRECTORS

The Board of Directors is composed of eight Directors elected by the Board of Governors from among Arab citizens of recognized experience and competence. They are elected for a renewable term of two years.

The Board of Directors is charged with all the activities of the Fund and exercises the powers delegated to it by the Board of Governors.

Director-General and Chairman of the Board of Directors: Abdlatif Yousuf al-Hamad (Kuwait).

FINANCIAL STRUCTURE

The Fund's authorized capital is 800m. Kuwaiti dinars (KD) divided into 80,000 shares having a value of KD 10,000 each. In April 2008 the Board of Governors approved a transfer of KD 1,337m. from the Fund's additional capital reserves to paid-up capital, increasing subscribed capital from KD 663m. to KD 2,000m. At 31 December 2010 shareholders' equity amounted to KD 2,617.5m. (including KD 617.5m. in reserves).

Activities

Pursuant to the Agreement Establishing the Fund (as amended in 1997 by the Board of Governors), the purpose of the Fund is to contribute to the financing of economic and social development projects in the Arab states and countries by:

1. Financing economic development projects of an investment character by means of loans granted on concessionary terms to governments and public enterprises and corporations, giving preference to projects which are vital to the Arab entity, as well as to joint Arab projects;

2. Financing private sector projects in member states by providing all forms of loans and guarantees to corporations and enterprises (possessing juridical personality), participating in their equity capital, and providing other forms of financing and the requisite financial, technical and advisory services, in accordance with such regulations and subject to such conditions as may be prescribed by the Board of Directors;

3. Forming or participating in the equity capital of corporations possessing juridical personality, for the implementation and financing of private sector projects in member states, including the provision and financing of technical, advisory and financial services;

4. Establishing and administering special funds with aims compatible with those of the Fund and with resources provided by the Fund or other sources;

5. Encouraging, directly or indirectly, the investment of public and private capital in a manner conducive to the development and growth of the Arab economy;

6. Providing expertise and technical assistance in the various fields of economic development.

The Fund co-operates with other Arab organizations such as the Arab Monetary Fund, the League of Arab States and the Organization of Arab Petroleum Exporting Countries in preparing regional studies and conferences, for example in the areas of human resource development, demographic research and private sector financing of infrastructure projects. It also acts as the secretariat of the Co-ordination Group of Arab National and Regional Development Financing Institutions. These organizations work together to produce a *Joint Arab Economic Report*, which considers economic and social developments in the Arab states. In March 2011 the Fund hosted the first in a series of annual Arab Development Symposiums, to be organized jointly with the World Bank. The inaugural Symposium concerned 'Water and Food Security in the Arab World'. In September the Fund endorsed the so-called Deauville Partnership, which had been established by the Group of Eight industrialized countries in May in order to assist countries in the Middle East and North Africa undergoing social and economic transformations. The Fund joined some nine other international financial institutions active in the region to establish a Co-ordination Platform to facilitate and promote collaboration among the institutions extending assistance under the Partnership.

During 2010 the Fund approved 14 loans, totalling KD 360.5m., to help finance projects in seven member countries, of which 13 loans were for the public sector and one for a private sector project (in Jordan). At the end of that year total lending since 1974 amounted to KD 6,879.1m., which had helped to finance 568 projects in 17 Arab countries. In 2010 39% of financing was for energy and electricity projects, while 38% was for projects in the transport and telecommunications sector. During the period 1974–2010 33% of project financing was for energy and electricity, 26% for transport and telecommunications, 15% for agriculture and rural development, 10% for water and sewerage, 7% for social services and 6% for industry and mining.

During 2010 the Fund extended 28 inter-Arab and national grants, totalling KD 9.6m., providing for technical assistance, training, research activities and other emergency assistance programmes. The cumulative total number of grants provided by the end of 2010 was 946, with a value of KD 162.5m.

In December 1997 AFESD initiated an Arab Fund Fellowships Programme, which aimed to provide grants to Arab academics to conduct university teaching or advanced research. During 2010 the Fund contributed US $100m. to a new Special Account to finance small and medium-sized private sector projects in Arab countries, which had first been proposed in January 2009. The Fund was to administer the Account, and hosted its inaugural meeting in October 2010.

Publications

Annual Report.

Joint Arab Economic Report (annually).

Statistics

LOANS BY SECTOR

	2010		1974–2010
Sector	Amount (US $ million)	%	%
Infrastructure sectors	307.0	85.2	69.0
Transport and telecommunications	135.0	37.5	25.6
Energy and electricity	142.0	39.4	33.0
Water and sewerage	30.0	8.3	10.4
Productive sectors	46.5	12.9	21.3
Industry and mining	34.5	9.6	6.4
Agriculture and rural development	12.0	3.3	14.9
Social services	0.0	0.0	7.4
Other	7.0	1.9	2.3
Total	360.5	100.0	100.0

Source: AFESD, *Annual Report 2010.*

ARAB MONETARY FUND

Address: Arab Monetary Fund Bldg, Corniche Rd, POB 2818, Abu Dhabi, United Arab Emirates.

Telephone: (2) 6171400; **fax:** (2) 6326454; **e-mail:** centralmail@amfad.org.ae; **internet:** www.amf.org.ae.

The Agreement establishing the Arab Monetary Fund was approved by the Economic Council of Arab States in Rabat, Morocco, in April 1976 and entered into force on 2 February 1977.

MEMBERS

Algeria	Morocco
Bahrain	Oman
Comoros	Palestine
Djibouti	Qatar
Egypt	Saudi Arabia
Iraq*	Somalia*
Jordan	Sudan*
Kuwait	Syria
Lebanon	Tunisia
Libya	United Arab Emirates
Mauritania	Yemen

* From July 1993 loans to Iraq, Somalia and Sudan were suspended as a result of non-repayment of debts to the Fund. Sudan was readmitted in April 2000, following a settlement of its arrears; a memorandum of understanding, to incorporate new loan repayments was concluded in September 2001. An agreement to reschedule Iraq's outstanding arrears was concluded in 2008.

Organization

(April 2012)

BOARD OF GOVERNORS

The Board of Governors is the highest authority of the Arab Monetary Fund. It formulates policies on Arab economic integration and the liberalization of trade among member states. With certain exceptions, it may delegate to the Board of Executive Directors some of its powers. The Board of Governors is composed of a governor and a deputy governor appointed by each member state for a term of five years. It meets at least once a year; meetings may also be convened at the request of half the members, or of members holding half of the total voting power.

BOARD OF EXECUTIVE DIRECTORS

The Board of Executive Directors exercises all powers vested in it by the Board of Governors and may delegate to the Director-General such powers as it deems fit. It is composed of the Director-General and eight non-resident directors elected by the Board of Governors. Each director holds office for three years and may be re-elected.

DIRECTOR-GENERAL

The Director-General of the Fund is appointed by the Board of Governors for a renewable five-year term, and serves as Chairman of the Board of Executive Directors.

The Director-General supervises Committees on Loans, Investments, and Administration. Other offices include the Economic and Technical Department, the Economic Policy Institute, the Investment Department, the Legal Department, an Internal Audit Office, and the Finance and Computer Department.

Director-General and Chairman of the Board of Executive Directors: Dr Jassim Abdullah al-Mannai.

FINANCE

The Arab Accounting Dinar (AAD) is a unit of account equivalent to three IMF Special Drawing Rights (SDRs). (The average value of the SDR in 2011 was US $1.57868.)

In April 1983 the authorized capital of the Fund was increased from AAD 288m. to AAD 600m. The new capital stock comprised 12,000 shares, each having the value of AAD 50,000. At the end of 2010 total paid-up capital was AAD 596.04m.

CAPITAL SUBSCRIPTIONS

(million Arab Accounting Dinars, 31 December 2010)

Member	Paid-up capital
Algeria	77.90
Bahrain	9.20
Comoros	0.45
Djibouti	0.45
Egypt	58.80
Iraq	77.90
Jordan	9.90
Kuwait	58.80
Lebanon	9.20
Libya	24.69
Mauritania	9.20

Member—*continued*	Paid-up capital
Morocco	27.55
Oman	9.20
Palestine	3.96
Qatar	18.40
Saudi Arabia	88.95
Somalia	7.35
Sudan	18.40
Syria	13.25
Tunisia	12.85
United Arab Emirates	35.30
Yemen	28.30
Total*	596.04

* Excluding Palestine's share (AAD 3.96m.), which was deferred by a Board of Governors' resolution in 1978.

Activities

The creation of the Arab Monetary Fund was seen as a step towards the goal of Arab economic integration. It assists member states in balance of payments difficulties, and also has a broad range of aims.

The Articles of Agreement define the Fund's aims as follows:

(*a*) to correct disequilibria in the balance of payments of member states;

(*b*) to promote the stability of exchange rates among Arab currencies, to render them mutually convertible, and to eliminate restrictions on current payments between member states;

(*c*) to establish policies and modes of monetary co-operation to accelerate Arab economic integration and economic development in the member states;

(*d*) to tender advice on the investment of member states' financial resources in foreign markets, whenever called upon to do so;

(*e*) to promote the development of Arab financial markets;

(*f*) to promote the use of the Arab dinar as a unit of account and to pave the way for the creation of a unified Arab currency;

(*g*) to co-ordinate the positions of member states in dealing with international monetary and economic problems; and

(*h*) to provide a mechanism for the settlement of current payments between member states in order to promote trade among them.

The Arab Monetary Fund functions both as a fund and a bank. It is empowered:

(*a*) to provide short- and medium-term loans to finance balance of payments deficits of member states;

(*b*) to issue guarantees to member states to strengthen their borrowing capabilities;

(*c*) to act as intermediary in the issuance of loans in Arab and international markets for the account of member states and under their guarantees;

(*d*) to co-ordinate the monetary policies of member states;

(*e*) to manage any funds placed under its charge by member states;

(*f*) to hold periodic consultations with member states on their economic conditions; and

(*g*) to provide technical assistance to banking and monetary institutions in member states.

Loans are intended to finance an overall balance of payments deficit and a member may draw up to 75% of its paid-up subscription, in convertible currencies, for this purpose unconditionally (automatic loans). A member may, however, obtain loans in excess of this limit, subject to agreement with the Fund on a programme aimed at reducing its balance of payments deficit (ordinary and extended loans, equivalent to 175% and 250% of its quota respectively). From 1981 a country receiving no extended loans was entitled to a loan under the Inter-Arab Trade Facility (discontinued in 1989) of up to 100% of its quota. In addition, a member has the right to borrow under a compensatory loan in order to finance an unexpected deficit in its balance of payments resulting from a decrease in its exports of goods and services or a large increase in its imports of agricultural products following a poor harvest. In 2009 the access limit was doubled to 100% of paid-up capital.

Automatic and compensatory loans are repayable within three years, while ordinary and extended loans are repayable within five and seven years, respectively. Loans are granted at concessionary and uniform rates of interest that increase with the length of the period of the loan. In 1996 the Fund established the Structural Adjustment Facility, initially providing up to 75% of a member's paid-up subscription and later increased to 175%. This may include a technical assistance component comprising a grant of up to 2% of the total loan. In 2009, in order to enhance the flexibility and effectiveness of its lending to meet the needs of member countries affected by the global financial crisis, the Fund determined to extend an access limit of 175% for lending for both the public finance sector and for the financial and banking sector under the Structural Adjustment Facility. In 2007 the Fund established an Oil Facility to assist petroleum-importing member countries to counter the effects of the escalation in global fuel prices. Eligible countries were entitled to borrow up to 200% of their paid-up subscription under the new Facility. A new Short Term Liquidity Facility was approved in 2009 to provide resources to countries with previously strong track records undergoing financial shortages owing to the sharp contraction in international trade and credit.

Over the period 1978–2010 the Fund extended 150 loans amounting to AAD 1,317m. During 2010 the Fund approved lending of AAD 118m. (compared with AAD 99m. in 2009), including two Structural Adjustment Loans, amounting to AAD 65m., for public finance reforms in Jordan and Morocco, an Extended Loan, amounting to AAD 43m., for Yemen, and a Compensatory Loan, amounting to AAD 10m., to Jordan.

The Fund's technical assistance activities are extended through either the provision of experts to the country concerned or in the form of specialized training of officials of member countries. In view of the increased importance of this type of assistance, the Fund established, in 1988, the Economic Policy Institute (EPI), which offers regular training courses and specialized seminars for middle-level and senior staff, respectively, of financial and monetary institutions of the Arab countries. During 2010 the EPI organized 17 training events, attended by 532 people. In April 1999 the Fund signed a Memorandum of Understanding with the International Monetary Fund (IMF) to establish a joint regional training programme. The Fund also co-operates with the IMF in conducting workshops and technical advice missions under the Arab Credit Reporting Initiative and the Arab Debt Markets Development Initiative.

AMF collaborates with Arab Fund for Economic and Social Development (AFESD), the Arab League and the Organization of Arab Petroleum Exporting Countries in writing and publishing a *Joint Arab Economic Report*. The Fund also co-operates with AFESD, with the technical assistance of the IMF and the World Bank, in organizing an annual seminar. The Fund provides the secretariat for the Council of Arab Central Banks, comprising the governors of central banks and the heads of the monetary agencies in Arab countries. In 1991 the Council established the Arab Committee on Banking Supervision. In 2005 the Council inaugurated a second technical grouping, the Arab Committee on Payments and Settlements Systems. In September 2011 the Fund endorsed the so-called Deauville Partnership, which had been established by the Group of Eight industrialized countries in May in order to assist countries in the Middle East and North Africa undergoing social and economic transformations. The Fund joined some nine other international financial institutions active in the region to establish a Co-ordination Platform to facilitate and promote collaboration among the institutions extending assistance under the Partnership.

TRADE PROMOTION

Arab Trade Financing Program (ATFP): POB 26799, Arab Monetary Fund Bldg, 7th Floor, Corniche Rd, Abu Dhabi, United Arab Emirates; tel. (2) 6316999; fax (2) 6316793; e-mail finadmin@atfp.ae; internet www.atfp.org.ae; f. 1989 to develop and promote trade between Arab countries and to enhance the competitive ability of Arab exporters; operates by extending lines of credit to Arab exporters and importers through national agencies (some 200 agencies designated by the monetary authorities of 19 Arab and five other countries); the Arab Monetary Fund provided 50% of ATFP's authorized capital of US $500m; participation was also invited from private and official Arab financial institutions and joint Arab/foreign institutions; administers the Inter-Arab Trade Information Network (IATIN), and organizes Buyers-Sellers meetings to promote Arab goods; by the end of 2010 the Program had extended lines of credit with a total value of $8,580m; Chair. and Chief Exec. Dr Jassim Abdullah al-Mannai; publ. *Annual Report* (Arabic and English).

Publications

Annual Report.

Arab Countries: Economic Indicators (annually).

Foreign Trade of the Arab Countries (annually).

Joint Arab Economic Report (annually).

Money and Credit in the Arab Countries.

National Accounts of the Arab Countries (annually).
Quarterly Bulletin.

Reports on commodity structure (by value and quantity) of member countries' imports from and exports to other Arab countries; other studies on economic, social, management and fiscal issues.

Statistics

LOANS APPROVED, 1978–2010

Type of loan	Number of loans	Amount (AAD '000)
Automatic	59	301,474
Ordinary	12	104,751
Compensatory	16	130,785
Extended	24	340,344
Structural Adjustment Facility	26	355,927
Oil Facility	2	18,814
Inter-Arab Trade Facility (cancelled in 1989)	11	64,730
Total	150	1,316,825

LOANS APPROVED, 2010

Borrower	Type of loan	Amount (AAD '000)
Jordan	Structural Adjustment Facility	17,185
	Automatic loan	9,820
Morocco	Structural Adjustment Facility	47,863
Yemen	Extended loan	43,000

Source: *Annual Report 2010*.

ASIA-PACIFIC ECONOMIC COOPERATION—APEC

Address: 35 Heng Mui Keng Terrace, Singapore 119616.

Telephone: 68919600; **fax:** 68919690; **e-mail:** info@apec.org; **internet:** www.apec.org.

The Asia-Pacific Economic Cooperation (APEC) was initiated in November 1989, in Canberra, Australia, as an informal consultative forum. Its aim is to promote multilateral economic co-operation on issues of trade and investment.

MEMBERS

Australia	Japan	Philippines
Brunei	Korea, Republic	Russia
Canada	Malaysia	Singapore
Chile	Mexico	Taiwan*
China, People's Republic	New Zealand	Thailand
Hong Kong	Papua New Guinea	USA
Indonesia	Peru	Viet Nam

* Admitted as Chinese Taipei.

Note: APEC has three official observers: the Association of Southeast Asian Nations (ASEAN) Secretariat; the Pacific Economic Cooperation Council; and the Pacific Islands Forum Secretariat. Observers may participate in APEC meetings and have full access to all related documents and information.

Organization

(April 2012)

ECONOMIC LEADERS' MEETINGS

The first meeting of APEC heads of government was convened in November 1993, in Seattle, Washington, USA. Subsequently, each annual meeting of APEC ministers of foreign affairs and of economic affairs has been followed by an informal gathering of the leaders of the APEC economies, at which the policy objectives of the grouping are discussed and defined. The 18th Economic Leaders' Meeting was convened in November 2011 in Honolulu, Hawaii.

MINISTERIAL MEETINGS

APEC ministers of foreign affairs and ministers of economic affairs meet annually. These meetings are hosted by the APEC Chair, which rotates each year, although it was agreed, in 1989, that alternate Ministerial Meetings were to be convened in an ASEAN member country. A Senior Officials' Meeting (SOM) convenes regularly between Ministerial Meetings to co-ordinate and administer the budgets and work programmes of APEC's committees and working groups. Other meetings of ministers are held on a regular basis to enhance co-operation in specific areas.

SECRETARIAT

In 1992 the Ministerial Meeting, held in Bangkok, Thailand, agreed to establish a permanent secretariat to support APEC activities. The Secretariat became operational in February 1993. In accordance with a decision of the 2007 Leaders' Meeting, from 1 January 2010 an Executive Director with a three-year fixed term of office was appointed (hitherto the Executive Director had served a one-year term). A Policy Support Unit was established within the Secretariat in 2008.

Executive Director: MUHAMAD NOOR YACOB (Malaysia).

COMMITTEES

Budget and Management Committee (BMC): f. 1993 as Budget and Administrative Committee, present name adopted 1998; advises APEC senior officials on budgetary, administrative and managerial issues. The Committee reviews the operational budgets of APEC committees and groups, evaluates their effectiveness and conducts assessments of group projects. In 2005 the APEC Support Fund (ASF) was established under the auspices of the BMC, with the aim of supporting capacity-building programmes for developing economies; subsidiary funds of the ASF have been established relating to human security and avian influenza.

Committee on Trade and Investment (CTI): f. 1993 on the basis of a Declaration signed by ministers meeting in Seattle, Washington, USA, in order to facilitate the expansion of trade and the development of a liberalized environment for investment among member countries; undertakes initiatives to improve the flow of goods, services and technology in the region. Supports Industry Dialogues to promote collaboration between public and private sector representatives in the following areas of activity: Automotive; Chemical; Non-ferrous Metal; and Life Sciences Innovation. An Investment Experts' Group was established in 1994, initially to develop non-binding investment principles. In May 1997 an APEC Tariff Database was inaugurated, with sponsorship from the private sector. A Market Access Group was established in 1998 to administer CTI activities concerned with non-tariff measures. In 2001 the CTI finalized a set of nine non-binding Principles on Trade Facilitation, which aimed to help eliminate procedural and administrative impediments to trade and to increase trading opportunities. A Trade Facilitation Action Plan (TFAP) was approved in 2002. By 2005 a strategy was adopted to systematize transparency standards. TFAP II, which aimed to reduce trade transaction costs by 5% during 2007–10, was endorsed by the APEC ministers responsible for trade in July 2007 and by APEC leaders in September; an assessment of achievements made under TFAP II was under way in 2011. In 2007 the Electronic Commerce Steering Group, established in 1999, became aligned to the CTI. An Investment Facilitation Action Plan (IFAP) was undertaken during 2008–10, with the aim of assisting investment flows into the region. The most recent (seventh) edition of the official *Guide to the Investment Regimes of the APEC Member Economies* was published in January 2011.

Economic Committee (EC): f. 1994 following an agreement, in November, to transform the existing ad hoc group on economic trends and issues into a formal committee; aims to enhance APEC's capacity to analyse economic trends and to research and report on issues affecting economic and technical co-operation in the region. In addition, the Committee is considering the environmental and development implications of expanding population and economic growth. During 2007–10 the EC implemented a work plan on the implementation of the Leaders' Agenda to Implement Structural Reform (LAISR, agreed in November 2004 by the 12th Economic Leaders' Meeting, see below).

SOM Steering Committee on ECOTECH (SCE): f. 1998 to assist the SOM with the co-ordination of APEC's economic and technical co-operation programme (ECOTECH); reconstituted in 2006, with an enhanced mandate to undertake greater co-ordination and oversee project proposals of the working groups; monitors and evaluates project implementation and also identifies initiatives designed to strengthen economic and technical co-operation in infrastructure.

ADVISORY COUNCIL

APEC Business Advisory Council (ABAC): Philamlife Tower, 43rd Floor, 8767 Paseo de Roxas, Makati City, 1226 Metro Manila, Philippines; tel. (2) 8454564; fax (2) 8454832; e-mail abacsec@pfgc.ph; internet www.abaconline.org; an agreement to establish ABAC, comprising up to three senior representatives of the private sector from each APEC member economy, was concluded at the Ministerial Meeting held in Nov. 1995. ABAC is mandated to advise member states on the implementation of APEC's Action Agenda and on other business matters, and to provide business-related information to APEC fora. ABAC meets three or four times each year and holds an annual CEO Summit alongside the annual APEC Economic Leaders' Meeting; Exec. Dir ZIYAVUDIN MAGOMEDOV (USA) (2012).

Activities

APEC is focused on furthering objectives in three key areas, or 'pillars': trade and investment liberalization; business facilitation; and economic and technical co-operation. It was initiated in 1989 as a forum for informal discussion between the then six ASEAN members and their six dialogue partners in the Pacific, and, in particular, to promote trade liberalization in the Uruguay Round of negotiations, which were being conducted under the General Agreement on Tariffs and Trade (GATT). The Seoul Declaration, adopted by ministers meeting in the Republic of Korea (South Korea) in November 1991, defined the objectives of APEC.

ASEAN countries were initially reluctant to support any more formal structure of the forum, or to admit new members, owing to concerns that it would undermine ASEAN's standing as a regional grouping and be dominated by powerful non-ASEAN economies. In August 1991 it was agreed to extend membership to the People's Republic of China, Hong Kong and Taiwan (subject to conditions imposed by China, including that a Taiwanese official of no higher than vice-ministerial level should attend the annual meeting of ministers of foreign affairs). Mexico and Papua New Guinea acceded to the organization in November 1993, and Chile joined in November 1994. The summit meeting held in November 1997 agreed that Peru, Russia and Viet Nam should be admitted to APEC at the 1998 meeting, but imposed a 10-year moratorium on further expansion of the grouping.

In September 1992 APEC ministers agreed to establish a permanent secretariat. In addition, the meeting created an 11-member non-governmental Eminent Persons Group (EPG), which was to assess trade patterns within the region and propose measures to promote co-operation. At the Ministerial Meeting in Seattle, Washington, USA, in November 1993, members agreed on a framework for expanding trade and investment among member countries, and to establish a permanent committee (the CTI, see above) to pursue these objectives.

In August 1994 the EPG proposed the following timetable for the liberalization of all trade across the Asia-Pacific region: negotiations for the elimination of trade barriers were to commence in 2000 and be completed within 10 years in developed countries, 15 years in newly industrialized economies and by 2020 in developing countries. Trade concessions could then be extended on a reciprocal basis to non-members in order to encourage world-wide trade liberalization, rather than isolate APEC as a unique trading bloc. In November 1994 the meeting of APEC heads of government adopted the Bogor Declaration of Common Resolve, which endorsed the EPG's timetable for free and open trade and investment in the region by the year 2020. Other issues incorporated into the Declaration included the implementation of GATT commitments in full and strengthening the multilateral trading system through the forthcoming establishment of the World Trade Organization (WTO), intensifying development co-operation in the Asia-Pacific region and expanding and accelerating trade and investment programmes. In November 1995 the Ministerial Meeting decided to dismantle the EPG, and to establish the APEC Business Advisory Council (ABAC), consisting of private sector representatives.

Meeting in Osaka, Japan, in November 1995, APEC heads of government adopted the Osaka Action Agenda as a framework to achieve the commitments of the Bogor Declaration. Part One of the Agenda identified action areas for the liberalization of trade and investment and the facilitation of business, for example, customs procedures, rules of origin and non-tariff barriers. It incorporated agreements that the process was to be comprehensive, consistent with WTO commitments, comparable among all APEC economies and non-discriminatory. Each member economy was to ensure the transparency of its laws, regulations and procedures affecting the flow of goods, services and capital among APEC economies and to refrain from implementing any trade protection measures. A second part of the Agenda was to provide a framework for further economic and technical co-operation between APEC members in areas such as energy, transport, infrastructure, small and medium-sized enterprises (SMEs) and agricultural technology. In order to resolve a disagreement concerning the inclusion of agricultural products in the trade liberalization process, a provision for flexibility was incorporated into the Agenda, taking into account diverse circumstances and different levels of development in APEC member economies. Liberalization measures were to be implemented from January 1997 (i.e. three years earlier than previously agreed). A Trade and Investment Liberalization and Facilitation Special Account was established to finance projects in support of the implementation of the Osaka Action Agenda. Each member economy was to prepare an Individual Action Plan (IAP) on efforts to achieve the trade liberalization measures, that were to be reviewed annually.

In November 1996 the Economic Leaders' Meeting, held in Subic Bay, Philippines, approved the Manila Action Plan for APEC (MAPA), which incorporated the IAPs and other collective measures aimed at achieving the trade liberalization and co-operation objectives of the Bogor Declaration, as well as the joint activities specified in the second part of the Osaka Agenda. Heads of government also endorsed a US proposal to eliminate tariffs and other barriers to trade in information technology products by 2000 and determined to support efforts to conclude an agreement to this effect at the forthcoming WTO conference; however, they insisted on the provision of an element of flexibility in achieving trade liberalization in this sector.

The 1997 Economic Leaders' Meeting, held in Vancouver, Canada, in November, was dominated by concern at the financial instability that had affected several Asian economies during that year. The final declaration of the summit meeting endorsed a framework of measures that had been agreed by APEC deputy ministers of finance and central bank governors at an emergency meeting convened in the previous week in Manila, Philippines (the so-called Manila Framework for Enhanced Asian Regional Cooperation to Promote Financial Stability). The meeting, attended by representatives of the IMF, the World Bank and the Asian Development Bank, committed all member economies receiving IMF assistance to undertake specified economic and financial reforms, and supported the establishment of a separate Asian funding facility to supplement international financial assistance (although this was later rejected by the IMF). APEC ministers of finance and governors of central banks were urged to accelerate efforts for the development of the region's financial and capital markets and to liberalize capital flows in the region. Measures were to include strengthening financial market supervision and clearing and settlement infrastructure, the reform of pension systems, and promoting co-operation among export credit agencies and financing institutions. The principal item on the Vancouver summit agenda was an initiative to enhance trade liberalization, which, the grouping insisted, should not be undermined by the financial instability in Asia. The following 15 economic sectors were identified for 'early voluntary sectoral liberalization' ('EVSL'): environmental goods and services; fish and fish products; forest products; medical equipment and instruments; toys; energy; chemicals; gems and jewellery; telecommunications; oilseeds and oilseed products; food; natural and synthetic rubber; fertilizers; automobiles; and civil aircraft. The implementation of EVSL was to encompass market opening, trade facilitation, and economic and technical co-operation activities.

In May 1998 APEC finance ministers met in Canada to consider the ongoing financial and economic crisis in Asia and to review progress in implementing efforts to alleviate the difficulties experienced by several member economies. The ministers agreed to pursue activities in the following three priority areas: capital market development; capital account liberalization; and strengthening financial systems (including corporate governance). The region's economic difficulties remained the principal topic of discussion at the Economic Leaders' Meeting held in Kuala Lumpur, Malaysia, in November. A final declaration reiterated their commitment to co-operation in pursuit of sustainable economic recovery and growth, in particular through the restructuring of financial and corporate sectors, promoting and facilitating private sector capital flows, and efforts to strengthen the global financial system. The meeting endorsed a proposal by ABAC to establish a partnership for equitable growth, with the aim of enhancing business involvement in APEC's programme of economic and technical co-operation. Other initiatives approved included an Agenda of APEC Science and Technology Industry Cooperation into the 21st Century (for which China announced it was to establish a special fund), and an Action Programme on Skills and Development in APEC. Japan's persisting opposition to a reduction of tariffs in the fish and forestry sectors prevented the conclusion of tariff negotiations under the EVSL scheme, and it was therefore agreed that responsibility for managing the tariff reduction element of the initiative should be transferred to the WTO.

In September 1999 political dialogue regarding civil conflict in East Timor (now Timor-Leste) dominated the start of the annual meetings of the grouping, held in Auckland, New Zealand, although the issue remained separate from the official agenda. The Economic Leaders' Meeting considered measures to sustain the economic recovery in Asia and endorsed the APEC Principles to Enhance Competition and Regulatory Reform (for example, transparency, accountability, non-discrimination) as a framework to strengthen APEC markets and to enable further integration and implementation of the IAPs. Also under discussion was the forthcoming round of multilateral trade negotiations, to be initiated by the WTO. The heads of government proposed the objective of completing a single package of trade agreements within three years and endorsed the abolition of export subsidies for agricultural products. The meeting determined to support the efforts of China, Russia, Taiwan and Viet Nam to accede to WTO membership. An APEC Business Travel Card scheme, to facilitate business travel within the region, was inaugurated in 1999, having been launched on a trial basis in 1997; card holders receive fast-track passage through designated APEC immigration processing lanes at major airports, and multiple short term-entry entitlements to participating economies. By 2012 more than 80,000 individuals were registered under the scheme, in which 18 economies were participating fully. The November 2011 Leaders' Meeting determined to launch an APEC Travel Facilitation Initiative, which was to address means of facilitating faster, easier and more secure travel through the region.

The Economic Leaders' Meeting for 2000, held in Brunei in November, urged that an agenda for the now-stalled round of multilateral trade negotiations should be formulated without further delay. The meeting endorsed a plan of action to promote the utilization of advances in information and communications technologies in member economies, for the benefit of all citizens. It adopted the aim of tripling the number of people in the region with access to the internet by 2005, and determined to co-operate with business and education sector interests to attract investment and expertise in the pursuit of this goal. A proposal that the Democratic People's Republic of Korea (North Korea) be permitted to participate in APEC working groups was approved at the meeting.

The 2001 Economic Leaders' Meeting, held in October, in Shanghai, China, condemned the terrorist attacks against targets in the USA of the previous month and resolved to take action to combat the threat of international terrorism. The heads of government declared terrorism to be a direct challenge to APEC's vision of free, open and prosperous economies, and concluded that the threat made the continuing move to free trade, with its aim of bolstering economies, increasing prosperity and encouraging integration, even more of a priority. Leaders emphasized the importance of sharing the benefits of globalization, and adopted the Shanghai Accord, which identified development goals for APEC during its second decade and clarified measures for achieving the Bogor goals within the agreed timetable. A process of IAP Peer Reviews was initiated. (By late 2005 the process had been concluded for each member economy.) The meeting also outlined the e-APEC Strategy developed by the e-APEC Task Force established after the Brunei Economic Leaders' meeting. Considering issues of entrepreneurship, structural and regulatory reform, competition, intellectual property rights and information security, the strategy aimed to facilitate technological development in the region. Finally, the meeting adopted a strategy document relating to infectious diseases in the Asia Pacific region, which aimed to promote a co-ordinated response to combating HIV/AIDS and other contagious diseases.

In September 2002 a meeting of APEC ministers of finance was held in Los Cabos, Mexico. Ministers discussed the importance of efforts to combat money-laundering and the financing of terrorism. The meeting also focused on ways to strengthen global and regional economic growth, to advance fiscal and financial reforms and to improve the allocation of domestic savings for economic development. The theme of the 2002 Economic Leaders' Meeting, held in the following month in Los Cabos, was 'Expanding the Benefits of Cooperation for Economic Growth and Development—Implementing the Vision'. The meeting issued a statement on the implementation of APEC standards of transparency in trade and investment liberalization and facilitation. Leaders also issued a statement on fighting terrorism and promoting growth. In February the first conference to promote the Secure Trade in the APEC Region (STAR) initiative was convened in Bangkok, Thailand, and attended by representatives of all APEC member economies as well as senior officers of private sector companies and relevant international organizations. The second STAR conference was held in Viña del Mar, Chile, in March 2004; the third in Incheon, South Korea, in February 2005; the fourth in Hanoi, Viet Nam, in February 2006; the fifth in Sydney, Australia, in June 2007; the sixth in Lima, Peru, in August 2008; the seventh in Singapore, in July 2009; and the eighth in Washington, DC, USA, in September 2011.

The 2003 Economic Leaders' Meeting, convened in October, in Bangkok, Thailand, considered means of advancing the WTO's stalled Doha round of trade negotiations, emphasizing the central importance of its development dimension, and noted progress made hitherto in facilitating intra-APEC trade. The meeting also addressed regional security issues, reiterating the Community's commitment to ensuring the resilience of APEC economies against the threat of terrorism. The Leaders adopted the Bangkok Declaration on Partnership for the Future, which identified the following areas as priority concerns for the group: the promotion of trade and investment liberalization; enhancing human security; and helping people and societies to benefit from globalization. The Bangkok meeting also issued a statement on health security, which expressed APEC's determination to strengthen infrastructure for the detection and prevention of infectious diseases, as well as the surveillance of other threats to public health, and to ensure a co-ordinated response to public health emergencies, with particular concern to the outbreak, earlier in the year, of Severe Acute Respiratory Syndrome (SARS).

The 12th Economic Leaders' Meeting was held in Santiago, Chile, in November 2004, on the theme 'One Community, Our Future'. The meeting reaffirmed the grouping's commitment to the Doha Development Agenda, and endorsed the package of agreements concluded by the WTO in July. The meeting approved a Santiago Initiative for Expanded Trade in APEC, to promote further trade and investment liberalization in the region and advance trade facilitation measures. Other areas discussed were human security, HIV/AIDS and other emerging infectious diseases, and energy security. Efforts to combat corruption and promote good governance included a Santiago Commitment to Fight Corruption and Ensure Transparency, the APEC Course of Action on Fighting Corruption and Ensuring Transparency, and a Leaders' Agenda to Implement Structural Reform (LAISR). LAISR covers the following five policy areas: regulatory reform; competition policy; public sector governance; corporate governance; and strengthening economic and legal infrastructure.

In September 2005 APEC finance ministers, meeting in Jeju, South Korea, discussed two main issues: the increased importance of capital flows among member economies, particularly those from worker remittances; and the challenge presented by the region's ageing population. The meeting resolved to promote capital account liberalization and to develop resilient and efficient capital markets. It also adopted the 'Jeju Declaration on Enhancing Regional Cooperation against the Challenges of Population Ageing', in which it acknowledged the urgency of such domestic reforms such as creating sustainable pension systems, providing an increased range of savings products and improving financial literacy. In November 2005 the 13th Economic Leaders' Meeting endorsed a Busan Roadmap to the Bogor Goals, based on an assessment of action plans, which outlined key priorities and frameworks. Particular focus was drawn to support for the multilateral trading system, efforts to promote high quality regional trade agreements and free trade agreements, and strengthened collective and individual action plans. It also incorporated a Busan Business Agenda and commitments to a strategic approach to capacity building and to a pathfinder approach to promoting trade and investment in the region, through work on areas such as intellectual property rights, anti-corruption, secure trade and trade facilitation.

The 14th Economic Leaders' Meeting, held in Hanoi, Viet Nam, in November 2006 on the theme 'Towards One Dynamic Community for Sustainable Development and Prosperity', reaffirmed support for the stalled negotiations on the WTO's Doha Development Agenda; adopted the Hanoi Action Plan on the implementation of the Busan Roadmap (endorsed by the 2005 Leaders' Meeting); endorsed the APEC Action Plan on Prevention and Response to Avian and Influenza Pandemics; and expressed strong concern at the nuclear test conducted by North Korea in October.

The participants at the 15th Economic Leaders' Meeting, convened in Sydney, Australia, in September 2007, on the theme 'Strengthening our Community, Building a Sustainable Future', adopted a Declaration on Climate Change, Energy Security and Clean Development, wherein they acknowledged the need to ensure energy supplies to support regional economic growth while also preserving the quality of the environment. The Declaration incorporated an Action Agenda and agreements to establish an Asia-Pacific Network for Energy Technology and an Asia-Pacific Network for Sustainable

Forest Management and Rehabilitation. The Economic Leaders also issued a statement once again affirming the need successfully to resolve the stalled WTO Doha Development Round; endorsed a report on means of further promoting Asia-Pacific economic integration; agreed to examine the options and prospects for the development of a Free Trade Area of the Asia-Pacific (FTAAP); welcomed efforts by the Economic Committee to enhance the implementation of the LAISR; endorsed the second Trade Facilitation Action Plan, which aimed to achieve a 5% reduction in business and trade transaction costs by 2010; determined to strengthen the protection and enforcement of intellectual property rights in the region; and approved the Anti-corruption Principles for the Public and Private Sectors, and related codes of conduct, that had been adopted in June 2007 by the Anti-corruption and Transparency Experts' Task Force and endorsed by the September 2007 Ministerial Meeting.

The 16th Economic Leaders' Meeting, held in November 2008, in Lima, Peru, under the theme 'A New Commitment to Asia-Pacific Development', addressed the implications for the region of the then deteriorating global economic situation. The APEC Leaders urged the promotion of good Corporate Social Responsibility (CSR) practices in the region; commended the progress made hitherto in examining the prospects for establishing the proposed FTAAP; and urged ministers of finance to examine more fully means of optimizing linkages between private infrastructure finance and economic growth and development. Expressing deep concern at the impact on the region of volatile global food prices, and at food shortages in some developing economies, the meeting determined to support the regional implementation of the Comprehensive Framework for Action of the UN Task Force on the Global Food Security Crisis, and to increase technical co-operation and capacity-building measures aimed at fostering the growth of the agricultural sector.

Convened in November 2009, in Singapore, the 17th Economic Leaders' Meeting expressed support for the goals of the G20 'Framework for Strong, Sustainable and Balanced Growth' (adopted in September), and adopted a Declaration on a New Growth Paradigm for a Connected Asia-Pacific in the 21st Century, aimed at navigating a future post-global economic crisis landscape; reaffirming commitment to addressing issues related to the threat of climate change; and welcoming the implementation of a peer review of energy efficiency in APEC economies.

The first APEC Ministerial Meeting on Food Security, held in October 2010, in Niigata, Japan, endorsed a new APEC Action Plan on Food Security. In November the 18th Economic Leaders' Meeting, held in Yokohama, Japan, adopted the APEC Leaders' Growth Strategy, representing a comprehensive long-term framework for promoting high-quality growth in the region. The Growth Strategy included an action plan, which was to outline work towards progress in the areas of structural reform; human resource and entrepreneurship development; human security; green growth; and the development of a knowledge-based economy. Progress in the implementation of the Growth Strategy was to be reviewed in 2015. The November 2010 Leaders' Meeting also endorsed a report and issued an assessment on the state of progress towards achieving the Bogor Goals,. Leaders reaffirmed strong commitment to pursuing the proposed FTAAP and towards achieving a successful conclusion to the Doha Development Agenda, while determining to refrain from adopting protectionist measures until 2014. In May 2011 APEC and the World Bank concluded a Memorandum of Understanding on strengthening collaboration on food safety in the Asia-Pacific region. In September a session of APEC ministers and senior government officials, and leaders from the private sector, meeting in San Francisco, USA, adopted the San Francisco Declaration on Women and the Economy, outlining means of realizing the as yet untapped full potential of women to contribute to the regional economy, and welcoming the establishment of an APEC Policy Partnership on Women and the Economy (PPWE), which had been endorsed by senior officials in May.

The 19th Leaders' Meeting, convened in Honolulu, Hawaii, in November 2011, adopted the Honolulu Declaration 'Toward a Seamless Regional Economy', which, *inter alia*, instructed regional officials to consider new approaches to the then stalled negotiations on concluding the Doha Development Round; reaffirmed commitment to anti-protectionism; determined to advance a set of policies to promote market-driven innovation policy; committed to implementing plans towards the establishment of an APEC New Strategy for Structural Reform and an APEC Cross Border Privacy Rules System; committed, further, to promoting green growth, including through encouraging member economies, in 2012, to develop an APEC list of environmental goods contributing directly to the Community's sustainable development objectives, to which applied tariff rates were to be reduced to 5% or less by end-2015; aspired to reduce regional energy intensity by 45% by 2035, to take specific steps to promote energy-smart low-carbon communities, and to incorporate low-emissions development strategies into national economic growth plans; welcomed the San Francisco Declaration on Women and the Economy and pledged to monitor its implementation; and determined to enhance the role of the private sector in APEC, through greater contribution to its working groups and the establishment of new public-private policy partnerships.

SPECIAL TASK GROUPS

These may be established by the Senior Officials' Meeting to identify issues and make recommendations on areas for consideration by the grouping.

Counter Terrorism Task Force (CTTF): established in February 2003 to co-ordinate implementation of the Leaders' Statement on Fighting Terrorism and Promoting Growth, which had been adopted in October 2002. It was subsequently mandated to implement all other APEC initiatives to enhance human security. The CTTF assists member economies to identify and assess counter-terrorism needs and co-ordinates individual Counter Terrorism Action Plans, which identify measures required and the level of implementation achieved to secure trade.

Mining Task Force (MTF): the first meeting of the MTF was convened in May 2008, in Arequipa, Peru. The Task Force was to provide a unified, cohesive mining, minerals and metals forum for APEC member economies. Its ongoing work programme includes undertaking a study on means of attracting investment to the regional mining sector, with a particular focus on investment; the regulatory framework; and the availability of skilled workforces. A Conference on Sustainable Development of the Mining Sector in the APEC Region was held in July 2009, in Singapore.

WORKING GROUPS

APEC's structure of working groups aims to promote practical and technical co-operation in specific areas, and to help implement individual and collective action plans in response to the directives of the Economic Leaders and meetings of relevant ministers.

Agricultural Technical Co-operation (ATCWG): formally established as an APEC expert's group in 1996, and incorporated into the system of working groups in 2000. The ATCWG aims to enhance the role of agriculture in the economic growth of the region and to promote co-operation in the following areas: conservation and utilization of plant and animal genetic resources; research, development and extension of agricultural biotechnology; processing, marketing, distribution and consumption of agricultural products; plant and animal quarantine and pest management; development of an agricultural finance system; sustainable agriculture; and agricultural technology transfer and training. The ATCWG has primary responsibility for undertaking recommendations connected with the implementation of the APEC Food System, which aims to improve the efficiency of food production, supply and trade within member economies. The ATCWG has conducted projects on human resource development in post-harvest technology and on capacity building, safety assessment and communication in biotechnology. A high-level policy dialogue on agricultural biotechnology was initiated in 2002. Following the outbreak of so-called avian flu and its impact on the region's poultry industry, in 2004 it was agreed that the ATCWG would develop the enhanced biosecurity planning and surveillance capacity considered by APEC's member economies as being essential to protect the region's agricultural sector from the effects of future outbreaks of disease. A quarantine regulators' seminar on Implementing Harmonised Arrangements for Ensuring Effective Quarantine Treatments, and an APEC Workshop on Avian Influenza Risks in the Live Bird Market System, were organized in 2008; and in August 2009 a symposium on the Approach of Organic Agriculture: New Markets, Food Security and a Clean Environment was held. In April 2010 a *Report on Developing and Applying a Traceability System in Agriculture Production and Trade* was issued. The ATCWG contributed to the development of the APEC Action Plan on Food Security, which was endorsed by the October 2010 APEC Ministerial Meeting on Food Security. The 15th ATCWG meeting, held in Washington, DC, USA, in February 2011, agreed to promote agricultural technical transfer and co-operation within the APEC region; consequently, in November 2011, an APEC Agricultural Technology Transfer Forum was held, in Beijing, China, on the theme 'Strengthening Agricultural Technology Transfer for Food Security in the APEC Region'. A workshop on developing a regional food security information platform, comprising general information and statistical data, was convened in February 2011; the platform was expected to be finalized in 2012. In 2011 an APEC Experts Group on Illegal Logging and Associated Trade was established to enhance co-operation in addressing concerns surrounding illegal logging, and to promote sustainable forest management.

Anti-corruption and Transparency (ACT): the ACT was upgraded to a working group in March 2011, having been established as a task force in 2004. The Ministerial Meeting, held in Santiago, Chile, in November 2004, endorsed the establishment of the ACT to implement an APEC Course of Action on Fighting Corruption and Ensuring Transparency. Following its establishment the ACT worked to promote ratification and implementation of the UN Convention against Corruption, to strengthen measures to prevent and combat corruption and to sanction public officials found guilty of corruption, to promote public-private partnerships, and to enhance co-operation within the region to combat problems of corruption. An APEC Anti-Counterfeiting and Piracy Initiative was launched in mid-2005. In June 2007 the ACT approved a Code of Conduct for Business, in collaboration with ABAC, a set of Conduct Principles for Public Officials, and Anti-corruption Principles for the Public and Private Sectors. In February 2010 the ACT endorsed the final result of a project entitled 'Stocktaking of Bilateral and Regional Arrangements on Anti-corruption Matters Between/Among APEC Member Economies'. An ACT Workshop on Successful Training Techniques for Implementing the Principles of Conduct for Public Officials was held in September 2010, in Sendai, Japan. The work plan for 2012 included promoting the implementation of existing APEC anti-corruption commitments; convening a workshop in July, in Phuket, Thailand, on Effectively Combating Corruption and Illicit Trade through Tracking Cross-Border Financial Flows, International Asset Recovery and Anti-Money-Laundering Efforts; and implementing a three-year project on enhancing anti-corruption and money-laundering efforts using financial flow tracking techniques.

Emergency Preparedness (EPWG): established in March 2005, as a special task force, in response to the devastating natural disaster that had occurred in the Indian Ocean in late December 2004; upgraded to a working group in 2010. The EPWG is mandated to co-ordinate efforts throughout APEC to enhance disaster management capacity building, to strengthen public awareness regarding natural disaster preparedness, prevention and survival, and to compile best practices. An APEC Senior Disaster Management Co-ordinator Seminar, convened in Cairns, Australia, in August 2007, and comprising representatives of APEC member economies and of international humanitarian organizations, determined to support the development of a three- to five-year emergency preparedness strategic plan. The fourth APEC Emergency Management CEOs' Forum was held in January 2010, in Kobe, Japan. In October 2011 the EPWG organized a workshop on 'school earthquake and tsunami safety in APEC economies'.

Energy (EWG): APEC ministers responsible for energy convened for the first time in August 1996 to discuss major energy challenges confronting the region. The main objectives of the EWG, established in 1990, are: the enhancement of regional energy security and improvement of the fuel supply market for the power sector; the development and implementation of programmes of work promoting the adoption of environmentally sound energy technologies and promoting private sector investment in regional power infrastructure; the development of energy efficiency guidelines; and the standardization of testing facilities and results. The EWG is supported by five expert groups, on clean fossil energy, efficiency and conservation, energy data and analysis, new and renewable energy technologies, and minerals and energy exploration and development; and by two task forces, on renewable energy and energy efficiency financing, and biofuels. In March 1999 the EWG resolved to establish a business network to improve relations and communications with the private sector. The first meeting of the network took place in April. In May 2000 APEC energy ministers meeting in San Diego, California, USA, launched the APEC 21st Century Renewable Energy Initiative, which aimed to encourage co-operation in and advance the utilization of renewable energy technologies, envisaging the establishment of a Private Sector Renewable Energy Forum. In June 2003 APEC energy ministers agreed on a framework to implement APEC's Energy Security Initiative. The first meeting of ministers responsible for mining was convened in Santiago, Chile, in June 2004. In 2004, amid challenges to energy security and unusually high oil prices, the EWG was instructed by APEC Economic Leaders to accelerate the implementation of the Energy Security Initiative, a strategy aimed at responding to temporary supply disruptions and at addressing the broader challenges facing the region's energy supply by means of longer-term policy. In October 2005 APEC ministers responsible for energy convened in Gyeongju, South Korea, to address the theme 'Securing APEC's Energy Future: Responding to Today's Challenges for Energy Supply and Demand'. Meeting in May 2007 in Darwin, Australia, under the theme 'Achieving Energy Security and Sustainable Development through Efficiency, Conservation and Diversity', energy ministers directed the EWG to formulate a voluntary Energy Peer Review Mechanism. The ministers welcomed the work of the Asia-Pacific Partnership on Clean Development and Climate, launched in January 2006 by Australia, China, India, Japan, South Korea and the USA. In June 2010 energy ministers gathered, in Fukui, Japan, under the theme 'Low Carbon Path to Energy Security'. Pursuant to the Osaka Action Agenda adopted by APEC Economic Leaders in 1995, the Asia Pacific Energy Research Centre (APERC) was established in July 1996 in Tokyo, Japan; APERC's mandate and programmes focus on energy sector development in APEC member states. APERC maintains a comprehensive regional Energy Database. Meeting in Kaohsiung, Taiwan, in October 2011, the EWG set a target to reduce APEC regional energy intensity by 45% by 2035; this was endorsed by the November 2011 Leaders' Meeting. In March 2012 the EWG, convened in Kuala Lumpur, Malaysia, discussed an 'Action Agenda to move APEC toward an Energy Efficient, Sustainable, Low-Carbon Transport Future', which had been adopted by the first APEC Joint Transportation and Energy Ministerial Conference, convened in September 2011, in San Francisco, USA.

Health: in October 2003 a Health Task Force (HTF) was established, on an ad hoc basis, to implement health-related activities as directed by APEC leaders, ministers and senior officials, including a Health Safety Initiative, and to address health issues perceived as potential threats to the region's economy, trade and security, in particular emerging infectious diseases. The HTF convened for the first time in Taiwan, in April 2004. It was responsible for enhancing APEC's work on preventing, preparing for and mitigating the effects of highly pathogenic avian influenza (avian flu) and any future related human influenza pandemic. APEC organized an intergovernmental meeting on Avian and Pandemic Influenza Preparedness and Response, convened in Brisbane, Australia, in October 2005. In May 2006 a Ministerial Meeting on Avian and Influenza Pandemics, held in Da Nang, Viet Nam, endorsed an APEC Action Plan on the Prevention of and Response to Avian and Influenza Pandemics. In June 2007 APEC ministers of health, meeting in Sydney, Australia, determined to reconstitute the HTF as the Health Working Group. The Group convened for its first official meeting in February 2008. Meeting in June 2010, the HWG identified the following priority areas: enhancing preparedness for combating vector-borne diseases, including avian and human pandemic influenza, and HIV/AIDS; capacity-building in the areas of health promotion and prevention of lifestyle-related diseases; improving health outcomes through advances in health information technologies; and strengthening health systems in each member economy. In September 2011 the HWG considered the development of an APEC Action Plan to Reduce the Economic Burden of Non-Communicable Disease.

Human Resources Development (HRD): established in 1990; comprises three networks: the Capacity Building Network, with a focus on human capacity building, including management and technical skills development and corporate governance; the Education Network, promoting effective learning systems and supporting the role of education in advancing individual, social and economic development; and the Labour and Social Protection Network, concerned with promoting social integration through the strengthening of labour markets, the development of labour market information and policy, and improvements in working conditions and social safety net frameworks. The HRD undertakes activities through these networks to implement ministerial and leaders' directives. A voluntary network of APEC study centres links higher education and research institutions in member economies. Private sector participation in the HRD has been strengthened by the establishment of a network of APEC senior executives responsible for human resources management. Recent initiatives have included a cyber-education co-operation project, a workshop on advanced risk management, training on the prevention and resolution of employment and labour disputes, and an educators' exchange programme on the use of information technology in education. In 2012 the HRD was to undertake a project on 'Advancing Inclusive Growth through Social Protection'. A seminar on strengthening the social protection system was to be convened in July 2012, in the Philippines. Meeting in February 2012, in Moscow, Russia, the HRD adopted the Moscow Initiative on fostering public-private partnership in the working group's work.

Industrial Science and Technology (ISTWG): aims to contribute to sustainable development in the region, improve the availability of information, enhance human resources development in the sector, improve the business climate, promote policy dialogue and review and facilitate networks and partnerships. Accordingly, the ISTWG has helped to establish an APEC Virtual Centre for Environmental Technology Exchange in Japan; a Science and Technology Industrial Parks Network; an International Molecular Biology Network for the APEC Region; an APEC Centre for Technology Foresight, based in Thailand; and the APEC Science and Technology Web, an online database. During 1997 and 1998 the ISTWG formulated an APEC Action Framework on Emerging Infectious Diseases and developed an Emerging Infections Network (EINet), based at the University of Washington, Seattle, USA. In March 2004 the fourth meeting of science ministers was held in Christchurch, New Zealand, the first since 1998. ISTWG's work plan for 2010–15 outlined the following goals: enhanced economic growth, trade and investment opportunities, and sustainable development; improved quality of life and a cleaner environment; a safe and secure society; human resource capacity building; enhanced international science and technology networks; improved interconnection between research and innovation; and strengthened technological co-operation.

Oceans and Fisheries (OFWG): formed in 2011 by the merger of the former Fisheries Working Group (FWG) and Marine Resource Conservation Working Group (MRCWG); promotes initiatives within APEC to protect the marine environment and its resources, and to maximize the economic benefits and sustainability of fisheries resources for all APEC members; previously the FWG and MRCWG had held a number of joint sessions focusing on areas of common interest, such as: management strategies for regional marine protected areas, fishery resources and aquaculture; exotic marine species introduction; capacity building in the fields of marine and fishery resources and coral reef conservation; combating destructive fishing practices; aquaculture; and information sharing. The OFWG was to implement the October 2010 Paracas Declaration on Healthy Oceans and Fisheries Management Towards Food Security, focusing on sustainable development and protection of the marine environment, which upon the previous Seoul Oceans Declaration (2002) and Bali Plan of Action (2005).

Policy Partnership on Women and the Economy (PPWE): established in May 2011 as a public-private mechanism to integrate gender considerations into APEC activities, replacing the former Gender Focal Point Network (GFPN, established in 2002); provides policy advice on gender issues and promotes gender equality; aims to provide linkages between the APEC secretariat, working groups, and economies, to advance the economic integration of women in the APEC region for the benefit of all members; at the inaugural meeting of the PPWE, convened in San Francisco, USA, in September 2011, member states address four policies areas regarded as key in increasing economic participation by women: access to capital; access to markets; capacity and skills building; and women's leadership; the meeting also adopted terms of reference and endorsed the San Francisco Declaration on Women and the Economy, urging APEC member states to take concrete actions to realize the full potential of women and integrate them more fully into APEC economies; an APEC Women's Entrepreneurship Summit was held in September–October 2010, in Gifu, Japan; in 2005, the GFPN recommended that women's participation in the APEC Business Advisory Council (ABAC) should be increased, following which several member economies have nominated at least one female delegate to ABAC; a *Gender Experts List* and a *Register of Best Practices on Gender Integration* are maintained.

Small and Medium Enterprises (SMEWG): established in 1995, as the Ad Hoc Policy Level Group on Small and Medium Enterprises (SMEs), with a temporary mandate to oversee all APEC activities relating to SMEs. It supported the establishment of an APEC Centre for Technical Exchange and Training for Small and Medium Enterprises, which was inaugurated at Los Baños, near Manila, Philippines, in September 1996. A five-year action plan for SMEs was endorsed in 1998. The group was redesignated as a working group, with permanent status, in 2000. In August 2002 the SMEWG's action plan was revised to include an evaluation framework to assist APEC and member economies in identifying and analysing policy issues. In the same month a sub-group specializing in micro-enterprises was established. The first APEC Incubator Forum was held in July–August 2003, in Taiwan, to promote new businesses and support their early development. During 2003 the SMEWG undertook efforts to develop a special e-APEC Strategy for SMEs. In 2004 the APEC SME Coordination Framework was finalized. The 12th APEC SME ministerial meeting, held in Daegu, South Korea, in September 2005, adopted the 'Daegu Initiative on SME Innovation Action Plan', which provided a framework for member economies to create economic and policy environments more suitable to SME innovation. In 2006 the APEC Private Sector Development Agenda was launched. The sixth APEC SME Technology Conference and Fair was convened in June–July 2010, in Fuzhou, China. In December 2011 the 33rd APEC SME meeting considered drafting a SME Strategic Plan to cover the period 2013–16; this was to have three main priority areas: improving the business environment; market access and internationalization; and capacity-building management.

Telecommunications and Information (TEL): incorporates three steering groups concerned with different aspects of the development and liberalization of the sector—Liberalization; ICT development; and Security and prosperity. Activities are guided by directives of ministers responsible for telecommunications, who first met in 1995, in South Korea, and adopted a Seoul Declaration on Asia Pacific Information Infrastructure (APII). The second ministerial meeting, held in Gold Coast, Australia, in September 1996, adopted more detailed proposals for liberalization of the sector in member economies. In June 1998 ministers, meeting in Singapore, agreed to remove technical barriers to trade in telecommunications equipment (although Chile and New Zealand declined to sign up to the arrangement). At their fourth meeting, convened in May 2000 in Cancún, Mexico, telecommunications ministers approved a programme of action that included measures to bridge the 'digital divide' between developed and developing member economies, and adopted the APEC Principles on International Charging Arrangements for Internet Services and the APEC Principles of Interconnection. The fifth ministerial meeting, held in May 2002, issued a Statement on the Security of Information and Communications Infrastructures; a compendium of IT security standards has been disseminated in support of the Statement. A Mutual Recognition Arrangement Task Force (MRATF) (under the Liberalization steering group) implements a mutual recognition arrangement for conformity assessment of telecommunications equipment. An APEC Digital Prosperity Checklist is under development, with the aim of promoting ICT as a means of fuelling economic growth; the first and second seminars on the implementation of the Checklist were conducted, respectively, in July 2009 and March 2010. An Asia-Pacific Information Infrastructure (APII) Testbed Network Project, which aimed to facilitate researchers' and engineers' work and to promote the use of new generation internet, and a Stock-Take on Regulatory Convergence are also ongoing. TEL is implementing a Strategic Action Plan over 2010–15, with a focus on universal broadband access.

Tourism (TWG): established in 1991, with the aim of promoting the long-term sustainability of the tourism industry, in both environmental and social terms. The TWG administers a Tourism Information Network and an APEC International Centre for Sustainable Tourism. The first meeting of APEC ministers of tourism, held in South Korea in July 2000, adopted the Seoul Declaration on the APEC Tourism Charter. The TWG's work plan is based on four policy goals inherent in the Seoul Declaration, namely: the removal of impediments to tourism business and investment; increased mobility of visitors and increased demand for tourism goods and services; sustainable management of tourism; and enhanced recognition of tourism as a vehicle for economic and social development. At a meeting of the TWG in April 2001, APEC and the Pacific Asia Travel Association (PATA) adopted a Code for Sustainable Tourism. The Code is designed for adoption and implementation by a variety of tourism companies and government agencies. It urges members to conserve the natural environment, ecosystems and biodiversity; respect local traditions and cultures; conserve energy; reduce pollution and waste; and ensure that regular environmental audits are carried out. In 2004 the TWG published a report on Best Practices in Safety and Security to Safeguard Tourism against Terrorism. In October 2004 the 'Patagonia Declaration on Tourism in the APEC region' was endorsed at the third tourism ministers' meeting in Punta Arenas, Chile. The Declaration set out a strategic plan to ensure the viability of the regional tourism industry by measuring sustainability, safety and security and developing niche projects such as sports and health tourism. The fourth meeting of tourism ministers, held in Hoi An, Viet Nam, in October 2006, adopted the 'Hoi An Declaration on Tourism', which aimed to promote co-operation in developing sustainable tourism and investment in the region, with a focus on the following areas: encouragement of private sector participation in a new APEC Tourism and Investment Forum, and the promotion of the APEC Tourism Fair, both of which were to be held on the sidelines of tourism sector ministerial meetings; and liberalization of the air routes between the cultural heritage sites of APEC member states. In April 2008 tourism ministers, meeting in Lima, Peru, adopted the 'Pachacamac Declaration on Responsible Tourism'. The TWG recognizes tourism as a vehicle of social development, as well as an economic force. The sixth meeting of APEC tourism ministers, convened in Nara, Japan, in September 2010 considered tourism as an engine for economic growth. Meeting in May 2011 the TWG agreed to increase private sector involvement in future meetings.

Transportation (TPTWG): undertakes initiatives to enhance the efficiency and safety of the regional transportation system, in order to facilitate the development of trade. The TPTWG focuses on three main areas: improving the competitiveness of the transportation industry; promoting a safe and environmentally sound regional transportation system; and human resources development, including training, research and education. The TPTWG has published surveys, directories and manuals on all types of transportation systems, and has compiled an inventory on regional co-operation on oil spills preparedness and response arrangements. A Road Transportation Harmonization Project aims to provide the basis for common standards in the automotive industry in the Asia-Pacific region. The TPTWG has established an internet database on ports and the internet-based Virtual Centre for Transportation Research, Development and Education. It plans to develop a regional action plan on the implementation of Global Navigation Satellite Systems, in consultation with the relevant international bodies. A Special Task Force was established by the TPTWG in 2003 to assist member economies to implement a new International Ship and Port Facility Security Code, sponsored by the International Maritime Organization, which entered into force on 1 July 2004. In April 2004 an Aviation Safety Experts' Group met for the first time since 2000. In July 2004 the fourth meeting of APEC ministers of transport directed the TPTWG to prepare a strategy document to strengthen its activities in transport liberalization and facilitation. A Seminar on Post Tsunami Reconstruction and Functions of Ports Safety was held in 2005. The fifth APEC Transportation ministerial meeting was held in Adelaide, Australia, in March 2007; the sixth, convened in Manila, Philippines, in April 2009, issued a joint ministerial statement detailing the following future focus areas for the TPTWG: liberalization and facilitation of transport services; seamless transportation services; aviation safety and security; land transport and mass transit safety and security; maritime safety and security; sustainable transport; industry involvement; and information sharing. The seventh meeting of APEC transport ministers, convened in September 2011, in San Francisco, USA, pledged to increase co-operation on greener, more energy-efficient co-operation. The first APEC Joint Transportation and Energy Ministerial Conference, also convened in September, in San Francisco, adopted an 'Action Agenda to move APEC toward an Energy Efficient, Sustainable, Low-Carbon Transport Future'.

Publications

ABAC Report to APEC Leaders (annually).

APEC at a Glance (annually).

APEC Business Travel Handbook.

APEC Economic Outlook (annually).

APEC Economic Policy Report.

APEC Energy Handbook (annually).

APEC Energy Statistics (annually).

APEC Outcomes and Outlook.

Guide to the Investment Regimes of the APEC Member Economies (every three years).

Key APEC Documents (annually).

Towards Knowledge-based Economies in APEC.

Trade and Investment Liberalization in APEC.

Working group reports, regional directories, other irregular surveys.

ASIAN DEVELOPMENT BANK—ADB

Address: 6 ADB Ave, Mandaluyong City, 0401 Metro Manila, Philippines; POB 789, 0980 Manila, Philippines.

Telephone: (2) 6324444; **fax:** (2) 6362444; **e-mail:** information@adb.org; **internet:** www.adb.org.

The ADB commenced operations in December 1966. The Bank's principal functions are to provide loans and equity investments for the economic and social advancement of its developing member countries, to give technical assistance for the preparation and implementation of development projects and programmes and advisory services, to promote investment of public and private capital for development purposes, and to respond to requests from developing member countries for assistance in the co-ordination of their development policies and plans.

MEMBERS

There are 48 member countries and territories within the ESCAP region and 19 others (see list of subscriptions below).

Organization

(April 2012)

BOARD OF GOVERNORS

All powers of the Bank are vested in the Board, which may delegate its powers to the Board of Directors except in such matters as admission of new members, changes in the Bank's authorized capital stock, election of Directors and President, and amendment of the Charter. One Governor and one Alternate Governor are appointed by each member country. The Board meets at least once a year. The 44th meeting was held in Ha Noi, Viet Nam, in May 2011; the 45th meeting was scheduled to be convened in Manila, Philippines, in May 2012.

BOARD OF DIRECTORS

The Board of Directors is responsible for general direction of operations and exercises all powers delegated by the Board of Governors, which elects it. Of the 12 Directors, eight represent constituency groups of member countries within the ESCAP region (with about 65% of the voting power) and four represent the rest of the member countries. Each Director serves for two years and may be re-elected.

Three specialized committees (the Audit Committee, the Budget Review Committee and the Inspection Committee), each comprising six members, assist the Board of Directors in exercising its authority with regard to supervising the Bank's financial statements, approving the administrative budget, and reviewing and approving policy documents and assistance operations.

The President of the Bank, though not a Director, is Chairman of the Board.

Chairman of Board of Directors and President: HARUHIKO KURODA (Japan).

Vice-Presidents: ZHAO XIAOYU (People's Republic of China), STEPHEN P. GROFF (USA), BINDU LOHANI (Nepal), LAKSHMI VENKATACHALAM (India), THIERRY DE LONGUEMAR (France).

ADMINISTRATION

The Bank had 2,833 staff, from 59 countries, at 31 December 2010.

Five regional departments cover Central and West Asia, East Asia, the Pacific, South Asia, and South-East Asia. Other departments and offices include Anti-corruption and Integrity, Central Operations Services, Co-financing Operations, Economics and Research, Private Sector Operations, Regional and Sustainable Development, Risk Management, Strategy and Policy, as well as other administrative units.

There are Bank Resident Missions in Afghanistan, Armenia, Azerbaijan, Bangladesh, Cambodia, the People's Republic of China, Georgia, India, Indonesia, Kazakhstan, Kyrgyzstan, Laos, Mongolia, Nepal, Pakistan, Papua New Guinea, Sri Lanka, Tajikistan, Thailand, Turkey, Uzbekistan and Viet Nam, all of which report to the head of the regional department. In addition, the Bank maintains a Country Office in the Philippines, a Special Liaison Office in Timor-Leste, a Pacific Liaison and Co-ordination Office in Sydney, Australia, and a South Pacific Sub-Regional Mission, based in Fiji. Representative Offices are located in Tokyo, Japan, Frankfurt am Main, Germany (for Europe), and Washington, DC, USA (for North America).

INSTITUTE

ADB Institute (ADBI): Kasumigaseki Bldg, 8th Floor, 2–5 Kasumigaseki 3-chome, Chiyoda-ku, Tokyo 100-6008, Japan; tel. (3) 3593-5500; fax (3) 3593-5571; e-mail info@adbi.org; internet www.adbi.org; f. 1997 as a subsidiary body of the ADB to research and analyse long-term development issues and to disseminate development practices through training and other capacity-building activities; Dean Dr MASAHIRO KAWAI (Japan).

FINANCIAL STRUCTURE

The Bank's ordinary capital resources (which are used for loans to the more advanced developing member countries) are held and used entirely separately from its Special Funds resources (see below). In May 2009 the Board of Governors approved a fifth General Capital Increase (GCI V), increasing the Bank's resources by some 200% to US $165,000m.

At 31 December 2010 the position of subscriptions to the capital stock was as follows: authorized US $163,843m.; subscribed $143,950m.

The Bank also borrows funds from the world capital markets. Total borrowings during 2010 amounted to US $14,940m. (compared with $10,359m. in 2009). At 31 December 2010 total outstanding debt amounted to $51,822m.

In July 1986 the Bank abolished the system of fixed lending rates, under which ordinary operations loans had carried interest rates fixed at the time of loan commitment for the entire life of the loan. Under the new system the lending rate is adjusted every six months, to take into account changing conditions in international financial markets.

Activities

Loans by the ADB are usually aimed at specific projects. In responding to requests from member governments for loans, the Bank's staff assesses the financial and economic viability of projects and the way in which they fit into the economic framework and priorities of development of the country concerned. In 1985 the Bank decided to expand its assistance to the private sector, hitherto comprising loans to development finance institutions, under government guarantee, for lending to small and medium-sized enterprises; a programme was formulated for direct financial assistance, in the form of equity and loans without government guarantee, to private enterprises. During the early 1990s the Bank aimed to expand its role as project financier by providing assistance for policy formulation and review and promoting regional co-operation, while placing greater emphasis on individual country requirements. During that period the Bank also introduced a commitment to assess development projects for their impact on the local population and to avoid all involuntary resettlement where possible and established a formal procedure for grievances, under which the Board may authorize an inspection of a project by an independent panel of experts, at the request of the affected community or group. The currency instability and ensuing financial crises affecting many Asian economies in 1997/98 prompted the Bank to reflect on its role in the region. The Bank resolved to strengthen its activities as a broad-based development institution, rather than solely as a project financier, through lending policies, dialogue, co-financing and technical assistance.

In November 1999 the Board of Directors approved a new overall strategy objective of poverty reduction, which was to be the principal consideration for all future Bank activities. The strategy incorporated key aims of supporting sustainable, grass-roots based economic growth, social development and good governance. From 2000 the Bank refocused its country strategies, projects and lending targets to complement the poverty reduction strategy. In addition, it initiated a process of consultation to formulate a long-term strategic framework, based on the target of reducing by 50% the incidence of extreme poverty by 2015, one of the so-called Millennium Development Goals (MDGs) identified by the UN General Assembly. The framework, establishing the operational priorities and principles for reducing poverty, was approved in March 2001. A review of the strategy, initiated at the end of 2003, concluded that more comprehensive, results-oriented monitoring and evaluation be put in place. It also recommended a closer alignment of Bank operations with national poverty reduction strategies and determined to include capacity development as a new overall thematic priority for the Bank, in addition to environmental sustainability, gender and development, private sector development and regional co-operation. In mid-2004 the Bank initiated a separate reform agenda to incorporate the strategy approach 'Managing for development results' throughout the organization. In April 2005 a Regional Monitoring Unit was replaced by an Office of Regional Economic Integration, which aimed to promote economic co-operation and integration among developing member countries and to contribute to economic growth throughout the whole region. In July 2006 the Bank adopted a strategy to promote regional co-operation and integration in order to combat poverty through collective regional and cross-border activities.

In June 2006 the Bank convened a panel of eminent persons to assess the Bank's future role within the region. The report of the panel, submitted in March 2007, prompted further wide-ranging consultations. In April 2008 the Bank published a new long-term strategic framework to cover the period 2008–20 ('Strategy 2020'), replacing the previous 2001–15 strategic framework, in recognition of the unprecedented economic growth of recent years and its associated challenges, including the effect on natural resources, inadequate infrastructure to support economic advances, and widening disparities both within and between developing member countries. The Bank determined to refocus its activities onto three critical agendas: inclusive economic growth; environmentally sustainable growth; and regional integration. It determined to initiate a process of restructuring its operations into five core areas of specialization: infrastructure; environment, including climate change; regional co-operation and integration; financial sector development; and education. Some 80% of Bank lending was to be allocated to these five areas by 2012. Under the strategy the Bank resolved to act as an agent of change, stimulating economic growth and widening development assistance, for example by supporting the private sector with more risk guarantees, investment and other financial instruments, placing greater emphasis on good governance, promoting gender equality and improving accessibility to and distribution of its knowledge services. It also committed to expanding its partnerships with other organizations, including with the private sector and other private institutions. The strategy was endorsed at the annual meeting of the Board of Governors, convened in Madrid, Spain, in May 2008.

In September 2008 the Bank organized a high level conference, attended by representatives of multilateral institutions, credit rating agencies, regulatory and supervisory bodies and banks to discuss and exchange ideas on measures to strengthen the region's financial markets and contain the global financial instability evident at that time. In March 2009 the Bank hosted a South Asia Forum on the Impact of the Global Economic and Financial Crisis, as the first of a proposed series of sub-regional conferences. At the end of that month the Bank expanded its Trade Finance Facilitation Program (TFFP, inaugurated in 2004) to support the private sector by increasing its exposure limit to guarantee trade transactions from US $150m. to $1,000m. In May 2009 the Board of Governors approved a general capital increase of some 200% to enable the Bank to extend the lending required to assist countries affected by the global economic downturn, as well as to support the longer-term development objectives of Strategy 2020. In June 2009 the Board of Directors approved a new Countercyclical Support Facility, with resources of $3,000m., to extend short-term, fast-disbursing loans to help developing member countries to counter the effects of the global financial crisis. Countries eligible for the funds were required to formulate a countercyclical development programme, to include plans for investment in public infrastructure or social safety net initiatives. The Board approved an additional $400m, to be made available through the Asian Development Fund (ADF), for countries with no access to the Bank's ordinary capital resources.

In 2010 the Bank's total financing operations amounted to US $17,514m, compared with $19,156m. in the previous year. Of the total amount approved in 2010, $11,463m. was for 118 loans, of which loans from ordinary capital resources totalled $9,250m., while loans from the ADF amounted to $2,213m. In 2010 the Bank approved 40 grants amounting to $982m. financed mainly by the ADF, as well as by other Special Funds (see below) and bilateral and multilateral sources. It also approved funding of $176m. for 243 technical assistance projects, $243m. for eight equity investments, and $982m. in guarantees for five projects. During 2010 $3,669m. of the total financing approved came from co-financing partners, for 155 investment and technical assistance projects, compared with $3,418m. in 2009.

An Operations Evaluation Office prepares reports on completed projects, in order to assess achievements and problems. In April 2000 the Bank announced that some new loans would be denominated in local currencies, in order to ease the repayment burden on recipient economies.

The Bank co-operates with other international organizations active in the region, particularly the World Bank, the IMF, UNDP and APEC, and participates in meetings of aid donors for developing member countries. In May 2001 the Bank and UNDP signed a Memorandum of Understanding (MOU) on strategic partnership, in order to strengthen co-operation in the reduction of poverty, for example the preparation of common country assessments and a common database on poverty and other social indicators. Also in 2001 the Bank signed an MOU with the World Bank on administrative arrangements for co-operation, providing a framework for closer co-operation and more efficient use of resources. In May 2004 the Bank signed a revised MOU with ESCAP to enhance co-operation activities to achieve the MDGs. In November 2011 the Bank signed an MOU with the EBRD to strengthen mutual co-operation in their mutual countries of operation. In early 2002 the Bank worked with the World Bank and UNDP to assess the preliminary needs of the interim administration in Afghanistan, in preparation for an International Conference on Reconstruction Assistance to Afghanistan, held in January, in Tokyo, Japan. The Bank pledged to work with its member governments to provide highly concessional grants and loans of some US $500m. over two-and-a-half years, with a particular focus on road reconstruction, basic education, and agricultural irrigation rehabilitation. In June 2008, at an international donors' conference held in Paris, France, the Bank pledged up to $1,300m. to finance infrastructure projects in Afghanistan in the coming five years. A new policy concerning co-operation with non-governmental organizations (NGOs) was approved by the Bank in 1998. The Bank administers an NGO Centre to provide advice and support to NGOs on involvement in country strategies and development programmes.

In June 2004 the Bank approved a new policy to provide rehabilitation and reconstruction assistance following disasters or other emergencies. The policy also aimed to assist developing member countries with prevention, preparation and mitigation of the impact of future disasters. At the end of December the Bank announced assistance amounting to US $325m. to finance immediate reconstruction and rehabilitation efforts in Indonesia, the Maldives and Sri Lanka, which had been severely damaged by the tsunami that had spread throughout the Indian Ocean as a result of a massive earthquake that had occurred close to the west coast of Sumatra, Indonesia. Of the total amount $150m. was to be drawn as new lending commitments from the ADF. Teams of Bank experts undertook to identify priority operations and initiated efforts, in co-operation with governments and other partner organizations, to prepare for more comprehensive reconstruction activities. In accordance with the 2004 policy initiative, an interdepartmental task force was established to co-ordinate the Bank's response to the disaster. In January 2005, at a Special ASEAN Leaders' Meeting, held in Jakarta, Indonesia, the Bank pledged assistance amounting to $500m.; later in that month the Bank announced its intention to establish a $600m. Multi-donor Asian Tsunami Fund to accelerate the provision of reconstruction and technical assistance to countries most affected by the disaster. In March 2006 the Bank hosted a high-level co-ordination meeting on rehabilitation and reconstruction assistance to tsunami-affected countries. In October the Bank, with representatives of the World Bank, undertook an immediate preliminary damage and needs assessment following a massive earthquake in north-western Pakistan, which also affected remote parts of Afghanistan and India. The report identified relief and reconstruction requirements totalling some $5,200m. The Bank made an initial contribution of $80m. to a Special Fund (see below) and also pledged concessional support of up to $1,000m. for rehabilitation and reconstruction efforts in the affected areas. In August 2010 the Bank announced that it was to extend up to $2,000m. in emergency rehabilitation and reconstruction assistance to Pakistan, large areas of which had been severely damaged by flooding. The Bank agreed to undertake, jointly with the World Bank, a damage and needs assessment to determine priority areas of action.

The Bank has actively supported regional, sub-regional and national initiatives to enhance economic development and promote economic co-operation within the region. The Bank is the main co-ordinator and financier of a Greater Mekong Sub-region (GMS) programme, initiated in 1992 to strengthen co-operation between Cambodia, the People's Republic of China, Laos, Myanmar, Thailand and Viet Nam. Projects undertaken have included transport and other infrastructure links, energy projects and communicable disease control. The first meeting of GMS heads of state was convened in Phnom-Penh, Cambodia, in November 2002. A second summit was held in Kunming, China, in July 2005, and a third summit in Vientiane, Laos, in March 2008, on the theme 'Enhancing Competitiveness through Greater Connectivity'. In June a GMS Economic Corridors Forum was held, in Kunming, to accelerate development of economic corridors in the sub-region. A second Forum was convened in Phnom-Penh, in September 2009, and a third in Vientiane, in June 2011. Other sub-regional initiatives supported by the Bank include the Central Asian Regional Economic Co-operation (CAREC) initiative, the South Asia Sub-regional Economic Cooperation (SASEC) initiative, the Indonesia, Malaysia, Thailand Growth Triangle (IMT-GT), and the Brunei, Indonesia, Malaysia, Philippines East ASEAN Growth Area (BIMP-EAGA).

SPECIAL FUNDS

The Bank is authorized to establish and administer Special Funds. The Asian Development Fund (ADF) was established in 1974 in order to provide a systematic mechanism for mobilizing and administering resources for the Bank to lend on concessionary terms to the least-developed member countries. In 1998 the Bank revised the terms of ADF. Since 1 January 1999 all new project loans are repayable within 32 years, including an eight-year grace period, while quick-disbursing programme loans have a 24-year maturity, also including an eight-year grace period. The previous annual service charge was redesignated as an interest charge, including a portion to cover administrative expenses. The new interest charges on all loans are 1%–1.5% per annum. In May 2008 30 donor countries pledged US $4,200m. towards the ninth replenishment of ADF resources (ADF X), which totalled $11,300m. to provide resources for the four-year period 2009–12. The total amount included replenishment of the Technical Assistance Special Fund (TASF—see below). During 2010 ADF loans approved amounted to $2,212.3m.

The Bank provides technical assistance grants from its TASF. A fourth replenishment of its resources was approved in August 2008 for the period 2009–12. By the end of 2010 the Fund's total resources amounted to US $1,759.7m. During 2010 $147.1m. was approved under the TASF project preparation, advisory and capacity development activities. The Japan Special Fund (JSF) was established in 1988 to provide finance for technical assistance by means of grants, in both the public and private sectors. The JSF aims to help developing member countries tp restructure their economies, enhance the opportunities for attracting new investment, and recycle funds. The Japanese Government had committed a total of 112,900m. yen (equivalent to some $973.7m.) to the JSF by the end of 2010. The Bank administers the ADB Institute Special Fund, which was established to finance the ADB Institute's operations. By 31 December 2010 cumulative commitments to the Special Fund amounted to 18,645m. yen and A$0.5m. (or $166.2m.).

In February 2005 the Bank established the Asian Tsunami Fund, with funds of US $600m., to accelerate the provision of reconstruction and technical assistance to countries most affected by the natural disaster that had affected several countries in the region in December 2004. At the end of 2010 the Fund's uncommitted resources amounted to $2.6m., of total resources amounting to $586.9m. The Pakistan Earthquake Fund was established in November 2005, with a commitment from the Bank of $80m., to help to deliver emergency grant financing and technical assistance required for immediate rehabilitation and reconstruction efforts following the massive earthquake that had occurred in October. At the end of 2010 the Fund's total resources amounted to some $145.2m., of which $3.9m. was uncommitted. In February 2007 the Bank established, with an initial $40.0m., the Regional Co-operation and Integration Fund to fund co-operation and integration activities. By the end of 2010 the Fund's total resources amounted to $53.0m., of which $10.4m. was uncommitted. In April 2008 the Bank established a Climate Change Fund, with an initial contribution of $40.0m. By 31 December 2010 total resources amounted to $51.0m., of which $19.1m. was uncommitted. In April 2009 the Bank's Board of Directors approved the establishment of an Asia Pacific Disaster Response Fund (APDRF) to extend rapid assistance to developing countries following a natural disaster. Some $40.0m. from the Asian Tsunami Fund was transferred to inaugurate the APDRF, which was mandated to provide grants of up to $3.0m. to fund immediate humanitarian relief operations. The APDRF was used in late September to provide assistance for more than 300,000 families in the Philippines affected by extensive flooding and damage to infrastructure caused by a tropical storm. In the following month the Bank approved $1.0m. from the Fund to support emergency efforts in Samoa, following an earthquake and tsunami. In August 2010 $3.0m. was approved under the APDRF to extend immediate emergency assistance following devastating flooding in Pakistan. At that time the Bank established a special flood reconstruction fund to administer donor contributions for relief and rehabilitation efforts in Pakistan.

TRUST FUNDS

The Bank also manages and administers several trust funds and other bilateral donor arrangements. The Japanese Government funds the Japan Scholarship Program, under which 2,696 scholarships had been awarded to recipients from 35 member countries between 1988 and 2010. In May 2000 the Japan Fund for Poverty Reduction was established, with an initial contribution of 10,000m. yen (approximately US $92.6m.) by the Japanese Government, to support ADB-financed poverty reduction and social development activities. During 2010 the Fund's mandate was expanded to provide for technical assistance grants. By the end of 2010 cumulative resources available to the Fund totalled $445.8m. In March 2004 a Japan Fund for Public Policy Training was established, with an initial contribution by the Japanese Government, to enhance capacity building for public policy management in developing member countries.

The majority of grant funds in support of the Bank's technical assistance activities are provided by bilateral donors under channel financing arrangements (CFAs), the first of which was negotiated in 1980. CFAs may also be processed as a thematic financing tool, for example concerned with renewable energy, water or poverty reduction, enabling more than one donor to contribute. A Co-operation Fund for Regional Trade and Financial Security Initiative was established in July 2004, with contributions by Australia, Japan and the USA, to support efforts to combat money laundering and the financing of terrorism. Other financing partnerships facilities may also be established to mobilize additional financing and investment by development partners. In November 2006 the Bank approved the establishment of an Asia Pacific Carbon Fund (within the framework of a Carbon Market Initiative) to finance clean energy projects in developing member countries. To complement this Fund a new Future Carbon Fund was established, in July 2008, to provide resources for projects beyond 2012 (when the Kyoto Protocol regulating trade in carbon credits was due to expire). In December 2006 the Bank established a Water Financing Partnership Facility to help to achieve the objectives of its Water Financing Program. In April 2007 a Clean Energy Financing Partnership Facility (CEFPF) was established, further to provide investment in clean energy projects for developing member countries. An Asian Clean Energy Fund and an Investment Climate Facilitation Fund were established in 2008 within the framework of the CEFPF. A separate Carbon Capture and Storage Fund was established, under the CEFPF, with funding from the Australian Government, in July 2009. In November the Bank, with funding from the United Kingdom, initiated a five-year strategic partnership to combat poverty in India. In the following month the Bank established a multi-donor Urban Financing Partnership Facility. In November 2010 the Board of Directors approved the establishment of an Afghanistan Infrastructure Trust Fund, to be administered by the Bank, to finance and co-ordinate donor funding for infrastructure projects in that country.

In April 2010 the Board of Directors agreed to allocate US $130m. to a new Credit Guarantee and Investment Facility, established by ASEAN + 3 governments, with a further capital contribution of some $570m., in order to secure longer-term financing for local businesses and to support the development of Asian bond markets.

Finance

Internal administrative expenses totalled an estimated US $496.3m. in 2011 and were budgeted at $544.8m. for 2012.

Publications

ADB Business Opportunities (monthly).

ADB Institute Newsletter.

ADB Review (monthly).

Annual Report.

Asia Bond Monitor (quarterly).

Asia Capital Markets Monitor (annually).

Asia Economic Monitor (2 a year).

Asian Development Outlook (annually; an *Update* published annually).

Asian Development Review (2 a year).

Basic Statistics (annually).

Development Asia (2 a year).

Key Indicators for Asia and the Pacific (annually).

Law and Policy Reform Bulletin (annually).

Sustainability Report.

Studies and technical assistance reports, information brochures, guidelines, sample bidding documents, staff papers.

Statistics

SUBSCRIPTIONS AND VOTING POWER
(31 December 2010)

Country	Voting power (% of total)	Subscribed capital (% of total)
Regional:		
Afghanistan	0.329	0.038
Armenia	0.570	0.339
Australia	5.555	6.571
Azerbaijan	0.703	0.505
Bangladesh	1.226	1.160
Bhutan	0.304	0.007
Brunei	0.405	0.133
Cambodia	0.343	0.056
China, People's Republic	6.153	7.318
Cook Islands	0.301	0.003
Fiji	0.360	0.077
Georgia	0.609	0.388
Hong Kong	0.793	0.618
India	6.050	7.190
Indonesia	5.246	6.185
Japan	14.477	17.723
Kazakhstan	1.031	0.916
Kiribati	0.302	0.005
Korea, Republic	4.875	5.721
Kyrgyzstan	0.570	0.340
Laos	0.311	0.016
Malaysia	2.772	3.092
The Maldives	0.302	0.005
Marshall Islands	0.301	0.003
Micronesia, Federated States	0.300	0.002
Mongolia	0.312	0.017
Myanmar	0.793	0.618
Nauru	0.302	0.005
Nepal	0.432	0.167
New Zealand	1.694	1.744
Pakistan	2.278	2.474
Palau	0.301	0.004
Papua New Guinea	0.384	0.107
Philippines	2.463	2.706
Samoa	0.299	0.001
Singapore	0.402	0.129
Solomon Islands	0.305	0.008
Sri Lanka	0.825	0.659
Taiwan	1.288	1.237
Tajikistan	0.559	0.325
Thailand	1.535	1.546
Timor-Leste	0.307	0.011
Tonga	0.302	0.005
Turkmenistan	0.529	0.288
Tuvalu	0.299	0.001
Uzbekistan	0.910	0.765
Vanuatu	0.305	0.008
Viet Nam	0.402	0.129
Sub-total	71.417	71.361
Non-regional:		
Austria	0.608	0.386
Belgium	0.608	0.386
Canada	5.051	5.940
Denmark	0.608	0.386
Finland	0.608	0.386
France	2.413	2.643
Germany	4.229	4.913
Ireland	0.402	0.129
Italy	1.940	2.052
Luxembourg	0.608	0.386
Netherlands	1.230	1.165
Norway	0.608	0.386
Portugal	0.402	0.129
Spain	0.608	0.386
Sweden	0.608	0.386
Switzerland	0.475	0.221
Turkey	0.402	0.129
United Kingdom	2.154	2.319
USA	5.025	5.908
Sub-total	29.583	28.639
Total	100.000	100.000

LOAN APPROVALS BY SECTOR

Sector	2010 Amount (US $ million)	2010 %	1968–2010 Amount
Agriculture and natural resources	613.9	5.4	19,624.2
Education	70.0	0.6	6,178.8
Energy	2,454.0	21.4	32,857.4
Finance	1,263.4	11.0	20,337.7
Health and social protection	177.0	1.5	3,832.9
Industry and trade	—	—	4,588.0
Public sector management	894.5	7.9	13,980.3
Transport and information and communication technology (ICT)	3,831.1	33.4	41,141.2
Water supply and other municipal infrastructure and services	607.0	5.3	14,060.8
Multi-sector	1,551.4	13.5	10,414.8
Total	11,462.3	100.0	167,116.2

APPROVALS BY COUNTRY, 2010
(US $ million)

Country	Ordinary Capital loans	ADF loans	Total approvals*
Afghanistan	—	—	362.4
Armenia	210.0	—	210.0
Azerbaijan	27.0	—	438.0
Bangladesh	800.0	449.0	2,967.5
Bhutan	—	—	30.4
Brunei	—	—	0.8
Cambodia	—	95.0	203.2
China, People's Republic	1,577.5	—	1,947.9
Cook Islands	—	—	0.3
Georgia	338.0	85.0	596.4
India	2,119.6	—	2,395.2
Indonesia	785.0	—	901.6
Kazakhstan	606.0	—	674.7
Kiribati	—	12.0	32.8
Kyrgyzstan	—	88.2	168.8
Laos	—	151.6	211.9
Maldives	—	—	0.7
Marshall Islands	—	9.5	11.7
Mongolia	—	48.0	110.4
Nepal	—	154.9	301.2
Pakistan	378.8	270.0	1,094.0
Palau	12.6	3.4	16.0
Papua New Guinea	40.9	29.4	77.5
Philippines	600.0	—	708.0
Samoa	—	16.0	16.0

Country—*continued*	Ordinary Capital loans	ADF loans	Total approvals*
Solomon Islands	—	—	78.6
Sri Lanka	350.0	107.2	507.1
Tajikistan	—	—	122.8
Thailand	504.3	—	509.1
Timor-Leste	—	—	1.8
Tonga	—	—	0.5
Turkmenistan	—	—	0.4
Uzbekistan	390.0	265.0	957.4
Vanuatu	—	—	0.5
Viet Nam	510.0	580.0	1,246.5
Total	9,249.7	2,212.6	17,513.5

* Includes guarantees, equity investments, grants, technical assistance financing and co-financing.

Source: Asian Development Bank, *Annual Report 2010*.

ASSOCIATION OF SOUTHEAST ASIAN NATIONS—ASEAN

Address: 70A Jalan Sisingamangaraja, POB 2072, Jakarta 12110, Indonesia.

Telephone: (21) 7262991; **fax:** (21) 7398234; **e-mail:** public@aseansec.org; **internet:** www.aseansec.org.

ASEAN was established in August 1967 in Bangkok, Thailand, to accelerate economic progress and to increase the stability of the South-East Asian region. In November 2007 its 10 members signed an ASEAN Charter, which, after ratification by all member states, was formally to accord the grouping the legal status of an intergovernmental organization. The Charter entered into force on 15 December 2008.

MEMBERS

Brunei	Malaysia	Singapore
Cambodia	Myanmar	Thailand
Indonesia	Philippines	Viet Nam
Laos		

Organization

(April 2012)

SUMMIT MEETING

The summit meeting is the highest authority of ASEAN, bringing together the heads of state or government of member countries. The first meeting was held in Bali, Indonesia, in February 1976. The new ASEAN Charter specified that summit meetings were to be convened at least twice a year, hosted by the member state holding the Chairmanship of the organization (a position that rotates on an annual basis). The 20th summit meeting was held in Phnom Penh, Cambodia, in April 2012.

ASEAN CO-ORDINATING COUNCIL

The inaugural meeting of the Council was convened in December 2008, upon the entering into force of the new ASEAN Charter. Comprising the ministers of foreign affairs of member states, the Council was to meet at least twice a year to assist in the preparation of summit meetings, to monitor the implementation of agreements and summit meeting decisions and to co-ordinate ASEAN policies and activities.

ASEAN COMMUNITY COUNCILS

Three new Community Councils were established within the framework of the ASEAN Charter in order to pursue the objectives of the different pillars of the grouping and to enhance regional integration and co-operation. The ASEAN Political-Security Community Council, the ASEAN Economic Community Council and the ASEAN Socio-Cultural Community Council each were to meet at least twice a year, chaired by the appropriate government minister of the country holding ASEAN Chairmanship. Each Council was to oversee a structure of Sectoral Ministerial Bodies, many of which had established mandates as ministerial meetings, councils or specialized bodies.

COMMITTEE OF PERMANENT REPRESENTATIVES

The Committee, according to the new Charter, was to comprise a Permanent Representative appointed, at ambassadorial level, by each member state. Its functions were to include supporting the work of ASEAN bodies, liaising with the Secretary-General, and facilitating ASEAN co-operation with external partners.

SECRETARIATS

A permanent secretariat was established in Jakarta, Indonesia, in 1976 to form a central co-ordinating body. The Secretariat comprises the Office of the Secretary-General and Bureaux relating to Economic Integration and Finance, External Relations and Co-ordination, and Resources Development. The Secretary-General holds office for a five-year term and is assisted by four Deputy Secretaries-General, increased from two in accordance with the new ASEAN Charter. Two were to remain as nominated positions, rotating among member countries for a non-renewable term of three years; the two new positions of Deputy Secretary-General were to be openly recruited on a renewable three-year term. Each member country is required to maintain an ASEAN National Secretariat to co-ordinate implementation of ASEAN decisions at the national level and to raise awareness of the organization and its activities within that country. In July 2009 the first ASEAN Secretariat Policy Forum was convened with the aim of promoting public debate on the activities of the Secretariat.

ASEAN Committees in Third Countries (composed of heads of diplomatic missions) may be established to promote ASEAN's interests and to support the conduct of relations with other countries and international organizations.

Secretary-General: Dr Surin Pitsuwan (Thailand).

Deputy Secretary-General, for the ASEAN Political Security Community: Nyan Lynn (Myanmar).

Deputy Secretary-General, for the ASEAN Economic Community: Sundram Pushpanathan (Singapore).

Deputy Secretary-General, for the ASEAN Socio-Cultural Community: Misran Karmain (Malaysia).

Deputy Secretary-General, for Community and Corporate Affairs: Bagas Hapsoro (Indonesia).

Activities

ASEAN was established in 1967 with the signing of the ASEAN Declaration, otherwise known as the Bangkok Declaration, by the ministers of foreign affairs of Indonesia, Malaysia, the Philippines, Singapore and Thailand. In February 1976 the first ASEAN summit meeting adopted the Treaty of Amity and Co-operation in South-East Asia and the Declaration of ASEAN Concord. Brunei joined the organization in January 1984, shortly after attaining independence. Viet Nam was admitted as the seventh member of ASEAN in July 1995. Laos and Myanmar joined in July 1997 and Cambodia was formally admitted in April 1999, fulfilling the organization's ambition to incorporate all 10 countries in the sub-region.

In December 1997 ASEAN heads of government agreed upon a series of commitments to determine the development of the grouping into the 21st century. The so-called Vision 2020 envisaged ASEAN as 'a concert of Southeast Asian nations, outward looking, living in peace, stability and prosperity, bonded together in partnership in dynamic development and in a community of caring societies'. In October 2003 ASEAN leaders adopted a declaration known as 'Bali Concord II', which committed signatory states to the creation of an ASEAN Economic Community, an ASEAN Security Community and an ASEAN Socio-Cultural Community. In December 2005 heads of state determined to establish a High Level Task Force to formulate a new ASEAN Charter. The finalized document, codifying the principles and purposes of the grouping and according it the legal status of an intergovernmental organization, was signed in November 2007 by ASEAN heads of government attending the 13th summit meeting, convened in Singapore. In July 2008 the ASEAN Ministerial Meeting of ministers of foreign affairs reaffirmed their commitment to ratifying the Charter by the 14th summit meeting, scheduled to be held in Bangkok, Thailand, in December. Early in that month, however, the summit meeting was postponed, owing to political instability in Thailand. None the less, the Charter entered into force on 15 December, having been ratified by each member state. The occasion was commemorated at a Special ASEAN Foreign Ministers' Meeting, convened at the Secretariat, which consequently became the inaugural meeting of the new ASEAN Co-ordinating Council.

In March 2009, at the end of the reconvened 14th summit meeting, held in Cha-am and Hua Hin, Thailand, ASEAN heads of state and government signed the Cha-am Hua Hin Declaration on the Roadmap for an ASEAN Community (2009–15), comprising Blueprints on ASEAN Political Security, Economic, and Socio-cultural Communities as well as a second Initiative for ASEAN Integration Work Plan. The meeting also issued a Statement on the Global Economic and Financial Crisis, which emphasised the need for co-ordinated policies and joint actions to restore financial stability and to safeguard economic growth in the region.

In October 2010 ASEAN heads of state, meeting in Hanoi, Viet Nam, adopted a Master Plan on ASEAN Connectivity, which identified priority projects to enhance communications and community-building in three dimensions: physical, institutional and people-to-people. The November 2011 summit meeting of ASEAN heads of state, held in Bali, agreed to consider the possibility of developing a 'Connectivity Master Plan Plus' in future, with the aim of expanding the Connectivity initiative beyond the immediate ASEAN region. The November 2011 meeting also adopted a declaration on 'Bali Concord III', promoting a common ASEAN platform on global issues of common interest and concern, based on a shared ASEAN global view.

TRADE AND ECONOMIC CO-OPERATION

In January 1992 heads of government, meeting in Singapore, signed an agreement to create an ASEAN Free Trade Area (AFTA) by 2008. In accordance with the agreement, a common effective preferential tariff (CEPT) scheme came into effect in January 1993. The CEPT covered all manufactured products, including capital goods, and processed agricultural products (which together accounted for two-thirds of intra-ASEAN trade), but was to exclude unprocessed agricultural products. Tariffs were to be reduced to a maximum of 20% within a period of five to eight years and to 0%–5% during the subsequent seven to 10 years. Fifteen categories were designated for accelerated tariff reduction. In October 1993 ASEAN trade ministers agreed to modify the CEPT, with only Malaysia and Singapore having adhered to the original tariff reduction schedule. The new AFTA programme, under which all member countries except Brunei were scheduled to begin tariff reductions from 1 January 1994, substantially enlarged the number of products to be included in the tariff reduction process (i.e. on the so-called 'inclusion list') and reduced the list of products eligible for protection. In September 1994 ASEAN ministers of economic affairs agreed to accelerate the implementation of AFTA, advancing the deadline for its entry into operation from 2008 to 1 January 2003. Tariffs were to be reduced to 0%–5% within seven to 10 years, or within five to eight years for products designated for accelerated tariff cuts. In July 1995, Viet Nam was admitted as a member of ASEAN and was granted until 2006 to implement the AFTA trade agreements. In December 1995 heads of government, at a meeting convened in Bangkok, Thailand, agreed to extend liberalization to certain service industries, including banking, telecommunications and tourism. In July 1997 Laos and Myanmar became members of ASEAN and were granted a 10-year period, from 1 January 1998, to comply with the AFTA schedule.

In December 1998, meeting in Hanoi, Viet Nam, heads of government approved a Statement on Bold Measures, detailing ASEAN's strategies to deal with the economic crisis that had prevailed in the region since late 1997. These included incentives to attract investors, for example a three-year exemption on corporate taxation, accelerated implementation of the ASEAN Investment Area (AIA, see below), and advancing the AFTA deadline, for the original six members, to 2002, with some 85% of products to be covered by the arrangements by 2000, and 90% by 2001. It was envisaged that the elimination of tariffs would be achieved by 2015, by the original six members, or by 2018, by the new members. The Hanoi Plan of Action, which was also adopted at the meeting as a framework for the development of the organization over the period 1999–2004, incorporated a series of measures aimed at strengthening macroeconomic and financial co-operation and enhancing economic integration. In April 1999 Cambodia, on being admitted as a full member of ASEAN, signed an agreement to implement the tariff reduction programme over a 10-year period, commencing 1 January 2000. Cambodia also signed a declaration endorsing the commitments of the 1998 Statement on Bold Measures. In May 2000 Malaysia was granted a special exemption to postpone implementing tariff reductions on motor vehicles for two years from 1 January 2003. In November 2000 a protocol was approved permitting further temporary exclusion of products from the CEPT scheme for countries experiencing economic difficulties. On 1 January 2002 AFTA was formally realized among the original six signatories (Brunei, Indonesia, Malaysia, the Philippines, Singapore and Thailand), which had achieved the objective of reducing to less than 5% trade restrictions on 96.24% of products on the inclusion list. By 1 January 2005 tariffs on just under 99% of products on the 2005 CEPT inclusion list had been reduced to the 0%–5% range among the original six signatory countries, with the average tariff standing at 1.93%. With regard to Cambodia, Laos, Myanmar and Viet Nam, some 81% of products fell within the 0%–5% range. On 1 August 2008 comprehensive revised CEPT rules of origin came into effect.

To complement AFTA in facilitating intra-ASEAN trade, member countries committed to the removal of non-tariff barriers (such as quotas), the harmonization of standards and conformance measures, and the simplification and harmonization of customs procedures. In June 1996 the Working Group on Customs Procedures completed a draft legal framework for regional co-operation, designed to simplify and harmonize customs procedures, legislation and product classification. The agreement was signed in March 1997 at the inaugural meeting of ASEAN finance ministers. (Laos and Myanmar signed the customs agreement in July and Cambodia assented to it in April 1999.) In 2001 ASEAN finalized its system of harmonized tariff nomenclature, implementation of which commenced in the following year. In November the summit meeting determined to extend ASEAN tariff preferences to ASEAN's newer members from January 2002, under the ASEAN Integration System of Preferences (AISP), thus allowing Cambodia, Laos, Myanmar and Viet Nam tariff-free access to the more developed ASEAN markets earlier than the previously agreed target date of 2010. In April 2002 ASEAN ministers of economic affairs signed an agreement to facilitate intra-regional trade in electrical and electronic equipment by providing for the mutual recognition of standards (for example, testing and certification). The agreement was also intended to lower the costs of trade in those goods, thereby helping to maintain competitiveness.

In November 2000 heads of government endorsed an Initiative for ASEAN Integration (IAI), which aimed to reduce economic disparities within the region through effective co-operation. In July 2002 the AMM endorsed an IAI Work Plan, which focused on the following priority areas: human resources development; infrastructure; information and communications technology (ICT); and regional economic integration. The Plan was to be implemented over the six-year period 2002–08. Much of the funding for the Initiative came from ASEAN's external partners, including Australia, India, Japan, Norway and the Republic of Korea (South Korea). A second IAI Work Plan, covering the period 2009–15, was adopted by ASEAN heads of state and government in March 2009.

The Bali Concord II, adopted in October 2003, affirmed commitment to existing ASEAN economic co-operation frameworks, including the Hanoi Plan of Action (and any subsequently agreed regional plans of action) and the IAI, and outlined plans for the creation, by 2020, of an integrated ASEAN Economic Community (AEC), entailing: the harmonization of customs procedures and technical regulations by the end of 2004; the removal of non-tariff trade barriers and the establishment of a network of free trade zones by 2005; and the progressive withdrawal of capital controls and strengthening of intellectual property rights. An ASEAN legal unit was to be established to strengthen and enhance existing dispute settlement systems. (A Protocol on Enhanced Dispute Settlement Mechanism was signed in November 2004.) The free movement of professional and skilled workers would be facilitated by standardizing professional requirements and simplifying visa procedures, with the adoption of a single ASEAN visa requirement envisaged by 2005. In 2004 ASEAN economic and trade ministers worked closely, in co-operation with the private sector, to produce a roadmap for the integration of 11 sectors identified as priority areas in the AEC plan of action. In July the ASEAN Ministerial Meeting reviewed progress in preparing the Vientiane Action Programme (VAP), the proposed successor to the Hanoi Plan of Action. In November the 10th meeting of ASEAN heads of state, held in Vientiane, Laos, endorsed the VAP with commitments to deepen regional integration and narrow the development gap within the grouping. An ASEAN Development Fund was to be established to support the implementation of the VAP and other action programmes. The leaders adopted two plans of action (concerning security and sociocultural affairs) to further the implementation of the Bali Concord II regarding the establishment of a three-pillared ASEAN Community, which included the AEC. An ASEAN Framework Agreement for Integration of the Priority Sectors and its Protocols was also signed. Import duties (on 85% of products) were to be eliminated by 2007 for the original members (including Brunei) and by 2012 for newer member states in 11 sectors, accounting for more than 50% of intra-ASEAN trade in 2003. A Blueprint and

Strategic Schedule for realizing the AEC by 2015 was approved by ASEAN ministers of economic affairs in August 2007 and was signed by ASEAN heads of state, meeting in November. During 2008 ASEAN developed a 'scorecard' mechanism to track the implementation of the Blueprint by member countries. The first AEC Scorecard was published in April 2010, which demonstrated that 73% of the targets set by the Blueprint had been achieved. In March 2009 heads of state agreed that the new Roadmap for an ASEAN Community should replace the VAP. In May 2010 an ASEAN Trade in Goods Agreement entered into force, which aimed to consolidate all trade commitments and tariff liberalization schedules.

In November 1999 an informal meeting of leaders of ASEAN countries, the People's Republic of China, Japan and South Korea (designating themselves 'ASEAN + 3') issued a Joint Statement on East Asian Co-operation, in which they agreed to strengthen regional unity, and addressed the long-term possibility of establishing an East Asian common market and currency. In July 2000 ASEAN + 3 ministers of foreign affairs convened an inaugural formal summit in Bangkok, Thailand, and in October ASEAN + 3 economic affairs ministers agreed to hold their hitherto twice-yearly informal meetings on an institutionalized basis. In November an informal meeting of ASEAN + 3 leaders approved further co-operation in various sectors and initiated a feasibility study into a proposal to establish a regional free trade area. In May 2001 ASEAN + 3 ministers of economic affairs endorsed a series of projects for co-operation in ICT, environment, small and medium-sized enterprises, Mekong Basin development, and harmonization of standards. In July 2002 ASEAN + 3 ministers of foreign affairs declared their support for other regional initiatives, namely an Asia Co-operation Dialogue, which was initiated by the Thai Government in June, and an Initiative for Development in East Asia (IDEA), which had been announced by the Japanese Government in January. An IDEA ministerial meeting was convened in Tokyo, in August. ASEAN + 3 ministers of labour convened in May 2003. In September the sixth consultation between ASEAN + 3 ministers of economic affairs was held, at which several new projects were endorsed, including two on e-commerce. During 2004 an ASEAN + 3 Unit was established in the ASEAN Secretariat. In November the ASEAN summit meeting agreed to convene a meeting of an East Asia grouping, to be developed in parallel with the ASEAN + 3 framework.

In October 2008 ASEAN heads of state held a special meeting, in Beijing, China, to consider the impact on the region of the deceleration of growth in the world's most developed economies and the ongoing instability of global financial markets. The meeting was followed by a specially convened ASEAN + 3 summit to discuss further regional co-operation to counter the impact of the crisis. In April 2010 ASEAN heads of state, convened in Hanoi, Viet Nam, adopted an ASEAN Strategy for Economic Recovery and Development to ensure sustainable recovery from the global financial and economic crisis. Leaders determined to strengthen efforts to enhance financial monitoring and surveillance, to foster infrastructure and sustainable development and to achieve regional economic integration. The Strategy determined to pursue the ASEAN Connectivity Initiative, which had been approved at the 15th summit in October 2009, as well as efforts to develop a Master Plan on ASEAN Connectivity.

In August 2010 an inaugural meeting of ministers of economic affairs of Cambodia, Laos, Myanmar and Viet Nam (the so-called 'CLMV' countries) was convened, in Da Nang, Viet Nam, further to strengthen intra-economic and trade relations. In particular, the meeting considered measures to enhance trade promotion and to narrow the development gap between the CLMV countries and other countries in the region.

FINANCE AND INVESTMENT

In 1987 heads of government agreed to accelerate regional financial co-operation in order to support intra-ASEAN trade and investment. They adopted measures to increase the role of ASEAN currencies in regional trade, to assist negotiations on the avoidance of double taxation, and to improve the efficiency of tax and customs administrators. An ASEAN Reinsurance Corporation was established in 1988, with initial authorized capital of US $10m. Other measures to attract greater financial resource flows in the region, including an ASEAN Plan of Action for the Promotion of Foreign Direct Investment and Intra-ASEAN Investment, were implemented during 1996.

In February 1997 ASEAN central bank governors agreed to strengthen efforts to combat currency speculation through the established network of foreign exchange repurchase agreements. However, from mid-1997 several Asian currencies were undermined by speculative activities. Subsequent unsuccessful attempts to support the foreign exchange rates contributed to a collapse in the value of financial markets in some countries and to a reversal of the region's economic growth, at least in the short term, while governments undertook macroeconomic structural reforms. In December ASEAN ministers of finance, meeting in Malaysia, agreed to liberalize markets for financial services and to strengthen surveillance of member country economies, to help prevent further deterioration of the regional economy. The ministers also endorsed a proposal for the establishment of an Asian funding facility to provide emergency assistance in support of international credit and structural reform programmes.

In October 1998 ministers of economic affairs, meeting in Manila, Philippines, signed a Framework Agreement on an ASEAN Investment Area (AIA), which was to provide for equal treatment of domestic and other ASEAN direct investment proposals within the grouping by 2010, and of all foreign investors by 2020. The meeting also confirmed that the proposed ASEAN Surveillance Process (ASP), to monitor the economic stability and financial systems of member states, would be implemented with immediate effect, and would require the voluntary submission of economic information by all members to a monitoring committee, to be based in Jakarta, Indonesia. The ASP and the Framework Agreement on the AIA were incorporated into the Hanoi Plan of Action, adopted by heads of state in December 1998. The summit meeting also resolved to accelerate reforms, particularly in the banking and financial sectors, in order to strengthen the region's economies, and to promote the liberalization of the financial services sector. In March 1999 ASEAN ministers of trade and industry, meeting in Phuket, Thailand, as the AIA Council, agreed to open their manufacturing, agriculture, fisheries, forestry and mining industries to foreign investment. Investment restrictions affecting those industries were to be eliminated by 2003 in most cases, although Laos and Viet Nam were granted until 2010. In addition, ministers adopted a number of measures to encourage investment in the region, including access to three-year corporate income tax exemptions, and tax allowances of 30% for investors. The AIA agreement formally entered into force in June 1999, having been ratified by all member countries. In September 2001 ministers agreed to accelerate the full realization of the AIA for non-ASEAN investors in manufacturing, agriculture, forestry, fishing and mining sectors. The date for full implementation was advanced to 2010 for the original six ASEAN members and to 2015 for the newer members. In August 2007 the AIA Council determined to revise the Framework Agreement on the AIA in order to implement a more comprehensive investment arrangement in support of the establishment of the AEC.

In May 2000, ASEAN + 3 ministers of economic affairs, meeting in Chiang Mai, Thailand, proposed the establishment of an enhanced currency swap mechanism, enabling countries to draw on liquidity support to defend their economies during balance of payments difficulties or speculative currency attacks and to prevent future financial crises. The so-called Chiang Mai Initiative Multilateralization (CMIM) on currency swap arrangements was formally approved by ASEAN + 3 finance ministers in May 2001. In August 2003 ASEAN + 3 finance ministers agreed to establish a Finance Co-operation Fund, to be administered by the ASEAN Secretariat; the Fund was to support ongoing economic reviews relating to projects such as the CMIM. An Asian Bond Markets Initiative (ABMI) was launched by ASEAN + 3 countries in 2003 to develop local currency denominated bond markets. In February 2009 ministers of finance of ASEAN + 3 countries convened a special meeting, in Phuket, Thailand, to consider the impact on the region of the global economic and financial crisis, and issued an Action Plan to Restore Economic and Financial Stability of the Asian Region. Ministers agreed to expand the CMIM (from US $80m. to $120m.) and to establish an independent regional surveillance unit to strengthen economic monitoring. The CMIM entered into force in March 2010. In May ASEAN + 3 finance ministers, convened in Tashkent, Uzbekistan, announced the launch, within the ABMI framework, of a Credit Guarantee and Investment Facility, with an initial capital of $700m., as a trust fund of the Asian Development Bank. Ministers also acknowledged that agreement had been reached on the establishment, in Singapore, of an ASEAN + 3 Macroeconomic Research Office, to monitor and analyse regional economies and to support the effectiveness of the CMIM. The Office was inaugurated in April 2011.

POLITICS AND SECURITY

In 1971 ASEAN members endorsed a declaration envisaging the establishment of a Zone of Peace, Freedom and Neutrality (ZOPFAN) in the South-East Asian region. This objective was incorporated in the Declaration of ASEAN Concord, which was adopted at the first summit meeting of the organization, held in Bali, Indonesia, in February 1976. Heads of state also signed a Treaty of Amity and Co-operation, establishing principles of mutual respect for the independence and sovereignty of all nations, non-interference in the internal affairs of one another and settlement of disputes by peaceful means. The Treaty was amended in December 1987 by a protocol providing for the accession of Papua New Guinea and other non-member countries in the region. In January 1992 ASEAN leaders agreed that there should be greater co-operation on security matters within the grouping, and that ASEAN's post-ministerial conferences (PMCs) should be used as a forum for discussion of questions relating to security with dialogue partners and other countries. In July 1992

Viet Nam and Laos signed ASEAN's Treaty of Amity and Co-operation. Cambodia acceded to the Treaty in January 1995 and Myanmar signed it in July.

In December 1995 ASEAN heads of government, meeting in Bangkok, Thailand, signed a treaty establishing a South-East Asia Nuclear-Weapon Free Zone (SEANWFZ). The treaty was also signed by Cambodia, Myanmar and Laos. It was extended to cover the offshore economic exclusion zones of each country. On ratification by all parties, the treaty was to prohibit the manufacture or storage of nuclear weapons within the region. Individual signatories were to decide whether to allow port visits or transportation of nuclear weapons by foreign powers through territorial waters. The treaty entered into force in March 1997. ASEAN senior officials were mandated to oversee implementation of the treaty, pending the establishment of a permanent monitoring committee. In July 1999 China and India agreed to observe the terms of the SEANWFZ.

In July 1992 the ASEAN Ministerial Meeting issued a statement calling for a peaceful resolution of the dispute concerning the strategically significant Spratly Islands in the South China Sea, which are claimed, wholly or partly, by China, Viet Nam, Taiwan, Brunei, Malaysia and the Philippines. In 1999 ASEAN established a special committee to formulate a code of conduct for the South China Sea to be observed by all claimants to the Spratly Islands. In November 2002 ASEAN and China's ministers of foreign affairs adopted a Declaration on the Conduct (DOC) of Parties in the South China Sea, agreeing to promote a peaceful environment and durable solutions for the area, to resolve territorial disputes by peaceful means, to refrain from undertaking activities that would aggravate existing tensions (such as settling unpopulated islands and reefs), and to initiate a regular dialogue of defence officials. In December 2004 in Kuala Lumpur, Malaysia, at the first senior officials' meeting between ASEAN and China on the implementation of the DOC, it was agreed to adopt the Terms of Reference of the newly established joint working group as a step towards enhancing security and stability in the South China Sea.

In July 1997 ASEAN ministers of foreign affairs reiterated their commitment to the principle of non-interference in the internal affairs of other countries. However, the group's efforts in negotiating a political settlement to the internal conflict in Cambodia marked a significant shift in diplomatic policy towards one of 'constructive intervention', which had been proposed by Malaysia's Deputy Prime Minister in recognition of the increasing interdependence of the region. At the Ministerial Meeting in July 1998 Thailand's Minister of Foreign Affairs, supported by his Philippine counterpart, proposed that the grouping formally adopt a policy of 'flexible engagement'. The proposal, based partly on concerns that the continued restrictions imposed by the Myanmar authorities on dissident political activists was damaging ASEAN relations with its dialogue partners, was to provide for the discussion of the affairs of other member states when they have an impact on neighbouring countries. While rejecting the proposal, other ASEAN ministers agreed to pursue a more limited version, referred to as 'enhanced interaction', and to maintain open dialogue within the grouping. In September 1999 the unrest prompted by the popular referendum on the future of East Timor (now Timor-Leste) and the resulting humanitarian crisis highlighted the unwillingness of some ASEAN member states to intervene in other member countries and undermined the political unity of the grouping. A compromise agreement, enabling countries to act on an individual basis rather than as representatives of ASEAN, was formulated prior to an emergency meeting of ministers of foreign affairs, held during the APEC meetings in Auckland, New Zealand. Malaysia, the Philippines, Singapore and Thailand declared their support for the establishment of a multinational force to restore peace in East Timor and committed troops to participate in the Australian-led operation. At their informal summit in November 1999 heads of state approved the establishment of an ASEAN Troika, which was to be constituted as an ad hoc body comprising the foreign ministers of the Association's current, previous and future chairmanship with a view to providing a rapid response mechanism in the event of a regional crisis.

On 12 September 2001 ASEAN issued a ministerial statement on international terrorism, condemning the attacks of the previous day in the USA and urging greater international co-operation to counter terrorism. The seventh summit meeting in November issued a Declaration on a Joint Action to Combat Terrorism. This condemned the September attacks, stated that terrorism was a direct challenge to ASEAN's aims, and affirmed the grouping's commitment to strong measures to counter terrorism. The summit encouraged member countries to sign (or ratify) the International Convention for the Suppression of the Financing of Terrorism, to strengthen national mechanisms against terrorism, and to work to deepen co-operation, particularly in the area of intelligence exchange; international conventions to combat terrorism would be studied to see if they could be integrated into the ASEAN structure, while the possibility of developing a regional anti-terrorism convention was discussed. The summit noted the need to strengthen security co-operation to restore investor confidence. In its Declaration and other notes, the summit explicitly rejected any attempt to link terrorism with religion or race, and expressed concern for the suffering of innocent Afghanis during the US military action against the Taliban authorities in Afghanistan. The summit's final Declaration was worded so as to avoid any mention of the US action, to which Muslim ASEAN states such as Malaysia and Indonesia were strongly opposed. In November 2002 the eighth summit meeting adopted a Declaration on Terrorism, reiterating and strengthening the measures announced in the previous year. (See, also, Transnational Crime, below.)

The ASEAN Charter that entered into force in December 2008 envisaged the establishment of a new ASEAN human rights body. It was to extend, for the first time within the grouping, a formal structure for the promotion and protection of human rights and fundamental freedoms. In July 2009 the ASEAN Ministerial Meeting of ministers of foreign affairs adopted the terms of reference of the body, which had been drafted by a High Level Panel. It was to be established as the ASEAN Intergovernmental Commission on Human Rights (AICHR) and composed of a national expert representative from each member state. At the same meeting, ASEAN ministers urged the authorities in Myanmar to release all political detainees, including the main opposition leader Aung San Suu Kyi, in order to enable them to participate freely in elections scheduled to be conducted in 2010. In August 2009 Thailand, acting in its capacity as the ASEAN Chair, expressed deep disappointment at the sentencing of Aung San Suu Kyi for allegedly breaching the terms of her house arrest. The inaugural meeting of the AICHR was held at the ASEAN Secretariat in March–April 2010. The Commission considered the formulation of rules of procedure, the development of a five-year work plan and priority activities for 2010/11.

In May 2011 ASEAN heads of state, meeting in Jakarta, Indonesia, urged ministers of foreign affairs to elaborate plans to establish an ASEAN Institute for Peace and Reconciliation.

ASEAN Regional Forum (ARF): In July 1993 the meeting of ASEAN ministers of foreign affairs sanctioned the establishment of a forum to discuss and promote co-operation on security issues within the region, and, in particular, to ensure the involvement of China in regional dialogue. The ARF was informally initiated during that year's PMC, comprising the ASEAN countries, its dialogue partners (at that time Australia, Canada, the European Community, Japan, South Korea, New Zealand and the USA), and China, Laos, Papua New Guinea, Russia and Viet Nam. The first formal meeting of the ARF was conducted in July 1994, following the Ministerial Meeting held in Bangkok, Thailand, and it was agreed that the ARF would be convened on an annual basis. The 1995 meeting, held in Brunei, in August, attempted to define a framework for the future of the Forum. It was perceived as evolving through three stages: the promotion of confidence-building (including disaster relief and peace-keeping activities); the development of preventive diplomacy; and the elaboration of approaches to conflict. The third ARF, convened in July 1996, which was attended for the first time by India and Myanmar, agreed a set of criteria and guiding principles for the future expansion of the grouping. In particular, it was decided that the ARF would only admit as participants countries that had a direct influence on the peace and security of the East Asia and Pacific region. The ARF held in July 1997 reviewed progress made in developing the first two 'tracks' of the ARF process, through the structure of inter-sessional working groups and meetings. The Forum's consideration of security issues in the region was dominated by concern at the political situation in Cambodia; support was expressed for ASEAN mediation to restore stability within that country. Mongolia was admitted into the ARF at its meeting in July 1998. India rejected a proposal that Pakistan attend the meeting to discuss issues relating to both countries' testing of nuclear weapons. The meeting ultimately condemned the testing of nuclear weapons in the region, but declined to criticize specifically India and Pakistan. In July 1999 the ARF warned the Democratic People's Republic of Korea (North Korea) not to conduct any further testing of missiles over the Pacific. At the seventh meeting of the ARF, convened in Bangkok, in July 2000, North Korea was admitted to the Forum. The meeting considered the positive effects and challenges of globalization, including the possibilities for greater economic interdependence and for a growth in transnational crime. The eighth ARF meeting in July 2001 in Hanoi, Viet Nam, pursued these themes, and also discussed the widening development gap between nations. The meeting agreed to enhance the role of the ARF Chairman, enabling him to issue statements on behalf of ARF participants and to organize events during the year. The ninth ARF meeting, held in Bandar Seri Begawan, Brunei, in July 2002, assessed regional and international security developments, and issued a statement of individual and collective intent to prevent any financing of terrorism. The statement included commitments by participants to freeze the assets of suspected individuals or groups, to implement international financial standards and to enhance co-operation and the exchange of information. In October the Chairman, on behalf of all ARF participants, condemned the terrorist bomb attacks committed against tourist targets in Bali, Indonesia. Pakistan joined the ARF in July 2004. In November the first ARF Security Policy Conference was held in Beijing, China. The Conference recommended developing various aspects of bilateral and multilateral co-operation, including with regard to non-traditional security threats. Timor-Leste and Bangladesh became participants in the ARF in July 2005. In July 2006 the ARF issued statements on 'co-operation in fighting cyber attacks and terrorist misuse of cyber space' and on disaster management and emergency responses, which determined to formulate guidelines for enhanced co-operation in humanitarian operations. In January 2007 an ARF maritime security shore exercise was conducted, in Singapore. In March the first ARF Defense Ministers Retreat was convened, in Bali. The 14th ARF, held in Manila, Philippines, in July, approved the establishment of a 'Friends of the Chair' mechanism, comprising three ministers, to promote preventive diplomacy and respond rapidly to political crises. In July 2008 the 15th ARF determined further to strengthen co-operation in natural disaster preparedness and relief operations and resolved to organize training in those areas and a disaster relief exercise. At that time North Korea acceded to ASEAN's Treaty of Amity and Co-operation. The USA acceded to the Treaty in July 2009; Canada and Turkey acceded to the Treaty in July 2010. In July 2009, the ARF marked its 15th anniversary by adopting a Vision Statement for the period up to 2020. It reaffirmed its commitment to 'building a region of peace, friendship and prosperity' and proposed measures to strengthen the ARF and to develop security-based partnerships. In the following 12-month period intersessional meetings of the ARF were held on disaster relief, maritime security, confidence-building measures and preventive diplomacy, counter-terrorism and transnational crime, and non-proliferation and disarmament. The 17th meeting of the ARF, convened in Hanoi, in July 2010, adopted a Plan of Action to implement the Vision Statement 2020. The meeting also discussed security in the South China Sea, preparations for a general election in Myanmar and efforts to achieve the denuclearization of the Korean Peninsula.

Since 2000 the ARF has published the *Annual Security Outlook*, to which participating countries submit assessments of the security prospects in the region.

In October 2010 the first so-called ASEAN Defence Ministers' Meeting (ADMM) Plus was held, in Hanoi, incorporating ASEAN ministers and their counterparts from eight dialogue partner countries, i.e. Australia, China, Japan, South Korea, New Zealand, Russia and the USA. The new body was intended to complement the work of the ARF.

TRANSNATIONAL CRIME

In June 1999 the first ministerial meeting to consider issues relating to transnational crime was convened. Regular meetings of senior officials and ministers were subsequently held. The third ministerial meeting, in October 2001, considered initiatives to combat transnational crime, which was defined as including terrorism, trafficking in drugs, arms and people, money-laundering, cyber-crime, piracy and economic crime. In May 2002 ministers responsible for transnational crime issues convened a Special Ministerial Meeting on Terrorism, in Kuala Lumpur, Malaysia. The meeting approved a work programme to implement a plan of action to combat transnational crime, including information exchange, the development of legal arrangements for extradition, prosecution and seizure, the enhancement of co-operation in law enforcement, and the development of regional security training programmes. In a separate initiative Indonesia, Malaysia and the Philippines signed an agreement on information exchange and the establishment of communication procedures. Cambodia acceded to the agreement in July. In November 2004 ASEAN leaders adopted an ASEAN Declaration against Trafficking in Persons, Particularly Women and Children, which aimed to strengthen co-operation to prevent and combat trafficking, through, *inter alia*, the establishment of a new regional focal network, information-sharing procedures and standardized immigration controls. In late May 2011 ASEAN leaders issued a joint statement on enhancing co-operation against trafficking in persons in South East Asia. The Plan of Action of the ASEAN Security Community (envisaged by the Bali Concord II—see above) had as its five key areas: political development; shaping and sharing of norms; conflict prevention; conflict resolution; and post-conflict peace building. In November 2004 eight member countries, namely Brunei, Cambodia, Indonesia, Malaysia, Laos, the Philippines, Singapore and Viet Nam, signed a Treaty on Mutual Legal Assistance in Criminal Matters in Kuala Lumpur, Malaysia.

In January 2007 ASEAN leaders, meeting in Cebu, Philippines, signed an ASEAN Convention on Counter Terrorism. The Convention entered into force in late May 2011, having received the required ratification by six member states: Brunei, Cambodia, the Philippines, Singapore, Thailand and Viet Nam.

INDUSTRY

The ASEAN-Chambers of Commerce and Industry (CCI) aims to enhance ASEAN economic and industrial co-operation and the participation in these activities of the private sector. In March 1996 a permanent ASEAN-CCI secretariat became operational at the ASEAN Secretariat. The first AIA Council-Business Sector Forum was convened in September 2001, with the aim of developing alliances between the public and private sectors. An ASEAN Business Advisory Council held its inaugural meeting in April 2003.

The ASEAN Industrial Co-operation (AICO) scheme, initiated in 1996, encourages companies in the ASEAN region to undertake joint manufacturing activities. Products derived from an AICO arrangement benefit immediately from a preferential tariff rate of 0%–5%. The AICO scheme superseded the ASEAN industrial joint venture scheme, established in 1983. The attractiveness of the scheme was expected slowly to diminish as ASEAN moves towards the full implementation of the CEPT scheme. ASEAN has initiated studies of new methods of industrial co-operation within the grouping, with the aim of achieving further integration. In April 2004 ASEAN economic ministers signed a Protocol to Amend the Basic Agreement on the AICO Scheme, which aimed to maintain its relevance. As from 1 January 2005 the tariff rate for Brunei, Cambodia, Indonesia, Laos, Malaysia and Singapore was 0%; for the Philippines 0%–1%, for Thailand 0%–3% and for Myanmar and Viet Nam 0%–5%.

The ASEAN Consultative Committee on Standards and Quality (ACCSQ) aims to promote the understanding and implementation of quality concepts, considered to be important in strengthening the economic development of a member state and in helping to eliminate trade barriers. ACCSQ comprises three working groups: standards and information; conformance and assessment; and testing and calibration. A Standards and Quality Bulletin is published regularly to disseminate information and promote transparency on standards, technical regulations and conformity assessment procedures. In September 1994 an ad hoc Working Group on Intellectual Property (IP) Co-operation was established, with a mandate to formulate a framework agreement on intellectual property co-operation and to strengthen ASEAN activities in intellectual property protection. An ASEAN Intellectual Property Right (IPR) Action Plan covering the period 2011–15 aims, *inter alia,* to promote a balanced IP system taking into account the varying levels of development of member states, to develop national or regional legal and policy infrastructures to address the evolving demands of the IP landscape, and to ensure that IP is utilized as a tool for innovation and development.

In 1988 the ASEAN Fund was established, with capital of US $150m., to provide finance for portfolio investments in ASEAN countries, in particular for small and medium-sized enterprises (SMEs). The Hanoi Plan of Action, which was adopted by ASEAN heads of state in December 1998, incorporated a series of initiatives to enhance the development of SMEs, including training and technical assistance, co-operation activities and greater access to information. In September 2004 ASEAN economic ministers approved an ASEAN Policy Blueprint for SME Development 2004–14, first proposed by a working group in 2001, which comprised strategic work programmes and policy measures for the development of SMEs in the region. The first meeting of a new ASEAM SME Advisory Board was held in Singapore, in June 2011.

In January 2007 senior officials concluded a five-year ASEAN plan of action to support the development and implementation of national occupational safety and health frameworks. In May 2010 ASEAN ministers responsible for labour adopted a Work Programme for the period 2010–15, which aimed to support the realization of the ASEAN Community and to further the objectives of achieving adequate social protection for all workers in the region and fostering productive employment.

FOOD, AGRICULTURE AND FORESTRY

In October 1983 a ministerial agreement on fisheries co-operation was concluded, providing for the joint management of fish resources, the sharing of technology, and co-operation in marketing. In July 1994 a Conference on Fisheries Management and Development Strategies in the ASEAN region resolved to enhance fish production through the introduction of new technologies, aquaculture development, improvements of product quality and greater involvement by the private sector. In June 2011 the ministerial session of the ASEAN-Southeast Asian Fisheries Development Center Conference on Sustainable Fisheries for Sustainable Development adopted a resolution on Sustainable Fisheries for Food Security for the ASEAN Region Towards 2020, to be implemented through individual and collective efforts among member states.

Co-operation in forestry is focused on joint projects, funded by ASEAN's dialogue partners, which include a Forest Tree Seed Centre, an Institute of Forest Management and the ASEAN Timber Technology Centre. In 2005 an Ad Hoc Experts Working Group on International Forest Policy Processes was created, to support the development of ASEAN joint positions and approaches on regional and international forest issues. An ASEAN Social Forestry Network was also established in that year. In November 2007 ASEAN ministers responsible for forestry issued a statement on strengthening forest law enforcement and governance.

There is an established ASEAN programme of training and study exchanges for farm workers, agricultural experts and members of agricultural co-operatives. Other areas of co-operation aim to enhance food security and the international competitiveness of ASEAN food, agriculture and forestry products, to promote the sustainable use and conservation of natural resources, to encourage greater involvement by the private sector in the food and agricultural industry, and to strengthen joint approaches on international and regional issues. An ASEAN Task Force has been formed to harmonize regulations on agricultural products derived from biotechnology. In December 1998 heads of state determined to establish an ASEAN Food Security Information Service to enhance the capacity of member states to forecast and manage food supplies. In 1999 agriculture ministers endorsed guidelines on assessing risk from genetically modified organisms (GMOs) in agriculture, to ensure a common approach. In 2001 work was undertaken to increase public and professional awareness of GMO issues, through workshops and studies. In October ASEAN + 3 ministers of agriculture and forestry met for the first time, and discussed issues of poverty alleviation, food security, agricultural research and human resource development. An East Asia Emergency Rice Reserve (enhancing the original emergency rice reserve scheme, established in 1979) was initiated by ASEAN + 3 ministers in 2003 as a pilot project. In October 2004 ministers of agriculture and forestry, meeting in Yangon, Myanmar, endorsed a Strategic Plan of Action on ASEAN Co-operation in Food, Agriculture and Forestry 2005–10. The ministers also approved certain regional food standards, endorsed the establishment of an ASEAN Animal Health Trust Fund, and resolved to establish a Task Force to co-ordinate regional co-operation for the control and eradication of highly pathogenic avian influenza (HPAI). A Regional Strategy for the Progressive Control and Eradication of HPAI, covering the period 2008–10, was endorsed at a meeting of ASEAN ministers of agriculture and forestry held in November 2007. The meeting also determined to establish an ASEAN Network on Aquatic Animal Health Centres to strengthen diagnostic and certification measures of live aquatic animals within the region. In October 2010 ASEAN ministers of agriculture and forestry endorsed a 'Roadmap Towards an HPAI-Free ASEAN Community by 2020', as a strategic framework to address avian influenza and other transboundary and zoonotic diseases of significant priority to the region.

In February–March 2009 ASEAN heads of state, meeting in Cha-am and Hua Hin, Thailand, adopted an Integrated Food Security Framework and a Strategic Plan of Action on Food Security in the ASEAN Region. An ASEAN-FAO Regional Conference on Food Security was held in Bangkok, Thailand, in May. In October 2010 ministers endorsed the transformation of the ASEAN + 3 Emergency Rice Reserve into a permanent scheme for meeting emergency food requirements and improving food security.

MINERALS AND ENERGY

The ASEAN Centre for Energy (ACE), based in Jakarta, Indonesia, provides an energy information network, promotes the establishment of interconnecting energy structures among ASEAN member countries, supports the development of renewable energy resources and encourages co-operation in energy efficiency and conservation. An ASEAN energy business forum is held annually and attended by representatives of the energy industry in the private and public sectors. In November 1999 a Trans-ASEAN Gas Pipeline Task Force was established and in April 2000 an ASEAN Interconnection Masterplan Study Working Group was established to formulate a study on the power grid. In July 2002 ASEAN ministers of energy signed a memorandum of understanding (MOU) to implement the pipeline project, involving seven interconnections. In early 2005 the Trans-Thai-Malaysia Gas Pipeline became operational. In June 2004 the first meeting of ASEAN + 3 energy ministers was also convened in June 2004. Later in that year a permanent Secretariat of the heads of ASEAN Power Utilities/Authorities was established on a three-year rotation basis. An MOU on the regional power grid initiative was signed by ministers of energy, meeting in August 2007. In July 2009 ministers of energy adopted an ASEAN Plan of Action for Energy Cooperation (APAEC) 2010–15.

A Framework of Co-operation in Minerals was adopted by an ASEAN working group of experts in August 1993. The group has also developed a programme of action for ASEAN co-operation in the development and utilization of industrial minerals, to promote the exploration and development of mineral resources, the transfer of mining technology and expertise, and the participation of the private sector in industrial mineral production. The programme of action is implemented by an ASEAN Regional Development Centre for Mineral Resources, which also conducts workshops and training programmes relating to the sector. In August 2005 ASEAN ministers responsible for minerals held an inaugural meeting, in Kuching, Malaysia. A second meeting was convened, in October 2008, in Manila, Philippines; and a third in December 2011, in Hanoi, Viet Nam. An ASEAN Minerals Co-operation Action Plan for 2011–15 aimed to promote information sharing on minerals; to facilitate and enhance trade and investment in the sector; and to promote environmentally and socially sustainable practices.

TRANSPORT

ASEAN objectives for the transport sector include developing multimodal transport, harmonizing road transport laws and regulations, improving air space management and developing ASEAN legislation for the carriage of dangerous goods and waste by land and sea. In September 1999 ASEAN ministers of transport and communications adopted a programme of action for development of the sector in 1999–2004. By September 2001, under the action programme, a harmonized road route numbering system had been completed, a road safety implementation work plan agreed, and two pilot courses, on port management and traffic engineering and safety, had been adopted. A Framework Agreement on Facilitation of Goods in Transit entered into force in October 2000. In September 2002 ASEAN transport ministers signed Protocol 9 on Dangerous Goods, one of the implementing protocols under the framework agreement, which provided for the simplification of procedures for the transportation of dangerous goods within the region using internationally accepted rules and guidelines. In November 2004 the ASEAN Transport Action Plan 2005–10 was adopted. A roadmap to support the development of an integrated and competitive maritime transport sector in the ASEAN region was signed by ministers of transport in November 2007. At the same time an agreement to strengthen co-operation in maritime cargo and passenger transport was signed with China. The November 2008 meeting of ministers of transport concluded an ASEAN Framework Agreement on the Facilitation of Inter-State Transport. In November 2010 ASEAN ministers of transport adopted a successor Transport Action Plan, for the period 2011–15, which incorporated measures to support the realization of the AEC by 2015 and the regional transport priorities of the Master Plan on ASEAN Connectivity.

In October 2001 ministers approved the third package of commitments for the air and transport sectors under the ASEAN framework agreement on services (according to which member countries were to liberalize the selling and marketing of air and maritime transport services). A protocol to implement the fourth package of commitments was signed by ministers in November 2004. In September 2002 ASEAN senior transport officials signed the MOU on air freight services, which represented the first stage in full liberalization of air freight services in the region. As one of the priority sectors within the ASEAN Framework Agreement for Integration of the Priority Sectors and its Protocols, air travel in the region was to be fully integrated by 2010. The Action Plan for ASEAN Air Transport Integration and Liberalization 2005–15 was adopted in November 2004. The Master Plan for ASEAN Connectivity, adopted by heads of state in October 2010, incorporated objectives for the development and implementation of an ASEAN Single Aviation Market, as well as an ASEAN Single Shipping Market, by 2015.

TELECOMMUNICATIONS

ASEAN aims to achieve interoperability and interconnectivity in the telecommunications sector. In November 2000 ASEAN heads of government approved an e-ASEAN Framework Agreement to promote and co-ordinate e-commerce and internet utilization. The Agreement incorporated commitments to develop and strengthen ASEAN's information infrastructure, in order to provide for universal and affordable access to communications services. Tariff reduction on information and communication technology (ICT) products was to be accelerated, with the aim of eliminating all tariffs in the sector by 2010. In July 2001 the first meeting of ASEAN ministers responsible for telecommunications (TELMIN) was held, in Kuala Lumpur, Malaysia, during which a Ministerial Understanding on ASEAN co-operation in telecommunications and ICT was signed. In September ASEAN ministers of economic affairs approved a list of ICT products eligible for the elimination of duties under the e-ASEAN Framework Agreement. This was to take place in three annual tranches, commencing in 2003 for the six original members of ASEAN and in 2008 for the newer member countries. During 2001 ASEAN continued to develop a reference framework for e-commerce legislation. In September 2003 the third ASEAN telecommunications ministerial meeting adopted a declaration incorporating commitments to harness ASEAN technological advances, create digital opportunities and enhance ASEAN's competitiveness in the field of ICT. The ministers also endorsed initiatives to enhance cybersecurity, including the establishment of computer emergency response teams in each member state. In August 2004 an ASEAN ICT Fund was established to accelerate implementation of the grouping's ICT objectives. At the fifth meeting of telecommunications ministers, held in Hanoi, Viet Nam, in September 2005, the Hanoi Agenda on Promoting Online Services and Applications was adopted. 'ASEAN-connect', a web portal collating all essential information and data regarding ICT activities and initiatives within ASEAN, was also launched. In August 2007 ASEAN telecommunications ministers, convened in Siem Reap, Cambodia, endorsed a commitment to enhance universal access of ICT services within ASEAN, in particular to extend the benefits of ICT to rural communities and remote areas. At the same time ministers met their counterparts from China, Japan and South Korea to strengthen co-operation in ICT issues. An ASEAN Connectivity Initiative, approved by ASEAN heads of state in October 2009, envisaged greater investment and targets for co-operation in ICT, as well as transport, energy and cross-border movement of goods and people. A Master Plan on ASEAN Connectivity (MPAC) was adopted by heads of state meeting in Hanoi, in October 2010. In September 2011 ASEAN and the ADB signed an agreement to establish the ASEAN Infrastructure Fund (AIF), which was to channel funding to support regional infrastructure development and MPAC. In January 2011 ASEAN telecommunications ministers adopted an ASEAN ICT Masterplan 2015 ('AIM2015').

SCIENCE AND TECHNOLOGY

ASEAN's Committee on Science and Technology (COST) supports co-operation in food science and technology, meteorology and geophysics, microelectronics and ICT, biotechnology, non-conventional energy research, materials science and technology, space technology applications, science and technology infrastructure and resources development, and marine science. There is an ASEAN Science Fund, used to finance policy studies in science and technology and to support information exchange and dissemination.

The Hanoi Plan of Action, adopted in December 1998, envisaged a series of measures aimed at promoting development in the fields of science and technology, including the establishment of networks of science and technology centres of excellence and academic institutions, the creation of a technology scan mechanism, the promotion of public and private sector co-operation in scientific and technological (particularly ICT) activities, and an increase in research on strategic technologies. In September 2001 the ASEAN Ministerial Meeting on Science and Technology, convened for its first meeting since 1998, approved a new framework for the implementation of ASEAN's Plan of Action on Science and Technology during the period 2001–04. The Plan aimed to help less developed member countries become competitive in the sector and integrate into regional co-operation activities. In September 2003 ASEAN and China inaugurated a Network of East Asian Think-tanks to promote scientific and technological exchange. In November 2004 a Ministerial Meeting on Science and Technology decided to establish an ASEAN Virtual Institute of Science and Technology with the aim of developing science and technology human resources in the region. In August 2006 an informal Ministerial Meeting on Science and Technology endorsed in principle a Plan of Action on Science and Technology for 2007–11, focusing on the following areas of activity: environment and disaster management; new and renewable energy; open source software system; and food safety and security. An ASEAN Plan of Action on Science and Technology for 2012–17 covered: food security; an early warning system for natural disasters; biofuels; development and application of open source software; and climate change.

ENVIRONMENT

An ASEAN Agreement on the Conservation of Nature and Natural Resources was signed in July 1985. In April 1994 a ministerial meeting on the environment approved long-term objectives on environmental quality and standards for the ASEAN region, aiming to enhance joint action in addressing environmental concerns. At the same time, ministers adopted standards for air quality and river water to be achieved by all ASEAN member countries by 2010. In June 1995 ministers agreed to co-operate to counter the problems of transboundary pollution. An ASEAN Regional Centre for Biodiversity Conservation (ARCBC) was established in February 1999.

In December 1997 ASEAN heads of state endorsed a Regional Haze Action Plan to address the environmental problems resulting from forest fires, which had afflicted several countries in the region throughout that year. A Haze Technical Task Force undertook to implement the plan, with assistance from the UN Environment Programme. Sub-regional fire-fighting arrangement working groups for Sumatra and Borneo were established in April 1998 and in May the Task Force organized a regional workshop to strengthen ASEAN capacity to prevent and alleviate the haze caused by the extensive fires. A pilot project of aerial surveillance of the areas in the region most at risk of forest fires was initiated in July. In December heads of government resolved to establish an ASEAN Regional Research and Training Centre for Land and Forest Fire Management. In March 2002 members of the working groups on sub-regional fire-fighting arrangements for Sumatra and Borneo agreed to intensify early warning efforts and surveillance activities in order to reduce the risks of forest fires. In June ASEAN ministers of the environment signed an Agreement on Transboundary Haze Pollution, which was intended to provide a legal basis for the Regional Haze Action Plan. The Agreement, which entered into force in November 2003, required member countries to co-operate in the prevention and mitigation of haze pollution, for example, by responding to requests for information by other states and facilitating the transit of personnel and equipment in case of disaster. The Agreement also provided for the establishment of an ASEAN Co-ordination Centre for Transboundary Haze Pollution Control. The first conference of parties to the Agreement was held in November 2004. An ASEAN Specialized Meteorological Centre (ASMC) based in Singapore, plays a primary role in long-range climatological forecasting, early detection and monitoring of fires and haze. In August 2005, guided by the ASEAN Agreement on Transboundary Haze Pollution, member countries activated bilateral and regional mechanisms to exchange information and mobilize resources to deal with severe fires in Sumatra (Indonesia), peninsular Malaysia and southern Thailand. In September 2007 ASEAN ministers agreed to establish a sub-regional Technical Working Group to focus on addressing land and forest fires in the northern part of the region.

In May 2001 environment ministers launched the ASEAN Environment Education Action Plan (AEEAP), with the aim of promoting public awareness of environmental and sustainable development issues. In November 2003 ASEAN + 3 ministers responsible for the environment agreed to prioritize environmental activities in the following areas: environmentally sustainable cities; global environmental issues; land and forest fires and transboundary haze pollution; coastal and marine environment; sustainable forest management; freshwater resources; public awareness and environmental education; promotion of green technologies and cleaner production; and sustainable development monitoring and reporting. The Vientiane Action Plan (see above) incorporated objectives for environmental and natural resource management for the period 2004–10. In September 2005 the ASEAN Centre for Biodiversity, funded jointly by ASEAN and the European Union (EU), was inaugurated in La Union, near Manila, the Philippines. In that month ministers of the environment approved an ASEAN Strategic Plan of Action on Water Resources Management. The ASEAN summit meeting convened in November 2007 was held on the theme of 'energy, environment, climate change, and sustainable development'. A final Declaration on Environmental Sustainability incorporated specific commitments to strengthen environmental protection management, to respond to climate change and to work towards the conservation and sustainable management of natural resources. A Special Ministerial Meeting on the environment was held in Hua Hin, Thailand, in September 2009. The meeting reviewed ongoing programmes and approved the establishment of an ASEAN Working Group on Climate Change. In the following month ASEAN environment ministers endorsed the terms of reference of an ASEAN Climate Change Initiative and adopted a Singapore Resolution on Environmental Sustainability and Climate Change, recognising the need for closer co-operation in responding to climate change. In April 2010 ASEAN heads of state, meeting in Hanoi, Viet Nam, adopted a Leaders' Statement on Joint Response to Climate Change, which reaffirmed ASEAN's commitment to securing a new legally binding agreement on carbon emissions and to strengthening ASEAN efforts to counter and respond to climate change.

SOCIAL WELFARE AND DEVELOPMENT

ASEAN is concerned with a range of social issues including youth development, the role of women, health and nutrition, education and labour affairs. In December 1993 ASEAN ministers responsible for social affairs adopted a Plan of Action for Children, which provided a framework for regional co-operation for the survival, protection and development of children in member countries. ASEAN supports efforts to combat drug abuse and illegal drugs-trafficking. It aims to promote education and drug-awareness campaigns throughout the region, and administers a project to strengthen the training of personnel involved in combating drug abuse. In July 1998 ASEAN ministers of foreign affairs signed a Joint Declaration for a Drug-Free ASEAN, which envisaged greater co-operation among member states, in particular in information exchange, educational resources and legal procedures, in order to eliminate the illicit production, processing and trafficking of narcotic substances by 2020. (This deadline was subsequently advanced to 2015.)

In December 1998 ASEAN leaders approved a series of measures aimed at mitigating the social impact of the financial and economic crises that had affected many countries in the region. Plans of Action were formulated on issues of rural development and poverty eradication, while Social Safety Nets, which aimed to protect the most vulnerable members of society, were approved. The summit meeting emphasized the need to promote job generation as a key element of strategies for economic recovery and growth. In November 2001 the leaders meeting considered the widening development gap between ASEAN members and concluded that bridging this gap was a priority. The meeting approved an Initiative for ASEAN Integration Work Plan, which identified infrastructure development, human resource development, access to ICT and the promotion of regional economic integration as priority areas of activity, in particular to assist the newer signatory states, i.e. Cambodia, Laos, Myanmar and Viet Nam. The Plan of Action for the ASEAN Socio-Cultural Community (envisaged in the Bali Concord II—see above) was adopted by ASEAN leaders in November 2004. The first ASEAN + 3 Ministerial Meeting for social welfare and development was convened in Bangkok, Thailand, in December, at which it was agreed that the three key areas of co-operation were to be: the promotion of a community of caring societies in the region; developing policies and programmes to address the issue of ageing; and addressing human resource development in the social sector. In July 2005 it was agreed to establish an ASEAN Development Fund, to which each member country would make an initial contribution of US $1m. An ASEAN Commission on the Promotion and Protection of the Rights of Women and Children was inaugurated in April 2010. A Strategic Framework and Plan of Action for Social Welfare, Family and Children for the period 2011–15 had the following objectives: promoting the welfare of children by safeguarding their rights, ensuring their survival and their full development; protecting children from abuse, discrimination and exploitation; protecting the elderly by supporting community-based support systems to supplement the role of the family as primary caregiver; strengthening regional co-operation to promote self-reliance of older persons and persons with disabilities; strengthening national social welfare and social protection national capacities; and developing family support and family life education programmes.

The seventh ASEAN summit meeting, held in November 2001, declared work on combating HIV and AIDS to be a priority. The second phase of a work programme to combat AIDS and provide help for sufferers was endorsed at the meeting. Heads of government expressed their readiness to commit the necessary resources for prevention and care, and to attempt to obtain access to cheaper drugs. An ASEAN task force on AIDS has been operational since March 1993. An ASEAN Co-operation Forum on HIV/AIDS was held in February 2003, in Bangkok. An East Asia and Pacific Consultation on Children and AIDS was convened in March 2006 and identified nine urgent actions to respond to children affected by HIV/AIDS. In April 2003 a Special ASEAN Leaders' Meeting on Severe Acute Respiratory Syndrome (SARS) endorsed the recommendations of ministers of health, who convened in special session a few days previously, and agreed to establish an ad hoc ministerial-level Joint Task Force to follow-up and monitor implementation of those decisions. Co-operation measures approved included public information and education campaigns, health and immigration control procedures, and the establishment of an early-warning system on emerging infectious diseases. In June 2006 ASEAN ministers responsible for health adopted a declaration entitled 'ASEAN Unity in Health Emergencies'. In June 2008 ASEAN inaugurated an internet-based information centre on emerging infectious diseases in the ASEAN + 3 countries to exchange data relating to infection outbreaks and surveillance. In May 2009 ASEAN +3 ministers of health convened a Special Meeting on Influenza A(H1N1), a new strain of swine flu that had recently emerged as a serious threat to humans. The meeting agreed to strengthen surveillance and effective responses; to implement national pandemic preparedness plans; and to ensure effective public communication. It urged regional co-operation to promote surveillance and the transfer of technology, in relation to the production of vaccines. An International Ministerial Conference on Animal and Pandemic Influenza was convened in Hanoi, Viet Nam, in April 2010. The meeting commended the efforts to counter infectious diseases, but noted the continued threat of highly pathogenic avian influenza (HPAI—see above).

In November 2011 ASEAN ministers approved a new framework action plan on rural development and poverty eradication, covering the period 2011–15, to address the following priorities: sustainable rural development and rural economic growth; food security and food sovereignty amid climate change; social protection and safety nets; development of infrastructure and human resources in rural areas; constituency building for rural development and poverty eradication; and monitoring and evaluation of the poverty reduction in the region.

In January 1992 the ASEAN summit meeting resolved to establish an ASEAN University Network (AUN) to hasten the development of a regional identity. A draft AUN Charter and Agreement were adopted in 1995. The Network aims to strengthen co-operation within the grouping, develop academic and professional human resources and transmit information and knowledge. The 17 universities linked by the Network carry out collaborative studies and research programmes. Three more universities became members of the AUN in November 2006. At the seventh ASEAN summit in November 2001 heads of government agreed to establish the first ASEAN University, in Malaysia. In August 2005 it was agreed to convene a regular ASEAN Ministerial Meeting on education; the first meeting was held in March 2006. In March 2007 education ministers determined to restart an ASEAN Student Exchange Programme.

In January 2007 ASEAN heads of government signed a Declaration on the Protection and Promotion of the Rights of Migrant Workers, which mandated countries to promote fair and appropriate employment protection, payment of wages, and adequate access to decent working and living conditions for migrant workers. A Committee on the Implementation of the ASEAN Declaration held its inaugural meeting in September 2008.

DISASTER MANAGEMENT

An ASEAN Committee on Disaster Management was established in early 2003 and worked to formulate a framework for co-operation in disaster management and emergency response. In January 2005 a Special ASEAN Leaders' Meeting was convened in Jakarta, Indonesia, to consider the needs of countries affected by an earthquake and devastating tsunami that had occurred in the Indian Ocean in late December 2004. The meeting, which was also attended by the UN Secretary-General, the President of the World Bank and other senior envoys of donor countries and international organizations, adopted a Declaration on Action to Strengthen Emergency Relief, Rehabilitation, Reconstruction and Prevention on the Aftermath of Earthquake and Tsunami Disaster. In July 2005 an ASEAN Agreement on Disaster Management and Emergency Response was signed in Vientiane, Laos. The Agreement stated as its objective the provision of mechanisms that would effectively reduce the loss of life and damage to the social, economic and environmental assets of the region and the response to disaster emergencies through concerted national efforts and increased regional and international co-operation. By October 2009 the Agreement had been ratified by each member state and it entered into force in December. In May 2009 ASEAN, with the World Bank and UN International Strategy for Disaster Reduction, announced a new co-operation programme to strengthen disaster reduction, including reducing vulnerability to natural hazards, and disaster management in South-East Asia.

TOURISM

National tourist organizations from ASEAN countries meet regularly to assist in co-ordinating the region's tourist industry, and a Tourism Forum is held annually to promote the sector. (In January 2012 the Forum was held in Manado, North Sulawesi, Indonesia.) The first formal meeting of ASEAN ministers of tourism was held in January 1998, in Cebu, Philippines. The meeting adopted a Plan of Action on ASEAN Co-operation in Tourism, which aimed to promote intra-ASEAN travel, greater investment in the sector, joint marketing of the region as a single tourist destination and environmentally sustainable tourism. In January 1999 the second meeting of ASEAN ministers of tourism agreed to appoint country co-ordinators to implement various initiatives, including research to promote the region as a tourist destination in the 21st century, and to develop a cruise ship industry; and the establishment of a network of ASEAN Tourism Training Centres to develop new skills and technologies in the tourist industry. The third meeting of tourism ministers, held in Bangkok, Thailand, in January 2000, agreed to reformulate the Visit ASEAN Millennium Year initiative as a long-term Visit ASEAN programme. This was formally launched in January 2001. The first phase of the programme promoted brand awareness through an intense marketing effort; the second phase, initiated at the fifth meeting of tourism ministers, held in Yogyakarta, Indonesia, in January 2002, was to direct campaigns towards end-consumers. Ministers urged member states to abolish all fiscal and non-fiscal travel barriers to encourage tourism, including intra-ASEAN travel. Tourism ministers from the ASEAN + 3 countries attended the meeting for the first time. In November the eighth summit of heads of state adopted a framework agreement on ASEAN co-operation in tourism, aimed at facilitating domestic and intra-regional travel. ASEAN national tourism organizations signed an implementation plan for the agreement in May 2003, when they also announced a Declaration on Tourism Safety and Security. In January 2011 ASEAN ministers of tourism approved a new ASEAN Tourism Strategic Plan for the period 2011–15. The Plan envisaged promoting the region as a single tourist destination, developing a set of ASEAN tourism standards with a certification process, and enabling visitors to travel throughout the region with a single visa.

CULTURE AND INFORMATION

Regular workshops and festivals are held in visual and performing arts, youth music, radio, television and films, and print and interpersonal media. In addition, ASEAN administers a News Exchange and provides support for the training of editors, journalists and information officers. In 2000 ASEAN adopted new cultural strategies, with the aim of raising awareness of the grouping's objectives and achievements, both regionally and internationally. The strategies included: producing ASEAN cultural and historical educational materials; promoting cultural exchanges; and achieving greater exposure of ASEAN cultural activities and issues in the mass media. An ASEAN Youth Camp was held for the first time in that year, and subsequently has been organized on an annual basis. ASEAN ministers responsible for culture and arts (AMCA) met for the first time in October 2003. The fourth ministerial meeting was convened, with their ministerial counterparts from the ASEAN + 3 countries, in Clark, Angelus City (Pampanga province), Philippines, in March 2010. The fourth ASEAN Festival of Arts was held concurrently, on the theme 'The Best of ASEAN', while Clark was named as the first ASEAN City of Culture.

In July 1997 ASEAN ministers of foreign affairs endorsed the establishment of an ASEAN Foundation to promote awareness of the organization and greater participation in its activities; this was inaugurated in July 1998 and is based at the ASEAN secretariat building (www.aseanfoundation.org).

EXTERNAL RELATIONS

ASEAN's external relations have been pursued through a dialogue system, initially with the objective of promoting co-operation in economic areas with key trading partners. The system has been expanded in recent years to encompass regional security concerns and co-operation in other areas, such as the environment. The ARF (see above) emerged from the dialogue system, and more recently the formalized discussions of ASEAN with China, Japan and South Korea (ASEAN + 3) has evolved as a separate process with its own strategic agenda. In February 2000 a meeting of ASEAN heads of state and the Secretary-General of the United Nations (UN) took place in Bangkok, Thailand. (A second ASEAN-UN summit was held in September 2005, in New York, USA, and a third was convened in October 2010, in Hanoi, Viet Nam.) In December 2006 the UN General Assembly granted ASEAN permanent observer status at its meetings.

In December 2005 the first East Asia Summit (EAS) meeting was convened, following the ASEAN leaders' meeting in Kuala Lumpur, Malaysia. It was attended by ASEAN member countries, tChina, Japan, South Korea (the '+ 3' countries), India, Australia and New Zealand; Russia participated as an observer. The meeting agreed to pursue co-operation in areas of common interest and determined to meet annually. It concluded a Declaration on Avian Influenza Prevention, Control and Response. At the second EAS meeting, held in Cebu, Philippines, in January 2007, a Declaration on East Asian Energy Security was adopted. An inaugural meeting of East Asian ministers of energy was convened in August. The third summit meeting was convened in Singapore, in November; it issued the Singapore Declaration on Climate Change, Energy and the Environment and held discussions on issues of mutual concern. The fourth EAS, scheduled to be held in Bangkok, in December 2008, was postponed owing to civil unrest, and was again deferred, in April 2009, owing to violent anti-government demonstrations at a new venue in Pattaya, Thailand. A statement by EAS heads of state, issued in June, declared their support for efforts to counter the global economic and financial crisis, including measures agreed by the G20, completion of the World Trade Organization's Doha Round, and a Comprehensive Economic Partnership in East Asia Initiative. Russia and the USA participated fully in the EAS for the first time at the sixth summit meeting, held in Bali, Indonesia, in November 2011.

European Union: In March 1980 a co-operation agreement was signed between ASEAN and the European Community (EC, as the EU was known prior to its restructuring on 1 November 1993), which provided for the strengthening of existing trade links and increased co-operation in the scientific and agricultural spheres. A Joint Co-operation Committee met in November (and annually thereafter). An ASEAN-EC Business Council was launched in December 1983 to promote private sector co-operation. The first meeting of ministers of economic affairs from ASEAN and EC member countries took place in October 1985. In December 1990 the Community adopted new guidelines on development co-operation, with an increase in assistance to Asia, and a change in the type of aid given to ASEAN members, emphasizing training, science and technology and venture capital, rather than assistance for rural development. In October 1992 the EC and ASEAN agreed to promote further trade between the regions, as well as bilateral investment, and made a joint declaration in support of human rights. An EU-ASEAN Junior Managers Exchange Programme was initiated in November 1996, as part of efforts to promote co-operation and understanding between the industrial and business sectors in both regions. In December 2000 an ASEAN-EU Ministerial Meeting was held in Vientiane, Laos. Both sides agreed to pursue dialogue and co-operation and issued a joint declaration that accorded support for the efforts of the UN Secretary-General's special envoy towards restoring political dialogue in Myanmar. Myanmar agreed to permit an EU delegation to visit the country and political opposition leaders in early 2001. In September the Joint Co-operation Committee, meeting for the first time since 1999, resolved to strengthen policy dialogue, in particular in areas fostering regional integration. An ASEAN-EU Business Network was established in Brussels, Belgium, in 2001, to develop political and commercial contacts between the two sides. An ASEAN-EU Business Summit meeting was convened for the first time in May 2011, in Jakarta, Indonesia.

In May 1995 ASEAN and EU senior officials endorsed an initiative to strengthen relations between the two economic regions within the framework of an Asia-Europe Meeting of heads of government (ASEM). The first ASEM was convened in Bangkok, Thailand, in March 1996, at which leaders approved a new Asia-Europe Partnership for Greater Growth. The second ASEM summit meeting, held in April 1998, focused heavily on economic concerns. In February 1997 ministers of foreign affairs of countries participating in ASEM met in Singapore. Despite ongoing differences regarding human rights issues, in particular concerning ASEAN's granting of full membership status to Myanmar and the situation in East Timor (which precluded the conclusion of a new co-operation agreement), the Ministerial Meeting issued a final joint declaration, committing both sides to strengthening co-operation and dialogue on economic, international and bilateral trade, security and social issues. The third ASEM summit meeting was convened in Seoul, South Korea in October 2000. At the 14th ASEAN-EU Ministerial Meeting, held in Brussels, in January 2003, delegates adopted an ASEAN-EU Joint Declaration on Co-operation to Combat Terrorism. An ASEM seminar on combating terrorism was held in Beijing, China, in October. In February 2003 the EU awarded €4.5m. under the ASEAN-EU Programme on Regional Integration Support (APRIS) to enhance progress towards establishing AFTA. (The first phase of the APRIS programme was concluded in September 2006, and a second three-year phase, APRIS II, was initiated in November with a commitment by the EU of €7.2m.) In April 2003 the EU proposed the creation of a regional framework, the Trans-Regional EU-ASEAN Trade Initiative (TREATI), to address mutual trade facilitation, investment and regulatory issues. It was suggested that the framework might eventually result in a preferential trade agreement. In January 2004 a joint statement was issued announcing a roadmap for implementing the TREATI and an EU-ASEAN work plan for that year. The fifth ASEM meeting of heads of state and government was held in Hanoi, Viet Nam, in October, attended for the first time by the 10 new members of the EU and by Cambodia, Laos, and Myanmar. At the session of the Joint Co-operation Committee held in February 2005, in Jakarta, Indonesia, it was announced that the European Commission's communication entitled 'A New Partnership with South-east Asia', issued in July 2003, would form the basis for the development of the EU's relations with ASEAN, along with Bali Concord II and the VAP. Under the new partnership, the TREATI would represent the framework for dialogue on trade and economic issues, whereas the READI (Regional EC ASEAN Dialogue Instrument) would be the focus for non-trade issues. The sixth ASEM, convened in Helsinki, Finland, in September 2006, on the theme '10 Years of ASEM: Global Challenges and Joint Responses', was attended for the first time by the ASEAN Secretariat, Bulgaria, India, Mongolia, Pakistan and Romania. The participants adopted a Declaration on Climate Change, aimed at promoting efforts to reach consensus in international climate negotiations, and the Helsinki Declaration on the Future of ASEM, detailing guidelines and practical recommendations for developing future ASEM co-operation. A Declaration on an Enhanced Partnership was endorsed in March 2007 and a plan of action to pursue strengthened co-operation was adopted at an ASEAN-EU summit meeting held in November. The seventh ASEM summit, convened in Beijing, China, in October 2008, issued a Declaration on Sustainable Development, focusing on the MDGs, climate change and energy security, and social cohesion. In May 2009 ASEAN and EU ministers of foreign affairs signed a declaration committing both sides to completing EU accession to the Treaty of Amity and Co-operation as a priority. The 18th ASEAN-EU Ministerial Meeting was held in Madrid, Spain, in May 2010, on the theme of 'Partners in Regional Integration'. The eighth ASEM summit took place in October, in Brussels. During the meeting Australia, New Zealand and Russia acceded to the grouping. The ninth ASEM summit was to be convened in Japan, in November 2012.

People's Republic of China: Efforts to develop consultative relations between ASEAN and China were initiated in 1993. Joint Committees on economic and trade co-operation and on scientific and technological co-operation were subsequently established. The first formal consultations between senior officials of the two sides were held in April 1995. In July 1996, in spite of ASEAN's continued concern at China's territorial claims to the Spratly Islands in the South China Sea, China was admitted to the PMC as a full dialogue partner. In February 1997 a Joint Co-operation Committee was established to co-ordinate the China-ASEAN dialogue and all aspects of relations between the two sides. Relations were further strengthened by the decision to form a joint business council to promote bilateral trade and investment. China participated in the informal summit meeting held in December, at the end of which both sides issued a joint statement affirming their commitment to resolving regional disputes through peaceful means. China was a participant in the first official ASEAN + 3 meeting of foreign ministers, which was convened in July 2000. An ASEAN-China Experts Group was established in November, to consider future economic co-operation and free trade opportunities. The Group held its first meeting in April 2001 and proposed a framework agreement on economic co-operation and the establishment of an ASEAN-China free trade area within 10 years (with differential treatment and flexibility for newer ASEAN members). Both proposals were endorsed at the seventh ASEAN summit meeting in November 2001. In November 2002 an agreement on economic co-operation was concluded by the ASEAN member states and China. The Framework Agreement on Comprehensive Economic Co-operation between ASEAN and China entered into force in July 2003, and envisaged the establishment of an ASEAN-China Free Trade Area (ACFTA) by 2010 (with the target for the newer member countries being 2015). The Agreement provided for strengthened co-operation in key areas including agriculture, information and telecommunications, and human resources development. It was also agreed to implement the consensus of the Special ASEAN-China Leaders' Meeting on SARS, held in April 2003, and to set up an ASEAN + 1 special fund for health co-operation. In October China acceded to the Treaty on Amity and Co-operation and signed a joint declaration with ASEAN on Strategic Partnership for Peace and Prosperity on strengthening co-operation in politics, economy, social affairs, security and regional and international issues. It was also agreed to continue consultations on China's accession to the SEANWFZ and to expedite the implementation of the Joint Statement on Co-operation in the Field of Non-Traditional Security Issues and the Declaration on the Conduct of Parties in the South China Sea. In November 2004 ASEAN and China signed the Agreement on Trade in Goods and the Agreement on Dispute Settlement Mechanism of the Framework Agreement on Comprehensive Economic Co-operation, to be implemented from 1 July 2005. A Plan of Action to Implement ASEAN-China Joint Declaration on Strengthening Strategic Partnership for Peace and Prosperity was also adopted by both parties at that time. In August 2005 ASEAN signed an MOU with China on cultural co-operation. An ASEAN-China Agreement on Trade in Services was signed in January 2007, within the Framework Agreement on Comprehensive Economic Co-operation, and entered into force on 1 July. The final component of the Framework Agreement, an ASEAN-China Investment Agreement, was signed in August 2009. Accordingly, ACFTA entered fully into effect on 1 January 2010. In November 2007 the ASEAN-China summit resolved that the environment should be included as a priority area for future co-operation and endorsed agreements concluded earlier in that month to strengthen co-operation in aviation and maritime transport. An ASEAN-China Environmental Co-operation Centre was formally inaugurated in Beijing, in May 2011. It was announced in October 2011 that China was to establish a mission to ASEAN during 2012.

Japan: The first meeting between the two sides at ministerial level was held in October 1992. At this meeting, and subsequently, ASEAN requested Japan to increase its investment in member countries and to make Japanese markets more accessible to ASEAN products, in order to reduce the trade deficit with Japan. Since 1993 ASEAN-Japanese development and cultural co-operation has expanded under schemes including the Inter-ASEAN Technical Exchange Programme, the Japan-ASEAN Co-operation Promotion Programme and the ASEAN-Japan Friendship Programme. In December 1997 Japan, attending the informal summit meeting in Malaysia, agreed to improve market access for ASEAN products and to provide training opportunities for more than 20,000 young people in order to help develop local economies. In December 1998 ASEAN heads of government welcomed a Japanese initiative to allocate US $30,000m. to promote economic recovery in the region. In mid-2000 a new Japan-ASEAN General Exchange Fund (JAGEF) was established to promote and facilitate the transfer of technology, investment and personnel. In November 1999 Japan, with China and South Korea, attending an informal summit meeting of ASEAN, agreed to strengthen economic and political co-operation with the ASEAN countries, to enhance political and security dialogue, and to implement joint infrastructure and social projects. Japan participated in the first official ASEAN + 3 meeting of foreign ministers, which was convened in July 2000. In recent years Japan has provided ICT support to ASEAN countries, and has offered assistance in environmental and health matters and for educational training and human resource development (particularly in engineering). In October 2003 ASEAN and Japan signed a Framework for Comprehensive Partnership. In December Japan concluded a joint action plan with ASEAN with provisions on reinforcing economic integration within ASEAN and enhancing competitiveness, and on addressing terrorism, piracy and other transnational issues. A joint declaration was also issued on starting discussions on the possibility of establishing an ASEAN-Japan FTA by 2012 (with the newer ASEAN countries participating from 2017). Negotiations on a Comprehensive Economic Partnership Agreement were initiated in April 2005 and concluded in November 2007. The accord was signed in April 2008 and entered into force on 1 December. In July 2004 Japan acceded to the Treaty on Amity and Co-operation. In November the ASEAN-Japan summit meeting adopted the ASEAN-Japan Joint Declaration for Co-operation in the Fight Against International Terrorism. In July 2008 ASEAN concluded a formal partnership agreement with the new Japan International Co-operation Agency, with the aim of working together to strengthen ASEAN integration and development. In April 2011 a Special ASEAN-Japan Ministerial Meeting was convened, in Jakarta, Indonesia, to reaffirm mutual support, in particular in respect to Japan's recovery from a massive earthquake in the previous month.

Australia and New Zealand: In 1999 ASEAN and Australia undertook to establish the ASEAN-Australia Development Co-operation Programme (AADCP), to replace an economic co-operation programme that had begun in 1974. In August 2002 the two sides signed a formal MOU on the AADCP. It was to comprise three core elements, with assistance amounting to $A45m.: a Program Stream, to address medium-term issues of economic integration and competitiveness; a Regional Partnerships Scheme for smaller collaborative activities; and the establishment of a Regional Economic Policy Support Facility within the ASEAN Secretariat. In July 2009 ASEAN and Australia signed an MOU on the implementation of a second phase of the AADCP.

In September 2001 ASEAN ministers of economic affairs signed a Framework for Closer Economic Partnership (CEP) with their counterparts from Australia and New Zealand (the Closer Economic Relations—CER—countries), and agreed to establish a Business Council to involve the business communities of all countries in the CEP. In November 2004 a Commemorative Summit, marking 30 years of dialogue between the nations, took place between ASEAN leaders and those of Australia and New Zealand at which it was agreed to launch negotiations on a free trade agreement. In July 2005 New Zealand signed ASEAN's Treaty of Amity and Co-operation; Australia acceded to the Treaty in December. In August 2007 the Australian and ASEAN ministers of foreign affairs signed a Joint Declaration on a Comprehensive Partnership, and in November they agreed upon a plan of action to implement the accord. An agreement establishing an ASEAN–Australia–New Zealand free trade area was negotiated during 2008 and signed in Cha-am/Hua Hin, Thailand, in February 2009. An ASEAN-New Zealand Joint Declaration on Comprehensive Partnership for the period 2010-2015 was signed by ministers of foreign affairs of both sides in July 2010.

South Asia: In July 1993 both India and Pakistan were accepted as sectoral partners, providing for their participation in ASEAN meetings in sectors such as trade, transport and communications and tourism. An ASEAN-India Business Council was established, and met for the first time, in New Delhi, in February 1995. In December 1995 the ASEAN summit meeting agreed to enhance India's status to that of a full dialogue partner; India was formally admitted to the PMC in July 1996. At a meeting of the ASEAN-India Working Group in March 2001 the two sides agreed to pursue co-operation in new areas, such as health and pharmaceuticals, social security and rural development. The fourth meeting of the ASEAN-India Joint Co-operation Committee in January 2002 agreed to strengthen co-operation in these areas and others, including technology. The first ASEAN-India consultation between ministers of economic affairs, which took place in September, resulted in the adoption as a long-term objective, of the ASEAN-India Regional Trade and Investment Area. The first ASEAN-India summit at the level of heads of state was held in Phnom-Penh, Cambodia, in November. In October 2003 India acceded to the Treaty of Amity and Co-operation and signed a joint Framework Agreement on Comprehensive Economic Co-operation, which was to enter into effect in July 2004. The objectives of the Agreement included: strengthening and enhancing economic, trade and investment co-operation; liberalizing and promoting trade in goods and services; and facilitating economic integration within ASEAN. It was also agreed that negotiations would begin on establishing an ASEAN-India Regional Trade and Investment Area (RTIA), including a free trade area, for Brunei, Indonesia, Malaysia, Singapore and Thailand. A Partnership for Peace, Progress and Shared Prosperity was signed at the third ASEAN-India summit, held in November 2004. At the sixth summit meeting, held in November 2007, it was noted that annual bilateral ASEAN-India trade had reached US $20,000m. ASEAN-India agreements on trade in goods and on a dispute settlement mechanism were concluded in August 2008. The agreement on trade in goods was signed by both sides in August 2009, enabling the RTIA to enter into force on 1 January 2010.

An ASEAN-Pakistan Joint Business Council met for the first time in February 2000. In early 2001 both sides agreed to co-operate in projects relating to new and renewable energy resources, ICT, agricultural research and transport and communications. Pakistan acceded to the Treaty on Amity and Co-operation in July 2004. In January 2007 Timor-Leste acceded to the Treaty; Sri Lanka and Bangladesh acceded in August.

Republic of Korea: In July 1991 the Republic of Korea (South Korea) was accepted as a 'dialogue partner' in ASEAN, and in December a joint ASEAN-Korea Chamber of Commerce was established. South Korea participated in ASEAN's informal summit meetings in December 1997 and November 1999 (see above), and took part in the first official ASEAN + 3 meeting of ministers of foreign affairs, convened in July 2000. South Korea's assistance in the field of ICT has become particularly valuable in recent years. In

March 2001, in a sign of developing co-operation, ASEAN and South Korea exchanged views on political and security issues in the region for the first time. South Korea acceded to the Treaty on Amity and Co-operation in November 2004. In that month an ASEAN-Korea summit meeting agreed to initiate negotiations on the establishment of a free trade area between the two sides. The Framework Agreement on Comprehensive Economic Co-operation, providing for the establishment of an ASEAN-Korea Free Trade Area, was signed in December 2005, eliminating tariffs on some 80% of products, with effect from 1 January 2010. In May 2006 governments of both sides (excluding Thailand, owing to a dispute concerning trade in rice) signed an Agreement on Trade in Goods. An ASEAN–Korea agreement on trade in services entered into force in May 2009. An ASEAN-Korea Investment Agreement was signed in June.

Russia: In March 2000 the first ASEAN-Russia business forum opened in Kuala Lumpur, Malaysia. In July 2004 ASEAN and Russia signed a Joint Declaration to Combat International Terrorism, while in November Russia acceded to the Treaty of Amity and Co-operation. The first ASEAN-Russia summit meeting was held in December 2005. The leaders agreed on a comprehensive programme of action to promote co-operation between both sides in the period 2005–15. This included commitments to co-operate in areas including counter-terrorism, human resources development, finance and economic activities and science and technology. In July 2008 both sides adopted a roadmap to further implementation of the comprehensive programme of action.

USA and Canada: In 1990 ASEAN and the USA established an ASEAN-US Joint Working Group, the purpose of which was to review ASEAN's economic relations with the USA and to identify measures by which economic links could be strengthened. In recent years, dialogue has increasingly focused on political and security issues. In August 2002 ASEAN ministers of foreign affairs met with their US counterpart, and signed a Joint Declaration for Co-operation to Combat International Terrorism. At the same time, the USA announced the ASEAN Co-operation Plan, which was to include activities in the fields of ICT, agricultural biotechnology, health, disaster response and training for the ASEAN Secretariat. In July 2009 the USA signed ASEAN's Treaty of Amity and Co-operation. The first official ASEAN meeting with the US President took place in November, in Singapore. Both sides resolved to enhance collaboration and to establish an ASEAN-US Eminent Persons Group. A second ASEAN-US leaders' meeting was held in September 2010, and a third in November 2011.

ASEAN-Canadian co-operation projects include fisheries technology, the telecommunications industry, use of solar energy, and a forest seed centre. A Working Group on the Revitalization of ASEAN-Canada relations met in February 1999. At a meeting in Bangkok, Thailand, in July 2000, the two sides agreed to explore less formal avenues for project implementation. A Work Plan for ASEAN-Canada Co-operation 2007–10 was adopted in August 2007.

Indo-China: In June 1996 ministers of ASEAN countries, and of Cambodia, China, Laos and Myanmar adopted a framework for ASEAN-Mekong Basin Development Co-operation. The initiative aimed to strengthen the region's cohesiveness, with greater co-operation on issues such as drugs-trafficking, labour migration and terrorism, and to facilitate the process of future expansion of ASEAN. Groups of experts and senior officials were to be convened to consider funding issues and proposals to link the two regions, including a gas pipeline network, rail links and the establishment of a common time zone. In December 1996 the working group on rail links appointed a team of consultants to conduct a feasibility study of the proposals. The completed study was presented at the second ministerial conference on ASEAN-Mekong Basin Development Co-operation, convened in Hanoi, Viet Nam, in July 2000. At the November 2001 summit China pledged US $5m. to assist with navigation along the upper stretches of the Mekong River, while other means by which China could increase its investment in the Mekong Basin area were considered. At the meeting South Korea was invited to become a core member of the grouping. Other growth regions sponsored by ASEAN include the Brunei, Indonesia, Malaysia, Philippines, East ASEAN Growth Area (BIMP-EAGA), the Indonesia, Malaysia, Singapore Growth Triangle (IMS-GT), and the West-East Corridor within the Mekong Basin Development initiative.

Gulf States: In June 2009 ASEAN ministers of foreign affairs held an inaugural meeting with their counterpart from the Co-operation Council for the Arab States of the Gulf (GCC). The meeting, convened in Manama, Bahrain, adopted a GCC-ASEAN Joint Vision as a framework for future co-operation between the two groupings. A second meeting, held in Singapore, in May–June 2010, approved an ASEAN–GCC Action Plan, which identified specific measures for closer co-operation to be undertaken in the two-year period 2010–12.

Publications

Annual Report.

Annual Security Report.

ASEAN Investment Report (annually).

ASEAN State of the Environment Report (1st report: 1997; 2nd report: 2000; 3rd report: 2006; 4th report: 2009).

Business ASEAN (quarterly).

ASEAN Updates.

Public Information Series, briefing papers, documents series, educational materials.

BANK FOR INTERNATIONAL SETTLEMENTS—BIS

Address: Centralbahnplatz 2, 4002 Basel, Switzerland.

Telephone: 612808080; **fax:** 612809100; **e-mail:** email@bis.org; **internet:** www.bis.org.

The Bank for International Settlements was founded pursuant to the Hague Agreements of 1930 to promote co-operation among national central banks and to provide additional facilities for international financial operations.

Organization

(April 2012)

GENERAL MEETING

The General Meeting is held annually in June and is attended by representatives of the central banks of countries in which shares have been subscribed. The central banks of the following 56 authorities are entitled to attend and vote at General Meetings of the BIS: Algeria, Argentina, Australia, Austria, Belgium, Bosnia and Herzegovina, Brazil, Bulgaria, Canada, Chile, the People's Republic of China, Croatia, the Czech Republic, Denmark, Estonia, Finland, France, Germany, Greece, Hong Kong SAR, Hungary, Iceland, India, Indonesia, Ireland, Israel, Italy, Japan, the Republic of Korea, Latvia, Lithuania, the former Yugoslav republic of Macedonia, Malaysia, Mexico, the Netherlands, New Zealand, Norway, the Philippines, Poland, Portugal, Romania, Russia, Saudi Arabia, Serbia, Singapore, Slovakia, Slovenia, South Africa, Spain, Sweden, Switzerland, Thailand, Turkey, the United Kingdom and the USA. The European Central Bank became a BIS shareholder in December 1999.

BOARD OF DIRECTORS

The Board of Directors is responsible for the conduct of the Bank's operations at the highest level. It comprises the Governors in office of the central banks of Belgium, France, Germany, Italy, and the United Kingdom, as well as the Chairman of the Board of Governors of the US Federal Reserve System. Each of those six *ex officio* members may appoint another director of the same nationality. The Bank's statutes provide for the election to the Board of not more than nine Governors of other member central banks. As at March 2012 those of Canada, People's Republic of China, Japan, Mexico, the Netherlands, Sweden and Switzerland and the President of the European Central Bank were elected members of the Board. In June 2005 an extraordinary general meeting amended the statutes to abolish the position of President of the Bank, which had been jointly vested with chairmanship of the Board since 1948.

Chairman of the Board: CHRISTIAN NOYER (France).

MANAGEMENT

At January 2012 the Bank employed some 589 staff members, from 54 countries. The main departments are the General Secretariat, the Monetary and Economic Department and the Banking Department. In July 1998 the BIS inaugurated its first overseas administrative unit, the Representative Office for Asia and the Pacific, which is based in Hong Kong. A Regional Treasury dealing room became operational at the Hong Kong office in October 2000, with the aim of improving access for Asian central banks to BIS financial services during their trading hours. In November 2002 a Representative Office for the Americas was inaugurated in Mexico City, Mexico.

General Manager: JAIME CARUANA (Spain).

Representative Office for Asia and the Pacific: Two International Finance Centre, 78th Floor, 8 Finance St, Central, Hong Kong, Special Administrative Region, People's Republic of China; tel. 28787100; fax 28787123.

Representative Office for the Americas: Torre Chapultepec, Rubén Darío 281, 17th Floor, Col. Bosque de Chapultepec, Del. Miguel Hidalgo, 11580 Mexico, D.F., Mexico; tel. (55) 91380290; fax (55) 91380299; e-mail americas@bis.org.

Activities

The BIS is an international financial institution whose role is to promote international monetary and financial co-operation, and to fulfil the function of a 'central banks' bank'. Although it has the legal form of a company limited by shares, it is an international organization governed by international law, and enjoys special privileges and immunities in keeping with its role (a Headquarters Agreement was concluded with Switzerland in 1987). The participating central banks were originally given the option of subscribing the shares themselves or arranging for their subscription in their own countries. In January 2001, however, an extraordinary general meeting amended the Bank's statutes to restrict ownership to central banks. Accordingly, all shares then held by private shareholders (representing 14% of the total share capital) were repurchased at a compensation rate of 16,000 Swiss francs per share. An additional compensation payment was required following a decision by the Hague Arbitral Tribunal (provided for in the 1930 Hague Agreements) in September 2003.

FINANCE

Until the end of the 2002/03 financial year the Bank's unit of account was the gold franc. An extraordinary general meeting in March 2003 amended the Bank's statutes to redenominate the Bank's share capital in Special Drawing Rights (SDRs), the unit of account of the IMF, with effect from 1 April 2003, in order to enhance the efficiency and transparency of the Bank's operations. The meeting decided that the nominal value of shares would be rounded down from SDR 5,696 at 31 March 2003 to SDR 5,000, entailing a reduction of 12.2% in the total share capital. The excess of SDR 92.1m. was transferred to the Bank's reserve funds. The authorized capital of the Bank at 31 March 2011 was SDR 3,000m., divided into 600,000 shares of equal value.

BANKING OPERATIONS

The BIS assists central banks in managing and investing their foreign exchange and gold reserves: in 2011 some 140 international financial institutions and central banks from all over the world had deposits with the BIS, representing around 3% of world foreign exchange reserves.

The BIS uses the funds deposited with it partly for lending to central banks. Its credit transactions may take the form of swaps against gold; covered credits secured by means of a pledge of gold or marketable short-term securities; credits against gold or currency deposits of the same amount and for the same duration held with the BIS; unsecured credits in the form of advances or deposits; or standby credits, which in individual instances are backed by guarantees given by member central banks.

The BIS also engages in traditional types of investment: funds not required for lending to central banks are placed in the market as deposits with commercial banks and purchases of short-term negotiable paper, including Treasury bills. Such operations constitute a major part of the Bank's business. Increasingly, the Bank has developed its own investment services for central banks, including short-term products and longer-term financial instruments.

Central banks' monetary reserves often need to be available at short notice, and need to be placed with the BIS at short term, for fixed periods and with clearly defined repayment terms. The BIS has to match its assets to the maturity structure and nature of its commitments, and must therefore conduct its business with special regard to maintaining a high degree of liquidity.

The Bank's operations must be in conformity with the monetary policy of the central banks of the countries concerned. It is not permitted to make advances to governments or to open current accounts in their name. Real estate transactions are also excluded.

INTERNATIONAL MONETARY CO-OPERATION

Governors of central banks meet for regular discussions at the BIS to co-ordinate international monetary policy and to promote stability in the international financial markets. There is close co-operation with the IMF and the World Bank. The BIS participates in meetings of the so-called Group of 10 (G10) industrialized nations (see IMF), which has been a major forum for discussion of international monetary issues since its establishment in 1962. Governors of central banks of the G10 countries convene for regular Basel Monthly Meetings. In 1971 a Standing Committee of the G10 central banks was established at the BIS to consider aspects of the development of Euro-currency markets. In February 1999 the G10 renamed the body the Committee on the Global Financial System, and approved a revised mandate to undertake systematic short-term monitoring of global financial system conditions; longer-term analysis of the functioning of financial markets; and the articulation of policy recommendations aimed at improving market functioning and promoting stability. A Markets Committee (formerly known as the Committee on Gold and Foreign Exchange, established in 1962) comprises senior officials responsible for market operations in the G10 central banks. It meets regularly to consider developments in foreign exchange and related financial markets, possible future trends and short-run implications of events on market functioning. In 1990 a Committee on Payment and Settlement Systems was established to monitor and analyse developments in domestic payment, settlement and clearing systems, and cross-border and multi-currency systems. It meets three times a year. The Irving Fisher Committee on Central Bank Statistics, a forum of central bank users and compilers of statistics, has operated under the auspices of the BIS since January 2006.

In 1974 the Governors of central banks of the G10 set up the Basel Committee on Banking Supervision (whose secretariat is provided by the BIS) to co-ordinate banking supervision at the international level. The Committee pools information on banking supervisory regulations and surveillance systems, including the supervision of banks' foreign currency business, identifies possible danger areas and proposes measures to safeguard the banks' solvency and liquidity. An International Conference of Banking Supervisors is held every two years. In 1997 the Committee published new guidelines, entitled Core Principles for Effective Banking Supervision, that were intended to provide a comprehensive set of standards to ensure sound banking. In 1998 the Committee was concerned with the development and implementation of the Core Principles, particularly given the ongoing financial and economic crisis affecting several Asian countries and instability of other major economies. A Financial Stability Institute was established in 1999, jointly by the BIS and Basel Committee, to enhance the capacity of central banks and supervisory bodies to implement aspects of the Core Principles, through the provision of training programmes and other policy workshops. In January 2001 the Committee issued preliminary proposals on capital adequacy rules. In June 2004 the Committee approved a revised framework of the International Convergence of Capital Measurement and Capital Standards (also known as Basel II), which aimed to promote improvements in risk management and strengthen the stability of the financial system. An updated version of the revised framework, as well as a new version of the Amendment to the Capital Accord to incorporate market risks, was issued in November 2005. The updated versions also incorporated a paper concerned with trading activities and the treatment of double default effects prepared by a joint working group of the Committee and the International Organization of Securities Commissions. In October 2006 the International Conference of Banking Supervisors endorsed an enhanced version of the Core Principles (and its associated assessment methodology), incorporating stricter guidelines to counter money-laundering and to strengthen transparency. The Basel II capital framework began to be implemented by countries and banks from 1 January 2007. The Committee's Accord Implementation Group undertook to promote full implementation of the accord, to provide supervisory guidance and review procedures. In January 2009 the Committee proposed a package of enhanced measures to strengthen the Basel II capital framework. In June the Committee agreed to broaden its membership to include representatives from the Group of 20 (G20) countries not currently in the Committee, i.e. Argentina, Indonesia, Saudi Arabia, South Africa and Turkey. In addition, Hong Kong, Special Administrative Region, and Singapore were invited to become members. The first meeting of the expanded Committee, convened in July, approved the enhancements to the Basel II capital framework. In July 2010 a reformed capital framework programme, Basel III, was agreed by Committee's Group of Central Bank Governors and Heads of Supervision. In accordance with an agreement concluded by G20 ministers of finance in the previous month, Basel III regulations were to be phased in gradually, with some elements, for example those concerning liquidity, not becoming mandatory until 2018. In September 2010 the Group announced further agreements substantially to strengthen global capital requirements, including raising common equity levels in relation to risk-weighted assets, and introducing capital conservation buffers from 2016. The regulatory framework was endorsed by a meeting of the G20 heads of state and government held in Seoul, Republic of Korea, in November 2010.

The BIS hosts the secretariat of the Financial Stability Board, which was established (as the Financial Stability Forum) following a meeting in February 1999 of ministers of finance and governors of the central banks of the Group of Seven (G7) industrialized nations. Its aim was to strengthen co-operation among the world's largest economies and economic bodies in order to improve the monitoring of international finance, to reduce the tendency for financial shocks to spread from one economy to another, and thus to prevent a recurrence of economic crises such as those that occurred in 1997 and 1998. Working groups have studied aspects of highly leveraged, or unregulated, institutions, offshore financial centres, short-term capital flows, deposit insurance schemes and measures to promote implementation of international standards. In March 2009 membership was expanded to include all G20 economies, as well as Spain and the European Commission. In the following month G20 heads of state and government, meeting in London, United Kingdom, determined to re-establish the Financial Stability Forum as the Financial Stability Board, with an expanded mandate to develop and implement strengthened financial regulation and supervision. The inaugural meeting of the Board was convened in June.

Since January 1998 the BIS has hosted the secretariat of the International Association of Insurance Supervisors, which aims to promote co-operation within the insurance industry with regard to effective supervision and the development of domestic insurance markets. It also hosts the secretariat of the International Association of Deposit Insurers, founded in May 2002.

RESEARCH

The Bank's Monetary and Economic Department conducts research, particularly into monetary and financial questions; collects and publishes data on securities markets and international banking developments; and administers a Data Bank for central banks. Examples of recent research and policy analysis include inflation targeting procedures, structural changes in foreign exchange markets, financial risks and the business cycle, international capital flows, and transmission mechanism of monetary policy. In 2004 the BIS established a Central Bank Research Hub to promote and facilitate the dissemination of economic research published by central banks. Statistics on aspects of the global financial system are published regularly, including details on international banking activities, international and domestic securities markets, derivatives, global foreign exchange markets, external debt, and payment and settlement systems. In September 2006 a three-year Asian research programme was initiated, concerned with monetary policy and exchange rates and analysing financial markets and institutions. Following the conclusion of the programme in August 2009, a more permanent research presence in the region was under consideration. The Bank is a co-sponsor, with the UN, Euro Banking Association, Eurostat, OECD, the IMF and the World Bank, of the Statistical Data and Metadata Exchange initiative, established in June 2002.

AGENCY AND TRUSTEE FUNCTIONS

Throughout its history the BIS has undertaken various duties as Trustee Fiscal Agent or Depository with regard to international loan agreements. In October 2005 the BIS served as an escrow agent role in a loan with the Central Bank of Nigeria; the arrangement was terminated upon the final release of funds in February 2007.

In April 1994 the BIS assumed new functions in connection with the rescheduling of Brazil's external debt, which had been agreed by the Brazilian Government in November 1993. In accordance with two collateral pledge agreements, the BIS acts in the capacity of Collateral Agent to hold and invest collateral for the benefit of the holders of certain US dollar-denominated bonds, maturing in 15 or 30 years, which have been issued by Brazil under the rescheduling arrangements. The Bank acts in a similar capacity for Peru, in accordance with external debt agreements concluded in November 1996 and a collateral agreement signed with the BIS in March 1997, and for Côte d'Ivoire, under a restructuring agreement signed in May 1997 and collateral agreement signed in March 1998.

Publications

Annual Report (in English, French, German, Italian and Spanish).

BIS Consolidated Banking Statistics (every 6 months).

BIS Papers (series).

Central Bank Survey of Foreign Exchange and Derivatives Market Activity (every 3 years).

International Journal of Central Banking (quarterly).

Joint BIS-IMF-OECD-World Bank Statistics on External Debt (quarterly).

Quarterly Review.

Regular OTC Derivatives Market Statistics (every 6 months).

Statistics

STATEMENT OF ACCOUNT
(In SDR millions; 31 March 2011)

Assets		%
Gold and gold deposits	36,637.2	14.0
Cash and on sight a/c with banks	329.8	0.1
Treasury bills	76,932.1	29.5
Loans and advances	24,170.4	9.3
Securities	108,451.9	41.5
Miscellaneous	14,597.4	5.6
Total	261,118.8	100.0

Liabilities		%
Deposits (gold)	21,269.9	8.1
Deposits (currencies)	207,085.6	79.3
Accounts payable	8,758.1	3.4
Other liabilities	7,334.9	2.8
Shareholders' equity	16,670.3	6.4
Total	261,118.8	100.0

Source: BIS, *Annual Report*.

CARIBBEAN COMMUNITY AND COMMON MARKET—CARICOM

Address: POB 10827, Georgetown, Guyana.

Telephone: (2) 222-0001; **fax:** (2) 222-0171; **e-mail:** info@caricom.org; **internet:** www.caricom.org.

CARICOM was formed in 1973 by the Treaty of Chaguaramas, signed in Trinidad, as a movement towards unity in the Caribbean; it replaced the Caribbean Free Trade Association (CARIFTA), founded in 1965. A revision of the Treaty of Chaguaramas (by means of nine separate Protocols), in order to institute greater regional integration and to establish a CARICOM Single Market and Economy (CSME), was instigated in the 1990s and completed in July 2001. The single market component of the CSME was formally inaugurated on 1 January 2006.

MEMBERS

Antigua and Barbuda
Bahamas*
Barbados
Belize
Dominica
Grenada
Guyana
Haiti
Jamaica
Montserrat
Saint Christopher and Nevis
Saint Lucia
Saint Vincent and the Grenadines
Suriname
Trinidad and Tobago

* The Bahamas is a member of the Community but not the Common Market.

ASSOCIATE MEMBERS

Anguilla
Bermuda
British Virgin Islands
Cayman Islands
Turks and Caicos Islands

Note: Aruba, Colombia, Dominican Republic, Mexico, Puerto Rico, and Venezuela have observer status with the Community.

Organization

(April 2012)

HEADS OF GOVERNMENT CONFERENCE AND BUREAU

The Conference is the final authority of the Community and determines policy. It is responsible for the conclusion of treaties on behalf of the Community and for entering into relationships between the Community and international organizations and states. Decisions of the Conference are generally taken unanimously. Heads of government meet annually, although inter-sessional meetings may be convened.

At a special meeting of the Conference, held in Trinidad and Tobago in October 1992, participants decided to establish a Heads of Government Bureau, with the capacity to initiate proposals, to update consensus and to secure the implementation of CARICOM decisions. The Bureau became operational in December, comprising the Chairman of the Conference, as Chairman, as well as the incoming and outgoing Chairmen of the Conference, and the Secretary-General of the Conference, in the capacity of Chief Executive Officer.

COMMUNITY COUNCIL OF MINISTERS

In October 1992 CARICOM heads of government agreed that a Caribbean Community Council of Ministers should be established to replace the existing Common Market Council of Ministers as the second highest organ of the Community. Protocol I amending the Treaty of Chaguaramas, to restructure the organs and institutions of the Community, was formally adopted at a meeting of CARICOM heads of government in February 1997 and was signed by all member states in July. The inaugural meeting of the Community Council of Ministers was held in Nassau, Bahamas, in February 1998. The Council consists of ministers responsible for community affairs, as well as other government ministers designated by member states, and is responsible for the development of the Community's strategic planning and co-ordination in the areas of economic integration, functional co-operation and external relations.

COURT OF JUSTICE

Caribbean Court of Justice (CCJ): 134 Henry St, POB 1768, Port of Spain, Trinidad and Tobago; tel. 623-2225; e-mail info@caribbeancourtofjustice.org; internet www.caribbeancourtofjustice.org; inaugurated in April 2005; an agreement establishing the Court was formally signed by 10 member countries in February 2001, and by two further states in February 2003; in January 2004 a revised agreement on the establishment of the CCJ, which incorporated provision for a Trust Fund, entered into force; serves as a tribunal to enforce rights and to consider disputes relating to the CARICOM Single Market and Economy; intended to replace the Judicial Committee of the Privy Council as the Court of Final Appeal (effective for Barbados, Belize and Guyana in 2010); Pres. Sir DENNIS BYRON (Saint Christopher and Nevis).

MINISTERIAL COUNCILS

The principal organs of the Community are assisted in their functions by the following bodies, established under Protocol I amending the Treaty of Chaguaramas: the Council for Trade and Economic Development (COTED); the Council for Foreign and Community Relations (COFCOR); the Council for Human and Social Development (COHSOD); and the Council for Finance and Planning (COFAP). The Councils are responsible for formulating policies, promoting their implementation and supervising co-operation in the relevant areas.

SECRETARIAT

The Secretariat is the main administrative body of the Caribbean Community. The functions of the Secretariat are to service meetings of the Community and of its Committees; to take appropriate follow-up action on decisions made at such meetings; to carry out studies on questions of economic and functional co-operation relating to the region as a whole; to provide services to member states at their request in respect of matters relating to the achievement of the objectives of the Community. The Secretariat incorporates Directorates, each headed by an Assistant Secretary-General, for Trade and Economic Integration; Foreign and Community Relations; Human and Social Development; and CARIFORUM.

Secretary-General: IRWIN LAROCQUE (Dominica).

Activities

The Heads of Government meeting, convened in Montego Bay, Jamaica, in July 2010, agreed to establish a seven-member high-level committee to draft proposals on a new governance structure for CARICOM, in order to address concerns regarding the implementation of community decisions. The report, entitled *Turning around CARICOM: Proposals to restructure the Secretariat*, was presented to heads of government, convened for an inter-sessional meeting in Paramaribo, Suriname, in March 2012.

ECONOMIC CO-OPERATION

The Caribbean Community's main field of activity is economic integration, by means of a Caribbean Common Market. The Secretariat and the Caribbean Development Bank undertake research on the best means of tackling economic difficulties, and meetings of the chief executives of commercial banks and of central bank officials are also held with the aim of strengthening regional co-operation. In March 2009 heads of government, meeting in Belize City, Belize, resolved to pursue a regional strategy to counter the effects on the region of the severe global economic and financial downturn. A new Heads of Government Task Force on the Regional Financial and Economic Crisis held its inaugural meeting in August, in Jamaica.

In July 1984 heads of government agreed to establish a common external tariff (CET) on certain products, in order to protect domestic industries. They urged structural adjustment in the economies of the region, including measures to expand production and reduce imports. In 1989 the Conference of Heads of Government agreed to implement, by July 1993, a series of measures to encourage the creation of a single Caribbean market. These included the establishment of a CARICOM Industrial Programming Scheme; the inauguration of the CARICOM Enterprise Regime; facilitation of travel for CARICOM nationals within the region; full implementation of the rules of origin and the revised scheme for the harmonization of fiscal incentives; free movement of skilled workers; removal of all remaining regional barriers to trade; establishment of a regional system of air and sea transport; and the introduction of a scheme for regional capital movement. A CARICOM Export Development Council, established in November 1989, undertook a three-year export development project to stimulate trade within CARICOM and to promote exports outside the region. In August 1990 CARICOM heads of government mandated the governors of CARICOM members' central banks to begin a study of the means to achieve monetary union within CARICOM; they also institutionalized biannual meetings of CARICOM ministers of finance and senior finance officials.

The initial deadline of 1991 for the establishment of a CET was not achieved. At a special meeting, held in October 1992, CARICOM heads of government agreed to reduce the maximum level of tariffs from 45% to between 30% and 35%, to be in effect by 30 June 1993 (the level was to be further lowered, to 25%–30% by 1995). The Bahamas, however, was not party to these trading arrangements (since it is a member of the Community but not of the Common Market), and Belize was granted an extension for the implementation of the new tariff levels. At the Heads of Government Conference, held in July 1995 in Guyana, Suriname was admitted as a full member of CARICOM and acceded to the treaty establishing the Common Market. It was granted until 1 January 1996 for implementation of the tariff reductions.

The 1995 Heads of Government Conference approved additional measures to promote the single market. The free movement of skilled workers (mainly graduates from recognized regional institutions) was to be permitted from 1 January 1996. At the same time an agreement on the mutual protection and provision of social security benefits was to enter into force. In July 1996 the heads of government agreed to extend the provisions of free movement to sports men and women, musicians and others working in the arts and media.

In July 1997 the Conference, meeting in Montego Bay, Jamaica, determined to accelerate economic integration, with the aim of completing a single market by 1999. At the meeting 11 member states signed Protocol II amending the Treaty of Chaguaramas, which constituted a central element of a CARICOM Single Market and Economy (CSME), providing for the right to establish enterprises, the provision of services and the free movement of capital and labour throughout participating countries. A regional collaborative network was established to promote the CSME. In July 1998, at the meeting of heads of government, held in Saint Lucia, an agreement was signed with the Insurance Company of the West Indies to accelerate the establishment of a Caribbean Investment Fund, which was to mobilize foreign currency from extra-regional capital markets for investment in new or existing enterprises in the region. Some 60% of all funds generated were to be used by CARICOM countries and the remainder by non-CARICOM members of the Association of Caribbean States.

In November 2000 a special consultation on the single market and economy was held in Barbados, involving CARICOM and government officials, academics, and representatives of the private sector, labour organizations, the media, and other regional groupings. In February 2001 heads of government agreed to establish a new high-level sub-committee to accelerate the establishment of the CSME and to promote its objectives. The sub-committee was to be supported by a Technical Advisory Council, comprising representatives of the public and private sectors. By June all member states had signed and declared the provisional application of Protocol II. By May 2007 12 countries had completed the fourth phase of the CET.

In October 2001 CARICOM heads of government, convened for a special emergency meeting, considered the impact on the region's economy of the terrorist attacks perpetrated against targets in the USA in the previous month. The meeting resolved to enhance aviation security, implement promotion and marketing campaigns in support of the tourist industry, and approach international institutions to assist with emergency financing. The economic situation, which had been further adversely affected by the reduced access to the European Union (EU) banana market, the economic downturn in the USA, and the effects on the investment climate of the OECD Harmful Taxation Initiative, was considered at the Heads of Government Conference, held in Guyana, in July 2002.

On 1 January 2006 the single market component of the CSME was formally inaugurated, with Barbados, Belize, Guyana, Jamaica, Suriname and Trinidad and Tobago as active participants. Six more countries (Antigua and Barbuda, Dominica, Grenada, Saint Christopher and Nevis, Saint Lucia, Saint Vincent and the Grenadines) formally joined the single market in July. At the same time CARICOM heads of government approved a contribution formula allowing for the establishment of a regional development fund. In February 2007 an inter-sessional meeting of the Conference of Heads of Government, held in Saint Vincent and the Grenadines, approved a timetable for the full implementation of the CSME: phase I (mid-2006–08) for the consolidation of the single market and the initiation of a single economy; phase II (2009–15) for the consolidation and completion of the single economy process, including the harmonization and co-ordination of economic policies in the region and the establishment of new institutions to implement those policies. In July 2007 CARICOM heads of government endorsed the report, *Towards a Single Development Vision and the Role of the Single Economy*, on which the elaboration of the CSME was based. In January 2008 a Caribbean Competition Commission was inaugurated, in Paramaribo, Suriname, to enforce the rules of competition within the CSME. In February Haiti signed the revised Treaty of Chaguaramas. The Caribbean Development Fund (CDF), launched in mid-2008, with initial finances of US $60m. commenced full operations in August 2009. A Convocation on the CSME was convened in Bridgetown, Barbados, in October, as part of a wider appraisal of the CSME. In February 2011 heads of government signed an agreement to enable the CDF to grant funds on preferential terms to low-income member countries.

In December 2007 a special meeting of the Conference of Heads of Government, convened in Georgetown, Guyana, considered issues relating to regional poverty and the rising cost of living in member states. The meeting resolved to establish a technical team to review the CET on essential commodities to determine whether it should be removed or reduced to deter inflationary pressures. The meeting also agreed to review the supply and distribution of food throughout the region, including transportation issues affecting the price of goods and services, and determined to expand agricultural production and agro-processing. Efforts to harness renewable energy sources were to be strengthened to counter rising fuel prices.

REGIONAL INTEGRATION

In 1989 CARICOM heads of government established the 15-member West Indian Commission to study regional political and economic integration. The Commission's final report, submitted in July 1992, recommended that CARICOM should remain a community of sovereign states (rather than a federation), but should strengthen the integration process and expand to include the wider Caribbean region. It recommended the formation of an Association of Caribbean States (ACS), to include all the countries within and surrounding the Caribbean Basin. In November 1997 the Secretaries-General of CARICOM and the ACS signed a Co-operation Agreement to formalize the reciprocal procedures through which the organizations work to enhance and facilitate regional integration. Suriname was admitted to CARICOM in July 1995. In July 1997 the Heads of Government Conference agreed to admit Haiti as a member, although the terms and conditions of its accession to the organization were not finalized until July 1999. In July 2001 the CARICOM Secretary-General formally inaugurated a CARICOM Office in Haiti, which aimed to provide technical assistance in preparation of Haiti's accession to the Community. In January 2002 a CARICOM special mission visited Haiti, following an escalation of the political violence that had started in the previous month. Ministers of foreign affairs emphasized the need for international aid for Haiti when they met their US counterpart in February. Haiti was admitted as the 15th member of CARICOM at the Heads of Government Conference, held in July.

During 1998 CARICOM was concerned by the movement within Nevis to secede from its federation with Saint Christopher. In July heads of government agreed to dispatch a mediation team to the country (postponed until September). The Heads of Government Conference held in March 1999 welcomed the establishment of a Constitutional Task Force by the local authorities to prepare a draft constitution, on the basis of recommendations of a previous constitutional commission and the outcome of a series of public meetings. In July 1998 heads of government expressed concern at the hostility between the Government and opposition groupings in Guyana. The two sides signed an agreement, under CARICOM auspices, and in September a CARICOM mediation mission visited Guyana to promote further dialogue. CARICOM has declared its support for Guyana in its territorial disputes with Venezuela and Suriname. An CARICOM electoral observer mission monitored the conduct of a general election in Guyana in November 2011.

In February 1997 Community heads of government signed a new Charter of Civil Society for the Community, which set out principles in the areas of democracy, government, parliament, freedom of the press and human rights. In July 2002 a conference was held, in Liliendaal, Guyana, attended by representatives of civil society and CARICOM heads of government. The meeting issued a statement of principles on 'Forward Together', recognizing the role of civil society in meeting the challenges to the region. It was agreed to hold regular meetings and to establish a task force to develop a regional strategic framework for pursuing the main recommendations of the conference. In February 2007 an inter-sessional meeting of CARICOM heads of government determined to add security (including crime) as a fourth pillar of regional integration, in addition to those identified: economic integration; co-ordination of foreign policy; and functional co-operation.

CO-ORDINATION OF FOREIGN POLICY

The co-ordination of foreign policies of member states is listed as one of the main objectives of the Community in its founding treaty. Activities include strengthening member states' position in international organizations; joint diplomatic action on issues of particular interest to the Caribbean; joint co-operation arrangements with third countries and organizations; and the negotiation of free trade agreements with third countries and other regional groupings. In April 1997 CARICOM inaugurated a Caribbean Regional Negotiating

Machinery (CRNM) body, based in Kingston, Jamaica, to co-ordinate and strengthen the region's presence at external economic negotiations. The main areas of activity were negotiations to establish a Free Trade Area of the Americas (FTAA—now stalled), ACP relations with the EU, and multilateral trade negotiations under the World Trade Organization (WTO). In July 2009 the CRNM was renamed the Office of Trade Negotiations, reporting directly to the Council for Trade and Economic Development; its mandate was expanded to include responsibility for all external trade negotiations on behalf of the Community, with immediate priority to be placed on negotiations with Canada. Since 2001 CARICOM has conducted regular meetings with representatives of the United Nations. The sixth meeting, convened in July 2011, agreed to revise the existing Regional Strategic Framework for co-operation and to initiate negotiations towards a more effective mechanism for UN activities in the region.

In July 1991 Venezuela applied for membership of CARICOM, and offered a non-reciprocal free trade agreement for CARICOM exports to Venezuela, over an initial five-year period. In October 1993 the newly established Group of Three (Colombia, Mexico and Venezuela) signed joint agreements with CARICOM and Suriname on combating drugs-trafficking and on environmental protection. In June 1994 CARICOM and Colombia concluded an agreement on trade, economic and technical co-operation, which, *inter alia*, gives special treatment to the least-developed CARICOM countries. CARICOM has observer status in the Latin American Rio Group.

In 1992 Cuba applied for observer status within CARICOM, and in July 1993 a joint commission was inaugurated to establish closer ties between CARICOM and Cuba and provide a mechanism for regular dialogue. In July 1997 the heads of government agreed to pursue consideration of a free trade accord between the Community and Cuba. A Trade and Economic Agreement was signed by the two sides in July 2000, and in February 2001 a CARICOM office was established in Cuba. At the first meeting of heads of state and government in December 2002, convened in Havana, Cuba, it was agreed to commemorate the start of diplomatic relations between the two sides, some 30 years previously, on 8 December each year as Cuba/CARICOM Day. The second summit meeting, held in December 2005 in Bridgetown, Barbados, agreed to strengthen co-operation in education, culture and the environment, access to health care and efforts to counter international terrorism. A second meeting of CARICOM-Cuba ministers of foreign affairs was convened in May 2007 (the first having taken place in July 2004). The third meeting at the level of heads of state and government was held in December 2008 in Santiago de Cuba, Cuba. CARICOM leaders urged the new US administration to reconsider its restrictions on trade with Cuba. A similar appeal was made at the fourth summit meeting, convened in December 2011, in Port-of-Spain, Trinidad and Tobago. The meeting also focused on collaboration with regard to the illegal trafficking of drugs and small arms.

In August 1998 CARICOM and the Dominican Republic signed a free trade accord, covering trade in goods and services, technical barriers to trade, government procurement, and sanitary and phytosanitary measures and standards. A protocol to the agreement was signed in April 2000, following the resolution of differences concerning exempted items. The accord was ratified by the Dominican Republic in February 2001 and entered partially into force on 1 December. A Task Force to strengthen bilateral relations was established in 2007 and held its first meeting in November 2008. In November 2001 the CARICOM Secretary-General formally inaugurated a Caribbean Regional Technical Assistance Centre (CARTAC), in Barbados, to provide technical advice and training to officials from member countries and the Dominican Republic in support of the region's development. The IMF was to manage the Centre's operations, while UNDP was to provide administrative and logistical support.

In March 2000 heads of government issued a statement supporting the territorial integrity and security of Belize in that country's ongoing border dispute with Guatemala. CARICOM subsequently urged both countries to implement the provisions of an agreement signed in November and has continued to monitor the situation regularly.

In February 2002 the first meeting of heads of state and of government of CARICOM and the Central American Integration System (SICA) was convened in Belize City, Belize. The meeting aimed to strengthen co-operation between the groupings, in particular in international negotiations, efforts to counter transnational organized crime, and support for the regions' economies. In late 2002 a joint CARICOM-Spain commission was inaugurated to foster greater co-operation between the two parties. In March 2004 CARICOM signed a free trade agreement with Costa Rica.

In January 2004 CARICOM heads of government resolved to address the escalating political crisis in Haiti. Following a visit by a high-level delegation to that country early in the month discussions were held with representatives of opposition political parties and civil society groups. At the end of January several CARICOM leaders met with Haiti's President Aristide and members of his Government and announced a Prior Action Plan, incorporating opposition demands for political reform. The Plan, however, was rejected by opposition parties since it permitted Aristide to complete his term-in-office. CARICOM, together with the OAS, continued to pursue diplomatic efforts to secure a peaceful solution to the crisis. On 29 February Aristide resigned and left the country and a provisional president was appointed. In March CARICOM heads of government determined not to allow representatives of the new interim administration to participate in the councils of the Community until constitutional rule had been reinstated. In July heads of government resolved to send a five-member ministerial team to Haiti to discuss developments in that country with the interim authorities. In July 2005 CARICOM heads of government expressed concern at the deterioration of the situation in Haiti, but reiterated their readiness to provide technical assistance for the electoral process, under the auspices of the UN mission. In March 2006 the CARICOM Chairman endorsed the results of the presidential election, conducted in February, and pledged to support Haiti's return to democratic rule. In August 2010 CARICOM sent a joint election observation mission (JEOM), with the OAS, to monitor presidential and legislative elections in Haiti, scheduled for November. Although the JEOM reported several procedural irregularities in the voting process, and expressed concern at allegations by some candidates and their supporters of fraudulence or intimidation at polling stations, it confirmed that the elections were valid. The mission remained in Haiti in early 2011 in order to monitor the second round of voting in the presidential election, held inMarch.

In March 2006 a CARICOM-Mexico Joint Commission signed an agreement to promote future co-operation, in particular in seven priority areas. The first summit level meeting between heads of state and government of Mexico and CARICOM was held in February 2010, in Riviera Maya, Mexico. In February 2007 the Secretaries-General of CARICOM and SICA signed a plan of action on future co-operation between the two groupings. A second CARICOM-SICA meeting of heads of state and of government was convened in May, in Belize. The meeting endorsed the plan of action and, in addition, instructed their ministers of foreign affairs and of trade to pursue efforts to negotiate a free trade agreement, to be based on that signed by CARICOM with Costa Rica (see above). Trade negotiations were formally inaugurated in August. The third CARICOM-SICA summit meeting was convened in El Salvador, in August 2011. A joint declaration recognized the need to develop transport and cultural links, and detailed measures to strengthen co-operation in international environmental negotiations, combating transnational crime, disaster management, the prevention of non-communicable diseases, and the management of migratory fish stocks in the Caribbean Sea.

In March 2006 CARICOM ministers of foreign affairs met with the US Secretary of State and agreed to strengthen co-operation and enhance bilateral relations. In June 2007 a major meeting, the 'Conference on the Caribbean: a 20/20 Vision', was held in Washington, DC, USA. A series of meetings was held to consider issues and challenges relating to CARICOM's development and integration efforts and to the strengthening of relations with other countries in the region and with the USA. An Experts' Forum was hosted by the World Bank, a Private Sector Dialogue was held at the headquarters of the Inter-American Development Bank, and a Diaspora Forum was convened at the OAS. A summit meeting of CARICOM heads of government and US President George W. Bush was held in the context of the Conference, at which issues concerning trade, economic growth and development, security and social investment were discussed. A second Conference on the Caribbean was held in New York, USA, in June 2008. A meeting of CARICOM foreign ministers with the US Secretary of State was held in June 2010, in Barbados, at which a series of commitments was concluded to enhance co-operation on a range of issues including energy security, climate change, health and trade relations.

CRIME AND SECURITY

In December 1996 CARICOM heads of government determined to strengthen comprehensive co-operation and technical assistance to combat illegal drugs-trafficking. The Conference decided to establish a Caribbean Security Task Force to help to formulate a single regional agreement on maritime interdiction, incorporating agreements already concluded by individual members. A Regional Drugs Control Programme at the CARICOM Secretariat aims to co-ordinate regional initiatives with the overall objective of reducing the demand and supply of illegal substances.

In July 2000 the Heads of Government meeting issued a statement strongly opposing the OECD Harmful Tax Initiative, under which punitive measures had been threatened against 35 countries, including CARICOM member states, if they failed to tighten taxation legislation. The meeting also condemned a separate list, issued by OECD's Financial Action Task Force on Money Laundering (FATF), which identified 15 countries, including five Caribbean states, of failing to counter effectively international money-laundering. The statement reaffirmed CARICOM's commitment to fighting financial crimes and support for any necessary reform of supervisory practices or legislation, but insisted that national taxation jurisdictions, and specifically competitive regimes designed to attract offshore business, was not a matter for OECD concern. CARICOM remained actively involved in efforts to counter the scheme, and in April 2001 presented its case to the US President. In September the FATF issued a revised list of 19 'unco-operative jurisdictions', including Dominica, Grenada, Saint Christopher and Nevis and Saint Vincent and the Grenadines. In early 2002 most Caribbean states concluded a provisional agreement with OECD to work to improve the transparency and supervision of offshore sectors.

In July 2001 heads of government resolved to establish a task force to be responsible for producing recommendations for a forthcoming meeting of national security advisers. In October heads of government convened an emergency meeting in Nassau, the Bahamas, to consider the impact of the terrorist attacks against the USA that had occurred in September. The meeting determined to convene immediately the so-called Task Force on Crime and Security in order to implement new policy directives. It was agreed to enhance co-ordination and collaboration of security services throughout the region, in particular in intelligence gathering, analysis and sharing in relation to crime, illicit drugs and terrorism, and to strengthen security at airports, seaports and borders. In July 2002 heads of government agreed on a series of initiatives recommended by the Task Force to counter the escalation in crime and violence. These included strengthening border controls, preparing national anti-crime master plans, establishing broad-based National Commissions on law and order and furthering the exchange of information and intelligence.

In July 2005 CARICOM heads of government endorsed a new Management Framework for Crime and Security, which provided for regular meetings of a Council of Ministers responsible for national security and law enforcement, a Security Policy Advisory Committee, and the establishment of an Implementation Agency for Crime and Security. Several co-ordinated security measures were implemented during the cricket world cup, which was held across the region in early 2007. In July CARICOM heads of government agreed in principle to extend these security efforts, including the introduction of a voluntary CARICOM Travel Card, CARIPASS, to facilitate the establishment of a single domestic space. An agreement to implement CARIPASS was signed by heads of state and government meeting in Dominica, in March 2010; the installation of the CARIPASS system was ongoing in 2012.

In April 2010 US President Barack Obama announced a Caribbean Basin Security Initiative (CBSI), which was to structure its regional security policy around a bilateral partnership with CARICOM, in particular to advance public safety and security, substantially to reduce trafficking of illicit substances and to promote social justice. In the following month an inaugural Caribbean-US Security Co-operation Dialogue was held, in Washington, DC, to pursue discussion of the CBSI. The first meeting of a CBSI Commission was convened in Kingston, Jamaica, in November. Also in November, at the second meeting of the CARICOM-US Security Co-operation Dialogue, held in the Bahamas, officials agreed to facilitate region-wide information sharing, and to develop a regional juvenile justice policy.

In September 2011 a delegation from the UN Office on Drugs and Crime met with officials from CARICOM's Implementation Agency for Crime and Security in Trinidad and Tobago. Discussions centred on strengthening regional forensics capacity, the proliferation of illegal guns, human trafficking, smuggling of migrants, and money-laundering.

INDUSTRY, ENERGY AND THE ENVIRONMENT

A protocol relating to the CARICOM Industrial Programming Scheme (CIPS), approved in 1988, is the Community's instrument for promoting the co-operative development of industry in the region. Protocol III amending the Treaty of Chaguaramas, with respect to industrial policy, was opened for signature in July 1998. The Secretariat has established a national standards bureau in each member country to harmonize technical standards. In 1999 members agreed to establish a new CARICOM Regional Organisation for Standards and Quality (CROSQ), as a successor to the Caribbean Common Market Standards Council. The agreement to establish CROSQ, to be located in Barbados, was signed in February 2002.

The CARICOM Alternative Energy Systems Project provides training, assesses energy needs and conducts energy audits. Efforts in regional energy development are directed at the collection and analysis of data for national energy policy documents. Implementation of a Caribbean Renewable Energy Development Programme, a project initiated in 1998, commenced in 2004. The Programme aimed to remove barriers to renewable energy development, establish a foundation for a sustainable renewable energy industry, and to create a framework for co-operation among regional and national renewable energy projects. A Caribbean Renewable Energy Fund was established to provide equity and development financing for renewable energy projects.

In January 2001 the Council for Trade and Economic Development approved the development of a specialized CARICOM agency to co-ordinate the gathering of information and other activities relating to climate change. The Caribbean Community Climate Change Centre became operational in early 2004 and was formally inaugurated, in Belmopan, Belize, in August 2005. It serves as an official clearing house and repository of data relating to climate change in the Caribbean region, provides advice to governments and other expertise for the development of projects to manage and adapt to climate change, and undertakes training. The results of the Centre's Mainstreaming Adaptation to Climate Change (MACC) Project were presented to governments at a Caribbean Climate Change Conference, held in Saint Lucia, in March 2009. In July 2008 CARICOM heads of government established a Task Force on Climate Change and Development to consider future action in relation to developments in energy and climate change, and in particular food insecurity caused by global rising food and fuel prices. The inaugural meeting of the Task Force was held in November, in Saint Lucia. In March 2012 CARICOM heads of government endorsed an 'Implementation Plan for the Regional Framework for Achieving Development Resilient to Climate Change', to cover the period 2011–21.

TRANSPORT, COMMUNICATIONS AND TOURISM

In 1997 CARICOM heads of government considered a number of proposals relating to air transportation, tourism, human resource development and capital investment, which had been identified by Community ministers of tourism as critical issues in the sustainable development of the tourist industry. The heads of government requested ministers to meet regularly to develop tourism policies, and in particular to undertake an in-depth study of human resource development issues in 1998. A regional summit on tourism was held in the Bahamas in December 2001. A new Caribbean passport was introduced in January 2005; all 12 member countries participating in the CSME were issuing the document by 2009.

A Caribbean Confederation of Shippers' Councils represents the interests of regional exporters and importers. A Multilateral Agreement Concerning the Operations of Air Services within the Caribbean Community entered into force in November 1998, providing a formal framework for the regulation of the air transport industry and enabling CARICOM-owned and -controlled airlines to operate freely within the region. In July 1999 heads of government signed Protocol VI amending the Treaty of Chaguaramas providing for a common transportation policy, with harmonized standards and practices, which was to be an integral component of the development of a single market and economy. In November 2001 representatives of national civil aviation authorities signed a memorandum of understanding, providing for the establishment of a regional body, the Regional Aviation Safety Oversight System. This was succeeded, in July 2008, by a Caribbean Aviation Safety and Security Oversight System upon the signing of an agreement by Barbados, Guyana, Saint Lucia and Trinidad and Tobago.

In 1989 the Caribbean Telecommunications Union was established to oversee developments in regional telecommunications. In July 2006 the Conference of Heads of Government, convened in Saint Christopher and Nevis, mandated the development of C@ribNET, a project to extend the availability of high speed internet access throughout the region. In May 2007 the inaugural meeting of a Regional Information Communications and Technology Steering Committee was held, in Georgetown, Guyana, to determine areas of activity for future co-operation in support of the establishment of a Caribbean Information Society.

AGRICULTURE AND FISHERIES

In July 1996 the CARICOM summit meeting agreed to undertake wide-ranging measures in order to modernize the agricultural sector and to increase the international competitiveness of Caribbean agricultural produce. The CARICOM Secretariat was to support national programmes with assistance in policy formulation, human resource development and the promotion of research and technology development in the areas of productivity, marketing, agri-business and water resources management. Protocol V amending the Treaty of Chaguaramas, which was concerned with agricultural policy, was opened for signature by heads of government in July 1998. In July 2002 heads of government approved an initiative to develop a CARIFORUM Special Programme for Food Security. CARICOM Governments have continually aimed to generate awareness of the economic and social importance of the banana industry to the region, in particular within the framework of the WTO multilateral trade negotiations.

In July 2005 CARICOM heads of government issued a statement protesting against proposals by the European Commission, issued in the previous month, to reform the EU sugar regime. Particular concern was expressed at a proposed price reduction in the cost of refined sugar of 39% over a four-year period. The heads of government insisted that, in accordance with the ACP-EU Cotonou Agreement, any review of the Sugar Protocol was required to be undertaken with the agreement of both parties and with regard to safeguarding benefits. In December CARICOM heads of government held a special meeting to discuss the EU sugar and banana regimes, in advance of a ministerial meeting of the WTO, held in Hong Kong that month. The Conference reiterated the potentially devastating effects on regional economies of the sugar price reduction and proposed new banana tariffs, and expressed the need for greater compensation and for the WTO multilateral negotiations to address fairly issues of preferential access. Negotiations between the ACP Caribbean signatory countries (the so-called CARIFORUM) and the EU on an Economic Partnership Agreement to succeed the Cotonou Agreement, which had commenced in April 2004, were concluded in December 2007. In January 2008 CARICOM's Council for Trade and Economic Development resolved to conduct an independent review of the new agreement. The agreement was signed (initially, with the exception of Guyana and Haiti) in October.

A Caribbean Regional Fisheries Mechanism was established in 2002 to promote the sustainable use of fisheries and aquaculture resources in the region. It incorporates a Caribbean Fisheries Forum, which serves as the main technical and scientific decision-making body of the Mechanism. In March 2010 a Caribbean Agricultural Health and Food Safety Agency (CAHFSA) was inaugurated in Paramaribo, Suriname.

HEALTH AND SOCIAL POLICY

In 1984 CARICOM and the Pan-American Health Organization launched 'Caribbean Co-operation in Health' with projects to be undertaken in six main areas: environmental protection, including the control of disease-bearing pests; development of human resources; chronic non-communicable diseases and accidents; strengthening health systems; food and nutrition; maternal and child health care; and population activities. A second phase of the initiative commenced in 1992. In 2001 CARICOM established the Pan-Caribbean Partnership against HIV/AIDS (PANCAP), with the aim of reducing the spread and impact of HIV and AIDS in member countries. In February 2002 PANCAP initiated regional negotiations with pharmaceutical companies to secure reductions in the cost of anti-retroviral drugs.

A Caribbean Environmental Health Institute (see below) aims to promote collaboration among member states in all areas of environmental management and human health. In July 2001 heads of government, meeting in the Bahamas, issued the Nassau Declaration on Health, advocating greater regional strategic co-ordination and planning in the health sector and institutional reform, as well as increased resources. In February 2006 PANCAP and UNAIDS organized a regional consultation on the outcomes of country-based assessments of the HIV/AIDS crisis that had been undertaken in the region, and formulated a Regional Roadmap for Universal Access to HIV and AIDS Prevention, Care, Treatment and Support over the period 2006–10. A special meeting of COHSOD, convened in June 2006, in Trinidad and Tobago, issued the Port of Spain Declaration on the Education Sector Response to HIV and AIDS, which committed member states to supporting the Roadmap through education policy. In September 2007 a special regional summit meeting on chronic non-communicable diseases was held in Port of Spain, Trinidad and Tobago. In July 2008 CARICOM heads of government endorsed a new Caribbean Regional Strategy Framework on HIV and AIDS for the period 2008–12. In March 2010 Caribbean heads of government approved the establishment of a Caribbean Public Health Agency (CARPHA), which was intended to promote a co-ordinated approach to public health issues, in accordance with the Nassau Declaration. CARPHA became a legally established entity in July 2011. The operational development of CARPHA, including the full integration of the core functions of the existing five regional health institutions, was scheduled to be completed by 2014.

CARICOM education programmes have included the improvement of reading in schools through assistance for teacher training and ensuring the availability of low-cost educational material throughout the region. In July 1997 CARICOM heads of government adopted the recommendations of a ministerial committee, which identified priority measures for implementation in the education sector. These included the objective of achieving universal, quality secondary education and the enrolment of 15% of post-secondary students in tertiary education by 2005, as well as improved training in foreign languages and science and technology. In March 2004 CARICOM ministers of education endorsed the establishment of a Caribbean Knowledge and Learning Network (CKLN) to strengthen tertiary education institutions throughout the region and to enhance knowledge sharing. The CKLN, which also co-ordinates and manages the development of C@ribNET, was formally inaugurated in July, in co-operation with the OECS, in Grenada. A Caribbean Vocational Qualification was introduced in 2007.

From the late 1990s youth activities have been increasingly emphasized by the Community. These have included new programmes for disadvantaged youths, a mechanism for youth exchange and the convening of a Caribbean Youth Parliament. CARICOM organizes a biennial Caribbean Festival of Arts (CARIFESTA). CARIFESTA X was staged in Georgetown, Guyana, in August 2008. As a result of the poor economic climate, the Bahamas withdrew its offer to hold the festival in 2010. In July 2011 Suriname announced that it was to host CARIFESTA XI, in 2013. A CARICOM Regional Sports Academy was inaugurated, in Paramaribo, Suriname, in March 2012.

EMERGENCY ASSISTANCE

A Caribbean Disaster Emergency Response Agency (CDERA) was established in 1991 to co-ordinate immediate disaster relief, primarily in the event of hurricanes. In January 2005, meeting on the sidelines of the fifth Summit of the Alliance of Small Island States, in Port Louis, Mauritius, the Secretaries-General of CARICOM, the Commonwealth, the Pacific Islands Forum and the Indian Ocean Commission determined to take collective action to strengthen the disaster preparedness and response capabilities of their member countries in the Caribbean, Pacific and Indian Ocean areas. In September 2006 CARICOM, the EU and the Caribbean ACP states signed a Financing Agreement for Institutional Support and Capacity Building for Disaster Management in the Caribbean, which aimed to support CDERA by providing €3.4m. to facilitate the implementation of revised legislation, improved co-ordination between countries in the region and the increased use of information and communications technology in emergency planning. A new Caribbean Catastrophe Risk Insurance Facility (CCRIF), a multi-country initiative enabling participating states to draw funds for responding immediately to adverse natural events, such as earthquakes and hurricanes, became operational in June 2007, with support from international donors, including the Caribbean Development Bank and the World Bank. In September 2009 a new Caribbean Disaster Emergency Management Agency (CDEMA) formally replaced the CDERA, which had 18 participating states.

In January 2010 CARICOM provided immediate assistance to Haiti, after a massive earthquake caused extensive damage and loss of life in the country. A Tactical Mission was deployed to assess relief requirements and logistics, in particular in providing health services. A Special Co-ordinator, to be based in Haiti, was appointed to ensure the effectiveness of the Community's assistance, working closely with CDEMA and other international relief efforts. At the International Donors' Conference Towards a New Future for Haiti, held in New York, USA, in March, UN member countries and other international partners pledged US $5,300m. in support of an Action Plan for the National Recovery and Development of the country. CARICOM pledged to support the Haitian Government in working with the international community and to provide all necessary institutional and technical assistance during the rehabilitation process. CARICOM was represented on the Board of the Interim Commission for the Reconstruction of Haiti, inaugurated in June, following a World Summit on the Future of Haiti, held to discuss the effective implementation of the Action Plan. In April 2011 CARICOM heads of government expressed serious concern at the slow disbursement of international pledges towards the reconstruction effort.

INSTITUTIONS

The following are among the institutions formally established within the framework of CARICOM:

Assembly of Caribbean Community Parliamentarians: c/o CARICOM Secretariat; an intergovernmental agreement on the establishment of a regional parliament entered into force in August 1994; inaugural meeting held in Barbados in May 1996. Comprises up to four representatives of the parliaments of each member country, and up to two of each associate member. It aims to provide a forum for wider community involvement in the process of integration and for enhanced deliberation on CARICOM affairs; authorized to issue recommendations for the Conference of Heads of Government and to adopt resolutions on any matter arising under the Treaty of Chaguaramas.

Caribbean Agricultural Research and Development Institute (CARDI): UWI Campus, St Augustine, Trinidad and Tobago; tel. 645-1205; fax 645-1208; e-mail infocentre@cardi.org; internet www.cardi.org; f. 1975; aims to contribute to the competitiveness and sustainability of Caribbean agriculture by generating and transferring new and appropriate technologies and by developing effective partnerships with regional and international entities; Exec. Dir Dr ARLINGTON CHESNEY; publs *CARDI Weekly*, *CARDI Review*, technical bulletin series.

Caribbean Centre for Development Administration (CARICAD): Weymouth Corporate Centre, 1st Floor, Roebuck St, St Michael, Barbados; tel. 427-8535; fax 436-1709; e-mail info@caricad.net; internet www.caricad.net; f. 1980; aims to assist governments in the reform of the public sector and to strengthen their managerial capacities for public administration; promotes the involvement of the private sector, non-governmental organizations and other bodies in all decision-making processes; Exec. Dir JENNIFER ASTAPHAN.

Caribbean Community Climate Change Centre: Lawrence Nicholas Bldg, 2nd Floor, Ring Rd, POB 563, Belmopan, Belize;

tel. 822-1094; fax 822-1365; e-mail kleslie1@caribbeanclimate.bz; internet www.caribbeanclimate.bz; f. 2005 to co-ordinate the region's response to climate change; Exec. Dir Dr KENRICK LESLIE.

Caribbean Competition Commission: Hendrikstraat 69, Paramaribo, Suriname; tel. 491480; f. 2008; to enforce the rules of competition of the CARICOM Single Market and Economy; Chair. KUSHA HARAKSINGH (Trinidad and Tobago); Exec. Dir BARBARA LEE (Jamaica).

Caribbean Disaster Emergency Management Agency (CDEMA): Bldg 1, Manor Lodge, Lodge Hill, St Michael, Barbados; tel. 425-0386; fax 425-8854; e-mail cdera@caribsurf.com; internet www.cdera.org; f. 1991; aims to respond with immediate assistance following a request by a participating state in the event of a natural or man-made disaster; co-ordinates other relief efforts; assists states to establish disaster preparedness and response capabilities; incorporates national disaster organizations, headed by a co-ordinator, in each participating state; Exec. Dir JEREMY COLLYMORE.

Caribbean Environmental Health Institute (CEHI): POB 1111, The Morne, Castries, St Lucia; tel. 4522501; fax 4532721; e-mail cehi@candw.lc; internet www.cehi.org.lc; f. 1980 (began operations in 1982); provides technical and advisory services to member states in formulating environmental health policy legislation and in all areas of environmental management (for example, solid waste management, water supplies, beach and air pollution, and pesticides control); promotes, collates and disseminates relevant research; conducts courses, seminars and workshops throughout the region; Exec. Dir PATRICIA AQUING (Trinidad and Tobago).

Caribbean Examinations Council: The Garrison, St Michael 20, Barbados; tel. 436-6261; fax 429-5421; e-mail cxcezo@cxc.org; internet www.cxc.org; f. 1972; develops syllabuses and conducts examinations for the Caribbean Advanced Proficiency Examination (CAPE), the Caribbean Secondary Education Certificate (CSEC) and the Caribbean Certificate of Secondary Level Competence (CCSLC); mems: govts of 16 English-speaking countries and territories; Registrar and CEO Dr DIDACUS JULES.

Caribbean Food and Nutrition Institute (CFNI): UWI Campus, POB 140, St Augustine, Trinidad and Tobago; tel. 645-2917; fax 663-1544; e-mail cfni@cablenett.net; internet www.paho.org/cfni; f. 1967 to serve the governments and people of the region and to act as a catalyst among persons and organizations concerned with food and nutrition through research and field investigations, training in nutrition, dissemination of information, advisory services and production of educational material; a specialized centre of the Pan American Health Organization; mems: all English-speaking Caribbean territories, including the mainland countries of Belize and Guyana; Dir Dr FITZROY HENRY; publs *CAJANUS* (quarterly), *Nyam News* (monthly), *Nutrient-Cost Tables* (quarterly), educational material.

Caribbean Meteorological Organization (CMO): POB 461, Port of Spain, Trinidad and Tobago; tel. 622-4711; fax 622-0277; e-mail cmohq@cmo.org.tt; internet www.cmo.org.tt; f. 1973 as successor to Caribbean Meteorological Service (founded 1951) to co-ordinate regional activities in meteorology, operational hydrology and allied sciences; became a specialized institution of CARICOM in 1973; comprises a Council of Government Ministers, a Headquarters Unit, the Caribbean Meteorological Foundation and the Caribbean Institute for Meteorology and Hydrology, located in Barbados; mems: govts of 16 countries and territories represented by the National Meteorological and Hydro-meteorological Services; Co-ordinating Dir TYRONE W. SUTHERLAND.

Caribbean Telecommunications Union (CTU): Victoria Park Suites, 3rd Floor, 14–17 Victoria Sq., Port of Spain, Trinidad and Tobago; tel. 627-0281; fax 623-1523; internet www.ctu.int; f. 1989; aims to co-ordinate the planning and development of telecommunications in the region; encourages the development of regional telecommunications standards, the transfer of technology and the exchange of information among national telecommunications administrations; membership includes mems of CARICOM and other countries in the region, private sector orgs and non-governmental orgs; Sec.-Gen. BERNADETTE LEWIS (Trinidad and Tobago).

CARICOM Implementation Agency for Crime and Security (IMPACS): Sagicor Bldg, Ground Floor, 16 Queen's Park West, Port of Spain, Trinidad and Tobago; tel. 622-0245; fax 628-9795; e-mail enquiries@caricomimpacs.org; internet www.caricomimpacs.org; f. 2006 as a permanent institution to co-ordinate activities in the region relating to crime and security; incorporates two sub-agencies: a Joint Regional Communications Centre and a Regional Intelligence Fusion Centre; Exec. Sec. a.i. FRANCIS FORBES (Jamaica).

CARICOM Regional Organisation for Standards and Quality: Baobab Towers, Warrens, St Michael, Barbados; tel. -622-7677; fax -622-7678; e-mail crosq.caricom@crosq.org; internet www.crosq.org; f. 2002; aims to enhance and promote the implementation of standards, infrastructure and quality verification throughout the region and liaise with international standards orgs; CEO WINSTON BENNETT.

Council of Legal Education: c/o Gordon St, St Augustine, Trinidad and Tobago; tel. 662-5860; fax 662-0927; internet www.clecaribbean.com; f. 1971; responsible for the training of members of the legal profession; administers law schools in Jamaica, Trinidad and Tobago, and the Bahamas; mems: govts of 12 countries and territories; Chair. E. ANN HENRY (Antigua and Barbuda).

ASSOCIATE INSTITUTIONS

Caribbean Development Bank: POB 408, Wildey, St Michael, Barbados; tel. 431-1600; fax 426-7269; e-mail info@caribank.org; internet www.caribank.org; f. 1969 to stimulate regional economic growth through support for agriculture, industry, transport and other infrastructure, tourism, housing and education; in 2008 new loans, grants and equity investments approved totalled US $348.2m., bringing the cumulative total to $3,305.7m.; in May 2010 the Board of Governors approved an ordinary capital increase of some $1,000m., including a paid-up component of $216m.; mems: CARICOM states, and Canada, the People's Republic of China, Colombia, Germany, Italy, Mexico, United Kingdom, Venezuela; Pres. Dr. WARREN SMITH (Jamaica).

Caribbean Law Institute: University of the West Indies, Cave Hill Campus, POB 64, Bridgetown, Barbados; tel. 417-4560; fax 417-4138; internet www.law.fsu.edu/centers/cli/index.html; f. 1988 to harmonize and modernize commercial laws in the region.

Other Associate Institutions of CARICOM, in accordance with its constitution, are the University of Guyana, the University of the West Indies and the Secretariat of the Organisation of Eastern Caribbean States.

Publications

CARICOM Perspective (annually).

CARICOM View (6 a year).

CENTRAL AMERICAN INTEGRATION SYSTEM

(SISTEMA DE LA INTEGRACIÓN CENTROAMERICANA—SICA)

Address: Final Blv. Cancillería, Ciudad Merliot, Antiguo Cuscatlán, La Libertad, San Salvador, El Salvador.

Telephone: 2248-8800; **fax:** 2248-8899; **e-mail:** info.sgsica@sica.int; **internet:** www.sica.int.

Founded in December 1991, when the heads of state of six Central American countries signed the Protocol of Tegucigalpa to the agreement establishing the Organization of Central American States (f. 1951), creating a new framework for regional integration. A General Secretariat of the Sistema de la Integración Centroamericana (SICA) was inaugurated in February 1993 to co-ordinate the process of political, economic, social cultural and environmental integration and to promote democracy and respect for human rights throughout the region.

MEMBERS

Belize	Guatemala	Nicaragua
Costa Rica	Honduras	Panama
El Salvador		

ASSOCIATE MEMBER

Dominican Republic

Note: Argentina, Australia, Brazil, Chile, France, Germany, Italy, Japan, the Republic of Korea, Mexico, Peru, Spain, Taiwan and the USA have observer status with SICA.

Organization

(April 2012)

SUMMIT MEETINGS

The meetings of heads of state of member countries serve as the supreme decision-making organ of SICA.

COUNCIL OF MINISTERS

Ministers of foreign affairs of member states meet regularly to provide policy direction for the process of integration.

Executive Committee

Comprises a government representative of each member state tasked with ensuring the implementation of decisions adopted by heads of state or the Council of Ministers, and with overseeing the activities of the General Secretariat.

CONSULTATIVE COMMITTEE

The Committee comprises representatives of business organizations, trade unions, academic institutions and other federations concerned with the process of integration in the region. It is a fundamental element of the integration system and assists the Secretary-General in determining the organization's policies.

GENERAL SECRETARIAT

The General Secretariat of SICA was established in February 1993 to co-ordinate the process of enhanced regional integration. It comprises Directorates-General of Social Integration, Economic Integration, and of Environmental Affairs.

In September 1997 Central American Common Market (CACM) heads of state, meeting in the Nicaraguan capital, signed the Managua Declaration in support of further regional integration and the establishment of a political union. In February 1998 heads of state resolved to establish a Unified General Secretariat to integrate the institutional aspects of the grouping in a single office, to be located in San Salvador, El Salvador. A new headquarters for the organization was inaugurated in July 2011.

Secretary-General: JUAN DANIEL ALEMÁN GURDIÁN.

CORE INSTITUTIONS

Central American Parliament (PARLACEN)

12 Avda 33-04, Zona 5, 01005 Guatemala City, Guatemala; tel. 2424-4600; fax 2424-4610; e-mail guatemala@parlacen.org.gt; internet www.parlacen.org.gt.; officially inaugurated in 1991; comprises 20 elected representatives of Domincan Republic, El Salvador, Guatemala, Honduras, Nicaragua and Panama, as well as former Presidents and Vice-Presidents of mem. countries; Haiti awarded observer status in Feb. 2012; Pres. MANOLO PICHARDO (Dominican Republic); publ. *Foro Parlamentario*.

Central American Court of Justice

Apdo Postal 907, Managua, Nicaragua; tel. 266-6273; fax 266-4604; e-mail cortecen@ccj.org.ni; internet portal.ccj.org.ni.; officially inaugurated in 1994; tribunal authorized to consider disputes relating to treaties agreed within the regional integration system; in February 1998 Central American heads of state agreed to limit the number of magistrates in the Court to one per country.

SPECIALIZED SECRETARIATS

In addition to those listed below, various technical or executive secretariat units support meetings of ministerial Councils, concerned *inter alia*with women, housing, health and finance.

Secretaría General de la Coordinación Educativa y Cultural Centroamericana (SG-CECC): 400m este y 25m norte de la Iglesia Santa Teresita en Barrio Escalante, 262-1007 San José, Costa Rica; tel. 2283-7630; e-mail sgcecc@racsa.co.cr; internet www.sica.int/cecc; f. 1982; promotes development of regional programmes in the fields of education and culture; Sec.-Gen. MARÍA EUGENIA PANIAGUA PADILLA.

Secretaría de Integración Económica Centroamericana (SIECA): 4A Avda 10–25, Zona 14, Apdo 1237, 01901 Guatemala City, Guatemala; tel. 2368-2151; fax 2368-1071; e-mail info@sieca.int; internet www.sieca.int; f. 1960 to assist the process of economic integration and the creation of a Central American Common Market (CACM—established by the organization of Central American States under the General Treaty of Central American Economic Integration, signed in December 1960 and ratified by Costa Rica, Guatemala, El Salvador, Honduras and Nicaragua in September 1963); supervises the correct implementation of the legal instruments of economic integration, conducts relevant studies at the request of the CACM, and arranges meetings; comprises departments covering the working of the CACM: negotiations and external trade policy; external co-operation; systems and statistics; finance and administration; also includes a unit for co-operation with the private sector and finance institutions, and a legal consultative committee; Sec.-Gen. ERNESTO TORRES CHICO (El Salvador); publs *Anuario Estadístico Centroamericano de Comercio Exterior*, *Carta Informativa* (monthly), *Cuadernos de la SIECA* (2 a year), *Estadísticas Macroeconómicas de Centroamérica* (annually), *Series Estadísticas Seleccionadas de Centroamérica* (annually), *Boletín Informativo* (fortnightly).

Secretaría Ejecutiva del Consejo Monetario Centroamericano (SECMCA) (Central American Monetary Council): 400m suroeste de la Rotonda La Bandera, Barrio Dent, Contiguo al BANHVI, San José, Costa Rica; tel. 2280-9522; fax 2524-1062; e-mail secma@secmca.org; internet www.secmca.org; f. 1964 by the presidents of Central American central banks, to co-ordinate monetary policies; Exec. Sec. WILLIAM CALVO VILLEGAS; publs *Boletín Estadístico* (annually), *Informe Económico* (annually).

Secretaría de la Integración Social Centroamericana (SISCA): Final Boulevard Cancillería, Distrito El Espino Ciudad Merliot, Antiguo Cuscatlán, La Libertad, El Salvador; tel. 2248-8857; fax 2248-8896; e-mail info.sisca@sica.int; internet www.sica.int/sisca; f. 1995; co-ordinates various inter-governmental secretariats, including regional councils concerned with social security, sport and recreation, and housing and human settlements; Sec. ANA HAZEL ESCRICH.

Secretaría Ejecutiva de la Comisión Centroamericana de Ambiente y Desarrollo (SE-CCAD): Final Boulevard Cancillería, Distrito El Espino Ciudad Merliot, Antiguo Cuscatlán, La Libertad, El Salvador; tel. 2248-8800; fax 2248-8894; e-mail info.ccad@sica.int; internet www.sica.int/ccad; f. 1989 to enhance collaboration in the promotion of sustainable development and environmental protection; Exec. Sec. NELSON ORLANDO TREJO AGUILAR (Honduras).

Secretaría de Integración Turística Centroamericana (SITCA): Final Bulevar Cancillería, Distrito El Espino, Ciudad Merliot, Antiguo Cuscatlán, La Libertad,, El Salvador; tel. 2248-8837; fax 2248-8897; e-mail info.stcct@sica.int; internet www.sica.int/cct; f. 1965 to develop regional tourism activities; provides administrative support to the Central American Tourism Council, comprising national ministers and directors of tourism; Dir MERCEDES MELÉNDEZ DE MENA.

Secretaría del Consejo Agropecuario Centroamericano (SCAC): 600m noreste del Cruce de Ipis-Coronado, San Isidro de Coronado, Apdo Postal 55-2200, San José, Costa Rica; tel. 2216-0303; fax 2216-0285; e-mail coreca@iica.ac.cr; internet www.sica.int/cac; f. 1991 to determine and co-ordinate regional policies and programmes relating to agriculture and agroindustry; Exec. Sec. JULIO O. CALDERÓN ARTIEDA.

OTHER SPECIALIZED INSTITUTIONS

Agriculture and Fisheries

Organismo Internacional Regional de Sanidad Agropecuaria (OIRSA) (International Regional Organization of Plant Protection and Animal Health): Calle Ramón Belloso, Final Pasaje Isolde, Colonia Escalón, Apdo (01) 61, San Salvador, El Salvador; tel. 2263-1123; fax 2263-1128; e-mail oirsa@oirsa.org; internet www.oirsa.org; f. 1953 for the prevention of the introduction of animal and plant pests and diseases unknown in the region; research, control and eradication programmes of the principal pests present in agriculture; technical assistance and advice to the ministries of agriculture and livestock of member countries; education and qualification of personnel; mems: Belize, Costa Rica, Dominican Republic, El Salvador, Guatemala, Honduras, Mexico, Nicaragua, Panama; Exec. Dir GUILLERMO ENRIQUE ALVARADO DOWNING.

Unidad Coordinadora de la Organización del Sector Pesquero y Acuícola del Istmo Centroamericano (OSPESCA) (Organization of Fishing and Aquaculture in Central America): Blv. Orden de Malta 470, Santa Elena, Antiguo Cuscatlán, San Salvador, El Salvador; tel. 2248-8841; fax 2248-8899; e-mail info.ospesca@sica.int; internet www.sica.int/ospesca; f. 1995, incorporated into SICA in 1999; Regional Co-ordinator MARIO GONZÁLEZ RECINOS.

Education, Health and Sport

Consejo Superior Universitario Centroamericano (CSUCA) (Central American University Council): Avda Las Américas 1–03, Zona 14, International Club Los Arcos, 01014 Guatemala City, Guatemala; tel. 2367-1833; fax 2367-4517; e-mail sg@listas.csuca.org; internet www.csuca.org; f. 1948 to guarantee academic, administrative and economic autonomy for universities and to encourage regional integration of higher education; maintains libraries and documentation centres; Council of 32 mems; mems: 18 universities, in Belize, Costa Rica (four), Dominican Republic, El

Salvador, Guatemala, Honduras (two), Nicaragua (four) and Panama (four); Sec.-Gen. JUAN ALFONSO FUENTES SORIA; publs *Estudios Sociales Centroamericanos* (quarterly), *Cuadernos de Investigación* (monthly), *Carta Informativa de la Secretaría General* (monthly).

Instituto de Nutrición de Centro América y Panamá (INCAP) (Institute of Nutrition of Central America and Panama): Calzada Roosevelt 6–25, Zona 11, Apdo Postal 1188-01901, Guatemala City, Guatemala; tel. 2472-3762; fax 2473-6529; e-mail email@incap.int; internet new.paho.org/incap; f. 1949 to promote the development of nutritional sciences and their application and to strengthen the technical capacity of member countries to reach food and nutrition security; provides training and technical assistance for nutrition education and planning; conducts applied research; disseminates information; maintains library (including about 600 periodicals); administered by the Pan American Health Organization and the World Health Organization; mems: CACM mems, Belize and Panama; Dir CAROLINA SIÚ; publ. *Annual Report*.

Consejo del Istmo Centroamericano de Deportes y Recreación (CODICADER) (Committee of the Central American Isthmus for Sport and Recreation): Blv. Orden de Malta 470, Santa Elena, Antiguo Cuscatlán, San Salvador, El Salvador; tel. 2248-8857; fax 2248-8899; internet www.sica.int/sisca/codicader; f. 1992.

Energy and the Environment

Secretaría Ejecutiva de la Comisión Regional de Recursos Hidráulicos (SE-CRRH): Apdo Postal 21–2300, Curridabat, San José, Costa Rica; tel. 2231-5791; fax 2296-0047; e-mail crrhcr@sol.racsa.co.cr; f. 1966; mems: Belize, Costa Rica, El Salvador, Guatemala, Honduras, Nicaragua, Panama.

Secretaría Ejecutiva del Consejo de Electrificación de América Central (CEAC) (Central American Electrification Council): 9A Calle Pte 950, Edif. CEL, Centro de Gobierno, San Salvador, El Salvador; tel. 2211-6175; fax 2211-6239; e-mail jmontesi@cel.gob.sv; f. 1985; Exec. Sec. JULIO ROBERTO ALVAREZ.

Finance

Banco Centroamericano de Integración Económica (BCIE) (Central American Bank for Economic Integration): Blv. Suyapa, Contigua a Banco de Honduras, Apdo 772, Tegucigalpa, Honduras; tel. 2240-2243; fax 2240-2185; e-mail MNunez@bcie.org; internet www.bcie.org; f. 1961 to promote the economic integration and balanced economic development of member countries; finances public and private development projects, particularly those related to industrialization and infrastructure; auth. cap. US $2,000m; regional mems: Costa Rica, El Salvador, Guatemala, Honduras, Nicaragua; non-regional mems: Argentina, Colombia, Dominican Republic, Mexico, Panama, Spain, Taiwan; Exec. Pres. NICK RISCHBIETH; publs *Annual Report*, *Revista de la Integración y el Desarrollo de Centroamérica*.

Organización Centroamericana y del Caribe de Entidades Fiscalizadores Superiores (OCCEFS) (Organization of Central American and Caribbean Supreme Audit Institutions): Tribunal Superior de Cuentas de la República de Honduras, Centro Cívico Gubernamental, Col. Las Brisas Comayagüela, Honduras; tel. and fax 234-5210; internet www.sica.int/occefs; f. 1995 as the Organización Centroamericana de Entidades Fiscalizadores Superiores, within the framework of the Organización Latinoamericana y del Caribe de Entidades Fiscalizadoras Superiores; assumed present name in 1998; aims to promote co-operation among members, facilitate exchange of information, and provide technical assistance; Exec. Sec. JORGE BOGRÁN RIVERA (Honduras).

Public Administration

Centro de Coordinación para la Prevención de Desastres Naturales en América Central (CEPREDENAC): Avda Hincapié 21–72, Zona 13 Guatemala City, Guatemala; tel. 2390-0200; fax 2390-0202; e-mail info.cepredenac@sica.int; internet www.sica.int/cepredenac; f. 1988, integrated into SICA in 1995; aims to strengthen the capacity of the region to reduce its vulnerability to natural disasters; Exec. Sec. IVAN MORALES.

Instituto Centroamericano de Administración Pública (ICAP) (Central American Institute of Public Administration): Apdo Postal 10025-1000, San José, Costa Rica; tel. 2234-1011; fax 2225-2049; e-mail info@icap.ac.cr; internet www.icap.ac.cr; f. 1954 by the five Central American Republics and the UN, with later participation by Panama; the Institute aims to train the region's public servants, provide technical assistance and carry out research leading to reforms in public administration.

Science and Technology

Comisión para el Desarrollo Científico y Tecnológico de Centroamérica y Panamá (CTCAP) (Committee for the Scientific and Technological Development of Central America and Panama): Pavas, Edificio 'Centro nacional de Alta Tecnología Franklin Chang Díaz', 1.3km al norte de la Embajada de Estados Unidos, San José, Costa Rica; tel. 290-1790; fax 290-3343; internet www.sica.int/ctcap; f. 1976; Pres. ROSA MARÍA AMAYA FABIÁN DE LÓPEZ.

Transport and Communications

Comisión Centroamericana de Transporte Marítimo (COCATRAM): Frente al costado oeste del Hotel Mansión Teodolinda, Barrio Bolonia, Apdo Postal 2423, Managua, Nicaragua; tel. 2222-3667; fax 222-2759; e-mail drojas@cocatram.org.ni; internet www.cocatram.org.ni; f. 1981; Exec. Dir OTTO NOACK SIERRA; publ. *Boletín Informativo*.

Comisión de Telecomunicaciones de Centroamérica (COMTELCA) (Commission for Telecommunications in Central America): Col. Palmira, Edif. Alpha 608, Avda Brasil, Apdo 1793, Tegucigalpa, Honduras; tel. 2220-6666; fax 2220-1197; e-mail sec@comtelca.org; internet www.comtelca.org; f. 1966 to co-ordinate and improve the regional telecommunications network; Dir-Gen. RAFAEL A. MARADIAGA.

Corporación Centroamericana de Servicios de Navegación Aérea (COCESNA) (Central American Air Navigation Services Corporation): Apdo 660, Aeropuerto de Toncontín, Tegucigalpa, Honduras; tel. 2234-3360; fax 2234-2550; e-mail sec-interna@cocesna.org; internet www.cocesna.org; f. 1960; offers radar air traffic control services, aeronautical telecommunications services, flight inspections and radio assistance services for air navigation; provides support in the areas of safety, aeronautical training and aeronautical software; Exec. Pres. BAYARDO PAGOADA FIGUEROA.

Activities

In June 1990 the presidents of the CACM countries (Costa Rica, El Salvador, Guatemala, Honduras and Nicaragua) signed a declaration welcoming peace initiatives in El Salvador, Guatemala and Nicaragua, and appealing for a revitalization of CACM, as a means of promoting lasting peace in the region. In December the presidents committed themselves to the creation of an effective common market, proposing the opening of negotiations on a comprehensive regional customs and tariffs policy by March 1991, and the introduction of a regional 'anti-dumping' code by December 1991. They requested the support of multilateral lending institutions through investment in regional development, and the cancellation or rescheduling of member countries' debts. In December 1991 the heads of state of the five CACM countries and Panama signed the Protocol of Tegucigalpa; in February 1993 the General Secretariat of SICA was inaugurated to co-ordinate the integration process in the region.

In June 2009 SICA ministers of foreign affairs, meeting in Managua, Nicaragua, issued a special declaration condemning the removal, by military force, of the Honduran President Manuel Zelaya and the illegal detention of members of his Government. SICA heads of state subsequently met in an extraordinary session and agreed a series of immediate measures, including the suspension of all meetings with the new Honduran authorities, the suspension—through the Central American Bank for Economic Integration—of all loans and disbursements to Honduras, and support for an Organization of American States (OAS) resolution demanding a reinstatement of the democratically elected government. Costa Rica and Panama recognized the results of a general election, held in November. In July 2010 SICA heads of state (excluding the Nicaraguan President) signed a Special Declaration on Honduras, permitting that country's full participation in the grouping and supporting its readmission into the OAS. The 16th meeting of SICA heads of state was convened in Belize, in December.

EXTERNAL RELATIONS

In February 1993 the European Community (now European Union—EU) signed a new framework co-operation agreement with the CACM member states extending the programme of economic assistance and political dialogue initiated in 1984; a further co-operation agreement with the EU was signed in early 1996. In May 2002 ministers of foreign affairs of Central America and the EU agreed a new agenda for a formalized dialogue and priority areas of action, including environmental protection, democracy and governance, and poverty reduction. The meeting determined to work towards the eventual conclusion of an Association Agreement, including an agreement on free trade, although the latter was to be conditional upon the completion of the Doha Round of multilateral negotiations on trade liberalization and upon the attainment of a sufficient level of economic integration in Central America. It was agreed that meetings between the two sides, at ministerial level, were to be held each year. In December 2003 an EU-Central America Political Dialogue and Co-operation Agreement was signed to replace an existing (1993) framework accord. A new Regional Strategy, for 2007–13, was concluded in March 2007, with an allocation of €75.0m.

A framework agreement with the Andean Community was signed with the SICA in November 2004 to strengthen dialogue and co-operation between the two blocs of countries. In January 2011 the Secretaries-General of the two organizations, meeting in San Salvador, El Salvador, determined to reactivate the agreement and pursue greater collaboration.

In May 2008 Brazil was invited to become an observer of SICA. In June 2009 the Council of Ministers agreed to admit Japan as an extra-regional observer of the grouping. The agreement was formalized with the Japanese Government in January 2010. The Republic of Korea was approved as an observer at the meeting of heads of state held in July 2011. In June, meanwhile, at the International Conference in Support of the Regional Strategy for Central America and Mexico, the US Secretary of State announced that the USA was to apply for regional observer status with SICA. This was granted at the SICA summit meeting held in December, while Australia and France became extra-regional observers. Peru was admitted with regional observer status in February 2012.

A meeting of SICA heads of state and the Secretary-General of the United Nations, Ban Ki-Moon, took place in Guatemala, in March 2011.

TRADE AGREEMENTS AND ECONOMIC INTEGRATION

In October 1993 the presidents of the CACM countries and Panama signed a protocol to the 1960 General Treaty, committing themselves to full economic integration in the region (with a common external tariff of 20% for finished products and 5% for raw materials and capital goods) and creating conditions for increased free trade. The countries agreed to accelerate the removal of internal non-tariff barriers, but no deadline was set. Full implementation of the protocol was to be 'voluntary and gradual', owing to objections on the part of Costa Rica and Panama. In May 1994, however, Costa Rica committed itself to full participation in the protocol. In March 1995 a meeting of the Central American Monetary Council discussed and endorsed a reduction in the tariff levels from 20% to 15% and from 5% to 1%. Efforts to adopt this as a common policy were hindered by the implementation of these tariff levels by El Salvador on a unilateral basis, from 1 April, and the subsequent modifications by Guatemala and Costa Rica of their external tariffs. In March 2002 Central American leaders adopted the San Salvador Plan of Action for Central American Economic Integration, establishing several objectives as the basis for the future creation of a regional customs union, with a single tariff. CACM heads of state, meeting in December in Costa Rica, adopted the 'Declaration of San José', supporting the planned establishment of the Central American customs union.

In May 1997 the heads of state of CACM member countries, together with the Prime Minister of Belize, conferred with the then US President, Bill Clinton, in Costa Rica. The leaders resolved to establish a Trade and Investment Council to promote trade relations; however, Clinton failed to endorse a request from CACM members that their products receive preferential access to US markets, on similar terms to those from Mexico agreed under the North American Free Trade Agreement (NAFTA). During the 1990s the Central American Governments pursued negotiations to conclude free trade agreements with Mexico, Panama and the members of the Caribbean Community and Common Market (CARICOM). Nicaragua signed a bilateral accord with Mexico in December (Costa Rica already having done so in 1994). El Salvador, Guatemala and Honduras jointly concluded a free trade arrangement with Mexico in May 2000. In November 1997, at a special summit meeting of CACM heads of state, an agreement was reached with the President of the Dominican Republic to initiate a gradual process of incorporating that country into the process of Central American integration, with the aim of promoting sustainable development throughout the region. A free trade accord with the Dominican Republic was concluded in April 1998, and formally signed in November.

In April 2001 Costa Rica concluded a free trade accord with Canada; the other four CACM countries commenced negotiations with Canada in November with the aim of reaching a similar agreement. In February 2002 Central American heads of state convened an extraordinary summit meeting in Managua, Nicaragua, at which they resolved to implement measures to further the political and economic integration of the region. The leaders determined to pursue initial proposals for a free trade accord with the USA, a Central American Free Trade Area (CAFTA), during the visit to the region of the then US President George W. Bush in the following month, and, more generally, to strengthen trading relations with the EU. They also pledged to resolve all regional conflicts by peaceful means. Earlier in February the first meeting of heads of state or government of Central American and CARICOM countries took place in Belize, with the aim of strengthening political and economic relations between the two groupings. The meeting agreed to work towards concluding common negotiating positions, for example in respect of the World Trade Organization.

Negotiations on CAFTA between the CACM countries and the USA were initiated in January 2003. An agreement was concluded between the USA and El Salvador, Guatemala, Honduras and Nicaragua in December, and with Costa Rica in January 2004. Under the resulting US-Central America Free Trade Agreement some 80% of US exports of consumer and industrial goods and more than 50% of US agricultural exports to CAFTA countries were to become duty-free immediately upon its entry into force, with remaining tariffs to be eliminated over a 10-year period for consumer and industrial goods and over a 15-year period for agricultural exports. Almost all CAFTA exports of consumer and industrial products to the USA were to be duty-free on the Agreement's entry into force. The Agreement was signed by the US Trade Representative and CACM ministers of trade and economy, convened in Washington, DC, USA, in May 2004. It required ratification by all national legislatures before entering into effect. Negotiations on a US-Dominican Republic free trade agreement, to integrate the Dominican Republic into CAFTA, were concluded in March and the agreement was signed in August. The so-called DR-CAFTA accord was formally ratified by the USA in August 2005. Subsequently the agreement has entered into force with El Salvador on 1 March 2006, Honduras and Nicaragua on 1 April, Guatemala on 1 July, the Dominican Republic on 1 March 2007, and Costa Rica on 1 January 2009.

In May 2006 a meeting of EU and Central American heads of state resolved to initiate negotiations to conclude an Association Agreement. The first round of negotiations was concluded in San José, Costa Rica, in October 2007; subsequent rounds were held in Brussels, Belgium, in February 2008, in San Salvador, in April, in Brussels in July, in Guatemala City, Guatemala, in October, and in Brussels, in January 2009. In April the seventh round of negotiations, being held in Tegucigalpa, Honduras, was suspended when the delegation from Nicaragua withdrew from the talks. The process was suspended in July owing to the political crisis in Honduras. Negotiations to conclude the accord resumed in February 2010; Panama participated in the negotiations as a full member for the first time in March. The Association Agreement was formally signed by both sides in May. It provided for immediate duty-free access into the EU for some 92% of Central American products into the EU (48% for EU goods entering Central America), with the remainder of tariffs (on all but 4% of products) being phased out over a 15-year period. The accord also incorporated new import quotas for meat, dairy products and rice, and market access agreements for car manufacturers and the service industry.

In February 2007 the Secretaries-General of SICA and CARICOM signed a plan of action to foster greater co-operation in areas including foreign policy, international trade relations, security and combating crime, and the environment. Meetings of ministers of foreign affairs and of the economy and foreign trade were convened in the same month at which preparations were initiated for trade negotiations between the two groupings. In May the second Central American-CARICOM summit meeting was convened, in Belize City, Belize. Heads of state and of government endorsed the efforts to enhance co-operation between the organizations and approved the elaboration of a free trade agreement, based on the existing bilateral accord signed between CARICOM and Costa Rica. Formal negotiations were inaugurated at a meeting of ministers of trade in August. In December 2010 SICA heads of state, meeting in Belize, resolved to strengthen co-operation with CARICOM and the Association of Caribbean States. The third meeting of SICA and CARICOM heads of state or government was held in August 2011, in San Salvador. Also in August, the OAS convened a high-level meeting of CEOs and business executives from the two blocs to discuss measures to expand trade and investment in the region following the global economic downturn.

In May 2008 SICA heads of state and government met their Brazilian counterparts in San Salvador. The summit meeting reaffirmed the willingness of both sides to enhance political and economic co-operation with the grouping of Southern Common Market (Mercosur) countries and determined to establish mechanisms, in particular, to promote trade and political dialogue.

FINANCIAL CO-OPERATION

In January 2007 the Treaty on Payment Systems and the Liquidation of Assets in Central America and the Dominican Republic was presented to the Secretary-General of SICA. The treaty aimed to increase greater financial co-operation and further develop the financial markets in the region.

In December 2008 a summit meeting, convened in San Pedro Sula, Honduras, adopted a plan of urgent measures to address the effects of the global economic and financial downturn, including a commitment of greater investment in infrastructure projects and the establishment of a common credit fund. Heads of state ratified an agreement to establish a Central American Statistical Commission (Centroestad) to develop a regional statistics service, provide technical statistical assistance to member countries and harmonize national and regional statistics.

INTEGRATED DISASTER RISK MANAGEMENT, ENERGY AND CLIMATE CHANGE

In December 1994 SICA member states and the USA signed a joint declaration (CONCAUSA), covering co-operation in the following areas: conservation of biodiversity; sound management of energy; environmental legislation; and sustainable economic development. In June 2001 both sides signed a renewed and expanded CONCAUSA, now also covering co-operation in addressing climate change, and in disaster preparedness.

In October 1999 SICA heads of state adopted a strategic framework for the period 2000–04 to strengthen the capacity for the physical, social, economic and environmental infrastructure of Central American countries to withstand the impact of natural disasters. In particular, programmes for the integrated management and conservation of water resources, and for the prevention of forest fires were to be implemented.

In June 2001 the heads of state and representatives of Belize, Costa, Rica, El Salvador, Guatemala, Honduras, Mexico, Nicaragua and Panama agreed to activate a Puebla-Panamá Plan (PPP) to promote sustainable social and economic development in the region and to reinforce integration efforts among Central America and the southern states of Mexico (referred to as Mesoamerica). The heads of state identified the principal areas for PPP initiatives, including tourism, road integration, telecommunications, energy interconnection, and the prevention and mitigation of disasters. In June 2002 the heads of state of seven countries, and the Vice-President of Panama, convened in Mérida, Mexico, during an investment fair to promote the Plan and reiterated their support for the regional initiatives. The meeting was also held within the framework of the 'Tuxtla dialogue mechanism', so-called after an agreement signed in 1991 between Mexico and Central American countries, to discuss co-ordination between the parties, in particular in social matters, health, education and the environment. Regular 'Tuxtla' summit meetings convened subsequently.

Representatives of SICA and of Colombia, the Dominican Republic and Mexico adopted the Declaration of Romana in June 2006, wherein they agreed to implement the Mesoamerican Energy Integration Program, aimed at developing regional oil, electricity and natural gas markets, promoting the use of renewable energy, and increasing electricity generation and interconnection capacity across the region. In the following month, at the eighth Tuxtla summit, convened in Panama, SICA member states approved the legal framework for the Central American Electrical Connection System (known as SIEPAC), which was to be co-funded by the Central American Bank for Economic Integration and the Inter-American Development Bank. In June 2008 the 10th Tuxtla summit meeting, convened in Villahermosa, Mexico, agreed to establish the Mesoamerican Integration and Development Project to supersede the PPP. The new Project was to incorporate ongoing initiatives on highways and infrastructure and implement energy, electricity and information networks.

In November 2007 SICA heads of state endorsed a Sustainable Energy Strategy for Central America 2020. Its main areas of concern were: access to energy by the least advantaged populations; the rational and efficient use of energy; renewable sources of energy; biofuels for the transport sector; and climate change. A joint summit on the environment and climate change in Central America and the Caribbean was held with CARICOM representatives in San Pedro Sula, Honduras, in May 2008.

SICA heads of state ratified an agreement, in July 2010, to accelerate efforts to reduce the region's vulnerability to natural disasters and the effects of climate change. They determined to establish a special regional fund to finance the initiative. At the third SICA-CARICOM meeting, held in San Salvador, El Salvador, in August 2011, heads of state welcomed an initiative by Panama to establish a Regional Humanitarian Logistic Assistance Centre to respond to emergency situations in the region within 24 to 48 hours. The meeting recognized the need to strengthen transport and cultural links and detailed measures to bolster co-operation in international environmental negotiations and disaster management. In December, at the summit meeting of SICA heads of state, environmental preservation and tackling natural disasters were central to the agenda, and members agreed to adopt the constitution of a Central American Fund for the Promotion of Integrated Risk Management to provide technical assistance and resources as needed.

HEALTH AND TOURISM

At the meeting of CACM heads of state in December 2002, the establishment of a new Central American Tourism Agency was announced. In July 2011 SICA heads of state declared 2012 to be the Central American Year of Sustainable Tourism.

In June 2008 the SICA summit meeting, convened in San Salvador, El Salvador, reiterated concerns regarding escalating petroleum and food prices, and welcomed several initiatives concerned with strengthening the region's food security (see above). During the SICA-CARICOM heads of state meeting in El Salvador, in August 2011, it was agreed that the two organizations would collaborate on the early detection (and prevention) of non-communicable diseases.

REGIONAL SECURITY

In March 2005 SICA ministers responsible for security, defence and the interior resolved to establish a special regional force to combat crime, drugs and arms trafficking and terrorism. In June 2008 SICA heads of state and government, convened in San Salvador, agreed to establish a peace-keeping operations unit within the secretariat in order to co-ordinate participation in international peace-keeping missions.

In June 2008 the US Congress approved US $65m. to fund a Central American initiative to counter drugs-trafficking and organized crime, as part of a larger agreement arranged with the Mexican Government (the so-called Mérida Initiative). The scheme was subsequently relaunched as the Central American Regional Security Initiative, with additional approved funds of some $100m. to provide equipment, training, and technical assistance to build the capacity of Central American institutions to counter crime. In February 2010, at a meeting of the Inter-American Development Bank (IDB), several countries and other multilateral organizations determined to establish a Group of Friends for Central American Security, in order to support the region to counter organized crime. In March 2011 US President Obama announced the establishment of a Central American Citizen Security Partnership to strengthen law enforcement and to provide young people with alternatives to organized crime.

In early 2011 an Ad Hoc Regional Expert Task Force was established to help to elaborate a regional security strategy, in advance of an international conference, convened in Guatemala City, Guatemala, in June. At the International Conference in Support of the Regional Security Strategy for Central America and Mexico, the US Secretary of State committed US $300m. in support of security initiatives, including more specialized police units and a new SICA Regional Crime Observatory. Negotiations to formulate a Central American Security Strategy (Estrategia de Seguridad de Centroamérica—ESCA), based on 22 priority projects identified at the International Conference, recommenced in September. ESCA's main activities were to incorporate combating crime and preventing violence, rehabilitation of offenders, prison management, and institutional strengthening. In February 2012 the IDB hosted a meeting of the SICA Security Commission and the so-called Group of Friends of the Central America Security Strategy to inaugurate an initial eight ESCA projects.

COMMON MARKET FOR EASTERN AND SOUTHERN AFRICA—COMESA

Address: COMESA Secretariat, Ben Bella Rd, POB 30051, 101101 Lusaka, Zambia.

Telephone: (1) 229725; **fax:** (1) 225107; **e-mail:** comesa@comesa.int; **internet:** www.comesa.int.

The COMESA treaty was signed by member states of the Preferential Trade Area for Eastern and Southern Africa (PTA) in November 1993. COMESA formally succeeded the PTA in December 1994. COMESA aims to strengthen the process of regional economic and social development that was initiated under the PTA, with the ultimate aim of merging with the other regional economic communities of the African Union.

MEMBERS

Burundi	Malawi
Comoros	Mauritius
Congo, Democratic Republic	Rwanda
Djibouti	Seychelles
Egypt	Sudan
Eritrea	Swaziland
Ethiopia	Uganda
Kenya	Zambia
Libya	Zimbabwe
Madagascar	

Organization

(April 2012)

AUTHORITY

The Authority of the Common Market is the supreme policy organ of COMESA, comprising heads of state or government of member countries. The inaugural meeting of the Authority took place in Lilongwe, Malawi, in December 1994. The 15th summit meeting was held in October 2011, in Lilongwe, Malawi, on the theme 'Harnessing Science and Technology for Development'.

COUNCIL OF MINISTERS

Each member government appoints a minister to participate in the Council. The Council monitors COMESA activities, including supervision of the Secretariat, recommends policy direction and development, and reports to the Authority.

A Committee of Governors of Central Banks advises the Authority and the Council of Ministers on monetary and financial matters.

COURT OF JUSTICE

The sub-regional Court is vested with the authority to settle disputes between member states and to adjudicate on matters concerning the interpretation of the COMESA treaty. The Court is composed of seven judges, who serve terms of five years' duration. The Court was restructured in 2005 to comprise a First Instance division and an Appellate division.

President: Nzamba Kitonga (Kenya).

SECRETARIAT

COMESA's Secretariat comprises the following divisions: Administration; Budget and finance; Gender and social affairs; Infrastructure development; Investment Promotion; Private Sector Development; and Trade customs and monetary affairs. There are also units at the Secretariat dealing with legal and institutional affairs, and climate change.

Secretary-General: Sindiso Nwengya (Zimbabwe).

Activities

COMESA aims to promote economic and social progress, co-operation and integration in member states. A strategic plan, endorsed by the COMESA Authority at its 14th summit meeting convened in August 2010, governs COMESA's medium-term goals and activities during the period 2011–15, prioritizing integration; enhancing productive capacity for global competitiveness; infrastructure development; cross-cutting issues such as gender and social development, climate change, statistics, peace and security, knowledge-based capacity and human capital; co-operation and partnership; and institutional development. COMESA supports capacity-building activities and the establishment of other specialized institutions (see below).

In May 1999 COMESA established a Free Trade Area (FTA) Committee to facilitate and co-ordinate preparations for the creation of the common market envisaged under the COMESA treaty. An extraordinary summit of COMESA heads of state or government, held in October 2000, inaugurated the FTA, with nine initial members: Djibouti, Egypt, Kenya, Madagascar, Malawi, Mauritius, Sudan, Zambia and Zimbabwe. Burundi and Rwanda became members of the FTA in January 2004, and Swaziland undertook in April to seek the concurrence of the Southern African Customs Union, of which it is also a member, to allow it to participate in the FTA. Trading practices within the FTA have been fully liberalized, including the elimination of non-tariff barriers, thereby enabling the free internal movement of goods, services and capital. The COMESA Customs Union (CU), with a common external tariff (CET) set at 0% for capital goods and raw materials, 10% for intermediate goods and 25% for finished products, was launched at the 13th annual summit meeting of the Authority, in June 2009. It was envisaged that the Customs Union would be fully operational by June 2012. A Protocol establishing the COMESA Fund, which assists member states in addressing structural imbalances in their economies, came into effect in November 2006. COMESA plans to form an economic community (entailing monetary union and the free movement of people between member states) by 2014. The COMESA Regional Investment Agency (RIA), based in Cairo, Egypt, was inaugurated in June 2006, its founding charter having been adopted in June 2005 by the 10th summit meeting of the Authority. An Agreement on the establishment of a COMESA Common Investment Area (CCIA) was adopted by the Authority at its May 2007 summit meeting. The May 2007 meeting also endorsed the establishment of an 'Aid for Trade' unit in the COMESA Secretariat, which was to assist countries with the identification and implementation of projects aimed at removing trade-related supply constraints. A COMESA Competition Commission, based in Blantyre, Malawi, was inaugurated in December 2008. In June 2009 a regional payments and settlement system (REPSS), headquartered in Lusaka, Zambia, was launched.

In February 2000 a COMESA economic forum was convened in Cairo, Egypt. The seventh COMESA Business Forum was organized in October 2011, in Lilongwe, Malawi, on the sidelines of the 15th summit of the Authority. The COMESA RIA sponsors annual investment fora: the fourth forum was convened in Dubai, United Arab Emirates, in March 2011.

Co-operation programmes have been implemented by COMESA in the financial, agricultural, transport and communications, industrial, and energy sectors. A regional food security programme aims to ensure continuous adequate food supplies. COMESA works with private sector interests through the African Union (AU) Comprehensive African Agricultural Development Programme (CAADP) to improve agricultural performance. The CAADP undertook efforts in 2008 to strengthen regional capacity to address food insecurity, promoting robust markets and long-term competitiveness. COMESA maintains a Food and Agricultural Marketing Information System (FAMIS), providing up-to-date data on the sub-regional food security situation. In 1997 COMESA heads of state advocated that the food sector be supported by the implementation of an irrigation action plan for the region. The organization supports the establishment of common agricultural standards and phytosanitary regulations throughout the region in order to stimulate trade in food crops. In March 2005 more than 100 standards on quality assurance, covering mainly agricultural products, were adopted. Meeting for the first time in November 2002, COMESA ministers of agriculture determined to formulate a regional policy on genetically modified organisms. At their second meeting, held in October 2004, ministers of agriculture agreed to prioritize agriculture in their development efforts, and—in accordance with a Declaration of the AU—the objective of allocating at least 10% of national budgets to agriculture and rural development. In September 2008 COMESA ministers of agriculture launched the Alliance for Commodity Trade in Eastern and Southern Africa (ACTESA), with the aim of integrating small farmers into national, regional and international markets. ACTESA became a specialized agency of COMESA in June 2009. In March 2010 COMESA and ACTESA signed an agreement aimed at accelerating the implementation of regional initiatives in agriculture, trade and investment. Other organization-wide initiatives include a road customs declaration document, a scheme for third-party motor vehicle insurance, a system of regional travellers cheques, and a regional customs bond guarantee scheme. A COMESA Telecommunications Company (COMTEL) was registered in May 2000. In January 2003 the Association of Regulators of Information and Communication for Eastern and Southern Africa was launched, under the auspices of COMESA. An Eastern Africa Power Pool (EAPP) has been established by COMESA, comprising Burundi, Democratic Republic of the Congo, Djibouti, Ethiopia, Kenya, Sudan, Tanzania and Uganda. COMESA and the Southern African Development Community (SADC) have the joint objective of eventually linking the EAPP and the Southern Africa Power Pool. COMESA maintains a priority list of regional infrastructure projects, and, in 2008, launched an interactive database recording the status of the projects.

In May 1999 the COMESA Authority resolved to establish a Committee on Peace and Security comprising ministers of foreign affairs from member states. It was envisaged that the Committee would convene at least once a year to address matters concerning regional stability. (Instability in certain member states was regarded as a potential threat to the successful implementation of the FTA.) The Committee met for the first time in 2000. It was announced in September 2002 that the COMESA Treaty was to be amended to provide for the establishment of a formal conflict prevention and resolution structure to be governed by member countries' heads of state. The seventh meeting of the Committee, held in November 2006, recommended the establishment of a COMESA Committee of Elders, which was to undertake preventive peace-building assignments; the Committee of Elders held its inaugural meeting in December 2011. The seventh meeting of COMESA ministers of foreign affairs also decided that COMESA's peace and security activities should focus in particular on the economic dimensions of conflicts.

Following a recommendation by the AU, in January 2007, that climate change adaptation strategies should be integrated into African national and sub-regional development planning and activities, COMESA launched a Climate Change Initiative, which aims to improve economic and social resilience to the impacts of climate change. In July 2010 COMESA, the EAC and SADC adopted a tripartite five-year Programme on Climate Change Adaptation and Mitigation in the COMESA-EAC-SADC region.

A joint COMESA-EAC-IGAD observer mission was dispatched to monitor presidential and legislative elections that took place in Uganda in February 2011. COMESA also sent an observer mission to monitor the conduct of the presidential, legislative and local government elections that were held in late September in Zambia.

From COMESA's establishment there were concerns on the part of member states, as well as other regional non-member countries, in particular South Africa, of adverse rivalry between COMESA and the SADC and of a duplication of roles. In 1997 Lesotho and Mozambique terminated their membership of COMESA owing to concerns that their continued participation in the organization was incompatible with their SADC membership. Tanzania withdrew from COMESA in September 2000, reportedly also in view of its dual commitment to that organization and to SADC. In June 2003 Namibia announced its withdrawal from the organization. The summit meeting of COMESA heads of state or government held in May 2000 expressed support for an ongoing programme of co-operation by the Secretariats of COMESA and SADC aimed at reducing the duplication of roles between the two organizations, and urged further mutual collaboration. A co-ordinating task force was established in 2001, and was joined by the EAC (becoming the COMESA-EAC-SADC Task Force) in 2005, as the EAC became involved in the regional economic community (REC) co-operation programme. The Regional Trade Facilitation Programme covering southern and eastern Africa, and based in Pretoria, South Africa, provides secretariat services to the Task Force.

In October 2008 the first tripartite COMESA-EAC-SADC summit was convened, in Kampala, Uganda, to discuss the harmonization of policy and programme work by the three RECs. Leaders of the 26 countries attending the Kampala summit approved a roadmap towards the formation of a common FTA and the eventual establishment of a single African Economic Community (a long-term objective of AU co-operation). A COMESA-EAC-SADC Joint Competition Authority was established at the tripartite summit. At the second tripartite summit, held in June 2011, in Johannesburg, South Africa, negotiations were initiated on the establishment of the proposed COMESA-EAC-SADC Tripartite FTA. In January 2012 AU leaders endorsed a new Framework, Roadmap and Architecture for Fast Tracking the Establishment of a Continental FTA (referred to as CFTA), and an Action Plan for Boosting Intra-African Trade, which planned for the consolidation of the COMESA-EAC-SADC Tripartite FTA with other regional FTAs into the CFTA initiative during 2015–16; and the establishment of an operational CFTA by 2017. COMESA has co-operated with other sub-regional organizations to finalize a common position on co-operation between African ACP countries and the European Union (EU) under the Cotonou Agreement (concluded in June 2000, see chapter on the EU).

In February 2010 COMESA and ECOWAS concluded a memorandum of understanding aimed at enhancing private sector development in their regions, and at advancing pan-African economic integration.

In June 2010 a consultative meeting was convened between COMESA, the AU, IGAD, and other regional partners, aimed at advancing co-ordination and harmonization of their activities related to the environment.

In September 2006 the COMESA Regional Economic and Trade Integration Program (CRETIP) was adopted by COMESA and the USA; under CRETIP, COMESA receives US assistance towards the implementation of programmes promoting COMESA–USA trade, regional trade, and the institutional strengthening of the COMESA Secretariat. In August 2007 COMESA appointed a Special Representative to the Middle East to establish partnerships with that region and to promote trade opportunities.

COMESA INSTITUTIONS

African Trade Insurance Agency (ATI): POB 10620, 00100-GPO, Nairobi, Kenya; tel. (20) 27269999; fax (20) 2719701; e-mail info@ati-aca.org; internet www.ati-aca.org; f. 2001 to promote trade and investment activities throughout the region; mems: 13 African countries; CEO George O. Otieno.

Alliance for Commodity Trade in Eastern and Southern Africa (ACTESA): Corporate Park, Alick Nkhata Rd, Lusaka, 10101 Zambia; tel. 211-253572; e-mail info@actesacomesa.org; internet www.actesacomesa.org; f. 2008, became a specialized agency of COMESA in June 2009; aims to integrate small farmers into national, regional and international markets; CEO Dr Chungu Mwila (acting).

COMESA Bankers Association: Private Bag 271, Kapeni House, 1st Floor, Blantyre, Malawi; tel. and fax (1) 674236; e-mail info@comesabankers.org; internet www.comesabankers.org; f. 1987 as the PTA Association of Commercial Banks; name changed as above in 1994; aims to strengthen co-operation between banks in the region; organizes training activities; conducts studies to harmonize banking laws and operations; implements a bank fraud prevention programme; mems: 55 commercial banking orgs in Burundi, Egypt, Eritrea, Ethiopia, Kenya, Malawi, Rwanda, Sudan, Swaziland; Exec. Sec. Eric C. Chinkanda (acting).

COMESA Leather and Leather Products Institute (LLPI): POB 2358, 1110 Addis Ababa, Ethiopia; tel. (11) 431318; fax (11) 431321; e-mail comesa.llpi@telecom.net.et; f. 1990 as the PTA Leather Institute; mems: 17 COMESA mem. states; Chair. Wilson Mazimba.

COMESA Regional Investment Authority (COMESA-RIA): 3 Salah Salem Rd, Nasr City, Cairo, Egypt; tel. (2) 405-5428; fax (2) 405-5421; e-mail info@comesaria.org; internet www.comesaria.org; Man. Heba Salama.

Compagnie de réassurance de la Zone d'échanges préférentiels (ZEP-RE) (PTA Reinsurance Co): ZEP-RE Place, Longonot Rd, Upper Hill, POB 42769, 00100 Nairobi, Kenya; tel. (20) 2738221; fax (20) 2738444; e-mail mail@zep-re.com; internet www.zep-re.com; f. 1992 (began operations on 1 Jan. 1993); provides local reinsurance services and training to personnel in the insurance industry; total assets US $103.1m. (2010); Chair. Dr Michael Gondwe; Man. Dir Jephita Gwatipedza.

East African Power Pool (EAPP): Bole Sub City, Gulz Aziz Bldg, Addis Ababa Ethiopia; tel. (11) 6183694; fax (11) 6183694; e-mail eapp@eappool.org; internet www.eappool.org/eng/about.html; in Feb. 2005 energy ministers from Burundi, DRC, Egypt, Ethiopia, Kenya, Rwanda and Sudan signed the Inter-Governmental Memorandum of Understanding on the establishment of the Eastern Africa Power Pool (EAPP); EAPP was adopted by COMESA as a specialized institution in 2006; Tanzania and Libya joined in 2010 and 2011, respectively; Exec. Sec. Jasper Oduor.

Eastern and Southern African Trade and Development Bank: NSSF Bldg, 22nd/23rd Floor, Bishop's Rd, POB 48596, 00100 Nairobi, Kenya; tel. (20) 2712250; fax (20) 2711510; e-mail official@ptabank.org; internet www.ptabank.org; f. 1983 as PTA Development Bank; aims to mobilize resources and finance COMESA activities to foster regional integration; promotes investment and co-financing within the region; in Jan. 2003 the US dollar replaced the UAPTA (PTA unit of account) as the Bank's reporting currency; shareholders: 15 COMESA mem. states, the People's Republic of China, Somalia, Tanzania and the African Development Bank; total assets US 1,055.9m. (Dec. 2010); Pres. Admassu Y. Tadesse (Ethiopia).

Federation of National Associations of Women in Business in Eastern and Southern Africa (FEMCOM): Off Queens Drive, Area 6, Plot No. 170, POB 1499, Lilongwe, Malawi; tel. (1) 205-908; e-mail info@femcomcomesa.org; internet www.femcomcomesa.org; f. 1993; self-standing secretariat launched in 2009; aims to promote programmes that integrate women into regional trade and development activities, with a particular focus on the areas of agriculture, fishing, energy, communications, industry, mining, natural resources, trade, services, and transport; has chapters in all COMESA mem. states; Exec. Dir KATHERINE ICHOYA.

Finance

COMESA is financed by member states.

Publications

Annual Report of the Council of Ministers.
Asycuda Newsletter.
COMESA Journal.
COMESA Trade Directory (annually).
COMESA Trade Information Newsletter (monthly).
e-comesa (monthly newsletter).
Demand/supply surveys, catalogues and reports.

THE COMMONWEALTH

Address: Commonwealth Secretariat, Marlborough House, Pall Mall, London, SW1Y 5HX, United Kingdom.

Telephone: (20) 7747-6500; **fax:** (20) 7930-0827; **e-mail:** info@commonwealth.int; **internet:** www.thecommonwealth.org.t

The Commonwealth is a voluntary association of 53 independent states, comprising about one-quarter of the world's population. It includes the United Kingdom and most of its former dependencies, and former dependencies of Australia and New Zealand (themselves Commonwealth countries).

The evolution of the Commonwealth began with the introduction of self-government in Canada in the 1840s; Australia, New Zealand and South Africa became independent before the First World War. At the Imperial Conference of 1926 the United Kingdom and the Dominions, as they were then called, were described as 'autonomous communities within the British Empire, equal in status', and this change was enacted into law by the Statute of Westminster, in 1931.

The modern Commonwealth began with the entry of India and Pakistan in 1947, and of Sri Lanka (then Ceylon) in 1948. In 1949, when India decided to become a republic, the Commonwealth Heads of Government agreed to replace allegiance to the British Crown with recognition of the British monarch as Head of the Commonwealth, as a condition of membership. This was a precedent for a number of other members (see Heads of State and Heads of Government, below).

MEMBERS*

Antigua and Barbuda	Kenya	Saint Vincent and the Grenadines
Australia	Kiribati	Samoa
Bahamas	Lesotho	Seychelles
Bangladesh	Malawi	Sierra Leone
Barbados	Malaysia	Singapore
Belize	The Maldives	Solomon Islands
Botswana	Malta	South Africa
Brunei	Mauritius	Sri Lanka
Cameroon	Mozambique	Swaziland
Canada	Namibia	Tanzania
Cyprus	Nauru	Tonga
Dominica	New Zealand	Trinidad and Tobago
The Gambia	Nigeria	Tuvalu
Ghana	Pakistan	Uganda
Grenada	Papua New Guinea	United Kingdom
Guyana	Rwanda	Vanuatu
India	Saint Christopher and Nevis	Zambia
Jamaica	Saint Lucia	

* Ireland, South Africa and Pakistan withdrew from the Commonwealth in 1949, 1961 and 1972, respectively. In October 1987 Fiji's membership was declared to have lapsed (following the proclamation of a republic there). It was readmitted in October 1997, but was suspended from participation in meetings of the Commonwealth in June 2000. Fiji was formally readmitted to Commonwealth meetings in December 2001 following the staging of free and fair legislative elections in August–September. However, following a further military coup in December 2006, Fiji was once again suspended from participation in meetings of the Commonwealth, and, in September 2009, Fiji's Commonwealth membership was fully suspended. Pakistan rejoined the Commonwealth in October 1989. However, it was suspended from participation in meetings during the period October 1999–May 2004 and, once again, during November 2007–May 2008. South Africa rejoined in June 1994. Nigeria's membership was suspended in November 1995; it formally resumed membership in May 1999, when a new civilian government was inaugurated. In 1995 Mozambique became a member, the first to have no historical or administrative connection with another Commonwealth country. Tuvalu, previously a special member of the Commonwealth with the right to participate in all activities except full Meetings of Heads of Government, became a full member in September 2000. In March 2002 Zimbabwe was suspended from participation in meetings of the Commonwealth. Zimbabwe announced its withdrawal from the Commonwealth in December 2003. Rwanda was admitted to membership of the Commonwealth in November 2009. In June 2011 Nauru was reinstated as a full member of the Commonwealth, having been classed as a 'member in arrears' from 2003. In 2012 the Commonwealth was considering possible future membership for South Sudan, which attained independence in July 2011.

Australian External Territories

Ashmore and Cartier Islands	Coral Sea Islands Territory
Australian Antarctic Territory	Heard Island and the McDonald Islands
Christmas Island	Norfolk Island
Cocos (Keeling) Islands	

New Zealand Dependent and Associated Territories

Cook Islands	Ross Dependency
Niue	Tokelau

United Kingdom Overseas Territories

Anguilla	Gibraltar
Bermuda	Isle of Man
British Antarctic Territory	Montserrat
British Indian Ocean Territory	Pitcairn Islands
British Virgin Islands	St Helena, Ascension, Tristan da Cunha
Cayman Islands	South Sandwich Islands
Channel Islands	Turks and Caicos Islands
Falkland Islands	

HEADS OF STATE AND HEADS OF GOVERNMENT

At April 2012 21 member countries were monarchies and 33 were republics. All Commonwealth countries accept Queen Elizabeth II as the symbol of the free association of the independent member nations and as such the Head of the Commonwealth. Of the 33 republics, the offices of Head of State and Head of Government were combined in 22: Botswana, Cameroon, Cyprus, The Gambia, Ghana, Guyana, Kenya, Kiribati, Malawi, the Maldives, Mozambique, Namibia, Nauru, Nigeria, Rwanda, Seychelles, Sierra Leone, South Africa, Sri Lanka, Tanzania, Uganda and Zambia. The two offices were separated in the remaining 11: Bangladesh, Dominica, Fiji, India, Malta, Mauritius, Pakistan, Samoa, Singapore, Trinidad and Tobago and Vanuatu.

Of the monarchies, the Queen is Head of State of the United Kingdom and of 15 others, in each of which she is represented by a Governor-General: Antigua and Barbuda, Australia, the Bahamas, Barbados, Belize, Canada, Grenada, Jamaica, New Zealand, Papua New Guinea, Saint Christopher and Nevis, Saint Lucia, Saint Vincent and the Grenadines, Solomon Islands and Tuvalu. Brunei, Lesotho, Malaysia, Swaziland and Tonga are also monarchies, where the traditional monarch is Head of State.

The Governors-General are appointed by the Queen on the advice of the Prime Ministers of the country concerned. They are wholly independent of the Government of the United Kingdom.

HIGH COMMISSIONERS

Governments of member countries are represented in other Commonwealth countries by High Commissioners, who have a status equivalent to that of Ambassadors.

Organization

(April 2012)

The Commonwealth is not a federation: there is no central government nor are there any rigid contractual obligations such as bind members of the United Nations.

Commonwealth members subscribe to the ideals of the Declaration of Commonwealth Principles unanimously approved by a meeting of heads of government in Singapore in 1971. Members also approved the Gleneagles Agreement concerning apartheid in sport (1977); the Lusaka Declaration on Racism and Racial Prejudice (1979); the Melbourne Declaration on relations between developed and developing countries (1981); the New Delhi Statement on Economic Action (1983); the Goa Declaration on International Security (1983); the Nassau Declaration on World Order (1985); the Commonwealth Accord on Southern Africa (1985); the Vancouver Declaration on World Trade (1987); the Okanagan Statement and Programme of Action on Southern Africa (1987); the Langkawi Declaration on the Environment (1989); the Kuala Lumpur Statement on Southern Africa (1989); the Harare Commonwealth Declaration (1991); the Ottawa Declaration on Women and Structural Adjustment (1991); the Limassol Statement on the Uruguay Round of multilateral trade negotiations (1993); the Millbrook Commonwealth Action Programme on the Harare Declaration (1995); the Edinburgh Commonwealth Economic Declaration (1997); the Fancourt Commonwealth Declaration on Globalization and People-centred Development (1999); the Coolum Declaration on the Commonwealth in the 21st Century: Continuity and Renewal (2002); the Aso Rock Commonwealth Declaration and Statement on Multilateral Trade (2003); the Malta Commonwealth Declaration on Networking for Development (2005); the Munyonyo Statement on Respect and Understanding (2007); the Marlborough House Statement on Reform of International Institutions (2008); the Commonwealth Climate Change Declaration (2009); and the Perth Declaration on Food Security Principles (2011). In October 2011 Commonwealth heads of government agreed that a non-binding Charter of the Commonwealth, embodying the principles contained in previous declarations, should be drafted.

MEETINGS OF HEADS OF GOVERNMENT

Commonwealth Heads of Government Meetings (CHOGMs) are private and informal and operate not by voting but by consensus. The emphasis is on consultation and exchange of views for co-operation. A communiqué is issued at the end of every meeting. Meetings are normally held every two years in different capitals in the Commonwealth. The 2011 meeting was convened in Perth, Australia, at the end of October. The 2013 and 2015 meetings were to be held, respectively, in Sri Lanka and in Mauritius.

OTHER CONSULTATIONS

The Commonwealth Ministerial Action Group on the Harare was formed in 1995 to support democracy in member countries (see Activities, below). It comprises a group of nine ministers of foreign affairs, with rotating membership.

Since 1959 Commonwealth finance ministers have met in the week prior to the annual meetings of the IMF and the World Bank. Ministers responsible for civil society, education, the environment, foreign affairs, gender issues, health, law, tourism and youth also hold regular meetings.

Senior officials—cabinet secretaries, permanent secretaries to heads of government and others—meet regularly in the year between meetings of heads of government to provide continuity and to exchange views on various developments.

COMMONWEALTH SECRETARIAT

The Secretariat, established by Commonwealth heads of government in 1965, operates as an intergovernmental organization at the service of all Commonwealth countries. It organizes consultations between governments and runs programmes of co-operation. Meetings of heads of government, ministers and senior officials decide these programmes and provide overall direction. A Board of Governors, on which all eligible member governments are represented, meets annually to review the Secretariat's work and approve its budget. The Board is supported by an Executive Committee which convenes four times a year to monitor implementation of the Secretariat's work programme. The Secretariat is headed by a secretary-general, elected by heads of government.

In 2002 the Secretariat was restructured, with a view to strengthening the effectiveness of the organization to meet the priorities determined by the meeting of heads of government held in Coolum, Australia, in March 2002. Under the reorganization the number of deputy secretaries-general was reduced from three to two. Certain work divisions were amalgamated, while new units or sections, concerned with youth affairs, human rights and good offices, were created to strengthen further activities in those fields. Accordingly, the Secretariat's divisional structure is as follows: Legal and constitutional affairs; Political affairs; Corporate services; Communications and public affairs; Strategic planning and evaluation; Economic affairs; Governance and institutional development; Social transformation programmes; Youth affairs (from 2004); and Special advisory services. (Details of some of the divisions are given under Activities, below.) In addition there are units responsible for human rights and project management and referrals, and an Office of the Secretary-General.

The Secretariat's strategic plan for 2008/09–2011/12, approved by the Board of Governors in May 2008, set out two main, long-term objectives for the Commonwealth. The first, 'Peace and Democracy', was to support member countries in preventing or resolving conflicts, to strengthen democracy and the rule of law, and to achieve greater respect for human rights. The second, 'Pro-Poor Growth and Sustainable Development', was to support policies for economic growth and sustainable development, particularly for the benefit of the poorest people, in member countries. Four programmes were to facilitate the pursuit of the first objective: Good Offices for Peace; Democracy and Consensus Building; Rule of Law; and Human Rights. The second objective was to be pursued through the following four programmes: Public Sector Development; Economic Development; Environmentally Sustainable Development; and Human Development.

Secretary-General: KAMALESH SHARMA (India).

Deputy Secretaries-General: MMASEKGOA MASIRE-MWAMBA (Botswana), RANSFORD SMITH (Jamaica).

Assistant Secretary-General for Corporate Affairs: STEPHEN CUTTS (United Kingdom).

Activities

PROMOTING DEMOCRACY, HUMAN RIGHTS AND DEVELOPMENT

In October 1991 heads of government, meeting in Harare, Zimbabwe, issued the Harare Commonwealth Declaration, in which they reaffirmed their commitment to the Commonwealth Principles declared in 1971, and stressed the need to promote sustainable development and the alleviation of poverty. The Declaration placed emphasis on the promotion of democracy and respect for human rights and resolved to strengthen the Commonwealth's capacity to assist countries in entrenching democratic practices. In November 1995 Commonwealth heads of government, convened in New Zealand, formulated and adopted the Millbrook Commonwealth Action Programme on the Harare Declaration, to promote adherence by member countries to the fundamental principles of democracy and human rights (as proclaimed in the 1991 Declaration). The Programme incorporated a framework of measures to be pursued in support of democratic processes and institutions, and actions to be taken in response to violations of the Harare Declaration principles, in particular the unlawful removal of a democratically elected government. A Commonwealth Ministerial Action Group on the Harare Declaration (CMAG) was established in December 1995 to implement this process and to assist the member country involved to comply with the Harare principles. In March 2002 Commonwealth leaders expanded CMAG's mandate to enable the Group to consider action against serious violations of the Commonwealth's core values perpetrated by elected administrations as well as by military regimes. In October 2011 the Perth summit of Commonwealth leaders agreed a series of reforms aimed at strengthening the role of CMAG in addressing serious violations of Commonwealth political values; these included clearer guidelines and time frames for engagement when the situation in a country causes concern, with a view to shifting from a reactive to a more proactive role.

The October 2011 heads of government reconstituted CMAG's membership to comprise over the next biennium the ministers responsible for foreign affairs of Australia, Bangladesh, Canada, Jamaica, the Maldives (suspended from the Group in February 2012), Sierra Leone, Tanzania, Trinidad and Tobago, and Vanuatu.

In February 2012 CMAG placed the Maldives on its formal agenda, having considered a report from a Commonwealth ministerial mission that reviewed an allegedly forced transfer of presidential power, in early February, between former President Mohamed Nasheed and the incumbent President Mohammed Waheed. CMAG urged the initiation of immediate dialogue between the two sides, with a view to setting a date for early elections, and welcomed the appointment of a Special Envoy of the Commonwealth Secretary-General to address the situation in the Maldives. CMAG also placed in abeyance the Maldives' ongoing Group membership, owing to its inclusion on the Group's formal agenda.

In December 2006, following the overthrow of the Fijian Government by the military, an extraordinary meeting of CMAG determined that Fiji should be suspended from meetings of the Commonwealth, pending the reinstatement of democratic governance. In September 2007 the Group urged the Fijian authorities to hold a democratic general election by March 2009 and determined to keep the situation in that country under review; the March 2009 election deadline was not, however, met by the Fijian authorities. CMAG expressed support at the March meeting for ongoing political dialogue in Fiji, jointly mediated by the Commonwealth and the UN. In April the Commonwealth Secretary-General condemned the unconstitutional conduct of the Fijian authorities in abrogating the Constitution, dismissing the judiciary and announcing that democratic elections were to be postponed to 2014, following a judgment by Fiji's Court of Appeal declaring the appointment of the current interim government to be unlawful and urging the prompt restoration of democracy. Meeting at the end of July, CMAG demanded that the Fijian regime reactivate by 1 September 2009 the Commonwealth- and UN-mediated political dialogue process, leading to the staging of elections no later than October 2010. At the beginning of September 2009 the Commonwealth Secretary-General announced that the Fijian regime had not acted to meet CMAG's demands and that Fiji's Commonwealth membership was consequently fully suspended with immediate effect. Meeting in September 2010 and April 2011 CMAG reiterated its concern at the situation in Fiji and maintained the suspension of Fiji's Commonwealth membership.

In March 2002, meeting in Coolum, near Brisbane, Australia, Commonwealth heads of government adopted the Coolum Declaration on the Commonwealth in the 21st Century: Continuity and Renewal, which reiterated commitment to the organization's principles and values. Leaders at the meeting condemned all forms of terrorism and endorsed a Plan of Action for combating international terrorism, establishing a Commonwealth Committee on Terrorism, convened at ministerial level, to oversee the implementation of the Plan. The leaders welcomed the Millennium Development Goals (MDGs) adopted by the UN General Assembly; requested the Secretary-General to constitute an expert group on implementing the objectives of the Fancourt Commonwealth Declaration on Globalization and People-Centred Development (see Economic Co-operation, below); pledged continued support for small states; and urged renewed efforts to combat the spread of HIV/AIDS. They also endorsed a Commonwealth Local Government Good Practice Scheme, to be managed by the Commonwealth Local Government Forum (established in 1995). The heads of government adopted a report on the future of the Commonwealth drafted by the High Level Review Group. The document recommended strengthening the Commonwealth's role in conflict prevention and resolution and support of democratic practices; enhancing the 'good offices' role of the Secretary-General; better promoting member states' economic and development needs; strengthening the organization's role in facilitating member states' access to international assistance; and promoting increased access to modern information and communications technologies.

In concluding the 2003 meeting heads of government issued the Aso Rock Commonwealth Declaration, which emphasized their commitment to strengthening development and democracy, and incorporated clear objectives in support of these goals. Priority areas identified included efforts to eradicate poverty and attain the MDGs, to strengthen democratic institutions, empower women, promote the involvement of civil society, combat corruption and recover assets (for which a working group was to be established), facilitate finance for development, address the spread of HIV/AIDS and other diseases, combat illicit trafficking in human beings, and promote education. The leaders also adopted a separate statement on multilateral trade, in particular in support of the stalled Doha Round of World Trade Organization (WTO) negotiations.

The 2007 meeting of Commonwealth heads of government, convened in Kampala, Uganda, in November, issued the Munyonyo Statement on Respect and Understanding, which commended the work of the Commonwealth Commission on Respect and Understanding (established in 2005) and endorsed its recently published report entitled *Civil Paths to Peace* aimed at building tolerance and understanding of diversity.

In November 2009 Commonwealth heads of government, meeting in Trinidad and Tobago, welcomed recent progress in the discussion of border disputes between Belize and Guatemala, and between Guyana and Venezuela. They expressed support for negotiations on the reunification of Cyprus, initiated in 2008, and welcomed the recent agreement on power-sharing in Zimbabwe. They urged the renewal of commitment to the non-proliferation of nuclear weapons at the next Non-Proliferation Treaty review conference (convened in May 2010), and the negotiation of a comprehensive Arms Trade Treaty (on conventional weapons) at a conference to be held in 2012. Heads of government also urged the conclusion of a UN treaty on international terrorism and discussed combating piracy and human trafficking. In July 2010, in view of a decision of the 2009 heads of government meeting, a new Commonwealth Eminent Persons Group (EPG) was inaugurated, with a mandate to make recommendations on means of strengthening the organization. During June 2010 the Commonwealth Secretariat hosted the first Small States Biennial Conference.

The summit of heads of Government held in Perth, Australia, in October 2011, issued the Perth Declaration on Food Security Principles, reaffirming the universal right to safe, sufficient and nutritious food. The summit agreed that a Charter of the Commonwealth, proposed by the EPG, should be drafted, embodying the principles contained in previous declarations; and that the appointment of a Commonwealth Commissioner for Democracy, Rule of Law and Human Rights, also recommended by the EPG, should be considered.

Political Affairs Division: assists consultation among member governments on international and Commonwealth matters of common interest. In association with host governments, it organizes the meetings of heads of government and senior officials. The Division services committees and special groups set up by heads of government dealing with political matters. The Secretariat has observer status at the United Nations, and the Division manages a joint office in New York to enable small states, which would otherwise be unable to afford facilities there, to maintain a presence at the United Nations. The Division monitors political developments in the Commonwealth and international progress in such matters as disarmament and the Law of the Sea. It also undertakes research on matters of common interest to member governments, and reports back to them. The Division is involved in diplomatic training and consular co-operation.

In 1990 Commonwealth heads of government mandated the Division to support the promotion of democracy by monitoring the preparations for and conduct of parliamentary, presidential or other elections in member countries at the request of national governments. In May 2010 a new Commonwealth Network of National Election Management Bodies was inaugurated; the Network aimed to enhance collaboration among institutions, thereby boosting standards. Commonwealth observer groups were dispatched to observe legislative and presidential elections in Uganda in February 2011; legislative and presidential elections in Nigeria in April; presidential elections in Seychelles in May, and legislative elections in Guyana in November of that year.

Under the reorganization of the Secretariat in 2002 a Good Offices Section was established within the Division to strengthen and support the activities of the Secretary-General in addressing political conflict in member states and in assisting countries to adhere to the principles of the Harare Declaration. The Secretary-General's good offices may involve discreet 'behind the scenes' diplomacy to prevent or resolve conflict and assist other international efforts to promote political stability.

Human Rights Unit: undertakes activities in support of the Commonwealth's commitment to the promotion and protection of fundamental human rights. It develops programmes, publishes human rights materials, co-operates with other organizations working in the field of human rights, in particular within the UN system, advises the Secretary-General, and organizes seminars and meetings of experts. It also provides training for police forces, magistrates and government officials in awareness of human rights. The Unit aims to integrate human rights standards within all divisions of the Secretariat.

Legal and Constitutional Affairs Division: promotes and facilitates co-operation and the exchange of information among member governments on legal matters and assists in combating financial and organized crime, in particular transborder criminal activities. It administers, jointly with the Commonwealth of Learning (see below), a distance training programme for legislative draftsmen and assists governments to reform national laws to meet the obligations of international conventions. The Division organizes the triennial meeting of ministers, Attorneys General and senior ministry officials concerned with the legal systems in Commonwealth countries. It has also initiated four Commonwealth schemes for co-operation on extradition, the protection of material cultural heritage, mutual assistance in criminal matters and the transfer of convicted offenders within the Commonwealth. It liaises with the Commonwealth Magistrates' and Judges' Association, the Commonwealth Legal Education Association, the Commonwealth Lawyers' Association (with which it helps to prepare the triennial Commonwealth Law Conference for the practising profession), the Commonwealth Association of Legislative Counsel, and with other international non-governmental organizations. The Division provides in-house legal advice for the Secretariat. The Commonwealth Law Bulletin, published four times a year, reports on legal developments in and beyond the Commonwealth. The Commonwealth Human Rights Law Digest (three a year) contains details of decisions relating to human rights cases from across the Commonwealth.

ECONOMIC AND ENVIRONMENTAL CO-OPERATION

In May 1998 the Commonwealth Secretary-General appealed to the Group of Eight industrialized nations (G8) to accelerate and expand the initiative to ease the debt burden of the most heavily indebted poor countries (HIPCs—see World Bank and the IMF). In October Commonwealth finance ministers reiterated their appeal to international financial institutions to accelerate the HIPC initiative. The meeting also issued a Commonwealth Statement on the global economic crisis and endorsed proposals to help to counter the difficulties experienced by several countries. These measures included a mechanism to enable countries to suspend payments on all short-term financial obligations at a time of emergency without defaulting, assistance to governments to attract private capital and to manage capital market volatility, and the development of international codes of conduct regarding financial and monetary policies and corporate governance. In March 1999 the Commonwealth Secretariat hosted a joint IMF-World Bank conference to review the HIPC scheme and initiate a process of reform. In November Commonwealth heads of government, meeting in South Africa, declared their support for measures undertaken by the World Bank and IMF to enhance the HIPC initiative. At the end of an informal retreat the leaders adopted the Fancourt Commonwealth Declaration on Globalization and People-Centred Development, which emphasized the need for a more equitable spread of wealth generated by the process of globalization, and expressed a renewed commitment to the elimination of all forms of discrimination, the promotion of people-centred development and capacity building, and efforts to ensure that developing countries benefit from future multilateral trade liberalization measures. In June 2002 the Commonwealth Secretary-General urged more generous funding of the HIPC initiative. Meetings of ministers of finance from Commonwealth member countries participating in the HIPC initiative are convened twice a year, as the Commonwealth Ministerial Debt Sustainability Forum. The Secretariat aims to assist HIPCs and other small economies through its Debt Recording and Management System (DRMS), which was first used in 1985 and updated in 2002; in July 2010 Liberia became the 60th country to join the System. In July 2005 the Commonwealth Secretary-General welcomed an initiative of the G8 to eliminate the debt of those HIPCs that had reached their completion point in the process, in addition to a commitment substantially to increase aid to Africa.

In February 1998 the Commonwealth Secretariat hosted a meeting of intergovernmental organizations to promote co-operation between small island states and the formulation of a unified policy approach to international fora. A second meeting was convened in March 2001, where discussions focused on the forthcoming WTO ministerial meeting and OECD's Harmful Tax Competition Initiative. In September 2000 Commonwealth ministers of finance, meeting in Malta, reviewed the OECD initiative and agreed that the measures, affecting many member countries with offshore financial centres, should not be imposed on governments. The ministers mandated the involvement of the Commonwealth Secretariat in efforts to resolve the dispute; a joint working group was subsequently established by the Secretariat with the OECD. In April 2002 a meeting on international co-operation in the financial services sector, attended by representatives of international and regional organizations, donors and senior officials from Commonwealth countries, was held under Commonwealth auspices in Saint Lucia. In September 2005 Commonwealth finance ministers, meeting in Barbados, considered new guidelines for Public Financial Management Reform.

In November 2005 Commonwealth heads of government issued the Malta Declaration on Networking the Commonwealth for Development, expressing their commitment to making available to all the benefits of new technologies and to using information technology networks to enhance the effectiveness of the Commonwealth in supporting development. The meeting endorsed a new Commonwealth Action Programme for the Digital Divide and approved the establishment of a special fund to enable implementation of the programme's objectives. Accordingly a Commonwealth Connects programme was established in August 2006 to develop partnerships and help to strengthen the use of and access to information technology in all Commonwealth countries; a Commonwealth Connects web portal—www.commonwealthconnects.org—was launched at the October 2011 heads of government summit. The 2005 Heads of Government Meeting also issued the Valletta Statement on Multilateral Trade, emphasizing their concerns that the Doha Round of WTO negotiations proceed steadily, on a development-oriented agenda, to a successful conclusion and reiterating their objectives of achieving a rules-based and equitable international trading system. A separate statement drew attention to the specific needs and challenges of small states and urged continued financial and technical support, in particular for those affected by natural disasters.

The Commonwealth Climate Change Action Plan, adopted by heads of government in November 2007, acknowledged that climate change posed a serious threat to the very existence of some small island states within the Commonwealth, and to the low-lying coastal areas of others. It offered unqualified support for the UN Framework Convention on Climate Change, and recognized the need to overcome technical, economic and policy-making barriers to reducing carbon emissions, to using renewable energy, and to increasing energy efficiency. The Plan undertook to assist developing member states in international negotiations on climate change; to support improved land use management, including the use of forest resources; to investigate the carbon footprint of agricultural exports from member countries; to increase support for the management of natural disasters in member countries; and to provide technical assistance to help least developed members and small states to assess the implications of climate change and adapt accordingly. A high-level meeting on climate finance, convened in London, in January 2011, determined to establish a working group to advance climate-related Commonwealth initiatives; and to integrate work on climate-related finance mechanisms into the next (2012–16) strategic plan.

In June 2008 the Commonwealth issued the Marlborough House Statement on Reform of International Institutions, declaring that ongoing global financial turbulence and soaring food and fuel prices highlighted the poor responsiveness of some international organizations mandated to promote economic stability, and determining to identify underlying principles and actions required to reform the international system. In November 2009 heads of government reiterated the need for reform in the UN system, demanding greater representation for developing countries in international economic decision-making, with particular reference to the IMF and the World Bank. They expressed concern that many Commonwealth countries were falling behind the MDG targets, and resolved to strengthen existing networks of co-operation: in particular, they undertook to take measures to improve the quality of data used in policy-making, and to strengthen the links between research and policy-making. A new Commonwealth Partnership Platform Portal was to provide practical support for sharing ideas and best practices. Heads of government also undertook to promote investment in science, technology and innovation.

Economic Affairs Division: organizes and services the annual meetings of Commonwealth ministers of finance and the ministerial group on small states and assists in servicing the biennial meetings of heads of government and periodic meetings of environment ministers. It engages in research and analysis on economic issues of interest to member governments and organizes seminars and conferences of government officials and experts. The Division actively supports developing Commonwealth countries to participate in the Doha Round of multilateral trade negotiations and is assisting the ACP group of countries to negotiate economic partnership agreements with the European Union. It continues to help developing countries to strengthen their links with international capital markets and foreign investors. The Division also services groups of experts on economic affairs that have been commissioned by governments to report on, among other things, protectionism; obstacles to the North-South negotiating process; reform of the international financial and trading system; the debt crisis; management of technological change; the impact of change on the development process; environmental issues; women and structural adjustment; and youth unemployment. A separate section within the Division addresses the specific needs of small states and provides technical assistance. The work of the section covers a range of issues including trade, vulnerability, environment, politics and economics. In 2000 a Commonwealth Secretariat/World Bank Joint Task Force on Small States finalized a report entitled *Small States: Meeting Challenges in the Global Economy*. A review of the report was issued in 2005. In June 2010 the first Commonwealth Biennial Small States Conference was convened, in London, comprising representatives of small states from the Africa, Asia-Pacific and Caribbean regions. In January 2011 a new Commonwealth Small States Office was inaugurated in Geneva, Switzerland; the Office was to provide subsidized office space for the Geneva-based diplomatic missions of Commonwealth small states, and business facilities for both diplomatic personnel and visiting delegations from small member states. The Economic Affairs Division also co-ordinates the Secretariat's environmental work and manages the Iwokrama International Centre for Rainforest Conservation and Development.

The Division supported the establishment of a Commonwealth Private Investment Initiative (CPII) to mobilize capital, on a regional basis, for investment in newly privatized companies and in small and medium-sized businesses in the private sector. The first regional fund under the CPII, the Commonwealth Africa Investment Fund (Comafin), was operational during the period July 1996–end-December 2006, and made 19 investments (of which three were subsequently written off) to assist businesses across nine sectors in seven countries in sub-Saharan Africa. A Pan-Commonwealth Africa Partners Fund was launched in 2002, which aimed to help existing businesses expand to become regional or pan-African in scope. In 1997 an investment fund for the Pacific Islands (known as the Kula Fund) was launched; a successor fund (Kula Fund II), with financing of some $20m., was launched in October 2005, with the aim of injecting capital into the smaller Pacific Island countries. A $200m. South Asia Regional Fund (SARF) was established in October 1997. In 1998 the Tiona Fund for the Commonwealth Caribbean was inaugurated, at a meeting of Commonwealth finance ministers; this was subsequently absorbed into the Caribbean Investment Fund (established in 1993 by member states of the Caribbean Community and Common Market—CARICOM).

SOCIAL WELFARE

Social Transformation Programmes Division: consists of three sections concerned with education, gender and health.

The **Education Section** arranges specialist seminars, workshops and co-operative projects, and commissions studies in areas identified by ministers of education, whose meetings it also services. Its areas of work include improving the quality of and access to basic education; strengthening science, technology and mathematics education in formal and non-formal areas of education; improving the quality of management in institutions of higher learning and basic education; improving the performance of teachers; strengthening examination assessment systems; and promoting the movement of students between Commonwealth countries. The Section also promotes the elimination of gender disparities in education, support for education in difficult circumstances, such as areas affected by conflict or natural disasters, and mitigating the impact of HIV and AIDS on education. It attempts to address the problems of scale particular to smaller member countries, and encourages collaboration between governments, the private sector and other non-governmental organizations.

The **Gender Affairs Section** is responsible for the implementation of the Commonwealth Plan of Action for Gender Equality, covering the period 2005–15, which succeeded the Commonwealth Plan of Action on Gender and Development (adopted in 1995 and updated in 2000). The Plan of Action supports efforts towards achieving the MDGs, and the objectives of gender equality adopted by the 1995 Beijing Declaration and Platform for Action and the follow-up Beijing + 5 review conference, held in 2000, and Beijing + 10 in 2005. Gender equality, poverty eradication, promotion of human rights, and strengthening democracy are recognized as intrinsically inter-related, and the Plan has a particular focus on the advancement of gender mainstreaming in the following areas: democracy, peace and conflict; human rights and law; poverty eradication and economic empowerment; and HIV/AIDS.

The **Health Section** organizes ministerial, technical and expert group meetings and workshops, to promote co-operation on health matters, and the exchange of health information and expertise. The Section commissions relevant studies and provides professional and technical advice to member countries and to the Secretariat. It also supports the work of regional health organizations and promotes health for all people in Commonwealth countries.

The **Youth Affairs Division**, reporting directly to a Deputy Secretary-General, was established within the Secretariat in 2002, acquiring divisional status in 2004.

The Division administers the Commonwealth Youth Programme (CYP), which was initiated in 1973 to promote the involvement of young people in the economic and social development of their countries. The CYP, funded through separate voluntary contributions from governments, was awarded a budget of £2.8m. for 2009/10. The Programme's activities are in three areas: Youth Enterprise and Sustainable Livelihoods; Governance, Development and Youth Networks; and Youth Work Education and Training. Regional centres are located in Zambia (for Africa), India (for Asia), Guyana (for the Caribbean), and Solomon Islands (for the Pacific). The Programme administers a Youth Study Fellowship scheme, a Youth Project Fund, a Youth Exchange Programme (in the Caribbean), and a Youth Development Awards Scheme. It also holds conferences and seminars, carries out research and disseminates information. The CYP Diploma in Youth Development Work is offered by partner institutions in 45 countries, primarily through distance education. The Commonwealth Youth Credit Initiative, initiated in 1995, provides funds and advice for young entrepreneurs setting up small businesses. A Plan of Action for Youth Empowerment, covering the period 2007–15, was approved by the sixth meeting of Commonwealth ministers responsible for youth affairs, held in Nassau, Bahamas, in May 2006. The first Commonwealth Youth Games was held in Edinburgh, United Kingdom in 2000, and has been convened every four years since. The eighth Commonwealth Youth Forum was convened in Freemantle, Australia, in October 2011.

TECHNICAL ASSISTANCE

Commonwealth Fund for Technical Co-operation (CFTC): f. 1971 to facilitate the exchange of skills between member countries and to promote economic and social development; it is administered by the Commonwealth Secretariat and financed by voluntary subscriptions from member governments. The CFTC responds to requests from member governments for technical assistance, such as the provision of experts for short- or medium-term projects, advice on economic or legal matters, and training programmes. Public sector development, allowing member states to build on their capacities, is the principal element in CFTC activities. This includes assistance for improvement of supervision and combating corruption; improving economic management, for example by advising on exports and investment promotion; strengthening democratic institutions, such as electoral commissions; and improvement of education and health policies. The CFTC also administers the Langkawi awards for the study of environmental issues, which is funded by the Canadian Government; the CFTC budget for 2009/10 amounted to £29.2m, supplemented by external resources through partnerships.

CFTC activities are mainly implemented by the following divisions:

Governance and Institutional Development Division: strengthens good governance in member countries, through advice, training and other expertise in order to build capacity in national public institutions. The Division administers the Commonwealth Service Abroad Programme (CSAP), which is funded by the CFTC. The Programme extends short-term technical assistance through highly qualified volunteers. The main objectives of the scheme are to provide expertise, training and exposure to new technologies and practices, to promote technology transfers and sharing of experiences and knowledge, and to support community workshops and other local activities.

Special Advisory Services Division: provides advice and technical assistance in four principal areas: debt management; economic and legal services; enterprise and agriculture; and trade.

Finance

The Secretariat's budget for 2009/10 amounted to £15.0m. Member governments meet the cost of the Secretariat through subscriptions on a scale related to income and population.

Publications

Advisory (annual newsletter of the Special Advisory Services Division).

Global (electronic magazine).

Commonwealth News (weekly e-mail newsletter).

Report of the Commonwealth Secretary-General (every 2 years).

Numerous reports, studies and papers (catalogue available).

Commonwealth Organizations

(in the United Kingdom, unless otherwise stated)

The two principal intergovernmental organizations established by Commonwealth member states, apart from the Commonwealth Secretariat itself, are the Commonwealth Foundation and the Commonwealth of Learning. In 2012 there were nearly 90 other professional or advocacy organizations bearing the Commonwealth's name and associated with or accredited to the Commonwealth, a selection of which are listed below.

PRINCIPAL INTERGOVERNMENTAL ORGANIZATIONS

Commonwealth Foundation: Marlborough House, Pall Mall, London, SW1Y 5HY; tel. (20) 7930-3783; fax (20) 7839-8157; e-mail geninfo@commonwealth.int; internet www.commonwealthfoundation.com; f. 1966; intergovernmental body promoting people-to-people interaction, and collaboration within the non-governmental sector of the Commonwealth; supports non-governmental organizations, professional associations and Commonwealth arts and culture; awards an annual Commonwealth Writers' Prize; funds are provided by Commonwealth govts; Chair. SIMONE DE COMARMOND (Seychelles); Dir Dr MARK COLLINS (United Kingdom); publ. *Commonwealth People* (quarterly).

Commonwealth of Learning (COL): 1055 West Hastings St, Suite 1200, Vancouver, BC V6E 2E9, Canada; tel. (604) 775-8200; fax (604) 775-8210; e-mail info@col.org; internet www.col.org; f. 1987 by Commonwealth Heads of Government to promote the devt and sharing of distance education and open learning resources, including materials, expertise and technologies, throughout the Commonwealth and in other countries; implements and assists with national and regional educational programmes; acts as consultant to international agencies and national governments; conducts seminars and studies on specific educational needs; core financing for COL is provided by Commonwealth governments on a voluntary basis; COL has an annual budget of approx. C $12m; Pres. and CEO Prof. ASHA KANWAR (India); publs *Connections*.

The following represents a selection of other Commonwealth organizations:

ADMINISTRATION AND PLANNING

Commonwealth Association for Public Administration and Management (CAPAM): 1075 Bay St, Suite 402, Toronto, ON M5S 2B1, Canada; tel. (416) 920-3337; fax (416) 920-6574; e-mail capam@capam.org; internet www.capam.org; f. 1994; aims to promote sound management of the public sector in Commonwealth countries and to assist those countries undergoing political or financial reforms; an international awards programme to reward innovation within the public sector was introduced in 1997, and is awarded every 2 years; more than 1,200 individual mems and 80 institutional memberships in some 80 countries; Pres. Geraldine Fraser-Moleketi (South Africa); Exec. Dir and CEO David Waung.

Commonwealth Association of Planners: c/o Royal Town Planning Institute in Scotland, 18 Atholl Crescent, Edinburgh, EH3 8HQ; tel. (131) 229-9628; fax (131) 229-9332; e-mail annette.odonnell@rtpi.org.uk; internet www.commonwealth-planners.org; aims to develop urban and regional planning in Commonwealth countries, to meet the challenges of urbanization and the sustainable development of human settlements.

Commonwealth Local Government Forum: 16A Northumberland Ave, London, WC2N 5AP; tel. (20) 7389-1490; fax (20) 7389-1499; e-mail info@clgf.org.uk; works to promote democratic local government in Commonwealth countries, and to encourage good practice through conferences, programmes, research and the provision of information; regional offices in Fiji, India and South Africa.

AGRICULTURE AND FORESTRY

Commonwealth Forestry Association: Crib, Dinchope, Craven Arms, Shropshire, SY7 9JJ; tel. (1588) 672868; fax (870) 0116645; e-mail cfa@cfa-international.org; internet www.cfa-international.org; f. 1921; produces, collects and circulates information relating to world forestry and promotes good management, use and conservation of forests and forest lands throughout the world; mems: 1,200; Pres. David Bills (Australia/UK); publs *International Forestry Review* (quarterly), *Commonwealth Forestry News* (quarterly), *Commonwealth Forestry Handbook* (irregular).

Royal Agricultural Society of the Commonwealth: Ingliston House, Royal Highland Centre, Edinburgh, EH28 8NB; tel. (131) 335-6200; fax (131) 335 6229; e-mail rasc@commagshow.org; internet www.commagshow.org; f. 1957 to promote development of agricultural shows and good farming practice, in order to improve incomes and food production in Commonwealth countries.

Standing Committee on Commonwealth Forestry: Forestry Commission, 231 Corstorphine Rd, Edinburgh, EH12 7AT; tel. (131) 314-6405; fax (131) 316-4344; e-mail jonathan.taylor@forestry.gsi.gov.uk; internet www.cfc2010.org; f. 1923 to provide continuity between Confs, and to provide a forum for discussion on any forestry matters of common interest to mem. govts which may be brought to the Cttee's notice by any mem. country or organization; 54 mems; June 2010 Conference: Edinburgh, United Kingdom; Sec. Jonathan Taylor.

BUSINESS

Commonwealth Business Council: 18 Pall Mall, London, SW1Y 5LU; tel. (20) 7024-8200; fax (20) 7024-8201; e-mail info@cbcglobal.org; internet www.cbcglobal.org; f. 1997 by the Commonwealth Heads of Government Meeting to promote co-operation between governments and the private sector in support of trade, investment and development; the Council aims to identify and promote investment opportunities, in particular in Commonwealth developing countries, to support countries and local businesses to work within the context of globalization, to promote capacity building and the exchange of skills and knowledge (in particular through its Information Communication Technologies for Development programme), and to encourage co-operation among Commonwealth members; promotes good governance; supports the process of multilateral trade negotiations and other liberalization of trade and services; represents the private sector at government level; Dir-Gen. and CEO Dr Mohan Kaul.

COMMONWEALTH STUDIES

Institute of Commonwealth Studies: South Block, 2nd Floor, Senate House, Malet Street, London, WC1E 7HU; tel. (20) 7862-8844; fax (20) 7862-8813; e-mail ics@sas.ac.uk; internet commonwealth.sas.ac.uk/; f. 1949 to promote advanced study of the Commonwealth; provides a library and meeting place for postgraduate students and academic staff engaged in research in this field; offers postgraduate teaching; Dir Prof. Philip Murphy; publs *Annual Report*, *Collected Seminar Papers*, *Newsletter*, *Theses in Progress in Commonwealth Studies*.

EDUCATION AND CULTURE

Association of Commonwealth Universities (ACU): Woburn House, 20-24 Tavistock Sq., London, WC1H 9HF; tel. (20) 7380-6700; fax (20) 7387-2655; e-mail info@acu.ac.uk; internet www.acu.ac.uk; f. 1913; promotes international co-operation and understanding; provides assistance with staff and student mobility and development programmes; researches and disseminates information about universities and relevant policy issues; organizes major meetings of Commonwealth universities and their representatives; acts as a liaison office and information centre; administers scholarship and fellowship schemes; operates a policy research unit; mems: c. 500 universities in 36 Commonwealth countries or regions; Sec.-Gen. Prof. John Tarrant; publs include *Yearly Review*, *Commonwealth Universities Yearbook*, *ACU Bulletin* (quarterly), *Who's Who of Executive Heads: Vice-Chancellors, Presidents, Principals and Rectors*, *International Awards*, student information papers (study abroad series).

Commonwealth Association of Museums: R.R.1, De Winton, Alberta, T0L 0X0, Canada; tel. and fax (403) 938-3190; e-mail rvinel@fclc.com; internet www.maltwood.uvic.ca/cam; f. 1985; professional asscn working for the improvement of museums throughout the Commonwealth; encourages links between museums and assists professional development and training through distance learning, workshops and seminars; general assembly held every three or four years; c. 700 mems in 32 Commonwealth countries; Pres. Prof. Lois Irvine.

Commonwealth Association of Science, Technology and Mathematics Educators (CASTME): c/o Dr Egan, Faculty of Education, University of Winchester, SO22 4NR; e-mail Bridget.Egan@winchester.ac.uk; internet www.castme.org; f. 1974; special emphasis is given to the social significance of education in these subjects; organizes an Awards Scheme to promote effective teaching and learning in these subjects, and biennial regional seminars; Chair. Bridget Egan; publ. *CASTME Journal* (3 a year).

Commonwealth Council for Educational Administration and Management: Suite 161, Private Bag X9, Melville 2109, Johannesburg, South Africa; tel. (18) 302200; fax (866) 312639; e-mail zandileK@mgsl.co.za; internet www.cceam.org; f. 1970; aims to foster quality in professional development and links among educational administrators; holds nat. and regional confs, as well as visits and seminars; mems: 24 affiliated groups representing 3,000 persons; Pres. Zandile Kunene; publ. *International Studies in Educational Administration* (2 a year).

Commonwealth Education Trust: New Zealand House, 80 Haymarket, London, SW1Y 4TQ; tel. (20) 7024-9822; fax (20) 7024-9833; e-mail info@cet1886.org; internet www.cet1886.org; f. 2007 as the successor trust to the Commonwealth Institute; funds the Centre of Commonwealth Education, established in 2004 as part of Cambridge University; supports the Lifestyle of Our Kids (LOOK) project initiated in 2005 by the Commonwealth Institute (Australia); Chief Exec. Judy Curry.

League for the Exchange of Commonwealth Teachers: 7 Lion Yard, Tremadoc Rd, London, SW4 7NQ; tel. (870) 7702636; fax (870) 7702637; e-mail info@lect.org.uk; internet www.lect.org.uk; f. 1901; promotes educational exchanges between teachers throughout the Commonwealth; Dir Anna Tomlinson; publ. *Annual Review*.

HEALTH AND WELFARE

Commonwealth Medical Trust (COMMAT): BMA House, Tavistock Sq., London, WC1H 9JP; tel. (20) 7272-8492; fax (1689) 890609; e-mail office@commat.org; internet www.commat.org; f. 1962 (as the Commonwealth Medical Association) for the exchange of information; provision of tech. co-operation and advice; formulation and maintenance of a code of ethics; promotes the Right to Health; liaison with WHO and other UN agencies on health issues; meetings of its Council are held every three years; mems: medical asscns in Commonwealth countries; Dir Marianne Haslegrave.

Commonwealth Nurses' Federation: c/o Royal College of Nursing, 20 Cavendish Sq., London, W1G 0RN; tel. (20) 7647-3593; fax (20) 7647-3413; e-mail jill@commonwealthnurses.org; internet www.commonwealthnurses.org; f. 1973 to link national nursing and midwifery asscns in Commonwealth countries; aims to influence health policy, develop nursing networks, improve nursing education and standards, and strengthen leadership; Exec. Sec. Jill Iliffe.

Commonwealth Organization for Social Work: Melbourne, Australia; tel. (3) 9489-3774; e-mail cosw@aasw.asn.au; internet www.sasw.org.sg/cosw; promotes communication and collaboration between social workers in Commonwealth countries; provides network for information and sharing of expertise.

Commonwealth Pharmacists Association: 1 Lambeth High St, London, SE1 7JN; tel. (20) 7572-2364; fax (20) 7572-2508; e-mail admin@commonwealthpharmacy.org; internet www.commonwealthpharmacy.org; f. 1970 (as the Commonwealth

Pharmaceutical Association) to promote the interests of pharmaceutical sciences and the profession of pharmacy in the Commonwealth; to maintain high professional standards, encourage links between members and the creation of nat. asscns; and to facilitate the dissemination of information; holds confs (every four years) and regional meetings; mems: pharmaceutical asscns from over 40 Commonwealth countries; Pres. IVAN KOTZÉ; publ. *Quarterly Newsletter*.

Commonwealth Society for the Deaf (Sound Seekers): 34 Buckingham Palace Rd, London, SW1W 0RE; tel. (20) 7233-5700; fax (20) 7233-5800; e-mail sound.seekers@btinternet.com; internet www.sound-seekers.org.uk; f. 1959; undertakes initiatives to establish audiology services in developing Commonwealth countries, including mobile clinics to provide outreach services; aims to educate local communities in aural hygiene and the prevention of ear infection and deafness; provides audiological equipment and organizes the training of audiological maintenance technicians; conducts research into the causes and prevention of deafness; Chief Exec. GARY WILLIAMS; publ. *Annual Report*.

Royal Commonwealth Ex-Services League: Haig House, 199 Borough High St, London, SE1 1AA; tel. (20) 3207-2413; fax (20) 3207-2115; e-mail mgordon-roe@commonwealthveterans.org.uk; internet www.commonwealthveterans.org.uk; links the ex-service orgs in the Commonwealth, assists ex-servicemen of the Crown who are resident abroad; holds conferences every 4 years; 56 mem. orgs in 48 countries; Grand Pres. HRH The Duke of EDINBURGH; publ. *Annual Report*.

Sightsavers (Royal Commonwealth Society for the Blind): Grosvenor Hall, Bolnore Rd, Haywards Heath, West Sussex, RH16 4BX; tel. (1444) 446600; fax (1444) 446688; e-mail info@sightsavers.org; internet www.sightsavers.org; f. 1950 to prevent blindness and restore sight in developing countries, and to provide education and community-based training for incurably blind people; operates in collaboration with local partners in some 30 developing countries, with high priority given to training local staff; Chair. Lord NIGEL CRISP; Chief Exec. Dr CAROLINE HARPER; publ. *Sight Savers News*.

INFORMATION AND THE MEDIA

Commonwealth Broadcasting Association: 17 Fleet St, London, EC4Y 1AA; tel. (20) 7583-5550; fax (20) 7583-5549; e-mail cba@cba.org.uk; internet www.cba.org.uk; f. 1945; gen. confs are held every two years (2010: Johannesburg, South Africa); mems: c. 100 in more than 50 countries; Pres. ABUBAKAR JIJIWA; Sec.-Gen. ELIZABETH SMITH; publs *Commonwealth Broadcaster* (quarterly), *Commonwealth Broadcaster Directory* (annually).

Commonwealth Journalists Association: c/o Canadian Newspaper Association, 890 Yonge St, Suite 200, Toronto, ON M4W 3P4, Canada; tel. (416) 575-5377; fax (416) 923-7206; e-mail cantleyb@commonwealthjournalists.com; internet www.commonwealthjournalists.com; f. 1978 to promote co-operation between journalists in Commonwealth countries, organize training facilities and confs, and foster understanding among Commonwealth peoples; Exec. Dir BRYAN CANTLEY; publ. *Newsletter* (3 a year).

CPU Media Trust (Association of Commonwealth Newspapers, News Agencies and Periodicals): e-mail webform@cpu.org.uk; internet www.cpu.org.uk; f. 2008 as a 'virtual' organization charged with carrying on the aims of the Commonwealth the Commonwealth Press Union (CPU, f. 1950, terminated 2008); promotes the welfare of the Commonwealth press; Chair. GUY BLACK.

LAW

Commonwealth Lawyers' Association: c/o Institute of Advanced Legal Studies, 17 Russell Sq., London, WC1B 5DR; tel. (20) 7862-8824; fax (20) 7862-8816; e-mail cla@sas.ac.uk; internet www.commonwealthlawyers.com; f. 1983 (fmrly the Commonwealth Legal Bureau); seeks to maintain and promote the rule of law throughout the Commonwealth, by ensuring that the people of the Commonwealth are served by an independent and efficient legal profession; upholds professional standards and promotes the availability of legal services; organizes the biannual Commonwealth Law Conference; Sec.-Gen. CLAIRE MARTIN; publs *The Commonwealth Lawyer*, *Clarion*.

Commonwealth Legal Advisory Service: c/o British Institute of International and Comparative Law, Charles Clore House, 17 Russell Sq., London, WC1B 5DR; tel. (20) 7862-5151; fax (20) 7862-5152; e-mail info@biicl.org; internet www.biicl.org; f. 1962; financed by the British Institute and by contributions from Commonwealth govts; provides research facilities for Commonwealth govts and law reform commissions; Chair. Rt Hon. Lord BROWNE-WILKINSON; publ. *New Memoranda* series.

Commonwealth Legal Education Association: c/o Legal and Constitutional Affairs Division, Commonwealth Secretariat, Marlborough House, Pall Mall, London, SW1Y 5HX; tel. (20) 7747-6415; fax (20) 7004-3649; e-mail clea@commonwealth.int; internet www.clea-web.com; f. 1971 to promote contacts and exchanges and to provide information regarding legal education; Gen. Sec. SELINA GOULBOURNE; publ. *Commonwealth Legal Education Association Newsletter* (3 a year).

Commonwealth Magistrates' and Judges' Association: Uganda House, 58–59 Trafalgar Sq., London, WC2N 5DX; tel. (20) 7976-1007; fax (20) 7976-2394; e-mail info@cmja.org; internet www.cmja.org; f. 1970 to advance the administration of the law by promoting the independence of the judiciary, to further education in law and crime prevention and to disseminate information; confs and study tours; corporate membership for asscns of the judiciary or courts of limited jurisdiction; assoc. membership for individuals; Pres. Hon. Mrs Justice NORMA WADE-MILLER; Exec. Vice-Pres. Sir PHILIP BAILHACHE; publs *Commonwealth Judicial Journal* (2 a year), *CMJA News*.

PARLIAMENTARY AFFAIRS

Commonwealth Parliamentary Association: Westminster House, Suite 700, 7 Millbank, London, SW1P 3JA; tel. (20) 7799-1460; fax (20) 7222-6073; e-mail hq.sec@cpahq.org; internet www.cpahq.org; f. 1911 to promote understanding and co-operation between Commonwealth parliamentarians; organization: Exec. Cttee of 35 MPs responsible to annual Gen. Assembly; 176 brs in national, state, provincial and territorial parliaments and legislatures throughout the Commonwealth; holds annual Commonwealth Parliamentary Confs and seminars; also regional confs and seminars; Sec.-Gen. Dr WILLIAM F. SHIJA; publ. *The Parliamentarian* (quarterly).

SCIENCE AND TECHNOLOGY

Commonwealth Association of Architects: POB 508, Edgware, Middx, HA8 9XZ; tel. and fax (20) 8951-0550; e-mail info@comarchitect.org; internet comarchitect.org; f. 1964; an asscn of 38 socs of architects in various Commonwealth countries; objectives: to facilitate the reciprocal recognition of professional qualifications; to provide a clearing house for information on architectural practice; and to encourage collaboration. Plenary confs every three years; regional confs are also held; Exec. Dir TONY GODWIN; publs *Handbook, Objectives and Procedures: CAA Schools Visiting Boards, Architectural Education in the Commonwealth* (annotated bibliography of research), *CAA Newsnet* (2 a year), a survey and list of schools of architecture.

Commonwealth Engineers' Council: c/o Institution of Civil Engineers, 1 Great George St, London, SW1P 3AA; tel. (20) 7665-2005; fax (20) 7223-1806; e-mail neil.bailey@ice.org.uk; internet www.ice.org.uk/cec; f. 1946; links and represents engineering institutions across the Commonwealth, providing them with an opportunity to exchange views on collaboration and mutual support; holds international and regional conferences and workshops; mems: 45 institutions in 44 countries; Pres. TOM FOULKES; Sec.-Gen. NEIL BAILEY.

Commonwealth Telecommunications Organization: 26–28 Hammersmith Grove, London, W6 7BA; tel. (870) 7777697; fax (870) 0345626; e-mail info@cto.int; internet www.cto.int; f. 1967 as an international development partnership between Commonwealth and non-Commonwealth governments, business and civil society organizations; aims to help to bridge the digital divide and to achieve social and economic development by delivering to developing countries knowledge-sharing programmes in the use of information and communication technologies in the specific areas of telecommunications, IT, broadcasting and the internet; CEO Dr EKWOW SPIO-GARBRAH; publs *CTO Update* (quarterly), *Annual Report*, *Research Reports*.

Conference of Commonwealth Meteorologists: c/o International Branch, Meteorological Office, FitzRoy Rd, Exeter, EX1 3PB; tel. (1392) 885680; fax (1392) 885681; e-mail commonwealth@metoffice.gov.uk; internet internet www.commonwealthmet.org; links national meteorological and hydrological services in Commonwealth countries; conferences held every four years.

SPORT AND YOUTH

Commonwealth Games Federation: 2nd Floor, 138 Piccadilly, London, W1J 7NR; tel. (20) 7491-8801; fax (20) 7409-7803; e-mail info@thecgf.com; internet www.thecgf.com; the Games were first held in 1930 and are now held every four years; participation is limited to competitors representing the mem. countries of the Commonwealth; 2010 games: New Delhi, India, in October; 2014 games: Glasgow, United Kingdom; mems: 72 affiliated bodies; Pres. MICHAEL FENNELL; CEO MICHAEL HOOPER.

Commonwealth Youth Exchange Council: 7 Lion Yard, Tremadoc Rd, London, SW4 7NQ; tel. (20) 7498-6151; fax (20) 7622-4365; e-mail mail@cyec.org.uk; internet www.cyec.org.uk; f. 1970; promotes contact between groups of young people of the United Kingdom and other Commonwealth countries by means of educational exchange visits, provides information for organizers and allocates grants; provides host governments with technical assistance for delivery of the Commonwealth Youth Forum, held every two years (2009: Trinidad and Tobago); mems: 222 orgs, 134 local authorities, 88 voluntary bodies; Chief Exec. V. S. G. CRAGGS; publs *Contact* (handbook), *Exchange* (newsletter), *Final Communiqués* (of the Commonwealth Youth Forums), *Safety and Welfare* (guidelines for Commonwealth Youth Exchange groups).

RELATIONS WITHIN THE COMMONWEALTH

Commonwealth Countries League: 37 Priory Ave, Sudbury, Middx, HA0 2SB; tel. (20) 8248- 3275; e-mail rennie158@btinternet.com; internet www.ccl-int.org; f. 1925; aims to secure equality of liberties, status and opportunities between women and men and to promote friendship and mutual understanding throughout the Commonwealth; promotes women's political and social education and links together women's organizations in most countries of the Commonwealth; an education sponsorship scheme was established in 1967 to finance the secondary education of bright but needy girls in their own Commonwealth countries; the CCL Education Fund was sponsoring more than 300 girls throughout the Commonwealth (2012); Exec. Chair. MARJORIE RENNIE; publs *News Update* (3 a year), *Annual Report*.

Commonwealth War Graves Commission: 2 Marlow Rd, Maidenhead, Berks, SL6 7DX; tel. (1628) 634221; fax (1628) 771208; internet www.cwgc.org; casualty and cemetery enquiries; e-mail casualty.enq@cwgc.org; f. 1917 (as Imperial War Graves Commission); responsible for the commemoration in perpetuity of the 1.7m. members of the Commonwealth Forces who died during the wars of 1914–18 and 1939–45; provides for the marking and maintenance of war graves and memorials at some 23,000 locations in 150 countries; mems: Australia, Canada, India, New Zealand, South Africa, United Kingdom; Pres. HRH The Duke of KENT; Dir-Gen. ALAN PATEMAN-JONES.

Council of Commonwealth Societies: c/o Royal Commonwealth Society, 25 Northumberland Ave, London, WC2N 5AP; tel. (20) 7766-9200; fax (20) 7930-9705; e-mail ccs@rcsint.org; internet www.rcsint.org/day; f. 1947; provides a forum for the exchange of information regarding activities of mem. orgs which promote understanding among countries of the Commonwealth; co-ordinates the distribution of the Commonwealth Day message by Queen Elizabeth II, organizes the observance of and promotes Commonwealth Day, and produces educational materials relating to the occasion; seeks to raise the profile of the Commonwealth; mems: 30 official and unofficial Commonwealth orgs; Chair. Lord ALAN WATSON; Sec. ALICE KAWOWA.

Royal Commonwealth Society: 25 Northumberland Ave, London, WC2N 5AP; tel. (20) 7766-9200; fax (20) 7930-9705; e-mail info@thercs.org; internet www.thercs.org; f. 1868; to promote international understanding of the Commonwealth and its people; organizes meetings and seminars on topical issues, projects for young people, a youth leadership programme, and cultural and social events; Chair. Baroness PRASHAR; Dir Dr DANNY SRISKANDARAJAH; publs *RCS Exchange* (3 a year), conference reports.

Royal Over-Seas League: Over-Seas House, Park Place, St James's St, London, SW1A 1LR; tel. (20) 7408-0214; fax (20) 7499-6738; e-mail info@rosl.org.uk; internet www.rosl.org.uk; f. 1910 to promote friendship and understanding in the Commonwealth; clubhouses in London and Edinburgh; membership is open to all British subjects and Commonwealth citizens; Dir-Gen. ROBERT F. NEWELL; publ. *Overseas* (quarterly).

Victoria League for Commonwealth Friendship: 55 Leinster Sq., London, W2 4PW; tel. (20) 7243-2633; fax (20) 7229-2994; e-mail victorialeaguehq@btconnect.com; internet www.victorialeague.co.uk; f. 1901; aims to further personal friendship among Commonwealth peoples and to provide hospitality for visitors; maintains Student House, providing accommodation for students from Commonwealth countries; has brs elsewhere in the UK and abroad; Chair. LYN D. HOPKINS; Gen. Sec. JOHN M. W. ALLAN; publ. *Annual Report*.

THE COMMONWEALTH OF INDEPENDENT STATES—CIS

Address: 220000 Minsk, Kirava 17, Belarus.

Telephone: (17) 222-35-17; **fax:** (17) 227-23-39; **e-mail:** postmaster@www.cis.minsk.by; **internet:** www.cis.minsk.by.

The Commonwealth of Independent States (CIS) is a voluntary association of 11 states, established at the time of the collapse of the USSR in December 1991.

MEMBERS

Armenia	Moldova
Azerbaijan	Russia
Belarus	Tajikistan
Kazakhstan	Ukraine
Kyrgyzstan	Uzbekistan

Note: Azerbaijan formally became a member of the CIS in September 1993. Georgia was admitted to the CIS in December 1993. In August 2009 Georgia's membership was terminated. Ukraine ratified the foundation documents that established the CIS in 1991 but has not yet ratified the CIS Charter. Turkmenistan has associate membership, reduced from full membership in August 2005.

Organization

(April 2012)

COUNCIL OF HEADS OF STATE

This is the supreme body of the CIS, on which all the member states of the Commonwealth are represented at the level of head of state, for discussion of issues relating to the co-ordination of Commonwealth activities and the development of the Minsk Agreement. Decisions of the Council are taken by common consent, with each state having equal voting rights. The Council meets at least once a year. An extraordinary meeting may be convened on the initiative of the majority of Commonwealth heads of state. The chairmanship of the Council is normally rotated among member states.

COUNCIL OF HEADS OF GOVERNMENT

This Council convenes for meetings at least once every three months; an extraordinary sitting may be convened on the initiative of a majority of Commonwealth heads of government. The two Councils may discuss and take necessary decisions on important domestic and external issues, and may hold joint sittings.

Working and auxiliary bodies, composed of authorized representatives of the participating states, may be set up on a permanent or interim basis on the decision of the Council of Heads of State and the Council of Heads of Government.

EXECUTIVE COMMITTEE

The Executive Committee was established by the Council of Heads of State in April 1999 to supersede the previous Secretariat, the Interstate Economic Committee and other working bodies and committees, in order to improve the efficient functioning of the organization. The Executive Committee co-operates closely with other CIS bodies including the councils of foreign ministers and defence ministers; the Economic Council; Council of Border Troops Commanders; the Collective Security Council; the Secretariat of the Council of the Interparliamentary Assembly; and the Inter-state Committee for Statistics.

Executive Secretary and Chairman of the Executive Committee: SERGEI N. LEBEDEV (Russia).

Activities

On 8 December 1991 the heads of state of Belarus, Russia and Ukraine signed the Minsk Agreement, providing for the establishment of a Commonwealth of Independent States. Formal recognition of the dissolution of the USSR was incorporated in a second treaty (the Alma-Ata Declaration), signed by 11 heads of state in the then Kazakh capital, Alma-Ata (Almatı), later in that month.

In March 1992 a meeting of the CIS Council of Heads of Government decided to establish a commission to examine the resolution that 'all CIS member states are the legal successors of the rights and obligations of the former Soviet Union'. Documents relating to the legal succession of the Soviet Union were signed at a meeting of heads of state in July. In April an agreement establishing an Inter-parliamentary Assembly (IPA), signed by Armenia, Belarus, Kazakhstan, Kyrgyzstan, Russia, Tajikistan and Uzbekistan, was published. The first Assembly was held in Bishkek, Kyrgyzstan, in September, attended by delegates from all these countries, with the exception of Uzbekistan.

A CIS Charter was adopted at the meeting of the heads of state in Minsk, Belarus, in January 1993. The Charter, providing for a defence alliance, an inter-state court and an economic co-ordination committee, was to serve as a framework for closer co-operation and was signed by all of the members except for Turkmenistan and Ukraine; by 2012 Ukraine had still not signed the Charter.

In May 1994 the CIS and UNCTAD signed a co-operation accord. A similar agreement was concluded with the UN Economic Commission for Europe in June 1996. Working contacts have also been established with the ILO, UNHCR, WHO and the European Union (EU). In June 1998 the IPA approved a decision to sign the European Social Charter (see Council of Europe); a declaration of co-operation between the Assembly and the OSCE Parliamentary Assembly was also signed.

In April 1996 the Council of Heads of Government approved a long-term plan for the integrated development of the CIS, incorporating measures for further socio-economic, military and political co-operation. Meeting in April 1999 the Council of Heads of Government adopted guidelines for restructuring the CIS and for the future development of the organization. Economic co-operation was to be a priority area of activity, and in particular, the establishment of a free trade zone. In June 2000 the Councils of Heads of State and Government issued a declaration concerning the maintenance of strategic stability, approved a plan and schedule for pursuing economic integration, and adopted a short-term programme for combating international terrorism (perceived to be a significant threat in central Asia). An informal CIS 10-year 'jubilee' summit, convened in November 2001, adopted a statement identifying the collective pursuit of stable socio-economic development and integration on a global level as the organization's principal objectives. A summit of heads of state convened in January 2003 agreed that the position of Chairman of the Council of Heads of State (hitherto held by consecutive Russian presidents) should be rotated henceforth among member states. Leonid Kuchma, then President of Ukraine, was elected as the new Chairman. (In September 2004, however, Russia's then President Vladimir Putin was reappointed temporarily as the Chairman of the Council, owing to a perceived deterioration in the international security situation and a declared need for experienced leadership.) A summit meeting convened in September 2003, in Yalta, Ukraine, focused on measures to combat crime and terrorism, and endorsed an economic plan for 2003–10.

In September 2004 the CIS Council of Heads of State, meeting in Astana, Kazakhstan, was dominated by consideration of measures to combat terrorism and extremist violence, following a month in which Russia, including North Ossetia, had experienced several atrocities committed against civilian targets. As part of a wider consideration of a reorganization of the CIS, the Council resolved to establish a Security Council.

Member states of the CIS have formed alliances of various kinds among themselves, thereby potentially undermining the unity of the Commonwealth. In March 1996 Belarus, Kazakhstan, Kyrgyzstan and Russia signed the Quadripartite Treaty for greater integration. This envisaged the establishment of a 'New Union', based, initially, on a common market and customs union, and was to be open to all CIS members and the Baltic states. Consequently, these countries (with Tajikistan) became founding members of the Eurasian Economic Community (EURASEC), inaugurated in October 2001. In April 1996 Belarus and Russia signed the Treaty on the Formation of a Community of Sovereign Republics (CSR), which provided for extensive economic, political and military co-operation. In April 1997 the two countries signed a further Treaty of Union and, in addition, initialled the Charter of the Union, which detailed the procedures and institutions designed to develop a common infrastructure, a single currency and a joint defence policy within the CSR, with the eventual aim of 'voluntary unification of the member states'. The Charter was signed in May and ratified by the respective legislatures the following month. The Union's Parliamentary Assembly, comprising 36 members from the legislature of each country, convened in official session for the first time shortly afterwards. Progress within the framework of the CSR stalled, however, in the early 2000s. Azerbaijan, Georgia, Moldova and Ukraine co-operated increasingly from the late 1990s as the so-called GUAM group, which envisaged implementing joint economic and transportation initiatives (such developing a Eurasian Trans-Caucasus transportation corridor) and establishing the GUAM Free Trade Zone. Uzbekistan was a member of the group during the period April 1999–May 2005, during which time it was known as 'GUUAM'. The group agreed in September 2000 to convene regular annual summits of member countries' heads of state and to organize meetings of ministers of foreign affairs at least twice a year. Meeting in Kyiv, Ukraine, in May 2006 the heads of state of Azerbaijan, Georgia, Moldova and Ukraine adopted a charter formally inaugurating GUAM as a full international organization and renaming it Organization for Democracy and Economic Development—GUAM. The heads of state suggested at that time that the GUAM countries might withdraw from the CIS. In April 2003 Armenia, Belarus, Kazakhstan, Kyrgyzstan, Tajikistan and Russia established the Collective Security Treaty Organization (see below). In 1994 Kazakhstan, Kyrgyzstan, Tajikistan and Uzbekistan formed the Central Asian Economic Community. In February 2002 those countries relaunched the grouping as the Central Asian Co-operation Organization (CACO), to indicate that co-operation between member states had extended to political and security matters. Russia joined the organization in 2004. In October 2005, at a summit of CACO leaders in St Petersburg, Russia, it was announced that the organization would be merged with EURASEC. This was achieved in January 2006 with the accession to EURASEC of Uzbekistan, which had hitherto been the only member of CACO that did not also belong to the Community. In November 2008 Uzbekistan announced a temporary withdrawal from EURASEC.

The CIS regularly sends observer teams to monitor legislative and presidential elections in member states. In March 2005 Ukraine announced that it was to suspend its participation in the CIS Election Monitoring Organization (CIS-EMO, registered as a non-governmental organization in December 2003), owing to discrepancies in the findings of the observers of that body with those of the OSCE during the Ukrainian presidential election that was held in October and December 2004. The CIS Convention on Democratic Elections Standards, Electoral Rights and Freedoms in Member States, adopted in October 2002, has been ratified by Armenia, Kyrgyzstan, Moldova, Russia and Tajikistan.

In August 2005 a number of recommendations aimed at restructuring the organs of the CIS, with a view to increasing the overall efficiency of the organization, were presented to the summit of the Council of Heads of State, which was held in Kazan, Russia. Several declarations were signed at the Kazan summit, including a document on co-operation in humanitarian projects and combating illegal migration; however, a consensus on far-reaching reform of the organization failed to be reached by CIS leaders at that time. The heads of state of Armenia, Georgia, Turkmenistan (which had downgraded its full membership of the CIS to associate membership in 2005) and Ukraine did not attend an informal summit of CIS leaders convened in Moscow, Russia, in July 2006.

At the 2007 CIS summit meeting, held in Dushanbe, Tajikistan, in October, CIS heads of state (excluding those of Georgia and Turkmenistan) adopted the 'Concept for Further Development of the CIS' and an action plan for its implementation. Azerbaijan endorsed the document, but reserved the right to abstain from implementing certain clauses. The Concept cited the 'long-term formation of an integrated economic and political association' as a major objective of the Commonwealth, and determined that the multi-sector nature of the organization should be retained and that the harmonized development of its interacting spheres should continue to be promoted. Further goals detailed in the Concept included: supporting regional socio-economic stability and international security; improving the economic competitiveness of member states; supporting the accession of member states to the World Trade Organization (WTO); improving regional living standards and conditions; promoting inter-parliamentary co-operation; increasing co-operation between national migration agencies; harmonizing national legislation; and standardizing CIS structures and bodies. The state chairing the Council of Heads of State was to have responsibility for co-ordinating the implementation of the Concept. Leaders attending the Dushanbe summit also determined to establish a special body to oversee migration in the region and adopted an agreement aimed at promoting the civil rights of migrants.

In mid-August 2008, following a period of conflict between Georgian and Russian forces earlier in that month, Georgia announced its intention to withdraw from the CIS; this came into effect in August 2009. The 2008 regular CIS summit meeting was convened in Bishkek, Kyrgyzstan, in October, without the participation of Azerbaijan, (outgoing) Georgia, or Ukraine. Leaders attending the summit meeting considered—and determined to send for revision—a draft 'CIS Economic Development Strategy until 2020' and also discussed means of alleviating the regional impact of the ongoing global financial crisis. The 2009 CIS summit meeting was hosted by the Moldovan Government in Chişinău, in October, without participation by the heads of state of Tajikistan, Turkmenistan or Uzbekistan. The meeting endorsed the 'CIS Economic Development Strategy until 2020', discussed strengthening member states' co-operation in combating the impact of the global financial crisis, and adopted a joint action plan of related measures. It also addressed advancing co-operation in the humanitarian and collective security spheres. The heads of state adopted a Declaration on the forthcoming 65th anniversary commemorating the end of the Second World War, and declared 2010 as CIS Year of Veterans. Leaders participating in the 2010 summit meeting, convened in December, in Moscow, signed an agreement on advancing military co-operation until 2015, as well as concluding agreements addressing CIS common border policy; trafficking in humans and drugs; terrorism; and combating extremist terrorist activity. The 2011 summit meeting was held in September, in Dushanbe; participation by Azerbaijan, Belarus and Uzbekistan was at only prime ministerial level. The summit gave consideration to a report analysing progress during the first 20 years of the CIS, and to a draft programme on co-operation in combating illegal migration during 2012–14. Food security was a priority area of focus for CIS member states at that time. The 2012 summit meeting was to be held in November, in Aşgabat, Turkmenistan.

In May 2009 the heads of state or government of Armenia, Azerbaijan, Belarus, Georgia, Moldova and Ukraine, and representatives of the EU and the heads of state or government, and other representatives, of its member states, convened in Prague, Czech Republic, issued a Joint Declaration on establishing an Eastern Partnership. The main goal of the Eastern Partnership (to be facilitated through a specific Eastern dimension of the EU's European Neighbourhood Policy) was, through EU support for political and socio-economic reforms in interested partner countries, to create the necessary conditions to accelerate political association and further economic integration with the EU.

ECONOMIC AFFAIRS

At a meeting of the Council of Heads of Government in March 1992 agreement was reached on repayment of the foreign debt of the former USSR. Agreements were also signed on pensions, joint tax policy and the servicing of internal debt. In May an accord on repayment of inter-state debt and the issue of balance of payments statements was adopted by the heads of government, meeting in Tashkent, Uzbekistan. In July it was decided to establish an economic court in Minsk, Belarus.

The CIS Charter, adopted in January 1993, provided for the establishment of an economic co-ordination committee. In February, at a meeting of the heads of foreign economic departments, a foreign economic council was formed. In May all member states, with the exception of Turkmenistan, adopted a declaration of support for increased economic union and, in September, agreement was reached by all states except Ukraine and Turkmenistan on a framework for economic union, including the gradual removal of tariffs and creation of a currency union. Turkmenistan was subsequently admitted as a full member of the economic union in December 1993 and Ukraine as an associate member in April 1994.

At the Council of Heads of Government meeting in September 1994 all member states, except Turkmenistan, agreed to establish an Inter-state Economic Committee to implement economic treaties adopted within the context of an economic union. The establishment of a payments union to improve the settlement of accounts was also agreed. In April 1998 CIS heads of state resolved to incorporate the functions of the Inter-state Economic Committee, along with those of other working bodies and sectional committees, into a new CIS Executive Committee.

Guidelines adopted by the Council of Heads of State in April 1999 concerning the future development of the CIS identified economic co-operation and the establishment of a free trade zone (see Trade) as priority areas for action. Improving the economic competitiveness of member states was a primary focus of the 'Concept for the Integrated Economic Development of the CIS' that was adopted by the organization's October 2007 summit meeting. A 'CIS Economic Development Strategy until 2020' was adopted by the October 2009 Chişinău summit.

TRADE

Agreement was reached on the free movement of goods between republics at a meeting of the Council of Heads of State in February 1992, and in April 1994 an agreement on the creation of a CIS free trade zone (envisaged as the first stage of economic union) was concluded. In July a council of the heads of customs committees, meeting in Moscow, approved a draft framework for customs legislation in CIS countries, to facilitate the establishment of a free trade zone. The framework was approved by all the participants, with the exception of Turkmenistan. Draft customs union legislation was approved by the first session of the Inter-state Economic Committee, held in November 1994. In April 1999 CIS heads of state signed a protocol to the 1994 free trade area accord, which aimed to accelerate co-operation. In June 2000 the Council of Heads of State adopted a plan and schedule for the implementation of priority measures related to the creation of the free trade zone, and at the September 2003 summit meeting Russia, Belarus, Kazakhstan and Ukraine signed the Union of Four agreement establishing the framework for a Common Economic Space (CES, see below).

The development of a customs union and the strengthening of intra-CIS trade were objectives endorsed by all participants, with the exception of Georgia, at the Council of Heads of Government meeting held in March 1997. In March 1998 Russia, Belarus, Kazakhstan and Kyrgyzstan signed an agreement establishing a customs union, which was to be implemented in two stages: firstly, the removal of trade restrictions and the unification of trade and customs regulations; followed by the integration of economic, monetary and trade policies. In February 1999 Tajikistan signed the 1998 agreement to become the fifth member of the customs union. In October 1999 the heads of state of the five member states of the customs union reiterated their political determination to implement the customs union and approved a programme to harmonize national legislation to create a single economic space. In May 2000 the heads of state announced their intention to raise the status of the customs union to that of an inter-state economic organization, and, in October, the leaders signed the founding treaty of EURASEC. Under the new structure member states aimed to formulate a unified foreign economic policy, and, taking into account existing customs agreements, collectively to pursue the creation of the planned single economic space. In the following month the five member governments signed an agreement enabling visa-free travel within the new Community. (Earlier in 2000 Russia had withdrawn from a CIS-wide visa-free travel arrangement agreed in 1992. Kazakhstan, Turkmenistan and Uzbekistan subsequently withdrew from the agreement, and Belarus announced its intention to do so in late 2005.) In December 2000 member states of the Community adopted several documents aimed at facilitating economic co-operation. EURASEC, governed by an inter-state council based in Astana, Kazakhstan, was formally inaugurated in October 2001. In October 2003 the Community was granted observer status at the UN. The Union of Four agreement on establishing the framework for a CES, adopted in September 2003 by the leaders of Belarus, Kazakhstan, Russia and Ukraine, envisaged the creation of a free trade zone and the gradual harmonization of tariffs, customs and transport legislation. While participation at each stage would remain optional, decisions would be obligatory and certain areas of sovereignty would eventually be ceded to a council of heads of state and a commission. The Union of Four accord entered into force in April 2004. Meeting on the sidelines of the CIS summit held in October 2007, EURASEC leaders determined to establish a fully operational customs union over the next three years, with Belarus, Kazakhstan and Russia as the founding members, and Kyrgyzstan, Tajikistan and Uzbekistan to join at a later date, once they had achieved the requisite accession conditions. Ukraine, which was also committed to participation in the GUAM Free Trade Zone, was not at that time participating actively in the negotiating process on the CES. It was envisaged that the CES, open to accession by other CIS member states, would form the basis of the planned wider EURASEC economic integration. Despite significant growth in the gross domestic product of the poorer states of the CIS at that time (Armenia, Azerbaijan, Georgia, Kyrgyzstan, Moldova, Tajikistan and Uzbekistan, then known as the 'CIS-7'), in April 2005 the IMF called for greater harmonization of trade rules within the CIS, as well as liberalization of transit policies and the removal of non-tariff barriers. The customs union between Russia, Belarus and Kazakhstan entered into formal existence on 1 January 2010, when a common external tariff was adopted; on 1 July 2010 a harmonized customs code came into force. In December of that year the heads of state of Russia, Belarus and Kazakhstan signed several agreements aimed at finalizing the establishment of the planned CES, and in November 2011 they signed a declaration on Eurasian economic integration and adopted a roadmap outlining integration processes aimed at creating a Eurasian Economic Union, to be established, provisionally, by 1 Jan. 2015, and to be based on the customs union and proposed CES. In October 2011, in St Petersburg, the leaders of Russia, Armenia, Belarus, Kazakhstan, Kyrgyzstan, Moldova, Tajikistan, and Ukraine (therefore all CIS states except for Azerbaijan, Uzbekistan and Turkmenistan) signed an agreement establishing the CIS Free Trade Area—CISFTA; this aimed to simplify trade and economic relations, and to regulate a free trade regime, replacing several previous multilateral agreements and around 100 bilateral agreements. The CIS leaders also adopted an accord on basic principles of currency regulation and currency controls within the CIS.

The CIS maintains a 'loose co-ordination' on issues related to applications by member states to join the WTO. Supporting the accession of member states to the WTO was a primary focus of the Concept for Further Development of the CIS that was adopted by the October 2007 summit meeting of the Commonwealth. Russia, Belarus and Kazakhstan, whose customs union entered into formal existence in 2010, see above, aim to synchronize their positions on WTO accession.

BANKING AND FINANCE

In February 1992 CIS heads of state agreed to retain the rouble as the common currency for trade between the republics. However, in July 1993, in an attempt to control inflation, notes printed before 1993 were withdrawn from circulation and no new ones were issued until January 1994. Despite various agreements to recreate the 'rouble zone', including a protocol agreement signed in September 1993 by six states, it effectively remained confined to Tajikistan, which joined in January 1994, and Belarus, which joined in April. Both those countries proceeded to introduce national currencies in May 1995. In

January 1993, at the signing of the CIS Charter, the member countries endorsed the establishment of an inter-state bank to facilitate payments between the republics and to co-ordinate monetary credit policy. Russia was to hold 50% of shares in the bank, but decisions were to be made only with a two-thirds' majority approval. In December 2000, in accordance with the CSR and Treaty of Union (see above), the Presidents of Belarus and Russia signed an agreement providing for the adoption by Belarus of the Russian currency from 1 January 2005, and for the introduction of a new joint Union currency by 1 January 2008; the adoption by Belarus of the Russian currency was, however, subsequently postponed. Following the entry into formal existence on 1 January 2010 of the customs union between Belarus, Russia and Kazakhstan (see above), the introduction of a new common currency unit for the members of the union was under consideration.

In October 2004 Russia and Kazakhstan announced a proposal to establish a CIS Development Bank, with capital of €1m.

REGIONAL SECURITY

At a meeting of heads of government in March 1992 agreements on settling inter-state conflicts were signed by all participating states (except Turkmenistan). At the same meeting an agreement on the status of border troops was signed by five states. In May a five-year Collective Security Treaty was signed. In July further documents were signed on collective security and it was agreed to establish joint peace-making forces to intervene in CIS disputes. (CIS peace-keeping forces were sent into Tajikistan, and Abkhazia, Georgia during 1993–2000, and 1994–2009, respectively.) In December 1993 the Council of Defence Ministers agreed to establish a secretariat to co-ordinate military co-operation. In November 1995 the Council of Defence Ministers authorized the establishment of a Joint Air Defence System, to be co-ordinated largely by Russia. In the context of the CSR (see above) Russia and Belarus also agreed to develop a joint air defence unit, although implementation of this was postponed. (In February 2009 the two states announced plans to proceed with the establishment of a joint integrated air defence system.) In April 1999 Armenia, Belarus, Kazakhstan, Kyrgyzstan, Russia and Tajikistan signed a protocol to extend the Collective Security Treaty (while Azerbaijan, Georgia and Uzbekistan withdrew from the agreement). In April 1998 the Council proposed drawing up a draft programme for military and technical co-operation between member countries and also discussed procedures advising on the use and maintenance of armaments and military hardware. The programme was approved by CIS heads of state in October 2002.

In October 2000 the six signatory states to the Collective Security Treaty signed an agreement on the Status of Forces and Means of Collective Security Systems, establishing a joint rapid deployment function. The so-called CIS Collective Rapid Reaction Force was to be assembled to combat insurgencies, with particular reference to transborder terrorism from Afghanistan, and also to deter transborder illegal drugs-trafficking. In June 2001 a CIS Anti-terrorism Centre was established in Moscow. A Central Asian subdivision of the CIS Anti-Terrorism Centre was established in Bishkek, Kyrgyzstan, in October 2002. In October 2001, in response to the major terrorist attacks perpetrated in September against targets in the USA—allegedly co-ordinated by militant fundamentalist Islamist leader Osama bin Laden—the parties to the Collective Security Treaty adopted a new anti-terrorism plan. In December 2002 the committee of the Collective Security Treaty member countries adopted a protocol on the exchange of expertise and information on terrorist organizations and their activities. In April 2003 the signatory states determined to establish the Collective Security Treaty Organization (CSTO); ratification of its founding documents was completed by September, when it applied for UN observer status (granted in December 2004). The CIS summit in September 2003 approved draft decisions to control the sale of portable anti-aircraft missiles and to set up a joint co-ordination structure to address illegal immigration. During September 2004 the CIS Council of Heads of State determined to establish a Security Council, comprising the ministers responsible for foreign affairs and for defence, and heads of security and border control.

The signatory countries to the Collective Security Treaty participate in regular so-called CIS Southern Shield joint military exercises. A summit meeting of CSTO leaders held in October 2007 endorsed documents enabling the future establishment of CSTO joint peace-keeping forces and the creation of a co-ordination council for the heads of member states' emergency response agencies. In July 2008 the Council of Defence Ministers, convened in Bishkek, discussed strengthening air defence co-operation until 2015. In February 2009 the participating states in the CSTO determined to develop a rapid reaction military force, which would be deployed to combat terrorists and in response to regional emergencies. A meeting of the Council of Defence Ministers held in June 2009, in Moscow, addressed conceptual approaches to the development of military co-operation among CIS countries until 2015.

An Agreement on the Co-operation of the CIS Member States in Combating Trafficking in Persons, Human Organs and Tissues was adopted in November 2005 and has been ratified by Azerbaijan, Armenia, Belarus, Kyrgyzstan and Russia. In August 2005 CIS member states adopted a blueprint on joint co-operation in combating terrorism and extremism; the blueprint provided for the exchange of relevant information between member states and for the extradition of individuals suspected of financing or committing terrorist acts. In October 2009 CIS heads of states approved a number of additional measures for strengthening border control.

OTHER ACTIVITIES

An agreement on legislative co-operation was signed at an Inter-Parliamentary Conference in January 1992; joint commissions were established to co-ordinate action on economy, law, pensions, housing, energy and ecology. The CIS Charter, formulated in January 1993, provided for the establishment of an inter-state court. In October 1994 a Convention on the rights of minorities was adopted at the meeting of the heads of state; this has been ratified by Azerbaijan, Armenia, Belarus, Kyrgyzstan and Tajikistan. In May 1995, at the sixth plenary session of the IPA, several acts to improve co-ordination of legislation were approved, relating to migration of labour, consumer rights, and the rights of prisoners of war; revised legislation on labour migration and the social protection of migrant workers was adopted in November 2005. A CIS Convention on Human Rights and Fundamental Freedoms, adopted at that time, and incorporating the Statute of a proposed CIS Commission on Human Rights, has been ratified by Belarus, Kyrgyzstan, Russia and Tajikistan. In November 2006 an agreement on the protection of participants in the criminal justice system was signed by eight member states. In November 2008 the CIS Convention on the Legal Status of Working Migrants and their Families was signed by the heads of member states.

The creation of a Council of Ministers of Internal Affairs was approved at the heads of state meeting in January 1996; the Council was to promote co-operation between the law enforcement bodies of member states. The IPA has approved a number of model laws, relating to areas including banking and financial services; charity; defence; ecology, the economy; education; the regulation of refugee problems; combating terrorism; and social issues, including obligatory social insurance against production accidents and occupational diseases.

The CIS has held a number of discussions relating to the environment. In July 1992 agreements were concluded to establish an Inter-state Ecological Council. It was also agreed in that month to establish *Mir*, an inter-state television and radio company. In October 2002 a decision was made by CIS heads of government to enhance mutual understanding and co-operation between members countries through *Mir* radio and television broadcasts. In February 1995 the IPA established a Council of Heads of News Agencies, in order to promote the concept of a single information area. CIS leaders meeting in Moscow in May 2005 agreed to sign a declaration aimed at enhancing co-operation between CIS members in the humanitarian, cultural and scientific spheres.

A Connect CIS Summit was convened by the International Telecommunications Union and partners in Minsk, Belarus, in November 2009, with participation by CIS leaders and representatives from businesses and financial institutions, with the aim of mobilizing the financial and technical resources required to facilitate a swift regional transition towards a digital infrastructure and services. The Summit urged greater investment in regional ICT broadband access.

COOPERATION COUNCIL FOR THE ARAB STATES OF THE GULF

Address: POB 7153, Riyadh 11462, Saudi Arabia.

Telephone: (1) 482-7777; **fax:** (1) 482-9089; **internet:** www.gcc-sg.org.

More generally known as the Gulf Cooperation Council (GCC), the organization was established on 25 May 1981 by six Arab states.

MEMBERS*

Bahrain	Oman	Saudi Arabia
Kuwait	Qatar	United Arab Emirates

* In December 2001 the Supreme Council admitted Yemen (which applied to join the organization as a full member in 1996) as a member of the GCC's Arab Bureau of Education for the Gulf States, as a participant in meetings of GCC ministers of health and of labour and social affairs, and, alongside the GCC member states, as a participant in the biennial Gulf Cup football tournament. In September 2008 Yemen's inclusion in future GCC development planning was approved and Yemen was admitted to GCC control and auditing apparatuses. Negotiations are ongoing on the full accession of Yemen to the GCC by 2016. In May 2011 the GCC invited Jordan and Morocco to submit membership applications.

Organization

(April 2012)

SUPREME COUNCIL

The Supreme Council is the highest authority of the GCC. It comprises the heads of member states and holds one regular session annually, and in emergency session if demanded by two or more members. The Council also convenes an annual consultative meeting. The Presidency of the Council is undertaken by each state in turn, in alphabetical order. The Supreme Council draws up the overall policy of the organization; it discusses recommendations and laws presented to it by the Ministerial Council and the Secretariat General in preparation for endorsement. The GCC's charter provided for the creation of a commission for the settlement of disputes between member states, to be attached to and appointed by the Supreme Council. The Supreme Council convenes the commission for the settlement of disputes on an ad hoc basis to address altercations between member states as they arise. The 32nd annual meeting of the Supreme Council was convened in December 2011 in Riyadh, Saudi Arabia.

CONSULTATIVE COMMISSION

The Consultative Commission, comprising 30 members (five from each member state) nominated for a three-year period, acts as an advisory body, considering matters referred to it by the Supreme Council.

COMMISSION FOR THE SETTLEMENT OF DISPUTES

The Commission for the Settlement of Disputes is formed by the Supreme Council for each case, on an ad hoc basis in accordance with the nature of each specific dispute.

MINISTERIAL COUNCIL

The Ministerial Council consists of the ministers of foreign affairs of member states (or other ministers acting on their behalf), meeting every three months, and in emergency session if demanded by two or more members. It prepares for the meetings of the Supreme Council, and draws up policies, recommendations, studies and projects aimed at developing co-operation and co-ordination among member states in various spheres. GCC ministerial committees have been established in a number of areas of co-operation; sectoral ministerial meetings are held periodically.

SECRETARIAT GENERAL

The Secretariat assists member states in implementing recommendations by the Supreme and Ministerial Councils, and prepares reports and studies, budgets and accounts. The Secretary-General is appointed by the Supreme Council for a three-year term renewable once. The position is rotated among member states in order to ensure equal representation. The Secretariat comprises the following divisions and departments: Political Affairs; Economic Affairs; Human and Environmental Affairs; Military Affairs; Security; Legal Affairs; the Office of the Secretary-General; Finance and Administrative Affairs; a Patent Bureau; an Administrative Development Unit; an Internal Auditing Unit; an Information Centre; and a Telecommunications Bureau (based in Bahrain). Assistant Secretaries-General, in charge of Political Affairs; Economic Affairs; Human and Environmental Affairs; Military Affairs; Security, are appointed by the Ministerial Council upon the recommendation of the Secretary-General. All member states contribute in equal proportions towards the budget of the Secretariat. There is a GCC delegation office in Brussels, Belgium, of which the head is appointed by the Ministerial Council for a three-year term of office.

Secretary-General: ABDUL LATIF BIN RASHID AL-ZAYANI (Bahrain).

Activities

The GCC was established following a series of meetings of foreign ministers of the states concerned, culminating in an agreement on the basic details of its charter on 10 March 1981. The Charter was signed by the six heads of state on 25 May. It describes the organization as providing 'the means for realizing co-ordination, integration and co-operation' in all economic, social and cultural affairs. In December 2012 the 32nd summit of the Supreme Council welcomed a proposal by King Abdullah of Saudi Arabia specifying that the basis of GCC collaboration should progress from the stage of co-operation to full union. The summit directed the Ministerial Council to form in 2012 a specialized commission, to comprise three members from each member state, to study the proposal.

COMPREHENSIVE DEVELOPMENT STRATEGY FOR 2010–25

In December 1998 the Supreme Council approved a long-term strategy for regional development, covering the period 2000–25, and aimed at achieving integrated, sustainable development in all member states and the co-ordination of national development plans. Meeting in December 2010 the 31st summit of GCC heads of state adopted a revised comprehensive development strategy for member states, covering 2010–25. The updated strategy identified several ongoing challenges including: promoting integration over competition, and collective over national development efforts, within the grouping; scarcity of water resources in the region, the high salinity content in local water, and the high cost of alternative water resources; limitations on cultivating farming lands; the disproportionate engagement of national citizens in state employment and dependence on foreign workers in the non-governmental labour market; incompatibility between educational and training goals and the needs of the labour market (the region has a large non-resident population); investment decline in certain sectors, and migration of national capital abroad owing to limited local investment opportunities; the existence of budgetary deficits; the potential impacts of climate change on the environment; and global development, security and economic challenges. The following strategic goals were outlined: pursuing a framework enabling sustainable development; ensuring adequate water for development needs; achieving self-sufficiency in meeting the security and defence needs of the GCC development process; achieving integrated economic partnership; eliminating sources of vulnerability from the GCC economic environment; deriving maximum benefit from infrastructure facilities; technical and scientific capacity building; enhancing social development in the areas of education and training, health, and intellectual and cultural development; and enhancing the productivity of the GCC labour force.

ECONOMIC CO-OPERATION

In November 1981 GCC ministers drew up a Unified Economic Agreement covering freedom of movement of people and capital, the abolition of customs duties, technical co-operation, harmonization of banking regulations and financial and monetary co-ordination. At the same time GCC heads of state approved the formation of a Gulf Investment Corporation, to be based in Kuwait (see below). In March 1983 customs duties on domestic products of the Gulf states were abolished, and new regulations allowing free movement of workers and vehicles between member states were also introduced. A common minimum customs levy (of between 4% and 20%) on foreign imports was imposed in 1986. In February 1987 the governors of the member states' central banks agreed in principle to co-ordinate their rates of exchange, and this was approved by the Supreme Council in November. It was subsequently agreed to link the Gulf currencies to a 'basket' of other currencies. In April 1993 the Gulf central bank governors decided to allow Kuwait's currency to become part of the GCC monetary system that was established following Iraq's invasion of Kuwait in order to defend the Gulf currencies. In May 1992 GCC trade ministers announced the objective of establishing a GCC common market. Meeting in September GCC ministers reached agreement on the application of a unified system of tariffs by March 1993. A meeting of the Supreme Council, held in December 1992, however, decided to mandate GCC officials to formulate a plan for the introduction of common external tariffs, to be presented to the Council in December 1993. Only the tax on tobacco products was to be standardized from March 1993, at a rate of 50% (later increased to 70%). In April 1994 ministers of finance agreed to pursue a gradual approach to the unification of tariffs. A technical committee, which had been constituted to consider aspects of establishing a customs union, met for the first time in June 1998. In November 1999 the Supreme Council concluded an agreement to establish the customs union by 1 March 2005. However, in December 2001 the Supreme Council, meeting in Muscat, Oman, adopted a new agreement on regional economic union ('Economic Agreement Between the Arab GCC States'), which superseded the 1981 Unified Economic Agreement. The new accord brought forward the deadline for the establishment of the proposed customs union to 1 January 2003 and provided for a standard tariff level of 5% for foreign imports (with the exception of 53 essential commodities previously exempted by the Supreme Council). The agreement also provided for the introduction, by January 2010, of a GCC single currency, linked to the US dollar (this deadline, however, was not met—see below). The Supreme Council also authorized the creation of a new independent authority for overseeing the unification of specifications and standards throughout member states.

The GCC customs union was launched, as planned, on 1 January 2003. In July the GCC entered into negotiations with Yemen on harmonizing economic legislation. In December 2005 the Supreme Council approved standards for the introduction of the planned single currency. The GCC Common Market was inaugurated on 1 January 2008. Oman and the United Arab Emirates (UAE) withdrew from the process to introduce a single currency in 2007 and 2009, respectively. An accord on Gulf Monetary Union was signed in June 2009 by Bahrain, Kuwait, Qatar and Saudi Arabia, and was approved by the 30th meeting of the Supreme Council, held in Kuwait in December. In May 2010 the GCC Secretary-General stated that the introduction of the single currency was unlikely to occur for at least five years.

In April 1993 GCC central bank governors agreed to establish a joint banking supervisory committee, in order to devise rules for GCC banks to operate in other member states. In December 1997 GCC heads of state authorized guidelines to this effect. These were to apply only to banks established at least 10 years previously with a share capital of more than US $100m.

The 29th summit meeting of heads of state, held in Muscat, Oman, in December 2008, discussed the ongoing global financial crisis, and directed relevant ministerial committees to intensify co-ordination among member states to mitigate the negative impact of the global situation on the region's economies.

The sixth GCC Economic Forum was held in Dubai, United Arab Emirates, in February 2010.

TRADE AND INDUSTRY

In 1982 a ministerial committee was formed to co-ordinate trade policies and development in the region. Technical subcommittees were established to oversee a strategic food reserve for the member states, and joint trade exhibitions (which were generally held every year until responsibility was transferred to the private sector in 1996). In 1986 the Supreme Council approved a measure whereby citizens of GCC member states were enabled to undertake certain retail trade activities in any other member state, with effect from 1 March 1987. In September 2000 GCC ministers of commerce agreed to establish a technical committee to promote the development of electronic commerce and trade among member states.

In 1976 the GCC member states formed the Gulf Organization for Industrial Consulting, based in Doha, Qatar, which promotes regional industrial development. In 1985 the Supreme Council endorsed a common industrial strategy for the Gulf states. It approved regulations stipulating that priority should be given to imports of GCC industrial products, and permitting GCC investors to obtain loans from GCC industrial development banks. In November 1986 resolutions were adopted on the protection of industrial products, and on the co-ordination of industrial projects, in order to avoid duplication. In 1989 the Ministerial Council approved the Unified GCC Foreign Capital Investment Regulations, which aimed to attract foreign investment and to co-ordinate investments amongst GCC countries. Further guidelines to promote foreign investment in the region were formulated during 1997. In December 1999 the Supreme Council amended the conditions determining rules of origin on industrial products in order to promote direct investment and intra-Community trade. In December 1992 the Supreme Council endorsed Patent Regulations for GCC member states to facilitate regional scientific and technological research. A GCC Patent Office for the protection of intellectual property in the region was established in 1998. In December 2006 the Supreme Council endorsed a system to unify trademarks in GCC states.

In December 2001 the Supreme council adopted unified procedures and measures for facilitating the intra-regional movement of people and commercial traffic, as well as unified standards in the areas of education and health care. In August 2003 the GCC adopted new measures permitting nationals of its member states to work in, and to seek loans from financial institutions in, any other member state. In December 2005 the Supreme Council approved a plan to unify member states' trade policies. The Council adopted further measures aimed at facilitating the movement of people, goods and services between member countries, with consideration given to environmental issues and consumer protection, and agreed to permit GCC citizens to undertake commercial activities in all member states.

AGRICULTURE

The GCC states aim to achieve food security through the best utilization of regional natural resources. A unified agricultural policy for GCC countries was endorsed by the Supreme Council in November 1985, and revised in December 1996. Efforts were also made to harmonize legislation relating to water conservation, veterinary vaccines, insecticides, fertilizers, fisheries and seeds. Unified agricultural quarantine laws were adopted by the Supreme Council in December 2001. In 2006 an agreement was entered into with the FAO on the regional implementation of a technical programme on agricultural quarantine development, aimed at protecting the agricultural sector from plant disease epidemics. A permanent committee on fisheries aims to co-ordinate national fisheries policies, to establish designated fishing periods and to undertake surveys of the fishing potential in the Arabian (Persian) Gulf. In December 2010 the summit meeting of GCC leaders called for a comprehensive review of agricultural sector development, with a focus on policies aimed at preserving water resources; the regional scarcity of water, and its high saline content, have been an area of concern.

COMMUNICATIONS, INFORMATION AND TRANSPORT

GCC ministers responsible for telecoms, posts and information technology, and ministers of information, convene regularly. The 2001 Economic Agreement provided for member states to take all necessary means to ensure the integration of their telecommunication policies, including telephone, post and data network services. A simplified passport system was approved in 1997 to facilitate travel between member countries. In December 2006 the Supreme Council requested that all GCC members conclude studies on the implementation of a GCC rail network, which was to interconnect all member states, with a view to enhancing economic development. It was announced in 2010 that the GCC states would invest nearly US $119,600m. in infrastructure projects during 2010–20, with developing the regional rail infrastructure accounting for some 90% of the investment. A report, issued in April 2011, on the status of GCC infrastructure development schemes, stated that some $452m. of infrastructure projects were under way in the region. It was envisaged that increased expenditure on infrastructure projects, representing a diversification from petroleum-based growth, might strengthen the regional economy during the ongoing global economic slowdown.

ENERGY AND ENVIRONMENT

The 1981 Unified Economic Agreement stated that member states should harmonize their policies in hydrocarbons industry, with regard to extraction, refining, marketing, processing, pricing, exploitation and development of energy resources; and that member states should develop common oil policies and take common positions at the international level. The 2001 Economic Agreement expanded upon this.

In 1982 a ministerial committee was established to co-ordinate hydrocarbons policies and prices. Ministers adopted a petroleum security plan to safeguard individual members against a halt in their production, to form a stockpile of petroleum products, and to organize a boycott of any non-member country when appropriate. In December 1987 the Supreme Council adopted a plan whereby a member state whose petroleum production was disrupted could 'borrow' petroleum from other members, in order to fulfil its export obligations. GCC petroleum ministers hold occasional co-ordination meetings to discuss the agenda and policies of OPEC, to which all six member states belong. In December 1988 the Supreme Council authorized the development of a long-term petroleum policy, and adopted a regional emergency policy for oil products. In November 2003 ministers of petroleum determined to develop a GCC Common Mining Law.

The Unified Economic Agreement provided for the establishment and co-ordination of an infrastructure of power-generating stations and desalination plans. The 2001 Economic Agreement also stressed that member states should adopt integrated economic policies with regard to developing the basic utilities infrastructure. During the early 1990s proposals were formulated to integrate the electricity networks of the six member countries. In December 1997 GCC heads of state declared that work should commence on the first stage of the plan, under the management of an independent authority. The estimated cost of the project was more than US $6,000m. However, it was agreed not to invite private developers to participate in construction of the grid, but that the first phase of the project should be financed by member states (to contribute 35% of the estimated $2,000m. required), and by loans from commercial banking and international monetary institutions. The Gulf Council Interconnection Authority was established in 1999, with its headquarters in Dammam, Saudi Arabia. In 2001 a GCC Electric Interconnection Commission was established, which was to support the project. The first phase of the project was completed, and in trial operation, by 2009.

In February 2001 GCC ministers responsible for water and electricity determined to formulate a common water policy for the region. Ministers responsibility for electricity and water approved an Electric Interconnection Agreement in November 2009, setting out the relations between the contracting parties. A GCC conference on Power and Water Desalination was convened in Qatar in October 2011. A Common Water Emergency Plan is under development.

In December 2006 the Supreme Council declared its intention to pursue the use of nuclear energy technology in the GCC region. The Council commissioned a study to develop a joint nuclear energy programme, but emphasized that any development of this technology would be for peaceful purposes only and fully disclosed to the international community. In February 2009 representatives of GCC member states attended a workshop organized by the IAEA.

In December 2001 GCC member states adopted the Convention on the Conservation of Wildlife and their Natural Habitats in the Countries of the GCC; the Convention entered into force in April 2003. In December 2007 the Supreme Council adopted a green environment initiative, aimed at improving the efficiency and performance of environmental institutions in member states.

CULTURAL CO-OPERATION

The GCC Folklore Centre, based in Doha, Qatar, was established in 1983 to collect, document and classify the regional cultural heritage, publish research, sponsor and protect regional folklore, provide a database on Gulf folklore, and to promote traditional culture through education. The December 2005 summit of heads of state adopted the 'Abu Dhabi Declaration', which stressed that member states should place a strong focus on education and on the development of human resources in order better to confront global challenges. Periodically cultural fora are held, including on: folklore (most recently in 2001); poetry (2004); drama (2009); and intellectual matters (2006). An occasional Exhibition of Creative Arts and Arabic Calligraphy is convened, most recently in 2006.

REGIONAL SECURITY

Although no mention of defence or security was made in the original charter, the summit meeting which ratified the charter also issued a statement rejecting any foreign military presence in the region. The Supreme Council meeting in November 1981 agreed to include defence co-operation in the activities of the organization: as a result, defence ministers met in January 1982 to discuss a common security policy, including a joint air defence system and standardization of weapons. In November 1984 member states agreed to form the Peninsula ('Al Jazeera') Shield Force for rapid deployment against external aggression, comprising units from the armed forces of each country under a central command to be based in north-eastern Saudi Arabia.

In December 1987 the Supreme Council approved a joint pact on regional co-operation in matters of security. In August 1990 the Ministerial Council condemned Iraq's invasion of Kuwait as a violation of sovereignty, and demanded the withdrawal of all Iraqi troops from Kuwait. The Peninsula Shield Force was not sufficiently developed to be deployed in defence of Kuwait. During the crisis and the ensuing war between Iraq and a multinational force which took place in January and February 1991, the GCC developed closer links with Egypt and Syria, which, together with Saudi Arabia, played the most active role among the Arab countries in the anti-Iraqi alliance. In March the six GCC nations, Egypt and Syria formulated the 'Declaration of Damascus', which announced plans to establish a regional peace-keeping force. The Declaration also urged the abolition of all weapons of mass destruction in the area, and recommended the resolution of the Palestinian question by an international conference. In June Egypt and Syria, whose troops were to have formed the largest proportion of the proposed peace-keeping force, announced their withdrawal from the project, reportedly as a result of disagreements with the GCC concerning the composition of the force and the remuneration involved. In December 1997 the Supreme Council approved plans for linking the region's military telecommunications networks and establishing a common early warning system. In December 2000 GCC leaders adopted a joint defence pact aimed at enhancing the grouping's defence capability. The pact formally committed member states to defending any other member state from external attack, envisaging the expansion of the Peninsula Shield Force from 5,000 to 22,000 troops and the creation of a new rapid deployment function within the Force. In March 2001 the GCC member states inaugurated the first phase of the long-envisaged joint air defence system. In December GCC heads of state authorized the establishment of a supreme defence council, comprising member states' ministers of defence, to address security-related matters and supervise the implementation of the joint defence pact. The council was to convene on an annual basis. Meeting in emergency session in early February 2003 GCC ministers of defence and foreign affairs agreed to deploy the Peninsula Field Force in Kuwait, in view of the then impending US military action against neighbouring Iraq. The full deployment of 3,000 Peninsula Shield troops to Kuwait was completed in early March; the force was withdrawn two months later. In December 2005 the Supreme Council, meeting in Abu Dhabi, UAE, agreed that the Peninsula Shield Force should be reconstituted. Proposals to develop the Force were endorsed by the 2006 heads of state summit, held in December, in Riyadh. In December 2009 the 30th Supreme Council meeting ratified a new defence strategy that included upgrading the capabilities of the Peninsula Shield, undertaking joint military projects, and pursuing co-operation in combating the illegal trade of armaments to GCC member states.

In November 1994 a security agreement, to counter regional crime and terrorism, was concluded by GCC states. The pact, however, was not signed by Kuwait, which claimed that a clause concerning the extradition of offenders was in contravention of its constitution. The GCC welcomed a judgement made in March 2001 by the International Court of Justice awarding Bahrain sovereignty of the Hawar islands, while supporting Qatar's sovereignty over certain other territories; this settled a territorial dispute that had been a long-term cause of tension between the two GCC member countries.

In December 1997 the Council expressed concern at the escalation of tensions owing to Iraq's failure to co-operate with the UN Special Commission (UNSCOM). In February 1998 the US Secretary of Defense visited each of the GCC countries in order to generate regional support for any punitive military action against Iraq, given that country's obstruction of UN weapons inspectors. Kuwait was the only country to declare its support for the use of force (and to permit the use of its bases in military operations against Iraq), while other member states urged a diplomatic solution to the crisis. The GCC supported an agreement concluded between the UN Secretary-General and the Iraqi authorities at the end of February 1998, and urged Iraq to co-operate with UNSCOM in order to secure an end to the problem and a removal of the international embargo against the country. This position was subsequently reiterated by the Supreme Council. In September 2002 the US Secretary of State met representatives of the GCC to discuss ongoing US pressure on the UN Security Council to draft a new resolution insisting that Iraq comply with previous UN demands, setting a time frame for such compliance and authorizing the use of force against Iraq in response to non-compliance. In March 2003, in response to the initiation of US-led military action against Iraq for perceived non-compliance with the resulting Security Council resolution (1441, adopted in November 2002), the GCC Secretary-General urged the resumption of negotiations in place of military conflict. The GCC summit meeting held in Kuwait, in December 2003, issued a statement accepting the USA's policies towards Iraq at that time, emphasizing the importance of UN participation there, condemning ongoing operations by terrorist forces, and denoting the latter as anti-Islamic. In December 2009 the 30th Supreme Council meeting emphasized the GCC's support for Iraq's sovereignty, independence and territorial integrity, on non-interference in Iraq's internal affairs, and on the preservation of its Arab and Islamic identity; and urged inclusive national reconciliation.

In 1992 Iran extended its authority over the island of Abu Musa, which it had administered under a joint arrangement with the UAE since 1971. In September 1992 the GCC Ministerial Council condemned Iran's continued occupation of the island and efforts to consolidate its presence, and reiterated support of UAE sovereignty over Abu Musa, as well as the largely uninhabited Greater and Lesser Tunb islands (also claimed by Iran). All three islands are situated in the approach to the Strait of Hormuz, through which petroleum exports are transported. The GCC has condemned repeated military exercises conducted by Iran in the waters around the disputed islands as a threat to regional security and a violation of the UAE's sovereignty. Successive GCC summit meetings have restated support for the UAE's right to regain sovereignty over the three islands (and over their territorial waters, airspace, continental shelf and economic zone). In December 2010 the 31st summit meeting stated disappointment at the failure of repeated contacts with Iran over the matter. The meeting welcomed international efforts to engage with Iran over its controversial nuclear programme, particularly by the 5+1 Group (comprising the People's Republic of China, France, Germany, Russia and the United Kingdom).

In March 2011, in response to a request from the Bahrain Government following a series of violent clashes between opposition protesters and security forces in that country, the GCC dispatched a contingent of Peninsula Shield Force troops (numbering some 1,000 from Saudi Arabia and 500 from the UAE, with more than 100 armoured vehicles), to Bahrain to protect strategic facilities and help maintain order.

The December 2005 summit of GCC heads of state issued a statement declaring that the Gulf region should be a zone free of weapons of mass destruction.

The December 2009 meeting of the Supreme Council stated concern over acts of marine piracy in the Gulf of Aden, the Red Sea and other regional waterways, and emphasized the need to intensify co-operation in challenging the perpetrators. The December 2010 summit meeting expressed appreciation at efforts made by the GCC naval forces in combating maritime piracy and protecting shipping corridors.

In July 2007 the Ministerial Council determined to establish a GCC Disaster Control Center; a team of experts in disaster management was to be established there. In December 2010 the GCC summit approved a regional plan of action to prepare for and respond to radiation risks.

EXTERNAL RELATIONS

In June 1988 an agreement was signed by GCC and European Community (EC) ministers on economic co-operation; this took effect from January 1990. Under the accord a joint ministerial council (meeting on an annual basis) was established, and working groups were subsequently created to promote co-operation in several specific areas, including business, energy, the environment and industry. In October 1990 GCC and EC ministers of foreign affairs commenced negotiations on formulating a free trade agreement. GCC heads of state, meeting in December 1997, condemned statements issued by the European Parliament, as well as by other organizations, regarding human rights issues in member states and insisted they amounted to interference in GCC judicial systems. In January 2003 the GCC established a customs union (see above), which was a precondition of the proposed GCC-European Union (EU, as the restructured EC was now known) free trade agreement. Negotiations on the agreement, initiated in 2003, had, by early 2012, still not been concluded. In June 2010 the GCC and EU adopted a Joint Action Programme for 2010–13, aimed at strengthening economic, financial and monetary co-operation, as well as co-operation in other key strategic areas of investment, including trade, energy and the environment, transport, industry, telecommunications and information technology, education and scientific research. In April 2008 the GCC and the European Free Trade Association (EFTA) finalized negotiations on the conclusion of a bilateral free trade agreement; the agreement was signed in July 2009, in Norway.

In September 1994 GCC ministers of foreign affairs decided to end the secondary and tertiary embargo on trade with Israel. In December 1996 the foreign ministers of the Damascus Declaration states, convened in Cairo, Egypt, requested the USA to exert financial pressure on Israel to halt the construction of settlements on occupied Arab territory. In December 2001 GCC heads of state issued a statement holding Israeli government policy responsible for the escalating crisis in the Palestinian territories. The consultative meeting of heads of state held in May 2002 declared its support for a Saudi-proposed initiative aimed at achieving a peaceful resolution of the crisis. GCC heads of state summits have repeatedly urged the international community to encourage Israel to sign the Nuclear Non-Proliferation Treaty.

In June 1997 ministers of foreign affairs of the Damascus Declaration states agreed to pursue efforts to establish a free trade zone throughout the region, which they envisaged as the nucleus of a future Arab common market. Meanwhile, the Greater Arab Free Trade Area, an initiative of the League of Arab States, entered into effect on 1 January 2005.

The GCC-USA Economic Dialogue, which commenced in 1985, convenes periodically as a government forum to promote co-operation between the GCC economies and the USA. Since the late 1990s private sector interests have been increasingly represented at sessions of the Dialogue. It was announced in March 2001 that a business forum was to be established under the auspices of the Dialogue, to act as a permanent means of facilitating trade and investment between the GCC countries and the USA.

In January 2008 the last of four rounds of negotiations between the GCC member states and Singapore on the creation of a GCC-Singapore Free Trade Area (GSFTA) was concluded; the agreement establishing the GSFTA was signed, in Doha, Qatar, in December 2008. An inaugural meeting of ministers of foreign affairs of the GCC and the Association of Southeast Asian Nations (ASEAN) was held in June 2009, in Manama, Bahrain. The meeting adopted a GCC-ASEAN Joint Vision as a framework for future co-operation between the two groupings. A second meeting, held in Singapore, in May–June 2010, approved an ASEAN-GCC Action Plan, which identified specific measures for closer co-operation to be undertaken in the two-year period 2010–12.

The GCC Secretary-General denounced the major terrorist attacks that were perpetrated in September 2001 against targets in the USA. Meeting in an emergency session in mid-September, in Riyadh, Saudi Arabia, GCC ministers of foreign affairs agreed to support the aims of the developing international coalition against terrorism. Meanwhile, however, member states urged parallel international resolve to halt action by the Israeli security forces against Palestinians. In December the Supreme Council declared the organization's full co-operation with the anti-terrorism coalition. In December 2006 the Supreme Council determined to establish a specialized security committee to counter terrorism.

In March 2011 GCC leaders issued a statement urging the League of Arab States to take measures to protect citizens in Libya from the effects of violent measures against opposition elements being taken at that time by the regime of the then Libyan leader Col Muammar al-Qaddafi. In October 2011 the Council met in emergency session to discuss ongoing violent unrest in Syria, where suppression by the regime of anti-government protests during that year had resulted in more than 3,000 civilian fatalities. By March 2012 all of the GCC member states had withdrawn their diplomatic presence from Syria in protest at the Syrian regime's violent suppression of mass anti-government protests.

INVESTMENT CORPORATION

Gulf Investment Corporation (GIC): POB 3402, Safat 13035, Kuwait; tel. 2225000; fax 2225010; e-mail gic@gic.com.kw; internet www.gic.com.kw; f. 1983 by the six member states of the GCC, each contributing 16.6% of the total capital; total assets US $5,776m. (Dec. 2010); investment chiefly in the Gulf region, financing industrial projects (including pharmaceuticals, chemicals, steel wire, aircraft engineering, aluminium, dairy produce and chicken-breeding); provides merchant banking and financial advisory services, and in 1992 was appointed to advise the Kuwaiti Government on a programme of privatization; CEO and Chief Investment Officer HISHAM ABDULRAZZAQ AL-RAZZUQI; publ. *The GIC Gazetteer* (annually).

Gulf International Bank: POB 1017, ad-Dowali Bldg, 3 Palace Ave, Manama 317, Bahrain; tel. 17534000; fax 17522633; e-mail info@gibbah.com; internet www.gibonline.com; f. 1976 by the six GCC states and Iraq; became a wholly owned subsidiary of the GIC (without Iraqi shareholdings) in 1991; in April 1999 a merger with Saudi Investment Bank was concluded; cap. US $2,500m. (Dec. 2010); CEO Dr YAHYA ALYAHYA.

Publications

GCC News (monthly, available online in Arabic).

GCC: A Statistical Glance.

Statistical Bulletin on Water.

At-Ta'awun (periodical).

COUNCIL OF ARAB ECONOMIC UNITY

Address: 1113 Corniche el-Nil, 4th Floor, POB 1 Mohammed Fareed, 11518 Cairo, Egypt.

Telephone: (2) 5755321; **fax:** (2) 5754090.

Established in 1957 by the Economic Council of the League of Arab States. The first meeting of the Council of Arab Economic Unity was held in 1964.

MEMBERS

Egypt	Palestine
Iraq	Somalia
Jordan	Sudan
Libya	Syria
Mauritania	Yemen

Organization

(April 2012)

COUNCIL

The Council consists of representatives of member states, usually ministers of economy, finance and trade. It meets twice a year; meetings are chaired by the representative of each country for one year.

GENERAL SECRETARIAT

Entrusted with the implementation of the Council's decisions and with proposing work plans, including efforts to encourage participation by member states in the Arab Economic Unity Agreement. The Secretariat also compiles statistics, conducts research and publishes studies on Arab economic problems and on the effects of major world economic trends.

Secretary-General: MOHAMMED AL-RABEE (Yemen).

COMMITTEES

The following permanent committees have been established: customs issues; monetary and finance; economic; permanent representatives; and follow-up.

Activities

The Council undertakes to co-ordinate measures leading to a customs union subject to a unified administration; conduct market and commodity studies; assist with the unification of statistical terminology and methods of data collection; conduct studies for the formation of new joint Arab companies and federations; and to formulate specific programmes for agricultural and industrial co-ordination and for improving road and railway networks.

ARAB ECONOMIC INTEGRATION

Based on a resolution passed by the Council in August 1964, an Arab Common Market was to be established, with its implementation to be supervised by the Council. Customs duties and other taxes on trade between the member countries were to be eliminated in stages prior to the adoption of a full customs union, and ultimately all restrictions on trade between the member countries, including quotas, and restrictions on residence, employment and transport, were to be abolished. In practice, however, little progress was achieved in the development of an Arab common market during 1964–2000. In 2001 the Council's efforts towards liberalizing intra-Arab trade were intensified. A meeting of Council ministers of economy and trade convened in Baghdad, Iraq, in June, approved an executive programme for developing the proposed common market, determined to establish a compensation fund to support the integration of the least developed Arab states into the regional economy, and agreed to provide technical assistance for Arab states aiming to join the World Trade Organization. In May 2001 Egypt, Jordan, Morocco and Tunisia (all then participants in the Euro-Mediterranean Partnership, re-launched in 2008 as the Union for the Mediterranean—see European Union), while convened in Agadir, Morocco, had issued the 'Agadir Declaration' in which they determined to establish an Arab Mediterranean Free Trade Zone. The so-called Agadir Agreement on the establishment of a Free Trade Zone between the Arabic Mediterranean Nations was signed in February 2004, came into force in July 2006, and entered its implementation phase in March 2007. Tariff-free trade between the 17 participants in the Greater Arab Free Trade Area (GAFTA, implemented by the Arab League, also known as the 'Pan-Arab Free Trade Area') entered into force on 1 January 2005. The signatories to the Agadir Agreement are also members of GAFTA. Progress towards achieving Arab economic integration was considered at the first ever Economic, Development and Social summit meeting of Arab leaders, convened in January 2009 in Kuwait, under the auspices of the Arab League; a second summit was held in January 2011, in Sharm el-Sheikh, Egypt.

Council agreements aimed at encouraging Arab investment include an accord on Non-Double Taxation, Tax Evasion, and Establishing Common Rules on Income and Capital (adopted in December 1997); an accord on Non-Double Taxation and Income Tax Evasion (December 1998); an accord on Investment Promotion and Protection (June 2000); and an accord on Investment Dispute Settlement in Arab Countries (December 2000).

Publications

Annual Bulletin for Arab Countries' Foreign Trade Statistics.
Annual Bulletin for Official Exchange Rates of Arab Currencies.
Arab Economic Unity Bulletin (2 a year).
Demographic Yearbook for Arab Countries.
Economic Report (2 a year).
Guide to Studies prepared by Secretariat.
Progress Report (2 a year).
Statistical Yearbook for Arab Countries.
Yearbook for Intra-Arab Trade Statistics.
Yearbook of National Accounts for Arab Countries.

COUNCIL OF THE BALTIC SEA STATES—CBSS

Address: Slussplan 9, POB 2010, 103 11 Stockholm, Sweden.

Telephone: (8) 440-19-20; **fax:** (8) 440-19-44; **e-mail:** cbss@cbss.org; **internet:** www.cbss.org.

The Council of the Baltic Sea States (CBSS) was established in 1992 to develop co-operation between member states.

MEMBERS

Denmark	Iceland	Poland
Estonia	Latvia	Russia
Finland	Lithuania	Sweden
Germany	Norway	

The European Commission also has full membership status.

Observers: Belarus, France, Italy, the Netherlands, Romania, Slovakia, Spain, Ukraine, United Kingdom, USA.

Organization

(April 2012)

PRESIDENCY

The presidency is occupied by member states for one year (1 July 2011–30 June 2012: Germany), on a rotating basis. Summit meetings of heads of government are convened every two years. The eighth summit meeting was convened in Vilnius, Lithuania, in June 2010. The ninth summit meeting was to be held in Germany, in May 2012.

MINISTERIAL COUNCIL

The Council comprises the ministers of foreign affairs of each member state and a representative of the European Commission. The Council meets every two years and aims to serve as a forum for guidance, direction of work and overall co-ordination among participating states. The 17th, extraordinary, session of the Council was convened in Plön, Germany, in February 2012. Chairmanship of the Council rotates annually among member states and is responsible for co-ordinating the Council's activities between ministerial sessions, with assistance from the Committee of Senior Officials. (Other ministers also convene periodically, on an ad hoc basis by their own decision.)

COMMITTEE OF SENIOR OFFICIALS—CSO

The Committee consists of senior officials of the ministries of foreign affairs of the member states and of the European Commission. It serves as the main discussion forum and decision-making body for matters relating to the work of the Council, and monitors, facilitates and aims to co-ordinate the activities of all structures for CBSS co-operation. The Chairman of the Committee, from the same country serving as President of the CBSS, meets regularly with the previous and future Chairmen. The so-called Troika aims to maintain information co-operation, promote better exchange of information, and ensure more effective decision-making. The CSO monitors the work of the Expert Group on Nuclear and Radiation Safety, the Task Force against Trafficking in Human Beings, the Expert Group on Co-operation on Children at Risk, the Expert Group on Youth Affairs, the Lead Country Function of the EuroFaculty Project in Pskov (in Russia, see below), the Expert Group on Maritime Policy, and the Expert Group on Sustainable Development—Baltic 21.

SECRETARIAT

The tasks of the secretariat include providing technical and organizational support to the chairmanship, structures and working bodies of the Ministerial Council; co-ordinating CBSS activities; managing the CBSS archives and information databases; and maintaining contacts with governments and other organizations operational in the region. The Secretariat includes a Children's Unit, and it hosts the Secretariat of Northern Dimension Partnership in Public Health and Social Well-being.

Director: JAN LUNDIN (Sweden).

Activities

The CBSS was established in March 1992 as a forum to enhance and strengthen co-operation between countries in the Baltic Sea region. At a meeting of the Council in Kalmar, Sweden, in July 1996, ministers adopted an Action Programme as a guideline for CBSS activities. The main programme areas covered stable and participatory political development; economic integration and prosperity; and protection of the environment. The third summit meeting of CBSS heads of government, held at Kolding, Denmark, in April 2000, recommended a restructuring of the organization to consolidate regional intergovernmental, multilateral co-operation in all sectors. In June the ninth meeting of the CBSS Council approved the summit's recommendations. The 10th ministerial session, held in Hamburg, Germany, in June 2001, adopted a set of guidelines regarding the strengthening of the CBSS. Heads of government attending the seventh summit of Baltic Sea States, held in Riga, Latvia, in June 2008, endorsed a Declaration on the Reform of the CBSS, listing the following five future priority areas of co-operation for member states: environment (which may include climate change); economic development; energy; education and culture; and civil security and the human dimension. The 15th ministerial session, held in Helsingør, Denmark, in June 2009, endorsed new terms of reference of the CBSS and of its Secretariat, updated in view of the 2008 Declaration on the Reform of the CBSS. Meeting in Vilnius, Lithuania, in June 2010, the eighth summit of heads of government adopted the Vilnius Declaration on 'A Vision for the Baltic Region by 2020'.

The ministerial session held in May 1994 determined to appoint an independent Commissioner on Democratic Development, concerned with democratic institutions and human rights, to serve a three-year term of office, from October of that year. The Commissioner's mandate was subsequently twice extended for three years, in July 1997 and June 2000, and was terminated in December 2003.

At the first Baltic Sea States summit, held in Visby, Sweden, in May 1996, heads of government agreed to establish a Task Force on Organized Crime to counter drugs-trafficking, strengthen judicial co-operation, increase the dissemination of information, impose regional crime-prevention measures, improve border controls and provide training. The Task Force's mandate has been successively renewed, most recently, by the 10th Baltic Sea States summit, until 31 December 2016. In January 1998 the second summit meeting, convened in Riga, Latvia, agreed to enhance co-operation in the areas of civic security and border control. The third Baltic Sea summit, held in April 2000, authorized the establishment of a Task Force on Communicable Disease Control, which was mandated to formulate a joint plan aimed at improving disease control throughout the region, and also to strengthen regional co-operation in combating the threat to public health posed by a significant increase in communicable diseases, in particular HIV/AIDS. The Task Force presented its final report to the CBSS summit meeting held in June 2004. It was recognized that some of the structures of the Task Force could be pursued through the Northern Dimension Partnership in Public Health and Social Well-Being (NDPHS, see below). A Task Force against Trafficking in Human Beings was established in November 2006.

The Council has founded a number of groups, comprising experts in specific fields, which aim to report on and recommend action on issues of concern to the Council (see under the Committee of Senior Officials). In January 2009 the Council inaugurated the CBSS EuroFaculty Pskov programme, aimed at upgrading business/economics education at two higher education institutions in the western Russian Pskov region (bordering Estonia and Latvia) over a two-year period. A CBSS EuroFaculty programme was implemented during 2000–07 at the Immanuel Kant State University in Kaliningrad, Russia.

A Baltic Business Advisory Council was established in 1996 with the aim of facilitating the privatization process in the member states in transition and promoting small and medium-sized enterprises. A Roadmap on Investment Promotion, drafted by the Working Group on Economic Co-operation, was approved by the sixth summit meeting of CBSS heads of government, held in Reykjavik, Iceland, in June 2006. A Ministerial Conference on Trade and Economy was held in Stockholm, Sweden, in May 2007.

The environmental state of the Baltic Sea, which is one of the world's busiest shipping routes, and associated issues such as eutrophication, overfishing, unsustainable production, and marine littering, are of great concern to the Council. In January 2001 the CBSS Council agreed to establish a unit in the CBSS secretariat to implement Baltic 21, the regional variant (adopted by the CBSS in 1998) of Agenda 21, the programme of action agreed by the UN Conference on Environment and Development, held in Rio de Janeiro, Brazil, in June 1992. From January 2010 Baltic 21 was integrated into the structure of the CBSS as the Expert Group on Sustainable Development—Baltic 21. The 16th session of the Ministerial Council, held in June 2011, in Oslo, Norway, endorsed a new CBSS Strategy on Sustainable Development for 2010–15, with a focus on the following four strategic areas of co-operation: climate change; sustainable urban and rural development; sustainable consumption and production; and innovation and education for sustainable development. In June 2010 funding was approved by the Baltic Sea Region Programme of the European Union (EU) for a new Baltic Sea Region Climate Change Adaptation Strategy (BALTADAPT), to be implemented, with participation by 11 partners from seven countries, under the auspices of Baltic 21. The CBSS was to convene a high-level Policy Forum on Climate Change Adaptation in Berlin, Germany, in April 2012. The Baltic Sea Region Energy Co-operation (BASREC) has its own secretariat function and council of senior energy officials, administered by the CBSS secretariat. BASREC also has ad hoc groups on electricity markets, gas markets, energy efficiency and climate change. The 17th, extraordinary, ministerial session, held February 2012, adopted a Declaration on Energy Security, highlighting future areas of policy focus; these included: diversification; reciprocity; security of supplies; environmental aspects and sustainability; and nuclear safety standards. The promotion of the sustainable and balanced spatial development of the region is addressed within the framework of the Visions and Strategies around the Baltic Sea (VASAB) co-operation.

The CBSS organizes annual co-ordination meetings to provide a forum and framework of co-operation for its strategic partners in the Baltic Sea area, including the B7 Baltic Island Network (comprising the seven largest Baltic Sea islands), the Baltic Development Forum, the Baltic Sea Forum, the Helsinki Commission and the Union of the Baltic Cities. The CBSS seeks synergies with the Arctic Council, the Barents Euro-Arctic Council, the Nordic Council of Ministers, and the EU's Northern Dimension co-operation framework. The Council contributed to the implementation of Northern Dimension Action Plans (NDAPs) for 2000–03 and 2004–06. In 2006 the CBSS prepared and presented to the European Commission a survey on the future of Northern Dimension co-operation. This contributed to the development of a long-term Northern Dimension Policy Framework Document that was adopted, alongside a Political Declaration on the Northern Dimension, in November 2006, in place of the previous NDAPs, with a view to renewing the co-operation. The first ministerial meeting of the renewed Northern Dimension co-operation was convened in St Petersburg, Russia, in October 2008. Ongoing Northern Dimension initiatives that are supported by CBSS member states include the Northern Dimension Environment Partnership (NDEP), established in 2001; the NDPHS, which was established in 2003; and the development of a Northern Dimension Partnership on Transport and Logistics, approved in October 2008. An EU Strategy for the Baltic Sea Region (EUSBSR) was adopted by the European Council in October 2009. In January 2012 the CBSS Secretariat became lead partner of a EUSBSR flagship project on macro-regional risk scenarios and gaps identification.

Finance

The Secretariat is financed by contributions of the governments of the Council's 11 member states. Ongoing activities and co-operation projects are funded through voluntary contributions from member states on the basis of special contribution schemes.

Publication

Balticness Light (quarterly).

THE COUNCIL OF EUROPE

Address: Ave de l'Europe, 67075 Strasbourg Cedex, France.

Telephone: 3-88-41-20-33; **fax:** 3-88-41-27-45; **e-mail:** infopoint@coe.int; **internet:** www.coe.int.

The Council was founded in May 1949 to achieve a greater unity between its members, to facilitate their social progress and to uphold the principles of parliamentary democracy, respect for human rights and the rule of law. Membership has risen from the original 10 to 47.

MEMBERS*

Albania	Lithuania
Andorra	Luxembourg
Armenia	Macedonia, former Yugoslav republic
Austria	Malta
Azerbaijan	Moldova
Belgium	Montenegro†
Bosnia and Herzegovina	Monaco
Bulgaria	Netherlands
Croatia	Norway
Cyprus	Poland
Czech Republic	Portugal
Denmark	Romania
Estonia	Russia
Finland	San Marino
France	Serbia†
Georgia	Slovakia
Germany	Slovenia
Greece	Spain
Hungary	Sweden
Iceland	Switzerland
Ireland	Turkey
Italy	Ukraine
Latvia	United Kingdom
Liechtenstein	

* Belarus is a state candidate for membership of the Council of Europe. Canada, the Holy See, Japan, Mexico and the USA have observer status with the Committee of Ministers. The parliaments of Canada, Israel and Mexico have observer status with the Parliamentary Assembly.

† Following the division of Serbia and Montenegro into separate sovereign states in June 2006, Serbia retained the seat hitherto held by Serbia and Montenegro. Montenegro was admitted as a member in May 2007.

Organization

(April 2012)

COMMITTEE OF MINISTERS

The Committee consists of the ministers of foreign affairs of all member states (or their deputies, who are usually ministers' permanent diplomatic representatives in Strasbourg); it decides all matters of internal organization, makes recommendations to governments and draws up conventions and agreements with binding effect; it also discusses matters of political concern, such as European co-operation, compliance with member states' commitments, in particular concerning the protection of human rights, and considers possible co-ordination with other institutions, such as the European Union (EU) and the Organization for Security and Co-operation in Europe (OSCE). The Committee meets weekly at deputy ministerial level and once a year (in May or November) at ministerial level. Six two-day meetings are convened each year to supervise the execution of judgments of the European Court of Human Rights (see below).

CONFERENCES OF SPECIALIZED MINISTERS

There are 20 Conferences of specialized ministers, meeting regularly for intergovernmental co-operation in various fields.

PARLIAMENTARY ASSEMBLY

President: JEAN-CLAUDE MIGNON (France).

Secretary-General of the Parliamentary Assembly: WOJCIECH SAWICKI (Poland).

Chairman of the Socialist Group: ANDREAS GROSS (Switzerland).

Chairman of the Group of the European People's Party: LUCA VOLONTÈ (Italy).

Chairman of the Alliance of Liberals and Democrats for Europe: ANNE BRASSEUR (Luxembourg).

Chairman of the European Democrat Group: ROBERT WALTER (United Kingdom).

Chairman of the Unified European Left Group: TINY KOX (Netherlands).

Members are elected or appointed by their national parliaments from among the members thereof; political parties in each delegation follow the proportion of their strength in the national parliament. Members do not represent their governments, speaking on their own behalf. At April 2012 the Assembly had 318 members (and 318 substitutes): 18 each for France, Germany, Italy, Russia and the United Kingdom; 12 each for Poland, Spain, Turkey and Ukraine; 10 for Romania; seven each for Belgium, the Czech Republic, Greece, Hungary, the Netherlands, Portugal and Serbia; six each for Austria, Azerbaijan, Bulgaria, Sweden and Switzerland; five each for Bosnia and Herzegovina, Croatia, Denmark, Finland, Georgia, Moldova, Norway and Slovakia; four each for Albania, Armenia, Ireland and Lithuania; three each for Cyprus, Estonia, Iceland, Latvia, Luxembourg, the former Yugoslav republic of Macedonia, Malta, Montenegro and Slovenia; and two each for Andorra, Liechtenstein, Monaco and San Marino. The parliaments of Canada, Israel and Mexico have permanent observer status. (Belarus's special 'guest status' was suspended in January 1997.)

The Assembly meets in ordinary session once a year. The session is divided into four parts, generally held in the last full week of January, April, June and September. The Assembly submits Recommendations to the Committee of Ministers, passes Resolutions, and discusses reports on any matters of common European interest. It is also a consultative body to the Committee of Ministers, and elects the Secretary-General, the Deputy Secretary-General, the Secretary-General of the Assembly, the Council's Commissioner for Human Rights, and the members of the European Court of Human Rights.

The parliament of Morocco (since June 2011) and the Palestine National Council (since October 2011) hold 'Partner for Democracy' status at the Parliamentary Assembly, which aims to provide democracy-building support to national legislatures in regions neighbouring the Council of Europe area.

Standing Committee: represents the Assembly when it is not in session, and may adopt Recommendations to the Committee of Ministers and Resolutions on behalf of the Assembly. Consists of the President, Vice-Presidents, Chairmen of the Political Groups, Chairmen of the Ordinary Committees and Chairmen of national delegations. Meetings are usually held at least twice a year.

Ordinary Committees: political affairs; legal and human rights; economic affairs and development; social, health and family affairs; culture, science and education; environment, agriculture, and local and regional affairs; migration, refugees and population; rules of procedure and immunities; equal opportunities for women and men; honouring of obligations and commitments by member states of the Council of Europe.

SECRETARIAT

The Secretariat incorporates the Secretariats and Registry of the institutions of the Council. There are Directorates of Communication and Research, Strategic Planning, Protocol and Internal Audit, and the following Directorates-General: Political Affairs; Legal Affairs;

Human Rights; Social Cohesion; Education, Culture and Heritage, Youth and Sport; and Administration and Logistics.

Secretary-General: THORBJØRN JAGLAND (Norway).

Deputy Secretary-General: MAUD DE BOER-BUQUICCHIO (Netherlands).

EUROPEAN COURT OF HUMAN RIGHTS

The Court was established in 1959 under the European Convention on Human Rights. It has compulsory jurisdiction and is competent to consider complaints lodged by states party to the European Convention and by individuals, groups of individuals or non-governmental organizations (NGOs) claiming to be victims of breaches of the Convention's guarantees. The Court comprises one judge for each contracting state. The Court sits in three-member Committees, empowered to declare applications inadmissible in the event of unanimity and where no further examination is necessary, seven-member Chambers, and a 17-member Grand Chamber. Chamber judgments become final three months after delivery, during which period parties may request a rehearing before the Grand Chamber, subject to acceptance by a panel of five judges. Grand Chamber judgments are final. The Court's final judgments are binding on respondent states and their execution is supervised by the Committee of Ministers. Execution of judgments includes payment of any pecuniary just satisfaction awarded by the Court, adoption of specific individual measures to erase the consequences of the violations found (such as striking out of impugned convictions from criminal records, reopening of judicial proceedings, etc.), and general measures to prevent new similar violations (e.g. constitutional and legislative reforms, changes of domestic case-law and administrative practice, etc.). When the Committee of Ministers considers that the measures taken comply with the respondent state's obligation to give effect to the judgment, a final resolution is adopted that terminates the supervision of the case. In June 2009 the Court adopted a new policy establishing seven categories of case, and aiming to focus resources on the cases ('priority applications') deemed to be most important. The EU Treaty of Lisbon, which entered into force in December 2009, committed the EU to pursuing accession to the Court. During 2011 the Court delivered 1,511 judgments, and some 149,450 cases were pending at 31 March 2012.

President: Sir NICHOLAS BRATZA (United Kingdom).

Registrar: ERIK FRIBERGH (Sweden).

CONGRESS OF LOCAL AND REGIONAL AUTHORITIES OF THE COUNCIL OF EUROPE (CLRAE)

The Congress was established in 1994, incorporating the former Standing Conference of Local and Regional Authorities, in order to protect and promote the political, administrative and financial autonomy of local and regional European authorities by encouraging central governments to develop effective local democracy. The Congress comprises two chambers—a Chamber of Local Authorities and a Chamber of Regions—with a total membership of 318 elected representatives (and 318 elected substitutes). Annual sessions are mainly concerned with local government matters, regional planning, protection of the environment, town and country planning, and social and cultural affairs. A Standing Committee, drawn from all national delegations, meets between plenary sessions of the Congress. Four Statutory Committees (Institutional; Sustainable Development; Social Cohesion; Culture and Education) meet twice a year in order to prepare texts for adoption by the Congress.

The Congress advises the Council's Committee of Ministers and the Parliamentary Assembly on all aspects of local and regional policy and co-operates with other national and international organizations representing local government. The Congress monitors implementation of the European Charter of Local Self-Government, which was opened for signature in 1985 and provides common standards for effective local democracy. Other legislative guidelines for the activities of local authorities and the promotion of democracy at local level include the 1980 European Outline Convention on Transfrontier Co-operation, and its Additional Protocol which was opened for signature in 1995; a Convention on the Participation of Foreigners in Public Life at Local Level (entered into force in 1997); and the European Charter for Regional or Minority Languages (entered into force 1998). In addition, the European Urban Charter (adopted 1992) defines citizens' rights in European towns and cities, for example in the areas of transport, urban architecture, pollution and security; the European Landscape Convention (entered into force in March 2004) details an obligation for public authorities to adopt policies and measures at local, regional, national and international level for the protection, management and planning of landscapes; and the Charter on the Participation of Young People in Municipal and Regional Life (adopted in 1992 and revised in 2003), sets out guidelines for encouraging the active involvement of young people in the promotion of social change in their municipality or region. In May 2005 the Congress concluded an agreement with the EU Committee of the Regions on co-operation in ensuring local and regional democracy and self-government.

The Congress produces 'monitoring reports' on the state of local democracy in member countries, and is responsible for the monitoring of local and regional elections and for setting standards in electoral matters. It was envisaged that during 2011–12 the Congress would enhance its monitoring activities, broaden the scope of election observation, develop the provision of targeted post-monitoring and post-observation assistance, streamline its thematic activities, and introduce as a new priority area of focus the local dimension of human rights.

In September 2011 the Congress convened a Summit of Mayors on Roma, in Strasbourg, with participation by representatives of European municipalities, regions, institutions and networks, and Roma and traveller organizations. The Summit issued a final Declaration which supported the establishment of a new European Alliance of Cities and Regions for Roma Inclusion, with a view to enhancing future co-operation.

President: KEITH WHITMORE (United Kingdom).

Activities

In an effort to harmonize national laws, to put the citizens of member countries on an equal footing and to pool certain resources and facilities, the Council of Europe has concluded a number of conventions and agreements covering particular aspects of European co-operation. Since 1989 the Council has undertaken to increase co-operation with all countries of the former Eastern bloc and to facilitate their accession to the organization. In October 1997 heads of state or government of member countries convened for only the second time (the first meeting took place in Vienna, in October 1993) with the aim of formulating a new social model to consolidate democracy throughout Europe. The meeting endorsed a Final Declaration and an Action Plan, which established priority areas for future Council activities, including fostering social cohesion; protecting civilian security; promoting human rights; enhancing joint measures to counter cross-border illegal trafficking; and strengthening democracy through education and other cultural activities. In addition, the meeting generated renewed political commitment to the Programme of Action against Corruption, which has become a key element of Council activities. A third meeting of heads of state or government was held in Warsaw, Poland, in May 2005. In a Final Declaration and an Action Plan the meeting defined the principal tasks of the Council in the coming years, i.e. promoting human rights and the rule of law, strengthening the security of European citizens and fostering co-operation with other international and European organizations. The Council's activities have three cross-cutting themes: children; democracy; and combating violence. In January 2011 the Parliamentary Assembly adopted a resolution recommending that a Council of Europe summit should be convened with the aim of redefining the role of the Council and giving it a new political impetus.

HUMAN RIGHTS

The protection of human rights is one of the Council of Europe's basic goals, to be achieved in four main areas: the effective supervision and protection of fundamental rights and freedoms; identification of new threats to human rights and human dignity; development of public awareness of the importance of human rights; and promotion of human rights education and professional training. The most significant treaties in this area include: the European Convention for the Protection of Human Rights and Fundamental Freedoms (European Convention on Human Rights) (which was adopted in 1950 and entered into force in 1953); the European Social Charter; the European Convention for the Prevention of Torture and Inhuman or Degrading Treatment or Punishment; the Framework Convention for the Protection of National Minorities; the European Charter for Regional or Minority Languages; and the Convention on Action against Trafficking in Human Beings.

The Steering Committee for Human Rights is responsible for intergovernmental co-operation in the field of human rights and fundamental freedoms; it works to strengthen the effectiveness of systems for protecting human rights and to identify potential threats and challenges to human rights. The Committee has been responsible for the elaboration of several conventions and other legal instruments including the following protocols to the European Convention on Human Rights: Protocol No. 11, which entered into force in November 1998, resulting in the replacement of the then existing institutions—the European Commission of Human Rights and the European Court of Human Rights—by a single Court, working on a full-time basis; Protocol No. 12, which entered into force in April 2005, enforcing a general prohibition of discrimination; No. 13, which entered into force in July 2003, guaranteeing the abolition of the death penalty in all circumstances (including in time of war); and No.

14, which entered into force on 1 June 2010, aiming to enhance the effectiveness of the Court by improving implementation of the European Convention on Human Rights at national level and the processing of applications, and accelerating the execution of the Court's decisions.

The Steering Committee for Human Rights was responsible for the preparation of the European Ministerial Conference on Human Rights, held in Rome in November 2000, to commemorate the 50th anniversary of the adoption of the European Convention on Human Rights. The Conference highlighted, in particular, 'the need to reinforce the effective protection of human rights in domestic legal systems as well as at the European level'.

The Council of Europe Commissioner for Human Rights (whose office was established by a resolution of the Council's Committee of Ministers in May 1999) promotes respect for human rights in member states.

Commissioner for Human Rights: THOMAS HAMMARBERG (Sweden).

European Committee for the Prevention of Torture and Inhuman or Degrading Treatment or Punishment (CPT)

The Committee was established under the 1987 Convention for the Prevention of Torture as an integral part of the Council of Europe's system for the protection of human rights. The Committee, comprising independent experts, aims to examine the treatment of persons deprived of their liberty with a view to strengthening, if necessary, the protection of such persons from torture and from inhuman or degrading treatment or punishment. It conducts periodic visits to police stations, prisons, detention centres, and all other sites where persons are deprived of their liberty by a public authority, in all states parties to the Convention, and may also undertake ad hoc visits when the Committee considers them necessary. After each visit the Committee drafts a report of its findings and any further advice or recommendations, based on dialogue and co-operation. By March 2012 the Committee had published 267 reports and had undertaken 316 visits (192 periodic and 124 ad hoc).

President: LATIF HÜSEYNOV (Azerbaijan).

European Social Charter

The European Social Charter, in force since 1965, is the counterpart of the European Convention on Human Rights, in the field of protection of economic and social rights. A revised Charter, which amended existing guarantees and incorporated new rights, was opened for signature in May 1996, and entered into force on 1 July 1999. By April 2012 27 member states had ratified the Charter and 31 had ratified the revised Charter. Rights guaranteed by the Charter concern all individuals in their daily lives in matters of housing, health, education, employment, social protection, movement of persons and non-discrimination. The European Committee of Social Rights considers reports submitted to it annually by member states. It also considers collective complaints submitted in the framework of an Additional Protocol (1995), providing for a system which entered into force in July 1998, permitting trade unions, employers' organizations and NGOs to lodge complaints on alleged violations of the Charter. The Committee, composed of 15 members, decides on the conformity of national situations with the Charter. When a country does not bring a situation into conformity, the Committee of Ministers may, on the basis of decisions prepared by a Governmental Committee (composed of representatives of each Contracting Party), issue recommendations to the state concerned, inviting it to change its legislation or practice in accordance with the Charter's requirements.

President of the European Committee of Social Rights: LUIS JIMENA QUESADA (Spain).

FRAMEWORK CONVENTION FOR THE PROTECTION OF NATIONAL MINORITIES

In 1993 the first summit meeting of Council of Europe heads of state and government, held in Vienna, mandated the Committee of Ministers to draft 'a framework convention specifying the principle that States commit themselves to respect in order to assure the protection of national minorities'. A special committee was established to draft the so-called Framework Convention for the Protection of National Minorities, which was then adopted by the Committee in November 1994. The Convention was opened for signature in February 1995, entering into force in February 1998. Contracting parties (39 states at November 2011) are required to submit reports on the implementation of the treaty at regular intervals to an Advisory Committee composed of 18 independent experts. The Advisory Committee adopts an opinion on the implementation of the Framework Convention by the contracting party, on the basis of which the Committee of Ministers adopts a resolution. A Conference entitled 10 Years of Protecting National Minorities and Regional or Minority Languages was convened in March 2008 to review the impacts of, and the role of regional institutions in implementing, both the Framework Convention and the Convention on Minority Languages. In October 2010 a high-level meeting of the Council of Europe adopted the Strasbourg Declaration on Roma, detailing guiding principles and priorities to encourage the empowerment and inclusion of Roma/Gypsy people in Europe (who were estimated to number 10m.–12m. at that time); the Declaration outlined the establishment of a new European Training Programme for Roma Mediators, which was to enable the provision of legal and administrative advice to Roma communities.

Head, Secretariat: MICHÈLE AKIP.

RACISM AND INTOLERANCE

In October 1993 heads of state and of government, meeting in Vienna, resolved to reinforce a policy to combat all forms of intolerance, in response to the increasing incidence of racial hostility and intolerance towards minorities in European societies. A European Commission against Racism and Intolerance (ECRI) was established by the summit meeting to analyse and assess the effectiveness of legal, policy and other measures taken by member states to combat these problems. It became operational in March 1994. The European conference against racism, held in October 2000, requested that ECRI should be reinforced and, in June 2002, the Committee of Ministers of the Council of Europe adopted a new Statute for ECRI that consolidated its role as an independent human rights monitoring body focusing on issues related to racism and racial discrimination. Members of ECRI are appointed on the basis of their recognized expertise in the field; they are independent and impartial in fulfilling their mandate. ECRI undertakes activities in three programme areas: country-by-country approach; work on general themes; and relations with civil society. In the first area of activity, ECRI analyses the situation regarding racism and intolerance in each of the member states, in order to advise governments on measures to combat these problems. In December 1998 ECRI completed a first round of reports for all Council members. A second series of country reports was completed in December 2002 and a third monitoring cycle, focusing on implementation and 'specific issues', was undertaken during 2003–07. The fourth series of country reports was being compiled during 2008–12. ECRI's work on general themes includes the preparation of policy recommendations and guidelines on issues of importance to combating racism and intolerance. ECRI also collects and disseminates examples of good practices relating to these issues. Under the third programme area ECRI aims to disseminate information and raise awareness of the problems of racism and intolerance among the general public.

EQUALITY BETWEEN WOMEN AND MEN

The Steering Committee for Equality between Women and Men (CDEG—an intergovernmental committee of experts) is responsible for encouraging action at both national and Council of Europe level to promote equality of rights and opportunities between the two sexes. Assisted by various specialist groups and committees, the CDEG is mandated to establish analyses, studies and evaluations, to examine national policies and experiences, to devise concerted policy strategies and measures for implementing equality and, as necessary, to prepare appropriate legal and other instruments. It is also responsible for preparing the European Ministerial Conferences on Equality between Women and Men. The main areas of CDEG activities are the comprehensive inclusion of the rights of women (for example, combating violence against women and trafficking in human beings) within the context of human rights; the issue of equality and democracy, including the promotion of the participation of women in political and public life; projects aimed at studying the specific equality problems related to cultural diversity, migration and minorities; positive action in the field of equality between men and women and the mainstreaming of equality into all policies and programmes at all levels of society. In October 1998 the Committee of Ministers adopted a Recommendation to member states on gender mainstreaming; in May 2000 it approved a Recommendation on action against trafficking in human beings for the purpose of sexual exploitation; and in May 2002 it adopted a Recommendation on the protection of women from violence. Following a decision of the meeting of heads of state or government convened in Warsaw in May 2005, a Council of Europe Task Force to Combat Violence against Women, including Domestic Violence was established. In June 2006 the Committee of Ministers adopted the Blueprint of the Council of Europe Campaign to Combat Violence against Women, including Domestic Violence, which had been drafted by the Task Force. In May 2009 the Council of Europe published a *Handbook on the Implementation of Gender Budgeting*.

MEDIA AND COMMUNICATIONS

Article 10 of the European Convention on Human Rights (freedom of expression and information) forms the basis for the Council of

Europe's activities in the area of mass media. Implementation of the Council of Europe's work programme concerning the media is undertaken by the Steering Committee on the Media and New Communication Services (CDMC), which comprises senior government officials and representatives of professional organizations, meeting in plenary session twice a year. The CDMC is mandated to devise concerted European policy measures and appropriate legal instruments. Its underlying aims are to further freedom of expression and information in a pluralistic democracy, and to promote the free flow of information and ideas. The CDMC is assisted by various specialist groups and committees. Policy and legal instruments have been developed on subjects including: exclusivity rights; media concentrations and transparency of media ownership; protection of journalists in situations of conflict and tension; independence of public-service broadcasting, protection of rights holders; legal protection of encrypted television services; media and elections; protection of journalists' sources of information; the independence and functions of broadcasting regulatory authorities; and coverage of legal proceedings by the media. These policy and legal instruments (mainly in the form of non-binding recommendations addressed to member governments) are complemented by the publication of studies, analyses and seminar proceedings on topics of media law and policy. The CDMC has also prepared a number of international binding legal instruments, including the European Convention on Transfrontier Television (adopted in 1989 and ratified by 34 countries by April 2012), the European Convention on the Legal Protection of Services Based on or Consisting of Conditional Access (ratified by nine countries at April 2012), and the European Convention Relating to Questions on Copyright Law and Neighbouring Rights in the Context of Transfrontier Broadcasting by Satellite (ratified by two countries at April 2012).

In March 2005 the Council's Committee of Ministers adopted a declaration on freedom of expression and information in the media in the context of the fight against terrorism. A declaration on the independence and functions of regulatory authorities for the broadcasting sector was adopted by the Committee of Ministers in March 2008. In that month the Committee also adopted a Recommendation on the Use of Internet Filters aimed at promoting a balance between freedom of expression and the protection of children against harmful material published on the internet.

SOCIAL COHESION

In June 1998 the Committee of Ministers established the European Committee for Social Cohesion (CDCS). The CDCS has the following responsibilities: to co-ordinate, guide and stimulate co-operation between member states with a view to promoting social cohesion in Europe; to develop and promote integrated, multidisciplinary responses to social issues; and to promote the social standards embodied in the European Social Charter and other Council of Europe instruments, including the European Code of Social Security. In 2002 the CDCS published the *Report on Access to Social Rights in Europe*, concerning access to employment, housing and social protection. The Committee supervises an extensive programme of work on children, families and the elderly. In March 2004 the Committee of Ministers approved a revised version of the Council's Strategy for Social Cohesion (adopted in July 2000).

The European Code of Social Security and its Protocol entered into force in 1968; by April 2012 the Code had been ratified by 21 states and the Protocol by seven states. These instruments set minimum standards for medical care and the following benefits: sickness; old age; unemployment; employment injury; family; maternity; invalidity; and survivor's benefit. A revision of these instruments, aiming to provide higher standards and greater flexibility, was completed for signature in 1990 and had been ratified by one member state (the Netherlands) at April 2012.

The European Convention on Social Security, in force since 1977, currently applies in Austria, Belgium, Italy, Luxembourg, the Netherlands, Portugal, Spain and Turkey; most of the provisions apply automatically, while others are subject to the conclusion of additional multilateral or bilateral agreements. The Convention is concerned with establishing the following four fundamental principles of international law on social security: equality of treatment; unity of applicable legislation; conservation of rights accrued or in course of acquisition; and payment of benefits abroad. In 1994 a Protocol to the Convention, providing for the enlargement of the personal scope of the Convention, was opened for signature; by April 2012 it had been ratified only by Portugal.

In May 2011 a Group of Eminent Persons, appointed by the Secretary-General, released a report entitled 'Living Together: Combining Freedom and Diversity in 21st Century Europe', which identified threats to the values of the Council of Europe deriving from rising intolerance and increasing diversity in European populations, and outlined proposed responses.

HEALTH

Through a series of expert committees, the Council aims to ensure constant co-operation in Europe in a variety of health-related fields, with particular emphasis on health services and patients' rights, for example: equity in access to health care; quality assurance; health services for institutionalized populations (prisoners, elderly in homes); discrimination resulting from health status; and education for health. These efforts are supplemented by the training of health personnel. Recommendations adopted by the Committee of Ministers in the area of health cover blood, cancer control, disabilities, health policy development and promotion, health services, the protection of human rights and dignity of persons with mental disorder, the organization of palliative care, the role of patients, transplantation, access to health care by vulnerable groups, and the impact of new information technologies on health care.

A Partial Agreement in the Social and Public Health Field aims to protect the consumer from potential health risks connected with commonplace or domestic products, including asbestos, cosmetics, flavouring substances, pesticides, pharmaceuticals and products that have a direct or indirect impact on the human food chain, and also has provisions on the integration of people with disabilities. Two European treaties have been concluded within the framework of this Partial Agreement: the European Agreement on the Restriction of the use of Certain Detergents in Washing and Cleaning Products, and the Convention on the Elaboration of a European Pharmacopoeia (establishing legally binding standards for medicinal substances, auxiliary substances, pharmaceutical preparations, vaccines for human and veterinary use and other articles). The latter Convention entered into force in eight signatory states in May 1974 and, by April 2012 had been ratified by 36 states and the EU. WHO, and eight European and 15 non-European states, participate (as at April 2012) as observers in the sessions of the European Pharmacopoeia Commission. In 1994 a procedure on certification of suitability to the European Pharmacopoeia monographs for manufacturers of substances for pharmaceutical use was established. A network of official control laboratories for human and veterinary medicines was established in 1995, open to all signatory countries to the Convention and observers at the Pharmacopoeia Commission. The seventh edition of the European Pharmacopoeia, in force since 1 January 2011, is updated regularly in its electronic version, and includes more than 2,000 harmonized European standards, or 'monographs', 268 general methods of analysis and 2,210 reagents.

The 1992 Recommendation on A Coherent Policy for People with Disabilities contains the policy principles for the rehabilitation and integration of people with disabilities. This model programme recommends that governments of all member states develop comprehensive and co-ordinated national disability policies taking account of prevention, diagnosis, treatment education, vocational guidance and training, employment, social integration, social protection, information and research. It has set benchmarks, both nationally and internationally. The 1995 Charter on the Vocational Assessment of People with Disabilities states that a person's vocational abilities and not disabilities should be assessed and related to specific job requirements. The 2001 Resolution on Universal Design aims to improve accessibility, recommending the inclusion of Universal Design principles in the training for vocations working on the built environment. The 2001 Resolution on New Technologies recommends formulating national strategies to ensure that people with disabilities benefit from new technologies. In April 2006 the Council of Europe Committee of Ministers adopted a Recommendation endorsing a recently drafted Council of Europe action plan for 2006–15, with the aim of promoting the rights and full participation of people with disabilities in society and of improving the quality of life of people with disabilities in Europe.

In the co-operation group to combat drug abuse and illicit drugs trafficking (Pompidou Group), 35 states work together, through meetings of ministers, officials and experts, to counteract drug abuse. The Group follows a multidisciplinary approach embracing, in particular, legislation, law enforcement, prevention, treatment, rehabilitation and data collection. In January 2007 the Group initiated an online register of ongoing drug research projects; a revised version of the register was launched in April 2008.

A new Council of Europe Convention on the Counterfeiting of Medical Products and Similar Crimes Involving Threats to Public Health ('Medicrime Convention') was opened for signature in October 2011 and had 15 signatories at April 2012.

Improvement of blood transfusion safety and availability of blood and blood derivatives has been ensured through European Agreements and guidelines. Advances in this field and in organ transplantation are continuously assessed by expert committees.

In April 1997 the first international convention on biomedicine was opened for signature at a meeting of health ministers of member states, in Oviedo, Spain. The so-called Convention for the Protection of Human Rights and the Dignity of Human Beings with Respect to the Applications of Biology and Medicine incorporated provisions on scientific research, the principle of informed patient consent, organ and tissue transplants and the prohibition of financial gain and disposal of a part of the human body. It entered into force on 1 November 1999 (see below).

POPULATION AND MIGRATION

The European Convention on the Legal Status of Migrant Workers, in force since 1983, has been ratified by Albania, France, Italy, Moldova, the Netherlands, Norway, Portugal, Spain, Sweden, Turkey and the Ukraine. The Convention is based on the principle of equality of treatment for migrant workers and the nationals of the host country as to housing, working conditions, and social security. It also upholds the principle of the right to family reunion. An international consultative committee, representing the parties to the Convention, monitors the application of the Convention.

In 1996 the European Committee on Migration concluded work on a project entitled 'The Integration of Immigrants: Towards Equal Opportunities' and the results were presented at the sixth conference of European ministers responsible for migration affairs, held in Warsaw. At the conference a new project, entitled 'Tensions and Tolerance: Building better integrated communities across Europe' was initiated; it was concluded in 1999. During the period 1977–2005 an ad hoc committee of experts on the Legal Aspects of Territorial Asylum Refugees and Stateless Persons (CAHAR) assisted the Committee on Migration with examining migration issues at the pan-European level. In 2002 CAHAR prepared a Recommendation relating to the detention of asylum seekers. In May 2005 the Committee of Ministers adopted *Twenty Guidelines on Forced Return of Illegal Residents*, which had been drafted by CAHAR. The European Committee on Migration was responsible for activities concerning Roma/Gypsies in Europe, in co-ordination with other relevant Council of Europe bodies. In December 2004 a European Roma and Travellers Forum, established in partnership with the Council of Europe, was inaugurated. The eighth Council of Europe conference of ministers responsible for migration affairs, convened in Kyiv, Ukraine, in September 2008, adopted a final declaration on pursuing an integrated approach to addressing economic migration, social cohesion and development. In May 2011 a consultation meeting on Council of Europe activities in the area of migration, addressing the human rights dimension of migration; procedures for asylum and return; and questions relating to the social integration of migrants, was convened in Athens, Greece, with participation by experts and representatives of UNHCR and the EU Fundamental Rights Agency.

In May 2006 the Council of Europe adopted a Convention on the avoidance of statelessness in relation to state succession. It was reported in August 2011 by the Council's Commissioner for Human Rights that there were at that time up to 589,000 stateless people in Europe.

The European Population Committee, an intergovernmental committee of scientists and government officials responsible for population matters, monitors and analyses population trends throughout Europe and informs governments, research centres and the public of demographic developments and their impact on policy decisions. It compiles an annual statistical review of regional demographic developments and publishes the results of studies on population issues.

COUNCIL OF EUROPE DEVELOPMENT BANK

The Council of Europe Development Bank was established in April 1956 by the Committee of Ministers, initially as the Resettlement Fund, and later as the Council of Europe Social Development Fund, and then renamed again in November 1999. It is a multilateral development bank with a social mandate, promoting social development by granting loans for projects with a social purpose. Projects aimed at solving social problems related to the presence of refugees, displaced persons or forced migrants are a priority. In addition, the Bank finances projects in other fields that contribute directly to strengthening social cohesion in Europe: job creation and preservation in small and medium-sized enterprises; social housing; improving urban living conditions; health and education infrastructure, protection of the environment, and rural modernization; protection and rehabilitation of the historic heritage. At December 2010 the Bank had total assets of €24,721m. In 2010 the Bank approved 31 new projects with a value of €2,267m. Its lending activities have been increasingly targeted at Central and Eastern European countries.

LEGAL AFFAIRS

The European Committee on Legal Co-operation develops co-operation between member states in the field of law, with the objective of harmonizing and modernizing public and private law, including administrative law and the law relating to the judiciary. The Committee is responsible for expert groups which consider issues relating to administrative law, efficiency of justice, family law, nationality, information technology and data protection.

Numerous conventions and Recommendations have been adopted, and followed up by appropriate committees or groups of experts, on matters which include: efficiency of justice; nationality; legal aid; rights of children; data protection; information technology; children born out of wedlock; animal protection; adoption; information on foreign law; and the legal status of NGOs.

In December 1999 the Convention for the Protection of Human Rights and the Dignity of Human Beings with Respect to the Applications of Biology and Medicine: Convention on Human Rights and Biomedicine entered into force, as the first internationally binding legal text to protect people against the misuse of biological and medical advances. It aims to preserve human dignity and identity, rights and freedoms, through a series of principles and rules. Additional protocols develop the Convention's general provisions by means of specialized texts. A Protocol prohibiting the medical cloning of human beings was approved by Council heads of state and government in 1998 and entered into force on 1 March 2001. A Protocol on the transplantation of human organs and tissue was opened for signature in January 2002 and entered into force in May 2006, and a Protocol concerning biomedical research opened for signature in January 2005 and entered into force in September 2007. Work on draft protocols relating to protection of the human embryo and foetus, and genetics is ongoing. A Recommendation on xenotransplantation was adopted by the Committee of Ministers in 2003.

In 2001 an Additional Protocol to the Convention for the protection of individuals with regard to automatic processing of personal data was adopted. The Protocol, which opened for signature in November, concerned supervisory authorities and transborder data flows. It entered into force in July 2004.

In 2001 the European Committee for Social Cohesion (CDCS) approved three new conventions on contact concerning children, legal aid, and 'Information Society Services'. In 2002 the CDCS approved a Recommendation on mediation on civil matters and a resolution establishing the European Commission for the Efficiency of Justice (CEPEJ). The aims of the CEPEJ are: to improve the efficiency and functioning of the justice system of member states, with a view to ensuring that everyone within their jurisdiction can enforce their legal rights effectively, increasing citizen confidence in the system; and to enable better implementation of the international legal instruments of the Council of Europe concerning efficiency and fairness of justice.

A Convention on Contact concerning Children was adopted in May 2003. It entered into force in September 2005 and by April 2012 had been ratified by seven states. A new convention on the Protection of Children against Sexual Exploitation and Sexual Abuse was adopted in July 2007 and entered into force in July 2010; by April 2012 it had received 18 ratifications.

A Convention on Preventing and Combating Violence against Women and Domestic Violence was adopted in May 2011, and was to enter into force following its 10th ratification (it had 18 signatories and one ratification at April 2012).

The Consultative Council of European Judges has prepared a framework global action plan for judges in Europe. In addition, it has contributed to the implementation of this programme by the adoption of opinions on standards concerning the independence of the judiciary and the irremovability of judges, and on the funding and management of courts.

A Committee of Legal Advisers on Public and International Law (CAHDI), comprising the legal advisers of ministers of foreign affairs of member states and of several observer states, is authorized by the Committee of Ministers to examine questions of public international law, and to exchange and, if appropriate, to co-ordinate the views of member states. The CAHDI functions as a European observatory of reservations to international treaties. Recent activities of the CAHDI include the preparation of a Recommendation on reactions to inadmissible reservations to international treaties, the publication of a report on state practice with regard to state succession and recognition, and another on expression of consent of states to be bound by a treaty.

With regard to crime, expert committees and groups operating under the authority of the European Committee on Crime Problems have prepared conventions on such matters as extradition, mutual assistance, recognition and enforcement of foreign judgments, transfer of proceedings, suppression of terrorism, transfer of prisoners, compensation payable to victims of violent crime, money-laundering, confiscation of proceeds from crime and corruption.

A Convention on Cybercrime, adopted in 2001, entered into force in July 2004 and by April 2012 had received 32 ratifications. In 2003 member states concluded an additional Protocol to the Convention relating to the criminalization of acts of a racist and xenophobic nature committed through computer systems; this entered into force in March 2006 and had been ratified by 20 countries at April 2012. The Council of Europe organizes an annual conference on cybercrime (in 2011 held in November, in Strasbourg). The 2008 conference, convened in April, adopted guidelines aimed at improving co-operation between crime investigators and internet service providers.

A Multidisciplinary Group on International Action against Terrorism, established in 2001, elaborated a protocol that updated the 1977 European Convention on the Suppression of Terrorism. In 2002 the Council's Committee of Ministers adopted a set of 'guidelines on Human Rights and the Fight against Terrorism'. In 2003 a Committee of Experts on Terrorism (CODEXTER) was inaugurated, with a mandate to oversee and co-ordinate the Council's counter-terrorism activities in the legal field. CODEXTER formulated the Council of Europe Convention for the Prevention of Terrorism, which was opened for signature in May 2005 and entered into force in June 2007. By April 2012 the Convention for the Prevention of Terrorism had been ratified by 29 member states. In 2006 the Council of Europe launched a campaign to combat trafficking, which seeks to raise awareness of the extent of trafficking in present-day Europe and to emphasize the measures that can be taken to prevent it. The campaign also promotes participation in the Convention on Action against Trafficking in Human Beings; the Convention entered into force in February 2008 and, by April 2012, had been ratified by 35 countries.

The Group of States Against Corruption (GRECO) became operational in 1999 and became a permanent body of the Council in 2002. At April 2012 it had 49 members (including the USA). A monitoring mechanism, based on mutual evaluation and peer pressure, GRECO assesses members' compliance with Council instruments for combating corruption, including the Criminal Law Convention on Corruption, which entered into force in July 2002 (and by April 2012 had been ratified by 43 states), and its Additional Protocol (which entered into force in February 2005). The evaluation procedure of GRECO is confidential but it has become practice to make reports public after their adoption. GRECO's First Evaluation Round was completed during 2001–02, and the Second Evaluation Round was conducted during 2003–06. The Third Evaluation Round, which was undertaken during 2007–11, covered member states' compliance with, *inter alia*, requirements of the Criminal Law Convention on Corruption and its Additional Protocol, and the area of transparency of political party funding. GRECO's Fourth Evaluation Round commenced in January 2012.

The Select Committee of Experts on the Evaluation of Anti-Money Laundering Measures (MONEYVAL) became operational in 1998. It is responsible for mutual evaluation of the anti-money-laundering measures in place in 20 Council of Europe states that are not members of the Financial Action Task Force (FATF). The MONEYVAL mechanism is based on FATF practices and procedures. States are evaluated against the relevant international standards in the legal, financial and law enforcement sectors. In the legal sector this includes evaluation of states' obligations under the Council of Europe Convention on Laundering, Search, Seizure and Confiscation of the Proceeds from Crime and on the Financing of Terrorism, which entered into force in May 2008. With effect from 1 January 2011 MONEYVAL was elevated to the status of an independent monitoring mechanism, reporting directly to the Committee of Ministers. After the terrorist attacks against targets in the USA on 11 September 2001, the Committee of Ministers adopted revised terms of reference, which specifically include the evaluation of measures to combat the financing of terrorism. MONEYVAL undertook its first round of on-site visits during 1998–2000. Its second round, focusing even more closely on the effectiveness of national systems, began in 2001 and was completed in 2004. MONEYVAL's third evaluation round, covering the period 2005–10, was being conducted in accordance with a comprehensive global methodology agreed with the FATF, FATF-style regional bodies, the IMF and the World Bank, and was evaluating the effectiveness of enforcement measures in place to combat the financing of terrorism as well as money laundering. The evaluations of MONEYVAL are confidential, but summaries of adopted reports are made public.

A Criminological Scientific Council, composed of specialists in law, psychology, sociology and related sciences, advises the Committee and organizes criminological research conferences and colloquia. A Council for Penological Co-operation organizes regular high-level conferences of directors of prison administrations and is responsible for collating statistical information on detention and community sanctions in Europe. The Council prepared the European Prison Rules in 1987 and the European Rules on Community Sanctions (alternatives to imprisonment) in 1992. A council for police matters was established in 2002.

In May 1990 the Committee of Ministers adopted a Partial Agreement to establish the European Commission for Democracy through Law, to be based in Venice, Italy. The so-called Venice Commission was enlarged in February 2002 and in April 2012 comprised all Council of Europe member states in addition to Kyrgyzstan (which joined in 2004), Chile (2005), the Republic of Korea (2006), Algeria and Morocco (2007), Israel and Tunisia (2008), Peru and Brazil (2009), and Mexico (2010). The Commission is composed of independent legal and political experts, mainly senior academics, supreme or constitutional court judges, members of national parliaments, and senior public officers. Its main activity is constitutional assistance and it may supply opinions upon request, made through the Committee of Ministers, by the Parliamentary Assembly, the Secretary-General or any member states of the Commission. Other states and international organizations may request opinions with the consent of the Committee of Ministers. The Commission is active throughout the constitutional domain, and has worked on issues including legislation on constitutional courts and national minorities, electoral law and other legislation with implications for national democratic institutions. The creation of the Council for Democratic Elections institutionalized co-operation in the area of elections between the Venice Commission, the Parliamentary Assembly of the Council of Europe, and the Congress of Regional and Local Authorities of the Council of Europe. The Commission disseminates its work through the UniDem (University for Democracy) programme of seminars, the CODICES database, and the *Bulletin of Constitutional Case-Law*. In May 2005 Council heads of state decided to establish a new Forum for the Future of Democracy, with the aim of strengthening democracy and citizens' participation.

The promotion of local and regional democracy and of transfrontier co-operation constitutes a major aim of the Council's intergovernmental programme of activities. The Steering Committee on Local and Regional Democracy (CDLR) serves as a forum for representatives of member states to exchange information and pursue co-operation in order to promote the decentralization of powers, in accordance with the European Charter on Local Self-Government. The CDLR's principal objectives are to improve the legal, institutional and financial framework of local democracy and to encourage citizen participation in local and regional communities. In December 2001 the Committee of Ministers adopted a Recommendation on citizens' participation in public life at local level, drafted on the basis of the work conducted by the CDLR. The CDLR publishes comparative studies and national reports, and aims to identify guidelines for the effective implementation of the principles of subsidiarity and solidarity. Its work also constitutes a basis for the provision of aid to Central and Eastern European countries in the field of local democracy. The CDLR is responsible for the preparation and follow-up of Conferences of Ministers responsible for local and regional government.

Intergovernmental co-operation with the CDLR is supplemented by specific activities aimed at providing legislative advice, supporting reform and enhancing management capabilities and democratic participation in European member and non-member countries. These activities are specifically focused on the democratic stability of Central and Eastern European countries. The programmes for democratic stability in the field of local democracy draw inspiration from the European Charter of Local Self-Government, operating at three levels of government: at intergovernmental level, providing assistance in implementing reforms to reinforce local or regional government, in compliance with the Charter; at local or regional level, co-operating with local and regional authorities to build local government capacity; and at community level, co-operating directly with individual authorities to promote pilot initiatives. Working methods include: awareness-raising conferences; legislative opinion involving written opinions, expert round-tables and working groups; and seminars, workshops and training at home and abroad.

In February 2005 the 14th session of the conference of European ministers responsible for local and regional government adopted the Budapest Agenda for Delivering Good Local and Regional Governance in 2005–10, which identified challenges confronting local and regional democracy in Europe and actions to be taken in response to them. In October 2007 the 15th session of the conference adopted the Valencia Declaration, recommitting to the implementation of the Budapest Agenda and endorsing a new Council of Europe Strategy on Innovation and Good Governance at Local Level. The 15th session also determined to draft an additional protocol to the European Charter on Local Self-Government consolidating at European level the right to democratic participation, citizens' right to information, and the duties of authorities relating to these rights; this was opened for signature in November 2009. The 16th session, held in Utrecht, Netherlands, in October 2009, adopted the 'Utrecht Declaration on Good Local and Regional Governance in Turbulent Times: The Challenge of Change'.

The policy of the Council of Europe on transfrontier co-operation between territorial communities or authorities is implemented through two committees. The Committee of Experts on Transfrontier Co-operation, working under the supervision of the CDLR, aims to monitor the implementation of the European Outline Convention on Transfrontier Co-operation between Territorial Communities or Authorities; to make proposals for the elimination of obstacles, in particular of a legal nature, to transfrontier and interterritorial co-operation; and to compile 'best practice' examples of transfrontier co-operation in various fields of activity. In 2002 the Committee of Ministers adopted a Recommendation on the mutual aid and assistance between central and local authorities in the event of disasters affecting frontier areas. A Committee of Advisers for the development of transfrontier co-operation in Central and Eastern Europe is composed of six members appointed or elected by the Secretary-General, the Committee of Ministers and the Congress of Local and Regional Authorities of Europe. Its task is to guide the promotion of transfrontier co-operation in Central and Eastern European countries, with a view to fostering good neighbourly relations between the frontier populations, especially in particularly sensitive regions. Its programme comprises: conferences and colloquies designed to raise awareness on the Outline Convention; meetings in border regions between representatives of local communities with a view to strengthening mutual trust; and legal assistance to, and restricted meetings with, national and local representatives responsible for preparing the legal texts for ratification and/or implementation of the Outline Convention. The priority areas outlined by the Committee of Advisers include South-East Europe, northern Europe around the Baltic Sea, the external frontiers of an enlarged EU, and the Caucasus.

EDUCATION, CULTURE AND HERITAGE

The European Cultural Convention covers education, culture, heritage, sport and youth. Programmes on education, higher education, culture and cultural heritage are managed by four steering committees. A new Council of Europe cultural governance observatory, CultureWatchEurope is under development, with a mandate to monitor the follow-up to all relevant Council of Europe Conventions; to act as a forum for the exchange of information on culture, and on cultural and natural heritage; to observe ongoing relevant policies, practices, trends and emerging issues; to highlight good practice; and to analyse and advise on policy.

The education programme consists of projects on education for democratic citizenship and human rights, history teaching, intercultural dialogue, instruments and policies for plurilingualism, the education of European Roma/Gypsy children, teaching remembrance—education for the prevention of crimes against humanity, and the 'Pestalozzi' training programme for education professionals. The Council of Europe's main focus in the field of higher education is, in co-operation with the EU, on the Bologna Process, which was launched in 1999 with the aim of establishing a European Higher Education Area, including education networks and student exchanges at all levels. In May 2007 the Council of Europe and the EU signed a memorandum of understanding confirming mutual co-operation in the promotion of democratic citizenship and human rights education and reaffirming commitment to the Bologna Process. In April 2009 ministers responsible for higher education in the member countries of the Bologna Process adopted the priorities for the European Higher Education Area until 2020, with an emphasis on the importance of life long learning, expanding access to higher education, and mobility. In March 2010 the Bologna Process ministers for higher education adopted the Budapest-Vienna Declaration officially launching the European Higher Education Area. Other Council of Europe activities in the area of education include the partial agreement for the European Centre for Modern Languages located in Graz, Austria, the Network for School Links and Exchanges, and the European Schools Day competition, organized in co-operation with the EU.

In December 2000 the Committee of Ministers adopted a Declaration on Cultural Diversity, formulated in consultation with other organizations (including the EU and UNESCO), which created a framework for developing a European approach to valuing cultural diversity. A European Charter for Regional or Minority Languages entered into force in 1998, with the aim of protecting regional or minority languages, which are considered to be a threatened aspect of Europe's cultural heritage. It was intended to promote the use in private and public life of languages traditionally used within a state's territory. The Charter provides for a monitoring system enabling states, the Council of Europe and individuals to observe and follow up its implementation. The meeting of heads of state or government convened in Warsaw, Poland, in May 2005 identified intercultural dialogue as a means of promoting tolerance and social cohesion; this was supported by the Faro Declaration on the Council of Europe's Strategy for Developing Intercultural Dialogue adopted by ministers of culture convened in Faro, Portugal, in October of that year. In May 2008 the Council of Europe organized, in Liverpool, United Kingdom, a conference on intercultural cities, which addressed replacing a multicultural approach to cultural diversity with an intercultural outlook, encouraging interaction between and hybridization of cultures, with a view to generating a richer common cultural environment. A new Council of Europe Intercultural Cities Programme was launched at the conference. In that month the Committee of Ministers adopted a *White Paper on Intercultural Dialogue* which stated that clear reference to the universal values of democracy, human rights, and the rule of law must underpin the use of intercultural dialogue as a means of addressing the complex issues raised by increasingly culturally diverse societies.

The Framework Convention on the Value of Cultural Heritage for Society (known as the Faro Framework Convention), which entered into force in June 2011, establishes principles underpinning the use and development of heritage in Europe in the globalization era.

The European Audiovisual Observatory, established in 1992, collates and circulates information on legal, production, marketing and statistical issues relating to the audiovisual industry in Europe, in the four sectors of film, television, video and DVD, and new media. The European Convention for the Protection of Audiovisual Heritage and its Protocol were opened for signature in November 2001; the first document entered into force in January 2008, and had been ratified by eight countries at April 2012. The Eurimages support fund, in which 36 member states participate, helps to finance co-production of films. The Convention for the Protection of the Architectural Heritage and the Protection of the Archaeological Heritage provide a legal framework for European co-operation in these areas. The European Heritage Network is being developed to facilitate the work of professionals and state institutions and the dissemination of good practices in more than 30 countries of the states party to the European Cultural Convention.

YOUTH

In 1972 the Council of Europe established the European Youth Centre (EYC) in Strasbourg. A second residential centre was created in Budapest in 1995. The centres, run with and by international non-governmental youth organizations representing a wide range of interests, provide about 50 residential courses a year (study sessions, training courses, symposia). A notable feature of the EYC is its decision-making structure, by which decisions on its programme and general policy matters are taken by a Programming Committee composed of an equal number of youth organizations and government representatives. The ninth Council of Europe Conference of Ministers responsible for Youth was scheduled to take place in St Petersburg, Russia, in September 2012.

The European Youth Foundation (EYF) aims to provide financial assistance to European activities of non-governmental youth organizations and began operations in 1973. Since that time more than 300,000 young people have benefited directly from EYF-supported activities. The Steering Committee for Youth conducts research in youth-related matters and prepares for ministerial conferences.

In 1997 the Council of Europe and the European Youth Information and Counselling Agency (EYRICA) concluded a partnership agreement on developing the training of youth information workers. EYRICA maintains SHEYRICA, an online platform supporting youth information workers. In November 2004 the EYRICA General Assembly adopted the European Youth Information Charter; in 2012 some 13,000 EYRICA youth workers were providing young people with general information in accordance with the principles of the Charter. EYRICA comprises 26 member organizations, as well as five affiliated and four co-operating organizations, which were active in more than 8,000 youth information centres in 31 countries.

SPORT

The Committee for the Development of Sport, founded in 1977, oversees sports co-operation and development on a pan-European basis, bringing together all the 50 (as at April 2012) states party to the European Cultural Convention. Its activities focus on the implementation of the European Sport Charter and Code of Sports Ethics (adopted in 1992 and revised in 2001), the role of sport in society, the provision of assistance in sports reform to new member states in Central and Eastern Europe, and the practice of both recreational and high-level sport. A Charter on Sport for Disabled Persons was adopted in 1986. The Committee also prepares the Conferences of European Ministers responsible for Sport (usually held every four years) and has been responsible for drafting two important conventions to combat negative influences on sport. The European Convention on Spectator Violence and Misbehaviour at Sport Events (1985) provides governments with practical measures to ensure crowd security and safety, particularly at football matches. The Anti-Doping Convention (1989) has been ratified by 51 countries (as at April 2012); it is also open to non-European states. In October 2004 the ministerial conference, convened in Budapest, Hungary, adopted principles of good governance in sport. In May 2007 the Committee of Ministers adopted the Enlarged Partial Agreement on Sport (EPAS), which aimed to develop a framework for a pan-European platform of intergovernmental sports co-operation and to set international standards.

ENVIRONMENT AND SUSTAINABLE DEVELOPMENT

In 1995 the Pan-European Biological and Landscape Diversity Strategy (PEBLDS), formulated by the Committee of Ministers, was endorsed at a ministerial conference of the UN Economic Commission for Europe, which was held in Sofia, Bulgaria. The Strategy is implemented jointly by the Council of Europe and UNEP, in close co-operation with the European Community. In particular, it provides for implementation of the Convention on Biological Diversity.

It promotes the development of the Pan-European Ecological Network (PEEN), supporting the conservation of a full range of European ecosystems, habitats, species and landscapes, and physically linking core areas through the preservation (or restoration) of ecological corridors.

The Convention on the Conservation of European Wildlife and Natural Habitats (Bern Convention), which was signed in 1979 and entered into force in June 1982, gives total protection to 693 species of plants, 89 mammals, 294 birds, 43 reptiles, 21 amphibians, 115 freshwater fishes, 113 invertebrates and their habitats. The Convention established a network of protected areas known as the 'Emerald Network'. The Council awards the European Diploma for protection of sites of European significance, supervises a network of biogenetic reserves, and co-ordinates conservation action for threatened animals and plants. A European Convention on Landscape, to provide for the management and protection of the natural and cultural landscape in Europe, was adopted by the Committee of Ministers in 2000 and entered into force in July 2004.

Regional disparities constitute a major obstacle to the process of European integration. Conferences of ministers responsible for regional/spatial planning (CEMAT) are held to discuss these issues. In 2000 they adopted guiding principles for sustainable development of the European continent and, in 2001, a resolution detailing a 10-point programme for greater cohesion among the regions of Europe. In September 2003 the 13th CEMAT, convened in Ljubljana, Slovenia, agreed on strategies to promote the sustainable spatial development of the continent, including greater public participation in decision-making, an initiative to revitalize the countryside and efforts to prevent flooding. The 14th meeting was held in Portugal, in October 2006, and the 15th was convened in July 2010, in Moscow, Russia, on the theme 'Challenge of the Future: Sustainable Spatial Development of the European Continent in a Changing World'.

EXTERNAL RELATIONS

Agreements providing for co-operation and exchange of documents and observers have been concluded with the UN and its agencies, and with most of the European intergovernmental organizations and the Organization of American States. Relations with non-member states, other organizations and NGOs are co-ordinated by the Directorate-General of Political Affairs. In 2001 the Council and European Commission signed a joint declaration on co-operation and partnership, which provided for the organization and funding of joint programmes.

Israel, Canada and Mexico are represented in the Parliamentary Assembly by observer delegations, and certain European and other non-member countries participate in or send observers to certain meetings of technical committees and specialized conferences at intergovernmental level. Full observer status with the Council was granted to the USA in 1995, to Canada and Japan in 1996 and to Mexico in 1999. The Holy See has had a similar status since 1970.

The European Centre for Global Interdependence and Solidarity (the 'North-South Centre') was established in Lisbon, Portugal, in 1990, in order to provide a framework for European co-operation in this area and to promote pluralist democracy and respect for human rights. The Centre is co-managed by parliamentarians, governments, NGOs and local and regional authorities. Its activities are divided into three programmes: public information and media relations; education and training for global interdependence; and dialogue for global partnership. The Centre organizes workshops, seminars and training courses on global interdependence and convenes international colloquies on human rights.

The partial European and Mediterranean Major Hazards Agreement (EUR-OPA), adopted in 1987, facilitates co-operation between European and non-European southern Mediterranean countries in the field of major natural and technological disasters, covering knowledge of hazards, risk prevention, risk management, post-crisis analysis and rehabilitation.

Since 1993 the Council of Europe and EU have jointly established a co-operative structure of programmes to assist the process of democratic reform in Central and Eastern European countries that were formerly under communist rule. The majority of ongoing joint programmes are country-specific (for example, programmes focused on Albania (inaugurated in 1993), on Armenia, Azerbaijan and Georgia (1999), on Bosnia and Herzegovina (2003), Moldova (1997), Russia (1996), Serbia (2001), and Ukraine (1995). Sub-regional multilateral thematic programmes have also been implemented, for example on combating organized crime and corruption, and on the protection of national minorities. A scheme of Democratic Leadership Programmes for the training of political leaders has been implemented. Within the framework of the co-operation programme 21 information and documentation offices have been established in Central and Eastern European countries.

Finance

The budget is financed by contributions from members on a proportional scale of assessment (using population and gross domestic product as common indicators). The 2012 budget totalled €240m.

Publications

Activities Report (in English and French).

The Bulletin (newsletter of the CLRAE, quarterly).

Bulletin On Constitutional Case-Law (3–4 times a year, in English and French).

The Council of Europe: 800 million Europeans (introductory booklet).

Education Newsletter (3 a year).

The Europeans (electronic bulletin of the Parliamentary Assembly).

The Fight Against Terrorism, Council of Europe Standards (in English and French).

Human Rights and the Environment (in English, French and Italian).

Human Rights Information Bulletin (3 a year, in English and French).

The Independent (newsletter of the North-South Centre, 3 a year).

Iris (legal observations of the European audiovisual observatory, monthly).

Naturopa (2 a year, in 15 languages).

Penological Information Bulletin (annually, in English and French).

The Pompidou Group Newsletter (3 a year).

Recent Demographic Developments in Europe (annually, in English and French).

Social Cohesion Developments (3 a year).

Yearbook of Film, Television and Multimedia in Europe (in English and French).

ECONOMIC COMMUNITY OF WEST AFRICAN STATES—ECOWAS

Address: ECOWAS Executive Secretariat, 101 Yakubu Gowon Crescent, PMB 401, Asokoro, Abuja, Nigeria.

Telephone: (9) 3147647; **fax:** (9) 3147646; **e-mail:** info@ecowas.int; **internet:** www.ecowas.int.

The Treaty of Lagos, establishing ECOWAS, was signed in May 1975 by 15 states, with the object of promoting trade, co-operation and self-reliance in West Africa. Outstanding protocols bringing certain key features of the Treaty into effect were ratified in November 1976. Cape Verde joined in 1977. A revised ECOWAS treaty, designed to accelerate economic integration and to increase political co-operation, was signed in July 1993.

MEMBERS

Benin	Ghana	Niger
Burkina Faso	Guinea	Nigeria
Cape Verde	Guinea-Bissau	Senegal
Côte d'Ivoire	Liberia	Sierra Leone
The Gambia	Mali	Togo

Mauritania withdrew from the organization in December 2001.

Organization

(April 2012)

AUTHORITY OF HEADS OF STATE AND GOVERNMENT

The Authority is the supreme decision-making organ of the Community, with responsibility for its general development and realization of its objectives. The Chairman is elected annually by the Authority from among the member states. The Authority meets at least once a year in ordinary session. The 40th ordinary session was convened in February 2012, in Abuja, Nigeria.

COUNCIL OF MINISTERS

The Council consists of two representatives from each member country; the chairmanship is held by a minister from the same member state as the Chairman of the Authority. The Council meets at least twice a year, and is responsible for the running of the Community.

ECOWAS COMMISSION

The ECOWAS Commission, formerly the Executive Secretariat, was inaugurated in January 2007, following a decision to implement a process of structural reform taken at the January 2006 summit meeting of the Authority. Comprising a President, a Vice-President and seven Commissioners, the Commission is elected for a four-year term, which may be renewed once only.

President: Kadré Désiré Ouédraogo (Burkina Faso).

TECHNICAL COMMITTEES

There are nine technical committees, formerly specialized technical commissions, which prepare Community projects and programmes in the following areas:

(i) Administration and Finance;

(ii) Agriculture, Environment and Water Resources;

(iii) Communication and Information Technology;

(iv) Human Development and Gender;

(v) Infrastructure;

(vi) Legal and Judicial Affairs;

(vii) Macro-economic Policy;

(viii) Political Affairs, Peace and Security; and

(ix) Trade, Customs and Free Movement of Persons.

ECOWAS PARLIAMENT

The inaugural session of the 120-member ECOWAS Parliament, based in Abuja, Nigeria, was held in November 2000. The January 2006 summit meeting of the Authority determined to restructure the Parliament, in line with a process of wider institutional reform. The number of seats was reduced from 120 to 115 and each member of the Parliament was to be elected for a four-year term (reduced from five years). The second legislature was inaugurated in November 2006. There is a co-ordinating administrative bureau, comprising a speaker and four deputy speakers, and there are also eight standing committees (reduced in number from 13) covering each of the Parliament's areas of activity.

Speaker: Ike Ekweremadu (Nigeria).

ECOWAS COURT OF JUSTICE

The Court of Justice, established in January 2001, is based in Abuja, and comprises seven judges who serve a five-year renewable term of office. At the January 2006 summit meeting the Authority approved the creation of a Judicial Council, comprising qualified and experienced persons, to contribute to the establishment of community laws. The Authority also approved the inauguration of an appellate division within the Court. The judges will hold (non-renewable) tenure for four years.

President: Nana Awa Daboya (Togo).

Activities

ECOWAS aims to promote co-operation and development in economic, social and cultural activities, to raise the standard of living of the people of the member countries, to increase and maintain economic stability, to improve relations among member countries and to contribute to the progress and development of Africa. ECOWAS is committed to abolishing all obstacles to the free movement of people, services and capital, and to promoting: harmonization of agricultural policies; common projects in marketing, research and the agriculturally based industries; joint development of economic and industrial policies and elimination of disparities in levels of development; and common monetary policies.

Initial slow progress in achieving many of ECOWAS's aims was attributed *inter alia* to the reluctance of some governments to implement policies at the national level and their failure to provide the agreed financial resources; to the high cost of compensating loss of customs revenue; and to the existence of numerous other intergovernmental organizations in the region (in particular the Union économique et monétaire ouest-africaine—UEMOA, which replaced the francophone Communauté économique de l'Afrique de l'ouest in 1994). In respect of the latter obstacle to progress, however, ECOWAS and UEMOA resolved in February 2000 to create a single monetary zone (see below). In October ECOWAS and the European Union (EU) held their first joint high-level meeting, at which the EU pledged financial support for ECOWAS's economic integration programme, and in April 2001 it was announced that the IMF had agreed to provide technical assistance for the programme.

A revised treaty for the Community was drawn up by an ECOWAS Committee of Eminent Persons in 1991–92, and was signed at the ECOWAS summit conference that took place in Cotonou, Benin, in July 1993. The treaty designated the achievement of a common market and a single currency as economic objectives, while in the political sphere it envisaged the establishment of an ECOWAS parliament, an economic and social council, and an ECOWAS court of justice to enforce Community decisions (see above). The treaty also formally assigned the Community with the responsibility of preventing and settling regional conflicts. At a summit meeting held in Abuja, in August 1994, ECOWAS heads of state and government signed a protocol agreement for the establishment of a regional parliament. The meeting also adopted a Convention on Extradition of non-political offenders. The new ECOWAS treaty entered into effect in August 1995, having received the required number of ratifications. A draft protocol providing for the creation of a mechanism for the prevention, management and settlement of conflicts, and for the maintenance of peace in the region, was approved by ECOWAS heads of state and government in December 1999.

In May 2002 the ECOWAS Authority met in Yamoussoukro, Côte d'Ivoire, to develop a regional plan of action for the implementation of the New Partnership for Africa's Development (NEPAD). In January 2006 the Authority, meeting in Niamey, Niger, commended the recent establishment of an ECOWAS Project Development and Implementation Unit, aimed at accelerating the implementation of regional infrastructural projects in sectors such as energy, telecommunications and transport. Also at that meeting the Authority approved further amendments to the revised ECOWAS treaty to provide for institutional reform.

Meeting in Abuja, in June 2007, the Authority adopted a long-term ECOWAS Strategic Vision, detailing the proposed establishment by

2020 of a West African region-wide borderless, stateless space and single economic community. In January 2008 the Authority adopted a comprehensive strategy document proposing a number of initiatives and programmes aimed at reducing poverty in West Africa. The Authority also approved the establishment of a statistics development support fund, and the ECOWAS Common Approach on Migration.

TRADE AND MONETARY UNION

In 1990 ECOWAS heads of state and government agreed to adopt measures that would create a single monetary zone and remove barriers to trade in goods that originated in the Community. ECOWAS regards monetary union as necessary to encourage investment in the region, since it would greatly facilitate capital transactions with foreign countries. In September 1992 it was announced that, as part of efforts to enhance monetary co-operation and financial harmonization in the region, the West African Clearing House was to be restructured as the West African Monetary Agency (WAMA). As a specialized agency of ECOWAS, WAMA was to be responsible for administering an ECOWAS exchange rate system (EERS) and for establishing the single monetary zone. In July 1996 the Authority agreed to impose a common value-added tax (VAT) on consumer goods, in order to rationalize indirect taxation and to stimulate greater intra-Community trade. In August 1997 ECOWAS heads of state and government authorized the introduction of a regional travellers' cheque scheme. (The scheme was formally inaugurated in October 1998, and the cheques, issued by WAMA in denominations of a West African Unit of Account and convertible into each local currency at the rate of one Special Drawing Right—SDR—see IMF—entered into circulation on 1 July 1999.) In December 1999 the ECOWAS Authority determined to pursue a 'Fast Track Approach' to economic integration, involving a two-track implementation of related measures. In April 2000 seven, predominantly anglophone, ECOWAS member states—Cape Verde, The Gambia, Ghana, Guinea, Liberia, Nigeria and Sierra Leone—issued the 'Accra Declaration', in which they agreed to establish a second West African monetary union (the West African Monetary Zone—WAMZ) to co-exist initially alongside UEMOA, which unites eight, mainly francophone, ECOWAS member states. As preconditions for adopting a single currency and common monetary and exchange rate policy, the member states of the second West African monetary union were (under the supervision of a newly established ECOWAS Convergence Council, comprising member states' ministers of finance and central bank governors) to attain a number of convergence criteria, including: a satisfactory level of price stability; sustainable budget deficits; a reduction in inflation; and the maintenance of an adequate level of foreign exchange reserves. The two complementary monetary unions were expected to harmonize their economic programmes, with a view to effecting an eventual merger, as outlined in an action plan adopted by ECOWAS and UEMOA in February 2000. The ECOWAS Authority summit held in December 2000, in Bamako, Mali, adopted an Agreement Establishing the WAMZ, approved the establishment of a West African Monetary Institute to prepare for the formation of a West African Central Bank (WACB), and determined that the harmonization of member countries' tariff structures should be accelerated to facilitate the implementation of the planned customs union. In December 2001 the Authority determined that the currency of the WAMZ (and eventually the ECOWAS-wide currency) would be known as the 'eco' and authorized the establishment during 2002 of an exchange rate mechanism. This was achieved in April. Meeting in November 2002 the heads of state and government determined that a forum of WAMZ ministers of finance should be convened on a regular basis to ensure the effective implementation of fiscal policies. In May 2004 ECOWAS and UEMOA signed an agreement that provided for the establishment of a Joint Technical Secretariat to enhance the co-ordination of their programmes.

Owing to slower-than-anticipated progress in achieving the convergence criteria required for monetary union, past deadlines for the inauguration of the WAMZ and launch of the 'eco' were not met. In May 2009 the Convergence Council adopted a new roadmap towards realizing the single currency for West Africa by 2020. Under the roadmap (of which an updated version was released in March 2010), the harmonization of the regulatory and supervisory framework for banking and other financial institutions, the establishment of the payment system infrastructure for cross-border transactions and of the payment system infrastructure in Guinea, The Gambia and Sierra Leone, and also the ongoing integration of regional financial markets, were all to be finalized during 2009–early 2013. The roadmap envisaged that, by 2014, ratification of the legal instruments for the creation of the WAMZ would have been achieved, and that during 2014 the WACB, WAMZ Secretariat and West African Financial Supervisory Agency would be established. The WAMZ monetary union was finally to enter into effect before or at the start of 2015, with the 'eco' scheduled to enter into circulation in January 2015. In October 2011 the Convergence Council adopted supplementary acts to facilitate the process of establishing the single currency. The documents included: the Guideline on the Formation of a Multi-year Programme on Convergence with ECOWAS; and the Draft Supplementary Act on Convergence and Macroeconomic Stability Pact among Member States, the latter constituting a formal commitment by signatories to ensure economic policy co-ordination, to strengthen economic convergence and to increase macroeconomic stability.

In January 2006 the Authority approved the implementation of a four-band common external tariff (CET) that was to align the WAMZ tariff structure with that of UEMOA, as follows: a 0% tariff would be applied to social goods (for example, educational and medical equipment); 5% would be levied on raw materials and most agricultural inputs; 10% on intermediate goods and rice; and 20% on finished consumer products. At the inaugural meeting of the Joint ECOWAS–UEMOA Management Committee of the ECOWAS CET, convened in July 2006, members agreed on a roadmap for implementing the uniform tariff system. The roadmap also outlined the legal framework for the introduction of the CET. In December 2011 a meeting of the Joint Committee agreed on a timetable for concluding the draft CET, in order to be able to present it for adoption by the ECOWAS Council of Ministers in June 2012.

In December 1992 ECOWAS ministers agreed on the institutionalization of an ECOWAS trade fair, in order to promote trade liberalization and intra-Community trade. The first trade fair was held in Dakar, Senegal, in 1995; the sixth was held in Lomé, Togo, in November–December 2011, on the theme 'Strengthening intra-Community trade through public private partnership'. In September an ECOWAS Investment Forum was held in Lagos, Nigeria (following an inaugural event held in Brussels, Belgium, in the previous year), during which member states were called upon to implement measures to reduce risk and improve investor confidence and the business climate.

An extraordinary meeting of ministers of trade and industry was convened in May 2008 to discuss the impact on the region of the rapidly rising cost at that time of basic food items. In December the ECOWAS Authority warned that the ongoing global financial crisis might undermine the region's economic development, and called for a regional strategy to minimize the risk.

TRANSPORT AND COMMUNICATIONS

In July 1992 the ECOWAS Authority formulated a Minimum Agenda for Action for the implementation of Community agreements regarding the free movement of goods and people, for example the removal of non-tariff barriers, the simplification of customs and transit procedures and a reduction in the number of control posts on international roads. However, implementation of the Minimum Agenda was slow. In April 1997 Gambian and Senegalese finance and trade officials concluded an agreement on measures to facilitate the export of goods via Senegal to neighbouring countries, in accordance with ECOWAS protocols relating to inter-state road transit arrangements. An Inter-state Road Transit Authority has been established. A Brown Card scheme provides recognized third-party liability insurance throughout the region. In January 2003 Community heads of state and government approved the ECOWAS passport; by 2011 the passport was being issued by Benin, Guinea, Liberia, Niger, Nigeria and Senegal.

In February 1996 ECOWAS and several private sector partners established ECOAir Ltd, based in Abuja, Nigeria, which was to develop a regional airline. In December 2007, following a recommendation by the Authority, a new regional airline, ASKY (Africa Sky) was established, which initiated operations in January 2010. A regional shipping company, ECOMARINE, commenced operations in February 2003. In October 2011 West African ministers of transported concluded a series of measures to establish a common regulatory regime for the airline industry in order to improve the viability of regional airlines and to support regional integration.

An ECOWAS programme for the development of an integrated regional road network comprises: the Trans-West African Coastal Highway, linking Lagos, Nigeria, with Nouackchott, Mauritania (4,767 km), and envisaged as the western part of an eventual Pan-African Highway; and the Trans-Sahelian Highway, linking Dakar, Senegal, with N'Djamena, Chad (4,633 km). By 2006 about 83% of the coastal route was reportedly complete, and by 2001 about 87% of the trans-Sahelian route had reportedly been built. It was reported in January 2009 that construction companies were tendering to complete the Nigerian section of the Coastal Highway. In 2003 the African Development Bank agreed to finance a study on interconnection of the region's railways.

In August 1996 the initial phase of a programme to improve regional telecommunications was reported to have been completed. A second phase of the programme (INTELCOM II), which aimed to modernize and expand the region's telecommunications services, was initiated by ECOWAS heads of state in August 1997. A West African Telecommunications Regulators' Association was established, under the auspices of ECOWAS, in September 2000. The January 2006 summit meeting of the Authority approved a new

Special Fund for Telecommunications to facilitate improvements to cross-border telecommunications connectivity. In May ECOWAS ministers of information and telecommunications agreed guidelines for harmonizing the telecommunications sector. In January 2007 ECOWAS leaders adopted a regional telecommunications policy and a regulatory framework that covered areas including interconnection to ICT and services networks, license regimes, and radio frequency spectrum management. A common, liberalized ECOWAS telecommunications market is envisaged. In October 2008 ECOWAS ministers responsible for telecommunications and ICT adopted regional legislation on combating cybercrime. In October 2011 ECOWAS ministers of ICT and telecommunications, meeting in Yamoussoukro, Côte d'Ivoire, adopted a series of priority projects to be undertaken in the next five years, including the elaboration of a regulation on access to submarine cable landing stations and national rights of way. The meeting recommended the establishment of a Directorate of Telecoms-ICT and Post sectors by late 2012, in order to improve ECOWAS's operational capacity and to enhance the planning and monitoring of these sectors at the Community level.

ECONOMIC AND INDUSTRIAL DEVELOPMENT

In June 2010 the Council of Ministers adopted the West African Common Industrial Policy (WACIP), and a related action plan and supplementary acts. WACIP aimed to diversify and expand the regional industrial production base by supporting the creation of new industrial production capacities as well as developing existing capacities. WACIP envisaged the expansion of intra-ECOWAS trade from 13% to 40% by 2030, through enhancing skills, industrial competitiveness and quality infrastructure, with a particular focus on the areas of information, communications and transport.

The West African Industrial Forum, sponsored by ECOWAS, is held every two years to promote regional industrial investment. In September 2008 the inaugural meeting was convened of an ECOWAS–People's Republic of China economic and trade forum, which aimed to strengthen bilateral relations and discuss investment possibilities in the development of infrastructure, financial services, agriculture and the exploitation of natural resources. A second forum was convened in March 2012, in Accra, Ghana.

In November 1984 ECOWAS heads of state and government approved the establishment of a private regional investment bank, Ecobank Transnational Inc. ECOWAS has a 10% share in the bank, which is headquartered in Lomé, Togo.

In September 1995 Nigeria, Ghana, Togo and Benin resolved to develop a gas pipeline to connect Nigerian gas supplies to the other countries. In August 1999 the participating countries, together with two petroleum companies operating in Nigeria, signed an agreement on the financing and construction of the 600-km West African Gas Pipeline, which was to extend from the Nigerian capital, Lagos, to Takoradi, Ghana. It became operational in late 2007. The implementation of a planned energy exchange scheme, known as the West African Power Pool Project (WAPP), is envisaged as a means of efficiently utilizing the region's hydro-electricity and thermal power capabilities by transferring power from surplus producers to countries unable to meet their energy requirements. An ECOWAS Energy Protocol, establishing a legal framework for the promotion of long-term co-operation in the energy sector, was adopted in 2003. In May of that year the Community decided to initiate the first phase of WAPP, to be implemented in Benin, Côte d'Ivoire, Ghana, Niger, Nigeria and Togo, at an estimated cost of US $335m. In January 2005 the Authority endorsed a revised masterplan for the implementation of WAPP, which was scheduled to be completed by 2020. In July 2005 the World Bank approved a $350m. facility to support the implementation of WAPP, which became fully operational in January 2006.

In November 2008 the Authority approved the establishment of a Regional Centre for Renewable Energy and Energy Efficiency (ECREEE), to be based in Praia, Cape Verde, and also endorsed the establishment of an ECOWAS Regional Electricity Regulatory Authority, to be based in Accra. The Authority also adopted a joint ECOWAS/UEMOA action plan on priority regional infrastructure projects. ECREEE was inaugurated in 2009, and a Secretariat was established in July 2010. In September 2011 the ECOWAS Commission signed a €2.3m. grant contract with the EU for an ECREEE project on energy efficiency in West Africa.

In April 2009 ministers responsible for the development of mineral resources endorsed an ECOWAS Directive on the Harmonization of Guiding Principles and Policies in the Mining Sector. An ad hoc committee to monitor the implementation of the Directive convened in May 2011.

REGIONAL SECURITY

The revised ECOWAS treaty, signed in July 1993, incorporates a separate provision for regional security, requiring member states to work towards the maintenance of peace, stability and security. In December 1997 an extraordinary meeting of ECOWAS heads of state and government was convened in Lomé, Togo, to consider the future stability and security of the region. It was agreed that a permanent mechanism should be established for conflict prevention and the maintenance of peace. ECOWAS leaders also reaffirmed their commitment to pursuing dialogue to prevent conflicts, co-operating in the early deployment of peace-keeping forces and implementing measures to counter trans-border crime and the illegal trafficking of armaments and drugs. At the meeting ECOWAS leaders acknowledged the role of the ECOWAS Cease-fire Monitoring Group (ECOMOG) in restoring constitutional order in Liberia and expressed their appreciation of the force's current efforts in Sierra Leone (see below). In March 1998 ECOWAS ministers of foreign affairs, meeting in Yamoussoukro, Côte d'Ivoire, resolved that ECOMOG should become the region's permanent peace-keeping force, and agreed to undertake a redefinition of the command structure within the organization in order to strengthen decision-making and the legal status of the ECOMOG force.

In December 1999 ECOWAS heads of state and government, meeting in Lomé, Togo, approved a draft protocol to the organization's treaty, providing for the establishment of a Permanent Mechanism for the Prevention, Management and Settlement of Conflicts and the Maintenance of Peace in the Region, and for the creation of a Mediation and Security Council, to comprise representatives of 10 member states, elected for two-year terms. The Council was to be supported by an advisory Council of Elders (also known as the Council of the Wise), comprising 32 eminent statesmen from the region; this was inaugurated in July 2001. ECOMOG was to be transformed from an ad hoc cease-fire monitoring group into a permanent standby force available for immediate deployment to avert emerging conflicts in the region. In January 2003 the Council of Elders was recomposed as a 15-member body with a representative from each member state. In December 2006 a Technical Committee of Experts on Political Affairs, Peace and Security was established as a subsidiary body of the Mediation and Security Council.

In October 1998 the ECOWAS Authority determined to implement a renewable three-year moratorium on the import, export or manufacture of small armaments in order to enhance the security of the sub-region. In March 1999 the Programme of Co-ordination and Assistance for Security and Development (PCASED) was launched to complement the moratorium. The moratorium was renewed for a further three years in July 2001. (In 2004 ECOWAS announced its intention to transform the moratorium into a convention and PCASED was decommissioned.) In June 2006 the Authority adopted the ECOWAS Convention on Small Arms and Light Weapons, their Ammunitions and other Materials, with the aim of regulating the importation and manufacture of such weapons. The ECOWAS Small Arms Control Programme (ECOSAP) was inaugurated in that month, based in Bamako, Mali, aimed at improving the capacity of national and regional institutions to reduce the proliferation of small weapons across the region. During 1999 ECOWAS member states established the Intergovernmental Action Group Against Money Laundering in Africa (GIABA), which was mandated to combat drug-trafficking and money laundering throughout the region; a revised regulation for GIABA adopted by the Authority in January 2006 expanded the Group's mandate to cover regional responsibility for combating terrorism. Representatives from ECOWAS member states met in Ouagadougou, Burkina Faso, in September 2007 to draft a new West African strategy for enhanced drug control. In October 2008—during a High-level Conference on Drugs Trafficking as a Security Threat to West Africa, convened by ECOWAS jointly with the UN Office on Drugs and Crime (UNODC) and the Cape Verde Government, in Praia, Cape Verde—the Executive Director of UNODC warned that West Africa was at risk of becoming an epicentre for drugs trafficking, representing a serious threat to public health and security in the region. He proposed the establishment of a West African intelligence-sharing centre, and urged the promotion of development and the strengthening of the rule of law as a means of reducing regional vulnerability to drugs and crime. At the Conference ECOWAS adopted a Political Declaration on Drugs Trafficking and Organized Crime in West Africa, and approved an ECOWAS Regional Response Plan. In April 2009 ECOWAS ministers with responsibility for issues relating to trafficking in persons adopted a policy aimed at establishing a legal mechanism for protecting and assisting victims of trafficking. In July 2009 ECOWAS, UNODC, other UN agencies, and INTERPOL launched the West Africa Coast Initiative (WACI), which aimed to build national and regional capacities to combat drugs trafficking and organized crime in, initially, four pilot post-conflict countries: Côte d'Ivoire, Guinea-Bissau, Liberia and Sierra Leone. In February 2010 the pilot countries signed the 'WACI- Freetown Commitment', endorsing the implementation of the initiative, and agreeing to establish specialized transnational crime units on their territories. WACI activities were to be expanded to Guinea during 2012. In March 2010 ECOWAS, the African Union, the International Organization for Migration and UNODC launched an initiative to develop a roadmap for implementing in West Africa the Ouagadougou Action Plan to Combat Trafficking in Human Beings (adopted by the AU in 2006).

An ECOWAS Warning and Response Network (ECOWARN) asseses threats to regional security. In June 2004 the Community approved the establishment of the ECOWAS Standby Force (ESF), comprising 6,500 troops, including a core rapid reaction component, the ECOWAS Task Force, numbering around 2,770 soldiers (deployable within 30 days). The ECOWAS Defence and Security Commission approved the operational framework for the ESF in April 2005. A training exercise for the logistics component of the ESF was conducted, in Ouagadougou, Burkina Faso, in June 2009.

In January 2005 the Authority authorized the establishment of humanitarian depot, to be based in Bamako, Mali, and a logistics depot, to be based in Freetown, Sierra Leone, with a view to expanding regional humanitarian response capacity. In December 2009 the Sierra Leone Government allocated land for the construction on the planned Freetown depot, and, in February 2011, ECOWAS signed memoranda of understanding with WFP and with the Government of Mali relating to the planned creation of the Bamako ECOWAS Humanitarian Depot, which, once established, was to provide storage for food and non-food items, and for emergency equipment. An ECOWAS Emergency Response Team (EERT) was established in 2007.

In October 2006 it was reported that ECOWAS planned to introduce a series of initiatives in each of the member states under a Peace and Development Project (PADEP). The Project intended to foster a 'culture of peace' among the member states of ECOWAS, strengthening social cohesion and promoting economic integration, democracy and good governance.

In March 2008 an ECOWAS Network of Electoral Commissions, comprising heads of member states' institutions responsible for managing elections, was established with the aim of ensuring the transparency and integrity of regional elections and helping to entrench a culture of democracy.

Guinea's membership of ECOWAS was suspended in January 2009, following a *coup d'état* in December 2008. The inaugural meeting of an International Contact Group on Guinea (ICG-G), co-chaired by ECOWAS and the AU Commission, and also comprising representatives of other regional and international organizations, was held in February 2009. Meeting in October, in its eighth session, the ICG-G strongly condemned brutal acts perpetrated by armed troops in Guinea against women and other unarmed civilians in late September. The ICG-G also invited ECOWAS, with support from partners, to establish an international observer and protection mission to contribute to the establishment of an atmosphere of security in Guinea. An extraordinary summit of the ECOWAS Authority, held in mid-October, urged the establishment of a transitional regime in Guinea. Also in October 2009, Niger's ECOWAS membership was suspended, following the refusal of that country's authorities to respond to a request by ECOWAS to postpone a controversial presidential election. ECOWAS condemned a *coup d'état* which took place in Niger in February 2010. In June 2010 the Mediation and Security Council expressed satisfaction with progress being made towards the restoration of democracy in both Guinea (where a presidential election was held, in two rounds, in June and November 2010) and Niger (where a 12-month timetable outlining the return to democratic rule had been adopted, in April, by the military regime). A meeting of the Authority in March 2011 ended the membership suspensions of both Guinea and Niger.

The President of the ECOWAS Commission participated in an AU High-level Panel appointed in January 2011 to address ongoing unrest in Côte d'Ivoire, where the security situation had deteriorated following the refusal of the outgoing President Laurent Gbagbo to acknowledge the outcome of presidential elections held in 2010, and consequently to cede power. The legitimately elected President, Alassane Ouattara, was eventually inaugurated in May 2011. In September the President of the Commission led an ECOWAS delegation to Côte d'Ivoire to assess that country's post-conflict humanitarian and economic needs. The President appointed Oluwole Coker as his Special Representative to Côte d'Ivoire in order to facilitate the provision and distribution of ECOWAS assistance. In the same month five ECOWAS heads of state met to consider the deteriorating security situation along the borders between Côte d'Ivoire and Liberia.

In April 2011 ECOWAS initiated a series of regional measures to combat the increased incidence of piracy, in co-operation with the Communauté économique des états de l'Afrique centrale (CEEAC—Economic Community of Central African States). In October the UN Security Council adopted Resolution 2018 which urged ECOWAS, the CEEAC and the Gulf of Guinea Commission to develop a comprehensive regional action plan against piracy and armed robbery at sea.

In October 2011 ECOWAS dispatched a 150-member observer mission to monitor the presidential and legislative elections in Liberia. An enlarged mission, comprising 200 observers, returned to the country in November in order to monitor the second round of voting in the presidential poll. In February 2012 ECOWAS heads of state and government authorized a Joint AU–ECOWAS high-level mission to Senegal, in order to promote political dialogue and to ensure peaceful, fair and transparent forthcoming elections. An observer mission was dispatched to Senegal in late February to monitor the presidential poll.

In March 2009 ECOWAS Chiefs of Defence agreed to deploy a multidisciplinary group to monitor and co-ordinate security sector reforms in Guinea-Bissau, following the assassinations of the military Chief of Staff and President of that country at the beginning of the month. The ECOWAS Chiefs of Defence also demanded a review of ECOWAS legislation on conflict prevention and peace-keeping. In March 2012 an 80-member ECOWAS observation mission monitored the first round of a presidential election held in Guinea-Bissau following the death in office, in January, of the most recent President. In mid-April, before the planned second round of the Guinea-Bissau presidential election, scheduled for later in that month, a military junta usurped power by force and established a Transitional National Council (TNC), comprising military officers and representatives of political parties that had been in opposition to the legitimate government. The ECOWAS Commission strongly condemned the military coup and denounced the establishment of the TNC. An ECOWAS high-level delegation visited Guinea-Bissau in mid-April to hold discussions with the military leadership.

In mid-March 2012 the President of the ECOWAS Commission led a fact-finding mission to Mali, in view of escalating unrest in northern areas of that country arising from attacks by separatist militants of the National Movement for the Liberation of Azawad (MNLA). The Commission condemned all acts of violence committed by the MNLA. In late March ECOWAS heads of state and government convened an extraordinary summit to discuss the recent illegal overthrow, by the Comité National de Redressement pour la Démocratie et la Restauration de l'Etat (CNRDRE), of the legitimate government of Mali's elected President Amadou Touré, and also to address the separatist violence ongoing in the north of the country. The regional leaders suspended Mali from participating in all decision-making bodies of ECOWAS pending the restoration of constitutional order, and imposed sanctions (including a ban on travel and an assets freeze) on members of the CNRDRE and their associates. The summit appointed President Blaise Compaoré of Burkina Faso as ECOWAS mediator, with a mandate to facilitate dialogue between the legitimate Mali Government and the CNRDRE regime on achieving a return to civilian rule, and also on means of terminating the northern rebellion. Meanwhile, in early April, MNLA rebels, assisted by Islamist forces, seized land in the Kidal, Gao and Tombouctou regions of northern Mali, unilaterally declaring this to be the independent entity of Azawad. At that time the Commission denounced a 'Declaration of Independence by the MNLA for the North of Mali', reminding all militants that Mali is an 'indivisible entity', and stating that ECOWAS would be prepared to use all necessary measures, including force, to ensure Mali's territorial integrity. An emergency meeting of ECOWAS Joint Chiefs of Defence Staff, held in early April, adopted preparatory measures for the rapid deployment of the ESF to Mali if necessary. On 6 April representatives of the CNRDRE and the ECOWAS mediation team, under the chairmanship of Compaoré, signed an accord that was intended to lead to a return to full constitutional rule; the accord entailed the appointment of a new interim president, who was to lead a transitional administration pending the staging of democratic elections. Accordingly, an interim president, Dioncounda Traoré, was sworn in on 12 April, and ECOWAS sanctions against Mali were withdrawn. The CNRDRE, however, subsequently appeared to influence the political process: in late April Traoré announced a new government, which included three posts held by military officers and no ministers from the former Touré government. From mid-April Compaoré continued to mediate negotiations on finalizing the restoration of civilian rule, as well as means of resolving the conflict in northern Mali.

An extraordinary summit meeting of ECOWAS heads of state and government convened in late April 2012 decided immediately to deploy troops from the ESF to both Guinea-Bissau and Mali to support in both countries a swift restoration of constitutional order. Sanctions, including economic measures and targeted individual penalties, were to be imposed if the military in either country continued to obstruct the democratic process. The summit meeting urged military leaders in both countries to release civilians who had been detained during the coups and to ensure the safety of officials from the former legitimate administrations. The meeting stipulated that democratic elections should be held in both Guinea-Bissau and Mali within 12 months. It was reported at that time that the ESF contingent in Guinea-Bissau would comprise up to 300 troops, and that the ESF presence in Mali would number at least 3,000.

Past Peace-keeping Operations

The ECOWAS cease-fire monitoring group, ECOMOG, was established in 1990, when it was dispatched to Liberia in an attempt to enforce a cease-fire between conflicting factions there and to help restore public order. It remained in that country until October 1999, undertaking roles including disarmament of rebel soldiers, maintaining security during presidential and legislative elections, and restructuring the national security forces. A second military force, the ECOWAS Mission in Liberia, ECOMIL, was authorized in July 2003 to protect civilians following political disturbances in the Liberian capital, Monrovia. The 3,500 ECOMIL troops transferred to a UN-mandated mission in October.

In August 1997 ECOMOG was mandated by ECOWAS heads of state and government to monitor a cease-fire in Sierra Leone negotiated with the dissident Armed Forces Revolutionary Council (ARFC), which had removed the president, Ahmed Tejan Kabbah, from office earlier in that year. ECOMOG was also mandated to upholding international sanctions against the new authorities. In February 1999 ECOMOG troops assumed control of Freetown from ARFC and the rebel Revolutionary United Front (RUF) control. Following the return of Kabbah in March, it was agreed that ECOMOG forces, then numbering some 10,000, were to remain in the country in order to ensure the full restoration of peace and security, to assist in the restructuring of the armed forces and to help to resolve the problems of the substantial numbers of refugees and internally displaced persons. ECOMOG's mandate in Sierra Leone was further adapted, following the signing of a political agreement in July, to support the consolidation of peace in that country and national reconstruction. In October a new UN mission, UNAMSIL, assumed many of the functions then being performed by ECOMOG, including the provision of security at Lungi international airport and at other key installations, buildings and government institutions in the Freetown area. In consequence the ECOMOG contingent was withdrawn in April 2000.

In February 1999 a 600-strong ECOMOG Interposition Force was dispatched to Guinea-Bissau to help uphold a cease-fire agreement between government and rebel factions in that country, to supervise the border region with Senegal and to facilitate the delivery of humanitarian assistance. The Force was withdrawn, however, in June following the removal from office of President João Vieira.

In September 2002 an extraordinary summit meeting of ECOWAS heads of state and government was convened in Accra, Ghana, to address the violent unrest that had erupted in Côte d'Ivoire during that month. The meeting condemned the attempt to overthrow democratic rule and constitutional order and established a high-level contact group, comprising the heads of state of Ghana, Guinea-Bissau, Mali, Niger, Nigeria and Togo, to prevail upon the rebel factions to end hostilities, and to negotiate a general framework for the resolution of the crisis. The contact group helped to mediate a cease-fire in the following month; this was to be monitored by an ECOWAS military mission in Côte d'Ivoire (ECOMICI), which was also to be responsible for ensuring safe passage for deliveries of humanitarian assistance. In March 2003, following the conclusion in January by the parties to the conflict of a peace agreement, signed at Marcoussis, France, ECOWAS chiefs of staff endorsed the expansion of ECOMICI from 1,264 to a maximum of 3,411 troops, to monitor the implementation of the peace agreement in co-operation with the UN Mission in Côte d'Ivoire (MINUCI), and French forces. In April 2004 authority was transferred from ECOMICI and MINUCI to the newly established UN Operation in Côte d'Ivoire (UNOCI). In mid-June ECOWAS heads of state and government convened at a summit to address means of reviving the implementation of the stalled Marcoussis peace accord. A high-level meeting of ECOWAS heads of state and government, other African leaders, the Chairperson of the AU, and the parties to the Côte d'Ivoire conflict, held in Accra in late July, affirmed that a monitoring mechanism, comprising representatives of ECOWAS, the AU, Côte d'Ivoire and the UN, should produce regular reports on progress towards peace in Côte d'Ivoire.

AGRICULTURE AND THE ENVIRONMENT

The Community enforces a certification scheme for facilitating the monitoring of animal movement and animal health surveillance and protection in the sub-region. In February 2001 ECOWAS ministers of agriculture adopted an action plan for the formulation of a common agricultural policy, as envisaged under the ECOWAS treaty. An ECOWAS Regional Agricultural Policy (ECOWAP) was endorsed by the January 2005 Authority summit. In January 2006 the Authority approved an action plan for the implementation of ECOWAP. The Policy was aimed at enhancing regional agricultural productivity with a view to guaranteeing food sufficiency and standards. In October 2011 a high-level consultative meeting of ECOWAS and FAO officials determined that ECOWAP was the most effective means of countering the effects of food price increases and volatility.

ECOWAS promotes implementation of the UN Convention on Desertification Control and supports programmes initiated at national and sub-regional level within the framework of the treaty. Together with the Permanent Inter-State Committee on Drought Control in the Sahel—CILSS, ECOWAS has been designated as a project leader for implementing the Convention in West Africa. Other environmental initiatives include a regional meteorological project to enhance meteorological activities and applications, and in particular to contribute to food security and natural resource management in the sub-region. ECOWAS pilot schemes have formed the basis of integrated control projects for the control of floating (or invasive aquatic) weeds in five water basins in West Africa, which had hindered the development of the local fishery sectors. A rural water supply programme aims to ensure adequate water for rural dwellers in order to improve their living standards. The first phase of the project focused on schemes to develop village and pastoral water points in Burkina Faso, Guinea, Mali, Niger and Senegal, with funds from various multilateral donors.

In September 2009 a regional conference, convened in Lomé, Togo, to address the potential effects of rapid climate change on regional stability, issued the Lomé Declaration on Climate Change and Protection of Civilians in West Africa, and recommended the establishment of a fund to support communities suffering the negative impact of climate change. In March 2010 ECOWAS ministers responsible for agriculture, environment and water resources adopted a Framework of Strategic Guidelines on the Reduction of Vulnerability and Adaptability to Climate Change in West Africa, outlining the development of regional capacities to build up resilience and adaptation to climate change and severe climatic conditions. ECOWAS supports the development and implementation by member states of Nationally Appropriate Mitigation Actions (NAMAs).

SOCIAL PROGRAMME

The following organizations have been established within ECOWAS: the Organization of Trade Unions of West Africa, which held its first meeting in 1984; the West African Universities' Association, the ECOWAS Youth and Sports Development Centre (EYSDC), the ECOWAS Gender Development Centre (EGDC), and the West African Health Organization (WAHO), which was established in 2000 by merger of the West African Health Community and the Organization for Co-ordination and Co-operation in the Struggle against Endemic Diseases. ECOWAS and the European Commission jointly implement the West African Regional Health Programme, which aims to improve the co-ordination and harmonization of regional health policies, with a view to strengthening West African integration. In December 2001 the ECOWAS summit of heads of state and government adopted a plan of action aimed at combating trafficking in human beings and authorized the establishment of an ECOWAS Criminal Intelligence Bureau. In March 2009 ECOWAS ministers of education, meeting in Abuja, Nigeria, identified priority activities for advancing the regional implementation of regional activities relating to the AU-sponsored Second Decade of Education in Africa (2006–15). In the following month ECOWAS ministers responsible for labour and employment adopted a regional labour policy. In February 2012 the ECOWAS Commission and the International Labour Organization determined to collaborate in order to address the challenges of child labour in West Africa. The Commission resolved to harmonize national action plans relating to child labour and to formulate a regional strategy.

SPECIALIZED AGENCIES

ECOWAS Bank for Investment and Development (EBID) : BP 2704, 128 blvd du 13 janvier, Lomé, Togo; tel. 22-21-68-64; fax 22-21-86-84; e-mail bidc@bidc-ebid.org; internet www.bidc-ebid.org; f. 2001, replacing the former ECOWAS Fund for Co-operation, Compensation and Development; comprises two divisions, a Regional Investment Bank and a Regional Development Fund; Pres. BASHIR M. IFO.

West African Monetary Agency (WAMA): 11–13 ECOWAS St, PMB 218, Freetown, Sierra Leone; tel. 224485; fax 223943; e-mail wamao@amao-wama.org; internet www.wama-amao.org; f. 1975 as West African Clearing House; agreement founding WAMA signed by governors of ECOWAS central banks in March 1996; administers transactions between its eight member central banks in order to promote sub-regional trade and monetary co-operation; administers ECOWAS travellers' cheques scheme. Mems: Banque Centrale des Etats de l'Afrique de l'Ouest (serving Benin, Burkina Faso, Côte d'Ivoire, Guinea-Bissau, Mali, Niger, Senegal, Togo) and the central banks of Cape Verde, The Gambia, Ghana, Guinea, Liberia, Nigeria and Sierra Leone; Dir-Gen. Prof. MOHAMED BEN OMAR NDIAYE; publ. *Annual Report*.

West African Monetary Institute (WAMI): Gulf House, Tetteh Quarshie Interchange, Cantonments 75, Accra, Ghana; tel. (30) 2743801; fax (30) 2743807; e-mail info@wami-imao.org; internet www.wami-imao.org; f. by the ECOWAS Authority summit in December 2000 to prepare for the establishment of a West African Central Bank, currently scheduled for 2014; Dir-Gen. TEI KITCHER (acting).

West African Health Organization (WAHO): 01 BP 153 Bobo-Dioulasso 01, Burkina Faso; tel. and fax (226) 975772; e-mail wahooas@wahooas.org; internet www.wahooas.org; f. 2000 by merger of the West African Health Community (f. 1978) and the Organization for Co-ordination and Co-operation in the Struggle against Endemic Diseases (f. 1960); aims to harmonize member states' health policies and to promote research, training, the sharing of resources and diffusion of information; Dir-Gen. Dr PLACIDO MONTEIRO CARDOSO (Guinea-Bissau); publ. *Bulletin Bibliographique* (quarterly).

West African Power Pool (WAPP): 06 BP 2907, Zone des Ambassade, PK 6 Cotonou, Benin; tel. 21-37-41-95; fax 21-37-41-96; e-mail info@ecowapp.org; internet www.ecowapp.org; f. 1999; new organization approved as a Specialized Agency in Jan. 2006; inaugural meeting held in July 2006; aims to facilitate the integration of the power systems of member nations into a unified regional electricity market; Gen. Sec. AMADOU DIALLO; publ. *WAPP Newsletter* (intermittent).

Finance

Under the revised treaty, signed in July 1993, ECOWAS was to receive revenue from a community tax, based on the total value of imports from member countries. In July 1996 the summit meeting approved a protocol on a community levy, providing for the imposition of a 0.5% tax on the value of imports from a third country. In August 1997 the Authority of Heads of State and Government determined that the community levy should replace budgetary contributions from member states as the organization's principal source of finance. The protocol came into force in January 2000, having been ratified by nine member states, with the substantive regime entering into effect on 1 January 2003. The January 2006 meeting of the Authority approved a budget of US $121m. for the operations of the Community in that year.

Publications

Annual Report.
Contact.
ECOWAS National Accounts.
ECOWAS News.
ECOWAS Newsletter.
West African Bulletin.

ECONOMIC COOPERATION ORGANIZATION—ECO

Address: 1 Golbou Alley, Kamranieh St, POB 14155-6176, Tehran, Iran.

Telephone: (21) 22831733; **fax:** (21) 22831732; **e-mail:** registry@ecosecretariat.org; **internet:** www.ecosecretariat.org.

The Economic Cooperation Organization (ECO) was established in 1985 as the successor to the Regional Cooperation for Development, founded in 1964.

MEMBERS

Afghanistan	Kyrgyzstan	Turkey
Azerbaijan	Pakistan	Turkmenistan
Iran	Tajikistan	Uzbekistan
Kazakhstan		

The 'Turkish Republic of Northern Cyprus' has been granted special guest status.

Organization

(April 2012)

SUMMIT MEETING

The first summit meeting of heads of state and of government of member countries was held in Tehran, Iran, in February 1992. Summit meetings are generally held at least once every two years. The 11th summit meeting was held in Istanbul, Turkey, in December 2010.

COUNCIL OF MINISTERS

The Council of Ministers, comprising ministers of foreign affairs of member states, is the principal policy- and decision-making body of ECO. It meets at least once a year.

REGIONAL PLANNING COUNCIL

The Council, comprising senior planning officials or other representatives of member states, meets at least once a year. It is responsible for reviewing programmes of activity and evaluating results achieved, and for proposing future plans of action to the Council of Ministers.

COUNCIL OF PERMANENT REPRESENTATIVES

Permanent representatives or Ambassadors of member countries accredited to Iran meet regularly to formulate policy for consideration by the Council of Ministers and to promote implementation of decisions reached at ministerial or summit level.

SECRETARIAT

The Secretariat is headed by a Secretary-General, who is supported by two Deputy Secretaries-General. The following Directorates administer and co-ordinate the main areas of ECO activities: Trade and investment; Transport and communications; Energy, minerals and environment; Agriculture, industry and tourism; Project and economic research and statistics; Human resources and sustainable development; and International relations. The Secretariat services regular ministerial meetings held by regional ministers of agriculture; energy and minerals; finance and economy; industry; trade and investment; and transport and communications.

Secretary-General: YAHYA P. MAROOFI (Afghanistan).

Activities

The Regional Cooperation for Development (RCD) was established in 1964 as a tripartite arrangement between Iran, Pakistan and Turkey, which aimed to promote economic co-operation between member states. ECO replaced the RCD in 1985, and seven additional members were admitted to the Organization in November 1992. The main areas of co-operation are transport (including the building of road and rail links, of particular importance as seven member states are landlocked), telecommunications and post, trade and investment, energy (including the interconnection of power grids in the region), minerals, environmental issues, industry, and agriculture. ECO priorities and objectives for each sector are defined in the Quetta Plan of Action and the Istanbul Declaration; an 'Almaty Outline Plan', which was adopted in 1993, is specifically concerned with the development of regional transport and communication infrastructure. Meeting in October 2005, in Astana, Kazakhstan, the ECO Council of Ministers adopted a document entitled *ECO Vision 2015*, detailing basic policy guidelines for the organization's activities during 2006–15, and setting a number of targets to be achieved in the various areas of regional co-operation. The 10th ECO summit meeting, convened in Tehran, Iran, in March 2009, reaffirmed commitment to ongoing co-operation, and observed that the global financial crisis had originated in factors such as world-wide systemic weaknesses, unsound practices, and excessive use of resources, necessitating closer future co-operation among member states. At the 11th summit meeting, held in Istanbul, Turkey, in December 2010, it was reported that Iraq had applied to join the Organization.

In 1990 an ECO College of Insurance was inaugurated. A joint Chamber of Commerce and Industry was established in 1993. The third ECO summit meeting, held in Islamabad, Pakistan, in March 1995, concluded formal agreements on the establishment of several other regional institutes and agencies: an ECO Trade and Development Bank, headquartered in Istanbul (with main branches in Tehran and Islamabad) (the Bank's headquarters was inaugurated in late 2006, and commenced operations in 2008); a joint shipping company (now operational), airline (project abandoned, see below), and an ECO Cultural Institute (inaugurated in 2000), all based in Iran; and an ECO Reinsurance Company (draft articles of agreement relating to its creation were finalized in May 2007) and an ECO Science Foundation, with headquarters in Pakistan. In addition, heads of state and of government endorsed the creation of an ECO eminent persons group and signed the following two agreements in order to enhance and facilitate trade throughout the region: the Transit Trade Agreement (which entered into force in December 1997) and the Agreement on the Simplification of Visa Procedures for Businessmen of ECO Countries (which came into effect in March 1998). In May 2001 the Council of Ministers agreed to terminate the ECO airline project, owing to its unsustainable cost, and to replace it with a framework agreement on co-operation in the field of air transport.

In September 1996, at an extraordinary meeting of the ECO Council of Ministers, held in Izmir, Turkey, member countries signed a revised Treaty of Izmir, the Organization's founding charter. An extraordinary summit meeting, held in Aşgabat, Turkmenistan, in May 1997, adopted the Aşgabat Declaration, emphasizing the importance of the development of the transport and communications infrastructure and the network of transnational petroleum and gas pipelines through bilateral and regional arrangements in the ECO area. In May 1998, at the fifth summit meeting, held in Almatı, Kazakhstan, ECO heads of state and of government signed a Transit Transport Framework Agreement (TTFA) and a memorandum of understanding (MOU) to help combat the cross-border trafficking of illegal goods. (The TTFA entered into force in May 2006.) The meeting also agreed to establish an ECO Educational Institute in Ankara, Turkey; in April 2012 the Institute was formally inaugurated. In June 2000 the sixth ECO summit encouraged member states to participate in the development of information and communication technologies through the establishment of a database of regional educational and training institutions specializing in that field. The seventh ECO summit, held in Istanbul, in October 2002, adopted the Istanbul Declaration, which outlined a strengthened and more proactive economic orientation for the Organization.

Convening in conference for the first time in March 2000, ECO ministers of trade signed a Framework Agreement on ECO Trade Cooperation (ECOFAT), which established a basis for the expansion of intra-regional trade. The Framework Agreement envisaged the eventual adoption of an accord providing for the gradual elimination of regional tariff and non-tariff barriers between member states. The so-called ECO Trade Agreement (ECOTA) was endorsed at the eighth ECO summit meeting, held in Dushanbe, Tajikistan, in September 2004. Heads of state and government urged member states to ratify ECOTA at the earliest opportunity, in order to achieve their vision of an ECO free trade area by 2015. The meeting also requested members to ratify and implement the Transit Transport Framework Agreement (see above), to support economic co-operation throughout the region. In May 2011 the Permanent Steering Committee on Economic Research, meeting for the first time, adopted the ECO Plan of Action for Economic Research.

ECO ministers of agriculture, convened in July 2002, in Islamabad, adopted a declaration on co-operation in the agricultural sector, which specified that member states would contribute to agricultural rehabilitation in Afghanistan, and considered instigating a mechanism for the regional exchange of agricultural and cattle products. In December 2004, meeting in Antalya, Turkey, agriculture ministers approved the Antalya Declaration on ECO Cooperation in Agriculture and adopted an ECO plan of action on drought management and mitigation. In March 2007, meeting in Tehran, ECO ministers of agriculture approved the concept of an ECO Permanent Commission for Prevention and Control of Animal Diseases and Control of Animal Origin Food-Borne Diseases (ECO-PCPCAD). ECO implements a Regional Programme for Food Security (RPFS), supported by FAO, which comprises nine regional components, as well as a country programme for community-based food production in Afghanistan. In April 2007 an ECO experts' group convened to develop a work plan on biodiversity in the ECO region with the aim of promoting co-operation towards achieving a set of agreed biodiversity targets over the period 2007–15. The ECO member states agreed, in July 2008, to establish the ECO Seed Association (ECOSA); ECOSA hosted its first international seed trade conference in December 2009, and a second in October 2010; a third was held in November 2011. In December 2008 the first ECO expert meeting on tourism adopted a plan of action on ECO co-operation in the field of ecotourism, covering 2009–13. In September 2007 the ECO Regional Center for Risk Management of Natural Disasters was inaugurated in Mashhad, Iran; the Center was to promote co-operation in drought monitoring and early warning. The sixth ECO International Conference on Disaster Risk Management was convened in February 2012, in Kabul, Afghanistan. In February 2006 a high-level group of experts on health was formed; its first meeting, held in the following month, focused on the spread of avian influenza in the region. The first ECO ministerial meeting on health, convened in February 2010, considered means of enhancing co-operation on health issues with regard to attaining relevant UN Millennium Development Goals, and addressed strengthening co-operation in the areas of blood transfusion and pharmaceuticals. The meeting adopted the Baku Declaration, identifying key priority areas for future ECO area health co-operation. In June 2011 ECO environment ministers adopted a Framework Plan of Action on Environmental Cooperation and Global Warming, covering the period 2011–15.

A meeting of ministers of industry, convened in November 2005, approved an ECO plan of action on privatization, envisaging enhanced technical co-operation between member states, and a number of measures for increasing cross-country investments; and adopted a declaration on industrial co-operation. The first meeting of the heads of ECO member states' national statistics offices, convened in January 2008 in Tehran, adopted the ECO Framework of Cooperation in Statistics and a related plan of action. An ECO Trade Fair was staged in Pakistan, in July 2008. The Organization maintains ECO TradeNet, an internet-based repository of regional trade information.

ECO has co-operation agreements with several UN agencies and other international organizations in development-related activities. In December 2007 the ECO Secretary-General welcomed, as a means of promoting regional peace and security, the inauguration of the UN Regional Centre for Preventive Diplomacy in Central Asia (UNRCCA), based in Aşgabat. In that month ECO and the Shanghai Cooperation Organization signed an MOU on mutual co-operation in areas including trade and transportation, energy and environment, and tourism. An ECO-International Organization on Migration MOU on co-operation was concluded in January 2009. In March 2011 ECO, the UN Economic Commission for Europe and the Islamic Development Bank signed a trilateral MOU on co-operation. ECO has been granted observer status at the UN, OIC and WTO.

ECO prioritizes activities aimed at combating the cultivation of and trade in illicit drugs in the region (which is the source of more than one-half of global seizures of opium, with more than 90% of global opium production occuring in Afghanistan, and many ECO member states are used in transit for its distribution). An ECO-UNODC Drug Control and Co-ordination Unit was inaugurated, in Tehran, in July 1999. In 2011 the ECO Secretariat and European Commission were jointly implementing a project entitled 'Fight against Illicit Drug Trafficking from/to Afghanistan'. The inaugural meeting of heads of INTERPOL of ECO member states was held in June 2010, in Tehran, and, in August, the first conference of ECO police chiefs with responsibility for anti-narcotics was convened, also in Tehran.

In November 2001 the UN Secretary-General requested ECO to take an active role in efforts to restore stability in Afghanistan and to co-operate closely with his special representative in that country. In June 2002 the ECO Secretary-General participated in a tripartite ministerial conference on co-operation for development in Afghanistan that was convened under the auspices of the UN Development Programme and attended by representatives from Afghanistan, Iran and Pakistan. ECO operates a Special Fund for the Reconstruction of Afghanistan, which was established in April 2004; at December 2011 US $11.2m. had been pledged to the Fund. By that time the Fund had approved four ECO projects targeted towards the education and health sectors. ECO envisages connecting Afghanistan to the regional rail road system. In January 2010 the ECO Secretary-General participated in a Regional Summit Meeting of Afghanistan and Neighbours, hosted by the Turkish Government in Istanbul, with participation by representatives of regional governments and organizations; and, in July 2010, he attended the first International Conference on Afghanistan to be convened on that country's territory, in the Afghan capital, Kabul.

Finance

Member states contribute to a centralized administrative budget.

Publications

ECO Annual Economic Report.

ECO Bulletin (quarterly).

ECO Environment Bulletin.

EUROPEAN BANK FOR RECONSTRUCTION AND DEVELOPMENT—EBRD

Address: One Exchange Square, London, EC2A 2JN, United Kingdom.

Telephone: (20) 7338-6000; **fax:** (20) 7338-6100; **e-mail:** generalenquiries@ebrd.com; **internet:** www.ebrd.com.

The EBRD was founded in May 1990 and inaugurated in April 1991. Its object is to contribute to the progress and the economic reconstruction of the countries of Central and Eastern Europe, and, from 2011–12, transitional economies in the Middle East and North Africa, that undertake to respect and put into practice the principles of multi-party democracy, pluralism, the rule of law, respect for human rights and a market economy.

MEMBERS

Countries of Operations:

Albania	Moldova
Armenia	Mongolia
Azerbaijan	Montenegro
Belarus	Poland
Bosnia and Herzegovina	Romania
Bulgaria	Russia
Croatia	Serbia
Estonia	Slovakia
Georgia	Slovenia
Hungary	Tajikistan
Kazakhstan	Turkey
Kyrgyzstan	Turkmenistan
Latvia	Ukraine
Lithuania	Uzbekistan
Macedonia, former Yugoslav republic	

Other EU members*:

Austria	Ireland
Belgium	Italy
Cyprus	Luxembourg
Czech Republic	Malta
Denmark	Netherlands
Finland	Portugal
France	Spain
Germany	Sweden
Greece	United Kingdom

EFTA† members:

Iceland	Norway
Liechtenstein	Switzerland

Other countries:

Australia	Republic of Korea
Canada	Mexico
Egypt‡	Morocco‡
Israel	New Zealand
Japan	Tunisia‡
Jordan‡	USA

* The European Union (EU) and the European Investment Bank (EIB) are also shareholder members in their own right.

† European Free Trade Association.

‡ Jordan and Tunisia were admitted as members of the EBRD in January 2012; during 2012 a process was under way to enable those two countries, as well as Egypt and Morocco (both founding members of the Bank), to become countries of operations.

Organization

(April 2012)

BOARD OF GOVERNORS

The Board of Governors, to which each member appoints a Governor (normally the minister of finance of that country) and an alternate, is the highest authority of the EBRD. It elects the President of the Bank. The Board meets each year. The 2011 meeting was held in Astana, Kazakhstan, in May. The 2012 meeting was to be held in London, United Kingdom, also in May.

BOARD OF DIRECTORS

The Board, comprising 23 directors, elected by the Board of Governors for a three-year term, is responsible for the organization and operations of the EBRD.

ADMINISTRATION

The EBRD's operations are conducted by its Banking Department, headed by the First Vice-President. Three other Vice-Presidents oversee departments of Finance; Risk Management, Human Resources and Nuclear Safety; and Environment, Procurement and Administration. Other offices include Internal Audit; Communications; the Evaluation Department; and Offices of the President, the Secretary-General, the General Counsel, the Chief Economist and the Chief Compliance Officer. A structure of country teams, industry teams and operations support units oversee the implementation of projects. The EBRD has 34 local offices in 26 countries. At December 2010 there were 1,172 staff at the Bank's headquarters (77%) and 354 staff in the Resident Offices.

President: THOMAS MIROW (Germany).

First Vice-President: VAREL FREEMAN (USA).

FINANCIAL STRUCTURE

In May 2010 EBRD shareholders agreed to increase the Bank's capital from €20,000m. to €30,000m., through use of a temporary increase in callable capital of €9,000m. and a €1,000m. transfer from reserves to paid-in capital. At 31 December 2010 paid-in capital amounted to €6,197m.

Activities

The Bank was founded to assist the transition of the economies of Central Europe, Southern and Eastern Europe and the Caucasus, and Central Asia and Russia towards a market economy system, and to encourage private enterprise. The Agreement establishing the EBRD specifies that 60% of its lending should be for the private sector, and that its operations do not displace commercial sources of finance. The Bank helps the beneficiaries to undertake structural and sectoral reforms, including the dismantling of monopolies, decentralization, and privatization of state enterprises, to enable these countries to become fully integrated in the international economy. To this end, the Bank promotes the establishment and improvement of activities of a productive, competitive and private nature, particularly small and medium-sized enterprises (SMEs), and works to strengthen financial institutions. It mobilizes national and foreign capital, together with experienced management teams, and helps to develop an appropriate legal framework to support a market-orientated economy. The Bank provides extensive financial services, including loans, equity and guarantees, and aims to develop new forms of financing and investment in accordance with the requirements of the transition process. In 2006 the Bank formally began to implement a strategy to withdraw, by 2010, from countries where the transition to a market economy was nearing completion, i.e. those now members of the European Union (EU, see below), and strengthen its focus on and resources to Russia, the Caucasus and Central Asia. New operations in the Czech Republic were terminated at the end of 2007. Mongolia and Montenegro became new countries of operations in 2006. In November 2008 Turkey, which had been a founding member of the Bank, became the 30th country of operations. In May 2011 the Group of Eight major industrialized nations (G8) declared their support for an expansion of the Bank's geographical mandate to support transitional economies in the Middle East and North Africa. In March the Bank signed a new Memorandum of Understanding (MOU) with the European Investment Bank (EIB) and European Commission to enhance co-operation in activities outside of the EU region. MOUs with the African Development Bank and the Islamic Development Bank were signed in September. At that time the EBRD joined other international financial institutions active in the Middle East and North Africa region to endorse the so-called Deauville Partnership, established by G8 in May to support political and economic reforms being undertaken by several countries, notably Egypt, Jordan, Morocco and Tunisia. Jordan and Tunisia were admitted as members of the EBRD in January 2012; during that year a process was under way to enable those two countries, as well as Egypt and Morocco (both founding members of the Bank), to become countries of operations. It was envisaged that the EBRD would be able to invest up to €2,500m. annually across the four countries. Initial flows of grant-funded technical assistance to the planned four new countries of operations commenced in late 2011; a dedicated fund to enable investments in the four countries was to be established in 2012.

During 2010 the Bank continued to support its countries of operations affected by the global financial and economic crisis by approving its largest ever amount of investment commitments. During the crisis the Bank aimed, in particular, to maintain the flow of credit to SMEs, to uphold investor confidence in local economies, to ensure the continuation of projects providing essential jobs and economic stimulus, and to initiate the restructuring of private and public institutions.

In the year ending 31 December 2010 the EBRD approved 386 operations, involving funds of €9,009m., compared with €7,861m. for 311 operations in the previous year. During 2010 some 34% of all project financing committed was allocated to the financial sector, including loans to SMEs through financial intermediaries, while 25% was for the corporate sector, including agribusiness, manufacturing, property, tourism, telecommunications and new media, 21% for energy projects, comprising natural resources and the power sector, and 20% was infrastructure projects. Some 26% of the Bank's commitments in 2010 was for projects in Russia, 24% for countries in South-Eastern Europe, 17% for Eastern Europe and the Caucasus, 16% for Central Europe and the Baltic states, 11% for Central Asia, and 6% for Turkey. By the end of 2010 the Bank had approved 3,119 projects since it commenced operations, for which financing of €61,975m. had been approved. In addition, the Bank had mobilized resources amounting to an estimated €115,012m., bringing the total project value to €178,832m.

In 1999 the Bank established a Trade Facilitation Programme to extend bank guarantees in order to promote trading capabilities, in particular for SMEs. An increasing number of transactions are intra-regional arrangements. In December 2008 the Bank's Board of Directors agreed to expand the Programme's budget for 2009, from €800m. to €1,500m., in order to provide exceptional assistance to countries affected by the global deceleration of economic growth and contraction in credit markets. During 2009, however, the Programme was less widely used than anticipated, owing to a sharp decline in foreign trade transactions and a reluctance on the part of local banks to expose themselves to more risk. In 2010 the Bank financed 1,274 trade transactions under the Programme, amounting to €774m. (compared with 886 transactions amounting to €576m. in the previous year). In February 2009 the Bank established a Corporate Support Facility, with funds of €250m., to assist medium-sized businesses to counter the economic downturn. In the same month the EBRD, with the World Bank and the EIB, inaugurated a Joint International Financial Institutions (IFI) Action Plan to support the banking systems in Central and Eastern Europe and to finance lending to businesses in the region affected by the global economic crisis. Under the Plan the Banks initially committed €24,500m. over a two-year period. The IFI Action Plan concluded in March 2011, at which time €33,200m. had been provided under the joint initiative, of which €8,100m. was provided by the EBRD. A parallel plan, the European Banking Co-ordination Initiative (the 'Vienna Initiative'), was established in early 2009 to promote dialogue between authorities in emerging European economies, official multilateral donors and private banks. In early 2010 the Bank initiated a Local Currency and Capital Market Initiative ('Vienna Plus') aimed at addressing the regional impact of new global regulatory standards on bank capital adequacy and liquidity, as well as the challenges confronting emerging economies in managing non?-performing loans. The EBRD chaired a committee, established under the Initiative framework, concerning local currency finance development, and in 2011 co-chaired, with the World Bank, a new committee on the challenges of implementing the Basel III capital framework programme.

From 2002 the EBRD, together with the World Bank, the IMF and the Asian Development Bank, sponsored the CIS-7 initiative, which aimed to generate awareness of the difficulties of transition for seven low-income countries of the Commonwealth of Independent States (Armenia, Azerbaijan, Georgia, Kyrgyzstan, Moldova, Tajikistan, Uzbekistan), strengthen international and regional co-operation, and promote reforms to achieve economic growth. A review of the scheme was published in April 2004. In that month a new initiative was launched to increase activities in those CIS states, designated 'Early Transition Countries' (ETCs), in particular to stimulate private sector business development, market activity and financing of small-scale projects. In November the Bank established a multi-donor ETC Fund to administer donor pledges and grant financing in support of EBRD projects in those countries. In 2006 Mongolia was incorporated into the ETC grouping. In 2007 the Bank's resident office in Tbilisi, Georgia, was transformed into a regional focal point for specialized activities in the Caucasus and Moldova. Belarus and Turkmenistan joined the ETC programme in 2009 and 2010 respectively. During 2010 Bank commitments for the ETCs increased substantially to €920m. for 114 projects, while financing from the ETC Fund amounted to €11m.

High priority is given to attracting external finance for Bank-sponsored projects, in particular in countries at advanced stages of transition, from government agencies, international financial institutions, commercial banks and export credit agencies. The EBRD's Technical Co-operation Funds Programme (TCFP) aims to facilitate access to the Bank's capital resources for countries of operations by providing support for project preparation, project implementation and institutional development. Resources for technical co-operation originate from regular TCFP contributions, specific agreements and contributions to Special Funds. The Baltic Investment Programme, which is administered by Nordic countries, consists of two special funds to co-finance investment and technical assistance projects in the private sectors of Baltic states. The Funds are open to contributions from all EBRD member states. The Russia Small Business Fund (RSBF) was established in 1994 to support local SMEs through similar investment and technical co-operation activities. In November 2006 a new Western Balkans Fund was established as a multi-donor facility to support economic growth and the business environment in Albania, Bosnia and Herzegovina, the former Yugoslav republic of Macedonia, Montenegro and Serbia (including Kosovo). A Western Balkans Local Enterprise Facility was also established in 2006. In November 2009 a Western Balkans Investment Framework was inaugurated by the EBRD, the European Commission, the European Investment Bank and the Council of Europe Development Bank, to co-ordinate the leverage and use of donor funds in support of priority projects in the region. In mid-2008 the Bank established a Neighbourhood Investment Facility to provide technical assistance and grants mainly for infrastructure projects. An Investment Facility for Central Asia was launched in June 2010 to provide additional grant funding for energy and environmental sustainability projects in Kazakhstan, Kyrgyzstan, Tajikistan, Turkmenistan and Uzbekistan. Other financing mechanisms that the EBRD uses to address the needs of the region include Regional Venture Funds, which invest equity in privatized companies, in particular in Russia, and provide relevant management assistance, and the Central European Agency Lines, which disburse lines of credit to small-scale projects through local intermediaries.

A TurnAround Management (TAM) initiative provides practical assistance to senior managers of industrial enterprises to facilitate the expansion of businesses in a market economy. A Business Advisory Services (BAS) scheme complements TAM by undertaking projects to improve competitiveness, strategic planning, marketing and financial management in SMEs. During 2010 93 TAM and 1,365 BAS projects were initiated in 20 countries. A new strategy for the TAM/BAS programme for the period 2011–15 was approved during 2010. In May 2008 the Bank agreed to establish a Shareholders Special Fund (SSF), with resources of €115m., in order to support technical co-operation and grant operations. Further allocations of resources, including of €150m. in May 2010, brought the total committed by the Bank to €295m. by the end of that year.

In 2001 the EBRD collaborated with other donor institutions and partners to initiate a Northern Dimension Environmental Partnership (NDEP) to strengthen and co-ordinate environmental projects in northern Europe. The Partnership, which became operational in November 2002, includes a 'nuclear window' to address the nuclear legacy of the Russian Northern Fleet. The Bank administers the NDEP Support Fund, as well as a number of other funds specifically to support the promotion of nuclear safety: the Nuclear Safety Account (NSA), a multilateral programme of action established in 1993; the Chornobyl (Chernobyl) Shelter Fund (CSF), established in 1997; and International Decommissioning Support Funds (IDSFs), which have enabled the closure of nuclear plants for safety reasons where this would otherwise have been prohibitively costly, in Bulgaria, Lithuania and Slovakia. In 1997 a CSF-financed Chornobyl Unit 4 Shelter Implementation Plan (SIP) was initiated to assist Ukraine in stabilizing the protective sarcophagus covering the damaged Chornobyl reactor. The first-stage Unit 4 shelter was completed in December 2006. A contract for construction of a New Safe Confinement of the destroyed Unit 4 was signed in 2007.

The EBRD's founding Agreement specifies that all operations are to be undertaken in the context of promoting environmentally sound and sustainable development. It undertakes environmental audits and impact assessments in areas of particular concern, which enable the Bank to incorporate environmental action plans into any project approved for funding. An Environment Advisory Council assists with the development of policy and strategy in this area. In May 2006 the Bank launched a Sustainable Energy Initiative (SEI), which commits the Bank to doubling investments in energy efficiency and renewable energy projects to some €1,500m. within three years. A second phase of the SEI was initiated in 2009, with enhanced activities in areas including transport energy efficiency, climate change adaptation and the stationary use of biomass. By early 2012 €6,600m. had been committed under the SEI in support of 369 projects in 29 countries. A separate Multilateral Carbon Credit Fund was established, in December 2006, in co-operation with the EIB, providing a means by which countries may obtain carbon credits from emission-related projects. By early 2012 the Fund was fully subscribed with resources totalling €208.5m. In December 2009 the Bank contributed €25m. to a new joint Southeast Europe Energy Efficiency Fund (SE4F), which aimed to expand the availability of and access to sustainable energy finance in the western Balkans and Turkey. A new multi-donor EBRD Water Fund, with a particular focus on water projects in Central Asia, was established in July 2010.

Publications

Annual Report.
Donor Report (annually).
Economics of Transition (quarterly).
Law in Transition (2 a year).
People and Projects (annually).
Sustainability Report (annually).
Transition Report (annually).
Working papers, fact sheets.

Statistics

BANK COMMITMENTS BY SUB-REGION AND COUNTRY
(in € million)

	2010	Cumulative to 31 Dec. 2010
Central Europe and the Baltic States		
Croatia	386	2,463
Czech Republic	0	1,135
Estonia	8	518
Hungary	178	2,483
Latvia	104	557
Lithuania	99	596
Poland	643	4,662
Slovakia	63	1,544
Slovenia	3	634
Sub-total	1,485	14,592
South-Eastern Europe		
Albania	75	575
Bosnia and Herzegovina	190	1,308
Bulgaria	546	2,422
Macedonia, former Yugoslav republic	44	716
Montenegro	135	240
Romania	593	5,101
Serbia	598	2,432
Sub-total	2,182	12,794
Eastern Europe and the Caucasus		
Armenia	53	403
Azerbaijan	59	1,224
Belarus	60	551
Georgia	349	1,453
Moldova	97	549
Ukraine	952	6,435
Sub-total	1,570	10,614
Central Asia		
Kazakhstan	668	3,942
Kyrgyzstan	86	338
Mongolia	185	306
Tajikistan	22	214
Turkmenistan	6	135
Uzbekistan	4	743
Sub-total	970	5,678
Russia	2,309	17,671
Turkey	494	627
Total	9,009	61,975

Note: Financing for regional projects is allocated to the relevant countries.

Source: EBRD, *Annual Report 2010*.

EUROPEAN SPACE AGENCY—ESA

Address: 8–10 rue Mario Nikis, 75738 Paris Cedex 15, France.

Telephone: 1-53-69-76-54; **fax:** 1-53-69-75-60; **e-mail:** contactesa@esa.int; **internet:** www.esa.int.

ESA was established in 1975 to provide for, and to promote, European co-operation in space research and technology, and their applications, for exclusively peaceful purposes. It replaced the European Space Research Organisation (ESRO) and the European Launcher Development Organisation (both founded in 1962).

MEMBERS*

Austria
Belgium
Czech Republic
Denmark
Finland
France
Germany
Greece
Ireland
Italy
Luxembourg
Netherlands
Norway
Portugal
Romania
Spain
Sweden
Switzerland
United Kingdom

* Estonia, Hungary, Poland, and Slovenia have 'European Co-operating State' status. Canada has signed an agreement for close co-operation with ESA, including representation on the ESA Council. Cyprus, Israel, Latvia, and Slovakia have also signed Co-operation Agreements.

Organization

(April 2012)

COUNCIL

The Council is composed of representatives of all member states. It is responsible for formulating policy and meets at ministerial or delegate level.

ADMINISTRATION

ESA's activities are divided into the following 10 Directorates, each headed by a Director who reports directly to the Director-General: Earth Observation Programmes; Technical and Quality Management; Launchers; Human Spaceflight; Resources Management; Legal Affairs and External Relations; Science and Robotic Exploration; Telecommunications and Integrated Applications; Galileo Programme and Navigation-related Activites; Operations; and Infrastructure.

Director-General: JEAN-JACQUES DORDAIN (France).

ESA CENTRES

European Astronaut Centre (EAC): Cologne, Germany. As a subsidiary of the Directorate of Human Spaceflight, manages all European astronaut activities and trains European and international partner astronauts on the European elements of the International Space Station. The Centre employs 16 European astronauts.

European Space Astronomy Centre (ESAC): Villafranca del Castillo, Spain. A centre of excellence for space science and a base for ESA astrophysics and solar system missions. Hosts a virtual observatory.

European Space Operations Centre (ESOC): Darmstadt, Germany. Responsible for all satellite operations and the corresponding ground facilities and communications networks.

European Space Research and Technology Centre (ESTEC): Noordwijk, Netherlands. ESA's principal technical establishment, at which the majority of project teams are based, together with the space science department and the technological research and support engineers; provides the appropriate testing and laboratory facilities.

European Space Research Institute (ESRIN): Frascati, Italy. Responsible for the corporate exploitation of Earth observation data from space.

ESA has liaison offices in Brussels, Belgium, Moscow, Russia and Washington, DC, USA, as well as offices in Houston, Texas, USA, to support International Space Station activities, and at the Guyana Space Centre, located in Kourou, French Guyana. ESA owns the launch and launcher production facilities at Kourou. The Agency also operates ground/tracking stations around the world.

Activities

ESA's tasks are to define and put into effect a long-term European space policy of scientific research and technological development and to encourage all members to co-ordinate their national programmes with those of ESA to ensure that Europe maintains a competitive position in the field of space technology. ESA's basic activities cover studies on future projects; technological research; and shared technical investments, information systems and training programmes. These, and the science programme, are mandatory activities to which all members must contribute; other programmes are optional and members may determine their own level of participation. In November 2000 the ESA Council and the Council of the European Union (EU) adopted parallel resolutions endorsing a European strategy for space. The strategy, which had been jointly prepared in 1999 and was entitled *Europe and Space: A New Chapter*, aimed to strengthen the foundation for European space activities; advance scientific knowledge; and to use the technical capabilities developed in connection with space activities to secure wider economic and social benefits. ESA collaborated with the European Commission in the preparation of a Green Paper on EU Space Policy, which assessed Europe's strengths and weaknesses in the sector. In May 2004 a framework agreement entered into force providing the legal basis for structured co-operation between ESA and the European Commission. The framework agreement provides for a co-ordinating ESA-European Commission secretariat, and for joint consultations between the ESA Council and the EU Council (known as the Space Council). The European Space Policy (based on an EU White Paper, drafted with ESA support, and adopted in 2004) was adopted in May 2007, providing a common political framework for space activities in Europe. In June 2011 ESA and the European Defence Agency concluded an administrative arrangement on co-operation.

ESA is committed to pursuing international co-operation to achieve its objective of developing the peaceful applications of space technology. ESA works closely with both the US National Aeronautics and Space Administration (NASA) and the Russian Federal Space Agency ('Roscosmos'). In 2003 ESA and the Russian Government signed an Agreement on Co-operation and Partnership in the Exploration and Use of Outer Space for Peaceful Purposes, succeeding a similar agreement concluded with the USSR in 1990. Also, 'European Co-operating State Agreements' (a legal instrument designed to replace existing co-operation agreements between ESA and European states seeking closer relations with the Agency) are in force with Estonia, Hungary, Poland and Slovenia, providing for technical training and joint projects in the fields of space science, Earth observation and telecommunications. ESA assists other transitional and developing countries to expand their space activities. It works closely with other international organizations, in particular the EU and EUMETSAT. ESA has observer status with the UN Committee on the Peaceful Uses of Outer Space and co-operates closely with the UN's Office of Outer Space Affairs, in particular through the organization of a training and fellowship programme. ESA has also developed a co-operative relationship with Japan, with a special focus on data relay satellites and the exchange of materials for the International Space Station.

In March–April 2009 ESA convened the fifth European Conference on Space Debris.

SCIENCE AND ROBOTIC EXPLORATION

The first European scientific space programmes were undertaken under the aegis of ESRO, which launched seven satellites during 1968–72. The Science Programme is a mandatory activity of the Agency and forms the basis of co-operation between member states. Among the most successful scientific satellites and probes subsequently launched by ESA are the Giotto probe, launched in 1985 to study the composition of Halley's comet and reactivated in 1990 to observe the Grigg-Skjellerup comet in July 1992; and Hipparcos, which, between 1989 and 1993, determined the precise astronomic positions and distances of more than 1m. stars. In November 1995 ESA launched the Infrared Space Observatory (the operational phase of which lasted until April 1998, and was followed by a post-operational period ending in 2006), which successfully conducted pre-planned scientific studies providing data on galaxy and star formation and on interstellar matter. ESA collaborated with NASA in the Ulysses space project (a solar polar mission that was launched in October 1990 and terminated in June 2009, as the spacecraft's orbital path became too far removed from the Earth to allow sufficient transmission of data); the Solar and Helispheric Observatory (SOHO, launched in December 1995 to study the internal structure of the sun); and the Hubble Space Telescope. The Agency is committed to co-operation with NASA on the JWST (James Webb Space Telescope), the successor of the Hubble Space telescope, scheduled to be launched in 2014. In October 1997 the Huygens space probe was launched under the framework of a joint NASA–ESA project (the Cassini/Huygens mission) to study the planet Saturn and its largest moon, Titan, where it landed in January 2005. In August 2009 ESA and NASA agreed in principle to establish a Mars Exploration Joint Initiative (MEJI), which was to launch (in 2016, 2018 and 2020) landers and orbiters to conduct astrobiological, geological, geophysical and other investigations; samples were to be returned to Earth from Mars during the 2020s. The LISA Pathfinder mission (see below) is to be conducted with NASA.

In December 1999 the X-Ray Multimirror Mission (XMM–Newton) was launched from Kourou, French Guyana. It was envisaged that XMM–Newton, the most powerful X-ray telescope ever placed in orbit, would investigate the origin of galaxies, the formation of black holes, etc. Four cluster satellites, launched from Baikonur, Russia, in July–August 2000, were, in association with SOHO (see above), to explore the interaction between the Earth's magnetic field and electrically charged particles transported on the solar wind. In October 2002 INTEGRAL (International Gamma-Ray Astrophysical Laboratory) was successfully launched by a Russian Proton vehicle, to study the most violent events perceptible in the Universe.

ESA's space missions are an integral part of its long-term science programme, Horizon 2000, which was initiated in 1984. In 1994 a new set of missions was defined, to enable the inclusion of projects using new technologies and participation in future international space activities, which formed the Horizon 2000 Plus extension covering the period 2005–16. Together they were called Horizons 2000.

In November 2003 the Science Programme Committee initiated a new long-term space science programme, Cosmic Vision, initially to cover the period 2004–14. Under the programme three main projects—Astrophysics, Solar System Science, and Fundamental Physics—were to be developed in production groups, missions within each to be built synergistically, where possible using common technologies and engineering teams. Projects included: Herschel, exploring the infrared and microwave Universe (the Herschel Space Observatory, designed to investigate the formation of stars and galaxies, was launched in mid-May 2009); Planck, studying the cosmic microwave background (launched in May 2009); GAIA, the ultimate galaxy mapper (to be launched no later than 2012); Rosetta, launched in March 2004, to rendez vous with and land on a comet; Mars Express, a Mars orbiter carrying the Beagle 2 lander (launched in 2003; contact with Beagle 2 was, however, lost in January 2004); Venus Express, a Venus orbiter (launched 2005, entered into orbit around Venus in April 2006); SMART-1, which was to demonstrate solar propulsion technology while on course to the Moon (launched 2003); BepiColombo, a mission to Mercury (to be launched in 2014); and SMART-2, a technology demonstration mission.

In accordance with a new phase of Cosmic Vision, focusing on 2015–25, further missions are to be undertaken, including LISA Pathfinder, a joint mission with NASA, searching for gravitational waves (to be launched in 2012); and Solar Orbiter, which aims to take a closer look at the Sun (to be launched in 2017). Other missions under consideration include: Cross-Scale (Investigating Multi-scale Coupling in Space Plasmas); Euclid (mapping the geometry of the dark universe; to be launched in 2019); Plato (next generation planet finder); Spica (an infrared space telescope for cosmology and astrophyics), Laplace/EJSM (mission to Europa and Jupiter system); and Xeus/Ixo (X-ray observatory for the extreme and evolving universe).

EARTH OBSERVATION

ESA has contributed to the understanding and monitoring of the Earth's environment through its satellite projects. Since 1977 ESA has launched seven Meteosat spacecraft into geosynchronous orbit, which have provided continuous meteorological data, mainly for the purposes of weather forecasting. The Meteosat systems are financed and owned by EUMETSAT, but were operated by ESA until December 1995. ESA and EUMETSAT have collaborated on the development of a successor to the Meteosat weather satellites (Meteosat Second Generation—MSG) to provide enhanced geostationary data coverage. The first satellite, MSG-1, was launched in August 2002. ESA and EUMETSAT have also collaborated on the METOP/EPS (EUMETSAT Polar System) programme, to provide observations from polar orbit. The first METOP satellite was launched in October 2006.

In 1991 ESA launched the ERS-1 satellite, which carried sophisticated instruments to measure the Earth's surface and its atmosphere. A second ERS satellite was launched in April 1995 with the specific purpose of measuring the stratospheric and tropospheric ozone. ENVISAT, the largest and most advanced European-built observation satellite, was launched in February 2002 from Kourou, French Guyana. ENVISAT aims to provide a detailed assessment of the impact of human activities on the Earth's atmosphere, and land and coastal processes, and to monitor exceptional natural events, such as volcanic eruptions.

ESA Earth Explorer missions aim to enhance understanding of the Earth's system with a view to supporting efforts to address the challenges posed by ongoing global change, i.e. climate change and also the large-scale impact on Earth of the growing human population and continued economic expansion. The Agency has selected six such missions, of which three are 'Core' (responding to specific areas of public concern) and three are 'Opportunity' (quick implementation missions aimed at addressing areas of immediate environmental concern). The Core missions are as follows: GOCE (see below); the Atmospheric Dynamics Mission (ADM)-Aeolus, which, when launched in 2013, will aim to demonstrate measurements of vertical wind profiles from space; and the Earth Clouds Aerosols and Radiation Explorer (EarthCARE), which, once launched in 2013, will aim to improve the representation and understanding of the Earth's radiative balance in climate and numerical forecast models. The Opportunity missions are: the Soil Moisture and Ocean Salinity (SMOS) mission, launched in November 2009, which aims to further understanding of the Earth's water cycle; CryoSat-2 (see below); and Swarm, scheduled to be launched in 2012, which was to produce the best survey to date of the geomagnetic field and its temporal evolution.

In June 1998 the ESA Council approved the initiation of activities related to the Living Planet Programme, designed to increase understanding of environmental issues. In May 1999 the Council committed funds for a research mission, CryoSat, to be undertaken, in order to study the impact of global warming on polar ice caps. However, the launch of CryoSat was aborted in October 2005. A CryoSat recovery plan, completed in February 2006, provided for the development of a CryoSat-2 mission, with the same objectives; CryoSat-2 was eventually launched in April 2010. The Gravity Field and Steady-State Ocean Circulation Explorer (GOCE) mission, launched in March 2009, was to use a unique measurement technique to recover geodetic precision data on the Earth's gravity field. ESA is responsible for the space component of the European Commission's Global Monitoring for Environment and Security (GMES) programme and aimed to launch an earth observation satellite, Sentinel-2, specifically to monitor the land environment, in 2012. In November 2008 the Council approved a Space Situational Awareness (SSA) preparatory programme, for an initial three-year period, to develop a capability to monitor potentially hazardous objects and natural phenomena.

As part of the Treaty Enforcement Services using Earth Observation (TESEO) initiative, agreed in 2001, ESA satellites provide data for a wide range of environmental activities including monitoring wetlands, ensuring compliance with Kyoto Protocol emission targets and combating desertification. Similarly, ESA has agreements with UNESCO to protect wildlife and sites of historic interest, in support of the Convention Concerning the Protection of the World Cultural and Natural Heritage.

TELECOMMUNICATIONS AND INTEGRATED APPLICATIONS

ESA commenced the development of communications satellites in 1968. These have since become the largest markets for space use and have transformed global communications, with more than 100 satellites circling the Earth for the purposes of telecommunications. The main series of operational satellites developed by ESA are the European Communications Satellites (ECS), based on the original orbital test satellite and used by EUTELSAT, and the Maritime Communications Satellites (MARECS), which have been leased for operations to Inmarsat.

An Advanced Relay and Technology Mission Satellite (ARTEMIS) has been developed by ESA to test and operate new telecommunications techniques, and in particular to enable the relay of information directly between satellites. ARTEMIS was launched in July 2001. In 1998 ESA, together with the EU and EUROCONTROL continued to implement a satellite-based navigation system to be used for civilian aircraft and maritime services, similar to the two existing systems operational for military use. ESA was also working with the EU and representatives of the private sector to enhance the region's role in the development of electronic media infrastructure to meet the expanding global demand. In May 1999 the Council approved funding for a satellite multimedia programme, Advanced Research in Telecommunications Systems (Artes), which aimed to support the development of satellite systems and services for delivering information through high-speed internet access. Ongoing in 2012 were: Artes-1 (focused on strategic analysis); Artes-3–4 (seeking to improve the near-term competitiveness of the satcom industry through the development of equipment including terminals, processors and antennas for ground or space); Artes-5 (seeking to develop a more sustained long-term technological basis for European industrial effectiveness, and divided into Artes-5.1, involving projects initiated by and also fully funded by the Agency, and Artes-5.2, comprising projects initiated by industry and 75% ESA-funded); Artes-7, dedicated to the implementation of an European Data Relay Satellite (EDRS) system; Artes-8, focused on the development of the Alphasatis satellite that, with Inmarsat, was to incorporate the first stage of the Alphabus multi-purpose geostationary communications platform; Artes-10, a satellite-based communication system that was to complement a new EU air traffic management system; Artes-11, aimed at developing the Small GEO System, a satellite incorporating advanced payload technology; Artes-20, dedicated to the development, implementation and pilot operations of Integrated Applications (combined satellite operations); Artes-21, developing the Automatic Identification System, a short-range coastal tracking system.

GALILEO PROGRAMME AND NAVIGATION-RELATED ACTIVITIES

ESA and the European Commission are collaborating to design and develop a European global satellite and navigation system, *Galileo*. The project, scheduled to be fully deployed during 2013, will provide a highly accurate global positioning service by means of 30 satellites (of which 27 will be operational and three active spares), a global network of 20 Galileo Sensor Stations (GSSs), and two Galileo Control Centres (GCCs), based in Europe. ESA, in co-operation with the European Commission and Eurocontrol, is implementing the EGNOS System. EGNOS is the European contribution to the Global Navigation Satellite System phase 1 (GNSS-1) and will provide an improved navigation and positioning service for all users of the (American) GPS and (Russian) GLONASS systems. It is envisaged that EGNOS will serve as a major regional component of a seamless, world-wide augmentation system for navigation, aimed at meeting the demanding requirements for aircraft navigation, and comprising (in addition to EGNOS in Europe): WAAS in the USA; MSAS in Japan; and GAGAN in India. The GNSS aims to use the *Galileo*, GPS and GLONASS systems to provide an integrated satellite navigation service of unprecedented accuracy and global coverage under civilian control.

LAUNCHERS

The European requirement for independent access to space first manifested itself in the early 1970s against the background of strategic and commercial interests in telecommunications and Earth observation. As a consequence, and based on knowledge gained through national programmes, ESA began development of a space launcher. The resulting Ariane rocket was first launched in December 1979. The project, which incorporated four different launchers; Ariane-1 to Ariane-4, subsequently became an essential element of ESA's programme activities and, furthermore, developed a successful commercial role in placing satellites into orbit. The last flight of Ariane-4 took place in February 2003. From 1985 ESA worked to develop the more powerful Ariane-5 launcher, which has been in commercial operation since 1999, launched from the ESA facility at the Guyana Space Centre. In December 2000 the ESA Council approved the Vega Small Launcher Development and the P80 Advanced Solid Propulsion Stage programmes. The first Vega launch took place in February 2012. A Future Launcher Preparatory Programme is being defined.

HUMAN SPACEFLIGHT

In the 1980s and 1990s Europe gained access to human space technology and operations through Spacelab, which ESA developed as the European contribution to the US Space Shuttle Programme, and through two joint Euromir missions on the Russian space station, Mir. Since the mid-1980s ESA has supported space research in the life and physical sciences through its microgravity programmes. A considerable scientific output has been achieved in key areas such as crystal growth, solidification physics, fluid sciences, thermophysical properties, molecular and cell biology, developmental biology, exobiology and human physiology. The latest microgravity programme, approved in November 2001, is the ESA Programme in Life and Physical Sciences and Applications (ELIPS). ESA is a partner in the International Space Station (ISS), which was initiated by the US Government in 1984, and subsequently developed as a joint project between five partners—Canada, Europe, Japan, Russia and the USA. ESA's main contributions to the ISS are the Columbus Laboratory (launched in February 2008); and the 'Jules Verne' Automated Transfer Vehicle—ATV (launched by Ariane-5 in March 2008), which was designed to provide logistical support to the ISS. The Columbus laboratory accommodates European multi-user research facilities: Biolab; Fluid Science Laboratory, European Physiology Modules, Material Science Laboratory (all developed within the Microgravity Facilities for the Columbus Programme); and European Drawer Rack and European Stowage Rack (both within the ISS Utilization Programme). In the framework of the ISS agreements with the USA, ESA is allocated 51% usage of Columbus, the remainder being allocated to NASA. In addition to the experiment accommodation capabilities on Columbus, the European Zero-G Airbus, operated under ESA contract by Novespace, provides European researchers short-duration access to microgravity conditions for a wide variety of experiments, ranging from precursor experiments for the ISS to student experiments. Droptowers and sounding rockets provide additional short-duration opportunities. The ESA Directorate of Human Spaceflight also provides European researchers with flight opportunities on unmanned Russian Foton and Bion capsules.

Finance

All member states contribute to ESA's mandatory programme activities (studies on future projects; technological research; shared technical investments, information systems and training programmes; and the science programme) on a scale based on their national income, and are free to decide on their level of commitment in optional programmes. The total budget for 2012 amounted to about €4,020m., with €861.4m. (21.4%) allocated to earth observation (an optional programme), €720.7m. (17.9%) to navigation (optional), €570.0m. (14.4%) to launchers (optional), €479.7m. (11.9%) to space science (mandatory), and €413.3m. (10.3%) to human spaceflight (optional).

Publications

CONNECT.

ECSL News.

ESA Annual Report.

ESA Bulletin (quarterly).

Eurocomp (newsletter).

PFF—Preparing for the Future.

Monographs and conference proceedings.

EUROPEAN UNION—EU

The European Coal and Steel Community (ECSC) was created by a treaty signed in Paris on 18 April 1951 (effective from 25 July 1952) to pool the coal and steel production of the six original members. It was seen as a first step towards a united Europe. The European Economic Community (EEC) and European Atomic Energy Community (Euratom) were established by separate treaties signed in Rome, Italy, on 25 March 1957 (effective from 1 January 1958), the former to create a common market and to approximate economic policies, the latter to promote growth in nuclear industries. The common institutions of the three Communities were established by a treaty signed in Brussels, Belgium, on 8 April 1965 (effective from 1 July 1967).

The EEC was formally changed to the European Community (EC) under the Treaty on European Union (effective from 1 November 1993, and renamed from December 2009, see below), although in practice the term EC had been used for several years to describe the three Communities together. The new Treaty established a European Union (EU), which introduced citizenship thereof and aimed to increase intergovernmental co-operation in economic and monetary affairs; to establish a common foreign and security policy; and to introduce co-operation in justice and home affairs. The EU was placed under the supervision of the European Council (comprising heads of state or of government of member countries), while the EC continued to exist, having competence in matters relating to the Treaty of Rome and its amendments.

The Treaty of Paris establishing the ECSC expired on 23 July 2002, resulting in the termination of the ECSC legal regime and procedures and the dissolution of the ECSC Consultative Committee. The ECSC's assets and liabilities were transferred to the overall EU budget, while rights and obligations arising from international agreements drawn up between the ECSC and third countries were devolved to the EC.

With the entry into force, on 1 December 2009, of the Treaty of Lisbon amending the Treaty on European Union and the Treaty establishing the European Community, the Treaty on European Union was renamed the Treaty on the Functioning of the European Union, with all references to the European 'Community' changed to the 'Union'. Euratom continued to exist, alongside the EU.

Meetings of the principal organs take place in Brussels, Luxembourg and Strasbourg, France. The Treaty of Lisbon provided for the posts of President of the European Council and High Representative of the Union for Foreign Affairs and Security Policy; and for an 18-month troika comprising groups of three successive governments holding the rotating six-month presidency of the Council of the European Union.

Presidency of the Council of the European Union: Denmark (January–June 2012); Cyprus (July–December 2012); Ireland (January–June 2013).

President of the European Council: HERMAN VAN ROMPUY (Belgium).

High Representative of the Union for Foreign Affairs and Security Policy: CATHERINE ASHTON (United Kingdom).

Secretary-General of the Council of the European Union: UWE CORSEPIUS (Germany).

President of the European Commission: JOSÉ MANUEL DURÃO BARROSO (Portugal).

President of the European Parliament: MARTIN SCHULZ (Germany).

MEMBERS

Austria	Germany*	Netherlands*
Belgium*	Greece	Poland
Bulgaria	Hungary	Portugal
Cyprus	Ireland	Romania
Czech Republic	Italy*	Slovakia
Denmark	Latvia	Slovenia
Estonia	Lithuania	Spain
Finland	Luxembourg*	Sweden
France*	Malta	United Kingdom

* Original members.

ENLARGEMENT

The six original members (Belgium, France, Germany, Italy, Luxembourg and the Netherlands) were joined in the European Communities (later the European Union—EU) on 1 January 1973 by Denmark, Ireland and the United Kingdom, and on 1 January 1981 by Greece. In a referendum held in February 1982, the inhabitants of Greenland voted to end their membership of the Community, entered into when under full Danish rule. Greenland's withdrawal took effect from 1 February 1985. Portugal and Spain became members on 1 January 1986. Following the reunification of Germany in October 1990, the former German Democratic Republic immediately became part of the Community, although a transitional period was allowed before certain Community legislation took effect there. Austria, Finland and Sweden became members on 1 January 1995.

At the Copenhagen summit on 13 December 2002, an historic agreement was reached when the European Council agreed that 10 candidate countries, comprising eight in Central and Eastern Europe (the Czech Republic, Estonia, Hungary, Latvia, Lithuania, Poland, Slovakia and Slovenia), and Malta and Cyprus, should join the EU on 1 May 2004. The leaders of the 10 new member states signed the accession treaty in Athens, Greece, on 16 April 2003. The Treaty of Athens had to be ratified by all 25 states prior to accession on 1 May 2004. The 15 existing member states opted to ratify the Treaty in parliament whereas the future member states, except Cyprus (the Cypriot Parliament unanimously approved accession to the EU on 14 July 2003), adopted the Treaty by referendum. A referendum took place in Malta on 8 March 2003, Slovenia on 23 March, Hungary on 12 April, Lithuania on 10 and 11 May, Slovakia on 16 and 17 May, Poland on 7 and 8 June, the Czech Republic on 15 and 16 June, Estonia on 14 September and Latvia on 20 September; each poll recorded a majority in favour of accession. Under the terms of the Treaty, only the Greek Cypriot sector of Cyprus was to be admitted to the EU in the absence of a settlement on the divided status of the island, although the EU made clear its preference for the accession of a united Cyprus. In April 2004, however, in a referendum on a UN-proposed reunification settlement held only a few days before Cyprus was scheduled to join the EU, some 76% of Greek Cypriot voters rejected the proposal. At the same time, some 65% of Turkish Cypriot voters endorsed the settlement. Both communities would have had to approve the proposed reunification in order for Cyprus to commence its membership of the EU undivided. Consequently, only the Greek sector of the island assumed EU membership from 1 May.

Romania submitted its formal application for EU membership on 22 June 1995, while Bulgaria applied for membership on 14 December. Following the Helsinki European Council's decision in December 1999, accession negotiations started with Romania and Bulgaria in February 2000. The Commission concluded in November 2003 that Bulgaria had a functioning market economy and would be able to perform within the EU in the near future provided it continued to implement its reform programme. In October 2004 a report by the European Commission described Romania as a functioning market economy, although it confirmed that endemic corruption, ethnic minority rights and human trafficking remained, *inter alia*, areas of concern in both countries. In the same strategy document, the Commission proposed a new clause in accession treaties under which membership negotiations could be suspended if candidate countries failed to fulfil the economic and political criteria established in Copenhagen, Denmark, in December 2002, according to which a prospective member must: be a stable democracy, respecting human rights, the rule of law, and the protection of minorities; have a functioning market economy; and adopt the common rules, standards and policies that make up the body of EU law. Bulgaria and Romania provisionally completed formal negotiations in June and December 2004, respectively, and this was confirmed at the Brussels European Council meeting of 17 December. The Commission formally approved the accession applications of Romania and Bulgaria on 22 February 2005. Bulgaria and Romania signed a joint accession treaty on 25 April. In September 2006 the Commission recommended that Romania and Bulgaria should accede to the EU as planned; both countries formally became members of the Union on 1 January 2007, with the entry into force of their joint accession treaty.

Croatia submitted its application for membership of the EU in February 2003, and membership negotiations finally commenced in October 1995. Negotiations were completed in June 2011, and Croatia signed an accession treaty on 9 December. Croatia was expected to accede to full membership of the EU in July 2013, following approval of EU membership by a referendum held in that country in January 2012.

Turkey, which had signed an association agreement with the EC in 1963 (although this was suspended between 1980 and 1986, following a military coup), applied for membership of the EU on 14 April 1987. As a populous, predominantly Muslim nation, with a poor record on human rights and low average income levels, Turkey encountered objections to its prospective membership, which opponents claimed would disturb the balance of power within the EU and place an intolerable strain on the organization's finances. The Helsinki European Council of 1999, however, granted Turkey applicant status and encouraged it to undertake the requisite political and economic reforms for eventual membership. By accelerating the pace of reforms, Turkey had made significant progress towards achieving compliance with the Copenhagen criteria by 2004, including far-reaching reforms of the Constitution and the penal code. Turkish ambitions for EU membership were adversely affected in April 2004 by the failure of the UN plan for the reunification of Cyprus, which was rejected in a referendum by the Greek Cypriots in the south of the island (see above). Cyprus has been divided since 1974 when Turkey invaded the northern third of the country in response to a Greek-sponsored coup aiming to unite the island with Greece. Turkey refuses to recognize the Greek Cypriot Government and is the only country to recognize the Government of the northern section of the country, known as the 'Turkish Republic of Northern Cyprus', where it has 30,000 troops deployed. The requirement for the successful resolution of all territorial disputes with members of the EU meant that failure to reach a settlement in Cyprus remained a significant impediment to Turkey's accession to the EU, although the Turkish authorities had expressed strong support for the peace plan. In December 2004, however, the EU agreed to begin accession talks with Turkey in early October 2005, although it specified a number of conditions, including the right to impose 'permanent safeguard' clauses in any accession accord. The safeguard clauses related to the freedom of movement of Turkish citizens within the EU (seeking to allay fears about large numbers of low-paid Turkish workers entering other EU member states) and restrictions on the level of subsidy available to Turkey for its infrastructure development or agriculture. The EU warned that negotiations could last between 10 and 15 years and that eventual membership was not guaranteed. Turkey was also obliged to sign a protocol to update its association agreement with the EU prior to accession negotiations in October, to cover the 10 new members that had joined the organization in May 2004, including Cyprus. The Turkish Government had previously refused to grant effective recognition to the Greek Cypriot Government and, although it signed the protocol at the end of July 2005, it still insisted that the extension of the association agreement did not constitute formal recognition. In a report issued in November 2006, the Commission demanded that Turkey open its ports to Cypriot ships by mid-December, in compliance with its agreement to extend its customs union to the 10 new member states in 2005. Turkey announced that there could be no progress on this issue until the EU implemented a regulation drafted in 2004 to end the economic isolation of the 'Turkish Republic of Northern Cyprus', the adoption of which had been blocked by Cyprus. In December 2006, therefore, the EU Council stipulated that talks would not commence in eight policy areas affected by the restrictions placed on Cypriot traffic by Turkey. In its 2011 annual report on enlargement strategy and progress, the Commission expressed regret that negotiations had not opened in any new policy areas for over a year. By March 2012 negotiations had opened in 13 of the total of 33 policy areas, with talks provisionally closed in one area; 18 areas remained blocked.

At a summit of EU leaders in Brussels in December 2005, the former Yugoslav Republic of Macedonia (FYRM) was granted candidate status, joining Croatia and Turkey. However, no date was established for the initiation of accession negotiations. A summit of the Council convened in June 2008 determined that, as a precondition of the FYRM's accession, an ongoing dispute with Greece concerning its name (Macedonia also being the name of a region of Greece) must be satisfactorily resolved. Montenegro applied for EU membership in December 2008, and the European Council confirmed Montenegro's status as a candidate country in December 2010. In October 2011 the European Commission declared that Montenegro had fulfilled the political and economic criteria needed to begin EU membership negotiations. Upon the Commission's recommendation, the European Council agreed in December to initiate the accession process, and negotiations were expected to commence in June 2012, dependent on further progress in combating corruption and organized crime in that country. In July 2009 Iceland's legislature voted to apply for EU membership, and membership negotiations commenced in July 2010. By December 2011 talks had opened in 11 policy areas.

Serbia applied for EU membership in December 2009, and in October 2011 the European Commission recommended to the Council that Serbia should be granted candidate status. On 1 March 2012 the European Council agreed officially to give Serbia the status of a candidate country for EU membership. Albania submitted a membership application in April 2009. In November 2010 the European Commission adopted an Opinion on Albanian membership of the EU, which recommended that Albania should be considered as a candidate for membership once it had fulfilled the necessary political and economic criteria.

INSTITUTIONAL REFORM

In February 2002 a Convention on the Future of Europe was opened in Brussels, Belgium, chaired by former French President Valéry Giscard d'Estaing. The Convention, which had been agreed upon at the Laeken summit in December 2001, when the European Council adopted the Declaration on the Future of the European Union, included in its remit 60 or more topics aimed at reforming EU institutions to ensure the smooth functioning of the Union after enlargement. The full text of the draft constitutional treaty was submitted to the Council of the European Union in July 2003. The draft was discussed at the Intergovernmental Conference (IGC), which was composed of the representatives of the member states and the accession countries, from October to December.

Heads of state and of government attending an EU summit held in Brussels, in December 2003, failed to agree the final text of the proposed constitution, owing to conflicting views over the issue of voting rights. At a summit meeting held in Brussels, in June 2004, the heads of state and of government of the then 25 EU member states approved a draft constitutional treaty, having reached a compromise over voting rights. The draft constitutional treaty was formally signed in Rome, Italy, in October by the heads of state or of government of the 25 member states and the three candidate countries of Bulgaria, Romania and Turkey, although it remained subject to ratification by each member nation (either by a vote in the national legislature or by a popular referendum). The future of the constitutional treaty became uncertain following its rejection in national referendums held in France and the Netherlands, in May and June 2005, respectively, and seven countries (the Czech Republic, Denmark, Finland, Ireland, Portugal, Sweden and the United Kingdom) announced plans to postpone a national referendum.

In June 2007, at a summit in Brussels, the European Council agreed to convene an IGC to draft a new treaty. At an informal summit of the European Council held in Lisbon, Portugal, in mid-October, agreement was reached on the final text of a new reform treaty. The resulting Treaty of Lisbon amending the Treaty on European Union and the Treaty establishing the European Community was signed in Lisbon, on 13 December, by the heads of state or of government of the now 27 member states. The Treaty of Lisbon revised existing treaties, and retained much of the content of the abandoned constitutional treaty, including its scheme for Council of the European Union voting rights (whereby measures would require the support of at least 55% of EU states, representing at least 65% of the total population, see below; this aimed to ensure that smaller member states—particularly the new Eastern European members—could not be overruled by a small but powerful group of senior members). During 2008 the parliaments of most member states voted to ratify the Treaty. However, in June 2008 voters in Ireland, which was constitutionally bound to conduct a popular referendum on the issue, rejected ratification. In December the European Council agreed to a number of concessions, including the removal of a provision in the Treaty for a reduction in the number of European Commissioners (see below), and relating to taxation, the family, and state neutrality, with the aim of securing its ratification by all EU member states by the end of 2009. A new referendum, held in Ireland in early October 2009, approved the Treaty. In early November, following a ruling by the Constitutional Court of the Czech Republic that its provisions were compatible with the country's Constitution, the Czech Republic became the final EU country to ratify the Treaty of Lisbon. The Treaty entered into force on 1 December 2009.

Principal Elements of the Treaty of Lisbon

The Treaty of Lisbon (formally known as the Treaty of Lisbon amending the Treaty on European Union and the Treaty establishing the European Community) sought to redefine the functions and procedures of the institutions of the EU. It created a High Representative of the Union for Foreign Affairs and Security Policy (appointed by the European Council by qualified majority with the agreement of the President of the Commission) to represent the EU internationally, combining the former roles of EU Commissioner responsible for external relations and EU High Representative for the Common Foreign and Security Policy (although foreign policy remains subject to a national veto). The High Representative of the Union for Foreign Affairs and Security Policy is mandated by the Council, but is also one of the Vice-Presidents of the Commission and chairs the External Relations Council. The Lisbon Treaty also provides for the creation of a new permanent president of the European Council, elected by the European Council for a period of two and one-half years, renewable once; the creation of this role aims to promote coherence and continuity in policy-making. The system of a six-month rotating presidency has been retained for the different Council formations (except for the External Relations Council, chaired by the new High Representative of the Union for Foreign Affairs and Security Policy). A new system of fixed 18-month troikas (groups of three presidencies) has been introduced, sharing the presidencies of most configurations of the Council, to facilitate overall co-ordination and continuity of work. The Lisbon Treaty provides for a revised system of qualified majority voting in the Council (see Council of the European Union). The European Parliament's legislative powers are consolidated under the Treaty, which grants the Parliament the right of co-decision with the Council of the European Union in an increased number of policy areas, giving it a more prominent role in framing legislation. The maximum number of seats in the European Parliament is raised to 751 (to be fully effective from 2014, see European Parliament). The European Commission retains its composition of one commissioner for each member state. The Treaty establishing the European Community (also known as the Treaty of Rome) is renamed as the Treaty on the Functioning of the European Union, with references to the 'Community' replaced by 'Union'. The Lisbon Treaty attempts to improve democracy and transparency within the Union, introducing the right for EU citizens to petition the Commission to introduce new legislation and enshrining the principles of subsidiarity (that the EU should only act when an objective can be better achieved at the supranational level, implying that national powers are the norm) and proportionality (that the action should be proportional to the desired objective). National parliaments are given the opportunity to examine EU legislation to ensure that it rests within the EU's remit, and legislation may be returned to the Commission for reconsideration if one-third of member states find that a proposed law breaches these principles. The Treaty of Lisbon enables enhanced co-operation for groups numbering at least one-third (i.e. currently nine) of the member states. The Treaty provides a legal basis for the EU defence force, with a mutual defence clause, and includes the stipulation that the EU has the power to sign treaties and sit on international bodies as a legal entity in its own right. The new framework also provides for the establishment of a European public prosecutor's office to combat EU fraud and cross-border crime and the right to dual citizenship (i.e. of the EU as well as of a member state), and includes arrangements for the formal withdrawal of a member state from the EU.

Union Institutions

The EU provides an information service, Europe Direct, online at europa.eu/europedirect/index_en.htm.

EUROPEAN COMMISSION

Address: 200 rue de la Loi, 1049 Brussels, Belgium.

Telephone: (2) 299-11-11; **fax:** (2) 295-01-38; **e-mail:** forename.surname@ec.europa.eu; **internet:** ec.europa.eu.

Please note: in an e-mail address, when the forename and/or the surname are composed of more than one word, the different words are linked by a hyphen. If help is needed, you may send a message to address-information@ec.europa.eu requesting the correct e-mail address of the correspondent.

MEMBERS OF THE COMMISSION
(2010–14)

President: JOSÉ MANUEL DURÃO BARROSO (Portugal).

Vice-President and High Representative of the Union for Foreign Affairs and Security Policy: CATHERINE ASHTON (United Kingdom).

Vice-President, responsible for Justice, Fundamental Rights and Citizenship: VIVIANE REDING (Luxembourg).

Vice-President, responsible for Competition: JOAQUÍN ALMUNIA (Spain).

Vice-President, responsible for Transport: SIIM KALLAS (Estonia).

Vice-President, responsible for the Digital Agenda: NEELIE KROES (Netherlands).

Commissioner, responsible for Industry and Entrepreneurship: ANTONIO TAJANI (Italy).

Commissioner, responsible for Inter-Institutional Relations and Administration: MAROŠ ŠEFČOVIČ (Slovakia).

Commissioner, responsible for the Environment: JANEZ POTOČNIK (Slovenia).

Commissioner, responsible for Economic and Monetary Affairs and the Euro: OLLI REHN (Finland).

Commissioner, responsible for Development: ANDRIS PIEBALGS (Latvia).

Commissioner, responsible for Internal Market and Services: MICHEL BARNIER (France).

Commissioner, responsible for Education, Culture, Multilingualism and Youth: ANDROULLA VASSILIOU (Cyprus).

Commissioner, responsible for Taxation and Customs Union, Audit and Anti-Fraud: ALGIRDAS ŠEMETA (Lithuania).

Commissioner, responsible for Trade: KAREL DE GUCHT (Belgium).

Commissioner, responsible for Health and Consumer Policy: JOHN DALLI (Malta).

Commissioner, responsible for Research, Innovation and Science: MÁIRE GEOGHEGAN-QUINN (Ireland).

Commissioner, responsible for Financial Programming and Budget: JANUSZ LEWANDOWSKI (Poland).

Commissioner, responsible for Maritime Affairs and Fisheries: MARIA DAMANAKI (Greece).

Commissioner, responsible for International Co-operation, Humanitarian Aid and Crisis Response: KRISTALINA GEORGIEVA (Bulgaria).

Commissioner, responsible for Energy: GÜNTHER H. OETTINGER (Austria).

Commissioner, responsible for Regional Policy: JOHANNES HAHN (Austria).

Commissioner, responsible for Climate Action: CONNIE HEDEGAARD (Denmark).

Commissioner, responsible for Enlargement and European Neighbourhood Policy: ŠTEFAN FÜLE (Czech Republic).

Commissioner, responsible for Employment, Social Affairs and Inclusion: LÁSZLÓ ANDOR (Hungary).

Commissioner, responsible for Home Affairs: CECILIA MALMSTRÖM (Sweden).

Commissioner, responsible for Agriculture and Rural Development: DACIAN CIOLOŞ (Romania).

The European Commission, like the European Parliament and Council of the European Union, was established in the 1950s under the EU's founding Treaties. The functions of the Commission are four-fold: to propose legislation to the European Parliament and the Council of the European Union; to implement EU policies and programmes adopted by the European Parliament and to manage and implement the budget; to enforce European law, in conjunction with the Court of Justice, in all the member states; and to represent the EU in international affairs and to negotiate agreements between the EU and other organizations or countries.

A new Commission is appointed for a five-year term, normally within six months of the elections to the European Parliament. The Governments of the member states agree on an individual to designate as the new Commission President. The President-designate then selects the other members of the Commission, following discussions with the member state Governments. In the performance of their duties, the members of the Commission are forbidden to seek or accept instructions from any government or other body, or to engage in any other paid or unpaid professional activity. The nominated President and other members of the Commission must be approved as a body by the European Parliament before they can take office. Once approved, the Commission may nominate a number of its members as Vice-President. Any member of the Commission, if he or she no longer fulfils the conditions required for the performance of his or her duties, or commits a serious offence, may be declared removed from office by the Court of Justice. The Court may, furthermore, on the petition of the Council of the European Union or of the Commission itself, provisionally suspend any member of the Commission from his or her duties. The European Parliament has the authority to dismiss the entire Commission by adopting a motion of censure. The number of members of the Commission may be amended by a unanimous vote of the Council of the European Union.

The members of the Commission, also known as the College, meet once a week and a collective decision is made on policy following a presentation by the relevant Commissioner. The Commission's staff is organized into Directorates-General and Services. The Directorates-General are each responsible for a particular policy area and they devise and draft the Commission's legislative proposals, which become official when adopted by the Commission.

In January 1999 Commissioners accused of mismanagement and corruption retained their positions following a vote of censure by Parliament. However, Parliament appointed a five-member Committee of Independent Experts to investigate allegations of fraud, mismanagement and nepotism within the Commission. In March two new codes of conduct for Commissioners were announced, and the Committee published a report that criticized the Commission's failure to control the administration of the budget and other measures implemented by each department. As a consequence of the report the Commission agreed, collectively, to resign, although Commissioners retained their positions, and exercised limited duties, until their successors were appointed. In late March EU heads of state and of government nominated Romano Prodi, the former Italian Prime Minister, as the next President of the Commission. His appointment, and that of his interim team of Commissioners, were duly ratified by Parliament in September, subject to conditions that formed the foundation of a future inter-institutional agreement between Parliament and the Commission. The Commission retained its powers, but undertook to be more open in its dealings with the Parliament.

In January 2004 the Commission launched legal proceedings against the Economic and Financial Council of Ministers (ECOFIN—which comprises the national ministers responsible for finance). The Commission sought a ruling from the European Court of Justice on the legality of ECOFIN's decision to suspend disciplinary procedures against France and Germany, both of which intended to exceed the budget deficit limit of 3% of gross domestic product (GDP), imposed under the Stability and Growth Pact, for the third consecutive year. In July the European Court of Justice ruled that ECOFIN's intervention was not compatible with EU legislation but that ministers retained ultimate control over the implementation of the pact. In November 2005, in response to diminishing public confidence in EU institutions, the Commission launched the European Transparency Initiative, with the aim of strengthening ethical rules for EU policy-makers, increasing the transparency of lobbying and ensuring the openness of the institutions.

Meanwhile, on 1 May 2004, following the accession of 10 new member states, the 20 existing members of the Commission were joined by 10 new members (one from each new member state). For the first six months of their term of office, although considered full members, they worked alongside existing Commissioners and were not allocated their own departments. From 1 November, when a new Commission was to begin its mandate, there were to be 25 members of the Commission, one from each member state as stipulated by the Treaty of Nice (prior to 1 May, large countries had been permitted two Commissioners, while smaller countries had one). In late October, however, the incoming President of the European Commission, José Manuel Durão Barroso, withdrew his proposed team of commissioners, in order to avoid defeat in the investiture vote in the European Parliament. The reconstituted Commission (two members were replaced and one was allocated a new portfolio) was approved by the European Parliament and took office on 22 November. In January 2007, following the accession of Bulgaria and Romania, the number of Commissioners increased to 27. As it was feared that too large an increase in the number of Commissioners would be prejudicial to collective responsibility, it was initially determined that from 2014 the number would be reduced to a level determined by the Council. However, in December 2008, in response to Ireland's rejection of the Lisbon Treaty in a national referendum in June, the European Council agreed a number of legal guarantees intended to address voters' objections, including a commitment that every member state would have one Commissioner. (The Irish electorate approved the Treaty in October 2009, and it entered into force in December of that year.)

The second Barroso Commission, for 2010–14, was approved by the European Parliament in January 2010 and inaugurated in the following month. The mandate of the previous commission (that should have expired in October 2009) had been lengthened temporarily to accommodate delays in the appointment of the new Commission that were caused by the later than anticipated entry into force of the Lisbon Treaty.

DIRECTORATES-GENERAL AND SERVICES

Policies

Directorate-General for Agriculture and Rural Development: 130 rue de la Loi, 1049 Brussels; tel. (2) 295-32-40; fax (2) 295-01-30; e-mail agri-library@ec.europa.eu; internet ec.europa.eu/dgs/agriculture; Dir-Gen. JOSÉ MANUEL SILVA RODRIGUEZ.

Directorate-General for Budget: 45 ave d'Auderghem, 1049 Brussels; tel. (2) 299-11-11; fax (2) 295-95-85; e-mail budget@ec.europa.eu; internet ec.europa.eu/dgs/budget; Dir-Gen. HERVÉ JOUANJEAN.

Directorate-General for Climate Action: 1049 Brussels; e-mail ec.europa.eu/dgs/clima/contact_en.htm (contact form); internet ec.europa.eu/dgs/climateaction/index_en.htm; f. Feb. 2010; Dir-Gen. JOS DELBEKE.

Directorate-General for Competition: 70 rue Joseph II, 1049 Brussels; tel. (2) 299-11-11; fax (2) 295-01-28; e-mail infocomp@ec.europa.eu; internet ec.europa.eu/competition; f. 1958; Dir-Gen. ALEXANDER ITALIANER.

Directorate-General for Economic and Financial Affairs: 1049 Brussels; tel. (2) 299-11-11; fax (2) 298-08-23; e-mail staffdir@ec.europa.eu; internet ec.europa.eu/economy_finance; Dir-Gen. MARCO BUTI.

Directorate-General for Education and Culture: 200 rue de la Loi, 1049 Brussels; tel. (2) 299-11-11; fax (2) 295-60-85; e-mail eac-info@ec.europa.eu; internet ec.europa.eu/dgs/education_culture; Dir-Gen. JAN TRUSZCZYŃSKI.

Directorate-General for Employment, Social Affairs and Inclusion: 200 rue de la Loi, 1049 Brussels; tel. (2) 299-11-11; e-mail ec.europa.eu/social/contact (contact form); internet ec.europa.eu/social; Dir-Gen. JACOBUS RICHELLE.

Directorate-General for Energy: 200 rue de la Loi, 1049 Brussels; tel. (2) 299-11-11; fax (2) 295-01-50; e-mail ec.europa.eu/energy/contact/index_en.htm (contact form); internet ec.europa.eu/energy/index_en.htm; Dir-Gen. PHILIP LOWE.

Directorate-General for Health and Consumers: 4 rue Breydel, 1049 Brussels; tel. (2) 299-11-11; fax (2) 296-62-98; e-mail sanco-mailbox@ec.europa.eu; internet ec.europa.eu/dgs/health_consumer/index_en.htm; Dir-Gen. PAULA TESTORI COGGI.

Directorate-General for Home Affairs: 46 rue du Luxembourg, 1050 Brussels; tel. (2) 299-11-11; fax (2) 296-74-81; e-mail forename.surname@ec.europa.eu; internet ec.europa.eu/dgs/home-affairs/index_en.htm; Dir-Gen. STEFANO MANSERVISI.

Directorate-General for Internal Market and Services: rue de Spa, 1000 Brussels; e-mail markt-info@ec.europa.eu; internet ec.europa.eu/dgs/internal_market; Dir-Gen. JONATHAN FAULL.

Directorate-General for Justice: 200 rue de la Loi, 10549 Brussels; tel. (2) 299-11-11; fax (2) 296-74-81; e-mail forename.surname@ec.europa.eu; internet ec.europa.eu/justice/index_en.htm; Dir-Gen. FRANÇOISE LE BAIL.

Directorate-General for Maritime Affairs and Fisheries: 99 rue de Joseph II, 1000 Brussels; tel. (2) 299-11-11; fax (2) 299-30-40; e-mail fisheries-info@ec.europa.eu; internet ec.europa.eu/fisheries; Dir-Gen. LOWRI EVANS.

Directorate-General for Mobility and Transport (DG Move) : 24–28 rue Demot, 1040 Brussels; tel. (2) 299-11-11; fax (2) 295-01-50; e-mail ec.europa.eu/transport/contact/index_en.htm (contact form); internet ec.europa.eu/transport/index_en.htm; Dir-Gen. MATTHIAS RUETE.

Directorate-General for Regional Policy: 23 rue Père de Deken, 1040 Brussels; tel. (2) 296-06-34; fax (2) 296-60-03; e-mail regio-info@ec.europa.eu; internet ec.europa.eu/dgs/regional_policy; Dir-Gen. WALTER DEFFAA.

Directorate-General for Research: 21 rue de Champ de Mars, 1050 Brussels; tel. (2) 299-11-11; fax (2) 295-82-20; e-mail research@cec.eu.int; internet ec.europa.eu/dgs/research; Dir-Gen. ROBERT-JAN SMITS.

Enterprise and Industry Directorate-General: 45 ave d'Auderghem, 1049 Brussels; tel. (2) 299-11-11; fax (2) 296-99-30; e-mail info-enterprises@ec.europa.eu; internet ec.europa.eu/enterprise; Dir-Gen. DANIEL CALLEJA CRESPO.

Environment Directorate-General: 5 ave de Beaulieu, 1160 Brussels; tel. (2) 299-11-11; fax (2) 299-11-05; e-mail envinfo@ec.europa.eu; internet ec.europa.eu/environment; Dir-Gen. KARL FALKENBERG.

Information Society and Media Directorate-General: 24 ave de Beaulieu, 1049 Brussels; tel. (2) 299-93-99; fax (2) 299-94-99; e-mail infso-desk@ec.europa.eu; internet ec.europa.eu/dgs/information_society; Dir-Gen. ROBERT MADELIN.

Taxation and the Customs Union Directorate-General: 59 rue Montoyer, 1000 Brussels; tel. (2) 299-11-11; fax (2) 295-07-56; e-mail librarian-information@ec.europa.eu; internet ec.europa.eu/taxation_customs/index_en.htm; Dir-Gen. HEINZ ZOUREK.

External Relations

Directorate-General for Enlargement: 200 rue de la Loi, 1049 Brussels; tel. (2) 299-96-96; fax (2) 296-84-90; e-mail elarg-info@ec.europa.eu; internet ec.europa.eu/dgs/enlargement; Dir-Gen. STEFANO SAFFINO.

Directorate-General for Trade (DG Trade): 200 rue de la Loi, 1049 Brussels; tel. (2) 299-11-11; fax (2) 299-10-29; e-mail trade-unit3@ec.europa.eu; internet ec.europa.eu/dgs/trade; Dir-Gen. JEAN-LUC DEMARTY.

Directorate-General for Development and Co-operation (EuropeAid): 15 rue de la Science, 1049 Brussels; tel. (2) 299-21-23; fax (2) 296-49-26; e-mail development@ec.europa.eu; internet ec.europa.eu/development/AboutGen_en.cfm; Dir-Gen. FOKIAN FOTIADIS.

Humanitarian Aid Office (ECHO): 88 rue d'Arlon, 1040 Brussels; tel. (2) 299-11-11; fax (2) 295-45-78; e-mail echo-info@ec.europa.eu; internet ec.europa.eu/echo; Dir CLAUS SØRENSEN.

General Services

Directorate-General for Communication: 45 ave d'Auderghem, SDME 2/2, 1049 Brussels; tel. (2) 299-11-11; fax (2) 295-01-43; e-mail comm-web@ec.europa.eu; internet ec.europa.eu/dgs/communication; Dir-Gen. GREGORY PAULGER.

European Anti-Fraud Office: 30 rue Joseph II, 1000 Brussels; tel. (2) 296-29-76; fax (2) 296-08-53; e-mail olaf-courrier@ec.europa.eu; internet ec.europa.eu/anti_fraud/index_en.htm; Dir-Gen. GIOVANNI KESSLER.

Eurostat (Statistical Office of the European Communities): Bâtiment Joseph Bech, 5 Rue Alphonse Weicker, 2721 Luxembourg; tel. 43-01-33-444; fax 43-01-35-349; e-mail eurostat-pressoffice@ec.europa.eu; internet epp.eurostat.ec.europa.eu; Dir-Gen. WALTER RADERMACHER.

Joint Research Centre (JRC): 200 rue de la Loi, 1049 Brussels; tel. (2) 297-41-81; fax (2) 299-63-22; e-mail jrc-info@ec.europa.eu; internet ec.europa.eu/dgs/jrc; Dir-Gen. DOMINIQUE RISTORI.

Office for Official Publications of the European Communities (Publications Office): 2 rue Mercier, 2985 Luxembourg; tel. 29-291; fax 29-29-44-619; e-mail info@publications.europa.eu; internet www.publications.europa.eu; Dir-Gen. MARTINE REICHERTS.

Secretariat-General: 45 ave d'Auderghem, 1049 Brussels; tel. (2) 299-11-11; fax (2) 296-05-54; e-mail sg-info@ec.europa.eu; internet ec.europa.eu/dgs/secretariat_general; Sec.-Gen. CATHERINE DAY.

Internal Services

Bureau of European Policy Advisers (BEPA): 200 rue de la Loi, 1049 Brussels; tel. (2) 299-11-11; fax (2) 295-23-05; e-mail bepa-info@ec.europa.eu; internet ec.europa.eu/dgs/policy_advisers; Head JEAN-CLAUDE THÉBAULT.

Data Protection Officer of the European Commission: 1049 Brussels; tel. (2) 226-87-50; fax (2) 296-38-91; e-mail data-protection-officer@ec.europa.eu; internet ec.europa.eu/dataprotectionofficer; Data Protection Officer PHILIPPE RENAUDIÈRE.

Directorate-General for Human Resources and Security: 200 rue de la Loi, 1040 Brussels; tel. (2) 299-11-11; fax (2) 299-62-76; e-mail forename.surname@ec.europa.eu; internet ec.europa.eu/dgs/human-resources/index_en.htm; Dir-Gen. IRÈNE SOUKA.

Directorate-General for Informatics (DIGIT): rue Alcide de Gasperi, 2920 Luxembourg; e-mail digit-europa@ec.europa.eu; internet ec.europa.eu/dgs/informatics; Dir-Gen. FRANCISCO GARCÍA MORÁN.

Directorate-General for Interpretation: 200 rue de la Loi, 1040 Brussels; tel. (2) 299-11-11; e-mail scic-euroscic@ec.europa.eu; internet scic.ec.europa.eu/europa/jcms/j_8/home; Head of Service MARCO BENEDETTI.

Directorate-General for Translation (DGT): 200 rue de la Loi, 1040 Brussels; rue de Genève, 1140 Brussels; tel. (2) 299-11-11; fax (2) 296-97-69; e-mail dgt-webmaster@ec.europa.eu; internet ec.europa.eu/dgs/translation; Dir-Gen. RYTIS MARTIKONIS (acting).

Internal Audit Service (IAS): 200 rue de la Loi, 1049 Brussels; tel. (2) 299-11-11; fax (2) 295-41-40; e-mail ias-europa@ec.europa.eu; internet ec.europa.eu/dgs/internal_audit/index_en.htm; Internal Auditor of the European Commission BRIAN GRAY.

Legal Service: 85 ave des Nerviens, 1049 Brussels; tel. (2) 299-11-11; fax (2) 296-30-86; e-mail oib-info@ec.europa.eu; internet ec.europa.eu/dgs/legal_service; Dir-Gen. LUIS ROMERO REQUENA.

Office for Infrastructure and Logistics in Brussels (OIB): Garderie Wilson, 16 rue Wilson, 1040 Brussels; fax (2) 295-76-41; e-mail oib-info@ec.europa.eu; internet ec.europa.eu/oib; Dir GÁBOR ZUPKÓ.

Office for Infrastructure and Logistics in Luxembourg (OIL): Luxembourg; e-mail oil-cad@ec.europa.eu; internet ec.europa.eu/oil; Dir MARIAN O'LEARY.

EUROPEAN COUNCIL

Address: Justus Lipsius Bldg, 175 rue de la Loi, 1048 Brussels, Belgium.

Telephone: (2) 281-61-11; **fax:** (2) 281-69-34; **internet:** www.european-council.europa.eu.

The European Council was the name used to describe summit meetings of the heads of state or of government of the EU member states, their ministers of foreign affairs, and senior officials of the European Commission. The Council met at least twice a year, in the member state that exercised the Presidency of the Council of the European Union, or in Brussels. Until 1975 summit meetings were held less frequently, on an ad hoc basis, usually to adopt major policy decisions regarding the future development of the Community. In answer to the evident need for more frequent consultation at the highest level, it was decided at the summit meeting held in Paris in December 1974 to convene the meetings on a regular basis, under the rubric of the European Council. There was no provision made for the existence of the European Council in the Treaty of Rome, but its position was acknowledged and regularized in the Single European Act (1987). Its role was further strengthened in the Treaty on European Union, which entered into force on 1 November 1993. As a result of the Treaty, the European Council became directly responsible for common policies within the fields of common foreign and security policy and justice and home affairs.

Under the Treaty of Lisbon, which came into force at the beginning of December 2009, the European Council became an institution shaping the EU's development and defining its political priorities. In November 2009, prior to the entry into force of the Treaty, an informal meeting of EU heads of state and of government elected Herman Van Rompuy of Belgium to the new position of President of the European Council, for a period of two years and six months, renewable once. He took office upon the entry into force of the Treaty. The European Council comprises the heads of state or of government of the member states, together with its President and the President of the Commission; the High Representative is also involved in the activities of the European Council, which performs no legislative function, and meets twice every six months, as convened by its President. If required, the President may convene special meetings of the European Council.

COUNCIL OF THE EUROPEAN UNION

Address: Justus Lipsius Bldg, 175 rue de la Loi, 1048 Brussels, Belgium.

Telephone: (2) 281-61-11; **fax:** (2) 281-69-34; **e-mail:** press.office@consilium.europa.eu; **internet:** www.consilium.europa.eu.

The Council of the European Union (until November 1993 known formally as the Council of Ministers of the European Communities and still sometimes referred to as the Council of Ministers) is the only institution that directly represents the member states. It is the Community's principal decision-making body, acting, as a rule, only on proposals made by the Commission, and has six main responsibilities: to approve EC legislation (in many fields it legislates jointly with the European Parliament); to co-ordinate the broad economic policies of the member states; to conclude international agreements between the EU and one or more states or international organizations; to approve the EU budget (in conjunction with the European Parliament); to develop the EU's Common Foreign and Security Policy (CFSP), on the basis of guidelines drawn up by the European Council; and to co-ordinate co-operation between the national courts and police forces in criminal matters. The Council is composed of representatives of the member states, each Government delegating to it one of its members, according to the subject to be discussed (the Council has nine different configurations). These meetings are generally referred to as the Agriculture and Fisheries Council, the Transport, Telecommunications and Energy Council, etc. The General Affairs and External Relations Council, the Economic and Financial Affairs Council (ECOFIN) and the Agriculture and Fisheries Council each normally meet once a month. The Presidency is exercised for a term of six months by each member of the Council in rotation. A new, fixed 18-month troika system (groups of three presidencies) was introduced under the Treaty of Lisbon, which entered into force on 1 December 2009. The current group of presidencies is as follows: Denmark, January–June 2012; Cyprus, July–December 2012; Ireland, January–June 2013). The troika shares the presidencies of most configurations of the Council, with the aim of facilitating overall co-ordination and continuity of work.

The Treaty of Rome prescribed three types of voting (depending on the issue under discussion): simple majority, qualified majority and unanimity. Amendments to the Treaty of Rome (the Single European Act), effective from July 1987, restricted the right of veto, and were expected to accelerate the development of a genuine common market: they allowed proposals relating to the dismantling of barriers to the free movement of goods, persons, services and capital to be approved by a majority vote in the Council, rather than by a unanimous vote. Unanimity was still required, however, for certain areas, including harmonization of indirect taxes, legislation on health and safety, veterinary controls, and environmental protection; individual states retained control over immigration rules and the prevention of terrorism and of drugs-trafficking. The Treaty of Amsterdam, which came into force on 1 May 1999, extended the use of qualified majority voting (QMV) to a number of areas previously subject to unanimous decision. Under the terms of the Treaty of Nice, which came into force on 1 February 2003, a further range of areas (mostly minor in nature and relating to appointments to various EU institutions) that had previously been subject to national vetoes became subject to QMV. With the expansion of the EU to 25 members in 2004, and subsequently to 27 members in 2007, and the consequent reduced likelihood of unanimity in Council decisions, the use of QMV in an even broader range of decisions was intended to minimize so-called policy drag. The 2009 Lisbon Treaty provided for the further extension of QMV, which was newly defined, to areas that had previously been subject to national vetoes (from 2014, see below).

The Single European Act introduced a 'co-operation procedure' whereby a proposal adopted by a qualified majority in the Council must be submitted to the European Parliament for approval: if the Parliament rejects the Council's common position, unanimity shall be required for the Council to act on a second reading, and, if the Parliament suggests amendments, the Commission must re-examine the proposal and forward it to the Council again. A 'co-decision procedure' was introduced in 1993 by the Treaty on European Union. The procedure allowed a proposal to be submitted for a third reading by a so-called Conciliation Committee, composed equally of Council representatives and members of the European Parliament. The Treaty of Amsterdam simplified the co-decision procedure, and extended it to matters previously resolved under the co-operation procedure, although the latter remained in place for matters concerning economic and monetary union.

Under the Treaty of Amsterdam, the Secretary-General of the Council also took the role of High Representative, responsible for the co-ordination of the common foreign and security policy. The Council Secretary-General is supported by a policy planning and early warning unit.

The Treaty of Nice, which came into force in February 2003, addressed institutional issues that remained outstanding under the Treaty of Amsterdam and that had to be settled before the enlargement of the EU in 2004, and various other issues not directly connected with enlargement. The main focus of the Treaty was the establishment of principles governing the new distribution of seats in the European Parliament, the new composition of the Commission and a new definition of QMV within the Council of the European Union. From 1 May 2004 (when the 10 accession states joined the EU) until 31 October, there were transitional arrangements for changing the weighting of votes in the Council. In accordance with the provisions incorporated in the Treaty of Nice, from 1 November the new weighting system was as follows: France, Germany, Italy and the United Kingdom 29 votes each; Poland and Spain 27 votes each; the Netherlands 13 votes; Belgium, the Czech Republic, Greece, Hungary and Portugal 12 votes each; Austria and Sweden 10 votes each; Denmark, Finland, Ireland, Lithuania and Slovakia seven votes each; Cyprus, Estonia, Latvia, Luxembourg and Slovenia four votes each; and Malta three votes. A qualified majority was reached if a majority of member states (in some cases a two-thirds' majority) approved and if a minimum of 232 votes out of a total of 321 was cast in favour (which was 72.3% of the total—approximately the same share as under the previous system). In addition, a member state could request confirmation that the votes in favour represented at least 62% of the total population of the EU. Should this not be the case, the decision would not be adopted by the Council. The number of weighted votes required for the adoption of a decision (referred to as the 'qualified majority threshold') was to be reassessed on the accession of any additional new member state. Accordingly, in January 2007, with the accession of Romania and Bulgaria, which were allocated, respectively, 14 and 10 votes, the 'qualified majority threshold' was increased to 255 votes, which represented 73.9% of the new total of 345 votes. It was widely held that the voting system according to the Treaty of Nice was overly complicated and that it gave undue power to certain less populous countries, notably Spain and Poland (which both held 27 votes each, compared with Germany, which, with a population of at least twice the size of those in Spain and Poland, controlled 29 votes).

Reforms approved under the 2009 Treaty of Lisbon made provision for the extension and redefinition of QMV in the Council of the European Union and the ending of the system of national vetoes in a number of further policy areas (including combating climate change, energy, emergency aid, and security). Under a system to be gradually introduced during 2014–17, a qualified majority was to be defined as representing at least 55% of the members of the Council, composed of at least 15 of them and representing member states comprising at least 65% of the EU's population (although a blocking minority would have to include at least four member states). The Lisbon Treaty includes a provision allowing the European Council to agree, by unanimity and subject to prior unanimous approval by national legislatures, to introduce QMV in an area currently requiring unanimity (except in a small number of areas including defence, foreign policy and taxation), thus obviating the need for treaty change.

GENERAL SECRETARIAT

Secretary-General of the Council of the European Union: Uwe Corsepius (Germany).

Secretary-General's Private Office: Head of Cabinet Marek Mora.

Legal Service: Dir-Gen./Legal Adviser Hubert Legal.

Directorates-General:

A (Administration): Dir-Gen. William Shapcott.

B (Agriculture, Fisheries, Social Affairs and Health): Dir-Gen. Ángel Boixareu Carrera.

C (Foreign Affairs, Enlargement and Civil Protection): Dir-Gen. Leonardo Schiavo.

D (Justice and Home Affairs): Dir-Gen. Rafael Fernández-Pita y González (acting).

E (Environment, Education, Transport and Energy): Dir-Gen. Jarosław Pietras.

F (Communication and Transparency): Dir-Gen. Reijo Kemppinen.

G (Economic and Social Affairs): Dir-Gen. Carsten Pillath.

PERMANENT REPRESENTATIVES OF MEMBER STATES

(April 2012)

Austria: Walter Grahammer; 30 ave de Cortenberg, 1040 Brussels; tel. (2) 234-51-00; fax (2) 235-63-00; e-mail bruessel-ov@bmeia.gv.at.

Belgium: Dirk Wouters; 61–63 rue de la Loi, 1040 Brussels; tel. (2) 233-21-11; fax (2) 231-10-75; e-mail dispatch.belgoeurop@diplobel.fed.be.

Bulgaria: Boyko Vassilev Kotzev; 49 sq. Marie-Louise, 1000 Brussels; tel. (2) 235-83-00; fax (2) 374-91-88; e-mail info@bg-permrep.eu; internet www.bg-permrep.eu.

Cyprus: Kornelios S. Korneliou; 61 ave de Cortenberg, 1000 Brussels; tel. (2) 739-51-11; fax (2) 735-45-52; e-mail cy.perm.rep@mfa.gov.cy.

Czech Republic: Milena Vicenová; 15 rue Caroly, 1050 Brussels; tel. (2) 213-91-11; fax (2) 213-91-86; e-mail eu.brussels@embassy.mzv.cz; internet www.czechrep.be.

Denmark: Jeppe Tranholm-Mikkelsen; 73 rue d'Arlon, 1040 Brussels; tel. (2) 233-08-11; fax (2) 230-93-84; e-mail brurep@um.dk.

Estonia: Matti Maasikas; 11–13 rue Guimard, 1040 Brussels; tel. (2) 227-39-10; fax (2) 227-39-25; e-mail permrep.eu@mfa.ee; internet www.eu.estemb.be.

Finland: Jan Store; 100 rue de Trèves, 1040 Brussels; tel. (2) 287-84-11; fax (2) 287-84-05; e-mail forename.surname@formin.fi; internet www.finland.eu.

France: Philippe Etienne; 14 place de Louvain, 1000 Brussels; tel. (2) 229-82-11; fax (2) 230-99-50; e-mail courrier.bruxelles-dfra@diplomatie.gouv.fr; internet www.rpfrance.org.

Germany: Peter Tempel; 8–14 rue Jacques de Lalaing, 1040 Brussels; tel. (2) 787-10-00; fax (2) 787-20-00; e-mail info@eu-vertretung.de; internet www.eu-vertretung.de.

Greece: Theodoros N. Sotiropoulos; 19–21 rue Jacques de Lalaing, 1040 Brussels; tel. (2) 551-56-11; fax (2) 551-56-51; e-mail mea.bruxelles@rp-grece.be; internet www.greekembassy-press.be.

Hungary: PÉTER GYÖRKÖS; 92–98 rue de Trèves, 1040 Brussels; tel. (2) 234-12-00; fax (2) 372-07-84; e-mail sec.beu@kum.hu; internet www.hunrep.be.

Ireland: RORY MONTGOMERY; 50 rue Froissart, 1040 Brussels; tel. (2) 230-85-80; fax (2) 230-32-03; e-mail irlprb@dfa.ie; internet www.irelandrepbrussels.be.

Italy: FERDINANDO NELLI FEROCI; 5–11 rue du Marteau, 1000 Brussels; tel. (2) 220-04-11; fax (2) 219-34-49; e-mail rpue@rpue.esteri.it; internet www.italiaue.esteri.it.

Latvia: ILZE JUHANSONE; 23 ave des Arts, 1000 Brussels; tel. (2) 238-31-00; fax (2) 238-32-50; e-mail permrep.eu@mfa.gov.lv; internet www.mfa.gov.lv/brussels.

Lithuania: RAIMUNDAS KAROBLIS; 41–43 rue Belliard, 1040 Brussels; tel. (2) 771-01-40; fax (2) 401-98-77; e-mail office@eurep.mfa.lt; internet www.eurep.mfa.lt.

Luxembourg: CHRISTIAN BRAUN; 75 ave de Cortenberg, 1000 Brussels; tel. (2) 737-56-00; fax (2) 737-56-10; e-mail forename.surname@rpue.etat.lu.

Malta: RICHARD CACHIA CARUANA; 25 rue d'Archimède, 1000 Brussels; tel. (2) 343-01-95; fax (2) 343-01-06; e-mail maltarep@gov.mt.

Netherlands: PIETER DE GOOIJER; 4–10 ave de Cortenberg, 1040 Brussels; tel. (2) 679-15-11; fax (2) 679-17-75; e-mail BRE@minbusa.nl; internet eu.nlvertegenwoordiging.org.

Poland: JAN TOMBIŃSKI; 139 rue Stevin, 1000 Brussels; tel. (2) 780-42-00; fax (2) 780-42-97; e-mail bebrustpe@msz.gov.pl; internet www.brukselaeu.polemb.net.

Portugal: MANUEL LOBO ANTUNES; 12 ave de Cortenberg, 1040 Brussels; tel. (2) 286-42-11; fax (2) 231-00-26; e-mail reper@reper-portugal.be; internet www.reper-portugal.be.

Romania: MIHNEA IOAN MOTOC; 12 rue Montoyer, 1000 Brussels; tel. (2) 700-06-40; fax (2) 700-06-41; e-mail bru@rpro.eu; internet www.ue.mae.ro.

Slovakia: IVAN KORČOK; 79 ave de Cortenberg, 1000 Brussels; tel. (2) 743-68-11; fax (2) 743-68-88; e-mail eu.brussels@mzv.sk; internet www.mzv.sk/szbrusel.

Slovenia: RADO GENORIO; 44 rue du Commerce, 1000 Brussels; tel. (2) 213-63-00; fax (2) 213-63-01; e-mail pr.spbr@gov.si; internet www.mzz.gov.si.

Spain: ALFONSO DASTIS QUECEDO; 52 blvd du Régent, 1000 Brussels; tel. (2) 509-86-11; fax (2) 511-19-40; e-mail reperue@reper.maec.es; internet www.es-ue.org.

Sweden: DAG HARTELIUS; 30 place de Meeûs, 1000 Brussels; tel. (2) 289-56-11; fax (2) 289-56-00; e-mail representationen.bryssel@foreign.ministry.se; internet www.sweden.gov.se/sb/d/2250.

United Kingdom: JON CUNLIFFE; 10 ave d'Auderghem, 1040 Brussels; tel. (2) 287-82-11; fax (2) 282-89-00; e-mail ukrep@fco.gov.uk; internet ukeu.fco.gov.uk/en.

Preparation and co-ordination of the Council's work (with the exception of agricultural issues, which are handled by the Special Committee on Agriculture) is entrusted to a Committee of Permanent Representatives (COREPER), which meets in Brussels on a weekly basis and which consists of the permanent representatives of the member countries to the Union (who have senior ambassadorial status). A staff of national civil servants assists each ambassador.

EUROPEAN EXTERNAL ACTION SERVICE—EEAS

Address: 1 ave de Cortenberg, Brussels, 1046 Belgium.

Telephone: (2) 584-11-11; **internet:** www.eeas.europa.eu.

The Treaty of Lisbon, which entered into force at the beginning of December 2009, created the new position of High Representative of the Union for Foreign Affairs and Security, to which Catherine Ashton was appointed for a five-year term. In July 2010 the European Parliament approved the creation of the European External Action Service (EEAS), which was formally established at the beginning of December, as the EU's foreign policy and diplomatic service. The High Representative of the Union for Foreign Affairs and Security Policy, who is also a Vice-President of the Commission, is responsible for the co-ordination of the EEAS, and chairs monthly meetings of the Foreign Affairs Council, which comprises EU ministers of foreign affairs, of defence and of development. The EEAS, an independent body, combines the functions of the Commission and the Council hitherto responsible for foreign affairs.

High Representative of the Union for Foreign Affairs and Security Policy: CATHERINE ASHTON (United Kingdom).

Executive Secretary-General: PIERRE VIMONT (France).

Chief Operating Officer: DAVID O'SULLIVAN (Ireland).

EUROPEAN PARLIAMENT

Address: Centre Européen, Plateau du Kirchberg, BP 1601, 2929 Luxembourg.

Telephone: 4300-1; **fax:** 4300-29494; **internet:** www.europarl.europa.eu.

PRESIDENT AND MEMBERS

President: MARTIN SCHULZ (Germany).

Members: Members of the Parliament are elected for a five-year term by direct universal suffrage and proportional representation by the citizens of the member states. Members sit in the Chamber in transnational political, not national, groups. The Parliament elected in June 2009 was initially composed of 736 members; the Treaty of Lisbon, which entered into force on 1 December 2009, however, makes provision for a total of 751 seats.

The European Parliament has three main roles: sharing with the Council of the European Union the power to legislate; holding authority over the annual Union budget (again, jointly with the Council), including the power to adopt or reject it in its entirety; and exercising a measure of democratic control over the executive organs of the European Communities, the Commission and the Council. Notably, it has the power to dismiss the European Commission as a whole by a vote of censure (requiring a two-thirds' majority of the votes cast, which must also be a majority of the total parliamentary membership). The Parliament does not exercise the authority, however, to dismiss individual Commissioners. Increases in parliamentary powers were brought about through amendments to the Treaty of Rome. The Single European Act, which entered into force on 1 July 1987, introduced, in certain circumstances where the Council normally adopts legislation through majority voting, a co-operation procedure involving a second parliamentary reading, enabling the Parliament to amend legislation. Community agreements with third countries require parliamentary approval. The Treaty on European Union, which came into force in November 1993, introduced the co-decision procedure, permitting a third parliamentary reading (see the Council of the European Union). The Treaty also gives the Parliament the right potentially to veto legislation, and allows it to approve or reject the nomination of Commissioners (including the President of the Commission). The Parliament appoints the European Ombudsman from among its members, who investigates reports of maladministration in Community institutions. The Treaty of Amsterdam, which entered into force in May 1999, expanded and simplified the Parliament's legislative role. The co-decision procedure between the Parliament and the Council was extended into a wider range of policy areas. The Treaty also stipulated that the President of the Commission must be formally approved by the Parliament. In addition, international agreements, treaty decisions and the accession of new member states all require the assent of the Parliament. The Treaty of Nice, which came into force in February 2003, further extended the use of co-decision and introduced a new distribution of seats in the Parliament. The Treaty of Lisbon again extended the Parliament's right of co-decision with the Council, and made provision for a maximum number of seats of 751 (750 voting members and the President), with each member state being entitled to a minimum of six and a maximum of 96 seats, on a proportional basis (see below). Under the Treaty 18 additional seats were allocated to 12 member states, while Germany was to lose three of its former seats.

The Parliament elected in June 2009, prior to the entry into force of the Lisbon Treaty in December, initially comprised the 736 members provided for by the Nice Treaty. However, in December 2008 EU heads of state and of government had agreed a compromise composition for the 2009–14 Parliament, which was to comprise the 736 members elected in June 2009 (including the three extra German representatives elected legitimately under the terms of the Nice Treaty), plus the 18 additional members provided for by the Lisbon Treaty (see below for distribution), thereby temporarily raising the total number of members to 754, until the election of the next, 751-member Parliament in 2014. In order to enable the 18 additional members (who would technically hold observer status, to enable their participation in the 2009–14 Parliament) to assume their responsibilities, a transitional change to the Lisbon Treaty was required. On 17 June 2010 the European Council agreed to launch an Intergovernmental Conference to negotiate the required amendment. The amendment was adopted six days later, subject to ratification by the national legislatures of member states. Ratification was completed in November 2011, and the amendment entered into force on 1 December 2011. Moreover, from April 2012 Croatia sent a further 12 members, with observer status, to the Parliament; they would become full members in July 2013, upon Croatia's admission to the EU.

The distribution of seats among the 27 members provided for by the Lisbon Treaty is as follows: Germany 96 members (with, exceptionally, 99, in accordance with the provisions of the Nice Treaty, to hold seats during 2009–14); France 74 (compared with 72 provided for under the Nice Treaty); the United Kingdom 73 (including one additional member); Italy 73 (one additional member); Spain 54 (four); Poland 51 (one); Romania 33; the Netherlands 26 (one); Portugal (with one additional member), Belgium, the Czech Republic, Greece and Hungary 22 each; Sweden 20 (two additional members); Austria 19 (two); Bulgaria 18 (one additional member); Denmark, Finland and Slovakia 13 each; Ireland and Lithuania 12 each; Latvia nine (one); Slovenia eight (one); and Malta (with one additional member), Cyprus, Estonia and Luxembourg six each.

Political Groups

	Distribution of seats (March 2012)
Group of the European People's Party (Christian Democrats) (EPP)	271
Group of the Progressive Alliance of Socialists and Democrats (S/D)	190
Group of the Alliance of Liberals and Democrats for Europe (ALDE)	85
Group of the Greens/European Free Alliance (Verts/EFA)	58
European Conservatives and Reformists Group (ECR)	53
Confederal Group of the European United Left/ Nordic Green Left (GUE/NGL)	34
Europe of Freedom and Democracy Group (EFD)	33
Non-affiliated (NA)	30
Total	754

With effect from June 2009 the minimum number of members required to form a political group under the Parliament's rules of procedure has been fixed at 25, from a minimum of seven member states (previously 20 members were required from a minimum of six member states).

The Parliament has an annual session, divided into around 12 one-week meetings, attended by all members and normally held in Strasbourg, France. The session opens with the March meeting. Committee meetings, political group meetings and additional plenary sittings of the Parliament are held in Brussels, while the parliamentary administrative offices are based in Luxembourg.

The budgetary powers of the Parliament (which, together with the Council of the European Union, forms the Budgetary Authority of the Communities) were increased to their present status by a treaty of 22 July 1975. Under this treaty the Parliament can amend non-agricultural spending and reject the draft budget, acting by a majority of its members and two-thirds of the votes cast. The Parliament debates the draft budget in two successive readings, and it does not come into force until it has been signed by the President of the Parliament. The Parliament's Committee on Budgetary Control (COCOBU) monitors how the budget is spent, and each year the Parliament decides whether to approve the Commission's handling of the budget for the previous financial year (a process technically known as 'granting a discharge').

The Parliament is run by a Bureau comprising the President, 14 Vice-Presidents elected from its members by secret ballot to serve for two-and-a-half years, and the five members of the College of Quaestors. The Conference of Presidents is the political governing body of the Parliament, with responsibility for formulating the agenda for plenary sessions and the timetable for the work of parliamentary bodies, and for establishing the terms of reference and the size of committees and delegations. It comprises the President of the Parliament and the Chairmen of the political groups.

The majority of the Parliament's work is conducted by 22 Standing Parliamentary Committees, which correspond to different policy areas and various European Commission agencies: Foreign Affairs; Development; International Trade; Budgets; Budgetary Control; Economic and Monetary Affairs; Employment and Social Affairs; Environment, Public Health and Food Safety; Industry, Research and Energy; Internal Market and Consumer Protection; Transport and Tourism; Regional Development; Agriculture and Rural Development; Fisheries; Culture and Education; Legal Affairs; Civil Liberties, Justice and Home Affairs; Constitutional Affairs; Women's Rights and Gender Equality; Petitions; Human Rights; and Security Defence.

The first direct elections to the European Parliament took place in June 1979, and Parliament met for the first time in July. The second elections were held in June 1984 (with separate elections held in Portugal and Spain in 1987, following the accession of these two countries to the Community), the third in June 1989, and the fourth in June 1994. Direct elections to the European Parliament were held in Sweden in September 1995, and in Austria and Finland in October 1996. The fifth European Parliament was elected in June 1999, and the sixth in June 2004, following the mass accession of 10 new member states in May of that year. Elections to the seventh European Parliament were held on 4–7 June 2009; the rate of participation by the electorate was 43.1%.

EUROPEAN OMBUDSMAN

Address: 1 ave du Président Robert Schuman, BP 30403, 67001 Strasbourg Cedex, France.

Telephone: 3-88-17-23-13; **fax:** 3-88-17-90-62; **e-mail:** euro-ombudsman@europarl.eu.int; **internet:** www.ombudsman.europa.eu/home/en/default.htm.

The position was created by the Treaty on European Union (the Maastricht Treaty), and the first Ombudsman took office in July 1995. The Ombudsman is appointed by the European Parliament (from among its own members) for a renewable five-year term (to run concurrently with that of the European Parliament). He is authorized to receive complaints (from EU citizens, businesses and institutions, and from anyone residing or having their legal domicile in an EU member state) regarding maladministration in Community institutions and bodies (except in the Court of Justice and Court of First Instance), to make recommendations, and to refer any matters to the Parliament. The Ombudsman submits an annual report on his activities to the European Parliament.

European Ombudsman: Prof. NIKIFOROS DIAMANDOUROS (Greece).

COURT OF JUSTICE OF THE EUROPEAN UNION

Address: Cour de justice de l'Union européenne, 2925 Luxembourg.

Telephone: 4303-1; **fax:** 4303-2600; **e-mail:** info@curia.europa.eu; **internet:** curia.europa.eu/jcms/jcms/Jo2_7024.

As the EU's judicial institution, the Court of Justice acts as a safeguard of EU legislation and has jurisdiction over cases concerning member states, EU institutions, undertakings or individuals. EU legislation has been technically known as European Union law since the entry into force in December 2009 of the Treaty of Lisbon, which invested the EU with legal personality; prior to that it was known as Community law. The Court ensures uniform interpretation and application of European Union law throughout the EU. The 27 Judges and the eight Advocates-General are each appointed for a term of six years, after which they may be reappointed for one or two further periods of three years. The role of the Advocates-General is—publicly and impartially—to deliver reasoned opinions on the cases brought before the Court. There is normally one Judge per member state, whose name is put forward by the Government of that member state. These proposed appointments are then subject to a vote in the Council of the European Union. For the sake of efficiency, when the Court holds a plenary session only 13 Judges—sitting as a 'Grand Chamber'—have to attend. The President of the Court, who has overall charge of the Court's work and presides at hearings and deliberations, is elected by the Judges from among their number for a renewable term of three years. The majority of cases are dealt with by one of the eight chambers, each of which consists of a President of Chamber and three or five Judges. The Court may sit in plenary session in cases of particular importance or when a member state or Union institution that is a party to the proceedings so requests. Judgments are reached by a majority vote and are signed by all Judges involved in the case, irrespective of how they voted. The Court has jurisdiction to award damages. It may review the legality of acts (other than recommendations or opinions) of the Council, the Commission or the European Central Bank, of acts adopted jointly by the European Parliament and the Council, and of Acts adopted by the Parliament and intended to produce legal effects vis-à-vis third parties. It is also competent to give judgment on actions by a member state, the Council or the Commission on grounds of lack of competence, of infringement of an essential procedural requirement, of infringement of a Treaty or of any legal rule relating to its application, or of misuse of power. The Court of Justice may hear appeals, on a point of law only, from the Court of First Instance.

The Court is empowered to hear certain other cases concerning the contractual and non-contractual liability of the Communities and disputes between member states in connection with the objects of the Treaties. It also gives preliminary rulings at the request of national courts on the interpretation of the Treaties, of Union legislation, and of the Brussels Convention on Jurisdiction and the Enforcement of Judgments in Civil and Commercial Matters.

President of the Court of Justice: VASSILIOS SKOURIS (Greece).

Registrar: ALFREDO CALOT ESCOBAR (Spain).

GENERAL COURT

Address: Cour de justice de l'Union européenne, 2925 Luxembourg.

Telephone: 4303-1; **fax:** 4303-2600; **internet:** curia.europa.eu/jcms/jcms/Jo2_7033.

The General Court was established, as the Court of First Instance of the European Communities, by the European Council by a decision of October 1988, and began operations in 1989. Its current name was adopted following the entry into force of the Treaty of Lisbon on 1 December 2009. In order to help the Court of Justice deal with the thousands of cases brought before it and to offer citizens better legal protection, the General Court (which, although independent, is attached to the Court of Justice) deals with cases brought by individuals, legal entities and member states against the actions of EU institutions. The decisions of the General Court may be subject to appeal to the Court of Justice, on issues of law, within two months. As with the Court of Justice, the composition of the General Court is based on 27 Judges (one from each member state, appointed for a renewable term of six years), one President (elected from among the 27 Judges for a renewable period of three years) and eight chambers. The General Court has no permanent Advocates-General.

Within the framework of the Treaty of Nice, which provided for the creation of additional judicial panels in specific areas, in November 2004 the Council decided to establish the Civil Service Tribunal in order to reduce the number of cases brought before the Tribunal of First Instance. The specialized tribunal, which had been fully constituted by December 2005, exercises jurisdiction in the first instance in disputes between the EU and its staff. Its decisions are subject to appeal on questions of law only to the General Court and, in exceptional cases, to review by the European Court of Justice. The Council appoints the tribunal's seven Judges for a period of six years, and the President is elected by the Judges from among their number for a period of three years. The Council is charged with ensuring that as many member states as possible are represented in the tribunal.

President of the General Court: MARC JAEGER (Luxembourg).

Registrar: EMMANUEL COULON (France).

President of the Civil Service Tribunal: SEAN VAN RAEPENBUSCH (Belgium).

EUROPEAN COURT OF AUDITORS

Address: 12 rue Alcide de Gasperi, 1615 Luxembourg.

Telephone: 4398-1; **fax:** 4393-42; **e-mail:** eca-info@eca.europa.eu; **internet:** www.eca.europa.eu.

The European Court of Auditors (ECA) was created by the Treaty of Brussels, which was signed on 22 July 1975, and commenced its duties in late 1977. It was given the status of an institution on a par with the Commission, the Council, the Court of Justice and the Parliament by the Treaty on European Union. It is the institution responsible for the external audit of the resources managed by the EU. It consists of 27 members (one from each member state) who are appointed for renewable six-year terms (under a qualified majority voting system) by the Council of the European Union, after consultation with the European Parliament (in practice, however, the Council simply endorses the candidates put forward by the member states). The members elect the President of the Court from among their number for a renewable term of three years.

The Court is organized and acts as a collegiate body. It adopts its decisions by a majority of its members. Each member, however, has a direct responsibility for the audit of certain sectors of Union activities.

The Court examines the accounts of all expenditure and revenue of the EU and of any body created by them in so far as the relevant constituent instrument does not preclude such examination. It examines whether all revenue has been received and all expenditure incurred in a lawful and regular manner and whether the financial management has been sound. The audit is based on records, and if necessary is performed directly in the institutions of the Union, in the member states and in other countries. In the member states the audit is carried out in co-operation with the national audit bodies. The Court of Auditors draws up an annual report after the close of each financial year. The Court provides the Parliament and the Council with a statement of assurance as to the reliability of the accounts, and the legality and regularity of the underlying transactions. It may also, at any time, submit observations on specific questions (usually in the form of special reports) and deliver opinions at the request of one of the institutions of the Union. It assists the European Parliament and the Council in exercising their powers of control over the implementation of the budget, in particular within the framework of the annual discharge procedure, and gives its prior opinion on financial regulations, on the methods and procedure whereby budgetary revenue is made available to the Commission, and on the formulation of rules concerning the responsibility of authorizing officers and accounting officers and concerning appropriate arrangements for inspection.

President: VÍTOR MANUEL SILVA CALDEIRA (Portugal).

Secretary-General: EDUARDO RUIZ GARCÍA (Spanish).

EUROPEAN CENTRAL BANK

Address: Kaiserstr. 29, 60311 Frankfurt am Main, Germany; Postfach 160319, 60066 Frankfurt am Main, Germany.

Telephone: (69) 13440; **fax:** (69) 13446000; **e-mail:** info@ecb.europa.eu; **internet:** www.ecb.int/home/html/index.en.html.

The European Central Bank (ECB) was formally established on 1 June 1998, replacing the European Monetary Institute, which had been operational since January 1994. The Bank has the authority to issue the single currency, the euro, which replaced the European Currency Unit (ECU) on 1 January 1999, at the beginning of Stage III of Economic and Monetary Union (EMU), in accordance with the provisions of the Treaty on European Union (the Maastricht Treaty). One of the ECB's main tasks is to maintain price stability in the euro area (i.e. in those member states that have adopted the euro as their national currency). This is achieved primarily by controlling the money supply and by monitoring price trends. The Bank's leadership is provided by a six-member Executive Board, appointed by common agreement of the presidents or prime ministers of the 17 euro area countries for a non-renewable term of eight years (it should be noted that the Statute of the European System of Central Banks—ESCB—provides for a system of staggered appointments to the first Executive Board for members other than the President in order to ensure continuity). The Executive Board is responsible for the preparation of meetings of the Governing Council, the implementation of monetary policy in accordance with the guidelines and decisions laid down by the Governing Council and for the current business of the ECB. The ECB and the national central banks of all EU member states together comprise the ESCB. The Governing Council, which is the ECB's highest decision-making body and which consists of the six members of the Executive Board and the governors of the central banks of countries participating in EMU, meets twice a month. The prime mission of the Governing Council is to define the monetary policy of the euro area, and, in particular, to fix the interest rates at which the commercial banks can obtain money from the ECB. The General Council is the ECB's third decision-making body; it comprises the ECB's President, the Vice-President and the governors of the central banks of all EU member states.

President: MARIO DRAGHI (Italy).

Vice-President: VITOR MANUEL RIBEIRO CONSTÂNCIO (Portugal).

EUROPEAN INVESTMENT BANK

Address: 100 blvd Konrad Adenauer, 2950 Luxembourg.

Telephone: 4379-1; **fax:** 4377-04; **e-mail:** info@eib.org; **internet:** www.eib.org.

The European Investment Bank (EIB) is the EU's international financing institution, and was created in 1958 by the six founder member states of the European Economic Community. The shareholders are the member states of the EU, which have all subscribed to the bank's capital. The bulk of the EIB's resources comes from borrowings, principally public bond issues or private placements on capital markets inside and outside the Union.

The EIB's principal task, defined by the Treaty of Rome, is to work on a non-profit basis, making or guaranteeing loans for investment projects that contribute to the balanced and steady development of EU member states. Throughout the Bank's history, priority has been given to financing investment projects that further regional development within the Union. The EIB also finances projects that improve communications, protect and improve the environment, promote urban development, strengthen the competitive position of industry and encourage industrial integration within the Union, support the activities of small and medium-sized enterprises (SMEs), and help ensure the security of energy supplies. Following a recommendation of the Lisbon European Council in March 2000 for greater support for SMEs, the Board of Governors set up the EIB Group, consisting of the EIB and the European Investment Fund. The EIB also provides finance for developing countries in Africa, the Caribbean and the Pacific, under the terms of the Cotonou Agreement (see p. 328), the successor agreement to the Lomé Convention; for countries in the Mediterranean region, under a new Euro-Mediterranean investment facility established in 2002; and for accession countries in Central and Eastern Europe. Lending outside the EU is usually based on Union agreements, but exceptions have been made for specific projects in certain countries, such as Russia.

The Board of Governors of the EIB, which usually meets once a year, lays down general directives on credit policy, approves the annual report and accounts and decides on capital increases. The Board of Directors meets once a month, and has sole power to take decisions in respect of loans, guarantees and borrowings. The Bank's President presides over meetings of the Board of Directors. The day-to-day management of operations is the responsibility of the Management Committee, which is the EIB's collegiate executive body and recommends decisions to the Board of Directors. The Audit Committee, which reports to the Board of Governors regarding the management of operations and the maintenance of the Bank's accounts, is an independent body comprising three members who are appointed by the Board of Governors for a renewable three-year term.

Board of Governors: The Board of Governors comprises one minister (usually the minister with responsibility for finance or economic affairs) from each member state.

Chair.: JEAN-CLAUDE JUNCKER (Luxembourg).

Board of Directors: The Board of Directors consists of 28 directors, appointed for a renewable five-year term, with one director appointed by each member state and one by the European Commission. There are 16 alternates, also appointed for a renewable five-year term, meaning that some of these positions will be shared by groupings of countries. Since 1 May 2004 decisions have been taken by a majority consisting of at least one-third of members entitled to vote and representing at least 50% of the subscribed capital.

Management Committee: Comprises the President and seven Vice-Presidents, nominated for a renewable six-year term by the Board of Directors and approved by the Board of Governors. The President presides over the meetings of the Management Committee but does not vote.

President: WERNER HOYER (Germany).

Audit Committee: The Audit Committee is composed of three members and three observers, appointed by the Governors for a term of office of three years.

Chair.: ERIC MATHAY (Belgium).

EUROPEAN INVESTMENT FUND

Address: 96 blvd Konrad Adenauer, 2968 Luxembourg.

Telephone: 2485-1; **fax:** 2485-81301; **e-mail:** info@eif.org; **internet:** www.eif.org.

The European Investment Fund was founded in 1994 as a specialized financial institution to support the growth of small and medium-sized enterprises (SMEs). Its operations are focused on the provision of venture capital, through investment in funds that support SMEs, and on guarantee activities to facilitate access to finance for SMEs. In all its activities the Fund aims to maintain a commercial approach to investment, and to apply risk-sharing principles. The Fund manages the SME Guarantee Facility. The Joint European Resources for Micro to Medium Enterprises (JEREMIE) initiative, which was launched in May 2006, enables EU member countries and regions to use part of their allocation of structural funds to obtain financing that is specifically targeted to support SMEs. The European Investment Fund is operational in the member states of the EU and in accession countries.

Chief Executive: RICHARD PELLY (United Kingdom).

EUROPEAN ECONOMIC AND SOCIAL COMMITTEE

Address: 99 rue Belliard, 1040 Brussels.

Telephone: (2) 546-90-11; **fax:** (2) 513-48-93; **e-mail:** info@eesc.europa.eu; **internet:** www.eesc.europa.eu.

The Committee was set up by the 1957 Rome Treaties. It is advisory and is consulted by the Council of the European Union or by the European Commission, particularly with regard to agriculture, free movement of workers, harmonization of laws and transport, as well as legislation adopted under the Euratom Treaty. In certain cases consultation of the Committee by the Commission or the Council is mandatory. In addition, the Committee has the power to deliver opinions on its own initiative.

The Committee has a tripartite structure with members belonging to one of three groupings: the Employers' Group; the Workers' Group; and the Various Interests' Group, which includes representatives of social, occupational, economic and cultural organizations. The Committee is appointed for a renewable term of four years by the unanimous vote of the Council of the European Union. The 344 members are nominated by national governments, but are appointed in their personal capacity and are not bound by any mandatory instructions. Germany, France, Italy and the United Kingdom have 24 members each, Spain and Poland have 21, Romania 15, Belgium, Bulgaria, Greece, the Netherlands, Portugal, Austria, Sweden, the Czech Republic and Hungary 12, Denmark, Ireland, Finland, Lithuania and Slovakia nine, Estonia, Latvia and Slovenia seven, Luxembourg and Cyprus six, and Malta five. The Committee is served by a permanent and independent General Secretariat, headed by the Secretary-General.

President: STAFFAN NILSSON (Italy) (Various Interests' Group).

Secretary-General: MARTIN WESTLAKE (United Kingdom).

COMMITTEE OF THE REGIONS—COR

Address: 99–101 rue Belliard, 1040 Brussels.

Telephone: (2) 282-22-11; **fax:** (2) 282-23-25; **e-mail:** info@cor.europa.eu; **internet:** www.cor.europa.eu.

The Treaty on European Union provided for a committee to be established, with advisory status, comprising representatives of regional and local bodies throughout the EU. The first meeting of the CoR was held in March 1994. It may be consulted on EU proposals concerning economic and social cohesion, trans-European networks, public health, education and culture, and may issue an opinion on any issue with regional implications. The CoR meets in plenary session five times a year.

The entry into force of the Lisbon Treaty, in December 2009, empowered the CoR, on the basis of a simple majority vote, to challenge at the European Court of Justice any new EU legislation—relating to the policy areas where the Committee may be consulted—that is deemed to infringe the principle of 'subsidiarity', i.e. that decisions should be taken as closely as possible to the citizens.

The number of members of the CoR is equal to that of the European Economic and Social Committee. Members are appointed for a renewable term of four years by the Council, acting unanimously on the proposals from the respective member states. The Committee elects its principal officers from among its members for a two-year term.

President: MERCEDES BRESSO (Italy).

First Vice-President: RAMÓN LUIS VALCÁRCEL SISO (Spain).

AGENCIES

Agency for the Co-operation of Energy Regulators—ACER

1000 Ljubljana, Trg republike 3, Slovenia; tel. 082-053400; e-mail info@acer.europa.eu; internet www.acer.europa.eu; f. 2011; ACER aims to facilitate cross-border energy trade, to co-ordinate the activities of national energy regulators and to help to prevent conflict between them, in order to encourage competition and to ensure fair prices for both consumers and businesses. The agency's opening coincided with the entry into force of the EU's third energy package on the internal market.

President: ALBERTO POTOTSCHNIG (Italy).

Body of European Regulators for Electronic Communications—BEREC

2nd Floor, Z. A. Meierovica Bulv. 14, Riga 1050, Latvia; tel. 6611-7590; e-mail berec@berec.europa.eu; internet erg.eu.int/Default.htm.

Established by a regulation of the European Parliament in Nov. 2009, replacing the European Regulators Group (ERG).

Administrative Manager: ANDO REHEMAA (Estonia).

Community Plant Variety Office—CPVO

POB 10121, 49101 Angers Cédex 2, France; 3 blvd Maréchal Foch, 49000 Angers, France; tel. 2-41-25-64-00; fax 2-41-25-64-10; e-mail cpvo@cpvo.europa.eu; internet www.cpvo.europa.eu.

Began operations in April 1995, with responsibility for granting intellectual property rights for plant varieties. Supervised by an Administrative Council, and managed by a President, appointed by the Council of the European Union. A Board of Appeal has been established to consider appeals against certain technical decisions taken by the Office. Publishes an annual report listing valid Community plant variety rights, their owners and their expiry dates.

President: BART P. KIEWIET (Netherlands).

Euratom Supply Agency

Euroforum Bldg, 10 rue Robert Stumper, 2920 Luxembourg; tel. 4301-36738; fax 4301-38139; internet ec.europa.eu/euratom/index.html.

The Euratom Supply Agency commenced operations in 1960, having been established by the Euuratom Treaty to ensure the regular and equitable supply of nuclear energy throughout EU member states.

Director: STAMATIOS TSALAS (Belgium).

European Agency for the Management of Operational Co-operation at the External Borders—FRONTEX

Rondo ONZ 1, 00-124 Warsaw, Poland; tel. (22) 5449500; fax (22) 5449501; e-mail frontex@frontex.europa.eu; internet www.frontex.europa.eu.

Established by a regulation of the European Parliament in October 2004, the Agency's primary responsibility is the creation of an integrated border management system, in order to ensure a high and uniform level of control and surveillance. The Agency began operations on 1 May 2005.

Executive Director: Col ILKKA PERTTI JUHANI LAITINEN (Finland).

European Agency for Safety and Health at Work—EU-OSHA
Gran Vía 33, 48009 Bilbao, Spain; tel. (94) 4794360; fax (94) 4794383; e-mail information@osha.europa.eu; internet osha.europa.eu.

Began operations in 1996. Aims to encourage improvements in the working environment, and to make available all necessary technical, scientific and economic information for use in the field of health and safety at work. The Agency supports a network of Focal Points in the member states of the EU, in the member states of the European Free Trade Association (EFTA) and in the candidate states of the EU.

Director: Dr CHRISTA SEDLATSCHEK (Austria).

European Aviation Safety Agency—EASA
Postfach 101253, 50452 Köln, Germany; Ottoplatz 1, 50679 Köln, Germany; tel. (221) 89990000; fax (221) 89990999; e-mail info@easa.europa.eu; internet easa.europa.eu/home.php.

Established by a regulation of the European Parliament in July 2002; the mission of the agency is to establish and maintain a high, uniform level of civil aviation safety and environmental protection in Europe. The Agency commenced full operations in September 2003, and moved to its permanent seat, in Köln, Germany, in November 2004.

Executive Director: PATRICK GOUDOU (France).

European Centre for the Development of Vocational Training—Cedefop
POB 22427, 551 02 Thessaloníki, Greece; Evropis 123, 570 01 Thessaloníki, Greece; tel. (30) 2310490111; fax (30) 2310490049; e-mail info@cedefop.europa.eu; internet www.cedefop.europa.eu.

Established in 1975, Cedefop assists policy-makers and other officials in member states and partner organizations in issues relating to vocational training policies, and assists the European Commission in the development of these policies. Manages a European Training Village internet site (www.trainingvillage.gr/etv/default.asp).

Director: CHRISTIAN F. LETTMAYR (Austria) (acting).

European Centre for Disease Prevention and Control—ECDC
17183 Stockholm, Sweden; Tomtebodavägen 11A, Solna, Sweden; tel. (8) 586-01000; fax (8) 586-01001; e-mail info@ecdc.europa.eu; internet www.ecdc.europa.eu.

Founded in 2005 to strengthen European defences against infectious diseases. It works with national health protection bodies to develop disease surveillance and early warning systems across Europe.

Director: Dr MARC SPRENGER (Netherlands).

European Chemicals Agency—ECHA
Annankatu 18, Helsinki, Finland; POB 400, 00121 Helsinki, Finland; tel. (9) 686180; e-mail press@echa.europa.eu; internet echa.europa.eu.

The European Chemicals Agency (ECHA) was established by regulations of the European Parliament and the European Council in 2006, and became fully operational in June 2008. The objective of the ECHA is to supervise and undertake the technical, scientific and administrative aspects of the Registration, Evaluation, Authorization and Restriction of Chemicals (REACH) throughout the EU and in Iceland, Liechtenstein and Norway. It also supports and runs a national helpdesk, and disseminates information on chemicals to the public.

Executive Director: GEERT DANCET (Finland).

European Defence Agency—EDA
17–23 rue des Drapiers, 1050 Brussels, Belgium; tel. (2) 504-28-00; fax (2) 504-28-15; e-mail info@eda.europa.eu; internet www.eda.europa.eu.

Founded in July 2004 and became operational in 2005; aims to help member states to improve their defence capabilities for crisis management under the European Security and Defence Policy. The Steering Board is composed of the ministers responsible for defence of 26 member states (all states except Denmark).

Head of the Agency and Chairman of the Steering Board: CATHERINE ASHTON (United Kingdom).

Chief Executive: CLAUDE-FRANCE ARNOULD (France).

European Environment Agency—EEA
6 Kongens Nytorv, 1050 Copenhagen K, Denmark; tel. 33-36-71-00; fax 33-36-71-99; e-mail eea@eea.europa.eu; internet www.eea.europa.eu.

Became operational in 1994, having been approved in 1990, to gather and supply information to assist the drafting and implementation of EU policy on environmental protection and improvement. Iceland, Liechtenstein, Norway, Switzerland and Turkey are also members of the Agency. The Agency publishes frequent reports on the state of the environment and on environmental trends.

Executive Director: Prof. JACQUELINE MCGLADE (United Kingdom).

European Fisheries Control Agency—CFCA
Edificio Odriozola, Avda García Barbón, 36201 Vigo, Spain; tel. (98) 6120610; e-mail efca@efca.europa.eu; internet cfca.europa.eu/pages/home/home.htm.

Established in April 2005 to improve compliance with regulations under the 2002 reform of the Common Fisheries Policy. The EFCA aims to ensure the effectiveness of enforcement by sharing EU and national methods of fisheries' control, monitoring resources and co-ordinating activities.

Executive Director: PASCAL SAVOURET (France).

European Food Safety Authority—EFSA
Via Carlo Magno 1A, 43126 Parma, Italy; tel. (39-0521) 036111; fax (39-0521) 036110; e-mail info@efsa.europa.eu; internet www.efsa.europa.eu.

Established by a regulation of the European Parliament in February 2002 and began operations in May 2003; the primary responsibility of the Authority is to provide independent scientific advice on all matters with a direct or indirect impact on food safety. The Authority will carry out assessments of risks to the food chain and scientific assessment on any matter that may have a direct or indirect effect on the safety of the food supply, including matters relating to animal health, animal welfare and plant health. The Authority will also give scientific advice on genetically modified organisms (GMOs), and on nutrition in relation to European Union law.

Executive Director: CATHERINE GESLAIN-LANÉELLE (France).

European Foundation for the Improvement of Living and Working Conditions—CCP
Wyattville Rd, Loughlinstown, Dublin 18, Ireland; tel. (1) 2043100; fax (1) 2826456; e-mail postmaster@eurofound.europa.eu; internet www.eurofound.europa.eu.

Established in 1975, the Foundation aims to provide information and advice on European living and working conditions, industrial relations, and the management of change to employers, policy-makers, governments and trade unions, by means of comparative data, research and analysis. In 2001 the Foundation established the European Monitoring Centre on Change (EMCC) to help disseminate information and ideas on the management and anticipation of change in industry and enterprise.

Director: JORMA KARPPINEN (Finland).

European GNSS Supervisory Authority—GSA
56 Rue de la Loi, 1049 Brussels, Belgium; tel. (2) 297-16-16; fax (2) 296-72-38; e-mail news@gsa.europa.eu; internet www.gsa.europa.eu.

The European GNSS Supervisory Authority (GSA) was established in July 2004, to oversee all public interests relating to European Global Navigation Satellite System (GNSS) programmes. On 1 January 2007 the GSA officially took over the tasks previously assigned to the Galileo Joint Undertaking (GJU), which had been established in May 2002 by the EU and the European Space Agency to manage the development phase of the Galileo programme. The strategic objectives of the GSA include the achievement of a fully operational Galileo system, capable of becoming the world's leading civilian satellite navigation system, and Europe's only GNSS.

Executive Director: CARLO DES DORIDES (Italy).

European Institute for Gender Equality
Švitrigailos g. 11M, Vilnius, Lithuania; tel. (5) 239-4140; internet eige.europa.eu.

The European Institute for Gender Equality was established in May 2007, initially in Brussels, Belgium, to help EU member states and institutions to promote gender equality, combat gender discrimination and disseminate information on gender issues. The institute collects and interprets relevant data, to develop methodologies and tools to help integrate gender across all policy areas, to facilitate discussion and the adoption of best practices, and to raise awareness of gender issues. The institute comprises a management board, which is the decision-making body, together with a consultative experts' forum. The budget for 2007–13 is €52.5m.

Director: VIRGINIJA LANGBAKK (Sweden).

European Institute of Innovation and Technology
Infopark 1/E, 1117 Budapest, Neumann Janos ut., Hungary; tel. (1) 481-93-00.

The Agency was established in 2008 with the aim of increasing sustainable growth and competitiveness in Europe by reinforcing the EU's innovation capacity.

Director: JOSÉ MANUEL LECETA (Spain).

European Joint Undertaking for ITER and the Development of Fusion Energy—Fusion for Energy
2 Josep Pla, Torres Diagonal Litoral, Edificio B3, 08019 Barcelona, Spain; tel. (93) 320-18-00; fax (93) 489-75-37; e-mail info@f4e.europa.eu; internet fusionforenergy.europa.eu.

The Agency was established in 2007, as a Joint Undertaking under the European Atomic Energy Community (Euratom) Treaty, by a decision of the Council of the European Union (see Energy). Its members comprise the EU member states, Euratom and Switzerland.

Director: FRANK BRISCOE (United Kingdom).

European Judicial Co-operation Unit—EUROJUST

Maanweg 174, 2516 The Hague, the Netherlands; tel. (70) 4125000; fax (70) 4125005; e-mail info@eurojust.europa.eu; internet www.eurojust.europa.eu.

Established in 2002 to improve co-operation and co-ordination between member states in the investigation and prosecution of serious cross-border and organized crime. The EUROJUST College is composed of one member (a senior prosecutor or judge) nominated by each member state.

President of the College: ALED WILLIAMS (United Kingdom).

Administrative Director: KLAUS RACKWITZ (Germany).

European Maritime Safety Agency—EMSA

Cais do Sodré, 1249-206 Lisbon, Portugal; tel. (21) 1209200; fax (21) 1209210; e-mail information@emsa.europa.eu; internet www.emsa.europa.eu.

Established by a regulation of the European Parliament in June 2002; the primary responsibility of the Agency is to provide technical and scientific advice to the Commission in the field of maritime safety and prevention of pollution by ships, and, from April 2012, oil and gas rigs. The Agency held its inaugural meeting in December 2002, and in December 2003 it was decided that the permanent seat of the Agency would be Lisbon, Portugal. Norway and Iceland are also members of EMSA.

Executive Director: LEENDERT BAL (acting).

European Medicines Agency—EMA

7 Westferry Circus, Canary Wharf, London, E14 4HB, United Kingdom; tel. (20) 7418-8400; fax (20) 7418-8416; e-mail infol@ema.europa.eu; internet www.ema.europa.eu.

Established in 1995 for the evaluation, authorization and supervision of medicinal products for human and veterinary use.

Executive Director: GUIDO RASI (Sweden).

European Monitoring Centre for Drugs and Drug Addiction—EMCDDA

Cais do Sodré, 1249-289 Lisbon, Portugal; tel. (21) 1210200; fax (21) 8131711; e-mail info@emcdda.europa.eu; internet www.emcdda.europa.eu.

Founded in 1993 and became fully operational at the end of 1995, with the aim of providing member states with objective, reliable and comparable information on drugs and drug addiction in order to assist in combating the problem. The Centre co-operates with other European and international organizations and non-EU countries. The Centre publishes an *Annual Report on the State of the Drugs Problem in Europe*. A newsletter, *Drugnet Europe*, is published quarterly.

Executive Director: WOLFGANG GÖTZ (Germany).

European Network and Information Security Agency—ENISA

POB 1309, 710 01 Heraklion, Crete, Greece; Science and Technology Park of Crete, Vassilika Vouton, 700 13 Heraklion, Crete, Greece; tel. (2810) 391280; fax (2810) 391410; e-mail info@enisa.europa.eu; internet www.enisa.europa.eu.

Established by a regulation of the European Parliament in March 2004; commenced operations in 2005. The primary responsibilities of the Agency are to promote closer European co-ordination on the security of communications networks and information systems and to provide assistance in the application of EU measures in this field. The agency publishes a quarterly magazine.

Executive Director: Dr UDO HELMBRECHT (Germany).

European Police College—CEPOL

CEPOL House, Bramshill, Hook, Hampshire, RG27 0JW, United Kingdom; tel. (1256) 60-26-68; fax (1256) 60-29-96; e-mail secretariat@cepol.europa.eu; internet www.cepol.europa.eu.

Founded in 2005 to help create a network of senior police officers throughout Europe, to encourage cross-border co-operation in combating crime, and to improve public security and law and order through the organization of training activities and research.

Director: Dr FERENC BÁNFI (Hungary).

European Police Office—EUROPOL

POB 90850, 2509 The Hague, the Netherlands; Raamweg 47, The Hague, the Netherlands; tel. (70) 3025000; fax (70) 3025896; e-mail info@europol.europa.eu; internet www.europol.europa.eu.

Established in 1992, EUROPOL is a law enforcement organization that aims to aid EU member states to combat organized crime, by handling criminal intelligence throughout Europe and promoting co-operation between the law enforcement bodies of member countries; became a full EU agency, with an enhanced mandate for combating international crime, in Jan. 2010.

Director: ROB WAINWRIGHT (United Kingdom).

European Railway Agency—ERA

120 rue Marc Lefrancq, 59300 Valenciennes, France; tel. 3-27-09-65-00; fax 3-27-33-40-65; e-mail press-info@era.europa.eu; internet www.era.europa.eu.

Established by a regulation of the European Parliament in April 2004; the primary responsibility of the Agency is to reinforce the safety and interoperability of railways in the EU.

Executive Director: MARCEL VERSLYPE (Belgium).

European Training Foundation—ETF

Villa Gualino, Viale Settimio Severo 65, 10133 Turin, Italy; tel. (011) 630-22-22; fax (011) 630-22-00; e-mail info@etf.europa.eu; internet www.etf.europa.eu.

The Foundation, which was established in 1990 and became operational in 1994, provides policy advice to the European Commission and to the EU's partner countries, to support vocational education and training reform. The ETF works in the countries surrounding the EU, which are involved either in the European Neighbourhood Partnership Instrument, or in the enlargement process under the Instrument for Pre-accession Assistance. The ETF also works in a number of other countries from Central Asia. The ETF also gives technical assistance to the European Commission for the implementation of the Trans-European Mobility Programme for University Studies (TEMPUS), which focuses on the reform of higher education systems in partner countries.

Director: MADLEN SERBAN (Romania).

European Union Agency for Fundamental Rights—FRA

Schwarzenbergplatz 11, 1040 Vienna, Austria; tel. (1) 580300; fax (1) 58030699; e-mail information@fra.europa.eu; internet fra.europa.eu.

Founded in March 2007, replacing the European Monitoring Centre on Racism and Xenophobia (EUMC). The Agency aims to provide assistance to EU member states on fundamental rights matters during the application of EU law. The FRA continues the work of the EUMC on racism, xenophobia, anti-Semitism and related intolerance, and utilizes its experience of data collection methods and co-operation with governments and international organizations. In addition, the FRA gives significant emphasis to increasing public awareness of rights issues and to co-operation with civil society.

Director: MORTEN KJAERUM (Denmark).

European Union Institute for Security Studies—EUISS

100 ave de Suffren, 75015 Paris, France; tel. 1-56-89-19-30; fax 1-56-89-19-31; e-mail institute@iss.europa.eu; internet www.iss.europa.eu.

Established by a Council Joint Action in July 2001, and inaugurated in January 2002. The Institute aims to help implement and develop the EU's Common Foreign and Security Policy (CFSP), and carries out political analysis and forecasting. The Institute produces several publications: the Chaillot Papers, Occasional Papers and a quarterly Newsletter, as well as books containing in-depth studies of specialized topics.

Director: ÁLVARO DE VASCONCELOS (Portugal).

European Union Satellite Centre—EUSC

Apdo de Correos 511, Torréjon de Ardoz, 28850 Madrid, Spain; tel. (91) 6786000; fax (91) 6786006; e-mail info@eusc.europa.eu; internet www.eusc.europa.eu.

Established by a Council Joint Action in July 2001 and operational from 1 January 2002. The Centre is dedicated to providing material derived from the analysis of satellite imagery in support of the Common Foreign and Security Policy.

Director: TOMAŽ LOVRENČIČ (Slovenia).

Office for Harmonization in the Internal Market (Trade Marks and Designs)—OHIM

Apdo. de Correos 77, 03080 Alicante, Spain; Avda de Europa 4, 03008 Alicante, Spain; tel. (96) 5139100; fax (96) 5131344; e-mail information@oami.europa.eu; internet www.oami.europa.eu.

Established in 1993 to promote and control trade marks and designs throughout the EU.

President: ANTÓNIO CAMPINOS (Portugal).

Translation Centre for the Bodies of the European Union—CdT

Bâtiment Nouvel Hémicycle, 1 rue du Fort Thüngen, 1499 Luxembourg; tel. 4217-11-1; fax 4217-11-220; e-mail cdt@cdt.europa.eu; internet www.cdt.europa.eu.

Established in 1994 to meet the translation needs of other decentralized Union agencies.

Director: GAILĖ DAGILIENĖ (Lithuania).

Activities of the Community

STRATEGIC FRAMEWORK

Meeting in March 2000, the European Council launched the Lisbon Strategy, which was elaborated at subsequent meetings of the Council and rested on three pillars: an economic pillar preparing for a transition to a competitive, knowledge-based economy, with a focus on research and development; a social pillar that covered investment in human resources and combating social exclusion, with a focus on education, training and employment policy; and an environmental pillar, focused on disconnecting economic growth from the depletion of natural resources.

On 17 June 2010 the Council adopted the Europe 2020 strategic policy framework, the successor to the Lisbon Strategy, which seeks to consolidate the Lisbon Strategy's achievements with respect to economic growth and the creation of jobs. EU-wide targets were agreed in five policy areas. By 2020 at least 75% of those aged between 20 and 64 years are to be in employment; 3% of the EU's total gross domestic product (GDP) is to be invested in research and innovation; greenhouse gas emissions are to be reduced by at least 20%, compared with levels in 1990, with 20% of energy produced to be renewable, and with energy efficiency to be increased by 20%; at least 40% of those aged 30–34 years are to have completed higher education, and 10% more children are to complete their schooling; and there are to be at least 20m. fewer people living in, or threatened by, poverty and social exclusion.

AGRICULTURE

Agriculture (including rural development) is by far the largest single item on the EU budget, accounting for 42% of annual expenditure in 2010, although this represented a significant reduction compared with 1984, when agriculture accounted for 70% of expenditure.

Co-operation in the EU has traditionally been at its most highly organized in the area of agriculture. The Common Agricultural Policy (CAP), which took effect from 1962, was originally devised to ensure food self-sufficiency for Europe following the food shortages of the post-war period and to ensure a fair standard of living for the agricultural community. Its objectives are described in the Treaty of Rome. The markets for agricultural products have been progressively organized following three basic principles: unity of the market (products must be able to circulate freely within the Union and markets must be organized according to common rules); EU preference (products must be protected from low-cost imports and from fluctuations on the world market); and common financial responsibility: the European Agricultural Guarantee Fund (which replaced the European Agricultural Guidance and Guarantee Fund in 2007) finances the export of agricultural products to third countries, intervention measures to regulate agricultural markets, and direct payments to farmers.

Agricultural prices are, in theory, fixed each year at a common level for the EU as a whole, taking into account the rate of inflation and the need to discourage surplus production of certain commodities. Export subsidies are paid to enable farmers to sell produce at the lower world market prices without loss. When market prices of certain cereals, sugar, some fruits and vegetables, dairy produce and meat fall below a designated level, the Community intervenes, and buys a quantity, which is then stored until prices recover.

Serious reform of the CAP began in 1992, following strong criticism of the EC's agricultural and export subsidies during the Uruguay Round of negotiations on the General Agreement on Tariffs and Trade (GATT, see World Trade Organization—WTO) in 1990. In May 1992 ministers adopted a number of reforms, which aimed to transfer the Community's agricultural support from upholding prices to maintaining farmers' incomes, thereby removing the incentive to over-produce. Intervention prices were reduced, and farmers were compensated by receiving additional grants, which, in the case of crops, took the form of a subsidy per hectare of land planted. To qualify for these subsidies, arable farmers (except for those with the smallest farms) were obliged to remove 15% of their land from cultivation (the 'set-aside' scheme). Incentives were given for alternative uses of the withdrawn land (e.g. forestry).

In March 1999, at the Berlin European Council, the EU Heads of Government concluded an agreement on a programme, Agenda 2000, which aimed to reinforce Community policies and to restructure the financial framework of the EU with a view to enlargement. In terms of agriculture, it was decided to continue the process of agricultural reform begun in 1992 with particular emphasis on environmental concerns, safeguarding a fair income for farmers, streamlining legislation and decentralizing its application. A further element of reform was the increased emphasis on rural development, which was described as the 'second pillar' of the CAP in Agenda 2000. The objective was to restore and increase the competitiveness of rural areas, through supporting employment, diversification and population growth. In addition, producers were to be rewarded for the preservation of rural heritage. Forestry was recognized as an integral part of rural development (previous treaties of the EU had made no provision for a comprehensive common forestry policy).

The accession of 10 new states to the EU in May 2004 had major implications for the CAP, in that the enlargement doubled the EU's arable land area and its farming population. In October 2002 it was agreed that the enlargement process would be part-funded by a deal to maintain farm subsidies at 2006 levels until 2013, with a 1% annual correction for inflation, and that the new members would be offered direct farm payments at 25% of the level paid to existing member states, rising in stages to 100% over 10 years.

In July 2002 the Commissioner responsible for Agriculture, Rural Development and Fisheries proposed directing more funds towards the rural development policy and severing the link between direct payments to farmers and production (a policy styled 'decoupling'). The reforms suggested were, however, vigorously opposed by the main beneficiaries of the existing system, notably France. A revised plan was submitted, which restored the link between subsidies and production for certain products while still adhering to the principle of decoupling.

The compromise deal for CAP reform was agreed in June 2003, and the agreement was ratified by the Council of the European Union and the accession states in September. Production-linked subsidies were to be replaced by a Single Farm Payment, subsidies previously received, rather than tied to current production levels, and was also to be linked to environmental, food safety and animal welfare standards. Obligatory decoupling was only partial for beef, cereal and mutton, with production still accounting for as much as 25% of payments for cereals and as much as 40% for beef. Overall, however, 90% of payments would no longer be linked to production. The agreement contained a commitment to reduce all payments above €5,000 a year by 3% in 2005, by 4% in 2006 and by 5% in 2007. Increased resources were to be directed towards rural development projects, protecting the environment and improvements to food quality; organic farmers and those offering high-quality produce with special guarantees were to receive grants of up to €3,000 a year for five years. Under the principle of 'modulation', an increasing percentage of direct farm subsidies was to be retained by individual member states to finance rural development measures. The equivalent of at least 80% of the funds gathered in each member state (90% in Germany) was to be spent in that country. Implementation of the CAP reforms agreed in June 2003 commenced on 1 January 2005.

Meanwhile, in April 2004 the EU Council of Ministers of Agriculture reached agreement for CAP reform of the olive oil, cotton, hops and tobacco sectors. The principle of decoupling aid from production was to be extended to these commodities. A significant share of the existing production-linked payments was to be transferred to the Single Farm Payment (which was provided independently of production), although production-linked subsidies were permitted of up to 60% for tobacco, 40% for olive oil, 35% for cotton and 25% for hops. Moreover, full decoupling in the tobacco sector was to be introduced progressively over the four years to 2010 and rural development aid was to finance conversion to other crops in tobacco-producing areas. The remaining production aid for olive oil was to be directed at maintaining olive groves with environmental or social value. In September 2006 the European Court of Justice annulled the CAP provisions on cotton, proposing a slightly revised reform of the support scheme in November 2007. The new proposal maintained the support arrangements agreed in 2004 (i.e. production-linked subsidies of up to 35%), but provided for additional funding for support measures in cotton-producing regions and the creation of a 'label of origin' to enhance the promotion of EU cotton.

The EU finally agreed on reforms to the sugar industry in November 2005, following a WTO ruling earlier in the year (after an action brought by Brazil, Australia and Thailand) that the current level of subsidy breached legal limits. In 2005 the EU sugar sector was still characterized by large subsidies, high internal prices, and imports by African, Caribbean and Pacific (ACP) countries on favourable terms under quotas. The EU produced large surpluses of sugar, which were disposed of on the world market to the detriment of more competitive producers, notably developing countries. The reforms, which were implemented from July 2006, included the gradual reduction of the internal EU market price (which was three times the international price for the commodity in 2005) by 36% by 2009, and direct aid payments of €6,300m. over the four years of the phased introduction of the reforms to EU sugar producers as compensation. A fundamental element in the reform of the EU sugar sector was the establishment of a restructuring fund, financed by sugar producers, to ease the transition to greater competitiveness. The objective was to remove a total of some 6m. metric tons of sugar quota during the four-year reform period. Amendments to the sugar-restructuring scheme were adopted in October 2007 in an attempt to encourage greater participation, and, by the conclusion of the reform period, in early 2009, some 5.8m. metric tons of sugar quota had been renounced.

At the Doha Round of the WTO in Hong Kong in December 2005, agreement was reached on the elimination of export subsidies on farm goods by the end of 2013. This represented a concession by the EU but was three years later than the date sought by the USA and developing countries.

A new regulation laying down specific rules concerning the fruit and vegetables sector was adopted in September 2007 and entered into force in January 2008. Notable reforms included: the integration of the sector into the Single Farm Payment scheme; the requirement that producer organizations allocate at least 10% of their annual expenditure to environmental concerns; an increase in EU funding for the promotion of fruit and vegetable consumption and for organic production; and the abolition of export subsidies for fruit and vegetables. In April ministers of agriculture adopted a new regulation on the reform of the wine sector. The regulation provided, *inter alia*, for the inclusion of the sector in the Single Farm Payment scheme, while distillation subsidies were to be gradually withdrawn by 2012, releasing funds for measures such as wine promotion in third countries and the modernization of vineyards and cellars. In addition, the regulation provided for the introduction of a voluntary, three-year scheme, under which wine producers were to receive subsidies over a three-year period, with the aim of removing surplus and uncompetitive wine from the market.

In May 2008 the European Commission proposed a number of regulations to reform and simplify the CAP further in 2009–13, including additional reductions in production-linked payments and increased funding for rural development. In November 2008 the European Council reached agreement on the proposed reforms, which: raised the rate of decoupling in those countries that maintained the link between subsidy and production; provided for reform of the dairy sector; abolished the set-aside scheme from 2009; and provided for payments to farms qualifying for subsidies of at least €5,000 a year to be reduced gradually, so that by 2012 10% of funds (compared with the existing 5%) would be transferred to the rural development budget (large-scale farms would be required to transfer a greater proportion of funds). Milk quotas were to be increased by 1% per year in 2009–13, before their eventual expiry in 2015.

As a result of severe decline in dairy prices from 2008, in June 2009 the Commissioner for Agriculture and Rural Development established a High Level Experts' Group on Milk (HLG), comprising representatives of the 27 EU member states, and chaired by the Director-General for Agriculture and Rural Development. The HLG sought to identify medium- and long-term measures for stabilizing the market and incomes, and increasing transparency, given the expiry of milk quotas from 1 April 2015. The HLG held 10 meetings between October 2009 and June 2010, and identified significant problems in the supply chain. In late September 2010 its proposals for addressing the problems were endorsed by the Council's Presidency. These required endorsement by the Council of Agriculture Ministers and the European Parliament, and were expected to enter into effect in 2012.

In mid-November 2010 the European Commission launched the consultation process on further reform of the CAP with the adoption of a communication entitled 'The CAP towards 2020: meeting the food, natural resources and territorial challenges of the future', based on the results of public debate on the issue of CAP reform, which were summarized at a conference held in Brussels, Belgium, in July 2010. In mid-October 2011 the Commission announced a set of legislative proposals aimed at simplifying the CAP from 2014, while ensuring greater transparency, and the long-term sustainability, competitiveness and diversity of the agricultural sector. Income support was to be available only to economically active farmers, and was to be subject to a fixed maximum rate, and distributed more evenly. Improved tools for managing economic crises were to be introduced, to reduce the impact of volatility in the prices of raw agricultural materials; the Commission proposed the introduction of 'safety nets' (specifically intervention and storage arrangements), and the establishment of insurance and mutual funds. There were also plans to introduce a 'green' component to reward environmental competitiveness by directing up to 30% of the value of direct payments towards encouraging better use of natural resources. The budget for agricultural research and innovation was to be increased two-fold, supported by the creation of a new European Innovation Partnership. The Commission proposed increasing support for producer organizations, developing inter-professional organizations, and encouraging direct sales by producers to customers. Sugar quotas were to be removed by the end of 2015. Two targeted Rural Development policy objectives were to seek to develop, maintain and improve ecosystems; and help maximize the efficiency of resources and combat climate change. Farmers under 40 years of age were to receive inducements to enter the sector (some 65% of farmers were aged at least 55 years). The administration of the CAP was also to be simplified.

Food safety is a significant issue in the EU, especially since the first case of bovine spongiform encephalopathy (BSE), a transmissible disease that causes the brain tissue to degenerate, was diagnosed in cattle in the United Kingdom in 1986. The use of meat and bone meal (MBM) in animal feed was identified as possibly responsible for the emergence of the disease, and was banned for use in cattle feed in the United Kingdom in 1988. MBM was banned throughout the EU from 1994 for ruminants and in December 2000 for all animals. The possible link between BSE and new variant Creutzfeldt-Jakob disease (vCJD), a degenerative brain disease that affects humans, led to a collapse in consumer confidence in the European beef market in 1996. By January 2011 176 people were believed to have contracted vCJD in the United Kingdom, the location of the vast majority of cases.

In July 1997 ministers of agriculture voted to introduce a complete ban on the use for any purpose of 'specified risk materials' (SRMs—i.e. those parts and organs most likely to carry the BSE prion disease agent) from cattle, sheep and goats. The ban was implemented in January 1999. The scope of legislation on undesirable substances in animal feed was extended in May 2002, to cover additives. In May 2001 new legislation was adopted by the European Parliament and the Agriculture Council that consolidated much of the existing legislation on BSE and other transmissible spongiform encephalopathies (TSEs) in bovine, ovine and caprine animals. The new TSE Regulation, which replaced previous emergency legislation and clarified the rules for the prevention, control and eradication of TSEs, came into force on 1 July 2001. Every year the Commission approves programmes aimed at monitoring, controlling and eradicating animal diseases, with a special focus on zoonoses, which are transmissible from animal carriers to humans.

The EU's Food and Veterinary Office was established in April 1997 to ensure that the laws on food safety, animal health and welfare, and plant health are applied in all member states. The office carries out audits and checks on food safety in member states and in third countries exporting agricultural produce to the EU. Legislation establishing the European Food Safety Authority (EFSA) was signed in January 2002; the new body was to provide independent scientific advice and support on matters with a direct or indirect impact on food safety. It was to have no regulatory or judicial power, but would co-operate closely with similar bodies in the member states. The first meeting of the EFSA management board took place in September, and its Advisory Forum was convened for the first time in March 2003. In September 2007 the European Commission adopted a communication setting out the EU's animal health strategy for 2007–13. The aims of the new strategy were: to ensure a high level of public health and food safety by reducing the risks posed to humans by problems with animal health; to promote animal health by preventing or reducing the incidence of animal diseases, thus also protecting farming and the rural economy; to improve economic growth, cohesion and competitiveness in animal-related sectors; and to promote farming and animal welfare practices that prevent threats to animal health and minimize the environmental impact of raising animals. In January 2012 the European Commission adopted a new animal health strategy for 2012–15, the objective of which is to improve animal welfare throughout the EU, by adopting new, comprehensive legislation on animal welfare, while strengthening existing actions.

In June 1995 the Agriculture Council agreed to new rules on the welfare of livestock during transport. The agreement, which came into effect in 1996, limited transport of livestock to a maximum of eight hours in any 24-hour period, and stipulated higher standards for their accommodation and care while in transit. In January 1996 the Commission proposed a ban on veal crates, which came into effect from January 1998. In April 2001 the Commission adopted new rules for long-distance animal transport, setting out the required standards of ventilation, temperature and humidity control. A new regulation aimed at further enhancing the welfare of animals during transport was adopted in December 2004. To ensure improved enforcement of the rules, a satellite navigation system was to be introduced from January 2007 to track vehicles carrying livestock. In June 1999 EU agriculture ministers agreed to end battery egg production within the EU by 2012; in December 2000 a regulation was adopted requiring EU producers to indicate the rearing method on eggs and egg-packaging. A new directive laying out minimum standards for the protection of pigs, including provisions banning the use of individual stalls for pregnant sows and gilts, increasing their living space, and allowing them to have permanent access to materials for rooting, was applicable from January 2003 to holdings newly built or rebuilt and from January 2013 to all holdings. A similar directive was adopted in June 2007 for the protection of chickens kept for meat production, laying out minimum standards in areas such as stocking density, lighting, litter and ventilation; it was to be implemented by member states within three years. Following 13 years of negotiations, in November 2002 agreement was finally reached between the European Parliament and the member states to ban the sale, import and export of virtually all cosmetic products tested after 11 March 2009 on animals in the EU, and to halt from 11 March 2013 all animal testing for cosmetics. Accordingly, on 11 March 2009 testing on animals was outlawed in seven mandatory tests of toxicity following a single application (namely tests for absorption through the skin, skin irritancy, sensitivity to light, eye irritancy, corrosivity, genetic toxicity and acute toxicity), with eight further tests, designed to establish longer-term toxicity following multiple applications (e.g. tendency to cause cancer or birth defects), to be banned by the 2013 deadline. In October 2009 the European Commission adopted a report (compiled with a view to facilitating political debate with other institutions) that outlined options for labelling products with the objective of enabling consumers to identify good animal welfare practices and to provide an economic incentive to producers to make advances in the area of animal welfare. The report considered the possible future establishment of an animal welfare-orientated European Network of Reference Centres to provide technical support for the development and implementation of animal welfare policies, including in the areas of certification and labelling.

The EU has adopted a number of protective measures to prevent the introduction of organisms harmful to plants and plant products. Regulations governing the deliberate release of genetically modified organisms (GMOs) into the environment have been in force since October 1991, with an approval process based on a case-by-case analysis of the risks to human health and the environment. A total of 18 GMOs were authorized for use in the EU under this directive. An updated directive took effect in October 2002, which introduced principles for risk assessment, long-term monitoring requirements and full labelling and traceability obligations for food and feed containing more than 0.9% GM ingredients. A further regulation adopted by the Commission in January 2004 specified a system to identify and trace each GMO product used in the production of all food and animal feeds, completing the EU's regulatory framework on the authorization, labelling and traceability of GMOs. All of the accession states had adopted EU regulations on GM products by 2004, despite fears raised by environmental groups that inadequate testing facilities would prevent the implementation of effective labelling procedures. By June 2009 15 EU member states had adopted specific legislation on the co-existence of GMOs with conventional and organic crops. In March 2010 the European Commission announced that Amflora, a genetically modified potato, had been authorized for cultivation in the EU for industrial use.

In 2004 the Commission, with support from the Council, presented a European action plan for organic food and farming, comprising 21 measures, aimed at promoting the development of organic farming in the EU. The Council also adopted a regulation improving legal protection for organic farming methods and established a programme on the conservation, collection and utilization of genetic resources in agriculture. In 2005 the Commission adopted a proposal for new regulations defining objectives and principles for organic production, clarifying labelling rules and regulating imports. The new regulation on production and labelling was adopted in June 2007 and came into force on 1 January 2009. The new rules concerning imports of organic foods were approved in December 2006. From July 2010 all pre-packaged EU organic products were required to carry an EU organic food logo.

FISHERIES

The Common Fisheries Policy (CFP) came into effect in January 1983 after seven years of negotiations, particularly concerning the problem of access to fishing grounds. The CFP confirmed a 200-mile (370-km) zone around the regional coastline (excluding the Mediterranean) within which all members had access to fishing, and allowed exclusive national zones of six miles with access between six and 12 miles from the shore for other countries according to specified historic rights. Rules furthering conservation (e.g. standards for fishing tackle) were imposed under the policy, with checks by a Community fisheries inspectorate. A body of inspectors answerable to the Commission monitored compliance with the quotas and with technical measures in Community and some international waters.

In December 1992 EC ministers agreed to extend the CFP for a further 10-year period. Two years later ministers concluded a final agreement on the revised CFP, allowing Spain and Portugal to be integrated into the policy by 1 January 1996. A compromise accord was reached regarding access to waters around Ireland and off south-west Great Britain (referred to as the 'Irish box'), by means of which up to 40 Spanish vessels were granted access to 80,000 sq miles of the 90,000 sq mile area. However, the accord was strongly opposed by Irish and British fishermen. In October 1995 fisheries ministers agreed a regime to control fishing in the 'Irish box', introducing stricter controls and instituting new surveillance measures.

The organization of fish marketing involves common rules on size, weight, quality and packing and a system of guide prices established annually by the Council of the European Union. Fish are withdrawn from the market if prices fall too far below the guide price, and compensation may then be paid to the fishermen. Export subsidies are paid to enable the export of fish onto the lower-priced world market, and import levies are imposed to prevent competition from low-priced imports. A new import regime took effect from May 1993. This enabled regional fishermen's associations to increase prices to a maximum of 10% over the Community's reference price, although this applied to both EU and imported fish.

In June 1998 the Council of the European Union overcame long-standing objections from a number of member states and adopted a ban on the use of drift nets in the Atlantic Ocean and the Mediterranean Sea, in an attempt to prevent the unnecessary deaths of marine life such as dolphins and sharks. The ban, which was introduced in January 2002, partially implemented a 1992 UN resolution demanding a complete cessation of drift-net fishing. A series of compensatory measures aimed to rectify any short-term detrimental impact on EU fishing fleets. In March 2004 the Council approved a ban on the use of drift nets in the Baltic Sea, and, in April, it adopted a regulation stipulating the use of active acoustic deterrent devices on fishing nets throughout most EU waters to prevent dolphins and porpoises from becoming fatally entangled in the nets.

With concern over stocks continuing to mount (it was calculated in the early 2000s that cod stocks in the North Sea had fallen to one-10th of their level at 1970), in June 2002 the Commission proposed to establish a procedure for setting total allowable catches (TACs) so as to achieve a significant increase in mature fish stocks, with limits on the fishing effort fixed in accordance with the TACs. The Commission also proposed the temporary closure of areas where endangered species had congregated, and more generous EU aid for the decommissioning of vessels (aid for the modernization of vessels, which tends to increase the fishing catch, was to be reduced). By 2002 the Commission had also been alerted to the critical depletion of deep-sea species, the commercialization of which had become increasingly attractive in the 1990s as other species became less abundant. For the first time, in December 2002, the Commission introduced catch limits for deep-water fish species, complemented by a system of deep-sea fishing permits. In 2004 the Commission extended the scope of the use of TACs to more fish stocks and introduced a number of closed areas for heavily depleted species.

Initially structural assistance actions for fisheries were financed by the European Agricultural Guidance and Guarantee Fund (which was replaced by the European Agricultural Guarantee Fund in 2007). Following the reform of funding programmes in 1993, a separate fund, the Financial Instrument for Fisheries Guidance (FIFG), was set up. The instrument's principal responsibilities included the decommissioning of vessels and the creation, with foreign investors, of joint ventures designed to reduce the fishing effort in EU waters. The fund also supported the building and modernizing of vessels, developments in the aquaculture sector, and the creation of protected coastal areas. From January 2007 the FIFG was replaced by the simplified European Fisheries Fund, covering the period 2007–13, which grants financial support to facilitate the implementation of the CFP (see below).

Radical reform of the CFP, aimed at ensuring the sustainable development of the industry, was announced during 2002. The Commission proposed a new multi-annual framework—which was to replace the existing Multi-Annual Guidance Programme—MAGP—for the efficient conservation of resources and the management of fisheries, incorporating environmental concerns. The new measures were introduced on 1 January 2003, replacing the basic rules that had governed the CFP since 1993, and substantially amending structural assistance in the fisheries sector under the FIFG. The new framework provided for a long-term approach to attaining and maintaining fish stocks, designed to encourage member states to achieve a better balance between the fishing capacity of their fleets and available resources. Under the terms of the new framework quotas for catches of cod, whiting and haddock were substantially reduced, fishermen were guaranteed only nine days a month at sea (with provision to extend this to 15 days in some circumstances), and public funding for the renewal or modernization of fishing boats was abolished after 2004 (with the exception of funding for the provision of aid to improve security and working conditions on board). In addition, measures were announced to develop co-operation among the various fisheries authorities and to strengthen the uniformity of control and sanctions throughout the EU. The Commission inspectors had their powers extended to ensure the equity and efficacy of the enforcement of EU regulations. In an attempt to compensate for the ongoing decline of the EU fishing fleet, a number of socio-economic measures were introduced, including the provision of aid from member states to fishermen and vessel owners who had temporarily to halt their fishing activities and the granting of aid to fishermen to help them retrain to convert to professional activities outside the fisheries sector, while permitting them to continue fishing on a part-time basis. A new regulation setting up an emergency fund to encourage the decommissioning of vessels (known as the 'Scrapping Fund') was also adopted.

In July 2004 the Council adopted a common framework on the establishment of regional advisory councils (RACs), as part of the 2002 reform, to enable scientists, fishermen and other interested parties to work together to identify ways of maintaining sustainable fisheries. In November 2004 the first RAC, for the North Sea, was instituted in Edinburgh, Scotland. The Pelagic RAC and the North Western Waters RAC, based, respectively, in Amsterdam, Netherlands, and Dublin, Ireland, were created in August and September 2005. A Baltic Sea RAC, based in Copenhagen, Denmark, was set up in March 2006. The RAC for Long Distance Waters and the RAC for the South Western Waters were established in March and April 2007, while the last RAC (for the Mediterranean Waters) was established in September 2008. During 2006, for the first time, TACs and quotas for the Baltic Sea were discussed separately from those covering other Community waters. Meanwhile, in March 2005 the European Commission announced its decision to initiate a consultation process on a new integrated EU maritime policy aimed at developing the potential of the maritime economy in an environmentally sustainable manner. In October 2007 the Commission presented a communication on integrated maritime policy, which was endorsed by the Council in December. An accompanying action plan included fisheries-related initiatives such as a scheme to strengthen international co-operation against destructive deep-sea fishing practices and measures to halt imports of illegal fisheries products.

In April 2005, in order to improve further compliance with the CFP as reformed in 2002, the Council of Ministers agreed to establish a Community Fisheries Control Agency (CFCA). The Agency, through the implementation of joint deployment plans, aims to strengthen the uniformity and effectiveness of enforcement of fisheries regulations by pooling EU and individual countries' means of control and monitoring and by co-ordinating enforcement activities. The CFCA (now the European Fisheries Control Agency—EFCA) adopted five joint deployment plans for 2009, three of which covered the regulated fisheries in the North Atlantic, and cod fisheries in the Baltic, North Sea and adjacent areas; and two of which covered the cod fisheries in Western Waters, and the regulated fisheries in waters beyond the national fisheries jurisdiction in the North Eastern Atlantic.

In July 2006, in order to facilitate, within the framework of the CFP, a sustainable European fishing and aquaculture industry, the Agriculture and Fisheries Council adopted a regulation on the establishment of a European Fisheries Fund (EFF), which replaced the FIFG on 1 January 2007. The Fund was to support the industry as it adapted its fleet in order to make it more competitive, and to promote measures to protect the environment. It was also to assist the communities that were most affected by the resulting changes to diversify their economic base. The EFF was to remain in place for seven years, with a total budget of some €3,800m. The regulation also set forth detailed rules and arrangements regarding structural assistance, including an obligation on all member states to draw up a national strategic plan for their fisheries sectors. Assistance was henceforth to be channelled through a single national EFF programme.

In January 2009 the European Commission adopted the first EU Plan of Action for the Conservation and Management of Sharks, which also aimed to protect related species, such as skates and rays, and was to apply wherever the EU fleet operates, both within and outside European waters. At the beginning of January 2010 a framework of new rules to strengthen the CFP control system entered into force, in accordance with which no country was to be given preferential treatment over another, thereby promoting, it was envisaged, a culture of compliance throughout the sector. The framework comprised three separate, yet inter-related, regulations on: combating illegal, unreported and unregulated (IUU) fishing; authorizations for the EU fleet operating outside EU waters; and establishing a control system for ensuring compliance with CFP rules. Under the new IUU regulation, all marine fishery products traded with the EU were to be certified and their origin traceable under a comprehensive catch certification scheme.

Legally bound to review some areas of the CFP by 2012, and concerned to address depleted stock levels and fleet overcapacity, the European Commission launched a consultation process on CFP reform in April 2009; following the termination of the consultations in December, the Commission published a report in April 2010. Five structural failings of the CFP were identified: the issue of fleet overcapacity; the need to refocus the CFP on the ecological sustainability of fish stocks and the minimization of 'discards' (dead fish or other marine organisms caught in excess of quotas that are dumped overboard, having been caught unintentionally); the desire to adapt fisheries governance away from centralized control, towards regionalized implementation of principles; involving the sector in resource management and implementation of the CFP; and developing a culture of compliance with rule. The Commission published its draft proposals for reform in July 2011. The proposals provided for returning fish stocks to sustainable levels by 2015, using a multi-annual, ecosystem approach. The discard system was to be gradually abandoned. The proposals provided for the establishment of clear targets and timetables to prevent overfishing, and to benefit small-scale fisheries, while providing transferrable fishing concessions. The Commission intended the new framework for fisheries policy to enter into force in 2013, following its approval by the European Parliament and the Council. In December 2011 the European Commission proposed the establishment of a new European Maritime and Fisheries Fund (EMFF) to co-ordinate the EU's maritime and fisheries policies in 2014–20. The EMFF, which was expected to have a budget of some €6,500m., was to be responsible for implementing the objectives of the revised CFP, assisting fishermen to adapt to more sustainable methods of fishing and helping coastal areas to diversify their economies.

Bilateral fisheries agreements have been signed with other countries (Norway, Iceland and the Faroe Islands) allowing limited reciprocal fishing rights and other advantages ('reciprocity agreements'), and with some African and Indian Ocean countries and Pacific Islands that receive technical and financial assistance in strengthening their fishing industries in return for allowing EU boats to fish in their waters ('fisheries partnership agreements'). Following the withdrawal of Greenland from the Community in February 1985, Community vessels retained fishing rights in Greenland waters, in exchange for financial compensation. In recent years, however, owing to growing competition for scarce fish resources, it has become increasingly difficult for the EU to conclude bilateral fisheries agreements giving its fleets access to surplus fish stocks in the waters of third countries.

Of the 10 new states that joined the EU in 2004, only four had sizeable fishing industries (Poland, Estonia, Latvia and Lithuania); the combined total annual catch of these four states in the early 2000s was equivalent to less than 7% of the EU total. Prior to their membership, the accession states were obliged to establish the necessary administrative capacity for applying the obligations arising from the CFP, including the modernization and renewal of old fishing vessels, the joint conservation of resources, the training of fisheries inspectors, the implementation and monitoring of common marketing standards, the introduction of EU health and hygiene standards, the management of structural policy in fisheries and aquaculture, and the compilation of a register of fishing vessels. In December 2005 the International Baltic Sea Fishery Commission (IBSFC) ceased its activities. Following the accession of Estonia, Latvia, Lithuania and Poland to the EU in 2004, membership of the IBSFC had been reduced to only two parties, the EU and Russia, and the negotiations that had formerly been conducted within its framework could now be undertaken bilaterally.

RESEARCH AND INNOVATION

In the amendments to the Treaty of Rome, effective from July 1987, a section on research and technology (subsequently restyled 'research and innovation') was included for the first time, defining the extent of Community co-operation in this area. Most of the funds allocated to research and innovation are granted to companies or institutions that apply to participate in EU research programmes.

A new Competitiveness and Innovation Framework Programme (CIP) was formally approved by the Council of the European Union in October 2006. The CIP for 2007–13 has an overall budget of €3,621m., and is divided into three operational programmes: the Entrepreneurship and Innovation Programme (EIP); the Information Communication Technologies Policy Support Programme (ICT-PSP); and the Intelligent Energy Europe Programme (IEE). In December 2006 the Council adopted a decision establishing the Seventh Framework Programme for research and technological development (FP7), and also established the Seventh Framework Programme of Euratom, for nuclear research and training activities in 2007–11, with a budget of €2,702m. A budget of €48,770m. was approved for the four specific programmes into which FP7 had been structured: co-operation (€32,413m.); ideas (to be implemented by the European Research Council—ERC—€7,510m.); people (€4,750m.); and capacities (€4,097m.). Joint technology initiatives (JTIs), in which industry, research organizations and public authorities would form public-private partnerships to pursue common research objectives, were a major new element of FP7. In December 2007 the Council adopted resolutions establishing ARTEMIS, a JTI involving research into embedded computer systems (specialized computer components dedicated to a specific task that are part of a larger system); the Clean Sky JTI, which aimed to develop environmentally sound and reasonably priced aircraft; the Innovative Medicines Initiative (IMI), which aimed to attract pharmaceutical research and development to Europe, in order to improve access to the newest and most effective medicines; and Nanoelectronics Technologies 2020 (ENIAC), a JTI which aimed to develop European nanoelectronic capabilities. In May 2008 the Council approved the establishment of the Fuel Cells and Hydrogen JTI, which aims to develop new hydrogen energy and fuel cell technologies for use in transport, and stationary and portable applications.

In February 2006 the Commission recommended the establishment of a European Institute of Technology (EIT), to promote excellence in higher education, research and innovation, and based on a Europe-wide network of 'knowledge and innovation communities' (KIC—partnerships comprising higher education institutions, research organizations, companies and other interested parties). The EU's contribution to the EIT was forecast at €308.7m. during 2008–13. A directive on the establishment of the EIT (now known as the European Institute of Innovation and Technology) came into force in April 2008, and the inaugural meeting of the EIT's 18-member governing board took place in September. The first KICs were chosen in December 2009, focusing on: climate change mitigation and adaptation; sustainable energy; and the information and communication society. In April 2010 the EIT's headquarters moved to Budapest, Hungary.

In October 2010 the Commission adopted a communication on the new Innovation Union, part of the 10-year Europe 2020 Strategy, designed to help steer the EU economy out of the economic crisis, by encouraging global competitiveness and innovation. From 2014 FP7 was to be superseded by Horizon 2020, a financial instrument to aid implementation of the Innovation Union. Horizon 2020, which was to have a budget of €80,000m., was to combine all the research and innovation funding now provided through the FP7, the CIP and the EIT. The CIP was to be replaced by a new Programme for the Competitiveness of Enterprises and Small and Medium-sized Enterprises (COSME), which was to have an individual budget of €2,500m. for 2014–20.

In January 2000 the Commission launched an initiative to establish a European Research Area (ERA). The aim was to promote the more effective use of scientific resources within a single area, in order to enhance the EU's competitiveness and create jobs. Detailed plans for the creation of the ERC, as an independent funding body for science, were incorporated in the FP7 agenda. The 22 founding members of a Scientific Council, responsible for determining the scientific funding strategy of the ERC and defining methods of peer review and proposal evaluation, held their inaugural meeting in October 2005. The ERC commenced operations in February 2007, with a budget of €7,500m. The ERC's Dedicated Implementation Structure, the Council's executive agency responsible for applying the strategies and methodologies defined by the Scientific Council, became operational in July 2009. The mandate of a new European Research Area Committee (ERAC) was approved by the Council in May 2010; the Committee, which replaced the Scientific and Technical Research Committee (CREST) established in 1995, provides strategic policy advice to the Council, the Commission and the EU member states on research and innovation issues of relevance to the ERA.

In July 1997 the European Parliament approved the Life Patent Directive, a proposal aiming to harmonize European rules on gene patenting in order to promote research into genetic diseases, despite objections over the ethical implications. In December 2004, at a meeting of the Council of the European Union, Germany, Austria and Italy reiterated their strong opposition to proposed EU funding of embryo research; consequently, the proposal was blocked and a moratorium on central funding was extended indefinitely, although the Commission remained free to approve stem cell research projects on a case-by-case basis and in accordance with strict ethical guidelines.

The EU is making efforts to integrate space science into its research activities, and has increasingly been collaborating with the European Space Agency (ESA). In September 2000 the EU and ESA adopted a joint European strategy for space, and in the following year the two bodies established a joint task force. In November 2003 negotiations on a framework agreement for structured co-operation between the EU and ESA were concluded. The European Space Policy, providing a common political framework for space activities in Europe, was adopted in May 2007. The European Commission, ESA and Eurocontrol developed the European Geostationary Navigation Overlay Service (EGNOS), the first pan-European satellite navigation system, which extends the US GPS system, and is suitable for use in challenging navigational situations in which safety is critical (for example, guiding boats through narrow channels). In April 2009 ownership of EGNOS was transferred to the European Commission. In October the European Commission announced the launch of the free EGNOS Open Service. The European Commission and ESA are also collaborating to design and develop a European satellite and navigation system, Galileo, to consist of about 30 satellites, a global network of tracking stations, and central control facilities in Europe. The European Global Navigation Satellite System (GNSS) Supervisory Authority (GSA) aims to use the Galileo, GPS and Global Navigation Satellite (GLONASS) systems to provide a global, integrated satellite navigation service under civilian control.

The Joint Research Centre (JRC) was established under the European Atomic Energy Community. Directed by the European Commission, but relying for much of its funding on individual contracts, the JRC is a collection of seven institutes, based at five different sites around Europe—Ispra, Italy; Geel, Belgium; Karlsruhe, Germany; Seville, Spain; and Petten, Netherlands. While nuclear research and development remain major concerns of the institutes, their research efforts have diversified substantially over the years. The JRC identified seven priority areas to be addressed under FP7: food safety; biotechnology, chemicals and health; the environment (including climate change and natural disasters); energy and transport; nuclear energy, safety and security; the Lisbon Strategy, information society and rural development; and internal and external security, anti-fraud measures and development aid. Nuclear work accounts for about one-quarter of all JRC activities, with the share accounted for by non-nuclear work increasing. The JRC also provides technical assistance to applicant countries. The JRC's budget for the FP7 period was €1,751m. for non-nuclear activities and €517m. for nuclear activities.

In 2005 the Enterprise and Industry Directorate-General launched the PRO INNO ('Promoting innovation in Europe') initiative, which aimed to foster trans-European co-operation between national and sub-national innovation programmes and activities. The INNO-Policy TrendChart provides detailed information about innovation trends in 39 countries in Europe, the Mediterranean region, North America and Asia. In order to analyse the EU's performance, the Commission used a set of performance indicators to draw up a so-called European Innovation Scoreboard (EIS). After the adoption by the Commission of the Innovation Union in October 2010, the EIS was re-established as the Innovation Union Scoreboard (IUS), in order to monitor implementation of the Innovation Union. The IUS for 2011, published in February 2012, uses 25 research and innovation-related indicators, and covers the 27 EU member states, as well as Croatia, Iceland, the former Yugoslav republic of Macedonia, Norway, Serbia, Switzerland and Turkey. Denmark, Finland, Germany and Sweden were designated 'European innovation leaders', outperforming the rest of Europe. However, when compared with major global competitor nations, a significant gap remained between the EU and the superior performance in innovation of Japan, the Republic of Korea and the USA.

The EU also co-operates with non-member countries in bilateral research projects. The Commission and 38 (mainly European) countries—including EU members as individuals—participate, as full members, in the EUREKA programme of research and development in market-orientated industrial technology, which was launched in 1985; in addition to the full members, the Republic of Korea is designated a EUREKA associated country, and Albania and Bosnia and Herzegovina participate in EUREKA projects through a network of National Information Points (NIPs). EUREKA (the acronym of the European Research Co-ordination Agency), sponsors projects focusing on robotics, engineering, information technology and environmental science, allows resources to be pooled and promotes collaboration. Most of EUREKA's funding is provided by private sources. The Community research and development information service (CORDIS) disseminates findings in the field of advanced technology.

ENERGY

The treaty establishing the European Atomic Energy Community (Euratom) came into force on 1 January 1958. This was designed to encourage the growth of the nuclear energy industry in the Community by conducting research, providing access to information, supplying nuclear fuels, building reactors and establishing common laws and procedures. A common market for nuclear materials was introduced in 1959 and there is a common insurance scheme against nuclear risks. In 1977 the Commission began granting loans on behalf of Euratom to finance investment in nuclear power stations and the enrichment of fissile materials. An agreement with the International Atomic Energy Agency (IAEA) entered into force in the same year, to facilitate co-operation in research on nuclear safeguards and controls. The EU's Joint Research Centre (JRC, see Research and Innovation) conducts research on nuclear safety and the management of radioactive waste.

The Joint European Torus (JET) is an experimental thermonuclear machine designed to pioneer new processes of nuclear fusion, using the 'Tokamak' system of magnetic confinement to heat gases to very high temperatures and bring about the fusion of tritium and deuterium nuclei. Fusion powers stars and is viewed as a 'cleaner' approach to energy production than nuclear fission and fossil fuels. Switzerland is also a member of the JET project (formally inaugurated in 1984), which is based at Culham in the United Kingdom and which is funded by the European Commission. In 1991 JET became the first fusion facility in the world to achieve significant production of controlled fusion power. The European Fusion Development Agreement (EFDA), which entered into force in March 1999, and a new JET implementing agreement, which came into force in January 2000, provide the framework for the collective use of the JET facilities. In 1988 work began with representatives of Japan, the former USSR and the USA on the joint design of an International

Thermonuclear Experimental Reactor (ITER), based on JET but with twice its capacity. In mid-2005 the six participant teams in the ITER project (the People's Republic of China, the EU—represented by Euratom, Japan, the Republic of Korea, Russia and the USA), organized under the auspices of the IAEA, agreed that the vast trial reactor would be located in Cadarache, in southern France. In late 2005 India also became a full partner in the project. The main aim of ITER is to demonstrate the potential for fusion to generate electrical power (ITER would be the first fusion experiment with a net output of power) as well as to collect the data required to design and operate the first electricity-producing plant. In March 2007 the Council established the European Joint Undertaking for ITER and the Development of Fusion Energy (Fusion for Energy) to manage the EU's contribution to ITER. Overall responsibility for ITER was formally assumed by the newly established ITER International Fusion Energy Organization in November, following the ratification of a joint implementation agreement by all seven participants in the project. The construction of the project was expected to be accomplished during 2011–16, after which the reactor would remain operational for 20 years, at a total estimated cost of €10,000m., of which the EU was to contribute about 50%.

Legislation on the completion of the 'internal energy market', adopted in 1990, aimed to encourage the sale of electricity and gas across national borders in the Community by opening national networks to foreign supplies, obliging suppliers to publish their prices and co-ordinating investment in energy. Energy ministers reached agreement in June 1996 on rules for the progressive liberalization of the electricity market. In December 1997 the Council agreed rules to allow the gas market to be opened up in three stages, over a 10-year period.

In 2000 European electricity and gas energy regulators established the Council of European Energy Regulators (CEER), a not-for-profit association that promotes voluntary co-operation. In 2001 the Commission amended the timetable for liberalizing the electricity and gas markets: by 2003 all non-domestic consumers were to have the freedom to choose their electricity supplier; by 2004 non-domestic consumers were to have the freedom to choose their gas supplier; and by 2005 all consumers, domestic and non-domestic, would be able to choose both suppliers. In June 2002 the European Council confirmed amended target dates for the complete two-stage liberalization of the markets: opening up by July 2004 for non-domestic users and by July 2007 for domestic users. The European Regulators Group for electricity and gas (ERGEG) was established in November 2003 to act as an advisory group of independent national regulatory authorities to assist the European Commission in consolidating the internal market for electricity and gas. In early 2006 the ERGEG launched a regional initiative which created three gas and seven electricity zones within the EU. The initiative focused on removing barriers to market integration at a regional level, in order to facilitate the creation of a single competitive market. In October 2009 the CEER helped to organize the fourth World Forum on Energy Regulation, convened in Athens, Greece.

In October 2005 the EU signed a treaty establishing an Energy Community, which entered into force in July 2006. The contracting parties to the treaty comprise Albania, Bosnia and Herzegovina, Croatia, the former Yugoslav Republic of Macedonia, Montenegro, Serbia and the UN Interim Administration Mission in Kosovo. Moldova subsequently became a member in May 2010, and Ukraine joined in February 2011. Georgia, Norway and Turkey have been admitted as observers. The treaty, which aimed to facilitate the creation of an integrated pan-European market for electricity and gas, required the signatories to adopt EU energy regulations. The treaty provided for the liberalization of electricity and gas markets within participating countries by 2008 for non-domestic users, and by 2015 for domestic users. The World Bank estimated that this planned extension of the single European market for electricity and gas would lead to investment of €21,000m. in energy infrastructure in South-Eastern Europe over 15 years. In March 2006 the Commission adopted a Green Paper on developing a common European energy policy, which included recommendations on the appointment of a single energy regulator, the creation of an integrated European power grid and the negotiation of a new long-term pact with Russia on energy supplies. In December the Commission issued a final warning ('reasoned opinion') to 16 member states, including Germany, the United Kingdom, Spain, France and Italy, for having failed to open up sufficiently their energy markets. The final report of a competition inquiry, published in January 2007, identified high levels of market concentration, vertical integration of supply, production and infrastructure and collusion between operators to share markets as the main obstacles to the effective integration of the energy market. The Commission recommended the more stringent enforcement of regulations within an improved regulatory framework for energy liberalization.

The Commission has consistently urged the formation of an effective overall energy policy. The five-year programmes, SAVE and SAVE II, introduced respectively in 1991 and 1995, aimed to establish energy efficiency (e.g. reduction in the energy consumption of vehicles and the use of renewable energy) as a criterion for all EU projects. SAVE was integrated into Energy, Environment and Sustainable Development (EESD), initiated under the Fifth Framework Programme (FP5) for 1998–2002 and subsequently incorporated into a new, overarching plan, Intelligent Energy for Europe (IEE), which was adopted by the Commission for 2003–06 as part of the Sixth Framework Programme (FP6). IEE aimed to strengthen the security of supply and to promote energy efficiency and renewable energy sources (RES) such as wind, solar, biomass and small-scale hydropower. IEE has continued and expanded under a new Competitiveness and Innovation Framework Programme (CIP), in conjunction with the Seventh Framework Programme (FP7) for research during 2007–13. Under CIP, the so-called IEE 2 incorporated three separate elements: energy efficiency (SAVE); RES for the production of electricity and heat (ALTENER); and the energy aspects of transport (STEER); IEE 2 was allocated a budget of €730m. The EU Sustainable Energy Europe Campaign, covering 2005–11, and including an annual European Sustainable Energy Week, aims to accelerate private investment in sustainable energy technologies, to spread best practices, and to encourage alliances among sustainable energy stakeholders. A European Council Directive issued in April 2006 required each member state to submit a National Energy Efficiency Action Plan (NEEAP) to the European Commission by the end of June 2007, demonstrating means of achieving an energy savings target of 9% by 2016.

In order to help the EU to meet its joint commitment under the Kyoto Protocol to reduce greenhouse gas emissions by 8% from 1990 levels by 2012, and to encourage the use of more efficient energy technologies, in July 2003 the Council established the Emissions Trading Scheme, now Emissions Trading System (ETS). Under the scheme, which came into force in January 2005, individual companies were allocated a free greenhouse gas emission allowance by national governments. If they reduced emissions beyond their allocated quota, they would be allowed to sell their credits on the open market. During the first phase, covering 2005–07, ETS was only applied to large industrial and energy undertakings in certain sectors and only covered carbon dioxide emissions. Several member states opted to extend the scope of ETS for the second trading period (2008–12), and it incorporated revised rules for monitoring and reporting, more stringent restrictions on emissions, and an increased number of combustion sources. The third trading period (2013–20) will introduce significant changes, including harmonized allocation methodologies and additional emissions and installations.

In January 2007 the Commission attempted to initiate a more coherent integration of the EU energy and climate policies by incorporating in its proposals a comprehensive series of measures addressing the issue of climate change, while emphasizing the interdependency between security of supply and the promotion of sustainable energy sources. The measures included the establishment of a biennial Strategic Energy Review (SEER) to monitor progress in all aspects of energy policy, which was to constitute the basis for future action plans to be adopted by the Council and the Parliament. The Council endorsed the proposals in March; it also stated that its strategic objective was to limit the increase in the average global temperature to no more than 2°C above pre-industrial levels. The EU was to commit itself to reducing its greenhouse gas emissions by 20% (compared with their 1990 levels) by 2020. At the same time, the renewable energy sector was to supply 20% of EU energy by 2020, compared with 6.6% in 1990, and the share of biofuels in overall consumption of energy by the transport sector was to increase by 10%, also by 2020. New legislation was to facilitate the market penetration of renewable energy sources, while individual member states were to decide whether to develop their nuclear electricity sectors. The development of a European strategic energy technology plan was agreed. It was to be instrumental in increasing research into sustainable technologies (including low-carbon technology) by 50% by 2014. In November 2007 the Commission duly launched the European Strategic Energy Technology Plan (SET-Plan), in which it outlined plans to introduce six new industrial initiatives, focusing on wind power; solar power; biofuels; carbon dioxide capture, transport and storage; the electricity grid (including the creation of a centre to implement a research programme on the European transmission network); and sustainable nuclear fission.

Energy ministers from the EU member states and 12 Mediterranean countries agreed at a meeting held in June 1996 in Trieste, Italy, to develop a Euro-Mediterranean gas and electricity network. The first Euro-Med Energy Forum was held in May 1997, and an action plan for 1998–2002 was adopted in May 1998. In May 2003 the energy ministers of the Euro-Med partnership (including the ministers from the 10 accession states) adopted a declaration launching the Second Regional Energy Plan (2003–06). The Energy Forum that took place in September 2006, to agree on priorities for 2007–10, advocated the continued integration of Euro-Med energy markets, the development of energy projects of common interest, and of sustainable energy. The fifth Euro-Med ministerial conference on energy, held in Cyprus in December 2007, endorsed an action plan for further energy co-operation, covering 2008–13, which was to receive funding of €12,400m. from the European Investment Bank. Priorities included: the harmonization of regional energy markets and legislation; the promotion of sustainable development in the energy sector; and the development of initiatives of common interest in areas such as infrastructure, investment financing and research and development.

In 1997 the Community agreed to help a number of newly independent Eastern European countries to overcome energy problems by means of the Interstate Oil and Gas Transport to Europe programme (INOGATE). The overall aim of this programme was to improve the security of Europe's energy supply by promoting the regional integration of the oil and gas pipeline systems both within Eastern Europe itself and towards the export markets of Europe and the West in general, while acting as a catalyst for attracting private investors and international financial institutions to these pipeline projects. INOGATE originally formed part of the TACIS (Technical Assistance to the Commonwealth of Independent States) programme (see External Relations). However, under the Umbrella Agreement of INOGATE, which officially came into force as an international treaty in February 2001, the programme is open to all interested countries. In November 2006, as a continuation of the Baku initiative inaugurated in November 2004 under the umbrella of INOGATE, the EU and the governments of countries in the Caspian and Black Sea regions adopted a new Energy Road Map, which established a long-term plan of action. The Road Map provided for enhanced energy co-operation between all of the partners involved in such areas as the integration of energy markets on the basis of the EU internal energy market; the improvement of energy security by addressing issues of energy exports/imports; supply diversification; energy transit; sustainable energy development; and the securing of investment for projects of common interest.

At the sixth EU-Russia summit, held in Paris in October 2000, the two sides agreed to institute an energy dialogue on a regular basis with a view to establishing a strategic EU-Russia energy partnership. The dialogue was subsequently structured around joint thematic research groups to analyse issues of common interest, notably in the areas of energy strategies and balances, investment, technology transfers, energy infrastructures and energy efficiency and the environment. From 2001 annual progress reports were presented to EU-Russia summit meetings. However, following the disruption in January 2006 of Russian gas supplies to the EU via Ukraine, which demonstrated the extent of the EU's dependency on Russian gas (about one-quarter of gas supplied to the EU is from Russia), a European Parliament resolution emphasized that there was an urgent need to secure a more stable, reciprocal and transparent EU-Russia energy framework. Reductions in crude oil supplies from Russia to the EU in early 2007, resulting from a dispute between Russia and the transit country, Belarus, led to further demands for measures to enhance the security of the Union's energy supply. In April a restructuring of the thematic groups of the EU-Russia energy dialogue was agreed, to cover energy strategies, forecasts and scenarios; market developments; and energy efficiency. At an EU-Russia summit meeting held in Mafra, Portugal, in October it was agreed to establish a system to provide early warnings of threats to the supply of natural gas and petroleum to the EU.

In addition, the EU promotes trans-European networks (TENs, see also Transport), with the aim of developing European energy, telecommunications and transport through the interconnection and opening-up of national networks. In 2003 a revision of the guidelines for the TEN-Energy (TEN-E) programme was undertaken to take into account the priorities of the enlarged EU. The revised guidelines, adopted by the Council in July 2006, sought: to enhance the security of energy supplies in Europe; to strengthen the internal energy market of the enlarged EU; to support the modernization of energy systems in partner countries; to increase the share of renewable energies, in particular in electricity generation; and to facilitate the realization of major new energy infrastructure projects. The TEN-E networks policy, in particular, aimed to secure and diversify additional gas import capacity from sources in Russia, the Caspian Basin, northern Africa and the Middle East. The budget agreed for the TEN-E programme for 2007–13 totalled €155m. In October 2011 the European Commission published a proposal for a regulation on guidelines for trans-European energy infrastructure, which aimed to ensure the completion of energy networks (12 priority corridors were identified) and storage facilities by 2020.

In November 1999 the Commission indicated the need to strengthen the EU's Northern Dimension energy policy (covering Scandinavia, the Baltic states and north-west Russia) through the reinforcement of international co-operation, the opening-up of markets, the promotion of competition and the improvement of nuclear safety. In a communication in September 2000, the Commission set out a new EU strategy on nuclear safety in Central and Eastern Europe and the former Soviet states. The strategy entailed supporting those countries in their efforts to improve operating safety, strengthening their regulatory frameworks, and closing reactors that could not be upgraded to an acceptable standard. The fifth enlargement of the EU, completed in January 2007 with the accession of Bulgaria and Romania, had implications for nuclear safety, since seven of the 12 new member states had nuclear reactors, mostly of the old Soviet design. The closure of two ageing reactors was one of the preconditions for Bulgaria's accession to the EU. In June 2009 the European Council issued a Directive that established a common binding legal framework for the safety of nuclear installations.

EU member states are required to maintain minimum stocks of crude oil and/or petroleum products. In accordance with a European Council Directive issued in September 2009 member states were to ensure, by 31 December 2012, that these correspond to, at the very least, 90 days of average daily net imports or to 61 days of average daily internal consumption. A Green Paper of March 2006, entitled 'Towards a European strategy for the security of energy supply', re-emphasized the links between security of supply, the creation of a liberalized, integrated EU energy market and the development of sustainable energy. To protect energy supplies against the risk of natural catastrophes, terrorist threats, political risks and rising oil and gas prices, it recommended the following measures: the development of smart electricity networks; the establishment of a European Energy Supply observatory to monitor supply and demand patterns in EU energy markets; improved network security through increased collaboration and exchange of information between transmission system operators under an overarching European centre of energy networks; a solidarity mechanism to ensure rapid assistance to any member state confronted by damage to its essential infrastructure; and common standards to protect infrastructure and the development of a common European voice to promote partnerships with third countries. In May 2007 an EU Network of Energy Security Correspondents (NESCO) was launched to provide early warnings, and so enhance the Community's ability to react to pressure on external energy security.

In October 2008 the first meeting of a new Citizens' Energy Forum, organized by the Commission, took place in London, United Kingdom, bringing together consumer associations, industry representatives, national regulators, and government authorities to discuss issues affecting energy consumers, including billing, smart metering and the protection of vulnerable consumers, in order to serve as a platform to ensure consumer rights in the EU energy market; the Forum met annually thereafter.

In mid-June 2009 the Council formally adopted a new liberalization agreement for the EU's gas and electricity markets, known as the Third Energy Package (the Second Energy Package had been agreed in 2003), which was to enter into effect in 2011–13, and which established common rules for the internal markets in gas and electricity; included regulations on conditions for access to natural gas transmission networks and the network for cross-border exchanges in electricity; and provided for the establishment of an Agency for the Co-operation of Energy Regulators. The Third Energy Package aimed to: separate energy supply and production from network operations; ensure fair competition both within the EU, and with respect to third countries; strengthen the national energy regulators; and create a new Agency for the Co-operation of Energy Regulators (ACER), together with European Networks of Transmission System Operators for electricity (ENTSO-E) and for gas (ENTSO-G). In July the new ENTSO-E took over all the operational tasks of the six existing European Transmission System Operators associations. The new ENTSO-G was established at the beginning of December, and comprises 33 Transmission System Operators from 22 European countries in an effort to facilitate progress towards the creation of a single energy market.

In November 2010 the European Commission adopted a communication entitled 'Energy 2020: a strategy for competitive, sustainable and secure energy', which defined the Commission's energy priorities for the next 10 years, focusing on the need to save energy; to ensure a competitive market with secure energy supplies; to promote technological advances; and to encourage effective international negotiation. In early February 2011 the first EU energy summit was held, in Brussels, Belgium, at which an agreement was adopted on a number of strategic energy-related areas. In particular, the summit concluded that work should be undertaken to develop a transparent, rule-governed relationship with Russia. The summit also made clear its intention to promote investment in renewable energy, and sustainable low-carbon technologies; to accelerate the liberalization of energy markets, in order to bring them into accordance with EU law (about one-half of the EU member states had liberalized their energy markets, but only Denmark had fully implemented the latest legislation; some 60 infringement proceedings had been brought against member states for failing to open up their markets); to improve adherence to the 2020 20% energy-efficiency target (which aimed to reduce the use of greenhouse gases by 20%, to increase the proportion of renewable energy used to 20%, and to improve overall energy efficiency by 20% by 2020); and to investigate the potential extraction and use of unconventional fossil fuel sources, such as shale gas and oil shale, favoured, in particular, by Poland.

Since June 2005 annual formal ministerial meetings of the EU-Organization of the Petroleum Exporting Countries (OPEC) Energy Dialogue have been convened; the eighth ministerial Dialogue, convened in Vienna, Austria, in June 2011, agreed to conduct a workshop to review the findings of a study on technological development in the road transport sector; to finalize preparations for a proposed EU-OPEC Energy Technology Centre; and to address the major challenges affecting oil and gas exploration and production activities, such as the safety of offshore operations and the shortage of human resources.

ENTERPRISE AND INDUSTRY

Industrial co-operation was the earliest activity of the Community. The treaty establishing the European Coal and Steel Community (ECSC) came into force in July 1952, and by the end of 1954 nearly all barriers to trade in coal, coke, steel, pig iron and scrap iron had been removed. The ECSC treaty expired in July 2002, and the provisions of the ECSC treaty were incorporated in the EEC treaty, on the grounds that it was no longer appropriate to treat the coal and steel sectors separately.

In the late 1970s and 1980s measures were adopted radically to restructure the steel industry in response to a dramatic reduction in world demand for steel. During the 1990s, however, new technologies and modern production processes were introduced, and the European steel sector showed signs of substantial recovery. Privatization and cross-border mergers also improved the industry's competitive performance, and by the 2000s Europe was a competitive global exporter. In March 2004 the European Commission and major stakeholders in the European steel industry launched the European Steel Technology Platform, the long-term aim of which was to help the sector meet the challenges of the global marketplace, changing supply and demand patterns, environmental objectives, and the simplification of EU and national legislation and regulation in this field. In addition, the May 2004 enlargement of the EU increased the need for extensive restructuring of the steel industries. The steel industry played a relatively larger role in the 10 new member states, compared with the existing 15 members. In 2008 the European steel industry produced 198m. metric tons of steel, compared with some 160m. tons in the early 2000s. The industry directly employed around 420,000 EU citizens (with several times this number employed in the steel-processing, -usage and -recycling industries) in 2008. A decrease in production resulting from the global economic downturn, however, caused up to 170,000 steel sector employees to be laid off, either temporarily or permanently, or to adopt short-time working patterns in 2009.

The European textiles and clothing industry has been seriously affected by overseas competition over an extended period. From 1974 the Community participated in the Multi-Fibre Arrangement (MFA, see World Trade Organization), to limit imports from low-cost suppliers overseas. However, as a result of the Uruguay Round of GATT (General Agreement on Tariffs and Trade) trade negotiations, the quotas that existed under the MFA were progressively eliminated during 1994–2004 in accordance with an Agreement on Textiles and Clothing. An action plan for the European textiles and clothing industry was drawn up in 1997. A report published by the Commission in 2000 established future priorities for the sector, focusing on preparations for the enlargement of the EU and systems for co-operation in the 'new economy'. Particular importance was attached to ensuring a smooth transition to the quota-free world environment (from 1 January 2005), to enable third countries currently exporting to the EU to maintain their competitive position, and to secure for EU textiles and clothing industries in third countries market access conditions similar to those offered by the EU. A high-level group on textiles and clothing, established by the Commission in order to encourage debate on initiatives to facilitate the sectors' adjustment to major challenges, and to improve their competitiveness, published its first report in 2004.

In May 2005, in response to a dramatic increase in clothing exports from the People's Republic of China since 1 January, the EU imposed limits on textiles imports from that country. In June the EU and the Chinese Government agreed import quotas on 10 clothing and textiles categories until 2008, but by August several of the quotas for 2005 had already been breached. In September the dispute was resolved when it was agreed that one-half of the estimated 80m. Chinese garments that had been impounded at European ports would be released and the remainder counted against the quotas for 2006. In September 2006 the high-level group on textiles and clothing published its second report, which sought, *inter alia*, to chart the likely development of the sector up to 2020. In October 2007 the European Commission and China agreed that, following the expiry in 2008 of the agreement on import quotas, a monitoring system would be introduced to track, but not limit, the issuing of export licences in China and the import of goods into the EU for eight clothing and textiles categories. Trade in textiles and clothing was fully liberalized from January 2009, following which China continued to increase its market share in Europe.

Production in EU member states' shipyards fell drastically from the 1970s, mainly as a result of competition from shipbuilders in the Far East. In the first half of the 1980s a Council directive allowed for subsidies to help reorganize the shipbuilding industry and to increase efficiency, but subsequently rigorous curbs on state aid to the industry were introduced. State aid was eventually withdrawn in early 2001. From 2000 construction activity increased somewhat. However, the number of new orders declined sharply from the latter half of 2008 as a result of the global economic downturn.

In April 2002 the Commission adopted its fifth report on the state of global shipbuilding. It confirmed previous observations that, in the absence of an international agreement, the market was in crisis, owing to the extremely low prices offered by shipyards in the Republic of Korea (South Korea). In May the EU agreed to launch WTO procedures against South Korea, and to establish a 'temporary defensive mechanism' (TDM) of state subsidies to protect European shipbuilding against unfair South Korean practices.

Harmonization of national company law to form a common legal structure within the Community has led to the adoption of directives on disclosure of information, company capital, internal mergers, the accounts of companies and of financial institutions, the division of companies, the qualification of auditors, single-member private limited companies, mergers, take-over bids, and the formation of joint ventures.

The European Patent Convention (EPC) was signed in 1973 and entered into force in 1977. Revisions to the Convention were agreed in November 2000, and a revised EPC entered into force on 13 December 2007. In June 1997 the Commission published proposals to simplify the European patent system through the introduction of a unitary Community patent, to remove the need to file patent applications with individual member states. Upon the entry into force in December 2009 of the Lisbon Treaty, which provided a new legal basis for the establishment of unitary intellectual property titles within the EU, the proposed Community patent was renamed the EU patent. During that month the European Council agreed a draft regulation on the EU patent, in accordance with which it was envisaged that the EU would accede to the EPC (which would require further revision to the Convention), and the European Patent Office (EPO, based in Munich, Germany) would grant EU patents with unitary effect throughout the territory of the EU. Infringement and validity issues relating to the planned EU patent were to be addressed by a proposed European and EU Patents Court. In June 2011 the EU Council agreed to draw up two EU regulations on the unitary patent, concerning increased co-operation on unitary patent protection, and the associated translation arrangements.

An Office for Harmonization in the Internal Market (OHIM), based in Alicante, Spain, was established in December 1993, and is responsible for the registration of Community trademarks and for ensuring that these receive uniform protection throughout the EU.

The liberalization of Community public procurement has played an important role in the establishment of the internal market. From January 1993 the liberalization of procurement was extended to include public utilities in the previously excluded sectors of energy, transport, drinking water and telecommunications. In 1996 the Commission launched the Système d'information pour les marchés publics (SIMAP) programme, to give information on rules, procedures and opportunities in the public procurement market, and to encourage the optimum use of information technology in public procurement. In 2002 the European Parliament adopted a regulation aimed at simplifying the rules on procurement of contract notices, by introducing a single system for classifying public procurement, to be used by all public authorities; a regulation updating the classification system was adopted in November 2007. The European Public Procurement Network was established in January 2003. The objective of this network, which comprises all EU member states, EU candidate countries, European Economic Area (EEA) members, Switzerland and other European countries, was to strengthen the application of public procurement rules through a mutual exchange of experience. Reforms to the EU's public procurement directives were adopted in 2004 in an attempt to make the often complex rules more transparent, efficient and comprehensible. In November 2007 a directive was adopted with the aim of improving the effectiveness of review procedures concerning the award of public contracts.

In 1990 the European Council adopted two directives with the aim of removing the tax obstacles encountered by companies operating across borders: the Merger Directive was designed to reduce tax measures that could hamper business reorganization and the Parent-Subsidiary Directive abolished double taxation of profit distributed between parent companies in one member state and their subsidiaries in others. In October 2001 the European Council adopted two legislative instruments enabling companies to form a European Company (known as a Societas Europaea—SE). A vital element of the internal market, the legislation gave companies operating in more than one member state the option of establishing themselves as single companies, thereby able to function throughout the EU under one set of rules and through a unified management system; companies might be merged to establish an SE. The legislation was aimed at making cross-border enterprise management more flexible and less bureaucratic, and at helping to improve competitiveness. In July 2003 the Council adopted similar legislation enabling co-operatives to form a European Co-operative Society (Societas Cooperativa Europaea—SCE). In September 2004 the Commission established a working group to advance the development of a common consolidated corporate tax base (CCCTB). In February 2005 the Council approved an amendment to the Merger Directive of 1990, extending its provisions to cover a wider range of companies, including SEs and SCEs. A directive aimed at facilitating cross-border mergers of limited liability companies was adopted by the European Parliament and the Council in October 2005. The establishment of SPEs from mid-2008 (see below) aimed to facilitate the operation of small and medium-sized enterprises (SMEs) across borders.

In September 1995 a Commission report outlined proposals to improve the business environment for SMEs. In March 1996 the Commission agreed new guidelines for state aid to SMEs. Aid for the acquisition of patent rights, licences, expertise, etc., was to be allowed at the same level as that for tangible investment. A Charter for Small Enterprises, approved in June 2000, aimed to support SMEs in areas such as education and training, the development of regulations, and taxation and financial matters, and to increase representation of the interests of small businesses at national and EU level. In November 2005 the Commission launched a new policy framework for SMEs, proposing specific actions in five areas: promoting entrepreneurship and skills; improving SMEs' access to markets; simplifying regulations; improving SMEs' growth potential; and strengthening dialogue and consultation with SME stakeholders. In January 2007 the Commission launched an action programme aimed at reducing unnecessary administrative burdens on companies, primarily SMEs, by one-quarter by 2012, focusing on 13 priority areas, including company law, employment relations, taxation, agriculture and transport. In addition, 10 'fast-track' measures were identified, which, it was estimated, would reduce the burden on businesses by €1,300m. per year. A high-level group of experts was appointed in November 2007 to advise the Commission on the implementation of the action programme, which had been endorsed by the Council in March. In June 2008 the Commission adopted the Small Business Act for Europe (SBA), which was endorsed by the EU Council of Ministers in December. The SBA aimed further to streamline bureaucratic procedures for SMEs, and to enable businesses to establish a European Private Company (Societas Privata Europaea—SPE), which would operate according to uniform principles in all member states, thereby simplifying procedures for SMEs operating across borders. By 2010 there were more than 20m. SMEs in the EU, accounting for 99% of all EU enterprises. In February 2011 the results of a review of the SBA's work in 2008–10 was published. The review concluded that some 100,000 SMEs had benefited from the Competitiveness and Innovation Framework Programme 2007–13; a new late payment directive required public authorities to pay suppliers within 30 days, improving cash flow; the resources (both financial and in terms of time taken) required to establish a new SME had been reduced; simplified online procedures and opportunities for joint bidding had facilitated the participation of SMEs in public procurement; and the establishment of a new EU SME Centre in China had helped SMEs to access Chinese markets. The review also identified a number of priority areas for further action: the need to assist SMEs in accessing finance, for investment and growth, for example by improving access to loan guarantees and venture capital markets, as well as targeted measures aimed at making investors more aware of the benefits of SMEs; improving regulation; enhancing the ability of SMEs fully to utilize the common market, with proposals for a Common Consolidated Corporate Tax Base, measures to facilitate cross-border debt recovery, and a revision of the European standardization system to make it more accessible to SMEs; and assisting SMEs in dealing with the issues of globalization and climate change.

The European Investment Bank provides finance for small businesses by means of 'global loans' to financial intermediaries. A mechanism providing small businesses with subsidized loans was approved by ministers in April 1992.

The Enterprise Europe Network, launched in February 2008, comprises contact points providing information and advice to businesses, in particular SMEs, on EU matters, in 51 countries, including the EU member states, EU candidate countries, members of the EEA, and other participating third countries. The EU's other information services for business include the Community Research and Development Information Service (CORDIS, see Research and Innovation) and the internet-based Your Europe: Business, which brings together advice and data from various sources. In addition, around 147 accredited Business and Innovation Centres (BICs) were operating in the 27 EU countries by 2008, with a mission to promote entrepreneurship and the creation of innovative businesses, and to assist existing companies to enhance their prospects through innovation.

In January 2000 the EU's Directorates-General for Industry and SMEs and for Innovation were transformed into one Directorate-General for Enterprise Policy (subsequently restyled the Enterprise and Industry Directorate-General). The Commission subsequently adopted a Multiannual Programme for Enterprise and Entrepreneurship (MAP) covering 2001–05, aimed particularly at SMEs. Stronger measures were proposed for the protection of intellectual property rights (IPRs), and the harmonization of legislation on IPRs was advocated (differences between national laws in this respect could constitute protectionist barriers to the EU's principle of free movement of goods and services). In April 2004 a directive was adopted on the enforcement of IPRs, to make it easier to enforce copyrights, patents and trademarks in the EU and to punish those who tampered with technical mechanisms designed to prevent copying or counterfeiting. In July 2005 the Commission proposed a second directive on the enforcement of IPRs, which would impose criminal penalties for infringements, to supplement the civil and administrative measures contained in the 2004 directive; the draft directive remained under consideration. Meanwhile, in November 2004 the Commission announced plans to commence monitoring certain countries (particularly China, Ukraine and Russia) to check that they were making genuine efforts to halt the production of counterfeit goods. In October 2005 the Commission launched a new industrial policy, proposing eight new initiatives or actions targeted at specific sectors, including pharmaceuticals, defence, and information and communication technologies, as well as cross-sectoral initiatives on: competitiveness; energy and the environment; IPRs; improved regulation; research and innovation; market access; skills; and managing structural change. In January 2007 the MAP, which had been extended until the end of 2006, was succeeded by an Entrepreneurship and Innovation Programme under a wider Competitiveness and Innovation Framework Programme for 2007–13, with a budget of some €3,600m. In January 2009 the EU and China agreed an action plan on advancing closer customs co-operation relating to IPR protection, and signed an agreement aimed at enhancing co-operation in monitoring trade and preventing trafficking in chemicals used in the illicit manufacture of narcotic drugs.

The European Business Angels Network (EBAN) provides a means of introduction between SMEs and investors and encourages the exchange of expertise. The Commission also promotes inter-industry co-operation between enterprises in the EU and in third countries through the TransAtlantic Business Dialogue (TABD), the Canada-Europe Round Table, the EU-Japan Business Round Table, the Mercosur-Europe Business Forum (MEBF), the EU-Russia Industrialists' Round Table, the EU-India Business Dialogue, the EU-Indonesia Business Dialogue and the European-Israeli Business Dialogue.

COMPETITION

The Treaty of Rome establishing the European Economic Community provided for the creation of a common market based on the free movement of goods, persons, services and capital. The EU's competition policy aims to guarantee the unity of this internal market, by providing access to a range of high-quality goods and services, at competitive prices. It seeks to prevent anti-competitive practices by companies or national authorities, and to outlaw monopolization, protective agreements and abuses of dominant positions. Overall, it aims to create a climate favourable to innovation, while protecting the interests of consumers.

The Commission has wide investigative powers in the area of competition policy. It may act on its own initiative, or after a complaint from a member state, firm or individual, or after being notified of agreements or planned state aid. Before taking a decision, the Commission organizes hearings; its decisions can be challenged before the Court of First Instance and the Court of Justice, or in national courts.

The Treaty of Rome prohibits any state aid that distorts or threatens to distort competition in the common market (e.g. by discriminating in favour of certain firms or the production of certain goods); however, some exceptions are permitted where the proposed aid may have a beneficial impact in overall Union terms. As an integral part of competition policy, control of state aid, including balancing the negative effects of aid on competition with its positive effects on the common interest, helps to maintain competitive markets. The procedural rules on state aid were consolidated and clarified in a regulation in 1999, and provided for several exemptions, notably regarding the provision of aid to small and medium-sized enterprises (SMEs) and for training. The EU has drawn up 'regional aid maps' designed to concentrate aid in those regions with the most severe development problems. A State Aid Action Plan (SAAP), covering the five-year period 2005–09, was adopted by the Commission in June 2005 as a roadmap for the reform of state aid policy. The SAAP streamlined procedures (which had become increasingly complex, and challenged by EU enlargement) to provide member states with a clear and predictable state aid framework. It promoted targeting state aid towards improving the competitiveness of European industry and towards the creation of sustainable jobs, thereby advancing the Lisbon Strategy. It provided for aid to be utilized as a means of achieving objectives of common interest, such as services of general economic interest, social and regional cohesion, employment, research and development, sustainable development, and promotion of cultural diversity, and for redressing inefficiencies in the functioning of markets ('market failures') with a view to promoting growth. Amid widespread recession, in December 2008 the European Commission adopted a Temporary Framework for State Aid, which aimed to assist member states in co-ordinating the provision of credit facilities to businesses until 2010, in order to protect and restore their viability in the long term. The Temporary Framework was subsequently extended until the end of 2011. In February 2012 the Commission published a guidance paper on state aid-compliant financing, and restructuring and privatization of state-owned enterprises. Since 2001 the Commission has analysed state aid granted by member states in its State Aid Scoreboard. According to the Scoreboard published in December 2011, and excluding targeted crisis measures, the total amount of state aid granted by EU member states in 2010 was some €73,700m., equivalent to 0.6% of EU gross domestic product (GDP). In the same year, crisis-support measures, such as the recapitalization of the financial sector, totalled €121,300m. (equivalent to some 1% of EU GDP); some €11,700m. of aid (equivalent to some 0.9% of EU GDP) was granted under the Temporary Framework. By the beginning of October 2011, the Commission had approved financial crisis measures for 22 member states, and aid measures for 26 member states had been approved under the temporary framework. The Commission acts to recover any illegal or incompatible state aid: recovery of such aid disbursed since 1 January 2000 exceeded €11,500m. by the end of June 2011.

The Treaty of Rome prohibits agreements and concerted practices between firms resulting in the prevention, restriction or distortion of competition within the common market. This ban applies both to horizontal agreements (between firms at the same stage of the production process) and vertical agreements (between firms at different stages). The type of agreements and practices that are prohibited include: price-fixing; imposing conditions on sale; seeking to isolate market segments; imposing production or delivery quotas; agreements on investments; establishing joint sales offices; market-sharing agreements; creating exclusive collective markets; agreements leading to discrimination against other trading parties; collective boycotting; and voluntary restraints on competitive behaviour. Certain types of co-operation considered to be positive, such as agreements promoting technical and economic progress, may be exempt.

In addition, mergers that would significantly impede competition in the common market are banned. The Commission examines prospective mergers in order to decide whether they are compatible with competition principles. In July 2001 the EU blocked a merger between two US companies for the first time, on the grounds that EU companies would be adversely affected. In December the Commission launched a review of its handling of mergers and acquisitions, focusing on the speed of decisions and on bringing European competition standards in line with those in the USA and elsewhere. A new merger regulation was adopted in January 2004 and came into force in May, introducing some flexibility into the time frame for investigations into proposed mergers.

The Commission is attempting to abolish monopolies in the networks supplying basic services to member states. In June 2002 the Council adopted a directive on the opening up of postal services. Liberalization has also been pursued in the gas and electricity, telecommunications and transport sectors. In July 2002 the Commission approved a plan to open the car industry to greater competition, by applying new EU-wide rules for car sales, giving car dealers the freedom to operate anywhere in the EU. The reforms, which were strongly opposed by car manufacturers and by the French and German Governments, came into effect in October 2005. In June the Commission launched inquiries into competition in the electricity and gas markets and in the retail banking and business insurance sectors. In January 2007 the Commission adopted the final report of the inquiry into the gas and electricity markets, concluding that consumers and businesses were disadvantaged by inefficiency and expense. Particular problems that were identified by the final report were high levels of market concentration; vertical integration of supply, generation and infrastructure, leading to a lack of equal access to and insufficient investment in infrastructure; and possible collusion between incumbent operators to share markets. The Commission announced its intention to pursue action in individual cases, within the framework of anti-trust, merger control and state aid regulations, and to act to improve the regulatory framework for energy liberalization. The adoption of the final report was accompanied by the adoption of a comprehensive package of measures to establish a New Energy Policy for Europe, with the aim of combating climate change and prompting energy security and competitiveness within the EU. The final report of the inquiry into the retail banking sector, published in January 2007, indicated a number of concerns in the markets for payment cards, payments systems and retail banking products. In particular, the report noted that there were large variations in merchant and interchange fees for payment cards, barriers to entry into the markets for payment systems and credit registers, impediments to customer mobility and product tying. In response to these findings, the Commission announced that it would use its powers, within the framework of competition regulations and in close collaboration with national authorities, to combat serious abuses. The final report of the inquiry into the business insurance sector, published in September, raised concerns about the widespread practice of premium alignment in the reinsurance and coinsurance markets when more than one insurer is involved in covering a single risk and about lack of transparency in the remuneration of insurance brokers, as well as the risk of conflicts of interest jeopardizing the objectivity of brokers' advice to clients.

In February 2006, in a first reading, the European Parliament adopted a draft directive aimed at opening up the services sector to cross-border competition. The directive had proved controversial, with opponents fearing it would lead to lower wages, lower standards of social and environmental protection and an influx of foreign workers. The Parliament notably amended the directive so that a company offering services in another country would be governed by the rules and regulations of the country in which the service was being provided (rather than those of the company's home country, as the Commission had favoured). The Parliament excluded a number of areas from the future directive's scope, including broadcasting, audiovisual services, legal services, social services, gambling and public health, and also agreed a list of legitimate reasons that a country could cite for restricting the activities of foreign service providers, such as national security, public health and environmental protection. Those in favour of the directive claimed that it had been severely weakened by the Parliament. In December, having been approved by the Parliament at its second reading earlier in that month, the directive was adopted by the Parliament and the Council of the European Union and entered into force.

In 2003 the Commission worked to establish detailed provisions for a modernized framework for anti-trust and merger control in advance of the enlargement of the EU in May 2004. In that month major changes to EU competition law and policy (including substantive and procedural reform of the European Community Merger Regulation) entered into force. As part of the reforms, national competition authorities, acting as a network, and national courts were to become much more involved in the enforcement of competition rules, and companies were to be required to conduct more self-assessment of their commercial activities. In March the US Department of Justice had criticized the EU's anti-trust action against the US computer software company Microsoft. The European Commission imposed a fine of €497m. and instructed the company to disclose elements of its programming (within 120 days) to facilitate the development of competitive products. Microsoft appealed against the decision in the Court of First Instance in Luxembourg in June and the EU penalties were temporarily suspended. In December, however, the Court rejected Microsoft's appeal to delay the implementation of the EU sanctions pending the final outcome of the company's main appeal against the Commission's anti-trust decision. In July 2006 the Commission imposed a fine of €280.5m. on Microsoft, and threatened to impose heavier penalties on the company in future, for its failure to comply with the EU's demand that it should provide complete and accurate information to permit interoperability between its Windows operating system and rivals' work-group servers. The Commission was also legally entitled to impose a further daily fine of €0.5m., backdated to December 2005, on the company if the royalty fees it charged for the use of its technical information were found to be excessive. In March 2007 the Commission communicated a statement of objection to Microsoft, stating its preliminary view that there was no significant innovation in submissions made by the company from December 2005 in respect of compliance with the Commission's anti-trust action of March 2004, and that the royalty fees proposed were therefore unreasonable. In September 2007 the Court of First Instance rejected Microsoft's appeal against the 2004 anti-trust decision. Microsoft announced in October 2007 that it would accept the Court's ruling and comply with the Commission's demands. In December 2009 the Commission made legally binding, for five years from March 2010, a commitment offered by Microsoft in October 2009 to give consumers of its Windows operating system a choice of web browser beyond Microsoft's own Internet Explorer, and, thereby, to remove a long-term obstacle to competition and innovation. Meanwhile, in May 2009 the Commission imposed a fine of €1,060m. on the Intel Corporation, after concluding that it had abused its strong position in the central processing unit (CPU) market by making reimbursements to computer manufacturers, provided that they bought CPUs from Intel, and by making direct payments to Europe's largest computer retailer, Media Saturn Holding, on condition that its stock solely comprised computers containing Intel CPUs. In addition, Intel made direct payments to computer manufacturers to postpone or halt the launch of specific products containing competitors' CPUs and to restrict the sales avenues available to such products.

In October 2004 the USA initiated dispute procedures at the World Trade Organization (WTO) in protest at alleged massive state subsidies to the civil aircraft manufacturer Airbus. However, the EU took retaliatory action regarding state subsidies to the US aircraft manufacturer Boeing. An attempt, from January 2005, to settle the dispute through bilateral talks failed, and both sides renewed their cases at the WTO in May. In July the WTO agreed to establish two panels to examine the complaints of the USA and the EU; members of the panels were appointed in October. In November 2006 the US case against Airbus was formally presented; a preliminary report on the situation, issued by the WTO in September 2009, determined that Airbus had received illegal subsidies totalling US $13,000m., but did not find the EU systematically to have abused global trade rules. The case of the EU against Boeing was presented in March 2007, and in March 2011 the WTO ruled that Boeing had received illegal US subsidies worth more than $5,000m.

In mid-January 2008 the Commission initiated an inquiry into the pharmaceuticals sector, in response to indications that fewer new medicines were entering the market, and that the launch of generic medicines appeared to be subject to unnecessary delays. In July 2009 the Commission adopted the final report of the sector inquiry into pharmaceuticals, which confirmed that originator companies use a variety of methods to extend the commercial life of their products prior to generic entry, and which confirmed a decline in the number of new medicines reaching the market and indicated that pharmaceutical companies might have created obstacles to market entry. The Commission planned to increase monitoring of pharmaceuticals companies in order to identify breaches of anti-trust legislation in the sector, and to identify defensive patenting strategies. To reduce the risk that settlements between originator and generic companies are concluded at the expense of consumers, the Commission undertakes to carry out further focused monitoring of settlements that limit or delay the market entry of generic drugs.

The international affairs unit of the Directorate-General for Competition co-operates with foreign competition authorities and promotes competition instruments in applicant countries, where it also provides technical assistance. The unit works within the framework of international organizations such as the WTO, the Organisation for Economic Co-operation and Development (OECD) and the United Nations Conference on Trade and Development (UNCTAD). Dedicated co-operation agreements on competition policy have been signed with the USA, Canada and Japan, while other forms of bilateral co-operation on competition issues exist with a number of other countries and regions. In addition, in 2001 the European Commission was a founding member of the International Competition Network, an informal forum for competition authorities from around the world.

TELECOMMUNICATIONS, INFORMATION TECHNOLOGY AND BROADCASTING

In 1991 the Council adopted a directive requiring member states to liberalize their rules on the supply of telecommunications terminal equipment, thus ending the monopolies of national telecommunications authorities. In the same year, the Council adopted a plan for the gradual introduction of a competitive market in satellite communications; a directive relating to the liberalization of satellite telecommunications equipment and services came into force in late 1994, but allowed for deferment until 1 January 1996. In October 1995 the European Commission adopted a directive liberalizing the use of cable telecommunications, requiring member states to permit a wide range of services, in addition to television broadcasts, on such networks. The EU market for mobile telephone networks was opened to full competition as a result of a directive adopted by the Commission in January 1996, which obliged member states to abolish all exclusive and special rights in this area, and establish open and fair licensing procedures for digital services. All the major EU telecommunications markets were, in principle, open to competition from 1998.

In February 2000 the Commission requested that national competition authorities, telecommunications regulators, mobile network operators and service providers give information on conditions and price structures for national and international mobile services. In response to concerns regarding the increased cost for EU citizens of using a mobile telephone when travelling in another EU country, a new regulation fixing a maximum rate for so-called roaming charges entered into force in June 2007. In order to enhance the transparency of retail prices, mobile telephony providers were also required to inform their customers of the charges applicable to them when making and receiving calls in another member state. In July 2011 the Commission published a proposal to further amend the application of roaming charges for EU mobile telephone users, by imposing new maximum rates, increasing competition, and allowing consumers to sign a separate, additional contract for data roaming with a company other than their contracted domestic mobile service provider.

In July 2000 a comprehensive reform of the regulatory framework for telecommunications—the 'telecoms package'—was launched. The reform aimed to update EU regulations to take account of changes in the telecommunications, media and information technology (IT) sectors. Noting the continuing convergence of these sectors, the Commission aimed to develop a single regulatory framework for all transmission networks and associated services, in order to exploit the full potential for growth, competition and job creation. The Commission recommended, as a priority, the introduction of a regulation on unbundled access to the local loop (the final connection of telephone wires into the home). The lack of competition in this part of the network was considered a significant obstacle to the widespread provision of low-cost internet access. The regulation obliged incumbent operators to permit shared and full access to the local loop by the end of 2000. In December 2001 the European Parliament voted to adopt a compromise telecoms package. This gave the Commission powers to oversee national regulatory regimes and, in some cases, to overrule national regulatory authorities. The package included a framework directive and three specific directives (covering issues of authorization, access and interconnection, universal service and users' rights) and measures to ensure harmonized conditions in radio spectrum policy. By the end of 2003 the EU regulatory framework for electronic communications had been completely implemented; during subsequent years, however, the Commission initiated legal proceedings against a number of member states for either their failure fully to transpose the new rules of competition in their national laws or for incorrect implementation of the framework. In November 2009 the European Parliament and the Council of Ministers agreed a reform of the EU's telecommunications rules; the new rules, which were to be fully incorporated into national legislation by June 2011, aimed to provide consumers with more choice by reinforcing competition between operators; to promote investment in new communication infrastructures, notably by freeing radio spectrum for wireless broadband services; and to make communication networks more reliable and more secure, for example by introducing new measures to combat unsolicited e-mail, viruses, etc. To improve regulation and competition, and reinforce co-operation between national telecommunications regulators in an attempt to facilitate the creation of pan-European services, a new Body of European Regulators for Electronic Communications (BEREC) was inaugurated in January 2010.

The '.eu' top-level domain name, aimed at giving individuals, organizations and companies the option of having a pan-European identity for their internet presence, was launched in December 2005, when registration commenced for applicants with prior rights, such as trademark holders and public bodies; registration was open to all from April 2006. The European Registry of Internet Domain Names (ERID) reported in February 2010 that the number of registered '.eu' domain names had exceeded 3.2m.

Information and communication technologies (ICT) was one of the main themes of the co-operation programme of the Seventh Framework Programme for research, technological development and demonstration activities (FP7, covering 2007–13)—see Research and Innovation. The development of ICT was allocated €9,050m. in the budget for 2007–13. Aims included strengthening Europe's scientific and technology base in ICTs; stimulating innovation through ICT use; and ensuring that progress in ICTs is rapidly transformed into benefits for citizens, businesses, industry and governments. The Interchange of Data between Administrations (IDA) initiative supported the rapid electronic exchange of information between EU administrations—in January 2005 the IDA was renamed the Interoperable Delivery of pan-European eGovernment Services to Public Administrations, Businesses and Citizens (IDAbc) programme. An action plan promoting safer use of the internet, extended in March 2002 until December 2004, aimed to combat illegal and harmful content on global networks. In December 2004 the EU approved a new programme, called Safer Internet Plus (2005–08), to promote safer use of the internet and new online technologies and to combat illegal and harmful content (particularly child pornography and violent and racist material). The renewed Safer Internet programme for 2009–13 was awarded a budget of €55m., and aimed to combat both illegal content and harmful conduct such as the 'grooming' of children by paedophiles (where an adult establishes contact with a child via the internet, under false pretences, with the intention of arranging a meeting with that child for the purposes of committing a sexual offence) and bullying.

In 1992 a White Paper proposed the establishment of trans-European networks (TENs) in telecommunications, energy and transport, in order to improve infrastructure and assist in the development of the common market. Following the liberalization of the telecommunications market in 1998, efforts in this area were concentrated on support (through the eTEN programme) for the development of broadband networks and multimedia applications. The eTEN programme, which expired in 2006, focused strongly on public services and its objectives were based on the EU's stated aim of 'an information society for all'. The ICT Policy Support Programme (ICT PSP), part of the wider Competitiveness and Innovation Framework Programme (CIP, covering 2007–13), was designed to build on the former eTEN programme by stimulating innovation and competitiveness through the wider uptake and best use of ICT by citizens, governments and businesses. A budget of €728m. was allocated to the ICT PSP for 2007–13.

In October 2003 new digital privacy legislation aimed at combating unwanted commercial e-mails (known collectively as 'spam') came into force across the EU. The new rules required companies to gain consent before sending e-mails and introduced a ban on the use of 'spam' throughout the EU. It was widely recognized, however, that concerted international action was required, since most of the 'spam' entering Europe originated from abroad (particularly from the USA). In February 2005 13 European countries agreed to share information and pursue complaints across borders in an effort to combat unsolicited e-mails. A European Network and Information Security Agency (ENISA) became fully operational in October 2004. The main aims of the Agency, which is based in Heraklion, Greece, are to promote closer European co-ordination on information security and to provide assistance in the application of EU measures in this field. ENISA periodically monitors anti-spam activities. A 2009 ENISA survey of measures taken by European e-mail service providers to combat spam in their networks found that less than 5% of EU e-mail traffic at that time was delivered to inboxes. In February 2010 ENISA, which reported that 211m. internet users in Europe were regularly accessing online social networking sites (SNSs), released a list of 17 'golden rules' to enable consumers to protect themselves from online risk.

In 1991 a directive ('Television without Frontiers') came into force, establishing minimum standards for television programmes to be broadcast freely throughout the Community: limits were placed on the amount of time devoted to advertisements, a majority of programmes broadcast were to be from the Community, where practicable, and governments were allowed to forbid the transmission of programmes considered morally harmful. In November 2002 the Commission adopted a communication on the promotion and distribution of television programmes. In July 2003 the Commission reiterated proposals (originally presented at the Lisbon summit in March 2000) to help film and audiovisual production companies to have access to external funding from banks and other financial institutions by covering some of the costs of the guarantees demanded by these institutions and/or part of the cost of a loan ('discount contract loan') for financing the production of their works. In May 2005 the Commission urged EU member states to accelerate the changeover from analogue to digital broadcasting, setting a target of 2012 for shutting down analogue services. In December 2005 the Commission proposed a modernization of the Television without Frontiers directive in view of rapid technological and market developments in the audiovisual sector. A reduction in the regulatory burden on providers of television and similar services was envisaged, as well as the introduction of more flexible rules on advertising. National rules on the protection of minors, against incitement to hatred and against surreptitious advertising would be replaced with an EU-wide minimum standard of protection. The proposals distinguished between so-called 'linear' services (e.g. scheduled broadcasting via traditional television, the internet or mobile cellular telephones) and 'non-linear' services, such as on-demand films or news, which would be subject only to a basic set of minimum principles. The modernized Television without Frontiers directive, renamed the Audiovisual Media Services without Frontiers directive, was adopted by the European Parliament in November 2007. The deadline for implementation of the legislation by member states was December 2009, although this was not universally met. In July 2007 the Commission adopted a strategy urging member states and industry to facilitate and accelerate the introduction of mobile television (the transmission of traditional and on-demand audiovisual content to a mobile device), encouraging the use of DVB-H (Digital Video Broadcasting for Handhelds) technology as the single European standard. This strategy was endorsed by the Council in November.

The MEDIA programme was introduced in 1991 to provide financial support to the television and film industry. MEDIA 2007, covering the period 2007–13, was formally adopted by the European Parliament and the Council in November 2007, with a budget of €755m. MEDIA 2007's principal objectives are: to preserve and enhance European cultural diversity and its cinematographic and audiovisual heritage, and to guarantee Europeans' access to it and foster intercultural dialogue; to increase the circulation of European audiovisual works both within and outside the EU; and to reinforce the competitiveness of the European audiovisual sector within the framework of an open and competitive market. In January 2011 the Commission launched a loan guarantee mechanism, the MEDIA Production Guarantee Fund, within the framework of MEDIA 2007; the Fund was to facilitate access to bank credits for European audiovisual companies during 2011–13.

In October 2009 the European Commission published a report on cross-border consumer e-commerce that detailed concerns with ongoing barriers to completing online purchases across EU borders and so to achieving progress towards the creation of a digital single market. Difficulties were, in particular, caused by traders not shipping their products to certain countries or not offering suitable means for cross-border payment; the countries where consumers were least able to buy cross-border products online were Belgium, Bulgaria, Latvia and Romania. The number of broadband subscribers in the EU had reached 120m. by July 2009, equivalent to 24% of the population, compared with 48.4m. subscribers (10.6%) at July 2005.

In March 2010 the European Commission launched the Europe 2020 strategy, which established the Digital Agenda for Europe as one of seven principal initiatives. The Digital Agenda for Europe, which replaced the i2010 initiative, aimed to exploit the full economic and social potential of ICT resources, in particular the internet, in order to promote innovation and economic growth, through the creation of a digital single market. The Commission identified seven principal objectives: the creation of a new single, online market; improved standards and interoperability for ICT; enhanced trust and security for those using the internet; improved access to very fast internet speeds; improved research and innovation; improved digital literacy; and using ICT to address issues of importance to society throughout Europe, such as mitigating rising health costs and digitising the EU's cultural heritage.

TRANSPORT

The establishment of a common transport policy is stipulated in the Treaty of Rome, with the aim of gradually standardizing the national regulations that hinder the free movement of traffic within the Community, such as the varying safety and licensing rules, diverse restrictions on the size of lorries, and frontier-crossing formalities. A White Paper in 1992 set out a common transport policy for the EU. The paper proposed the establishment of trans-European networks (TENs) to improve transport, telecommunications and energy infrastructure throughout the Community, as well as the integration of transport systems and measures to protect the environment and improve safety.

The overall aim of the EU's trans-European transport network (TEN-T) policy, which included so-called intelligent transport systems and services, was to unite the various national networks into a single European network, by eliminating bottlenecks and adding missing links. As a result of the accession of 10 new member states in 2004, a further 16 TEN-T projects, in addition to 14 ongoing projects, were identified as being priorities for the enlarged Union. The Commission estimated that all 30 TEN-T projects would require investment of €225,000m. for completion by 2020, of which around €140,000m. would be required in 2007–13. The total cost of completing the TEN-T was estimated at €600,000m. In July 2005 the Commission nominated six co-ordinators with a four-year mandate to facilitate dialogue between member states on transnational TEN-T projects in an attempt to accelerate their completion; two further co-ordinators were appointed in 2007, and in July 2009 the co-ordinators' mandate was extended for a further four-year term. A Trans-European Transport Network Executive Agency was established in November 2006 to manage priority projects. The first annual ministerial conference on the future of TEN-T, held in October 2009, with participation by delegates from the EU member states, the Balkans, the Western Mediterranean and Africa, and from Norway, Switzerland, Russia and Turkey, determined to strengthen co-operation to facilitate the creation of a sustainable infrastructure network, and outlined common priorities until 2020. In October 2010 the Commission published the first mid-term review of the TEN-T programme. Of the 92 large-scale infrastructure projects under way, 48 were deemed to be making sufficient progress to reach completion in December 2013, as planned; a further 39 projects were given a revised deadline, of 2015, while the remaining five were to be cancelled. It has been estimated that the completion of TEN-T could reduce transport-generated carbon dioxide emissions by 6.3m. metric tons per year by 2020.

The EU has increasingly focused on integrating environmental issues and questions of sustainable development into transport policy. In September 2001 the Commission adopted a White Paper on Transport Policy for 2010, setting out a framework designed to accommodate the forecast strong growth in demand for transport on a sustainable basis. The policy aimed to shift the balance between modes of transport by 2010, by revitalizing railways, promoting maritime and inland waterway transport systems, and by linking up different kinds of transport. The paper proposed an action plan and a strategy designed gradually to break the link between economic and transport growth, with the aim of reducing pressure on the environment and relieving congestion. A communication on an action plan for the deployment of intelligent transport systems in Europe, issued by the Commission in December 2008, promoted the use of information and communications technologies to enable the development of cleaner, more efficient (including energy efficient) and safer transport systems.

In March 2011 the Commission published a new White Paper on Transport Policy for a Single European Transport Area, which aimed to create a competitive and environmentally efficient transport system by 2050. The Commission detailed 40 separate initiatives for the next decade with the objective of building a competitive transport system to increase mobility; removing barriers; and aiding economic growth and employment. The proposals sought to reduce substantially Europe's dependence on imported petroleum and to reduce carbon emissions in the transport sector by 60% by 2050. Principal goals for fulfilment by 2050 included: removing conventionally fuelled cars from cities; ensuring that 40% of aviation fuels used were sustainable, low-carbon fuels; and reducing shipping emissions by at least 40%.

In 1991 directives were adopted by the Council on the compulsory use of safety belts in vehicles weighing less than 3.5 metric tons. Further regulations applying to minibuses and coaches were introduced in 1996. In June 2000 the Commission issued a communication setting out measures to improve the safety and efficiency of road transport and to ensure fair competition. These included road traffic monitoring, the regulation of employed drivers' working time, and regularity of employment conditions. In November 2002 the European Parliament adopted a directive on speed limitation devices for certain categories of motor vehicles, including haulage vehicles and passenger vehicles carrying more than eight passengers. In March 2006 the European Parliament and Council adopted a regulation reducing maximum driving times and increasing obligatory rest periods for professional drivers and a directive increasing the number of checks on lorries; the new legislation entered into force in April 2007.

In 1992 ministers of transport approved an 'open skies' arrangement that would allow any EC airline to operate domestic flights within another member state (with effect from 1 April 1997). In November 2002 the European Court of Justice ruled that bilateral open skies treaties, or Air Services Agreements (ASAs), between countries were illegal if they discriminated against airlines from other member states; the ruling was in response to a case brought by the Commission against eight member states that had concluded such agreements with the USA. In response to the ruling, in June 2003 the Commission and member states identified two ways of resolving the issues: either bilateral negotiations between each member state concerned and its partners, amending each bilateral ASA separately, or single 'horizontal' agreements negotiated by the Commission on behalf of the member states. Each horizontal agreement aims to amend the relevant provisions of all existing bilateral ASAs in the context of a single negotiation with one third country. By May 2006 separate bilateral negotiations had led to changes with 39 partner states, representing the correction of 69 bilateral agreements, while by December 2007 horizontal negotiations had led to changes with 32 partner states. In 2004–05 the Commission initiated infringement proceedings against a number of member states that were persisting in maintaining discriminatory bilateral air agreements with the USA. At the same time the Commission was conducting negotiations with the USA in an attempt to conclude an overall open skies agreement, under which a common aviation area would be created. In November 2005 a preliminary agreement was concluded with the USA, and in early March 2007 EU and US negotiators concluded a draft accord. The EU-US aviation agreement, encompassing some 60% of global air traffic, was approved by EU ministers of transport later in March and formally signed in April.

In June 2006 the European Commission signed a political agreement with the eight new EU member states from Central and South-Eastern Europe, Bulgaria, Romania, Norway, Iceland and the countries of the Western Balkans on the creation of a European Common Aviation Area (ECAA). The establishment of the ECAA involved the harmonization of standards and regulations on safety, security, competition policy, social policy and consumer rights, as well as the establishment of a single market for aviation.

In July 1994, despite EU recommendations for tighter controls on subsidies awarded to airlines, as part of efforts to increase competitiveness within the industry, the Commission approved substantial subsidies that had been granted by the French and Greek governments to their respective national airlines. Subsequently the Commission specified that state assistance could be granted to airlines 'in exceptional, unforeseen circumstances, outside the control of the company'. Following the terrorist attacks perpetrated against targets in the USA in September 2001, and the consequent difficulties suffered by the air transport sector, the EU ruled that a degree of aid or compensation was permissible, but stressed that this must not lead to distortion of competition. In October the Commission proposed to establish common rules in the field of civil aviation security, to strengthen public confidence in air transport following the terrorist attacks on the USA. Issues addressed included securing cockpits, improving air-ground communications and using video cameras in aircraft. Member states also agreed to incorporate into Community law co-operation arrangements on security measures. These measures covered control of access to sensitive areas of airports and aircraft, control of passengers and hand luggage, control and monitoring of hold luggage, and training of ground staff. In October 2006 the Commission adopted a regulation restricting the liquids that air passengers were allowed to carry beyond certain screening points at airports and onto aircraft. The new regulation, introduced in response to the threat posed to civil aviation security by home-made liquid explosives, was to be applied to all flights departing from member states' airports.

In July 2002 the European Parliament adopted a regulation creating a European Aviation Safety Agency (EASA). The EASA (which officially opened its permanent seat in Köln, Germany, in December 2004) was to cover all aircraft registered in member states, unless agreed otherwise. The Commission has also formulated ground rules for inquiries into civil air incidents and has issued proposals for assessing the safety of aircraft registered outside the EU. In April 2008 a regulation entered into force that extended the responsibilities of the EASA, particularly regarding control over pilots' licences and the regulation of airlines based in third countries operating in the EU. In December 2005 EU ministers of transport approved a regulation introducing a Europe-wide 'blacklist' of unsafe airlines and granting passengers the right to advance information about the identity of the air carrier operating their flight.

In December 1999 the Commission presented a communication on streamlining air traffic management (ATM) to create a Single European Sky (SES), of which the overall aim was to restructure the EU's airspace on the basis of traffic, rather than national frontiers. In December 2002 EU ministers of transport agreed on a package of measures under which the separate European ATM providers would be regulated as a single entity, and EU airspace over 28,500 ft (approximately 8,690 m) would be under unified control. A first package of SES legislation (SES I), bringing ATM under the common transport policy, was adopted by the European Parliament and Council in April 2004. In November 2005 the European Commission launched SESAR, a Single European Sky industrial and technological programme to develop a new ATM system. The project consisted of three phases: the definition phase (2005–07), costing €60m. (co-funded by the Commission and the European Organisation for the Safety of Air Navigation—EUROCONTROL); the development phase (2008–13), estimated to cost around €300m. per year (co-funded by the Commission, EUROCONTROL and the industry); and the deployment phase (2014–20), to be financed by the industry. A regulation creating the SESAR Joint Undertaking, a public-private entity managing the development stage of the project, was formally approved by the Council and Parliament in February 2007. Meanwhile, in April 2006 a directive was adopted on the introduction of a Community air traffic controller licence, with the aim of raising safety standards and improving the operation of the ATM system. In March 2009 the Council adopted a decision endorsing a new SESAR ATM Master Plan as the initial version of a planned European ATM Master Plan. Also during that month the European Parliament approved a second package of SES legislation (SES II), incorporating improvements aimed at addressing environmental challenges and fuel cost efficiency.

In 1986 progress was made towards the establishment of a common maritime transport policy, with the adoption of regulations on unfair pricing practices, safeguard of access to cargoes, application of competition rules and the eventual elimination of unilateral cargo reservation and discriminatory cargo-sharing arrangements. In December 1990 the Council approved, in principle, the freedom for shipping companies to provide maritime transport anywhere within the Community. Cabotage by sea began to be introduced from January 1993 and was virtually complete by January 1999. Cabotage was also introduced in the inland waterways transport sector in 1993. By January 2000 the inland waterways market had been liberalized, although obstacles to the functioning of the single market subsequently persisted, including differing technical regulations among member states. The 2001 White Paper on European Transport Policy proposed the development of Motorways of the Sea, which aimed to shift a proportion of freight traffic from the road system to short sea shipping, or to a combination of short sea shipping and other modes of transport in which road journeys were minimized. In March 2005 the European Commission launched a consultation process on a new integrated EU maritime policy aimed at developing the potential of the maritime economy in an environmentally sustainable manner. The commissioners responsible for sea-related policies were charged with preparing a consultation paper addressing all economic and recreational maritime activities, such as shipping, fishing, oil and gas extraction, use of wind and tidal power, shipbuilding, tourism and marine research. The resultant Green Paper was adopted by the Commission in June 2006. Following the conclusion of a consultation process based on the document, in October 2007 the Commission presented a communication on its vision for the integrated maritime policy, which was endorsed by the Council in December. An accompanying action plan included initiatives such as a European strategy for marine research; national integrated maritime policies; an integrated network for maritime surveillance; a European marine observation and data network; and a strategy to mitigate the effects of climate change on coastal regions.

In March 2000 the Commission adopted a communication on the safety of the seaborne oil trade. It proposed the introduction of a first package of short-term measures to strengthen controls, including the right to refuse access to substandard ships, more stringent inspections and a generalization of the ban on single-hull oil tankers. In

May the Commission adopted a proposal to harmonize procedures between bulk carriers and terminals, in order to reduce the risk of accidents caused by incorrect loading and unloading. In the same month the Commission signed a memorandum of understanding (MOU) with several countries on the establishment of the Equasis database, intended to provide information on the safety and quality of ships. In December the Commission set out a second package of safety measures, broad agreement was reached on the first package, and the EU agreed to accelerate the gradual introduction of double-hull tankers (single-hull tankers were being phased out from the end of 2010). In June 2002 the European Parliament established by regulation the European Maritime Safety Agency (the permanent seat of which was to be located in Lisbon, Portugal); its tasks were to include preparing legislation in the field of maritime safety, co-ordination of investigations following accidents at sea, assisting member states in implementing maritime safety measures, and providing assistance to candidate countries. In March 2004 the Agency was given additional responsibility for combating pollution caused by ships. In November 2005 the Commission proposed a third package of maritime safety measures, including a requirement that member states ensure that ships flying their flags comply with international standards; an improvement in the quality and effectiveness of ship inspections, with increased targeting of vessels deemed to pose the greatest risk and less frequent inspections of high-quality ships; and an obligation that member states designate an independent authority responsible for the prior identification of places of refuge for ships in distress. The Commission noted that the EU had become a major maritime power, accounting for some 25% of the world's fleet.

In April 1998 the Commission published a report on railway policy, with the aim of achieving greater harmonization, the regulation of state subsidies and the progressive liberalization of the rail-freight market. In October 1999 EU ministers of transport concluded an agreement that was regarded as a precursor to the full liberalization and revitalization of the rail-freight market. Rail transport's share of the total freight market had declined substantially since the 1970s, but it was widely recognized that, in terms of environmental protection and safety, transport of freight by rail was greatly preferable to road haulage. The agreement provided for the extension of access to a planned core Trans-European Rail Freight Network (TERFN, covering some 50,000 km), with a charging system designed to ensure optimum competitiveness. During 2000–04 the EU adopted three 'railway packages', which dealt with the progressive deregulation of the rail market. However, a number of EU member states vehemently opposed granting full access to their national railway networks. Other measures incorporated in the packages included developing a common approach to rail safety; upholding principles of interoperability; and setting up a European Railway Agency (ERA). The ERA was established by a regulation of the European Parliament in April 2004. The main aim of the Agency, the permanent seat of which was inaugurated in Lille/Valenciennes, France, in June 2005, was to reinforce the safety and interoperability of railways in the EU. In March 2005 the European Commission and representatives of the rail industry signed an MOU on the deployment of a European Rail Traffic Management System (ERTMS) on a major part of the European network. The ERTMS, a single European rail signalling system, was intended to enhance safety and reduce infrastructure costs in the longer term; existing national systems were to be gradually withdrawn within 10–12 years. In December 2006 the Commission presented a communication proposing measures to remove technical and operational barriers to international rail activities, with the aim of making the rail industry more competitive, particularly in relation to road and air transport; the simplification of procedures for the approval of locomotives for operational service across the EU; and the extension of the powers of the ERA.

The Marco Polo II programme, which was being implemented during 2007–13 (having succeeded the original Marco Polo programme, covering 2003–06, which, in turn, had replaced an earlier PACT—pilot action for combined transport—scheme), was allocated a budget of €400m. Marco Polo II, the scope of which extended to countries bordering the EU, aimed to reduce road congestion by increasing the utilization of sea, rail and inland waterways routes for freight traffic, and to improve the environmental performance of the intermodal network within the EU, thereby contributing to an efficient and sustainable transport system.

A directive adopted in April 2004 aimed to establish an electronic toll collection system across the EU that would apply to roads, tunnels, bridges, ferries and urban congestion-charging schemes. Notably, all new electronic toll systems brought into service from 1 January 2007 were required to use at least one of three prescribed existing technologies.

JUSTICE AND HOME AFFAIRS

Under the Treaty on European Union, EU member states undertook to co-operate in the areas of justice and home affairs, particularly in relation to the free movement of people between member states. Issues of common interest were defined as asylum policy; border controls; immigration; drug addiction; fraud; judicial co-operation in civil and criminal matters; customs co-operation; and police co-operation for the purposes of combating terrorism, drugs-trafficking and other serious forms of international crime. In view of the sensitivity of many of the issues involved in this sphere, the EU affords great weight to the positions and opinions of individual states. There tends to be a greater degree of flexibility than in other areas, and requirements are frequently less stringent.

The EU's draft Charter of Fundamental Rights, which was signed in December 2000, outlines the rights and freedoms recognized by the EU. It includes civil, political, economic and social rights, with each based on a previous charter, convention, treaty or jurisprudence. The charter may be used to challenge decisions taken by the Community institutions and by member states when implementing EU law. A reference to the charter, making it legally binding, was included in the Treaty of Lisbon amending the Treaty on European Union and the Treaty establishing the European Community (previously known as the Reform Treaty), which was signed in December 2007 and entered into force in December 2009. A protocol to the Treaty of Lisbon limited the application of the charter in the United Kingdom and Poland to rights recognized by national legislation in those countries. In June 2005 the European Commission adopted a proposal for a regulation establishing an EU Agency for Fundamental Rights. The regulation was adopted in its final form in February 2007, allowing the establishment of the Agency, as the successor to the European Monitoring Centre on Racism and Xenophobia, on 1 March. In April the specific programme 'Fundamental Rights and Citizenship' was established under the framework programme 'Fundamental Rights and Justice'. With a budget of €94m. for 2007–13, the Programme aimed to promote the development of a European society based on respect for fundamental rights; to strengthen civil society organizations and to encourage a dialogue with them regarding fundamental rights; to combat racism, xenophobia and anti-Semitism; and to improve contacts between legal, judicial and administrative authorities and the legal professions.

In July 2010 the Directorate-General for Justice, Freedom and Security was divided into the Directorate-General for Justice and the Directorate-General for Home Affairs. The new Directorate-General for Justice comprises three directorates: Civil Justice; Criminal Justice; and Fundamental Rights and Citizenship.

In December 2009 the European Council adopted the Stockholm Programme, which aimed to provide a framework in 2010–14 for the creation of an 'open and secure Europe serving and protecting its citizens'. The Programme's objectives were to promote European citizenship and fundamental rights; to achieve a Europe of law and justice; to develop an internal EU security strategy; to promote, through integrated border management and visa policies, access to Europe; to develop a forward-looking and comprehensive European migration and asylum policy; and to develop the external dimension of EU freedom, security and justice policy. Cyber-security (developing a single system for the protection of personal data), combating terrorism and organized crime, and border control were all to be addressed by the new agenda. Ensuring equal rights for migrants, finer monitoring of migration patterns and labour trends, and closer co-operation with non-EU countries on managing migration flows were areas of focus.

A European Police Office (Europol), facilitating the exchange of information between police forces, operates from The Hague, Netherlands. A special Europol unit dealing with the trafficking of illicit drugs and nuclear and radioactive materials began work in 1994. Europol's mandate has been extended to cover illegal immigrants, stolen vehicles, paedophilia and terrorist activities, money-laundering and counterfeiting of the euro and other means of payment. From 1 January 2010 Europol became a full EU agency, with a stronger mandate and enhanced capability for combating serious international crime and terrorism.

The EU convention on extradition, signed by ministers of justice in September 1996 prior to ratification by national governments, simplified and accelerated procedures in this area, reduced the number of cases where extradition could be refused, and made it easier to extradite members of criminal organizations. In November 1997 the Commission proposed an extension to European law to allow civil and commercial judgments made in the courts of member states to be enforced throughout the whole of the EU. A regulation on the mutual recognition and enforcement of such judgments came into force in March 2001 across the EU, with the exception of Denmark. In 2000 a convention on mutual assistance in criminal matters (such as criminal hearings by video and telephone conference and cross-border investigations) was adopted.

The Grotius-Civil programme of incentives and exchanges for legal practitioners was established in 1996. It was designed to aid judicial co-operation between member states by improving reciprocal knowledge of legal and judicial systems. The successor programme, Grotius II, focused on general and criminal law. In February 2002 the EU established a 'Eurojust' unit, composed of prosecutors, magistrates and police officers from member states, to help co-ordinate prosecutions and support investigations into incidences of serious organized crime. A European Police College (CEPOL) has also been created, initially consisting of a network of existing national training institutes; in December 2003, however, the European Council decided that a permanent CEPOL institution would be established at Bramshill in the United Kingdom. CEPOL was formally established as an EU agency in 2005.

In March 2000 an action programme to develop a European strategy for the prevention and control of organized crime was adopted. A European crime prevention network was formally established in May 2001. There are also agreements within the EU on co-operation between financial intelligence units and between police forces for the purposes of combating child pornography. In addition, the EU has a common strategy designed to help Russia combat organized crime. The EU ran the FALCONE programme—a series of incentives, training opportunities and exchanges for those responsible for the fight against organized crime in individual member states. The STOP (sexual treatment of persons) programme operated a similar system for those responsible for combating trade in humans and the sexual exploitation of children. Several programmes, including Grotius II, STOP and FALCONE, were merged into a single framework programme, called AGIS, in January 2003. In 2006 AGIS, which covered police and judicial co-operation in criminal matters, was terminated and succeeded by new programmes, adopted by the Council in February 2007 and covering the period 2007–13, with a focus on internal security (with an overall budget of €745m.) and criminal justice (with an overall budget of some €196m.).

In September 2001 member states harmonized their definitions of human trafficking and set common minimum prison sentences. In January 2005 the European Commission adopted a proposal for a framework decision on the fight against organized crime, in which it sought to harmonize the definition of what constitutes a criminal organization. A White Paper on exchanges of information on criminal convictions in the EU was also adopted, proposing, notably, that a computerized mechanism be established to allow the criminal record offices of the member states to share information. In June, in a communication on developing a 'strategic concept' on tackling organized crime, the Commission recommended the development of common methodologies among national and EU bodies involved in combating organized crime, as well as an EU crime statistics system.

The European Monitoring Centre for Drugs and Drug Addiction (EMCDDA) is based in Lisbon, Portugal. In 2000 Norway became the first non-EU state to be admitted to EMCDDA. The EU is working with other third countries to tackle issues of drugs demand and supply. In December 2004 the European Council endorsed an EU strategy on drugs (2005–12), which set out the framework, objectives and priorities for two consecutive four-year action plans. A drug prevention and information programme was adopted in September 2007. With a budget of €21m. for 2007–13, the programme's general objectives were to prevent and reduce drugs use and dependence; to enhance information on the effects of drugs use; and to support the implementation of the EU drugs strategy and action plans.

Measures related to the abolition of customs formalities at intra-community frontiers were completed by mid-1991, and entered into force in January 1993. In June 1990 Belgium, France, Germany, Luxembourg and the Netherlands, meeting in Schengen, Luxembourg, signed a convention to implement an earlier agreement (concluded in 1985 at the same location), abolishing frontier controls on the free movement of persons from 1993. Delay in the establishment of the Schengen Information System (SIS), providing a computer network on suspect persons or cargo for use by the police forces of signatory states, resulted in the postponement of the implementation of the new agreement. Seven countries (Belgium, France, Germany, Luxembourg, the Netherlands, Portugal and Spain) agreed to implement the agreement with effect from March 1995. Frontier controls at airports on those travelling between the seven countries were dismantled during a three-month transition period, which ended on 1 July 1995 (although France retained all of its land-border controls until March 1996, when border controls with Spain and Germany were lifted, although controls on borders with the Benelux countries were retained owing to fear over the transportation of illicit drugs). Italy joined the 'Schengen Group' in October 1997, and Austria in December. Border controls for both countries were removed in 1998. Denmark, Finland and Sweden (and non-EU members Norway and Iceland) were admitted as observers of the accord from 1 May 1996, and all five countries joined the Schengen Group in March 2001. Meanwhile, in March 1999 signatories of the Schengen accords on visa-free border crossings began to waive visa requirements with Estonia, Latvia and Lithuania. The Treaty of Amsterdam, which came into effect on 1 May, incorporated the so-called Schengen *acquis* (comprising the 1985 agreement, 1990 convention and additional accession protocols and executive decisions), in order to integrate it into the framework of the EU. The Treaty permitted the United Kingdom and Ireland to maintain permanent jurisdiction over their borders and rules of asylum and immigration. Countries acceding to the EU after 2000 were automatically to adhere to the Schengen arrangements. In February 2002 the Council approved Ireland's participation in some of the provisions of the Schengen *acquis*.

Following the enlargement of the EU in May 2004, border controls between the 15 existing members and the 10 new members remained in force until 2007. Although the 10 new states technically belonged to the Schengen agreement, the Commission decided that the SIS computer network was not large enough to incorporate data from 10 more countries. Work on a new computerized information system, SIS II, began in 2002 but suffered delays and is not expected to be completed until 2013. Pending deployment of SIS II, a modified version of SIS, named SISone4ALL, was introduced to allow the extension of the Schengen area to proceed. In December 2007 the provisions of the Schengen agreement were applied to the land and sea borders of nine of the 10 countries that joined the EU in 2004, with controls at airports removed, accordingly, in March 2008. The inclusion of Cyprus in the Schengen area was postponed. The admission of Bulgaria and Romania (which were both subject to ongoing concerns regarding their progress in combating corruption and organized crime) to the Schengen area was vetoed in both December 2010 and September 2011. Switzerland, a non-EU member, joined the Schengen area in December 2008, and Liechtenstein was expected to join in the future.

In November 2000 the Commission adopted a communication outlining a common asylum procedure and providing for a uniform status, valid throughout the EU, for persons granted asylum. In March 2001 a common list of countries whose citizens required visas to enter the EU was adopted. The EU has also developed the so-called Eurodac database for co-ordinating information on the movements of asylum seekers; Eurodac allows for the comparison of fingerprints of refugees. In April 2004 the Council adopted a directive establishing a common European definition of a refugee, aimed at curtailing movement from state to state until one is reached that is prepared to give protection. In February 2002 the European Council adopted a comprehensive plan to combat illegal immigration. Priority areas included visa policy, readmission and repatriation policies, the monitoring of borders, the role of Europol and penalties. A European Agency for the Management of Operational Co-operation at the External Borders of the European Union (FRONTEX) was established by a regulation of the European Parliament in October 2004, the primary responsibility of which was the creation of an integrated border management system. The Agency commenced operations on 1 May 2005, with its seat at Warsaw, Poland. The role of FRONTEX was to be enhanced during 2010–14, under the Stockholm Programme. In June 2004 the Council adopted a decision concerning the development of a system for the exchange of visa data between member states, the Visa Information System (VIS). The VIS was intended to enhance the internal security of member states and contribute to the fight against illegal immigration. In September 2005 the Commission presented a package of measures on asylum and immigration. The proposals included the application of common standards to the return of illegal immigrants, the adoption of a more coherent approach to the integration of migrants, the encouragement of migrants to contribute to the development of their home countries, and the introduction of Regional Protection Programmes to assist refugees remaining in their regions of origin and their host countries. In December, in a move towards the creation of a common European asylum system, the Justice and Home Affairs Council adopted a directive on asylum procedures, setting minimum standards for granting and withdrawing refugee status, as well as an action plan on preventing human trafficking. A new framework programme entitled 'Solidarity and Management of Migration Flows' was adopted in December 2006 with the aim of improving management of migratory flows at EU level. Allocated an overall budget of €4,020m. for 2007–13, the programme was divided into four specific policy areas, each with its own financial instrument: the control and surveillance of external borders (External Borders Fund, €1,820m.); the return of third country nationals residing illegally in the EU (European Return Fund, €676m.); the integration of legally resident third country nationals (European Integration Fund, €825m.); and asylum (European Refugee Fund—first established in 2000—€699m.). In June 2008 the Commission adopted a communication on principles, actions and tools relating to a common immigration policy for Europe, and a policy plan on asylum. The latter provided the framework for the second phase of the creation of the common European asylum system. In December the European Parliament and Council of the EU adopted a directive on determining common standards and procedures for returning illegally staying third country nationals from member states, and, in May 2009, the Council adopted a directive on the enforcement of sanctions and measures against employers engaging illegal immigrants. It was estimated at that time that up to 8m. illegal immigrants were residing in the EU. A new European Migration Network, fully established following a directive of the Council adopted in May 2008, having been launched in 2003 as a pilot project, aims to provide current and comparable information on migration and asylum. In November 2011 the EU Immigration Portal was launched, to provide practical information for foreign nationals interested in moving to the EU, or seeking to move between EU countries. In December the Single Permit Directive was adopted, establishing rights for non-EU workers residing lawfully in an EU member state.

EDUCATION, TRAINING AND CULTURE

The Treaty of Rome, although not covering education directly, gave the Community the role of establishing general principles for implementing a common vocational training policy. The Treaty on European Union urged greater co-operation on education policy, including encouraging exchanges and mobility for students and teachers, distance learning and the development of European studies. The Bologna Process was launched in 1999 with the aim of establishing a European Higher Education Area, including education networks and student exchanges. In May 2007 the EU and the Council of Europe signed a memorandum of understanding confirming mutual co-operation in the promotion of democratic citizenship and human rights education and their joint commitment to the Bologna Process. In November 2007 the Council adopted a resolution on modernising universities to aid Europe's competitiveness in the global knowledge economy. In April 2009 ministers responsible for higher education in the member countries of the Bologna Process adopted the priorities for the European Higher Education Area until 2020, with an emphasis on the importance of lifelong learning, expanding access to higher education, and mobility. In March 2010 the Bologna Process ministers for higher education adopted the Budapest-Vienna Declaration officially launching the European Higher Education Area. Meanwhile, in May 2009 the Council had adopted Education and Training 2020 (ET 2020), a strategic framework for European co-operation in education and training, which identified four principal objectives: to facilitate lifelong learning and mobility; to improve the quality of education and training; to promote equality, social cohesion and citizenship; and to help develop creativity and innovation in education and training. ET 2020 also provided for support for the Bologna intergovernmental process, which focuses on higher education.

The postgraduate European University Institute (EUI) was founded in Florence, Italy, in 1972, with departments of history and civilization, economics, law, and political and social sciences. The EUI is also the depository for the historical archives of the EC institutions. Approximately 140 new research students enrol at the Institute each year. An Academy of European Law was founded within the EUI in 1990, and in 1992 the Robert Schuman Centre for Advanced Studies was established to develop inter-disciplinary and comparative postdoctoral research. The Jean Monnet programme, which supports institutions and activities in the field of European integration, finances the establishment of Jean Monnet chairs at universities throughout the world; the programme targets disciplines in which EU developments are an increasingly important part of the subject studied—e.g. European law, European economic and political integration, and the history of the European construction process. The establishment of a network of Jean Monnet Centres of Excellence was approved in 1998; the network was extended beyond Europe in 2001, and by 2012 it was active in 72 countries world-wide.

The EU's Lifelong Learning Programme, an integrated action programme covering 2007–13, and with an overall budget of €6,970m., incorporated as sub-programmes four existing educational and training initiatives—Comenius (for schools), Erasmus (for higher education), Grundtvig (for adult education) and the Leonardo da Vinci programme (see below)—as well as the Jean Monnet programme, and introduced a new Transversal programme to facilitate activities involving more than one area of education, such as language learning and innovation in information and communication technologies. An educational information network, Eurydice, which began operations in 1980, provides data on and analyses of European national education systems and policies. Eurydice is co-ordinated by an Education, Audiovisual and Culture Executive Agency in Brussels, Belgium, and comprises national units based in the 33 Lifelong Learning programme countries.

The Erasmus educational exchange programme, which was launched in 1987, enables students throughout Europe to travel to other EU countries to study and work as part of their degree programme. The first Erasmus Mundus programme ran from 2004–08 as a global mobility programme, promoting inter-cultural co-operation, and the EU as a centre of academic excellence, by enabling highly qualified students and academics living outside the EU to pursue Masters or doctorate programmes at EU universities. In October 2008 the European Parliament approved a second Erasmus Mundus programme for 2009–13, with an estimated budget of €950m.

The EU's Youth in Action programme, with a total budget of €885m., covers the period 2007–13, replacing the previous Youth programme for 2000–06. Objectives of Youth in Action include: fostering a sense of citizenship, solidarity and mutual understanding in young people; enhancing the quality of support systems for youth activities; and promoting European co-operation in youth policy. In March 2005 the Council adopted a European Pact for Youth, which focused on improving the education, training, mobility, vocational integration and social inclusion of young Europeans, while facilitating the reconciliation of family life and working life.

In November 2011 the European Commission proposed a new EU programme for education, training, youth and sport, Erasmus for All, which was intended to replace both the Lifelong Learning and the Youth in Action programmes. The Commission intended to introduce the new programme in 2014, with a budget of €19,000m. The proposal required approval by the European Council and the European Parliament.

Covering 2007–13, the fourth phase of the Trans-European Mobility Scheme for University Studies (TEMPUS, the first phase of which was launched in 1990) aims to support the modernization of higher education, and to create an area of co-operation between institutions in EU member countries and partner countries surrounding the EU. TEMPUS IV covers 27 partner countries in Central and Eastern Europe, Central Asia, North Africa and the Middle East. The European Training Foundation (ETF), which was established in Turin, Italy, in 1995, and the mandate of which was revised in December 2008, aims to support developing and transition countries in the promotion of human capital development, i.e. advancing skills and competences through the improvement of vocational education and training systems.

The European Centre for the Development of Vocational Training (Centre Européen pour le Développement de la Formation Professionnelle—CEDEFOP) was established in Berlin, Germany, in 1975. The centre relocated to Thessaloníki, Greece, in 1995. Much of CEDEFOP's recent work has focused on the employment problems encountered by women, especially those who wish to return to work after a long absence, on encouraging the participation of older workers in vocational training, and on addressing the needs of low-skilled people. The Leonardo da Vinci programme was introduced in 1994 to help European citizens to enhance their skills and to improve the quality and accessibility of vocational training. The programme supports lifelong learning policies and promotes transnational projects in an effort to increase mobility and foster innovation in European vocational education and training. The EUROPASS programme, which was officially launched in February 2005 and which brought into a single framework several existing tools for the transparency of diplomas, certificates and competences, was aimed at promoting both occupational mobility, between countries as well as across sectors, and mobility for learning purposes. In September 2006 the Commission proposed the establishment of a European qualifications framework (EQF), based on eight reference levels of qualifications, with the aim of further promoting mobility and lifelong learning. Member states were required to relate their own qualifications systems to the EQF by 2010, and by 2012 every new qualification issued in the EU was to have a reference to the appropriate EQF level. The EQF was formally adopted in April 2008.

The EU's Culture 2007 programme, covering the period 2007–13, and with a total budget of some €400m., replaced a previous Culture 2000 agenda, and focused on three priorities: the mobility of those working in the cultural sector; the transnational circulation of works of art; and intercultural dialogue. In November 2007 the Council endorsed the first European strategy for culture policy, which had three main objectives: the promotion of cultural diversity and intercultural dialogue; the promotion of culture as a catalyst for creativity; and the promotion of culture as a vital element in the EU's international relations. The EU's Culture programme supports several prizes, which are awarded in recognition of excellence in architecture, cultural heritage, literature and music. In November 2008 the Europeana project was launched, funded by the European Commission, with the aim of creating an online digital library to make Europe's cultural heritage accessible to the public (www.europeana.net). By July 2010 the collection comprised some 10m. items.

The European City of Culture initiative was launched in 1985 (and renamed the European Capital of Culture initiative in 1999). Member states nominate one or more cities in turn, according to an agreed chronological order. The capitals of culture are then formally selected by the Council on the recommendation of the Commission, taking into account the view of a selection panel. Since 2009 there have been two annual capitals of culture from member states, including one from the new, post-May 2004, membership, plus a maximum of one city from European non-member countries. Guimarães (Portugal) and Maribor (Slovenia) were selected as capitals for culture for 2012; Marseille (France) and Košice (Slovakia) for 2013; and Umeå (Sweden) and Rīga (Latvia) for 2014.

EMPLOYMENT, SOCIAL AFFAIRS AND INCLUSION

The Single European Act, which entered into force in 1987, added to the original Treaty of Rome articles that emphasized the need for 'economic and social cohesion' in the Community, i.e. the reduction of disparities between the various regions. This was to be achieved principally through the existing 'structural funds'—the European

Regional Development Fund, the European Social Fund, and the Guidance Section of the European Agricultural Guidance and Guarantee Fund, which was replaced by the European Fund for Agricultural Development in 2007. In 1988 the Council declared that Community operations through the structural funds, the European Investment Bank and other financial instruments should have five priority objectives: (i) promoting the development and structural adjustment of the less-developed regions (where gross domestic product per head was less than 75% of the Community average); (ii) converting the regions, frontier regions or parts of regions seriously affected by industrial decline; (iii) combating long-term unemployment among people above the age of 25; (iv) providing employment for young people (under the age of 25); and (v) with a view to the reform of the common agricultural policy (CAP), speeding up the adjustment of agricultural structures and promoting the development of rural areas.

In 1989 the Commission proposed a Charter of Fundamental Social Rights of Workers (later known as the Social Charter), covering freedom of movement, fair remuneration, improvement of working conditions, the right to social security, freedom of association and collective wage agreements, the development of participation by workers in management, and sexual equality. The Charter was approved (with some modifications) by the heads of government of all Community member states, except the United Kingdom, in December. On the insistence of the United Kingdom, the chapter on social affairs of the Treaty on European Union, negotiated in December 1991, was omitted from the Treaty to form a separate protocol (the Community Charter of Fundamental Social Rights for Workers, or so-called Social Charter, complete with an opt-out arrangement for the United Kingdom). In September 1994 ministers adopted the first directive to be approved under the Social Charter, concerning the establishment of mandatory works councils in multinational companies; this came into force in September 1996. In April 1996 the Commission proposed that part-time, fixed-term and temporary employees should receive comparable treatment to permanent, full-time employees. A directive ensuring equal treatment for part-time employees was adopted by the Council in December 1997. A directive on parental leave, the second directive to be adopted under the Social Charter, provided for a statutory minimum of three months' unpaid leave to allow parents to care for young children, and was adopted in June 1996. In May 1997 the new Government of the United Kingdom approved the Social Charter, which was to be incorporated into the Treaty of Amsterdam. The Treaty, which entered into force in May 1999, consequently removed the opt-out clause and incorporated the Social Chapter in the revised Treaty of Rome. In December the Council adopted amendments extending the two directives adopted under the Charter to include the United Kingdom.

The Treaty of Amsterdam authorized the European Council to take action against all types of discrimination. Several directives and programmes on gender equality and equal opportunities have been approved and the Commission has initiated legal proceedings against a number of member states before the European Court of Justice for infringements. In December 2006 the Council and Parliament approved the establishment of a European Institute for Gender Equality, which was founded in 2007; initially temporarily located in Brussels, Belgium, it is now based in Vilnius, Lithuania. In June 2000 the Council adopted a directive implementing the principle of equal treatment regardless of racial or ethnic origin in employment, education, social security, health care and access to goods and services. This was followed in November by a directive establishing a framework for equal treatment regardless of religion or belief, disability, age or sexual orientation. A joint seminar was held in February 2004, in Brussels, by the Commission and the European Jewish Congress, to discuss Jewish community concerns that anti-Semitism was increasing in Europe. In June 2005 the Commission presented a framework strategy on non-discrimination and equal opportunities, aimed at ensuring the full implementation and enforcement by member states of anti-discrimination legislation. In March 2007 the EU Agency for Fundamental Rights (FRA), based in Vienna, replaced the former European Monitoring Centre on Racism and Xenophobia (EUMC). The FRA, which immediately assumed the mandate of the EUMC regarding racism and xenophobia, was gradually to develop knowledge, expertise and work programmes in respect of other fundamental rights. The Agency maintains an information network (the European Information Network on Racism and Xenophobia—RAXEN) and a database.

Numerous directives on health and safety in the workplace have been adopted by the Community. The Major Accident Hazards Bureau (MAHB), which was established in 1996 and is based at the Joint Research Centre in Ispra, Italy, helps to prevent and to mitigate industrial accidents in the EU. To this end, MAHB maintains a Major Accident Reporting System database and a Community Documentation Centre on Industrial Risk. There is also a European Agency for Health and Safety at Work, which was established in 1995 in Bilbao, Spain. The Agency has a health and safety information network composed of 'focal points' in each member state, in the candidate countries and in the four European Free Trade Association (EFTA) states. In February 2007 the Commission adopted a new five-year strategy for health and safety at work, which aimed to reduce work-related illness and accidents by 25% by 2012.

In June 1993 the Working Time Directive (WTD) was approved, restricting the working week to a maximum duration of 48 hours, except where overtime arrangements are agreed with trade unions. The WTD also prescribed minimum rest periods and a minimum of four weeks' paid holiday a year. However, certain categories of employee were exempt from the maximum 48-hour week rule, including those in the transport sector, those employed in offshore oil extraction, fishermen and junior hospital doctors. In April 2000 agreement was reached on gradually extending some or all of the rights of the WTD to cover most excluded workers. A Road Transport Directive, which applies to mobile workers who participate in road transport activities covered by EU drivers' hours rules, was adopted in March 2002 and took effect in March 2005. In January 2004 the Commission launched a review of the WTD following an increase in the use of its opt-out clause by a number of member states. In May 2005, however, in a first reading, the European Parliament voted in favour of proposals to phase out the opt-out clause (except for the police, army and emergency services, and chief executive officers and senior managers) and to count all on-call time as working time, although members agreed with the Commission regarding the use of a one-year reference period for calculating the average working week. In December 2008 the European Parliament voted to phase out the WTD opt-out clause within three years of the entry into force of a revised directive; however, negotiations on WTD reform subsequently broke down. A European Commission report published in December 2010 indicated that five member states (Bulgaria, Cyprus, Estonia, Malta and the United Kingdom) permitted the opt-out to be used, without restriction on sector, while 11 further member states allowed, or were introducing, limited use of the opt-out clause. In contrast, four member states made use of the opt-out clause in 2003.

The European Foundation for the Improvement of Living and Working Conditions (Eurofound), which was established in Dublin, Ireland, in 1975, undertakes four-year research and development programmes in the fields of employment, sustainable development, equal opportunities, social cohesion, health and well-being, and participation. Prior to the EU's enlargement in May 2004, Eurofound made available wide-ranging new data and analysis on living and working conditions in the existing member states and in the accession and candidate states. The Foundation utilizes monitoring tools including the European Industrial Relations Observatory (EIRO), the European Working Conditions Observatory (EWCO), and the European Monitoring Centre on Change (EMCC). Every four years Eurofound conducts surveys on Quality of Life in Europe; and surveys are also carried out on European Working Conditions; and on European companies.

An employment body, European Employment Services (EURES), launched in 1994, maintains a web portal and operates as a network of more than 750 specialist advisers across Europe, who (with the co-operation of national public employment services, trade unions, employers' organizations, local authorities, etc., and with access to a detailed database) provide the three basic EURES services of information, guidance and placement to both job seekers and employers interested in the European job market. EURES has a particularly effective role to play in cross-border regions where there are significant degrees of cross-border commuting by employees. EURES, which covers the countries of the European Economic Area (EEA) and Switzerland, also provides a public database of employment vacancies and a database through which job seekers can make their curricula vitae available to a wide range of employers.

Under the European employment strategy, initiated in 1997 and incorporated in the Treaty of Amsterdam, an Employment Committee was established in 2000 to oversee the co-ordination of the employment strategies of the member states and an employment package was to be presented (as a joint effort by the Council of the European Union and the Commission) each year. The package contains reports on member states' performances, individual recommendations and policy guidelines for the future. In December 2007 EU ministers responsible for employment and social affairs adopted a set of common principles of 'flexicurity' (a combination of flexibility and security) that member states should follow when developing labour market policies. This new approach was based on four components: effective labour market policies; flexible and reliable contractual arrangements; comprehensive lifelong learning strategies; and modern and adequate social protection systems. At an EU summit in Brussels at the end of January 2012 the European Council pledged to increase efforts to provide jobs for young people, in particular by identifying EU member states with the highest rates of unemployment among young people, and diverting funds to facilitate the provision of training or access to employment, and establish apprenticeship schemes. The Council also sought the completion of the single market, and the promotion of cross-border labour mobility; and the provision of assistance to small and medium-sized enterprises (SMEs). The overall EU unemployment rate was

9.9% in December 2011, while the rate of employment in the euro area was 10.4%.

All 15 of the longer-standing members of the EU (EU-15), except the United Kingdom, Ireland and Sweden, had planned to impose at least a two-year period of restriction on immigrants from the eight formerly communist new member states (EU-8—the Czech Republic, Estonia, Hungary, Latvia, Lithuania, Poland, Slovenia and Slovakia) after their accession to the EU in May 2004, to prevent their labour markets being saturated with inexpensive labour. Workers from the new member states Malta and Cyprus were allowed into existing EU countries without any restrictions. All EU-15 states were required to apply EU legislation on free movement and open their labour markets to the EU-8 in 2011, and to Bulgaria and Romania by 2014. By early 2012 work restrictions on citizens of Bulgaria and Romania remained in place in Austria, France, Germany, Ireland, Holland, Luxembourg, Malta and the United Kingdom. A European Commission report published in 2009 estimated that the number of EU-8 nationals residing in EU-15 countries had risen from around 900,000 before enlargement to some 1.9m. in 2007, with Ireland and the United Kingdom as the main destination for new workers; meanwhile, over the same period, the number of Bulgarian and Romanian workers resident in EU-15 states was estimated to have increased from about 700,000 to nearly 1.9m., with Italy and Spain as the principal destination countries.

A European Social Protection Committee was established in June 2000. In addition, the EU administers MISSOC—the Mutual Information System on Social Protection in the EU member states and the EEA. Switzerland is also included in MISSOC. In February 2005 the European Commission launched its Social Agenda (2005–10) for modernizing the EU's social model. The Agenda focused on providing jobs and equal opportunities for all and ensuring that the benefits of the EU's growth and employment creation schemes reached all levels of society. A renewed Agenda was adopted by the European Commission in July 2008, focusing on seven priority areas: children and youth; investment in people; mobility; longer, healthier lives; combating poverty and social exclusion; fighting discrimination and promoting equality; and global opportunities, access and solidarity. Meanwhile, a new programme for employment and social solidarity (PROGRESS) had been established to provide financial support for the implementation of the objectives set out in the Social Agenda. With an overall budget of €743m. for 2007–13, PROGRESS replaced four previous programmes that had expired in 2006 and was to cover the policy areas of social protection and inclusion, employment, non-discrimination, gender equality and working conditions.

The Charter of Fundamental Rights (CFR) was proclaimed at the Nice Summit of the European Council in December 2000. The text of the CFR consists of seven chapters, covering dignity, freedoms, equality, solidarity, citizens' rights, justice and general provisions. No new rights were actually created as part of the CFR; rather, it presents in a single document the existing rights and freedoms enjoyed by EU citizens through the European Convention on Human Rights, the Charter of Fundamental Social Rights of Workers and various other EU treaties. The CFR became legally binding following the entry into force in December 2009 of the Treaty of Lisbon. (A protocol limited the application of the CFR in the Czech Republic, Poland and the United Kingdom.) In February 2010 the EU, a single legal entity under the terms of the Lisbon Treaty, acceded to the European Convention on Human Rights (ECHR), thereby enabling the European Court of Human Rights to verify future EU compliance with the provisions of the ECHR.

The EU disability strategy has three main focuses: co-operation between the Commission and the member states; the full participation of people with disabilities; and ensuring disability issues are fully recognized in policy formulation (particularly with regard to employment). Ongoing EU activities relating to disability include dialogue with the European Disability Forum and a European Day of Disabled People, which takes place in December each year. A disability action plan for 2004–10 aimed to enhance the economic and social integration of people with disabilities. In November 2010 the Commission launched the EU Disability Strategy 2010–20, which established plans for the forthcoming decade. In the Strategy's first five years the Commission aimed to: improve accessibility to goods and services for people with disabilities, and to consider proposing a European Accessibility Act; help disabled people to exercise their right to vote; use the European Platform Against Poverty to reduce the risk of poverty; ensure that the European Social Fund offered ongoing support to disability-related projects; carry out data collection with the aim of improving opportunities for the employment of disabled people; develop policies to ensure inclusive education; facilitate the mutual recognition of disability cards and related entitlements throughout Europe; and promote the rights of people with disabilities through the EU's external action.

CONSUMER PROTECTION AND HEALTH

Consumer protection is one of the stated priorities of EU policy, and has been implemented via a series of action programmes covering areas such as safety of products and services (e.g. food additives, safety of toys and childcare articles, packaging and labelling of goods), protecting consumers' economic and legal interests, and promoting consumer representation. A number of measures have been taken to strengthen consumer power, by promoting consumer associations and drawing up a requirement for fair commercial practices. The EU consumer policy strategy for 2007–13 was adopted in March 2007, subtitled 'Empowering consumers, enhancing their welfare, effectively protecting them'.

In December 2009 the European Commission adopted a new set of Rapid Alert System for Non-Food Consumer Products (known as RAPEX) guidelines. The RAPEX system (inaugurated in 2004) facilitates the rapid exchange of information between member states of measures taken to restrict or prevent the marketing or use of products deemed to pose a serious risk to the health and safety of consumers. The Commission publishes a weekly report of recent RAPEX notifications. In July 2009 a new Toy Safety Directive entered into force, which aimed to ensure that toys produced in and/or sold to consumers in the EU meet the highest safety requirements, and included limiting the amounts of certain chemicals that may be contained in materials used in the production of toys.

The Dolceta—Online Consumer Education initiative of the European Commission (launched in June 2005; managed by the European Association for University Lifelong Learning in co-operation with the European Association for Adult Education, and national teams; and accessible at www.dolceta.eu) aims to educate European consumers in areas including consumer rights; financial services; product safety; sustainable consumption; and services (utilities, telecommunications, transport and postal services).

In February 1997 the Commission extended the function of its directorate-general on consumer policy to incorporate consumer health protection. This decision (which followed widespread consumer concerns regarding the bovine spongiform encephalopathy (BSE) crisis—see Agriculture) was designed to ensure that sufficient importance was given to food safety. The European Food Safety Authority was established to assume responsibility for providing the Commission with scientific advice on food safety. With a wide brief to cover all stages of food production and supply right through to consumers, the Authority has been based in Parma, Italy, since June 2005. In March 2004 the Commission adopted a decision to establish three new scientific steering committees in the fields of consumer products, health and environmental risks, and emerging and newly identified health risks. In July 1998 an Institute for Health and Consumer Protection (IHCP), attached to the Commission's Joint Research Centre, was established (see ihcp.jrc.ec.europa.eu).

In July 2001 the Commission developed its rules on the labelling and tracing of genetically modified organisms (GMOs, see Agriculture). During 2004 a framework was developed for the creation of international guidelines on the measurement of chemical and biological elements in food and other products. The system would facilitate the detection of GMOs and the measurement of sulphur content in motor fuels. New legislation on the safety of food and animal feed came into force in January 2005. Business operators were required to ensure the safety of their products and apply appropriate systems and procedures to establish the traceability of food, feed, food-producing animals and all substances incorporated into foodstuffs at all stages of production, processing and distribution. An Advisory Group on the Food Chain and Animal and Plant Health was established by the Commission in March and held its inaugural meeting in July. A Community Register of Feed Additives was first published in November, in accordance with a regulation on additives for use in animal nutrition. A regulation requiring that all health claims on food, drinks or food supplements be substantiated by independent experts was adopted in December 2006. In January of that year new regulations on food and animal feed hygiene, applying to every stage of the food chain, entered into force. At the same time, an EU-wide ban on the use of antibiotics in animal feed to stimulate growth took effect, as part of efforts to reduce the non-essential use of antibiotics in order to address the problem of micro-organisms becoming resistant to traditional medical treatments. In November 2009 the European Commission published, as a basis for future discussion, a working paper on means of addressing so-called anti-microbial resistance (AMR) which, it was reported, was causing annually around 25,000 human fatalities in the EU region.

In January 2005 a European Consumer Centres Network (ECC-Net) was established to provide a single point of contact in each member state for consumers to obtain information about their rights and assistance in pursuing complaints, particularly in cases concerning cross-border purchases. The ECC-NET handled 71,292 cases in 2010, of which 12,622 related to the rights of air travellers. Legislation increasing the compensation rights of air travellers took effect in February 2005. New rights to compensation and assistance in the event of cancellations or long delays were introduced, compensation was increased for passengers unable to board a flight owing to overbooking by the airline and cover was extended to passengers travelling on charter or domestic flights. In November

2009 the European Commission launched a public consultation on revising EU legislation relating to package travel, to take account of advances made in recent years in internet and low-cost airline usage. Also in that month the Commission published a report on airline charges which found that frequently it had been airline practice to incorporate some basic operational costs (including handling charges, fuel charges and booking fees) into the 'taxes and charges' category, rendering it difficult for consumers to make comparisons between offers or to identify the value of national taxes and airport charges that might be refunded against unused tickets.

The Consumer Protection Co-operation Network (CPC), comprising public authorities responsible for enforcing legislation to protect the interests of consumers in the event of cross-border disputes, was officially launched in February 2007. The first of a series of EU 'sweeps'—joint investigations and enforcement actions aimed at evaluating compliance with consumer laws in particular markets—was conducted in September 2007, into misleading advertising and unfair practices on airline ticket-selling websites, and in November it was revealed that irregularities had been discovered on more than 50% of the sites checked. Following such investigations, national enforcement authorities act to ensure that companies found to have been compromising consumer rights improve their practices. The results of a 'sweep' focusing on the provision of online mobile cellular telephone services, initiated in June 2008, were published in November 2009. In September 2010 the results of the second phase of a 'sweep' investigating online distributors of electronic goods (such as mobile cellular telephones, digital cameras and personal music players) were published; 84% of the websites checked for breach of EU consumer legislation in 26 member states, plus Iceland and Norway, were found to comply with EU laws, compared with 44% in 2009. The breaches identified involved misleading information on consumer rights, incorrect tariffs, and failures to provide traders' contact details; such sites were compelled to make adjustments, and, if necessary, penalties were imposed. In July 2009 the European Commission published a blueprint for a proposed standardized EU-wide method for classifying and reporting consumer complaints. In November 2011 the Commission adopted a directive on Alternative Dispute Resolution (ADR), which sought to ensure that all contractual disputes between consumers and providers could be resolved without recourse to the courts. A new Regulation on Online Dispute Resolution sought to create an online presence ('ODR platform') throughout the EU, which could be consulted by both consumers and businesses in order to enable them to settle disputes concerning the online purchase of goods from other EU member countries.

In February 2005 the European Parliament approved a new directive to harmonize the framework across the EU for banning unfair commercial practices. The new legislation, which clarified consumers' rights, banned pressure selling and misleading marketing and facilitated cross-border trade, took effect in December 2007, although only 14 member states had implemented the directive by that time. In February 2003 the Commission adopted an action plan for a more coherent and standardized European contract law. Substantive work towards the long-term aim of developing a Common Frame of Reference, which would contain clear definitions of legal terms, fundamental principles and coherent model rules of contract law, was ongoing.

A programme of action in the field of health, for the period 2008–13, entitled 'Together for Health', was adopted in October 2007, with a budget of €321.5m. Its three general objectives were: to improve citizens' health security; to promote health, including the reduction of health inequalities; and to generate and disseminate health information and knowledge. Meanwhile, the Commission adopted a new health strategy for the same period with the aims of fostering good health in an ageing Europe, protecting citizens from health threats, and supporting dynamic health systems and new technologies.

In December 2008—in view of estimates that annually 8%–12% of patients admitted to EU hospitals suffered largely preventable harm from the health care they received, including contracting health care-associated infections, such as those caused by the bacterium MRSA (methicillin-resistant staphylococcus aureus)—the Commission adopted a Communication and proposal for a Council Recommendation on specific actions that member states could take, either individually, collectively or with the Commission, to improve the safety of patients.

In September 2009 the European Commission determined to limit health risks to consumers derived from exposure to noise from personal music players; it was decided that default settings on personal music players should be set at safe exposure levels, and that clear warnings should be provided alerting consumers to the possible adverse effects of excessive exposure to high sound levels.

Various epidemiological surveillance systems are in operation, covering major communicable diseases. An early warning and response system (EWRS) to help member states deal with outbreaks of diseases was in place by the end of 2000. In April 2004 the European Parliament and the Council adopted a regulation establishing a European Centre for Disease Prevention and Control (ECDC), to enable the EU to share its disease control expertise more effectively and to allow multinational investigation teams to be drawn up quickly and efficiently. The Centre, based in Sweden, became operational in May 2005. The ECDC's European Programme for Intervention Epidemiology Training (EPIET) provides training and practical experience in intervention epidemiology at national centres for surveillance and communicable diseases control within the EU. In late April 2009 an extraordinary meeting of EU health ministers was convened, in Luxembourg, to address the emergence of a new variant of swine influenza (A/H1N1), referred to from June as pandemic (H1N1) 2009. The directorate-general with responsibility for Health took control of the co-ordinated response to pandemic (H1N1) 2009 within the framework of the EWRS. In September 2009 the European Commission adopted the EU Strategy on Pandemic (H1N1) 2009, aimed at supporting member states in their efforts to respond efficiently to it, and focusing on the importance of co-ordination across sectors and between states.

In September 2009 the European Commission launched a new European Partnership for Action against Cancer, which was to bring together relevant organizations to pool expertise with the aim of lowering the number of new cancer cases arising in the EU by some 15%, by 2020. During 2006–08 the EU member states, and Iceland and Norway, implemented the Vaccine European New Integrated Collaboration Effort (VENICE) project, which aimed to broaden knowledge and best practices on vaccination; a follow-up project, VENICE II, was launched in December 2008. The first European conference on vaccination and immunization—Eurovaccine 2009, organized and funded by the ECDC, and convened in Stockholm, Sweden, in December 2009—addressed topics including vaccinating against pandemic (H1N1) 2009 and the formulation of strategies for eliminating measles throughout Europe.

Under the Treaty on European Union, the EU assumed responsibility for the problem of drug addiction; a European Monitoring Centre for Drugs and Drug Addiction (EMCDDA, see Justice and Home Affairs) was established in Lisbon, Portugal, in 1995. In March 2005 an EU Platform for Action on Diet, Physical Activity and Health was launched, as part of an overall strategy on nutrition and physical activity being developed by the Commission to address rising levels of obesity. The Commission initiated a public consultation in December on how to reduce obesity levels and the prevalence of associated chronic diseases in the EU. In May 2007 the Commission adopted a White Paper on nutrition- and obesity-related health issues, in which it urged food manufacturers to reduce levels of salt, fat and sugar in their products and emphasized the need to encourage Europeans to undertake more physical activity. A European Alcohol and Health Forum, comprising more than 40 businesses and non-governmental organizations, was formed in June 2007 to focus on initiatives to protect European citizens from the harmful use of alcohol. In October 2006 the Commission had adopted a communication setting out an EU strategy to support member states in reducing alcohol-related harm.

The European Commission states that tobacco use is the largest single cause of premature death and disease in the EU. In July 2005 an EU directive came into effect that prohibited tobacco advertising in the print media, on radio and over the internet, as well as the sponsorship by tobacco companies of cross-border cultural and sporting events. The directive applied only to advertising and sponsorship with a cross-border dimension. Tobacco advertising on television had already been banned in the EU in the early 1990s. In June 2009, after extensive consultation, the Commission adopted a proposal for a Council recommendation on the introduction by 2012 of national legislation to protect citizens from exposure to tobacco smoke. At February 2011 comprehensive legislation on providing a smoke-free environment had been enacted in 10 EU countries, with complete bans on smoking in enclosed public places, on public transport and in workplaces in force in Ireland and the United Kingdom.

The Food Supplements Directive, which was approved in 2002 and was designed to strengthen controls on the sale of natural remedies, vitamin supplements and mineral plant extracts, came into effect in August 2005. Under the legislation, only vitamins and minerals on an approved list could be used in supplements and restrictions were to be placed on the upper limits of vitamin doses. In July 2005 the European Court of Justice had confirmed the validity of the directive, which had been challenged by a group of consumers' and retail associations in the United Kingdom.

In June 2008 an EU high-level conference entitled 'Together for Mental Health and Well-being' launched the European Pact for Mental Health and Well-being, to be implemented through thematic conferences during 2009–10 focusing on five priority areas: prevention of suicide and depression; mental health in youth and education; mental health in workplace settings; mental health in older people; and combating stigma and social exclusion.

In October 2009 the European Commission adopted a strategy and action plan for combating HIV/AIDS in the EU and neighbouring countries in 2009–13, with a focus on the following principal areas: HIV prevention and testing; targeting priority groups most at risk of HIV; and targeting regions with a higher proportion of people at risk.

The strategy had the following overall objectives: to reduce new HIV infections across all European countries by 2013; to improve patients' access to prevention, treatment and support; and to ameliorate the quality of life of those living with, affected by or most vulnerable to HIV/AIDS in Europe and neighbouring countries.

It was envisaged that the enlargement of the EU in May 2004, and again in January 2007, providing for the incorporation of 12 new member states, would cause a number of problems for the Union with regard to public health policy given that, in general, the health status indicators of the majority of the accession states compared poorly with the EU average. Some of the new member states, which (with only one or two exceptions) had few resources to spend on health, had serious problems with communicable diseases (particularly HIV/AIDS), and the health systems of most were in need of improvement. In October 2009 the European Commission announced a series of actions aimed at helping member states and other actors to address inequalities in health provision and life expectancy within and between individual EU member states. Member states and stakeholders were to be helped to identify best practices; and the Commission was to publish regular relevant statistics, and also to issue reports on inequalities and their impact and on successful strategies for addressing them. It was to support countries by using EU funds towards improving primary care facilities, water provision, sanitation and housing renewal. An initial report on progress towards combating health inequalities was to be released in 2012.

Since 1 January 2006 EU member states have issued European Health Insurance Cards (EHICs), which entitle residents to receive state-provided medical treatment in the event of suffering either an accident or illness while visiting temporarily states within the European Economic Area (EEA) and Switzerland.

ENVIRONMENT

Environmental action by the EU was initiated in 1972. The Maastricht Treaty on European Union, which entered into force in November 1993, gave environmental action policy status, and the Treaty of Amsterdam identified sustainable development as one of the Community's overall aims. In June 1998 European heads of state and government launched the Cardiff Process, requiring the integration of environmental considerations into all EU policies.

The EU's sixth environmental action programme (2002–12), Environment 2010: Our Future, Our Choice, emphasized the continuing importance of the integration of environmental considerations into other EU policies, focusing on four priority areas: climate change, nature and biodiversity; environment; health and quality of life; and the management of natural resources and waste. The programme also identified explicitly the measures required to implement successfully the EU's sustainable development strategy. In addition, it sought to encourage greater public participation in environmental debates.

The environment was one of the 10 themes of the 'co-operation' specific programme of the Seventh Framework Programme (FP7) for research, technological development and demonstration activities covering 2007–13 (see Research and Innovation). With a budget of €1,900m., a wide range of environmental research activities were allocated funding under FP7, grouped into four areas: climate change, pollution and risks; sustainable management of resources; environmental technologies; and earth observation and assessment tools for sustainable development. The Institute for Environment and Sustainability, located in Ispra, Italy, was created in 2001 as part of the Joint Research Centre to provide research-based support to the development and implementation of European environmental policies.

In 1990 the EC established the European Environment Agency (EEA, see p. 286) to monitor environmental issues and provide advice. The agency, which is located in Copenhagen, Denmark, and which became operational in November 1994, also provides targeted information to policy-makers and the public and disseminates comparable environmental data. The agency is open to non-EU countries and it was the first EU body to have members from the accession states.

From November 2009 the online European Pollutant Release and Transfer Register (E-PRTR) replaced the former European Pollutant Emission Register (EPER). The E-PRTR provides data (updated annually, with records commencing in 2007) for EU member states on 91 substances released to air, water and land and 65 sectors of industrial activity, including data on transfers of waste and wastewater from industrial facilities to other locations, and data on emissions caused by accidents at industrial facilities. The European Parliament approved legislation in April 2004 aimed at making firms causing pollution liable for the costs of repairing the damage caused to natural habitats, water resources and wildlife. In December 2007 the Commission adopted a new directive on reducing industrial emissions, which was to replace seven existing directives. The directive was intended, *inter alia*, to tighten emission limits in certain industrial sectors, to introduce minimum standards for environmental inspections of industrial installations and to extend the scope of legislation to cover other polluting activities, such as medium-sized combustion plants.

In May 2007 the Council and Parliament adopted a new funding programme, LIFE+, following on from a LIFE programme established in 1992; LIFE+ was to be the EU's single financial instrument targeting only the environment. With a budget of €2,143m. for the period 2007–13, LIFE+ consists of three thematic components: nature and biodiversity; environment policy and governance; and information and communication. LIFE+ supports projects throughout the EU, as well as in some candidate, acceding and neighbouring countries. Between 1992 and 2009 some 3,316 projects were co-financed by LIFE/LIFE+.

The EU has approved numerous international instruments relating to the environment, including the Vienna Convention for the Protection of the Ozone Layer, and its protocol, controlling the production of chlorofluorocarbons (CFCs); the Stockholm Convention on Persistent Organic Pollutants; and the Kyoto Protocol. In June 2000 the Commission launched the European Climate Change Programme (ECCP), which aimed to identify and develop a strategy needed to meet commitments under the Kyoto Protocol, and to incorporate climate change concerns into various EU policies. A second phase of the ECCP (under which more than 30 measures had been implemented since its establishment in 2000), ECCP II, was launched in October 2005, with the aim of reviewing the progress of individual member states towards achieving their individual targets on reducing emissions, and developing a framework for EU climate change policy beyond the expiry of the Kyoto Protocol in 2012. In January 2007, in a communication ('Limiting Global Climate Change to 2° Celsius: The Way Ahead for 2020 and Beyond'), the Commission set out proposals for climate change management, which were aimed at limiting the increase in the average global temperature to no more than 2°C above pre-industrial levels. In March 2007, at a summit meeting, EU leaders set a number of joint targets as part of the continued effort to combat the effects of global warming, which, together, it was claimed, constituted the Union's first ever comprehensive agreement on climate and energy policy. Consequently, in April 2009, the Council adopted new climate change legislation, committing EU member states to reducing carbon dioxide emissions by 20% in 2013–20, compared with emissions levels in 1990. The Council also agreed to increase the use of renewable energy sources to 20% (10% for transport energy consumption) by 2020, and to increase energy efficiency by 20% by the same date. Meeting in January 2010, the European Council and the European Commission published a joint letter in which they formally stated the willingness of the EU to adhere to emission reduction targets detailed in the non-binding Copenhagen Accord, which had been agreed in December 2009 by heads of state and government and other delegates attending the UN Climate Change Conference that had been convened in Copenhagen, originally with the objective of finalizing negotiations on a successor instrument to the Kyoto Protocol. The Copenhagen Accord determined that international co-operative action should be taken, in the context of sustainable development, to reduce global greenhouse gas emissions so as to hold the ongoing increase in global temperature below 2°C; in accordance with its April 2009 commitments, the EU had pledged a unilateral commitment to reduce the overall emissions by 20% of 1990 levels by 2020, and made a conditional offer to increase this reduction in emissions to 30%, provided that other major emitters agreed to assume their fair share of global emissions reduction efforts.

In February 2010 a Directorate-General for Climate Action was established, to help mitigate the consequences of climate change, to ensure targets on climate change are met, and to oversee the EU Emissions Trading System (ETS). The ETS, which was launched in January 2005, obliges companies that exceed their allocation of carbon dioxide emissions to buy extra allowances from more efficient companies or incur considerable fines. In November 2006 the Commission initiated a review of the EU ETS, proposing an expansion of its coverage to new sectors and emissions and the further harmonization of its application between member states. Legislation on a revised ETS was adopted by the Commission in April 2009. The revised ETS was to be effective from 2013–20, capping the overall level of permissible emissions, while allowing allowances to be traded as required. The total annual allowance was to decline each year, in order to reduce gradually the overall emissions level; 12% of ETS revenues were to be invested in a fund designed to encourage poorer member states to modernize their industry. Exemptions were to apply to industrial sectors considered to be at risk of 'carbon leakage', through the relocation of factories to countries located outside the EU, or the acquisition of EU industries by non-EU competitors. A directive incorporating the aviation sector into the EU ETS, with a view to capping aviation sector emissions, entered into force in February 2009. In October 2007 the European Commission announced that it had reached an agreement with the three countries of the EEA on linking their respective emissions trading systems. In the same month the Commission became a founding member of the International Carbon Action Partnership (ICAP), which convenes a Global Carbon Market Forum for countries and regions with mandatory emissions capping and trading systems.

Europe 2020 is the EU's strategy for growth until 2020, as part of which the Commission's flagship initiative for a resource-efficient Europe focuses on sustainable growth and a move towards a resource-efficient, low-carbon economy. In March 2011 the Commission adopted detailed proposals concerned with bringing about the transition to a competitive, low-carbon EU economy, by reducing domestic carbon emissions by between 80% and 95% by 2050. A so-called roadmap for a resource-efficient Europe was adopted by the Commission in September.

In June 1996 the Commission agreed a strategy, drawn up in collaboration with the European petroleum and car industries and known as the Auto-Oil Programme, for reducing harmful emissions from road vehicles by between 60% and 70% by 2010 in an effort to reduce air pollution. The programme committed member states to the progressive elimination of leaded petrol by 2000 (with limited exemptions until 2005). From 2000 petrol-powered road vehicles were to be fitted with 'on-board diagnostic' (OBD) systems to monitor emissions. Diesel vehicles were to be installed with OBD systems by 2005. Under Auto-Oil II, the directive was revised in 2003, establishing specifications to come into force on 1 January 2005, with new limits on sulphur content of both petrol and diesel. Moreover, lower limits would come into force for all fuel marketed from December 2009, although there would be limited availability from 2005. In July 1998 the Commission announced plans to reduce pollution from nuclear power stations by reducing emissions of sulphur dioxides, nitrogen oxides and dust by one-half. A new directive limiting the sulphur content of marine fuel came into force in August 2005. In April 2009 the Council and the European Parliament adopted a regulation on setting carbon dioxide emissions performance standards for new passenger cars, as part of an integrated approach to reducing carbon dioxide emissions from light-duty vehicles to no more than 120g per km by 2012.

In September 2005 the European Commission presented a thematic strategy on air pollution, prepared under the auspices of Clean Air for Europe (CAFE), a programme of technical analysis and policy development launched in March 2001. While covering all major pollutants, the new air quality policy focused on particulates and ground-level ozone pollution, which were known to pose the greatest risk to human health. The strategy aimed to cut the annual number of premature deaths from pollution-related diseases by almost 40% by 2020, compared with the 2000 level, and also to reduce the area of forests and other ecosystems suffering damage from airborne pollutants. In April 2008 a new air quality directive was approved by the Council, which merged five existing pieces of legislation into a single directive, and imposed limits on fine particle emissions (PM2.5) from vehicles, agriculture and small-scale industry for the first time. Emissions of PM2.5 in urban areas were to be reduced by 20% by 2020, compared with 2010 levels. The European Commission estimated that some 370,000 EU citizens died each year from conditions linked to air pollution.

In October 2005 the Commission proposed a strategy to protect the marine environment, which aimed to ensure that all EU marine waters were environmentally healthy by 2021. This was the second of seven thematic strategies to be adopted under the sixth environmental action programme (2002–12). The Commission proposed strategies on the prevention and recycling of waste and the sustainable use of natural resources in December 2005, and on the urban environment in January 2006. In July the Commission proposed a directive aimed at establishing a framework for achieving a more sustainable use of pesticides by reducing the risks posed by pesticides to human health and the environment (its sixth thematic strategy). In September the Commission adopted a comprehensive strategy dedicated to soil protection, including a proposal for a directive setting forth common principles for soil protection across the EU. A directive on the assessment and management of flood risks entered into force in November 2007, requiring member states to conduct preliminary assessments by 2011 to identify river basins and associated coastal areas at risk of flooding, to develop flood-risk maps by 2013 for areas deemed to be at risk, and to establish flood-risk management plans for these areas by 2015. In March 2009 the European Commission finalized an EU-wide review of the safety—to consumers, farmers, local residents, passers-by and animals—of existing pesticides used in plant protection products that were on the market before 1993; the review had resulted in the removal from sale of more than two-thirds of the substances assessed.

In September 2000 the EU adopted a directive on end-of-life vehicles (ELVs), containing measures for the collection, treatment, recovery and disposal of such waste. The ruling forced manufacturers to pay for the disposal of new cars from July 2002 and of old cars from January 2007. The directive set recycling and recovery targets, restricted the use of heavy metals in new cars from 2003, and specified that ELVs might only be dismantled by authorized agencies. EU directives on waste electronic and electrical equipment and the restriction of the use of certain hazardous substances in electronic and electrical equipment came into force in February 2003. The directives were based on the premise of producer responsibility and aimed to persuade producers to improve product design in order to facilitate recycling and disposal. Increased recycling of electrical and electronic equipment would limit the total quantity of waste going to final disposal. Under the legislation consumers would be able to return equipment free of charge from August 2005. In order to prevent the generation of hazardous waste, the second directive required the substitution of various heavy metals (lead, mercury, cadmium, and hexavalent chromium) and brominated flame retardants in new electrical and electronic equipment marketed from July 2006. In January 2005 the Commission adopted a new strategy on reducing mercury pollution, which was endorsed by EU ministers of the environment in June. A regulation banning mercury exports from the EU by 2011 was proposed by the Commission in October 2006. In September 2007 a directive was adopted on phasing out, by April 2009, the use of toxic mercury in measuring devices in cases where it could be substituted by safer alternatives; this was expected to lead to an annual reduction of 33 metric tons in mercury emissions in the EU.

A regulation revising EU laws on trade in wild animals and plants was adopted by ministers of the environment in December 1996. A series of directives adopted in 2002 formulated new EU policy on the conservation of wild birds, fishing and protection for certain species of whales. Every three years the Commission publishes an official report on the conservation of wild birds. In January 2010 the Commission issued a communication detailing possible future options for biodiversity policy after 2010, to succeed a previous agenda of halting biodiversity loss in the Union by 2010. The communication envisaged a long-term vision, towards 2050, for preserving and, as far as possible, restoring biodiversity, to be preceded by medium-term objectives to be achieved by 2020.

As part of the EU's efforts to promote awareness of environmental issues and to encourage companies to do likewise, the voluntary Eco-Management and Audit Scheme (EMAS) was launched in April 1995. Under the scheme, participating industrial companies undergo an independent audit of their environmental performance. In addition, the EU awards 'eco-labels' for products that limit harmful effects on the environment (including foodstuffs, beverages and pharmaceutical products, among others). The criteria to be met are set by the EU Eco-Labelling Board (EUEB).

In October 2003 the Commission presented a new environmental policy—the Registration, Evaluation and Authorisation of Chemicals system (REACH)—which was originally intended to collate crucial safety information on tens of thousands of potentially dangerous chemicals used in consumer goods industries. However, following intensive lobbying by the chemical industry sector, the scope of REACH was reduced (for example, the number of chemicals to be tested was cut and the number of chemicals that would require licences was also substantially curtailed). The European Parliament approved the proposed legislation in a first reading in November 2005, and in December the Council reached a political agreement on REACH. Environmentalists criticized ministers for weakening the legislation by relaxing the conditions set by the Parliament for authorization of the most dangerous chemicals. The REACH regulation was formally adopted in December 2006. The European Chemicals Agency, which is responsible for managing REACH, commenced operations in Helsinki, Finland, in June 2007. In December 2008 the Commission adopted a regulation aligning the EU system of classification, labelling and packaging of chemical substances and mixtures to the UN Globally Harmonized System of Classification and Labelling of Chemicals.

SECURITY AND DEFENCE

Under the Single European Act, which came into force on 1 July 1987 (amending the Treaty of Rome), it was formally stipulated for the first time that member states should inform and consult each other on foreign policy matters (as was already, in practice, often the case). In June 1992 the Petersberg Declaration of Western European Union (WEU) defined the role of WEU as the defence component of the EU and outlined the 'Petersberg tasks' relating to crisis management, including humanitarian, peace-keeping and peace-making operations, which could be carried out under WEU authority (now EU authority). In 1992 France and Germany established a joint force called Eurocorps, based in Strasbourg, France, which was later joined by Belgium, Spain and Luxembourg. An agreement was signed in January 1993 that specified that Eurocorps troops could serve under the command of the North Atlantic Treaty Organization (NATO), thus relieving concern, particularly from the United Kingdom and the USA, that the Eurocorps would undermine NATO's role in Europe. In May member states of the Eurocorps agreed to make the Eurocorps available to WEU. WEU also ratified in May 1995 the decision by Spain, France, Italy and Portugal to establish land and sea forces, the European Operational Rapid Force (EUROFOR) and the European Maritime Force (EUROMARFOR) respectively, which were also to undertake the Petersberg tasks under the auspices of WEU. Several other multinational forces also belonged to Forces

Answerable to the WEU (FAWEU). At the EU summit in Köln, Germany, in June 1999, EU member states accepted a proposal for the Eurocorps to be placed at the disposal of the EU for crisis response operations. At the end of that year Eurocorps member states agreed to transform the Eurocorps into a rapid reaction corps headquarters available both to the EU and NATO. In 2002 NATO certified the Eurocorps as a NATO high readiness force, which required the headquarters (Eurocorps HQ) to be open to all NATO members as well as those from the EU; thus representatives from Austria, Canada, Finland, Greece, Italy, the Netherlands, Poland, Turkey and the United Kingdom are integrated into Eurocorps HQ. During early 2004–early 2005 an HQ Eurocorps European staff took the lead of the NATO International Security Assistance Force in Afghanistan (ISAF) for the duration of its sixth mandate.

The Maastricht Treaty on European Union, which came into force on 1 November 1993, provided for joint action by member governments in matters of common foreign and security policy (CFSP), and envisaged the formation of a European security and defence policy (ESDP), with the possibility of a common defence force, although existing commitments to NATO were to be honoured. The Treaty raised WEU to the rank of an 'integral part of the development of the Union', while preserving its institutional autonomy, and gave it the task of elaborating and implementing decisions and actions with defence implications.

The Treaty of Amsterdam, which entered into force in May 1999, aimed to strengthen the concept of a CFSP within the Union and incorporated a process of common strategies to co-ordinate external relations with a third party. Under the Amsterdam Treaty, WEU was to provide the EU with access to operational capability for undertaking the so-called Petersberg tasks. In March 1999 representatives of the Commission and NATO held a joint meeting, for the first time, to discuss the conflict in the southern Serbian province of Kosovo. The Treaty introduced the role of High Representative for the CFSP. In April a meeting of NATO Heads of State and of Government determined that NATO's equipment, personnel and infrastructure would be available to any future EU military operation. In June the European Council, meeting in Köln, determined to strengthen the ESDP, stating that the EU needed a capacity for autonomous action, without prejudice to actions by NATO and acknowledging the supreme prerogatives of the UN Security Council. The European Council initiated a process of assuming direct responsibility for the Petersberg tasks, which were placed at the core of the ESDP process. In December, following consultation with NATO, the European Council, meeting in Helsinki, Finland, adopted the European Defence Initiative, comprising the following goal: by 2003 the EU should be able to deploy within 60 days and for a period of up to one year a rapid reaction force, comprising up to 60,000 national troops from member states, capable of implementing the full range of Petersberg tasks. At the Helsinki meeting, the establishment of three permanent military institutions was proposed: a Political and Security Committee (PSC); a Military Committee; and a Military Staff. The PSC, which was fully established by 2001, monitors the international situation, helps to define policies and assess their implementation, encourages dialogue and, under the auspices of the Council, takes responsibility for the political direction of capability development. In the event of a crisis situation, it oversees the strategic direction of any military response, proposes political objectives and supervises their enactment. The Military Committee gives military advice to the PSC, and comprises the chiefs of defence of member states, represented by military delegates. It serves as a forum for military consultation and co-operation and deals with risk assessment, the development of crisis management and military relations with non-EU European NATO members, accession countries, and NATO itself. Meanwhile, the Military Staff, comprising experts seconded by the member states, provides the EU with an early-warning capability, takes responsibility for strategic planning for the Petersberg tasks and implements the Military Committee's policies. Permanent arrangements have been agreed for EU-NATO consultation and co-operation in this area. The process of transferring the crisis management responsibilities of WEU to the EU was finalized by July 2001. From January 2007 a new EU Operations Centre (OpsCentre), located in Brussels, Belgium, was available as a third option for commanding EU crisis management missions. Hitherto autonomous EU operations were commanded either with recourse to NATO's command structure or from the national operational headquarters of one of five member states (France, Germany, Greece, Italy and the United Kingdom). Although the EU OpsCentre was to have a permanent staff of only eight core officers, it was envisaged that a total of 89 officers and civilians would be able to begin planning an operation within five days of the Council deciding to activate the centre, achieving full capability to command the operation within 20 days.

In December 2001 the EU announced that the rapid reaction force was ready to undertake small-scale crisis management tasks. A deal was agreed at the Copenhagen summit in December 2002 on sharing planning resources with NATO. In January 2003 EU forces were deployed for the first time in an international peace-keeping role (when 500 police officers were dispatched to Bosnia and Herzegovina to take over policing duties from the existing UN force). In March the European Parliament voted to approve the EU's first military mission, allowing 450 lightly armed EU troops to take over from NATO peace-keepers in the former Yugoslav republic of Macedonia.

In June 2004 the European Council approved the creation of a European Defence Agency, which commenced operations later that year. The European Defence Agency was to be responsible for improving the EU's defence capabilities in relation to crisis management and for promoting co-operation on research and procurement, strengthening the European defence industrial and technological base and developing a competitive European defence equipment market. In November 2007 EU ministers responsible for defence adopted a framework for a joint strategy on defence research and technology.

In June 2000 the EU established a civilian crisis management committee. In the same month the European Council defined four priority areas for civilian crisis management: developing the role of the police; strengthening the rule of law; strengthening civilian administrations; and improving civil protection. In February 2001 the Council adopted a regulation creating a rapid reaction mechanism (RRM) to improve the EU's civilian capacity to respond to crises. The mechanism bypassed cumbersome decision-making processes, to enable civilian experts in fields such as mine clearance, customs, police training, election-monitoring, institution-building, media support, rehabilitation and mediation to be mobilized speedily. In November 2006 the Council and Parliament adopted a regulation establishing an Instrument for Stability for 2007–13, replacing the RRM.

The common security and defence policy (CSDP), as the ESDP was renamed, remained an integral part of the CFSP under the Treaty of Lisbon, which entered into force, becoming the new legal basis for the CFSP, in December 2009. According to the Lisbon Treaty, the progressive framing of a common defence policy was intended to lead to a common defence, following a unanimous decision of the European Council. A mutual defence clause and a solidarity clause (in the event of a member state becoming the victim of a terrorist attack or natural or man-made disaster) were included, and joint disarmament operations, military advice and assistance, conflict prevention and post-conflict stabilization were added to the Petersberg tasks. The Lisbon Treaty introduced the office of High Representative of the Union for Foreign Affairs and Security Policy (uniting the previous roles of High Representative for the CFSP and External Affairs Commissioner), and provided for the establishment of the European External Action Service (with a diplomatic function, and supporting the work of and reporting to the High Representative). The High Representative leads the External Relations Council, is also a Vice-President of the European Commission, and heads political dialogue with international partners. Most decisions on the CFSP are to continue to be adopted at intergovernmental level and by consensus of all member states.

In November 2004 EU ministers responsible for defence agreed to create several Battlegroups (BGs) for eventual deployment to crisis areas. BGs were to comprise up to 1,500 troops and were to be capable of being deployed within 10 days of a unanimous decision from EU member states and the creation of a battle plan and would be equipped to stay in an area for up to four months. Each group was to be commanded by a 'lead nation' and associated with a force headquarters. The BGs reached initial operational capacity in January 2005, meaning that at least one was on standby every six months. France, Italy, Spain and the United Kingdom set up their own BGs. The creation of the BGs was partly to compensate for the inadequacies of the rapid reaction force of 60,000 troops, which, while theoretically declared ready for action in May 2003, in practice was adversely affected by shortfalls in equipment, owing to a lack of investment in procurement and research and a failure to co-ordinate purchases among member states. In November 2005 it was announced that 15 BGs would be created, and additional groups were subsequently proposed. In January 2007 the BGs reached full operational capacity, meaning that two BG operations could be undertaken concurrently; no BG deployments had, however, taken place by mid-2012.

The Justice and Home Affairs Council held an emergency meeting in September 2001 following the terrorist attacks on the USA. It determined a number of measures to be taken to improve security in the Community. First, the Council sought to reach a common definition of acts of terrorism, and to establish higher penalties for such acts. The new definition included 'cyber' and environmental attacks. The Council decided that, for the perpetrators of terrorist attacks, as well as those involved in other serious crimes (including trafficking in arms, people and drugs and money-laundering), the process of extradition would ultimately be replaced by a procedure for handover based on a European arrest warrant. In the mean time, member states were urged to implement the necessary measures to allow the existing conventions on extradition to enter into force. The member states reached agreement on the arrest warrant in December; under the agreement, covering 32 serious offences, EU countries may no longer refuse to extradite their own nationals. The warrant entered into force in eight of the then 15 EU member states on 1 January 2004 (the seven other member states having failed to meet the implementation deadline of 31 December 2003). The European arrest warrant had been implemented in all member states by mid-2005. The Council also determined to accelerate the implementation of the convention on mutual assistance in criminal matters and to establish a joint investigation team. Member states were encouraged to ratify the convention on combating the financing of terrorism and to exercise greater rigour in the issuing of travel documents. The heads of the security and intelligence services of member states met in October 2001, in the first EU-wide meeting of this kind, to discuss the co-ordinated action to be taken to curb terrorism. They were to meet in regular sessions thereafter. A team of counter-terrorist specialists, established within Europol, was to produce an assessment of terrorist threats to EU states, indicating the likely nature and location of any such attacks. Rapid links were forged with US counterparts—in December Europol signed a co-operation agreement on the exchange of strategic information (excluding personal data) with the USA; in December 2002 the agreement was extended to include the exchange of personal data. The heads of the EU's anti-terrorist units also held a meeting following the September 2001 attacks, to discuss issues such as joint training exercises, equipment sharing, the joint procurement of equipment and possible joint operations. Prior to these emergency meetings, intelligence and security information had been shared bilaterally and on a small scale. Terrorist bombings in Madrid, Spain, in March 2004 gave added impetus to EU initiatives aimed at improving travel-document security and impeding the cross-border movements of terrorists. Following the attacks, the EU created the new position of Counter-terrorist Co-ordinator, the principal responsibilities of whom included enhancing intelligence-sharing among EU members and promoting the implementation of agreed EU anti-terrorism measures, some of which had been impeded by the legislative processes of individual member states. The Justice and Home Affairs Council held an extraordinary meeting following the terrorist attacks in London, United Kingdom, in July 2005, at which ministers pledged to accelerate the adoption and implementation of enhanced counter-terrorism measures, focusing on issues such as the financing of terrorism, information-sharing by law enforcement authorities, police co-operation and the retention of telecommunications data by service providers. In December the Council adopted a new EU counter-terrorism strategy focused on preventing people embracing terrorism, protecting citizens and infrastructure, pursuing and investigating suspects, and responding to the consequences of an attack. A specific strategy for combating radicalization and the recruitment of terrorists was approved at the same time. Despite concerns over privacy rights, the Council also reached agreement on a draft directive on the retention of telecommunications data for a period of between six months and two years for use in anti-terrorism investigations. Police would have access to information about telephone calls, text messages and internet data, but not to the exact content. The directive was approved by the European Parliament later that month. In November 2007 the Commission adopted a series of proposals on the criminalization of terrorist training, recruitment and public provocation to commit terrorist offences, on the prevention of the use of explosives by terrorists and on the use of airline passenger information in law enforcement investigations.

Under the European code of conduct on arms exports, the EU publishes an annual report on defence exports based on confidential information provided by each member state. EU member states must withhold export licences to countries where it is deemed that arms sales might lead to political repression or external aggression. The Community funds projects aimed at the collection and destruction of weapons in countries emerging from conflict. The EU is strongly committed to nuclear non-proliferation. Under its programme of co-operation with Russia, the Union works to dismantle or destroy nuclear, chemical and biological weapons and weapons of mass destruction.

In September 2004 five European ministers responsible for defence signed an agreement in Noordwijk, Netherlands, to establish a police force, which could be deployed internationally for post-conflict peace-keeping duties and maintaining public order. The European Gendarmerie Force (EGF), which was officially inaugurated at its headquarters (EGF HQ) in Vicenza, Italy, in January 2006, was to be capable of deploying a mission of up to 800 gendarmes within 30 days, which could be reinforced. EGF HQ has developed a comprehensive operational system for crisis management, to be at the prompt disposal of EU and other international organizations, including the UN, NATO and the Organization for Security and Co-operation in Europe (OSCE). In 2007 the EGF became involved with EUFOR-Althea (in Bosnia and Herzegovina), and in February 2010 the EGF commenced an operational commitment within the NATO Training Mission in Afghanistan, to contribute to the development of the Afghan National Police. From December 2008 the EGF comprised members from France, Italy, the Netherlands, Portugal, Romania and Spain; Poland's military gendarmerie is also a partner.

For details of military operations that the EU has undertaken in third countries, see the specific regional information.

FINANCIAL SERVICES AND CAPITAL MOVEMENTS

Freedom of capital movement and the creation of a uniform financial area were regarded as vital for the completion of the EU's internal market by 1992. In 1987, as part of the liberalization of the flow of capital, a Council directive came into force whereby member states were obliged to remove restrictions on three categories of transactions: long-term credits related to commercial transactions; acquisition of securities; and the admission of securities to capital markets. In June 1988 the Council of Ministers approved a directive whereby all restrictions on capital movements (financial loans and credits, current and deposit account operations, transactions in securities and other instruments normally dealt in on the money market) were to be removed by 1 July 1990. A number of countries were permitted to exercise certain restrictions until the end of 1992, and further extensions were then granted to Portugal and Greece. With the entry into force of the Maastricht Treaty in November 1993, the principle of full freedom of capital movements was incorporated into the structure of the EU.

The EU worked to develop a single market in financial services throughout the 1990s. In October 1998 the Commission drew up a framework for action in the financial services sector. This communication was followed by a Financial Services Action Plan (FSAP) in May 1999, with three strategic objectives: to establish a single market in wholesale financial services; to make retail markets open and secure; and to strengthen the rules on prudential supervision in order to keep pace with new sources of financial risk. The prudential supervision of financial conglomerates (entities offering a range of financial services in areas such as banking, insurance and securities), which were developing rapidly, was identified as an area of particular importance. During 2002 a directive was drawn up on the supplementary supervision of such businesses, in recognition of the increasing consolidation in the financial sector and the emergence of cross-sector financial groups. Individual targets specified in the 1999 FSAP included removing the outstanding barriers to raising capital within the EU; creating a coherent legal framework for supplementary pension funds; and providing greater legal certainty in cross-border securities trading.

In November 2003 the Commission adopted a package of seven measures aiming to establish a new organizational architecture in all financial services sectors. The Commission stressed that this initiative was required urgently if the FSAP was to be implemented and enforced effectively. The deadline of 2005 for the adoption of the FSAP measures was largely met, with 98% of the measures having been completed, and their implementation by member states was being closely monitored by the Commission. In December 2005 the Commission presented its financial services policy for 2005–10, identifying five priorities: to consolidate progress and ensure effective implementation and enforcement of existing rules; to extend the 'better regulation principles' (i.e. transparency, wide consultation and thorough evaluation) to all policy-making; to enhance supervisory co-operation and convergence; to create greater competition between service providers, especially those active in retail markets; and to expand the EU's external influence in globalizing capital markets.

In July 2001 progress towards the creation of a single financial market was impeded by the European Parliament's rejection of a proposed takeover directive that had been under negotiation for 12 years. The directive had aimed to ensure that shareholders were treated in the same way throughout the EU after takeover bids, and had sought to create a single Community framework governing takeovers. The proposed directive was eventually approved by the European Parliament (with a number of strategic amendments) in December 2003. The Council gave its final approval to the directive in March 2004, and it came into force in May. The takeover directive was due to be incorporated into member states' national laws by 20 May 2006. In February 2007 a report by the Commission on the implementation of the takeover directive indicated that the continued use by a large number of member states of exemptions from the directive's main provisions (which were not mandatory) might bring about new barriers in the EU takeover market, rather than eliminate existing ones. A directive enhancing the rights of shareholders of listed companies was adopted in June; member states were to implement the directive within two years.

A directive on Community banking, adopted in 1977, laid down common prudential criteria for the establishment and operation of banks in member states. A second banking directive, adopted in 1989, aimed to create a single community licence for banking, thereby permitting a bank established in one member country to open branches in any other. The directive entered into force on 1 January 1993. Related measures were subsequently adopted, with the aim of ensuring the capital adequacy of credit institutions and the prevention of money-laundering by criminals. In September 1993 ministers approved a directive on a bank deposit scheme to protect account holders. These directives were consolidated into one overall banking directive in March 2000. Non-bank institutions may be granted a 'European passport' once they have complied with the principles laid down in the EU's first banking directive on the mutual recognition of licences, prudential supervision and supervision by the home member state. Non-bank institutions must also comply with the directive on money-laundering. In May 2001 a directive on the reorganization and closure of failed credit institutions with branches in more than one member state was agreed; it entered into force in May 2004. The capital requirements directive, which was adopted in June 2006, provided for the introduction of a supervisory framework on capital measurement and capital standards in accordance with the Basel II rules agreed by the Basel Committee on Banking Supervision (see Bank for International Settlements). The new framework aimed to enhance consumer protection and strengthen the stability of the financial system by fostering improved risk management among financial institutions. In October 2008, in response to the ongoing crisis in global financial markets, the European Commission proposed amendments to the existing capital requirement directive, revising the rules on bank capital requirements with the aim of reinforcing the stability of the financial system; under the revised directive, banks were to be restricted in lending beyond a specified limit to any one party, while national supervisory authorities were to have a better overview of cross-border banking group activities.

In September 2000 a directive was issued governing the actions of non-bank institutions with regard to the issuance of 'electronic money' (money stored on an electronic device, for example a chip card or in a computer memory). The directive authorized non-bank institutions to issue electronic money on a non-professional basis, with the aim of promoting a 'level playing field' with other credit institutions. Other regulations oblige the institutions to redeem electronic money at par value in coins and bank notes, or by transfer without charge. A review of this directive, prompted by various market developments since its introduction, such as the use of pre-paid telephone cards, which some member states considered as electronic money and others did not, was proposed by the Commission in July 2006 and was to follow the approval of the directive on payment services. The directive on payment services, which was adopted in November 2007, provided the legal framework for the creation of the Single Euro Payments Area (SEPA), an initiative designed to make all electronic payments across the euro area, for example by credit card, debit card, bank transfer or direct debit, as straightforward, efficient and secure as domestic payments within a single member state. From November 2009 non-bank institutions were also permitted to provide payment services under the new directive, thus opening the market to competition.

In July 1994 the third insurance co-ordination directives, relating to life assurance and non-life insurance, came into effect, creating a framework for an integrated Community insurance market. The directive on the reorganization and winding-up of insurance undertakings was adopted by the EU in February 2001 and came into force in April 2003. The main aim of the directive was to provide greater consumer protection and it formed part of a wider drive to achieve a consistent approach to insolvency proceedings across the EU. A new directive on life assurance was adopted in November 2002, superseding all previous directives in this field. In May 2005 the EU adopted a fifth motor insurance directive, which considerably increased the minimum amounts payable for personal injuries and damage to property and designated pedestrians and cyclists as specific categories of victims who are entitled to compensation. A directive on reinsurance was adopted in November; companies specializing in this area had not previously been specifically regulated by EU legislation. In July 2007 the Commission proposed a thorough reform of EU insurance legislation, which was designed to improve consumer protection, modernize supervision, deepen market integration and increase the international competitiveness of European insurers. The new system, known as Solvency II, would introduce more extensive solvency requirements for insurers, in order to guarantee that they have sufficient capital to withstand adverse events, covering not only traditional insurance risks, but also economic risks, including market risk (such as a fall in the value of an insurer's investments), credit risk (for example when debt obligations are not met) and operational risk (such as malpractice or system failure). In addition, insurers would be compelled to devote significant resources to the identification, measurement and pro-active management of risks. The directive on Solvency II (replacing 14 existing directives), was adopted in May 2009 and it was envisaged that the new system would be operational by 1 January 2013. The European Insurance and Occupational Pensions Committee works to improve co-operation with national supervisory authorities.

In September 2007 the Council and Parliament adopted a directive designed to harmonize procedural rules and assessment criteria throughout the Community with regard to acquisitions and increases of shareholdings in the banking, insurance and securities sectors. A directive aimed at modernizing and simplifying rules on value-added tax (VAT) for financial and insurance services was proposed by the Commission in November. It was noted that although these services were generally exempt from VAT, the exemption was not being applied uniformly by member states and that a clear definition of exempt services was therefore required.

In May 1993 ministers adopted a directive on investment services, which (with effect from 1 January 1996) allowed credit institutions to offer investment services in any member state, on the basis of a licence held in one state. The 1999 FSAP aimed to achieve the further convergence of national approaches to investment, in order to increase the effectiveness of the 1993 directive. The directive on the market in financial services, which was adopted in April 2004 to replace the 1993 directive, aimed to allow investment firms to operate throughout the EU on the basis of authorization in their home member state and to ensure that investors enjoyed a high level of protection when employing investment firms, regardless of their location in the EU. The directive entered into force in November 2007.

In late 1999 the Commission put forward proposals to remove tax barriers and investment restrictions affecting cross-border pension schemes, as variations among member states in the tax liability of contributions to supplementary pension schemes were obstructing the transfer of pension rights from one state to another, contradicting the Treaty of Rome's principles of free movement. In October 2000 a specific legal framework for institutions for occupational retirement provision (IORPs) was proposed. This seeks to abolish barriers to investment by pension funds and would permit the cross-border management of IORP pension schemes, with mutual recognition of the supervisory methods in force. In September 2003 the occupational pensions directive (IORP directive), which was designed to allow workers of multinational companies to have access to cross-border employer pension schemes, became EU law. Implementation, which had been due within two years, was subject to delays.

In November 1997 the Commission adopted proposals to co-ordinate tax policy among member states. The measures aimed to simplify the transfer of royalty and interest payments between member states and to prevent the withholding of taxes. In February 1999 the European Parliament endorsed a proposal by the Commission to harmonize taxation further, through the co-ordination of savings taxes. In November 2000 ministers of finance agreed on a proposed savings tax directive, the details of which were endorsed in July 2001. This directive set out rules on the exchange of information on savings accounts of individuals resident in one EU country and receiving interest in another. However, in December Austria, Luxembourg and Belgium abandoned the agreement, insisting that they would only comply if other tax havens in Europe, such as Monaco, Liechtenstein and Switzerland, were compelled to amend their banking secrecy laws.

Two proposed directives were issued in November 2000, the first relating to interest and royalties and the second concerning the code of conduct for business taxation. Together with the savings tax directive, these were known as the EU tax package. The EU ministers of finance finally reached agreement on the terms of the package in June 2003. The package consisted of a political code of conduct to eliminate harmful business tax regimes; a legislative measure to ensure an effective minimum level of taxation of savings income; and a legislative measure to eliminate source taxes on cross-border payments of interest and royalties between associated companies. The Council of the EU reached agreement on the controversial savings tax directive (after 15 years of negotiation) in June 2004; the directive entered into force on 1 July 2005. The aim of the directive was to prevent EU citizens from avoiding taxes on savings by keeping their money in foreign bank accounts. Under the directive, each member state would ultimately be expected to provide information to other member states on interest paid from that member state to individual savers resident in those other member states. For a transitional period, Belgium, Luxembourg and Austria were to be allowed to apply a withholding tax instead, at a rate of 15% for the first three years (2005–07), 20% for the subsequent three years (2008–10) and 35% from 1 July 2011. Negotiations had been concluded with Switzerland, Liechtenstein, Monaco, Andorra and San Marino to ensure the adoption of equivalent measures in those countries to allow effective taxation of savings income paid to EU residents.

The May 2000 convention on mutual assistance in criminal matters (see Justice and Home Affairs) committed member states to co-operation in combating economic and financial crime. In May 2001 the Council adopted a framework decision on preventing fraud and counterfeiting in non-cash means of payment, recognizing this as a criminal offence. An EU conference in Paris, France, in February 2002 (which was also attended by representatives of seven candidate countries and Russia) agreed to tackle money-laundering by setting minimum secrecy levels and compelling internet service providers to identify operators of suspect financial deals. Following the terrorist attacks on the USA in September 2001, the EU attempted to accelerate the adoption of the convention combating the financing of terrorism, and began work on a new directive on 'freezing' assets or evidence related to terrorist crimes. In October 2005 a regulation on the compulsory declaration at EU borders of large amounts (i.e. more than €10,000) of cash (including banknotes and cheques) entered into force. The aim of this measure, which applied only to the external borders of the Union, was to prevent the entry into the EU of untraceable money, which could then be used to fund criminal or terrorist activities. A third money-laundering directive (which was extended to cover terrorist financing as well as money-laundering) was also adopted in that month. In November 2006 the Council and Parliament adopted a regulation aimed at ensuring that law enforcement authorities have access to basic information on the payer of transfers of funds in the context of investigating terrorists and tracing their assets.

In February 2001 the Commission launched a complaints network for out-of-court settlements in the financial sector (FIN-NET), to help consumers find amicable solutions in cases where the supplier is in another member state. A directive establishing harmonized rules on the cross-border distance-selling of financial services was adopted in June 2002. The first meeting took place in June 2006 of the Financial Services Consumer Group, a permanent committee, comprising representatives of consumer organizations from each of the member states as well as those active at EU level, established by the Commission to discuss financial services policies and proposals of particular relevance to consumers. In December 2007 the Commission published a White Paper proposing measures to improve the competitiveness and efficiency of European residential mortgage markets by facilitating the cross-border supply and funding of mortgage credit and by increasing the diversity of products available.

The European Commission convened regularly from late 2008 to address the crisis. In October 2008 the President of the European Commission established a high-level group on financial supervision in the EU to decide means of building more effective European and global supervision for financial institutions. Shortly afterwards the heads of state or government of the euro area countries issued a Declaration on a Concerted European Action Plan of the Euro Area Countries, outlining measures to ensure liquidity for financial institutions and co-operation among European states. In mid-October the European Commission proposed a revision to the deposit guarantee schemes directive, which would increase the minimum protection for bank deposits to €100,000. A summit of the Council held in mid-October urged further concerted and global action to protect the financial market system and the best interests of tax-payers. It emphasized the need for further action to strengthen European and international financial market rules and supervision. In mid-December the European Council approved a European Economic Recovery Plan (EERP), outlining a co-ordinated European response to the crisis, involving a three-part approach, based on a new European financial market architecture; a framework plan for the recovery of the real economy, to stimulate jobs and economic growth; and a global response to the financial crisis (see Economic Co-operation). In January 2009 the European Commission adopted decisions aimed at strengthening the supervisory framework for the EU financial markets. The high-level group on financial supervision in the EU, established in October 2008, published a report in February 2009 that analysed the complexity and principal causes of the financial crisis; identified priority areas requiring regulatory change; detailed proposals for far-reaching reforms within the EU aimed at stabilizing the financial markets; and proposals for changes at international level to prevent the recurrence of such a crisis. In mid-March the European Council adopted a common European position, based on constructing a rules- and values-based form of globalization, for a summit of the Group of Twenty (G20), which was held in early April. The Commission participated in the Financial Stability Forum which the April G20 meeting determined to establish, with a mandate to strengthen world-wide financial regulation and supervision; the Forum's inaugural meeting was held in June.

In September 2009, with a view to strengthening EU financial supervision, the Commission adopted proposals for the creation of a European Systemic Risk Board (ESRB), which was to monitor and assess risks to the stability of the financial system as a whole; and a European System of Financial Supervisors (ESFS), which would have the capacity to address recommendations and warnings issued to member states and to the European supervisory authorities. The ESFS was to comprise three European Supervisory Authorities (ESAs): a European Banking Authority; a European Securities and Markets Authority; and a European Insurance and Occupational Pensions Authority. These authorities were to be responsible for helping to rebuild confidence, develop a single set of financial rules, seek solutions to problems involving cross-border firms, and prevent the accumulation of risks that could undermine the stability of the financial system. In September 2010 the European Parliament endorsed the new supervisory framework, which was confirmed by ministers of the economy and of finance (the ECOFIN Council) in mid-November. The three ESAs and the ESRB were established in January 2011 to replace the supervisory committees hitherto in place.

ECONOMIC CO-OPERATION

A review of the economic situation is presented annually by the Commission, analysing recent developments and short- and medium-term prospects. Economic policy guidelines for the following year are adopted annually by the Council.

The following objectives for the end of 1973 were agreed by the Council in 1971, as the first of three stages towards European economic and monetary union: the narrowing of exchange rate margins to 2.25%; creation of a medium-term pool of reserves; co-ordination of short- and medium-term economic and budgetary policies; a joint position on international monetary issues; harmonization of taxes; creation of the European Monetary Co-operation Fund (EMCF); and creation of the European Regional Development Fund.

The narrowing of exchange margins (the 'snake') came into effect in 1972; however, Denmark, France, Ireland, Italy and the United Kingdom later floated their currencies, with only Denmark permanently returning to the arrangement. Sweden and Norway also linked their currencies to the 'snake', but Sweden withdrew from the arrangement in August 1977, and Norway withdrew in December 1978.

The European Monetary System (EMS) came into force in March 1979, with the aim of creating closer monetary co-operation, leading to a zone of monetary stability in Europe, principally through an Exchange Rate Mechanism (ERM), supervised by the ministries of finance and the central banks of member states. Not all Community members participated in the ERM: Greece did not join, Spain joined only in June 1989, the United Kingdom in October 1990 and Portugal in April 1992. To prevent wide fluctuations in the value of members' currencies against each other, the ERM fixed for each currency a central rate in European Currency Units (ECUs, see below), based on a 'basket' of national currencies; a reference rate in relation to other currencies was fixed for each currency, with established fluctuation margins. Central banks of the participating states intervened by buying or selling currencies when the agreed margin was likely to be exceeded. Each member placed 20% of its gold reserves and dollar reserves, respectively, into the EMCF, and received a supply of ECUs to regulate central bank interventions. Short- and medium-term credit facilities were given to support the balance of payments of member countries. The EMS was initially put under strain by the wide fluctuations in the exchange rates of non-Community currencies and by the differences in economic development among members, which led to nine realignments of currencies in 1979–83. Subsequently greater stability was achieved, with only two realignments of currencies between 1984 and 1988. In 1992–93, however, there was great pressure on currency markets, necessitating further realignments; in September 1992 Italian and British membership of the ERM was suspended. In July 1993, as a result of intensive currency speculation on European financial markets (forcing the weaker currencies to the very edge of their permitted margins), the ERM almost collapsed. In response to the crisis, EC ministers of finance decided to widen the fluctuation margins allowed for each currency, except in the cases of Germany and the Netherlands, which agreed to maintain their currencies within the original limits. The new margins were regarded as allowing for so much fluctuation in exchange rates as to represent a virtual suspension of the ERM, although some countries, notably France and Belgium, expressed their determination to adhere as far as possible to the original 'bands' in order to fulfil the conditions for eventual monetary union. In practice, most currencies remained within the former narrower bands during 1994. Austria became a member of the EMS in January 1995, and its currency was subject to ERM conditions. While Sweden decided to remain outside the EMS, Finland joined in October 1996. In November of that year the Italian lira was readmitted to the ERM.

The Intergovernmental Conference on Economic and Monetary Union, initiated in December 1990, was responsible for the drafting of the economic and monetary provisions of the Treaty on European Union, which came into force on 1 November 1993. The principal feature of the Treaty's provisions on Economic and Monetary Union (EMU), which was to be implemented in three stages, was the gradual introduction of a single currency, to be administered by a single central bank.

In December 1995 the European Council confirmed that Stage III of EMU was to begin on 1 January 1999 and confirmed the economic conditions for member states wishing to participate in it. The meeting decided that the proposed single currency would be officially known as the euro. Member countries remaining outside the monetary system, whether or not by choice, would still be part of the single market. Technical preparations for the euro were confirmed during a meeting of the European Council in Dublin, Ireland, in December 1996. The heads of government endorsed the new ERM and the legal framework for the euro, and approved the Stability and Growth Pact (SGP), intended to ensure that member countries maintained strict budgetary discipline. In March 1998 Greece was admitted to the ERM, causing a 14% devaluation of its national currency. In May of that year it was confirmed by a meeting of heads of state and of government that Greece failed to fulfil the conditions required for the adoption of a single currency from 1999. The meeting agreed that existing ERM central rates were to be used to determine the final rates of exchange between national currencies and the euro. A European Central Bank (ECB) was established in June 1998, which was to be accountable to a European Forum, comprising members of the European Parliament (MEPs) and chairmen of the finance committees of the national parliaments of EU member countries.

Although all of the then 15 members of the EU endorsed the principle of monetary union, with France and Germany the most ardent supporters, some countries had political doubts about joining. In October 1997 both the United Kingdom and Sweden confirmed that they would not participate in EMU from 1999. Denmark was also to remain outside the single currency. In May 1998 heads of state and government confirmed that 11 countries would take part in Stage III of EMU. It was agreed that existing ERM central rates were to be used to determine the final rates of exchange between national currencies and the euro. A European Central Bank (ECB) was established in June 1998.

On 31 December 1998 the ECOFIN Council adopted the conversion rates for the national currencies of the countries participating in the single currency. The euro was formally launched on 1 January 1999. ERM-II, the successor to the ERM, was launched on the same day. Both Greece and Denmark joined ERM-II, but in September 2000 some 53% of Danish voters participating in a national referendum rejected the adoption of the euro. On 1 January 2001 Greece became the 12th EU member state to adopt the euro. In September 2003 the majority of Swedish voters—some 56%—participating in a national referendum chose to reject Sweden's adoption of the euro.

The SGP, endorsed by the European Council in 1996, was instituted with the intention of ensuring that member countries maintain strict budgetary discipline during Stage III of monetary union, of which it was regarded as the cornerstone. Under its original terms, member states were obliged to keep budget deficits within 3% of gross domestic product (GDP), or face fines, and to bring their budgets close to balance by 2004. However, during 2002 the Pact was strongly criticized for being inflexible, when a number of countries could not meet its requirements. In September 2002 the 2004 deadline for reaching a balanced budget was extended by two years, although the 3% limit for budgetary deficit remained, while some concessionary provision was introduced to allow countries with low levels of long-term debt to increase investment spending by running larger short-term budget deficits.

In November 2003 France and Germany, which were both likely to breach the budget deficit of 3% for a third consecutive year, persuaded the EU ministers responsible for finance to suspend the disciplinary procedure (triggered by their failure to meet the 3% limit in 2002) under which they could have faced punitive fines. The refusal of France and Germany to restrict their expenditure provoked anger among some smaller EU countries that had implemented strict austerity programmes in order to comply with the Pact. In January 2004 the European Commission launched a legal action against the Council of Finance Ministers in the European Court of Justice, seeking clarification of whether the Council had acted illegally in temporarily suspending the budget rules. The SGP faced additional pressure with the pending enlargement of the EU, as its framework would have to apply to the 10 candidate countries, even though their economies were very diverse.

All 10 countries that joined the EU on 1 May 2004 (Cyprus, the Czech Republic, Estonia, Hungary, Latvia, Lithuania, Malta, Poland, Slovakia and Slovenia) were obliged to participate in EMU; however, adoption of the euro was dependent on the fulfilment of the same Maastricht convergence criteria as the initial entrants, which comprised conditions regarding inflation, debt, budget deficit, long-term interest rates and exchange rate stability. The exchange rate criteria included the requirement to spend at least two years in ERM-II. Although the currency was permitted to fluctuate 15% either side of a central rate or, by common agreement, within a narrower band, the ECB specified that the limit of 2.25% would be applied when judging whether countries had achieved sufficient stability to join the euro area. The entry into the euro area of the new member states was not expected to affect the ECB's monetary policy, as the new member states only accounted for about 5% of the GDP of the enlarged EU. Although many of the new member countries were keen to adopt the euro as soon as possible, the ECB warned of the risks associated with early membership of ERM-II, sharing widespread concerns that the required fiscal austerity and loss of flexibility over exchange rate policy would stifle economic growth in the accession countries. Moreover, currencies would also become vulnerable to speculative attacks once they entered ERM-II. Owing to differences in the economies of the new member states, progress towards adoption of the euro varied significantly. In June 2004 Estonia, Lithuania and Slovenia joined ERM-II. In May 2006, in a specific convergence report drawn up at the request of Slovenia and Lithuania to assess their readiness to adopt the euro, the Commission concluded that Slovenia met all of the conditions for admission to the euro area, while Lithuania should retain its current status as a member state with a derogation. Slovenia duly adopted the euro on 1 January 2007. Cyprus, Latvia and Malta joined ERM-II on 2 May 2005, followed by Slovakia on 28 November. Cyprus and Malta were admitted to the euro area on 1 January 2008, and Slovakia adopted the euro on 1 January 2009. Estonia adopted the euro on 1 January 2011, increasing the number of countries in the euro area to 17.

In September 2004 revised figures released by Greece revealed previous gross under-reporting of the country's national budgetary deficit and debt figures. It was subsequently established that Greece had not complied with membership rules for the single currency in 2000, the year in which it qualified to join. Greece received a formal warning from the Commission in December 2004 for publishing inaccurate data concerning its public finances for 1997–2003. In April 2009 the Council placed Greece under excessive deficit procedures, setting a deadline of 2010 for correction of the deficit to below 3%, on the basis of a Commission proposal which, in turn, had been based on an estimated Greek budgetary deficit equivalent to 3.7% of GDP in 2008. In December 2009—by which time Greece's 2008 budgetary deficit had been revised up to 7.7% and the 2009 deficit was being estimated at 12.7%, attributable to factors such as the effects of the ongoing economic crisis, absence of corrective measures and fiscal slippage—the Council determined that the Greek authorities had not taken sufficient effective action to correct the deficit. The estimated 12.7% Greek budgetary deficit for 2009 was deemed potentially destabilizing to markets and to the entire euro area, and the unreliable reporting of public finance statistics was a significant cause of concern: in this respect it was reported in early 2010 that the Commission was considering reforms that would in future enable Eurostat to audit national statistical agencies.

In January 2010 the ECOFIN Council advised the Greek Government to embrace a far-reaching economic reform plan aimed at gradually reducing Greece's budget deficit (by 4% by the end of 2010, initially); the plan was endorsed by the Commission in early February 2010. In early February the European Commission also, using new powers given under the Treaty of Lisbon, imposed a new 'quasi-permanent' surveillance system on the management of Greece's public finances. Furthermore, the Commission issued a formal warning to the Greek authorities regarding the need to pursue policies consistent with the broad economic guidelines adopted by the Council, and launched infringement proceedings against Greece relating to the submission of erroneous statistical data. Soon afterwards EU heads of state and government issued a statement emphasizing that all euro area members were required to conduct sound national policies in line with agreed rules, while committing the euro area member states to taking determined and co-ordinated action, if need be, to safeguard financial stability in the euro area as a whole. In mid-February 2010 the Council gave notice to Greece to correct its excessive deficit (to below 3% of GDP) by 2012, setting out a timetable for corrective measures, and issued a formal recommendation to Greece to bring its economic policies into line with broad EU economic policy guidelines and thereby remove the risk of jeopardizing the overall proper functioning of economic and monetary union. In May 2010 the European Commission, the European Central Bank (ECB) and the IMF reached agreement with Greece on a programme intended to stabilize the Greek economy, in accordance with which funding of €110,000m. would be provided over a period of three years, of which €80,000m. was to originate from the countries of the euro area. In accordance with the terms of the programme, Greece was required to implement further budget cuts, increase taxation, and carry out substantial reforms of the pensions and social security systems.

In early July 2011 EU ministers of finance approved the disbursement of further lending to Greece, temporarily alleviating the threat of default. In late October 2011 EU leaders agreed further emergency measures designed to help resolve the euro area debt crisis. The agreement provided for the recapitalization of private banks; provided for losses of one-half of the banks' holdings of Greek debt; and sought to increase the financial strength of the European Financial Stability Facility (EFSF—see below). In February 2012 the EU, the ECB and the IMF approved further lending to Greece, worth some €130,000m. However, its disbursement remained dependent on the rapid adoption of further reductions in expenditure and guarantees of their implementation, despite the approval of a series of austerity measures by Greece.

Meanwhile, in 2008 a sharp contraction in global credit markets had prompted EU Governments to offer widespread financial assistance to support failing banks amid the onset of recession throughout the EU. In mid-November a Group of Twenty (G20) summit meeting was held in Washington, DC, USA, at the EU's instigation, in order to discuss measures to help stimulate economic recovery world-wide, improve the regulation of financial markets, aid international governance, and reject protectionism. In December the European Council adopted a European Economic Recovery Plan (EERP), worth around €200,000m., equivalent to some 1.5% of the EU's total GDP, and representing a co-ordinated response to the situation. The plan aimed to restore consumer and business confidence, to restart lending, and to stimulate investment in EU economies and create jobs, by increasing investments in infrastructure and important sectors of the economy—including the automotive industry, construction and green technologies—while making full use of the flexibility offered in the SGP. The EERP proposed that member states should co-ordinate national budgetary stimulus packages in order to optimize their impact and avoid secondary consequences, as negative effects spread from one country to another. A Commission report on the EU economy issued in September 2009 found the ongoing recession to be the deepest since the 1930s, and stated that a comprehensive, co-ordinated recession 'exit strategy' (emphasizing investment in renewable energy sources and green infrastructure) should be developed, for implementation as soon as economic recovery was apparent.

In early May 2010 euro area member states agreed to the establishment of a new, temporary institution, the EFSF, with a lending capacity of €4,400m., which aimed to maintain financial stability in the euro area through the provision of rapid financial assistance to member countries. In late June heads of state and of government agreed to expand the EFSF's remit and increase its guarantee commitments from €4,400m. to €7,800m., equivalent to a lending capacity of €4,400m. The EFSF's scope was further expanded in late July, and all amendments to the EFSF Framework entered into force in mid-October 2011. The EFSF is based in Luxembourg, and is backed by guarantees from 14 of the euro area's 17 members (Greece, Ireland and Portugal were exempted). Meanwhile, in October 2010 the European Council had agreed to establish a permanent crisis mechanism, the European Stability Mechanism (ESM), to safeguard the financial stability of the euro area. Combined with strengthened economic governance and monitoring, the ESM, which was to have an overall lending capacity of €500,000m., aimed to prevent the development of future crises. In late July 2011 EU heads of state and of government taking part in an emergency Euro Area Summit in Brussels, Belgium, agreed to reduce EFSF interest rates and extend the maturities of future loans issued to Greece, Ireland and Portugal, in an effort to strengthen their financial programmes.

On 9 December 2011 the majority of EU member states reached agreement in principal on new fiscal arrangements, designed to increase fiscal discipline and convergence in the euro area. The so-called fiscal compact, *inter alia*, required member states to maintain a balanced budget (or a deficit of no more than 0.5% of nominal GDP). Agreement was reached on increased co-operation on economic policy, and an acceleration of arrangements for the introduction of the ESM. In March 2012 25 heads of state and of government signed the new fiscal compact, which required ratification by 12 euro area member states; the United Kingdom and the Czech Republic refused to sign the agreement. In Ireland, the fiscal compact was to be subject to approval by a referendum, scheduled to take place at the end of May.

In mid-December 2011 new rules, comprising five regulations and one directive (the 'six-pack'), came into effect, applying to both the procedures within the SGP that are designed to prevent excessive deficits, and the excessive deficit procedure (EDP), which is the corrective branch of the pact. New measures, specifically financial disincentives and fines, were to be applied to non-compliant euro area members in an effort to strengthen the efficacy of the SGP. At January 2012 23 of the 27 EU member states were subject to an EDP (with the exception of Estonia, Finland, Luxemburg and Sweden).

The Euro

With the creation of the European Monetary System (EMS) in 1979, a new monetary unit, the European Currency Unit (ECU), was adopted. Its value and composition were identical to those of the European Unit of Account (EUA) already used in the administrative fields of the Community. The ECU was a composite monetary unit, in which the relative value of each currency was determined by the gross national product and the volume of trade of each country. Assigned the function of the unit of account used by the European Monetary Co-operation Fund, the ECU was also used as the denominator for the Exchange Rate Mechanism (ERM); as the denominator for operations in both the intervention and the credit mechanisms; and as a means of settlement between monetary authorities of the European Community. From April 1979 the ECU was also used as the unit of account for the purposes of the Common Agricultural Policy (CAP). From 1981 it replaced the EUA in the general budget of the Community; the activities of the European Development Fund (EDF) under the Lomé Convention; the balance sheets and loan operations of the European Investment Bank (EIB); and the activities of the European Coal and Steel Community (ECSC). In June 1985 measures were adopted by the governors of the Community's central banks, aiming to strengthen the EMS by expanding the use of the ECU, for example, by allowing international monetary institutions and the central banks of non-member countries to become 'other holders' of ECUs. From September 1989 the Portuguese and Spanish currencies were included in the composition of the ECU. The composition of the ECU 'basket' of national currencies was 'frozen' with the entry into force of the Treaty on European Union on 1 November 1993, and remained unchanged until the termination of the ECU on 31 December 1998. (Consequently the currencies of Austria, Finland and Sweden, on those countries' accession to the EU, were not represented in the ECU 'basket'.)

As part of Stage III of the process of Economic and Monetary Union (EMU), the ECU was replaced by a single currency, the euro (€), on 1 January 1999, at a conversion rate of 1:1. Initially the euro was used for cashless payments and accounting purposes, while the traditional national currencies, then considered as 'sub-units' of the euro, continued to be used for cash payments. On 1 January 2002 euro coins and banknotes entered into circulation in the then 12 participating countries, and, by the end of February, the former national currencies of all of the participating countries had been withdrawn. The euro's value in national currencies is calculated and published daily, and stood at €1 = US $1.322 on 26 April 2012, at which time there were 17 participating countries.

A payments settlement system, known as TARGET (Trans-European Automated Real-time Gross Settlement Express Transfer), was introduced for countries participating in EMU on 4 January 1999. An upgraded version of the system, TARGET2, was launched in November 2007. The Single Euro Payments Area (SEPA), which was introduced gradually from 2008, was designed to enable all electronic payments across the euro area to be made as efficiently and securely as domestic payments within a single member state.

Three interest rates are set for the euro area: the rate on the main refinancing operations, providing most of the banking system's liquidity; the rate on the deposit facility, which may be used by banks making overnight deposits with the euro system; and the rate on the marginal lending facility, which offers overnight credit to banks from the euro system. From October 2008 refinancing operations were conducted through a fixed-rate tender procedure, having been conducted as variable rate tenders since June 2000. During the second half of 2008 and early 2009 the ECB considerably reduced interest rates with the aim of stimulating non-inflationary growth and contributing to financial stability. The ECB reduced the fixed refinancing rate progressively from 3.75% in October 2008 to 1.0% at 13 May 2009 (that rate remaining in force until 13 April 2011). The rates set in 2009 represented the lowest euro area rates (whether variable or fixed) set in the decade since January 1999. On 13 April 2011 the fixed refinancing rate was increased to 1.25%. From 14 December 2011 the fixed refinancing rate was 1.0%.

External Relations

CENTRAL AND SOUTH-EASTERN EUROPE

During the late 1980s the extensive political changes and reforms in Eastern European countries led to a strengthening of links with the EC. Agreements on trade and economic co-operation were concluded with several countries. Community heads of government agreed in December 1989 to establish a European Bank for Reconstruction and Development—EBRD, with participation by member states of the Organisation for Economic Co-operation and Development—OECD and the Council for Mutual Economic Assistance, to promote investment in Eastern Europe; the EBRD began operations in April 1991. In the 1990s 'Europe Agreements' were signed with Czechoslovakia, Hungary and Poland (1991), Bulgaria and Romania (1993), Estonia, Latvia and Lithuania (1995), and Slovenia (1996), which led to formal applications for membership of the EU. On 1 May 2004 the Czech Republic, Estonia, Hungary, Latvia, Lithuania, Poland, Slovakia and Slovenia acceded to the EU. Bulgaria and Romania formally joined the EU on 1 January 2007.

In July 2006 an Instrument for Pre-Accession Assistance (IPA) was adopted by the Council, which replaced the former PHARE (Poland/Hungary Aid for Restructuring of Economies) and other such programmes (Instrument for Structural Policies for Pre-Accession—ISPA; Special Accession Programme for Agriculture and Rural Development—SAPARD; Community Assistance for Reconstruction, Development and Stabilisation, with reference to the Western Balkans—CARDS; and the Turkey instrument) from January 2007. The IPA aims to provide targeted assistance to candidate countries for membership of the EU (Croatia, Iceland, the former Yugoslav republic of Macedonia—FYRM, Montenegro, Serbia and Turkey by April 2012) or those that are potential candidate countries (e.g. Albania and Bosnia and Herzegovina). In March 2008 the Commission launched the Civil Society Facility, a new financing arrangement under the IPA, which aims to support the development of civil society in South-Eastern Europe, by strengthening the political role of civil society organizations; developing cross-border projects; and familiarizing representatives of civil society with EU affairs. In November the Commission adopted the IPA Multi-Annual Financial Framework for 2010–12, comprising five components: transition and institution building; cross-border co-operation; regional development; human resources development; and rural development. Candidate countries Croatia and the FYRM were allocated €471.8m. and €296.8m. for 2010–12, respectively; Albania was to receive €285.1m.; Bosnia and Herzegovina €324.3m.; Kosovo €4,631.4m.; Montenegro €104.1m.; and Serbia €608.2m. (Turkey was also eligible for funding under the IPA.)

In June 1999 the EU, in conjunction with the Group of Seven industrialized nations and Russia (the Group of Eight—G8), regional governments and other organizations concerned with the stability of the region, launched the Stability Pact for South Eastern Europe, a comprehensive conflict-prevention strategy, which was placed under the auspices of the Organization for Security and Co-operation in Europe (OSCE). The Stability Pact aimed to strengthen the efforts of the countries of South-Eastern Europe in fostering peace, democracy, respect for human rights and economic prosperity. In April 2008 the Stability Pact was replaced by a Regional Co-operation Council, based in Sarajevo, Bosnia and Herzegovina.

In March 1997 the EU sent two advisory delegations to Albania to help to restore order after violent unrest and political instability erupted in that country. It was announced in early April that the EU was to provide humanitarian aid of some ECU 2m., to be used for emergency relief. In September 2002 the European Parliament voted in support of opening negotiations for a Stabilization and Association Agreement (SAA) with Albania, following satisfactory progress in that country, with regard to presidential voting and electoral reform. In November 2005 the Commission urged Albania to increase its efforts to combat organized crime and corruption, to enhance media freedom and to conduct further electoral reform. Negotiations on the signature of an SAA with Albania, which officially commenced at the end of January 2003, were completed in February 2006. The SAA was formally signed in June and entered into force in April 2009. In April 2009 Albania applied for the status of a candidate country for EU membership. In November 2010 the European Commission agreed to introduce visa liberalization for Albania, with effect from mid-December. The Commission considered that Albania had made substantial efforts to meet the EU's political, economic and legislative criteria during the preceding year, but that further reform was required before it could be considered suitable for candidate status, owing, in particular, to the inefficacy of the public administration and the political impasse that had followed the legislative elections of June 2009. In January 2011 more than 20,000 people took part in an anti-Government demonstration in the Albanian capital, Tirana, which led to violent clashes between police and protesters. EU officials condemned the excessive use of force, and urged political dialogue. Following local elections in May, the EU's Commissioner responsible for Enlargement and European Neighbourhood Policy criticized the conduct of the elections (which were marred by controversy and disputes between the two main political parties), declaring that they demonstrated the urgent need for electoral reform. In October the European Commission again failed to recommend candidate status for Albania, citing insufficient progress in meeting the EU's political criteria.

A co-operation agreement was signed with Yugoslavia in 1980 (but was not ratified until April 1983), allowing tariff-free imports and Community loans. New financial protocols were signed in 1987 and 1991. However, EC aid was suspended in July 1991, following the declarations of independence by the Yugoslav republics of Croatia and Slovenia, and the subsequent outbreak of civil conflict. Efforts were made in the ensuing months by EC ministers of foreign affairs to negotiate a peaceful settlement, and a team of EC observers was maintained in Yugoslavia from July, to monitor successive cease-fire agreements. In October the EC proposed a plan for an association of independent states, to replace the Yugoslav federation: this was accepted by all of the Yugoslav republics except Serbia, which demanded a redefinition of boundaries to accommodate within Serbia all predominantly Serbian areas. In November the application of the Community's co-operation agreements with Yugoslavia was suspended (with exemptions for the republics which co-operated in the peace negotiations). In January 1992 the Community granted diplomatic recognition to the former Yugoslav republics of Croatia and Slovenia, and in April it recognized Bosnia and Herzegovina, while withholding recognition from Macedonia (owing to pressure from the Greek Government, which feared that the existence of an independent Macedonia would imply a claim on the Greek province of the same name). In May EC ambassadors were withdrawn from the Yugoslav capital, Belgrade, in protest at Serbia's support for aggression by Bosnian Serbs against other ethnic groups in Bosnia and Herzegovina, and in the same month the Community imposed a trade embargo on Serbia and Montenegro.

In April 1994, following a request from EU ministers of foreign affairs, a Contact Group, consisting of France, Germany, the United Kingdom, the USA and Russia, was initiated to undertake peace negotiations. In the following month ministers of foreign affairs of the USA, Russia and the EU (represented by five member states) jointly endorsed a proposal to divide Bosnia and Herzegovina in proportions of 49% to the Bosnian Serbs and 51% to the newly established Federation of Muslims and Croats. The proposal was rejected by the Bosnian Serb assembly in July and had to be abandoned after the Muslim-Croat Federation also withdrew its support. In July the EU formally assumed political control of Mostar, in southern Bosnia and Herzegovina, in order to restore the city's administrative infrastructure.

In September 1995 the EU supported US-led negotiations in Geneva, Switzerland, to devise a plan to end the conflict in Bosnia and Herzegovina. The plan closely resembled the previous proposals of the Contact Group: two self-governing entities were to be created within Bosnia and Herzegovina, with 51% of territory being allocated to the Muslim-Croat Federation and 49% to Bosnian Serbs. The proposals were finally agreed after negotiations in Dayton, OH, USA, in November 1995, and an accord was signed in Paris, France, in December.

In January 1996 the EU announced its intention to recognize Yugoslavia (Serbia and Montenegro). During 1996–99 the EU allocated ECU 1,000m. for the repatriation of refugees, restructuring the economy and technical assistance, in addition to ECU 1,000m. in humanitarian aid provided since the beginning of the conflict in the former Yugoslavia.

In 2000 the EU published a roadmap for Bosnia and Herzegovina, outlining measures that must be undertaken by the Government prior to the initiation of a feasibility study on the formulation of an SAA. In September 2002 the Commission reported that Bosnia and Herzegovina had essentially adhered to the terms of the roadmap. In January 2003 a new EU Police Mission (EUPM) took over from the UN peace-keeping force in Bosnia and Herzegovina. This was the first operation under the common European Security and Defence Policy. The EUPM was re-established in 2006, and aimed to support the police-reform process and continue to help to combat organized crime. Meanwhile, on 28 January 2004 the Bosnian Government issued a decree providing for the reunification of Mostar (divided between Croat- and Bosnian-controlled municipalities since 1993) into a single administration, thereby fulfilling one of the major preconditions for the signature of an SAA with the EU. In December 2004 7,000 troops (EUFOR) were deployed under EU command in Bosnia and Herzegovina, taking over from NATO, with a mission (Operation Althea) to ensure stability in the country. From the end of March 2007 EUFOR-Althea was downsized to comprise the Multinational Maneuver Battalion, of around 2,000 troops. Negotiations on an SAA officially commenced in November 2005, and an SAA with the EU was initialled in December 2007, and signed in mid-June 2008. In November 2010 the European Commission agreed to introduce visa liberalization for Bosnia and Herzegovina, with effect from mid-December. Following state and entity elections in October, the failure to establish a state-level government was cited by the European Commission in October 2011 as a major obstacle to progress in reforms. In November the Commission announced that it was to grant pre-accession funds of some €200m. during 2012–13 to support government reform efforts. (A new state Council of Ministers was finally formed in February 2012.)

An SAA was signed with Croatia in October 2001. In February 2003 Croatia submitted a formal application for membership of the EU. In December 2004 the European Council announced that negotiations on membership would commence in mid-March 2005, provided that Croatia co-operated fully with the International Criminal Tribunal for the former Yugoslavia (ICTY). The SAA entered into force in February 2005. In early 2005 the only outstanding issue between Croatia and the ICTY was the need for the arrest and transfer to The Hague of the retired Gen. Ante Gotovina, who went into hiding in 2001 when the ICTY charged him with war crimes against ethnic Serbs during a military operation in 1995. The planned accession talks with Croatia were postponed in March 2005, following an official report by the Chief Prosecutor at the ICTY, Carla Del Ponte, which stated that the Croatian authorities had failed to demonstrate full co-operation with the ICTY. However, in early October Del Ponte issued an assessment stating that Croatia's co-operation with the ICTY had improved, and negotiations were initiated. In December Gotovina was apprehended in the Canary Islands, Spain, thereby removing the main perceived obstacle to EU membership. A border dispute with Slovenia threatened progress towards membership from late 2008; however, a referendum held in Slovenia in early June 2010 secured support for the resolution of the dispute by international arbitration. In November the Commission praised Croatia's progress towards meeting the criteria for EU membership, but urged that further efforts be made to combat corruption and organized crime, to undertake administrative reform, protect ethnic minorities and to aid the repatriation of refugees. Croatia completed membership negotiations on 30 June 2011, and signed the Treaty of Accession on 9 December. Accession was due to take place in 2013, following popular approval of Croatian membership of the EU in a referendum held in late January 2012.

In December 1993 six member states of the EU formally recognized the FYRM as an independent state, but in February 1994 Greece imposed a commercial embargo against the FYRM, on the grounds that the use of the name and symbols (e.g. on the state flag) of 'Macedonia' was a threat to Greek national security. In March, however, ministers of foreign affairs of the EU decided that the embargo was in contravention of EU law, and in April the Commission commenced legal proceedings in the European Court of Justice against Greece. In September 1995 Greece and the FYRM began a process of normalizing relations, after the FYRM agreed to change the design of its state flag. In October Greece ended its economic blockade of the FYRM. A trade and co-operation agreement with the FYRM entered into force in January 1998. In April 2001 an SAA was signed with the FYRM. At the same time, an interim agreement was adopted, allowing for trade-related matters of the SAA to enter into effect in June, without the need for formal ratification by the national parliaments of the EU member states. (The SAA provided for the EU to open its markets to 95% of exports from the FYRM.) However, the Macedonian Government was informed that it would be required to deliver concessions to the ethnic Albanian minority population prior to entering into the agreement. In 2002 the remit of the European Agency for Reconstruction, which had been originally established to implement aid programmes in Kosovo, was extended to include the FYRM. On 31 March 2003 a NATO contingent in the FYRM was replaced by an EU-led mission, Operation Concordia, comprising 350 military personnel. It was replaced in December by a 200-member EU police mission, Operation Proxima, which, in addition to maintaining security and combating organized crime, was to advise the Macedonian police forces. Operation Proxima's mandate expired at the end of 2005. The SAA entered into force in April 2004. A formal application for membership of the EU was submitted in March of that year, and the FYRM was granted candidate status in December 2005. In October 2009 the European Commission recommended that accession negotiations with the FYRM commence; however, Greece objected to the initiation of membership negotiations while the dispute over the country's name remained unresolved. In mid-December visa liberalization entered into force for travel within the Schengen area. In progress reports in November 2010 and October 2011, the European Commission confirmed that the FYRM's unresolved dispute with Greece remained the only main obstacle to the commencement of accession negotiations. Despite the continued impasse, in March 2012 the FYRM began a preliminary dialogue with the EU, which was designed to reduce the length of any future official membership negotiations.

In 1998 the escalation of violence in the Serbian province of Kosovo (Federal Republic of Yugoslavia—FRY), between Serbs and the ethnic Albanian majority, prompted the imposition of sanctions by EU ministers of foreign affairs. In March ministers agreed to impose an arms embargo, to halt export credit guarantees to Yugoslavia and to restrict visas for Serbian officials. A ban on new investment in the region was imposed in June. In the same month, military observers from the EU, Russia and the USA were deployed to Kosovo. During October the Yugoslav Government allowed a team of international experts to investigate atrocities in the region, under an EU mandate. Several EU countries participated in the NATO military offensive against Yugoslavia, which was initiated in March 1999 owing to the continued repression of ethnic Albanians in Kosovo by Serbian forces. Ministers approved a new series of punitive measures in April, including an embargo on the sale or supply of petroleum to the Yugoslav authorities and an extension of a travel ban on Serbian officials and business executives. Humanitarian assistance was extended to provide relief for the substantial numbers of refugees who fled Kosovo amid the escalating violence, in particular to assist the Governments of Albania and the FYRM.

In September 1999 EU ministers responsible for foreign affairs agreed to ease sanctions against Kosovo and Montenegro. In October the EU began to implement an Energy for Democracy initiative, with the objective of supplying some €5m.-worth of heating oil to Serbian towns controlled by groups in opposition to the Yugoslav President, Slobodan Milošević. In February 2000 the EU suspended its ban on the Yugoslav national airline. However, the restrictions on visas for Serbian officials were reinforced. Kosovo received a total of €474.7m. under EU programmes in 2000 and the EU was the largest financial contributor to the province in 2001.

In May 2000 the EU agreed an emergency aid package to support Montenegro against destabilization by Serbia. Following the election of a new administration in the FRY in late 2000, the EU immediately withdrew all remaining sanctions, with the exception of those directed against Milošević and his associates, and pledged financial support of €200m. The FRY was welcomed as a full participant in the stabilization and association process (see below). The EU insisted that the FRY must co-operate fully with the ICTY. Following the arrest of Milošević by the FRY authorities in April 2001, the first part of the EU's aid package for that year (amounting to €240m.) was released. During 2002 EU humanitarian aid to Serbia totalled €37.5m., to assist the large numbers of refugees and displaced persons. Negotiations on an SAA between the State Union of Serbia and Montenegro (as the FRY became known in February 2003) and the EU commenced in November 2005, but were terminated in May 2006, owing to the country's failure fully to co-operate with the ICTY. Following Montenegro's declaration of independence on 3 June 2006, the Narodna skupština Republike Srbije (National Assembly of the Republic of Serbia) confirmed that Serbia was the official successor state of the State Union of Serbia and Montenegro. On 12 June the EU recognized Montenegrin independence, and the Serbian Government officially recognized Montenegro as an independent state three days later. At the end of September the Narodna skupština adopted a new Constitution, which was confirmed by referendum in late October. In early June 2007 the President of the European Commission invited Serbia to resume negotiations on an SAA, following the arrest, within Serbia, of Zdravko Tolimir, a former Bosnian Serb army officer. A visa facilitation and readmission agreement between Serbia and the EU came into force at the beginning of 2008. In late February the EU suspended negotiations with Serbia on an SAA, after violence broke out in Belgrade following the declaration of independence by Kosovo (see below). However, on 29 April EU ministers of foreign affairs signed the SAA, in what was widely perceived as an effort to strengthen popular support for reformist parties contesting the forthcoming elections. The SAA with Serbia was accompanied by a provisional document granting Serbia access to benefits based on the SAA before all EU members had ratified the Agreement; however, its implementation was to be suspended until EU member states agreed unanimously on Serbia's full co-operation with the ICTY. In late July Radovan Karadžić, a former President of Republika Srpska, Bosnia and Herzegovina, whose arrest on charges of war crimes, including genocide, had long been sought by the ICTY, was apprehended in Belgrade. In mid-December 2009 visa liberalization was implemented for Serbian citizens travelling within the Schengen area. In late December Serbia formally applied for membership of the EU. At the end of March 2010 the Narodna skupština passed a resolution condemning the massacre of up to 8,000 Muslim male civilians by Serb forces in July 1995, in Srebrenica, Bosnia and Herzegovina. In June 2010 the EU agreed to begin the ratification process for the SAA with Serbia, following a positive assessment of Serbia's co-operation with the ICTY. In late July the International Court of Justice (ICJ) issued a non-binding, advisory opinion that Kosovo's declaration of independence on 17 February 2008 had not breached international law, Security Council Resolution 1244 or the constitutional framework. Serbia reaffirmed its intention to continue to withhold recognition of independence for Kosovo. In early September 2010, however, the UN General Assembly adopted a joint, non-binding, EU-Serbia resolution, according to which Serbia agreed to participate in direct talks with Kosovo, under the aegis of the EU. Subsequently, in late October EU ministers of foreign affairs agreed to request that the Commission assess Serbia's application for candidacy. In late May 2011 the Serbian authorities arrested the Bosnian Serb former military leader Ratko Mladić in northern Serbia. The arrest of the final major war crimes suspect to be indicted by the ICTY, the Croatian Serb Goran Hadžić, was announced in late July. In October the European Commission issued a report stating that Serbia had made sufficient progress towards meeting EU criteria for a formal recommendation to be made that it become a candidate country. In December, nevertheless, Serbia failed to secure membership status at an EU summit meeting in Brussels owing to the insistence of a number of EU leaders that the issue of Serbia's refusal to recognize Kosovo first be resolved. At the end of February 2012, the Romanian Government unexpectedly presented objections to Serbia's candidacy relating to the treatment of the Vlach ethnic minority in Serbia, which were withdrawn following an agreement between Serbian and Romanian officials. EU heads of state and government officially approved Serbia's candidate status on 1 March (following significant progress in dialogue between Serbian and Kosovo representatives in Brussels), although no date for the beginning of accession negotiations was announced.

Following the declaration of independence by Montenegro in June 2006, the EU Council pledged to develop the relationship of the EU with Montenegro as a sovereign state. The first Enhanced Permanent Dialogue meeting between Montenegro and the EU was held in the Montenegrin capital, Podgorica, in late July. On the same day the Council adopted a mandate for the negotiation of an SAA with Montenegro (based on the previous mandate for negotiations with the State Union of Serbia and Montenegro). Negotiations were initiated in September, and in October 2007 Montenegro signed an SAA with the EU, which entered into force on 1 May 2010. Meanwhile, Montenegro had applied for membership of the EU in December 2008. A visa facilitation and readmission agreement between Montenegro and the EU came into force at the beginning of 2008, and from 19 December 2009 Montenegrin citizens were no longer required to hold a visa to travel within the Schengen area. Following a recommendation by the European Commission in the previous month, in mid-December 2010, at a meeting of the EU Council, held in Brussels, Montenegro was formally granted the status of a candidate country for EU membership. In March 2011 the European Parliament adopted a resolution commending Montenegro's progress towards EU integration. In October the Commission recommended that accession negotiations be opened with Montenegro, stating that the Government had made satisfactory progress towards meeting the criteria for EU membership, although stipulating that sustained efforts were necessary in the area of the rule of law, particularly in combating corruption and organized crime.

On 17 February 2008 the Assembly of Kosovo endorsed a declaration establishing the province as a sovereign state, independent from Serbia. Serbia immediately protested that the declaration of independence contravened international law and demanded that it be annulled. The USA extended recognition to Kosovo on the following day, and a large number of EU member nations announced their intention to do so. A supervisory EU mission in Kosovo (the EU Rule of Law Mission in Kosovo—EULEX), to comprise some 1,900 foreign personnel, became operational after a 120-day transition period (although full deployment was delayed). Following the deployment of EULEX, UNMIK had been scheduled to transfer authority to government institutions in Kosovo. However, after both Serbia and Russia challenged the legality of EULEX, it was agreed that the two missions would co-exist under joint command. It was also anticipated that a NATO presence would remain in Kosovo for a period of five years, in order to oversee Kosovo's security. On 15 June a new Constitution came into force in Kosovo (Serbia refused to accept its introduction in Serb-dominated northern Kosovo). In late October an agreement was signed with the USA, providing for its participation in EULEX. EULEX assumed responsibility from UNMIK for police and judicial functions in December. In December 2008 EULEX Kosovo became operational, and by April 2009 the mission was being deployed to full operational capacity. At April 2012 90 UN member nations, including 22 EU member states, had formally recognized Kosovo, and many diplomatic missions in Prishtina had become embassies. However, several EU member states (Cyprus, Greece, Romania, Slovakia and Spain) had announced their intention to withhold recognition of Kosovo as an independent state. In July 2010 the European Parliament adopted a resolution that reiterated its desire for all EU member states to recognize Kosovo's independence, the legality of which was upheld by the advisory opinion of the ICJ later that month. In February 2012 the European Commission proposed the undertaking of a feasibility study for an SAA with Kosovo.

EASTERN EUROPE, RUSSIA AND THE CIS

In the late 1980s the extensive political changes and reforms in Eastern Europe led to a strengthening of links with the EC. In December 1989 EC heads of government agreed to establish the European Bank for Reconstruction and Development (EBRD) to promote investment in Eastern Europe, with participation by member states of the Organisation for Economic Co-operation and Development (OECD) and the Council for Mutual Economic Assistance (CMEA), which provided economic co-operation and co-ordination in the communist bloc between 1949 and 1991. The EBRD began operations in April 1991. In the same year the EC established the Technical Assistance to the Commonwealth of Independent States (TACIS) programme, to promote the development of successful market economies and to foster democracy in the countries of the former USSR through the provision of expertise and training. (TACIS initially extended assistance to the Baltic states; in 1992, however, these became eligible for assistance under PHARE and withdrew from TACIS. Mongolia was eligible for TACIS assistance in 1991–2003, but was subsequently covered by the Asia Latin America—ALA programme.)

In March 2003 the European Commission launched a European Neighbourhood Policy (ENP) with the aim of enhancing co-operation with countries adjacent to the enlarged Union. A new European Neighbourhood and Partnership Instrument (ENPI) replaced TACIS and MEDA (which was concerned with EU co-operation with Mediterranean countries) from 2007. All countries covered by the ENP (Armenia, Azerbaijan, Belarus, Georgia, Moldova, Ukraine and several Mediterranean countries) were to be eligible for support under the ENPI. Russia was not covered by the ENP, and the relationship between Russia and the EU was described as a Strategic Partnership, which was also to be funded by the ENPI. In accordance with the ENP, in December 2004 the EU agreed Action Plans with Moldova and Ukraine, establishing targets for political and economic co-operation. These Plans were adopted by EU ministers of foreign affairs and the two countries concerned in February 2005. ENP Action Plans for Armenia, Azerbaijan and Georgia were developed in 2005 and published in late 2006. A visa facilitation and readmission agreement with Georgia was concluded in January 2011. The EU did not enter into discussions on a Plan with Belarus, stating that it first required the country to hold free and fair elections in order to establish a democratic form of government (see below). The eventual conclusion of more ambitious relationships with partner countries achieving sufficient progress in meeting the priorities set out in the Action Plans (through the negotiation of European Neighbourhood Agreements) was envisaged.

In June 2007 the European Council adopted The EU and Central Asia: Strategy for a New Partnership, which aimed to develop bilateral and regional co-operation in a wide number of areas. An initial progress report was published in June 2008. In May 2009 the heads of state or government of Armenia, Azerbaijan, Belarus, Georgia, Moldova and Ukraine, and representatives of the EU and the heads of state or government, and other representatives, of its member states, convened in Prague, Czech Republic, issued a joint declaration on establishing an Eastern Partnership. The Eastern Partnership (facilitated through a specific Eastern dimension of the ENP) aimed, through support for political and socio-economic reforms in interested partner countries, to create the necessary conditions to accelerate political association and further economic integration with the EU.

In 1992 EU heads of government decided to replace the agreement on trade and economic co-operation that had been concluded with the USSR in 1989 with new Partnership and Co-operation Agreements (PCAs), providing a framework for closer political, cultural and economic relations between the EU and the former republics of the USSR. An Interim Agreement with Russia on trade concessions came into effect in February 1996, giving EU exporters improved access to the Russian market for specific products, and at the same time abolishing quantitative restrictions on some Russian exports to the EU; a PCA with Russia came into effect in December 1997. In January 1998 the first meeting of the Co-operation Council for the EU-Russia PCA was held, and in July an EU-Russia Space Dialogue was established. In June 1999 the EU adopted a Common Strategy on Russia. This aimed to promote the consolidation of democracy and rule of law in the country; the integration of Russia into the common European economic and social space; and regional stability and security. At the sixth EU-Russia summit, held in October 2000, both parties agreed to initiate a regular energy dialogue, with the aim of establishing an EU-Russia Energy Partnership. However, the status of Kaliningrad, a Russian enclave situated between Poland and Lithuania, became an increasing source of contention as the EU prepared to admit those two countries. Despite opposition from Russia, the EU insisted that residents of Kaliningrad would need a visa to cross EU territory. In November 2002, at an EU-Russia summit meeting held in Brussels, Belgium, a compromise agreement was reached, according to which residents of the enclave were to be issued with multiple-transit travel documentation; the new regulations took effect in July 2003. Also in November 2002, the EU granted Russian exporters market economy status, in recognition of the progress made by Russia to liberalize its economy. At a summit held in St Petersburg, Russia, in May 2003, the EU and Russia agreed to improve their co-operation by creating four 'common spaces' within the framework of the PCA. The two sides agreed to establish a common economic space; a common space for freedom, security and justice; a space for co-operation on external security; and for research, education and culture. However, relations between the EU and Russia remained strained by Russia's opposition to EU enlargement, partly owing to fears of a detrimental effect on the Russian economy, as some of its neighbouring countries (significant markets for Russian goods) were obliged to introduce EU quotas and tariffs. In February 2004 the European Commission made proposals to improve the efficacy of EU-Russia relations, given their increased dependence, the enlargement due to take place in May, and unresolved territorial conflicts in a number of countries close to the Russian and EU borders (Azerbaijan, Georgia and Moldova). In May, at a bilateral summit held in the Russian capital, Moscow, the EU agreed to support Russia's membership of the World Trade Organization (WTO), following Russia's extension in April of its PCA with the EU to 10 accession states. The Russian President, Vladimir Putin, signed legislation ratifying the Kyoto Protocol of the UN Convention on Climate Change in November, following EU criticism of the country's failure to do so. The Kyoto Protocol entered into force in February 2005. Consultations on human rights took place between the EU and Russia for the first time in March of that year, in Luxembourg. At a summit held in Moscow in May the two sides adopted a single package of 'roadmaps', to facilitate the creation of the four common spaces in the medium term. As part of the common space on freedom, security and justice, agreements on visa facilitation (simplifying the procedures for issuing short-stay visas) and on readmission (setting out procedures for the return of people found to be illegally resident in the territory of the other party) were reached in October, and were signed at the EU-Russia summit held in Sochi, Russia, in May 2006. In July the Commission approved draft negotiating directives for a new EU-Russia Agreement to replace the PCA, which was to come to the end of its initial 10-year period in December 2007. The PCA remained in force pending the conclusion of a new agreement. In March 2007 the Commission published a Country Strategy Paper for EU-Russia relations in 2007–13. Associated with the paper was a National Indicative Programme for Russia for 2007–10, which envisaged that financial allocations from the EU to Russia during that period would amount to €30m. annually. Financial co-operation was intended to focus on the common spaces and the package of road maps for their creation. At an EU-Russia summit meeting held in Mafra, Portugal, in October 2007, it was agreed to establish a system to provide early warning of threats to the supply of natural gas and petroleum to the EU, following the serious disruption of supplies to EU countries from Russia, via

Belarus, in previous years. In November 2008 the European Commission, the USA and 15 other countries attending an energy summit in Baku, Azerbaijan, signed a declaration urging increased co-operation in projects aimed at improving co-operation in energy projects in the Caspian Sea region, in order to diversify supply routes. In January 2009 the European Commission proposed to contribute €250m. towards funding the planned Nabucco gas pipeline, which was to channel about 5%–10% of Europe's gas requirements (originating in the Caspian region and the Middle East, including Azerbaijan, Egypt, Iraq and Turkmenistan) from Erzurum, Turkey, to Baumgarten an der March, Austria, possibly also with an extension pipeline to Poland. Construction of the Nabucco pipeline was scheduled to commence in 2013, and gas was scheduled to start flowing through it in 2017.

On 8 August 2008 Georgia launched a military offensive in the separatist republic of South Ossetia, prompting retaliatory intervention by Russia. A cease-fire agreement was brokered four days later, with the assistance of French President Nicolas Sarkozy, whose country held the rotating Presidency of the Council of the European Union. However, Russia's failure to withdraw its troops from Georgian territory by the end of August, and its decision to recognize the independence of the republics of South Ossetia and Abkhazia, resulted, at the beginning of September, in an agreement by EU leaders to postpone talks with Russia on the new EU-Russia agreement, which had been scheduled to commence later that month. Following further negotiations with Sarkozy, Russia subsequently agreed to withdraw its troops from Georgia by 10 October. Meanwhile, in early September EU ministers responsible for foreign affairs reached agreement on the deployment of an EU Monitoring Mission (EUMM) to Georgia from 1 October. EUMM comprised some 350 personnel from 22 countries, and was mandated to monitor adherence to peace agreements signed in Georgia in August and September 2008, and to contribute to stability throughout Georgia and the surrounding region. EUMM's field office structure was strengthened in September 2009. An EU-Russia summit meeting took place in Nice, France, in November. The EU noted that Russia had fulfilled most of its obligations in Georgia, but that further progress was needed with regard to the withdrawal of troops from two locations in South Ossetia. In November 2008 EU ministers of foreign affairs agreed to resume talks with Russia on the new EU-Russia agreement, which remained ongoing.

In February 1994 the EU Council of Ministers agreed to pursue closer economic and political relations with Ukraine, following an agreement by that country to renounce control of nuclear weapons on its territory. A PCA was signed by the two sides in June. In December EU ministers of finance approved a loan totalling ECU 85m., conditional on Ukraine's implementation of a strategy to close the Chernobyl (Chornobyl) nuclear power plant. An Interim Trade Agreement with Ukraine came into force in February 1996; this was replaced by a PCA in March 1998. In December 1999 the EU adopted a Common Strategy on Ukraine, aimed at developing a strategic partnership on the basis of the PCA. The Chernobyl plant closed in December 2000. The EU has provided funding to cover the interim period prior to the completion of two new reactors (supported by the EBRD and the European Atomic Energy Community—Euratom) to replace the plant's generating capacity. The EU Action Plan for Ukraine adopted in February 2005 envisaged enhanced co-operation in many areas. At a summit held in the Ukrainian capital, Kyiv, in December, the EU and Ukraine signed agreements on aviation and on Ukraine's participation in the EU's Galileo civil satellite navigation and positioning system and a memorandum of understanding (MOU) on increased co-operation in the energy sector. Ukraine reiterated its strategic goal to be integrated fully into the EU, and the EU pledged support for Ukraine's bid to join the WTO (Ukraine became a member of the WTO in May 2008). Meanwhile, in November 2005 an EU Border Assistance Mission to monitor Ukraine's border with Moldova (EUBAM) was launched at the request of both countries' Governments (deployed for an initial period of two years, subsequently extended, and ongoing at 2012). In February 2008 EU ministers of foreign affairs attended a conference on the EU's Black Sea Synergy programme, held in Kyiv, Ukraine. Following the accession to the EU of the littoral states Bulgaria and Romania, the programme aims to improve co-operation between countries bordering the Black Sea, as well as between members of the Black Sea region and the EU. In September, at an EU-Ukraine summit, held in Paris, France, the EU announced plans to commence negotiations towards an Association Agreement with Ukraine, which would supersede the PCA. In November 2009 an EU-Ukraine Association Agenda was adopted, replacing the EU Action Plan. In March 2011 an MOU on the National Indicative Programme for Ukraine for 2011–13 was signed, allocating some €470m. to Ukraine, focusing on three principal areas: good governance and the rule of law; progress pertaining to the EU-Ukraine Association Agreement (including plans for the creation of a deep and comprehensive free trade area—DCFTA); and sustainable development. An EU-Ukraine free trade agreement was finalized in late October 2011, but the signature of the agreement, which was to form part of the EU-Ukraine Association Agreement, risked delay, owing to EU concerns over the prosecution of opposition politicians in that country. In mid-October Yuliya Tymoshenko, a former Prime Minister and the principal political opponent of the President of Ukraine, Viktor Yanukovych, had been sentenced to seven years' imprisonment for abuse of office, after a trial that she claimed was politically motivated. In December the European Parliament urged the EU-Ukraine association agreement to be initialled rapidly, asserting that the agreement could help to bring about political change. The Agreement was initialled at the end of March 2012.

Prior to 2009 Russia and Ukraine held annual negotiations on the renewal of gas supply contracts. A dispute between Russia and Ukraine over gas prices in January 2006 was of considerable concern to the EU, which relied on Russia for some 25% of its gas (with some member states entirely dependent on imports from Russia), most of which passed through Ukraine. In January 2009, owing to the failure of negotiations to agree the 2009 prices for Ukraine's consumption and Russia's gas transit through Ukraine, Russia suspended gas supplies to Ukraine, stating that it would pump only sufficient gas for customers further down the pipeline. Later in January a 10-year deal on prices was concluded between Russia and Ukraine and supplies to Ukraine were resumed. In March 2009 the EU, Ukraine, international financial institutions, gas industry representatives and other partners participated in a Joint EU-Ukraine International Investment Conference on the Rehabilitation of Ukraine's Gas Transit System, to discuss the future modernization of the system, with a view to improving the sustainability, reliability and efficiency of the infrastructure and helping to secure long-term supplies of gas to the rest of Europe.

In April 2008, following a visit to Turkmenistan by the Commissioner for External Relations and European Neighbourhood Policy, the Turkmenistani authorities pledged to supply some 10,000m. cu m of natural gas per year to the EU from 2009 (thereby enabling EU member states to reduce their reliance on Russian gas supplies). A memorandum of mutual understanding and co-operation on energy issues was signed between the EU and Turkmenistan in May.

In January 2011 the Commission signed a joint declaration on gas delivery for Europe, in Baku. According to the agreement, Azerbaijan guaranteed substantial, long-term gas supplies to EU markets, while the EU provided access to its markets for Azerbaijani gas, via a planned Southern Gas Corridor.

An Interim Agreement with Belarus was signed in March 1996. However, in February 1997 the EU suspended negotiations for the conclusion of the Interim Agreement and for a PCA in view of serious reverses to the development of democracy in that country. EU technical assistance programmes were suspended, with the exception of aid programmes and those considered directly beneficial to the democratic process. In 1999 the EU announced that the punitive measures would be withdrawn gradually upon the attainment of certain benchmarks. In 2000 the EU criticized the Belarusian Government for failing to accept its recommendations on the conduct of the legislative elections held in October. In November 2002 EU member states imposed a travel ban on President Alyaksandr Lukashenka and other senior Belarusian officials, in protest against the lack of democracy and the declining human rights situation in the country; the ban was lifted in April 2003. In September 2004 the European Parliament condemned Lukashenka's attempt to secure a third term of office by scheduling a referendum to change the country's Constitution, which permitted a maximum of two terms. The EU subsequently imposed a travel ban on officials responsible for the allegedly fraudulent legislative elections and the referendum held in Belarus in October, which abolished limits on the number of terms that the President was permitted to serve. The Council, nevertheless, reiterated the EU's willingness to develop closer relations with Belarus if Lukashenka were to introduce fundamental democratic and economic reforms. As part of efforts to support civil society and democratization, in September the European Commission initiated a €2m. project to increase access in Belarus to independent sources of news and information. In April 2006, following Lukashenka's re-election in the previous month, the EU extended the travel ban imposed in 2004 to include Lukashenka and 30 government ministers and other officials. In November 2006, in a communication to the Belarusian authorities, the EU detailed the benefits that Belarus could expect to gain, within the framework of the European Neighbourhood Policy, were the country to embark on a process of democratization and to show due respect for human rights and the rule of law. In October 2008 EU ministers of foreign affairs agreed to soften sanctions against Belarus, which released three high-profile political prisoners from detention in August, by suspending the travel ban on Lukashenka and other officials. In November 2009 the Council noted positive developments in EU-Belarus relations, with the development of an EU-Belarus Human Rights Dialogue, increased technical co-operation and the country's active participation in the Eastern Partnership. However, owing to a lack of progress with regard to human rights and democracy, the Council agreed to retain restrictive measures in place against a number of Belarusian officials. At the end of September 2011

Belarusian officials failed to attend a summit meeting of the Eastern Partnership, held in Warsaw, Poland. The meeting was attended by representatives of Armenia, Azerbaijan, Georgia, Moldova and Ukraine, but the EU was unable to secure support for a statement demanding the safeguarding of human rights and democracy in Belarus. In October 2011 the EU agreed to retain restrictive measures against Belarusian officials for a further 12-month period. In January 2012 the EU noted a worsening in the human rights situation in Belarus, and announced that it was to expand its list of banned officials (then numbering 210) to some 336; in response, in February Belarus expelled EU diplomats and the Polish ambassador from the country, and recalled its own ambassadors.

In May 1997 an Interim Agreement with Moldova entered into force; this was replaced by a PCA in July 1998. The first EU-Moldova Co-operation Council meeting was held in the same month in Brussels. Interim Agreements entered into force during 1997 with Kazakhstan (April), Georgia (September) and Armenia (December). An Interim Agreement with Azerbaijan entered into force in March 1999. A PCA with Turkmenistan was signed in May 1998 and an Interim Agreement with Uzbekistan entered into force in June. By the end of that year PCAs had been signed with all the countries of the CIS, except Tajikistan, owing to political instability in that country. All remaining Agreements had entered into force by 1 July 1999, with the exception of those negotiated with Belarus and Turkmenistan. A PCA with Tajikistan was eventually signed in October 2004, and entered into force in January 2010.

OTHER EUROPEAN COUNTRIES

The members of the European Free Trade Association (EFTA) concluded bilateral free trade agreements with the EEC and the ECSC during the 1970s. On 1 January 1984 the last tariff barriers were eliminated, thus establishing full free trade for industrial products between the Community and EFTA members. Some EFTA members subsequently applied for membership of the EC: Austria in 1989, Sweden in 1991, and Finland, Switzerland and Norway in 1992. Formal negotiations on the creation of a European Economic Area (EEA), a single market for goods, services, capital and labour among EC and EFTA members, began in June 1990, and were concluded in October 1991. The agreement was signed in May 1992 (after a delay caused by a ruling of the Court of Justice of the EC that a proposed joint EC-EFTA court, for adjudication in disputes, was incompatible with the Treaty of Rome; EFTA members then agreed to concede jurisdiction to the Court of Justice on cases of competition involving both EC and EFTA members, and to establish a special joint committee for other disputes). In a referendum in December, Swiss voters rejected ratification of the agreement, and the remaining 18 countries signed an adjustment protocol in March 1993, allowing the EEA to be established without Switzerland (which was to have observer status). The EEA entered into force on 1 January 1994. Despite the rejection of the EEA by the Swiss electorate, the Swiss Government declared its intention to continue to pursue its application for membership of the EU. Formal negotiations on the accession to the EU of Austria, Finland and Sweden began on 1 February, and those on Norway's membership started on 1 April. Negotiations were concluded in March 1994. Heads of government of the four countries signed treaties of accession to the EU in June, which were to come into effect from 1995, subject to approval by a national referendum in each country. Accession to the EU was endorsed by the electorates of Austria, Finland and Sweden in June, October and November 1994, respectively. Norway's accession, however, was rejected in a national referendum (by 52.4% of voters) conducted at the end of November. The success of the campaign opposing Norway's entry to the EU was attributed to several factors: in particular, fears that an influx of cheaper agricultural goods from the EU would lead to bankruptcies and unemploymen, and that stocks of fish would be severely depleted if EU boats were granted increased access to Norwegian waters. There was also widespread concern that national sovereignty would be compromised by the transfer to the EU of certain executive responsibilities. From 1994 Norway's relations with the EU were based on full participation in the EEA as well as involvement (at non-signatory level) in the EU's Schengen Agreement. Austria, Finland and Sweden became members of the EU on 1 January 1995. Liechtenstein, which became a full member of EFTA in September 1991, joined the EEA on 1 May 1995.

In 1999 Switzerland signed seven bilateral free trade agreements with the EU, mainly relating to trade liberalization (known together as Bilateral I). A referendum was held in March 2001 on whether to begin 'fast-track' accession negotiations with the EU. Participation in the ballot was high and the motion was rejected by 77% of voters; however, the Swiss application remains open. The first EU-Switzerland summit meeting took place in Brussels, Belgium, in May 2004, after which nine sectoral agreements (together known as Bilateral II, and covering areas such as savings tax, fraud, the Schengen Agreement on border controls and the environment) were signed by the two parties. The participation of Switzerland in the Schengen area and the extension of the agreement on the free movement of persons to the 10 states that joined the EU in May 2004 were approved by Swiss voters in public referendums in June and September 2005. A protocol on these measures and on Bilateral II was signed in October 2004 and entered into force in April 2006.

Despite the fact that Iceland joined EFTA in 1970 and ratified the EEA in 1993 (although the extension of the single market legislation excluded agriculture and fisheries management, as in Norway and Liechtenstein), it did not thereafter apply for EU membership. Although opposition to Iceland's joining the EU persisted at government level in the first half of the 2000s, relations between the EU and Iceland had generally developed smoothly since 1993—notably, Iceland negotiated participation in the Schengen Agreement (although, as a signatory, it was not involved in decision-making within the agreement). Following a serious economic crisis in Iceland in 2008, in July 2009 the Icelandic Parliament voted in favour of making an application for membership of the EU. Accession negotiations with Iceland opened in July 2010, and by December 2011 talks had opened in 11 of the total of 33 policy areas.

In November 2008 the European Commission adopted a communication on the EU and the Arctic Region, which emphasized the adverse effects of climate change and technological activities in that region. The Commission identified three principal goals: to preserve the region, in co-operation with its indigenous population; to encourage the sustainable use of natural resources; and to aid improved multilateral governance. In January 2011 the European Parliament adopted a resolution on EU policy in the High North, which emphasized the need for a co-ordinated approach to EU activity in the Arctic Region.

The EU's Northern Dimension programme covers the Baltic Sea, Arctic Sea and north-west Russia regions. It aims to address the specific challenges of these areas and to encourage co-operation with external states. The Northern Dimension programme operates within the framework of the EU-Russia PCA and the TACIS programme, as well as other agreements and financial instruments. An Action Plan for the Northern Dimension in the External and Cross-border Policies of the EU, covering 2000–03, was adopted in June 2000. The Plan detailed objectives in the following areas of co-operation: environmental protection; nuclear safety and nuclear waste management; energy; transport and border-crossing infrastructure; justice and internal affairs; business and investment; public health and social administration; telecommunications; and human resources development. The first conference of Northern Dimension foreign ministers was held in Helsinki, Finland, in November 1999. At a ministerial conference on the Northern Dimension held in October 2002, guidelines were adopted for a second Action Plan for the Northern Dimension in the External and Cross-border Policies of the EU, covering 2004–06. The second Action Plan, which was formally adopted in October 2003, set out strategic priorities and objectives in five priority areas: economy and infrastructure; social issues (including education, training and public health); environment, nuclear safety and natural resources; justice and home affairs; and cross-border co-operation. Under the Northern Dimension programme, priority was given to efforts to integrate Russia into a common European economic and social area through projects dealing with environmental pollution, nuclear risks and cross-border organized crime. At a Northern Dimension summit meeting held in Helsinki, Finland, in November 2006, the leaders of the EU, Iceland, Norway and Russia endorsed a new Policy Framework Document and Northern Dimension Political Declaration, replacing the three-year action plans hitherto in place with a new common regional policy. In October 2009 a memorandum of understanding was signed in Naples, Italy, by the European Commission and 11 northern European countries, establishing the Northern Dimension Partnership on Transport and Logistics, which sought to develop important transport links in northern Europe.

A trade agreement with Andorra entered into force on 1 January 1991, establishing a customs union for industrial products, and allowing duty-free access to the EC for certain Andorran agricultural products. A wide-ranging co-operation agreement with Andorra and an agreement on the taxation of savings income were signed in November 2004 and entered into force in July 2005. Similar agreements on the taxation of savings income also took effect in Liechtenstein, Monaco and San Marino in July 2005. Negotiations on a co-operation and customs union agreement between the EC and San Marino were concluded in December 1991; the agreement entered into force in May 2002. The euro became the sole currency in circulation in Andorra, Monaco, San Marino and the Vatican City at the beginning of 2002.

THE MIDDLE EAST AND THE MEDITERRANEAN

A scheme to negotiate a series of parallel trade and co-operation agreements encompassing almost all of the non-member states on the coast of the Mediterranean was formulated by the European Community (EC) in 1972. Association Agreements, intended to lead to customs union or the eventual full accession of the country concerned, had been signed with Greece (which eventually became a member of the Community in 1981) in 1962, Turkey in 1964 and Malta in 1971; a fourth agreement was signed with Cyprus in 1972. (In May 2004 Malta and Cyprus became members of the European Union—EU, as the EC became known in May 2003.) These established free access to the Community market for most industrial products and tariff reductions for most agricultural products. Annexed were financial protocols under which the Community was to provide concessional finance. During the 1970s a series of agreements covering trade and economic co-operation were concluded with the Arab Mediterranean countries and Israel, all establishing free access to EC markets for most industrial products. Access for agricultural products was facilitated, although some tariffs remained. In 1982 the Commission formulated an integrated plan for the development of its own Mediterranean regions and recommended the adoption of a new policy towards the non-Community countries of the Mediterranean. This was to include greater efforts towards diversifying agriculture, in order to avoid surpluses of items such as citrus fruits, olive oil and wine (which the Mediterranean countries all wished to export to the Community) and to reduce these countries' dependence on imported food. From 1 January 1993 the majority of agricultural exports from Mediterranean non-Community countries were granted exemption from customs duties.

In June 1995 the European Council endorsed a proposal by the Commission to reform and strengthen the Mediterranean policy of the EU. In November a conference of ministers of foreign affairs of the EU member states, 11 Mediterranean non-member countries (excluding Libya) and the Palestinian authorities was convened in Barcelona, Spain. The conference issued the Barcelona Declaration, outlining the main objective of the partnership, which was to create a region of peace, security and prosperity. The Declaration set the objective of establishing a Euro-Mediterranean free trade area. The process of co-operation and dialogue under this agreement became known as the Euro-Mediterranean Partnership (or Barcelona Process, until 2008, when this was renamed as the Union for the Mediterranean, see below).

In March 2008 the European Council approved a proposal formally to transform the Barcelona Process into a Union for the Mediterranean. In mid-July heads of state and of government from the 27 EU member states and from the member states and observers of the Barcelona Process attended the Paris Summit for the Mediterranean, at which the new Union for the Mediterranean was officially launched. Bosnia and Herzegovina, Croatia, Monaco and Montenegro were also admitted to the Union for the Mediterranean. Six co-operation projects were approved at the summit, which were to focus on: improving pollution levels in the Mediterranean; constructing maritime and land highways; civil protection; the creation of a Mediterranean Solar Plan; the establishment of a Euro-Mediterranean University (which was established in Slovenia in June 2008); and the launch of a Mediterranean Business Development Initiative. Various institutions were to be established to support the Union for the Mediterranean, including a joint Secretariat and a Joint Permanent Committee, to be based in Brussels. A meeting of Euro-Mediterranean ministers of foreign affairs, convened in Marseilles, in November, endorsed the new Union. A Euro-Mediterranean Regional and Local Assembly (ARLEM) held its inaugural meeting in Barcelona in January 2010, and a Secretariat was established in Barcelona in March.

The European Neighbourhood Policy (ENP) was established by the European Commission in 2004, to enhance co-operation with 16 countries neighboured the EU following its enlargement. Algeria, Egypt, Israel, Jordan, Lebanon, Libya, Morocco, the Palestinian Autonomous Areas, Syria and Tunisia were covered by the ENP (which became known as the Southern Neighbourhood), which was intended to complement the Barcelona Process, in addition to several countries to the east of the Union (the Eastern Neighbourhood). Under the ENP, the EU has negotiated bilateral Action Plans with 12 neighbouring countries, establishing targets for further political and economic co-operation over a three- to five-year period. The Action Plans aimed to build on existing contractual relationships between the partner country and the EU (e.g. an Association Agreement or a Partnership and Co-operation Agreement). The eventual conclusion of more ambitious relationships with partner countries achieving sufficient progress in meeting the priorities set out in the Action Plans (through the negotiation of European Neighbourhood Agreements) was envisaged.

The EU's primary financial instrument for the implementation of the Euro-Mediterranean Partnership was the MEDA programme, providing support for the reform of economic and social structures within partnership countries. It was followed by MEDA II, which was granted a budget of €5,350m. for 2000–06. In 2007 a new European Neighbourhood and Partnership Instrument (ENPI) replaced MEDA and the Technical Assistance to the Commonwealth of Independent States (TACIS) programme (which was concerned with EU co-operation with the countries of the former USSR). ENPI was conceived as a flexible, policy-orientated instrument to target sustainable development and conformity with EU policies and standards. In 2007–13 some €12,000m. was to be made available, within its framework, to support ENP Action Plans and the Strategic Partnership with Russia. An ENPI cross-border co-operation programme was to cover activities across the external borders of the EU in the south and the east, supported by funds totalling €1,180m. in 2007–13.

Turkey, which had signed an Association Agreement with the EC in 1963 (although this was suspended between 1980 and 1986 following a military coup), applied for membership of the EU in April 1987. Accession talks began in October 2005 (see Enlargement).

Co-operation agreements concluded in the 1970s with the Maghreb countries (Algeria, Morocco and Tunisia), the Mashreq countries (Egypt, Jordan, Lebanon and Syria) and Israel covered free access to the Community market for industrial products, customs preferences for certain agricultural products, and financial aid in the form of grants and loans from the EIB. A co-operation agreement negotiated with the Republic of Yemen was non-preferential. In June 1992 the EC approved a proposal to conclude new bilateral agreements with the Maghreb countries, incorporating the following components: political dialogue; financial, economic, technical and cultural co-operation; and the eventual establishment of a free trade area. A Euro-Mediterranean Association Agreement with Tunisia was signed in July 1995 and entered into force in March 1998. A similar agreement with Morocco (concluded in 1996) entered into force in March 2000. (In July 1987 Morocco applied to join the Community, but its application was rejected on the grounds that it is not a European country.) In March 1997 negotiations were initiated between the European Commission and representatives of the Algerian Government on a Euro-Mediterranean Association Agreement that would incorporate political commitments relating to democracy and human rights; this was signed in December 2001 and entered into force in September 2005. An Association Agreement with Jordan was signed in November 1997 and entered into force in May 2002. A Euro-Mediterranean Association Agreement with Egypt (which has been a major beneficiary of EU financial co-operation since the 1970s) was signed in June 2001 and was fully ratified in June 2004. In May 2001 Egypt, together with Jordan, Tunisia and Morocco, issued the Agadir Declaration, in which they determined to establish an Arab Mediterranean Free Trade Zone. The so-called Agadir Agreement on the establishment of a Free Trade Zone between the Arabic Mediterranean Nations was signed in February 2004, entered into force in July 2006, and entered its implementation phase in March 2007. An interim EU Association Agreement with Lebanon was signed in June 2002, and entered into force in April 2006. Protracted negotiations on an Association Agreement with Syria were concluded in October 2004 and a revised version of the Agreement was initialled in December 2008.

In January 1989 the EC and Israel eliminated the last tariff barriers to full free trade for industrial products. A Euro-Mediterranean Association Agreement with Israel was signed in 1995, providing further trade concessions and establishing an institutional political dialogue between the two parties. The agreement entered into force in June 2000. In late 2004 an ENP Action Plan on further co-operation was agreed by the EU and Israel; it was adopted by the EU in February 2005 and by the Israeli authorities in April of that year.

Following the signing of the September 1993 Israeli-Palestine Liberation Organization (PLO) peace agreement, the EC committed substantial funds in humanitarian assistance for the Palestinians. A Euro-Mediterranean Interim Association Agreement on Trade and Co-operation was signed with the PLO in February 1997 and entered into force in July. In April 1998 the EU and the Palestinian (National) Authority (PA) signed a security co-operation agreement. The escalation of violence between Israel and the Palestinians from September 2000 resulted in a deterioration in EU-Israel relations. The EU formed part of the Quartet (alongside the UN, the USA and Russia), which was established in July 2002 to monitor and aid the implementation of Palestinian civil reforms, and to guide the international donor community in its support of the Palestinian reform agenda. In September the Quartet put forward a peace plan aiming at a final settlement, which was published in April 2003. In late 2004 the EU agreed an Action Plan with the PA; it was adopted by the EU in February 2005 and by the PA in May. In November, on the basis of an agreement reached by Israel and the PA following Israel's withdrawal from Gaza and the northern West Bank, the EU established an EU Border Assistance Mission (EU BAM Rafah), which monitored operations at the Rafah border crossing between Egypt and the Gaza Strip until June 2007. An EU Police Mission for the Palestinian Territories (EUPOL COPPS) commenced operations in January 2006, with an initial three-year mandate, subsequently extended to 2012, to support the PA in establishing sustainable and effective policing arrangements. At March 2012 the mission comprised 41 international staff and 70 local personnel. EU observation missions monitored Palestinian presidential and legislative elections in January 2005 and January 2006, respectively. In June 2006 EU member states and the European Commission established the Temporary International Mechanism (TIM), an emergency assistance mechanism to provide support directly to the Palestinian people. After the formation of a new, interim Government under Dr Salam Fayyad, the EU renewed co-operation with, and assistance to, the PA. The militant Islamist group Hamas refused to recognize the legitimacy of the interim administration. On 1 February 2008 the European Commission launched a new mechanism, known as PEGASE, to support the PRDP, with a wider remit than the TIM. PEGASE aimed to support activities in four principal areas: governance (including fiscal reform, security and the rule of law); social development (including social protection, health and education); economic and private-sector development; and development of public infrastructure (in areas such as water, the environment and energy). In February 2009 the European Commission's Humanitarian Aid Office (ECHO) agreed to allocate €58m. towards a global plan to assist the most vulnerable population groups affected by the Israeli–Palestinian conflict. Meeting in Trieste, Italy, in June 2009, the Quartet issued a statement welcoming commitments made by the new Israeli Prime Minister, Binyamin Netanyahu, and President Mahmud Abbas to seek a two-state solution, and stressed the need for the conclusion of peace agreements between Israel and Syria and between Israel and Lebanon. In December 2010 some 26 prominent political figures, including the former High Representative of the Common Foreign and Security Policy and Secretary-General of the Council of the European Union and of the Western European Union Javier Solana and 10 former heads of state, wrote to the EU Council President Herman Van Rompuy, the High Representative of the Union for Foreign Affairs and Security Policy Catherine Ashton, and all EU heads of state and of government, urging the EU to strengthen its response to Israel's continued construction of settlements in the Palestinian Autonomous Areas.

Talks were held with Iran in April 1992 on the establishment of a co-operation accord. In December the Council of Ministers recommended that a 'critical dialogue' be undertaken with Iran, owing to the country's significance to regional security. In April 1997 the 'critical dialogue' was suspended and ambassadors were recalled from Iran, after a German court found the Iranian authorities responsible for having ordered the murder of four Kurdish dissidents in Berlin in 1992. Later that month ministers of foreign affairs resolved to restore diplomatic relations with Iran, in order to protect the strong trading partnership. In November 2000 an EU-Iran Working Group on Trade and Investment met for the first time to discuss the possibility of increasing and diversifying trade and investment. During 2002 attempts were made to improve relations with Iran, as negotiations began in preparation for a Trade and Co-operation Agreement. An eventual trade deal was to be linked to progress in political issues, including human rights, weapons proliferation and counter-terrorism. In mid-2003 the EU (in conformity with US policy) warned Iran to accept stringent new nuclear inspections, and threatened the country with economic repercussions (including the abandonment of the proposed trade agreement) unless it restored international trust in its nuclear programme. A 'comprehensive dialogue' between the EU and Iran (which replaced the 'critical dialogue' in 1998) was suspended by Iran in December 2003. In January 2005 the EU resumed trade talks with Iran after the Iranian authorities agreed to suspend uranium enrichment. However, these talks were halted by the Commission in August, following Iran's resumption of uranium conversion to gas (the stage before enrichment). Following Iran's removal of international seals from a nuclear research facility in January 2006, the EU supported moves to refer Iran to the UN Security Council. In mid-2006, during a visit to Tehran, Javier Solana presented to the Iranian authorities new proposals by the international community on how negotiations on Iran's nuclear programme could be initiated. In December, in a declaration on Iran, the Council criticized the country's failure to implement measures required by both the International Atomic Energy Agency (IAEA) and the UN Security Council in respect of its nuclear programme, and warned that this failure would be to the detriment of EU-Iran relations. EU trade sanctions against Iran were strengthened in August 2008, after Iran failed to halt its uranium-enrichment programme. In July 2010 EU ministers of foreign affairs adopted a new set of sanctions, prohibiting investment, technical assistance and technology transfers to Iran's energy sector, and also targeting the country's financial services, insurance and transport sectors. Sanctions were strengthened in May 2011. In October an IAEA report expressed strong concern that Iran's nuclear programme related to military technology. EU sanctions were strengthened in January 2012, when a ban on imports of Iranian crude oil was imposed and the assets of the Iranian central bank within the EU were frozen. The EU also has strong concerns over the human rights situation in Iran, particularly following the increased repression that followed the presidential election of 2009. As a consequence, the EU has imposed sanctions on 61 people believed to be responsible for significant human rights abuses; in March 2012 EU ministers of foreign affairs expanded these sanctions to cover a further 17 individuals.

A co-operation agreement between the EC and the countries of the Gulf Co-operation Council (GCC), which entered into force in January 1990, provided for co-operation in industry, energy, technology and other fields. Negotiations on a full free trade pact began in October, but it was expected that any agreement would involve transition periods of some 12 years for the reduction of European tariffs on 'sensitive products' (i.e. petrochemicals). In November 1999 the GCC Supreme Council agreed to establish a customs union (a precondition of the proposed EU-GCC free trade agreement); the union was established in January 2003. At the 20th EU-GCC Joint Council and Ministerial Meeting, held in Luxembourg in June 2010, an EU-GCC Joint Action Programme for 2010–13 was adopted, with the aim of strengthening co-operation in a number of areas, principally economic and financial co-operation; trade and industry; energy and the environment; transport, telecommunications and information technology; education and research; and culture.

The increased tension in the Middle East prior to the US-led military action in Iraq in March 2003 placed considerable strain on relations between member states of the EU, and exposed the lack of a common EU policy on Iraq. In February 2003 the European Council held an extraordinary meeting to discuss the crisis in Iraq, and issued a statement reiterating its commitment to the UN. In April, however, the EU leaders reluctantly accepted a dominant role for the USA and the United Kingdom in post-war Iraq, and Denmark, Spain and the Netherlands announced plans to send peace-keeping troops to Iraq. At the Madrid Donors' Conference in October the EU and its accession states pledged more than €1,250m. (mainly in grants) for Iraq's reconstruction. In March 2004 the Commission adopted a programme setting three priorities for reconstruction assistance to Iraq in that year: restoring the delivery of principal public services; increasing employment and reducing poverty; and strengthening governance, civil society and human rights. The EU welcomed the handover of power by the Coalition Provisional Authority to the Iraqi Interim Government in June 2004 and supported the holding of elections to the Transitional National Assembly in Iraq in January 2005. An EU integrated rule-of-law mission for Iraq, to provide training in management and criminal investigation to staff and senior officials from the judiciary, the police and the penitentiary, commenced operations in July, with an initial mandate of 12 months. In December 2006 an agreement was signed on the establishment of a European Commission delegation office in the Iraqi capital, Baghdad. In June of that year, in response to the formation of a new Iraqi Government, the Commission set forth its proposals for an EU-wide strategy to govern EU relations with Iraq. The strategy comprised five objectives: overcoming divisions within Iraq and building democracy; promoting the rule of law and human rights; supporting the Iraqi authorities in the delivery of basic services; supporting the reform of public administration; and promoting economic reform. In November negotiations commenced on a trade and co-operation agreement with Iraq; at a round of negotiations on the agreement held in February 2009, participants agreed to upgrade the draft accord to a more comprehensive draft partnership agreement, which would provide for annual ministerial meetings and the establishment of a joint co-operation council. In November the EU and Iraq completed negotiations on the partnership and co-operation agreement, which had still to be signed. A memorandum of understanding on a strategic energy partnership between the EU and the Iraqi Government was signed in January 2010. Between 2003 and the end of 2008 the EU provided €933m. in reconstruction and humanitarian assistance to Iraq. The EU allocated €66m. towards development co-operation with Iraq during 2009–10 (€42m. for 2009 and €24m. for 2010). In November 2010 the EU adopted a Joint Strategy Paper for Iraq for 2011–13, which aimed to assist Iraq in making optimum use of its resources through: capacity-building activities relating to good governance; promoting education in order to aid socio-economic recovery; building institutional capacity; water management and agriculture.

A series of large-scale demonstrations in Tunisia, prompted by the self-immolation of a young Tunisian man in protest at state restrictions in mid-December 2010, led President Zine al-Abidine Ben Ali to flee the country in mid-January 2011. An EU-Tunisia Task Force was established to ensure the improved co-ordination of support for Tunisia's political and economic transition, the first meeting of which took place in late September in the capital, Tunis. Negotiations towards the agreement of a Deep and Comprehensive Free Trade Area (DCFTA) were due to be initiated in 2012.

Mass protests also took place in Egypt in early 2011, which resulted in the resignation of the Egyptian President Lt-Gen. Muhammad Hosni Mubarak on 11 February. In mid-February a series of violent clashes broke out between anti-Government protesters in Libya and armed forces loyal to the Libyan leader, Col Muammar al-Qaddafi. By 22 February it was reported that protesters had taken control of Benghazi and large parts of eastern Libya. At the end of February the Council of the EU adopted a UN Security Council Resolution on Libya, prohibiting the sale to that country of arms and ammunition, and agreed to impose additional sanctions against those responsible for the violent repression of the civilian protests, halting trade in any equipment that could be utilized for such purposes. The Council also imposed a visa ban on several people, including al-Qaddafi and other members of his family, and froze the assets of al-Qaddafi and 25 other people. On 1 April 2011 the Council agreed to establish EUFOR Libya to help support the provision of humanitarian assistance, and to facilitate the movement of displaced people, in response to the crisis situation in Libya, if its deployment were requested by the UN Office for the Coordination of Humanitarian Affairs. After al-Qaddafi went into hiding in late August, and forces in support of the opposition National Transitional Council (NTC) took control of the capital, Tripoli, the European Council agreed measures to support the Libyan economy and to assist the UN mission in Libya. Some €30m. was to be provided to aid the NTC in its efforts to stabilize the country. A number of hitherto frozen assets were released in support of humanitarian and civilian needs, and a ban on the use of European air space by Libyan aircraft was removed. At the end of August the EU opened an office in Tripoli. At an international conference held in Paris, France, in early September, the EU agreed to initiate assessments of the needs of the NTC in the fields of security, communication, civil society, border management and procurement, and a further €50m. was to be made available for longer-term support programmes. On 20 October it was confirmed that Qaddafi had been captured and killed during fighting in his home city of Sirte; three days later the NTC formally declared 'national liberation'. In mid-November the EU's Tripoli office was formally upgraded, becoming the headquarters of the new EU delegation to Libya.

Meanwhile, from mid-March 2011 anti-Government protests in Syria were violently suppressed by the authorities. In response, the EU imposed a number of restrictive measures, including an arms embargo and targeted sanctions, comprising a travel ban and the freezing of assets, against those deemed to be responsible for, or involved with, the repression. In May bilateral EU-Syria co-operation programmes were suspended, as were preparations for new areas of co-operation. The Syrian authorities continued to implement harsh measures in an attempt to quell demonstrations against the rule of President Bashar al-Assad; by mid-October the Office of the UN High Commissioner for Human Rights estimated that more than 3,000 people had been killed in Syria since protests began. In March 2012 the EU imposed its 13th set of sanctions on the Syrian authorities since the protests began.

Unrest also developed in Yemen in early 2011, with escalating conflict between forces loyal to Saleh and tribal groups, and ongoing protests against Field Marshal Ali Abdullah Saleh's rule in several cities. In late November the EU expressed satisfaction at the signature in Riyadh of the agreement for political transition signed by President Saleh and senior Yemeni officials, under the auspices of the GCC. The EU provided some €20m. in additional humanitarian aid to Yemen in 2011, and welcomed the presidential election that took place in late February 2012, and the subsequent inauguration of President Field Marshal Abd al-Rabbuh Mansur al-Hadi, prior to legislative elections in 2014.

After demonstrations commenced in the capital of Bahrain, Manama, in early 2011, the EU urged restraint, and exhorted all parties to take part in negotiations. None the less, protests were violently repressed, and the EU's High Representative dispatched a senior EU envoy to Bahrain for talks. The EU welcomed the establishment, in June, of the Bahrain Independent Commission of Inquiry (BICI)—an independent, international commission of judicial and human rights experts—to investigate both the causes of the unrest and allegations of human rights violations.

In late February 2011, at a Senior Officials' meeting to discuss the instability in the Middle East (which became widely known as the 'Arab Spring'), EU High Representative Catherine Ashton identified the need to respond in three ways: by helping to develop 'deep democracy', through a process of political reform, democratic elections, institution-building, measures to combat corruption, and support for the independent judiciary and civil society; through economic development; and by facilitating the movement of people and of communications, while avoiding mass migration. In late September the European Commission agreed to new economic support for the Middle East. The Support for Partnership Reform and Inclusive Growth (SPRING) programme was to be allocated a budget of €350m. in additional funds for 2011–12, and was to provide support on a so-called more-for-more basis to those countries that demonstrated progress in implementing democratic reforms. The Civil Society Facility was to be established, with a budget of €26.4m., with the objective of strengthening the capacity of civil society to promote reform and increase public accountability. By December 2011 the European Commission had provided funds amounting to some €80.5m. to help the refugee crisis in North Africa, while EU member states had provided a further €73.0m.

SUB-SAHARAN AFRICA

The first Africa-EU summit, representing the institutionalization of Africa-EU dialogue, was convened in April 2000, in Cairo, Egypt. The second summit was held in December 2007, in Lisbon, Portugal (having been postponed from 2003 owing to concerns over the participation of President Mugabe of Zimbabwe, see below). The 2007 Lisbon summit adopted a Joint Africa-EU Strategy as a vision and road map, providing an overarching long-term framework for future political co-operation, to be implemented through successive short-term action plans. The First Action Plan of the Joint Strategy identified eight areas for strategic partnership during 2008–10: peace and security; democratic governance and human rights; trade, regional integration and infrastructure; achievement of the UN Millennium Development Goals; energy; climate change; migration, mobility and employment; and science, information society and space. The third Africa-EU summit, with the theme of 'investment, economic growth and job creation' was held in Tripoli, Libya, in November 2010. An action plan for 2011–13 was adopted, focusing on the following principal areas of co-operation: peace and security; democratic governance and human rights; regional integration, trade and infrastructure; the UN's eight Millennium Development Goals; energy; climate change and the environment; migration, mobility and employment; and science, the information society and space.

In June 2004 the European Commission activated for the first time its newly established Africa Peace Facility (APF), which provided €12m. in support of African Union (AU) humanitarian and peace-monitoring activities in Darfur (Sudan). In 2007 the EU and the AU agreed to expand the APF to cover the prevention of conflict and post-conflict stabilization, and to facilitate decision-making and co-ordination. APF funds were allocated accordingly: €600m. for Peace Support Operations, the principal focus of the APF; €100m. to aid capacity-building efforts, specifically in the context of the African Peace and Security Architecture (APSA) and Africa-EU dialogue; €15m. to support the Early Response Mechanism; and €40m. for contingencies.

During 2002 the European Council condemned the worsening human rights situation in Zimbabwe, and imposed a range of targeted sanctions, including a travel ban on and freezing of the assets of certain members of the leadership, an arms embargo, and the suspension of development aid. Sanctions relating to Zimbabwe have been extended repeatedly on an annual basis. In September 2009 an EU delegation visited Zimbabwe for the first time since the imposition of sanctions, and indicated that further progress was needed to end human rights violations there. The majority of the sanctions were extended in February 2010 and February 2011. In February 2012 the EU welcomed developments towards the formation of a Government of National Unity, and agreed to remove sanctions from 51 people and 20 entities with immediate effect.

The EU, together with, *inter alia*, the UN Secretary-General, US President Barack Obama, the IMF and the Economic Community of West African States (ECOWAS), recognized Alassane Ouattara as the legitimate victor of a run-off election to decide the presidency of Côte d'Ivoire in November 2010; however, in early December the country's constitutional council released results indicating that incumbent President Laurent Gbagbo had won the election. Widespread disruption and violence followed the disputed elections. In mid-January 2011 the EU imposed sanctions against Côte d'Ivoire, which were subsequently strengthened at the end of that month. Ouattara was officially sworn in as President in May. In July the EU adopted five programmes, which allocated some €125m. to Côte d'Ivoire to support vocational training, road maintenance, health and the management of public finances, and to strengthen civil society organizations.

The EU maintains several missions in Africa. During June–September 2003 an EU military operation, codenamed Artemis, was conducted in the Democratic Republic of the Congo (DRC). In June 2005 1,400 EUSEC RD Congo peace-keepers were dispatched to attempt to curb ongoing ethnic violence in the DRC; the mandate of EUSEC RD Congo was scheduled to terminate at the end of September 2012. In October 2007 the Council approved a EUFOR operation (EUFOR Chad/CAR), comprising 3,300 troops, to support a UN mission in eastern Chad and north-eastern Central African Republic (MINURCAT) in efforts to improve security in those regions, where more than 200,000 people from the Darfur region of western Sudan had sought refuge from violence in their own country. The force began deployment in early 2008. In March 2009 EUFOR Chad/CAR's mandate expired and MINURCAT assumed the EU force's military and security responsibilities. In December 2008 Operation EU NAVFOR Somalia—Operation Atalanta, the EU's first maritime military operation, reached its initial operational capacity; Operation EU NAVFOR Somalia was established in support of UN Security Council resolutions aimed at deterring and repressing acts of piracy and armed robbery in waters off the coast of Somalia, and protecting vulnerable vessels in that area (including vessels delivering humanitarian aid to displaced persons in Somalia). The mandate of EU NAVFOR Somalia was due to expire in December 2012, subsequently extended to December 2014. In February 2010 the Council of the European Union established the EU Training Mission for Somalia (EUTM Somalia), to help strengthen the Somali transitional federal Government, in particular through providing military training to 2,000 security force recruits; EUTM

Somalia became operational in April. An EU mission in support of security sector reform in Guinea-Bissau was established in February 2008, and its mandate expired in September 2010.

There are EU Special Representatives to the African Union and for the Great Lakes Region.

LATIN AMERICA

A non-preferential trade agreement was signed with Uruguay in 1974, and economic and commercial co-operation agreements with Mexico in 1975 and with Brazil in 1980. A five-year co-operation agreement with the members of the Central American Common Market and with Panama entered into force in 1987, as did a similar agreement with the member countries (see below) of the Andean Group (now the Andean Community). Co-operation agreements were signed with Argentina and Chile in 1990, and in that year tariff preferences were approved for Bolivia, Colombia, Ecuador and Peru, in support of those countries' efforts to combat drugs-trafficking. In May 1992 an inter-institutional co-operation agreement was signed with the Southern Common Market (Mercado Común del Sur—Mercosur); in the following month the European Community (EC) and the member states of the Andean Group (Bolivia, Colombia, Ecuador, Peru and Venezuela) initialled a new co-operation agreement, which was to broaden the scope of economic and development co-operation and enhance trade relations, and a new co-operation agreement was signed with Brazil. In July 1993 the EC introduced a tariff regime to limit the import of bananas from Latin America, in order to protect the banana-producing countries of the African, Caribbean and Pacific (ACP) group, then linked to the EC by the Lomé Convention. (In December 2009, in resolution to a long dispute over the tariff regime, the EU and Latin American states initialled the EU-Latin America Bananas Agreement, which provided for a gradual reduction in the tariff rate.)

From 1996 the European Union (EU, as the EC became in 1993) forged closer links with Latin America, by means of strengthened political ties, an increase in economic integration and free trade, and co-operation in other areas. In April 1997 the EU extended further trade benefits to the countries of the Andean Community. In September 2009 the Commission adopted 'The European Union and Latin America: Global Players in Partnership', updating an earlier communication, published in 2005, on 'A Stronger Partnership between the European Union and Latin America'.

In July 1997 the EU and Mexico concluded an Economic Partnership, Political Co-ordination and Co-operation Agreement (the Global Agreement) and an interim agreement on trade. The accords were signed in December, and entered into effect in 2000. In November 1999 the EU and Mexico concluded a free trade agreement, which provided for the removal of all tariffs on bilateral trade in industrial products by 2007. The first meeting of the Joint Council established by the Economic Partnership, Political Co-ordination and Co-operation Agreement between the EU and Mexico was held in February 2001; further meetings have since been held on a regular basis. In July 2008, in acknowledgement of the gradual strengthening of EU-Mexico relations, the European Commission proposed the establishment of a Strategic Partnership with Mexico. An EU-Mexico summit meeting was held in Comillas, Spain, in May 2010.

In June 1996 the EU and Chile signed a framework agreement on political and economic co-operation, which provided for a process of bilateral trade liberalization, as well as co-operation in other industrial and financial areas. An EU-Chile Joint Council was established. In November 1999 the EU and Chile commenced practical negotiations on developing closer political and economic co-operation, within the framework of a proposed Association Agreement. In November 2002 the EU and Chile signed an association and free trade agreement, which entered into force in March 2005; it provided for the liberalization of trade within seven years for industrial products and 10 years for agricultural products. The first meeting of the Association Council set up by the agreement took place in Athens, Greece, in March 2003, and the second was held in Luxembourg in May 2005. Representatives of civil society met within the framework of the Association Agreement for the first time in late 2006. In May 2008 the EU and Chile determined to establish a joint Association for Development and Innovation. The fourth EU-Chile summit meeting was held in Madrid, Spain, in May 2010.

In May 2007 the European Commission proposed to launch a Strategic Partnership with Brazil, in recognition of its increasing international prominence and strong bilateral ties with Europe. The first EU-Brazil summit was duly held in Lisbon, Portugal, in July; the fifth EU-Brazil summit took place in Brussels, Belgium, in October 2011.

In late December 1994 the EU and Mercosur signed a joint declaration that aimed to promote trade liberalization and greater political co-operation. In September 1995, at a meeting in Montevideo, Uruguay, a framework agreement on the establishment of a free trade regime between the two organizations was initialled. The agreement was formally signed in December. In July 1998 the European Commission voted to commence negotiations towards an interregional Association Agreement with Mercosur, which would strengthen existing co-operation agreements. Negotiations were initiated in April 2000 (focusing on the three pillars of political dialogue, co-operation, and establishing a free trade area), and were extended in May 2008 to cover the additional pillars of science and technology, infrastructure, and renewable energy.

The first ministerial conference between the EC and the Rio Group of Latin American and Caribbean states took place in April 1991; since then high-level joint ministerial meetings have been held every two years. The first summit meeting of all EU and Latin American and Caribbean heads of state or government was held in Rio de Janeiro, Brazil, in June 1999, when a strategic partnership was launched. A second EU-Latin America/Caribbean (EU-LAC) summit took place in Madrid, in May 2002, and covered co-operation in political, economic, social and cultural fields. A political dialogue and co-operation agreement with the Andean Community and its member states was signed in December 2003. At the third EU-LAC summit meeting, held in Guadalajara, Mexico, in May 2004 it was agreed by the two parties that an Association Agreement, including a free trade area, was a common objective. In December 2005 the European Commission proposed a renewed strategy for strengthening the strategic partnership with Latin America, ahead of the fourth EU-LAC summit, held in Vienna, Austria, in May 2006. Its proposals included increasing political dialogue between the two regions, stimulating economic and commercial exchanges, encouraging regional integration, addressing inequality and adapting the EU's development and aid policy to correspond more closely to conditions in Latin America. At the fourth EU-LAC summit it was decided that negotiations for Association Agreements with Central America and with the Andean Community should be initiated. The summit also endorsed a proposal to establish an EU-Latin America parliamentary assembly. The assembly met for the first time in November 2006. In May 2010 the sixth EU-LAC summit was convened, in Madrid, on the theme 'Innovation and Technology for Sustainable Development and Social Inclusion'. In June 2007 the EU and the Andean Community initiated negotiations on the planned Association Agreement in Tarija, Bolivia. However, negotiations were suspended in June 2008, reportedly owing to divergent views of the aims and scope of the trade provisions. In January 2009 negotiations recommenced between three of the Andean Community countries, Colombia, Ecuador and Peru, with the goal of concluding a multi-party trade agreement; Ecuador provisionally suspended its participation in the negotiations in July. Negotiations were concluded on 1 March 2010, with an agreement on trade between the EU and Colombia and Peru, providing for the liberalization of trade in 65% of industrial products with Colombia, and 80% with Peru. Talks on an Association Agreement between the EU and the countries of Central America (Costa Rica, El Salvador, Guatemala, Honduras, Nicaragua and Panama) commenced in Costa Rica in October 2007, but negotiations were suspended temporarily during 2009 owing to the unstable political situation in Honduras. In May 2010 the EU concluded negotiations on an Association Agreement with Central America, covering three areas: trade; political dialogue; and co-operation. The European Commission was expected to provide total funding of some €3,000m. to Latin America, some €840m. to the countries of Central America, and some €50m. to the Andean Community in 2007–13. In 2007 the EU also concluded negotiations for an Economic Partnership Agreement with the Caribbean Forum (CARIFORUM) grouping of 16 Caribbean states.

Cuba remained the only Latin American country that did not have a formal economic co-operation agreement with the EU. In June 1995 a Commission communication advocated greater economic co-operation with Cuba; this policy was criticized by the US Government, which maintained an economic embargo against Cuba. Later that year the EU agreed to make the extent of economic co-operation with Cuba (a one-party state) contingent on progress towards democracy. An EU legation office opened in the Cuban capital, Havana, in March 2003, and the EU supported a renewed application by Cuba to join the successor to the Lomé Convention, the Cotonou Agreement. However, human rights abuses perpetrated by the Cuban regime in April (the imprisonment of a large number of dissidents) led to the downgrading of diplomatic relations with Cuba by the EU, the instigation of an EU policy of inviting dissidents to embassy receptions in Havana (the so-called cocktail wars) and the indefinite postponement of Cuba's application to join the Cotonou Agreement. In May Cuba withdrew its application for membership, and in July the Cuban President, Fidel Castro, announced that the Government would not accept aid from the EU and would terminate all political contact with the organization. In December 2004 the EU proposed a compromise—namely not to invite any Cubans, whether government ministers or dissidents, to future embassy receptions—but reiterated its demand that Cuba unconditionally release all political prisoners who remained in detention (several dissidents had already been released). Cuba announced in January 2005 that it was restoring diplomatic ties with all EU states. At the end of that month the EU temporarily suspended the diplomatic sanctions imposed on Cuba in mid-2003 and announced its intention to resume a 'constructive dialogue' with the Cuban authorities. In March 2005 the European Commissioner responsible for Development and Humanitarian Aid visited Cuba, and held meetings with the Cuban President, as well as several dissidents. The EU extended the temporary suspension of diplomatic sanctions against Cuba for one year in June, and again in mid-2006 and mid-2007, in the hope that constructive dialogue would bring about reform in the areas of human rights and democratization and the release of further political prisoners. Sanctions were lifted in June 2008, although the decision was to be subject to an annual review. In May 2010 the European Commission adopted a country strategy paper on Cuba, which identified three priority areas for intervention: food security; the environment, and adaptation to climate change; and exchanges of expertise, training and studies. Some €20m. was allocated to Cuba for the period 2011–13.

The EU's natural disaster prevention and preparedness programme (Dipecho) has targeted earthquake, flood, hurricane, and volcanic eruption preparedness throughout Latin America and the Caribbean. By March 2010 EU humanitarian assistance for Haiti (including planned pledges), in the aftermath of the earthquake that devastated the country's infrastructure, totalled more than €320m. (from member states and the European Commission). Emergency relief from the European Commission was worth over €120m., including €3m. in emergency funding allocated within 24 hours of the earthquake taking place. Following an outbreak of cholera in October 2010, an alert system was put in place, and the Commission approved new funding of some €10m. at the end of December to help fund the efforts of the European Commission's Humanitarian Aid Office (ECHO) to provide support for health staff; to implement preventive strategies, such as the promotion of chlorination and a hygiene-awareness campaign; and to improve the collection and analysis of health-related data.

FAR EAST AND AUSTRALASIA

Relations between the EU and the Association of Southeast Asian Nations (ASEAN) were based on a Co-operation Agreement of 1980. In March 2007, at an EU-ASEAN ministerial meeting held in Nuremberg, Germany, ASEAN and the EU made the Nuremberg Declaration on an EU-ASEAN Enhanced Partnership, and a Plan of Action was approved to strengthen co-operation during 2007–12. In September an EU-ASEAN commemorative summit took place in Singapore, to mark 30 years of co-operation between the two organizations.

In May 1995 ASEAN and EU senior officials endorsed an initiative to convene an Asia-Europe Meeting of heads of government (ASEM), which takes places every two years. The first ASEM summit was held in March 1996 in Bangkok, Thailand. The second ASEM summit, convened in the United Kingdom in April 1998, established an ASEM Trust Fund, under the auspices of the World Bank, to alleviate the social impact of financial crisis. Other initiatives adopted by ASEM were an Asia-Europe Co-operation Framework (AECF) to co-ordinate political, economic and financial co-operation, a Trade Facilitation Action Plan, and an Investment Promotion Action Plan, which incorporated a new Investment Experts Group. ASEM VI, convened in Helsinki, Finland, in September 2006, addressed the theme '10 Years of ASEM: Global Challenges and Joint Responses'. The participants adopted a Declaration on Climate Change, aimed at promoting efforts to reach consensus in international climate negotiations, and the Helsinki Declaration on the Future of ASEM, detailing practical recommendations for developing future ASEM co-operation. ASEM VII was held in Beijing, People's Republic of China, in October 2008. The meeting had the theme 'Vision and Action: Towards a Win-Win Solution', focusing on advancing dialogue regarding mutually beneficial co-operation on economic and social and cultural issues, and on sustainable development. The meeting resulted in the Beijing Declaration on Sustainable Development, which recognized the challenges posed to sustainable development by increasing global population, environmental degradation, depletion of resources, and deteriorating ecological 'carrying' capacity. The eighth ASEM summit meeting took place in Brussels, Belgium, in October 2010.

A trade agreement was signed with China in 1978 and renewed in May 1985. In June 1989, following the violent repression of the Chinese pro-democracy movement by Chinese Government, the EC imposed economic sanctions and an embargo on arms sales to that country. In October 1990 it was decided that relations with China should be 'progressively normalized'. The EU has supported China's increased involvement in the international community and, in particular, supported its application for membership of the WTO. The first EU-China meeting of heads of government was convened in April 1998. In November the President of the Commission made an official visit to China and urged that country to remove trade restrictions imposed on European products. In the same month the EU and Hong Kong signed a co-operation agreement to combat drugs-trafficking and copyright piracy. A bilateral trade agreement between the EU and China was concluded in May 2000, removing a major barrier to China's accession to the World Trade Organization; this was approved in November 2001. A third EU-China summit meeting was held in Beijing in October 2000. At the fourth summit, convened in September 2001, the two sides agreed to strengthen and widen political dialogue and to continue discussions on human rights issues. In March 2002 the European Commission approved a strategy document setting out a framework for co-operation between the EU and China in 2002–06, and in September the fifth EU-China summit discussed trade relations and future co-operation on illegal immigrants and tourism. At the sixth EU-China summit, held in Beijing in October 2003, two agreements were signed establishing a new dialogue on industrial policy and confirming China's participation in the 'Galileo' project; in addition, a memorandum of understanding (MOU) was initialled, paving the way for Chinese tourist groups to travel to the EU more easily. At the seventh EU-China summit, which took place in The Hague, Netherlands, in December 2004, the two sides further strengthened their maturing strategic partnership. A joint declaration was signed on nuclear non-proliferation and arms control, and agreements were also concluded on customs co-operation, and science and technology. The eighth summit, held in Beijing in September 2005, marked the 30th anniversary of the establishment of EU-China diplomatic relations. During the meeting, the establishment of an EU-China partnership on climate change was confirmed. The two sides also agreed to move towards early negotiations on a new framework agreement, and two MOUs were signed on labour, employment and social affairs and on the initiation of a dialogue on energy and transport strategies. The ninth EU-China summit, convened in September 2006, agreed that negotiations should be initiated on concluding a comprehensive Partnership and Co-operation Agreement (PCA) and on updating the 1985 trade and economic co-operation agreement. In October 2006, in a strategy communication, the Commission set forth details of a new agenda for EU-China relations, the priorities of which included support for China's transition towards greater openness and political pluralism and co-operation on climate change. In a separate policy paper, the Commission detailed a new strategy for expanding EU-China relations in the areas of trade and investment. Negotiations for a comprehensive PCA were launched in January 2007. The 10th EU-China summit took place in Beijing in November 2007. At the meeting, heads of state and of government witnessed the signature of a €500m. framework loan from the European Investment Bank to support efforts to tackle climate change. In January 2009 China and EU adopted nine agreements aimed at strengthening joint co-operation. Convened in Prague, Czech Republic, in May, the 11th EU-China summit addressed issues including the ongoing global financial and economic crisis and climate change. At the 12th EU-China summit, held in Nanjing in November, the two sides agreed to make efforts to facilitate the further implementation of the EU-China Joint Declaration on Climate Change, and agreed to strengthen the existing Partnership on Climate Change. The 13th EU-China summit took place in Brussels in October 2010, at which it was decided to designate 2011 as the EU-China Year of Youth.

A framework agreement on trade and co-operation between the EU and the Republic of Korea was signed in 1996 and entered into force in April 2001. In September 1997 the EU joined the Korean Peninsula Energy Development Organization, an initiative founded in 1995 to increase nuclear safety and reduce the risk of nuclear proliferation from the energy programme of the Democratic People's Republic of Korea (DPRK). Meanwhile, in May 2007 the EU and the Republic of Korea had commenced negotiations towards the adoption of a free trade agreement, and an agreement was initialled in October 2009. The deal, which provided for the elimination of almost all duties in the agricultural and industrial sectors, was signed formally at an EU-Republic of Korea summit meeting, held in Brussels in October 2010. The agreement was approved by the European Parliament in February 2011, with the addition of a clause ensuring that new Korean legislation on carbon dioxide limits from cars would not damage the interests of European car-makers. The free trade agreement entered into force in July of that year. Meanwhile, in June 2008 negotiations had commenced, aimed at updating the mutual framework agreement. In May 2010 the EU and the Republic of Korea signed a new framework agreement on bilateral relations. At the EU-Korea summit meeting of October 2010 the EU and the Republic of Korea also agreed further to strengthen their relationship, by forming a Strategic Partnership, which provided for increased commitment to co-operation by both parties.

In September 1999, for the first time, ministerial-level discussions took place between the EU and the DPRK at the UN General Assembly. In May 2001 the EU announced that it was to establish diplomatic relations with the DPRK to facilitate the Union's efforts in support of reconciliation in the Korean Peninsula and, in particular, in support of economic reform and the easing of the acute food and health problems in the DPRK. However, the implementation of a Country Strategy Paper, adopted in March 2002, was suspended, and there no plan for its renewal. In October 2002 the EU expressed its deep concern after the DPRK admitted that it had conducted a clandestine nuclear weapons programme, in serious breach of the country's international non-proliferation commitments. In the following month the EU stated that failure to resolve the nuclear issue would jeopardize the future development of EU-DPRK relations. In response to the DPRK's announcement in October 2006 that it had conducted a nuclear test, the EU strongly condemned the 'provocative' action and urged the DPRK to abandon its nuclear programme. In April 2009 the EU strongly condemned the DPRK for launching a rocket in contravention of relevant UN Security Council resolutions. In December 2010 the Council reinforced sanctions in place against a number of individuals and entities in the DPRK.

In June 1992 the EC signed trade and co-operation agreements with Mongolia and Macao, with respect for democracy and human rights forming the basis of envisaged co-operation. The 10th EU-Mongolia joint committee, held in Brussels in September 2007, focused on political and economic issues, and concluded that negotiations would be initiated on a PCA. An agreement on aviation was also reached, as a result of which legal certainty was to be restored to 11 air service agreements between Mongolia and individual EU member states. The 13th EU-Macao joint committee met in Brussels in December. A co-operation accord was formally signed with Viet Nam in July 1995, under which the EU agreed to increase quotas for Vietnamese textiles products, to support the country's efforts to join the WTO and to provide aid for environmental and public management projects. The agreement entered into force in June 1996. A permanent EU mission to Viet Nam was established in February 1996. In October 2004 the EU and Viet Nam concluded a bilateral agreement on market access in preparation for Viet Nam's accession to the WTO, which took place in January 2007. In addition, an agreement signed in December 2004 lifted all EU quantitative restrictions for Vietnamese textiles with effect from 1 January 2005. In May 2007 the EU and Viet Nam commenced negotiations on a new PCA, to replace that of 1995. Non-preferential co-operation agreements were signed with Laos and Cambodia in April 1997. The agreement with Laos (which emphasized development assistance and economic co-operation) entered into force on 1 December; the agreement with Cambodia was postponed owing to adverse political developments in that country. The EU concluded a textiles agreement with Laos, which provisionally entered into force in December 1998; as a result of the agreement, exports of textiles to the EU from Laos increased significantly. In 1998 the EU provided financial assistance to support preparations for a general election in Cambodia, and dispatched observers to monitor the election, which was held in July. The EU co-operation agreement with Cambodia entered into force in November 1999. EU-Cambodia relations were further enhanced with the opening of an EU delegation in Phnom-Penh in early 2002 and a Cambodian embassy in Brussels in late 2004. In September 1999 the EU briefly imposed an arms embargo against Indonesia, which was at that time refusing to permit the deployment of an international peace-keeping force in East Timor (now Timor-Leste). In April 2005 the EU extended preferential trade conditions to Indonesia, which meant that the country would benefit from lower customs duties in certain sectors. From September of that year the EU, together with contributing countries from ASEAN, as well as Norway and Switzerland, deployed a monitoring mission in the Indonesian province of Aceh to supervise the implementation of a peace agreement between the Government of Indonesia and the separatist Gerakan Aceh Merdeka (Free Aceh Movement). Having achieved its aims, the mission was concluded in December 2006. In November 2009 an EU-Indonesia PCA was signed.

In October 1996 the EU imposed strict limits on entry visas for Myanma officials, because of Myanmar's refusal to allow the Commission to send a mission to the country to investigate allegations of forced labour. In March 1997 EU ministers of foreign affairs agreed to revoke Myanmar's special trade privileges under the Generalized System of Preferences (GSP). The EU successively extended its ban on arms exports to Myanmar and its prohibition on the issuing of visas. In April 2003 a new 'Common Position' was adopted by the EU, which consolidated and extended the scope of existing sanctions against Myanmar and strengthened the arms embargo; EU sanctions were further extended in April 2004 in view of the military regime's failure to make any significant progress in normalizing the administration of the country and addressing the EU's concerns with regard to human rights. EU ministers of foreign affairs agreed to Myanmar's participation in ASEM V in October at a level below head of government. Following the summit, however, the EU revised the Common Position, further broadening sanctions against Myanmar, as the military regime had failed to comply with certain demands, including the release from house arrest of the opposition leader Aung San Suu Kyi. The Common Position was renewed in April 2006, November 2007, and April 2009. In August 2009 an amended Common Position was adopted, extending sanctions to the Myanmar judiciary, following proceedings against Aung San Suu Kyi related to alleged violation of the terms of her house arrest. Restrictive measures against Myanmar were renewed in April 2010. Legislative elections in Myanmar in November of that year (which were followed by the release of Suu Kyi) were criticized by the EU and other international observers. However, a civilian Government took power, and a degree of reform was being undertaken. In April 2012 the EU agreed to suspend most of the sanctions in place against Myanmar, in recognition of the significant political changes in that country; an arms embargo remained in place.

The EU's long-term assistance strategy for Timor-Leste has focused on stabilization and dialogue, combating poverty, and humanitarian support. Under the EU country strategy for Timor-Leste during 2008–13, rural development was to be strengthened, with a view to achieving sustained poverty reduction and food security, and the health sector and capacity building were to be supported.

Textiles exports by Asian countries have caused concern in the EU, owing to the depressed state of its textiles industry. In 1982 bilateral negotiations were held under the former Multi-Fibre Arrangement (MFA, see WTO) with Asian producers, notably Hong Kong, the Republic of Korea and Macao. Agreements were eventually reached involving reductions in clothing quotas and 'anti-surge' clauses to prevent flooding of European markets. In 1986 new bilateral negotiations were held and agreements were reached with the principal Asian textiles exporters, for the period 1987–91 (later extended to December 1993, when the Uruguay Round of GATT negotiations was finally concluded): in most cases a slight increase in quotas was permitted. Under the conclusions of the Uruguay Round, the MFA was replaced by an Agreement on Textiles and Clothing (ATC), which provided for the progressive elimination of the quotas that existed under the MFA during 1994–2004. In January 1995 bilateral textiles agreements, signed by the EU with India, Pakistan and China, specified certain trade liberalization measures to be undertaken, including an increase of China's silk export quota. In May 2005 the EU imposed limits on textiles imports from China, in response to a dramatic increase in Chinese clothing exports since the expiry of the ATC on 1 January. In June the EU and the Chinese Government agreed import quotas on 10 clothing and textiles categories until 2008, but by August several of the quotas for 2005 had already been breached. In September the dispute was resolved when it was agreed that one-half of the estimated 80m. Chinese garments that had been impounded at European ports would be released and the remainder counted against the quotas for 2006. Also in September 2005 a report published by the high-level group on textiles and clothing—established by the Commission in 2003—sought, *inter alia*, to chart the likely development of the sectors up to 2020. With regard to the quota-free environment for textiles and clothing that had been introduced at the beginning of 2005, the report noted that a Commission statement released in mid-2006 had indicated that the disruptive impact of liberalization of Chinese textiles exports to the EU had been confined to a fairly restricted range of product categories. None the less, China's share of exports to the EU of products in the liberalized categories had risen markedly, to the detriment of traditional EU suppliers. Overall, however, only a modest increase in EU imports of textiles and clothing (in both the liberalized categories and in total) had occurred. The statement noted, too, that China was becoming a key growth market for exports of textiles and clothing from the EU. In October 2007 the European Commission agreed not to renew quotas on textiles from China, but instead to introduce a system of monitoring imports.

Numerous discussions have been held since 1981 on the EU's increasing trade deficit with Japan, and on the failure of the Japanese market to accept more European exports. In July 1991 the heads of government of Japan and of the EC signed a joint declaration on closer co-operation in both economic and political matters. The European office of the EU-Japan Industrial Co-operation Centre was opened in Brussels in June 1996; the Centre, which was established in 1987 as a joint venture between the Japanese Government and the European Commission, sought to increase industrial co-operation between the EU and Japan. In October 1996 the WTO upheld a long-standing complaint brought by the EU that Japanese taxes on alcoholic spirits discriminated against certain European products. In January 1998 an EU-Japan summit meeting was held, followed by a meeting at ministerial level in October. Subsequent summits (the 19th was held in Brussels in April 2011) have aimed to strengthen dialogue.

Regular consultations are held with Australia at ministerial and senior official level. In January 1996 the Commission proposed a framework agreement to formalize the EU's trade and political relationship with that country. In September, however, after the Australian Government had objected to the human rights clause contained in all EU international agreements, negotiations were suspended. In June 1997 a joint declaration was signed, committing both sides to greater political, cultural and economic co-operation. In 2001 a National Europe Centre, based at the Australian National University in Canberra, was established jointly by the EU and the University to consolidate EU-Australia relations. The EU-Australia ministerial consultations convened in Melbourne, Australia, in April 2003, adopted a five-year Agenda for Co-operation. In October 2008 ministers of foreign affairs from the EU and Australia, meeting in Paris, France, adopted a Partnership Framework, outlining future co-operation in the areas of: foreign policy and security issues; trade; relations with Asia and the Pacific; environment; and science, technology and education. The Partnership Framework was updated at a meeting of ministers of foreign affairs held in Stockholm, Sweden, in October 2009. In March 1997 New Zealand took a case relating to import duties to the WTO, which later ruled against the EU. A joint declaration detailing areas of co-operation and establishing a consultative framework to facilitate the development of these was signed in May 1999. Mutual recognition agreements were also signed with Australia and New Zealand in 1999, with the aim of facilitating bilateral trade in industrial products. In March 2004 a European Commission Delegation was inaugurated in Wellington, New Zealand. In September 2007 a new joint declaration on relations and co-operation was adopted by the EU and New Zealand, replacing the 1999 joint declaration and 2004 action plan.

SOUTH ASIA

Bilateral non-preferential co-operation agreements were signed with Bangladesh, India, Pakistan and Sri Lanka between 1973 and 1976. A further agreement with India, extended to include co-operation in trade, industry, energy, science and finance, came into force in December 1981. A third agreement, which entered into effect in August 1994, included commitments to develop co-operation between the two sides and improve market access, as well as on the observance of human rights and democratic principles. The first EU-India summit meeting was held in Lisbon, Portugal, in June 2000. In November 2004 the EU and India signed a 'strategic partnership' agreement, which was expected significantly to improve their relationship; the agreement—described as a reflection of 'India's growing stature and influence'—meant that India became a special EU partner alongside the USA, Canada, the People's Republic of China and Russia. The sixth EU-India summit meeting, held in New Delhi, India, in September 2005, adopted a joint action plan to implement the strategic partnership. It was agreed to establish a dialogue on security issues, disarmament and non-proliferation, to increase co-operation in efforts to combat terrorism, and to create a high-level trade group to examine ways of strengthening economic relations. An agreement on India's participation in the EU's Galileo civil satellite navigation and positioning system was also signed. The country strategy paper for 2007–13 allocated funds totalling some €470m. to India, focusing on the implementation of the joint action plan and the country's pursuit of the Millennium Development Goals agreed by UN member Governments in 2000, concentrating on health and education. The 10th EU-India summit was held in Brussels, Belgium, in December 2010, and a joint declaration on international terrorism was adopted. The first India-EU Joint Working Group on Counter-Terrorism met in New Delhi in January 2012. The most recent EU-India summit was held in New Delhi in February, at which participants welcomed the progress that had been made in ongoing negotiations towards the finalization of an India-EU Broad-based Trade and Investment Agreement (BTIA).

A new accord with Sri Lanka, designed to promote co-operation in areas such as trade, investment and protection of the environment, entered into force in April 1995. In mid-August 2010 the EU temporarily withheld certain trade preferences for Sri Lanka, after an investigation confirmed that three UN conventions relating to human rights had failed to be fully implemented.

The EU has provided support for democracy and peace in Nepal, which formally abolished the monarchy in May 2008, following multi-party legislative elections. In January 2011 an EU-Nepal memorandum of understanding on the Multi-Annual Indicative Programme for 2011–13 was signed. Bilateral co-operation focuses on three principal areas: education; stability and peace-building; and trade and strengthening of economic capacity building.

A new agreement with Pakistan on commercial and economic co-operation entered into force in May 1986; in May 1992 an agreement was signed on measures to stimulate private investment in Pakistan. A draft co-operation agreement was initialled with Pakistan in April 1998. However, following a military coup in Pakistan in October 1999, the agreement was suspended. Political dialogue with Pakistan recommenced on an ad hoc basis in November 2000, and the co-operation agreement was signed in November 2001; a joint statement was issued on the occasion, in which Pakistan reiterated its firm commitment to return to democratic government. The co-operation agreement with Pakistan entered into force in April 2004. The EU pledged assistance for Pakistan amounting to €398m. in 2007–13, compared with €125m. in development co-operation funding granted in 2002–06. In February 2008 the EU deployed an Election Observation Mission to Pakistan, to monitor the conduct of the general election. The first EU-Pakistan summit was held in June 2009, and a second EU-Pakistan summit was held in Brussels, Belgium, in June 2010. In February 2012 the Council adopted a five-year EU-Pakistan engagement plan, which aimed to promote peace and stability in the region.

Meanwhile, the new co-operation accord with Bangladesh (which replaced the 1976 commercial co-operation agreement) was signed in May 2000 and came into force in March 2001. In 2007–13, within the framework of a country strategy paper, assistance pledged to Bangladesh totalled €403m.

The EU pledged assistance for the reconstruction of Afghanistan following the removal of the Taliban regime in late 2001, and in 2002 announced development aid of €1,000m. for 2002–06, in addition to humanitarian aid. (By the end of 2006 the total of €1,000m. had been exceeded.) In March 2003 the European Commission hosted, along with the World Bank, the Afghanistan High Level Strategic Forum. The Government of Afghanistan convened the meeting to discuss with its principal partners, donors and multilateral organizations the progress and future vision for state-building in Afghanistan, as well as the long-term funding requirements for reconstruction. In 2004–05 the EU provided substantial support for the election process in Afghanistan, dispatching a Democracy and Election Support Mission to assess the presidential election, which was held in October 2004, and a full Election Observation Mission to monitor legislative and provincial elections, which took place in September 2005. In November the EU and Afghanistan adopted a joint declaration on a new partnership aimed at promoting Afghanistan's political and economic development and strengthening EU-Afghan relations. Increased co-operation was envisaged in areas such as political and economic governance, judicial reform, counter-narcotics measures, and human rights, while the declaration also provided for a regular political dialogue, in the form of annual meetings at ministerial level. The EU welcomed the launch by the UN-sponsored London Conference on Afghanistan, held on 31 January–1 February 2006, of the Afghanistan Compact, representing a framework for co-operation between the Government of Afghanistan, the UN and the international community for a five-year period. The EU pledged €1,030m. in development assistance to Afghanistan over 2007–13. In May 2007 the Council adopted a Joint Action on an EU police mission to Afghanistan; EUPOL, comprising some 160 police officers, was officially launched on 15 June, and aimed to help develop a police force in Afghanistan that would work to respect human rights and operate within the framework of the rule of law, and to address the issue of police reform at central, regional and provincial levels. In May 2010 the Council extended EUPOL's mandate for a three-year period, terminating at the end of May 2013. Assistance provided by the EU focused on the principal areas of concern identified in the National Development Strategy for Afghanistan, which was adopted by the Paris Declaration at a donors' conference held in France on 12 June 2008, and which included strengthening the judicial system; rural development, to combat narcotics production by promoting alternatives to poppy cultivation; and supporting the health sector. The EU agreed to provide food and other humanitarian assistance amounting to €35m. in 2009 to vulnerable civilians in Afghanistan and to Afghan refugees sheltering in Pakistan and Iran. An EU Election Observation Mission was dispatched to monitor the presidential and provincial elections held in Afghanistan in August. In October a Plan for Enhanced EU Engagement in Afghanistan and Pakistan was approved by EU ministers of foreign affairs. The Plan emphasized the need to strengthen sub-national governance, the police and the judiciary in Afghanistan; the importance of co-ordinated EU support for national programmes and the process of reintegration; and support for the electoral structure and the development of democratic institutions.

THE USA AND CANADA

A framework agreement for commercial and economic co-operation between the Community and Canada was signed in Ottawa in 1976. It was superseded in 1990 by a Declaration on EC-Canada Relations. In February 1996 the Commission proposed closer ties with Canada and an action plan including early warning to avoid trade disputes, elimination of trade barriers, and promotion of business contacts. An action plan and joint political declaration were signed in December.

Canadian and EU leaders meet regularly at bilateral summits. At the Ottawa summit meeting held in December 1996, a political declaration on EU-Canada relations was adopted, specifying areas for co-operation. At a summit held in Ottawa in March 2004, Canada and the EU adopted a Partnership Agenda to promote political and economic co-operation. In November 2005 Canada and the EU signed an agreement creating a framework for Canada's participation in the EU's crisis management operations.

A number of specific agreements were concluded between the Community and the USA: a co-operation agreement on the peaceful use of atomic energy entered into force in 1959, and agreements on environmental matters and on fisheries came into force in 1974 and 1984, respectively. Additional agreements provide for co-operation in other fields of scientific research and development, while bilateral contacts take place in many areas not covered by a formal agreement. A Transatlantic Declaration on EC-US relations was concluded in November 1990: the two parties agreed to consult each other on important matters of common interest, and to increase formal contacts. A new Transatlantic Agenda for EU-US relations was signed by the US President and the Presidents of the European Commission and the European Council at a meeting in Madrid, Spain, in December 1995. In May 1998, at an EU-US summit held in London, the United Kingdom, a new Transatlantic Economic Partnership (TEP) was launched, to remove technical trade barriers, eliminate industrial tariffs, establish a free trade area in services, and further liberalize measures relating to government procurement, intellectual property and investment. (The agricultural and audiovisual sectors were excluded from the TEP.) In June 2005 an EU-US economic summit reached agreement on an initiative to enhance transatlantic economic integration and growth; the first informal EU-US economic ministerial meeting took place in Brussels in November. In January 2006 the Commission hosted the first high-level EU-US Regulatory Co-operation Forum, which aimed to minimize barriers to bilateral trade. At an EU-US summit held in April 2007, in Washington, DC, USA, a new Framework for Advancing Transatlantic Economic Integration between the USA and the EU was adopted. A new Transatlantic Economic Council, a political body established to monitor and facilitate bilateral co-operation in order to promote economic integration, met for the first time in November. In November 2009, at an EU-US summit held in Washington, DC, the EU and the US agreed to re-launch their High Level Consultative Group on Development and to hold annual ministerial meetings to increase co-operation on development policy, initially focused on three areas: food security and agricultural development; climate change; and the Millennium Development Goals. On the margins of the summit, the first meeting of a ministerial-level EU-US Energy Council, which had been launched in September, and aimed to strengthen transatlantic dialogue on energy matters, took place. An EU-US summit was held in Lisbon, Portugal, in November 2010. The summit focused on three principal issues: economic growth and the creation of employment, including in new and emerging business areas; addressing global challenges, such as climate change and international development; and strengthening security for citizens. At the summit meeting held in Washington, DC, in November 2011 the EU and the USA agreed to expand the work of the Transatlantic Economic Council, and to maintain and increase work on energy security and research in the EU-US Energy Council.

The USA has frequently criticized the Common Agricultural Policy, which it regards as creating unfair competition for US exports by its system of export refunds and preferential agreements. In 1998 the World Trade Organization (WTO) upheld a US complaint about the EU ban on imports of hormone-treated beef, which had led to a retaliatory US ban on meat imports from the EU. Following the EU's refusal to repeal the ban by May 1999, the WTO authorized the imposition by the USA and Canada of retaliatory sanctions for each year that the ban was in place. In March 2008 a WTO panel ruled that scientific evidence did not support the imposition of the import ban by the EU; Canada and the USA were also criticized for their failure to repeal their retaliatory measures against the EU. Meanwhile, in June 2003, at a US-EU summit in Washington, DC, it was acknowledged that agriculture remained a major obstacle to agreement in the Doha Round of the WTO. In May the USA had further strained relations by filing a WTO complaint, supported by Argentina and Canada, to end the EU's de facto moratorium on genetically modified food, which began in 1998 and was based on European safety concerns, on the grounds that it was an unfair trade barrier. Another issue of contention between the USA and the EU was the EU's banana import regime (see African, Caribbean and Pacific countries). At a WTO Ministerial Conference held in Hong Kong in December 2005 to advance the Doha Round of negotiations, agreement was reached on the elimination of export subsidies on agricultural goods by the end of 2013.

In October 1996 EU ministers of foreign affairs agreed to pursue in the WTO a complaint regarding the effects on European businesses of the USA's trade embargo against Cuba, formulated in the Helms-Burton Act. In April 1997 the EU and the USA approved a temporary resolution of the Helms-Burton dispute, whereby the US Administration was to limit the application of sanctions in return for a formal suspension of the WTO case. In mid-1996 the US Congress had adopted legislation imposing an additional trade embargo (threatening sanctions against any foreign company investing more than US $40m. in energy projects in a number of prescribed states, including Iran and Libya), the presence of which further complicated the EU-US debate in September 1997, when a French petroleum company, Total, provoked US anger, owing to its proposed investment in an Iranian natural gas project. In May 1998 an EU-US summit meeting reached agreement on the Transatlantic Economic Partnership (see above). The USA agreed to exempt European companies from the trade embargo on Iran and Libya, and to seek congressional approval for an indefinite waiver for the Helms-Burton Act, thereby removing the threat of sanctions from Total. The EU had allowed the WTO case to lapse in April, but it warned that a new WTO panel would be established if the USA took action against European companies trading with Cuba. In return, the EU agreed to increase co-operation in combating terrorism and the proliferation of weapons of mass destruction and to discourage investment in expropriated property.

In July 1997 the EU became involved in intensive negotiations with the US aircraft company Boeing over fears that its planned merger with McDonnell Douglas would harm European interests. In late July the EU approved the merger, after Boeing accepted concessions including an agreement to dispense with exclusivity clauses for 20-year supply contracts and to maintain McDonnell Douglas as a separate company for a period of 10 years. In June the EU and the USA agreed to introduce a mutual recognition agreement, which was to enable goods (including medicines, pharmaceutical products, telecommunications equipment and electrical apparatus) undergoing tests in Europe to be marketed in the USA or Canada without the need for further testing. In August 2004 a fresh trade dispute erupted between the USA and the EU over the subsidies that the two sides paid to their respective aircraft industries. The USA claimed that the financial support European governments provided to aircraft manufacturer Airbus was in breach of world trade rules, while the EU stated that the same was true of the US Administration's subsidies for Boeing. The USA made a formal complaint to the WTO over the EU's support for Airbus in October; the EU immediately responded in kind by filing a complaint regarding the US financial assistance to Boeing. Following the failure of bilateral talks to resolve the dispute, in July 2005 the WTO agreed to establish two panels to examine the complaints of the USA and the EU; members of the panels were appointed in October. In November 2006 the US case against Airbus was formally presented. In May 2011 a WTO appeals panel ruled that some EU subsidies to Airbus had been illegal. The case of the EU against Boeing was presented in March 2007. In March 2012 a WTO panel of appeal ruled that subsidies granted to Boeing by the US Government were incompatible with international trade rules.

In July 2002 the Commission submitted a complaint to the WTO regarding tax exemptions granted to US companies exporting goods via subsidiaries established in tax-free countries (foreign sales corporations). The WTO found in favour of the Commission and authorized the EU to levy punitive tariffs of up to US $4,000m. in compensation for the US tax exemptions, which benefited large companies, including Boeing and Microsoft, and which the WTO ruled were discriminatory and should be abolished. In February 2003 the EU released a final list of about 50,000 goods that would be subjected to tariffs of 100%, but postponed implementation of the sanctions, pending the progress of a bill to amend the tax law in the US Congress. In March 2004, however, the legislation remained in place and the EU began the phased imposition of duties (initially at 5%, but increasing by 1% every month) on a range of US exports. This represented the first time that the EU had taken retaliatory action against the USA in a trade dispute. In October the US President, George W. Bush, signed legislation that repealed the tax exemptions from 1 January 2005 but contained transitional provisions allowing for exemptions to be maintained for some exporters until the end of 2006 and for an indefinite period on certain binding contracts. The EU appealed to the WTO regarding the transitional provisions, suspending sanctions from January 2005 pending a ruling. In September a WTO panel concluded that, despite the changes to its legislation, the USA had not fully abided by previous rulings and that the tax exemptions maintained under transitional provisions violated WTO rules. In February 2006 the WTO upheld this ruling, rejecting an appeal from the USA. The USA amended its legislation in May and EU sanctions were terminated in the same month.

From 1 May 2005 the EU imposed an additional 15% duty on a range of US goods (including paper, farm goods, textiles and machinery) as punishment for the failure of the USA to revoke a clause in its anti-dumping legislation, known as the Byrd Amendment. The Byrd Amendment, which was promulgated in October 2000, made provision for funds accruing from the payment of anti-dumping and anti-subsidy duties to be paid to the US companies that filed the complaint. The WTO ruled the Amendment illegal in 2002, but the USA failed to repeal the legislation by the deadline of December 2003. In February 2006 the European Commission welcomed the enactment in the USA of legislation repealing the Byrd Amendment (however, under a transition clause, duties imposed on goods imported into the USA until 30 September 2007 were to be distributed after their collection, which, under US practice, could take place several years after the import).

Some member states criticized the USA's objections to the establishment of the International Criminal Court (which came into effect in The Hague, Netherlands, in 2003), while there was also criticism of the USA's strategy towards Iraq in early 2003 (see the Middle East and the Mediterranean), as the EU emphasized that only the UN Security Council could determine whether military action in Iraq was justified. The EU-US annual summit held in June, however, emphasized the need for transatlantic co-operation following the overthrow by a US-led coalition force of Saddam Hussain's regime in Iraq, stressing the need to unite against global terrorism and the proliferation of weapons of mass destruction.

A visit to several European countries by the US Secretary of State, Condoleezza Rice, in December 2005 was largely overshadowed by allegations, published in November, that the USA's Central Intelligence Agency (CIA) had used European airports to transport suspected Islamist militants to secret detention centres in Eastern Europe for interrogation in an illegal programme of so-called extraordinary rendition. Rice acknowledged the practice of rendition, but denied that prisoners were tortured and refused to comment on the alleged existence of CIA prisons in Eastern Europe. In late November the EU requested clarification from the USA about the alleged secret prisons and transfer flights, while the Council of Europe established an inquiry into the matter. Meanwhile, the European Parliament formed its own 46-member committee to investigate the allegations. The final report of the Parliament's inquiry, published in February 2007, rejected extraordinary rendition as an illegal instrument used by the USA in the fight against terrorism. The report noted that secret detention facilities may have been located at US military bases in Europe, and deplored the acquiescence of some member states in illegal CIA operations and the failure of the EU Council of Ministers to co-operate with the inquiry.

AFRICAN, CARIBBEAN AND PACIFIC (ACP) COUNTRIES

In June 2000, meeting in Cotonou, Benin, heads of state and of government of the EU and African, Caribbean and Pacific (ACP) countries concluded a new 20-year partnership accord between the EU and ACP states. The EU-ACP Partnership Agreement, known as the Cotonou Agreement, entered into force on 1 April 2003 (although many of its provisions had been applicable for a transitional period since August 2000), following ratification by the then 15 EU member states and more than the requisite two-thirds of the ACP countries. Previously, the principal means of co-operation between the Community and developing countries were the Lomé Conventions. The First Lomé Convention (Lomé I), which was concluded at Lomé, Togo, in February 1975 and came into force on 1 April 1976, replaced the Yaoundé Conventions and the Arusha Agreement. Lomé I was designed to provide a new framework of co-operation, taking into account the varying needs of developing ACP countries. The Second Lomé Convention entered into force on 1 January 1981 and the Third Lomé Convention on 1 March 1985 (trade provisions) and 1 May 1986 (aid). The Fourth Lomé Convention, which had a 10-year commitment period, was signed in December 1989: its trade provisions entered into force on 1 March 1990, and the remainder entered into force in September 1991.

The Cotonou Agreement was to cover a 20-year period from 2000 and was subject to revision every five years. A financial protocol was attached to the Agreement, which indicated the funds available to the ACP through the European Development Fund (EDF), the main instrument for Community aid for development co-operation in ACP countries. The ninth EDF, covering the initial five-year period from March 2000, provided a total budget of €13,500m., of which €1,300m. was allocated to regional co-operation and €2,200m. was for the new investment facility for the development of the private sector. In addition, uncommitted balances from previous EDFs amounted to a further €2,500m. The new Agreement envisaged a more participatory approach with more effective political co-operation to encourage good governance and democracy, increased flexibility in the provision of aid to reward performance, and a new framework for economic and trade co-operation. Its objectives were to alleviate poverty, contribute to sustainable development and integrate the ACP economies into the global economy. Negotiations to revise the Cotonou Agreement were initiated in May 2004 and concluded in February 2005. The political dimension of the Agreement was broadly strengthened and a reference to co-operation in counter-terrorism and the prevention of the proliferation of weapons of mass destruction was included. The revised Cotonou Agreement was signed on 24 June 2005.

Under the provisions of the new accord, the EU was to finalize free trade arrangements (replacing the previous non-reciprocal trade preferences) with the most-developed ACP countries during 2000–08; these would be structured around a system of six regional free trade zones, and would be designed to ensure full compatibility with World Trade Organization (WTO) provisions. Once in force, the agreements would be subject to revision every five years. The first general stage of negotiations for the Economic Partnership Agreements (EPAs), involving discussions with all ACP countries regarding common procedures, began in September 2002. The regional phase of EPA negotiations to establish a new framework for trade and investment commenced in October 2003. Negotiations had been scheduled for completion in mid-2007 to allow for ratification by 2008, when the WTO exception for existing arrangements expired. However, the negotiation period was subsequently extended. Some 36 ACP states have signed full or interim EPAs, covering the liberalization of goods and agricultural products. The EPAs have attracted some criticism for their focus on trade liberalization and their perceived failure to recognize the widespread poverty of ACP countries.

In March 2010 negotiations were concluded on the second revision of the Cotonou Agreement, which sought to take into account various factors, including the increasing importance of enhanced regional co-operation and a more inclusive partnership in ACP countries; the need for security; efforts to meet the Millennium Development Goals; the new trade relationship developed following the expiry of trade preferences at the end of 2007; and the need to ensure the effectiveness and coherence of international aid efforts. The second revised Cotonou Agreement was formally signed in Ouagadougou, Burkina Faso, in June 2010, and entered into effect, on a provisional basis, at the beginning of November.

Meanwhile, the EU had launched an initiative to allow free access to the products of the least-developed ACP nations by 2005. Stabex and Sysmin, instruments under the Lomé Conventions designed to stabilize export prices for agricultural and mining commodities, respectively, were replaced by a system called FLEX, introduced in 2000, to compensate ACP countries for short-term fluctuations in export earnings. In February 2001 the EU agreed to phase out trade barriers on imports of everything but military weapons from the world's 48 least-developed countries, 39 of which were in the ACP group. Duties on sugar, rice, bananas and some other products were to remain until 2009 (these were withdrawn from October of that year). In May 2001 the EU announced that it would cancel all outstanding debts arising from its trade accords with former colonies of member states.

One major new programme set up on behalf of the ACP countries and financed by the EDF was Pro€Invest, which was launched in 2002, with funding of €110m. over a seven-year period. In October 2003 the Commission proposed to incorporate the EDF into the EU budget (it had previously been a fund outside the EU budget, to which the EU member states made direct voluntary contributions). The cost-sharing formula for the 25 member states would automatically apply, obviating the need for negotiations about contributions for the 10th EDF. The Commission proposal was endorsed by the European Parliament in April 2004. Despite the fears of ACP countries that the enlargement of the EU could jeopardize funding, the 10th EDF was agreed in December 2005 by the European Council and provided funds of €22,682m. for 2008–13.

On 1 July 1993 the EC introduced a regime to allow the preferential import into the Community of bananas from former French and British colonies in the Caribbean. This was designed to protect the banana industries of ACP countries from the availability of cheaper bananas, produced by countries in Latin America. Latin American and later US producers brought a series of complaints before the WTO, claiming that the EU banana import regime was in contravention of free trade principles. The WTO upheld their complaints on each occasion leading to adjustments of the complex quota and tariffs systems in place. Following the WTO authorization of punitive US trade sanctions, in April 2001 the EU reached agreement with the USA and Ecuador on a new banana regime. Under the new accord, the EU was granted the so-called Cotonou waiver, which allowed it to maintain preferential access for ACP banana exports, in return for the adoption of a new tariff-only system for bananas from Latin American countries from 1 January 2006. The Latin American producers were guaranteed total market access under the agreement and were permitted to seek arbitration if dissatisfied with the EU's proposed tariff levels. Following the WTO rejection of EU proposals for tariff levels of €230 and €187 per metric ton (in comparison with existing rates of €75 for a quota of 2.2m. tons and €680 thereafter), in November 2005 the EU announced that a tariff of €176, with a duty-free quota of 775,000 metric tons for ACP producers, would be implemented on 1 January 2006. In late 2006 Ecuador initiated a challenge to the EU's proposals at the WTO. Twelve other countries subsequently initiated third-party challenges to the proposals at the WTO, in support of the challenge by Ecuador. In April 2008 the WTO upheld the challenge by Ecuador, and ordered the EU to align its tariffs with WTO regulations. In December 2009 representatives from the EU and Latin American countries initialled the Geneva Agreement on Trade in Bananas (GATB), which aimed to end the dispute. Under the Agreement, which made no provision for import quotas, the EU was gradually to reduce its import tariff on bananas from Latin American countries, from €176 per metric ton to €114 per ton by 2017. In March 2010 The EU also approved the implementation of Banana Accompanying Measures, which aimed to mobilize €190m. to support the 10 main ACP banana-exporting countries in adjusting to the anticipated increase in market competition from Latin America during 2010–13. (ACP countries would continue to benefit from duty- and quota-free access to EU markets.) For their part, Latin American banana-producing countries undertook not to demand further tariff reductions; and to withdraw several related cases against the EU that were pending at the WTO. In response to the Agreement, the US authorities determined to settle ongoing parallel complaints lodged with the WTO against the EU relating to bananas.

Following a WTO ruling at the request of Brazil, Australia and Thailand in 2005 that the EU's subsidized exports of sugar breached legal limits, reform of the EU's sugar regime was required by May 2006. Previously, the EU purchased fixed quotas of sugar from ACP producers at two or three times the world price, the same price that it paid to sugar growers in the EU. In November 2005 the EU agreed to reform the sugar industry through a phased reduction of its prices for white sugar of 36% by 2009 (which was still twice the market price in 2005). Compensation to EU producers amounted to €6,300m. over the four years beginning in January 2006, but compensation to ACP producers was worth just €40m. in 2006. Development campaigners and impoverished ACP countries, notably Jamaica and Guyana, condemned the plans.

In June 1995 negotiations opened with a view to concluding a wide-ranging trade and co-operation agreement with South Africa, including the eventual creation of a free trade area (FTA). The accord was approved by heads of state and of government in March 1999, after agreement was reached to eliminate progressively, over a 12-year period, the use of the terms 'port' and 'sherry' to describe South African fortified wines. The accord provided for the removal of duties from about 99% of South Africa's industrial exports and some 75% of its agricultural products within 10 years, while South Africa was to liberalize its market for some 86% of EU industrial goods (with protection for the motor vehicle and textiles industries), within a 12-year period. The accord also introduced increased development assistance for South Africa after 1999. The long-delayed agreement was finally signed in January 2002, allowing South African wines freer access to the EU market. Under the terms of the agreement, South Africa was allowed to export 42m. litres of wine a year duty-free to the EU, in exchange for abandoning the use of names such as 'sherry', 'port', 'ouzo' or 'grappa'. In March 1997 the Commission approved a Special Protocol for South Africa's accession to the Lomé Convention, and in April South Africa attained partial membership. Full membership was withheld, as South Africa was not regarded as, in all respects, a developing country, and was therefore not entitled to aid provisions. The EU and South Africa launched a strategic partnership in November 2006. In May 2007 the two sides agreed an Action Plan, which aimed to develop political dialogue and increase co-operation on a range of economic, social and other issues. The first EU-South Africa summit meeting was held in Bordeaux, France, in July 2008.

In May 2003 Timor-Leste joined the ACP and the ACP-EC Council of Ministers approved its accession to the ACP-EC Partnership Agreement. Cuba, which had been admitted to the ACP in December 2000, was granted observer status. Cuba withdrew its application to join the Cotonou Agreement in July 2003.

Article 96 of the Cotonou Agreement, which provides for suspension of the Agreement in specific countries in the event of violation of one of its essential elements (respect for human rights, democratic principles and the rule of law), was invoked against Haiti in 2001, and this was extended annually to December 2004. However, relations with Haiti were in the process of normalization from September of that year.

ACP-EU Institutions

The three institutions of the Cotonou Agreement are the Council of Ministers, the Committee of Ambassadors and the Joint Parliamentary Assembly.

Council of Ministers: comprises the members of the Council of the European Union and members of the EU Commission and a member of the Government of each ACP signatory to the Cotonou Agreement; meets annually.

Committee of Ambassadors: comprises the Permanent Representative of each member state to the European Union and a representative of the EU Commission and the Head of Mission (ambassador) of each ACP state accredited to the EU; assists the Council of Ministers and meets regularly, in particular to prepare the session of the Council of Ministers.

Joint Parliamentary Assembly: EU and ACP countries are equally represented; attended by parliamentary delegates from each of the ACP countries and an equal number of members of the European Parliament; two co-presidents are elected by the Assembly from each of the two groups; meets twice a year; 24 vice-presidents (12 EU and 12 ACP) are also elected by the Assembly and with the co-presidents constitute the Bureau of the Joint Parliamentary Assembly, which meets several times a year; Co-Pres LOUIS MICHEL, MUSIKARI KOMBO.

Secretariat of the ACP-EC Council of Ministers: 175 rue de la Loi, 1048 Brussels, Belgium; tel. (2) 281-61-11; fax (2) 281-69-34; Co-Secretaries ALDA SILVEIRA REIS, Dr MOHAMED IBN CHAMBAS.

Centre for the Development of Enterprise (CDE): 52 ave Herrmann Debroux, 1160 Brussels, Belgium; tel. (2) 679-18-11; fax (2) 679-26-03; e-mail info@cde.int; internet www.cde.int/index.aspx; f. 1977 to encourage and support the creation, expansion and restructuring of industrial companies (mainly in the fields of manufacturing and agro-industry) in the ACP states by promoting co-operation between ACP and European companies, in the form of financial, technical or commercial partnership, management contracts, licensing or franchise agreements, sub-contracts, etc.; manages the Pro€Invest programme; Dir JEAN-ERICK ROMAGNE.

Technical Centre for Agricultural and Rural Co-operation (CTA): Postbus 380, 6700 AJ Wageningen, Netherlands; tel. (317) 467100; fax (317) 460067; e-mail cta@cta.int; internet www.cta.int/index.htm; f. 1984 to improve the flow of information among agricultural and rural development stakeholders in ACP countries; Dir MICHAEL HAILU.

ACP Institutions

ACP Council of Ministers: composed of a member of Government for each ACP state or a government-designated representative; the principal decision-making body for the ACP group; meets twice annually; ministerial sectoral meetings are held regularly.

ACP Committee of Ambassadors: the second decision-making body of the ACP Group; it acts on behalf of the Council of Ministers between ministerial sessions and is composed of the ambassadors or one representative from every ACP State.

ACP Secretariat: ACP House, 451 ave Georges Henri, Brussels, Belgium; tel. (2) 743-06-00; fax (2) 735-55-73; e-mail info@acpsec.org; internet www.acpsec.org; Sec.-Gen. Dr MOHAMED IBN CHAMBAS (Ghana).

On 15 April 2005 27 ACP countries signed a charter creating the ACP Consultative Assembly, which formalized the existing inter-parliamentary co-operation between the ACP member states.

The ACP States

Angola
Antigua and Barbuda
Bahamas
Barbados
Belize
Benin
Botswana
Burkina Faso
Burundi
Cameroon
Cape Verde
Central African Republic
Chad
Comoros
Congo, Democratic Republic
Congo, Republic
Cook Islands
Côte d'Ivoire
Cuba
Djibouti
Dominica
Dominican Republic
Equatorial Guinea
Eritrea
Ethiopia
Fiji
Gabon
The Gambia
Ghana
Grenada
Guinea
Guinea-Bissau
Guyana
Haiti
Jamaica
Kenya
Kiribati
Lesotho
Liberia
Madagascar
Malawi
Mali
Marshall Islands
Mauritania
Mauritius
Federated States of Micronesia
Mozambique
Namibia
Nauru
Niger
Nigeria
Niue
Palau
Papua New Guinea
Rwanda
Saint Christopher and Nevis
Saint Lucia
Saint Vincent and the Grenadines
Samoa
São Tomé and Príncipe
Senegal
Seychelles
Sierra Leone
Solomon Islands
Somalia
South Africa
Sudan
Suriname
Swaziland
Tanzania
Timor-Leste
Togo
Tonga
Trinidad and Tobago
Tuvalu
Uganda
Vanuatu
Zambia
Zimbabwe

GENERALIZED PREFERENCES

In July 1971 the Community introduced a generalized system of preferences (GSP) for tariffs in favour of developing countries, ensuring duty-free entry to the EC of all manufactured and semi-manufactured industrial products, including textiles, but subject in certain circumstances to preferential limits. Preferences, usually in the form of a tariff reduction, are also offered on some agricultural products. In 1980 the Council agreed to the extension of the scheme for a second decade (1981–90): at the same time it adopted an operational framework for industrial products, giving individual preferential limits based on the degree of competitiveness of the developing country concerned. From the end of 1990 an interim scheme was in operation, pending the introduction of a revised scheme based on the outcome of the Uruguay Round of GATT negotiations on international trade (which were finally concluded in December 1993). Since 1977 the Community has progressively liberalized GSP access for the least-developed countries by according them duty-free entry on all products and by exempting them from virtually all preferential limits. In 1992–93 the GSP was extended to Albania, the Baltic states, the CIS and Georgia; in September 1994 it was extended to South Africa.

In December 1994 the European Council adopted a revised GSP to operate during 1995–98. It provided additional trade benefits to encourage the introduction by governments of environmentally sound policies and of internationally recognized labour standards. Conversely, a country's preferential entitlement could be withdrawn, for example, if it permitted forced labour. Under the new scheme, preferential tariffs amounted to 85% of the common customs duty for very sensitive products (for example, most textiles products), and 70% or 35% for products classified as sensitive (for example, chemicals and electrical goods). The common customs duty was suspended for non-sensitive products (for example, paper, books and cosmetics). In accordance with the EU's foreign policy objective of focusing on the development of the world's poorest countries, duties were eliminated in their entirety (with the exception of arms and ammunition) for 49 least-developed countries (LDCs). Duties were also suspended for a further five Latin American countries, conditional on the implementation of campaigns against the production and trade of illegal drugs. The GSP for 1999–2001 largely extended the existing scheme unchanged. The next GSP regulation, for 2002–04 (subsequently extended until the end of 2005), was revised to expand product coverage and improve preferential margins. In May 2003 new regulations were adopted enabling certain countries to be exempted from the abolition of tariff preferences on export of their products to the EU if that sector was judged to be in crisis.

Under the GSP for 2006–08, the coverage of the general arrangement was extended to a further 300 products, mostly in the agriculture and fishery sectors, bringing the total number of products covered to some 7,200. The focus of the new regime was on developing countries most in need. Additional preferences were granted under a new GSP+ incentive scheme to particularly vulnerable countries pursuing good governance and sustainable development policies (judged by their ratification and implementation of relevant international conventions). Bolivia, Colombia, Costa Rica, Ecuador, El Salvador, Georgia, Guatemala, Honduras, Moldova, Mongolia, Nicaragua, Panama, Peru, Sri Lanka and Venezuela were declared eligible for GSP+, which took effect, exceptionally, on 1 July 2005, replacing the special arrangements to combat drugs production and trafficking in force under the previous GSP. Under the GSP for 2009–11, the GSP+ scheme was also retained, as was an initiative in support of LDCs, Everything but Arms (introduced in 2001), which granted those countries duty- and quota-free access to EU markets.

In May 2011 the Commission agreed that the existing GSP should remain in place ('roll over') until the end of 2013, in order to avoid the system lapsing and to enable applications for GSP+ to continue to be submitted, while a new, revised GSP was agreed. The objectives of the new system, which was to come into effect by January 2014, were to target fewer countries, focusing on the most needy; to strengthen GSP+ and to bolster the effectiveness of trade concessions for LDCs through the Everything but Arms scheme; and to increase the system's transparency and stability, while removing the need for its renewal every three years.

AID TO DEVELOPING AND NON-EU COUNTRIES

The main channels for EU aid to developing countries are the Cotonou Agreement and the Mediterranean Financial Protocols, but technical and financial aid and assistance for refugees, training, trade promotion and co-operation in industry, energy, science and technology are also provided to about 30 countries in Asia and Latin America. The European Commission's Humanitarian Aid Office (ECHO) was established in 1991, with a mandate to co-ordinate the provision of emergency humanitarian assistance and food aid. ECHO, which became fully operational in 1993 and is based in Brussels, finances operations conducted by non-governmental organizations and international agencies, with which it works in partnership. Relations between ECHO and its partners are governed by Framework Partnership Agreements (FPAs), which define roles and responsibilities in the implementation of humanitarian operations financed by the EU. In December 2003 ECHO signed an FPA with the International Committee of the Red Cross, the International Federation of Red Cross and Red Crescent Societies, and the national Red Cross societies of the EU member states and Norway. A new FPA with non-governmental organizations entered into force on 1 January 2004; this agreement expired on 30 December 2007, and a revised FPA came into force on 1 January 2008. ECHO's relations with UN agencies are covered by a Financial and Administrative Framework Agreement signed in April 2003. ECHO aims to meet the immediate needs of victims of natural and man-made disasters world-wide, in such areas as assisting displaced persons, health, and mine-clearing programmes. In 2010 ECHO committed funds totalling €1,115m. to humanitarian assistance.

In December 2008 the European Council and European Parliament endorsed a new €1,000m. EU Food Facility, aimed at alleviating the global crisis in food security in 2009–11, by supporting agricultural sector programmes and projects in 23 developing countries. In March 2009 the European Commission made its first EU Food Facility financing decision, adopting a €314m. package of projects.

Allocations by ECHO towards sub-Saharan Africa in 2010 included €131m. to distribute food and aid the implementation of other life-saving activities (for example, in the areas of sanitation, hygiene and shelter) in Sudan, €47m. to help refugees in the Democratic Republic of the Congo, €38m. to support vulnerable refugee populations, to combat a cholera epidemic and to aid drought in the Sahel region in Chad, and €96m. to provide support to populations affected by drought in the Horn of Africa (Djibouti, Ethiopia, Kenya, Somalia and Uganda). In January–September 2011 the EU also contributed some €160m. in emergency funding to help those affected by the continuing severe drought throughout the Horn of Africa region.

In 2010 ECHO provided €51m. in humanitarian and food aid to support populations in the Occupied Palestinian Territories; €18m. to respond to humanitarian needs in and around Iraq; €10m. to Western Sahara; €10m. to Yemen; and €7m. to aid Palestinian refugees in Lebanon.

Funds totalling €150m. were allocated by ECHO in 2010 for those displaced by conflict and the aftermath of large-scale flooding in Pakistan; €36m. for those affected by the crisis in Afghanistan; €18m. to people affected by natural disasters and crisis in Bangladesh (including the aftermath of a cyclone in 2009, a severe rodent infestation and flash floods); and €10m. to aid the return of refugees and support health care in Sri Lanka.

Finance

BUDGET

The EU budget, which funds EU policies and finances all the EU institutions, is limited by agreement of all the member states. The Commission puts forward spending proposals, which have to be approved by the European Parliament and the Council of the European Union. The Parliament signs the agreed budget into law. Revenue for the budget comes from customs duties, sugar levies, payments based on value-added tax (VAT) and contributions from the member states based on their gross national income (GNI). The Commission is accountable each year to the European Parliament for its use of EU funds. External audits are carried out by the European Court of Auditors. To combat fraud, the European Anti-Fraud Office (OLAF) was established in June 1999.

The general budget contains the expenditure of the six main EU institutions—the Commission, the Council, Parliament, the Court of Justice, the Court of Auditors, and the Economic and Social Committee and the Committee of the Regions—of which Commission expenditure (covering administrative costs and expenditure on operations) forms the largest proportion. Expenditure is divided into two categories: that necessarily resulting from the Treaties (compulsory expenditure) and other (non-compulsory) expenditure. The budgetary process is aided by the establishment of Financial Perspectives, which are spending plans covering a number of years, thus guaranteeing the security of long-term EU projects and activities. Although the Financial Perspective limits expenditure in each policy area for each of the years covered, a more detailed annual budget still has to be agreed each year. The Commission presents the preliminary draft annual budget in late April or early May of the preceding year and the adopted budget is published in February of the relevant year. If the budget has not been adopted by the beginning of the financial year, monthly expenditure may amount to one-12th of the appropriations adopted for the previous year's budget. The Commission may (even late in the year during which the budget is being executed) revise estimates of revenue and expenditure, by presenting supplementary and/or amending budgets. Expenditure under the general budget is financed by 'own resources', comprising agricultural duties (on imports of agricultural produce from non-member states), customs duties, application of VAT on goods and services, and (since 1988) a levy based on the GNI of member states. Member states are obliged to collect 'own resources' on the Community's behalf.

In January 2006 the European Commission proposed an action plan to simplify the audit system, following the Court of Auditors' failure to approve the EU's accounts for the 11th consecutive year. The Commission criticized member states, which supervise about 80% of EU spending, and suggested the harmonization of audit systems across the member states.

In May 2006 a new financial framework for the enlarged EU was formally adopted, when the European Parliament, the Council and the Commission signed an inter-institutional agreement on budgetary discipline and sound financial management, which entered into force at the beginning of January 2007. According to the framework, the EU was to focus on three main priority areas in 2007–13:

integrating the single market to achieve sustainable growth by promoting competitiveness, cohesion and the preservation and management of natural resources; promoting the concept of European citizenship by prioritizing freedom, justice and security, and ensuring access to basic public goods and services; and establishing a strong global influence for Europe through its regional responsibilities, through emphasizing sustainable development, and by contributing to security. According to the agreement, which was amended in December 2007, the average annual upper limit on payment appropriations for 2007–13 amounted to 1.03% of the GNI of the 27 member states. Meanwhile, in mid-December 2006 the Council adopted new financial regulations, which aimed to improve the management of EU expenditure; the regulations demanded the publication of a list of all those receiving EU funds. All provisions of the Financial Regulation and its Implementing Rules had entered into force by 1 May 2007.

On 1 December 2011 the European Parliament endorsed the 2012 EU budget, which provided for payment appropriations of €129,100m., (representing 0.98% of the member states' GNI) and commitment appropriations of €147,200m. (1.12% of GNI). The largest proportion of spending, 45.9%, was to be allocated towards the promotion of increased economic competitiveness and greater cohesion between the 27 member states in the pursuit of growth and employment, with the aim of reactivating economic activity and overcoming the adverse economic and financial climate.

In late June 2011 the European Commission, in the course of preparations for the 2014–20 Multi-annual Financial Framework, proposed to increase the transparency and fairness of the system for financing the EU budget by introducing a new financial transaction tax (FTT). In late September the Commission presented a directive on the proposed FTT, which would be levied on all transactions between financial institutions, provided that at least one of those institutions was located in the EU; it was proposed that the exchange of shares and bonds be taxed at a rate of 0.1%, and derivatives at a rate of 0.01%, with effect from 1 January 2014. Two-thirds of revenue from the FTT was to be directed to the EU budget, thereby reducing the GNI-based contributions of member states, while the remaining one-third would be retained by individual member states.

FUNDING PROGRAMMES

In July 2006 the Council and the European Parliament adopted five new regulations that were to constitute the legal basis for the pursuit of cohesion objectives in 2007–13. A general regulation indicated common principles and standards for the implementation of three 'structural funds' (principal instruments for financing EU-wide economic and social restructuring, addressing regional disparities and supporting regional development): the European Regional Development Fund (ERDF), the European Social Fund (ESF) and the Cohesion Fund. The regulation on the ERDF defined the scope of its interventions, among them the promotion of private and public investments assisting in the reduction of regional disparities across the EU. Funding priorities were identified as research, innovation, environmental protection and risk prevention. The regulation concerning the ESF determined that it should be implemented in accordance with European employment strategy in 2007–13, and that it should focus on increasing the flexibility of workers and enterprises, enhancing access to and participation in the labour market, reinforcing social inclusion—by such means as combating discrimination—and promoting partnership for reform in the areas of employment and inclusion. In view of its application to member states with a GNI of less than 90% of the Community average, the new regulation concerning the Cohesion Fund extended eligibility for its support to the new member states, in addition to Greece and Portugal. Spain was also to qualify for the Cohesion Fund, but on a transitional basis. A fifth regulation established a European Grouping of Territorial Co-operation, whose aim was to facilitate cross-border and transnational/inter-regional co-operation between regional and local authorities.

In 2007–13 the ERDF, the ESF and the Cohesion Fund were to contribute to three objectives: convergence (ERDF, ESF and the Cohesion Fund); regional competitiveness and employment (ERDF and ESF); and European territorial co-operation (ERDF). The convergence objective was to concern 84 regions in 17 of the 27 member states and, on a 'phasing-out' basis, a further 16 regions where per head gross domestic product was only slightly more than the threshold of 75% of the EU average. Indicative allocations for the convergence objective in 2007–13 (expressed in 2004 prices) were to total €251,100m. The regional competitiveness and employment objective was to apply to 168 regions in the 27 member states, 13 of which were so-called 'phasing-in' regions, eligible for special financial allocations. Indicative allocations for the regional competitiveness and employment objective were to total €49,100m., including €10,400m. for the phasing-in regions. A total of €7,750m. was to be made available for the European territorial co-operation objective in 2007–13.

In addition to the funds listed below, four financial instruments were created in 2007. Jasper and Jasmine were developed to provide technical assistance, Jeremie to improve access to finance for small and medium-sized businesses, and Jessica to provide support for urban development.

Cohesion Fund

The Treaty on European Union and its protocol on economic and social cohesion provided for the establishment of a Cohesion Fund, which began operating on 1 April 1993, with a mandate to subsidize projects in the fields of the environment and trans-European energy and communications networks in member states with a per-head gross national income of less than 90% of the Community average. The Fund's total budget 2007–13 was €61,590m.

European Agricultural Fund for Rural Development—EAFRD

The EAFRD was created in September 2005 and came into operation at the beginning of 2007. It replaced the Guidance Section of the European Agricultural Guidance and Guarantee Fund (which previously financed the Common Agricultural Policy–CAP) and the rural development measures previously financed under the Guarantee section. It is responsible for the single financial contribution under the CAP to rural development programmes.

European Agricultural Guarantee Fund—EAGF

The EAGF was created in September 2005 to replace the Guarantee Section of the European Agricultural Guidance and Guarantee Fund. It came into operation at the beginning of 2007 and, *inter alia*, provides direct payments to farmers under the CAP, finance for the export of agricultural products to third countries, and intervention measures to regulate agricultural markets.

European Fisheries Fund—EFF

The EFF, covering the period 2007–13, came into operation on 1 January 2007, replacing, with a simplified programming process, the former Financial Instrument for Fisheries Guidance (established in 1993). The EFF grants financial support to facilitate the implementation of the Common Fisheries Policy.

European Regional Development Fund—ERDF

Payments began in 1975. The Fund is intended to compensate for the unequal rate of development in different EU regions. It finances investment leading to the creation or maintenance of jobs, improvements in infrastructure, local development initiatives and the business activities of small and medium-sized enterprises in 'least favoured regions'.

European Social Fund—ESF

The Fund (established in 1960) provides resources with the aim of combating long-term unemployment and facilitating the integration into the labour market of young people and the socially disadvantaged. It also supports schemes to help workers to adapt to industrial changes.

European Union Solidarity Fund—EUSF

The EUSF was established in 2002 to support disaster response activities in member states.

BUDGET EXPENDITURE: COMMITMENT APPROPRIATIONS
(€ million)

	2011	2012
Sustainable growth	53,629.0	55,336.7
Preservation and growth of natural resources	55,945.9	57,034.2
Citizenship, freedom, security and justice	1,738.1	1,484.3
EU as a global player	7,242.5	6,955.1
Administration	8,171.5	8,277.7
Total	126,727.1	129,088.0

Source: Official Journal of the European Union, *Definitive Adoption of the European Union's General Budget for the Financial Year 2012*.

REVENUE
(€ million)

Source of revenue	2011	2012
Customs duties and sugar levies	16,667.0	19,294.6
VAT-based resource	14,126.0	14,498.9
GNI-based resource	87,496.5	93,718.8
Other revenue	8,437.6	1,575.7
Total	126,727.1	129,088.0

Source: Official Journal of the European Union, *Definitive Adoption of the European Union's General Budget for the Financial Year 2012*.

NATIONAL CONTRIBUTION TO THE EU BUDGET

Country	Contribution for 2011 (€ million)	% of total
Austria	2,505.3	2.3
Belgium	3,342.9	3.1
Bulgaria	328.7	0.3
Cyprus	165.3	0.2
Czech Republic	1,318.1	1.2
Denmark	2,247.6	2.1
Estonia	130.4	0.1
Finland	1,707.2	1.6
France	19,075.6	17.6
Germany	21,189.9	19.6
Greece	2,183.1	2.0
Hungary	922.9	0.9
Ireland	1,264.0	1.2
Italy	14,517.6	13.4
Latvia	157.2	0.1
Lithuania	259.0	0.2
Luxembourg	277.6	0.3
Malta	54.9	0.1
Netherlands	4,263.7	3.9
Poland	3,501.5	3.2
Portugal	1,552.8	1.4
Romania	1,170.3	1.1
Slovakia	630.7	0.6
Slovenia	338.5	0.3
Spain	9,625.7	8.9
Sweden	2,679.8	2.5
United Kingdom	12,918.3	11.9
Total	108,328.7	100.0

Source: European Commission.

Publications*

The Courier ACP-EU (every 2 months, in English, French, Portuguese and Spanish on ACP-EU affairs).

EUR-Lex (treaties, legislation and judgments; internet europa.eu .int/eur-lex/lex).

European Economy Research Letter (3 a year).

General Report on the Activities of the European Union (annually; internet europa.eu/generalreport/en/welcome.htm).

Official Journal of the European Union (website on which all contracts from the public sector that are valued above a certain threshold must be published; internet www.ojec.com).

Publications of the European Communities (quarterly).

Information sheets, background reports and statistical documents.

* Most publications are available in all of the official languages of the Union and are available free of charge online. They can be obtained from the Office for Official Publications of the European Communities (Publications Office), 2 rue Mercier, 2985 Luxembourg; tel. 29291; fax 495719; e-mail info@publications.europa.eu; internet publications.europa.eu/index_en.htm.

THE FRANC ZONE

Address: c/o Direction de la Communication (Service de Presse), Banque de France, 48 rue Croix-des-Petits-Champs, 75049, Paris Cedex 01, France.

Telephone: 1-42-92-39-08; **fax:** 1-42-92-39-40; **e-mail:** infos@banque-france.fr; **internet:** www.banque-france.fr/en/eurosystem-international/franc-zone-and-development-financing .html.

MEMBERS*

Benin
Burkina Faso
Cameroon
Central African Republic
Chad
Comoros
Republic of the Congo
Côte d'Ivoire
Equatorial Guinea
French Overseas Territories
Gabon
Guinea-Bissau
Mali
Niger
Senegal
Togo

* Prior to 1 January 2002, when the transition to a single European currency (euro) was finalized (see below), the Franc Zone also included Metropolitan France, the French Overseas Departments (French Guiana, Guadeloupe, Martinique and Réunion), the French Overseas Collectivité Départementale (Mayotte) and the French Overseas Collectivité Territoriale (St Pierre and Miquelon). The French Overseas Territory (French Polynesia) and the French Overseas Countries (New Caledonia and the Wallis and Futuna Islands) have continued to use the franc CFP (franc des Comptoirs français du Pacifique, 'French Pacific franc').

Apart from Guinea and Mauritania (see below), all of the countries that formerly comprised French West and Equatorial Africa are members of the Franc Zone. The former West and Equatorial African territories are still grouped within the two currency areas that existed before independence, each group having its own variant on the CFA, issued by a central bank: the franc de la Communauté Financière d'Afrique ('franc CFA de l'Ouest'), issued by the Banque centrale des états de l'Afrique de l'ouest—BCEAO, and the franc Coopération financière en Afrique centrale ('franc CFA central'), issued by the Banque des états de l'Afrique centrale—BEAC.

The following states withdrew from the Franc Zone during the period 1958–73: Guinea, Tunisia, Morocco, Algeria, Mauritania and Madagascar. Equatorial Guinea, formerly a Spanish territory, joined the Franc Zone in January 1985, and Guinea-Bissau, a former Portuguese territory, joined in May 1997.

The Comoros, formerly a French Overseas Territory, did not join the Franc Zone following its unilateral declaration of independence in 1975. However, the franc CFA was used as the currency of the new state and the Institut d'émission des Comores continued to function as a Franc Zone organization. In 1976 the Comoros formally assumed membership. In July 1981 the Banque centrale des Comores replaced the Institut d'émission des Comores, establishing its own currency, the Comoros franc.

The Franc Zone operates on the basis of agreements concluded between France and each group of member countries, and the Comoros. The currencies in the Franc Zone were formerly linked with the French franc at a fixed rate of exchange. However, following the introduction of the euro (European single currency) in January 1999, within the framework of European economic and monetary union, in which France was a participant, the Franc Zone currencies were effectively linked at fixed parity to the euro (i.e. parity was based on the fixed conversion rate for the French franc and the euro). From 1 January 2002, when European economic and monetary union was finalized and the French franc withdrawn from circulation, the franc CFA, Comoros franc and franc CFP became officially pegged to the euro, at a fixed rate of exchange. (In accordance with Protocol 13 on France, appended to the 1993 Maastricht Treaty on European Union, France was permitted to continue issuing currencies in its Overseas Territories—i.e. the franc CFP—following the completion of European economic and monetary union.) All the convertability arrangements previously concluded between France and the Franc Zone remained in force. Therefore, Franc Zone currencies are freely convertible into euros, at the fixed exchange rate, guaranteed by the

French Treasury. Each group of member countries, and the Comoros, has its own central issuing bank, with overdraft facilities provided by the French Treasury. (The issuing authority for the French Overseas Territories is the Institut d'émission d'outre-mer, based in Paris, France.) Monetary reserves are held mainly in the form of euros. The BCEAO and the BEAC are authorized to hold up to 35% of their foreign exchange holdings in currencies other than the euro. Franc Zone ministers of finance normally meet twice a year to review economic and monetary co-operation. The meeting is normally attended by the French Minister of Co-operation and Francophony.

In August 1993, in view of financial turmoil related to the continuing weakness of the French franc and the abandonment of the European exchange rate mechanism, the BCEAO and the BEAC determined to suspend repurchasing of francs CFA outside the Franc Zone. Effectively this signified the temporary withdrawal of guaranteed convertibility of the franc CFA with the French franc. Devaluations of the franc CFA and the Comoros franc (by 50% and 33.3%, respectively) were implemented in January 1994. Following the devaluation the CFA countries embarked on programmes of economic adjustment, including restrictive fiscal and wage policies and other monetary, structural and social measures, designed to stimulate growth and to ensure eligibility for development assistance from international financial institutions. France established a special development fund of FFr 300m. to alleviate the immediate social consequences of the devaluation, and announced substantial debt cancellations. The IMF, which had strongly advocated a devaluation of the franc CFA, and the World Bank approved immediate soft-credit loans, technical assistance and cancellations or rescheduling of debts. In June 1994 heads of state (or representatives) of African Franc Zone countries convened in Libreville, Gabon, to review the effects of the currency realignment. The final communiqué of the meeting urged further international support for the countries' economic development efforts. In April 1995 Franc Zone ministers of finance, meeting in Paris, recognized the positive impact of the devaluation on agricultural export sectors, in particular in West African countries. In January 1996 Afristat, a research and training institution based in Bamako, Mali, commenced activities to support national statistical organizations in participating states in order to strengthen their economic management capabilities. The IMF and the World Bank have continued to support economic development efforts in the Franc Zone. France provides debt relief to Franc Zone member states eligible under the World Bank's initiative for heavily indebted poor countries (HIPCs). In April 2001 the African Franc Zone member states determined jointly to develop anti-money-laundering legislation.

In February 2000 the Union économique et monétaire ouest-africaine (UEMOA) and the Economic Community of West African States (ECOWAS) adopted an action plan for the creation of a single West African Monetary Zone and consequent replacement of the franc Communauté financière africaine by a single West African currency (see below).

CURRENCIES OF THE FRANC ZONE

1 franc CFA = €0.00152. CFA stands for Communauté financière africaine in the West African area and for Coopération financière en Afrique centrale in the Central African area. Used in the monetary areas of West and Central Africa, respectively.

1 Comoros franc = €0.00201. Used in the Comoros, where it replaced the franc CFA in 1981.

1 franc CFP = €0.00839. CFP stands for Comptoirs français du Pacifique. Used in New Caledonia, French Polynesia and the Wallis and Futuna Islands.

WEST AFRICA

Union économique et monétaire ouest-africaine (UEMOA): BP 543, Ouagadougou 01, Burkina Faso; tel. 31-88-73; fax 31-88-72; e-mail commission@uemoa.int; internet www.uemoa.int; f. 1994; promotes regional monetary and economic convergence, and envisages the eventual creation of a sub-regional common market. A preferential tariff scheme, eliminating duties on most local products and reducing by 30% import duties on many Union-produced industrial goods, became operational on 1 July 1996; in addition, from 1 July, a community solidarity tax of 0.5% was imposed on all goods from third countries sold within the Union, in order to strengthen UEMOA's capacity to promote economic integration. (This was increased to 1% in December 1999.) In June 1997 UEMOA heads of state and government agreed to reduce import duties on industrial products originating in the Union by a further 30%. An inter-parliamentary committee, recognized as the predecessor of a UEMOA legislature, was inaugurated in Mali in March 1998. In September Côte d'Ivoire's stock exchange was transformed into the Bourse regionale des valeurs mobilières, a regional stock exchange serving the Union, in order to further economic integration. On 1 January 2000 internal tariffs were eliminated on all local products (including industrial goods) and a joint external tariff system, in five bands of between 0% and 20%, was imposed on goods deriving from outside the new customs union. Guinea-Bissau was excluded from the arrangement owing to its unstable political situation. The UEMOA member countries also belong to ECOWAS and, in accordance with a decision taken in April 2000, aim to harmonize UEMOA's economic programme with that of a planned second West African monetary union (the West African Monetary Zone—WAMZ), to be established by the remaining—mainly anglophone—ECOWAS member states by January 2015 (as currently scheduled). A merger of the two complementary monetary unions, and the replacement of the franc Communauté financière africaine by a new single West African currency (the 'eco', initially to to be adopted by the WAMZ), is eventually envisaged. In January 2003 member states adopted a treaty on the establishment of a UEMOA parliament. During 2006–10 UEMOA implemented a regional economic programme aimed at developing regional infrastructures. Mems: Benin, Burkina Faso, Côte d'Ivoire, Guinea-Bissau, Mali, Niger, Senegal and Togo; Pres. CHEIKH HADJIBOU SOUMARÉ (Senegal).

Banque centrale des états de l'Afrique de l'ouest (BCEAO): ave Abdoulaye Fadiga, BP 3108, Dakar, Senegal; tel. 839-05-00; fax 823-93-35; e-mail webmaster@bceao.int; internet www.bceao.int; f. 1962; central bank of issue for the mems of UEMOA; total assets 8,370.1m. francs CFA (31 Dec. 2009); mems: Benin, Burkina Faso, Côte d'Ivoire, Guinea-Bissau, Mali, Niger, Senegal and Togo; Gov. TIEMOKO MEYLIET KONE (Côte d'Ivoire); publs *Annual Report, Notes d'Information et Statistiques* (monthly), *Annuaire des banques, Bilan des banques et établissements financiers* (annually).

Banque ouest-africaine de développement (BOAD): 68 ave de la Libération, BP 1172, Lomé, Togo; tel. 221-42-44; fax 221-52-67; e-mail boadsiege@boad.org; internet www.boad.org; f. 1973 to promote the balanced development of mem. states and the economic integration of West Africa; a Guarantee Fund for Private Investment in West Africa, established jtly by BOAD and the European Investment Bank in Dec. 1994, aims to guarantee medium- and long-term credits to private sector businesses in the region; auth. cap. 1,050,000m. francs CFA (30 June 2010); mems: Benin, Burkina Faso, Côte d'Ivoire, Guinea-Bissau, Mali, Niger, Senegal, Togo; Pres. CHRISTIAN ADOVELANDE (Benin); publs *Rapport Annuel*, *BOAD en Bref* (quarterly).

Bourse Régionale des Valeurs Mobilières (BRVM): 18 rue Joseph Anoma, BP 3802, Abidjan 01, Côte d'Ivoire; tel. 20-32-66-85; fax 20-32-66-84; e-mail brvm@brvm.org; internet www.brvm.org; f. 1998; regional electronic stock exchange; Dir-Gen. JEAN-PAUL GILLET.

CENTRAL AFRICA

Communauté économique et monétaire de l'Afrique centrale (CEMAC): BP 969, Bangui, Central African Republic; tel. and fax 21-61-47-81; fax 70-14-15-66; e-mail secemac@cemac.int; internet www.cemac.int; f. 1998; formally inaugurated as the successor to the Union douanière et économique de l'Afrique centrale (UDEAC, f. 1966) at a meeting of heads of state held in Malabo, Equatorial Guinea, in June 1999; aims to promote the process of sub-regional integration within the framework of an economic union and a monetary union; CEMAC was also to comprise a parliament and sub-regional tribunal; UDEAC established a common external tariff for imports from other countries and administered a common code for investment policy and a Solidarity Fund to counteract regional disparities of wealth and economic development; mems: Cameroon, Central African Republic, Chad, Republic of the Congo, Equatorial Guinea, Gabon; Pres. ANTOINE NTSIMI (Cameroon).

At a summit meeting in December 1981, UDEAC leaders agreed in principle to form an economic community of Central African states (Communauté économique des états de l'Afrique centrale—CEEAC), to include UDEAC members and Burundi, Rwanda, São Tomé and Príncipe and Zaire (now Democratic Republic of the Congo). CEEAC began operations in 1985.

Banque de développement des états de l'Afrique centrale (BDEAC): place du Gouvernement, BP 1177, Brazzaville, Republic of the Congo; tel. 281-18-85; fax 281-18-80; e-mail bdeac@bdeac.org; internet www.bdeac.org; f. 1975; total assets 31,620m. francs CFA (31 Dec. 2008); shareholders: Cameroon, Central African Republic, Chad, Republic of the Congo, Gabon, Equatorial Guinea, AfDB, BEAC, France, Germany and Kuwait; Pres. MICHAËL ADANDÉ.

Banque des états de l'Afrique centrale (BEAC): 736 ave Mgr François Xavier Vogt, BP 1917, Yaoundé, Cameroon; tel. 223-40-30; fax 223-33-29; e-mail beac@beac.int; internet www.beac.int; f. 1973 as the central bank of issue of Cameroon, the Central African Republic, Chad, Republic of the Congo, Equatorial Guinea and Gabon; a monetary market, incorporating all national financial institutions of the BEAC countries, came into effect on 1 July 1994; Gov. LUCAS ABAGA NCHAMA (Equatorial Guinea); publs *Rapport annuel*, *Etudes et statistiques* (monthly).

CENTRAL ISSUING BANKS

Banque centrale des Comores: place de France, BP 405, Moroni, Comoros; tel. (773) 1814; fax (773) 0349; e-mail bancecom@snpt.km; internet www.bancecom.com; f. 1981; Gov. ABOUDOU MOHAMED CHAFIOUN.

Banque centrale des états de l'Afrique de l'ouest: see above.

Banque des états de l'Afrique centrale: see above.

Institut d'émission d'outre-mer (IEOM): 5 rue Roland Barthes, 75012 Paris Cedex 12, France; tel. 1-53-44-41-41; fax 1-43-47-51-34; e-mail direction@iedom-ieom.fr; internet www.ieom.fr; f. 1966; issuing authority for the French Overseas Territories; Dir-Gen. NICOLAS DE SEZE.

FRENCH ECONOMIC AID

France's connection with the African Franc Zone countries involves not only monetary arrangements, but also includes comprehensive French assistance in the forms of budget support, foreign aid, technical assistance and subsidies on commodity exports.

Official French financial aid and technical assistance to developing countries is administered by the following agencies:

Agence française de développement (AFD): 5 rue Roland Barthes, 75598 Paris Cedex 12, France; tel. 1-53-44-31-31; fax 1-44-87-99-39; e-mail com@afd.fr; internet www.afd.fr; f. 1941; fmrly the Caisse française de développement—CFD; French development bank that lends money to member states and former member states of the Franc Zone and several other states, and executes the financial operations of the FSP (see below). Following the devaluation of the franc CFA in January 1994, the French Government cancelled some FFr 25,000m. in debt arrears owed by member states to the CFD. The CFD established a Special Fund for Development and the Exceptional Facility for Short-term Financing to help to alleviate the immediate difficulties resulting from the devaluation. Serves as the secretariat for the Fonds français pour l'environnement mondial (f. 1994). Since 2000 the AFD has been implementing France's support of the World Bank's HIPC initiative; Pres. PIERRE-ANDRÉ PERISSOL; CEO DOV ZERAH.

Fonds de Solidarité Prioritaire (FSP): c/o Ministry of Foreign and European Affairs, 37 quai d'Orsay, 75351 Paris, France; tel. 1-43-17-53-53; fax 1-43-17-52-03; internet www.diplomatie.gouv.fr; f. 2000, taking over from the Fonds d'aide et de coopération (f. 1959) the administration of subsidies from the French Government to 54 countries of the Zone de solidarité prioritaire; FSP is administered by the French Ministry of Foreign and European Affairs, which allocates budgetary funds to it.

INTER-AMERICAN DEVELOPMENT BANK—IDB

Address: 1300 New York Ave, NW, Washington, DC 20577, USA.

Telephone: (202) 623-1000; **fax:** (202) 623-3096; **e-mail:** pic@iadb.org; **internet:** www.iadb.org.

The Bank was founded in 1959 to promote the individual and collective development of Latin American and Caribbean countries through the financing of economic and social development projects and the provision of technical assistance. From 1976 membership was extended to include countries outside the region.

MEMBERS

Argentina	Ecuador	Nicaragua
Austria	El Salvador	Norway
Bahamas	Finland	Panama
Barbados	France	Paraguay
Belgium	Germany	Peru
Belize	Guatemala	Portugal
Bolivia	Guyana	Slovenia
Brazil	Haiti	Spain
Canada	Honduras	Suriname
Chile	Israel	Sweden
China, People's Rep.	Italy	Switzerland
Colombia	Jamaica	Trinidad and Tobago
Costa Rica	Japan	United Kingdom
Croatia	Republic of Korea	USA
Denmark	Mexico	Uruguay
Dominican Republic	Netherlands	Venezuela

Organization

(April 2012)

BOARD OF GOVERNORS

All the powers of the Bank are vested in a Board of Governors, consisting of one Governor and one alternate appointed by each member country (usually ministers of finance or presidents of central banks). The Board meets annually, with special meetings when necessary. The 53nd annual meeting was held in Montevideo, Uruguay, in March 2012.

BOARD OF EXECUTIVE DIRECTORS

The Board of Executive Directors is responsible for the operations of the Bank. It establishes the Bank's policies, approves loan and technical co-operation proposals that are submitted by the President of the Bank, and authorizes the Bank's borrowings on capital markets.

There are 14 executive directors and 14 alternates. Each Director is elected by a group of two or more countries, except the Directors representing Canada and the USA. The USA holds 30% of votes on the Board, in respect of its contribution to the Bank's capital. The Board has five permanent committees, relating to: Policy and evaluation; Organization, human resources and board matters; Budget, financial policies and audit; Programming; and a Steering Committee.

ADMINISTRATION

In December 2006 the Board of Executive Directors approved a new structure which aimed to strengthen the Bank's country focus and improve its operational efficiency. Three new positions of Vice-Presidents were created. Accordingly the executive structure comprised the President, Executive Vice-President and Vice-Presidents for Countries (with responsibility for four regional departments); Sectors and Knowledge; Private Sector and Non-sovereign Guaranteed Operations; and Finance and Administration. The principal Offices were of the Auditor-General, Outreach and Partnerships, External Relations, Risk Management, and Strategic Planning and Development Effectiveness. An Independent Consultation and Investigation Mechanism to monitor compliance with the Bank's environmental and social policies, was established in February 2010. The Bank has country offices in each of its borrowing member states, and special offices in Paris, France and in Tokyo, Japan. There are some 1,800 Bank staff (excluding the Board of Executive Directors and the Evaluation Office), of whom almost 30% are based in country offices. The total Bank group administrative expenses for 2011 amounted to US $618m.

President: LUIS ALBERTO MORENO (Colombia).

Executive Vice-President: JULIE T. KATZMAN (USA).

Activities

Loans are made to governments and to public and private entities for specific economic and social development projects and for sectoral reforms. These loans are repayable in the currencies lent and their terms range from 12 to 40 years. Total lending authorized by the Bank amounted to US $207,122m. by the end of 2011. During 2011 the Bank approved loans and guarantees amounting to $10,671m., of which Ordinary Capital loans totalled $10,400m. (compared with a total of $12,136m. in 2010). Disbursements on Ordinary Capital loans amounted to $7,902m. in 2011, compared with $10,341m. in the previous year. Some 167 projects were approved in 2011, of which 142 were investment projects. In October 2008 the Bank announced measures to help to counter the effects on the region of the downturn in the world's major economies and the restrictions on the availability of credit. It resolved to accelerate lending and establish an emergency liquidity facility, with funds of up to $6,000m., in order to sustain regional economic growth and to support social welfare programmes.

In March 2009 the Board of Governors agreed to initiate a capital review, in recognition of unprecedented demand for Bank resources owing to the sharp contraction of international capital markets. An agreement to increase the Bank's authorized capital by US $70,000m. was concluded in March 2010 and endorsed, as the Ninth General Capital Increase (IDB-9), by the Board of Governors in July. Of the total increase, $1,700m. was expected to be paid in by member countries over a five-year period. At the end of 2011 the subscribed Ordinary Capital stock, including inter-regional capital, which was merged into it in 1987, totalled $104,980m., of which $4,339m. was paid-in and $100,641m. was callable. The callable capital constitutes, in effect, a guarantee of the securities that the Bank issues in the capital markets in order to increase its resources available for lending.

In 2011 operating income amounted to US $836m. At the end of 2011 total borrowings outstanding amounted to $58,015m., compared with $57,874m. at the end of the previous year.

The Fund for Special Operations (FSO) enables the Bank to make concessional loans for economic and social projects where circumstances call for special treatment, such as lower interest rates and longer repayment terms than those applied to loans from the ordinary resources. Assistance may be provided to countries adversely affected by economic crises or natural disasters through an Emergency Lending Program. In March 2007 the Board of Governors approved a reform of the Bank's concessional lending (at the same time as endorsing arrangements for participation in the Multilateral Debt Relief Initiative, see below), and resolved that FSO lending may be 'blended' with Ordinary Capital loans by means of a parallel lending mechanism. At 31 December 2011 cumulative FSO lending amounted to $19,204m., and in 2011 FSO lending totalled $181m. The terms and conditions of IDB-9, approved by the Board of Governors in July 2010, incorporated a commitment to replenish FSO resources by $479m.

On 1 January 2012 a new Flexible Financing Facility (FFF) entered into effect, which was, thereafter, to be the only financial product platform for approval of all new Ordinary Capital sovereign guaranteed loans.

In June 2007 a new IDB Grant Facility (GRF) was established, funded by transfers from the FSO, to make available resources for specific projects or countries in specific circumstances. By the end of 2011 resources had only been granted to support reconstruction and development in Haiti. In accordance with IDB-9 the Board of Governors may approve transfers of Ordinary Capital to the GRF. Accordingly, in March 2011 the Board approved the transfer of US $200m. from Ordinary Capital. During 2011 the Bank approved grants to Haiti from the GRF totalling $241m. In May 2011 the Board of Governors approved a new Small and Medium-sized Enterprises (SME) Financing Facility, with funds of up to $100m. in order to improve access to finance for SMEs, to promote job creation and stimulate economic growth.

In 1998 the Bank agreed to participate in an initiative of the IMF and the World Bank to assist heavily indebted poor countries (HIPCs) to maintain a sustainable level of debt. Also in 1998, following projections of reduced resources for the FSO, borrowing member countries agreed to convert about US $2,400m. in local currencies held by the Bank, in order to maintain a convertible concessional Fund for poorer countries, and to help to reduce the debt-servicing payments under the HIPC initiative. In mid-2000 a committee of the Board of Governors endorsed a financial framework for the Bank's participation in an enhanced HIPC initiative, which aimed to broaden the eligibility criteria and accelerate the process of debt reduction. The Bank was to provide $896m. (in net present value), in addition to $204m. committed under the original scheme, of which $307m. was for Bolivia, $65m. for Guyana, $391m. for Nicaragua and $133m. for Honduras. The Bank assisted the preparation of national Poverty Reduction Strategy Papers, a condition of reaching the 'completion point' of the process. In January 2007 the Bank concluded an agreement to participate in the Multilateral Debt Relief Initiative (MDRI), which had been approved by the World Bank and IMF in 2005 as a means of achieving 100% cancellation of debts for eligible HIPCs. The agreement to support the MDRI was endorsed by the Bank's Board of Governors in March 2007. Under the initiative the eligible completion point countries, along with Haiti (which had reached 'decision point' in November 2006), were to receive additional debt relief amounting to some $3,370m. in principal payments and $1,000m. in future interest payments, cancelling loan balances with the FSO (outstanding as of 31 December 2004). Haiti reached 'completion point' under the HIPC initiative in June 2009. Accordingly, FSO delivered debt relief under the enhanced HIPC initiative and the MDRI amounting to some $419m. The general capital increase, approved in 2010, intended to provide for cancellation of all Haiti's outstanding debts to the Bank. In September 2010 the US Government made available an advance contribution of $204m. to the FSO, enabling the Bank to announce the cancellation of Haiti's outstanding debts, amounting to $484m.

In June 2006 the Bank inaugurated a new initiative, Opportunities for the Majority, to improve conditions for low-income communities throughout the region. Under the scheme the Bank was to support the development of partnerships between communities, private sector bodies and non-governmental organizations to generate employment, deliver services and integrate poorer members of society into the productive economy. During 2011 a total of 11 projects were approved under the initiative with a value of US $48.4m. By the end of that year the initiative was supporting 32 projects in low-income communities in the region, with a total commitment of $190.2m.

In March 2007 the Bank's Board of Governors endorsed the Sustainable Energy and Climate Change Initiative (SECCI), which aimed to expand the development and use of biofuels and other sources of renewable energy, to enhance energy efficiency and to facilitate adaptation to climate change. A Bank fund, with an initial US $20m. in resources, was established to finance feasibility studies and technical co-operation projects. In November 2009 the Bank signed a memorandum of understanding with the Asian Development Bank to support projects and programmes that promote sustainable, low-carbon transport in both regions. In accordance with the priorities of the lending agreement approved along with IDB-9 in July 2010, support for climate change adaptation initiatives and other projects concerned with renewable energy and environmental sustainability was expected to reach 25% of total lending by the end of 2015.

The Bank supports a range of consultative groups in order to strengthen donor co-operation with countries in the Latin America and Caribbean region, in particular to co-ordinate emergency relief and reconstruction following a natural disaster or to support peace efforts within a country. In November 2001 the Bank hosted the first meeting of a Network for the Prevention and Mitigation of Natural Disasters in Latin America and the Caribbean, which was part of a regional policy dialogue, sponsored by the Bank to promote broad debate on strategic issues. In April 2006 the Bank established the Disaster Prevention Fund, financed through Ordinary Capital funds, to help countries to improve their disaster preparedness and reduce their vulnerability to natural hazards. A separate Multi-donor Disaster Prevention Trust Fund was established at the end of 2006 to finance technical assistance and investment in preparedness projects.

In July 2004 the Bank co-hosted an international donor conference, together with the World Bank, the EU and the UN, to consider the immediate and medium-term needs for Haiti following a period of political unrest. Some US $1,080m. was pledged at the conference, of which the Bank's contribution was $260m. In April 2009 international donors, meeting under the Bank's auspices, pledged further contributions of $324m. to Haiti's economic and social development. In January 2010 the Bank determined to redirect undisbursed funds of up to $90m. to finance priority emergency assistance and reconstruction efforts in Haiti following a devastating earthquake. In March the Board of Governors agreed to cancel Haiti's outstanding debt and to convert undisbursed loans in order to provide grant assistance amounting to $2,000m. over the coming 10 years. In mid-March the Bank organized a conference of representatives of the private sector in Haiti, in preparation for the International Donors' Conference, which was then held at the end of that month in New York, USA. The Bank also supported the Haitian Government in preparing, jointly with the UN, World Bank and European Commission, a Preliminary Damage and Needs Assessment report for presentation at the Conference. During 2011 the Bank committed some $241m. in grants to Haiti, in particular to fund the provision of basic services, education reform, and to support small farmers; of this, some $175m. was disbursed.

An increasing number of donor countries have placed funds under the Bank's administration for assistance to Latin America, outside the framework of the Ordinary Resources and the Bank's Special Operations. These include the Social Progress Trust Fund (set up by the USA in 1961); the Venezuelan Trust Fund (set up in 1975); the Japan Special Fund (1988); and other funds administered on behalf of Austria, Belgium, Canada, Chile, Denmark, Finland, France, Israel, Italy, Japan, the Netherlands, Norway, Portugal, Spain, Sweden, Switzerland, the United Kingdom and the EU. A Program for the Development of Technical Co-operation was established in 1991, which is financed by European countries and the EU. During 2011 co-financing by bilateral and multilateral sources amounted to some US $2,010.48m.

The Bank provides technical co-operation to help member countries to identify and prepare new projects, to improve loan execution, to strengthen the institutional capacity of public and private agencies, to address extreme conditions of poverty and to promote small- and micro-enterprise development. The Bank has established a special co-operation programme to facilitate the transfer of experience and technology among regional programmes. Technical co-operation operations are mainly financed by income from the FSO and donor trust funds. The Bank supports the efforts of the countries of the region to achieve economic integration and has provided extensive technical support for the formulation of integration strategies in the Andean, Central American and Southern Cone regions. In June 2010 the Bank agreed to collaborate with the Spanish Government, the Bill and Melinda Gates Foundation and the Carlos Slim Health Institute in administering a new 'Salud Mesoamérica 2015' initiative, which aimed to support efforts to achieve the millennium development health objectives in the region over a five-year period. The Bank is a member of the technical co-ordinating committee of the Integration of Regional Infrastructure in South America initiative, which aimed to promote multinational development projects, capacity building and integration in that region. In September 2006 the Bank established a new fund to support the preparation of infrastructure projects, InfraFund, with an initial US $20m. in resources. In 2005 the Bank inaugurated a Trade Finance Facilitation Program (TFFP) to support economic growth in the region by expanding the financing available for international trade activities. The programme was given permanent status in November 2006. In May 2008 the Bank launched a training initiative within the framework of the TFFP. In January 2009 the Bank determined to expand the TFFP to include loans, as well as guarantees, and to increase the programme limit from $400m. to $1,000m. By April 2012 there were 77 issuing banks from 20 Latin American and Caribbean countries participating in the programme, and 248 confirming banks from 52 countries world-wide. In September 2009 the Bank supported the establishment, jointly with the MIF, IIC, Andean Development Corporation, the US private investment corporation and a Swiss investment management company, of a Microenterprise Growth Facility (MIGROF), which aimed to provide up to $250m. to microfinance institutions in Latin America and the Caribbean.

AFFILIATES

Inter-American Investment Corporation (IIC): 1350 New York Ave, NW, Washington, DC 20577, USA; tel. (202) 623-3900; fax (202) 623-2360; e-mail iicmail@iadb.org; internet www.iic.int; f. 1986 as a legally autonomous affiliate of the Inter-American Development Bank, to promote the economic development of the region; commenced operations in 1989; initial capital stock was US $200m., of which 55% was contributed by developing member nations, 25.3% by the USA, and the remainder by non-regional members; in 2001 the Board of Governors of the Bank agreed to increase the IIC's capital to $500m; places emphasis on investment in small and medium-sized enterprises without access to other suitable sources of equity or long-term loans; developed FINPYME as an online service to support SMEs and to improve their access to potential sources of financing; in 2011 the IIC approved 71 operations with commitments amounting to $465m., with an additional $463m. mobilized from other sources; mems: 44 countries as shareholders; Gen. Man. JACQUES ROGOZINSKI; publ. *Annual Report* (in English, French, Portuguese and Spanish).

Multilateral Investment Fund (MIF) (Fondo Multilateral de Inversiones (FOMIN): 1300 New York Ave, NW, Washington, DC 20577, USA; tel. (202) 942-8211; fax (202) 942-8100; e-mail mifcontact@iadb.org; internet www.iadb.org/mif; f. 1993 as an autonomous fund administered by the Bank, to promote private sector development in the region; the 21 Bank members who signed the initial draft agreement in 1992 to establish the Fund pledged to contribute US $1,200m.; the Fund's activities are undertaken through three separate facilities concerned with technical co-operation, human resources development and small enterprise development; in 2000 a specialist working group, established to consider MIF operations, recommended that it target its resources on the following core areas of activity: small business development; market functioning; and financial and capital markets; the Bank's Social Entrepreneurship Program makes available credit to individuals or groups without access to commercial or development loans; some $10m. is awarded under the programme to fund projects in 26 countries; a Microenterprise Forum, 'Foromic', is held annually (Oct. 2012: Barbados); in April 2005 38 donor countries agreed to establish MIF II, and replenish the Fund's resources with commitments totalling $502m.; MIF II came into effect in March 2007; in mid-2010 MIF supported the establishment of an Emergency Liquidity Program for Haiti; during 2011 MIF approved $108m. to finance 74 operations; Gen. Man. NANCY LEE; publ. *MicAméricas*.

INSTITUTIONS

Instituto para la Integración de América Latina y el Caribe (INTAL) (Institute for the Integration of Latin America and the Caribbean): Esmeralda 130, 17°, 1035 Buenos Aires, Argentina; tel. (11) 4320-1850; fax (11) 4320-1865; e-mail intal@iadb.org; internet www.iadb.org/intal; f. 1965 under the auspices of the Inter-American Development Bank; undertakes research on all aspects of regional integration and co-operation and issues related to international trade, hemispheric integration and relations with other regions and countries of the world; activities come under four main headings: regional and national technical co-operation projects on integration; policy fora; integration fora; and journals and information; hosts the secretariat of the Integration of Regional Infrastructure in South America (IIRSA) initiative; maintains an extensive Documentation Center and various statistical databases; Dir RICARDO CARCIOFI; publs *Integración y Comercio/Integration and Trade* (2 a year), *INTAL Monthly Newsletter, Informe Andino/Andean Report, CARICOM Report, Informe Centroamericano/Central American Report, Informe Mercosur/Mercosur Report* (2 a year).

Inter-American Institute for Social Development (INDES): 1350 New York Ave, NW, Washington, DC 20057, USA; fax (202) 623-2008; e-mail indes@iadb.org; internet indes.iadb.org; commenced operations in 1995; aims to support the training of senior officials from public sector institutions and organizations involved with social policies and social services; organizes specialized sub-regional courses and seminars and national training programmes; produces teaching materials and also serves as a forum for the exchange of ideas on social reform.

Publications

Annual Report (in English, French, Portuguese and Spanish).

Development in the Americas (series).

Development Effectiveness Overview (annually).

IDB Edu (quarterly).

Puentes (periodic civil society newsletter).

Revelation of Expectations in Latin America (periodic analysis of market expectations of inflation and growth).

Brochure series, occasional papers, working papers, reports.

Statistics

DISTRIBUTION OF OPERATIONS BY SECTOR, 2011*

Sector	Amount (US $ million)	% of total	Number of projects
Infrastructure and Environment	6,711	62	71
Agriculture and rural development	565	5	11
Energy	1,585	15	22
Environmental protection and natural disasters	410	4	8
Tourism	115	1	3
Transportation	2,249	21	11
Water and sanitation	1,788	16	16
Institutional capacity and finance	3,3163	29	62
Capital markets	707	6	22
Industry	252	2	2
Microenterprises	52	0	2
Multisector credit and preinvestment	55	1	2
Private sector development	31	0	2
Reform/modernization of the state	1,226	11	24
Urban development and housing	841	8	8
Integration and trade	94	1	13
Social sector	943	21	9
Education	465	7	12
Health	128	2	5
Science and technology	—	—	—
Social investment	350	3	11
Total	10,911	100.0	167

* Includes loans, guarantees, and operations financed by the IDB Grant Facility.

YEARLY AND CUMULATIVE LOANS AND GUARANTEES, 1961–2011
(US $ million; after cancellations and exchange adjustments)

Country	Total Amount* 2011	Total Amount* 1961–2011	Ordinary Capital 1961–2011	Fund for Special Operations 1961–2011	Funds in Administration 1961–2011
Argentina	1,312.7	31,434.1	30,740.0	644.9	49.2
Bahamas	131.0	633.4	620.4	—	2.0
Barbados	70.0	696.4	635.4	41.7	19.0
Belize	10.0	183.7	183.7	—	—
Bolivia	259.1	4,646.1	1,961.9	2,612.0	72.2
Brazil	2,188.0	42,004.6	40,314.4	1,555.9	134.3
Chile	91.8	6,472.2	6,221.1	206.3	44.8
Colombia	785.2	18,184.7	17,330.6	767.6	86.5
Costa Rica	132.4	3,642.1	3,133.7	371.1	137.2
Dominican Republic	464.8	4,668.9	3,826.5	753.4	89.0
Ecuador	568.8	6,837.3	5,744.5	998.1	97.7
El Salvador	263.1	4,562.9	3,609.9	806.2	146.8
Guatemala	50.3	4,450.5	3,651.3	729.5	69.7
Guyana	17.0	1,232.9	209.2	1,016.8	6.9
Haiti	241.0	2,018.3	—	1,154.3	864.0
Honduras	172.0	3,728.3	1,200.5	2,462.7	65.1
Jamaica	328.0	3,244.9	2,871.8	174.6	198.9
Mexico	1,638.3	30,093.4	29,376.9	559.0	157.5
Nicaragua	107.0	4,696.7	651.8	2,447.2	68.0
Panama	228.2	4,054.3	3,716.6	296.6	41.4
Paraguay	170.0	3,000.4	2,298.1	690.0	12.3
Peru	450.0	10,241.9	9,580.0	440.8	221.1
Suriname	80.0	292.5	286.1	6.4	—
Trinidad and Tobago	290.0	1,657.1	1,601.3	30.6	25.2
Uruguay	317.6	5,537.4	5,391.4	104.2	41.8
Venezuela	120.0	7,229.0	7,054.7	101.4	72.9
Regional	425.0	4,076.5	3,828.9	233.6	14.0
Total	12,464.2	197,025.4	176,179.9	19,054.1	1,791.4

* Includes non-sovereign guaranteed loans, net of participations, and guarantees, as applicable. Excludes the IDB Grant Facility or lines of credit approved and guarantees issued under the Trade Finance Facilitation Program.

Source: Inter-American Development Bank, *Annual Report 2011*.

INTERGOVERNMENTAL AUTHORITY ON DEVELOPMENT—IGAD

Address: Ave Georges Clemenceau, BP 2653, Djibouti.

Telephone: 354050; **fax:** 356994; **internet:** igad.int.

The Intergovernmental Authority on Development (IGAD), established in 1996 to supersede the Intergovernmental Authority on Drought and Development (IGADD, founded in 1986), aims to co-ordinate the sustainable socio-economic development of member countries, to combat the effects of drought and desertification, and to promote regional food security.

MEMBERS*

Djibouti	Kenya	South Sudan	Uganda
Ethiopia	Somalia	Sudan	

* In April 2007 Eritrea suspended its IGAD membership; the IGAD Council of Ministers has subsequently engaged with Eritrea to promote its return to the organization. South Sudan was admitted as the seventh member of the organization in November 2011.

Organization

(April 2012)

ASSEMBLY

The Assembly, consisting of heads of state and of government of member states, is the supreme policy-making organ of the Authority. It holds a summit meeting at least once a year. The chairmanship of the Assembly rotates among the member countries on an annual basis.

Chairman: MELES ZENAWI (Ethiopia).

COUNCIL OF MINISTERS

The Council of Ministers is composed of the minister of foreign affairs and one other minister from each member state. It meets at least twice a year and approves the work programme and the annual budget of the Secretariat.

COMMITTEE OF AMBASSADORS

The Committee of Ambassadors comprises the ambassadors or plenipotentiaries of member states to Djibouti. It convenes as regularly as required to advise and assist the Executive Secretary concerning the interpretation of policies and guidelines and the realization of the annual work programme.

SECRETARIAT

The Secretariat, the executive body of IGAD, is headed by the Executive Secretary, who is appointed by the Assembly for a term of four years, renewable once. In addition to the Office of the Executive Secretary, the Secretariat comprises the following three divisions: Agriculture and Environment; Economic Co-operation; and Political and Humanitarian Affairs, each headed by a director. A workshop was convened in September 2011 to discuss the future organizational restructuring of IGAD.

Executive Secretary: MAHBOUB MAALIM (Kenya).

Activities

IGADD was established in 1986 by Djibouti, Ethiopia, Kenya, Somalia, Sudan and Uganda, to combat the effects of aridity and desertification arising from the severe drought and famine that has periodically affected the Horn of Africa. Eritrea became a member of IGADD in September 1993, following its proclamation as an independent state. In April 1995, at an extraordinary summit meeting held in Addis Ababa, Ethiopia, heads of state and of government resolved to reorganize and expand the Authority. In March 1996 IGAD was endorsed to supersede IGADD, at a second extraordinary summit meeting of heads of state and of government, held in Nairobi, Kenya. The meeting led to the adoption of an agreement for a new organizational structure and the approval of an extended mandate to co-ordinate and harmonize policy in the areas of economic co-operation and political and humanitarian affairs, in addition to its existing responsibilities for food security and environmental protection.

IGAD aims to achieve regional co-operation and economic integration. To facilitate this, IGAD assists the governments of member states to maximize resources and co-ordinates efforts to initiate and implement regional development programmes and projects. In this context, IGAD promotes the harmonization of policies relating to agriculture and natural resources, communications, customs, trade and transport; the implementation of programmes in the fields of social sciences, research, science and technology; and effective participation in the global economy. Meetings between IGAD ministers of foreign affairs and the IGAD Partners' Forum (IPF), comprising the grouping's donors, are convened periodically to discuss issues such as food security and humanitarian affairs. In October 2001 delegates from IGAD and representatives of government and civil society in member states initiated a process to establish an IGAD-Civil Society Forum; the founding assembly of the Forum was convened in Nairobi, in July 2003. In August 2008 a meeting was held with the UN Development Programme (UNDP) on mobilizing resources and capacity building for the regional organization. Negotiations were conducted during 2008 on formulating a regional Integration Plan to cover all sectors of IGAD's activity. In February 2009 the IGAD Executive Secretary chaired a technical meeting, in Djibouti, which aimed to chart a road map for future integration.

In October 2003 the 10th IGAD summit meeting ratified a decision of the eighth summit, held in November 2000, to absorb the Harare, Zimbabwe- and Nairobi-based Drought Monitoring Centre (an initiative of 24 eastern and southern African states inaugurated in 1989 under the auspices of UNDP and the World Meteorological Organization) as a specialized institution of IGAD; the Centre was renamed the IGAD Climate Prediction and Applications Centre (ICPAC). In April 2007 ICPAC was fully integrated into IGAD.

A Protocol establishing the Inter-parliamentary Union of IGAD (IPU-IGAD), signed in February 2004 by the participants in the first meeting of regional speakers of parliament, entered into force in November 2007; IPU-IGAD was to be based in Addis Ababa.

In January 2008 the IGAD Regional AIDS Partnership Program (IRAPP) was launched, with a particular focus on protecting mobile communities (for example pastoralists, internally displaced persons, and refugees) at risk of HIV/AIDS. IRAPP was implementing a common regional strategic plan for combating HIV/AIDS, targeting cross-border and mobile populations, over the period 2011–16. Jointly with the World Bank the IGAD Secretariat is developing a mechanism for monitoring the occurrence of HIV/AIDS in member states.

In June 2006 IGAD launched the IGAD Capacity Building Program Against Terrorism (ICPAT), a four-year programme based in Addis Ababa, which aimed to combat the reach of international terrorism through the enhancement of judicial measures and interdepartmental co-operation, improving border control activities, supporting training and information-sharing, and promoting strategic co-operation. In April 2009 a meeting of IGAD justice ministers, organized by ICPAT, approved a draft IGAD Convention on Extradition, and also a draft Convention on Mutual Legal Assistance. In October 2011 a new IGAD Security Sector Program (ISSP) was launched, focusing on initiatives in the areas of counter-terrorism; organized crime; maritime security; and capacity building of security institutions.

A draft framework for an IGAD Gender Peer Review Mechanism is under consideration; it is envisaged that the Mechanism would be a means of addressing the issue of violence against women in the region as well as other matters relating to women's progress. In December 2009 the first IGAD Women's Parliamentary Conference, convened in Addis Ababa, adopted a declaration on the Enhancement of Women's Participation and Representation in Decision-Making Positions. In April 2011 IGAD convened a conference on women and peace, considering the engagement of women in peace-building and security initiatives in the region.

In October 2011 IGAD was granted observer status at the UN General Assembly.

FOOD SECURITY AND ENVIRONMENTAL PROTECTION

IGAD seeks to achieve regional food security, the sustainable development of natural resources and environmental protection, and to encourage and assist member states in their efforts to combat the consequences of drought and other natural and man-made disasters. The region suffers from recurrent droughts, which severely impede crop and livestock production. Natural and man-made disasters increase the strain on resources, resulting in annual food deficits. About 80% of the IGAD sub-region is classified as arid or semi-arid, and some 40% of the region is unproductive, owing to severe environmental degradation. Activities to improve food security and preserve natural resources have included: the introduction of remote-sensing services; the development of a Marketing Information System and of a Regional Integrated Information System (RIIS); the establishment of training and credit schemes for fishermen; research into the sustainable production of drought-resistant, high-yielding crop varieties; transboundary livestock disease control and vaccine production; the control of environmental pollution; the promotion of alternative sources of energy in the home; the management of integrated water resources; the promotion of community-based land husbandry; training programmes in grain marketing; and the implementation of the International Convention to Combat Desertification. IGAD's Livestock Marketing Information System (LMIS) aims to improve food security in the sub-region.

In June 2008 the IGAD Assembly, meeting in a climate of escalating global food prices and shortfalls in regional imports of foodstuffs, issued a Declaration on the Current High Food Price Crisis, in which it resolved to pursue policies aimed at improving sustainable food production; urged IGAD's partners to support regional agricultural development programmes; determined to enhance the regional drought, climate change monitoring, and early warning mechanisms; and announced that a regional emergency reserve fund would be established. In addition the Authority decided to establish a ministerial task force to assess regional emergency food aid requirements with a view to launching an international appeal for assistance. In July an IGAD meeting on regional food security and risk management, held in Nairobi, Kenya, addressed means of improving social protection and disaster risk management strategies and policies. In December 2009 IGAD and the World Food Programme (WFP) concluded a memorandum of understanding (MOU) aimed at enhancing mutual co-operation with a view to improving food and nutrition security in the IGAD region. An executive body, technical committee and co-ordination office were to be established to facilitate the implementation of the MOU.

In November 2011 IGAD and partner countries held a consultative meeting entitled 'Ending Drought Emergencies in the Horn of Africa', in response to ongoing severe drought and an ensuing food security crisis, that had resulted in some 13m. people in the region requiring food assistance. The meeting determined the institutional arrangements for implementing a Horn of Africa Disaster Resilience and Sustainability Initiative, which had been launched by regional heads of state in September. The meeting also agreed to establish an IGAD Platform, intended as an enhanced partnership with donors facilitating long-term investment—particularly in regional arid and semi-arid lands—to end the recurrence of drought emergencies.

IGAD adopted an Environment and Natural Resources Strategy in April 2007, identifying a number key strategic objectives that were to guide future sub-regional environmental programmes. In June 2010 a consultative meeting was convened between IGAD, the African Union (AU), the Common Market for Eastern and Southern African (COMESA), and other regional partners, aimed at advancing the co-ordination and harmonization of their activities governing the environment.

ECONOMIC CO-OPERATION

The Economic Co-operation division concentrates on the development of a co-ordinated infrastructure for the region, in particular in the areas of transport and communications, to promote foreign, cross-border and domestic trade and investment opportunities. IGAD seeks to harmonize national transport and trade policy and thereby to facilitate the free movement of people, goods and services. The improvements to infrastructure also aim to facilitate more timely interventions in conflicts, disasters and emergencies in the sub-region. Projects under way include: the construction of missing segments of the Trans-African Highway and the Pan African Telecommunications Network; the removal of barriers to trade and communications; improvements to ports and inland container terminals; and the modernization of railway and telecommunications services. In November 2000 the IGAD Assembly determined to establish an integrated rail network connecting all member countries. In addition, the heads of state and government considered the possibility of drafting legislation to facilitate the expansion of intra-IGAD trade. The development of economic co-operation has been impeded by persisting conflicts in the sub-region (see below). In August 2010 an IGAD Business Forum was held, in Kampala, Uganda.

POLITICAL AND HUMANITARIAN AFFAIRS

The field of political and humanitarian affairs focuses on conflict prevention, management and resolution through dialogue. The division's primary aim is to restore peace and stability to member countries affected by conflict, in order that resources may be diverted for development purposes. Efforts have been pursued to strengthen capacity for conflict prevention and to relieve humanitarian crises. The ninth IGAD summit meeting, held in Khartoum, Sudan, in January 2002, adopted a protocol to IGAD's founding agreement establishing a conflict early warning and response mechanism (CEWARN). CEWARN, which is based in Addis Ababa, Ethiopia, collects and analyses information for the preparation of periodic early warning reports concerning the potential outbreak of violent conflicts in the region. In February 2006 IGAD convened a ministerial conference on refugees, returnees and internally displaced persons, to consider means of addressing the burden posed by population displacement in member states; at that time it was estimated that 11m. people had been forcibly displaced from their homes in the region. In May 2008 IGAD, the AU and the International Organization for Migration (IOM) jointly organized a workshop, held in Addis Ababa, on inter-state and intra-regional co-operation on migration; an IGAD Regional Consultative Process (IGAD-RCP) on migration was launched, with the aim of building member countries' management capacities. In February 2012 a meeting of the IGAD-RCP considered the possibility of developing a regional action plan for Diaspora engagement in development. IGAD contributes to efforts to raise awareness of the AU's 2006 Ouagadougou Action Plan to Combat Trafficking in Human Beings, and supports the AU COMMIT campaign, launched in June 2009 to combat human trafficking.

The Executive Secretary of IGAD participated in the first summit meeting of all East African heads of state and government, convened in April 2005 in Addis Ababa; the meeting agreed to establish an Eastern African Standby Brigade (EASBRIG). EASBRIG, the development of which is co-ordinated by IGAD, will form the regional component of the AU African Standby Force. In November 2009 EASBRIG undertook a field training exercise ('Exercise Amani Carana') in Djibouti.

In 2008 a new IGAD Peace and Security Strategy was devised. In August IGAD chaired the first meeting of the steering committee on Conflict Prevention Management and Resolution (CPMR), comprising IGAD, COMESA and the East African Community (EAC), which aimed to promote a co-ordinated approach to peace and security in the region.

In September 1995 negotiations between the Sudanese Government and opposition leaders were initiated, under the auspices of IGAD, with the aim of resolving the conflict in southern Sudan; these were subsequently reconvened periodically. In March 2001 IGAD's mediation committee on southern Sudan, chaired by (then) President Daniel arap Moi of Kenya, publicized a seven-point plan for a peaceful settlement of the conflict. In June, at a regional summit on the situation in Sudan convened by IGAD, it was agreed that a permanent negotiating forum comprising representatives of the parties to the conflict would be established at the Authority's secretariat. In July 2002 the Sudanese Government and the main rebel grouping in that country signed, under IGAD auspices, in Machakos, Kenya, a protocol providing for a six-year period of autonomy for southern Sudan to be followed by a referendum on self-determination, and establishing that northern Sudan would be governed in accordance with *Shari'a* law and southern Sudan by a secular judicial system. Peace negotiations subsequently continued under IGAD auspices. A cease-fire agreement was concluded by the parties to the conflict in October, to which an addendum was adopted in February 2003, recommending the deployment of an IGAD verification and monitoring team to oversee compliance with the agreement. In September of that year the parties to the conflict signed an accord on interim security arrangements. During 2003–04 IGAD mediated several further accords that paved the way for the conclusion, in January 2005, of a final Comprehensive Peace Agreement (CPA). An extraordinary session of the IGAD Council of Ministers, convened in January 2010, in Addis Ababa, expressed concern regarding the ongoing status of the implementation of the CPA and directed the IGAD Secretariat to develop programmes and seminars aimed at promoting a culture of peace in Sudan. An extraordinary summit meeting of the IGAD Assembly, held in March, *inter alia* emphasized the centrality of IGAD's role in the full implementation of the CPA; directed the IGAD Secretariat to open immediately a liaison office in Juba, Sudan, to follow up the implementation of the CPA; directed the IGAD Secretariat to accept an invitation to observe the April 2010 Sudanese elections; and directed the IGAD Secretariat to convene, in collaboration with the IPF and the parties to the CPA, an international Donors' Conference for Sudan. The IGAD monitoring team dispatched to observe the presidential and legislative elections in Sudan, in April, found them to be 'credible', while noting that technical problems had occurred and that the electoral authorities had been overwhelmed by the magnitude of their task. Following the referendum on self-determination for South Sudan, held in January 2011, and South Sudan's consequent attainment of independence in July, the new nation was admitted to IGAD in November 2011. The 20th extraordinary session of the Authority, held in January 2012, noted with concern deteriorating relations between Sudan and South Sudan, and strongly urged both states to refrain from actions that might undermine the resolution of outstanding issues under the CPA. In February 2012 the IGAD Executive Secretary reiterated the position of the AU that a warrant issued in November 2011 by the Kenyan High Court for the arrest of Sudanese President Omar Al-Bashir—indicted by the International Criminal Court on charges of including crimes against humanity and genocide—contravened the interests of peace, stability and economic development in the region, and risked undermining the peace process being undertaken by IGAD in Sudan.

In May–August 2000 a conference aimed at securing peace in Somalia was convened in Arta, Djibouti, under the auspices of IGAD. The conference appointed a transitional Somali legislature, which then elected a transitional national president. The eighth summit of IGAD heads of state and government, held in Khartoum, in November, welcomed the conclusion in September of an agreement on reconciliation between the new Somali transitional administration and a prominent opposition alliance, and determined that those member countries that neighboured Somalia (the 'frontline states' of Djibouti, Ethiopia and Kenya) should co-operate in assisting the process of reconstruction and reconciliation in that country. The summit appointed a special envoy to implement IGAD's directives concerning the Somali situation. In January 2002 the ninth IGAD summit meeting determined that a new conference for promoting reconciliation in Somalia (where insecurity continued to prevail) should be convened, under IGAD's auspices. The leaders also issued a statement condemning international terrorism and urged Somalia, in particular, to make a firm commitment to eradicating terrorism. The second Somalia reconciliation conference, initiated in October, in Eldoret, Kenya, under IGAD auspices, issued a Declaration on Cessation of Hostilities, Structures and Principles of the Somalia National Reconciliation Process, as a basis for the pursuit of a peace settlement. In February 2003 the conference was relocated to Nairobi, Kenya. In January 2004 the Nairobi conference determined to establish a new parliament; this was inaugurated in August. In January 2005 IGAD heads of state and government authorized the deployment of a Peace Support Mission to Somalia (IGASOM) to assist the transitional federal authorities there, pending the subsequent deployment of an AU peace force; this arrangement was endorsed in the same month by the AU. In mid-March 2006 the IGAD Assembly reiterated its support for the planned deployment of IGASOM, and urged the UN Security Council to grant an exemption to the UN arms embargo applied to Somalia in order to facilitate the regional peace support initiative. At a consultative meeting on the removal of the arms embargo, convened in mid-April, in Nairobi, representatives of the Somali transitional federal authorities presented for consideration by IGAD and the AU a draft national security and stabilization plan. It was agreed that a detailed mission plan should be formulated to underpin the proposed IGAD/AU peace missions. In January 2007 the AU Peace and Security Council authorized the deployment of the AU Mission in Somalia (AMISOM) in place of the proposed IGASOM.

An extraordinary meeting of the IGAD Council of Ministers, held in New York, USA, in September 2008, noted with serious concern the ongoing escalation in acts of piracy in waters off the Somalian coast, and urged the international community to take co-ordinated action to safeguard maritime safety in the region. In December a new IGAD Facilitator for the Somali peace process was appointed. Meeting in May 2009 an extraordinary session of the IGAD Council of Ministers urged the UN Security Council to impose (except for humanitarian personnel) a no-fly zone over Somalia and blockades on identified Somali seaports, and also to impose targeted sanctions against all those providing assistance to extremists—including foreign forces—who were continuing to attack AMISOM and otherwise to destabilize that country. A further extraordinary meeting of IGAD leaders, convened in June 2009, on the sidelines of the AU summit, in Sirte, Libya, noted with deep concern the continuing poor security situation in Somalia; urged the UN Security Council to consider enabling front-line states to deploy troops to Somalia if necessary; committed IGAD member states individually and collectively to establishing an internal mechanism to effect the sanctions called for in May and to enact legislation aimed at combating piracy; and directed the IGAD Secretariat to accord full support to the grouping's Facilitator for the Somali peace process. In mid-September IGAD, the UN, the European Union (EU), the League of Arab States and the respective Governments of Norway and the USA issued a joint statement strongly condemning suicide car bomb attacks that were perpetrated by Islamic extremists against the AMISOM headquarters in Mogadishu, Somalia, killing more than 20 people, including the Deputy Force Commander of the Mission, and injuring a further 40. The January 2010 IGAD extraordinary summit gathering determined to send a ministerial delegation to selected partner countries and organizations to solicit their support for the Somali transitional federal authorities; and welcomed the imposition by the UN Security Council in December 2009 of punitive sanctions against the Eritrean political and military leadership, who were found to have provided political, financial and logistical support to armed groups engaged in undermining the reconciliation process in Somalia, and to have acted aggressively towards Djibouti. The Kampala Accord, signed in June 2011 by the President of the Somali transitional federal authorities and the Speaker of the transitional legislature, and related Roadmap on its implementation, outlined a schedule for national elections, and determined that the IGAD and EAC heads of state, with UN and AU co-operation, should establish a political bureau to oversee and advance the Somali peace process. The January 2012 extraordinary session of the Authority endorsed a new IGAD Somalia Inland Strategy and Action Plan to Prevent and Counter Piracy.

At the beginning of February 2008 IGAD heads of state and government convened in Addis Ababa, on the sidelines of the 10th Assembly of the AU, to discuss the violent unrest that had erupted in Kenya in the aftermath of that country's December 2007 disputed general election; following the meeting an IGAD ministerial delegation was dispatched to Kenya as a gesture of regional solidarity with the Kenyan people and with a peace initiative led by the former UN Secretary-General, Kofi Annan. IGAD sent an observer mission to monitor the national referendum on a new draft constitution held in Kenya in August 2010.

Publications

Annual Report.

IGAD News (2 a year).

Proceedings of the Summit of Heads of State and Government; Reports of the Council of Ministers' Meetings.

INTERNATIONAL CHAMBER OF COMMERCE—ICC

Address: 38 cours Albert 1er, 75008 Paris, France.

Telephone: 1-49-53-28-28; **fax:** 1-49-53-28-59; **e-mail:** webmaster@iccwbo.org; **internet:** www.iccwbo.org.

The ICC, founded in 1919, is the primary world business organization, representing enterprises world-wide from all business sectors. The ICC aims to promote cross-border trade and investment and to support enterprises in meeting the challenges and opportunities presented by globalization. The ICC regards trade as a force for peace and prosperity. In the 2000s the ICC underwent an extensive process of reform.

MEMBERS

ICC membership comprises corporations, national professional and sectoral associations, business and employer federations, chambers of commerce, and individuals involved in international business from more than 130 countries. National Committees or Groups have been formed in some 85 countries and territories to co-ordinate ICC objectives and functions at the national level.

Organization

(April 2012)

ICC WORLD COUNCIL

The ICC World Council is the governing body of the organization. It meets twice a year and is composed of members nominated by the National Committees. Ten direct members, from countries where no National Committee exists, may also be invited to participate. The Council elects the Chairman and Vice-Chairman for terms of two years. Ten 'direct' members originating in countries that do not have a national committee may also be invited to participate in the meetings of the World Council.

Chairman: GÉRARD WORMS (France).

EXECUTIVE BOARD

The Executive Board consists of up to 30 business leaders and ex officio members appointed by the ICC World Council upon recommendation of the Chairman. Members serve for a three-year term, one-third of the members retiring at the end of each year. It ensures the strategic direction of ICC activities and the implementation of its policies, and meets at least three times each year.

INTERNATIONAL SECRETARIAT

The ICC International Secretariat, based in Paris, is the operational arm of the ICC. It implements the work programme approved by the ICC World Council, providing intergovernmental organizations with commercial views on issues that directly affect business operations. The International Secretariat is led by the Secretary-General, who is appointed by the World Council on the recommendation of the Executive Board. A regional office for Asia, based in Singapore, was inaugurated in January 2010.

Secretary-General: JEAN-GUY CARRIER (Canada).

NATIONAL COMMITTEES AND GROUPS

Each affiliate is composed of leading business organizations and individual companies. It has its own secretariat, monitors issues of concern to its national constituents, and draws public and government attention to ICC policies.

WORLD CHAMBERS CONGRESS

The ICC's World Chambers Federation (WCF) organizes the ICC's supreme World Chambers Congress every two years; the seventh was convened in Mexico City, Mexico, in June 2011.

CONFERENCES

Regular ICC topical conferences and seminars, organized by ICC Events, disseminate ICC expertise in various fields including international arbitration, trade, banking and commercial practice.

COMMISSIONS

Policy Commissions:

Commission on Arbitration;
Commission on Banking Technique and Practice;
Commission on Commercial Practice;
Corporate Responsibility and Anti-corruption;
Commission on Competition;
Commission on Customs and Trade Regulations;
Commission on E-business, IT and Telecoms;
Commission on Environment and Energy;
Commission on Financial Services and Insurance;
Commission on Intellectual Property;
Commission on Marketing and Advertising;
Commission on Taxation;
Commission on Trade and Investment Policy;
Commission on Transport and Logistics.

ADVISORY GROUPS

Corporate Economist Advisory Group;
G20 Advisory Group.

OTHER BODIES

ICC Commercial Crime Services;
ICC Services (incorporates ICC Events and ICC Publications);
ICC World Chambers Federation.

ICC Commercial Crime Services Divisions:

International Maritime Bureau (IMB): a Piracy Reporting Centre provides the most accurate and up-to-date information to shippers regarding pirate activity on the world's oceans.

Financial Investigation Bureau (FIB): works to detect financial fraud before it occurs by allowing banks and other financial institutions access to a database of shared information.

Counterfeiting Intelligence Bureau (CIB): runs a number of initiatives to protect against counterfeiting including Counterforce, Countertech and Countersearch international networks, the Counterfeit Pharmaceutical Initiative, the IHMA's Hologram Image Register and the Universal Hologram Scanner.

Activities

The ICC's main activities are setting voluntary rules guiding the conduct of international trade, arbitrating trade disputes, and establishing policy.

The various Commissions of the ICC (listed above) are composed of more than 500 practising business executives and experts from all sectors of economic life, nominated by National Committees. ICC recommendations must be adopted by a Commission following consultation with National Committees, and then approved by the ICC World Council or Executive Board, before they can be regarded as official ICC policies. Meetings of Commissions are generally held twice a year. Task Forces are frequently constituted by Commissions to undertake specific projects and report back to their parent body. The Commissions produce a wide array of specific codes and guidelines of direct use to the world business community; formulate statements and initiatives for presentation to governments and international bodies; and comment constructively and in detail on proposed actions by intergovernmental organizations and governments that are likely to affect business.

The ICC works closely with other international organizations. It has undertaken a broad range of activities with the UN, the World Trade Organization (WTO), the European Union (EU) and many other intergovernmental bodies. The ICC presidency meets annually with the leader of the country hosting the Group of Eight (G8) summit to discuss business aspects of the meeting. A G20 Advisory Group, comprising chief executives from major global corporations and other business leaders, aims to support the effective targeting of G20 policy development.

The ICC plays a part in combating international crime connected with commerce through its Commercial Crime Services (CCS). Based in London, United Kingdom, the CCS operates according to two basic principles: to prevent and investigate commercial crime and to facilitate the prosecution of criminals involved in such crimes. In July 2008 the ICC issued guidelines on establishing and implementing internal whistleblowing programmes within businesses, aimed at exposing fraud. In March 2009 the ICC, in partnership with Transparency International, the UN Global Compact and the World Economic Forum, launched RESIST (Resisting Extortions and Solicitations in International Transactions), a tool providing recommendations to assist businesses with responding to attempted solicitation and extortion from clients.

Following the launch of the ICC's Business Action to Stop Counterfeiting and Piracy (BASCAP) initiative in November 2004, more than 150 companies and trade associations have become actively engaged in a set of projects designed to combat counterfeiting and piracy and increase awareness of the economic and social harm such activities cause. In March 2008 chief executive officers and senior corporate executives participating in BASCAP convened in New York, USA, with representatives of the World Customs Organization, World Intellectual Property Organization and US Government to discuss means of co-operation in addressing counterfeiting and piracy. The BASCAP delegates urged the prompt negotiation of an Anti-Counterfeiting Trade Agreement (ACTA). In October BASCAP published a set of intellectual property (IP) guidelines aimed at supporting businesses in managing copyright and branded materials, and deterring trade in counterfeit goods. In March 2010 BASCAP noted that jobs in creative industries were under threat from piracy, increasingly caused by illicit use of the internet (so-called digital piracy). In June 2010 BASCAP released an Arabic version of its IP guidelines for businesses. In February 2011 the ICC warned that the global economic and social impacts of counterfeiting and piracy would reach US $1,700,000m. by 2015, putting at risk 2.5m. legitimate jobs annually. The ICC issues an annual *Intellectual Property Roadmap*.

The International Maritime Bureau of the ICC compiles an annual *Global Piracy Report*, detailing incidents of maritime piracy. The 2012 Report, issued in April, reported an increase in the first quarter of that year in cases (totalling 10) of armed robbery at sea off the coast of West Africa, attributing this to the activities of Nigerian pirates, who were reported to be widening their range. Some 43 attacks by armed pirates were reported off the coast of Somalia over that period.

The ICC provides a framework for settling international commercial disputes. The Commission on Arbitration acts as a forum for experts and also reviews the ICC's dispute settlement services, for example regarding the deployment of new technologies. In 2011 the ICC International Court of Arbitration, which was established in 1923, received 796 requests for arbitration, concerning 2,293 parties from 139 countries. Other ICC services for dispute resolution include its Rules of Arbitration (updated Rules entered into force from 1 January 2012, the Rules having previously been revised in 1998), its Alternative Dispute Resolution, and the International Centre for Expertise, which administers ICC Rules of Expertise and Rules for Documentary Credit and Dispute Resolution Expertise (DOCDEX). In June 2008 the ICC's Dispute Resolution Library was migrated to the internet, providing online access to ICC documentation on international dispute resolution.

The ICC's World Chambers Federation (WCF), a global network of chambers of commerce, acts as a platform for interaction and exchange of best practice. It is responsible for the ATA Carnet temporary export document system. The WCF also organizes the biennial World Chambers Federation Congresses. At the sixth Congress, convened in Kuala Lumpur, Malaysia, in June 2009, the WCF signed a co-operation agreement with the UN. The seventh WCF Congress was held in June 2011, in Mexico City, Mexico, on the theme 'Enterprise—Network—Prosperity; and the eighth was scheduled to be held in Doha, Qatar, in April 2013, themed as 'Opportunities for All'. In June 2008, in Stockholm, Sweden, the ICC launched the first ICC World Business Summit, as a forum for business decision makers in government and in the private sector. The Summit was convened on the theme 'World Economy at a Crossroads', and addressed the risks to the global economy posed by rising protectionism and increasing threats to IP rights. The second World Business Summit was held in June 2010, on the theme 'New Global Economic Realities: Asia-Pacific Perspectives'.

The ICC has developed rules and guidelines relating to electronic transactions, including guidelines for ethical advertising on the internet and for data protection. The ICC has devised a system of standard trade definitions most commonly used in international sales contracts ('Incoterms') and the Uniform Customs and Practice (UCP) for Documentary Credits, used by banks to finance international trade. An updated set of Incoterms ('Incoterms 2010') entered into force in January 2011. The UCP for Documentary Credits were most recently updated in 2007 (the 'UCP 600' edition). There are also ICC voluntary codes for eliminating extortion and bribery, and for promoting sound environmental management practices. The first ICC Trade Finance Summit was held in Beijing, People's Republic of China, in October 2011. A new Consolidated ICC Code of Advertising and Marketing Communications was launched in September 2011, detailing standards for marketers selling over the internet, and aimed also at strengthening protection for online consumers.

In mid-2006 the ICC launched the Business Action to Support the Information Society (BASIS) initiative, which aims to project, at international fora, the global business outlook on issues relating to the information society, such as internet governance, and the use of information and communications technologies in promoting development. BASIS contributes to the annual policy-setting Internet Governance Forum, established in 2005 by the World Summit on the Information Society.

In January 2010 the ICC launched a new global framework for responsible environmental marketing communications. In early 2012 the ICC was leading the engagement of the global business sector in preparations for the UN Conference on Sustainable Development (Rio+20), to be held in Rio de Janeiro, Brazil, in June.

In co-operation with the Ifo Institute for Economic Research, the ICC has since 1981 compiled a quarterly *World Economic Survey*. The *Survey* edition that was issued in February 2009 reported the lowest ever recorded global economic index, confirming the prevalence of global recession; the *Survey* index rose, however, in subsequent quarters; by the February 2012 edition, which was based on the input of more than 1,129 economic experts in 120 countries, it stood at significantly below its long-term average.

Finance

The ICC is a private, non-profit-making organization financed partly by contributions from National Committees and other members, according to the economic importance of the country that each represents, and partly by revenue from fees for various services and from sales of publications.

Publications

Annual Report.

Documentary Credits Insight (quarterly).

Global Piracy Report (annually).

ICC Banking Commission Opinions.

ICC International Court of Arbitration Bulletin.

Intellectual Property Roadmap (annually).

World Economic Survey (jointly with the Ifo Institute for Economic Research, quarterly).

Publications on general and technical business and trade-related subjects are also available online.

INTERNATIONAL CRIMINAL COURT

Address: Maanweg 174, 2516 AB The Hague, Netherlands.

Telephone: (70) 515-8097; **fax:** (70) 515-8376; **e-mail:** asp@asp.icc-cpi.int; **internet:** www.icc-cpi.int.

The International Criminal Court (ICC) was established by the Rome Statute of the International Criminal Court, adopted by 120 states participating in a UN Diplomatic Conference in July 1998. The Rome Statute (and therefore the temporal jurisdiction of the ICC) entered into force on 1 July 2002, 60 days after ratification by the requisite 60th signatory state in April. The ICC is a permanent, independent body, in relationship with the UN, that aims to promote the rule of law and punish the most serious international crimes. The Rome Statute reaffirmed the principles of the UN Charter and stated that the relationship between the Court and the UN system should be determined by a framework relationship agreement between the states parties to the Rome Statute and the UN General Assembly: under the so-called negotiated relationship agreement, which entered into force in October 2004, upon signature by the Court's President and the Secretary-General of the UN, there was to be mutual exchange of information and documentation to the fullest extent and co-operation and consultation on practical matters, and it was stipulated that the Court might, if deemed appropriate, submit reports on its activities to the UN Secretary-General and propose to the Secretary-General items for consideration by the UN.

The Court comprises the Presidency (consisting of a President and first and second Vice-Presidents), Chambers (including a Pre-Trial Chamber, Trial Chamber and Appeals Chamber) with 18 permanent judges, Office of the Prosecutor (comprising the Chief Prosecutor and up to two Deputy Prosecutors), and Registry. The judges must each have a different nationality and equitably represent the major legal systems of the world, a fair geographical distribution, and a fair proportion of men and women. They are elected by the Assembly of States Parties to the Rome Statute from two lists, the first comprising candidates with established competence in criminal law and procedures and the second comprising candidates with established competence in relevant areas of international law, to terms of office of three, six or nine years. The President and Vice-Presidents are elected by an absolute majority of the judges for renewable three-year terms of office. The Chief Prosecutor is elected by an absolute majority of states parties to the Rome Statute to an unrenewable nine-year term of office. The first judges were elected to the Court in February 2003, the first Presidency in March, and the first Chief Prosecutor in April.

The Court has established a Victims Trust Fund to finance compensation, restitution or rehabilitation for victims of crimes (individuals or groups of individuals). The Fund is administered by the Registry and supervised by an independent board of directors.

By April 2012 14 cases in seven situations had been brought before the Court. Three cases were being pursued by the Court that had been referred to it by states party to the Rome Statute relating to situations occurring on their territories; two cases were being pursued that had been referred by the UN Security Council; and investigations *proprio motu* were being conducted into situations in Kenya and Côte d'Ivoire (see below).

Situation in Uganda: referred to the Court in January 2004 by the Ugandan Government; the Chief Prosecutor agreed to open an investigation into the situation in July 2004; relates to the long-term unrest in the north of the country; in October 2005 the Court unsealed warrants of arrest (issued under seal in July) against five commanders of the Ugandan Lord's Resistance Army (LRA), including the LRA leader, Joseph Kony; in July 2007 the Court's proceedings against one of the named commanders were terminated on the grounds that he had been killed during LRA rebel activities in August 2006; the other four suspects remained at large at April 2012.

Situation in the Democratic Republic of the Congo (DRC): referred in April 2004 by the DRC Government; the Chief Prosecutor agreed to open an investigation into the situation in June 2004; relates to alleged war crimes; in March 2006 Thomas Lubanga Dyilo, a DRC militia leader, was arrested by the Congolese authorities and transferred to the Court, thereby becoming the first ICC indictee to be captured; Lubanga was charged with conscripting child soldiers, a sealed warrant for his arrest having been issued in February; in July 2007 warrants of arrest were issued for the DRC rebel commanders Germain Katanga and Mathieu Ngudjolo Chui; Katanga was transferred into the custody of the Court in October 2007 and Ngudjolo Chui in February 2008; in April 2008 the Court unsealed a warrant of arrest for the rebel leader Bosco Ntaganda; Lubanga's trial—the first conducted by the Court—commenced in January 2009; the Prosecution concluded its presentation of its case in the trial of Lubanga in July 2009; Lubanga was found guilty in mid-March 2012, in the first verdict given by the Court; the trial in the case of Katanga and Ngudjolo Chui (the Court's second trial) commenced in November 2009; in December 2011 charges relating to crimes against humanity and other war crimes were withdrawn against Callixte Mbarushimana, an alleged rebel leader who had been arrested by the French authorities in October 2010 and transferred to the custody of the Court in January 2011; Ntaganda remained at large at April 2012.

Situation in the Central African Republic (CAR): referred in January 2005 by the CAR Government; the Chief Prosecutor agreed to open an investigation into the situation in May 2005; relates to war crimes and crimes against humanity allegedly committed during the period October 2002–March 2003; in May 2008 the Court issued a warrant of arrest for Jean-Pierre Bemba Gombo, the leader of the Mouvement du Libération du Congo (the 'Banyamulenge'); Bemba Gombo was transferred into the custody of the Court in July 2008, and his trial commenced in November 2010.

Situation in Darfur, Sudan: referred to the Court in March 2005 by the UN Security Council on the basis of the recently issued report of an International Commission of Inquiry on Darfur; the Chief Prosecutor agreed to open an investigation into the situation in June 2005; relates to the situation prevailing in Darfur since 1 July 2002; the UN Secretary-General handed the Chief Prosecutor a sealed list of 51 names of people identified in the report as having committed crimes under international law; in April 2007 the Court issued warrants for the arrests of Ahmad Harun, a former Sudanese government minister, and Ali Kushayb, a leader of the Sudanese Janjaweed militia, who were both accused of perpetrating war crimes and crimes against humanity; both remained at large at April 2012; in July 2008 the Chief Prosecutor presented evidence that Sudan's President Omar Al-Bashir had been responsible for committing alleged war crimes, including crimes against humanity and genocide, in Darfur; an arrest warrant for President Al-Bashir was issued by the Court in March 2009; a second arrest warrant for President Al-Bashir was issued in July 2010, charging him with genocide against three ethnic groups in Darfur; Al-Bashir had not surrendered to the Court at April 2012; in May 2009 a summons was issued against the militia leader Bahr Idriss Abu Garda, who appeared voluntarily before the Court later in that month; the Pre-Trial Chamber examining the Garda case declined, in February 2010, to confirm the charges against him; in June 2010 Abdallah Banda Abakaer Nourain and Saleh Mohammed Jerbo Jamus surrendered voluntarily to the Court, having been accused, with Abu Garda, of attacking the Haskanita African Union (AU) camp in September–October 2007 and causing the deaths of 12 peace-keeping troops deployed to the former AU Mission in Sudan; on 1 March 2012 the Court issued an arrest warrant for the Sudanese Minister of Defence, Abdelrahim Mohamed Hussein, for crimes against humanity and war crimes committed during August 2003–March 2004, when he was the country's Minister for the Interior, as detailed in the case of Harun and Kushayb (see above).

Situation in Kenya: in November 2009 the Presidency of the Court decided to assign the situation in Kenya (relating to violent unrest following the December 2007 presidential elections there) to a Pre-Trial Chamber; in July 2009 the International Commission of Inquiry on Post-Election Violence (known also as the Waki Commission), which had been established by the Kenyan Government in February 2008, presented the Court Prosecutor with documentation, supporting materials, and a list of people suspected of being implicated in the violent unrest; on 31 March 2010 Pre-Trial Chamber II granted the Prosecution authorization to open an investigation *proprio motu* into the situation of Kenya; in March 2011 the ICC issued summonses for six Kenyans alleged to be criminally responsible for crimes against humanity; charges against five of the six: William Samoei Ruto, Joshua Arap Sang, Henry Kiprono Kosgey, Francis Kirimi Muthaura, and Uhuru Muigai Kenyatta were confirmed in January 2012.

Situation in Libya: referred to the Court in February 2011 by the UN Security Council; in the following month the Prosecutor agreed to open an investigation into the situation in Libya since February 2011; in late June 2011 the Court issued arrest warrants against the Libyan leader Col Muammar al-Qaddafi, Saif al-Islam (his son), and Abdullah Al-Senussi (his former Head of Military Intelligence), regarding crimes against humanity (murder and persecution) committed in Libya—through the state apparatus and security forces—from 15 February until at least 28 February; in September 2011 the ICC Prosecutor requested INTERPOL to issue a Red Notice for the arrest of the three Libyan indictees; Col Qaddafi was killed during fighting with opposition forces on 20 October; in late November Saif al-Islam was detained in southern Libya; it was subsequently reported that, despite the ICC indictment, the Libyan authorities intended to bring al-Islam to trial within Libya on charges of relating to murder and rape; Abdullah Al-Senussi was also detained by Libyan security forces in mid-March 2012.

Situation in Côte d'Ivoire: in early October 2011 an ICC Pre-Trial Chamber agreed, at the request of the Prosecutor, to commence an investigation into alleged crimes committed in Côte d'Ivoire between 28 November 2010 and 12 April 2011, during a period of civil unrest resulting from disputed presidential election results, and to consider also any crimes that may be committed in the future in the context of this situation; in late November 2011 the former president, Laurent Gbagbo, who had been in Ivorian custody since April, was transferred to the Court to face charges of crimes against humanity; in February 2012 the Court expanded the scope of the Côte d'Ivoire investigation also to include crimes within the jurisdiction of the Court allegedly committed during the period 19 September 2002–28 November 2010.

The Office of the Prosecutor also receives communications from civilian individuals and organizations relating to alleged crimes that come under the Court's jurisdiction; by 31 May 2011 9,214 such communications had been received since July 2002.

The Court also conducts an Outreach Programme, which pursues activities (through community, legal, academic, and media divisions) aimed at raising awareness and understanding of the Court's mandate in the communities most affected by the situations and cases being addressed (i.e. currently in the CAR, Darfur—Sudan, the DRC, and Uganda). During 1 October 2009–1 October 2010 more than 46,499 individuals participated in 422 Outreach Programme activities.

By April 2012 121 states had ratified the Rome Statute.

THE JUDGES
(April 2012)

	Term ends*
President: Sang-Hyun Song (Republic of Korea)	2015
First Vice-President: Sanji Mmasenono Monageng (Botswana)	2018
Second Vice President: Cuno Jakob Tarfusser (Italy)	2018
Hans-Peter Kaul (Germany)	2015
Akua Kuenyehia (Ghana)	2015
Erkki Kourula (Finland)	2015
Anita Ušacka (Latvia)	2015
Ekaterina Trendafilova (Bulgaria)	2015
Joyce Aluoch (Kenya)	2018
Christine van den Wyngaert (Belgium)	2018
Silvia Alejandra Fernández de Gurmendi (Argentina)	2018
Kuniko Ozaki (Japan)	2018
Miriam-Defensor Santiago (Philippines)	2021
Howard Morrison (United Kingdom)	2021
Anthony T. Carmona (Trinidad and Tobago)	2021
Olga Herrera Carbuccia (Dominican Republic)	2021
Robert Fremr (Czech Republic)	2021
Chile Eboe-Osuji (Nigeria)	2021

* Each term ends on 10 March of the year indicated.

Chief Prosecutor: Luis Moreno Ocampo (Argentina) (until 15 June 2012), Fatou B. Bensouda (The Gambia) (designate).

Registrar: Silvana Arbia (Italy).

Finance

The proposed budget for the International Criminal Court for 2012 amounted to €111m.

Publication

ICC Weekly Update (electronic publication).

Other International Criminal Tribunals

EXTRAORDINARY CHAMBERS IN THE COURTS OF CAMBODIA—ECCC

Address: National Rd 4, Chaom Chau Commune, Dangkao District, POB 71, Phnom-Penh, Cambodia.

Telephone: (23) 219824; **fax:** (23) 219841; **e-mail:** info@eccc.gov.kh; **internet:** www.eccc.gov.kh.

Formally established as the Extraordinary Chambers in the Courts of Cambodia for the Prosecution of Crimes Committed during the Period of Democratic Kampuchea, the ECCC was inaugurated in July 2006 on the basis of an agreement concluded in June 2003 between the Cambodian Government and the UN. The ECCC is mandated to prosecute senior leaders of the former Khmer Rouge regime for serious contraventions of Cambodian and international law—including crimes against humanity, genocide and war crimes—committed during the period 17 April 1975–6 January 1979. The ECCC is a hybrid Cambodian tribunal with international participation, combining Cambodian and international judges and personnel. It applies international standards and acts independently of the Cambodian Government and the UN. The ECCC comprises a Pre-Trial Chamber, Trial Chamber and Supreme Court Chamber; an Office of the Co-Prosecutors; an Office of the Co-Investigating Judges; a Defence Support section; a Victims' Unit; and an Office of Administration. The UN Assistance to the Khmer Rouge Trials (UNAKRT) provides technical assistance to the ECCC. Victims may file complaints before the ECCC, and may apply to become Civil Parties to the proceedings. By October 2011 some 3,866 people had been admitted as Civil Parties in Case 002 (ongoing, see below). In February 2009 the ECCC initiated proceedings ('Case 001') against its first defendent, Kaing Guek Eav (also known as 'Duch'), who had been charged under international law with crimes against humanity and grave breaches of the Geneva Conventions, and under Cambodian national law with homicide and torture offences, in relation to his former role under the Khmer Rouge regime as director of Tuol Sleng prison, where at least 15,000 prisoners had been tortured and executed. The presentation of evidence in the Kaing Guek Eav case was concluded in September 2009, closing statements were made in November. In July 2010 Kaing Guek Eav was found guilty and sentenced to 35 years of imprisonment; in February 2012, following an appeal in that case, lodged in March 2011, Kaing Guek Eav's sentence was increased to life imprisonment. In September 2010 four other senior figures in the Khmer Rouge regime (Nuon Chea, formerly the Deputy Secretary of the Party of Democratic Kampuchea; Ieng Sary, formerly Minister of Foreign Affairs; Khieu Samphan, formerly President of the State Presidium; and Ieng Thirith, formerly Minister of Social Affairs and Action) were indicted on charges of crimes against humanity, grave breaches of the Geneva Conventions, genocide, and offences under the Cambodian criminal code ('Case 002'). In January 2011 the Pre-Trial Chamber ordered the case to be sent for trial. In September the Trial Chamber ordered the division of Case 002 into a series of smaller trials, which were to be tried and adjudicated separately. The first trial was to focus on the forced movement of population and related charges of crimes against humanity. In November the Trial Chamber ordered the unconditional release from detention of Ieng Thirith on the grounds that she was unfit to stand trial; trial proceedings against the remaining three defendants commenced on 21 November. In September 2009 the International Prosecutor, submitting to investigating judges a confidential list of the names of five additional suspects, requested a formal judicial investigation into two further cases ('Case 003' and 'Case 004', the subject matter of which also remained confidential). In October 2011 the Court's then International Co-Investigating Judge resigned, citing attempted interference by government officials in the investigation into Cases 003 and 004. His successor submitted his resignation on similar grounds in March 2012.

National Co-Prosecutor: CHEA LEANG (Cambodia).

International Co-Prosecutor: ANDREW T. CAYLEY (United Kingdom).

National Co-Investigating Judge: YOU BUNLENG (Cambodia).

International Co-Investigating Judge: LAURENT KASPER-ANSERMET (Switzerland) (until 4 May 2012).

SPECIAL TRIBUNAL FOR LEBANON

Address: POB 115, 2260 AC Leidschendam, Netherlands.

Telephone: (70) 800-3400; **e-mail:** stl-pressoffice@un.org; **internet:** www.stl-tsl.org.

In March 2006 the UN Security Council adopted a resolution requesting the UN Secretary-General to negotiate an agreement with the Lebanese Government on the establishment of an international tribunal to try those suspected of involvement in a terrorist attack that, in February 2005, had killed 23 people, including the former Prime Minister of Lebanon, Rafik Hariri. The resulting agreement on the Special Tribunal for Lebanon was endorsed by the Security Council in May 2007. The Tribunal, which became operational on 1 March 2009, comprises both international and Lebanese judges and applies Lebanese (not international) law. On its establishment the Tribunal took over the mandate of a terminated UN International Independent Investigation Commission (UNIIIC), which had been created by a resolution of the Security Council in April 2005 in order to gather evidence and assist the Lebanese authorities in their investigation into the February 2005 attacks, and whose mandate had later been expanded to investigate other assassinations that had occurred before and after the February 2005 attack. A Defence Office has been established within the Tribunal to protect the rights of the suspects, accused and their counsel, providing legal assistance and support where necessary. In June 2011 the Tribunal passed to the Lebanese authorities arrest warrants for four Lebanese suspects, Salim Jamil Ayyash, Mustafa Amine Badreddine, Hussein Hassan Oneissi and Assad Hassan Sabra, who were indicted on charges of conspiracy to commit a terrorist act; in February 2012 the Tribunal announced that it would try the four suspects *in absentia*, as it appeared that they had absconded. Also in February 2012, the UN Secretary-General extended the mandate of the Special Tribunal for a further three years, with effect from 1 March. The Tribunal maintains an office in Beirut, Lebanon.

President of the Court: Sir DAVID BARAGWANATH (New Zealand).

Chief Prosecutor: NORMAN FARELL (Canada).

Registrar: HERMAN VON HEBEL (Netherlands).

Head of Defence Office: FRANÇOIS ROUX (France).

SPECIAL COURT FOR SIERRA LEONE

Address: Jomo Kenyatta Rd, New England, Freetown, Sierra Leone.

Telephone: (22) 297000; **fax:** (22) 297001; **e-mail:** scsl-mail@un.org; **internet:** www.sc-sl.org.

The Court was established in January 2002 by agreement of the UN and the government of Sierra Leone, pursuant to a UN Security Council resolution of August 2000 to establish an independent Special Court to prosecute those 'bearing the greatest responsibility for committing violations against humanitarian law' committed in the territory of Sierra Leone since 20 November 1996. The Court is funded entirely by voluntary contributions. The Court indicted in total some 13 people, although two indictments were withdrawn in December 2003 following the deaths of two of the accused, and, following the death of another of the accused, a further indictment was terminated in May 2007. Trial proceedings commenced in June 2004. Three cases involving eight defendants have been completed. In April 2006 the Special Court for Sierra Leone and the ICC concluded a memorandum of understanding in accordance with which the Special Court was to use the courtroom and detention facilities of the ICC for the planned trial of Charles Taylor, the former President of Liberia, who had been indicted in March 2003 on 17 counts (subsequently reduced to 11) of crimes against humanity and violations of international law, relating to his 'acts or omissions' in relation to the activities of the rebel forces of the Sierra Leone Revolutionary United Front. Taylor, who had been arrested in Nigeria and transferred to the Special Court in March 2006, was taken to the ICC's detention centre in The Hague, Netherlands, in June of that year. Taylor's trial commenced in June 2007. It was adjourned shortly afterwards and reconvened in January 2008. In February 2009 the Prosecution formally closed its case. The Defence case was conducted during July 2009–March 2011. In late April 2012 Taylor was found guilty of aiding and abetting the crimes on which he had been indicted, while acquitted of bearing criminal responsibility and 'joint enterprise' in the commission of the crimes. Taylor, who was the first former head of state to be found guilty of charges relating to war crimes by an international court, was to be sentenced in mid-May.

President of the Court: JON KAMANDA (Sierra Leone).

Chief Prosecutor: BRENDA HOLLIS (USA).

Registrar: BINTA MANSARAY (Sierra Leone).

INTERNATIONAL OLYMPIC COMMITTEE

Address: Château de Vidy, 1001 Lausanne, Switzerland.

Telephone: 216216111; **fax:** 216216216; **internet:** www.olympic.org.

The International Olympic Committee was founded in 1894 to ensure the regular celebration of the Olympic Games.

Organization

(April 2012)

INTERNATIONAL OLYMPIC COMMITTEE

The International Olympic Committee (IOC) is a non-governmental international organization comprising 115 members—who are representatives of the IOC in their countries and not their countries' delegates to the IOC, and include 15 active Olympic athletes, 15 National Olympic Committee presidents, 15 International Sports Federation presidents, and 70 other individuals—as well as 24 Honorary members and three Honor members. The members meet in session at least once a year. A Nomination Commission examines and reports to the Executive Board on each candidate for membership of the IOC.

The IOC is the final authority on all questions concerning the Olympic Games and the Olympic Movement. There are 205 recognized National Olympic Committees, which are the sole authorities responsible for the representation of their respective countries at the Olympic Games. The IOC may give recognition to International Federations which undertake to adhere to the Olympic Charter, and which govern sports that comply with the IOC's criteria.

An International Council of Arbitration for Sport (ICAS) has been established. ICAS administers the Court of Arbitration for Sport which hears cases brought by competitors.

EXECUTIVE BOARD

The session of the IOC delegates to the Executive Board the authority to manage the IOC's affairs. The President of the Board is elected for an eight-year term, and is eligible for re-election once for an additional term of four years. The Vice-Presidents are elected for four-year terms, and may be re-elected after a minimum interval of four years. Members of the Board are elected to hold office for four years. The Executive Board generally meets four to five times per year.

President: Dr JACQUES ROGGE (Belgium).

Vice-Presidents: THOMAS BACH (Germany), ZAIQING YU (People's Republic of China), MARIO PESCANTE (Italy), SER MIANG NG (Singapore).

Members of the Board: DENIS OSWALD (Switzerland), RENÉ FASEL (Switzerland), MARIO VÁZQUEZ RAÑA (Mexico), FRANK FREDERICKS (Namibia), NAWAL EL MOUTAWAKEL (Morocco), RICHARD L. CARRIÓN (Puerto Rico), CRAIG REEDIE (United Kingdom), JOHN D. COATES (Australia), SAM RAMSAMY (South Africa), GUNILLA LINSBERG (Sweden).

IOC COMMISSIONS

Athletes' Commission: f. 1981; comprising active and retired athletes, represents their interests; convenes an Athletes' Forum every two years; may issue recommendations to the Executive Board.

Commission for Culture and Olympic Education: f. 2000 by merger of the Culture Commission (f. 1968) and the IOC Commission for the International Olympic Academy and Olympic Education (f. 1961).

Entourage Commission: f. 2010 to address issues relating to members of Olympic athletes' entourages, such as sports coaches and trainers.

Ethics Commission: f. 1999 to develop and monitor rules and principles to guide the selection of hosts for the Olympic Games, and the organization and execution of the Games; the activities of the Ethics Commission are funded by the Foundation for Universal Olympic Ethics, inaugurated in 2001.

Evaluation Commission: prepares a technical assessment of candidate cities' bids to host the Olympic Games, analysing their suitability.

Finance Commission: aims to ensure the efficient management of the IOC's financial resources.

International Relations Commission: f. 2002 to promote a positive relationship between the Olympic Movement and national governments and public authorities.

Juridical Commission: f. 1974 to provide legal opinions and perform other tasks of a legal nature.

Marketing Commission: helps to perpetuate the work of the Olympic Movement through the provision of financial resources and programmes aimed at protecting and enhancing the Olympic image and Olympic values.

Medical Commission: f. 1967; concerned with the protection of the health of athletes, respect for medical and sport ethics, and equality for all competing athletes; a new Olympic Movement Medical Code entered into force in October 2009.

Nominations Commission: f. 1999 to institute a procedure for electing and re-electing IOC members.

Olympic Philately, Numismatic and Memorabilia Commission: f. 1993; aims to increase awareness of the Olympic ideal through the promotion of Olympic commemorative paraphenalia.

Olympic Programme Commission: reviews, and analyses the Olympic programme of sports, disciplines and events; develops recommendations on the principles and structure of the programme.

Olympic Solidarity Commission: f. 1971; assists National Olympic Committees (NOCs); responsible for managing and administering the share of television rights allocated to NOCs.

Press Commission: advises Olympic Games organizing committees on the provision of optimum working conditions for the written and photographic media.

Radio and Television Commission: advises Olympic Games organizing committees and national broadcasting organizations on the provision of the optimum working conditions for the broadcast media.

Sport and Environment Commission: f. 1995 to promote environmental protection and sustainable development.

Sport and Law Commission: f. 1996 to act as a forum for discussion of legal issues concerning the Olympic Movement.

Sport for All Commission: f. 1983 to encourage and support the principles of Sport for All.

TV Rights and New Media Commission: prepares and implements overall IOC strategy for future broadcast rights negotiations.

Women and Sport Commission: f. 2004 (by transformation of a working group, f. 1995 to advise the Executive Board on policies to promote women in sport).

In addition, co-ordination commissions for specific Olympic Games are founded after the election of a host city to oversee and assist the organizing committee in the planning and management of the Games: in March 2012 co-ordination commissions were in force for London Summer Olympic Games 2012; Sochi Winter Olympic Games 2014; Nanjing Youth Olympic Games 2014; Rio de Janeiro Summer Olympic Games 2016; and PyeongChang Winter Olympic Games 2018.

OLYMPIC CONGRESS

Olympic Congresses are held periodically, on particular themes, to gather together the different components of the Olympic Movement with the aim of analysing the Movement's strengths and weaknesses and evaluating ongoing opportunities and challenges. The first Congress (Paris, France, 1894) addressed the theme 'Re-establishment of the Olympic Games'; the most recent, the 13th Congress (Copenhagen, Denmark, October 2009) was convened on the theme 'The Role of the Olympic Movement in Society and in all Regions of the World'.

ADMINISTRATION

The administration of the IOC is under the authority of the Director-General, who is appointed by the Executive Board, on the proposal of the President, and is assisted by Directors responsible for the following administrative sectors: international co-operation; Olympic Games co-ordination; finance, marketing and legal affairs; technology; control and co-ordination of operations; communications; and medical.

Director-General: CHRISTOPHE DE KEPPER.

Activities

The fundamental principles of the Olympic movement are:

Olympism is a philosophy of life, exalting and combining, in a balanced whole, the qualities of body, will and mind. Blending sport with culture, education and respect for the environment, Olympism seeks to create a way of life based on the joy found in effort, the educational value of good example and respect for universal fundamental ethical principles.

Under the supreme authority of the IOC, the Olympic movement encompasses organizations, athletes and other persons who agree to be guided by the Olympic Charter. The criterion for belonging to the Olympic movement is recognition by the IOC.

The goal of the Olympic movement is to contribute to building a peaceful and better world by educating youth through sport practised without discrimination of any kind and in the Olympic spirit, which requires mutual understanding with a spirit of friendship, solidarity and fair play.

The activity of the Olympic movement is permanent and universal. It reaches its peak with the bringing together of the athletes of the world at the great sport festival, the Olympic Games.

The Olympic Charter is the codification of the fundamental principles, rules and bye-laws adopted by the IOC. It governs the organization and operation of the Olympic movement and stipulates the conditions for the celebration of the Olympic Games. In March 1999, following the publication in January of the results of an investigation into allegations of corruption and bribery, an extraordinary session of the IOC was convened, at which the six Committee members were expelled for violating rules relating to Salt Lake City's bid to host the Olympic Winter Games in 2002; four other members had already resigned, while an Executive Board member had received disciplinary action. The President of the IOC retained his position after receiving a vote of confidence. The session approved a number of reform measures, including the establishment of a new independent Ethics Commission to oversee cities' bids to host the Olympic Games, and the establishment of a commission mandated to recommend far-reaching reforms to the internal structure of the organization and to the bidding process. In December 1999, having considered the recommendations of the Commission, the IOC adopted 50 reforms aimed at creating a more open, responsive and accountable organization. These included a new permanent procedure for the elimination of member visits to bid cities, the application of terms of office, limiting the expansion of the Summer Games, and the election of 15 active athletes to the IOC membership.

In response to ongoing concern at drugs abuse in sport an independent World Anti-Doping Agency (WADA) was established by the IOC in November 1999 and, on 1 January 2000, an Anti-Doping Code entered into effect. Participants attending the World Conference on Doping in Sport, held in Copenhagen, Denmark, in March 2003, adopted the Copenhagen Declaration on Doping in Sport and promoted the World Anti-Doping Code, formulated by WADA, as the basis for combating such abuses.

In July 2000 the IOC established a subsidiary International Olympic Truce Foundation, and an International Olympic Truce Centre, based in Athens, Greece, with the aim of promoting a culture of peace through the pursuit of sport and the Olympic ideals. In early 2002 the Olympic Games Study Commission was established to address means of reducing the cost and complexity of the Games. The Commission presented a full report of its findings, incorporating several recommendations for the future organization of the Games, to the 115th Session of the IOC, held in Prague, Czech Republic, in July 2003. The Commission was subsequently dissolved. In November 2002 the Olympic Programme Commission made a full review of the sports programme for the first time since 1936. It decided to cap the number of sports at 28, the number of events at 300, and the number of participating athletes at 10,500.

In July 2007 the IOC determined to establish Summer and Winter Youth Olympic Games (YOG); the first Summer YOG were held in August 2010, in Singapore, and the first Winter YOG were staged in January 2012, in Innsbrück, Austria. In October 2009 the IOC was granted observer status at the UN. The 13th Olympic Congress, convened in that month, in Copenhagen, approved a set of 66 recommendations with a particular emphasis on youth and athletes, including proposals to promote greater engagement by young people in sport; to improve the protection of athletes medically, psychologically, and in retirement; to make full use of new digital technology, and to establish a digital task force in this respect; and to utilize the YOG as a model for youth competition.

ASSOCIATED BODIES

International Committee for Fair Play: Istvánmezei út 1-3, 1146 Budapest, Hungary; tel. (1) 460-6057; fax (1) 460-6956; e-mail cifp@fairplayinternational.org; internet www.fairplayinternational.org; f. 1963 to defend and promote good sportsmanship; organizes annual World Fair Play Awards; Pres. Dr Jenö Kamuti; Sec.-Gen. Jean Durry (France).

World Anti-Doping Agency (WADA): Stock Exchange Tower, Suite 1700, 800 Place Victoria, POB 120 Montréal, QC H4Z 1B7, Canada; tel. (514) 904-9232; fax (514) 904-8650; e-mail info@wada-ama.org; internet www.wada-ama.org; f. 1999; aims to promote and co-ordinate efforts to achieve drug-free sport; principal areas of activity are: code compliance monitoring; co-operation with law enforcement; science and medicine; anti-doping co-ordination; anti-doping development; education; and athlete outreach; Pres. John Fahey; Dir-Gen. David Howman.

THE GAMES OF THE OLYMPIAD

The Olympic Summer Games take place during the first year of the Olympiad (period of four years) that they are to celebrate. They are the exclusive property of the IOC, which entrusts their organization to a host city seven years in advance.

1896 Athens
1900 Paris
1904 St Louis
1908 London
1912 Stockholm
1920 Antwerp
1924 Paris
1928 Amsterdam
1932 Los Angeles
1936 Berlin
1948 London
1952 Helsinki
1956 Melbourne
1960 Rome
1964 Tokyo
1968 Mexico City
1972 Munich
1976 Montreal
1980 Moscow
1984 Los Angeles
1988 Seoul
1992 Barcelona
1996 Atlanta
2000 Sydney
2004 Athens
2008 Beijing
2012 London
2016 Rio de Janeiro

The programme of the Games must include at least 15 of the total number of Olympic sports (sports governed by recognized International Federations and admitted to the Olympic programme by decision of the IOC at least seven years before the Games). The Olympic summer sports are: aquatics (including swimming, diving and water polo); archery; athletics; badminton; baseball; basketball; boxing; canoeing; cycling; equestrian sports; fencing, football; gymnastics; handball; field hockey; judo; modern pentathlon; rowing; sailing; shooting; softball; table tennis; tae kwondo; tennis; triathlon; volleyball; weight-lifting; wrestling.

OLYMPIC WINTER GAMES

The Olympic Winter Games comprise competitions in sports practised on snow and ice. Since 1994 they have been held in the second calendar year following that in which the Games of the Olympiad take place.

1924 Chamonix
1928 St Moritz
1932 Lake Placid
1936 Garmisch-Partenkirchen
1948 St Moritz
1952 Oslo
1956 Cortina d'Ampezzo
1960 Squaw Valley
1964 Innsbrück
1968 Grenoble
1972 Sapporo
1976 Innsbrück
1980 Lake Placid
1984 Sarajevo
1988 Calgary
1992 Albertville
1994 Lillehammer
1998 Nagano
2002 Salt Lake City
2006 Turin
2010 Vancouver
2014 Sochi
2018 Pyeongchang

The Winter Games may include biathlon, bobsleigh, curling, ice hockey, luge, skating, skiing, ski jumping, and snowboarding.

YOUTH OLYMPIC GAMES

Athletes aged between 14 and 18 years may compete in the Youth Olympic Games.

2010 Singapore (Summer)
2012 Innsbrück (Winter)
2014 Nanjing (Summer)
2016 Lillehammer (Winter)

Finance

The IOC derives marketing revenue from the sale of broadcast rights, the Olympic Partners sponsorship Programme, local sponsorship, ticketing, and licensing. Some 8% of this is retained for the Committee's operational budget, with the remainder allocated to Olympic organizing committees, National Olympic Committees and teams, and international sports federations.

Publications

IOC Newsletter (weekly).

Olympic Review (quarterly).

INTERNATIONAL ORGANIZATION FOR MIGRATION—IOM

Address: 17 route des Morillons, CP 71, 1211 Geneva 19, Switzerland.

Telephone: 227179111; **fax:** 227986150; **e-mail:** info@iom.int; **internet:** www.iom.int.

The Intergovernmental Committee for Migration (ICM) was founded in 1951 as a non-political and humanitarian organization with a predominantly operational mandate, including the handling of humane, orderly and planned migration to meet specific needs of emigration and immigration countries; and the processing and movement of refugees, displaced persons and other individuals in need of international migration services to countries offering them resettlement opportunities. In 1989 ICM's name was changed to the International Organization for Migration (IOM). IOM was admitted as an observer to the UN General Assembly in 1992.

MEMBERS

Afghanistan
Albania
Algeria
Angola
Antigua and Barbuda
Argentina
Armenia
Australia
Austria
Azerbaijan
Bahamas
Bangladesh
Belarus
Belgium
Belize
Benin
Bolivia
Bosnia and Herzegovina
Botswana
Brazil
Bulgaria
Burkina Faso
Burundi
Cambodia
Cameroon
Canada
Cape Verde
Central African Republic
Chad
Chile
Colombia
Comoros
Congo, Democratic Republic
Congo, Republic
Costa Rica
Côte d'Ivoire
Croatia
Cyprus
Czech Republic
Denmark
Djibouti
Dominican Republic
Ecuador
Egypt
El Salvador
Estonia
Ethiopia
Finland
France
Gabon
The Gambia
Georgia
Germany
Ghana
Greece
Guatemala
Guinea
Guinea-Bissau
Guyana
Haiti
Holy See
Honduras
Hungary
India
Iran
Ireland
Israel
Italy
Jamaica
Japan
Jordan
Kazakhstan
Kenya
Korea, Republic
Kyrgyzstan
Latvia
Lesotho
Liberia
Libya
Lithuania
Luxembourg
Madagascar
Mali
Maldives
Malta
Mauritania
Mauritius
Mexico
Micronesia, Federated States
Moldova
Mongolia
Montenegro
Morocco
Mozambique
Namibia
Nauru
Nepal
Netherlands
New Zealand
Nicaragua
Niger
Nigeria
Norway
Pakistan
Panama
Paraguay
Peru
Philippines
Poland
Portugal
Romania
Rwanda
Senegal
Serbia
Seychelles
Sierra Leone
Slovakia
Slovenia
Somalia
South Africa
South Sudan
Spain
Sri Lanka
Sudan
Swaziland
Sweden
Switzerland
Tajikistan
Tanzania
Thailand
Timor-Leste
Togo
Trinidad and Tobago
Tunisia
Turkey
Uganda
Ukraine
United Kingdom
USA
Uruguay
Vanuatu
Venezuela
Viet Nam
Yemen
Zambia
Zimbabwe

Observers: Bahrain, Bhutan, People's Republic of China, Cuba, Indonesia, former Yugoslav republic of Macedonia, Papua New Guinea, Qatar, Russia, San Marino, São Tomé and Príncipe, Saudi Arabia and Turkmenistan. In addition, 85 international, governmental and non-governmental organizations hold observer status with IOM.

Organization

(April 2012)

IOM is governed by a Council that is composed of representatives of all member governments, and has the responsibility for making final decisions on policy, programmes and financing. An Executive Committee of nine member governments elected by the Council examines and reviews the organization's work; considers and reports on any matter specifically referred to it by the Council; advises the Director-General on any matters that he may refer to it; makes, between sessions of the Council, any urgent decisions on matters falling within the competence of the Council, which are then submitted for approval by the Council; and presents advice or proposals to the Council or the Director-General on its own initiative. The Director-General is responsible to the Council and the Executive Committee. Alongside the Director-General's Office there are offices of International Migration Law and Legal Affairs; Management Co-ordination; Information Technology and Communications; and Gender Co-ordination. In recent years IOM has transferred some administrative functions from its headquarters to two administrative centres, located in Manila, Philippines, and Ciudad del Saber, Panama. Plans are under way to establish a Capacity-Building Office in Africa. In July 2010 a Field Implementation Team was established, mandated to oversee a reorganization of IOM's field activities, including the establishment of eight new regional offices.

Director-General: WILLIAM LACY SWING (USA).

Deputy Director-General: LAURA THOMPSON CHACÓN (Costa Rica).

Activities

IOM aims to provide assistance to member governments in meeting the operational challenges of migration, to advance understanding of migration issues, to encourage social and economic development through migration and to work towards effective respect of the human dignity and well-being of migrants. It provides a full range of migration assistance to, and sometimes de facto protection of, migrants, refugees, displaced persons and other individuals in need of international migration services. This includes recruitment, selection, processing, medical examinations, and language and cultural orientation courses, placement, activities to facilitate reception and integration and other advisory services. IOM co-ordinates its refugee activities with the UN High Commissioner for Refugees (UNHCR) and with governmental and non-governmental partners. In May 1997 IOM and UNHCR signed a memorandum of understanding that aimed to facilitate co-operation between the two organizations. Since it commenced operations in February 1952 IOM is estimated to have provided assistance to more than 12m. migrants. IOM estimates that migrants comprise some 3% of the global population, and that some 15%–20% of migrant movements are unregulated. In 2010 IOM provided movement assistance to 269,931 individuals, including the resettlement of 101,685 refugees, and repatriation of a further 13,196. During 2010 IOM undertook 2,302 active projects, of which 690 were initiated in that year; some 33% of the total number of projects were implemented in Europe, 21% in Africa, and 19% in Asia and Oceania. In 2010 38% of ongoing projects related to regulating migration (38%), 28% to movement, emergency and post-crisis migration management, and 10% to facilitating migration.

IOM's International Migration Law (IML) and Legal Affairs Department promotes awareness and knowledge of the legal instruments that govern migration at national, regional and international level; provides training and capacity-building services connected with IML; and researches IML. IOM maintains an international database of IML.

IOM provides information and advice to support the efforts of governments and other stakeholders to formulate effective national, regional and global migration management policies and strategies; and conducts research, aimed at guiding migration policy and practice, in areas including migration trends and data, IML, migration and development, health and migration, counter-trafficking, labour migration, trade, remittances, irregular migration, integration and return migration.

IOM was a founder member with other international organizations of the inter-agency Global Migration Group (GMG, established as the Geneva Migration Group in April 2003 and renamed in 2006). The GMG provides a framework for discussion among the heads of member organizations on the application of decisions and norms relating to migration, and for stronger leadership in addressing related issues. Since 2007 the GMG has organized an annual Global Forum for Migration and Development (GFMD). The 2010 GFMD, convened in Puerto Vallarta, Mexico, in November, addressed the theme 'Partnerships for Migration and Human Development—Shared Prosperity, Shared Responsibility'. The 2011 GFMD took the form of a series of decentralized small-scale action-oriented meetings world-wide, focused on the theme 'Action on Migration and Development—Coherence, Capacity and Co-operation', and culminated in a final conference of Friends of the GFMD, held in Geneva, in December. GFMD 2012 was to be hosted by Mauritius, in accordance with the traditional centralized format, with a main meeting to be convened towards the end of the year.

In October 2005 IOM's Director-General inaugurated a new Business Advisory Board, comprising 13 business leaders representing a cross section of global concerns. It was envisaged that the initiative would promote an effective partnership between IOM and the private sector aimed at supporting the planning, development and implementation of improved mobility policies and practices.

IOM acknowledges a direct link between migration and both climate change and environmental degradation; so-called 'environmental migration' (both cross-border and internal) is particularly prevalent in the world's poorest countries. In March 2011 IOM organized a workshop aimed at assisting the international community in preparing for environmental migration.

In June 2007 the IOM Council adopted a comprehensive 12-point strategy, which was to be incorporated into all of the activities of the organization.

IOM operates within the framework of the main service areas outlined below.

MIGRATION AND DEVELOPMENT

IOM places a strategic focus on advancing a positive relationship between migration and development; on fostering a deeper understanding of the linkages between migration and development; and on enhancing the benefits that well-managed migration can have for the development, growth and prosperity of migrants' countries of origin and of destination, as well as for the migrants personally. IOM's activities in this area include strengthening the capacity of governments and other stakeholders to engage expatriate migrant communities in development processes in their countries of origin; promoting economic and community development in places from which there is a high level of emigration; enhancing the development impact of remittances; and facilitating the return and reintegration of qualified nationals. There are two main branches of Migration and Development programming: Migration and Economic/Community Development; and Capacity Building Through Qualified Human Resources and Experts.

IOM's Migration and Economic/Community Development programme area covers three principal fields of activity. First, IOM seeks to maximize the positive potential from migration for the development of countries of origin and destination, promoting an increase in more development-oriented migration policies, and implementing initiatives aimed at building the capacity of governments and other stakeholders in countries of origin to involve their migrant populations in home country development projects. Second, IOM aims to address the root causes of economically motivated migration by assisting governments and other actors with the strategic focusing of development activities to expand economic opportunities and improve social services and infrastructures in regions experiencing outward or returning migration. Third, IOM promotes data collection, policy dialogue and dissemination of good practices, and pilot project implementation, in the area of remittances (funds sent home by migrant workers, mainly in the form of private money transfers), with the aim of improving the development impact of remittances. IOM helped to organize the Global Consultation on Migration, Remittances and Development: Responding to the Global Economic Crisis from a Gender Perspective, which was convened in June–July 2009, in Switzerland; the meeting adopted a communiqué detailing policy recommendations.

IOM's Capacity Building Through Qualified Human Resources and Experts programme area focuses on the return from abroad and socio-economic reintegration of skilled and qualified nationals. Return and Reintegration of Qualified Nationals (RQN) and similar projects include recruitment, job placement, transport and limited employment support services, and aim to influence the economic and social environment in countries of origin in a manner conducive to further returns. IOM also focuses on the recruitment and selection of highly trained workers and professionals to fill positions in priority sectors of the economy in developing countries for which qualified persons are not available locally, taking into account national development priorities as well as the needs and concerns of receiving communities.

A programme to encourage the Return and Reintegration of Qualified Afghan Nationals (RQAFN), co-funded by the European Commission, and a Return and Reintegration of Qualified Nationals to Sudan programme, were ongoing in 2012. In 2005 IOM, the United Nations Volunteers (UNV) and the Iraqi Government established an ongoing RQN–Transfer of Knowledge Through Expatriate Nationals (TOKTEN) programme for Iraq, known as 'Iraqis Rebuilding Iraq', with funding from the International Reconstruction Fund Facility for Iraq. In addition, IOM operates the Migration for Development in Africa (MIDA) institutional capacity-building programme, which provides a framework for transferring skills and resources from African migrants to their countries of origin. For example, in 2012 a MIDA project was encouraging expatriate Ghanaian health professionals to provide training to health workers in Ghana. IOM and the UN Development Programme (UNDP) jointly implement the Qualified Expatriate Somali Technical Support (QUESTS)-MIDA scheme, which aims to engage technical expertise in the areas of policy and legislation, human resources management, and public financial management, among the Somali diaspora, to support the rebuilding of key governance foundations in parts of Somalia. IOM and the European Union jointly fund a scheme to support Rwandan students abroad and encourage their return to Rwanda.

In 2010 migrants were estimated to have remitted some US $325,000m. to developing countries of origin. In March 2009 IOM and FAO agreed to collaborate on supporting agricultural projects in home countries funded by remittances from migrants in OECD member states.

From April 2006–June 2008 IOM and the Netherlands Government undertook the Temporary Return of Qualified Nationals (TRQN) project, with the aim of supporting reconstruction and development efforts in Afghanistan, Bosnia and Herzegovina, Kosovo, Montenegro, Serbia, Sierra Leone and Sudan. Under the TRQN, IOM provided logistical and financial assistance to experts originating in any of the target countries who were also nationals of or had residence in the Netherlands, to help them participate in projects aimed at enriching the target countries. TRQN II was undertaken during July 2009–July 2011, in support of development efforts in Afghanistan, Bosnia and Herzegovina, Ethiopia, Georgia, Sierra Leone and Sudan.

IOM offers Assisted Voluntary Return (AVR) services to migrants and governments, with the aim of facilitating the efficient and humane return and reintegration of migrants who wish to repatriate voluntarily to their countries of origin. Pre-departure, transportation and post-arrival assistance is provided to unsuccessful asylum seekers, migrants in irregular situations, migrants stranded in transit, stranded students, etc. AVR services can be tailored to the particular needs of specific groups, such as vulnerable migrants. IOM established a Stranded Migrant Facility in 2005.

During October 2006–October 2007 IOM implemented the pilot Return and Reintegration in Countries of Origin (IRRiCO) project, which aimed to establish an internet-based database of relevant information in support of voluntary returns and reintegration, for use both by service providers and by migrants considering returning home. IRRiCO II, with the participation of 20 countries of origin and nine European countries, was launched in September 2008.

The IOM Development Fund (founded in 2001 as the '1035 Facility', and renamed in January 2012) supports developing member states and member states with economies in transition with the implementation of migration management capacity-building projects. By March 2012 some 370 projects in 112 member states had been supported by the Facility, at a cost of US $32m.

FACILITATING MIGRATION

Integrated world markets, transnational business networks and the rapid growth of ICTs have contributed to large-scale movements of workers, students, family members, and other migrants. IOM implements programmes that assist governments and migrants with recruitment, language training, pre-departure cultural orientation, pre-consular support services, arrival reception, and integration, and has introduced initiatives in areas including document verification, migrant information, interviews, applicant testing and logistical support. There are three main branches of Facilitating Migration programming: Labour Migration; Migrant Processing and Assistance; and Migrant Integration.

Through its Labour Migration activities, IOM aims to promote regulated orderly labour migration while combating illegal, often clandestine, migration; and and to foster the economic and social development of countries of origin, transit and destination. Jointly with governments and other agencies, IOM has developed specific labour migration programmes that include elements such as capacity building; pre-departure training; return and reintegration support; and regional dialogue and planning.

Through its Migrant Processing and Assistance activities IOM provides assistance to facilitate migration under organized and regular migration schemes that are tailored to meet specific programme needs and cover the different stages of the migration process: information and application, interview and approval, and post-approval (including pre-departure counselling and cultural orientation). Similar assistance is also provided to experts participating in international technical co-operation activities, to students studying abroad and, in some cases, to their dependents.

IOM's Migration Integration activities promote strategies aimed at enabling migrants to adjust easily to new environments abroad and focus on the dissemination of information on the rights and obligations of migrants and refugees in home and in host countries, the provision of advisory and counselling services, and the reinforcement of their skills. In addition IOM promotes awareness-raising activities in host societies that highlight the positive contributions that migrants can make, with a view to reducing the risks of discrimination and xenophobia.

REGULATING MIGRATION

IOM aims to counter the growing problem of smuggling and trafficking in migrants, which has resulted in several million people being exploited by criminal agents and employers. IOM aims to provide shelter and assistance for victims of trafficking; to provide legal and medical assistance to migrants uncovered in transit or in the receiving country; and to offer voluntary return and reintegration assistance. The organization maintains the IOM Global Human Trafficking Information Management System (also known as the IOM Global Database), which aims to facilitate the management of assistance for victims of trafficking. IOM organizes mass information campaigns in countries of origin, in order to highlight the risks of smuggling and trafficking, and aims to raise general awareness of the problem. The most common countries of origin covered in the database are Belarus, Bulgaria, the Dominican Republic, Moldova, Romania and Ukraine. IOM also provides training to increase the capacity of governments and other organizations to counter irregular migration. Since 1996 IOM has worked in Cambodia and Thailand to help victims of trafficking to return home. A transit centre has been established on the border between the two countries, where assessments are carried out, advice is given, and the process of tracing families is undertaken. IOM has campaigned for the prevention of trafficking in women from the Baltic states. IOM launched a series of new training modules in November 2006, designed to enhance the knowledge and understanding of the issues of human trafficking.

Through its Technical Co-operation on Migration Division, IOM offers advisory services to governments on the optimum administrative structures, policy, legislation, operational systems and human resource systems required to regulate migration. IOM technical co-operation also focuses on capacity-building projects such as training courses for government migration officials, and analysis of and suggestions for solving emerging migration problems. Throughout these activities, IOM aims to maintain an emphasis on the rights and well-being of migrants, and in particular to ensure that the specific needs of migrant women are incorporated into programmes and policies.

In October 2009 IOM launched a campaign entitled 'What Lies Behind the Things We Buy?', which aimed to draw attention to the use of trafficked and exploited labour in the manufacture of cheap goods.

MOVEMENT, EMERGENCY AND POST-CRISIS RESPONSE

IOM provides services to assist with the resettlement of individuals accepted under regular national immigration programmes; these include: supporting the processing of relevant documentation; medical screening; arranging safe transportation; and, in some cases, the provision of language training and cultural orientation. IOM also assists with the voluntary repatriation of refugees, mainly in support of UNHCR's voluntary repatriation activities.

In emergency situations IOM provides transportation and humanitarian assistance to individuals requiring evacuation, as well as providing support to countries of temporary protection. IOM supports internally displaced populations through the provision of emergency shelter and relief materials. Post-emergency movement assistance for returning displaced populations is also provided (mainly internally displaced perons—IDPs, demobilized soldiers and persons affected by natural disasters). In post-crisis situations it actively supports governments in the reconstruction and rehabilitation of affected communities and offers short-term community and micro-enterprise development programmes. In such situations IOM's activities may include health sector assistance and counter-trafficking awareness activities, psycho-social support, capacity building for disaster transportation and logistics; and registration and information management of affected populations.

During 2005 the UN developed a concept of organizing humanitarian agency assistance to IDPs through the institutionalization of a 'Cluster Approach', currently comprising 11 core areas of activity. IOM was designated the lead humanitarian agency for the cluster on Camp Co-ordination and Management in natural disaster situations (UNHCR was to lead that cluster in conflict situations).

Since April 2003, following the launching in March of US-led military action against the Saddam Hussain regime in Iraq, IOM has been lead organization for emergency distributions of food and non-food items (NFIs) for the displaced population inside Iraq, and has co-ordinated the assessment and monitoring of Iraqi IDPs, including providing data on their numbers, locations and needs. IOM works to restore essential services, including the provision of drinking water, good sanitation, health, and education, in central and southern Iraq. By 2012 IOM had established community management teams and technical consultative boards in Iraq, with a view to empowering local communities to identify and implement sustainable long-term development structures. In April 2009 IOM was appointed the partner with responsibility for transportation of NFIs in the UN-managed 'common pipeline' operation for Darfur and northern Sudan; by December IOM had delivered about 2.3m. NFIs in Darfur. IOM was responsible for organizing the out-of-country registration and voting process for the referendum on independence for southern Sudan that took place in January 2011; following its attainment of independence in July 2011, South Sudan became a member of IOM.

CLAIMS PROGRAMMES

IOM was designated as one of the implementing organizations of the settlement agreement concluded between survivors of the Nazi Holocaust and Swiss banks. IOM established the Holocaust Victim Assets Programme (HVAP) to process claims made by certain target groups. A German Forced Labour Compensation Programme (GFLCP) was founded to process applications for claims of forced labour and personal injury and for property loss. By September 2005 IOM had recommended payment in respect of 18,431 of a total of 49,371 claims received under the HVAP, while claims received under the GFLCP included 332,307 for slave and forced labour, 41,837 for personal injury and 34,997 for property loss. Under the terms of the settlement agreement, with regard to 'looted assets', IOM was mandated to distribute US $20.5m. to humanitarian programmes, specifically to assist elderly Roma and Sinti, Jehovah's Witnesses, disabled and homosexual victims and targets of Nazi persecution. The HVAP and GFLCP were terminated in December 2006.

IOM provides assistance and advice to the Commission for Resolution of Real Property Disputes (CRRPD), an independent agency of the Government of Iraq that was established in March 2006 to resolve claims on property in Iraq relating to the period 17 July 1968–9 April 2003.

In 2012 IOM was implementing a 'Technical Assistance to the Administrative Reparation Programme in Colombia' initiative, launched in January 2008, with the aim of supporting the Colombian authorities in compensating—as an act of solidarity—the victims of violence inflicted by illegal armed militia in that country.

MIGRATION HEALTH

IOM's Migration Health Department aims to ensure that migrants are fit to travel, do not pose a danger to those travelling with them, and that they receive medical attention and care when necessary. IOM also undertakes research and other technical support and policy development activities in the field of health care. Medical screening of prospective migrants is routinely conducted, along with immunizations and specific counselling, e.g. for HIV/AIDS. IOM administers programmes for disabled refugees and undertakes medical evacuation of people affected by conflict. Under its programmes for health assistance and advice, IOM conducts health education programmes, training for health professionals in post-conflict regions, and assessments of availability and access to health care for migrant populations. IOM provides assistance for post-emergency returning populations, through the rehabilitation of health infrastructures; provision of medical supplies; mental health programmes, including psychosocial support; and training of personnel.

IOM collaborates with government health authorities and relevant intergovernmental and non-governmental organizations. In September 1999 IOM and UNAIDS signed a co-operation framework to promote awareness on HIV/AIDS issues relating to displaced populations, and to ensure that the needs of migrants are incorporated into national and regional AIDS strategies. In October IOM and the World Health Organization (WHO) signed an agreement to strengthen collaborative efforts to improve the health care of migrants. IOM maintains a database of its tuberculosis diagnostic and treatment programmes, which facilitates the management of the disease. An information system on immigration medical screening data was being developed to help to analyse disease trends among migrants.

International Centre for Migration and Health

11 route du Nant-d'Avril, 1214 Geneva, Vernier, Switzerland; tel. 227831080; fax 227831087; e-mail secretariat@icmhd.ch; internet www.icmhd.ch.

Established in March 1995, by IOM and the University of Geneva, with the support of WHO, to respond to the growing needs for information, documentation, research, training and policy development in migration health; designated as a WHO collaborating centre for health-related issues among people displaced by disasters.

Executive Director: Dr MANUEL CARBALLO.

Finance

IOM's proposed operational budget for 2012 totalled US $615.4m.

Publications

Global Eye on Human Trafficking (quarterly).
International Migration (quarterly).
IOM Harare Newsletter.
IOM News (quarterly, in English, French and Spanish).
Migration (2 a year).
Migration and Climate Change.
Migration Health Annual Report.
Report by the Director-General (in English, French and Spanish).
Trafficking in Migrants (quarterly).
World Migration Report (annually).
Research reports, *IOM Info Sheets* surveys and studies.

INTERNATIONAL RED CROSS AND RED CRESCENT MOVEMENT

The International Red Cross and Red Crescent Movement is a world-wide independent humanitarian organization, comprising three main components: the International Committee of the Red Cross (ICRC), founded in 1863; the International Federation of Red Cross and Red Crescent Societies (the Federation), founded in 1919; and National Red Cross and Red Crescent Societies in 185 countries; as well as Magen David Adom, an Israeli society equivalent to the Red Cross and Red Crescent Societies. In 1997 all constituent parts of the Movement adopted the Seville Agreement on co-operation in the undertaking of international relief activities. The Agreement excludes activities that are entrusted to individual components by the statutes of the Movement or the Geneva Conventions.

Organization

INTERNATIONAL CONFERENCE

The supreme deliberative body of the Movement, the Conference comprises delegations from the ICRC, the Federation and the National Societies, and of representatives of States Parties to the Geneva Conventions (see below). The Conference's function is to determine the general policy of the Movement and to ensure unity in the work of the various bodies. It usually meets every four to five years, and is hosted by the National Society of the country in which it is held. The 30th International Conference was held in Geneva, Switzerland, in November 2007.

The 29th International Conference, held in Geneva in June 2006, approved membership of the Palestinian Red Crescent Society and the Israeli society Magen David Adom. A Third Additional Protocol (Protocol III—see below) to the Geneva Conventions was adopted in December 2005 and entered into force in January 2007. Protocol III recognizes as third emblem of the Movement a red crystal, which is deemed to be a neutral symbol devoid of political or religious connotations.

STANDING COMMISSION

The Commission meets at least twice a year in ordinary session. It promotes harmony in the work of the Movement, and examines matters which concern the Movement as a whole. It is formed of two representatives of the ICRC, two of the Federation, and five members of National Societies elected by the Conference.

COUNCIL OF DELEGATES

The Council comprises delegations from the National Societies, from the ICRC and from the Federation. The Council is the body where the representatives of all the components of the Movement meet to discuss matters that concern the Movement as a whole.

In November 1997 the Council adopted an Agreement on the organization of the activities of the Movement's components. The Agreement aimed to promote increased co-operation and partnership between the Movement's bodies, clearly defining the distribution of tasks between agencies. In particular, the Agreement aimed to ensure continuity between international operations carried out in a crisis situation and those developed in its aftermath.

Fundamental Principles of the Movement

Humanity: The International Red Cross and Red Crescent Movement, born of a desire to bring assistance without discrimination to the wounded on the battlefield, endeavours, in its international and national capacity, to prevent and alleviate human suffering wherever it may be found. Its purpose is to protect life and health and to ensure respect for the human being. It promotes mutual understanding, friendship, co-operation and lasting peace among all peoples.

Impartiality: It makes no discrimination as to nationality, race, religious beliefs, class or political opinions. It endeavours to relieve the suffering of individuals, being guided solely by their needs, and to give priority to the most urgent cases of distress.

Neutrality: In order to continue to enjoy the confidence of all, the Movement may not take sides in hostilities or engage in controversies of a political, racial, religious or ideological nature.

Independence: The Movement is independent. The National Societies, while auxiliaries in the humanitarian services of their governments and subject to national laws, must retain their autonomy so that they may always be able to act in accordance with the principles of the Movement.

Voluntary Service: It is a voluntary relief movement not prompted by desire for gain.

Unity: There can be only one Red Cross or Red Crescent Society in any one country. It must be open to all. It must carry on its humanitarian work throughout the territory.

Universality: The International Red Cross and Red Crescent Movement, in which all National Societies have equal status and share equal responsibilities and duties in helping each other, is world-wide.

International Committee of the Red Cross—ICRC

Address: 19 ave de la Paix, 1202 Geneva, Switzerland.

Telephone: 227346001; **fax:** 227332057; **e-mail:** press.gva@icrc.org; **internet:** www.icrc.org.

Founded in 1863, the ICRC is at the origin of the Red Cross and Red Crescent Movement, and co-ordinates all international humanitarian activities conducted by the Movement in situations of conflict. New statutes of the ICRC, incorporating a revised institutional structure, entered into force in July 1998.

The ICRC is an independent institution of a private character composed exclusively of Swiss nationals. Members are co-opted, and their total number may not exceed 25. The international character of the ICRC is based on its mission and not on its composition.

Organization

(April 2012)

ASSEMBLY

The Assembly is the supreme governing body of the ICRC. It formulates policy, defines the Committee's general objectives and strategies, oversees its activities, and approves its budget and accounts. The Assembly is composed of the members of the ICRC, and is collegial in character. The President and Vice-Presidents of the ICRC hold the same offices in the Assembly.

President: Jakob Kellenberger.

Vice-Presidents: Christine Beerli, Olivier Vodoz.

ASSEMBLY COUNCIL

The Council (formerly the Executive Board) is a subsidiary body of the Assembly, to which the latter delegates certain of its responsibilities. It prepares the Assembly's activities and takes decisions on matters within its competence. The Council is composed of five members elected by the Assembly and is chaired by the President of the ICRC.

Members: Jakob Kellenberger, Christine Beerli, Claude le Coultre, Rolf Soiron, Bruno Staffelbach.

DIRECTORATE

The Directorate is the executive body of the ICRC, overseeing the efficient running of the organization and responsible for the application of the general objectives and institutional strategies decided by the Assembly. Members are appointed by the Assembly to serve a four-year term.

Director-General: Yves Daccord.

Members: Pierre Krähenbühl (Director of Operations), Helen Alderson (Director of Financial Resources and Logistics), Charlotte Lindsey-Curtet (Director of Communication and Information Management), Philip Spoerri (Director for International Law and Co-operation within the Movement), Caroline Welch-Ballentine (Director of Human Resources).

Activities

The International Committee of the Red Cross was founded in 1863 in Geneva, by Henry Dunant and four of his friends. The original purpose of the Committee was to promote the foundation, in every country, of a voluntary relief society to assist wounded soldiers on the battlefield (the origin of the National Societies of the Red Cross or Red Crescent), as well as the adoption of a treaty protecting wounded soldiers and all those who come to their rescue. The mission of the ICRC was progressively extended through the Geneva Conventions (see below). The present activities of the ICRC consist in giving legal protection and material assistance to military and civilian victims of wars (international wars, internal strife and disturbances), in promoting and monitoring the application of international humanitarian law (IHL), and, in recent years, in providing humanitarian assistance in situations of violence other than armed conflicts: in 2011 the ICRC provided emergency assistance to civilians affected by violent disturbances in Egypt, Syria, Tunisia and Yemen. The ICRC takes into account the legal standards and the specific cultural, ethical and religious features of the environment in which it operates. It aims to influence the conduct of all actual and potential perpetrators of violence by seeking direct dialogue with combatants. In 1990 the ICRC was granted observer status at the UN General Assembly. The ICRC overall programme of activities covers the following areas:

The protection of vulnerable individuals and groups under IHL, including activities related to ensuring respect for detainees (monitoring prison conditions), respect for civilians, reuniting relatives separated in conflict situations and restoring family links, and tracing missing persons;

The implementation of assistance activities, aimed at restoring a sufficient standard of living to victims of armed conflict, including the provision of medical aid and emergency food supplies, initiatives to improve water supply, basic infrastructure and access to health care, and physical rehabilitation assistance (for example to assist civilians injured by landmines);

Preventive action, including the development and implementation of IHL and dissemination of humanitarian principles, with a view to protecting non-combatants from violence;

The use of humanitarian diplomacy to raise awareness of humanitarian issues among states and within international organizations;

Building private sector relations;

Co-operation with National Societies.

The ICRC Advisory Service, established in 1996, offers legal and technical assistance to national authorities with incorporating IHL into their national legislation, assists them in their implementation of IHL, maintains a database on IHL, and publishes specialist documents. A Documentation Centre has also been established for exchanging information on national measures and activities aimed at promoting humanitarian law in countries. The Centre is open to all states and National Societies, as well as to interested institutions and the general public. In 2010 the ICRC maintained contact with the military in some 160 countries, with nearly 80 armed militia, and with a number of private military and security companies with the intention of ensuring that they are knowledgable about and comply with IHL. A Senior Workshop on International Rules Governing Military Operations is organized annually by the ICRC to provide guidance to combatants.

In April 1998 the Assembly endorsed a plan of action, based on the following four priorities identified by the 'Avenir' project to define the organization's future role, that had been launched in 1996: improving the status of international humanitarian action and knowledge of and respect for IHL; carrying out humanitarian action in closer proximity to victims, with long-term plans and identified priorities; strengthening dialogue with all parties (including launching joint appeals with other organizations if necessary); and increasing the ICRC's efficiency. In December 2003 the 28th International Conference of the Red Cross and Red Crescent adopted an Agenda for Humanitarian Action. The main components of the Agenda, which had the overall theme 'protecting human dignity', were: respecting and restoring the dignity of persons and families missing as a result of conflict situations; strengthening controls on weapons development, proliferation and use; lessening the impact of disasters through the implementation of disaster risk reduction measures and improving preparedness and response mechanisms; and reducing vulnerability to the effects of disease associated with lack of access to comprehensive prevention, care and treatment.

The ICRC's Institutional Strategy covering the period 2011–14 focused on the following four priority areas: reinforcing the ICRC's scope of action; strengthening the Committee's contextualized, multidisciplinary response; shaping the debate on legal and policy issues related to the Committee's mission; and optimizing the Committee's performance. The ICRC has noted in recent years that, while some conflicts remain underpinned by territorial or ideological disputes, increasing numbers of conflicts and so-called situations of violence are being fuelled by pressure to secure control over natural resources, and that there is evidence of increasing activity by economically predatory armed elements. Fragile humanitarian situations are complicated by other factors, including weapons proliferation; environmental degradation; mass migration to cities and increased urban violence; and acts of terrorism and anti-terrorism operations. The ICRC has identified two principal challenges to the neutral and independent implementation of its humanitarian activities: developing a refined understanding of the diversity and specificity of armed conflicts and other situations of violence; and addressing meaningfully the many needs of affected civilian populations. During 2011–15 the ICRC was undertaking a Health Care in Danger project, which aimed to enhance protection of the sick and wounded, and address other negative impacts, in cases where illegal and violent acts obstruct the delivery of health provision or endanger health care staff, during armed conflict and other situations of violence.

The ICRC consistently reviews the 1980 UN Convention on prohibitions or restrictions on the use of certain conventional weapons which may be deemed to be excessively injurious or to have indiscriminate effects and its protocols. In September 1997 the ICRC participated in an international conference, held in Oslo, Norway, which adopted the Convention on the Prohibition of the Use, Stockpiling, Production and Transfer of Anti-personnel Mines and on their Destruction. The Convention entered into force on 1 March 1999. In April 1998 the Swiss Government established a Geneva International Centre for Humanitarian Demining, in co-operation with the UN and the ICRC, to co-ordinate the destruction of landmines world-wide. The ICRC was a principal advocate for the formulation of the Convention on Cluster Munitions, which was opened for signature in December 2008, and entered into force on 1 August 2010.

In 1995 the ICRC adopted a Plan of Action concerning Children in Armed Conflicts, to promote the principle of non-recruitment and non-participation in armed conflict of children under the age of 18 years. A co-ordinating group was established, with representatives of the individual National Societies and the International Federation of Red Cross and Red Crescent Societies. The ICRC participated in drafting the Optional Protocol to the Convention on the Rights of the Child, which was adopted by the UN General Assembly in May 2000 and entered into force in February 2002, raising from 15 to 18 years the minimum age for recruitment in armed conflict.

The ICRC's presence in the field is organized under the following three categories: responsive action, aimed at addressing the immediate effects of crises; remedial action, with an emphasis on rehabilitation; and environment-building activities, aimed at creating political, institutional, humanitarian and economic situations that are suitable for generating respect for human rights. ICRC operational delegations focus on responsive action and remedial action, while environment-building is undertaken by ICRC regional delegations. The regional delegations undertake humanitarian diplomacy efforts (e.g. networking, promoting IHL and distributing information), logistical support to operational delegations, and their own operations; they also have an early warning function, alerting the ICRC to developing conflict situations. The ICRC targets its activities at the following groups: 'victims', comprising civilians affected by violent crises, people deprived of their freedom, and the wounded and sick (whether civilians or weapon-bearers); and institutions and individuals with influence, i.e. national and local authorities, security forces, representatives of civil society, and ICRC National Societies. Children, women, internally displaced people and missing persons are of particular concern to the ICRC.

The ICRC's 'Family Links' internet pages (accessible at www.familylinks.icrc.org) aim to reunite family members separated by conflict or disaster situations. In February 2003 the ICRC launched 'The Missing', a major initiative that aimed to raise awareness of the issue of persons unaccounted for owing to armed conflict or internal violence. The ICRC assisted with the preparation of the International Convention for the Protection of all Persons from Enforced Disappearance, adopted by the UN General Assembly in December 2006, and representing the first international treaty to prohibit practices facilitating enforced disappearance. Meeting in November 2007 prior to the 30th International Conference, the Council of Delegates adopted the Restoring Family Links Strategy for the International Red Cross and Red Crescent Movement, covering the period 2008–18.

In 2007 the ICRC adopted a rapid deployment and response approach. During 2010 this was used to meet large-scale humanitarian requirements following the devastating earthquake that struck Haiti in January, and following the eruption in June of violent inter-ethnic unrest in Kyrgyzstan. In 2011 rapid deployment and response were deployed in Côte d'Ivoire, affected by serious unrest early in the year following a disputed presidential election result in November 2010, and also in Libya, where unrest and conflict also prevailed from early 2011, and where the ICRC had no previous operational framework.

During 2010 ICRC representatives visited some 500,928 prisoners (30,674 individually) held in 1,783 places of detention in 71 countries world-wide. A total of 160,338 messages were collected from and 145,114 distributed to family members separated by conflict; and 12,795 phone calls were facilitated between family members. Some 3,822 individuals who were the subject of other tracing requests were located; 1,983 unaccompanied minors and separated children were reunited with their families; and some 614 demobilized child soldiers were reunited with their families. Regular substantial assistance was provided to 294 hospitals, 351 health care facilities, and to 81 physical rehabilitation centres world-wide. Food was distributed by the ICRC in that year to more than 4.9m. beneficiaries and essential household and hygiene items to more than 4.7m. ICRC activities in the areas of water, sanitation and construction benefited some 10m. people and ICRC sustainable food production programmes and micro-economic initiatives supported more than 3.2m. people.

In 2012 the ICRC was actively concerned with around 80 conflicts and was undertaking major operations in (in order of budgetary priority): Afghanistan (provisionally allocated 88.9m. Swiss francs), Somalia (70.2m.), Iraq (67.3m.), Pakistan (66.2m.), the Democratic Republic of the Congo (54.1m.), Sudan (54.6m.), Israel and the Palestinian territories (52.6), Yemen (37.6m.), Colombia (33.1m.), and South Sudan (which attained independence in July 2011) (25.0m.).

In 2011 around 1,780 ICRC personnel were deployed in Afghanistan. Activities included protecting detainees and enabling them to maintain contact with their families; monitoring the conduct of hostilities and supporting the implementation of IHL; assisting the disabled and wounded; supporting the provision of hospital care; improving water and sanitation services; and building the capacity of the Afghan Red Crescent Society. From October 2010 Somalia was affected by severe drought, prompting the ICRC, working with the Somali Red Crescent Society (SCRS), to provide food assistance to more than 800,000 people. During June–October 2011 the ICRC and SCRS launched 11 new outpatient therapeutic feeding programmes and nine mobile health teams; the ICRC also delivered water to 11 drought-affected areas of Somalia, benefiting up to 700,000 persons and their livestock, as well as renovating 46 water supply infrastructures, with a view to improving groundwater sources and surface water storage facilities. During 2011 the ICRC also distributed essential household items to more than 260,000 new Somali IDPs, displaced by conflict, and provided seeds and tools to nearly 100,000 farmers, with the aim of boosting food production.

In April 2009 the ICRC and IFRC launched a joint website, www.ourworld-yourmove.org, which aimed to highlight ongoing humanitarian crises.

THE GENEVA CONVENTIONS

Since its inception the ICRC has been a leader in the process of improving and complementing IHL. In 1864, one year after its foundation, the ICRC submitted to the states called to a Diplomatic Conference in Geneva a draft international treaty for 'the Amelioration of the Condition of the Wounded in Armies in the Field'. This treaty was adopted and signed by 12 states, which thereby bound themselves to respect as neutral wounded soldiers and those assisting them. This was the first Geneva Convention.

With the development of technology and weapons, the introduction of new means of waging war, and the manifestation of certain phenomena (the great number of prisoners of war during World War I; the enormous number of displaced persons and refugees during World War II; the internationalization of internal conflicts in recent years), it was considered necessary to develop other international treaties to protect new categories of war victims.

There are now four Geneva Conventions, adopted on 12 August 1949: I—to protect wounded and sick in armed forces on land, as well as medical personnel; II—to protect the same categories of people at sea, as well as the shipwrecked; III—concerning the treatment of prisoners of war; IV—for the protection of civilians in time of war. Two Additional Protocols were adopted on 8 June 1977, for the protection of victims in international armed conflicts (Protocol I) and in non-international armed conflicts (Protocol II). A Third Additional Protocol (Protocol III), endorsing the red crystal as an additional emblem of the Movement, was adopted on 8 December 2005 and entered into force on 14 January 2007.

By April 2012 194 states were parties to the Geneva Conventions; 171 were parties to Protocol I, 166 to Protocol II and 59 to Protocol III.

Finance

The ICRC's work is financed by a voluntary annual grant from governments parties to the Geneva Conventions, the European Commission, voluntary contributions from National Red Cross and Red Crescent Societies and by gifts and legacies from private donors. The ICRC's provisional budget for 2012 allocated 180.8m. Swiss francs to headquarters, and 969.5m. Swiss francs to field operations.

In October 2005, as part of a long-term strategy to diversify funding sources, the ICRC launched a Corporate Support Group in partnership with seven Swiss-based companies, which had been selected in accordance with ethical guidelines based on ICRC's mandate and on the principles and statutes of the International Red Cross and Red Crescent Movement. Contributions from Corporate Support Group Partners is used to fund both staff training and operational activities.

Publications

Annual Report (editions in English, French and Spanish).

FORUM series.

The Geneva Conventions (texts and commentaries).

ICRC News (weekly, English, French, German and Spanish editions).

International Review of the Red Cross (quarterly in English and French; annually in Arabic, Russian and Spanish).

The Additional Protocols (texts and commentaries).

The Missing.

Various publications on subjects of Red Cross interest (medical studies, IHL, etc.), some in electronic form.

International Federation of Red Cross and Red Crescent Societies

Address: 17 chemin des Crêts, Petit-Saconnex, CP 372, 1211 Geneva 19, Switzerland.

Telephone: 227304222; **fax:** 227330395; **e-mail:** secretariat@ifrc.org; **internet:** www.ifrc.org.

The Federation was founded in 1919 (as the League of Red Cross Societies). It works on the basis of the Principles of the Red Cross and Red Crescent Movement to inspire, facilitate and promote all forms of humanitarian activities by the National Societies, with a view to the prevention and alleviation of human suffering, and thereby contribute to the maintenance and promotion of peace in the world. The Federation acts as the official representative of its member societies in the field. The Federation maintains close relations with many inter-governmental organizations, the UN and its Specialized Agencies, and with non-governmental organizations. It has permanent observer status with the UN.

MEMBERS

National Red Cross and Red Crescent Societies in 187 countries, and Magen David Adom, Israel's equivalent of the Red Cross Society (at March 2012).

Organization

(April 2012)

GENERAL ASSEMBLY

The General Assembly is the highest authority of the Federation and meets every two years in commission sessions (for development, disaster relief, health and community services, and youth) and plenary sessions. It is composed of representatives from all National Societies that are members of the Federation.

GOVERNING BOARD

The Board (formerly the Executive Council) meets every six months and is composed of the President of the Federation, nine Vice-Presidents, representatives of 16 National Societies elected by the Assembly, and the Chairman of the Finance Commission. Its functions include the implementation of decisions of the General Assembly; it also has powers to act between meetings of the Assembly.

President: TADATERU KONOÉ (Japan).

COMMISSIONS

Development Commission;

Disaster Relief Commission;

Finance Commission;

Health and Community Services Commission;

Youth Commission.

The Commissions meet, in principle, twice a year, before the Governing Board meeting. Members are elected by the Assembly under a system that ensures each Society a seat on one Commission.

SECRETARIAT

The Secretariat assumes the statutory responsibilities of the Federation in the field of relief to victims of natural disasters, refugees and civilian populations who may be displaced or exposed to abnormal hardship. In addition, the Secretariat promotes and co-ordinates assistance to National Societies in developing their basic structure and their services to the community. The Secretariat has the following main departments: co-operation and governance support and risk management and audit; and the following divisions: support services, co-ordination and programmes, and policy and communications. The Secretary-General nominates honorary and special envoys for specific situations.

Secretary-General: BEKELE GELETA (Canada and Ethiopia).

Activities

In November 2005 the Assembly adopted a Global Agenda, comprising the following objectives which aimed to contribute to the attainment of the UN Millennium Development Goals: to reduce the deaths, injuries and impact of disasters on peoples' lives; to improve methods of dealing with public health crises; to combat intolerance and discrimination; and to build Red Cross and Red Crescent capacity at the community level to prepare for and cope with threats to lives and livelihoods.

In April 2008, in response to rapidly increasing food prices worldwide, the Federation launched a new five-year community-based food security initiative in 15 countries in Africa, with the aim of fostering resilience to fluctuating food prices by supporting local agriculture projects in the areas of microfinance, sustainable farming, small-scale irrigation and the development of food security early alert systems. Addressing the Group of Eight summit of industrialized nations in July, the Federation's Secretary-General urged participating states to support such long-term community-based food insecurity prevention programmes, stating that the ongoing food crisis represented a long-term phenomenon.

In November 2009, following extensive consultation within the Movement, the Assembly adopted Strategy 2020, outlining the Federation's objectives and strategies for the next 10 years, and replacing the previous Strategy 2010 (adopted in 1999). Strategy 2020 focused on a common vision (inspiring, encouraging, facilitating and promoting at all times all forms of humanitarian activities by national societies, with a view to preventing and alleviating suffering and thereby promoting dignity and world peace), and detailed three strategic aims for the Federation and its member national societies: saving lives, protecting livelihoods, and strengthening recovery from disasters and crises; enabling healthy and safe living; and promoting social inclusion and a culture of non-violence and peace. These were to be delivered through three enabling actions: building strong national Red Cross and Red Crescent societies; pursuing humanitarian diplomacy to prevent and reduce vulnerability in a globalized world; and functioning effectively as the International Federation.

DISASTER RESPONSE

The Federation supports the establishment of emergency response units, which aim to act effectively and independently to meet the needs of victims of natural or man-made disasters. The units cover basic health care provision, referral hospitals, water sanitation, logistics, telecommunications and information units. The Federation advises National Societies in relief health. A Disaster Relief Emergency Fund (DREF) was established in 1985 to ensure the availability of immediate financial support for emergency response actions. In 2012 DREF's budget totalled 18m. Swiss francs. In the event of a disaster the following areas are covered: communicable disease alleviation and vaccination; psychological support and stress management; health education; the provision of medicines; and the organization of mobile clinics and nursing care. The Societies also distribute food and clothing to those in need and assist in the provision of shelter and adequate sanitation facilities and in the management of refugee camps. The 2005 Global Agenda provided for a significant increase in Federation activities, in particular in the provision of emergency shelter, following natural disasters.

During 2005 the UN's Inter-Agency Standing Committee (IASC), concerned with co-ordinating the international response to humanitarian disasters, developed a concept of organizing agency assistance to IDPs through the institutionalization of a 'Cluster Approach', comprising nine core areas of activity. The Federation was designated the lead agency for the Emergency Protection (in natural disasters) cluster.

DEVELOPMENT

The Federation undertakes capacity-building activities with the National Societies to train and develop staff and volunteers and to improve management structures and processes, in particular in the area of disaster-preparedness. Blood donor programmes are often undertaken by National Societies, sometimes in conjunction with the World Health Organization. The Federation supports the promotion of these programmes and the implementation of quality standards. Other activities in the health sector aim to strengthen existing health services and promote community-based health care and first aid; the prevention of HIV/AIDS and substance abuse; and health education and family planning initiatives. The Federation also promotes the establishment and development of education and service programmes for children and for other more vulnerable members of society, including the elderly and disabled. Education projects support the promotion of humanitarian values.

Finance

The permanent Secretariat of the Federation is financed by the contributions of member Societies on a pro-rata basis. Each relief action is financed by separate, voluntary contributions, and development programme projects are also financed on a voluntary basis.

Publications

Annual Report.

Handbook of the International Red Cross and Red Crescent Movement (with the ICRC).

Red Cross, Red Crescent Magazine (quarterly, in English, French and Spanish).

Weekly News.

World Disasters Report (annually).

Newsletters on several topics; various guides and manuals for Red Cross and Red Crescent activities.

INTERNATIONAL SEABED AUTHORITY

Address: 14–20 Port Royal St, Kingston, Jamaica.

Telephone: 922-9105; **fax:** 922-0195; **e-mail:** webmaster@isa.org.jm; **internet:** www.isa.org.jm.

The Authority is an autonomous international organization established in accordance with the United Nations Convention on the Law of the Sea—UNCLOS (which was adopted in April 1982 and entered into force in November 1994) and the Agreement Relating to the Implementation of Part XI of the Convention (which was adopted in 1994 and entered into force in July 1996). The Authority was founded in November 1994 and became fully operational in June 1996.

Organization

(April 2012)

ASSEMBLY

The Assembly is the supreme organ of the Authority, consisting of representatives of all member states. In conjunction with the Council, it formulates the Authority's general policies. It elects Council members and members of the Finance Committee. It also approves the budget, submitted by the Council on the recommendation of the Finance Committee. The 17th session of the Assembly was convened in July 2011. The 18th session was to be convened in July 2012.

COUNCIL

The Council, elected by the Assembly for four-year terms, acts as the executive organ of the Authority. It consists of 36 members, comprising the four states that are the largest importers or consumers of seabed minerals, the four largest investors in seabed minerals, the four major exporters of seabed minerals, six developing countries representing special interests, and 18 members covering all the geographical regions.

LEGAL AND TECHNICAL COMMISSION

The Legal and Technical Commission, comprising 25 experts elected for five-year terms, assists the Council by making recommendations concerning seabed activities, assessing the environmental implications of activities in the area, proposing measures to protect the marine environment, and reviewing the execution of exploration contracts.

FINANCE COMMITTEE

The Committee, comprising 15 experts, was established to make recommendations to the Assembly and the Council on all financial and budgetary issues.

SECRETARIAT

The Secretariat provides administrative services to all the bodies of the Authority and implements the relevant work programmes. It comprises the Office of the Secretary-General, Offices of Resources and Environmental Monitoring, Legal Affairs, and Administration and Management. Under the terms of the 1994 Agreement Relating to the Implementation of Part XI of the Convention, the Secretariat is performing the functions of the Enterprise, the organ through which the Authority carries out deep-seabed mining operations (directly or through joint ventures). It is envisaged that the Enterprise will eventually operate independently of the Secretariat.

Secretary-General: NII ALLOTEY ODUNTON (Ghana).

Activities

The Authority, functioning as an autonomous international organization in relationship with the UN, implements UNCLOS. All states party to the Convention (161 and the European Union as at April 2012) are members. The Convention covers the uses of ocean space: navigation and overflight, resource exploration and exploitation, conservation and pollution, and fishing and shipping; as well as governing conduct on the oceans; defining maritime zones; establishing rules for delineating sea boundaries; assigning legal rights, duties and responsibilities to states; and providing machinery for the settlement of disputes. Its main provisions are as follows:

Coastal states are allowed sovereignty over their territorial waters of up to 12 nautical miles in breadth; foreign vessels are to be allowed 'innocent passage' through these waters;

Ships and aircraft of all states, including landlocked states, are allowed 'transit passage' through straits used for international navigation; states bordering these straits can regulate navigational and other aspects of passage;

Archipelagic states (composed of islands and interconnecting waters) have sovereignty over a sea area enclosed by straight lines drawn between the outermost points of the islands;

Coastal states and inhabited islands are entitled to proclaim a 200-mile exclusive economic zone (EEZ) with respect to natural resources and jurisdiction over certain activities (such as protection and preservation of the environment), and rights over the adjacent continental shelf, up to 350 miles from the shore under specified circumstances;

All states have freedom of navigation, overflight, scientific research and fishing within the EEZ, in addition to the right to lay submarine cables and pipelines, but must co-operate in measures to conserve living resources;

A 'parallel system' is to be established for exploiting the international seabed, where all activities are to be supervised by the International Seabed Authority (ISA); landlocked and geographically disadvantaged states have the right to participate, on an equitable basis, in the exploitation of an appropriate part of the surplus of living resources of the EEZs of coastal states of the same region or sub-region;

Coastal states have sovereign rights over the continental shelf (the national area of the seabed, which can extend up to 200 nautical miles from the shore) for exploring and exploiting its natural resources; the UN Commission on the Limits of the Continental Shelf shall make recommendations to states on the shelf's outer boundaries when it extends beyond 200 miles;

All states party to the Convention share, through the Authority, the revenue generated from exploiting non-living resources from any part of the continental shelf extending beyond 200 miles; the distribution of revenue is determined according to equitable sharing criteria, taking into account the interests and needs of developing and landlocked states;

States are bound to control pollution and co-operate in forming preventive rules, and incur penalties for failing to combat pollution; states bordering enclosed, or semi-enclosed, waters are bound to co-operate in managing living resources, environmental policies and research activities;

Marine scientific research in the zones under national jurisdiction is subject to the prior consent of the coastal state, but consent may be denied only under specific circumstances;

States are bound to co-operate in the development and transfer of marine technology 'on fair and reasonable terms and conditions' and with proper regard for all legitimate interests;

States are obliged to settle by peaceful means disputes on the application and interpretation of the Convention; disputes must be submitted to a compulsory procedure entailing decisions binding on all parties.

The Convention provides for the establishment of an International Tribunal for the Law of the Sea (see below), which has exclusive jurisdiction over disputes relating to the international seabed area. In July 1994 the UN General Assembly adopted the Agreement Relating to the Implementation of Part XI of the Convention. At April 2012 there were 141 states party to the Agreement. The original Part XI, concerning the exploitation of the international ocean bed, and particularly the minerals to be found there (chiefly manganese, cobalt, copper and nickel), envisaged as the 'common heritage of mankind', had not been supported by the USA and other industrialized nations on the grounds that countries possessing adequate technology for deep sea mining would be insufficiently represented in the ISA; that the operations of private mining consortia would be unacceptably limited by the stipulations that their technology should be shared with the Authority's 'Enterprise'; and that production should be limited in order to protect land-based mineral producers. Under the 1994 Agreement there was to be no mandatory transfer of technology, the Enterprise was to operate according to commercial principles; and there were to be no production limits, although a compensation fund was to assist land-based producers adversely affected by seabed mining. By April 2012 the USA had not yet ratified either the Convention or the Agreement. An agreement on the implementation of the provisions of the Convention relating to the conservation and management of straddling and highly migratory fish stocks was opened for signature in December 1995 and entered into force in December 2001; by April 2012 it had been ratified by 78 states.

The comprehensive set of rules, regulations and procedures being developed by the ISA to govern prospecting, exploration and exploitation of marine minerals in the international seabed 'Area' (defined as the seabed and subsoil beyond the limits of national jurisdictions) are known as the 'Mining Code'. So far the Mining Code comprises the Regulations for Prospecting and Exploration for Polymetallic Nodules in the Area, adopted by the Authority in July 2000; and the Regulations for Prospecting and Exploration for Polymetallic Sulphides, adopted in May 2010 by the 16th session of the Authority. A third set of regulations, on prospecting and exploration for cobalt-rich crusts, were drafted in 2011, and were to be endorsed in July 2012 by the 18th session of the Assembly. The Legal and Technical Commission has also issued recommendations for the guidance of contractors on regarding the assessment of the environmental impacts of exploration for polymetallic nodules. In November 2011 ISA organized a workshop on 'environmental management needs for exploration and exploitation of deep seabed minerals'.

Pursuant to the Regulations for Prospecting and Exploration for Polymetallic Nodules in the Area, eight exploration contracts have been signed: the first seven contracts were signed, between 2001–02, with registered pioneer investors who had submitted plans of work for deep seabed exploration; the eighth was signed, in July 2006, with the Federal Institute for Geosciences and Natural Resources of the Federal Republic of Germany. The Authority maintains a database on polymetallic nodules (POLYDAT) and a central data repository (CDR) for all marine minerals in the seabed. In November 2008 the ISA organized another seminar, jointly with the Government of Brazil, to address the challenges relating to the development of marine mineral resources of the South and Equatorial Atlantic Oceans.

In 2005 the ISA launched a project to make a geological model (comprising a set of digital and hard copy maps and tables describing predicted metal content and abundance of deposits, as well as related error estimates) of the Clarion-Clipperton Fracture Zone (CCZ), which is located south-east of Hawaii in the Pacific Ocean and has the largest known deposits world-wide of seabed polymetallic nodules. In December 2009 the Authority organized a workshop aimed at finalizing the CCZ geological model as well as a Prospector's Guide for the Zone. An international workshop was held in November 2010 to advise on the formulation of a CCZ environmental management plan and strategic environmental assessment. A geological model project was also planned for the Central Indian Ocean.

In February 2008 the ISA launched a new Endowment Fund aimed at promoting and supporting collaborative marine scientific research in the international seabed area. The Fund awards fellowships to scientists and technical personnel from developing countries through its Technical Assistance Programme-Marine Scientific Research (TAP-MAR). By end-2011 the Fund was financing training and research activities for 16 scientists and technicians from 14 developing countries. Following the conclusion in June 2009 of a Memorandum of Understanding between the Authority and the People's Republic of China, in November China agreed to fund postgraduate studies in marine science at a Chinese university for up to five candidates from ISA developing member states.

Finance

The Authority's budget is adopted by the Assembly on the recommendations of both the Council and the Finance Committee. The budget for the Authority for the biennium 2011–12 was US $13.0m. The administrative expenses of the Authority are met by assessed contributions from its members.

Publications

Basic Texts of the ISA (in English, French and Spanish).

Handbook (annually).

The Law of the Sea: Compendium of Basic Documents.

Selected decisions of sessions of the Authority, consultations, documents, rules of procedure, technical reports and studies, etc.

Associated Institutions

The following were also established under the terms of the Convention:

Commission on the Limits of the Continental Shelf: Division for Ocean Affairs and the Law of the Sea, Room DC2-0450, United Nations, New York, NY 10017, USA; tel. (212) 963-3966; fax (212) 963-5847; e-mail doalos@un.org; internet www.un.org/Depts/los/clcs_new/clcs_home.htm; 21 members, serving a five-year term (the most recent election of members took place in June 2007); responsible for making recommendations regarding the establishment of the outer limits of the continental shelf of a coastal state, where the limit extends beyond 200 nautical miles (370 km); Chair. ALEXANDRE TAGORE MEDEIROS DE ALBUQUERQUE.

International Tribunal for the Law of the Sea: Am internationalen Seegerichtshof 1, 22609 Hamburg, Germany; tel. (40) 35607-0; fax (40) 35607-245; e-mail itlos@itlos.org; internet www.itlos.org; inaugurated in 1996; 21 judges; responsible for interpreting the Convention and ruling on disputes brought by states parties to the Convention on matters within its jurisdiction; Registrar PHILIPPE GAUTIER (Belgium).

International Trade Union Confederation—ITUC

Address: 5 blvd du Roi Albert II, bte 1, 1210 Brussels, Belgium.

Telephone: (2) 224-02-10; **fax:** (2) 201-58-15; **e-mail:** info@ituc-csi.org; **internet:** www.ituc-csi.org.

ITUC was established in November 2006 by the merger of the International Confederation of Free Trade Unions (ICFTU, founded in 1949 by trade union federations that had withdrawn from the World Federation of Trade Unions), the World Confederation of Labour (WCL, founded in 1920 as the International Federation of Christian Trade Unions and reconstituted and renamed in 1968), and eight national trade union organizations. ITUC aims to defend and promote the rights of working people by encouraging co-operation between trade unions, and through global campaigning and advocacy. The principal areas of activity are: trade union and human rights; the economy, society and the workplace; equality and non-discrimination; and international solidarity. The principles of trade union democracy and independence are enshrined in ITUC's Constitution. In November 2006, following its establishment, ITUC ratified an agreement with the so-called Global Unions (global trade union federations, see list below) and the Trade Union Advisory Committee to the OECD (TUAC) to form a Council of Global Unions, with the aims of promoting trade union membership and advancing common trade union interests world-wide. In 2007 ITUC, UNEP and the ILO launched the Green Jobs Initiative (the International Organisation of Employers joined the partnership in 2008). The Initiative aims to promote the creation of decent jobs as a consequence of new environmental policies required to transform ongoing global environmental challenges.

MEMBERS

There were 308 member organizations in 153 countries and territories with 175m. members (at April 2012).

Organization

(April 2012)

WORLD CONGRESS

The Congress, the highest authority of ITUC, meets in ordinary session at least once every four years. The first Congress was held in Vienna, Austria, in November 2006; and the second was convened in Vancouver, Canada, in June 2010.

Delegations from national federations vary in size on the basis of their paying membership. The Congress examines past activities and financial reports of the Confederation; reports on the activities of ITUC's regional organizations and on the Council of Global Unions (the structured partnership with the global union federations and TUAC); addresses general policy questions; maps out future plans; considers proposals for amendments to the Constitution and any other proposals submitted by member organizations; and elects the General Council, the General Secretary and the Confederation's three auditors. The General Secretary leads the Secretariat and is an ex officio member of the General Council and of the Executive Bureau.

GENERAL COUNCIL

Elected by the Congress, the General Council comprises 78 members, of whom 70 represent regions (Europe: 24; the Americas: 18; Asia-Pacific: 15; Africa: 11; 'open' regional membership: two); six members are nominated by the Women's Committee; and two members are nominated by the Youth Committee. The Council meets at least once a year and acts as the supreme authority of the Confederation between World Congresses, with responsibility for directing the activities of the Confederation and effecting decisions and recommendations of the Congress. The Council's agenda is prepared by the General Secretary.

The Council has appointed the following Committees:

Human and Trade Union Rights Committee;

Women's Committee;

Youth Committee.

EXECUTIVE BUREAU

At its first meeting after the regular World Congress the General Council elects an Executive Bureau, comprising the President, the General Secretary and up to 25 members of the General Council. The Executive Bureau is authorized to address questions of urgency that arise between meetings of the General Council, or which are entrusted to it by the General Council. The Bureau meets at least twice a year.

President: MICHAEL SOMMER (Germany).

SECRETARIAT

General Secretary: SHARAN BURROW (Australia).

The General Secretary is supported by two Deputy General Secretaries.

BRANCH OFFICES

ITUC Amman Office: POB 925875, Amman 11190, Jordan; tel. (6) 5603181; fax (6) 5603185; e-mail ituc-jor@orange.jo; Co-ordinator NEZAM QAHOUSH; ITUC Co-ordinator of the Iraqi Workers Project RALF ERBEL.

ITUC CIS Office: Leninsky Prospect 42, Office 2139, 117119 Moscow, Russia; tel. (495) 938-7356; fax (495) 938-7304; e-mail ituc.mos@gmail.com.

ITUC Geneva Office: 46 ave Blanc, 1202 Geneva, Switzerland; tel. 227384202; fax 227381082; e-mail genevaoffice@ituc-csi.org; Dir RAQUEL GONZALEZ.

ITUC South-East European Office: 71000 Sarajevo, Topal Osman paše 26/iv, Bosnia and Herzegovina; tel. (33) 715346; fax (33) 664606; Rep. JASMIN RADZEPOVIC.

There are also Permanent Representatives accredited to FAO (Rome), IMO (London), UNIDO and IAEA (Vienna), and to UNEP and UN-Habitat (Nairobi).

REGIONAL ORGANIZATIONS

African Regional Organisation of ITUC (ITUC-Africa): route Internationale d'Atakpamé, POB 44101, Lomé, Togo; tel. and fax 225-07-10; e-mail info@ituc-africa.org; internet www.ituc-africa.org; f. 2007; Gen. Sec. KWASI ADU-AMANKWAH.

ITUC Regional Organisation for Asia-Pacific (ITUC-AP): 9th Floor, NTUC Centre, One Marina Blvd, Singapore 018989; tel. 63273590; fax 63273576; e-mail gs@ituc-ap.org; internet www.ituc-ap.org; f. 2007; Gen. Sec. NORIYUKI SUZUKI.

Pan-European Regional Council (PERC): 5 blvd du Roi Albert II, bte 1, 1210, Brussels, Belgium; tel. (2) 224-02-11; fax (2) 201-58-15; e-mail perc@ituc-sci.org; Gen. Sec. BERNADETTE SEGOL.

Trade Union Confederation of the Americas (TUCA): Rua Formosa 367, Centro CEP 01049-000, São Paulo, Brazil; tel. (11) 21040750; fax (11) 21040751; internet www.csa-csi.org; f. 2008; Gen. Sec. VICTOR BAEZ MOSQUEIRA.

Finance

Affiliated organizations pay an affiliation fee per 1,000 members per annum, which finances ITUC's activities. The Confederation's budget amounts to some €11m. annually.

A Solidarity Fund, financed by contributions from affiliated organizations, supports the development and practice of democratic trade unionism world-wide and assists workers and trade unionists victimized by repressive political measures.

Global Union Federations

Building and Wood Workers International (BWI): 54 route des Acacias, 1227 Carouge, Switzerland; tel. 228273777; fax 228273770; e-mail info@bwint.org; internet www.bwint.org; f. 2005 by merger of International Federation of Building and Woodworkers (f. 1934) and World Federation of Building and Wood Workers (f. 1936); mems: 318 national unions with a membership of around 12m. workers in 130 countries; organization: Congress, World Council, World Board; Pres. KLAUS WIESEHÜGEL (Germany); Gen. Sec. AMBET YUSON (Philippines); publ. *BWI Online on the web* (daily).

Education International (EI): 5 blvd du Roi Albert II, 1210 Brussels, Belgium; tel. (2) 224-06-11; fax (2) 224-06-06; e-mail info@ei-ie.org; internet www.ei-ie.org; f. 1993; the fmr World Confederation of Teachers (f. 1962) merged with EI in 2006; aims to represent the causes of teachers and education employees and to promote the development of education; advocates for free quality public education for all, deeming education to be a 'human right and a public good'; regards literacy as the cornerstone of all sustainable societies, and the key to breaking the poverty cycle and halting the spread of HIV/AIDS; mems: 401 organizations representing 30m. teachers and education workers in 172 countries; Pres. SUSAN HOPGOOD (Australia); Gen. Sec. FRED VAN LEEUWEN (Netherlands).

International Federation of Chemical, Energy, Mine and General Workers' Unions (ICEM): 20 rue Adrien Lachenal, 1207 Geneva, Switzerland; tel. 223041840; fax 223041841; e-mail info@icem.org; internet www.icem.org; f. 1995 by merger of the International Federation of Chemical, Energy and General Workers' Unions (f. 1907) and the Miners' International Federation (f. 1890); mems: 355 trade unions covering more than 20m. workers in 115 countries; main sectors cover energy industries; chemicals; pharmaceuticals and biotechnology; mining and extraction; pulp and paper; rubber; ceramics; glass; building materials; and environmental services; Pres. SENZENI ZOKWANA; Gen. Sec. MANFRED WARDA (Germany); publs *ICEM Info* (quarterly), *ICEM Focus on Health, Safety and Environment* (2 a year), *ICEM Update* (irregular).

International Federation of Journalists (IFJ): International Press Centre, 155 rue de la Loi, 1040 Brussels, Belgium; tel. (2) 235-22-00; fax (2) 235-22-19; e-mail ifj@ifj.org; internet www.ifj.org; f. 1952 to link national unions of professional journalists dedicated to the freedom of the press, to defend the rights of journalists, and to raise professional standards; it conducts surveys, assists in trade union training programmes, organizes seminars and provides information; it arranges fact-finding missions in countries where press freedom is under pressure, and issues protests against the persecution and detention of journalists and the censorship of the mass media; holds Congress every three years (May 2010: Cadiz, Spain); mems: 156 unions in more than 100 countries, comprising 600,000 individuals; Pres. JIM BOUMELHA (United Kingdom); Gen. Sec. ELIZABETH (BETH) COSTA (Brazil); publ. *IFJ Direct Line* (every 2 months).

International Metalworkers' Federation (IMF): 54 bis route des Acacias, CP 1516, 1227 Geneva, Switzerland; tel. 223085050; fax 223085055; e-mail info@imfmetal.org; internet www.imfmetal.org; f. 1893; mems: represents the collective interests of 25m. metalworkers from more than 200 unions in 100 countries; holds Congress every four years (May 2009: Göteborg, Sweden); has five regional offices; six industrial departments; World Company Councils for unions in multinational corporations; Pres. BERTHOLD HUBER (Germany); Gen. Sec. JYRKI RAINA; publs *IMF News Briefs* (weekly), *Metal World* (quarterly).

International Textile, Garment and Leather Workers' Federation (ITGLWF): 8 rue Joseph Stevens (bte 4), 1000 Brussels, Belgium; tel. (2) 512-26-06; fax (2) 511-09-04; e-mail office@itglwf.org; internet www.itglwf.org; f. 1970; mems: 217 unions covering 10m. workers in 110 countries; normally holds Congress every five years (Dec. 2009: Frankfurt, Germany); Pres. HISANOBU SHIMADA (Japan); Gen. Sec. KLAUS PRIEGNITZ (acting).

International Transport Workers' Federation (ITF): 49–60 Borough Rd, London, SE1 1DR, United Kingdom; tel. (20) 7403-2733; fax (20) 7357-7871; e-mail mail@itf.org.uk; internet www.itfglobal.org; f. 1896; hosts the Seafarers' Rights International Centre (f. 2010); scheduled to convene in Sept. 2012, in Casablanca, Morocco, the first of a series of Maritime Roundtables, focusing on building links between dockers' and seafarers unions; organizes and negotiates on behalf of crews working on ships flying Flags of Convenience (FOCs); mems: national trade unions covering 4.5m. workers in 654 unions in 153 countries; holds Congress every four years; has eight Industrial Sections; Pres. PADDY CRUMLIN (Australia); Gen. Sec. DAVID COCKROFT (United Kingdom); publ. *Transport International* (quarterly).

International Union of Food, Agricultural, Hotel, Restaurant, Catering, Tobacco and Allied Workers' Associations: 8 rampe du Pont-Rouge, 1213 Petit-Lancy, Switzerland; tel. 227932233; fax 227932238; e-mail iuf@iuf.org; internet www.iuf.org; f. 1920; mems: 336 affiliated organizations covering about 12m. workers in 120 countries; holds Congress every five years (May 2012: Geneva, Switzerland); Gen. Sec. RON OSWALD; publ. bi-monthly bulletins.

Public Services International (PSI): 45 ave Voltaire, BP9, 01211 Ferney-Voltaire Cédex, France; tel. 4-50-40-64-64; fax 4-50-40-73-20; e-mail psi@world-psi.org; internet www.world-psi.org; f. 1907; represents 20m. people working in the public services around the world; PSI is an officially recognized non-governmental organization for the public sector within the ILO; mems: 690 unions and professional associations covering 20m. workers in 161 countries; holds Congress every five years (Nov. 2012: Durban, South Africa); Pres. DAVE PRENTIS (United Kingdom); Gen. Sec. PETER WALDORFF (Denmark); publ. *Focus* (quarterly).

Union Network International (UNI): 8–10 ave Reverdil, 1260 Nyon, Switzerland; tel. 223652100; fax 223652121; e-mail contact@uniglobalunion.org; internet www.uniglobalunion.org; f. 2000 by merger of Communications International (CI), the International Federation of Commercial, Clerical, Professional and Technical Employees (FIET), the International Graphical Federation (IGF), and Media and Entertainment International (MEI); mems: 900 unions in more than 140 countries, representing 20m. people; activities cover the following sectors: cleaning and security, commerce, finance, gaming, graphical and packaging, hair and beauty, IT and services, media, entertainment and arts, post and logistics, social insurance, telecommunications, tourism, temporary and agency work; third World Congress was held in Nagasaki, Japan, in Nov. 2010, and the fourth was scheduled to be held in Cape Town, South Africa, in 2014; Pres. JOSEPH DE BRUYN (Australia); Gen. Sec. PHILIP J. JENNINGS (United Kingdom); publs *UNIinfo* (quarterly), *UNInet News* (monthly).

INTER-PARLIAMENTARY UNION—IPU

Address: 5 chemin du Pommier, CP 330, 1218 Le Grand Saconnex/Geneva, Switzerland.

Telephone: 229194150; **fax:** 229194160; **e-mail:** postbox@mail.ipu.org; **internet:** www.ipu.org.

Founded in 1889, the IPU aims to promote peace, co-operation and representative democracy by providing a forum for multilateral political debate between representatives of national parliaments.

MEMBERS

National parliaments of 153 sovereign states; eight international parliamentary associations (associate members). Most member states are affiliated to one of six geopolitical groupings, known as the African, Arab, Asia-Pacific, Eurasia, Latin American and '12-Plus' (European) groups.

Organization

(April 2012)

ASSEMBLY

The Assembly (formerly known as the Inter-Parliamentary Conference and renamed in April 2003) is the main statutory body of the IPU, comprising eight to 10 representatives from each member parliament. It meets twice a year to discuss current issues in world affairs and to make political recommendations. Other specialized meetings of parliamentarians may also be held, on a global or regional basis. The Assembly is assisted by the following three plenary Standing Committees: on Peace and International Security; Sustainable Development, Finance and Trade; and Democracy and Human Rights. The 126th Assembly was convened in Kampala, Uganda, in March–April 2012.

GOVERNING COUNCIL

The Governing Council (formerly the Inter-Parliamentary Council, renamed in April 2003) comprises two representatives of each member parliament, usually from different political groups. It is responsible for approving membership and the annual programme and budget of the IPU, and for electing the Secretary-General. The Council may consider substantive issues and adopt resolutions and policy statements, in particular on the basis of recommendations from its subsidiary bodies.

President: ABDELWAHAD RADI (Morocco).

MEETING OF WOMEN PARLIAMENTARIANS

The Meeting is a mechanism for co-ordination between women parliamentarians. Convened twice a year, on the occasion of IPU statutory meetings, the Meeting aims to address subjects of common interest, to formulate strategies to develop the IPU's women's programme, to strengthen their influence within the organization and to ensure that women are elected to key positions. The Meeting is assisted by a Co-ordinating Committee.

SUBSIDIARY BODIES

In addition to the thematic Standing Committees of the IPU Assembly, various other committees and groups undertake and co-ordinate IPU activities in specific areas. The following bodies are subsidiary to the IPU Council:

Standing Committee on Peace and International Security;

Standing Committee on Sustainable Development, Finance and Trade;

Standing Committee on Democracy and Human Rights;

Committee on the Human Rights of Parliamentarians;

Committee on Middle East Questions;

Committee on UN Affairs;

Group of Facilitators for Cyprus;

Ad Hoc Committee to Promote Respect for International Humanitarian Law;

Co-ordinating Committee of the Meeting of Women MPs;

Gender Partnership Group.

The Association of Secretaries-General of Parliaments (ASGP), an autonomous, self-managing body that meets during the IPU Assembly, has consultative status at the IPU.

EXECUTIVE COMMITTEE

The Committee, comprising 17 members and presided over by the President of the Council, oversees the administration of the IPU and advises the Council on membership, policy and programme, and any other matters referred to it.

SECRETARIAT

Secretary-General: ANDERS B. JOHNSSON (Sweden).

Activities

PROMOTION OF REPRESENTATIVE DEMOCRACY

This is one of the IPU's core areas of activity, and covers a wide range of concerns, such as democracy, gender issues, human rights and ethnic diversity, parliamentary action to combat corruption, and links between democracy and economic growth. The IPU sets standards and guidelines, provides technical assistance for strengthening national representative institutions, promotes human rights and the protection of members of parliament, supports partnership between men and women in politics, and promotes knowledge of the functioning of national parliaments. In September 1997 the Council adopted a Universal Declaration on Democracy. The IPU subsequently published a study entitled *Democracy: Its Principles and Achievements*.

The IPU aims to improve knowledge of the functioning of national parliaments by gathering and disseminating information on their constitutional powers and responsibilities, structure, and membership, and on the electoral systems used. The IPU also organizes international seminars and gatherings for parliamentarians, officials, academics and other experts to study the functioning of parliamentary institutions. A Technical Co-operation Programme aims to mobilize international support in order to improve the capabilities, infrastructure and technical facilities of national parliaments and enhance their effectiveness. Under the Programme, the IPU may provide expert advice on the structure of legislative bodies, staff training, and parliamentary working procedures, and provide technical equipment and other resources. There is a Parliamentary Resource Centre at IPU headquarters.

In 1993 the Council resolved that the IPU be present at all national elections organized, supervised or verified by the UN. The IPU has reported on the rights and responsibilities of election observers and issued guidelines on the holding of free and fair elections. These include the 1994 *Declaration on Criteria for Free and Fair Elections*, a study entitled *Free and Fair Elections* (initially published in 1994, and re-issued in a new, expanded version in 2006), *Codes of Conduct for Elections*, and *Tools for Parliamentary Oversight* (issued in 2008).

The IPU maintains a special database (PARLINE) on parliaments of the world, giving access to information on the structure and functioning of all existing parliaments, and on national elections. It conducts regular world studies on matters regarding the structure and functioning of parliaments. It also maintains a separate database (PARLIT) comprising literature from around the world on constitutional, electoral and parliamentary matters.

In August–September 2000 the IPU organized the first international conference of presiding officers of national parliaments. The second speakers' conference took place in September 2005, and the third in July 2010. The sixth annual meeting of women speakers of parliament, organized by the IPU jointly with the Swiss Government, also took place in July 2010.

INTERNATIONAL PEACE AND SECURITY

The IPU aims to promote conflict resolution and international security through political discussion. Certain areas of conflict are monitored by the Union on an ongoing basis (for example, Cyprus and the Middle East), while others are considered as they arise. In February 2011 the IPU President strongly condemned the use of military force by the Libyan authorities against political demonstrators in that country, and, in the following month, he similarly condemned the use by the Côte d'Ivoire authorities of force against political protesters. In early April 2012 the 126th IPU Assembly issued a statement expressing profound concern at the overthrow, in late March, of Mali's legitimate authorities by the military; and adopted a resolution demanding the immediate cessation of violence and human rights violations in Syria, and requesting the IPU to dispatch an international parliamentary fact-finding mission to that country to assess the situation there. The 126th Assembly also adopted a resolution inviting all states and parliaments to consider the lessons to be drawn from the Middle East, North Africa, Europe, the USA, and elsewhere, on the need for democratic reform, and on the need for governments to provide their citizens with basic employment and economic opportunities, and to guarantee equal opportunities for all; and urged that an international parliamentary conference should be convened, under IPU auspices, on the role of youth in politics and current technological developments.

The objectives outlined at the first Conference on Security and Co-operation in the Mediterranean (CSCM), held in June 1992, were integrated as a structured process of the IPU. A second CSCM was held in Valletta, Malta, in November 1995, and a third was convened in Marseilles, France, in March–April 2000. In February 2005 participants attending the fourth CSCM, held in Nafplion, Greece, agreed to terminate the process and establish in its place a Parliamentary Assembly of the Mediterranean (PAM); the inaugural session of the PAM was convened in Amman, Jordan, in September 2006.

The IPU has worked constantly to promote international and regional efforts towards disarmament, as part of the process of enhancing peace and security. Issues that have been discussed by the Assembly include nuclear non-proliferation, a ban on testing of nuclear weapons, and a global register of arms transfers.

SUSTAINABLE DEVELOPMENT

The Standing Committee for Sustainable Development, Finance and Trade guides the IPU's work in this area, with a broad approach of linking economic growth with social, democratic, human welfare and environmental considerations. Issues of world economic and social development on which the IPU has approved recommendations include employment in a globalizing world, the globalization of economy and liberalization of trade, Third World debt and its impact on the integration of those countries affected into the process of globalization, international mass migration and other demographic problems, and the right to food. The IPU co-operates with programmes and agencies of the UN, in particular in the preparation and follow-up of major socio-economic conferences, including the World Summit for Social Development, which was held in Copenhagen, Denmark, in March 1995; the Fourth World Conference on Women, held in Beijing, People's Republic of China, in September 1995; and the World Food Summit, held in Rome, Italy, in November 1996. In September 1996 a tripartite meeting of parliamentary, governmental and inter-governmental representatives, convened at the UN headquarters in New York, USA, considered legislative measures to pursue the objectives of the World Summit for Social Development. The IPU and the European Parliament jointly organize an annual parliamentary conference on the World Trade Organization (WTO), which addresses issues including access to markets, the development dimension of the multilateral trading system, agriculture and subsidies. The conference aims to add a parliamentary dimension to multilateral co-operation on trade matters and thereby to enhance the transparency of the WTO's activities and to strengthen democracy at international level. The 2012 session was to take place in Geneva, Switzerland, in May.

Activities to protect the environment are undertaken within the framework of sustainable development. In 1984 the first Inter-Parliamentary Conference on the Environment, convened in Nairobi, Kenya, advocated the inclusion of environmental considerations into the development process. The IPU was actively involved in the preparation of the UN Conference on Environment and Development (UNCED), which was held in Rio de Janeiro, Brazil, in June 1992. Subsequently the IPU's environment programme focused on implementing the recommendations of UNCED, and identifying measures to be taken at parliamentary level to facilitate that process. The IPU monitors the actual measures taken by national parliaments to pursue the objective of sustainable development, as well as emerging environmental problems. In 1997 the IPU published the *World Directory of Parliamentary Bodies for Environment*. In April 2005 the Assembly held an emergency debate on the role of parliaments in the prevention of natural disasters and the protection of vulnerable groups. In October 2011 the 125th Assembly debated sustainable development, and in 2011–12 the IPU was participating in the preparations for the June 2012 UN Conference on Sustainable Development.

In November 2007 the IPU, in co-operation with the UN Development Programme (UNDP), UNAIDS and the Philippines legislature, convened the first Global Parliamentary Meeting on HIV/AIDS, at which participating parliamentary representatives addressed the role of national legislatures in responding to the HIV/AIDS pandemic.

The IPU and UNDP concluded a comprehensive Memorandum of Understanding in November 2007 aimed at expanding mutual co-operation in support of world-wide democratic governance; future areas of co-operation were to cover national budgetary processes; and parliamentary activities aimed at advancing the achievement of the UN Millennium Development Goals (MDGs) and at implementing UN treaties and conventions, and strategies aimed at poverty reduction and the empowerment of women. The IPU welcomed a resolution adopted in December 2010 by the UN General Assembly on co-operation between the UN, national parliaments and the IPU.

In May 2009, in Geneva, the IPU convened a parliamentary conference on the ongoing global financial and economic crisis. The role of parliaments in developing South-South and 'triangular' (where two countries form a partnership to assist a third country) co-operation, with a view to accelerating achievement of the MDGs, and parliamentary action to ensure global food security, were addressed by the IPU Assembly in October.

IPU co-ordinated a two-year consultation process aimed at incorporating the concerns of national parliaments into the outcome of the Fourth UN Conference for the Least Developed Countries (LDV IV), convened in Istanbul, Turkey, in May 2011. LDC IV approved the Istanbul Programme of Action, which included a provision that national parliaments should be engaged in debating development strategies as well as in overseeing their implementation.

HUMAN RIGHTS AND HUMANITARIAN LAW

The IPU aims to incorporate human rights concerns, including employment, the rights of minorities, and gender issues, in all areas of activity. The Assembly and specialized meetings of parliamentarians frequently consider and make relevant recommendations on human rights issues. A five-member Committee on the Human Rights of Parliamentarians is responsible for the consideration of complaints relating to alleged violations of the human rights of members of parliament, for example state harassment, arbitrary arrest and detention, unfair trail and violation of parliamentary immunity, based on a procedure adopted by the IPU in 1976, when the Committee was established. The Committee conducts hearings and site missions to investigate a complaint and communicates with the authorities of the country concerned. If no settlement is reached at that stage, the Committee may then publish a report for the Governing Council and submit recommendations on specific measures to be adopted. During 2010 the Committee addressed cases of allegations of human rights violations against 306 current or former members of parliament in 35 countries.

The IPU works closely with the International Committee of the Red Cross to uphold respect for international humanitarian law (IHL). It supports the implementation of the Geneva Conventions and their Additional Protocols, and the adoption of appropriate national legislation. In 1995 the Council adopted a special resolution to establish a reporting mechanism at the parliamentary level to ensure respect for IHL. Consequently IPU initiated a world survey on legislative action regarding the application of IHL, as well as efforts to ban anti-personnel landmines. In April and September 1998 the Council adopted special resolutions on parliamentary action to secure the entry into force (achieved in March 1999) and implementation of the Convention on the Prohibition of the Use, Stockpiling, Production and Transfer of Anti-personnel Mines and on their Destruction, which had been signed by representatives of some 120 countries meeting in Ottawa, Canada, in December 1997.

In February 2008 the IPU and the UN Office on Drugs and Crime (UNODC) jointly organized a Parliamentary Forum on Human Trafficking, convened in Vienna, Austria, in the context of the global Vienna Forum to Fight Human Trafficking; in April 2009 the IPU and UNODC jointly issued *Combating Trafficking in Persons: a Handbook for Parliamentarians*. In April 2010 the Assembly issued a declaration on 'Co-operation and shared responsibility in the global fight against organized crime, in particular drug trafficking, illegal arms trafficking, trafficking in persons, and cross-border terrorism'.

In November 2010 participants in the international parliamentary conference on 'Parliaments, minorities and indigenous peoples', convened in Chiapas, Mexico, adopted the 'Chiapas Declaration' aimed at improving the situation of minorities and indigenous peoples.

WOMEN IN POLITICS

In conjunction with UN Women, IPU publishes an annual survey on progress made towards increasing female representation in parliament since the 1995 Fourth World Conference on Women (see above). The March 2012 *Women in Politics* survey reported that, at 1 January of that year, only 27 countries world-wide had achieved female parliamentary representation of 30% or more, and that there were at that time only 17 female elected heads of state or government. In September 2008 the IPU noted that Rwanda had become the first country with more than 50% female parliamentary representation, and, by 2012 Andorra also had also reached that benchmark.

The IPU aims to promote the participation of women in the political and parliamentary decision-making processes, and, more generally, in all aspects of society. It organizes debates and events on these issues and maintains an online statistical database on women in politics, compiled by regular world surveys, as well as a women in politics bibliographic database. The IPU also actively addresses wider issues of concern to women, such as literacy and education, women in armed conflicts, women's contribution to development, and women in the electoral process. The eradication of violence against women was the subject of a special resolution adopted by the Conference in 1991. The Meeting of Women MPs has monitored efforts by national authorities to implement the recommendations outlined in the resolution. In 1996 the IPU promoted the Framework for Model Legislation on Domestic Violence, formulated by the UN Special Rapporteur on the issue, which aimed to assist national parliaments in preparing legislation to safeguard women. At the Fourth World Conference on Women, held in Beijing, People's Republic of China, in September 1995, the IPU organized several events to bring together parliamentarians and other leading experts, diplomats and officials to promote the rights of women and of children. In February 1997 the IPU organized a Specialized Inter-Parliamentary Conference, in New Delhi, India, entitled 'Towards partnership between men and women in politics'. Following the Conference the IPU established a Gender Partnership Group, comprising two men and two women, within the Executive Committee, to ensure that IPU activities and decisions serve the interests and needs of all members of the population. The Group was authorized to report to the IPU Council.

The IPU aims to promote the importance of women's role in economic and social development and their participation in politics as a democratic necessity, and recognizes the crucial role of the media in presenting the image of women. Within the context of the 1997 New Delhi Conference, the IPU organized a second Round Table on the Image of Women Politicians in the Media (the first having been convened in November 1989). The debate urged fair and equal representation of women politicians by the media and for governments to revise their communications policies to advance the image of female parliamentarians.

In March 2007 IPU, jointly with UNDP, UNIFEM (from 2011 part of UN Women) and other partners, launched the International Knowledge Network of Women in Politics (iKNOW Politics), an online workspace aimed at supporting government officials, researchers, etc., in achieving the objective of advancing female participation in politics.

In 2008 the IPU launched a three-year programme to support parliaments to make ending violence against women a priority at the national level.

In April 2009 the IPU Assembly discussed means of accelerating progress towards securing the rights of adolescent girls to survival, education, health care, and protection, while emphasizing that the empowerment of adolescent girls belongs at the core of the development agenda and efforts towards achieving the UN Millennium Development Goals. In April 2012 the Assembly adopted a resolution on Access to Health as a Basic Right: the Role of Parliaments in Addressing Challenges to Securing the Health of Women and Children.

EDUCATION, SCIENCE AND CULTURE

Activities in these sectors are often subject to consideration by statutory meetings of the Assembly. Assembly resolutions have focused on the implementation of educational and cultural policies designed to foster greater respect for demographic values, adopted in April 1993; on bioethics and its implications world-wide for human rights protection, adopted in April 1995; and on the importance of education and culture as prerequisites for securing sustainable development (with particular emphasis on the education of women and the application of new information technologies), necessitating their high priority status in national budgets, adopted in April 2001. Specialized meetings organized by the IPU have included the Asia and Pacific Inter-Parliamentary Conference on 'Science and technology for regional sustainable development', held in Tokyo, Japan, in June 1994, and the Inter-Parliamentary Conference on 'Education, science, culture and communication on the threshold of the 21st century', organized jointly with UNESCO, and held in Paris, France, in June 1996. In October 2003 the IPU and UNESCO launched a network of national focal points linking the IPU's member parliaments and UNESCO, with the aim of circulating information and improving co-operation in the area of education, science, culture and communications.

In November 2006, the IPU and the UN Department of Economic and Social Affairs inaugurated the Rome, Italy-based Global Centre for Information and Communication Technologies in Parliament. The Centre, whose establishment was endorsed at the World Summit of the Information Society held in November 2005 in Tunis, Tunisia, is mandated to act as a clearing house for information, research, innovation, technology and technical assistance, and to promote a structured dialogue among parliaments, centres of excellence, international organizations, civil society, private sector interests, and international donors.

In October 2007 IPU, in conjunction with the UN Department for Economic and Social Affairs and the Association of Secretaries-General of Parliament, with support from the Global Centre for ICT in Parliament, convened the first World e-Parliament Conference, with participation by members of parliament, parliamentary officials, academics, and representatives of international organizations and of civil society. The e-Conference aimed to identify best practices in the use of new technologies to modernize parliamentary processes and communications. The IPU has, since 2008, issued an annual *World e-Parliament Report*.

Finance

The IPU is financed by its members, mainly from assessed contributions from member states. In addition, external financial support, primarily from voluntary donor contributions and UNDP, is received for some special activities. The 2012 annual budget amounted to 13.7m. Swiss francs.

Publications

Activities of the Inter-Parliamentary Union (annually).

Chronicle of Parliamentary Elections (annually).

Free and Fair Elections.

Global Parliamentary Report.

IPU Information Brochure (annually).

World Directory of Parliamentary Human Rights Bodies.

World Directory of Parliaments (annually).

World e-Parliament Report (annually).

The World of Parliaments (quarterly).

Other handbooks, reports and surveys, documents, proceedings of the Assembly.

ISLAMIC DEVELOPMENT BANK

Address: POB 5925, Jeddah 21432, Saudi Arabia.

Telephone: (2) 6361400; **fax:** (2) 6366871; **e-mail:** idbarchives@isdb.org; **internet:** www.isdb.org.

The Bank was established following a conference of Ministers of Finance of member countries of the then Organization of the Islamic Conference (now Organization of Islamic Cooperation—OIC), held in Jeddah in December 1973. Its aim is to encourage the economic development and social progress of member countries and of Muslim communities in non-member countries, in accordance with the principles of the Islamic *Shari'a* (sacred law). The Bank formally opened in October 1975. The Bank and its associated entities—the Islamic Research and Training Institute, the Islamic Corporation for the Development of the Private Sector, the Islamic Corporation for the Insurance of Investment and Export Credit, and the International Islamic Trade Finance Corporation—constitute the Islamic Development Bank Group.

MEMBERS

There are 56 members.

Organization

(April 2012)

BOARD OF GOVERNORS

Each member country is represented by a governor, usually its Minister of Finance, and an alternate. The Board of Governors is the supreme authority of the Bank, and meets annually. The 36th meeting was held at the Bank's headquarters in Jeddah, in June–July 2011. The 37th and 38th meetings were scheduled to be convened in Sudan and Yemen, respectively.

BOARD OF EXECUTIVE DIRECTORS

The Board consists of 18 members, half of whom are appointed by the eight largest subscribers to the capital stock of the Bank; the remaining eight are elected by Governors representing the other subscribers. Members of the Board of Executive Directors are elected for three-year terms. The Board is responsible for the direction of the general operations of the Bank.

ADMINISTRATION

President of the Bank and Chairman of the Board of Executive Directors: Dr AHMAD MOHAMED ALI AL-MADANI (Saudi Arabia).

Vice-President Corporate Services: Dr AHMET TIKTIK (Turkey).

Vice-President Finance: Dr ABDULAZIZ BIN MOHAMED BIN ZAHIR AL HINAI (Oman).

Vice-President Operations: BIRAMA BOUBACAR SIDIBE (Mali).

REGIONAL OFFICES

Kazakhstan: 050000 Almatı, Aiteki bi 67; tel. (727) 272-70-00; fax (727) 250-13-02; e-mail idbroa@isdb.org; Dir HISHAM TALEB MAAROUF.

Malaysia: Menara Bank Pembangunan Bandar Wawasan, Level 13, Jalan Sultan Ismail, 508250 Kuala Lumpur; tel. (3) 26946627; fax (3) 26946626; e-mail ROKL@isdb.org.

Morocco: Km 6.4, Ave Imam Malik Route des Zaers, POB 5003, Rabat; tel. (3) 7757191; fax (3) 7775726.

Senegal: 18 blvd de la République, Dakar; tel. (33) 889-1144; fax (33) 823-3621; e-mail RODK@isdb.org; Dir SIDI MOHAMED OULD TALEB.

FINANCIAL STRUCTURE

The Bank's unit of account is the Islamic Dinar (ID), which is equivalent to the value of one Special Drawing Right (SDR) of the IMF (average value of the SDR in 2010 was US $1.52571; and in 2011 it was US $1.57868). In May 2006 the Bank's Board of Governors approved an increase in the authorized capital from ID 15,000m. to ID 30,000m. An increase in subscribed capital, from ID 15,000m. to ID 16,000m. was approved by the Board of Governors in June 2008. In June 2010 the Board of Governors approved a further increase in subscribed capital to ID 18,000m. At 6 December total committed subscriptions amounted to ID 17,471.4m.

SUBSCRIPTIONS
(million Islamic Dinars, as at 6 December 2010)

Afghanistan	9.93	Maldives	9.23
Albania	9.23	Mali	18.19
Algeria	459.22	Mauritania	9.77
Azerbaijan	18.19	Morocco	91.69
Bahrain	25.88	Mozambique	9.23
Bangladesh	182.16	Niger	24.63
Benin	20.80	Nigeria	1,384.00
Brunei	45.85	Oman	50.92
Burkina Faso	24.63	Pakistan	459.22
Cameroon	45.85	Palestine	19.55
Chad	9.77	Qatar	1,297.50
Comoros	4.65	Saudi Arabia	4,249.60
Côte d'Ivoire	4.65	Senegal	52.80
Djibouti	4.96	Sierra Leone	4.96
Egypt	1,278.67	Somalia	4.96
Gabon	54.58	Sudan	83.21
The Gambia	9.23	Suriname	9.23
Guinea	45.85	Syria	18.49
Guinea-Bissau	4.96	Tajikistan	4.96
Indonesia	406.48	Togo	4.96
Iran	1,491.20	Tunisia	19.55
Iraq	48.24	Turkey	1,165.86
Jordan	78.50	Turkmenistan	4.96
Kazakhstan	19.29	Uganda	24.63
Kuwait	985.88	United Arab Emirates	1,045.96
Kyrgyzstan	9.23	Uzbekistan	4.80
Lebanon	9.77	Yemen	92.38
Libya	1,704.46		
Malaysia	294.01		

Activities

The Bank adheres to the Islamic principle forbidding usury, and does not grant loans or credits for interest. Instead, its methods of project financing are: provision of interest-free loans, mainly for infrastructural projects which are expected to have a marked impact on long-term socio-economic development; provision of technical assistance (e.g. for feasibility studies); equity participation in industrial and agricultural projects; leasing operations, involving the leasing of equipment such as ships, and instalment sale financing; and profit-sharing operations. Funds not immediately needed for projects are used for foreign trade financing. Under the Bank's trade financing operations funds are used for importing commodities for development purposes (i.e. raw materials and intermediate industrial goods, rather than consumer goods), with priority given to the import of goods from other member countries. In AH 1424 (2003/04) the Bank adopted a new group strategic framework, which identified three principal objectives: the promotion of Islamic financial industry and institutions; poverty alleviation; and the promotion of co-operation among member countries. In 2005 the Bank initiated a consultation process, led by a commission of eminent persons, to develop a new long-term strategy for the Bank. A document on the AH 1440 (2020) Vision was published in March 2006. It recommended that the Bank redefine its mandate and incorporate a broad focus on comprehensive human development, with priority concerns to be the alleviation of poverty and improvements to health, education and governance. The Vision also envisaged greater community involvement in Bank operations and more support given to local initiatives. In October 2008 the Bank organized a forum to consider the impact of the international economic and financial crisis on the Islamic financial system. The meeting resolved to establish a Task Force for Islamic Finance and Global Financial Stability, which met for the first time in January 2009, in Kuala Lumpur, Malaysia. In May the Board of Executive Directors agreed to double ordinary capital resources operations over a three-year period in order to support economic recovery in member countries. In the following month the Board of Governors approved the measure, along with others in support of mitigating the effects of the global financial crisis. During that year the Bank resolved to accelerate implementation of a major reform programme to enhance its relevance and impact in member countries, in accordance with the AH 1440 (2020) Vision. The Bank also adopted a Thematic Strategy for Poverty Reduction and Comprehensive Human Development to focus efforts to achieve the Vision's objectives. In September 2011 the Bank participated in a meeting of ministers of finance of the Group of Eight industrialized nations (G8) and high-level representatives of international financial institutions active in the Middle East and North Africa region to further support of the so-called Deauville Partnership, which had been established in May in order to assist countries in the region undergoing social and economic transformations. The Bank was a founding member of the new Co-ordination Platform to facilitate and promote collaboration among the institutions extending assistance under the Partnership.

By 6 December 2010 the Bank had approved a total of ID 22,313.0m. (equivalent to some US $32,316.0m.) for project financing since operations began in 1976, ID 246.1m. ($343.7m.) for technical assistance, ID 26,583.4m. ($36,959.3m.) for foreign trade financing, and ID 541.9m. ($702.1m.) for special assistance operations, excluding amounts for cancelled operations. Total net approved operations amounted to ID 49,684.3m. ($70,320.9m.) at that time.

During the Islamic year 1431 (17 December 2009–6 December 2010) the Bank approved a net total of ID 4,547.3m., for 363 operations, compared with ID 4,558.8m. for 469 operations in the previous year. Of the total approved in the Islamic year 1431 ID 245.4m. was approved for 43 loans, supporting projects concerned with the education and health sectors, infrastructural improvements, and agricultural developments. During that year the Bank's total disbursements totalled ID 2,548.0m., bringing the total cumulative disbursements since the Bank began operations to ID 33,266.0m. The Bank approved 82 technical assistance operations during that year in the form of grants and loans, amounting to ID 12.3m. Trade financing approved during the Islamic year 1431 amounted to ID 1,729.0m. for 77 operations.

During AH 1427 the Bank's export financing scheme was formally dissolved, although it continued to fund projects pending the commencement of operations of the International Islamic Trade Finance Corporation (ITFC). The Bank also finances other trade financing operations, including the Islamic Corporation for the Development of the Private Sector (ICD, see below), the Awqaf Properties Investment Fund and the Treasury Department. In addition, a Trade Co-operation and Promotion Programme supports efforts to enhance trade among OIC member countries. In June 2005 the Board of Governors approved the establishment of the ITFC as an autonomous trade promotion and financing institution within the Bank Group. The inaugural meeting of the ITFC was held in February 2007. In May 2006 the Board of Governors approved a new fund to reduce poverty and support efforts to achieve the UN Millennium Development Goals, in accordance with a proposal of the OIC. It was inaugurated, as the Islamic Solidarity Fund for Development, in May 2007; at that time 28 countries had pledged US $1,600m. to the Fund. The Fund became operational in early 2008.

In AH 1407 (1986/87) the Bank established an Islamic Bank's Portfolio for Investment and Development (IBP) in order to promote the development and diversification of Islamic financial markets and to mobilize the liquidity available to banks and financial institutions. During AH 1428 resources and activities of the IBP were transferred to the newly established ITFC. The Bank's Unit Investment Fund (UIF) became operational in 1990, with the aim of mobilizing additional resources and providing a profitable channel for investments conforming to *Shari'a*. The initial issue of the UIF was US $100m., which was subsequently increased to $325m. The Fund finances mainly private sector industrial projects in middle-income countries and also finances short-term trade operations. In October 1998 the Bank announced the establishment of a new fund to invest in infrastructure projects in member states. The Bank committed $250m. to the fund, which was to comprise $1,000m. equity capital and a $500m. Islamic financing facility. In January 2009 the Bank launched a second phase of the infrastructure fund. In November 2001 the Bank signed an agreement with Malaysia, Bahrain, Indonesia and Sudan for the establishment of an Islamic financial market. In April 2002 the Bank, jointly with governors of central banks and the Accounting and Auditing Organization for Islamic Financial Institutions, concluded an agreement, under the auspices of the IMF, for the establishment of an Islamic Financial Services Board. The Board, which was to be located in Kuala Lumpur, Malaysia, was intended to elaborate and harmonize standards for best practices in the regulation and supervision of the Islamic financial services industry. In August 2003 the Bank mobilized some $400m. from the international financial markets through the issue of the International Islamic Sukuk bond.

The Bank's Special Assistance Programme was initiated in AH 1400 to support the economic and social development of Muslim communities in non-member countries, in particular in the education and health sectors. It also aimed to provide emergency aid in times of natural disasters, and to assist Muslim refugees throughout the world. Operations undertaken by the Bank are financed by the Waqf Fund (formerly the Special Assistance Account). By the end of AH 1431 some ID 541.9m. (US $702.1m.) had been approved under the Waqf Fund Special Assistance Programme for 1,341 operations. Other assistance activities include scholarship programmes, technical co-operation projects and the sacrificial meat utilization project (see below). In January 2005 the Bank allocated $500m. to assist the survivors of the Indian Ocean earthquake and tsunami that struck coastal areas in 14 countries in late December 2004. The Bank dispatched missions to provide emergency relief to Indonesia, the Maldives and Sri Lanka, and planned to send further teams to assess the requirements for reconstruction. The Bank approved an assistance programme amounting to $501.6m. following a massive earthquake in north-western Pakistan in October 2005. The funds aimed to support recovery, rehabilitation and reconstruction efforts. The Bank increasingly has worked to assist post-conflict member countries in rehabilitation and reconstruction. It is a member of the management committee of the Afghanistan Reconstruction Trust Fund, which was established in 2001; during 2003 the Bank approved an operation to assist Afghan refugees. In December 2003 the Bank approved a Programme for Reconstruction of Iraq, with funding of ID 365.5m. ($500m.) to be implemented over a five-year period. In October 2002 the Bank's Board of Governors, meeting in Burkina Faso, adopted the Ouagadougou Declaration on the co-operation between the Bank group and Africa, which identified priority areas for Bank activities, for example education and the private sector. The Bank pledged $2,000m. to finance implementation of the Declaration over the five year period 2004–08. A successor initiative, the IDB Special Programme for the Development of Africa, was endorsed at a summit meeting of the OIC held in March 2008. The Bank committed $4,000m. to the Programme for the next five-year period, 2008–12. In June 2008 the Board of Governors inaugurated the Jeddah Declaration Initiative, with an allocation of $1,500m. in funds over a five-year period, to assist member countries to meet the escalating costs of food and to attain greater food security. In November 2009 the Bank concluded a co-financing agreement with IFAD, with funds of up to $1,500m., to support priority projects concerned with food security and rural development in the poorest member countries in Africa and Asia. The agreement was signed by the presidents of the two organizations in February 2010.

In AH 1404 (1983/84) the Bank established a scholarship programme for Muslim communities in non-member countries to provide opportunities for students to pursue further education or other professional training. The programme also assists 12 member countries on an exceptional basis. By the end of the Islamic year 1431 6,314 people had graduated and 4,022 were undertaking studies under the scheme. The Merit Scholarship Programme, initiated in AH 1412 (1991/92), aims to develop scientific, technological and research capacities in member countries through advanced studies and/or research. A total of 660 scholarships had been awarded by the end of AH 1431. In AH 1419 (1998/99) a Scholarship Programme in Science and Technology for IDB Least Developed Member Countries became operational for students in 20 eligible countries. The Bank awards annual prizes for science and technology to promote excellence in research and development and in scientific education.

The Bank's Programme for Technical Co-operation aims to mobilize technical capabilities among member countries and to promote the exchange of expertise, experience and skills through expert missions, training, seminars and workshops. In December 1999 the Board of Executive Directors approved two technical assistance grants to support a programme for the eradication of illiteracy in the Islamic world, and one for self-sufficiency in human vaccine production. The Bank also undertakes the distribution of meat sacrificed by Muslim pilgrims. The Bank was the principal source of funding of the International Centre for Biosaline Agriculture, which was established in Dubai, UAE, in September 1999.

BANK GROUP ENTITIES

International Islamic Trade Finance Corporation: Jeddah, Saudia Arabia; tel. (2) 6361400; fax (2) 6371064; e-mail info@itfc-idb.org; internet www.itfc-idb.org; f. 2007; commenced operations Jan. 2008; aims to promote trade and trade financing in Bank member countries, to facilitate access to public and private capital, and to promote investment opportunities; auth. cap. US $3,000m.; subs. cap. $750m. (Dec. 2010); CEO Dr WALID AL-WOHAIB.

Islamic Corporation for the Development of the Private Sector (ICD): POB 54069, Jeddah 21514, Saudi Arabia; tel. (2) 6441644; fax (2) 6444427; e-mail icd@isdb.org; internet www.icd-idb.org; f. 1999; to identify opportunities in the private sector, provide financial products and services compatible with Islamic law, mobilize additional resources for the private sector in member countries, and encourage the development of Islamic financing and capital markets; the Bank's share of the capital is 50%, member countries 30% and public financial institutions of member countries 20%; auth. cap. US $2,000m., cap. p.u. $460m. (Dec. 2010); mems: 47 countries, the Bank, and 5 public financial institutions; CEO and Gen. Man. KHALID M. AL-ABOODI.

Islamic Corporation for the Insurance of Investment and Export Credit (ICIEC): POB 15722, Jeddah 21454, Saudi Arabia; tel. (2) 6445666; fax (2) 6379504; e-mail idb.iciec@isdb.org.sa; internet www.iciec.com; f. 1994; aims to promote trade and the flow of investments among member countries of the OIC through the provision of export credit and investment insurance services; a representative office was opened in Dubai, UAE, in May 2010; auth. cap. increased from ID 150m. to ID 400m. in July 2011; subs. cap. ID 149m. (Aug. 2010); mems: 40 member states and the Islamic Development Bank (which contributes two-thirds of its capital); Gen. Man. Dr ABDEL RAHMAN A. TAHA.

Islamic Research and Training Institute: POB 9201, Jeddah 21413, Saudi Arabia; tel. (2) 6361400; fax (2) 6378927; e-mail irti@isdb.org; internet www.irti.org; f. 1982 to undertake research enabling economic, financial and banking activities to conform to Islamic law, and to provide training for staff involved in development activities in the Bank's member countries; the Institute also organizes seminars and workshops, and holds training courses aimed at furthering the expertise of government and financial officials in Islamic developing countries; Dir-Gen. a.i. LAMINE BEN ALI DOGHRI; publs *Annual Report*, *Islamic Economic Studies* (2 a year), various research studies, monographs, reports.

Publication

Annual Report.

Statistics

OPERATIONS APPROVED, ISLAMIC YEAR 1431
(17 December 2009–6 December 2010)

Type of operation	Number of operations	Amount (million Islamic Dinars)
Total project financing	233	2,806.0
Project financing	151	2,793.7
Technical assistance	82	12.3
Trade financing operations*	77	1,729.0
Special assistance operations	53	12.5
Total†	363	4,547.3

* Including operations by the ITFC, the ICD, the UIF, Treasury operations, and the Awqaf Properties Investment Fund.
† Excluding cancelled operations.

DISTRIBUTION OF PROJECT FINANCING AND TECHNICAL ASSISTANCE BY SECTOR, ISLAMIC YEAR 1431
(17 December 2009–6 December 2010)

Sector	Number of operations	Amount (million Islamic Dinars)	%
Agriculture	29	242.2	10.1
Education	19	80.2	3.3
Energy	14	792.4	33.1
Finance	48	93.9	3.9
Health	26	98.0	4.1
Industry and mining	8	213.4	8.9
Information and communications	7	0.4	0.0
Public administration	1	0.1	0.0
Transportation	11	651.9	27.2
Water, sanitation and urban services	16	224.1	9.4
Total*	179	2,396.6	100.0

* Excluding cancelled operations.

Source: Islamic Development Bank, *Annual Report 1431 H*.

LATIN AMERICAN INTEGRATION ASSOCIATION—LAIA

(ASOCIACIÓN LATINOAMERICANA DE INTEGRACIÓN—ALADI)

Address: Cebollatí 1461, Casilla 20.005, 11200 Montevideo, Uruguay.

Telephone: (2) 410-1121; **fax:** (2) 419-0649; **e-mail:** sgaladi@aladi.org; **internet:** www.aladi.org.

The Latin American Integration Association was established in August 1980 to replace the Latin American Free Trade Association, founded in February 1960.

MEMBERS

Argentina	Cuba	Paraguay
Bolivia	Ecuador	Peru
Brazil	Mexico	Uruguay
Chile	Panama	Venezuela
Colombia		

Observers: People's Republic of China, Costa Rica, Dominican Republic, El Salvador, Guatemala, Honduras, Italy, Japan, Republic of Korea, Nicaragua, Pakistan, Portugal, Romania, Russia, San Marino, Spain, Switzerland and Ukraine; also the UN Economic Commission for Latin America and the Caribbean, the UN Development Programme, the Andean Development Corporation, the European Union, the Ibero-American General Secretariat (SEGIB), the Inter-American Development Bank, the Inter-American Institute for Co-operation on Agriculture, the Latin American Economic System, the Organization of American States, and the Pan American Health Organization/World Health Organization.

Organization

(April 2012)

COUNCIL OF MINISTERS

The Council of Ministers of Foreign Affairs is responsible for the adoption of the Association's policies. It meets when convened by the Committee of Representatives.

CONFERENCE OF EVALUATION AND CONVERGENCE

The Conference, comprising plenipotentiaries of the member governments, assesses the integration process and encourages negotiations between members. It also promotes the convergence of agreements and other actions on economic integration. The Conference meets when convened by the Committee of Representatives.

COMMITTEE OF REPRESENTATIVES

The Committee, the permanent political body of the Association, comprises a permanent and a deputy representative from each member country. The Committee is the main forum for the negotiation of ALADI's initiatives and is responsible for the correct implementation of the Treaty and its supplementary regulations. There are the following auxiliary bodies:

Advisory Commission for Financial and Monetary Affairs.
Advisory Commission on Customs Valuation.
Advisory Council for Enterprises.
Advisory Council for Export Financing.
Advisory Council for Customs Matters.
Budget Commission.
Commission for Technical Support and Co-operation.
Council for Financial and Monetary Affairs: comprises the Presidents of member states' central banks, who examine all aspects of financial, monetary and exchange co-operation.
Council of National Customs Directors.
Council on Transport for Trade Facilitation.
Labour Advisory Council.
Nomenclature Advisory Commission.
Sectoral Councils.
Tourism Council.

GENERAL SECRETARIAT

The General Secretariat is the technical body of the Association; it submits proposals for action, carries out research and evaluates activities. The Secretary-General is elected for a three-year term, which is renewable. There are two Assistant Secretaries-General.

Secretary-General: CARLOS ÁLVAREZ (Argentina).

Activities

The Latin American Free Trade Association (LAFTA) was an inter-governmental organization, created by the Treaty of Montevideo in February 1960 with the object of increasing trade between the Contracting Parties and of promoting regional integration, thus contributing to the economic and social development of the member countries. The Treaty provided for the gradual establishment of a free trade area, which would form the basis for a Latin American Common Market. Reduction of tariff and other trade barriers was to be carried out gradually until 1980. In June 1980, however, it was decided that LAFTA should be replaced by a less ambitious and more flexible organization, the Latin American Integration Association (Asociación Latinoamericana de Integración—ALADI), established by the 1980 Montevideo Treaty, which came into force in March 1981, and was fully ratified in March 1982. The Treaty envisaged an area of economic preferences, comprising a regional tariff preference for goods originating in member states (in effect from 1 July 1984) and regional and partial scope agreements (on economic complementation, trade promotion, trade in agricultural goods, scientific and technical co-operation, the environment, tourism, and other matters), taking into account the different stages of development of the members, and with no definite timetable for the establishment of a full common market. By 2010 intra-ALADI exports were estimated to total US $133,151m., an increase of almost 25% from the previous year, when trade declined owing to adverse global economic conditions. The estimated total of intra-ALADI trade in 2011 amounted to $160,000m.

Certain LAFTA institutions were retained and adapted by ALADI, e.g. the Reciprocal Payments and Credits Agreement (1965, modified in 1982) and the Multilateral Credit Agreement to Alleviate Temporary Shortages of Liquidity, known as the Santo Domingo Agreement (1969, extended in 1981 to include mechanisms for counteracting global balance of payments difficulties and for assisting in times of natural disaster).

Agreements concluded under ALADI auspices include a regional tariff preference agreement, whereby members allow imports from other member states to enter with tariffs 20% lower than those imposed on imports from other countries, and a Market Opening Lists agreement in favour of the three least developed member states, which provides for the total elimination of duties and other restrictions on imports of certain products. Other 'partial scope agreements' (in which two or more member states participate), include: renegotiation agreements (pertaining to tariff cuts under LAFTA); trade agreements covering particular industrial sectors; the agreements establishing the Southern Common Market (Mercosur) and the Group of Three (G-3); and agreements covering agriculture, gas supply, tourism, environmental protection, books, transport, sanitation and trade facilitation. A new system of tariff nomenclature, based on the 'harmonized system', was adopted from 1 January 1990 as a basis for common trade negotiations and statistics. General regimes on safeguards and rules of origin entered into force in 1987. The Secretariat convenes meetings of entrepreneurs in various private industrial sectors, to encourage regional trade and co-operation.

ALADI has worked to establish multilateral links or agreements with Latin American non-member countries or integration organizations, and with other developing countries or economic groups outside the continent. In February 1994 the Council of Ministers of Foreign Affairs urged that ALADI should become the co-ordinating body for the various bilateral, multilateral and regional accords (with the Andean Community, Mercosur and G-3, etc.), with the aim of eventually forming a region-wide common market. The General Secretariat initiated studies in preparation for a programme to undertake this co-ordinating work. At the same meeting in February there was a serious disagreement regarding the proposed adoption of a protocol to the Montevideo Treaty to enable Mexico to participate in the North American Free Trade Agreement (NAFTA), while remaining a member of ALADI. However, in June the first Interpretative Protocol to the Montevideo Treaty was signed by the Ministers of Foreign Affairs: the Protocol allows member states to establish preferential trade agreements with developed nations, with a temporary waiver of the most favoured nation clause, subject to the negotiation of unilateral compensation. In December 2011 the Secretary-General of ALADI welcomed the establishment of the Community of Latin American and Caribbean States as further means of strengthening regional integration and of formulating a unified regional position in global fora. In March 2012 ALADI hosted a ministerial meeting, attended by high-level representatives of other regional organizations, which discussed current approaches to development in Latin America.

Mercosur (comprising Argentina, Brazil, Paraguay and Uruguay) aims to conclude free trade agreements with the other members of ALADI. In March 2001 ALADI signed a co-operation agreement with the Andean Community to facilitate the exchange of information and consolidate regional and sub-regional integration. In December 2003 Mercosur and the Andean Community signed an Economic Complementary Agreement, and in April 2004 they concluded a free trade agreement, to come into effect on 1 July 2004 (although later postponed). Those ALADI member states remaining outside Mercosur and the Andean Community would be permitted to apply to join the envisaged larger free trade zone.

Publications

Noticias ALADI (monthly, in Spanish).

Estadísticas y Comercio (quarterly, in Spanish).

Reports, studies, brochures, texts of agreements.

LEAGUE OF ARAB STATES

Address: POB 11642, Arab League Bldg, Tahrir Sq., Cairo, Egypt.
Telephone: (2) 575-0511; **fax:** (2) 574-0331; **internet:** www.arableagueonline.org.

The League of Arab States (more generally known as the Arab League) is a voluntary association of sovereign Arab states, designed to strengthen the close ties linking them and to co-ordinate their policies and activities and direct them towards the common good of all the Arab countries. It was founded in March 1945.

MEMBERS

Algeria	Lebanon	Somalia
Bahrain	Libya*	Sudan
Comoros	Mauritania	Syria*
Djibouti	Morocco	Tunisia
Egypt	Oman	United Arab Emirates
Iraq	Palestine†	Yemen
Jordan	Qatar	
Kuwait	Saudi Arabia	

* Libya was suspended from participation in meetings of the League in February 2011. It was readmitted in August following an agreement that the new Libyan Transitional Council would represent the country at the League. In mid-November Syria was suspended from meetings of the League.

† Palestine is considered to be an independent state, and therefore a full member of the League.

Organization

(April 2012)

COUNCIL

The supreme organ of the Arab League, the Council consists of representatives of the member states, each of which has one vote, and a representative for Palestine. The Council meets ordinarily every March, normally at the League headquarters, at the level of heads of state ('kings, heads of state and emirs'), and in March and September at the level of ministers of foreign affairs. The summit level meeting reviews all issues related to Arab national security strategies, co-ordinates supreme policies of the Arab states towards regional and international issues, reviews recommendations and reports submitted to it by meetings at foreign minister level, appoints the Secretary-General of the League, and is mandated to amend the League's Charter. Decisions of the Council at the level of heads of state are passed on a consensus basis. Meetings of ministers of foreign affairs assess the implementation of summit resolutions, prepare relevant reports, and make arrangements for subsequent summits. Committees comprising a smaller group of foreign ministers may be appointed to follow up closely summit resolutions. Extraordinary summit meetings may be held at the request of one member state or the Secretary-General, if approved by a two-thirds' majority of member states. Extraordinary sessions of ministers of foreign affairs may be held at the request of two member states or of the Secretary-General. The presidency of ordinary meetings is rotated in accordance with the alphabetical order of the League's member states. Unanimous decisions of the Council are binding upon all member states of the League; majority decisions are binding only on those states that have accepted them.

The Council is supported by technical and specialized committees advising on financial and administrative affairs, information affairs and legal affairs. In addition, specialized ministerial councils have been established to formulate common policies for the regulation and the advancement of co-operation in the following sectors: communications; electricity; environment; health; housing and construction; information; interior; justice; social affairs; tourism; transportation; and youth and sports.

GENERAL SECRETARIAT

The administrative and financial offices of the League. The Secretariat carries out the decisions of the Council, and provides financial and administrative services for the personnel of the League. General departments comprise: the Bureau of the Secretary-General, Arab Affairs, Economic Affairs, Information Affairs, Legal Affairs, Palestine Affairs, Political International Affairs, Military Affairs, Social Affairs, Administrative and Financial Affairs, and Internal Audit. In addition, there is a Documentation and Information Centre, an Arab League Centre in Tunis, Tunisia, an Arab Fund for Technical Assistance in African States, a Higher Arab Institute for Translation in Algiers, Algeria, a Music Academy in Baghdad, Iraq, and a Central Boycott Office, based in Damascus, Syria (see below). The following bodies have also been established: an administrative court; an investment arbitration board; and a higher auditing board.

The Secretary-General is appointed at summit meetings of the Council by a two-thirds' majority of the member states, for a five-year, renewable term. He appoints the Assistant Secretaries-General and principal officials, with the approval of the Council. He has the rank of ambassador, and the Assistant Secretaries-General have the rank of ministers plenipotentiary.

Secretary-General: NABIL AL-ARABI (Egypt).

DEFENCE AND ECONOMIC CO-OPERATION

Groups established under the Treaty of Joint Defence and Economic Co-operation, concluded in 1950 to complement the Charter of the League.

Arab Unified Military Command: f. 1964 to co-ordinate military policies for the liberation of Palestine.

Economic and Social Council: compares and co-ordinates the economic policies of the member states; supervises the activities of the Arab League's specialized agencies. The Council is composed of ministers of economic affairs or their deputies; decisions are taken by majority vote. The first meeting was held in 1953. In February 1997 the Economic and Social Council adopted the Executive Programme of the League's (1981) Agreement to Facilitate and Develop Trade Among Arab Countries, with a view to establishing a Greater Arab Free Trade Area (see below).

Joint Defence Council: supervises implementation of those aspects of the treaty concerned with common defence. Composed of ministers of foreign affairs and of defence; decisions by a two-thirds' majority vote of members are binding on all.

Permanent Military Commission: f. 1950; composed of representatives of army general staffs; main purpose: to draw up plans of joint defence for submission to the Joint Defence Council.

ARAB TRANSITIONAL PARLIAMENT

Inaugurated in December 2005, the Arab Transitional Parliament, based in Damascus, Syria, comprises 88 members (four delegates from each Arab state, including some representing non-elected bodies). The Transitional Parliament is eventually to be replaced by a Permanent Arab Parliament, a Statute for which remains under discussion. The interim body (which has no legislative function) aims to encourage dialogue between member states and to provide a focal point for joint Arab action.

OTHER INSTITUTIONS OF THE LEAGUE

Other bodies established by resolutions adopted by the Council of the League:

Administrative Tribunal of the Arab League: f. 1964; began operations 1966.

Arab Fund for Technical Assistance to African Countries: f. 1975 to provide technical assistance for development projects by providing African and Arab experts, grants for scholarships and training, and finance for technical studies.

Central Boycott Office: POB 437, Damascus, Syria; f. 1951 to prevent trade between Arab countries and Israel, and to enforce a boycott by Arab countries of companies outside the region that conduct trade with Israel.

Higher Auditing Board: comprises representatives of seven member states, elected every three years; undertakes financial and administrative auditing duties.

Investment Arbitration Board: examines disputes between member states relating to capital investments.

SPECIALIZED AGENCIES

All member states of the Arab League are also members of the Specialized Agencies, which constitute an integral part of the Arab League. (See also the Arab Fund for Economic and Social Development, the Arab Monetary Fund, Council of Arab Economic Unity and the Organization of Arab Petroleum Exporting Countries.)

Arab Academy for Science, Technology and Maritime Transport (AASTMT): POB 1029, Alexandria, Egypt; tel. (3) 5622388; fax (3) 5622525; internet www.aast.edu; f. 1975 as Arab Maritime Transport Academy; provides specialized training in marine transport, engineering, technology and management; Pres. Prof. Dr ISMAIL ABDEL GHAFAR ISMAIL; publs *Maritime Research Bulletin* (monthly), *Journal of the Arab Academy for Science, Technology and Maritime Transport* (2 a year).

Arab Administrative Development Organization (ARADO): 2 El-Hegaz St, POB 2692 al-Horreia, Heliopolis, Cairo, Egypt; tel. (2)

22580006; fax (2) 22580077; e-mail arado@arado.org.eg; internet www.arado.org.eg; f. 1961 (as Arab Organization of Administrative Sciences), became operational in 1969; administration development, training, consultancy, research and studies, information, documentation; promotes Arab and international co-operation in administrative sciences; includes Arab Network of Administrative Information; maintains an extensive digital library; 20 Arab state members; Dir-Gen. Prof. REFAT ABDELHALIM ALFAOURI; publs *Arab Journal of Administration* (biannual), *Management Newsletter* (quarterly), research series, training manuals.

Arab Atomic Energy Agency (AAEA): POB 402, El-Manzah 1004, 1004 Tunis, Tunisia; tel. (71) 808400; fax (71) 808450; e-mail aaea@aaea.org.tn; internet www.aaea.org.tn; f. 1988; Dir-Gen. Prof. Dr ABDELMAJID MAHJOUB (Tunisia); publs *The Atom and Development* (quarterly), other publs in the field of nuclear sciences and their applications in industry, biology, medicine, agriculture, food irradiation and seawater desalination.

Arab Bank for Economic Development in Africa (Banque arabe pour le développement économique en Afrique—BADEA): Sayed Abd ar-Rahman el-Mahdi St, POB 2640, Khartoum 11111, Sudan; tel. (1) 83773646; fax (1) 83770600; e-mail badea@badea.org; internet www.badea.org; f. 1973 by Arab League; provides loans and grants to African countries to finance development projects; paid-up cap. US $2,800m. (Dec. 2010); in 2010 the Bank approved loans and grants totalling $192.0m. and technical assistance for feasibility studies and institutional support amounting to $30m.; by the end of 2010, total net loan and grant commitments approved since funding activities began in 1975 amounted to $2,223.6m; during 2010 the Bank contributed $13.91m. to the heavily indebted poor countries initiative, bringing the cumulative total to $186.3. since the scheme commenced in 1997; subscribing countries: all countries of the Arab League, except the Comoros, Djibouti, Somalia and Yemen; recipient countries: all countries of the African Union, except those belonging to the Arab League; Chair. YOUSEF IBRAHEM AL-BASSAM (Saudi Arabia); Dir-Gen. ABDELAZIZ KHELEF (Algeria); publs *Annual Report Co-operation for Development* (quarterly), studies on Afro-Arab co-operation, periodic brochures.

Arab Center for the Studies of Arid Zones and Dry Lands (ACSAD): POB 2440, Damascus, Syria; tel. (11) 5743039; fax (11) 5743063; e-mail email@acsad.org; internet www.acsad.org; f. 1968 to conduct regional research and development programmes related to water and soil resources, plant and animal production, agro-meteorology, and socio-economic studies of arid zones; holds conferences and training courses and encourages the exchange of information by Arab scientists; Dir-Gen. RAFIK ALI SALEH.

Arab Industrial Development and Mining Organization: rue France, Zanagat al-Khatawat, POB 8019, Rabat, Morocco; tel. (37) 772600; fax (37) 772188; e-mail id@aidmo.org; internet www.aidmo.org; f. 1990 by merger of Arab Industrial Development Organization, Arab Organization for Mineral Resources and Arab Organization for Standardization and Metrology; comprises a 13-member Executive Council, a High Consultative Committee of Standardization, a High Committee of Mineral Resources and a Co-ordination Committee for Arab Industrial Research Centres; a Council of ministers of member states responsible for industry meets every two years; in Sept. 2011 organized, jointly with ESCWA, a conference on 'The Role of Green Industries in Promoting Socio-Economic Development in the Arab Countries'; Dir-Gen. MOHAMED BIN YOUSEF; publs *Arab Industrial Development* (monthly and quarterly newsletters).

Arab Investment & Export Credit Guarantee Corporation: POB 23568, Safat 13096, Kuwait; tel. 4959000; fax 4959596; e-mail operations@dhaman.org; internet www.dhaman.org; f. 1974; insures Arab investors for non-commercial risks, and export credits for commercial and non-commercial risks; undertakes research and other activities to promote inter-Arab trade and investment; total assets US $354.5m. (Dec. 2010); mems: 21 Arab countries and four multilateral Arab financial institutions; Dir-Gen. FAHAD RASHID AL-IBRAHIM; publs *News Bulletin* (quarterly), *Arab Investment Climate Report* (annually).

Arab Labour Organization: POB 814, Cairo, Egypt; tel. (2) 3362721; fax (2) 3484902; internet www.alolabor.org; f. 1965 for co-operation between member states in labour problems; unification of labour legislation and general conditions of work wherever possible; research; technical assistance; social insurance; training, etc; the organization has a tripartite structure: governments, employers and workers; Dir-Gen. AHMAD MUHAMMAD LUQMAN; publs *ALO Bulletin* (monthly), *Arab Labour Review* (quarterly), *Legislative Bulletin* (annually), series of research reports and studies concerned with economic and social development issues in the Arab world.

Arab League Educational, Cultural and Scientific Organization (ALECSO): ave Mohamed V, POB 1120, Tunis, Tunisia; tel. (71) 784-466; fax (71) 784-496; e-mail alecso@email.ati.tn; internet www.alecso.org.tn; f. 1970 to promote and co-ordinate educational, cultural and scientific activities in the Arab region; 21 mem. states; regional units: Arab Centre for Arabization, Translation, Authorship, and Publication—Damascus, Syria; Institute of Arab Manuscripts—Cairo, Egypt; Institute of Arab Research and Studies—Cairo, Egypt; Khartoum International Institute for Arabic Language—Khartoum, Sudan; and the Arabization Co-ordination Bureau—Rabat, Morocco; Dir-Gen. MOHAMED-EL AZIZ BEN ACHOUR; publs *Arab Journal of Culture* (2 a year), *Arab Journal of Education* (2 a year), *Arab Journal of Science and Information* (2 a year), *Arab Bulletin of Publications* (annually), *ALECSO Newsletter* (monthly).

Arab Organization for Agricultural Development (AOAD): 7 al-Amarat St, POB 474, Khartoum 11111, Sudan; tel. (1) 83472176; fax (1) 83471402; e-mail info@aoad.org; internet www.aoad.org; f. 1970; began operations in 1972 to contribute to co-operation in agricultural activities, and in the development of natural and human resources for agriculture; compiles data, conducts studies, training and food security programmes; includes Information and Documentation Centre, Arab Centre for Studies and Projects, and Arab Institute of Forestry and Biodiversity; Dir-Gen. Dr TARIQ MOOSA AL-ZADJALI; publs *Agricultural Statistics Yearbook*, *Annual Report on Agricultural Development*, *the State of Arab Food Security* (annually), *Agriculture and Development in the Arab World* (quarterly), *Accession Bulletin* (every 2 months), *AOAD Newsletter* (monthly), *Arab Agricultural Research Journal*, *Arab Journal for Irrigation Water Management* (2 a year).

Arab Satellite Communications Organization (ARABSAT): POB 1038, Diplomatic Quarter, Riyadh 11431, Saudi Arabia; tel. (1) 4820000; fax (1) 4887999; e-mail info@arabsat.com; internet www.arabsat.com; f. 1976; regional satellite telecommunications organization providing television, telephone and data exchange services to members and private users; operates five satellites, which cover all Arab and Western European countries; Pres. and CEO KHALID AHMED BALKHEYOUR.

Arab States Broadcasting Union (ASBU): POB 250, 1080 Tunis Cedex; rue 8840, Centre Urbain Nord, Tunisia; tel. (71) 843505; fax (71) 843054; e-mail asbu@asbu.intl.tn; internet www.asbu.net; f. 1969 to promote and study broadcasting subjects, to exchange expertise and technical co-operation in broadcasting; conducts training and audience research; 28 active mems, seven participating mems, 19 assoc. mems; Pres. of Exec. Council MOHAMED HATEM SULEIMAN (Sudan); publ. *Arab Broadcasters* (quarterly).

Activities

The League was founded in 1945 with the signing of the Pact of the Arab League. A Cultural Treaty was signed in the following year. In 1952, agreements were concluded on extradition, writs, letters of request and the nationality of Arabs outside their country of origin, and in the following year a Convention was adopted on the privileges and immunities of the League. At an emergency summit meeting held in 1985, two commissions were established to mediate in disagreements between Arab states (between Jordan and Syria, Iraq and Syria, Iraq and Libya, and Libya and the Palestine Liberation Organization (PLO). The League's headquarters, which had been transferred from Cairo, Egypt, to Tunis, Tunisia, in 1979, were relocated back to Cairo in 1990. At a meeting of the Council held in September 2000, ministers of foreign affairs of member states adopted an Appendix to the League's Charter that provided for the Council to meet ordinarily every March at the level of a summit conference of heads of state ('kings, heads of state and emirs'). The Council was to continue to meet at foreign ministerial level every March and September. In October 2002 Libya announced plans to withdraw from the League, although these were subsequently suspended. In July the Egyptian Government unveiled a series of measures aimed at strengthening the League, including the adoption of majority voting and the establishment of a body to resolve conflicts in the region (previously agreed at the 1996 summit and sanctioned by member states' foreign ministers in 2000). The 2004 summit meeting of Arab League heads of state, scheduled to be held in Tunis in late March, was postponed by the Tunisian Government two days in advance following disagreements among member states over a number of issues on the summit's agenda, including democratic reforms in Arab states and the proposed reforms to the League. The meeting, which was eventually held in May, approved a *Pledge of Accord and Solidarity* that committed the League heads of state to implementing in full decisions of the League. The Arab leaders also stated their commitment to conducting political, economic and social reforms, respect for human rights, and to strengthening the role of women, despite continuing opposition from several member states. In March 2007 the summit meeting of heads of state, held in Riyadh, Saudi Arabia, determined that in future Arab consultative summits should be convoked when deemed necessary to address specific issues. The 22nd Arab League summit meeting, held in Sirte, Libya, in March 2010, approved the formation of a committee comprising the Egyptian, Iraqi, Libyan, Qatari and Yemeni heads of state, and the League Secretary-General, with a mandate to oversee the development of a new structure for joint Arab action. The committee prepared documentation on proposed reforms for consideration by an extraordinary summit of the League that was held in early October, also in Sirte.

From February–August 2011 the League suspended Libya from participation in its meetings owing to the use of military force against opposition movements in that country (see below). In mid-November Syria was suspended from meetings of the League, on similar grounds. The emerging civil unrest in countries in the region, notably, in addition, in Egypt, Tunisia and Yemen, led to the 23rd summit meeting, initially scheduled to be held in March 2011, being postponed until March 2012.

In mid-May 2011 a meeting of League ministers of foreign affairs unanimously elected Nabil al-Arabi, hitherto the Egyptian minister of foreign affairs, as the new Secretary-General of the League.

The 23rd summit meeting of Arab League heads of state, convened in Baghdad, Iraq, in late March 2012, endorsed, and called for the immediate implementation of, a six-point plan on resolving the Syrian crisis that had been recently proposed by the UN-Arab League Joint Special Envoy on the Syrian Crisis. The UN Secretary-General attended the summit, owing to the inclusion of the Syrian crisis on its agenda. Saudi Arabia, seeking the imposition of stronger measures against the Syrian regime, and having reportedly failed to secure the agreement of the Iraqi Government to invite Syrian opposition representatives to the summit meeting, was represented at the gathering at the level of Ambassador. Egypt and Qatar also sent delegates lower than the level of head of state. The Amir of Kuwait participated in the meeting, representing the first visit by a Kuwaiti leader to Baghdad since prior to the 1990 invasion Kuwait by Iraq. Regional water shortages and means of coping with natural disasters were also discussed by the summit.

SECURITY

In 1950 Arab League member states concluded a Joint Defence and Economic Co-operation Treaty. An Arab Deterrent Force was established by the Arab League Council in June 1976 to supervise attempts at that time to cease hostilities in Lebanon; the Force's mandate was terminated in 1983. In April 1998 Arab League ministers of the interior and of justice adopted the Arab Convention for the Suppression of Terrorism, which incorporated security and judicial measures, such as extradition arrangements and the exchange of evidence. The agreement entered into effect in May 2000, 30 days after being ratified by at least seven member countries. In August 1998 the League denounced terrorist bomb attacks against the US embassies in Kenya and Tanzania. Nevertheless, it condemned US retaliatory military action, a few days later, against suspected terrorist targets in Afghanistan and Sudan, and endorsed a request by the Sudanese Government that the Security Council investigate the incident. An emergency meeting of the League's Council, convened in mid-September 2001 in response to major terrorist attacks on the USA, perpetrated by militant Islamist fundamentalists, condemned the atrocities, while urging respect for the rights of Arab and Muslim US citizens. The Secretary-General subsequently emphasized the need for co-ordinated global anti-terrorist action to have clearly defined goals and to be based on sufficient consultations and secure evidence. He also deplored anti-Islamic prejudice, and stated that US-led action against any Arab state would not be supported and that Israeli participation in an international anti-terrorism alliance would be unacceptable. A meeting of League ministers of foreign affairs in Doha, Qatar, in early October condemned international terrorism but did not express support for retaliatory military action by the USA and its allies. In December a further emergency meeting of League foreign affairs ministers was held to discuss the deepening Middle East crisis. In January 2002 the League appointed a commissioner responsible for promoting dialogue between civilizations. The commissioner was mandated to encourage understanding in Western countries of Arab and Muslim civilization and viewpoints, with the aim of redressing perceived negative stereotypes (especially in view of the Islamist fundamentalist connection to the September 2001 terrorist atrocities). In April 2003 the Secretary-General expressed his regret that the Arab states had failed to prevent the ongoing war in Iraq, and urged the development of a new regional security order. In November the UN Secretary-General appointed the Secretary-General of the League to serve as the Arab region's representative on the UN High-Level Panel on Threats, Challenges and Change. In March 2007 the League's summit meeting resolved to establish an expert-level task force to consider national security issues.

In December 2010 the Arab League and the UN Office on Drugs and Crime jointly launched a five-year Regional Programme on Drug Control, Crime Prevention and Criminal Justice Reform for the Arab States, covering the period 2011–15, and based on the following pillars: countering illicit trafficking, organized crime and terrorism; promoting justice and integrity; and drug prevention and improving health.

LIBYA

In December 1991 the League expressed solidarity with Libya, which was under international pressure to extradite two government agents who were suspected of involvement in the explosion which destroyed a US passenger aircraft over Lockerbie, United Kingdom, in December 1988. In March 1992 the League appointed a committee to seek to resolve the disputes between Libya and the USA, the United Kingdom and France over the Lockerbie bomb and the explosion which destroyed a French passenger aircraft over Niger in September 1989. The League condemned the UN's decision, at the end of March, to impose sanctions against Libya, and appealed for a negotiated solution. In September 1997 Arab League ministers of foreign affairs advocated a gradual removal of international sanctions against Libya, and agreed that member countries should permit international flights to leave Libya for specific humanitarian and religious purposes and when used for the purpose of transporting foreign nationals. In August 1998 the USA and United Kingdom accepted a proposal of the Libyan Government, supported by the Arab League, that the suspects in the Lockerbie case be tried in The Hague, Netherlands, under Scottish law. In March 1999 the League's Council determined that member states would suspend sanctions imposed against Libya, once arrangements for the trial of the suspects in the Lockerbie case had been finalized. (The suspects were transferred to a detention centre in the Netherlands in early April, whereupon the UN Security Council suspended its sanctions against Libya.) At the end of January 2001, following the completion of the trial in The Hague of the two Libyans accused of complicity in the Lockerbie case (one of whom was found guilty and one of whom was acquitted), the Secretary-General of the League urged the UN Security Council fully to terminate the sanctions against Libya that had been suspended in 1999. Meeting in mid-March, the League's Council pledged that member states would not consider themselves bound by the (inactive) UN sanctions. In early September 2002 the Council deplored the USA's continuing active imposition of sanctions against Libya and endorsed Libya's right to claim compensation in respect of these.

In mid-February 2011, in protest against violent measures taken by the regime of the Libyan leader Col Muammar al-Qaddafi against opposition groupings, the Libyan delegate to the League resigned his representative position. An emergency session of the League convened soon afterwards suspended Libya from participation in meetings of the League. The League supported the adoption by the UN Security Council, in March, of Resolution 1973, which imposed a no-fly zone in Libya's airspace, strengthened sanctions against the Qaddafi regime, demanded an immediate cease-fire, and authorized member states to take 'all necessary measures to protect civilians and civilian populated areas under threat of attack' by forces loyal to Qaddafi, 'while excluding a foreign occupation force of any form on any part of Libyan territory'. Following the instigation of the UN-mandated military action in Libya, the League Secretary-General reportedly emphasized that the focus of the military intervention ought to be on the protection of civilians and ought not to exceed the mandate to impose a no-fly zone. In August, as opposition forces captured the Libyan capital, Tripoli, the League Secretary-General offered full solidarity to the new Libyan National Transitional Council, as the legitimate representative of the Libyan people. Libya was readmitted to full League membership at the end of that month. The League at that time urged the international community to release all assets and property of the Libyan state, previously blocked by economic sanctions. Following the death of al-Qaddafi in October the Secretary-General urged unity and extended the League's full support for the country's transition.

SYRIA

By August 2011 it was estimated that around 2,200 anti-government street protesters had been killed by security forces—deploying tanks and snipers—during several months of unrest in Syria. A meeting of Arab League foreign ministers convened in that month issued a statement urging the Syrian regime to act reasonably, stop the ongoing bloodshed, and respect the 'legitimate demands' of the Syrian people. The meeting also determined that the League Secretary-General, Nabil al-Arabi, would visit the Syrian authorities with a peace initiative aimed at resolving the situation through dialogue. Accordingly, talks were held between the Secretary-General and President Bashar al-Assad in the Syrian capital, Damascus, in early September. It was reported that al-Arabi and al-Assad discussed measures aimed at accelerating political reforms in Syria, and that the League Secretary-General stated his rejection of foreign intervention in the Syrian situation. The League's peace initiative was, however, reportedly rejected by both the Syrian authorities and protesters. In October al-Arabi led a further delegation to the country, amid an escalation of attacks by the security forces. In mid-November the League, meeting in emergency session, voted to suspend Syria from participation in meetings of the League, and to impose economic and diplomatic sanctions in protest at the violent repression of political opponents and civilian demonstrators by the government, and its failure to implement a peace initiative. The resolution was endorsed by 18 members; Syria, Lebanon and Yemen voted against the suspension (Iraq abstained). The measures came into effect four days later, when no concessions had been made by the Syrian authorities. By mid-December the UN estimated that at least 5,000 Syrians had died in the uprising. On 19 December the Syrian authorities reportedly agreed to the League's peace plan to withdraw security forces and heavy weapons from civilian areas, to initiate negotiations with the opposition movement and to release political prisoners. The Arab League was to send an observer mission to the country, with an initial mandate of one month, in order to monitor compliance with the measures. However, within days of the arrival of the first 50 observers, on 26 December, the mission was strongly criticized for its ineffectiveness in preventing further government attacks and its inability to act independently of the authorities to assess accurately the level of violence. On 9 January 2012 Arab League ministers of foreign affairs met to consider the mission's initial findings and to discuss demands for its withdrawal. The meeting agreed to maintain and to reinforce the mission and demanded that the Syrian authorities co-operate fully. On 22 January Arab League ministers agreed on a plan of action to end the conflict, requiring President Assad to transfer his authority to an interim government within two months, and democratic parliamentary and presidential elections to be conducted within six months. The proposals were to be submitted for approval by the UN Security Council. They were rejected, the following day, by the Syrian authorities. The ministerial meeting agreed to extend the monitoring mission. Saudi Arabia, however, decided to withdraw from the operation. On 24 January members of the Gulf Cooperation Council also resolved to withdraw their monitors. A few days later the League announced that it was suspending the mission owing to a sharp deterioration in the security situation in Syria. In early February Russia and the People's Republic of China vetoed a draft resolution at the UN Security Council to endorse the League's peace plan for Syria. In mid-February League ministers adopted a resolution providing for the termination of the suspended monitoring mission; ending diplomatic co-operation with the Syrian regime; and proposing the creation of a joint Arab-UN peace-keeping mission to Syria. Later in that month the Secretaries-General of the League and of the UN appointed Kofi Annan—formerly the UN Secretary-General (until 2006)—as their Joint Special Envoy on the Syrian Crisis; in March Nasser al-Kidwa, a former minister of foreign affairs in the Palestine National Authority, and Jean-Marie Guéhenno, a former UN Under-Secretary-General for Peace-keeping Operations, were appointed as Deputy Joint Special Envoys. Towards the end of February an international conference on the situation in Syria, which had escalated significantly, was convened in Tunis, Tunisia, by the 'Friends of Syria', a coalition initiated by France and the USA, with League support (specifically, with endorsement from Qatar and Saudi Arabia), following China and Russia's veto of the Security Council's draft resolution on Syria. The conference urged the UN to consider establishing a peace-keeping mission for Syria. In late March the Syrian Government announced its acceptance of a six-point peace plan proposed earlier in that month by Annan. The plan envisaged: (i) a commitment to working with the Joint Envoy in an inclusive Syrian-led political process aimed at addressing the legitimate aspirations and concerns of the Syrian people; (ii) a UN-monitored cease-fire by all parties, including a commitment by the Syrian regime to withdraw troops and heavy weaponry from population centres; (iii) a commitment to enabling the timely provision of humanitarian assistance to all areas affected by the fighting, and the immediate implementation of a daily two-hour humanitarian pause; (iv) the expedited release of arbitrarily arrested detainees; (v) free access and movement for journalists; and (vi) freedom of association and the right to demonstrate peacefully for all. The plan did not demand explicitly the resignation of Syrian President Assad. Shortly afterwards Arab League heads of state, gathered at a summit meeting in Baghdad, Iraq, endorsed the plan, and called for its immediate and full implementation. In mid-April the UN Security Council—taking note of an assessment by the League-UN Joint Special Envoy that the parties to the Syrian violence appeared to be observing a cessation of fire, and that the Syrian Government had begun to implement its commitments under the plan—authorized an advance team of up to 30 unarmed military observers to monitor the cease-fire, pending the deployment of a full cease-fire supervision mission. Soon afterwards, as violence had escalated since the attempt to impose a cease-fire, and Syrian forces had not withdrawn from urban areas, the UN Secretary-General requested that a full team of 300 unarmed observers should be promptly deployed. Consequently, on 21 April, the UN Security Council unanimously authorized the establishment of the UN Supervision Mission in Syria (UNSMIS), initially for a period of 90 days, with a mandate to monitor the cessation of violence and to observe and support the full implementation of the six-point peace plan. By mid-April the number of civilians killed in the Syrian conflict since March 2011 was estimated at more than 9,000; many more people were estimated to have been displaced from their homes.

Joint Special Envoy of the League of Arab States and the UN on the Syrian Crisis: KOFI ANNAN (Ghana).

TRADE AND ECONOMIC CO-OPERATION

In 1953 Arab League member states formed an Economic and Social Council. In 1956 an agreement was concluded on the adoption of a Common Tariff Nomenclature. In 1962 an Arab Economic Unity Agreement was concluded. The first meeting of the Council of Arab Economic Unity took place in June 1964. An Arab Common Market Agreement was endorsed by the Council in August. In February 1997 the Economic and Social Council adopted the Executive Programme of the (1981) Agreement to Facilitate and Develop Trade Among Arab Countries, with a view to creating a Greater Arab Free Trade Area (GAFTA), which aimed to facilitate and develop trade among participating countries through the reduction and eventual elimination of customs duties over a 10-year period (at a rate of 10% per year), with effect from January 1998. In February 2002 the Economic and Social Council agreed to bring forward the inauguration of GAFTA to 1 January 2005. Consequently customs duties, which, according to schedule, had been reduced by 50% from January 1998–January 2002, were further reduced by 10% by January 2003, 20% by January 2004, and a final 20% by January 2005. GAFTA entered into force, as planned, with 17 participating countries (accounting for about 94% of the total volume of intra-Arab trade). The Council agreed to supervise the implementation of the free trade agenda and formally to review its progress twice a year.

The first ever Economic, Development and Social summit meeting of Arab leaders was held in January 2009, in Kuwait, under the auspices of the Arab League. The second Economic, Development and Social summit meeting was convened in January 2011, in Sharm el-Sheikh, Egypt.

WATER RESOURCES

In April 1993 the Council approved the creation of a committee to consider the political and security aspects of water supply in Arab countries. In March 1996, following protests by Syria and Iraq that extensive construction work in southern Turkey was restricting water supply in the region, the Council determined that the waters of the Euphrates and Tigris rivers be shared equitably between the three countries. In April an emergency meeting of the Council issued a further endorsement of Syria's position in the dispute with Turkey.

The inaugural session of a new Arab Ministerial Water Council was convened in June 2009. The Council gave consideration to the development of an Arab Water Strategy; this was launched in March 2011.

ARAB–ISRAELI AFFAIRS

The League regards Palestine as an independent state and therefore as a full League member. In 1951 a Central Boycott Office was established, in Damascus, Syria, to oversee the prevention of trade between Arab countries and Israel, and to enforce a boycott by Arab countries of companies outside the region that conduct trade with Israel. The second summit conference of Arab heads of state, convened in 1964, welcomed the establishment of the PLO.

In April 1993 the League pledged its commitment to the ongoing US-sponsored Middle East Peace Process. Following the signing of the Israeli-PLO Oslo peace accords in September the Council convened in emergency session, at which it approved the agreement. In 1994 the League condemned a decision of the Gulf Cooperation Council (GCC), announced in late September, to end the secondary and tertiary trade embargo against Israel, by which member states refuse to trade with international companies that have investments in Israel. A statement issued by the League insisted that the embargo could be removed only on the decision of the Council.

In March 1995 Arab ministers of foreign affairs approved a resolution urging Israel to renew the Nuclear Non-Proliferation Treaty. The resolution stipulated that failure by Israel to do so would cause Arab states to seek to protect legitimate Arab interests by alternative means. In May an extraordinary session of the Council condemned a decision by Israel to confiscate Arab-owned land in East Jerusalem for resettlement. The Israeli Government announced the suspension of its expropriation plans. The 2009 Arab League summit stated that the International Atomic Energy Agency (IAEA) should provide guarantees on Israel's nuclear facilities and activities.

In June 1996 an extraordinary summit conference of Arab League heads of state was convened, the first since 1990, in order to formulate a united Arab response to the election, in May 1996, of a new government in Israel. The conference (from which Iraq was excluded from the meeting in order to ensure the attendance of the Gulf member states) urged Israel to honour its undertaking to withdraw from the Occupied Territories, including Jerusalem, and to respect the establishment of an independent Palestinian state, in order to ensure the success of the peace process. A final communiqué of the meeting warned that Israeli co-operation was essential to prevent Arab states from reconsidering their participation in the peace process and the re-emergence of regional tensions. In September the League met in emergency session following an escalation of civil unrest in Jerusalem and the Occupied Territories. The League urged the UN Security Council to prevent further alleged Israeli aggression against the Palestinians. In November the League criticized Israel's settlement policy, and at the beginning of December it convened in emergency session to consider measures to end any expansion of the Jewish population in the West Bank and Gaza. In March 1997 the Council met in emergency session in response to the Israeli Government's decision to proceed with construction of a new settlement at Har Homa (Jabal Abu-Ghunaim) in East Jerusalem. At the end of March ministers of foreign affairs of Arab League states agreed to end all efforts to secure normal diplomatic relations with Israel (although binding agreements already in force with Egypt, Jordan and Palestine were exempt) and to close diplomatic offices and missions while construction work continued in East Jerusalem.

In March 1999 a meeting of the League's Council expressed support for a UN resolution convening an international conference to facilitate the implementation of agreements applying to Israel and the Occupied Territories, condemned Israel's refusal to withdraw from the Occupied Territories without a majority vote in favour from its legislature, as well as its refusal to resume peace negotiations with Lebanon and Syria that had ended in 1996, and advocated the publication of evidence of Israeli violence against Palestinians. The Council considered other issues, including the need to prevent further Israeli expansion in Jerusalem and the problem of Palestinian refugees, and reiterated demands for international support to secure Israel's withdrawal from the Golan Heights. In June the League condemned an Israeli aerial attack on Beirut and southern Lebanon. In November the League demanded that Israel compensate Palestinians for alleged losses incurred by their enforced use of the Israeli currency. In late December, prior to a short-lived resumption of Israeli-Syrian peace negotiations, the League reaffirmed its full support for Syria's position.

In February 2000 the League strongly condemned an Israeli aerial attack on southern Lebanon; the League's Council changed the venue of its next meeting, in March, from the League's Cairo headquarters to Beirut as a gesture of solidarity with Lebanon. The League welcomed the withdrawal of Israeli forces from southern Lebanon in May, although it subsequently condemned continuing territorial violations by the Israeli military. At a meeting of the Council in early September resolutions were passed urging international bodies to avoid participating in conferences in Jerusalem, reiterating a threatened boycott of a US chain of restaurants that was accused of operating a franchise in an Israeli settlement in the West Bank, and opposing an Israeli initiative for a Jewish emblem to be included as a symbol of the International Red Cross and Red Crescent Movement. At an emergency summit meeting convened in late October in response to mounting insecurity in Jerusalem and the Occupied Territories, 15 Arab heads of state, senior officials from six countries and Yasser Arafat, the then Palestinian National Authority (PA) leader, strongly rebuked Israel, which was accused of inciting the ongoing violent disturbances by stalling the progress of the peace process. The summit determined to 'freeze' co-operation with Israel, requested the formation of an international committee to conduct an impartial assessment of the situation, urged the UN Security Council to establish a mechanism to bring alleged Israeli 'war criminals' to trial, and requested the UN to approve the creation of an international force to protect Palestinians residing in the Occupied Territories. The summit also endorsed the establishment of an 'al-Aqsa Fund', with a value of US $800m., which was to finance initiatives aimed at promoting the Arab and Islamic identity of Jerusalem, and a smaller 'Jerusalem Intifada Fund' to support the families of Palestinians killed in the unrest. A follow-up committee was subsequently established to implement the resolutions adopted by the emergency summit.

In January 2001 a meeting of Arab League ministers of foreign affairs reviewed a proposed framework agreement, presented by outgoing US President Clinton, which aimed to resolve the continuing extreme tension between the Israeli and Palestinian authorities. The meeting agreed that the issues dominating the stalled Middle East peace process should not be redefined, strongly objecting to a proposal that, in exchange for Palestinian assumption of control over Muslim holy sites in Jerusalem, Palestinians exiled at the time of the foundation of the Israeli state in 1948 should forgo their claimed right to return to their former homes. In March 2001 the League's first ordinary annual summit-level Council was convened, in Amman, Jordan. The summit issued the Amman Declaration, which emphasized the promotion of Arab unity, and demanded the reversal of Israel's 1967 occupation of Arab territories. Heads of state attending the summit requested that the League consider means of reactivating the now relaxed Arab economic boycott of Israel. In May 2001 League ministers of foreign affairs determined that all political contacts with Israel should be suspended in protest at aerial attacks by Israel on Palestinian targets in the West Bank. In July representatives of 13 member countries met in Damascus, Syria, under the auspices of the Central Boycott Office. The meeting declared unanimous support for reactivated trade measures against Israeli companies and foreign businesses dealing with Israel. In August an emergency meeting of ministers of foreign affairs of the member states was convened at the request of the Palestinian authorities to address the recent escalation of hostilities and Israel's seizure of institutions in East Jerusalem. The meeting, which was attended by the League's Secretary-General and the leader of the PA, Yasser Arafat, aimed to formulate a unified Arab response to the situation.

In early March 2002 a meeting of League foreign ministers agreed to support an initiative proposed by Crown Prince Abdullah of Saudi Arabia aimed at brokering a peaceful settlement to the, by then, critical Palestinian–Israeli crisis. The Saudi-backed plan—entailing the restoration of 'normal' Arab relations with Israel and acceptance of its right to exist in peace and security, in exchange for a full Israeli withdrawal from the Occupied Territories, the establishment of an independent Palestinian state with East Jerusalem at its capital, and the return of refugees—was unanimously endorsed, as the first-ever pan-Arab Palestinian-Israeli peace initiative, by the summit-level Council held in Beirut in late March. The plan urged compliance with UN Security Council Resolution 194 concerning the return of Palestinian refugees to Israel, or appropriate compensation for their property; however, precise details of eligibility criteria for the proposed return, a contentious issue owing to the potentially huge numbers of refugees and descendants of refugees involved, were not elaborated. Conditions imposed by Israel on Yasser Arafat's freedom of movement deterred him from attending the summit. At the end of March the League's Secretary-General condemned the Israeli military's siege of Arafat's presidential compound in Ramallah (initiated in retaliation against a succession of Palestinian bomb attacks on Israeli civilians). In April an extraordinary Council meeting, held at the request of Palestine to consider the 'unprecedented deterioration' of the situation in the Palestinian territories, accused certain states (notably the USA) of implementing a pro-Israeli bias that enabled Israel to act outside the scope of international law and to ignore relevant UN resolutions, and accused Israel of undermining international co-operation in combating terrorism by attempting to equate its actions towards the Palestinian people with recent anti-terrorism activities conducted by the USA. A meeting organized by the Central Boycott Office at the end of April agreed to expand boycott measures and assessed the status of 17 companies believed to have interests in Israel. Israel's termination of its siege of Arafat's Ramallah compound in early May was welcomed by the Secretary-General. Following an aerial raid by the Israeli military on targets in Gaza in late July, the League urged a halt to the export of weaponry, particularly F-16 military aircraft, to Israel. A Council meeting held in early September agreed to intensify Arab efforts to expose Israeli atrocities against the Palestinians and urged the international community to provide protection and reparations for Palestinians. The Council authorized the establishment of a committee to address the welfare of imprisoned Palestinians and urged the USA and the United Kingdom to reconsider their policies on exporting weaponry to Israel, while issuing a resolution concerning the danger posed by Israel's possession of weapons of mass destruction. In early October the Secretary-General expressed concern at new US legislation aimed at securing the relocation of the USA's embassy in Israel from Tel-Aviv to Jerusalem, stating that this represented a symbolic acceptance of Jerusalem as the Israeli capital, in contravention of relevant UN resolutions.

In November 2003 the League welcomed the adoption by the UN Security Council of a resolution endorsing the adoption in April by the so-called 'Quartet', comprising envoys from the UN, the European Union (EU), Russia and the USA, of a 'performance-based roadmap to a permanent two-state solution to the Israeli–Palestinian conflict'. In January 2004 the International Court of Justice (ICJ) authorized the participation of the League in proceedings relating to a request for an advisory opinion on the *Legal Consequences of the Construction of a Wall in the Occupied Palestinian Territory*, referred to the ICJ by the UN General Assembly in late 2003; the League welcomed the ICJ's conclusions on the case, published in July 2004. The 2004 summit meeting of Arab League heads of state, held in Tunis, Tunisia, in May, condemned contraventions of international law by the Israeli Government, in particular continuing settlement activities and the use of unjudicial killings and other violence, and focused on the humanitarian situation of Palestinians recently displaced by large-scale house demolitions in Rafah, Gaza. In January 2005 the League welcomed the election of Mahmud Abbas as the new Executive President of the PA, following the death in November 2004 of Yasser Arafat.

In March 2007 the annual summit meeting of the League reaffirmed the League's support for the 2002 peace initiative proposed by Crown Prince Abdullah of Saudi Arabia, and urged the Israeli authorities to resume direct negotiations based on the principles of the initiative. In July 2007 the ministers of foreign affairs of Egypt and Jordan, representing the League, visited Israel to promote the 2002 initiative. The March 2009 League summit meeting condemned the intensive military assault on Gaza perpetrated by Israeli forces (with the stated aim of ending rocket attacks launched by

Hamas and other militant groups on Israeli targets) during late December 2008–mid-January 2009. The summit urged Israel to establish a time frame for committing to the peace process. In October an emergency meeting of the League condemned attacks by the Israeli armed forces on the al-Aqsa Mosque in Jerusalem.

The March 2010 summit meeting, held in Sirte, Libya, agreed, in its final declaration, all Israeli measures seeking to alter the features and demographic, humanitarian and historic situation of occupied Jerusalem to be invalid and unacceptable, while appealing to the international community (particularly the UN Security Council, the EU and UNESCO) to act to save East Jerusalem and maintain the al-Aqsa Mosque. The meeting's declaration urged that a special session of the UN General Assembly should be held with a view to halting Israeli measures that contravened international law, and mandated the formation of a League legal committee to follow up the issue of the 'judaization' of East Jerusalem and the confiscation of Arab property, and to take these issues before national and international courts with appropriate jurisdiction.

In June 2010, in response to an Israeli raid at the end of May on a flotilla of vessels carrying humanitarian aid through international waters towards the Gaza Strip, resulting in nine civilian fatalities and wounding at least 40 further people, the League Secretary-General visited Gaza in a gesture of solidarity towards the Palestinian people. During the visit he demanded the termination of the blockade imposed since 2006 by Israel against Gaza. The League was critical of a UN-commissioned report on the flotilla incident, released in September 2011, which, while concluding that the Israeli army had used 'excessive and unreasonable' force, also found the Israeli naval blockade of Gaza to have been imposed as a 'legitimate security measure' to prevent weapons from reaching Gaza by sea, and found that the flotilla had acted recklessly in attempting to breach the naval blockade.

In July 2011 the recently appointed League Secretary-General, Nabil al-Arabi, announced that the League would request the UN to grant full membership—and consequently recognition as an independent state—to Palestine; in September the Executive President of the Palestinian Authority submitted a formal application to the UN Secretary-General for Palestine's admission to that organization.

CONFLICT IN SUB-SAHARAN AFRICA

In 1992 the League attempted to mediate between the warring factions in Somalia. In early June 2002 the League appointed a special representative to Somalia to assist with the ongoing reconciliation efforts in that country.

In early September 2002 the Council established a committee to encourage peace efforts in Sudan. In May 2004 representatives of the League participated in an African Union (AU) fact-finding mission to assess the ongoing humanitarian crisis in Darfur, Sudan. In August an emergency meeting of League ministers of foreign affairs, convened to address the situation in Darfur, declared support for the Sudanese Government's measures to disarm Arab militias and punish human rights violations there. In November the League was asked to join a panel appointed to monitor the cease-fire agreement that had been adopted in April by the parties to the Darfur conflict. In March 2006 the meeting of heads of state agreed to offer financial support to the AU Mission in Sudan, deployed to the Darfur region of that country. The summit meeting in March 2007 expressed continued support for all peace accords signed between conflicting parties in Sudan. In March 2009 the summit of heads of state expressed full support and solidarity with Sudan in rejecting the legitimacy of the arrest warrant that had been issued earlier in that month by the International Criminal Court against President Omar Al-Bashir of Sudan.

In October 2010 the League and the AU jointly organized an Afro-Arab summit, held in Sirte, Libya; leaders attending the summit endorsed a new Strategic Plan of the Afro-Arab Co-operation, covering the period 2011–15. The next Afro-Arab summit was scheduled to be held in Kuwait, during 2013.

Finance

The League's budget for 2010 totalled US $61.2m., including $58.8m. for the League Secretariat and $5m. allocated to the Arab Fund for Technical Assistance in African States.

Publications

Arab Perspectives—Sh'oun Arabiyya (monthly).

Journal of Arab Affairs (monthly).

Bulletins of treaties and agreements concluded among the member states, essays, regular publications circulated by regional offices.

NORTH AMERICAN FREE TRADE AGREEMENT—NAFTA

Address: *(Canadian section)* 111 Sussex Drive 5th Floor Ottawa, ON K1N 1J1.

Telephone: (613) 992-9388; **fax:** (613) 992-9392; **e-mail:** canada@nafta-sec-alena.org; **internet:** www.nafta-sec-alena.org/canada.

Address: *(Mexican section)* Blvd Adolfo López Mateos 3025, 2°, Col Héroes de Padierna, 10700 México, DF.

Telephone: (55) 5629-9630; **fax:** (55) 5629-9637; **e-mail:** mexico@nafta-sec-alena.org.

Address: *(US section)* 14th St and Constitution Ave, NW, Room 2061, Washington, DC 20230.

Telephone: (202) 482-5438; **fax:** (202) 482-0148; **e-mail:** usa@nafta-sec-alena.org; **internet:** www.nafta-sec-alena.org.

The North American Free Trade Agreement (NAFTA) grew out of the free trade agreement between the USA and Canada that was signed in January 1988 and came into effect on 1 January 1989. Negotiations on the terms of NAFTA, which includes Mexico in the free trade area, were concluded in October 1992 and the Agreement was signed in December. The accord was ratified in November 1993 and entered into force on 1 January 1994; the full implementation of the provisions of the accord was achieved in January 2008. The NAFTA Secretariat is composed of national sections in each member country.

MEMBERS

Canada Mexico USA

MAIN PROVISIONS OF THE AGREEMENT

Under NAFTA almost all restrictions on trade and investment between Canada, Mexico and the USA were removed during the period 1 January 1994–1 January 2008. Tariffs on trade between the USA and Mexico in 94% of agricultural products were eliminated immediately, with trade restrictions on further agricultural products initially protected by tariff-rate quotas (TRQs) and eliminated more gradually; tariffs on the most import-sensitive staple agricultural commodities, including Mexican exports to the USA of sugar and selected horticultural products and US exports to Mexico of corn, high fructose corn syrup, dry edible beans and non-fat dry milk, were abolished on 1 January 2008.

NAFTA also provided for the phasing out by 2004 of tariffs on automobiles and textiles between all three countries; and for Mexico to open its financial sector to US and Canadian investment, with all restrictions to be removed by 2008. Mexico was to liberalize government procurement, removing preferential treatment for domestic companies over a 10-year period. Barriers to investment were removed in most sectors, with exemptions for petroleum in Mexico, culture in Canada and airlines and radio communications in the USA. In April 1998 the fifth meeting of the three-member ministerial Free Trade Commission (see below), held in Paris, France, agreed to remove tariffs on some 600 goods, including certain chemicals, pharmaceuticals, steel and wire products, textiles, toys, and watches, from 1 August. As a result of that agreement, a number of tariffs were eliminated as much as 10 years earlier than had been originally planned.

In transport, it was initially planned that heavy goods vehicles would have complete freedom of movement between the three countries by 2000. However, owing to concerns on the part of the US Government relating to the implementation of adequate safety standards by Mexican truck drivers, the 2000 deadline for the free circulation of heavy goods vehicles was not met. In February 2001 a five-member NAFTA panel of experts appointed to adjudicate on the dispute ruled that the USA was violating the Agreement. In December the US Senate approved legislation entitling Mexican long-haul trucks to operate anywhere in the USA following compliance with rigorous safety checks to be enforced by US inspectors.

In the case of a sudden influx of goods from one country to another that adversely affects a domestic industry, the Agreement makes provision for the imposition of short-term 'snap-back' tariffs.

Disputes are to be settled in the first instance by intergovernmental consultation. If a dispute is not resolved within 30 to 40 days, a government may call a meeting of the Free Trade Commission. The Commission's Advisory Committee on Private Commercial Disputes and its Advisory Committee on Private Commercial Disputes Regarding Agricultural Goods recommend procedures for the resolution of such complex disputes. If the Commission is unable to settle an issue a panel of experts in the relevant field is appointed to adjudicate. In June 1996 Canada and Mexico announced their decision to refer the newly enacted US 'Helms-Burton' legislation on trade with Cuba to the Commission. They claimed that the legislation, which provides for punitive measures against foreign companies that engage in trade with Cuba, imposed undue restrictions on Canadian and Mexican companies and was, therefore, in contravention of NAFTA. However, at the beginning of 1997 certain controversial provisions of the Helms-Burton legislation were suspended for a period of six months by the US Administration. The relevant provisions have continued subsequently to be suspended at six-monthly intervals.

In December 1994 NAFTA members issued a formal invitation to Chile to seek membership of the Agreement. Formal discussions on Chile's entry began in June 1995, but were stalled in December when the US Congress failed to approve 'fast-track' negotiating authority for the US Government, which was to have allowed the latter to negotiate a trade agreement with Chile, without risk of incurring a line-by-line veto from the US Congress. In February 1996 Chile began high-level negotiations with Canada on a wide-ranging bilateral free trade agreement. Chile, which already had extensive bilateral trade agreements with Mexico, was regarded as advancing its position with regard to NAFTA membership by means of the proposed accord with Canada. The bilateral agreement, which provided for the extensive elimination of customs duties by 2002, was signed in November 1996 and ratified by Chile in July 1997. However, in November 1997 the US Government was obliged to request the removal of the 'fast-track' proposal from the legislative agenda, owing to insufficient support within Congress.

In April 1998 heads of state of 34 countries, meeting in Santiago, Chile, agreed formally to initiate the negotiating process to establish a Free Trade Area of the Americas (FTAA). The US Government had originally proposed creating the FTAA through the gradual extension of NAFTA trading privileges on a bilateral basis. However, the framework agreed upon by ministers of trade of the 34 countries, meeting in March, provided for countries to negotiate and accept FTAA provisions on an individual basis and as part of a sub-regional economic bloc. It was envisaged that the FTAA would exist alongside the sub-regional associations, including NAFTA. At a special summit of the Americas, held in January 2004 in Monterrey, Mexico, the leaders adopted a declaration committing themselves to the eventual establishment of the FTAA; however, they did not specify a completion date for the negotiations. In March the negotiations were suspended, and in early 2012 they remained so.

ADDITIONAL AGREEMENTS

During 1993, as a result of domestic pressure, the new US Government negotiated two 'side agreements' with its NAFTA partners, which were to provide safeguards for workers' rights and the environment. A Commission for Labor Cooperation was established under the North American Agreement on Labor Cooperation (NAALC) to monitor implementation of labour accords and to foster co-operation in that area. Panels of experts, with representatives from each country, were established to adjudicate in cases of alleged infringement of workers' rights or environmental damage. The panels were given the power to impose fines and trade sanctions, but only with regard to the USA and Mexico; Canada, which was opposed to such measures, was to enforce compliance with NAFTA by means of its own legal system. The Commission for Environmental Cooperation (CEC), initiated in 1994 under the provisions of the 1993 North American Agreement on Environmental Cooperation (which complements the relevant environmental provisions of NAFTA), addresses regional environmental concerns, assists in the prevention of potential trade and environmental conflicts, advises on the environmental impact of trade issues, encourages private sector investment in environmental trade issues, and promotes the effective enforcement of environmental law. In co-operation with mapping agency partners CEC produces the *North American Environmental Atlas*. During 1994–early 2012 the CEC adopted numerous resolutions, including on the sound management of chemicals, the environmentally sound management and tracking of hazardous wastes and hazardous recyclable materials, the conservation of butterflies and birds, the availability of pollutant release and transfer data, and on co-operation in the conservation of biodiversity. The CEC-financed North American Fund for Environmental Cooperation (NAFEC), established in 1995, supports community environmental projects.

With regard to the NAALC, National Administration Offices have been established in each of the three NAFTA countries in order to monitor labour issues and to address complaints about non-compliance with domestic labour legislation. However, punitive measures in the form of trade sanctions or fines (up to US $20m.) may only be imposed in the specific instances of contravention of national legislation regarding child labour, a minimum wage or health and safety standards.

In August 1993 the USA and Mexico agreed to establish a Border Environmental Cooperation Commission (BECC) to assist with the co-ordination of projects for the improvement of infrastructure and to monitor the environmental impact of the Agreement on the US–Mexican border area, where industrial activity was expected to intensify. The Commission is located in Ciudad Juárez, Mexico. By March 2012 the BECC had certified 191 projects, at a cost of US $4,314.9m. The North American Development Bank (NADB or NADBank), established by an agreement concluded between the USA and Mexico in October 1993, is mandated to finance environmental and infrastructure projects along the US–Mexican border.

Commission for Environmental Cooperation (CEC): 393 rue St Jacques Ouest, Bureau 200, Montréal, QC H2Y IN9, Canada; tel. (514) 350-4300; fax (514) 350-4314; e-mail info@cec.org; internet www.cec.org; f. 1994; Exec. Dir EVAN LLOYD; publs *Annual Report*, *Taking Stock* (annually), industry reports, policy studies.

Commission for Labor Cooperation: 1211 Connecticut Ave, NW Suite 400, Washington, DC 20036, USA; tel. (202) 464-1100; fax (202) 464-9490; e-mail info@naalc.org; internet www.naalc.org; f. 1994; Exec. Dir (vacant); publ. *Annual Report*.

North American Development Bank (NADB/NADBank): 203 South St Mary's, Suite 300, San Antonio, TX 78205, USA; tel. (210) 231-8000; fax (210) 231-6232; internet www.nadbank.org; at March 2012 the NADB had authorized capital of US $3,000m., subscribed equally by Mexico and the USA, of which $450m. was paid-up; Man. Dir GERÓNIMO GUTIÉRREZ FERNÁNDEZ (Mexico); publs *Annual Report*, *NADBank News*.

NORTH ATLANTIC TREATY ORGANIZATION—NATO

Address: blvd Léopold III, 1110 Brussels, Belgium.

Telephone: (2) 707-41-11; **fax:** (2) 707-45-79; **e-mail:** natodoc@hq.nato.int; **internet:** www.nato.int.

The Atlantic Alliance was established on the basis of the 1949 North Atlantic Treaty as a defensive political and military alliance of a group of European states (then numbering 10) and the USA and Canada. The Alliance aims to provide common security for its members through co-operation and consultation in political, military and economic fields, as well as scientific, environmental, and other non-military aspects. The objectives of the Alliance are implemented by NATO. Since the collapse of the communist governments in Central and Eastern Europe, from 1989 onwards, and the dissolution, in 1991, of the Warsaw Treaty of Friendship, Co-operation and Mutual Assistance (the Warsaw Pact), which had hitherto been regarded as the Alliance's principal adversary, NATO has undertaken a fundamental transformation of its structures and policies to meet the new security challenges in Europe.

MEMBERS*

Albania	Greece	Poland
Belgium	Hungary	Portugal
Bulgaria	Iceland	Romania
Canada	Italy	Slovakia
Croatia	Latvia	Slovenia
Czech Republic	Lithuania	Spain
Denmark	Luxembourg	Turkey
Estonia	Netherlands	United Kingdom
France	Norway	USA
Germany		

* Greece and Turkey acceded to the Treaty in 1952, and the Federal Republic of Germany in 1955. France withdrew from the integrated military structure of NATO in 1966, although remaining a member of the Atlantic Alliance; in 1996 France resumed participation in some, but not all, of the military organs of NATO. Spain acceded to the Treaty in 1982, but remained outside the Alliance's integrated military structure until 1999. The Czech Republic, Hungary and

Poland were formally admitted as members of NATO in March 1999. In March 2003 protocols of accession, amending the North Atlantic Treaty, were adopted by the 19 NATO member states with a view to admitting Bulgaria, Estonia, Latvia, Lithuania, Romania, Slovakia and Slovenia to the Alliance. In March 2004, the protocols of accession having been ratified by all of the member states, those seven countries were formally invited to join NATO and, on 29 March, they acceded to the Treaty. On 1 April 2009 Albania and Croatia acceded to the Treaty.

Organization

(April 2012)

NORTH ATLANTIC COUNCIL

The Council, the highest authority of the Alliance, is composed of representatives of the 28 member states. It meets at the level of Permanent Representatives, ministers of foreign affairs, or heads of state and government, and, at all levels, has effective political and decision-making authority. Ministerial meetings are held at least twice a year. Occasional meetings of defence ministers are also held. At the level of Permanent Representatives the Council meets at least once a week. A meeting of heads of state and government was convened in Lisbon, Portugal, in November 2010.

The Secretary-General of NATO is Chairman of the Council, and each year a minister of foreign affairs of a member state is nominated honorary President, following the English alphabetical order of countries.

Decisions are taken by common consent and not by majority vote. The Council is a forum for wide consultation between member governments on major issues, including political, military, economic and other subjects, and is supported by the Senior or regular Political Committee, the Military Committee and other subordinate bodies.

PERMANENT REPRESENTATIVES

Albania: Artur Kuko.

Belgium: Rudolf Huygelen.

Bulgaria: Todor Churov.

Canada: Yves Brodeur.

Croatia: Igor Pokaz.

Czech Republic: Martin Povejšil.

Denmark: Carsten Søndergaard.

Estonia: Jüri Luik.

France: Philippe Errera.

Germany: Martin Erdmann.

Greece: Tryphon Paraskevopoulos.

Hungary: István Kovács.

Iceland: Thorstein Ingolfsson.

Italy: Riccardo Sessa.

Latvia: Māris Riekstiņš.

Lithuania: Kęstutis Jankauskas.

Luxembourg: Jean-Jacques Welfring.

Netherlands: Frank Majoor.

Norway: Vegard Ellefsen.

Poland: Jacek Najder.

Portugal: João Mira Gomes.

Romania: Sorin Dumitru Ducaru.

Slovakia: František Kašický.

Slovenia: Andrej Benedejčič.

Spain: José de Carvajal.

Turkey: Haydar Berk.

United Kingdom: Mariot Leslie.

USA: Ivo H. Daalder.

Note: NATO partner countries are represented by heads of diplomatic missions or liaison officers located at NATO headquarters.

DEFENCE PLANNING COMMITTEE

Most defence matters are dealt with in the Defence Planning Committee, composed of representatives of all member countries except France. The Committee provides guidance to NATO's military authorities and, within the field of its responsibilities, has the same functions and authority as the Council. Like the Council, it meets regularly at ambassadorial level and assembles twice a year in ministerial sessions, when member countries are represented by their ministers of defence.

NUCLEAR PLANNING GROUP

Defence ministers of countries participating in the Defence Planning Committee meet regularly in the Nuclear Planning Group (NPG) to discuss specific policy issues relating to nuclear forces, such as safety, deployment issues, nuclear arms control and proliferation. The NPG is supported by a Staff Group, composed of representatives of all members participating in the NPG, which meets at least once a week. The NPG High Level Group, chaired by the USA and comprising national policy-makers and experts, exists as a senior advisory body to the NPG in respect of nuclear policy and planning issues.

OTHER COMMITTEES

There are also committees for political affairs, economics, military medical services, armaments, defence review, science, infrastructure, logistics, communications, civil emergency planning, information and cultural relations, and civil and military budgets. In addition, other committees consider specialized subjects such as NATO pipelines, air traffic management, etc. Since 1992 most of these committees have consulted on a regular basis with representatives from central and eastern European countries.

INTERNATIONAL SECRETARIAT

The Secretary-General is Chairman of the North Atlantic Council, the Defence Planning Committee and the Nuclear Planning Group. He is the head of the International Secretariat, with staff drawn from the member countries. He proposes items for NATO consultation and is generally responsible for promoting consultation and co-operation in accordance with the provisions of the North Atlantic Treaty. He is empowered to offer his help informally in cases of disputes between member countries, to facilitate procedures for settlement.

Secretary-General: Anders Fogh Rasmussen (Denmark).

Deputy Secretary-General: Alexander Vershbow (USA).

There is an Assistant Secretary-General for each of the operational divisions listed below.

PRINCIPAL DIVISIONS

Division of Defence Investment: responsible for enhancing NATO's defence capacity (including armaments planning, air defence and security investment) by developing and investing in the Alliance's assets and capabilities; Asst Sec.-Gen. Patrick Auroy (France).

Division of Defence Policy and Planning: responsible for defence planning, nuclear policy and defence against weapons of mass destruction; Asst Sec.-Gen. Hüseyin Diriöz (Turkey).

Division of Emerging Security Challenges: co-ordinates the Alliance approach to security issues, including terrorism, the proliferation of weapons of mass destruction, cyber threats, and energy security challenges; Asst Sec.-Gen. Gábor Iklódy (Hungary).

Division of Political Affairs and Security Policy: is concerned with regional, economic and security affairs and relations with other international organizations and partner countries; Asst Sec.-Gen. Dirk Brengelmann (Germany).

Division of Public Diplomacy: responsible for dissemination of information on NATO's activities and policies through the media, the official website and print publications as well as seminars and conferences; manages the Science for Peace and Security programme and the information offices in Russia and Ukraine; Asst Sec.-Gen. Kolinda Grabar Kitarović (Croatia).

Executive Management Division: ensures the efficient running of the International Secretariat and provides support to elements such as conference services, information management and human and financial resources; Asst Sec.-Gen. William A. Eaton (USA).

Operations Division: responsible for the Alliance's crisis management and peace-keeping activities and civil emergency planning and exercises; incorporates the Euro-Atlantic Disaster Response Coordination Centre (EADRCC) and the NATO Situation Centre; Asst Sec.-Gen. Stephen Evans (United Kingdom).

Military Organization

MILITARY COMMITTEE

Composed of the allied Chiefs-of-Staff, or their representatives, of all member countries: the highest military body in NATO under the authority of the Council. Meets at least twice a year at Chiefs-of-Staff level and remains in permanent session with Permanent Military Representatives. It is responsible for making recommendations to the Council and Defence Planning Committee and Nuclear Planning Group on military matters and for supplying guidance on military questions to Supreme Allied Commanders and subordinate military authorities. The Committee is supported by an International Military Staff.

Chairman: Gen. KNUD BARTELS (Denmark).

COMMANDS

In June 2011 NATO ministers of defence approved a reform of the existing command structure, in order to enhance its effectiveness and affordability, with the number of command headquarters and personnel to be significantly reduced. In addition to the two strategic commands, of Operations and Transformation, there were to be two main Joint Force Headquarters, each able to deploy a major joint operation into theatre, comprising a Combined Air Operations Centre and static air, land and maritime commands. The Command Structure was to be supported by a Communication and Information Systems Group.

Allied Command Operations: Casteau, Belgium—Supreme Headquarters Allied Powers Europe—SHAPE; Supreme Allied Commander Europe—SACEUR Adm. JAMES G. STAVRIDIS (USA).

Allied Command Transformation: Norfolk, Virginia, USA; Supreme Allied Commander Transformation—SACT Lt-Gen. STÉPHANE ABRIAL (France).

Activities

The common security policy of the members of the North Atlantic Alliance is to safeguard peace through the maintenance of political solidarity and adequate defence at the lowest level of military forces needed to deter all possible forms of aggression. Each year, member countries take part in a Defence Review, designed to assess their contribution to the common defence in relation to their respective capabilities and constraints. Allied defence policy is reviewed periodically by ministers of defence.

Political consultations within the Alliance take place on a permanent basis, under the auspices of the North Atlantic Council (NAC), on all matters affecting the common security interests of the member countries, as well as events outside the North Atlantic Treaty area.

Co-operation in environmental, scientific and technological fields takes place in the NATO Science Committee and in its Committee on the Challenges of Modern Society. Both these bodies operate an expanding international programme of science fellowships, advance study institutes and research grants. NATO has also pursued co-operation in relation to civil emergency planning. These activities represent NATO's 'Third Dimension'.

Since the 1980s the Alliance has been actively involved in co-ordinating policies with regard to arms control and disarmament issues designed to bring about negotiated reductions in conventional forces, intermediate and short-range nuclear forces and strategic nuclear forces. A Verification Co-ordinating Committee was established in 1990. In April 1999 the summit meeting determined to improve co-ordination on issues relating to weapons of mass destruction through the establishment of a separate centre at NATO headquarters. At a summit meeting of the Conference on Security and Co-operation in Europe (CSCE), later renamed the Organization for Security and Co-operation in Europe (OSCE), in November 1990 the member countries of NATO and the Warsaw Pact signed an agreement limiting Conventional Armed Forces in Europe (CFE), whereby conventional arms would be reduced to within a common upper limit in each zone. The two groups also issued a Joint Declaration, stating that they were no longer adversaries and that none of their weapons would ever be used 'except in self-defence'. In March 1992, under the auspices of the CSCE, the ministers of foreign affairs of the NATO and of the former Warsaw Pact countries (with Russia, Belarus, Ukraine and Georgia taking the place of the USSR) signed the 'Open Skies' treaty. Under this treaty, aerial reconnaissance missions by one country over another were to be permitted, subject to regulation. The eight former Soviet republics with territory in the area of application of the CFE Treaty committed themselves to honouring its obligations in June. At the summit meeting of the OSCE in December 1996 the signatories of the CFE Treaty agreed to begin negotiations on a revised treaty governing conventional weapons in Europe. In July 1997 the CFE signatories concluded an agreement on Certain Basic Elements for Treaty Adaptation, which provided for substantial reductions in the maximum levels of conventional military equipment at national and territorial level, replacing the previous bloc-to-bloc structure of the Treaty. The Adapted CFE Treaty was concluded and signed in November 1999, at an OSCE meeting held in Istanbul, Turkey. At the same time, a series of agreements or Commitments, was approved which required Russia to withdraw forces from and reduce levels of military equipment in Georgia and Moldova, a process to be monitored by NATO. In April 2007 NATO ministers of foreign affairs held immediate discussions following an announcement by Russia's President that it intended to suspend unilaterally its implementation of CFE obligations. An extraordinary conference of parties to the CFE was convened in June to consider Russia's security concerns; in the following month, however, the Russian Government announced that it was to suspend obligations under the Treaty, with effect from mid-December. In April 2008 NATO heads of state and government urged Russia to resume its implementation of the Treaty. The Lisbon Summit Declaration, issued by NATO heads of state and government in November 2010, reaffirmed political commitment to the CFE process, but insisted that the existing *impasse* could not continue indefinitely.

In January 1994 NATO heads of state and government welcomed the entry into force of the Maastricht Treaty, establishing the European Union (EU, superseding the EC). The Treaty included an agreement on the development of a common foreign and security policy, which was intended to be a mechanism to strengthen the European pillar of the Alliance. NATO subsequently co-operated with Western European Union (WEU, now defunct) in support of the development of a European Security and Defence Identity. In June 1996 NATO ministers of foreign affairs reached agreement on the implementation of a 'Combined Joint Task Force (CJTF) concept'. Measures were to be taken to establish the 'nuclei' of these task forces at certain NATO headquarters, which would provide the basis for missions that could be activated at short notice for specific purposes such as crisis management and peace-keeping. The summit meeting held in April 1999 confirmed NATO's willingness to establish a direct NATO-EU relationship. The first formal meeting of the Military Committees of the EU and NATO took place in June 2001 to exchange information relating to the development of EU-NATO security co-operation. In November 2003 NATO and the EU conducted a joint crisis management exercise for the first time. In order to support an integrated security structure in Europe, NATO also co-operates with the OSCE and has provided assistance for the development of the latter's conflict prevention and crisis management activities. In September 2008 a Joint Declaration on UN/NATO Secretariat Co-operation was signed by the Secretaries-General of the two organizations to strengthen practical co-operation, in particular in crisis management. In November 2010 NATO heads of state and government endorsed an Action Plan to incorporate into all aspects of Alliance planning, training and operations the provisions of the UN Security Council Resolution 1325 on Women, Peace and Security.

On 12 September 2001 the NAC agreed to invoke, for the first time, Article 5 of the North Atlantic Treaty, providing for collective self-defence, in response to terrorist attacks against targets in the USA that had taken place on the previous day. The measure was formally implemented in early October after the US authorities presented evidence substantiating claims that the attacks had been directed from abroad. The NAC endorsed eight specific US requests for logistical and military support in its efforts to counter terrorism, including enhanced sharing of intelligence and full access to airfields and ports in member states. It also agreed to dispatch five surveillance aircraft to help to patrol US airspace and directed the standing naval force to the Eastern Mediterranean (see 'Operation Active Endeavour', below). In December NATO ministers of defence initiated a review of military capabilities and defences with a view to strengthening its ability to counter international terrorism.

In November 2002 NATO heads of state and government, convened in Prague, Czech Republic, approved a comprehensive reform of the Alliance's capabilities in order to reflect a new operational outlook and enable the transition to smaller, more flexible forces. The command structure was to be reduced and redefined, under operational and functional strategic commands, while a NATO Response Force (NRF), comprising a flexible and interoperable force of readily deployable land, sea and air elements, was to be established. The meeting agreed on further measures to strengthen NATO's capabilities to defend against terrorism and approved a broader commitment to improve and develop modern warfare capabilities. The Prague Summit initiatives were endorsed by a meeting of NATO defence ministers in June 2003. In March 2005 the NAC approved a charter formally to establish an organization to manage an Active Layered Theatre Ballistic Missile Defence programme, which aimed to establish a new collective defence capability. The NRF was inaugurated in October 2003, with a force strength of 9,500 troops. It was intended to enable NATO to react swiftly and efficiently in new areas of operation, such as evacuations, disaster management and counter-terrorism. By October 2004 the NRF had reached its initial operating capacity, comprising some 17,000 troops. It reached its full capacity, of 25,000 troops, in November 2006.

In April 2003 an agreement was signed by six member states—the Czech Republic, Denmark, Germany, the Netherlands, Norway and Poland—formally establishing the Civil-Military Co-operation Group North. The group was to be based at Budel, Netherlands, and was intended to provide NATO commanders with a co-ordinated approach to civil-military co-operation during crises and in post-conflict areas.

Periodic reviews of NATO's structures have been undertaken in response to changes in the security environment. In November 1991 NATO heads of government, convened in Rome, Italy, recommended a radical restructuring of the organization in view of the fundamental changes then taking place in Central and Eastern Europe; the restructuring entailed further reductions in military forces in Europe, active involvement in international peace-keeping operations, increased co-operation with other international institutions and close co-operation with its former adversaries, the USSR and the countries of Eastern Europe. The basis for NATO's revised force structure was incorporated into a Strategic Concept, which was adopted in the Rome Declaration issuing from the summit meeting. The concept provided for the maintenance of a collective defence capability, with a reduced dependence on nuclear weapons. Substantial reductions in the size and levels of readiness of NATO forces were undertaken, in order to reflect the Alliance's strictly defensive nature, and forces were reorganized within a streamlined integrated command structure. Forces were categorized into immediate and rapid reaction forces (including the ACE Rapid Reaction Corps—ARRC, which was inaugurated in October 1992), main defence forces and augmentation forces, which may be used to reinforce any NATO region or maritime areas for deterrence, crisis management or defence. During 1998 work was undertaken on the formulation of an updated Strategic Concept, reflecting the changing security environment and defining NATO's future role and objectives, which recognized a broader sphere of influence and confirmed NATO to be the principal generator of security in the Euro-Atlantic area. It emphasized NATO's role in crisis management and a renewed commitment to partnership and dialogue. The document was approved at a special summit meeting, convened in Washington, DC, USA, in April 1999, to commemorate the 50th anniversary of the Alliance. A separate initiative was approved to assist member states to adapt their defence capabilities to meet changing security requirements, for example improving the means of troop deployment and equipping and protecting forces. A summit meeting convened in Istanbul, Turkey in June 2004, evaluated progress made in transforming the Alliance's capabilities. In November 2006 NATO heads of state and government, meeting in Riga, Latvia, endorsed and made public a Comprehensive Political Guidance document which aimed to provide a framework and direction for the Alliance in the next 10–15 years. In particular, it identified the likely capability requirements of future operations, the need to respond to new threats and challenges, such as terrorism and the spread of weapons of mass destruction, and the development of relations with non-NATO countries. In June 2007 NATO ministers of defence, meeting to review the transformation of the Alliance's operational capabilities, agreed to assess the political and military implications of a possible redeployment of US missile defences in Europe. In April 2008 a NATO summit meeting, convened in Bucharest, Romania, reviewed progress in transforming the Alliance. It endorsed an Action Plan of proposals to develop and implement a NATO strategy for a comprehensive approach to existing and future security challenges. The meeting recognized the importance of working in partnership with the UN and EU and of strengthening co-operation with other countries and regional alliances. The meeting highlighted issues of arms control, nuclear non-proliferation and disarmament as being of particular concern. NATO's 60th anniversary summit meeting, convened in early April 2009, in Strasbourg, France and Kehl, Germany, adopted a Declaration on Alliance Security, reaffirming the basic values, principles and purposes of the Alliance, and determined to develop a new Strategic Concept that was to define NATO's longer-term role in the 21st century. The process of defining a new Strategic Concept was launched in July at a security conference attended by representatives of allied and partner governments, international organizations, the private sector, and civil society, including non-governmental organizations, academia and the media. In May 2010 a Group of Experts, appointed by the Secretary-General, presented a report to the NAC incorporating an analysis and recommendations for the new Strategic Concept. Further detailed deliberations were pursued over the next few months. The Strategic Concept, entitled *Active Engagement, Modern Defence*, was adopted by NATO heads of state and government, meeting in Lisbon, Portugal, in November. The document identified the challenges posed by the contemporary security environment and sought to enhance NATO's defence and deterrence capacities accordingly, while reaffirming its core tasks of collective defence, crisis management and co-operative security. NATO leaders approved the development of a new European missile defence capability, as well as measures to enhance cyber defence capabilities. They also endorsed an extensive reform of NATO's civil and military command structures, in order to enhance the organization's efficiency and flexibility.

In January 2012 the Secretary-General's first Annual Report (covering 2011) was published. In March 2012 the Secretary-General presented 'NATO 2020', a vision for the Alliance's medium-term future; this focused on the vigorous pursuit of so-called 'smart defence': acquiring, and maintaining, capabilities by means of greater collaboration, coherence and focus of effort, rather than through greater resources. During 2012, in accordance with the new Strategic Concept, a NATO rapid reaction team against cyber attack was under development; it was envisaged that this would be operational by the end of that year. A NATO summit meeting was scheduled to take place in May 2012, in Chicago, USA.

PARTNERSHIPS

In May 1997 a Euro-Atlantic Partnership Council (EAPC) was inaugurated as a successor to the North Atlantic Co-operation Council (NACC), that had been established in December 1991 to provide a forum for consultation on political and security matters with the countries of central and eastern Europe, including the former Soviet republics. An EAPC Council was to meet monthly at ambassadorial level and twice a year at ministerial level. It was to be supported in its work by a steering committee and a political committee. The EAPC was to pursue the NACC Work Plan for Dialogue, Partnership and Co-operation and incorporate it into a new Work Plan, which was to include an expanded political dimension of consultation and co-operation among participating states. The Partnership for Peace (PfP) programme, which was established in January 1994 within the framework of the NACC, was to remain an integral element of the new co-operative mechanism. The PfP incorporated practical military and defence-related co-operation activities that had originally been part of the NACC Work Plan. Participation in the PfP requires an initial signature of a framework agreement, establishing the common principles and objectives of the partnership, the submission of a presentation document, indicating the political and military aspects of the partnership and the nature of future co-operation activities and the development of individual partnership programmes establishing country-specific objectives. In June 1994 Russia, which had previously opposed the strategy as being the basis for future enlargement of NATO, signed the PfP framework document, which included a declaration envisaging an 'enhanced dialogue' between the two sides. Despite its continuing opposition to any enlargement of NATO, in May 1995 Russia agreed to sign a PfP Individual Partnership Programme, as well as a framework document for NATO-Russian dialogue and co-operation beyond the PfP. During 1994 a Partnership Co-ordination Cell (PCC), incorporating representatives of all partnership countries, became operational in Mons, Belgium. The PCC, under the authority of the NAC, aims to co-ordinate joint military activities and planning in order to implement PfP programmes. The first joint military exercises with countries of the former Warsaw Pact were conducted in September. NATO began formulating a PfP Status of Forces Agreement (SOFA) to define the legal status of Allies' and partners' forces when they are present on each other's territory; the PfP SOFA was opened for signature in June 1995. The new EAPC was to provide a framework for the development of an enhanced PfP programme, which NATO envisaged would become an essential element of the overall European security structure. Accordingly, the military activities of the PfP were to be expanded to include all Alliance missions and incorporate all NATO committees into the PfP process, thus providing for greater co-operation in crisis management, civil emergency planning and training activities. In addition, all PfP member countries were to participate in the CJTF concept through a structure of Partners Staff Elements, working at all levels of the Alliance military structure. Defence ministers of NATO and the 27 partner countries were to meet regularly to provide the political guidance for the enhanced Planning and Review Process of the PfP. In December 1997 NATO ministers of foreign affairs approved the establishment of a Euro-Atlantic Disaster Response Co-ordination Centre (EADRCC), and a non-permanent Euro-Atlantic Disaster Response Unit. The EADRCC was inaugurated in June 1998 and immediately commenced operations to provide relief to ethnic Albanian refugees fleeing the conflict in the Serbian province of Kosovo. In November the NAC approved the establishment of a network of PfP training centres, the first of which was inaugurated in Ankara, Turkey. The centres were a key element of a Training and Education Programme, which was endorsed at the summit meeting in April 1999. A policy of establishing individual PfP Trust Funds was approved in September 2000. These aimed to provide support for military reform and demilitarization activities in partners countries, in particular the destruction of anti-personnel landmines. In November 2002 heads of state and government, meeting in Prague, Czech Republic, endorsed a new initiative to formulate Individual Partnership Action Plans (IPAPs) designed to strengthen bilateral relations with a partner country, improve the effectiveness of NATO assistance in that country, and provide for intensified political dialogue. The Istanbul summit meeting in June 2004 agreed to strengthen co-operation with partner countries in the Caucasus and Central Asia. A Special Representative of the Secretary-General to the two regions was appointed in September. In October the first IPAP was signed with Georgia, with the aim of defining national security and defence objectives, reforms and country-specific NATO assistance. IPAPs were concluded with Azerbaijan in May 2005, Armenia in December, Kazakhstan in January 2006 and with Moldova in May. Bosnia and Herzegovina and Montenegro joined the PfP process in December 2006. (Serbia also joined at that time.) In April 2008 both countries were invited to begin an Intensified Dialogue with NATO. Monte-gro concluded an IPAP in June and held its first consultation under the Intensified Dialogue in that month. The IPAP with Bosnia and Herzegovina was concluded in September. In December 2009 NATO ministers of foreign affairs agreed to invite Montenegro to join the Membership Action Plan (MAP—see below), and determined that Bosnia and Herzegovina join MAP once further institutional reforms had been implemented.

The enlargement of NATO, through the admission of new members from the former USSR and Central and Eastern European countries, was considered to be a progressive means of contributing to the enhanced stability and security of the Euro-Atlantic area. In December 1996 NATO ministers of foreign affairs announced that invitations to join the Alliance would be issued to some former eastern bloc countries during 1997. The NATO Secretary-General and member governments subsequently began intensive diplomatic efforts to secure Russia's tolerance of these developments. It was agreed that no nuclear weapons or large numbers of troops would be deployed on the territory of any new member country in the former Eastern bloc. In May 1997 NATO and Russia signed the Founding Act on Mutual Relations, Co-operation and Security, which provided for enhanced Russian participation in all NATO decision-making activities, equal status in peace-keeping operations and representation at the Alliance headquarters at ambassadorial level, as part of a recognized shared political commitment to maintaining stability and security throughout the Euro-Atlantic region. A NATO-Russian Permanent Joint Council (PJC) was established under the Founding Act, and met for the first time in July; the Council provided each side with the opportunity for consultation and participation in the other's security decisions, but without a right of veto. In March 1999 Russia condemned NATO's military action against the Federal Republic of Yugoslavia and announced the suspension of all relations within the framework of the Founding Act, as well as negotiations on the establishment of a NATO mission in Moscow. The PJC convened once more in May 2000, and subsequent meetings were held in June and December. In February 2001 the NATO Secretary-General agreed with the then acting Russian President a joint statement of commitment to pursuing dialogue and co-operation. A NATO information office was opened in Moscow in that month. In December an agreement was concluded by NATO ministers of foreign affairs and their Russian counterpart to establish an eventual successor body to the PJC. The new NATO-Russia Council (NRC), in which NATO member states and Russia were to have equal status in decision-making, was inaugurated in May 2002. The Council aimed to strengthen co-operation in issues including counter-terrorism, crisis management, nuclear non-proliferation, and arms control. The third NATO-Russia conference on the role of the military in combating terrorism was convened in April 2004. In September the Council issued a joint statement condemning atrocities committed against civilians in North Ossetia and other parts of the Russian Federation. In April 2005, at an informal meeting of the ministers of foreign affairs of the NATO-Russia Council, Russia signed the PfP Status of Forces Agreement that provides a legal framework for the movement to and from Allied countries, partner countries and Russia of military personnel and support staff. In June a meeting of the Council endorsed Political-Military Guidance towards Enhanced Interoperability between Russian and NATO forces, thereby facilitating the preparation of those forces for possible joint operations. In April 2006 an informal meeting of the Council's ministers of foreign affairs reviewed NATO-Russia co-operation to date and adopted recommendations identifying interoperability, a pilot Afghanistan counter-narcotics project, a co-operative airspace initiative (CAI) and intensified political dialogue as the priority areas for future co-operation. In April 2008 the NRC, meeting at the level of heads of state, determined to extend on a permanent basis the joint project on counter-narcotics training of Afghan and Central Asian personnel and to accelerate the CAI project to ensure it reaches full operational capability by the end of 2009. In June 2008 NATO's Secretary-General urged Russia to withdraw some 400 troops from the Abkhazian region of Georgia and to respect that country's territorial integrity. In August meetings of the NRC were suspended owing to Russia's military action in Georgia, which the Alliance deemed to be 'disproportionate'. In December NATO ministers of foreign affairs agreed to initiate a gradual resumption of contacts with Russia. In April 2009 the meeting of NATO heads of state and government determined to resume normal relations with Russia. A meeting of the NRC at ministerial level was convened in June, in Corfu, Greece, at which all sides agreed to resume full political and military co-operation within the framework of the NRC. In September NATO's new Secretary-General, Anders Fogh Rasmussen, spoke on the importance of renewing and revitalizing NATO's strategic partnership with Russia. Later in that month he met with the Russian Minister of Foreign Affairs, in New York, USA, to discuss areas in which practical co-operation could be strengthened. In December the NRC, meeting at the level of foreign ministers, agreed on an extensive 2010 work programme, including renewed military co-operation, and initiated a Joint Review of 21st Century Common Security Challenges. At a meeting of the NRC, held in September 2010, discussions focused on strengthening practical co-operation and enhancing security in Europe. In November the NRC met at the level of heads of state. Both sides agreed on the need for a new strategic partnership, based on the presumption that they no longer posed a mutual threat. The declaration issued by NATO heads of state and government, meeting at that time in Lisbon, Portugal, incorporated an invitation to Russia to co-operate with the development of a new European missile defence capability. In June 2011 the first joint exercise was conducted under the CAI. In early July the NRC met in Sochi, Russia. The meeting reaffirmed the commitment of both sides to pursuing co-operation in missile defence, as well as other areas of mutual concern.

In May 1997 NATO ministers of foreign affairs, meeting in Sintra, Portugal, concluded an agreement with Ukraine providing for enhanced co-operation between the two sides; the so-called Charter on a Distinctive Relationship was signed at the NATO summit meeting held in Madrid, Spain, in July. In May 1998 NATO agreed to appoint a permanent liaison officer in Ukraine to enhance co-operation between the two sides and assist Ukraine to formulate a programme of joint military exercises. The first NATO-Ukraine meeting at the level of heads of state took place in April 1999. A NATO-Ukraine Commission (NUC) met for the first time in March 2000. In February 2005, at a NATO-Ukraine summit meeting, NATO leaders expressed support for Ukraine's reform agenda and agreed to strengthen co-operation with the country. In view of its commitment to strengthened co-operation, NATO announced that it would launch a project, the largest of its kind ever undertaken, to assist Ukraine in the decommissioning of old ammunitions, small arms and light weapons stockpiles. In April NATO invited Ukraine to begin an 'Intensified Dialogue' on its aspirations to NATO membership and on the necessary relevant reforms that it would be required to undertake. In the same month NATO and Ukraine effected an exchange of letters preparing the way for Ukraine to support 'Operation Active Endeavour' (see below). In June talks held between NATO ministers of defence and their Ukrainian counterpart focused on NATO's assistance to Ukraine in the reform of its defence and security sectors. In October the NATO-Ukraine Commission held its first meeting within the framework of the Intensified Dialogue initiated in April. A meeting of the ministers of defence of the NATO-Ukraine Commission held in June 2006 discussed Ukraine's defence policy and the ongoing transformation of the Ukrainian armed forces. In this context, ministers confirmed that the NATO-Ukraine Joint Working Group on Defence Reform should remain a key mechanism. In April 2008 NATO heads of state and government approved, in principle, Ukraine's future membership of the Alliance. The NAC, headed by the Secretary-General, visited Ukraine for a series of meetings in June. In August 2009 a Declaration to Complement the Charter on a Distinctive Partnership between NATO and Ukraine was signed, which emphasized the NUC's role in strengthening political dialogue and co-operation between the two sides and in securing reforms necessary for Ukraine to join the Alliance.

In August 2008 an extraordinary meeting of the NAC was convened to discuss an escalation of conflict in Georgia. The meeting expressed solidarity with Georgia's actions to counter attacks by separatist forces in Abkhazia and South Ossetia and deplored as disproportionate the use of force by Russia. Several days later the NAC held a special ministerial meeting to demand a peaceful, lasting solution to the conflict based on respect for Georgia's independence, sovereignty and territorial integrity. The meeting agreed that NATO would support Georgia in assessing damage to civil infrastructure, as well as in re-establishing an air traffic system and advising on cyber defence issues. Ministers also determined to establish a NATO-Georgia Commission, to strengthen co-operation and political dialogue between the two sides and to oversee Georgia's future application for NATO membership. A Framework Document to establish the Commission was signed by NATO's Secretary-General and Georgia's Prime Minister in the Georgian capital, Tbilisi, in September; the inaugural session of the Commission was convened immediately. The first meeting of the Commission at ministerial level was convened in December. In that month NATO ministers of foreign affairs agreed to establish a NATO Liaison Office in Tbilisi. The Office was inaugurated in October 2010 during a visit by the Secretary-General to Georgia. In December 2008 NATO foreign ministers also determined that Georgia should develop an Annual National Programme, replacing its existing IPAP, as a framework for co-operation with the Alliance and the implementation of reforms needed to fulfil membership criteria.

The Madrid summit meeting in July 1997 endorsed the establishment of a Mediterranean Co-operation Group to enhance NATO relations with Egypt, Israel, Jordan, Mauritania, Morocco and Tunisia. The Group was to provide a forum for regular political dialogue between the two groupings and to promote co-operation in training, scientific research and information exchange. In April 1999 NATO heads of state endorsed measures to strengthen the so-called Mediterranean Dialogue. Algeria joined the Mediterranean Dialogue in February 2000. The June 2004 summit meeting determined to enhance the Mediterranean Dialogue and launched a new 'Istanbul

Co-operation Initiative' aimed at promoting broader co-operation with the Middle East. By April 2007 Bahrain, Kuwait, Qatar and the UAE had joined the Istanbul Co-operation Initiative (ICI). In February 2012 an ICI seminar was convened to consider means of deepening the partnership, and to discuss ongoing security challenges in the Middle East and North Africa. In February 2006 NATO and Mediterranean Dialogue partner countries convened their first meeting at the level of ministers of defence. In April, under the chairmanship of NATO's Deputy Secretary-General, the NAC and representatives of the seven Mediterranean Dialogue countries met in Rabat, Morocco, in order to review their co-operation to date and to discuss its future prospects. All countries were encouraged to formulate Individual Co-operation Programmes (ICPs) as a framework for future co-operation. In November NATO heads of state and government, meeting in Riga, Latvia, inaugurated a NATO Training Co-operation Initiative to extend defence and specialist training and expertise with Mediterranean Dialogue and Istanbul Co-operation Initiative partner countries. The Initiative aimed to help those countries to strengthen their defence structures and enhance the interoperability of their armed forces with those of the Alliance. Egypt signed an ICP with NATO in October 2007, and Jordan concluded its ICP in April 2009.

In July 1997 heads of state and government formally invited the Czech Republic, Hungary and Poland to begin accession negotiations. Accession Protocols for the admission of those countries were signed in December and required ratification by all member states. The three countries formally became members of NATO in March 1999. In April the NATO summit meeting, held in Washington, DC, USA, initiated a new Membership Action Plan (MAP) to extend practical support to aspirant member countries and to formalize a process of reviewing applications. In March 2003 protocols of accession, amending the North Atlantic Treaty, were adopted by the then 19 NATO member states with a view to admitting Bulgaria, Estonia, Latvia, Lithuania, Romania, Slovakia and Slovenia to the Alliance. In March 2004, the protocols of accession having been ratified by all of the member states, those seven countries were formally invited to join NATO and, on 29 March, they acceded to the Treaty. In April 2008 NATO heads of state and government, meeting in Bucharest, Romania, invited Albania and Croatia to commence accession negotiations and declared support for Georgia and Ukraine to apply for MAP status. It was also agreed that accession negotiations with the former Yugoslav republic of Macedonia, which joined the MAP programme in 1999, would be initiated as soon as a mutually acceptable solution to the issue over the country's name has been reached with Greece. The Accession Protocols for Albania and Croatia were signed by NATO ministers of foreign affairs in July, and those countries formally acceded to the Treaty on 1 April 2009. Montenegro was invited to join MAP in December; at that time NATO ministers confirmed that Bosnia and Herzegovina would participate in MAP as soon as further institutional reforms had been implemented. In April 2010 NATO ministers of foreign affairs invited Bosnia and Herzegovina to join MAP, conditional on full registration of its defence properties.

In November 2010 the Lisbon summit meeting determined to reform NATO's structure of partnership mechanisms, in order to enhance the flexibility and efficiency of co-operation arrangements.

OPERATIONS

During the 1990s NATO increasingly developed its role as a mechanism for peace-keeping and crisis management. In June 1992 NATO ministers of foreign affairs, meeting in Oslo, Norway, announced the Alliance's readiness to support peace-keeping operations under the aegis of the CSCE on a case-by-case basis: NATO would make both military resources and expertise available to such operations. In July NATO, in co-operation with WEU, undertook a maritime operation in the Adriatic Sea to monitor compliance with the UN Security Council's resolutions imposing sanctions against the Yugoslav republics of Serbia and Montenegro. In December NATO ministers of foreign affairs expressed the Alliance's readiness to support peace-keeping operations under the authority of the UN Security Council. From April 1993 NATO fighter and reconnaissance aircraft began patrolling airspace over Bosnia and Herzegovina in order to enforce the UN prohibition of military aerial activity over the country. In addition, from July NATO aircraft provided protective cover for troops from the UN Protection Force in Yugoslavia (UNPROFOR) operating in the 'safe areas' established by the UN Security Council. In February 1994 NATO conducted the first of several aerial strikes against artillery positions that were violating heavy weapons exclusion zones imposed around 'safe areas' and threatening the civilian populations. Throughout the conflict the Alliance also provided transport, communications and logistics to support UN humanitarian assistance in the region.

The peace accord for the former Yugoslavia, which was initialled in Dayton, USA, in November 1995, and signed in Paris, France, in December, provided for the establishment of a NATO-led Implementation Force (IFOR) to ensure compliance with the treaty, in accordance with a strictly defined timetable and under the authority of a UN Security Council mandate. In December a joint meeting of allied foreign and defence ministers endorsed the military structure for the peace mission, entitled 'Operation Joint Endeavour', which was to involve approximately 60,000 troops from 31 NATO and non-NATO countries. IFOR, which constituted NATO's largest military operation ever, formally assumed responsibility for peace-keeping in Bosnia and Herzegovina from the UN on 20 December.

By mid-1996 the military aspects of the Dayton peace agreement had largely been implemented under IFOR supervision. Substantial progress was achieved in the demobilization of soldiers and militia and in the cantonment of heavy weaponry. During 1996 IFOR personnel undertook many activities relating to the civilian reconstruction of Bosnia and Herzegovina, including the repair of roads, railways and bridges, reconstruction of schools and hospitals, delivery of emergency food and water supplies, and emergency medical transportation. IFOR also co-operated with, and provided logistical support for, the Office of the High Representative of the International Community in Bosnia and Herzegovina, which was charged with overseeing implementation of the civilian aspects of the Bosnian peace accord. IFOR assisted the OSCE in preparing for and overseeing the all-Bosnia legislative elections that were held in September, and provided security for displaced Bosnians who crossed the inter-entity boundary in order to vote in their towns of origin. In December NATO ministers of foreign affairs approved a follow-on operation, with an 18-month mandate, to be known as the Stabilization Force (SFOR). SFOR was to be about one-half the size of IFOR, but was to retain 'the same unity of command and robust rules of engagement' as the previous force. Its principal objective was to maintain a safe environment at a military level to ensure that the civil aspects of the Dayton peace accord could be fully implemented, including the completion of the de-mining process, the repatriation of refugees, rehabilitation of local infrastructure and preparations for municipal elections. In December 1997 NATO ministers of defence confirmed that SFOR would be maintained at its current strength of some 31,000 troops, subject to the periodic six-monthly reviews. In February 1998 NATO resolved to establish within SFOR a specialized unit to respond to civil unrest and uphold public security. At the same time the NAC initiated a series of security co-operation activities to promote the development of democratic practices and defence mechanisms in Bosnia and Herzegovina. In October 1999 the NAC agreed to implement a reduction in SFOR's strength to some 20,000 troops, as well as a revision of its command structure, in response to the improved security situation in Bosnia and Herzegovina. In May 2002 NATO determined to reduce SFOR to 12,000 troops by the end of that year, and in December 2003 NATO defence ministers undertook to reduce NATO's presence to some 7,000 troops by mid-2004. The June 2004 summit meeting determined to terminate SFOR's mandate at the end of 2004, and endorsed a new European Union (EU) mission, EUFOR, in Bosnia and Herzegovina. NATO maintains a military headquarters in Sarajevo, in order to continue to assist the authorities in Bosnia and Herzegovina in matters of defence reform.

In March 1998 an emergency session of the NAC was convened at the request of the Albanian Government, which was concerned at the deteriorating security of its border region with the Serbian province of Kosovo and Metohija. In June NATO defence ministers authorized the formulation of plans for air-strikes against Serbian targets, which were finalized in early October. However, the Russian Government remained strongly opposed to the use of force and there was concern among some member states over whether there was sufficient legal basis for NATO action without further UN authorization. Nevertheless, in mid-October, following Security Council condemnation of the humanitarian situation in Kosovo, the NAC agreed on limited air-strikes against Serbian targets, with a 96-hour delay on the 'activation order'. At the same time the US envoy to the region, Richard Holbrooke, concluded an agreement with President Milošević to implement the conditions of a UN resolution (No. 1199). A 2,000-member international observer force, under the auspices of the OSCE, was to be established to monitor compliance with the agreement, supported by a NATO Co-ordination Unit, based in the former Yugoslav republic of Macedonia (FYRM), to assist with aerial surveillance. In mid-November NATO ambassadors approved the establishment of a 1,200–1,800-strong multinational force, under French command, to assist in any necessary evacuation of OSCE monitors. A NATO Kosovo Verification Command Centre was established in Kumanovo, north-east FYRM, later in that month.

On 24 March 1999 an aerial offensive against the Federal Republic of Yugoslavia (which was renamed 'Serbia and Montenegro' in 2003 and divided into separate states of Montenegro and Serbia in 2006) was initiated by NATO, with the declared aim of reducing that country's capacity to commit attacks on the Albanian population. The first phase of the allied operation was directed against defence facilities, followed, a few days later, by the second phase which permitted direct attacks on artillery positions, command centres and other military targets in a declared exclusion zone south of the 44th parallel. The escalation of the conflict prompted thousands of Albanians to flee Kosovo, while others were reportedly forced from their homes by Serbian security personnel, creating massive refugee populations in neighbouring countries. In early April 1999 NATO ambassadors agreed to dispatch some 8,000 troops, as an ACE Mobile Force Land operation (entitled 'Operation Allied Harbour'), to provide humanitarian assistance to the estimated 300,000 refugees in Albania at that time and to provide transportation to relieve overcrowded camps, in particular in border areas. Refugees in the FYRM were to be assisted by the existing NATO contingent (numbering some 12,000 troops by early April), which was permitted by the authorities in that country to construct new camps for some 100,000 displaced Kosovans. An additional 1,000 troops were transferred from the FYRM to Albania in mid-May in order to construct a camp to provide for a further 65,000 refugees. NATO's 50th anniversary summit meeting, held in Washington, DC, USA, in late April, was dominated by consideration of the conflict and of the future stability of the region. A joint statement declared the determination of all Alliance members to increase economic and military pressure on President Milošević to withdraw forces from Kosovo. In particular, the meeting agreed to prevent shipments of petroleum reaching Serbia through Montenegro, to complement the embargo imposed by the EU and a new focus of the bombing campaign which aimed to destroy the fuel supply within Serbia. However, there was concern on the part of several NATO governments with regard to the legal and political aspects of implementing the embargo. The meeting failed to adopt a unified position on the use of ground forces. Following further intensive diplomatic efforts to secure a cease-fire in Kosovo, on 9 June a Military Technical Agreement was signed between NATO and the Federal Republic of Yugoslavia, incorporating a timetable for the withdrawal of all Serbian security personnel. On the following day the UN Security Council adopted Resolution 1244, which authorized an international security presence in Kosovo, the Kosovo Peace Implementation Force (KFOR), under NATO command, and an international civilian presence, the UN Interim Administration Mission in Kosovo (UNMIK). The NAC subsequently suspended the air-strike campaign, which, by that time, had involved some 38,000 sorties. An initial 20,000 KFOR troops entered Kosovo on 12 June. A few days later an agreement was concluded with Russia, providing for the joint responsibility of Pristina airport with a NATO contingent and for the participation of some 3,600 Russian troops in KFOR, reporting to the country command in each sector. On 20 June the withdrawal of Yugoslav troops from Kosovo was completed, providing for the formal ending of NATO's air campaign. KFOR's immediate responsibility was to create a secure environment to facilitate the safe return of refugees, and, pending the full deployment of UNMIK, to assist the reconstruction of infrastructure and civil and political institutions. In addition, NATO troops were to assist personnel of the international tribunal to investigate sites of alleged violations of human rights and mass graves. In January 2000 NATO agreed that the Eurocorps defence force would assume command of KFOR headquarters in April. In February an emergency meeting of the NAC was convened to review the situation in the divided town of Mitrovicë (Kosovska Mitrovica), northern Kosovo, where violent clashes had occurred between the ethnic populations and five people had died during attempts by KFOR to impose order. The NAC expressed its determination to reinforce KFOR's troop levels. In October KFOR worked with OSCE and UN personnel to maintain a secure environment and provide logistical assistance for the holding of municipal elections in Kosovo. During the year KFOR attempted to prevent the movement and stockpiling of illegal armaments in the region. A Weapons Destruction Programme was successfully conducted by KFOR between April 2000–December 2001; a second programme was initiated in March 2002, while an Ammunition Destruction Programme commenced in January. In May the NAC approved a modification of KFOR's mission that was designed to facilitate the introduction of a more regional approach to operations and permit a reduction in KFOR's strength from 38,000 troops to some 33,200 by the end of the year. In July 2003, in view of progress made in the security situation, the withdrawal of the Russian contingent from KFOR was effected. In March 2004, in response to renewed inter-ethnic violence in Kosovo, NATO deployed additional troops from previously designated operational and strategic reserve forces in order to support operations undertaken by KFOR to protect Kosovar Serbs and other ethnic minorities in addition to ethnic Albanians. In February 2006 direct UN-led talks between Serbian and Kosovo Albanian officials on the future status of Kosovo commenced in Vienna, Austria. By the end of 2007, however, the two sides had failed to reach agreement. NATO's ministers of foreign affairs, meeting in December 2007, agreed that KFOR would remain in the province, at current troop levels, unless the UN Security Council decided otherwise. In February 2008 Kosovo's newly elected government issued a unilateral declaration of independence from Serbia, supported by many EU countries. NATO's Secretary-General and NAC reaffirmed the commitment to maintain a force in Kosovo and to support any future arrangements. In June 2009 NATO defence ministers announced a gradual reduction in KFOR troop numbers, given improvements in the security environment, and envisaged the force becoming a 'deterrent presence'. In February 2010 NATO ministers of defence reviewed the situation in Kosovo and welcomed the conclusion of the first phase adjusting KFOR to a deterrent force. At that time there were some 10,700 troops under NATO command in Kosovo (compared with some 15,500 in January 2009).

In September 2001, following the terrorist attacks against targets in the USA and the decision to invoke Article 5 of the North Atlantic Treaty, NATO redirected the standing naval force to provide an immediate Alliance presence in the Eastern Mediterranean. In the following month 'Operation Active Endeavour' was formally launched, to undertake surveillance and monitoring of maritime trade in the region and to detect and deter terrorist activity, including illegal trafficking. In February 2003 the NAC agreed to extend the operation to escort non-military vessels through the Strait of Gibraltar; this aspect of the mission was suspended in May 2004. In March 2004 the NAC determined to expand the operation to the whole of the Mediterranean and to seek the support of this extension, through their active participation in the operation, by participants in the EAPC and the PfP programme. An Exchange of Letters between NATO and Russia, concluded in December 2004, facilitated the implementation from February 2006 of joint training activities. In September 2006 NATO authorized the participation of a Russian naval ship in the operation. The NAC approved the active involvement of a Ukrainian ship in the operation in May 2007. By early 2012 more than 100,000 vessels had been monitored under the operation, and some 155 compliant boardings had taken place.

In August 2003 NATO undertook its first mission outside of the Euro-Atlantic area when it assumed command of the UN-mandated International Security Assistance Force (ISAF) in Afghanistan. In October the office of a Senior Civilian Representative was established to liaise with the national government and representatives of the international community and advance NATO's politico-military objectives in the country. In December NATO ministers of defence agreed progressively to extend ISAF's mission in Afghanistan beyond the capital, Kabul. The transfer of command of the Kunduz Provincial Reconstruction Team (PRT) to NATO in January 2004 represented the first step of that expansion. In June the summit meeting, held in Istanbul, Turkey, determined to expand the ISAF in order to assist the Afghan authorities to extend and exercise authority across the country. A first phase of the mission's expansion, involving the establishment of PRTs in Baghlan, Feyzabad, Mazar-e-Sharif and Meymana, had been completed by October of that year. In December the NAC authorized a second expansionary phase, which envisaged the establishment of four PRTs in western provinces of Afghanistan. This was undertaken in 2005. In September an additional 2,000 NATO troops were temporarily deployed to Afghanistan to provide security during provincial and parliamentary elections, held in that month. In December NATO ministers of foreign affairs endorsed a revised operational plan to incorporate a Stage 3 and Stage 4 Expansion of ISAF. The Stage 3 and Stage 4 Expansions, achieved, respectively, in July and October 2006, entailed extending operations to cover the entire country and establishing 15 additional PRTs, five regional commands and two forward support bases (in Kandahar and Khost). Additional ISAF officers were dispatched to mentor and liaise with national army units, support government programmes to disarm rebel groups and support government and international programmes to counter illicit narcotic production. NATO continued to emphasize immediate reconstruction and development activities, through its civil military co-operation units, working closely with government and local and community leaders, and co-operated with the Pakistani military and Afghan National Army through a Tripartite Commission and a Joint Intelligence and Operations Centre. In September 2006 NATO's Secretary-General signed a declaration with the Afghan President establishing a Framework for Enduring Co-operation in Partnership, committing NATO to long-term support for the country's efforts to secure democratic government and territorial integrity. In April 2008 NATO heads of state and government, meeting in Bucharest, Romania, confirmed that ISAF remained a priority for the Alliance and expressed a long-term commitment to achieving peace and security in Afghanistan. In June the Secretary-General participated in an International Conference in Support of Afghanistan, hosted by the French Government in Paris. In April 2009 heads of state and government, and leaders of partner countries contributing to ISAF, attending the NATO summit, issued a Declaration on Afghanistan, in which they stated their long-term commitment to that country, pledged the deployment there of additional military forces for electoral support and for training and mentoring the Afghan National Army, and announced the establishment of a NATO Training Mission in Afghanistan (NTM-A). Further initiatives to enhance the training for Afghan National Security Forces, to improve the command and control structure of ISAF and to deploy NATO airborne warning and control aircraft to Afghanistan, were approved by NATO defence ministers meeting in June. In October NATO defence ministers and ministers from non-NATO contributing countries agreed a set of key priorities for the coming year: placing the Afghan population at the core of Alliance activities in that country; building further the capacity of the national security forces; promoting better governance; and engaging with Afghanistan's neighbours, in particular with Pakistan. NTM-A was formally established in that month. In February 2010 ISAF initiated a joint military offensive with Afghan national security forces, entitled Operation Moshtarak, in order to reassert government authority and to protect the civilian population in southern Helmand province. In April an informal meeting of NATO and ISAF ministers of foreign affairs agreed on a roadmap to structure a transition process of handing over full sovereignty to the Afghan authorities. At the same time ministers adopted an Afghan First Policy to strengthen the local Afghan economy. A joint framework for transition to full Afghan ownership of its national security by the end of 2014 was endorsed at an international conference on Afghanistan, convened in Kabul, in July 2010. The transition process, was endorsed at the NATO summit meeting in November 2010. At that time ISAF 's troop strength totalled 130,930 from 40 contributing nations. NATO heads of state and government also reaffirmed their long-term commitment to ensuring the stability of Afghanistan. In March 2011 the Afghan President confirmed that from July troops would be withdrawn and power transferred to local authorities in a first tranche of areas. Accordingly, responsibility for security of Bamiyan province, central Lashkar Gah, and Mehter Lam in eastern Afghanistan was transferred to Afghan forces in July. The transition process started in a second tranche of Afghan areas in December 2011. In early February 2012 a meeting of NATO and ISAF defence ministers determined that the process of transition to Afghan security ownership was on course, and reaffirmed the objective that the Afghan security forces should have full responsibility for security across the country by end-2014. Later in February 2012 ISAF personnel were temporarily withdrawn from government ministries in and around Kabul following the killing of two ISAF officers inside the Afghan Ministry of Interior; violent protests had erupted at that time over reports that US troops based in Afghanistan had unintentionally burned copies of the Koran. The 2012 NATO summit, to be held in May, was to assess the degree of additional support still required by the Afghan security forces, and how much further training and education would be required before the 2014 transfer of power.

In June 2004 NATO heads of state and government, meeting in Istanbul, Turkey, agreed to offer assistance to the newly inaugurated Iraqi Interim Government with the training of its security forces. The meeting also endorsed a new NATO Policy on Combating Trafficking in Human Beings, with the aim of supporting the efforts of countries and international organizations to counter the problem. In July a NATO Training Implementation Mission was initiated to undertake the training commitments in Iraq. In December the NAC authorized an expansion of the Mission, of up to 300 personnel, and the establishment of an Iraq Training, Education and Doctrine Centre. The expanded operation was to be called the NATO Training Mission–Iraq (NTM-I). In September 2005 an Iraqi Joint Staff College was inaugurated. In July 2009 NATO and the Iraqi Government signed a long-term agreement regarding the training of Iraqi Security Forces. NTM-I expanded its remit in 2010 to include training of border personnel. NTM-1 was terminated in December 2011. In April 2011 Iraq was granted NATO partner status.

In April 2005 the African Union (AU) requested NATO assistance to support its peace-keeping mission in Darfur, western Sudan, where civil conflict had caused a severe humanitarian crisis. In May the NAC provisionally agreed to provide logistical support for the mission. Further consultations were held with the AU, UN and EU. In June the NAC confirmed that it would assist in the expansion of the AU mission (AMIS) by airlifting supplementary AU peace-keepers into the region. No NATO combat troops were to be deployed to Darfur. The first airlifts were undertaken in July and in August NATO agreed to transport civilian police officers. NATO established a Senior Military Liaison Officer team, in Addis Ababa, Ethiopia, to liaise with the AU. In June 2006 the AU requested enhanced NATO assistance for its peace-keeping mission in Darfur, including the certification of troops allocated to the peace-keeping force, assistance with lessons learned and support in the establishment of a joint operations centre. NATO undertook staff training to further the mission's capacity-building activities. In November NATO ministers extended its support for proposals by the AU and UN to undertake a hybrid peace-keeping mission in Darfur. NATO support to AMIS was concluded on 31 December 2007 when the mission was transferred to the UN/AU operation. In June 2007 NATO agreed to support an AU mission in Somalia by providing strategic airlifts for deployment of personnel and equipment. In October 2008 NATO ministers of defence, meeting in Budapest, Hungary, agreed to initiate a temporary assignment, Operation Allied Provider, in support of a request by the UN Secretary-General, to protect ships chartered by the World Food Programme to deliver humanitarian aid to Somalia. The mission was also mandated to conduct patrols to deter piracy and other criminal acts against merchant shipping in the high risk areas in the Gulf of Aden. The Operation was concluded in mid-December. NATO resumed its counter-piracy operations in that region in March 2009, under Operation Allied Protector. A successor mission, Operation Ocean Shield, was approved in August and incorporated a new training element to enable countries in the region to strengthen their counter-piracy capabilities. In March 2012 the mandate of Operation Ocean Shield was extended to the end of 2014.

From October 2005 until 1 February 2006 NATO undertook a mission to provide relief to areas of north-west Pakistan severely damaged and isolated by a massive earthquake. NATO airlifted relief supplies into the region, transported civilians and official personnel, and deployed some 1,200 engineers and troops to assist with road clearance and the construction of shelters and other local infrastructure. In August 2010 the NAC agreed to a request from the Pakistani Government to provide assistance in the delivery of humanitarian supplies, donated by international organizations following extensive flooding in large parts of the country.

In March 2011 NATO initiated Operation Unified Protector, using ships and aircraft operating in the Central Mediterranean, in order to monitor and enforce an arms embargo against the Libyan authorities, which had been imposed by the UN Security Council (Resolution 1973, adopted on 17 March) in response to the violent oppression of an opposition movement in that country. Later in that month NATO members determined to enforce the UN-sanctioned no-fly zone over Libya, alongside a military operation to prevent further attacks on civilians and civilian-populated areas, undertaken by a multinational coalition under British, France and US command. A few days later, on 27 March, NATO member states agreed to assume full command of the operation to protect civilians in Libya (formal transfer of command took place on 31 March). On 28 March NATO's Secretary-General attended an international conference on Libya, held in London, United Kingdom, at which it was agreed to establish a Contact Group to give political guidance to the international community's response to the situation. The first meeting of the Contact Group was held in Doha, Qatar, in April. (The Contact Group was replaced in September by a Group of Friends of the New Libya.) In early June NATO ministers extended Operation Unified Protector for a further 90 days (from 27 June); in September the Operation was extended once again for 90 days. In late October, following the capture by opposition forces of the last remaining government-controlled city, Sirte, and the arrest (and subsequent death) of the Libyan leader, Col Muammar al-Qaddafi, the North Atlantic Council resolved to conclude the Operation with effect from the end of that month. By the time of its conclusion NATO and its partners had conducted more than 26,500 air sorties over Libya, including 9,700 strike missions. Nineteen vessels were deployed during the Operation to monitor and enforce the arms embargo, supported by patrol aircraft. Over 3,100 ships were hailed, 300 boarded and 11 denied transit to port under the Operation.

NATO Agencies

In November 2010 NATO heads of state and government agreed to consolidate the functions and programmes of the various NATO Agencies and realign the structure along three major programmatic themes: procurement; support; and communications and information systems. The Agency Reform plan was approved in June 2011. Accordingly, there were to be Agencies for Communications and Information, Standardization, Procurement and Support, and a new Science and Technology Organization (to be established from June 2012).

Central Europe Pipeline Management Agency (CEPMA): BP 552, 78005 Versailles Cedex, France; tel. 1-39-24-49-00; fax 1-39-55-65-39; e-mail registry@cepma.nato.int; f. 1957; responsible for the 24-hour operation of the Central Europe Pipeline System and its storage and distribution facilities, on behalf of the Central Europe Pipeline Management Organization (CEPMO).

NATO Air Command and Control System Management Agency (NACMA): Bâtiment Z, blvd Leopold III, 1110 Brussels, Belgium; tel. (2) 707-8536; fax (2) 707-8777; e-mail hrab@nacma.nato.int; internet www.nacma.nato.int; conducts planning, system engineering, implementation and configuration management for NATO's ACCS programme; Gen. Man. JAN FLEDDERUS (Netherlands).

NATO Airborne Early Warning and Control Programme Management Organisation (NAPMO): Akerstraat 7, 6445 CL Brunssum, Netherlands; fax (45) 5254373; f. 1978; responsible for the management and implementation of the NATO Airborne Early Warning and Control Programme.

NATO Consultation, Command and Control Agency (NC3A): 1110 Brussels, Belgium; tel. (2) 707-41-11; fax (2) 707-87-70; internet www.nc3a.nato.int; works within the framework of the NATO C3 Organization (f. 1996 by restructuring of the NATO Communications and Information Systems Organization and the Tri-Service Group on Communications and Electronics, incorporating the former Allied

Data Systems Interoperability Agency, the Allied Naval Communications Agency and the Allied Tactical Communications Agency); provides scientific advice and assistance to NATO military and political authorities; helps to develop, procure and implement cost-effective system capabilities to support political consultations and military command and control functions; also maintains an office in The Hague, Netherlands; Gen. Man. GEORGES D'HOLLANDER.

NATO CIS Operating and Support Agency (NACOSA): maintains NATO's communications and information system (CIS); supervised by the NC3 Board.

NATO Communications and Information Systems (NCISS) School: 04010 Borgo Piave, Latina, Italy; tel. (0773) 6771; fax (0773) 662467; e-mail tc@nciss.nato.int; internet www.nciss.nato.int; f. 1959; provides advanced training to civilian and military personnel in the operation and maintenance of NATO's communications and information systems; conducts orientation courses for partner countries; scheduled to be moved to Portugal, in accordance with the June 2011 reforms; Commandant MARCELLO TURCHETTA (Italy).

NATO EF 2000 and Tornado Development, Production and Logistics Management Agency (NETMA): Insel Kammerstrasse 12–14, Postfach 1302, 82008 Unterhaching, Germany; tel. (89) 666800; fax (89) 66680555; replaced the NATO Multirole Combat Aircraft (MRCA) Development and Production Management Agency (f. 1969) and the NATO European Fighter (EF) Aircraft Development, Production and Logistics Management Agency (f. 1987); responsible for the joint development and production of the European Fighter Aircraft and the MRCA (Tornado).

NATO HAWK Management Office: 26 rue Galliéni, 92500 Rueil-Malmaison, France; tel. 1-47-08-75-00; fax 1-47-52-10-99; e-mail bgohnhmo@csi.com; f. 1959 to supervise the multinational production and upgrading programmes of the HAWK surface-to-air missile system in Europe.

NATO Helicopter Design and Development Production and Logistics Management Agency (NAHEMA): Le Quatuor, Bâtiment A, 42 route de Galice, 13082 Aix-en-Provence Cedex 2, France; tel. 4-42-95-92-00; fax 4-42-64-30-50.

NATO Maintenance and Supply Agency (NAMSA): 11 rue de la Gare, 8325 Capellen, Luxembourg; tel. 30-631; fax 30-87-21; e-mail contact@namsa.nato.int; internet www.namsa.nato.int; f. 1958; provides logistics services to NATO and NATO nations; headquarters to be assumed by the new NATO Support Agency, approved in June 2011; Gen. Man. ANTONIOS CHATZIDAKIS.

Responsible to the Military Committee:

NATO Civil/Military Frequency Management Sub-Committee (Civ./Mil. FMSC): 1110 Brussels, Belgium; tel. (2) 707-55-28; e-mail chsmb@hq.nato.int; replaced the Allied Radio Frequency Agency (f. 1951); the Civ./Mil. FMSC is the frequency authority of the Alliance and establishes and co-ordinates in close co-operation with civil Authorities all policy concerned with the military use of the radio frequency spectrum.

NATO Defense College (NDC): Via Giorgio Pelosi 1, 00143 Rome, Italy; tel. (06) 50525255; fax (06) 50525794; e-mail research@ndc.nato.int; internet www.ndc.nato.int; f. 1951; conducts education, research and outreach activites; Commandant Lt-Gen. ARNE BARD DALHAUG.

NATO (SHAPE) School: Am Rainenbichl 54, 82487 Oberammergau, Germany; tel. (8822) 94811052; fax (8822) 94811396; e-mail pao@natoschool.nato.int; internet www.natoschool.nato.int; f. 1975; acts as a centre for training military and civilian personnel of NATO countries, and, since 1991, for officials from partner countries, in support of NATO policies, operations and objectives; Commandant Col MARK D. BAINES.

NATO Standardization Agency (NSA): 1110 Brussels, Belgium; tel. (2) 707-55-56; fax (2) 707-57-18; e-mail nsa@nsa.nato.int; internet nas.nato.int; lead agent for the development, co-ordination and assessment of operational standardization, in order to enhance interoperability; initiates, co-ordinates, supports and administers standardization activities conducted under the authority of the NATO Committee for Standardization; one of the major Agencies to be retained after the June 2011 reform, although to be reviewed in early 2014.

NATO Undersea Research Centre (NURC): Viale San Bartolomeo 400, 19126 La Spezia, Italy; tel. (0187) 527370; fax (0187) 527700; e-mail pao@nurc.nato.int; internet www.nurc.nato.int; f. 1959; conducts maritime research in response to NATO's operational and transformational requirements, in particular through its science programme; focuses on the undersea domain and on solutions to maritime security problems; brings researchers together through rotational scientific staffing and through extensive partnering with NATO mem. states; scheduled to be incorporated into a new NATO Science and Technology Organization in 2012; Dir Dr DIRK TIELBUERGER.

Research and Technology Organisation (RTO): BP 25, 7 rue Ancelle, 92201 Neuilly-sur-Seine Cedex, France; tel. 1-55-61-22-00; fax 1-55-61-22-99; e-mail mailbox@rta.nato.int; internet www.rto.nato.int; f. 1998 by merger of the Advisory Group for Aerospace Research and Development and the Defence Research Group; brings together scientists and engineers from member countries for exchange of information and research co-operation (formally established 1998); provides scientific and technological advice for the Military Committee, for other NATO bodies and for member nations; comprises a Research and Technology Board and a Research and Technology Agency, responsible for implementing RTO's work programme.

Finance

As NATO is an international, not a supra-national, organization, its member countries themselves decide the amount to be devoted to their defence effort and the form which the latter will assume. Thus, the aim of NATO's defence planning is to develop realistic military plans for the defence of the Alliance at reasonable cost. Under the annual defence planning process, political, military and economic factors are considered in relation to strategy, force requirements and available resources. The procedure for the co-ordination of military plans and defence expenditures rests on the detailed and comparative analysis of the capabilities of member countries. All installations for the use of international forces are financed under a common-funded infrastructure programme. In accordance with the terms of the Partnership for Peace strategy, partner countries undertake to make available the necessary personnel, assets, facilities and capabilities to participate in the programme. The countries also share the financial cost of military exercises in which they participate.

Publications

NATO publications (in English and French, with some editions in other languages) include:

NATO Basic Texts.

NATO Handbook.

NATO Ministerial Communiqués.

NATO Review (quarterly, in 24 languages).

NATO Update (monthly, electronic version only).

Secretary-General's Annual Report.

Economic and scientific publications.

ORGANISATION FOR ECONOMIC CO-OPERATION AND DEVELOPMENT—OECD

Address: 2 rue André-Pascal, 75775 Paris Cedex 16, France.
Telephone: 1-45-24-82-00; **fax:** 1-45-24-85-00; **e-mail:** webmaster@oecd.org; **internet:** www.oecd.org.

OECD was founded in 1961, replacing the Organisation for European Economic Co-operation (OEEC) which had been established in 1948 in connection with the Marshall Plan. It constitutes a forum for governments to discuss, develop and attempt to co-ordinate their economic and social policies. The organization aims to promote policies designed to achieve the highest level of sustainable economic growth, employment and increase in the standard of living, while maintaining financial stability and democratic government, and to contribute to economic expansion in member and non-member states and to the expansion of world trade.

MEMBERS

Australia	Hungary	Norway
Austria	Iceland	Poland
Belgium	Ireland	Portugal
Canada	Israel	Slovakia
Chile	Italy	Slovenia
Czech Republic	Japan	Spain
Denmark	Republic of Korea	Sweden
Estonia	Luxembourg	Switzerland
Finland	Mexico	Turkey
France	Netherlands	United Kingdom
Germany	New Zealand	USA
Greece		

Note: Accession talks were ongoing with Russia in 2012.
The European Commission also takes part in OECD's work. Brazil, the People's Republic of China, India, Indonesia and South Africa are regarded as 'enhanced engagement countries'.

Organization

(April 2012)

COUNCIL

The governing body of OECD is the Council, at which each member country is represented. The Council meets from time to time (usually once a year) at the level of government ministers, with the chairmanship rotated among member states. It also meets regularly at official level, when it comprises the Secretary-General and the Permanent Representatives of member states to OECD. It is responsible for all questions of general policy and may establish subsidiary bodies as required, to achieve the aims of the organization. Decisions and recommendations of the Council are adopted by mutual agreement of all its members.

Heads of Permanent Delegations
(with ambassadorial rank)

Australia: Christopher Barrett.
Austria: Wolfgang Petritsch.
Belgium: Yves Haesendonck.
Canada: Judith LaRocque.
Chile: Raul Saez.
Czech Republic: Karel Dyba.
Denmark: Poul Eric Dam Kristensen.
Estonia: Marten Kokk.
Finland: Antti Kuosmanen.
France: Roger Karoutchi.
Germany: Johannes Westerhoff.
Greece: Konstantina (Tina) Birmpili.
Hungary: Istvan Mikola.
Iceland: Berglind Asgeirstdottir.
Ireland: Michael Forbes.
Italy: Carlo Maria Oliva.
Japan: Motohide Yoshikawa.
Republic of Korea: Kyung-wook Hur.
Luxembourg: Georges Santer.
Mexico: Agustín García-López Loaeza.
Netherlands: Edmond H. Wellenstein.
New Zealand: Rosemary Bank.
Norway: Harald Neple.
Poland: Pawel Wojciechowski.
Portugal: Eduardo Ferro Rodrigues.
Slovakia: Ingrid Brocková.
Slovenia: Andrej Rant.
Spain: Ricardo Díez-Hochleitner.
Sweden: Anders Ahnlid.
Switzerland: Stefan Fluckinger.
Turkey: Ahmet Kamil Erozan.
United Kingdom: Nicholas (Nick) Mark Bridge.
USA: Karen Kornbluh.
European Union: Maria-Francesca Spatolisano.

EXECUTIVE COMMITTEE

The Executive Committee prepares the work of the Council. It is also called upon to carry out specific tasks where necessary. In addition to its regular meetings, the Committee meets occasionally in special sessions attended by senior government officials.

SECRETARIAT

The Council, the committees and other bodies in OECD are assisted by an independent international secretariat headed by the Secretary-General. An Executive Director is responsible for the management of administrative support services. There are OECD Centres in Berlin, Germany; Mexico City, Mexico; Tokyo, Japan; and Washington, DC, USA.

Secretary-General: José Ángel Gurría Treviño (Mexico).
Deputy Secretaries-General: Pier Carlo Padoan (Italy) (OECD Chief Economist), Rintaro Tamaki (Japan), Richard A. Boucher (USA), Yves Leterme (Belgium).
Chief of Staff and 'Sherpa to the G20': Gabriela Ramos (Mexico).

SPECIAL BODIES

African Partnership Forum.
Centre for Educational Research and Innovation (CERI).
Development Centre.
Financial Action Task Force.
Global Project 'Measuring the Progress of Societies'.
International Energy Agency.
International Transport Forum.
Nuclear Energy Agency.
Partnership for Democratic Governance Advisory Unit.
Sahel and West Africa Club.

Activities

In 2011 OECD resolved to strengthen its multilateral policy approach in order to fulfil its founding ambitions, and adopted a new directive entitled 'Better Policies for Better Lives'. In its 50th Anniversary Vision Statement, published in May, OECD also resolved to adopt a New Paradigm for Development, with greater collaboration within the organization and strengthened partnerships with non-member countries, and to work Towards a Global Policy Network.

ECONOMIC POLICY

OECD aims to promote stable macroeconomic environments in member and non-member countries. The Economics Department works to identify priority concerns for governments and to assess the economic implications of a broad range of structural issues, such as ageing, labour market policies, migration, public expenditure and financial market developments. *Economic Outlook*, analysing the major trends in short-term economic prospects and key policy issues, is published twice a year. The main organ for the consideration and direction of economic policy is the Economic Policy Committee, which comprises governments' chief economic advisers and central bankers, and meets two or three times a year.

The Economic and Development Review Committee, comprising all member countries, is responsible for surveys of the economic situation and macroeconomic and structural policies of each member country. A report, including specific policy recommendations, is issued every 12 to 18 months on each country, after an examination carried out by the Committee.

In December 2008 OECD published a *Strategic Response to the Global Financial and Economic Crisis* (developed collectively by the OECD Council, Committees and Secretariat), which aimed to address regulatory and policy failures in a comprehensive manner, and focused on strengthening and implementing principles and guidelines, and on identifying regulatory gaps in, the areas of finance, competition and governance; and monitoring developments and identifying policy options to promote the restoration of sustainable long-term growth. From early 2009 OECD co-ordinated an initiative, also comprising the ILO, the IMF, the World Bank and the World Trade Organization (WTO), to compile *A 'Global Charter'/ 'Legal Standard', Inventory of Possible Policy Instruments*; this audit of the existing range of economic and social policy instruments, a preliminary version of which was issued in March, was to be a single, coherent repository of policy recommendations, guidelines and principles of best practice, and was regarded as a work in progress aimed at strengthening the regulatory framework. The five organizations contributing to the *Inventory* had been invited by the G8 summit held in Hokkaido, Japan, in June 2008, to enhance their co-operation. The meeting of G20 heads of state and government held, for the first time with OECD participation, in April 2009, determined to re-launch the Financial Stability Board, which comprises senior representatives of national financial authorities, international financial institutions, international regulatory and supervisory groupings, and committees of central bank experts, and aims to stabilize and strengthen the functioning of the financial markets. The meeting issued as its final communiqué a global plan for recovery and reform, outlining commitments that included strengthening financial supervision and regulation and reforming global financial institutions, and supporting consideration of a new charter for promoting sustainable economic development. In June G8 ministers responsible for finance, meeting in Lecce, Italy, endorsed a 'Global Standard for the 21st Century' through the adoption of the Lecce Framework of Common Principles and Standards for Propriety, Integrity and Transparency; the Lecce Framework, as the Global Standard was known thereafter, was supported by OECD and was approved by G8 heads of state and government held in L'Aquila, Italy, in July. It was envisaged that OECD would continue to play a leading role in its development. In April 2011 OECD reported that global economic recovery was advancing and was reaching self-sustaining levels throughout the OECD area. Owing to the devastating earthquake and tsunami that struck Japan in mid-March, projections for economic growth in that country were excluded at that time. In November, in the context of a serious debt crisis within several euro area countries, OECD's *Economic Outlook* urged member countries to implement decisive policies, including a substantial increase in the capacity of the European Financial Stability Fund, in order to prevent sovereign defaults, credit contraction and bank failures.

STATISTICS

Statistical data and related methodological information are collected from member governments and, where possible, consolidated, or converted into an internationally comparable form. The Statistics Directorate maintains and makes available data required for macroeconomic forecasting, i.e. national accounts, the labour force, foreign trade, prices, output, and monetary, financial, industrial and other short-term statistics. Work is also undertaken to develop new statistics and new statistical standards and systems in areas of emerging policy interest (such as sustainable development). In addition, the Directorate shares with non-member countries member states' experience in compiling statistics. In the early 2000s a new Statistical Information System, incorporating new technical infrastructure, was developed which aimed to improve the efficiency of data collection, processing, storage etc., to improve the quality of OECD statistics, and to enhance accessibility to the data. The first World Forum on Statistics, Knowledge and Policy was held in November 2004, in Palermo, Italy. At the second Forum, held in Istanbul, Turkey, in June 2007, on the theme 'Measuring and Fostering the Progress of Societies', OECD, the European Commission, the OIC, the UN, UNDP and the World Bank issued the Istanbul Declaration, in which they made a commitment to measuring and fostering the progress of societies with a view to improving policy-making and advancing democracy and the well-being of citizens. The Declaration was subsequently opened to wider signature. A Global Project on Measuring the Progress of Societies, with OECD participation, was launched in 2008. The third World Forum on Statistics, Knowledge and Policy was convened in Busan, Republic of Korea (South Korea), in October 2009, on the theme 'Charting Progress, Building Visions, Improving Life'; the fourth Forum was to be convened in October 2012, in New Delhi, India.

In September 2010 OECD launched the iLibrary, a new platform providing comprehensive access to statistical data, working papers, books and journals.

DEVELOPMENT CO-OPERATION

The Development Assistance Committee (DAC) is the principal body through which OECD deals with issues relating to co-operation with developing countries and is one of the key forums in which the major bilateral donors work together to increase their effectiveness in support of sustainable development. The DAC is supported by the Development Co-operation Directorate, which monitors aid programmes and resource flows, compiles statistics and seeks to establish codes of practice in aid. There are also working parties on statistics, aid evaluation, gender equality and development co-operation and environment; and networks on poverty reduction, good governance and capacity development, and conflict, peace and development co-operation. The DAC holds an annual high-level meeting of ministers responsible for international aid, and heads of aid agencies from member governments, with senior officials from the World Bank, the IMF and UNDP.

The DAC's mission is to foster co-ordinated, integrated, effective and adequately financed international efforts in support of sustainable economic and social development. Recognizing that developing countries themselves are ultimately responsible for their own development, the DAC concentrates on how international co-operation can contribute to the population's ability to overcome poverty and participate fully in society. Principal activities include: adopting authoritative policy guidelines; conducting periodic critical reviews of members' programmes of development co-operation; providing a forum for dialogue, exchange of experience and the building of international consensus on policy and management issues; and publishing statistics and reports on aid and other resource flows to developing countries and countries in transition. A working set of indicators of development progress has been established by the DAC, in collaboration with experts from UN agencies (including the World Bank) and from developing countries.

In February 2003 OECD/DAC co-sponsored a High-Level Forum on Aid Effectiveness, held in Rome, Italy. The second High-Level Forum, convened in February–March 2005, in Paris, France, endorsed the Paris Declaration on Aid Effectiveness, and agreed a number of country-based action plans, for donor and recipient countries, aimed at improving aid effectiveness. In addition, the meeting reviewed OECD's contribution to achieving the UN Millennium Development Goals, issues relating to development, peace and security, and a report on development effectiveness in the context of the New Partnership for Africa's Development (NEPAD). The Accra Agenda for Action, adopted in September 2008 by the third High-Level Forum convened in Accra, Ghana, included further country-based action plans tailored to advance progress in aid effectiveness. In November–December 2011 the fourth High-Level Forum, convened in Busan, South Korea, reviewed progress in implementing the principles of the Paris Declaration. A Busan Partnership for Effective Development Co-operation was signed to foster a framework for co-operation by developed and developing countries, emerging economies, civil society and private funders.

In 2010 official development assistance (ODA) from DAC donor countries totalled US $129,000m. The five largest ODA donors in 2010 were France, Germany, Japan, the United Kingdom and the USA.

Development Centre: f. 1962; acts as a forum for dialogue and undertakes research and policy analysis in order to assist the development of policy to stimulate economic and social growth in developing and emerging economies; membership open to both OECD and non-OECD countries.

Sahel and West Africa Club: f. 1976, initially to support countries affected by drought in the Sahel region of Africa; expanded to include other countries in West Africa in 2001; acts as an informal discussion grouping between some 17 African countries and OECD members.

African Partnership Forum: f. 2003, following a meeting of heads of state of the G8, in Evian, France; comprises representatives of G8 countries, NEPAD and major bilateral and multilateral development partners; meets twice a year; aims to strengthen efforts in support of Africa's development.

PUBLIC GOVERNANCE AND TERRITORIAL DEVELOPMENT

The Public Governance and Territorial Development Directorate is concerned with identifying changing needs in society and in markets, and with helping countries to adapt their governmental systems and territorial policies. One of the Directorate's primary functions is to provide a forum for exchanging ideas on how to meet the challenges countries face in the area of governance. It is concerned with improving public sector governance through comparative data and analysis, the setting and promotion of standards, and the facilitation of transparency and peer review, as well as to encourage the participation of civil society in public governance. The Public Management Committee (PUMA) serves as a forum for senior officials responsible for the central management systems of government, providing information, analysis and recommendations on public management and governing capacity. A Working Party of Senior Budget Officials is the principal international forum for issues concerning international budgeting. In 1992 a joint initiative of OECD and the European Union (EU), operating within OECD, was established to support good governance in the countries of Central and Eastern Europe that were to accede to, or were candidates for either accession to or association with, the EU. The so-called Support for Improvement in Governance and Management (SIGMA) programme assists in the reform and modernization of public institutions in those countries and assesses their progress in those areas. OECD undertakes Reviews of Public Sector Integrity in member and non-member states to assist policy makers to improve policies, adopt good practices and implement established principles and standards. In March 2012 OECD hosted, in Mexico City, Mexico, a high-level meeting on e-government, which reviewed new digital public sector management tools.

In October 2007 OECD, with UNDP, the Organization of American States and the Inter-American Development Bank, inaugurated the Partnership for Democratic Governance (PDG), to assist developing countries to improve governance and strengthen their accountability and effectiveness. OECD hosts an advisory unit of the initiative. The OECD Secretary-General acts as chairperson of the PDG.

The Territorial Development Policy Committee assists central governments with the design and implementation of more effective, area-based strategies, encourages the emergence of locally driven initiatives for economic development, and promotes better integration of local and national approaches. Generally, the Committee's work programme emphasizes the need for innovative policy initiatives and exchange of knowledge in a wide range of policies, such as entrepreneurship and technology diffusion and issues of social exclusion and urban deprivation. National and regional territorial reviews are undertaken to analyse economic and social trends and highlight governance issues.

TRADE AND AGRICULTURE

Through the Trade and Agriculture Directorate OECD works to support a rules-based multilateral trading system with the objective of promoting further trade liberalization; and to assess government support to the agricultural sector in OECD and principal emerging economies, while assessing the medium-term outlook for agricultural markets and advising on policies for the sustainable use of farm and fisheries resources.

The OECD Trade Committee supports the continued liberalization and efficient operation of the multilateral trading system, with the aim of contributing to the expansion of world trade on a non-discriminatory basis, and thereby advancing standards of living and sustainable development. Its activities include examination of issues concerning trade relations among member countries as well as relations with non-member countries, and consideration and discussion of trade measures taken by a member country which adversely affect another's interests. The Committee holds regular consultations with civil society organizations.

A Working Party on Export Credits and Credit Guarantees serves as a forum for the discussion and co-ordination of export credit policies. OECD maintains an Export Credit Arrangement, which provides a framework for the use of officially supported export credits, stipulating the most generous financial terms and conditions available. Governments participating in the Arrangement meet regularly. In 2000 the Working Party agreed an Action Statement on Bribery and Officially Supported Export Credits; this was strengthened and converted into an OECD Recommendation in December 2006. In June 2007 the OECD Council adopted a Revised Recommendation on Common Approaches to the Environment and Officially Supported Export Credits (updated from 2003).

The Trade Committee considers the challenges that are presented to the existing international trading system by financial or economic instability, the process of globalization of production and markets and the ensuing deeper integration of national economies. OECD is committed to the Doha Development Agenda, the framework for the multilateral trade negotiations currently being pursued by the WTO. OECD and the WTO have established a joint database that provides information about trade-related technical assistance and capacity building in respect of trade policy and regulation; trade development; and infrastructure. In accordance with the Doha Agenda OECD is undertaking analysis of the implications on business of the growing number of regional trade agreements and the relationship between those agreements and the multilateral system. OECD hosts an annual Global Forum on Trade. The 2011 event was convened in November, in Paris, to highlight the initial work of an International Collaborative Initiative on Trade and Employment.

OECD undertakes analysis of relevant issues and advises governments, in particular in relation to policy reform, trade liberalization and sustainable agriculture and fisheries. OECD is also a focal point for global efforts in the certification and standardization of products, packaging and testing procedures, though its agricultural codes and schemes. A Committee for Agriculture reviews major developments in agricultural policies, deals with the adaptation of agriculture to changing economic conditions, elaborates forecasts of production and market prospects for the major commodities, identifies best practices for limiting the impact of agricultural production on the environment, promotes the use of sustainable practices in the sector and considers questions of agricultural development in emerging and transition economies. A separate Fisheries Committee carries out similar tasks in its sector, and, in particular, analyses the consequences of policy measures with a view to promoting responsible and sustainable fisheries. The Directorate administers a Biological Resources in Agriculture programme, which sponsors research fellowships as well as workshops and conferences, to enhance international co-operation in priority areas of agro-food research.

In February 2010 ministers of agriculture from OECD states met, for the first time since 1998, to discuss global food security in relation to issues such as population growth, food demand in affluent industrialized societies, pressure on land and water, and climate change; agriculture ministers from non-member countries with significant agricultural sectors or food markets also participated in the meeting. In January 2011 the OECD Secretary-General stated that volatility in food and commodity prices was undermining efforts to address global poverty and hunger, and was threatening economic growth, and urged governments to co-operate in mitigating extreme swings in market prices. The *OECD-FAO Agricultural Outlook 2011–20*, published in June 2011, found that while a good harvest in the near future might lead to a reduction in commodity prices compared with extremely high levels reached earlier in 2011, nevertheless cereal prices might average up to 20% higher and meat prices up to 30% higher during 2011–20, compared with 2001–10 price levels. It was noted that higher commodity prices were leading to rising consumer price inflation in many countries, raising concern for food security and economic stability in some developing countries. Boosting investment in agriculture and reinforcing rural development in developing countries were urged.

ENTREPRENEURSHIP AND LOCAL DEVELOPMENT

In June 2000 OECD convened a Ministerial Conference on Small and Medium-sized Enterprises (SMEs), in Bologna, Italy, and initiated a process to promote SMEs and entrepreneurship policies. Within the context of the so-called Bologna Process, an OECD Global Conference on SME and Entrepreneurship Funding was held in March 2006, in Brasilia, Brazil. In July 2004 OECD established a Centre for Entrepreneurship, SMEs and Local Development, responsible for promoting OECD work on entrepreneurship and for bringing together experts in the field. In addition, it disseminates best practices on the design, implementation and evaluation of initiatives to promote entrepreneurship, SMEs and local economic and employment development. The Centre administers OECD's Local Economic and Employment Development (LEED) programme, which aims to promote the creation of employment through innovative strategies and recommendations to local governments and communities.

A Tourism Committee promotes sustainable growth in the tourism sector and encourages the integration of tourism issues into other policy areas. A Global Forum on Tourism Statistics is convened every two years.

FINANCIAL AND ENTERPRISE AFFAIRS

Promoting the efficient functioning of markets and enterprises and strengthening the multilateral framework for trade and investment is the responsibility of the main OECD committees and working groups supported by the Directorate for Financial and Enterprise Affairs. The Directorate analyses emerging trends, provides policy guidelines and recommendations, gives examples of best practice and maintains benchmarks to measure progress.

The Committee on Capital Movements and Invisible Transactions monitors the implementation of the Codes of Liberalization of Invisible Transactions and of Current Invisible Operations as legally binding norms for all member countries. The Committee on International Investment and Multinational Enterprises monitors the OECD Guidelines for Multinational Enterprises, a corporate Code of Conduct recommended by OECD member governments, business and labour units. A Declaration on International Investment and Multinational Enterprises, while non-binding, contains commitments on the conduct and treatment of foreign-owned enterprises established in member countries. It is subject to periodic reviews, the most recent of which was concluded in May 2011. By the end of that year 43 countries had subscribed to the Declaration. Negotiations on a Multilateral Agreement on Investment (MAI), initiated by OECD ministers in 1995 to provide a legal framework for international investment, broke down in October 1998, although 'informal consultation' on the issue was subsequently pursued. In June 2008 the OECD Council, meeting at ministerial level, adopted a declaration on sovereign wealth funds (SWFs) and policies for recipient countries, to ensure a fair and transparent investment environment. The declaration was also endorsed by the governments of Chile, Estonia and Slovenia. The development of a non-binding 'Model Investment Treaty', to facilitate negotiations and foster more consistency in investment procedures, is under consideration by OECD.

The Committee on Competition Law and Policy promotes the harmonization of national competition policies, co-operation in competition law enforcement, common merger reporting rules and pro-competitive regulatory reform, the development of competition laws and institutions, and efforts to change policies that restrain competition. The Committee on Financial Markets exercises surveillance over recent developments, reform measures and structural and regulatory conditions in financial markets. It aims to promote international trade in financial services, to encourage the integration of non-member countries into the global financial system, and to improve financial statistics. The Insurance Committee monitors structural changes and reform measures in insurance markets, for example the liberalization of insurance markets, financial insolvency, co-operation on insurance and reinsurance policy, the monitoring and analysis of regulatory and structural developments, and private pensions and health insurance. A working party on private pensions meets twice a year. In 2002 OECD member governments approved guidelines for the administration of private pension funds, the first initiative they had taken to set international standards for the governance and supervision of collective pension funds. Specialized work on public debt is undertaken by the Working Party on Government Debt Management. An OECD Global Forum on Public Debt Management and Emerging Government Securities Markets is convened each year.

In May 1997 the OECD Council endorsed plans to introduce a global ban on the corporate bribery of public officials. The OECD Convention on Bribery of Foreign Public Officials in International Business Transactions entered into force in February 1999 and, by March 2012, had been ratified by all OECD member states and five non-member countries (Argentina, Brazil, Bulgaria, Russia and South Africa). All signatory states were required to undergo a 'phase I' review of legislation conformity with anti-bribery standards and help to compile a 'phase II' country report assessing the structures in place to enforce these laws and their effectiveness. In May 2009 the OECD Council adopted a Recommendation on the Non-Tax Deductibility of Bribes and in December adopted a Recommendation for Further Combating Bribery of Foreign Public Officials in order to strengthen the existing legal framework for combating bribery and corruption. All signatory states were required to implement the new measures. In 2010, OECD member states, and enhanced partner countries, adopted a Declaration on Propriety, Integrity and Transparency in the Conduct of International Business and Finance.

In March 2011 it was announced that OECD was developing a new initiative, entitled 'clean.gov.biz', to improve the co-ordination of anti-corruption and transparency initiatives, firstly within member countries, and then, in an expanded version, to incorporate all other relevant players, including governments, international organizations, and the private sector.

In May 1999 ministers endorsed a set of OECD Principles for Corporate Governance, covering ownership and control of corporate entities, the rights of shareholders, the role of stakeholders, transparency, disclosure and the responsibilities of boards. In 2000 these became one of the 12 core standards of global financial stability, and they are used as a benchmark by other international financial institutions. A revised set of Principles was published in 2004. OECD collaborates with the World Bank and other organizations to promote good governance world-wide, for example through regional round tables and the Global Corporate Governance Forum. OECD provides the secretariat for the Financial Action Task Force on Money Laundering (FATF), which develops and promotes policies to combat money-laundering. In February 2011 the G20 ministers of finance and central bank governors tasked OECD and the Financial Stability Board with developing a new set of principles on consumer protection in financial services. The resulting draft guidelines were agreed at a meeting of G20 ministers in October, and were to be incorporated into a broader regulatory framework.

TAXATION

OECD promotes internationally accepted standards and practices of taxation, and provides a forum for the exchange of information and experience of tax policy and administration. The Committee on Fiscal Affairs is concerned with promoting the removal of tax barriers, monitoring the implementation and impact of major tax reforms, developing a neutral tax framework for electronic commerce, and studying the tax implications of the globalization of national economies. A Centre for Tax Policy and Administration supports the work of the Committee. Other activities include the publication of comparable statistics on taxation and guidelines on transfer pricing, and the study of tax evasion and tax and electronic commerce. OECD is a sponsor, with the IMF and the World Bank, of an International Tax Dialogue. OECD administers a network of Multilateral Tax Centres that provide workshops and a venue for exchanges between national officials and OECD experts.

Since 1998 OECD has promoted co-ordinated action for the elimination of so-called 'harmful' tax practices, designed to reduce the incidence of international money-laundering, and the level of potential tax revenue lost by OECD members. In mid-2000 OECD launched an initiative to abolish 'harmful tax systems', identifying a number of offshore jurisdictions as tax havens lacking financial transparency, and inviting these to co-operate by amending national financial legislation. Several of the countries and territories named agreed to follow a timetable for reform, with the aim of eliminating such practices by the end of 2005. Others, however, were reluctant to participate. (The USA also strongly opposed the initiative.) In April 2002 OECD announced that co-ordinated defensive measures would be implemented against non-complying jurisdictions ('un-co-operative tax havens') from early 2003. OECD has also highlighted examples of preferential tax regimes in member countries. In May 2009 the Committee removed the remaining three jurisdictions, Andorra, Liechtenstein and Monaco, from the list of un-co-operative tax havens, following commitments made by those authorities to implement recommended standards of transparency and effective exchange of information.

OECD convenes a Global Forum on Transparency and Exchange of Information for Tax Purposes to promote co-operation and dialogue with non-member countries. In September 2009 the Global Forum determined to implement a strengthened global monitoring and peer review process to ensure full implementation by members of their commitments. The Forum agreed to expand its membership, emphasizing that all members shared an equal footing; agreed to accelerate negotiations processes; and decided to establish a co-ordinated technical assistance programme aimed at supporting smaller jurisdictions rapidly to implement standards. In October 2011 the Global Forum, by that time comprising 105 member jurisdictions, agreed guidelines on the co-ordination of technical assistance and adopted a progress report on international compliance with standards of exchange of tax information. Reviews of 59 tax jurisdictions were presented to the G20 meeting of heads of state in November. At the meeting G20 countries signed together the amended Convention on Mutual Administrative Assistance in Tax Matters (first developed by OECD and the Council of Europe in 1988), which aimed to promote exchange of information on tax examinations, evasion and collection between member and non-member states. By March 2012 the Convention had 34 signatories.

ENVIRONMENT

The OECD Environment Directorate works in support of the Environment Policy Committee (EPOC) on environmental issues. EPOC assesses performance; encourages co-operation on environmental policy; promotes the integration of environmental and economic policies; works to develop principles, guidelines and strategies for effective environmental management; provides a forum for member states to address common problems and share data and experience; and promotes the sharing of information with non-member states. The Directorate conducts peer reviews of environmental conditions and progress. A first cycle of 32 Environmental Performance Reviews of member and selected non-member countries was completed in 2000, and a second cycle was undertaken during 2001–09. A third cycle, initiated in 2009, was ongoing in 2012. The Directorate aims to improve understanding of past and future trends through the collection and dissemination of environmental data.

OECD programmes and working parties on the environment consider a range of issues, including the harmonization of biotechnology regulation, the environmental impact of production and consumption, natural resource management, trade and investment and the environment, and chemical safety. In some cases working parties collaborate with other Directorates (for example, the working parties on Trade and Environment and on Agriculture and Environment). An Experts Group on Climate Change, based in the Environment Directorate, undertakes studies related to international agreements on climate change.

In May 2001 OECD ministers of the environment, convened in Paris, France, adopted the OECD Environmental Strategy for the 21st Century, containing recommendations for future work, with a focus on fostering sustainable development, and strengthening co-operation with non-member countries and partnerships with the private sector and civil society. The strategy identified several issues requiring urgent action, such as the generation of municipal waste, increased car and air travel, greenhouse gas emissions, groundwater pollution, and the exploitation of marine fisheries. The meeting endorsed guidelines for the provision of environmentally sustainable transport, as well as the use of a set of key environmental indicators. A review of the key indicators was presented to a meeting of environment ministers, convened in April 2004. The *Global Environment Outlook to 2030*, issued in March 2008, indicated that wide-ranging climate change might be achieved without negatively impacting economic growth, if efficient policy instruments were employed. In June 2009 OECD member countries, candidate countries, and 'enhanced engagement countries' issued a declaration on 'Green Growth', urging the adoption of targeted policy instruments to promote green investment, and emphasizing their commitment to the realization of an ambitious and comprehensive post-2012 global climate agreement. In March 2012 OECD published *Global Environment Outlook to 2050: Consequences of Inaction*. OECD ministers of the environment meeting in that month considered the following main concerns identified by the report: energy demands, air pollution, natural resources and biodiversity, and global water demand. The meeting was convened on the theme 'Making Green Growth Deliver', which aimed to secure sustainable socio-economic development, in accordance with OECD's Green Growth Strategy, launched in May 2011. In January 2012 OECD, jointly with UNEP, the World Bank and the Global Green Growth Institute, established a Green Growth Knowledge Platform to compile and disseminate research and policy experience concerning green growth.

SCIENCE, TECHNOLOGY AND INDUSTRY

The Directorate for Science, Technology and Industry aims to assist member countries in formulating, adapting and implementing policies that optimize the contribution of science, technology, industrial development and structural change to economic growth, employment and social development. It provides indicators and analysis on emerging trends in these fields, identifies and promotes best practices, and offers a forum for dialogue. In February 2008 OECD, as part of its then International Futures Programme (which was merged into the Directorate in April 2011) inaugurated a Global Forum on Space Economics to provide a focus for international debate and co-operation on economic issues affecting the development of space infrastructure and other space-related activities.

Areas considered by the Committee for Scientific and Technological Policy include the management of public research, technology and innovation, and intellectual property rights. A Working Party on Biotechnology was established in 1993 to pursue study of biotechnology and its applications, including issues such as scientific and technological infrastructure, and the relation of biotechnology to sustainable industrial development. Statistical work on biotechnology is undertaken by a Working Party of National Experts on Science and Technology Indicators. In 1992 a megascience forum was established to bring together senior science policy officials to identify and pursue opportunities for international co-operation in scientific research. It was succeeded, in 1999, by the Global Science Forum which meets two times a year. A Global Biodiversity Information Facility (GBIF) began operations in 2001 to connect global biodiversity databases in order to make available a wide range of data online. In September 2011 OECD hosted a Global Forum on the Knowledge Economy, which focused on improving national science and innovation policies, and science and innovation for inclusive development.

The Committee for Information, Computer and Communications Policy monitors developments in telecommunications and information technology and their impact on competitiveness and productivity, with an emphasis on technological and regulatory convergence. It also promotes the development of new guidelines and analyses trade and liberalization issues. The Committee maintains a database of communications indicators and telecommunications tariffs. A Working Party on Information Security and Privacy promotes a co-ordinated approach to efforts to enhance trust in the use of electronic commerce. In August 2004 an OECD Task Force was established to co-ordinate efforts to counter unsolicited e-mail ('spam'). OECD supports the Digital Opportunities Task Force (Dot.force) which was established in June 2000 by the G8 to recommend action with a view to eliminating the so-called 'digital divide' between developed and less developed countries and between different population sectors within nations. OECD's Global Conference on Telecommunications Policy for the Digital Environment, held in January 2002, emphasized the importance of competition in the sector and the need for regulatory reform. A ministerial meeting on the Future of the Internet Economy was held in Seoul, South Korea, in June 2008. A follow-up High-Level Meeting on the Internet Economy: Generating Innovation and Growth, was convened in June 2011, in Paris.

The Committee on Industry and the Business Environment focuses on industrial production, business performance, innovation and competitiveness in industrial and services sectors, and policies for private sector development in member and selected non-member economies. In recent years the Committee has addressed issues connected with globalization, regulatory reform, SMEs, and the role of industry in sustainable development. Business and industry policy fora explore a variety of issues with the private sector, for example new technologies or environmental strategies for industry, and develop recommendations. The Working Party on SMEs and Entrepreneurship conducts an ongoing review of the contribution of SMEs to growth and employment and carries out a comparative assessment of best practice policies. (See also the Bologna Process.)

The Transport Division of the Directorate for Science, Technology and Industry considers aviation, maritime, shipbuilding, road and intermodal transport issues. Maritime Transport and Steel Committees aim to promote multilateral solutions to sectoral friction and instability based on the definition and monitoring of rules. The Working Party on Shipbuilding seeks to establish normal competitive conditions in that sector, especially through dialogue with non-OECD countries. In January 2004 a new Transport Research Centre was established by merger of OECD's road transport and intermodal linkages research programme and the economic research activities of the European Conference of Ministers of Transport. A new report, entitled *Strategic Transport Infrastructure Needs to 2030* was published in March 2012.

International Transport Forum (ITF): in May 2006 the European Conference of Ministers of Transport agreed to establish and become integrated into a new International Transport Forum; the inaugural meeting of the Forum was held in May 2008, in Leipzig, Poland.

EMPLOYMENT, LABOUR AND SOCIAL AFFAIRS

The Employment, Labour and Social Affairs Committee is concerned with the development of the labour market and selective employment policies to ensure the utilization of human capital at the highest possible level and to improve the quality and flexibility of working life, as well as the effectiveness of social policies; it plays a central role in addressing OECD's concern to reduce high and persistent unemployment through the creation of high-quality jobs. The Committee's work covers such issues as the role of women in the economy, industrial relations, measurements of unemployment, and the development of an extensive social database. The Committee also carries out single-country and thematic reviews of labour market policies and social assistance systems. It has assigned a high priority to work on the policy implications of an ageing population and on indicators of human capital investment. In May 2011 OECD and the ILO signed an MOU on strengthening mutual co-operation. Both organizations provided analysis and support to the G20 meeting of ministers of labour and employment, held in September 2011, in Cannes, France. The heads of both organizations expressed concern that world unemployment was almost 200m. and urged G20 members to prioritize employment and social protection in the policy debate.

OECD undertakes analysis of health care and health expenditure issues, and reviews the organization and performance of health systems. In May 2004 OECD ministers responsible for health reviewed a three-year project to evaluate and analyse the performance of health care systems in member countries. Upon their recommendation a new Group on Health was established in January 2005 to direct a further programme of work, to be supported by a new Health Division within the Directorate of Employment, Labour and Social Affairs. Social policy areas of concern include benefits and wages, family-friendly policies, and the social effects of population ageing. In 2011 OECD launched a Better Life Index to enhance understanding of the impact of policy options on quality of life.

A Non-Member Economies and International Migration Division works on social policy issues in emerging economies and economies in transition, especially relating to education and labour market reforms and to the economic and social aspects of migration. The Directorate undertakes regular analysis of trends in international migration, including consideration of its economic and social impact, the integration of immigrants, and international co-operation in the control of migrant flows.

In January 2011 OECD issued a study entitled *Housing and the Economy: Policies for Renovation*, which offered governments a roadmap for developing sounder housing policy through the promotion of reforms in areas such as financial sector regulation, taxation, the regulation of rental markets, and the provision of social housing. The study also found that national policies favouring home ownership over renting had reduced residential and labour mobility, which in turn undermined recovery in employment levels.

EDUCATION

The Directorate for Education was created in 2002 in order to raise the profile of OECD's work, which is conducted in the context of its view of education as a lifelong activity. The Directorate comprises Divisions on Education and Training, Indicators and Analysis, Education Management, and Infrastructure. Programmes undertaken by the Directorate include a Programme for Co-operation with non-member Economies, the Programme of International Student Assessments (PISA), the Programme on Institutional Management in Higher Education and the Programme on Education Building, as well as regular peer reviews of education systems. A Programme for the International Assessment of Adult Competencies (PIAAC) was launched in 2011 to measure skills and comptencies of individuals to contribute to society. The results were expected to be published in

2013. In February 2012 OECD published a report which encouraged governments to increase investment in disadvantaged schools in order to reduce school failure, increase economic growth and help to contribute to a fairer society.

Centre for Educational Research and Innovation (CERI): f. 1968; an independently funded programme within the Directorate for Education; promotes the development of research activities in education, together with experiments of an advanced nature, designed to test innovations in educational systems and to stimulate research and development.

CO-OPERATION WITH NON-MEMBER ECONOMIES

The Centre for Co-operation with Non-Members (CCNM) was established in January 1998, by merger of the Centre for Co-operation with Economies in Transition (founded in 1990) and the Liaison and Co-ordination Unit. It serves as the focal point for the development of policy dialogue with non-member economies, managing multi-country, thematic, regional and country programmes. These include a Baltic Regional Programme, Programmes for Russia and for Brazil, an Emerging Asian Economies Programme and the OECD Programme of Dialogue and Co-operation with China. The Centre also manages OECD's various Global Forums, which discuss a wide range of specific issues that defy resolution in a single country or region, for example international investment, sustainable development, biotechnology, and trade. The Centre co-ordinates and maintains OECD's relations with other international organizations. An integral part of the CCNM is the joint venture with the EU, the Support for Improvement in Governance and Management (SIGMA) programme, which is directed towards the transition economies of Central and Eastern Europe.

Non-member economies are invited by the CCNM, on a selective basis, to participate in or observe the work of certain OECD committees and working parties. The Centre also provides a limited range of training activities in support of policy implementation and institution building. In 1994 the OECD Centre for Private Sector Development, based in Istanbul, Turkey, commenced operations as a joint project between the OECD and the Turkish Government to provide policy advice and training to administrators from transitional economies in Eastern Europe, Central Asia and Transcaucasus. Subsequently, the Centre has evolved into a regional forum for policy dialogue and co-operation with regard to issues of interest to transitional economies. The CCNM is also a sponsor of the Joint Vienna Institute, which offers a variety of administrative, economic and financial management courses to participants from transition economies. In May 2007 OECD invited Chile, Estonia, Israel, Russia and Slovenia to initiate discussions with a view to future membership of the organization. So-called 'roadmaps' for negotiations were agreed with those five 'accession countries' in December. Chile, Slovenia, Israel and Estonia formally acceded to the Organization in May, July, September and December 2010, respectively.

In 2007 OECD launched an Enhanced Engagement Initiative. Participating countries—Brazil, China, India, Indonesia and South Africa—are encouraged to participate directly in the work of the Organisation and are important partners in dialogue.

In November 2006 OECD's Trade Union Advisory Committee (TUAC) ratified an agreement with the International Trade Union Confederation and the so-called Global Unions (global trade union federations) to form a Council of Global Unions, with the aims of promoting trade union membership and advancing common trade union interests world-wide.

OECD administered a support unit to the Heiligendamm L'Aquila Process, which was launched, with a two-year mandate, in July 2009, to follow on from the Heiligendamm Process (inaugurated in June 2007 with the aim of strengthening relations between the G8 and principal emerging economies). The Heiligendamm L'Aquila Process aimed to broaden the thematic framework addressed by the Heiligendamm Process: cross-border investment; innovation and intellectual property; energy and climate change; and development, in particular in Africa.

Finance

OECD's total budget for 2011 amounted to €342m.

Publications

OECD Annual Report.

African Economic Outlook (annually).

Agricultural Policies in Emerging Economies (annually).

Agricultural Policies in OECD Countries.

Development Co-operation Report (annually).

Economic Policy Reforms (annually).

Education at a Glance (annually).

Energy Balances of Non-OECD Countries (annually).

Energy Balances of OECD Countries (annually).

Geographical Distribution of Financial Flows to Developing countries (annually).

Going for Growth (annually).

Health at a Glance.

Information Technology Outlook (every two years).

International Migration Outlook (annually).

Labour Force Statistics.

Latin American Economic Outlook (annually).

Measuring Globalisation.

Measuring Innovation.

National Accounts at a Glance.

OECD Economic Surveys (every 12 to 18 months for each country).

OECD Employment Outlook (annually).

OECD Environmental Outlook to 2030.

OECD Factbook (annually).

OECD Information Technology Outlook.

OECD Observer (every 2 months).

OECD Transfer Pricing Guidelines for Multinational Enterprises and Tax Administrations.

OECD Yearbook.

Perspectives on Global Development (annually).

Regions at a Glance.

Southeast Asian Economic Outlook (annually).

Society at a Glance.

Tax Co-operation.

Numerous specialized reports, working papers, books and statistics on economic and social subjects are also published.

International Energy Agency—IEA

Address: 9 rue de la Fédération, 75739 Paris Cedex 15, France.

Telephone: 1-40-57-65-00; **fax:** 1-40-57-65-09; **e-mail:** info@iea.org; **internet:** www.iea.org.

The Agency was established by the OECD Council Decision Establishing an International Energy Agency to develop co-operation on energy questions among participating countries.

MEMBERS

Australia	Hungary	Portugal
Austria	Ireland	Slovakia
Belgium	Italy	Spain
Canada	Japan	Sweden
Czech Republic	Republic of Korea	Switzerland
Denmark	Luxembourg	Turkey
Finland	Netherlands	United Kingdom
France	New Zealand	USA
Germany	Norway*	
Greece	Poland	

* Norway participates in the IEA under a special Agreement.

In October 2010 the Governing Board determined that negotiations should commence on the future admission of Chile to the IEA.

The European Commission also takes part in the IEA's work as an observer.

Organization

(April 2012)

GOVERNING BOARD

Composed of ministers or senior officials of the member governments. Meetings are held every two years at ministerial level and five times a year at senior official level. Decisions may be taken by a special weighted majority on a number of specified subjects, particularly concerning emergency measures and emergency reserve commitments; a simple weighted majority is required for procedural decisions and decisions implementing specific obligations in the agreement. Unanimity is required only if new obligations, not already specified in the agreement, are to be undertaken.

SECRETARIAT

The Secretariat comprises the following Directorates: Energy Markets and Security (with three divisions: Oil Industry and Markets; Emergency Policy; and Energy Diversification); Global Energy Dialogue (four divisions: an office on co-operation with dialogue countries in the Asia-Pacific region, Latin America, and sub-Saharan Africa; an office on co-operation with dialogue countries in Europe, the Middle East and North Africa; Country Studies; and Energy Technology Collaboration); Sustainable Energy Policy and Technology (two divisions: Energy Efficiency and Environment; and Energy Technology Policy); and Employment at the IEA. There are also the following Standing Groups and Committees: Standing Group on Long-Term Co-operation; Standing Group on the Oil Market; Standing Group on Emergency Questions; Committee on Energy Research and Technology (with working parties); and the Standing Group on Global Energy Dialogue.

Executive Director: MARIA VAN DER HOEVEN (Netherlands).

Activities

The Agreement on an International Energy Programme was signed in November 1974 and formally entered into force in January 1976. The Agreement commits the participating countries of the IEA to share petroleum in certain emergencies, to strengthen co-operation in order to reduce dependence on petroleum imports, to increase the availability of information on the petroleum market, to co-operate in the development and co-ordination of energy policies, and to develop relations with the petroleum-producing and other petroleum-consuming countries. In mid-2011 IEA countries possessed total reserves of petroleum totalling more than 4,100m. barrels, of which 1,600m. barrels were in public stocks kept exclusively for emergency purposes.

The IEA collects, processes and disseminates statistical data and information on all aspects of the energy sector, including production, trade, consumption, prices and greenhouse gas emissions. The IEA promotes co-operation among policy-makers and energy experts to discuss common energy issues, to enhance energy technology and research and development, in particular projects concerned with energy efficiency, conservation and protection of the environment, and to engage major energy producing and consuming non-member countries.

The IEA has developed a system of emergency measures to be used in the event of a reduction in petroleum supplies. Under the International Energy Programme, member states are required to stock crude oil equivalent to 90 days of the previous year's net imports. These measures, which also include demand restraint, were to take effect in disruptions exceeding 7% of the IEA or individual country average daily rate of consumption. A more flexible system of response to oil supply disruption has also been developed under the Co-ordinated Energy Response Measures in 1984. By July 2011 IEA member states had collectively made available to the market additional supplies of petroleum three times. Firstly in the lead-up to the 1991 Gulf War. Secondly in September 2005, in response to concerns at interruptions to the supply of petroleum from the Gulf of Mexico, following extensive hurricane damage to oil rigs, pipeline and refineries (that action was terminated in December). In June 2011 IEA member states agreed for the third time collectively to release emergency oil stocks (60m. barrels over an initial period of 30 days), in response to ongoing disruption of oil supplies from Libya; it was feared that continuing pressure on petroleum markets at that time might undermine the fragile global economic recovery.

The IEA undertakes emergency response reviews and workshops, and publishes an Emergency Management Manual to facilitate a co-ordinated response to a severe disruption in petroleum supplies. The Oil Markets and Emergency Preparedness Office monitors and reports on short-term developments in the petroleum market. It also considers other related issues, including international crude petroleum pricing, petroleum trade and stock developments and investments by major petroleum-producing countries.

Through its Energy Technology Office the IEA promotes international collaboration in this field and the participation of energy industries to facilitate the application of new technologies, through effective transfer of knowledge, technology innovation and training. Member states have initiated over 40 Multilateral Technology Initiatives (also referred to as Implementing Agreements), which provide a framework for international collaboration and information exchange in specific areas, including renewable energy, fossil fuels, end-use technologies and fusion power. OECD member states, non-member states, the energy producers and suppliers are encouraged to participate in these Agreements. The Committee on Energy Research and Technology, which supports international collaboration, is serviced by four expert bodies: Working Parties on Fossil Fuels, Renewable Energy Technologies and Energy End-Use Technologies and a Fusion Power Co-ordinating Committee. In May 2011 the IEA issued two roadmaps on solar electricity: the Solar Photovoltaic Roadmap and the Concentrating Solar Power Roadmap; the Agency predicted at that time that by 2050 solar energy could represent up to 25% of global electricity production. In April 2011 the IEA produced its first *Clean Energy Progress Report*, providing an overview of key policy developments in the field of clean energy technologies. Later in April the IEA issued a roadmap on *Biofuels for Transport*, assessing that by 2050 biofuels could provide up to 27% of world transportation fuel. In October 2011 OECD and the IEA released a joint statement in support of reform of fossil fuel subsidies, in order to promote investment in renewable energy and encourage greater energy efficiency.

The IEA Long-Term Co-operation Programme is designed to strengthen the security of energy supplies and promote stability in world energy markets. It provides for co-operative efforts to conserve energy, to accelerate the development of alternative energy sources by means of both specific and general measures, to strengthen research and development of new energy technologies and to remove legislative and administrative obstacles to increased energy supplies. Regular reviews of member countries' efforts in the fields of energy conservation and accelerated development of alternative energy sources assess the effectiveness of national programmes in relation to the objectives of the Agency.

The IEA actively promotes co-operation and dialogue with non-members and international organizations in order to promote global energy security, environmental protection and economic development. The IEA holds bilateral and regional technical meetings and conducts surveys and reviews of the energy situation in non-member countries. Co-operation agreements with key energy-consuming countries, including India and China, are a priority. The Agency also has co-operation agreements with Russia and the Ukraine and works closely with the petroleum-producing countries of the Middle East. In the latter states the IEA has provided technical assistance for the development of national energy legislation, regulatory reform and energy efficiency projects. The IEA is represented on the Executive Committee of the International Energy Forum (formerly the Oil Producer-Consumer Dialogue) to promote greater co-operation and understanding between petroleum producing and consuming countries. It is also active in the Joint Oil Data Initiative (JODI), a collaborative initiative of seven international organizations to improve oil data transparency.

Recognizing that ongoing energy trends are not sustainable and that an improved balance should be sought between energy security, economic development, and protection of the environment, the IEA supports analysis of actions to mitigate climate change; studies of the implications of the Kyoto Protocol to the UN Framework Convention on Climate Change (UNFCCC), and the development of new international commitments on climate change alleviation following the end of the Kyoto Protocol's first commitment period in 2012; and analysis of policies designed to reduce greenhouse gas emissions, including emissions trading. It is a partner in the Global Bioenergy Partnership and is active in the Renewable Energy and Efficiency Partnership (REEEP). Since 2001 the IEA has organized, with the International Emissions Trading Association and the Electric Power Research Institute, an annual workshop of greenhouse gas emissions trading. The Agency also analyses the regulation and reform of energy markets, especially for electricity and gas. The IEA Regulatory Forum held in February 2002 considered the implications for security of supply and public service of competition in energy markets. In July 2005 heads of state of the Group of Eight industrialized nations (G8) approved a plan of action mandating a clean, competitive and sustainable energy future. The IEA was requested to make recommendations towards achieving the plan of action and has submitted reports to each subsequent annual summit meeting. In July 2008 the G8 heads of state, convened in Hokkaido, Japan, endorsed an IEA initiative to develop roadmaps for new energy technologies, in particular carbon capture and storage projects. The IEA participated in the 2009 G8 summit, held in L'Aquila, Italy, in July. In December 2009 the IEA presented to the UN Climate Change Conference (the 15th conference of parties of the UNFCCC), held in Copenhagen, Denmark, a blueprint for delivering in future on ambitious climate change goals; the Agency also urged participating governments to promote new investment in clean energy. At the 2010 Climate Change Conference, held in December, in Cancún, Mexico, the IEA urged the increased adoption world-wide of clean energy solutions.

In March 2009 the IEA inaugurated a new Energy Business Council, which was mandated to meet twice a year to assess the impact of the global financial crisis on energy markets, and to address climate change and other energy issues.

Publications

CO² Emissions from Fuel Combustion (annually).

Coal Information (annually).

Electricity Information (annually).

Energy Balances and Energy Statistics of OECD and non-OECD Countries (annually).

Energy Policies of IEA Countries (annually).

Key World Energy Statistics.

Natural Gas Information (annually).

Natural Gas Market Review (annually).

Oil Information (annually).

Oil Market Report (monthly).

Renewables Information (annually).

World Energy Outlook (annually).

Other reports, studies, statistics, country reviews.

OECD Nuclear Energy Agency—NEA

Address: Le Seine Saint-Germain, 12 blvd des Îles, 92130 Issy-les-Moulineaux, France.

Telephone: 1-45-24-82-00; **fax:** 1-45-24-11-10; **e-mail:** nea@oecd-nea.org; **internet:** www.oecd-nea.org.

The NEA was established in 1958 to further the peaceful uses of nuclear energy. Originally a European agency, it has since admitted OECD members outside Europe.

MEMBERS

The NEA has 30 member states.

Organization

(April 2012)

STEERING COMMITTEE FOR NUCLEAR ENERGY

Meets twice a year. Comprises senior representatives of member governments, presided over by a chairman. Reports directly to the OECD Council.

SECRETARIAT

Director-General: LUIS ENRIQUE ECHÁVARRI (Spain).

MAIN COMMITTEES

Committee on Nuclear Regulatory Activities.

Committee on Radiation Protection.

Committee on the Safety of Nuclear Installations.

Committee for Technical and Economic Studies on Nuclear Development and the Fuel Cycle (Nuclear Development Committee).

Nuclear Law Committee.

Nuclear Science Committee.

Radioactive Waste Management Committee.

NEA DATA BANK

The Data Bank was established in 1978, as a successor to the Computer Programme Library and the Neutron Data Compilation Centre. The Data Bank develops and supplies data and computer programmes for nuclear technology applications to users in laboratories, industry, universities and other areas of interest. Under the supervision of the Nuclear Science Committee, the Data Bank collates integral experimental data, and functions as part of a network of data centres to provide direct data services. It was responsible for co-ordinating the development of the Joint Evaluation Fission and Fusion (JEFF) data reference library, and works with the Radioactive Waste Management Division of the NEA on the Thermonuclear Database project (see below).

Activities

The NEA's mission is to assist its member countries in maintaining and further developing, through international co-operation, the scientific, technological and legal bases required for the safe, environmentally friendly and economical use of nuclear energy for peaceful purposes. It maintains a continual survey with the co-operation of other organizations, notably the International Atomic Energy Agency (IAEA), of world uranium resources, production and demand, and of economic and technical aspects of the nuclear fuel cycle.

A major part of the Agency's work is devoted to the safety and regulation of nuclear power, including co-operative studies and projects related to the prevention of nuclear accidents and the long-term safety of radioactive waste disposal systems. The Committee on Nuclear Regulatory Activities contributes to developing a consistent and effective regulatory response to current and future challenges. These challenges include operational experience feedback, increased public expectations concerning safety in the use of nuclear energy, industry initiatives to improve economics and inspection practices, the necessity to ensure safety over a plant's entire life cycle, and new reactors and technology. The Committee on the Safety of Nuclear Installations contributes to maintaining a high level of safety performance and safety competence by identifying emerging safety issues through the analysis of operating experience and research results, contributing to their resolution and, when needed, establishing international research projects. The Radioactive Waste Management Committee assists member countries in the management of radioactive waste and materials, focusing on the development of strategies for the safe, sustainable and broadly acceptable management of all types of radioactive waste, in particular long-lived waste and spent fuel. The Committee on Radiation Protection and Public Health, comprising regulators and protection experts, aims to identify new and emerging issues, analyse their impact and recommend action to address issues and to enhance protection regulation and implementation. It is served by various expert groups and a working party on nuclear emergency matters. The Nuclear Development Committee supports member countries in formulating nuclear energy policy, addressing issues of relevance for governments and the industry at a time of nuclear technology renaissance and sustained government interest in ensuring long-term security of energy supply, reducing the risk of global climate change and pursuing sustainable development. The aim of the NEA nuclear science programme is to help member countries identify, share, develop and disseminate basic scientific and technical knowledge used to ensure safe and reliable operation of current nuclear systems, as well as to develop next-generation technologies. The main areas covered are reactor physics, fuel behaviour, fuel cycle physics and chemistry, critical safety and radiation shielding. The Nuclear Law Committee (NLC) promotes the harmonization of legislation governing the peaceful uses of nuclear energy in member countries and in selected non-member countries. It supports the modernization and strengthening of national and international nuclear liability regimes. Under the supervision of the NLC, the NEA also compiles, analyses and disseminates information on nuclear law through a regular publications programme and organizes the International School of Nuclear Law educational programme. The NEA co-operates with non-member countries of Central and Eastern Europe and the CIS in areas such as nuclear safety, radiation protection and nuclear law.

In January 2005 a policy group of the Generation IV International Forum (GIF) confirmed arrangements under which the NEA would provide technical secretariat support to the GIF, including the funding of this activity by GIF members through voluntary contributions. The GIF is a major international initiative aimed at developing the next generation of nuclear energy systems. In September 2006 the NEA was selected to perform the technical secretariat functions for the Multinational Design Evaluation Programme (MDEP), which had been established to share the resources and knowledge accumulated by national nuclear regulatory authorities during their assessment of new reactor designs, with the aim of improving both the efficiency and the effectiveness of the process.

The NEA offered its support to the Government of Japan in mid-March 2011, following the destabilization of the Fukushima nuclear power plant by an earthquake and tsunami in that month. In response to the Fukushima incident the Agency activated its Flash-news system, facilitating the swift exchange of information among nuclear regulators, and also established a senior-level task group to exchange information, co-ordinate activities and examine the implications for future nuclear plant management. In June the NEA and the French G8 presidency jointly organized a *Forum on the Fukushima Daiichi Accident: Insights and Approaches*. In January 2012 an NEA panel of experts met with members of the Japanese Advisory Committee for the Prevention of Nuclear Accidents and the special Japanese Task Force for the Reform of Nuclear Safety Regulations and Organizations to discuss improving approaches to the regulation and oversight of nuclear facilities.

JOINT PROJECTS

Joint projects and information exchange programmes enable interested countries to share the costs of pursuing research or the sharing of data, relating to particular areas or problems, with the support of the NEA.

Nuclear Safety

OECD/NEA Behaviour of Iodine Project Phase 2: initiated in April 2011, with a mandate until March 2014; aims to examine iodine behaviour in a nuclear reactor containment building following a severe accident.

OECD/NEA Loss of Forced Coolant (LOFC) Project: initiated in March 2011, with a mandate until March 2013; conducting an integrated large-scale test of LOFC in the Japan Atomic Energy Agency high temperature test reactor.

OECD/NEA Cabri Water Loop Project: initiated in 2000, with a mandate until 2015; conducted at the Institute for Protection and Nuclear Safety (IPNS), based in France; investigates the capacity of high burn-up fuel to withstand sharp power peaks that may occur in power reactors owing to rapid reactivity insertion in the reactor core (i.e. reactivity-initiated accidents); 19 participating orgs.

OECD Halden Reactor Project: initiated in Jan. 2009, with an initial mandate until Dec. 2011, extended until 2014; based in Halden, Norway; experimental boiling heavy water reactor, which became an OECD project in 1958; from 1964, under successive agreements with participating countries, the reactor has been used for long-term testing of water reactor fuels and for research into automatic computer-based control of nuclear power stations; the main focus is on nuclear fuel safety and man-machine interface; some 130 nuclear energy research institutions and authorities in 19 countries participate in the project.

OECD/NEA PKL-2 Project: initiated in April 2008 with a mandate until Sept. 2011; investigated safety issues relating to current pressurised water reactor (PWR) plants and new PWR design concepts; a concluded workshop was scheduled for Oct. 2012, and a three-and-a-half year follow-up project was expected to commence during that year.

OECD/NEA Fire Propagation in Elementary, Multi-rooms Scenarios (PRISME) Project-2: initiated in Jan. 2006, with a mandate until Dec. 2010; PRISME-2 was mandated to operate from July 2011–June 2016; aims to support the qualification of fire codes and the development of fire protection strategies; eight participating countries.

OECD/NEA Studsvik Cladding Integrity Project: phase 2 covers July 2009–June 2014 (phase 1 covered July 2004–June 2009); aims to generate high quality experimental data to improve understanding of the dominant failure mechanisms for water reactor fuels, and to devise means for reducing fuel failures

OECD/NEA Rig of Safety Assessment (ROSA-2) Project: initiated in April 2009, with a mandate until 31 March 2012; aims to resolve key safety issues relating to light water reactor (LWR) thermal hydraulics.

OECD/NEA Sandia Fuel Project (SFP): launched in July 2009, with a mandate until Feb. 2013; aims to provide experimental data relevant to the hydraulic and ignition phenomena of prototypic water reactor fuel assemblies.

OECD/NEA Source Term Evaluation and Mitigation (STEM) Project: initiated in July 2011, with a mandate until June 2015; aims to improve the general evaluation of the source term, to provide better information for diagnosis and prognosis of the progression of an accident, to allow for better evaluation of the potential release of radioactive materials; seven participating countries.

OECD/NEA Steam Explosion Resolution for Nuclear Applications (SERENA) Project: launched in October 2007, with a mandate until March 2012; established to assess the capabilities of fuel-coolant interaction computer codes to predict steam explosion-induced loads in reactor situations; 11 participating countries.

OECD/NEA Thermal-hydraulics, Hydrogen, Aerosols, Iodine (ThAI) Project-2: launched in January 2007, with a mandate until December 2009; ThAI-2 was launched in July 2011, and mandated until June 2014; the initial project was designed to provide data for the evaluation and simulation of hydrogen and fission product interactions, supporting accident simulation models; phase 2 was aimed at addressing remaining questions and providing experimental data for relevant HTGR graphite dust transport issues, specific Water Cooled Reactors aerosol and iodine issues and hydrogen mitigation under accidental circumstances; 11 participating countries.

Radioactive Waste Management

International Co-operative Programme on Decommissioning: initiated in 1985; promotes exchange of technical information and experience for ensuring that safe, economic and optimum environmental options for decommissioning are used; 12 participating countries.

Thermochemical Database (TDB) Project: aims to develop a quality-assured, comprehensive thermodynamic database of selected chemical elements for use in the safety assessment of radioactive waste repositories; data are selected by review teams; phase II commenced in 1998 and phase III commenced in Feb. 2003; phase IV, studying inorganic species and compounds of iron, was ongoing during 2008–12; 12 participating countries and 17 participating organizations.

Radiation Protection

Information System on Occupational Exposure (ISOE): initiated in 1992 and co-sponsored by the IAEA; maintains largest database world-wide on occupational exposure to ionizing radiation at nuclear power plants; participants: 323 reactors (some of which are either defunct or actively decommissioning) in 29 countries.

Finance

The Agency's annual budget amounts to some €10.4m., while funding of €3.0m. is made available for the Data Bank. These sums may be supplemented by members' voluntary contributions.

Publications

Annual Report.

NEA News (2 a year).

Nuclear Energy Data (annually).

Nuclear Law Bulletin (2 a year).

Publications on a range of issues relating to nuclear energy, reports and proceedings.

ORGANIZATION FOR SECURITY AND CO-OPERATION IN EUROPE—OSCE

Address: Wallnerstrasse 6, 1010 Vienna, Austria.

Telephone: (1) 514-36-0; **fax:** (1) 514-36-96; **e-mail:** info@osce.org; **internet:** www.osce.org.

The OSCE was established in 1972 as the Conference on Security and Co-operation in Europe (CSCE), providing a multilateral forum for dialogue and negotiation. It produced the Helsinki Final Act of 1975 on East–West relations (see below). The areas of competence of the CSCE were expanded by the Charter of Paris for a New Europe (1990), which transformed the CSCE from an ad hoc forum into an organization with permanent institutions, and the Helsinki Document 1992. In December 1994 the summit conference adopted the new name of OSCE, in order to reflect the organization's changing political role and strengthened secretariat.

PARTICIPATING STATES

Albania	Greece	Portugal
Andorra	Hungary	Romania
Armenia	Iceland	Russia
Austria	Ireland	San Marino
Azerbaijan	Italy	Serbia
Belarus	Kazakhstan	Slovakia
Belgium	Kyrgyzstan	Slovenia
Bosnia and Herzegovina	Latvia	Spain
Bulgaria	Liechtenstein	Sweden
Canada	Lithuania	Switzerland
Croatia	Luxembourg	Tajikistan
Cyprus	Macedonia, former Yugoslav republic	Turkey
Czech Republic	Malta	Turkmenistan
Denmark	Moldova	Ukraine
Estonia	Monaco	United Kingdom
Finland	Montenegro	USA
France	Netherlands	Uzbekistan
Georgia	Norway	Vatican City (Holy See)
Germany	Poland	

Organization

(April 2012)

SUMMIT CONFERENCES

Heads of state or government of OSCE participating states convene periodically to set priorities and the political orientation of the organization. The sixth conference was held in Istanbul, Turkey, in November 1999. A seventh summit meeting was convened, in Astana, Kazakhstan, in December 2010.

MINISTERIAL COUNCIL

The Ministerial Council (formerly the Council of Foreign Ministers) comprises ministers of foreign affairs of member states. It is the central decision-making and governing body of the OSCE and meets every year in which no summit conference is held. The 18th Ministerial Council was held in Vilnius, Lithuania, in December 2011, and the 19th was to be held in Dublin, Ireland, in December 2012. The first informal meeting of ministers was held in Corfu, Greece, in June 2009. A second informal ministerial meeting was convened in Almatı, Kazakhstan, in July 2010.

PERMANENT COUNCIL

The Council, which is based in Vienna, Austria, is responsible for day-to-day operational tasks. Members of the Council, comprising the permanent representatives of member states to the OSCE, convene weekly. The Council is the regular body for political consultation and decision-making, and may be convened for emergency purposes.

FORUM FOR SECURITY CO-OPERATION

The Forum for Security Co-operation (FSC), comprising representatives of delegations of member states, meets weekly in Vienna to negotiate and consult on measures aimed at strengthening security and stability throughout Europe. Its main objectives are negotiations on arms control, disarmament, and confidence- and security-building measures (CSBMs); regular consultations and intensive co-operation on matters related to security; and the further reduction of the risks of conflict. The FSC is also responsible for the implementation of CSBMs; the preparation of seminars on military doctrine; the holding of annual implementation assessment meetings; and the provision of a forum for the discussion and clarification of information exchanged under agreed CSBMs.

CHAIRPERSON-IN-OFFICE

The Chairperson-in-Office (CiO) is vested with overall responsibility for executive action. The position is held by a minister of foreign affairs of a member state for a one-year term. The CiO is assisted by a Troika, consisting of the preceding, current and incoming chairpersons; ad hoc steering groups; and special or personal representatives, who are appointed by the CiO with a clear and precise mandate to assist in dealing with specific issues, crises or conflicts.

Chairperson-in-Office: EAMON GILMORE (Ireland) (2012).

SECRETARIAT

The Secretariat comprises the following principal units: the Conflict Prevention Centre; the Action against Terrorism Unit; the Anti-trafficking Assistance Unit; the Office of the Co-ordinator of OSCE Economic and Environmental Activities; External Co-operation, the Strategic Police Matters Unit; the Training Section; a Department of Human Resources; and the Department of Management and Finance, responsible for technical and administrative support activities. The OSCE maintains an office in Prague, Czech Republic, which assists with documentation and information activities.

The position of Secretary-General was established in December 1992 and the first appointment to the position was made in June 1993. The Secretary-General is appointed by the Ministerial Council for a three-year term of office. The Secretary-General is the representative of the CiO and is responsible for the management of OSCE structures and operations.

Secretary-General: LAMBERTO ZANNIER (Italy).

Co-ordinator of OSCE Economic and Environmental Activities: GORAN SVILANOVIĆ (Serbia).

Director of Conflict Prevention Centre: ADAM KOBIERACKI (Poland).

Senior Police Advisor: KNUT DREYER (Sweden).

Special Representative and Co-ordinator for Combating Trafficking in Human Beings: MARIA GRAZIA GIAMMARINARO (Italy).

OSCE Specialized Bodies

High Commissioner on National Minorities

POB 20062, 2500 EB The Hague, Netherlands; tel. (70) 3125500; fax (70) 3635910; e-mail hcnm@hcnm.org; internet www.osce.org/hcnm.

The office of High Commissioner on National Minorities was established in December 1992. The High Commissioner is an instrument for conflict prevention, tasked with identifying ethnic tensions that have the potential to develop into conflict, thereby endangering peace, stability or relations between OSCE participating states, and to promote their early resolution. The High Commissioner works in confidence and provides strictly confidential reports to the OSCE CiO. The High Commissioner is appointed by the Ministerial Council, on the recommendation of the Senior Council, for a three-year term.

High Commissioner: KNUT VOLLEBAEK (Norway).

Office for Democratic Institutions and Human Rights (ODIHR)

Aleje Ujazdowskie 19, 00-557 Warsaw, Poland; tel. (22) 520-06-00; fax (22) 520-06-05; e-mail office@odihr.pl; internet www.osce.org/odihr.

Established in July 1999, the ODIHR has responsibility for promoting human rights, democracy and the rule of law. The Office provides a framework for the exchange of information on and the promotion of democracy-building, respect for human rights and elections within OSCE states. In addition, it co-ordinates the monitoring of elections and provides expertise and training on constitutional and legal matters.

Director: JANEZ LENARČIČ (Slovenia).

Office of the Representative on Freedom of the Media

Wallnerstrasse 6, 1010 Vienna, Austria; tel. (1) 512-21-450; fax (1) 512-21-459; e-mail pm-fom@osce.org; internet www.osce.org/fom.

The office was established by a decision of the Permanent Council in November 1997 to strengthen the implementation of OSCE commitments regarding free, independent and pluralistic media.

Representative: DUNJA MIJATOVIĆ (Bosnia and Herzegovina).

Parliamentary Assembly

Radhusstraede 1, 1466 Copenhagen K, Denmark; tel. 33-37-80-40; fax 33-37-80-30; e-mail osce@oscepa.dk; internet www.oscepa.org.

In April 1991 parliamentarians from the CSCE countries agreed on the creation of a pan-European parliamentary assembly. Its inaugural session was held in Budapest, Hungary, in July 1992. The Parliamentary Assembly, which is composed of 320 members from 55 parliaments, meets annually. It comprises a Standing Committee, a Bureau and three General Committees and is supported by a Secretariat in Copenhagen, Denmark.

President: PETROS EFTHYMIOU (Greece).

Secretary-General: R. SPENCER OLIVER (USA).

OSCE Related Bodies

Court of Conciliation and Arbitration

Villa Rive-Belle, 266 route de Lausanne, 1292 Chambésy, Geneva, Switzerland; tel. 227580025; fax 227582510; e-mail cca.osce@bluewin.ch; internet www.osce.org/cca.

An OSCE Convention on Conciliation and Arbitration, providing for the establishment of the Court, was concluded in 1992 and entered into effect in December 1994. The first meeting of the Court was convened in May 1995. OSCE states that have ratified the Convention may submit a dispute to the Court for settlement by the Arbitral Tribunal or the Conciliation Commission.

President: ROBERT BADINTER (France).

Joint Consultative Group (JCG)

The states that are party to the Treaty on Conventional Armed Forces in Europe (CFE), which was concluded within the CSCE framework in 1990, established the Joint Consultative Group (JCG). The JCG, which meets in Vienna, addresses questions relating to compliance with the Treaty; enhancement of the effectiveness of the Treaty; technical aspects of the Treaty's implementation; and disputes arising out of its implementation. There are currently 30 states participating in the JCG.

Open Skies Consultative Commission

The Commission promotes implementation of the Treaty on Open Skies, which was signed by members of NATO and the former members of the Warsaw Pact (with Russia, Belarus, Ukraine and Georgia taking the place of the USSR) in March 1992. Under the accord, aerial reconnaissance missions by one country over another were permitted, subject to regulation. Regular meetings of the Commission are serviced by the OSCE secretariat.

Activities

In July 1990 heads of government of the member countries of the North Atlantic Treaty Organization (NATO) proposed to increase the role of the CSCE 'to provide a forum for wider political dialogue in a more united Europe'. The Charter of Paris for a New Europe, which undertook to strengthen pluralist democracy and observance of human rights, and to settle disputes between participating states by peaceful means, was signed in November. At the summit meeting the Treaty on Conventional Armed Forces in Europe (CFE), which had been negotiated within the framework of the CSCE, was signed by the member states of NATO and of the Warsaw Pact. The Treaty limits non-nuclear air and ground armaments in the signatory countries. The summit conference that was held in Lisbon, Portugal, in December 1996 agreed to adapt the CFE Treaty, in order to further arms reduction negotiations on a national and territorial basis. In November 1999 a revised CFE Treaty was signed, providing for a stricter system of limitations and increased transparency, which was to be open to other OSCE states not currently signatories. The US and European Union (EU) governments determined to delay ratification of the Agreement of the Adaptation of the Treaty until Russian troop levels in the Caucasus had been reduced.

The Council of Foreign Ministers met for the first time in Berlin, Germany, in June 1991. The meeting adopted a mechanism for consultation and co-operation in the case of emergency situations, to be implemented by the Council of Senior Officials (CSO; subsequently renamed the Senior Council, which was dissolved in 2006, with all functions transferred to the Permanent Council). A separate mechanism regarding the prevention of the outbreak of conflict was also adopted, whereby a country can demand an explanation of 'unusual military activity' in a neighbouring country. These mechanisms were utilized in July in relation to the armed conflict in Yugoslavia between the Republic of Croatia and the Yugoslav Government. In August a meeting of the CSO resolved to reinforce the CSCE's mission in Yugoslavia and in September the CSO agreed to impose an embargo on the export of armaments to Yugoslavia. In October the CSO determined to establish an observer mission to monitor the observance of human rights in Yugoslavia.

In January 1992 the Council of Foreign Ministers agreed to alter the Conference's rule of decision-making by consensus in order to allow the CSO to take appropriate action against a participating state 'in cases of clear and gross violation of CSCE commitments'. This development was precipitated by the conflict in Yugoslavia, where the Yugoslav Government was held responsible by the majority of CSCE states for the continuation of hostilities and was suspended from the grouping. The meeting also agreed that the CSCE should undertake fact-finding and conciliation missions to areas of tension, with the first such mission to be sent to Nagornyi Karabakh, the largely Armenian-populated enclave in Azerbaijan.

The meeting of heads of state and government, held in Helsinki, Finland, in July 1992, adopted the Helsinki Document, in which participating states defined the terms of future CSCE peace-keeping activities. Conforming broadly to UN practice, operations would be undertaken only with the full consent of the parties involved in any conflict and only if an effective cease-fire were in place. The CSCE may request the use of the military resources of NATO, the Commonwealth of Independent States (CIS), the EU or other international bodies. The Helsinki Document declared the CSCE a 'regional arrangement' in the sense of Chapter VIII of the UN's Charter, which states that such a regional grouping should attempt to resolve a conflict in the region before referring it to the Security Council.

In 1993 the First Implementation Meeting on Human Dimension Issues (the CSCE term used with regard to issues concerning human rights and welfare) took place. The Meeting, for which the ODIHR serves as a secretariat, provides a now annual forum for the exchange of news regarding OSCE commitments in the fields of human rights and democracy. Also in 1993 the first annual Economic Forum was convened to focus on the transition to and development of free market economies as an essential aspect of democracy-building. It was renamed the Economic and Environment Forum in 2007 to incorporate consideration of environmental security matters. The first Preparatory Meeting of the 20th Forum was convened in February 2012 (in Vienna Austria), and the second was held in April (in Dublin, Ireland). The theme of the 20th Forum was 'Promoting Security and Stability through Good Governance'.

In December 1993 a Permanent Committee (later renamed the Permanent Council) was established in Vienna, providing for greater political consultation and dialogue through its weekly meetings. In December 1994 the summit conference redesignated the CSCE as the Organization for Security and Co-operation in Europe (OSCE) and endorsed the role of the organization as the primary instrument for early warning, conflict prevention and crisis management in the region. The conference adopted a 'Code of Conduct on Politico-Military Aspects of Security', which set out principles to guide the role of the armed forces in democratic societies. In December 1996 the summit conference convened in Lisbon, Portugal, adopted the 'Lisbon Declaration on a Common and Comprehensive Security Model for Europe for the 21st Century', committing all parties to pursuing measures to ensure regional security. A Security Model Committee was established and began to meet regularly during 1997 to consider aspects of the Declaration. In November the Office of the Representative on Freedom of the Media was established in Vienna, to support the OSCE's activities in this field. In the same month a new position of Co-ordinator of OSCE Economic and Environmental Activities was created.

In November 1999 OSCE heads of state and of government, convened in Istanbul, Turkey, signed a new Charter for European Security, which aimed to formalize existing norms regarding the observance of human rights and to strengthen co-operation with other organizations and institutions concerned with international security. The Charter focused on measures to improve the operational capabilities of the OSCE in early warning, conflict prevention, crisis management and post-conflict rehabilitation. Accordingly, Rapid Expert Assistance and Co-operation (REACT) teams were to be established to enable the organization to respond rapidly to requests from participating states for assistance in crisis situations. The REACT programme became operational in April 2001. The 1999 summit meeting also adopted a revised Vienna Document on confidence- and security-building measures and a

Platform for Co-operative Security as a framework for co-operation with other organizations and institutions concerned with maintaining security in the OSCE area.

In April 2000 the OSCE High Commissioner on National Minorities issued a report reviewing the problems confronting Roma and Sinti populations in OSCE member states. In April 2001 the ODIHR launched a programme of assistance for the Roma communities of south-eastern Europe. In November 2000 an OSCE Document on Small Arms and Light Weapons was adopted, aimed at curtailing the spread of armaments in member states. A workshop on implementation of the Document was held in February 2002. In mid-November 2000 the Office of the Representative on Freedom of the Media organized a conference, staged in Dushanbe, Tajikistan, of journalists from Kazakhstan, Kyrgyzstan, Tajikistan and Uzbekistan. In February 2001 the ODIHR established an Anti-Trafficking Project Fund to help to finance its efforts to combat trafficking in human beings.

In September 2001 the Secretary-General condemned terrorist attacks perpetrated against targets in the USA, by militant Islamist fundamentalists. In early October OSCE member states unanimously adopted a statement in support of the developing US-led global coalition against international terrorism. In December the Ministerial Council, meeting in Romania, approved the 'Bucharest Plan of Action' outlining the organization's contribution to countering terrorism. An Action against Terrorism Unit was established within the Secretariat to co-ordinate and help to implement the counter-terrorism initiatives. A Personal Representative for Terrorism was appointed by the CiO in January 2002. Also in December 2001 the OSCE sponsored, with the then UN Office for Drug Control and Crime Prevention (ODCCP), an International Conference on Security and Stability in Central Asia, held in Bishkek, Kyrgyzstan. The meeting, which was attended by representatives of more than 60 countries and organizations, was concerned with strengthening efforts to counter terrorism and providing effective support to the Central Asian states. At a Ministerial Council meeting held in Porto, Portugal, in December 2002, the OSCE issued a Charter on Preventing Terrorism, which condemned terrorism 'in all its forms and manifestations' and called upon member states to work together to counter, investigate and prosecute terrorist acts. The charter also acknowledged the links between terrorism, organized crime and trafficking in human beings. At the same time, a political declaration entitled 'Responding to Change' was adopted, in which member states pledged their commitment to mutual co-operation in combating threats to security. The OSCE's first Annual Security Review Conference was held in Vienna, in July 2003. The meeting elaborated a range of practical options for addressing the new threats and challenges, including the introduction of common security features on travel documentation, stricter controls on manual portable air defence systems and the improvement of border security and policing methods. Security issues were also the subject of the Rotterdam Declaration, adopted by some 300 members of the Parliamentary Assembly in July, which stated that it was imperative for the OSCE to maintain a strong field presence and for field missions to be provided with sufficient funding and highly trained staff. It also recommended that the OSCE assume a role in unarmed peacekeeping operations.

In July 2003 the Permanent Council adopted a new Action Plan to Combat Trafficking in Human Beings. The Plan was endorsed by the Ministerial Council, held in Maastricht, Netherlands, in December. The Council approved the appointment of a Special Representative on Combating Trafficking in Human Beings, mandated to raise awareness of the issues and to ensure member governments comply with international procedures and conventions, and the establishment of a special unit within the Secretariat. In July 2004 the Special Representative organized an international conference to consider issues relating to human trafficking, including human rights, labour, migration, organized crime, and minors. Participants agreed to establish an Alliance against Trafficking in Persons, which aimed to consolidate co-operation among international and non-governmental organizations.

During July 2003 the first OSCE conference on the effects of globalization was convened in Vienna, attended by some 200 representatives from international organizations. Participants called for the advancement of good governance in the public and private sectors, the development of democratic institutions and the creation of conditions that would enable populations to benefit from the global economy. At a meeting of the Ministerial Council, convened in Maastricht, in December, member states endorsed a document that aimed to address risks to regional security and stability arising from stockpiles of conventional ammunition through, *inter alia*, detailing practical steps for their destruction. In December 2004 the Ministerial Council, meeting in Sofia, Bulgaria, condemned terrorist attacks that had been committed during the year, including in Madrid, Spain, in March, and in Beslan, Russia, in September. The meeting issued a statement expressing determination to pursue all measures to prevent and combat international terrorism, while continuing to protect and uphold human rights. In order to consider OSCE's capacity to address new security challenges, and to provide a new strategic vision for the organization, the Council resolved to establish a Panel of Eminent Persons on Strengthening the Effectiveness of the OSCE. The Panel presented its report, comprising some 70 recommendations, to the Permanent Council in June 2005. In December 2008 the Ministerial Council, convened in Helsinki, determined to pursue a high-level dialogue on strengthening the legal framework of OSCE. In June 2009 OSCE ministers of foreign affairs, meeting in an informal session in Greece, inaugurated the Corfu Process to structure further dialogue on future European security. A Ministerial Declaration on the Corfu Process was adopted by the Ministerial Council in December, which determined to use it to strengthen a free, democratic and integrated Europe. The Declaration was to serve as a roadmap for dialogue focusing on: OSCE norms, principles and commitments; conflict resolution; arms control and confidence- and security-building regimes; transnational and multidimensional threats and challenges; common economic and environmental challenges; human rights and fundamental freedoms, as well as democracy and the rule of law; and enhancing the OSCE's effectiveness and interaction with other organizations and institutions. In July 2010 a second informal ministerial meeting, convened in Almatı, Kazakhstan, reviewed progress in implementing the Corfu Process, as well as the Organization's response to insecurity in Kyrgyzstan. Later in that month the Permanent Council endorsed a decision to deploy a 52-member Police Advisory Group to Kyrgyzstan in order to facilitate law enforcement efforts in areas of ethnic unrest. In December OSCE and the ILO jointly published a study entitled *Strengthening Migration Governance*.

In December 2010 OSCE heads of state and government, meeting in Astana, Kazakhstan, adopted the 'Astana Commemorative Declaration: Towards a Security Community', which reaffirmed the core principles and commitments of the organization. The Declaration asserted that commitments in the three security dimensions, i.e. human, politico-military, and economic and environmental, are matters of direct and legitimate concern to all participating states. In spite of a lack of full consensus to adopt a framework for future action, the Declaration urged greater efforts to resolve conflicts and to undertake conflict prevention, to update the Vienna Document 1999 (concerning confidence- and security-building measures), and to enhance energy security dialogue.

In December 2011 the Ministerial Council, convened in Vilnius, Lithuania, adopted a decision on 'enhancing OSCE capabilities in early warning, early action, dialogue facilitation, mediation support and post-conflict rehabilitation on an operational level', tasking the Secretary-General with ensuring that the Secretariat's Conflict Prevention Centre assumes the role of focal point for the systematic collection, collation, analysis and assessment of relevant early warning signals, and calling for increased exchange of information and co-ordination between the OSCE executive structures. Other decisions made by the Council included: enhancing engagement with Afghanistan and Partners for Co-operation; promoting equal opportunities for women in the economic sphere; addressing transnational threats; strengthening dialogue on transport; and addressing small arms, light weapons and stockpiles of conventional ammunition. A declaration on combating all forms of human trafficking was adopted.

The OSCE maintains regular formal dialogue and co-operation with certain nominated countries. Afghanistan, Australia, Japan, the Republic of Korea, Mongolia and Thailand have the status of 'Asian Partners for Co-operation' with the OSCE, while Algeria, Egypt, Israel, Jordan, Morocco and Tunisia are 'Mediterranean Partners for Co-operation'. Regular consultations are held with these countries in order to discuss security issues of common concern. In October 2004 OSCE deployed a team of observers to monitor the presidential election in Afghanistan, representing the organization's first election mission in a partner country. In October 2008 OSCE participating states and Mediterranean partner countries convened, in Amman, Jordan, at conference level, to discuss regional security. In the following month a conference was held in the Afghan capital, Kabul, to strengthen co-operation between the OSCE and its Asian partner countries. An OSCE-Japan conference, convened in Tokyo, Japan, in June 2009, considered how the OSCE and Asian partner states should best address global security challenges. In December 2010 OSCE heads of state and government resolved to enhance interaction with its Partners for Co-operation. The annual conference of all OSCE Asian Partners for Co-operation was convened in 2011 in Ulan Bator, Mongolia, in May. The December 2011 Ministerial Conference adopted a decision on Partners for Co-operation, which commended the voluntary reform processes ongoing in some Mediterranean partner countries; reaffirmed the OSCE's readiness, through its executive structures, when requested, to assist the Partners for Co-operation in their voluntary implementation of OSCE norms, principles and commitments; decided to enhance the Partnership for Co-operation by broadening dialogue, intensifying political consultations, strengthening practical co-operation and further sharing best practices, according to the needs and priorities identified by the Partners; and determined to strengthen regular high-level dialogue with the Partners for Co-operation.

OSCE provides technical assistance to the Southeast European Co-operative Initiative.

FIELD OPERATIONS IN CENTRAL AND SOUTH-EASTERN EUROPE

OSCE Mission in Kosovo: 38000 Priština, Beogradska 32; tel. (38) 500162; fax (38) 240711; e-mail press.omik@osce.org; internet www.osce.org/kosovo; f. July 1999 as an integral component of an international operation, led by the UN, with specific responsibility for democracy- and institution-building; in 2012 the Mission was operating five regional centres: in Mitrovica/Mitrovice, Pejë/Peć, Prizren, Gjilan/Gnjilane, and Prishtinë/Priština, as well as more than 30 municipal teams throughout Kosovo; succeeded a 2,000-member OSCE Kosovo Verification Mission (KVM), established to monitor compliance with the terms of a cease-fire between Serbian authorities and ethnic Albanian separatists in the formerly autonomous province of Kosovo and Metohija; helped to establish and/or administer a police training school and inspectorate, an Institute for Civil Administration, the Department for Democratic Governance and Civil Society, the Office of the Ombudsperson, a Kosovo Centre for Public Safety Education and Development and a Press Council; in early 2002 the Mission initiated training sessions for members of the new Kosovo Assembly; in mid-2004 the Mission initiated an Out-of-Kosovo voting scheme to update the voter registration for forthcoming Assembly elections and, following the election in Oct., the Mission, with other partner organizations co-ordinated under an Assembly Support Initiative, again undertook an induction programme for newly elected members; the Mission provided technical assistance for the preparation of national and municipal assembly elections, held in Nov. 2007, and, following the new government's unilateral declaration of independence, issued in Feb. 2008, determined to support the country's new institutions, and monitor their work for compliance with human rights standards; following the reconfiguration of the UN operation in Kosovo, and reduction of its field presence, the OSCE Mission has assumed greater responsibility for monitoring and reporting on the security situation and compliance with human rights standards; in mid-2010 the Head of Mission condemned violent attacks in northern Mitrovica/Mitrovice; a Mission report on the functioning of the Kosovo justice system, released in Jan. 2012, found that improvements were still required to establish a fully independent judiciary; in Feb. 2012 the Head of the Misson expressed concern over recent security incidents affecting the Kosovo Serb community in the eastern Gjilan/Gnjilane region; Head of Mission WERNER ALMHOFER (Austria).

OSCE Mission to Bosnia and Herzegovina: 71000 Sarajevo, Fra Andjela Zvizdovica 1; tel. (33) 752100; fax (33) 442479; e-mail info .ba@osce.org; internet www.oscebih.org; f. Dec. 1995 to achieve the objectives of the peace accords for the former Yugoslavia, in particular to oversee the process of democratization; in 2012 had 13 field offices, and an additional office in Brcko (the so-called 'Brcko Team'); helped to organize and monitor national elections, held in Sept. 1996, municipal elections, held in Sept. 1997, elections to the National Assembly of the Serb Republic and to the Bosnian Serb presidency in Nov., a general election, conducted in Sept. 1998, and legislative elections held in Nov. 2000; the Mission's responsibility for elections in the country ended in Nov. 2001 when a new permanent Election Commission was inaugurated, to which the Mission was to provide support; other key areas of Mission activity are the promotion of democratic values, monitoring and promoting respect for human rights, strengthening the legal system, assisting with the creation of a modernized, non-discriminatory education system and establishing democratic control over the armed forces; in Sept. 2004 the agreement on confidence- and security-building measures, mandated under the Dayton peace accords, was suspended in acknowledgement of the country's extensive political reforms and in Dec. the Mission transferred its co-chairmanship of the country's Defence Reform Commission (DRC) to the new NATO headquarters in Sarajevo, although representatives of the Mission continued to be involved in work of the DRC; in June 2008 the Mission concluded a long-term legislative strengthening programme, which included the development of an intranet system for the country's Parliamentary Assembly; responsibility for a project to promote greater legislative transparency and accessibility, Open Parliament, was transferred to the national Parliament in July 2009; the Mission supports implementation of the sub-regional arms control agreement, although responsibility for inspection missions was assumed by the national armed forces from Jan. 2010; during 2011–12 the Mission was implementing a Citizens' Academy project, aimed at encouraging citizens to engage with local government; Head of Mission FLETCHER M. BURTON (USA).

OSCE Mission to Montenegro: 81000 Podgorica, Bul. Svetog Petra Cetinjskog bb; tel. (81) 401401; fax (81) 406431; internet www.osce.org/montenegro; f. June 2006 following the country's declaration of independence from Serbia; supports the reform processes required to achieve European and Euro-Atlantic integration, i.e. democratization processes, legislative reform and institution-building, police and media reform, and activities to promote environmental protection and economic development; in March 2011 the Mission organized a regional conference of ministers responsible for justice and interior affairs in order to strengthen co-operation in judicial and policing matters; the Head of Mission and the Montenegro Ministry of Justice concluded a Memorandum of Understanding on judicial reform in Dec. 2011; Head of Mission ŠARŪNAS ADOMAVIČIUS (Lithuania).

OSCE Mission to Serbia: 11000 Belgrade, Čakorska 1; tel. (11) 3606100; fax (11) 3606119; e-mail ppiu-serbia@osce.org; internet www.osce.org/serbia; f. Jan. 2001 as the OSCE Mission to the Federal Republic of Yugoslavia (FRY, renamed the OSCE Mission to Serbia and Montenegro in 2003 and divided into two separate Missions in June 2006); the initial mandate of the Mission was to assist in the areas of democracy and protection of human rights and in the restructuring and training of law enforcement agencies and the judiciary, to provide advice to government authorities with regard to reform of the media, and, in close co-operation with the United Nations High Commissioner for Refugees, to facilitate the return of refugees to and from neighbouring countries as well as within the FRY; until Dec. 2011 the Mission provided on-site field support to the Basic Police Training Centre in Sremska Kamenica; in March 2002 the Mission facilitated the census process in southern Serbia; in June 2003 the Mission initiated an Outreach Campaign, to ensure regular visits by Mission representatives to more remote municipalities, and undertook a border-policing project in an effort to reduce human trafficking and organized crime in Serbia and Montenegro; the Mission supported the formulation and implementation of new procedures to counter organized crime; a seminar on effective and transparent methods for managing temporarily-seized assets was organized by the Mission in April 2011; in 2012 the Mission aimed to support Serbia's efforts to build accountable and effective democratic institutions, to uphold human rights, to establish a stable and inclusive civil society, and to enhance environmental protection measures; supports the activities of the Citizen's Protector/Ombudsman, the Commissioner for the Protection of Equality and the Judicial Training Academy; in 2012 the Mission had an office in Bujanovac, southern Serbia, a training facility in Novi Pazar, and an advanced police training centre in Zemun; Head of Mission DIMITRIOS KYPREOS (Greece).

OSCE Presence in Albania: Sheraton Tirana Hotel & Towers, 1st Floor, Sheshi 'Italia', Tirana; tel. (4) 2235993; fax (4) 2235994; e-mail post.albania@osce.org; internet www.osce.org/albania; f. in March 1997 to help to restore political and civil stability, which had been undermined by the collapse of national pyramid saving schemes at the start of the year; in 2012 the Presence had four field stations, in Gjirokaster, Kukes, Shkoder and Vlora; from March 1998 to the conclusion of a political settlement for Kosovo and Metohija in mid-1999 the Presence was mandated to monitor the country's borders with the Kosovan region of southern Serbia and to prevent any spillover effects from the escalating crisis; from Sept. 1998 the Presence became the Co-Chair, with the EU, of the Friends of Albania group, which brought together countries and international bodies concerned with the situation in Albania; in accordance with an updated mandate, approved in Dec. 2003, the Presence provides advice and support to the Albanian Government regarding democratization, the rule of law, the media, human rights, anti-trafficking, weapons collection, election preparation and monitoring, and the development of civil society; it supports an Economics and Environment Unit and an Elections Unit, which, since the parliamentary elections of 2001, has facilitated the process of electoral reform, including modernization of the civil registration system; in 2010 the Presence assisted the Albanian Government with drafting legislation concerning parliamentary oversight of the intelligence and security services and in 2011 extended technical assistance to the Central Elections Commission in preparing for local government elections, that were conducted in May; Head of Presence EUGEN WOLLFARTH (Germany).

OSCE Spillover Monitor Mission to Skopje: MK-1000 Skopje, 11 Oktomvri str. 25, QBE Building; tel. (2) 3234000; fax (2) 3234234; e-mail info-MK@osce.org; f. Sept. 1992 to help to prevent the conflict in the former Yugoslavia from destabilizing the former Yugoslav republic of Macedonia (FYRM), with an initial mandate of overseeing the border region, monitoring human rights and promoting the development of democratic institutions, including an independent media; supports implementation of the Ohrid framework political agreement, signed in August 2001, initially through the deployment of international confidence-building monitors and police advisers, the recruitment and training of police cadets, and measures to strengthen local self-government; since

2002 the Mission has supported the Office of the Ombudsman, and in June 2007 initiated a second phase of the support project, including a new public awareness campaign; in early 2009 the Mission worked to strengthen the integrity of the electoral process for presidential and municipal elections that were conducted in March; in April 2010 Skopje missions of the OSCE, EU, NATO and USA reiterated the need for full commitment to the Ohrid Framework Agreement and for reinforced political dialogue; a short-term OSCE observer mission monitored parliamentary elections held in June 2011; in July the Mission organized a regional conference on the introduction of legal aid and the improvement of practices to promote access to justice throughout south-eastern Europe; in Jan. 2012 the Mission organized a workshop aimed at strengthening regional co-operation and dialogue to promote an effective response to human- and child-trafficking; in March 2012 the Head of Mission condemned recent violent incidents in Skopje; Head of Mission RALF BRETH (Germany).

In January 2012 the OSCE closed its Office in Zagreb, which had been established in January 2008, replacing a former OSCE Mission to Croatia.

FIELD OPERATIONS IN EASTERN EUROPE AND CENTRAL ASIA

An OSCE Mission to Georgia was established in 1992 to work towards a political settlement between disputing factions within the country. Since 1994 the Mission has contributed to efforts to define the political status of South Ossetia and has supported UN peace-keeping and human rights activities in Abkhazia. In 1997 the Mission established a field office in Tskhinvali (South Ossetia). In December 1999 the Permanent Council, at the request of the Government of Georgia expanded the mandate of the existing OSCE Mission to Georgia to include monitoring that country's border with the Chechen Republic of Ichkeriya (Chechnya). The first permanent observation post opened in February 2000 and the monitoring team was fully deployed by July. In December 2001 the Permanent Council approved an expansion in the border monitoring mission to cover the border between Georgia and Ingushetia. A further expansion, to include monitoring Georgia's border with Dagestan, was effected from January 2003. A special envoy of the OSCE Chairperson visited Georgia in July 2004 following a deterioration in the security situation. In November the Mission assisted the Georgian Government to develop an Action Plan to combat trafficking in human beings. In the same month the Mission helped to organize a national workshop on combating money-laundering and suppressing the financing of terrorism. In April 2005 the OSCE Permanent Council established a Training Assistance Programme for some 800 Georgian border guards. In June 2006 OSCE participating states pledged more than €10m. in support of projects for social and economic rehabilitation in the zone of the Georgian–Ossetian conflict. The donors' conference was the first of its kind to be organized by the OSCE. During 2007 the Mission continued to support activities concerned with police reform, human rights monitoring and education, munitions disposal, border control and management, counter-trafficking, and strengthening local democracy. OSCE observers participated in an international mission to monitor parliamentary elections held in May 2008. In July the Mission signed a memorandum of understanding with the Georgian Ministry of Defence to implement a three-year plan to strengthen local capacity for the dismantling and disposal of munitions. In the same month the Mission organized a training course for officials on the protection of human rights and fundamental freedoms. At that time the OSCE expressed concern at escalating tensions between the Georgian and Ossetian authorities. In August intensive fighting broke out when Georgian forces entered the territory and attempted to seize control of Tskhinvali. The resulting counter-attack by Ossetian troops, supported by additional Russian land and air forces, contributed to extensive civilian casualties, population displacement and damage to the region's infrastructure. The OSCE participated in diplomatic efforts to secure a cease-fire and convened a special meeting of the Permanent Council to discuss the organization's contribution to stabilizing the post-conflict situation. Members agreed to expand the Mission to Georgia by 100 military monitoring officers, of whom 20 were to be deployed immediately to the areas adjacent to South Ossetia. In late August the CiO and the Head of the Mission to Georgia visited the worst affected areas. In the following month the Head of Mission met the Russian Minister of Foreign Affairs to discuss issues relating to the freedom of movement of the Mission's unarmed monitors and the need for the effective delivery of humanitarian aid. In October the OSCE met with senior representatives of the UN and EU, in Geneva, Switzerland, to consider the stability and security of the region and the situation of displaced persons. The Mission to Georgia was terminated upon the expiry of its mandate on 31 December 2008, as agreement had not been reached by that time on continuing it into 2009, owing to Russia's insistence on a new mandate for the mission that excluded any arrangement sustaining Georgia's territorial claims on South Ossetia and Abkhazia, and Georgia's opposition to this. In February 2009 the OSCE Permanent Council agreed to extend, until 30 June, the mandate of the OSCE unarmed monitors in Georgia. During the first six months of 2009 intensive diplomatic efforts were undertaken to conclude an agreement on a continued OSCE presence in Georgia; there was failure, however, to achieve consensus by the end of June when, as planned, the unarmed monitors were withdrawn.

OSCE Centre in Aşgabat: 744005 Aşgabat, Türkmenbasi Shayoly 15, Turkmenistan; tel. (12) 35-30-92; fax (12) 35-30-41; e-mail info_tm@osce.org; internet www.osce.org/ashgabat/; f. Jan. 1999 (following a decision of the Permanent Council, in July 1998, to establish a permanent presence in the country); works to support greater collaboration between the authorities and the OSCE and the implementation of OSCE principles, to facilitate contacts with other local and international institutions and organizations working in the region and to assist in arranging regional seminars, events and visits by OSCE personnel; courses and workshops organized by the Centre in 2011 included best practices in police training, travel document security, anti-corruption measures, protecting human rights while countering terrorism, and contemporary global journalism; Head of Centre SERGEI BELYAEV (Russia).

OSCE Centre in Astana: 010000 Astana, Beibitshilik 10, Kazakhstan; tel. (7172) 32-68-04; fax (7172) 32-83-04; internet www.osce.org/astana; f. June 2007, as successor to an OSCE Centre in Almatı (f. Jan. 1999); mandated to support greater co-operation between the authorities and the OSCE, as well as the implementation of OSCE principles, to facilitate contacts with other local and international institutions and organizations working in the region, to assist in arranging regional seminars, events and visits by OSCE personnel, and to support the Government of Kazakhstan, for example by training officials and raising awareness of OSCE activities; matters addressed by seminars and courses organized by the Centre in 2010/11 included freedom of peaceful assembly, corporate social accountability, environmental protection, criminal justice reform, including the development of a probation system, the establishment of a national preventive mechanism to monitor the use of torture in detention centres, and gender equality; in June 2011 hosted a regional forum on internet development in Central Asia; Head of Centre ALEXANDRE KELTCHEWSKY (France).

OSCE Centre in Bishkek: 720001 Bishkek, Toktogula 139, Kyrgyzstan; tel. (312) 66-50-15; fax (312) 66-31-69; e-mail pm-kg@osce.org; internet www.osce.org/bishkek/; f. Jan. 1999 (following a decision of the Permanent Council, in July 1998, to establish a permanent presence in the country); works to support greater collaboration between the authorities and the OSCE and the implementation of OSCE principles, to facilitate contacts with other local and international institutions and organizations working in the region and to assist in arranging regional seminars, events and visits by OSCE personnel; established a field office in Osh, in 2000, to oversee operations in Kyrgyzstan's southern provinces; supports the OSCE Academy in Bishkek, which was inaugurated in Dec. 2002 as a regional centre for training, research and dialogue, in particular in security-related issues; following an escalation of civil and political tensions after legislative elections in Feb.–March 2005, the Centre offered to provide a forum for dialogue between the authorities and opposition groups; following political upheaval and civil and ethnic violence in April and June 2010 the Centre worked closely with the interim authorities to alleviate political tension and to promote dialogue and reconciliation; in Sept. the Centre facilitated contacts between political and non-governmental groups and the Head of an OSCE Police Advisory Group, which was deployed from Jan. 2011 in a primarily consultative role; prior to parliamentary elections, held in Oct. 2010, the Centre worked to ensure compliance with an electoral Code of Conduct signed by representatives of 26 political parties, to advise on the role of prosecutors, to promote impartial media reporting and to ensure the safety of journalists; organized a training course on multi-ethnic policing in July 2011; also in July, supported a meeting on the development of a new national action plan to combat human trafficking; in March 2012 co-hosted, jointly with the World Bank, UNODC and the Kyrgyz Government, a workshop on assessing the risk of money laundering; in 2012 the Centre aimed to focus its activities on six strategic priority areas: border security and management, including customs training; rule of law; good governance; legislation; environmental protection; and regional co-operation; Head of Centre ANDREW TESORIERE (United Kingdom).

OSCE Mission to Moldova: 2012 Chişinău, str. Mitropolit Dosoftei 108; tel. (22) 22-34-95; fax (22) 22-34-96; e-mail moldova@osce.org; internet www.osce.org/moldova/; f. Feb. 1993, in order to assist conflicting parties in that country to pursue negotiations on a political settlement for the Transniestrian region, as well as to observe the military situation in the region and to provide advice on issues of human and minority rights, democratization and the repatriation of refugees; the Mission's mandate was expanded in Dec. 1999 to ensure the full removal and destruction of Russian ammunition and armaments and to co-ordinate financial and technical assistance for the withdrawal of foreign troops and the destruction of weapons; in June 2001 the Mission established a tripartite working group, with representatives of the Russian Ministry of Defence and the local authorities in Transnistria, to assist and support the process of disposal of munitions; destruction of heavy weapons began in mid-2002, under the supervision of the Mission; in Sept. 2004 the OSCE Mission financed a workshop as part of a two-year project concerned with 'strengthening protection and assistance to victims of trafficking, adults and minors'; during 2005 the OSCE Mission hosted negotiations which resulted in the Transnistrian authorities extending permanent registration to four Moldovan schools; in March 2006 the OSCE CiO expressed concern at the situation along the Transnistrian section of the Moldovan–Ukrainian state border and instructed the Mission to pursue a solution by consulting with all relevant parties; in Jan. 2007 representatives of the OSCE, Russia and Ukraine met, with observers from the EU and USA (i.e. the so-called 5+2 negotiation format), to consider the future of the settlement process and invited chief negotiators from the Moldovan and Transnistrian authorities to initiate mediated discussions in the following month; in Oct. the Mission organized a high-level seminar on confidence- and security-building measures, in support of peace negotiations between Moldova and Transnistria, and in April 2008 the Mission organized a seminar on economic and environmental confidence-building measures, held in Odesa, Ukraine; in Feb. 2009 a Special Representative of the CiO for Protracted Conflicts visited Moldova to promote a resumption of the Transnistrian peace negotiations; an agreement to revive the process was signed by leaders of both sides, meeting in Moscow, Russia, in March; in April the Head of Mission condemned violent demonstrations that occurred following legislative elections; the Mission and the OSCE CiO convened a seminar in June on confidence- and security-building measures in Moldova, with participation by experts and 5+2 process participants; a Trial Monitoring Programme was conducted by the Mission with ODIHR, between March 2006 and Dec. 2009, to observe and enhance Moldova's compliance with OSCE commitments and international legal standards; in June 2010 the Mission signed a memorandum of understanding with the Moldovan Government to implement a four-year social integration project for ex-military personnel from the Transniestrian region; the initiative commenced in Sept; in Feb. 2011 an informal meeting of participants in the 5+2 settlement process agreed a work plan for that year, which included greater bilateral contact, pursuing other confidence-building measures, and resolving outstanding problems of freedom of movement; a further informal round of consultations was held in June, in Moscow; a limited OSCE/ODIHR election observation team was dispatched in May to monitor local elections conducted in the following month; in Sept. an agreement was concluded to restart official talks between the political leaders within the 5+2 framework, which were then initiated, at a meeting in Vilnius, Lithuania, in Nov.; a second formal meeting was convened in Dublin, Ireland, in Feb. 2012 (both the first and second meetings were concerned with the principles and procedures for the negotiating process); Mission offices opened in Tiraspol, in Feb. 1995, and in Bender, in May 2003; Head of Mission JENNIFER LEIGH BRUSH (USA).

OSCE Office in Baku: 1005 Baku, Nizami küç 96, The Landmark III, Azerbaijan; tel. (12) 497-23-73; fax (12) 497-23-77; e-mail office-az@osce.org; internet www.osce.org/baku/; f. Nov. 1999 (began operations in July 2000) to undertake activities concerned with democratization, human rights, economy and the environment, and media; supports a police assistance programme, including a police training school; supports the training of legal professionals and monitors court proceedings and conditions in prisons; during 2010 the Office worked to secure democratic principles in the preparation of legislative elections, held in Nov., including initiatives to promote political dialogue, media impartiality, and public confidence in the electoral process; workshops and seminars organized by the Office in early 2012 were concerned with community policing, countering money laundering and financing of terrorism, training detention facility officers, and the prevention of domestic violence; Head of Office KORAY TARGAY (Turkey).

OSCE Office in Tajikistan: 734017 Dushanbe, Zikrullo Khojaev 12, Tajikistan; tel. (372) 24-33-38; fax (372) 24-91-59; e-mail cid-tj@osce.org; internet www.osce.org/tajikistan/; f. June 2008, as successor to the OSCE Centre in Dushanbe, with an expanded mandate to support the country in efforts to promote the implementation of OSCE principles and commitments, to maintain peace and security, to counter crime, to undertake economic and environmental activities and to develop democratic political and legal institutions, incorporating respect for human rights; a Task Force Meeting, comprising OSCE officials, and representatives of the Tajik Government and civil society, convenes annually to consider the strategic partnership between the OSCE and Tajikistan; the Office implements a Mine Action Programme, initiated in 2004, and in April 2010 inaugurated a new integrated landmine clearance project along the border with Afghanistan; the Office supported the establishment of a human rights ombudsman, and hosts monthly inter-agency human rights sector meetings and an annual Human Dimension Implementation Meeting, attended by representatives of Government and civil society; a counter-terrorism and police unit assists the local law enforcement agencies to combat organized crime, including drugs-trafficking, and terrorism; in May 2009 an OSCE Border Management Staff College (BMSC) was established in Dushanbe to train border security managers and to promote co-operation between OSCE member states and partner countries; in April 2012 the BMSC organized a training course on the implementation of UN Security Council Resolution 1540 concerning the non-proliferation of weapons of mass destruction; in March 2010 the Office signed a memorandum of understanding with Tajikistan's Ministry of Economic Development and Trade establishing a Co-ordination Council on Free Economic Zones; the Office facilitates a Dialogue on Human Trafficking, which during 2010, developed a National Action Plan to Combat Human Trafficking; in Sept. 2011 the Office conducted a training course for election observers; Head of Office IVAR VIKKI (Norway).

OSCE Office in Yerevan: 0009 Yerevan, ul. Terian 89, Armenia; tel. (10) 54-58-45; fax (10) 54-10-61; e-mail yerevan-am@osce.org; internet www.osce.org/yerevan/; f. July 1999 (began operations in Feb. 2000); the Office works independently of the Minsk Group to promote OSCE principles within the country in order to support political and economic stability, the development of democratic institutions and the strengthening of civil society; a police assistance programme was initiated in 2004, which oversaw the renovation of a police training centre; promotes awareness of human rights, assists the Human Rights Defender's Office and supports Public Monitoring Groups concerned with detention centres; other areas of activity concern legislative reform and good governance, freedom of the media, gender issues and counter-terrorism and money-laundering; in May 2009 the Office, with other partners, organized a high-level forum concerned with discussing Armenian economic policy and addressing the local impact of the global financial crisis; during 2011 the Office, *inter alia*, supported electoral reform, the development of a new criminal procedure code, upholding human rights in the armed forces, and the process of transferring to digital broadcasting; in March 2012 the Head of Office signed a Memorandum of Understanding with Yerevan State University on establishing a Sustainable Development Centre within the University, to support Armenia in implementing UN declarations on sustainable development; Head of Office ANDREY SOROKIN (Russia).

OSCE Project Co-ordinator in Ukraine: 01054 Kyiv, vul. Striletska 16; tel. (44) 492-03-82; fax (44) 492-03-83; internet www.osce.org/ukraine/; f. June 1999, as a successor to the OSCE Mission to Ukraine (which had been established in Nov. 1994); responsible for pursuing co-operation between Ukraine and the OSCE and providing technical assistance in areas including legal and electoral reform, freedom of the media, trafficking in human beings, and the work of the human rights Ombudsman; the Project Co-ordinator has developed a Cross-Dimensional Economic-Environmental/Politico-Military Programme, in co-operation with the Ukrainian authorities, in support of the country's objectives of closer integration into European structures; the Programme incorporates activities such as strengthening border security, enhancing national capacity to combat illegal transboundary transportation of hazardous waste, promoting the sustainable management of the Dniestr River basin, and supporting the retraining and integration into civil society of military personnel; a new draft unified Election Code, developed with the support of the Project Co-ordinator, was presented to the Ukrainian parliament in April 2010; convenes an annual roundtable meeting (most recently in Dec. 2011) aimed at promoting joint efforts in combating human trafficking between the Ukrainian authorities and diplomatic missions based in Kyiv; Project Co-ordinator ĽUBOMÍR KOPAJ (Slovakia).

OSCE Project Co-ordinator in Uzbekistan: 100000 Tashkent, Afrosiab ko'ch 12B, 4th Floor; tel. (71) 140-04-70; fax (71) 140-04-66; e-mail osce-cit@osce.org; internet www.osce.org/tashkent/; f. July 2006; works to assist the Government to uphold security and stability, to strengthen socio-economic development and protection of the environment, and to implement other OSCE principles; in Feb. 2011 the Project Co-ordinator formally provided the Uzbek authorities with equipment to implement improvements to the national passport system; training courses and seminars organized by the Project Co-ordinator in early 2012 were concerned with the development of entrepreneurship, efforts to eliminate trafficking in human beings, combating the illegal trade in narcotics, access to information, and building ministerial press services; Project Co-ordinator GYÖRGY SZABÓ (Hungary).

Personal Representative of the OSCE Chairperson-in-Office on the Conflict Dealt with by the OSCE Minsk Conference (Nagornyi Karabakh): Tbilisi, Zovreti 15, Georgia; tel. (32) 37-61-61; fax (32) 98-85-66; e-mail persrep@access.sanet.ge; appointed in August 1995 to represent the CiO in the 11-nation Minsk Group process concerned with the conflict between Armenia and Azerbaijan in relation to the Nagornyi Karabakh region; in 2005–06 the Minsk Group undertook intensive negotiations to formulate a set of basic principles for a peaceful settlement of the conflict, including proposals for the redeployment of Armenian troops, demilitarization of formally occupied territories and a popular referendum to determine the final legal status of the region; in Nov. 2007 the Co-Chairs of the Minsk Group presented a Document of Basic Principles for the Peaceful Settlement of the Nagornyi Karabakh Conflict, which has been the basis of subsequent discussions with both sides; in Sept. 2011 the Minsk Group Co-Chairs announced a work plan focused on delineating ongoing differences concerning the basic principles; and drafting additional measures aimed at strengthening implementation of the cease-fire implemented since May 1994 in Nagornyi Karabakh; the Personal Representative is mandated to assist a High Level Planning Group, which was established in Vienna, Austria, to develop a plan for a multinational OSCE peace-keeping operation in the disputed region; Field Assistants of the Personal Representative have been deployed to Baku, Yerevan and Stepanakert/Khankendi; Personal Rep. ANDRZEJ KASPRZYK (Poland).

Finance

All activities of the institutions, negotiations, ad hoc meetings and missions are financed by contributions from member states. The unified budget for 2012 amounted to €148.1m.

Publications

Annual Report of the Secretary-General.

The Caucasus: In Defence of the Future.

Decision Manual (annually).

OSCE Handbook.

OSCE Highlights (regular electronic newsletter).

OSCE Newsletter (quarterly, in English and Russian).

Factsheets on OSCE missions, institutions and other structures are published regularly.

ORGANIZATION OF AMERICAN STATES—OAS

(ORGANIZACIÓN DE LOS ESTADOS AMERICANOS—OEA)

Address: 17th St and Constitution Ave, NW, Washington, DC 20006, USA.

Telephone: (202) 458-3000; **fax:** (202) 458-6319; **e-mail:** pi@oas.org; **internet:** www.oas.org.

The ninth International Conference of American States (held in Bogotá, Colombia, in 1948) adopted the Charter of the Organization of American States; the OAS succeeded the Commercial Bureau of American Republics, founded in 1890, and the Pan-American Union. The Charter was subsequently amended by the Protocol of Buenos Aires (creating the annual General Assembly), signed in 1967 and enacted in 1970; by the Protocol of Cartagena de Indias, which was signed in 1985 and enacted in 1988; and by the Protocol of Washington, signed in 1992 and enacted in 1997. The purpose of the OAS is to strengthen the peace and security of the continent; to promote human rights and to promote and consolidate representative democracy, with due respect for the principle of non-intervention; to prevent possible causes of difficulties and to ensure the peaceful settlement of disputes that may arise among the member states; to provide for common action in the event of aggression; to seek the solution of political, juridical and economic problems that may arise among the member states; to promote, by co-operative action, their economic, social and cultural development; to achieve an effective limitation of conventional weapons; to devote the largest amount of resources to the economic and social development of the member states; and to confront shared problems such as poverty, terrorism, the trade in illegal drugs, and corruption. The OAS is the principal regional multilateral forum. It plays a leading role in implementing mandates established by the hemisphere's leaders through the Summits of the Americas.

MEMBERS

Antigua and Barbuda	Guyana
Argentina	Haiti
Bahamas	Honduras
Barbados	Jamaica
Belize	Mexico
Bolivia	Nicaragua
Brazil	Panama
Canada	Paraguay
Chile	Peru
Colombia	Saint Christopher and Nevis
Costa Rica	Saint Lucia
Cuba*	Saint Vincent and the Grenadines
Dominica	Suriname
Dominican Republic	Trinidad and Tobago
Ecuador	USA
El Salvador	Uruguay
Grenada	Venezuela
Guatemala	

*The Cuban Government was suspended from OAS activities in 1962; the suspension was revoked by the OAS General Assembly in June 2009, although Cuba's participation in the organization was to be subject to further review.

Permanent Observers: Albania, Algeria, Angola, Armenia, Austria, Azerbaijan, Belgium, Benin, Bosnia and Herzegovina, Bulgaria, People's Republic of China, Croatia, Cyprus, Czech Republic, Denmark, Egypt, Equatorial Guinea, Estonia, Finland, France, Georgia, Germany, Ghana, Greece, Holy See, Hungary, Iceland, India, Ireland, Israel, Italy, Japan, Kazakhstan, Republic of Korea, Latvia, Lebanon, Lithuania, Luxembourg, Monaco, Morocco, Netherlands, Nigeria, Norway, Pakistan, Philippines, Poland, Portugal, Qatar, Romania, Russia, Saudi Arabia, Serbia, Slovakia, Slovenia, Spain, Sri Lanka, Sweden, Switzerland, Thailand, Tunisia, Turkey, Ukraine, United Kingdom, Yemen and the European Union.

Organization

(April 2012)

GENERAL ASSEMBLY

The Assembly meets annually and may also hold special sessions when convoked by the Permanent Council. As the highest decision-making body of the OAS, it decides general action and policy. The 41st General Assembly was convened in San Salvador, El Salvador, in June 2011; the 42nd General Assembly was scheduled to be held in Cochabamba, Bolivia, in June 2012.

MEETINGS OF CONSULTATION OF MINISTERS OF FOREIGN AFFAIRS

Meetings are convened, at the request of any member state, to consider problems of an urgent nature and of common interest to member states, or to serve as an organ of consultation in cases of armed attack or other threats to international peace and security. The Permanent Council determines whether a meeting should be convened and acts as a provisional organ of consultation until ministers are able to assemble.

PERMANENT COUNCIL

The Council meets regularly throughout the year at OAS headquarters. It is composed of one representative of each member state with the rank of ambassador; each government may accredit alternate representatives and advisers and when necessary appoint an interim representative. The office of Chairman is held in turn by each of the representatives, following alphabetical order according to the names of the countries in Spanish. The Vice-Chairman is determined in the same way, following reverse alphabetical order. Their terms of office are three months.

The Council guides ongoing policies and actions and oversees the maintenance of friendly relations between members. It supervises the work of the OAS and promotes co-operation with a variety of other international bodies including the United Nations. It comprises a General Committee and Committees on Juridical and Political Affairs, Hemispheric Security, Inter-American Summits Management and Civil Society Participation in OAS Activities, and Administrative and Budgetary Affairs. There are also ad hoc working groups. The official languages are English, French, Portuguese and Spanish.

In January 2012 the Secretary-General presented to the Permanent Council 'A Strategic Vision of the OAS', proposing a refocusing of the Organization's core tasks, prioritizing mandates in accordance with the principal strategic objectives, and a rationalization of the Organization's use of its financial resources.

INTER-AMERICAN COUNCIL FOR INTEGRAL DEVELOPMENT (CIDI)

The Council was established in 1996, replacing the Inter-American Economic and Social Council and the Inter-American Council for Education, Science and Culture. Its aim is to promote co-operation among the countries of the region, in order to accelerate economic and social development. An Executive Secretariat for Integral Development provides CIDI with technical and secretarial services and co-ordinates a Special Multilateral Fund of CICI (FEMCIDI), the New Programming Approaches programme, a Hemispheric Integral Development Program, a Universal Civil Identity Program in the Americas, and Migration and Development Innovative Programs. Technical co-operation and training programmes are managed by a subsidiary body of the Council, the Inter-American Agency for Co-operation and Development, which was established in 1999.

Executive Secretary: MAURICIO EDUARDO CORTÉS COSTA.

INTER-AMERICAN JURIDICAL COMMITTEE (IAJC)

The Committee's purposes are to serve as an advisory body to the OAS on juridical matters; to promote the progressive development and codification of international law; and to study juridical problems relating to the integration of the developing countries in the hemisphere, and, in so far as may appear desirable, the possibility of attaining uniformity in legislation. It comprises 11 jurists, nationals of different member states, elected for a period of four years, with the possibility of re-election.

Chairman: GUILLERMO FERNÁNDEZ DE SOTO (Colombia); Av. Marechal Floriano 196, 3° andar, Palácio Itamaraty, Centro, 20080-002, Rio de Janeiro, Brazil; tel. (21) 2206-9903; fax (21) 2203-2090; e-mail cjioea.trp@terra.com.br.

INTER-AMERICAN COMMISSION ON HUMAN RIGHTS

The Commission was established in 1960 to promote the observance and protection of human rights in the member states of the OAS. It examines and reports on the human rights situation in member countries and considers individual petitions relating to alleged human rights violations by member states. A Special Rapporteurship on the Rights of People of Afro-Descendants, and against Racial Discrimination was established in 2005. Other rapporteurs analyse and report on the rights of children, women, indigenous peoples, migrant workers, prisoners and displaced persons, and on freedom of expression.

Executive Secretary: SANTIAGO A. CANTON; 1889F St, NW, Washington, DC 20006, USA; tel. (202) 458-6002; fax (202) 458-3992; e-mail cidhoea@oas.org; internet www.cidh.oas.org.

GENERAL SECRETARIAT

The Secretariat, the central and permanent organ of the Organization, performs the duties entrusted to it by the General Assembly, Meetings of Consultation of Ministers of Foreign Affairs and the Councils. There is an Administrative Tribunal, comprising six elected members, to settle staffing disputes.

Secretary-General: JOSÉ MIGUEL INSULZA (Chile).

Assistant Secretary-General: ALBERT R. RAMDIN (Suriname).

INTER-AMERICAN COMMITTEES AND COMMISSIONS

Inter-American Committee Against Terrorism (Comité Interamericano Contra el Terrorismo—CICTE): 1889 F St, NW, Washington, DC 20006, USA; tel. (202) 458-6960; fax (202) 458-3857; e-mail cicte@oas.org; internet www.cicte.oas.org; f. 1999 to enhance the exchange of information via national authorities, formulate proposals to assist member states in drafting counter-terrorism legislation in all states, compile bilateral, sub-regional, regional and multilateral treaties and agreements signed by member states and promote universal adherence to international counter-terrorism conventions, strengthen border co-operation and travel documentation security measures, and develop activities for training and crisis management; Exec. Sec. GORDON DUGUID (USA).

Inter-American Committee on Ports (Comisión Interamericana de Puertos—CIP): 1889 F St, NW, Washington, DC 20006, USA; tel. (202) 458-3871; fax (202) 458-3517; e-mail cip@oas.org; internet www.oas.org/cip; f. 1998; serves as the permanent inter-American forum to strengthen co-operation on port-related issues among the member states, with the active participation of the private sector; the Committee, comprising 34 mem. states, meets every two years; its Executive Board, which executes policy decisions, meets annually; four technical advisory groups have been established to advise on logistics and competition (formerly port operations), port security, navigation control, and environmental protection; Sec. CARLOS M. GALLEGOS.

Inter-American Court of Human Rights (IACHR) (Corte Interamericana de Derechos Humanos): Ave 10, St 45-47 Los Yoses, San Pedro, San José; Postal 6906-1000, San José, Costa Rica; tel. (506) 2234-0581; fax (506) 2234-0584; e-mail corteidh@corteidh.or.cr; internet www.corteidh.or.cr; f. 1979 as an autonomous judicial institution whose purpose is to apply and interpret the American Convention on Human Rights (which entered into force in 1978); comprises seven jurists from OAS member states; Pres. DIEGO GARCÍA SAYÁN (Peru); Exec. Sec. PABLO SAAVEDRA ALESSANDRI (Chile); publ. *Annual Report*.

Inter-American Defense Board (Junta Interamericana de Defensa—JID): 2600 16th St, NW, Washington, DC 20441, USA; tel. (202) 939-6041; fax (202) 387-2880; e-mail iadc-registrar@jid.org; internet www.jid.org; promotes co-operative security interests in the Western Hemisphere; new statutes adopted in 2006 formally designated the Board as an OAS agency; works on issues such as disaster assistance and confidence-building measures directly supporting the hemispheric security goals of the OAS and of regional ministers of defence; also provides a senior-level academic programme in security studies for military, national police and civilian leaders at the Inter-American Defense College; Dir-Gen. Maj.-Gen. JUAREZ APARECIDO DE PAULA CUNHA (Brazil).

Inter-American Drug Abuse Control Commission (Comisión Interamericana para el Control del Abuso de Drogas—CICAD): 1889 F St, NW, Washington, DC 20006, USA; tel. (202) 458-3178; fax (202) 458-3658; e-mail oidcicad@oas.org; internet www.cicad.oas.org; f. 1986 by the OAS to promote and facilitate multilateral co-operation in the control and prevention of the trafficking, production and use of illegal drugs, and related crimes; reports regularly, through the Multilateral Evaluation Mechanism, on progress against illegal drugs in each member state and region-wide; mems: 34 countries; Exec. Sec. PAUL E. SIMONS; publs *Statistical Survey* (annually), *Directory of Governmental Institutions Charged with the Fight Against the Illicit Production, Trafficking, Use and Abuse of Narcotic Drugs and Psychotropic Substances*, *Evaluation of Progress in Drug Control*, *Progress Report on Drug Control—Implementation and Recommendations* (2 a year).

Inter-American Telecommunication Commission (Comisión Interamericana de Telecomunicaciones—CITEL): 1889 F St, NW, Washington, DC 20006, USA; tel. (202) 458-3004; fax (202) 458-6854; e-mail citel@oas.org; internet www.citel.oas.org; f. 1993 to promote the development and harmonization of telecommunications in the region, in co-operation with governments and the private sector; CITEL has more than 200 associate members representing private associations or companies, permanent observers, and international organizations; under its Permanent Executive Committee specialized consultative committees focus on telecommunication standardization and radiocommunication, including broadcasting; mems: 35 countries; Exec. Sec. CLOVIS JOSÉ BAPTISTA NETO.

Activities

STRENGTHENING DEMOCRACY

The OAS promotes and supports good governance in its member states through various activities, including electoral observations, crisis-prevention missions, and programmes to strengthen government institutions and to support a regional culture of democracy. In September 2001 the member states adopted the Inter-American Democratic Charter, which details the essential elements of representative democracy, including free and fair elections; respect for human rights and fundamental freedoms; the exercise of power in accordance with the rule of law; a pluralistic political party system; and the separation and independence of the branches of government. Transparency and responsible administration by governments, respect for social rights, freedom of expression and citizen participation are among other elements deemed by the Charter to define democracy. The 41st General Assembly, held in June 2011, in San Salvador, El Salvador, approved a final Declaration on Citizen Security in the Americas, which incorporated a request to ministers to draft a hemispheric plan of action for consideration the following year.

The observation of elections is one of the most important tasks of the OAS. Depending on the specific situation and the particular needs of each country, missions vary from a few technical experts sent for a limited time to a large country-wide team of monitors dispatched to observe the full electoral process for an extended period commencing with the political parties' campaigns. The missions present their observations to the OAS Permanent Council, along with recommendations for how each country's electoral process might be strengthened. In August 2010 a joint electoral observation mission (JEOM), with representatives from CARICOM, was deployed to oversee the presidential and legislative electoral processes in Haiti, where polling was scheduled to take place in November. The mission remained in the country after the elections to monitor the second round of voting in the presidential poll, which took place in late March 2011. The JEOM was reinforced in December 2010 by two expert missions, which were dispatched, following disputed preliminary first round results, to verify statistical procedures and to strengthen legal technical assistance. Other electoral observation missions in 2011 were dispatched to Peru, to oversee voting in presidential and legislative elections, which were conducted in April and June, to Ecuador to observe a national referendum, conducted in May, to Saint Christopher and Nevis, for legislative elections conducted in July, to Guatemala, to monitor voting in a general election, conducted in September, to Nicaragua, in November, to monitor presidential and legislative elections, to St Lucia and Guyana, also in November, to oversee legislative elections, and to Jamaica, in December, to monitor legislative elections. In March 2012 OAS observer teams monitored legislative and municipal elections held in Belize and in El Salvador.

The OAS has responded to numerous political crises in the region. In some cases, at the request of member states, it has sent special missions to provide critical support to the democratic process. During 2005–06 the OAS was particularly active in Nicaragua. In June 2005, responding to issues raised by the Government of President Enrique Bolaños, the OAS General Assembly expressed concern about developments that posed a threat to the separation and independence of branches of government. Citing the Inter-American Democratic Charter and the OAS Charter, the General Assembly authorized an OAS mission to help establish a broad national dialogue in that country; accordingly, the OAS Secretary-General led a high-level mission to Nicaragua to support efforts to find democratic solutions to the situation, and also appointed a special envoy to facilitate dialogue there. In 2006 the OAS Special Mission to Accompany the Democratic and Electoral Process in Nicaragua monitored regional elections, conducted in March, and a general election in November. In a subsequent report to the OAS Permanent Council, the Chief of Mission noted that Nicaragua had made significant steps forward in its democratic development and that its elections were 'increasingly clean and competitive'.

In 2005, following an institutional crisis in Ecuador, the OAS offered support for the establishment of an impartial, independent Supreme Court of Justice. The OAS Secretary-General appointed two distinguished jurists as his special representatives to observe the selection process; members of Ecuador's new Supreme Court were sworn in during November. The OAS also played a role in Bolivia in 2005, following the resignation in June of President Carlos Mesa. The OAS Secretary-General appointed a special representative to facilitate political dialogue and to head the OAS observation mission on the electoral process that resulted in Evo Morales winning the presidency.

In August 2000 the OAS Secretary-General undertook the first of several high-level missions to negotiate with the authorities in Haiti in order to resolve the political crisis resulting from a disputed general election in May. In January 2001, following a meeting with the Haitian Prime Minister, the Assistant Secretary-General recommended that the OAS renew its efforts to establish a dialogue between the Government, opposition parties and representatives of civil society in that country. In May and June the OAS and the Caribbean Community and Common Market (CARICOM) undertook joint missions to Haiti in order to assess and promote prospects for a democratic resolution to the political uncertainties. Following political and social unrest in Haiti in December, the OAS and CARICOM pledged to conduct an independent investigation into the violence, and in March 2002 an agreement to establish a Special OAS Mission for Strengthening Democracy in Haiti was signed in the capital, Port-au-Prince. The independent commission of inquiry reported to the OAS at the beginning of July, and listed a set of recommendations relating to law reform, security and other confidence-building measures to help to secure democracy in Haiti. In January 2004 the OAS Special Mission condemned the escalation of political violence in Haiti and in February took a lead in drafting a plan of action to implement a CARICOM-brokered action plan to resolve the crisis. In late February the Permanent Council met in special session, and urged the UN to take necessary and appropriate action to address the deteriorating situation in Haiti. On 29 February President Jean-Bertrand Aristide resigned and left the country; amid ongoing civil unrest, a provisional leader was sworn in. The OAS Mission continued to attempt to maintain law and order, in co-operation with a UN-authorized Multinational Interim Force, and facilitated political discussions on the establishment of a transitional government. From March the Special Mission participated in the process to develop an Interim Co-operation Framework, identifying the urgent and medium-term needs of Haiti, which was presented to a meeting of international donors held in July. In June the OAS General Assembly adopted a resolution instructing the Permanent Council to undertake all necessary diplomatic initiatives to foster the restoration of democracy in Haiti, and called upon the Special Mission to work with the new UN Stabilization Mission in Haiti in preparing, organizing and monitoring future elections. During 2005 OAS technical experts, together with UN counterparts, assisted Haiti's Provisional Electoral Council (PEC) with the process of voter registration for legislative and presidential elections, initially scheduled for later in that year, as well as to formulate an electronic vote tabulation system, which was to serve as the basis for a permanent civil registry. In January 2006 the OAS Permanent Council declared its grave concern at a further postponement of the elections. In the following month, however, the Council expressed its satisfaction that polling had taken place in a free and fair manner. The Secretary-General visited Haiti to meet with officials and offer his support for the declared President-elect, Réné Préval. The OAS has continued to extend support to the country and to co-ordinate international assistance, mainly through its Haiti Task Force, chaired by the Assistant Secretary-General. In February 2008 a special mission of the Permanent Council visited Haiti to assess priorities for future support. In July the Assistant Secretary-General announced the establishment of an OAS Haiti Fund to support the organization's mandate and priorities in that country. In September the Assistant Secretary-General, visiting Haiti after it had been struck by a series of tropical cyclones, reiterated OAS commitment to Haiti's socio-economic development and stability. In early 2009 the OAS pledged to support the electoral process in Haiti, and to monitor the forthcoming senate elections.

In April 2002 a special session of the General Assembly was convened to discuss the ongoing political instability in Venezuela. The Assembly applied its authority granted under the Inter-American Democratic Charter to condemn the alteration of the constitutional order in Venezuela which forced the temporary eviction of President Hugo Chávez from office. In January 2003 the OAS announced the establishment of a Group of Friends, composed of representatives from Brazil, Chile, Mexico, Spain, Portugal and the USA, to support its efforts to resolve the ongoing crisis in Venezuela. In March the OAS Secretary-General was invited by Venezuelan opposition groupings to mediate negotiations with the Government. The talks culminated in May with the signing of an OAS-brokered agreement which, it was hoped, would lead to mid-term referendums on elected officials, including the presidency. The OAS, with the Carter Center, subsequently oversaw and verified the collection of signatures to determine whether referendums should be held. Following the staging of a recall referendum on the Venezuelan presidency in August 2004, OAS member states urged that there should be a process of reconciliation in that country.

In June 2009 the OAS Secretary-General and Permanent Council condemned the forced expulsion from power of President José Manuel Zelaya of Honduras by members of that country's armed forces. A special session of the General Assembly was convened, which urged the Secretary-General to pursue diplomatic efforts to restore constitutional order and the rule of law. When this was not achieved within the required 72 hour period, the Assembly, on 4 July, resolved to suspend the membership rights of Honduras to participate in the organization. President Oscar Arias of Costa Rica agreed to lead efforts on behalf of the OAS to mediate with the new authorities in Honduras in order to resolve the crisis. In August the OAS organized a delegation of ministers of foreign affairs to visit Honduras and promote a settlement based on the San José Accord formulated by President Arias, which envisaged Zelaya returning to the country as head of a government of national unity, and the holding of a general election a month earlier than scheduled, in late October. Political amnesty was to be offered to all sides under the proposed agreement. The interim authorities permitted the delegation's visit conditional on the OAS Secretary-General participating only as an observer. The opposing leaders signed an accord in October, although it was soon rejected by Zelaya after he was excluded from an interim national unity government. A special session of the Permanent Council was convened in December to consider the political situation in Honduras following a general election conducted in late November. The Council urged the newly elected leader, Porfirio Lobo, fully to re-establish respect for human rights, to end 'persecution' of Zelaya, and to establish a national unity government to serve until the original presidential term ended in January 2010. In June the OAS General Assembly determined to establish a high-level commission to assess the political and human rights situation in Honduras. The commission's report, issued in late July, included the following recommendations: the termination of legal proceedings initiated against former President Zelaya; support for Zelaya's application for membership of the Central American Parliament with the status of a former constitutional president; continued investigation into alleged human rights violations; and implementation, by the new government, of further measures to protect activists, journalists, judges and others who had opposed the *coup d'etat*. The suspension of Honduras' OAS membership was removed in June 2011.

In special situations, when both or all member states involved in a dispute ask for its assistance, the OAS plays a longer-term role in supporting countries to resolve bilateral or multilateral issues. In September 2005 Belize and Guatemala signed an agreement at the OAS establishing a framework for negotiations and confidence-building measures to help to maintain good bilateral relations while they sought a permanent solution to a long-standing territorial dispute. Following a series of negotiations under OAS auspices, both sides signed a Special Agreement to resolve the dispute in December 2008. In April 2006 another OAS-supported effort was concluded successfully when El Salvador and Honduras signed an accord settling differences over the demarcation of their common border. In March 2008 a Meeting of Consultation of OAS ministers of foreign affairs was convened following an escalation of diplomatic tension between Colombia and Ecuador resulting from a violation of Ecuador's borders by Colombian soldiers in pursuit of opposition insurgents. The meeting approved a resolution to establish a Good Offices Mission to restore confidence between the two countries and to negotiate an appropriate settlement to the dispute. A Verification Commission of the Good Offices Mission presented a report in July 2009, which included proposals to strengthen bilateral relations. In November 2010 a special meeting of the Permanent Council was convened, at the request of the Costa Rican government, to consider a border dispute with Nicaragua in the San Juan river area. The Council adopted a resolution in support of recommendations of the OAS Secretary-General, who had recently visited the area, to implement various confidence-building measures, including the resumption of bilateral talks on boundary demarcation, the convening of a Binational Committee and strengthening collaborative mechanisms to counter organized crime and arms- and drugs-trafficking.

The OAS places a high priority on combating corruption in recognition of the undermining effect this has on democratic institutions. In 1996 the OAS member states adopted the Inter-American Convention against Corruption, which by 2012 had been ratified or acceded to by 33 member states. In 2002 the treaty's signatory states initiated a peer review process to examine their compliance with the treaty's key provisions. The Follow-Up Mechanism for the Implementation of the Inter-American Convention against Corruption assesses progress and recommends concrete measures that the states parties can implement to improve compliance. Representatives of civil society organizations are also given the opportunity to meet with experts and present information for their consideration. A second round of the review process commenced in 2006 and was concluded in December 2008, at which time 28 country reports had been adopted. All participating countries have been assessed at least once and the completed progress reports are available to the public. The OAS has also held seminars and training sessions in the region on such matters as improving transparency in government and drafting model anti-corruption legislation. In May 2010 the Follow-up Mechanism organized a Conference on the Progress and Challenges in Hemispheric Co-operation against Corruption, held in Lima, Peru. A second conference was convened in Cali, Colombia, in June 2011.

In recent years, the OAS has expanded its outreach to civil society. More than 200 non-governmental organizations (NGOs) are registered to take part in OAS activities. Civil society groups are encouraged to participate in workshops and round tables in advance of the OAS General Assembly to prepare proposals and recommendations to present to the member states. This is also the case with Summits of the Americas and the periodic ministerial meetings, such as those on education, labour, culture, and science and technology. NGOs contributed ideas to the development of the Inter-American Democratic Charter and have participated in follow-up work on hemispheric treaties against corruption and terrorism.

The OAS has also focused on strengthening ties with the private sector. In 2006 it concluded a co-operation agreement with the business forum Private Sector of the Americas which aimed to promote dialogue and to support public–private alliances with a view to creating jobs, combating poverty and strengthening development. Business leaders from the region develop proposals and recommendations to present to the OAS General Assembly and to the Summits of the Americas.

Under the Democratic Charter a 'respect for human rights and fundamental freedoms' is deemed to be an essential element of a democracy. The Inter-American Commission on Human Rights and the Inter-American Court of Human Rights are the pillars of a system designed to protect individuals in the Americas who have suffered violations of their rights. A key function of the Commission is to consider petitions from individuals who claim that a state has violated a protected right and that they have been unable to find justice. The Commission brings together the petitioner and the state to explore a 'friendly settlement'. If such an outcome is not possible, the Commission may recommend specific measures to be carried out by the state to remedy the violation. If a state does not follow the recommendations the Commission has the option to publish its report or take the case to the Inter-American Court of Human Rights, as long as the state involved has accepted the Court's compulsory jurisdiction. The Commission convenes for six weeks each year.

In addition to hearing cases the Court may exercise its advisory jurisdiction to interpret the human rights treaties in effect in the region. The Commission, for its part, may conduct an on-site visit to a country, at the invitation of its Government, to analyse and report on the human rights situation. The Commission has also created rapporteurships focusing on particular human rights issues. In 2005 it created a rapporteurship on the rights of persons of African descent and against racial discrimination. Other rapporteurs analyse and report on the rights of children, women, indigenous peoples migrant workers, prisoners and displaced persons, and on freedom of expression. The Commission also has a special unit on human rights defenders. The OAS also works beyond the inter-American human rights system to promote the rights of vulnerable groups. The member states are in the process of negotiating the draft American Declaration on the Rights of Indigenous Peoples, which is intended to promote and protect a range of rights covering such areas as family, spirituality, work, culture, health, the environment, and systems of knowledge, language and communication. A special fund was established for voluntary contributions by member states and permanent observers in order to help cover the costs involved in broadening indigenous participation. The OAS also works to promote and protect women's rights. The Inter-American Commission of Women (CIM), established in 1928, has had an impact on shaping laws and policies in many countries. One of its key initiatives led to the adoption of the Inter-American Convention on the Prevention, Punishment and Eradication of Violence against Women, also known as the Convention of Belém do Pará, which was adopted in 1994 by the OAS General Assembly and, by 2010, had been ratified by 32 OAS member states. Since 2005 parties to the Belém do Pará Convention have participated in a follow-up mechanism designed to determine how the countries are complying with the treaty and progress achieved in preventing and punishing violence against women. In 2006 the CIM also initiated an examination of strategies for reversing the spread of HIV/AIDS among women in the region. The Commission has urged greater efforts to integrate a gender perspective into every aspect of the OAS agenda. An Inter-American Year of Women was inaugurated in February 2010.

SOCIAL AND ECONOMIC DEVELOPMENT

Combating poverty and promoting social equity and economic development are priority concerns of the OAS. In 2007 the member states were negotiating the text of a new Social Charter of the Americas. The OAS works on a number of fronts to combat poverty and promote development, in partnership with regional and global agencies, the private sector and the international community. In 2006 the OAS General Assembly approved a new Strategic Plan for Partnership for Integral Development 2006–09, which was to guide OAS actions in this area. (In June 2009 the General Assembly resolved to extend the Strategic Plan by one year, until 31 December 2010.) OAS development policies and priorities are determined by the organization's political bodies, including the General Assembly, the Permanent Council and the Inter-American Council for Integral Development (CIDI), with direction from the Summits of the Americas. The OAS Executive Secretariat for Integral Development (SEDI) implements the policies through projects and programmes. Specialized departments within SEDI focus on education, culture, science and technology; sustainable development; trade, tourism and competitiveness; and social development and employment. SEDI also supports the regional ministerial meetings on topics such as culture, education, labour and sustainable development that are held periodically as part of the Summit of the Americas process. These regional meetings foster dialogue and strengthen co-operation in specific sectors and ensure that Summit policies are implemented at the national level. The OAS convenes the ministerial meetings, prepares documents for discussion and tracks the implementation of Summit mandates. In June 2009 the General Assembly adopted a resolution committing members to strengthening co-operation to control the spread of communicable diseases, in particular the outbreak of the swine influenza variant pandemic (H1N1), through greater surveillance and other disease control methods.

In June 2008 a technical secretariat was established in Panama City, Panama, to co-ordinate the implementation of an action plan in support of the Decade of the Americas for the Rights and Dignity of Persons with Disabilities (2006–16). The theme of the Decade, which had been inaugurated in Santo Domingo, Dominican Republic, was 'Equality, Dignity, and Participation'. In July 2008 the first Meeting of Ministers and High Authorities of Social Development, within the framework of CIDI, was convened in Valparaiso, Chile.

The OAS Department of Sustainable Development assists member states with formulating policies and executing projects that are aimed at integrating environmental protection with rural development and poverty alleviation, and that ensure high levels of transparency, public participation and gender equity. Its projects, which receive substantial external funding, focus on several key areas. In December 2006 regional ministers of the environment met in Santa Cruz de la Sierra, Bolivia, to define strategies and goals related to sustainable development, environmental protection, the management of resources and the mitigation of natural disasters. Water resource management projects include initiatives that support member states in managing transboundary water resources in the major river basins of South and Central America, in partnership with UNEP, the World Bank and the Global Environment Facility (GEF). The OAS is also active in various international fora that address water-related issues.

Projects focusing on natural disasters and climate adaptation include a new programme, launched in April 2006, which is aimed at assisting member countries to reduce the risk of natural disasters, particularly those related to climatic variations that have been linked to rises in sea levels. The OAS also works with CARICOM on the Mainstreaming Adaptation to Climate Change project. Activities include incorporating risk reduction into development and economic planning; supporting good governance in such areas as the use of appropriate building codes and standards for public and residential buildings; supporting innovative financial instruments related to risk transfer; and supporting regional collaboration with different agencies and organizations.

The OAS serves as the technical secretariat for the Renewable Energy in the Americas initiative, which offers governments access to information on renewable energy and energy-efficient technologies, and facilitates contacts between the private sector and state energy entities in the Americas. The OAS also provides technical assistance for developing renewable energy projects and facilitating their funding.

Various OAS-supported activities help member countries to improve the management of biological diversity. The Inter-American Biodiversity Information Network (IABIN), which has been supported since 2004 by the GEF, the World Bank and other sources, is a principal focus of OAS biodiversity efforts. The Department of Sustainable Development also supports the work of national conservation authorities in areas such as migratory species and biodiversity corridors. It co-operates with the private sector to support innovative financing through payment for ecological services, and maintains a unique online portal regarding land tenure and land title, which is used throughout the Americas.

In the areas of environmental law, policy and economics the OAS conducts environmental and sustainability assessments to help member states to identify key environmental issues that impact trade. Efforts include working with countries to develop priorities for capacity building in such areas as domestic laws, regulations and standards affecting market access of goods and services. Other initiatives include supporting countries in water and renewable energy legislation; supporting efforts towards the more effective enforcement of domestic laws; and facilitating natural disaster risk reduction and relief.

In mid-2006 the OAS launched a programme aimed at supporting countries with managing pesticides and industrial chemicals. The programme was to co-ordinate its work closely with UNEP Chemicals, the UN Stockholm Convention and other entities.

The OAS supports member states at national, bilateral and multilateral level to cope with trade expansion and economic integration. Through its Department of Trade, Tourism and Competitiveness the OAS General Secretariat provides support in strengthening human and institutional capacities; and in enhancing trade opportunities and competitiveness, particularly for micro, small and medium-sized enterprises. One of the Department's key responsibilities is to help member states (especially smaller economies) to develop the capacity they need to negotiate, implement and administer trade agreements and to take advantage of the benefits offered by free trade and expanded markets. Many member states seek assistance from the OAS to meet successfully the challenges posed by increasing globalization and the need to pursue multiple trade agendas. The OAS also administers an Inter-American Foreign Trade Information System (SICE), which acts as a repository for information about trade and trade-related issues in the region, including the texts of trade agreements, information on trade disciplines, data, and national legislation. In October 2008 a meeting of Ministers and High Authorities on Science and Technology, convened in Mexico City, Mexico, declared their commitment to co-ordinating activities to promote and enhance policies relating to science, technology, engineering and innovation as tools of development, increasing productivity, and sustainable natural resource management.

The OAS provided support to the Free Trade Area of the Americas (FTAA) process, endorsed by the First Summit of the Americas, held in December 1994 (see below), as well as supporting sub-regional and bilateral trade agreements. A trade unit was established in 1995 in order to strengthen the organization's involvement in trade issues and the process of economic integration, which became a priority area following the First Summit of the Americas. The trade unit provided technical assistance in support of the establishment of the FTAA and co-ordinated activities between regional and sub-regional integration organizations. At the Special Summit of the Americas, held in January 2004 in Monterrey, Mexico, the leaders failed to specify a completion date for the negotiations, although they adopted a declaration committing themselves to its eventual establishment. Negotiations on the FTAA subsequently stalled. The unit also supports a Hemispheric Co-operation Programme, which was established by ministers of trade of the Americas, meeting in November 2002, to assist smaller economies to gain greater access to resources and technical assistance.

MULTIDIMENSIONAL SECURITY

The promotion of hemispheric security is a fundamental purpose of the OAS. In October 2003, at a Special Conference on Security convened in Mexico City, Mexico, the member states established a 'multidimensional' approach that recognized both traditional security concerns and newer threats such as international terrorism, drugs-trafficking, money-laundering, illegal arms dealing, trafficking in persons, institutional corruption and organized crime. In some countries problems such as poverty, disease, environmental degradation and natural disasters increase vulnerability and undermine human security. In March 2006, during a special session of the OAS General Assembly, the member states determined to enhance co-operation on defence issues by formally designating the Inter-American Defense Board (IADB) as an OAS agency. Under its new mandate the operations and structure of the IADB were to be in keeping with the OAS Charter and the Inter-American Democratic Charter, including 'the principles of civilian oversight and the subordination of military institutions to civilian authority'. The IADB provides technical and educational advice and consultancy services to the OAS and its member states on military and defence matters. The OAS Secretary-General chairs the Inter-American Committee on Natural Disaster Reduction, which was established in 1999 comprising the principal officers of regional and international organizations concerned with the prevention and mitigation of natural disasters. In January 2010 the OAS established an emergency committee to help to co-ordinate relief efforts for Haiti, which had suffered extensive damage and loss of life as a result of a massive earthquake. A joint mission of the OAS and representatives of four inter-American institutions visited Haiti at the end of that month to assess its immediate relief and reconstruction needs. In March the OAS hosted a Haiti Diaspora Meeting, with the collaboration of the Haitian Government, which made recommendations, in particular concerning nation-building, recovery and development, for the forthcoming International Donors' Conference, held in New York, USA, at the end of that month.

Following the 11 September 2001 terrorist attacks perpetrated against targets in the USA, the OAS member states strengthened their co-operation against the threat of terrorism. The Inter-American Convention against Terrorism, which seeks to prevent the financing of terrorist activities, strengthen border controls and increase co-operation among law enforcement authorities in different countries, was opened for signature in June 2002 and entered into force in July 2003. At mid-2009 it had been signed by all 34 active member states and ratified or acceded to by 24. The Inter-American Committee against Terrorism (CICTE) offers technical assistance and specialized training in key counter-terrorism areas including port security, airport security, customs and border security, and legislation and legal assistance. In 2006 CICTE provided training to security officials in the Caribbean countries that were preparing to host the 2007 Cricket World Cup. Through CICTE member countries have also improved co-operation in improving the quality of identification and travel documents, strengthening cyber-security and adopting financial controls to prevent money-laundering and the funding of terrorist activities. In October 2008 the first meeting of ministers responsible for public security in the Americas was convened, in Mexico City. In June 2009 the General Assembly, meeting in Honduras, adopted the Declaration of San Pedro Sula, promoting the theme 'Towards a Culture of Non-violence'.

The Inter-American Drug Abuse Control Commission (CICAD) seeks to reduce the supply of and demand for illegal drugs, building on the 1996 Anti-Drug Strategy in the Hemisphere. The CICAD Executive Secretariat implements programmes aimed at preventing and treating substance abuse; reducing the supply and availability of illicit drugs; strengthening national drug control institutions; improving practices to control firearms and money-laundering; developing alternate sources of income for growers of coca, poppy and marijuana; and helping member governments to improve the gathering and analysis of data. The Multilateral Evaluation Mechanism (MEM) measures drug control progress in the member states and the hemisphere as a whole, based on a series of objective indicators. The national reports on the third evaluation round, completed in 2006, included 506 specific recommendations designed to help countries strengthen their policies to combat drugs-related activities, and to increase multilateral co-operation. Following each evaluation round the MEM process examines how countries are carrying out the recommendations. In June 2009 the OAS General Assembly agreed to initiate a review of the organization's anti-drug strategy and its instruments to counter drugs-trafficking and abuse.

In 1997 the member states adopted the Inter-American Convention against the Illicit Manufacturing of and Trafficking in Firearms, Ammunition, Explosives, and other Related Materials (known as CIFTA), which, by early 2009, had been ratified by 29 member states. These countries have strengthened co-operation and information sharing on CIFTA-related issues. In 2005 the OAS convened the first meeting of national authorities that make operational decisions on granting export, import and transit licenses for firearms, with a view to creating an information-exchange network to prevent illegal manufacturing and trafficking. In June 1999 20 member states signed an Inter-American Convention on Transparency in Conventional Weapons Acquisition; it had been ratified by 15 members by early 2012.

Since the 1990s the OAS has co-ordinated a comprehensive international programme to remove many thousands of anti-personnel landmines posing a threat to civilians in countries that have been affected by conflict. The OAS co-ordinates activities, identifying, obtaining and delivering the necessary resources, including funds, equipment and personnel; the IADB oversees technical demining operations, working with field supervisors from various countries; and the actual demining is executed by teams of trained soldiers, security forces or other personnel from the affected country. In addition to supporting landmine clearance the OAS Program for Comprehensive Action against Anti-personnel Mines helps with mine risk education; victim assistance and the socio-economic reintegration of formerly mined zones; the establishment of a mine action database; and support for a ban on the production, use, sale, transfer and stockpiling of anti-personnel landmines. It has also helped to destroy more than 1m. stockpiled mines in Argentina, Colombia, Chile, Ecuador, Honduras, Nicaragua and Peru. By mid-2009 Costa Rica, El Salvador, Guatemala, Honduras and Suriname had declared their territory to be clear of anti-personnel landmines. Nicaragua was officially declared to be free of landmines in June 2010.

The OAS Trafficking in Persons Section organizes seminars and training workshops for law enforcement officials and others to raise awareness on human trafficking, which includes human exploitation, smuggling and other human rights violations. In March 2006 the Venezuelan Government hosted the first Meeting of National Authorities on Trafficking in Persons in order to study ways to strengthen co-operation and to develop regional policies and strategies to prevent human trafficking. Gang violence is another growing public security concern in the region. A second Meeting was convened in Buenos Aires, Argentina, in March 2009.

In June 2010 the 40th meeting of the OAS General Assembly, meeting in Lima, Peru, adopted the Declaration of Lima, aimed at strengthening collective commitment to peace, security and co-operation, as the principal means of confronting threats to the region.

SUMMITS OF THE AMERICAS

Since December 1994, when the First Summit of the Americas was convened in Miami, USA (see below), the leaders of the region's 34 democracies have met periodically to examine political, economic and social development priorities and to determine common goals and forge a common agenda. This process has increasingly shaped OAS policies and priorities and many OAS achievements, for example the adoption of the Inter-American Democratic Charter and the creation of mechanisms to measure progress against illicit drugs and corruption, have been attained as a result of Summit mandates. The Summits of the Americas have provided direction for the OAS in the areas of human rights, hemispheric security, trade, poverty reduction, gender equity and greater civil society participation. The OAS serves as the institutional memory and technical secretariat to the Summit process. It supports the countries in follow-up and planning, and provides technical, logistical and administrative support. The OAS Summits Secretariat co-ordinates the implementation of mandates assigned to the OAS and chairs the Joint Summit Working Group, which includes the institutions of the inter-American system. The OAS also has responsibility for strengthening outreach to civil society to ensure that NGOs, academic institutions, the private sector and other interests can contribute ideas and help to monitor and implement Summit initiatives.

In December 1994 the First Summit of the Americas was convened in Miami, USA. The meeting endorsed the concept of a Free Trade Area of the Americas, and also approved a Plan of Action to strengthen democracy, eradicate poverty and promote sustainable development throughout the region. The OAS subsequently embarked on an extensive process of reform and modernization to strengthen its capacity to undertake a lead role in implementing the Plan. The organization realigned its priorities in order to respond to the mandates emerging from the Summit and developed a new institutional framework for technical assistance and co-operation, although many activities continued to be undertaken by the specialized or associated organizations of the OAS (see below). In 1996 the OAS member states participated in the interim Summit of the Americas on Sustainable Development, convened in Santa Cruz de la Sierra, Bolivia, which established sustainable development goals that incorporated economic, social and environmental concerns. The Second Summit of the Americas, which took place in 1998 in Santiago, Chile, focused on education, as well as such issues as strengthening democracy, justice and human rights; promoting integration and free trade; and eradicating poverty and discrimination. In 1998, following the Second Summit, the OAS established an Office of Summit Follow-Up, in order to strengthen its servicing of the meetings, and to co-ordinate tasks assigned to it. The Third Summit, convened in Québec, Canada, in April 2001, reaffirmed the central role of the OAS in implementing decisions of the summit meetings and instructed the organization to pursue the process of reform in order to enhance its operational capabilities, in particular in the areas of human rights, combating trade in illegal drugs, and enforcement of democratic values. The Summit declaration stated that commitment to democracy was a requirement for a country's participation in the summit process. The Third Summit urged the development of an Inter-American Democratic Charter to reinforce OAS instruments for defending and promoting democracy; the Democratic Charter was adopted in September of that year. The Third Summit also determined that the OAS was to be the technical secretariat for the summit process, assuming many of the responsibilities previously incumbent on the host country. Further to its mandate, the OAS established a Summits of the Americas Secretariat, which assists countries in planning and follow-up and provides technical, logistical and administrative support for the Summit Implementation Review Group and the summit process. An interim Special Summit of the Americas was held in January 2004, in Monterrey, Mexico, to reaffirm commitment to the process. The Fourth Summit of the Americas was convened in Mar del Plata, Argentina, in November 2005, on the theme 'Creating jobs to fight poverty and strengthen democracy'. The meeting approved a plan of action to achieve employment growth and security. The Fifth Summit was held in Port of Spain, Trinidad and Tobago, in April 2009, focusing on the theme 'Securing our citizens' future by promoting human prosperity, energy security and environmental sustainability'. All governments determined to enhance co-operation to restore global economic growth and to reduce social inequalities. The meeting mandated the OAS to pursue various objectives, including the establishment of an Inter-American Social Protection Network, to facilitate the exchange of information with regard to policies, programmes and best practices; the convening of a Conference on Development; organizing regional consultations on climate change; and strengthening the leadership of the Joint Summit Working Group. A Summits of the Americas follow-up and implementation system was inaugurated in January 2010. The Sixth Summit was held in Cartagena, Colombia, in April 2012, on the theme 'Connecting the Americas: Partners for Prosperity'. The meeting mandated the OAS to review its strategies to counter the trafficking of illegal drugs. However, no unanimity was reached on the admission of Cuba to the next summit, scheduled to be convened in Panama, in 2015.

TOURISM AND CULTURE

A specialized unit for tourism was established in 1996 in order to strengthen and co-ordinate activities for the sustainable development of the tourism industry in the Americas. The unit supports regional and sub-regional conferences and workshops, as well as the Inter-American Travel Congress, which serves as a forum to consider and formulate region-wide tourism policies. The unit also undertakes research and analysis of the industry. In April 2006 the OAS, the Caribbean Tourism Organization and the Caribbean Hotel Association signed an agreement on the provision of training and assistance aimed at improving the capacity of the Caribbean tourism industry. In June 2011 a draft regional strategy for sustainable tourism development was formulated at a preparatory meeting for the 19th Inter-American Travel Congress, which was convened in San Salvador, El Salvador, in late September. The Travel Congress adopted, by consensus, the 'Declaration of San Salvador for Sustainable Tourism Development in the Americas', recognizing the contribution of the tourism sector towards national efforts to reduce poverty and inequality, to advance standards of living in host communities, and to promote sustainable economic development. The Congress approved the establishment of a Hemispheric Tourism Fund, which was to support poor communities in developing their tourism potential.

In 1998 the OAS approved an Inter-American Programme of Culture to support efforts being undertaken by member states and to promote co-operation in areas such as cultural diversity; protection of cultural heritage; training and dissemination of information; and the promotion of cultural tourism. The OAS also assists with the preparation of national and multilateral cultural projects, and co-operates with the private sector to protect and promote cultural assets and events in the region. In July 2002 the first Inter-American meeting of ministers of culture approved the establishment of an Inter-American Committee on Culture, within the framework of CIDI, to co-ordinate high-level dialogue and co-operation on cultural issues. In November 2006 regional ministers of culture met in Montréal, Canada, to address the contribution of the cultural sector towards promoting development and combating poverty. In 2009 the General Assembly declared 2011 as the Inter-American Year of Culture.

Finance

The OAS regular budget for 2012, approved by the General Assembly in October 2011, amounted to US $85.4m.

Publications

(in English and Spanish)

Américas (6 a year).

Annual Report.

Numerous cultural, legal and scientific reports and studies.

Specialized Organizations and Associated Agencies

Inter-American Children's Institute (Instituto Americano del Niño, la Niña y Adolescentes—IIN): Avda 8 de Octubre 2904, POB 16212, Montevideo 11600, Uruguay; tel. (2) 487-2150; fax (2) 487-3242; e-mail iin@oas.org; internet www.iin.oea.org; f. 1927; promotes the regional implementation of the Convention on the Rights of the Child, assists in the development of child-oriented public policies; promotes co-operation between states; and aims to develop awareness of problems affecting children and young people in the region. The Institute organizes workshops, seminars, courses, training programmes and conferences on issues relating to children, including, for example, the rights of children, children with disabilities, and the child welfare system. It also provides advisory services, statistical data and other relevant information to authorities and experts throughout the region. The 20th Pan American Child Congress was convened in Lima, Peru, in September 2009; Dir-Gen. MARÍA DE LOS DOLORES AGUILAR MARMOLEJO; publ. *iinfancia* (annually).

Inter-American Commission of Women (Comisión Interamericana de Mujeres—CIM): 1889 F St, NW, Suite 350 Washington, DC 20006, USA; tel. (202) 458-6084; fax (202) 458-6094; e-mail spcim@oas.org; internet www.oas.org/cim; f. 1928 as the first ever official intergovernmental agency created expressly to ensure recognition of the civil and political rights of women; the CIM is the principal forum for generating hemispheric policy to advance women's rights and gender equality; comprises 34 principal delegates; the Assembly of Delegates, convened every two years, is the highest authority of the Commission, establishing policies and a plan of action for each biennium and electing the seven-member Executive Committee; Pres. MARÍA DEL ROCÍO GARCÍA GAYTÁN (Mexico); Exec. Sec. CARMEN MORENO TOSCANO (Mexico).

Inter-American Indigenous Institute (Instituto Indigenista Interamericano—III): Avda de las Fuentes 106, Col. Jardines del Pedregal, Delegación Álvaro Obregón, 01900 México, DF, Mexico; tel. (55) 5595-8410; fax (55) 5595-4324; e-mail ininin@data.net.mx; internet www.indigenista.org; f. 1940; conducts research on the situation of the indigenous peoples of America; assists the exchange of information; promotes indigenous policies in member states aimed at the elimination of poverty and development within Indian communities, and to secure their position as ethnic groups within a democratic society; Hon. Dir Dr GUILLERMO ESPINOSA VELASCO (Mexico); publs *América Indígena* (quarterly), *Anuario Indigenista*.

Inter-American Institute for Co-operation on Agriculture (IICA) (Instituto Interamericano de Cooperación para la Agricultura): Apdo Postal 55–2200, San Isidro de Coronado, San José, Costa Rica; tel. (506) 216-0222; fax (506) 216-0233; e-mail iicahq@iica.ac.cr; internet www.iica.int; f. 1942 (as the Inter-American Institute of Agricultural Sciences, present name adopted 1980); supports the efforts of member states to improve agricultural development and rural well-being; encourages co-operation between regional organizations, and provides a forum for the exchange of experience; Dir-Gen. VÍCTOR M. VILLALOBOS (Mexico).

Justice Studies Center of the Americas (Centro de Estudios de Justicia de las Américas): Rodó 1950, Providencia, Santiago, Chile; tel. (2) 2742933; fax (2) 3415769; e-mail info@cejamericas.org; internet www.cejamericas.org; f. 1999; aims to support the modernization of justice systems in the region; Exec. Dir CRISTIÁN RIEGO RAMÍREZ (Chile).

Pan American Development Foundation (PADF) (Fundación Panamericana para el Desarrollo): 1889 F St, NW, Washington, DC 20006, USA; tel. (202) 458-3969; fax (202) 458-6316; e-mail padf-dc@padf.org; internet www.padf.org; f. 1962 to promote and facilitate economic and social development in Latin America and the Caribbean by means of innovative partnerships and integrated involvement of the public and private sectors; provides low-interest credit for small-scale entrepreneurs, vocational training, improved health care, agricultural development and reafforestation, and strengthening local non-governmental organizations; provides emergency disaster relief and reconstruction assistance; Exec. Dir JOHN A. SANBRAILO.

Pan American Health Organization (PAHO) (Organización Panamericana de la Salud): 525 23rd St, NW, Washington, DC 20037, USA; tel. (202) 974-3000; fax (202) 974-3663; e-mail webmaster@paho.org; internet www.paho.org; f. 1902; co-ordinates regional efforts to improve health; maintains close relations with national health organizations and serves as the Regional Office for the Americas of the World Health Organization; Dir Dr MIRTA ROSES PERIAGO (Argentina).

Pan American Institute of Geography and History (PAIGH) (Instituto Panamericano de Geografía e Historia–IPGH): Ex-Arzobispado 29, 11860 México, DF, Mexico; tel. (55) 5277-5888; fax (55) 5271-6172; e-mail secretariageneral@ipgh.org; internet www.ipgh.org.mx; f. 1928; co-ordinates and promotes the study of cartography, geophysics, geography and history; provides technical assistance, conducts training at research centres, distributes publications, and organizes technical meetings; Sec.-Gen. SANTIAGO BORRERO MUTIS (Colombia); Publs *Revista Cartográfica* (2 a year), *Revista Geográfica* (2 a year), *Revista de Historia de América* (2 a year), *Revista Geofísica* (2 a year), *Revista de Arqueología Americana* (annually), *Folklore Americano* (annually), *Boletín de Antropología Americana* (annually).

ORGANIZATION OF ARAB PETROLEUM EXPORTING COUNTRIES—OAPEC

Address: POB 20501, Safat 13066, Kuwait.

Telephone: 24959000; **fax:** 24959755; **e-mail:** oapec@oapecorg.org; **internet:** www.oapecorg.org.

OAPEC was established in 1968 to safeguard the interests of members and to determine ways and means for their co-operation in various forms of economic activity in the petroleum industry. In 2009 OAPEC member states contributed 28.4% of total world petroleum production and 13.2% of total global marketed natural gas. At end-2009 OAPEC member states accounted for an estimated 56.6% of total global oil reserves and 28.1% of total global reserves of natural gas.

MEMBERS

Algeria	Kuwait	Saudi Arabia
Bahrain	Libya	Syria
Egypt	Qatar	United Arab Emirates
Iraq		

Organization

(April 2012)

MINISTERIAL COUNCIL

The Council consists normally of the ministers of petroleum of the member states, and forms the supreme authority of the Organization, responsible for drawing up its general policy, directing its activities and laying down its governing rules. It meets twice yearly, and may hold extraordinary sessions. Chairmanship is on an annual rotating basis.

EXECUTIVE BUREAU

Assists the Council to direct the management of the Organization, approves staff regulations, reviews the budget, and refers it to the Council, considers matters relating to the Organization's agreements and activities and draws up the agenda for the Council. The Bureau comprises one senior official from each member state. Chairmanship is by rotation on an annual basis, following the same order as the Ministerial Council chairmanship. The Bureau convenes at least three times a year.

GENERAL SECRETARIAT

Secretary-General: ABBAS ALI NAQI (Kuwait).

Besides the Office of the Secretary-General, there are four departments: Finance and Administrative Affairs; Information and Library; Technical Affairs; and Economics. The last two form the Arab Centre for Energy Studies (which was established in 1983).

JUDICIAL TRIBUNAL

The Tribunal comprises seven judges from Arab countries. Its task is to settle differences in interpretation and application of the OAPEC Agreement, arising between members and also between OAPEC and its affiliates; disputes among member countries on petroleum activities falling within OAPEC's jurisdiction and not under the sovereignty of member countries; and disputes that the Ministerial Council decides to submit to the Tribunal.

President: Dr MOUSTAFA ABDUL HAYY AL-SAYED.

Activities

OAPEC co-ordinates different aspects of the Arab petroleum industry through the joint undertakings described below. It co-operates with the League of Arab States and other Arab organizations, and attempts to link petroleum research institutes in the Arab states. It organizes or participates in conferences and seminars, many of which are held jointly with non-Arab organizations in order to enhance Arab and international co-operation. OAPEC collaborates with the Arab Fund for Economic and Social Development (AFESD), the Arab Monetary Fund and the League of Arab States in compiling the annual *Joint Arab Economic Report*, which is issued by the Arab Monetary Fund.

OAPEC provides training in technical matters and in documentation and information. The General Secretariat also conducts technical and feasibility studies and carries out market reviews. It provides information through a library, databank and the publications listed below.

In association with AFESD, OAPEC organizes the Arab Energy Conference every four years. The conference is attended by OAPEC ministers of petroleum and energy, senior officials from other Arab states, and representatives of invited institutions and organizations concerned with energy issues. The ninth Arab Energy Conference, focusing on the theme 'Energy and Arab Co-operation', was held in Doha, Qatar, in May 2010. The 10th was scheduled to take place in early 2014, in Beirut, Lebanon. OAPEC, with other Arab organizations, participates in the Higher Co-ordination Committee for Higher Arab Action.

Finance

The combined General Secretariat and Judicial Tribunal budget for 2010 was 2.1m. Kuwaiti dinars.

Publications

Annual Statistical Report.

Energy Resources Monitor (quarterly, Arabic).

OAPEC Monthly Bulletin (Arabic and English editions).

Oil and Arab Co-operation (quarterly, Arabic).

Secretary-General's Annual Report (Arabic and English editions).

Papers, studies, conference proceedings.

OAPEC-Sponsored Ventures

Arab Maritime Petroleum Transport Company (AMPTC): POB 22525, Safat 13086, Kuwait; tel. 24959400; fax 24842996; e-mail amptc.kuwait@amptc.net; internet www.amptc.net; f. 1973 to undertake transport of crude petroleum, gas, refined products and petro-chemicals, and thus to increase Arab participation in the tanker transport industry; owns and operates a fleet of oil tankers and other carriers; also maintains an operations office in Giza, Egypt; auth. cap. US $200m.; Gen. Man. SULAYMAN AL-BASSAM.

Arab Petroleum Investments Corporation (APICORP): POB 9599, Dammam 31423, Saudi Arabia; tel. (3) 847-0444; fax (3) 847-0022; e-mail apicorp@apicorp-arabia.com; internet www.apicorp-arabia.com; f. 1975 to finance investments in petroleum and petrochemicals projects and related industries in the Arab world and in developing countries, with priority being given to Arab joint ventures; projects financed include gas liquefaction plants, petrochemicals, tankers, oil refineries, pipelines, exploration, detergents, fertilizers and process control instrumentation; auth. cap. US $1,200m.; paid-up cap. $550m.; shareholders: Kuwait, Saudi Arabia and United Arab Emirates (17% each), Libya (15%), Iraq and Qatar (10% each), Algeria (5%), Bahrain, Egypt and Syria (3% each); CEO and Gen. Man. AHMAD BIN HAMAD AL-NUAIMI.

Arab Detergent Chemicals Company (ARADET): POB 27064, el-Monsour, Baghdad, Iraq; tel. (1) 541-9893; fax (1) 543-0265; e-mail info@aradetco.com; internet www.aradetco.com; f. 1981; produces and markets linear alkyl benzene; construction of a sodium multiphosphate plant is under way; APICORP holds 32% of shares in the co; auth. cap. 72m. Iraqi dinars; subs. cap. 60m. Iraqi dinars.

Arab Petroleum Services Company (APSCO): POB 12925, Tripoli, Libya; tel. (21) 4445860; fax (21) 3335816; e-mail info@apsco.com.ly; internet apsco.com.ly; f. 1977 to provide petroleum services through the establishment of companies specializing in various activities, and to train specialized personnel; auth. cap. 100m. Libyan dinars; subs. cap. 15m. Libyan dinars.

Arab Drilling and Workover Company: POB 680, Suani Rd, km 3.5, Tripoli, Libya; tel. (21) 48004854; fax (21) 4804998; e-mail info@adwoc.com; internet www.adwoc.com; f. 1980; 40% owned by APSCO; auth. cap. 12m. Libyan dinars; Gen. Man. OMRAN ABUKRAA.

Arab Geophysical Exploration Services Company (AGESCO): POB 84224, Tripoli, Libya; tel. (21) 4804863; fax (21) 4803199; e-mail agesco@agesco-ly.com; internet agesco-ly.com; f. 1985; 40% owned by APSCO; auth. cap. 12m. Libyan dinars; subs. cap. 4m. Libyan dinars; Gen. Man. AHMED ESSED.

Arab Well Logging Company (AWLCO): POB 6225, Baghdad, Iraq; tel. (1) 541-8259; f. 1983 to provide well-logging services and data interpretation; wholly owned subsidiary of APSCO; auth. cap. 7m. Iraqi dinars.

Arab Petroleum Training Institute (APTI): POB 6037, Al-Tajeyat, Baghdad, Iraq; tel. (1) 523-4100; fax (1) 521-0526; f. 1978 to provide instruction in many technical and managerial aspects of the oil industry.

Arab Shipbuilding and Repair Yard Company (ASRY): POB 50110, Hidd, Bahrain; tel. 17671111; fax 17670236; e-mail asryco@batelco.com.bh; internet www.asry.net; f. 1974 to undertake repairs and servicing of vessels; operates a 500,000-dwt dry dock in Bahrain; two floating docks operational since 1992, and two slipways became operational in 2008; has recently diversified its activities, e.g. into building specialized service boats and upgrading oil rigs; cap. (auth. and subsidized) US $170m.; CEO CHRIS POTTER (United Kingdom); Gen. Man. RALF ERIKSSON (Sweden).

ORGANIZATION OF THE BLACK SEA ECONOMIC COOPERATION—BSEC

Address: Sakıp Sabancı Cad., Müşir Fuad Paşa Yalısı, Eski Tersane 34460 İstinye-İstanbul, Turkey.

Telephone: (212) 229-63-30; **fax:** (212) 229-63-36; **e-mail:** info@bsec-organization.org; **internet:** www.bsec-organization.org.

The Black Sea Economic Cooperation (BSEC) was established in 1992 to strengthen regional co-operation, particularly in the field of economic development. In June 1998, at a summit meeting held in Yalta, Ukraine, participating countries signed the BSEC Charter, thereby officially elevating BSEC to regional organization status. The Charter entered into force on 1 May 1999, at which time BSEC formally became the Organization of the Black Sea Economic Co-operation, retaining the same acronym.

MEMBERS

Albania	Georgia	Russia
Armenia	Greece	Serbia
Azerbaijan	Moldova	Turkey
Bulgaria	Romania	Ukraine

Note: Observer status has been granted to Austria, Belarus, Croatia, the Czech Republic, Egypt, France, Germany, Israel, Italy, Poland, Slovakia, Tunisia and the USA. The Black Sea Commission, the BSEC Business Council, the Energy Charter Conference, the European Commission, and the International Black Sea Club also have observer status. Sectoral Dialogue Partnership status has been granted to: Hungary, Iran, Japan, Jordan, Montenegro, Slovenia, the United Kingdom, and seven intergovernmental organizations.

Organization

(April 2012)

PRESIDENTIAL SUMMIT

The Presidential Summit, comprising heads of state or government of member states, represents the highest authority of the body.

COUNCIL

The Council of Ministers of Foreign Affairs is BSEC's principal decision-making organ. Ministers meet twice a year to review progress and to define new objectives. Chairmanship of the Council rotates among members every six months (1 January–1 July 2012: Serbia); the Chairman-in-Office co-ordinates the activities undertaken by BSEC. The Council is supported by a Committee of Senior Officials. Upon request of the Chairman-in-Office a Troika, comprising the current, most recent and next Chairman-in-Office, or their representatives, is convened to consider BSEC's ongoing and planned activities.

PERMANENT INTERNATIONAL SECRETARIAT

The Secretariat's tasks are, primarily, of an administrative and technical nature, and include the maintenance of archives, and the preparation and distribution of documentation. Much of the organization's activities are undertaken by 15 working groups, each headed by an Executive Manager, and by various ad hoc groups and meetings of experts.

Secretary-General: LEONIDAS CHRYSANTHOPOULOS (Greece).

Activities

In June 1992, at a summit meeting held in Istanbul, heads of state and of government signed the summit declaration on BSEC, and adopted the Bosphorus statement, which established a regional structure for economic co-operation. The grouping attained regional organization status in May 1999 (see above). The Organization's main areas of co-operation include transport; communications; trade and economic development; banking and finance; energy; tourism; agriculture and agro-industry; health care and pharmaceuticals; environmental protection; science and technology; the exchange of statistical data and economic information; collaboration between customs authorities; and combating organized crime, drugs-trafficking, trade in illegal weapons and radioactive materials, and terrorism. In order to promote regional co-operation, the Organization also aims to strengthen the business environment by providing support for small and medium-sized enterprises; facilitating closer contacts between businesses in member countries; progressively eliminating obstacles to the expansion of trade; creating appropriate conditions for investment and industrial co-operation, in particular through the avoidance of double taxation and the promotion and protection of investments; encouraging the dissemination of information concerning international tenders organized by member states; and promoting economic co-operation in free trade zones. A Working Group on Culture was established in November 2006 to promote and protect the cultural identity of the region.

A BSEC Business Council was established in Istanbul in December 1992 by the business communities of member states. It has observer status at the BSEC, and aims to identify private and public investment projects, maintain business contacts and develop programmes in various sectors. A Black Sea Trade and Development Bank has been established, in Thessaloníki, Greece, as the Organization's main funding institution, to finance and implement joint regional projects. It began operations in July 1999 (see below). A BSEC Coordination Center for the Exchange of Statistical Data and Economic Information is located in Ankara, Turkey. An International Centre for Black Sea Studies (ICBSS) was established in Athens, Greece, in March 1998, in order to undertake research concerning the BSEC, in the fields of economics, industry and technology.

In recent years BSEC has undergone a process of reform aimed at developing a more project-based orientation. In April 2001 the Council adopted the so-called BSEC Economic Agenda for the Future Towards a More Consolidated, Effective and Viable BSEC Partnership, which provided a roadmap for charting the implementation of the Organization's goals. Meeting in June 2011 the Council established an Ad Hoc Group of Experts, with a mandate to revise and update the BSEC Economic Agenda for the Future; the document was to constitute a basis for discussions during the BSEC 20th anniversary summit, scheduled to be held in 2012. In 2002 a Project Development Fund (PDF) was established and a regional programme of governance and institutional renewal was launched. A project aimed at developing renewable energy sources, and a project entitled 'Introducing climate change in the environmental strategy for the protection of the Black Sea' (ICEBS) were approved for PDF funding in 2010. Under the new orientation the roles of BSEC's Committee of Senior Officials and network of country co-ordinators were to be enhanced. In April 2008 the BSEC Council inaugurated a new €2m. BSEC Hellenic Development Fund to support regional co-operation; guidelines for the operation of the Fund were adopted at a meeting of the Council in late October. The Council also adopted the modalities for BSEC fast-track co-operation, aimed at enabling sub-groups of member states to proceed with policies that other member states were unwilling or unable to pursue. The October 2008 meeting of the Council adopted new guidelines on improving the efficiency of the grouping.

BSEC aims to foster relations with other international and regional organizations, and has been granted observer status at the UN General Assembly. BSEC supports the Stability Pact for South-Eastern Europe, initiated in June 1999 as a collaborative plan of action by the European Union (EU), the Group of Seven industrialized nations and Russia (the G8), regional governments and other organizations concerned with the stability of the region. In 1999 BSEC agreed upon a platform of co-operation for future structured relations with the European Union (EU). The main areas in which BSEC determined to develop co-operation with the EU were transport, energy and telecommunications infrastructure; trade and the promotion of foreign direct investment; sustainable development and environmental protection, including nuclear safety; science and technology; and combating terrorism and organized crime. The Declaration issued by BSEC's decennial anniversary summit, held in Istanbul in June 2002, urged that collaboration with the EU should be enhanced. In April 2005 representatives of BSEC and the EU met in Brussels, Belgium, to address possibilities for such co-operation, focusing in particular on the EU's policy in the Black Sea region and on the development of regional transport and energy networks (see Alexandroupolis Declaration, below). In June 2007 BSEC heads of state confirmed their commitment to an enhanced relationship with the EU, based on a communication of the European Commission, published in April, entitled 'Black Sea Synergy—a New Regional Cooperation Initiative'. In February 2008 a special meeting of the BSEC Council adopted a Declaration on a BSEC-EU Enhanced Relationship. Consideration of the prospects of enhanced interaction between the two organizations was pursued at a round-table discussion hosted by the European Policy Centre (and jointly organized with the BSEC International Secretariat and the International Centre for Black Sea Studies) in April 2009. A BSEC-EU Black Sea Regional Strategy was prepared, promoting BSEC-EU interaction during 2010–13. In March 2010 a Black Sea Environmental Partnership was launched by the EU, to support its efforts, and those of regional partners, including BSEC, to find co-operative approaches towards addressing environmental challenges in areas such as biodiversity conservation, integrated coastal zone and river basin management, and sources of pollution, and towards promoting environmental integration, monitoring and research.

BSEC has supported implementation of the Bucharest Convention on the Protection of the Black Sea Against Pollution, adopted by Bulgaria, Georgia, Romania, Russia, Turkey and Ukraine in April 1992. In October 1996 those countries adopted the Strategic Action Plan for the Rehabilitation and Protection of the Black Sea (BSSAP), to be implemented by the Commission of the Bucharest Convention. In March 2001 the ministers of transport of BSEC member states adopted a Transport Action Plan, which envisaged reducing the disparities in regional transport systems and integrating the BSEC regional transport infrastructure with wider international networks and projects. In November 2006 BSEC signed a Memorandum of Understanding (MOU) with the International Road Federation. In April 2007 BSEC governments signed an agreement for the co-ordinated development of a 7,100 km-long Black Sea Ring Highway (BSRH). An MOU relating to the development of 'Motorways of the Sea' was also signed. Both accords entered into effect in late 2008. In March 2005 ministers of BSEC member states responsible for energy adopted the Alexandroupolis Declaration, approving a common framework for future collaboration on the creation of a regional energy market, and urging the liberalization of electricity and natural gas markets in accordance with EU directives as a basis for this.

In April 2009 a BSEC Working Group on Banking and Finance convened in Yerevan, Armenia, to consider how the global financial and economic crisis had affected banking and finance sectors in the region and to review national stabilization measures and other efforts being undertaken to contain the crisis. The meeting preceded a regular meeting of the Council of Ministers of Foreign Affairs which also discussed the implications for the region of the instability of the world's financial markets and the economic downturn.

Finance

BSEC is financed by annual contributions from member states on the following scale: Greece, Russia, Turkey and Ukraine each contribute 15% of the budget; Bulgaria, Romania and Serbia contribute 7.5%; the remaining members each contribute 3.5%.

Publication

Black Sea News (quarterly).

Related Bodies

Parliamentary Assembly of the Black Sea: 1 Hareket Kösku, Dolmabahçe Sarayi, Besiktas, 80680 İstanbul, Turkey; tel. (212) 227-6070; fax (212) 227-6080; e-mail pabsec@pabsec.org; internet www.pabsec.org; f. 1993; the Assembly, consisting of the representatives of the national parliaments of member states, aims to provide a legal basis for the implementation of decisions within the BSEC framework; comprises three committees concerning economic, commercial, technological and environmental affairs; legal and political affairs; and cultural, educational and social affairs; the presidency rotates every six months; Sec.-Gen. KYRYLO TRETIAK (Ukraine).

Black Sea Trade and Development Bank: 1 Komninon str., 54624 Thessaloníki, Greece; tel. (2310) 290400; fax (2310) 221796; e-mail info@bstdb.org; internet www.bstdb.org; f. 1999; the Bank supports economic development and regional co-operation by providing trade and project financing, guarantees, and equity for development projects supporting both public and private enterprises in its member countries, in sectors including energy, infrastructure, finance, manufacturing, transport, and telecommunications; by 31 Dec. 2011 the Bank had approved 265 approved operations with funding exceeding €2,000m; auth. cap. SDR 3,000m. (March 2012); Pres. ANDREY KONDAKOV (Russia); Sec.-Gen. ORSALIA KALANTZOPOULOS (Greece).

BSEC Business Council: Müsir Fuad Pasa Yalisi, Eski Tersane, 80860 Istinye, İstanbul, Turkey; tel. (212) 229-1144; fax (212) 229-0332; e-mail info@bsec-business.org; internet www.bsec-business.org; f. 1992; aims to secure greater economic integration and to promote investment in the region; Sec.-Gen. EFTYCHIA BACOPOULOU.

International Centre for Black Sea Studies: 4 Xenophontos Str., 10557 Athens, Greece; tel. (210) 3242321; fax (210) 3242244; e-mail icbss@icbss.org; internet www.icbss.org; f. 1998; aims to foster co-operation among BSEC member states and with international partners through applied research and advocacy; hosts the International Black Sea Symposium, an Annual Lecture and other events; Dir-Gen. Dr ZEFI DIMADAMA (Greece); publs *Xenophon Paper* series, Policy Briefs, *Black Sea Monitor* (quarterly).

ORGANIZATION OF ISLAMIC COOPERATION—OIC

Address: Medina Rd, Sary St, POB 178, Jeddah 21411, Saudi Arabia.

Telephone: (2) 690-0001; **fax:** (2) 275-1953; **e-mail:** info@oic-oci.org; **internet:** www.oic-oci.org.

The Organization was formally established, as the Organization of the Islamic Conference, at the first conference of Muslim heads of state convened in Rabat, Morocco, in September 1969; the first conference of Muslim foreign ministers, held in Jeddah in March 1970, established the General Secretariat; the latter became operational in May 1971. In June 2011 the 38th ministerial conference agreed to change the name of the Organization, with immediate effect, to the Organization of Islamic Cooperation (abbreviated, as hitherto, to OIC).

MEMBERS

Afghanistan	Indonesia	Qatar
Albania	Iran	Saudi Arabia
Algeria	Iraq	Senegal
Azerbaijan	Jordan	Sierra Leone
Bahrain	Kazakhstan	Somalia
Bangladesh	Kuwait	Sudan
Benin	Kyrgyzstan	Suriname
Brunei	Lebanon	Syria
Burkina Faso	Libya	Tajikistan
Cameroon	Malaysia	Togo
Chad	Maldives	Tunisia
Comoros	Mali	Turkey
Côte d'Ivoire	Mauritania	Turkmenistan
Djibouti	Morocco	Uganda
Egypt	Mozambique	United Arab Emirates
Gabon	Niger	Uzbekistan
The Gambia	Nigeria	Yemen
Guinea	Oman	
Guinea-Bissau	Pakistan	
Guyana	Palestine	

Note: Observer status has been granted to Bosnia and Herzegovina, the Central African Republic, Russia, Thailand, the Muslim community of the 'Turkish Republic of Northern Cyprus', the Moro National Liberation Front (MNLF) of the southern Philippines, the UN, the African Union, the Non-Aligned Movement, the League of Arab States, the Economic Cooperation Organization, the Union of the Arab Maghreb and the Cooperation Council for the Arab States of the Gulf. The revised OIC Charter, endorsed in March 2008, made future applications for OIC membership and observer status conditional upon Muslim demographic majority and membership of the UN.

Organization

(April 2012)

SUMMIT CONFERENCES

The supreme body of the Organization is the Conference of Heads of State ('Islamic summit'), which met in 1969 in Rabat, Morocco, in 1974 in Lahore, Pakistan, and in January 1981 in Mecca, Saudi Arabia, when it was decided that ordinary summit conferences would normally be held every three years in future. An extraordinary summit conference was convened in Doha, Qatar, in March 2003, to consider the situation in Iraq. A further extraordinary conference, held in December 2005, in Mecca, determined to restructure the OIC. The 11th ordinary Islamic summit was convened in Dakar, Senegal, in March 2008. The summit conference troika comprises member countries equally representing the OIC's African, Arab and Asian membership.

CONFERENCE OF MINISTERS OF FOREIGN AFFAIRS

Conferences take place annually, to consider the means of implementing the general policy of the Organization, although they may also be convened for extraordinary sessions. The ministerial conference troika comprises member countries equally representing the OIC's African, Arab and Asian membership.

SECRETARIAT

The executive organ of the organization, headed by a Secretary-General (who is elected by the Conference of Ministers of Foreign Affairs for a five-year term, renewable only once) and four Assistant Secretaries-General (similarly appointed).

Secretary-General: Prof. Dr EKMELEDDIN IHSANOGLU (Turkey).

At the summit conference in January 1981 it was decided that an International Islamic Court of Justice should be established to adjudicate in disputes between Muslim countries. Experts met in January 1983 to draw up a constitution for the court; however, by 2012 it was not yet in operation.

EXECUTIVE COMMITTEE

The third extraordinary conference of the OIC, convened in Mecca, Saudi Arabia, in December 2005, mandated the establishment of the Executive Committee, comprising the summit conference and ministerial conference troikas, the OIC host country, and the OIC Secretariat, as a mechanism for following up resolutions of the Conference.

STANDING COMMITTEES

Al-Quds Committee: f. 1975 to implement the resolutions of the Islamic Conference on the status of Jerusalem (Al-Quds); it meets at the level of foreign ministers; maintains the Al-Quds Fund; Chair. King MUHAMMAD VI OF MOROCCO.

Standing Committee for Economic and Commercial Co-operation (COMCEC): f. 1981; Chair. ABDULLAH GÜL (Pres. of Turkey).

Standing Committee for Information and Cultural Affairs (COMIAC): f. 1981; Chair. MACKY SALL (Pres. of Senegal).

Standing Committee for Scientific and Technological Co-operation (COMSTECH): f. 1981; Chair. ASIF ALI ZARDARI (Pres. of Pakistan).

Other committees comprise the Islamic Peace Committee, the Permanent Finance Committee, the Committee of Islamic Solidarity with the Peoples of the Sahel, the Eight-Member Committee on the Situation of Muslims in the Philippines, the Six-Member Committee on Palestine, the Committee on UN reform, and the ad hoc Committee on Afghanistan. In addition, there is an Islamic Commission for Economic, Cultural and Social Affairs, and there are OIC contact groups on Bosnia and Herzegovina, Iraq, Kosovo, Jammu and Kashmir, Sierra Leone, and Somalia. A Commission of Eminent Persons was inaugurated in 2005.

Activities

The Organization's aims, as proclaimed in the Charter (adopted in 1972, with revisions endorsed in 1990 and 2008), are:

(i) To promote Islamic solidarity among member states;

(ii) To consolidate co-operation among member states in the economic, social, cultural, scientific and other vital fields, and to arrange consultations among member states belonging to international organizations;

(iii) To endeavour to eliminate racial segregation and discrimination and to eradicate colonialism in all its forms;

(iv) To take necessary measures to support international peace and security founded on justice;

(v) To co-ordinate all efforts for the safeguard of the Holy Places and support of the struggle of the people of Palestine, and help them to regain their rights and liberate their land;

(vi) To strengthen the struggle of all Muslim people with a view to safeguarding their dignity, independence and national rights;

(vii) To create a suitable atmosphere for the promotion of co-operation and understanding among member states and other countries.

The first summit conference of Islamic leaders (representing 24 states) took place in 1969 following the burning of the al-Aqsa Mosque in Jerusalem. At this conference it was decided that Islamic governments should 'consult together with a view to promoting close co-operation and mutual assistance in the economic, scientific, cultural and spiritual fields, inspired by the immortal teachings of Islam'. Thereafter the foreign ministers of the countries concerned met annually, and adopted the Charter of the Organization of the Islamic Conference in 1972.

At the second Islamic summit conference (Lahore, Pakistan, 1974), the Islamic Solidarity Fund was established, together with a committee of representatives that later evolved into the Islamic Commission for Economic, Cultural and Social Affairs. Subsequently, numerous other subsidiary bodies have been set up (see below).

ECONOMIC CO-OPERATION

A general agreement on economic, technical and commercial co-operation came into force in 1981, providing for the establishment of joint investment projects and trade co-ordination. This was followed by an agreement on promotion, protection and guarantee of investments among member states. A plan of action to strengthen economic co-operation was adopted at the third Islamic summit conference in 1981, aiming to promote collective self-reliance and the development of joint ventures in all sectors. The fifth summit conference, held in 1987, approved proposals for joint development of modern technology, and for improving scientific and technical skills in the less developed Islamic countries. In 1994 the 1981 plan of action was revised to place greater emphasis on private sector participation in its implementation. In October 2003 a meeting of COMCEC endorsed measures aimed at accelerating the hitherto slow implementation of the plan of action. A new 10-year plan of action for fostering member states' development and strengthening economic and trade co-operation was launched in December 2005.

In 1991 22 OIC member states signed a Framework Agreement on a Trade Preferential System among the OIC Member States (TPS-OIC); this entered into force in 2003, following the requisite ratification by more than 10 member states, and was envisaged as representing the first step towards the eventual establishment of an Islamic common market. A Trade Negotiating Committee (TNC) was established following the entry into force of the Framework Agreement. The first round of trade negotiations on the establishment of the TPS-OIC, concerning finalizing tariff-reduction modalities and an implementation schedule for the Agreement, was held during April 2004–April 2005, and resulted in the conclusion of a Protocol on the Preferential Tariff Scheme for TPS-OIC (PRETAS). In November 2006, at the launch of the second round of negotiations, ministers adopted a roadmap towards establishing the TPS-OIC; the second round of negotiations ended in September 2007 with the adoption of rules of origin for the TPS-OIC. PRETAS entered into force in February 2010. By April 2012 the Framework Agreement had been ratified by 28 OIC member states, and PRETAS had 15 ratifications.

In March 2008 the summit adopted a five-year Special Programme for the Development of Africa, covering the period 2008–12, which aimed to promote the economic development of OIC African member states and to support these countries in achieving the UN Millennium Development Goals.

The first OIC Anti-Corruption and Enhancing Integrity Forum was convened in August 2006 in Kuala Lumpur, Malaysia. The 13th Trade Fair of the OIC member states was staged in Sharjah, Saudi Arabia, in April 2011. The second OIC Tourism Fair was to take place in Cairo, Egypt, in December 2012. The seventh World Islamic Economic Forum was convened in Astana, Kazakhstan, in June 2011. In November 2009 a COMCEC Business Forum was held, in Istanbul, Turkey. An International Islamic Business and Finance Summit has been organized annually since 2009, in Kazan, Russia, by the OIC and the Russian Government; 'KAZANSUMMIT 2012' was to be convened in May 2012.

CULTURAL AND TECHNICAL CO-OPERATION

The Organization supports education in Muslim communities throughout the world, and was instrumental in the establishment of Islamic universities in Niger and Uganda. It organizes seminars on various aspects of Islam, and encourages dialogue with the other monotheistic religions. Support is given to publications on Islam both in Muslim and Western countries. In June 1999 an OIC Parliamentary Union was inaugurated; its founding conference was convened in Tehran, Iran. An inaugural Conference of Muslim Women Parliamentarians was convened in January 2012, in Palembang, Indonesia.

The OIC organizes meetings at ministerial level to consider aspects of information policy and new technologies. An OIC Digital Solidarity Fund was inaugurated in May 2005. Participation by OIC member states in the Fund was promoted at the 11th OIC summit meeting in March 2008, and the meeting also requested each member state to establish a board to monitor national implementation of the Tunis Declaration on the Information Society, adopted by the November 2005 second phase of the World Summit on the Information Society. The first OIC Conference on Women was held in November 2006, on the theme 'The role of women in the development of OIC member states'. In January 2009 the OIC and the League of Arab States signed an agreement providing for the strengthening of co-operation and co-ordination in the areas of politics, media, the economy, and in the social and scientific spheres. In August 2011 the OIC organized a Decorative Arts and Calligraphy Exhibition, at its headquarters in Jeddah.

HUMANITARIAN ASSISTANCE

Assistance is given to Muslim communities affected by violent conflict and natural disasters, in co-operation with UN organizations, particularly UNCHR. The OIC has established trust funds to assist vulnerable people in Afghanistan, Bosnia and Herzegovina, and Sierra Leone. Humanitarian assistance provided by OIC member states has included aid to the Muslim population affected by the conflict in Chechnya; to victims of conflict in Darfur, southern Sudan; to Indonesia following the tsunami disaster in December 2004; and to Pakistan following the major earthquake there in October 2005. In October 2009 an OIC humanitarian mission was sent to support survivors of the earthquake that struck Padang, Indonesia, at the end of September. In mid-August 2010, at the request of the Pakistan Government, the OIC organized an emergency meeting to review the ongoing humanitarian relief operation supporting survivors of the severe floods that had devastated northern and central areas of Pakistan during that month (seriously adversely affecting at least 15m. people, of whom 8m. were believed to be at high risk of contracting waterborne diseases, and including 2m. people who had been displaced from their homes). By the end of August OIC member countries had pledged US $1,000m. in support of the flood-affected communities. It was announced at that time that an OIC Emergency Fund for Natural Disasters would be established, to assist survivors of any natural disaster occurring in future in a Muslim country. The countries of the Sahel region (Burkina Faso, Cape Verde, Chad, The Gambia, Guinea, Guinea-Bissau, Mali, Mauritania, Niger and Senegal) receive particular attention as victims of drought. In mid-March 2012 a joint OIC-UN team of technical experts was dispatched to Syria to assess the humanitarian impact of the ongoing unrest there and to prepare an evaluation of the level of humanitarian aid required.

In March 2008 the OIC launched a humanitarian support operation for Palestinians in Gaza; an initial 'assistance caravan' transported medical supplies and equipment to the area. An expanded extraordinary meeting of the Executive Committee, convened, at the level of ministers of foreign affairs, in January 2009 to address the ongoing intensive bombardment of the Gaza Strip that was initiated by Israeli forces in late December 2008 with the stated aim of ending rocket attacks launched by Hamas and other militant groups on Israeli targets, requested the OIC Secretariat to co-ordinate with member states' civil society organizations to provide urgent humanitarian relief to the Palestinian people. OIC convoys of humanitarian aid, including medical supplies, food and clothing, were subsequently dispatched to Gaza.

In August 2011 OIC governments pledged US $350m. in aid to combat famine in Somalia, where some 3.7m. people were reported at that time to be at risk of starvation. The OIC Secretary-General urged donor nations to help to rehabilitate Somalia's infrastructure and agricultural production with a view to improving the long-term prospects for food security. In early October 2011 the OIC convened a conference on the theme 'Water for Life in Somalia', with participation by 32 non-governmental humanitarian relief agencies; the conference adopted a declaration pledging to drill 682 boreholes in 11 provinces of Somalia, with a view to alleviating the acute shortage of water that had contributed to the famine.

The first conference of Islamic humanitarian organizations was convened by the OIC in March 2008, and a second conference, bringing together 32 organizations, took place in April 2009. The third conference of Islamic humanitarian organizations, held in March 2010, established a working group to draft a plan aimed at strengthening co-operation between the OIC and other humanitarian organizations active in Afghanistan, Gaza, Darfur, Iraq, Niger, Somalia, and Sudan; and also approved the formation of a joint commission which was to study the structure and mechanism of co-operation and co-ordination between humanitarian organizations. The fourth conference was convened in June 2011, with the theme 'Civil Society Organizations in the Muslim World: Responsibilities and Roles'.

POLITICAL CO-OPERATION

In April 2009 an intergovernmental group of experts met to discuss the formation of an OIC Independent Human Rights Commission. In June 2011 OIC foreign ministers adopted the Astana Declaration on Peace, Co-operation and Development, in which they recognized emerging challenges presented by unfolding significant political developments in the Middle East and North Africa (the so-called 'Arab Spring') and appealed for engagement in constructive dialogue towards peaceful solutions. The Declaration expressed grave concern at the then ongoing conflict in Libya, and at the humanitarian consequences thereof. The foreign ministers also adopted the OIC Action Plan for Cooperation with Central Asia, which aimed to establish centres of excellence with a view to encouraging scientific innovation; and to promote job training and public-private partnership; to promote a reduction in the incidence of HIV/AIDS, polio, malaria and TB in the region; to build cultural understanding; and to combat trafficking in human beings and in illegal drugs. The OIC gives support to member countries in regaining or maintaining political stability. During 2011, for example, it participated in International Contact Groups on Afghanistan, Libya, and Somalia, co-operating with the UN and other international organizations and national governments in supporting efforts to restore constitutional rule in those countries. A delegation of the OIC was dispatched to observe legislative elections in Tunisia, in October 2011 and the OIC also monitored legislative elections held in Morocco, in November. In December the OIC Executive Committee convened a ministerial open-ended meeting on the ongoing unrest in Syria.

Israel/Palestine: Since its inception the OIC has called for the vacation of Arab territories by Israel, recognition of the rights of Palestinians and of the Palestine Liberation Organization (PLO) as their sole legitimate representative, and the restoration of Jerusalem to Arab rule. The 1981 summit conference called for a *jihad* (holy war—though not necessarily in a military sense) 'for the liberation of Jerusalem and the occupied territories'; this was to include an Islamic economic boycott of Israel. In 1982 Islamic ministers of foreign affairs decided to establish Islamic offices for boycotting Israel and for military co-operation with the PLO. In view of the significant deterioration in relations between Israel and the Palestinian (National) Authority (PA) during late 2000, in December of that year the ninth summit conference of heads of state and of government, held in Doha, Qatar, issued a Declaration pledging solidarity with the Palestinian cause and accusing the Israeli authorities of implementing large-scale systematic violations of human rights against Palestinians. In June 2002 OIC ministers of foreign affairs endorsed the peace plan for the region that had been adopted by the summit meeting of the League of Arab States in March. In early January 2009 an expanded extraordinary meeting of the Executive Committee, at the level of ministers of foreign affairs, convened to address the ongoing intensive bombardment of the Gaza Strip that was initiated by Israeli forces in late December 2008 with the stated aim of ending rocket attacks launched by Hamas and other militant groups on Israeli targets. The meeting strongly condemned the Israeli attacks and ensuing destruction and loss of civilian life, and requested the OIC Secretariat to co-ordinate with member states' civil society organizations to provide urgent humanitarian relief to the Palestinian people. In March 2009, while visiting the affected area, the OIC Secretary-General urged the reconciliation of the different Palestinian political factions. In June 2010 an expanded extraordinary ministerial meeting of the Executive Committee condemned the attack by Israeli security forces, at the end of May, against a flotilla of vessels carrying humanitarian aid to Gaza, which had resulted in nine civilian deaths and caused injuries to at least 40 people. The OIC rejected a UN-commissioned report on the flotilla incident, released in September 2011, which—while concluding that the Israeli army had used 'excessive and unreasonable' force—also found the Israeli naval blockade of Gaza to have been imposed as a 'legitimate security measure' to prevent weapons from reaching Gaza by sea, and found that the flotilla had acted recklessly in attempting to breach the naval blockade. The OIC Secretary-General supported efforts to bring the issue of the blockade of Gaza before competent international legal authorities. In late September the OIC Secretary-General condemned a decision by Israel to build 1,100 new housing units in occupied East Jerusalem. During that month the OIC expressed support for the formal request by the Executive President of the Palestinian Authority for Palestine's admission to the UN, and recognition of its independent statehood.

Iraq: In August 1990 a majority of OIC member states' ministers of foreign affairs condemned Iraq's recent invasion of Kuwait, and demanded the withdrawal of Iraqi forces. The sixth summit conference, held in Senegal in December 1991, reflected the divisions in the Arab world that resulted from Iraq's invasion of Kuwait and the ensuing war. Twelve heads of state did not attend, reportedly to register protest at the presence of Jordan and the PLO at the conference, both of which had given support to Iraq. In December 1994 OIC heads of state supported the decision by Iraq to recognize Kuwait. In December 1998 the OIC appealed for a diplomatic solution to the tensions arising from Iraq's withdrawal of co-operation with UN weapons inspectors, and criticized subsequent military airstrikes, led by the USA, as having been conducted without renewed UN authority. An extraordinary summit conference of Islamic leaders convened in Doha, in early March 2003, to consider the ongoing Iraq crisis, welcomed the Saddam Hussain regime's acceptance of UN Security Council Resolution 1441 and consequent co-operation with UN weapons inspectors, and emphatically rejected military action against Iraq or threats to the security of any other Islamic state. The conference also urged progress towards the elimination of all weapons of mass destruction in the Middle East, including those held by Israel. In mid-May 2004 the OIC Secretary-General urged combat forces in Iraq to respect the inviolability of that country's holy places. In December 2005 he appealed to the people of Iraq to participate peacefully in the legislative elections that took place later in that month. In October 2006 a meeting of Iraqi Islamic scholars from all denominations issued a declaration on the Iraqi situation, in which they urged unity between different Islamic factions in that country. During 2008–11 the OIC Secretary-General repeatedly appealed for an end to sectarian strife in Iraq, and in October 2008 he condemned the persecution of Christians in northern Iraq.

Afghanistan: In October 2001 OIC ministers of foreign affairs established a fund to assist Afghan civilians, following US-led military attacks on targets in Afghanistan. In mid-2010 the OIC determined to appoint a permanent representative for Afghanistan, to be based in an OIC office in Kabul, the Afghan capital. The OIC Kabul office was inaugurated in January 2011. In March the OIC Secretary-General, addressing the International Contact Group on Afghanistan, stressed OIC support for the High Peace Council, established in Afghanistan in 2010 as a platform for dialogue between the Afghan administration and the Taliban, and stated the willingness of the Organization to contribute to peace in that country. In December 2011, attending the International Conference on Afghanistan, convened in Bonn, Germany, the OIC Secretary-General emphasized that the Organization would continue to support Afghanistan beyond 2014, when NATO forces were scheduled to leave the country.

Combating Terrorism: In December 1994 OIC heads of state adopted a Code of Conduct for Combating International Terrorism, in an attempt to control Muslim extremist groups. The code commits states to ensuring that militant groups do not use their territory for planning or executing terrorist activity against other states, in addition to states refraining from direct support or participation in acts of terrorism. An OIC Convention on Combating International Terrorism was adopted in 1998. In September 2001 the OIC Secretary-General strongly condemned major terrorist attacks perpetrated against targets in the USA. Soon afterwards the US authorities rejected a proposal by the Taliban regime that an OIC observer mission be deployed to monitor the activities of the Saudi Arabian-born exiled militant Islamist fundamentalist leader Osama bin Laden, who was accused by the US Government of having co-ordinated the attacks from alleged terrorist bases in the Taliban-administered area of Afghanistan. An extraordinary meeting of OIC ministers of foreign affairs, convened in early October, in Doha, Qatar, to consider the implications of the terrorist atrocities, condemned the attacks and declared its support for combating all manifestations of terrorism within the framework of a proposed collective initiative co-ordinated under the auspices of the UN. The meeting, which did not pronounce directly on the recently-initiated US-led military retaliation against targets in Afghanistan, urged that no Arab or Muslim state should be targeted under the pretext of eliminating terrorism. In February 2002 the Secretary-General expressed concern at statements of the US administration describing Iran and Iraq (as well as the Democratic People's Republic of Korea) as belonging to an 'axis of evil' involved in international terrorism and the development of weapons of mass destruction. In April OIC ministers of foreign affairs convened an extraordinary session on terrorism, in Kuala Lumpur, Malaysia. The meeting issued the Kuala Lumpur Declaration, which reiterated member states' collective resolve to combat terrorism, recalling the organization's 1994 code of conduct and 1998 convention to this effect; condemned attempts to associate terrorist activities with Islam or any other particular creed, civilization or nationality, and rejected attempts to associate Islamic states or the Palestinian struggle with terrorism; rejected the implementation of international action against any Muslim state on the pretext of combating terrorism; urged the organization of a global conference on international terrorism; and urged an examination of the root causes of international terrorism. The meeting adopted a plan of action on addressing the issues raised in the declaration. Its implementation was to be co-ordinated by a 13-member committee on international terrorism. Member states were encouraged to sign and ratify the Convention on Combating International Terrorism in order to accelerate its implementation. In June 2002 ministers of foreign affairs issued a declaration reiterating the OIC call for an international conference to be convened, under UN auspices, in order clearly to define terrorism and to agree on the international procedures and mechanisms for combating terrorism through the UN. In May 2003 the 30th session of the Conference of Ministers of Foreign Affairs, entitled 'Unity and Dignity', issued the Tehran Declaration, in which it resolved to combat terrorism and to contribute to preserving peace and security in Islamic countries. The Declaration also pledged its full support for the Palestinian cause and rejected the labelling as 'terrorist' of those Muslim states deemed to be resisting foreign aggression and occupation.

Supporting Muslim Minorities and Combating Anti-Islamic Feeling: In December 1995 OIC ministers of foreign affairs determined that an intergovernmental group of experts should be established to address the situation of minority Muslim communities residing in non-OIC states. The OIC committee of experts responsible for formulating a plan of action for safeguarding the rights of Muslim communities and minorities met for the first time in 1998. In June 2001 the OIC condemned attacks and ongoing discrimination against the Muslim community in Myanmar. In October 2005 the OIC Secretary-General expressed concern at the treatment of Muslims in the southern provinces of Thailand. The first tripartite meeting between the OIC, the Government of the Philippines and

Muslim separatists based in the southern Philippines took place in November 2007, and in April 2009 the OIC Secretary-General announced the appointment of an OIC special envoy to assist in negotiating a peaceful solution to the conflict in the southern Philippines.

In January 2006 the OIC strongly condemned the publication in a Norwegian newspaper of a series of caricatures of the Prophet Muhammad that had originally appeared in a Danish publication in September 2005 and had caused considerable offence to many Muslims. An Islamic Observatory on Islamophobia was established in September 2006; in April 2011 the Observatory released its fourth annual report on Islamophobia. In December 2007 the OIC organized the first International Conference on Islamophobia, aimed at addressing concerns that alleged instances of defamation of Islam appeared to be increasing world-wide (particularly in Europe). Responding to a reported rise in anti-Islamic attacks on Western nations, OIC leaders denounced stereotyping and discrimination, and urged the promotion of Islam by Islamic states as a 'moderate, peaceful and tolerant religion'. In June 2011 the OIC Secretary-General issued a statement strongly condemning 'attacks on Islam and insult and vilification of the Prophet Muhummad and his wives' by the right-wing Dutch politician Geert Wilders.

Reform of the OIC: In March 1997, at an extraordinary meeting of heads of state and of government, held in Islamabad, Pakistan, an Islamabad Declaration was adopted, which pledged to increase co-operation between members of the OIC. In November 2000 OIC heads of state attended the ninth summit conference, held in Doha, Qatar, and issued the Doha Declaration, which reaffirmed commitment to the OIC Charter and undertook to modernize the organization. The 10th OIC summit meeting, held in October 2003, in Putrajaya, Malaysia, issued the Putrajaya Declaration, in which Islamic leaders resolved to enhance Islamic states' role and influence in international affairs. The leaders adopted a plan of action that entailed: reviewing and strengthening OIC positions on international issues; enhancing dialogue among Muslim thinkers and policy-makers through relevant OIC insitutions; promoting constructive dialogue with other cultures and civilizations; completing an ongoing review of the structure and efficacy of the OIC Secretariat; establishing a working group to address means of enhancing the role of Islamic education; promoting among member states the development of science and technology, discussion of ecological issues, and the role of information communication technology in development; improving mechanisms to assist member states in post-conflict situations; and advancing trade and investment through data-sharing and encouraging access to markets for products from poorer member states. In January 2005 the inaugural meeting of an OIC Commission of Eminent Persons was convened in Putrajaya. The Commission was mandated to make recommendations in the following areas: the preparation of a strategy and plan of action enabling the Islamic community to meet the challenges of the 21st century; the preparation of a comprehensive plan for promoting enlightened moderation, both within Islamic societies and universally; and the preparation of proposals for the future reform and restructuring of the OIC system. In December the third extraordinary OIC summit, convened in Mecca, Saudi Arabia, adopted a Ten-Year Programme of Action to Meet the Challenges Facing the Ummah (the Islamic world) in the 21st Century, a related Mecca Declaration and a report by the Commission of Eminent Persons. The summit determined to restructure the OIC, and mandated the establishment of an Executive Committee, comprising the summit conference and ministerial conference troikas (equally reflecting the African, Arab and Asian member states), the OIC host country, and the OIC Secretariat, to implement Conference resolutions.

The 11th OIC heads of state summit meeting, held in Dakar, Senegal, in March 2008, endorsed a revised OIC Charter.

Finance

The OIC's activities are financed by mandatory contributions from member states.

Subsidiary Organs

Islamic Centre for the Development of Trade: Complexe Commercial des Habous, ave des FAR, BP 13545, Casablanca, Morocco; tel. (522) 314974; fax (522) 310110; e-mail icdt@icdt-oic.org; internet www.icdt-oic.org; f. 1983 to encourage regular commercial contacts, harmonize policies and promote investments among OIC mems; Dir-Gen. Dr EL HASSANE HZAINE; publs *Tijaris: International and Inter-Islamic Trade Magazine* (bi-monthly), *Inter-Islamic Trade Report* (annually).

Islamic Jurisprudence (Fiqh) Academy: POB 13917, Jeddah, Saudi Arabia; tel. (2) 667-1664; fax (2) 667-0873; internet www.fiqhacademy.org.sa; f. 1982; Gen. Sec. MAULANA KHALID SAIFULLAH RAHMANI.

Islamic Solidarity Fund: c/o OIC Secretariat, POB 1997, Jeddah 21411, Saudi Arabia; tel. (2) 698-1296; fax (2) 256-8185; e-mail info@isf-fsi.org; internet www.isf-fsi.org; f. 1974 to meet the needs of Islamic communities by providing emergency aid and the finance to build mosques, Islamic centres, hospitals, schools and universities; Exec. Dir IBRAHIM BIN ABDALLAH AL-KHOZAIM.

Islamic University in Uganda: POB 2555, Mbale, Uganda; tel. (35) 2512100; fax (45) 433502; e-mail info@iuiu.ac.ug; internet www.iuiu.ac.ug/; f. 1988 to meet the educational needs of Muslim populations in English-speaking African countries; second campus in Kampala; mainly financed by OIC; Rector Dr AHMAD KAWESA SENGENDO.

Islamic University of Niger: BP 11507, Niamey, Niger; tel. 20-72-39-03; fax 20-73-37-96; e-mail unislam@intnet.ne; internet www.universite_say.ne/; f. 1984; provides courses of study in *Shari'a* (Islamic law) and Arabic language and literature; also offers courses in pedagogy and teacher training; receives grants from Islamic Solidarity Fund and contributions from OIC member states; Rector Prof. ABDELJAOUAD SEKKAT.

Islamic University of Technology (IUT): Board Bazar, Gazipur 1704, Dhaka, Bangladesh; tel. (2) 9291250; fax (2) 9291260; e-mail vc@iut-dhaka.edu; internet www.iutoic-dhaka.edu; f. 1981 as the Islamic Centre for Technical and Vocational Training and Resources, named changed to Islamic Institute of Technology in 1994, current name adopted in 2001; aims to develop human resources in OIC mem. states, with special reference to engineering, technology, and technical education; 145 staff and 800 students; library of 30,450 vols; Vice-Chancellor Prof. Dr M. IMTIAZ HOSSAIN; publs *Journal of Engineering and Technology* (2 a year), *News Bulletin* (annually), *News Letter* (6 a year), annual calendar and announcement for admission, reports, human resources development series.

Research Centre for Islamic History, Art and Culture (IRCICA): POB 24, Beşiktaş 34354, İstanbul, Turkey; tel. (212) 2591742; fax (212) 2584365; e-mail ircica@ircica.org; internet www.ircica.org; f. 1980; library of 60,000 vols; Dir-Gen. Prof. Dr HALIT EREN; publs *Newsletter* (3 a year), monographical studies.

Statistical, Economic and Social Research and Training Centre for Islamic Countries (SESRIC): Attar Sokak No. 4, GOP 06700, Ankara, Turkey; tel. (312) 4686172; fax (312) 4673458; e-mail oicankara@sesric.org; internet www.sesric.org; became operational in 1978; has a three-fold mandate: to collate, process and disseminate socio-economic statistics and information on, and for the utilization of, its member countries; to study and assess economic and social developments in member countries with the aim of helping to generate proposals for advancing co-operation; and to organize training programmes in selected areas; the Centre also acts as a focal point for technical co-operation activities between the OIC system and related UN agencies; and prepares economic and social reports and background documentation for OIC meetings; Dir-Gen. Dr SAVAŞ ALPAY (Turkey); publs *Annual Economic Report on the OIC Countries*, *Journal of Economic Cooperation and Development* (quarterly), *Economic Cooperation and Development Review* (semi-annually), *InfoReport* (quarterly), *Statistical Yearbook* (annually), *Basic Facts and Figures on OIC Member Countries* (annually).

Specialized Institutions

International Islamic News Agency (IINA): King Khalid Palace, Madinah Rd, POB 5054, Jeddah 21422, Saudi Arabia; tel. (2) 665-8561; fax (2) 665-9358; e-mail iina@islamicnews.org; internet www.iina.me; f. 1972; distributes news and reports daily on events in the Islamic world, in Arabic, English and French; Dir-Gen. ERDEM KOK.

Islamic Educational, Scientific and Cultural Organization (ISESCO): BP 2275 Rabat 10104, Morocco; tel. (37) 772433; fax (37) 772058; e-mail cid@isesco.org.ma; internet www.isesco.org.ma; f. 1982; Dir-Gen. Dr ABDULAZIZ BIN OTHMAN ALTWAIJRI; publs *ISESCO Newsletter* (quarterly), *Islam Today* (2 a year), *ISESCO Triennial*.

Islamic Broadcasting Union (IBU): POB 6351, Jeddah 21442, Saudi Arabia; tel. (2) 672-1121; fax (2) 672-2269; e-mail ibu@ibuj.org; internet www.ibuj.org; f. 1975; Gen. Man. ZAINAL ABIDIN IBERAHIM (Malaysia).

Affiliated Institutions

International Association of Islamic Banks (IAIB): King Abdulaziz St, Queen's Bldg, 23rd Floor, Al-Balad Dist, POB 9707, Jeddah 21423, Saudi Arabia; tel. (2) 651-6900; fax (2) 651-6552; f. 1977 to link financial institutions operating on Islamic banking principles; activities include training and research; mems: 192 banks and other financial institutions in 34 countries.

Islamic Chamber of Commerce and Industry: POB 3831, Clifton, Karachi 75600, Pakistan; tel. (21) 5874910; fax (21) 5870765; e-mail icci@icci-oic.org; internet www.iccionline.net/en/icci-en/index.aspx; f. 1979 to promote trade and industry among member states; comprises nat. chambers or feds of chambers of commerce and industry; Sec.-Gen. Dr BASSEM AWADALLAH.

Islamic Committee for the International Crescent: POB 17434, Benghazi, Libya; tel. (61) 9095824; fax (61) 9095823; e-mail info@icic-oic.org; internet www.icic-oic.org; f. 1979 to attempt to alleviate the suffering caused by natural disasters and war; Pres. ALI MAHMOUD BUHEDMA.

Islamic Solidarity Sports Federation: POB 5844, Riyadh 11442, Saudi Arabia; tel. (1) 480-9253; fax (1) 482-2145; e-mail issf@awalnet.net.sa; internet issf-fssi.org; f. 1981; organizes the Islamic Solidarity Games (2005: Jeddah, Saudi Arabia, in April; the next Games were to have been held in April 2010, in Tehran, Iran, but were postponed); Sec.-Gen. Dr MOHAMMAD SALEH QAZDAR.

Organization of Islamic Capitals and Cities (OICC): POB 13621, Jeddah 21414, Saudi Arabia; tel. (2) 698-1953; fax (2) 698-1053; e-mail webmaster@oicc.org; internet www.oicc.org; f. 1980; aims to preserve the identity and the heritage of Islamic capitals and cities; to achieve and enhance sustainable development in member capitals and cities; to establish and develop comprehensive urban norms, systems and plans to serve the growth and prosperity of Islamic capitals and cities and to enhance their cultural, environmental, urban, economic and social conditions; to advance municipal services and facilities in the member capitals and cities; to support member cities' capacity-building programmes; and to consolidate fellowship and co-ordinate the scope of co-operation between members; comprises 157 capitals and cities as active members, eight observer members and 18 associate members, in Asia, Africa, Europe and South America; Sec.-Gen. OMAR KADI.

Organization of the Islamic Shipowners' Association: POB 14900, Jeddah 21434, Saudi Arabia; tel. (2) 663-7882; fax (2) 660-4920; e-mail mail@oisaonline.com; internet www.oisaonline.com; f. 1981 to promote co-operation among maritime cos in Islamic countries; in 1998 mems approved the establishment of a new commercial venture, the Bakkah Shipping Company, to enhance sea transport in the region; Sec.-Gen. Dr ABDULLATIF A. SULTAN.

World Federation of Arab-Islamic Schools: 2 Wadi el-Nile St, Maadi, Cairo, Egypt; tel. (2) 358-3278; internet www.wfais.org; f. 1976; supports Arab-Islamic schools world-wide and encourages co-operation between the institutions; promotes the dissemination of the Arabic language and Islamic culture; supports the training of personnel.

ORGANIZATION OF THE PETROLEUM EXPORTING COUNTRIES—OPEC

Address: Helferstorferstrasse 17, 1010 Vienna, Austria.

Telephone: (1) 211-12-0; **fax:** (1) 216-43-20; **e-mail:** prid@opec.org; **internet:** www.opec.org.

OPEC was established in 1960 to link countries whose main source of export earnings is petroleum; it aims to unify and co-ordinate members' petroleum policies and to safeguard their interests generally. In 1976 OPEC member states established the OPEC Fund for International Development.

OPEC's share of world petroleum production was 41.8% in 2010 (compared with 54.7% in 1974). OPEC members were estimated to possess 81.3% of the world's known reserves of crude petroleum in 2010. In that year OPEC members also possessed about 49% of known reserves of natural gas, and accounted for 18% of total production of marketed natural gas.

MEMBERS

Algeria	Iraq	Qatar
Angola	Kuwait	Saudi Arabia
Ecuador	Libya	United Arab Emirates
Iran	Nigeria	Venezuela

Organization

(April 2012)

CONFERENCE

The Conference is the supreme authority of the Organization, responsible for the formulation of its general policy. It consists of representatives of member countries, who examine reports and recommendations submitted by the Board of Governors. It approves the appointment of Governors from each country and elects the Chairman of the Board of Governors. It works on the unanimity principle, and meets at least twice a year. In September 2000 the Conference agreed that regular meetings of heads of state or government should be convened every five years.

BOARD OF GOVERNORS

The Board directs the management of the Organization; it implements resolutions of the Conference and draws up an annual budget. It consists of one governor for each member country, and meets at least twice a year.

MINISTERIAL MONITORING COMMITTEE

The Committee (f. 1982) is responsible for monitoring price evolution and ensuring the stability of the world petroleum market. As such, it is charged with the preparation of long-term strategies, including the allocation of quotas to be presented to the Conference. The Committee consists of all national representatives, and is normally convened four times a year. A Ministerial Monitoring Sub-committee, reporting to the Committee on production and supply figures, was established in 1993.

ECONOMIC COMMISSION

A specialized body operating within the framework of the Secretariat, with a view to assisting the Organization in promoting stability in international prices for petroleum at equitable levels; consists of a Board, national representatives and a commission staff; meets at least twice a year.

SECRETARIAT

Secretary-General: ABDALLA SALEM EL-BADRI (Libya).

Legal Office: Provides legal advice, supervises the Secretariat's legal commitments, evaluates legal issues of concern to the Organization and member countries, and recommends appropriate action; General Legal Counsel ASMA MUTTAWA.

Office of the Secretary-General: provides the Secretary-General with executive assistance in maintaining contacts with governments, organizations and delegations, in matters of protocol and in the preparation for and co-ordination of meetings; Head ABDULLAH AL-SHAMERI.

Research Division: comprises the Data Services Department; the Energy Studies Department; and the Petroleum Market Analysis Department; Dir Dr HASAN M. QABAZARD.

Support Services Division: responsible for providing the required infrastructure and services to the whole Secretariat, in support of its programmes; has three departments: Administration and IT Services; Finance and Human Resources; and Public Relations and Information; Dir. (vacant).

Activities

OPEC's principal objectives, according to its Statute, are to co-ordinate and unify the petroleum policies of member countries and to determine the best means for safeguarding their individual and collective interests; to seek ways and means of ensuring the stabilization of prices in international oil markets, with a view to eliminating harmful and unnecessary fluctuations; and to provide a steady income to the producing countries, an efficient, economic and regular supply of petroleum to consuming nations, and a fair return on capital to those investing in the petroleum industry.

The first OPEC conference was held in Baghdad, Iraq, in September 1960. It was attended by representatives from Iran, Iraq, Kuwait, Saudi Arabia and Venezuela, the founder members. These were joined by Qatar in the following year, when a Board of Governors was formed and statutes agreed. Indonesia and Libya were admitted to membership in 1962, Abu Dhabi in 1967, Algeria in 1969, Nigeria in 1971, Ecuador in 1973 and Gabon in 1975; Abu Dhabi's membership was transferred to the United Arab Emirates (UAE) in 1974. Ecuador resigned from OPEC in 1992 and Gabon did so in 1996. Angola became a member in 2007, and Ecuador rejoined the organization in the same year. Indonesia withdrew from OPEC in 2009.

PRICES AND PRODUCTION

OPEC's five original members first met following the imposition of price reductions by petroleum companies in the previous month (August 1960). During the 1960s members sought to assert their rights in an international petroleum market that was dominated by multinational companies. Between 1965 and 1967 a two-year joint production programme limited annual growth in output so as to secure adequate prices. During the 1970s member states increased their control over their domestic petroleum industries, and over the pricing of crude petroleum on world markets. In 1971 the five-year Tehran Agreement on pricing was concluded between the six producing countries from the Arabian Gulf region and 23 petroleum companies. In January 1972 petroleum companies agreed to adjust the petroleum revenues of the largest producers after changes in currency exchange rates (Geneva Agreement), and in 1973 OPEC and the petroleum companies agreed to raise posted prices of crude petroleum by 11.9% and installed a mechanism to make monthly adjustments to prices in future (Second Geneva Agreement). In October of that year a pricing crisis occurred when Arab member states refused to supply petroleum to nations that had supported Israel in its conflict with Egypt and Syria earlier in that month. Negotiations on the revision of the Tehran Agreement failed in the same month, and the Gulf states unilaterally declared increases of 70% in posted prices, from US $3.01 to $5.11 per barrel. In December the OPEC Conference decided to increase the posted price to $11.65 per barrel from the beginning of 1974 (despite Saudi Arabian opposition): almost a four-fold increase in three months. During 1974 royalties and taxes imposed on petroleum companies were increased in all member states except Saudi Arabia. OPEC's first summit meeting of heads of state or government was held in March 1975, and in September a ministerial meeting agreed to increase prices by 10% for the period to June 1976. During 1976 and 1977 disagreements between 'moderate' members (principally Saudi Arabia and Iran) and 'radical' members (led by Algeria, Iraq and Libya) caused discrepancies in pricing: a 10% increase was agreed by 11 member states as of 1 January 1977, but Saudi Arabia and the UAE decided to limit their increase to 5%. A further increase of 5% by Saudi Arabia and the UAE in July restored a single level of pricing, but in December the Conference was unable to agree on a new increase, and prices remained stable until the end of 1978, when it was agreed that during 1979 prices should increase by an average of 10% in four instalments over the year, to compensate for the effects of the depreciation of the US dollar. The overthrow of the Iranian Government in early 1979, however, led to a new steep increase in petroleum prices.

In June 1980 the Conference decided to set the price for a 'marker' crude at US $32 per barrel, and stipulated that the value differentials which could be added to this (on account of quality and geographical location) should not exceed $5 per barrel. Prices continued to vary, however, and in May 1981 Saudi Arabia refused to increase its price of $32 per barrel unless the higher prices charged by other members were lowered. Members agreed to reduce surplus production during the year, and in October the marker price was increased to $34 per barrel, with a 'ceiling' price of $38 per barrel. In March 1982 an emergency meeting of ministers of petroleum agreed (for the first time in OPEC's history) to defend the Organization's price structure by imposing an overall production ceiling of 18m. barrels per day (b/d), reducing this to 17.5m. b/d at the beginning of 1983, although ministers initially failed to agree on production quotas for individual members, or on adjustments to the differentials in prices charged for the high-quality crude petroleum produced by Algeria, Libya and Nigeria compared with that produced by the Gulf States. In February 1983 Nigeria reduced its price to $30 per barrel, and to avoid a 'price war' OPEC set the official price of marker crude at $29 per barrel. Quotas were allocated for each member country except Saudi Arabia, which was to act as a 'swing producer' to supply the balancing quantities to meet market requirements. In October 1984 the production ceiling was lowered to 16m. b/d, and in December price differentials for light (more expensive) and heavy (cheaper) crudes were altered in an attempt to counteract price-cutting by non-OPEC producers, particularly Norway and the United Kingdom. During 1985, however, most members effectively abandoned the marker price system, and production in excess of quotas, unofficial discounts and barter deals by members, and price cuts by non-members (such as Mexico, which had hitherto kept its prices in line with those of OPEC) contributed to a weakening of the market. During the first half of 1986 petroleum prices dropped to below $10 per barrel. Discussions were held with non-member producing countries (Angola, Egypt, Malaysia, Mexico and Oman) which agreed to co-operate in limiting production, although the United Kingdom declined. In August all members except Iraq agreed upon a return to production quotas (Iraq declined to co-operate after its request to be allocated the same quota as Iran had been refused): total production was to be limited to 14.8m. b/d (16.8m. b/d including Iraq). This measure resulted in an increase in prices to about $15 per barrel. In December members (except Iraq) agreed to return to a fixed pricing system, at a level of $18 per barrel as the OPEC Reference Basket (ORB) price (based on a 'basket' of seven crudes, not, as hitherto, on a 'marker' crude, Arabian Light) with effect from 1 February 1987, setting a total production limit of 15.8m. b/d for the first half of the year. OPEC's role of actually setting crude oil prices had come to an end, however, and from the late 1980s prices were determined by movements in the international markets, with OPEC's role being to increase or restrain production in order to prevent harmful fluctuations in prices. In June 1987, with prices having stabilized, the Conference decided to limit production to 16.6m. b/d (including Iraq's output) for the rest of the year. In April 1988, following a further reduction in prices below $15 per barrel, non-OPEC producers offered to reduce the volume of their petroleum exports by 5% if OPEC members would do the same. Saudi Arabia insisted that existing quotas should be more strictly observed before it would reduce its production. The production limit was increased to 18.5m. b/d for the first half of 1989 and, after prices had recovered to about $18 per barrel, to 19.5m. b/d for the second half of 1989, and to 22m. b/d for the first half of 1990.

In May 1990 members resolved to adhere more strictly to the agreed production quotas, in response to a decline in prices, which stood at about US $14 per barrel in June. In August Iraq invaded Kuwait (which it had accused, among other grievances, of violating production quotas). Petroleum exports by the two countries were halted by an international embargo, and petroleum prices immediately increased to exceed $25 per barrel. OPEC ministers promptly allowed a temporary increase in production by other members, of between 3m. and 3.5m. b/d (mostly by Saudi Arabia, the UAE and Venezuela), to stabilize prices, and notwithstanding some fluctuations later in the year, this was achieved. During 1991 and 1992 ministers attempted to reach a minimum ORB price of $21 per barrel by imposing production limits that varied between 22.3m. b/d and 24.2m. b/d. Kuwait, which resumed production in 1992 after extensive damage had been inflicted on its oil wells during the conflict with Iraq, was granted a special dispensation to produce without a fixed quota until the following year. Ecuador withdrew from OPEC in November 1992, citing the high cost of membership and the organization's refusal to increase Ecuador's production quota. In 1993 a Ministerial Monitoring Sub-committee was established to supervise compliance with quotas, because of members' persistent over-production. A production ceiling of 24.46m. b/d was set for the first quarter of 1993 and was reduced to 23.5m. b/d from 1 March (including a fixed quota for Kuwait for the first time since the Iraqi invasion). In July discussions between Iraq and the UN on the possible supervised resumption of Iraqi petroleum exports depressed petroleum prices to below $16 per barrel, and at the end of the year prices fell below $14, after the Conference rejected any further reduction in the current limit (imposed from 1 October) of 24.52m. b/d, which remained in force during 1994 and 1995, although actual output continued to be well in excess of quotas. In March 1996 prices reached $21 per barrel (largely owing to unusually cold weather in the northern hemisphere). In May the UN and Iraq concluded an agreement allowing Iraq to resume exports of petroleum in order to fund humanitarian relief efforts within Iraq, and OPEC's overall production ceiling was accordingly raised to 25.03m. b/d from June, remaining at this level until the end of 1997. Gabon withdrew from OPEC in June 1996, citing difficulties in meeting its budgetary contribution. Prices declined during the first half of 1997, falling to a low point of $16.7 per barrel in April, owing to the resumption of Iraqi exports, depressed world demand and continuing over-production: an escalation in political tension in the Gulf region, however, and in particular Iraq's reluctance to co-operate with UN weapons inspectors, prompted a price increase to about $21.2 per barrel in October. The overall production ceiling was raised by about 10%, to 27.5m. b/d, with effect from the beginning of 1998, but during that year prices declined, falling below $12 per barrel from August (demand having been affected by the current economic difficulties in South-East Asia), and OPEC imposed a succession of reductions in output, down to 24.387m. b/d from 1 July. Non-member countries (chiefly Mexico) also concluded agreements with OPEC to limit their production in that year, and in March 1999 Mexico, Norway, Oman and Russia agreed to decrease production by a total of 388,000 b/d, while OPEC's own production limit was reduced to 22.976m. b/d. Evidence of almost 90% compliance with the new production quotas contributed to market confidence that stockpiles of petroleum would be reduced, and resulted in sustained price increases during the second half of the year: the ORB price for petroleum rose above $24 per barrel in September.

By March 2000 petroleum prices had reached their highest level since 1990, briefly exceeding US $34 per barrel. In that month OPEC ministers agreed to raise output by 1.45m. b/d, in order to ease supply shortages, and introduced an informal price band mechanism that was to signal the need for adjustments in production should prices deviate for more than 20 days from an average bracket of $22–$28 per barrel. Further increases in production, totalling 1.8m. b/d, took effect in the second half of the year (with five non-OPEC members, Angola, Mexico, Norway, Oman and Russia, also agreeing to raise their output), but prices remained high and there was intense international pressure on OPEC to resolve the situation: in September both the Group of Seven industrialized countries (G7) and the IMF issued warnings about the potential economic and social consequences of sustained high petroleum prices. In that month OPEC heads of state and government, convened in their first summit meeting since 1975, responded by issuing the Caracas Declaration, in which they resolved (among other things) to promote market stability through their policies on pricing and production, to increase co-operation with other petroleum exporters, and to improve communication with consumer countries. During the first half of 2001, with a view to stabilizing prices that by January had fallen back to around $25 per barrel, the Conference agreed to implement reductions in output totalling 2.5m. b/d, thereby limiting overall production to 24.2m. b/d, with a further reduction of 1m. b/d from 1 September. Terrorist attacks on targets in the USA in September gave rise to market uncertainty, and prices declined further, averaging $17–$18 per barrel in November and December. In September the Conference announced the establishment of a working group of experts from OPEC and non-OPEC petroleum-producing countries, to evaluate future market developments and advance dialogue and co-operation. In December the Conference announced a further reduction in output by 1.5m. b/d (to 21.7m. b/d) from 1 January 2002, provided that non-OPEC producers also reduced their output, which they agreed to do by 462,500 b/d. This output limit was maintained throughout 2002, and the ORB price averaged $24.4 per barrel during the year, with temporary increases caused partly by a one-month suspension of Iraq's exports in April (in protest at Israeli military intervention in Palestinian-controlled areas), and by a strike in the Venezuelan petroleum industry. From 1 January 2003 the production ceiling was raised to 23m. b/d, but stricter compliance with individual quotas meant a reduction in actual output, and prices rose above the target range, with the ORB price reaching $32 per barrel in February, as a result of the continued interruption of the Venezuelan supply, together with the market's reaction to the likelihood of US-led military action against Iraq. In January the Conference agreed to raise the production ceiling to 24.5m. b/d from 1 February, and in March (when Venezuelan production had resumed) members agreed to make up from their available excess capacities any shortfall that might result following military action against Iraq. In the event the war on Iraq that commenced later in that month led to such a rapid overthrow of Saddam Hussain's regime that there were fears that a petroleum surplus, driving down prices, would result, and a production ceiling of 25.4m. b/d was set with effect from the beginning of June: although higher than the previous limit, it represented a 2m. b/d reduction in actual output at that time. The production ceiling of 24.5m. b/d was reinstated from 1 November, in view of the gradual revival of Iraqi exports. The ORB price averaged $28.1 per barrel in 2003. In 2004, however, petroleum prices increased considerably, with the ORB price averaging $36 per barrel over the year, despite OPEC's raising its production ceiling (excluding Iraq's output), in several stages, from the 23.5m. b/d limit imposed from 1 April to 27m. b/d with effect from 1 November. In January 2005 the Conference suspended the $22–$28 price band mechanism, acknowledging this to be unrealistic at the present time. The production ceiling was increased to 27.5m. b/d in March and to 28m. b/d in June, but the ORB price nevertheless averaged $50.6 per barrel over the year. The March Conference attributed the continuing rise in prices to expectations of strong demand, speculation on the futures markets, and geopolitical tensions; it expressed particular concern that a shortage of effective global refining capacity was also contributing to higher prices by causing 'bottlenecks' in the downstream sector, and announced that members had accelerated the implementation of existing capacity expansion plans. In June the Conference approved an increase in the composition of the ORB from seven to 12 crudes, representing the main export crudes of all member countries, weighted according to production and exports to the main markets: the new composition was intended to reflect more accurately the average quality of crude petroleum in OPEC's member states. In September the Conference adopted a first Long-Term Strategy for OPEC, setting objectives concerning members' long-term petroleum revenues, fair and stable prices, the role of petroleum in meeting future energy demand, the stability of the world oil market, and the security of regular supplies to consumers. During 2006 petroleum prices continued to rise, with the ORB price averaging $61.08 per barrel for the year. The rise was partly attributable to uncertainty about Iran's future output (since there was speculation that international sanctions might be imposed on that country as a penalty for continuing its nuclear development programme), and to a reduction in Nigeria's production as a result of internal unrest. Existing production targets were maintained until November, when the production ceiling was lowered to 26.3m. b/d, and a further reduction of 500,000 b/d was announced in December. In March 2007 the Conference agreed to maintain the current level of production. Concern over fuel supplies and distribution contributed to steadily rising prices, in spite of OPEC's statements estimating that there were sufficient stock levels to meet demand. In November the ORB price reached a monthly average of $88.99 per barrel, despite an increase in OPEC's output by 500,000 b/d from the start of that month (agreed by the Conference in September). In October OPEC's Secretary-General reiterated that the market was well supplied, and attributed the rising prices chiefly to market speculators, with persistent refinery bottlenecks, seasonal maintenance work, ongoing geopolitical problems in the Middle East and fluctuations in the US dollar also continuing to play a role in driving oil prices higher. In November the third OPEC summit meeting of heads of state and government agreed on principles concerning the stability of global energy markets, the role of energy in sustainable development, and the relationship between energy and environmental concerns. In December the Conference observed that, despite the current volatility of prices, the petroleum market continued to be well supplied, with stocks at comfortable levels, and decided to leave the production ceiling unchanged for the time being.

Meeting in March 2008, the Conference again determined to maintain the current production ceiling and in September, once again, the Conference resolved to maintain the production allocations agreed in September 2007 (with an adjustment to include the admission to the Organization in late 2007 of both Angola and Ecuador while excluding Indonesia, whose membership was being terminated, resulting in an overall production ceiling of 28.8m. b/d). At 11 July 2008 the ORB price reached a record high of US $147.27 per barrel, although by late October it had fallen below $60 per barrel. An extraordinary meeting of the Conference, convened at that time, observed that the ongoing global financial crisis was suppressing demand for petroleum. The Conference determined to decrease the production ceiling by 1.5m. b/d, with effect from 1 November. A further extraordinary Conference meeting, held in mid-December, agreed to reduce production further, by 4.7m. b/d from the actual total production in September (29.0m. b/d), with effect from 1 January 2009. By 24 December 2008 the ORB price had fallen to $33.36 per barrel.

The ORB price stabilized in early 2009, fluctuating at around US $40 per barrel during January–mid-March (when a meeting of the Conference determined to maintain current production levels, but urged member states' full compliance with them: this had stood at 79% in February), and rising to around $50 per barrel during mid-March–early May. By mid-June the ORB price had risen to $70.89 per barrel. Meeting in late May the Conference noted that the impact of the ongoing global economic crisis had resulted in a reduction in the global demand for petroleum, this having declined during the second half of 2008 for the first time since the early 1980s. The Conference welcomed the positive effect of recent production decisions in redressing the balance of supply and demand, and decided to maintain current production levels. Reviewing the situation at the next meeting, convened in early September 2009, the Conference observed that the global economic situation continued to be very fragile and that the petroleum market remained over-supplied, and determined once more to maintain existing production levels. When convened again, in December, the Conference expressed concern at the gravity of the global economic contraction, noting that the worldwide demand for petroleum had now declined for two successive years. Production levels were kept unchanged, and remained unaltered by the next (March 2010) gathering of the Conference. The March 2010 Conference observed some improvement in the global economy, and projected marginal improvements in global demand for petroleum, but observed, also, that serious threats remained to the economic situation, and that, owing to a forecast increase in petroleum supplies from non-OPEC sources, a third successive year of declining demand for the Organization's crude oil was envisaged. The next ordinary meeting of the Conference, held in October, adopted a second Long-Term Strategy for the Organization, setting objectives relating to member countries' long-term petroleum revenues; fair and stable prices; future energy demand and OPEC's share in world oil supply; stability of the global oil market; security of regular supply to consumers, and of global demand; and enhancing the collective interests of member states in global negotiations and future multilateral agreements. An extraordinary meeting of the Conference, convened in December, observed that the global economic outlook remained fragile, and, on that basis, agreed to maintain current oil production levels. The next ordinary meeting of the Conference, held in June 2011—following, in the first half of that year, the unforeseen eruption of unrest and uncertainty in several Middle Eastern and North African countries, including Libya (where a significant decline in production was recorded), and a sharp increase in petroleum prices—failed to reach consensus on a proposed agreement to raise output. In December OPEC ministers agreed to maintain the production ceiling at current output levels (some 30m. b/d). The ORB price (still including 12 crudes) stood at $116.46 on 20 April 2012.

ENERGY DIALOGUES

Annual 'workshops' are convened jointly by OPEC, the International Energy Agency and the International Energy Forum, bringing together experts, analysts and government officials to discuss aspects of energy supply and demand. A workshop was staged by the three organizations in November 2010 on the theme 'Understanding the new dynamic: how the physical and financial markets for energy interact', alongside a forum on 'Energy market regulation: clarity and co-ordination'; and, in January 2011, they organized a symposium on energy outlooks.

The first annual formal ministerial meeting of the European Union (EU)-OPEC Energy Dialogue took place in June 2005, with the aim of exchanging views on energy issues of common interest, including petroleum market developments, and thus contributing to stability, transparency and predictability in the market. A round-table meeting was held in November to discuss recent petroleum market developments and future prospects, and a conference was held in 2006 to discuss energy technologies, with a particular focus on carbon capture and storage. The fifth EU-OPEC Energy Dialogue ministerial meeting, convened in June 2008, agreed to hold a round table on carbon capture and storage (this took place in October); to finalize a joint study on the impacts of financial markets on oil prices and market volatility, to be followed by an international workshop; to undertake a feasibility study on the establishment of an EU-OPEC Energy Technology Centre; and to prepare terms of reference for a joint study on the impacts of biofuels on oil refining. The sixth ministerial Dialogue, convened in June 2009, agreed to implement the joint study on the impacts of biofuels on oil refining and to conduct a workshop to review the findings of the study; to organize a round table on the impacts on the petroleum sector of the ongoing financial crisis; and to finalize the planned feasibility study on the proposed EU-OPEC Energy Technology Centre. In June 2010 a summary of the conclusions of the feasibility study was presented to the seventh ministerial Dialogue. The June 2010 Dialogue meeting determined, in 2011, to commission a study to explore the potential of technological advances in transportation, and to assess their impact on demand for petroleum; and also to arrange a round table to examine the causes of an ongoing shortage of skilled labour shortage in the energy and oil industries. The June 2011 Dialogue decided to organize, during 2011–12, a joint workshop to discuss the findings of the study on technological advances in the road transportation sector; to complete preparations for the proposed Energy Technology Centre; and to hold a round-table on the key challenges confronting oil and gas exploration and production activities.

Russia (a major producer of petroleum) was given OPEC observer status in 1992, and was subsequently represented at a number of ministerial and other meetings. A formal Energy Dialogue was established in December 2005, providing for annual ministerial meetings, together with technical exchanges, seminars and joint research, on such subjects as petroleum market developments and prospects, data flow, investments across the supply chain, and energy policies.

In March 2005 the Chinese Government proposed the creation of an official dialogue between OPEC and the People's Republic of China (a major customer of OPEC members) and this was formally established in December, with the aim of exchanging views on energy issues, particularly security of supply and demand, through annual ministerial meetings, technical exchanges and energy round-tables.

ENVIRONMENTAL CONCERNS

OPEC has frequently expressed its concern that any measures adopted to avert climate change by reducing the emission of carbon dioxide caused by the consumption of fossil fuels would seriously affect its members' income. In 1998, for example, OPEC representatives attending a conference of the parties to the UN Framework Convention on Climate Change warned that OPEC would claim compensation for any lost revenue resulting from initiatives to limit petroleum consumption, and at subsequent sessions, while expressing support for the fundamental principles of the Convention, OPEC urged that developing countries whose economies were dependent on the export of fossil fuels should not be unfairly treated. In June 2007 OPEC's Secretary-General criticized the industrialized nations' efforts to increase production of biofuel (derived from agricultural commodities) in order to reduce consumption of fossil fuels: he warned that OPEC might reduce its future investment in petroleum production accordingly. In November the third summit meeting of OPEC heads of state and government acknowledged the long-term challenge of climate change, but emphasized the continuing need for stable petroleum supplies to support global economic growth and development, and urged that policies aimed at combating climate change should be balanced, taking into account their impact on developing countries, including countries heavily dependent on the production and export of fossil fuels. The meeting stressed the importance of cleaner and more efficient petroleum technologies, and the development of technologies such as carbon capture and storage.

Finance

OPEC has an annual budget of about €25m.

Publications

Annual Report.
Annual Statistical Bulletin.
Environmental Newsletter (quarterly).
Monthly Oil Market Report.
OPEC Bulletin (10 a year).
OPEC Review (quarterly).
World Oil Outlook (annually).
Reports, information papers, press releases.

OPEC FUND FOR INTERNATIONAL DEVELOPMENT

Address: POB 995, 1011 Vienna, Austria.

Telephone: (1) 515-64-0; **fax:** (1) 513-92-38; **e-mail:** info@ofid.org; **internet:** www.ofid.org.

The OPEC Fund for International Development (initially referred to as 'the Fund', more recently as 'OFID') was established 1976 by OPEC member countries, in order to assist developing countries and to promote South-South co-operation. A revised agreement to establish the Fund as a permanent international agency was signed in May 1980.

MEMBERS

Algeria	Iraq	Qatar
Gabon	Kuwait	Saudi Arabia
Indonesia	Libya	United Arab Emirates
Iran	Nigeria	Venezuela

Organization

(April 2012)

ADMINISTRATION

OFID is administered by a Ministerial Council and a Governing Board. Each member country is represented on the Council by its minister of finance. The Board consists of one representative and one alternate for each member country.

Chairman, Ministerial Council: YOUSEF HUSSAIN KAMAL (Qatar).

Chairman, Governing Board: JAMAL NASSER LOOTAH (UAE).

Director-General of the Fund: SULEIMAN JASIR AL-HERBISH (Saudi Arabia).

FINANCIAL STRUCTURE

The resources of OFID, whose unit of account is the US dollar, consist of contributions by OPEC member countries, and income received from operations or otherwise accruing to the Fund.

The initial endowment of OFID amounted to US $800m. Its resources have been replenished three times, and have been further increased by the profits accruing to seven OPEC member countries through the sales of gold held by the International Monetary Fund (IMF). The total pledged contributions by member countries amounted to $3,435.0m. at the end of 2010, and paid-in contributions totalled some $3,050.0m.

Activities

The OPEC Fund for International Development (OFID) is a multilateral agency for financial co-operation and assistance. Its objective is to reinforce financial co-operation between OPEC member countries and other developing countries through the provision of financial support to the latter on appropriate terms, to assist them in their economic and social development. OFID was conceived as a collective financial facility which would consolidate the assistance extended by its member countries; its resources are additional to those already made available through other bilateral and multilateral aid agencies of OPEC members. It is empowered to:

(i) Provide concessional loans for balance of payments support;

(ii) Provide concessional loans for the implementation of development projects and programmes;

(iii) Contribute to the resources of other international development agencies;

(iv) Finance technical assistance, research, food aid and humanitarian emergency relief through grants; and

(v) Participate in the financing of private sector activities in developing countries.

The eligible beneficiaries of OFID's assistance are the governments of developing countries other than OPEC member countries, and international development agencies whose beneficiaries are developing countries. OFID gives priority to the countries with the lowest income.

OFID may undertake technical, economic and financial appraisal of a project submitted to it, or entrust such an appraisal to an appropriate international development agency, the executing national agency of a member country, or any other qualified agency. Most projects financed by the organization have been co-financed by other development finance agencies. In each such case, one of the co-financing agencies may be appointed to administer the loan in association with its own. This practice has enabled OFID to extend its lending activities to more than 100 countries over a short period of time and in a simple way, with the aim of avoiding duplication and complications. As its experience grew, OFID increasingly resorted to parallel, rather than joint financing, taking up separate project components to be financed according to its rules and policies. In addition, it started to finance some projects completely on its own. These trends necessitated the issuance in 1982 of guidelines for the procurement of goods and services under the Fund's loans, allowing for a margin of preference for goods and services of local origin or originating in other developing countries: the general principle of competitive bidding is, however, followed by OFID. The loans are not tied to procurement from OFID member countries or from any other countries. The margin of preference for goods and services obtainable in developing countries is allowed on the request of the borrower and within defined limits. OFID assistance in the form of programme loans has a broader coverage than project lending. Programme loans are used to stimulate an economic sector or sub-sector, and assist recipient countries in obtaining inputs, equipment and spare parts. In 2004 a supplementary lending mechanism, a Blend Facility, was established to make available additional resources at higher rates than the standard concessional lending terms. Besides extending loans for project and programme financing and balance of payments support, OFID also undertakes other operations, including grants in support of technical assistance and other activities (mainly research), emergency relief and humanitarian aid, and financial contributions to other international institutions. In 1998 the Fund began to extend lines of credit to support private sector activities in beneficiary countries. The so-called Private Sector Facility aims to encourage the growth of private enterprises, in particular small and medium-sized enterprises, and to support the development of local capital markets. A new Trade Finance Facility, to provide loans, lines of credit and guarantees in support of international trade operations in developing countries, was launched in December 2006.

In March 2009 OFID participated in a meeting of international finance institutions and development banks to discuss closer co-operation in order to respond more effectively to the global financial and economic crisis. OFID agreed to provide US $30m. to an African sub-fund of the International Finance Corporation's Recapitalization Fund, which aimed to support banks in developing countries. It also participated in a Microfinance Enhancement Facility and, though its Trade Finance Facility, in the World Bank's Global Trade Liquidity Programme. During 2010 OFID continued to work to alleviate the impact of the crisis on low-income developing countries, and to refocus efforts on achieving the UN Millennium Development Goals. In October OFID signed a Memorandum of Understanding (MOU) with the World Bank Group in order to strengthen their joint efforts to meet new development challenges, with a particular focus on the need to counter energy poverty, to improve the management of natural resources, to facilitate trade and to strengthen financial institutions. In May 2011 OFID signed an MOU with the Asian Development Bank, in order to enhance co-operation between the two organizations, and in July signed an MOU with the Arab Bank for Economic Development in Africa. In December of that year OFID's Director-General, addressing the 20th World Petroleum Congress, convened in Doha, Qatar, recommended that the Fund might act as a hub for efforts by the petroleum sector to promote the global Sustainable Energy for All by 2030 initiative that had been launched by the UN Secretary-General in September 2011.

By the end of December 2010 OFID had approved a total of US $13,056.1m. since operations began in 1976, of which $8,595.5m. was for public sector loans. Included in the public sector lending is the Fund's contribution to the Heavily Indebted Poor Countries (HIPC) initiative (see World Bank), which by the end of 2010 amounted to $155m. Private sector financing totalled $1,383.1m. committed in the same period, while loans committed under the Trade Finance Facility, amounted to $963.8m. At that time cumulative disbursements of all loans and operations amounted to $7,966.1m.

Direct loans are supplemented by grants to support technical assistance, food aid and research. By the end of December 2010 grants amounting to US $504.0m., had been committed since operations commenced, including $20m. as a special contribution to the International Fund for Agricultural Development (IFAD) and a further $20.0m. approved under a new Food Aid Special Grant Account, which was established in 2003 to combat famine in Africa. In addition, by the end of 2010 OFID had committed $1,021.8m. to the resources of IFAD, an IMF Trust Fund and the IMF's Poverty Reduction and Growth Facility (PRGF) Trust.

During the year ending 31 December 2010 the Fund's total commitments amounted to US $1,374.3m. (compared with $1,382.4m. in the previous year). These commitments included public sector loans, amounting to $637.9m., supporting 45 projects in 38 countries. The largest proportion of loans (33% of the total) was for transportation projects, for example the construction or rehabilitation of roads (in Albania, Grenada, Kenya and Niger), construction of a light rail system in Turkey, and the rehabilitation of a ship yard in Cameroon. The energy sector accounted for 24% of the total for projects including the improvement of electricity generation, transmission and distributions in Cuba, Ethiopia, Tanzania and Uganda, and the construction of a gas turbine power plant in Egypt. Public sector loans for the water supply and sewerage sector, amounting to 19% of the total, financed projects to improve water supply infrastructure in Belize, Côte d'Ivoire, Nepal, Sierra Leone and Swaziland, sewerage facilities in Panama and irrigation infrastructure in Cambodia. Health sector loans (10%) included projects to construct new health centres or hospitals in Burkina Faso, Ghana, the Maldives and Viet Nam. Agriculture and agro-industry loans (9%) financed irrigation schemes (in Egypt, Lebanon and Mali), other food security efforts (in Niger), and market access initiatives (in Cuba and Guatemala). Three loans (4%), were allocated to education projects (in The Gambia, Grenada and Yemen), while one loan (1%) was for the development of the industry sector in Lesotho.

Private sector operations approved during 2010 amounted to US $227.3m., which funded projects in the infrastructure, industry and telecommunications sectors and to the financial sector in order to enhance the availability of credit for small and medium-sized enterprises. During that year the Bank aimed to expand its trade financing activities in order to counter the effects on beneficiary countries of the global financial crisis. Approvals under the Trade Financing Facility amounted to $481.0m. in 2010 (compared with $364.0m. in 2009). Risk-sharing guarantee arrangements totalling $225.0m. were also concluded during 2010 ($480.0m. in the previous year).

During 2010 OFID approved US $28.1m. in grants for 45 projects. Of the total $10.3m. was committed from the Special Grant Account for Palestine to improve living conditions in the poorest communities and to support the work of some 65 local organizations to deliver essential social services. A further $9.4m. was approved from the HIV/AIDS Special Account to support regional or global partnership initiatives, $4.7m. for technical assistance projects, $2.0m. to provide emergency humanitarian aid (to Burkina Faso, Chile, Egypt, Haiti, Mongolia, Niger and Pakistan), and $1.8m. to fund research projects and other related activities.

Publications

Annual Report (in Arabic, English, French and Spanish).
OFID Quarterly.
Pamphlet series, author papers, books and other documents.

Statistics

TOTAL APPROVALS IN 2010, BY SECTOR AND REGION
(US $ million)

	Financing approved	%
Sector:		
Agriculture	186.2	13.5
Education	27.6	2.0
Energy	324.2	23.6
Finance	251.6	18.3
Health	73.5	5.3
Industry	90.8	6.6
Telecommunications	32.7	2.4
Transportation	257.0	18.7
Water supply	118.6	8.6
Palestine and emergency grants	12.3	0.9
Total	1,374.3	100.0
Region:		
Africa	737.0	53.6
Asia	261.3	19.0
Latin America and the Caribbean	342.7	24.9
Europe and multi-regional	33.3	2.4

Source: OFID, *Annual Report 2010*.

PACIFIC COMMUNITY

Address: BP D5, 98848 Nouméa Cedex, New Caledonia.
Telephone: 26-20-00; **fax:** 26-38-18; **e-mail:** spc@spc.int; **internet:** www.spc.int.

In February 1947 the Governments of Australia, France, the Netherlands, New Zealand, the United Kingdom, and the USA signed the Canberra Agreement establishing the South Pacific Commission, which came into effect in July 1948. (The Netherlands withdrew from the Commission in 1962, when it ceased to administer the former colony of Dutch New Guinea, now Papua, formerly known as Irian Jaya, part of Indonesia.) In October 1997 the 37th South Pacific Conference, convened in Canberra, Australia, agreed to rename the organization the Pacific Community, with effect from 6 February 1998. The Secretariat of the Pacific Community (SPC) services the Community, and provides research, technical advice, training and assistance in economic, social and cultural development to 22 countries and territories of the Pacific region. It serves a population of about 6.8m., scattered over some 30m. sq km, more than 98% of which is sea.

MEMBERS

American Samoa	Niue
Australia	Northern Mariana Islands
Cook Islands	Palau
Fiji	Papua New Guinea
France	Pitcairn Islands
French Polynesia	Samoa
Guam	Solomon Islands
Kiribati	Tokelau
Marshall Islands	Tonga
Federated States of Micronesia	Tuvalu
Nauru	USA
New Caledonia	Vanuatu
New Zealand	Wallis and Futuna Islands

Organization

(April 2012)

CONFERENCE OF THE PACIFIC COMMUNITY

The Conference is the governing body of the Community (replacing the former South Pacific Conference) and is composed of representatives of all member countries and territories. The main responsibilities of the Conference, which meets every two years, are to appoint the Director-General, to determine major national or regional policy issues in the areas of competence of the organization and to note changes to the Financial and Staff Regulations approved by the Committee of Representatives of Governments and Administrations (CRGA). The sixth Conference of the Pacific Community was convened in Majuro, Marshall Islands, in November 2011.

COMMITTEE OF REPRESENTATIVES OF GOVERNMENTS AND ADMINISTRATIONS (CRGA)

The CRGA comprises representatives of all member states and territories, having equal voting rights. It meets annually to consider the work programme evaluation conducted by the Secretariat and to discuss any changes proposed by the Secretariat in the context of regional priorities; to consider and approve any policy issues for the organization presented by the Secretariat or by member countries and territories; to consider applicants and make recommendations for the post of Director-General; to approve the administrative and work programme budgets; to approve amendments to the Financial and Staff Regulations; and to conduct annual performance evaluations of the Director-General.

SECRETARIAT

The Secretariat of the Pacific Community (SPC) is headed by a Director-General, a Senior Deputy Director-General and a Deputy Director-General, based in Suva, Fiji. In October 2009 the CRGA approved a reorganization which was completed by January 2011 and included the transfer to SPC of activities from the Pacific Islands Applied Geoscience Commission (SOPAC), with a view to making

SPC the lead co-ordinating agency for the Pacific regional energy sector. The reorganization provided for Secretariat divisions of Applied Geoscience and Technology; Economic Development; Land Resources; Fisheries, Aquaculture and Marine Ecosystems; Public Health; and Social Resources; and for the merger into the SPC of the South Pacific Board for Educational Assessment (SPBEA), initially as a stand-alone programme. The Secretariat provides information services, including library facilities, publications, translation and computer services. During February–April 2012 a review of the SPC's role in regional development was being undertaken.

Director-General: Dr JIMMIE RODGERS (Solomon Islands).

Deputy Directors-General: FEKITAMOELOA KATOA 'UTOIKAMANU (Tonga), RICHARD MANN (Germany).

North Pacific Regional Office: POB 2299, Botanical Garden 2, Kolonia, Pohnpei, Federated States of Micronesia; tel. 320-7523; fax 320-5854; e-mail amenay@spc.int.

Suva Regional Office: Private Mail Bag, Suva, Fiji; tel. 3370733; fax 3370021; e-mail spcsuva@spc.org.fj.

Activities

SPC provides, on request of its member countries, technical assistance, advisory services, information and clearing house services aimed at developing the technical, professional, scientific, research, planning and management capabilities of the regional population. SPC also conducts regional conferences and technical meetings, as well as training courses, workshops and seminars at the regional or country level. It provides small grants-in-aid and awards to meet specific requests and needs of members. In November 1996 the Conference agreed to establish a specific Small Islands States (SIS) fund to provide technical services, training and other relevant activities. The Pacific Community oversees the maritime programme and telecommunications policy activities of the Pacific Islands Forum Secretariat.

The 1999 Conference, held in Tahiti in December, adopted the Déclaration de Tahiti Nui, a mandate that detailed the operational policies and mechanisms of the Pacific Community, taking into account operational changes not covered by the founding Canberra Agreement. The Declaration was regarded as a 'living document' that would be periodically revised to record subsequent modifications of operational policy.

SPC has signed memoranda of understanding with the World Health Organization (WHO), the Forum Fisheries Agency, the South Pacific Regional Environment Programme (SPREP), and several other partners. The organization participates in meetings of the Council of Regional Organizations in the Pacific (CROP). Representatives of SPC and SPREP have in recent years convened periodic meetings to develop regional technical co-operation and harmonization of work programmes.

SPC aims to develop joint country strategies with each of the Pacific Community's member countries and territories, detailing the full scope of its assistance over a defined period.

APPLIED GEOSCIENCE AND TECHNOLOGY

The reorganization of SPC implemented during 2010 provided for the core work programme of SOPAC (see above) to be absorbed into SPC as a new Applied Geoscience and Technology Division. The Division has responsibility for ensuring the productive regional utilization of earth sciences (geology, geophysics, oceanography and hydrology), and comprises the following three technical work programmes: ocean and islands; water and sanitation; and disaster reduction.

ECONOMIC DEVELOPMENT

The Economic Development Division (EDD) has the following four pillars: programmes in the areas of Transport, Energy, Infrastructure and Information and Communications Technology (ICT). An inaugural Regional Meeting of Ministers for Energy, ICT and Transport was held in April 2011, on the theme of 'strategic engagement for economic development'.

The Transport Programme comprises the work of the former Regional Maritime Programme (RMP—amalgamated into the main Transport Programme in mid-2011), as well as research and advisory services relating to specific capacity in aviation, and research into transport research. In 2002 the RMP launched the model Pacific Islands Maritime Legislation and Regulations as a framework for the development of national maritime legislation. Since 2006 the Transport programme has provided the secretariat of the Pacific Maritime Transport Alliance. The inaugural regional meeting of ministers responsible for maritime transport was convened in April 2007. In April 2011 SPEC transport ministers adopted a Framework for Action on Transport Services (FATS) to support all Pacific Islands and Territories (PICTs) to provide regular, safe and affordable air and sea transport services

The Energy Programme comprises related activities transferred from SOPAC (see above), including its advisory functions and activities relating to petroleum data and information. The Programme co-ordinates and leads work on: energy policy, planning, legislation and regulation; petroleum, including procurement, transport, storage and pricing mechanisms; renewable energy production; energy efficiency and conservation; and support for the Pacific Power Association and other relevant bodies regarding to power generation and electric utilities. In April 2011 ministers responsible for energy adopted a Framework for Action on Energy Security in the Pacific (FAESP) and an implementation plan.

The Pacific ICT Outreach (PICTO) Programme, established in January 2010, implements the 'Framework for Action on ICT for Development in the Pacific', endorsed in June 2010 by ministers responsible for ICT; and takes into account initiatives such as the Pacific Regional Infrastructure facility; to implement the Pacific Plan Digital Strategy; to take over work on ICT policy and regulations hitherto undertaken by the Pacific Islands Forum Secretariat; to continue ongoing SPC work relating to submarine cable and satellite communication technology; and to support the ongoing Oceania 'one laptop per child' (OLPC) initiative. In October SPC launched the e-Pacific Island Countries (e-PIC), an online portal providing access to information including country profiles; downloadable documents relating to policy, legal and regulatory matters, publications, news and research materials; a regional forum; and a register of ICT professionals and policy makers. In April 2011 SPC hosted a Pacific ICT Ministerial Forum, and signed an agreement with the International Telecommunications Union to enhance co-operation between the two organizations and facilitate the implementation of ICT and cyber protection programmes throughout the region. A Pacific Regional Workshop on Cybercrime, was held in Nukúalofa, Tonga, in May.

With other regional partners, including the Pacific Islands Forum and Asian Development Bank, the SPC supported the Pacific Conference on the Human Face of the Global Economic Crisis, hosted by the Vanuatu Government in February 2010, in Port Vila.

In 2012 the SPC was supporting a Tonga Government project, being implemented in connection with the Australian Government's Pacific Adaptation Strategy Assistance Program (PASAP), to assess vulnerability and adaptation to sea level rises on the small island of Lifuka.

LAND RESOURCES

The Land Resources Division (LRD) comprises three major programmes: the sustainable management of integrated forest and agriculture systems programme; the biosecurity and trade support programme; and the food security and health programme. In September 2008 ministers of agriculture and forestry of Pacific Island countries, convened in Apia, Samoa, approved a second LRD strategic plan, following on from a first strategic plan that had been implemented during 2005–08. The second plan, covering the period 2009–12, emphasized three primary objectives: strengthened regional food and nutritional security (identified in view of recently soaring global food prices); integrated and sustainable agriculture and forestry resource management and development; and improved biosecurity and increased trade in agriculture and forestry products. The LRD has increasingly decentralized the delivery of its services, which are co-ordinated at the country level by personnel within national agricultural systems. The LRD aims to develop the capacity of PICTs in initiatives such as policy analysis and advice, and support for agricultural science and technology. In December 2011 a regional meeting on biosecurity urged increased surveillance concerning alien pest and disease invasion, which at once can derive from international trade, and also risks undermining trade. In February 2012 the LRD organized a workshop aimed at supporting PICTs in strengthening crop production through improved pest management methods, and, at that time, a new regional project on building capacities to develop integrated crop management strategies was launched. SPC hosts the Centre for Pacific Crops and Trees (CePaCT, known prior to 2007 as the Regional Germplasm Centre), which assists PICTs in efforts to conserve and access regional genetic resources. In 2001 the Pacific Community endorsed the Pacific Agricultural Plant Genetic Resources Network (PAPGREN), which is implemented by the LRD and other partners. The Pacific Animal Health Information System (PAHIS) provides data on regional livestock numbers and the regional status of animal diseases, and the Pacific Islands Pest List Database provides a register of regional agriculture, forestry and environmental pests. In 2003 a European Union-funded Development of Sustainable Agriculture in the Pacific (DSAP) project was initiated to assist 10 member countries to implement sustainable agriculture measures and to improve food production and security. A further six Pacific countries joined the programme in 2004. The LRD co-ordinates the development of organic agriculture in the Pacific region. In 2008 it adopted the

Pacific Organic Standard, and it supports the Pacific Organic and Ethical Trade Community (POETCom), which was launched in 2009 to replace a previous Regional Organic Task Force (established in 2006). In December 2009 a POETCom technical experts' group met to finalize a farmers' version of the Pacific Organic Standard. IFAD and the International Federation of Organic Agricultural Movement (IFOAM) contributed to the development of the Pacific Regional Organic Strategic Plan for 2009–13. In September 2009 SPC organized a meeting of heads of forestry agencies in the Pacific, on the theme 'Forests, Climate Change and Markets'. In October 2010 a multi-agency Food Secure Pacific (FSP) working group, established in 2008 by SPC, Pacific Islands Forum Secretariat, FAO, UNICEF and WHO, began implementing a new Framework for Action on Food Security in the Pacific, which had been endorsed by a Pacific Food Summit, convened in April 2010, in Port Vila, Vanuatu. The seventh Conference of the Pacific Community was held, in November 2011, on the theme 'Climate change and food security: Managing risks for sustainable development'.

FISHERIES, AQUACULTURE AND MARINE ECOSYSTEMS

The Fisheries, Aquaculture and Marine Ecosystems (FAME) Division aims to support and co-ordinate the sustainable development and management of inshore fisheries resources in the region, to undertake scientific research in order to provide member governments with relevant information for the sustainable development and management of tuna and billfish resources in and adjacent to the South Pacific region, and to provide data and analytical services to national fisheries departments. The principal programmes under FAME are the Coastal Fisheries Programme (CFP) and the Oceanic Fisheries Programme (OFP). The development and advisory activities of the CFP are focused within the near territorial and archipelagic waters of the PICTs. The CFP is divided into the following sections: the Reef Fisheries Observatory; sustainable fisheries development; fisheries management; fisheries training; and aqualculture. SPC administers the Pacific Island Aquaculture Network, a forum for promoting regional aquaculture development. During 2007 a Pacific Regional Aquatic Biosecurity Initiative was initiated. In contrast to the CFP, the OFP focuses it activities within 200-mile exclusive economic zones and surrounding waters, and is mandated to equip PICTs with the necessary scientific information and advice for rationally managing and exploiting the regional resources of tuna, billfish and related species. The OFP consists of the following three sections: statistics and monitoring; tuna ecology and biology; and stock assessment and modelling. The statistics and monitoring section maintains a database of industrial tuna fisheries in the region. The OFP contributed research and statistical information for the formulation of the Convention for the Conservation and Management of Highly Migratory Fish Stocks in the Western and Central Pacific, which entered into force in June 2004 and aims to establish a regime for the sustainable management of tuna reserves. In March 2002 SPC and European Commission launched a Pacific Regional Oceanic and Coastal Fisheries Project (PROCFISH). The oceanic component of the project aimed to assist the OFP with advancing knowledge of tuna fisheries ecosystems, while the coastal element was to produce the first comparative regional baseline assessment of reef fisheries. Since 2006 the OFP has organized annual tuna Stock Assessment Workshops (SAW) with participation by senior regional fishery officers; some 30 officials from 23 Pacific countries attended in 2011. The theme of the fifth Pacific Community Conference, convened in November 2007, was 'The future of Pacific fisheries'; a set of recommendations on managing the regional fisheries was endorsed by the Conference.

SPC hosts the Pacific Office of the WorldFish Center (the International Centre for Living Aquatic Resources Management—ICLARM); SPC and the WorldFish Center have jointly implemented a number of projects. SPC also hosts the Co-ordination Unit of the Coral Reef Initiative for the South Pacific (CRISP), which was launched in January 2005 to address the protection and management of the region's coral reefs.

PUBLIC HEALTH

The Public Health Division aims to implement health promotion programmes; to assist regional authorities to strengthen health information systems and to promote the use of new technology for health information development and disease control; to promote efficient health services management; and to help all Pacific Islanders to attain a level of health and quality of life that will enable them to contribute to the development of their communities. The three main areas of focus of the Public Health Division are: noncommunicable diseases (such as heart disease, cerebrovascular disease and diabetes, which are prevalent in parts of the region); communicable diseases (such as HIV/AIDS, other sexually tranmitted infections—STIs, TB, and vector-borne diseases such as malaria and dengue fever); and public health policy. A Healthy Pacific Lifestyle section aims to assist member countries to improve and sustain health, in particular through advice on nutrition, physical activity and the damaging effects of alcohol and tobacco. The Public Health Surveillance and Communicable Disease Control section is the focal point of the Pacific Public Health Surveillance Network (PPHSN), a regional framework established in 1996 jointly by SPC and WHO, with the aim of sustainably advancing regional public health surveillance and response. SPC operates a project (mainly funded by Australia and New Zealand), to prevent AIDS and STIs among young people through peer education and awareness. SPC is the lead regional agency for co-ordinating and monitoring the implementation of the Pacific Regional Strategy on HIV/AIDS and other STIs, endorsed by both the Community and the Pacific Islands Forum, and covering the period 2009–13. In March 2007 the Pacific Community launched the Oceania Society for Sexual Health and HIV Medicine, a new Pacific network aimed at ensuring access to best practice prevention, treatment, care and support services in the area of sexual health and HIV/AIDS. SPC and WHO jointly organize regular meetings aimed at strengthening TB control in the region. In February 2006 SPC established a Pacific Regional Infection Control Network, based in Fiji, to improve communication and access to expert technical advice on all aspects of infectious diseases and control. During 2006 SPC, in partnership with FAO, WHO and the World Organisation for Animal Health, established the Pacific Regional Influenza Pandemic Preparedness Project (PRIPPP), with the aim of supporting the PICTs in elaborating plans to prepare for outbreaks of avian influenza or other rapidly contagious diseases. A Pacific Community Pandemic Task Force, established under the PRIPPP and comprising human and animal health experts from Pacific governments and international and regional organizations, met for the first time in March 2007 at the Pacific Community headquarters. In July 2009 Pacific ministers of health met to discuss issues including the development of strategies to control and prevent escalating diseases in the region, and the impact on regional nutrition and health of reduced household incomes in view of the global economic crisis. A Pacific Non-communicable Disease (NCD) Forum, held in Nadi, Fiji, in August, agreed recommendations on action to address the increasing regional prevalence of NCDs (also referred to as 'lifestyle diseases'). In June 2011 SPC, with WHO, organized the ninth meeting of Pacific Island ministers of health, at which it was acknowledged that the escalation in incidence of NCDs remained a priority for all regional governments.

SOCIAL RESOURCES

The Social Resources Division comprises the Human Development Programme (HDP), the Regional Media Centre, the Pacific Regional Rights Resource Team, and the Statistics and Demography Programmes.

The HDP focuses on the areas of gender; youth; culture; and community education. The HDP's Pacific Women's Bureau (PWB) aims to promote the social, economic and cultural advancement of women in the region by assisting governments and regional organizations to include women in the development planning process. The PWB also provides technical and advisory services, advocacy and management support training to groups concerned with women in development and gender and development, and administers the Pacific Women's Information Network (PACWIN). A new adviser for gender equality was appointed in September 2008. The SPC hosted the 11th Triennial Conference of Pacific Women, at its Nouméa, New Caledonia headquarters, in August 2010. The Pacific Youth Bureau (PYB) co-ordinates the implementation of the Pacific Youth Strategy (PYS), which is updated at five-yearly intervals, most recently to cover the period 2011–15, and aims to develop opportunities for young people to play an active role in society. The PYB provides non-formal education and support for youth, community workers and young adults in community development subjects and provides grants to help young people find employment. It also advises and assists the Pacific Youth Council in promoting a regional youth identity. At the first Pacific Youth Festival, held in Tahiti in July 2006, a Pacific Youth Charter was formulated, to be incorporated into the PYS. A Pacific Youth Mapping Exercise (PYME) was undertaken in 2007, with the aim of establishing a complete picture of youth programmes being implemented across the region. The second Pacific Youth Festival, held in Suva, Fiji, in July 2009, included discussions on the following issues: promoting healthy living; Pacific identity; adaptation to climate change; and governance, peace and security. In September 2011 the Community published a *State of Pacific Youth Report*, which had been prepared with the Pacific Office of the UN Children's Fund.

The HDP works to preserve and promote the cultural heritage of the Pacific Islands. The Programme assists with the training of librarians, archivists and researchers and promotes instruction in local languages, history and art at schools in the PICTs. SPC acts as the secretariat of the Council of Pacific Arts, which organizes the Festival of Pacific Arts on a four-yearly basis. The 11th Festival was to be held in July 2012, in Solomon Islands, on the theme 'Culture in Harmony with Nature'. In March 2010 representatives of cultural interests from PICTs met to consider means of strengthening the profile of Pacific culture, including developing a regional cultural strategy, incorporating culture into educational programmes, establishing partnerships at national, regional and international level, and accessing funding for cultural projects. In November 2006 the HDP published *Guidelines for developing national legislation for the protection of traditional knowledge and expressions of culture*, with the aim of protecting indigenous Pacific knowledge and cultures. The SPC regional office in Fiji administers a Community Education Training Centre (CETC), which conducts a seven-month training course for up to 40 female community workers annually, with the objective of training women in methods of community development so that they can help others to achieve better living conditions for island families and communities.

The Pacific Regional Rights Resource Team provides training, technical support, and policy and advocacy services specifically tailored towards the Pacific region.

The Regional Media Centre provides training, technical assistance and production materials in all areas of the media for member countries and territories, community work programmes, donor projects and regional non-governmental organizations. The Centre comprises a radio broadcast unit, a graphic design and publication unit and a TV and video unit.

The Statistics Programme assists governments and administrations in the region to provide effective and efficient national statistical services through the provision of training activities, a statistical information service and other advisory services. A Regional Meeting of Heads of Statistics facilitates the integration and co-ordination of statistical services throughout the region, while the Pacific Regional Information System (PRISM), initiated by the National Statistics Office of the Pacific Islands and developed with British funding, provides statistical information about member countries and territories. The first regional meeting concerned with cultural statistics was convened in May 2011.

The Demography Programme provides technical support in population, demographic and development issues to member governments, other SPC programmes, and organizations active in the region. The Programme aims to assist governments effectively to analyse data and utilize it into the formulation of national development policies and programmes. The Programme organizes national workshops in population and development planning, provides short-term professional attachments, undertakes demographic research and analysis, and disseminates information.

SOUTH PACIFIC BOARD FOR EDUCATIONAL ASSESSMENT

Under the 2010 reorganization of SPC, the South Pacific Board for Educational Assessment (SPBEA, established in 1980 to develop procedures for assessing national and regional secondary education certificates) merged into the Community, in January 2010, initially as a stand-alone programme.

Finance

SPC has an annual budget of around US $65m., to be funded jointly by Community member states and international donors.

Publications

Annual Report.
Fisheries Newsletter (quarterly).
Pacific Aids Alert Bulletin (quarterly).
Pacific Island NCDs.
Pacific Island Nutrition (quarterly).
Regional Tuna Bulletin (quarterly).
Report of the Conference of the Pacific Community.
Women's Newsletter (quarterly).
Technical publications, statistical bulletins, advisory leaflets and reports.

PACIFIC ISLANDS FORUM

Address: Private Mail Bag, Suva, Fiji.
Telephone: 3312600; **fax:** 3301102; **e-mail:** info@forumsec.org.fj; **internet:** www.forumsec.org.

The Pacific Islands Forum (which in October 2000 changed its name from South Pacific Forum, in order to reflect the expansion of its membership since its establishment) was founded as the gathering of Heads of Government of the independent and self-governing states of the South Pacific; the first annual Forum meeting was held on 5 August 1971, in Wellington, New Zealand. The Pacific Islands Forum Secretariat was established (as the South Pacific Bureau for Economic Co-operation—SPEC) by an agreement signed on 17 April 1973, at the third Forum meeting, in Apia, Western Samoa (now Samoa). SPEC was redesignated as the South Pacific Forum Secretariat in 1988, and the present name was adopted in October 2000. The Secretariat aims to enhance the economic and social well-being of the Pacific Islands peoples, in support of the efforts of national governments. In October 2005 the 36th Forum adopted an Agreement Establishing the Pacific Islands Forum, which aimed to formalize the grouping's status as a full intergovernmental organization.

Members

Australia
Cook Islands
Fiji*
Kiribati
Marshall Islands
Federated States of Micronesia
Nauru
New Zealand
Niue
Palau
Papua New Guinea
Samoa
Solomon Islands
Tonga
Tuvalu
Vanuatu

* In May 2009 Fiji was suspended from participation in the Forum.

Note: French Polynesia and New Caledonia were admitted to the Forum as associate members in 2006. The Asian Development Bank, the Commonwealth, the UN, Timor-Leste, Tokelau, Wallis and Futuna, the Western and Central Pacific Fisheries Commission, and the World Bank are observers. In September 2011 the 42nd Forum offered observer status to the ACP Group.

Organization

(April 2012)

FORUM OFFICIALS COMMITTEE

The Forum Officials Committee is the Secretariat's executive board, overseeing its activities. It comprises representatives and senior officials from all member countries. It meets twice a year, immediately before the meetings of the Pacific Islands Forum and at the end of the year, to discuss in detail the Secretariat's work programme and annual budget.

FORUM MEETING

Each annual leaders' Forum is chaired by the Head of Government of the country hosting the meeting, who remains as Forum Chairperson until the next Forum. The Forum has no written constitution or international agreement governing its activities nor any formal rules relating to its purpose, membership or conduct of meeting. Decisions are always reached by consensus, it never having been found necessary or desirable to vote formally on issues. In October 1994 the Forum was granted observer status by the General Assembly of the United Nations. The 42nd Forum was convened in Auckland, New Zealand, in September 2011. The 43rd Forum was to be held in August 2012, in Rarotonga, Cook Islands.

DIALOGUE PLENARY MEETING

From 1989–2006 each annual Pacific Islands Forum meeting was followed by individual dialogues with representatives of selected countries considered to have a long-term interest in the region. A review of the post-Forum dialogues, undertaken in August 2006, recommended that the individual dialogues should be replaced by a new single Post-Forum Dialogue Plenary Meeting, to enable structured communication at ministerial level between Forum and Dialogue countries; and that 'core' dialogue partners, with a special engagement in and commitment to the region, should be identified. The findings of the review were approved in October 2006 by the 37th Forum meeting, and the new post-Forum dialogue structure was initiated following the 38th Forum. In 2012 Canada, the People's Republic of China, France, India, Indonesia, Italy, Japan, the

Republic of Korea, Malaysia, Philippines, Thailand, the United Kingdom, the USA, and the European Union (EU) had dialogue partner status. A separate post-Forum session is convened between the Republic of China (Taiwan) and six of the Forum member states. In August 2010 leaders attending the 41st Forum determined to establish a review process to reassess the status of Post-Forum Dialogue partners; it was announced in September 2011 that implementation would begin during 2012.

SECRETARIAT

The Secretariat acts as the administrative arm of the Forum. It is headed by a Secretary-General, assisted by two Deputy Secretaries-General, and has a staff of some 70 people drawn from the member countries. The Secretariat comprises the following four Divisions: Corporate Services; Development and Economic Policy; Trade and Investment; and Political, International and Legal Affairs. The Secretariat's Pacific Plan Office services the Pacific Plan Action Committee and supports the overall implementation of the Pacific Plan. A Pacific ACP/EU Co-operation unit assists member states and regional organizations with submitting projects to the EU. A Smaller Island States (SIS) unit was established within the Secretariat in 2006. The Secretariat chairs the Council of Regional Organizations in the Pacific (CROP), an ad hoc committee comprising the heads of 10 regional organizations, which aims to discuss and co-ordinate the policies and work programmes of the various agencies in order to avoid duplication of or omissions in their services to member countries.

Secretary-General: Tuiloma Neroni Slade (Samoa).

Deputy Secretary-General (Strategic Partnership and Co-ordination): Feleti Penitala Teo (Tuvalu).

Deputy Secretary-General (Economic Governance and Security: Andie Fong Toy (New Zealand).

Activities

The Pacific Islands Forum provides an opportunity for informal discussions to be held on a wide range of common issues and problems and meets annually or when issues require urgent attention.

The Pacific Islands Forum Secretariat organizes Forum-related events, implements decisions by the Leaders, facilitates the delivery of development assistance to member states, and undertakes the political and legal mandates of Forum meetings.

In February 2007 a Regional Institutional Framework (RIF) Taskforce, comprising representatives of the member states of the Council of Regional Organizations in the Pacific agencies, convened for the first time, under Secretariat auspices. The RIF Taskforce was mandated by the October 2006 Forum to develop an appropriate institutional framework for supporting the implementation of the Pacific Plan. It was envisaged that the Pacific regional institutions would be reorganized under the following three 'pillars': a political and general policy institution; an activity sector-focused technical institution; and academic/training organizations. Lourdes Pangelinan, a former Director-General of the Pacific Community, was given responsibility for overseeing the development of the RIF.

In December 2008 the Forum Officials Committee approved a Forum corporate plan, covering the period 2008–12, and focusing on the following strategic areas: economic governance; political governance and security; regional co-ordination; and corporate services.

PACIFIC PLAN

In August 2003 regional leaders attending the 34th Forum, held in Auckland, New Zealand, authorized the establishment of an Eminent Persons Group to consider the future activities and development of the Forum. In April 2004 a Special Leaders' Retreat, also convened in Auckland, in order to review a report prepared by the Group, mandated the development of a new Pacific Plan on Strengthening Regional Co-operation and Integration as a means of addressing the challenges confronting the Pacific Island states. Consequently a Pacific Plan Task Force, managed by the Forum Secretary-General in consultation with a core leaders' group, undertook work to formulate the document. The finalized Pacific Plan, which was endorsed by the October 2005 Forum, incorporates development initiatives that are focused around the four 'pillars' of economic growth, sustainable development, good governance, and regional security and partnerships. It also recognizes the specific needs of SIS. The Pacific Plan is regarded as a 'living document', which can be amended and updated continuously to accommodate emerging priorities. The Pacific Plan Action Committee (PPAC), comprising representatives of the Forum member states and chaired by the Forum Chairperson, has met regularly since January 2006. Regional organizations, working in partnership with national governments and other partners, are responsible for co-ordinating the implementation of—and compiling reports on—many of the specific Pacific Plan initiatives. The 37th Forum leaders' meeting in October 2006 adopted the Nadi Decisions on the Pacific Plan, prioritizing several key commitments in the four pillar areas; these were consequently incorporated into the ('living') Plan during 2007. In October 2007 the 38th Forum adopted a further set of key commitments, the Vava'U Decisions on the Pacific Plan. More key commitments and priority areas, to advance the Pacific Plan over the period 2010–13, were adopted by the 40th Forum, in August 2009. The five main themes of the Plan during 2010–13 were: fostering economic development and promoting opportunities for broad-based growth; improving the livelihoods and the well-being of the Pacific peoples; addressing the impacts of climate change; achieving stronger national development through better governance; and ensuring improved social, political and legal conditions to enable future stability, safety and security.

POLITICAL AND SOCIAL AFFAIRS AND REGIONAL SECURITY

The Political, International and Legal Affairs Division of the Secretariat organizes and services the meetings of the Forum, disseminates its views, administers the Forum's observer office at the United Nations, and aims to strengthen relations with other regional and international organizations, in particular APEC and ASEAN. The Division's other main concern is to promote regional co-operation in law enforcement and legal affairs, and it provides technical support for the drafting of legal documents and for law enforcement capacity building.

In recent years the Forum Secretariat has been concerned with assessing the legislative reforms and other commitments needed to ensure implementation of the 1992 Honiara Declaration on Law Enforcement Co-operation. The Secretariat assists member countries to ratify and implement the 1988 UN Convention against Illicit Trafficking in Narcotic Drugs and Psychotropic Substances. At the end of 2001 a conference of Forum immigration ministers expressed concern at rising levels of human-trafficking and illegal immigration in the region, and recommended that member states become parties to the 2000 UN Convention Against Transnational Organized Crime. A Pacific Transnational Crime Co-ordination Centre was established in Suva, Fiji, in 2004, to enhance and gather law enforcement intelligence. In September 2006 the Forum, in co-operation with the USA and the UN Global Programme Against Money Laundering (administered by the UN Office on Drugs and Crime), launched the Pacific Anti-Money Laundering Programme (PALP). PALP provides technical assistance to member states for the development of their national anti-money laundering and counter-terrorism financing regimes, in accordance with the Pacific Plan's development priority of regional security. Under the Pacific Plan, the Forum Secretariat requested the establishment of a Pacific Islands Regional Security Technical Co-operation Unit to support legislative efforts regarding, *inter alia*, transnational organized crime, counter-terrorism and financial intelligence.

In July 1995, following a decision of the French Government to resume testing of nuclear weapons in French Polynesia, members of the Forum resolved to increase diplomatic pressure on the Governments of France, the United Kingdom, and the USA to accede to the 1986 South Pacific Nuclear-Free Zone Treaty (Treaty of Rarotonga), prohibiting the acquisition, stationing or testing of nuclear weapons in the region. Following France's decision, announced in January 1996, to end the programme four months earlier than scheduled, representatives of the Governments of the three countries signed the Treaty in March.

Since 2001 the Forum has sent election observer groups to monitor elections taking place in member states, and, since 2004, joint election observer missions have been undertaken with the Commonwealth.

In September 2008 the first Pacific Islands-EU troika ministerial meeting was convened, in Brussels, Belgium, under a new Forum-EU enhanced political dialogue framework, which was to cover areas including regional security and governance, development co-operation, economic stability and growth, the environment and trade.

In October 2000 leaders attending the 31st Forum, convened in Tarawa, Kiribati, adopted the Biketawa Declaration, which outlined a mechanism for responding to any security crises that might occur in the region, while also urging members to undertake efforts to address the fundamental causes of potential instability. In August 2003 regional leaders convened at the 34th Forum commended the swift response by member countries and territories in deploying a Regional Assistance Mission in Solomon Islands (RAMSI), which had been approved by Forum ministers of foreign affairs at a meeting held in Sydney, Australia, in June, in accordance with the Biketawa Declaration. In December 2011 the Solomon Islands Government agreed to lead a process under which RAMSI would be phased out. In January 2009 Forum heads of state and government convened a Special Leaders' Retreat, in Port Moresby, Papua New Guinea, to consider the political situation in Fiji. The meeting resolved to suspend Fiji from the Forum if no date for democratic elections had been set by the interim authorities in that country by 1 May. Fiji's suspension was confirmed in May.

The 33rd Forum, held in Suva, Fiji, in August 2002, adopted the Nasonini Declaration on Regional Security, which recognized the need for immediate and sustained regional action to combat international terrorism and transnational crime, in view of the perceived increased threat to global and regional security following the major terrorist attacks perpetrated against targets in the USA in September 2001. In October 2007 the 37th Forum determined to develop a Regional Co-operation for Counter-Terrorism Assistance and Response model.

In August 2003 regional leaders attending the 34th Forum adopted a set of Forum Principles of Good Leadership, establishing key requirements for good governance, including respect for law and the system of government, and respect for cultural values, customs and traditions, and for freedom of religion.

In December 2009 the Forum Secretariat and the World Intellectual Property Organization launched a Traditional Knowledge Action Plan for Forum Island Countries, which sought to protect Pacific traditional knowledge from misuse without compensation to its owners.

In October 2005 the 36th Forum urged the adoption of national and regional avian influenza preparedness measures and considered a proposal to establish a Pacific Health Fund to address issues such as avian influenza, HIV/AIDS, malaria, and non-communicable diseases. In June 2011 regional ministers of health issued the Honiara Communiqué on the Pacific NCD Crisis, highlighting the impact of a rapid increase in non-communicable diseases (NCDs) in the region (the estimated cause of three-quarters of adult deaths). In September 2011 the 42nd Forum issued a Leaders' Statement on Non-Communicable Diseases.

In August 2010 the 41st Forum welcomed the outcome of the Pacific Conference on the Human Face of the Global Economic Crisis, which had been convened in February of that year, with participation by policy-makers and civil society and private sector delegates from 16 Pacific Island countries, as well as development partners and representatives of UN agencies and regional organizations, including the Forum Secretariat.

In October 2010 a multi-agency Food Secure Pacific (FSP) working group, established in 2008 by the Forum Secretariat, the Secretariat of the Pacific Community, FAO, UNICEF and WHO, began implementing a new Framework for Action on Food Security in the Pacific, which had been endorsed by a Pacific Food Summit, convened in April 2010, in Port Vila, Vanuatu.

TRADE, ECONOMIC CO-OPERATION AND SUSTAINABLE DEVELOPMENT

The Secretariat's Trade and Investment Division extends advice and technical assistance to member countries in policy, development, export marketing, and information dissemination. Trade policy activities are mainly concerned with improving private sector policies, for example investment promotion, assisting integration into the world economy (including the provision of information and technical assistance to member states on WTO-related matters and supporting Pacific Island ACP states with preparations for negotiations on trade partnership with the EU under the Cotonou Agreement), and the development of businesses. During 2004–09 the Secretariat was supported in these activities through PACREIP (see below). The Secretariat aims to assist both island governments and private sector companies to enhance their capacity in the development and exploitation of export markets, product identification and product development. A regional trade and investment database is being developed. The Secretariat co-ordinates the activities of the regional trade offices located in Australia, New Zealand and Japan (see below). A representative trade office in Beijing, People's Republic of China, opened in January 2002. A Forum office was opened in Geneva, Switzerland, in 2004 to represent member countries at the WTO. In April 2005 the Pacific Islands Private Sector Organisation (PIPSO), representing regional private sector interests, was established. The PIPSO Secretariat, hosted by the Forum Secretariat, was inaugurated in April 2007. In August of that year PIPSO organized the first Pacific Islands Business Forum, convened in Nadi, Fiji.

In 1981 the South Pacific Regional Trade and Economic Co-operation Agreement (SPARTECA) came into force. SPARTECA aimed to redress the trade deficit of the Pacific Island countries with Australia and New Zealand. It is a non-reciprocal trade agreement under which Australia and New Zealand offer duty-free and unrestricted access or concessional access for specified products originating from the developing island member countries of the Forum. In 1985 Australia agreed to further liberalization of trade by abolishing (from the beginning of 1987) duties and quotas on all Pacific products except steel, cars, sugar, footwear and garments. In August 1994 New Zealand expanded its import criteria under the agreement by reducing the rule of origin requirement for garment products from 50% to 45% of local content. In response to requests from Fiji, Australia agreed to widen its interpretation of the agreement by accepting as being of local content manufactured products that consist of goods and components of 50% Australian content. A new Fiji/Australia Trade and Economic Relations Agreement (AFTERA) was concluded in March 1999 to complement SPARTECA and compensate for certain trade benefits that were in the process of being withdrawn.

Two major regional trade accords signed by Forum heads of state in August 2001 entered into force in April 2003 and October 2002, respectively: the Pacific Island Countries Trade Agreement (PICTA), providing for the establishment of a Pacific Island free trade area (FTA); and the related Pacific Agreement on Closer Economic Relations (PACER), incorporating trade and economic co-operation measures and envisaging the phased establishment of a regional single market comprising the PICTA FTA and Australia and New Zealand. The FTA was to be implemented over a period of eight years for developing member countries and 10 years for SIS and least developed countries. It was envisaged that negotiations on free trade agreements between Pacific Island states and Australia and New Zealand, with a view to establishing the larger regional single market envisaged by PACER, would commence within eight years of PICTA's entry into force. SPARTECA (see above) would remain operative pending the establishment of the larger single market, into which it would be subsumed. Under the provisions of PACER, Australia and New Zealand were to provide technical and financial assistance to PICTA signatory states in pursuing the objectives of PACER. In August 2003 regional leaders attending the 34th Forum agreed, in principle, that the USA and France should become parties to both PICTA and PACER. In September 2004 Forum trade officials adopted a Regional Trade Facilitation Programme (RTFP), within the framework of PACER, which included measures concerned with customs procedures, quarantine, standards and other activities to harmonize and facilitate trade between Pacific Island states and Australia and New Zealand, as well as with other international trading partners. It was announced in August 2007 that a review of the RTFP was to be undertaken. In March 2008 negotiations commenced on expanding PICTA to include provisions for trade in services as well as trade in goods; the seventh round of negotiations was convened in February 2012. In August leaders attending the 40th Forum, convened in Cairns, Australia, endorsed the Cairns Compact on Strengthening Development Co-ordination in the Pacific, aimed at improving regional economic and development progress despite the ongoing global economic crisis; and agreed that negotiations on a new regional trade and economic integration agreement (PACER-Plus) should commence forthwith. The participants in the PACER-Plus negotiations (which were ongoing in 2012) are Australia, the Cook Islands, Kiribati, the Marshall Islands, the Federated States of Micronesia, Nauru, New Zealand, Niue, Palau, Papua New Guinea, Samoa, the Solomon Islands, Tonga, Tuvalu and Vanuatu. A meeting of Forum ministers of trade, convened in April 2010, proposed that a shared 10-year strategy for trade and investment promotion should be developed. The April 2010 meeting established a new umbrella body, Pacific Islands Trade and Invest, to cover and develop a co-ordinated corporate strategy for the former Pacific Islands Trade and Investment Commissions, based in Auckland, New Zealand and Sydney, Australia; and trade offices in Beijing, People's Republic of China and Tokyo, Japan.

In April 2001 the Secretariat convened a meeting of seven member island states—the Cook Islands, the Marshall Islands, Nauru, Niue, Samoa, Tonga and Vanuatu—as well as representatives from Australia and New Zealand, to address the regional implications of the OECD's Harmful Tax Competition Initiative. (OECD had identified the Cook Islands, the Marshall Islands, Nauru and Niue as so-called 'tax havens' lacking financial transparency and had demanded that they impose stricter legislation to address the incidence of international money-laundering on their territories.) The meeting requested the OECD to engage in conciliatory negotiations with the listed Pacific Island states. The August 2001 Forum reiterated this stance, proclaiming the sovereign right of nations to establish individual tax regimes, and supporting the development of a new co-operative framework to address financial transparency concerns.

The Development and Economic Policy Division of the Secretariat aims to co-ordinate and promote co-operation in development activities and programmes throughout the region. The Division administers a Short Term Advisory Service, which provides consultancy services to help member countries meet economic development priorities, and a Fellowship Scheme to provide practical training in a range of technical and income-generating activities. A Small Island Development Fund aims to assist the economic development of the SIS sub-group of member countries (see below) through project financing. A separate fellowship has also been established to provide training to the Kanak population of New Caledonia, to assist in their social, economic and political development. During 2004–09 a Pacific Regional Assistance to Nauru (PRAN) initiative was implemented. The Division aims to assist regional organizations to identify development priorities and to provide advice to national governments on economic analysis, planning and structural reforms.

In November 2008 the Forum and the EU approved a Pacific Regional Strategy Paper (RSP) and Regional Indicative Programme (RIP), representing the framework for co-operation between the Pacific ACP States and European Commission over the period 2008–13.

In August 2008 the 39th Forum welcomed a new Pacific Region Infrastructure Facility initiated by the World Bank, Asian Development Bank and Governments of Australia and New Zealand.

ENVIRONMENT

The Forum actively promotes the development of effective international legislation to reduce emissions by industrialized countries of so-called 'greenhouse gases'. Such gases contribute to the warming of the earth's atmosphere (the 'greenhouse effect') and to related increases in global sea levels, and have therefore been regarded as a major threat to low-lying islands in the region. The Secretariat has played an active role in supporting regional participation at meetings of the Conference of the Parties to the UN Framework Convention on Climate Change (UNFCCC), and helps to co-ordinate Forum policy on the environment. With support from the Australian Government, it administers a network of stations to monitor sea levels and climate change throughout the Pacific region. The 29th Forum, held in Pohnpei, Federated States of Micronesia, in August 1998, adopted a Statement on Climate Change, which urged all countries to ratify and implement the gas emission reductions agreed upon by UN member states in December 1997 (the so-called Kyoto Protocol of the UNFCCC), and emphasized the Forum's commitment to further measures for verifying and enforcing emission limitation. In October 2005 the 36th Forum approved the Pacific Islands Framework for Action on Climate Change 2006–15, and noted the need to implement national action plans to address climate change issues. In October 2007 leaders attending the 38th Forum reiterated deep concern over the economic, social and environmental impact of climate change, noting the recent findings of the IPCC's *Fourth Assessment Report* and the importance of negotiating a comprehensive international framework to tackle climate change after the expiry of the Kyoto Protocol in 2012. In August 2008 the 39th Forum, held in Alofi, Niue, endorsed the Niue Declaration on Climate Change, which urged international partners to undertake immediate and effective measures to reduce emissions, to use cleaner fuels, and to increase use of renewable energy sources, and directed the Forum Secretariat to work with relevant agencies and member countries and territories in support of a number of commitments, including examining the potential for regional climate change insurance arrangements, and advancing regional expertise in the development and deployment of adaptation technologies. In November 2008 the EU and the Forum Secretariat adopted a joint declaration on co-operating in combating the challenges posed by climate change. The 40th Forum, in August 2009, adopted the Pacific Leaders Call for Action on Climate Change. A mid-term review of the Pacific Islands Framework for Action on Climate Change was undertaken in 2010.

In August 2002 regional leaders attending the 33rd Forum approved a Pacific Island Regional Ocean Policy, which aimed to ensure the future sustainable use of the ocean and its resources by Pacific Island communities and external partners. A Declaration on Deep Sea Bottom Trawling to Protect Biodiversity on the High Seas was adopted in October 2005 by the 36th Forum. In October 2007 leaders attending the 38th Forum urged increased efforts among Forum members to foster a long-term strategic approach to ensuring the effective management of fish stocks, with a particular focus on tuna, and adopted a related Declaration on Pacific Fisheries Resources. In August 2010 the 41st Forum endorsed both a new Regional Monitoring Control and Surveillance Strategy, adopted by Forum ministers responsible for fisheries in July, as the overarching framework to support regional fisheries management, and also endorsed a new Framework for a Pacific Oceanscape, aimed at ensuring the long-term, co-operative sustainable development, management and conservation of the Pacific.

In September 1995 the 26th Forum adopted the Waigani Convention, banning the import into the region of all radioactive and other hazardous wastes, and providing controls for the transboundary movement and management of these wastes. Forum leaders have frequently reiterated protests against the shipment of radioactive materials through the region.

In January 2005, meeting on the fringes of the fifth Summit of the Alliance of Small Island States, in Port Louis, Mauritius, the Secretaries-General of the Pacific Islands Forum Secretariat, the Commonwealth, CARICOM, and the Indian Ocean Commission determined to take collective action to strengthen the disaster preparedness and response capacities of their member countries in the Pacific, Caribbean and Indian Ocean areas. In October 2005 the 36th Forum endorsed the Pacific Regional Framework for Action for Building the Resilience of Nations and Communities to Disasters during 2005–15.

TRANSPORT

The Forum established the Pacific Forum Line and the Association of South Pacific Airlines (see below), as part of its efforts to promote co-operation in regional transport. In May 1998 ministers responsible for aviation in member states approved a new regional civil aviation policy, which envisaged liberalization of air services, common safety and security standards and provisions for shared revenue. The Pacific Islands Air Services Agreement (PIASA) was opened for signature in August 2003, and entered into effect in October 2007, having been ratified by six Pacific Island countries. In August 2004 the Pacific Islands Civil Aviation and Security Treaty (PICASST) was opened for signature, and, in June 2005 PICASST entered into force, establishing a Port Vila, Vanuatu-based Pacific Aviation Security Office. In accordance with the Principles on Regional Transport Services, which were adopted by Forum Leaders in August 2004, the Secretariat was to support efforts to enhance air and shipping services, as well as develop a regional digital strategy.

In August 2004 the 35th Forum adopted a set of Principles on Regional Transport Services, based on the results of a study requested by the 34th Forum, 'to improve the efficiency, effectiveness and sustainability of air and shipping services'.

SMALLER ISLAND STATES

In 1990 the Cook Islands, Kiribati, Nauru, Niue and Tuvalu, among the Forum's smallest island member states, formed the Forum SIS economic sub-group, which convenes an annual summit meeting to address their specific smaller island concerns. These include, in particular, economic disadvantages resulting from a poor resource base, absence of a skilled work-force and lack of involvement in world markets. Small island member states have also been particularly concerned about the phenomenon of global warming and its potentially damaging effects on the region. In September 1997 the Marshall Islands was admitted as the sixth member of SIS, and Palau was subsequently admitted as the seventh member. In February 1998 senior Forum officials, for the first time, met with representatives of the Caribbean Community and the Indian Ocean Commission, as well as other major international organizations, to discuss means to enhance consideration and promotion of the interests of small island states. An SIS unit, established within the Forum Secretariat in 2006, aims to enable high-profile representation of the SIS perspective, particularly in the development of the Pacific Plan, and to enable the small island member states to benefit fully from the implementation of the Plan. In August 2010 the 41st Forum welcomed the outcome of a Pacific High Level Dialogue (convened in February of that year) on the five-year review conference of the 2005 Mauritius Strategy for the further Implementation of the 1994 Barbados Programme of Action for the Sustainable Development of SIS, which was convened in September 2010.

Recent Meetings of the Pacific Islands Forum

The 41st Forum, which took place in Port Vila, Vanuatu, in August 2010, endorsed the Port Vila Declaration on Accelerating Progress on the Achievement of the UN Millennium Development Goals; endorsed a new Regional Monitoring Control and Surveillance Strategy for fisheries (see above); stated strong support for the Pacific Regional Strategy on Disability covering 2010–15, which had been approved by Forum disability ministers in October 2009; endorsed a Framework for Action on Energy Security in the Pacific; and endorsed the Framework for a Pacific Oceanscape (see above).

In early September 2011 the 42nd Forum, held in Auckland, New Zealand, endorsed the Waiheke Declaration on Sustainable Economic Development—recognizing the importance of focusing regional efforts on sectors such as tourism, fisheries and agriculture, in which there is comparative advantage; and a Forum Leaders' Statement on Non-Communicable Diseases (NCDs). Leaders emphasized maximizing the economic benefit from fisheries, expressed concern at the effect of illegal, unreported and unregulated fishing, and stressed the importance of transport links and secure access to energy. The leaders recalled the Honiara Communiqué on the Pacific NCD Crisis, issued by regional health ministers in June 2011, which highlighted the impact of a rapid increase in NCDs in the region (the estimated cause of three-quarters of adult deaths). Leaders undertook to support the Marshall Islands in raising the profile of the issue of international contaminants at international fora.

Finance

The Governments of Australia and New Zealand each contribute some one-third of the annual budget and the remaining amount is shared by the other member Governments. Extra-budgetary funding is contributed mainly by Australia, New Zealand, Japan, the EU and France. The Forum's 2010 budget amounted to $F43.5m. Following a decision of the 36th Forum a Pacific Fund was established to support the implementation of the Pacific Plan, under the management of the Pacific Plan Action Committee.

Publications

Annual Report.

Forum News (quarterly).

Forum Trends.

Forum Secretariat Directory of Aid Agencies.

Pacific Plan Progress Report.

South Pacific Trade Directory.

SPARTECA (guide for Pacific island exporters).

Reports of meetings; profiles of Forum member countries.

Overseas Agencies and Affiliated Organizations

Association of South Pacific Airlines (ASPA): POB 9817, Nadi Airport, Nadi, Fiji; tel. 6723526; fax 6720196; e-mail georgefaktaufon@aspa.aero; internet aspa.aero/index.php; f. 1979 at a meeting of airlines in the South Pacific, convened to promote co-operation among the member airlines for the development of regular, safe and economical commercial aviation within, to and from the South Pacific; mems: 16 regional airlines, two associates; Sec.-Gen. Dr Lee Kwon.

Forum Fisheries Agency (FFA): POB 629, Honiara, Solomon Islands; tel. (677) 21124; fax (677) 23995; e-mail info@ffa.int; internet www.ffa.int; f. 1979 to promote co-operation in fisheries among coastal states in the region; collects and disseminates information and advice on the living marine resources of the region, including the management, exploitation and development of these resources; provides assistance in the areas of law (treaty negotiations, drafting legislation, and co-ordinating surveillance and enforcement), fisheries development, research, economics, computers, and information management; implements a Vessel Monitoring System, to provide automated data collection and analysis of fishing vessel activities throughout the region; on behalf of its 16 member countries, the FFA administers a multilateral fisheries treaty, under which vessels from the USA operate in the region, in exchange for an annual payment; the FFA is implementing the FFA Strategic Plan 2005–20, detailing the medium-term direction of the Agency; Dir Su'a N. F. Tanielu; publs *FFA News Digest* (every two months), *FFA Reports*, *MCS Newsletter* (quarterly), *Tuna Market Newsletter* (monthly).

Pacific Forum Line: POB 105-612, Auckland 1143, New Zealand; tel. (9) 356-2333; fax (9) 356-2330; e-mail info@pflnz.co.nz; internet www.pflnz.co.nz; f. 1977 as a joint venture by South Pacific countries, to provide shipping services to meet the special requirements of the region; operates three container vessels; conducts shipping agency services in Australia, Fiji, New Zealand and Samoa, and stevedoring in Samoa; CEO Henning Hansen.

Pacific Islands Centre (PIC): Meiji University, 1-1 Kanda-Surugadai, Chiyoda-ku, Tokyo 101-8301, Japan; tel. (3) 3296-4545; e-mail info@pic.or.jp; internet www.pic.or.jp; f. 1996 to promote and to facilitate trade, investment and tourism among Forum members and Japan; Dir K. Sohma.

Pacific Islands Forum Trade Office: 5-1-3-1 Tayuan Diplomatic Compound, 1 Xin Dong Lu, Chaoyang District, Beijing 100600, People's Republic of China; tel. (10) 6532-6622; fax (10) 6532-6360; e-mail answers@pifto.org.cn; internet www.pifto.org.cn; f. 2001.

Pacific Islands Private Sector Organization (PIPSO): c/o Pacific Islands Forum Secretariat, Private Mail Bag, Suva, Fiji; tel. 3312600; fax 3301102; e-mail info@pipso.org.fj; internet www.pipso.org; f. 2005 to represent regional private sector interests; organizes Pacific Islands Business Forum; Chair. Hafiz Khan (Fiji).

Pacific Islands Trade and Invest (Sydney): Level 11, 171 Clarence St, Sydney, NSW 20010, Australia; tel. (2) 9290-2133; fax (2) 9299-2151; e-mail info@pitic.org.au; internet www.pitic.org.au; f. 1979 as Pacific Islands Trade and Investment Commission (Sydney), current name adopted 2010; assists Pacific Island Governments and business communities to identify market opportunities in Australia and promotes investment in the Pacific Island countries.

Pacific Islands Trade and Invest (New Zealand): POB 109-395, 5 Short St, Level 3, Newmarket, Auckland, New Zealand; tel. (9) 5295165; fax (9) 5231284; e-mail info@pitic.org.nz; internet www.pacifictradeinvest.com; f. 1988 as Pacific Islands Trade and Investment Commission (New Zealand), current name adopted 2010; Trade Commr Adam Denniss.

SOUTH ASIAN ASSOCIATION FOR REGIONAL COOPERATION—SAARC

Address: POB 4222, Tridevi Marg, Kathmandu, Nepal.

Telephone: (1) 4221785; **fax:** (1) 4227033; **e-mail:** saarc@saarc-sec.org; **internet:** www.saarc-sec.org.

The South Asian Association for Regional Cooperation (SAARC) was formally established in 1985 in order to strengthen and accelerate regional co-operation, particularly in economic development.

MEMBERS

Afghanistan	Maldives
Bangladesh	Nepal
Bhutan	Pakistan
India	Sri Lanka

Observers: People's Republic of China, Iran, Japan, the Republic of Korea, the European Union.

Organization

(April 2012)

SUMMIT MEETING

Heads of state and of government of member states represent the body's highest authority, and a summit meeting is normally held annually. The 17th summit was held in Addu City, Maldives, in November 2011.

COUNCIL OF MINISTERS

The Council of Ministers comprises the ministers of foreign affairs of member countries, who meet twice a year. The Council may also meet in extraordinary session at the request of member states. The responsibilities of the Council include formulation of policies, assessing progress and confirming new areas of co-operation.

STANDING COMMITTEE

The Committee consists of the ministers of foreign affairs of member states. It has overall responsibility for the monitoring and co-ordination of programmes and financing, and determines priorities, mobilizes resources and identifies areas of co-operation. It usually meets twice a year, and submits its reports to the Council of Ministers. The Committee is supported by an ad hoc Programming Committee made up of senior officials, who meet to examine the budget of the Secretariat, confirm the Calendar of Activities and resolve matters assigned to it by the Standing Committee.

TECHNICAL COMMITTEES

SAARC's six Technical Committees cover: Agriculture and rural development; Environment; Health and population activities; Science and technology; Transport; and Women, Youth and Children; and are responsible for forming, co-ordinating, implementing and monitoring programmes in their respective areas of focus. Each committee comprises representatives of member states and meets annually.

SECRETARIAT

The Secretariat comprises the Secretary-General and eight Directors, from each member country, responsible for the following working divisions: Media and Integration of Afghanistan; Agriculture and Rural Development; Environment and Science and Technology; Economic, Trade and Finance; Social Affairs; Information and Publications; Administration, Energy and Tourism; and Human Resource Development, Transport and the SAARC Charter. The Secretary-General is appointed by the Council of Ministers, after being nominated by a member state, and serves a three-year term of office.

Secretary-General: AHMED SALEEM (Maldives).

Activities

The first summit meeting of SAARC heads of state and government, held in Dhaka, Bangladesh, in December 1985, resulted in the signing of the Charter of the South Asian Association for Regional Cooperation. The SAARC Charter stipulates that decisions should be made unanimously, and that 'bilateral and contentious issues' should not be discussed. In August 1993 ministers of foreign affairs of seven countries, meeting in New Delhi, India, adopted a Declaration on South Asian Regional Cooperation. In April 2010 the 16th SAARC summit meeting noted the need to develop a SAARC 'Vision Statement', and determined to organize a South Asia Forum in which to exchange ideas on future regional development. In April 2011 a steering committee for the establishment of the South Asia Forum finalized the 'Objectives, Scope and Guidelines' for the Forum. The 16th summit also directed SAARC to establish a working group to organize the creation of a Conclave of SAARC Parliamentarians, and determined to focus more strongly on people-centric development, preservation of environment and better governance. The 17th SAARC summit, convened in November 2011, in Addu City, Maldives, adopted the Addu Declaration on 'Building Bridges', urging, *inter alia*, the promotion of the region in terms of trade and tourism as 'Destination South Asia'; the elimination of terrorism and combating of maritime piracy in the region; the establishment of a regional mechanism to ensure the empowerment of women and gender equality in the region; the finalization of work to elaborate a new SAARC Regional Convention on Preventing and Combating Trafficking in Women and Children for Prostitution; the commemoration of a new SAARC Media Day and staging of a Regional Conference on Media; and the promotion of regional co-operation in other areas including trade, transport, and energy.

A priority objective is the eradication of poverty in the region, and in 1993 SAARC endorsed a conceptual framework to help achieve this. The 11th SAARC summit meeting, held in Kathmandu, Nepal, in January 2002, adopted a convention on regional arrangements for the promotion of child welfare in South Asia. The 11th summit also determined to reinvigorate regional poverty reduction activities in the context of the UN General Assembly's Millennium Development Goal of halving extreme poverty by 2015, and of other internationally agreed commitments. The meeting reconstituted the Independent South Asian Commission on Poverty Alleviation—ISACPA, which had been established in 1991. ISACPA reported to the 12th summit meeting of heads of state, held in Islamabad, Pakistan, in January 2004. The 12th summit meeting declared poverty alleviation to be the overarching goal of all SAARC activities and requested ISACPA to continue its work in an advocacy role and to prepare a set of SAARC Development Goals (SDGs). At the meeting heads of state endorsed a Plan of Action on Poverty Alleviation, and also adopted a SAARC Social Charter that had been drafted with assistance from representatives of civil society, academia, non-governmental organizations and government, under the auspices of an intergovernmental expert group, and incorporated objectives in areas including poverty alleviation, promotion of health and nutrition, food security, water supply and sanitation, children's development and rights, participation by women, and human resources development. The 13th SAARC summit meeting, held in Dhaka, in November 2005, declared the SAARC Decade of Poverty Alleviation covering the period 2006–15 and determined to replace SAARC's Three-tier Mechanism on Poverty Alleviation (established in 1995) with a Two-tier Mechanism on Poverty Alleviation, comprising ministers and secretaries responsible for poverty alleviation at national level. The 14th summit meeting, held in New Delhi, in April 2007, acknowledged ISACPA's efforts in elaborating the SDGs and entrusted the Two-tier Mechanism with monitoring progress towards the achievement of these. The 16th summit, held in Thimphu, Bhutan, in April 2010, urged the mainstreaming of the SDGs into member states' national processes.

An agreement establishing a Food Security Reserve to meet emergency food requirements was signed in November 1987, and entered into force in August 1988. In 2004 the 12th summit meeting determined to establish a Food Bank, incorporating a Food Reserve of wheat and/or rice; the Food Bank was to act as a regional food security reserve during times of normal food shortages as well as during emergencies. The Intergovernmental Agreement establishing the SAARC Food Bank (SFB) was signed by leaders attending the 14th summit meeting in April 2007. A meeting of the SFB executive board, convened in October 2010, determined to raise the SFB's then authorized total reserve of 241,580 metric tons of food grains to 400,000 metric tons, in view of ongoing acute regional food insecurity. SAARC's 15th summit meeting, held in Colombo, Sri Lanka, in August 2008, issued the 'Colombo Statement on Food Security', urging the region—in response to the ongoing global crisis of reduced food availability and rising food prices—to forge greater co-operation with the international community to ensure regional food availability and nutrition security. An extraordinary meeting of SAARC ministers of agriculture, convened in November 2008, adopted a guiding 'SAARC Agriculture Vision 2020', and a roadmap for its achievement. In November 2011 the 17th SAARC summit adopted an agreement on the establishment of a SAARC Seed Bank, aimed at enhancing regional agricultural productivity.

The eighth SAARC summit meeting, held in New Delhi in May 1996, established a South Asian Development Fund, comprising a Fund for Regional Projects, a Regional Fund and a fund for social development and infrastructure building. A meeting of SAARC financial experts, held in September 2005, submitted for further consideration by the Association proposals that the South Asian Development Fund should be replaced by a new SAARC Development Fund (SDF), comprising a Social Window (to finance poverty alleviation projects), an Infrastructure Window (for infrastructure development) and an Economic Window (for non-infrastructure commercial programmes). The meeting also considered the possibility of establishing a South Asian Development Bank. A roadmap for the establishment of the SDF was endorsed by the SAARC Council of Ministers in August 2006, and the Fund was eventually launched in April 2010; its secretariat was to be based in Thimphu, Bhutan. In October 2010 the Japanese Government suspended new financing to a SAARC-Japan Special Fund, established in September 1993, through which funds (cumulatively totalling US $4.73m. by 2010) had been channelled to support SAARC symposia and expert meetings on socio-economic matters, especially relating to energy and disaster reduction; the Fund was to terminate operations following the allocation of some $100,000 that remained deposited at that time.

In April 2003 SAARC ministers of health convened an emergency meeting to consider the regional implications of the spread of Severe Acute Respiratory Syndrome (SARS), a previously unknown atypical pneumonia. In November of that year SAARC ministers of health determined to establish a regional surveillance and rapid reaction system for managing health crises and natural disasters; the August 2008 summit meeting approved the development of a Natural Disaster Rapid Response Mechanism. In November 2011 ministers of foreign affairsattending the 17th SAARC summit signed a regional Agreement on Rapid Response to Natural Disasters. A SAARC Regional Strategy on HIV/AIDS aims to combat the spread of the infection.

A Committee on Economic Cooperation (CEC), comprising senior trade officials of member states, was established in July 1991 to monitor progress concerning trade and economic co-operation issues. In the same year the summit meeting approved the creation of an inter-governmental group to establish a framework for the promotion of specific trade liberalization measures. A SAARC Chamber of Commerce (SCCI) became operational in 1992. In April 1993 ministers signed a SAARC Preferential Trading Arrangement (SAPTA), which came into effect in December 1995. In December 1995 the Council resolved that the ultimate objective for member states should be the establishment of a South Asian Free Trade Area (SAFTA), superseding SAPTA. An Agreement on SAFTA was signed in January 2004, at the 12th summit, and on 1 January 2006 it entered into force, providing for the phased elimination of tariffs: these were to be reduced to 30% in least developed member countries and to 20% in the others over an initial two-year period, and subsequently to 0%–5% over a period of five years. The Agreement established a mechanism for administering SAFTA and for settling disputes at ministerial level. In August 2008 the 15th summit adopted a protocol on Afghanistan's admission to SAFTA. In February 2009 the Council of Ministers issued a Statement on the Global Economic Crisis. In November 2011 the 17th SAARC summit urged the intensification of efforts to implement SAFTA effectively, and also directed SAARC finance ministers to draft a proposal on means of facilitating greater regional flow of financial capital and intra-regional long-term investment.

In January 1996 the first SAARC Trade Fair was held, in New Delhi, to promote intra-SAARC commerce. At the same time SAARC ministers of commerce convened for their first meeting to discuss regional economic co-operation. The 11th SAARC Trade Fair and Tourism Mart was to be held in Dhaka, in March–April 2012, and the 12th Fair and Tourism Mart was to be held in Kulhudhuffushi, Maldives, later in 2012.

Since 2007 a SAARC Youth Camp has been periodically convened (2007: Bangladesh; 2008: Sri Lanka; 2010–11: the Maldives). A

Youth Awards Scheme to reward, annually, outstanding achievements by young people has been operational since 1996. Under the SAARC Agenda for Culture, approved in April 2007, the online promotion of regional culture, a SAARC website on culture, and a SAARC exchange programme on culture were to be developed. SAARC film festivals have been convened. The SAARC Consortium of Open and Distance Learning was established in 2000. A Visa Exemption Scheme, exempting 21 specified categories of person from visa requirements, with the aim of promoting closer regional contact, became operational in March 1992. A SAARC citizens forum promotes interaction among the people of South Asia. In addition, SAARC operates a fellowships, scholarships and chairs scheme and a scheme for the promotion of organized tourism.

In June 2005 SAARC ministers of the environment met in special session to consider the impact of the devastating earthquake and subsequent massive ocean movements, or tsunamis, that struck in the Indian Ocean at the end of 2004. The meeting reviewed an assessment of the extent of loss and damage in each country, and of the relief and rehabilitation measures being undertaken. Ministers resolved to strengthen early warning and disaster management capabilities in the region, and determined to support the rehabilitation of members' economies, in particular through the promotion of the tourism sector. In July 2008 SAARC ministers of the environment, meeting to discuss climate change, adopted a SAARC Action Plan and 'Dhaka Declaration on Climate Change', urging close co-operation in developing projects and raising mass awareness of climate change. In April 2010 leaders attending the 16th SAARC summit meeting issued the 'Thimphu Statement on Climate Change', in which they determined to review the implementation of the 2008 SAARC Action Plan and Dhaka Declaration, and agreed, *inter alia*, to establish an Inter-governmental Expert Group on Climate Change, with the aim of developing clear policy direction and guidelines for regional co-operation; to direct the Secretary-General to commission a study on 'Climate risks in the region: ways comprehensively to address the related social, economic and environmental challenges'; to implement advocacy and awareness programmes on climate change; to organize for 10m. trees to be planted in the region during 2010–15; to formulate national plans, and, when appropriate, regional projects, aimed at protecting and safeguarding the SAARC region's archeological and historical infrastructure from the adverse effects of climate change; to commission SAARC inter-governmental initiatives on the marine and mountain ecosystems, and on evolving monsoon patterns; and to organize a SAARC Inter-governmental Climate-related Disasters Initiative, aimed at integrating climate change adaptation and disaster risk reduction planning mechanisms.

From October 2004 SAARC implemented, under supervision from the Asian Development Bank (ADB), a Regional Multimodal Transport Study; this was extended in 2007 to cover Afghanistan. The first South Asia Energy dialogue was convened in March 2007 in New Delhi. The November 2011 SAARC summit urged the conclusion of a new Regional Railways Agreement; and also the conclusion of an Inter-governmental Framework Agreement for Energy Cooperation, and of a Study on Regional Power Exchange.

At the third SAARC summit, held in Kathmandu, in November 1987, member states signed a regional convention on measures to counteract terrorism. The convention, which entered into force in August 1988, commits signatory countries to the extradition or prosecution of alleged terrorists and to the implementation of preventative measures to combat terrorism. A convention on narcotic drugs and psychotropic substances was signed during the fifth SAARC summit meeting, held in Malé, Maldives, in 1990, and entered into force in September 1993. It is implemented by a co-ordination group of drug law enforcement agencies. At the 11th SAARC summit member states adopted a convention on the prevention of trafficking of women and children for prostitution. The 12th summit adopted an Additional Protocol on Suppression of Terrorism with a view to preventing the financing of terrorist activities. In February 2009 the Council of Ministers issued a Declaration on Cooperation in Combating Terrorism.

There is a wide network of SAARC Regional Centres. In 1998 an Agricultural Information Centre was established, in Dhaka, to serve as a central institution for the dissemination of knowledge and information in the agricultural sector. It maintains a network of centres in each member state, which provide for the efficient exchange of technical information and for strengthening agricultural research. Other regional centres include the SAARC Tuberculosis and HIV/AIDS Centre (inaugurated in November 2007, replacing the former SAARC Tuberculosis Centre, which had been established in 1992); a SAARC Documentation Centre, established in New Delhi in 1994; a SAARC Meteorological Research Centre, which opened in Dhaka in 1995; a Human Resources Development Centre, established in Islamabad, Pakistan in 1999; a SAARC Coastal Zone Management Centre, established in 2005 in the Maldives; a SAARC Information Centre, inaugurated in Nepal in 2005; and a SAARC Cultural Centre, which opened in Colombo, in 2009. In July 2005 the Council of Ministers approved the establishment of additional regional centres for forestry, to be based in Bhutan, and for energy, to be located in Pakistan. In January 2008 a new SAARC database on gender data (the SAARC 'Genderbase') was launched. Construction of a SAARC University campus, to be based in South Delhi, India, was to commence in 2012.

SAARC has signed Memoranda of Understanding (MOUs) with UNICEF and UNCTAD (in 1993); ESCAP (1994); the Asia Pacific Telecommunity (1994); UNDP (1995); the UN Drug Programme (1995); the European Commission (1996); the International Telecommunication Union (1997); the Canadian International Development Agency (1997); WHO (2000); the ADB, FAO, the Joint UN Programme on HIV/AIDS and the UN Population Fund (2004); UNEP and UNESCO (2007); and the UN International Strategy for Disaster Reduction (2008). An informal dialogue at ministerial level has been conducted with ASEAN and the European Union since 1998. SAARC and the WTO hold regular consultations. SAARC's Secretary-General participates in regular consultative meetings of executive heads of sub-regional organizations (including ESCAP, ASEAN, the Economic Cooperation Organization, and the Pacific Islands Forum).

Finance

The national budgets of member countries provide the resources to finance SAARC activities. The Secretariat's annual budget is shared among member states according to a specified formula.

Publications

SAARC News (3 or 4 a year).

Other official documents, regional studies, reports.

Regional Apex Bodies

Association of Persons of the Legal Communities of the SAARC Countries (SAARCLAW): 495 HSIDC, Udyog Vihar Phase V, N. H. 8, Gurgaon 122016, National Capital Region, India; tel. (124) 4040193; fax (124) 4040194; e-mail info@saarclaw.com; internet www.saarclaw.com; f. 1991; recognized as a SAARC regional apex body in July 1994; aims to enhance exchanges and co-operation among the legal communities of the sub-region and to promote the development of law; Pres. SONAM TOBGYE; Sec.-Gen. HERMANT K. BATRA.

SAARC Chamber of Commerce and Industry (SCCI): House 397, St 64, I-8/3, Islamabad, Pakistan; tel. (51) 4860611; fax (51) 4860610; e-mail info@saarcchamber.org; internet www.saarcchamber.org; f. 1992; promotes economic and trade co-operation throughout the sub-region and greater interaction between the business communities of member countries; organizes SAARC Economic Cooperation Conferences and Trade Fairs; Pres. SHRI VIKRAMJIT S. SAHNEY; Sec.-Gen. MUHAMMAD IQBAL TABISH.

South Asian Federation of Accountants (SAFA): c/o Institute of Chartered Accountants of India, ICAI Bhavan, POB 7100, Indraprastha Marg, New Delhi 110002, India; tel. (11) 23370195; fax (11) 23379334; e-mail safa@icai.org; internet www.esafa.org; f. 1984; recognized as a SAARC regional apex body in Jan. 2002; aims to develop regional co-ordination for the accountancy profession; Pres. Muhammad RAFI; Sec. T. KARTHIKEYAN.

Other recognized regional bodies include the South Asian Association for Regional Cooperation of Architects, the Association of Management Development Institutions, the SAARC Federation of University Women, the SAARC Association of Town Planners, the SAARC Cardiac Society, the Association of SAARC Speakers and Parliamentarians, the Federation of State Insurance Organizations of SAARC Countries, the Federation of State Insurance Organizations of SAARC Countries, the SAARC Diploma Engineers Forum, the Radiological Society of SAARC Countries, the South Asia Initiative to End Violence Against Children (SAIEVAC), the SAARC Teachers' Federation, the SAARC Surgical Care Society and the Foundation of SAARC Writers and Literature.

SOUTHERN AFRICAN DEVELOPMENT COMMUNITY—SADC

Address: SADC HQ, Plot No. 54385, Private Bag 0095, Gaborone, Botswana.

Telephone: 3951863; **fax:** 3972848; **e-mail:** registry@sadc.int; **internet:** www.sadc.int.

The first Southern African Development Co-ordination Conference (SADCC) was held at Arusha, Tanzania, in July 1979, to harmonize development plans and to reduce the region's economic dependence on South Africa. In August 1992 the 10 member countries of the SADCC signed the Treaty establishing the Southern African Development Community (SADC), which replaced SADCC upon its entry into force in October 1993. The Treaty places binding obligations on member countries, with the aim of promoting economic integration towards a fully developed common market. The Community Tribunal, envisaged in the Treaty, was inaugurated in 2005. The Protocol on Politics, Defence and Security Co-operation, regulating the structure, operations and functions of the Organ on Politics, Defence and Security, established in June 1996 (see under Regional Security), entered into force in March 2004. A troika system, comprising the current, incoming and outgoing SADC chairmanship, operates at the level of the summit, Council of Ministers and Standing Committee of Officials, and co-ordinates the Organ on Politics, Defence and Security. Other member states may be co-opted into the troika as required. A system of SADC national committees, comprising representatives of government, civil society and the private sector, oversees the implementation of regional programmes at country level and helps to formulate new regional strategies. In recent years SADC institutions have undergone a process of intensive restructuring.

MEMBERS

Angola	Malawi	South Africa
Botswana	Mauritius	Swaziland
Congo, Democratic Republic	Mozambique	Tanzania
Lesotho	Namibia	Zambia
Madagascar*	Seychelles	Zimbabwe

* In March 2009 Madagascar was suspended from meetings of SADC, following the forced resignation of the elected President and transfer of power to the military.

Organization

(April 2012)

SUMMIT MEETING

The meeting is held at least once a year and is attended by heads of state and government or their representatives. It is the supreme policy-making organ of SADC and is responsible for the appointment of the Executive Secretary. A report on the restructuring of SADC, adopted by an extraordinary summit held in Windhoek, Namibia, in March 2001, recommended that biannual summit meetings should be convened. The 2011 regular SADC summit meeting was convened in Luanda, Angola, in August.

COUNCIL OF MINISTERS

Representatives of SADC member countries at ministerial level meet at least once a year.

INTEGRATED COMMITTEE OF MINISTERS

The Integrated Committee of Ministers (ICM), which is responsible to the Council of Ministers, meets at least once a year and comprises at least two ministers from each member state. The ICM facilitates the co-ordination and harmonization of cross-sectoral areas of regional integration; oversees the activities of the Community Directorates; and provides policy guidance to the Secretariat. The ICM formulated and supervises the implementation of the Regional Indicative Strategic Development Plan (RISDP—see below).

STANDING COMMITTEE OF OFFICIALS

The Committee, comprising senior officials, usually from the ministry responsible for economic planning or finance, acts as the technical advisory body to the Council. It meets at least once a year. Members of the Committee also act as a national contact point for matters relating to SADC.

SECRETARIAT

Executive Secretary: Tomás Augusto Salomão (Mozambique).

The Secretariat comprises permanently staffed Directorates covering the following priority areas of regional integration: Trade, Industry, Finance and Investment; Infrastructure and Services; Food, Agriculture and Natural Resources; Social and Human Development and Special Programmes; and Policy, Planning and Resource Mobilization.

SADC TRIBUNAL

The establishment of the SADC Tribunal was provided for under the Treaty establishing the SADC and facilitated by a protocol adopted in 2000. The Windhoek, Namibia-based 10-member Tribunal was inaugurated in November 2005 and is mandated to arbitrate in the case of disputes between member states arising from the Treaty.

Activities

In July 1979 the first Southern African Development Co-ordination Conference (SADCC) was attended by delegations from Angola, Botswana, Mozambique, Tanzania and Zambia, with participation by representatives from donor governments and international agencies. In April 1980 a regional economic summit conference was held in Lusaka, Zambia, and the Lusaka Declaration, a statement of strategy entitled 'Southern Africa: Towards Economic Liberation', was approved, with the aim of reducing regional economic dependence on South Africa, then in its apartheid period. The 1986 SADCC summit meeting recommended the adoption of economic sanctions against South Africa but failed to establish a timetable for doing so.

In January 1992 a meeting of the SADCC Council of Ministers approved proposals to transform the organization (by then expanded to include Lesotho, Malawi, Namibia and Swaziland) into a fully integrated economic community, and in August the Treaty establishing SADC was signed. Post-apartheid South Africa became a member of SADC in August 1994, thus strengthening the objective of regional co-operation and economic integration. Mauritius became a member in August 1995. In September 1997 SADC heads of state agreed to admit the Democratic Republic of the Congo (DRC) and Seychelles as members of the Community; Seychelles withdrew, however, in July 2004. In August 2005 Madagascar was admitted as a member.

A task force to co-ordinate a programme of co-operation between SADC and the Common Market for Eastern and Southern Africa (COMESA) was established in 2001, and in 2005 the East African Community (EAC) became incorporated into the process, which was led thereafter by the COMESA-EAC-SADC Task Force. In October 2008 the first tripartite COMESA-EAC-SADC summit was convened, in Kampala, Uganda, to discuss the harmonization of policy and programme work by the three regional economic communities (RECs). The Kampala summit approved a roadmap towards the formation of a single free trade area and the eventual establishment of a single African Economic Community (a long-term objective of African Union (AU) co-operation). At the second tripartite summit, held in June 2011, in Johannesburg, South Africa, negotiations were initiated on the establishment of the proposed COMESA-EAC-SADC Tripartite Free Trade Area. In January 2012 AU leaders endorsed a new Framework, Roadmap and Architecture for Fast Tracking the Establishment of a Continental FTA (referred to as CFTA), and an Action Plan for Boosting Intra-African Trade, which planned for the consolidation of the COMESA-EAC-SADC Tripartite FTA with other regional FTAs into the CFTA initiative during 2015–16; and the establishment of an operational CFTA by 2017. In July 2010 the SADC, COMESA and the EAC adopted a tripartite five-year Programme on Climate Change Adaptation and Mitigation in the COMESA-EAC-SADC region.

In September 1994 the first conference of ministers of foreign affairs of SADC and the European Union (EU) was held in Berlin, Germany, instigating the so-called Berlin Initiative on SADC-EU Dialogue. The participants agreed to establish working groups to promote closer trade, political, regional and economic co-operation. In particular, a declaration issued from the meeting specified joint objectives, including a reduction of exports of weapons to southern Africa and of the arms trade within the region, promotion of investment in the region's manufacturing sector and support for democracy at all levels. A second SADC-EU ministerial conference, held in Namibia in October 1996, endorsed a Regional Indicative Programme (RIP) to enhance co-operation between the two organizations over the next five years. The third ministerial conference under the Berlin Initiative took place in Vienna, Austria, in November 1998. In September 1999 SADC signed a co-operation agreement with the US Government, which incorporated measures to promote US investment in the region, and commitments to support HIV/AIDS assessment and prevention programmes and to assist member states to develop environmental protection capabilities. The fourth SADC–EU ministerial conference, convened in Gaborone, in November 2000, adopted a joint declaration on the control of small arms and light weapons in the SADC region. The fifth SADC-EU ministerial conference was held in Maputo, Mozambique, in November 2002. In July SADC and the EU approved a roadmap to guide future co-operation, and in October of that year an EU-SADC ministerial 'double troika' meeting took place in The Hague, Netherlands, to mark 10 years of dialogue between the two organizations under the Berlin Initiative. At the meeting both SADC and the EU reaffirmed their commitment to reinforcing co-operation with regard to peace and security in Africa. In November 2006, at an EU-SADC double troika meeting held in Maseru, Lesotho, SADC representatives agreed to the development of institutional support to the member states through the establishment of a Human Rights Commission and a new SADC Electoral Advisory Council (SEAC). SEAC became operational in April 2011. The 14th SADC-EU double troika ministerial conference under the Berlin initiative, convened in Brussels, Belgium, in November 2008, discussed, *inter alia*, the ongoing global financial crisis and means of addressing volatility in commodity prices and food insecurity in southern Africa. The ongoing EU-SADC Investment Promotion Programme (ESIPP) aims to mobilize foreign capital and technical investment in southern Africa. SADC has co-operated with other sub-regional organizations to finalize a common position on co-operation between African ACP countries and the EU under the Cotonou Agreement (concluded in June 2000, see chapter on the EU).

In July 1996 the SADC Parliamentary Forum was inaugurated, with the aim of promoting democracy, human rights and good governance throughout the region. Membership of the Forum, which is headquartered in Windhoek, Namibia, is open to national parliaments of all SADC countries, and offers fair representation for women. Representatives serve for a period of five years. The Forum receives funds from member parliaments, governments and charitable and international organizations. In September 1997 SADC heads of state endorsed the establishment of the Forum as an autonomous institution. The Forum frequently deploys missions to monitor parliamentary and presidential elections in the region (most recently to observe legislative and presidential elections held in Zambia in September 2011). A regional women's parliamentary caucus was inaugurated in April 2002. In 2005 a training arm of the Forum, the SADC Parliamentary Leadership Centre, was established.

The August 2004 summit meeting of heads of state and government, held in Grand Baie, Mauritius, adopted a new Protocol on Principles and Guidelines Governing Democratic Elections, which advocated: full participation by citizens in the political process; freedom of association; political tolerance; elections at regular intervals; equal access to the state media for all political parties; equal opportunity to exercise the right to vote and be voted for; independence of the judiciary; impartiality of the electoral institutions; the right to voter education; the respect of election results proclaimed to be free and fair by a competent national electoral authority; and the right to challenge election results as provided for in the law.

At the summit meeting of heads of state and government held in Maseru, Lesotho, in August 2006, a new Protocol on Finance and Investment was adopted. Amendments to SADC protocols on the Tribunal, trade, immunities and privileges, transport, communications and meteorology, energy and mining, combating illicit drugs and education and training were also approved at the meeting. The summit emphasized the need to scale up implementation of SADC's agenda for integration, identifying the RISDP (see below) and the Strategic Indicative Plan for the Organ (SIPO) as the principal instruments for achieving this objective. In pursuit of this aim, the summit established a task force—comprising ministers responsible for finance, investment, economic development, trade and industry—charged with defining the measures necessary for the eradication of poverty and how their implementation might be accelerated.

In accordance with a decision of an extraordinary summit meeting convened in March 2001, SADC's institutions were extensively restructured during 2001–03, with a view to facilitating the more efficient and effective application of the objectives of the organization's founding Treaty and of the SPA. The March 2001 summit meeting endorsed a Common Agenda for the organization, which covered the promotion of poverty reduction measures and of sustainable and equitable socio-economic development, promotion of democratic political values and systems, and the consolidation of peace and security. Furthermore, the establishment of an integrated committee of ministers was authorized; this was mandated to formulate and oversee a Regional Indicative Strategic Development Plan (RISDP), intended as the key policy framework for managing, over a period of 15 years, the SADC Common Agenda. A draft RISDP was approved by the summit meeting convened in Dar es Salaam, Tanzania, in August 2003. In April 2006 SADC adopted the Windhoek Declaration on a new relationship between the Community and its international co-operating partners. The declaration provides a framework for co-operation and dialogue between SADC and international partners, facilitating the implementation of the SADC Common Agenda. A Consultative Conference on Poverty and Development, organized by SADC and attended by its international co-operating partners, was convened in April 2008, in Port Louis, Mauritius.

A high-level meeting concerned with integrating the objectives of the New Partnership for Africa's Development (NEPAD) into SADC's regional programme activities was convened in August 2004. SADC and NEPAD determined in late 2008 to launch a joint business hub, aimed at consolidating regional private sector investment.

REGIONAL SECURITY

In November 1994 SADC ministers of defence, meeting in Arusha, Tanzania, approved the establishment of a regional rapid-deployment peace-keeping force, which could be used to contain regional conflicts or civil unrest in member states. An SADC Mine Action Committee is maintained to monitor and co-ordinate the process of removing anti-personnel land devices from countries in the region. The summit meeting of heads of state and government held in August 2007 authorized the establishment of the SADC Standby Brigade (SADCBRIG), with the aim of ensuring collective regional security and stability. SADCBRIG is a pillar of the African Union's African Standby Force (ASF). SADC's Regional Peacekeeping Training Centre (SADC-RPTC) was established in June 1999 and since August 2005 has been directed by the SADC Secretariat.

In June 1996 SADC heads of state and government, meeting in Gaborone, Botswana, inaugurated an Organ on Politics, Defence and Security (OPDS), with the aim of enhancing co-ordination of national policies and activities in these areas. The stated objectives of the body were, *inter alia*, to safeguard the people and development of the region against instability arising from civil disorder, inter-state conflict and external aggression; to undertake conflict prevention, management and resolution activities, by mediating in inter-state and intra-state disputes and conflicts, pre-empting conflicts through an early warning system and using diplomacy and peace-keeping to achieve sustainable peace; to promote the development of a common foreign policy, in areas of mutual interest, and the evolution of common political institutions; to develop close co-operation between the police and security services of the region; and to encourage the observance of universal human rights, as provided for in the charters of the UN and the Organization of African Unity (OAU—now AU). The extraordinary summit held in March 2001 determined to develop the OPDS as a substructure of SADC, with subdivisions for defence and international diplomacy, to be chaired by a member country's head of state, working within a troika system. A Protocol on Politics, Defence and Security Co-operation—to be implemented by an Interstate Politics and Diplomacy Committee—regulating the structure, operations and functions of the Organ, was adopted and opened for signature in August 2001 and entered into force in March 2004.

The March 2001 extraordinary SADC summit adopted a Declaration on Small Arms, promoting the curtailment of the proliferation of and illicit trafficking in light weapons in the region. A Protocol on the Control of Firearms, Ammunition and Other Related Materials was adopted in August of that year. In July SADC ministers of defence approved a draft regional defence pact, providing for a mechanism to prevent conflict involving member countries and for member countries to unite against outside aggression. In January 2002 an extraordinary summit of SADC heads of state, held in Blantyre, Malawi, adopted a Declaration against Terrorism.

An extraordinary SADC summit meeting convened in March 2007, in Dar es Salaam, Tanzania, mandated the OPDS to assess the political and security situations in the DRC and Lesotho (see below). The ministerial committee of the OPDS troika stressed to the summit the need for SADC support to the ongoing post-conflict reconstruction process in the DRC. An extraordinary meeting of the ministerial committee of the OPDS troika convened in October of that year resolved to mobilize humanitarian assistance for eastern areas of the DRC in view of an escalation in the violent unrest there, with a particular focus on assisting internally displaced civilians. In November 2008 SADC convoked an extraordinary summit of heads of state or government in response to mounting insecurity in eastern areas of the DRC. The summit determined to assist the government of the DRC, if necessary by sending a regional peace-keeping force to the province of North Kivu. In February 2009 it was reported that SADCBRIG was ready to intervene if required in the DRC situation. A large team of SADC observers, comprising more than 200 representatives of Community member states, was sent to monitor the presidential and legislative elections that were held in the DRC in November 2011.

In August 2001 SADC established a task force, comprising representatives of five member countries, to address the ongoing political crisis in Zimbabwe. The Community sent two separate observer teams to monitor the controversial presidential election held in Zimbabwe in March 2002; the SADC Council of Ministers team found the election to have been conducted freely and fairly, while the Parliamentary Forum group was reluctant to endorse the poll. Having evaluated both reports, the Community approved the election. An SADC Council of Ministers group was convened to observe the parliamentary elections held in Zimbabwe in March 2005; however, the Zimbabwean Government refused to invite a delegation from the SADC Parliamentary Forum. The Zimbabwean Government claimed to have enacted electoral legislation in accordance with the provisions of the August 2004 SADC Protocol on Principles and Guidelines Governing Democratic Elections (see above). The extraordinary summit meeting of SADC heads of state and government, convened in Dar es Salaam, Tanzania, in March 2007, to address the political, economic, and security situation in the region, declared 'solidarity with the government and people of Zimbabwe' and mandated then President Thabo Mbeki of South Africa to facilitate dialogue between the Zimbabwean government and opposition. Mbeki reported to the ordinary SADC summit held in August of that year that restoring Zimbabwe's capacity to generate foreign exchange through balance of payments support would be of pivotal importance in promoting economic recovery and that SADC should assist Zimbabwe with addressing the issue of international sanctions.

In early March 2008 an SADC election observer team was sent to monitor preparations for and the conduct of presidential and national and local legislative elections that were staged in Zimbabwe at the end of that month. In mid-April, at which time the Zimbabwe Electoral Commission had failed to declare the results of the presidental election, prompting widespread international criticism, SADC convened an extraordinary summit to address the electoral outcome. The OPDS presented to the summit a report by the observer team on the presidential and legislative elections which claimed that the electoral process had been acceptable to all parties. The summit urged the Zimbabwe Electoral Commission to verify and release the results of the elections without further delay and requested President Mbeki of South Africa to continue in his role as facilitator of dialogue with the Zimbabwe authorities. In June an emergency meeting of the OPDS troika, at the level of heads of state, was convened following an announcement by the main opposition candidate, Morgan Tsvangirai, that he was withdrawing from a forthcoming second round of voting in the presidential election owing to an escalation of violence against opposition supporters in that country. In July Mugabe and the leaders of the two main opposition parties signed a memorandum of understanding, brokered by President Mbeki, confirming their commitment to pursuing dialogue and forming an inclusive government. An agreement to share executive responsibilities in a government of national unity was concluded and signed in September. In December 2008 SADC launched a new Zimbabwe Humanitarian and Development Assistance Framework (ZHDAF), and in January 2009 it established an All Stakeholders Working Committee to implement the ZHDAF. The extraordinary SADC summit convened in March commended political progress recently achieved in Zimbabwe, and established a committee to co-ordinate SADC support, and to mobilize international support for, Zimbabwe's recovery process. The SADC summit held in September urged the termination of all forms of international sanctions against Zimbabwe. It was reported in that month that Zimbabwe had withdrawn from participation in the SADC Tribunal. Responsibility for managing the ZHDAF was transferred to the Zimbabwe Government in December 2009.

The March 2009 extraordinary summit strongly condemned the unconstitutional actions that led to the forced resignation during that month of the elected President of Madagascar, Mark Ravalomanana, and ensuing transfer of power to the military in that country; the summit suspended Madagascar from participation in the activities of the Community and urged the immediate restoration of constitutional order. In June SADC appointed the former President of Mozambique, Joachim Chissano, as the Community's mediator in the Madagascar consitutional crisis. Negotiations subsequently facilitated by Chissano, under SADC auspices, in Maputo, Mozambique, led, in August, to the conclusion of an agreement on the establishment of a power-sharing administration in Madagascar; the power-sharing accord was not, however, subsequently implemented. In March 2011 SADC mediators proposed a new 'Roadmap Out of The Crisis' for Madagascar, again envisaging a power-sharing interim government; this was approved by SADC heads of state and government at a summit convened in June 2011.

TRADE, INDUSTRY AND INVESTMENT

Under the Treaty establishing SADC, efforts were to be undertaken to achieve regional economic integration. The Directorate of Trade, Industry, Finance and Investment aims to facilitate such integration, and poverty eradication, through the creation of an enabling investment and trade environment in SADC countries. Objectives include the establishment of a single regional market; the progressive removal of barriers to the movement of goods, services and people; and the promotion of cross-border investment. SADC supports programmes for industrial research and development and standardization and quality assurance, and aims to mobilize industrial investment resources and to co-ordinate economic policies and the development of the financial sector. In August 1996, at a summit meeting held in Lesotho, SADC member states signed the Protocol on Trade, providing for the establishment of a regional free trade area (FTA), through the gradual elimination of tariff barriers. (Angola and the DRC are not yet signatories to the Protocol.) In October 1999 representatives of the private sector in SADC member states established the Association of SADC Chambers of Commerce, based in Mauritius. The Protocol on Trade entered into force in January 2000, and an Amendment Protocol on Trade came into force in August, incorporating renegotiated technical details on the gradual elimination of tariffs, rules of origin, customs co-operation, special industry arrangements and dispute settlement procedures. The implementation phase of the Protocol on Trade commenced in September. In accordance with a revised schedule, some 85% of intra-SADC trade tariffs were withdrawn by 1 January 2008. (The remaining intra-SADC trade tariffs were to be removed by 2012.) The SADC Free Trade Area was formally inaugurated, under the theme 'SADC FTA for Growth, Development and Wealth Creation', at the meeting of heads of state and government, held in Sandton, South Africa, in August 2008; Angola, the DRC, Malawi and Seychelles, however, had not implemented all requirements of the Protocol on Trade and were not yet participating in the FTA. According to the schedule, reaffirmed at the EU–SADC ministerial meeting in 2006, an SADC customs union was to be implemented by 2010 (however, this deadline was not achieved), a common market by 2015, monetary union by 2016, and a single currency was to be introduced by 2018. Annual meetings are convened to review the work of expert teams in the areas of standards, quality, assurance, accreditation and metrology. At an SADC Extraordinary Summit convened in October 2006 it was determined that a draft roadmap was to be developed to facilitate the process of establishing a customs union. In November 2007 the Ministerial Task Force on Regional Economic Integration approved the establishment of technical working groups to facilitate the development of policy frameworks in legal and institutional arrangements; revenue collection, sharing and distribution; policy harmonization; and a common external tariff. A strategic forum of the Ministerial Task Force, to review the regional economic integration agenda, was convened in February 2010, in Johannesburg, South Africa, immediately prior the Task Force's ninth meeting.

The mining sector contributes about 10% of the SADC region's annual GDP. The principal objective of SADC's programme of action on mining is to stimulate increased local and foreign investment in the sector, through the assimilation and dissemination of data, prospecting activities, and participation in promotional fora. In December 1994 SADC held a mining forum, jointly with the EU, in Lusaka, Zambia, with the aim of demonstrating to potential investors and promoters the possibilities of mining exploration in the region. A second mining investment forum was held in Lusaka in December 1998; and a third ('Mines 2000'), also in Lusaka, in October 2000. In April 2006 SADC and the EU launched a new initiative, in the framework of the EU-SADC Investment Promotion Programme, to facilitate European investment in some 100 mining projects in southern Africa. Other objectives of the mining sector are the improvement of industry training, increasing the contribution of small-scale mining, reducing the illicit trade in gemstones and gold, increasing co-operation in mineral exploration and processing, and minimizing the adverse impact of mining operations on the environment. In February 2000 a Protocol on Mining entered into force, providing for the harmonization of policies and programmes relating to the development and exploitation of mineral resources in the region. SADC supports the Kimberley Process Certification Scheme aimed at preventing illicit trade in illegally mined rough diamonds. (The illicit trade in so-called 'conflict diamonds' and other minerals is believed to have motivated and financed many incidences of rebel activity in the continent, for example in Angola and the DRC.)

In July 1998 a Banking Association was officially constituted by representatives of SADC member states. The Association was to establish international banking standards and regional payments systems, organize training and harmonize banking legislation in the region. In April 1999 governors of SADC central banks determined to strengthen and harmonize banking procedures and technology in order to facilitate the financial integration of the region. Efforts to harmonize stock exchanges in the region were also initiated in 1999.

The summit meeting of heads of state and government held in Maseru, Lesotho, in August 2006 adopted a new Protocol on Finance and Investment. The document, regarded as constituting the main framework for economic integration in southern Africa, outlined, *inter alia*, how the region intended to proceed towards monetary union, and was intended to complement the ongoing implementation of the SADC Protocol on Trade and targets contained in the RISDP.

INFRASTRUCTURE AND SERVICES

The Directorate of Infrastructure and Services focuses on transport, communications and meteorology, energy, tourism and water. At SADC's inception transport was regarded as the most important area to be developed, on the grounds that, as the Lusaka Declaration noted, without the establishment of an adequate regional transport and communications system, other areas of co-operation become impractical. The SADC Protocol on Transport, Communications and Meteorology, adopted in August 1996, provides, *inter alia*, for an integrated regional transport policy, an SADC Regional Trunk Road Network (RTRN), and harmonized regional policies relating to maritime and inland waterway transport; civil aviation; regional telecommunications; postal services; and meterology. An Integrated Transport Committee, and other sub-committees representing the sectors covered by the Protocol, have been established. In January 1997 the Southern African Telecommunications Regional Authority (SATRA), a regulatory authority, was established. In March 2001 the Association of Southern African National Road Agencies (ASANRA) was created to foster the development of an integrated regional road transportation system.

SADC development projects have aimed to address missing links and over-stretched sections of the regional network, as well as to improve efficiency, operational co-ordination and human resource development, such as management training projects. Other objectives have been to ensure the compatibility of technical systems within the region and to promote the harmonization of regulations relating to intra-regional traffic and trade. SADC's road network, whose length totals more than 1m. km, constitutes the regions's principal mode of transport for both freight and passengers and is thus vital to the economy. Unsurfaced, low-volume roads account for a substantial proportion of the network and many of these are being upgraded to a sealed standard as part of a wider strategy that focuses on the alleviation of poverty and the pursuit of economic growth and development. In July 1999 a 317-km rail link between Bulawayo, Zimbabwe, and the border town of Beitbridge, administered by SADC as its first build-operate-transfer project, was opened.

SADC policy guidelines on 'making information and communications technology a priority in turning SADC into an information-based economy' were adopted in November 2001. Policy guidelines and model regulations on tariffs for telecommunications services have also been adopted. An SADC Regional Information Infrastructure (SRII) was adopted in December 1999, with the aim of linking member states by means of high capacity digital land and submarine routes. In May 2010 SADC ministers responsible for telecommunications, postal services and ICT adopted a regional e-SADC Strategy Framework, which aimed to utilize ICT for regional socio-economic development and integration. Proposed priorities for the period 2011–12 under the e-SADC initiative included creating national and regional internet exchange points; harmonizing cyber security regulatory frameworks in member countries; and implementing a regional project aimed at improving interconnection of the electronic, physical and financial postal networks. In September 2011 SADC endorsed the inaugural Southern Africa Internet Governance Forum (SAIGF), hosted by the South African Government, in Pretoria, and jointly convened by NEPAD and other agencies.

The SADC Drought Monitoring Centre organizes an annual Southern African Regional Climate Outlook Forum (SARCOF), which assesses seasonal weather prospects. SARCOF-15 was convened in Windhoek, Namibia, in August 2011.

Areas of activity in the energy sector include: joint petroleum exploration, training programmes for the petroleum sector and studies for strategic fuel storage facilities; promotion of the use of coal; development of hydroelectric power and the co-ordination of SADC generation and transmission capacities; new and renewable sources of energy, including pilot projects in solar energy; assessment of the environmental and socio-economic impact of wood-fuel scarcity and relevant education programmes; and energy conservation. In July 1995 SADC energy ministers approved the establishment of the Southern African Power Pool (SAPP), whereby all member states were to be linked into a single electricity grid. Utilities participating in SAPP aim to provide to consumers in the region an economical and reliable electricity supply. SADC and COMESA have the joint objective of eventually linking SAPP and COMESA's Eastern Africa Power Pool. In July 1995 ministers also endorsed a protocol to promote greater co-operation in energy development within SADC, providing for the establishment of an Energy Commission, responsible for 'demand-side' management, pricing, ensuring private sector involvement and competition, training and research, collecting information, etc.; the protocol entered into force in September 1998. In September 1997 heads of state endorsed an Energy Action Plan to proceed with the implementation of co-operative policies and strategies in four key areas of energy: trade; information exchange; training and organizational capacity building; and investment and financing. There are two major energy supply projects in the region: utilities from Angola, Botswana, the DRC, Namibia and South Africa participate in the Western Power Corridor project, approved in October 2002, while a Zambia–Tanzania Inter-connector project was under development in 2012. In July 2007 it was announced that a Regional Petroleum and Gas Association (REPGA) would be established, with the aim of promoting a common investment destination with harmonized environmental standards.

The tourism sector operates within the context of national and regional socio-economic development objectives. It comprises four components: tourism product development; tourism marketing and research; tourism services; and human resources development and training. SADC has promoted tourism for the region through trade fairs and investment fora. In September 1997 the legal charter for the establishment of the Regional Tourism Organization for Southern Africa (RETOSA), administered jointly by SADC officials and private sector operators, was signed by ministers of tourism. RETOSA assists member states to formulate tourism promotion policies and strategies. The development is under way of a region-wide common visa (UNI-VISA) system, aimed at facilitating tourism.

In June 2005 the SADC Council of Ministers endorsed the Transfrontier Conservation Area (TFCA) 2010 Development Strategy, aimed at establishing and promoting TFCAs, conservation parks straddling international borders, as premier regional tourist and investment destinations. Phase 1 of the Strategy, up to 2010, focused on the following TFCAs: Ais/Richtersveld (in Namibia and South Africa), Kgalagadi (Botswana, Namibia and South Africa), Limpopo-Shashe (Botswana, South Africa, Zimbabwe), the Great Limpopo Transfrontier Park (GLTP) (Mozambique, South Africa, Zimbabwe), Lubombo (Mozambique, South Africa, Swaziland), Maloti-Drakensburg (Lesotho, South Africa), and Kavango-Zambezi (envisaged as the largest conservation area in the world, straddling the borders of Angola, Botswana, Namibia, Zambia and Zimbabwe); while Phase 2 ('Beyond 2010') focused on Iona-Skeleton Coast (Angola, Namibia), Liuwa Plain-Kamela (Zambia, Angola), Lower Zambezi-Mana Pools (Zambia, Zimbabwe), Malawi-Zambia, Niassa-Selous (a woodland ecosystem) (Mozambique and Tanzania), Mnazi Bay-Quirimbas (Mozambique and Tanzania), and Chimanimani (Zimbabwe, Mozambique).

SADC aims to promote equitable distribution and effective management of the region's water resources, around 70% of which are shared across international borders. A Protocol on Shared Watercourse Systems entered into force in April 1998, and a Revised Protocol on Shared Watercourses came into force in September 2003. An SADC Regional Water Policy was adopted in August 2005 as a framework for providing the sustainable and integrated development, protection and utilization of national and transboundary water resources.

A first Regional Strategic Action Plan (RASP I) on Integrated Water Resources Development and Management was implemented during 1999–2004; RASP II was undertaken in 2005–10; and RASP III was ongoing during 2011–15, covering three strategic areas: water governance; infrastructure development; and water management.

FOOD, AGRICULTURE AND NATURAL RESOURCES

The Directorate of Food, Agriculture and Natural Resources aims to develop, co-ordinate and harmonize policies and programmes on agriculture and natural resources with a focus on sustainability. The Directorate covers the following sectors: agricultural research and training; inland fisheries; forestry; wildlife; marine fisheries and resources; food security; livestock production and animal disease control; and environment and land management. According to SADC figures, agriculture contributes one-third of the region's gross national product (GNP), accounts for about one-quarter of total earnings of foreign exchange and employs some 80% of the labour force. The principal objectives in this field are regional food security, agricultural development and natural resource development.

The Southern African Centre for Co-operation in Agricultural Research (SACCAR), was established in Gaborone, in 1985. It aims to strengthen national agricultural research systems, in order to improve management, increase productivity, promote the development and transfer of technology to assist local farmers, and improve training. Examples of activity include: a sorghum and millet improvement programme; a land and water management research programme; a root crop research network; agroforestry research, implemented in Malawi, Tanzania, Zambia and Zimbabwe; and a grain legume improvement programme, comprising separate research units for groundnuts, beans and cowpeas. SADC's Plant Genetic Resources Centre, based near Lusaka, Zambia, aims to collect, conserve and utilize indigenous and exotic plant genetic resources and to develop appropriate management practices. In November 2009 scientists from SADC member states urged the Community to strengthen and support regional capacity to screen for and detect genetically modified organisms (GMOs), with a view to preventing the uncontrolled influx into the region of GMO products; the results of a survey conducted across the region, released in February 2011, concluded that most Southern African countries lacked sufficient technological capacity to screen for and detect GMOs.

SADC aims to promote inland and marine fisheries as an important, sustainable source of animal protein. Marine fisheries are also considered to be a potential source of income of foreign exchange. In May 1993 the first formal meeting of SADC ministers of marine fisheries convened in Namibia, and it was agreed to hold annual meetings. Meeting in May 2002 ministers of marine fisheries expressed concern about alleged ongoing illegal, unregulated and unreported (IUU) fisheries activities in regional waters. The development of fresh water fisheries is focused on aquaculture projects, and their integration into rural community activities. The SADC Fisheries Protocol entered into force in September 2003. Environment and land management activities have an emphasis on sustainability as an essential quality of development. SADC aims to protect and improve the health, environment and livelihoods of people living in the southern African region; to preserve the natural heritage and biodiversity of the region; and to support regional economic development on a sustainable basis. There is also a focus on capacity building, training, regional co-operation and the exchange of information in all areas related to the environment and land management. SADC operates an Environmental Exchange Network and implements a Land Degradation and Desertification Control Programme. Projects on the conservation and sustainable development of forestry and wildlife are under implementation. An SADC Protocol on Forestry was signed in October 2002, and in November 2003 the Protocol on Wildlife Conservation and Law Enforcement entered into force.

Under the food security programme, the Regional Early Warning System (REWS) aims to anticipate and prevent food shortages through the provision of information relating to the food security situation in member states. As a result of frequent drought crises, SADC member states have agreed to inform the food security sector of their food and non-food requirements on a regular basis, in order to assess the needs of the region as a whole. A programme on irrigation development and water management aims to reduce regional dependency on rain-fed agricultural production, while a programme on the promotion of agricultural trade and food safety aims to increase intra-regional and inter-regional trade with a view to improving agriculture growth and rural incomes. An SADC extraordinary summit on agriculture and food security, held in May 2004 in Dar es Salaam, Tanzania, considered strategies for accelerating development in the agricultural sector and thereby securing food security and reducing poverty in the region. In July 2008 the inaugural meeting was convened of a Task Force of ministers of trade, finance and agriculture, which was established by SADC heads of government earlier in that year in response to rising food prices and production costs. The Task Force agreed upon several measures to improve the food security situation of the SADC region, including increased investment in agriculture and the establishment of a Regional Food Reserve Facility. It also directed the SADC secretariat to develop a regional policy on the production of biofuels. The first Food, Agriculture and Natural Resources cluster ministerial meeting was held in November 2008, in Gaborone, to assess the regional food security situation in view of the ongoing global food security crisis.

The Livestock Sector Unit of the Directorate of Food, Agriculture and Natural Resource co-ordinates activities related to regional livestock development, and implements the Promotion of Regional INTegration (PRINT) livestock sector capacity-strengthening programme; the SADC foot-and-mouth disease (FMD) Programme; and the SADC Transboundary Animal Diseases (TADs) project, which aims to strengthen capacity (with a special focus on Angola, Malawi, Mozambique, Tanzania, and Zambia) to control TADs such as FMD, rinderpest, contagious bovine pleuropneumonia, African swine fever, Newcastle disease, avian influenza, Rift Valley Fever, and lumpy skin disease.

SOCIAL AND HUMAN DEVELOPMENT AND SPECIAL PROGRAMMES

SADC helps to supply the region's requirements in skilled manpower by providing training in the following categories: high-level managerial personnel; agricultural managers; high- and medium-level technicians; artisans; and instructors. Human resources development activities focus on determining active labour market information systems and institutions in the region, improving education policy analysis and formulation, and addressing issues of teaching and learning materials in the region. SADC administers an Intra-regional Skills Development Programme, and the Community has initiated a programme of distance education to enable greater access to education, as well as operating a scholarship and training awards programme. In July 2000 a Protocol on Education and Training, which was to provide a legal framework for co-operation in this sector entered into force. In September 1997 SADC heads of state, meeting in Blantyre, Malawi, endorsed the establishment of a Gender Department within the Secretariat to promote the advancement and education of women. A Declaration on Gender and Development was adopted. SADC leaders adopted an SADC Protocol on Gender Equality in August 2008.

An SADC Protocol on Combating Illicit Drugs entered into force in March 1999. In October 2000 an SADC Epidemiological Network on Drug Use was established to enable the systematic collection of narcotics-related data. SADC operates a regional drugs control programme, funded by the EU.

In August 1999 an SADC Protocol on Health was adopted. In December 1999 a multisectoral sub-committee on HIV/AIDS (which are endemic in the region) was established. In August 2000 the Community adopted a set of guidelines to underpin any future negotiations with major pharmaceutical companies on improving access to and reducing the cost of drugs to combat HIV/AIDS. In July 2003 an SADC special summit on HIV/AIDS, convened in Maseru, Lesotho, and attended by representatives of the World Bank, UNAIDS and WHO, issued the Maseru Declaration on HIV/AIDS, identifying priority areas for action, including prevention, access to testing and treatment, and social mobilization. The implementation of the priority areas outlined in the Maseru Declaration is co-ordinated through an SADC Business Plan on HIV/AIDS (currently in a phase covering the period 2010–15), with a focus on harmonizing regional guidelines on mother-to-child transmission and anti-retroviral therapy; and on issues relating to access to affordable essential drugs, including bulk procurement and regional production. The SADC summit held in September 2009 urged member states to intensify their efforts to implement the Maseru Declaration. An SADC Model Law on HIV/AIDS was adopted by the SADC Parliamentary Forum in 2008; the Forum is implementing a Strategic Framework for HIV/AIDS during 2010–15. The SADC aims to achieve, by 2015, an 'HIV-Free Generation' and no new infections. Since 2008 SADC has celebrated an annual Healthy Lifestyles Day, during the last week in February (25 February in 2012). SADC is implementing a Strategic Plan for the Control of TB In the SADC Region, 2007–15, which aims to address challenges posed by the emergence of Multidrug Resistant TB (MDR-TB) and Extensive Drug Resistant TB (XDR-TB) strains. SADC supports the Southern Africa Roll Back Malaria Network (SARN), which was established in November 2007. SADC member states met in October 2011 to address the elimination of malaria from the region by 2015.

SADC seeks to promote employment and harmonize legislation concerning labour and social protection. Activities include: the implementation of International Labour Standards; the improvement of health and safety standards in the workplace; combating child labour; and the establishment of a statistical database for employment and labour issues. In February 2007 a task force was mandated to investigate measures for improving employment conditions in member countries.

Following the ratification of the Treaty establishing the Community, regional socio-cultural development was emphasized as part of the process of greater integration. Public education initiatives have been undertaken to encourage the involvement of people in the process of regional integration and development, as well as to promote democratic and human rights' values. Two SADC Artists AIDS Festivals have been organized, the first in Bulawayo, Zimbabwe, in August 2007; and the second in Lilongwe, Malawi, in December 2009. The first SADC Poetry Festival was convened in November 2009, in Windhoek, Namibia, with the second held in August 2010, in Gaborone. The creation of an SADC Culture Trust Fund is planned.

Finance

SADC's administrative budget for 2012–13 amounted to US $78.4m., to be financed by contributions from member states (45%) and by international development partners (55%).

Publications

SACCAR Newsletter (quarterly).

SADC Annual Report.

SADC Energy Bulletin.

SADC Food Security Update (monthly).

SADC Today (six a year).

SOUTHERN COMMON MARKET—MERCOSUR/MERCOSUL

(MERCADO COMÚN DEL SUR/MERCADO COMUM DO SUL)

Address: Edif. Mercosur, Luis Piera 1992, 1°, 11200 Montevideo, Uruguay.

Telephone: 2412-9024; **fax:** 2418-0557; **e-mail:** secretaria@mercosur.org.uy; **internet:** www.mercosur.int.

Mercosur (known as Mercosul in Portuguese) was established in March 1991 by the heads of state of Argentina, Brazil, Paraguay and Uruguay with the signature of the Treaty of Asunción. The primary objective of the Treaty is to achieve the economic integration of member states by means of a free flow of goods and services between member states, the establishment of a common external tariff, the adoption of common commercial policy, and the co-ordination of macroeconomic and sectoral policies. The Ouro Preto Protocol, which was signed in December 1994, conferred on Mercosur the status of an international legal entity with the authority to sign agreements with third countries, groups of countries and international organizations.

MEMBERS

Argentina	Brazil	Paraguay	Uruguay

Note: Venezuela was admitted as a full member of Mercosur in July 2006, pending ratification by each country's legislature. At April 2012 ratification by the Paraguayan Congress remained outstanding. Bolivia, Chile, Colombia, Ecuador and Peru are associate members.

Organization

(April 2012)

COMMON MARKET COUNCIL

The Common Market Council (Consejo del Mercado Común) is the highest organ of Mercosur and is responsible for leading the integration process and for taking decisions in order to achieve the objectives of the Treaty of Asunción. In December 2010 the Council decided to establish the position of High Representative, with a three-year term-in-office, in order to support the integration process, to promote trade and investment and to represent the grouping internationally. The first High Representative took office on 1 February 2011.

High Representative: SAMUEL PINHEIRO GUIMARÃES (Brazil).

COMMON MARKET GROUP

The Common Market Group (Grupo Mercado Común) is the executive body of Mercosur and is responsible for implementing concrete measures to further the integration process.

TRADE COMMISSION

The Trade Commission (Comisión de Comercio del Mercosur) has competence for the area of joint commercial policy and, in particular, is responsible for monitoring the operation of the common external tariff (see below). The Brasília Protocol may be referred to for the resolution of trade disputes between member states.

CONSULTATIVE ECONOMIC AND SOCIAL FORUM

The Consultative Economic and Social Forum (Foro Consultivo Económico-Social) comprises representatives from the business community and trade unions in the member countries and has a consultative role in relation to Mercosur.

PARLIAMENT

Parlamento del Mercosur: Pablo de María 827, 11200 Montevideo, Uruguay; tel. 2410-9797; e-mail secadministrativa@parlamentodelmercosur.org; internet www.parlamentodelmercosur.org; f. 2005, as successor to the Joint Parliamentary Commission (Comisión Parlamentaria Conjunta); aims to facilitate implementation of Mercosur decisions and regional co-operation.

ADMINISTRATIVE SECRETARIAT

Director: Dr AGUSTÍN COLOMBO SIERRA (Argentina).

Activities

Mercosur's free trade zone entered into effect on 1 January 1995, with tariffs removed from 85% of intra-regional trade. A regime of gradual removal of duties on a list of special products was agreed, with Argentina and Brazil given four years to complete this process while Paraguay and Uruguay were allowed five years. Regimes governing intra-zonal trade in the automobile and sugar sectors remained to be negotiated. Mercosur's customs union also came into force at the start of 1995, comprising a common external tariff (CET) of 0%–20%. A list of exceptions from the CET was also agreed; these products were to lose their special status and were to be subject to the general tariff system concerning foreign goods by 2006.

In December 1995 Mercosur presidents affirmed the consolidation of free trade as Mercosur's 'permanent and most urgent goal'. To this end they agreed to prepare norms of application for Mercosur's customs code, accelerate paper procedures and increase the connections between national computerized systems. It was also agreed to increase co-operation in the areas of agriculture, industry, mining, energy, communications, transport and tourism, and finance. At this meeting Argentina and Brazil reached an accord aimed at overcoming their dispute regarding the trade in automobiles between the two countries. They agreed that cars should have a minimum of 60% domestic components and that Argentina should be allowed to complete its balance of exports of cars to Brazil, which had earlier imposed a unilateral quota on the import of Argentine cars. In June 1995 Mercosur ministers responsible for the environment agreed to harmonize environmental legislation and to form a permanent sub-group of Mercosur.

In May 1996 Mercosur parliamentarians met with the aim of harmonizing legislation on patents in member countries. In December Mercosur heads of state, meeting in Fortaleza, Brazil, approved agreements on harmonizing competition practices (by 2001), integrating educational opportunities for postgraduates and human resources training, standardizing trading safeguards applied against third country products (by 2001) and providing for intra-regional cultural exchanges. An Accord on Sub-regional Air Services was signed at the meeting (including by the heads of state of Bolivia and Chile) to liberalize civil transport throughout the region. In addition, the heads of state endorsed texts on consumer rights that were to be incorporated into a Mercosur Consumers' Defence Code.

In June 1996 Mercosur heads of state, meeting in San Luis de Mendoza, Argentina, endorsed a 'Democratic Guarantee Clause', whereby a country would be prevented from participation in Mercosur unless democratic, accountable institutions were in place. At the summit meeting, the presidents approved the entry into Mercosur of Bolivia and Chile as associate members. An Economic Complementation Accord with Bolivia, which includes Bolivia in Mercosur's free trade zone, but not in the customs union, was signed in December 1995 and was to come into force on 1 January 1997, later extended until 30 April 1997. Measures of the free trade agreement, which was signed in October 1996, were to be implemented over a transitional period commencing on 28 February 1997 (revised from 1 January). Chile's Economic Complementation Accord with Mercosur entered into effect on 1 October 1996, with duties on most products to be removed over a 10-year period (Chile's most sensitive products were given 18 years for complete tariff elimination). Chile was also to remain outside the customs union, but was to be involved in other integration projects, in particular infrastructure projects designed to give Mercosur countries access to both the Atlantic and Pacific Oceans (Chile's Pacific coast was regarded as Mercosur's potential link to the economies of the Far East).

In June 1997 the first meeting of tax administrators and customs officials of Mercosur member countries was held, with the aim of enhancing information exchange and promoting joint customs inspections. During 1997 Mercosur's efforts towards regional economic integration were threatened by Brazil's adverse external trade balance and its Government's measures to counter the deficit, which included the imposition of import duties on certain products. In November the Brazilian Government announced that it was to increase its import tariff by 3%, in a further effort to improve its external balance. The measure was endorsed by Argentina as a means of maintaining regional fiscal stability. The new external tariff, which was to remain in effect until 31 December 2000, was formally adopted by Mercosur heads of state at a meeting held in Montevideo, in December 1997. At the summit meeting a separate Protocol was signed providing for the liberalization of trade in services and government purchases over a 10-year period. In order to strengthen economic integration throughout the region, Mercosur leaders agreed that Chile, while still not a full member of the organization, should be integrated into the Mercosur political structure, with equal voting rights. In December 1998 Mercosur heads of state agreed on the establishment of an arbitration mechanism for disputes between members, and on measures to standardize human, animal and plant health and safety regulations throughout the grouping. In March 1998 the ministers of the interior of Mercosur countries, together with representatives of the Governments of Chile and Bolivia, agreed to implement a joint security arrangement for the border region linking Argentina, Paraguay and Brazil. In particular, the initiative aimed to counter drugs-trafficking, money-laundering and other illegal activities in the area.

Tensions within Mercosur were compounded in January 1999 owing to economic instability in Brazil and its Government's decision effectively to devalue the national currency, the real. In March the grouping's efforts at integration were further undermined by political instability in Paraguay. Argentina imposed tariffs on imports of Brazilian steel and demanded some form of temporary safeguards on certain products as compensation for their perceived loss of competitiveness resulting from the devalued real. An extraordinary meeting of the Common Market Council was convened, at Brazil's request, in August, in order to discuss the dispute, as well as measures to mitigate the effects of economic recession throughout the sub-region. However, little progress was made and the bilateral trade dispute continued to undermine Mercosur's integration objectives. Argentina imposed new restrictions on textiles and footwear, while, in September, Brazil withdrew all automatic import licences for Argentine products, which were consequently to be subject to the same quality control, sanitary measures and accounting checks applied to imports from non-Mercosur countries. In January 2000, however, the Argentine and Brazilian Governments agreed to refrain from adopting potentially divisive unilateral measures and resolved to accelerate negotiations on the resolution of ongoing differences. In March Mercosur determined to promote and monitor private accords to cover the various areas of contention, and also established a timetable for executing a convergence of regional macroeconomic policies. In June Argentina and Brazil signed a bilateral automobile agreement. The motor vehicle agreement, incorporating new tariffs and a nationalization index, was endorsed by all Mercosur leaders at a meeting convened in Florianópolis, Brazil, in December. (In July 2002 the summit meeting, convened in Buenos Aires, Argentina, adopted an agreement providing for reduced tariffs and increased quotas in the grouping's automotive sector, with a view to establishing a fully liberalized automotive market by 2006.) The summit meeting held in December 2000 approved criteria, formulated by Mercosur finance ministers and central bank governors, determining monetary and fiscal targets which aimed to achieve economic convergence, to promote economic stability throughout the region, and to reduce competitive disparities affecting the unity of the grouping. The Florianópolis summit meeting also recommended the formulation of social indicators to facilitate achieving targets in the reduction of poverty and the elimination of child labour. However, political debate surrounding the meeting was dominated by the Chilean Government's announcement that it had initiated bilateral free trade discussions with the USA, which was considered, in particular by the Brazilian authorities, to undermine Mercosur's unified position at multilateral free trade negotiations. Procedures to incorporate Chile as a full member of Mercosur were suspended. (Chile and the USA concluded negotiations on a bilateral free trade agreement in December 2002.) In July 2008 Mercosur and Chile concluded a protocol on trade in services.

In early 2001 Argentina imposed several emergency measures to strengthen its domestic economy, in contradiction of Mercosur's external tariffs. In March Brazil was reported to have accepted the measures, which included an elimination of tariffs on capital goods and an increase in import duties on consumer goods, as an exceptional temporary trade regime; this position was reversed by mid-2001 following Argentina's decision to exempt certain countries from import tariffs. In February 2002, at a third extraordinary meeting of the Common Market Council, held in Buenos Aires, Mercosur heads of state expressed their support for Argentina's application to receive international financial assistance, in the wake of that country's economic crisis. Although there were fears that the crisis might curb trade and stall economic growth across the region, Argentina's adoption of a floating currency made the prospect of currency harmonization between Mercosur member countries appear more viable. In December Mercosur ministers of justice signed an agreement permitting citizens of Mercosur member and associate member states to reside in any other Mercosur state, initially for a two-year period. At a summit convened in June 2003, in Asunción, Paraguay, heads of state of the four member countries agreed to strengthen integration of the bloc and to harmonize all import tariffs by 2006, thus creating the basis for a single market. They also agreed to establish a directly elected Mercosur legislature, as a successor to the Joint Parliamentary Commission. The July 2004 summit of Mercosur heads of state announced that an Asunción-based five-member tribunal (comprising one legal representative from each of Mercosur's four member countries, plus one 'consensus' member) responsible for ruling on appeals in cases of disputes between member countries was to become operational in the following month. In September 2006 the tribunal criticized the Argentine Government for allowing blockades of international bridges across the River Uruguay by protesters opposing the construction of two pulp mills on the Uruguayan side of the river. (In April 2010 the International Court of Justice delivered a judgment supporting the ongoing operations of the mills; both sides subsequently agreed to co-operate in the implementation of environmental protection measures to limit pollution of the River Uruguay.)

In June 2005 Mercosur heads of state announced a US $100m. structural convergence fund to support education, job creation and infrastructure projects in the poorest regions, in particular in Paraguay and Uruguay, in order to remove some economic disparities within the grouping. The meeting also endorsed a multilateral energy project to link gasfields in Camisea, Peru, to existing supply pipelines in Argentina, Brazil and Uruguay, via Tocopilla, Chile. In July 2008 Mercosur heads of state considered the impact of escalating food costs and the production of biofuels. In December a summit meeting, convened in Bahia, Brazil, agreed to establish a $100m. guarantee fund to facilitate access to credit for small and medium-sized businesses operating in the common market in order to alleviate the impact of the global financial crisis. In August 2010 Mercosur heads of state, meeting in San Juan, Argentina, endorsed a new common customs code, incorporating agreements on the redistribution of external customs revenue and elimination of the double taxation on goods imported from outside the group. In December Mercosur heads of state, meeting in Foz do Iguaçú, Brazil, concluded further agreements to accelerate regional integration. These included the appointment of a new High Representative, a Customs Union Consolidation Program, a Strategic Social Action Plan, which aimed to support the eradication of poverty and greater social equality, and a roadmap for the formation of a Mercosur citizenship statute in order to facilitate the free movement of persons throughout the region. A common Mercosur vehicle license plate was endorsed by the summit meeting.

In May 2007 the Mercosur parliament, the so-called Parlasur, which initially was to serve as an advisory committee, held its inaugural session in Montevideo. In April 2009 a new agreement was concluded providing for representation in the parliament to be proportionally allocated based on each country's population and introduced in two stages, in 2010 and in 2014. Thus the distribution of seats was envisaged as 36 (75 in 2014) for Brazil, 26 (43) for Argentina and 18 each for Paraguay and Uruguay. The accord required ratification by the Common Market Council. In July final consideration of the proposal was postponed owing to a demand by the Paraguayan authorities that it should be conditional on a parallel approval to establish a supranational justice tribunal to adjudicate on trade disputes.

EXTERNAL RELATIONS

During 1997 negotiations to establish a free trade accord with the Andean Community were hindered by differences regarding schedules for tariff elimination and Mercosur's insistence on a local content of 60% to qualify for rules of origin preferences. However, in April 1998 the two groupings signed an accord that committed them to the establishment of a free trade area by January 2000. Negotiations in early 1999 failed to conclude an agreement on preferential tariffs between the two blocs, and the existing arrangements were extended on a bilateral basis. In March the Andean Community agreed to initiate free trade negotiations with Brazil; a preferential tariff agreement was concluded in July. In August 2000 a similar agreement between the Community and Argentina entered into force. In September leaders of Mercosur and the Andean Community, meeting at a summit of Latin American heads of state, determined to relaunch negotiations. The establishment of a mechanism to support political dialogue and co-ordination between the two groupings, was approved at the first joint meeting of ministers of foreign affairs in July 2001. In April 2004 Mercosur and the Andean Community signed a free trade accord, providing for tariffs on 80% of trade between the two groupings to be phased out by 2014, and for tariffs to be removed from the remaining 20% of, initially protected, products by 2019. The entry into force of the accord, scheduled for 1 July 2004, was postponed owing to delays in drafting the tariff reduction schedule. Peru became an associate member of Mercosur in December 2003, and Colombia and Ecuador were granted associate membership in December 2004. In July 2004 Mexico was invited to attend all meetings of the organization with a view to future accession to associate membership. Bilateral negotiations on a free trade agreement between Mexico and Mercosur were initiated in 2001. In 2005 Mercosur and the Andean Community formulated a reciprocal association agreement, to extend associate membership to all member states of both groupings. In February 2010 foreign ministers agreed to establish an Andean Community-Mercosur Mixed Commission to facilitate and strengthen co-operation between member countries of both organizations. In December 2005 Bolivia was invited to join as a full member. At the summit meeting of heads of state held in January 2007 in Rio de Janeiro, Brazil, Bolivia stated two conditions on which its membership would be dependent: continued membership of the Andean Community and exemption from Mercosur's CET. Also in December 2005 Mercosur heads of state agreed to a request by Venezuela (which had been granted associate membership in December 2004) to become a member with full voting rights. The leaders signed a protocol, in July 2006, formally to admit Venezuela to the group. The accord, however, required ratification by each country's legislature. In August 2010 Mercosur heads of state urged a quick conclusion to Venezuela's incorporation into the organization in order to enhance regional integration. By December 2011 the Paraguayan parliament had yet to endorse the protocol, as it was blocked by the country's senate.

In December 1995 Mercosur and the European Union (EU) signed a framework agreement for commercial and economic co-operation, which provided for co-operation in the economic, trade, industrial, scientific, institutional and cultural fields and the promotion of wider political dialogue on issues of mutual interest. In June 1997 Mercosur heads of state, convened in Asunción, Paraguay, reaffirmed the group's intention to pursue trade negotiations with the EU, Mexico and the Andean Community, as well as to negotiate as a single economic bloc in discussions with regard to the establishment of a Free Trade Area of the Americas (FTAA). Chile and Bolivia were to be incorporated into these negotiations. Negotiations between Mercosur and the EU on the conclusion of an Interregional Association Agreement commenced in 1999. Specific discussion of tariff reductions and market access commenced at the fifth round of negotiations, held in July 2001, at which the EU proposed a gradual elimination of tariffs on industrial imports over a 10-year period and an extension of access quotas for agricultural products; however, negotiations stalled in 2005 owing to differences regarding farm subsidies. In July 2008 Mercosur heads of state condemned a new EU immigration policy that would permit the detention and forcible return of illegal immigrants. Leaders attending a Mercosur-EU summit meeting, convened in Madrid, Spain, in May 2010, determined to restart promptly the Association Agreement negotiations. The first discussions took place in Buenos Aires, in July, and subsequently at regular intervals. The seventh round of discussions was held in Montevideo, in November 2011, the eighth was convened in Brussels, Belgium, in March 2012, and a ninth round was to take place in July 2012, in Brazil.

In March 2003 Argentina and Brazil, with the support of other Mercosur member states, formed the Southern Agricultural Council (CAS), which was to represent the interests of the grouping as a whole in negotiations with third countries. In December 2004 leaders from 12 Latin American countries (excluding Argentina, Ecuador, Paraguay and Uruguay) attending a pan-South American summit, convened in Cusco, Peru, approved in principle the creation of a new South American Community of Nations (SACN). It was envisaged that negotiations on the formation of the new Community, which was to entail the merger of Mercosur, the Andean Community and the Latin American Integration Association (ALADI), would be completed within 15 years. In April 2005 a region-wide meeting of ministers of foreign affairs was convened within the framework of establishing the SACN. A joint SACN communiqué was released, expressing concern at the deterioration of constitutional rule and democratic institutions in Ecuador, and announcing its intention to send a ministerial mission to that country. The first SACN summit meeting was convened in September, in Brasília, Brazil. In April 2007, at the first South American Energy Summit, convened on Margarita Island, Venezuela, heads of state endorsed the establishment of a Union of South American Nations (UNASUR), to replace SACN as the lead organization for regional integration. UNASUR was to have political decision-making functions, supported by a small permanent secretariat, to be located in Quito, Ecuador, and was to co-ordinate economic and trade matters with Mercosur, the Andean Community and ALADI. A summit meeting formally to inaugurate UNASUR, scheduled to be convened in December, was postponed. A rescheduled meeting, to be convened in March 2008, was also postponed, owing to a diplomatic dispute between Ecuador and Colombia. It was later convened in May, in Brasília, Brazil, when the constitutional document formally establishing UNASUR was signed. In December Brazil hosted a Latin American and Caribbean Summit on Integration and Development, which aimed to strengthen the commitment in the region to support sustainable development. It issued the Salvador Declaration, which pledged support to strengthen co-operation among the regional and sub-regional groupings, to pursue further consultation and joint efforts to counter the effects of the global financial crisis on the region, and to promote closer collaboration on a range of issues including energy, food security, social development, physical infrastructure and natural disaster management. In February 2010 a summit meeting of the Rio Group, convened in Cancún, Mexico, approved in principle the establishment of a new Community of Latin American and Caribbean States, excluding Canada and the USA, to strengthen regional co-operation. The Community was formally established at a summit meeting held in Caracas, Venezuela, in December 2011 (postponed from July, owing to the Venezuelan president's ill health).

In March 1998 ministers of trade of 34 countries agreed a detailed framework for negotiations on the establishment of the FTAA. Mercosur secured support for its request that a separate negotiating group be established to consider issues relating to agriculture, as one of nine key sectors to be discussed. The FTAA negotiating process was formally initiated by heads of state of the 34 countries meeting in Santiago, Chile, in April 1998. In June Mercosur and Canada signed a Trade and Investment Co-operation Arrangement, which aimed to remove obstacles to trade and to increase economic co-operation between the two signatories. The summit meeting held in December 2000 was attended by the President of South Africa, and it was agreed that Mercosur would initiate free trade negotiations with that country. (These commenced in October 2001.) In June 2001 Mercosur leaders agreed to pursue efforts to conclude a bilateral trade agreement with the USA, an objective previously opposed by the Brazilian authorities, while reaffirming their commitment to the FTAA process. Leaders attending a special summit of the Americas, convened in January 2004 in Monterrey, Mexico, failed to specify a completion date for the FTAA process, although they adopted a declaration committing themselves to its eventual establishment. Negotiations were suspended in March, and remained stalled in 2012. Regional integration and co-operation were the principal focus of the sixth summit of the Americas, held in Catagena, Colombia, in April, on the theme 'Connecting the Americas: Partners for Prosperity'.

In December 2007 Mercosur signed a free trade accord with Israel, which entered into effect in January 2010. At the meeting of heads of state, held in San Miguel de Tucumán, Argentina, in July 2008, a preferential trade agreement was signed with the Southern African Customs Union. Framework agreements on the preparation of free trade accords were also signed with Turkey and Jordan. In June 2009 a preferential trade agreement with India entered into force. A framework agreement on trade with Morocco entered into effect in April 2010. In August Mercosur signed a free trade agreement with Egypt, and in December Mercosur signed a trade and economic co-operation agreement with the Palestinian National Authority and a framework agreement to establish a free trade agreement with Syria. Agreements to establish mechanisms for political dialogue and co-operation were signed with Cuba and Turkey at that time.

In July 2009 Mercosur heads of state, meeting in Asunción, issued a joint statement condemning the removal by military force of President Manuel Zelaya of Honduras, demanding the immediate restoration of democratic and constitutional order, and refusing to recognize the legitimacy of the interim authorities in that country.

Finance

The annual budget for the secretariat is contributed by the four full member states.

Publication

Boletín Oficial del Mercosur (quarterly).

WORLD COUNCIL OF CHURCHES—WCC

Address: 150 route de Ferney, POB 2100, 1211 Geneva 2, Switzerland.

Telephone: 227916111; **fax:** 227910361; **e-mail:** infowcc@wcc-coe.org; **internet:** www.oikoumene.org.

The Council was founded in 1948 to promote co-operation between Christian Churches and to prepare for a clearer manifestation of the unity of the Church.

MEMBERS

There are 349 member Churches in more than 110 countries. Chief denominations: Anglican; Baptist; Congregational; Lutheran; Methodist; Moravian; Old Catholic; Orthodox; Presbyterian; Reformed; and Society of Friends. The Roman Catholic Church is not a member but sends official observers to meetings.

Organization

(April 2012)

ASSEMBLY

The governing body of the World Council, consisting of delegates of the member Churches, it meets every seven years to frame policy and consider some main themes. It elects the Presidents of the Council, who serve as members of the Central Committee. The ninth Assembly was held in Porto Alegre, Brazil, in February 2006; the 10th Assembly was scheduled to be held in Busan, Republic of Korea, in October–November 2013.

Presidium: Archbishop Dr Anastasios of Tirana and all Albania, John Taroanui Doom (French Polynesia), Rev. Dr Simon Dossou (Benin), Rev. Dr Soritua Nababan (Indonesia), Rev. Dr Ofelia Ortega (Cuba), Abune Paulos (Ethiopia), Rev. Dr Bernice Powell Jackson (USA), Dr Mary Tanner (United Kingdom).

CENTRAL COMMITTEE

Appointed by the Assembly to carry out its policies and decisions, the Committee consists of 150 members chosen from Assembly delegates. It meets every 12 to 18 months.

The Central Committee comprises the Programme Committee and the Finance Committee. Within the Programme Committee there are advisory groups on issues relating to communication, women, justice, peace and creation, youth, ecumenical relations, and inter-religious relations. There are also five commissions and boards.

Moderator: Rev. Dr Walter Altmann (Armenian Apostolic Church, Lebanon).

Vice-Moderators: Prof. Dr Gennadios of Sassima (Turkey), Rev. Dr Margaretha M. Hendriks-Ririmasse (Indonesia).

EXECUTIVE COMMITTEE

Consists of the Presidents, the Officers and 20 members chosen by the Central Committee from its membership to prepare its agenda, expedite its decisions and supervise the work of the Council between meetings of the Central Committee. Meets every six months.

CONSULTATIVE BODIES

Various bodies, including advisory groups, commissions and reference groups, comprising members from WCC governing bodies and member churches, advise the secretariat on policy direction, implementation and evaluation. The main bodies are the Commissions on Faith and Order (plenary and standing bodies), on World Mission and Evangelism, on Education and Ecumenical Formation, of the Churches on International Affairs, and the Echos Commission on Youth in the Ecumenical Movement.

GENERAL SECRETARIAT

The General Secretariat implements the policies laid down by the WCC and co-ordinates the Council's work. The General Secretariat is also responsible for an Ecumenical Institute, at Bossey, Switzerland, which provides training in ecumenical leadership.

General Secretary: Rev. Dr Olav Fykse Tveit (Norway).

Activities

The ninth WCC Assembly, held in February 2006, approved a reorganization of the WCC's work programme, based on six key areas of activity.

THE WCC AND THE ECUMENICAL MOVEMENT IN THE 21ST CENTURY

The WCC aims to support co-operation among member churches and their involvement in the activities of the organization. It also works to enhance partnerships with other regional and international ecumenical organizations to support the ecumenical movement as a whole, and aims to facilitate communication and consultation among relevant bodies with regard to the future of the ecumenical movement. The WCC supported the development of a Global Christian Forum, which initiated regional consultations among churches in 2004 and convened its first global meeting in November 2007. Within this work programme was a commitment to promote the active participation of young adults in the life of churches and the ecumenical movement, for example through an internship programme at the WCC secretariat, and to ensure that women are and specific issues concerning them are fully considered and represented.

UNITY, MISSION, EVANGELISM AND SPIRITUALITY

This work programme is directed and supported by the Commissions on Faith and Order and on World Mission and Evangelism. It aims to promote a 'visible unity' among member churches and to encourage them to address potentially divisive issues and develop mutually acceptable positions. The WCC produces materials to share among churches information on worship and spiritual life practices and to co-ordinate and promote the annual Week of Prayer for Christian Unity. Other activities aim to confront and overcome any discrimination against ethnic minorities, people with disabilities or other excluded groups within the church and society as a whole. A project to study how to hold commitment to unity together with mission and evangelism was being undertaken within the work programme.

PUBLIC WITNESS: ADDRESSING POWER, AFFIRMING PEACE

The Public Witness programme aims to ensure that the Council's concerns relating to violence, war, human rights, economic injustice, poverty and exclusion are raised and addressed at an international level, including at meetings of UN or other intergovernmental bodies. At a regional and local level the Council aims to accompany churches in critical situations in their efforts to defend human rights and dignity, overcome impunity, achieve accountability and build just and peaceful societies. An Ecumenical Accompaniment Programme in Palestine and Israel (EAPPI) was inaugurated in August 2002 to provide for individuals to support and protect vulnerable groups in the Occupied Territories and to accompany the Israeli Peace movement. The WCC has established an Israeli/Palestine Ecumenical Forum to bring together churches in the region to develop unified policy positions in support of peace and justice. The WCC supported a range of activities within the framework of its Decade to Overcome Violence (2001–10); the Decade culminated in an International Ecumenical Peace Convocation, held in May 2011, in Kingston, Jamaica. An International Day of Prayer for Peace is held each year on 21 September.

JUSTICE, *DIAKONIA* AND RESPONSIBILITY FOR CREATION

The Council supports its members efforts to combat injustice and meet human needs. It aims to strengthen churches' organizational capacities and to strengthen and monitor accountability (and greater understanding) between donors and recipients of resources. It is also committed to strengthening the role of churches in the fields of health and healing, in particular in HIV/AIDS and mental health-related issues. The Council undertakes networking and advocacy activities at an international level and promotes dialogue among church health networks and those of civil society. In 2002 the Council inaugurated the Ecumenical HIV and AIDS Initiative in Africa (EHAIA) to inform and assist churches in Africa in their efforts to support communities affected by HIV/AIDS. The WCC participated in the first Summit of High Level Religious Leaders on HIV and AIDS, which was convened in Den Dolder, Netherlands, in late March 2010. A WCC Ecumenical Solidarity Fund (ESF) provides grants in support of capacity-building efforts, activities to combat racism and other strategic initiatives. The Council aims to strengthen activities relating to migration and racism and to develop new advocacy strategies. The Council provides a forum for discussion and exchange of information on the use of science and new technologies, for example genetically modified seeds and stem cell research. As part of a wider concern for challenges facing the planet, the WCC has formulated a public campaign to raise awareness of climate change, its impact and the need to address the related problems. It hosts the secretariat of the Ecumenical Water Network, which aims to highlight issues relating to the scarcity of water resources in many parts of the work and to advocate community-based initiatives to manage resources more effectively.

EDUCATION AND ECUMENICAL FORMATION

The WCC is committed to supporting ecumenical and faith formation, as well as providing educational opportunities itself. The Ecumenical Institute, in Bossey, Switzerland, offers academic courses, research opportunities and residential programmes, including one for the promotion of inter-faith dialogue. The WCC organizes seminars and workshops to promote good practices in ecumenical formation and leadership training. The Council aims to strengthen theological education through accreditation standards, exchange programmes and modifying curricula. It administers a sponsorship programme to provide opportunities for ecumenical learning in different cultures. In September 2011 the WCC, with Globethics.net, launched the Global Digital Library on Theology and Ecumenism (GlobeTheoLib, accessible at www.globethics.net/gtl), a multi-lingual theological resource providing access to research materials in theology and related disciplines.

INTER-RELIGIOUS DIALOGUE AND CO-OPERATION

This work programme aims to promote the peaceful co-existence of different faiths and communities within society. It supports inter-faith dialogue and opportunities to develop mutual trust and respect, in particular among women and young people of different faiths. It promotes best practices in inter-religious dialogue and co-operation. The Council encourages reflection on Christianity in an inter-faith society. In 2006 it inaugurated, with the Roman Catholic Church, a process of consultations on religious freedom, to result in the definition of a code of conduct on religious conversion. The Council supports churches in conflict situations to counter religious intolerance or discrimination. It undertakes research, field visits, advocacy work and capacity building in support of churches or communities affected by conflict.

Finance

The main contributors to the WCC's budget are the churches and their agencies, with funds for certain projects contributed by other organizations. The 2011 budget amounted to 32.9m. Swiss francs.

Publications

Current Dialogue (2 a year).
Ecumenical News International (weekly).
Ecumenical Review (quarterly).
EEF-NET (2 a year).
International Review of Mission (quarterly).
Ministerial Formation (quarterly).
WCC News (electronic publication).
WCC Yearbook.
Catalogue of periodicals, books and audio-visuals.

WORLD FEDERATION OF TRADE UNIONS—WFTU

Address: 40 Zan Moreas St, 11745 Athens, Greece.

Telephone: (21) 09236700; **fax:** (21) 09214517; **e-mail:** info@wftucentral.org; **internet:** www.wftucentral.org.

The Federation was founded in 1945, on a world-wide basis. A number of members withdrew from the Federation in 1949 to establish the International Confederation of Free Trade Unions (now the International Trade Union Confederation).

MEMBERS

Affiliated or associated national federations (including the six Trade Unions Internationals) in 126 countries representing some 135m. individuals.

Organization

(April 2012)

WORLD TRADE UNION CONGRESS

The Congress meets every five years. It reviews WFTU's work, endorses reports from the executives, and elects the General Council. The size of the delegations is based on the total membership of national federations. The Congress is also open to participation by non-affiliated organizations. The 16th Congress was held in Athens, Greece, in April 2011.

GENERAL COUNCIL

The General Council meets three times between Congresses, and comprises members and deputies elected by Congress from nominees of national federations. Every affiliated or associated organization and Trade Unions International has one member and one deputy member.

The Council receives reports from the Presidential Council, approves the plan and budget and elects officers.

PRESIDENTIAL COUNCIL

The Presidential Council meets twice a year and conducts most of the executive work of WFTU. It comprises a President, elected each year from among its members, the General Secretary and 18 Vice-Presidents.

SECRETARIAT

The Secretariat consists of the General Secretary, and six Deputy General Secretaries. It is appointed by the General Council and is responsible for general co-ordination, regional activities, national trade union liaison, press and information, administration and finance.

WFTU has regional offices in New Delhi, India (for the Asia-Pacific region); Havana, Cuba (covering the Americas); Dakar, Senegal (for Africa); Damascus, Syria (for the Middle East); Nicosia, Cyprus (for Europe); and in Moscow, Russia (covering the CIS countries).

General Secretary: GEORGE MAVRIKOS (Greece).

Activities

The April 2011 World Trade Union Congress adopted the Athens Pact, concerning the impact on the 'international working class' of the global economic crisis from 2008, regarded by the Congress as a 'deep and multifaceted crisis of the capitalist system', burdening the global labouring class most. In February 2012, meeting in Johannesburg, South Africa, the Presidential Council adopted an action plan for 2012, aiming: to address unemployment by combating anti-labour policies and urging governments and public institutions to support the survival of unemployed workers and their families, respecting their needs for affordable food, housing, clean water, and free health care and education; to organize on 3 October WFTU's annual militant International Action Day; to promote trade union education; to promote WFTU in Africa; and to support working youth and women.

Finance

Income is derived from affiliation dues, which are based on the number of members in each trade union federation.

Publication

Comments.
From the World (electronic news).
Reflects

Trade Unions Internationals

The following autonomous Trade Unions Internationals (TUIs) are associated with WFTU:

Trade Unions International of Public and Allied Employees: off 10A Shankharitola St, Kolkata 700014, India; tel. (33) 2217-7721; fax (33) 2265-9450; e-mail aisgef@dataone.in; internet www.tradeunionindia.org; f. 1949; mems: 34m. in 152 unions in 54 countries; Branch Commissions: State, Municipal, Postal and

Telecommunications, Health, Banks and Insurance; Pres. LULAMILE SOTAKA (South Africa); Gen. Sec. SUKOMAL SEN (India); publ. *Information Bulletin* (in three languages).

Trade Unions International of Transport Workers (TUI-Transport) : Rua Serra do Japi 31, 03309–000 Sao Paulo, Brazil; tel. (11) 209-536-05; fax (11) 229-633-03; e-mail info@tui-transport.org; f. 1949; holds International Trade Conference (every 4 years) and General Council (annually); mems: 95 unions from 37 countries; publ. *TUI Reporter* (every 2 months, in English and Spanish).

Trade Unions International of Workers of the Building, Wood and Building Materials Industries (Union Internationale des Syndicats des Travailleurs du Bâtiment, du Bois et des Matériaux de Construction—UITBB): POB 281, 00101 Helsinki, Finland; tel. (9) 693-1130; fax (9) 693-1020; e-mail rguitbb@kaapeli.fi; internet www.uitbb.org; f. 1949; mems: unions in 60 countries, grouping 2.5m. workers; Pres. ANTONIO LOPÉS DE CARBALHO (Brazil); Gen. Sec. DEBANJAN CHAKRABARTI (India); publ. *Bulletin*.

Trade Unions International of Workers in the Energy, Chemical, Oil and Related Industries: c/o 3A Calle Maestro Antonio Caso 45, Col. Tabacalera, 06470 Mexico City, Mexico; tel. and fax (55) 5546-3200; e-mail uis-temqpia@sme.org; f. 1998; Gen. Sec. MARTIN ESPARZA FLORES (Mexico); publ. *Bulletin*.

Trade Union International Union of Workers in the Mining, the Metallurgy and the Metal industries (TUI-Metal): f. 2008; Sec.-Gen. JESÚS GETE OLARRA (Mexico); publ. *Bulletin*.

World Federation of Teachers' Unions: 6/6 Kalicharan Ghosh Rd, Kolkata 700 050, India; tel. (33) 2528-4786; fax (33) 2557-1293; f. 1946; mems: 132 national unions of teachers and educational and scientific workers in 78 countries, representing over 24m. individuals; Pres. LESTURUGE ARIYAWANSA (Sri Lanka); Gen. Sec. MRINMOY BHATTACHARYYA (India); publ. *Teachers of the World* (quarterly, in English).

The foundation congress of a new TUI for Tourism and Hotels (TUI-HOTUR) was held in December 2009, in Athens.

WORLD TRADE ORGANIZATION—WTO

Address: Centre William Rappard, rue de Lausanne 154, 1211 Geneva, Switzerland.

Telephone: 227395111; **fax:** 227314206; **e-mail:** enquiries@wto.org; **internet:** www.wto.org.

The WTO is the legal and institutional foundation of the multilateral trading system. It was established on 1 January 1995, as the successor to the General Agreement on Tariffs and Trade (GATT).

MEMBERS*

Albania
Angola
Antigua and Barbuda
Argentina
Armenia
Australia
Austria
Bahrain
Bangladesh
Barbados
Belgium
Belize
Benin
Bolivia
Botswana
Brazil
Brunei
Bulgaria
Burkina Faso
Burundi
Cambodia
Cameroon
Canada
Cape Verde
Central African Republic
Chad
Chile
China, People's Republic
China, Republic†
Colombia
Congo, Democratic Republic
Congo, Republic
Costa Rica
Côte d'Ivoire
Croatia
Cuba
Cyprus
Czech Republic
Denmark
Djibouti
Dominica
Dominican Republic
Ecuador
The Gambia
Georgia
Germany
Ghana
Greece
Grenada
Guatemala
Guinea
Guinea-Bissau
Guyana
Haiti
Honduras
Hong Kong
Hungary
Iceland
India
Indonesia
Ireland
Israel
Italy
Jamaica
Japan
Jordan
Kenya
Korea, Republic
Kuwait
Kyrgyzstan
Latvia
Lesotho
Liechtenstein
Lithuania
Luxembourg
Macao
Macedonia, former Yugoslav republic
Madagascar
Malawi
Malaysia
Maldives
Mali
Malta
Mauritania
Mauritius
Mexico
Moldova
Mongolia
Morocco
Niger
Nigeria
Norway
Oman
Pakistan
Panama
Papua New Guinea
Paraguay
Peru
Philippines
Poland
Portugal
Qatar
Romania
Rwanda
Saint Christopher and Nevis
Saint Lucia
Saint Vincent and the Grenadines
Saudi Arabia
Senegal
Sierra Leone
Singapore
Slovakia
Slovenia
Solomon Islands
South Africa
Spain
Sri Lanka
Suriname
Swaziland
Sweden
Switzerland
Tanzania
Thailand
Togo
Tonga
Trinidad and Tobago
Tunisia
Turkey
Uganda
Ukraine
United Arab Emirates
United Kingdom
Egypt
El Salvador
Estonia
Fiji
Finland
France
Gabon
Mozambique
Myanmar
Namibia
Nepal
Netherlands
New Zealand
Nicaragua
USA
Uruguay
Vanuatu
Venezuela
Viet Nam
Zambia
Zimbabwe

* The European Union also has membership status, and negotiates and acts within the WTO as a single body on behalf of its 27 member states, which are individually members of the WTO.

† Admitted as the Separate Customs Territory of Taiwan, Penghu, Kinmen and Matsu (referred to as Chinese Taipei).

Note: At April 2012 26 applications to join the WTO were either under consideration or awaiting consideration by accession working parties. In December 2011 the eighth Ministerial Conference approved the terms of entry of Montenegro, Russia, and Samoa; these countries were expected to become full members of the WTO in 2012, in each case 30 days following domestic ratification of the accession agreements. Vanuatu was admitted as a WTO member in February 2012.

Organization

(April 2012)

MINISTERIAL CONFERENCE

The Ministerial Conference is the highest authority of the WTO. It is composed of representatives of all WTO members at ministerial level, and may take decisions on all matters under any of the multilateral trade agreements. The Conference is normally required to meet at least every two years. The eighth Conference was convened in December 2011, in Geneva, Switzerland, on the themes 'Importance of the Multilateral Trading System and the WTO', 'Trade and Development' and 'the Doha Development Agenda'.

GENERAL COUNCIL

The General Council, which is also composed of representatives of all WTO members, is required to report to the Ministerial Conference and conducts much of the day-to-day work of the WTO. The Council convenes as the Dispute Settlement Body, to oversee the trade dispute settlement procedures, and as the Trade Policy Review Body, to conduct regular reviews of the trade policies of WTO members. The Council delegates responsibility to three other major Councils: for trade-related aspects of intellectual property rights, for trade in goods and for trade in services.

TRADE NEGOTIATIONS COMMITTEE

The Committee was established in November 2001 by the Declaration of the fourth Ministerial Conference, held in Doha, Qatar, to supervise the agreed agenda of trade negotiations. It operates under the authority of the General Council and was mandated to establish negotiating mechanisms and subsidiary bodies for each subject under consideration. A structure of negotiating groups and a declaration of principles and practices for the negotiations were formulated by the Committee in February 2002.

SECRETARIAT

The WTO Secretariat comprised some 629 staff in 2012. Its responsibilities include the servicing of WTO delegate bodies, with respect to negotiations and the implementation of agreements, undertaking accession negotiations for new members and providing technical support and expertise to developing countries.

The WTO Institute for Training and Technical Co-operation, based at the Secretariat, offers courses on trade policy; introduction to the WTO for least developed countries; WTO dispute settlement rules and procedures; and other specialized topics. Other programmes include training-of-trainers schemes and distance-learning services.

Director-General: PASCAL LAMY (France).

Deputy Directors-General: ALEJANDRO JARA (Chile), VALENTINE SENDANYOYE RUGWABIZA (Rwanda), HARSHA VARDHANA SINGH (India), RUFUS YERXA (USA).

Activities

The Final Act of the Uruguay Round of GATT multilateral trade negotiations, which were concluded in December 1993, provided for extensive trade liberalization measures and for the establishment of a permanent structure to oversee international trading procedures. The Final Act was signed in April 1994, in Marrakesh, Morocco. At the same time a separate accord, the Marrakesh Declaration, was signed by the majority of GATT contracting states, endorsing the establishment of the WTO. The essential functions of the WTO are: to administer and facilitate the implementation of the results of the Uruguay Round; to provide a forum for multilateral trade negotiations; to administer the trade dispute settlement procedures; to review national trade policies; and to co-operate with other international institutions, in particular the IMF and the World Bank, in order to achieve greater coherence in global economic policy-making.

The WTO Agreement contains some 29 individual legal texts and more than 25 additional Ministerial declarations, decisions and understandings, which cover obligations and commitments for member states. All these instruments are based on a few fundamental principles, which form the basis of the WTO Agreement. An integral part of the Agreement is 'GATT 1994', an amended and updated version of the original GATT Agreement of 1947, which was formally concluded at the end of 1995. Under the 'most-favoured nation' (MFN) clause, members are bound to grant to each other's products treatment no less favourable than that accorded to the products of any third parties. A number of exceptions apply, principally for customs unions and free trade areas and for measures in favour of and among developing countries. The principle of 'national treatment' requires goods, having entered a market, to be treated no less favourably than the equivalent domestically produced goods. Secure and predictable market access, to encourage trade, investment and job creation, may be determined by 'binding' tariffs, or customs duties. This process means that a tariff level for a particular product becomes a commitment by a member state, and cannot be increased without compensation negotiations with its main trading partners. Other WTO agreements also contribute to predictable trading conditions by demanding commitments from member countries and greater transparency of domestic laws and national trade policies. By permitting tariffs, while adhering to the guidelines of being non-discriminatory, the WTO aims to promote open, fair and undistorted competition.

The WTO aims to encourage development and economic reform among the increasing number of developing countries and countries with economies in transition participating in the international trading system. These countries, particularly the least developed states, have been granted transition periods and greater flexibility to implement certain WTO provisions. Industrial member countries are encouraged to assist developing nations by their trading conditions and by not expecting reciprocity in trade concession negotiations. In addition, the WTO operates a limited number of technical assistance programmes, mostly relating to training (including online courses) and the provision of information technology.

Finally, the WTO Agreement recognizes the need to protect the environment and to promote sustainable development. A Committee on Trade and Environment examines the relationship between trade policies, environmental measures and sustainable development and to recommend any appropriate modifications of the multilateral trading provisions.

With the planned accession of Russia to the WTO in 2012, all members of the so-called BRICS informal grouping of large emerging economies, comprising Brazil, Russia, India, People's Republic of China, and South Africa (which together accounted for some 20% of global GDP in 2011), were to be members of the Organization. BRICS (known as BRIC prior to the accession of South Africa in December 2010) convened an inaugural summit of heads or states and government in June 2009, in Yekaterinburg, Russia, at which principles for future co-operation and development were adopted; a second summit was held in April 2010, in Brasília, Brazil; a third in Sanya, China, in April 2011, which adopted the Sanya Declaration, outlining the future deepening of co-operation in areas including trade, energy, finance and industry; and a fourth in New Delhi, India, in March 2012. The fourth summit directed member state finance ministers to examine the feasibility of establishing a new Development Bank to mobilize resources in support of infrastructure and sustainable development projects in BRICS economies, other emerging economies, and developing countries, with the aim of supplementing the existing efforts of multilateral and regional financial institutions.

At the 1996 Conference representatives of some 29 countries signed an Information Technology Agreement (ITA), which aimed to eliminate tariffs on the significant global trade in IT products by 2000. By February 1997 some 39 countries, then representing the required 90% share of the world's IT trade, had consented to implement the ITA. It was signed in March, and was to cover the following main product categories: computers; telecommunications products; semiconductors or manufacturing equipment; software; and scientific instruments. Tariff reductions in these sectors were to be undertaken in four stages, commencing in July, and subsequently on 1 January each year, providing for the elimination of all tariffs by the start of 2000. By April 2012 there were 74 participants in the ITA, representing some 97% of world trade in IT products. In February 1999 the WTO announced plans to investigate methods of removing non-tariff barriers to trade in IT products, such as those resulting from non-standardization of technical regulations. A work programme on non-tariff measures was approved by the Committee of Participants on the Expansion of Trade in IT Products in November 2000.

At the end of the Uruguay Round a 'built-in' programme of work for the WTO was developed. In addition, the Ministerial Conferences in December 1996 and May 1998 addressed a range of issues. The final declaration issued from the Ministerial Conference in December 1996 incorporated a text on the contentious issue of core labour standards, although it was emphasized that the relationship between trade and labour standards was not part of the WTO agenda. The text recognized the International Labour Organization's competence in establishing and dealing with core labour standards and endorsed future WTO/ILO co-operation. The declaration also included a plan of action on measures in favour of the world's least developed countries, to assist these countries in enhancing their trading opportunities. The second Conference, convened in May 1998, decided against imposing customs duties on international electronic transactions, and agreed to establish a comprehensive work programme to address the issues of electronic commerce. The Conference also supported the creation of a framework of international rules to protect intellectual property rights and provide security and privacy in transactions. Developing countries were assured that their needs in this area would be taken into account. Members agreed to begin preparations for the launch of comprehensive talks on global trade liberalization. In addition, following repeated mass public demonstrations against free trade, it was agreed to try to increase the transparency of the WTO and improve public understanding of the benefits of open global markets.

Formal negotiations on the agenda of a new multilateral trade 'round', which was initially scheduled to be launched at the third Ministerial Conference, to be held in Seattle, USA, in late November–December 1999, commenced in September 1998. While it was confirmed that further liberalization of agriculture and services was to be considered, no consensus was reached (in particular between the Cairns Group of countries and the USA, and the European Union—EU, supported by Japan) on the terms of reference or procedures for these negotiations prior to the start of the Conference. In addition, developing countries criticized renewed efforts, mainly by the USA, to link trade and labour standards and to incorporate environmental considerations into the discussions. Efforts by the EU to broaden the talks to include investment and competition policy were also resisted by the USA. The conduct of the Ministerial Conference was severely disrupted by public demonstrations by a diverse range of interest groups concerned with the impact of WTO accords on the environment, workers' rights and developing countries. The differences between member states with regard to a formal agenda failed to be resolved during extensive negotiations, and the Conference was suspended. At a meeting of the General Council, convened later in December, member countries reached an informal understanding that any agreements concluding on 31 December would be extended. Meanwhile, the Director-General attempted to maintain a momentum for proceeding with a new round of trade negotiations. In February 2000 the General Council agreed to resume talks with regard to agriculture and services, and to consider difficulties in implementing the Uruguay Accord, which was a main concern of developing member states. The Council also urged industrialized nations to pursue an earlier initiative to grant duty-free access to the exports of least developed countries. In May the Council resolved to initiate a series of Special Sessions to consider implementation of existing trade agreements, and approved more flexible provisions for implementation of TRIPS (see below), as part of ongoing efforts to address the needs of developing member states and strengthen their confidence in the multilateral trading system.

During 2001 negotiations were undertaken to reach agreement on further trade liberalization. A draft accord was approved by the General Council in October. The fourth Ministerial Conference, held in Doha, Qatar, in November, adopted a final declaration providing a mandate for a three-year agenda for negotiations on a range of subjects, commencing on 1 January 2002. Most of the negotiations were initially scheduled to be concluded, on 1 January 2005, as a single undertaking, i.e. requiring universal agreement on all matters under consideration. (The deadline was subsequently advanced to end-2006, and in July 2006 was postponed indefinitely—see below.) A new Trade Negotiations Committee (TNC) was established to supervise the process, referred to as the Doha Development Round. Several aspects of existing agreements were to be negotiated, while new issues included WTO rules, such as subsidies, regional trade agreements and anti-dumping measures, and market access. The Declaration incorporated a commitment to negotiate issues relating to trade and the environment, including fisheries subsidies, environmental labelling requirements, and the relationship between trade obligations of multilateral environment agreements and WTO rules. The Conference approved a separate decision on implementation-related issues, to address the concerns of developing countries in meeting their WTO commitments. Several implementation issues were agreed at the meeting, while others were incorporated into the Development Agenda. Specific reference was made in the Declaration to providing greater technical co-operation and capacity-building assistance to WTO developing country members. A Doha Development Agenda Global Trust Fund was established in late 2001, with a core budget of CHF 15m., to help finance technical support for trade liberalization in less developed member states. In July 2011 Spain donated €350,000 to the Fund. In September 2002 the WTO Director-General announced that, in support of the ongoing trade negotiations, the following four 'pillars' of the organization should be strengthened: beneficial use of the legal framework binding together the multilateral system; technical and capacity-building assistance to least developed and developing countries; greater coherence in international economic policy-making; and the WTO's functioning as an institution.

The fifth Ministerial Conference, convened in Cancún, Mexico, in September 2003 to advance the Doha Development Round, failed to achieve consensus on a number of issues, in particular investment and competition policy. Senior officials from member states met in December to discuss the future of the Doha Round, but no major breakthrough was achieved. Members did, however, indicate their willingness to recommence work in negotiating groups, which had been suspended after the Cancún conference. The General Council, meanwhile, was to continue working to explore the possibilities of agreements on a multilateral approach on trade facilitation and transparency in government procurement.

In July 2004 the General Council presented for consideration and revision by WTO member states a new draft Doha Agenda Work Programme (the so-called 'July Package' of framework trade agreements) aimed at reviving the stalled Doha Development Round. Following intensive negotiations, the finalized July Package was adopted by the General Council at the beginning of August. The Package included an interim accord on agricultural subsidies that established guidelines for future Doha Round negotiations, entailing a key commitment by rich developed nations eventually to eliminate all agricultural export subsidies. Although no deadline was set for the completion of this process, it was agreed that maximum permitted subsidies would be reduced by 20% in the first year of the implementation of the new regime. The EU would remove some US $360m. of annual export subsidies, with similar concessions also to be made by the USA. The EU's subsidies to its milk and sugar producers and the USA's subsidies to its cotton farmers were withdrawn from the Package and were to be addressed by separate negotiations. Under the July Package all countries were to be required to reduce tariffs on agricultural imports, but the poorest countries would be set lower reduction targets and longer periods for their implementation.

The sixth Ministerial Conference, convened in Hong Kong, in December 2005, set a deadline of 30 April 2006 for finalizing details of the methods of reducing tariffs and subsidies (the 'modalities') in agriculture and industrial goods, with a view to concluding the Doha Round at the end of 2006. It was also agreed that duty- and quota-free access for at least 97% of least developed countries' exports should be achieved by 2008. However, in July 2006 the Doha Development Round of negotiations was suspended across all sectors, with all related deadlines postponed, owing to failure by the participating countries to reach a satisfactory final agreement on agricultural trade, and, in particular, deadlock on the issues of reductions in market access restrictions and domestic support mechanisms in the agriculture sector. Participants were urged by the WTO Director-General to reconsider their negotiating positions. In February 2007 the Director-General announced that negotiations across all sectors had been resumed. In June discussions between the EU, USA, India and Brazil, which were aimed at bridging the gaps in their negotiating positions and had been regarded as a basis for advancing the wider negotiations, failed to reach any agreement on the main areas of dispute i.e. farm subsidies and market access. In July the WTO Director-General endorsed compromise texts that had been negotiated for trade in agriculture and for non-agricultural market access.

The 2005 Ministerial Conference launched the Aid for Trade initiative, which provides a platform for developing countries to build the supply capacity and trade-related infrastructure necessary for implementing and benefiting from WTO agreements. In December 2011 the eighth Ministerial Conference determined to maintain, beyond 2011, Aid for Trade levels reflecting the average of the period 2006-08, and to pursue efforts with development banks to ensure the availability of trade finance to low-income states. In February 2012 WTO organized a workshop on Aid for Trade, sustainable development and the green economy.

Addressing the IMF in April 2008, the WTO Director-General urged WTO member governments to agree at ministerial level by the end of May a framework for cutting agricultural tariffs, agricultural subsidies and industrial tariffs. He emphasized the role of the WTO's rules-based trading system as a source of economic stability for governments, businesses and consumers, and indicated that the prompt finalization of the Doha Round would provide reassurance to international markets given the emerging climate of increased global financial uncertainty. Revised negotiating texts for trade in agriculture and non-agricultural market access were presented in May and two further revisions of the documents was released in July, prior to a formal meeting of the TNC held at end of that month. The Committee meeting failed, however, to reach agreement on the formal establishment of modalities in agriculture and non-agricultural market access, although the WTO Director-General reported that positions had converged in 18 of the 20 areas under discussion. Positions on the development of a special safeguard mechanism on farm products for developing countries reportedly remained in conflict. The seventh (Geneva) Ministerial Conference, held in late November–early December 2009, agreed that progress in the Doha Round should be assessed in the first quarter of 2010; accordingly, the TNC oversaw a phase of 'stocktaking' discussions in March. The eighth Ministerial Conference, held in Geneva in December 2011, acknowledged that, despite strong engagement to conclude the Doha Round, the negotiations remained at an *impasse*, and urged a refocusing of the discussions.

In October 2008 a task force was established within the WTO secretariat to address the effects of the ongoing global financial crisis. In January 2009 the WTO Director-General announced that WTO was to issue periodic reports on trends in global trade, and was to organize future meetings on trade finance, in order to support members with dealing with the global situation. During that month the WTO launched a database on regional trade agreements; a database on non-reciprocal preferential schemes was launched in July 2011. WTO, with UNCTAD, jointly lead an initiative on promoting trade—through combating protectionism, including through the conclusion of the Doha round, and by strengthening aid-for-trade financing-for-trade initiatives—the third of nine activities that were launched in April 2009 by the UN System Chief Executives Board for Co-ordination (CEB), with the aim of alleviating the impact on poor and vulnerable populations of the global crisis. From early 2009 WTO contributed, with the ILO, the IMF, the World Bank, and OECD (the co-ordinating agency), to the compilation of *A 'Global Charter'/'Legal Standard', Inventory of Possible Policy Instruments*, which aimed to stocktake the current range of financial policy instruments, as part of a united response to the financial crisis that involved establishing a shared 'global standard' of propriety and transparency for the future development of the global economic framework. The five organizations contributing to the *Inventory* had been invited by the G8 summit held in Hokkaido, Japan, in June 2008, to enhance their co-operation. In November–December 2009 the seventh WTO Ministerial Conference addressed the impact of the global financial crisis on least developed countries (numbering 49 at that time, of which 32 were WTO member states). In September 2011 WTO and the ILO jointly issued a publication entitled *Making Globalization Socially Sustainable*. In March 2012 WTO and OECD agreed to develop statistics on trade in 'value added'; accordingly, both organizations were to produce a publicly accessible database of trade flows estimated in value-added terms.

AGRICULTURE

The Final Act of the Uruguay Round extended previous GATT arrangements for trade in agricultural products through new rules and commitments to ensure more predictable and fair competition in the sector. All quantitive measures limiting market access for agricultural products were to be replaced by tariffs (i.e. a process of 'tariffication'), enabling more equal protection and access opportunities. All tariffs on agricultural items were to be reduced by 36% by developed countries, over a period of six years, and by 24% by developing countries (excluding least developed member states) over 10 years. A special treatment clause applied to 'sensitive' products (mainly rice) in four countries, for which limited import restrictions could be maintained. Efforts to reduce domestic support measures for agricultural products were to be based on calculations of total aggregate measurements of support (Total AMS) by each member state. A 20% reduction in Total AMS was required by developed countries over six years, and 13% over 10 years by developing countries. No reduction was required of least developed countries. Developed member countries were required to reduce the value and quantity of direct export subsidies by 36% and 21% respectively (on 1986–90 levels) over six years. For developing countries these reductions were to be two-thirds those of developed nations, over 10 years. A specific concern of least developed and net-food importing developing countries, which had previously relied on subsidized food products, was to be addressed through other food aid mechanisms and assistance for agricultural development. The situation was to be monitored by WTO's Committee on Agriculture. Negotiations on the further liberalization of agricultural markets were part of the WTO 'built-in' programme for 2000 or earlier, but remained a major area of contention. In March 2000 negotiations on market access in the agricultural sector commenced, under an interim chairman owing to a disagreement among participating states. The Doha Declaration, approved in that month, established a timetable for further negotiations on agriculture, which were initially scheduled to be concluded as part of the single undertaking on 1 January 2005. (The deadline was subsequently postponed indefinitely.) A compromise agreement was reached with the EU to commit to a reduction in export subsidies, with a view to phasing them out (without a firm deadline for their elimination). Member states agreed to aim for further reductions in market access restrictions and domestic support mechanisms, and to incorporate non-trade concerns, including environmental protection, food security and rural development, into the negotiations. In December 2005 the sixth Ministerial Conference set a deadline of 2013 for the elimination of agricultural export subsidies; a deadline of end-2006 was established for the elimination of export subsidies for cotton by developed countries. The Doha Round of negotiations and all associated deadlines have, however, subsequently been subject to delay (see above).

TEXTILES AND CLOTHING

From 1974–94 the former Multi-Fibre Arrangement (MFA) provided the basis of international trade concerning textiles and clothing, enabling the major importers to establish quotas and protect their domestic industries, through bilateral agreements, against more competitive low-cost goods from developing countries. MFA restrictions that were in place on 31 December 1994 were carried over into a new transitional 10-year Agreement on Textiles and Clothing (ATC) and were phased out through integration into GATT 1994, in four planned stages: products accounting for 16% of the total volume of textiles and clothing imports (at 1990 levels) to be integrated from 1 January 1995; a further 17% on 1 January 1998; not less than a further 18% on 1 January 2002; and all remaining products by 1 January 2005. Since the expiry on that date of the ATC, international trade in clothing and textiles has, as envisaged, been governed by general rules and disciplines embodied in the multilateral trading system.

TRADE IN SERVICES

The General Agreement on Trade in Services (GATS), which was negotiated during the GATT Uruguay Round, is the first set of multilaterally agreed and legally enforceable rules and disciplines ever negotiated to cover international trade in services. The GATS comprises a framework of general rules and disciplines, annexes addressing special conditions relating to individual sectors and national schedules of market access commitments. A Council for Trade in Services oversees the operation of the agreement.

The GATS framework consists of 29 articles, including the following set of basic obligations: total coverage of all internationally traded services; national treatment, i.e. according services and service suppliers of other members no less favourable treatment than that accorded to domestic services and suppliers; MFN treatment (see above), with any specific exemptions to be recorded prior to the implementation of the GATS, with a limit of 10 years' duration; transparency, requiring publication of all relevant national laws and legislations; bilateral agreements on recognition of standards and qualifications to be open to other members who wish to negotiate accession; no restrictions on international payments and transfers; progressive liberalization to be pursued; and market access and national treatment commitments to be bound and recorded in national schedules. These schedules, which include exemptions to the MFN principles, contain the negotiated and guaranteed conditions under which trade in services is conducted and are an integral part of the GATS.

Annexes to the GATS cover the movement of natural persons, permitting governments to negotiate specific commitments regarding the temporary stay of people for the purpose of providing a service; the right of governments to take measures in order to ensure the integrity and stability of the financial system; the role of telecommunications as a distinct sector of economic activity and as a means of supplying other economic activities; and air transport services, excluding certain activities relating to traffic rights.

At the end of the Uruguay Round governments agreed to continue negotiations in the following areas: basic telecommunications; maritime transport; movement of natural persons; and financial services. The Protocol to the GATS relating to movement of natural persons was concluded in July 1995. In May 1996 the USA withdrew from negotiations to conclude an agreement on maritime transport services. At the end of June the participating countries agreed to suspend the discussions and to recommence negotiations in 2000 (see below).

In July 1995 some 29 members signed an interim agreement to grant greater access to the banking, insurance, investment and securities sectors from August 1996. Negotiations to strengthen the agreement and to extend it to new signatories (including the USA, which had declined to sign the agreement, claiming lack of reciprocity by some Asian countries) commenced in April 1997. A final agreement was successfully concluded in December: 102 countries endorsed the elimination of restrictions on access to the financial services sectors from 1 March 1999, and agreed to subject those services to legally binding rules and disciplines. In late January 1999 some 35 signatory states had yet to ratify the financial services agreement, and its entry into force was postponed. Negotiations on trade in basic telecommunications began in May 1994 and were scheduled to conclude in April 1996. Before the final deadline, however, the negotiations were suspended, owing to US concerns, which included greater access to satellite telecommunications markets in Asia and greater control over foreign companies operating from the domestic markets. An agreement was finally concluded by the new deadline of 15 February 1997. Accordingly the largest telecommunications markets, i.e. the USA, the EU and Japan, were to eliminate all remaining restrictions on domestic and foreign competition in the industry by 1 January 1998 (although delays were granted to Spain, until December 1998, Ireland, until 2000, and Greece and Portugal, until 2003). The majority of the signatories to the accord also agreed on common rules to ensure that fair competition could be enforced by the WTO disputes settlement mechanism, and pledged their commitment to establishing a regulatory system for the telecommunications sector and guaranteeing transparency in government licensing. The agreement eventually entered into force in February 1998.

The negotiations to liberalize trade in services, suspended in 1996, were formally reopened in January 2000, with new guidelines and procedures for the negotiations approved in March 2001. The negotiations were incorporated into the Doha Agenda and were to be concluded as part of a single undertaking, initially by 1 January 2005, although the deadline was subsequently postponed.

INTELLECTUAL PROPERTY RIGHTS

The WTO Agreement on Trade-Related Aspects of Intellectual Property Rights (TRIPS), which entered into force on 1 January 1995, recognizes that widely varying standards in the protection and enforcement of intellectual property rights and the lack of multilateral disciplines dealing with international trade in counterfeit goods have been a growing source of tension in international economic relations. The TRIPS agreement aims to ensure that nationals of member states receive equally favourable treatment with regard to the protection of intellectual property and that adequate standards of intellectual property protection exist in all WTO member countries. These standards are largely based on the obligations of the Paris and Berne Conventions of WIPO, however, and the agreement aims to expand and enhance these where necessary, for example: computer programmes, to be protected as literary works for copyright purposes; definition of trade marks eligible for protection; stricter rules of geographical indications of consumer products; a 10-year protection period for industrial designs; a 20-year patent protection available for all inventions; tighter protection of layout design of integrated circuits; and protection for trade secrets and 'know-how' with a commercial value.

Under the agreement member governments are obliged to provide procedures and remedies to ensure the effective enforcement of intellectual property rights. Civil and administrative procedures outlined in the TRIPS include provisions on evidence, injunctions, judicial authority to order the disposal of infringing goods, and criminal procedures and penalties, in particular for trademark counterfeiting and copyright piracy. A one-year period from TRIPS' entry into force was envisaged for developed countries to bring their legislation and practices into conformity with the agreement. Developing countries were to do so in five years (or 10 years if an area of technology did not already have patent protection) and least developed countries in 11 years. A Council for Trade-Related Property Rights monitors the compliance of governments with the agreement and its operation. During 2000 the implementation of TRIPS was one the key areas of contention among WTO members. In November WTO initiated a review of TRIPS, although this was expected to consider alteration of the regime rather than of its implementation. At that time some 70 developing countries were failing to apply TRIPS rules. In November 2001 the Doha Ministerial Conference sought to resolve the ongoing dispute regarding the implementation of TRIPS in respect of pharmaceutical patents in developing countries. A separate declaration aimed to clarify a flexible interpretation of TRIPS in order for governments to meet urgent public health priorities. The deadline for some of the poorest countries to apply provisions on pharmaceutical patents was extended to 1 January 2016. The TRIPS Council was mandated to undertake further consideration of problems concerning compulsory licensing. The Doha Declaration also committed the Council to concluding, by the next (2003) Ministerial Conference, negotiations on a multilateral registration system for geographical indications for wines and spirits; however, this deadline was not achieved, and was subsequently postponed indefinitely. In November 2005 the original deadline of 1 January 2006 for least developed countries to bring their legislation and practices into conformity with TRIPS was extended by the Council for Trade-Related Property Rights to 1 July 2013; the Council also determined that technical assistance to support the application of the agreement in those member countries should be enhanced.

LEGAL FRAMEWORK

In addition to the binding agreements mentioned above, WTO aims to provide a comprehensive legal framework for the international trading system. Under GATT 1994 'anti-dumping' measures were permitted against imports of a product with an export price below its normal value, if these imports were likely to cause damage to a domestic industry. The WTO agreement provides for greater clarity and more detailed rules determining the application of these measures and determines settlement procedures in disputes relating to anti-dumping actions taken by WTO members. In general, anti-dumping measures were to be limited to five years. WTO's Agreement on Subsidies and Countervailing Measures is intended to expand on existing GATT agreements. It classifies subsidies into three categories: prohibited, which may be determined by the Dispute Settlement Body and must be immediately withdrawn; actionable, which must be withdrawn or altered if the subsidy is found to cause adverse effects on the interests of other members; and non-actionable, for example subsidies involving assistance to industrial research, assistance to disadvantaged regions or adaptation of facilities to meet new environmental requirements; non-actionable subsidies, however, were terminated in 1999. The Agreement also contains provisions on the use of duties to offset the effect of a subsidy (so-called countervailing measures) and establishes procedures for the initiation and conduct of investigations into this action. Countervailing measures must generally be terminated within five years of their imposition. Least developed countries, and developing countries with gross national product per capita of less than US $1,000, are exempt from disciplines on prohibited export subsidies; however, it was envisaged that these would be eliminated by 2003 in all other developing countries and by 2002 in countries with economies in transition. In November 2001 the Doha Ministerial Conference agreed to permit developing countries individually to request an extension of the interim period prior to elimination; consequently, a number of such member countries were granted extensions.

WTO members may take safeguard actions to protect a specific domestic industry from a damaging increase of imported products. However, the WTO agreement aims to clarify criteria for imposing safeguards, their duration (normally to be no longer than four years, which may be extended to eight years) and consultations on trade compensation for the exporting countries. Safeguard measures are not applicable to products from developing countries as long as their share of imports of the product concerned does not exceed 3%.

Further legal arrangements act to ensure the following: that technical regulations and standards (including testing and certification procedures) do not create unnecessary obstacles to trade; that import licensing procedures are transparent and predictable; that the valuation of goods for customs purposes are fair and uniform; that GATT principles and obligations apply to import preshipment inspection activities; the fair and transparent administration of rules of origin; and that no investment measures which may restrict or distort trade may be applied. A Working Group on Notification Obligations and Procedures aims to ensure that members fulfil their notification requirements, which facilitate the transparency and surveillance of the trading rules.

PLURILATERAL AGREEMENT

The majority of GATT agreements became multilateral obligations when the WTO became operational in 1995; however, four agreements, which had a selective group of signatories, remained in effect. These so-called plurilateral agreements, the Agreement on Trade in Civil Aircraft, the Agreement on Government Procurement, the International Dairy Agreement and the International Bovine Meat Agreement, aimed to increase international co-operation and fair and open trade and competition in these areas. The bovine meat and dairy agreements were terminated in 1997. The remaining two plurilateral agreements establish their own management bodies, which are required to report to the General Council.

TRADE POLICY REVIEW MECHANISM

The mechanism, which was established provisionally in 1989, was given a permanent role in the WTO. Through regular monitoring and surveillance of national trade policies the mechanism aims to increase the transparency and understanding of trade policies and practices and to enable assessment of the effects of policies on the world trading system. In addition, it records efforts made by governments to bring domestic trade legislation into conformity with WTO provisions and to implement WTO commitments. Reviews are conducted in the Trade Policy Review Body on the basis of a policy statement of the government under review and an independent report prepared by the WTO Secretariat. Under the mechanism the world's four largest traders, the EU, the USA, Japan and Canada, were to be reviewed every two years. Special groups were established to examine new regional free trade arrangements and the trade policies of acceding countries. In February 1996 a single Committee on Regional Trade Agreements was established, superseding these separate working parties. The Committee aimed to ensure that these groupings contributed to the process of global trade liberalization and to study the implications of these arrangements on the multilateral system.

SETTLEMENT OF DISPUTES

A separate annex to the WTO agreement determines a unified set of rules and procedures to govern the settlement of all WTO disputes, substantially reinforcing the GATT procedures. WTO members are committed not to undertake unilateral action against perceived violations of the trade rules, but to seek recourse in the dispute settlement mechanism and abide by its findings. By March 2012 434 trade complaints had been notified to the WTO since 1995.

The agreements that may be cited in the bilateral consultations (first stage, see below) of the disputes process relate to: Establishing the WTO (cited in 44 cases by March 2012); Agriculture (cited in 67 cases by March 2012); Anti-dumping (Article VI of GATT 1994) (90 cases); Civil Aircraft (no citations); Customs Valuation (Article VII of GATT 1994) (cited in 15 cases); Dispute Settlement Understanding (15 cases); GATT 1947 (one case); GATT 1994 (345 cases); Government Procurement (four cases); Import Licensing (34 cases); Intellectual Property (TRIPS) (30 cases); Preshipment Inspection (no citations); Rules of Origin (seven cases); Safeguards (39 cases); Sanitary and Phytosanitary Measures (SPS) (38 cases); Services (GATS) (22 cases); Subsidies and Countervailing Measures (89 cases); Technical Barriers to Trade (TBT) (42 cases); Textiles and Clothing (16 cases); Trade-Related Investment Measures (TRIMs) (28 cases); Protocol of Accession (23 cases).

The first stage of the process requires bilateral consultations between the members concerned in an attempt to conclude a mutually acceptable solution to the issue. These may be undertaken through the good offices and mediation efforts of the Director-General. Only after a consultation period of 60 days may the complainant ask the General Council, convened as the Dispute Settlement Body (DSB), to establish an independent panel to examine the case, which then does so within the terms of reference of the agreement cited. Each party to the dispute submits its arguments and then presents its case before the panel. Third parties which notify their interest in the dispute may also present views at the first substantive meeting of the panel. At this stage an expert review group may be appointed to provide specific scientific or technical advice. The panel submits sections and then a full interim report of its findings to the parties, who may then request a further review involving additional meetings. A final report should be submitted to the parties by the panel within six months of its establishment, or within three months in cases of urgency, including those related to perishable goods. Final reports are normally adopted by the DSB within 60 days of issuance. In the case of a measure being found to be inconsistent with the relevant WTO agreement, the panel recommends ways in which the member may bring the measure into conformity with the agreement. However, under the WTO mechanism either party has the right to appeal against the decision and must notify the DSB of its intentions before adoption of the final report. Appeal proceedings, which are limited to issues of law and the legal interpretation covered by the panel report, are undertaken by three members of the Appellate Body within a maximum period of 90 days. The report of the Appellate Body must be unconditionally accepted by the parties to the dispute (unless there is a consensus within the DSB against its adoption). If the recommendations of the panel or appeal report are not implemented immediately, or within a 'reasonable period' as determined by the DSB, the parties are obliged to negotiate mutually acceptable compensation pending full implementation. Failure to agree compensation may result in the DSB authorizing the complainant to suspend concessions or obligations against the other party. In any case the DSB monitors the implementation of adopted recommendations or rulings, while any outstanding cases remain on its agenda until the issue is resolved.

In late 1997 the DSB initiated a review of the WTO's understanding on dispute settlement, as required by the Marrakesh Agreement. The Doha Declaration, adopted in November 2001, mandated further that negotiations to be conducted on the review and on additional proposals to amend the dispute procedure as a separate undertaking from the rest of the work programme.

The Agreement on the Application of Sanitary and Phytosanitary Measures aims to regulate world-wide standards of food safety and animal and plant health in order to encourage the mutual recognition of standards and conformity, so as to facilitate trade in these products. The Agreement includes provisions on control inspection and approval procedures. In September 1997, in the first case to be brought under the Agreement, a dispute panel of the WTO ruled that the EU's ban on imports of hormone-treated beef and beef products from the USA and Canada was in breach of international trading rules. In January 1998 the Appellate Body upheld the panel's ruling, but expressed its support for restrictions to ensure food standards if there was adequate scientific evidence of risks to human health. The EU maintained the ban, against resistance from the USA, while it carried out scientific risk assessments.

In December 2009 representatives of the EU and Latin American countries initialled the EU-Latin America Bananas Agreement, under which (with a view to ending a 15-year dispute) the EU was gradually to reduce its import tariff on bananas from Latin American countries, from €176 to €114 per metric ton, by 2017. On their side, Latin American banana-producing countries undertook not to demand further tariff reductions; and to withdraw several related cases against the EU pending at the WTO. In response to the Agreement, the US authorities determined to settle a parallel dispute with the EU at the WTO relating to bananas.

CO-OPERATION WITH OTHER ORGANIZATIONS

WTO is mandated to pursue co-operation with the IMF and the World Bank, as well as with other multilateral organizations, in order to achieve greater coherence in global economic policy-making. In November 1994 the preparatory committee of the WTO resolved not to incorporate the new organization into the UN structure as a specialized agency. Instead, co-operation arrangements with the IMF and the World Bank were to be developed. In addition, efforts were pursued to enhance co-operation with UNCTAD in research, trade and technical issues. The Directors-General of the two organizations agreed to meet at least twice a year in order to develop the working relationship. In particular, co-operation was to be undertaken in WTO's special programme of activities for Africa, which aimed to help African countries expand and diversify their trade and benefit from the global trading system. Since 1997 WTO has co-operated with the IMF, ITC, UNCTAD, UNDP and the World Bank in an Integrated Framework for trade-related technical assistance to least developed countries. An enhanced Integrated Framework (EIF) was adopted in May 2007. Annually (most recently in March 2011) WTO, the IMF, the World Bank, UNCTAD and ECOSOC participate in high-level consultations.

From early 2009 WTO, the ILO, the IMF, the World Bank, and OECD entered into co-operation on the establishment of a new global standard for future economic development, in response to the ongoing global financial crisis (see above); it was announced in April 2010 that the inter-agency collaboration would be intensified. In June 2009 WTO and UNEP jointly issued a report entitled *Trade and Climate Change*, reviewing the intersections between trade and climate change from the perspectives of: the science of climate change; economics; multilateral efforts to combat climate change; and the effects on trade of national climate change policies.

In July 2010 WTO, WIPO and WHO organized a symposium to initiate a process of co-operation in addressing means of improving the access of poorer populations to necessary medicines.

International Trade Centre (UNCTAD/WTO): Palais des Nations, 1211 Geneva 10, Switzerland; tel. 227300111; fax 227334439; e-mail itcreg@intracen.org; internet www.intracen.org; f. 1964 by GATT; jointly operated with the UN (through UNCTAD) since 1968; ITC works with developing countries in product and market development, the development of trade support services, trade information, human resource development, international purchasing and supply management, and needs assessment and programme design for trade promotion; allocated US $41.3m. under the proposed UN budget for 2012–13; publs *International Trade Forum* (quarterly), market studies, handbooks, etc.

Executive Director: PATRICIA R. FRANCIS (Jamaica).

Finance

The WTO's 2012 budget amounted to 196m. Swiss francs, financed mainly by contributions from members in proportion to their share of total trading conducted by WTO members.

Publications

Annual Report (2 volumes).
Annual Report of the Appellate Body.
International Trade Statistics (annually).
World Trade Report (annually).
World Trade Review (3 a year).
World Trade Report (annually).
WTO Focus (monthly).

OTHER INTERNATIONAL ORGANIZATIONS

Agriculture, Food, Forestry and Fisheries

(for organizations concerned with agricultural commodities, see Commodities)

African Agricultural Technology Foundation: POB 30709, Nairobi 00100, Kenya; tel. (20) 4223700; fax (20) 4223701; e-mail aatf@aatf-africa.org; internet www.aatf-africa.org; f. 2002; aims to facilitate and promote public/private partnerships for the access and delivery of agricultural technologies for use by resource poor smallholder farmers; Exec. Dir DENIS TUMWESIGYE KYETERE (Uganda).

African Timber Organization (ATO): BP 1077, Libreville, Gabon; tel. 732928; fax 734030; e-mail oab-gabon@internetgabon.com; f. 1976 to enable members to study and co-ordinate ways of ensuring the optimum utilization and conservation of their forests; mems: 13 African countries; publs *ATO Information Bulletin* (quarterly), *International Magazine of African Timber* (2 a year).

Arab Authority for Agricultural Investment and Development (AAAID): POB 2102, Khartoum, Sudan; tel. (18) 7096100; fax (18) 7096295; e-mail info@aaaid.org; internet www.aaaid.org; f. 1976 to accelerate agricultural development in the Arab world and to ensure food security; acts principally by equity participation in agricultural projects in member countries; AAAID has adopted new programmes to help raise productivity of food agricultural products and introduced zero-tillage farming technology for developing the rain-fed sector, which achieved a substantial increase in the yields of grown crops, including sorghum, cotton, sesame, and sunflower; mems: 20 countries; Pres. and Chair. ALI BIN SAEED AL-SHARHAN; publs *Journal of Agricultural Investment* (English and Arabic), *Extension and Investment Bulletins*, *Annual Report* (Arabic and English), *AAAID Newsletter* (quarterly).

Association of Agricultural Research Institutions in the Near East and North Africa: POB 950764, 11195 Amman, Jordan; tel. (6) 5525750; fax (6) 5525930; e-mail icarda-jordan@cgiar.org; internet www.aarinena.org; f. 1985; aims to strengthen co-operation among national, regional and international research institutions; operates the internet-based Near East and North Africa Rural and Agricultural Knowledge and Information Network (NERAKIN); Exec. Sec. IBRAHIM YUSUF HAMDAN (Jordan).

AVRDC—the World Vegetable Center: POB 42, Shanhua, Tainan 74199, Taiwan; tel. (6) 5837801; fax (6) 5830009; e-mail info@worldveg.org; internet www.avrdc.org; f. 1971 as the Asian Vegetable Research and Development Center; aims to enhance the nutritional well-being and raise the incomes of the poor in rural and urban areas of developing countries, through improved varieties and methods of vegetable production, marketing and distribution; runs an experimental farm, laboratories, gene-bank, greenhouses, quarantine house, insectarium, library and weather station; provides training for research and production specialists in tropical vegetables; exchanges and disseminates vegetable germplasm through regional offices in the developing world; serves as a clearing-house for vegetable research information; and undertakes scientific publishing; mems: Japan, Republic of Korea, Philippines, Taiwan, Thailand, USA; Dir-Gen. Dr DYNO KEATINGE; publs *Annual Report*, *Technical Bulletin*, *Proceedings*.

CAB International (CABI): Nosworthy Way, Wallingford, Oxon, OX10 8DE, United Kingdom; tel. (1491) 832111; fax (1491) 829292; e-mail enquiries@cabi.org; internet www.cabi.org; f. 1929 as the Imperial Agricultural Bureaux (later Commonwealth Agricultural Bureaux), current name adopted in 1985; aims to improve human welfare world-wide through the generation, dissemination and application of scientific knowledge in support of sustainable development; places particular emphasis on sustainable agriculture, forestry, human health and the management of natural resources, with priority given to the needs of developing countries; a separate microbiology centre, in Egham, Surrey (UK), undertakes research, consultancy, training, capacity-building and institutional development measures in sustainable pest management, biosystematics and molecular biology, ecological applications and environmental and industrial microbiology; compiles and publishes extensive information (in a variety of print and electronic forms) on aspects of agriculture, forestry, veterinary medicine, the environment and natural resources, and Third World rural development; maintains regional centres in the People's Republic of China, India, Kenya, Malaysia, Pakistan, Switzerland, Trinidad and Tobago, and the USA; mems: 45 countries and territories; Chair. JOHN RIPLEY (United Kingdom); CEO Dr TREVOR NICHOLLS (United Kingdom).

Collaborative International Pesticides Analytical Council Ltd (CIPAC): c/o Dr Ralf Hänel, Referat 206, Messeweg 11/12 38104, Braunschweig, Germany; tel. (531) 2993506; fax (531) 2993002; e-mail cipac@acw.admin.ch; internet www.cipac.org; f. 1957 to organize international collaborative work on methods of analysis for pesticides used in crop protection; 25 mems, 8 hon. life mems; Chair. Dr RALF HÄNEL (Germany); Sec. Dr LÁZLÓ BURA (Hungary).

Desert Locust Control Organization for Eastern Africa (DLCOEA): POB 4255, Addis Ababa, Ethiopia; tel. (1) 461477; fax (1) 460296; e-mail dlc@ethionet.et; internet www.dlcoea.org.et; f. 1962 to promote effective control of desert locust in the region and to conduct research into the locust's environment and behaviour; also assists member states in the monitoring, forecasting and extermination of other migratory pests; mems: Djibouti, Eritrea, Ethiopia, Kenya, Somalia, Sudan, Tanzania, Uganda; Dir GASPAR ATTMAN MALLYA; Co-ordinator JAMES M. GATIMU; publs *Desert Locust Situation Reports* (monthly), *Annual Report*, technical reports.

European and Mediterranean Plant Protection Organization (EPPO): 21 blvd Richard Lenoir, 75011 Paris, France; tel. 1-45-20-77-94; fax 1-70-76-65-47; e-mail hq@eppo.fr; internet www.eppo.org; f. 1951, present name adopted in 1955; aims to promote international co-operation between government plant protection services to prevent the introduction and spread of pests and diseases of plants and plant products; mems: govts of 50 countries and territories; Dir-Gen. RINGOLDS ARNITIS; publs *EPPO Bulletin*, *Data Sheets on Quarantine Organisms*, *Guidelines for the Efficacy Evaluation of Pesticides*, *Crop Growth Stage Keys*, *Summary of the Phytosanitary Regulations of EPPO Member Countries*, *Reporting Service*.

European Association for Animal Production (EAAP) (Fédération européenne de zootechnie): Via G. Tomassetti 3 A/1, 00161 Rome, Italy; tel. (06) 44202639; fax (06) 44266798; e-mail eaap@eaap.org; internet www.eaap.org; f. 1949 to help improve the conditions of animal production and meet consumer demand; holds annual meetings; mems: asscns in 41 countries; Sec.-Gen. ANDREA ROSATI (Italy); publs *Animal* (International Journal of Animal Biosciences), *EAAP News*.

European Association for Research on Plant Breeding (EUCARPIA): c/o Agricultural Research Institute of the Hungarian Academy of Sciences, 2462 Martonvásár, Brunszvik u2, Hungary; tel. (22) 569550; fax (22) 460213; e-mail eucarpia@mgki.hu; internet www.eucarpia.org; f. 1956 to promote scientific and technical co-operation in the plant breeding field; mems: 1,100 individuals, 65 corporate mems; Pres. Dr ZOLTÁN BEDŐ (Hungary); Sec.-Gen. Dr LÁSZLÓ LÁNG (Hungary); publ. *EUCARPIA Bulletin*.

European Grassland Federation (EGF): Dr Willy Kessler, c/o Agroscope Reckenholz-Tänikon Research Station ART, Reckenholzstr. 191, 8046, Zürich, Switzerland; tel. 443777376; fax 443770201; e-mail fedsecretary@europeangrassland.org; internet www.europeangrassland.org; f. 1963 to facilitate and maintain liaison between European grassland organizations and to promote the interchange of scientific and practical knowledge and experience; holds General Meeting every two years and a Symposium in the intervening year; mems: 31 full and 4 corresponding member countries in Europe; Pres. Prof. Dr PIOTR STYPINSKI; Sec. Dr WILLY KESSLER (Switzerland); publ. *Grassland Science in Europe*.

European Livestock and Meat Trading Union (UECBV): 81A rue de la Loi, 4th floor, 1040 Brussels, Belgium; tel. (2) 230-46-03; fax (2) 230-94-00; e-mail info@uecbv.eu; internet www.uecbv.eu; f. 1952 to study problems of the European livestock and meat trade and inform members of all relevant legislation; acts as an international arbitration commission; conducts research on agricultural markets, quality of livestock, and veterinary regulations; incorporates the European Association of Livestock Markets and the Young European Meat Committee; mems: 50 national orgs in 31 countries, representing some 20,000 companies; Pres. LAURENT SPANGHERO NUTRINAT; Sec.-Gen. JEAN-LUC MERIAUX.

European Society for Sugar Technology (ESST): Lückhoffstr. 16, 14129 Berlin, Germany; tel. (30) 8035678; fax (30) 8032049; e-mail mail@esst-sugar.org; internet www.esst-sugar.org; Pres. DENIS BOURÉE (France); Sec. Dr JÜRGEN BRUHNS (Germany).

Indian Ocean Tuna Commission (IOTC): POB 1011, Victoria, Mahé, Seychelles; tel. 4225494; fax 4224364; e-mail iotc.secretary@iotc.org; internet www.iotc.org; f. 1996 as a regional fisheries organization with a mandate for the conservation and management of tuna and tuna-like species in the Indian Ocean; mems: Australia, Belize, People's Republic of China, the Comoros, European Union, Eritrea, France, Guinea, India, Indonesia, Iran, Japan, Kenya, Republic of Korea, Madagascar, Malaysia, Maldives, Mauritius, Mozambique, Oman, Pakistan, Philippines, Seychelles, Sudan, Sri Lanka, Tanzania, Thailand, United Kingdom, Vanuatu; co-operating non-contracting parties: Senegal, South Africa; Exec. Sec. ALEJANDRO ANGANUZZI (Argentina).

Inter-American Association of Agricultural Librarians, Documentalists and Information Specialists (Asociación Interamericana de Bibliotecarios, Documentalistas y Especialistas en Información Agrícolas—AIBDA): c/o IICA-CIDIA, Apdo 55-2200 Coronado, Costa Rica; tel. 2216-0222; fax 2216-0291; e-mail info@aibda.com; internet www.aibda.com; f. 1953 to promote professional improvement through technical publications and meetings, and to promote improvement of library services in agricultural sciences; mems: 653 in 31 countries and territories; Pres. RUBÉN URBIZAGÁSTEGUI (Peru); publ. *Revista AIBDA* (2 a year).

Inter-American Tropical Tuna Commission (IATTC): 8604 La Jolla Shores Drive, La Jolla, CA 92037-1508, USA; tel. (858) 546-7100; fax (858) 546-7133; e-mail info@iattc.org; internet www.iattc.org; f. 1950; administers two programmes, the Tuna-Billfish Programme and the Tuna-Dolphin Programme. The principal responsibilities of the Tuna-Billfish Programme are: to study the biology of the tunas and related species of the eastern Pacific Ocean to estimate the effects of fishing and natural factors on their abundance; to recommend appropriate conservation measures in order to maintain stocks at levels which will afford maximum sustainable catches; and to collect information on compliance with Commission resolutions. The principal functions of the Tuna-Dolphin Programme are: to monitor the abundance of dolphins and their mortality incidental to purse-seine fishing in the eastern Pacific Ocean; to study the causes of mortality of dolphins during fishing operations and promote the use of fishing techniques and equipment that minimize these mortalities; to study the effects of different fishing methods on the various fish and other animals of the pelagic ecosystem; and to provide a secretariat for the International Dolphin Conservation Programme; mems: Belize, Canada, People's Republic of China, Colombia, Costa Rica, Ecuador, El Salvador, European Union, France, Guatemala, Japan, Kiribati, Republic of Korea, Mexico, Nicaragua, Panama, Peru, Chinese Taipei (Taiwan), USA, Vanuatu, Venezuela; co-operating non-contracting party: Cook Islands; Dir GUILLERMO A. COMPEÁN; publs *Bulletin* (irregular), *Annual Report*, *Fishery Status Report*, *Stock Assessment Report* (annually), *Special Report* (irregular).

International Association for Cereal Science and Technology (ICC): Marxergasse 2, 1030 Vienna, Austria; tel. (1) 707-72-020; fax (1) 707-72-040; e-mail office@icc.or.at; internet www.icc.or.at; f. 1955 (as the International Association for Cereal Chemistry, name changed 1986); aims to promote international co-operation in the field of cereal science and technology through the dissemination of information and the development of standard methods of testing and analysing products; mems: 49 mem. and 6 observer mem. states; Pres. Prof. MARINA CARCEA (Italy) (2011–12); Pres. Elect JOEL ABECASSIS (France) (2013–14); Sec.-Gen. and CEO Dr ROLAND POMS (Austria).

International Association for Vegetation Science (IAVS): c/o Nina A.C. Smits, IAVS Administration, Wes Beekhuizenweg 3, 6871 VJ Renkum, Netherlands; tel. (317) 477914; fax (317) 424988; e-mail admin@iavs.org; internet www.iavs.org; f. 1938; mems: 1,500 in 70 countries; Pres. MARTIN DIEKMANN (Germany); Sec. SUSAN WISER (New Zealand); publs *Journal of Vegetation Science*, *Applied Vegetation Science*.

International Association of Agricultural Economists (IAAE): 555 East Wells St, Suite 1100, Milwaukee, WI 53202, USA; tel. (414) 918-3199; fax (414) 276-3349; e-mail iaae@execinc.com; internet www.iaae-agecon.org; f. 1929 to foster development of agricultural economic sciences; aims to further the application of research into agricultural processes; works to improve economic and social conditions for agricultural and rural life; mems: in 83 countries; Pres. KEIJIRO OTSUKA (Japan); Pres. Elect Prof. JOHAN SWINNEN (Belgium); Sec. and Treas. WALTER J. ARMBRUSTER (USA); publs *Agricultural Economics* (8 a year), *IAAE Newsletter* (2 a year).

International Association of Agricultural Information Specialists: c/o Toni Greider, POB 63, Lexington, KY 40588-0063, USA; fax (859) 257-8379; e-mail info@iaald.org; internet www.iaald.org; f. 1955 to provide educational and networking opportunities for agricultural information professionals world-wide; aims to enable its members to create, capture, access and disseminate information to achieve a more productive and sustainable use of the world's land, water, and renewable natural resources and to contribute to improved livelihoods of rural communities through educational programmes, conferences, and networking opportunities; affiliated to INFITA; mems: 400 in 84 countries; Pres. FREDERICO SANCHO (Costa Rica); Sec.-Treas. TONI GREIDER (USA); publ. *Agricultural Information Worldwide*.

International Association of Horticultural Producers: Oude Herenweg 10, 2215 RZ Voorhout, Netherlands; e-mail sg@aiph.org; internet www.aiph.org; f. 1948; represents the common interests of commercial horticultural producers in the international field; authorizes international horticultural exhibitions; mems: national asscns in 25 countries; Pres. DOEKE FABER (Netherlands); Sec.-Gen. SJAAK LANGESLAG (Netherlands); publ. *Statistical Yearbook*.

International Bee Research Association (IBRA): 16 North Rd, Cardiff, CF10 3DY, United Kingdom; tel. (29) 2037-2409; fax (56) 0113-5640; e-mail mail@ibra.org.uk; internet www.ibra.org.uk; f. 1949 to further bee research and provide an information service for bee scientists and beekeepers world-wide; mems: 1,200 in 130 countries; Exec. Dir SARAH JONES (United Kingdom); publs *Apicultural Abstracts* (quarterly), *Journal of Apicultural Research* (quarterly), *Bee World* (quarterly).

International Centre for Agricultural Research in the Dry Areas (ICARDA): POB 5466, Aleppo, Syria; tel. (21) 2213433; fax (21) 2213490; e-mail icarda@cgiar.org; internet www.icarda.org; f. 1977; aims to improve the production of lentils, barley and fava beans throughout the developing world; supports the improvement of on-farm water-use efficiency, rangeland and small-ruminant production in all dry-area developing countries; within the West and Central Asia and North Africa region promotes the improvement of bread and durum wheat and chickpea production and of farming systems; undertakes research, training and dissemination of information, in co-operation with national, regional and international research institutes, universities and ministries of agriculture, in order to enhance production, alleviate poverty and promote sustainable natural resource management practices; member of the network of 15 agricultural research centres supported by the Consultative Group on International Agricultural Research (CGIAR); Dir-Gen. Dr MAHMOUD MOHAMED BASHIR EL-SOLH; publs *Annual Report*, *Caravan Newsletter* (2 a year).

International Centre for Tropical Agriculture (Centro Internacional de Agricultura Tropical—CIAT): Apdo Aéreo 6713, Cali, Colombia; tel. (2) 445-0000; fax (2) 445-0073; e-mail ciat@cgiar.org; internet www.ciat.cgiar.org; f. 1967 to contribute to the alleviation of hunger and poverty in tropical developing countries by using new techniques in agriculture research and training; focuses on production problems in field beans, cassava, rice and tropical pastures in the tropics; Dir-Gen. RUBEN G. ECHEVERRÍA; publs *Annual Report*, *Growing Affinities* (2 a year), *Pasturas Tropicales* (3 a year), catalogue of publications.

International Commission for the Conservation of Atlantic Tunas (ICCAT): Calle Corazón de María 8, 28002 Madrid, Spain; tel. (91) 4165600; fax (91) 4152612; e-mail info@iccat.es; internet www.iccat.int; f. 1969 under the provisions of the International Convention for the Conservation of Atlantic Tunas (1966) to maintain the populations of tuna and tuna-like species in the Atlantic Ocean and adjacent seas at levels that permit the maximum sustainable catch; collects statistics; conducts studies; mems: 48 contracting parties; Chair. M. MIYAHARA (Japan); Exec. Sec. DRISS MESKI (Morocco); publs *ICCAT Biennial Report*, *ICCAT Collective Vol. of Scientific Papers*, *Statistical Bulletin* (annually), *Data Record* (annually).

International Committee for Animal Recording (ICAR): Via Tomassetti 3-1/A, 00161, Rome, Italy; tel. (06) 44202639; fax (06) 44266798; e-mail icar@icar.org; internet www.icar.org; f. 1951 to extend and improve the work of recording and to standardize methods; mems: in 58 countries; Pres. UFFE LAURITSEN (Denmark); Sec. REINHARD REENTS (Germany).

International Crops Research Institute for the Semi-Arid Tropics (ICRISAT): Patancheru, Andhra Pradesh 502 324, India; tel. (40) 30713071; fax (40) 30713074; e-mail icrisat@cgiar.org; internet www.icrisat.org; f. 1972 to promote the genetic improvement of crops and for research on the management of resources in the world's semi-arid tropics, with the aim of reducing poverty and protecting the environment; research covers all physical and socio-economic aspects of improving farming systems on unirrigated land; maintains regional centres in Nairobi, Kenya (for eastern and southern Africa) and in Niamey, Niger (for western and central Africa); Dir-Gen. Dr WILLIAM D. DAR (Philippines); publs *ICRISAT Report* (annually), *Journal of Semi-Arid Tropical Agricultural Research* (2 a year), information and research bulletins.

International Dairy Federation (IDF): 70/B blvd Auguste Reyers, 1030 Brussels, Belgium; tel. (2) 733-98-88; fax (2) 733-04-13; e-mail info@fil-idf.org; internet www.fil-idf.org; f. 1903 to link all dairy asscns, in order to encourage the solution of scientific, technical and economic problems affecting the dairy industry; holds annual World Dairy Summit (2012: Cape Town, South Africa, in Nov.); mems: national cttees in 53 countries; Pres. RICHARD DOYLE; publs *Bulletin of IDF*, *IDF-ISO Standard Methods of Analysis*.

International Federation of Agricultural Producers (IFAP): 60 rue St-Lazare, 75009 Paris, France; tel. 1-45-26-05-53; fax 1-48-74-72-12; e-mail ifap@ifap.org; internet www.ifap.org; f. 1946 to represent, in the international field, the interests of agricultural producers; encourages the exchange of information and ideas; works to develop understanding of world problems and their effects upon agricultural producers; encourages sustainable patterns of agricultural development; holds conference every two years; mems: national farmers' orgs and agricultural co-operatives of 83 countries; Pres. AJAY VASHEE (Zambia); Sec.-Gen. DAVID KING; publs *The World Farmer* (monthly), *Proceedings of General Conferences*.

International Federation of Beekeepers' Associations (APIMONDIA): Corso Vittorio Emanuele II 101, 00186 Rome, Italy; tel. (06) 6852286; fax (06) 6852287; e-mail apimondia@mclink.it; internet www.apimondia.com; f. 1949; collects and brings up to date documentation on international beekeeping; carries out studies into the particular problems of beekeeping; organizes international congresses, seminars, symposia and meetings; co-operates with other international organizations interested in beekeeping, in particular, with the FAO; mems: 112 asscns from 75 countries; Pres. GILLES RATIA (France); Sec.-Gen. RICCARDO JANNONI-SEBASTIANINI (Italy); publs *Dictionary of Beekeeping Terms*, *AGROVOC* (thesaurus of agricultural terms), studies.

International Food Policy Research Institute (IFPRI): 2033 K St, NW, Washington, DC 20006, USA; tel. (202) 862-5600; fax (202) 467-4439; e-mail ifpri@cgiar.org; internet www.ifpri.org; f. 1975; co-operates with academic and other institutions in further research; develops policies for cutting hunger and malnutrition; committed to increasing public awareness of food policies; Dir-Gen. SHENGGEN FAN (People's Republic of China).

International Service for National Agricultural Research (ISNAR): IFPRI, ISNAR Division, ILRI, POB 5689, Addis Ababa, Ethiopia; tel. (11) 646-3215; fax (11) 646-2927; e-mail ifpri-addisababa@cgiar.org; fmrly based in The Hague, Netherlands, the ISNAR Program relocated to Addis Ababa in 2004, under the governance of IFPRI; Dir Dr WILBERFORCE KISAMBA-MUGERWA.

International Hop Growers' Convention: Malgajeva 18, 3000 Celje, Slovenia; tel. (3) 712-16-00; fax (3) 712-16-20; e-mail martin.pavlovic@guest.arnes.si; internet www.ihgc.org; f. 1950; acts as a centre for the collection of national reports and global data on hop production and information management on the hop industry among member countries, estimates the world crop and promotes scientific research; mems: national hop producers' asscns and hop trading companies in 19 countries world-wide; Sec.-Gen. Dr MARTIN PAVLOVIČ.

International Institute for Beet Research (IIRB): 40 rue Washington, 1050 Brussels, Belgium; Holtenser Landstr. 77, 37079 Göttingen, Germany; tel. (551) 500-65-84; fax (551) 500-65-85; e-mail mail@iirb.org; internet www.iirb.org; f. 1932 to promote research and the exchange of information; organizes congresses and study group meetings; mems: 400 in 28 countries; Sec.-Gen. STEPHANIE KLUTH (Germany).

International Institute of Tropical Agriculture (IITA): Oyo Rd, PMB 5320, Ibadan, Oyo State, Nigeria; tel. (2) 7517472; fax (2) 2412221; e-mail iita@cgiar.org; internet www.iita.org; f. 1967; principal financing arranged by the Consultative Group on International Agricultural Research—CGIAR and several NGOs for special projects; research programmes comprise crop management, improvement of crops and plant protection and health; conducts a training programme for researchers in tropical agriculture; maintains a virtual library and an image database; administers Research Stations, Research Sites, and Regional Administrative Hubs in 41 African countries; Dir-Gen. Dr NTERANYA SANGINGA (Democratic Repub. of the Congo); publs *Annual Report*, *R4DReview*, *MTP Fact Sheets*, *BOT Newsletter* (quarterly), technical bulletins, research reports.

International Livestock Research Institute (ILRI): POB 30709, Nairobi 00100, Kenya; tel. (20) 4223000; fax (20) 4223001; e-mail ilri-kenya@cgiar.org; internet www.ilri.org; f. 1995 to supersede the International Laboratory for Research on Animal Diseases and the International Livestock Centre for Africa; conducts laboratory and field research on animal health and other livestock issues, focusing on the following global livestock development challenges: developing vaccine and diagnostic technologies; conservation and reproductive technologies; adaptation to and mitigation of climate change; addressing emerging diseases; broadening market access for the poor; sustainable intensification of smallholder crop-livestock systems; reducing the vulnerability of marginal systems and communities; carries out training programmes for scientists and technicians; maintains a specialized science library; Dir-Gen. JIMMY SMITH (Guyana); publs *Annual Report*, *Livestock Research for Development* (newsletter, 2 a year).

International Maize and Wheat Improvement Centre (CIMMYT): Apdo Postal 6-641, 06600 México, DF, Mexico; tel. (55) 5804-7502; fax (55) 5804-7558; e-mail cimmyt@cgiar.org; internet www.cimmyt.org; conducts world-wide research programme for sustainable maize and wheat cropping systems to help the poor in developing countries; Dir-Gen. Dr THOMAS A. LUMPKIN (USA).

International Organization for Biological Control of Noxious Animals and Plants: c/o Prof. Dr Joop C. van Lenteren, Laboratory of Entomology, Wageningen University, POB 8031, 6700 EH Wageningen, The Netherlands; e-mail Joop.vanLenteren@wur.nl; internet www.iobc-global.org; f. 1955 to promote and co-ordinate research on the more effective biological control of harmful organisms; reorganized in 1971 as a central council with world-wide affiliations and six largely autonomous regional sections; Pres. Prof. Dr JACQUES BRODEUR (Canada); Gen. Sec. Prof. Dr JOOP C. VAN LENTEREN (Netherlands); publs *BioControl*, *Newsletter*.

International Organization of Citrus Virologists (IOCV): c/o C. N. Roistacher, Dept of Plant Pathology, University of California, Riverside, CA 92521-0122, USA; tel. (909) 684-0934; fax (909) 684-4324; e-mail iocvsecretary@gmail.com; internet www.ivia.es/iocv/; f. 1957 to promote research on citrus virus diseases at international level by standardizing diagnostic techniques and exchanging information; mems: 250; Chair. NURIA DURAN-VILA; Sec. GIORGIOS VIDALAKIS.

International Red Locust Control Organization for Central and Southern Africa (IRLCO-CSA): POB 240252, Ndola, Zambia; tel. (2) 651251; fax (2) 650117; e-mail locust@zamnet.zm; f. 1971 to control locusts in eastern, central and southern Africa; also assists in the control of African army-worm and quelea-quelea; mems: 6 countries; Dir MOSES M. OKHOBA; publs *Annual Report*, *Quarterly Report*, *Monthly Report*, scientific reports.

International Rice Research Institute (IRRI): Los Baños, Laguna, DAPO Box 7777, Metro Manila, Philippines; tel. (2) 5805600; fax (2) 5805699; e-mail irri@cgiar.org; internet www.irri.org; f. 1960; conducts research on rice, with the aim of developing technologies of environmental, social and economic benefit; works to enhance national rice research systems and offers training; operates Riceworld, a museum and learning centre about rice; maintains a library of technical rice literature; organizes international conferences and workshops (third International Rice Congress held in Hanoi, Viet Nam, in Nov. 2010; sixth International Hybrid Rice Symposium: Sept. 2012, Hyderabad, India; seventh Rice Genetics Symposium: 2013, Philippines); Dir-Gen. Dr ROBERT S. ZEIGLER; publs *Rice Literature Update*, *Rice Today* (quarterly), *Hotline*, *Facts about IRRI*, *News about Rice and People*, *International Rice Research Notes*.

International Seed Testing Association (ISTA): Zürichstrasse 50, 8303 Bassersdorf, Switzerland; tel. 448386000; fax 448386001; e-mail ista.office@ista.ch; internet www.seedtest.org; f. 1924 to promote uniformity and accurate methods of seed testing and evaluation in order to facilitate efficiency in production, processing, distribution and utilization of seeds; organizes meetings, workshops, symposia, training courses and triennial congresses; mems: 76 countries; Pres. JOËL LÉCHAPPÉ (France); Sec.-Gen. Dr MICHAEL MUSCHICK; publs *Seed Science and Technology* (3 a year), *Seed Testing International (ISTA News Bulletin)* (2 a year), *International Rules for Seed Testing* (annually).

International Sericultural Commission (ISC): 26 rue Bellecordière, 69002 Lyon, France; tel. 4-78-50-41-98; fax 4-78-86-09-57; e-mail info@inserco.org; internet www.inserco.org; f. 1948 to encourage the development of silk production; mems: 13 states; Sec.-Gen. CHRISTIAN FRESQUET (France); publ. *Sericologia* (quarterly).

International Society for Horticultural Science (ISHS): Corbeekhoeve Pastoriestraat 2, 3360 Korbeek-Lo, Belgium; POB 500, 3001 Leuven 1, Belgium; tel. (16) 22-94-27; fax (16) 22-94-50; e-mail info@ishs.org; internet www.ishs.org; f. 1959 to promote co-operation in horticultural science research; mems: 54 countries, 300 orgs, 6,000 individuals; Pres. Dr ANTÓNIO A. MONTEIRO (Portugal); Exec. Dir JOZEF VAN ASSCHE (Belgium); publs *Chronica Horticulturae* (quarterly), *Acta Horticulturae*, *Horticultural Research International*.

International Union for the Protection of New Varieties of Plant (Union internationale pour la protection des obtentions végétales—UPOV): 34 chemin des Colombettes, 1211 Geneva 20, Switzerland; tel. 223389111; fax 227330336; e-mail upov.mail@upov.int; internet www.upov.int; f. 1961 by the International Convention for the Protection of New Varieties of Plants (entered into force 1968, revised in 1972, 1978 and 1991); aims to encourage the development of new plant varieties and provide an effective system of intellectual property protection for plant breeders. Admin. support provided by the World Intellectual Property Organization; mems: 70 states; Pres. of the Council KEUN-JIN CHOI; Sec.-Gen. FRANCIS GURRY.

International Union of Forest Research Organizations (IUFRO): Mariabrunn (BFW), Hauptstrasse 7, 1140 Vienna, Austria; tel. (1) 877-01-51-0; fax (1) 877-01-51-50; e-mail office@iufro.org; internet www.iufro.org; f. 1892; aims to promote global co-operation in forest-related research and enhance the understanding of the ecological, economic and social aspects of forests and trees; disseminates scientific knowledge to stakeholders and decision-makers and aims to contribute to forest policy and on-the-ground forest management; mems: more than 600 orgs in more than 100 countries, involving some 15,000 scientists; Pres. NIELS ELERS KOCH (Denmark); Exec. Dir Dr ALEXANDER BUCK (Austria); publs *Annual Report*, *IUFRO News* (10 a year, electronic format only), *IUFRO World Series*, *IUFRO Occasional Paper Series*, *IUFRO Research Series*.

International Whaling Commission (IWC): The Red House, 135 Station Rd, Impington, Cambridge, CB24 9NP, United Kingdom; tel. (1223) 233971; fax (1223) 232876; e-mail secretariat@iwcoffice.com; internet www.iwcoffice.org; f. 1946 under the International Convention for the Regulation of Whaling, for the conservation of world whale stocks; reviews the regulations covering whaling operations; encourages research; collects, analyses and disseminates statistical and other information on whaling. A ban on commercial whaling was passed by the Commission in July 1982, to take effect three years subsequently (in some cases, a phased reduction of commercial operations was not completed until 1988). A revised whale-management procedure was adopted in 1994, to be implemented after the development of a complete whale management scheme; mems: 88 countries; Sec. Dr SIMON BROCKINGTON; publs *Annual Report*, *Journal of Cetacean Research and Management*.

North Pacific Anadromous Fish Commission: 889 W. Pender St, Suite 502, Vancouver, BC V6C 3B2, Canada; tel. (604) 775-5550; fax (604) 775-5577; e-mail secretariat@npafc.org; internet www.npafc.org; f. 1993; mems: Canada, Japan, Republic of Korea, Russia, USA; Exec. Dir VLADIMIR FEDORENKO; publs *Annual Report*, *Newsletter* (2 a year), *Statistical Yearbook*, *Scientific Bulletin*, *Technical Report*.

Northwest Atlantic Fisheries Organization (NAFO): 2 Morris Drive, POB 638, Dartmouth, NS B2Y 3Y9, Canada; tel. (902) 468-5590; fax (902) 468-5538; e-mail info@nafo.int; internet www.nafo.int; f. 1979 (fmrly International Commission for the Northwest Atlantic Fisheries); aims at optimum use, management and conservation of resources; an amended Convention, adopted in 2007, was being ratified in 2012; promotes research and compiles statistics; Pres. VERONIKA VEITS; Exec. Sec. Dr VLADIMIR SHIBANOV; publs *Annual Report*, *Statistical Bulletin* (electronic format only), *Journal of Northwest Atlantic Fishery Science* (in electronic and print formats), *Scientific Council Reports*, *Scientific Council Studies*, *Sampling Yearbook*, *Meeting Proceedings*.

Western and Central Pacific Fisheries Commission: Kaselehie St, POB 2356, Kolonia, Pohnpei State 96941, Federated States of Micronesia; tel. 3201992; fax 3201108; e-mail wcpfc@wcpfc.int; internet www.wcpfc.int; f. 2004 under the Convention for the Conservation and Management of Highly Migratory Fish Stocks in the Western and Central Pacific, which entered into force in June of that year, six months after the deposit of the 13th ratification; inaugural session convened in December, in Pohnpei, Federated States of Micronesia; mems: 31 countries and the European Community; Exec. Dir Prof. GLENN HURRY; publs *Secretariat Quarterly Report*, *Newsletter*.

World Association for Animal Production (WAAP): Via Tomassetti 3A/1, 00161 Rome, Italy; tel. (06) 44202639; fax (06) 86329263; e-mail waap@waap.it; internet www.waap.it; f. 1965; holds world conference on animal production every five years; encourages, sponsors and participates in regional meetings, seminars and symposia; mems: 17 mem. orgs; Pres. NORMAN H. CASEY (South Africa); Sec.-Gen. ANDREA ROSATI (Italy); publ. *WAAP Newsletter*.

WorldFish Center (International Centre for Living Aquatic Resources Management—ICLARM): Jalan Batu Maung, Batu Maung, 11960 Bayan Lepas, Penang, Malaysia; POB 500, GPO, 10670 Penang; tel. (4) 626-1606; fax (4) 626-5530; e-mail worldfishcenter@cgiar.org; internet www.worldfishcenter.org; f. 1973; became a mem. of the Consultative Group on International Agricultural Research (CGIAR) in 1992; aims to contribute to food security and poverty eradication in developing countries through the sustainable development and use of living aquatic resources; carries out research and promotes partnerships; Dir-Gen. Dr STEPHEN J. HALL.

World Organisation of Animal Health: 12 rue de Prony, 75017 Paris, France; tel. 1-44-15-18-88; fax 1-42-67-09-87; e-mail oie@oie.int; internet www.oie.int; f. 1924 as Office International des Epizooties (OIE); objectives include promoting international transparency of animal diseases; collecting, analysing and disseminating scientific veterinary information; providing expertise and promoting international co-operation in the control of animal diseases; promoting veterinary services; providing new scientific guidelines on animal production, food safety and animal welfare; launched in May 2005, jointly with FAO and WHO, a Global Strategy for the Progressive Control of Highly Pathogenic Avian Influenza (H5N1), and, in partnership with other organizations, has convened conferences on avian influenza; experts in a network of 156 collaborating centres and reference laboratories; mems: 178; Dir-Gen. BERNARD VALLAT (France); publs *Disease Information* (weekly), *World Animal Health* (annually), *Scientific and Technical Review* (3 a year), other manuals, codes, etc.

World Ploughing Organization (WPO): Grolweg 2, 6964 BL Hall, Netherlands; tel. (313) 619634; fax (313) 619735; e-mail hans.spieker@worldploughing.org; internet www.worldploughing.org; f. 1952 to promote the World Ploughing Contest in a different country each year, to improve techniques and promote better understanding of soil cultivation practices through research and practical demonstrations; arranges tillage clinics world-wide; mems: affiliates in 30 countries; Gen. Sec. HANS SPIEKER; publ. *WPO Handbook* (annually).

World Veterinary Association: 1B rue Defacqz, 1000 Brussels, Belgium; tel. (2) 533-70-22; fax (2) 537-28-28; e-mail secretariat@worldvet.org; internet www.worldvet.org; f. 1959 as a continuation of the International Veterinary Congresses (f. 1863); organizes congress every three years (2011: Cape Town, South Africa); mems: orgs in more than 80 countries, 19 orgs of veterinary specialists as assoc. mems; Pres. Dr FAOUZI KECHRID (Tunisia); Exec. Sec. JAN VAARTEN; publ. *WVA Newsletter* (every 2 months).

World's Poultry Science Association (WPSA): c/o Dr Roel Mulder, POB 31, 7360 AA Beekbergen, Netherlands; tel. (55) 506-3250; fax (55) 506-4858; e-mail roel.mulder@wpsa.com; internet www.wpsa.com; f. 1912 (as the International Asscn of Poultry Instructors); aims to advance and exchange knowledge relating to poultry science and the poultry industry; organizes World Poultry Congress every four years (2012: Salvador, Brazil, in Aug.); mems: 7,500 individuals in more than 100 countries, branches in 77 countries; Pres. Dr BOB PYM (Australia); Sec. Dr ROEL MULDER (Netherlands); publ. *The World's Poultry Science Journal* (quarterly).

Arts and Culture

Association of Baltic Academies of Music: c/o Musikhochschule Lübeck, Grosse Petersgrube 21, 23552 Lübeck, Germany; tel. (451) 1505303; fax (451) 15050; e-mail info@mh-luebeck.de; internet www.abamusic.org; f. 1995 as a regional network of music academies in the Baltic Sea region; organizes annual summer campuses, orchestral seminars, other regular seminars and festivals; Pres. JÖRG LINOWITZKI (Germany).

Europa Nostra—Pan-European Federation for Cultural Heritage: Lange Voorhout 35, 2514 EC The Hague, Netherlands; tel. (70) 3024051; fax (70) 3617865; e-mail info@europanostra.org; internet www.europanostra.org; f. 1963; groups, organizations and individuals concerned with the protection and enhancement of the European architectural and natural heritage and of the European environment; has consultative status with the Council of Europe; mems: some 250 mem. orgs, around 170 supporting bodies, more than 1,200 individual mems; Pres. PLÁCIDO DOMINGO (Spain); Exec. Pres. DENIS DE KERGORLAY (France); Sec.-Gen. SNESKA QUAEDVLIEG-MIHAILOVIĆ.

European Association of Conservatoires, Music Academies and Music High Schools: POB 805, 3500 AV Utrecht, Netherlands; tel. (30) 2361242; fax (30) 2361290; e-mail aecinfo@aecinfo.org; internet www.aecinfo.org; f. 1953; aims to establish and foster contacts and exchanges between and represent the interests of members; initiates and supports international collaboration through research projects, congresses and seminars; mems: 273 mem institutions in 55 countries; Pres. PASCALE DE GROOTE (Belgium); Sec.-Gen. JÖRG LINOWITZKI (Germany); publs e-mail newsletters (2–3 a year), project newsletters (3 a year), conference proceedings, research findings, various other publs and websites.

European Cultural Foundation: Jan van Goyenkade 5, 1075 HN Amsterdam, Netherlands; tel. (20) 5733868; fax (20) 6752231; e-mail eurocult@eurocult.org; internet www.eurocult.org; f. 1954 as a non-governmental organization, supported by private sources, to promote cultural co-operation in Europe; aims to give culture a stronger voice and presence in local communities and on the European political stage; supports closer ties among Europe's richly diverse population through joint artistic and cultural exploration; promotes good cultural policy-making that improves peoples' quality of life across Europe and its neighbouring regions; Chair. Dr WOLFGANG PETRITSCH (Austria); Dir KATHERINE WATSON; publs *Annual Report*, *electronic newsletter* (7 a year).

European Society of Culture: 10 rue de la Science, 1000 Brussels, Belgium; tel. (2) 534-40-02; fax (2) 534-11-50; e-mail advocate@cultureactioneurope.org; internet www.cultureactioneurope.org; f. 1950 to unite artists, poets, scientists, philosophers and others through mutual interests and friendship in order to safeguard and improve the conditions required for creative activity; maintains a library of 10,000 volumes; mems: national and local centres, and

1,500 individuals, in 60 countries; Pres. MERCEDES GIOVINAZZO (Italy); Gen. Sec. LUCA BERGAMO.

International Association of Art Critics: 32 rue Yves Toudic, 75010 Paris, France; tel. 1-47-70-17-42; e-mail aica.office@gmail.com; internet www.aica-int.org; f. 1949 to increase co-operation in plastic arts, promote international cultural exchanges and protect the interests of mems; mems: 4,600 in 70 countries; Pres. MAREK BARTELIK (USA); Sec.-Gen. BRANE KOVIC (Slovenia); publs *Annuaire*, *Newsletter* (quarterly).

International Association of Bibliophiles: Réserve des livres rares, Quai François Mauriac, 75706 Cedex 13, France; tel. 1-53-79-54-52; fax 1-53-79-54-60; f. 1963 to create contacts between bibliophiles and encourage book-collecting in different countries; organizes and encourages congresses, meetings, exhibitions and the award of scholarships; mems: 450; Sec.-Gen. JEAN-MARC CHATELAIN (France); publs *Le Bulletin du Bibliophile* (2 a year), yearbooks.

International Association of Film and Television Schools (Centre international de liaison des écoles de cinéma et de television—CILECT): c/o Stanislav Semerdjiev, 1000 Sofia, ul. Rakosky 108A, Bulgaria; tel. (88) 7-64-63-70 (mobile); fax (2) 989-73-89; e-mail executive.director@cilect.org; internet www.cilect.org; f. 1955 to link higher teaching and research institutes and improve education of makers of films and television programmes; organizes conferences and student film festivals; runs a training programme for developing countries; mems: 122 institutions in 56 countries; Pres. Dr MARIA DORA MOURÃO (Brazil); Exec. Dir. Dr STANISLAV SEMERDJIEV (Bulgaria); publ. *Newsletter*.

International Board on Books for Young People (IBBY): Nonnenweg 12, Postfach, 4003 Basel, Switzerland; tel. 612722917; fax 612722757; e-mail ibby@ibby.org; internet www.ibby.org; f. 1953 to support and link bodies in all countries connected with children's book work; encourages the distribution of good children's books; promotes scientific investigation into problems of juvenile books; presents the Hans Christian Andersen Award every two years to a living author and a living illustrator whose work is an outstanding contribution to juvenile literature; presents the IBBY-Asahi Reading Promotion Award (every two years) to an organization that has made a significant contribution towards the encouragement of reading; sponsors International Children's Book Day (2 April); mems: national sections and individuals in more than 70 countries; Pres. AHMAD REDZA AHMAD KHAIRUDDIN (Malaysia); Exec. Dir LIZ PAGE; publs *Bookbird* (quarterly, in English), *Congress Papers*, *IBBY Honour List* (every 2 years), special bibliographies.

International Centre for the Study of the Preservation and Restoration of Cultural Property (ICCROM): Via di San Michele 13, 00153 Rome, Italy; tel. (06) 585531; fax (06) 58553349; e-mail iccrom@iccrom.org; internet www.iccrom.org; f. 1959; assembles documents on the preservation and restoration of cultural property; stimulates research and proffers advice; organizes missions of experts; undertakes training of specialists; mems: 117 countries; Dir-Gen. STEFANO DE CARO (Italy); publ. *Newsletter* (annually, in Arabic, English, French and Spanish).

International Centre of Films for Children and Young People (Centre international du film pour l'enfance et la jeunesse—CIFEJ): CIFEJ, End of Seif St, phase 3, Shahrak-e Gharb, Tehran 1466893311, Iran; tel. (21) 88087870; fax (21) 88085847; e-mail info@cifej.com; internet www.cifej.com; f. 1955; serves as a clearing house for information about: films for children and young people, the influence of films on the young, and the regulations in force for the protection and education of young people; promotes production and distribution of suitable films and their appreciation; awards the CIFEJ prize at selected film festivals; mems: 150 mems in 55 countries; Pres. FIRDOZE BULBULIA; Exec. Dir MARYAM BAFEKRPOUR; publ. *CIFEJ Info* (every 3 months).

International Comparative Literature Association (ICLA) (Association Internationale de Littérature Comparée): Brigham Young University, 3168 JFSB, Provo, UT 84602, USA; tel. (801) 422-5598; e-mail ailc.icla@gmail.com; internet www.ailc-icla.org/site/; f. 1954 to work for the development of the comparative study of literature in modern languages; mems: 35 regional asscns; Pres. STEVEN SONDRUP.

International Confederation of Societies of Authors and Composers—World Copyright Summit: 20–26 blvd du Parc, 92200 Neuilly-sur-Seine, France; tel. 1-55-62-08-50; fax 1-55-62-08-60; e-mail cisac@cisac.org; internet www.cisac.org; f. 1926 to protect the rights of authors and composers; organizes biennial summit; mems: 232 mem. societies from 121 countries; Pres. ROBIN GIBB; Dir Gen. OLIVIER HINNEWINKEL.

International Council of Museums (ICOM): Maison de l'UNESCO, 1 rue Miollis, 75732 Paris Cedex 15, France; tel. 1-47-34-05-00; fax 1-43-06-78-62; e-mail secretariat@icom.museum; internet icom.museum; f. 1946; committed to the conservation and communication to society of the world's natural and cultural heritage; achieves its major objectives through its 30 international committees, each devoted to the study of a particular type of museum or to a specific museum-related discipline; maintains with UNESCO the organization's documentation centre; mems: 26,000 individuals and institutions in 140 countries; Pres. HANS-MARTIN HINZ (Germany); Gen. Dir JULIEN ANFRUNS (France); publ. *ICOM News—Nouvelles de l'ICOM—Noticias del ICOM* (quarterly).

International Committee of Museums and Collections of Arms and Military History (ICOMAM): Parc du Cinquantenaire 3, 1000 Brussels, Belgium; tel. (2) 737-79-00; e-mail chairman@icomam.icom.museum; internet www.icomam.icom.museum; f. 1957 as International Association of Museums of Arms and Military History (IAMAM); present name assumed in 2004; links museums and other scientific institutions with public collections of arms and armour and military equipment, uniforms, etc; holds triennial conferences and occasional specialist symposia; mems: over 260 institutions in more than 60 countries; Chair. PIET DE GRYSE (Belgium); Sec.-Gen. MATHIEU WILLEMSEN (Netherlands); publs *The Mohonk Courier*, *The Magazine* (online).

International Council on Monuments and Sites (ICOMOS): 49–51 rue de la Fédération, 75015 Paris, France; tel. 1-45-67-67-70; fax 1-45-66-06-22; e-mail secretariat@icomos.org; internet www.international.icomos.org; f. 1965 to promote the study and preservation of monuments and sites and to arouse and cultivate the interest of public authorities and people of every country in their cultural heritage; disseminates the results of research into the technical, social and administrative problems connected with the conservation of architectural heritage; holds triennial General Assembly and Symposium; mems: 24 international cttees, 116 national cttees; Pres. GUSTAVO ARAOZ (USA); Sec.-Gen. KIRSTI KOVANEN (Finland); publs *ICOMOS Newsletter* (quarterly), *Scientific Journal* (quarterly).

International Federation for Theatre Research (IFTR) (Fédération Internationale pour la Recherche Théâtrale): c/o Jan Clarke, School of Modern Languages and Culture, University of Durham, Durham, DH1 3JT, United Kingdom; e-mail jan.clarke@durham.ac.uk; internet www.firt-iftr.org; f. 1955 by 21 countries at the International Conference on Theatre History, London; Pres. CHRISTOPHER BALME (Germany); Joint Secs-Gen. Prof. JAN CLARKE (United Kingdom), PAUL MURPHY (United Kingdom).

International Federation of Film Archives (Fédération Internationale des Archives du Film—FIAF): 1 rue Defacqz, 1000 Brussels, Belgium; tel. (2) 538-30-65; fax (2) 534-47-74; e-mail info@fiafnet.org; internet www.fiafnet.org; f. 1938 to encourage the creation of audio-visual archives for the collection and conservation of the moving image heritage of every country; facilitates co-operation and exchanges between film archives; promotes public interest in the art of the cinema; aids and conducts research; compiles new documentation; holds annual congress; mems: c. 150 archives in 77 countries; Pres. ERIC LE ROY (France); Sec.-Gen. MEG LABRUM (Australia); publs *Journal of Film Preservation* (2 a year), *FIAF International Film Archive Database* (2 a year).

International Federation of Film Producers' Associations (Fédération Internationale des associations de Producteurs de Films—FIAPF): 9 rue de l'Echelle, 75001 Paris, France; tel. 1-44-77-97-50; fax 1-42-56-16-55; e-mail info@fiapf.org; internet www.fiapf.org; f. 1933 to represent film production internationally, to defend its general interests and promote its development; studies all cultural, legal, economic, technical and social problems related to film production; mems: 26 producers' orgs in 23 countries; Pres. LUIS ALBERTO SCALELLA.

International Institute for Children's Literature and Reading Research (Internationales Institut für Jugendliteratur und Leseforschung): Mayerhofgasse 6, 1040 Vienna, Austria; tel. (1) 505-03-59; fax (1) 50503-5917; e-mail office@jugendliteratur.net; internet www.jugendliteratur.net; f. 1965 as an international documentation, research and advisory centre of juvenile literature and reading; maintains specialized library; arranges conferences and exhibitions; compiles recommendation lists; mems: individual and group members in 28 countries; Pres. Prof. RENATE WELSH; Dir KARIN HALLER; publ. *1000 & 1 Buch* (quarterly).

International Institute for Conservation of Historic and Artistic Works: 3 Birdcage Walk, Westminster, London, SW1H 9JJ, United Kingdom; tel. (20) 7799-5500; fax (20) 7799-4961; e-mail iic@iiconservation.org; internet www.iiconservation.org; f. 1950; mems: 2,400 individual, 400 institutional mems; Pres. JERRY PODANY (USA); Sec.-Gen. JOSEPHINE KIRBY; publs *Studies in Conservation* (quarterly), *Reviews in Conservation* (annually), *News in Conservation* (every 2 months), *Congress Preprints* (every 2 years).

International Music Council (IMC): Maison de l'UNESCO, 1 rue Miollis, 75732 Paris Cedex 15, France; tel. 1-45-68-48-50; fax 1-43-06-87-98; e-mail info@imc-cim.org; internet www.imc-cim.org; f. 1949; mems: regional music councils, international music orgs, national and specialized orgs in some 150 countries; Pres. FRANS DE RUITER; Sec.-Gen. SILJA FISCHER.

Members of IMC include:

European Festivals Association: Kasteel Borluut, Kleine Gentstraat 46, 9051 Ghent, Belgium; tel. (9) 241-80-80; fax (9) 241-80-89; e-mail info@efa-aef.eu; internet www.efa-aef.eu; f. 1952 to maintain high artistic standards and the representative character of art festivals; holds annual General Assembly; mems: more than 100 regular international performing arts festivals in 38 countries; Pres. DARKO BRLEK; Sec.-Gen. KATHRIN DEVENTER; publ. *Festivals* (annually).

International Association of Music Libraries, Archives and Documentation Centres (IAML): c/o Music and Drama Library, Göteborg University Library, POB 201, SE 405 30 Göteborg, Sweden; tel. (31) 786-40-57; fax (31) 786-40-59; e-mail secretary@iaml.info; internet www.iaml.info; f. 1951; mems: 1,742 institutions and individuals in 49 countries; Pres. ROGER FLURY (New Zealand); Sec.-Gen. PIA SHEKHTER (Sweden); publ. *Fontes artis musicae* (quarterly).

International Council for Traditional Music (ICTM): Dept of Musicology, Faculty of Arts, University of Ljubljana, 1000 Ljubljana, Slovenia; tel. (2) 6125-1449; e-mail secretariat@ictmusic.org; internet www.ictmusic.org; f. 1947 (as International Folk Music Council) to further the study, practice, documentation, preservation and dissemination of traditional music of all countries; holds ICTM World Conference every two years; mems: 1,885; Pres. Dr ADRIENNE L. KAEPPLER (USA); Sec.-Gen. Dr SVANIBOR PETTAN (Slovenia); publs *Yearbook for Traditional Music*, *ICTM Bulletin* (2 a year).

International Federation of Musicians: 21 bis rue Victor Massé, 75009 Paris, France; tel. 1-45-26-31-23; fax 1-45-26-31-57; e-mail office@fim-musicians.com; internet www.fim-musicians.com/; f. 1948 to promote and protect the interests of musicians in affiliated unions; mems: 75 unions in 64 countries; Pres. JOHN F. SMITH (United Kingdom); Gen. Sec. BENOÎT MACHUEL (France).

International Music and Media Centre (Internationales Musik + Medienzentrum): Stiftgasse 29, 1070 Vienna, Austria; tel. (1) 889 03-15; fax (1) 889 03-1577; e-mail office@imz.at; internet www.imz.at; f. 1961 for the study and dissemination of music through technical media (film, television, radio, gramophone); organizes congresses, seminars and screenings on music in audio-visual media; holds courses and competitions designed to strengthen the relationship between performing artists and audio-visual media; mems: 180 ordinary mems and 30 associate mems in 35 countries, including 50 broadcasting orgs; Pres. CHRIS HUNT (United Kingdom); Sec.-Gen. FRANZ A. PATAY (Austria).

International Society for Contemporary Music (ISCM): c/o Muziek Centrum Nederland, Rokin 111, 1012 KN Amsterdam, Netherlands; tel. (20) 3446060; e-mail info@iscm.org; internet www.iscm.org; f. 1922 to promote the development of contemporary music; organizes annual World Music Day; mems: orgs in 50 countries; Pres. JOHN DAVIS; Sec.-Gen. ARTHUR VAN DER DRIFT.

Jeunesses Musicales International (JMI): 1 rue Defacqz, 1000 Brussels, Belgium; tel. (2) 513-97-74; fax (2) 514-47-55; e-mail mail@jmi.net; internet www.jmi.net; f. 1945 to enable young people to develop, through music, and to stimulate contacts between member countries; mems: orgs in 40 countries; Sec.-Gen. BLASKO SMILEVSKI; publ. *JMI News* (6 a year).

World Federation of International Music Competitions (WFIMC): 104 rue de Carouge, 1205 Geneva, Switzerland; tel. 223213620; fax 227811418; e-mail fmcim@fmcim.org; internet www.wfimc.org; f. 1957 to co-ordinate the arrangements for affiliated competitions and to exchange experience; holds General Assembly annually; mems: 129 international music competitions; Pres. GLEN KWOK (USA); Sec.-Gen. LOTTIE CHALUT.

International PEN (World Association of Writers): Brownlow House, 50–51 High Holborn, London, WC1V 6ER, United Kingdom; tel. (20) 7405-0338; fax (20) 7405-0339; e-mail info@pen-international.org; internet www.internationalpen.org.uk; f. 1921 to promote co-operation between writers; mems: 144 centres in 102 countries; International Pres. JOHN RALSTON SAUL; Exec. Dir LAURA MCVEIGH; publ. *PEN International* (2 a year, in English, French and Spanish, with the assistance of UNESCO).

International Theatre Institute (ITI): Maison de l'UNESCO, 1 rue Miollis, 75732 Paris Cedex 15, France; tel. 1-45-68-48-80; fax 1-45-66-50-40; e-mail iti@iti-worldwide.org; internet iti-worldwide.org; f. 1948 to facilitate cultural exchanges and international understanding in the domain of the theatre and performing arts; promotes performing arts/theatre on a national and international level and facilitates international collaboration; mems: around 100 national centres and co-operating mems world-wide; Pres. RAMENDU MAJUMDAR (Bangladesh); Sec.-Gen. TOBIAS BIANCONE (Switzerland); publs *ITI News* (3 times a year in English and French), *World Theatre Directory* (every 2 years), *The World of Theatre* (every 2 years).

Nordic Cultural Fund (Nordisk Kulturfond): Ved Stranden 18, 1061 Copenhagen K, Denmark; tel. 3396-0200; fax 3332-5636; e-mail kulturfonden@norden.org; internet www.nordiskkulturfond.org; f. 1967; aims to support a broad spectrum of Nordic cultural co-operation activities; awards around 28m. Danish kroner annually towards cultural projects being implemented in the Nordic Region, and Nordic projects being undertaken outside the region; projects are designated by the Fund as 'Nordic' if a minimum of three Nordic countries (Denmark, Iceland, Finland, Norway and Sweden) or self-governing areas (Faroe Islands, Greenland, and the Åland Islands) are involved, either as participants, organizers, or as the project subject area; Dir KAREN BUE.

Organization of World Heritage Cities: 15 rue Saint-Nicolas, Québec, QC G1K 1M8, Canada; tel. (418) 692-0000; fax (418) 692-5558; e-mail secretariat@ovpm.org; internet www.ovpm.org; f. 1993 to assist cities inscribed on the UNESCO World Heritage List to implement the Convention concerning the Protection of the World Cultural and Natural Heritage (1972); promotes co-operation between city authorities, in particular in the management and sustainable development of historic sites; holds an annual General Assembly, comprising the mayors of member cities; mems: 238 cities world-wide; Sec.-Gen. DENIS RICARD; publ. *OWHC Newsletter* (2 a year, in English, French and Spanish).

Pan-African Writers' Association (PAWA): PAWA House, Roman Ridge, POB C456, Cantonments, Accra, Ghana; tel. (21) 773062; fax (21) 773042; e-mail pawahouse@gmail.com; f. 1989 to link African creative writers, defend the rights of authors and promote awareness of literature; mems: 52 national writers' associations on the continent; Sec.-Gen. ATUKWEI OKAI (Ghana).

Royal Asiatic Society of Great Britain and Ireland: 14 Stephenson Way, London, NW1 2HD, United Kingdom; tel. (20) 7388-4539; fax (20) 7391-9429; e-mail info@royalasiaticsociety.org; internet www.royalasiaticsociety.org; f. 1823 for the study of history and cultures of the East; mems: c. 700, branch societies in Asia; Pres. Prof. GORDON JOHNSON; Dir ALISON OHTA; publ. *Journal* (3 a year).

World Crafts Council International (WCC): 98A Dr. Radhakrishnan Salai, Chennai 600004, India; tel. (44) 28478500; fax (44) 28478509; e-mail wcc.sect.in@gmail.com; internet www.worldcraftscouncil.org; f. 1964; aims to strengthen the status of crafts as a vital part of cultural and economic life, to link crafts people around the world, and to foster wider recognition of their work; mems: national orgs in more than 89 countries; Pres. USHA KRISHNA (India).

Commodities

Africa Rice Center (AfricaRice): 01 BP 2031, Cotonou, Benin; tel. 21-35-01-88; fax 21-35-05-56; e-mail AfricaRice@cgiar.org; internet www.africarice.org/; f. 1971 (as the West Africa Rice Development Association—WARDA, present name adopted in 2009); participates in the network of agricultural research centres supported by the Consultative Group on International Agricultural Research (CGIAR); aims to contribute to food security and poverty eradication in poor rural and urban populations, through research, partnerships, capacity strengthening and policy support on rice-based systems; promotes sustainable agricultural development based on environmentally sound management of natural resources; maintains research stations in Nigeria and Senegal; provides training and consulting services; from 2007 expanded scope of membership and activities from West African to pan-African; mems: 24 African countries; Dir-Gen. Dr PAPA ABDOULAYE SECK (Senegal); publs *Program Report* (annually), *Participatory Varietal Selection* (annually), *Rice Interspecific Hybridization Project Research Highlights* (annually), *Inland Valley Newsletter*, *ROCARIZ Newsletter*, training series, proceedings, leaflets.

African Groundnut Council (AGC): C43, Wase Satellite Town, Rjiyar Zaki, Kano, Kano State, Nigeria; tel. (1) 8970605; e-mail info@afgroundnutcouncil.org; internet www.afgroundnutcouncil.org; f. 1964 to advise producing countries on marketing policies; mems: The Gambia, Mali, Niger, Nigeria, Senegal, Sudan; Exec. Sec. ELHADJ MOUR MAMADOU SAMB (Senegal); publ. *Groundnut Review*.

African Oil Palm Development Association (AFOPDA): 15 BP 341, Abidjan 15, Côte d'Ivoire; tel. 21-25-15-18; fax 20-25-47-00; f. 1985; seeks to increase production of, and investment in, palm oil; mems: Benin, Cameroon, Democratic Republic of the Congo, Côte d'Ivoire, Ghana, Guinea, Nigeria, Togo.

African Petroleum Producers' Association (APPA): POB 1097, Brazzaville, Republic of the Congo; tel. 665-38-57; fax 669-99-13; e-mail appa@appa.int; f. 1987 by African petroleum-producing countries to reinforce co-operation among regional producers and to stabilize prices; council of ministers responsible for the hydrocarbons sector meets twice a year; holds regular Congress and Exhibition: March 2010, Kinshasa, Democratic Republic of the Congo; mems: Algeria, Angola, Benin, Cameroon, Democratic

Republic of the Congo, Republic of the Congo, Côte d'Ivoire, Egypt, Equatorial Guinea, Gabon, Libya, Nigeria; Exec. Sec. GABRIEL DANSOU LOKOSSOU; publ. *APPA Bulletin* (2 a year).

Asian and Pacific Coconut Community (APCC): 3rd Floor, Lina Bldg, Jalan H. R. Rasuna Said Kav. B7, Kuningan, Jakarta 12920, Indonesia; POB 1343, Jakarta 10013; tel. (21) 5221712; fax (21) 5221714; e-mail apcc@indo.net.id; internet www.apccsec.org; f. 1969 to promote and co-ordinate all activities of the coconut industry, to achieve higher production and better processing, marketing and research; organizes annual Coconut Technical Meeting (COCOTECH); mems: Fiji, India, Indonesia, Kiribati, Malaysia, Marshall Islands, Federated States of Micronesia, Papua New Guinea, Philippines, Samoa, Solomon Islands, Sri Lanka, Thailand, Vanuatu, Viet Nam; Exec. Dir ROMULO N. ARANCON, Jr; publs *Cocomunity* (monthly), *CORD* (2 a year), *CocoInfo International* (2 a year), *Coconut Statistical Yearbook*, guidelines and other ad hoc publications.

Association of Natural Rubber Producing Countries (ANRPC): Bangunan Getah Asli, 148 Jalan Ampang, 7th Floor, 50450 Kuala Lumpur, Malaysia; tel. (3) 21611900; fax (3) 21613014; e-mail anrpc.secretariat@gmail.com; internet www.anrpc.org; f. 1970 to co-ordinate the production and marketing of natural rubber, to promote technical co-operation among members and to bring about fair and stable prices for natural rubber; holds seminars, meetings and training courses on technical and statistical subjects; a joint regional marketing system has been agreed in principle; mems: Cambodia, People's Republic of China, India, Indonesia, Malaysia, Papua New Guinea, Philippines, Singapore, Sri Lanka, Thailand, Viet Nam; Sec.-Gen. Dr KAMARUL BAHARAIN BIN BASIR; publs *NR Trends & Statistics* (monthly), *Qtrly NR Market Review, Market and Industry Update*.

Cocoa Producers' Alliance (CPA): National Assembly Complex, Tafawa Balewa Sq., POB 1718, Lagos, Nigeria; tel. (9) 8141735; fax (9) 8141734; e-mail info@copal-cpa.org; internet www.copal-cpa.org; f. 1962 to exchange technical and scientific information, to discuss problems of mutual concern to producers, to ensure adequate supplies at remunerative prices and to promote consumption; mems: Brazil, Cameroon, Côte d'Ivoire, Dominican Republic, Gabon, Ghana, Malaysia, Nigeria, São Tomé and Príncipe, Togo; Sec.-Gen. HOPE SONA EBAI.

Common Fund for Commodities (CFC): POB 74656, 1070 BR, Amsterdam, Netherlands; tel. (20) 5754949; fax (20) 6760231; e-mail managing.director@common-fund.org; internet www.common-fund.org; f. 1989 as the result of an UNCTAD negotiation conference; finances commodity development measures including research, marketing, productivity improvements and vertical diversification, with the aim of increasing the long-term competitiveness of particular commodities; paid-in capital US $181m; mems: 105 countries and 10 institutional members; Man. Dir (also Chief Exec.) ALI MCHUMO.

European Aluminium Association (EAA): 12 ave de Broqueville, 1150 Brussels, Belgium; tel. (2) 775-63-50; fax (2) 779-05-31; e-mail eaa@eaa.be; internet www.eaa.net; f. 1981 to encourage studies, research and technical co-operation, to make representations to international bodies and to assist national asscns in dealing with national authorities; mems: individual producers of primary aluminium, 18 national groups for wrought producers, the Organization of European Aluminium Smelters, representing producers of recycled aluminium, and the European Aluminium Foil Association, representing foil rollers and converters; Sec.-Gen. PATRICK DE SCHRYNMAKERS; publs *Annual Report*, *EAA Quarterly Report*.

European Association for the Trade in Jute and Related Products: POB 93002, 2509 AA The Hague, Netherlands; tel. (70) 3490750; fax (70) 3490775; e-mail info@eurojute.com; internet www.eurojute.com; f. 1970 to maintain contacts between national asscns, permit the exchange of information and represent the interests of the trade; carries out scientific research; mems: enterprises in 9 European countries.

European Committee of Sugar Manufacturers (CEFS): 182 ave de Tervuren, 1150 Brussels, Belgium; tel. (2) 762-07-60; fax (2) 771-00-26; e-mail cefs@cefs.org; internet www.cefs.org; f. 1954 to collect statistics and information, conduct research and promote co-operation between national organizations; mems: national asscns in 22 European countries and other associate members world-wide; Pres. JOHANN MARIHART; Dir-Gen. MARIE-CHRISTINE RIBERA.

Gas Exporting Countries Forum: POB 23753, 47-48th Floors, Tornado Tower, West Bay, Doha, Qatar; tel. 44048410; fax 44048416; e-mail gecfsg@gmail.com; internet www.gecf.org; f. 2001 to represent and promote the mutual interests of gas exporting countries; aims to increase the level of co-ordination among member countries and to promote dialogue between gas producers and consumers; a ministerial meeting is convened annually; the seventh ministerial meeting, convened in Moscow, Russia, in Dec. 2008, agreed on a charter and a permanent structure for the grouping; mems: Algeria, Bolivia, Egypt, Equatorial Guinea, Iran, Libya, Nigeria, Oman, Qatar, Russia, Trinidad and Tobago, Venezuela; observers: Kazakhstan, Netherlands, Norway.

Inter-African Coffee Organization (IACO) (Organisation Inter-Africaine du Café—OIAC): BP V210, Abidjan, Côte d'Ivoire; tel. 20-21-61-31; fax 20-21-62-12; e-mail sg@iaco-oiac.org; internet www.iaco-oiac.org; f. 1960 to adopt a common policy on the marketing and consumption of coffee; aims to foster greater collaboration in research technology transfer through the African Coffee Research Network (ACRN); seeks to improve the quality of coffee exports, and implement poverty reduction programmes focusing on value added product (VAP) and the manufacturing of green coffee; mems: 25 coffee-producing countries in Africa; Sec.-Gen. JOSEFA LEONEL CORREIA SACKO (Angola).

International Cadmium Association: 168 ave Tervueren, 1150 Brussels, Belgium; tel. (2) 777-05-60; fax (2) 777-05-65; e-mail info@cadmium.org; internet www.cadmium.org; f. 1976; covers all aspects of the production and use of cadmium and its compounds; includes almost all producers and users of cadmium; Exec. Dir MICHAEL TAYLOR.

International Cocoa Organization (ICCO): Commonwealth House, 1–19 New Oxford St, London, WC1A 1NU, United Kingdom; tel. (20) 7400-5050; fax (20) 7421-5500; e-mail info@icco.org; internet www.icco.org; f. 1973 under the first International Cocoa Agreement, 1972; the ICCO supervises the implementation of the agreements, and provides member governments with up-to-date information on the world cocoa economy; the sixth International Cocoa Agreement (2001) entered into force in October 2003; the seventh International Cocoa Agreement was signed in June 2010 and was to enter into force in October 2012; mems: 13 exporting countries and 28 importing countries; and the EU; Exec. Dir a.i. Dr JEAN-MARC ANGA (Côte d'Ivoire); publs *Quarterly Bulletin of Cocoa Statistics*, *Annual Report*, *World Cocoa Directory*, *Cocoa Newsletter*, studies on the world cocoa economy.

International Coffee Organization (ICO): 22 Berners St, London, W1T 3DD, United Kingdom; tel. (20) 7612-0600; fax (20) 7612-0630; e-mail info@ico.org; internet www.ico.org; f. 1963 under the International Coffee Agreement, 1962, which was renegotiated in 1968, 1976, 1983, 1994 (extended in 1999), 2001 and 2007; aims to improve international co-operation and provide a forum for intergovernmental consultations on coffee matters; to facilitate international trade in coffee by the collection, analysis and dissemination of statistics; to act as a centre for the collection, exchange and publication of coffee information; to promote studies in the field of coffee; and to encourage an increase in coffee consumption; mems: 33 exporting countries and six importing countries, plus the European Union; Chair. of Council EWALD WERMUTH (Netherlands); Exec. Dir JOSÉ SETTE (Brazil).

International Confederation of European Beet Growers (Confédération internationale des betteraviers européens—CIBE): 111/9 blvd Anspachlaan, 1000 Brussels; tel. (2) 504-60-90; fax (2) 504-60-99; e-mail cibeoffice@cibe-europe.eu; internet www.cibe-europe.eu; f. 1927 to act as a centre for the co-ordination and dissemination of information about beet sugar production; to represent the interests of beet growers at an international level; mems in Austria, Belgium, Czech Republic, Denmark, Finland, France, Germany, Greece, Hungary, Italy, Netherlands, Poland, Romania, Slovakia, Sweden, Switzerland, Turkey, United Kingdom; Pres. JOS VAN CAMPEN (Netherlands); Gen. Sec. ELISABETH LACOSTE (France).

International Cotton Advisory Committee (ICAC): 1629 K St, NW, Suite 702, Washington, DC 20006-1636, USA; tel. (202) 463-6660; fax (202) 463-6950; e-mail secretariat@icac.org; internet www.icac.org; f. 1939 to observe developments in world cotton; to collect and disseminate statistics; to suggest measures for the furtherance of international collaboration in maintaining and developing a sound world cotton economy; and to provide a forum for international discussions on cotton prices; mems: 44 countries; Exec. Dir Dr TERRY TOWNSEND (USA); publs *Cotton This Week!* (internet/e-mail only), *Cotton This Month*, *Cotton: Review of the World Situation* (every 2 months), *Cotton: World Statistics* (annually), *The ICAC Recorder*, *World Textile Demand* (annually), other surveys, studies, trade analyses and technical publications.

International Energy Forum (IEF): POB 94736, Diplomatic Quarter, Riyadh-11614, Saudi Arabia; tel. (1) 4810022; fax (1) 4810055; e-mail info@ief.org; internet www.ief.org; f. 1991; annual gathering of ministers responsible for energy affairs from states accounting for about 90% of global oil and gas supply and demand; the IEF is an intergovernmental arrangement aimed at promoting dialogue on global energy matters among its membership; the annual IEF is preceded by a meeting of the International Business Energy Forum (IEBF), comprising energy ministers and CEOs of leading energy companies; 13th IEF and 5th IEBF: March 2012, Kuwait; 87 mem. states, including the mems of OPEC and the International Energy Agency; Sec.-Gen. ALDO FLORES-QUIROGA.

International Gas Union (IGU): c/o Statoil, 0246 Oslo, Norway; tel. 51-99-00-00; fax 22-53-43-40; e-mail secrigu@statoil.com; internet www.igu.org; f. 1931; represents the gas industry worldwide; organizes World Gas Conference every three years (2012: Kuala Lumpur, Malaysia); mems: 75 Charter mems, 35 Associate mems; Pres. ABDUL RAHIM HASHIM (Malaysia); Sec.-Gen. TORSTEIN INDREBØ (Norway).

International Grains Council (IGC): 1 Canada Sq., Canary Wharf, London, E14 5AE, United Kingdom; tel. (20) 7513-1122; fax (20) 7513-0630; e-mail igc@igc.int; internet www.igc.int; f. 1949 as International Wheat Council, present name adopted in 1995; responsible for the administration of the International Grains Agreement, 1995, comprising the Grains Trade Convention (GTC) and the Food Aid Convention (FAC, under which donors pledge specified minimum annual amounts of food aid for developing countries in the form of grain and other eligible products); aims to further international co-operation in all aspects of trade in grains, to promote international trade in grains, and to achieve a free flow of this trade, particularly in developing member countries; seeks to contribute to the stability of the international grain market; acts as a forum for consultations between members; provides comprehensive information on the international grain market (with effect from 1 July 2009 the definition of 'grain' was extended to include rice); mems: 26 countries and the EU; Exec. Dir ETSUO KITAHARA; publs *World Grain Statistics* (annually), *Wheat and Coarse Grain Shipments* (annually), *Report for the Fiscal Year* (annually), *Grain Market Report* (monthly), *IGC Grain Market Indicators* (weekly), *Rice Market Bulletin* (weekly).

International Jute Study Group (IJSG): 145 Monipuriparu, Tejgaon, Dhaka 1215, Bangladesh; tel. (2) 9125581; fax (2) 9125248; e-mail info@jute.org; internet www.jute.org; f. 2002 as successor to International Jute Organization (f. 1984 in accordance with an agreement made by 48 producing and consuming countries in 1982, under the auspices of UNCTAD); aims to improve the jute economy and the quality of jute and jute products through research and development projects and market promotion; Sec.-Gen BHUPENDRA SINGH (India).

International Lead and Zinc Study Group (ILZSG): Rua Almirante Barroso 38, 5th Floor, Lisbon 1000-013, Portugal; tel. (21) 3592420; fax (21) 3592429; e-mail root@ilzsg.org; internet www.ilzsg.org; f. 1959 for intergovernmental consultation on world trade in lead and zinc; conducts studies and provides information on trends in supply and demand; mems: 29 countries accounting for more than 85% of world production and usage of lead and zinc; Sec.-Gen. DON SMALE; publ. *Lead and Zinc Statistics* (monthly).

International Lead Association (also, International Lead Association—Europe): 17A Welbeck Way, London, W1G 9YJ, United Kingdom; tel. (20) 7499-8422; fax (20) 7493-1555; e-mail enq@ila-lead.org; internet www.ila-lead.org; f. 1956 as Lead Development Asscn International; provides authoritative information on the use of lead and its compounds; financed by lead producers and users in the United Kingdom, Europe and elsewhere; Dir (ILA) Dr DAVID WILSON (United Kingdom); Dir (ILA—Europe) Dr ANDY BUSH (United Kingdom).

International Molybdenum Association (IMOA): 4 Heathfield Terrace, London, W4 4JE, United Kingdom; tel. (20) 7871-1580; fax (2) 8994-6067; e-mail info@imoa.info; internet www.imoa.info; f. 1989; collates statistics; promotes the use of molybdenum; monitors health and environmental issues in the molybdenum industry; mems: 70; Pres. VICTOR PEREZ; Sec.-Gen. TIM OUTTERIDGE.

International Olive Council: Príncipe de Vergara 154, 28002 Madrid, Spain; tel. (91) 5903638; fax (91) 5631263; e-mail iooc@internationaloliveoil.org; internet www.internationaloliveoil.org; f. 1959 to administer the International Agreement on Olive Oil and Table Olives, which aims to promote international co-operation in connection with problems of the world economy for olive products; works to prevent unfair competition, to encourage the production and consumption of olive products, and their international trade, and to reduce the disadvantages caused by fluctuations of supplies on the market; also takes action to foster a better understanding of the nutritional, therapeutic and other properties of olive products, to foster international co-operation for the integrated, sustainable development of world olive growing, to encourage research and development, to foster the transfer of technology and training activities in the olive products sector, and to improve the interaction between olive growing and the environment; mems: of the International Agreement on Olive Oil and Table Olives, 2005 (fifth Agreement, in force until 31 Dec. 2014): 14 countries, and the European Union; Exec. Dir JEAN-LOUIS BARJOL; publ. *OLIVAE* (2 a year, in Arabic, English, French, Italian and Spanish).

International Organisation of Vine and Wine (Organisation Internationale de la Vigne et du Vin—OIV): 18 rue d'Aguesseau, 75008 Paris, France; tel. 1-44-94-80-80; fax 1-42-66-90-63; e-mail contact@oiv.int; internet www.oiv.int; f. 2001 (agreement establishing an International Wine Office signed Nov. 1924, name changed to International Vine and Wine Office in 1958); researches vine and vine product issues in the scientific, technical, economic and social areas, disseminates knowledge, and facilitates contacts between researchers; mems: 44 countries and 3 countries with observer status; Dir-Gen. FEDERICO CASTELLUCCI (Italy); publs *Bulletin de l'OIV* (every 2 months), *Lexique de la Vigne et du Vin*, *Recueil des méthodes internationales d'analyse des vins*, *Code international des Pratiques oenologiques*, *Codex oenologique international*, numerous scientific publications.

International Organization of Spice Trading Associations (IOSTA): c/o American Spice Trade Association, 2025 M St, NW, Suite 800, Washington, DC 20036, USA; tel. (202) 367-1127; fax (202) 367-2127; e-mail info@astaspice.org; internet www.astaspice.org; f. 1999; mems: 8 national and regional spice orgs.

International Pepper Community (IPC): 4th Floor, Lina Bldg, Jalan H. R. Rasuna Said, Kav. B7, Kuningan, Jakarta 12920, Indonesia; tel. (21) 5224902; fax (21) 5224905; e-mail mail@ipcnet.org; internet www.ipcnet.org; f. 1972 for promoting, co-ordinating and harmonizing all activities relating to the pepper economy; mems: Brazil, India, Indonesia, Malaysia, Sri Lanka, Viet Nam; Exec. Dir SUBRAMANIAM KANNAN; publs *Pepper Statistical Yearbook*, *International Pepper News Bulletin* (quarterly), *Directory of Pepper Exporters*, *Directory of Pepper Importers*, *Weekly Prices Bulletin*, *Pepper Market Review*.

International Platinum Group Metals Association (IPA): Schiess-Staett-Str. 30, Munich, 80339 Germany; tel. (89) 51996770; fax (89) 51996719; e-mail info@ipa-news.com; internet www.ipa-news.com/index.php; links principal producers and fabricators of platinum; Pres. WILLIAM SANDFORD; Man. Dir GABRIELE RANDLSHOFER.

International Rubber Study Group: 111 North Bridge Rd, 23-06 Peninsula Plaza, Singapore 179098; tel. 68372411; fax 63394369; e-mail irsg@rubberstudy.com; internet www.rubberstudy.com; f. 1944 to provide a forum for the discussion of problems affecting synthetic and natural rubber and to provide statistical and other general information on rubber; mems: 16 governments and the EU; Sec.-Gen. Dr STEPHEN V. EVANS; publs *Rubber Statistical Bulletin* (every 2 months), *Rubber Industry Report* (every 2 months), *Proceedings of International Rubber Forums* (annually), *World Rubber Statistics Handbook*, *Key Rubber Indicators*, *Rubber Statistics Yearbook*, *Outlook for Elastomers* (annually).

International Sugar Organization: 1 Canada Sq., Canary Wharf, London, E14 5AA, United Kingdom; tel. (20) 7513-1144; fax (20) 7513-1146; e-mail exdir@isosugar.org; internet www.isosugar.org; administers the International Sugar Agreement (1992), with the objectives of stimulating co-operation, facilitating trade and encouraging demand; aims to improve conditions in the sugar market through debate, analysis and studies; serves as a forum for discussion; holds annual seminars and workshops; sponsors projects from developing countries; mems: 84 countries producing some 83% of total world sugar; Exec. Dir Dr PETER BARON; publs *Sugar Year Book*, *Monthly Statistical Bulletin*, *Market Report and Press Summary*, *Quarterly Market Outlook*, seminar proceedings.

International Tea Committee Ltd (ITC): 1 Carlton House Terrace, London, SW1Y 5DB, United Kingdom; tel. (20) 7839-5090; e-mail info@inttea.com; internet www.inttea.com; f. 1933 to administer the International Tea Agreement; now serves as a statistical and information centre; in 1979 membership was extended to include consuming countries; producer mems: national tea boards or asscns in Bangladesh, People's Republic of China, India, Indonesia, Kenya, Malawi, Sri Lanka and Tanzania; consumer mems: Tea Asscn of the USA Inc., Irish Tea Trade Asscn, and the Tea Asscn of Canada; assoc. mems: Netherlands Ministry of Agriculture, Nature and Food Quality and United Kingdom Dept for Environment Food and Rural Affairs, and national tea boards/asscns in 10 producing and 4 consuming countries; Chief Exec. MANUJA PEIRIS; publs *Annual Bulletin of Statistics*, *Monthly Statistical Summary*.

International Tobacco Growers' Association (ITGA): Av. Gen. Humberto Delgado 30A, 6001-081 Castelo Branco, Portugal; tel. (272) 325901; fax (272) 325906; e-mail itga@tobaccoleaf.org; internet www.tobaccoleaf.org; f. 1984 to provide a forum for the exchange of views and information of interest to tobacco producers; holds annual meeting; mems: 23 countries producing over 80% of the world's internationally traded tobacco; Chief Exec. ANTÓNIO ABRUNHOSA (Portugal); publs *Tobacco Courier* (quarterly), *Tobacco Briefing*.

International Tropical Timber Organization (ITTO): International Organizations Center, 5th Floor, Pacifico-Yokohama, 1-1-1, Minato-Mirai, Nishi-ku, Yokohama 220-0012, Japan; tel. (45) 223-1110; fax (45) 223-1111; e-mail itto@itto.or.jp; internet www.itto.int; f. 1985 under the International Tropical Timber Agreement (1983); subsequently a new treaty, ITTA 1994, came into force in 1997, and this was replaced by ITTA 2006, which entered into force in Dec. 2011; provides a forum for consultation and co-operation between countries that produce and consume tropical timber, and is dedicated to the sustainable development and conservation of tropical forests;

facilitates progress towards 'Objective 2000', which aims to move as rapidly as possible towards achieving exports of tropical timber and timber products from sustainably managed resources; encourages, through policy and project work, forest management, conservation and restoration, the further processing of tropical timber in producing countries, and the gathering and analysis of market intelligence and economic information; mems: 25 producing and 36 consuming countries and the EU; Exec. Dir EMMANUEL ZE MEKA (Cameroon); publs *Annual Review and Assessment of the World Timber Situation*, *Tropical Timber Market Information Service* (every 2 weeks), *Tropical Forest Update* (quarterly).

International Tungsten Industry Association (ITIA): 4 Heathfield Terrace, London, W4 4JE, United Kingdom; tel. (20) 8996-2221; fax (20) 8994-8728; e-mail info@itia.info; internet www.itia.info; f. 1988 (fmrly Primary Tungsten Asscn, f. 1975); promotes use of tungsten; collates statistics; prepares market reports; monitors health and environmental issues in the tungsten industry; mems from 18 countries; Pres. STEPHEN LEAHY; Sec.-Gen. BURGHARD ZEILER.

International Zinc Association (IZA): 168 ave de Tervueren, Boîte 4, 1150 Brussels, Belgium; tel. (2) 776-00-70; fax (2) 776-00-89; e-mail contact@zinc.org; internet www.zinc.org; f. 1990 to represent the world zinc industry; provide a forum for senior executives to address global issues requiring industry-wide action; consider new applications for zinc and zinc products; foster understanding of zinc's role in the environment; build a sustainable development policy; mems: 33 zinc-producing countries; Exec. Dir STEPHEN R. WILKINSON; publ. *Zinc Protects* (quarterly).

Petrocaribe: internet www.petrocaribe.org; f. June 2005; an initiative of the Venezuelan Government to enhance the access of countries in the Caribbean region to petroleum on preferential payment terms; aims to co-ordinate the development of energy policies and plans regarding natural resources among signatory countries; 6th summit held in Saint Christopher and Nevis in June 2009; mems: Antigua and Barbuda, Bahamas, Belize, Cuba, Dominica, Dominican Republic, Grenada, Guatemala, Guyana, Haiti, Honduras, Jamaica, Nicaragua, Saint Christopher and Nevis, Saint Lucia, Saint Vincent and the Grenadines, Suriname, Venezuela.

Regional Association of Oil and Natural Gas Companies in Latin America and the Caribbean (Asociación Regional de Empresas de Petróleo y Gas Natural en Latinoamérica y el Caribe—ARPEL): Javier de Viana 2345, Casilla de correo 1006, 11200 Montevideo, Uruguay; tel. 2410 6993; fax 2410 9207; e-mail arpel@arpel.org.uy; internet www.arpel.org; f. 1965 as the Mutual Assistance of the Latin American Oil Companies; aims to initiate and implement activities for the development of the oil and natural gas industry in Latin America and the Caribbean; promotes the expansion of business opportunities and the improvement of the competitive advantages of its members; promotes guidelines in support of competition in the sector; and supports the efficient and sustainable exploitation of hydrocarbon resources and the supply of products and services. Works in co-operation with international organizations, governments, regulatory agencies, technical institutions, universities and non-governmental organizations; mems: 28 state-owned enterprises, representing more than 90% of regional operations, in Argentina, Bolivia, Brazil, Canada, Chile, Colombia, Costa Rica, Cuba, Ecuador, Jamaica, Mexico, Nicaragua, Paraguay, Peru, Suriname, Trinidad and Tobago, Uruguay, Venezuela; Exec. Sec. CÉSAR GONZALEZ NEWMAN; publ. *Boletín Técnico*.

Sugar Association of the Caribbean (Inc.): c/o Caroni, Brechin Castle, Trinidad and Tobago; f. 1942; administers the West Indies Central Sugar Cane Breeding Station (in Barbados) and the West Indies Sugarcane Breeding and Evaluation Network; mems: national sugar cos of Barbados, Belize, Guyana, Jamaica and Trinidad and Tobago, and Sugar Asscn of St Kitts–Nevis–Anguilla; publs *SAC Handbook*, *SAC Annual Report*, *Proceedings of Meetings of WI Sugar Technologists*.

Union of Banana-Exporting Countries (Unión de Paises Exportadores de Banano—UPEB): Apdo 4273, Bank of America, 7°, Panamá 5, Panama; tel. 263-6266; fax 264-8355; e-mail iicapan@pan.gbm.net; f. 1974 as an intergovernmental agency to assist in the cultivation and marketing of bananas and to secure prices; collects statistics; mems: Colombia, Costa Rica, Guatemala, Honduras, Nicaragua, Panama, Venezuela; publs *Informe UPEB*, *Fax UPEB*, *Anuario de Estadísticas*, bibliographies.

West Indian Sea Island Cotton Association (Inc.): c/o Barbados Agricultural Development Corporation, Fairy Valley, Christ Church, Barbados; mems: organizations in Antigua and Barbuda, Barbados, Jamaica, Montserrat and Saint Christopher and Nevis; Pres. LEROY ROACH; Sec. MICHAEL I. EDGHILL.

World Association of Beet and Cane Growers (WABCG): c/o IFAP, 60 rue St Lazare, 75009 Paris, France; tel. 1-45-26-05-53; fax 1-48-74-72-12; e-mail wabcg@ifap.org; internet www.ifap.org/wabcg; f. 1983 (formal adoption of Constitution, 1984); groups national organizations of independent sugar beet and cane growers; aims to boost the economic, technical and social development of the beet- and cane-growing sector; works to strengthen professional representation in international and national fora; serves as a forum for discussion and exchange of information; mems: 21 beet-growing organizations, 14 cane-growing organizations, from 30 countries; Pres. ROGER STEWART (South Africa); Sec. DAVID LOUIS JOHN KING; publs *World Sugar Farmer News* (quarterly), *World Sugar Farmer Fax Sheet*, *WABCG InfoFlash*, study reports.

World Federation of Diamond Bourses (WFDB): 62 Pelikaanstraat, 2018 Antwerp, Belgium; tel. (3) 234-91-21; fax (3) 226-40-73; e-mail info@worldfed.com; internet www.worldfed.com; f. 1947 to protect the interests of affiliated bourses and their individual members and to settle disputes through international arbitration; mems: 25 bourses world-wide; Pres. AVI PAZ (South Africa); Sec.-Gen. RONY UNTERMAN (acting).

World Gold Council (WGC): 55 Old Broad St, London, EC2M 1RX, United Kingdom; tel. (20) 7826-4700; fax (20) 7826-4799; e-mail info@gold.org; internet www.gold.org; f. 1987 as world-wide international asscn of gold producers, to promote the demand for gold; Chair. IAN TELFER; Chief Exec. ADAM SHISHMANIAN.

World Petroleum Council (WPC): 1 Duchess St, 4th Floor, Suite 1, London, W1W 6AN, United Kingdom; tel. (20) 7637-4958; fax (20) 7637-4965; e-mail info@world-petroleum.org; internet www.world-petroleum.org; f. 1933 to serve as a forum for petroleum science, technology, economics and management; undertakes related information and liaison activities; 20th Congress: Doha, Qatar, Dec. 2011; mems: Council includes 66 mem. countries; Pres. Dr RENATO BERTANI (Brazil); Dir-Gen. Dr PIERCE W. F. RIEMER (United Kingdom).

World Sugar Research Organisation (WSRO): 70 Collingwood House, Dolphin Sq., London, SW1V 3LX, United Kingdom; tel. (20) 7821-6800; fax (20) 7834-4137; e-mail wsro@wsro.org; internet www.wsro.org; an alliance of sugar producers, processors, marketers and users; monitors and communicates research on role of sugar and other carbohydrates in nutrition and health; organizes conferences and symposia; operates a database of information; serves as a forum for exchange of views; mems: 67 orgs in 30 countries; Dir-Gen. Dr RICHARD COTTRELL; publs *WSRO Research Bulletin* (online, monthly), *WSRO Newsletter*, papers and conference proceedings.

Development and Economic Co-operation

African Capacity Building Foundation (ACBF): ZB Life Towers, 7th Floor, cnr Jason Moyo Ave/Sam Nujoma St, POB 1562, Harare, Zimbabwe; tel. (4) 702931; fax (4) 702915; e-mail root@acbf-pact.org; internet www.acbf-pact.org; f. 1991 by the World Bank, UNDP, the African Development Bank, African governments and bilateral donors; aims to build sustainable human and institutional capacity for sustainable growth, poverty reduction and good governance in Africa; mems: 44 African and non-African govts, the World Bank, UNDP, AfDB, the IMF; Exec. Sec. Dr FRANNIE A. LÉAUTIER.

African Training and Research Centre in Administration for Development (Centre Africain de Formation et de Recherche Administratives pour le Développement—CAFRAD): POB 1796, Tangier, 90001 Morocco; tel. (661) 307269; fax (539) 325785; e-mail cafrad@cafrad.org; internet www.cafrad.org; f. 1964 by agreement between Morocco and UNESCO; undertakes research into administrative problems in Africa and documents results; provides a consultation service for governments and organizations; holds workshops to train senior civil servants; prepares the Biennial Pan-African Conference of Ministers of the Civil Service; mems: 37 African countries; Chair. MOHAMED SAÂD EL-ALAMI; Dir-Gen. Dr SIMON MAMOSI LELO; publs *African Administrative Studies* (2 a year), *Research Studies*, *Newsletter* (internet), *Collection: Etudes et Documents*, *Répertoires des Consultants et des institutions de formation en Afrique*.

Afro-Asian Rural Development Organization (AARDO): No. 2, State Guest Houses Complex, Chanakyapuri, New Delhi 110 021, India; tel. (11) 24100475; fax (11) 24672045; e-mail aardohq@nde.vsnl.net.in; internet www.aardo.org; f. 1962 to act as a catalyst for the co-operative restructuring of rural life in Africa and Asia and to explore opportunities for the co-ordination of efforts to promote rural welfare and to eradicate hunger, thirst, disease, illiteracy and poverty; carries out collaborative research on development issues; organizes training; encourages the exchange of information; holds international conferences and seminars; awards 150 individual training fellowships at 12 institutes in Bangladesh, Egypt, India, Japan, the Republic of Korea, Malaysia, Nigeria, Taiwan and Zambia; mems: 15 African countries, 14 Asian countries, 1 African associate; Sec.-Gen. WASSFI HASSAN EL-SREIHIN (Jordan); publs *Afro-Asian Journal of Rural Development* (2 a year), *Annual Report*, *AARDO Newsletter* (2 a year).

Agadir Agreement: Fifth Circle, Hanna Qa'war St, Bldg 3, POB 830487, 11183 Amman, Jordan; tel. (6) 5935305; fax (6) 5935306; e-mail atu@agadiragreement.org; internet www.agadiragreement.org; a Declaration made in Agadir, in May 2001, by the governments of Egypt, Jordan, Morocco and Tunisia on the establishment of a common free trade area was followed, in February 2004, by the adoption of the Agadir Agreement on the establishment of a Free Trade Zone between the Arabic Mediterranean Nations, as a means of implementing the Agadir Declaration; the Agadir Agreement entered into force in July 2006 and its implementation commenced in March 2007; mems: Egypt, Jordan, Morocco, Tunisia; Technical Unit Exec. Pers. WALID ELNOZAHY.

Amazon Co-operation Treaty Organization: SHIS-QI 05, Conjunto 16, casa 21, Lago Sul, Brasília, DF 71615-160, Brazil; tel. (61) 3248-4119; fax (61) 3248-4238; internet www.otca.org.br; f. 1978, permanent secretariat established 1995; aims to promote the co-ordinated and sustainable development of the Amazonian territories; there are regular meetings of ministers of foreign affairs; there are specialized co-ordinators of environment, health, science technology and education, infrastructure, tourism, transport and communications, and of indigenous affairs; mems: Bolivia, Brazil, Colombia, Ecuador, Guyana, Peru, Suriname, Venezuela; Sec.-Gen. ALEJANDRO A. GORDILLO (Peru); Exec. Dir. MAURICIO DORFLER.

Arab Gulf Programme for the United Nations Development Organizations (AGFUND): POB 18371, Riyadh 11415, Saudi Arabia; tel. (1) 4418888; fax (1) 4412962; e-mail info@agfund.org; internet www.agfund.org; f. 1981 to provide grants for projects in mother and child care carried out by United Nations organizations, Arab non-governmental organizations and other international bodies, and to co-ordinate assistance by the nations of the Gulf; financing comes mainly from member states, all of which are members of OPEC; mems: Bahrain, Kuwait, Oman, Qatar, Saudi Arabia, UAE; Pres. HRH Prince TALAL BIN ABDAL-AZIZ.

Arctic Council: c/o Polarmiljøsenteret, 9296 Tromsø, Norway; tel. 77-75-01-40; fax 77-75-05-01; e-mail ac-chair@arctic-council.org; internet www.arctic-council.org; f. 1996 to promote co-ordination of activities in the Arctic region, in particular in the areas of education, development and environmental protection; working groups, supported by scientific and technical expert groups, focus on the following six areas: action on Arctic contaminants; Arctic monitoring and assessment; conservation of Arctic flora and fauna; emergency prevention, preparedness and response; protection of the Arctic marine environment; and sustainable development; ministerial meetings are normally convened at two-year intervals, most recently in Nuuk, Greenland, in May 2011; Senior Arctic Officials meet annually; mems: Canada, Denmark, Finland, Iceland, Norway, Russia, Sweden, USA; in addition the following 6 orgs representing Arctic indigenous peoples have Permanent Participant status: the Arctic Athabaskan Council, Aleut International Association, Gwich'in Council International, Inuit Circumpolar Council, Russian Arctic Indigenous Peoples of the North, and Saami Council, these are supported by an Indigenous People's Secretariat, based in Copenhagen, Denmark; chairmanship of the Council rotates on a 2-yearly basis (2011–13: Sweden); Chair. of Senior Arctic Officials GUSTAF LIND; Head of Secretariat NINA BUVANG VAAJA.

Association of Caribbean States (ACS): 5–7 Sweet Briar Rd, St Clair, POB 660, Port of Spain, Trinidad and Tobago; tel. 622-9575; fax 622-1653; e-mail mail@acs-aec.org; internet www.acs-aec.org; f. 1994 by the Governments of the 13 CARICOM countries and Colombia, Costa Rica, Cuba, Dominican Republic, El Salvador, Guatemala, Haiti, Honduras, Mexico, Nicaragua, Suriname and Venezuela; aims to promote economic integration, sustainable development and co-operation in the region; to preserve the environmental integrity of the Caribbean Sea which is regarded as the common patrimony of the peoples of the region; to undertake concerted action to protect the environment, particularly the Caribbean Sea; and to co-operate in the areas of trade, transport, sustainable tourism, and natural disasters. Policy is determined by a Ministerial Council and implemented by a Secretariat based in Port of Spain. In December 2001 a third Summit of Heads of State and Government was convened in Venezuela, where a Plan of Action focusing on issues of sustainable tourism, trade, transport and natural disasters was agreed. The fourth ACS Summit was held in Panama, in July 2005. A final Declaration included resolutions to strengthen co-operation mechanisms with the EU and to promote a strategy for the Caribbean Sea Zone to be recognized as a special area for the purposes of sustainable development programmes, support for a strengthened social agenda and efforts to achieve the Millennium Development Goals, and calls for member states to sign or ratify the following accords: an ACS Agreement for Regional Co-operation in the area of Natural Disasters; a Convention Establishing the Sustainable Tourism Zone of the Caribbean; and an ACS Air Transport Agreement; mems: 25 signatory states, 5 associate mems, 19 observers, 6 founding observer countries; Sec.-Gen. ALFONSO MUÑERA CAVADÍA (Colombia).

Association of Development Financing Institutions in Asia and the Pacific (ADFIAP): Skyland Plaza, 2nd Floor, Sen. Gil J. Puyat Ave, Makati City, Metro Manila, 1200 Philippines; tel. (2) 8161672; fax (2) 8176498; e-mail info@adfiap.org; internet www.adfiap.org; f. 1976 to promote the interests and economic development of the respective countries of its member institutions, through development financing; mems: 113 institutions in 42 countries; Chair. NIHAL FONSEKA (Sri Lanka); Sec.-Gen. OCTAVIO B. PERALTA; publs *Asian Banking Digest*, *Journal of Development Finance* (2 a year), *ADFIAP Newsletter*, *ADFIAP Accompli*, *DevTrade Finance*.

Barents Euro-Arctic Council: International Secretariat, POB, 9915, Rådhusgt. 8, Kirkenes, Norway; tel. 78-97-08-70; fax 78-97-70-79; e-mail ibs@beac.st; internet www.beac.st; f. 1993 as a forum for Barents regional intergovernmental co-operation; mems: Denmark, Finland, Iceland, Norway, Russia, Sweden, European Commission; chairmanship of the Council rotates on a 2-yearly basis between the member states (2011–13:Norway); Head of Int. Secretariat ARI SIRÉN.

Benelux Economic Union: 39 rue de la Régence, 1000 Brussels, Belgium; tel. (2) 519-38-11; fax (2) 513-42-06; e-mail info@benelux.int; internet www.benelux.int; f. 1960 to bring about the economic union of Belgium, Luxembourg and the Netherlands; in June 2008 a new Benelux Treaty was adopted to enter into force upon the expiry in 2010 of the treaty establishing the Union; under the new legal framework cross-border co-operation between the member states and co-operation within a broader European context were to be advanced and the name of the organization was to be changed to Benelux Union; the Union aims to introduce common policies in the field of cross-border co-operation and harmonize standards and intellectual property legislation; structure comprises: Committee of Ministers; Council; Court of Justice; Consultative Inter-Parliamentary Council; the Economic and Social Advisory Council; the General Secretariat; a Benelux Organisation for Intellectual Property was established in Sept. 2006; Sec.-Gen. Dr J. P. R. M. VAN LAARHOVEN (Netherlands); publs *Benelux Newsletter*, *Bulletin Benelux*.

Caribbean-Britain Business Council: 2 Belgrave Sq., London, SW1X 8PJ, United Kingdom; tel. (20) 7235-9484; fax (20) 7823-1370; e-mail david.jessop@caribbean-council.org; internet www.caribbean-council.org; f. 2001; promotes trade and investment development between the United Kingdom, the Caribbean and the European Union; Man. Dir DAVID JESSOP; publs *Caribbean Insight* (weekly), *Cuba Briefing* (weekly).

Central Asia Regional Economic Co-operation (CAREC): CAREC Unit, 6 ADB Ave, Mandaluyong City, 1550 Metro Manila, Philippines; tel. (2) 6326134; fax (2) 6362387; e-mail rabutiong@adb.org; internet www.carecprogram.org; f. 1997; a sub-regional alliance supported by several multilateral institutions (ADB, EBRD, the IMF, IDB, the UNDP, and the World Bank) to promote economic co-operation and development; supports projects in the following priority areas: transport, energy, trade policy, trade facilitation; a Cross-Border Transport Agreement was signed by Kyrgyzstan and Tajikistan in Oct. 2010 (an agreement for Afghanistan to accede to the Agreement was concluded in Aug. 2011); mems: Afghanistan, Azerbaijan, Kazakhstan, Kyrgyzstan, Mongolia, Tajikistan, Uzbekistan, Xinjiang Uygur Autonomous Region (of the People's Republic of China); Unit Head RONALD ANTONIO Q. BUTIONG.

Central European Free Trade Association: 12–16 rue Joseph II, 1000 Brussels; tel. (2) 229-10-11; fax (2) 229-10-19; e-mail cefta@cefta.int; internet www.cefta2006.com; f. 1992, Central European Free Trade Agreement (CEFTA) entered into force 1993; enlarged CEFTA signed 19 Dec. 2006; free trade agreement covering a number of sectors; mems: Albania, Bosnia and Herzegovina, Croatia, former Yugoslav republic of Macedonia, Moldova, Montenegro, Serbia, UNMIK (representing Kosovo); Dir. RENATA VITEZ.

Centre on Integrated Rural Development for Asia and the Pacific (CIRDAP): Chameli House, 17 Topkhana Rd; GPO Box 2883, Dhaka 1000, Bangladesh; tel. (2) 9558751; fax (2) 9562035; e-mail infocom@cirdap.org; internet www.cirdap.org.sg; f. 1979 to support integrated rural development; promotes regional co-operation; mems: Afghanistan, Bangladesh, Fiji, India, Indonesia, Iran, Laos, Malaysia, Myanmar, Nepal, Pakistan, Philippines, Sri Lanka, Thailand, Viet Nam; Dir Dr DURGA PRASAD PAUDYAL.

Coalition for Dialogue on Africa (CoDA): POB 3001, Addis Ababa, Ethiopia; tel. (11) 15443277; e-mail coda@uneca.org; internet www.uneca.org/coda; f. 2009; brings together African stakeholders and policy-makers; policy-oriented, working in collaboration with regional and international organizations to address issues relating to security, peace, governance and development; sponsored by, but not a programme of, the AU Commission, the UN Economic Commission for Africa and the AfDB; Chair. FESTUS MOGAE.

Colombo Plan: POB 596, 31 Wijerama Rd, Colombo 7, Sri Lanka; tel. (11) 2684188; fax (11) 2684386; e-mail info@colomboplan.org; internet www.colombo-plan.org; f. 1950, as the Colombo Plan for Co-operative Economic and Social Development in Asia and the Pacific, by seven Commonwealth countries, to encourage economic and social development in that region, based on principles of partnership and collective effort; the Plan comprises four training programmes: the Drug Advisory Programme, to enhance the capabilities of officials, in government and non-governmental organizations, involved in drug abuse prevention and control; the Programme for Public Administration, to develop human capital in the public sector; the Programme for Private Sector Development, which implements skill development programmes in the area of small and medium-sized enterprises and related issues; and the Staff College for Technician Education (see below); all training programmes are voluntarily funded, while administrative costs of the organization are shared equally by all member countries; developing countries are encouraged to become donors and to participate in economic and technical co-operation activities; mems: 26 countries; Sec.-Gen. ADAM MANIKU (Maldives); publs *Annual Report*, *Colombo Plan Focus* (quarterly), *Consultative Committee Proceedings and Conclusions* (every 2 years).

Colombo Plan Staff College for Technician Education: blk C, DepEd Complex, Meralco Ave, Pasig City 1600, Metro Manila, Philippines; tel. (2) 6310991; fax (2) 6310996; e-mail cpsc@cpsctech.org; internet www.cpsctech.org; f. 1973 with the support of member governments of the Colombo Plan; aims to enhance the development of technician education systems in developing mem. countries; Dir MOHAMMAD NAIM BIN YAAKUB (Malaysia); publ. *CPSC Quarterly*.

Communauté économique des états de l'Afrique centrale (CEEAC) (Economic Community of Central African States): BP 2112, Libreville, Gabon; tel. (241) 44-47-31; fax (241) 44-47-32; e-mail secretariat@ceeac-eccas.org; internet www.ceeac-eccas.org; f. 1983, operational 1 January 1985; aims to promote co-operation between member states by abolishing trade restrictions, establishing a common external customs tariff, linking commercial banks, and setting up a development fund, over a period of 12 years; works to combat drug abuse and to promote regional security; has since July 2008 deployed the Mission for the Consolidation of Peace in the CAR—MICOPAX; mems: 10 African countries; Sec.-Gen. NASSOUR GUELENGDOUSKSIA OUAIDO.

Community of Sahel-Saharan States (Communauté des états Sahelo-Sahariens—CEN-SAD): Place d'Algeria, POB 4041, Tripoli, Libya; tel. (21) 361-4832; fax (21) 334-3670; e-mail info@cen-sad.org; internet www.uneca.org/cen-sad; f. 1998; fmrly known as COMESSA; aims to strengthen co-operation between signatory states in order to promote their economic, social and cultural integration and to facilitate conflict resolution and poverty alleviation; partnership agreements concluded with many orgs, including the AU, UN and ECOWAS; mems: Benin, Burkina Faso, Central African Republic, Chad, Côte d'Ivoire, Djibouti, Egypt, Eritrea, The Gambia, Ghana, Guinea-Bissau, Liberia, Libya, Mali, Morocco, Niger, Nigeria, Senegal, Sierra Leone, Somalia, Sudan, Togo, Tunisia; Sec.-Gen. Dr MOHAMMED AL-MADANI AL-AZHARI (Libya).

Conseil de l'Entente (Entente Council): 01 BP 3734, angle ave Verdier/rue de Tessières, Abidjan 01, Côte d'Ivoire; tel. 20-33-28-35; fax 20-33-11-49; e-mail fegece@conseil-entente.org; f. 1959 to promote economic development in the region; the Council's Mutual Aid and Loan Guarantee Fund (Fonds d' entraide et de garantie des emprunts) finances development projects, including agricultural projects, support for small and medium-sized enterprises, vocational training centres, research into new sources of energy and building of hotels to encourage tourism; a Convention of Assistance and Co-operation was signed in Feb. 1996; holds annual summit; mems: Benin, Burkina Faso, Côte d'Ivoire, Niger, Togo; publ. *Rapport d'activité* (annually).

Council of American Development Foundations (Consejo de Fundaciones Americanas de Desarrollo—SOLIDARIOS): Calle 6 No. 10 Paraíso, Apdo Postal 620, Santo Domingo, Dominican Republic; tel. 549-5111; fax 544-0550; e-mail solidarios@claro.net.do; internet www.redsolidarios.org; f. 1972; exchanges information and experience, arranges technical assistance, raises funds to organize training programmes and scholarships; administers development fund to finance programmes carried out by members through a loan guarantee programme; provides consultancy services. Mem. foundations provide technical and financial assistance to low-income groups for rural, housing and microenterprise development projects; mems: 18 institutional mems in 9 Latin American and Caribbean countries; Pres. Dr CESAR ALARCÓN COSTTA; Sec.-Gen. ZULEMA BREA DE VILLAMÁN; publs *Solidarios* (quarterly), *Annual Report*.

Developing Eight (D-8): Maya Aka Center, Buyukdere Cad. 100–102, Esentepe, 34390, Istanbul, Turkey; tel. (212) 3561823; fax (212) 3561829; e-mail secretariat@developing8.org; internet www.developing8.org; inaugurated at a meeting of heads of state in June 1997; aims to foster economic co-operation between member states and to strengthen the role of developing countries in the global economy; project areas include trade (with Egypt as the co-ordinating member state), agriculture (Pakistan), human resources (Indonesia), communication and information (Iran), rural development (Bangladesh), finance and banking (Malaysia), energy (Nigeria), and industry, and health (Turkey); seventh Summit meeting: convened in Abuja, Nigeria, July 2010; mems: Bangladesh, Egypt, Indonesia, Iran, Malaysia, Nigeria, Pakistan, Turkey; Sec.-Gen. Dr WIDI PRATIKTO (Indonesia).

Earth Council Alliance: 1250 24th St, NW Suite 300, Washington, DC 20037, USA; tel. (202) 467-2786; e-mail admin@earthcouncilalliance.org; internet www.earthcouncilalliance.org; f. 1992, as the Earth Council, in preparation for the UN Conference on Environment and Development; supported the establishment of National Councils for Sustainable Development (NCSDs) and administers a programme to promote co-operation and dialogue and to facilitate capacity-building and training, with NCSDs; works, with other partner organizations, to generate support for an Earth Charter (adopted in 2000); since 2002 supports other Earth Councils world-wide to promote and support sustainable development; Chair. MAURICE STRONG (Canada); Pres. Dr MARCELO CARVALHO DE ANDRADE (Brazil).

East African Community (EAC): AICC Bldg, Kilimanjaro Wing, 5th Floor, POB 1096, Arusha, Tanzania; tel. (27) 2504253; fax (27) 2504255; e-mail eac@eachq.org; internet www.eac.int; f. 2001, following the adoption of a treaty on political and economic integration (signed in November 1999) by the heads of state of Kenya, Tanzania and Uganda, replacing the Permanent Tripartite Commission for East African Co-operation (f. 1993) and reviving the former East African Community (f. 1967; dissolved 1977); initial areas for co-operation were to be trade and industry, security, immigration, transport and communications, and promotion of investment; further objectives were the elimination of trade barriers and ensuring the free movement of people and capital within the grouping; a customs union came into effect on 1 Jan. 2005; a Court of Justice and a Legislative Assembly have been established; in April 2006 heads of state agreed that negotiations on a common market would commence in July; the Protocol on the Establishment of the EAC Common Market entered into force on 1 July 2010; Rwanda and Burundi formally became members of the Community on 1 July 2007; has aimed, since 2005, to advance regional co-operation through the 'COMESA-EAC-SADC Task Force'; participated, in October 2008, in the first tripartite COMESA-EAC-SADC summit, convened in Kampala, Uganda; the summit approved a roadmap towards the formation of a single free trade area (FTA) and the eventual establishment of a single African Economic Community; at the second tripartite summit, held in June 2011, in Johannesburg, South Africa, negotiations were initiated on the establishment of the proposed COMESA-EAC-SADC Tripartite FTA; in accordance with a Framework, Roadmap and Architecture for Fast Tracking the Establishment of a Continental FTA (referred to as CFTA), and an Action Plan for Boosting Intra-African Trade, adopted by AU leaders in January 2012, the COMESA-EAC-SADC Tripartite FTA was to be finalized by 2014 and, during 2015–16, consolidated with other regional FTAs into the CFTA initiative, with the aim of establishing by 2017 an operational CFTA; Sec.-Gen. RICHARD SEZIBERA (Rwanda).

Economic Community of the Great Lakes Countries (Communauté économique des pays des Grands Lacs—CEPGL): POB 58, Gisenyi, Rwanda; tel. 61309; fax 61319; f. 1976 main organs: annual Conference of Heads of State, Council of Ministers of Foreign Affairs, Permanent Executive Secretariat, Consultative Commission, Security Commission, three Specialized Technical Commissions; there are four specialized agencies: a development bank, the Banque de Développement des Etats des Grands Lacs (BDEGL) at Goma, Democratic Republic of the Congo; an energy centre at Bujumbura, Burundi; the Institute of Agronomic and Zootechnical Research, Gitega, Burundi; and a regional electricity company (SINELAC) at Bukavu, Democratic Republic of the Congo; mems: Burundi, Democratic Republic of the Congo, Rwanda; Exec. Sec. HERMAN TUYAGA (Burundi); publs *Grands Lacs* (quarterly review), *Journal* (annually).

Eurasian Economic Community (EURASEC): 105066 Moscow, 1-i Basmannyi per. 6/4, Russia; tel. (495) 223-90-00; fax (495) 223-90-23; e-mail evrazes@evrazes.ru; internet www.evrazes.com; f. 2000; formerly a Customs Union agreed between Belarus, Kazakhstan, Kyrgyzstan, Russia and Tajikistan in 1999; the merger of EURASEC with the Central Asian Co-operation Organization (CACO) was agreed in Oct. 2005, and achieved in Jan. 2006 with the accession to EURASEC of Uzbekistan, which had hitherto been the only mem. of CACO that did not also belong to EURASEC; aims to create a Common Economic Space (CES) with a single currency; a free trade zone was established at the end of 2002; in Oct. 2007 EURASEC leaders approved the legal basis for establishing a new customs union, initially to comprise Belarus, Kazakhstan and Russia, with

Kyrgyzstan, Tajikistan and Uzbekistan expected to join subsequently; the customs union entered into formal existence on 1 Jan. 2010; in Dec. 2010 the heads of state of Belarus, Kazakhstan and Russia signed several agreements aimed at finalizing the establishment of the planned CES, and, in Nov. 2011, they signed a declaration on Eurasian economic integration and adopted a roadmap outlining integration processes aimed at creating a Eurasian Economic Union, to be established by 1 Jan. 2015, and to be based on the Customs Union and CES; in March 2012 the Russian President urged the EURASEC observer states to join the ongoing economic integration process; mems co-operate on issues including customs tariff harmonization, migration, border security and negotiating admission to the WTO; Uzbekistan announced the suspension of is membership of EURASEC in Nov. 2008; Armenia, Moldova and Ukraine have observer status; Sec.-Gen. TAIR A. MANSUROV.

European Free Trade Association (EFTA): 9–11 rue de Varembé, 1211 Geneva 20, Switzerland; tel. 223322600; fax 223322677; e-mail mail.gva@efta.int; internet www.efta.int; f. 1960 to bring about free trade in industrial goods and to contribute to the liberalization and expansion of world trade; EFTA states (except Switzerland) participate in the European Economic Area (EEA) with the 27 member countries of the European Union; has concluded free trade agreements with, *inter alia*, Canada, Chile, Colombia, Croatia, Egypt, Israel, Jordan, Republic of Korea, Lebanon, Macedonia, Mexico, Morocco, Palestinian Authority, Singapore, Southern African Customs Union (SACU), Tunisia and Turkey; mems: Iceland, Liechtenstein, Norway, Switzerland; Sec.-Gen. KÅRE BRYN (Norway); publs *EFTA Annual Report*, *EFTA Bulletin*.

Food Aid Committee: c/o International Grains Council, 1 Canada Sq., Canary Wharf, London, E14 5AE, United Kingdom; tel. (20) 7513-1122; fax (20) 7513-0630; e-mail fac@foodaidconvention.org; internet www.foodaidconvention.org; f. 1967; responsible for administration of the Food Aid Convention—FAC (1999), a constituent element of the International Grains Agreement (1995); aims to make appropriate levels of food aid available on a consistent basis to maximize the impact and effectiveness of such assistance; provides a framework for co-operation, co-ordination and information-sharing among members on matters related to food aid. The 23 donor members pledge to supply a minimum of 5m. metric tons of food annually to developing countries and territories, mostly as gifts: in practice aid has usually exceeded 8m. tons annually. Secretariat support is provided by the International Grains Council; Chair. LESLIE NORTON; publ. *Report on shipments* (annually).

G-20 (Doha Round negotiating group): e-mail g-20@mre.gov.br; f. 2003 with the aim of defending the interests of developing countries in the negotiations on agriculture under the WTO's Doha Development Round and meets regularly to address WTO-related agricultural trade issues; now comprises 23 developing countries; mems: Argentina, Bolivia, Brazil, Chile, People's Republic of China, Cuba, Ecuador, Egypt, Guatemala, India, Indonesia, Mexico, Nigeria, Pakistan, Paraguay, Peru, Philippines, South Africa, Tanzania, Thailand, Uruguay, Venezuela, Zimbabwe.

Gambia River Basin Development Organization (Organisation pour la mise en valeur du fleuve Gambie—OMVG): BP 2353, 13 passage Leblanc, Dakar, Senegal; tel. 822-31-59; fax 822-59-26; e-mail omvg@omvg.sn; f. 1978 by Senegal and The Gambia; Guinea joined in 1981 and Guinea-Bissau in 1983. A masterplan for the integrated development of the Kayanga/Geba and Koliba/Corubal river basins has been developed, encompassing a projected natural resources management project; a hydraulic development plan for the Gambia river was formulated during 1996–98; a pre-feasibility study on connecting the national electric grids of the four member states has been completed, and a feasibility study for the construction of the proposed Sambangalou hydroelectric dam, was undertaken in the early 2000s; maintains documentation centre; Exec. Sec. JUSTINO VIEIRA.

Group of Three (G-3): c/o Secretaría de Relaciones Exteriores, 1 Tlatelolco, Del. Cuauhtémoc, 06995 México, DF, Mexico; e-mail gtres@sre.gob.mx; f. 1990 by Colombia, Mexico and Venezuela to remove restrictions on trade between the three countries; in November 2004 Panama joined the Group, which briefly became the Group of Four until Venezuela's withdrawal in November 2006; the trade agreement covers market access, rules of origin, intellectual property, trade in services, and government purchases, and entered into force in early 1994. Tariffs on trade between member states were to be removed on a phased basis. Co-operation was also envisaged in employment creation, the energy sector and the fight against cholera. The secretariat function rotates between the member countries on a two-yearly basis; mems: Colombia, Mexico and Panama.

Group of 15 (G15): G15 Technical Support Facility, 1 route des Morillons, CP 2100, 1218 Grand Saconnex, Geneva, Switzerland; tel. 227916701; fax 227916169; e-mail tsf@g15.org; internet www.g15.org; f. 1989 by 15 developing nations during the ninth summit of the Non-Aligned Movement; retains its original name although current membership totals 17; convenes biennial summits to address the global economic and political situation and to promote economic development through South-South co-operation and North-South dialogue; mems: Algeria, Argentina, Brazil, Chile, Egypt, India, Indonesia, Iran, Jamaica, Kenya, Malaysia, Mexico, Nigeria, Senegal, Sri Lanka, Venezuela, Zimbabwe; Head of Office AUDU A. KADIRI.

Group of 77 (G77): c/o UN Headquarters, Rm NL-2077, New York, NY 10017, USA; tel. (212) 963-0192; fax (212) 963-1753; e-mail secretariat@g77.org; internet www.g77.org; f. 1964 by the 77 signatory states of the 'Joint Declaration of the Seventy-Seven Countries' (the G77 retains its original name, owing to its historic significance, although its membership has expanded since inception); first ministerial meeting, held in Algiers, Algeria, in Oct. 1967, adopted the Charter of Algiers as a basis for G77 co-operation; subsequently G77 Chapters were established with liaison offices in Geneva (UNCTAD), Nairobi (UNEP), Paris (UNESCO), Rome (FAO/IFAD), Vienna (UNIDO), and the Group of 24 (G24) in Washington, DC (IMF and World Bank); as the largest intergovernmental organization of developing states in the United Nations the G77 aims to enable developing nations to articulate and promote their collective economic interests and to improve their negotiating capacity with regard to global economic issues within the United Nations system; in Sept. 2006 G77 ministers of foreign affairs, and the People's Republic of China, endorsed the establishment of a new Consortium on Science, Technology and Innovation for the South (COSTIS); a chairperson, who also acts as spokesperson, co-ordinates the G77's activities in each Chapter; the chairmanship rotates on a regional basis between Africa, Asia, and Latin America and the Caribbean; the supreme decision-making body of the G77 is the South Summit, normally convened at five-yearly intervals (2005: Doha, Qatar; the third Summit was scheduled to be convened in Africa, during 2012); the annual meeting of G77 ministers of foreign affairs is convened at the start (in September) of the regular session of the UN General Assembly; periodic sectoral ministerial meetings are organized in preparation for UNCTAD sessions and prior to the UNIDO and UNESCO General Conferences, and with the aim of promoting South-South co-operation; other special ministerial meetings are also convened from time to time; the first G77 Ministerial Forum on Water Resources was convened in February 2009, in Muscat, Oman; mems: 132 developing countries.

Indian Ocean Commission (IOC) (Commission de l'Océan Indien—COI): Q4, Ave Sir Guy Forget, BP 7, Quatre Bornes, Mauritius; tel. 427-3366; fax 425-2709; e-mail secretariat@coi-ioc.org; internet www.coi-ioc.org; f. 1982 to promote regional co-operation, particularly in economic development; projects include tuna-fishing development, protection and management of environmental resources and strengthening of meteorological services; tariff reduction is also envisaged; organizes an annual regional trade fair; mems: the Comoros, France (representing the French Overseas Department of Réunion), Madagascar, Mauritius, Seychelles; Sec.-Gen. CALLIXTE D'OFFAY; publ. *La Lettre de l'Océan Indien*.

Indian Ocean Rim Association for Regional Co-operation (IOR–ARC): Nexteracom Tower 1, 3rd Floor, Ebene, Mauritius; tel. 454-1717; fax 468-1161; e-mail iorarcsec@iorarc.org; internet www.iorarc.org; the first intergovernmental meeting of countries in the region to promote an Indian Ocean Rim initiative was convened in March 1995; charter to establish the Asscn was signed at a ministerial meeting in March 1997; aims to promote the sustained growth and balanced devt of the region and of its mem. states and to create common ground for regional economic co-operation, *inter alia* through trade, investment, infrastructure, tourism, and science and technology; 10th meeting of Council of Ministers held in San'a, Yemen, Aug. 2010; mems: Australia, Bangladesh, India, Indonesia, Iran, Kenya, Madagascar, Malaysia, Mauritius, Mozambique, Oman, Singapore, South Africa, Sri Lanka, Tanzania, Thailand, United Arab Emirates and Yemen. Dialogue Partner countries: People's Republic of China, Egypt, France, Japan, United Kingdom. Observers: Indian Ocean Research Group (IORG) Inc., Indian Ocean Tourism Org; Sec.-Gen. K. V. BHAGIRATH.

Inter-American Planning Society (Sociedad Interamericana de Planificación—SIAP): c/o Revista Interamericana de Planificación, Casilla 01-05-1978, Cuenca, Ecuador; tel. (7) 823860; fax (7) 823949; e-mail siap1@siap.org.ec; f. 1956 to promote development of comprehensive planning; mems: institutions and individuals in 46 countries; Exec. Sec. LUIS E. CAMACHO (Colombia); publs *Correo Informativo* (quarterly), *Inter-American Journal of Planning* (quarterly).

International Co-operation for Development and Solidarity (Co-opération Internationale pour le Développement et la Solidarité—CIDSE): 16 rue Stévin, 1000 Brussels, Belgium; tel. (2) 230-77-22; fax (2) 230-70-82; e-mail postmaster@cidse.org; internet www.cidse.org; f. 1967; an international alliance of Catholic development agencies, whose members share a common strategy in their efforts to eradicate poverty and establish global justice. CIDSE's advocacy work covers trade and food security, climate change, resources for development, global governance, and EU development policy; promotes co-operation and the development of common strategies on advocacy work, development projects and programmes and development education; mems: 16 Catholic agencies in 15 countries and territories; Pres. CHRIS BAIN; Sec.-Gen. BERND NILLES.

Inuit Circumpolar Council: Aqqusinersuaq 3 A, 1st Floor, POB 204, 3900 Nuuk Greenland; tel. 323632; fax 323001; e-mail iccgreenland@inuit.org; internet www.inuit.org; f. 1977 (as the Inuit Circumpolar Conference, name changed 2006) to protect the indigenous culture, environment and rights of the Inuit people, and to encourage co-operation among the Inuit; has adopted a Circumpolar Inuit Declaration on Sovereignty in the Arctic (in April 2009), and a Circumpolar Inuit Declaration on Resource Development Principles in Inuit Nunaat (May 2011); the Nuuk Declaration, adopted in June 2010 by the 11th General Assembly, directed the Council, *inter alia*, to implement a 2010–14 Circumpolar Inuit Health Strategy; to keep environmental stewardship of the Inuit homeland as a priority activity during 2010–14; to organize an Inuit leaders' summit on resource development; to continue to participate in international bodies to defend and promote the right of the Inuit to harvest marine mammals and to trade their products on a sustainable basis; and instructed the Council to organize a pan-Arctic Inuit leaders' summit during 2012; General Assemblies held every four years (2010: Nuuk, Greenland, in June); mems: Inuit communities in Canada, Greenland, Alaska and Russia; Chair. AQQALUK LYNGE; Exec. Dir ALFRED JAKOBSEN; publ. *Silarjualiriniq*.

Lake Chad Basin Commission (LCBC): BP 727, N'Djamena, Chad; tel. 52-41-45; fax 52-41-37; e-mail lcbc@intnet.td; internet www.cblt.org; f. 1964 to encourage co-operation in developing the Lake Chad region and to promote the settlement of regional disputes; work programmes emphasize the regulation of the utilization of water and other natural resources in the basin; the co-ordination of natural resources development projects and research; holds annual summit of heads of state; mems: Cameroon, Central African Republic, Chad, Niger, Nigeria; Exec. Sec. MUHAMMAD SANI ADAMU; publ. *Bibliographie générale de la CBLT* (2 a year).

Latin American Association of Development Financing Institutions (Asociación Latinoamericana de Instituciones Financieras para el Desarrollo—ALIDE): Apdo Postal 3988, Paseo de la República 3211, Lima 27, Peru; tel. (1) 4422400; fax (1) 4428105; e-mail sg@alide.org.pe; internet www.alide.org.pe; f. 1968 to promote co-operation among regional development financing bodies; programmes: technical assistance; training; studies and research; technical meetings; information; projects and investment promotion; mems: more than 70 active, 3 assoc. and 5 collaborating (banks and financing institutions and development organizations in 22 Latin American countries, Canada, Germany and Spain); Pres. RODRIGO SÁNCHEZ MÚJICA; Sec.-Gen. ROMMEL ACEVEDO; publs *ALIDE Bulletin* (6 a year), *ALIDENOTICIAS Newsletter* (monthly), *Annual Report*, *Latin American Directory of Development Financing Institutions*.

Latin American Economic System (Sistema Económico Latinoamericano—SELA): Torre Europa, 4°, Urb. Campo Alegre, Avda Francisco de Miranda, Caracas 1060, Venezuela; Apdo 17035, Caracas 1010-A, Venezuela; tel. (212) 955-7111; fax (212) 951-5292; e-mail sela@sela.org; internet www.sela.org; f. 1975 in accordance with the Panama Convention; aims to foster co-operation and integration among the countries of Latin America and the Caribbean, and to provide a permanent system of consultation and co-ordination in economic and social matters; conducts studies and other analysis and research; extends technical assistance to sub-regional and regional co-ordination bodies; provides library, information service and databases on regional co-operation. The Latin American Council, the principal decision-making body of the System, meets annually at ministerial level and high-level regional consultation and co-ordination meetings are held; there is also a Permanent Secretariat; mems: 28 countries; Perm. Sec. JOSÉ RIVERA BANUET (Mexico); publs *Capítulos del SELA* (3 a year), *Bulletin on Latin America and Caribbean Integration* (monthly), *SELA Antenna in the United States* (quarterly).

Liptako-Gourma Integrated Development Authority (LGA): POB 619, ave M. Thevenond, Ouagadougou, Burkina Faso; tel. (3) 30-61-48; f. 1970; scope of activities includes water infrastructure, telecommunications and construction of roads and railways; in 1986 undertook study on development of water resources in the basin of the Niger river (for hydroelectricity and irrigation); mems: Burkina Faso, Mali, Niger; Chair. SEYDOU BOUDA (Mali).

Mano River Union: Private Mail Bag 133, Delco House, Lightfoot Boston St, Freetown, Sierra Leone; tel. (22) 226883; e-mail sg@manoriveruniononline.org; internet www.manoriveruniononline.org; f. 1973 to establish a customs and economic union between member states to accelerate development via integration; a common external tariff was instituted in 1977. Intra-union free trade was officially introduced in May 1981, as the first stage in progress towards a customs union. A non-aggression treaty was signed by heads of state in 1986. The Union was inactive for three years until mid-1994, owing to regional conflict and disagreements regarding funding. In Jan. 1995 a Mano River Centre for Peace and Development was established, to provide a permanent mechanism for conflict prevention and resolution, and monitoring of human rights violations, and to promote sustainable peace and development. A new security structure was approved in 2000. In Aug. 2001 ministers of foreign affairs, security, internal affairs, and justice, meeting as the Joint Security Committee, resolved to deploy joint border security and confidence-building units, and to work to re-establish the free movement of people and goods; implements programmes in the following areas: institutional revitalisation, restructuring and development; peace and security; economic development and regional integration; and social development; mems: Guinea, Liberia, Sierra Leone; Sec.-Gen. Dr HADJA SARAN DARABA KABBA.

Mekong River Commission (MRC): POB 6101, Unit 18 Ban Sithane Neua, Sikhottabong District, Vientiane, Laos 01000; tel. (21) 263263; fax (21) 263264; e-mail mrcs@mrcmekong.org; internet www.mrcmekong.org; f. 1995 as successor to the Committee for Co-ordination of Investigations of the Lower Mekong Basin ('Mekong Committee' f. 1957); aims to promote and co-ordinate the sustainable development and use of the water and related resources of the Mekong River Basin for navigational and non-navigational purposes, in order to assist the social and economic development of member states and preserve the ecological balance of the basin; provides scientific information and policy advice; supports the implementation of strategic programmes and activities; organizes an annual donor consultative group meeting; maintains regular dialogue with Myanmar and the People's Republic of China; the first meeting of heads of government was convened in Hua Hin, Thailand, in April 2010; mems: Cambodia, Laos, Thailand, Viet Nam; CEO HANS GUTTMAN; publs *Annual Report*, *Catch and Culture* (3 a year), *Mekong News* (quarterly).

Mesoamerican Integration and Development Project (Proyecto de Integración y Desarrollo de Mesoamérica): Torre Roble, 8º, San Salvador, El Salvador; tel. 2261-5444; fax 2260-9176; e-mail e.whyte@proyectomesoamerica.org; internet www.proyectomesoamerica.org; f. 2001 as the Puebla-Panamá Plan (PPP); relaunched with formal institutionalized structure in 2004; current name and mandate approved in June 2008 by the Tuxtla summit meeting; aims to promote economic development and reduce poverty in member countries; eight key areas of activity: energy, transport, telecommunications, tourism, trade environment and competitiveness, human development, sustainable development, prevention and mitigation of natural disasters; administers the Mesoamerica Biological Corridor initiative to enhance the management of the region's biodiversity; mems: Belize, Colombia, Costa Rica, El Salvador, Guatemala, Honduras, Mexico, Nicaragua, Panama; Exec. Dir ELAYNE WHYTE GÓMEZ.

Niger Basin Authority (Autorité du Bassin du Niger): BP 729, Niamey, Niger; tel. 20724395; fax 20724208; e-mail sec-executif@abn.ne; internet www.abn.ne; f. 1964 (as River Niger Commission; name changed 1980) to harmonize national programmes concerned with the River Niger Basin and to execute an integrated development plan; compiles statistics; regulates navigation; runs projects on hydrological forecasting, environmental control; infrastructure and agro-pastoral development; mems: Benin, Burkina Faso, Cameroon, Chad, Côte d'Ivoire, Guinea, Mali, Niger, Nigeria; Exec. Sec. MOHAMMED BELLO TUGA (Nigeria); publ. *NBA-INFO* (quarterly).

Nile Basin Initiative: POB 192, Entebbe, Uganda; tel. (41) 321329; fax (41) 320971; e-mail nbisec@nilebasin.org; internet www.nilebasin.org; f. 1999; aims to achieve sustainable socio-economic development through the equitable use and benefits of the Nile Basin water resources and to create an enabling environment for the implementation of programmes with a shared vision. Highest authority is the Nile Basin Council of Ministers (Nile-COM); other activities undertaken by a Nile Basin Technical Advisory Committee (Nile-TAC); mems: Burundi, Democratic Republic of the Congo, Egypt, Eritrea, Ethiopia, Kenya, Rwanda, Sudan, Tanzania, Uganda; Chair. CHARITY K. NGILU.

Nordic Development Fund: POB 185, 00171 Helsinki, Finland; tel. (10) 618-002; fax (9) 622-1491; e-mail info.ndf@ndf.fi; internet www.ndf.fi; f. 1989; supports activities by national administrations for overseas development, with resources amounting to €330m; Man. Dir HELGE SEMB.

Organization for the Development of the Senegal River (Organisation pour la mise en valeur du fleuve Sénégal—OMVS): c/o Haut-Commissariat, 46 rue Carnot, BP 3152, Dakar, Senegal; tel. 859-81-81; fax 864-01-63; e-mail omvssphc@omvs.org; internet www.omvs.org; f. 1972 to promote the use of the Senegal river for hydroelectricity, irrigation and navigation; the Djama dam in Senegal provides a barrage to prevent salt water from moving upstream, and the Manantali dam in Mali is intended to provide a reservoir for irrigation of about 375,000 ha of land and for production of hydroelectricity and provision of year-round navigation for ocean-going vessels. In 1997 two companies were formed to manage the dams: Société de gestion de l'énergie de Manantali (SOGEM) and Société de gestion et d'exploitation du barrage de Djama (SOGED); mems: Guinea, Mali, Mauritania, Senegal; High Commissioner MOHAMED SALEM OULD MERZOUG (Mauritania).

Organization for the Management and Development of the Kagera River Basin (Organisation pour l'aménagement et le développement du bassin de la rivière Kagera—OBK): BP 297, Kigali, Rwanda; tel. (7) 84665; fax (7) 82172; f. 1978; envisages joint development and management of resources, including the construction of an 80-MW hydroelectric dam at Rusumo Falls, on the Rwanda-Tanzania border, a 2,000-km railway network between the four member countries, road construction (914 km), and a telecommunications network between member states; mems: Burundi, Rwanda, Tanzania, Uganda.

Organization of the Co-operatives of America (Organización de las Cooperativas de América): Apdo Postal 241263, Carrera 11, No 86-32, Of. 101, Bogotá, Colombia; tel. (1) 6103296; fax (1) 6101912; f. 1963 for improving socio-economic, cultural and moral conditions through the use of the co-operatives system; works in every country of the continent; regional offices sponsor plans and activities based on the most pressing needs and special conditions of individual countries; mems: national or local orgs in 23 countries and territories; Exec. Sec. Dr CARLOS JULIO PINEDA SUÁREZ; publs *América Cooperativa* (monthly), *OCA News* (monthly).

Pacific Basin Economic Council (PBEC): 2803–04, 28/F, Harbour Centre, 25 Harbour Rd Wanchai, Hong Kong SAR; tel. 2815-6550; fax 2545-0499; e-mail info@pbec.org; internet www.pbec.org; f. 1967; an asscn of business representatives aiming to promote business opportunities in the region, in order to enhance overall economic development; advises governments and serves as a liaison between business leaders and government officials; encourages business relationships and co-operation among members; holds business symposia; mems: 20 economies (Australia, Canada, Chile, People's Republic of China, Colombia, Ecuador, Hong Kong, Indonesia, Japan, Republic of Korea, Malaysia, Mexico, New Zealand, Peru, Philippines, Russia, Singapore, Taiwan, Thailand, USA); Chair. WILFRED WONG YING-WAI; publs *PBEC Update* (quarterly), *Executive Summary* (annual conference report).

Pacific Economic Cooperation Council (PECC): 29 Heng Mui Keng Terrace, Singapore 119620; tel. 67379823; fax 67379824; e-mail info@pecc.org; internet www.pecc.org; f. 1980; an independent, policy-orientated organization of senior research, government and business representatives from 26 economies in the Asia-Pacific region; aims to foster economic development in the region by providing a forum for discussion and co-operation in a wide range of economic areas; PECC is an official observer to APEC; holds a General Meeting annually; mems: Australia, Brunei, Canada, Chile, the People's Republic of China, Colombia, Ecuador, Hong Kong, Indonesia, Japan, the Republic of Korea, Malaysia, Mexico, Mongolia, New Zealand, Peru, Philippines, Singapore, Taiwan, Thailand, USA, Viet Nam and the Pacific Islands Forum; assoc. mem.: France (Pacific Territories); Sec.-Gen. EDUARDO PEDROSA; publs *Issues PECC* (quarterly), *Pacific Economic Outlook* (annually), *Pacific Food Outlook* (annually).

Pan-African Institute for Development (PAID): BP 1756, Ouagadougou 01, Burkina Faso; tel. 5036-4807; fax 5036-4730; e-mail ipdaos@fasonet.bf; internet www.ipd-aos.org; f. 1964; gives training to people from African countries involved with development at grassroots, intermediate and senior levels; emphasis is given to: development management and financing; agriculture and rural development; issues of gender and development; promotion of small and medium-sized enterprises; training policies and systems; environment, health and community development; research, support and consultancy services; and specialized training. There are four regional institutes: Central Africa (Douala, Cameroon), Sahel (Ouagadougou, Burkina Faso), West Africa (Buéa, Cameroon), Eastern and Southern Africa (Kabwe, Zambia) and a European office in Geneva; publs *Newsletter* (2 a year), *Annual Progress Report*, *PAID Report* (quarterly).

Partners in Population and Development (PPD): IPH Bldg, 2nd Floor, Mohakhali, Dhaka 1212, Bangladesh; tel. (2) 988-1882; fax (2) 882-9387; e-mail partners@ppdsec.org; internet www.partners-popdev.org; f. 1994; aims to implement the decisions of the International Conference on Population and Development, held in Cairo, Egypt in 1994, in order to expand and improve South-South collaboration in the fields of family planning and reproductive health; administers a Visionary Leadership Programme, a Global Leadership Programme, and other training and technical advisory services; mems: 24 developing countries; Exec. Dir Dr JOE THOMAS.

Permanent Interstate Committee on Drought Control in the Sahel (Comité permanent inter états de lutte contre la sécheresse au Sahel—CILSS): POB 7049, Ouagadougou 03, Burkina Faso; tel. 50-37-41-25; fax 50-37-41-32; e-mail cilss.se@cilss.bf; internet www.cilss.bf; f. 1973; works in co-operation with UNDP Drylands Development Centre; aims to combat the effects of chronic drought in the Sahel region, by improving irrigation and food production, halting deforestation and creating food reserves; initiated a series of projects to improve food security and to counter poverty, entitled Sahel 21; the heads of state of all members had signed a convention for the establishment of a Fondation pour le Développement Durable du Sahel; maintains Institut du Sahel at Bamako (Mali) and centre at Niamey (Niger); mems: Burkina Faso, Cape Verde, Chad, The Gambia, Guinea-Bissau, Mali, Mauritania, Niger, Senegal; Pres. BA MAMADOU MBARE (Mauritania); Exec. Sec. ALHOUSSEÏNI BRETAUDEAU (The Gambia); publ. *Reflets Sahéliens* (quarterly).

Population Council: 1 Dag Hammarskjöld Plaza, New York, NY 10017, USA; tel. (212) 339-0500; fax (212) 755-6052; e-mail pubinfo@popcouncil.org; internet www.popcouncil.org; f. 1952; the council is organized into three programmes: HIV and AIDS; Poverty, Gender, and Youth; and Reproductive Health; aims to improve reproductive health and achieve a balance between people and resources; analyses demographic trends; conducts biomedical research to develop new contraceptives; works with private and public agencies to improve the quality and scope of family planning and reproductive health services; helps governments to design and implement population policies; communicates results of research. Four regional offices, in India, Mexico, Egypt and Ghana, and 18 country offices in the developing world, with programmes in more than 65 countries. Additional office in Washington, DC, USA, carries out world-wide operational research and activities for reproductive health and the prevention of HIV and AIDS; Pres. PETER J. DONALDSON; publs *Momentum* (2 a year), *Studies in Family Planning* (quarterly), *Population and Development Review* (quarterly), *Population Briefs* (3 a year).

Society for International Development: Via Panisperna 207, 00184 Rome, Italy; tel. (06) 4872172; fax (06) 4872170; e-mail info@sidint.org; internet www.sidint.net; f. 1957; a global network of individuals and institutions wishing to promote participative, pluralistic and sustainable development; builds partnerships with civil society groups and other sectors; fosters local initiatives and new forms of social experimentation; mems: 3,000 individual mems and 55 institutional mems in 125 countries, 65 local chapters; Pres. JUMA V. MWAPACHU (Tanzania); Man. Dir STEFANO PRATO (Italy); publ. *Development* (quarterly).

South Centre: 17–19 Chemin du Champ-d'Anier, CP 228, 1211 Geneva 19, Switzerland; tel. 227918050; fax 227988531; e-mail south@southcentre.org; internet www.southcentre.org; f. 1990 as a follow-up mechanism of the South Commission (f. 1987); in 1995 established as an intergovernmental body to promote South-South solidarity and co-operation by generating ideas and action-oriented proposals on major policy issues; mems: 50 mem. countries; Chair. BENJAMIN WILLIAM MKAPA (Tanzania); Exec. Dir MARIN KHOR (Malaysia); publs *South Bulletin* (every 2 weeks), *Policy Brief* (monthly).

Southeast European Co-operative Initiative (SECI): Heldenplatz 1, 1010 Vienna, Austria; tel. (1) 514-36-64-22; fax (1) 531-37-420; e-mail seci2@osce.org; internet www.secinet.info; f. 1996 in order to encourage co-operation among countries of the sub-region and to facilitate their integration into European structures; receives technical support from the ECE and OSCE; ad hoc Project Groups have been established to undertake preparations for the following selected projects: commercial arbitration and mediation; co-operation between the Danube countries (particularly in the areas of policy harmonization, transport, energy, culture and education); electricity grids; energy efficiency; environmental recovery; combating organized crime; regional road transport; securities markets; trade and transport facilitation; and transport infrastructure; activities are overseen by a SECI Agenda Committee, a SECI Business Advisory Council (based in Thessaloniki, Greece) and a SECI Regional Centre for Combating Transborder Crime (based in Bucharest, Romania); mems: Albania, Bosnia and Herzegovina, Bulgaria, Croatia, Greece, Hungary, former Yugoslav republic of Macedonia, Moldova, Romania, Serbia, Slovenia, Turkey; Co-ordinator ERHARD BUSEK.

Union of the Arab Maghreb (Union du Maghreb arabe—UMA): 73 rue Tensift, Agdal, Rabat, Morocco; tel. (53) 7681371; fax (53) 7681377; e-mail sg.uma@maghrebarabe.org; internet www.maghrebarabe.org; f. 1989; aims to encourage joint ventures and to create a single market; structure comprises a council of heads of state (meeting annually), a council of ministers of foreign affairs, a follow-up committee, a consultative council of 30 delegates from each country, a UMA judicial court, and four specialized ministerial commissions. Chairmanship rotates annually between heads of state. A Maghreb Investment and Foreign Trade Bank, funding joint agricultural and industrial projects, has been established and a customs union created; mems: Algeria, Mauritania, Morocco, Tunisia; Sec.-Gen. HABIB BEN YAHIA (Tunisia).

Vienna Institute for International Dialogue and Co-operation (Wiener Institut für internationalen Dialog und Zusammenarbeit): Möllwaldplatz 5/3, 1040 Vienna, Austria; tel. (1) 713-35-94;

fax (1) 713-35-73; e-mail office@vidc.org; internet www.vidc.org; f. 1987 (as Vienna Institute for Development and Co-operation; fmrly Vienna Institute for Development, f. 1964); manages development policy research on sectoral, regional and cross-cutting issues (for example, gender issues); arranges cultural exchanges between Austria and countries from Africa, Asia and Latin America; deals with conception and organization of anti-racist and integrative measures in sport, in particular football; Pres. BARBARA PRAMMER; Dir WALTER POSCH; publs *Report Series*, *Echo*.

World Economic Forum: 91–93 route de la Capite, 1223 Cologny/Geneva, Switzerland; tel. 228691212; fax 227862744; e-mail contact@weforum.org; internet www.weforum.org; f. 1971; the Forum comprises commercial interests gathered on a non-partisan basis, under the stewardship of the Swiss Government, with the aim of improving society through economic development; convenes an annual meeting in Davos, Switzerland; organizes the following programmes: Technology Pioneers; Women Leaders; and Young Global Leaders; and aims to mobilize the resources of the global business community in the implementation of the following initiatives: the Global Health Initiative; the Disaster Relief Network; the West-Islamic World Dialogue; and the G20/International Monetary Reform Project; the Forum is governed by a guiding Foundation Board; an advisory International Business Council; and an administrative Managing Board; regular mems: representatives of 1,000 leading commercial companies in 56 countries world-wide; selected mem. companies taking a leading role in the movement's activities are known as 'partners'; Chair. KLAUS SCHWAB.

Economics and Finance

African Insurance Organization (AIO): 30 ave de Gaulle, BP 5860, Douala, Cameroon; tel. 33-42-01-63; fax 33-43-20-08; e-mail info@africaninsurance.net; internet www.african-insurance.org; f. 1972 to promote the expansion of the insurance and reinsurance industry in Africa, and to increase regional co-operation; holds annual conference, periodic seminars and workshops, and arranges meetings for reinsurers, brokers, consultant and regulators in Africa; has established African insurance 'pools' for aviation, petroleum and fire risks, and created asscns of African insurance educators, supervisory authorities and insurance brokers and consultants; Sec.-Gen. P. M. G. SOARES; publ. *African Insurance Annual Review*.

African Reinsurance Corporation (Africa-Re): Africa Re House, Plot 1679, Karimu Kotun St, Victoria Island, PMB 12765, Lagos, Nigeria; tel. (1) 2626660; fax (1) 2663282; e-mail info@africa-re.com; internet www.africa-re.com; f. 1976; its purpose is to foster the development of the insurance and reinsurance industry in Africa and to promote the growth of national and regional underwriting capacities; auth. cap. US $100m., of which the African Development Bank holds 10%; mems: 41 countries, 5 development finance institutions, and some 110 insurance and reinsurance companies; Chair. MUSA AL-NAAS; Man. Dir and CEO CORNEILLE KAREKEZI; publ. *The African Reinsurer* (annually).

African Rural and Agricultural Credit Association (AFRACA): ACK Garden House, 2nd Floor, POB 41378–00100, Nairobi, Kenya; tel. (20) 2717911; fax (20) 2710082; e-mail afraca@africaonline.co.ke; internet www.afraca.org; f. 1977 to develop the rural finance environment by adopting and promoting policy frameworks and assisting sustainable financial institutions to increase outreach; 86 mems in 27 African countries, including central, commercial and agricultural banks, micro-finance institutions, and national programmes working in the area of agricultural and rural finance in the continent; Chair. JEAN MARIE EMUNGU; publ. *Afraca Workshop Reports*; *Rural Finance Reports*.

Asian Clearing Union (ACU): Pasdaran Ave, POB 15875-7177, 16646 Tehran, Iran; tel. (21) 22842076; fax (21) 22847677; e-mail acusecret@cbi.ir; internet www.asianclearingunion.org; f. 1974; provides a facility to settle payments, on a multilateral basis, for international transactions among participating central banks, thereby contributing to the expansion of trade and economic activity among ESCAP countries; the Central Bank of Iran is the agent for the Union; units of account are, with effect from 1 Jan. 2009, denominated as the ACU dollar and the ACU euro; mems: central banks of Bangladesh, Bhutan, India, Iran, Myanmar, Nepal, Pakistan, Sri Lanka; Chair. Dr D. SUBBARAO; Sec.-Gen. LIDA BORHAN-AZAD; publs *Annual Report*, *Monthly Newsletter*.

Asian Reinsurance Corporation: 17th Floor, Tower B, Chamnan Phenjati Business Center, 65 Rama 9 Rd, Huaykwang, Bangkok 10320, Thailand; tel. (2) 245-2169; fax (2) 248-1377; e-mail asianre@asianrecorp.com; internet www.asianrecorp.com; f. 1979 under ESCAP auspices; aims to operate as a professional reinsurer serving the needs of the Asia Pacific region; also aims to provide technical assistance to national insurance markets; cap. (auth.) US $100m., (subscribed and p.u.) $30.2m. (Dec. 2010); mems: Afghanistan, Bangladesh, Bhutan, People's Republic of China, India, Iran, Republic of Korea, Philippines, Sri Lanka, Thailand; Pres. and CEO S. A. KUMAR.

Association of African Central Banks (AACB): Ave Abdoulaye Fadiga, BP 3108, Dakar, Senegal; tel. 839-05-00; fax 839-08-01; e-mail akangni@bceao.int; internet www.aacb.org; f. 1968 to promote contacts in the monetary and financial sphere, in order to increase co-operation and trade among member states; aims to strengthen monetary and financial stability on the African continent; since 2002 administers an African Monetary Co-operation Programme; mems: 40 African central banks representing 47 states; Chair. Dr PERKS LIGOYA; Exec. Sec. SAMUEL MÉANGO.

Association of African Development Finance Institutions (AADFI): Immeuble AIAFD, blvd Latrille, rue J61, Cocody Deux Plateaux, Abidjan 0, Côte d'Ivoire; tel. 22-52-33-89; fax 22-52-25-84; e-mail info@adfi-ci.org; internet www.aadfi.org; f. 1975; aims to promote co-operation among financial institutions in the region in matters relating to economic and social development, research, project design, financing and the exchange of information; mems: 92 in 43 African and non-African countries; Chair. PETER M. NONI; Sec.-Gen. JOSEPH AMIHERE; publs *Annual Report*, *AADFI Information Bulletin* (quarterly), *Finance and Development in Africa* (2 a year).

Association of Asian Confederations of Credit Unions (AACCU): U Tower Bldg 411, 8th Floor, Srinakarin Rd, Suanluang, Bangkok 10250, Thailand; tel. (2) 704-4253; fax (2) 704-4255; e-mail accu@aaccu.coop; internet www.aaccu.asia; links and promotes credit unions and co-operatives in Asia, provides research facilities and training programmes; mems: in credit union leagues and federations in 24 Asian countries; CEO RANJITH HETTIARACHCHI (Thailand); publs *ACCU News* (every 3 months), *Annual Report*, *ACCU Directory*.

Association of European Institutes of Economic Research (AIECE) (Association d'instituts européens de conjoncture économique): 3 pl. Montesquieu, 1348 Louvain-la-Neuve, Belgium; tel. (10) 47-34-26; fax (10) 47-39-45; e-mail olbrechts@aiece.org; internet www.aiece.org; f. 1957; provides a means of contact between member institutes; organizes two meetings annually, at which discussions are held on the economic situation and on a special theoretical subject; mems: 43 institutes in 20 European countries and 5 int. orgs; Admin. Sec. PAUL OLBRECHTS.

Banco del Sur (South American Bank): Caracas, Venezuela; f. Dec. 2007; formal agreement establishing the bank signed in Sept. 2009; aims to provide financing for social and investment projects in South America; auth. cap. US $20,000m.; mems: Argentina, Brazil, Bolivia, Ecuador, Paraguay, Uruguay, Venezuela.

Centre for Latin American Monetary Studies (Centro de Estudios Monetarios Latinoamericanos—CEMLA): Durango 54, Col. Roma, Del. Cuauhtémoc, 06700 México, DF, Mexico; tel. (55) 5061-6640; fax (55) 5061-6695; e-mail cemla@cemla.org; internet www.cemla.org; f. 1952; organizes technical training programmes on monetary policy, development finance, etc; runs applied research programmes on monetary and central banking policies and procedures; holds regional meetings of banking officials; mems: 30 assoc. mems (Central Banks of Latin America and the Caribbean), 23 co-operating mems (supervisory institutions of the region and non-Latin American Central Banks); Dir-Gen. JAVIER GUZMÁN CALAFELL; publs *Bulletin* (every 2 months), *Monetaria* (quarterly), *Money Affairs* (2 a year).

East African Development Bank: 4 Nile Ave, POB 7128, Kampala, Uganda; tel. (417) 112900; fax (41) 259763; e-mail info@eadb.org; internet www.eadb.org; f. 1967 by the former East African Community to promote regional development within Kenya, Tanzania and Uganda, which each hold 24.07% of the equity capital; Kenya, Tanzania and Uganda each hold 27.2% of the equity capital; the remaining equity is held by the African Development Bank (6.8%), Rwanda (4.3%) and other institutional investors; Dir-Gen. VIVIENNE YEDA APOPO.

Eastern Caribbean Central Bank (ECCB): POB 89, Basseterre, St Christopher and Nevis; tel. 465-2537; fax 465-9562; e-mail info@eccb-centralbank.org; internet www.eccb-centralbank.org; f. 1983 by OECS governments; maintains regional currency (Eastern Caribbean dollar) and advises on the economic development of member states; mems: Anguilla, Antigua and Barbuda, Dominica, Grenada, Montserrat, Saint Christopher and Nevis, Saint Lucia, Saint Vincent and the Grenadines; Gov. Sir K. DWIGHT VENNER; Man. Dir JENNIFER NERO.

Econometric Society: Dept of Economics, New York University, 19 West Fourth St, 6th Floor, New York, NY 10012, USA; tel. (212) 998-3820; fax (212) 995-4487; e-mail sashi@econometricsociety.org; internet www.econometricsociety.org; f. 1930 to promote studies aiming at a unification of the theoretical-quantitative and the empirical-quantitative approaches to economic problems; mems: c.

7,000; Pres. Bengt Holmström; Chair. Oliver Hart; publ. *Econometrica* (6 a year).

Equator Principles Association: tel. (1621) 853-900; fax (1621) 731-483; e-mail secretariat@equator-principles.com; internet www.equator-principles.com; f. July 2010; aims to administer and develop further the Equator Principles, first adopted in 2003, with the support of the International Finance Corporation, as a set of industry standards for the management of environmental and social risk in project financing; a Strategic Review conference was convened in Beijing, People's Republic of China, in Dec. 2010; 70 signed-up Equator Principles Financial Institutions (EPFIs); Administrators Joanna Clark, Samantha Hoskins.

Eurasian Development Bank: 050051 Almatı, ul. Dostık 51, Kazakhstan; tel. (727) 244-40-44; fax (727) 250-81-58; e-mail info@eabr.org; internet www.eabr.org; f. 2006; aims to facilitate the economic development of the region through investment and the promotion of trade; mems: Armenia, Belarus, Kazakhstan, Kyrgyzstan, Russia; Chair. Igor Finogenov.

European Federation of Finance House Associations (Eurofinas): 87 blvd Louis Schmidt, 1040 Brussels, Belgium; tel. (2) 778-05-60; fax (2) 778-05-78; e-mail i.vermeersch@eurofinas.org; internet www.eurofinas.org; f. 1959 to study the development of instalment credit financing in Europe, to collate and publish instalment credit statistics, and to promote research into instalment credit practice; mems: finance houses and professional asscns in 17 European countries; Chair. Pedro Guijarro; Dir-Gen. Tanguy van de Werve; publs *Eurofinas Newsletter* (monthly), *Annual Report*, *Study Reports*.

European Federation of Financial Analysts Societies (EFFAS): Mainzer Landstr. 47a, Frankfurt-am-Main, Germany; tel. (69) 264848300; fax (69) 264848335; e-mail claudia.stinnes@effas.com; internet www.effas.com; f. 1962 to co-ordinate the activities of European asscns of financial analysts; aims to raise the standard of financial analysis and improve the quality of information given to investors; encourages unification of national rules and draws up rules of profession; holds biennial congress; mems: asscns in 25 European countries; Chair. Giampaolo Trasi; Gen. Sec. Claudia Stinnes.

European Financial Management and Marketing Association (EFMA): 8 rue Bayen, 75017 Paris, France; tel. 1-47-42-52-72; fax 1-47-42-56-76; e-mail info@efma.com; internet www.efma.com; f. 1971 to link financial institutions by organizing seminars, conferences and training sessions and an annual Congress and World Convention, and by providing information services; mems: more than 3,000 financial institutions world-wide; Chair. Roberto Nicastro; Sec.-Gen. Patrick Desmarès; publ. *Newsletter*.

European Private Equity and Venture Capital Association (EVCA): Bastion Tower, 5 pl. du Champ de Mars, 1050 Brussels, Belgium; tel. (2) 715-00-20; fax (2) 725-07-04; e-mail info@evca.eu; internet www.evca.eu; f. 1983 to link private equity and venture capital companies within Europe; mems: over 950; Sec.-Gen. Dörte Höppner (Germany); publs *Yearbook*, research and special papers, legal documents, industry guidelines.

Financial Action Task Force (FATF) (Groupe d'action financière—GAFI): 2 rue André-Pascal, 75775 Paris Cédex 16, France; tel. 1-45-24-79-45; fax 1-44-30-61-37; e-mail contact@fatf-gafi.org; internet www.fatf-gafi.org; f. 1989, on the recommendation of the Group of Seven industrialized nations (G7), to develop and promote policies to combat money laundering and the financing of terrorism; formulated a set of recommendations (40+9) for countries world-wide to implement; established partnerships with regional task forces in the Caribbean, Asia-Pacific, Central Asia, Europe, East and South Africa, the Middle East and North Africa and South America; mems: 34 state jurisdictions, the European Commission, and the Cooperation Council for the Arab States of the Gulf; observers: India, Basel Committee on Banking Supervision, Eurasian Group (EAG) on combating money laundering and financing of terrorism; Pres. Giancarlo Del Bufalo (Italy); Exec. Sec. Rick McDonell; publs *Annual Report*, *e-Bulletin*.

Financial Stability Board: c/o BIS, Centralbahnplatz 2, 4002 Basel, Switzerland; tel. 612808298; fax 612809100; e-mail fsb@bis.org; internet www.financialstabilityboard.org; f. 1999 as the Financial Stability Forum, name changed in April 2009; brings together senior representatives of national financial authorities, international financial institutions, international regulatory and supervisory groupings and committees of central bank experts and the European Central Bank; aims to promote international financial stability and strengthen the functioning of the financial markets; in March 2009 agreed to expand its membership to include all Group of 20 (G20) economies, as well as Spain and the European Commission; in April 2009 the meeting of G20 heads of state and government determined to re-establish the then Forum as the Financial Stability Board, strengthen its institutional structure (to include a plenary body, a steering committee and three standing committees concerned with Vulnerabilities Assessment; Supervisory and Regulatory Co-operation; and Standards Implementation) and expand its mandate to enhance its effectiveness as an international mechanism to promote financial stability; the Board was to strengthen its collaboration with the International Monetary Fund, and conduct joint 'early warning exercises'; in Dec. 2009 the Board initiated a peer review of implementation of the Principles and Standards for Sound Compensation Practices; in Nov. 2010 determined to establish six FSB regional consultative groups; Chair. Mark Carney (Canada).

Fonds Africain de Garantie et de Co-opération Economique (FAGACE) (African Guarantee and Economic Co-operation Fund): 01 BP 2045 RP, Cotonou, Benin; tel. 30-03-76; fax 30-02-84; e-mail fagace_dg@yahoo.fr; internet www.le-fagace.org; commenced operations in 1981; guarantees loans for development projects, provides loans and grants for specific operations and supports national and regional enterprises; mems: 13 African countries; Dir-Gen. Henri Marie Jeanneney Dondra.

Group of Seven (G7): f. 1975 as an informal framework of co-operation; despite the formation in 1998 of the Group of Eight (G8), incorporating Russia, and the inclusion of Russia in all G8 sectoral areas from 2003, the Group of Seven major industrialized countries (G7) remains a forum for regular discussion (at the level of ministers of finance and central bank governors) of developments in the global economy and of economic policy; the IMF Managing Director is normally invited to participate in G7 meetings; mems: ministers of finance and central bank governors of Canada, France, Germany, Italy, Japan, United Kingdom and the USA; European Union representation.

Group of 20 (G20): internet www.g20.org; f. Sept. 1999 as an informal deliberative forum of finance ministers and central bank governors representing both industrialized and 'systemically important' emerging market nations; aims to strengthen the international financial architecture and to foster sustainable economic growth and development; in 2004 participating countries adopted the G20 Accord for Sustained Growth and stated a commitment to high standards of transparency and fiscal governance; the IMF Managing Director and IBRD President participate in G20 annual meetings; an extraordinary Summit on Financial Markets and the World Economy was convened in Washington, DC, USA, in November 2008, attended by heads of state or government of G20 member economies; a second summit meeting, held in London, United Kingdom, in April 2009, issued as its final communiqué a *Global Plan for Recovery and Reform* outlining commitments to restore economic confidence, growth and jobs, to strengthen financial supervision and regulation, to reform and strengthen global financial institutions, to promote global trade and investment and to ensure a fair and sustainable economic recovery; detailed declarations were also issued on measures agreed to deliver substantial resources (of some US $850,000m.) through international financial institutions and on reforms to be implemented in order to strengthen the financial system; as a follow-up to the London summit, G20 heads of state met in Pittsburgh, USA, in Sept. 2009; the meeting adopted a *Framework for Strong, Sustainable, and Balanced Growth* and resolved to expand the role of the G20 to be at the centre of future international economic policymaking; summit meetings were held in June 2010, in Canada (at the G8 summit), and in Seoul, Republic of Korea, in November; the sixth G20 summit, held in Cannes, France, in Nov. 2011, concluded an *Action Plan for Growth and Jobs* but was dominated by discussion of measures to secure financial stability in the 'eurozone' countries; seventh summit to be convened in Los Cabos, Baja California Sur, Mexico, in June 2012; mems: Argentina, Australia, Brazil, Canada, People's Republic of China, France, Germany, India, Indonesia, Italy, Japan, Republic of Korea, Mexico, Russia, Saudi Arabia, South Africa, Turkey, United Kingdom, USA and the European Union; observers: Netherlands, Spain.

Insurance Europe: 51 rue Montoyer, 1000 Brussels, Belgium; tel. (2) 894-30-00; fax (2) 894-30-01; e-mail info@insuranceeurope.eu; internet www.insuranceeurope.eu; f. 1953 as the CEA (Comité Européen de Assurances) to represent the interests of European insurers, to encourage co-operation between members, to allow the exchange of information and to conduct studies; mems: national insurance asscns of 33 full mems, Russia and Ukraine observers; Pres. Sergio Balbinot (Italy); Dir-Gen. Michaela Koller (Germany); publs *European Insurance in Figures* (annually), *Indirect Taxation on Insurance Contracts* (annually).

Intergovernmental Group of 24 (G24) on International Monetary Affairs and Development: 700 19th St, NW, Rm 3-600 Washington, DC 20431, USA; tel. (202) 623-6101; fax (202) 623-6000; e-mail g24@g24.org; internet www.g24.org; f. 1971; aims to co-ordinate the position of developing countries on monetary and development finance issues; operates at the political level of ministers of finance and governors of central banks, and also at the level of government officials; mems (Africa): Algeria, Côte d'Ivoire, DRC, Egypt, Ethiopia, Gabon, Ghana, Nigeria, South Africa; (Latin America and the Caribbean): Argentina, Brazil, Colombia, Guatemala, Mexico, Peru, Trinidad and Tobago and

Venezuela; (Asia and the Middle East): India, Iran, Lebanon, Pakistan, Philippines, Sri Lanka and Syrian Arab Republic; the People's Republic of China has the status of special invitee at G24 meetings; G77 participant states may attend G24 meetings as observers.

International Accounting Standards Board (IASB): 30 Cannon St, London, EC4M 6XH, United Kingdom; tel. (20) 7246-6410; fax (20) 7246-6411; e-mail info@ifrs.org; internet www.iasb.org.uk; f. 1973 as International Accounting Standards Committee, reorganized and present name adopted 2001; aims to develop, in the public interest, a single set of high-quality, uniform, clear and enforceable global accounting standards requiring the submission of high-quality, transparent and comparable information in financial statements and other financial reporting, in order to assist participants in world-wide capital markets and other end-users to make informed decisions on economic matters; aims also to promote the use and rigorous application of these global accounting standards, and to bring about the convergence of these with national accounting standards; Chair. and CEO Hans Hoogervorst; publs *IASB Insight* (quarterly), *Bound Volume of International Accounting Standards* (annually), *Interpretations of International Accounting Standards*.

International Association for Research in Income and Wealth: 151 Slater St, Suite 710, Ottawa, Ontario, K1P 5H3, Canada; tel. (613) 233-8891; fax (613) 233-8250; e-mail info@iariw.org; internet www.iariw.org; f. 1947 to further research in the general field of national income and wealth and related topics by the organization of biennial conferences and other means; mems: approx. 400; Chair. Peter van de Ven (Netherlands); Exec. Dir Andrew Sharpe (Canada); publ. *Review of Income and Wealth* (quarterly).

International Association of Deposit Insurers: c/o BIS, Centralbahnplatz 2, 4002 Basel, Switzerland; tel. 612809933; fax 612809554; e-mail service.iadi@bis.org; internet www.iadi.org; f. 2002; aims to contribute to the stability of the international financial system by promoting co-operation among deposit insurers and establishing effective systems; mems: 64 orgs, 8 assoc. and 12 partners; Acting Chair. Martin J. Gruenberg; Sec.-Gen. Carlos Isoard.

International Association of Insurance Supervisors: c/o BIS, Centralbahnplatz 2, 4002 Basel, Switzerland; tel. 612257300; fax 612809151; e-mail iais@bis.org; internet www.iaisweb.org; f. 1994 to improve supervision of the insurance industry and promote global financial stability; Sec.-Gen. Yoshihiro Kawai.

International Bureau of Fiscal Documentation (IBFD): H. J. E. Wenckebachweg 210, 1096 AS Amsterdam, Netherlands; tel. (20) 5540100; fax (20) 6228658; e-mail info@ibfd.org; internet www.ibfd.org; f. 1938 to supply information on fiscal law and its application; maintains library on international taxation; Chair. S. R. B. van der Feltz; publs *Bulletin for International Fiscal Documentation*, *Asia Pacific Tax Bulletin*, *Derivatives and Financial Instruments*, *European Taxation*, *International VAT Monitor*, *International Transfer Pricing Journal*, *Supplementary Service to European Taxation* (all monthly), *Tax News Service* (weekly); studies, databases, regional tax guides.

International Capital Market Association (ICMA): Talacker 29, 8001 Zürich, Switzerland; tel. 443634222; fax 443637772; e-mail info@icma-group.org; internet www.icma-group.org; f. 2005 by merger of International Primary Market Association (IPMA) and International Securities Association (ISMA), f. 1969; maintains and develops an efficient and cost-effective market for capital; mems: 400 banks and major financial institutions in 47 countries; Chair. Martin Scheck; publs reports and market surveys.

International Centre for Local Credit: Tour Dexia 2, 92919 La Défense, France; tel. 1-58-58-75-69; fax 1-58-58-87-40; e-mail estelle.ricque-mathien@dexia.com; internet www.iclc.eu; f. 1958 to promote local authority credit by gathering, exchanging and distributing information and advice on member institutions and on local authority credit and related subjects; studies important subjects in the field of local authority credit; mems: 14 financial institutions; Gen. Sec. Pierre Mariani (France); publs *Bulletin*, *Newsletter* (quarterly).

International Economic Association: c/o Instituto de Análisis Económico, Campus de la UAB, 08193 Barcelona, Spain; tel. (93) 5806612; fax (93) 5805214; e-mail iea@iea-world.org; internet www.iea-world.com; f. 1949 to promote international collaboration for the advancement of economic knowledge and develop personal contacts between economists, and to encourage the provision of means for the dissemination of economic knowledge; mems: asscns in 59 countries; Pres. Joseph Stiglitz; Sec.-Gen. Joan Esteban.

International Federation of Accountants: 529 Fifth Ave, 6th Floor, New York, NY 10017, USA; tel. (212) 286-9344; fax (212) 286-9570; e-mail communications@ifac.org; internet www.ifac.org; f. 1977 to develop a co-ordinated world-wide accounting profession with harmonized standards; mems: 167 accountancy bodies in 127 countries; Pres. Göran Tidström (Sweden); Chief Exec. Ian Ball.

International Fiscal Association (IFA): World Trade Center, POB 30215, 3001 DE Rotterdam, Netherlands; tel. (10) 4052990; fax (10) 4055031; e-mail a.gensecr@ifa.nl; internet www.ifa.nl; f. 1938 to study international and comparative public finance and fiscal law, especially taxation; holds annual congresses; mems in 106 countries and branches in 62 countries; Pres. M. E. Tron (Mexico); Sec.-Gen. Prof. H. A. Kogels (Netherlands); publs *Cahiers de Droit Fiscal International*, *Yearbook of the International Fiscal Association*, *IFA Congress Seminar Series*.

International Institute of Public Finance e.V.: POB 860446, 81631 Munich, Germany; tel. (89) 9224-1281; fax (89) 907795-2281; e-mail info@iipf.org; internet www.iipf.org; f. 1937; a private scientific organization aiming to establish contacts between people of every nationality, whose main or supplementary activity consists in the study of public finance; holds annual congress devoted to a specific scientific subject; 800 mems; Pres. Robin Boadway (Canada).

International Organization of Securities Commissions (IOSCO): Calle Oquendo 12, 28006 Madrid, Spain; tel. (91) 417-5549; fax (91) 555-9368; e-mail mail@iosco.org; internet www.iosco.org; f. 1983 to facilitate co-operation between securities and futures regulatory bodies at the international level; in 1998 adopted the Objectives and Principles of Securities Regulation (the IOSCO Principles); mems: 188 agencies; Chair. Jane Diplock (New Zealand); Sec.-Gen. David Wright; publs *Annual Report*, *IOSCO News* (3 a year).

International Union for Housing Finance (IUHF): 71 ave de Cortenbergh, 8th Floor, 1000 Brussels, Belgium; tel. (2) 285- 40-30; fax (2) 285-40-31; e-mail info@housingfinance.org; internet www.housingfinance.org; f. 1914 to foster world-wide interest in savings and home ownership and co-operation among members; encourages comparative study of methods and practice in housing finance; promotes development of appropriate legislation on housing finance; mems: 108 in over 49 countries; Sec.-Gen. Annik Lambert (Belgium); publ. *Housing Finance International* (quarterly).

Islamic Financial Services Board: Level 5, Sasana Kijang, Bank Negara Malaysia, 2 Jalan Dato Onn, 50840 Kuala Lumpur, Malaysia; tel. (3) 91951400; fax (3) 91951405; e-mail ifsb_sec@ifsb.org; internet www.ifsb.org; f. 2002; aims to formulate standards and guiding principles for regulatory and supervisory agencies working within the Islamic financial services industry; mems: 27 full mems (incl. Islamic Development Bank), 26 assoc. mems (incl. Asian Development Bank, the Bank for International Settlements, the IMF and the World Bank), and 136 observer mems; Sec.-Gen. Jaseem Ahmed.

Latin American Banking Federation (Federación Latinoamericana de Bancos—FELABAN): Cra 11A No. 93-67 Of. 202 A.A 091959, Bogotá, Colombia; tel. (1) 6215848; fax (1) 6217659; e-mail mangarita@felaban.com; internet www.felaban.com; f. 1965 to co-ordinate efforts towards wide and accelerated economic development in Latin American countries; mems: 19 Latin American national banking asscns, representing more than 500 banks and financial institutions; Pres. Oscar Rivera (Peru); Sec.-Gen. Giorgio Trettenero Castro (Peru).

Nordic Investment Bank (NIB) (Nordiska Investeringsbanken): Fabianinkatu 34, POB 249, 00171 Helsinki, Finland; tel. (10) 618001; fax (10) 6180725; e-mail info@nib.int; internet www.nib.int; f. 1975; provides long-term loans and guarantees for both public and private projects in and outside its member countries; main focus areas of the Bank are energy, environment, transport, logistics, communications, and innovation; mems: Governments of Denmark, Estonia, Finland, Iceland, Latvia, Lithuania, Norway and Sweden; Pres. and CEO Henrik Normann.

Nordic Project Fund (Nopef): POB 241, 00171 Helsinki, Finland; tel. (9) 6840570; fax (9) 650113; e-mail ib.sonnerstad@nopef.com; internet www.nopef.com; f. 1982; aims to strengthen the international competitiveness of Nordic exporting cos, and to promote industrial co-operation in international projects (e.g. in environmental protection); grants loans to Nordic cos for feasibility expenses relating to projects; with effect from 1 Jan. 2008 Nopef's geographical target area expanded to include Bulgaria, Romania and countries outside the EU and EFTA; Chair. Bo Jerlström; Man. Dir Ib Sønnerstad.

Union of Arab Banks (UAB): POB 11-2416, Riad El-Solh 1107 2210, Beirut, Lebanon; tel. (1) 377800; fax (1) 364927; e-mail uab@uabonline.org; internet www.uabonline.org; f. 1972; aims to foster co-operation between Arab banks and to increase their efficiency; prepares feasibility studies for projects; 2007 Arab Banking Conference: Tripoli, Libya; mems: more than 300 Arab banks and financial institutions; Chair. Adnan Youssif (Bahrain); Sec.-Gen. Wissam Hassan Fattouh (Lebanon).

World Council of Credit Unions (WOCCU): POB 2982, 5710 Mineral Point Rd, Madison, WI 53705-4493, USA; tel. (608) 395-2000; fax (608) 395-2001; e-mail mail@woccu.org; internet www.woccu.org; f. 1970 to link credit unions and similar co-operative financial institutions and assist them in expanding and improving their services; provides technical and financial assistance to credit union asscns in developing countries; mems: 54,000 credit unions in 97 countries; Pres. and CEO BRIAN BRANCH; publs *WOCCU Annual Report*, *Credit Union World* (3 a year), *Spotlights On Development*; technical monographs and brochures.

World Federation of Exchanges: 176 rue de Rivoli, 75001 Paris, France; tel. 1-58-62-54-00; fax 1-58-62-50-48; e-mail secretariat@world-exchanges.org; internet www.world-exchanges.org; f. 1961; fmrly Fédération Internationale des Bourses de Valeurs—FIBV; central reference point for the securities industry; offers member exchanges guidance in business strategies, and improvement and harmonization of management practices; works with public financial authorities to promote increased use of regulated securities and derivatives exchanges; mems: 57 full mems, 21 affiliates and 34 corresponding exchanges; Chair. RONALDI ARCULLI; Sec.-Gen. THOMAS KRANTZ.

World Savings Banks Institute: 11 rue Marie Thérèse, 1000 Brussels, Belgium; tel. (2) 211-11-11; fax (2) 211-11-99; e-mail info@savings-banks.com; internet www.wsbi.org; f. 1924 as International Savings Banks Institute, present name and structure adopted in 1994; promotes co-operation among members and the development of savings banks world-wide; mems: 104 banks and asscns in 86 countries; Pres. and Chair. JOSÉ ANTONIO OLAVARRIETA ARCOS (Spain); Man. Dir CHRIS DE NOOSE; publs *Annual Report*, *International Savings Banks Directory*, *Perspectives* (4–5 a year).

Education

Agence Universitaire de la Francophonie (AUF): Case postale du Musée, CP 49714, Montréal, QC H3T 2A5, Canada; tel. (514) 343-6630; fax (514) 343-2107; e-mail rectorat@auf.org; internet www.auf.org; f. 1961; aims to develop a francophone university community, through building partnerships with students, teachers, institutions and governments; mems: 67 institutions in 40 countries; Pres. YVON FONTAINE (Canada); Exec. Dir. BERNARD CERQUIGLINI; publ. *Le Français à l'Université* (quarterly).

AMSE-AMCE-WAER (Association mondiale des sciences de l'éducation) (Asociación mundial de ciencias de la educación) (World Association for Educational Research): c/o Yves Lenoir, Faculty of Education, Sherbrooke Univ., 2500 blvd de l'Université Sherbrooke, QC J1K 2R1, Canada; tel. (819) 821-8000; fax (819) 829-5343; e-mail wera@aera.net; internet www.weraonline.org; f. 1953, present title adopted 2004; aims to encourage research in educational sciences by organizing congresses, issuing publications and supporting the exchange of information; mems: 27 research associations; Pres. EVA BAKER (until 30 June 2012), YIN CHEONG CHENG (elect, 1 July 2012–30 June 2014), Dr SARI LINDBLOM-YLÄNNE (Finland) (elect, 1 July 2014–30 June 2016); Sec.-Gen. FELICE LEVINE; publ. *Educational Research around the World*.

Asian Institute of Technology (AIT): POB 4, Klong Luang, Pathumthani 12120, Thailand; tel. (2) 516-0144; fax (2) 516-2126; e-mail president@ait.ac.th; internet www.ait.ac.th; f. 1959; Master's, Doctor's and Diploma programmes are offered in four schools: Advanced Technologies, Civil Engineering, Environment, Resources and Development, and Management; specialized training is provided by the Center for Library and Information Resources (CLAIR), the Continuing Education Center, the Center for Language and Educational Technology, the Regional Computer Center, the AIT Center in Viet Nam (based in Hanoi) and the Swiss-AIT-Viet Nam Management Development Program (in Ho Chi Minh City); other research and outpost centres are the Asian Center for Engineering Computations and Software, the Asian Center for Research on Remote Sensing, the Regional Environmental Management Center, the Asian Center for Soil Improvement and Geosynthetics and the Urban Environmental Outreach Center; there are four specialized information centres (on ferro-cement, geotechnical engineering, renewable energy resources, environmental sanitation) under CLAIR; the Management of Technology Information Center conducts short-term courses in the management of technology and international business; Pres. Prof. SAID IRANDOUST; publs *AIT Annual Report*, *Annual Report on Research and Activities*, *AIT Review* (3 a year), *Prospectus*, other specialized publs.

Asian South Pacific Bureau of Adult Education (ASPBAE): c/o MAAPL, Eucharistic Congress Bldg No. 3, 9th Floor, 5 Convent St, Colaba, Mumbai 400 039, India; tel. (22) 22021391; fax (22) 22832217; e-mail aspbae@vsnl.com; internet www.aspbae.org; f. 1964 to assist non-formal education and adult literacy; organizes training courses and seminars; provides material and advice relating to adult education; mems in 31 countries and territories; Sec.-Gen. MARIA-LOURDES ALMAZAN-KHAN; publ. *ASPBAE News* (3 a year).

Association for Childhood Education International: 17904 Georgia Ave, Suite 215, Olney, MD 20832, USA; tel. (301) 570-2111; fax (301) 570-2212; e-mail headquarters@acei.org; internet www.acei.org; f. 1892 to work for the education of children (from infancy through early adolescence) by promoting desirable conditions in schools, raising the standard of teaching, co-operating with all groups concerned with children, informing the public of the needs of children; mems: 12,000; Pres. DEBORAH WISNESKI; Exec. Dir DIANE WHITEHEAD; publs *Childhood Education* (6 a year), *Professional Focus Newsletters*, *Journal of Research in Childhood Education* (quarterly), books on current educational subjects.

Association for the Development of Education in Africa: c/o Temporary Relocation Agency, 13 ave du Ghana, BP 323, 1002 Tunis, Tunisia; tel. 71-10-39-00; e-mail adea@afdb.org; internet www.adeanet.org; f. 1988 as Donors to African Education, adopted present name in 1995; aims to enhance collaboration in the support of African education; promotes policy dialogue and undertakes research, advocacy and capacity-building in areas of education in sub-Saharan Africa through programmes and working groups comprising representatives of donor countries and African ministries of education; Exec. Sec. AHLIN BYLL-CATARIA.

Association Montessori Internationale: Koninginneweg 161, 1075 CN Amsterdam, Netherlands; tel. (20) 6798932; fax (20) 6767341; e-mail info@montessori-ami.org; internet www.montessori-ami.org; f. 1929 to propagate the ideals and educational methods of Dr Maria Montessori on child development, without racial, religious or political prejudice; organizes training courses for teachers in 18 countries; world congress held every four years (2013: Portland, OR, USA, in July–Aug.); Pres. ANDRÉ ROBERFROID (Belgium); Exec. Dir LYNNE LAWRENCE (United Kingdom); publs *Communications* (2 a year), *AMI Bulletin*.

Association of African Universities (AAU) (Association des universités africaines): POB 5744, Accra-North, Ghana; tel. (21) 774495; fax (21) 774821; e-mail info@aau.org; internet www.aau.org; f. 1967 to promote exchanges, contact and co-operation among African university institutions and to collect and disseminate information on research and higher education in Africa; mems: 225 in 44 countries; Acting Pres. GEORGE ALBERT MAGOHA (Kenya); Sec.-Gen. Prof. OLUGBEMIRO JEGEDE (Nigeria); publs *AAU Newsletter* (3 a year), *Directory of African Universities* (every 2 years).

Association of Arab Universities: POB 2000, Amman, Jordan 13110; tel. (6) 5345131; fax (6) 5332994; e-mail secgen@aaru.edu.jo; internet www.aaru.edu.jo; f. 1964; a scientific conference is held every three years; council meetings held annually; mems: 163 universities; Sec.-Gen. Prof. Dr SALEH HASHEM; publ. *AARU Bulletin* (annually and quarterly, in Arabic).

Association of Caribbean University and Research Institutional Libraries (ACURIL): Apdo postal 21609, San Juan 00931-1906, Puerto Rico; tel. 763-6199; e-mail executivesecretariat@acuril.org; internet www.acuril.uprrp.edu; f. 1968 to foster contact and collaboration between mem. universities and institutes; holds conferences, meetings and seminars; circulates information through newsletters and bulletins; facilitates co-operation and the pooling of resources in research; encourages exchange of staff and students; mems: 250; Pres. FRANCOISE THYBULLE; Exec.-Sec. LUISA VIGO-CEPEDA; publ. *Cybernotes*.

Association of South-East Asian Institutions of Higher Learning (ASAIHL): Secretariat, Rm 113, Jamjuree 1 Bldg, Chulalongkorn University, Phyathai Rd, Bangkok 10330, Thailand; tel. (2) 251-6966; fax (2) 253-7909; e-mail ninnat.o@chula.ac.th; internet www.seameo.org/asaihl; f. 1956 to promote the economic, cultural and social welfare of the people of South-East Asia by means of educational co-operation and research programmes; and to cultivate a sense of regional identity and interdependence; collects and disseminates information, organizes discussions; mems: 170 university institutions in 20 countries; Pres. NARCISO ERGUIZA; Sec.-Gen. Dr NINNAT OLANVORAVUTH; publs *Newsletter*, *Handbook* (every 3 years).

Catholic International Education Office: 718 ave Houba de Strooper, 1020 Brussels, Belgium; tel. (2) 230-72-52; fax (2) 230-97-45; e-mail info@infoiec.org; internet www.infoiec.org; f. 1952 for the study of the problems of Catholic education throughout the world; co-ordinates the activities of members; represents Catholic education at international bodies; mems: 102 countries, 18 assoc. mems, 13 collaborating mems, 6 corresponding mems; Pres. Mgr CARLOS PELLEGRIN; Sec.-Gen. ÁNGEL ASTORGANO; publs *OIEC Bulletin* (every 3 months, in English, French and Spanish), *OIEC Tracts on Education*.

Comparative Education Society in Europe (CESE): European University of Cyprus, POB 22006, 6 Diogenes Street, 1516 Nicosia, Cyprus; e-mail e.klerides@euc.ac.cy; internet www.cese-europe.org; f. 1961 to promote teaching and research in comparative and international education; organizes conferences and promotes literature; mems: in 49 countries; Pres. MIGUEL PEREYRA (Spain); Sec. and Treas. ELEFTHERIOS KLERIDES (Cyprus); publ. *Newsletter* (quarterly).

Council of Legal Education (CLE): c/o Registrar, POB 323, Tunapuna, Trinidad and Tobago; tel. 662-5860; fax 662-0927; f. 1971; responsible for the training of members of the legal profession; mems: govts of 12 countries and territories.

Education Action International: 14 Dufferin St, London, EC1Y 8PD, United Kingdom; tel. (20) 7426 5800; e-mail international@education-action.org; f. 1920, as European Student Relief; focuses on improving the lives of people in conflict-affected countries and fragile states and refugees from war living in the UK through education.

European Association for Education of Adults (EAEA): 40 rue d'Arlon, 1000 Brussels, Belgium; tel. (2) 234-37-63; fax (2) 235-05-39; e-mail eaea-info@eaea.org; internet www.eaea.org; f. 1953; aims to create a 'learning society' by encouraging demand for learning, particularly from women and excluded sectors of society; seeks to improve response of providers of learning opportunities and authorities and agencies; mems: 127 orgs in 43 countries; Pres. SUSAN WADDINGTON; Gen. Sec. GINA EBNER; publs *EAEA Monograph Series*, newsletter.

European Federation for Catholic Adult Education (Federation Européene pour l'Éducation Catholique des Adultes—FEECA): Joachimstr. 1, 53113 Bonn, Germany; tel. (228) 9024710; fax (228) 9024729; e-mail hoffmeier@kbe-bonn.de; internet www.feeca.org; f. 1963 to strengthen international contact between mems and to assist with international research and practical projects in adult education; holds conference every two years; Vice-Pres. ANDREA HOFFMEIER (Germany).

European Foundation for Management Development (EFMD): 88 rue Gachard, 1050 Brussels, Belgium; tel. (2) 629-08-10; fax (2) 629-08-11; e-mail info@efmd.org; internet www.efmd.org; f. 1971 through merger of European Association of Management Training Centres and International University Contact for Management Education; aims to help improve the quality of management development, disseminate information within the economic, social and cultural context of Europe and promote international co-operation; mems: over 500 institutions in 65 countries world-wide (28 in Europe); Pres. ALAIN DOMINQUE PERRIN; Dir-Gen. ERIC CORNUEL; publs *Forum* (3 a year), *The Bulletin* (3 a year), *Guide to European Business Schools and Management Centres* (annually).

European Union of Arabic and Islamic Scholars (Union Européenne des Arabisants et Islamisants—UEAI): c/o Bernadette Martel-Thoumian, Université de Grenoble, BP 47, 38040 Grenoble, Cédex 9, France; e-mail info@ueai.eu; internet www.ueai.eu; f. 1962 to organize congresses of Arabic and Islamic Studies; holds congress every two years; mems: 300 in 28 countries; Pres. SEBASTIAN GÜNTHER (Germany); Sec.-Gen. Prof. BERNADETTE MARTEL-THOUMIAN (France).

European University Association (EUA): Ave de l'Yser 24, 1040 Brussels, Belgium; tel. (2) 230-55-44; fax (2) 230-57-51; e-mail info@eua.be; internet www.eua.be; f. 2001 by merger of the Association of European Universities and the Confederation of EU Rectors' Conferences; represents European universities and national rectors' conferences; promotes the development of a coherent system of European higher education and research through projects and membership services; provides support and guidance to mems; mems: more than 850 in 47 countries; Pres. Prof. MARIA HELENA NAZARÉ; Sec.-Gen. LESLEY WILSON; publs *Thema*, *Directory*, *Annual Report*.

Graduate Institute of International and Development Studies (Institut universitaire de hautes études internationales—HEI): POB 136, 132 rue de Lausanne, 1211 Geneva 21, Switzerland; tel. 229085700; fax 229085710; e-mail info@graduateinstitute.ch; internet graduateinstitute.ch; f. 1927, as the Graduate Institute of International Studies, to establish a centre for advanced studies in international relations of the present day; merged with the Graduate Institute of Development Studies in 2008; maintains a library of 147,000 vols; Dir Prof. PHILIPPE BURRIN.

Inter-American Centre for Research and Documentation on Vocational Training (Centro Interamericano de Investigación y Documentación sobre Formación Profesional—CINTERFOR): Avda Uruguay 1238, Casilla de correo 1761, Montevideo, Uruguay; tel. 2902 0557; fax 2902 1305; e-mail oitcinterfor@oitcinterfor.org; internet wwww.oitcinterfor.org; f. 1964 by the International Labour Organization for mutual help among the Latin American and Caribbean countries in planning vocational training; services are provided in documentation, research, exchange of experience; holds seminars and courses; Dir MARTHA PACHECA; publs *Bulletin CINTERFOR/OIT Heramientas para la transformación*, *Trazos de la formación*, studies, monographs and technical papers.

Inter-American Confederation for Catholic Education (Confederación Interamericana de Educación Católica—CIEC): Carrera 24, No. 34, Bogotá 37 DC, Colombia; tel. (1) 2871036; e-mail asistente@ciec.edu.co; internet www.ciec.edu.co; f. 1945 to defend and extend the principles and rules of Catholic education, freedom of education, and human rights; organizes congress every three years (2010: Santo Domingo, Dominican Republic); Sec.-Gen. PADRE JOSÉ LEONARDO RINCÓN CONTRERAS (Colombia); publ. *Educación Hoy*.

Inter-American Organization for Higher Education (IOHE): 475 rue du Parvis, bureau 1338, Québec, QC G1K 9H7, Canada; tel. (418) 657-4350; fax (418) 657-4150; e-mail sec.general@oui-iohe.org; internet www.oui-iohe.org; f. 1980 to promote co-operation among universities of the Americas and the development of higher education; mems: some 265 institutions and 34 national and regional higher education asscns; Exec. Dir PATRICIA GUDIÑO.

International Anti-Corruption Academy (IACA): Muenchendorfer Strasse 2, 2361 Laxenburg, Austria; tel. (2236) 710-71-81-00; fax (2236) 710-71-83-11; e-mail mail@iaca.int; internet www.iaca.int; f. March 2011, as a joint initiative by the United Nations Office on Drugs and Crime (UNODC), the European Anti-Fraud Office (OLAF) and others; aims to expand existing knowledge and practice in the field of anti-corruption; Pres. EUGENIO M. CURIA (Argentina); Exec. Sec. MARTIN KREUTNER.

International Association for Educational and Vocational Guidance (IAEVG): 119 Ross Ave, Suite 202, Ottawa, ON K1Y 0N6, Canada; tel. (613) 729-6164; fax (613) 729-3515; e-mail membership@iaevg.org; internet www.iaevg.org; f. 1951 to contribute to the development of vocational guidance and promote contact between persons associated with it; mems: over 22,000 individuals; Pres. LESTER OAKES (New Zealand); Sec.-Gen. SUZANNE BULTHEEL (France); publs *IAEVG Journal* (2 a year), *Newsletter* (3 a year).

International Association for the Development of Documentation, Libraries and Archives in Africa: Villa 2547 Dieuppeul II, BP 375, Dakar, Senegal; tel. 824-09-54; f. 1957 to organize and develop documentation and archives in all African countries; mems: national asscns, institutions and individuals in 48 countries; Sec.-Gen. ZACHEUS SUNDAY ALI (Nigeria).

International Association of Educators for World Peace: POB 3282, Mastin Lake Station, Huntsville, AL 35810-0282, USA; tel. (256) 534-5501; fax (256) 536-1018; e-mail mercieca@knology.net; internet www.iaewp.org; f. 1969 to develop education designed to contribute to the promotion of peaceful relations at personal, community and international levels; aims to communicate and clarify controversial views in order to achieve maximum understanding; organizes annual World Peace Congress; helps put into practice the Universal Declaration of Human Rights; mems: 55,000 in 80 countries; Pres. Dr CHARLES MERCIECA (USA); Sec.-Gen. NENAD JAVORNIK (Croatia); publs *Diplomacy Journal* (every 3 months), *Peace Education Journal* (annually), other articles and irregular publications.

International Association of Papyrologists (Association Internationale de Papyrologues): Association Egyptologique Reine Elisabeth, Parc du Cinquantenaire 10, 1000 Brussels, Belgium; tel. (2) 741-73-64; e-mail amartin@ulb.ac.be; internet www.ulb.ac.be/assoc/aip; f. 1947; links all those interested in Graeco-Roman Egypt, especially Greek texts; mem. of the International Federation of the Societies of Classical Studies; mems: about 400; Pres. Prof. ROGER S. BAGNALL (USA); Sec./Treas. Prof. ALAIN MARTIN (Belgium).

International Association of Physical Education in Higher Education (Association Internationale des Écoles Supérieures d'Éducation Physique—AIESEP): Department of Sport Sciences, University of Liège, Allée des Sports, 4 Bât B-21 B-4000 Liège, Belgium; tel. (4) 366-38-80; fax (4) 366-29-01; e-mail marc.cloes@ulg.ac.be; internet www.aiesep.org; f. 1962; organizes congresses, exchanges, and research in physical education; mems: institutions in 51 countries; Sec.-Gen. Dr MARC CLOES.

International Association of Universities (IAU): 1 rue Miollis, 75732 Paris cédex 15, France; tel. 1-45-68-48-00; fax 1-47-34-76-05; e-mail iau@iau-aiu.net; internet www.iau-aiu.net; f. 1948 to allow co-operation at the international level among universities and other institutions and organizations of higher education; provides clearing-house services and operates the joint IAU/UNESCO Information Centre on Higher Education; brings together institutions and organizations from some 160 countries for reflection and action on common concerns, and collaborates with various international, regional and national bodies active in higher education; incorporates the International Universities Bureau (IUB); mems: more than 600 institutions of higher education and other organizations concerned with higher education in some 160 countries; Pres. JUAN RAMON DE LA FUENTE (Mexico); Sec.-Gen. and Exec. Dir EVA EGRON-POLAK; *Higher Education Policy* (quarterly), *IAU Horizons* (3 a year), *International Handbook of Universities* (annually), *World Higher Education Database (WHED) CD-ROM* (annually).

International Association of University Professors and Lecturers (IAUPL) (Association Internationale des Professeurs et Maîtres de Conférence Universitaires): c/o Prof. Michel Gay, 4 rue de Trévise, 75009, Paris, France; tel. 1-44-90-01-01; fax 1-46-59-01-23; e-mail migay@laposte.net; f. 1945 for the development of academic fraternity among university teachers and research workers; the protection of independence and freedom of teaching and research; the furtherance of the interests of all university teachers; and the consideration of academic problems; mems: federations in 13 countries and territories.

International Baccalaureate Organization (IBO): 15 route des Morillons, Grand-Saconnex 1218, Geneva, Switzerland; tel. 227917740; fax 227910277; e-mail ibhq@ibo.org; internet www.ibo.org; f. 1968 to plan curricula and an international university entrance examination, the International Baccalaureate diploma, recognized by major universities world-wide; offers the Primary Years Programme for children aged 3–12, the Middle Years Programme for students in the 11–16 age range, and the Diploma Programme for 17–18-year-olds; mems: 2,217 participating schools in 125 countries; Pres. of Bd of Governors MONIQUE SEEFRIED (France/USA); Dir-Gen. JEFFREY BEARD.

International Catholic Federation for Physical and Sports Education (Fédération Internationale Catholique d'Education Physique et Sportive—FICEP): 22 rue Oberkampf, 75011 Paris, France; tel. 1-513-77-14; fax 1-513-40-36; e-mail info@ficep.org; internet www.ficep.org; f. 1911 to group Catholic asscns for physical education and sport of different countries and to develop the principles and precepts of Christian morality by fostering meetings, study and international co-operation; mems: 14 affiliated national federations representing about 3.5m. members; Pres. GERHARD HAUER; Sec.-Gen. ANNE CORDIER.

International Centre for Minority Studies and Inter-Cultural Relations (IMIR): 1303 Sofia, ul. I Antim 55, Bulgaria; tel. (2) 832-31-12; fax (2) 931-05-83; e-mail marko@imir-bg.org; internet www.imir-bg.org; f. 1992 to carry out scientific research and humanitarian work with minority communities in Bulgaria; works with experts in the study of ethnic relations and religious issues in the wider Balkan region; Chair. ANTONINA ZHELYAZKOVA; publ. research, analyses, forecasts and policy recommendations.

International Council for Adult Education (ICAE): Ave. 18 de Julio 2095/301, CP 11200, Montevideo, Uruguay; tel. and fax 2409 7982; e-mail secretariat@icae.org.uy; internet www.icae2.org; f. 1973 as a partnership of adult learners, teachers and organizations; General Assembly meets every four years; mems: 7 regional orgs and over 700 literacy, adult and lifelong learning asscns in more than 50 countries; Pres. ALAN TUCKETT; Sec.-Gen. CELITA ECCHER; publs *Convergence*, *ICAE News*.

International Council for Open and Distance Education (ICDE): Lilleakerveien 23, 0283 Oslo, Norway; tel. 22-06-26-30; fax 22-06-26-31; e-mail icde@icde.no; internet www.icde.org; f. 1938 (name changed 1982); furthers distance education by promoting research, encouraging regional links, providing information and organizing conferences; mems: institutions, corporations and individuals world-wide; Pres. TIAN BELAWATI (Indonesia); Sec.-Gen. GARD TITLESTAD (Norway); publ. *Open Praxis* (online, at www.openpraxis.com).

International Federation for Parent Education (IFPE) (Fédération internationale pour l'éducation des parents—FIEP): 1 ave Léon Journault, 92318 Sèvres Cédex, France; tel. 4-77-21-67-43; fax 1-46-26-69-27; e-mail fiep.ifpe@gmail.com; internet www.fiep-ifpe.fr; f. 1964 to gather in congresses and colloquia experts from different scientific fields and those responsible for family education in their own countries and to encourage the establishment of family education where it does not exist; mems: 60 nat. and local mem. orgs, 35 individual mems and 4 int. or regional orgs; Sec.-Gen. HABIB ABDENNEBI; publ. *Lettre de la FIEP* (2 a year).

International Federation of Catholic Universities (Fédération internationale d'universités catholiques—FIUC): 21 rue d'Assas, 75270 Paris Cédex 06, France; tel. 1-44-39-52-26; fax 1-44-39-52-28; e-mail sgfiuc@bureau.fiuc.org; internet www.fiuc.org; f. 1948; aims to ensure a strong bond of mutual assistance among all Catholic universities in the search for truth; to help to solve problems of growth and development, and to co-operate with other international organizations; mems: some 200 in 53 countries; Pres. ANTHONY J. CERNERA (USA); Sec.-Gen. GUY-RÉAL THIVIERGE (Canada); publ. *Monthly Newsletter*.

International Federation of Library Associations and Institutions (IFLA): POB 95312, 2509 CH The Hague, Netherlands; tel. (70) 3140884; fax (70) 3834827; e-mail ifla@ifla.org; internet www.ifla.org; f. 1927 to promote international co-operation in librarianship and bibliography; mems: over 1,700 members in 150 countries; Pres. (2011-13) INGRID PARENT (Canada); Sec.-Gen. JENNEFER NICHOLSON (Australia); publs *IFLA Annual Report*, *IFLA Directory*, *IFLA Journal*, *International Cataloguing and Bibliographic Control* (quarterly), *IFLA Professional Reports*.

International Federation of Physical Education (Fédération internationale d'éducation physique—FIEP): Foz do Iguaçu, PR, Brazil; tel. (45) 3574-1949; fax (45) 3525-1272; e-mail fiep.brasil@uol.com.br; internet www.fiep.net; f. 1923; studies physical education on scientific, pedagogic and aesthetic bases, with the aim of stimulating health, harmonious development or preservation, healthy recreation, and the best adaptation of the individual to the general needs of social life; organizes international congresses and courses; awards research prize; mems: from 112 countries; Sec. ALMIR GRUHN; publ. *FIEP Bulletin* (3 a year, in English, French, and Spanish).

International Federation of Teachers of Modern Languages (Fédération des Professeurs de Langues Vivantes): POB 216, Belgrave 3160, Australia; tel. (6139) 754-4714; fax (6139) 416-9899; e-mail djc@netspace.net.au; internet www.fiplv.org; f. 1931; holds meetings on every aspect of foreign-language teaching; has consultative status with UNESCO; mems: 28 national and regional language asscns and 9 international unilingual asscns (teachers of Arabic, English, Esperanto, French, German, Portuguese, Russian); Pres. TERRY LAMB; Sec.-Gen. DENIS CUNNINGHAM.

International Federation of University Women (IFUW): 10 rue du Lac, 1207 Geneva, Switzerland; e-mail ifuw@ifuw.org; internet www.ifuw.org; f. 1919; to promote life-long learning; to work for improvement of the status of women and girls; to encourage and enable women as leaders and decision-makers; Affiliates: 63 national asscns and feds; Pres. MARIANNE HASLEGRAVE.

International Federation of Workers' Education Associations: c/o Labour Research Service, POB 376, Woodstock 7915, Cape Town, South Africa; tel. (21) 447-1677; fax (21) 447-9244; e-mail ifweasecretariat@lrs.org.za; internet www.ifwea.org; f. 1947 to promote co-operation between non-governmental bodies concerned with workers' education; organizes clearing house services; promotes exchange of information; holds international seminars, conferences and summer schools; Pres. SUE SCHURMAN (USA); Gen. Sec. SAHRA RYKLIEF (South Africa); publ. *Worker's Education* (quarterly).

International Institute of Philosophy (IIP) (Institut international de philosophie): 8 rue Jean-Calvin, 75005 Paris, France; tel. 1-43-36-39-11; e-mail inst.intern.philo@wanadoo.fr; f. 1937 to clarify fundamental issues of contemporary philosophy and to promote mutual understanding among thinkers of different backgrounds and traditions; mems: 107 in 45 countries; Pres. ENRICO BERTI (Italy); Sec.-Gen. BERNARD BOURGEOIS (France); publs *Bibliography of Philosophy* (quarterly), *Proceedings of annual meetings*, *Chroniques*, *Philosophy and World Community* (series), *Philosophical Problems Today*, *Open Problems*, *Philosophy of Education*.

International Reading Association: 800 Barksdale Rd, POB 8139, Newark, DE 19714-8139, USA; tel. (302) 731-1600; fax (302) 731-1057; e-mail pubinfo@reading.org; internet www.reading.org; f. 1956 to improve the quality of reading instruction at all levels, to promote the habit of lifelong reading, and to develop every reader's proficiency; mems: 85,000 in 118 countries; Pres. VICTORIA J. RISKO (USA); Exec. Dir. MARCIE CRAIG POST; publs *The Reading Teacher* (8 a year), *Journal of Adolescent and Adult Literacy* (8 a year), *Reading Research Quarterly*, *Lectura y Vida* (quarterly), *Reading Today* (6 a year).

International Schools Association (ISA): 10333 Diego Drive South, Boca Raton, FL 33428, USA; tel. (561) 883-3854; fax (561) 483-2004; e-mail info@isaschools.org; internet www.isaschools.org; f. 1951 to co-ordinate work in international schools and to promote their development; convenes biennial Conferences and annual Youth Leadership Seminars on topics of global concern, and organizes specialist seminars on internationalism and international-mindedness; a not-for-profit international non-governmental org; has consultative status at ECOSOC; mems: 100 schools world-wide; Chair. LUIS MARTINEZ ZORZO.

International Society for Business Education (Société Internationale pour l'Enseignement Commercial—SIEC): 6302 Mineral Point Rd, 100 Madison, Wisconsin, USA 53705; tel. (608) 273-8467; e-mail secretary@siec-isbe.org; internet www.siec-isbe.org; f. 1901; encourages international exchange of information; organizes international courses and congresses on business education; mems: 2,200 national orgs and individuals in 23 countries; Pres. Dr TAMRA S. DAVIS (USA); Gen. Sec. Dr JUDITH OLSON-SUTTON (USA); publ. *International Review for Business Education*.

International Society for Education through Art (INSEA): e-mail secretary@insea.org; internet www.insea.org; f. 1951 to unite art teachers throughout the world, to exchange information and to co-ordinate research into art education; organizes international congresses and exhibitions of children's art; Pres. RITA IRWIN (Canada); Sec. GRAHAM NASH (Australia); publ. *International Journal for Education through Art* (3 a year).

International Society for Music Education (ISME): POB 909, Nedlands, WA 6909, Australia; tel. (8) 9386-2654; fax (8) 9386-2658; e-mail isme@isme.org; internet www.isme.org; f. 1953 to organize international conferences, seminars and publications on matters pertaining to music education; acts as advisory body to UNESCO in matters of music education; mems: national committees and individuals in more than 70 countries; Pres. YASUHARU TAKAHAGI (Japan); Sec.-Gen. JUDY THÖNELL (Australia); publs *ISME Newsletter*, *International Journal of Music Education*.

International Society for the Study of Medieval Philosophy (SIEPM): Albert-Ludwigs-Universität Freiburg, Philosophisches Seminar, Platz der Universität 3, 79085 Freiburg, Germany; tel. (10) 47-48-07; fax (10) 47-82-85; internet www.siepm.uni-freiburg.de; f. 1958 to promote the study of medieval thought and the collaboration between individuals and institutions in this field; organizes International Congress of Medieval Philosophy every five years; mems: 700; Sec. Prof. MAARTEN J. F. M. HOENEN; publ. *Bulletin de Philosophie Médiévale* (annually).

International Youth Library (Internationale Jugendbibliothek): Schloss Blutenburg, 81247 Munich, Germany; tel. (89) 8912110; fax (89) 8117553; e-mail info@ijb.de; internet www.ijb.de; f. 1949, since 1953 an associated project of UNESCO; promotes the international exchange of children's literature; provides study opportunities for specialists in childrens' books; maintains a library of 600,000 volumes in about 130 languages; Dir Dr CHRISTIANE RAABE; publs *The White Ravens*, *Das Buecherschloss*, catalogues.

Italian-Latin American Institute: Via Giovanni Paisiello 24, 00198 Rome, Italy; tel. (06) 684921; fax (06) 6872834; e-mail info@iila.org; internet www.iila.org; f. 1966; aims to promote Italian culture in Latin America; awarded observer status at the UN General Assembly in 2007; Dir-Gen. SIMONETTA CAVALIERI; Sec.-Gen. GIORGIO MALFATTI DI MONTE TRETTO.

LIBER (Association of European Research Libraries) (Ligue des Bibliothèques Européennes de Recherche): National Library of the Netherlands, POB 90407, 2509 LK, The Hague, Netherlands; tel. (70) 314-07-67; fax (70) 314-01-97; e-mail liber@kb.nl; internet www.libereurope.eu; f. 1971 to encourage collaboration between the general research libraries of Europe, and national and university libraries in particular; gives assistance in finding practical ways of improving the quality of the services provided; mems: 400 libraries, library orgs and individuals in 40 countries; Pres. PAUL AYRIS; Sec.-Gen. ANN MATHESON; publ. *LIBER Quarterly*.

Organization of Ibero-American States for Education, Science and Culture (Organización de Estados Iberoamericanos para la Educación, la Ciencia y la Cultura—OEI): Centro de Recursos Documentales e Informáticos, Calle Bravo Murillo 38, 28015 Madrid, Spain; tel. (91) 5944382; fax (91) 5944622; internet www.oei.es; f. 1949 (as the Ibero-American Bureau of Education); promotes peace and solidarity between member countries, through education, science, technology and culture; provides information, encourages exchanges and organizes training courses; the General Assembly (at ministerial level) meets every four years; mems: govts of 20 countries; Sec.-Gen. ÁLVARO MARCHESI ULLASTRES; publ. *Revista Iberoamericana de Educación* (quarterly).

Organization of the Catholic Universities of Latin America (Organización de Universidades Católicas de América Latina—ODUCAL): Av. Libertador Bernardo O'Higgins 340, Of. 242, 2° piso, Santiago, Chile; tel. and fax (2) 354-1866; e-mail oducal@uc.cl; internet www.oducal.uc.cl; f. 1953 to assist the social, economic and cultural development of Latin America through the promotion of Catholic higher education in the continent; mems: 43 Catholic universities in 15 Latin American countries; Pres. Dr PEDRO PABLO ROSSO; Sec.-Gen. ANTONIO DAHER HECHEM; publs *Anuario*, *Sapientia*, *Universitas*.

Pan-African Association for Literacy and Adult Education: Rue 10, Bldg. 306, POB 21783, Ponty, Dakar, Senegal; tel. 825-48-50; fax 824-44-13; e-mail anafa@sentoo.sn; f. 2000 to succeed African Asscn for Literacy and Adult Education (f. 1984); Co-ordinator Dr LAMINE KANE.

Southeast Asian Ministers of Education Organization (SEAMEO): M. L. Pin Malakul Bldg, 920 Sukhumvit Rd, Bangkok 10110, Thailand; tel. (2) 391-0144; fax (2) 381-2587; e-mail secretariat@seameo.org; internet www.seameo.org; f. 1965 to promote co-operation among the Southeast Asian nations through projects in education, science and culture; SEAMEO has 19 regional centres including: BIOTROP for tropical biology, in Bogor, Indonesia; INNOTECH for educational innovation and technology, in Philippines; SEAMOLEC, an open-learning centre, in Indonesia; RECSAM for education in science and mathematics, in Penang, Malaysia; RELC for languages, in Singapore; RIHED for higher education development, in Bangkok, Thailand; SEARCA for graduate study and research in agriculture, in Los Baños, Philippines; SPAFA for archaeology and fine arts, in Bangkok, Thailand; TROPMED for tropical medicine and public health, with regional centres in Indonesia, Malaysia, Philippines and Thailand and a central office in Bangkok; VOCTECH for vocational and technical education; QITEPs, regional centres for quality improvement of teachers and education personnel, for language, based in Jakarta, Indonesia, for mathematics, in Yogyakarta, Indonesia, and for science, in Bandung, Indonesia; RETRAC, a training centre, in Ho Chi Minh City, Viet Nam; and the SEAMEO Regional Centre for History and Tradition (CHAT) in Yangon, Myanmar; mems: Brunei, Cambodia, Indonesia, Laos, Malaysia, Philippines, Singapore, Thailand, Timor-Leste and Viet Nam; assoc. mems: Australia, Canada, France, Germany, Netherlands, New Zealand, Norway and Spain; Dir Dr WITAYA JERADECHAKUL (Thailand); publs *Annual Report*, *SEAMEO Education Agenda*.

Union of Universities of Latin America and the Caribbean (Unión de Universidades de América Latina y el Caribe—UDUAL): Edificio UDUAL, Apdo postal 70-232, Ciudad Universitaria, Del. Coyoacán, 04510 México, DF, Mexico; tel. (55) 5616-2386; fax (55) 5622-0092; e-mail contacto@udual.org; internet www.udual.org; f. 1949 to organize exchanges between professors, students, research fellows and graduates and generally encourage good relations between the Latin American universities; arranges conferences; conducts statistical research; maintains centre for university documentation; mems: 180 universities and 8 university networks; Pres. Dr GUSTAVO GARCÍA DE PAREDES (Panama); Sec.-Gen. Dr ROBERTO ESCALANTE SEMERENA (Mexico); publs *Universidades* (2 a year), *Gaceta UDUAL* (quarterly), *Censo* (every 2 years).

Universal Esperanto Association (Universala Esperanto-Asocio): Nieuwe Binnenweg 176, 3015 BJ Rotterdam, Netherlands; tel. (10) 4361044; fax (10) 4361751; e-mail info@co.uea.org; internet www.uea.org; f. 1908 to assist the spread of the international language, Esperanto, and to facilitate the practical use of the language; organizes World Congresses (2012: Hanoi, Viet Nam); mems: 70 affiliated national asscns and 15,800 individuals in 118 countries; Pres. PROBAL DASGUPTA (India); Dir-Gen. OSMO BULLER (Finland); publs *Esperanto* (monthly), *Kontakto* (every 2 months), *Jarlibro* (annually).

World Education Fellowship: 54 Fox Lane, London, N13 4AL, United Kingdom; tel. (20) 8245-4561; e-mail generalsecretary@wef-international.org; internet www.wef-international.org; f. 1921 to promote education for international understanding, and the exchange and practice of ideas, together with research into progressive educational theories and methods; mems: sections and groups in 20 countries; Pres. Prof. SHINJO OKUDA (Japan); Gen. Sec. GUADALUPE G. DE TURNER; publ. *The New Era in Education* (3 a year).

World Union of Catholic Teachers (Union mondiale des enseignants catholiques—UMEC): Palazzo San Calisto 16, 00120 Vatican City, Vatican; tel. (06) 69887286; fax (06) 69887207; e-mail umec@org.va; f. 1951; encourages the grouping of Catholic teachers for the greater effectiveness of Catholic schools, distributes documentation on Catholic doctrine with regard to education, and facilitates personal contacts through congresses, and seminars, etc; nationally and internationally; mems: 32 orgs in 29 countries; Pres, MARK PHILPOT; publ. *Nouvelles de l'UMEC*.

Environmental Conservation

BirdLife International: Wellbrook Ct, Girton Rd, Cambridge, CB3 0NA, United Kingdom; tel. (1223) 277318; fax (1223) 277200; e-mail birdlife@birdlife.org; internet www.birdlife.org; f. 1922 as the International Council for Bird Preservation; a global partnership of organizations that determines status of bird species throughout the world and compiles data on all endangered species; identifies conservation problems and priorities; initiates and co-ordinates conservation projects and international conventions; mems: partners or representatives in more than 100 countries; Chair. PETER JOHAN SCHEI; Dir Dr MARCO LAMBERTINI (Italy); publs *Bird Red Data Book*, *World Birdwatch* (quarterly), *Bird Conservation Series*.

Caspian Environment Programme: c/o Kazhydromet Bldg, 7th floor, Orynbor St, Astana, 010000 Kazakhstan; tel. (7172) 798317; e-mail msgp.meg@undp.org; internet www.caspianenvironment.org; f. 1998 by Azerbaijan, Iran, Kazakhstan, Russia and Turkmenistan with the aim of halting the deterioration of environmental conditions in the area of the Caspian Sea and also with a view to promoting sustainable development in the region; supported the efforts of the Caspian states to negotiate and conclude, in 2003, a Framework Convention for the Protection of the Marine Environment of the Caspian Sea (the Tehran Convention).

Coalition Clean Baltic (CCB): Östra Ågatan 53, SE-753 22 Uppsala, Sweden; tel. (18) 71-11-55; fax (18) 71-11-75; e-mail secretariat@ccb.se; internet www.ccb.se; f. 1990, network of environmental non-governmental organizations from countries bordering the Baltic Sea; Exec. Sec. GUNNAR NORÉN.

Commission for the Conservation of Antarctic Marine Living Resources (CCAMLR): POB 213, North Hobart, Tasmania 7002, Australia; tel. (3) 6210-1111; fax (3) 6224-8744; e-mail ccamlr@ccamlr.org; internet www.ccamlr.org; established under the 1982 Convention on the Conservation of Antarctic Marine Living Resources to manage marine resources in the Antarctic region; Exec. Sec. ANDREW WRIGHT.

Commission on the Protection of the Black Sea Against Pollution: Orman Bolge Müdürlüğü, Büyükdere Cad. 265, 34398 Maslak Şişli, Istanbul, Turkey; tel. (212) 2992940; fax (212)

2992944; e-mail secretariat@blacksea-commission.org; internet www.blacksea-commission.org; established under the 1992 Convention on the Protection of the Black Sea Against Pollution (Bucharest Convention) to implement the Convention and its Protocols; also oversees the 1996 Strategic Action Plan for the Rehabilitation and Protection of the Black Sea; Exec. Dir Prof. HALIL IBRAHIM SUR.

Consortium for Ocean Leadership: 1201 New York Ave, NW, Suite 420, Washington, DC 20005, USA; tel. (202) 232-3900; fax (202) 462-8754; e-mail info@oceanleadership.org; internet www.oceanleadership.org; f. 2007, following the merger of the Consortium for Oceanographic Research and Education (CORE, f. 1999) and the Joint Oceanographic Institutions (JOI); aims to promote, support and advance the science of oceanography; Pres. ROBERT B. GAGOSIAN.

Friends of the Earth International: POB 19199, 1000 GD, Amsterdam, Netherlands; tel. (20) 6221369; fax (20) 6392181; internet www.foei.org; f. 1971 to promote the conservation, restoration and rational use of the environment and natural resources through public education and campaigning; mems: 77 national groups; Chair. NNIMMO BASSEY (Nigeria); publ. *Link* (quarterly).

Global Coral Reef Monitoring Network: POB 772, Townsville MC 4810, Australia; tel. (7) 4721-2699; fax (7) 4772-2808; e-mail clive.wilkinson@rrrc.org.au; internet www.gcrmn.org; f. 1994, as an operating unit of the International Coral Reef Initiative; active in more than 80 countries; aims include improving the management and sustainable conservation of coral reefs, strengthening links between regional organizations and ecological and socioeconomic monitoring networks, and disseminating information to assist the formulation of conservation plans; Global Co-ordinator Dr CLIVE WILKINSON (Australia); publ. *Status of Coral Reefs of the World*.

Global Wind Energy Council: Wind Power House, 80 rue d'Arlon, 1040 Brussels, Belgium; tel. (2) 213-18-97; fax (2) 213-18-90; e-mail info@gwec.net; internet www.gwec.net; represents the main national, regional and international institutions, companies and asscns related to wind power; aims to promote the development and growth of wind as a major source of energy; organizes a Global Wind Power Conference every two years (2011: India); Chair. KLAUS RAVE; Sec.-Gen. STEVE SAWYER; publs *Global Wind Energy Outlook*, *Wind Force 12*, other reports, surveys.

Greencross International: 160A route de Florissant, 1231 Conches/Geneva, Switzerland; tel. 227891662; fax 227891695; e-mail gcinternational@gcint.org; internet www.greencrossinternational.net; f. 1993; aims to promote Earth Charter, to mitigate the environmental legacy of conflicts, to deter conflict in water-stressed regions, to combat desertification, to promote new energy consumption patterns, and to promote international conferences on and awareness of environmental issues; Chair. JAN KULCZYK (Poland); Pres. ALEXANDER LIKHOTAL (Russia).

Greenpeace International: Ottho Heldringstraat 5, 1066 AZ Amsterdam, Netherlands; tel. (20) 718-2000; fax (20) 718-2002; e-mail supporter.services.int@greenpeace.org; internet www.greenpeace.org; f. 1971 to campaign for the protection of the environment through non-violent direct action, and to offer solutions for positive change; aims to change attitudes and behaviour, to protect and conserve the environment, to promote peace by working for solutions for positive change; to maintain its independence Greenpeace does not accept donations from governments or corporations but relies on contributions from individual supporters and foundation grants; mems: representation in more than 40 countries across Europe, the Americas, Africa, Asia and the Pacific; Chair. Bd of Dirs ANA TONI (Brazil); Exec. Dir KUMI NAIDOO (South Africa).

International Commission for the Protection of the Rhine: Postfach 200253, 56002 Koblenz; Hohenzollernstrasse 18, 56068 Koblenz, Germany; tel. (261) 94252; fax (261) 9425252; e-mail sekretariat@iksr.de; internet www.iksr.org; f. 1950; prepares and commissions research on the nature of the pollution of the Rhine; proposes protection, ecological rehabilitation and flood prevention measures; mems: 23 delegates from France, Germany, Luxembourg, Netherlands, Switzerland and the EU; Chair. ANDRÉ WEIDENHAUPT; Sec.-Gen. BEN VAN DE WETERING; publ. *Annual Report*.

International Coral Reef Initiative: c/o Australia/Great Barrier Reef Marine Park Authority (GBRMPA), 2–68 Flinders St, POB 1379, Townsville, QLD, 4810, Australia; e-mail icri@gbrmpa.gov.au; internet www.icriforum.org; f. 1994 at the first Conference of the Parties of the Convention on Biological Diversity; a partnership of governments, non-governmental organizations, scientific bodies and the private sector; aims to highlight the degradation of coral reefs and provide a focus for action to ensure the sustainable management and conservation of these and related marine ecosystems; in 1995 issued a Call to Action and a Framework for Action; the Secretariat is co-chaired by a developed and a developing country, on a rotational basis among mem. states (2012–13, Australia and Belize); Co-Chair. MARGARET JOHNSON (Australia), BEVERLEY WADE (Belize).

International Emissions Trading Association: 24 rue Merle d'Aubigné, 1207 Geneva, Switzerland; tel. 227370500; fax 227370508; e-mail secretariat@ieta.org; internet www.ieta.org; f. 1999 to establish a functional international framework for trading greenhouse gas emissions, in accordance with the objectives of the UN Framework Convention on Climate Change; serves as a specialized information centre on emissions trading and the greenhouse gas market; mems: 179 international companies; Pres. and CEO HENRY DERWENT.

International Fund for Saving the Aral Sea: 050020 Almatı, Dostyk Av. 280, Kazakhstan; tel. (727) 387-34-31; fax (727) 387-34-33; e-mail mail@ec-ifas.org; internet www.ec-ifas.org/russian_version/about.html; f. 1993 by Central Asian heads of state; incorporates an Intergovernmental Sustainable Development Commission and an Interstate Commission for Water Co-ordination; granted observer status at the UN General Assembly in Nov. 2008; in Oct. 2011 organized a conference, in Kyzylorda, southern Kazakhstan, on biodiversity conservation, climate change response, sustainable development and comprehensive integrated water resources management in the Aral Sea Basin Area; aims to incorporate the Syrdarya River Delta Wetlands into the Ramsar List of Wetlands of International Importance; mems: Kazakhstan, Kyrgyzstan, Tajikistan, Turkmenistan, Uzbekistan; Chair. SAGHIT IBATULLIN.

International Renewable Energy Agency: C67 Office Bldg, Khalidiyah (32nd) St, POB 236, Abu Dhabi, United Arab Emirates; tel. (2) 4179000; internet www.irena.org; f. 2009 at a conference held in Bonn, Germany; aims to promote the development and application of renewable sources of energy; to act as a forum for the exchange of information and technology transfer; and to organize training seminars and other educational activities; inaugural Assembly convened in April 2011; mems: 91 states and the EU; at April 2012 a further 65 countries had signed but not yet ratified the founding agreement to become full mems; Dir-Gen. ADNAN AMIN (Kenya).

IUCN—International Union for Conservation of Nature: 28 rue Mauverney, 1196 Gland, Switzerland; tel. 229990000; fax 229990002; e-mail press@iucn.org; internet www.iucn.org; f. 1948, as the International Union for Conservation of Nature and Natural Resources; supports partnerships and practical field activities to promote the conservation of natural resources, to secure the conservation of biological diversity as an essential foundation for the future; to ensure wise use of the earth's natural resources in an equitable and sustainable way; and to guide the development of human communities towards ways of life in enduring harmony with other components of the biosphere, developing programmes to protect and sustain the most important and threatened species and eco-systems and assisting governments to devise and carry out national conservation strategies; incorporates the Species Survival Commission (SSC), a science-based network of volunteer experts aiming to ensure conservation of present levels of biodiversity; compiles annually updated Red List of Threatened Species, comprising in 2011 some 59,508 species, of which 19,265 were threatened with extinction; maintains a conservation library and documentation centre and units for monitoring traffic in wildlife; mems: more than 1,000 states, government agencies, non-governmental organizations and affiliates in some 140 countries; Pres. ASHOK KHOSLA (India); Dir-Gen. JULIA MARTON-LEFÈVRE (USA); publs *World Conservation Strategy*, *Caring for the Earth*, *Red List of Threatened Plants*, *Red List of Threatened Species*, *United Nations List of National Parks and Protected Areas*, *World Conservation* (quarterly), *IUCN Today*.

Nordic Environment Finance Corporation (NEFCO): Fabianinkatu 34, POB 249, 00171 Helsinki, Finland; tel. (10) 618003; fax (9) 630976; e-mail info@nefco.fi; internet www.nefco.org; f. 1990; finances environmentally beneficial projects in Central and Eastern Europe with transboundary effects that also benefit the Nordic region; Man. Dir MAGNUS RYSTEDT.

Permanent Commission of the South Pacific (Comisión Permanente del Pacífico Sur): Av. Carlos Julio Arosemena, Km 3 Edificio Inmaral, Guayaquil, Ecuador; tel. (4) 222-1202; fax (4) 222-1201; e-mail sgeneral@cpps-int.org; internet www.cpps-int.org; f. 1952 to consolidate the presence of the zonal coastal states; Sec.-Gen. HÉCTOR SOLDI SOLDI (Peru).

Secretariat of the Antarctic Treaty: Maipú 757, piso 4, C1006ACI Buenos Aires, Argentina; tel. (11) 4320-4250; fax (11) 4320-4253; e-mail ats@ats.aq; internet www.ats.aq; f. 2004 to administer the Antarctic Treaty (signed in 1959); has developed an Electronic Information Exchange System; organizes annual Consultative Meeting (2012: Hobart, Australia, in June); mems: 49 states party to the Treaty; Exec. Sec. MANFRED REINKE.

Secretariat of the Pacific Regional Environment Programme (SPREP): POB 240, Apia, Samoa; tel. 21929; fax 20231; e-mail sprep@sprep.org; internet www.sprep.org; f. 1978 by the South Pacific Commission (where it was based, now Pacific Community), the South Pacific (now Pacific Islands) Forum, ESCAP and UNEP;

formally established as an independent institution in 1993; SPREP's mandate is to promote co-operation in the Pacific islands region and to provide assistance in order to protect and improve the environment and to ensure sustainable development for present and future generations; has the following four strategic priorities: Bio-diversity and Ecosystems Management, Climate Change, Environmental Monitoring and Governance, Waste Management and Pollution Control; in March 2010 letters of agreement were signed relating to the transfer and integration to SPREP from the Pacific Islands Applied Geoscience Commission of the following functions: the Pacific Islands Global Ocean Observing System (PI-GOOS); the Islands Climate Update (ICU); the Climate and Meteorological Databases (CMD); and climate change-associated energy activities; mems: 21 Pacific islands, Australia, France, New Zealand, USA; Dir DAVID SHEPPARD (Australia).

South Asia Co-operative Environment Programme (SACEP): 10 Anderson Rd, Colombo 05, Sri Lanka; tel. (11) 2589787; fax (11) 2589369; e-mail info@sacep.org; internet www.sacep.org; f. 1982; aims to promote regional co-operation in the protection and management of the environment, in particular in the context of sustainable economic and social development; works closely with governmental and non-governmental national, regional and international institutions in conservation and management efforts; Governing Council meets regularly; working to establish a South Asia Biodiversity Clearing House Mechanism; also actively developing specific projects: the conservation and integrated management of marine turtles and their habitats in the South Asia Seas region; reef-based corals management; accelerated penetration of cost effective renewable energy technologies; the establishment of a Basel Convention Sub-regional Centre for South Asia; protected areas management of world heritage sites and implementation of the Ramsar Strategic Plan at a sub-regional level; mems: Afghanistan, Bangladesh, Bhutan, India, Maldives, Nepal, Pakistan, Sri Lanka; Officiating Dir-Gen. JACINTHA S. TISSERA; publs *SACEP Newsletter*, *South Asia Environmental and Education Action Plan*, other reports.

Wetlands International: POB 471, 6700 AL Wageningen, Netherlands; tel. (318) 660910; fax (318) 660950; e-mail post@wetlands.org; internet www.wetlands.org; f. 1995 by merger of several regional wetlands organizations; aims to protect and restore wetlands, their resources and biodiversity through research, information exchange and conservation activities; promotes implementation of the 1971 Ramsar Convention on Wetlands; Chair. JAN ERNST DE GROOT (Netherlands); CEO JANE MADGWICK.

World Association of Zoos and Aquariums (WAZA): IUCN Conservation Centre, 28 rue Mauverney, 1196 Gland, Switzerland; tel. 229990790; fax 229990791; e-mail secretariat@waza.org; internet www.waza.org; f. 1946, current name adopted 2000; aims to provide leadership and support for zoos and aquariums and to promote biodiversity, environmental education, and global sustainability; adopted WAZA Code of Ethics and Animal Welfare, and a Consensus Document on Responsible Reproductive Management, in 2003; in 2005 WAZA launched a World Zoo and Aquarium Conservation Strategy, adopted Research Guidelines, and participated for the first time in Conferences of the Parties to the Ramsar Convention and the Convention of Migratory Species; mems: leading zoos and aquariums and related regional and national asscn; affiliate conservation orgs; Pres. JORG JUNHOLD; Exec. Dir GERALD DICK.

World Ocean Observatory: 1 Oak St, Boothbay Harbor, Maine 04538, USA; e-mail info@thew2o.net; internet www.thew2o.net; f. 2004; recommendation of the final report of the Independent World Commission on the Oceans; serves as a focal point for ocean-related information from governments, non-governmental organizations and other networks; aims to enhance public awareness of the importance of oceans and facilitate the dissemination of information; maintains an online radio station and organizes other online events; Dir PETER NEILL; publ. *World Ocean Observer* (monthly).

World Rainforest Movement (WRM): Maldonado 1858, Montevideo 11200, Uruguay; tel. 2413 2989; fax 2410 0985; e-mail wrm@wrm.org.uy; internet www.wrm.org.uy; f. 1986; aims to secure the lands and livelihoods of rainforest peoples and supports their efforts to defend rainforests from activities including commercial logging, mining, the construction of dams, the development of plantations, and shrimp farming; issued the Penang Declaration in 1989 setting out the shared vision of an alternative model of rainforest development based on securing the lands and livelihoods of forest inhabitants; released in 1998 the Montevideo Declaration, campaigning against large-scale monocrop plantations, for example of pulpwood, oil palm and rubber; and issued the Mount Tamalpais Declaration in 2000, urging governments not to include tree plantations as carbon sinks in international action against climate change; Co-ordinator WINFRIDUS OVERBEEK; publ. *WRM Bulletin* (monthly).

World Society for the Protection of Animals (WSPA): 222 Grays Inn Rd, London WC1X 8HB, United Kingdom; tel. (20) 7239-0500; fax (20) 7793-0208; e-mail wspa@wspa.org; internet www.wspa-international.org; f. 1981, incorporating the World Federation for the Protection of Animals (f. 1950) and the International Society for the Protection of Animals (f. 1959); promotes animal welfare and conservation by humane education, practical field projects, international lobbying and legislative work; mems: over 850 member societies in 150 countries; Pres. HANJA MAIJ-WEGGEN; Dir-Gen. MICHAEL BAKER.

World Water Council: Espace Gaymard, 2–4 pl. d'Arvieux, 13002 Marseille, France; tel. 4-91-99-41-00; fax 4-91-99-41-01; internet www.worldwatercouncil.org; f. 1996; aims to facilitate the efficient conservation, protection, development, planning, management and use of water resources on an environmentally sustainable basis; organizes a World Water Forum held every three years since 1997 (2012: Marseilles, France, in March); Pres. LOÏC FAUCHON; Gen. Dir (vacant).

World Water Organization: 1350 Ave of the Americas, 2nd Floor, New York, NY 10019, USA; tel. (212) 759-1639; fax (646) 666-4349; e-mail info@theworldwater.org; internet www.theworldwater.org; organizes conferences and special projects to highlight issues related to water security and to seek means of protecting the global water infrastructure; arranged High-Level Symposium on Water Security at UN headquarters, New York, in Oct. 2010; mems: experts from government, business, medical, and academic backgrounds; Chair. HAROLD HYUNSUK OH; Exec. Dir Dr ELAINE VALDOV.

WWF International: 27 ave du Mont-Blanc, 1196 Gland, Switzerland; tel. 223649111; fax 223648836; e-mail info@wwfint.org; internet www.wwf.panda.org; f. 1961 (as World Wildlife Fund), name changed to World Wide Fund for Nature in 1986, current nomenclature adopted 2001; aims to stop the degradation of natural environments, conserve bio-diversity, ensure the sustainable use of renewable resources, and promote the reduction of both pollution and wasteful consumption; addresses six priority issues: forests, freshwater, marine, species, climate change, and toxics; has identified, and focuses its activities in, 200 'ecoregions' (the 'Global 200'), believed to contain the best part of the world's remaining biological diversity; actively supports and operates conservation programmes in more than 90 countries; mems: 54 offices, 5 associate orgs, c. 5m. individual mems world-wide; Pres. YOLANDA KAKABADSE (Ecuador); Dir-Gen. JAMES P. LEAPE; publs *Annual Report*, *Living Planet Report*.

Government and Politics

African Association for Public Administration and Management (AAPAM): Britak Centre, Ragati and Mara Rds, POB 48677, 00100 GPO, Nairobi, Kenya; tel. (20) 2730555; fax (22) 310102; e-mail aapam@aapam.org; internet www.aapam.org; f. 1971 to promote good practices, excellence and professionalism in public administration through training, seminars, research, publications; convenes regular conferences to share learning experiences among members, and an annual Roundtable Conference; funded by membership contributions, government and donor grants; mems: 500 individual, 50 corporate; Pres. ABDON AGAW JOK NHIAL (South Sudan); Sec.-Gen. Dr YOLAMU R. BARONGO (Uganda); publs *Newsletter* (quarterly), *Annual Seminar Report*, *African Journal of Public Administration and Management* (2 a year), books.

African Parliamentary Union: BP V314, Abidjan, Côte d'Ivoire; tel. 20-30-39-70; fax 20-30-44-05; e-mail upa1@aviso.ci; internet www.african-pu.org; f. 1976 (as Union of African Parliaments); holds annual conf. (2012: Kigali, Rwands, in Nov.); mems: 40 parliaments; Chair, ANGEL SERAFIN SERICHE DOUGAN MALABO (Equatorial Guinea); Sec.-Gen. N'ZI KOFFI.

Afro-Asian Peoples' Solidarity Organization (AAPSO): 89 Abdel Aziz Al-Saoud St, POB 11559-61 Manial El-Roda, Cairo, Egypt; tel. (2) 3636081; fax (2) 3637361; e-mail aapso@idsc.net.eg; f. 1958; acts among and for the peoples of Africa and Asia in their struggle for genuine independence, sovereignty, socio-economic development, peace and disarmament; mems: national committees and affiliated organizations in 66 countries and territories, assoc. mems in 15 European countries; Sec.-Gen. NOURI ABDEL RAZZAK HUSSEIN (Iraq); publs *Solidarity Bulletin* (monthly), *Socio-Economic Development* (3 a year).

Agency for the Prohibition of Nuclear Weapons in Latin America and the Caribbean (Organismo para la Proscripción de las Armas Nucleares en la América Latina y el Caribe—OPANAL): Schiller 326, 5°, Col. Chapultepec Morales, 11570 México, DF, Mexico; tel. (55) 5255-2914; fax (55) 5255-3748; e-mail info@opanal.org; internet www.opanal.org; f. 1969 to ensure compliance with the Treaty for the Prohibition of Nuclear Weapons in Latin America (Treaty of Tlatelolco), 1967; to ensure the absence of all nuclear weapons in the application zone of the Treaty; to contribute to the movement against proliferation of nuclear weapons; to promote general and complete disarmament; to prohibit all testing, use, manufacture, acquisition, storage, installation and any form of possession, by any means, of nuclear weapons; the organs of the Agency comprise the General Conference, meeting every two years, the Council, meeting every two months, and the secretariat; a General Conference is held every two years; mems: 33 states that have fully ratified the Treaty; the Treaty has two additional Protocols: the first signed and ratified by France, the Netherlands, the United Kingdom and the USA, the second signed and ratified by People's Republic of China, the USA, France, the United Kingdom and Russia; Sec.-Gen. GIOCONDA UBEDA RIVERA (until 31 Dec. 2013).

Alliance of Small Island States (AOSIS): c/o 800 Second Ave, Suite 400K, New York, NY 10017, USA; tel. (212) 599-0301; fax (212) 599-1540; e-mail grenada@un.int; internet www.aosis.info; f. 1990 as an ad hoc intergovernmental grouping to focus on the special problems of small islands and low-lying coastal developing states; mems: 43 island nations; Chair. MARLENE MOSES (Nauru); publ. *Small Islands, Big Issues*.

ANZUS: c/o Dept of Foreign Affairs and Trade, R. G. Casey Bldg, John McEwen Crescent, Barton, ACT 0221, Australia; tel. (2) 6261-1111; fax (2) 6271-3111; internet www.dfat.gov.au; the ANZUS Security Treaty was signed in 1951 by Australia, New Zealand and the USA, and ratified in 1952 to co-ordinate partners' efforts for collective defence for the preservation of peace and security in the Pacific area, through the exchange of technical information and strategic intelligence, and a programme of exercises, exchanges and visits. In 1984 New Zealand refused to allow visits by US naval vessels that were either nuclear-propelled or potentially nuclear-armed, and this led to the cancellation of joint ANZUS military exercises: in 1986 the USA formally announced the suspension of its security commitment to New Zealand under ANZUS. Instead of the annual ANZUS Council meetings, ministerial consultations (AUSMIN) were subsequently held every year between Australia and the USA on policy and political-military issues. ANZUS continued to govern security relations between Australia and the USA, and between Australia and New Zealand; security relations between New Zealand and the USA were the only aspect of the treaty to be suspended. Senior-level contacts between New Zealand and the USA resumed in 1994. The Australian Govt invoked the ANZUS Security Treaty for the first time following the international terrorist attacks against targets in the USA that were perpetrated in September 2001.

Association of Pacific Islands Legislatures (APIL): Carl Rose Bldg, Suite 207, 181 E. Marine Corps Drive, Hagatna, Guam; tel. (671) 477-2719; fax (671) 473-3004; e-mail apil@guam.net; internet www.apilpacific.com; f. 1981 to provide a permanent structure of mutual assistance for representatives of the people of the Pacific Islands; comprises legislative representatives from 12 Pacific Island Govts; Pres. REBLUUD KESOLEI (Palau).

Association of Secretaries General of Parliaments: c/o Committee Office, House of Commons, London, SW1, United Kingdom; tel. (20) 7219-3498; fax (20) 7219-2681; e-mail asgp@parliament.uk; internet www.asgp.info; f. 1938; studies the law, practice and working methods of different Parliaments; proposes measures for improving those methods and for securing co-operation between the services of different Parliaments; operates as a consultative body to the Inter-Parliamentary Union, and assists the Union on subjects within the scope of the Association; mems: c. 200 representing 145 countries; 5 assoc. institutions; Pres. MARC BOSC (Canada); Jt Secs STEVEN MARK (United Kingdom), AGATHE LE NAHÉNEC (France); publ. *Constitutional and Parliamentary Information* (2 a year).

Atlantic Treaty Association: Quartier Prince Albert, 20 rue des Petits Carmes, 1000 Brussels, Belgium; tel. (2) 502-31-60; fax (2) 502-48-77; e-mail info@ata-sec.org; internet www.ata-sec.org; f. 1954 to inform public opinion on the North Atlantic Alliance and to promote the solidarity of the peoples of the North Atlantic; holds annual assemblies, seminars, study conferences for teachers and young politicians; mems: national asscns in 28 member countries of NATO; 12 assoc. mems from Central and Eastern Europe, 2 observer mems; Pres. Dr KARL A. LAMERS (Germany); Sec.-Gen. TROELS FRØLING (Denmark).

Baltic Council: f. 1993 by the Baltic Assembly, comprising 60 parliamentarians from Estonia, Latvia and Lithuania; the Council of Ministers of the member countries co-ordinates policy in the areas of foreign policy, justice, the environment, education and science.

Bolivarian Alliance for the Americas (Alianza Bolivariana para las Américas—ALBA): internet www.alianzabolivariana.org; f. 2002 (as the Bolivarian Alternative for the Americas) by the President of Venezuela, Hugo Chávez, to promote an alternative model of political, economic and social co-operation and integration between Caribbean and Latin American countries sharing geographic, historical and cultural bonds; aims to reduce disparities in development between countries in the region and to combat poverty and social exclusion; in June 2007 ministers of foreign affairs convened for the inaugural meeting of ALBA's Council of Ministers agreed to the establishment of joint enterprises, as an alternative to transnational corporations, a joint bank to finance projects supported by the grouping and to develop bilateral agreements; the establishment of a Bank of ALBA was endorsed at the 6th summit meeting of heads of state, convened in January 2008; an emergency summit meeting was convened in April to consider the global food crisis; summit meeting convened in Caracas, Venezuela, in Feb. 2012; mems: Antigua and Barbuda, Bolivia, Cuba, Dominica, Ecuador, Nicaragua, Saint Vincent and the Grenadines, Venezuela.

Celtic League: c/o Mark Lockerby, 12 Magherdonnag, Ponyfields, Port Erin IM9 6BY, United Kingdom; internet www.celticleague.net; f. 1961 to foster co-operation between the six Celtic nations (Ireland, Scotland, Isle of Man, Wales, Cornwall and Brittany), especially those actively working for political autonomy by non-violent means; campaigns politically on issues affecting the Celtic countries; monitors military activity in the Celtic countries; co-operates with national cultural organizations to promote the languages and culture of the Celts; mems: approx. 1,400 individuals in the Celtic communities and elsewhere; Gen. Sec. RHISIART TAL-E-BOT; publ. *Carn* (quarterly).

Central European Initiative (CEI): CEI Executive Secretariat, Via Genova 9, 34121 Trieste, Italy; tel. (040) 7786777; fax (040) 360640; e-mail cei-es@cei-es.org; internet www.ceinet.org; f. 1989 as 'Quadragonal' co-operation between Austria, Italy, Hungary and Yugoslavia, became 'Pentagonal' in 1990 with the admission of Czechoslovakia, and 'Hexagonal' with the admission of Poland in 1991, present name adopted in 1992, when Bosnia and Herzegovina, Croatia and Slovenia were admitted; the Czech Republic and Slovakia became separate mems in January 1993, and Macedonia also joined in that year; Albania, Belarus, Bulgaria, Romania and Ukraine joined the CEI in 1995 and Moldova in 1996; the Federal Republic of Yugoslavia (now the separate sovereign states of Montenegro and Serbia) admitted in 2000; encourages regional political and economic co-operation with a focus on the following nine areas of activity: climate, environment and sustainable energy; enterprise development (incl. tourism); human resource development; information society and media; intercultural co-operation (incl. minorities); multimodal transport; science and technology; sustainable agriculture; interregional and cross-border co-operation; economic forum held annually since 1998; Sec.-Gen. GERHARD PFANZELTER; publ. *Newsletter* (monthly).

Centrist Democrat International: 10 rue du Commerce, 1000 Brussels, Belgium; tel. (2) 285-41-45; fax (2) 300-80-13; e-mail idc@cdi-idc.org; internet www.cdi-idc.com; f. 1961 (as Christian Democrat and Peoples' Parties International); serves as an asscn of political groups adhering to Christian humanist and democratic theology; mems: parties in 64 countries (of which 47 in Europe); Pres. PIER FERDINANDO CASINI (Italy); Exec. Sec. ANTONIO LÓPEZ ISTÚRIZ (Spain); publs *DC-Info* (quarterly), *Human Rights* (5 a year), *Documents* (quarterly).

Club of Madrid: Carrera de San Jerónimo 15, 3A planta, 28014 Madrid, Spain; tel. (91) 1548230; fax (91) 1548240; e-mail clubmadrid@clubmadrid.org; internet www.clubmadrid.org; f. 2001, following Conference on Democratic Transition and Consolidation; forum of former Presidents and Prime Ministers; aims to strengthen democratic values and leadership; maintains office in Brussels, Belgium; 87 mems. from 60 countries; Pres. WIM KOK (Netherlands); Sec.-Gen. CARLOS WESTENDORP (Spain).

Collective Security Treaty Organization (CSTO): 103012 Moscow, Varvarka 7, Russia; tel. (495) 606-97-71; fax (495) 625-76-20; e-mail odkb@gov.ru; internet www.dkb.gov.ru; f. 2003 by signatories to the Treaty on Collective Security (signed Tashkent, Uzbekistan, May 1992); aims to co-ordinate and strengthen military and political co-operation and to promote regional and national security; maintains a joint rapid deployment force; the Oct. 2007 leaders' summit endorsed documents enabling the establishment of CSTO joint peace-keeping forces and the creation of a co-ordination council for the heads of member states' emergency response agencies; the leaders' summit convened in Sept. 2008 issued a joint declaration stating that conflicts should be settled preferably through political and diplomatic means in line with international law and stating the following as immediate priorities: strengthening efforts to promote nuclear non-proliferation; to combat terrorism, drugs-trafficking and weapon-smuggling; to expand co-operation with international bodies; and to promote international efforts to establish 'anti-drug and financial security belts' around Afghanistan; the CSTO became an observer in the UN General Assembly in 2004; in April 2006 it signed a protocol with the UN Office on Drugs and Crime to develop joint projects to combat drugs-trafficking, terrorism and transborder crime; in Feb. 2009 agreed to establish a rapid reaction force and conducted a joint military exercise (without the participation of Uzbekistan) in Aug.–Oct; mems: Armenia, Belarus, Kazakhstan, Kyrgyzstan, Russia, Tajikistan, Uzbekistan; Sec.-Gen. NIKOLAY BORDYUZHA.

Community of Latin American and Caribbean States (CELAC) (Comunidad de Estados de América Latina y el Caribe): 3841 NE 2nd Ave, Suite 203A, Miami, FL 33137, USA; e-mail cumbre.calc@mppre.gob.ve; internet www.celac.gob.ve; f. 2010; aim to build regional co-operation on political, cultural, social and economic issues in the countries of Latin America and the Caribbean; inaugural summit held in Dec. 2011 (2012 summit to be hosted by Chile); 32 Latin American and Caribbean states; Interim Pres. SEBASTIÁN PIÑERA (Chile).

Comunidade dos Países de Língua Portuguesa (CPLP) (Community of Portuguese-Speaking Countries): rua S. Caetano 32, 1200-829 Lisbon, Portugal; tel. (21) 392-8560; fax (21) 392-8588; e-mail comunicacao@cplp.org; internet www.cplp.org; f. 1996; aims to produce close political, economic, diplomatic and cultural links between Portuguese-speaking countries and to strengthen the influence of the Lusophone Commonwealth within the international community; dispatched an observer mission to oversee presidential elections held in Timor-Leste in May 2007; mems: Angola, Brazil, Cape Verde, Guinea-Bissau, Mozambique, Portugal, São Tomé and Príncipe, Timor-Leste; assoc. observers: Equatorial Guinea, Mauritius, Senegal; Exec. Sec. DOMINGOS SIMÕES PEREIRA (Guinea-Bissau).

Conference on Interaction and Confidence-building Measures in Asia: 050000, Almatı, Aiteke Bi 65, Kazakhstan; tel. (727) 272-01-08; fax (727) 272-40-96; e-mail s-cica@s-cica.kz; internet www.s-cica.org; f. 1999 at first meeting of 16 Asian ministers for foreign affairs, convened in Almatı; aims to provide a structure to enhance co-operation, with the objectives of promoting peace, security and stability throughout the region; first meeting of heads of state held in June 2002, adopted the Almatı Act; activities focused on a catalogue of confidence-building measures grouped into five areas: economic dimension; environmental dimension; human dimension; fight against new challenges and threats; and military-political dimension; mems: Afghanistan, Azerbaijan, People's Republic of China, Egypt, India, Iran, Israel, Jordan, Kazakhstan, Republic of Korea, Kyrgyzstan, Mongolia, Pakistan, Palestine, Russia, Tajikistan, Thailand, Turkey, United Arab Emirates, Uzbekistan; observers: Indonesia, Japan, Malaysia, Qatar, Viet Nam, Ukraine, USA, and the UN, OSCE and League of Arab States; Exec. Dir DULAT BAKISHEV.

Eastern Regional Organization for Public Administration (EROPA): National College of Public Administration, Univ. of the Philippines, Diliman, Quezon City 1101, Philippines; tel. and fax (2) 9297789; e-mail eropa@eropa.org.ph; internet www.eropa.org.ph; f. 1960 to promote regional co-operation in improving knowledge, systems and practices of governmental administration, to help accelerate economic and social development; organizes regional conferences, seminars, special studies, surveys and training programmes; accredited, in 2000, as an online regional centre of the UN Public Administration Network for the Asia and Pacific region; there are three regional centres: Training Centre (New Delhi), Local Government Centre (Tokyo), Development Management Centre (Seoul); mems: 10 countries, 63 groups, 266 individuals; Sec.-Gen. ORLANDO S. MERCADO (Philippines); publs *EROPA Bulletin* (quarterly), *Asian Review of Public Administration* (2 a year).

The Elders: c/o POB 60837, London, W6 6GS, United Kingdom; e-mail info@theelders.org; internet www.theelders.org; f. 2001; aims to alleviate human suffering world-wide by offering a catalyst for the peaceful resolution of conflicts, seeking new approaches to unresolved global issues, and sharing wisdom; comprises: Martti Ahtisaari (Finland), Kofi Annan (Ghana), Ela Bhatt (India), Lakhdar Brahimi (Algeria), Gro Brundtland (Norway), Jimmy Carter (USA), Fernando H Cardoso (Brazil), Graça Machel (Mozambique), Nelson Mandela (South Africa), Desmond Tutu (South Africa), Mary Robinson (Ireland), Aung San Suu Kyi (Myanmar); CEO MABEL VAN ORANJE.

European Movement: 25 sq. de Meeûs, 1000 Brussels, Belgium; tel. (2) 508-30-88; fax (2) 508-30-89; e-mail secretariat@europeanmovement.eu; internet www.europeanmovement.eu; f. 1947 by a liaison committee of representatives from European organizations, to study the political, economic and technical problems of a European Union and suggest how they could be solved and to inform and lead public opinion in the promotion of integration; Conferences have led to the creation of the Council of Europe, College of Europe, etc; mems: national councils and committees in 42 European countries, and several international social and economic orgs, 25 assoc. mems; Sec.-Gen. DIOGO PINTO.

European Union of Women (EUW): Blenheim House, Henry St, Bath BA1 1JR, United Kingdom; tel. (20) 79244124; e-mail euw@euw-uk.co.uk; internet www.euw-uk.co.uk; f. 1953 to increase the influence of women in the political and civic life of their country and of Europe; mems: national organizations in 21 countries; Chair. LYNNE FAULKNER.

Group of Eight (G8): an informal meeting of developed nations, originally comprising France, Germany, Italy, Japan, United Kingdom and the USA, first convened in Nov. 1975, at Rambouillet, France, at the level of heads of state and government; Canada became a permanent participant in 1976, forming the Group of Seven major industrialized countries—G7; from 1991 Russia was invited to participate in the then G7 summit outside the formal framework of co-operation; from 1994 Russia contributed more fully to the G7 political dialogue and from 1997 Russia became a participant in nearly all of the summit process scheduled meetings, excepting those related to finance and the global economy; from 1998 the name of the co-operation framework was changed to Group of Eight—G8, and since 2003 Russia has participated fully in all scheduled summit meetings, including those on the global economy; the EU is also represented at G8 meetings, although it may not chair fora; G8 heads of government and the President of the European Commission and President of the European Council convene an annual summit meeting, the chairmanship and venue of which are rotated in the following order: France, USA, United Kingdom, Russia, Germany, Japan, Italy, Canada; G8 summit meetings address and seek consensus, published in a final declaration, on social and economic issues confronting the international community; the following ('+8') nations: Australia, Brazil, People's Republic of China, India, Indonesia, Mexico, Republic of Korea and South Africa were guest participants at the June 2008 G8 summit; G8 sectoral ministerial meetings (covering areas such as energy, environment, finance and foreign affairs) are held on the fringes of the annual summit, and further G8 sectoral ministerial meetings are convened through the year; mems: Canada, France, Germany, Italy, Japan, Russia, United Kingdom and the USA; European Union representation.

Gulf of Guinea Commission (Commission du Golfe de Guinée—CGG): f. 2001 to promote co-operation among mem; countries and the peaceful and sustainable development of natural resources in the sub-region; mems: Angola, Cameroon, the Repub. of the Congo, Equatorial Guinea, Gabon, Nigeria, São Tomé and Príncipe.

Hansard Society: 40–43 Chancery Lane, London, WC2A 1JA, United Kingdom; tel. (20) 7438-1222; fax (20) 7438-1229; e-mail contact@hansardsociety.org.uk; internet www.hansardsociety.org.uk; f. 1944 as Hansard Society for Parliamentary Government; aims to promote political education and research and the informed discussion of all aspects of modern parliamentary government; presidency is held jointly by the incumbent Speakers of the United Kingdom House of Commons and House of Lords; Co-Pres JOHN BERCOW, Baroness FRANCES D'SOUZA; CEO FIONA BOOTH; publ. *Parliamentary Affairs* (quarterly).

Ibero-American General Secretariat (Secretaría General Iberoamericana—SEGIB): Paseo de Recoletos 8, 28001 Madrid, Spain; tel. (91) 5901980; e-mail info@segib.org; internet www.segib.org; f. 2003; aims to provide institutional and technical support to the annual Iberoamerican summit meetings, to monitor programmes agreed at the meetings and to strengthen the Ibero-American community; meetings of Ibero-American heads of state and government (the first of which was convened in Guadalajara, Mexico in 1991, and the 21st in Oct. 2011, in Asunción, Paraguay) aim to promote political, economic and cultural co-operation among the 19 Spanish- and Portuguese-speaking Latin American countries and three European countries; Sec.-Gen. ENRIQUE IGLESIAS (Uruguay).

International Alliance of Women (Alliance Internationale des Femmes): Aaloekken 11, 5250 Odense, Denmark; tel. 65-96-08-68; e-mail iawsec@womenalliance.org; internet www.womenalliance.org; f. 1904 to obtain equality for women in all fields and to encourage women to assume decision-making responsibilities at all levels of society; lobbies at international organizations; mems: 58 national affiliates and associates; Pres. ROSY WEISS; Sec.-Gen. LENE PIND; publs *International Women's News* (3 a year), electronic newsletter (monthly).

International Association for Community Development (IACD): The Stables, Falkland, Fife, KY15 7AF, United Kingdom; e-mail info@iacdglobal.org; internet www.iacdglobal.org; f. 1952; promotes community development across international policies and programmes, supports community development practitioners and encourages the exchange of research and information; membership open to individuals and organizations working in or supporting community development across eight world regions; organizes annual international colloquium for community-based organizations; Pres. Dr INGRID BURKETT; publs *IACD Newsletter* (2 a year), monthly e-bulletins.

International Commission for the History of Representative and Parliamentary Institutions (ICHRPI): c/o Lothar Höbelt, Department of History, University of Vienna, Dr-Karl-Lueger-Ring 1, 1010 Vienna, Austria; fax (1) 4277 40821; e-mail lothar.hoebelt@univie.ac.at; internet www.ichrpi.com; f. 1936; promotes research into the origin and development of representative and parliamentary institutions world-wide; encourages wide and comparative study of such institutions, both current and historical; facilitates the exchange of information; 63rd Conference to be held in Cádiz, Spain (Sept. 2012); mems: 300 individuals in 31 countries; Pres. MARIA SOFIA CORCIULO (Italy); Sec.-Gen. Prof. LOTHAR HÖBELT (Austria); publs *Parliaments, Estates and Representation* (annually), studies.

International Conference on the Great Lakes Region, (ICGLR) (Conference Internationale sur la region des grands lacs): POB 7076, Bujumbura, Burundi; e-mail secretariat@icglr

.org; internet www.icglr.org; f. 2006 following the signing of the Security, Stability and Development Pact for the Great Lakes Region at the second summit meeting of the International Conference on the Great Lakes Region, held in December, in Nairobi, Kenya; the UN Security Council proposed in 2000 the organization of a Great Lakes Conference to initiate a process that would bring together regional leaders to pursue agreement on a set of principles and to articulate programmes of action to help end the cycle of regional conflict and establish durable peace, stability, security, democracy and development in the whole region; runs the Special Fund for Reconstruction and Development (SFRD) which is hosted and managed by the African Development Bank (AfDB); the first summit meeting of the Conference was convened in Dar es Salaam, Tanzania, in November 2004; executive secretariat created in May 2007; mems: Angola, Burundi, Central African Republic, Democratic Republic of the Congo, Republic of the Congo, Kenya, Rwanda, Sudan, Tanzania, Uganda, Zambia; Exec. Sec. Prof. ALPHONSE LUMU NTUMBA LUABA.

International Democrat Union: POB 1536, Vika, 0117 Oslo, Norway; tel. 22-82-90-00; fax 22-82-90-80; e-mail secretariat@idu.org; internet www.idu.org; f. 1983 as a group of centre and centre-right political parties; facilitates the exchange of information and views; promotes networking; organizes campaigning seminars for politicians and party workers; holds Party Leaders' meetings every three years, also executive meetings and a Young Leaders' Forum; mems: political parties in some 60 countries, 46 assoc. mems in regions; Exec. Sec. EIRIK MOEN.

International Federation of Resistance Fighters (FIR): Franz Mehring Platz 1, 10243 Berlin, Germany; tel. (30) 29784174; fax (30) 29784179; e-mail office@fir.at; internet www.fir.at; f. 1951; supports the medical and social welfare of former victims of fascism; works for peace, disarmament and human rights, and against fascism and neo-fascism; mems: 76 national orgs; Pres. VILMOS HANTI (Hungary); Sec.-Gen. Dr ULRICH SCHNEIDER (Germany).

International Institute for Democracy and Electoral Assistance (IDEA): Strömsborg, 103 34 Stockholm, Sweden; tel. (8) 698-3700; fax (8) 20-2422; e-mail info@idea.int; internet www.idea.int; f. 1995; aims to promote sustainable democracy in new and established democracies; works with practitioners and institutions promoting democracy in Africa, Asia, Arab states and Latin America; 27 mem. states and one observer; Sec.-Gen. VIDAR HELGESEN (Norway).

International Institute for Peace: Möllwaldplatz 5/2, 1040 Vienna, Austria; tel. (1) 504-64-37; fax (1) 505-32-36; e-mail secretariat@iip.at; internet www.iip.at; f. 1957; non-governmental organization with consultative status at ECOSOC and UNESCO; studies conflict prevention; new structures in international law; security issues in Europe and world-wide; mems: individuals and corporate bodies invited by the executive board; Pres. Dr PETER SCHIEDER (Austria); Dir PETER STANIA (Austria); Sec.-Gen. Dr GRIGORI LOKSHIN; publ. *Peace and Security* (quarterly).

International Institute for Strategic Studies (IISS): Arundel House, 13–15 Arundel St, London, WC2R 3DX, United Kingdom; tel. (20) 7379-7676; fax (20) 7836-3108; e-mail iiss@iiss.org; internet www.iiss.org; f. 1958 as an independent institution concerned with the study of the role of force in international relations, including problems of international strategy, the ethnic, political and social sources of conflict, disarmament and arms control, peace-keeping and intervention, defence economics, etc.; mems: c. 3,000; Dir-Gen. Dr JOHN M. W. CHIPMAN; Chair. FLEUR DE VILLIERS; publs *Survival* (quarterly), *The Military Balance* (annually), *Strategic Survey* (annually), *Adelphi Papers* (10 a year), *Strategic Comments* (10 a year).

International Lesbian and Gay Association (ILGA): 17 rue de la Charité, 1020 Brussels, Belgium; tel. and fax (2) 502-24-71; fax (2) 223-48-20; e-mail information@ilga.org; internet www.ilga.org; f. 1978; works to abolish legal, social and economic discrimination against homosexual and bisexual women and men, and transexuals, throughout the world; co-ordinates political action at an international level; co-operates with other supportive movements; 2012 world conference: Stockholm. Sweden; mems: 750 national and regional asscns in 110 countries; Co-Secs-Gen. GLORIA CAREAGA, RENATO SABBADINI; publs *ILGA Bulletin* (quarterly), *GBLT Human Rights Annual Report*.

International Peace Bureau (IPB): 41 rue de Zürich, 1201 Geneva, Switzerland; tel. 227316429; fax 227389419; e-mail mailbox@ipb.org; internet www.ipb.org; f. 1891; promotes international co-operation for general and complete disarmament and the non-violent solution of international conflicts; co-ordinates and represents peace movements at the UN; conducts projects on Disarmament for Development and the abolition of nuclear weapons; mems: 300 peace orgs and 150 individual mems in 70 countries; Co-Pres TOMAS MAGNUSSON, INGEBORG BREINES; Sec.-Gen. COLIN ARCHER (United Kingdom); publs *IPB News* (every 2 weeks, by e-mail), *IPB Geneva News*.

International Political Science Association (IPSA) (Association Internationale de Science Politique—AISP): c/o Concordia Univ., 331 ave Docteur Penfield, Montréal, QC H3G 1C5, Canada; tel. (514) 848-8717; fax (514) 848-4095; e-mail info@ipsa.org; internet www.ipsa.org; f. 1949; aims to promote the development of political science; organizes Annual International Congress of Political Science (2012: Belfast, Ireland); mems: 41 national asscns, 100 institutions, 1,350 individual mems; Pres. LEONARDO MORLINO (Italy); Sec.-Gen. GUY LACHAPELLE (Canada); publs *Participation* (3 a year), *International Political Science Abstracts* (6 a year), *International Political Science Review* (quarterly).

Jewish Agency for Israel (JAFI): POB 92, 48 King George St, Jerusalem 91000 Israel; tel. (2) 6202251; fax (2) 6202577; e-mail barbaram@jafi.org; internet www.jafi.org.il; f. 1929; reconstituted 1971 as an instrument through which world Jewry can work to develop a national home; constituents are: World Zionist Organization, United Israel Appeal, Inc. (USA), and Keren Hayesod; Chair. Exec. NATAN SHARANSKY; Chair. of the Bd JAMES TISCH; Dir-Gen. ALAN HOFFMANN.

Latin American Parliament (Parlamento Latinoamericano): Casilla 1527, Edif. 1111-1113, Apdo 4, ave. Principal de Amador, Panama; tel. 512-8500; e-mail secgeneral@parlatino.org; internet www.parlatino.org; f. 1965; permanent democratic institution, representative of all existing political trends within the national legislative bodies of Latin America; aims to promote the movement towards economic, political and cultural integration of the Latin American republics, and to uphold human rights, peace and security; Sec.-Gen. SONIA ESCUDERO; publs *Acuerdos, Resoluciones de las Asambleas Ordinarias* (annually), *Parlamento Latinoamericano–Actividades de los Órganos*, *Revista Patria Grande* (annually), statements and agreements.

Liberal International: 1 Whitehall Pl., London, SW1A 2HD, United Kingdom; tel. (20) 7839-5905; fax (20) 7925-2685; e-mail all@liberal-international.org; internet www.liberal-international.org; f. 1947; co-ordinates foreign policy work of member parties, and promotes freedom, tolerance, democracy, international understanding, protection of human rights and market-based economics; has consultative status at ECOSOC of United Nations and the Council of Europe; mems: 101 mem. parties and 10 co-operating orgs in 63 countries; Pres. HANS VAN BAALEN; Sec.-Gen. EMIL KIRJAS; publ. *Liberal Aerogramme* (quarterly).

NATO Parliamentary Assembly: 3 pl. du Petit Sablon, 1000 Brussels, Belgium; tel. (2) 513-28-65; fax (2) 514-18-47; internet www.nato-pa.int; f. 1955 as the NATO Parliamentarians' Conference; name changed 1966 to North Atlantic Assembly; renamed as above 1999; the inter-parliamentary assembly of the North Atlantic Alliance; holds two plenary sessions a year and meetings of committees (Political, Defence and Security, Economics and Security, Civil Dimension of Security, Science and Technology) to facilitate parliamentary awareness and understanding of key Alliance security issues, to provide the Alliance governments with a collective parliamentary voice, to contribute to a greater degree of transparency of NATO policies, and to strengthen the transatlantic dialogue; Pres. Dr KARL A. LAMERS (Germany); Sec.-Gen. DAVID HOBBS (United Kingdom).

Non-aligned Movement (NAM): c/o Ministry of Foreign Affairs, Arab Republic of Egypt, Corniche el-Nil, Cairo, Egypt; tel. (2) 25749820; fax (2) 25748822; e-mail namsummit@mfa.gov.eg; internet www.namegypt.org; f. 1961 by a meeting of 25 heads of state, with the aim of linking countries that had refused to adhere to the main East/West military and political blocs; co-ordination bureau established in 1973; works for the establishment of a new international economic order, and especially for better terms for countries producing raw materials; maintains special funds for agricultural development, improvement of food production and the financing of buffer stocks; South Commission promotes co-operation between developing countries; seeks changes at the United Nations to give developing countries greater decision-making power; holds summit conference every three years (2012: Iran); a 50th anniversary conference was convened in Bali, Indonesia, in May 2011; mems: 118 countries, 16 observer countries and 9 observer orgs.

Nordic Council: Ved Stranden 18, 1061 Copenhagen, Denmark; tel. 33-96-04-00; fax 33-11-18-70; e-mail nordisk-rad@norden.org; internet www.norden.org; f. 1952 to facilitate co-operation between Nordic parliaments and governments; 87 elected mems; Pres. KIMMO SASI (Finland); Sec.-Gen. JAN-ERIK ENESTAM (Finland); publs *Norden the Top of Europe* (monthly newsletter in English and Russian), *Norden this week* (weekly newsletter).

Nordic Council of Ministers: Ved Stranden 18, 1061, Copenhagen, Denmark; tel. 33-96-020-0; e-mail nmr@norden.org; internet www.norden.org; the Nordic Council of Ministers co-ordinates the activities of the governments of the Nordic countries when decisions are to be implemented; co-operation with adjacent areas includes the Baltic States, where Nordic governments are committed to furthering democracy, security and sustainable development, to contribute to peace, security and stability in Europe; the Nordic–Baltic Scholarship Scheme awards grants to students, teachers, scientists, civil servants and parliamentarians; Sec.-Gen. HALLDÓR ASGRÍMSSON (Iceland).

Northern Forum: 716 W 4th Ave, Suite 100, Anchorage, Alaska, USA; tel. (907) 561-3280; fax (907) 561-6645; e-mail nForum@northernforum.org; internet www.northernforum.org; f. 1991; aims to improve the quality of life of Northern peoples through support for sustainable development and socio-economic co-operation throughout the region; Exec. Dir PRISCILLA P. WOHL.

Organisation for the Prohibition of Chemical Weapons (OPCW): Johan de Wittlaan 32, 2517JR The Hague, Netherlands; tel. (70) 4163300; fax (70) 3063535; e-mail media@opcw.org; internet www.opcw.org; f. April 1997, on the entry into force of the Chemical Weapons Convention (CWC)—an international, multilateral disarmament treaty banning the development, production, stockpiling, transfer and use of chemical weapons—to oversee its implementation; verifies the irreversible destruction of declared chemical weapons stockpiles, as well as the elimination of all declared chemical weapons production facilities; OPCW member states undertake to provide protection and assistance if chemical weapons have been used against a state party, or if such weapons threaten a state party, and, together with OPCW inspectors, monitor the non-diversion of chemicals for activities prohibited under the CWC and verify the consistency of industrial chemical declarations; CWC states parties are obligated to declare any chemical weapons-related activities, to secure and destroy any stockpiles of chemical weapons within the stipulated deadlines, as well as to inactivate and eliminate any chemical weapons production capacity within their jurisdiction; mems: states party to the Convention (188 at April 2012); 2012 budget: €71m.; Dir-Gen. AHMET ÜZÜMCÜ (Turkey).

Organisation Internationale de la Francophonie (La Francophonie): 19-21 ave Bosquet, 75007 Paris, France; tel. 1-44-11-12-50; fax 1-44-11-12-80; e-mail oif@francophonie.org; internet www.francophonie.org; f. 1970 as l'Agence de coopération culturelle et technique; promotes co-operation among French-speaking countries in the areas of education, culture, peace and democracy, and technology; implements decisions of the Sommet francophone; technical and financial assistance has been given to projects in every member country, mainly to aid rural people; mems: 56 states and govts; 19 countries with observer status; Sec.-Gen. ABDOU DIOUF (Senegal); publ. *Journal de l'Agence de la Francophonie* (quarterly).

Organisation of Eastern Caribbean States (OECS): Morne Fortune, POB 179, Castries, Saint Lucia; tel. 455-6327; fax 453-1628; e-mail oecss@oecs.org; internet www.oecs.org; f. 1981 by the seven states which formerly belonged to the West Indies Associated States (f. 1966); aims to promote the harmonized development of trade and industry in member states; single market created on 1 January 1988; principal institutions are: the Authority of Heads of Government (the supreme policy-making body), the Foreign Affairs Committee, the Defence and Security Committee, and the Economic Affairs Committee; other functional divisions include an Export Development and Agricultural Diversification Unit (EDADU, based in Dominica), a Pharmaceutical Procurement Service (PPS), a Regional Integration Unit, a Regional E-Government Unit and an HIV/AIDS Project Unit; an OECS Technical Mission to the World Trade Organization in Geneva, Switzerland, was inaugurated in June 2005; in Aug. 2008 heads of government determined to achieve economic union by 2011 and political union by 2013; an agreement to establish an economic union was signed in December 2009; a Revised Treaty of Basseterre Establishing the OECS Economic Union was signed by heads of government of six member states (Antigua and Barbuda, Grenada, Dominica, Saint Christopher and Nevis, Saint Vincent and the Grenadines and Saint Lucia) in June 2010; the Treaty envisaged a new governance structure, in which an OECS Commission was to be established as a supranational executive institution; the Revised Treaty entered into force in February 2011, having been ratified by four of the signatory states; mems: Antigua and Barbuda, Dominica, Grenada, Montserrat, Saint Christopher and Nevis, Saint Lucia, Saint Vincent and the Grenadines; assoc. mems: Anguilla, British Virgin Islands; Dir-Gen. Dr LEN ISHMAEL.

Organization for Democracy and Economic Development (GUAM): 01001 Kyiv, str. Sofievska 2, Ukraine; tel. (44) 2063737; fax (44) 2063006; e-mail secretariat@guam-organization.org; internet www.guam-organization.org; f. 1997 as a consultative alliance of Georgia, Ukraine, Azerbaijan and Moldova (GUAM); Uzbekistan joined the grouping in April 1999, when it became known as GUUAM, but withdrew in May 2005, causing the grouping's name to revert to GUAM; formally inaugurated as a full international organization and current name adopted by heads of state at a summit held in Kyiv in May 2006; objectives include the promotion of a regional space of democracy, security, and stable economic and social development; strengthening relations with the EU and NATO; developing a database on terrorism, organized crime, drugs-trafficking, and related activities; establishing a GUAM energy security council; creating the GUAM Free-Trade Zone, in accordance with an agreement signed by heads of state at a meeting in Yalta, Ukraine, in July 2002; further economic development, including the creation of an East–West trade corridor and transportation routes for petroleum; and participation in conflict resolution and peace-keeping activities, with the establishment of peace-keeping forces and civilian police units under consideration; Sec.-Gen. VALERI CHECHELASHVILI (Georgia).

Organization of Solidarity of the Peoples of Africa, Asia and Latin America (OSPAAAL) (Organización de Solidaridad de los Pueblos de Africa, Asia y América Latina): Calle C No 670 esq. 29, Vedado, Havana 10400, Cuba; tel. (7) 830-5136; fax (7) 833-3985; e-mail secretario.general@tricontinental.cu; internet www.tricontinental.cu; f. 1966 at the first Conference of Solidarity of the Peoples of Africa, Asia and Latin America, to unite, co-ordinate and encourage national liberation movements in the three continents, to oppose foreign intervention in the affairs of sovereign states, colonial and neo-colonial practices, and to fight against racialism and all forms of racial discrimination; favours the establishment of a new international economic order; mems: 76 orgs in 46 countries; Sec.-Gen. ALFONSO FRAGA; publ. *Tricontinental* (quarterly).

Parliamentary Association for Euro-Arab Co-operation (PAEAC) (Institut européen de recherche sur la coopération euro-arabe): 24 Sq. de Meeus, 5th Floor, 1000 Brussels, Belgium; tel. (2) 231-13-00; fax (2) 231-06-46; e-mail secretariat@medeainstitute.org; internet www.medea.be; f. 1974 as an asscn of 650 parliamentarians of all parties from the national parliaments of the Council of Europe countries and from the European Parliament, to promote friendship and co-operation between Europe and the Arab world; Executive Committee holds annual joint meetings with Arab Inter-Parliamentary Union; represented in Council of Europe, Western European Union and European Parliament; works for the progress of the Euro-Arab Dialogue and a settlement in the Middle East that takes into account the national rights of the Palestinian people; Pres. FRANÇOIS-XAVIER DE DONNEA; Sec.-Gen. CHARLES KLEINERMANN; publs *Information Bulletin* (quarterly), *Euro-Arab and Mediterranean Political Fact Sheets* (2 a year), conference notes.

Party of European Socialists (PES): 98 rue du Trône, 1050 Brussels, Belgium; tel. (2) 548-90-80; fax (2) 230-17-66; e-mail info@pes.org; internet www.pes.org; f. 1992 to replace the Confederation of the Socialist Parties of the EC (f. 1974); affiliated to Socialist International; mems: 33 parties, 11 associate parties and 5 observer parties; 5 mem. orgs, 3 associate orgs and 10 observer orgs; Interim Pres. SERGEI STANISHEV; Sec.-Gen. PHILIP CORDERY; publs various, including *The New Social Europe*, *The EU on the international scene: Promoting sustainable peace*, statutes, manifestos and Congress documents.

Polynesian Leaders Group (PLG): c/o Govt of Samoa, POB L 1861, Apia, Samoa; tel. 24799; e-mail presssecretariat@samoa.ws; f. 2011 in Apia with the MOU signed by 8 states; to represent the collective interests of the Polynesian islands; first formal meeting to be held in the Cook Islands in August 2012; mems: American Samoa, Cook Islands, French Polynesia, Niue, Samoa, Tokelau, Tonga and Tuvalu; Chair. TUILA'EPA SAILELE MALIELEGAOI (Samoa).

Regional Co-operation Council: 71000 Sarajevo, Trg Bosne i Hercegovine 1/V, Bosnia and Herzegovina; tel. (33) 561700; fax (33) 561701; e-mail rcc@rcc.int; internet www.rcc.int; f. 2008, as successor to the Stability Pact for South Eastern Europe; serves as a focus for co-operation in the region; its six priority areas of activity cover: economic and social development, energy and infrastructure, justice and home affairs, security co-operation, and building human capital, with parliamentary co-operation as an overarching theme; maintains a Liaison Office in Brussels, Belgium; 50 mem. countries and orgs; Sec.-Gen. HIDO BIŠČEVIĆ.

Rio Group: f. 1987 at a meeting in Acapulco, Mexico, of eight Latin American government leaders, who agreed to establish a 'permanent mechanism for joint political action'; additional countries subsequently joined the Group (see below); holds annual summit meetings at presidential level. At the ninth presidential summit (Quito, Ecuador, September 1995) a 'Declaration of Quito' was adopted, which set out joint political objectives, including the strengthening of democracy; combating corruption, drugs-production and -trafficking and money-laundering; and the creation of a Latin American and Caribbean free trade area (supporting the efforts of the various regional groupings). Opposes US legislation (the 'Helms-Burton' Act), which provides for sanctions against foreign companies that trade with Cuba; admitted Cuba as a member in Nov. 2008; also concerned with promoting sustainable development in the region, the elimination of poverty, and economic and financial stability. The Rio Group holds regular ministerial conferences with the EU; summit meeting in Cancún, Mexico, in Feb. 2010, determined to establish a new regional grouping, the Community of Latin American and Caribbean States (inaugurated in Dec. 2011, q.v.); mems: Argentina, Belize, Bolivia, Brazil, Chile, Colombia, Costa Rica, Cuba, Dominican Republic, Ecuador, El Salvador, Guatemala, Guyana, Haiti,

Honduras, Jamaica, Mexico, Nicaragua, Panama, Paraguay, Peru, Suriname, Uruguay, Venezuela.

Shanghai Cooperation Organization (SCO): 41 Liangmaqiao Rd, Chaoyang District, Beijing, People's Republic of China; tel. (10) 65329806; fax (10) 65329808; e-mail sco@sectsco.org; internet www.sectsco.org; f. 2001, replacing the Shanghai Five (f. 1996 to address border disputes); aims to achieve security through mutual co-operation: promotes economic co-operation and measures to eliminate terrorism and drugs-trafficking; agreement on combating terrorism signed June 2001; a Convention on the Fight against Terrorism, Separatism and Extremism signed June 2002; Treaty on Long-term Good Neighbourliness, Friendship and Co-operation was signed August 2007; maintains an SCO anti-terrorism centre in Tashkent, Uzbekistan; holds annual summit meeting (2012: China); mems: People's Republic of China, Kazakhstan, Kyrgyzstan, Russia, Tajikistan and Uzbekistan; Sec.-Gen. MURATBEK IMANALIEV (Kyrgyzstan).

Socialist International: Maritime House, Clapham, London, SW4 0JW, United Kingdom; tel. (20) 7627-4449; fax (20) 7720-4448; e-mail secretariat@socialistinternational.org; internet www.socialistinternational.org; f. 1864; re-established in 1951; the world's oldest and largest asscn of political parties, grouping democratic socialist, labour and social democratic parties from every continent; provides a forum for political action, policy discussion and the exchange of ideas; works with many international orgs and trades unions (particularly members of ITUC; established a Commission for a Sustainable World Society in Nov. 2006; holds Congress every three years (23rd Congress held in Athens, Greece, in June–July 2008); the Council meets twice a year, and regular conferences and meetings of party leaders are also held; committees and councils on a variety of subjects and in different regions meet frequently; mems: 115 full member, 37 consultative and 18 observer parties in 122 countries; there are 3 fraternal orgs and 9 associated orgs, including: the Party of European Socialists (PES), the Group of the PES at the European Parliament and the International Federation of the Socialist and Democratic Press; Pres. GEORGE A. PAPANDREOU (Greece); Gen. Sec. LUIS AYALA (Chile); publ. *Socialist Affairs* (quarterly).

International Falcon Movement—Socialist Educational International: 98 rue du Trône, 2nd Floor, 1050 Brussels, Belgium; tel. (2) 215-79-27; fax (2) 245-00-83; e-mail contact@ifm-sei.org; internet www.ifm-sei.org; f. 1924 to help children and adolescents develop international understanding and a sense of social responsibility and to prepare them for democratic life; co-operates with several institutions concerned with children, youth and education; mems: 62 mems world-wide; Pres. TIM SCHOLZ (Germany); Sec.-Gen. TAMSIN PEARCE (United Kingdom); publs *IFM-SEI Newsletter* (quarterly), *IFM-SEI World News*, *EFN Newsletter*, *Asian Regional Bulletin*, *Latin American Regional Bulletin*.

International Union of Socialist Youth (IUSY): Amtshausgasse 4, 1050 Vienna, Austria; tel. (1) 523-12-67; fax (1) 523-12-679; e-mail iusy@iusy.info; internet www.iusy.info; f. 1907 as Socialist Youth International (present name adopted 1946), to educate young people in the principles of free and democratic socialism and further the co-operation of democratic socialist youth orgs; conducts international meetings, symposia, etc; mems: 149 youth and student orgs in 100 countries; Pres. JACINTA ARDERN; Gen. Sec. JOHAN HASSEL (Sweden); publs *IUSY Newsletter*, *FWG News*.

Stockholm International Peace Research Institute (SIPRI): Signalistgatan 9, 169 70 Solna, Sweden; tel. (8) 655-97-00; fax (8) 655-97-33; e-mail sipri@sipri.org; internet www.sipri.org; f. 1966; researches regional and global security, armed conflict and conflict management, military spending, armaments, arms control, disarmament and non-proliferation; provides data, analysis and recommendations to policy-makers, researchers, the media, and the interested public; has recently established programmes on China and Global Security and on Global Health and Security; maintains a number of databases on international arms transfers, military expenditure, multilateral peace operations, and international arms embargoes; mems: about 50 staff mems, about 30 of whom are researchers; Dir Dr GILL BATES (USA); publs *SIPRI Yearbook: Armaments, Disarmament and International Security*, monographs and research reports.

Transparency International: Alt Moabit 96, 10559 Berlin, Germany; tel. (30) 3438200; fax (30) 34703912; e-mail ti@transparency.org; internet www.transparency.org; f. 1993; aims to promote governmental adoption of anti-corruption practices and accountability at all levels of the public sector; works to ensure that international business transactions are conducted with integrity and without resort to corrupt practices; raises awareness of the damaging effects of corruption; produces an annual Corruption Perceptions Index, a Bribe Payers Index, a Global Corruption Barometer and an annual Global Corruption Report; holds International Anti-Corruption Conference every two years; some 90 chapters world-wide; Chair. Dr HUGUETTE LABELLE.

Trilateral Commission: 1156 15th St, NW, Washington, DC 20005, USA; tel. (202) 467-5410; fax (202) 467-5415; e-mail contactus@trilateral.org; internet www.trilateral.org; also offices in Paris and Tokyo; f. 1973 by private citizens of western Europe, Japan and North America, to encourage closer co-operation among these regions on matters of common concern; through analysis of major issues the Commission seeks to improve public understanding of problems, to develop and support proposals for handling them jointly, and to nurture the habit of working together in the 'trilateral' area. The Commission issues 'task force' reports on such subjects as monetary affairs, political co-operation, trade issues, the energy crisis and reform of international institutions; mems: about 335 individuals eminent in academic life, industry, finance, labour, etc.; those currently engaged as senior government officials are excluded; Chair. YOTARO KOBYASHI, JOSEPH S. NYE, Jr ; Dirs MICHAEL J. O'NEIL, PAUL RÉVAY, TADASHI YAMAMOTO; publs *Task Force Reports*, *Triangle Papers*.

Union for the Mediterranean Secretariat (UfMS): Palacio de Pedralbes, Pere Duran Farell, 11, 08034 Barcelona, Spain; tel. (93) 5214100; fax (93) 5214102; e-mail info@ufmsecretariat.org; internet www.ufmsecretariat.org; f. 2008 as a continuation of the Euro-Mediterranean Partnership ('Barcelona Process'), which had been launched in 1995; the statutes of the UfMS were adopted in March 2010; the UfMS's mandate is defined by the July 2008 'Paris Declaration' of the Euro-Mediterranean summit, and by the subsequent 'Marseilles Declaration', adopted in Nov. of that year; the Union was established as a framework for advancing relations (political, economic and social) between the EU and countries of the Southern and Eastern Mediterranean, in accordance with the goals detailed in the 1995 Barcelona Declaration: i.e. working to create an area of stability and shared economic prosperity, underpinned by full respect for democratic principles, human rights and fundamental freedoms; mems: 27 EU member states, the European Commission and 16 Mediterranean countries; Sec.-Gen. FATHALLAH SIJILMASSI (Morocco).

Union of International Associations (UIA): 40 rue Washington, 1050 Brussels, Belgium; tel. (2) 640-18-08; fax (2) 643-61-99; e-mail uia@uia.org; internet www.uia.org; f. 1907, present title adopted 1910; aims to facilitate the evolution of the activities of the world-wide network of non-profit orgs, especially non-governmental and voluntary asscns; collects and disseminates information on such orgs; promotes research on the legal, administrative and other problems common to these asscns; mems: 115 individuals in 28 countries and 71 assoc. corp. bodies or individuals; Sec.-Gen. JACQUES DE MÉVIUS; publs *International Congress Calendar* (quarterly), *Yearbook of International orgs*, *International Organization Participation* (annually), *Global Action Network* (annually), *Encyclopedia of World Problems and Human Potential*, *Documents for the Study of International Non-Governmental Relations*, *International Congress Science* series, *International Association Statutes* series, *Who's Who in International Organizations*.

Union of South American Nations (UNASUR): Avda 6 de Diciembre, Quito, Ecuador; tel. (2) 2554034; e-mail secretaria.general@unasursg.org; internet www.unasursg.org; in Dec. 2004 leaders from 12 Latin American countries attending a pan-South American summit, convened in Cusco, Peru, approved in principle the creation of a new South American Community of Nations (SACN), to entail the merger of the Andean Community, Mercosur and Aladi (with the participation of Chile, Guyana and Suriname); the first South American Community meeting of heads of state was held in September, in Brasília, Brazil; in April 2007, at the first South American Energy Summit, convened in Margarita Island, Venezuela, heads of state endorsed the establishment of a Union of South American Nations (UNASUR), to replace SACN as the lead organization for regional integration; it was envisaged that UNASUR would have political decision-making functions, supported by a small permanent secretariat, to be located in Quito, and would co-ordinate on economic and trade matters with the Andean Community, Mercosur and Aladi; a regional parliament was to be established in Cochabamba, Bolivia; summit meetings formally to inaugurate UNASUR were scheduled to be held in December 2007, then March 2008; both were postponed; the constituent treaty to establish UNASUR was signed by heads of state meeting in Brasília, Brazil, in May; a South American Defence Council (Consejo de Defensa Suramericano—CDS) was inaugurated in Santiago, Chile, in March 2009; in April 2009 UNASUR ministers of health approved the establishment of a South American Council on Health; the third ordinary summit meeting of heads of state was held in Quito, in August, followed by an extraordinary summit at the end of that month, in Bariloche, Argentina, to consider a military agreement between Colombia and the USA; a summit meeting in May 2010 elected the organization's first Secretary-General (deceased Oct. 2010); the fourth summit meeting was held in Georgetown, Guyana, in November; the constituent treaty entered into force on 11 March

2011, having received the required nine ratifications; in May a UNASUR centre for strategic defence studies (Centro de Estudios Estratégicos de la Defensa—CEED) was inaugurated in Buenos Aires, Argentina; the first meeting of a South American Economic and Financial Council, comprising UNASUR ministers of finance and central bank officials, was held in Buenos Aires, in August; Sec.-Gen. MARÍA EMMA MEJÍA (Colombia).

United Cities and Local Governments (UCLG): Carrer Avinyó 15, 08002 Barcelona, Spain; tel. (93) 3428750; fax (93) 3428760; e-mail info@cities-localgovernments.org; internet www.cities-localgovernments.org; f. 2004 by merger of the Int. Union of Local Authorities and the World Federation of United Cities; aims to increase the role and influence of local governments, promotes democratic local governance, and facilitates partnerships and networks among cities and local authorities; initiated a Millennium Towns and Cities Campaign to encourage civic authorities to support implementation of the Millennium Development Goals; launched the Global Observatory on Local Democracy and Decentralisation (GOLD) to provide information on the situation and evolution of decentralisation, self-government and local government across the world; mems: 112 local government asscns, more than 1,000 mem. cities in 95 countries; Pres. KADIR TOPBAS (Turkey); Sec.-Gen. ELISABETH GATEAU; publ. *Global Report on Decentralisation and Local Democracy*.

Unrepresented Nations and Peoples Organization (UNPO): Laan van Meerdervoort 70, 2517 AN, The Hague, Netherlands; tel. (70) 3646504; fax (70) 3646608; e-mail unpo@unpo.org; internet www.unpo.org; f. 1991; an international, non-violent, and democratic membership organization representing indigenous peoples, minorities, and unrecognised or occupied territories united in the aim of protecting and promoting their human and cultural rights, preserving their environments, and finding non-violent solutions to conflicts that affect them; mems: 60 orgs representing occupied nations, indigenous peoples and minorities; Pres. NGAWANG CHOEPHEL; Gen. Sec. MARINO BUSDACHIN; publ. *UNPO Yearbook*.

War Resisters' International: 5 Caledonian Rd, London, N1 9DX, United Kingdom; tel. (20) 7278-4040; fax (20) 7278-0444; e-mail info@wri-irg.org; internet www.wri-irg.org; f. 1921; encourages refusal to participate in or support wars or military service, collaborates with movements that work for peace and non-violent social change; mems: approx. 150,000; Chair. HOWARD CLARK; Treasurer DOMINIC SAILLARD (Spain); publs *The Broken Rifle* (quarterly), *warprofiteers-news* (every 2 months) *co-update* (monthly).

Women's International Democratic Federation (WIDF): Guimarães Passos 422, Vila Mariana, São Paulo, SP, Brazil, 04107-031; tel. (11) 2892-3087; e-mail fdim.sec@terra.com.br; internet www.fdim-widf.org; f. 1945 to unite women regardless of nationality, race, religion or political opinion; to enable them to work together to win and defend their rights as citizens, mothers and workers; to protect children; and to ensure peace and progress, democracy and national independence; structure: Congress, Secretariat and Executive Committee; mems: 660 affiliated orgs in 160 countries; Pres. MARCIA CAMPOS (Brazil); publs *Women of the Whole World* (6 a year), *Newsletter*.

World Disarmament Campaign: POB 28209, Edinburgh, EH9 1ZR, United Kingdom; tel. (20) 7377-2111; fax (20) 7377-2999; e-mail editor.worlddisarm@ntlworld.com; internet www.world-disarm.org.uk; f. 1980 to encourage governments to take decisive action to reduce armaments and military expenditure; promotes measures for disarmament, to secure peace and security in a great and sustainable global community; encourages inter-faith work for world peace; acts on the four main commitments called for in the Final Document of the UN's First Special Session on Disarmament; Co-ordinator Rev. BRIAN G. COOPER; publ. *World Disarm!* (quarterly).

World Federalist Movement (WFM): 708 Third Ave, 24th Floor, New York, NY 10017, USA; tel. (212) 599-1320; fax (212) 599-1332; e-mail info@wfm-igp.org; internet www.wfm-igp.org; f. 1947; aims to acquire for the UN the authority to make and enforce laws for the peaceful settlement of disputes, and to raise revenue under limited taxing powers; to establish better international co-operation in the areas of environment, development and disarmament; and to promote federalism throughout the world; an Institute for Global Policy was established in 1983 as the research and policy analysis mechanism of the WFM; Congress meetings held every five years (July 2012: Winnipeg, Canada); mems: 20 mem. orgs and 16 assoc. orgs; Pres. LLOYD AXWORTHY; Exec. Dir WILLIAM R. PACE; publs *World Federalist News* (quarterly), *International Criminal Court Monitor* (quarterly).

World Federation of United Nations Associations (WFUNA) (Fédération Mondiale des Associations Pour les Nations Unies—FMANU): 1 United Nations Plaza, Rm 1177, New York, NY 10017, USA; tel. (212) 963-0569 (temporary); e-mail info@wfuna.org; internet www.wfuna.org; f. 1946 to encourage popular interest and participation in United Nations programmes, discussion of the role and future of the UN, and education for international understanding; Plenary Assembly meets every three years; mems: national asscns in more than 100 countries; Pres. PARK SOO-GIL (Republic of Korea); Sec.-Gen. BONIAN GOLMOHAMMADI (Sweden); publ. *WFUNA News*.

World Peace Council: Othonos 10, Athens 10557, Greece; tel. (210) 331-6326; fax (210) 322-4302; e-mail info@wpc-in.org; internet www.wpc-in.org; f. 1950 at the Second World Peace Congress, Warsaw; principles: the prevention of nuclear war; the peaceful co-existence of the various socio-economic systems in the world; settlement of differences between nations by negotiation and agreement; complete disarmament; elimination of colonialism and racial discrimination; and respect for the right of peoples to sovereignty and independence; mems: representatives of national orgs, groups and individuals from 140 countries, and of 30 international orgs; Executive Committee of 40 mems elected by world assembly held every three years; Pres. SOCORRO GOMES; Exec. Sec. THANASSIS PAFILIS; publ. *Peace Courier* (monthly).

Youth of the European People's Party (YEPP): 10 Rue du Commerce, 1000 Brussels, Belgium; tel. (2) 285-41-63; fax (2) 285-41-65; e-mail yepp@epp.eu; internet www.yepp-online.net; f. 1997 to unite national youth orgs of member parties of European Young Christian Democrats and Democrat Youth Community of Europe; aims to develop contacts between youth movements and advance general political debate among young people; mems: 56 orgs in some 38 European countries; Pres. CSABA DÖMÖTÖR (Hungary); Sec.-Gen. JUHA-PEKKA NURVALA (Finland).

Industrial and Professional Relations

Association of Mutual Insurers and Insurance Co-operatives in Europe (AMICE): 98 rue de Trone, 1050 Brussels, Belgium; tel. (2) 503-38-78; fax (2) 503-30-55; e-mail secretariat@amice-eu.org; internet www.amice-eu.org; f. 2008 through the merger of the International Association of Mutual Insurance Companies (AISAM) and the Association of European Co-operative and Mutual Insurers (ACME), to raise the profile of the mutual and co-operative insurance sector in Europe; convenes congress every two years (2012: Gdańsk, Poland); mems: 100 direct mems and 1,600 indirect mems, representing one-third of the insurance companies in Europe; Pres. ASMO KALPALA (Finland); Sec.-Gen. GREGOR POZNIAK; publs *Annual Report*, *Newsletter*.

European Association for Personnel Management: c/o CIPD, 151 The Broadway, Wimbledon, London, SW19 1JQ, United Kingdom; tel. (20) 8612-6000; fax (20) 8612-6201; e-mail eapmsecretary@cipd.co.uk; internet www.eapm.org; f. 1962 to disseminate knowledge and information concerning the personnel function of management, to establish and maintain professional standards, to define the specific nature of personnel management within industry, commerce and the public services, and to assist in the development of national asscns; mems: 27 national asscns; Pres. FILIPPO ABRAMO (Italy); Sec.-Gen. EILEEN PEVREALL (United Kingdom).

European Cities Marketing: 29D rue de Talant, 21000 Dijon, France; tel. 3-80-56-02-04; fax 3-80-56-02-05; e-mail headoffice@europeancitiesmarketing.com; internet www.europeancitiesmarketing.com; European Cities Marketing is the network of City Tourist Offices and Convention Bureaus; aims to strengthen city tourism by providing sales and marketing opportunities, communicating information, sharing knowledge and expertise, educating and working together on an operational level; Pres. DIETER HARDT-STREMAYR.

European Civil Service Federation (ECSF) (Fédération de la Fonction Publique Européenne—FFPE): 200 rue de la Loi, L 102 6/14,1049 Brussels, Belgium; tel. (2) 295-00-12; fax (2) 298-17-21; e-mail secretariat.politique@ffpe.org; internet www.ffpe-bxl.eu; f. 1962 to foster the idea of a European civil service of staff of international organizations operating in western Europe or pursuing regional objectives; upholds the interests of civil service members; mems: local cttees in 12 European countries and individuals in 66 countries; Pres. BACRI PIERRE-PHILIPPE; Political Sec. TOSON MYRIAM; publ. *Eurechos*.

European Construction Industry Federation (Fédération de l'Industrie Européenne de la Construction—FIEC): 225 ave Louise, 1050 Brussels, Belgium; tel. (2) 514-55-35; fax (2) 511-02-76; e-mail info@fiec.eu; internet www.fiec.org; f. 1905 as International European Construction Federation, present name adopted 1999; mems: 33 national employers' organizations in 27 countries; Pres. LUISA TODINI (Italy); Dir-Gen. ULRICH PAETZOLD; publs *FIEC News* (2 a year), *Annual Report*, *Construction Activity in Europe*.

European Industrial Research Management Association (EIRMA): 46 rue Lauriston, 75116 Paris, France; tel. 1-53-23-83-10; fax 1-47-20-05-30; e-mail info@eirma.asso.fr; internet www.eirma.asso.fr; f. 1966 under auspices of the OECD; a permanent body in which European science and technology firms meet to consider approaches to industrial innovation, support research and development, and take joint action to improve performance in their various fields; mems: 120 in 20 countries; Pres. LEOPOLD DEMIDDELEER; Sec.-Gen. MICHEL JUDKIEWICZ; publs *Annual Report*, *Conference Reports*, *Working Group Reports*, *Workshop Reports*.

European Trade Union Confederation (ETUC) (Confédération européenne des syndicats): 5 blvd du Roi Albert II, 1210 Brussels, Belgium; tel. (2) 224-04-11; fax (2) 224-04-54; e-mail etuc@etuc.org; internet www.etuc.org; f. 1973; comprises 85 national trade union confederations and 12 European industrial federations in 36 European countries, representing 60m. workers; co-operates closely with the International Trade Union Confederation; Pres. IGNACIO FERNÁNDEZ TOXO (Spain); Gen. Sec. BERNADETTE SÉGOL.

Federation of International Civil Servants' Associations (FICSA): Palais des Nations, Office BOC 74, 1211 Geneva 10, Switzerland; tel. 229173150; fax 229170660; e-mail ficsagensec@unog.ch; internet www.ficsa.org; f. 1952 to co-ordinate policies and activities of member asscns and unions, to represent staff interests before inter-agency and legislative organs of the UN and to promote the development of an international civil service; mems: 30 asscns and unions consisting of staff of UN orgs, 9 associate mems from non-UN orgs, 16 consultative asscns and 21 inter-organizational federations with observer status; Pres. MAURO PACE; Gen. Sec. MARIE-THÉRÈSE CONILH DE BEYSSAC; publs *Annual Report*, *FICSA Newsletter*, *FICSA Update*, *FICSA circulars*.

INSOL International: 6–7 Queen St, London, EC4N 1SP, United Kingdom; tel. (20) 7248-3333; fax (20) 7248-3384; e-mail heather@insol.ision.co.uk; internet www.insol.org; f. 1982 as International Federation of Insolvency Professionals; comprises national asscns of accountants and lawyers specializing in corporate turnaround and insolvency; holds oneday seminars, an annual conference and congress every four years; mems: 36 asscns, with more than 9,500 individual members in 60 countries; Pres. GORDON STEWART (United Kingdom); Exec. Dir CLAIRE BROUGHTON; publs *INSOL World* (quarterly newsletter), *International Insolvency Review* (2 a year).

International Association of Conference Interpreters: 46 ave Blanc, 1202 Geneva, Switzerland; tel. 229081540; fax 227324151; e-mail info@aiic.net; internet www.aiic.net; f. 1953 to represent professional conference interpreters, ensure the highest possible standards and protect the legitimate interests of mems; establishes criteria designed to improve the standards of training; recognizes schools meeting the required standards; has consultative status with the UN and several of its agencies; mems: 3,004 in more than 105 countries; Pres. LINDA FITCHETT; publs *Code of Professional Conduct*, *Yearbook* (listing interpreters), etc.

International Association of Conference Translators: 15 route des Morillons, 1218 Le Grand-Saconnex, Geneva, Switzerland; tel. 227910666; fax 227885644; e-mail secretariat@aitc.ch; internet www.aitc.ch; f. 1962; represents revisers, translators, précis writers and editors working for international conferences and organizations; aims to protect the interests of those in the profession and help maintain high standards; establishes links with international organizations and conference organizers; mems: c. 450 in 33 countries; Pres. MICHEL BOUSSOMMIER; Exec. Sec. CORALIE GOURDON; publs *Directory*, *Bulletin*.

International Confederation of Energy Regulators: e-mail office@icer-regulators.net; internet www.iern.net; f. 2009; mems: 11 regional energy regulatory asscns, representing more than 200 regulatory authorities world-wide; Interim Pres. JEAN-MICHEL GLACHANT.

International Federation of Actors (Fédération internationale des acteurs—FIA): 31 rue de l'Hôpital, 1000 Brussels, Belgium; tel. (2) 234-56-53; fax (2) 235-08-61; e-mail office@fia-actors.com; internet www.fia-actors.com; f. 1952; Exec. Cttee meets annually, Congress convened every four years; mems: 97 performers' unions in 71 countries; Pres. AGNETE HAALAND (Norway); Gen. Sec. DOMINICK LUQUER.

International Federation of Air Line Pilots' Associations (IFALPA): Interpilot House, Gogmore Lane, Chertsey, Surrey, KT16 9AP, United Kingdom; tel. (1932) 571711; fax (1932) 570920; e-mail ifalpa@ifalpa.org; internet www.ifalpa.org; f. 1948 to represent pilots world-wide; aims to promote the highest level of aviation safety world-wide and to provide services, support and representation to all its Member Associations; mems: 102 asscns, representing more than 100,000 pilots; Pres. Capt. DON WYKOFF; publs *Interpilot* (6 a year), safety bulletins and news-sheets.

International Federation of Biomedical Laboratory Science (IFBLS): POB 2830, Hamilton, Ontario, ON L8N 3N8, Canada; tel. (905) 667-8695; fax (905) 528-4968; e-mail communications@ifbls.org; internet www.ifbls.org; f. 1954 to allow discussion of matters of common professional interest; fmrly the International Association of Medical Laboratory Technologists (f. 1954); aims to promote globally the highest standards in the delivery of care, of professional training, and ethical and professional practices; develops and promotes active professional partnerships in health care at the international level; promotes and encourages participation of members in international activities; holds international congress every second year; mems: 180,000 in 37 countries; Pres. VINCENT GALLICCHIO (USA); publ. *Biomedical Laboratory Science International* (quarterly).

International Federation of Business and Professional Women (BPW International): BPW International, POB 2040, Fitzroy, Victoria 3065, Australia; e-mail presidents.office@bpw-international.org; internet www.bpw-international.org; f. 1930 to promote interests of business and professional women and secure combined action by such women; mems: national federations, associate clubs and individual associates, totalling more than 100,000 mems in over 100 countries; Pres. FREDA MIRIKLIS (Australia); Exec. Sec. Dr YASMIN DARWICH (Mexico); publ. *BPW News International* (every 2 months).

International Labour and Employment Relations Association (ILERA): c/o International Labour Office, 1211 Geneva 22, Switzerland; tel. 227997371; fax 227998749; e-mail ilera@ilo.org; internet www.ilo.org/ilera; f. 1966 as the International Industrial Relations Association (IIRA); to encourage development of national asscns of specialists, facilitate the spread of information, organize conferences, and promote internationally planned research, through study groups and regional meetings; a World Congress is held every three years; mems: 39 asscns, 47 institutions and 1,100 individuals; Pres. Prof. JANICE BELLACE (USA); Sec. MOUSSA OUMAROU (Niger); publs *IIRA Bulletin* (3 a year), *IIRA Membership Directory*, *IIRA Congress proceedings*.

International Organisation of Employers (IOE): 26 chemin de Joinville, BP 68, 1216 Cointrin/Geneva, Switzerland; tel. 229290000; fax 229290001; e-mail ioe@ioe-emp.org; internet www.ioe-emp.org; f. 1920; aims to establish and maintain contacts between mems and to represent their interests at the international level; works to promote free enterprise; joined in 2008 the Green Jobs Initiative, a partnership launched in 2007 by UNEP, the ILO and the International Confederation of Trade Unions; and to assist the development of employers' organizations; General Council meets annually; there is a Management Board and a General Secretariat; mems: 150 federations in 143 countries; Pres. Dato' AZMAN SHAH SERI HARON (Malaysia); Acting Sec.-Gen. BRENT WILTON; publ. *IOE.net*.

International Organization of Experts (ORDINEX): 19 blvd Sébastopol, 75001 Paris, France; tel. 1-40-28-06-06; fax 1-40-28-03-13; e-mail contact@ordinex.net; internet www.ordinex.net; f. 1961 to establish co-operation between experts on an international level; mems: 600; Sec.-Gen. PIERRE ROYER (France); publ. *General Yearbook*.

International Public Relations Association (IPRA): POB 6945, London W1A 6US, United Kingdom; tel. (1903) 744442; e-mail info@ipra.org; internet www.ipra.org; f. 1955 to provide an exchange of ideas, technical knowledge and professional experience among those engaged in public relations, and to foster the highest standards of professional competence; mems: 700 in 80 countries; Pres. JOHANNA MCDOWELL (South Africa); publs *Frontline* (every 2 months), *Directory of Members* (annually).

International Society of City and Regional Planners (ISOCARP): POB 983, 2501 CZ, The Hague, Netherlands; tel. (70) 3462654; fax (70) 3617909; e-mail isocarp@isocarp.org; internet www.isocarp.org; f. 1965 to promote better planning practice through the exchange of professional knowledge; holds annual world congress (Sept. 2012: Perm, Russia); mems: 653 in 87 countries; Pres. ISMAEL FERNÁNDEZ MEJÍA (Mexico); Sec.-Gen. ALEX MACGREGOR (United Kingdom); publs *Newsletter* (3 a year), *ISoCaRP REVIEW* (annually), seminar and congress reports.

International Union of Architects (Union internationale des architectes—UIA): Tour Maine Montparnasse, BP 158, 33 ave du Maine, 75755 Paris Cédex 15, France; tel. 1-45-24-36-88; fax 1-45-24-02-78; e-mail uia@uia-architectes.org; internet www.uia-architectes.org; f. 1948; holds triennial congress (2011: Tokyo, Japan); mems: professional orgs in 124 countries; Pres. ALBERT DUBLER (France); Gen. Sec. MICHEL BARMAKI (Lebanon); publ. *Lettre d'informations* (monthly).

Latin American Federation of Agricultural Workers (Federación Latinoamericana de Trabajadores Agrícolas, Pecuarios y Afines—FELTRA): Antiguo Local Conadi, B° La Granja, Comayaguela, Tegucigalpa, Honduras; tel. 2252526; fax 2252525; e-mail feltra@123.hn; f. 1999 by reorganization of FELTACA (f. 1961) to represent the interests of workers in agricultural and related industries in Latin America; mems: national unions in 28 countries and territories; Sec.-Gen. MARCIAL REYES CABALLERO; publ. *Boletín Luchemos* (quarterly).

Nordic Innovation (Nordisk InnovationsCenter): Stensberggt. 25, 0170 Oslo, Norway; tel. 47-61-44-00; fax 22-56-55-65; e-mail info@nordicinnovation.org; internet www.nordicinnovation.org; f. 1973; provides grants, subsidies and loans for industrial research and development projects of interest to Nordic countries; Chair. KARIN WIKMAN; Man. Dir KARI WINQUIST.

Organisation of African Trade Union Unity (OATUU): POB M386, Accra, Ghana; tel. (21) 508855; fax (21) 508851; e-mail oatuu@ighmail.com; f. 1973 as a single continental trade union org., independent of international trade union organizations; has affiliates from all African trade unions. Congress, the supreme policy-making body, is composed of four delegates per country from affiliated national trade union centres, and meets at least every four years; the General Council, composed of one representative from each affiliated trade union, meets annually to implement Congress decisions and to approve the annual budget; mems: trade union movements in 53 independent African countries; Sec.-Gen. Gen. HASSAN A. SUNMONU (Nigeria); publ. *The African Worker*.

Pan-African Employers' Confederation (PEC): c/o Mauritius Employers' Federation (MEF), Ebene Cyber City Ebene, Mauritius; tel. 466-3600; fax 465-8200; e-mail mefmim@intnet.mu; internet www.pec-online.org; f. 1986 to link African employers' organizations and represent them at the AU, UN and the ILO; mems: representation in 39 countries on the continent; Pres. THABO MAKEKA; Sec.-Gen. AZAD JEETUN (Mauritius).

Society of European Affairs Professionals (SEAP): Brussels, Belgium; tel. 478996025; e-mail secretariat@seap.be; internet www.seap.be; f. 1997; aims to establish an open non-profit making organization of European affairs professionals dealing with European institutions; Pres. SUSANNA DI FELICIANTONIO; Sec.-Gen. GARY HILLS.

World Federation of Scientific Workers (WFSW) (Fédération mondiale des travailleurs scientifiques—FMTS): Case 404, 263 rue de Paris, 93516 Montreuil Cédex, France; tel. 1-48-18-81-75; fax 1-48-18-80-03; e-mail fmts@fmts-wfsw.org; internet www.fmts-wfsw.org; f. 1946 to improve the position of science and scientists, to assist in promoting international scientific co-operation and to promote the use of science for beneficial ends; studies and publicizes problems of general, nuclear, biological and chemical disarmament; surveys the position and activities of scientists; mems: orgs in 28 countries; Pres. JEAN-PAUL LAINÉ (France); Sec.-Gen. PASCAL JANOTS (France).

World Movement of Christian Workers (WMCW): 124 blvd du Jubilé, 1080 Brussels, Belgium; tel. (2) 421-58-40; fax (2) 421-58-49; e-mail info@mmtc-infor.com; internet www.mmtc-infor.com; f. 1961 to unite national movements that advance the spiritual and collective well-being of workers; holds General Assembly every four years; mems: more than 50 affiliated movements in 39 countries; Sec.-Gen. PAUL EDWARDS; publ. *Infor-WMCW*.

World Union of Professions (Union mondiale des professions libérales): 46 blvd de la Tour-Maubourg, 75007 Paris, France; tel. 1-44-05-90-15; fax 1-44-05-90-17; e-mail info@umpl.org; internet www.umpl.com; f. 1987 to represent and link members of the liberal professions; mems: 27 national inter-professional orgs, 2 regional groups and 12 international federations; Chair. FRANCISCO ANTÔNIO FEIJO; Sec.-Gen. Dr GÉRARD GOUPIL.

Law

African Society of International and Comparative Law (ASICL): Private Bag 520, Kairaba Ave, KSMD, Banjul, The Gambia; tel. 375476; fax 375469; e-mail asicl_un@freesurf.ch; f. 1986; promotes public education on law and civil liberties; aims to provide a legal aid and advice system in each African country, and to facilitate the exchange of information on civil liberties in Africa; Sec. EMILE YAKPO (Ghana); publs *Newsletter* (every 2 months), *African Journal of International and Comparative Law* (quarterly).

Asian-African Legal Consultative Organization (AALCO): 29-C, Rizal Marg, Diplomatic Enclave, Chanakyapuri, New Delhi 110057, India; tel. (11) 24197000; fax (11) 26117640; e-mail mail@aalco.int; internet www.aalco.int; f. 1956 to consider legal problems referred to it by member countries and to serve as a forum for Afro-Asian co-operation in international law, including international trade law, and economic relations; provides background material for conferences, prepares standard/model contract forms suited to the needs of the region; promotes arbitration as a means of settling international commercial disputes; trains officers of member states; has permanent UN observer status; has established four International Commercial Arbitration Centres in Kuala Lumpur, Malaysia; Cairo, Egypt; Lagos, Nigeria; and Tehran, Iran; mems: 47 countries; Sec.-Gen. Prof. Dr RAHMAT BIN MOHAMAD (Malaysia).

Centre for International Environmental Law (CIEL): 1350 Connecticut Ave, NW, Suite 1100, Washington, DC 20036, USA; tel. (202) 785-8700; fax (202) 785-8701; e-mail info@ciel.org; internet www.ciel.org; f. 1989; aims to solve environmental problems and promote sustainable societies through use of law; works to strengthen international and comparative environmental law and policy and to incorporate fundamental ecological principles into international law; provides a range of environmental legal services; educates and trains environmental lawyers; Pres. and CEO CARROLL MUFFETT.

Comité maritime international (CMI): Everdijstraat 43, 2000 Antwerp, Belgium; tel. (3) 203-45-00; fax (3) 203-45-01; e-mail admin@cmi-imc.org; internet www.comitemaritime.org; f. 1897 to contribute to the unification of maritime law and to encourage the creation of national asscns; work includes drafting of conventions on collisions at sea, salvage and assistance at sea, limitation of shipowners' liability, maritime mortgages, etc; mems: national asscns in more than 59 countries; Pres. KARL-JOHAN GOMBRII; Sec.-Gen. NIGEL FRAWLEY (Canada); publs *CMI Newsletter*, *Year Book*.

Council of the Bars and Law Societies of Europe (CCBE): 1–5 ave de la Joyeuse Entrée, 1040 Brussels, Belgium; tel. (2) 234-65-10; fax (2) 234-65-11; e-mail ccbe@ccbe.eu; internet www.ccbe.eu; f. 1960; the officially recognized representative organization for the legal profession in the European Union and European Economic Area; liaises between the bars and law societies of member states and represents them before the European institutions; also maintains contact with other international organizations of lawyers; principal objective is to study all questions affecting the legal profession in member states and to harmonize professional practice; mems: 31 delegations (representing some 1m. European lawyers), and observer/associate delegations from 11 countries; Pres. JOSÉ MARÍA DAVÓ FERNÁNDEZ; Sec.-Gen. JONATHAN GOLDSMITH.

East African Court of Justice: AICC Bldg, Kilimanjaro Wing, 6th Floor, POB 1096, Arusha, Tanzania; tel. (27) 2504253; fax (27) 2504255; e-mail eacj@eachq.org; internet www.eacj.org/index.php; f. 2001; organ of the East African Community (EAC), established under the Treaty for the Establishment of the EAC with responsibility for ensuring compliance with the Treaty; Registrar Dr JOHN RUHANGISA.

Eastern Caribbean Supreme Court: Heraldine Rock Bldg, Block B, Waterfront, POB 1093, Castries; tel. 457-3600; fax 457-3601; e-mail offices@eccourts.org; internet www.eccourts.org; f. 1967 as the West Indies Associated States Supreme Court, in 1974 as the Supreme Court of Grenada and the West Indies Associated States, present name adopted in 1979; composed of the High Court of Justice and the Court of Appeal, High Court is composed of the Chief Justice and 16 High Court Judges. The Court of Appeal is itinerant and presided over by the Chief Justice and three other Justices of Appeal; jurisdiction of the court extends to fundamental rights and freedoms, membership of the parliaments, and matters concerning the interpretation of constitutions; Chief Justice HUGH ANTHONY RAWLINS.

Hague Conference on Private International Law: Scheveningseweg 6, 2517 KT, The Hague, Netherlands; tel. (70) 3633303; fax (70) 3604867; e-mail secretariat@hcch.net; internet www.hcch.net; f. 1893 to work for the unification of the rules of private international law; Permanent Bureau f. 1955; mems: 72 (incl. the European Union); Sec.-Gen. J. H. A. VAN LOON; publs *Proceedings of Diplomatic Sessions* (every 4 years), *Collection of Conventions*, *The Judges' Newsletter on International Child Protection*.

Institute of International Law (Institut de Droit international): 132 rue de Lausanne, CP 136, 1211 Geneva 21, Switzerland; tel. 229085720; fax 229086277; e-mail joe.verhoeven@uclouvain.be; internet www.idi-iil.org; f. 1873 to promote the development of international law through the formulation of general principles, in accordance with civilized ethical standards; provides assistance for the gradual and progressive codification of international law; mems: limited to 132 members and associates world-wide; Pres. EMMANUEL ROUCOUNAS; Sec.-Gen. JOE VERHOEVEN (Belgium); publ. *Annuaire de l'Institut de Droit international*.

Inter-African Union of Lawyers (IAUL) (Union interafricaine des avocats): BP14409, Libreville, Gabon; tel. 76-41-44; fax 74-54-01; f. 1980; holds congress every three years; publ. *L'avocat africain* (2 a year).

Inter-American Bar Association (IABA): 1211 Connecticut Ave, NW, Suite 202, Washington, DC 20036, USA; tel. (202) 466-5944; fax (202) 466-5946; e-mail iaba@iaba.org; internet www.iaba.org; f. 1940 to promote the rule of law and to establish and maintain relations between asscns and organizations of lawyers in the Americas; mems: 90 asscns and 3,500 individuals in 27 countries; Pres. BEATRIZ MARTORELLO; Sec.-Gen. HUGO CHAVIANO; publs *Newsletter* (quarterly), *Conference Proceedings*.

Intergovernmental Committee of the Universal Copyright Convention: Section for the Diversity of Cultural Expressions, UNESCO, 1 rue Miollis, 75700 Paris, France; tel. 1-45-68-47-45; fax 1-45-68-55-89; e-mail convention2005@unesco.org; established to study the application and operation of the Universal Copyright Convention and to make preparations for periodic revisions of this Convention; studies other problems concerning the international protection of copyright, in co-operation with various international organizations; mems: 24 states; Dir GALIA SAOUMA-FORERO; publ. *Copyright Bulletin* (quarterly: digital format in English, French and Spanish; print format in Chinese and Russian).

International Association for the Protection of Industrial Property (AIPPI): Tödistrasse 16, 8027 Zürich 27, Switzerland; tel. 442805880; fax 442805885; e-mail mail@aippi.org; internet www.aippi.org; f. 1897 to encourage the development of legislation on the international protection of industrial property and the development and extension of international conventions, and to make comparative studies of existing legislation with a view to its improvement and unification; holds triennial congress; mems: 8,200 (national and regional groups and individual mems) in 108 countries; Pres. YOON BAE KIM; Sec.-Gen. STEPHAN FREISCHEM; publs *Yearbook*, reports.

International Association of Chiefs of Police (IACP): 515 North Washington St, Alexandria, VA, 22314, USA; tel. (703) 836-6767; fax (703) 836-4543; e-mail rosenblatt@theiacp.org; internet www.theiacp.org; f. 1893 to advance the science and art of police services; Pres. MARK A. MARSHALL; Exec. Dir DANIEL N. ROSENBLATT.

International Association of Democratic Lawyers: 21 rue Brialmont, 1210 Brussels, Belgium; tel. and fax (2) 223-33-10; e-mail jsharma@vsnl.com; internet www.iadllaw.org; f. 1946 to facilitate contacts and exchange between lawyers, encourage study of legal science and international law and support the democratic principles favourable to the maintenance of peace and co-operation between nations; promotes the preservation of the environment; conducts research on labour law, private international law, agrarian law, etc; has consultative status with UN; mems: in 96 countries; Pres. JEANNE MIRER (USA); Sec.-Gen. OSAMU NIIKURA (Japan); publ. *International Review of Contemporary Law* (2 a year, in French, English and Spanish).

International Association of Law Libraries (IALL): POB 5709, Washington, DC 20016-1309, USA; e-mail xtl5d@virginia.edu; internet www.iall.org; f. 1959 to encourage and facilitate the work of librarians and others concerned with the bibliographic processing and administration of legal materials; mems: over 600 from more than 50 countries (personal and institutional); Pres. PETAL KINDER (Australia); Sec. BARBARA GARVAGLIA (USA); publ. *International Journal of Legal Information* (3 a year).

International Association of Legal Sciences (IALS) (Association internationale des sciences juridiques): c/o CISS, 1 rue Miollis, 75015 Paris, France; tel. 1-45-68-25-59; fax 1-45-66-76-03; e-mail info@aisj-ials.org; internet aisj-ials.org; f. 1950 to promote the mutual knowledge and understanding of nations and the increase of learning by encouraging throughout the world the study of foreign legal systems and the use of the comparative method in legal science; governed by a president and an executive committee of 11 members known as the International Committee of Comparative Law; sponsored by UNESCO; mems: national cttees in 47 countries; Pres. ERGUN ÖSZUNAY (Turkey); Sec.-Gen. M. LEKER (Israel).

International Association of Penal Law: 15 rue Charles Fourier, 75013 Paris, France; tel. 1-45-88-72-42; fax 1-55-04-92-89; e-mail secretariat@penal.org; internet www.penal.org; f. 1924 to promote collaboration between those from different countries working in penal law, studying criminology, or promoting the theoretical and practical development of international penal law; mems: 1,800; Pres. Prof. JOSÉ LUIS DE LA CUESTA (Spain); Sec.-Gen. KATALIN LIGETI (Luxembourg); publs *Revue Internationale de Droit Pénal* (2 a year), *Nouvelles Etudes Penales*.

International Association of Youth and Family Judges and Magistrates (IAYFJM): Lagergasse 6–8, 1030 Vienna, Austria; tel. (1) 713-18-25; e-mail nesrinlushta@yahoo.com; internet www.judgesandmagistrates.org; f. 1928 to support the protection of youth and family, and criminal behaviour and juvenile maladjustment; members exercise functions as juvenile and family court judges or within professional services linked to youth and family justice and welfare; organizes study groups, meetings and an international congress every four years (April 2010: Tunis, Tunisia); mems: 12 national asscns and mems in more than 80 countries; Pres. RENATE WINTER (Austria); Sec.-Gen. NESRIN LUSHTA (Kosovo).

International Bar Association (IBA): 1 Stephen St, 10th Floor, London, W1T 1AT, United Kingdom; tel. (20) 7691-6868; fax (20) 7691-6544; e-mail iba@int-bar.org; internet www.ibanet.org; f. 1947; a non-political federation of national bar asscns and law societies; aims to discuss problems of professional organization and status; to advance the science of jurisprudence; to promote uniformity and definition in appropriate fields of law; to promote administration of justice under law among peoples of the world; to promote in their legal aspects the principles and aims of the UN; mems: 198 orgs in 194 countries, 30,000 individual members; Pres. AKIRA KAWAMURA (Japan); Exec. Dir MARK ELLIS; publs *Business Law International* (3 a year), *International Bar News* (6 a year), *Competition Law International* (2 a year), *Journal of Energy and Natural Resources Law* (quarterly).

International Commission of Jurists (ICJ): POB 91, 33 rue des Bains, 1211 Geneva 8, Switzerland; tel. 229793800; fax 229793801; e-mail info@icj.org; internet www.icj.org; f. 1952 to promote the implementation of international law and principles that advance human rights; provides legal expertise to ensure that developments in international law adhere to human rights principles and that international standards are implemented at the national level; disseminates reports and other legal documents through the ICJ Legal Resource Centre; maintains Centre for the Independence of Judges and Lawyers (f. 1978); in Oct. 2005 established an Eminent Jurists' Panel on Terrorism, Counter-terrorism and Human Rights; mems: 82 sections and affiliated orgs in 62 countries; Pres. MARY ROBINSON (Ireland); Sec.-Gen. WILDER TAYLER (Uruguay); publs special reports.

International Commission on Civil Status: 3 pl. Arnold, 67000 Strasbourg, France; e-mail ciec-sg@ciec1.org; internet www.ciec1.org; f. 1950 for the establishment and presentation of legislative documentation relating to the rights of individuals; carries out research on means of simplifying the judicial and technical administration with respect to civil status; mems: governments of Belgium, Croatia, France, Germany, Greece, Hungary, Italy, Luxembourg, Mexico, Netherlands, Poland, Portugal, Spain, Switzerland, Turkey, United Kingdom; Pres. DUNCAN MACNIVEN; Sec.-Gen. WALTER PINTENS; publs *Guide pratique international de l'état civil* (available online), various studies on civil status.

International Copyright Society (Internationale Gesellschaft für Urheberrecht e.V.—INTERGU): Rosenheimer Strasse 11, 81667 Munich, Germany; tel. (89) 48003-00; fax (89) 48003-969; f. 1954 to enquire scientifically into the natural rights of the author and to put the knowledge obtained to practical application worldwide, in particular in the field of legislation; mems: 187 individuals and corresponding orgs in 37 countries; CEO Dr HARALD HEKER; publs *Schriftenreihe* (61 vols), *Yearbook*.

International Council for Commercial Arbitration (ICCA): c/o International Centre for Settlement of Investment Disputes, 1818 H St, NW, Washington, DC 20433, USA; tel. (202) 744-8801; fax (202) 522-2615; e-mail arparra@earthlink.net; internet www.arbitration-icca.org; promotes international arbitration and other forms of dispute resolution; convenes Congresses and Conferences for discussion and the presentation of papers; mems: 42 mems, 17 advisory mems; Pres. Prof. JAN PAULSSON (USA); Sec.-Gen. KAP-YOU (KEVIN) KIM (Republic of Korea); publs *Yearbook on Commercial Arbitration*, *International Handbook on Commercial Arbitration*, *ICCA Congress Series*.

International Council of Environmental Law (ICEL): Godesberger Allee 108–112, 53175 Bonn, Germany; tel. (228) 2692-240; fax (228) 2692-251; e-mail icel@intlawpol.org; internet www.i-c-e-l.org; f. 1969 to promote the exchange of information and expertise on legal, administrative and policy aspects of environmental conservation and sustainable development; in has consultative status with the ECOSOC; Exec. Governors Dr WOLFGANG E. BURHENNE (Germany), AMADO TOLENTINO, Jr (Philippines); publs *Directory*, *References*, *Environmental Policy and Law*, *International Environmental Law—Multilateral Treaties*, etc.

International Criminal Police Organization (INTERPOL): 200 quai Charles de Gaulle, 69006 Lyon, France; tel. 4-72-44-70-00; fax 4-72-44-71-63; e-mail info@interpol.int; internet www.interpol.int; f. 1923, reconstituted 1946; aims to promote and ensure mutual assistance between police forces in different countries; coordinates activities of police authorities of member states in international affairs; works to establish and develop institutions with the aim of preventing transnational crimes; centralizes records and information on international criminals; operates a global police communications network linking all member countries; holds General Assembly annually; mems: 188 countries; Sec.-Gen. RONALD K. NOBLE (USA); publ. *Annual Report*.

International Development Law Organization (IDLO): Viale Vaticano, 106 00165 Rome, Italy; tel. (06) 40403200; fax (06) 404032327; e-mail idlo@idlo.int; internet www.idlo.int; f. 1983; aims to promote the rule of law and good governance in developing countries, transition economies and nations emerging from conflict and to assist countries to establish effective infrastructure to achieve sustainable economic growth, security and access to justice; activities include Policy Dialogues, Technical Assistance, Global Network of Alumni and Partners, Training Programs, Research and Publications; maintains Regional Offices in Cairo, Egypt, covering Arabic-speaking countries and in Sydney, Australia, covering the Asia Pacific area; also operates Project Offices in Afghanistan, Indonesia, Sudan and Kyrgyzstan; mems: 22 mems (21 states and OPEC Fund for International Development); Dir-Gen. ANTONIO BADINI (Italy).

International Federation for European Law (Fédération Internationale pour le Droit Européen—FIDE): 113 ave Louise, 1050 Brussels, Belgium; tel. (2) 534-71-63; fax (2) 534-28-58; e-mail fide2008@jku.at; f. 1961 to advance studies on European law among members of the European Community by co-ordinating activities of member societies; organizes conferences every two years; mems: 12 national asscns; Pres. GIL CARLOS RODRÍGUEZ RODRÍGUEZ IGLESIAS (Spain); Sec.-Gen. LUIS ORTIZ BLANCO (Spain).

International Federation of Senior Police Officers (Federation Internationale des Fonctionnaires Superieures de Police—FIFSP): FIFSP, Ministère de l'Intérieur, 127 rue Faubourg Saint Honoré, 75008 Paris, France; tel. 1-49-27-40-67; fax 1-45-62-48-52; f. 1950 to unite policemen of different nationalities, adopting the general principle that prevention should prevail over repression, and that the citizen should be convinced of the protective role of the police; established International Centre of Crime and Accident Prevention, 1976 and International Association against Counterfeiting, 1994; mems: 34 national orgs; Pres. JUAN GARCÍA LLOVERA; Sec.-Gen. JEAN-PIERRE HAVRIN (France); publ. *International Police Information* (quarterly, in English, French and German).

International Humanitarian Fact-Finding Commission (IHFFC): Fed. Palace N, 3003 Bern, Switzerland; tel. 313250768; fax 313250767; e-mail info@ihffc.org; internet www.ihffc.org; f. 1992 in response to the First Additional Protocol (1977) of the Geneva Conventions, to establish an autonomous body to address the enforcement of int. humanitarian law; operates through a declaration of recognition, signed by 71 states; first constitutional meeting convened in March 1992; organizes annual meetings (2012: Geneva); mems: 15 individuals elected by state parties; Pres. MICHAEL BOTHE.

International Institute for the Unification of Private Law (UNIDROIT): Via Panisperna 28, 00184 Rome, Italy; tel. (06) 696211; fax (06) 69941394; e-mail info@unidroit.org; internet www.unidroit.org; f. 1926 to undertake studies of comparative law, to prepare for the establishment of uniform legislation, to prepare drafts of international agreements on private law and to organize conferences and publish works on such subjects; holds international congresses on private law and meetings of organizations concerned with the unification of law; maintains a library of 215,000 vols; mems: govts of 63 countries; Pres. Prof. BERARDINO LIBONATI (Italy); Sec.-Gen. JOSÉ ANGELO ESTRELLA FARIA; publs *Uniform Law Review* (quarterly), *Digest of Legal Activities of International Organizations*, etc.

International Institute of Space Law (IISL): 8–10 rue Mario Nikis, 75015 Paris, France; tel. 1-45-67-42-60; fax 1-42-73-21-20; e-mail president@iafastro-iisl.com; internet www.iafastro-iisl.com; f. 1959 at the XI Congress of the International Astronautical Federation; organizes annual Space Law colloquium; studies juridical and sociological aspects of astronautics; makes awards; Pres. Dr NANDASIRI JASENTULIYANA (USA); publs *Proceedings of Annual Colloquium on Space Law*, *Survey of Teaching of Space Law in the World*.

International Juridical Institute (IJI): Permanent Office for the Supply of International Legal Information, Spui 186, 2511 BW, The Hague, Netherlands; tel. (70) 3460974; fax (70) 3625235; e-mail info@iji.nl; internet www.iji.nl; f. 1918 to supply information on any non-secret matter of international interest, respecting international, municipal and foreign law and the application thereof; Pres. E M. WESSELING VAN GENT; Dir J M J. KELTJENS.

International Law Association (ILA): Charles Clore House, 17 Russell Sq., London, WC1B 5DR, United Kingdom; tel. (20) 7323-2978; fax (20) 7323-3580; e-mail info@ila-hq.org; internet www.ila-hq.org; f. 1873 for the study and advancement of international law, both public and private and the promotion of international understanding and goodwill; mems: 3,700 in 50 regional branches; 25 international cttees; Pres. EDUARDO GREBLER (Brazil); Chair. Exec. Council Lord MANCE (United Kingdom); Sec.-Gen. DAVID J. C. WYLD (United Kingdom).

International Nuclear Law Association (INLA): 29 sq. de Meeûs, 1000 Brussels, Belgium; tel. (2) 547-58-41; fax (2) 503-04-40; e-mail info@aidn-inla.be; internet www.aidn-inla.be; f. 1972 to promote international studies of legal problems related to the peaceful use of nuclear energy; holds conference every two years; mems: 650 in 40 countries; Sec.-Gen. PATRICK REYNERS; publ. *Congress reports*.

International Penal and Penitentiary Foundation (IPPF) (Fondation internationale pénale et pénitentiaire—FIPP): c/o Prof. P.H.P.H.M.C. van Kempen, Radboud University, 6500 Nijmegen, Netherlands; tel. (24) 3615538; fax (24) 3612185; e-mail info@InternationalPenalandPenitentiaryFoundation.org; internet fondationinternationalepenaleetpenitentiaire.org/; f. 1951 to encourage studies in the field of prevention of crime and treatment of delinquents; mems in 23 countries (membership limited to 3 people from each country) and corresponding mems and fellows in another 20 countries; Pres. PHILLIP RAPOZA (USA); Sec.-Gen. PIET HEIN VAN KEMPEN (Netherlands).

International Police Association (IPA): Arthur Troop House, 1 Fox Rd, West Bridgford, Nottingham, NG2 6AJ, United Kingdom; tel. (115) 945-5985; fax (115) 982-2578; e-mail isg@ipa-iac.org; internet www.ipa-iac.org; f. 1950 to permit the exchange of professional information, create ties of friendship between all sections of the police service and organize group travel and studies; mems: 375,000 in more than 63 countries; International Pres. MICHAEL ODYSSEOS (Cyprus); International Sec.-Gen. GEORGIOS KATSAROPOULOS (Greece).

International Society for Labour and Social Security Law (ISLSSL): CP 500, CH-1211 Geneva 22, Switzerland; tel. 227996961; fax 227998749; e-mail sidtss@ilo.org; internet www.asociacion.org.ar/ISLLSS; f. 1958 to encourage collaboration between labour law and social security specialists; holds World Congress every three years, as well as irregular regional congresses (Europe, Africa, Asia and Americas); mems: 66 national asscns of labour law officers; Pres. MICHAL SEWERYNSKI (Poland); Sec.-Gen. ARTURO BRONSTEIN (Argentina).

International Union of Latin Notaries (Union Internationale du Notariat Latin—UINL): Alsina 2280, 2°, 1090 Buenos Aires, Argentina; tel. (11) 4952-8848; fax (11) 4952-7094; e-mail onpiuinl@onpi.org.ar; internet www.uinl.org; f. 1948 to study and standardize notarial legislation and promote the progress, stability and advancement of the Latin notarial system; mems: organizations and individuals in 81 countries; Pres. Dr EDUARDO GALLINO; publs *Revista Internacional del Notariado* (quarterly), *Notarius International*.

Law Association for Asia and the Pacific (LAWASIA): LAWASIA Secretariat, GPO Box 980, Brisbane, Qld 4001, Australia; tel. (7) 3222-5888; fax (7) 3222-5850; e-mail lawasia@lawasia.asn.au; internet www.lawasia.asn.au; f. 1966; provides an international, professional network for lawyers to update, reform and develop law within the region; comprises six Sections and 21 Standing Committees in Business Law and General Practice areas, which organize speciality conferences; also holds an annual conference (2012: Singapore, in May); mems: national orgs in 23 countries; 1,500 mems in 55 countries; CEO JANET NEVILLE; publs *Directory* (annually), *Journal* (annually), *LAWASIA Update* (3 a year).

Permanent Court of Arbitration: Peace Palace, Carnegieplein 2, 2517 KJ, The Hague, Netherlands; tel. (70) 3024165; fax (70) 3024167; e-mail bureau@pca-cpa.org; internet www.pca-cpa.org; f. 1899 (by the Convention for the Pacific Settlement of International Disputes); provides for the resolution of disputes involving combinations of states, private parties and intergovernmental organizations, under its own rules of procedure, by means of arbitration, conciliation and fact-finding; operates a secretariat, the International Bureau, which provides registry services and legal support to ad hoc tribunals and commissions; mems: governments of 110 countries; Sec.-Gen. CHRISTIAAN M. J. KRÖNER (Netherlands).

SECI Center: calea 13 Septembrie 3–5, Sector 5, 050711 Bucharest, Romania; tel. (21) 303-60-09; fax (21) 303-60-77; internet www.secicenter.org; f. 2000 by the Southeast European Co-operative Initiative; an operative collaboration of customs and police officials working under the guidance of recommendations and directives from INTERPOL and the World Customs Organization; Task Force on Illegal Human Beings Trafficking established May 2000, Task Force on Illegal Drugs Trafficking established July 2000, Task Force on Commercial Fraud established February 2001; the Center was to be transformed into the Southeast European Law Enforcement Co-operation Centre (SELEC) upon ratification by two-thirds of member states of a Convention establishing SELEC, signed in Dec. 2009; mems: Albania, Bosnia and Herzegovina, Bulgaria, Croatia, Greece, Hungary, former Yugoslav Republic of Macedonia, Moldova, Romania, Serbia, Slovenia, Turkey; Dir-Gen. GÜRBÜZ BAHADIR.

Society of Comparative Legislation: 28 rue Saint-Guillaume, 75007 Paris, France; tel. 1-44-39-86-23; fax 1-44-39-86-28; e-mail slc@legiscompare.com; internet www.legiscompare.com; f. 1869 to study and compare laws of different countries, and to investigate practical means of improving the various branches of legislation; mems: 600 in 48 countries; Pres. EMMANUEL PIWNICA (France); Sec.-Gen. BÉNÉDICTE FAUVARQUE-COSSON (France); publ. *Revue Internationale de Droit Comparé* (quarterly).

Union Internationale des Avocats (International Association of Lawyers): 25 rue du Jour, 75001 Paris, France; tel. 1-33-88-55-66; fax 1-33-88-55-77; e-mail uiacentre@uianet.org; internet www.uianet.org; f. 1927 to promote the independence and freedom of lawyers, and defend their ethical and material interests on an international level; aims to contribute to the development of international order based on law; mems: over 200 asscns and 3,000 lawyers in over 110 countries; Pres. PASCAL MAURER; Exec. Dir MARIE-PIERRE RICHARD.

Union of Arab Jurists (UAJ): POB 6026, Al-Mansour, Baghdad, Iraq; tel. (1) 537-2371; fax (1) 537-2369; f. 1975 to facilitate contacts between Arab lawyers, to safeguard the Arab legislative and judicial heritage, to encourage the study of Islamic jurisprudence; and to defend human rights; mems: national jurists asscns in 15 countries; Sec.-Gen. SHIBIB LAZIM AL-MALIKI; publ. *Al-Hukuki al-Arabi* (Arab Jurist).

West African Bar Association: Abuja, Nigeria; fax (229) 21305271; e-mail info@wabalaw.org; internet wabalaw.org; f. 2004; Sec.-Gen. OLAWOLE FAPOHUNDA.

World Jurist Association (WJA): 7910 Woodmont Ave, Suite 1440, Bethesda, Maryland 20814, USA; tel. (202) 466-5428; fax (202) 452-8540; e-mail wja@worldjurist.org; internet www.worldjurist.org; f. 1963; promotes the continued development of international law and the legal maintenance of world order; holds biennial world conferences, World Law Day and demonstration trials; organizes research programmes; mems: lawyers, jurists and legal scholars in 155 countries; Pres. VALERIY YEVDOKYMOV (Ukraine); Exec. Vice-Pres. MARGARETHA M. HENNEBERRY (USA); publs *The World Jurist* (6 a year), Research Reports, *Law and Judicial Systems of Nations*, 4th revised edn (directory), *World Legal Directory*, *Law / Technology* (quarterly), *World Law Review* Vols I–V (World Conference Proceedings), *The Chief Justices and Judges of the Supreme Courts of Nations* (directory), work papers, newsletters and journals.

World Association of Judges: 7910 Woodmont Ave, Suite 1440, Bethesda, Maryland 20814, USA; tel. (202) 466-5428; fax (202) 452-8540; e-mail wja@worldjurist.org; f. 1966 to advance the administration of judicial justice through co-operation and communication among ranking jurists of all countries; Pres. Prince BOLA AJIBOLA (Nigeria).

World Association of Law Professors (WALP): 7910 Woodmont Ave, Suite 1440, Bethesda, Maryland 20814, USA; tel. (202) 466-5428; fax (202) 452-8540; e-mail wja@worldjurist.org; internet www.worldjurist.org; f. 1975 to improve scholarship and education in matters related to international law; Pres. HILARIO G. DAVIDE, Jr (Philippines).

World Association of Lawyers (WAL): 7910 Woodmont Ave, Suite 1440, Bethesda, Maryland 20814, USA; tel. (202) 466-5428; fax (202) 452-8540; e-mail wja@worldjurist.org; internet www.worldjurist.org; f. 1975 to develop international law and improve lawyers' effectiveness in this field; Pres. ALEXANDER BELOHLAVEK (Czech Republic).

Medicine and Health

Aerospace Medical Association (AsMA): 320 S. Henry St, Alexandria, VA 22314-3579, USA; tel. (703) 739-2240; fax (703) 739-9652; e-mail inquiries@asma.org; internet www.asma.org; f. 1929 as Aero Medical Association; aims to advance the science and art of aviation and space medicine; establishes and maintains co-operation between medical and allied sciences concerned with aerospace medicine; works to promote, protect, and maintain safety in aviation and astronautics; mems: individual, constituent and corporate in 75 countries; Pres. FANANCY L. ANZALONE; Exec. Dir JEFFREY SVENTEK; publ. *Aviation Space and Environmental Medicine* (monthly).

Asia Pacific Academy of Ophthalmology (APAO): c/o Dept of Ophthalmology and Visual Sciences, Chinese University of Hong Kong, 3/F 147 K Argyle St, Kowloon, Hong Kong, SAR; tel. 27623040; fax 27159490; e-mail secretariat@apaophth.org; internet www.apaophth.org; f. 1956; holds Congress annually since 2006 (previously every two years); mems: 17 mem. orgs; Pres. FRANK MARTIN; Sec.-Gen and CEO DENNIS LAM.

Asia Pacific Dental Federation (APDF): c/o 242 Tanjong Katong Rd, Singapore 437030; tel. 6345-3125; fax 6344-2116; e-mail droliver@singnet.com.sg; internet www.apdfederation.com; f. 1955 to establish closer relationships among dental asscns in Asia Pacific countries and to encourage research on dental health in the region; administers the International College of Continuing Dental Education (ICCDE); holds congress every year; mems: 27 national dental asscns; Sec.-Gen. Dr OLIVER HENNEDIGE.

Association of National European and Mediterranean Societies of Gastroenterology (ASNEMGE): Wienerbergstrasse 11/12A, 1100 Vienna, Austria; tel. and fax (1) 997-16-43; fax (1) 997-16-39; e-mail info@asnemge.org; internet www.asnemge.org; f. 1947 to facilitate the exchange of ideas between gastroenterologists and to disseminate knowledge; organizes International Congress of Gastroenterology every four years; mems: in 43 countries, national societies and sections of national medical societies; Pres. MARK HULL (United Kingdom); Gen. Sec. JOOST DRENTH (Netherlands).

Council for International Organizations of Medical Sciences (CIOMS): c/o WHO, ave Appia, 1211 Geneva 27, Switzerland; tel. 227913413; fax 227914286; e-mail cioms@who.int; internet www.cioms.ch; f. 1949 to serve the scientific interests of the international biomedical community; aims to facilitate and promote activities in biomedical sciences; runs long-term programmes on bioethics, health policy, ethics and values, drug development and use, and the international nomenclature of diseases; maintains collaborative relations with the UN; holds a general assembly every three years; mems: 66 orgs; Pres. Prof. J. J. M. VAN DELDEN; Sec.-Gen. Dr GUNILLA SJÖLIN-FORSBERG; publs *Bioethics and Health Policy' Reports on Drug Development and Use*, *Proceedings of CIOMS Conferences*, *International Nomenclature of Diseases*.

Cystic Fibrosis Worldwide: 210 Park Ave, Suite 267, Worcester, MA 01609, USA; tel. (508) 762-4232; e-mail information@cfww.org; internet www.cfww.org; f. 2003 by merger of the International Association of Cystic Fibrosis Adults and International Cystic Fibrosis (Muscoviscidosis) Association (f. 1964); promotes the development of lay organizations and the advancement of knowledge among medical, scientific and health professionals in underdeveloped areas; convenes annual conference; Pres. MITCH MESSER (Australia); Exec. Dir CHRISTINE NOKE (USA); publs *Annual Report*, *CFW Newsletter* (quarterly), *Joseph Levy Lecture*, booklet on physiotherapy.

European Association for Cancer Research (EACR): c/o Pharmacy School Bldg, University of Nottingham, University Park, Nottingham, NG7 2RD, United Kingdom; tel. (115) 9515116; fax (115) 9515115; e-mail eacr@nottingham.ac.uk; internet www.eacr.org; f. 1968 to facilitate contact between cancer research workers and to organize scientific meetings in Europe; operates a number of fellowship and award programmes; mems: more than 8,000 in 76 countries world-wide, incl. 10 affiliated mem. societies in Croatia, France, Germany, Hungary, Ireland, Israel, Italy, Spain, Turkey and United Kingdom; Pres. JULIO CELIS; Sec.-Gen. RICHARD MARAIS (United Kingdom).

European Association for Paediatric Education (EAPE) (Association Européene pour l'Enseignement de la Pédatrie): c/o Dr Claude Billeaud, Dept Néonatal Médicine, Hôpital des Enfants-CHU Pellegrin, 33076 Bordeaux Cédex, France; tel. 5-56-79-56-35; fax 5-57-82-02-48; e-mail claude.billeaud@chu-bordeaux.fr; internet www.aeep.asso.fr; f. 1970 to promote research and practice in educational methodology in paediatrics; mems: 120 in 20 European countries; Pres. Dr CLAUDE BILLEAUD (France); Sec.-Gen. ELIE SALIBA (France).

European Association for Palliative Care (EAPC Onlus): National Cancer Institute Milano Via Venezian 1, 20133 Milan, Italy; e-mail amelia.giordano@istitutotumori.mi.it; internet www.eapcnet.eu; f. 1988; aims to promote palliative care in Europe and to act as a focus for all of those who work, or have an interest, in the field of palliative care at the scientific, clinical and social levels; 12th Congress: May 2011, Lisbon, Portugal; mems: 47 national asscns in 29 countries, individual mems from 48 countries world-wide; Pres. SHEILA PAYNE (United Kingdom); Chief Exec. HEIDI BLUMHUBER; publs *European Journal of Palliative Care*, *Palliative Medicine*.

European Association for the Study of Diabetes (EASD): Rheindorfer Weg 3, 40591 Düsseldorf, Germany; tel. (211) 7584690; fax (211) 75846929; e-mail secretariat@easd.org; internet www.easd.org; f. 1965 to support research in the field of diabetes, to promote the rapid diffusion of acquired knowledge and its application; holds annual scientific meetings within Europe; mems: approx. 6,000 in 101 European and other countries; Pres. A. BOLTON (United Kingdom); Exec. Dir Dr VIKTOR JÖRGENS (Germany); publ. *Diabetologia* (13 a year).

European Brain and Behaviour Society (EBBS): Einsteinweg 55, 2333 CC, Leiden, Netherlands; tel. (71) 5276289; fax (71) 5274277; e-mail vjb@st-and.ac.uk; internet www.ebbs-science.org; f. 1968; holds an annual conference and organizes workshops; Pres. CARMEN SANDI (Switzerland); Sec.-Gen. VERITY BROWN (United Kingdom); publ. *Newsletter* (annually).

European Federation of Internal Medicine (EFIM): 287 ave. Louise, 4th Floor, 1050 Brussels, Belgium; tel. (2) 643-20-40; fax (2) 645-26-71; e-mail info@efim.org; internet www.efim.org; f. 1969 as European Asscn of Internal Medicine (present name adopted 1996); aims to bring together European specialists, and establish communication between them, to promote internal medicine; organizes congresses and meetings; provides information; mems: 34 European societies of internal medicine; Pres. RAMON PUJOL FARRIOLS (Spain); Sec. Dr JAN WILLEM F. ELTE (Netherlands); publ. *European Journal of Internal Medicine* (8 a year).

European Health Management Association (EHMA): rue Belliar 15–17, 6th Floor, 1040 Brussels, Belgium; tel. (2) 502-65-25; fax (2) 503-10-07; e-mail info@ehma.org; internet www.ehma.org; f. 1966; aims to improve health care in Europe by raising standards of managerial performance in the health sector; fosters co-operation between managers, academia, policy-makers and educators to understand health management in different European contexts and to influence both service delivery and the policy agenda in Europe; mems: more than 160 institutions in 30 countries; Pres. Prof. AAD DE ROO; Dir JENNIFER BREMNER; publs *Newsletter*, *Eurobriefing* (quarterly).

European League against Rheumatism (EULAR): Seestrasse 240, 8802 Kilchberg-Zürich, Switzerland; tel. 447163030; fax 447163039; e-mail eular@eular.org; internet www.eular.org;

f. 1947 to co-ordinate research and treatment of rheumatic complaints; holds an annual Congress in Rheumatology; mems: in 41 countries; Pres. Prof. MAXIME DOUGADOS (France); Exec. Dir HEINZ MARCHESI; publ. *Annals of the Rheumatic Diseases*.

European Organization for Caries Research (ORCA): c/o Academic Centre for Dentistry Amsterdam (ACTA), Gustav Mahlerlaan 3004, 1081 LA Amsterdam, Netherlands; tel. (20) 5980437; e-mail m.vd.veen@acta.nl; internet www.orca-caries-research.org; f. 1953 to promote and undertake research on dental health, encourage international contacts, and make the public aware of the importance of care of the teeth; mems: research workers in 23 countries; Pres. Prof. CAROLINA GANSS (Germany); Sec.-Gen. Dr M. H. VAN DER VEEN (Netherlands); publ. *Caries Research*.

European Orthodontic Society (EOS): Flat 20, 49 Hallam St, London, W1W 6JN, United Kingdom; tel. (20) 7637-0367; fax (20) 7323-0410; e-mail eoslondon@aol.com; internet www.eoseurope.org; f. 1907 (name changed in 1935), to advance the science of orthodontics and its relations with the collateral arts and sciences; mems: more than 2,500 in 85 countries; Pres. DAVID SUÁREZ QUINTANILLA (Spain); publ. *European Journal of Orthodontics* (6 a year).

European Society of Radiology: c/o ESR Office, Neutorgasse 9/2A, Vienna, Austria; tel. (1) 533-40-64-0; fax (1) 533-40-64-44-8; e-mail communications@myesr.org; internet www.myesr.org; f. 2005 by merger of European Society of Radiology (f. 1962) and European Congress of Radiology; aims to harmonize and improve training programmes throughout Europe and develop a new research institute; organizes an Annual Congress; mems: some 29,300 individual mems; Pres. GABRIEL P. KRESTIN (Netherlands).

European Union of Medical Specialists (Union Européenne des Médecins Spécialistes—UEMS): 20 ave de la Couronne, Kroonlaan, 1050 Brussels, Belgium; tel. (2) 649-51-64; fax (2) 640-37-30; e-mail sg@uems.net; internet www.uems.net; f. 1958 to harmonize and improve the quality of medical specialist practices in the EU and safeguard the interests of medical specialists; seeks formulation of common training policy; mems: 27 full mems, 7 assoc. mems; Pres. Dr ZLATKO FRAS (Slovenia); Sec.-Gen. Dr BERNARD MAILLET (Belgium).

Eurotransplant International Foundation: POB 2304, 2301 CH Leiden, Netherlands; tel. (71) 5795700; fax (71) 5790057; e-mail mfranzen@eurotransplant.org; internet www.eurotransplant.org; f. 1967; co-ordinates the exchange of organs for transplants in Austria, Belgium, Croatia, Germany, Luxembourg, Netherlands and Slovenia; keeps register of c. 16,000 patients with all necessary information for matching with suitable donors in the shortest possible time; organizes transport of the organ and transplantation; collaborates with similar orgs in western and eastern Europe; Pres. Dr BRUNO MEISER; Dirs ARIE OOSTERLEE, AXEL RAHMEL.

FDI World Dental Federation: Tour de Cointrin, 84 ave Louis Casaï, CP 3, 1216 Genève-Cointrin, Switzerland; tel. 225608150; fax 225608140; e-mail info@fdiworldental.org; internet www.fdiworldental.org; f. 1900; aims to bring together the world of dentistry, to represent the dental profession of the world and to stimulate and facilitate the exchange of information; mems: about 200 national dental asscns and groups; Pres. Dr ROBERTO VIANNA (Brazil); Exec. Dir JEAN-LUC EISELÉ; publs *International Dental Journal*, *Developing Dentistry*, *European Journal of Prosthodontics and Restorative Dentistry*.

Federation of the European Dental Industry (Fédération de l'Industrie Dentaire en Europe—FIDE): Aachener Str. 1053–1055, 50858 Cologne, Germany; tel. (221) 50068723; fax (221) 50068721; e-mail m.heibach@fide-online.org; internet www.fide-online.org; f. 1957 to promote the interests of dental industry manufacturers; mems: almost 550 dental manufacturers and national asscns in 13 European countries; Pres. and Chair. Dr JÜRGEN EBERLEIN (Germany); Sec.-Gen. Dr MARKUS HEIBACH (Germany).

Global Fund to Fight AIDS, Tuberculosis and Malaria: 8 chemin de Blandonnet, 1214 Vernier-Geneva, Switzerland; tel. 587911700; fax 587911701; e-mail info@theglobalfund.org; internet www.theglobalfund.org; f. 2002 as a partnership between governments, civil society, private sector interests, UN bodies (including WHO, UNAIDS, the IBRD and UNDP), and other agencies to raise resources for combating AIDS, tuberculosis and malaria; the Fund supports but does not implement assistance programmes; US $11,700m. was pledged by international donors at a conference convened in Oct. 2010 to replenish the Fund during 2011–13; by Dec. 2011, US $22,900m. had been approved for over 1,000 grants in 150 countries; Gen. Man. GABRIEL JARAMILLO (Colombia/Brazil).

Inter-American Association of Sanitary and Environmental Engineering (Asociación Interamericana de Ingeniería Sanitaria y Ambiental—AIDIS): Av. Angélica 2355, 01227-200 São Paulo, SP, Brazil; tel. (11) 3812-4080; fax (11) 3814-2441; e-mail aidis@aidis.org.br; internet www.aidis.org.br; f. 1948 to assist in the development of water supply and sanitation; aims to generate awareness on environmental, health and sanitary problems and assist in finding solutions; mems: 32 countries; Pres. RAFAEL DAUTANT (Venezuela); Sec.-Gen. CÉLIA G. CASTELLÓ (Brazil); publs *Revista Ingeniería Sanitaria* (quarterly), *Desafío* (quarterly).

International Academy of Aviation and Space Medicine (IAASM): c/o Dr C. Thibeault, 502-8500 rue St Charles, Brossard, QC J4X2Z8, Canada; tel. (450) 923-6826; fax (450) 923-1236; e-mail ctebo@videotron.ca; internet www.iaasm.org; f. 1955 to facilitate international co-operation in research and teaching in the fields of aviation and space medicine; mems: in 45 countries; Pres. Prof. ANTHONY BATCHELOR (United Kingdom); Sec.-Gen. Dr CLAUDE THIBEAULT (Canada).

International Academy of Cytology: POB 1347, Burgunderstr. 1, 79013 Freiburg, Germany; tel. (761) 292-3801; fax (761) 292-3802; e-mail centraloffice@cytology-iac.org; internet www.cytology-iac.org; f. 1957 to facilitate the international exchange of information on specialized problems of clinical cytology, to stimulate research and to standardize terminology; mems: 2,400; Pres. Prof. DIANE SOLOMON (USA); publs *Acta Cytologica*, *Analytical and Quantitative Cytology and Histology* (both every 2 months).

International Agency for the Prevention of Blindness (IAPB): c/o London School of Hygiene & Tropical Medicine, Keppel St, London, WC1E 7HT, United Kingdom; e-mail cgarms@iapb.org; internet www.iapb.org; f. 1975; promotes advocacy and information sharing on the prevention of blindness; aims to encourage the formation of national prevention of blindness committees and programmes; with WHO launched VISION 2020 initiative to eliminate the main causes of avoidable blindness by 2020; Pres. CHRISTIAN G. GARMS; CEO PETER ACKLAND; publ. *IAPB News*.

International Association for Child and Adolescent Psychiatry and Allied Professions (IACAPAP): c/o Daniel Fung, Duke-NUS Graduate Medical School and Division of Psychology, Nanyang Technological University, Singapore; tel. 63892309; e-mail daniel_fung@imh.com.sg; internet www.iacapap.org; f. 1937; aims to promote the study, treatment, care and prevention of mental and emotional disorders and disabilities of children, adolescents and their families. The emphasis is on practice and research through collaboration between child psychiatrists and the allied professions of psychology, social work, pediatrics, public health, nursing, education, social sciences and other relevant fields; IACAPAP developed the guidelines and principles of Ethics in Child and Adolescent Mental Health; IACAPAP also develops and adopts other Declarations, Statements and Position Papers of help to mental health professionals in their work; mems: national asscns and individuals in 45 countries; Pres. Dr OLAYINKA OMIGBODUN (Nigeria); Sec.-Gen. Dr DANIEL FUNG (Singapore); publs *The Child in the Family* (Yearbook of the IACAPAP), *Newsletter (IACAPAP Bulletin)*, Monographs.

International Association for Dental Research (IADR): 1619 Duke St, Alexandria, VA 22314-3406, USA; tel. (703) 548-0066; fax (703) 548-1883; e-mail research@iadr.org; internet www.dentalresearch.org; f. 1920; aims to advance research and increase knowledge for the improvement of oral health world-wide; holds annual meetings, triennial conferences and divisional meetings; Pres. Dr DIANNE REKOW; Exec. Dir Dr CHRISTOPHER H. FOX.

International Association for Group Psychotherapy and Group Processes (IAGP): IAGP, rua Sergipe 401 conjunto 808, São Paulo, SP CEP 01243-906, Brazil; tel. and fax (11) 31591653; e-mail office@iagp.com; internet www.iagp.com; f. 1973; holds a congress every three years and regional congresses at more frequent intervals; mems: in 49 countries; Pres. JORGE BURMEISTER (Switzerland/Spain); Sec. IVAN URLIC (Croatia); publs *Forum* (annually), *Globeletter* (2 a year).

International Association for the Study of Obesity (IASO): Charles Darwin House, 12 Roger St, London, WCIN 2JU, United Kingdom; tel. (20) 7685-2580; fax (20) 7685-2581; e-mail enquiries@iaso.org; internet www.iaso.org; f. 1986; supports research into the prevention and management of obesity throughout the world and disseminates information regarding disease and accompanying health and social issues; incorporates the International Obesity Task Force; international congress every four years (2010: Stockholm, Sweden); mems: 52 asscns representing 56 countries; Pres. PHILIP JAMES; Exec. Dir CHRISTINE TRIMMER.

International Association of Agricultural Medicine and Rural Health (IAAMRH): Pravara Medical Trust, Loni-413736, Maharashtra State, India; tel. and fax (24) 2273600; fax (24) 2273413; e-mail contact@pmtpims.org; internet www.iaamrh.org; f. 1961 to study the problems of medicine in agriculture in all countries and to prevent the diseases caused by the conditions of work in agriculture; mems: 405 in 51 countries; Pres. Dr ASHOK PATIL (India); Gen. Sec. Dr SYUSUKE NATSUKAWA (Japan).

International Association of Applied Psychology (IAAP): c/o Prof. José M. Prieto, Colegio Oficial de Psicólogos, Cuesta de San Vicente 4–5, 28008 Madrid, Spain; tel. (91) 3943236; fax (91) 3510091; e-mail iaap@psy.ulaval.ca; internet www.iaapsy.org;

f. 1920, present title adopted in 1955; aims to establish contacts between those carrying out scientific work on applied psychology, to promote research and to encourage the adoption of measures contributing to this work; organizes International Congress of Applied Psychology every four years (2010: Melbourne, Australia, in July) and co-sponsors International Congress of Psychology (2008: Berlin, Germany) and European Congress of Psychology (2009: Oslo, Norway); mems: 2,200 in 94 countries; Pres. Prof. JOSÉ MARIA PÉIRO (Spain); Sec.-Gen. Prof. JANEL GAUTHIER (Canada); publ. *Applied Psychology: An International Review* (quarterly).

International Association of Asthmology (INTERASMA): (no permanent secretariat); internet www.interasma.org; f. 1954 to advance medical knowledge of bronchial asthma and allied disorders; mems: 1,100 in 54 countries; Pres. KIM YOU-YOUNG (Republic of Korea); Sec.-Gen. CARLOS NUÑES (Portugal); publs *Interasma News, Journal of Investigative Allergology and Clinical Immunology* (every 2 months), *Allergy and Clinical Immunology International* (every 2 months).

International Association of Bioethics: POB 280, University of the Philippines, Diliman, Quezon City 1101, Philippines; tel. and fax (2) 426-9590; e-mail secretariat@bioethics-international.org; internet www.bioethics-international.org; f. 1992; aims to facilitate contact and to promote exchange of information among people working in the bioethics field; aims to promote the development of research and training in bioethics; organizes international conferences every two years (11th World Congress of Bioethics: June 2012, Rotterdam); mems: over 1,000 individuals and institutions in more than 40 countries; Pres. Prof. NIKOLA BILLER-ANDORNO (Switzerland); Sec. Prof. LEONARDO DE CASTRO (Philippines); publ. *Bioethics Journal*.

International Association of Gerontology and Geriatrics (IAGG): c/o Faculté de Médecine, Institut du Vieillissement, 37 Allées Jules Guesde, 31000 Toulouse, France; tel. 5-61-14-56-39; fax 5-61-14-56-40; e-mail contact@iagg.info; internet www.iagg.info; f. 1950 as the International Association of Gerontological Societies to promote research and training in all fields of gerontology and to protect the interests of gerontological societies and institutions; assumed current name in 2005, with the aim of promoting and developing Geriatrics as a medical specialism; holds World Congress every four years; mems: more than 40,000 in some 60 countries; Pres. Prof. BRUNO VELLAS (France); Sec.-Gen./Vice-Pres. ALAIN FRANCO (France); publ. *IAGG Newsletter* (quarterly).

International Association of Logopedics and Phoniatrics (IALP): c/o Robbin King, University of Illinois, 1206 S Fourth St, Champaign, IL 61820, USA; tel. (217) 333-2129; fax (217) 333-0404; e-mail office@ialp.info; internet www.ialp.info; f. 1924 to promote standards of training and research in human communication disorders, to establish information centres and communicate with kindred organizations; 28th International Congress on Logopedics and Phoniatrics: Athens, Greece, in Aug. 2010; mems: 125,000 in 56 societies from 30 countries; Pres. Dr TANYA GALLAGHER; publ. *Folia Phoniatrica et Logopedica* (6 a year).

International Association of Medicine and Biology of the Environment (IAMBE): c/o 115 rue de la Pompe, 75116 Paris, France; tel. 1-45-53-45-04; fax 1-45-53-41-75; e-mail aimbe.world@free.fr; f. 1971 with assistance from the UN Environment Programme; aims to contribute to the solution of problems caused by human influence on the environment; structure includes 13 technical commissions; mems: individuals and orgs in 79 countries; Pres. CÉLINE ABBOU.

International Association of Oral and Maxillofacial Surgeons (IAOMS): 17 W 220, 22nd St, Suite 420, Oakbrook Terrace, IL 60181, USA; tel. (630) 833-0945; fax (630) 833-1382; e-mail info@iaoms.org; internet www.iaoms.org; f. 1962 to advance the science and art of oral and maxillofacial surgery; organizes biennial international conference; mems: over 5,000; Pres. Dr LARRY NISSEN (USA); Exec. Dir Dr JOHN F. HELFRICK (USA); publs *International Journal of Oral and Maxillofacial Surgery* (2 a year), *Newsletter*.

International Brain Research Organization (IBRO): 255 rue St Honoré, 75001 Paris, France; tel. 1-46-47-92-92; fax 1-45-20-60-06; e-mail stephanie@ibro.info; internet www.ibro.org; f. 1960 to further all aspects of brain research; Exec. Dir STEPHANIE DE LA ROCHEFOUCAULD; publs *IBRO News*, *Neuroscience* (every 2 months).

International Bronchoesophagological Society (IBES): Mayo Clinic Arizona, 13400 E. Shea Blvd, Scottsdale, AZ 85259, USA; tel. (480) 301-9692; fax (480) 301-9088; e-mail hillard.julie@mayo.edu; internet www.ibesociety.org; f. 1951 to promote the progress of bronchoesophagology and to provide a forum for discussion among bronchoesophagologists with various medical and surgical specialities; holds Congress every two years; mems: over 700 in 30 countries; Exec. Sec./Treas. PAUL F. CASTELLANOS.

International Bureau for Epilepsy (IBE): 11 Priory Hall, Stillorgan, Blackrock, Co Dublin, Ireland; tel. (1) 2108850; fax (1) 2108450; e-mail ibedublin@eircom.net; internet www.ibe-epilepsy.org; f. 1961; collects and disseminates information about social and medical care for people with epilepsy; organizes international and regional meetings; advises and answers questions on social aspects of epilepsy; has special consultative status with ECOSOC; mems: 126 national epilepsy orgs; Pres. MIKE GLYNN; Exec. Dir Dr CARLOS ACEVEDO; publ. *International Epilepsy News* (quarterly).

International Catholic Committee of Nurses and Medico-Social Assistants (Comité International Catholique des Infirmières et Assistantes Médico-Sociales—CICIAMS): St. Mary's Bloomfield Ave, Donnybrook, Dublin 4, Ireland; tel. (1) 668-9150; e-mail ciciams@eircom.net; internet www.ciciams.org; f. 1933 to group professional Catholic nursing asscns; to represent Christian thought in the general professional field at international level; to co-operate in the general development of the profession and to promote social welfare; mems: 30 full, 10 corresponding mems; Pres. MARYLEE MEEHAN; Acting Sec. JOSEPHINE BARTLEY; publ. *Nouvelles/News/Nachrichten* (3 a year).

International Cell Research Organization (ICRO) (Organisation Internationale de Recherche sur la Cellule): c/o UNESCO, SC/BES/LSC, 1 rue Miollis, 75732 Paris, France; fax 1-45-68-58-16; e-mail icro@unesco.org; internet www.unesco.org/icro; f. 1962 to create, encourage and promote co-operation between scientists of different disciplines throughout the world for the advancement of fundamental knowledge of the cell, normal and abnormal; organizes international laboratory courses on modern topics of cell and molecular biology and biotechnology for young research scientists; mems: 400; Pres. Prof. QI-SHUI LIN (People's Republic of China); Exec. Sec. Prof. GEORGES N. COHEN (France).

International Centre for Diarrhoeal Disease Research, Bangladesh, B: Centre for Health and Population Research (ICDDR,B): GPO Box 128, Dhaka 1000, Bangladesh; tel. (2) 8860523; fax (2) 8823116; e-mail communications@icddrb.org; internet www.icddrb.org; f. 1960 as Pakistan-SEATO Cholera Research Laboratory, international health research institute since 1978; undertakes research, training and information dissemination on diarrhoeal diseases, child health, nutrition, emerging infectious diseases, environmental health, sexually transmitted diseases, HIV/AIDS, poverty and health, vaccine evaluation and case management, with particular reference to developing countries; supported by 55 governments and international orgs; Exec. Dir Dr ALEJANDRO CRAVIOTO; publs *Annual Report*, *Journal of Health, Population and Nutrition* (quarterly), *Glimpse* (quarterly), *Shasthya Sanglap* (3 a year), *Health and Science Bulletin* (quarterly), *SUZY* (newsletter, 2 a year), scientific reports, working papers, monographs, special publications.

International Chiropractors' Association: 6400 Arlington Blvd, Suite 800, Falls Church, VA 22042, USA; tel. (703) 528-5000; fax (703) 528-5023; e-mail chiro@chiropractic.org; internet www.chiropractic.org; f. 1926 to promote advancement of the art and science of chiropractors; mems: 7,000 individuals, and affiliated asscns; Pres. Dr GARY WALSEMANN; Int. Dir PINCHAS NOYMAN; publs *International Review of Chiropractic* (every 2 months), *ICA Today* (every 2 months), *The Chiropractic Choice*.

International College of Angiology: 161 Morin Dr., Jay, VT 05859-9283, USA; tel. (802) 988-4065; fax (802) 988-4066; e-mail denisemrossignol@cs.com; internet www.intlcollegeofangiology.org; f. 1958, as an association of scientists working in the field of vascular medicine and surgery; aims to encourage, support, and facilitate research and education in the problems of vascular disease; Chair. JOHN B. CHANG (USA); Exec. Dir DENISE M. ROSSIGNOL (USA); publ.*International Journal of Angiology*.

International College of Surgeons (ICS): 1516 N. Lake Shore Drive, Chicago, IL 60610, USA; tel. (312) 642-3555; fax (312) 787-1624; e-mail info@icsglobal.org; internet www.icsglobal.org; f. 1935, as a world-wide federation of surgeons and surgical specialists for the advancement of the art and science of surgery; aims to create a common bond among the surgeons of all nations and promote the highest standards of surgery, without regard to nationality, creed, or colour; sends teams of surgeons to developing countries to teach local surgeons; provides research and scholarship grants, organizes surgical congresses around the world; manages the International Museum of Surgical Science in Chicago; mems: c. 8,000 in 100 countries and regions; Pres. Dr. SAID A. DAEE (USA); Exec. Dir MAX C. DOWNHAM (USA); publ. *International Surgery* (every 2 months).

International Commission on Occupational Health (ICOH): Via Fontana Candida 1, 1-00040 Monteporzio Catone (Rome), Italy; tel. (06) 94181407; fax (06) 94181556; e-mail icoh@ispesl.it; internet www.icohweb.org; f. 1906, present name adopted 1985; aims to study and prevent pathological conditions arising from industrial work; arranges congresses on occupational medicine and the protection of workers' health; provides information for public authorities and learned societies; mems: 1,800 in 94 countries; Pres. Dr KAZUTAKA KOGI (Japan); Sec.-Gen. Dr SERGIO IAVICOLI (Italy); publ. *Newsletter* (electronic version).

International Commission on Radiological Protection (ICRP): POB 1046, Station B, 280 Slater St, Ottawa, Ontario, Canada, K1P 5S9; tel. (613) 947-9750; fax (613) 944-1920; e-mail sci.sec@icrp.org; internet www.icrp.org; f. 1928 to provide technical guidance and promote international co-operation in the field of radiation protection; committees on Radiation Effects, Doses from Radiation Exposure, Protection in Medicine, Application of Recommendations, and Radiological Protection of the Environment; mems: c. 85; Exec. Sec. LYNNE LEMAIRE; Scientific Sec. Dr CHRISTOPHER CLEMENT (Canada); publ. *Annals of the ICRP*.

International Committee of Military Medicine (ICMM) (Comité international de médecine militaire—CIMM): Hôpital Militaire Reine Astrid, rue Bruyn, 1120 Brussels, Belgium; tel. (2) 264-43-48; fax (2) 264-43-67; e-mail info@cimm-icmm.org; internet www.cimm-icmm.org; f. 1921 as Permanent Committee of the International Congresses of Military Medicine and Pharmacy; name changed 1990; aims to increase co-operation and promote activities in the field of military medicine; considers issues relating to mass medicine, dentistry, military pharmacy, veterinary sciences and the administration and organization of medical care missions, among others; mems: official delegates from 110 countries; Chair. Brig.-Gen. Dr HILARY M. A. AGADA (Nigeria); Sec.-Gen. Maj.-Gen. Dr ROGER VAN HOOF (Belgium); publ. *International Review of the Armed Forces Medical Services* (quarterly).

International Council for Laboratory Animal Science (ICLAS): c/o School of Veterinary Medicine, University of Pennsylvania, 3800 Spruce St, Philadelphia, PA 19104, USA; tel. (215) 728-2525; fax (215) 214-4040; e-mail rozmiar@pobox.upenn.edu; internet www.iclas.org; f. 1956; promotes the ethical care and use of laboratory animals in research, with the aim of advancing human and animal health; establishes standards and provides support resources; encourages international collaboration to develop knowledge; Pres. Dr PATRI VERGARA (Spain); Sec.-Gen. Dr HARRY ROZMIAREK (USA).

International Council for Physical Activity and Fitness Research (ICPAFR): c/o Prof. F. G. Viviani, Faculty of Psychology, University of Padua, via Venezia 8, 35131 Padua, Italy; tel. (049) 880-4668; fax (049) 827-6600; e-mail franco.viviani@unipd.it; internet icpafr.psy.unipd.it; f. 1964 to construct international standardized physical fitness tests, to encourage research based upon the standardized tests and to enhance participation in physical activity; organizes biennial symposiums on topics related to physical activity and fitness; mems: 34 countries; Pres. Prof. FRANCO G. VIVIANI (Italy); Sec./Treas. ALISON MACMANUS; publs *International Guide to Fitness and Health*, biennial proceedings of seminars and symposia, other fitness and health publs.

International Council of Nurses (ICN): 3 pl. Jean-Marteau, 1201 Geneva, Switzerland; tel. 229080100; fax 229080101; e-mail icn@icn.ch; internet www.icn.ch; f. 1899 to allow national asscns of nurses to work together to develop the contribution of nursing to the promotion of health; holds quadrennial Congresses; mems: more than 130 national nurses' asscns; Pres. ROSEMARY BRYANT (Australia); CEO DAVID BENTON; publ. *The International Nursing Review* (quarterly).

International Council of Ophthalmology: 945 Green St, San Francisco, CA 94133, USA; tel. (415) 409-8410; fax (415) 409-8403; e-mail info@icoph.org; internet www.icoph.org; f. 1927; works to support and develop ophthalmology, especially in developing countries; carries out education and assessment programmes; promotes clinical standards; holds World Ophthalmology Congress every two years (June 2010: Berlin, Germany); Pres. Dr BRUCE E. SPIVEY; Sec.-Gen. JEAN-JACQUES DE LAEY (France).

International Diabetes Federation (IDF): 166 Chaussée de la Hulpe, 1170 Brussels, Belgium; tel. (2) 538-55-11; fax (2) 538-51-14; e-mail info@idf.org; internet www.idf.org; f. 1949 to help in the collection and dissemination of information on diabetes and to improve the welfare of people suffering from diabetes; mems: more than 200 asscns in more 160 countries; Pres. JEAN CLAUDE MBANYA (Cameroon); Exec. Dir ANN KEELING; publs *Diabetes Voice*, *Bulletin of the IDF* (quarterly).

International Epidemiological Association (IEA): 1500 Sunday Dr., Suite 102, Raleigh, NC 27607, USA; tel. (919) 861-5586; fax (919) 787-4916; e-mail nshore@firstpointresources.com; internet www.ieaweb.org; f. 1954; mems: 1,500; promotes epidemiology and organizes international scientific meetings and region-specific meetings; Pres. Dr CESAR VICTORA (Brazil); Sec. Dr MATHIAS EGGER; publ. *International Journal of Epidemiology* (6 a year).

International Federation for Medical and Biological Engineering (IFMBE): 10000 Zagreb, Unska 3, Faculty of Electrical Engineering and Computing, University of Zagreb, Croatia; tel. (1) 6129938; fax (1) 6129652; e-mail office@ifmbe.org; internet www.ifmbe.org; f. 1959; mems: 58 societies; Pres. HERBERT F. VOIGT; Sec.-Gen. Prof. RATKO MAGJAREVIC (Croatia).

International Federation for Psychotherapy: c/o Cornelia Erpenbeck, Department of Psychiatry, University Hospital Zurich. Culmannstrasse 8, 8091 Zürich, Switzerland; tel. 442555251; fax 442554408; e-mail secretariat@ifp.name; internet www.ifp.name; f. 1935 (as General Medical Society for Psychotherapy); aims to further research and teaching of psychotherapy; encourages and supports development within psychotherapy; organizes international congresses; mems: c. 6,000 psychotherapists from around 40 countries, 36 societies; Pres. Prof. FRANZ CASPAR (Switzerland); publ. *Newsletter*, *Psychotherapy and Psychosomatics*.

International Federation of Association of Anatomists: c/o Friedrich P. Paulsen, Dept of Anatomy and Cell Biology, Martin Luther University of Halle-Wittenberg, Grosse Steinstrasse 52, 06097 Germany; e-mail friedrich.paulsen@medizin.uni-halle.de; internet www.ifaa.net; f. 1903 as the Federative International Anatomical Congress; 18th Conference: Beijing, People's Republic of China, 2014; Pres. BERNARD MOXHAM (United Kingdom); Sec.-Gen. FRIEDRICH P. PAULSEN (Germany); publ. *Plexus* (2 a year).

International Federation of Clinical Chemistry and Laboratory Medicine (IFCC): via Carlo Farini 81, 20159 Milan, Italy; tel. (02) 6680-9912; fax (02) 6078-1846; e-mail ifcc@ifcc.org; internet www.ifcc.org; f. 1952; mems: 86 national societies (about 35,000 individuals) and 46 corporate mems; Pres. Dr GRAHAM BEASTALL (United Kingdom); Sec. Dr SERGIO BERNARDINI (Italy); publs *IFCC eNews*, *eIFCC* (electronic journal), *Annual Report*.

International Federation of Clinical Neurophysiology: c/o Venue West Conference Services Ltd, 100–873 Beatty St, Vancouver, BC, Canada, V6B 2M6; tel. (604) 681-5226; fax (604) 681-2503; e-mail sstevenson@venuewest.com; internet www.ifcn.info; f. 1949 to attain the highest level of knowledge in the field of electro-encephalography and clinical neurophysiology in all the countries of the world; mems in 58 countries; Pres. Prof. PAOLO M. ROSSINI; Sec. Prof. REINHARD DENGLER (Germany); publs *Clinical Neurophysiology* (monthly), *Evoked Potentials* (every 2 months), *EMG and Motor Control* (every 2 months).

International Federation of Fertility Societies (IFFS): 19 Mantua Rd, Mount Royal, NJ 08061, USA; tel. (856) 423-7222; fax (856) 423-3420; e-mail secretariat@iffs-reproduction.org; internet www.iffs-reproduction.org; f. 1951 to study problems of fertility and sterility; mems: approx. 40,000 world-wide; Pres. Prof. DAVID HEALY (Australia); Sec.-Gen. RICHARD KENNEDY (United Kingdom); publ. *Newsletter* (2 a year).

International Federation of Gynecology and Obstetrics (FIGO): FIGO House, Suite 3, Waterloo Court, 10 Theed St, London, SE1 8ST, United Kingdom; tel. (20) 7928-1166; fax (20) 7928-7099; e-mail figo@figo.org; internet www.figo.org; f. 1954; aims to improve standards in gynaecology and obstetrics, promote better health care for women, facilitate the exchange of information, and perfect methods of teaching; mems in 124 countries and territories; Pres. Prof. GAMAL SEROUR (Egypt); CEO Prof. HAMID RISHWAN; publ. *International Journal of Obstetrics and Gynecology*.

International Federation of Oto-Rhino-Laryngological Societies (IFOS): Antolská 11, 851 07, Bratislava Slovakia; e-mail info@ifosworld.org; internet www.ifosworld.org; f. 1965 to initiate and support programmes to protect hearing and prevent hearing impairment; holds Congresses every four years; mems: societies in 120 countries; Pres. Dr PAULO PONTES (Brazil); Gen. Sec. MILAN PROFANT (Slovakia); publ. *IFOS Newsletter* (quarterly).

International Federation of Surgical Colleges: c/o Royal College of Surgeons in Ireland, 123 St Stephen's Green, Dublin 2, Ireland; tel. (1) 4022707; fax (1) 4022230; e-mail ifsc@rcsi.ie; internet www.ifsc-net.org; f. 1958 to encourage high standards in surgical training; accepts volunteers to serve as surgical teachers in developing countries and co-operates with WHO in these countries; provides journals and text books for needy medical schools; conducts international symposia; offers grants; mems: colleges or asscns in 77 countries, 420 individual associates; Pres. Prof. PETER MCLEAN (Ireland); Hon. Sec. Prof. S. WILLIAM. A. GUNN (Switzerland); publ. *IFSC News*.

International Hospital Federation (IHF) (Fédération Internationale des Hôpitaux—FIH): Hôpital de Löex, 151 route de Löex, 1233 Bern, Switzerland; tel. 228509420; fax 227571016; e-mail info@ihf-fih.org; internet www.ihf-fih.org; f. 1947 for information exchange and education in hospital and health service matters; represents institutional health care in discussions with WHO; conducts conferences and courses on management and policy issues; mems in three categories: national hospital and health service organizations; assoc. mems, regional organizations and individual hospitals; honorary mems; Pres. THOMAS C. DOLAN (USA); CEO Dr ERIC DE ROODENBEKE; publs *World Hospitals and Health Services Journal* (quarterly), *IHF e-Newsletter* (5 a year).

International League against Epilepsy (ILAE): 342 North Main St, West Hartford, CT 06117-2507, USA; tel. (860) 586-7547; fax (860) 586-7550; internet www.ilae-epilepsy.org; f. 1909 to link national professional asscns and to encourage research, including classification and the development of anti-epileptic drugs; collaborates with the International Bureau for Epilepsy and with WHO; mems: 103 chapters; Pres. SOLOMON MOSHE; Sec.-Gen. SAMUEL WIEBE.

International League of Associations for Rheumatology (ILAR): All India Institute of Medical Sciences, Ansari Nagar, New Delhi 110029, India; e-mail ilar@rheumatology.org; internet www.ilar.org; f. 1927 to promote international co-operation for the study and control of rheumatic diseases; to encourage the foundation of national leagues against rheumatism; to organize regular international congresses and to act as a connecting link between national leagues and international organizations; mems: 13,000; Chair. ROHINI HANDA (India); publs *Annals of the Rheumatic Diseases* (in the United Kingdom), *Revue du Rhumatisme* (in France), *Reumatismo* (in Italy), *Arthritis and Rheumatism* (in the USA), etc.

International Leprosy Association (ILA): c/o Diana N. J. Lockwood, Dept of Clinical Sciences, London School of Hygiene and Tropical Medicine, Keppel St, London WC1E 7HT, United Kingdom; e-mail diana.lockwood@lshtm.ac.uk; internet www.leprosy-ila.org; f. 1931 to promote international co-operation in work on leprosy; holds congress every five years (2008: Hyderabad, India); Pres. Dr MARCOS VIRMOND (Brazil); Sec. Dr INDIRA NATH (India); publ. *The International Journal of Leprosy and Other Mycobacterial Diseases* (quarterly).

International Narcotics Control Board (INCB): Vienna International Centre, Rm E-1339, 1400 Vienna, POB 500, Austria; tel. (1) 260-60-0; fax (1) 260-60-58-67; e-mail secretariat@incb.org; internet www.incb.org; f. 1961 by the Single Convention on Narcotic Drugs, to supervise implementation of drug control treaties by governments; mems: 13 individuals; Pres. Prof. HAMID GHODSE (Iran); Sec. JONATHAN LUCAS; publ. *Annual Report* (with 3 technical supplements).

International Opticians' Association: c/o Association of British Dispensing Opticians, 199 Gloucester Terrace, London, W2 6LD, United Kingdom; tel. (20) 7298-5100; fax (20) 7298-5111; e-mail bdoris@abdo.org.uk; internet www.abdo.org.uk; f. 1951 to promote the science of opthalmic dispensing, and to maintain and advance standards and effect co-operation in optical dispensing; Pres. JENNIFER BROWER; Gen. Sec. Sir ANTHONY GARRETT.

International Organization for Medical Physics (IOMP): Fairmount House, 230 Tadcaster Rd, York, YO24 1ES, United Kingdom; tel. (0) 7787563913; e-mail nuesslin@lrz.tu-muenchen.de; internet www.iomp.org; f. 1963; aims to advance medical physics practice world-wide by disseminating scientific and technical information, fostering the educational and professional development of medical physicists, and promoting the highest quality medical services for patients; mems: represents more than 16,000 medical physicists world-wide and 75 adhering national orgs of medical physics; Pres. Prof. FRIDTJOF NÜSSLIN (Germany); Sec.-Gen. Dr MADAN REHANI (United Kingdom); publ. *Medical Physics World*.

International Pediatric Association (IPA): 1–3 rue de Chantepoulet, POB 1726,1211 Geneva 1, Switzerland; tel. 229069152; fax 227322852; e-mail adminoffice@ipa-world.org; internet www.ipa-world.org; f. 1912; holds triennial congresses and regional and national workshops; mems: national paediatric societies in 136 countries, 10 regional affiliate societies, 11 paediatric specialty societies; Pres. SERGIO AUGUSTO CABRAL (Brazil); Exec. Dir Dr WILLIAM J. KEENAN (USA); publ. *International Child Health* (quarterly).

International Pharmaceutical Federation (Fédération Internationale Pharmaceutique—FIP): POB 84200, 2508 AE, The Hague, Netherlands; tel. (70) 302-1970; fax (70) 302-1999; e-mail fip@fip.org; internet www.fip.org; f. 1912; aims to represent and serve pharmacy and pharmaceutical sciences world-wide and to improve access to medicines; holds World Congress of Pharmacy and Pharmaceutical Sciences annually; mems: 86 national pharmaceutical orgs in 62 countries, 55 associate, supportive and collective mems, 4,000 individuals; Gen. Sec. and CEO A. J. M. (TON) HOEK (Netherlands); Exec. Sec. RACHEL VAN KESTEREN; publ. *International Pharmacy Journal* (2 a year).

International Psychoanalytical Association (IPA): Broomhills, Woodside Lane, London, N12 8UD, United Kingdom; tel. (20) 8446-8324; fax (20) 8445-4729; e-mail ipa@ipa.org.uk; internet www.ipa.org.uk; f. 1908; aims to assure the continued vigour and development of psychoanalysis; acts as a forum for scientific discussions; controls and regulates training; contributes to the interdisciplinary area common to the behavioural sciences; mems: 11,500 in 34 countries; Pres. Prof. CHARLES M. T. HANLY; Sec.-Gen. H. GUNTHER PERDIGAO; publs *Bulletin*, *Newsletter*.

International Rhinologic Society: c/o Prof. Dr Metin Önerci, Hacettepe University Faculty of Medicine, Dept of Otorhinolaryngology, 06100 Hacettepe, Ankara, Turkey; tel. (532) 393-8668; fax (312) 311-3500; e-mail metin@tr.net; f. 1965; holds congress every two years; Pres. HIROSHI MORIYAMA; Gen. Sec. METIN ÖNERCI (Turkey); publ. *Rhinology*.

International Society for the Psychopathology of Expression and Art Therapy (SIPE): Hôpital La Grave-Casselardit, 170 ave de Casselardit, TSA 40031, 31059 Toulouse Cédex 9, France; tel. 4-90-03-92-12; fax 4-90-03-92-25; e-mail contact@sipe-art-therapy.com; internet www.sipe-art-therapy.com; f. 1959 to bring together specialists interested in the problems of expression and artistic activities in connection with psychiatric, sociological and psychological research; mems: 625; Pres. LAURENT SCHMITT (France); Sec.-Gen. JEAN-LUC SUDRES (France); publ. *Newsletter* (quarterly).

International Society for Vascular Surgery: 11 Scott Drive, Smithtown, NY 11787, USA; tel. (631) 979-3780; e-mail info@isvs.com; internet www.isvs.com; f. 1950 as the International Society for Cardiovascular Surgery (ISCVS) to stimulate research on the diagnosis and therapy of cardiovascular diseases and to exchange ideas on an international basis; present name adopted in 2005; Pres. Dr ENRICO. ASCHER (USA); Sec. Dr TIMUR SARAC (USA).

International Society of Audiology: 121 Anchor Drive, Halifax, Nova Scotia, Canada B3N 3B9; tel. (902) 477-5360; e-mail info@isa-audiology.org; internet www.isa-audiology.org; f. 1952 to facilitate the knowledge, protection and rehabilitation of human hearing and to represent the interests of audiology professionals and of the hearing-impaired; organizes biannual Congress and workshops and seminars; mems: 500 individuals; Pres. JOSÉ JUAN BARAJAS DE PRAT (Spain); Gen. Sec. Dr GEORGE MENCHER; publ. *International Journal of Audiology* (monthly).

International Society of Blood Transfusion (ISBT): Marnixstraat 317, 1016 TB Amsterdam, Netherlands; tel. and fax (20) 7601761; e-mail office@isbtweb.org; internet www.isbtweb.org; f. 1935; mems: c. 2,000 in over 97 countries; Pres. SILVANO WENDEL (Germany); Sec.-Gen. GEOFF DANIELS; publ. *Transfusion Today* (quarterly).

International Society of Developmental Biologists (ISDB): c/o Marianne Bronner, Biology Div., California Institute of Technology, 1200 E. California Blvd, Pasadena, CA 91125, USA; tel. (626) 395-4952; fax (626) 449-0756; e-mail mbronner@caltech.edu; internet www.developmental-biology.org; f. 1911 as International Institute of Embryology; aims to promote the study of developmental biology and to encourage international co-operation among investigators in the field; mems: 850 in 33 countries; Pres. CLAUDIO STERN (United Kingdom); International Sec. MARIANNE BRONNER-FRASER (USA); publs *Mechanisms of Development* (monthly), *Gene Expression Patterns* (6 a year).

International Society of Internal Medicine (ISIM): Dept of Internal Medicine, RSZ-Bern Hospitals, Zieglerspital, Morillonstrasse 75-91, 3001 Bern, Switzerland; tel. 319707178; fax 319707763; e-mail hanspeter.kohler@spitalnetzbern.ch; internet www.acponline.org/isim; f. 1948 to encourage research and education in internal medicine; mems: 61 national societies; Pres. Prof. WILLIAM J. HALL (USA); Sec.-Gen. Prof. HANS-PETER KOHLER (Switzerland).

International Society of Lymphology: POB 245066, Tucson, AZ 85724-5066, USA; tel. (520) 626-6118; e-mail lymph@u.arizona.edu; internet www.u.arizona.edu/~witte/ISL.htm; f. 1966 to further progress in lymphology through personal contacts and the exchange of ideas; mems: 375 in 42 countries; Pres. R. BAUMEISTER (Germany); Sec.-Gen. MARYLS H. WITTE (USA); publ. *Lymphology* (quarterly).

International Society of Neuropathology: c/o David Hilton, Dept of Neuropathology, Derriford Hospital, Plymouth, PL6 8DH, United Kingdom; fax (117) 9753765; e-mail davidhilton@nhs.net; internet www.intsocneuropathol.com; f. 1950 as International Committee of Neuropathology; renamed as above in 1967; Pres. Dr HERBERT BUDKA (Austria); Sec.-Gen. Dr DAVID HILTON (United Kingdom); publ. *Brain Pathology* (quarterly).

International Society of Orthopaedic Surgery and Traumatology (Société Internationale de Chirurgie Orthopédique et de Traumatologie): 40 rue Washington, bte 9, 1050 Brussels, Belgium; tel. (2) 648-68-23; fax (2) 649-86-01; e-mail hq@sicot.org; internet www.sicot.org; f. 1929; organizes Triennial World Congresses, Annual International Conferences and Trainees' Meetings; mems: 3,000 mems in 102 countries; Pres. Prof. MAURICE HINSENKAMP; Sec.-Gen. JOCHEN EULERT; publ. *International Orthopaedics* (scientific journal), *Newsletter* (quarterly), *e-Newsletter* (monthly).

International Society of Physical and Rehabilitation Medicine (ISPRM): ISPRM Central Office, Werner van Cleemputte, Medicongress, Kloosterstraat 5, 9960 Assenede, Belgium; tel. (9) 344-39-59; fax (9) 344-40-10; e-mail info@isprm.org; internet www.isprm.org; f. 1999 by merger of International Federation of Physical Medicine and Rehabilitation (f. 1952) and International Rehabilitation Medicine Association (f. 1968); sixth international congress: San Juan, Puerto Rico (June 2011); mems: in 68 countries; Pres. GEROLD STUCKI; Sec. JORGE LAINS; publs *Newsletter*, *Disability and Rehabilitation*, Journal of Rehabilitation Medicine.

International Society of Radiology (ISR): 7910 Woodmont Ave, Suite 400, Bethesda, Maryland 20814, USA; tel. (301) 657-2652 (ext.

22); fax (301) 907-8768; e-mail director@intsocradiology.org; internet www.isradiology.org; f. 1953 to promote radiology world-wide; International Commissions on Radiation Units and Measurements (ICRUM), on Radiation Protection (ICRP), and on Radiological Education (ICRE); organizes biannual International Congress of Radiology; collaborates with WHO and IAEA; mems: more than 80 national radiological societies; Pres. JAN LABASCAGNE (Australia); Sec.-Gen. LUIS DONOSO BACH (Spain); Exec. Dir OTHA W. LINTON; publ. *Newsletter*.

International Society of Surgery (ISS): Seltisbergerstr. 16, 4419 Lupsingen, Switzerland; tel. 618159666; fax 618114775; e-mail surgery@iss-sic.ch; internet www.iss-sic.com; f. 1902 to promote understanding between surgical disciplines; groups surgeons to address issues of interest to all surgical specialists; supports general surgery as a training base for abdominal surgery, surgery with integuments and endocrine surgery; organizes congresses, World Congress of Surgery: Yokohama, Japan (Aug.–Sept., 2011); mems: 4,000; Pres. GÖRAN AKERSTRÖM; Sec.-Gen. Prof. JEAN-CLAUDE GIVEL; publ. *World Journal of Surgery* (monthly).

International Society of Veterinary Dermatopathology (ISVD): c/o Sonja Bettenay, Tierdermatologie Deisenhofen, Schaeftlarner Weg 1A, Deisenhofen 82041, Germany; e-mail s-bettena@t-online.de; internet www.isvd.org; f. 1958; aims to advance veterinary and comparative dermatopathology, to group individuals with a professional interest in the histologic interpretation of animal skin diseases, to assist with and co-ordinate the adaptation and implementation of emerging technologies for the morphologic diagnosis of skin diseases in animals, and to provide an affiliation with physician dermatopathologists in order to exchange information on comparative dermatopathology; promotes professional training; Pres. Dr JUDITH NIMMO (Australia); Sec. SONJA BETTENAY (Germany).

International Spinal Cord Society (ISCoS): National Spinal Injuries Centre, Stoke Mandeville Hospital, Aylesbury, Bucks, HP21 8AL, United Kingdom; tel. (1296) 315866; fax (1296) 315870; e-mail admin@iscos.org.uk; internet www.iscos.org.uk; f. 1961; formerly the International Medical Society of Paraplegia (f. 1961); studies all problems relating to traumatic and non-traumatic lesions of the spinal cord, including causes, prevention, research and rehabilitation; promotes the exchange of information; assists in efforts to guide and co-ordinate research; Pres. FIN BIERING-SORENSEN (Denmark); Hon. Sec. SHINSUKE KATOH (Japan); publ. *Spinal Cord*.

International Union against Tuberculosis and Lung Disease (The Union): 68 blvd St Michel, 75006 Paris, France; tel. 1-44-32-03-60; fax 1-43-29-90-87; e-mail union@iuatld.org; internet www.theunion.org; f. 1920 to co-ordinate the efforts of anti-tuberculosis and respiratory disease asscns, to mobilize public interest, to assist control programmes and research around the world, to collaborate with governments and WHO and to promote conferences; mems: asscns in 145 countries, 10,000 individual mems; Pres. Dr JANE CARTER (USA); Sec.-Gen. Prof. CAMILO ROA, Jr (Philippines); publs *The International Journal of Tuberculosis and Lung Disease* (monthly), *Newsletter*.

International Union for Health Promotion and Education (IUHPE): 42 blvd de la Libération, 93203 St Denis Cédex, France; tel. 1-48-13-71-20; fax 1-48-09-17-67; e-mail iuhpe@iuhpe.org; internet www.iuhpe.org; f. 1951; provides an international network for the exchange of practical information on developments in health promotion and education; promotes research; encourages professional training for health workers, teachers, social workers and others; holds a World Conference on Health Promotion and Health Education every three years; organizes regional conferences and seminars; mems: in more than 90 countries; Pres. MICHAEL SPARKS (Australia); Exec. Dir MARIE-CLAUDE LAMARRE (France); publs *Health Promotion International*, *Promotion and Education* (quarterly, in English, French and Spanish).

Medical Women's International Association (MWIA): 7555 Morley Drive, Burnaby, B.C., V5E 3Y2, Canada; tel. (604) 522-1960; fax (604) 439-8994; e-mail secretariat@mwia.net; internet www.mwia.net; f. 1919 to facilitate contacts between women in medicine and to encourage co-operation in matters connected with international health problems; mems: national asscns in 48 countries, and individuals; Pres. Prof. AFUA HESSE (Japan); Sec.-Gen. Dr SHELLEY ROSS (Canada); publ. *MWIA UPDATE* (3 a year).

Multiple Sclerosis International Federation (MSIF): Skyline House, 3rd Floor, 200 Union St, London, SE1 0LX, United Kingdom; tel. (20) 7620-1911; fax (20) 7620-1922; e-mail info@msif.org; internet www.msif.org; f. 1967; promotes shared scientific research into multiple sclerosis and related neurological diseases; stimulates the active exchange of information; provides support for new and existing multiple sclerosis organizations; Pres. and Chair. WEYMAN JOHNSON (USA); CEO PEER BANEKE; publs *MSIF Annual Review*, *MS in Focus* (2 a year),.

Organisation panafricaine de lutte contre le SIDA (OPALS): 15–21 rue de L'École de Médecine, 75006 Paris, France; tel. 1-43-26-72-28; fax 1-43-29-70-93; internet www.opals.asso.fr; f. 1988; disseminates information relating to the treatment and prevention of AIDS; provides training of medical personnel; promotes co-operation between African medical centres and specialized centres in the USA and Europe; Pres. Prof. MARC GENTILINI; Sec.-Gen. Prof. DOMINIQUE RICHARD-LENOBLE; publ. *OPALS Liaison*.

Organization for Co-ordination in the Struggle against Endemic Diseases in Central Africa (Organisation de coordination pour la lutte contre les endémies en Afrique Centrale—OCEAC): BP 288, Yaoundé, Cameroon; tel. 23-22-32; fax 23-00-61; e-mail contact@oceac.org; internet www.oceac.org; f. 1965 to standardize methods of controlling endemic diseases, to co-ordinate national action, and to negotiate programmes of assistance and training on a regional scale; mems: Cameroon, Central African Republic, Chad, Republic of the Congo, Equatorial Guinea, Gabon; Exec. Sec. Dr JEAN JACQUES MOKA; publ. *Bulletin de Liaison et de Documentation* (quarterly).

Pan-American Association of Ophthalmology (PAAO): 1301 South Bowen Rd, Suite 450, Arlington, TX 76013, USA; tel. (817) 275-7553; fax (817) 275-3961; e-mail info@paao.org; internet www.paao.org; f. 1939 to promote friendship within the profession and the dissemination of scientific information; holds Congress every two years (2011: Buenos Aires, Argentina); mems: national ophthalmological societies and other bodies in 39 countries; Pres. MARK MANNIS; Exec. Dir TERESA BRADSHAW; publ. *Vision Panamerica* (quarterly).

Pan-Pacific Surgical Association: 1212 Punahou St, Suite 3506, Honolulu, HI 96826, Hawaii, USA; tel. (808) 941-1010; fax (808) 951-7004; e-mail ppsa.info@panpacificsurgical.org; internet www.panpacificsurgical.org; f. 1929 to bring together surgeons to exchange scientific knowledge relating to surgery and medicine, and to promote the improvement and standardization of hospitals and their services and facilities; congresses are held every two years; mems: 2,716 regular, associate and senior mems from 44 countries; Pres. Dr JEROME C. GOLDSTEIN.

Rehabilitation International: 25 East 21st St, 4th Floor, New York, NY 10010, USA; tel. (212) 420-1500; fax (212) 505-0871; e-mail ri@riglobal.org; internet www.riglobal.org; f. 1922 to improve the lives of people with disabilities through the exchange of information and research on equipment and methods of assistance; functions as a global network of disabled people, service providers, researchers and government agencies; advocates promoting and implementing the rights, inclusion and rehabilitation of people with disabilities; organizes international conferences and co-operates with UN agencies and other international organizations; mems: 700 orgs in more than 90 countries; Pres. ANNE HAWKER; Sec.-Gen. VENUS ILAGAN; publs *International Rehabilitation Review* (annually), *Rehabilitación* (2 or 3 a year).

Society of French-speaking Neuro-Surgeons (Société de neurochirurgie de langue française—SNCLF): Cabinet de Neurochirurgie, 4 ave de Vaudagne, 1217 Geneva, Switzerland; tel. 227830304; fax 227830308; e-mail daniel.may@bluewin.ch; internet www.snclf.com; f. 1949; holds annual convention and congress; mems: 700; Pres. FRANÇOIS-XAVIER ROUX (France); Sec.-Gen. DANIEL MAY; publ. *Neurochirurgie* (6 a year).

Transplantation Society (Société de Transplantation): 1255 University St, Suite 325, Montréal, QC, Canada H3B 3B4; tel. (514) 874-1717; fax (514) 874-1716; e-mail info@tts.org; internet www.transplantation-soc.org; f. 1966; aims to provide a focus for development of the science and clinical practice of transplantations, scientific communication, education, and guidance on ethics; mems: more than 3,000 in 65 countries; Pres. GERHARD OPELZ.

Union for International Cancer Control (Union internationale contre le cancer—UICC): 62 route de Frontenex, 1207 Geneva, Switzerland; tel. 228091811; fax 228091810; e-mail info@uicc.org; internet www.uicc.org; f. 1933 to promote the campaign to prevent and control cancer on an international level; aims to connect, mobilize and support organizations, leading experts, key stakeholders and volunteers in a community working together to eliminate cancer as a life-threatening disease for future generations; works closely with its member orgs and partners to implement a comprehensive strategy that includes: organizing the World Cancer Congress; promoting the World Cancer Declaration; raising awareness through the World Cancer Campaign; co-ordinating World Cancer Day annually, on 4 February; reviewing and disseminating the TNM (tumour-node-metastasis) classification of malignant tumours; developing effective cancer control programmes especially in low- and middle-income countries; changing cancer-related beliefs and behaviour through information and education; creating special initiatives in prevention, early detection, access to treatment and supportive care; awarding international cancer fellowships; producing scientific publications; mems: 470 orgs in 124 countries; Pres. Dr EDUARDO CAZAP (Argentina); CEO CARY ADAMS (United Kingdom); publs *International Journal of Cancer* (36 a year), *UICC News* (quarterly).

World Allergy Organization (IAACI): 555 East Wells St, Suite 1100, Milwaukee, WI 53202-3823, USA; tel. (414) 276-1791; fax (414)

276-3349; e-mail info@worldallergy.org; internet www.worldallergy.org; f. 1945, as International Association of Allergology and Clinical Immunology, to further work in the educational, research and practical medical aspects of allergic and immunological diseases; World Congresses held every two years (Dec. 2011: Cancún, Mexico); mems: 77 national and regional societies; Pres. RUBY PAWANKAR (India/Japan); Sec.-Gen. Prof. MARIO SÁNCHEZ BORGES (Venezuela); publ. *Allergy and Clinical Immunology International* (6 a year).

World Association for Disaster and Emergency Medicine (WADEM): International Office, POB 55158, Madison, WI 53705-8958, USA; tel. (608) 819-6604; fax (608) 819-6055; e-mail info@wadem.org; internet www.wadem.org; f. 1976; aims to improve prehospital and emergency health care, public health, and disaster health and preparedness; became a full partner in the Global Health Cluster of the UN Inter-Agency Standing Committee in April 2008; mems: 600 in 55 countries; Pres. PAUL ARBON (Australia); Sec. DARREN WALTER (United Kingdom); publs *International Disaster Nursing*, *Prehospital and Disaster Medicine*.

World Association of Societies of Pathology and Laboratory Medicine (WASPaLM): 2/F UI Bldg, 2-2 Kanda Ogawa-machi, Chiyoda-ku, Tokyo, 101-0052, Japan; tel. (3) 3295-0353; fax (3) 3295-0352; e-mail info@waspalm.org; internet www.waspalm.org; f. 1947 to link national societies and co-ordinate their scientific and technical means of action; promotes the development of anatomic and clinical pathology, especially by convening conferences, congresses and meetings, and through the interchange of publications and personnel; mems: 54 national asscns; Chair. Dr HENRY TRAVERS (USA); Exec. Dir. Dr MASSAMI MURAKAMI (Japan); publ. *Newsletter* (quarterly).

World Confederation for Physical Therapy (WCPT): Victoria Charity Centre, 11 Belgrave Rd,London, SW1V 1RB, United Kingdom; tel. (20) 7931-6465; fax (20) 7931-6494; e-mail info@wcpt.org; internet www.wcpt.org; f. 1951; represents physical therapy internationally; encourages high standards of physical therapy education and practice; promotes exchange of information among members, and the development of a scientific professional base through research; aims to contribute to the development of informed public opinion regarding physical therapy; holds seminars and workshops and quadrennial scientific congress showcasing advancements in physical therapy research, practice and education (June 2007: Vancouver, Canada); mems: 106 national physical therapy orgs; Pres. MARILYN MOFFAT; Sec.-Gen. BRENDA J. MYERS; publ. *WCPT News* (quarterly).

World Council of Optometry (WCO): 42 Craven St, London, WC2N 5NG, United Kingdom; tel. (20) 7839-6000; fax (20) 7839-6800; e-mail enquiries@worldoptometry.org; internet www.worldoptometry.org; f. 1927 to co-ordinate efforts to provide a good standard of ophthalmic optical (optometric) care throughout the world; enables exchange of ideas between different countries; focuses on optometric education; gives advice on standards of qualification; considers optometry legislation throughout the world; mems: 94 optometric orgs in 45 countries; Pres. TONE GARAAS-MAURDALEN (Norway).

World Federation for Medical Education (WFME) (Fédération mondiale pour l'enseignement de la medicine): Univ. of Copenhagen, Faculty of Health Sciences, Blegdamsvej 3, 2200 Copenhagen N, Denmark; tel. (353) 27103; fax (353) 27070; e-mail wfme@wfme.org; internet www.wfme.org; f. 1972; aims to promote and integrate medical education world-wide; links regional and international asscns; has official relations with WHO, UNICEF, UNESCO, UNDP and the World Bank; Pres. Prof. STEFAN LINDGREN; Sec. ANNA IVERSEN.

World Federation for Mental Health (WFMH): POB 807, Occoquan, VA 22125, USA; fax (703) 490-6926; e-mail info@wfmh.com; internet www.wfmh.org; f. 1948 to promote the highest standards of mental health; works with agencies of the UN in promoting global mental health needs; assists grassroots efforts to improve mental health services, treatment and stigma; voting, affiliate and individual members in more than 100 countries; Pres. DEBORAH WAN (Hong Kong SAR); Sec.-Gen. VIJAY GANJU; publs *Newsletter* (quarterly), *Annual Report*.

World Federation for Ultrasound in Medicine and Biology: 14750 Sweitzer Ln, Suite 100, Laurel, MD 20707-5906, USA; e-mail admin@wfumb.org; internet www.wfumb.org; f. 1973; Pres. MASATOSHI KUDO; Sec. DAVID EVANS; publs *Ultrasound in Medicine and Biology* (monthly), *Echoes* (2 a year).

World Federation of Associations of Paediatric Surgeons (WOFAPS): c/o Prof. J. Boix-Ochoa, Clinica Infantil 'Vall d'Hebron', Departamento de Cirugía Pediátrica, Valle de Hebron 119–129, Barcelona 08035, Spain; e-mail jboix99@hotmail.com; internet www.wofaps.org; f. 1974; World Congress (2010: New Delhi, India); mems: 80 asscns; Pres. Prof. PREM PURI; Sec.-Gen./Treas. Prof. PEPE BOIX-OCHOA.

World Federation of Hydrotherapy and Climatotherapy: Cattedra di Terapia Med. E Medic. Termal, Università degli Studi, via Cicognara 7, 20129 Milan, Italy; tel. (02) 50318458; fax (02) 50318461; e-mail crbbmn@unimi.it; internet www.femteconline.org; f. 1947 as International Federation of Thermalism and Climatism; recognized by WHO in 1986; present name adopted 1999; mems: in 44 countries; Pres. M. NIKOLAI A. STOROZHENKO (Russia); Gen. Sec. Prof. UMBERTO SOLIMENE (Italy).

World Federation of Neurology (WFN): Hill House, Heron Sq., Richmond, Surrey, TW9 1EP, United Kingdom; tel. (20) 8439-9556; fax (20) 8439-9499; e-mail info@wfneurology.org; internet www.wfneurology.org; f. 1955 as International Neurological Congress, present title adopted 1957; aims to assemble members of various congresses associated with neurology and promote co-operation among neurological researchers. Organizes Congress every four years; mems: 23,000 in 102 countries; Pres. VLADIMIR HACHINSKI (Canada); Sec.-Treas. Dr RAAD SHAKIR (United Kingdom); publs *Journal of the Neurological Sciences*, *World Neurology* (quarterly).

World Federation of Neurosurgical Societies (WFNS): 5 rue du Marché, 1260 Nyon Vaud, Switzerland; tel. 223624303; fax 223624352; e-mail teresachen@wfns.ch; internet www.wfns.org; f. 1957 to assist in the development of neurosurgery and to help the formation of asscns; facilitates the exchange of information and encourages research; mems: 116 societies; Pres. PETER M. BLACK; Sec. Dr HILDO AZEVEDO-FILHO.

World Federation of Occupational Therapists (WFOT): POB 30, Forrestfield, Western Australia 6058, Australia; fax (8) 9453-9746; e-mail admin@wfot.org.au; internet www.wfot.org; f. 1952 to further the rehabilitation of the physically and mentally disabled by promoting the development of occupational therapy in all countries; facilitates the exchange of information and publications; promotes research in occupational therapy; holds international congresses every four years; mems: national professional asscns in 69 countries, with total membership of c. 300,000; Pres. SHARON BRINTNELL (Canada); Exec. Dir MARILYN PATTISON (Australia); publ. *Bulletin* (2 a year).

World Federation of Public Health Associations: Office of the Secretariat, c/o Institute for Social and Preventive Medicine, University of Geneva CMU, 1 rue Michel Servet, 1211 Geneva 4, Switzerland; tel. 223970466; fax 223970452; e-mail bettina.borisch@unige.ch; internet www.wfpha.org; f. 1967; brings together researchers, teachers, health service providers and workers in a multidisciplinary environment of professional exchange, studies and action; endeavours to influence policies and to set priorities to prevent disease and promote health; holds aCongress every three years: Addis Ababa, Ethiopia (April 2012); mems: 68 national public health asscns and 5 regional asscns; Pres. JIM CHAUVIN (Canada); publs *WFPHA Report* (in English), occasional technical papers.

World Federation of Societies of Anaesthesiologists (WFSA): 21 Portland Pl., London, W1B 1PY, United Kingdom; tel. (20) 7631-8880; fax (20) 7631-8882; e-mail wfsahq@anaesthesiologists.org; internet www.anaesthesiologists.org; f. 1955; aims to make available the highest standards of anaesthesia, pain treatment, trauma management and resuscitation to all peoples of the world; mems: 122 national societies; Pres. Dr DAVID WILKINSON (United Kingdom); Sec. Dr GONZALO BARREIRO (Uruguay); publs *Update in Anaesthesia* (2 a year), *Annual Report*.

World Gastroenterology Organization (WGO): 555 East Wells St, Suite 1100, Milwaukee, WI 53202, USA; tel. (414) 918-9798; fax (414) 276-3349; e-mail info@worldgastroenterology.org; internet www.worldgastroenterology.org; f. 1958 as Organisation mondiale de gastro-entérologie—OMGE, to promote clinical and academic gastroenterological practice throughout the world, and to ensure high ethical standards; focuses on the improvement of standards in gastroenterology training and education on a global scale; renamed as above in 2007; a WGO Foundation, incorporated in 2007, is dedicated to raising funds to support WGO educational programs and activities; mems: 103 national societies, 4 regional asscns; Pres. Prof. HENRY COHEN (Uruguay); Sec.-Gen. Prof. CIHAN YURDAYDIN (Turkey).

World Heart Federation: 7 rue des Battoir, 1211 Geneva 4, Switzerland; tel. 228070320; fax 228070339; e-mail admin@worldheart.org; internet www.world-heart-federation.org; f. 1978 as International Society and Federation of Cardiology, name changed as above 1998; aims to help people to achieve a longer and better life through prevention and control of heart disease and stroke, with a focus on low- and middle-income countries; mems: 197 orgs in more than 100 countries; Pres. Dr SIDNEY C. SMITH,Jr (USA); Sec. JOHANNA RALSTON (Switzerland); publs *Nature Clinical Practice Cardiovascular Journal*, *Global Heart*.

World Medical Association (WMA): 13 chemin du Levant, CIB-Bâtiment A, 01210 Ferney-Voltaire, France; tel. 4-50-40-75-75; fax 4-50-40-59-37; e-mail wma@wma.net; internet www.wma.net; f. 1947 to achieve the highest international standards in all aspects of medical education and practice, to promote closer ties among doctors and national medical asscns by personal contact and all other means, to study problems confronting the medical profession, and to present its views to appropriate bodies; holds an annual General Assembly; mems: 83 national medical asscns; Pres. Dr JOSÉ LUIZ GOMES (Brazil); Sec.-Gen. Dr OTMAR KLOIBER (Germany); publ. *The World Medical Journal* (quarterly).

World Psychiatric Association (WPA): Psychiatric Hospital, 2 chemin du Petit-Bel-Air 1225, Chêne-Bourg, Switzerland; tel. 223055737; fax 223055735; e-mail wpasecretariat@wpanet.org; internet www.wpanet.org; f. 1961; aims to increase knowledge and skills necessary for work in the field of mental health and the care for the mentally ill; organizes World Psychiatric Congresses and regional and interregional scientific meetings; mems: 135 national psychiatric societies, representing some 200,000 psychiatrists, in 117 countries; Pres. PEDRO RUIZ (USA); Sec.-Gen. LEVENT KUEY (Turkey).

World Self-Medication Industry (WSMI): 13 chemin du Levant, 01210 Ferney-Voltaire, France; tel. 4-50-28-47-28; fax 4-50-28-40-24; e-mail admin@wsmi.org; internet www.wsmi.org; f. 1970; aims to promote understanding and development of responsible self-medication; Chair. ZHENYU GUO (People's Republic of China); Dir-Gen. Dr DAVID E. WEBBER.

Posts and Telecommunications

Arab Permanent Postal Commission: c/o Arab League Bldg, Tahrir Sq., Cairo, Egypt; tel. (2) 5750511; fax (2) 5779546; f. 1952; aims to establish stricter postal relations between the Arab countries than those laid down by the Universal Postal Union, and to pursue the development and modernization of postal services in member countries; publs *APU Bulletin* (monthly), *APU Review* (quarterly), *APU News* (annually).

Asia-Pacific Telecommunity (APT): No. 12/49, Soi 5, Chaengwattana Rd, Thungsonghong, Bangkok 10210, Thailand; tel. (2) 573-0044; fax (2) 573-7479; e-mail aptmail@apt.int; internet www.aptsec.org; f. 1979 to cover all matters relating to telecommunications in the region; serves as the focal organization for ICT in the Asia-Pacific region; contributes, through its various programmes and activities, to the growth of the ICT sector in the region and assists members in their preparation for global telecommunications conferences, as well as promoting regional harmonization for such events; mems: Afghanistan, Australia, Bangladesh, Bhutan, Brunei, Cambodia, People's Republic of China, Fiji, India, Indonesia, Iran, Japan, Democratic Republic of Korea, Republic of Korea, Laos, Malaysia, Maldives, Marshall Islands, Federated States of Micronesia, Mongolia, Myanmar, Nauru, Nepal, New Zealand, Pakistan, Palau, Papua New Guinea, Philippines, Samoa, Singapore, Sri Lanka, Thailand, Tonga, Tuvalu, Vanuatu, Viet Nam; assoc. mems: Cook Islands, Hong Kong, Macao, Niue; 130 affiliated mems; Sec.-Gen. TOSHIYUKI YAMADA.

Asian-Pacific Postal Union (APPU): APPU Bureau, POB 1, Laksi Post Office, 111 Chaeng Wattana Rd, Bangkok 10210, Thailand; tel. (2) 573-7282; fax (2) 573-1161; e-mail admin@appu-bureau.org; internet www.appu-bureau.org; f. 1962 to extend, facilitate and improve the postal relations between the member countries and to promote co-operation in the field of postal services; holds Congress every four years (2013: India); mems: postal administrations in 32 countries; Dir SOMCHAI REOPANICHKUL; publs *Annual Report*, *Exchange Program of Postal Officials*, *APPU Newsletter*.

European Conference of Postal and Telecommunications Administrations: Penblingehus, Nansensgade 19-3, 1366 Copenhagen, Denmark; tel. 33-89-63-00; fax 33-89-63-30; e-mail ceptpresidency@cept.org; internet www.cept.org; f. 1959 to strengthen relations between member administrations and to harmonize and improve their technical services; set up Eurodata Foundation, for research and publishing; supported by a separate European Communications Office (ECO); mems: 48 countries; Joint Chair. THOMAS EWERS, ULRICH DAMMANN, ANDERS JÖNSSON; Dir ECO MARK THOMAS (United Kingdom); publ. *Bulletin*.

European Telecommunications Satellite Organization (EUTELSAT): 33 ave du Maine, 75755 Paris, France; tel. 1-44-10-41-10; fax 1-44-10-41-11; e-mail secigo@eutelsat.fr; internet www.eutelsatigo.int; f. 1977 to operate satellites for fixed and mobile communications in Europe; EUTELSAT's in-orbit resource comprises 18 satellites; commercialises capacity in three satellites operated by other companies; mems: public and private telecommunications operations in 49 countries; Exec. Sec. CHRISTIAN ROISSE.

International Mobile Satellite Organization (IMSO): 99 City Rd, London, EC1Y 1AX, United Kingdom; tel. (20) 7728-1249; fax (20) 7728-1172; e-mail info@imso.org; internet www.imso.org; f. 1979 to provide (from Feb. 1982) global communications for shipping via satellites on a commercial basis; in 1985 the operating agreement was amended to include aeronautical communications, and in 1988 amendments were approved which allowed provision of global land mobile communications; in April 1999 the commercial functions of the organization became the limited company INMARSAT Ltd (the first intergovernmental org. to be transferred to the private sector); IMSO was maintained, initially to monitor, under a Public Services Agreement adopted in 1999, INMARSAT's public service obligations in respect of the Global Maritime Distress and Safety System (GMDSS); following amendments adopted in 2008 to the IMSO Convention, IMSO's oversight functions were extended to all satellite operators approved to provide GMDSS services, and IMSO was also mandated to oversee long range tracking and identification of ships (LRIT); mems: 97 states party to the founding Convention; Dir-Gen. Capt. ESTEBAN PACHA-VICENTE.

International Multinational Partnership against Cyber Threats (IMPACT): Jalan IMPACT, 63000 Cyberjaya, Malaysia; tel. (3) 83132020; fax (3) 83192020; e-mail contactus@impact-alliance.org; internet www.impact-alliance.org; f. 2006 as a global public-private partnership; aims to promote collaboration in order strengthen the capability of the international community and individual partner countries to prevent, defend against and respond to cyber threats; signed a Memorandum of Understanding with the ITU in Sept. 2008 to administer the Global Cyber Agenda; Chair. Datuk MOHD NOOR AMIN.

International Telecommunications Satellite Organization (ITSO): 3400 International Drive, NW, Washington, DC 20008-3098, USA; tel. (202) 243-5096; fax (202) 243-5018; internet www.itso.int; f. 1964 to establish a global commercial satellite communications system; Assembly of Parties attended by representatives of member governments, meets every two years to consider policy and long-term aims and matters of interest to members as sovereign states; meeting of Signatories to the Operating Agreement held annually; 24 INTELSAT satellites in geosynchronous orbit provide a global communications service; provides most of the world's overseas traffic; in 1998 INTELSAT agreed to establish a private enterprise, incorporated in the Netherlands, to administer six satellite services; mems: 150 govts; Dir-Gen. JOSÉ TOSCANO (USA).

Internet Corporation for Assigned Names and Numbers (ICANN): 4676 Admiralty Way, Suite 330, Marina del Rey, CA 90292-6601, USA; tel. (310) 823-9358; fax (310) 823-8649; e-mail icann@icann.org; internet www.icann.org; f. 1998; non-profit, private sector body; aims to co-ordinate the technical management and policy development of the Internet in relation to addresses, domain names and protocol; supported by an At-Large Advisory Committee (representing individual users of the Internet), a Country Code Names Supporting Organization (ccNSO), a Governmental Advisory Committee, a Generic Names Supporting Organization (GNSO), and a Security and Stability Advisory Committee; through its Internet Assigned Numbers Authority (IANA) department ICANN manages the global co-ordination of domain name system roots and Internet protocol addressing; at 30 June 2011 there were 310 top-level domains (TLDs), 30 of which were in non-Latin scripts, and the most common of which were generic TLDs (gTLDs) (such as .org or .com) and country code TLDs (ccTLDs); in June 2011 ICANN adopted an expanded gTLD programme, under which applications were to be accepted from 2012 from qualified orgs wishing to register domain names of their choosing, including the possibility of Internationalized Domain Names (IDNs) incorporating non-Latin character sets (Arabic, Chinese and Cyrillic), with a view to making the Internet more globally inclusive; Pres. and CEO ROD BECKSTROM (USA).

Pacific Telecommunications Council (PTC): 914 Coolidge St, Honolulu, HI 96826-3085, USA; tel. (808) 941-3789; fax (808) 944-4874; e-mail info@ptc.org; internet www.ptc.org; f. 1978 to facilitate the adoption of telecommunications and advanced information technologies throughout the Asia-Pacific region; enables the exchange of ideas and commerce through its annual conference each Jan; mems: 3,000 mem. representatives from more than 50 countries; Pres. RICHARD TAYLOR (USA); CEO SHARON NAKAMA.

Postal Union of the Americas, Spain and Portugal (PUASP) (Unión Postal de las Américas, España y Portugal): Cebollatí 1468/70, 1°, Casilla de Correos 20.042, Montevideo, Uruguay; tel. 2410 0070; fax 2410 5046; e-mail secretaria@upaep.com.uy; internet www.upaep.com.uy; f. 1911 to extend, facilitate and study the postal relationships of member countries; mems: 27 countries; Sec.-Gen. SERRANA BASSINI CASCO.

Press, Radio and Television

African Union of Broadcasting (AUB): 101 rue Carnot, BP 3237, Dakar, Senegal; tel. 821-16-25; fax 822-51-13; internet www.aub-uar.org/eng/; f. 1962 as Union of National Radio and Television Organizations of Africa (URTNA), new org. f. Nov. 2006; co-ordinates radio and television services, including monitoring and frequency allocation, the exchange of information and coverage of national and international events among African countries; mems: 48 orgs and 6 assoc. members; Pres. TEWFIK KHELLADI (Algeria), LAWRENCE ADDO-YAO ATIASE (Ghana).

Asia-Pacific Broadcasting Union (ABU): POB 1164, Lorong Maarof, 59000 Kuala Lumpur, Malaysia; tel. and fax (3) 22823592; e-mail info@abu.org.my; internet www.abu.org.my; f. 1964 to foster and co-ordinate the development of broadcasting in the Asia-Pacific area, to develop means of establishing closer collaboration and co-operation among broadcasting orgs, and to serve the professional needs of broadcasters in Asia and the Pacific; holds annual General Assembly; mems: more than 200 in 58 countries and territories; Pres. Dr KIM IN-KYU (Republic of Korea); Sec.-Gen. Dr JAVAD MOTTAGHI (Iran); publs *ABU News* (every 2 months), *ABU Technical Review* (every 2 months).

Association for the Promotion of International Press Distribution (DISTRIPRESS): Seefeldstrasse 35, 8008 Zürich, Switzerland; tel. 442024121; fax 442021025; e-mail info@distripress.net; internet www.distripress.net; f. 1955 to assist in the promotion of the freedom of the press throughout the world, supporting and aiding UNESCO in promoting the free flow of ideas; organizes meetings of publishers and distributors of newspapers, periodicals and paperback books, to promote the exchange of information and experience among members; mems: 470 in 95 countries; Pres. TONY JASHANMAL (UAE); Man. Dir DAVID OWEN (United Kingdom); publs *Distripress Gazette*, *Who's Who*.

Association of European Journalists (AEJ): 145 ave Baron Albert d'Huart, 1950 Kraainem, Belgium; tel. (478) 291985; e-mail npkramer@skynet.be; internet www.aej.org; f. 1963 to participate actively in the development of a European consciousness; to promote deeper knowledge of European problems and secure appreciation by the general public of the work of European institutions; to facilitate members' access to sources of European information; and to defend freedom of the press; mems: 2,100 individuals and national asscns in 25 countries; Pres. EILEEN DUNNE (Ireland); Sec.-Gen. N. PETER KRAMER (Belgium).

Cable Europe: 41 ave des Arts, 1040 Brussels, Belgium; tel. (2) 521-17-63; fax (2) 521-79-76; e-mail info@cable-europe.eu; internet www.cable-europe.eu; f. 1955 as European Cable Communications Associations (name changed in 2006); promotes the interests of the European cable industry and fosters co-operation among companies and national asscns; Pres. MANUEL KOHNSTAMM (Netherlands).

European Alliance of News Agencies: Norrbackagatan 23, 11341 Stockholm, Sweden; tel. and fax (8) 301-324; e-mail erik-n@telia.com; internet www.newsalliance.org; f. 1957 as European Alliance of Press Agencies (name changed 2002); aims to promote co-operation among members and to study and protect their common interests; annual assembly; mems: in 30 countries; Sec.-Gen. ERIK NYLÉN.

European Broadcasting Union (EBU): CP 45, 17A Ancienne-Route, 1218 Grand-Saconnex, Geneva, Switzerland; tel. 227172111; fax 227474000; e-mail ebu@ebu.ch; internet www.ebu.ch; f. 1950 in succession to the International Broadcasting Union; a professional asscn of broadcasting organizations, supporting the interests of members and assisting the development of broadcasting in all its forms; activities include the Eurovision news and programme exchanges and the Euroradio music exchanges; mems: 85 active in 56 countries, 37 assoc. mems; Pres. JEAN-PAUL PHILIPPOT (Belgium); Dir-Gen. INGRID DELTENRE; publs *EBU Technical Review* (annually), *Dossiers* (2 a year).

Inter-American Press Association (IAPA) (Sociedad Interamericana de Prensa): Jules Dubois Bldg, 1801 SW 3rd Ave, Miami, FL 33129, USA; tel. (305) 634-2465; fax (305) 635-2272; e-mail info@sipiapa.org; internet www.sipiapa.org; f. 1942 to guard the freedom of the press in the Americas; to promote and maintain the dignity, rights and responsibilities of the profession of journalism; to foster a wider knowledge and greater interchange among the peoples of the Americas; mems: 1,400; Exec. Dir JULIO E. MUÑOZ; publ. *IAPA News* (monthly).

International Amateur Radio Union: POB 310905, Newington, CT 06131-0905, USA; tel. (860) 594-0200; fax (860) 594-0259; e-mail iaru@iaru.org; internet www.iaru.org; f. 1925 to link national amateur radio societies and represent the interests of two-way amateur radio communication; mems: 161 national amateur radio societies; Pres. TIMOTHY ELLAM (Canada); Sec. RODNEY STAFFORD.

International Association of Sound and Audiovisual Archives: c/o Ilse Assmann, Radio Broadcast Facilities, SABC, POB 931, Auckland Park 2006, Johannesburg, South Africa; tel. (11) 714-4041; fax (11) 714-4419; e-mail assmanni@sabc.co.za; internet www.iasa-web.org; f. 1969; supports the professional exchange of sound and audiovisual documents, and fosters international co-operation between audiovisual archives in all fields, in particular in the areas of acquisition, documentation, access, exploitation, copyright, and preservation; holds annual conference; mems: 400 individuals and institutions in 64 countries; Pres. JACQUELINE VON ARB (Norway) (2011–14); Sec.-Gen. LYNN JOHNSON (South Africa); publs *IASA Journal* (2 a year), *IASA Information Bulletin* (2 a year), *eBulletin* (2 a year).

International Association of Women in Radio and Television (IAWRT): 3/F GIF Medical Bldg, 510C Raymundo Ave, Caniogan, Pasig City 1606, Philippines; tel. and fax (2) 6434583; e-mail secretariat@iawrt.org; internet www.iawrt.org; f. 1951; Pres. RACHEAL NAKITARE (Kenya); Sec. VIOLET GONDA (Zimbabwe).

International Catholics Organisation of the Media (ICOM) (World Forum of Professionals and Institutions in Secular and Religious Journalism): 37–39 rue de Vermont, CP 197, 1211 Geneva 20, Switzerland; tel. 227340017; fax 227340053; e-mail icom@bluewin.ch; internet www.IcomWorld.info; f. 2011, as a successor organization to the former International Catholic Union of the Press (f. 1927, dissolved 2011); focuses on inspiring and encouraging all media professionals world-wide, irrespective of differences, and on promoting the rights to information and freedom of opinion, and supports journalistic ethics; World Congress to be held in 2013, in Panama; mems: in 172 countries.

International Council for Film, Television and Audiovisual Communication (Conseil international du cinema de la television et de la communication audiovisuelle): 1 rue Miollis, 75732 Paris Cedex 15, France; tel. 1-45-68-48-55; fax 1-45-67-28-40; e-mail secretariat@cict-unesco.org; internet www.unesco.org/iftc; f. 1958 to support collaboration between UNESCO and professionals engaged in cinema, television and audiovisual communications; mems: 36 international film and television organizations; Pres. HISANORI ISOMURA; Sec.-Gen. LOLA POGGI GOUJON; publ. *Letter of Information* (monthly).

International Council of French-speaking Radio and Television Organizations (Conseil international des radios-télévisions d'expression française): 52 blvd Auguste-Reyers, 1044 Brussels, Belgium; tel. (2) 732-45-85; fax (2) 732-62-40; e-mail cirtef@rtbf.be; internet www.cirtef.org; f. 1978 to establish links between French-speaking radio and television organizations; mems: 46 orgs; Sec.-Gen. GUILA THIAM (Senegal).

International Federation of Film Critics (Fédération Internationale de la Presse Cinématographique—FIPRESCI): Schleissheimerstr. 83, 80797 Munich, Germany; tel. (89) 182303; fax (89) 184766; e-mail info@fipresci.org; internet www.fipresci.org; f. 1930 to develop the cinematographic press and promote cinema as an art; organizes international meetings and juries in film festivals; mems: national organizations or corresponding members in 68 countries; Pres. JEAN ROY (France); Gen. Sec. KLAUS EDER (Germany).

International Federation of Press Cutting Agencies (FIBEP) (Fédération Internationale des Bureaux D'Extraits de Presse): Chaussée de Wavre 1945, 1160 Brussels, Belgium; tel. (2) 508-17-13; fax (2) 513-82-18; internet www.fibep.info; f. 1953 to improve the standing of the profession, prevent infringements, illegal practices and unfair competition; and to develop business and friendly relations among press cuttings agencies throughout the world; Congress held every 18 months, Oct. 2012: Krakow, Poland; mems: 90 agencies in more than 40 countries; Pres. NOGUEIRA FRESCO; Gen. Sec. JOACHIM VON BEUST (Belgium).

International Federation of the Periodical Press (FIPP): Queen's House, 55/56 Lincoln's Inn Fields, London, WC2A 3LJ, United Kingdom; tel. (20) 7404-4169; fax (20) 7404-4170; e-mail info@fipp.com; internet www.fipp.com; f. 1925; works for the benefit of magazine publishers around the world by promoting the common editorial, cultural and economic interests of consumer and business-to-business publishers, both in print and electronic media; fosters formal and informal alliances between magazine publishers and industry suppliers; mems: 52 national asscns, 470 publishing cos, 180 assoc. mems and 6 individual mems; Pres. and CEO CHRIS LLEWELYN; publ. *Magazine World* (quarterly).

International Institute of Communications: 2 Printers Yard, 90A The Broadway, London, SW19 1RD, United Kingdom; tel. (20) 8417-0600; fax (20) 8417-0800; e-mail enquiries@iicom.org; internet www.iicom.org; f. 1969 (as the International Broadcast Institute) to link all working in the field of communications, including policy makers, broadcasters, industrialists and engineers; holds local, regional and international meetings; undertakes research; mems: over 1,000 corporate, institutional and individual; Pres. FABIO COLASANTI; Dir-Gen. ANDREA MILLWOOD HARGRAVE; publ. *Intermedia* (5 a year).

International Maritime Radio Association: South Bank House, Black Prince Rd, London, SE1 7SJ, United Kingdom; tel. (20) 7587-1245; fax (20) 7793-2329; e-mail secgen@cirm.org; internet www.cirm.org; f. 1928 to study and develop means of improving marine radio communications and radio aids to marine navigation; mems: some 75 orgs and companies from 21 maritime nations involved in marine electronics in the areas of radio communications and navigation; Pres. HANS RASMUSSEN; Sec.-Gen. MICHAEL RAMBAUT.

International Press Institute (IPI): Spiegelgasse 2, 1010 Vienna, Austria; tel. (1) 5129011; fax (1) 5129014; e-mail ipi@freemedia.at; internet www.freemedia.at; f. 1951 as a non-governmental organization of editors, publishers and news broadcasters supporting the principles of a free and responsible press; aims to defend press freedom; conducts research; maintains a library; holds regional meetings and an annual World Congress; mems: about 2,000 from 120 countries; Chair. CARL-EUGEN EBERLE (Germany); Exec. Dir ALISON BETHEL MCKENZIE (USA); publs *IPI Congress Report* (annually), *World Press Freedom Review* (annually).

International Press Telecommunications Council (IPTC): 20 Garrick St, London, WC2E 9BT, United Kingdom; tel. (20) 3178-4922; fax (20) 7664-7878; e-mail office@iptc.org; internet www.iptc.org; f. 1965 to safeguard the telecommunications interests of the world press; acts as the news industry's formal standards body; meets three times a year and maintains three committees and four working parties; mems: 65 news agencies, newspapers, news websites and industry vendors; Chair. VINCENT BABY; Man. Dir MICHAEL STEIDL; publs *IPTC Spectrum* (annually), *IPTC Mirror* (6 a year).

Organization of Asia-Pacific News Agencies (OANA): c/o Anadolu Ajansi, Gazi Mustafa Kemal Bulvari 128/C, Tandogan, Ankara, Turkey; tel. (312) 2317000; fax (231) 2312174; e-mail oana@aa.com.tr; internet www.oananews.org; f. 1961 to promote co-operation in professional matters and mutual exchange of news, features, etc. among the news agencies of Asia and the Pacific via the Asia-Pacific News Network (ANN); 14th General Assembly: Istanbul, Turkey, Nov. 2010; mems: 43 news agencies in 34 countries; Pres. KEMAL ÖZTÜRK (Turkey); Sec.-Gen. ERCAN GÖÇER (Turkey).

Pacific Islands News Association (PINA): Damodar Centre, 46 Gordon St, PMB, Suva, Fiji; tel. 3303623; fax 3317055; e-mail pina@connect.com.fj; internet www.pina.com.fj; f. 1991; regional press asscn; defends freedom of information and expression, promotes professional co-operation, provides training and education; mems: media orgs in 23 countries and territories; Man. MATAI AKAUOLA.

Pasifika Media Association (PasiMA): Apia, Samoa; internet www.pacific-media.org; f. 2010; Chair. SAVEA SANO MALIFA (Samoa); Sec./Treasurer JOHN WOODS (New Zealand).

Reporters sans Frontières: 47 rue Vivienne, 75002 Paris, France; tel. 1-44-83-84-84; fax 1-45-23-11-51; e-mail rsf@rsf.org; internet www.rsf.org; f. 1985 to defend press freedom throughout the world; generates awareness of violations of press freedoms and supports journalists under threat or imprisoned as a result of their work; mems in 77 countries; Sec.-Gen. OLIVIER BASILLE; publs *Annual Report*, *La Lettre de Reporters sans Frontières* (6 a year).

World Association for Christian Communication (WACC): 308 Main St, Toronto, ON M4C 4X7, Canada; tel. (416) 691-1999; fax (416) 691-1997; e-mail wacc@waccglobal.org; internet www.waccglobal.org; f. 1975 to promote human dignity, justice and peace through freedom of expression and the democratization of communication; offers professional guidance on communication policies; interprets developments in and the consequences of global communication methods; works towards the empowerment of women; assists the training of Christian communicators; mems: corporate and personal mems in 120 countries, organized in 8 regional asscns; Pres. Dr DENNIS SMITH; Gen. Sec. Rev. Dr KARIN ACHTELSTETTER (Germany); publs *Action*, *Newsletter* (10 a year), *Media Development* (quarterly), *Communication Resource*, *Media and Gender Monitor* (both occasional).

World Association of Newspapers and News Publishers (WAN-IFRA): Washingtonplatz 1, 64287 Darmstadt, Germany; tel. (6151) 7336; fax (6151) 733800; e-mail info@wan-ifra.org; internet www.wan-ifra.org; f. 2009 by merger of World Association of Newspapers (f. 1948) and IFRA (f. 1961); WAN-IFRA is the worldwide service and representative org of newspapers and the entire news publishing industry; aims to support this industry, as well as its technology and service; mems: more than 3,000 companies in 120 countries; Pres. JACOB MATHEW (India); CEO ANDREAS MUSIELAK (Germany); publ. *WAN-IFRA Magazine* (every 2 months, and online).

World Catholic Association for Communication (SIGNIS): 310 rue Royale, 1210 Brussels, Belgium; tel. (2) 734-97-08; fax (2) 734-70-18; e-mail sg@signis.net; internet www.signis.net; f. 2001; brings together professionals working in radio, television, cinema, video, media education, internet, and new technology; Sec.-Gen. ALVITO DE SOUZA.

Religion

Agudath Israel World Organisation: Hacherut Sq., POB 326, Jerusalem 91002, Israel; tel. (2) 5384357; fax (2) 5383634; f. 1912 to help solve the problems facing Jewish people all over the world in the spirit of the Jewish tradition; holds World Congress (every five years) and an annual Central Council; mems: over 500,000 in 25 countries; Secs Rabbi MOSHE GEWIRTZ, Rabbi CHAIM WEINSTOCK; publs *Hamodia* (Jerusalem, daily, in Hebrew; New York, daily, in English; Paris, weekly, in French), *Jedion* (Hebrew, monthly), *Jewish Tribune* (London, weekly), *Jewish Observer* (New York, monthly), *Dos Yiddishe Vort* (New York, monthly), *Coalition* (New York), *Perspectives* (Toronto, monthly), *La Voz Judia* (Buenos Aires, monthly), *Jüdische Stimme* (Zürich, weekly).

All Africa Conference of Churches (AACC): Waiyaki Way, POB 14205, 00800 Westlands, Nairobi, Kenya; tel. (20) 4441483; fax (20) 4443241; e-mail secretariat@aacc-ceta.org; internet www.aacc-ceta.org; f. 1963; an organ of co-operation and continuing fellowship among Protestant, Orthodox and independent churches and Christian Councils in Africa; 10th Assembly: Kampala, Uganda, in June 2013; mems: 173 churches and affiliated Christian councils in 40 African countries; Pres. Archbishop VALENTINE MOKIWA (Tanzania); Gen. Sec. Rev. Dr ANDRÉ KARAMAGA (Rwanda); publs *ACIS/APS Bulletin*, *Tam Tam*.

Bahá'í International Community: Bahá'í World Centre, POB 155, 31001 Haifa, Israel; tel. (4) 8358394; fax (4) 8313312; e-mail opi@bwc.org; internet www.bahai.org; f. 1844; promotes and applies the principles of the Bahá'í Faith, i.e. the abandonment of all forms of prejudice, the equality of women and men, recognition of the oneness of religion, the elimination of extremes of poverty and wealth, the realization of universal education and recognition that true religion is in harmony with reason and the pursuit of scientific knowledge, in order to contribute to the development of a peaceful, just, and sustainable society, and the resolution of the challenges currently facing humanity; Baha'is undertake to strengthen the moral and spiritual character of communities, for example by conducting classes that address the development of children and channel the energies of young people, and initiating study groups that enable people of varied backgrounds to explore the application of the Bahá'í teachings to their individual and collective lives; in some communities there is an annual election of a local council to administer affairs at that level; at the national level, there elected governing councils; the head of the Baha'i Faith is the Universal House of Justice, a body of nine members elected by the 186 National Spiritual Assemblies; has more than 5m. followers, living in more than 100,000 localities; 186 national governing councils; Sec.-Gen. ALBERT LINCOLN (USA); publs *Bahá'í World News Service* (online), *One Country* (quarterly, in 6 languages).

Baptist World Alliance: 405 North Washington St, Falls Church, VA 22046, USA; tel. (703) 790-8980; fax (703) 893-5160; e-mail bwa@bwanet.org; internet www.bwanet.org; f. 1905; aims to unite Baptists, lead in evangelism, respond to people in need, defend human rights, and promote theological reflection; mems: 37m. individuals and more than 200 Baptist unions and conventions representing about 105m. people world-wide; Pres. JOHN UPTON (USA); Gen. Sec. NEVILLE CALLAM (Jamaica); publ. *The Baptist World* (quarterly).

Caribbean Conference of Churches: POB 876, Port of Spain, Trinidad and Tobago; tel. 662-3064; fax 662-1303; e-mail ccchq@tstt.net.tt; internet www.ccc-caribe.org; f. 1973; governed by a General Assembly which meets every five years and appoints a 15-member Continuation Committee (board of management) to establish policies and direct the work of the organization between Assemblies; maintains two sub-regional offices in Antigua, Jamaica and Trinidad with responsibility for programme implementation in various territories; mems: 33 member churches in 34 territories in the Dutch-, English-, French-, and Spanish-speaking territories of the region; Gen. Sec. GERARD GRANADO; publ. *Ecuscope Caribbean*.

Christian Conference of Asia (CCA): c/o Payap Univ. Muang, Chiang Mai 50000, Thailand; tel. (53) 243906; fax (53) 247303; e-mail cca@cca.org.hk; internet www.cca.org.hk; f. 1957 (present name adopted 1973) to promote co-operation and joint study in matters of common concern among the Churches of the region and to encourage interaction with other regional Conferences and the World Council of Churches; mems: nearly 100 national churches, and 17 national councils in 21 countries; Gen. Sec. HENRIETTE HUTABARAT LEBANG (Indonesia); publ. *CCA News* (quarterly), *CTC Bulletin* (occasional).

Christian Peace Conference: POB 136, Prokopova 4, 130 00 Prague 3, Czech Republic; tel. 222781800; fax 222781801; e-mail christianpeace@volny.cz; internet www.volny.cz/christianpeace; f. 1958 as an international movement of theologians, clergy and lay people, aiming to bring Christendom to recognize its share of guilt in both world wars and to dedicate itself to the service of friendship, reconciliation and peaceful co-operation of nations, to concentrate on united action for peace and justice, and to co-ordinate peace groups in individual churches and facilitate their effective participation in the peaceful development of society; works through five continental asscns, regional groups and member churches in many countries; Moderator Dr SERGIO ARCE MARTÍNEZ; Co-ordinator Rev. BRIAN G. COOPER; publs *CPC Information* (8 a year, in English and German), occasional *Study Volume*.

Conference of European Churches (CEC): POB 2100, 150 route de Ferney, 1211 Geneva 2, Switzerland; tel. 227916228; fax 227916227; e-mail cec@cec-kek.org; internet www.ceceurope.org; f. 1959 as a regional ecumenical organization for Europe and a meeting-place for European churches, including members and non-members of the World Council of Churches; holds a General Assembly every six years; mems: 120 Protestant, Anglican, Orthodox and Old Catholic churches in all European countries; Gen. Sec. a.i. Rev. Dr GUY LIAGRE; publs *Monitor* (quarterly), CEC communiqués, reports.

Consultative Council of Jewish Organizations (CCJO): 420 Lexington Ave, New York, NY 10170, USA; tel. (212) 808-5437; f. 1946 to co-operate and consult with the UN and other international bodies directly concerned with human rights and to defend the cultural, political and religious rights of Jews throughout the world; Sec.-Gen. WARREN GREEN (USA).

European Baptist Federation (EBF): Nad Habrovkou 3, Jeneralka, 164 00 Prague 6, Czech Republic; tel. 296392250; fax 296392254; e-mail office@ebf.org; internet www.ebf.org; f. 1949 to promote fellowship and co-operation among Baptists in Europe; to further the aims and objects of the Baptist World Alliance; to stimulate and co-ordinate evangelism in Europe; to provide for consultation and planning of missionary work in Europe and elsewhere in the world; mems: 57 Baptist Unions in European countries and the Middle East; Pres. VALERIU GHILETCHI (Moldova); Gen. Sec. TONY PECK (United Kingdom).

European Evangelical Alliance: Hoofdstraat 51A, 3971 KB Driebergen, Netherlands; tel. (343) 513693; fax (343) 531488; e-mail office@europeanea.org; internet www.europeanea.org; f. 1953 to promote understanding and co-operation among evangelical Christians in Europe and to stimulate evangelism; mems: 15m. in 36 European countries; Gen. Sec. NIEK M. TRAMPER.

Federation of Jewish Communities of the CIS: 127055 Moscow, 2-i Vysheslavtsev per. 5A, Russia; tel. (495) 737-82-75; fax (495) 783-84-71; e-mail info@fjc.ru; internet www.fjc.ru; f. 1998 to restore Jewish society, culture and religion throughout the countries of the fmr Soviet Union through the provision of professional assistance, educational support and funding to member communities; Pres. LEV LEVAYEV.

Friends World Committee for Consultation: 173 Euston Rd, London, NW1 2AX, United Kingdom; tel. (20) 7663-1199; fax (20) 7663-1189; e-mail world@friendsworldoffice.org; internet www.fwccworld.org; f. 1937 to encourage and strengthen the spiritual life within the Religious Society of Friends (Quakers); to help Friends to a better understanding of their vocation in the world; and to promote consultation among Friends of all countries; representation at the United Nations as a non-governmental organization with general consultative status; mems: appointed representatives and individuals from 70 countries; Gen. Sec. NANCY IRVING; publs *Friends World News* (2 a year), *Calendar of Yearly Meetings* (annually), *Quakers around the World* (handbook).

Global Christian Forum: POB 306, 1290 Versoix, Switzerland; tel. 227554546; fax 227550108; e-mail gcforum@sunrise.ch; internet www.globalchristianforum.org; f. 1998 by the World Council of Churches, with an autonomous Continuation Committee, to provide opportunities for representatives of all the main Christian traditions to meet, foster mutual respect and address common challenges; a series of regional meetings was held during 2004–07 and the first Global Forum was convened in November 2007 in Limuru, near Nairobi, Kenya; Sec.-Gen. HUBERT VAN BEEK.

International Association for Religious Freedom (IARF): 3-8-21 Sangenya-Nishi, Taisho-ku, Osaka 551-0001, Japan; tel. (6) 7503-5602; e-mail hq@iarf.net; internet www.iarf.net; f. 1900 as a world community of religions, subscribing to the principle of openness and upholding the UN's Universal Declaration on freedom of religion or belief; conducts religious freedom programmes, focusing on inter-religious harmony; holds regional conferences and triennial congress; mems: 100 groups in 25 countries; Pres. MITSUO MIYAKE (Japan); Treas. JEFFREY TEAGLE (United Kingdom).

International Association of Buddhist Studies (IABS): c/o Prof. T. J. F. Tillemans, Section des langues et civilisations orientales, Université de Lausanne, 1015 Lausanne, Switzerland; fax 216923045; e-mail mail@iabsinfo.org; internet www.iabsinfo.net; f. 1976; supports studies of Buddhist religion, philosophy and literature; holds international conference every three or four years (16th Congress: Jinshan, Republic of China, June 2011); Pres. CRISTINA SCHERRER-SCHAUB (France); Gen. Sec. ULRICH PAGEL (Germany); publ. *Journal* (2 a year).

International Council of Christians and Jews (ICCJ): Martin Buber House, POB 1129, 64629 Heppenheim, Germany; tel. (6252) 6896810; fax (6252) 68331; e-mail info@iccj.org; internet www.iccj.org; f. 1947 to promote mutual respect and co-operation; holds annual international colloquium, seminars, meetings for young people and for women; maintains a forum for Jewish–Christian–Muslim relations; mems: 38 national councils world-wide; Pres. Dr DEBORAH WEISMAN; publs *ICCJ History*, *ICCJ Brochure*, conference documents.

International Council of Jewish Women: 5655 Silver Creek Valley Rd, 480 San Jose, CA 95138, USA; tel. and fax (408) 274-8020; fax (408) 274-0807; e-mail president@icjw.org; internet www.icjw.org; f. 1912 to promote friendly relations and understanding among Jewish women throughout the world; campaigns for human and women's rights, exchanges information on community welfare activities, promotes volunteer leadership, sponsors field work in social welfare, co-sponsors the International Jewish Women's Human Rights Watch and fosters Jewish education; mems: over 2m. mems in 52 orgs across 47 countries; Pres. SHARON SCOTT GUSTAFSON; Sec. VERA KRONENBERG; publs *Newsletter*, *Links around the World* (2 a year, English and Spanish), *International Jewish Women's Human Rights Watch* (2 a year).

International Fellowship of Reconciliation (IFOR): Spoorstraat 38, 1815 BK Alkmaar, Netherlands; tel. (72) 512-30-14; fax (72) 515-11-02; e-mail office@ifor.org; internet www.ifor-mir.org; f. 1919; international, spiritually based movement committed to active non-violence as a way of life and as a means of building a culture of peace and non-violence; maintains over 81 branches, affiliates and groups in more than 48 countries; Pres. HANS ULRICH GERBER (Netherlands); Int. Co-ordinator FRANCESCO CANDELARI; publs *IFOR in Action* (quarterly), *Patterns in Reconciliation*(2 a year), *International Reconciliation* (3–4 times a year), *Cross the Lines* (3 a year, in Arabic, English, French, Russian and Spanish), occasional paper series.

International Humanist and Ethical Union (IHEU): 1 Gower St, London, WC1E 6HD, United Kingdom; tel. and fax (20) 7636-4797; e-mail office-iheu@iheu.org; internet www.iheu.org; f. 1952 to bring into asscn all those interested in promoting ethical and scientific humanism and human rights; mems: national orgs and individuals in 40 countries; Pres. SONJA EGGERICKX; Int. Dir BABU GOGINENI; publ. *International Humanist News* (quarterly).

International Organization for the Study of the Old Testament: Dolnicarjeva 1, 1000 Ljubljana, Slovenia; tel. (1) 4340198; fax (1) 4330405; f. 1950; holds triennial congresses (20th Congress: Helskini, Finland, Aug. 2010); publ. *Vetus Testamentum* (quarterly).

Latin American Council of Churches (Consejo Latinoamericano de Iglesias—CLAI): Casilla 17-08-8522, Calle Inglaterra N.32–113 y Mariana de Jesús, Quito, Ecuador; tel. (2) 250-4377; fax (2) 256-8373; e-mail nilton@clailatino.org; internet www.clailatino.org; f. 1982; mems: some 150 churches in 21 countries; Pres. Rev. JULIO MURRAY (Panama); Gen. Sec. Rev. NILTON GUISE (Brazil); publs *Nuevo Siglo* (monthly, in Spanish), *Latin American Ecumenical News* (quarterly), *Signos de Vida* (quarterly), other newsletters.

Latin American Episcopal Council (Consejo Episcopal Latinoamericano—CELAM): Carrera 5A 118–31, Apartado Aéreo 51086, Bogotá, Colombia; tel. (1) 5879710; fax (1) 5879117; e-mail celam@celam.org; internet www.celam.org; f. 1955 to co-ordinate Church activities in and with the Latin American and the Caribbean Catholic Bishops' Conferences; mems: 22 Episcopal Conferences of Central and South America and the Caribbean; Pres. Archbishop RAYMUNDO DAMASCENO ASSIS (Brazil); publ. *Boletín* (6 a year).

Lutheran World Federation: 150 route de Ferney, POB 2100, 1211 Geneva 2, Switzerland; tel. 227916111; fax 227916630; e-mail info@lutheranworld.org; internet www.lutheranworld.org; f. 1947; provides inter-church aid and relief work in various areas of the globe; gives service to refugees, including resettlement; carries out theological research, advocates for human rights, organizes conferences and exchanges; grants scholarship aid in various fields of church life; conducts inter-confessional dialogue and conversation with the Anglican, Baptist, Methodist, Orthodox, Reformed, Roman Catholic and Seventh-day Adventist churches; mems: 70.3m. world-wide; groups 145 Lutheran Churches in 79 countries; Pres. Rev. MUNIB A. YOUNAN (Jordan); Gen. Sec. Rev. MARTIN JUNGE (Chile); publs *Lutheran World Information* (English and German, daily e-mail news service, online and monthly print edition), *LWF Annual Report*, *LWF Documentation* (in English and German).

Middle East Council of Churches: POB 5376, Beirut, Lebanon; tel. (1) 344896; fax (1) 344894; e-mail mecc@cyberia.net.lb; internet www.mec-churches.org; f. 1974; mems: 28 churches; Pres Catholicose ARAM I, Patriarch THEOPHILOS III, Archbishop BOULOS MATAR, Rev. Dr SAFWAT AL-BAYADI; Gen. Sec. GUIRGIS IBRAHIM SALEH; publs *MECC News Report* (monthly), *Al Montada News Bulletin* (quarterly, in Arabic), *Courrier oecuménique du Moyen-Orient* (quarterly), *MECC Perspectives* (3 a year).

Muslim World League (MWL) (Rabitat al-Alam al-Islami): POB 537, Makkah, Saudi Arabia; tel. (2) 5600919; fax (2) 5601319; e-mail mymwlsite@hotmail.com; internet www.muslimworldleague.org; f. 1962; aims to advance Islamic unity and solidarity, and to promote world peace and respect for human rights; provides financial assistance for education, medical care and relief work; has 45 offices throughout the world; Sec.-Gen. Prof. Dr ABDULLAH BIN ABDUL MOHSIN AL-TURKI; publs *Al-Aalam al Islami* (weekly, Arabic), *Dawat al-Haq* (monthly, Arabic), *Muslim World League Journal* (monthly, English), *Muslim World League Journal* (quarterly, Arabic).

Opus Dei (Prelature of the Holy Cross and Opus Dei): Viale Bruno Buozzi 73, 00197 Rome, Italy; tel. (06) 808961; e-mail info@opusdei .org; internet www.opusdei.org; f. 1928 by St Josemaría Escrivá de Balaguer to spread, at every level of society, an increased awareness of the universal call to sanctity and apostolate in the exercise of one's work; mems: 87,564 Catholic laypeople and 1,996 priests; Prelate Most Rev. JAVIER ECHEVARRÍA; publ. *Romana (Bulletin of the Prelature)* (2 a year).

Pacific Conference of Churches: POB 208, 4 Thurston St, Suva, Fiji; tel. 3311277; fax 3303205; e-mail pacific@pcc.org.fj; internet www.pcc.org.fj; f. 1961; organizes assembly every five years, as well as regular workshops, meetings and training seminars throughout the region; mems: 36 churches and councils; Moderator Bishop APIMELEKI QILIHO; Gen. Sec. FE'ILOAKITAU TEVI.

Pax Romana International Catholic Movement for Intellectual and Cultural Affairs (ICMICA); and International Movement of Catholic Students (IMCS): 3 rue de Varembé, 4th Floor, POB 161, 1211 Geneva 20, Switzerland; tel. 228230707; fax 228230708; e-mail international_secretariat@paxromana.org; internet www.icmica-miic.org; f. 1921 (IMCS), 1947 (ICMICA), to encourage in members an awareness of their responsibilities as people and Christians in the student and intellectual milieux; to promote contacts between students and graduates throughout the world and co-ordinate the contribution of Catholic intellectual circles to international life; mems: 80 student and 60 intellectual orgs in 80 countries; ICMICA—Pres. JAVIER MARÍA IGUIÑIZ ECHEVERRIA (Peru); Gen. Sec. LAURENCE KWARK (France); IMCS—Pres. MEHULBHAI KANTIBHAI DABHI; Sec.-Gen. CHRISTOPHER DERIGE MALANO.

Salvation Army: International HQ, 101 Queen Victoria St, London, EC4V 4EH, United Kingdom; tel. (20) 7332-0101; fax (20) 7236-4981; e-mail ihq-website@salvationarmy.org; internet www .salvationarmy.org; f. 1865 to spread the Christian gospel and relieve poverty; emphasis for members is placed on the need for personal Christian discipleship; to enhance the effectiveness of its evangelism and non-discriminatory practical ministry it has adopted a quasi-military form of organization; social, medical, educational and emergency relief activities are also performed in the 124 countries where the Army operates; Gen. LINDA BOND; Chief of Staff Commissioner BARRY SWANSON; publs *All the World*, *Revive*, *The Officer*, *The Yearbook of the Salvation Army*, *Words of Life*, various other publs, including the Army's *Handbook of Doctrine*, are published under its Salvation Books label.

Theosophical Society: Adyar, Chennai 600 020, India; tel. (44) 24912474; fax (44) 4902706; e-mail intl.hq@ts-adyar.org; internet www.ts-adyar.org; f. 1875; aims at universal brotherhood, without distinction of race, creed, sex, caste or colour; study of comparative religion, philosophy and science; investigation of unexplained laws of nature and powers latent in man; mems: 32,000 in 70 countries; Pres. RADHA S. BURNIER; Int. Sec. MARY ANDERSON; publs *The Theosophist* (monthly), *Adyar News Letter* (quarterly), *Brahmavidya* (annually), *Wake Up India* (quarterly).

United Bible Societies: World Service Centre, Reading Bridge House, Reading, RG1 8PJ, United Kingdom; tel. (118) 950-0200; fax (118) 950-0857; e-mail comms@ubs-wsc.org; internet www .unitedbiblesocieties.org; f. 1946; co-ordinates the translation, production and distribution of the Bible by Bible Societies world-wide; works with national Bible Societies to develop religious programmes; mems: 145 Bible Societies in more than 200 countries; Pres. Rev. Dr Robert CUNVILLE (India); Gen. Sec. MICHAEL PERREAU (United Kingdom); publs *The Bible Translator* (quarterly), *Publishing World* (3 a year), *Prayer Booklet* (annually).

Watch Tower Bible and Tract Society: 25 Columbia Heights, Brooklyn, NY 11201–2483, USA; tel. (718) 560-5600; fax (718) 560-5619; internet www.watchtower.org; f. 1881; 98 branches; serves as legal agency for Jehovah's Witnesses; publ. *The Watchtower* (in 188 languages).

World Alliance of Reformed Churches (Presbyterian and Congregational): Box 2100, 150 route de Ferney, 1211 Geneva 2, Switzerland; tel. 227916240; fax 227916505; e-mail warc@warc.ch; internet www.warc.ch; f. 1970 by merger of WARC (Presbyterian) (f. 1875) with International Congregational Council (f. 1891) to promote fellowship among Reformed, Presbyterian and Congregational churches; mems: 216 churches in 107 countries; Pres. CLIFTON KIRKPATRICK (USA); Gen. Sec. Rev. Dr SETRI NYOMI (Ghana); publs *Reformed World* (quarterly), *Up-Date*.

World Christian Life Community: Borgo Santo Spirito 8, 00193 Rome, Italy; tel. (06) 6869844; fax (06) 68132497; e-mail exsec@ cvx-clc.net; internet www.cvx-clc.net; f. 1953 as World Federation of the Sodalities of our Lady (first group f. 1563) as a lay organization based on the teachings of Ignatius Loyola, to integrate Christian faith and daily living; mems: groups in 60 countries representing about 100,000 individuals; Pres. DANIELA FRANK; Exec. Sec. FRANKLIN IBAÑEZ; publ. *Progressio* (in English, French and Spanish).

World Conference of Religions for Peace: 777 United Nations Plaza, New York, NY 10017, USA; tel. (212) 687-2163; fax (212) 983-0098; e-mail info@wcrp.org; internet www.religionsforpeace.org; f. 1970 to co-ordinate action of various world religions for world peace; mems: more than 80 inter-religious councils in Africa, Asia, Europe and Latin America; Sec.-Gen. Dr WILLIAM VENDLEY.

World Congress of Faiths: London Inter Faith Centre, 125 Salusbury Rd, London, NW6 6RG, United Kingdom; tel. (20) 8959-3129; fax (20) 7604-3052; e-mail enquiries@worldfaiths.org; internet www .worldfaiths.org; f. 1936 to promote a spirit of fellowship among mankind through an understanding of one another's religions, to bring together people of all nationalities, backgrounds and creeds in mutual respect and tolerance, to encourage the study and understanding of issues arising out of multi-faith societies, and to promote welfare and peace; sponsors lectures, conferences, retreats, etc.; works with other interfaith organizations; mems: about 400; Pres. Rev. MARCUS BRAYBROOKE; Chair. Rabbi JACQUELINE TABICK; publs *Interreligious Insight* (quarterly), *One Family*.

World Evangelical Alliance: 600 Alden Rd, Suite 300, Markham, ON L3R 0E7, Canada; tel. (905) 752-2164; fax (905) 479-4742; e-mail info@worldevangelical.org; internet www.worldevangelical.org; f. 1951 as World Evangelical Fellowship, on reorganization of World Evangelical Alliance (f. 1846), reverted to original name Jan. 2002; an int. grouping of national and regional bodies of evangelical Christians; encourages the organization of national fellowships and assists national mems in planning their activities; mems: 7 regional asscns and 128 national evangelical asscns; Int. Dir GEOFF TUNNICLIFFE; publs *Evangelical World* (monthly), *Evangelical Review of Theology* (quarterly).

World Fellowship of Buddhists (WFB): 616 Benjasiri Pk, Soi Medhinivet off Soi Sukhumvit 24, Bangkok 10110, Thailand; tel. (2) 661-1284-7; fax (2) 661-0555; e-mail wfb_hq@truemail.co.th; internet www.wfb-hq.org; f. 1950 to promote strict observance and practice of the teachings of the Buddha; holds General Conference every two years; 170 regional centres in 38 countries; Pres. PHAN WANNAMETHEE; Sec.-Gen. PHALLOP THAIARRY; publs *WFB Journal* (quarterly), *WFB Review* (quarterly), *WFB Newsletter* (monthly), documents, booklets.

World Hindu Federation: POB 20418, Kathmandu, Nepal; tel. (1) 470182; fax (1) 470131; e-mail whfintl@wlink.com.np; internet www .worldhindufederation; f. 1981 to promote and preserve Hindu philosophy and culture and to protect the rights of Hindus, particularly the right to worship; executive board meets annually; mems: in 45 countries and territories; Int. Pres. HEM BAHADUR KARKI; Sec.-Gen. Dr BINOD RAJBHANDARI (Nepal); publ. *Vishwa Hindu* (monthly).

World Jewish Congress: 501 Madison Ave, New York, NY 10022, USA; tel. (212) 755-5770; fax (212) 755-5883; e-mail info@ worldjewishcongress.org; internet www.worldjewishcongress.org; f. 1936 as a voluntary asscn of representative Jewish communities and organizations throughout the world; aims to foster the unity of the Jewish people and ensure the continuity and development of their heritage; mems: Jewish communities in 100 countries; Pres. RONALD LAUDER (USA); Sec.-Gen. DANIEL DIKER; publs *Dispatches*, *Jerusalem Review*, regular updates, policy studies.

World Methodist Council: International Headquarters, POB 518, Lake Junaluska, NC 28745, USA; tel. (828) 456-9432; fax (828) 456-9433; e-mail georgefreeman@mindspring.com; internet www .worldmethodistcouncil.org; f. 1881 to deepen the fellowship of the Methodist peoples, encourage evangelism, foster Methodist participation in the ecumenical movement and promote the unity of Methodist witness and service; mems: 76 churches in 132 countries, comprising 38m. individuals; Gen. Sec. GEORGE H. FREEMAN (USA); publ. *World Parish* (quarterly).

World Sephardi Federation: 13 rue Marignac, 1206 Geneva, Switzerland; tel. 223473313; fax 223472839; e-mail office@wsf.org .il; internet www.jafi.org.il/wsf; f. 1951 to strengthen the unity of Jewry and Judaism among Sephardi and Oriental Jews, to defend and foster religious and cultural activities of all Sephardi and Oriental Jewish communities and preserve their spiritual heritage, to provide moral and material assistance where necessary and to co-operate with other similar organizations; mems: 50 communities and orgs in 33 countries; Pres. NESSIM D. GAON; Sec.-Gen. AVI SHLUSH.

World Student Christian Federation (WSCF): Ecumenical Centre, POB 2100, 1211 Geneva 2, Switzerland; tel. 227916358; fax 227916152; e-mail wscf@wscf.ch; internet www.wscfglobal.org; f. 1895; aims to proclaim Jesus Christ as Lord and Saviour in the academic community, and to present students with the claims of the Christian faith over their whole life; has consultative status with the UN and advisory status at the World Council of Churches; holds General Assembly every four years; mems: more than 100 national

Student Christian Movements, and 6 regional officers; Chair. HORACIO MESONES (Uruguay); Gen. Sec. CHRISTINE HOUSEL (USA).

World Union for Progressive Judaism: 13 King David St, Jerusalem 94101, Israel; tel. (2) 6203447; fax (2) 6203525; e-mail wupj@wupj.org.il; internet www.wupj.org; f. 1926; promotes and co-ordinates efforts of Reform, Liberal, Progressive and Reconstructionist congregations throughout the world; supports new congregations; assigns and employs rabbis; sponsors seminaries and schools; organizes international conferences; maintains a youth section; mems: orgs and individuals in around 45 countries; Chair. MICHAEL GRABINER; Chief Operating Officer SHAI PINTO; publs *News Updates*, *International Conference Reports*, *European Judaism*.

World Union of Catholic Women's Organisations: 37 rue Notre-Dame-des-Champs, 75006 Paris, France; tel. 1-45-44-27-65; fax 1-42-84-04-80; e-mail wucwosecgen@gmail.com; internet www.wucwo.org; f. 1910 to promote and co-ordinate the contribution of Catholic women in international life, in social, civic, cultural and religious matters; General Assembly held every four or five years (2010: Jerusalem, Israel, in Oct.); mems: some 100 orgs representing 5m. women; Pres. MARIA GIOVANNA RUGGIERI (Italy); Sec.-Gen. LILIANE STEVENSON; publ. *Women's Voice* (quarterly, in 4 languages).

Science

Association for the Taxonomic Study of the Flora of Tropical Africa (Association pour l'Etude Taxonomique de la Flore d'Afrique Tropicale—AETFAT): c/o Herbarium, Royal Botanic Gardens, Kew, Surrey, TW9 3AR, United Kingdom; e-mail aetfat-sec@kew.org; internet www.kew.org/aetfat/index.html; f. 1951 to facilitate co-operation and liaison between botanists engaged in the study of the flora of tropical Africa south of the Sahara including Madagascar; holds Congress every three years (April 2010: Antananarivo, Madagascar); maintains a library; mems: c. 800 botanists in 63 countries; Sec.-Gen. Dr SYLVAIN RAZAFIMANDIMBISON; publs *AETFAT Bulletin* (annually), *Proceedings*.

Association of Geoscientists for International Development (AGID): c/o Geological Survey of Bangladesh, Segunbagicha, Dhaka 1000, Bangladesh; tel. (2) 8358144; e-mail afia@dhaka.agni.com; internet www.bgs.ac.uk/agid; f. 1974 to encourage communication and the exchange of knowledge between those interested in the application of the geosciences to international development; contributes to the funding of geoscience development projects; provides postgraduate scholarships; mems: 500 individual and institutional mems in 70 countries; Pres. AFIA AKHTAR (Bangladesh) (2009–12); Sec. Dr A. J. REEDMAN (United Kingdom); publ. *Geoscience and Development* (annually), *Geoscience Newsletter* (quarterly).

CIESM—The Mediterranean Science Commission (Commission internationale pour l'exploration scientifique de la mer Méditerranée): Villa Girasole, 16 blvd de Suisse, 98000 Monaco; tel. 93-30-38-79; fax 92-16-11-95; e-mail contact@ciesm.org; internet www.ciesm.org; f. 1919 for scientific exploration of the Mediterranean Sea; organizes multilateral research investigations, workshops, congresses; includes six permanent scientific committees; mems: 23 member countries, 4,300 scientists; Pres. HSH Prince ALBERT II of MONACO; Dir-Gen. Prof. FREDERIC BRIAND; publs White Papers, Congress reports.

Council for the International Congress of Entomology: c/o CSIRO Entomology, Private Bag No 5, PO Wembley, WA 6913, Australia; e-mail james.ridsdill-smith@csiro.au; f. 1910 to act as a link between quadrennial congresses and to arrange the venue for each congress held every four years (2012: Daegou, Republic of Korea); the Council is also the entomology section of the International Union of Biological Sciences; Chair. Dr HARI SHARMA (India); Sec. JAMES RIDSDILL-SMITH (Australia).

Council of Managers of National Antarctic Programs: Private Bag 4800, Gateway Antarctica, University of Canterbury, Ilam Rd, Christchurch, New Zealand; tel. (3) 364-2273; fax (3) 364-2297; e-mail sec@comnap.aq; internet www.comnap.aq; f. 1988; brings together National Antarctic Programs, developed by signatories to the Antarctic Treaty, with the aim of developing and promoting best practice in managing the support of scientific research in Antarctica; Chair. JOSÉ RETAMALES (Chile); Exec. Sec. MICHELLE ROGAN-FINNEMORE.

European Association of Geoscientists and Engineers (EAGE): De Molen 42, POB 59, 3990 DB Houten, Netherlands; tel. (30) 6354055; fax (30) 6343524; e-mail eage@eage.org; internet www.eage.org; f. 1997 by merger of European Asscn of Exploration Geophysicists and Engineers (f. 1951) and the European Asscn of Petroleum Geoscientists and Engineers (f. 1988); these two organizations have become, respectively, the Geophysical and the Petroleum Divisions of the EAGE; aims to promote the applications of geoscience and related subjects and to foster co-operation between those working or studying in the fields; organizes conferences, workshops, education programmes and exhibitions; seeks global co-operation with organizations with similar objectives; mems: approx. 8,500 in more than 100 countries; Pres. DAVIDE CALCAGNI; Exec. Dir ANTON VAN GERWEN; publs *Geophysical Prospecting* (6 a year), *First Break* (monthly), *Petroleum Geoscience* (quarterly).

European Atomic Forum (FORATOM): 65 rue Belliard, 1040 Brussels, Belgium; tel. (2) 502-45-95; fax (2) 502-39-02; e-mail foratom@foratom.org; internet www.foratom.org; f. 1960; promotes the peaceful use of nuclear energy; provides information on nuclear energy issues to the EU, the media and the public; represents the nuclear energy industry within the EU institutions; holds periodical conferences; mems: national nuclear asscns in 17 countries; Pres. Dr RALF GÜLDNER; Dir-Gen. SANTIAGO SAN ANTONIO.

European Molecular Biology Organization (EMBO): Meyerhofstr. 1, Postfach 1022.40, 69012 Heidelberg, Germany; tel. (6221) 8891-0; fax (6221) 8891-200; e-mail embo@embo.org; internet www.embo.org; f. 1962 to promote collaboration in the field of molecular biology and to establish fellowships for training and research; has established the European Molecular Biology Laboratory where a majority of the disciplines comprising the subject are represented; mems: 1,300 elected mems in Europe, 80 assoc. mems world-wide; Dir HERMANN BUJARD; publs *Annual Report*, *The EMBO Journal* (24 a year), *EMBO Reports* (monthly), *EMBO Molecular Medicine*, *Molecular Systems Biology*, *EMBO Encounters*.

European Organization for Nuclear Research (CERN): 1211 Geneva 23, Switzerland; tel. 227676111; fax 227676555; e-mail press.office@cern.ch; internet www.cern.ch; f. 1954 to provide for collaboration among European states in nuclear research of a pure scientific and fundamental character, for peaceful purposes only; Council comprises two representatives of each member state; major experimental facilities: Proton Synchrotron (of 25–28 GeV), Super Proton Synchrotron (of 450 GeV), and LHC (of 14 TeV); mems: 20 European countries; observers: India, Japan, Russia, Turkey, USA, European Commission, UNESCO; Dir-Gen. ROLF-DIETER HEUER; publs *CERN Courier* (monthly), *Annual Report*, *Scientific Reports*.

European-Mediterranean Seismological Centre (EMSC): c/o CEA, Bt. Sâbles Centre DAM, Ile de France, Bruyères le Châtel, 91297 Arpajon Cédex, France; fax 1-69-26-70-00; e-mail contact@emsc-csem.org; internet www.emsc-csem.org; f. 1976 for rapid determination of seismic hypocentres in the region; maintains database; mems: institutions in 45 countries; Pres. CHRIS BROWITT (United Kingdom); Sec.-Gen. RÉMY BOSSU (France); publ. *Newsletter* (2 a year).

Federation of Asian Scientific Academies and Societies (FASAS): c/o Australian Academy of Science, POB 783, Canberra ACT 2601, Australia; tel. (2) 6201-9456; fax (2) 6201-9494; e-mail fasas@science.org.au; internet www.fasas.org.au; f. 1984 to stimulate regional co-operation and promote national and regional self-reliance in science and technology, by organizing meetings, training and research programmes and encouraging the exchange of scientists and of scientific information; mems: 16 national scientific academies and societies from Afghanistan, Australia, Bangladesh, People's Republic of China, India, Republic of Korea, Malaysia, Nepal, New Zealand, Pakistan, Philippines, Singapore, Sri Lanka, Thailand; Pres. Tan Sri Datuk Dr OMAR ABDUL RAHMAN (Malaysia); Sec. Dato' IR LEE YEE CHEONG (Malaysia).

Federation of European Biochemical Societies: c/o Dept of Immunology, The Weizmann Institute of Science, POB 26, Rehovot 76100, Israel; tel. (8) 9344019; fax (8) 9465264; e-mail febs@weizmann.ac.il; internet www.febs.org; f. 1964 to promote the science of biochemistry through meetings of European biochemists, advanced courses and the provision of fellowships; mems: approx. 40,000 in 36 societies; Chair. Prof. WINNIE ESKILD (Norway); Sec.-Gen. ISRAEL PECHT (Israel); publs *The FEBS Journal*, *FEBS News*, *FEBS Letters*, *FEBS Newsletter*.

Foundation for International Scientific Co-ordination (Fondation 'Pour la science', Centre international de synthèse): Caphés-CNRS ENS, 45 rue d'Ulm, 75005 Paris, France; tel. 1-44-32-26-54; fax 1-44-32-26-56; e-mail revuedesynthese@ens.fr; internet www.ehess.fr/acta/synthese; f. 1925; Dir ERIC BRIAN; publs *Revue de Synthèse*, *Revue d'Histoire des Sciences*, *Semaines de Synthèse*, *L'Evolution de l'Humanité*.

Institute of General Semantics: 3000 A Landers St, Fort Worth, TX 76107, USA; tel. (817) 922-9950; fax (817) 922-9903; e-mail isgs@time-binding.org; internet time-binding.org; f. 1943 as the International Society for General Semantics to advance knowledge of and inquiry into non-Aristotelian systems and general semantics; merged with Institute of General Semantics (f. 1938) in 2004; mems: approx. 700 (100 int.); Pres. MARTIN H. LEVINSON (USA); Exec. Dir LANCE STRATE (USA).

Intergovernmental Oceanographic Commission: UNESCO, 1 rue Miollis, 75732 Paris Cédex 15, France; tel. 1-45-68-39-84; fax 1-45-68-58-12; e-mail ioc.secretariat@unesco.org; internet ioc.unesco.org; f. 1960 to promote scientific investigation of the nature and resources of the oceans through the concerted action of its members; mems: 129 govts; Chair. JAVIER A. VALLADARES (Argentina); Exec. Sec. WENDY WATSON-WRIGHT; publs *IOC Technical Series* (irregular), IOC *Manuals* and *Guides* (irregular), *IOC Workshop Reports* (irregular) and *IOC Training Course Reports* (irregular), annual reports.

International Academy of Astronautics (IAA): 6 rue Galilee, POB 1268–16, 75766 Paris Cédex 16, France; tel. 1-47-23-82-15; fax 1-47-23-82-16; e-mail sgeneral@iaamail.org; internet iaaweb.org; f. 1960; fosters the development of astronautics for peaceful purposes, holds scientific meetings and makes scientific studies, reports, awards and book awards; maintains 19 scientific cttees and a multilingual terminology database (20 languages); mems: 1,213 active mems, 5 hon. mems, in 75 countries; Pres. Dr MADHAVAN G. NAIR (India); Sec.-Gen. Dr JEAN-MICHEL CONTANT (France); publ. *Acta Astronautica* (monthly).

International Association for Biologicals (IABS): 79 ave Louis-Casaï, 1216 Geneva, Switzerland; tel. 223011036; fax 223011037; e-mail iabs@iabs.org; internet www.iabs.org; f. 1955 to connect producers and controllers of immunological products (sera, vaccines, etc.), for the study and development of methods of standardization; supports international organizations in their efforts to solve problems of standardization; mems: c. 400; Pres. and Sec. DANIEL GAUDRY (France); publs *Newsletter* (quarterly), *Biologicals* (6 a year).

International Association for Earthquake Engineering: Ken chiku-kaikan Bldg, 3rd Floor, 5-26-20, Shiba, Minato-ku, Tokyo 108-0014, Japan; tel. (3) 3453-1281; fax (3) 3453-0428; e-mail secretary@iaee.or.jp; internet www.iaee.or.jp; f. 1963 to promote international co-operation among scientists and engineers in the field of earthquake engineering through exchange of knowledge, ideas and results of research and practical experience; mems: national cttees in 49 countries; Pres. Prof. POLAT GÜLKAN (Turkey); Sec.-Gen. MANABU YOSHIMURA (Japan).

International Association for Ecology (INTECOL): c/o College of Forest Science, Department of Forest Resources, Kookmin Univ., Songbuk-gu, Seoul 136-702, Republic of Korea; tel. (10) 3785-4814; fax (2) 910-4809; e-mail kimeuns@kookmin.ac.kr; internet www.intecol.org; f. 1967 to provide opportunities for communication among ecologists world-wide; to co-operate with organizations and individuals having related aims and interests; to encourage studies in the different fields of ecology; affiliated to the International Union of Biological Sciences; mems: 35 national and international ecological societies, and 2,000 individuals; Pres. ALAN COVICH (USA); Sec.-Gen. EUN-SHIK KIM (Republic of Korea).

International Association for Mathematical Geology (IAMG): 5868 Westheimer Rd. Suite 537, Houston, TX 77057, USA; tel. (832) 380-8833; e-mail office@iamg.org; internet www.iamg.org; f. 1968 for the preparation and elaboration of mathematical models of geological processes; the introduction of mathematical methods in geological sciences and technology; assistance in the development of mathematical investigation in geological sciences; the organization of international collaboration in mathematical geology through various forums and publications; educational programmes for mathematical geology; affiliated to the International Union of Geological Sciences; mems: c. 600; Pres. VERA PAWLOWSKY GLAHN (Spain); Sec.-Gen. DANIEL M. TETZLAFF (USA); publs *Mathematical Geology* (8 a year), *Computers and Geosciences* (10 a year), *Natural Resources Research* (quarterly), *Newsletter* (2 a year).

International Association for Mathematics and Computers in Simulation: c/o Free University of Brussels, Automatic Control, CP 165/84, 50 ave F. D. Roosevelt, 1050 Brussels, Belgium; tel. (2) 650-20-85; fax (2) 650-45-34; e-mail Robert.Beauwens@ulb.ac.be; internet www.research.rutgers.edu/~imacs/; f. 1955 to further the study of mathematical tools and computer software and hardware, analogue, digital or hybrid computers for simulation of soft or hard systems; mems: 1,100 and 27 assoc. mems; Pres. ROBERT BEAUWENS (Belgium); Treas. ERNEST H. MUND; publs *Mathematics and Computers in Simulation* (6 a year), *Applied Numerical Mathematics* (6 a year), *Journal of Computational Acoustics*.

International Association for Plant Physiology (IAPP): c/o Dr D. Graham, Div. of Food Science and Technology, CSIRO, POB 52, North Ryde, NSW, Australia 2113; tel. (2) 9490-8333; fax (2) 9490-3107; e-mail douglasgraham@dfst.csiro.au; f. 1955 to promote the development of plant physiology at the international level through congresses, symposia and workshops, by maintaining communication with national societies and by encouraging interaction between plant physiologists in developing and developed countries; affiliated to the International Union of Biological Sciences; Pres. Prof. S. MIYACHI; Sec.-Treas. Dr D. GRAHAM.

International Association for Plant Taxonomy (IAPT): Institute of Botany, University of Vienna, Rennweg 14, 1030 Vienna, Austria; tel. (1) 4277-54098; fax (1) 4277-54099; e-mail office@iapt-taxon.org; internet www.botanik.univie.ac.at/iapt; f. 1950 to promote the development of plant taxonomy and encourage contacts between people and institutes interested in this work; maintains the International Bureau for Plant Taxonomy and Nomenclature; affiliated to the International Union of Biological Sciences; mems: institutes and individuals in 85 countries; Exec. Sec. Dr ALESSANDRA RICCIUTI LAMONEA; publs *Taxon* (quarterly), *Regnum vegetabile* (irregular).

International Association for the Physical Sciences of the Oceans (IAPSO): Johan Rodhe, POB 460, 40530 Göteborg, Sweden; e-mail johan.rodhe@gu.se; internet iapso.iugg.org; f. 1919 to promote the study of scientific problems relating to the oceans and interactions occurring at its boundaries, chiefly in so far as such study may be carried out by the aid of mathematics, physics and chemistry; to initiate, facilitate and co-ordinate oceanic research; and to provide for discussion, comparison and publication; affiliated to the International Union of Geodesy and Geophysics (IUGG); mems: 65 states; Pres. Dr EUGENE MOROZOV; Sec.-Gen. Prof JOHAN RODHE (Sweden).

International Association of Botanic Gardens (IABG): c/o Prof. J. E. Hernández-Bermejo, Córdoba Botanic Garden, Apdo 3048, 14071 Córdoba, Spain; tel. (957) 200355; fax (957) 295333; e-mail jardinbotcord@retemail.es; internet www.bgci.org/global/iabg; f. 1954 to promote co-operation between scientific collections of living plants, including the exchange of information and specimens; to promote the study of the taxonomy of cultivated plants; and to encourage the conservation of rare plants and their habitats; affiliated to the International Union of Biological Sciences; Pres. Prof. HE SHANAN (People's Republic of China); Sec. Prof. J. ESTEBAN HERNÁNDEZ-BERMEJO (Spain).

International Association of Geodesy: Deutsches Geodaetisches Forschungsinstitut (DGFI), Alfons-Goppel-Str. 11, 80539 Munich, Germany; tel. (89) 23031-1107; fax (89) 23031-1240; e-mail iag@dgfi.badw.de; internet www.iag-aig.org; f. 1922 to promote the study of all scientific problems of geodesy and encourage geodetic research; to promote and co-ordinate international co-operation in this field; to publish results; affiliated to the International Union of Geodesy and Geophysics; mems: national cttees in 73 countries; Pres. MICHAEL SIDERIS (Canada); Sec.-Gen. HERMANN DREWES (Germany); publs *Journal of Geodesy*, *Travaux de l'AIG*.

International Association of Geomagnetism and Aeronomy (IAGA): c/o Mioara Mandea, 50 blvd St Marcel, 75005 Paris, France; tel. 1-57-27-84-84; fax 1-57-27-84-82; e-mail iaga_sg@gfz-potsdam.de; f. 1919 for the study of questions relating to geomagnetism and aeronomy and the encouragement of research; holds General and Scientific Assemblies every two years; affiliated to the International Union of Geodesy and Geophysics; mems: countries that adhere to the IUGG; Pres. EIGEL FRIIS-CHRISTENSEN (Denmark); Sec.-Gen. MIOARA MANDEA (France); publs *IAGA Bulletin*, *IAGA News*, *IAGA Guides*.

International Association of Hydrological Sciences: Agrocampus Ouest, 65 rue de Saint-Brieuc, 35042 Rennes, France; tel. 2-23-48-55-58; e-mail cudennec@agrocampus-ouest.fr; internet iahs.info; f. 1922 to promote co-operation in the study of hydrology and water resources; Pres. Prof. GORDON YOUNG (Canada); Sec.-Gen. Prof. CHRISTOPHE CUDENNEC (France).

International Association of Meteorology and Atmospheric Sciences (IAMAS): Institut für Physik der Atmosphäre (IPA), Deutsches Zentrum für Luft und Raumfahrt, DLR-Oberpfaffenhofen, 82234 Wessling, Germany; tel. (8153) 282570; fax (8153) 281841; e-mail Hans.Volkert@dlr.de; internet www.iamas.org; f. 1919; maintains permanent commissions on atmospheric ozone, radiation, atmospheric chemistry and global pollution, dynamic meteorology, polar meteorology, clouds and precipitation, climate, atmospheric electricity, planetary atmospheres and their evolution, and meteorology of the upper atmosphere; holds general assemblies every four years, special assemblies between general assemblies; affiliated to the International Union of Geodesy and Geophysics; Pres. Dr GUOXIONG WU (People's Republic of China); Sec.-Gen. Dr HANS VOLKERT (Germany).

International Association of Sedimentologists: c/o Prof. Vincenzo Pascucci, Dipartimento di Scienze Botaniche, Ecologiche e Geologiche, Università di Sassari, Via Piandanna 4, Sassari, Italy; tel. (079) 228685; fax (079) 233600; e-mail pascucci@uniss.it; internet www.sedimentologists.org; f. 1952; affiliated to the International Union of Geological Sciences; mems: 2,200; Pres. POPPE DE BOER (Netherlands); Gen. Sec. VINCENZO PASCUCCI (Italy); publ. *Sedimentology* (every 2 months).

International Association of Volcanology and Chemistry of the Earth's Interior (IAVCEI): Institute of Earth Sciences 'Jaume Almera', CSIC, Lluis Sole Sabaris s/n, 08028 Barcelona, Spain; tel. (93) 4095410; fax (93) 4110012; e-mail joan.marti@ictja.csic.es; internet www.iavcei.org; f. 1919 to examine scientifically all aspects of volcanology; affiliated to the International Union of Geodesy and Geophysics; Pres. Prof. RAY CAS (Australia); Sec.-Gen. Prof. JOAN

MARTI (Spain); publs *Bulletin of Volcanology*, *Catalogue of the Active Volcanoes of the World*, *Proceedings in Volcanology*.

International Association of Wood Anatomists: USDA Forest Service, Forest Products Laboratory, 1 Gifford Pinchot Dr., Madison WI 53726-2398, USA; tel. (608) 231-9200; fax (608) 231-9508; e-mail rmiller1@facstaff.wisc.edu; internet www.iawa-website.org; f. 1931 for the purpose of study, documentation and exchange of information on the structure of wood; holds annual conference; mems: 650 in 68 countries; Exec. Sec. REGIS B. MILLER; publ. *IAWA Journal*.

International Astronautical Federation (IAF): 94 bis ave du Suffren, 75015 Paris, France; tel. 1-45-67-42-60; fax 1-42-73-21-20; e-mail secretariat.iaf@iafastro.org; internet www.iafastro.org; f. 1950; fosters the development of astronautics for peaceful purposes at national and international levels, encourages the advancement of knowledge about space and the development and application of space assets for the benefit of humanity; organizes an annual International Astronautical Congress in conjunction with its associates, the International Academy of Astronautics (IAA) and the International Institute of Space Law (IISL); mems: 227; Pres. BERNDT FEUERBACHER; Exec. Dir CHRISTIAN FEICHTINGER.

International Astronomical Union (IAU): 98 bis blvd d'Arago, 75014 Paris, France; tel. 1-43-25-83-58; fax 1-43-25-26-16; e-mail iau@iap.fr; internet www.iau.org; f. 1919 to facilitate co-operation between the astronomers of various countries and to further the study of astronomy in all its branches; organizes colloquia every two months; mems: orgs in 65 countries, and 9,000 individual mems; Pres. ROBERT WILLIAMS (USA); Gen. Sec. IAN F. CORBETT; publs *IAU Information Bulletin* (2 a year), *Symposia Series* (6 a year), *Highlights* (every 3 years).

International Biometric Society: International Business Office, 1444 I St, NW, Suite 700, Washington, DC 20005, USA; tel. (202) 712-9049; fax (202) 216-9646; e-mail ibs@tibs.org; internet www.tibs.org; f. 1947 for the advancement of quantitative biological science through the development of quantitative theories and the application, development and dissemination of effective mathematical and statistical techniques; the Society has 16 regional organizations and 17 national groups, is affiliated with the International Statistical Institute and WHO, and constitutes the Section of Biometry of the International Union of Biological Sciences; mems: over 6,000 in more than 70 countries; Pres. KAYE E. BASFORD; Exec. Dir DEE ANN WALKER; publs *Biometrics* (quarterly), *Biometric Bulletin* (quarterly), *Journal of Agricultural, Biological and Environmental Statistics* (quarterly).

International Botanical Congress: c/o Congress Secretariat, ICMS Australasia, GPO Box 5005, Melbourne, Victoria 3205, Australia; tel. (3) 9682-0500; fax (3) 9682-0344; e-mail info@ibc2011.com; internet www.ibc2011.com; f. 1864 to inform botanists of recent progress in the plant sciences; the Nomenclature Section of the Congress attempts to provide a uniform terminology and methodology for the naming of plants; other Divisions deal with developmental, metabolic, structural, systematic and evolutionary, ecological botany; genetics and plant breeding; 2011 Congress: Melbourne, Australia; affiliated to the International Union of Biological Sciences; Pres. Dr JUDY WEST; Sec.-Gen. KAREN WILSON.

International Bureau of Weights and Measures (Bureau international des poids et mesures—BIPM): Pavillon de Breteuil, 92312 Sèvres Cédex, France; tel. 1-45-07-70-70; fax 1-45-34-20-21; e-mail info@bipm.org; internet www.bipm.org; f. 1875; works to ensure the international unification of measurements and their traceability to the International System of Unification; carries out research and calibration; organizes international comparisons of national measurement standards; mems: 51 member states and 10 associates; Pres. J. KOVALEVSKY (France); Prof. A. J. WALLARD; publs *Le Système International d'Unités* (in English and French), *Metrologia* (6 a year), scientific articles, reports and monographs, committee reports.

International Cartographic Association (ICA) (Association Cartographique Internationale—ACI): c/o Eotvos University, Dept of Cartography and Geoinformatics, H-1117 Budapest, Pazmany Peter setany 1/A, Hungary; tel. (1) 372-2975; fax (1) 372-2951; e-mail lzentai@caesar.elte.hu; internet www.icaci.org; f. 1959 for the advancement, instigation and co-ordination of cartographic research involving co-operation between different nations; particularly concerned with furtherance of training in cartography, study of source material, compilation, graphic design, digital presentation of maps as artefacts communicating geographic information; organizes international conferences, symposia, meetings, exhibitions; mems: 80 countries; Pres. GEORG GARTNER (Austria); Sec.-Gen./Treas. LASZLO ZENTAI (Hungary); publ. *ICA Newsletter* (2 a year).

International Centre of Insect Physiology and Ecology: POB 30772-00100, Nairobi, Kenya; tel. (20) 8632000; fax (20) 8632001; e-mail icipe@icipe.org; internet www.icipe.org; f. 1970; aims to alleviate poverty, ensure food security and improve the overall health status of peoples of the tropics through developing and extending tools and strategies for managing harmful and useful arthropods, while preserving the natural resource base through research and capacity building; Dir-Gen. Prof. CHRISTIAN BORGEMEISTER (Germany); publs *International Journal of Tropical Insect Science* (quarterly), *Biennial Report*, training manuals, technical bulletins, newsletter.

International Commission for Optics (ICO): c/o Angela M. Guzman, Physics Dept, Florida Atlantic University, 777 Glades Rd, Boca Raton, FL 33431, USA; tel. (561) 297-1310; fax (561) 297-2662; e-mail angela.guzman@fau.edu; internet www.ico-optics.org; f. 1948; aims to contribute, on an international basis, to the progress and diffusion of knowledge in the field of optics; co-ordinates the dissemination and advancement of scientific and technical knowledge relating to optics; holds Gen. Assembly every three years; mems: cttees in 52 territories, and 6 int. societies; Pres. Prof. MARIA L. CALVO (Spain); Sec.-Gen. Prof. ANGELA M. GUZMAN; publ. *ICO Newsletter*.

International Commission for Plant-Bee Relationships (ICPBR): Hassellstr 23, 29223 Celle, Germany; e-mail icpbr@uoguelph.ca; internet www.uoguelph.ca/icpbr; f. 1950 to promote research and its application in the field of bee botany, and collect and spread information; to organize meetings, etc., and collaborate with scientific organizations; affiliated to the International Union of Biological Sciences; mems: 240 in 41 countries; Pres. Dr PETER KEVAN; Sec. Dr JOB VAN PRAAGH.

International Commission on Physics Education: e-mail elm@physics.unoquelph.ca; internet web.phys.ksu.edu/icpe/; f. 1960 to encourage and develop international collaboration in the improvement and extension of the methods and scope of physics education at all levels; collaborates with UNESCO and organizes international conferences; mems: appointed triennially by the International Union of Pure and Applied Physics; Chair. PRATIBHA JOLLY; Sec. DEAN ZOLLMAN.

International Commission on Radiation Units and Measurements, Inc (ICRU): 7910 Woodmont Ave, Suite 400, Bethesda, MD 20814-3095, USA; tel. (301) 657-2652; fax (301) 907-8768; e-mail icru@icru.org; internet www.icru.org; f. 1925 to develop internationally acceptable recommendations regarding: (1) quantities and units of radiation and radioactivity, (2) procedures suitable for the measurement and application of these quantities in clinical radiology and radiobiology, (3) physical data needed in the application of these procedures; makes recommendations on quantities and units for radiation protection (see International Radiation Protection Association); mems: from about 18 countries; Chair. HANS-GEORG MENZEL (acting); Exec. Sec. PATRICIA RUSSELL; publs reports.

International Commission on Zoological Nomenclature: c/o Natural History Museum, Cromwell Rd, London, SW7 5BD, United Kingdom; tel. (20) 7942-5653; e-mail iczn@nhm.ac.uk; internet www.iczn.org; f. 1895; has judicial powers to determine all matters relating to the interpretation of the International Code of Zoological Nomenclature and also plenary powers to suspend the operation of the Code where the strict application of the Code would lead to confusion and instability of nomenclature; also responsible for maintaining and developing the Official Lists and Official Indexes of Names and Works in Zoology; affiliated to the International Union of Biological Sciences; Pres. Dr JAN VAN TOL (Netherlands); Exec. Sec. Dr ELLINOR MICHEL (United Kingdom); publs *Bulletin of Zoological Nomenclature* (quarterly), *International Code of Zoological Nomenclature*, *Official Lists and Indexes of Names and Works in Zoology*, *Towards Stability in the Names of Animals*.

International Council for Science (ICSU): 5 rue Auguste Vacquerie 75116 Paris, France; tel. 1-45-25-03-29; fax 1-42-88-94-31; e-mail secretariat@icsu.org; internet www.icsu.org; f. 1919 as International Research Council; present name adopted 1998; revised statutes adopted 2011; incorporates national scientific bodies and International Scientific Unions, as well as 19 Interdisciplinary Bodies (international scientific networks established to address specific areas of investigation); through its global network co-ordinates interdisciplinary research to address major issues of relevance to both science and society; advocates for freedom in the conduct of science, promotes equitable access to scientific data and information, and facilitates science education and capacity-building; General Assembly of representatives of national and scientific members meets every three years to formulate policy. Interdisciplinary Bodies and Joint Initiatives: Future Earth; Urban Health and Well-being; Committee on Space Research (COSPAR); Scientific Committee on Antarctic Research (SCAR); Scientific Committee on Oceanic Research (SCOR); Scientific Committee on Solar-Terrestrial Physics (SCOSTEP); Integrated Research on Disaster Risk (IRDR); Programme on Ecosystem Change and Society (PECS); DIVERSITAS; International Geosphere-Biosphere Programme (IGBP); International Human Dimensions Programme on Global Environmental Change (IHDP); World Climate Research Programme (WCRP); Global Climate Observing System (GCOS); Global Ocean Observing System (GOOS); Global Terrestrial Observing System (GTOS); Committee on Data for Science and Technology (CODATA); International Network for the Availability of Scientific Publications

(INASP); Scientific Committee on Frequency Allocations for Radio Astronomy and Space Science (IUCAF); World Data System (WDS); mems: 120 national mems from 140 countries, 31 Int. Scientific Unions; Pres. LEE YUAN-TSEH (Taiwan); publs *Insight* (quarterly), *Annual Report*.

International Council for Scientific and Technical Information: 5 rue Ambroise Thomas, 75009 Paris, France; tel. 1-45-25-65-92; fax 1-42-15-12-62; e-mail icsti@icsti.org; internet www.icsti.org; f. 1984 as the successor to the International Council of Scientific Unions Abstracting Board (f. 1952); aims to increase accessibility to scientific and technical information; fosters communication and interaction among all participants in the information transfer chain; mems: 48 orgs; Pres. ROBERTA SHAFFER (USA); Gen. Sec. WENDY WARR (United Kingdom).

International Council for the Exploration of the Sea (ICES): H. C. Andersens Blvd 44–46, 1553 Copenhagen V, Denmark; tel. 33-38-67-00; fax 33-93-42-15; e-mail info@ices.dk; internet www.ices.dk; f. 1902 to encourage and facilitate research on the utilization and conservation of living resources and the environment in the North Atlantic Ocean and its adjacent seas; publishes and disseminates results of research; advises member countries and regulatory commissions; mems: 20 mem. countries, 5 affiliated institutes, 2 non-governmental orgs with observer status; Pres. MICHAEL SINCLAIR; Gen. Sec. ANNE CHRISTINE BRUSENDORFF; publs *ICES Journal of Marine Science*, *ICES Marine Science Symposia*, *ICES Fisheries Statistics*, *ICES Cooperative Research Reports*, *ICES Insight*, *ICES Techniques in Marine Environmental Sciences*, *ICES Identification Leaflets for Plankton*, *ICES Identification Leaflets for Diseases and Parasites of Fish and Shellfish*.

International Council of Psychologists: c/o Life Sq, Teshirogi A-101Matsushiro, 4-9-10 Tsukuba Science City, 305-0035 Japan; e-mail neditt33@yahoo.com; internet icpweb.org; f. 1941 to advance psychology and the application of its scientific findings throughout the world; holds annual conventions; mems: 1,200 qualified psychologists; Pres. ANN O'ROARK (USA); Sec.-Gen. Dr EDIT NAGY-TANAKA (Japan); publs *International Psychologist* (quarterly), *World Psychology* (quarterly).

International Council of the Aeronautical Sciences: c/o FOI, SE-16490 Stockholm, Sweden; tel. (8) 55503151; e-mail secr.exec@icas.org; internet www.icas.org; f. 1957 to encourage free interchange of information on aeronautical science and technology; holds biennial Congresses (2012: Brisbane, Australia; 2014: St Petersburg, Russia); mems: national assens in more than 30 countries; Pres. IAN POLL (United Kingdom); Exec. Sec. ANDERS GUSTAFSSON (Sweden).

International Earth Rotation and Reference Systems Service: Central Bureau, c/o Bundesamt für Kartographie und Geodäsie (BKG), Richard-Strauss-Allee 11, 60598 Frankfurt am Main, Germany; tel. (69) 6333273; fax (69) 6333425; e-mail central_bureau@iers.org; internet www.iers.org; f. 1988 (fmrly International Polar Motion Service and Bureau International de l'Heure); maintained by the International Astronomical Union and the International Union of Geodesy and Geophysics; defines and maintains the international terrestrial and celestial reference systems; determines earth orientation parameters (terrestrial and celestial co-ordinates of the pole and universal time) connecting these systems; monitors global geophysical fluids; organizes collection, analysis and dissemination of data; Chair. of Directing Bd Prof. CHOPO MA; Dir BERND RICHTER (Germany).

International Federation of Cell Biology (IFCB): c/o Dr Denys Wheatley, Leggat House, Keithhall, Inverurie, Aberdeen, AB51 0LX, United Kingdom; tel. and fax (1467) 670280; e-mail wheatley@abdn.ac.uk; internet www.ifcbiol.org; f. 1972 to foster international co-operation, and organize conferences; mems: some 30 full member societies, 20 associated and affiliated societies; Pres. Prof. DENYS WHEATLEY (United Kingdom); Sec.-Gen. Prof. HERNANDES CARVALHO (Brazil); publs *Cell Biology International* (monthly), reports.

International Federation of Operational Research Societies (IFORS): c/o Mary Magrogan, 7240 Parkway Drive, Suite 300 Hanover, MD 21076, USA; tel. (443) 757-3534; fax (443) 757-3535; e-mail secretary@ifors.org; internet www.ifors.org; f. 1959 for development of operational research as a unified science and its advancement in all nations of the world; mems: c. 30,000 individuals, 48 national societies, 5 kindred societies; Pres. DOMINIQUE DE WERRA; Sec. MARY MAGROGAN; publs *International Abstracts in Operational Research*, *IFORS News*, *International Transactions in Operational Research*.

International Federation of Societies for Microscopy (IFSM): c/o Centre for Microscopy and Microanalysis, University of Western Australia, 35 Stirling Hwy, Perth, WA 6008, Australia; tel. (8) 6488-2739; fax (8) 6488-1087; e-mail bjg@cmm.uwa.edu.au; internet www.ifsm.uconn.edu; f. 1955 to contribute to the advancement of all aspects of electron microscopy; promotes and co-ordinates research; sponsors meetings and conferences; holds International Congress every four years; mems: representative orgs of 40 countries; Pres. Prof. C. BARRY CARTER (USA); Gen. Sec. BRENDAN GRIFFIN (Australia).

International Food Information Service (IFIS): Lane End House, Shinfield Rd, Shinfield, Reading, RG2 9BB, United Kingdom; tel. (118) 988-3895; fax (118) 988-5065; e-mail ifis@ifis.org; internet www.ifis.org; f. 1968; board of governors comprises two members each from CAB-International (United Kingdom), Bundesministerium für Landwirtschaft, Ernährung und Forsten (represented by Deutsche Landwirtschafts-Gesellschaft e.V.) (Germany), and the Institute of Food Technologists (USA); collects and disseminates information on all disciplines relevant to food science, food technology and nutrition; Man. Dir RICHARD HOLLINGSWORTH; publ. *Food Science and Technology Abstracts* (monthly, also available online).

International Foundation of the High-Altitude Research Stations Jungfraujoch and Gornergrat: Sidlerstrasse 5, 3012 Bern, Switzerland; tel. 316314052; fax 316314405; e-mail louise.wilson@space.unibe.ch; internet www.ifjungo.ch; f. 1931; international research centre which enables scientists from many scientific fields to carry out experiments at high altitudes. Six countries contribute to support the station: Austria, Belgium, Germany, Italy, Switzerland, United Kingdom; Pres. Dr ERWIN FLÜCKIGER; Dir Prof. MARKUS LEUENBERGER.

International Geographical Union (IGU): Univ. of Cape Town, Department of Geographical and Environmental Science, Rondebosch 7701, South Africa; tel. (21) 6502873; fax (21) 6503456; e-mail mmeadows@mweb.co.za; internet www.igu-net.org; f. 1922 to encourage the study of problems relating to geography, to promote and co-ordinate research requiring international co-operation, and to organize international congresses and commissions; mems: 83 countries, 11 associates; Pres. RONALD F. ABLER (USA); Sec.-Gen. Prof. MICHAEL MEADOWS (South Africa); publ. *IGU Bulletin* (annually).

International Glaciological Society: Scott Polar Research Institute, Lensfield Rd, Cambridge, CB2 1ER, United Kingdom; tel. (1223) 355974; fax (1223) 354931; e-mail igsoc@igsoc.org; internet www.igsoc.org; f. 1936; aims to stimulate interest in and encourage research into the scientific and technical problems associated with snow and ice; mems: 850 in 30 countries; Pres. Dr ERIC BRUN; Sec.-Gen. MAGNÚS MÁR MAGNÚSSON; publs *Journal of Glaciology* (3 a year), *ICE* (News Bulletin, 3 a year), *Annals of Glaciology*.

International Hydrographic Organization (IHO): 4 quai Antoine 1er, BP 445, 98000 Monaco; tel. 93-10-81-00; fax 93-10-81-40; e-mail info@ihb.mc; internet www.iho.int; f. 1921 to link the hydrographic offices of member governments and co-ordinate their work, with a view to rendering navigation easier and safer; seeks to obtain, as far as possible, uniformity in charts and hydrographic documents; fosters the development of electronic chart navigation; encourages adoption of the best methods of conducting hydrographic surveys; encourages surveying in those parts of the world where accurate charts are lacking; provides IHO Data Centre for Digital Bathymetry; and organizes quinquennial conference; mems: 80 states; Directing Committee: Pres. Vice Adm. A. MARATOS (Greece); Dirs Capt. R. WARD (Australia), Capt. H. GORZIGLIA (Chile); publs *International Hydrographic Bulletin*, *IHO Yearbook*, other documents (available on the IHO website).

International Institute of Refrigeration: 177 blvd Malesherbes, 75017 Paris, France; tel. 1-42-27-32-35; fax 1-47-63-17-98; e-mail iif-iir@iifiir.org; internet www.iifiir.org; f. 1908 to further the science of refrigeration and its applications on a world-wide scale; to investigate, discuss and recommend any aspects leading to improvements in the field of refrigeration; mems: 60 nat., 1,200 associates; Pres. Prof. E. JOACHIM PAUL; Dir DIDIER COULOMB (France); publs *International Journal of Refrigeration* (8 a year), *Newsletter* (quarterly), books, proceedings, recommendations.

International Mathematical Union (IMU): Markgrafenstr. 32, 10117 Berlin, Germany; fax (30) 20372-439; e-mail office@mathunion.org; internet www.mathunion.org; f. 1952 to support and assist the International Congress of Mathematicians and other international scientific meetings or conferences and to encourage and support other international mathematical activities considered likely to contribute to the development of mathematical science—pure, applied or educational; mems: 78 countries; Pres. INGRID DAUBECHIES (USA); Sec.-Gen. MARTIN GRÖTSCHEL (Germany); publ. *IMU-Net Newsletter*.

International Mineralogical Association: c/o Robert Downs, Dept of Geosciences, Gould-Simpson Bldg 522, Univ. of Arizona, 1040 E 4th St. Tucson, AZ 8572-10077, USA; tel. 3-83-59-42-46; fax 3-83-51-17-98; e-mail downs@geo.arizona.edu; internet www.ima-mineralogy.org; f. 1958 to further international co-operation in the science of mineralogy; affiliated to the International Union of Geological Sciences; mems: national societies in 39 countries; Pres. Prof. EKKEHART TILLMANNS (Austria); Sec. RICHARD GÖD.

International Organization of Legal Metrology: 11 rue Turgot, 75009 Paris, France; tel. 1-48-78-12-82; fax 1-42-82-17-27; e-mail biml@oiml.org; internet www.oiml.org; f. 1955 to serve as documentation and information centre on the verification, checking, construction and use of measuring instruments, to determine characteristics and standards to which measuring instruments must conform for their use to be recommended internationally, and to determine the general principles of legal metrology; mems: governments of 59 countries; Pres. ALAN E. JOHNSTON (Canada); Dir JEAN-FRANÇOIS MAGAÑA; publ. *Bulletin* (quarterly).

International Palaeontological Association: c/o Paleontological Institute, 1475 Jayhawk Blvd, Rm 121, Lindley Hall, University of Kansas, Lawrence, KS 66045, USA; tel. (785) 864-3338; fax (785) 864-5276; e-mail rmaddocks@uh.edu; internet ipa.geo.ku.edu; f. 1933; affiliated to the International Union of Geological Sciences and the International Union of Biological Sciences; Pres. Dr MICHAEL BENTON (United Kingdom); Sec.-Gen. Prof. ROSALIE F. MADDOCKS (USA); publs *Lethaia* (quarterly), *Directory of Paleontologists of the World*, *Directory of Fossil Collectors of the World*.

International Peat Society: Vapaudenkatu 12, 40100 Jyväskylä, Finland; tel. (14) 3385440; fax (14) 3385410; e-mail ips@peatsociety.org; internet www.peatsociety.org; f. 1968 to encourage co-operation in the study and use of mires, peatlands, peat and related material, through international meetings, research groups and the exchange of information; mems: 21 National Cttees, research institutes and other orgs, and individuals from 37 countries; Pres. DONAL CLARKE (Ireland); Sec.-Gen. JAAKKO SILPOLA (Finland); publs *Peat News* (monthly electronic newsletter), *International Peat Journal* (annually), *Peatlands International* (2 a year).

International Permafrost Association: c/o Dr Hugues Lantuit, Alfred Wegener Institute for Polar and Marine Research, Telefrafenberg A43, 14473 Potsdam, Germany; tel. (331) 288-2162; fax (331) 288-2188; e-mail contact@ipa-permafrost.org; internet ipa.arcticportal.org; f. 1983; aims to foster dissemination and exchange of knowledge concerning permafrost and to promote co-operation among persons and organizations involved in scientific investigation and engineering work in permafrost; organizes the International Conference on Permafrost, held generally every five years (2012: Salekhard, Russia, in June); mems: Adhering Bodies from 26 countries; Pres. Prof. HANS-W. HUBBERTEN; Sec. Dr HUGUES LANTUIT; publs *Frozen Ground* (annually), conference proceedings, other scientific reports and assessments, reports in *Permafrost and Periglacial Process* (2 a year).

International Phonetic Association: Department of Theoretical and Applied Linguistics, School of English, Aristotle University of Thessaloniki, Thessaloniki 54124, Greece; tel. (2310) 997429; fax (2310) 997432; e-mail knicol@enl.auth.gr; internet www.langsci.ucl.ac.uk/ipa/l; f. 1886 to promote the scientific study of phonetics and its applications; organizes International Congress of Phonetic Sciences every four years (2011: Hong Kong, SAR, in August); mems: 550; Sec. Dr KATERINA NICOLAIDIS; publs *Journal of the International Phonetic Association* (3 a year), *Handbook of the International Phonetic Association*.

International Phycological Society: c/o Univ. of Adelaide School of Earth and Environmental Sciences, 112 Darling Bldg, Adelaide, SA 5005, Australia; tel. (8) 8222-9291; fax (8) 8222-9456; e-mail carlos.gurgel@adelaide.edu.au; internet www.intphycsoc.org; f. 1960 to promote the study of algae, the distribution of information, and international co-operation in this field; mems: about 1,000; Pres. JOE ZUCCARELLO (New Zealand); Sec. CARLOS F. GURGEL; publ. *Phycologia* (every 2 months).

International Primatological Society: c/o California State University San Marcos, San Marcos, CA 92096, USA; tel. (760) 750-4145; fax (760) 750-3418; e-mail ncaine@csusm.edu; internet www.internationalprimatologicalsociety.org; f. 1964 to promote primatological science in all fields; Congress held every two years (2012: Cancún, Mexico; 2014: Hanoi, Viet Nam); mems: about 1,500; Pres. JUICHI YAMAGIWA (Japan); Sec.-Gen. NANCY CAINE; publs *IPS Bulletin*, *International Journal of Primatology*, *Codes of Practice*.

International Radiation Protection Association (IRPA): c/o Jacques Lochard, CEPN, 28 rue de la Redoute, Fontenay-aux-Roses 92260, France; tel. 1-55-52-19-20; fax 1-55-52-19-21; e-mail irpa.exof@irpa.net; internet www.irpa.net; f. 1966 to link individuals and societies throughout the world concerned with protection against ionizing radiations and allied effects, and to represent doctors, health physicists, radiological protection officers and others engaged in radiological protection, radiation safety, nuclear safety, legal, medical and veterinary aspects and in radiation research and other allied activities; mems: 16,000 in 42 societies; Pres. KENNETH R. KASE (USA); Exec. Officer JACQUES LOCHARD (France); publ. *IRPA Bulletin*.

International Society for Human and Animal Mycology (ISHAM): c/o Dept of Haematology, Radboud University, Nijmegen Medical Centre & Nijmegen Institute for Infection, Inflammation and Immunity, Geert Grooteplein Zuid 8, 6525 GA Nijmegen, Netherlands; tel. (24) 361-9987; fax (24) 354-2080; e-mail p.donnelly@usa.net; internet www.isham.org; f. 1954 to pursue the study of fungi pathogenic for man and animals; holds congresses (2012: Berlin, Germany); mems: 1,100 in 70 countries; Pres. Prof. DAVID ELLIS (Australia); Gen. Sec. Dr PETER DONNELLY (Netherlands); publ. *Medical Mycology* (6 a year).

International Society for Rock Mechanics: c/o Laboratório Nacional de Engenharia Civil, 101 Av. do Brasil, 1700-066 Lisboa, Portugal; tel. (21) 8443419; fax (21) 8443021; e-mail secretariat.isrm@lnec.pt; internet www.isrm.net; f. 1962 to encourage and co-ordinate international co-operation in the science of rock mechanics; assists individuals and local organizations in forming national bodies; maintains liaison with organizations representing related sciences, including geology, geophysics, soil mechanics, mining engineering, petroleum engineering and civil engineering; organizes international meetings; encourages the publication of research; mems: c. 5,000 mems and 46 nat. groups; Pres. Prof. JOHN A. HUDSON; Sec.-Gen. Dr LUÍS LAMAS; publ. *News Journal* (3 a year).

International Society for Stereology: c/o Prof. Eric Pirard, Universite de Liege, GeMMe—Genie Mineral, Materiaux & Environnement, Sart Tilman B52, 4000 Liege, Belgium; fax (4) 366-91-98; e-mail mail@stereologysociety.org; internet www.stereologysociety.org; f. 1961; an interdisciplinary society gathering scientists from metallurgy, geology, mineralogy and biology to exchange ideas on three-dimensional interpretation of two-dimensional samples (sections, projections) of their material by means of stereological principles; mems: 300; Pres. Prof. JENS R. NYENGAARD (Denmark); Treas./Sec. Prof. ERIC PIRARD (Belgium); publs *Journal of Microscopy*, *Image Analysis & Stereology* (fmrly Acta Stereologica).

International Society for Tropical Ecology: c/o Botany Dept, Banaras Hindu University, Varanasi, 221 005 India; tel. (542) 2368399; fax (542) 2368174; e-mail singh.js1@gmail.com; internet www.tropecol.com; f. 1956 to promote and develop the science of ecology in the tropics in the service of humanity; to publish a journal to aid ecologists in the tropics in communication of their findings; and to hold symposia from time to time to summarize the state of knowledge in particular or general fields of tropical ecology; mems: 500; Sec. Prof. J. S. SINGH (India); publ. *Tropical Ecology* (3 a year).

International Society of Biometeorology: c/o Dept of Geography, Bolton 410, POB 413, University of Wisconsin-Milwaukee, Milwaukee, WI 53201-0413, USA; tel. (414) 229-3740; fax (414) 229-3981; e-mail mds@uwm.edu; internet www.biometeorology.org; f. 1956 to unite all biometeorologists working in the fields of agricultural, botanical, cosmic, entomological, forest, human, medical, veterinarian, zoological and other branches of biometeorology; mems: 250 individuals, nationals of 46 countries; Pres. PAUL BEGGS (Australia); Sec. MARK D. SCHWARTZ (USA); publs *Biometeorology* (Proceedings of the Congress of ISB), *International Journal of Biometeorology* (quarterly), *Biometeorology Bulletin*.

International Society of Criminology (ISC) (Société internationale de criminologie): 12 rue Charles Fourier, 75013 Paris, France; tel. 1-45-88-00-23; fax 1-45-88-96-40; e-mail crim.sic@wanadoo.fr; f. 1934 to promote the development of the sciences in their application to the criminal phenomenon; mems: in 63 countries; Pres. TONY PETERS (Belgium); Sec.-Gen. RACHIDA TOUAHRIA (France); publ. *Annales internationales de Criminologie*.

International Society of Limnology (Societas Internationalis Limnologiae—SIL): University of North Carolina at Chapel Hill, SPH, ESE, CB 7431, Rosenau Hall, Chapel Hill, NC 27599-7431, USA; tel. (336) 376-9362; fax (336) 376-8825; e-mail msondergaard@bi.ku.dk; internet www.limnology.org; f. 1922 (as the International Assen of Theoretical and Applied Limnology, name changed 2007) for the study of physical, chemical and biological phenomena of lakes and rivers; affiliated to the International Union of Biological Sciences; mems: c. 3,200; Pres. Dr BRIAN MOSS (United Kingdom); Gen. Sec. and Treas. Dr MORTEN SØNDERGAARD (Denmark).

International Union for Physical and Engineering Sciences in Medicine (IUPESM): c/o Dr Heikki Terio, Karolinska University Hospital, Dept of Biomedical Engineering, 14186 Stockholm, Sweden; tel. (8) 58580852; fax (8) 58586290; e-mail heikki.terio@karolinska.se; internet www.iupesm.org; f. 1980 by its two constituent orgs (International Federation for Medical and Biological Engineering, and International Organization for Medical Physics); promotes international co-operation in health care science and technology and represents the professional interests of members; organizes seminars, workshops, scientific conferences; holds World Congress every three years (2012: Beijing, People's Republic of China, in May); Pres. Prof. BARRY ALLEN (Australia); Sec.-Gen. Dr HEIKKI TERIO (Sweden); publs *IUPESM Newsletter* (2 a year), Congress proceedings.

International Union for Pure and Applied Biophysics (IUPAB): Bosch Institute, Anderson Stuart F13, The University of Sydney, Sydney, 2006 Australia; tel. (2) 9351-3209; fax (2) 9351-6546; e-mail dosremedios@iupab.org; internet www.iupab.org; f. 1961 to organize international co-operation in biophysics and promote communication between biophysics and allied subjects, to encourage national co-operation between biophysical societies, and to contribute to the advancement of biophysical knowledge; mems: 50 adhering bodies; Pres. KUNIAKI NAGAYAMA (Japan); Sec.-Gen. Prof. CRISTOBAL G. DOS REMEDIOS (Australia); publ. *Quarterly Reviews of Biophysics*.

International Union for Quaternary Research (INQUA): Dept of Geography, Museum Building, Trinity College, Dublin 2, Ireland; tel. (1) 6081213; e-mail pcoxon@tcd.ie; internet www.inqua.tcd.ie; f. 1928 to co-ordinate research on the Quaternary geological era throughout the world; holds congress every four years (2011: Bern, Switzerland); mems: in 48 countries and states; Pres. Prof. ALLAN R. CHIVAS (Australia); Sec.-Gen. Prof. PETER COXON (Ireland); publs *Quarternary International*, *Quarternary Perspectives*.

International Union of Biochemistry and Molecular Biology (IUBMB): c/o Dept of Biochemistry & Molecular Biology, University of Calgary, Faculty of Medicine, 3330 Hospital Drive, NW Calgary, Alberta, Canada T2N 4N1; tel. (403) 220-3021; fax (403) 270-2211; e-mail walsh@ucalgary.ca; internet www.iubmb.org; f. 1955 to sponsor the International Congresses of Biochemistry, to co-ordinate research and discussion, to organize co-operation between the societies of biochemistry and molecular biology, to promote high standards of biochemistry and molecular biology throughout the world and to contribute to the advancement of biochemistry and molecular biology in all its international aspects; mems: 76 bodies; Pres. Prof. ANGELO AZZI (USA); Gen. Sec. Prof. MICHAEL WALSH (Canada).

International Union of Biological Sciences (IUBS): Bâtiment 442, Université Paris-Sud 11, 91405 Orsay Cédex, France; tel. 1-69-15-50-27; fax 1-69-15-79-47; e-mail secretariat@iubs.org; internet www.iubs.org; f. 1919; serves as an international forum for the promotion of biology; administers scientific programmes on biodiversity, integrative biology (of ageing, bioenergy, and climate change), biological education, bioethics, bio-energy, and Darwin 200; carries out international collaborative research programmes; convenes General Assembly every three years; mems: 44 national bodies, 80 scientific bodies; Pres. Dr GIORGIO BERNARDI (Italy); Exec. Dir Dr NATHALIE FOMPROIX; publs *Biology International* (quarterly), *IUBS Monographs*, *IUBS Methodology*, *Manual Series*.

International Union of Crystallography: c/o M. H. Dacombe, 2 Abbey Sq., Chester, CH1 2HU, United Kingdom; tel. (1244) 345431; fax (1244) 344843; internet www.iucr.org; f. 1947 to facilitate the international standardization of methods, units, nomenclature and symbols used in crystallography; and to form a focus for the relations of crystallography to other sciences; mems: in 40 countries; Pres. Prof. G. R. DESIRAJU (India); Gen. Sec. L. VAN MEERWELT (Belgium); publs *IUCR Newsletter*, *Acta Crystallographica*, *Journal of Applied Crystallography*, *Journal of Synchroton Radiation*, *International Tables for Crystallography*, *World Directory of Crystallographers*, *IUCr / OUP Crystallographic Symposia*, *IUCr / OUP Monographs on Crystallography*, *IUCr / OUP Texts on Crystallography*.

International Union of Food Science and Technology (IUFoST): POB 61021, 511 Maplegrove Rd, Oakville, ON L6J 6X0, Canada; tel. (905) 815-1926; fax (905) 815-1574; e-mail secretariat@iufost.org; internet www.iufost.org; f. 1970; sponsors international symposia and congresses; mems: 60 national groups; Pres. GEOFFREY CAMPBELL-PLATT (United Kingdom); Sec.-Gen./Treas. JUDITH MEECH (Canada); publs *IUFOST Newsline* (3 a year), *International Review of Food Science and Technology*.

International Union of Geodesy and Geophysics (IUGG): IUGG Secretariat, Karlsruhe Institute of Technology (KIT), Geophysical Institute, Hertzstr. 16, 76187 Karlsruhe, Germany; tel. (721) 6084494; e-mail secretariat@iugg.org; internet www.iugg.org; f. 1919; federation of eight asscns representing Cryospheric Sciences, Geodesy, Geomagnetism and Aeronomy, Hydrological Sciences, Meteorology and Atmospheric Physics, Seismology and Physics of the Earth's Interior, Physical Sciences of the Ocean, and Volcanology and Chemistry of the Earth's Interior, which meet in committees and at the General Assemblies of the Union; organizes scientific meetings and sponsors various permanent services to collect, analyse and publish geophysical data; mems: 65 countries; Pres. Dr HARSH GUPTA (India); Sec.-Gen. Dr ALIK ISMAIL-ZADEH (Germany); publs *IUGG Yearbook*, *Journal of Geodesy* (quarterly), *IASPEI Newsletter* (irregular), *Bulletin of Volcanology* (8 a year), *Hydrological Sciences Journal* (6 a year), *IAMAS Newsletter* (irregular).

International Union of Geological Sciences (IUGS): IUGS Secretariat, c/o Richard Calnan, MS-917, US Geological Survey, Reston, Virginia 20192, USA; tel. (703) 648-6050; fax (703) 648-4227; e-mail IUGS@usgs.gov; internet www.iugs.org; f. 1961; aims to encourage the study of geoscientific problems, to facilitate international and inter-disciplinary co-operation in geology and related sciences, and to support the quadrennial International Geological Congress; organizes international meetings and co-sponsors joint programmes, including the International Geological Correlation Programme (with UNESCO); mems: in 121 countries; Pres. Prof. ALBERTO C. RICCARDI (Argentina); Sec.-Gen. Dr PETER T. BOBROWSKY (Canada).

International Union of Immunological Societies (IUIS): IUIS Central Office, c/o Vienna Academy of Postgraduate Medical Education and Research, Alser Strasse 4, 1090 Vienna, Austria; tel. (1) 405-13-83-18; fax (1) 407-82-87; e-mail iuis-central-office@medacad.org; internet www.iuisonline.org; f. 1969; holds triennial international congress; mems: national societies in 65 countries and territories; Pres. STEFAN H. E. KAUFMANN (Germany); Sec.-Gen. Dr SEPPO MERI (Finland); Exec. Man. GERLINDE JAHN.

International Union of Microbiological Societies (IUMS): c/o Dr Robert A. Samson, Centraalbureau voor Schimmelcultures Fungal Biodiversity Centre, POB 85167, 3508 AD, Utrecht, Netherlands; tel. (30) 2122600; fax (30) 2512097; e-mail samson@cbs.knaw.nl; internet www.iums.org; f. 1930; mems: 106 national microbiological societies; Pres. DANIEL O. SORDELLI (Argentina); Sec.-Gen. ROBERT A. SAMSON (Netherlands); publs *International Journal of Systematic Bacteriology* (quarterly), *International Journal of Food Microbiology* (every 2 months), *Advances in Microbial Ecology* (annually), *Archives of Virology*.

International Union of Nutritional Sciences (IUNS): c/o Dr Galal, UCLA School of Public Health, Community Health Sciences, POB 951772, Los Angeles, CA 90095-1772, USA; tel. (310) 206-9639; fax (310) 794-1805; e-mail info@iuns.org; internet www.iuns.org; f. 1946 to promote advancement in nutrition science, research and development through international co-operation at the global level; aims to encourage communication and collaboration among nutrition scientists as well as to disseminate information in nutritional sciences through modern communication technology; mems: 80 adhering bodies; Pres. Dr IBRAHIM ELMADFA (Austria); Sec.-Gen. Prof. REKIA BELAHSEN (Morocco); publs *Annual Report*, *IUNS Directory*, *Newsletter*.

International Union of Pharmacology: c/o Lindsay Hart, Dept of Pharmacology, College of Medicine, University of California, Irvine, CA 92697, USA; tel. (949) 824-1178; fax (949) 824-4855; e-mail l.hart@iuphar.org; internet www.iuphar.org; f. 1963 to promote co-ordination of research, discussion and publication in the field of pharmacology, including clinical pharmacology, drug metabolism and toxicology; co-operates with WHO in all matters concerning drugs and drug research; holds international congresses; mems: 54 national societies, 12 assoc. mem. societies, 3 corporate mems; Pres. PAUL M. VANHOUTTE (France); Sec.-Gen. Prof. SUE PIPER DUCKLES; publ. *PI (Pharmacology International)*.

International Union of Photobiology: c/o Dept of Dermatology, Medical University of Vienna, AKH-E07 Waehringer Guertel 18-20m, 1090 Vienna, Austria; tel. (1) 40400-7702; fax (1) 40400-7699; e-mail herbert.hoenigsmann@meduniwien.ac.at; internet www.pol-us.net/iupb/index.html; f. 1928 (frmly International Photobiology Asscn); stimulation of scientific research concerning the physics, chemistry and climatology of non-ionizing radiations (ultra-violet, visible and infra-red) in relation to their biological effects and their applications in biology and medicine; 18 national cttees represented; affiliated to the International Union of Biological Sciences. International Congresses held every four years; Pres. HENRY LIM (USA); Sec.-Gen./Treas. HERBERT HÖNIGSMANN (Austria).

International Union of Physiological Sciences (IUPS): IUPS Secretariat, LGN, Bâtiment CERVI, Hôpital de la Pitié-Salpêtrière, 83 blvd de l'Hôpital, 75013 Paris, France; tel. 1-42-17-75-37; fax 1-42-17-75-75; e-mail iups@case.edu; internet www.iups.org; f. 1955; mems: 51 national, 14 asscn, 4 regional, 2 affiliated mems; Pres. Prof. DENIS NOBLE; Sec.-Gen. WALTER BORON.

International Union of Psychological Science: c/o Prof. P. L.-J. Ritchie, Ecole de psychologie, Université d'Ottawa, 145 Jean-Jacques-Lussier, CP 450, Succ. A, Ottawa, ON KIN 6N5, Canada; tel. (613) 562-5800; fax (613) 562-5169; e-mail pritchie@uottawa.ca; internet www.iupsys.org; f. 1951 to contribute to the development of intellectual exchange and scientific relations between psychologists of different countries; mems: 68 national and 12 affiliate orgs; Pres. Prof. REINER SILBEREISEN (Germany); Sec.-Gen. Prof. P. L.-J. RITCHIE (Canada); publs *International Journal of Psychology* (quarterly), *The IUPsyS Directory* (irregular), *Psychology CD Rom Resource File* (annually).

International Union of Pure and Applied Chemistry (IUPAC): POB 13757, 104 T. W. Alexander Dr., Bldg 19, Research Triangle Park, NC 27709-3757, USA; tel. (919) 485-8700; fax (919) 485-8706; e-mail secretariat@iupac.org; internet www.iupac.org; f. 1919 to organize permanent co-operation between chemical asscns in the member countries, to study topics of international importance requiring standardization or codification, to co-operate with other international organizations in the field of chemistry and to contribute to the advancement of all aspects of chemistry; holds a biennial General Assembly; mems: in 56 countries; Pres. Prof. NICOLE MOREAU (France); Sec.-Gen. Dr DAVID BLACK (Australia).

International Union of Pure and Applied Physics (IUPAP): c/o Institute of Physics, 76 Portland Pl., London, W1B 1NT, United Kingdom; tel. (20) 7470-4849; fax (20) 7470-4861; e-mail admin.iupap@iop.org; internet www.iupap.org; f. 1922 to promote and encourage international co-operation in physics and facilitate the world-wide development of science; hosts a General Assembly every three years; mems: in 60 countries; Pres. CECILIA JARLSKOG (Sweden); Sec.-Gen. ROBERT KIRBY-HARRIS (United Kingdom).

International Union of Radio Science: c/o INTEC, Ghent University, Sint-Pietersnieuwstraat 41, 9000 Ghent, Belgium; tel. (9) 264-3320; fax (9) 264-4288; e-mail info@ursi.org; internet www.ursi.org; f. 1919 to stimulate and co-ordinate, on an international basis, studies, research, applications, scientific exchange and communication in the field of radio science; aims to encourage the adoption of common methods of measurement and the standardization of measuring instruments used in scientific work; represents radio science at national and international levels; mems: 44 national cttees; Pres. Dr Phil Wilkinson (Australia); Sec.-Gen. Prof. Paul Lagasse (Belgium); publs *The Radio Science Bulletin* (quarterly), *Records of General Assemblies* (every 3 years).

International Union of Soil Sciences: c/o Dept of Soil Science, University of Wisconsin-Madison, Madison, WI 53706, USA; tel. (608) 263-4947; e-mail hartemink@wisc.edu; internet www.iuss.org; f. 1924; mems: national academies or national soil science societies from 143 countries; Pres. Prof. Jae Yang (Republic of Korea); Sec.-Gen. Prof. Alfred Hartemink (USA); publ. *Bulletin* (2 a year).

International Union of the History and Philosophy of Science: Division of the History of Science and Technology (DHST): National Hellenic Research Foundation, 48 Vas. Constantinou av., 11635 Athens, Greece; e-mail e.nicolaidis@dhstweb.org; Division of the History of Logic, Methodology and Philosophy of Science (DLMPS): 161 rue Ada, 34392 Montpellier, France; f. 1956 to promote research into the history and philosophy of science; DHST has 50 national committees and DLMPS has 35 committees; DHST: Pres. Prof. Dun Liu (People's Republic of China); Sec.-Gen. Prof. Efthymios Nicolaïdes (Greece); DLMPS Council: Pres. Prof. Wilfrid Hodges; Sec.-Gen. Prof. Peter Clark.

International Union of Theoretical and Applied Mechanics (IUTAM): IUTAM-Secretariat, Centre de Mathématiques et de Leurs Applications, Ecole Normale Supérieure de Cachan, 94235 Cachan, France; tel. 1-47-40-59-00; fax 1-47-40-59-01; e-mail sg@iutam.net; internet www.iutam.net; f. 1947 to form links between those engaged in scientific work (theoretical or experimental) in mechanics or related sciences; organizes international congresses of theoretical and applied mechanics, through a standing Congress Committee, and other international meetings; engages in other activities designed to promote the development of mechanics as a science; mems: from 49 countries; Pres. Prof. Timothy Pedley (United Kingdom); Sec.-Gen. Prof. Frederic Dias (France); publs *Annual Report*, *Newsletter*.

International Union of Toxicology: IUTOX Headquarters, 1821 Michael Faraday Dr., Suite 300, Reston, VA 20190, USA; tel. (703) 438-3103; fax (703) 438-3113; e-mail iutoxhq@iutox.org; internet www.iutox.org; f. 1980 to foster international co-operation among toxicologists and promote world-wide acquisition, dissemination and utilization of knowledge in the field; sponsors International Congresses and other education programmes; mems: 47 national societies; Pres. Dr Daniel Acosta, Jr; Sec.-Gen. Prof. Elaine Faustman; publs *IUTOX Newsletter*, Congress proceedings.

International Water Association (IWA): Alliance House, 12 Caxton St, London, SW1H OQS, United Kingdom; tel. (20) 7654-5500; fax (20) 7654-5555; e-mail water@iwahq.org.uk; internet www.iwahq.org; f. 1999 by merger of the International Water Services Association and the International Association on Water Quality; aims to encourage international communication, co-operative effort, and exchange of information on water quality management, through conferences, electronic media and publication of research reports; mems: c. 9,000 in 130 countries; Pres. Dr Glen Daigger; Exec. Dir Paul Reiter; publs *Water Research* (monthly), *Water Science and Technology* (24 a year), *Water 21* (6 a year), *Yearbook*, *Scientific and Technical Reports*.

Nuclear Threat Initiative: 1747 Pennsylvania Ave NW, 7th Floor, Washington, DC 20006, USA; tel. (202) 296-4810; fax (202) 296-4810; e-mail contact@nti.org; internet www.nti.org; f. 2001 to help strengthen global security by reducing the risk of use of and preventing the spread of nuclear, biological and chemical weapons; promotes the objectives of the Nuclear Non-Proliferation Treaty; Co-Chair. R. E. (Ted) Turner; Co-Chair. and CEO Sam Nunn; Pres. and Chief Operating Officer Joan Rohlfing.

Pacific Science Association: 1525 Bernice St, Honolulu, HI 96817, USA; tel. (808) 848-4124; fax (808) 847-8252; e-mail info@pacificscience.org; internet www.pacificscience.org; f. 1920; a regional non-governmental organization that seeks to advance science, technology, and sustainable development in and of the Asia-Pacific region, by actively promoting interdisciplinary and international research and collaboration; sponsors Pacific Science Congresses and Inter-Congresses and scientific working groups and facilitates research initiatives on critical emerging issues for the region; 12th Inter-Congress: Suva, Fiji, in July, on the theme: 'Human Security in the Pacific'; 22nd Congress: Kuala Lumpur, Malaysia, June 2011; mems: institutional representatives from 35 areas, scientific societies, individual scientists; Pres. Prof. Nancy D. Lewis (USA); Sec-Gen. Makoto Tsuchiya (Japan); publs *Pacific Science* (quarterly), *Information Bulletin* (2 a year).

Pan-African Union of Science and Technology: POB 641, Brazzaville, Republic of the Congo; tel. 832265; fax 832185; f. 1987 to promote the use of science and technology in furthering the development of Africa; organizes triennial congress; Sec.-Gen. Prof. Lévy Makany.

Pugwash Conferences on Science and World Affairs: Ground Floor Flat, 63A Great Russell St, London, WC1B 3BJ, United Kingdom; tel. (20) 7405-6661; fax (20) 7831-5651; e-mail pugwash@mac.com; internet www.pugwash.org; f. 1957 to organize international conferences of scientists to discuss problems arising from the development of science, particularly the dangers to mankind from weapons of mass destruction; mems: national Pugwash groups in 38 countries; Pres. Jayantha Dhenapala; Sec.-Gen. Prof. Paolo Cotta-Ramusino; publs *Pugwash Newsletter* (2 a year), occasional papers, monographs.

Scientific, Technical and Research Commission of African Unity (OAU/STRC): Nigerian Ports Authority Bldg, PMB 2359, Marina, Lagos, Nigeria; tel. (1) 2633359; fax (1) 2636093; e-mail oaustrcl@hyperia.com; f. 1965 to succeed the Commission for Technical Co-operation in Africa (f. 1954); implements priority programmes of the African Union relating to science and technology for development; supervises the Inter-African Bureau for Animal Resources (Nairobi, Kenya), the Inter-African Bureau for Soils (Lagos, Nigeria) and the Inter-African Phytosanitary Commission (Yaoundé, Cameroon) and several joint research projects; provides training in agricultural management, and conducts pest control programmes; services various inter-African committees of experts, including the Scientific Council for Africa; publishes and distributes specialized scientific books and documents of original value to Africa; organizes training courses, seminars, symposia, workshops and technical meetings; Exec. Sec. Dr Mbaye Ndoye.

Unitas Malacologica (Malacological Union): c/o Dr Jackie Van Goethem, Royal Belgian Institute of Natural Sciences, Vautierstraat 29, 1000 Brussels, Belgium; tel. (2) 627-43-43; fax (2) 627-41-41; e-mail jackie.vangoethem@naturalsciences.be; internet www.unitasmalacologica.org; f. 1962 to further the study of molluscs world-wide; affiliated to the International Union of Biological Sciences; holds triennial world congress; mems: 400 in more than 35 countries; Pres. António de Frias Martins (Portugal); Sec. Jesús Troncoso (Spain); publ. *UM Newsletter* (2 a year).

World Institute for Nuclear Security (WINS): Graben 19 Vienna, 1010 Austria; tel. (1) 230-606-088; fax (1) 230-606-089; e-mail info@wins.org; internet www.wins.org; f. 2008; aims to strengthen the physical protection and security of nuclear materials and facilities world-wide; Exec. Dir Dr Roger Howsley (United Kingdom).

World Organisation of Systems and Cybernetics (WOSC): c/o Prof Raul Espejo, 3 North Pl., 30 Nettleham Rd, Lincoln, LN2 1RE, United Kingdom; tel. and fax (1522) 589252; e-mail r.espejo@syncho.org; internet www.wosc.co; f. 1969 to act as clearing-house for all societies concerned with cybernetics and systems, to aim for the recognition of cybernetics as fundamental science, to organize and sponsor international exhibitions of automation and computer equipment, congresses and symposia, and to promote and co-ordinate research in systems and cybernetics; sponsors an honorary fellowship and awards a Norbert Wiener memorial gold medal; mems: dirs. from 16 countries belonging to nat. and int. societies in 30 countries; Pres. Prof. R. Vallée (France); Dir-Gen. Prof. Raul Espejo; publs *Kybernetes*, *International Journal of Cybernetics and Systems*.

Social Sciences

African Social and Environmental Studies Programme: Box 4477, Nairobi, Kenya; tel. (20) 747960; fax (20) 747960; f. 1968; develops and disseminates educational material on social and environmental studies in eastern and southern Africa; mems: 18 African countries; Chair. Prof. William Senteza-Kajubi; Exec. Dir Prof. Peter Muyanda Mutebi; publs *African Social and Environmental Studies Forum* (2 a year), teaching guides.

Arab Towns Organization (ATO): POB 68160, Kaifan 71962, Kuwait; tel. 24849705; fax 24849319; e-mail ato@ato.net; internet www.ato.net; f. 1967; works to preserve the identity and heritage of Arab towns; to support the development and modernization of municipal and local authorities in member towns; to improve services and utilities in member towns; to support development schemes in member towns through the provision of loans and other assistance; to support planning and the co-ordination of development activities and services; to facilitate the exchange of service-related expertise among member towns; to co-ordinate efforts to modernize and standardize municipal regulations and codes among member towns; to promote co-operation in all matters related to Arab towns; manages the Arab Towns Development Fund, the Arab Institute for Urban Development, the Arab Towns Organization Award, the Arab Urban Environment Centre, the Arab Forum on Information Systems, and the Heritage and Arab Historic City Foundation; mems: 413 towns; Sec.-Gen. ABD AL-AZIZ Y. AL-ADASANI; publ. *Al-Madinah Al-Arabiyah* (every 2 months).

Association for the Study of the World Refugee Problem (AWR): POB 1241, 97201 Höchberg, Germany; e-mail awr_int_forschungsg@yahoo.de; internet www.awr-int.de; f. 1951 to promote and co-ordinate scholarly research on refugee problems; Pres. RAINER WIESTNER (Italy); Gen. Sec. Prof. MARKUS BABO; publs *AWR Bulletin* (quarterly, in English, French, Italian and German), treatises on refugee problems (17 vols).

Council for Research in Values and Philosophy (CRVP): 620 Michigan Ave, NE, Washington, DC 20064, USA; tel. and fax (202) 319-6089; e-mail cua-rvp@cua.edu; internet www.crvp.org; f. 1983; organizes conferences and an annual 10-week seminar; mems: 70 teams from 60 countries; Pres. Prof. KENNETH L. SCHMITZ (Canada); Sec.-Treas. Prof. GEORGE F. MCLEAN (USA); publs *Cultural Heritage and Contemporary Change* series (220 titles).

Council for the Development of Social Science Research in Africa (CODESRIA): Ave Cheikh, Anta Diop X Canal IV, BP 3304, CP 18524, Dakar, Senegal; tel. 825-98-22; fax 825-12-89; internet www.codesria.org; f. 1973; promotes research, organizes conferences, working groups and information services; mems: research institutes and university faculties and researchers in African countries; Exec. Sec. Dr EBRIMA SALL; publs *Africa Development* (quarterly), *CODESRIA Bulletin* (quarterly), *Index of African Social Science Periodical Articles* (annually), *African Journal of International Affairs* (2 a year), *African Sociological Review* (2 a year), *Afrika Zamani* (annually), *Identity, Culture and Politics* (2 a year), *Afro Arab Selections for Social Sciences* (annually), directories of research.

Eastern Regional Organisation for Planning and Housing: Ministry of Housing and Local Government, Aras 4, Block B (North), Pusat Bandar Damansara, Kuala Lumpur, Malaysia; tel. (3) 20925217; fax (3) 20924217; e-mail secretariat@earoph.info; internet www.earoph.info; f. 1956 to promote and co-ordinate the study and practice of housing and regional town and country planning; maintains offices in Japan, India and Indonesia; mems: 57 orgs and 213 individuals in 28 countries; Pres. MICHAEL HARBISON (Australia); Sec.-Gen. NORLIZA HASHIM (Malaysia); publs *EAROPH News and Notes* (monthly), *Town and Country Planning* (bibliography).

English-Speaking Union: Dartmouth House, 37 Charles St, Berkeley Sq., London, W1J 5ED, United Kingdom; tel. (20) 7529-1550; fax (20) 7495-6108; e-mail esu@esu.org; internet www.esu.org; f. 1918 to promote international understanding through the use of the English language; mems: 37 United Kingdom branches; 50 international affiliates; Chair. Dame MARY RICHARDSON; Dir-Gen. PETER KYLE.

European Association for Population Studies (EAPS): POB 11676, 2502 AR The Hague, Netherlands; Lange Houtst. 19, 2511 CV The Hague, Netherlands; tel. (70) 3565200; fax (70) 3647187; e-mail contact@eaps.nl; internet www.eaps.nl; f. 1983 to foster research and provide information on European population problems; organizes conferences, seminars and workshops; mems: demographers from 40 countries; Exec. Sec. HELGA DE VALK; publ. *European Journal of Population / Revue Européenne de Démographie* (quarterly).

European Society for Rural Sociology: c/o M. Lehtola, Swedish School of Social Science, POB 16, University of Helsinki, Finland; tel. (9) 19128483; fax (9) 19128485; e-mail minna.lehtola@helsinki.fi; internet www.ruralsociology.eu; f. 1957 to further research in, and co-ordination of, rural sociology and provide a centre for documentation of information; also involved in the study of agriculture and fisheries, food production and consumption, nature and environmental care, etc.; mems: 300 individuals, institutions and asscns in 29 European countries and 9 countries outside Europe; Pres. Dr JO LITTLE (United Kingdom); Sec. MINNA LEHTOLA (Finland); publ. *Sociologia Ruralis* (quarterly).

Federation EIL: 70 Landmark Hill, Suite 204, Brattleboro, VT 05301 USA; tel. (802) 246-1154; fax (802) 246-1154; e-mail federation@experiment.org; internet www.experiment.org; f. 1932 as Experiment in International Living; an international federation of non-profit educational and cultural exchange institutions; works to create mutual understanding and respect among people of different nations, as a means of furthering peace; mems: orgs in more than 20 countries; Dir ILENE TODD.

Fédération internationale des associations vexillologiques (International Federation of Vexillological Associations): 504 Branard St, Houston, TX 77006-5018, USA; tel. (713) 529-2545; e-mail sec.gen@fiav.org; internet www.fiav.org; f. 1969; unites associations and institutions throughout the world whose object is the pursuit of vexillology, i.e. the creation and development of a body of knowledge about flags of all types, their forms and functions, and of scientific theories and principles based on that knowledge; sponsors International Congresses of Vexillology every two years (2013: Rotterdam, Netherlands); mems: 52 institutions and asscns world-wide; Pres. Prof. MICHEL LUPANT (Belgium); Sec.-Gen. CHARLES A. SPAIN, Jr (USA); publs *Info FIAV* (annually), *Proceedings of the International Congresses of Vexillology* (every 2 years).

International African Institute (IAI): School of Oriental and African Studies, Thornhaugh St, Russell Sq., London, WC1H 0XG, United Kingdom; tel. (20) 7898-4420; fax (20) 7898-4419; e-mail iai@soas.ac.uk; internet www.internationalafricaninstitute.org; f. 1926 to promote the study of African peoples, their languages, cultures and social life in their traditional and modern settings; organizes an international seminar programme bringing together scholars from Africa and elsewhere; links scholars in order to facilitate research projects, especially in the social sciences; Chair. Prof. V. Y. MUDIMBE; Hon. Dir Prof. PHILIP BURNHAM; publs *Africa* (quarterly), *Africa Bibliography* (annually).

International Association for Media and Communication Research: c/o Annabelle Sreberny, Centre for Media and Film Studies, School of Oriental and African Studies, University of London, Russell Square, London, WC1 OXG, United Kingdom; tel. (20) 7898-4422; internet www.iamcr.org; f. 1957 (fmrly International Asscn for Mass Communication Research) to stimulate interest in mass communication research and the dissemination of information about research and research needs, to improve communication practice, policy and research and training for journalism, and to provide a forum for researchers and others involved in mass communication to meet and exchange information; mems: over 2,300 in c. 70 countries; Pres. Prof. ANNABELLE SREBERNY; publ. *Newsletter*.

International Association for the History of Religions (IAHR): c/o Prof. Tim Jensen, Institute of Philosophy, Education and the Study of Religion, Dept of the Study of Religions, Univ. of Southern Denmark, Odense, Campusvej 55, 5230 Odense M, Denmark; tel. 65-50-33-15; fax 65-50-26-68; e-mail t.jensen@ifpr.sdu.dk; internet www.iahr.dk; f. 1950 to promote international collaboration of scholars, to organize congresses and to stimulate research; mems: 37 nat. and 5 regional asscns; Pres. Prof. ROSALIND I. J. HACKETT; Gen. Sec. Prof. TIM JENSEN; publ. *Numen: International Review for the History of Religions* (annually).

International Association of Applied Linguistics (Association internationale de linguistique appliquée—AILA): Theaterstr. 15, 8401 Winterthur, Switzerland; tel. 589346060; e-mail secretariat@aila.info; internet www.aila.info; f. 1964; organizes seminars on applied linguistics, and a World Congress every three years (2011: Beijing, People's Republic of China, in Aug.; 2014: Brisbane, Australia, in April); mems: more than 8,000; Pres. Prof. BERND RUESCHOFF (Germany); Sec.-Gen. Prof. DANIEL PERRIN (Switzerland); publs *AILA Review* (annually),.

International Association of Metropolitan City Libraries (INTAMEL): c/o Frans Meijer, Bibliotheek Rotterdam, Hoogstraat 110, 3011 PV Rotterdam, Netherlands; tel. (10) 2816140; fax (10) 2816221; e-mail f.meijer@bibliotheek.rotterdam.nl; f. 1966; serves as a platform for libraries in cities of over 400,000 inhabitants or serving a wide and diverse geographical area; promotes the exchange of ideas and information on a range of topics including library networks, automation, press relations and research; mems: 98 libraries in 28 countries; Pres. FRANS MEIJER (Netherlands).

International Committee for Social Sciences Information and Documentation: c/o Clacso, Callao 875, 3rd Floor, Buenos Aires 1023, Argentina; e-mail saugy@clacso.edu.ar; internet www.unesco.org/most/icssd.htm; f. 1950 to collect and disseminate information on documentation services in social sciences, to help improve documentation, to advise societies on problems of documentation and to draw up rules likely to improve the presentation of documents; mems: from international asscns specializing in social sciences or in documentation, and from other specialized fields; Pres. KRISHANA G. TYAGI; Sec.-Gen. CATALINA SAUGY (Argentina); publs *International Bibliography of the Social Sciences* (annually), *Newsletter* (2 a year).

International Committee for the History of Art: c/o Prof. Dr P. J. Schneemann, Institut für Kunstgeschichte, Hodlerstr. 8, 3011 Bern, Switzerland; tel. 316314741; fax 316318669; e-mail ciha@unam.mx; internet www.esteticas.unam.mx/ciha; f. 1930 by the 12th International Congress on the History of Art, for collaboration in the scientific study of the history of art; holds international congress every four years, and at least two colloquia between congresses; mems: National Committees in 34 countries; Sec. Prof. Dr PETER JOHANNES SCHNEEMANN (Switzerland); publ. *Bibliographie d'Histoire de l'Art—Bibliography of the History of Art* (quarterly).

International Committee of Historical Sciences (Comité International des Sciences Historiques — CISH): Département d'histoire, UQAM, CP 8888, Succursale Centre-ville, Montréal, QC H3C 3P8,

Canada; e-mail cish@uqam.ca; internet www.cish.org; f. 1926 to work for the advancement of historical sciences by means of international co-ordination; holds international congress every five years, 2010: Amsterdam, Netherlands; mems: 53 national committees, 28 affiliated international orgs and 12 internal commissions; Pres. Prof. MARJATTA HIETALA (Finland); Sec.-Gen. Prof. ROBERT FRANK (France); publ. *Bulletin d'Information du CISH*.

International Council for Philosophy and Humanistic Studies (ICPHS): Maison de l'UNESCO, 1 rue Miollis, 75732 Paris Cédex 15, France; tel. 1-45-68-48-85; fax 1-40-65-94-80; e-mail cipsh@unesco.org; internet www.unesco.org/cipsh; f. 1949 under the auspices of UNESCO to encourage respect for cultural autonomy by the comparative study of civilization and to contribute towards international understanding through a better knowledge of humanity; works to develop international co-operation in philosophy, humanistic and kindred studies; encourages the setting up of international organizations; promotes the dissemination of information in these fields; sponsors works of learning, etc.; mems: 13 orgs representing 145 countries; Pres. IN SUK CHA; Sec.-Gen. MAURICE AYMARD; publs *Bulletin of Information* (biennially), *Diogenes* (quarterly).

International Council on Archives (ICA): 60 rue des Francs-Bourgeois, 75003 Paris, France; tel. 1-40-27-63-06; fax 1-42-72-20-65; e-mail ica@ica.org; internet www.ica.org; f. 1948 to develop relationships between archivists in different countries; aims to protect and enhance archives, to ensure preservation of archival heritage; facilitates training of archivists and conservators; promotes implementation of a professional code of conduct; encourages ease of access to archives; has 13 regional branches; mems: more than 1,465 in 198 countries; Pres. MARTIN BERENDSE (Netherlands); Sec.-Gen. DAVID LEITCH; publs *Comma* (2 a year), *Flash Newsletter* (2 a year), annual CD-Rom.

International Ergonomics Association (IEA): 1515 Engineering Drive, 3126 Engineering Centers Building, Madison, WI 53706, USA; tel. (608) 265-0503; fax (608) 263-1425; e-mail carayon@engr.wisc.edu; internet www.iea.cc; f. 1957 to bring together organizations and persons interested in the scientific study of human work and its environment; to establish international contacts among those specializing in this field, to co-operate with employers' asscns and trade unions in order to encourage the practical application of ergonomic sciences in industries, and to promote scientific research in this field; mems: 42 federated societies; Pres. ANDREW S. IMADA (USA); Sec.-Gen. Prof. Dr ERIC MIN-YANG WANG; publ. *Ergonomics* (monthly).

International Federation for Housing and Planning (IFHP): Binckhorstlaan 36, 2516 CG The Hague, Netherlands; tel. (70) 3244557; fax (70) 3282085; e-mail info@ifhp.org; internet www.ifhp.org; f. 1913 to study and promote the improvement of housing and the theory and practice of town planning; holds an annual World Congress (2012: Göteburg, Sweden, in Sept.); mems: 200 orgs and 300 individuals in 65 countries; Pres. JOHN ZETTER (United Kingdom); Sec.-Gen. DEREK MARTIN; publ. *Newsletter* (quarterly).

International Federation for Modern Languages and Literatures: c/o A. Pettersson, Dept of Culture and Media Studies, Umea University, 901 87 Umea, Sweden; tel. (90) 139-556; e-mail anders.pettersson@littvet.umu.se; internet www.fillm.ulg.ac.be; f. 1928 to establish permanent contact between historians of literature, to develop or perfect facilities for their work and to promote the study of modern languages and literature; holds Congress every three years; mems: 19 asscns, with individual mems in 98 countries; Pres. ROGER D. SELL (Finland); Sec.-Gen. ANDERS PETTERSSON (Sweden).

International Federation of Philosophical Societies (FISP): c/o Human Rights Centre, Maltepe University, 34857 Maltepe, Istanbul, Turkey; tel. (216) 6261132; fax (216) 6261125; e-mail kemp@dpu.dk; internet www.fisp.org; f. 1948 under the auspices of UNESCO, to encourage international co-operation in the field of philosophy; holds World Congress of Philosophy every five years (2008: Seoul, Republic of Korea); mems: 114 societies from 52 countries; 27 international societies; Pres. WILLIAM MCBRIDE (USA); Sec.-Gen. LUCA SCARANTINO (Italy); publs *Newsletter*, *International Bibliography of Philosophy*, *Chroniques de Philosophie*, *Contemporary Philosophy*, *Philosophical Problems Today*, *Philosophy and Cultural Development*, *Ideas Underlying World Problems*, *The Idea of Values*.

International Federation of Social Science Organizations (IFSSO): 245/69 Baromtrilokanart Rd, Muang District, Phitsanulok 65000, Thailand; tel. and fax (55) 244-240; e-mail sudakarn_p@yahoo.com; f. 1979 to assist research and teaching in the social sciences, and to facilitate co-operation and enlist mutual assistance in the planning and evaluation of programmes of major importance to members; mems: 31 national councils or academies in 29 countries; Sec.-Gen. Dr NESTOR CASTRO; publs *IFSSO Newsletter* (2 a year), *International Directory of Social Science Organizations*.

International Federation of Societies of Classical Studies: c/o Prof. P. Schubert, 7 rue des Beaux-Arts, 2000 Neuchatel, Switzerland; tel. 223797035; fax 223797932; e-mail paul.schubert@unige.ch; internet www.fiecnet.org; f. 1948 under the auspices of UNESCO; mems: 80 societies in 44 countries; Pres. Dame AVERIL CAMERON (United Kingdom); Sec.-Gen. Prof. PAUL SCHUBERT (Switzerland); publs *L'Année Philologique*, *Thesaurus linguae Latinae*.

International Institute for Ligurian Studies: Via Romana 39, 18012 Bordighera, Italy; tel. (0184) 263601; fax (0184) 266421; e-mail istituto@usl.it; f. 1947 to conduct research on ancient monuments and regional traditions in the north-west arc of the Mediterranean (France and Italy); maintains library of 80,000 vols; mems: in France, Italy, Spain, Switzerland; Dir Prof. CARLO VARALDO (Italy).

International Institute of Administrative Sciences (IIAS): 1 rue Defacqz, 1000 Brussels, Belgium; tel. (2) 536-08-80; fax (2) 537-97-02; e-mail iias@iias-iisa.org; internet www.iias-iisa.org; f. 1930 for the comparative examination of administrative experience; carries out research and programmes designed to improve administrative law and practices; has consultative status with UN, UNESCO and ILO; organizes international congresses, annual conferences, working groups; mems: 27 mem. states, 31 national sections, 3 international governmental orgs, 36 corporate mems; Pres. KIM PAN-SUK (Republic of Korea); Dir-Gen. ROLET LORETAN (Switzerland); publs *International Review of Administrative Sciences* (quarterly), *Newsletter* (3 a year).

International Institute of Sociology (IIS): c/o The Swedish Collegium for Advanced Study, Thunbergsvägen 2, 75238 Uppsala, Sweden; tel. (18) 55-70-85; e-mail info@iisoc.org; internet www.iisoc.org; f. 1893 to enable sociologists to meet and to study sociological questions; mems: c. 300 in 47 countries; Pres. BJÖRN WITTROCK (Sweden); Sec.-Gen. PETER HEDSTRÖM; publ. *The Annals of the IIS*.

International Musicological Society (IMS): POB 1561, CH-4001 Basel, Switzerland; tel. 449231022; fax 449231027; e-mail dorothea.baumann@ims-online.ch; internet www.ims-online.ch; f. 1927; holds international congresses every five years (2012: Rome, Italy); mems: c. 1,000 in 53 countries; Pres. DINKO FABRIS (Italy); Sec.-Gen. Dr DOROTHEA BAUMANN (Switzerland); publ. *Acta Musicologica* (2 a year).

International Numismatic Council (Conseil international de numismatique): Kunsthistorisches Museum, Coin Cabinet, Burgring 5, 1010 Vienna, Austria; tel. (1) 525-24-42-01; fax (1) 525-24-42-99; e-mail michael.alram@khm.at; internet www.inc-cin.org; f. 1934 as International Numismatic Commission; name changed to present in 2009; facilitates co-operation between scholars studying coins and medals; mems: 160 in 38 countries; Pres. Dr CARMEN ARNOLD-BIUCCHI; Sec. MICHAEL ALRAM.

International Peace Institute: 777 United Nations Plaza, New York, NY 10017-3521, USA; tel. (212) 687-4300; fax (212) 983-8246; e-mail ipi@ipinst.org; internet www.ipacademy.org; f. 1970 (as the International Peace Academy) to promote the prevention and settlement of armed conflicts between and within states through policy research and development; educates government officials in the procedures needed for conflict resolution, peace-keeping, mediation and negotiation, through international training seminars and publications; off-the-record meetings are also conducted to gain complete understanding of a specific conflict; Chair. RITA E. HAUSER; Pres. TERJE ROD-LARSEN.

International Peace Research Association (IPRA): University of Leuven, Van Evenstraat 2B, Leuven, Belgium; tel. (16) 32-32-41; fax (16) 32-30-88; e-mail luc.reychler@soc.kuleuven.ac.be; internet www.human.mie-u.ac.jp/~peace/; f. 1964 to encourage interdisciplinary research on the conditions of peace and the causes of war; mems: 150 corporate, 5 regional branches, 1,000 individuals, in 93 countries; Sec.-Gen. LUC REYCHLER (Belgium); publ. *IPRA Newsletter* (quarterly).

International Social Science Council (ISSC): Maison de l'UNESCO, 1 rue Miollis, 75732 Paris Cédex 15, France; tel. 1-45-68-48-60; fax 1-45-66-76-03; e-mail issc@unesco.org; internet www.unesco.org/ngo/issc; f. 1952; aims to promote the advancement of the social sciences throughout the world and their application to the major problems of the world; encourages co-operation at an international level between specialists in the social sciences; comprises programmes on International Human Dimensions of Global Environmental Change (IHDP), Gender, Globalization and Democratization, and Comparative Research on Poverty (CROP); mems: International Association of Legal Sciences, International Economic Association, International Federation of Social Science Organizations, International Geographical Union, International Institute of Administrative Sciences, International Peace Research Association, International Political Science Association, International Sociological Association, International Union for the Scientific Study of Population, International Union of Anthropological and Ethnological Sciences, International Union of Psychological Science, World Association for Public Opinion Research, World Federation for Mental Health; 28 national orgs; 16 associate members; Pres. Prof. GUDMUND HERNES (Norway); Sec.-Gen. Dr HEIDE HACKMANN (France).

International Society of Social Defence and Humane Criminal Policy (ISSD): c/o Centro nazionale di prevenzione e difesa sociale, Piazza Castello 3, 20121 Milan, Italy; tel. (02) 86460714; fax (02) 72008431; e-mail cnpds.ispac@cnpds.it; internet www.cnpds.it; f. 1945 to combat crime, to protect society and to prevent citizens from being tempted to commit criminal actions; mems: in 43 countries; Sec.-Gen. EDMONDO BRUTI LIBERATI (Italy); publ. *Cahiers de défense sociale* (annually).

International Sociological Association: c/o Faculty of Political Sciences and Sociology, Universidad Complutense, 28223 Madrid, Spain; tel. (91) 3527650; fax (91) 3524945; e-mail isa@isa-sociology.org; internet www.isa-sociology.org; f. 1949 to promote sociological knowledge, facilitate contacts between sociologists, encourage the dissemination and exchange of information and facilities and stimulate research; has 55 research committees on various aspects of sociology; holds World Congresses every four years (18th Congress: Yokohama, Japan, July 2014); Exec. Sec. IZABELA BARLINSKA; publs *Current Sociology* (6 a year), *International Sociology* (6 a year), *Sage Studies in International Sociology* (based on World Congress).

International Statistical Institute (ISI): POB 24070, 2490 AB The Hague, Netherlands; tel. (70) 3375737; fax (70) 3860025; e-mail isi@cbs.nl; internet www.isi-web.org; f. 1885; devoted to the development and improvement of statistical methods and their application throughout the world; executes international research programmes; mems: 2,000 ordinary mems, 11 hon. mems, 166 *ex officio* mems, 69 corporate mems, 45 affiliated orgs, 32 national statistical societies; Pres. LEE JAE-CHANG (Republic of Korea); Dir Permanent Office ADA VAN KRIMPEN; publs *Bulletin of the International Statistical Institute* (proceedings of biennial sessions), *International Statistical Review* (3 a year), *Short Book Reviews* (3 a year), *Statistical Theory and Method Abstracts–Z* (available on CD-Rom and online), *ISI Newsletter* (3 a year), *Membership Directory* (available online).

International Studies Association (ISA): Social Science 324, Univ. of Arizona, Tucson, AZ 85721, USA; tel. (520) 621-7715; fax (520) 621-5780; e-mail isa@u.arizona.edu; internet www.isanet.org; f. 1959; links those whose professional concerns extend beyond their own national boundaries (government officials, representatives of business and industry, and scholars); mems: 3,500 in 60 countries; Pres. THOMAS WEISS (USA); Exec. Dir THOMAS J. VOLGY; publs *International Studies Quarterly*, *International Studies Perspectives*, *International Studies Review*, *ISA Newsletter*.

International Union for the Scientific Study of Population (IUSSP): 3–5 rue Nicolas, 75980 Paris Cédex 20, France; tel. 1-56-06-21-73; fax 1-56-06-22-04; e-mail iussp@iussp.org; internet www.iussp.org; f. 1928 to advance the progress of quantitative and qualitative demography as a science (reconstituted in 1947); organizes International Population Conference every four years (27th Conference: Busan, Republic of Korea, Aug. 2013); mems: 1,917 in 121 countries; Pres. PETER MCDONALD (Australia); Sec.-Gen./Treas. EMILY GRUNDY (United Kingdom); publs *IUSSP Bulletin* and books on population.

International Union of Academies (IUA) (Union académique internationale—UAI): Palais des Académies, 1 rue Ducale, 1000 Brussels, Belgium; tel. (2) 550-22-00; fax (2) 550-22-05; e-mail info@uai-iua.org; internet www.uai-iua.org; f. 1919 to promote international co-operation through collective research in philology, archaeology, art history, history and social sciences; mems: academic institutions in 61 countries; Sec.-Gen. HERVÉ HASQUIN.

International Union of Anthropological and Ethnological Sciences (IUAES): Dept of Anthropology, Faculty of Human Sciences, Osaka University, 1–2 Yamadaoka, Suita, Osaka 565-0871; tel. (6) 6879-7002; e-mail iuaes@glocol.osaka-u.ac.jp; internet www.glocol.osaka-u.ac.jp/iuaes; f. 1948 under the auspices of UNESCO, to enhance exchange and communication between scientists and institutions in the fields of anthropology and ethnology; aims to promote harmony between nature and culture; organizes 22 international research commissions; mems: institutions and individuals in 100 countries; Pres. Dr PETER J. M. NAS (Netherlands); Sec.-Gen. JUNJI KOIZUMI (Japan); publ. *IUAES Newsletter* (3 a year).

International Union of Prehistoric and Protohistoric Sciences: GRI,Inst Politécnico de Tomar, ave Dr Cândido Madueira, 2300-531 Tomar, Portugal; tel. (249) 346363; fax (249) 346366; e-mail uispp@ipt.pt; internet www.uispp.ipt.pt; f. 1931 to promote congresses and scientific work in the fields of pre- and proto-history; mems: 120 countries; Sec.-Gen. LUIZ OOSTERBEEK.

Mensa International: c/o British Mensa, St John's House, St. John's Sq., Wolverhampton, WV2 4AH, United Kingdom; tel. (1902) 772771; fax (1902) 392500; e-mail enquiries@mensa.org; internet www.mensa.org; f. 1946 to identify and foster intelligence for the benefit of humanity; mems: individuals who score higher than 98% of people in general in a recognized intelligence test may become mems; there are 100,000 mems world-wide; Exec. Dir MICHAEL FEENAN (United Kingdom); publ. *Mensa International Journal* (monthly).

Permanent International Committee of Linguists: Postbus 3023, 2301 DA Leiden, Netherlands; tel. (71) 5211552; e-mail cipl.secretary-general@planet.nl; internet www.ciplnet.com; f. 1928; aims to further linguistic research, to co-ordinate activities undertaken for the advancement of linguistics, and to make the results of linguistic research known internationally; holds Congress every five years; mems: 34 countries and 2 int. linguistic orgs; Pres. F. KIEFER (Hungary); Sec.-Gen. P. G. J. VAN STERKENBURG (Netherlands); publ. *Linguistic Bibliography* (annually).

Third World Forum: 39 Dokki St, POB 43, Orman Giza, Cairo, Egypt; tel. (2) 7488092; fax (2) 7480668; e-mail 20sabry2@gega.net; internet www.forumtiersmonde.net; f. 1975 to link social scientists and others from the developing countries, to discuss alternative development policies and encourage research; maintains regional offices in Egypt, Mexico, Senegal and Sri Lanka; mems: individuals in more than 50 countries.

World Association for Public Opinion Research: c/o University of Nebraska-Lincoln, UNL Gallup Research Center, 201 N 13th St, Lincoln, NE 68588-0242, USA; tel. (402) 472-7720; fax (402) 472-7727; e-mail renae@wapor.org; internet www.wapor.org; f. 1947 to establish and promote contacts between persons in the field of survey research on opinions, attitudes and behaviour of people in the various countries of the world; works to further the use of objective, scientific survey research in national and international affairs; mems: 450 from 72 countries; Pres. Dr TOM W. SMITH; Gen. Sec. Prof. Dr ALLAN MCCUTCHEON; publs *WAPOR Newsletter* (quarterly), *International Journal of Public Opinion* (quarterly).

World Society for Ekistics: c/o Athens Center of Ekistics, 23 Strat. Syndesmou St, 106 73 Athens, Greece; tel. (210) 3623216; fax (210) 3629337; e-mail ekistics@otenet.gr; internet www.ekistics.org; f. 1965; aims to promote knowledge and ideas concerning human settlements through research, publications and conferences; encourages the development and expansion of education in ekistics; aims to recognize the benefits and necessity of an inter-disciplinary approach to the needs of human settlements; mems: 233 individuals; Pres. CALOGERO MUSCARA; Sec.-Gen. P. PSOMOPOULOS.

Social Welfare and Human Rights

African Commission on Human and Peoples' Rights: 31 Bijilo Annex Layout, POB 673, Banjul, The Gambia; tel. 4410505; fax 4410504; e-mail au-banjul@africa-union.org; internet www.achpr.org; f. 1987; mandated to monitor compliance with the African Charter on Human and People's Rights (ratified in 1986); investigates claims of human rights abuses perpetrated by govts that have ratified the Charter (claims may be brought by other African govts, the victims themselves, or by a third party); meets twice a year for 15 days in March and Oct; mems: 11; Exec. Sec. Dr MARY MABOREKE.

Aid to Displaced Persons (L'Aide aux Personnes Déplacées): 33 rue du Marché, 4500 Huy, Belgium; tel. (85) 21-34-81; fax (85) 23-01-47; e-mail aidepersdepl.huy@skynet.be; internet www.aideauxpersonnesdeplacees.be; f. 1949; aims to provide aid and support for refugees.

Amnesty International: 1 Easton St, London, WC1X ODW, United Kingdom; tel. (20) 7413-5500; fax (20) 7956-1157; e-mail amnestyis@amnesty.org; internet www.amnesty.org; f. 1961; an independent, democratic, self-governing world-wide movement of people who campaign for internationally recognized human rights, such as those enshrined in the Universal Declaration of Human Rights; undertakes research and action focused on preventing and ending grave abuses of the rights to physical and mental integrity, freedom of conscience and expression, and freedom from discrimination, within the context of its work impartially to promote and protect all human rights; mems: more than 2.2m. represented by 7,800 local, youth, student and other specialist groups, in more than 150 countries and territories; nationally organized sections in 58 countries and pre-section co-ordinating structures in another 22 countries; major policy decisions are taken by an International Council comprising representatives from all national sections; financed by donations; no funds are sought or accepted from governments; Sec.-Gen. SALIL SHETTY (India); publs *International Newsletter* (monthly), *Annual Report*, other country reports.

Anti-Slavery International: Thomas Clarkson House, The Stableyard, Broomgrove Rd, London, SW9 9TL, United Kingdom; tel. (20) 7501-8920; fax (20) 7738-4110; e-mail info@antislavery.org; internet www.antislavery.org; f. 1839; aims to eliminate all forms of slavery by exposing manifestations of it around the world and campaigning against it; supports initiatives by local organizations to release people from slavery, and develops rehabilitation programmes aimed at preventing people from re-entering slavery; pressures governments to implement international laws prohibiting slavery and to develop and enforce similar national legislation; maintains digital collection of 18th- and 19th-century documentation on the Transatlantic Slave

Trade at www.recoveredhistories.org; mems: c. 2,000 world-wide; Dir AIDAN MCQUADE; publs *Annual Review* (quarterly), *Reporter* (quarterly), special reports and research documentation.

Article 19: 60 Farringdon Rd, London, EC1R 3GA, United Kingdom; tel. (20) 7324-2500; e-mail info@article19.org; internet www.article19.org; f. 1987; an international human rights org., in particular dedicated to defending and promoting freedom of expression and of information; Exec. Dir Dr AGNÈS CALLAMARD.

Associated Country Women of the World (ACWW): Mary Sumner House, 24 Tufton St, London, SW1P 3RB, United Kingdom; tel. (20) 7799-3875; fax (20) 7340-9950; e-mail info@acww.org.uk; internet www.acww.org.uk; f. 1933; aims to aid the economic and social development of countrywomen and home-makers of all nations, to promote international goodwill and understanding, to work to alleviate poverty, and promote good health and education; Pres MAY KIDD; Gen. Sec. JO ELLEN ALMOND; publ. *The Countrywoman* (quarterly).

Association Internationale de la Mutualité (AIM) (International Association of Mutual Health Funds): 50 rue d'Arlon, 5th Floor, 1000 Brussels, Belgium; tel. (2) 234-57-00; fax (2) 234-57-08; e-mail aim.secretariat@aim-mutual.org; internet www.aim-mutual.org; f. 1950 as a grouping of autonomous health insurance and social protection bodies; aims to promote and reinforce access to health care by developing the sound management of mutualities; serves as a forum for exchange of information and debate; mems: 45 national federations in 28 countries; Pres. WILLI BUDDE (Germany); publs *AIMS* (newsletter), reports on health issues.

Aviation sans Frontières (ASF): Orly Fret 768, 94398 Orly Aérogare Cédex, France; tel. 1-49-75-74-37; fax 1-49-75-74-33; e-mail asfparis@asf-fr.org; internet www.asf-fr.org; f. 1983 to make available the resources of the aviation industry to humanitarian organizations, for carrying supplies and equipment at minimum cost, both on long-distance flights and locally; Pres. HUGUES GENDRE; Gen. Sec. PATRICK SAUMONT.

Caritas Internationalis (International Confederation of Catholic Organizations for charitable and social action): Palazzo San Calisto, 00120 Città del Vaticano; tel. (06) 6987-9799; fax (06) 6988-7237; e-mail caritas.internationalis@caritas.va; internet www.caritas.org; f. 1950 to study problems arising from poverty, their causes and possible solutions; national mem. organizations undertake assistance and development activities. The Confederation co-ordinates emergency relief and development projects, and represents mems at international level; mems: 162 national orgs; Pres. Cardinal OSCAR RODRIGUEZ MARADIAGA (Honduras); Sec.-Gen. MICHEL ROY (France); publs *Caritas Matters* (quarterly), *Emergency Calling* (2 a year).

CISV International Ltd: Mea House, Ellison Pl., Newcastle upon Tyne, NE1 8XS, United Kingdom; tel. (191) 232-4998; fax (191) 261-4710; e-mail international@cisv.org; internet www.cisv.org; f. 1950 as the International Association of Children's International Summer Villages to promote peace, education and cross-cultural friendship; conducts International Camps for children and young people mainly between the ages of 11 and 19; mems: c. 49,000; International Pres. ARNE-CHRISTIAN HAUKELAND; Sec.-Gen. GABRIELLE MANDELL.

CIVICUS (World Alliance for Citizen Participation): POB 933, Southdale, Johannesburg 2135, South Africa; tel. (11) 833-5959; fax (11) 833-7997; e-mail info@civicus.org; internet www.civicus.org; f. 1993; aims to protect and strengthen citizen action and civil society throughout the world, in particular in areas where participatory democracy and citizen freedoms are threatened; convenes a World Assembly every two years (2012: Montréal, Canada, in Sept.); mems: 450 orgs in 110 countries; Acting Sec.-Gen. KATSUJI IMATA (Japan).

Co-ordinating Committee for International Voluntary Service (CCIVS): Maison de l'UNESCO, 1 rue Miollis, 75732 Paris Cédex 15, France; tel. 1-45-68-49-36; fax 1-42-73-05-21; e-mail secretariat@ccivs.org; internet www.ccivs.org; f. 1948 to co-ordinate youth voluntary service organizations world-wide; organizes seminars and conferences; publishes relevant literature; undertakes planning and execution of projects in collaboration with UNESCO, the UN, the EU etc.; affiliated mems: 220 orgs in more than 100 countries; Pres. JINSU YOM; Dir FRANCESCO VOLPINI; publs *News from CCIVS* (3 a year), *The Volunteer's Handbook*, other guides, handbooks and directories.

Co-ordinator of the Indigenous Organizations of the Amazon Basin (COICA): Calle Sevilla 24–358 y Guipuzcoa, La Floresta, Quito, Ecuador; e-mail com@coica.org.ec; internet www.coica.org.ec; f. 1984; aims to co-ordinate the activities of national organizations concerned with the indigenous people and environment of the Amazon basin, and promotes respect for human rights and the self-determination of the indigenous populations; 9 member orgs; Co-ordinator-Gen. EDWIN VÁSQUEZ CAMPOS; publ. *Nuestra Amazonia* (quarterly, in English, Spanish, French and Portuguese).

EIRENE (International Christian Service for Peace): Postfach 1322, 56503 Neuwied, Germany; tel. (2631) 83790; fax (2631) 837990; e-mail eirene-int@eirene.org; internet www.eirene.org; f. 1957; carries out professional training, apprenticeship programmes, agricultural work and work to support co-operatives in Africa and Latin America; runs volunteer programmes in co-operation with peace groups in Europe and the USA; Gen. Sec. ANGELA KÖNIG.

European Federation of Older Persons (EURAG): Mozartgasse 14A, 8010 Graz, Austria; tel. (316) 380-29-64; fax (316) 380-92-12; e-mail dana_stein@volny.cz; internet eurageurope.org; f. 1962 as the European Federation for the Welfare of the Elderly (present name adopted 2002); serves as a forum for the exchange of experience and practical co-operation among member organizations; represents the interests of members before international organizations; promotes understanding and co-operation in matters of social welfare; draws attention to the problems of old age; mems: 148 orgs in 33 countries; Pres. Dr EVELINE HÖNIGSPERGER; Sec.-Gen. DANA STEINOVA (Czech Republic); publ. (in English, French, German and Italian) *EURAG Information* (monthly).

Federation of Asia-Pacific Women's Associations (FAWA): 962 Josefa Llanes Escoda St, Ermita, Manila, Philippines; tel. (2) 741-1675; e-mail nfwcp@yahoo.com; internet fawainternational.org; f. 1959 to provide closer relations, and bring about joint efforts among Asians, particularly women, through mutual appreciation of cultural, moral and socio-economic values; mems: 415,000; Pres. KRISTAL KOGA (USA); Sec. REBECCA STEPHENSON (USA); publ. *FAWA News Bulletin* (quarterly).

Global Migration Group: c/o UNICEF, 3 United Nations Plaza, New York, NY 10017, USA; tel. and fax (212) 906-5001; internet www.globalmigrationgroup.org; f. 2003, as the Geneva Migration Group; renamed as above in 2006; mems: ILO, IOM, UNCTAD, UNDP, United Nations Department of Economic and Social Affairs (UNDESA), UNFPA, OHCHR, UNHCR, UNODC, and the World Bank; holds regular meetings to discuss issues relating to int. migration, chaired by mem. orgs on a six-month rotational basis.

Inclusion Europe: Galeries de la Toison d'Or, 29 ch. d'Ixelles, bte 393/32, 1050 Brussels, Belgium; tel. (2) 502-28-15; fax (2) 502-80-10; e-mail secretariat@inclusion-europe.org; internet www.inclusion-europe.org; f. 1988 to advance the human rights and defend the interests of people with learning or intellectual disabilities, and their families, in Europe; mems: 46 societies in 34 European countries; Pres. MAUREEN PIGGOT (United Kingdom); publs *INCLUDE* (in English and French), *Information Letter* (weekly online, in English and French), *Human Rights Observer* (in English and French), *Enlargement Update* (online every 2 weeks, in English and French), other papers and publs.

Initiatives of Change International: 1 rue de Varembé, 1202 Geneva, Switzerland; tel. 227491620; fax 227330267; e-mail iofc-international@iofc.org; internet www.iofc.org; f. 1921; an international network specializing in conflict resolution that is open to people of all cultures, nationalities, religions and beliefs, and works towards change, both locally and globally, commencing at the personal level; has special consultative status with ECOSOC and participatory status with the Council of Europe; supports and publicizes the grassroots work of the National Societies of Initiatives of Change; works in 60 countries; fmrly the Moral Rearmament (MRA) movement; current name adopted in 2001; Pres. OMNIA MARZOUK; publs *Changer International* (French, 6 a year), *For a Change* (English, 6 a year), *Caux Information* (German, monthly).

Inter-American Conference on Social Security (Conferencia Interamericano de Seguridad Social—CISS): c/o F. Flores, Instituto Mexicano del Seguro Social, Paseo de la Reforma 476, 1°, Col. Juarez, Del. Cuauhtemoc, CP 06600, México, DF, Mexico; tel. (55) 5211-4853; fax (55) 5211-2623; e-mail ciss@ciss.org.mx; internet www.ciss.org.mx; f. 1942 to contribute to the development of social security in the countries of the Americas and to co-operate with social security institutions; CISS bodies are: the General Assembly, the Permanent Inter-American Committee on Social Security, the Secretariat General, six American Commissions of Social Security and the Inter-American Center for Social Security Studies; mems: 66 social security institutions in 36 countries; Pres. DANIEL KARAM TOUMEH (Mexico); Sec.-Gen. Dr GABRIEL MARTÍNEZ GONZÁLEZ (Mexico); publs *Social Security Journal/Seguridad Social* (every 2 months), *The Americas Social Security Report* (annually), *Social Security Bulleting* (monthly, online), monographs, study series.

International Association for Suicide Prevention: IASP Central Administrative Office, Sognsvannsveien 21, Bygg 12, 0372 Oslo, Norway; tel. 22-92-37-15; fax 22-92-39-58; e-mail office@iasp.info; internet www.iasp.info; f. 1960; serves as a common platform for interchange of acquired experience, literature and information about suicide; disseminates information; arranges special training; encourages and carries out research; organizes the Biennial International Congress for Suicide Prevention (Sept. 2013: Oslo, Norway); mems: 340 individuals and societies, in 55 countries of all continents; Pres. Dr LANNY BERMAN; publ. *Crisis* (quarterly).

International Association of Schools of Social Work: c/o A. Tasse, Graduate School of Social Work, University of Addis Ababa, POB 1176, Ethiopia; tel. (1) 231084; fax (1) 239768; e-mail abye

.tasse@ids.fr; internet www.iassw-aiets.org; f. 1928 to provide international leadership and encourage high standards in social work education; mems: 1,600 schools of social work in 70 countries, and 25 national asscns of schools; Pres. Prof. Dr ANGELINA YUEN (Hong Kong, SAR); Sec. HELLE STRAUSS; publs *Newsletters* (in English, French and Spanish), *Directory of Schools of Social Work*, *Journal of International Social Work*, reports and case studies.

International Association of Social Educators (AIEJI): Galgebakken Soender 5-4, DK-2620 Albertslund, Denmark; tel. 72486841; e-mail dee@sl.dk; internet www.aieji.net; f. 1951 (as International Asscn of Workers for Troubled Children and Youth); provides a centre of information about child welfare; encourages co-operation between members; 2013 Congress: Luxembourg, in April; mems: national and regional public or private asscns from 22 countries and individual members in many other countries; Pres. BENNY ANDERSEN (Denmark); Gen. Sec. LARS STEINOV (Denmark).

International Catholic Migration Commission (ICMC): 37–39 rue de Vermont, CP 96, 1211 Geneva 20, Switzerland; tel. 229191020; fax 229191048; e-mail info@icmc.net; internet www.icmc.net; f. 1951; serves and protects uprooted people (refugees, internationally displaced persons and migrants), regardless of faith, race, ethnicity or nationality; maintains staff and programmes in more than 40 countries; advocates for rights-based policies and durable solutions; Pres. JOHN KLINK (USA); Sec.-Gen. JOHAN KETELERS (Belgium).

International Civil Defence Organization (ICDO) (Organisation internationale de protection civile—OIPC): POB 172, 10–12 chemin de Surville, 1213 Petit-Lancy 2, Geneva, Switzerland; tel. 228796969; fax 228796979; e-mail icdo@icdo.org; internet www.icdo.org; f. 1931, present statutes in force 1972; aims to contribute to the development of structures ensuring the protection of populations and the safeguarding of property and the environment in the face of natural and man-made disasters; promotes co-operation between civil defence organizations in member countries; Sec.-Gen. NAWAF B. S. AL SLEIBI (Jordan); publ. *International Civil Defence Journal* (quarterly, in Arabic, English, French, Russian and Chinese).

International Commission for the Prevention of Alcoholism and Drug Dependency: 12501 Old Columbia Pike, Silver Spring, MD 20904-6600, USA; tel. (301) 680-6719; fax (301) 680-6707; e-mail the_icpa@hotmail.com; f. 1952 to encourage scientific research on intoxication by alcohol, its physiological, mental and moral effects on the individual, and its effect on the community; mems: individuals in 120 countries; Exec. Dir Dr PETER N. LANDLESS; publ. *ICPA Reporter*.

International Council of Voluntary Agencies (ICVA): 26–28 ave Guiseppe Motta, 1202 Geneva, Switzerland; tel. 229509600; fax 229509609; e-mail secretariat@icva.ch; internet www.icva.ch; f. 1962 as a global network of human rights and humanitarian non-governmental organizations; focuses on information exchange and advocacy, primarily in the areas of humanitarian affairs and refugee issues; mems: 74 non-governmental orgs; Chair. PAUL O'BRIEN; Co-ordinator ED SCHENKENBERG VAN MIEROP; publ. *Talk Back* (newsletter, available online).

International Council of Women (ICW) (Conseil International des Femmes—CIF): 13 rue Caumartin, 75009 Paris, France; tel. 1-47-42-19-40; fax 1-42-66-26-23; e-mail icw-cif@wanadoo.fr; internet www.icw-cif.org; f. 1888 to bring together in international affiliation Nat. Councils of Women from all continents, for consultation and joint action; promotes equal rights for men and women and the integration of women in development and decision-making; has five standing committees; mems: 65 national councils; Pres. COSIMA SCHENK; Sec.-Gen. RADOSVETA BRUZAUD; publ. *Newsletter*.

International Council on Alcohol and Addictions (ICAA): CP 189, 1001 Lausanne, Switzerland; tel. 213209865; fax 213209817; e-mail secretariat@icaa.ch; internet www.icaa.ch; f. 1907; provides an international forum for all those concerned with the prevention of harm resulting from the use of alcohol and other drugs; offers advice and guidance in development of policies and programmes; organizes training courses, congresses, symposia and seminars in different countries; mems: affiliated orgs in 74 countries, as well as individual members; Pres. Dr PETER A. VAMOS (Canada); publs *ICAA Newsflash*, *Alcoholism* (2 a year), *President's Letter*.

International Council on Social Welfare (ICSW): Berkerly Lane, Plot 4, Entebbe, POB 28957, Kampala, Uganda; tel. (414) 32-1150; e-mail dcorrell@icsw.org; internet www.icsw.org; f. 1928 to provide an international forum for the discussion of social work and related issues and to promote interest in social welfare; holds international conference every two years with the International Association of Schools of Social Work and the International Federation of Social Workers; provides documentation and information services; mems: 57 national cttees, 6 int. orgs, 34 other orgs in 87 countries; Pres. CHRISTIAN ROLLET; Exec. Dir DENYS CORRELL; publ. *Global Cooperation Newsletter Monthly*.

International Dachau Committee: 2 rue Chauchat, 75009 Paris, France; tel. 1-45-23-39-99; fax 1-48-00-06-13; e-mail info@comiteinternationaldachau.com; internet www.comiteinternationaldachau.com; f. 1958 to perpetuate the memory of the political prisoners of Dachau; to manifest the friendship and solidarity of former prisoners whatever their beliefs or nationality; to maintain the ideals of their resistance, liberty, tolerance and respect for persons and nations; and to maintain the former concentration camp at Dachau as a museum and international memorial; mems: national asscns in 20 countries; Pres. PIETER DIETZ DE LOOS; publ. *Bulletin Officiel du Comité International de Dachau* (2 a year).

International Federation for Human Rights Leagues (FIDH): 17 passage de la Main d'Or, 75011 Paris, France; tel. 1-43-55-25-18; fax 1-43-55-18-80; e-mail fidh@fidh.org; internet www.fidh.org; f. 1922; promotes the implementation of the Universal Declaration of Human Rights and other instruments of human rights protection; aims to raise awareness and alert public opinion to issues of human rights violations; undertakes investigation and observation missions; carries out training; uses its consultative and observer status to lobby international authorities; mems: 155 national leagues in over 100 countries; Pres. SOUHAYR BELHASSEN (Tunisia); Exec. Dir ANTOINE BERNARD; publs *Lettre* (2 a month), mission reports.

International Federation of Educative Communities (FICE): Vogelsbergstrasse 212, 63679 Schotten, Germany; tel. (60) 4460090; fax (60) 444394; e-mail info@fice.de; internet www.fice-europe.org; f. 1948 under the auspices of UNESCO to co-ordinate the work of national asscns, and to promote the international exchange of knowledge and experience in the field of childcare; Congress held every two years; mems: national asscns from 21 European countries, Canada, India, Israel, Morocco, South Africa and the USA; Pres. MONIKA NIEDERLE (Austria); Gen. Sec. ANDREW HOSIE (United Kingdom); publ. *Bulletin* (2 a year).

International Federation of Persons with Physical Disability (FIMITIC): Rákóczi út. 36, 2600 Vác, Hungary; tel. and fax (27) 502661; e-mail fimitic@invitel.hu; internet www.fimitic.org; f. 1953; an international, humanitarian, non-profit, politically and religiously neutral non-governmental umbrella federation of persons with physical disability under the guidance of the disabled themselves; focuses activities on ensuring the equalization of opportunities and full participation of persons with physical disabilities in society and fights against any kind of discrimination against persons with disabilities; mems: national groups from 28 European countries; Pres. MIGUEL ANGEL GARCÍA OCA (Spain); publs *Bulletin*, *Nouvelles*.

International Federation of Social Workers (IFSW): POB 6875, Schwarztorstrasse 22, 3001 Bern, Switzerland; tel. 225483625; fax 313808301; e-mail global@ifsw.org; internet www.ifsw.org; f. 1928 as International Permanent Secretariat of Social Workers; present name adopted 1956; aims to promote social work as a profession through international co-operation on standards, training, ethics and working conditions; organizes international conferences; represents the profession at the UN and other international bodies; supports national asscns of social workers; mems: national asscns in 90 countries; Pres. GARY BAILEY (USA); Sec.-Gen, Dr RORY G. TRUELL (New Zealand); publs *IFSW update* (available online), policy statements and manifestos.

International Federation of the Blue Cross: CP 6813, 3001 Bern, Switzerland; tel. 313005860; fax 313005869; e-mail office@ifbc.info; internet www.ifbc.info; f. 1877 to aid the victims of intemperance and drug addiction, and to take part in the general movement against alcoholism; mems: 40 orgs; Pres. GEIR GUNDERSEN (Norway); Sec.-Gen MARK MOSER.

International League against Racism and Antisemitism (La Ligue Internationale contre le Racisme et l'Antisémitisme—LICRA): 42 rue du Louvre, 75001 Paris, France; tel. 1-45-08-08-08; fax 1-45-08-18-18; e-mail licra@licra.org; internet www.licra.org; f. 1927; campaigns against all forms of racism in sport, culture, education, law etc.; Pres. ALAIN JAKUBOWICZ.

International League for Human Rights: 352 Seventh Ave, Suite 1234, New York, NY 10001, USA; tel. (212) 661-0480; fax (212) 661-0416; e-mail info@ilhr.org; internet www.ilhr.org; f. 1942 to implement political, civil, social, economic and cultural rights contained in the Universal Declaration of Human Rights adopted by the United Nations and to support and protect defenders of human rights world-wide; maintains offices in Geneva, Switzerland, and in Freetown, Sierra Leone; mems: individuals, national affiliates and correspondents throughout the world; Pres. ROBERT ARSENAULT; Exec. Dir DAVID TAM-BARYOH; publs various human rights reports.

International Planned Parenthood Federation (IPPF): 4 Newhams Row, London, SE1 3UZ, United Kingdom; tel. (20) 7939-8200; fax (20) 7939-8300; e-mail info@ippf.org; internet www.ippf.org; f. 1952; aims to promote and support sexual and reproductive health rights and choices world-wide, with a particular focus on the needs of young people; works to bring relevant issues to the attention of the media, parliamentarians, academics, governmental and non-governmental organizations, and the general public; mobilizes financial resources to fund programmes and information materials; offers technical assistance and training; collaborates with other international organizations; the International Medical Panel of the IPPF formulates guidelines and statements on current medical and scientific advice and best practices; mems: independent family planning asscns in over 151 countries; Pres. Dr JACQUELINE SHARPE; Dir-Gen. Dr GILL GREER.

International Prisoners' Aid Association: POB 7333, Arlington, VA 22207, USA; tel. (703) 836-0024; fax (703) 836-0024; e-mail desifl@aol.com; f. 1950; works to improve prisoners' aid services, with the aim of promoting the rehabilitation of the individual and increasing the protection of society; mems: national federations in 29 countries; Pres. Dr WOLFGANG DOLEISCH (Austria); Exec. Dir Dr ELIZABETH DESIDERIO GONDLES; publ. *Newsletter* (3 a year).

International Social Security Association (ISSA): 4 route des Morillons, CP 1, 1211 Geneva 22, Switzerland; tel. 227996617; fax 227998509; e-mail issa@ilo.org; internet www.issa.int; f. 1927 to promote the development of social security throughout the world, mainly through the improvement of techniques and administration, in order to advance social and economic conditions on the basis of social justice; collects and disseminates information on social security programmes throughout the world; undertakes research and policy analysis on the social security issues and distributes their results; encourages mutual assistance between member orgs; facilitates good practice collection and exchange; co-operates with other international or regional orgs exercising activities related to the field; communicates with its constituency and media and promotes social security through advocacy and information; and forges partnerships between the ISSA and other international orgs active in the area of social security to advance common strategies, including the ILO, the OECD and the World Bank; organizes a World Social Security Forum (2013: Doha, Qatar, in Nov.) and four Regional Social Security Forums (in Africa, the Americas, Asia/Pacific and Europe); convenes topic-related technical seminars in various regions; hosts international conferences, for example on information and communication technology in social security, social security actuaries and statisticians, and international policy research; co-organizes the World Congress on Occupational Safety and Health every three years; mems: 340 institutions in 150 countries; Pres. CORAZON DE LA PAZ-BERNARDO (Philippines); Sec.-Gen. HANS-HORST KONKOLEWSKY; publs *International Social Security Review* (quarterly, in English, French, German, Spanish), *Social Security Observer* (quarterly, in English, French, German, Spanish), *Social Security Worldwide*, online Social Security Observatory and other databases.

International Social Service (Service social international—SSI): 32 quai du Seujet, 1201 Geneva, Switzerland; tel. 229067700; fax 229067701; e-mail info@iss-ssi.org; internet www.iss-ssi.org; f. 1921 to aid families and individuals whose problems require services beyond the boundaries of the country in which they live, and where the solution of these problems depends upon co-ordinated action on the part of social workers in two or more countries; studies from an international standpoint the conditions and consequences of emigration in their effect on individual, family, and social life; operates on a non-sectarian and non-political basis; mems: 13 branches, 4 affiliated bureaux, and correspondents in more than 120 countries; Pres. a.i. DOUG LEWIS; Sec.-Gen. JEAN AYOUB.

International Union of Tenants: Box 7514, 10392 Stockholm, Sweden; tel. (8) 7910224; fax (8) 204344; e-mail info@iut.nu; internet www.iut.nu; f. 1955 to collaborate in safeguarding the interests of tenants; participates in activities of UN-Habitat; has working groups for EC matters, eastern Europe, developing countries and for future development; holds annual council meeting and triennial congress; mems: national tenant orgs in 29 European countries, and Australia, Benin, Canada, India, Japan, New Zealand, Nigeria, South Africa, Tanzania, Togo, Uganda, and USA; Chair. SVEN BERGENSTRÅHLE; Sec.-Gen. MAGNUS HAMMAR; publ. *The Global Tenant* (quarterly).

Inter-University European Institute on Social Welfare (IEISW): 179 rue du Débarcadère, 6001 Marcinelle, Belgium; tel. (71) 44-72-67; fax (71) 47-27-44; e-mail ieiasmayence@hotmail.com; f. 1970 to promote, carry out and publicize scientific research on social welfare and community work; Pres. JOSEPH GILLAIN; Gen. Dir SERGE MAYENCE; publ. *COMM*.

Lions Clubs International: 300 West 22nd St, Oak Brook, IL 60523-8842, USA; tel. (630) 571-5466; fax (630) 571-8890; e-mail lions@lionsclubs.org; internet www.lionsclubs.org; f. 1917 to foster understanding among people of the world; to promote principles of good government and citizenship and an interest in civic, cultural, social and moral welfare and to encourage service-minded people to serve their community without financial reward; mems: 1.35m. in over 45,000 clubs in 197 countries and geographic areas; Pres. WING-KUN TAM; publ. *The Lion* (10 a year, in 20 languages).

Médecins sans frontières (MSF): 78 rue de Lausanne, CP 116, 1211 Geneva 21, Switzerland; tel. 228498400; fax 228498404; internet www.msf.org; f. 1971; independent medical humanitarian org. composed of physicians and other members of the medical profession; aims to provide medical assistance to victims of war and natural disasters; operates longer-term programmes of nutrition, immunization, sanitation, public health, and rehabilitation of hospitals and dispensaries; awarded the Nobel Peace Prize in 1999; mems: national sections in 21 countries in Europe, Asia and North America; Pres. Dr UNNI KRISHNAN KARUNAKARA; Sec.-Gen. KRIS TORGESON; publ. *Activity Report* (annually).

Pan-Pacific and South East Asia Women's Association (PPSEAWA): POB 119, Nuku'alofa, Tonga; tel. 24003; fax 41404; e-mail info@ppseawa.org; internet www.ppseawa.org; f. 1928 to foster better understanding and friendship among women in the region, and to promote co-operation for the study and improvement of social conditions; holds international conference every three years (2013: Suva, Fiji, in Aug.); mems: 22 national member orgs; Pres. Dr VIOPAPA ANNANDALE; publ. *PPSEAWA Bulletin* (2 a year).

Relief International: 5455 Wilshire Blvd, Suite 1280 Los Angeles, CA 90024, USA; tel. (310) 478-1200; fax (310) 478-1212; e-mail info@ri.org; internet ri.org; f. 1990 to provide emergency relief, rehabilitation and development assistance to people suffering as a result of social conflict or natural disaster; CEO and Pres. FARSHAD RASTEGAR.

Rotary International: 1560 Sherman Ave, Evanston, IL 60201, USA; tel. (847) 866-3000; fax (847) 328-3000; e-mail ers@rotary.org; internet www.rotary.org; f. 1905 to carry out activities for the service of humanity, to promote high ethical standards in business and professions and to further international understanding, goodwill and peace; mems: 1.2m. in more than 32,000 Rotary Clubs in more than 200 countries; Pres. KALYAN BANERJEE (until 30 June 2012), SAKUJI TANAKA (Japan) (designate); Gen. Sec. EDWIN H. FUTA (USA); publs *The Rotarian* (monthly, English), *Rotary World* (5 a year, in 9 languages).

Service Civil International (SCI): St-Jacobsmarkt 82, 2000 Antwerp, Belgium; tel. (3) 226-57-27; fax (3) 232-03-44; e-mail info@sciint.org; internet www.sciint.org; f. 1920 to promote peace and understanding through voluntary service projects; more than 3,000 volunteers participate in SCI volunteer projects world-wide each year; SCI is also active in the field of peace education and organizes seminars, training activities and meetings; mems: 43 branches world-wide; Int. Pres. MIHAI CRISAN (Romania); publ. *Action* (quarterly).

Shack/Slum Dwellers International (SDI): POB 14038, Mowbray 7705 Cape Town, South Africa; tel. (21) 689-9408; fax (21) 689-3912; e-mail sdi@courc.co.za; internet www.sdinet.co.za; f. 1996; a transnational network of local shack/slum dweller orgs; Pres. ARPUTHAM JOCKIN.

Society of Saint Vincent de Paul: 6 rue du Londres, 75009 Paris, France; tel. 1-53-45-87-53; fax 1-42-61-72-56; e-mail cgi.information@ozanet.org; internet www.ssvpglobal.org; f. 1833 to conduct charitable activities such as childcare, youth work, work with immigrants, adult literacy programmes, residential care for the sick, handicapped and elderly, social counselling and work with prisoners and the unemployed, through personal contact; mems: over 700,000 in 141 countries; Pres. MICHAEL THIO; Sec.-Gen. BRUNO MENARD; publ. *Confeder@tioNews* (quarterly, in English, French and Spanish).

SOLIDAR: 22 rue de Commerce, 1000 Brussels, Belgium; tel. (2) 500-10-20; fax (2) 500-10-30; e-mail solidar@solidar.org; internet www.solidar.org; f. 1948 (fmrly International Workers' Aid); network of non-governmental orgs working to advance social justice in Europe and world-wide; mems: 52 orgs based in 25 countries, operating in more than 90 countries; Sec.-Gen. CONNY REUTER.

Soroptimist International: 87 Glisson Rd, Cambridge, CB1 2HG, United Kingdom; tel. (1223) 311833; fax (1223) 467951; e-mail hq@soroptimistinternational.org; internet www.soroptimistinternational.org; f. 1921; unites professional and business women in promoting a world where women and girls may achieve their individual and collective potential, attain equality, and establish strong, peaceful communities world-wide; aims, through a global network of members and international partnerships, to inspire action, and to create opportunities, that might transform the lives of women and girls; convention held every four years (2012: Porto Alegre, Brazil, in Jan., on the theme 'Capitalist Crisis, Social Justice and Environment'); mems: about 90,000 in 3,000 clubs in 124 countries and territories; International Pres. ALICE WELLS (USA) (2011–13); Exec. Officer (vacant); publ. *The International Soroptimist* (quarterly).

Women for Women International: 4455 Connecticut Ave, NW, Suite 200, Washington, DC 20008, USA; tel. (202) 737-7705; fax (202) 737-7709; e-mail general@womenforwomen.org; internet www.womenforwomen.org; f. 1993; aims to assist the recovery and rehabilitation of women in conflict and post-conflict environments, in order to promote sustainable and peaceful societies; Pres. and Chief Operating Officer ANDRÉE SIMON.

World Blind Union: 1929 Bayview Ave, Toronto, ON M4G 3E8, Canada; tel. (416) 486-9698; fax (416) 486-8107; e-mail info@wbuoffice.org; internet www.worldblindunion.org; f. 1984 (amalgamating the World Council for the Welfare of the Blind and the International Federation of the Blind) to work for the prevention of blindness and the welfare of blind and visually impaired people; encourages development of braille, talking book programmes and other media for the blind; organizes rehabilitation, training and employment; works on the prevention and cure of blindness in co-operation with the International Agency for the Prevention of Blindness; co-ordinates aid to the blind in developing countries; maintains the Louis Braille birthplace as an international museum; mems: in 190 countries; Pres. MARYANNE DIAMOND (Australia); Sec.-Gen. ENRIQUE PÉREZ (Spain); publ. *E-Bulletin* (quarterly).

World Family Organization (WFO): 28 pl. Saint-Georges, 75009 Paris, France; tel. 1-48-78-07-59; fax 1-42-82-95-24; e-mail info@worldfamilyorganization.org; internet www.worldfamilyorganization.org; f. 1947 as the International Union of Family Organizations (IUOF), to bring together all organizations throughout the world working for family welfare; present name adopted 1998; maintains commissions and working groups on issues including standards of living, housing, marriage guidance, rural families, etc.; there are six regional organizations: the Pan-African Family Organisation (Rabat, Morocco), the North America organization (Montréal, Canada), the Arab Family Organisation (Tunis, Tunisia), the Asian Union of Family Organisations (New Delhi, India), the European regional organization (Bern, Switzerland) and the Latin American Secretariat (Curitiba, Brazil); mems: national asscns, groups and governmental departments in over 55 countries; Pres. Dr DEISI NOELI WEBER KUSZTRA (Brazil).

World Federation of the Deaf (WFD): POB 65, 00401 Helsinki, Finland; tel. (9) 5803573; fax (9) 5803572; e-mail Info@wfdeaf.org; internet www.wfdeaf.org; f. 1951 to serve the interests of deaf people and their national organizations and represent these in international fora; works towards the goal of full participation by deaf people in society; encourages deaf people to set up and run their own organizations; priority is given to the promotion of the recognition and use of national sign languages, the education of deaf people and deaf people in the developing world; mems: 133 member countries; Pres. COLIN ALLEN; publ. *WFD Newsletter* (6 a year).

World ORT: ORT House, 126 Albert St, London, NW1 7NE, United Kingdom; tel. (20) 7446-8500; fax (20) 7446-8650; e-mail wo@ort.org; internet www.ort.org; f. 1880 for the development of industrial, agricultural and artisanal skills among Jews; conducts vocational training programmes for children and adults, including instructors' and teachers' education and apprenticeship training; implements technical assistance programmes in co-operation with interested governments; manages global network of schools, colleges, training centres and programmes; has assisted more than 3m. people; mems: committees in more than 40 countries; Pres. JEAN DE GUNZBURG; Dir-Gen. ROBERT SINGER; publs *Annual Report*, *World ORT Times*.

World Social Forum (WSF): Support Office: Rua General Jardim 660, 7° andar, São Paulo, Brazil 01223-010; tel. (11) 3258-8914; fax (11) 3258-8469; e-mail fsminfo@forumsocialmundial.org.br; internet www.forumsocialmundial.org.br; f. 2001 as an annual global meeting of civil society bodies; a Charter of Principles was adopted in June 2002; the WSF is a permanent global process which aims to pursue alternatives to neo-liberal policies and commercial globalization; its objectives include the development and promotion of democratic international systems and institutions serving social justice, equality and the sovereignty of peoples, based on respect for the universal human rights of citizens of all nations and for the environment; the 10th (2011) WSF was held in Dakar, Senegal, in February; an International Council, comprising more than 150 civil society orgs and commissions, guides the Forum and considers general political questions and methodology; the Support Office in São Paulo, Brazil, provides administrative assistance to the Forum process, to the International Council and to the specific organizing committees for each biannual event; mems: civil society orgs and movements world-wide.

World Veterans Federation: 17 rue Nicolo, 75116 Paris, France; tel. 1-40-72-61-00; fax 1-40-72-80-58; e-mail wvf@wvf-fmac.org; internet www.wvf-fmac.org; f. 1950 to maintain international peace and security by the application of the San Francisco Charter and work to help implement the Universal Declaration of Human Rights and related international conventions; aims to defend the spiritual and material interests of war veterans and war victims; promotes practical international co-operation in disarmament, legislation concerning war veterans and war victims, and development of international humanitarian law, etc.; maintains regional committees for Africa, Asia and the Pacific, and Europe and a Standing Committee on Women; mems: 173 national orgs in 90 countries, representing about 27m. war veterans and war victims; Pres. ABDUL HAMID IBRAHIM (Malaysia); Sec.-Gen. MOHAMMED BENJELLOUN (Morocco); publ. *WVF News*.

Zonta International: 1211 W 22nd St, Suite 900, Oak Brook, IL 60523, USA; tel. (630) 928-1400; fax (630) 928-1559; e-mail zontaintl@zonta.org; internet www.zonta.org; f. 1919; links executives in business and the professions, with the aim of advancing the status of women world-wide; carries out local and international projects; supports women's education and leadership; makes fellowship awards in various fields; mems: 30,000 in 63 countries and areas; Pres. DIANNE CURTIS; Exec. Dir JASON FRISKE; publ. *The Zontian* (quarterly).

Sport and Recreations

Badminton World Federation: Batu 3, 1/2 Jalan Cheras, 56000 Kuala Lumpur, Malaysia; tel. (3) 92837155; fax (3) 92847155; e-mail bwf@bwfbadminton.org; internet www.internationalbadminton.org; f. 1934, as International Badminton Federation, to oversee the sport of badminton world-wide; mems: affiliated national orgs in 164 countries and territories; Pres. Dr KANG YOUNG JOONG; Chief Operating Officer THOMAS LUND; publs *World Badminton* (available online), *Statute Book* (annually).

Confederation of African Football (Confédération africaine de football—CFA): 3 Abdel Khalek Sarwat St, El Hay El Motamayez, POB 23, 6th October City, Egypt; tel. (2) 38371000; fax (2) 38370006; e-mail info@cafonline.com; internet www.cafonline.com; f. 1957; promotes football in Africa; organizes inter-club competitions and Cup of Nations; General Assembly held every two years; mems: national asscns in 54 countries; Pres. ISSA HAYATOU (Cameroon); Sec.-Gen. HICHAM EL AMRANI (Morocco) (acting); publ. *CAF News* (quarterly).

Fédération Aéronautique Internationale (FAI) (World Air Sports Federation): 24 ave Mon Repos, 1005 Lausanne, Switzerland; tel. 213451070; fax 213451077; e-mail sec@fai.org; internet www.fai.org; f. 1905 to promote all aeronautical sports; sanctions world championships; develops rules through Air Sports Commissions; endorses world aeronautical and astronautical records; mems: in 100 countries and territories; Pres. PIERRE PORTMANN; Sec.-Gen. STÉPHANE DESPREZ (France).

Fédération Internationale de Philatélie (FIP): Biberlinstrasse 6, 8032 Zürich, Switzerland; tel. 444223839; fax 444223843; e-mail ats@f-i-p.ch; internet www.f-i-p.ch/; f. 1926 to promote philately internationally; also aims to establish and maintain close relations with the philatelic trade and postal administrations and to promote philatelic exhibitions; mems: 87 national federations, 3 associated mems (continental federations); Pres. JOSEPH WOLFF (Luxembourg); Sec.-Gen. ANDRÉE TROMMER (Luxembourg); publ. quarterly journal.

International Amateur Athletic Federation: 17 rue Princesse Florestine, BP 359, 98007 Monte Carlo Cédex, Monaco; tel. 93-10-88-88; fax 93-15-95-15; e-mail info@iaaf.org; internet www.iaaf.org; f. 1912 to ensure co-operation and fairness and to combat discrimination in athletics; compiles athletic competition rules and organizes championships at all levels; frames regulations for the establishment of World, Olympic and other athletic records; settles disputes between members; conducts a programme of development consisting of coaching, judging courses, etc.; and affiliates national governing bodies; mems: national asscns in 213 countries and territories; Pres. LAMINE DIACK (Senegal); Gen. Sec. PIERRE WEISS (France); publs *IAAF Handbook* (every 2 years), *IAAF Review* (quarterly), *IAAF Directory* (annually), *New Studies in Athletics* (quarterly).

International Automobile Federation (Fédération Internationale de l'Automobile—FIA): 2 chemin de Blandonnet, CP 296, 1215 Geneva, Switzerland; tel. 225444400; fax 225444450; e-mail admin@fiacommunications.com; internet www.fia.com; f. 1904; manages world motor sport and organizes international championships; mems: 213 national automobile clubs and asscns in 120 countries; Pres. JEAN TODT (France); Sec.-Gen. (Sport) PIERRE DE CONINCK; Sec.-Gen. (Mobility) SUSAN PIKRALLIDAS.

International Basketball Federation (Fédération Internationale de Basketball): 53 ave Louis Casai, 1216 Cointrin/Geneva, Switzerland; tel. 225450000; fax 225450099; e-mail info@fiba.com; internet www.fiba.com; f. 1932, as International Amateur Basketball Federation (present name adopted 1989); world governing body for basketball; mems: 213 affiliated national federations; Pres. YVAN MAININI (France); Sec.-Gen. PATRICK BAUMANN (Switzerland); publ. *FIBA Assist* (monthly).

International Boxing Association (AIBA): Maison du Sport International, 54 ave de Rhodanie, 1007 Lausanne, Switzerland; tel. 213212777; fax 213212772; e-mail info@aiba.org; internet www.aiba.org; f. 1946 as the world body controlling amateur boxing for the Olympic Games, continental, regional and inter-nation championships and tournaments in every part of the world; mems: 195 national assns; Pres. Dr CHING-KUO WU (Republic of China); publ. *World Amateur Boxing Magazine* (quarterly).

International Canoe Federation (ICF): 54 ave de Rhodanie, 1007, Lausanne, Switzerland; tel. 216120290; fax 216120291; e-mail info@canoeicf.com; internet www.canoeicf.com; f. 1924; administers canoeing at the Olympic Games; promotes canoe/kayak activity in general; mems: 148 national federations; Pres. JOSÉ PERURENA LÓPEZ (Spain); Sec.-Gen. SIMON TOULSON.

International Council for Health, Physical Education, Recreation, Sport and Dance (ICHPERSD): 1900 Association Drive, Reston, VA 20191, USA; tel. (800) 213-7193; e-mail ichper@aaperd.org; internet www.ichpersd.org; f. 1958 to encourage the development of programmes in health, physical education, recreation, sport and dance throughout the world, by linking teaching professionals in these fields; Sec.-Gen. Dr ADEL M. ELNASHAR (Bahrain); publ. *Journal* (quarterly).

International Cricket Council: POB 500070, St 69, Dubai Sports City, Emirates Rd, Dubai, UAE; tel. (4) 382-8800; fax (4) 382-8600; e-mail enquiry@icc-cricket.com; internet www.icc-cricket.com; f. 1909 as the governing body for international cricket; holds an annual conference; mems: Australia, Bangladesh, England, India, New Zealand, Pakistan, South Africa, Sri Lanka, West Indies, Zimbabwe, and 23 associate and 13 affiliate mems; Pres. SHARAD PAWAR; CEO HAROON LORGAT.

International Cycling Union (UCI): 12 ch. de la Mêlée, 1860 Aigle, Switzerland; tel. 244685811; fax 244685812; e-mail admin@uci.ch; internet www.uci.ch; f. 1900 to develop, regulate and control all forms of cycling as a sport; mems: 160 federations; Pres. PATRICK MCQUAID (Ireland); publs *International Calendar* (annually), *Velo World* (6 a year).

International Equestrian Federation (Fédération Equestre Internationale—FEI): 37 ave Rumine, 1005 Lausanne, Switzerland; tel. 213104747; fax 213104760; e-mail info@fei.org; internet www.fei.org; f. 1921; international governing body of equestrian sport recognized by the International Olympic Committee; establishes rules and regulations for conduct of international equestrian events, including on the health and welfare of horses; mems: 135 mem. countries; Pres. HRH Princess HAYA BINT AL HUSSEIN (Jordan); Sec.-Gen. ALEXANDER MCLIN.

International Federation of Associated Wrestling Styles: 6 rue du Château, 1804 Corsier-sur-Vevey, Switzerland; tel. 213128426; fax 213236073; e-mail fila@fila-wrestling.com; internet www.fila-wrestling.com; f. 1912 to encourage the development of amateur wrestling and promote the sport in countries where it is not yet practised and to further friendly relations between all members; mems: 168 federations; Pres. RAPHAËL MARTINETTI; Sec.-Gen. MICHEL DUSSON; publs *News Bulletin*, *Wrestling Revue*.

International Federation of Association Football (Fédération internationale de football association—FIFA): FIFA-Str. 20, POB 8044, Zürich, Switzerland; tel. 432227777; fax 432227878; e-mail media@fifa.org; internet www.fifa.com; f. 1904 to promote the game of association football and foster friendly relations among players and national assns; to control football and uphold the laws of the game as laid down by the International Football Association Board; to prevent discrimination of any kind between players; and to provide arbitration in disputes between national assns; organizes World Cup competition every four years (2014: Brazil); the FIFA Executive Committee—comprising the Federation's President, eight vice-presidents and 15 members—meets at least twice a year; in May 2011 FIFA provisionally suspended, with immediate effect, one of the Federation's vice-presidents and a member of the Executive Committee in relation to alleged violations of the Federation's code of ethics relating to the election to the FIFA presidency held on 1 June 2011; mems: 208 national assns, 6 continental confederations; Pres. JOSEPH (SEPP) BLATTER (Switzerland); Gen. Sec. JÉRÔME VALCKE (France); publs *FIFA News* (monthly), *FIFA Magazine* (every 2 months) (both in English, French, German and Spanish), *FIFA Directory* (annually), *Laws of the Game* (annually), *Competitions' Regulations* and *Technical Reports* (before and after FIFA competitions).

International Federation of Park and Recreation Administration (IFPRA): Globe House, Crispin Close, Caversham, Reading, Berks, RG4 7JS, United Kingdom; tel. and fax (118) 946-1680; e-mail ifpraworld@aol.com; internet www.ifpra.org; f. 1957 to provide a world centre for members of government departments, local authorities, and all organizations concerned with recreational and environmental services to discuss relevant matters; mems: 550 in over 50 countries; Gen. Sec. ALAN SMITH (United Kingdom); publ. *IFPRA World* (monthly).

International Fencing Federation (Fédération internationale d'escrime—FIE): Maison du Sport International, 54 ave de Rhodanie, 1007 Lausanne, Switzerland; tel. 213203115; fax 213203116; e-mail info@fie.ch; internet www.fie.ch; f. 1913; promotes development and co-operation between amateur fencers; determines rules for international events; organizes World Championships; mems: 134 national federations; Pres. ALISHER USMANOV (Russia); Sec.-Gen. MAXIM PARAMONOV (Ukraine).

International Gymnastic Federation (Fédération internationale de Gymnastique—FIG): 12 ave de la Gare, 1003 Lausanne, Switzerland; tel. 213215510; fax 213215519; e-mail info@fig-gymnastics.org; internet www.fig-gymnastics.com; f. 1881 to promote the exchange of official documents and publications on gymnastics; mems: 120 affiliated federations; Pres. BRUNO GRANDI (Italy); Gen. Sec. ANDRÉ GUEISBUHLER (Switzerland); publs *FIG Bulletin* (3 a year), *World of Gymnastics* (3 a year).

International Hockey Federation: 61 rue du Valentin, Lausanne, Switzerland; tel. 216410606; fax 216410607; e-mail info@fih.ch; internet www.fih.ch; f. 1924; mems: 127 national assns; Pres. LEANDRO NEGRE (Spain); CEO KELLY G. FAIRWEATHER (South Africa).

International Judo Federation: Maison du Sport International, ave de Rhodanie 54, 1007 Lausanne, Switzerland; tel. 216017720; fax 216017727; e-mail office@ijf.org; internet www.ijf.org; f. 1951 to promote cordial and friendly relations between members; to protect the interests of judo throughout the world; to organize World Championships and the judo events of the Olympic Games; to develop and spread the techniques and spirit of judo throughout the world; and to establish international judo regulations; Pres. MARIUS VIZER (Hungary); Gen. Sec. JEAN-LUC ROUGE (France).

International Kung Fu Federation: 1073 Baku, 529 Block, Metbuat Ave, Azerbaijan; tel. (12) 470-14-65; e-mail office@internationalkungfu.com; internet www.internationalkungfu.com; f. 2003; governing authority of national and international kung fu and taichi organizations world-wide; established internationally recognized rules and regulations and promotes regional and world championships; Pres. DAVUD MAHMUDZADEH (Azerbaijan).

International Paralympic Committee (IPC): Adenauerallee 212–214, 53113 Bonn, Germany; tel. (228) 2097200; fax (228) 2097209; e-mail info@paralympic.org; internet www.paralympic.org; f. 1989 as the international governing body of the Paralympic Movement; supervises and co-ordinates the Paralympic Summer and Winter Games, and other multi-disability competitions, including the World and Regional Championships; promotes paralympic sports through the paralympic sport television channel (www.Paralympic-Sport.TV); mems: 160 National Paralympic Committees and 4 disability-specific sport orgs and several international sports federations; Pres. Sir PHILIP CRAVEN (United Kingdom); CEO XAVIER GONZALEZ (Spain); publ. *The Paralympian* (quarterly), *IPC Newsflash* (monthly), *Annual Report*.

International Rowing Federation (Fédération internationale des sociétés d'aviron—FISA): MSI, 54 ave de Rhodanie, 1007 Lausanne, Switzerland; tel. 216178373; fax 216178375; e-mail info@fisa.org; internet www.worldrowing.com; f. 1892; serves as the world controlling body of the sport of rowing; mems: 128 national federations; Pres. DENIS OSWALD (Switzerland); Sec.-Gen. and Exec. Dir MATT SMITH (USA); publs *World Rowing Directory* (annually), *World Rowing E-Magazine* (quarterly), *FISA Bulletins* (annually).

International Rugby Board: Huguenot House, 35-38 St Stephen's Green, Dublin 2, Ireland; tel. (1) 240-9200; fax (1) 240-9201; e-mail irb@irb.com; internet www.irb.com; f. 1886; serves as the world governing and law-making body for the game of rugby union; supports education and development of the game and promotes it through regional and world tournaments; since 1987 has organized a Rugby World Cup every four years (2011: New Zealand); holds General Assembly every two years; mems: 97 national unions as full mems, 20 assoc. mems and six regional assns; Chair. BERNARD LAPASSET; Acting CEO ROBERT BROPHY.

International Sailing Federation (ISAF): Ariadne House, Town Quay, Southampton, Hants, SO14 2AQ, United Kingdom; tel. (2380) 635111; fax (2380) 635789; e-mail secretariat@isaf.co.uk; internet www.sailing.org; f. 1907; world governing body for the sport of sailing; establishes and amends Racing Rules of Sailing; organizes the Olympic Sailing Regatta, the ISAF Sailing World Championships, the ISAF World Cup and other events; mems: 138 member national authorities, 105 classes, 9 affiliated members; Pres. GÖRAN PETERSSON; Sec.-Gen. JEROME PELS; publ. *Making Waves* (weekly).

International Shooting Sport Federation (ISSF): 80336 Munich, Bavariaring 21, Germany; tel. (89) 5443550; fax (89) 54435544; e-mail munich@issf-sports.org; internet www.issf-sports.org; f. 1907 to promote and guide the development of amateur shooting sports; organizes World Championships and controls the organization of continental and regional championships; supervises the shooting events of the Olympic and Continental Games under the auspices of the International Olympic Committee; mems: 157 nat. federations from 137 affiliated countries; Pres. OLEGARIO VÁZQUEZ RAÑA (Mexico); Sec.-Gen. FRANZ SCHREIBER (Germany); publs *ISSF News*, *International Shooting Sport* (6 a year).

International Skating Union (ISU): 2 chemin de Primerose, 1007 Lausanne, Switzerland; tel. 216126666; fax 216126677; e-mail info@isu.ch; internet www.isu.org; f. 1892; holds regular conferences; mems: 78 national federations in 61 countries; Pres. OTTAVIO CINQUANTA (Italy); Gen. Sec. FREDI SCHMID; publs Judges' manuals, referees' handbooks, general and special regulations.

International Ski Federation (Fédération Internationale de Ski—FIS): Marc Hodler House, Blochstr. 2, 3653 Oberhofen am Thunersee, Switzerland; tel. 332446161; fax 332446171; e-mail mail@fisski.ch; internet www.fis-ski.com; f. 1924 to further the sport of skiing; to prevent discrimination in skiing matters on racial, religious or political grounds; to organize World Ski Championships and regional championships and, as supreme international skiing authority, to establish the international competition calendar and rules for all ski competitions approved by the FIS, and to arbitrate in any disputes; mems: 108 national ski asscns; Pres. GIAN FRANCO KASPER (Switzerland); Sec.-Gen. SARAH LEWIS (United Kingdom); publs *Weekly Newsflash*, *FIS Bulletin* (2 a year).

International Swimming Federation (Fédération internationale de natation—FINA): POB 4, ave de l'Avant, 1005 Lausanne, Switzerland; tel. 213104710; fax 213126610; internet www.fina.org; f. 1908 to promote amateur swimming and swimming sports internationally; administers rules for swimming sports, competitions and for establishing records; organizes world championships and FINA events; runs a development programme to increase the popularity and quality of aquatic sports; mems: 201 federations; Pres. JULIO C. MAGLIONE (Uruguay); Exec. Dir CORNEL MARCULESCU; publs *Handbook* (every 4 years), *FINA News* (monthly), *World of Swimming* (quarterly).

International Table Tennis Federation: 11 chemin de la Roche, 1020 Renens/Lausanne, Switzerland; tel. 213407090; fax 213407099; e-mail ittf@ittf.com; internet www.ittf.com; f. 1926; Pres. ADHAM SHARARA (Canada); Exec. Dir JORDI SERRA; publs *Table Tennis Illustrated*, *Table Tennis News* (both every 2 months), *Table Tennis Legends*, *Table Tennis Fascination*, *Table Tennis: The Early Years*.

International Tennis Federation: Bank Lane, Roehampton, London, SW15 5XZ, United Kingdom; tel. (20) 8878-6464; fax (20) 8878-7799; e-mail communications@itftennis.com; internet www.itftennis.com; f. 1913 to govern the game of tennis throughout the world, promote its teaching and preserve its independence of outside authority; produces the Rules of Tennis; organizes and promotes the Davis Cup Competition for men, the Fed. Cup for women, the Olympic Games Tennis Event, wheelchair tennis, 16 cups for veterans, the ITF Sunshine Cup and the ITF Continental Connelly Cup for players of 18 years old and under, the World Youth Cup for players of 16 years old and under, and the World Junior Tennis Tournament for players of 14 years old and under; organizes entry-level professional tournaments as well as junior and senior circuits, monitors equipment and technology and oversees the education and advancement of officials; mems: 145 full and 65 associate; Pres. FRANCESCO RICCI BITTI.

International Volleyball Federation (Fédération internationale de volleyball—FIVB): Château Les Tourelles, Edouard-Sandoz 2–4, Lausanne 1, Switzerland; tel. 213453535; fax 213453545; e-mail info@fivb.org; internet www.fivb.org; f. 1947 to encourage, organize and supervise the playing of volleyball, beach volleyball, and park volley; organizes biennial congress; mems: 220 national federations; Pres. JIZHONG WEI (People's Republic of China); publs *VolleyWorld* (every 2 months), *X-Press* (monthly).

International Weightlifting Federation (IWF): 1146 Budapest, Istvanmezei út 1–3, Hungary; tel. (1) 3530530; fax (1) 3530199; e-mail iwf@iwfnet.net; internet www.iwf.net; f. 1905 to control international weightlifting; draws up technical rules; trains referees; supervises World Championships, Olympic Games, regional games and international contests of all kinds; registers world records; mems: 189 national orgs; Pres. Dr TAMÁS AJAN (Hungary); Gen. Sec. MA WENGUANG (People's Republic of China); publs *IWF Constitution and Rules* (every 4 years), *World Weightlifting* (quarterly).

International World Games Association: 10 Lake Circle, Colorado Springs, CO 80906, USA; tel. (719) 471-8096; fax (719) 471-8105; e-mail info@theworldgames.org; internet www.theworldgames.org; f. 1980; organizes World Games every four years (2013: Cali, Colombia), comprising 32 sports that are not included in the Olympic Games; Pres. RON FROEHLICH; CEO JOACHIM GOSSOW.

Olympic Council of Asia: POB 6706, Hawalli, 32042 Kuwait City, Kuwait; tel. 25734972; fax 25734973; e-mail info@ocasia.org; internet www.ocasia.org; f. 1982; organizes Asian Games and Asian Winter Games (held every four years), and Asian Indoor Games and Asian Beach Games (held every two years); mems: 45 national Olympic cttees; Dir-Gen. HUSAIN A. H. Z. AL-MUSALLAM.

SportAccord: Maison du Sport International, 54 ave de Rhodanie, 1007 Lausanne, Switzerland; tel. 216123070; fax 216123071; e-mail sportaccord@sportaccord.com; internet www.sportaccord.com; f. 1967 as the General Assembly of International Sports Federations (name changed in 1976 to General Association of International Sports Federations—GAISF, and in March 2009 renamed as above) to act as a forum for the exchange of ideas and discussion of common problems in sport; collects and circulates information; and provides secretarial, translation, documentation and consultancy services for members; mems: 104 international sports orgs; Pres. HEIN VERBRUGGEN (Netherlands); Dir NOLVENN DUFAY DE LAVALLAZ (France); publs *GAISF Calendar* (online), *Sports Insider* (weekly, electronic bulletin), *Sports Insider Magazine* (annually).

Union of Arab Olympic Committees: POB 62997, Riyadh 11595, Saudi Arabia; tel. (1) 482-4927; fax (1) 482-1944; e-mail olympiccommittees@gmail.com; f. 1976 as Arab Sports Confederation to encourage regional co-operation in sport; mems: 21 Arab national Olympic Committees, 53 Arab sports federations; Sec.-Gen. OTHMAN M. AL-SAAD; publ. *Annual Report*.

Union of European Football Associations (UEFA): 46 route de Genève, 1260 Nyon 2, Switzerland; tel. 848002727; fax 848012727; e-mail info@uefa.com; internet www.uefa.com; f. 1954; works on behalf of Europe's national football asscns to promote football; aims to foster unity and solidarity between national asscns; mems: 53 national asscns; Pres. MICHEL PLATINI (France); Gen. Sec. GIANNI INFANTINO (Italy); publ. *Magazine* (available online).

World Archery Federation (Fédération mondiale de tir à l'arc): 54 ave de Rhodanie, 1007 Lausanne, Switzerland; tel. 216143050; fax 216143055; e-mail info@archery.org; internet www.worldarchery.org; f. 1931 to promote international archery; organizes world championships, world cup events and Olympic tournaments; holds Biennial Congress; mems: national asscns in 147 countries; Pres. UGUR ERDENER; Sec.-Gen. TOM DIELEN (Switzerland); publs *World Archery News* (monthly), *The Target* (2 a year).

World Boxing Organization: First Federal Bldg, 1056 Muñoz Rivera Ave, Suite 711–714, San Juan, PR 00927, Puerto Rico; tel. (787) 765-4628; fax (787) 758-9053; e-mail boxing@wbo-int.com; internet www.wbo-int.com; f. 1962; regulates professional boxing; Pres. FRANCISCO VALCARCEL; Sec. ARNALDO SANCHEZ-RECIO.

World Bridge Federation: c/o 10 Ch. Des Charmilles, Les Roussets, 01210 Ornex, France; tel. 4-50-40-41-31; fax 4-50-40-42-57; internet www.worldbridge.org; e-mail office@worldbridge.org; f. 1958 to promote the game of contract bridge throughout the world; federates national bridge asscns in all countries; conducts world championships competitions; establishes standard bridge laws; mems: 89 countries; Pres. JOSÉ DAMIANI (France); Hon. Sec. DAN MORSE (USA); publ. *World Bridge News* (annually).

World Chess Federation (Fédération internationale des echecs—FIDE): 9 Syggrou Ave, Athens 11743, Greece; tel. (210) 9212047; fax (210) 9212859; e-mail office@fide.com; internet www.fide.com; f. 1924; controls chess competitions of world importance and awards international chess titles; mems: national orgs in more than 160 countries; Pres. KIRSAN ILYUMZHINOV; publ. *International Rating List* (2 a year).

World Curling Federation: 74 Tay St, Perth, PN2 8NP, Scotland, United Kingom; tel. (1738) 451630; fax (1738) 451641; e-mail info@worldcurling.org; internet www.worldcurling.org; f. 1991; mems: 48 mem. asscns; Sec.-Gen. COLIN GRAHAMSLAW.

World Squash Federation Ltd: 25 Russell St, Hastings, East Sussex, TN34 1QU, United Kingdom; tel. (1424) 447440; fax (1424) 430737; e-mail admin@worldsquash.org; internet www.worldsquash.org; f. 1966 to maintain quality and reputation of squash and increase its popularity; monitors rules and makes recommendations for change; trains, accredits and assesses international and world referees; sets standards for all technical aspects of squash; co-ordinates coaching training and awards; runs World Championships; mems: 147 national orgs; Pres. N. RAMACHANDRAN; Co Sec. Dr GEORGE MIERAS.

World Underwater Federation: Viale Tiziano 74, 00196 Rome, Italy; tel. (06) 32110594; fax (06) 32110595; e-mail cmas@cmas.org; internet www.cmas2000.org; f. 1959 to develop underwater activities; to form bodies to instruct in the techniques of underwater diving; to perfect existing equipment, encourage inventions and experiment with newly marketed products; and to organize international competitions; mems: orgs in 100 countries; Pres. ACHILLE FERRERO (Italy); Sec.-Gen. ALESSANDRO ZERBI; publs *International Year Book of CMAS*, *Scientific Diving: A Code of Practice*, manuals.

Technology

African Organization of Cartography and Remote Sensing: 5 route de Bedjarah, BP 102, Hussein Dey, Algiers, Algeria; tel. (21) 23-17-17; fax (21) 23-33-39; e-mail oact@wissal.dz; f. 1988 by amalgamation of African Association of Cartography and African Council for Remote Sensing; aims to encourage the development of cartography and of remote sensing by satellites; organizes conferences and other meetings, promotes establishment of training institutions; maintains four regional training centres (in Burkina Faso, Kenya, Nigeria and Tunisia); mems: national cartographic institutions of 24 African countries; Sec.-Gen. UNIS MUFTAH.

African Regional Centre for Technology: Imm. Fahd, 17th Floor, blvd Djilly Mbaye, BP 2435, Dakar, Senegal; tel. 823-77-12; fax 823-77-13; e-mail arct@sonatel.senet.net; f. 1977 to encourage the development of indigenous technology and to improve the terms of access to imported technology; assists the establishment of national centres; mems: govts of 31 countries; Exec. Dir. Dr OUSMANE KANE; publs *African Technodevelopment*, *Alert Africa*.

AIIM International: 1100 Wayne Ave, Suite 1100, Silver Spring, Maryland 20910, USA; tel. (301) 587-8202; fax (301) 587-2711; e-mail aiim@aiim.org; internet www.aiim.org; f. 1999 by merger of the Association for Information and Image Management (f. 1943) and the International Information Management Congress (f. 1962); serves as the international body of the document technologies industry; Chair. JOHN OPDYKE; Pres. JOHN F. MANCINI.

Bureau International de la Recupération et du Recyclage (Bureau of International Recycling): 24 ave Franklin Roosevelt, 1050 Brussels, Belgium; tel. (2) 627-57-70; fax (2) 627-57-73; e-mail bir@bir.org; internet www.bir.org; f. 1948 as the world federation of the reclamation and recycling industries; promotes international trade in scrap iron and steel, non-ferrous metals, paper, textiles, plastics and glass; mems: asscns in 70 countries; Pres. BJÖRN GRUFMAN (Sweden); Dir-Gen. FRANCIS VEYS (Belgium).

Ecma International: 114 rue de Rhône, 1204 Geneva, Switzerland; tel. 228496000; fax 228496001; e-mail istvan@ecma-international.org; internet www.ecma-international.org; f. 1961 to develop standards and technical reports, in co-operation with the appropriate national, European and international organizations, in order to facilitate and standardize the use of information processing and telecommunications systems; promulgates various standards applicable to the functional design and use of these systems; mems: 15 ordinary mems, 16 associate mems, 3 small and medium-sized enterprises, 32 not-for-profit mems, 3 small private company mems; Sec.-Gen. Dr ISTVAN SEBESTYEN; publs *Ecma Standards*, *Ecma Memento*, *Ecma Technical Reports*.

EURELECTRIC (Union of the Electricity Industry): 66 blvd de l'Impératrice, BP 2, 1000 Brussels, Belgium; tel. (2) 515-10-00; fax (2) 515-10-10; e-mail mdebois@euelectric.org; internet www.eurelectric.org; f. 1999 by merger of International Union of Producers and Distributors of Electrical Energy (UNIPEDE, f. 1925) and European Grouping of the Electricity Industry (EEIG, f. 1989); a sector asscn representing the common interests of the electricity industry at pan-European level; contributes to the competitiveness of the electricity industry, provides effective representation for the sector in public affairs, promotes the role of electricity both in the advancement of society and in helping tp provide solutions to the challenges of sustainable development; Pres. FULVIO CONTI; Sec.-Gen. HANS TEN BERGE; publ. *Watt's New* (newsletter).

EUREKA: 107 rue Neerveld, bte 5, 1200 Brussels, Belgium; tel. (2) 777-09-50; fax (2) 770-74-95; e-mail info@eurekanetwork.org; internet www.eurekanetwork.org; f. 1985; aims to promote industrial collaboration between member countries on non-military research and development activities; enables joint development of technology; supports innovation and systematic use of standardization in new technology sectors; administers Eurostars programme, with European Commission, to fund and support collaborative research and innovation projects; mems: 126 in 38 countries; Dir LUUK BORG; publs *Annual Report*, *Eureka Bulletin*.

European Convention for Constructional Steelwork (ECCS): 32 ave des Ombrages, bte 20, 1200 Brussels, Belgium; tel. (2) 762-04-29; fax (2) 762-09-35; e-mail eccs@steelconstruct.com; internet www.steelconstruct.com; f. 1955 for the consideration of problems involved in metallic construction; mems: 20 full mems, 6 assoc. mems, 3 int. mems and 2 supporting mems; Sec.-Gen. VÉRONIQUE BAES-DEHAN; publs Information sheets and documents, symposia reports, model codes.

European Federation of Chemical Engineering: c/o Institution of Chemical Engineers, Davis Bldg, 165–189 Railway Terrace, Rugby, Warwickshire, CV21 3HQ, United Kingdom; tel. (1788) 578214; fax (1788) 560833; e-mail dbrown@icheme.org.uk; internet www.efce.info; f. 1953 to encourage co-operation between non-profit-making scientific and technical societies, for the advancement of chemical engineering and its application in the processing industries; mems: 40 societies in 30 European countries, 15 corresponding societies in other countries; Pres. Prof. RICHARD DARTON.

European Federation of Corrosion: 1 Carlton House Terrace, London, SW1Y 5DB, United Kingdom; tel. (20) 7451-7336; fax (20) 8392-2289; e-mail info@efcweb.org; internet www.efcweb.org; f. 1955 to encourage co-operation in research on methods of combating corrosion; mems: societies in 26 countries; Pres. PHILIPPE MARCUS (France).

European Federation of National Engineering Associations (Fédération européenne d'associations nationales d'ingénieurs—FEANI): 18 ave R. Vandendriessche, 1150 Brussels, Belgium; tel. (2) 639-03-90; fax (2) 639-03-99; e-mail secretariat.general@feani.org; internet www.feani.org; f. 1951 to affirm the professional identity of the engineers of Europe and to strive for the unity of the engineering profession in Europe; mems: 32 mem. countries; Pres. LARS BYTOFT (Denmark); Sec.-Gen. DIRK BOCHAR; publs *FEANI News*, *INDEX*.

European Metal Union: 4 rue J. de Lalaing, 1040 Brussels, Belgium; tel. (2) 282-05-33; fax (2) 282-05-35; e-mail contact@emu-online.info; internet www.emu-online.info; f. 1954 as International Union of Metal; liaises between national craft organizations and small and medium-sized enterprises in the metal industry; represents members' interests at a European level; provides for the exchange of information and ideas; mems: national federations from Austria, Germany, Hungary, Luxembourg, Netherlands and Switzerland; Pres. ERWIN KOSTYRA; Sec. MARIETTE WENNMACHER (Belgium).

European Organisation for the Exploitation of Meteorological Satellites (EUMETSAT): 64295 Darmstadt, Eumetsat Allee 1, Germany; tel. (6151) 8077; fax (6151) 807555; e-mail ops@eumetsat.int; internet www.eumetsat.int; f. 1986; establishes, maintains and exploits European systems of operational meteorological satellites; projects include a second generation Meteosat programme for gathering weather data and satellite application facilities; mems: 26 European countries and 5 co-operating states; Dir-Gen. ALAIN RATIER; publs *Annual Report*, *IMAGE Newsletter* (2 a year), brochures, conference and workshop proceedings.

European Organization for Civil Aviation Equipment (EURO-CAE): 102 rue Etienne Dolet, 4th Floor, 92240 Malakoff, France; tel. 1-40-92-79-30; fax 1-46-55-62-65; e-mail eurocae@eurocae.net; internet www.eurocae.net; f. 1963; studies and advises on problems related to the equipment used in aeronautics; assists international bodies in the establishment of international standards; mems: 92 manufacturers, and regulatory and research bodies; Sec.-Gen. ABDOULAYE N'DIAYE; publs reports, documents and specifications on civil aviation equipment.

Eurospace: 15–17 ave de Ségur, 75005 Paris, France; tel. 1-44-42-00-70; fax 1-44-42-00-79; e-mail letterbox@eurospace.org; internet www.eurospace.org; f. 1961 as an asscn of European aerospace industrial companies responsible for promotion of European Space activity; carries out studies on the legal, economic, technical and financial aspects of space activity; acts as an industrial adviser to the European Space Agency, in particular with regard to future space programmes and industrial policy matters; mems: 60 in 13 European countries; Pres. EVERT DUDOK; Sec.-Gen. JEAN-JACQUES TORTORA.

CIRP—International Academy for Production Engineering: 9 rue Mayran, 75009 Paris, France; tel. 1-45-26-21-80; fax 1-45-26-92-15; e-mail cirp@cirp.net; internet www.cirp.net; f. 1951, as International Institution for Production Engineering Research, to promote by scientific research the study of the mechanical processing of all solid materials; mems: 580 in 40 countries; Sec.-Gen. DIDIER DUMUR (France); publ. *Annals* (2 a year).

International Association for Bridge and Structural Engineering (IABSE): ETH—Hönggerberg, 8093 Zürich, Switzerland; tel. 446332647; fax 446331241; e-mail secretariat@iabse.org; internet www.iabse.org; f. 1929 to exchange knowledge and advance the practice of structural engineering world-wide; mems: 4,000 government departments, local authorities, universities, institutes, firms and individuals in over 100 countries; Pres. PREDRAG POPOVIC (USA); Exec. Dir UELI BRUNNER; publs *Structural Engineering International* (quarterly), *Structural Engineering Documents*, *IABSE Report*, *e-newsletter*.

International Association of Hydraulic Engineering and Research (IAHR): Paseo Bajo Virgen del Puerto 3, 28005 Madrid, Spain; tel. (91) 3357908; fax (91) 3357935; e-mail iahr@iahr.org; internet www.iahr.org; f. 1935; promotes advancement and exchange of knowledge on hydraulic engineering; holds biennial congresses and symposia; mems: 1,850 individual, 300 corporate; Pres. ROGER FALCONER; Exec. Dir CHRISTOPHER GEORGE; publs *The International Journal of River Basin Management*, *IAHR Newsletter*, *Hydrolink*, *Journal of Hydraulic Research*, *Proceedings of Biennial Conferences*, *Fluvial Processes Monograph*, *Fluvial Processes Solutions Manual*, *Hydraulicians in Europe 1800–2000*.

International Association of Marine Aids to Navigation and Lighthouse Authorities: 20 ter rue Schnapper, 78100 St Germain en Laye, France; tel. 1-34-51-70-01; fax 1-34-51-82-05; e-mail contact@iala-aism.org; internet www.iala-aism.org; f. 1957; holds technical conference every four years; working groups study special problems and formulate technical recommendations, guidelines and manuals; mems in 80 countries; Pres. DAVID GORDON; Sec.-Gen. GARY PROSSER; publ. *Bulletin* (quarterly).

International Association of Scientific and Technological University Libraries (IATUL): c/o Paul Sheehan, Dublin City University Library, Dublin 9, Ireland; e-mail paul.sheehan@dcu.ie; internet www.iatul.org; f. 1955 to promote co-operation between member libraries and stimulate research on library problems; mems: 238 university libraries in 41 countries; Pres. AINSLIE DEWE (Australia); Sec. PAUL SHEEHAN (Ireland); publs *IATUL Proceedings*, *IATUL Newsletter* (electronic version only).

International Bridge, Tunnel and Turnpike Association: 1146 19th St, NW, Suite 800, Washington, DC 20036-3725, USA; tel. (202) 659-4620; fax (202) 659-0500; e-mail info@ibtta.org; internet www.ibtta.org; f. 1932 to serve as a forum for sharing knowledge, with the aim of promoting toll-financed transportation services; mems: 280 mems in 25 countries; Exec. Dir and CEO PATRICK D. JONES; publ. *Tollways* (monthly).

International Cargo Handling Co-ordination Association (ICHCA): Suite 2, 85 Western Rd, Romford, Essex, RM1 3LS, United Kingdom; tel. (1708) 735295; fax (1708) 735225; e-mail info@ichca.com; internet www.ichca.com; f. 1952 to foster economy and efficiency in the movement of goods from origin to destination; mems: 2,000 in 90 countries; Int. Chair. JOHN STRANG; Exec. Dir ROSEMARY NEILSON; publs *Cargo Tomorrow: Cargo Handling News* (every 2 months), *World of Cargo Handling* (annually), *Who's Who in Cargo Handling* (annually), technical publs and reviews.

International Colour Association: c/o Nick Harkness Pty Ltd, Birdcage 3.1, 65 Doody St, Alexandria, NSW 2015, Australia; e-mail nick@nhpl.com.au; internet www.aic-colour.org; f. 1967 to encourage research in colour in all its aspects, disseminate the knowledge gained from this research and promote its application to the solution of problems in the fields of science, art and industry; holds international congresses and symposia; mems: orgs in 26 countries; Pres. BERIT BERGSTRÖM (Sweden); Sec. and Treas. NICK HARKNESS (Australia).

International Commission of Agricultural and Biosystems Engineering (CIGR): Research Group of Bioproduction Engineering, Research Faculty of Agriculture, Hokkaido University, N–9, W–9, Kita-ku, Sapporo, Hokkaido 060-8589, Japan; tel. (11) 706-3885; fax (11) 706-4147; e-mail cigr_gs2010@bpe.agr.hokudai.ac.jp; internet www.cigr.org; f. 1930; aims to stimulate development of science and technology in agricultural engineering; encourages education, training and mobility of professionals; facilitates exchange of research; represents profession at international level; mems: asscns from 92 countries; Pres. Prof. FEDRO ZAZUETA (USA); Sec.-Gen. Prof. TOSHINORI KIMURA (Japan); publs *Bulletin de la CIGR*, *Newsletter* (quarterly), technical reports.

International Commission on Glass: Via Molinella 17, Piombino, 35017 Padova, Italy; e-mail spevetro@ve-nettuno.it; internet www.icg.group.shef.ac.uk; f. 1933 to co-ordinate research in glass and allied products, exchange information and organize conferences; mems: 30 orgs; Pres. FABIANO NICOLETTI; Exec. Sec. PETER ŞIMURKA.

International Commission on Illumination (CIE): Kegelgasse 27, 1030 Vienna, Austria; tel. (1) 714-31-87-0; fax (1) 714-31-87-18; e-mail ciecb@cie.co.at; internet www.cie.co.at; f. 1900 as International Commission on Photometry, present name adopted 1913; aims to provide an international forum for all matters relating to the science and art of light and lighting; serves as a forum for the exchange of information; develops and publishes international standards and provides guidance in their application; mems: 40 national cttees, 12 supportive; Gen. Sec. MARTINA PAUL; publs standards, technical reports, congress organization.

International Commission on Irrigation and Drainage (ICID) (Commission Internationale des Irrigations et du Drainage): 48 Nyaya Marg, Chanakyapuri, New Delhi 110 021, India; tel. (11) 26115679; fax (11) 26115962; e-mail icid@icid.org; internet www.icid.org; f. 1950; aims to enhance the world-wide supply of food and fibre by improving the productivity of irrigated and drained lands through the appropriate management of water and application of irrigation, drainage and flood management techniques; promotes the development and application of the arts, sciences and techniques of engineering, agriculture, economics, ecological and social sciences in managing water and land resources for irrigation, drainage and flood management and for river training applications; holds triennial congresses; mems: 105 national cttees; Pres. CHANDRA A. MADRAMOOTOO (Canada); Sec.-Gen. ER. M. GOPALAKRISHNAN (India); publs *Ir* (quarterly), *World Irrigation*, *Multilingual Technical Dictionary*, *Historical Dams*, *Indus Basin*, *Danube Valley*, *Application of Geosynthetics in Irrigation and Drainage Projects*, technical books.

International Commission on Large Dams (ICOLD): 61 ave Kléber, 75116 Paris, France; tel. 1-47-04-17-80; fax 1-53-75-18-22; e-mail secretaire.general@icold-cigb.org; internet www.icold-cigb.org; f. 1928; mems: in 85 countries; Pres. JIA JINSHENG (People's Republic of China); Sec.-Gen. MICHEL DE VIVO; publs *Technical Bulletin* (3 or 4 a year), *World Register of Dams*, *World Register of Mine and Industrial Wastes*, *Technical Dictionary on Dams*, studies.

International Committee on Aeronautical Fatigue (ICAF): c/o Prof. O. Buxbaum, Fraunhofer-Institut für Betriebsfestigkeit LBF, 64289 Darmstadt, Bartningstrasse 47, Germany; tel. (6151) 7051; fax (6151) 705214; f. 1951 for collaboration between aeronautical bodies and laboratories on questions of fatigue of aeronautical structures; organizes periodical conferences; mems: national centres in 13 countries; Sec. Dr ANDERS BLOM (Sweden).

International Council for Research and Innovation in Building and Construction: Kruisplein 25G, POB 1837, 3000 BV Rotterdam, Netherlands; tel. (10) 4110240; fax (10) 4334372; e-mail secretariat@cibworld.nl; internet www.cibworld.nl; f. 1953 to encourage and facilitate co-operation in building research, studies and documentation in all aspects; mems: governmental and industrial orgs and qualified individuals in 70 countries; Pres. JOHN MCCARTHY (Australia); Sec.-Gen. W. J. P. BAKENS; publs *Information Bulletin* (every 2 months), conference proceedings and technical, best practice and other reports.

International Council on Large High-Voltage Electric Systems (Conseil international des grands réseaux électriques—CIGRE): 21 rue d'Artois, 75008 Paris, France; tel. 1-53-89-12-90; fax 1-53-89-12-99; e-mail secretary-general@cigre.org; internet www.cigre.org; f. 1921 to facilitate and promote the exchange of technical knowledge and information in the general field of electrical generation and transmission at high voltages; holds general sessions (every two years) and symposia; mems: 5,157 in over 80 countries; Pres. ANDRÉ MERLIN (France); Sec.-Gen. F. MESLIER (France); publ. *Electra* (every 2 months).

International Electrotechnical Commission (IEC): 3 rue de Varembé, POB 131, 1211 Geneva 20, Switzerland; tel. 229190211; fax 229190300; e-mail info@iec.ch; internet www.iec.ch; f. 1906 as the authority for world standards for electrical and electronic engineering: its standards are used as the basis for regional and national standards, and are used in the preparation of specifications for international trade; mems: national cttees representing all branches of electrical and electronic activities in some 60 countries; CEO and Gen. Sec. A. AMIT; publs *International Standards and Reports*, *IEC Bulletin*, *Annual Report*, *Catalogue of Publications*.

International Federation for Information Processing (IFIP): Hofstrasse 3, 2361 Laxenburg, Austria; tel. (2236) 73616; fax (2236) 736169; e-mail ifip@ifip.org; internet www.ifip.org; f. 1960 to promote information science and technology; encourages research, development and application of information processing in science and human activities; furthers the dissemination and exchange of information on information processing; mems: 49 full mems, 10 hon. mems, 4 assoc. mems and 4 *ex officio* mems; Pres. LEON STROUS (Netherlands); Sec. MARIA RAFFAI.

International Federation for the Promotion of Machine and Mechanism Science: Laboratory of Robotics and Mechatronics, Univ. of Cassino, via di Biasio 43, 03043 Cassino, Italy; tel. (0776) 299-3663; fax (0776) 299-3711; e-mail ceccarelli@unicas.it; internet www.iftomm.org; f. 1969 to study mechanisms, robots, man-machine systems, etc.; promotes research and development in the field of machines and mechanisms by theoretical and experimental methods and practical application; Pres. M. CECCARELLI; Sec.-Gen. CARLOS LOPEZ-CAJUN; publs *Mechanism and Machine Theory*, *Problems of Mechanics*, *Journal of Gearing and Transmissions*, *Electronic Journal on Computational Kinematics*.

International Federation of Airworthiness (IFA): 14 Railway Approach, East Grinstead, West Sussex, RH19 1BP, United Kingdom; tel. (1342) 301788; fax (1342) 317808; e-mail sec@ifairworthy.com; internet www.ifairworthy.com; f. 1964 to provide a forum for the exchange of international experience in maintenance, design and operations; holds annual conference; awards international aviation scholarship annually; mems include 23 airlines, 10 airworthiness authorities, 11 aerospace manufacturing companies, 14 service and repair organizations, 2 consultancies, 5 professional societies, 2 aviation insurance companies, 1 aircraft leasing company, and the Flight Safety Foundation (USA); Exec. Dir JOHN W. SAULL (United Kingdom); publ. *IFA News* (quarterly).

International Federation of Automatic Control (IFAC): Schlosspl. 12, 2361 Laxenburg, Austria; tel. (2236) 71447; fax (2236) 72859; e-mail secretariat@ifac-control.org; internet www.ifac-control.org; f. 1957 to serve those concerned with the theory and application of automatic control and systems engineering; mems: 50 national asscns; Pres. Prof. ALBERTO ISIDORI (Italy); Sec. KURT SCHLACHER; publs *Annual Reviews in Control*, *Automatica*, *Control Engineering Practice*, *Journal of Process Control*, *Newsletter*, *Engineering Applications of AI*, IFAC journals and affiliated journals.

International Federation of Automotive Engineering Societies (FISITA): 30 Percy St, London, W1T 2DB, United Kingdom; tel. (20) 7299-6630; fax (20) 7299-6633; e-mail info@fisita.com; internet www.fisita.com; f. 1948 to promote the technical and sustainable development of all forms of automotive transportation; maintains electronic job centre for automotive engineers (www.fisitajobs.com); holds congresses every two years; mems: national orgs in 38 countries; Chief Exec. IAN DICKIE; publ. *AutoTechnology*.

International Federation of Consulting Engineers (Fédération internationale des ingénieurs-conseils—FIDIC): POB 311, 1215 Geneva 15, Switzerland; tel. 227994900; fax 227994901; e-mail fidic@fidic.org; internet www.fidic.org; f. 1913 to encourage international co-operation and the establishment of standards for consulting engineers; mems: 78 national asscns world-wide, comprising some 500,000 design professionals; Pres. GREGS THOMOPULOS; publs *FIDIC Report*, *Annual Survey*, *Annual Review*.

International Federation of Hospital Engineering: 2 Abingdon House, Cumberland Business Centre, Northumberland Rd, Portsmouth, PO5 1DS, United Kingdom; tel. (2392) 823186; fax (2392) 815927; e-mail ifhe@iheem.org.uk; internet www.ifhe.info; f. 1970 to promote internationally standards of hospital engineering and to provide for the exchange of knowledge and experience in the areas of hospital and health care facility design, construction, engineering, commissioning, maintenance and estate management; mems: 50 in more than 30 countries; Pres. YASUSHI NAGASAWA (Japan); Gen. Sec. BERNARD SHAPIRO (South Africa); publ. *Hospital Engineering* (quarterly).

International Institute of Seismology and Earthquake Engineering (IISEE): Building Research Institute, 1 Tatehara, Tsukuba City, Ibaraki 305-0802, Japan; tel. (298) 79-0677; fax (298) 64-6777; e-mail iisee@kenken.go.jp; internet iisee.kenken.go.jp; f. 1962 to work on seismology and earthquake engineering for the purpose of reducing earthquake damage in the world; trains seismologists and earthquake engineers from the earthquake-prone countries; undertakes surveys, research, guidance and analysis of information on earthquakes and related matters; mems: 75 countries; Dir Dr SHOICHI ANDO; publs *Bulletin* (annually), *Individual Studies* (annually).

International Institute of Welding: 90 rue des Vanesses, ZI Paris Nord II, 93420 Villepinte, France; tel. 1-49-90-36-08; fax 1-49-90-36-80; e-mail c.mayer@iiwelding.org; internet www.iiwelding.org; f. 1948; serves as the world-wide network for knowledge exchange of joining technologies; develops authorized education, training, qualification and certification programmes; mems: 53 mem. societies; Chief Exec. CÉCILE MAYER (France); publ. *Welding in the World* (6 a year).

International Iron and Steel Institute (IISI): 120 rue Col Bourg, 1140 Brussels, Belgium; tel. (2) 702-89-00; fax (2) 702-88-99; e-mail info@worldsteel.org; internet www.worldsteel.org; f. 1967 to promote the welfare and interests of the world's steel industries; undertakes research into all aspects of steel industries; serves as a forum for exchange of knowledge and discussion of problems relating to steel industries; collects, disseminates and maintains statistics and information; serves as a liaison body between international and national steel organizations; mems: in over 50 countries; Dir-Gen. IAN CHRISTMAS; publs *Worldsteel Newsletter*, policy statements and reports.

International Measurement Confederation (IMEKO): POB 457, 1371 Budapest 5, Hungary; tel. and fax (1) 353-1562; e-mail imeko.ime@mtesz.hu; internet www.imeko.org; f. 1958 as a federation of member organizations concerned with the advancement of measurement technology; aims to promote exchange of scientific and technical information in field of measurement and instrumentation and to enhance co-operation between scientists and engineers; holds World Congress every three years (2012: Busan, Republic of Korea, in Sept.); mems: 39 orgs; Pres. Dr DAE-IM KANG (Republic of Korea); Sec.-Gen. Prof. MLADEN BORSIC (Croatia); publs *Acta IMEKO* (proceedings of World Congresses), *IMEKO TC Events Series*, *Measurement* (quarterly), *IMEKO Bulletin* (2 a year).

International Organization for Standardization: POB 56, 1 rue de de la Voie-Creuse, 1211 Geneva 20, Switzerland; tel. 227490111; fax 227333430; e-mail central@iso.org; internet www.iso.org; f. 1947 to reach international agreement on industrial and commercial standards; mems: national standards bodies of 161 countries; Pres. Dr BORIS ALESHIN (Russia); Sec.-Gen. ROBERT STEELE; publs *ISO International Standards*, *ISO Memento* (annually), *ISO Management Systems* (6 a year), *ISO Focus* (11 a year), *ISO Catalogue* (annually, updated regularly online), *ISO Annual Report*.

International Research Group on Wood Protection: Drottning Kristinas väg 33A, Stockholm, Sweden; tel. (8) 10-14-53; fax (8) 10-80-81; e-mail irg@sp.se; internet www.irg-wp.com; f. 1965 as Wood Preservation Group by OECD; independent since 1969; consists of five sections; holds plenary annual meeting; mems: 358 in 54 countries; Pres. JACKD NORTON (Australia); Sec.-Gen. JÖRAN JERMER (Sweden); publs technical documents.

International Rubber Research and Development Board (IRRDB): POB 10150, 50908 Kuala Lumpur, Malaysia; tel. (3) 42521612; fax (3) 42560487; e-mail sec_gen@theirrdb.org; internet www.irrdb.com; f. 1960 following the merger of International Rubber Regulation Committee (f. 1934) and International Rubber Research Board (f. 1937); mems: 15 research institutes; Sec. Dr Datuk A. AZIZ.

International Society for Photogrammetry and Remote Sensing (ISPRS): c/o National Geomatics Centre of China, 28 Lianhuachixi Rd, Haidian District, Beijing 100830, People's Republic of China; tel. (10) 63881102; fax (10) 63881026; e-mail chenjun@nsdi.gov.cn; internet www.isprs.org/; f. 1910; holds congress every four years, and technical symposia; mems: 103 countries; Pres. ORHAN ALTAN (Turkey); Sec.-Gen. CHEN JUN (People's Republic of China); publs *Journal of Photogrammetry and Remote Sensing* (6 a year), *ISPRS Highlights* (quarterly), *International Archives of Photogrammetry and Remote Sensing* (every 2 years).

International Society for Soil Mechanics and Geotechnical Engineering: City University London, Northampton Sq., London, EC1V 0HB, United Kingdom; tel. (20) 7040-8154; fax (20) 7040-8832; e-mail secretariat@issmge.org; internet www.issmge.org; f. 1936 to promote international co-operation among scientists and engineers in the field of geotechnics and its engineering applications; maintains 30 technical committees; holds quadrennial international conference, regional conferences and specialist conferences; mems: 18,000 individuals, 85 national societies, 21 corporate members; Pres. Prof. JEAN LOUIS BRIAUD; Sec.-Gen. Prof. R. N. TAYLOR; publs *ISSMGE Bulletin* (quarterly), *Lexicon of Soil Mechanics Terms* (in 8 languages).

International Solar Energy Society: Villa Tannheim, Wiesentalstrasse 50, 79115 Freiburg, Germany; tel. (761) 459060; fax (761) 4590699; e-mail hq@ises.org; internet www.ises.org; f. 1954; addresses all aspects of renewable energy, including characteristics, effects and methods of use; undertakes projects in several countries on various aspects of renewable energy technology and implementation; organizes major international, regional and national congresses; mems: c. 30,000 in some 100 countries; Pres. DAVID RENNÉ (USA); publs *Solar Energy Journal* (monthly), *Renewable Energy Focus* (6 a year).

International Solid Waste Association (ISWA): Auerspergstrasse 15, Top 41, 1080 Vienna, Austria; tel. 253-6001; e-mail iswa@iswa.org; internet www.iswa.org; f. 1970 to promote the exchange of information and experience in solid waste management, in order to protect human health and the environment; promotes research and development activities; provides advice; organizes conferences (World Congress, Sept. 2012: Florence, Italy); Pres. JEFF COOPER; Man. Dir. HERMANN KOLLER; publs *Waste Management World*, *Waste Management and Research* (monthly).

International Special Committee on Radio Interference: 143 Jumping Brook Rd, Lincroft, NJ 07738-1442, USA; tel. (732) 741-7723; e-mail d.heirman@ieee.org; f. 1934; special committee of the IEC, promoting international agreement on the protection of radio reception from interference by equipment other than authorized transmitters; recommends limits of such interference and specifies equipment and methods of measurement; mems: national cttees of IEC and 7 other int. orgs; Sec. STEPHEN COLCLOUGH.

International Union for Electricity Applications: 5 rue Chante-Coq, 92808 Puteaux Cédex, France; tel. 1-41-26-56-48; fax 1-41-26-56-49; e-mail uie@uie.org; internet www.uie.org; f. 1953, present title adopted 1994; aims to study all questions relative to electricity applications, except commercial questions; links national groups and organizes international congresses on electricity applications; mems: national cttees, corporate, associated and individual mems in 18 countries; Sec. KOEN VAN REUSEL; publ. UIE proceedings.

International Union for Vacuum Science, Technique and Applications (IUVSTA): c/o Dr R. J. Reid, 84 Oldfield Drive, Vicars Cross, Chester, CH3 5LW, United Kingdom; tel. (1244) 342675; e-mail iuvsta.secretary.general@ronreid.me.uk; internet www.iuvsta.org; f. 1958; collaborates with the International Standards Organization in defining and adopting technical standards; holds triennial International Vacuum Congress, European Vacuum Conference, triennial International Conference on Thin Films, and International Conference on Solid Surfaces; administers the Welch Foundation scholarship for postgraduate research in vacuum science and technology; mems: orgs in 30 countries; Pres. Prof. JEAN-JACQUES PIREAUX; Sec.-Gen. Dr R. J. REID (United Kingdom); publ. *News Bulletins* (2 a year, electronic version).

International Union of Air Pollution Prevention and Environmental Protection Associations: Oakwood House, 11 Wingle Tye Rd, Burgess Hill, West Sussex RH15 9HR, United Kingdom; tel. (1444) 236848; e-mail secretariat@iuappa.org; internet www.iuappa.org; f. 1963; organizes triennial World Clean Air Congress and regional conferences for developing countries (several a year); undertakes policy development and research programmes on international environmental issues; World Congress: Cape Town, South Africa (Sept. 2013); Pres. HANLIE LIEBENBERG ENSLIN (South Africa); Dir-Gen. RICHARD MILLS; publ. *IUAPPA Newsletter*.

International Union of Laboratories and Experts in Construction Materials, Systems and Structures (Réunion Internationale des Laboratoires et Experts des Matériaux, systèmes de construction et ouvrages—RILEM): 157 rue des Blains, 92220 Bagneux, France; tel. 1-45-36-10-20; fax 1-45-36-63-20; e-mail sg@rilem.net; internet www.rilem.net; f. 1947 for the exchange of information and the promotion of co-operation on experimental research concerning structures and materials; promotes research with a view to improvement and standardization; mems: laboratories and individuals in 73 countries; Pres. Dr PETER RICHNER; Sec.-Gen. PASCALE DUCORNET; publs *Materials and Structures* (10 a year), *RILEM Technical Recommendations*, conference proceedings.

International Union of Technical Associations and Organizations (Union internationale des associations et organismes techniques—UATI): UNESCO House, 1 rue Miollis, 75732 Paris Cédex 15, France; tel. 1-45-68-48-29; fax 1-43-06-29-27; e-mail uati@uati.info; internet www.uati.info; f. 1951 (fmrly Union of International Technical Associations) under the auspices of UNESCO; aims to promote and co-ordinate activities of member organizations and represent their interests; facilitates relations with international organizations, notably UN agencies; receives proposals and makes recommendations on the establishment of new international technical asscns; mems: 16 orgs; Pres. PHILIPPE AUSSOURD (France); Sec.-Gen. ROGER FRANK; publ. *Convergence* (3 a year).

International Water Resources Association (IWRA): c/o Association Verseau Développement, 859 rue Jean-François Breton, 34093 Montpellier Cédex 5, France; tel. 4-4-67-61-29-45; fax 4-4-67-52-28-29; e-mail office@iwra.org; internet www.iwra.org; f. 1972 to promote collaboration in and support for international water resources programmes; holds conferences; conducts training in water resources management; Pres. JUN XIA (People's Republic of China); Exec. Dir. TOM SOO; publ. *Water International* (quarterly).

Latin-American Energy Organization (Organización Latinoamericana de Energía—OLADE): Avda Mariscal Antonio José de Sucre, No N58–63 y Fernándes Salvador, Edif. OLADE, Sector San Carlos, POB 17-11-6413 CCI, Quito, Ecuador; tel. (2) 2598-122; fax (2) 2531-691; e-mail oladel@olade.org.ec; internet www.olade.org.ec; f. 1973 to act as an instrument of co-operation in using and conserving the energy resources of the region; mems: 26 Latin-American and Caribbean countries; Exec. Sec. VICTORIO OXILIA DAVALOS; publ. *Enerlac Magazine*.

Latin American Steel Association (Asociación Latinamericana del Acero—Alacero): Benjamín 2944, 5°, Las Condes, Santiago, Chile; tel. (2) 233-0545; fax (2) 233-0768; e-mail alacero@alacero.org; internet wwww.alacero.org; f. 1959 as the Latin American Iron and Steel Institute (ILAFA) to help achieve the harmonious development of iron and steel production, manufacture and marketing in Latin America; conducts economic surveys on the steel sector; organizes technical conventions and meetings; disseminates industrial processes suited to regional conditions; prepares and maintains statistics on production, end uses, etc., of raw materials and steel products within this area; mems: 18 hon. mems; 49 active mems; 36 assoc. mems; Chair. RAÚL MANUEL GUTIÉRREZ MUGUERZA (Mexico); Sec. ROBERTO DE ANDRACA BARBAS (Chile); publs *Industry Year Book*, *Latin American Steel Directory* (now electronic); also technical books, bulletins and manuals.

NORDTEST: Stensberggt. 25, 0170 Oslo, Norway; tel. 47-61-44-00; fax 22-56-55-65; e-mail info@nordicinnovation.org; internet www.nordtest.info; f. 1973; inter-Nordic agency for technical testing and standardization of methods and of laboratory accreditation; Man.Dir IVAR H. KRISTENSEN.

Regional Centre for Mapping of Resources for Development (RCMRD): POB 632, 00618 Ruaraka, Nairobi, Kenya; tel. (20) 8560227; fax (20) 8561673; e-mail rcmrd@rcmrd.org; internet www.rcmrd.org; f. 1975; present name adopted 1997; provides services for the professional techniques of map-making and the application of satellite and remote sensing data in resource analysis and development planning; undertakes research and provides advisory services to African governments; mems: 15 signatory and 10 non-signatory govts; Dir-Gen. Dr HUSSEIN O. FARAH.

Regional Centre for Training in Aerospace Surveys (RECTAS) (Centre Regional de Formations aux Techniques des leves aerospatiaux): PMB 5545, Ile-Ife, Nigeria; tel. (803) 384-0581; e-mail info@rectas.org; internet www.rectas.org; f. 1972; provides training, research and advisory services in aerospace surveys and geoinformatics; administered by the ECA; mems: 8 govts; Exec. Dir Prof. ISI IKHUORIA.

World Association of Industrial and Technological Research Organizations (WAITRO): c/o SIRIM Berhad, 1 Persiaran Dato' Menteri, Section 2, POB 7035, 40911 Shah Alam, Malaysia; tel. 55446635; fax 55446735; e-mail info@waitro.sirim.my; internet www.waitro.org; f. 1970 by the UN Industrial Development Organization to organize co-operation in industrial and technological research; provides financial assistance for training and joint activities; arranges international seminars; facilitates the exchange of information; mems: 168 research institutes in 77 countries; Pres. Dr R.K. KHANDAL (India); Sec.-Gen. Dr ROHANI HASHIM; publ. *WAITRO News* (quarterly).

World Association of Nuclear Operators (WANO): Cavendish Court, First Floor, 11–15 Wigmore St, London, W1U 1PF, United Kingdom; tel. (20) 7478-9200; fax (20) 7495-4502; internet www.wano.org.uk; f. 1989 by operators of nuclear power plants; aims to improve the safety and reliability of nuclear power plants through the exchange of information; operates four regional centres (in Paris, France; Tokyo, Japan; Moscow, Russia; and Atlanta, USA) and a Co-ordinating Centre in the United Kingdom; mems: in 35 countries; Pres. VLADIMIR ASMOLOV; Man. Dir GEORGE FELGATE.

World Bureau of Metal Statistics: 27A High St, Ware, Herts, SG12 9BA, United Kingdom; tel. (1920) 461274; fax (1920) 464258; e-mail enquiries@world-bureau.co.uk; internet www.world-bureau.com; f. 1947; produces statistics of production, consumption, stocks, prices and international trade in copper, lead, zinc, tin, nickel, aluminium and several other minor metals; publs *World Metal Statistics* (monthly), *World Tin Statistics* (monthly), *World Nickel Statistics* (monthly), *World Metal Statistics Yearbook*, *World Metal Statistics Quarterly Summary*, *Annual Stainless Steel Statistics* (annually), *Metallstatistik* (annually).

World Energy Council: 5th Floor, Regency House, 1–4 Warwick St, London, W1B 5LT, United Kingdom; tel. (20) 7734-5996; fax (20) 7734-5926; e-mail info@worldenergy.org; internet www.worldenergy.org; f. 1924 to link all branches of energy and resources technology and maintain liaison between world experts; holds congresses every three years; mems: cttees in over 90 countries; Chair. PIERRE GADONNEIX (France); Sec.-Gen. Dr CHRISTOPH FREI (Switzerland); publs energy supply and demand projections, resources surveys, technical assessments, reports.

World Federation of Engineering Organizations (WFEO): Maison de l'UNESCO, 1 rue Miollis, 75732 Paris, Cédex 15, France; tel. 1-45-68-48-47; fax 1-45-68-48-65; e-mail info@wfeo.net; internet www.wfeo.net; f. 1968 to advance engineering as a profession; fosters co-operation between engineering organizations throughout the world; undertakes special projects in co-operation with other international bodies; mems: 90 national mems, 9 int. mems; Pres. Elect ADEL ALKHARAFI (Kuwait); Exec. Dir TAHANI YOUSSEF (France); publ. *WFEO Newsletter* (2 a year).

World Foundry Organization (WFO): Winton House, Lyonshall, Kington, Herefordshire, HR5 3JP, United Kingdom; tel. (121) 601-6976; fax (1544) 340-332; e-mail secretary@thewfo.com; internet www.thewfo.com; f. 1927, as International Committee of Foundry Technical Asscns; named changed to World Foundrymen Organization in 2000, and as above in 2010; Pres. XABIER GONZALES ASPIRI (Spain).

Tourism

Alliance Internationale de Tourisme: 2 Chemin de Blandonnet, CP 111, 1215 Geneva 15, Switzerland; tel. and fax 225444500; e-mail dsmith@fia.com; internet www.aitgva.ch; f. 1898, present title adopted 1919; represents motoring orgs and touring clubs around the world; aims to study all questions relating to automobile mobility; mems: 120 mem. asscns in 101 countries; Pres. WERNER KRAUS (Austria); Dir-Gen. SUSAN PIKRALLIDAS (France).

Caribbean Tourism Organization: One Financial Pl., Collymore Rock, St Michael, Barbados; tel. 427-5242; fax 429-3065; e-mail ctobar@caribsurf.com; internet www.onecaribbean.org; f. 1989, by merger of the Caribbean Tourism Association (f. 1951) and the Caribbean Tourism Research and Development Centre (f. 1974); aims to encourage tourism in the Caribbean region; organizes annual Caribbean Tourism Conference, Sustainable Tourism Development Conference and Tourism Investment Conference; conducts training and other workshops on request; maintains offices in New York, Canada and London; mems: 32 Caribbean govts, 400 allied mems; Sec.-Gen. HUGH RILEY; publs *Caribbean Tourism Statistical News* (quarterly), *Caribbean Tourism Statistical Report* (annually).

European Travel Commission: 61 rue du Marché aux Herbes, 1000 Brussels, Belgium; tel. (2) 548-90-00; fax (2) 514-18-43; e-mail info@visiteurope.com; internet www.etc-corporate.org; f. 1948; currently promotes and markets 'Destination Europe' around the world, through its operations groups in Canada, Brazil (for Latin America), Japan (for Asia), and the USA; mems: national tourist orgs in 33 European countries; Exec. Dir EDUARDO SANTANDER (Belgium).

International Association of Scientific Experts in Tourism: Dufourstr. 40A, 9000 St Gallen, Switzerland; tel. 712242530; fax 712242536; e-mail aiest@unisg.ch; internet www.aiest.org; f. 1949 to encourage scientific activity in tourism, to support tourist institutions of a scientific nature and to organize conventions; mems: 300 from more than 50 countries; Pres. Prof. Dr PETER KELLER (Switzerland); Gen. Sec. Prof. Dr CHRISTIAN LAESSER (Switzerland); publ. *The Tourism Review* (quarterly).

International Hotel and Restaurant Association: rue de Montbrillant 87, 1202 Geneva, Switzerland; tel. 227348041; fax 227348056; e-mail info@ih-ra.ch; internet www.ih-ra.com; f. 1869 to act as the authority on matters affecting the international hotel and restaurant industry, to promote its interests and to contribute to its growth, profitability and quality; membership extended to restaurants in 1996; mems: 130 national hospitality asscns, 200 national and international hotel and restaurant chains; Pres. and CEO GHASSAN AIDI; publs *Hotels* (monthly), *Yearbook and Directory* (annually).

International Tourism Trade Fairs Association: 1 Old Forge Cottage, Carrington Rd, Richmond, Surrey, TW10 5AA, United Kingdom; tel. (20) 8939-9000; e-mail info@ittfa.org; internet www.ittfa.org; f. 1992 as European Tourism Trade Fairs Asscn; Chair. TOM NUTLEY (United Kingdom); Pres. ANTONIO DELL' AQUILANO (Italy).

Latin-American Confederation of Tourist Organizations (Confederación de Organizaciones Turísticas de la América Latino—COTAL): Viamonte 640, 3°, 1053 Buenos Aires, Argentina; tel. (11) 4322-4003; fax (11) 5277-4176; e-mail cotal@cotal.org.ar; internet www.cotal.org.ar; f. 1957 to link Latin American national asscns of travel agents and their members with other tourist bodies around the world; mems: in 21 countries; Pres. LUIS FELIPE AQUINO; publ. *Revista COTAL* (every 2 months).

Pacific Asia Travel Association (PATA): Unit B1, 28th Floor, Siam Tower, 989 Rama 1 Rd, Pratumwan, Bangkok 10330, Thailand; tel. (2) 658-2000; fax (2) 658-2010; e-mail patabkk@pata.org; internet www.pata.org; f. 1951; aims to enhance the growth, value and quality of Pacific Asia travel and tourism for the benefit of PATA members; holds annual conference and travel fair; divisional offices in Germany (Frankfurt), Australia (Sydney), USA (Oakland, CA) and the People's Republic of China (Beijing); mems: more than 1,200 governments, carriers, tour operators, travel agents and hotels; Chair. HIRAN COORAY (Sri Lanka); CEO MARTIN CRAIGS (United Kingdom/Ireland); publs *PATA Compass* (every 2 months), *Statistical Report* (quarterly), *Forecasts Book*, research reports, directories, newsletters.

South Pacific Tourism Organization: POB 13119, Suva, Fiji; tel. 3304177; fax 3301995; e-mail tourism@spto.org; internet www.south-pacific.travel; fmrly the Tourism Council of the South Pacific; also known as south-pacific.travel; aims to foster regional co-operation in the development, marketing and promotion of tourism in the island nations of the South Pacific; receives EU funding and undertakes sustainable activities; mems: 13 govts in the South Pacific, more than 200 private sector members in 25 countries world-wide; CEO ILISONI VUIDREKETI (Fiji); publ. *Weekly Newsletter*.

United Federation of Travel Agents' Associations (UFTAA): 19 ave des Castelans, Entrée C, 98000 Monaco; tel. 92-05-28-29; fax 92-05-29-87; e-mail uftaa@uftaa.org; internet www.uftaa.org; f. 1966 to unite travel agents' asscns; represents the interests of travel agents at the international level; helps in international legal differences; issues literature on travel; mems: regional federations representing some 80 national asscns; Pres. WILLIAM TAN (Singapore).

World Association of Travel Agencies (WATA): 11 rue du Boiron, 1260 Nyon, Switzerland; tel. 229951545; fax 223620753; e-mail wata@wata.net; internet www.wata.net; f. 1949 to foster the development of tourism, to help the rational organization of tourism in all countries, to collect and disseminate information and to participate in commercial and financial operations to foster the development of tourism; mems: more than 100 individual travel agencies in some 50 countries; Exec. Dir CHRISTINE FOURNIER (Switzerland); publ. *WATA News* (online).

World Travel and Tourism Council (WTTC): 1–2 Queen Victoria Terrace, Sovereign Court, London, E1W 3HA, United Kingdom; tel. (20) 7481-8007; fax (20) 7488-1008; e-mail enquiries@wttc.org; internet www.wttc.org; f. 1989; promotes the development of the travel/tourism industry; analyses impact of tourism on employment levels and local economies and promotes greater expenditure on tourism infrastructure; administers a 'Green Globe' certification programme to enhance environmental management throughout the industry; mems: reps from 100 cos world-wide; Chair. GEOFFREY KENT; Pres. and CEO DAVID SCOWSILL; publs *WTTC Backgrounder*, *Travel and Tourism Review*, *Viewpoint* (quarterly), *Blueprint for New Tourism*, regional and country reports.

Trade and Industry

African Regional Organization for Standardization (ARSO): POB 57363-00200, Nairobi, Kenya; tel. (20) 224561; fax (20) 218792; e-mail info@arso-oran.org; internet www.arso-oran.org; f. 1977 to promote standardization, quality control, certification and metrology in the African region, to formulate regional standards, and to co-ordinate participation in international standardization activities; mems: 27 African states; Pres. KIOKO MANG'ELI (Kenya); Sec.-Gen. (vacant); publs *ARSO Bulletin* (2 a year), *ARSO Catalogue of Regional Standards* (annually), *ARSO Annual Report*.

Arab Iron and Steel Union (AISU): BP 4, Chéraga, Algiers, Algeria; tel. (21) 36-27-04; fax (21) 37-19-75; e-mail relex@solbarab.com; internet www.arabsteel.info; f. 1972 to develop commercial and technical aspects of Arab steel production by helping member asscns commercialize their production in Arab markets, guaranteeing them high quality materials and intermediary products, informing them of recent developments in the industry and organizing training sessions; also arranges two annual symposia; mems: 80 companies in 15 Arab countries; Gen. Sec. MUHAMMAD LAID LACHGAR; publs *Arab Steel Review* (monthly), *Information Bulletin*, *News Steel World* (2 a month), *Directory* (annually).

Asian Productivity Organization: Hirakawacho Daiichi Seimei Bldg 2F, 1-2-10 Hirakawa-cho, Chiyoda-ku, Tokyo 102–0093, Japan; tel. (3) 5226-3920; fax (3) 5226-3950; e-mail apo@apo-tokyo.org; internet www.apo-tokyo.org; f. 1961 as non-political, non-profit-making, non-discriminatory regional intergovernmental organization with the aim of contributing to the socio-economic development of Asia and the Pacific through productivity promotion; activities cover industry, agriculture and service sectors, with the primary focus on human resources development; five key areas are incorporated into its activities: knowledge management, green productivity, strengthening small and medium enterprises, integrated community development and development of national productivity organizations; serves its members as a think tank, catalyst, regional adviser, institution builder and clearing house; mems: 20 countries; Sec.-Gen. RYUICHIRO YAMAZAKI (Japan); publs *APO News* (monthly), *Annual Report*, *APO Productivity Databook*, *Eco-products Directory*, other books and monographs.

Association of European Chambers of Commerce and Industry (EUROCHAMBRES): The Chamber House, 19A/D ave des Arts, 1000 Brussels, Belgium; tel. (2) 282-08-50; fax (2) 230-00-38; e-mail eurochambres@eurochambres.eu; internet www.eurochambres.eu; f. 1958 to promote the exchange of experience and information among its members and to bring their joint opinions to the attention of the institutions of the European Union; conducts studies and seminars; co-ordinates EU projects; mems: 45 nat. asscns of Chambers of Commerce and Industry and 1 transnational Chamber org, 2,000 regional and local Chambers and 19m. mem. enterprises in Europe; Pres. ALESSANDRO BARBERIS (Italy); Sec.-Gen. ARNALDO ABRUZZINI (Italy).

BusinessEurope: 168 ave de Cortenbergh, 1000 Brussels, Belgium; tel. (2) 237-65-11; fax (2) 231-14-45; e-mail main@businesseurope.eu; internet www.businesseurope.eu; f. 1958 as Union of Industrial and Employers' Confederations of Europe (UNICE); name changed, as above, Jan. 2007; aims to ensure that European Union policy-making takes account of the views of European business; committees and working groups develop joint positions in fields of interest to business and submit these to the Community institutions concerned; the Council of Presidents (of member federations) lays down general policy; the Executive Committee (of Directors-General of member federations) is the managing body; and the Committee of Permanent Delegates, consisting of federation representatives in Brussels, ensures permanent liaison with mems; mems: 41 industrial and employers' federations from 35 countries; Pres. JÜRGEN THUMANN (Germany); Dir. Gen. PHILIPPE DE BUCK (Belgium); publ. *BusinessEurope Newsletter* (weekly, electronic).

CAEF—The European Foundry Association: Sohnstrasse 70, 40237 Düsseldorf, Germany; tel. (211) 6871217; fax (211) 6871347; e-mail info@caef.eu; internet www.caef.eu; f. 1953 to safeguard the common interests of European foundry industries and to collect and exchange information; mems: asscns in 20 countries; Sec.-Gen. MAX SCHUMACHER; publ. *The European Foundry Industry* (annually).

Cairns Group: (no permanent secretariat); e-mail agriculture.negotiations@dfat.gov.au; internet www.cairnsgroup.org; f. 1986 by major agricultural exporting countries; aims to bring about reforms in international agricultural trade, including reductions in export subsidies, in barriers to access and in internal support measures; represents members' interests in WTO negotiations; mems: Argentina, Australia, Bolivia, Brazil, Canada, Chile, Colombia, Costa Rica, Guatemala, Indonesia, Malaysia, New Zealand, Pakistan, Paraguay, Peru, Philippines, South Africa, Thailand, Uruguay; Chair. Dr CRAIG EMERSON (Australia).

Caribbean Association of Industry and Commerce (CAIC): Ground Floor, 27A Saddle Rd, Maraval, Trinidad and Tobago; tel. 628-9859; fax 622-7810; e-mail info@caic.org.tt; internet www.caic.org.tt; f. 1955; aims to encourage economic development through the private sector; undertakes research and training and gives assistance to small enterprises; encourages export promotion; mems: chambers of commerce and enterprises in 20 countries and territories; Pres. CAROL EVELYN (Saint Christopher and Nevis); publ. *Caribbean Investor* (quarterly).

CINOA—International Confederation of Art and Antique Dealers: 33 rue Ernest-Allard, 1000 Brussels, Belgium; tel. (2) 502-26-92; e-mail secretary@cinoa.org; internet www.cinoa.org; f. 1936; mems: 32 art and antique dealer asscns in 22 countries, representing 5,000 dealers; holds anuual conference (June 2012: Bruges, Belgium); Pres. JAN DE MAERE; Sec.-Gen. ERIKA BOCHEREAU.

Committee for European Construction Equipment (CECE): Diamant Bldg, blvd Reyers 80, 1030 Brussels, Belgium; tel. (2) 706-82-26; fax (2) 706-82-10; e-mail info@cece.eu; internet www.cece.eu; f. 1959 to further contact between manufacturers, to improve market conditions and productivity and to conduct research into techniques; mems: representatives from 12 European countries; Pres. JOHANN SAILER; Sec.-Gen. RALF WEZEL.

Confederation of Asia-Pacific Chambers of Commerce and Industry (CACCI): 14/F, 3 11 Songgao Rd, Taipei 11073, Taiwan; tel. (2) 27255663; fax (2) 27255665; e-mail cacci@cacci.org.tw; internet www.cacci.org.tw; f. 1966; holds biennial conferences to examine regional co-operation, and an annual Council meeting; liaises with governments to promote laws conducive to regional co-operation; serves as a centre for compiling and disseminating trade and business information; encourages contacts between businesses; conducts training and research; mems: 29 national chambers of commerce and industry from the region, also affiliate and special mems; Pres. BENEDICTO V. YUJUICO; Dir-Gen. Dr WEBSTER KIANG; publs *CACCI Profile* (monthly), *CACCI Journal of Commerce and Industry* (2 a year).

Consumers International: 24 Highbury Cres., London, N5 1RX, United Kingdom; tel. (20) 7226-6663; fax (20) 7354-0607; e-mail consint@consint.org; internet www.consumersinternational.org; f. 1960 as International Organization of Consumers' Unions—IOCU; links consumer groups world-wide through information networks and international seminars; supports new consumer groups and represents consumers' interests at the international level; maintains four regional offices; mems: over 220 orgs in 115 countries; Dir-Gen. HELEN MCCALLUM; publs *World Consumer Rights Day Kit* (annually, English, French and Spanish), *Annual Report*, Policy Briefing Papers and Issue-specific reports.

CropLife International: 326 ave Louise, POB 35, 1050 Brussels, Belgium; tel. (2) 542-04-10; fax (2) 542-04-19; e-mail croplife@croplife.org; internet www.croplife.org; f. 1960 as European Group of National Asscns of Pesticide Manufacturers, international body since 1967, present name adopted in 2001, evolving from Global Crop Protection Federation; represents the plant science industry, with the aim of promoting sustainable agricultural methods; aims to harmonize national and international regulations concerning crop protection products and agricultural biotechnology; promotes observation of the FAO Code of Conduct on the Distribution and Use of Pesticides; holds an annual General Assembly; mems: 8 cos, regional bodies and national asscns in 91 countries; Pres. and CEO HOWARD MINIGH.

Energy Charter Conference: 56 blvd de la Woluwe, 1200 Brussels, Belgium; tel. (2) 775-98-00; fax (2) 775-98-01; e-mail info@encharter.org; internet www.encharter.org; f. 1995 under the provisions of the Energy Charter Treaty (1994); provides a legal framework for promotion of trade and investment across Eurasia in the energy industries; mems: 51 states; Sec.-Gen. URBAN RUSNÁK (Slovakia); publs *Putting a Price on Energy: International Pricing Mechanisms for Oil and Gas*, *The Energy Charter Treaty—A Reader's Guide*, reports.

ESOMAR—World Association of Opinion and Marketing Research Professionals: Eurocenter 2, 11th Floor, Barbara Strozzilaan 384, 1083 HN Amsterdam, Netherlands; tel. (20) 6642141; fax (20) 5897885; e-mail customerservice@esomar.org; internet www.esomar.org; f. 1948 (as European Society for Opinion and Marketing Research); aims to further professional interests and encourage high technical standards in the industry; creates and manages a comprehensive programme of industry-specific and thematic conferences, publications and communications, as well as actively advocating self-regulation and the world-wide code of practice; mems: over 4,500 in 100 countries; Pres. DIETER KORCZAK; publs *Research World* (monthly), *Global Market Research* (annually).

European Association of Communications Agencies (EACA): 152 blvd Brand Whitlock, 1200 Brussels, Belgium; tel. (2) 740-07-10; fax (2) 740-07-17; e-mail dominic.lyle@eaca.be; internet www.eaca.eu; f. 1959 (as European Association of Advertising Agencies) to maintain and raise the standards of service of all European advertising, media and sales promotions agencies; aims to promote honest, effective advertising, high professional standards, and awareness of the contribution of advertising in a free market economy and to encourage close co-operation between agencies, advertisers and media in European advertising bodies; mems: 30 national advertising agency asscns and 17 multinational agency networks; Pres. MORAY MACLENNAN; Dir-Gen. DOMINIC LYLE.

European Association of National Productivity Centres (EANPC): c/o Prevent, 88 rue de la Gachard, 1050 Brussels, Belgium; tel. (2) 643-44-51; fax (2) 643-44-50; e-mail ingrid.dhondt@prevent.be; internet www.eanpc.eu; f. 1966 to enable members to pool knowledge about their policies and activities; mems: 15 European centres; Pres. JOHN HEAP (United Kingdom); Sec.-Gen. MARC DE GREEF (Belgium); publs *EPI* (3 a year), *Europroductivity* (3 a year).

European Brewery Convention: c/o The Brewers of Europe, 23–25 rue Caroly, 1050 Brussels, Belgium; tel. (2) 551-18-28; fax (2) 660-09-02; e-mail info@europeanbreweryconvention.org; internet www.europeanbreweryconvention.org; f. 1947; aims to promote scientific co-ordination in malting and brewing; mems: national asscns in 20 European countries; Pres. Dr STEFAN LUSDIG; publs *Analytica*, *Thesaurus*, *Dictionary of Brewing*, monographs, conference proceedings, manuals of good practice.

European Chemical Industry Council: 4 ave E. van Nieuwenhuyse, Box 1, 1160 Brussels, Belgium; tel. (2) 676-72-11; fax (2) 676-73-00; e-mail apy@cefic.be; internet www.cefic.org; f. 1972; represents and defends the interests of the chemical industry in legal and trade policy, internal market, environmental and technical matters; liaises with intergovernmental organizations; provides secretariat for some 100 product sector groups; mems: 22 national federations, incl. 6 assoc. mem. feds; Pres. GIORGIO SQUINZI; Dir-Gen. HUBERT MANDERY.

European Committee for Standardization (Comité européen de normalisation—CEN): 17 ave Marnix, 1000 Brussels, Belgium; tel. (2) 550-08-11; fax (2) 550-08-19; e-mail infodesk@cenorm.be; internet www.cenorm.be; f. 1961 to promote European standardization; works to eliminate obstacles caused by technical requirements, in order to facilitate the exchange of goods and services; mems: 32 national standards bodies, 8 associated and 5 affiliated bodies in central and eastern Europe and 7 partnership standardization bodies; Pres. FRIEDRICH SMAXWIL; Dir. Gen. ELENA SANTIAGO CID; publs *Catalogue of European Standards* (2 a year), *CEN Networking* (newsletter, every 2 months), *Bulletin* (quarterly), *Directives and related standards* (in English, French and German), *Directions*, *European Standardization in a Global Context*, *The Benefits of Standards*, *Marking of Products and System Certification*.

European Committee of Associations of Manufacturers of Agricultural Machinery: 80 blvd A. Reyers, 1030 Brussels, Belgium; tel. (2) 706-82-16; e-mail info@cema-agri.org; internet www.cema-agri.org; f. 1959 to study economic and technical problems in field of agricultural machinery manufacture, to protect members' interests and to disseminate information; mems: 11 mem. countries; Pres. GILLES DRYANCOUR; Sec.-Gen. RALF WEZEL (Germany).

European Confederation of Iron and Steel Industries (EUROFER): Integrale Bldg, 3e étage, 5 ave Ariane, 1200 Brussels, Belgium; tel. (2) 738-79-20; fax (2) 738-79-55; e-mail g.moffat@eurofer.be; internet www.eurofer.eu; f. 1976 as a confederation of national federations and companies in the European steel industry; aims to foster co-operation between the member federations and companies and to represent their common interests to the EU and other international organizations; mems: 60 national federations and companies in 23 European countries; Gen. Dir GORDON MOFFAT.

European Confederation of Woodworking Industries: 24 rue Montoyer, Box 20, 1000 Brussels, Belgium; tel. (2) 556-25-85; fax (2) 287-08-75; e-mail info@cei-bois.org; internet www.cei-bois.org; f. 1952 to liaise between national organizations, undertake research and defend the interests of the industry; mems: national federations in 25 European countries, 8 branch feds; Chair. MATTI MIKKOLA (Finland); Sec.-Gen. FILIP DE JAEGER; publ. *Brochure*.

European Council of Paint, Printing Ink and Artists' Colours Industry: 6 ave E. van Nieuwenhuyse, 1160 Brussels, Belgium; tel. (2) 676-74-80; fax (2) 676-74-90; e-mail secretariat@cepe.org; internet www.cepe.org; f. 1951 to study questions relating to the paint and printing ink industries, to take or recommend measures for the development of these industries or to support their interests, and to exchange information; mems: company mems of national asscns in 23 European countries; Chair. JOAO SERRENHO; Man. Dir JAN VAN DER MEULEN; publs *Annual Review*, guidance documents.

European Crop Protection Association (ECPA): 6 ave E. van Nieuwenhuyse, 1160 Brussels, Belgium; tel. (2) 663-15-50; fax (2) 663-15-60; e-mail ecpa@ecpa.eu; internet www.ecpa.eu; aims to harmonize national and international regulations concerning crop protection products, to support the development of the industry and to promote observation of the FAO Code of Conduct on the Distribution and Use of Pesticides, forms part of Croplife International; mems: in 26 countries; Pres. VINCENT GROS; Dir-Gen. Dr FRIEDHELM SCHMIDER (Germany); publs *Annual Report*.

European Federation of Associations of Insulation Enterprises: c/o Thermal Insulation Contractors Asscn, TICA House, Allington Way, Darlington DL1 4QB, United Kingdom; tel. (1325) 734140; e-mail bfa.wksb@bauindustrie.de; f. 1970; groups organizations in Europe representing insulation firms; aims to facilitate contacts between member asscns; studies problems of interest to the profession; works to safeguard the interests of the profession and represent it in international fora; mems: professional orgs in 16 European countries; Sec.-Gen. JUERGEN SCHMOLDT.

European Federation of Associations of Marketing Research Organisations (EFAMRO): Bastion Tower, 20e étage, Pl. du Champ de Mars 5, 1050 Brussels, Belgium; tel. (2) 550-35-48; fax (2) 550-35-84; e-mail info@efamro.eu; internet www.efamro.eu; f. 1965 (frmly known as FEMRA) to facilitate contacts between researchers; maintains specialist divisions on European chemical marketing research, European technological forecasting, paper and related industries, industrial materials, automotives, textiles, methodology, and information technology; mems: nat. asscns in 9 countries; Pres. ANDREW CANNON; publs *EFAMRO Monitoring Report* (weekly).

European Federation of Insurance Intermediaries (BIPAR): 40 ave Albert-Elisabeth, 1200 Brussels, Belgium; tel. (2) 735-60-48; fax (2) 732-14-18; e-mail bipar@skynet.be; internet www.bipar.eu; f. 1937; represents, promotes and defends the interests of national asscns of professional insurance agents and brokers at the European and international level; works to co-ordinate members' activities; mems: 48 asscns from 30 countries, representing approx. 250,000 brokers and agents; Chair. ALESSANDRO DE BESI; Sec.-Gen. ANDRÉ LAMOTTE; publ. *BIPAR Press* (10 a year).

European Federation of Management Consultancies' Associations: 3–5 ave des Arts, 6e étage, 1210 Brussels, Belgium; tel. (2) 250-06-50; e-mail feaco@feaco.org; internet www.feaco.org; f. 1960; aims to promote networking within the management consultancy sector and its interests and promote a high standard of professional competence, by encouraging discussions of, and research into, problems of common professional interest; mems: 17 asscns; Chair. EZIO LATTANZIO (Italy); Sec.-Gen. DAVID IFRAH; publs *FEACO Newsletter* (quarterly), *Annual Survey of the European Management Consultancy Market*.

European Federation of Materials Handling and Storage Equipment: Diamant Bldg, 80 blvd A. Reyers, 1030 Brussels, Belgium; tel. (2) 706-82-37; fax (2) 706-82-53; e-mail olivier.janin@orgalime.org; internet www.fem-eur.com; f. 1953 to represent the technical, economic and political interests of one of the largest industrial sectors of the European mechanical engineering industry; mems: national orgs in 12 European countries; Pres. JOHN MEALE; Sec.-Gen. OLIVIER JANIN.

European Federation of the Plywood Industry (FEIC): 24 rue Montoyer, 1000 Brussels, Belgium; tel. (2) 556-25-84; fax (2) 287-08-75; e-mail info@europlywood.org; internet www.europlywood.org; f. 1957 to organize co-operation between members of the industry at the international level; mems: asscns in 18 European countries and 1 assoc. mem; Pres. JONI LUKKAROINEN; Sec.-Gen. K. WŸNENDAELE.

European Furniture Manufacturers Federation (Union européenne de l'ameublement—UEA): 163 rue Royale, Koningsstraat, 1210 Brussels, Belgium; tel. (2) 218-18-89; fax (2) 219-27-01; e-mail secretariat@uea.be; internet www.ueanet.com; f. 1950 to determine and support the general interests of the European furniture industry and facilitate contacts between members of the industry; mems: orgs in 25 European countries; Pres. MARTIN ČUDKA (Czech Republic); Sec.-Gen. BART DE TURCK; publs *UEA Newsletter* (every 2 months), *Focus on Issues*, *Strategy Survey*.

European General Galvanizers Association (EGGA): Maybrook House, Godstone Rd, Caterham, Surrey, CR3 6RE, United Kingdom; tel. (1883) 331277; fax (1883) 331287; e-mail mail@egga.com; internet www.egga.com; f. 1955 to promote co-operation between members of the industry, especially in improving processes and finding new uses for galvanized products; mems: asscns in 16 European countries; Dir MURRAY COOK (United Kingdom); Exec. Sec. FRANCES HOLMES.

European and International Booksellers Federation (EIBF): 10 rue de la science, 1000 Brussels, Belgium; tel. (2) 223-49-40; fax (2) 223-49-38; e-mail fran@ibf-booksellers.org; internet www.ibf-booksellers.org; f. 2010 by the merger of the former European Booksellers Federation and International Booksellers Federation (f. 1956) to promote the book trade and the exchange of information, and to protect the interests of booksellers when dealing with other international orgs; addresses pricing, book market research, advertising, customs and tariffs, the problems of young booksellers, etc.; mems: 200 in 25 countries; Pres. KARL PUS; Dir FRANÇOISE DUBRUILLE; publs *IBF Newsletter* (quarterly).

European Organization for Packaging and the Environment (EUROPEN): Le Royal Tervuren, ave de l'Armée 6 Legerlaan, B 1040 Brussels, Belgium; tel. (2) 736-36-00; fax (2) 736-35-21; e-mail packaging@europen.be; internet www.europen.be; provides policy support and a forum for the exchange of industry information related to packaging and the environment; mems: 42 corporate mems and 5 national orgs; Chair JOHN SWIFT; Man. Dir. VÉRONIQUE BAGGE; publs *EUROPEN Bulletin*(6 a year).

European Organization for Quality (EOQ): 36-38 rue Joseph II, 1000 Brussels, Belgium; tel. 474-24-08-00 (mobile); e-mail eoq@eoq-org.eu; internet www.eoq.org; f. 1956 to encourage the use and application of quality management, with the aim of improving quality, lowering costs and increasing productivity; organizes the exchange of information and documentation; mems: organizations in 34 European countries; Dir-Gen. ERIC JANSSENS.

European Panel Federation: 24 rue Montoyer, Box 20, 1000 Brussels, Belgium; tel. (2) 556-25-89; fax (2) 287-08-75; e-mail info@europanels.org; internet www.europanels.org; f. 1958 as European Federation of Associations of Particle Board Manufacturers; present name adopted 1999; works to develop and encourage international co-operation in the particle board and MDF industry; mems: in 23 countries; Pres. L. DÖRY; Sec.-Gen. K. WIJNENDALE (Belgium); publ. *Annual Report*.

European Patent Organisation: Erhardtstr. 27, 80469 Munich, Germany; tel. (89) 2399-0; fax (89) 2399-4560; e-mail info@epo.org; internet www.epo.org; f. 1977, in accordance with the European Patent Convention signed in Munich in 1973; conducts searches and examination of European patent applications; grants European patents; the Organisation comprises the European Patent Office (EPO) and an Administrative Council; mems: 38 European countries; Pres. EPO BENOÎT BATTISTELLI (France); Chair. Admin. Council JESPER KONGSTAD (Denmark).

European Photovoltaic Industry Association: 63–67 rue d'Arlon, 1040 Brussels, Belgium; tel. (2) 465-38-84; fax (2) 400-10-10; internet www.epia.org; f. 1985; promotes and represents the European photovoltaics industry and advises mems. in developing businesses within the EU and internationally; organizes annual conference (2012: Munich, Germany); mems: more than 230 cos; Pres. Dr WINFRIED HOFFMANN; Sec.-Gen REINHOLD BUTTGEREIT; publs reports, research documents and policy recommendations.

European Union of the Natural Gas Industry (EUROGAS): 172 ave de Cortenbergh, Box 6, 1000 Brussels, Belgium; tel. (2) 894-48-48; fax (2) 894-48-00; e-mail eurogas@eurogas.org; internet www.eurogas.org; f. 1910; mems: 50 orgs, federations and cos in 27 European countries; Pres. JEAN-FRANÇOIS CIRELLI (France); Sec.-Gen. BEATE RABBE; publs *Annual Report*, annual statistical brochures.

Fairtrade International: Bonner Talweg 177 53129 Bonn, Germany; tel. (228) 949230; fax (228) 2421713; e-mail info@fairtrade.net; internet www.fairtrade.net; f. 1997; co-ordinates Fairtrade labelling internationally, aims to set the strategic direction for Fairtrade, to produce the standards by which Fairtrade is conducted, and to support producers to gain Fairtrade certification and secure market opportunities; Producer Networks represent the interest of producers in the system while the Labelling Initiatives promote Fairtrade to business and consumers in the developed world; mems: 3 producer networks, 19 labelling initiatives and two marketing orgs in 26 countries; Chair. ESTHER GULUMA; CEO ROB CAMERON.

Federación de Cámaras de Comercio del Istmo Centroamericano (Federation of Central American Chambers of Commerce): 9A avda Norte y 5, Calle Poniente 333, San Salvador, El Salvador; tel. 2231-3065; e-mail aechevarria@fecamco.com; internet www.fecamco.com; f. 1961; plans and co-ordinates industrial and commercial exchanges and exhibitions; mems: Chambers of Commerce in 11 countries; Pres. MARIO GONZÁLEZ; Exec. Dir MARIA EUGENIA PACAS.

General Union of Chambers of Commerce, Industry and Agriculture for Arab Countries (GUCCIAAC): POB 11-2837, Beirut, Lebanon; tel. (1) 826020; fax (1) 826021; e-mail uac@uac.org.lb; internet www.gucciaac.org.lb; f. 1951 to enhance Arab economic development, integration and security through the co-ordination of industrial, agricultural and trade policies and legislation; mems: chambers of commerce, industry and agriculture in 22 Arab countries; Pres. ADNAN KASSAR; Sec.-Gen. Dr IMAD SHIHAB; publs *Arab Economic Report*, *Al-Omran Al-Arabi* (every 2 months), economic papers, proceedings.

Gulf Organization for Industrial Consulting (GOIC): POB 5114, Doha, Qatar; tel. 4858888; fax 4831465; e-mail goic@goic.org.qa; internet www.goic.org.qa; f. 1976 by the Gulf Arab states to encourage industrial co-operation among Gulf Arab states, to pool industrial expertise and to encourage joint development of projects; undertakes feasibility studies, market diagnosis, assistance in policy-making, legal consultancies, project promotion, promotion of small and medium industrial investment profiles and technical training; maintains industrial data bank; mems: mem. states of the Cooperation Council for the Arab States of the Gulf; Sec.-Gen. ABDULAZIZ BIN HAMAD AL-AGEEL; publs *GOIC Monthly Bulletin* (in Arabic), *Al Ta'awon al Sina'e* (quarterly, in Arabic and English).

Instituto Centroamericano de Administración de Empresas (INCAE) (Central American Institute for Business Administration): Apdo 960, 4050 Alajuela, Costa Rica; tel. 2443-9908; fax 2433-9983; e-mail costarica@incae.edu; internet www.incae.edu; f. 1964; provides a postgraduate programme in business administration; runs executive training programmes; carries out management research and consulting; maintains a second campus in Nicaragua; libraries of

85,000 vols; Pres. Dr ARTURO CONDO; publs *Alumni Journal* (in Spanish), *Bulletin* (quarterly), books and case studies.

Inter-American Commercial Arbitration Commission: OAS Administration Bldg, Rm 211, 19th and Constitution Ave, NW, Washington, DC 20006, USA; tel. (202) 458-3249; fax (202) 458-3293; f. 1934 to establish an inter-American system of arbitration for the settlement of commercial disputes by means of tribunals; mems: national committees, commercial firms and individuals in 22 countries; Dir-Gen. Dr ADRIANA POLANIA.

International Advertising Association Inc: World Service Center, 275 Madison Ave, Suite 2102, New York, NY 10016, USA; tel. (212) 557-1133; fax (212) 983-0455; e-mail iaa@iaaglobal.org; internet www.iaaglobal.org; f. 1938 as a global partnership of advertisers, agencies, the media and other marketing communications professionals; aims to protect freedom of commercial speech and consumer choice; holds World Congress every two years (2012: Manama, Bahrain); mems: 4,000 individuals, 55 corporate mems and 30 orgs in 76 countries; Chair. and World Pres. ALAN RUTHERFORD (United Kingdom); Exec. Dir MICHAEL LEE (USA); publs (electronic newsletters) *IAA EU News*, *IAA Intelligence*, *IAA Network News*, *Annual Report*.

International Association for Textile Professionals (American Association for Textile Chemists and Colourists): 1 Davis Dr., POB 12215, Research Triangle Park, NC 27709-2215, USA; tel. (919) 549-8141; fax (919) 549 8933; e-mail danielsj@aatcc.org; f. 1921 to establish industrial test methods, enable quality control and initiate networking between textile professionals globally; individual and corporate mems in 60 countries world-wide; Pres. R. MICHAEL TYNDALL.

International Association of Department Stores: 11-13 rue Guersant, 75017 Paris, France; tel. 1-42-94-02-02; fax 1-42-94-02-04; e-mail iads@iads.org; internet www.iads.org; f. 1928 to conduct research and exchange information and statistics on management, organization and technical problems; maintains a documentation centre; mems: large-scale retail enterprises operating department stores in 16 countries; Pres. PAUL DELAOUTRE (France); Gen. Sec. MAARTEN DE GROOT VAN EMBDEN (Netherlands).

International Association of the Soap, Detergent and Maintenance Products Industry (AISE) (Association internationale de la savonnerie, de la détergence et des produits d'entretien): 15 A ave Herrmann Debroux, 3rd Floor, 1160 Brussels, Belgium; tel. (2) 679-62-60; fax (2) 679-62-79; e-mail aise.main@aise.eu; internet www.aise.eu; f. 1952; aims to promote the manufacture and use of a wide range of cleaning products, polishes, bleaches, disinfectants and insecticides; mems: 37 national asscns in 42 countries; Dir-Gen. SUSANNE ZAENKER.

International Bureau for the Standardization of Man-Made Fibres (BISFA): 6 ave E. van Nieuwenhuyse, 1160 Brussels, Belgium; tel. (2) 676-74-55; fax (2) 676-74-54; e-mail secretariat@bisfa.org; internet www.bisfa.org; f. 1928 to examine and establish rules for the standardization, classification and naming of various categories of man-made fibres; mems: individual producers in 17 countries; Sec.-Gen. BERNARD DEFRAYE.

International Butchers' Confederation: Bte 10, 4 rue Jacques de Lalaing, 1040 Brussels, Belgium; tel. (2) 230-38-76; fax (2) 230-34-51; e-mail info@cibc.be; internet www.cibc.be; f. 1907; aims to defend the interests of small and medium-sized enterprises in the meat trading and catering industry; represents 16 asscns from the EU and EFTA; Pres. JEAN-MARIE OSWALD (Luxembourg); Sec.-Gen. MARTIN FUCHS.

International Confederation for Printing and Allied Industries (INTERGRAF): 7 pl. E. Flagey, Bte 5, 1050 Brussels, Belgium; tel. (2) 230-86-46; fax (2) 231-14-64; e-mail intergraf@intergraf.eu; internet www.intergraf.org; f. 1983 to work for the common interests of the printing and related industries in mem. countries through its lobbying, informing and networking activities; mems: 22 federations in 20 countries; Pres. HAVARD GRJOTHEIM; Sec.-Gen. BEATRICE KLOSE.

International Congress and Convention Association (ICCA): Toren A, De Entree 57, 1101 BH Amsterdam, Netherlands; tel. (20) 3981919; fax (20) 6990781; e-mail icca@icca.nl; internet www.iccaworld.com; f. 1963 to establish world-wide co-operation between all involved in organizing congresses, conventions and exhibitions; mems: more than 938 in 87 countries and territories; Pres. ARNALDO NARDONE; CEO MARTIN SIRK; publs *ICCA Intelligence* (5 a year, electronic), *ICCA Statistics* (annual).

International Co-operative Alliance (ICA): 150 route de Ferney, 1211Geneva 2, Switzerland; tel. 229298888; fax 227984122; e-mail ica@ica.coop; internet www.ica.coop; f. 1895 for the pursuit of co-operative aims; a General Assembly and four Regional Assemblies meet every two years, on an alternating basis; a 23-member ICA Board controls the affairs of the organization between meetings of the General Assembly; sectoral organisations and thematic committees have been established to promote co-operative activities in the following fields: agriculture; banking; fisheries; consumer affairs; tourism; communications; co-operative research; health; human resource development; housing; insurance; gender issues; and industrial, artisanal and worker co-operatives; mems: 267 affiliated national orgs, with a total membership of more than 1000m. individuals in 96 countries, and 4 int. orgs; Pres. Dame PAULINE GREEN (United Kingdom); Dir-Gen. CHARLES GOULD (USA); publs *Review of International Co-operation* (quarterly), *ICA Digest* (electronic newsletter, 2 a month), *Co-op Dialogue* (2 a year).

International Council of Communication Design (Icograda): 455 St Antoine Ouest, Suite SS 10, Montréal, QC H2Z 1J1, Canada; tel. (514) 448-4949; fax (514) 448-4948; e-mail info@icograda.org; internet www.icograda.org; f. 1963; aims to raise standards of communication design; promotes the exchange of information; organizes events; maintains archive; mems: 11 int. affiliated mems, 56 professional mems, 18 promotional mems, 86 educational mems, 5 corporate mems and 2 observers; Pres. LEIMEI JULIA CHIU (Japan); Sec.-Gen. IVA BRABAJA (Croatia); publs *Iridescent* (online) *electronic Newsletter* (weekly), *Regulations and Guidelines governing International Design Competitions*, *Model Code of Professional Conduct*, other professional documents.

International Council of Societies of Industrial Design (ICSID): 455 St Antoine Ouest, Suite SS 10, Montréal, QC H2Z 1J1, Canada; tel. (514) 448-4949; fax (514) 448-4948; e-mail office@icsid.org; internet www.icsid.org; f. 1957 to encourage the development of high standards in the practice of industrial design; works to improve and expand the contribution of industrial design throughout the world; mems: 8 assoc., 28 corporate, 61 educational, 24 professional and 54 promotional mems; Pres. LEE SOON-IN (South Korea); Sec.-Gen. DILKI DE SILVA; publs *ICSID News* (6 a year), *World Directory of Design Schools*.

International Council of Tanners: Leather Trade House, Kings Park Rd, Moulton Park, Northampton, NN3 6JD, United Kingdom; tel. (1604) 679917; fax (1604) 679998; e-mail sec@tannerscouncilict.org; internet www.tannerscouncilict.org; f. 1926 to study all questions relating to the leather industry and maintain contact with national asscns; mems: national tanners' orgs in 33 countries; Pres. WOLFGANG GOERLICH (Brazil).

International Council on Mining and Metals (ICMM): 35 Portman Sq., 6th Floor, London, W1H 6LR, United Kingdom; tel. (20) 7467-5070; fax (20) 7467-5071; e-mail info@icmm.com; internet www.icmm.com; f. 1991 (as the International Council on Metals and the Environment, present name adopted 2002); aims to promote sustainable development practices and policies in the mining, use, recycling and disposal of minerals and metals; mems: 19 cos, 30 asscns; Chair. MARIUS CLOPPERS (USA); publ. *ICMM Newsletter* (quarterly).

International Customs Tariffs Bureau: 15 rue des Petits Carmes, 1000 Brussels, Belgium; tel. (2) 501-87-74; fax (2) 501-31-47; e-mail dir@bitd.org; internet www.bitd.org; f. 1890; serves as the executive instrument of the International Union for the Publication of Customs Tariffs; translates and publishes all customs tariffs in five languages—English, French, German, Italian, Spanish; mems: 50 mem. countries; Pres. DIRK ACHTEN; Dir MICHEL GODFRIND; publs *International Customs Journal*, *Annual Report*.

International Exhibitions Bureau (Bureau International des Expositions): 34 ave d'Iéna, 75116 Paris, France; tel. 1-45-00-38-63; fax 1-45-00-96-15; e-mail info@bie-paris.org; internet www.bie-paris.org; f. 1931, revised by Protocol 1972, for the authorization and registration of international exhibitions falling under the 1928 Convention; mems: 160 states; Pres. JEAN-PIERRE LAFON; Sec.-Gen. VICENTE GONZALES LOSCERTALES; publs *BIE Bulletin*.

International Federation of Pharmaceutical Manufacturers and Associations (IFPMA): 15 chemin Louis-Dunant, POB 195, 1211 Geneva 20, Switzerland; tel. 223383200; fax 223383299; e-mail admin@ifpma.org; internet www.ifpma.org; f. 1968 for the exchange of information and international co-operation in all questions of interest to the pharmaceutical industry, particularly in the field of health legislation, science and research; represents the research-based pharmaceutical, biotech and vaccine sectors; develops ethical principles and practices and co-operates with national and international orgs; mems: 25 int. cos and 45 national and regional industry asscns; Pres. JOHN LECHLEITER (Japan); Dir-Gen. EDUARDO PISANI (Italy); publs *IFPMA Code of Pharmaceutical Marketing Practices*, action papers, occasional publications.

International Federation of the Phonographic Industry (IFPI): 10 Piccadilly, London W1J 0DD, United Kingdom; tel. (20) 7878-7900; fax (20) 7878-7950; e-mail info@ifpi.org; internet www.ifpi.org; f. 1933; represents the interests of record producers by campaigning for the introduction, improvement and enforcement of copyright and related rights legislation; co-ordinates the recording industry's anti-piracy activities; mems: around 1,400 members in 66 countries and nat. groups in 45 countries; CEO FRANCES MOORE; publs *Digital Music Report* (annually) *Recording Industry in Numbers* (annually); reports on digital music and commercial piracy, world sales.

International Fertilizer Industry Association (IFA): 28 rue Marbeuf, 75008 Paris, France; tel. 1-53-93-05-00; fax 1-53-93-05-45; e-mail ifa@fertilizer.org; internet www.fertilizer.org; f. 1927; represents companies involved in all aspects of the global fertilizer industry, including the production and distribution of fertilizers, their raw materials and intermediates; also represents organizations involved in agronomic research and training with regard to crop nutrition; mems: some 540 in more than 85 countries; Pres. WILLIAM J. DOYLE; Dir-Gen. LUC MAENE; publs *Fertilizers and Agriculture*.

International Fragrance Association (IFRA): 6 ave des Arts, 1210 Brussels, Belgium; tel. (2) 214-20-60; fax (2) 214-20-69; e-mail secretariat@ifraorg.org; internet www.ifraorg.org; f. 1973 to develop and advance the fragrance industry, to collect and study scientific data on fragrance materials and to make recommendations on their safe use; mems: national asscns of fragrance manufacturers in 19 countries; Chair. MICHEL BONGI; Pres. PIERRE SIVAC; publs *Code of Practice*, *Information Letters*.

International Fur Trade Federation: POB 495, Weybridge, Surrey, KT12 8WD, United Kingdom; tel. (1932) 850020; e-mail info@iftf.com; internet www.iftf.com; f. 1949 to promote and organize joint action by fur trade organizations in order to develop and protect the trade in fur skins and the processing of skins; mems: 42 orgs in 35 countries; Chair. ANDREAS LENHART.

International Meat Secretariat (Office international de la viande): 6 rue de la Victoire, 75009 Paris, France; tel. 1-45-26-68-97; fax 1-45-26-68-98; e-mail info@meat-ims.org; internet www.meat-ims.org; f. 1974; organizes World Meat Congress every two years (2012: Paris, France, in June); mems: in 28 countries; Pres. ARTURO LLAVALLOL (Argentina); Sec.-Gen. HSIN HUANG; publs *Newsletter* (fortnightly), *IMS-GIRA World Meat Facts Book* (annual).

International Organization of Motor Vehicle Manufacturers (Organisation internationale des constructeurs d'automobiles—OICA): 4 rue de Berri, 75008 Paris, France; tel. 1-43-59-00-13; fax 1-45-63-84-41; e-mail oica@oica.net; internet www.oica.net; f. 1919 to co-ordinate and further the interests of the automobile industry, to promote the study of economic and other matters affecting automobile construction, and to control automobile manufacturers' participation in international exhibitions in Europe; mems: 37 national trade asscns; Pres. PATRICK BLAIN (USA); Gen. Sec. YVES VAN DER STRAATEN; publ. *Yearbook of the World's Motor Industry*.

International Organization of the Flavour Industry (IOFI): 6 ave des Arts, 1210 Brussels, Belgium; tel. (2) 214-20-50; fax (2) 214-20-69; e-mail secretariat@iofiorg.org; internet www.iofi.org; f. 1969 to support and promote the flavour industry; active in the fields of safety evaluation and regulation of flavouring substances; mems: national asscns in 24 countries; Exec. Dir JOS STELDER; publs *Documentation Bulletin*, *Information Letters*, *Code of Practice*.

International Publishers' Association: 3 ave de Miremont, 1206 Geneva, Switzerland; tel. 227041820; fax 227041821; e-mail secretariat@internationalpublishers.org; internet www.internationalpublishers.org; f. 1896 to defend the freedom of publishers to publish, to defend publishers interests, and to foster international co-operation; promotes the international trade in books and literacy as a step to economic and social development; carries out work on international copyright; mems: 62 professional book publishers' orgs in 55 countries; Pres. YOUNGSUK CHI; Sec.-Gen. JENS BAMMEL.

International Rayon and Synthetic Fibres Committee (Comité international de la rayonne et des fibres synthétiques—CIRFS): 6 ave E. van Nieuwenhuyse, 1160 Brussels, Belgium; tel. (2) 676-74-55; fax (2) 676-74-54; e-mail info@cirfs.org; internet www.cirfs.org; f. 1950 to improve the quality and promote the use of man-made fibres and products made from fibres; mems: individual producers in 24 countries; Pres. ANDREAS EULE; Dir-Gen. FRÉDÉRIC VAN HOUTE; publs *Statistical Booklet* (annually), market reports, technical test methods.

International Shopfitting Organisation (ISO): Thornberg-Bailey AB, Torna Hällestad, 247 95 Lund, Sweden; tel. (46) 53-202; fax (46) 53-229; e-mail info@iso-shopfitting.com; internet www.iso-shopfitting.com; f. 1959 to promote the interchange of ideas between individuals and firms concerned with shopfitting; mems: national asscns and individuals in 20 countries; Pres. CARSTEN SCHEMBERG; Sec.-Gen. PREBEN BAILEY.

International Textile Manufacturers Federation (ITMF): Wiedingstrasse 9, 8055 Zürich, Switzerland; tel. 442836380; fax 442836389; e-mail secretariat@itmf.org; internet www.itmf.org; f. 1904, present title adopted 1978; aims to protect and promote the interests of its members, disseminate information, and encourage co-operation; mems: national textile trade asscns and companies in some 50 countries; Pres. BASHIR H. ALI MOHAMMAD (Pakistan); Dir-Gen. Dr CHRISTIAN P. SCHINDLER (Germany); publs *Annual Conference Report*, *Cotton Contamination Survey* (2 a year), *Country Statements* (annually), *International Textile Machinery Shipment Statistics* (annually), *International Cotton Industry Statistics* (annually), *International Production Cost Comparison* (2 a year), *State of Trade Report* (quarterly), *Directory*, various statistics, sectoral reports and guidelines.

International Union of Marine Insurance (IUMI): C.F. Meyer-Str. 14, POB 4288, 8022 Zürich, Switzerland; tel. 442082874; fax 442082800; e-mail simone.hirt@svv.ch; internet www.iumi.com; f. 1873 to collect and distribute information on marine insurance on a world-wide basis; mems: 54 asscns; organizes annual conference (Sept. 2012: San Diego, USA); Pres. OLE WIKBORG; Sec.-Gen. FRITZ STABINGER.

International Wool Textile Organisation (IWTO) (Fédération lanière internationale—FLI): 4 rue de l'Industrie, 1000 Brussels, Belgium; tel. (2) 505-40-10; fax (2) 503-47-85; e-mail info@iwto.org; internet www.iwto.org; f. 1929 to link wool textile organizations in member countries and represent their interests; holds annual Congress (May 2012: New York, USA); mems: in 27 countries; Pres. PETER ACKROYD (United Kingdom); Sec.-Gen. ELISABETH VAN DELDEN; publs *Wool Statistics* (annually), *Global Wool Supplies and Wool Textile Manufacturing Activity* (annually), *Blue Book*, *Red Book*.

International Wrought Copper Council: 55 Bryanston St, London, W1H 7AJ, United Kingdom; tel. (20) 7868-8930; fax (20) 7868-8819; e-mail iwcc@coppercouncil.org; internet www.coppercouncil.org; f. 1953 to link and represent copper fabricating industries and represent the views of copper consumers to raw material producers; organizes specialist activities on technical work and the development of copper; mems: 16 national groups in Europe, Australia, Japan and Malaysia, 9 corporate mems; Chair. JIN ROY RYU; Sec.-Gen. MARK LOVEITT; publs *Annual Report*, surveys.

Orgalime (European Engineering Industries Association): Diamant Bldg, 5th Floor, 80 blvd A Reyers, 1030 Brussels, Belgium; tel. (2) 706-82-35; fax (2) 706-82-50; e-mail secretariat@orgalime.org; internet www.orgalime.org; f. 1954 to provide a permanent liaison between the mechanical, electrical and electronic engineering, and metalworking industries of member countries; mems: 33 national trade asscns in 22 European countries; Pres. RICHARD DICK; Dir. Gen. ADRIAN HARRIS.

Southern African Customs Union: Private Bag 13285, Windhoek, Namibia; tel. (61) 243950; fax (61) 245611; e-mail info@sacu.int; internet www.sacu.int; f. 1969; provides common pool of customs, excise and sales duties, according to the relative volume of trade and production in each country; goods are traded within the union free of duty and quotas, subject to certain protective measures for less developed mems; the South African rand is legal tender in Lesotho, Namibia and Swaziland; the Customs Union Commission meets quarterly in each of the mems' capital cities in turn; mems: Botswana, Lesotho, Namibia, South Africa, Swaziland; Exec. Sec. TSWELOPELE CORNELIA MOREMI.

Tiles and Bricks Europe (TBE): 17 rue Montagne, 1000 Brussels, Belgium; tel. (2) 808-38-80; fax (2) 511-51-74; e-mail sykes@cerameunie.eu; internet www.tiles-bricks.eu; f. 1952 to co-ordinate research between members of the industry, improve technical knowledge and encourage professional training; mems: asscns in 24 European and East European countries; Sec.-Gen. CHRISTOPHE SYKES.

UFI (Global Association of the Exhibition Industry): 17 rue Louise Michel, 92300 Levallois-Perret, France; tel. 1-46-39-75-00; fax 1-46-39-75-01; e-mail info@ufi.org; internet www.ufi.org; f. 1925 as Union des Foires Internationales; works to increase co-operation between international trade fairs/exhibitions, safeguard their interests and extend their operations; imposes exhibition quality criteria and defines standards; approves 805 events; mems: 586 in 84 countries; Pres. ARIE BRIENAN; Man. Dir PAUL WOODWARD.

Union of European Beverages Associations (UNESDA): 79 blvd St Michel, 1040 Brussels, Belgium; tel. (2) 743-40-50; fax (2) 732-51-02; e-mail mail@unesda.org; internet www.unesda.org; f. 1958, as Confederation of International Soft Drinks Associations; aims to promote co-operation among the national asscns of non-alcoholic drinks manufacturers on all industrial and commercial matters, to stimulate the sales and consumption of soft drinks, to deal with matters of interest to all member asscns and to represent the common interests of member asscns; holds a congress every year; mems: 25 national asscns and 11 companies; Sec.-Gen. ALAIN BEAUMONT.

World Customs Organization (WCO): 30 rue du Marché, 1210 Brussels, Belgium; tel. (2) 209-92-11; fax (2) 209-92-62; e-mail communication@wcoomd.org; internet www.wcoomd.org; f. 1952 as Customs Co-operation Council (CCC); aims to enhance the effectiveness and efficiency of customs administrations by building capacity for more effective border enforcement, better application of international trade regulations, enhanced measures to protect society, and increased revenue security; mems: customs administrations of 177 countries and customs territories; Sec.-Gen. KUNIO MIKURIYA (Japan); publ. *WCO News* (3 a year).

World Fair Trade Organization: Prijssestraat 24, 4101 CR, Culemborg, Netherlands; tel. (34) 5535914; fax (84) 7474401; e-mail info@wfto.com; internet www.wfto.com; f. 1989 as the International Fair Trade Association; coalition of trading and producer organizations; prescribes 10 standards that fair trade organizations must follow in their day-to-day work and carries out monitoring to ensure these principles are upheld; mems: 450 alternative trade orgs from 75 countries; Pres. PAUL MYERS (USA); Sec. PAUL DEIGHTON (Australia).

World Federation of Advertisers: 120 ave Louise, Box 6, 1050 Brussels; tel. (2) 502-57-40; fax (2) 502-56-66; e-mail info@wfanet.org; internet www.wfanet.org; f. 1953; promotes and studies advertising and its related problems; mems: asscns in 56 countries and more than 60 international cos; Pres. CHRIS BURGGRAEVE; Man. Dir STEPHAN LOERKE; publ. *EU Brief* (weekly).

World Packaging Organisation: 1833 Centre Point Circle, Suite 123, Naperville IL 60563, USA; tel. (630) 596-9007; fax (630) 544-5055; e-mail wpo@kellencompany.com; internet www.worldpackaging.org; f. 1968 to provide a forum for the exchange of knowledge of packaging technology and, in general, to create conditions for the conservation, preservation and distribution of world food production; holds annual congress and competition; mems: Asian, North American, Latin American, European and African packaging federations; full mems in 44 countries, 7 affiliated mems; Pres. THOMAS SCHNEIDER (USA); Gen. Sec. KEITH PEARSON (South Africa).

World Trade Centers Association: 420 Lexington Ave, Suite 518, New York, NY 10170, USA; tel. (212) 432-2626; fax (212) 488-0064; e-mail wtca@wtca.org; internet www.wtca.org; f. 1968 to promote trade through the establishment of world trade centres, including education facilities, information services and exhibition facilities; operates an electronic trading and communication system (WTC Online); mems: 322 trade centres, chambers of commerce and other orgs in more than 107 countries; Pres. GUY F. TOZZOLI; Chair. GHAZI ABU NAHL; publ. *WTCA News* (monthly), *Trade Center Profiles* (annually), *World Business Directory* (annually).

Transport

African Airlines Association: POB 20116, Nairobi 00200, Kenya; tel. (20) 604855; fax (20) 601173; e-mail afraa@afraa.org; internet www.afraa.org; f. 1968 to give African air companies expert advice in technical, financial, juridical and market matters; to improve air transport in Africa through inter-carrier co-operation; and to develop manpower resources; mems: 34 national carriers; Pres. DIRSS BENHIMA (Morocco); Sec.-Gen. ELIJAH CHINGOSHO; publs *Newsletter*, reports.

Airports Council International (ACI): POB 16, 1215 Geneva 15-Airport, Switzerland; tel. 227178585; fax 227178888; e-mail aci@aci.aero; internet www.airports.org; f. 1991, following merger of Airport Operators Council International and International Civil Airports Association; aims to represent and develop co-operation among airports of the world; mems: 575 mems operating over 1,633 airports in 179 countries and territories; Chair. MAX MOORE-WILTON; Dir-Gen. ANGELA GITTENS; publs *World Report* (6 a year), *Airport World Magazine*, *Policy Handbook*, reports.

Arab Air Carriers' Organization (AACO): POB 13-5468, Beirut, Lebanon; tel. (1) 861297; fax (1) 863168; e-mail info@aaco.org; internet www.aaco.org; f. 1965 to promote co-operation in the activities of Arab airline companies; mems: 24 Arab air carriers; Pres. NABIL CHETTAOUI; Sec.-Gen. ABDUL WAHAB TEFFAHA; publs bulletins, reports and research documents.

Association of Asia Pacific Airlines: Kompleks Antarabangsa, 9th Floor, Jalan Sultan Ismail, 50250 Kuala Lumpur, Malaysia; tel. (3) 21455600; fax (3) 21452500; e-mail info@aapa.org.my; internet www.aapairlines.org; f. 1966 as Orient Airlines Asscn; present name adopted in 1997; as the trade association of the region's airlines, the AAPA aims to represent their interests and to provide a forum for all members to exchange information and views on matters of common concern; maintains international representation in Brussels, Belgium, and in Washington, DC, USA; mems: 17 scheduled international airlines (carrying approx. one-fifth of global passenger traffic and one-third of global cargo traffic); Dir-Gen. ANDREW J. HERDMAN; publs *Annual Report*, *Annual Statistical Report*, *Asia Pacific Perspectives*, *Orient Aviation* (10 a year).

Association of European Airlines: 350 ave Louise, 1050 Brussels, Belgium; tel. (2) 639-89-89; fax (2) 639-89-99; e-mail aea.secretariat@aea.be; internet www.aea.be; f. 1954 to carry out research on political, commercial, economic and technical aspects of air transport; maintains statistical data bank; mems: 35 airlines; Chair. WILLIAM WALSH (United Kingdom); Sec.-Gen. ULRICH SCHULTE-STRATHAUS (Germany).

Baltic and International Maritime Council (BIMCO): Bagsvaerdvej 161, 2880 Bagsvaerd, Denmark; tel. 44-36-68-00; fax 44-36-68-68; e-mail mailbox@bimco.org; internet www.bimco.org; f. 1905 to unite shipowners and other persons and organizations connected with the shipping industry; mems: 2,500 in 123 countries, representing over 65% of world merchant tonnage; Pres. ROBERT LORENZ-MEYER (Germany); Sec.-Gen. TORBEN SKAANILD; publs *BIMCO Review* (annually), *BIMCO Bulletin* (6 a year), *Vessel*, manuals.

Central Commission for the Navigation of the Rhine: Palais du Rhin, 2 Pl. de la République, 67082 Strasbourg, France; tel. 3-88-52-20-10; fax 3-88-32-10-72; e-mail ccnr@ccr-zkr.org; internet www.ccr-zkr.org; f. 1815 to ensure free movement of traffic and standard river facilities for ships of all nations; draws up navigational rules; standardizes customs regulations; arbitrates in disputes involving river traffic; approves plans for river maintenance work; there is an administrative centre for social security for boatmen; mems: Belgium, France, Germany, Netherlands, Switzerland; Sec.-Gen. JEAN-MARIE WOEHRLING (France); publs guides, rules and directives (in French and German).

Danube Commission: Benczúr utca 25, 1068 Budapest, Hungary; tel. (1) 352-1835; fax (1) 352-1839; e-mail secretariat@danubecom-intern.org; internet www.danubecommission.org; f. 1948; supervises implementation of the Belgrade Convention on the Regime of Navigation on the Danube; approves projects for river maintenance; supervises a uniform system of traffic regulations on the whole navigable portion of the Danube and on river inspection; mems: Austria, Bulgaria, Croatia, Germany, Hungary, Moldova, Romania, Russia, Serbia, Slovakia, Ukraine; Pres. DIMITAR IKONOMOV (Bulgaria); Dir-Gen. Dr ISTVÁN VALKÁR; publs *Basic Regulations for Navigation on the Danube*, *Hydrological Yearbook*, *Statistical Yearbook*, proceedings of sessions.

European Civil Aviation Conference (ECAC): 3 bis Villa Emile-Bergerat, 92522 Neuilly-sur-Seine Cédex, France; tel. 1-46-41-85-44; fax 1-46-24-18-18; e-mail secretariat@ecac-ceac.org; internet www.ecac-ceac.org; f. 1955; aims to promote the continued development of a safe, efficient and sustainable European air transport system; mems: 44 European states; Pres. CATALIN RADU; Exec. Sec. SALVATORE SCIACCHITANO.

European Organisation for the Safety of Air Navigation (EUROCONTROL): 96 rue de la Fusée, 1130 Brussels, Belgium; tel. (2) 729-90-11; fax (2) 729-90-44; e-mail infocentre@eurocontrol.int; internet www.eurocontrol.int; f. 1960; aims to develop a coherent and co-ordinated air traffic control system in Europe. A revised Convention was signed in June 1997, incorporating the following institutional structure: a General Assembly (known as the Commission in the transitional period), a Council (known as the Provisional Council) and an Agency under the supervision of the Director-General; there are directorates, covering human resources and finance matters and a general secretariat. A special organizational structure covers the management of the European Air Traffic Management Programme. EUROCONTROL also operates the Experimental Centre (at Brétigny-sur-Orge, France), the Institute of Air Navigation Services (in Luxembourg), the Central Route Charges Office, the Central Flow Management Unit (both in Brussels) and the Upper Area Control Centre (in Maastricht, Netherlands); mems: 38 European countries; Dir-Gen. DAVID MCMILLAN (United Kingdom).

Forum Train Europe FTE: Mittelstrasse 43, 3000 Bern 65, Switzerland; tel. 512202715; fax 512201242; e-mail mailbox@forumtraineurope.org; internet www.forumtraineurope.org; f. 1923 as the European Passenger Train Time-Table Conference to arrange international passenger connections by rail and water; since 1997 concerned also with rail freight; mems: 98 mems from 35 European countries; Pres. HANS-JÜRG SPILLMANN; Sec.-Gen. PETER JÄGGY.

Inland Waterways International: Crabtree Hall, Mill Lane, Lower Beeding, Horsham, West Sussex, RH13 6PX, United Kingdom; e-mail info@inlandwaterwaysinternational.org; internet www.inlandwaterwaysinternational.org; f. 1995; promotes the use, conservation and development of inland waterways world-wide; hosts the steering commitee to choose the venue of the annual World Canals Conference; mems: 18 countries; Pres. DAVID BALLINGER (Canada).

Institute of Air Transport: 103 rue la Boétie, 75008 Paris, France; tel. 1-43-59-38-68; fax 1-43-59-47-37; e-mail contact@ita-paris.com; internet www.ita-paris.com; f. 1945 as an international centre of research on economic, technical and policy aspects of air transport, and on the economy and sociology of transport and tourism; acts as economic and technical consultant in research requested by members on specific subjects; maintains a data bank, a library and a consultation and advice service; organizes training courses on air transport economics; mems: orgs involved in air transport, production and equipment, universities, banks, insurance companies, private individuals and government agencies in 79 countries; publs (in French and English), *ITA Press* (2 a month), *ITA Studies and Reports* (quarterly), *Aviation Industry Barometer* (quarterly).

Intergovernmental Organization for International Carriage by Rail: Gryphenhübeliweg 30, 3006 Bern, Switzerland; tel. 313591010; fax 313591011; e-mail info@otif.org; internet www.otif .org; f. 1893 as Central Office for International Carriage by Rail, present name adopted 1985; aims to establish and develop a uniform system of law governing the international carriage of passengers and goods by rail in member states; mems: 44 states; Sec.-Gen. STEFAN SCHIMMING; publ. *Bulletin des Transports Internationaux ferroviaires* (quarterly, in English, French and German).

International Air Transport Association (IATA): 33 route de l'Aéroport, CP 416, 1215 Geneva 15, Switzerland; tel. 227702525; fax 227983553; e-mail info.ch@iata.org; internet www.iata.org; f. 1945 to represent and serve the airline industry; aims to promote safe, reliable and secure air services; to assist the industry to attain adequate levels of profitability while developing cost-effective operational standards; to promote the importance of the industry in global social and economic development; and to identify common concerns and represent the industry in addressing these at regional and international level; maintains regional offices in Amman, Brussels, Dakar, London, Nairobi, Santiago, Singapore and Washington, DC; mems: c. 335 airline cos; Dir-Gen. and CEO GIOVANNI BISIGNANI; publ. *Airlines International* (every 2 months).

International Association of Ports and Harbors (IAPH): 7F, New Pier Takeshiba South Tower, 1-16-1, Kaigan, Minato-ku, Tokyo 105-0022, Japan; tel. (3) 5403-2770; fax (3) 5403-7651; e-mail info@ iaphworldports.org; internet www.iaphworldports.org; f. 1955 to increase the efficiency of ports and harbours through the dissemination of information on port organization, management, administration, operation, development and promotion; encourages the growth of waterborne commerce; holds conference every two years; mems: 350 in 90 states; Pres. GERALDINE KNATZ (USA); Sec.-Gen. SUSUMU NARUSE (Japan); publs *Ports and Harbors* (6 a year), *Membership Directory* (annually).

International Association of Public Transport: 6 rue Sainte-Marie, Quai de Charbonnages, 1080 Brussels, Belgium; tel. (2) 673-61-00; fax (2) 660-10-72; e-mail info@uitp.org; internet www.uitp .org; f. 1885 to study all problems connected with the urban and regional public passenger transport industry; serves as an international network for public transport authorities and operators, policy decision-makers, scientific institutes and the public transport supply and service industry; mems: 3,400 in 92 countries; Pres. OUSMANE THIAM; Sec.-Gen. ALAIN FLAUSCH; publs *Public Transport International* (every 2 months), *EUExpress*, *Mobility News* (monthly, electronic), statistics reports.

International Bureau of Containers and Intermodal Transport: 38 rue des Blancs Manteaux, 75004 Paris, France; tel. 1-47-66-03-90; fax 1-47-66-08-91; e-mail bis@bic-code.org; internet www .bic-code.org; f. 1933 to group representatives of all means of transport and activities concerning containers, to promote combined door-to-door transport by the successive use of several means of transport, to examine and bring into effect administrative, technical and customs advances, and to centralize data on behalf of mems; mems: 1,700; Chair. MICHEL HENNEMAND; Sec.-Gen. BERTRAND GEOFFRAY; publs *Containers Bulletin*, *Containers Bic-Code* (annually).

International Chamber of Shipping: Carthusian Court, 12 Carthusian St, London, EC1M 6EZ, United Kingdom; tel. (20) 7417-8844; fax (20) 7417-8877; e-mail ics@marisec.org; internet www.marisec.org; f. 1921 to co-ordinate the views of the international shipping industry on matters of common interest, in the policy-making, technical and legal fields of shipping operations; mems: national asscns representing free-enterprise shipowners and operators in 34 countries; Chair. SPYROS POLEMIS (Greece); Sec.-Gen. PETER HINCHLIFFE.

International Federation of Freight Forwarders Associations (FIATA): Schaffhauserstr. 104, 8152 Glattbrugg, Switzerland; tel. 432116500; fax 432116565; e-mail info@fiata.com; internet www.fiata.com; f. 1926 to protect and represent its members at international level; mems: 110 national orgs and some 5,500 individual members in 150 countries; Pres. JEAN-CLAUDE DELEN (Belgium); Dir MARCO A. SANGALETTI; publ. *FIATA Review* (every 2 months).

International Rail Transport Committee (Comité international des transports ferroviaires—CIT): Weltpoststr. 20, 3015 Bern, Switzerland; tel. 313500190; fax 313500199; e-mail info@cit-rail.org; internet www.cit-rail.org; f. 1902 for the development of international law relating to railway transport, on the basis of the Convention concerning International Carriage by Rail (COTIF) and its Appendices (CIV, CIM), and for the adoption of standard rules on other questions relating to international transport law; mems: 120 transport undertakings in 42 countries; Pres. JEAN-LUC DUFOURNAUD; Sec.-Gen. CESARE BRAND (Switzerland).

International Road Federation (IRF): Geneva Programme Centre: 2 chemin de Blandonnet 1214, Vernier, Geneva, Switzerland; tel. 223060260; fax 223060270; e-mail info@irfnet.org; internet www.irfnet.org; f. 1948 to encourage the development and improvement of highways and highway transportation; Programme Centres in Geneva, Switzerland, Brussels, Belgium and Washington, DC, USA; organizes IRF world and regional meetings; mems: 70 national road asscns and 500 individual firms and industrial asscns; Chair. KIRAN KAPILA; Dir-Gen. SIBYLLE RUPPRECHT; publs *World Road Statistics* (annually), *World Highways* (8 a year).

International Road Safety Organization (La prevention routière internationale—PRI): Rietgors 1, 3755 GA Eemnes, Netherlands; tel. (69) 8908758; fax (67) 1354578; e-mail contact@lapri.info; internet www.lapri.info; f. 1959 for exchange of ideas and material on road safety; organizes international action and congresses; assists non-member countries; mems: 50 national orgs; Pres. JOOP GOOS; publ. *Newsletter* (6 a year), also annual reports, news, brochures, booklets and manuals.

International Road Transport Union (IRU): Centre International, 3 rue de Varembé, BP 44, 1211 Geneva 20, Switzerland; tel. 229182700; fax 229182741; e-mail iru@iru.org; internet www.iru .org; f. 1948 to study all problems of road transport, to advocate harmonisation and simplification of regulations relating to road transport, and to promote the use of road transport for passengers and goods; represents, promotes and upholds the interests of the road transport industry at an international level; mems: 180 national asscns in 70 countries; Pres. JANUSZ LACNY; Sec.-Gen. MARTIN MARMY.

International Shipping Federation: Carthusian Court, 12 Carthusian St, London, EC1M 6EZ, United Kingdom; tel. (20) 7417-8844; fax (20) 7417-8877; e-mail isf@marisec.org; internet www.marisec.org; f. 1909 to consider all personnel questions affecting the interests of shipowners; responsible for Shipowners' Group at conferences of the International Labour Organisation; represents shipowners at the International Maritime Organization; mems: national shipowners' orgs in 32 countries; Pres. SPYROS POLEMIS (Greece); Sec.-Gen. PETER HINCHLIFFE; publs conference papers, guidelines and training records.

International Transport Forum: 2 rue André Pascal, 75775 Paris Cédex 16, France; tel. 1-45-24-97-10; fax 1-45-24-97-42; e-mail itf .contact@oecd.org; internet www.internationaltransportforum.org; f. 2006 by a decision of the European Conference of Ministers of Transport (f. 1953) to broaden membership of the org; aims to create a safe, sustainable, efficient, integrated transport system; provides an annual Forum in Liepzig, Germany (May 2012: 'Seamless Transport: Making Connections'); holds round tables, seminars and symposia; shares Secretariat staff with OECD; mems: 44 full member countries, 7 associate; 1 observer; Sec.-Gen. CAROLE COUNE (Belgium); publs *Annual Report*, various statistical publications and surveys.

International Union of Railways (Union internationale des chemins de fer—UIC): 16 rue Jean-Rey, 75015 Paris, France; tel. 1-44-49-20-20; fax 1-44-49-20-29; e-mail loubinoux@uic.org; internet www.uic.org; f. 1922 for the harmonization of railway operations and the development of international rail transport; aims to ensure international interoperability of the rail system; compiles information on economic, management and technical aspects of railways; co-ordinates research and collaborates with industry and the EU; organizes international conferences; mems: 196 in 92 countries; Chair. YOSHIO ISHIDA; Dir-Gen. JEAN-PIERRE LOUBINOUX; publs *International Railway Statistics* (annually), *Activities Reports*, *UIC News* (newsletter).

IVR: Vasteland 12E, 3011 BL Rotterdam (POB 23210, 3001 KE Rotterdam), Netherlands; tel. (10) 4116070; fax (10) 4129091; e-mail info@ivr.nl; internet www.ivr.nl; f. 1947 for the classification of Rhine ships, the organization and publication of a Rhine ships register, the unification of general average rules, and the harmonization of European inland navigation law; mems: shipowners and asscns, insurers and asscns, shipbuilding engineers, average adjusters and others interested in Rhine traffic; Gen. Sec. THERESIA HACKSTEINER; publs *IVR Report* (2 a year), *Registre de l'IVR* (annually).

Nordisk Defence Club (Nordisk Skibsrederforening): Kristinelundv. 22, POB 3033, Elisenberg, 0207 Oslo, Norway; tel. 22-13-56-00; fax 22-43-00-35; e-mail post@nordisk.no; internet www .nordisk.no; f. 1889 to assist members in disputes over charter parties, contracts and sale and purchase, taking the necessary legal steps on behalf of members and bearing the cost of such claims; mems: mainly Finnish, Swedish and Norwegian and some non-Scandinavian shipowners, representing about 2,150 ships and drilling rigs with gross tonnage of about 53m.; Man. Dir GEORGE SCHEEL; Chair. NILS P. DYVIK; publ. *A Law Report of Scandinavian Maritime Cases* (annually), *Medlemsbladet (Membership Circular)* (2 a year), *Annual Report*.

Organisation for Co-operation Between Railways: Hozà 63–67, 00681 Warsaw, Poland; tel. (22) 6573600; fax (22) 6219417; e-mail osjd@osjd.org.pl; internet osjd.org; f. 1956; aims to improve standards and co-operation in railway traffic between countries of Europe and Asia; promotes co-operation on issues relating to traffic policy and economic and environmental aspects of railway traffic; ensures enforcement of a number of rail agreements; aims to elaborate and standardize general principles for international transport law. Conference of Ministers of mem. countries meets annually; Conference of Gen. Dirs of Railways meets at least once a year; mems: ministries of transport of 27 countries world-wide; Chair. TADEUSZ SZOZDA; publ. *OSShD Journal* (every 2 months, in Chinese, German and Russian), *Statistic Report on Railway Transport* (annually).

Pan American Railway Congress Association (Asociación del Congreso Panamericano de Ferrocarriles): Av. Dr José María Ramos Mejía 1302, Planta Baja, 1104 Buenos Aires, Argentina; tel. (11) 4315-3445; fax (11) 4312-3834; e-mail acpf@acpf.com.ar; internet www.acpf.com.ar; f. 1907, present title adopted 1941; aims to promote the development and progress of railways in the American continent; holds Congresses every three years; mems: govt representatives, railway enterprises and individuals in 20 countries; Pres. LORENZO PEPE; Gen. Sec. JULIO SOSA; publ. *Boletín ACPF* (5 a year).

PIANC (World Association for Waterborne Transport Infrastructure): Bât Graaf de Ferraris, 11e étage, 20 blvd Roi Albert II, bte 3, 1000 Brussels, Belgium; tel. (2) 553-71-61; fax (2) 553-71-55; e-mail info@pianc-aipcn.org; internet www.pianc.org; f. 1885; fmrly Permanent International Asscn of Navigation Congresses; fosters progress in the construction, maintenance and operation of inland and maritime waterways, of inland and maritime ports and of coastal areas; holds International Navigation Congress every four years (2010: Liverpool, United Kingdom); mems: 33 govts, 3,400 others; Sec.-Gen. L. VAN SCHEL; publs *On Course* (quarterly), *Illustrated Technical Dictionary* (in 6 languages), *Sailing Ahead* (electronic newsletter), technical reports, Congress papers.

Union of European Railway Industries (UNIFE): 221 ave Louise, bte 11, 1050 Brussels, Belgium; tel. (2) 626-12-60; fax (2) 626-12-61; e-mail info@unife.org; internet www.unife.org; f. 1975 to represent companies concerned in the manufacture of railway equipment in Europe to European and international organizations; mems: 60 cos and 18 national asscns in 14 countries; Chair. HANS-JÖRG GRUNDMANN; Dir-Gen. MICHAEL CLAUSECKER; publ. *Newsletter* (quarterly).

World Airlines Clubs Association (WACA): c/o IATA, 800 Pl. Victoria, POB 113, Montréal, Québec, QC H4Z 1M1, Canada; tel. (514) 874-0202; fax (514) 874-1753; e-mail info@waca.org; internet www.waca.org; f. 1966; holds a General Assembly annually, regional meetings, social programmes, international events and sports tournaments; mems: clubs in 35 countries; Man. KEITH MILLER; publs *WACA Contact*, *WACA World News* (2 a year), *Annual Report*.

World Road Association (PIARC): La Grande Arche, Paroi Nord, Niveau 5, 92055 La Défense Cédex, France; tel. 1-47-96-81-21; fax 1-49-00-02-02; e-mail info@piarc.org; internet www.piarc.org; f. 1909 as the Permanent International Association of Road Congresses; aims to promote the construction, improvement, maintenance, use and economic development of roads; organizes technical committee and study sessions; mems: 113 govts; public bodies, orgs and private individuals in 142 countries; Pres. ANNE-MARIE LECLERC (Canada); Sec.-Gen. JEAN-FRANÇOIS CORTÉ (France); publs *Bulletin*, *Technical Dictionary*, *Lexicon*, technical reports.

Youth and Students

AIESEC International: Teilingerstraat 126, 3032 Rotterdam, Netherlands; tel. (10) 4434383; fax (10) 2651386; e-mail info@ai.aiesec.org; internet www.aiesec.org; f. 1948 as International Association of Students in Economics and Management; provides an international platform for young people to discover and develop their potential; enters into partnerships with selected organizations; mems: 60,000 students in more than 2,100 universities in c. 110 countries and territories; Pres. FLORENT MEIYI (People's Republic of China) (2012–13).

Asian Students Association: 2 Jordan Rd, Kowloon, Hong Kong, SAR; tel. 23880515; fax 27825535; e-mail asasec@netvigator.com; internet www.asianstudents.blogspot.com/; f. 1969; aims to promote students' solidarity in struggling for democracy, self-determination, peace, justice and liberation; conducts campaigns, training of activists, and workshops on human rights and other issues of importance; there are Student Commissions for Peace, Education and Human Rights; mems: 40 national or regional student unions in 25 countries and territories; publs *Movement News* (monthly), *ASA News* (quarterly).

Council on International Educational Exchange (CIEE): 300 Fore St, Portland, ME 04101, USA; tel. (207) 553-4000; fax (207) 553-4299; e-mail contact@ciee.org; internet www.ciee.org; f. 1947; issues International Student Identity Card entitling holders to discounts and basic insurance; arranges overseas work and study programmes for students; co-ordinates summer work programme in the USA for foreign students; administers programmes for teachers and other professionals and sponsors conferences on educational exchange; operates a voluntary service programme; mems: over 350 colleges, universities and international educational orgs in 22 countries; CEO JAMES P. PELLOW (USA); publs include *The Knowledge Series*, *Annual Report*, Occasional Papers in International Education.

European Law Students' Association (ELSA): 239 blvd Général Jacques, 1050 Brussels, Belgium; tel. (2) 646-26-26; fax (2) 646-29-23; e-mail elsa@elsa.org; internet www.elsa.org; f. 1981 to foster mutual understanding and promote social responsibility of law students and young laywers; mems: c. 30,000 students and lawyers in more than 300 law faculties in 42 countries; Pres. NIOUSHA NADEMI (Sweden); Sec.-Gen. JAANA SAARIJÄRVI (Finland); publs *Synergy* (2 a year), *Legal Studies in Europe*.

European Students' Forum (Association des Etats Généraux des Etudiants de l'Europe—AEGEE): 15 rue Nestor de Tière, 1030 Schaarbeek/Brussels, Belgium; tel. (2) 246-03-20; fax (2) 246-03-29; e-mail headoffice@aegee.org; internet www.aegee.org; promotes cross-border communication, co-operation and integration between students; fosters inter-cultural exchange; holds specialized conferences; mems: 13,000 students in 200 university cities in 40 countries; Sec.-Gen. ALMA MOZGOVAJA.

European Youth Forum: 120 rue Joseph II, 1000 Brussels, Belgium; tel. (2) 230-64-90; fax (2) 230-21-23; e-mail youthforum@youthforum.org; internet www.youthforum.org; f. 1996; represents and advocates for the needs and interests of all young people in Europe; promotes their active participation in democratic processes, as well as understanding and respect for human rights; consults with international organizations and governments on issues relevant to young people; mems: 98 national youth councils and international non-governmental youth orgs; Pres. PETER MATJASIC; Sec.-Gen. GIUSEPPE PORCARO.

Hostelling International: Gate House, 2nd Floor, Fretherne Rd, Welwyn Garden City, Herts., AL8 6RD, United Kingdom; tel. (1707) 324170; fax (1707) 323980; e-mail info@hihostels.com; internet www.hihostels.com; f. 1932 as International Youth Hostel Federation, present name adopted 2006; facilitates international travel by members of the various youth hostel asscns; advises and helps in the formation of youth hostel asscns in countries where no such organizations exist; records over 35m. overnight stays annually in some 4,000 youth hostels; mems: 90 national asscns with over 3.2m. national mems and 1m. international guest mems; 12 associated national orgs; CEO MIKAEL HANSSON; publs *Annual Report*, *Guidebook on World Hostels* (annually), *Manual*, *News Bulletin*.

International Association for the Exchange of Students for Technical Experience (IAESTE): POB 35-05, Belgrade, Serbia; tel. (11) 303-1677; fax (11) 303-1675; e-mail general.secretary@iaeste.org; internet www.iaeste.org; f. 1948; operates an exchange programme between students and employers; launched a web-based alumni network in 2011, accessible at alumni.iaeste.org; mems: 88 national cttees and co-operating institutions in 85 countries; Sec.-Gen. GORAN RADNOVIÇ (Serbia) (2010–14); publs *Activity Report*, *Annual Report*, *IAESTE Bulletin* (quarterly).

International Association of Dental Students (IADS): c/o FDI World Dental Federation, Tour de Cointrin, Ave Louis Casaï 84, CP 3, 1216 Genève-Cointrin, Switzerland; tel. 225608150; fax 225608140; e-mail info@fdiworldental.org; internet www.iads-web.org; f. 1951 to represent dental students and their opinions internationally, to promote dental student exchanges and international congresses; mems: 60,000 students in 45 countries, 15,000 corresponding mems; Pres. STEFÁNIA ZSUZSANNA RADÓ (Hungary); Sec. PAVEL SCARLAT (Moldova); publ. *IADS Newsletter* (2 a year).

International Federation of Medical Students' Associations (IFMSA): c/o WMA, BP 63, 01212 Ferney-Voltaire Cedex, France; fax 4-50-40-59-37; e-mail gs@ifmsa.org; internet www.ifmsa.org; f. 1951 to promote international co-operation in professional treatment and the achievement of humanitarian ideals; provides forum for medical students; maintains standing committees on professional and research exchange, medical education, public health, refugees and reproductive health, including AIDS; organizes annual General Assembly; mems: 94 asscns; Pres. CHRISTOPHER PLEYER; Gen. Sec. MIRJANA SPASOJEVIC (2011–12); publ. *IFMSA Newsletter* (quarterly).

International Pharmaceutical Students' Federation (IPSF): POB 84200, 2508 AE The Hague, Netherlands; tel. (70) 3021992; fax (70) 3021999; e-mail ipsf@ipsf.org; internet www.ipsf.org; f. 1949 to study and promote the interests of pharmaceutical students and to encourage international co-operation; mems: represents some 350,000 pharmacy students and recent graduates in 70 countries world-wide; Pres. SANNE TOFTE RASMUSSEN (Denmark); Sec.-Gen. LAERKE ARNFAST (Denmark); publ. *IPSF News Bulletin* (2 a year).

International Scout and Guide Fellowship (ISGF): 38 ave de la Porte de Hal, 1060 Brussels, Belgium; tel. and fax (2) 511-46-95; e-mail worldbureau@isgf.org; internet www.isgf.org; f. 1953 to help adult scouts and guides to keep alive the spirit of the Scout and Guide Promise and Laws in their own lives and to bring that spirit into the communities in which they live and work; promotes liaison and co-operation between national organizations for adult scouts and guides; encourages the founding of an organization in any country where no such organization exists; mems: 90,000 in 61 mem. states; Chair. of Cttee MIDÁ RODRIGUES; Sec.-Gen. FAOUZIA KCHOUK.

International Young Christian Workers: 4 ave G. Rodenbach, 1030 Brussels, Belgium; tel. (2) 242-18-11; fax (2) 242-48-00; e-mail joci@jociycw.net; internet www.jociycw.net; f. 1925, on the inspiration of the Priest-Cardinal Joseph Cardijn; aims to educate young workers to take on present and future responsibilities in their commitment to the working class, and to gain personal fulfilment through their actions; Pres. GEETHANI PERIES (Sri-Lanka); publs *International INFO* (3 a year), *IYCW Bulletin* (quarterly).

International Young Democrat Union: e-mail iydu@iydu.com; internet www.iydu.org; f. 1991; a global alliance of centre right political youth organizations; mems: 127 orgs from 81 countries; Chair. ARIS KALAFATIS (Greece); Sec.-Gen. JAMES MARRIOTT (United Kingdom).

Junior Chamber International (JCI), Inc.: 15645 Olive blvd, Chesterfield, MO 63017, USA; tel. (636) 449-3100; fax (636) 449-3107; e-mail news@jci.cc; internet www.jci.cc; f. 1944 to encourage and advance international understanding and goodwill; aims to solve civic problems by arousing civic consciousness; Junior Chamber organizations throughout the world provide opportunities for leadership training and for the discussion of social, economic and cultural questions; mems: 200,000 in more than 100 countries; Pres. BERTOLD DAEMS (Netherlands) (2012); publs *JCI News* (monthly in English, French and Spanish), *Leader Magazine* (2 a year).

Latin American and Caribbean Alliance of Young Men's Christian Associations (la Alianza Latinoamericana y del Caribe de Asociaciones Cristianas de Jóvenes): Rua N Pestana 125, 10° andar, Conj. 103, São Paulo 01303-010, Brazil; tel. (11) 3257-5867; fax (11) 3151-2573; e-mail secretariogeneral@lacaymca.org; internet www.lacaymca.org; f. 1914; aims to encourage the moral, spiritual, intellectual, social and physical development of young men; to strengthen the work of national Asscns and to sponsor the establishment of new Asscns; mems: affiliated YMCAs in 94 countries; Pres. GERARDO VITUREIRA (Uruguay); Gen. Sec. MAURICIO DIAZ VANDORSEE (Brazil); publs *Diecisiete/21* (bulletin), *Carta Abierta*, *Brief*, technical articles and other studies.

Pan-African Youth Union (Union pan-africaine de la jeunesse): Khartoum, Sudan; tel. 8037038097 (mobile); f. 1962; aims to encourage the participation of African youth in socio-economic and political development and democratization; organizes conferences and seminars, youth exchanges and youth festivals; 2011 Congress: Khartoum, Sudan, in Dec; mems: youth groups in 52 African countries and liberation movements; Pres. ANDILE LUNGISA (South Africa) (2012–14); publ. *MPJ News* (quarterly).

Round Table International: e-mail secretary@rtinternational.org; internet www.rtinternational.org; f. 1947 to promote international fellowship and co-operation among national Round Table groupings aimed at young business people 18–40 years of age; mems: some 2,700 clubs in 65 countries; Pres. STIJN DE FRENE (Belgium) (2011–12).

WFUNA Youth: c/o WFUNA, 1 United Nations Plaza, Room DC1-1177, New York, NY 10017, USA; tel. (212) 963-5610; fax (212) 963-0447; e-mail info@wfuna-youth.net; internet www.wfuna.org/youth; f. 1948 by the World Federation of United Nations Associations (WFUNA) as the International Youth and Student Movement for the United Nations (ISMUN), independent since 1949; an international non-governmental organization of students and young people dedicated especially to supporting the principles embodied in the United Nations Charter and Universal Declaration of Human Rights; encourages constructive action in building economic, social and cultural equality and in working for national independence, social justice and human rights on a world-wide scale; organizes periodic regional WFUNA International Model United Nations (WIMUN) conferences; maintains regional offices in Austria, France, Ghana, Panama and the USA; mems: asscns in over 100 mem. states of the UN.

World Alliance of Young Men's Christian Associations: 12 Clos. Belmont, 1208 Geneva, Switzerland; tel. 228495100; fax 228495110; e-mail office@ymca.int; internet www.ymca.int; f. 1855; organizes World Council every four years (2010: Hong Kong, SAR; 2014: Estes Park, USA); mems: federation of YMCAs in 125 countries with a membership of over 45m.; Pres. KEN COLLOTON (USA) (2010–14); Sec.-Gen. Rev. JOHAN VILHELM ELTVIK (Norway) (2010–14); publ. *YMCA World* (quarterly).

World Assembly of Youth: World Youth Complex, Lebuh Ayer Keroh, Ayer Keroh, 75450 Melaka, Malaysia; tel. (6) 2321871; fax (6) 2327271; e-mail info@way.org.my; internet www.way.org.my; f. 1949 as co-ordinating body for national youth councils and organizations; organizes conferences, training courses and practical development projects; has consultative status with the UN Economic and Social Council; mems: 120 mem. orgs; Pres. Datuk Wira IDRIS HARON; Sec.-Gen. EDIOLA PASHOLLARI; publs *WAY Information* (every 2 months), *Youth Roundup* (every 2 months), *WAY Forum* (quarterly).

World Association of Girl Guides and Girl Scouts (WAGGGS): World Bureau, Olave Centre, 12C Lyndhurst Rd, London, NW3 5PQ, United Kingdom; tel. (20) 7794-1181; fax (20) 7431-3764; e-mail wagggs@wagggsworld.org; internet www.wagggsworld.org; f. 1928 to enable girls and young women to develop their full potential as responsible citizens, and to support friendship and mutual understanding among girls and young women world-wide; operates four 'World Centres': Pax Lodge (United Kingdom), and a Sangam (India), Cabaña (Mexico), and Chalet (Switzerland), which provide residential training programmes to enable girls and young women to develop leadership skills and friendships; World Conference meets every three years; mems: about 10m. individuals in 145 orgs; Chair. World Board NADINE EL-ACHY (Lebanon); Chief Exec. MARY MCPHAIL (Ireland); publs *Triennial Review*, *Annual Report*, *Trefoil Round the World* (every 3 years), *Our World News* (quarterly).

World Federation of Democratic Youth (WFDY): 1139 Budapest, Frangepán u. 16, Hungary; tel. (1) 350-2202; fax (1) 350-1204; e-mail wfdy@wfdy.org; internet www.wfdy.org; f. 1945; promotes the unity, co-operation, organized action, solidarity and exchange of information and experiences of work and struggle among the progressive youth forces; campaigns against imperialism, fascism, colonialism, exploitation and war and for peace, internationalist solidarity, social progress and youth rights under the slogans Youth unite! and Forward for lasting peace!; mems: 152 members in 102 countries; publ. *World Youth*.

World Organization of the Scout Movement: CP 91, 1211 Geneva 4 Plainpalais, Switzerland; tel. 227051010; fax 227051020; e-mail worldbureau@world.scout.org; internet www.scout.org; f. 1922 to promote unity and understanding of scouting throughout the world; to develop good citizenship among young people by forming their characters for service, co-operation and leadership; and to provide aid and advice to members and potential member asscns. The World Scout Bureau (Geneva) has regional offices in Egypt, Kenya, Panama, the Philippines, Russia, Senegal, South Africa and Ukraine (the European Region has its offices in Brussels and Geneva); mems: over 30m. in 161 countries and territories; Sec.-Gen. LUC PANISSOD (France); publs *Worldinfo*, *Triennial Report*.

World Union of Jewish Students (WUJS): POB 39359, Tel Aviv 61392, Israel; tel. (2) 6251682; fax (2) 6251688; e-mail info@wujs.org.il; internet www.wujs.org.il; f. 1924 (with Albert Einstein as its first President); promotes dialogue and co-operation among Jewish university students world-wide; divided into six regions; organizes Congress every year; mems: 52 national unions representing over 1.5m. students; Chair. OLIVER WORTH; publs *The Student Activist Yearbook*, *Heritage and History*, *Forum*, *WUJS Report*.

World Young Women's Christian Association (World YWCA): 16 Ancienne Route, 1218 Grand-Saconnex, Geneva, Switzerland; tel. 229296040; fax 229296044; e-mail worldoffice@worldywca.org; internet www.worldywca.org; f. 1894; global movement which aims to empower women and girls to change their lives and communities; works to achieve social and economic justice through grassroots development and global advocacy; addresses critical issues affecting women, such as HIV and AIDS and violence; promotes the sharing of human and financial resources among member asscns; mems: in 106 countries; Pres. DEBORAH THOMAS-AUSTIN (Trinidad and Tobago); Gen. Sec. NYARADZAYI GUMBONZVANDA (Zimbabwe); publs *Annual Report*, *Common Concern*, *Week of Prayer* (booklet), other reports.

PART TWO

Afghanistan–Jordan

AFGHANISTAN

Introductory Survey

LOCATION, CLIMATE, LANGUAGE, RELIGION, FLAG, CAPITAL

The Islamic Republic of Afghanistan is a land locked country in south-western Asia. It is bordered by Turkmenistan, Uzbekistan and Tajikistan to the north, Iran to the west, the People's Republic of China to the north-east, and Pakistan to the east and south. The climate varies sharply between the highlands and lowlands; the temperature in the south-west in summer reaches 49°C (120°F), but in the winter, in the Hindu Kush mountains of the north-east, it falls to −26°C (−15°F). Of the many languages spoken in Afghanistan, the principal two are Pashto (Pakhto) and Dari (a dialect of Farsi or Iranian). The majority of Afghans are Muslims of the Sunni sect; there are also minority groups of Shi'a Muslims, Hindus, Sikhs and Jews. The state flag (proportions 1 by 2) has three equal vertical stripes from hoist to fly of black, red and green, bearing in the centre in white and red the state arms and an inscription reading 'There is no God but Allah, and Muhammad is his Prophet, and Allah is Great', in Arabic. The Islamic date 1298 appears under the inscription. The flag was first introduced in 1928, modified in 1964, and banned following the coup in 1978. The only difference featured in the current flag, which was introduced in June 2002 following the collapse of the Taliban regime, is the inscription bearing the word 'Afghanistan'. The capital is Kabul.

CONTEMPORARY POLITICAL HISTORY

Historical Context

The last King of Afghanistan, Mohammad Zahir Shah, reigned from 1933 to 1973. His country was neutral during both World Wars and became a staunch advocate of non-alignment. In 1953 the King's cousin, Lt-Gen. Sardar Mohammad Daoud Khan, was appointed Prime Minister and, securing aid from the USSR, initiated a series of economic plans for the modernization of the country. In 1963 Gen. Daoud resigned and Dr Mohammad Yusuf became the first Prime Minister not of royal birth. Dr Yusuf introduced a new democratic Constitution in the following year, which combined Western ideas with Islamic religious and political beliefs; however, the King did not permit political parties to operate. Afghanistan made little progress under succeeding Prime Ministers over the next 10 years or so.

In July 1973, while King Zahir was in Italy, the monarchy was overthrown by a coup, in which the main figure was Gen. Daoud. The 1964 Constitution was abolished and Afghanistan was declared a republic. Daoud renounced his royal titles and took office as Head of State, Prime Minister, and Minister of Foreign Affairs and Defence. A Loya Jirga (Grand National Council), appointed from among tribal elders by provincial governors, was convened in January 1977 and adopted a new Constitution, providing for presidential government and a one-party state. Daoud was elected to continue as President for six years and the Loya Jirga was then dissolved. In March President Daoud formed a new civilian Government, nominally ending military rule.

Domestic Political Affairs

Communist/PDPA rule (1978–92)

During 1977 there was growing discontent with Daoud, especially within the armed forces, and in April 1978 a coup, known (from the month) as the 'Saur Revolution', ousted the President, who was killed with several members of his family. Nur Mohammad Taraki, the imprisoned leader of the formerly banned People's Democratic Party of Afghanistan (PDPA), was released and installed as President of the Revolutionary Council and Prime Minister. The country was renamed the Democratic Republic of Afghanistan, the year-old Constitution was abolished and no political parties other than the communist PDPA were allowed to function. Afghanistan's already close relations with the USSR were further strengthened. However, opposition to the new regime led to armed insurrection, particularly by fiercely traditionalist Islamist rebel tribesmen (known, collectively, as the *mujahidin*), in almost all provinces, and the flight of thousands of refugees to Pakistan and Iran. In spite of purges of the army and civil service, Taraki's position became increasingly insecure, and in September 1979 he was ousted by Hafizullah Amin, an erstwhile Deputy Prime Minister and Minister of Foreign Affairs. Amin's imposition of rigorous communist policies proved unsuccessful and unpopular. In December he was killed in a coup, which was supported by the entry into Afghanistan of about 80,000 combat troops from the USSR. This incursion by Soviet armed forces into a traditionally non-aligned neighbouring country provoked world-wide condemnation. Babrak Karmal, a former Deputy Prime Minister under Taraki, was installed as the new head of state, having been flown into Kabul by a Soviet aircraft from virtual exile in Eastern Europe.

Riots, strikes and inter-factional strife and purges continued into 1980 and 1981. Sultan Ali Keshtmand, hitherto a Deputy Prime Minister, replaced Karmal as Prime Minister in June 1981. In the same month the regime launched the National Fatherland Front (NFF), incorporating the PDPA and other organizations, with the aim of promoting national unity. Despite a series of government reorganizations carried out in the early 1980s, the PDPA regime failed to win widespread popular support. Consequently, the Government attempted to broaden the base of its support: in April 1985 it summoned a Loya Jirga, which ratified a new Constitution for Afghanistan, and during the second half of 1985 and the first half of 1986 elections were held for new local government organs and several non-party members were appointed to high-ranking government posts.

In May 1986 Dr Najibullah (the former head of the state security service, KHAD) succeeded Karmal as General Secretary of the PDPA. Karmal retained the lesser post of President of the Revolutionary Council. In the same month Najibullah announced the formation of a collective leadership comprising himself, Karmal and Prime Minister Keshtmand. In November, however, Karmal was relieved of all party and government posts. Haji Muhammad Chamkani, formerly First Vice-President (and a non-PDPA member), became Acting President of the Revolutionary Council, pending the introduction of a new constitution and the establishment of a permanent legislature.

In December 1986 an extraordinary plenum of the PDPA Central Committee approved a policy of national reconciliation, involving negotiations with opposition groups, and the proposed formation of a government of national unity. In January 1987 a Supreme Extraordinary Commission for National Reconciliation, led by Abdul Rahim Hatif (the Chairman of the National Committee of the NFF), was formed to conduct the negotiations. The NFF was renamed the National Front (NF), and became a separate organization from the PDPA. The new policy of reconciliation won some support from former opponents, but the seven-party *mujahidin* alliance (Ittehad-i-Islami Afghan Mujahidin, Islamic Union of Afghan Mujahidin—IUAM), which was based in Peshawar, Pakistan, refused to observe the cease-fire or to participate in negotiations, while continuing to demand a complete and unconditional Soviet withdrawal from Afghanistan.

In July 1987, as part of the process of national reconciliation, the draft of a new Constitution was approved by the Presidium of the Revolutionary Council. The main innovations incorporated in the draft document were: the formation of a multi-party political system, under the auspices of the NF; the formation of a bicameral legislature, the Meli Shura (National Assembly), which was to be composed of a Sena (Senate) and a Wolasi Jirga (House of Representatives); the granting of a permanent constitutional status to the PDPA; the bestowal of unlimited power on the President, who was to hold office for seven years; and the reversion of the name of the country from the Democratic Republic to the Republic of Afghanistan. A Loya Jirga ratified the new Constitution in November.

On 30 September 1987 Najibullah was unanimously elected as President of the Revolutionary Council, and Chamkani resumed his former post as First Vice-President. In order to strengthen his position, Najibullah ousted all the remaining supporters of former President Karmal from the Central Committee and Politburo of the PDPA in October. In the following month a

Loya Jirga unanimously elected Najibullah as President of the State.

In April 1988 elections were held to both houses of the new National Assembly, which replaced the Revolutionary Council. Although the elections were boycotted by the *mujahidin*, the Government left vacant 50 of the 234 seats in the House of Representatives, and a small number of seats in the Senate, in the hope that the guerrillas would abandon their armed struggle and present their own representatives to participate in the new administration. The PDPA itself won only 46 seats in the House of Representatives, but was guaranteed support from the NF, which secured 45, and from the various newly recognized left-wing parties, which won a total of 24 seats. In May Dr Muhammad Hasan Sharq (a non-PDPA member and a Deputy Prime Minister since June 1987) replaced Keshtmand as Prime Minister, and in June a new Council of Ministers was appointed.

On 18 February 1989, following the completion of the withdrawal of Soviet troops from Afghanistan (see Soviet occupation and *mujahidin* resistance), Najibullah implemented a government reorganization, involving the replacement of non-communist ministers with loyal PDPA members. On the same day, Prime Minister Sharq (who had been one of the main promoters of the policy of national reconciliation) resigned from his post and was replaced by Keshtmand. Following the declaration of a state of emergency by Najibullah (citing allegations of repeated violations of the Geneva accords by Pakistan and the USA) on 19 February, a PDPA-dominated 20-member Supreme Council for the Defence of the Homeland was established. The Council, which was headed by President Najibullah and was composed of ministers, members of the PDPA Politburo and high-ranking military figures, assumed full responsibility for the country's economic, political and military policies (although the Council of Ministers continued to function).

In March 1990 the Minister of Defence, Lt-Gen. Shahnawaz Tanay, with the alleged support of the air force and some divisions of the army, led an unsuccessful coup attempt against Najibullah's Government. Najibullah subsequently enacted thorough purges of PDPA and army leaders, and decided to revert rapidly to some form of constitutional civilian government. On 20 May the state of emergency was lifted; the Supreme Council for the Defence of the Homeland was disbanded; and a new Council of Ministers, under the premiership of Fazle Haq Khalikyar, was appointed. At the end of the month a Loya Jirga was convened in Kabul, which ratified constitutional amendments, greatly reducing Afghanistan's socialist orientation; ending the PDPA's and the NF's monopoly over executive power and paving the way for fully democratic elections; introducing greater political and press freedom; encouraging the development of the private sector and further foreign investment; and lessening the role of the State and affording greater prominence to Islam. However, the extensive powers of the presidency were retained. In addition, in June the PDPA changed its name to the Homeland Party (HP—Hizb-i Watan), and dissolved the Politburo and the Central Committee, replacing them with an Executive Board and a Central Council, respectively. Najibullah was unanimously elected as Chairman of the HP. An important factor in Najibullah's decision to continue with, and to extend, the process of national reconciliation was the fact that the USSR's own internal problems meant that the Soviet administration was unwilling to sustain, for much longer, the supplies of weapons, goods and credits that were helping to support the Kabul regime.

Soviet occupation and mujahidin *resistance*

Fighting between the *mujahidin* and Afghan army units had begun in the eastern provinces after the 1978 coup and was aggravated by the implementation of unpopular social and economic reforms by the new administrations. The Afghan army relied heavily upon Soviet military aid in the form of weapons, equipment and expertise, but morale and resources were severely affected by defections to the rebels' ranks: numbers fell from around 80,000 men in 1978 to about 40,000 in 1985. During 1984–89 the guerrilla groups, which had been poorly armed at first, received ever-increasing military and financial support from abroad, notably from the USA (which began to supply them with sophisticated anti-aircraft weapons in 1986), the United Kingdom and the People's Republic of China. Despite the Government's decision to seal the border with Pakistan, announced in September 1985, and the strong presence of Soviet forces there, foreign weapons continued to reach the guerrillas via Pakistan. Many of the guerrillas established bases in the North-West Frontier Province of Pakistan (notably in the provincial capital, Peshawar). From 1985 the fighting intensified, especially in areas close to the Afghan–Pakistani border. There were many border violations, but the general pattern of the war remained the same: the regime held the main towns and a few strategic bases, and relied on bombing of both military and civilian targets, and occasional attacks in force, together with conciliatory measures such as the provision of funds for local development, while the rebel forces dominated rural areas and were able to cause serious disruption.

The civil war brought famine to parts of Afghanistan, and there was a mass movement of population from the countryside to Kabul, and of refugees to Pakistan and Iran. In mid-1988 the Office of the UN High Commissioner for Refugees (UNHCR) estimated the number of Afghan refugees in Pakistan at 3.15m., and the number in Iran at 2.35m. Supply convoys were often prevented from reaching the cities, owing to the repeated severing of major road links by the guerrillas. Kabul, in particular, began to suffer from severe shortages of food and fuel, which were only partially alleviated by airlifts of emergency aid supplies.

From 1980 extensive international negotiations took place to try to achieve the complete withdrawal of Soviet forces from Afghanistan. Between June 1982 and September 1987 seven rounds of indirect talks took place between the Afghan and Pakistani Ministers of Foreign Affairs in Geneva, Switzerland, under the auspices of the UN. In October 1986 the USSR made a token withdrawal of six regiments (6,000–8,000 men) from Afghanistan. As a result of the discussions in Geneva, an agreement was finally signed on 14 April 1988. The Geneva accords consisted of five documents: detailed undertakings by Afghanistan and Pakistan, relating to non-intervention and non-interference in each other's affairs; international guarantees of Afghan neutrality (with the USA and the USSR as the principal guarantors); arrangements for the voluntary and safe return of Afghan refugees; a document linking the preceding documents with a timetable for a Soviet withdrawal; and the establishment of a UN monitoring force, which was to oversee both the Soviet troop departures and the return of the refugees. The withdrawal of Soviet troops commenced on 15 May.

Neither the *mujahidin* nor Iran played any role in the formulation of the Geneva accords, and, in spite of protests by Pakistan, no agreement was incorporated regarding the composition of an interim coalition government in Afghanistan, or the cessation of Soviet aid to Najibullah's regime and US aid to the *mujahidin*. Therefore, despite the withdrawal of the Soviet troops, the supply of weapons to both sides was not halted, and the fighting continued. Pakistan repeatedly denied accusations that it had violated the accords by continuing to harbour Afghan guerrillas and to act as a conduit for the supply of weapons. In spite of the unabated violence, the USSR, adhering to the condition specified in the Geneva accords, withdrew all of its troops from Afghanistan by February 1989.

Meanwhile, the *mujahidin* had intensified their military activities in mid-1998, attacking small provincial centres and launching missiles against major cities. In February 1989 the IUAM convened its own *shura* (council) in Rawalpindi, Pakistan, at which an interim government-in-exile (known as the Afghan Interim Government—AIG) was elected. However, the AIG was officially recognized by only four countries. It also failed to gain any substantial support or recognition from the guerrilla commanders, who were beginning to establish their own unofficial alliances inside the country. In March, however, the AIG received a form of diplomatic recognition when it was granted membership of the Organization of the Islamic Conference (OIC). In addition, in June the US Government appointed a special envoy to the *mujahidin*, with the rank of personal ambassador. However, in mid-1989 the unity of the *mujahidin* forces was seriously weakened by an increase in internecine violence among the various guerrilla groups, while the AIG was riven by disputes between moderates and fundamentalists. The USA, Saudi Arabia and Pakistan began to reduce financial aid and military supplies to the IUAM in Peshawar, and to undertake the difficult task of delivering weapons and money directly to guerrilla commanders and tribal leaders inside Afghanistan. The *mujahidin* launched a series of new military campaigns in the second half of 1990 in an apparent attempt to impress their international supporters, disrupt the return of refugees and obstruct contacts between the Government and moderate guerrillas. In March 1991, following more than two weeks of heavy fighting, the south-eastern city of Khost was captured by the *mujahidin*, representing the most severe reversal sustained by the Government since the Soviet withdrawal.

An unexpected breakthrough towards resolving the Afghan crisis occurred in September 1991, when the USA and the USSR announced that they would stop supplying arms to the warring factions, and would encourage other countries (namely Pakistan, Saudi Arabia and Iran) to do likewise. Although both the Afghan Government and the *mujahidin* welcomed this pledge, neither side showed any sign of implementing the proposed cease-fire, and, indeed, the fighting intensified around Kabul. In February 1992, however, the peace process was given a major boost when Pakistan announced that it was urging all guerrilla factions to support a proposed UN peace plan, effectively abandoning its insistence on the installation of a fundamentalist government in Kabul. There were growing fears, none the less, that the peace process might be placed in jeopardy by an increase in ethnic divisions within both the government forces and a number of *mujahidin* groups, between the majority Pashtuns and minority groups such as the Tajiks and Uzbeks. As a result of a mutiny staged by Uzbek militia forces in the Afghan army, under the command of Gen. Abdul Rashid Dostam, the northern town of Mazar-i-Sharif was captured by the *mujahidin* in March.

The mujahidin *in power (1992–96)*

On 16 April 1992 Najibullah was unexpectedly forced to resign by his own ruling party, following the capture of the strategically important Bagram airbase and the nearby town of Charikar, about 50 km north of Kabul, by the Jamiat-i Islami guerrilla group under the command of the Tajik general Ahmad Shah Masoud. Najibullah went into hiding in the capital, under UN protection, while one of the Vice-Presidents, Abdul Rahim Hatif, assumed the post of acting President. Within a few days, every major town in Afghanistan was under the control of different coalitions of *mujahidin* groups co-operating with disaffected army commanders. On 25 April the forces of both Masoud and of Gulbuddin Hekmatyar, the leader of a rival guerrilla group, the Pashtun-dominated Hizb-i Islami (Islamic Party), whose men were massed to the south of the capital, entered Kabul. The army surrendered its key positions, and immediately the city was riven by *mujahidin* faction-fighting. The military council that had, a few days earlier, replaced the Government relinquished power to the *mujahidin*. Having discarded the UN's proposal to form a neutral ruling body, the guerrilla leaders in Peshawar agreed to establish a 51-member interim Islamic Jihad Council, composed of military and religious leaders, which was to assume power in Kabul. The leader of the small, moderate Jebha-i-Nejat-i-Melli (National Liberation Front), Prof. Sibghatullah Mojaddedi, was to chair the Islamic Jihad Council for two months, after which period a 10-member Leadership Council, comprising *mujahidin* chiefs and presided over by the head of the Jamiat-i Islami, Prof. Burhanuddin Rabbani, would be set up for a period of four months. Within the six months a special council was to meet to designate an interim administration, which was to hold power for up to a year pending elections.

However, the Islamic Jihad Council was not supported by Hekmatyar, whose radical stance differed substantially from Mojaddedi's more tolerant outlook. At the end of April 1992 Hekmatyar's forces lost control of their last stronghold in the centre of Kabul. Within a few weeks the Government of the newly proclaimed Islamic State of Afghanistan had won almost universal diplomatic recognition, and by May about one-half of the Islamic Jihad Council had arrived in the capital. An acting Council of Ministers was formed, in which Masoud was given the post of Minister of Defence and the premiership was set aside for Ustad Abdol Sabur Farid, a Tajik commander from the Hizb-i Islami (Hekmatyar declined to accept the post). As part of the process of 'Islamization', the death penalty was introduced, alcohol and narcotics were banned, and the wearing of strict Islamic dress by all women was enforced. Despite Mojaddedi's repeated pleas to Hekmatyar and his followers to lay down their arms, Hekmatyar, who was particularly angered by the presence of Gen. Dostam's Uzbek forces in the capital, continued to bombard Kabul with artillery and indiscriminate rocket launches from various strongholds around the city, killing and wounding scores of citizens.

On 28 June 1992 Mojaddedi surrendered power to the Leadership Council, which immediately offered Burhanuddin Rabbani the presidency of the country and the concomitant responsibility for the interim Council of Ministers for four months, as set forth in the Peshawar Agreement (see above). On assuming the presidency, Rabbani announced the adoption of a new Islamic flag, the establishment of an economic council, which was to address the country's severe economic problems, and the appointment of a commission to draw up a new constitution. In July Farid assumed the premiership, which had been held open for him since April. In August the withdrawal from the Leadership Council of the members of the Hizb-i Islami faction led by Maulvi Muhammad Yunus Khalis revealed serious rifts within the Government. A further problem was the continuing inter-*mujahidin* violence in Kabul, which within days had escalated into a full-scale ground offensive, launched by Hekmatyar's forces against the capital. The airport was closed, hundreds of people were killed or wounded, and tens of thousands of civilians fled the city. In response, President Rabbani expelled Hekmatyar from the Leadership Council and dismissed Prime Minister Farid. Hekmatyar demanded the expulsion of the 75,000 Uzbek militia from Kabul as a precondition to peace talks, alleging that Gen. Dostam was still closely allied to former members of the communist regime. At the end of August a cease-fire agreement was reached between Rabbani and Hekmatyar. However, sporadic fighting involving various *mujahidin* and militia groups (notably Gen. Dostam's Uzbek forces) continued in Kabul itself and in the provinces throughout the remainder of the year. In October the Leadership Council agreed to extend Rabbani's tenure of the presidency by two months. In December a special advisory body, the Resolution and Settlement Council (Shura-e Ahl-e Hal wa Aqd), comprising 1,335 tribal leaders, was convened in Kabul. The Council elected Rabbani, who was the sole candidate, as national President for a further two-year period. In January 1993 200 members of the advisory council were selected to constitute the future membership of the country's legislature.

The establishment of the advisory council and the re-election of President Rabbani provoked yet further heavy fighting in Kabul and other provinces in early 1993. Owing to the worsening violence, all Western diplomats had left the capital by the end of January. In March, however, President Rabbani, Hekmatyar, Mojaddedi and leaders of other major *mujahidin* factions held negotiations in Islamabad, Pakistan, at the end of which a peace accord was signed. Under the terms of the accord, an interim government was to be established, which would hold power for 18 months; President Rabbani was to remain as head of state, and Hekmatyar (or his nominee) was to assume the premiership of the acting Council of Ministers; a cease-fire was to be imposed with immediate effect; legislative elections were to be held within six months; a 16-member defence commission was to be formed, which would be responsible for the establishment of a national army; and all weaponry was to be seized from the warring factions in an attempt to restore peace and order. The peace accord was officially approved and signed by the Governments of Pakistan, Saudi Arabia and Iran.

Confronted with the difficult task of satisfying the demands of all the *mujahidin* groups, Hekmatyar was not able to present a new Council of Ministers until May 1993. Each *mujahidin* faction was allocated two ministerial posts, with further positions left vacant for other representatives. Members of Gen. Dostam's group of predominantly Uzbek militiamen—known collectively as the National Islamic Movement (NIM—Jonbesh-i Melli-i Islami)—were offered two posts in July. One of Hekmatyar's most noteworthy decisions in the formation of the new Council of Ministers was to remove Masoud, one of his most powerful rivals, from the crucial post of Minister of Defence. The new Prime Minister promised to hold a general election by October. The temporary headquarters of the Government were situated in Charasiab, Hekmatyar's military base, about 25 km south of Kabul.

Despite the signing of the Islamabad peace accord, the violence between the various *mujahidin* groups did not cease, and hundreds of people were killed and wounded. The interim Government was beset by internal dissension and proved relatively ineffectual. Hekmatyar refused to co-operate with Rabbani, and frequently demanded the President's resignation. In September 1993, however, it was reported that a new draft Constitution (known as the Basic Law) had been drawn up and approved by a special commission, in preparation for the holding of a general election. The fighting intensified in December, when Gen. Dostam transferred his allegiance to his hitherto arch-enemy, Hekmatyar, and the supporters of the two combined to confront the forces of Rabbani and Masoud. The violence spread throughout the provinces, resulting in large numbers of military and civilian casualties and the internal displacement of thousands of people. In June 1994 the Supreme Court ruled that Rabbani could retain the presidency for a further six months, but failed to grant a similar extension to Hekmatyar's premiership.

In the latter half of 1994 a new, hitherto unknown, militant grouping emerged in Afghanistan, known as the Taliban (the plural form of 'Talib', meaning 'seeker of religious knowledge'). The movement, which at the outset comprised an estimated 25,000 fighters (the majority of whom were reported to be young Pashtun graduates of fundamentalist Islamist schools established by Afghan refugees in Pakistan), advocated the adoption of extremist practices, including the complete seclusion of women from society. Although initially claiming that they had no interest in actually assuming power in Afghanistan, the Taliban, who were led by Mullah Mohammad Omar, captured the city of Qandahar from the forces of Hekmatyar in October. By February 1995 the Taliban had routed Hekmatyar's men from their headquarters in Charasiab and controlled 10 provinces, mostly in southern and south-eastern Afghanistan. However, the Taliban retreated from their advance on Kabul when Rabbani's troops launched a massive counter-offensive. By mid-1995, with both the Taliban and Hekmatyar's men held in check, President Rabbani and his supporters were enjoying an unprecedented level of authority and confidence in Kabul and its environs. This was reflected in Rabbani's reneging on his earlier promise of standing down from the presidency in March and in the growing number of countries that were considering reopening their embassies in the Afghan capital. However, the resurgence of the Taliban, which captured the key north-western city of Herat and the surrounding province from government forces in September, apparently provoked an attack on the Pakistani embassy in Kabul by hundreds of pro-Government demonstrators protesting against Pakistan's alleged support for the student militia; one embassy employee was killed and a number injured (including the ambassador himself). In response, the Afghan ambassador to Pakistan and six other Afghan diplomats were expelled from Islamabad. In October the Taliban launched a massive ground and air assault on Kabul; although this failed to breach the capital's defences, the constant bombardment of the besieged city resulted in hundreds of civilian deaths in late 1995 and early 1996.

In May 1996, in a critical development (known as the Mahipar Agreement), President Rabbani persuaded Hekmatyar to rejoin the Government. Hekmatyar's forces arrived in the capital later that month to defend the city against the Taliban. In June Hekmatyar resumed the post of Prime Minister.

The Taliban in power (1996–2001)

The political situation was radically altered in September 1996 when, as a culmination of two weeks of sweeping military advances (including the capture of the crucial eastern city of Jalalabad), the Taliban seized control of Kabul following fierce clashes with government troops, who fled northwards together with the deposed Government. One of the Taliban movement's first actions in the captured capital was the summary execution of former President Najibullah and his brother. On assuming power, the Taliban declared Afghanistan a 'complete' Islamic state and appointed an interim Council of Ministers, led by Mullah Mohammad Rabbani, to administer the country (of which it now controlled about two-thirds). Pakistan, which was widely suspected of actively aiding the Islamist militia, was the first of only three countries officially to recognize the new regime; formal recognition was subsequently also attained from Saudi Arabia and the United Arab Emirates. The Taliban imposed a strict and intimidatory Islamic code: women were not permitted to enter employment or be formally educated beyond the age of eight years; television, non-religious music and gambling were all banned; amputations and public stonings were enforced as forms of punishment; and compulsory attendance at mosques by all men was introduced.

In October 1996 a powerful military and logistical alliance was unexpectedly formed by Gen. Dostam, former Minister of Defence Masoud, who controlled six northern provinces, and Gen. Abdol Karim Khalili, leader of the Hizb-i Wahadat-i Islami (Islamic Unity Party—an alliance of eight Shi'a Afghan resistance groups). By late October the anti-Taliban forces, whose leaders were now collectively known as the Supreme Council for the Defence of Afghanistan (the headquarters of which were situated in Gen. Dostam's stronghold of Mazar-i-Sharif), had launched a concerted offensive against Kabul in the hope of ousting the Islamist militia. In January 1997, following the rapid collapse of UN-sponsored peace talks in Islamabad, the Taliban launched an unexpected offensive, advancing north and capturing Bagram airbase and the provincial capital of Charikar; by the end of the month the Taliban had made significant military gains and had pushed the front line to about 100 km north of Kabul. Following the defection of the Uzbek Gen. Abdul Malik and his men to the Taliban in May, the latter were able to capture the strategically important northern town of Mazar-i-Sharif. Gen. Dostam was reported to have fled to Turkey, and his position as leader of the Uzbek NIM militia was assumed by Gen. Malik. The Taliban now controlled about 80% of the country, including all of the major towns and cities. However, Taliban control of Mazar-i-Sharif was extremely brief, and within only three days of entering the town the movement was in full retreat. It appeared that Gen. Malik's tenuous alliance with the Taliban had collapsed almost immediately and his troops, together with Shi'a militia, forced the newcomers out after ferocious fighting.

The anti-Taliban alliance was reported to have been expanded and strengthened in June 1997 by the inclusion of the forces of Hekmatyar and of the Mahaz-i-Melli-i-Islami (National Islamic Front), led by Pir Sayed Ahmad Gailani. This new coalition—the United National Islamic Front for the Salvation of Afghanistan (commonly known as the United Front or the Northern Alliance)—superseded the Supreme Council for the Defence of Afghanistan. The United Front was the military wing of the exiled Government, the 'Islamic State of Afghanistan'. Despite the arrival of thousands of reinforcements from training camps in Pakistan (many of whom were inexperienced teenagers), the Taliban suffered a series of military defeats in northern Afghanistan, and by July the United Front forces were within firing range of Kabul, having recaptured Charikar and the airbase at Bagram. In the same month the UN Security Council demanded a cease-fire and an end to all foreign intervention in Afghanistan; it was widely believed that the Taliban were supported by Pakistan and Saudi Arabia; on the opposing side, to various degrees, were Iran, India, the Central Asian states (which feared the encroachment of Taliban fundamentalism) and Russia.

In August 1997 the United Front appointed a new Government, based in Mazar-i-Sharif, with Burhanuddin Rabbani continuing as President, Abdorrahim Ghafurzai as Prime Minister, Masoud as Minister of Defence and Gen. Malik as Minister of Foreign Affairs. However, within a few days of its appointment, Prime Minister Ghafurzai and six other members of the new Government (which Hekmatyar refused to recognize) were killed in an aeroplane crash. Later in August Abdolghaffur Rawanfarhadi was appointed Prime Minister.

Following his return from Turkey, in October 1997 Gen. Dostam was re-elected as commander of the United Front forces and concurrently appointed Vice-President of the anti-Taliban administration. Although a battle for supremacy between Gen. Dostam and Gen. Malik ensued, which sparked skirmishes between their respective forces, Gen. Dostam succeeded in ousting his rival to resume the leadership of the NIM militia. Meanwhile, in October the Taliban unilaterally decided to change the country's name to the Islamic Emirate of Afghanistan and altered the state flag, moves that were condemned by the opposition alliance and all of Afghanistan's neighbours except Pakistan.

In March 1998 the UN ceased operating aid programmes in the southern province of Qandahar (where the political headquarters of the Taliban were located) following attacks on staff and constant harassment by the Taliban. In the same month there were reports of factional fighting between rival members of the United Front in and around Mazar-i-Sharif, highlighting the fragile nature of the anti-Taliban alliance. In April, following the launch of a major diplomatic initiative by the USA, the Taliban and the United Front held talks, sponsored by the UN and the OIC, in Islamabad, the first formal peace negotiations between the two opposing sides for more than a year. However, the talks broke down in May, and fighting resumed to the north of Kabul.

In August 1998 the Taliban captured the northern city of Shiberghan, Gen. Dostam's new headquarters, after a number of his Uzbek commanders allegedly accepted bribes from the Taliban and switched allegiance. Gen. Dostam was reported to have fled to the Uzbek border and thence to Turkey. Following the recapture of Mazar-i-Sharif by the Taliban (who allegedly now included considerable numbers of extremist volunteers from various other Islamic countries, including Pakistan, Saudi Arabia, Algeria and Egypt) later in August, 10 Iranian diplomats and one Iranian journalist were reported to have been captured and killed by Taliban militia. In September Afghanistan and Iran appeared to be on the verge of open warfare, as 70,000 Iranian troops were deployed on the mutual border, and it emerged that nine of the missing Iranian nationals had, in fact, been murdered by members of the Taliban as they stormed Mazar-i-Sharif. (It was later reported that 2,000–6,000 Shi'a Hazara civilians had been systematically massacred by the guerrillas after recapturing the city.) Both Iran and Afghanistan massed more troops on the border, with 500,000 Iranian troops reportedly on full military alert. However, by the end of the year the situation appeared much calmer, with the Taliban having agreed to free all Iranian prisoners being held in Afghanistan and to punish those responsible for the killing of the nine Iranian diplomats (or military advisers, according to the Taliban), and Iran having scaled down its border forces and announced that it had no intention of invading Afghanistan.

Meanwhile, in August 1998 the USA launched simultaneous air-strikes against alleged terrorist bases in eastern Afghanistan and Sudan, reportedly operated by the Saudi-born militant leader of the al-Qa'ida organization, Osama bin Laden (who was supported by the Taliban), in retaliation for the bombing of two US embassies in East Africa earlier that month. Many aid agencies withdrew their remaining expatriate staff from Afghanistan, fearing terrorist acts of vengeance. In September the Taliban suffered a considerable set-back when Saudi Arabia withdrew its support and recalled its envoy from Kabul in response to the reported brutality of the guerrilla authorities and to their sheltering of bin Laden. In the following month the Taliban stated that, although they were not willing to extradite the Saudi-born dissident, in the event of a lawsuit being filed against him, they would be prepared to place him on trial in Afghanistan. The Taliban also insisted that bin Laden (who had reportedly been resident in Afghanistan for at least two years) was under close supervision, with his activities and media access suitably restricted. Evidence submitted by the US Government to the Afghan Supreme Court in November was deemed by the latter as inadequate grounds for bin Laden's arrest.

In September 1998 the Taliban captured the capital of Bamian province, a Shi'a stronghold; this victory meant that any substantial anti-Taliban opposition was effectively restricted to Masoud's stronghold in north-eastern Afghanistan. Taliban advances in the north alarmed Russia and the Central Asian states, which feared the unsettling potential of a militant Islamist army along their southern borders. In December the UN Security Council threatened the Taliban with the imposition of sanctions and appealed to the regime to commence negotiations with the opposition.

In January 1999 it was reported that the United Front had established a multi-ethnic Supreme Military Council, under the command of Masoud, the aim of which was to give fresh impetus to the anti-Taliban movement and to co-ordinate manoeuvres against Taliban forces in northern Afghanistan. UN-monitored direct peace talks between representatives of the Taliban and the United Front in February, March and July, ultimately achieved very little. In March, however, the first UN personnel returned to Afghanistan since their evacuation in August 1998 (following the murder of three UN employees), marking the beginning of a phased return of the organization's international staff to Afghanistan.

In July 1999, following reports that bin Laden was being sheltered in eastern Afghanistan, the USA imposed financial and economic sanctions on the Taliban regime in a further attempt to persuade it to hand over the militant leader (who the US authorities suspected of planning more atrocities) to stand trial in the USA. The Taliban claimed that the sanctions would have very little impact and again refused to extradite bin Laden.

At the 1999 session of the UN General Assembly (held in September–November) the UN again rejected the Taliban request to represent Afghanistan; the seat remained under the control of President Rabbani, the leader of the 'Islamic State of Afghanistan'. In October the UN Secretary-General's Special Envoy to Afghanistan, Lakhdar Brahimi, announced his withdrawal from his mission, owing to the lack of progress (and particularly to the alleged negative attitude of the Taliban). In November the UN Security Council imposed an embargo on all Taliban-controlled overseas assets and a ban on the international flights of the national airline, Ariana Afghan Airlines, as a result of the Afghan regime's continuing refusal to relinquish bin Laden. Following the imposition of the sanctions, large-scale demonstrations erupted throughout Afghanistan and international aid organizations again came under attack. In February 2000 Francesc Vendrell was appointed Head of the UN Special Mission to Afghanistan and Personal Representative of the UN Secretary-General, with the rank of Assistant Secretary-General. However, relations between the UN and Afghanistan remained tense, culminating in the UN's temporary withdrawal of its expatriate staff from Qandahar in March, following an assault on UN offices by the Taliban.

Heavy fighting between Taliban and United Front forces, concentrated in the north of Kabul, resumed in March 2000. During OIC-mediated peace negotiations in March and May, the two parties pledged to exchange prisoners of war; however, no agreement was reached on a cease-fire. In June there was renewed fighting in northern and central Afghanistan, and by September the Taliban had acquired more territory in the north, including, crucially, the capture of Taloqan, the capital of Takhar province and the headquarters of the United Front. In December the Taliban and the United Front entered into negotiations conducted by Francesc Vendrell. In the same month the UN Security Council approved a resolution, which stated that unless the Taliban surrendered bin Laden and closed down militant training camps by 19 January 2001, the international community would impose an arms embargo, tighten an existing embargo on flights and the freeze on Taliban assets abroad, restrict the sale of chemicals used to produce heroin from poppies, and close Ariana Afghan Airlines offices abroad. The Taliban refused to concede to the demands and, immediately after the UN's decision, shut down the UN special mission to Afghanistan and cancelled planned peace negotiations. The UN sanctions were duly imposed, and in May all UN political staff were expelled from Afghanistan.

In February 2001 the Taliban ordered the demolition of all statues in Afghanistan depicting living creatures, including the world's tallest standing Buddhas in Bamian. Despite widespread international condemnation, the destruction of much of Afghanistan's pre-Islamic cultural heritage was carried out in March. However, Hindu and Sikh statues, acknowledged as fundamental to the respective religious practices, were preserved. The order contravened a 1999 decree, which ordered the preservation of all ancient relics, thereby prompting speculation that members of bin Laden's al-Qa'ida had taken control of the Taliban by ousting the more moderate leaders.

In April 2001 the Chairman of the Taliban Interim Council of Ministers and Gen. Commander of the Armed Forces, Mullah Mohammad Rabbani, died. He was subsequently replaced as Gen. Commander by his brother, Mullah Ahmed. In July the Taliban issued another set of controversial edicts: the use of the internet was outlawed; women were banned from visiting picnic areas; and items such as tape recorders, telephone sets, musical instruments and lipstick were proscribed as non-Islamic.

In June 2001 the US ambassador to Pakistan issued a statement in which he warned the Taliban that they would be held accountable if bin Laden carried out an attack against US interests. In July the UN Security Council adopted a resolution that reinforced the sanctions imposed in January. Some 15 UN officials were to be posted in and around Afghanistan to monitor the success of the existing arms embargo. The resolution was censured for focusing solely on the Taliban and for failing to curb the United Front's arms supply.

Meanwhile, following the coup in Pakistan in October 1999 (see the chapter on Pakistan), there were indications that relations between the Taliban and the new Pakistani administration, headed by Gen. Pervez Musharraf, might not prove as amicable as they had been since 1996. In his first major address to the Pakistani nation shortly after assuming power, Gen. Musharraf pledged to work for a 'truly representative government' in Afghanistan, and in the following month the State Bank of Pakistan complied with the UN sanctions in ordering a freeze on all Taliban financial assets in Pakistan. However, Pakistan continued to offer economic aid and support to the Taliban and condemned the UN sanctions against Afghanistan.

The US-led military operation commences

The situation in Afghanistan drastically changed as a result of the terrorist attacks on New York and Washington, DC, USA, on 11 September 2001. Two days after the events the US Secretary of State publicly identified bin Laden and his al-Qa'ida organization as having been principally responsible for them. The Taliban initially claimed that neither bin Laden nor Afghanistan had the means to carry out the attacks, warning that they would retaliate if the USA attacked Afghanistan. On 16 September the UN imposed diplomatic sanctions and an arms embargo on the Taliban, while the USA began to form an anti-terrorism coalition, with the assistance of the United Kingdom.

Pakistan came under considerable pressure to reverse its policy of supporting the Taliban and agreed to co-operate with the US-led coalition. On 17 September 2001 a Pakistani delegation issued Taliban leaders with an ultimatum to surrender bin Laden or face retaliation from the USA. A few days later a *shura* of Afghan clerics, under the leadership of Mullah Mohammad Omar, issued an edict for bin Laden to leave Afghanistan voluntarily. The *shura* also demanded that the UN and OIC hold independent investigations, and threatened to instigate a *jihad* (holy war) if the USA attacked Afghanistan. US officials, demanding unconditional surrender, considered the edict insufficient. At the same time, US President George W. Bush warned that the Taliban would also be targeted if they refused to extradite bin Laden and other al-Qa'ida members.

Meanwhile, on 15 September 2001 Ahmad Shah Masoud died of injuries sustained during a suicide bombing, allegedly orchestrated by al-Qa'ida, two days before the terrorist attacks on the USA; his deputy, Gen. Muhammed Qasim Fahim, was subsequently appointed interim military leader of the United Front. In October there were reports that the USA was providing covert military aid to anti-Taliban groups within Afghanistan. The Taliban continued forcibly to conscript men to bolster their manpower, which in early October numbered an estimated 40,000 fighters. It was also reported that al-Qa'ida had provided the Taliban with several thousand troops.

The UN and other aid organizations had begun to withdraw their foreign staff from Afghanistan on 12 September 2001, in anticipation of retaliatory attacks by the USA against al-Qa'ida and the Taliban, while some reports estimated that 1.5m. Afghans had abandoned their homes in the latter half of September. Pakistan restricted entry at the border to those considered to be most in need of assistance. Nevertheless, thousands of refugees succeeded in entering Pakistan illegally. In October President Bush announced a humanitarian aid programme for Afghans, in an attempt to undermine the Taliban and to demonstrate to Muslim countries that the USA was planning war against terrorism and not Islam.

On 7 October 2001 US-led forces began the aerial bombardment of suspected al-Qa'ida camps and strategic Taliban positions in Afghanistan. In addition to military strikes, aircraft released food and medicine parcels to Afghan civilians near the southern border with Pakistan; leaflets were also dropped offering protection and a reward in return for information on the whereabouts of al-Qa'ida leaders. Mullah Mohammad Omar responded by appealing to all Muslims to help defend Afghanistan, and as a result several thousand pupils of *madrassas* (mosque schools) in Pakistan and a number of Arab countries arrived in Afghanistan during October. A pre-recorded videotape of bin Laden's response to the military strikes was broadcast by the Qatar-based satellite television company Al-Jazeera. In the recording, bin Laden declared war on the 'infidels' and warned the USA that counter-attacks would continue until it withdrew from the Middle East. Although he did not claim responsibility for the September attacks, bin Laden's comments were widely seen to be an implicit admission of his organization's involvement. Bin Laden also encouraged Muslims in countries that had offered assistance to the anti-terrorism coalition to rebel against their governments, thus reinforcing the impression that the US-led strikes were against Afghanistan and Islam, as opposed to terrorism.

The US-led military operation, named 'Operation Enduring Freedom', achieved rapid results. After 10 days President Bush announced that the Taliban regime's air defences had been destroyed. The nature of the attack changed when US and British ground forces, with Russian assistance, launched an assault on Afghanistan on 20 October 2001. Some three days later it was announced that all of the identified al-Qa'ida training camps had been destroyed by air-strikes. However, evidence of civilian casualties adversely affected support for the military action. Saudi Arabia, which had hitherto remained silent about the military strikes, voiced its discontent in mid-October. In addition, tension mounted in Pakistan, and thousands of pro-Taliban fighters attempted to cross the border into Afghanistan.

Initially, the US-led coalition avoided targeting Kabul in order to prevent the fractious United Front from seizing the capital. There were fears that while no alternative transitional government existed, the defeat of the Taliban in Kabul and other major cities would leave a power vacuum, resulting in anarchy. The USA, the United Kingdom, other UN Security Council members and countries neighbouring Afghanistan began discussions regarding the formation of a broad-based transitional government for Afghanistan. Meanwhile, the humanitarian situation worsened and in October 2001 the UN resumed the provision of food aid. At the same time, the number of Afghan refugees attempting to leave the country increased dramatically; in early November UNHCR estimated that 135,000 refugees had entered Pakistan since 11 September.

The fall of the Taliban and the restitution of a democratic system

Attacks against the Taliban in northern Afghanistan escalated from November 2001. On 9 November the United Front captured Mazar-i-Sharif and proceeded to seize almost all of northern Afghanistan at a rapid pace. The USA, the United Kingdom and Pakistan advised the United Front not to enter Kabul until a leadership council was formed; however, on 12 November the Taliban fled the capital and, facing very little resistance, the United Front took control of Kabul on the following day. Although the United Front (which was mainly composed of Tajiks, Uzbeks and Hazaras) immediately requested assistance from the US-led coalition to create a transitional government, it was impossible to do so while the majority Pashtun ethnic group remained under-represented. The USA and Pakistan had hitherto failed to attract defectors from the Pashtun Taliban leadership to join the council; in addition, US-led forces had given little support to anti-Taliban Pashtun leaders attempting to seize control in southern Afghanistan. Within a short time, the various commanders of the United Front were in disagreement over the running of provinces in northern Afghanistan. Anti-Taliban forces from all ethnic backgrounds swiftly advanced on southern Afghanistan and by the end of November had captured the Taliban stronghold of Kunduz. Unlike the factions belonging to the United Front, these groups were not united under a political alliance.

On 27 November 2001 the UN hosted a conference of 28 Afghan leaders representing the United Front, the Rome Group led by former monarch Zahir Shah, the pro-Iranian Cyprus Process and the Pakistan-backed Peshawar Process (composed of Pashtun exiles and headed by the moderate religious leader Pir Sayed Ahmad Gailani), as well as other leading figures, in Bonn, Germany. On 5 December the leaders signed the Agreement on Provisional Arrangements in Afghanistan Pending the Re-establishment of Permanent Government Institutions, also known as the Bonn Agreement, stipulating the establishment of a 30-member multi-ethnic Interim Authority that was to preside over the country for six months from 22 December. Hamid Karzai, a Pashtun tribal chief, was named Chairman of the Interim Authority, which was to comprise 11 Pashtuns, eight Tajiks, five Hazaras, three Uzbeks and three members of smaller tribal and religious groups. The United Front received the most seats; three of the leading members, Gen. Fahim, Younis Qanooni and Dr Abdullah Abdullah, were allocated the defence, interior and foreign affairs portfolios, respectively. Two female doctors were also granted posts in the executive council. Several leaders who were excluded from the government were dissatisfied with the outcome, including former President Rabbani.

The Taliban regime's sole official contact with the outside world ended in late November 2001, when Pakistan severed all diplomatic links with the Taliban and closed their last remaining embassy. On 7 December the Taliban finally surrendered Qandahar, thus marking the effective end of the Taliban regime. In the mean time, US ground forces were strengthened in an effort to locate bin Laden and his supporters. Following unconfirmed reports that bin Laden and Mullah Mohammad Omar were hiding in the Tora Bora caves with the remnants of the Islamist forces, the US-led coalition and United Front intensified the air and ground assault on the cave complex. However, after much of the region had been destroyed, there was no sign of the two leaders and their associates. On 9 December the World Food Programme began a massive aid distribution programme in Kabul. The reopening of the Friendship Bridge between Afghanistan and Uzbekistan on the same day provided humanitarian agencies with a vital route for the transport of supplies. However, poor weather conditions hampered the international relief campaign and most rural areas remained inaccessible, owing to safety concerns. Meanwhile, following the defeat of the Taliban regime, tens of thousands of refugees began to return to Afghanistan.

On 22 December 2001 the Interim Authority was inaugurated and Karzai was sworn in as Chairman. The new administration reinstated the Constitution of 1964, which combined *Shari'a* with Western concepts of justice. One of Karzai's first decisions was to appoint Gen. Dostam as Vice-Chairman and Deputy Minister of Defence. At the end of December the UN Security Council authorized, as envisaged in the Bonn Agreement, the deployment of an International Security Assistance Force (ISAF) to help maintain security in Kabul over the following six months.

Some 19 countries were authorized to form a 5,000-strong security force, headed by the United Kingdom.

In January 2002 the international community agreed to donate US $4,500m. over two-and-a-half years towards the reconstruction of Afghanistan. In the same month a 21-member Special Independent Commission for the Convening of the Emergency Loya Jirga (commonly known as the Loya Jirga Commission) was established to devise the selection process and conduct of the Emergency Loya Jirga. Deployment of ISAF began in mid-January and remained confined to Kabul, despite Karzai's requests for the number of ISAF troops to be increased and the international force's mandate to be expanded to include security operations for the entire country. In May a UN Security Council resolution approved the extension of ISAF for six months beyond June; the Force's mandate was subsequently extended on numerous occasions, most recently in October 2011, for a further 12 months. ISAF participated in joint patrols with Afghan police and assisted in creating and training a new Afghan National Army (ANA). Meanwhile, however, regional military commanders continued to reorganize their own armies, preventing scarce resources from being sent to the ANA and making the onerous task of creating a multi-ethnic national army even more difficult and reports emerged of fighting among ethnic groups. In February the Minister of Civil Aviation and Tourism, Abdul Rahman, was assassinated by a rival faction within the Interim Authority. The murder of Rahman, a staunch supporter of Zahir Shah, was evidently an attempt to deter the former monarch from returning to Afghanistan. Despite security concerns, Zahir Shah returned to Afghanistan as a 'private citizen' in April.

Internecine fighting escalated throughout Afghanistan as tribal commanders attempted to consolidate territorial and political influence in preparation for the Loya Jirga. Meanwhile, the US-led coalition continued its search for the leaders of al-Qa'ida and the Taliban. In February 2002 the former Taliban Minister of Foreign Affairs, Mawlawi Wakil Ahmad Motawakkil, surrendered himself to US forces in Qandahar. The search was often thwarted by the activities of regional Afghan (non-Taliban) military commanders. In January, for example, the Interim Authority confirmed that seven senior Taliban members, who had surrendered to a local Afghan commander, had been released without the approval of the Interim Authority or the US-led coalition forces. US forces depended heavily on information provided by military commanders regarding the whereabouts of militant Islamists. This tactic was often to the USA's detriment, as complex tribal allegiances and enmities regularly dictated the type of information given by tribal commanders. Indeed, it was widely believed that bin Laden had been allowed to escape from Tora Bora in December 2001 (see above) by Afghans who claimed to be US allies. The USA's policy of hiring and arming local soldiers in the hope of capturing Islamist militants at times compounded the unstable political situation.

The election of 1,051 delegates to attend the Emergency Loya Jirga by district representatives took place in May–June 2002 under the auspices of the UN and Loya Jirga Commission. International aid agencies, universities and other organizations selected by the Commission appointed an additional 600 members to ensure that the assembly was balanced in terms of gender, geography, ethnicity and political beliefs. The Emergency Loya Jirga convened on 11 June. Karzai was elected President, with around 80% of the votes cast. Former monarch Zahir Shah and former President Rabbani had both renounced their respective candidatures, reportedly under pressure from the USA. On 19 June the Loya Jirga approved the Transitional Authority cabinet, retaining most of the incumbent members of the Interim Authority. However, it failed to establish a Meli Shura (National Assembly). Instead, it was decided that a National Assembly Commission would be convened at a future date to discuss this matter. Karzai announced the creation of a number of other commissions to address the issues of defence, human rights, internal security reform and a new constitution.

In July 2002 the Vice-President and Minister of Reconstruction, Haji Abdul Qadir, was assassinated, raising new concerns over the Transitional Authority's stability. Many observers held the remnants of the Taliban or al-Qa'ida responsible for the attack. Later in July Karzai announced the establishment of a UN-supported security commission, which would begin the disarming of rebel troops and precipitate the creation of a national army. Despite commanding little control outside Kabul, Karzai warned military commanders that their powers would be removed unless they denounced factional fighting and joined the Government. In September Karzai escaped an assassination attempt in Qandahar; hours later a bomb explosion in Kabul killed 30 people and injured at least 160 others. Hekmatyar was reported to have joined forces with remaining Taliban and al-Qa'ida members in southern and eastern Afghanistan and to have perpetrated the attacks in an attempt to depose the Transitional Authority. Hekmatyar had allegedly also held negotiations with other discontented regional leaders in an effort to form a wider alliance against the Afghan Government and US military presence in Afghanistan. In November the President dismissed more than 20 senior regional officials—including Gen. Abdul Hamid, the military commander of Mazar-i-Sharif—in an attempt to consolidate the Transitional Authority's jurisdiction outside Kabul.

Concerns that Afghanistan was incapable of sustaining its population were elevated by reports indicating that less than one-third of the country's land was under cultivation in 2002, largely owing to a fourth successive year of drought and exacerbated by insufficient humanitarian assistance from the international donor community. The rapid return of refugees placed an even greater strain on the humanitarian programme. According to UNHCR, more than 1.5m. refugees returned from Pakistan and around 400,000 from Iran in 2002. An estimated 2.5m. refugees remained outside Afghanistan, including 1.1m. in Iran and 1.2m. in Pakistan. Some 80% of the funds provided by the international agencies had been allocated to humanitarian aid, thus leaving only 20% available for the country's reconstruction programme.

In January 2003 Karzai established four committees to accelerate the security commission's disarmament programme and to recruit personnel for the ANA. In October a three-year programme of disarmament, demobilization and reintegration, drawn up by the Transitional Authority and the USA, was launched. Shortly before, a law proscribing the participation of military commanders and armed factions in political life was approved by the authorities. Meanwhile, in March 2003 a number of new political parties were established and united under a single 'umbrella' movement: the National Front for Democracy in Afghanistan. In August supporters of former King Zahir Shah launched Jonbesh-i Wahadat-i Melli (the Afghan National Unity Movement). Later that month the activities of a new political organization, Hizb-i Muttahid-i Melli (the United National Party), established by supporters of the former communist PDPA, were proscribed by the Supreme Court after being deemed 'anti-Islamic'. A bill legalizing the formation of political parties was approved by the Government in September. In August, meanwhile, the North Atlantic Treaty Organization (NATO) assumed formal control of ISAF.

Meanwhile, in April 2003 the Afghan Constitutional Drafting Commission, which had been meeting since November 2002, completed its draft of a new constitution. A 35-member Constitutional Commission was established to review the draft and submit the proposed charter to a constitutional loya jirga for discussion and ratification. The charter, envisaging a strong presidential system of government and a bicameral legislature, was finally made public in November 2003. The draft provoked a wide range of reactions, including concerns about inadequate protection of women's rights and religious freedoms.

Following several weeks of intense negotiations, which were marred by ethnic divisions and arguments, Afghanistan's new Constitution was approved in January 2004, by consensus rather than an actual vote. In certain respects, the amended charter differed little from the earlier draft: it still provided for the introduction of a strongly presidential political system, despite a campaign by former *mujahidin* parties for the installation of a parliamentary state. However, the revised Constitution added a second vice-presidential post and gave the National Assembly powers of veto over major presidential appointments and policies. Pashto and Dari were identified as the national languages, with provision made for a third national language in areas where the language of the ethnic group forming the majority population differed. The charter also contained new human rights provisions and articulated the equal rights of men and women before the law. One of the most significant achievements was the ensuring of greater political representation for women: it was agreed that approximately 25% of seats in the Wolasi Jirga would be reserved for women; the President would appoint additional women to the Meshrano Jirga (House of Elders). However, following the ratification of the Constitution, the human rights organization Human Rights Watch expressed concern that military commanders, factional leaders and ministers had been involved in political intimidation and electoral fraud before and during the holding of the Constitutional Loya Jirga. Furthermore, the failure to address adequately the role of *Shari'a*, and its relation to human rights safeguards, generated concerns that conservative elements in the judiciary would be able to implement interpretations of Islam that might violate human rights values. In July it was announced that the presidential election would be held on 9 October 2004. However, legislative elections were to be deferred until 2005, owing to the ongoing unrest in the country.

Meanwhile, in May 2003 the US Secretary of Defense, Donald Rumsfeld, announced that major combat operations had ended in Afghanistan and that US forces had begun to concentrate on the stabilization and reconstruction of the country. Nevertheless, the security situation remained fragile. In June US-led forces launched a major assault on suspected Taliban and al-Qa'ida fighters along Afghanistan's border with Pakistan, in response to an increase in attacks on members of the Afghan Transitional Authority and ISAF. Attacks against foreign aid workers and contractors also increased, particularly in the weeks preceding the Constitutional Loya Jirga, which convened in December, comprising 502 delegates representing all of the provinces of Afghanistan, as well as the country's ethnic groups, minorities and refugees. In the same month US forces launched a new operation in southern and eastern Afghanistan against Taliban and al-Qa'ida members. However, the offensive was condemned following the deaths of 15 Afghan children and two adults in two separate miscalculated aerial attacks. In January 2004 ISAF assumed command of a Provincial Reconstruction Team (PRT) in Kunduz, as the pilot project for further expansion of the international security force. By the end of May 2005 ISAF controlled a total of nine PRTs, five in the north and four in the west of Afghanistan, allowing the US-led coalition to concentrate more on the volatile southern and eastern parts of the country.

Throughout 2004 violence and instability continued to affect significant areas of the country. In March the Minister of Civil Aviation and Tourism, Mirwais Sadiq, was killed in a reported grenade attack in Herat. Violent clashes ensued between rival forces in the province, and President Karzai subsequently deployed ANA troops to Herat in an attempt to restore order. In June the murder of 11 Chinese construction workers during an attack on a camp in the northern province of Kunduz, generally perceived to be one of the safer areas of the country, raised concerns regarding security for the forthcoming national elections. In the same month the killing of five Médecins Sans Frontières (MSF) workers prompted the international aid organization to withdraw completely from Afghanistan. MSF criticized the US-led coalition for endangering aid workers by failing to distinguish properly between humanitarian and military operations. In an attempt to increase security in the country, and to ensure its expansion outside Kabul, NATO pledged to increase the size of ISAF from 6,500 to 10,000. The Government expressed its concern that the additional forces would be deployed only in the north of the country, stressing that they were most urgently needed in the southern and eastern provinces.

In September 2004, in an apparent attempt to assert his jurisdiction outside Kabul in advance of the impending presidential election, President Karzai dismissed Ismail Khan, the powerful Governor of Herat province, and offered him the cabinet post of Minister of Mines and Industries. Khan's dismissal provoked rioting in the province as his supporters confronted US troops, reportedly resulting in the deaths of seven people. Khan subsequently rejected the ministerial portfolio, and Mohammed Khairkhwa was appointed to succeed him as Governor of Herat. Shortly afterwards President Karzai survived an assassination attempt when a rocket narrowly missed the US military helicopter in which he was travelling on an official visit to the south-east of the country. The Taliban claimed responsibility for the attack.

Democratic elections; rising instability and violence, 2004–08

On 9 October 2004 Afghanistan held its first direct presidential election. Despite some sporadic violence on the day of the election, no widespread disturbances were reported. Shortly after polling had begun, all 15 opposition candidates launched a boycott of the vote and demanded that it be abandoned, owing to alleged widespread electoral fraud. However, following an inquiry, international observers concluded in November that alleged irregularities during the poll were insufficient to have altered the final result. Interim President Hamid Karzai was subsequently declared the winner, receiving 55.4% of the votes. Former Minister of Education Younis Qanooni came second, with 16.3% of the votes, followed by Mohammad Mohaqqeq, with 11.7%, and Gen. Dostam, with 10.0%. A reported 83.7% of the electorate participated in the poll. However, concerns were raised by the regional nature of Karzai's victory, which seemed largely to have been secured by voters in the Pashtun-majority provinces, indicating that he had not succeeded in appealing to all ethnic groups.

In December 2004, following his inauguration, President Karzai announced the composition of his Cabinet. While Minister of Foreign Affairs Dr Abdullah Abdullah and Minister of Interior Affairs Ali Ahmad Jalali retained their portfolios, Marshal Fahim was replaced as Minister of Defence by Gen. Abdul Rahim Wardak, while Ismail Khan was transferred to the energy and water portfolio. However, several powerful regional commanders were not included in the new Cabinet, ostensibly owing to the fact that they did not satisfy a requirement that all cabinet ministers be educated to university level. Karzai was criticized for his failure to allocate more portfolios in the Pashtun-dominated Cabinet to other ethnic groups.

On 18 September 2005 an estimated 5,800 candidates, including several former Taliban officials, contested elections to the 249-member Wolasi Jirga and 34 provincial legislatures. A total of 68 seats in the Wolasi Jirga were reserved for women. The polls constituted Afghanistan's first democratic legislative elections since 1969. The nation-wide turn-out was an estimated 53% of the electorate, with the figure decreasing to only 36% in Kabul, a significant decline compared with the level of participation at the 2004 presidential election. The widespread disruption that al-Qa'ida and the Taliban had threatened to orchestrate on polling day did not materialize. A delegation from the European Union (EU) initially described the elections as having been 'free, fair and transparent', but concerns were later expressed as to possible instances of fraud and intimidation of voters. The results, which were announced in November, showed that many of those who had been elected were powerful factional figures, not aligned with any particular party, leading to fears that the country's legislature would be less a unified mechanism through which the central Government could assert its authority, and more a conduit for the re-emergence of provincial 'warlordism'. The newly elected National Assembly convened for the first time in December. Younis Qanooni, who was widely perceived to be the most prominent opposition figure in the legislature, was subsequently elected Speaker of the Wolasi Jirga, and Sibghatullah Mojaddedi Speaker of the Meshrano Jirga.

In the mean time, in September 2005 Minister of Interior Affairs Ali Ahmad Jalali announced his resignation from the Cabinet, citing personal reasons. However, it was rumoured that his departure was in part a result of disagreements concerning President Karzai's appointment of factional leaders to provincial posts. Zarar Ahmad Moqbel was subsequently appointed to replace Jalali, on an acting basis. In March 2006 Karzai announced an extensive reorganization of the Cabinet, including the replacement of Dr Abdullah Abdullah as Minister of Foreign Affairs by Dr Rangin Dadfar Spanta, and the allocation of the interior affairs portfolio to Moqbel on a permanent basis.

Provincial instability and violence, often co-ordinated by a resurgent Taliban, continued throughout 2005. More than 1,400 people were believed to have died over the course of the year during fighting with Taliban insurgents, while a number of US and British soldiers were also killed. Violence escalated towards the end of the year, with a number of suicide bombings, hitherto a rarity in Afghanistan, taking place. The attacks were believed to have been instigated by al-Qa'ida and the Taliban and carried out by foreign militants. The security situation deteriorated further in 2006, with frequent suicide bombings and clashes between Taliban forces and coalition troops leading to a rising death toll of combatants and civilians. Much of the conflict was centred on the southern and eastern provinces of the country, including Helmand and Qandahar, where regular attacks and raids were carried out by both sides. In September Abdul Hakim Taniwal, the Governor of Paktia province, was killed in a suicide bombing, and later that month the Director for Women's Affairs of Qandahar province, Safia Ama Jan, was assassinated. Meanwhile, in July NATO announced the expansion of the mandate of its 18,000 troops into the southern provinces, assuming control from US-led coalition forces therein, and in October NATO forces, which had now increased to number approximately 30,000, also assumed military command of the eastern provinces; ISAF thus became responsible for international military operations throughout Afghanistan. At the end of 2006 a number of reports were published estimating that up to 3,700 fatalities (around one-quarter of which were civilians) had occurred in Afghanistan that year as a result of the ongoing conflict, a significant and alarming increase compared with the previous year.

In March 2007 a senior Taliban commander confirmed that the insurgents were gathering strength for an imminent offensive. However, the Taliban suffered set-backs in the following months, with the deaths of several senior figures, including Mullah Dadullah, who was believed to have been the Taliban's most senior military commander and at the forefront of the planned offensive. None the less, attacks on government officials continued: Abdol Sabur Farid, a member of the Meshrano Jirga and former Prime Minister, was killed in May, and President Karzai survived another attempt on his life in June. Suicide bombings were an increasingly commonplace feature of insurgency activity from 2007. Furthermore, the alarming rate of civilian deaths was a cause for serious concern among Afghans and the international community, and garnered widespread media coverage. Both sides in the conflict were variously held responsible for the rising toll of casualties. According to the UN, an estimated 1,523 civilians died in 2007 as a result of military operations conducted by both coalition and insurgency forces; this was estimated to have increased by almost 40%, to 2,118, in 2008. Among the worst incidents was the reported bombing by US forces of a wedding party in Nangarhar province in July, which, according to the Afghan Government, killed 47 civilians, the majority of them women and children.

During 2007–08 there were also several instances of hostage-taking by the Taliban, most notably the kidnapping in July of 23 Christian missionaries from the Republic of Korea (South Korea)—who claimed to be involved in development projects rather than in work of a religious nature. Two of the missionaries were subsequently killed by their kidnappers. Following negotiations between the South Korean Government and the Taliban, the remaining 21 hostages were released by the end of August, amid unconfirmed reports of a ransom payment. Meanwhile, in May the Meshrano Jirga had adopted legislation aimed at opening lines of communication with the Taliban, and in September President Karzai expressed his willingness to enter into negotiations with the insurgents. Initially, the Taliban appeared ready to accept this offer; however, in late September the Taliban stipulated the withdrawal of foreign troops from Afghanistan as a precondition for the holding of bilateral talks, thereby stalling the nascent process indefinitely.

In 2007 Afghan government troops were reported to have carried out independent operations for the first time, and by May 2008 the strength of the ANA had reached more than 76,000 men. However, the Afghan Ministry of Defence had earlier stated that ideally the ANA should be expanded to 200,000 men in order to handle both external threats and the deteriorating security situation within Afghanistan itself. (The number of Afghan troops was reported to have increased to 180,000 by late 2011, with a further increase, to 195,000, expected by October 2012; however, observers noted that the ANA was still far from being able to function as an independent, effective fighting force.)

Former King Zahir Shah died in Kabul in July 2007, prompting three days of official mourning. In the mean time, in March a new political grouping entitled Jabhe-ye-Motahed-e-Milli (United National Front—UNF) was established, comprising senior government officials, members of parliament, and former members of the United Front (or Northern Alliance) and of communist parties. With former President Burhanuddin Rabbani as its Chairman and prominent figures such as Gen. Dostam, Marshal Fahim, Younis Qanooni and Vice-President Ahmad Zia Masoud within its ranks, the UNF was expected to have a significant impact on Afghan politics. Many of the Front's political objectives were reportedly in agreement with those of Karzai, but a number diverged considerably. Among these latter aims was the UNF's advocacy of the abolition of the presidential system of government in favour of a parliamentary system.

In February 2008 the assertion made by a senior US intelligence official that the Taliban controlled as much as 10% of Afghanistan while the Government was in charge of only 30% (with the remainder under the rule of tribal leaders) was greeted with disbelief in some quarters. Insurgents carried out a number of high-profile attacks throughout the year. The Deputy Governor of Helmand province, Haji Pir Mohammad, and the Governor of the eastern province of Loghar, Abdullah Wardak, were killed in separate bomb attacks, in January and September, respectively. In April President Karzai was the target of another failed assassination attempt, which took place at an official parade in Kabul, attended by foreign diplomats and senior government and military figures; three people, including a member of the National Assembly, were killed. Taliban forces executed a large-scale prison break in Qandahar in June, resulting in the escape of hundreds of Taliban detainees. Furthermore, in what was described as the worst attack to be carried out in Kabul since the defeat of the Taliban in 2001, a suicide bombing at the Indian embassy resulted in more than 40 fatalities in the capital in July 2008. In November President Karzai reportedly offered protection to Mullah Mohammad Omar in exchange for the commencement of peace negotiations; however, the Taliban dismissed the proposal, insisting instead on the withdrawal of foreign troops.

In October 2008, reportedly under pressure from the USA and its coalition partners to curb alleged endemic government corruption, President Karzai carried out a number of notable cabinet changes, including the replacement of Zarar Ahmad Moqbel as Minister of Interior Affairs by the incumbent Minister of Education, Dr Muhammad Hanif Atmar (Moqbel was transferred to the refugees and repatriation portfolio). In November the Minister of Transport and Aviation, Hamidullah Qaderi, was dismissed by Karzai on the grounds of 'negligence and ... suspicious activities', and in the following month the Minister of Commerce and Industry, Dr Mohammad Amin Farhang, was impeached by the Wolasi Jirga for corrupt activities regarding gas distribution and subsequently lost a parliamentary vote of no confidence.

Karzai returned to power; further escalation of unrest

In early 2009 the forthcoming presidential election and concurrent elections to the provincial councils were postponed from April until August, largely owing to a lack of stability in parts of the country, as well as the inaccessibility of some regions in winter. The presidential election, which was held on 20 August, saw incumbent President Karzai run against 41 rivals (including his main opponent, the independent candidate Dr Abdullah Abdullah); fears of attacks by Taliban insurgents were largely unmet, as voting took place throughout the country with few violent incidents, although the proceedings were marred by numerous allegations of electoral fraud. The Independent Election Commission of Afghanistan (IEC) released its final certified results for the election in October, following a two-month audit carried out by the UN-backed Electoral Complaints Commission (ECC), which had invalidated votes from hundreds of polling stations having found 'clear and convincing evidence of fraud relating to improperly recorded vote totals for candidates'. Consequently, Karzai's share of the vote fell from 54.6% (according to the initial uncertified results announced in September) to 49.7%, below the crucial 50% threshold required to avoid a run-off election. Accordingly, a second round of voting, between Karzai and Dr Abdullah, was scheduled to be held on 7 November, but the latter unexpectedly withdrew his candidacy on 1 November, claiming that the vote could be neither free nor fair. On the following day Karzai was officially declared the victor and was sworn in for his second term as President on 19 November, amid widespread concern about the validity of his victory. In his inauguration speech, Karzai pledged to work towards reconciliation with the Taliban, to hasten the transfer of responsibility for internal security to the ANA and police, and to tackle the problem of systematic government corruption.

In January 2010 the Meli Shura rejected 17 of the 23 cabinet ministers nominated by President Karzai in December 2009. Another 17 nominees were proposed by Karzai later in January 2010, but, of these, only seven were approved by the legislature. Following protracted delays, Karzai submitted another seven nominations for parliamentary approval in June; of these, five were approved—including a former Chief of Staff of the ANA, Gen. Bismillah Muhammadi, as Minister of Interior Affairs—leaving seven ministerial posts still to be filled. The posts remained vacant at early 2012.

In January 2010 the IEC announced the postponement of legislative elections from 22 May until 18 September, citing a lack of funds, logistical problems and security concerns. In February Karzai issued a presidential decree that gave him the power to appoint all five members of the ECC, which had previously included three foreign experts appointed by the UN. However, in March, in apparent response to widespread criticism of the decree, Karzai agreed to permit two UN-nominated foreign nationals to be included in the Commission. In April the resignations of the head of the IEC and his deputy were announced; the IEC had been broadly criticized for failing to control widespread electoral irregularities during the 2009 presidential election.

Largely owing to the Taliban's increasing use of indiscriminate roadside bombs and suicide attacks, the UN estimated that at least 2,412 civilians were killed in Afghanistan in 2009 as a result of the continuing conflict (a rise of 14% compared with 2008); around 70% of these deaths were caused by insurgent activity. An additional 30,000 US troops had been dispatched to Afghanistan during the first few months of 2010 (US army leaders had requested 40,000 for the planned military 'surge'), while NATO pledged that its other members would provide at least 5,000 more personnel to combat the Taliban. In February US officials reported the capture in Karachi, Pakistan, of the high-ranking Afghan Taliban military commander, Mullah Abdul Ghani Baradar, who was widely believed to be second-in-command to Mullah Mohammad Omar. In the following week the US-led coalition forces, together with ANA troops, launched 'Operation Moshtarak' in Helmand province, the largest offensive in Afghanistan since the ousting of the Taliban regime in 2001; the offensive (one of the main aims of which was to seize control of the town of Marjah, the Taliban's last remaining stronghold in Helmand) was widely publicized by the coalition forces prior to its inception in order to allow the province's civilian population sufficient time to leave the area if they so wished. As the operation progressed, there were reports that the Taliban fighters were increasingly using civilians as 'human shields'. A long-planned offensive in the Taliban stronghold of Qandahar commenced in June 2010, though had been adapted to move at a slower pace than originally envisaged, in order to secure local support. Reports that NATO troops had killed one of the Taliban's most senior commanders in Qandahar provided an early boost for the coalition forces in early June. However, a few days later, in one of the deadliest single days for the coalition forces since the start of the conflict in 2001, 10 NATO troops were killed in gun and bomb attacks across Afghanistan. As 2010 drew to a close, US and UK officials noted positive developments arising from the surge on Qandahar, but cautioned that the true extent of any progress would remain unclear for some time.

Meanwhile, an international conference on the future of Afghanistan was convened in London, United Kingdom, in January 2010 and was attended by officials from around 70 different countries and organizations, including President Karzai, the UN Secretary-General, Ban Ki-Moon, and the new US Secretary of State, Hillary Rodham Clinton. The key points covered at the summit meeting included the proposed establishment of a substantial Peace and Reintegration Fund to encourage the more moderate members of the Taliban to cease fighting in exchange for employment, land and training; provisions for the gradual handover of security duties from the coalition forces to the ANA and Afghan police commencing in late 2010 or early 2011; the more effective channelling and utilization of foreign aid through the appropriate government ministries and departments rather than through aid agencies and foreign contractors; and the proposed creation of an independent anti-corruption body with the power to investigate government officials. The Afghan President stressed that the establishment of peace in Afghanistan would not be possible without the support of neighbouring countries (principally Pakistan) and of influential Muslim states (notably Saudi Arabia). In February officials confirmed that shortly before the conference in London clandestine peace talks had been held between representatives of the Afghan Government and the Taliban (including the son of the warlord Gulbuddin Hekmatyar) in the Maldives. Further peace talks were held in Kabul in March between government officials and a delegation from Hekmatyar's Hizb-i Islami. The representatives of the militant group reportedly offered to act as a bridge between the Government and the Taliban in return for the setting of definite dates for the withdrawal of foreign troops from Afghanistan and the establishment of an interim administration.

During a brief visit to Kabul in March 2010, US President Barack Obama stressed the need for President Karzai to make further progress in tackling the corruption and cronyism that beset Afghan politics. In June Karzai staged a 'peace jirga' in Kabul, which, although boycotted by some Afghan leaders, was attended by more than 1,500 delegates, and constituted the first major public discussion within Afghanistan on the issue of how to bring an end to the conflict. Although little tangible progress was made during the three-day convention, delegates reached broad consensus on a number of issues, including proposals to release any Taliban suspects detained on 'doubtful evidence' as a goodwill gesture to precede the holding of peace negotiations with Taliban leaders.

Gen. David Petraeus replaced Gen. Stanley McChrystal as Commander of ISAF in July 2010, after negative comments pertaining to prominent figures within the Obama Administration were attributed to McChrystal in a prominent US publication. Relations with the USA were compromised following the online release by WikiLeaks, an organization publishing leaked private and classified information, of a series of leaked US diplomatic cables in late 2010; one such communiqué, released in December, revealed US concerns about the political abilities of Karzai and widespread allegations of corruption among the Afghan authorities. On the following day President Obama made an unannounced second visit to Afghanistan; however, a planned visit to Kabul to meet with Karzai was cancelled, ostensibly owing to bad weather. Meanwhile, in August the Netherlands formally ended its military mission in Afghanistan after four years' deployment, despite requests from NATO for the mission to be extended; the request had instigated a political crisis that resulted in the Dutch coalition Government being ousted from power (see the chapter on the Netherlands), and it was feared that mounting public opposition to the conflict might result in other European countries withdrawing their contingents from Afghanistan ahead of schedule. However, NATO officials insisted that the rest of the alliance remained entirely committed to the mission.

The 2010 parliamentary elections

Following the widespread allegations of fraud during the 2009 presidential poll, the 2010 legislative elections, due to be held in September, were widely regarded by international observers as a critical test of President Karzai's commitment to democratic reform. Reports in mid-September of the apparent circulation of more than 1m. fraudulent voter registration cards did little to allay concerns of widespread fraud, and prompted calls for the elections to be postponed. Shortly thereafter the IEC announced that more than 1,000 polling stations (of a total of 6,835) across Afghanistan were to remain closed, following threats by the Taliban to target anyone participating in the election process. At least 19 people, including four electoral candidates, were reported to have been killed in election-related violence prior to the polls, while more than 30 candidates were disqualified in advance of the ballot, owing to suspected links with militia groups.

In the event, the elections were held as scheduled on 18 September 2010, and concerns regarding the possibility of large-scale, co-ordinated attacks were largely unrealized, although at least 14 people were reported to have been killed in numerous incidents, including sporadic rocket and bomb attacks in Kabul and other cities, for which the Taliban claimed responsibility. More than 2,500 candidates (including 406 women) contested the 249 seats in the Wolasi Jirga, primarily as independent candidates; as in 2005, one-quarter of the legislative seats were reserved for female candidates. Turn-out was low, at an estimated 40% of the registered electorate. In October the IEC announced that 1.3m. votes—nearly one-quarter of the total ballot—had been cancelled, owing to fraud or other irregularities, while more than 200 candidates were being investigated for alleged malpractice; the UN-backed ECC was reported to be investigating more than 4,000 official complaints, including numerous claims of voter intimidation. In the following month the ECC disqualified 21 candidates, including seven existing legislators, having determined that the majority of the votes that they had received were fraudulent; of this number, 19 had won or were leading their respective electoral contests, according to provisional results. A further five winning candidates were subsequently disqualified, also on the grounds of alleged fraud. Final, certified results were released by the IEC later in November. Given that the vast majority of candidates had stood as independents, it was difficult to analyse the results in terms of political ramifications; however, Dr Abdullah claimed that more than 90 of his supporters had secured seats in the Wolasi Jirga and would put pressure on the Government 'to bring reforms, positive changes, and to implement and strengthen the rule of law'. The majority Pashtun ethnic group saw its representation decrease to 88 seats, from 112 previously. While the IEC declared the election a success, the response of the international community to a vote that had, to most observers, appeared neither free nor fair was rather more muted; however, the UN security council did welcome the final results as constituting an 'important milestone' in Afghanistan's development.

In December 2010 it was announced that the Supreme Court was to establish a special tribunal to investigate the widespread allegations of electoral fraud. While election officials insisted that the Supreme Court did not have the authority to revise official election results, the IEC did concede that the tribunal would have the power to bring criminal charges against individuals found to have engaged in corrupt practices. At the recommendation of the tribunal, on 19 January 2011 President Karzai announced a one-month postponement of the inauguration of the new Wolasi Jirga—which had been scheduled to convene on 23 January—in order to allow the tribunal additional time in which to investigate some 300 outstanding cases of alleged corruption. However, the announcement prompted the censure of many newly elected legislators, who threatened to inaugurate the parliament without Karzai's approval, and also elicited criticism from Afghanistan's international allies, some of whom expressed fears that the postponement would exacerbate already fraught tensions and could trigger a major political crisis. Appearing to capitulate to these dual domestic and foreign pressures, Karzai revoked his earlier decision, and the new parliament was sworn in on 26 January; hundreds of unsuccessful election candidates staged protests at the presidential palace, appealing for the election results to be annulled and for fresh, legitimate elections to be held.

The fractious nature of the new parliament was exemplified by a one-month political impasse, during which the Wolasi Jirga failed on several occasions to elect a new Speaker. Owing to numerous abstentions, none of the leading candidates obtained sufficient votes to be elected and, in all, at least eighteen candidates participated in several rounds of voting. In February 2011 Abdul Rauf Ibrahimi, a little-known former Uzbek militia commander from Kunduz province, was elected Speaker of the lower house. Meanwhile, despite opposition from legislators and the IEC, the Supreme Court's special tribunal completed its investigations into alleged electoral fraud, ordering that 62 winning candidates—nearly one-quarter of the total—be removed from the legislature on account of electoral fraud, effectively overruling the IEC. The ruling prompted vociferous criticism from members of the IEC and of parliament, and the latter responded with a vote of no confidence in the Attorney-General, Muhammad Aloko. With the ongoing crisis severely undermining the legitimacy of both the executive and the legislative branches of the Afghan Government, in August Karzai issued a presidential decree that appeared to reinforce the status of the IEC as the ultimate authority on electoral proceedings, ordering the IEC to finalize the results of the election 'immediately'. Later in the month, in what was hoped would bring an end to the protracted dispute, the IEC announced that nine of the 62 candidates identified for removal by the Supreme Court's special tribunal were to be replaced within the legislature by nine new candidates, all of whom had been among those disqualified for electoral fraud by the ECC in November 2010. The majority of those removed from their seats protested against the IEC's decision; however, eight of the nine newly proclaimed winning candidates were inaugurated in early September 2011. None the less, the issue continued to divide the legislature, with many parliamentarians arguing against the constitutionality of the IEC's decision.

Meanwhile, in September 2010 Kabul Bank, the country's largest bank, was placed under the direct supervision of the Central Bank following allegations of widespread fraud and mismanagement. It was reported that several hundred million dollars worth of irregular loans had been issued to shareholders. Media reports in early 2011 identified several prominent politicians and businessmen with links to Karzai's Government, including the brothers of Karzai and of Vice-President Marshal Muhammed Qasim Fahim, as alleged beneficiaries in the scandal, which by January was reported to have resulted in losses of around US $900m. The revelations triggered the near-collapse of the bank and prompted the IMF to suspend its credit programme for Afghanistan. In June 2011 it was announced that a payment of $70m. due to have been disbursed to the Afghan Government by the World Bank's Afghanistan Reconstruction Trust Fund, as a reward for achieving stipulated standards in, *inter alia*, public administration reform, was to be withheld. Donor nations were reported to have frozen payments to the trust fund since mid-2011. In an attempt to persuade the IMF to resume its funding, in April the Government had proposed splitting the stricken bank into two units, one of which was to set up as a receivership to try to collect the irregular loans. This, together with a series of other government measures intended to shore up the financial sector, including the implementation of a full deposit guarantee scheme, resulted in the approval by the IMF, in November, of a new, three-year, US $134m. credit programme for Afghanistan, which included the immediate disbursement of an initial loan of $18.9m. However, the Fund cautioned that the Afghan Government would need to continue its efforts to recover assets and prosecute those responsible for the Kabul Bank scandal. A commission of inquiry established by President Karzai to investigate the scandal had published its findings in May, absolving the brothers of the President and the Vice-President of any wrongdoing; however, the commission did report that members of the Cabinet and of parliament were among the 207 borrowers found to have taken out undocumented loans, and two former executives of the bank were arrested in June on charges of embezzlement.

Recent developments: the ongoing transition of security responsibilities to the Afghan authorities

In July 2010, during an international conference in Kabul on the security situation within Afghanistan, President Karzai announced ambitious plans for Afghan forces to have assumed control of all military and law enforcement operations throughout Afghanistan by 2014. The 60 or so foreign delegates in attendance, who included Ban Ki-Moon and US Secretary of State Clinton, adopted a statement endorsing the plan and urging the Afghan Government to accelerate reforms aimed at improving governance. Clinton stated that the target date of late 2014 underscored the need to transfer greater responsibility to the Afghan authorities on an ongoing basis. Karzai's plan gained the formal support of NATO in November 2010 when the Afghan President and NATO leaders signed a long-term security partnership agreement pledging to transfer leadership of all security operations to Afghanistan by the end of 2014; however, NATO's Secretary-General stressed that the coalition would remain committed in Afghanistan in a training and supportive capacity indefinitely.

In preparation for the transition of security responsibilities to the Afghan authorities, which was to commence in July 2011, officials of the US-led coalition sought to emphasize military successes in southern provinces and around Kabul. During a visit to the Afghan capital in January US Vice-President Joseph Biden claimed that Taliban momentum had been 'largely arrested' in key areas, including Helmand and Qandahar, although he also acknowledged that such gains were 'fragile and reversible'. The killing of senior al-Qa'ida leader Abu Hafs al-Najdi (alias Abdul Ghani) in a NATO air-strike in Kunar province in April 2011 was hailed as a significant success by ISAF, which claimed to have killed more than 25 al-Qa'ida operatives in April alone. Abdul Ghani was believed to have controlled a network of insurgents throughout Kunar and to have orchestrated attacks on tribal leaders and foreigners, including US officials. The killing in May of al-Qa'ida founder Osama bin Laden in the Pakistani town of Abbottabad, following his eventual discovery earlier in the year by US intelligence forces (see Pakistan), provided further cause for celebration within the alliance.

However, a steady deterioration in security conditions during 2010–11 appeared to run counter to any optimism, however cautious, regarding the prospects for peace and stability in Afghanistan. The year 2010 proved to be the most costly yet for the NATO alliance, with 711 NATO troops reported to have been killed (of which 499 were US soldiers). Although the number of NATO fatalities decreased in 2011, to 566 (of which 418 were US soldiers), this still represented the second highest number of deaths incurred by NATO personnel in a single year since the beginning of the campaign in 2001. Violent attacks by Taliban insurgents against security targets intensified during 2011. An attack on the provincial headquarters of the Afghan police in Qandahar killed 19 people, including 15 police officers, in February; in the same month suicide bombers launched an attack on a branch of Kabul Bank in Jalalabad, killing an estimated 38 people and injuring more than 70 others—many of those killed were members of the Afghan security forces who were collecting their wages. A series of devastating suicide bomb attacks in February and March in Kunduz province targeted local government offices, police stations and army recruitment centres, killing dozens of people, including a district governor and the provincial police chief. The Qandahar police chief was also killed, in April, in a suicide bomb attack on the provincial police headquarters. On the following day five ANA and five ISAF troops were killed when a suicide bomber targeted an army base near Jalalabad. Later in the month some 470 inmates escaped from Qandahar prison through a tunnel that appeared to have been dug from outside the gaol; many of the escaped prisoners were reported to be Taliban insurgents. In June Taliban militants conducted an intensive raid on the heavily guarded Intercontinental Hotel in Kabul, which was regularly frequented by foreign and local officials and business people; 22 people, including nine insurgents, were killed during the incident.

Nevertheless, the first phase of the security transition commenced, as scheduled, in July 2011, and involved the handing over of seven NATO-held areas to Afghan control—Bamiyan and Panjshir provinces, the majority of Kabul province (excluding the restive Surobi district) and four provincial capitals, Herat, Lashkar Gah, Mazar-i-Sharif and Mehter Lam. Shortly prior to the commencement of the transition, President Obama announced that 10,000 US forces were to leave Afghanistan by the end of the year, with a further 23,000 scheduled to depart by the end of 2012 and all remaining combat troops to withdraw in 2014. The pace of the announced withdrawal was quicker than had been anticipated by most observers, and Gen. Petraeus was reported not to have endorsed Obama's decision, having recommended a more limited initial troop withdrawal. US Secretary of Defense Leon Panetta, who had replaced Robert Gates at the beginning of July 2011, stressed that the US-led coalition would remain firmly committed to assisting the Afghan authorities in developing a skilled military, police force and local militias that would be sufficiently equipped to take over full responsibility for national security from 2014. The first stage in a phased withdrawal of French soldiers commenced in October 2011, and in January 2012 French President Nicolas Sarkozy, apparently in response to domestic political pressure, announced plans to accelerate the French withdrawal—the last of approximately 4,000 serving French troops were to leave Afghanistan by the end of 2013. Canada, meanwhile, officially concluded its involvement in the NATO combat mission at the beginning of December 2011; a deployment of 950 Canadian troops was to provide training assistance in Kabul until 2014.

However, a wave of violent incidents served to underscore concerns about the deteriorating security situation amid the ongoing transition of responsibilities to the Afghan authorities. In July 2011 Ahmad Wali Karzai, the chairman of the Qandahar provincial council and a half-brother of President Karzai, was assassinated at his home in Qandahar by the head of his own security team. The killing of the provincial leader, who had enjoyed an effective monopoly of power in Qandahar, provoked considerable shock and anger. Wali Karzai had done much to galvanize support for President Karzai in southern Afghanistan and, despite a contentious background, with widespread allegations that he had been involved in various criminal activities, Wali Karzai had also proven a key ally for the US-led coalition, serving as a stabilizing force by curbing, to a degree, simmering tribal tensions in the south. The Taliban immediately claimed responsibility for the assassination, but, with the controversial leader having had many tribal and business rivals, the veracity of the claims remained uncertain. Two other prominent allies of President Karzai—Jan Mohammad Khan, a senior adviser to the President and former Governor of Uruzgan province, and Ghulam Haidar Hameedi, the mayor of Qandahar—were killed in two separate attacks later in July. The Taliban claimed responsibility for both attacks. In Kabul, at least 12 security personnel were killed in August when insurgents attacked the compound of the British Council, an agency partly funded by the British Government that organizes primarily cultural programmes. In September a small but well-organized group of insurgents launched a series of rocket-propelled attacks on Western targets in Kabul, including the US embassy and the NATO headquarters. Five Afghan police officers and 11 civilians were killed during the attacks and a subsequent gun battle between the insurgents and the security authorities. All of the assailants were also killed.

The assassination of former Afghan President Burhanuddin Rabbani in September 2011 represented a severe set-back to hopes of a negotiated settlement of the Afghan insurgency. Rabbani had been appointed as the head of the Afghan High Peace Council, an agency inaugurated by President Karzai in October 2010, which was charged with brokering an end to the war and opening up a dialogue with the Taliban and other insurgents. Rabbani was killed in a suicide bomb attack during a meeting with members of the Taliban at his home in Kabul. Three days of official mourning were proclaimed for Rabbani, who was given a state funeral, and the Government broke off discussions with the Taliban as a result of the assassination. (In April 2012 Rabbani's son, Salahuddin Rabbani, Afghanistan's ambassador to Turkey, was appointed to succeed his father as head of the High Peace Council.) A UN report released in late September 2011 stated that there had been a 39% increase in the number of violent incidents (primarily gunfights and attacks using improvised bombs) in Afghanistan during the first eight months of the year compared with the corresponding period of 2010. More than 7,000 violent incidents were reported during June–August 2011 alone. An alleged assassination plot against President Karzai was reported to have been foiled in October; Afghan intelligence officials claimed that the apparent plot had possible links to the Haqqani network, an influential, Taliban-affiliated insurgent group led by former *mujahidin* fighter Jalaluddin Haqqani and based in North Waziristan, Pakistan. Later in October 'Operation Knife Edge' was launched by NATO and Afghan forces in south-eastern Afghanistan; the military operation was intended to target members of the Haqqani network, which, the alliance alleged, was sheltering al-Qa'ida operatives in the Pakistani border region. In December a suicide bomb attack on a Shi'a mosque in Kabul killed at least 56 people, while, in an apparently co-ordinated attack, a second suicide bomber detonated explosives at a Shi'a mosque in Mazar-i-Sharif, claiming the lives of a further four people. Observers noted that the attacks, which coincided with the Shi'a festival of Ashura—the most important day in the Shi'a calendar—were of a sectarian nature unprecedented in recent Afghan history, prompting concerns that insurgents might be adopting a new strategy intended to foment further divisions within the country.

Despite the series of high-profile attacks and assassinations, the second phase of the transition of security responsibilities from NATO to the Afghan authorities was initiated in November 2011, following which local forces were afforded complete or partial control of approximately half of the country. Among the previously NATO-held areas handed over were: Balkh, Day Kundi, Nimroz, Samangan and Takhar provinces, which were transferred to Afghan control in their entirety; seven provincial capitals, including Chaghcharan (Ghor province) Ghazni (Ghazni province), Jalalabad (Nangarhar province) and Maidan Shah (Wardak province); and more than 40 districts in provinces across the country, including the Marjah, Nadi Ali and Nawa districts of Helmand province, and Surobi, the final district in Kabul province to be handed over to the Afghan authorities.

Meanwhile, according to the UN, the number of civilian casualties in Afghanistan increased in 2010, to an estimated 2,777 (a rise of 15% compared with 2009); some 75% of these deaths were attributed to insurgent activity—following an escalation in targeted killings of civilians, including government officials and employees of non-governmental organizations—while 16% were caused by pro-Government forces. A UN report published in February 2012 estimated that civilian casualties rose for a fifth successive year in 2011, to 3,021 (an increase of about 8% compared with revised figures of 2,790 for 2010); of these, some 77% were attributed to insurgent activity, with almost 14% caused by pro-Government forces. According to the report, almost one-third of all civilian casualties were caused by the frequent use by insurgents of improvised explosive devices to target coalition patrols, which could just as easily be detonated by non-combatants. The death toll also included 431 civilians killed in suicide attacks, an increase of 80% compared with the previous year. Despite a slight decrease in the number of casualties attributed to pro-Government forces in 2011, the high level of civilian casualties caused by NATO forces continued severely to undermine popular support for the alliance's mission in Afghanistan. In particular, the number of civilian casualties in 2011 resulting from NATO aerial attacks (187) and nocturnal search operations (63) was a source of growing tension between coalition officials and President Karzai. Allegations that a NATO operation in Kunar province had resulted in the deaths of up to 65 civilians during a four-day period in February 2011 were strenuously denied by NATO officials, who insisted that the victims had been insurgents. In April demonstrations against the foreign military presence were staged in towns throughout the country, several of which escalated into violent unrest. Three UN staff members from European countries and four Nepalese security guards were killed when demonstrators attacked a UN compound during protests in Mazar-i-Sharif; at least four Afghans were also reported to have been killed during the unrest. The killings, in what was normally a peaceful city, represented the deadliest attack on UN personnel since the beginning of the conflict in Afghanistan. Further fatalities were reported following subsequent protests in Qandahar and Jalalabad.

In June 2011 President Obama was forced to apologize to the Karzai administration following a series of incidents in which Afghan civilians had been killed during NATO operations, including an errant air raid that had claimed the lives of nine Afghan children in Kunar in March, and an air-strike targeting insurgents who had taken cover in a residential compound in Helmand province, which killed at least nine other civilians in May. A further 13 civilian fatalities, including eight women and three children, were reported in July, following an errant NATO air-strike in Khost. Of further consternation to critics of the US-led coalition was the publication, in June, of a US military report revealing that almost 90% of those captured by US forces on suspicion of being members of the Taliban had, in fact, been civilians. In November Gen. John Allen, who had replaced Gen. Petraeus as Commander of ISAF in July following Petraeus' appointment in June as Director of the USA's Central Intelligence Agency (CIA), wrote to President Karzai expressing his regret following a further series of NATO air-strikes in which civilians had been killed during the latter half of 2011, and informed the Afghan President that he had issued a directive ordering all ISAF units to conduct retraining on methods of avoiding civilian casualties.

In November 2011, amid heightened security arrangements, a meeting of the Loya Jirga, which was attended by more than 2,300 tribal elders, local and regional leaders, and government officials, was held in Kabul. President Karzai used the occasion to outline his vision for a long-term strategic partnership with the USA, which, he argued, remained in the best interests of Afghanistan; however, he stressed that any pact must respect Afghan sovereignty. Thus, while the Afghan Government was prepared to allow the USA to base military facilities within Afghanistan beyond 2014, Karzai demanded that foreign forces cease house searches and night raids, and that all foreign-run detention facilities within the country be shut down. Karzai also tendered implicit criticism of Pakistan and Iran for not doing more to curb insurgents. On the closing day of the four-day meeting, the Loya Jirga elected to support Karzai's outline for negotiating a strategic agreement with the USA. However, the second primary issue of debate—namely, how to reignite peace negotiations with the Taliban—was reported to have been largely inconclusive.

An international conference held in Bonn in December 2011 on the future of Afghanistan was intended as a forum for discussions on the country's development following the planned withdrawal in 2014 of all foreign troops. However, the conference, which was attended by Afghan and international leaders, failed to produce any tangible results, beyond general expressions of continuing support for Afghanistan beyond 2014. President Karzai stated that Afghanistan would require some US $10,000m. annually for the next 10 years to bolster its security and reconstruction efforts. Notably absent from the proceedings were any representatives from Pakistan, the Government of which had in November announced a boycott of the conference following the killing of 24 Pakistani soldiers during an ISAF air-strike on the Afghan–Pakistani border earlier in the month. (Despite the issuance of a formal apology for the incident, which NATO insisted had been inadvertent, the Pakistani Government severed communications and blocked ISAF's two supply routes running through Pakistan.) With many insurgents, including al-Qa'ida leaders, widely believed to be located in safe havens within Pakistan's borders, the failure of a Pakistani delegation to attend the conference was widely seen as a considerable set-back for hopes of furthering discussions on reaching a negotiated settlement to the conflict in Afghanistan.

In January 2012 the Taliban announced that it had reached a provisional agreement with the Qatari Government to open a political office in the Middle Eastern country, in a development that was interpreted by some observers as a precursor to the staging of peace talks between the Taliban and the US Administration. At the same time the Taliban demanded the release of prisoners from the US detention centre in Guantánamo Bay, Cuba. Secretary of State Clinton stated in response that the US Administration had not yet made any decisions regarding the potential release of Taliban prisoners, adding that reconciliation could only occur if the Taliban renounced violence, ceased its support of al-Qa'ida and recognized the Afghan Constitution.

In early February 2012 Secretary of Defense Panetta stated that the US authorities aimed to conclude active combat operations in Afghanistan by the end of 2013, up to one year sooner than previously envisaged. US combat troops would, however, remain in Afghanistan in a supporting role during 2014. This apparent acceleration of US military disengagement in Afghanistan appeared to reflect the growing domestic unpopularity of the military campaign in the USA and other NATO countries, not least as a result of extensive coalition casualties and the apparently intractable security problems in the country. Moreover, several incidents in which members of the Afghan security forces attacked and killed NATO personnel served further to erode popular support for the campaign. In late March 2012 it was reported that at least 13 NATO soldiers had been killed in such circumstances since the beginning of the year.

Several events in early 2012 served to exacerbate tensions between ISAF and both the Afghan Government and the general populace. In January NATO officials issued an apology following the online release of video footage that appeared to show four US soldiers urinating on the corpses of Taliban fighters. On 21 February Secretary of Defense Panetta issued a further apology following reports that copies of the Koran had inadvertently been burned and improperly disposed of at Bagram airbase. The holy books had reportedly been confiscated from Taliban prisoners. The revelation provoked a massive wave of anti-US protests, violent unrest and attacks on Western military bases and diplomatic offices throughout the country. In an effort to calm tension, President Obama conveyed his 'deep apologies' in a letter to the Afghan President. However, within five days at least 30 people were reported to have been killed in the unrest. Following the killing of two NATO officials at the headquarters of the Ministry of the Interior in Kabul on 25 February, several NATO countries temporarily withdrew their civilian staff from Afghan government institutions. On 11 March up to 17 civilians, including nine children, were killed when a man, believed to be a US soldier, carried out a violent and apparently indiscriminate attack on villagers in Panjwai district, Qandahar province. The deaths prompted renewed public protests, although on a lesser scale than those following the Koran-burning incident. President Karzai issued a demand that all NATO troops should return to their main bases and cease operations in rural outposts in order to prevent further civilian casualties. Despite Afghan demands that the perpetrator be tried in an Afghan court, the chief suspect, Sergeant Robert Bales, was transported to a military base in the USA where he was charged with 17 counts of premeditated murder. In mid-March it was reported that the Taliban had suspended its involvement in nascent peace negotiations with the US authorities, although it was not clear whether this was in direct response to the massacre in Panjwai or simply a tactical measure.

Meanwhile, in early March the long-running political impasse regarding President Karzai's ministerial nominees was finally resolved when the Wolasi Jirga voted to approve nine cabinet ministers nominated by the President; these included six nominees that had been rejected by parliament in early 2010 but who, in the meantime, had served as ministers in an acting capacity. However, several other important officials, including the Chief Justice and the Attorney-General, remained in their posts beyond the expiry of their tenure or without parliamentary approval.

In general, Afghanistan has experienced a relative lull in militant attacks during the winter, as heavy snows render mountain passes along the border with Pakistan impassable; consequently, the spring thaw has often coincided with a period of renewed militant activity. In mid-April 2012 the Taliban signalled the commencement of its so-called 'spring offensive' by launching a dramatic series of co-ordinated gun and rocket attacks on foreign and government targets in Kabul and several other provincial towns. The assault in Kabul, which was even more extensive than similar attacks in September 2011, targeted the Afghan parliament, NATO's headquarters and foreign embassies. Following the attacks, which lasted for some 18 hours, it was reported that eight Afghan security personnel and 36 militants had been killed. The attacks served further to exacerbate concerns about the security situation amid the ongoing security transition.

In late April 2012, after lengthy and difficult negotiations, it was reported that the Afghan Government had agreed on the conditions for a long-term strategic partnership with the USA, which would provide for a continued US military and civil presence in Afghanistan for a further ten years after 2014.

Under the agreement, it was anticipated that the US military would continue to support the Afghan security forces in a training and advisory capacity, but would also be permitted to mount counter-terrorism and intelligence-gathering operations within the country. The agreement, which also provided for ongoing US financial support for education and governance in Afghanistan, was scheduled for formal approval at a NATO summit in the USA in May.

Production of Illicit Drugs

In January 2002 the Interim Authority issued a decree banning poppy cultivation and the processing, trafficking and abuse of opiates. In February, however, reports were emerging that the large-scale planting of poppies had already taken place during the collapse of law and order in late 2001. In April 2002 the Interim Authority introduced a radical programme to eradicate the crop. In accordance with the scheme, farmers would receive compensation for destroying their opium crops; those who refused would have their land seized by the Government and risk prosecution. However, the offer of compensation did not compare well with the lucrative sale of opium, and farmers carried out violent demonstrations throughout the country against the initiative. Despite attempts by the Government and the UN to curb the drugs trade, the annual survey conducted by the UN Office on Drugs and Crime (UNODC), published in October, reported that, owing to the planting of poppies in late 2001, Afghanistan had resumed its place as the world's largest producer of opium.

In an attempt to address Afghanistan's continuing problems with the widespread cultivation of opium, President Karzai, following his inauguration in December 2004, announced the formation of a Ministry of Counter Narcotics. According to the UN, in 2004 the total area under poppy cultivation had increased by 64%, compared with the previous year.

In 2008, however, there was a 6% decrease in opium production; further success was reported in 2009 when the area under poppy cultivation decreased to 123,000 ha, from 157,000 ha in 2008. In 2010 the area under poppy cultivation remained unchanged, at 123,000 ha, although opium production declined by about 50% year-on-year; however, the decline was attributed to a naturally occurring plant disease that had affected the crop in that year. Owing to rising global opium prices, coupled with the declining price of wheat (one of Afghanistan's main crop alternatives to opium) and the deteriorating security situation, the area under poppy cultivation increased, by 7%, to 131,000 ha in 2011, while opium production increased by some 61%, rising from 3,600 metric tons to 5,800 tons.

Following a detailed study in 2009, UNODC issued a report in April 2010 which concluded that Afghanistan was also the world's largest producer of hashish resin, an illegal derivative of the cannabis plant. The area under cultivation was estimated at 10,000–24,000 ha, spread over 17 provinces and yielding an estimated 1,500–3,500 metric tons of hashish. The report stated that some two-thirds of cannabis farmers were also involved in the cultivation of opium. Furthermore, the report noted that cultivation of both opium poppy and cannabis was concentrated in regions of instability and, through the levying of taxes on production and trafficking, served as an important source of revenue for militia groups.

Foreign Affairs

On 22 December 2002 the Governments of Afghanistan, the People's Republic of China, Iran, Pakistan, Tajikistan, Turkmenistan and Uzbekistan signed the Kabul Declaration on Good-Neighbourly Relations, in which they pledged never again to interfere in each other's affairs. On paper, the agreement signalled a new era of regional co-operation, yet, in reality, the situation was somewhat different. Afghan officials claimed that Iranian Revolutionary Guards were continuing to provide financial and military assistance to Ismail Khan; Russia was reportedly supporting Marshal Fahim and his army; and certain Saudis had allegedly resumed sending financial assistance to the remnants of the Taliban in Pakistan. In addition, the Uzbekistani President had provided Uzbek Gen. Dostam with his own bodyguards. Publicly, the Pakistani President supported Karzai and the USA's campaign against al-Qa'ida; however, at the same time, Pakistan's Inter-Services Intelligence (ISI) was reportedly giving sanctuary to senior Taliban members and other anti-Government military commanders, such as Gulbuddin Hekmatyar, leader of the Hizb-i Islami guerrilla group.

Despite repeated efforts to engender a lasting amelioration in bilateral ties, relations between Afghanistan and Pakistan encountered numerous setbacks during the early 2000s, and suffered a further deterioration from 2005 with President Karzai and his Pakistani counterpart engaging in protracted public recriminations over cross-border activities and the fight against the Taliban. Relations between the two countries appeared to improve with the holding of a joint 'peace jirga' in Kabul in August 2007; the four-day meeting, which was attended by some 650 tribal leaders from both countries, along with Karzai, Pakistani President Gen. Pervez Musharraf, and other senior government officials, was convened with the aim of addressing shared issues such as security and terrorism. However, tensions resurfaced in February 2008, when the Pakistani ambassador to Afghanistan was abducted by suspected Taliban militants in the Khyber Agency in Pakistan's Federally Administered Tribal Areas; he was released unharmed in May. In the following month relations between Afghanistan and Pakistan deteriorated further following the assertion by Karzai that Afghan troops had the right to enter Pakistani territory, which he claimed was being used as a base for cross-border attacks.

However, a significant thawing in Afghan-Pakistani relations was apparent from 2009. In February the new US Secretary of State, Hillary Rodham Clinton, hosted a meeting with the foreign ministers of Pakistan and Afghanistan in Washington, DC, and announced that these trilateral negotiations would be held on a regular basis to discuss mutually strategic issues. In August an official meeting took place between President Karzai and the Pakistani Prime Minister, Yousaf Raza Gilani, during which the two leaders agreed to co-operate in combating terrorism and militancy. Subsequent Pakistani anti-insurgency efforts led to the arrest, in early 2010, of a number of high-ranking Afghan Taliban figures (including Mullah Abdul Ghani Baradar—see Domestic Political Affairs). The growing strength and influence of the Tehrik-e-Taliban Pakistan, or the so-called Pakistani Taliban—the stated objectives of which were resistance against the Pakistani state, enforcement of their version of *Shari'a* and support to the insurgency in Afghanistan—was a disturbing development for both Governments from 2008; despite a successful army offensive against the militants in the Swat valley in mid-2009, the Pakistani Taliban remained a tangible force at early 2012. In October 2010 a long-anticipated Afghanistan-Pakistan Trade Transit Agreement (APTTA) was signed between the two countries; the APTTA would, *inter alia*, allow Afghan trade vehicles to carry Afghan exports across Pakistan to the border with India, via the Pakistani port cities of Karachi and Gwadar; pending an improvement in the security situation in Afghanistan, Pakistani trade vehicles would also be granted right of passage through Afghanistan to trading partners in Central Asia. Trade ties were further bolstered in late November by the establishment of a bilateral chamber of commerce. However, in February 2011 scheduled implementation of the APTTA was postponed owing to disagreements over the interpretation of several clauses, most notably a requirement for bank guarantees to ensure that imports to Afghanistan reach their designated destination.

In January 2011 representatives of the Afghan High Peace Council (see Domestic Political Affairs) visited the Pakistani capital, Islamabad, to discuss Pakistan's involvement in the Afghan reconciliation process. During its visit, the Afghan delegation, which was led by former President Burhanuddin Rabbani, met with representatives of Hizb-i Islami, whereupon the insurgency group presented the delegation with a 15-point peace plan: the proposals included demands for all US-led foreign troops to leave Afghanistan and for the current Afghan parliament to be replaced by an interim government, with fresh local and national elections to be held within 12 months, and the drafting of a new Constitution; in return, Hizb-i Islami would pledge its full support to efforts to restore peace. The delegation also met with the Pakistani Chief of Army Staff, Gen. Ashfaq Pervez Kayani, and the Minister of State for Foreign Affairs; the discussions were described by both sides as 'harmonious'. Following discussions between President Karzai and Prime Minister Gilani in Kabul in April, the two leaders announced an agreement to establish a joint peace and reconciliation commission as part of efforts to end the Taliban insurgency. Karzai travelled to Islamabad in June 2011 to attend the inaugural session of the commission. During his visit, Karzai also met with the Pakistani President, Asif Ali Zardari, and the two heads of state signed a 23-point agreement intended to bolster counter-terrorism co-operation and to facilitate a more general improvement in bilateral relations, including enhanced co-operation in the fields of communications, energy, infrastructure, and trade and commerce. The so-called Islamabad Declaration also included an agreement to establish a rail link between Peshawar in Pakistan and Jalalabad. Furthermore, Karzai and Zardari pledged to enforce the terms of the stalled APTTA. However, a series of cross-border attacks in July raised concerns that the apparent amelioration in bilateral relations would prove short-lived. Afghan officials claimed that Pakistani forces had fired hundreds of rockets into Afghan territory, killing dozens of border police and civilians; conversely, the Pakistani authorities contested that militants in the border regions of Afghanistan were launching frequent attacks on Pakistani border posts and villages. Following the assassination of Burhanuddin Rabbani in September (see Domestic Political Affairs), in November the Afghan and Pakistani Governments—meeting on the sidelines of a regional conference on the security situation in Afghanistan held in İstanbul, Turkey—announced an agreement jointly to investigate the killing of the former Afghan President. In October Karzai had accused elements within the Pakistani establishment of supporting the insurgency within Afghanistan, claims that were adamantly denied by the Pakistani Government. At the İstanbul conference, a security agreement was signed by representatives of more than a dozen countries in South and Central Asia and the Middle East pledging to adhere to a policy of non-interference in Afghanistan's internal affairs.

President Karzai returned to Islamabad in February 2012 for further talks concerning regional security and Pakistan's potential role in facilitating direct negotiations between the Taliban and the Karzai administration. Following the bilateral discussions, trilateral talks on trade and security, also involving President Mahmoud Ahmadinejad of Iran, took place. The summit was interpreted by many analysts as an attempt by the participants to reclaim a leading role in the search for a political solution in Afghanistan, following the initiation of exploratory negotiations, hosted by Qatar, between the Taliban and the USA (see Domestic Political Affairs). In late February, in what appeared to be a significant tactical shift, Prime Minister Gilani publicly urged the Taliban to enter direct peace negotiations with the Afghan Government. However, the Taliban has consistently viewed the Karzai administration as an illegitimate entity and refused to entertain direct talks.

A quadrilateral summit on anti-terrorism and anti-narcotics efforts was held between Afghanistan, Pakistan, Russia and Tajikistan in the Russian capital, Moscow, in August 2010. The four states agreed to pursue joint economic projects in an attempt to introduce stability to the region. In January 2011 President Karzai visited Moscow, where he met with Russian Prime Minister Dmitrii Medvedev. Medvedev pledged Russian support for Afghan energy and infrastructure projects, including the long-running plan (first proposed in 1990 but subsequently delayed owing to security concerns) to construct a Turkmenistan–Afghanistan–Pakistan–India (TAPI) natural gas pipeline; Afghan, Pakistani and Indian officials had convened in Turkmenistan to sign a framework agreement on the pipeline project in December 2010. The Afghan Government pledged to commit about 7,000 troops to guard the pipeline during its construction, which was due to commence in 2012; upon completion of the project, Afghanistan would receive an estimated 700m. cu ft of Turkmen natural gas via the pipeline annually.

Meanwhile, in August 2005 Indian Prime Minister Manmohan Singh visited Afghanistan, the first such visit by an Indian premier since 1975. During his visit the two countries signed several agreements relating to a wide range of issues and stressed the need for greater bilateral co-operation. In July 2008 a suicide bombing at the Indian embassy in Kabul resulted in more than 40 fatalities; the Indian Government intimated that the plot had originated in Pakistan. Another suicide bombing targeted the Indian embassy in the Afghan capital in October 2009, killing at least 17 people. During a visit by President Karzai to India in February 2011 Prime Minister Singh pledged to increase Indian aid and investment in Afghanistan: during a reciprocal visit to Kabul in May 2011, Singh announced the provision of US $500m. in aid to Afghanistan, taking the collective total pledged by India to some $2,000m.; priority was to be afforded to agriculture, infrastructure and social programmes. The two leaders signed a strategic partnership agreement in October, the first such partnership that Afghanistan had entered into in its history. Under the terms of the pact, Afghanistan and India agreed to deepen co-operation in the fields of trade, counter-terrorism, and political and cultural engagement, while India pledged to offer support in the form of security training and equipment as Afghanistan prepared to assume full responsibility for national security by 2014. India also agreed to work to improve Afghanistan's economic integration within the South Asian region as a whole. The deepening mistrust of Pakistan shared by both the Afghan and Indian Governments was widely believed to have accelerated the successful conclusion of negotiations on the partnership agreement. In November 2011 it was announced that the development rights for three blocks at the Hajigak iron ore concession in central Afghanistan had been awarded to the state-run Steel Authority of India; the Hajigak deposit contained around 1,800m. metric tons of iron ore, according to estimates by the Afghan Government.

In March 2010 Karzai paid an official visit to China, during which the Afghan leader and his Chinese counterpart, President Hu Jintao, signed agreements on trade and economic co-operation aimed at supporting the recovery of the war-ravaged Afghan economy. In December 2011 the two countries concluded an oil agreement potentially worth an estimated US $7,000m. to Afghanistan over the course of a 25-year period. Under the terms of the agreement, the state-owned China National Petroleum Corporation was to develop three oilfields along the Amu Darya river in northern Afghanistan; the concession was believed to contain around 87m. barrels of oil.

Seeking to counter US influence in Afghanistan, Iran has appeared increasingly anxious to exert its own influence upon its neighbour. Iran remains one of Afghanistan's most important sources of foreign aid and has been responsible for increasing levels of investment into the country, as well as providing assistance to the Afghan Government's counter-narcotic efforts and constructing outposts for Afghan border posts. However, US officials have voiced concerns about perceived Iranian efforts to influence the Afghan political arena by means of bribery and collusion. In October 2010 the office of President Karzai admitted to having received sizeable monetary payments from Iran on a relatively regular basis; such payments were widely believed to be intended to promote Iranian interests within Afghanistan to the detriment of US and other Western interests. Senior US officials and NATO commanders have frequently alleged that Iran has sought to undermine the Western mission in Afghanistan through the supply of munitions and the facilitation of training camps for Taliban and other militants in south-western Afghanistan. The Iranian Government adamantly refutes such claims, dismissing the allegations as crude attempts to discredit its reputation. Meanwhile, the Iranian authorities have expressed concern regarding the expansion of US military facilities in Herat province, in close proximity to the border with Iran.

CONSTITUTION AND GOVERNMENT

In December 2001 28 Afghan leaders signed the Agreement on Provisional Arrangements in Afghanistan Pending the Re-establishment of Permanent Government Institutions (also known as the Bonn Agreement), stipulating a timetable for the creation of a permanent constitution and the holding of free national elections. In accordance with the Agreement, Afghanistan temporarily reverted to the Constitution of 1964. In June 2002 an Emergency Loya Jirga (Grand National Council), comprising an estimated 1,650 delegates, appointed a head of state and the principal staff of a broad-based, gender-sensitive Transitional Authority. A new Constitution providing for a presidential system of government and a bicameral legislature following eventual elections by universal suffrage was approved by a Constitutional Loya Jirga in January 2004. Under the terms of the new charter, the President is elected for a five-year term, while the 249-member Wolasi Jirga (House of Representatives)—the lower house of the Meli Shura (National Assembly)—is elected on a provincial basis, with members also serving for five years; one-third of the 102-member Meshrano Jirga (House of Elders)—the upper house of the Meli Shura—is elected by the provincial councils, one-third by district councils, and the remaining members appointed by the President. The election of the President and the Meli Shura in October 2004 and September 2005, respectively, signified the end of the transitional period of government (the Bonn Process) that had been initiated in 2002.

Afghanistan is divided into 34 provinces. Each province is administered by a provincial council, which is headed by a governor and which is elected for a term of four years. The governor of each province is appointed by the President. Every village and town in the country also has a local council, with members serving for a three-year term.

REGIONAL AND INTERNATIONAL CO-OPERATION

Afghanistan is a member of the UN Economic and Social Commission for Asia and the Pacific (ESCAP, see p. 40), the Colombo Plan (see p. 449), which seeks to promote economic and social development in Asia and the Pacific, the Asian Development Bank (ADB, see p. 210) and the Economic Cooperation Organization (ECO, see p. 269). It was approved as a full member of the South Asian Association for Regional Cooperation (SAARC, see p. 420) in November 2005 and formally admitted as the eighth member of the regional organization in April 2007. Afghanistan was admitted as a member of the UN in November 1946. In April 2003 Afghanistan applied for membership to the World Trade Organization (WTO, see p. 433); the country formally initiated its accession process in November 2004, and the first Working Party meeting on its accession was convened in January 2011.

ECONOMIC AFFAIRS

In 2008, according to estimates by the World Bank, Afghanistan's gross national income (GNI), measured at average 2006–08 prices, was US $9,504m. In 2009/10, according to IMF estimates, Afghanistan's gross domestic product (GDP), excluding the illegal cultivation of poppies and production of drugs, was $16,631m. This implied a per head GDP of $561. During 2001–10, according to the Asian Development Bank (ADB), the population increased at an estimated average annual rate of 2.0%. According to the ADB, GDP increased at an average annual rate of 9.1% during 2002–09; growth was 21.0% in 2009, 8.4% in 2010 and 5.7% in 2011.

Agriculture (including hunting, forestry and fishing) contributed 32.5% of GDP in 2009/10. According to FAO estimates, 59.0% of the economically active population were employed in the agricultural sector in mid-2012. Livestock plays an important role in the traditional Afghan economy and is normally a major source of income for the country's numerous nomadic groups. However, the total livestock population has been seriously depleted, owing to the many years of conflict and prolonged drought conditions. Wheat production was estimated at 4.5m. tons in 2007, but this figure decreased to 2.6m. tons in 2008, owing to the ongoing drought in some regions of the country. Afghanistan thus continued to be dependent on food assistance. In 2008/09 the drought caused a major decline in the output of the agricultural sector; according to FAO estimates, cereal production decreased from 5.8m. tons in 2007 to around 3.7m. tons in 2008. According to ADB estimates, the GDP of the agricultural sector increased at an average annual rate of 5.0% during 2002–09; growth was 20.6% in 2007, but 2008 saw a massive decline of 21.3% owing to the severe drought conditions. The situation improved markedly in 2009 when cereal production recovered to 6.5m. tons, including wheat production estimated at 5.1m. tons, and the agricultural sector expanded by 23.3%. This was largely due to an increase in arable land devoted to wheat cultivation, favourable levels of rainfall, and the provision of seeds and fertilizers to farmers.

The industrial sector (including mining, manufacturing, construction and power) contributed an estimated 22.1% of GDP in 2009/10. The sector employed 6.2% of the economically active population in 2004/05, according to ADB figures. According to ADB estimates, sectoral GDP increased at an average annual rate of 12.4% between 2002 and 2009; the sector decreased by 4.1% in 2008, but grew by 5.5% in 2009.

Mining and quarrying, according to official estimates, contributed 0.5% of GDP in 2009/10. Natural gas was the major mineral export (accounting for about 23.6% of total export earnings, according to the IMF, in 1988/89). However, production of natural gas decreased from a high of 8.2m. cu m per day in the mid-1980s to around 600,000 cu m per day in 2001. Gas reserves were estimated at 150,000m. cu m in 2002. Salt, hard coal, copper, lapis lazuli, emeralds, barytes and talc are also mined. In addition, Afghanistan has sizeable reserves of iron ore, notably at Hajigak, which, according to government estimates, contained some 1,800m. metric tons of iron ore; development rights for three blocks in the concession were awarded to the state-run Steel Authority of India in November 2011, in a contract worth US $10,3000m., while rights for a fourth block were awarded to Kilo Goldmines of Canada. Afghanistan also has modest reserves of petroleum. In June 2010 Minister of Mines Waheedullah Shahrani claimed that Afghanistan's mineral wealth amounted to some US $3,000,000m. According to ADB estimates, mining GDP increased at an average annual rate of 27.1% during 2002–09; the sector increased by 42.5% in 2008 and by 13.2% in 2009.

Manufacturing, according to official estimates, contributed 13.3% of GDP in 2009/10. According to IMF estimates, the sector together with mining and utilities, employed about 4.9% of the labour force in 2002/03. Afghanistan's major manufacturing industries included food products, cotton textiles, chemical fertilizers, cement, leather and plastic goods. In 1999 only one of the four existing cement plants in Afghanistan and about 10% of the textile mills remained in operation (prior to the Soviet invasion in 1979 there were about 220 state-owned factories operating in Afghanistan). In July 2006 the Government advised that licences had been issued for the construction of four new private sector cement factories, the combined production of which was projected to provide around one-half of Afghanistan's total requirements. The traditional handicraft sector has better survived the devastating effects of war, and carpets, leather, embroidery and fur products continue to be produced. According to ADB estimates, manufacturing GDP increased at an average annual rate of 6.0% during 2002–09; the sector decreased by 14.3% in 2008, but increased by 4.0% in 2009.

The construction sector contributed 8.2% of GDP in 2009/10, and employed an estimated 1.3% of the economically active population in 2002/03. The sector has performed particularly well in recent years, owing to the extensive post-war reconstruction activity in the country. The GDP of the construction sector increased at an average annual rate of 24.8% during 2002–09; according to ADB figures, growth was 10.0% in 2008 and 6.7% in 2009.

Energy is derived principally from petroleum (which is imported from Iran and republics of the former USSR, notably Turkmenistan) and coal. It has been estimated that Afghanistan has some 73m. metric tons of coal reserves. Further work remains to be undertaken to assess petroleum reserves. The discovery in August 2010 of an oilfield believed to contain some 1,800m. barrels of oil, between Balkh and Jawzjan provinces in northern Afghanistan, represented a significant boon for the country's energy sector. In December the Government awarded its first private oil contract; the contract for the sale of crude petroleum, at a price of US $80 per barrel, from Angot oilfield in the province of Sar-e Pol was awarded to a local Afghan company.

Services contributed 45.4% of GDP in 2009/10. The sector employed an estimated 24.2% of the economically active population in 2004/05, according to ADB figures. The GDP of the service sector increased at an average annual rate of 10.8% in 2002–09; the sector declined by 13.9% in 2008, but grew by 17.9% in 2009, according to ADB figures. Sectoral growth was mainly driven by the expansion of the trade and financial activities.

In 2010/11 there was a surplus of an estimated US $267m. on the current account of the balance of payments. In the same year a trade deficit of $6,303m. (excluding opium-related exports) was recorded. In 2010/11 the principal exports were carpets and handicrafts, dried and fresh fruit and medicinal plants; the principal imports were machinery and equipment, household items and medicine, petroleum and petroleum products, food and metals. In 2010/11, according to official estimates, the principal market for exports was Pakistan (which purchased an estimated 38.7% of the total), followed by India, Turkey, Iran and Russia. In that year the principal source of imports was Uzbekistan (providing an estimated 21.1%), followed by the People's Republic of China, Pakistan, Japan, Germany and Iran. These official statistics do not, however, include illegal trade and smuggling. According to estimates by the UN Office on Drugs and Crime (UNODC), exports of opiates from Afghanistan totalled $2,800m. in 2009; the value of opiate exports fell by 50%, to $1,400m., in 2010, equivalent to around 11% of the country's overall GDP. This decline was due in part to falling production levels, owing to a naturally occurring plant disease, and stable cross-border prices. However, it was anticipated that opiate exports in 2011 would recover to earlier high levels. In 2011 UNODC estimated that opium production in Afghanistan accounted for about 90% of the global supply.

In the financial year ending 20 March 2011 there was an estimated budgetary deficit of 30,100m. afghanis, which was expected to be covered by financial assistance. In 2009/10, according to budget estimates, donor grants and loans totalled an estimated 54,500m. afghanis and development assistance grants and loans totalled an estimated 25,500m. afghanis. According to the ADB, the fiscal deficit of the central Government was equivalent to 0.2% of GDP in 2009/10, compared with 3.7% in 2007/08. Afghanistan's total external debt was US $2,328m. at the end of 2009, of which $2,203m. was public and publicly guaranteed debt. In that year the cost of debt-servicing was equivalent to 1.1% of earnings from the exports of goods, services and income. The ADB estimated that consumer prices in Afghanistan rose by 26.8% in 2008, compared with the previous year; however, consumer prices fell by 12.2% in 2009, before increasing again, by 8.2%, in 2010.

It is difficult to provide an accurate economic profile of Afghanistan, after many years of conflict, intermittent droughts and earthquakes, and constant population movements. However, more reliable statistics have become available in recent years as government and financial institutions have been re-established. Improvements in the domestic banking system have led to an increase in the levels of remittances from Afghans working abroad; according to UN estimates, remittances totalled around US $3,300m. in 2006. According to the ADB, foreign direct investment in Afghanistan increased by 9.4%, from $201m. in 2008/09 to $220m. in 2009/10. The opening in December 2011 of Afghanistan's first major rail link, between Mazar-i-Sharif and the border town of Hairatan (on the Afghan–Uzbek border) constituted the initial phase of a project intended to link Afghanistan to the extensive rail networks in its neighbouring countries; it was hoped that the initiative would eventually lead to the emergence of Afghanistan as a regional trade hub. However, several serious risks to the economy remained. A high proportion of economic activity involved informal undertakings, including the illegal trade in arms and poppy cultivation, which greatly hampered the authorities' ability to regulate the economy and collect tax revenues. Unemployment (standing at around 40%) and endemic government corruption remained obstacles to economic stability and threatened to derail consistent progress. Meanwhile, reconstruction efforts were severely hampered by the ongoing security crisis. Moreover, the transition of security responsibilities to the Afghan security forces (see Contemporary Political History)—and the concomitant withdrawal from Afghanistan of the international military presence, together with an expected decline in foreign aid (which in 2011 was estimated to account for more than 90% of Afghanistan's total $17,100m. budget)—was likely to pose significant economic and policy challenges for the Government, which would have to assume the financial burden of activities previously funded by donors, including a greater proportion of national security spending. The World Bank projected a fiscal deficit of some $7,000m. annually from 2014 through to 2021. None the less, according to the ADB, despite declining for a second successive year, in 2011 GDP growth remained relatively durable at 5.7%, and this was projected to increase, to 7.1%, in 2012. Inflation was forecast to average 9.1% in 2011/12, down from an estimated 9.8% in 2010/11, although the projection was dependent upon the Government proving able to mitigate successfully the impact of rising international commodity prices. In November 2011 the IMF approved funding of $133.6m. under its Extended Credit Facility to support Afghanistan's economic programme during 2011–14.

PUBLIC HOLIDAYS

The Afghan year 1391 runs from 21 March 2012 to 20 March 2013, and the year 1392 runs from 21 March 2013 to 20 March 2014.

2013: 23 January* (Roze-Maulud, Birth of Prophet Muhammad), 15 February (Liberation Day, commemoration of *mujahidin* struggle against Soviet occupation and withdrawal of Soviet troops in 1989), 21 March (Nauroz: New Year's Day, Iranian calendar), 28 April (Victory Day, commemoration of *mujahidin* victory over the communist regime in 1992), 1 May (Workers' Day), 8 July* (first day of Ramadan), 7 August* (Id al-Fitr, end of Ramadan), 19 August (Jeshen, Independence Day), 14 October* (Id al-Adha, Feast of the Sacrifice), 13 November* (Ashura, Martyrdom of Imam Husayn).

* These holidays are dependent on the Islamic lunar calendar and may vary by one or two days from the dates given.

Statistical Survey

Sources (unless otherwise stated): Central Statistics Authority, Block 4, Microrayon, Kabul; tel. (93) 24883; Central Statistics Office, Ansari Wat, Kabul; e-mail info@cso.gov.af; internet www.cso.gov.af.

Area and Population

AREA, POPULATION AND DENSITY

Area (sq km)	652,864*
Population (census results)	
23 June 1979†	
Males	6,712,377
Females	6,338,981
Total	13,051,358
Population (official estimates of settled population)‡	
2008	23,511,400
2009	23,993,500
2010§	24,485,600
Density (per sq km) at 2010	37.5

* 252,072 sq miles.

† Figures exclude nomadic population, estimated to total 2,500,000. The census data also exclude an adjustment for underenumeration, estimated to have been 5% for the urban population and 10% for the rural population.

‡ Figures are rounded to the nearest 100 persons and take no account of the nomadic population (estimated at 1.5m. in 2002) or emigration by refugees (at the end of 2010 UNHCR estimated that the total Afghan refugee and 'refugee-like' population numbered 3.1m., of whom 1,900,000 were located in Pakistan and 1,028,000 in Iran).

§ Males 12,524,700, females 11,960,900.

Mid-2012 (UN estimate): Total population 33,397,058 (Source: UN, *World Population Prospects: The 2010 Revision*).

POPULATION BY AGE AND SEX

(UN estimates at mid-2012)

	Males	Females	Total
0–14	7,873,178	7,385,118	15,258,296
15–64	9,033,639	8,347,302	17,380,941
65 and over	368,917	388,904	757,821
Total	17,275,734	16,121,324	33,397,058

Source: UN, *World Population Prospects: The 2010 Revision*.

PROVINCES

(2010, estimates of settled population)

	Area (sq km)	Population ('000)	Density (per sq km)	Capital
Kabul	4,524	3,691.4	816.0	Kabul
Kapisa	1,908	406.2	212.9	Mahmud-e-Iraqi
Parvan (Parwan)	5,715	610.3	106.8	Charikar
Wardak	10,348	549.2	53.1	Maidanshahr
Loghar (Logar)	4,568	360.9	79.0	Pul-i-Alam
Ghazni	22,461	1,130.1	50.3	Ghazni
Paktika	19,516	400.5	20.5	Sharan
Paktia (Paktya)	5,583	507.8	91.0	Gardez
Khost	4,235	528.9	124.9	Khost
Nangarhar	7,641	1,383.9	181.1	Jalalabad
Kunar (Kunarha)	4,926	414.7	84.2	Asadabad
Laghman	3,978	410.3	103.1	Mehter Lam
Nuristan (Nooristan)	9,267	136.3	14.7	Nuristan
Badakhshan	44,836	874.8	19.5	Faizabad
Takhar	12,458	901.9	72.4	Taloqan
Baghlan	18,255	833.3	45.6	Pul-e-Khomri
Kunduz	8,081	917.9	113.6	Kunduz
Samangan	13,438	356.3	26.5	Aybak
Balkh	16,186	1,194.0	73.8	Mazar-i-Sharif

—continued	Area (sq km)	Population ('000)	Density (per sq km)	Capital
Jawzjan (Juzjan)	11,292	494.2	43.8	Shiberghan
Sar-e Pol (Sar-e-Pul)	16,386	514.1	31.4	Sar-e Pol
Faryab	20,798	915.8	44.0	Maymana
Badghis	20,794	456.4	21.9	Qaleh-ye-Now
Herat	55,869	1,710.1	30.6	Herat
Farah	49,339	466.3	9.5	Farah
Nimroz	42,410	151.1	3.6	Zaranj
Helmand	58,305	850.2	14.6	Lashkar Gah
Qandahar (Kandahar)	54,845	1,103.4	20.1	Qandahar
Zabul	17,472	279.8	16.0	Qalat
Uruzgan (Urizan)	11,474	322.6	28.1	Tarin Kowt
Ghor	36,657	635.7	17.3	Chaghcharan
Bamian (Bamyan)	18,029	411.7	22.8	Bamian
Panjshir (Panjsher)	3,772	141.4	37.5	Bazarat
Daikundi (Daykundy)	17,501	424.1	24.2	Neli
Total	652,864	24,485.6	37.5	

Note: Totals may not be exactly equal to the sum of components, owing to rounding.

PRINCIPAL TOWNS
(2006, estimates of settled population, rounded figures)

Kabul (capital)	2,536,300	Pul-e-Khomri	180,800
Qandahar	450,300	Jalalabad	168,600
Herat	349,000	Baghlan	149,300
Mazar-i-Sharif	300,600	Ghazni	141,000
Kunduz	264,100	Maymana	67,800

Mid-2010 (incl. suburbs, UN estimate): Kabul (capital) 3,731,312 (Source: UN, *World Urbanization Prospects: The 2009 Revision*).

BIRTHS AND DEATHS
(annual averages, UN estimates)

	1995–2000	2000–05	2005–10
Birth rate (per 1,000)	52.4	48.4	45.1
Death rate (per 1,000)	20.1	18.3	16.8

Source: UN, *World Population Prospects: The 2010 Revision*.

Life expectancy (years at birth, WHO estimates): 48 (males 47; females 50) in 2009 (Source: WHO, *World Health Statistics*).

ECONOMICALLY ACTIVE POPULATION*
(ISIC major divisions, '000 persons aged 15–59 years, year ending 20 March, estimates)

	2000/01	2001/02	2002/03
Agriculture, hunting, forestry and fishing	4,986.1	5,082.6	5,181.4
Mining, quarrying, manufacturing and utilities	348.6	355.3	362.2
Construction	94.9	96.7	98.6
Wholesale and retail trade	490.4	499.9	509.6
Transport, storage and communications	163.1	166.3	169.5
Other services	1,083.6	1,104.5	1,126.0
Total	7,166.6	7,305.4	7,447.3

* Figures refer to settled population only.

2004/05 ('000 persons): Agriculture 5,534; Industry 492; Services 1,203; Others 725; *Total employed* 7,954; Unemployed and unclassified 277; *Total labour force* 8,231 (Source: Asian Development Bank).

Mid-2012 ('000 persons, FAO estimates): Agriculture, etc. 6,405; Total labour force 10,861 (Source: FAO).

Health and Welfare

KEY INDICATORS

Total fertility rate (children per woman, 2009)	6.5
Under-5 mortality rate (per 1,000 live births, 2009)	199
HIV/AIDS (% of persons aged 15–49, 2005)	<0.01
Physicians (per 1,000 head, 2005)	0.2
Hospital beds (per 1,000 head, 2003)	0.4
Health expenditure (2008): US $ per head (PPP)	57
Health expenditure (2008): % of GDP	7.4
Health expenditure (2008): public (% of total)	21.5
Total carbon dioxide emissions ('000 metric tons, 2007)	714.5
Carbon dioxide emissions per head (metric tons, 2007)	<0.1
Access to water (% of persons, 2008)	48
Access to sanitation (% of persons, 2008)	37
Human Development Index (2011): ranking	172
Human Development Index (2011): value	0.398

For sources and definitions, see explanatory note on p. vi.

Agriculture

PRINCIPAL CROPS
('000 metric tons)

	2008	2009	2010
Wheat	2,623	5,064	4,532
Rice, paddy	612	645	672
Barley	333	486	437
Maize	280	300	301
Millet	22	19	15
Potatoes	280	302	334*
Sesame seed†	32	32	32
Seed cotton	35	43	54†
Watermelons	200	250*	282*
Cantaloupes and other melons*	29	28	26
Grapes	364	394*	447*
Sugar cane	63	70*	70*
Plums and sloes*	35	35	35
Apricots*	57	60	66

* FAO estimate(s).
† Unofficial figure(s).

Aggregate production ('000 metric tons, may include official, semi-official or estimated data): Total cereals 3,870 in 2008, 6,514 in 2009, 5,957 in 2010; Total roots and tubers 280 in 2008, 302 in 2009, 334 in 2010; Total pulses 43 in 2008–09, 46 in 2010; Total vegetables (incl. melons) 875 in 2008, 964 in 2009, 1,145 in 2010; Total fruits (excl. melons) 765 in 2008–09, 848 in 2010.

Source: FAO.

LIVESTOCK
('000 head)

	2008	2009	2010*
Horses	162	177	180
Asses	1,209	1,322	1,350
Mules	24	26	24
Cattle	4,745	4,721	4,697
Camels	183	190	190
Sheep	10,710	12,287	12,500
Goats	6,386	5,810	5,500
Chickens	10,689	10,193	10,000

* FAO estimates.

Source: FAO.

LIVESTOCK PRODUCTS
('000 metric tons)

	2008	2009	2010*
Cattle meat	133	135	134
Sheep meat	87*	100*	100
Goat meat	42*	38*	38
Chicken meat	21*	21*	21
Cows' milk	1,391	1,413	1,482
Sheep's milk	162*	186*	207
Goats' milk	113	113	123
Hen eggs	17	17	17
Wool, greasy	13*	15*	15

* FAO estimate(s).

Source: FAO.

Forestry

ROUNDWOOD REMOVALS
('000 cubic metres, excl. bark, FAO estimates)

	2007	2008	2009
Sawlogs, veneer logs and logs for sleepers*	856	856	856
Other industrial wood†	904	904	904
Fuel wood	1,531	1,564	1,598
Total	3,291	3,324	3,358

* Assumed to be unchanged from 1976.
† Assumed to be unchanged from 1999.

2010: Production assumed to be unchanged from 2009 (FAO estimates).

Source: FAO.

SAWNWOOD PRODUCTION
('000 cubic metres, incl. railway sleepers, FAO estimates)

	1974	1975	1976
Coniferous (softwood)	360	310	380
Broadleaved (hardwood)	50	20	20
Total	410	330	400

1977–2010: Annual production as in 1976 (FAO estimates).

Source: FAO.

Fishing

(metric tons, live weight, FAO estimates)

	2002	2003	2004
Total catch (freshwater fishes)	900	900	1,000

2005–09: Catch assumed to be unchanged from 2004 (FAO estimates).

Source: FAO.

Mining

('000 metric tons unless otherwise indicated, estimates)

	2008	2009	2010
Hard coal	347	500	725
Natural gas (million cu m)*	155	142	142
Salt (unrefined)	158	180	186
Gypsum (crude)	49	46	63

* Figures refer to gross output. Estimated marketed production was 145m. cu m in 2008 and 140m. cu m per year in 2009–10.

Source: US Geological Survey.

2010/11 ('000 metric tons unless otherwise indicated): Coal 724.9; Natural gas (million cu m) 141.9; Salt 186.1; Marble 29.9.

Industry

SELECTED PRODUCTS
(year ending 20 March, '000 metric tons, unless otherwise indicated)

	1986/87	1987/88	1988/89
Margarine	3.5	3.3	1.8
Vegetable oil	4	n.a.	n.a.
Wheat flour*	187	203	166
Wine ('000 hectolitres)*	289	304	194
Soft drinks ('000 hectolitres)	8,500	10,300	4,700
Woven cotton fabrics (million sq metres)	58.1	52.6	32.1
Woven woollen fabrics (million sq metres)	0.4	0.3	0.3
Footwear—excl. rubber ('000 pairs)*	613	701	607
Rubber footwear ('000 pairs)*	2,200	3,200	2,200
Nitrogenous fertilizers†	56	57	55
Cement	103	104	70
Electric energy (million kWh)*‡	1,171	1,257	1,109

* Production in calendar years 1986, 1987 and 1988.
† Production in year ending 30 June.
‡ Provisional.

Wheat flour ('000 metric tons): 1,832 in 1994; 2,029 in 1995; 2,145 in 1996.

Nitrogenous fertilizers (provisional, year ending 30 June, '000 metric tons): 49 in 1994/95; 50 in 1995/96; 50 in 1996/97; 5 in 1997/98; 5 in 1998/99; 5 in 1999/2000.

Cement (year ending 20 March, '000 metric tons): 37.3 in 2008/09; 31.5 in 2009/10; 35.6 in 2010/11.

Electric energy (year ending 20 March, million kWh): 827.0 in 2008/09; 937.1 in 2009/10; 936.1 in 2010/11.

Sources: mainly UN, *Industrial Commodity Statistics Yearbook* and *Statistical Yearbook for Asia and the Pacific*, FAO, US Geological Survey and IMF, *Islamic Republic of Afghanistan: Statistical Appendix* (February 2008).

Finance

CURRENCY AND EXCHANGE RATES

Monetary Units:
100 puls (puli) = 2 krans = 1 afghani (Af).

Sterling, Dollar and Euro Equivalents (30 November 2011):
£1 sterling = 75,184 afghanis;
US $1 = 48,170 afghanis;
€1 = 64.635 afghanis;
1,000 afghanis = £13.30 = $20.76 = €15.47.

Average Exchange Rate (afghanis per US $):
2008 50.250
2009 50.233
2010 46.453

Note: The foregoing information refers to the official exchange rate. A new afghani, equivalent to 1,000 of the old currency, was introduced in October 2002

OPERATING BUDGET

(million afghanis, year ending 20 March)

Revenue*	2009/10	2010/11	2011/12†
Tax revenue	51,500	66,400	82,100
Taxes on income, profits and capital gains	15,600	19,400	23,700
Taxes on international trade and transactions	21,800	27,700	33,800
Taxes on goods and services	12,300	16,300	21,000
Other taxes	1,800	3,000	3,600
Non-tax revenue	12,000	14,000	16,700
Total	63,500	80,400	98,800

Expenditure‡	2009/10	2010/11	2011/12†
Wages and salaries	64,300	86,500	113,700
Purchase of goods and services	14,900	17,200	23,300
Transfers and subsidies	3,000	3,300	3,800
Pensions	5,300	1,900	6,100
Capital expenditure	1,500	1,600	3,400
Interest	100	0,100	1,000
Total	89,100	110,500	151,400

* Excluding donor assistance grants and loans (million afghanis): 32,800 in 2009/10; 54,500 in 2010/11; 65,900 in 2011/12 (budget projection), and development assistance grants and loans: 30,100 in 2009/10; 25,500 in 2010/11; 39,600 in 2011/12 (budget projection).

† Budget projections.

‡ Excluding development spending (million afghanis): 47,000 in 2009/10; 43,400 in 2010/11; 53,400 in 2011/12 (budget projection).

Source: IMF, *Islamic Republic of Afghanistan: 2011 Article IV Consultation and Request for a Three-Year Arrangement Under the Extended Credit Facility—Staff Report; Staff Supplement–A Joint World Bank/IMF Debt Sustainability Analysis; Staff Statement; Public Information Notice and Press Release on the Executive Board Discussion; and Statement by the Executive Director for Islamic Republic of Afghanistan* (November 2011).

FOREIGN EXCHANGE RESERVES

(million afghanis at 20 March)

	2005/06	2006/07*	2007/08†
Gold‡	19,230	23,006	23,006
Other	63,765	80,370	96,087
Total	82,995	103,376	119,093

* Estimates.

† Projections.

‡ Excluding gold held in palace vaults.

Source: IMF, *Islamic Republic of Afghanistan: Statistical Appendix* (February 2008).

MONEY SUPPLY

(million afghanis at 31 December)

	2008	2009	2010
Currency outside depository corporations	70,142.5	85,921.6	116,952.9
Transferable deposits	77,306.7	106,255.2	123,304.3
Other deposits	4,552.9	10,054.5	15,945.2
Broad money	152,002.1	202,231.3	256,202.4

Source: IMF, *International Financial Statistics*.

COST OF LIVING

(Consumer Price Index; base: March 2004 = 100)

	2008	2009	2010
Food	198.8	168.0	169.7
Non-food	149.5	153.8	167.6
All items	179.7	162.5	168.9

Source: Asian Development Bank.

NATIONAL ACCOUNTS

(million afghanis at current prices, year ending 20 March)

Expenditure on the Gross Domestic Product

	2007/08	2008/09	2009/10
Public consumption expenditure	50,727	69,100	87,324
Private consumption expenditure	569,208	566,554	616,369
Gross fixed capital investment	97,418	97,970	110,054
Total domestic expenditures	717,353	733,624	813,747
Exports of goods and services	87,408	93,417	90,463
Less Imports of goods and services	286,150	285,929	276,816
Gross domestic product (GDP) in market prices	518,611	541,112	627,394
GDP at constant 2002/03 prices	312,436	319,726	374,367

Gross Domestic Product by Economic Activity

	2007/08	2008/09	2009/10
Agriculture, hunting, forestry and fishing	174,343	150,133	196,990
Mining and quarrying	2,213	2,481	2,921
Manufacturing	86,148	91,879	80,435
Electricity, gas and water	630	527	629
Construction	41,500	43,741	49,955
Trade, restaurants and hotels	44,850	48,097	49,812
Transport, storage and communications	71,926	91,481	111,784
Finance, insurance, real estate and business	7,249	9,222	11,745
Government services	46,920	57,136	67,170
Community, social and personal services	4,012	4,413	4,854
Ownership of dwellings	12,925	14,476	15,074
Other services	12,701	13,195	14,243
Sub-total	505,417	526,782	605,612
Taxes on imports	13,194	14,330	21,782
GDP at market prices	518,611	541,112	627,394

BALANCE OF PAYMENTS

(US $ million, year ending 20 March)

	2008/09	2009/10	2010/11*
Exports of goods†	2,465	2,517	2,836
Imports of goods	–8,945	–8,872	–9,139
Trade balance	–6,480	–6,354	–6,303
Services and other income (net)	–240	–370	–408
Balance on goods, services and income	–6,720	–6,724	–6,711
Current transfers (net)	6,812	6,377	6,978
Current balance	92	–347	267
Capital and financial account (net)	338	–287	612
Net errors and omissions	541	190	–81
Overall balance	972	–445	797

* Preliminary.

† Excludes opium exports and flows associated with US Army and International Security Assistance Force activities.

Source: IMF, *Islamic Republic of Afghanistan: 2011 Article IV Consultation and Request for a Three-Year Arrangement Under the Extended Credit Facility—Staff Report; Staff Supplement–A Joint World Bank/IMF Debt Sustainability Analysis; Staff Statement; Public Information Notice and Press Release on the Executive Board Discussion; and Statement by the Executive Director for Islamic Republic of Afghanistan* (November 2011).

OFFICIAL DEVELOPMENT ASSISTANCE
(US $ million)

	1998	1999	2000
Bilateral	88.5	104.2	88.2
Multilateral	65.7	38.3	52.7
Total received	154.2	142.5	140.9
Grants	154.3	140.9	140.9
Loans	–0.1	1.6	—
Per caput assistance (US $)	7.4	6.7	6.5

Total received (US $ million): 3,965 in 2007; 4,865 in 2008; 1,010 in 2009.

Source: UN, *Statistical Yearbook for Asia and the Pacific*.

2010/11 (US $ million): Total bilateral 10,081; Total multilateral 819; *Total received* 10,900.

External Trade

PRINCIPAL COMMODITIES
(US $ million, year ending 20 March)

Imports c.i.f.	2008/09	2009/10	2010/11
Machinery and equipment	576	688	1,235
Petroleum and petroleum products	547	740	999
Metals	433	317	566
Chemical materials	120	45	57
Food	500	587	722
Fabrics, clothing and footwear	112	148	205
Household items and medicine	594	646	1,003
Total (incl. others)	3,020	3,336	5,154

Exports f.o.b.*	2008/09	2009/10	2010/11
Fresh fruits	41	23	28
Dried fruit	245	181	106
Medicinal plants	21	29	39
Animal skins	21	6	15
Carpets and handicrafts	199	148	156
Total (incl. others)	545	403	388

* Officially recorded transactions only.

PRINCIPAL TRADING PARTNERS
(US $ million, year ending 20 March)

Imports	2008/09	2009/10	2010/11
China, People's Republic	430	360	704
Germany	65	145	422
India	106	106	113
Iran	200	177	386
Japan	368	337	494
Kazakhstan	165	291	208
Korea, Republic	50	57	57
Malaysia	78	23	53
Pakistan	489	308	598
Russia	98	198	181
Saudi Arabia	29	47	54
Tajikistan	40	69	98
Turkey	51	71	109
Turkmenistan	81	76	117
United Arab Emirates	89	47	106
USA	19	45	78
Uzbekistan	501	876	1,088
Total (incl. others)	3,020	3,336	5,154

Exports*	2008/09	2009/10	2010/11
China, People's Republic	2	4	12
Egypt	—	1	4
Finland	6	—	3
India	136	76	65
Iran	18	41	32
Iraq	6	7	9
Netherlands	—	—	9
Pakistan	264	191	151
Russia	37	26	30
Tajikistan	6	6	7
Turkey	18	6	35
Turkmenistan	11	6	9
United Arab Emirates	19	7	6
USA	2	17	4
Total (incl. others)	545	403	388

* Officially recorded transactions only.

Transport

ROAD TRAFFIC
(year ending 20 March, motor vehicles in use)

	2008/09	2009/10	2010/11
Passenger cars	558,495	621,937	691,573
Lorries	156,469	169,737	184,799
Buses	65,471	71,581	74,834
Motorcycles	132,130	134,596	141,833
Rickshaws	10,349	10,351	10,647
Foreign vehicles	26,722	27,823	28,602

CIVIL AVIATION
('000)

	2008/09	2009/10	2010/11
Kilometres flown	9,150	10,444	12,074
Passengers carried	665	714	1,159
Freight ton-km	19,560	22,913	21,561

Tourism

	1996	1997	1998
Tourist arrivals ('000)	4	4	4
Tourism receipts (US $ million)	1	1	1

Source: World Tourism Organization, *Yearbook of Tourism Statistics*.

Communications Media

	2008	2009	2010
Telephones ('000 main lines in use)	101.1	129.3	140.0
Mobile cellular telephones ('000 subscribers)	7,898.9	12,000.0	13,000.0
Internet subscribers ('000)	n.a.	2.0	n.a.
Broadband subscribers	500	1,000	1,500

Personal computers: 100,000 (3.6 per 1,000 persons) in 2006.

Radio receivers ('000 in use): 2,400 in 1995; 2,550 in 1996; 2,750 in 1997.

Television receivers ('000 in use): 290 in 1998; 300 in 1999.

Sources: mainly UNESCO, *Statistical Yearbook*, UN, *Statistical Yearbook* and International Telecommunication Union.

Daily newspapers: *Number*: 15 in 1995, 12 in 1996; *Average circulation* ('000 copies): 200 in 1995 (estimate), 113 in 1996.

Education

(2010/11 unless otherwise indicated)

	Institutions	Teachers	Pupils
Pre-primary	358	2,673	23,917
Primary	5,571	40,131	5,112,931
Secondary*	7,213	122,142	1,988,733
Higher	24	3,023	63,837

* Figures refer to general secondary education only, excluding vocational education and teacher training.

Sources: Ministries of Education, of Higher Education and of Labour, Social Affairs, Martyrs and the Disabled, Kabul, and UNICEF.

Enrolment (2009/10 unless otherwise indicated): Pre-primary 25,372 (2003/04); Primary 5,279,326; Total secondary 2,044,157; Tertiary 95,185 (2008/09) (Source: UNESCO Institute for Statistics).

Teachers (2009/10 unless otherwise indicated): Pre-primary 3,510 (2003/04); Primary 118,858; Secondary general 46,622; Secondary vocational 621 (2006/07); Tertiary 3,342 (2008/09) (Source: UNESCO Institute for Statistics).

Pupil-teacher ratio (primary education, UNESCO estimate): 44.4 in 2009/10 (Source: UNESCO Institute for Statistics).

Adult literacy rate (UNESCO estimates): 28.0% (males 43.1%; females 12.6%) in 2000 (Source: UNESCO Institute for Statistics).

Directory

The Government

HEAD OF STATE

President: HAMID KARZAI (inaugurated as Chairman of Interim Authority 22 December 2001; elected as President of Transitional Authority by Loya Jirga 13 June 2002 and as President of the Islamic Republic of Afghanistan by direct popular vote 9 October 2004; sworn in as the country's President for a second term on 19 November 2009).

Vice-Presidents: Marshal MUHAMMED QASIM FAHIM, KARIM KHALILI.

CABINET
(May 2012)

Minister of Defence: Gen. MOHAMMAD ABDUL RAHIM WARDAK.

Minister of Foreign Affairs: Dr ZALMAI RASSOUL.

Minister of Finance: Dr OMAR ZAKHILWAL.

Minister of Interior Affairs: Gen. BISMILLAH MUHAMMADI.

Minister of Economy: ABDUL HADI ARGHANDIWAL.

Minister of Information and Culture: Dr SAYED MAKHDUM RAHEEN.

Minister of Public Works: NAJIBULLAH OZHAN.

Minister of Refugees and Repatriation: JAMAHIR ANWARI.

Minister of Border and Tribal Affairs: ASADULLAH KHALID.

Minister of Commerce and Industry: ANWAR-UL HAQ AHDI.

Minister of Mines: WAHEEDULLAH SHAHRANI.

Minister of Agriculture, Irrigation and Livestock: MUHAMMAD ASIF RAHIMI.

Minister of Justice: HABIBULLAH GHALEB.

Minister of Hajj and Islamic Affairs: MOHAMMAD YOUSUF NEYAZI.

Minister of Labour, Social Affairs, Martyrs and the Disabled: AMINA AFZALI.

Minister of Education: Dr GHULAM FAROOQ WARDAK.

Minister of Rural Rehabilitation and Development: WAIS AHMAD BARMAK.

Minister of Counter Narcotics: ZARAR AHMAD MOQBEL.

Minister of Communications and Information Technology: AMIRZAI SANGIN.

Minister of Public Health: Dr SURAYA DALIL.

Minister of Higher Education: OBAIDULLAH OBAID.

Minister of Urban Development: HASAN ABDULLAHI.

Minister of Women's Affairs: HOSNA BANU GHAZANFAR.

Minister of Transport and Civil Aviation: DAOUD ALI NAJAFI.

Minister of Water and Energy: MOHAMMED ISMAIL KHAN.

MINISTRIES

Office of the President: Gul Khana Palace, Presidential Palace, Kabul; tel. 706005528 (mobile); e-mail feroz.mohmand@gmic.gov.af; internet www.president.gov.af.

Ministry of Agriculture, Irrigation and Livestock: Jamal Mena, Kart-i-Sakhi, Kabul; tel. 752034204 (mobile); e-mail info@mail.gov.af; internet www.mail.gov.af.

Ministry of Border and Tribal Affairs: Shah Mahmud Ghazi Wat, Kabul; tel. (20) 2101365.

Ministry of Commerce and Industry: Darulaman Wat, Kabul; tel. 700225718 (mobile); fax (20) 2500356; e-mail fawad.it@commerce.gov.af; internet moci.gov.af.

Ministry of Communications and Information Technology: 6th Floor, ICT Directorate, Mohammad Jan Khan Wat, Kabul; tel. (20) 2101113; fax (20) 2101708; internet www.mcit.gov.af.

Ministry of Counter Narcotics: Kabul-Jalalabad Rd, Banaiey, Macroyan, Kabul; tel. 798242837 (mobile); e-mail spokesman@mcn.gov.af; internet www.mcn.gov.af.

Ministry of Defence: Shash Darak, Kabul; tel. (20) 2100451; fax (20) 2104172; internet www.mod.gov.af.

Ministry of Economy: Malik Asghar Sq., Kabul; tel. (20) 2100394; internet www.moec.gov.af.

Ministry of Education: Mohammad Jan Khan Wat, Kabul; tel. 798801066 (mobile); e-mail attaullah.wahidyar@moe.gov.af; internet www.moe.gov.af.

Ministry of Finance: Pashtunistan Wat, Kabul; tel. 752004199 (mobile); fax (20) 2103280; e-mail info@mof.gov.af; internet www.mof.gov.af.

Ministry of Foreign Affairs: Malek Asghar St, Kabul; tel. (20) 2100372; fax (20) 2100360; e-mail contact@mfa.gov.af; internet mfa.gov.af.

Ministry of Hajj and Islamic Affairs: nr District 10, Shir Pur, Shar-i-Nau, Kabul; tel. (20) 2201338.

Ministry of Higher Education: Karte Char, Kabul; tel. (20) 2500324; e-mail afmohe@hotmail.com; internet www.mohe.gov.af.

Ministry of Information and Culture: Mohammad Jan Khan Wat, Kabul; tel. (20) 2101301; fax (20) 2290088; e-mail znawabi2011@moic.gov.af; internet moic.afghanistan.af.

Ministry of Interior Affairs: Shar-i-Nau, Kabul; tel. (20) 32441; internet www.moi.gov.af.

Ministry of Justice: Pashtunistan Wat, Kabul; tel. (20) 2100325; e-mail info@moj.gov.af; internet www.moj.gov.af.

Ministry of Labour, Social Affairs, Martyrs and the Disabled: opp. First Makroryan Market, Kabul; tel. (20) 2300369; e-mail info@molsamd.gov.af; internet www.molsamd.gov.af.

Ministry of Mines: Pashtunistan Wat, Kabul; tel. (20) 2100309; e-mail info@mom.gov.af; internet www.mom.gov.af.

Ministry of Public Health: Wazir Akbar Khan, Sub-district 9, Kabul; tel. (20) 2301377; e-mail ahmadzaih@moph.gov.af; internet www.moph.gov.af.

Ministry of Public Works: Microrayon 1, Kabul; tel. (20) 2301363; fax (20) 2301362; internet www.mopws.gov.af.

Ministry of Refugees and Repatriation: Jungaluk, off Darulaman Wat, Kabul; e-mail afgmorr@afgmorr.com; internet morr.gov.af.

Ministry of Rural Rehabilitation and Development: Shah Mahmud Ghazi Wat, Kabul; tel. 778813167 (mobile); e-mail hashmat.nasiri@yahoo.com; internet www.mrrd.gov.af.

Ministry of Transport and Civil Aviation: Ansari Wat, Kabul; tel. (20) 2103064; e-mail arasikh@motca.gov.af; internet motca.gov.af.

Ministry of Urban Development: Microrayon 3, Kabul; tel. 799682833 (mobile); e-mail info@moud.gov.af; internet www.moud.gov.af.

Ministry of Water and Energy: Darulaman Wat, Kabul; tel. (75) 2004813; e-mail tawabmir@yahoo.com; internet mew.gov.af.

Ministry of Women's Affairs: beside Cinema Zainab, Shar-i-Nau, Kabul; tel. and fax (20) 2201378; e-mail spokesman.mowa@gmail.com; internet www.mowa.gov.af.

President and Legislature

PRESIDENT

Presidential Election, 20 August 2009 (revised figures)

Candidates	Votes	% of votes
Hamid Karzai	2,283,907	49.7
Dr Abdullah Abdullah	1,406,242	30.6
Ramazan Bashardost	481,072	10.5
Ashraf Ghani Ahmadzai	135,106	2.9
Mirwais Yasini	47,511	1.0
Shahnawaz Tanai	29,648	0.6
Others	214,243	4.7
Total	4,597,729	100.0

Note: On 21 October 2009 the Independent Election Commission (IEC) released its final certified results for the presidential election held on 20 August, following a two-month audit carried out by the UN-supported, independent Electoral Complaints Commission, which invalidated votes from hundreds of polling stations having found 'clear and convincing evidence of fraud relating to improperly recorded vote totals for candidates'. The number of votes awarded to Hamid Karzai was reduced from 3,093,256 (54.6% of the ballot) in the uncertified results, published on 16 September, to 2,283,907 (49.7% of the vote). With Karzai securing less than 50% of the vote, a second round of polling between Karzai and the second highest-polling candidate, Dr Abdullah Abdullah, was scheduled to take place on 7 November. However, following the withdrawal from the proceedings of Abdullah, who insisted that the vote would be neither free nor fair, on 2 November the IEC cancelled the run-off election and declared Karzai to be President for a second term.

MELI SHURA
(National Assembly)

Meshrano Jirga
(House of Elders)

The Meshrano Jirga, the upper house of the Meli Shura, comprises 102 members (three times the number of provinces in Afghanistan). One-third are elected by provincial councils (for a four-year term), one-third by district councils (for a three-year term) and the remaining members are nominated by the President (for a five-year term). The Constitution requires that one-half of the members nominated by the President must be women.

Speaker: ABDUL RAUF IBRAHIMI.

Wolasi Jirga
(House of Representatives)

The Wolasi Jirga, the lower house of the Meli Shura, comprises 249 directly elected members, all of whom serve a five-year term. Sixty-eight seats are reserved for women. The most recent election was held on 18 September 2010. In mid-January 2011 a Supreme Court special tribunal, established to investigate allegations of widespread electoral fraud, recommended postponing for one month the inauguration of the lower house. However, following intense opposition to the measure, the new Wolasi Jirga was sworn in on 26 January.

Speaker: ABDUL RAUF IBRAHIMI.

Election Commission

Independent Election Commission of Afghanistan (IEC): IEC Compound, Jalalabad Rd, Paktia Kot, POB 979, Kabul; tel. (75) 2035203; e-mail info@iec.org.af; internet iec.org.af; established by 2004 Constitution; appointed by the President; functions performed by Joint Electoral Management Body (JEMB) during transitional period of govt; following elections to the Wolasi Jirga and provincial councils in 2005, the JEMB was dissolved and the IEC assumed regulation and supervision of all election activities from 2006; Chair. FAZAL AHMAD MANAWI; Chief Electoral Officer ABDULLAH AHMADZAI.

Political Organizations

In September 2003 a new law allowing the formation of political parties was approved. In early 2012 more than 80 parties were registered with the Ministry of Justice, including the following:

Afghan Mellat (Afghan Social Democratic Party): National Bank Club, 3rd Floor, Nader Pashtoon Jadah, Kabul; tel. 70224793 (mobile); e-mail afghanmellat2@yahoo.com; f. 1966; Pres. Prof. Dr ANWAR-UL-HAQ AHADI; a breakaway faction, led by AJMAL SHAMS gained official recognition in 2007 (internet www.afghanmillat.org).

Da Afghanistan Da Solay Ghorzang Gond (Afghanistan Peace Movement): Kolola Poshta (adjacent to Dost Hotel), Kabul; tel. 799311523 (mobile); Leader SHAHNAWAZ TANAI.

Harakat-i Islami i Afghanistan (Islamic Movement of Afghanistan): St 4, Qala-i Fathullah, Shar-i-Nau, Kabul; tel. 799343998 (mobile); Leader SAYYED MOHAMMAD ALI JAWED.

Hizb-i Adalat-i Islami Afghanistan (Islamic Justice Party of Afghanistan): nr Aryub Cinema, Bagh-e-Bala, District 4, Kabul; tel. 799566386 (mobile); f. 2001; Leader MOHAMMAD KABIR MARZBAN.

Hizb-i Afghanistan-i Naween (New Afghanistan Party): 1st Rd, Khair Khana Phase One, Parwan Hotel Rd, District 11, Kabul; tel. 799342942 (mobile); f. 2005; Leader YOUNIS QANOONI.

Hizb-i Hambastagi-yi Melli-yi Jawanan-i Afghanistan (National Youth Solidarity Party of Afghanistan): House 2, St 3, Haji Yaqub Sq., towards Shaheed, Kabul; tel. 799424290 (mobile); f. 2004; Leader MOHAMMAD JAMIL KARZAI.

Hizb-i Haq wa Edalat (Right and Justice Party): Kabul; f. 2011; multi-ethnic; in early 2012 the party was awaiting registration and was administered by a 53-mem. interim council.

Hizb-i Harakat-i-Islami Mardum-i Afghanistan (Islamic Movement Party of the People of Afghanistan): Rd 2–3, Qala-i-Fathullah, Kabul; tel. 799183484 (mobile); f. 2004; Leader Al-Hajj SAYYED HUSSAIN ANWARI.

Hizb-i Harakat-i-Melli Wahdat-i-Afghanistan (National Movement for the Unity of Afghanistan): Jamia Mosque, 6th Floor, Karte 4, District 3, Kabul; tel. 70204847 (mobile); f. 2004; Chair. MOHAMMAD NADIR ATASH.

Hizb-i Islami Afghanistan (Islamic Party of Afghanistan): Area A, Khushal Mena, Kabul; tel. 799421474 (mobile); Pashtun/Turkmen/Tajik; breakaway faction of Hizb-i Islami org., est. to participate in parliamentary politics; nature of relationship with Gulbuddin Hekmatyar's proscribed Hizb-i Islami org. is unclear; Chair. ABDUL HADI ARGHANDIWAL; Leader KHALID FAROOQI.

Hizb-i Isteqlal-i Afghanistan (Freedom Party of Afghanistan): Khair Khana, nr Al-Farooq Healthcare Clinic, Kabul; tel. 799333448 (mobile); f. 2004; Leader Dr GHULAM FAROOQ NAJRABI.

Hizb-i Jumhuri-i Khwahan-i Afghanistan (Republican Party of Afghanistan): Zainaba St, 6th Rd, Qala-i-Fathullah, Kabul; tel. 70275107 (mobile); f. 2003; supporter of presidential system of govt; Leader SEBGHATULLAH SANGAR; c. 35,000 mems.

Hizb-i Junbesh-i Melli-i Islami (National Islamic Movement): St 4, Rd 15, Wazir Akbar Khan, Kabul; tel. 70511511 (mobile); f. 1992; formed mainly from troops of fmr Northern Command of the Afghan army; predominantly Uzbek/Tajik/Turkmen/Ismaili and Hazara Shi'a; Leader SAYED NOORULLAH; 65,000–150,000 supporters.

Hizb-i Kar wa Tawse'ah Afghanistan (Labour and Progress of Afghanistan Party): Karte 4, Rd 2, Kabul; tel. 70293176 (mobile); f. 1999 in Pakistan; fmrly known as the National Reconciliation Party; Leader ZULFIQAR OMID.

Hizb-i Nizat-i Azady Wa Demokrasi-ye Afghanistan (Movement for Democracy and Freedom in Afghanistan): Karte 4, adjacent to Suraya Lycee, Kabul; tel. 70281953 (mobile); f. 2004; Leader ABDUL RAQIB JAWED KOHESTANI.

Hizb-e Paiwand-e Melli-ye Afghanistan (National Solidarity Party of Afghanistan): Western Rd, Taimani Sq., Kabul; tel. 799182016 (mobile); predominantly Ismaili supporters; Leader SAYYED MANSUR NADERI.

Hizb-i Sahadat-i Mardum-i-Afghanistan (Welfare Popular Party of Afghanistan): Apt 1, Block 13, Air Force Blocks, Kabul; tel. 70204847 (mobile); f. 1998; Leader MOHAMMAD ZUBAIR PAYROZ.

Hizb-i-Wahdat-i Islami Afghanistan (Islamic Unity Party of Afghanistan): opp. Hawzeh 3 Police, Karte 4, Kabul; tel. 796358868 (mobile); e-mail info@wahdat.net; internet www.wahdat.net; f. 1989; Leader MOHAMMAD KARIM KHALILI.

Hizb-i Wahdat-i Islami Mardum-i Afghanistan (People's Islamic Unity Party of Afghanistan): House 3, Mohammadia St, Tapa-i-Salaam, Karte Sakhi, Kabul; tel. 70278276 (mobile); represents Hazaras; advocate of equal rights, freedom and social justice; Leader Haji MUHAMMAD MOHAQEQ.

Hizb-i Wahdat-i Melli-i Afghanistan (National Unity Party of Afghanistan): Qaisar Market, 2nd Floor, adjacent to Gul-i-Surkh Hotel, Old Kolola Poshta Sq., Kabul; tel. 799210998 (mobile); Leader ABDUL RASHID JALILI.

Jamiat-i Islami (Islamic Society): Karte Parwan, Phase 2, Badaam Bagh; tel. 70278950 (mobile); f. 1967; Turkmen/Uzbek/Tajik; Leaders MUHAMMAD ISMAEL KHAN, Gov. ATTA MUHAMMAD NUR; Chair. SALAHUDDIN RABBANI (acting); Gen. Sec. MUHAMMAD NASIM FAQIRI; c. 60,000 supporters.

Kangra-i Melli Afghanistan (National Congress of Afghanistan): Kabul; tel. 70290067 (mobile); e-mail mcnafghan@hotmail.com; internet mouv.national.afghan.free.fr; f. 2004; Leader ABDUL LATIF PEDRAM.

Mahaz-i-Melli-i-Islami (National Islamic Front): Malalai Wat, Interior Ministry Rd, Kabul; tel. 70204265 (mobile); Pashtun; Leader SAYED AHMAD GAILANI; Dep. Leader HAMED GAILANI; c. 15,000 supporters.

Nizat-i Hambastagi Melli (National Solidarity Movement): St 6, Taimani, Kabul; tel. 799300045 (mobile); Chair. Pir SAYED ISHAQ GAILANI.

Nizat-i Melli-i Afghanistan (National Movement of Afghanistan): St 1, Taimani, Kabul; tel. 70277938 (mobile); f. 2002; Leader AHMAD WALI MASOUD.

Tanzim-i Dawat-i Islami (Organization for Invitation to Islam): Ansari Sq., Rd 1, District 4, Kabul; tel. 70277007 (mobile); Pashtun; fmrly Ittihad-i Islami; name changed as above 2005; Leader Prof. ABDUL RASUL SAYEF.

There are, in addition, a number of influential opposition coalitions, including:

Jabhe-ye-Motahed-e-Milli (National Front of Afghanistan): internet www.jabhaemelli.com; f. 2007; informal political grouping incl. fmr mems of United Front; advocates parliamentary system of govt rather than presidential system; fmrly known as the United National Front; relaunched as above in late 2011 following the assassination of fmr Chair. Burhanuddin Rabbani; mems incl. Younis Qanooni, Gen. Abdul Rashid Dostam and Muhammad Mohaqeq; Chair. Prof. AHMAD ZIA MASOUD.

National Coalition of Afghanistan: Kabul; internet www.nca.af; f. 2010 as Omid wa Taghir (National Coalition of Hope and Change); expanded and renamed, as above, Dec. 2011; advocates transition to a fully parliamentary system of government; Leader Dr ABDULLAH ABDULLAH.

The following political organizations have been proscribed:

Hizb-i Islami Gulbuddin (Islamic Party Gulbuddin): originally est. as Hizb-i Islami in the mid-1970s to oppose the Soviet-backed communist regime; known as Hizb-i Islami Gulbuddin following a split in the org. around 1979; played a prominent role in the *mujahidin* guerrilla war against Soviet forces during 1980s, while based in North-West Frontier Province, Pakistan; engaged in violent power struggle between various *mujahidin* factions 1992–96; latterly, launched a campaign of violent opposition to the International Security Assistance Force and the Government of Hamid Karzai; has reportedly formed alliances with al-Qa'ida and the Taliban; promotes establishment of an Islamic state in accordance with Qu'ran, Sunnah and Shari'a doctrines; Leader GULBUDDIN HEKMATYAR.

Hizb-i Islami Khalis (Islamic Party Khalis): f. c. 1979, following a split in the Hizb-i Islami movt; Pashtun; Islamist; based in Nangarhar Province; est. by MAULVI MUHAMMAD YUNUS KHALIS (died 2006); current activities uncertain.

Taliban: emerged in 1994; Islamist fundamentalist; mainly Sunni Pashtuns; in power 1996–2001; also active in the Federally Administered Tribal Areas of Pakistan; Leader Mullah MOHAMMAD OMAR; c. 25,000 active supporters.

Diplomatic Representation

EMBASSIES IN AFGHANISTAN

Australia: Kabul; Ambassador PAUL FOLEY; (the Australian mission operates from a number of locations that, due to security reasons, are not publicly disclosed).

Bulgaria: St 15, Wazir Akbar Khan, Kabul; tel. (20) 2103148; fax (20) 2101089; e-mail bgembkabul@yahoo.com; internet www.mfa.bg/kabul; Ambassador VALERIY ARZHENTINSKI.

Canada: House 256, St 15, Wazir Akbar Khan, POB 2052, Kabul; tel. 799742800 (mobile); fax 799742805 (mobile); e-mail kabul@international.gc.ca; internet www.afghanistan.gc.ca/canada-afghanistan; Ambassador WILLIAM CROSBIE.

China, People's Republic: Sardar Shah Mahmoud Ghazi Wat, Kabul; tel. (20) 2102545; fax (20) 2102728; e-mail chinaemb_af@mfa.gov.cn; Ambassador XU FEIHONG.

Czech Republic: House 337, Rd 10, Wazir Akbar Khan, Kabul; tel. 798417418 (mobile); e-mail kabul@embassy.mzv.cz; internet www.mzv.cz/kabul; Ambassador PETR PELZ.

Denmark: House 35–36, Rd 13, Lane 1, Wazir Akbar Khan, Kabul; tel. (20) 2304545; fax (20) 2302838; e-mail kblamb@um.dk; internet www.ambkabul.um.dk; Ambassador RENÉ DINESEN.

Egypt: Road 15, Wazir Akbar Khan, Kabul; tel. 794500515 (mobile); e-mail egypt_kabul@mfa.gov.eg; Ambassador MAGED ABDUL REHMAN.

Finland: House 39, St 10, Lane 1, Wazir Akbar Khan, Kabul; tel. (20) 2103051; e-mail sanomat.kab@formin.fi; internet www.finland.org.af; Ambassador PAULI JÄRVENPÄÄ.

France: Cherpour Ave, Shar-i-Nau, POB 62, Kabul; tel. 799327238 (mobile); e-mail chancellerie.kaboul-amba@diplomatie.gouv.fr; internet www.ambafrance-af.org; Ambassador BERNARD BAJOLET.

Germany: Zanbaq Sq., Wazir Akbar Khan, Mena 6, POB 83, Kabul; tel. (20) 2101512; fax (4930) 50007518 (Germany); e-mail regl@kabu.auswaertiges-amt.de; internet www.kabul.diplo.de; Ambassador RÜDIGER KÖNIG.

Hungary: c/o Embassy of the Federal Republic of Germany, Zanbaq Sq., Wazir Akbar Khan, Mena 6, POB 83, Kabul; tel. 797035375 (mobile); e-mail huembkbl@gmail.com; Ambassador KÁROLY PEIMLI.

India: Malalai Wat, Shar-i-Nau, Kabul; tel. (20) 2200185; fax 763095561 (mobile); e-mail embassy@indembassy-kabul.com; internet meakabul.nic.in; Ambassador GAUTAM MUKHOPADHAYA.

Indonesia: Interior Ministry St, Shar-i-Nau, POB 532, Kabul; tel. (20) 2201066; fax (20) 2201735; e-mail kbrikabul@neda.af; internet www.kabul.deplu.go.id; Ambassador Brig.-Gen. ERMAN HIDAYAT.

Iran: Charahi Shir Pur, Kabul; tel. (20) 2101393; fax (20) 2101397; e-mail kabul@mfa.gov.ir; internet kabul.mfa.gov.ir; Ambassador FADA HOSSEIN MALEKI.

Italy: Great Masoud Rd, Wazir Akbar Khan, Kabul; tel. and fax (20) 2103144; e-mail ambasciata.kabul@esteri.it; internet www.ambkabul.esteri.it; Ambassador LUCIANO PEZZOTTI.

Japan: St 15, Wazir Akbar Khan, Kabul; tel. 799363827 (mobile); fax 761218272 (mobile); e-mail plt1@eoj-af.org; internet www.afg.emb-japan.go.jp; Ambassador REIICHIRO TAKAHASHI.

Kazakhstan: House 11, 1st Alley, Indira Gandhi St, Wazir Akbar Khan, Kabul; tel. (20) 2300960; e-mail kazembkb@multinet.af; Ambassador Maj.-Gen. OMIRTAI BITIMOV.

Korea, Republic: House 34, St 10, Wazir Akbar Khan, Kabul; tel. (20) 2102481; fax 762728481 (mobile); e-mail kabul@mofat.go.kr; internet afg.mofat.go.kr; Ambassador AHN SEONG-DOO.

Netherlands: Malalai Wat, Interior Ministry Rd, Shar-i-Nau, Kabul; tel. 700286641 (mobile); e-mail kab@minbuza.nl; internet www.mfa.nl/kab-en; Ambassador RADINCK VAN VOLLENHOVEN.

New Zealand: St 15 Roundabout, Wazir Akbar Khan, Kabul; tel. 700102000 (mobile); e-mail mea@mfat.govt.nz; Ambassador JUSTIN FEPULEAI (designate).

Norway: St 15, Lane 4, Wazir Akbar Khan, Kabul; tel. 701105000 (mobile); fax 701105090 (mobile); e-mail emb.kabul@mfa.no; internet www.norway.org.af; Ambassador TORE HATTREM.

Pakistan: 10 Nijat Wat Rd, Wazir Akbar Khan, Kabul; tel. (20) 2300911; fax (20) 2300912; e-mail embassy@pakembassykbl.com; internet www.mofa.gov.pk/afghanistan; Ambassador MOHAMMAD SADIQ.

Poland: House 2, Sarake Shora, Karte 3, Kabul; tel. 798292170 (mobile); e-mail kabul.amb.sekretariat@msz.gov.pl; internet www.kabul.polemb.net; Ambassador MACIEJ LANG.

Russia: Darulaman Wat, Ayub Khan Mena, Kabul; tel. (20) 2500255; fax 762743497 (mobile); e-mail rusembafg@multinet.af; internet www.afghanistan.mid.ru/en; Ambassador ANDREI AVETISYAN.

Saudi Arabia: Shah Darak, Kabul; tel. (20) 2102064; e-mail ksa_kemb@hotmail.com; Ambassador MANSOUR BIN SALEH ALSAFI.

Spain: Main St, Lane 3, Shir Pur, Kabul; tel. (20) 2203787; e-mail emb.kabul@maec.es; internet www.maec.es/subwebs/embajadas/kabul; Ambassador JUAN JOSÉ RUBIO DE URQUÍA.

Sweden: MoI St, Opp. the MoI, Shar-e Naw, Kabul; tel. (20) 2104912; fax (20) 2104913; e-mail ambassaden.kabul@foreign.ministry.se; internet www.swedenabroad.com/Start____81558.aspx; Ambassador TORBJÖRN PETTERSON.

Tajikistan: House 41, St 15, Wazir Akbar Khan, Kabul; tel. (20) 2300541; fax (20) 2300392; e-mail kabultj@tojikistan.com; Ambassador IMOMOV SHAROFIDDIN.

Turkey: House 134, 13 Shah Mahmoud Ghazi Khan St, Kabul; tel. (20) 2101581; fax (20) 2101579; e-mail turkemb.kabul@mfa.gov.tr; internet kabil.be.fscnet.net; Ambassador BASAT ÖZTÜRK.

Turkmenistan: House 280, St 13, Lane 3, Wazir Akbar Khan, Kabul; tel. (20) 2300541; e-mail kabulemb@neda.af; Ambassador ATAJAN MOVLAMOV.

United Arab Emirates: Charahi Zambak, Wazir Akbar Khan, Kabul; tel. 799003555 (mobile); e-mail uaemkbl@hotmail.com; Ambassador YUSOUF SAIF KHAMES AL-ALI.

United Kingdom: St 15 Roundabout, Wazir Akbar Khan, POB 334, Kabul; tel. 700102000 (mobile); fax 700102250 (mobile); e-mail britishembassy.kabul@fco.gov.uk; internet ukinafghanistan.fco.gov.uk; Ambassador Sir RICHARD STAGG (designate).

USA: Great Masoud Rd, Wazir Akbar Khan, Kabul; tel. 700108001 (mobile); fax (20) 2300546; e-mail usambassadorkabul@state.gov; internet kabul.usembassy.gov; Ambassador RYAN C. CROCKER.

Uzbekistan: House 14, St 13, Wazir Akbar Khan, Kabul; tel. (20) 2300124; e-mail mirnodir@hotmail.com; Ambassador PARVEZ MIRIYEVICH ALIYEV.

Judicial System

The new Constitution that was introduced in early 2004 made no specific reference to the role of *Shari'a* but stated that Afghan laws should not contravene the main tenets of Islam. The Constitution made provision for the creation of a Supreme Court (Stera Mahkama) as the highest judicial organ in Afghanistan. The Court was inaugurated shortly after the Meli Shura (National Assembly) was officially opened on 19 December 2005.

The Supreme Court comprises nine members, including the Chief Justice, who are appointed by the President, subject to the approval of the Wolasi Jirga (House of Representatives).

Supreme Court: Masood Sq., Kabul; tel. (20) 2300359; e-mail info@supremecourt.gov.af; internet www.supremecourt.gov.af.

Chief Justice: ABDUL SALAM AZIMI.

Attorney-General: MUHAMMAD ISHAQ ALOKO.

Religion

The official religion of Afghanistan is Islam. Muslims comprise 99% of the population, approximately 84% of them of the Sunni sect and the remainder of the Shi'ite sect. There are small minority groups of Hindus, Sikhs and Jews.

ISLAM

The High Council of Ulema and Clergy of Afghanistan: Kabul; f. 1980; 7,000 mems; Head Maulvi QIAMUDDIN KASHAF (acting).

The Press

Many newspapers and periodicals stopped appearing on a regular basis or, in a large number of cases, ceased publication during the civil war. Following the defeat of the Taliban in late 2001, a number of newspapers and periodicals resumed publication or were established for the first time. By early 2005 more than 250 publications had been registered with the then Ministry of Information and Culture.

PRINCIPAL DAILIES

Anis (Friendship): 3rd Floor, Azadi Printing Press Bldg, Microrayon 2, Kabul; tel. (20) 2301342; e-mail anisdaily@yahoo.com; f. 1927; evening; Dari and Pashto; state-owned; news and literary articles; Editor-in-Chief MOHAMMAD QASIM SOROSH; circ. 5,000.

Arman-e Melli (Hope of the Nation): 4 Muslim St, Shar-i-Nau, Kabul; tel. 700282673 (mobile); internet www.armanemili.af; f. 2002 by the Afghan Interim Authority; now independent; Dari and Pashto; Editor-in-Chief MIR HAYDAR MOTAHAR; circ. 4,200.

Cheragh Daily (Light): 112 Shar-i-Nau, Dist. 10, Kabul; tel. 700220222 (mobile); e-mail cheragh_daily@yahoo.com; f. 2004; Dari, Pashto and English; independent; Editor-in-Chief KATRINE WADA; circ. 17,000.

The Daily Afghanistan: Karta-e-Seh, House 263, St 4, District 6, Kabul; tel. 777005019 (mobile); e-mail mail@outlookafghanistan.com; internet www.dailyafghanistan.com; f. 2006; owned by the Afghanistan Group of Newspapers; Dari and Pashto; Editor-in Chief MAHMOUD HAKIMI; circ. 7,000.

Daily Outlook Afghanistan: St 1, Pul-e-Surkh, Kartai Seh, Dist. 3, Kabul; tel. (20) 2501306; e-mail outlookafghanistan@gmail.com; internet outlookafghanistan.net; f. 2004; publ. of the Afghanistan Group of Newspapers; English; Editor-in-Chief Dr HUSSAIN ALI YASA.

Erada (Intention): Nr Cinema Barikot, Dehmazang, Dist. 2, Kabul; tel. 700244384 (mobile); e-mail eradadaily@hotmail.com; f. 2000 as weekly in Pakistan; relaunched as daily in Afghanistan 2002; independent; Dari and Pashto; Editor-in-Chief KHADEM AHMAD.

Eslah (Reform): Azadi Printing Press, 4th Floor, Microrayon Part II, Kabul; e-mail islahdaily@yahoo.com; f. 1921; Dari and Pashto; state-owned; Editor-in-Chief SHAMSOLHAQ ARIANFAR.

Hasht-e Subh (Daily 8 AM): House 384, St 5, Kartai Seh, Kabul; tel. 799037083 (mobile); e-mail afghanistan_8am@yahoo.com; internet www.8am.af; f. 2006; Dari and Pashto; publ. in Kabul, Mazar-e-Sharif, Herat, Bamiyan, Baghlan, Kunduz, Takkar, Badakshan, Jowzjan, Jalalabad and Ghazni; Publr SANJER SOHAIL.

Hewad (Homeland): Azadi Press Centre, Microrayon,Dist. 16, Kabul; tel. (20) 2302130; f. 1949; Pashto and Dari; state-owned; Editor-in-Chief NAJIBULLAH SHINWARI; circ. 5,000.

Jahan-e-Naw (New World): Mazar-i-Sharif; Editor QAYOUM BAABAK.

Kabul Times: Macrorayon Azadi Printing Press, Kabul; tel. (20) 2301675; e-mail thekabultimes@yahoo.com; f. 1962 as Kabul Times, renamed Kabul New Times in 1980; ceased publication in 2001; revived in 2002 under new management; English; state-owned; Editor-in-Chief MOHAMMAD SHAFIQ AHMAD ZAI.

Mandegar Daily: tel. 799336075 (mobile); e-mail mandegardaily@gmail.com; internet mandegardaily.af; Dari; Editor-in-Chief NAZARI PARIANI.

Rah-e Nejat: Kabul; tel. 706747184 (mobile); e-mail info@rahenejat.com; internet www.rahenejatdaily.com; fmrly weekly, daily from 2005; Dari and Pashto; independent; Editor-in-Chief SAYED MOHAMMAD ALEMI.

Sarnavesht Daily: Kabul; Editor ASADULLAH WAHEEDI.

Tolo-e Afghan: Qandahar; e-mail afghan.tolo@yahoo.com; Pashto and Dari; Editor-in-Chief JANAN MOMIN.

Weesa Daily: House 11, St 9, Hesa-e-Du, Kartai Parwan, Dist. 4, Kabul; tel. 799878224 (mobile); internet www.dailyweesa.com; f. 2006; Dari and Pashto; Editor-in-Chief FAZAL ELAHI SHAFIQI; 5,000.

PERIODICALS

Afghan Scene: House 3, St 12, Wazir Akbar Khan, Kabul; tel. 799321010 (mobile); e-mail info@afghanscene.com; internet www.afghanscene.com; f. 2005; monthly; English; free magazine; owned by MOBY Group; Editor SAAD MOHSENI.

Aina-e Zan (Women's Mirror): House 26, Muslim Wat, Shahr-i-Nau, Dist. 10, Kabul; tel. 700281864 (mobile); e-mail womensmirror@hotmail.com; f. 2002; weekly; women's; Dari, Pashto and English; Chief Editor SHUKRIA BARAKZAI; circ. 3,000.

Eqtedar-e Melli: POB 4024, Kartai Char, University Rd, Kabul; tel. 799348791 (mobile); e-mail eqtedaremelli@yahoo.com; internet www.eqmweekly.com.af; f. 2002; weekly; Dari and Pashto; Editor SEYED MOHAMMAD ALI REZVANI.

Farda (Tomorrow): POB 1758, Kabul; tel. (20) 2100199; fax (20) 2100699; e-mail farda-news@yahoo.com; weekly; Publr ABDUL GHAFUR AITEQAD; circ. 4,000.

Killid (The Key): House 442, St 6, Chardehi Watt, Kabul; tel. (20) 2500717; fax (20) 2200574; e-mail info@tkg.af; internet www.tkg.af; weekly; current affairs; Editor SEDIQULLAH BADR; circ. 25,000.

Malalai: Afghan Visual Communication Institute, Malik Ashgar Crossroads, Kabul; internet www.ainaworld.org; f. 2002; monthly; women's; Dari, Pashto and English; publ. of Aïna humanitarian org.; Chief Editor JAMILA MUJAHID; circ. 3,000.

Mursal: House 442, St 6, Chardehi Watt, Kartai Seh, Kabul; tel. (20) 2500717; fax (20) 2200574; e-mail info@tkg.af; internet www.tkg.af/english/divisions/publishing/mursal-weekly; f. 2003; weekly; women's issues; Pashto and Dari; circ. 15,000.

Les Nouvelles de Kaboul (Kabul News): Afghan Visual Communication Institute, Malik Ashgar Crossroads, Kabul; tel. 70286215 (mobile); e-mail dimitri.beck@ainaworld.org; internet www.ainaworld.org; f. 2002; monthly; Dari, Pashto and French; publ. of

Aïna humanitarian org.; Chief Editor DIMITRI BECK; Propr and Dir SHAFIQA HABIBI.

Parvaz (Flight): Afghan Visual Communication Institute, Malik Ashgar Crossroads, Kabul; e-mail communication@ainaworld.org; internet www.ainaworld.org; f. 2002; Dari and Pashto; every two months; children's; Editor CLAUDINE BOEGLIN; circ. 25,000.

Payam-e-Mujahid (Holy Warrior's Message): POB 5051, Kabul; e-mail payamemojahed@yahoo.com; internet www.payamemojahed.com; f. 1996; weekly; Dari and Pashto; sponsored by the Northern Alliance; Editor ABDUL HAFIZ MANSOOR.

Roz (The Day): Kabul; internet www.rozmagazine.com; f. 2002; monthly; women's; Dari, Pashto, French and English; Editor-in-Chief LAILOMA AHMADI.

Sada-e-Azadi: Kabul; e-mail newspaper@sada-e-azadi.net; internet sada-e-azadi.net; bi-weekly; run by the International Security Assistance Force; English, Dari and Pashto.

Takhassos (Experts): Jadai Baghi Azadi, Herat; tel. 70280258 (mobile); monthly; Dari; published by Council of Professionals.

Zanbil-e-Gham: Afghan Visual Communication Institute, Malik Ashgar Crossroads, Kabul; f. 1997; monthly; satirical; Editor OSMAN AKRAM; circ. 2,000.

NEWS AGENCIES

Afghan Islamic Press (AIP): POB 520, GPO, Peshawar, North-West Frontier Province, Pakistan; tel. (91) 5701100 (Peshawar); fax (91) 5842544 (Peshawar); e-mail info@afghanislamicpress.com; internet www.afghanislamicpress.com; f. 1982; English and Pashto.

Bakhtar News Agency (BNA): Ministry of Communications and Information Technology, Mohammad Jan Khan Wat, Kabul; tel. 700202282 (mobile); e-mail info@bakhtarnews.com.af; internet www.bakhtarnews.com.af; f. 1939; govt news agency; correspondents in 32 provinces; English, Dari and Pashto; Dir-Gen. KHALIL MENAVI.

Pajhwok Afghan News: House 130/138, St 8, Taimani, Kabul; tel. (20) 2201814; fax (20) 2201813; e-mail feedback@pajhwok.com; internet www.pajhwok.com; f. 2004; independent; eight regional bureaux incl. Mazar-i-Sharif, Qandahar, Herat and Jalalabad; news service provided in English, Pashto and Dari; Dir and Editor-in-Chief DANISH KAROKHEL; Man. Editor FARIDA NEKZAD.

Wakht News Agency: Darul Aman Rd, Kabul; internet www.wakht.af; f. 2008; private news agency; correspondents in 34 provinces; Dari, Pashto and English; Dir RAHIMULLAH SAMANDER.

PRESS ASSOCIATIONS

Afghanistan Independent Journalists' Association (AIJA): 6th District, Darulaman Wat, opposite Habibia High School, Karta Seh, Kabul; tel. 752001623 (mobile); f. 2003; Pres. ABDULHAMID MUBAREZ.

Afghanistan Journalists Center (AFJC): Bagh-e-Azadi, 2 Baghmorad St, Herat; tel. 798816124 (mobile); e-mail info@afjc.af; internet afjc.af; f. 2009; licensed by the Ministry of Information and Culture; fmrly known as Center for Support of Journalists of Afghanistan, renamed as above 2011; publishes statements and studies on the status of Afghan media, job opportunities and freedom of the press; Dir AHMAD QURAISHI.

Publishers

Afghanistan Today Publishers: c/o The Kabul Times, Ansari Wat, POB 983, Kabul; tel. (20) 61847; e-mail www.afghanistan-today.org; publicity materials; answers enquiries about Afghanistan.

Ariana Press: Poli Jarkhi, Kabul; under the supervision of the Ministry of Information and Culture; Dir ABDUL KADER.

Azady (Freedom) Press: Azady Printing Press Bldg, 2nd Microrayon, Dist. 16, Kabul; tel. (20) 2100113; under supervision of the Ministry of Information and Culture; Dir MOHAMMAD RUSTAM ASHRAFI.

Beihagi Publishers: Azady Press Centre, Microrayon, Dist. 9, Kabul; tel. (20) 2302361; f. 1964; books on Afghan culture; also prints information related to the Govt and its plans; Dir FAIZULLAH MUHTAJ.

Book Publishing Institute: Qandahar; f. 1970; supervised by Government Printing House; mainly books in Pashto language.

Danish Press: Milli Market, opp. Marwarid Hotel, Kolola Poshta St, Kabul; tel. 93700639383 (mobile); e-mail danish2k2000@yahoo.com; internet www.danishpress.com; publishes dictionaries, translated works, guides and magazines; Dir ASADULLAH DANISH.

Educational Publications: Ministry of Education, Mohammad Jan Khan Wat, Kabul; tel. and fax (20) 200000; textbooks for primary and secondary schools in the Pashto and Dari languages; also three monthly magazines in Pashto and in Dari.

Historical Society of Afghanistan: Kabul; tel. (20) 30370; f. 1931; mainly historical and cultural works and two quarterly magazines: *Afghanistan* (English and French), *Aryana* (Dari and Pashto); Pres. AHMAD ALI MOTAMEDI.

International Center for Pashto Studies: Kabul; f. 1975 by the Afghan Govt with the assistance of UNESCO; research work on the Pashto language and literature and on the history and culture of the Pashtun people; Pres. and Assoc. Chief Researcher J. K. HEKMATY; publs *Pashto* (quarterly).

Kabul University Press: Kabul; tel. (20) 42433; f. 1950; textbooks; two quarterly scientific journals in Dari and in English, etc.

Research Center for Linguistics and Literary Studies: Afghanistan Academy of Sciences, Akbar Khan Mena, Kabul; tel. (20) 26912; f. 1978; research on Afghan languages (incl. Pashto, Dari, Balochi and Uzbek) and Afghan folklore; publs *Kabul* (Pashto), *Zeray* (Pashto weekly) and *Khurasan* (Dari); Pres. Prof. MOHAMMED R. ELHAM.

Shah M. Book Co: 12 Charahi Sadarat, Kabul 111; tel. (20) 2101569; e-mail info@shahmbookco.com; internet www.shahmbookco.com; f. 1974; books on Afghan history, economics, sciences, fine arts, religion and various other topics; Man. Dir IRAJ MUHAMMAD RAIS.

GOVERNMENT PUBLISHING HOUSE

Government Printing House: Kabul; tel. (93) 26851; f. 1870; under supervision of the Ministry of Communications and Information Technology; Dir SAID AHMAD RAHAA.

PUBLISHERS' ASSOCIATION

Afghan Libraries' and Publishers' Association: Chari Ansari, between Ansari Crossroads and Popo Lano Restaurant, Kabul.

Broadcasting and Communications

TELECOMMUNICATIONS

At the end of 2001 telecommunications services in Afghanistan were severely limited: outside the capital, Kabul, access to fixed-line services was negligible, while mobile telephone services were virtually non-existent throughout the country. The first mobile service provider, the Afghan Wireless Communication Co, was launched in 2002. In 2005 the Government approved the establishment of privately owned, independent telecommunications companies. By 2011 the mobile telephone market had expanded to 16.2m. users, with a penetration rate of some 61% of the population.

Afghanistan Telecom Regulatory Authority (ATRA): Ministry of Communications and Information Technology, MOC Headquarters Tower, 10th Floor, Mohammad Jan Khan Wat, Kabul; tel. (20) 2101179; fax (20) 2103700; e-mail z.hamidy@atra.gov.af; internet www.atra.gov.af; succeeded Telecom Regulatory Board; Chair. ABDUL WAKIL SHIRGUL.

Afghan Telecom (AfghanTel): Post Parcel Bldg, 4th Floor, Mohammad Jan Khan Wat, Kabul; tel. 752012345 (mobile); e-mail info@afghantelecom.af; internet www.afghantelecom.af; f. 2004; state-owned; provides wireless and digital fixed-line services; 80% of shares offered for sale in March 2008; Dir AMIRZAI SANGIN.

Afghan Wireless Communication Co (AWCC): Khuja Mullah, nr Hajari Najari Bus Station, Darulaman Wat, Kabul; tel. and fax 70830830 (mobile); e-mail info@afghanwireless.com; internet www.afghan-wireless.com; f. 2002; jt venture between the Ministry of Communications and Information Technology (20% ownership) and Telephone Systems International, Inc of the USA (80% ownership); reconstruction of Afghanistan's national and international telecommunications network; covers 95 major cities and towns; 1.3m. subscribers (July 2007); Chair. EHSAN BAYAT.

Etisalat Afghanistan: Ehsan Plaza, Shar-i-Nau, POB 800, Kabul; tel. 786786786 (mobile); e-mail info@etisalat.af; internet www.etisalat.af; commenced operations in Afghanistan in 2007; GSM operator; 100% owned by Etisalat UAE; 3m. subscribers (June 2010); CEO AHMED ALHOSANI.

MTN Afghanistan: House 35, Moslem St, Shar-i-Nau, POB 700, Central Post Office, Kabul; tel. 772222779 (mobile); internet www.mtn.com.af; provides mobile telecommunications services; fmrly Areeba, renamed as above in 2008; CEO HASSAN JABER.

Telecom Development Co Afghanistan Ltd (Roshan): Roshan Shop, St 13, off Main St, Wazir Akbar Khan, Kabul; tel. 799971333 (mobile); e-mail roshanca@roshan.af; internet www.roshan.af; f. 2002 by an international consortium comprising the Aga Khan Fund for Economic Development (AKFED), French cos Monaco Telecom International (MTI) and Alcatel, and US co MCT Corpn; 51% owned by AKFED, 36.75% by MTI and 12.25% by MCT Corpn; provides mobile telecommunications services; CEO KARIM KHOJA.

Wasel Telecom Co: House 33, Charahy Kamal Nabezada, Azizabad St, POB 06, Mazar-e-Sharif; tel. 750999888 (mobile); internet www.wasel.af; since 2007, licensed to provide voice and internet services in northern Afghanistan via CDMA technology; CEO MOHAMMAD GUL KHOLMI.

BROADCASTING

In 2009 Reporters Without Borders estimated that about 15 television stations and more than 100 privately owned radio stations were in operation. By 2011 there were 42 radio stations and 30 terrestrial television stations broadcasting in Kabul.

Radio

Radio-Television Afghanistan: St 10, Lane 2, Wazir Akbar Khan, POB 544, Kabul; tel. (20) 2101086; e-mail rta_afg@yahoo.com; internet rta.org.af; state broadcaster; revived in 2001; programmes in Dari, Pashto, Turkmen and Uzbek; Dir-Gen. MUHAMMAD ZAREEN ANZUR; Head of Radio GHULAM HASSAN HAZRATI.

Balkh Radio and TV: Mazar-i-Sharif; Pashto and Dari; Chair. ABDORRAB JAHED.

Radio Azadi: Kabul; c/o Radio Free Europe/Radio Liberty, Inc, Vinohradská 159A, 110 00 Prague 10, Czech Republic; internet pa.azadiradio.org; f. 1985 as Radio Free Afghanistan; service resumed and renamed as above 2002; outlet of Radio Free Europe/Radio Liberty (USA—based in the Czech Republic); Pashto, Dari; broadcasts 12 hours daily; Dir AKBAR AYAZI.

Radio Kabul: Ansari Wat, Kabul; tel. (20) 2101087; f. 1940; Dir GHULAM HASSAN HAZRATI.

Independent

Arman FM: POB 1045, Central Post Office, Kabul; tel. 799222229 (mobile); e-mail armanfm98.1@gmail.com; internet www.arman.fm; f. 2003; Afghanistan's first privately owned independent FM radio station; broadcasts in Kabul, Mazar-i-Sharif, Herat, Qandahar and Jalalabad; broadcasts popular music and culture 24 hours a day; Dari and Pashto; part of the Moby Media Group; Dir SAAD MOHSENI.

Radio Bakhtar: Kabul; e-mail info@bakhtarradio.com; internet bakhtarradio.com; live Afghan folk and alternative music.

Radio Killid: The Killid Group House 442, St 6, Chardehi Wat, nr Uzbekha Mosque, Karta Seh, Kabul; tel. (20) 2500717; fax (20) 2200574; e-mail info@tkg.af; internet www.tkg.af; f. 2003 by Development and Humanitarian Services for Afghanistan; broadcasts 24 hours daily; stations in Kabul, Mazar, Kandahar, Jelalabad, Ghazni, Khost and Herat; Chair. SHAHIR ZAHINE; Man. NAJIBA AYUBI.

Radio Rabia Balkhi: Mazar-i-Sharif; tel. 700656464 (mobile); e-mail info@rrb.af; internet rrb.af; f. 2003; broadcasts aimed at women in Balkh province; Head WAHEED SULTANI.

Radio Sahar: Herat; f. 2003; Dari; women's; broadcasts 12 hours daily; Dir HULAN KHATIBI; Station Man. HUMAIRA HABIB.

Radio Sharq: Jalalabad; e-mail info@sharq.radio-connect.af; internet www.sharq.radioconnect.af; f. 2003; broadcasts 12 hours daily.

Radio Tiraj Mir: Pol-e-Khomri; f. 2003; broadcasts 16 hours daily.

Voice of Afghan Women: Kabul; f. 2003; relaunched in 2005 following closure owing to lack of funds; dedicated to interests of women; Dir JAMILA MUJAHID.

Television

Radio-Television Afghanistan: see Radio.

Balkh Radio and TV: see Radio.

Herat TV: Herat; state-owned.

Kabul TV: Kabul; revived in 2001; broadcasts four hours daily; Dir HUMAYUN RAWI.

Independent

1 TV (Yak TV): 17 Wazir Akbar Khan, Kabul; e-mail info@1tvmedia.com/; internet www.1tvmedia.com; f. 2010; privately owned; entertainment-based programmes, hourly news broadcasts and periodicals on Islamic doctrine; Dari and Pashto; Dir FAHIM HASHIMI.

Afghan TV: Kabul; tel. (37) 99257750; e-mail afghantv1@gmail.com; internet www.afghantv.af; f. 2004; broadcasts 24 hours daily; CEO AHMED SHAH AFGHANZAI.

Ayna (Mirror): Shebarghan; f. 2003; broadcasts to Jawzjan, Sar-e Pol and Balkh provinces and to the bordering areas of Turkmenistan and Uzbekistan; entertainment, news and political propaganda; mainly in Uzbek; Pres. ABDUL RASHID DOSTUM.

Ariana Radio and Television Network: 318 Darulaman Wat, Kabul; tel. 700111000 (mobile); e-mail feedback@arianatelevision.com; internet arianatelevision.com; broadcasts to 34 provinces in Afghanistan, as well as Europe, the USA, Canada and the Middle East; f. 2005; Chair. EHSANULLAH BAYAT.

Lemar TV: House 3, St 12, Wazir Akbar Khan, Kabul 1000; tel. 799321010 (mobile); e-mail info@lemar.tv; internet www.lemar.tv; f. 2006; broadcasts in Pashto, Dari, English and Urdu; part of the Moby Media Group; Man. LAL AQA SHIRZAD.

Noorin TV: St 4, Silo, Kabul; tel. 786606010 (mobile); e-mail info@noorintv.net; internet www.noorintv.net; f. 2007; privately owned; has coverage in 34 provinces; also operates a radio station; Dir MOHAMMAD ARIF NOORI.

Saba TV: House 47, St 2, Pul-e-Sorkh, Karte 3, POB 475, Kabul; tel. 752023756 (mobile); fax 752023757 (mobile); f. 2008; features two channels; accessible through satellite, covering 11 provinces; Man. ZAINAB NADIRI.

Shamshad TV: Chaman Huzuri, nr Ghazi Stadium, Kabul; tel. 799322129 (mobile); internet www.shamshadtv.com; f. 2006; broadcasts 24 hours daily; mainly in Pashto; Dir FAZAL KARIM FAZAL.

Tamadon TV: St 1, Kartai Chahar, Dist 3, Kabul; tel. (20) 2500434; internet www.tamaddon.tv; live entertainment-based programmes.

Tolo TV: POB 225, Central Post Office, Kabul; tel. 799321010 (mobile); e-mail info@tolo.tv; internet tolo.tv; f. 2004; commercial station; broadcasts news, current affairs, entertainment, lifestyle and culture programmes in Dari and Pashto; launched Afghanistan's first 24-hour news satellite channel, Tolo News, in July 2010; part of the Moby Media Group; Dir SAAD MOHSENI; Head (Tolo News) MUJAHID KAKAR.

Zhwandoon TV (Life TV): Kabul; internet www.zhwandoon.tv; f. 2011; Pashto; Dir ISMAIL YOON.

Finance

(cap. = capital; res = reserves; dep. = deposits; m. = million; brs = branches; amounts in afghanis unless otherwise stated)

BANKING

In September 2003 the President approved a law allowing foreign banks to open branches in Afghanistan. By 2009 there were 17 licensed commercial banks operating in Afghanistan, of which six were branches of foreign banks.

Central Bank

Da Afghanistan Bank (Central Bank of Afghanistan): Ibne Sina Wat, Kabul; tel. (20) 2104146; fax (20) 2100305; e-mail info@centralbank.gov.af; internet www.centralbank.gov.af; f. 1939; cap. and res 27,891m., dep. 82,950m. (March 2010); main functions: banknote issue, modernize the banking system, re-establish banking relations with international banks, create a financial market system, foreign exchange regulation, govt and private depository; granted complete independence in September 2003; Gov. NOORULLAH DILAWARI; 47 brs.

Other Banks

Afghan United Bank: Turabaz Khan Watt, Shar-i-Nau, POB 425, Kabul; tel. (20) 2203836; fax (20) 2203837; e-mail info@aub.af; internet www.afghanunitedbank.com; f. 2007; cap. 875.758m., dep. 11,580m. (Dec. 2010); Chair. FAZAL AHMAD JOYA; CEO SHAHZAD HAIDER YOUSAFZAI; 14 brs.

Afghanistan International Bank: Haji Yaqoob Sq., Shahabudin Watt, Shar-i-Nau, POB 2074, Kabul; tel. (20) 2550255; fax (20) 2550256; e-mail info@aib.af; internet www.aib.af; f. 2004; established and managed by the ING Institutional and Government Advisory Group (Netherlands) on behalf of a consortium of Afghan and US investors; 75% owned by Afghan nationals, 25% owned by Asian Development Bank; cap. 1,465m., res 6m., dep 29,940m. (Dec. 2011); CEO KHALILULLAH SEDIQ; 23 brs.

Azizi Bank: Zambaq Sq., opp. Turkish Embassy, Main Rd, Kabul; tel. 799700900 (mobile); e-mail customercare@azizibank.af; internet www.azizibank.com; f. 2006; cap. US $58.8m., dep. 502m. (Dec. 2010); Pres. and CEO INAYATULLAH FAZLI; Gov. MIRWAIS AZIZI; 63 brs.

Bank-e-Millie Afghan (Afghan National Bank): Jade Ibne Sina, POB 522, Kabul; tel. (20) 2102221; fax (20) 2101801; e-mail info@bma.com.af; internet www.bma.com.af; f. 1933 as private bank, nationalized in 1976; Chair. KHAN AFZAL HADAWAL; 27 brs.

BRAC Afghanistan Bank: Charahi Turabaz Khan, Zarghona Maidan, Shar-i-Nau, Kabul; tel. 708274092 (mobile); fax (20) 2203870; e-mail info@bracafbank.com; internet www.bracafbank.com; f. 2006; cap. 379m., dep. 327m. (Dec. 2010); business with retail sector and small and medium-sized enterprises; managed by a Bangladeshi team; Chair. FAZLE HASAN ABED; four brs.

Export Promotion Bank of Afghanistan: Park-e-Timor Shahi, Kabul; tel. (20) 2100284; fax (20) 2103947; e-mail epbafghan@yahoo.com; f. 1976; provides financing for exports and export-orientated investments; state-owned; operations suspended under Taliban rule in 1996–2001; CEO ABDUL HAMEED MOHIBBI; three brs.

First Micro Finance Bank (FMFB): Plot No 174, Ashraf Watt, 2nd St, Ansari Sq., Shar-i-Nau, Kabul; tel. (20) 2201733; e-mail info@fmfb.com.af; f. 2004; 51% owned by Aga Khan Agency for Microfinance, 32% by Kreditanstalt fur Wiederaufbau, 17% by International Finance Corpn; provides sustainable financial services to the poor in order to contribute to poverty alleviation and economic development; CEO MUSLIM UL-HAQ.

Ghazanfar Bank: 866/A, Wazir Akbar Khan, Kabul; tel. (20) 2101111; e-mail info@ghazanfarbank.com; internet ghazanfarbank.com; f. 2009; cap. 667.6m., dep. 3,797.9m. (Dec. 2010); conducts business under conventional and Islamic banking systems; CEO RAVINDER SINGH YADAV; Dir HAJI MOHAMMED ISMAIL GHAZANFAR.

Maiwand Bank: Charahi Turabaz Khan, Shar-i-Nau, Kabul; tel. 752004000 (mobile); e-mail info@maiwandbank.com; internet www.maiwandbank.com; f. 2009; provides Islamic banking services; cap. US $15m.; Chair. and Man. Dir FRAIDOON NOORZAD; Pres. and CEO P. V. V. RAMA RAJU; 33 brs.

New Kabul Bank: 10–42 Turabaz Khan, Shar-i-Nau, Kabul; tel. 700222666 (mobile); e-mail info@newkabulbank.af; internet www.kabulbank.af; f. 2004 as Kabul Bank; in 2010 heavy losses and allegations of financial irregularities resulted in state intervention in the administration of the bank; restructured and renamed, as above, in 2011; cap. 27m., res 68m., dep. 976m. (Dec. 2009); CEO MASOOD KHAN MUSA GHAZI; 68 brs.

Pashtany Bank: Mohammad Jan Khan Watt, Kabul; tel. (20) 2105550; fax (20) 2102905; e-mail info@pashtanybank.com; internet www.pashtanybank.com; f. 1955 to provide short-term credits, forwarding facilities, opening letters of credit, purchase and sale of foreign exchange; nationalized in 1975; Pres. and CEO GUL MAQSOOD SABIT; 22 brs.

Banking Association

Afghanistan Banks Association (ABA): 718, St No 13, Lane 3, Wazir Akbar Khan, Kabul; tel. 799852497 (mobile); e-mail contact@aba.org.af; internet www.aba.org.af; f. 2004; represents 17 local and commercial banks; Gen. Sec. NAJIBULLAH AMIRI.

INSURANCE

In mid-2006 the Afghanistan Insurance Authority was established by the Ministry of Finance; the Commission was to oversee the development of the insurance sector within Afghanistan.

Afghan National Insurance Co: Second Ave, Kartai Parwan, nr fmr British Embassy, POB 329, Kabul; tel. and fax (20) 2200189; fax (20) 2200189; e-mail insuranceafghan@yahoo.com; f. 1964; government-owned; mem. of Asian Reinsurance Corpn; marine, aviation, fire, motor and accident insurance; Pres. AHMAD SHAH ALIZAI; Claims Man. S. OMAR SHIRZAD.

Insurance Corporation of Afghanistan (ICA): Naser Khusraw Balkhi Bldg, Charrahi Sarsabai, Taimani, Kabul; tel. 798242455 (mobile); e-mail info@icaaf.com; internet www.icaaf.co; f. 2007; privately owned; aviation, banking, construction, mining and accident insurance; Chair. LEONARD DELUNAS; CEO SADAT M. NADERI.

Trade and Industry

GOVERNMENT AGENCIES

Afghanistan Investment Support Agency (AISA): opposite Ministry of Foreign Affairs, Kabul; tel. (20) 2103404; fax (20) 2103402; e-mail invest@aisa.org.af; internet www.aisa.org.af; f. 2003; promotes and regulates domestic and foreign investment in the private sector; Pres. and CEO NOORULLAH DELAWARI.

Afghanistan Reconstruction and Development Services (ARDS): 4th and 5th Floors, Ministry of Economy Bldg, Malik Asghar Sq, Kabul; tel. 799385712 (mobile); e-mail ards.procurement@ards.org.af; internet www.ards.gov.af; f. 2003; co-ordination of procurement activities and recruitment of technical staff for govt ministries.

Export Promotion Agency of Afghanistan (EPAA): off Karte Char 2nd St, Kabul; tel. (20) 2504837; e-mail info@epaa.org.af; internet www.epaa.org.af; f. 2006; provides guidance for traders, collects and disseminates trade information; CEO AHMAD JAWED.

CHAMBERS OF COMMERCE AND INDUSTRY

Afghan Chamber of Commerce and Industries (ACCI): Chaman-e-Huzuri, next to Kabul Nendari, Kabul; tel. 700296771 (mobile); e-mail info@acci.org.af; internet www.acci.org.af; f. 1931; privately owned; merged with Afghanistan International Chamber of Commerce; Chair. ABDUL HOSSAIN FAHEEM; CEO MOHAMMAD QURBAN HAQJO.

Federation of Afghan Chambers of Commerce and Industry: Darulaman Wat, Kabul; f. 1923; includes chambers of commerce and industry in Ghazni, Qandahar, Kabul, Herat, Mazar-i-Sharif, Fariab, Jawzjan, Kunduz, Jalalabad and Andkhoy.

INDUSTRIAL AND TRADE ASSOCIATIONS

Afghan Carpet Exporters' Guild: POB 3159, Darulaman Wat, Kabul; tel. 70224575 (mobile); f. 1967; non-profit, independent organization of carpet manufacturers and exporters; Pres. ZIAUDDIN ZIA; c. 1,000 mems.

Afghanistan Builders Association: House 7, St 1, Kart-i-Si, Kabul; tel. 700224822 (mobile); e-mail aba@aba.af; internet www.aba.af; f. 2004; Pres. NAEEM YASSIN.

Afghanistan Karakul Institute: Puli Charkhi, POB 506, Kabul; tel. (20) 61852; f. 1967; exporters of furs; Pres. G. M. BAHEER.

Animal Products Trading and Industrial Association: Ayub Khan Mina, South of Habibia High School, 2nd St, Darulaman Wat, Kabul; tel. and fax 752023490 (mobile); e-mail mohsin_ataie@yahoo.com; f. 1979; promotes and exports animal products, incl. wool and animal skins; Chief Officer M. MOHSIN ATAIE.

TRADE UNIONS

Afghanistan National Union of Journalists: f. 2006; formed through merger of Afghanistan Gen. Union of Journalists, Free Journalist Union of Afghanistan and Nat. Union of Afghan Journalists; Pres. SAYYID HUSSAIN FAZIL SANCHARAKI.

All Afghanistan Federation of Trade Unions (AAFTU): Karte Nau, First St, Kabul; tel. 799340196 (mobile); Chair. Dr LIAQUAT ADIL.

Lawyers Union of Afghanistan (LUA): Apt 1, 2nd Floor, Iqbal Amiri Plaza, Airport Hwy, Kabul; tel. 752004342 (mobile); e-mail lawyers_union@yahoo.com; Pres. Prof. GUL RAHMAN.

National Union of Afghanistan Employees (NUAE): POB 756, Kabul; tel. (20) 23040; internet www.nuae.info; f. 1978 as Central Council of Afghanistan Trade Unions, to establish and develop the trade union movement; name changed in 1990; composed of seven vocational unions; 300,000 mems; Pres. of Cen. Council MOHAMMAD QASIM EHSAS; Vice-Pres. ASAD KHAN NACEIRY.

Transport

RAILWAYS

At the end of the 20th century there were no active railways in Afghanistan. Since 2002 the Afghan Government and its international partners have initiated various projects to develop a rail network, with the aim of establishing the country as a major regional transportation hub. In early 2007 construction began on a 202-km railway line, funded by the Iranian Government, from Torbat Heidarieh, Iran, to Herat. In early 2009 Iran announced that it would help to construct a 1,200-km rail link from Herat to the Sher Khan Bandar crossing, in north-eastern Afghanistan, at the border with Tajikistan. Work was scheduled to be completed within five years. Plans to connect Andkhoy, in Faryab Province, with the rail network of Turkmenistan were finalized in mid-2011. In early 2012 cargo services commenced on a 75-km railway connecting the northern town of Mazar-i-Sharif with Hairatan, on the border with Uzbekistan. The project was completed with assistance from the Asian Development Bank. A further expansion of the network, to connect the Mazar-i-Sharif–Hairatan line with Kabul and Torkham, on the border with Pakistan, was planned.

ROADS

In 2006 there were an estimated 42,150 km of roads, of which more than 70% were unpaved. All-weather highways link Kabul with Qandahar and Herat in the south and west, Jalalabad in the east, and Mazar-i-Sharif and the Amu-Dar'ya (Oxus) river in the north. A massive reconstruction programme of the road system in Afghanistan began in 2002. The Salang Highway was rehabilitated, thus reconnecting Kabul with the north. By late 2004 the reconstruction of the important 482-km highway linking Kabul and Qandahar had been completed. In 2005 Afghanistan, Iran and Uzbekistan signed an agreement concerning construction of a trans-Afghan transportation corridor, a 2,400-km road that would link the Uzbek city of Termez and the Iranian port of Bandar Abbas with Mazar-i-Sharif and Herat. Construction of a bridge across the Amu-Dar'ya river, linking Sher Khan Bandar in Kunduz province with Tajikistan, was completed in 2007. Reconstruction of the 557-km highway linking Qandahar and Herat was completed in 2009. The Asian Development Bank (ADB), through its Central Asia Regional Economic Cooperation (CAREC) initiative, provides substantial financing for the development of Afghanistan's road and rail networks. In early 2011 the ADB provided US $340m. to fund the construction of 233-

km road connecting the towns of Qaisar, Bala Murghab and Laman in north-western Afghanistan, which will form the final part of a 2,700-km national ring-road system connecting major cities including Kabul, Kandahar, Herat and Mazar-i-Sharif.

Afghan Container Transport Company Ltd (ACTCO): House 43, St 2, Shar-i-Nau, POB 3165, Kabul; tel. 70214666 (mobile); e-mail kabul@afghancontainers.com; internet www.afghancontainers.com; f. 1974; Vice-Pres. Ali Dad Beigh Zad.

AFSOTR: Kabul; tel. (20) 2102358; e-mail afsotr@svt.ru; founded as Afghan Soviet Transportation Company; resumed operations in 1998; transport co; 90 vehicles.

Milli Bus Enterprise: Ministry of Transport and Civil Aviation, Ansari Wat, Kabul; tel. (20) 2101032; state-owned; 900 buses; Pres. Eng. Aziz Naghaban.

INLAND WATERWAYS

There are 1,200 km of navigable inland waterways, including the Amu-Dar'ya (Oxus) river, which is capable of handling vessels of up to about 500 dwt. River ports on the Amu-Dar'ya are linked by road to Kabul.

CIVIL AVIATION

In 2011 there were two international airports in Afghanistan, at Kabul and Qandahar, four major domestic airports, at Herat, Jalalabad, Mazar-i-Sharif and Kunduz, and numerous regional domestic airports. Plans were under way to relocate and upgrade the airport at Kabul and to upgrade the airports at Herat, Mazar-i-Sharif and Jalalabad to international standards.

Ariana Afghan Airlines: POB 76, Kabul; tel. 752041013 (mobile); e-mail info@flyariana.com; internet www.flyariana.com; f. 1955; merged with Bakhtar Afghan Airlines Co Ltd in 1985; state-owned; flights to India, Germany, the Middle East and Russia; Pres. and CEO Capt. Moin Khan Wardak.

KamAir: Kabul Business Centre, Shar-i-Nau, Kabul; tel. (20) 2200447; e-mail info@flykamair.com; internet www.flykamair.com; f. 2003; privately owned; domestic and regional flights; Pres. Zamaria Kamgar.

Safi Airways: Quai-e-Markaz, Shar-e-Naw, nr Kabul City Centre, Kabul; tel. (20) 2222222; fax (20) 2202058; e-mail info@safiairways.aero; internet www.safiairways.aero; f. 2006; privately owned; international flights, scheduled and charter passenger services; Chair. Ghulam Hazrat Safi; Exec.-Dir Hamid Safi.

Tourism

Afghanistan's potential tourism attractions include: Bamian, with its thousands of painted caves; Bandi Amir, with its suspended lakes; the Blue Mosque of Mazar; Herat, with its Grand Mosque and minarets; the towns of Qandahar and Girishk; Balkh (ancient Bactria), 'Mother of Cities', in the north; Bagram, Hadda and Surkh Kotal (of interest to archaeologists); and the high mountains of the Hindu Kush. Furthermore, ruins of a Buddhist city (known locally as Kaffir Got—'Fortress of the Infidels') dating from the second century were discovered in July 2002 in a remote valley in southern Afghanistan. The restoration of cultural heritage, sponsored by UNESCO, began in 2002. In 1998 an estimated 4,000 tourists visited Afghanistan and receipts from tourism amounted to around US $1m.

Afghan Tour Organization (ATO): Asmaie Wat, next to National Gallery, Kabul; tel. 752016907 (mobile); e-mail jamalharoun@yahoo.fr; internet afghan-tours.com; f. 1958; Pres. Mohammad Zaher Ghauss.

Defence

Following the defeat of the Taliban in late 2001, an International Security Assistance Force (ISAF) was deployed in Kabul and at Bagram airbase to help maintain security in the area. In August 2003 the North Atlantic Treaty Organization (NATO) assumed command of the force and in December NATO began to expand its presence in the country by assuming command of a number of Provincial Reconstruction Teams (PRTs) in the north and west of Afghanistan. ISAF was also responsible for the training of the first battalion of the Afghan National Guard, which became operational in April 2003. By October 2006 ISAF, numbering some 30,000 troops from more than 35 countries, had assumed control of international military operations throughout Afghanistan. Four committees were established in January of that year to accelerate the disarmament of private armies and to establish a new multi-ethnic Afghan National Army (ANA) and Afghan National Police (including a border police contingent and an élite national civil order unit). In January 2010 the Joint Coordination and Monitoring Board, composed of representatives of the Afghan Government and various international bodies, agreed to increase the size of the ANA from the existing total of around 97,000 to 171,600 by the end of 2011. The Board stated that the Afghan authorities aimed to expand the country's security forces to 240,000 troops and 160,000 police officers by 2015. In July 2010, at a major international conference in Kabul, President Karzai announced that his Government aimed to restore full control of the country's security to the Afghan armed forces and police by 2014. The first phase of the transition of security responsibilities to the Afghan authorities commenced in July 2011, with the handover of seven NATO-held areas to Afghan control. Meanwhile, in June President Obama announced that 10,000 US forces were to leave Afghanistan by the end of the year, with a further 23,000 scheduled to depart by the end of 2012 and all remaining foreign forces to withdraw in 2014. As assessed at November 2011, while undergoing rapid expansion, the ANA had 165,700 troops. In the same month, the strength of the Afghan Air Force was 5,000 while the Afghan National Police numbered 136,100.

Defence Expenditure: Domestic budgetary expenditure on defence totalled an estimated 4,330m. afghanis in 2012.

Chief of Staff of the Afghan National Army: Gen. Sher Mohammad Karimi.

Education

Before the Taliban rose to power in 1996, primary education began at seven years of age and lasted for six years. Secondary education, beginning at 13 years of age, lasted for a further six years. As a proportion of the school-age population, the total enrolment at primary and secondary schools was equivalent to 36% (males 49%; females 22%) in 1995. Following their seizure of power, the Taliban banned education for girls over the age of eight, closed all the women's institutes of higher education and drew up a new Islamic curriculum for boys' schools. UNICEF reported that by December 1998 about 90% of girls and 66% of boys were not enrolled in school.

After the Taliban regime was defeated in late 2001, the Afghan Government, with the help of foreign governments, UNICEF and humanitarian organizations, began to rehabilitate the education system. By 2003/04 the boy-girl ratio in education had returned to pre-Taliban levels. However, female attendance varied significantly throughout the country and the attendance of girls at schools in parts of southern and eastern Afghanistan remained very low. In the mid-2000s the Afghan Ministry of Education, assisted by UNICEF, launched an initiative to establish community-based education, in order to provide basic educational opportunities for those with no access to formal schools. By 2011 3,843 community-based schools had been created, attended by approximately 125,000 children. According to statistics issued by the Afghan Ministry of Education, by 2011 the number of children enrolled in primary and secondary levels of education had increased to some 7.3m. (of whom 38% were girls), compared to about 1m. in 2001; although around 4.2m. children of school age (at least 60% of whom were girls) remained outside the education system. During the same period (2001–11) more than 9,000 new schools had been established. According to UNESCO, the total enrolment at primary and secondary schools in 2009/10 was equivalent to an estimated 74% (males 89%; females 57%) of children in the relevant age-groups.

Higher education was disrupted by the departure of many teaching staff from Afghanistan during more than 20 years of civil war. In 1991 there were six institutions of higher education (including Kabul University, which was founded in 1931) in Afghanistan. Kabul University reopened for men and women in March 2002. In 2008 there were an estimated 50,000 students enrolled in tertiary institutions in Afghanistan. By 2011 there were 17 institutions of higher education operating under the supervision of the Ministry of Higher Education. In 2011 there were 98 technical and vocational schools attended by an estimated 26,000 students (of whom 16% were females).

In 2003 UNESCO and the Afghan Transitional Authority launched a major project to boost literacy rates throughout Afghanistan. In that year an estimated 57% of men and 86% of women were illiterate in Afghanistan. According to UNICEF, in 2011 literacy rates in Afghanistan remained among the lowest in the world: 61% of all adults (aged 15 or older) and 87% of women were deemed illiterate.

ALBANIA

Introductory Survey

LOCATION, CLIMATE, LANGUAGE, RELIGION, FLAG, CAPITAL

The Republic of Albania lies in south-eastern Europe. It is bordered by Montenegro to the north, by Kosovo to the north-east, by the former Yugoslav republic of Macedonia (FYRM) to the east, by Greece to the south and by the Adriatic and Ionian Seas (parts of the Mediterranean Sea) to the west. The climate is Mediterranean throughout most of the country. The sea plays a moderating role, although frequent cyclones in the winter months make the weather unstable. The average temperature is 14°C (57°F) in the north-east and 18°C (64°F) in the south-west. The language is Albanian, the principal dialects being Gheg (north of the Shkumbin river) and Tosk, which is spoken in the south and has been the official dialect since 1952. Islam is the predominant faith, but there are small groups of Christians (mainly Catholic in the north and Eastern Orthodox in the south). The national flag (proportions 5 by 7) is red, with a two-headed black eagle in the centre. The capital is Tirana (Tiranë).

CONTEMPORARY POLITICAL HISTORY

Historical Context

On 28 November 1912, after more than 400 years of Turkish rule, Albania declared its independence under a provisional Government. Although the country was occupied by Italy in 1914, its independence was re-established in 1920. Albania was declared a republic in 1925 and Ahmet Beg Zogu was elected President; proclaimed King Zog I in 1928, he reigned until he was forced into exile by the Italian occupation of Albania in April 1939. Albania was united with Italy for four years, before being occupied by German forces in 1943; the Germans withdrew one year later.

The communist-led National Liberation Front (NLF), established in 1941, was the most successful wartime resistance group and took power on 29 November 1944. Elections in December 1945 were contested by only communist candidates. The new regime was headed by Enver Hoxha, the leader of the Albanian Communist Party (ACP). King Zog was declared deposed, and the People's Republic of Albania was proclaimed on 11 January 1946. The ACP was renamed the Party of Labour of Albania (PLA) in 1948, the NLF having been succeeded by the Democratic Front of Albania (DFA) in 1945.

The communist regime developed close relations with Yugoslavia until the latter's expulsion from the Cominform (a Soviet-sponsored body co-ordinating the activities of European communist parties) in 1948. Albania, fearing Yugoslav expansionism, became a close ally of the USSR and joined the Moscow-based Council for Mutual Economic Assistance (CMEA) in 1949. Hoxha resigned as Head of Government in 1954, but retained effective national leadership as First Secretary of the PLA. Albania joined the Warsaw Treaty Organization (Warsaw Pact) in 1955, but relations with the USSR deteriorated when Soviet leaders attempted a rapprochement with Yugoslavia. The Albanian leadership declared its support for the People's Republic of China in the Sino–Soviet ideological dispute, prompting the USSR to suspend relations with Albania in 1961. Albania established increasingly close relations with China, ended participation in the CMEA in 1962 and withdrew from the Warsaw Pact in 1968. However, following the improvement of relations between China and the USA after 1972, and the death of Mao Zedong, the Chinese leader, in 1976, Sino-Albanian relations progressively deteriorated. In 1978 Albania declared its support for Viet Nam in its dispute with China, prompting the Chinese Government to suspend all economic and military co-operation with Albania.

A new Constitution was adopted in December 1976, and the country was renamed the People's Socialist Republic of Albania. In December 1981 Mehmet Shehu, the Chairman of the Council of Ministers (Prime Minister) since 1954, was shot dead. Although officially reported to have committed suicide, there were suggestions of a leadership struggle with Hoxha, and subsequent allegations that he had been executed. Following the death of Shehu, a new Government, headed by Adil Çarçani, hitherto the First Deputy Chairman, was established. In November 1982 Ramiz Alia replaced Haxhi Lleshi as the head of state, as President of the Presidium of the Kuvendi Popullor (People's Assembly). A number of former state and PLA officials were reportedly executed in September 1983.

Hoxha died in April 1985, and was succeeded as First Secretary of the PLA by Alia. In March 1986 Hoxha's widow, Nexhmije, was elected to the chairmanship of the General Council of the DFA. Alia was re-elected as First Secretary of the PLA and as President of the Presidium of the Kuvendi Popullor in November 1986 and February 1987, respectively. In the latter month Çarçani was reappointed Chairman of the Council of Ministers.

In November 1989 an amnesty for certain prisoners (including some political prisoners) was declared. From December a number of anti-Government demonstrations were reportedly staged, particularly in the northern town of Shkodër. In January 1990 Alia announced proposals for limited political and economic reform, including the introduction of a system of multi-candidate elections (although the leading role of the PLA was to be maintained). The judicial system was reorganized, the number of capital offences considerably reduced, the practice of religion (prohibited since 1967) again tolerated, and Albanians were granted the right to foreign travel. Following renewed unrest in July more than 5,000 Albanians took refuge in foreign embassies, and were subsequently granted permission to leave the country. Meanwhile, the membership of both the Council of Ministers and the Political Bureau of the PLA had been reorganized. In December 1990 it was announced that the establishment of independent political parties was to be permitted, prior to elections to the Kuvendi Popullor, scheduled for February 1991. None the less, there was further unrest in several cities in mid-December 1990. Nexhmije Hoxha resigned from the chairmanship of the General Council of the DFA, and was replaced by Çarçani (who was, in turn, replaced in mid-1991).

Domestic Political Affairs

On 20 February 1991, following widespread anti-Government demonstrations, Alia declared presidential rule. An eight-member Presidential Council and a provisional Council of Ministers was established. Çarçani was replaced as Chairman of the Council of Ministers by Fatos Nano, a liberal economist, who had been appointed Deputy Chairman in late January. In late February the unrest finally ended. Following opposition pressure, elections were postponed until the end of March. In mid-March a general amnesty for all political prisoners was declared. The first round of the multi-party legislative elections took place on 31 March, with second and third ballots on 7 and 14 April, respectively. The PLA and affiliated organizations won 169 of the 250 seats, while the Democratic Party of Albania (DPA) secured 75 seats and the Democratic Union of the Greek Minority (OMONIA) five seats. The victory of the PLA, amid allegations of electoral malpractice, prompted dismay in some urban areas, where support for the DPA had been strong. Widespread protests ensued, and in Shkodër security forces opened fire on demonstrators, killing four.

In April 1991 an interim Constitution replaced that of 1976, pending the drafting of a new constitution. The country was renamed the Republic of Albania, and the post of executive President, to be elected by two-thirds of the votes cast in the Kuvendi Popullor, was created. Alia was subsequently elected to the new post, defeating the only other candidate, Namik Dokle, also of the PLA; opposition deputies abstained from voting. In May 1991 Nano was reappointed Chairman of the Council of Ministers. In accordance with the provisions of the interim Constitution, Alia resigned from the leadership of the PLA. In June a continuing general strike forced the resignation of Nano's administration. A subsequent Government of National Stability included representatives of the PLA, the DPA, the Republican Party of Albania (RPA), the Social Democratic Party (SDP) and the Agrarian Party of Albania (APA). Ylli Bufi became Chairman of the Council of Ministers, while Gramoz Pashko, a prominent member of the DPA, was appointed Deputy Chairman and Minister of the Economy. At a party congress later in June, the PLA was renamed the Socialist Party of Albania (SPA). In December the Chairman of the DPA, Sali Berisha, announced the withdrawal of the seven party representatives from the coalition Government, which, following the dismissal of three RPA ministers, forced the resignation of Bufi's administration. Pending elections, Alia appointed an interim Government of non-party 'technocrats', under a new Prime Minister, Vilson Ahmeti.

A new electoral law, approved by the legislature in February 1992, reduced the number of deputies in the Kuvendi Popullor from 250 to 140. Under provisions that defined legitimate political parties, organizations that represented ethnic minorities, such as OMONIA, were prohibited from contesting the forthcoming general election, prompting widespread protests from the Greek minority. At the general election, conducted in two rounds on 22 and 29 March, the DPA secured 92 of the 140 seats, the SPA 38, the SDP seven, the Union for Human Rights Party (UHRP—supported by the minority Greek and Macedonian communities) two and the RPA one seat. Following the resignation of Alia, the new Kuvendi Popullor elected Berisha to the presidency on 9 April. Berisha subsequently appointed a coalition Government dominated by the DPA, with Aleksander Meksi, of that party, as Prime Minister. The SDP and the RPA were each allocated one ministerial portfolio. In July the DPA secured 43% of the votes cast at multi-party local elections, while the SPA received 41%. In September divisions within the DPA resulted in the defection of a number of prominent party members, who formed a new political grouping, the Democratic Alliance Party (DAP).

During 1992–93 a number of former communist officials were arrested on various charges of corruption and abuse of power. Nexhmije Hoxha was imprisoned for nine years in January 1993, having been convicted of embezzling state funds. (She was released in January 1997.) In August Ahmeti was sentenced to two years' imprisonment. Despite an international campaign on his behalf, organized by the SPA, in April 1994 Nano (by this time Chairman of the SPA) was convicted of the misappropriation of state funds during his premiership in 1991, and was sentenced to 12 years' imprisonment. In July 1994 Alia was sentenced to nine years' imprisonment, but was released in 1995.

In October 1994 a draft Constitution was finally presented to Berisha, and was submitted for endorsement at a national referendum, after it failed to obtain the requisite two-thirds' majority approval in the Kuvendi Popullor. As a result of Berisha's support for the draft Constitution (which was to vest additional powers in the President), the referendum was widely perceived as a vote of confidence in his leadership. At the referendum, which took place on 6 November, with the participation of 84.4% of the electorate, the draft Constitution was rejected by 53.9% of the voters, precipitating demands for a general election. In December Berisha effected an extensive reorganization of the Council of Ministers. The RPA, which held only one seat in the Kuvendi Popullor, withdrew from the governing coalition. The SDP split into two factions; of these, only a new grouping, the Union of Social Democrats, remained in the coalition. In March 1995 the Chairman of the DPA, Eduard Selami, who had accused Berisha of abuse of power, was removed from his post.

In September 1995 the Kuvendi Popullor adopted legislation prohibiting those in power under the former communist regime from holding public office until 2002 (thereby banning a large number of prospective candidates, including incumbent SPA deputies, from contesting legislative elections in 1996). In November 1995 a parliamentary commission initiated an inquiry, following the discovery of a mass grave near the border town of Shkodër. Families of the deceased urged the prosecution service to initiate charges against former members of the communist regime, including Alia, who had allegedly been responsible for the killing by border guards of nationals attempting to flee the country in 1990–92; Alia was detained in February 1996. Meanwhile, in December 1995 the Kuvendi Popullor approved legislation requiring senior civil servants to be investigated for their activities under the communist regime. In December 14 prominent former members of the communist regime were arrested on charges of involvement in the execution, internment and deportation of citizens. (In May 1996 three of the former officials received death sentences, which were later commuted to terms of imprisonment, while the remaining defendants received custodial sentences.)

The first round of the legislative elections took place on 26 May 1996. Following alleged electoral irregularities, the principal opposition parties, including the SPA, the SDP and the DAP, withdrew from the poll and announced their rejection of the election results. A subsequent demonstration by the SPA was violently dispersed by the security forces. The second round of the elections took place on 2 June; as a result of opposition demands for a boycott, only 59% of the electorate participated in the poll (compared with 89% in the first round). According to official results, the DPA secured 101 of the 115 directly elected seats (25 seats were to be allocated on the basis of proportional representation). However, international observers, who included representatives of the Organization for Security and Co-operation in Europe (OSCE, see p. 388), formerly the Conference on Security and Co-operation in Europe (CSCE), reported that widespread malpractice and intimidation of voters had been perpetrated, and urged the Government to conduct fresh elections, while SPA deputies staged a hunger strike in protest at the results. Berisha rejected the allegations, but agreed to conduct further elections in 17 constituencies. With the principal opposition parties continuing their electoral boycott, the DPA won all the seats contested in the partial elections, held on 16 June, and secured a total of 122 of the 140 elective seats. The SPA won 10 of the remaining seats, while the UHRP and the RPA each secured three and the National Front two. (The SPA, however, began a boycott of the new legislature.) In early July Meksi, who had been reappointed to the office of Prime Minister, formed a new Council of Ministers. In August the Government established a permanent Central Election Commission (CEC), prior to proposed local government elections. Despite continued division within the SPA, Nano (who remained in prison) was re-elected as Chairman at a party congress in late August. In local government elections, which took place in two rounds in October, the DPA secured the highest number of votes in 58 of the 65 municipalities and in 267 of the 305 communes. Although the OSCE had withdrawn its observers, monitors from the Council of Europe (see p. 256) declared that, despite some irregularities, the elections had been conducted fairly.

Civil uprising

In January 1997 the collapse of several popular 'pyramid' financial investment schemes, resulting in huge losses of individual savings, prompted violent anti-Government demonstrations, particularly in Tirana and the southern town of Vlorë. It was widely believed that members of the Government were associated with the pyramid schemes, which had allegedly financed widespread illegal activities; legislation was subsequently adopted prohibiting the schemes. In late January the Kuvendi Popullor granted Berisha emergency powers to restore order. Several people were reported to have been killed in ensuing violent clashes between security forces and protesters. None the less, on 3 March Berisha was re-elected unopposed by the Kuvendi Popullor for a second five-year term.

Following an escalation in hostilities between insurgents (who seized armaments from military depots) and government troops in the south of the country, Berisha declared a state of emergency in early March 1997. However, insurgent groups gained control of the southern towns of Vlorë, Sarandë and Gjirokastër, and it was reported that members of government forces had deserted or defected. Following negotiations with representatives of nine opposition parties, Berisha signed an agreement providing for the installation of an interim coalition government, pending elections in June, and offered an amnesty to rebels who surrendered to the authorities. A former SPA mayor of Gjirokastër, Bashkim Fino, was appointed as Prime Minister. Berisha subsequently approved the formation of a Government of National Reconciliation, which included representatives of eight opposition parties. None the less, the insurgency continued, reaching the northern town of Tropojë and Tirana. Those detained in Tirana central prison, including Nano and Alia, were released; Berisha subsequently granted Nano an official pardon. Extreme hardship and fears of civil conflict prompted thousands of Albanians to flee to Italy, although later in March Italian naval authorities were ordered to intercept boats transporting Albanian refugees, in an effort to halt the exodus. By late March government forces had regained control of Tirana, although insurgent groups controlled the south of the country. The Government requested military assistance in the restoration of civil order, and Fino appealed to the European Union (EU, see p. 276) for the establishment of a multinational force to supervise aid operations in Albania. At the end of March the UN Security Council endorsed an OSCE proposal that member states be authorized to contribute troops to the force. The 5,915-member Multinational Protection Force for Albania was established in

April, with a three-month mandate to facilitate the distribution of humanitarian assistance.

In early April 1997 the SPA ended its boycott of the legislature. Later in April the National Council of the DPA endorsed Berisha's leadership of the party and removed a number of dissident members who had demanded his resignation. The son of King Zog I and claimant to the throne, Leka Zogu, returned to Albania in April, with the support of the monarchist Movement of Legality Party. In May the Kuvendi Popullor adopted legislation regulating the operation of pyramid investment schemes, and approved a proposal submitted by the DPA on the introduction of a new electoral system, under which the number of legislative deputies was to be increased from 140 to 155. The SPA and its allied parties agreed to participate in the elections, after Berisha complied with the stipulation that the CEC be appointed by the interim Government (rather than by himself).

The legislative elections of 1997: the SPA gains power

Election campaigning was marred by violence, including several bomb explosions in Tirana. On 29 June 1997 the first round of voting in the legislative elections took place; a referendum on the restoration of the monarchy was conducted on the same day. Despite the presence of the Multinational Protection Force (the mandate of which had been extended to mid-August), three people were reportedly killed in violent incidents on polling day. A further ballot took place in 32 constituencies on 6 July. Observers from the OSCE subsequently declared the elections to have been conducted satisfactorily. Later in July the CEC announced that the SPA had secured 101 seats in the Kuvendi Popullor, while the DPA had won 29 seats; the SPA and its allied parties (the SDP, the DAP, the APA and the UHRP) thereby secured the requisite two-thirds' majority for the approval of constitutional amendments that they had proposed earlier in the month. At the referendum held on 29 June, 66.7% of the electorate voted in favour of retaining a republic. On 24 July, following Berisha's resignation as President, the Kuvendi Popullor elected the Secretary-General of the SPA, Rexhep Mejdani, to that position. Parliamentary deputies also voted to end the state of emergency. The SPA proposed Nano to the office of Prime Minister, and a new Council of Ministers, comprising representatives of the SPA and its allied parties, was appointed. At the end of July the new Government's programme for the restoration of civil order and economic reconstruction received a legislative vote of confidence. The Kuvendi Popullor also voted in favour of auditing existing pyramid schemes and investigating those that had been dissolved, in an attempt to reimburse lost savings. In August the Government dispatched troops to the south of the country, in an effort to restore order in major towns that were under the control of rebel forces. It was subsequently announced that Vlorë had been recaptured and a number of rebel forces arrested. By mid-August the Multinational Protection Force had left Albania.

In September 1997 the Kuvendi Popullor established a parliamentary commission to draft a new constitution, in accordance with the amendments proposed by the SPA. Later that month an SPA deputy shot and wounded Azem Hajdari, a prominent DPA official and close associate of Berisha, in the parliamentary building. The DPA subsequently initiated a boycott of the legislature. In October Berisha was re-elected Chairman of the DPA. Intermittent violent unrest continued in early 1998. In February an armed revolt by civilians and disaffected members of the local security forces in Shkodër was suppressed by government troops. In March the DPA announced that it was to end its boycott of the Kuvendi Popullor, to express support within the legislature for ethnic Albanians in the Serbian province of Kosovo (see below). In early July a parliamentary commission into the unrest of 1997 recommended that several senior DPA officials, including Berisha, be charged in connection with the deployment of the armed forces to suppress the protests.

In early September 1998 Hajdari was assassinated in Tirana. Berisha accused Nano of involvement in the killing, and the DPA resumed its boycott of the legislature. The incident prompted violent protests by DPA supporters, who seized government offices and occupied the state television and radio buildings. Government security forces regained control of the capital, after clashes with protesters, in which about seven people were reported to have been killed. Although Berisha denied government claims that the uprising constituted a coup attempt, the Kuvendi Popullor voted to revoke Berisha's exemption (as a parliamentary deputy) from prosecution, allowing him to be charged with attempting to overthrow the Government. An OSCE delegation, which mediated subsequent discussions between the political parties, condemned Berisha for inciting unrest, but also criticized Nano for the continued corruption within his administration. At the end of September the Minister of Public Order resigned, amid widespread criticism of the Government's failure to improve public security. Shortly afterwards Nano tendered his resignation, following a meeting of the SPA leadership, having failed to reach agreement with the government coalition on the composition of a new Council of Ministers. Mejdani subsequently requested that the Secretary-General of the SPA, Pandeli Majko, form a new government. In October a new coalition Council of Ministers, headed by Majko, was installed. Later that month the Kuvendi Popullor approved the draft Constitution (with opposition deputies boycotting the vote). The new Constitution was submitted for endorsement at a national referendum, monitored by OSCE observers, on 22 November. The Government announced that 50.1% of the registered electorate had participated in the referendum, of whom 93.1% had voted in favour of adopting the draft. Berisha disputed the results of the referendum and announced that the DPA would refuse to recognize the new Constitution. None the less, on 28 November the new Constitution was officially adopted. In July 1999 a DPA congress voted in favour of ending the boycott of the legislature.

At an SPA party congress in September 1999 Nano was re-elected as party Chairman, narrowly defeating Majko. In October Majko resigned as Prime Minister. Mejdani subsequently nominated Ilir Meta (hitherto Deputy Prime Minister) as Prime Minister. In early November the new Government was formally approved in the Kuvendi Popullor, despite a boycott by the DPA.

Local government elections took place in two rounds in October 2000, following the preparation of a new voters' register, with assistance from the UN Development Programme (UNDP, see p. 63). Official results indicated that the SPA had obtained control of a total of 252 communes and municipalities, while the DPA had secured 118. In February 2001 the DPA and the SPA reached agreement on the adoption of a new electoral code.

In April 2001 President Mejdani announced that the first round of elections to the Kuvendi Popullor would take place on 24 June, with a second round in early July. Despite a number of minor violent incidents, the first round of elections on 24 June was judged by international observers to have been conducted satisfactorily. The second round took place on 8 July in 45 constituencies. Ballots were repeated in eight constituencies in July–August, after opposition complaints of irregularities were upheld by the Constitutional Court. According to the final results, which were announced by the CEC on 21 August, the SPA won 73 seats and a DPA-led coalition, the Union for Victory, won 46 seats in the Kuvendi Popullor (which had reverted to a total of 140 deputies).

Following Meta's re-appointment as Prime Minister, a reorganized Council of Ministers, nominated by President Mejdani, was approved in early September 2001. The new Government retained representatives of the SDP, notably the party Chairman, Skender Gjinushi, as Deputy Prime Minister and Minister of Labour and Social Affairs; Majko became Minister of Defence. (Deputies belonging to the Union for Victory boycotted the new Kuvendi Popullor, in continued protest at the outcome of the elections, which Berisha alleged had been characterized by widespread fraud.) A vote expressing confidence in the new Government and its political and social programme was adopted by 84 deputies in the Kuvendi Popullor.

In December 2001 severe divisions emerged within the SPA, after Nano publicly accused the Government of engaging in corrupt practices. In that month the Ministers of Finance and of the Public Economy and Privatization (both members of the SPA) resigned from the Government, after being implicated in the corruption allegations. Two further SPA members also resigned their ministerial portfolios. Later in December Berisha was re-elected to the leadership of the DPA. At the end of that month attempts by Meta to appoint new ministers to the four vacant posts in the Government proved unsuccessful, since his nominees were repeatedly rejected by supporters of Nano in the Kuvendi Popullor. On 29 January 2002 Meta tendered his resignation, after the two SPA factions failed to reach agreement on a government reorganization. Majko (a compromise candidate, who was supported by Meta), the SPA's candidate for Prime Minister, was appointed to the office on 7 February. Following protracted negotiations between the two SPA factions and allied parties, the Kuvendi Popullor approved a new Council of Ministers, in which portfolios were divided between supporters of Nano and Meta, on 22 February.

Following the establishment of the new, transitional Council of Ministers, deputies from the Union for Victory agreed to resume participation in the Kuvendi Popullor. As the end of Mejdani's term of office approached, it became apparent that Nano would be unable to secure majority support in the legislature, owing to strong opposition from Berisha. Following prolonged negotiations between the SPA and the DPA, Alfred Moisiu, a retired general who had served in the Berisha administration, was selected as the candidate of both parties. He was elected by 97 of the 140 legislative deputies on 24 June 2002, and was inaugurated on 24 July. On the following day Majko resigned as Prime Minister. Moisiu subsequently appointed Nano to the premiership, and a new administration, again including members of both SPA factions, was approved at the end of the month, with Majko returning to his post as Minister of Defence; Meta became Deputy Prime Minister and Minister of Foreign Affairs. A new electoral code was adopted in June 2003. Despite efforts towards reconciliation of the two SPA factions, continuing differences culminated in Meta's resignation from the Government in mid-July, citing authoritarian behaviour by Nano. The Minister of State for Integration, an ally of Meta, also tendered his resignation.

Local government elections, conducted on 12 October 2003, prompted reports by OSCE observers of irregularities; the rate of participation by the electorate was reported to be less than 50%. Although the SPA claimed to have secured control of 36 municipalities, the DPA immediately contested the results and accused the authorities of malpractice. Later that month Nano removed the Minister of Public Order, Luan Rama, who had reportedly assaulted the editor of a local television station critical of the Government. Meta declared that his faction would obstruct further ministerial appointments in the Kuvendi Popullor until Nano agreed to reorganize the Government, and the offices remained vacant. In early November the SPA leadership adopted amendments to its statute, whereby the Chairman would automatically obtain the premiership. At the end of November Nano finally conceded the need for a government reorganization, and commenced negotiations to secure the support of smaller parties within the Kuvendi Popullor. On 14 December, at the SPA annual congress, Nano was re-elected as party Chairman. Later that month Nano signed agreements with the leaders of the SDP, the DAP, the APA, the UHRP, and a breakaway faction of the SDP, establishing the Coalition for Integration, which adopted the principal objective of supporting Albania's rapid accession to the EU and the North Atlantic Treaty Organization (NATO, see p. 370). A government reorganization, which included the appointment of Namik Dokle as Deputy Prime Minister, was approved by the Kuvendi Popullor on 29 December. Meanwhile, further municipal elections were conducted in parts of the country in December, after a court of appeal upheld DPA allegations and declared the results in a number of districts to be invalid; OSCE monitors reported further irregularities at some ballots.

In February 2004 large demonstrations were organized by the DPA in Tirana, accusing the Government of having failed to improve living standards and demanding Nano's resignation. In June the approval by the Kuvendi Popullor, following protracted debate, of legislation on restitution and compensation of property (providing for the payment of recompense to citizens whose property had been transferred to state ownership after the accession to power of the NLF in November 1944) was welcomed by the OSCE.

The legislative elections of 2005: the DPA returns to government

In September 2004 the ruling coalition was severely weakened by Meta's resignation from the SPA, following continued disputes with Nano, and his establishment of a new political party, the Socialist Movement for Integration (SMI). The SPA subsequently lost its parliamentary majority, following the defection of several deputies to the new group. In February 2005, following protracted negotiations between the SPA and the DPA, with OSCE mediation, the parties signed a bilateral agreement on a new division of electoral zones, prior to legislative elections. The elections took place on 3 July, with the participation of some 56% of voters. A second round of voting was held in three constituencies on 21 August, following complaints of electoral irregularities. According to the final results, announced in early September, the DPA and its allies won 80 of the 140 seats in the Kuvendi Popullor, while the SPA and allied parties secured 60 seats. Nano duly conceded defeat and resigned as Chairman of the SPA, but continued to declare the results illegitimate. The final report of the OSCE, which monitored the elections, concluded that the ballot only partly met international standards for democratic elections, although it noted some improvements. The new Kuvendi Popullor, at its inaugural session on 2 September, elected Jozefina Topalli as parliamentary Speaker. On the same day President Moisiu nominated Berisha as Prime Minister. On 10 September the Kuvendi Popullor approved the new DPA-led, coalition Government in which the RPA, the New Democratic Party (NDP), the APA and the UHRP each received one portfolio. Notably, the Chairman of the RPA, Fatmir Mediu, was appointed Minister of Defence. In early October the Mayor of Tirana, Edi Rama, was elected leader of the SPA.

In December 2006, following the failure of parliamentary parties to agree on the adoption of electoral reform legislation, Moisiu decreed that local government elections would take place on 20 January 2007. However, opposition parties continued to demand a postponement, claiming that the Government had reneged on an agreement to prevent electoral malpractice. Later in January, following an agreement between political parties, which included provisions on voter identification, Moisiu rescheduled the local government elections for 18 February (narrowly meeting a deadline stipulated by the Constitution).

The CEC announced that a number of irregularities were reported during the elections; an OSCE observer mission and the EU concluded that preparations for, and the conduct of, the elections had failed to meet international standards. According to official results, the ruling coalition secured some 51.1% of the votes cast, and the SPA-led opposition alliance (known as Together for the Future) 42.9% (with about 48% of the registered electorate participating). Individually, however, the SPA won the greatest proportion of votes, with 23.2%, while the DPA received 20.6%. SPA candidates secured control of several principal municipalities; notably, Edi Rama was re-elected as Mayor of Tirana, defeating the DPA candidate (Sokol Olldashi, hitherto the Minister of the Interior). In March Berisha announced a number of government changes (among them the replacement of the Deputy Prime Minister), which were approved in the Kuvendi Popullor on 19 March. In mid-April Majko resigned as Secretary-General of the SPA. Later that month the Minister of Foreign Affairs, Besnik Mustafaj, announced his resignation; he was replaced by Lulzim Basha (hitherto the Minister of Public Works, Transport and Telecommunications). In May Rama was re-elected as Chairman of the SPA.

In June 2007 the scheduled election by the Kuvendi Popullor of a new President, to succeed Moisiu on the expiry of his second term in office on 24 July, was postponed, owing to dissent between the parties. The SPA objected to the DPA's nomination, without consultation, of Bamir Topi as its presidential candidate, and boycotted three rounds of voting in the Kuvendi Popullor, in which Topi was unable to secure the support of the three-fifths of deputies required for election. The prolonged impasse was finally resolved by a fourth round of voting on 20 July, when five members of the SPA voted for Topi, who narrowly obtained the required majority. Topi was inaugurated on 24 July.

In November 2007 the Minister of Justice, Ilir Rusmajli, tendered his resignation, shortly after that of the head of the prison service, who had made allegations of corruption involving Rusmajli's brother. Later that month Topi dismissed the Prosecutor-General, Theodhori Sollaku, who had been criticized for his perceived failure to address organized crime. He was succeeded by Ina Rama, who was the first woman to hold the post. In December the Kuvendi Popullor voted in favour of removing the parliamentary immunity of Basha, who was accused of abuse of office in the award of a road-construction contract in his previous ministerial post (Basha, who maintained that the charges were politically motivated, was officially cleared in December 2008). In March 2008 Mediu resigned as Minister of Defence and three state officials were arrested, after 26 people were killed and some 300 injured in an explosion at an army munitions depot at Gerdec, near Tirana.

On 21 April 2008 the Kuvendi Popullor adopted significant constitutional amendments, which, notably, abolished the partial majority voting system in favour of proportional representation within each of the country's 12 administrative regions (counties), and revised parliamentary procedures for the election of the President. In June Topi dismissed the Chief of the General Staff, Lt-Gen. Luan Hoxha, after indications that the explosion at the Gerdec depot had been caused by negligence. In a government reorganization in July, Genc Pollo of the NDP, hitherto Minister of Education and Science, was appointed to the office of

Deputy Prime Minister. In September SPA supporters demonstrated in Tirana to demand the resignation of the Government following the explosion at Gerdec.

The adoption of a new electoral code prior to forthcoming legislative elections, under discussion since April 2008, was protracted; smaller parliamentary parties opposed it on the grounds that they were to be excluded from electoral committees and were also expected to be disadvantaged by the new system of proportional representation. On 18 November the new code was finally approved, with the support of the SPA, by 112 of the 140 deputies in the Kuvendi Popullor. A hunger strike staged by a number of opposition deputies, including former Prime Minister Meta, in protest at the amendments, ended after some eight days. On 22 December a lustration law, which required all public officials to be investigated to determine whether they had co-operated with the secret police during the communist era, obtained parliamentary approval; however, in February 2009 the Constitutional Court voted in favour of suspending the legislation. Also in February it was announced that Mediu and 13 others were to be charged in connection with the explosion at the munitions depot.

The disputed 2009 legislative elections

A number of violent incidents were reported prior to legislative elections in mid-2009, including the killing of a parliamentary deputy belonging to the SPA in May. The elections to the Kuvendi Popullor were conducted on 28 June. An OSCE observer mission report stated that the organization of the elections demonstrated significant improvements, but noted irregularities in the vote-counting process. The SPA accused the authorities of extensive malpractice in the counting of votes, particularly in the town of Fier, and, following a recount there, gained an additional seat. According to the official results, announced in early August, the DPA-led Alliance for Change secured a total of 70 seats (68 of which were obtained by the DPA), with some 46.9% of the votes cast, while the SPA-led Unification for Change coalition won 66 seats (65 of which were received by the SPA), with about 45.3% of the votes. In early July it had been announced that the DPA was to establish a coalition with the SMI, which won some 4.9% of the votes and four seats, in order to form a new government. The new Kuvendi Popullor was convened in early September; however, the SPA began a parliamentary boycott, in protest against the rejection of its demands for an investigation into alleged electoral irregularities. Topalli of the DPA was re-elected as Speaker. On 9 September President Topi formally reappointed Berisha as Prime Minister. A new Government was established on 17 September; the DPA received 12 portfolios, the SMI was allocated four and the RPA obtained one ministerial post. Basha was appointed Minister of the Interior. Mediu (the RPA representative) was returned to the Government as Minister of the Environment; the Supreme Court suspended legal proceedings against him owing to his consequent immunity from prosecution. The SPA continued to organize demonstrations in Tirana, in protest against the election results, and in mid-November boycotted elections to fill five vacant seats. In January 2010 it was announced that the Parliamentary Assembly of the Council of Europe (PACE) was to assist Topi in mediating inter-party discussions with the aim of ending the ongoing SPA boycott. At the beginning of February the DPA announced that a revised draft of the suspended lustration law was to be submitted to the Kuvendi Popullor and subsequently referred for approval at a national referendum. In late February the 65 SPA deputies finally returned to the Kuvendi Popullor; however, dissent between the Government and the SPA concerning the 2009 elections continued, with the former favouring the establishment of a parliamentary commission to investigate the allegations of malpractice and the latter insisting on a recount of the electoral ballots in disputed regions.

In April 2010 the SPA organized a large anti-Government demonstration in Tirana. At the beginning of May some 22 SPA parliamentary deputies and 180 supporters of the party commenced a hunger strike in protest against the Government's refusal to allow a recount of the votes cast in the legislative elections. The hunger strike ended on 19 May, following the intervention of the European Parliament, which emphasized that Albania risked hindering its application for EU candidate status (see Foreign Affairs). The SPA subsequently resumed participation in parliamentary sessions, but, with a lack of progress in negotiations with the Government, continued to boycott votes on general and reform legislation. In September Meta (Deputy Prime Minister and Minister of Foreign Affairs since September 2009) was appointed as Deputy Prime Minister and Minister of Economy, Trade and Energy, replacing Dritan Prifti, who had resigned owing to corruption allegations. Edmond Haxhinasto was appointed as Minister of Foreign Affairs. In October 2010 the SPA deputies again withdrew from a parliamentary session, and presented further conditions for their participation, demanding *inter alia* that the Government abandon plans to demolish the 'Pyramid' in Tirana (regarded as a symbol of the communist era). In November the SPA resumed the organization of anti-Government protests, additionally denouncing the Government for failing to secure EU candidate status for Albania. In December an SPA proposal for the establishment of a parliamentary commission to investigate the disputed elections, which it maintained was in accordance with a July resolution by the European Parliament urging the two sides to end the impasse, was defeated in the Kuvendi Popullor.

Recent developments: political impasse

In January 2011 Meta resigned from the Government, after a local television channel broadcast video footage in which he appeared to apply pressure on Prifti in an attempt to influence the outcome of a public tender for a hydroelectric plant. Haxhinasto became Deputy Prime Minister and Minister of Foreign Affairs. Although Meta denied any wrongdoing, the European Commission urged an investigation, and Edi Rama reiterated accusations of government corruption and demanded that Berisha's administration resign. On 21 January more than 20,000 people took part in an anti-Government demonstration in Tirana organized by the SPA, which led to clashes between police and SPA supporters, as a result of which four protesters died, and several were injured. Berisha accused the opposition of attempting to overthrow his Government through violent means; meanwhile, EU officials condemned the excessive use of force, and urged a resumption of political dialogue. An arrest warrant issued by Prosecutor-General Ina Rama against six senior members of the Republican Guard, including its commander, in connection with the deaths was not implemented owing to alleged technical errors. Later in January former Slovakian Minister of Foreign Affairs Miroslav Lajčák, who had been appointed as the EU special envoy on the political crisis, began to mediate negotiations between the Government and the SPA. In early February a parliamentary session ended in a violent altercation between deputies of the DPA and the SPA (which temporarily withdrew from the Kuvendi Popullor). Later in February thousands of people attended a pro-Government rally in Tirana. In April, as part of a government reorganization, Bujar Nishani, hitherto the Minister of Justice, was appointed as Minister of the Interior, replacing Basha, who had resigned in order to stand as a mayoral candidate in forthcoming local elections. (In July Berisha appointed Eduard Halimi as Minister of Justice.)

Despite the continued unstable political environment, local government elections were conducted on 8 May 2011, as scheduled. The electoral campaign was marred by violence, with frequent clashes between supporters of rival political groups. A protracted dispute (owing to controversy over the validity of ballots that had not been cast in the designated boxes) ensued over the result of the mayoral election in Tirana, which initially indicated that SPA Chairman and incumbent Mayor Edi Rama had won. In late June, however, after ruling that the disputed ballots be included, the CEC declared that DPA candidate Basha had been elected as the new Mayor, defeating Rama. (The SPA, which again boycotted the Kuvendi Popullor, nevertheless submitted a further challenge against Basha's election, which was rejected by the Electoral College—the highest election-related court in the country—on 8 July.) Overall, the SPA-led coalition secured control of 35 municipalities (although winning about 48% of votes cast), and the DPA-led coalition the remaining 30 (with some 52% of the votes). The EU's Commissioner responsible for Enlargement and European Neighbourhood Policy subsequently criticized the conduct of the elections, considering them to demonstrate the need for reform of electoral legislation. Meanwhile, an OSCE report, issued in August, noted that acrimony between the two main political groupings, including disputes within the CEC, had adversely affected administration of the poll. Following an unfavourable progress report by the European Commission in mid-October (see below), in mid-November the DPA and the SPA, which had returned to the Kuvendi Popullor in the previous month, agreed to co-operate in meeting the Commission's requirements, and subsequently established a joint parliamentary committee for electoral reform, increasing hopes that the adoption of important legislation could proceed. In mid-January 2012 the Supreme Court dismissed the corruption charges brought against Meta in the previous year, announcing that there was no evidence to convict him.

Foreign Affairs

Regional relations

Albania's relations with both Greece and Serbia (formerly part of the State Union of Serbia and Montenegro, and prior to that, Yugoslavia) have been strained. In August 1987 Greece formally ended the technical state of war with Albania that had been in existence since 1945. However, the status of the Greek minority in Albania, officially numbering some 59,000 at the 1989 census, but estimated to number some 300,000 by the Greek authorities, remained a sensitive issue. Relations between Albania and Greece deteriorated in 1993, owing to Greece's deportation of some 20,000 Albanian immigrants and to the alleged mistreatment of the Greek minority in southern Albania. Tensions were exacerbated further in April 1994, following a border incident in which two Albanian guards were killed; diplomatic expulsions ensued on both sides, and the border situation remained tense. In May six prominent members of the ethnic Greek organization OMONIA were arrested. Greece subsequently vetoed the provision of EU funds to Albania and increased the deportation of illegal Albanian immigrants. In September five of the OMONIA detainees were convicted on charges including espionage and the illegal possession of weapons, and received custodial sentences. Following the verdict, Greece and Albania both recalled their ambassadors. In addition, Greece submitted formal protests to the UN and the EU regarding Albania's perceived maltreatment of its ethnic Greek population and closed the Kakavija border crossing, which had hitherto been used by Albanian migrant workers. One of the OMONIA defendants was pardoned in December, after Greece withdrew its veto on EU aid to Albania in November. In February 1995 the four remaining prisoners were released, allowing a subsequent improvement in bilateral relations. In June the Albanian Government approved a new education law, which recognized the right of ethnic minorities to their own language and culture. In March 1996 a co-operation agreement was signed, with the aim of resolving outstanding issues of concern between the two nations. In August 1997 the Greek Government agreed to grant temporary work permits to illegal Albanian immigrants in Greece, in exchange for assistance from Albania in combating cross-border crime. A new border crossing between Albania and Greece was opened in May 1999. In late 2006 the Albanian and Greek authorities announced a joint plan for increased surveillance measures to combat endemic cross-border trafficking.

Relations with Yugoslavia deteriorated sharply from 1989, when many ethnic Albanian demonstrators were killed during renewed unrest in the predominantly ethnic Albanian province of Kosovo. In early 1998 Albania condemned increased Serbian military activity against the ethnic Albanian majority in Kosovo, while clashes were reported on the Albanian border with Kosovo between Serbian troops and suspected members of the paramilitary Kosovo Liberation Army (KLA). The Albanian administration initiated measures to prevent the illicit transportation of armaments from northern Albania to KLA forces in Kosovo. By mid-1998 some 10,000 ethnic Albanian refugees had fled to northern Albania, following continued Serbian military reprisals against the ethnic Albanian population in Kosovo.

In March 1999, following the failure of diplomatic efforts to compel the Yugoslav President, Slobodan Milošević, to accede to NATO demands, NATO forces commenced an intensive aerial bombardment of Yugoslavia. The Albanian Government expressed support for the NATO military action, and allowed Albania's air and sea facilities to be used for NATO operations. Further Albanian troops were deployed on the northern border with Serbia in preparation for a possible Serbian retaliatory offensive. NATO troops (which later numbered about 8,000, and became known as AFOR) were dispatched to Albania to support humanitarian aid operations. The Government appealed for international financial assistance for the Kosovo refugee population. In early April Yugoslav forces bombarded Albanian border villages during heavy fighting with the KLA in Kosovo, increasing international concern that a broader regional conflict might develop. Later that month Serbian troops advanced into Albanian territory, but were repelled by the armed forces. Following the deployment of a NATO-led peace-keeping Kosovo Force (KFOR) in the province, under the terms of a peace agreement agreed with Milošević in June, refugees began rapidly to return to Kosovo from Albania. In September NATO announced that AFOR, which had been gradually withdrawing from the country, was to be replaced by a 1,200-member contingent, Communications Zone West (COMMZ-W), which was mandated to maintain civil order in Albania and to support the KFOR mission in Kosovo. (In June 2002 COMMZ-W was officially dissolved, when a NATO headquarters was established at Tirana.) Following the removal from power of Milošević in September 2000, Albania and Yugoslavia formally restored diplomatic relations in January 2001. Bilateral diplomatic relations were upgraded to ambassadorial level in September 2002.

In February 1993 Albania refused to accept an application by the former Yugoslav republic of Macedonia (FYRM) for membership of the CSCE; in April it officially recognized the existence of the republic as an independent state. Albania was concerned at the perceived oppression there of the ethnic Albanian minority, which constituted about 21% of the population. Following the civil unrest in Albania in early 1997 (see above), a number of incursions into FYRM territory by armed groups of Albanian rebels were reported; an agreement providing for increased security at the joint border between the two countries was signed in October. The outbreak of conflict between government forces and ethnic Albanian rebels, known as the National Liberation Army (NLA), in the FYRM in February 2001 prompted large numbers of ethnic Albanian civilians to take refuge in Albania. Relations between Albania and the FYRM became strained, although the Albanian authorities maintained their opposition to the NLA's reported aim of creating a 'Greater Albania'. In August the FYRM Government and NLA leaders signed a peace agreement, but the region remained unstable. In November 2003 the Ministries of Defence of Albania, Greece and the FYRM pledged to increase military co-operation to address the issues of illegal immigration and cross-border organized crime.

Negotiations between Kosovo Albanian and Serbian delegations on the final status of Kosovo commenced in early 2006 (see the chapter on Serbia). Despite the extension of the period of discussions, however, the two negotiating sides proved unable to reach a settlement, and the UN Security Council failed to approve a resolution on the future of Kosovo. Consequently, a newly installed Kosovo Government adopted a unilateral declaration of independence on 17 February 2008 (which was rapidly approved by the USA and a number of EU member states). The declaration prompted public celebrations in Tirana, and Berisha announced that Albania officially recognized Kosovo as an independent and sovereign state. On 19 February the Council of Ministers approved the establishment of diplomatic relations with Kosovo at ambassadorial level. In November the President of Kosovo, Fatmir Sejdiu, made his first official visit to Albania. In October 2009 Berisha made an official visit to Kosovo's capital, Prishtina, where a number of bilateral co-operation agreements were signed, including protocols on customs and border policing.

In December 2010 Swiss senator and Council of Europe rapporteur Dick Marty presented a report (which was subsequently adopted by PACE) claiming that human organ trafficking operations had occurred on Albanian territory during and after the 1999 conflict in Kosovo, and implicating the Kosovo Prime Minister, Hashim Thaçi. The Albanian Government pledged its readiness to co-operate with any investigation related to the allegations, which were strongly denied by Albanian officials. In July 2011 the Governments of Albania and Serbia approved an agreement to end visa requirements between the two states. In October the Albanian Government announced a decision to merge the Albanian and Kosovo consular services abroad, prompting renewed concerns from some regional commentators over the potential for the creation of a 'Greater Albania'.

Other external relations

The gradual relaxation of Albania's isolationist policies culminated in 1990 in a declaration of its intention to establish good relations with all countries, irrespective of their social system. In July of that year Albania and the USSR formally agreed to restore diplomatic relations. Diplomatic relations between Albania and the USA (suspended since 1946) were re-established in March 1991.

Negotiations on the signature of a Stabilization and Association Agreement (SAA) with the EU officially commenced at the end of January 2003. Following a positive recommendation issued by the European Commission in March 2006, the SAA was officially signed between the Albanian Government and the EU on 12 June. The Kuvendi Popullor ratified the Agreement in late July. At a NATO summit meeting, convened in Bucharest, Romania, on 2 April 2008, it was announced that official invitations to begin accession negotiations were to be extended to Albania and Croatia. In November a European Commission report cited high-level corruption, deficiencies in the judiciary, political influence in the civil service and organized crime as the main obstacles to Albania's EU accession aspirations. After member states of the Alliance completed the process of ratifying its accession protocols in February 2009, Albania acceded to membership of NATO on 1 April. In that month the SAA with the EU entered into effect, and on 28 April Albania submitted a formal application for membership of the Union.

In May 2010 the European Commission adopted a recommendation that visa restrictions for Albanian citizens be removed, but stipulated that this was conditional on the requirements that the Government present a reintegration strategy for returning immigrants, ensure effective application of a 2009 law on confiscating criminal assets, and increase efforts to combat organized crime and corruption. In November 2010 the European Commission issued a progress report stating that Albania had not fulfilled the criteria to receive official candidate status; however, following a favourable vote by the European Parliament in early October, it confirmed the recommendation that the visa requirement for Albanians entering the EU be removed (with effect from mid-December). The EU Commissioner for Enlargement emphasized that the continuing impasse over the 2009 elections (see Contemporary Political History), which had resulted in the legislature failing to function effectively and prevented the adoption of EU-required reforms, was the principal reason for Albania being denied EU candidate status. In October 2011 the European Commission issued a further report that again failed to recommend candidate status for Albania, citing continued lack of progress in fully meeting the EU's political criteria.

CONSTITUTION AND GOVERNMENT

Under the Constitution adopted in November 1998, legislative power is vested in the unicameral Kuvendi Popullor (People's Assembly). The Kuvendi Popullor, which is elected for a term of four years, comprises 140 deputies, 100 of whom are directly elected in single-member constituencies. Parties receiving 2.5% or more of the votes cast, and party coalitions obtaining 4.0% or more in the first round of voting, are allocated further deputies in proportion to the number of votes secured, on the basis of multi-name lists of parties or party coalitions. The President of the Republic is head of state, and is elected by the Kuvendi Popullor for a term of five years. Executive authority is held by the Council of Ministers, which is led by the Prime Minister as head of government. The Prime Minister is appointed by the President and appoints a Council of Ministers, which is presented for approval to the Kuvendi Popullor. Judicial power is exercised by the High Court, as well as by the Courts of Appeal and the Courts of First Instance. The Chairman and members of the High Court are nominated by the President of the Republic, subject to the approval of the Kuvendi Popullor, for a term of nine years. For the purposes of local government, Albania is divided into 12 counties (*qarqe*—also called prefectures), 36 districts (*rrethe*), 65 municipalities and 309 communes. The representative organs of the basic units of local government are councils, which are elected by direct election for a period of three years. The Council of Ministers appoints a Prefect as its representative in each of the 12 counties.

REGIONAL AND INTERNATIONAL CO-OPERATION

Albania is a member of the European Bank for Reconstruction and Development (EBRD, see p. 271), the Organization for Security and Co-operation in Europe (OSCE, see p. 388), the Council of Europe (see p. 256) and the Organization of the Black Sea Economic Co-operation (see p. 402). Albania is also a member of the Organization of Islamic Cooperation (see p. 404).

Albania became a member of the UN in 1955, and was admitted to the World Trade Organization (see p. 433) in 2000. Albania acceded to the North Atlantic Treaty Organization (NATO, see p. 370) on 1 April 2009.

ECONOMIC AFFAIRS

In 2010, according to World Bank estimates, Albania's gross national income (GNI), measured at average 2008–10 prices, was US $12,677m., equivalent to $3,960 per head (or $8,740 on an international purchasing-power parity basis). During 2001–10, it was estimated, the population increased by an annual average of 0.5%, while gross domestic product (GDP) per head increased, in real terms, by an average of 4.6% per year. According to World Bank estimates, overall GDP increased, in real terms, at an average annual rate of 3.8% in 2001–10; growth of 3.5% was recorded in 2010.

Agriculture contributed 20.5% of GDP in 2010, according to World Bank estimates. According to official estimates, in 2010 the sector (including fishing) engaged 55.3% of the employed labour force. Increased private enterprise was permitted from 1990, and agricultural land was subsequently redistributed to private ownership. The principal crops are wheat, maize, watermelons, potatoes, tomatoes and grapes. Agricultural GDP increased at an average annual rate of 1.5%, in real terms, in 2001–05, according to the World Bank; growth in the sector was 2.6% in 2005.

Industry (comprising mining, manufacturing and construction) contributed 19.6% of GDP in 2010, according to World Bank estimates. In 2010 the sector (including utilities) engaged an estimated 13.5% of the employed labour force. Principal contributors to industrial output include mining, energy generation and food-processing. According to World Bank estimates, industrial GDP increased at an average rate of 3.3% per year, in real terms, during 2001–10; the GDP of the sector increased by 7.0% in 2010.

Mining and quarrying contributed 0.9% of GDP in 2009, according to provisional figures, and engaged some 0.7% of the employed labour force in 2010. Albania is one of the world's largest producers of chromite (chromium ore), possessing Europe's only significant reserves (an estimated 33m. metric tons of recoverable ore in 2008). The mining sector was centred on chromite and copper, following the closure of nickel and iron ore operations, together with more than one-half of the country's coal mines, in 1990. By 2000 the output of copper was no longer significant. Annual chromite production was 290,000 metric tons in 2010 (compared with 587,000 tons in 1991). Albania has petroleum resources and its own refining facilities, and since 1991 there has been considerable foreign interest in the exploration of both onshore and offshore reserves. Proven reserves of petroleum were estimated at 199m. barrels in 2011; production of petroleum declined to 324,000 tons in 2008, compared with 378,000 tons in 2007.

The manufacturing sector contributed an estimated 19.6% of GDP in 2010, according to World Bank estimates. In 2010 the sector engaged some 5.8% of the employed labour force. The sector is based largely on the processing of building materials, agricultural products, minerals and chemicals. According to the World Bank, manufacturing GDP decreased, in real terms, at an average annual rate of 1.5% during 2001–04; the GDP of the sector declined by 4.5% in 2002 and remained constant in 2003 and 2004.

The construction sector has been the fastest growing sector in recent years, contributing 14.2% of GDP in 2009, according to provisional estimates, and engaging an estimated 4.3% of the employed labour force in 2010.

By 2008 all of the electricity generated in the country was produced from hydroelectric sources. In 2010 imports of mineral fuels and electricity accounted for 15.9% of the value of total merchandise imports. In 2011 a new, 97-MW thermal power plant opened some six km from the southern Albanian port of Vlorë. A US-funded oil pipeline terminal to deliver Russian petroleum to Vlorë via the Bulgarian Black Sea port of Burgas is also planned.

Services contributed 59.9% of GDP in 2010, according to World Bank estimates. Official estimates indicated that the sector engaged 31.2% of the employed labour force in 2010. The GDP of the services sector increased, in real terms, by an average of 7.0% per year during 2000–08; growth was 6.1% in 2008.

In 2010 Albania recorded a visible trade deficit of US $2,757.5m., and there was a deficit of $1,403.9m. on the current account of the balance of payments. In 2010 the principal source of imports (accounting for some 28.6%) was Italy; other major suppliers were Greece, Turkey and Germany. Italy was also the principal market for exports (accounting for 51.0% of the total); Turkey and Greece were also important purchasers. The principal exports in 2010 were textiles and footwear, mineral fuels and electricity, construction materials and metals, and food, beverages and tobacco. The main imports in that year were machinery equipment and spare parts, food, beverages and tobacco, construction materials and metals, mineral fuels and electricity, chemical and plastic products, and textiles and footwear.

Albania's overall budget deficit in 2009 was 85,500m. lekë, equivalent to 7.4% of GDP. Albania's general government gross debt was 720,645m. lekë in 2010, equivalent to 58.2% of GDP. Albania's total external debt in 2009 was US $4,719m., of which $2,829m. was public and publicly guaranteed debt. In that year, the cost of debt servicing was equivalent to 4.3% of the value of exports of goods, services and income. According to official figures, during 2001–10 the average annual rate of inflation was 3.0%; consumer prices increased by 3.6% in 2010. The rate of unemployment was 13.5% in 2010.

From the beginning of the 1990s Albania underwent an extensive transition to a more open market economy. In January 2009 the IMF issued a favourable review of Albania's economic performance, commending fiscal reforms and progress in privatization. In March a Czech corporation, CEZ Group, signed an agreement with the Government for the purchase of a 76% stake in the state electricity distribution company OSSH; proceeds were allocated to funding the rehabilitation of the energy sector and addressing longstanding electricity supply difficulties. Despite adverse effects resulting from the international economic crisis, growth was recorded in 2009, albeit at a reduced level, and the country was considered to have performed relatively well, compared with other regional economies. Meanwhile, following Albania's application for full membership of the European Union (EU) in April, the opposition Socialist Party of Albania's protracted boycott of the legislature (see Contemporary Political History) began to obstruct Albania's accession process. In October 2010 a report by Transparency International noted a slight improvement in Albania's efforts to fight corruption (also identified as a major obstacle to EU integration). In July 2011, after local elections in May that reportedly depleted the state budget, the Government announced plans for the complete privatization of remaining state assets, initially to involve four hydropower plants. The EU's Commissioner for Enlargement and European Neighbourhood Policy criticized the conduct of the local elections (which were marred by controversy and disputes between the two main political parties), declaring that they demonstrated the urgent need for electoral reform. Following the continuing impasse between the Government and the opposition, the European Commission issued a report in October, reiterating its belief that Albania had made insufficient progress to be granted candidate status (with the consequence that it also failed to qualify for additional EU funding). In compliance with an EU directive designed to improve competitiveness in energy markets, legislation was approved in November to allow large consumers to purchase electricity from suppliers other than the state utility KESH. In October an IMF report commended the Albanian authorities for withstanding the global crisis, but emphasized the continuing negative effects arising from the country's divisive political system, and the importance of fiscal consolidation in view of Albania's vulnerability to further adverse developments in the euro area; a reduced rate of growth, of some 2.5%, was expected for 2011.

PUBLIC HOLIDAYS

2013: 1 January (New Year's Day), 20–22 March (Nevruz, Spring Holiday), 1 April (Catholic Easter), 1 May (International Labour Day), 6 May (Eastern Orthodox Easter), 7 August* (Small Bayram, end of Ramadan), 14 October* (Great Bayram, Feast of the Sacrifice), 19 October (Mother Theresa Day), 28 November (Independence and Liberation Day), 25 December (Christmas Day).

* These holidays are dependent on the Islamic lunar calendar and may vary by one or two days from the dates given.

Statistical Survey

Sources (unless otherwise indicated): Institute of Statistics (Instituti i Statistikës), POB 8194, Tirana; tel. (4) 2222411; fax (4) 2228300; e-mail root@instat.gov.al; internet www.instat.gov.al; Bank of Albania (Banka e Shqipërisë), Sheshi Skënderbej 1, Tirana; tel. (4) 2222152; fax (4) 2223558; e-mail public@bankofalbania.org; internet www.bankofalbania.org.

Area and Population

AREA, POPULATION AND DENSITY

Area (sq km)	
Land	27,398
Inland water	1,350
Total	28,748*
Population (census results)	
2 April 1989	3,182,417
1 April 2001	
Males	1,530,443
Females	1,538,832
Total	3,069,275
Population (official estimates of annual averages)	
2007	3,161,337
2008	3,181,950
2009	3,194,417
Density (per sq km) in 2009	111.1

* 11,100 sq miles.

Population (UN estimates at mid-year): 3,204,284 in 2010; 3,215,987 in 2011; 3,227,373 in 2012 (Source: UN, *World Population Prospects: The 2010 Revision*).

POPULATION BY AGE AND SEX
(2009, official estimates)

	Males	Females	Total
0–14	388,901	358,535	747,436
15–64	1,069,596	1,077,017	2,146,613
65 and over	140,550	159,818	300,368
Total	1,599,047	1,595,370	3,194,417

COUNTIES (PREFECTURES)
(official estimates of annual averages, 2009)

County	Area (sq km)	Population	Density (per sq km)	Capital
Berat	1,798	170,815	95.0	Berat
Dibër	2,586	140,007	54.1	Peshkopi
Durrës	766	310,441	405.3	Durrës
Elbasan	3,199	343,053	107.2	Elbasan
Fier	1,890	374,004	197.9	Fier
Gjirokastër	2,884	102,531	35.6	Gjirokastër
Korçë	3,711	257,530	69.4	Korçë
Kukës	2,374	79,289	33.4	Kukës
Lezhë	1,620	158,800	98.0	Lezhë
Shkodër	3,562	246,016	69.1	Shkodër
Tiranë	1,652	800,197	484.4	Tiranë
Vlorë	2,706	211,734	78.2	Vlorë
Total	28,748	3,194,417	111.1	

PRINCIPAL TOWNS
(population at 2001 census, preliminary results)

Tiranë (Tirana, the capital)	343,078	Korçë (Koritsa)	55,130
Durrës (Durazzo)	99,546	Berat	40,112
Elbasan	87,797	Lushnjë	32,580
Shkodër (Scutari)	82,455	Kavajë	24,817
Vlorë (Vlonë or Valona)	77,691	Pogradec	23,843
Fier	56,297	Gjirokastër	20,630

Mid-2009 (incl. suburbs, UN estimate): Tirana 432,652 (Source: UN, *World Urbanization Prospects: The 2009 Revision*).

BIRTHS, MARRIAGES AND DEATHS

	Registered live births		Registered marriages		Registered deaths	
	Number	Rate (per 1,000)	Number	Rate (per 1,000)	Number	Rate (per 1,000)
2002	45,515	14.7	26,202	8.4	16,248	5.3
2003	47,012	15.1	27,342	8.7	17,967	5.8
2004	43,022	13.8	20,949	6.5	17,749	5.7
2005	39,612	12.6	21,795	6.9	17,124	5.5
2006	34,229	10.9	21,332	6.8	16,935	5.4
2007	33,163	10.5	22,371	7.0	14,528	4.6
2008	36,251	11.4	21,290	6.7	15,926	5.0
2009*	29,189	9.1	17,875	5.6	15,662	4.9

* Preliminary.

Life expectancy (years at birth, WHO estimates): 73 (males 72; females 75) in 2009 (Source: WHO, *World Health Statistics*).

ECONOMICALLY ACTIVE POPULATION
('000, official estimates)

	2008	2009	2010
Agriculture, hunting, forestry and fishing	568	496	507
Mining and quarrying	5	5	6
Manufacturing	56	53	53
Electricity, gas and water	25	26	26
Construction	46	40	39
Wholesale and retail trade	53	58	58
Hotels and restaurants	12	12	13
Transport, storage and communications	26	23	24
Education	37	40	42
Health and social work	28	26	27
Other activities	118	120	122
Total employed	974	899	916
Registered unemployed	140	142	143
Total labour force	1,114	1,041	1,059
Males	680	619	623
Females	434	422	436

Note: Totals may not be equal to the sum of components, owing to rounding.

Health and Welfare

KEY INDICATORS

Total fertility rate (children per woman, 2009)	1.9
Under-5 mortality rate (per 1,000 live births, 2009)	15
HIV/AIDS (% of persons aged 15–49, 2007)	<0.02
Physicians (per 1,000 head, 2006)	1.20
Hospital beds (per 1,000 head, 2006)	3
Health expenditure (2008): US $ per head (PPP)	569
Health expenditure (2008): % of GDP	6.8
Health expenditure (2008): public (% of total)	39.4
Access to water (% of total population, 2008)	97
Access to sanitation (% of total population, 2008)	98
Total carbon dioxide emissions ('000 metric tons, 2007)	4,239.3
Carbon dioxide emissions per head (metric tons, 2007)	1.4
Human Development Index (2011): ranking	70
Human Development Index (2011): value	0.739

For sources and definitions, see explanatory note on p. vi.

Agriculture

PRINCIPAL CROPS
('000 metric tons)

	2008	2009	2010
Wheat	335.0	333.1	294.9
Barley	3.6	4.5	7.3
Maize	245.0	265.1	362.0
Rye	3.1	3.2	2.3
Oats	21.8	25.0	27.3
Potatoes	190.0	200.0	208.0
Sugar beet	40.0*	40.0*	40.0†
Beans, dry	21.8	23.0	24.0
Olives	56.2	78.0	70.0
Sunflower seed	2.2	2.3	2.6
Tomatoes	162.5	162.4	199.3
Beans, green	7.1	6.9	9.3
Watermelons	142.9	195.4	199.4
Oranges	4.5	5.8	6.6
Apples	45.0	47.2	54.6
Pears	5.6	7.2	7.3
Sour (Morello) cherries†	14.1	15.4	15.0
Sweet cherries	8.0	10.9	12.5
Peaches and nectarines	9.0	11.0	11.5
Plums and sloes	22.0	23.8	26.1
Grapes	153.9	162.8	184.9
Figs	18.0	19.5	18.4
Tobacco, unmanufactured	1.3	1.6	1.7

* Unofficial figure.
† FAO estimates.

Aggregate production ('000 metric tons, may include official, semi-official or estimated data): Total cereals 608.5 in 2008, 630.9 in 2009, 693.8 in 2010; Total roots and tubers 190.0 in 2008, 200.0 in 2009, 208.0 in 2010; Total vegetables (incl. melons) 723.6 in 2008, 738.0 in 2009, 855.1 in 2010; Total fruits (excl. melons) 310.1 in 2008, 338.6 in 2009, 370.2 in 2010.

Source: FAO.

LIVESTOCK
('000 head, year ending September)

	2008	2009	2010
Horses	43	38	35
Asses	60*	56*	64†
Cattle	541	494	493
Pigs	161	160	164
Sheep	1,800	1,768	1,806
Goats	820	772	775
Chickens	5,000	5,138	5,245

* Unofficial figure.
† FAO estimate.

Source: FAO.

LIVESTOCK PRODUCTS
('000 metric tons)

	2008	2009	2010
Cattle meat*	39.6	39.0	40.8
Sheep meat*	14.9	15.6	13.9
Goat meat*	5.8	6.0	7.2
Pig meat*	12.5	12.5	12.5
Chicken meat	16.0	17.0	17.0
Cows' milk	895.0	908.0	930.0
Sheep's milk	77.0	75.0	77.0
Goats' milk	68.0	62.0	63.0
Hen eggs*	29.7	29.8	31.3
Wool, greasy	3.0	3.2	3.3

* Unofficial figures.

Source: FAO.

Forestry

ROUNDWOOD REMOVALS
('000 cubic metres, excl. bark)

	2005*	2006*	2007†
Sawlogs, veneer logs and logs for sleepers	62.1	62.1	15.0
Other industrial wood	13.1	13.1	65.0
Fuel wood	221.0	221.0	350.0
Total	296.2	296.2	430.0

* FAO estimates.
† Unofficial figures.

2008–10: Figures assumed to be unchanged from 2007 (FAO estimates).

Source: FAO.

SAWNWOOD PRODUCTION
('000 cubic metres, incl. railway sleepers)

	2005*	2006*	2007†
Coniferous (softwood)	47	47	4
Broadleaved (hardwood)	50	50	4
Total	97	97	8

* FAO estimates.
† Unofficial figures.

2008–10: Figures assumed to be unchanged from 2007 (FAO estimates).

Source: FAO.

Fishing

(metric tons, live weight)

	2007	2008	2009
Capture	5,497	5,506	5,945
Common carp	435	371	214
Bleak	504	190	530
Crucian carp	431	380	208
Silver carp	169	125	183
Salmonoids	58	58	49
Common sole	63	63	69
European hake	275	275	336
Gilthead seabream	51	110	67
Bogue	132	132	154
Surmullets	154	162	187
Mullets	325	320	278
European pilchard (sardines)	95	110	120
Aquaculture	2,008	1,858	2,182
Mediterranean mussel	1,360	950	1,250
Rainbow trout	221	254	300
Gilthead seabream	402	343	370
Total catch	7,505	7,364	8,127

Note: Figures exclude Sardinia coral (metric tons): 0.4 in 2007; 1.0 in 2008–09.

Source: FAO.

Mining

('000 metric tons unless otherwise indicated)

	2008	2009	2010
Lignite (brown coal)	1.5	7.8*	3.5
Crude petroleum ('000 barrels)*	4,000	4,200	5,000
Natural gas (gross production, million cu m)	6	8*	8*
Chromium ore (gross weight)	207	289	290
Kaolin	724	296	968
Dolomite*	1,000	1,000	n.a.
Olivinite (metric tons)*	200	n.a.	n.a.

* Estimate(s).

Source: US Geological Survey.

Industry

SELECTED PRODUCTS
('000 metric tons unless otherwise indicated)

	2005	2006	2007
Wheat flour	123	388	191
Beer ('000 hectolitres)	285	348	366
Wine ('000 hectolitres)	15	15	15
Cigarettes (metric tons)	4	n.a.	n.a.
Veneer sheets ('000 cubic metres)*	37	37	—
Paper and paperboard*	2.8	—	—
Cement†	489	525	889
Petroleum bitumen (asphalt)†	86	83	69
Petroleum coke†	60	64	59
Ferro-chromium†	34	17	n.a.
Crude steel†	180	206	263
Motor spirit (petrol)	14	—	—
Kerosene	9	10	10
Gas-diesel (distillate fuel) oil	72	99	82
Residual fuel oils	68	48	32
Electric energy (million kWh)‡	5,443	5,551	2,947

* Source: FAO.
† Source: US Geological Survey.
‡ Source: Institute of Statistics, Tirana.

Source (unless otherwise indicated): UN Industrial Commodity Statistics Database.

Electric energy (million kWh): 3,850 in 2008.

2008 ('000 metric tons): Cement 918 (estimate); Petroleum bitumen (asphalt) 92; Petroleum coke 47; Ferro-chromium 12; Crude steel 380 (Source: US Geological Survey).

2009 ('000 metric tons): Cement 1,110 (estimate); Petroleum bitumen (asphalt) 92; Petroleum coke 47 (estimate); Ferro-chromium 8; Crude steel 440 (Source: US Geological Survey).

2010 ('000 metric tons): Cement 1,300 (estimate); Petroleum bitumen (asphalt) 92; Petroleum coke 47 (estimate); Ferro-chromium 8; Crude steel 440 (estimate) (Source: US Geological Survey).

Finance

CURRENCY AND EXCHANGE RATES

Monetary Units
100 qindarka (qintars) = 1 new lek.

Sterling, Dollar and Euro Equivalents (30 November 2011)
£1 sterling = 164.243 lekë;
US $1 = 105.230 lekë;
€1 = 141.198 lekë;
1,000 lekë = £6.09 = $9.50 = €7.08.

Average Exchange Rate (lekë per US $)
2008 83.895
2009 94.978
2010 103.936

STATE BUDGET
('000 million lekë)

Revenue*	2009	2010†	2011†
Tax revenue	270.8	278.8	296.4
Tax revenue from Tax and Customs Directorate	211.3	216.9	229.5
Value-added tax	110.1	113.1	119.7
Profit tax	17.1	18.1	19.3
Excise taxes	33.5	35.4	37.6
Small business tax	2.5	2.6	2.8
Income tax	26.8	25.5	27.4
Customs duties	7.9	7.9	7.5
Other taxes	13.4	14.3	15.2
Property and local taxes	9.7	10.7	11.9
Social security contributions	49.8	51.2	55.0
Other revenue	24.3	21.3	21.0
Total	295.1	300.1	317.3

Expenditure‡	2009	2010†	2011†
Current expenditure	282.9	302.0	327.4
Wages	72.7	76.7	81.7
Interest	36.3	40.6	49.3
Operational and maintenance	27.9	27.8	28.6
Subsidies	2.0	1.9	2.0
Social security	96.7	103.7	110.3
Local government expenditure	32.8	29.3	32.2
Social protection transfers	19.1	20.5	21.8
Other	1.7	1.4	1.4
Capital expenditure	101.6	61.9	67.6
Reserve and contingency funds	0.0	5.2	7.6
Total	384.6	369.2	402.5

* Excluding grants received ('000 million lekë): 4.0 in 2009; 6.3 in 2010 (projection); 6.4 in 2011 (projection).

† Projections.

‡ Excluding lending minus repayments ('000 million lekë): 0.1 in 2009; 0.0 in 2010 (projection); 0.0 in 2011 (projection).

Source: IMF, *Albania: 2010 Article IV Consultation—Staff Report; Staff Statement; Public Information on the Executive Board Discussion; and Statement by the Executive Director for Albania* (July 2010).

INTERNATIONAL RESERVES

(US $ million at 31 December)

	2008	2009	2010
Gold*	43.93	55.83	71.37
IMF special drawing rights	7.24	79.02	78.10
Reserve position in IMF	5.17	5.26	5.17
Foreign exchange	2,307.37	2,229.63	2,386.28
Total	2,363.71	2,369.74	2,540.92

* Valued at market-related prices.

Source: IMF, *International Financial Statistics*.

MONEY SUPPLY

('000 million lekë at 31 December)

	2008	2009	2010
Currency outside depository corporations	195.82	209.04	195.06
Transferable deposits	116.70	115.89	130.03
Other deposits	503.19	546.54	655.20
Broad money	815.70	871.47	980.28

Source: IMF, *International Financial Statistics*.

COST OF LIVING

(Consumer Price Index; annual averages; base: December 2007 = 100)

	2008	2009	2010
Food and non-alcoholic beverages	100.9	105.9	111.4
Alcoholic beverages and tobacco	100.7	104.2	109.9
Clothing and footwear	96.5	94.6	93.2
Rent, water, fuel and power	103.3	105.1	108.9
Household goods and maintenance	100.1	100.5	101.0
Medical care	100.8	102.6	111.3
Transport	104.7	102.5	107.3
Communication	94.4	80.8	81.1
Recreation and culture	103.5	110.7	110.9
Education	100.3	102.6	105.7
All items (incl. others)	101.1	103.4	107.1

NATIONAL ACCOUNTS

(million lekë at current prices)

Expenditure on the Gross Domestic Product

	2006	2007	2008
Final consumption expenditure	771,105	874,937	974,504
Households	680,323	775,081	861,890
Non-profit institutions serving households	1,371	1,504	1,691
General government	89,411	98,352	110,922
Gross fixed capital formation	343,882	374,058	415,121
Changes in inventories	–24,712	–22,805	–10,266
Total domestic expenditure	1,090,275	1,226,190	1,379,359
Exports of goods and services	219,974	272,164	319,931
Less Imports of goods and services	428,040	530,683	609,997
GDP in market prices	882,209	967,670	1,089,293

Gross Domestic Product by Economic Activity

	2007	2008	2009*
Agriculture, hunting and forestry	165,748	182,118	193,730
Mining and quarrying	8,005	11,223	9,729
Manufacturing	73,687	84,006	92,860
Construction	129,585	145,451	146,015
Wholesale and retail trade, hotels and restaurants	185,037	205,498	215,505
Transport	47,325	53,117	56,236
Post and communications	37,208	40,695	41,217
Other services	226,044	251,719	276,165
Sub-total	872,639	973,827	1,031,456
Less Financial intermediation services indirectly measured	38,681	40,902	43,344
Gross value added in basic prices	833,960	932,925	988,113
Taxes on products	136,789	158,712	164,717
Less Subsidies on products	3,079	2,344	1,810
GDP in market prices	967,670	1,089,293	1,151,020

* Provisional.

BALANCE OF PAYMENTS

(US $ million)

	2008	2009	2010
Exports of goods f.o.b.	1,355.6	1,048.0	1,547.9
Imports of goods f.o.b.	–4,907.5	–4,264.1	–4,305.3
Trade balance	–3,551.7	–3,216.1	–2,757.5
Exports of services	2,478.2	2,482.8	2,243.2
Imports of services	–2,379.4	–2,231.2	–2,010.3
Balance on goods and services	–3,452.9	–2,964.6	–2,524.6
Other income received	473.0	377.2	377.6
Other income paid	–418.1	–557.5	–478.7
Balance on goods, services and income	–3,398.1	–3,144.9	–2,625.7
Current transfers received	1,643.2	1,528.1	1,426.3
Current transfers paid	–263.8	–221.2	–204.5
Current balance	–2,018.7	–1,838.0	–1,403.9
Capital account (net)	115.3	118.7	112.3
Direct investment abroad	–84.2	–39.2	–0.2
Direct investment from abroad	958.7	963.7	1,109.6
Portfolio investment assets	–83.5	18.7	–118.4
Portfolio investment liabilities	45.7	8.5	421.0
Other investment assets	286.8	62.1	–212.6
Other investment liabilities	370.3	–351.0	–383.0
Net errors and omissions	14.2	415.8	411.0
Overall balance	–395.4	–640.7	–64.3

Source: IMF, *International Financial Statistics*.

External Trade

PRINCIPAL COMMODITIES
(million lekë)

Imports c.i.f.	2008	2009	2010
Food, beverages and tobacco	73,160	74,692	80,449
Mineral fuels and electricity	78,705	61,990	72,673
Chemical and plastic products	45,465	50,971	54,855
Wood manufactures	15,016	17,446	19,847
Textiles and footwear	39,582	39,557	43,688
Construction materials and metals	67,827	66,693	73,499
Machinery equipment and spare parts	97,059	98,381	88,383
Total (incl. others)	439,894	431,107	458,429

Exports f.o.b.	2008	2009	2010
Food, beverages and tobacco	7,215	7,498	9,318
Mineral fuels and electricity	20,339	20,648	44,858
Chemical and plastic products	1,177	1,644	1,695
Wood manufactures	3,619	3,431	4,796
Textiles and footwear	48,813	48,345	55,623
Construction materials and metals	22,492	12,914	31,881
Machinery equipment and spare parts	4,578	4,894	6,766
Total (incl. others)	112,572	103,244	160,962

PRINCIPAL TRADING PARTNERS
(million lekë)*

Imports c.i.f.	2008	2009	2010
Austria	5,636	5,391	7,630
Brazil	6,122	4,633	4,233
Bulgaria	8,406	8,116	8,164
Croatia	4,378	4,237	9,122
France	5,259	9,023	10,226
Germany	26,724	27,868	25,182
Greece	64,353	66,955	60,080
Italy	116,462	112,610	131,106
Macedonia, former Yugoslav republic	9,686	7,845	7,266
Russia	19,241	11,635	10,304
Serbia and Montenegro†	18,644	12,239	17,433
Slovenia	3,938	3,936	5,137
Spain	6,121	6,841	7,217
Turkey	26,245	27,743	25,476
Ukraine	6,570	6,994	4,338
United Kingdom	4,568	5,312	6,832
USA	5,607	6,293	7,072
Total (incl. others)	439,894	431,107	458,429

Exports f.o.b.	2008	2009	2010
Austria	762	891	1,664
Germany	3,016	3,520	4,436
Greece	9,904	7,615	8,733
Italy	69,593	64,795	82,090
Macedonia, former Yugoslav republic	3,225	2,866	2,667
Serbia and Montenegro†	4,353	2,195	3,459
Turkey	2,164	570	9,116
Sweden	469	106	129
Switzerland	399	1,210	6,692
USA	425	845	2,379
Total (incl. others)	112,572	103,244	160,962

* Imports by country of origin; exports by country of destination.

† Although the State Union of Serbia and Montenegro was dissolved in 2006, official reporting of Albanian trade data with the successor states has continued to be aggregated.

Transport

RAILWAYS
(traffic)

	2008	2009	2010
Passengers carried ('000)	822	645	430
Passenger-km (million)	41	32	19
Freight carried ('000 metric tons)	355	343	403
Freight ton-km (million)	52	46	66

ROAD TRAFFIC
(motor vehicles in use at 31 December)

	2008	2009	2010
Passenger cars	264,828	281,236	294,729
Buses and coaches	6,645	6,594	7,032
Lorries and vans	79,054	79,905	84,314
Road tractors	1,987	1,969	1,997
Motorcycles and mopeds	18,329	20,874	24,022
Trailers	7,217	7,403	7,799

SHIPPING

Merchant Fleet
(registered at 31 December)

	2007	2008	2009
Number of vessels	73	74	71
Displacement ('000 gross registered tons)	67.5	65.7	67.2

Source: IHS Fairplay, *World Fleet Statistics*.

International Sea-borne Freight Traffic
('000 metric tons)

	2003	2004	2005
Goods loaded	276	324	372
Goods unloaded	3,144	3,300	3,588

Source: UN, *Monthly Bulletin of Statistics*.

Goods loaded and unloaded ('000 metric tons): 4,705 in 2008; 4,193 in 2009; 4,170 in 2010.

CIVIL AVIATION
(traffic on scheduled services)

	2008	2009	2010
Passengers ('000):			
arrivals	615	687	752
departures	645	708	784
Freight (metric tons):			
loaded	1,408	1,217	249
unloaded	1,152	647	1,691

Tourism

FOREIGN TOURIST ARRIVALS BY COUNTRY OF ORIGIN*

	2006	2007	2008
Germany	27,364	31,181	38,428
Greece	56,219	58,217	85,505
Italy	68,240	84,680	98,573
Macedonia, former Yugoslav republic	187,554	224,348	341,801
Montenegro	n.a.	105,636	120,125
Serbia	n.a.	336,322	384,328
Serbia and Montenegro†	352,707	n.a.	n.a.
Turkey	14,286	21,812	32,575
United Kingdom	48,886	52,918	60,043
USA	36,057	43,779	50,354
Total (incl. others)	937,038	1,126,524	1,419,191

* Figures refer to arrivals at frontiers of visitors from abroad, and include same-day visitors.

† From 2007 data are attributed to independent successor states of Serbia and Montenegro.

Tourist arrivals ('000): 1,775 in 2009; 2,229 in 2010 (provisional).

Tourism receipts (US $ million, incl. passenger transport, unless otherwise indicated): 1,057 in 2006; 1,055 in 2007; 1,849 in 2008; 1,816 in 2009 (excl. passenger transport); 1,626 in 2010 (provisional, excl. passenger transport).

Source: World Tourism Organization.

Communications Media

	2008	2009	2010
Telephones ('000 main lines in use)	343.6	363.0	331.5
Mobile cellular telephones ('000 subscribers)	3,141.2	4,161.6	4,547.8
Internet subscribers ('000)	84	105	n.a.
Broadband subscribers ('000)	64.0	92.0	110.0

Personal computers: 145,000 (46.1 per 1,000 persons) in 2008.

Television receivers ('000 in use): 480 in 2000.

Radio receivers ('000 in use): 810 in 1997.

Book production (1991): 381 titles (including 18 pamphlets).

Daily newspapers (2006): Titles 5; Average circulation ('000 copies) 116.

Sources: UN, *Statistical Yearbook*; UNESCO, *Statistical Yearbook*; International Telecommunication Union.

Education

(2008/09 unless otherwise indicated)

	Institutions	Teachers	Students*
Pre-primary	1,774	3,949	74,914†
Primary and lower secondary	1,605	27,724	439,995
Upper secondary	502	8,046	140,657
General	403‡	n.a.	120,651
Vocational	89	1,508§	20,006
Higher education	26	2,885	116,292

* 2009/10.

† Figure includes enrolment in public schools only.

‡ 2006/07.

§ 2003/04.

Source: Ministry of Education, Tirana.

Pupil-teacher ratio (primary education, UNESCO estimate): 19.7 in 2009/10 (Source: UNESCO Institute for Statistics).

Adult literacy rate (UNESCO estimates): 95.9% (males 97.3 females 94.7%) in 2008 (Source: UNESCO Institute for Statistics).

Directory

The Government

HEAD OF STATE

President of the Republic: BAMIR TOPI (elected by vote of the Kuvendi Popullor 20 July 2007; inaugurated 24 July 2007).

COUNCIL OF MINISTERS

(May 2012)

A coalition of the Democratic Party of Albania (DPA), the Socialist Movement for Integration (SMI) and the Republican Party of Albania (RPA).

Prime Minister: Prof. SALI BERISHA (DPA).

Deputy Prime Minister and Minister of Foreign Affairs: EDMOND HAXHINASTO (SMI).

Minister of European Integration: MAJLINDA BREGU (DPA).

Minister of the Interior: BUJAR NISHANI (DPA).

Minister of Defence: ARBEN IMAMI (DPA).

Minister of Finance: RIDVAN BODE (DPA).

Minister of Justice: EDUARD HALIMI (DPA).

Minister of Public Works and Transport: SOKOL OLLDASHI (DPA).

Minister of Education and Science: MYQEREM TAFAJ (DPA).

Minister of Health: PETRIT VASILI (SMI).

Minister of Labour, Social Affairs and Equal Opportunities: SPIRO KSERA (SMI).

Minister of Agriculture, Food and Consumer Protection: GENC RULI (DPA).

Minister of Tourism, Culture, Youth and Sports: ALDO BUMÇI (DPA).

Minister of the Environment: FATMIR MEDIU (RPA).

Minister of Innovation and Information and Communication Technologies: GENC POLLO (DPA).

Minister of Economy, Trade and Energy: NASIP NAÇO (SMI).

MINISTRIES

Office of the President: Bulevardi Dëshmorët e Kombit, Tirana; tel. (4) 2389811; e-mail gen_sec@president.al; internet www.president.al.

Office of the Prime Minister: Bulevardi Dëshmorët e Kombit 1, 1000 Tirana; tel. (4) 2277404; fax (4) 2237501; e-mail info@km.gov.al; internet www.km.gov.al.

Ministry of Agriculture, Food and Consumer Protection: Sheshi Skënderbej 2, 1001 Tirana; tel. and fax (4) 2226551; e-mail info@mbumk.gov.al; internet www.mbumk.gov.al.

Ministry of Defence: Bulevardi Dëshmorët e Kombit, Tirana; tel. (4) 2226601; fax (4) 2228325; e-mail kontakt@mod.gov.al; internet www.mod.gov.al.

Ministry of Economy, Trade and Energy: Bulevardi Dëshmorët e Kombit 2, 1001 Tirana; tel. (4) 2227617; fax (4) 2234052; e-mail kabineti@mete.gov.al; internet www.mete.gov.al.

Ministry of Education and Science: Rruga Durrësit 23, Tirana; tel. and fax (4) 2230289; e-mail webmaster@mash.gov.al; internet www.mash.gov.al.

Ministry of the Environment: Rruga Durrësit 27, Tirana; tel. (4) 2224537; fax (4) 2270627; e-mail info@moe.gov.al; internet www.moe.gov.al.

Ministry of European Integration: Rruga Papa Gjon Pali II 3, POB 8302, Tirana; tel. (4) 2228623; fax (4) 2256267; e-mail albert.gajo@mie.gov.al; internet www.mie.gov.al.

Ministry of Finance: Bulevardi Dëshmorët e Kombit 4, 1001 Tirana; tel. (4) 2227937; fax (4) 2226111; e-mail dteliti@minfin.gov.al; internet www.minfin.gov.al.

Ministry of Foreign Affairs: Bulevardi Gjergj Fishta 6, Tirana; tel. (4) 2364090; fax (4) 2362084; e-mail info@mfa.gov.al; internet www.mfa.gov.al.

Ministry of Health: Bulevardi Bajram Curri 1, Tirana; tel. and fax (4) 2364908; e-mail ministri@moh.gov.al; internet www.moh.gov.al.

Ministry of Innovation and Information and Communication Technologies: Bulevardi Dëshmorët e Kombit 1, 1000 Tirana; tel. and fax (4) 2277306; fax (4) 2248298; e-mail genc.pollo@km.gov.al; internet www.mitik.gov.al.

Ministry of the Interior: Sheshi Skënderbej 3, Tirana; tel. (4) 2247155; e-mail ministria.brendshme@moi.gov.al; internet www.moi.gov.al.

Ministry of Justice: Bulevardi Dëshmorët e Kombit, Tirana; tel. (4) 2259388; fax (4) 2228359; e-mail gerdjan.xhanari@justice.gov.al; internet www.justice.gov.al.

Ministry of Labour, Social Affairs and Equal Opportunities: Rruga e Kavajës, 1001 Tirana; tel. (4) 2226132; fax (4) 2233429; e-mail kontakt@mpcs.gov.al; internet www.mpcs.gov.al.

Ministry of Public Works and Transport: Sheshi Skënderbej 5, Tirana; tel. and fax (4) 2380833; e-mail stela.basha@mppt.gov.al; internet www.mpptt.gov.al.

Ministry of Tourism, Culture, Youth and Sports: Rruga e Kavajës, Tirana; tel. (4) 2224204; fax (4) 2232488; e-mail informacion@mtkrs.gov.al; internet www.mtkrs.gov.al.

President

The first three rounds of voting for a President, conducted by members of the Kuvendi Popullor (People's Assembly) in July 2007, proved unsuccessful, as in each case fewer deputies than the required quorum of 85 participated (with 84 votes being required of the successful candidate). In the first round of polling, held on 8 July, BAMIR TOPI obtained 75 votes, and FATOS NANO won three votes. In a second round, conducted on 11 July, Topi obtained 75 votes, and Nano five. In a third round, held on 14 July, Topi obtained 50 votes, NERITAN CEKA 32 votes and Nano three. (The candidacy of Nano was thereby eliminated.) The fourth round of voting, held on 20 July, proved conclusive, as Topi obtained 85 votes, compared to the five awarded to Ceka. Topi was inaugurated on 24 July.

Legislature

Kuvendi Popullor
(People's Assembly)

Bulevardi Dëshmorët e Kombit 4, Tirana; tel. (4) 2278259; fax (4) 2221764; e-mail llleshi@parlament.al; internet www.parlament.al.

Speaker: JOZEFINA TOPALLI.

General Election, 28 June 2009

	Votes	%	Seats
Alliance for Change coalition	712,745	46.92	70
Democratic Party of Albania	610,463	40.18	68
Republican Party of Albania	31,990	2.11	1
Party for Justice and Integration	14,477	0.95	1
Unification for Change coalition	688,748	45.34	66
Socialist Party of Albania	620,586	40.85	65
Union for Human Rights Party	18,078	1.19	1
Socialist Alliance for Integration coalition	84,407	5.56	4
Socialist Movement for Integration	73,678	4.85	4
Pole of Freedom coalition	27,655	1.82	—
Independent candidates	5,621	0.37	—
Total	1,519,176	100.00	140

Election Commission

Komisioni Qendror i Zgjyedhjeve (KQZ) (Central Election Commission—CEC): Pallati i Kongreseve, Tirana; tel. and fax (4) 2235362; e-mail infosec@cec.org.al; internet www.cec.org.al; f. 1996; seven members: two elected by the Kuvendi Popullor, two by the President and three by the High Council of Justice; Chair. ARBEN RISTANI.

Political Organizations

Albanian Communist Party (ACP) (Partia Komuniste e Shqipërisë—PKSh): Tirana; fax (4) 2233164; f. 1991; granted legal recognition 1998; Chair. HYSNI MILLOSHI.

Albanian Green Party (Partia Gjelbërite e Shqipërisë): Rruga Bajram Curri Pall. 31/1/4, Tirana; tel. and fax (4) 2230676; e-mail office@pgj.al; internet www.pgj.al; f. 2001; ecologist; observer mem. of European Greens; contested 2009 legislative elections as mem. of Socialist Alliance; Chair. EDLIR PETANAJ.

Christian Democratic Party of Albania (CDPA) (Partia Demokristiane e Shqipërisë—PDK): Rruga Dëshmorët e 4 Shkurtit, Tirana; tel. (4) 2240574; fax (4) 2233024; e-mail partia.demokristiane@pdk.al; f. 1991; contested 2009 legislative elections as mem. of Pole of Freedom; Leader NARD NDOKA.

Democratic Alliance Party (DAP) (Partia Aleanca Demokratike—PAD): Tirana; tel. and fax (4) 2251971; e-mail aleancademokratikeal@yahoo.com; internet www.aleancademokratike.al; f. 1992 by fmr mems of the Democratic Party of Albania; contested 2009 legislative elections as mem. of Alliance for Change; Chair. NERITAN CEKA; Sec.-Gen. EDMOND DRAGOTI.

Democratic Party of Albania (DPA) (Partia Demokratike e Shqipërisë—PDSh): Rruga Punëtorët e Rilindjes 1, 1001 Tirana; tel. (4) 2228091; fax (4) 2223525; e-mail profsberisha@albaniaonline.net; internet www.pd.al; f. 1990; centre-right, pro-democracy, pro-market; merged with the New Democratic Party (f. 2001 by fmr mems of the DPA) in 2008; contested 2009 legislative elections as mem. of Alliance for Change; Chair. Prof. SALI BERISHA; Sec.-Gen. RIDVAN BODE.

Environmentalist Agrarian Party (EAP) (Partia Agrare Ambientaliste—PAA): Rruga Budi 6, Tirana; tel. and fax (4) 2231904; e-mail lufterxhuveli@yahoo.com; f. 1991; Chair. LUFTER XHUVELI.

Justice and Unity Party (Partisë për Drejtësi dhe Unitet): Rruga e Elbasanit, Tirana; internet www.pdu.al; tel. (4) 2235449; f. 2009; Chair. SHPËTIM IDRIZI.

Liberal Democratic Union Party (LDUP) (Partia Bashkimi Liberal Demokrat—PBLD): Tirana; contested 2009 legislative elections as mem. of Alliance for Change; Chair. ARJAN STAROVA.

Movement for Solidarity: Tirana; f. Sept. 2007 by fmr leader of the SPA; Leader FATOS NANO.

Movement of Legality Party (MLP) (Partia Lëvizja e Legalitetit—PLL): Bulevardi Zog I, Tirana; tel. and fax (4) 2230076; e-mail levizja_legalitetit@yahoo.com; internet www.legaliteti.org; f. 1992; monarchist; contested 2009 legislative elections as mem. of Alliance for Change; Chair. EKREM SPAHIA; Sec.-Gen. ARTAN TUJANI.

Party for Justice, Integration and Unity (PDIU) (Partia Drejtesi Integrim dhe Unitet): Rruga e Elbasanit, Tirana; tel. (4) 2235449; e-mail info@pdiu.al; internet www.pdiu.al; f. 2011 by merger of the Party for Justice and Integration and the Party for Justice and Unity; centre-right; concerned with issues affecting the Cham minority, an ethnic group of Greek origin; Chair. SHPËTIM IDRIZI.

Republican Party of Albania (RPA) (Partia Republika e Shqipërisë—PRSh): Tirana; f. 1991; contested 2009 legislative elections as mem. of Alliance for Change; Chair. FATMIR MEDIU.

Social Democracy Party (Partia Demokracia Sociale): Bulevardi Dëshmorët e Kombit 4, Tirana; tel. and fax (4) 2228526; f. 2003 by breakaway faction of the SDP; contested 2009 legislative elections as mem. of Unification for Change; Chair. Prof. Dr PASKAL MILO.

Social Democratic Party (SDP) (Partia Socialdemokrate—PSD): Rruga Asim Vokshi 26, Tirana; tel. (4) 2226540; fax (4) 2223338; f. 1991; contested 2009 legislative elections as mem. of Unification for Change; Chair. SKËNDER GJINUSHI.

Socialist Movement for Integration (SMI) (Lëvizja Socialiste për Integrim—LSI): Rruga Sami Frasheri, Godina 20/10, Tirana; tel. (4) 2270412; fax (4) 2270413; e-mail secretariat@lsi.al; internet www.lsi.al; f. 2004 by fmr mems of the SPA; moderate socialist; contested 2009 legislative elections as mem. of Socialist Alliance; Chair. ILIR META; c. 40,000 mems (April 2005).

Socialist Party of Albania (SPA) (Partia Socialiste e Shqipërisë—PSSh): Tirana; tel. (4) 2227409; fax (4) 2227417; e-mail info@ps.al; internet www.ps.al; f. 1941 as Albanian Communist Party; renamed Party of Labour of Albania in 1948, adopted present name in 1991; now rejects Marxism-Leninism and claims commitment to democratic socialism and a market economy; contested 2009 legislative elections as mem. of Unification for Change; Chair. EDI RAMA; 110,000 mems.

Union for Human Rights Party (UHRP) (Partia Bashkimi për të Drejtat e Njeriut—PBDNj): Bulevardi Bajram Curri 32, Tirana; tel. and fax (4) 2377921; e-mail contact@pbdnj.com; internet www.pbdnj.com; f. 1992; represents the Greek and Macedonian minorities; contested 2009 legislative elections as mem. of Unification for Change; Leader VANGJEL DULE.

Diplomatic Representation

EMBASSIES IN ALBANIA

Austria: Rruga Frederik Shiroka 3, Tirana; tel. (4) 2274855; fax (4) 2233140; e-mail tirana-ob@bmeia.gv.al; Ambassador FLORIAN RAUNIG.

Bulgaria: Rruga Skënderbej 12, Tirana; tel. (4) 2233155; fax (4) 2232272; e-mail embassy.tirana@mfa.bg; internet www.mfa.bg/bg/11/; Ambassador TEODOR S. RUSINOV.

China, People's Republic: Rruga Skënderbej 57, Tirana; tel. (4) 2232385; fax (4) 2233159; e-mail chinaemb_al@mfa.gov.cn; internet al.china-embassy.org; Ambassador YE HAO.

Croatia: Rruga A. Toptani, Torre Drin 4, Tirana; tel. (4) 2256948; fax (4) 2230578; e-mail croemb.tirana@mvpei.hr; Ambassador ALEKSANDER STIPETIĆ.

Czech Republic: Rruga Skënderbej 10, Tirana; tel. (4) 2234004; fax (4) 2232759; e-mail tirana@embassy.mzv.cz; internet www.mzv.cz/tirana; Chargé d'affaires VLADIMÍR VÁLKY.

Denmark: Rruga Nikolla Tupe 1/4, POB 1743, Tirana; tel. (4) 2280600; fax (4) 2280630; e-mail tiaamb@um.dk; internet www.ambtirana.um.dk; Ambassador KARSTEN ANKJÆR JENSEN.

Egypt: Rruga Skënderbej 1, Tirana; tel. (4) 2233022; fax (4) 2232295; e-mail egyemb@albaniaonline.net; Ambassador AMINA EMAM GOMAA.

France: Rruga Skënderbej 14, Tirana; tel. (4) 2234250; fax (4) 2234442; e-mail ambafrance.tr@adanet.com.al; internet www.ambafrance-al.org; Ambassador CHRISTINE MORO.

Germany: Rruga Skënderbej 8, Tirana; tel. (4) 2274505; fax (4) 2233497; e-mail info@tira.diplo.de; internet www.tirana.diplo.de; Ambassador CAROLA MÜLLER-HOLTKEMPER.

Greece: Rruga Frederik Shiroka 3, Tirana; tel. (4) 2274670; fax (4) 2234290; e-mail gremb.tir@mfa.gr; internet www.mfa.gr/tirana; Ambassador NICOLAS PAZIOS.

Holy See: Rruga e Durrësit 13, POB 8355, Tirana; tel. (4) 2233516; fax (4) 2232001; e-mail nunapal@icc-al.org; Apostolic Nuncio Most Rev. MOLINER INGLÉS RAMIRO (Titular Archbishop of Sardanensis).

Hungary: Rruga Skënderbej 16, Tirana; tel. (4) 2232238; fax (4) 2233211; e-mail mission.tia@kum.hu; internet www.mfa.gov.hu/emb/tirana; Ambassador JÁNOS HUSZÁR.

Iran: Rruga Mustafa Matohiti 20, Tirana; tel. (4) 2255038; fax (4) 2254621; Ambassador ALI AMOEE.

Italy: Rruga Papa Gjon Pali II 2, Tirana; tel. (4) 2275900; fax (4) 2250921; e-mail segreteriaambasciata.tirana@esteri.it; internet www.ambtirana.esteri.it; Ambassador MASSIMO GAIANI.

Kosovo: Rruga Skënderbej, Pallati 6, Tirana; tel. and fax (4) 2261650; e-mail embassy.albania@ks-gov.net; Chargé d'affaires GANI VESELAJ.

Libya: Rruga e Elbasanit, përballë Pallatit të Brigadave 9, Tirana; tel. (4) 2347816; fax (4) 2343434; e-mail lib_emb_al@foreign.gov.ly; Chargé d'affaires ZOHEIL EL-AZZABI.

Macedonia, former Yugoslav republic: Rruga Kavajës 116, Tirana; tel. (4) 2230909; fax (4) 2232514; e-mail tirana@mfa.gov.mk; internet www.missions.gov.mk/tirana; Ambassador VELE TRPEVSKI.

Montenegro: Rruga Abdi Toptani, Pallati Tore Drin, kati 8, Tirana; tel. (4) 2261309; fax (4) 2257406; e-mail mnembassy@albmail.com; Ambassador FERHAT DINOSHA.

Netherlands: Rruga Asim Zeneli 10, Tirana; tel. (4) 2240828; fax (4) 2232723; e-mail tir@minbuza.nl; internet www.mfa.nl/tir; Ambassador HENK G. C. VAN DEN DOOL.

Poland: Rruga e Durrësit 123, Tirana; tel. (4) 2234190; fax (4) 2233364; e-mail tirana.amb.sekretariat@msz.gov.pl; internet www.tirana.polemb.net; Ambassador IRENA TATARZYŃSKA.

Romania: Rruga Themistokli Gërmeni 1, Tirana; tel. (4) 2256071; fax (4) 2256072; e-mail roemb@adanet.co.al; Ambassador VIOREL STANILĂ.

Russia: Rruga Donika Kastrioti 2, Tirana; tel. (4) 2256040; fax (4) 2256046; e-mail rusemb@albmail.com; Ambassador LEONID ABRAMOV.

Saudi Arabia: Rruga Kavaja 116, Tirana; tel. (4) 2248306; fax (4) 2229982; e-mail embsaudarab@albaniaonline.net; Ambassador ABDULLAH A. AL-ABDULKARIM.

Serbia: Rruga Donika Kastrioti 9/1, Tirana; tel. (4) 2232091; fax (4) 2232089; e-mail ambatira@icc-al.org; internet www.tirana.mfa.gov.rs; Ambassador MIROLJUB ZARIĆ.

Slovenia: Rruga Abdyl Frashëri, EGT Tower, 3rd Floor, Tirana; tel. (4) 2274858; fax (4) 2221311; e-mail vti@gov.si; Ambassador BOJAN BERTONCELJ.

Spain: Rruga Skënderbej 43, Tirana; tel. (4) 2274960; fax (4) 2225383; e-mail emb.tirana@maec.es; Ambassador RAFAEL TORMO PÉREZ.

Switzerland: Rruga Dëshmorët e 4 Shkurtit 3/1, Tirana; tel. (4) 2234888; fax (4) 2234889; e-mail tir.vertretung@eda.admin.ch; internet www.eda.admin.ch/tirana; Ambassador YVANA ENZLER.

Turkey: Rruga e Elbasanit 65, Tirana; tel. (4) 2380350; fax (4) 2347767; e-mail embassy.tirana@mfa.gov.tr; internet www.tirana.emb.mfa.gov.tr; Ambassador HASAN S. AŞAN.

United Kingdom: Rruga Skënderbej 12, Tirana; tel. (4) 2234973; fax (4) 2247697; e-mail information.tiran@fco.gov.uk; internet www.ukinalbania.fco.gov.uk; Ambassador FIONA MCILWHAM.

USA: Rruga e Elbasanit 103, Tirana; tel. (4) 2247285; fax (4) 2232222; e-mail wm_tirana@pd.state.gov; internet tirana.usembassy.gov; Ambassador Dr ALEXANDER A. ARVIZU.

Judicial System

The judicial structure comprises the Supreme Court, the Courts of Appeal and the Courts of First Instance. The Chairman and members of the Supreme Court are appointed by the President of the Republic, with the approval of the legislature, for a term of nine years. Other judges are appointed by the President upon the proposal of the High Council of Justice. The High Council of Justice comprises the President of the Republic (who is its Chairman), the Chief Justice of the Supreme Court, the Minister of Justice, three members elected by the legislature for a term of five years, and nine judges of all levels who are elected by a national judicial conference. The Supreme Court consists of 17 members, appointed to office by the President, with the approval of the legislature, for a single, nine-year term. The Constitutional Court arbitrates on constitutional issues, and determines, *inter alia*, the conformity of proposed legislation with the Constitution. It is empowered to prohibit the activities of political organizations on constitutional grounds, and also formulates legislation regarding the election of the President of the Republic. The Constitutional Court comprises nine members, who are appointed by the President, with the approval of the legislature, for a term of nine years.

High Council of Justice: Bulevardi Zogu I, Tirana; tel. (4) 2280804; fax (4) 2259822; e-mail office@kld.al; internet www.kld.al; Chair. President of the Republic ; Dep. Chair. KRESHNIK SPAHIU.

Supreme Court (Gjykata e Larte): Rruga Dëshmorët e 4 Shkurtit, Tirana; tel. (4) 2228327; fax (4) 2228837; e-mail supremecourt@gjykataelarte.gov.al; internet www.gjykataelarte.gov.al; Chief Justice SHPRESA BEÇAJ.

Constitutional Court (Gjykata Kushtetuese): Bulevardi Dëshmoret e Kombit, Tirana; tel. and fax (4) 2228357; e-mail kujtim.osmani@gjk.gov.al; internet www.gjk.gov.al; Pres. BASHKIM DEDJA.

Office of the Prosecutor-General (Zyra e Prokurorit te Pergjithshem): Rruga Qemal Stafa 1, Tirana; tel. (4) 2234850; fax (4) 2229085; e-mail admin@pp.com; internet www.pp.gov.al; Prosecutor-General INA RAMA.

Religion

In May 1990 a prohibition on religious activities, enforced since 1967, was revoked, religious services were permitted and, from 1991, mosques and churches began to be reopened. Under the Constitution of November 1998, Albania is a secular state, which respects freedom of religious belief. On the basis of declared affiliation in 1945, it is estimated that some 70% of the population are of Muslim background, of whom about 75% are associated with Sunni Islam; many of the remainder are associated with the Bektashi sect, a Sufi dervish order. Muslims are mainly concentrated in the middle and, to some extent, the south of the country. Some 20% of the population are of Eastern Orthodox Christian background (mainly in the south) and some 13% are associated with the Roman Catholic Church (mainly in the north).

ISLAM

Albanian Islamic Community (AIC) (Bashkesia Islame e Shqipërisë): Rruga Puntoret e Rilindjes 50, Tirana; tel. and fax (22) 230492; e-mail icalb@yahoo.com; f. 1991 as Albanian Muslim Community; renamed as above in 2005; Chair. and Grand Mufti of Albania SELIM MUÇA.

Bektashi Sect

Albania is the world centre of the Bektashi sect.

World Council of Elders of the Bektashis (Kryegjyshata Boterore e Bektashinjve): Tirana; f. 1991; Chair. (vacant).

CHRISTIANITY

The Eastern Orthodox Church

Orthodox Autocephalous Church of Albania (Kisha Orthodhokse Autoqefale e Shqipërisë): Rruga e Kavajes 151, Tirana; tel. (4) 2234117; fax (4) 2232109; e-mail orthchal@orthodoxalbania.org; internet www.orthodoxalbania.org; the Albanian Orthodox Church was proclaimed autocephalous at the Congress of Berat in 1922, and it was recognized by the Ecumenical Patriarchate of Constantinople (İstanbul), Turkey, in 1937; Archbishop of Tirana, Durrës and all Albania ANASTASIOS YANNOULATOS.

The Roman Catholic Church

Many Roman Catholic churches have been reopened since 1990, and in September 1991 diplomatic relations were restored with the Holy See. Albania comprises two archdioceses, three dioceses and one apostolic administration. Some 12.8% of the population are Roman Catholics.

Bishops' Conference: Rruga Don Bosko 1, POB 2950, Tirana; tel. and fax (4) 2247159; e-mail cealbania@albmail.com; Pres. Most Rev. ROK K. MIRDITA (Archbishop of Tirana-Durrës).

Archbishop of Shkodër-Pult: Most Rev. ANGELO MASSAFRA, Sheshi Gjon Pali II, Shkodër; tel. (22) 242744; fax (22) 243673; e-mail curiashkoder@hotmail.com.

Archbishop of Tirana-Durrës: Most Rev. ROK K. MIRDITA, Bulevardi Zhan d'Ark, Tirana; tel. (4) 2232082; fax (4) 2230727; e-mail arq@icc.al.org.

The Press

PRINCIPAL NEWSPAPERS

Albania: Rruga Don Bosko, Tirana; tel. (4) 2229243; fax (4) 2223198; e-mail albaniakryeredaktor@yahoo.com; internet www.gazeta-albania.net; independent; politics, society, culture; pro-Democratic Party of Albania (DPA); Dir YLLI RAKIPI; Editor-in-Chief ARMAND META.

Albanian Daily News: Rruga Dervish Hima 1, ADA Tower, Tirana; tel. (4) 2256112; fax (4) 2240888; e-mail editoradn@albnet.net; internet www.albaniannews.com; f. 1995; in English, subscription-based online edition updated daily, printed weekly newspaper; Editor ARBEN LESKAJ.

Biznesi (Business): Rruga Don Bosko, Vilat e Reja, POB 2423, Tirana; tel. (4) 2251422; fax (4) 2233526; e-mail kontakt@biznesi.com.al; in Albanian; Editor-in-Chief ORJETA ZHUPA.

Gazeta 55 (Newspaper 55): Rruga Medar Shtylla; tel. (4) 2321364; fax (4) 2321365; e-mail info@gazeta55.net; internet www.gazeta55.net; f. 1997; independent; right-wing; English summary; Editor-in-Chief ILIR NIKOLLA.

Gazeta Ballkan: Rruga Durresit 61, Tirana; tel. and fax (4) 2229954; e-mail info@ballkan.com; internet www.ballkan.com; Editor-in-Chief ROMIR SARACI.

Gazeta Shqiptare (The Albanian Newspaper): Ish-Drejtoria e Uzines se AutoTraktoreve, Tirana; tel. (4) 2359104; fax (4) 2359116; e-mail gazetashqiptare@hotmail.com; internet www.balkanweb.com; f. 1927; re-established 1993; independent; politics, economics, culture; local news section; Editor-in-Chief ERL MURATI.

Gazeta Start: Tirana; e-mail info@gazetastart.com; internet www.gazetastart.com; Editor-in-Chief KLODIAN SHEHI; circ. 10,000 (Jan. 2010).

Integrimi (Integration): Rruga Sami Frasheri, 20/10, Tirana 1001; tel. (4) 2270413; fax (4) 2270412; e-mail breguz@gmail.com; internet www.integrimi.com; organ of the Socialist Movement for Integration.

Koha Jonë (Our Time): Rruga Aleksandër Moisiu 1, Tirana; tel. (4) 2347805; fax (4) 2347808; e-mail edisonkurani@kohajone.com; internet www.kohajone.com; f. 1991; independent; Editor-in-Chief EDISON KURANI; circ. 400,000.

Korrieri (The Courier): Rruga Dervish Hima 1, Tirana; tel. (4) 2253574; fax (4) 2253575; e-mail posta@korrieri.com; internet www.korrieri.com; independent; Editor-in-Chief ALFRED PEZA.

Metropol: Rruga Dull Keta 5, Tirana; tel. (4) 2233991; fax (4) 2233998; e-mail gazetametropol@yahoo.com; internet www.gazetametropol.com; Editor-in-Chief BRAHIM SHIMA.

Panorama (Panorama): Rruga Jordan Misja, prapa shkollës Harry Fultz, Pallati 1, Kati i II-të, Tirana; tel. (4) 2273207; fax (4) 2273206; e-mail info@panorama.com.al; internet www.panorama.com.al; independent; politics, economics, culture, sports, arts; Editor-in-Chief ROBERT RAKIPLLARI.

Rilindja Demokratike (Democratic Revival): Rruga Punëtorët e Rilindjes, pranë selisë së PD, Tirana; tel. (4) 2232355; fax (4) 2230329; e-mail gazetard@albaniaonline.net; internet www.rilindjademokratike.com; f. 1991; organ of the DPA; Editor-in-Chief BLEDI KASMI; circ. 50,000.

Shekulli (Century): Rruga Ismail Qemali, Pallati Abissnet, Tirana; tel. (4) 2256025; fax (4) 2256016; e-mail kryeredaktor.shekulli@abissnet.al; internet www.shekulli.com.al; independent; national and international politics, economics, culture; English summary; Editor-in-Chief ENED JANINA.

Sot (Today): Rruga Donika Kastrioti 9/1; tel. (4) 2382019; fax (4) 2382020; e-mail gazeta@sot.com.al; internet www.sot.com.al; Albanian and English; current affairs; Editor-in-Chief DRITAN YLLI.

Sporti Shqiptar (Albanian Sports): Rruga Aleksandër Moisiu, ish-Kinostudio, Tirana; tel. and fax (4) 2368322; e-mail sportishqiptar@live.com; internet www.sportishqiptar.com.al; f. 1935; national and international sports; Publr KOÇO KOKËDHIMA; Editor BASHKIM TUFA; circ. 10,000.

Tema: Zayed Business Center, Rruga Sulejman Delvina, 3rd Floor, Tirana; tel. and fax (4) 2251073; e-mail info@tema.al; internet www.gazetatema.net; independent; liberal; Editor-in-Chief MERO BAZE.

Tirana Observer: Rruga Irfan Tomini, Pallati Biorn, Kati i 2-të, Tirana; tel. (4) 2419002; fax (4) 2419000; e-mail kontakti@tiranaobserver.al; internet www.tiranaobserver.al; Editor ALTIN SINANI.

Tirana Times: Rruga Dëshmorët e 4 Shkurtit 7/1, Tirana; tel. (4) 2274203; fax (4) 2274204; e-mail editor@tiranatimes.com; internet www.tiranatimes.com; f. 2005; weekly (hard copy), daily (online); in English; news, analysis, politics, business, culture; Dir and Man. Editor JERINA ZALOSHNJA.

Zëri i Popullit (The Voice of the People): Bulevardi Zhan D'Ark, Tirana; tel. (4) 2222192; fax (4) 2227813; e-mail info@zeri-popullit.com; internet www.zeri-popullit.com; f. 1942; daily, except Mon.; organ of the Socialist Party of Albania (SPA); English summary; Editor-in-Chief ERION BRACE; circ. 105,000.

PERIODICALS

Albanian Journal of Natural and Technical Sciences (AJNTS): Akademia e Shkencave e Shqipërisë, Sheshi Fan S. Noli 7, Tirana; tel. (4) 2259657; fax (4) 2227476; e-mail sbushati@akad.edu.al; two a year; publ. by the Academy of Sciences of Albania Publishing House; in English; all fields of natural and technical sciences; Editor-in-Chief Prof. Dr SALVATORE BUSHATI.

Bujqesia Shqiptare (Albanian Agriculture): Ministria e Bujqësisë, Ushqimit dhe Mbrojtjes së Konsumatorit, Sheshi Skënderbej 2, Tirana; tel. (4) 2232796; fax (4) 2227924; e-mail gjana@hotmail.com; monthly; organ of the Ministry of Agriculture, Food and Consumer Protection; agriculture, cattle-breeding and gardening.

Fjala Review: Rruga M. Gjollesha 48, Tirana; tel. (4) 2273413; e-mail fjala2003@yahoo.com; internet www.fjalareview.com; f. 2001; weekly; literature and culture; in Albanian; Editor-in-Chief ELVANA TUFA.

Gazeta Drita Islame: Tirana; e-mail gazeta@dritaislame.com; monthly; owned by Islamic Community Organization of Albania; in Albanian; Editor HAXHI LIKA.

Gjuha Jonë (Our Language): Akademia e Shkencave e Shqipërisë, Sheshi Fan Noli 7, Tirana; tel. (4) 2256777; fax (4) 2227476; e-mail elafe@akad.edu.al; f. 1981; quarterly; publ. by the Institute of Linguistics and Literature, Academy of Sciences of Albania Publishing House; Albanian language issues; Editor-in-Chief Prof. Dr EMIL LAFE.

Iliria: Instituti i Arkeologjisë, Sheshi Nënë Tereza, Tirana; tel. and fax (4) 2240712; e-mail instark@albmail.com; f. 1971; two a year; publ. by the Archaeological Institute, Academy of Sciences of Albania Publishing House; concerned with archaeology studies in the fields of prehistory, antiquity and the early Middle Ages; in English and French, or in Albanian with English or French summaries; Editor-in-Chief Prof. Dr MUZAFER KORKUTI.

Jeta (Life): Rruga Gjergj Fishta, Pranë Ekspozites Shqiperia Sot, Tirana; tel. (4) 2270913; fax (4) 2270914; e-mail e.toni@jetamediacompany.com; f. 2000; monthly; general interest; illustrated; Gen. Dir ESMERALDA T. ÇOMACKA; circ. 14,000 (2009).

Klan: Rruga Dervish Hima 1, Tirana; tel. (4) 2256111; fax (4) 2234424; e-mail info@revistaklan.com; internet www.revistaklan.com; f. 1997.

Kultura Popullore (Folk Culture Magazine): Instituti i Kultures Popullore, Rruga Kont Urani 3, Tirana; tel. (4) 2222323; e-mail ikp.alb@icc.al.org; f. 1980; annually; publ. by the Institute of Folk Culture, Academy of Sciences of Albania Publishing House; folk culture, anthropology; English summary; Editor-in-Chief Prof. Dr AFËRDITA ONUZI.

Mapo: Rruga Gjin Bue Shpata 9A; tel. (4) 2223110; e-mail info@revistamapo.com; internet www.revistamapo.com; weekly; current affairs, economy, society, culture.

Mbrojtja (The Defence): Bulevardi Dëshmorët e Kombit, Tirana; tel. and fax (4) 2226701; internet www.mod.gov.al/botime/html/revista/revista.htm; f. 1931; monthly; publ. by the Ministry of Defence; Editor-in-Chief TEUTA REXHEPI; circ. 1,500.

Mesuesi (The Teacher): Rruga Durrësit, pranë Ministrise se Arsimit dhe Shkences, Tirana; tel. (4) 2227206; e-mail mesuesi@mash.gov.al; weekly; organ of the Ministry of Education and Science; Editor-in-Chief ANDON ANDONI.

Monitor: Media Union, Pallati 13-katësh për. Stacionit të Trenit, POB 129, Tirana; tel. (4) 2250653; fax (4) 2250654; e-mail revista@monitor.al; internet www.monitor.al; business and economic news; Editor-in-Chief ORNELA LIPERI.

Ngjallja (The Resurrection): Kisha Orthodhokse Autoqefale e Shqipërisë, Rruga e Kavajës 151, Tirana; tel. (4) 2234117; fax (4) 2232109; e-mail orthchal@orthodoxalbania.org; internet www.orthodoxalbania.org; f. 1992; monthly; organ of the Orthodox Autocephalous Church of Albania; Editor-in-Chief THOMA DHIMA.

Revista Pedagogjike: Rruga Naim Frashëri 37, Tirana; tel. (4) 2256440; e-mail sekretaria@izha.edu.a; internet www.izha.edu.al; f. 1945; quarterly; organ of the Institute i Studimeve Pedagogjike (Institute of Pedagogical Studies); educational development, psychology, pedagogy; Editor TIDITA ABDURRAHMANI; circ. 4,000.

Shqip: Bulevardi Zog I Pallati 13-katësh; e-mail info@shqip.al; internet www.shqip.al; monthly; information and culture; Editor NERITANA KRAJA.

Universi i Librit Shqiptar (Universe of the Albanian Book): Botimet Toena, Rruga Muhamet Gjollesha, POB 1420, Tirana; tel. (4) 2240116; fax (4) 2240117; e-mail toena@toena.com.al; internet www.toena.com.al; quarterly review of books publ. in Albanian and of foreign-language books about Albania, Albanian affairs, etc.; Editor-in-Chief IRENA TOÇI.

Ushtria (Army): Bulevardi Dëshmorët e Kombit, Tirana; tel. (4) 2226701; e-mail kontakt@mod.gov.al; internet www.mod.gov.al/botime/html/ushtria/ushtria.htm; f. 1945; weekly; publ. by the Ministry of Defence; Editor-in-Chief ERNEST TUSHE; circ. 3,200.

NEWS AGENCIES

Albanian Telegraphic Agency (ATA) (Agjencia Telegrafike Shqiptare—ATSh): Bulevardi Zhan D'Ark 23, Tirana; tel. (4) 2251152; fax (4) 2234393; e-mail director@ata.gov.al; internet www.ata.gov.al; f. 1929; state-owned; domestic and foreign news; brs in provincial towns and in Kosovo; Dir-Gen. ANTONETA MALJA.

Alna (Albanian News Agency—Agjensi Private e pavarur Lajmesh në Shqiperi): Rruga Ismail Qemali, Tirana; tel. (4) 2257001; fax (4) 2256002; f. 2001.

TIR-FAX Albanian Independent News Agency (AINA TIR-FAX) (Agjensia e Lajmeve të Pavarura Shqiptare): Rruga 4 Dëshmorët Villa 80, Tirana; tel. (4) 2241727; fax (4) 2230094; e-mail aina@abissnet.com.al; internet www.tirfaxnews.org; f. 1996; Albanian and English; Dir ZENEL ÇELIKU.

PRESS ASSOCIATIONS

Albanian Media Institute: Rruga Gjin Bue Shpata 8, Tirana; tel. and fax (4) 2229800; fax (4) 2267084; e-mail info@institutemedia.org; internet www.institutemedia.org; f. 1995; independent; produces books and publications on the Albanian and international media, incl. the *Albanian Media Newsletter* (monthly); Dir REMZI LANI.

Asscn of Professional Journalists of Albania: Rruga Dervish Hima 1, Tirana; e-mail ashkullaku@hotmail.com; affiliated to International Federation of Journalists (Brussels, Belgium); Pres. ARMAND SHKULLAKU.

League of Albanian Journalists: Bulevardi Dëshmorët e Kombit, Tirana; tel. and fax (4) 2228563; e-mail albania@albaniaonline.net; affiliated to International Federation of Journalists (Brussels, Belgium); Pres. YLLI RAKIPI.

Publishers

Academy of Sciences of Albania Publishing House (SHKENCA—Botime të Akademisë së Shkencave të RSH): Sheshi Fan S. Noli 7, Tirana; tel. and fax (4) 2230305; e-mail botimet_acad@yahoo.com; publs include *Studia Albanica*, *Studime Filologjike* and *New and Technical Journal of Natural Sciences*; Chair. GUDAR BEQIRAJ.

Dituria: Rruga Frederik Shiroka 31, POB 1441, Tirana; tel. and fax (4) 2236635; e-mail dituria@icc.al.org; f. 1991; dictionaries, calendars, encyclopedias, social sciences, biographies, fiction and non-fiction; Gen. Dir PETRIT YMERI.

Dudaj: Rruga Sami Frashëri 41, Tirana; tel. and fax (4) 2250156; e-mail info@botimedudaj.com; internet www.botimedudaj.com; f. 2001; fiction and non-fiction; CEO ARLINDA HOVI DUDAJ.

Fan Noli: Rruga Bulev Shekip. Ere, Tirana; tel. (4) 2242739; f. 1991; Albanian and foreign literature; Pres. REXHEP HIDA.

Neraida: Rruga Myslym Shyri 54/4/1, Tirana; tel. (4) 2243310; fax (4) 2262312; e-mail neraida@albaniaonline.net; fiction and non-fiction; f. 1995; Dir JANI MALO.

Ombra GVG: Rruga Gjergj Fishta, Kompleksi Tirana 2000 4/2, Tirana; tel. (4) 2224173; fax (4) 2224986; e-mail info@ombragvg.com; internet www.ombragvg.com; f. 1998; Pres. GËZIM TAFA.

Omsca: Rruga Frederik Shiroka, Tirana; tel. (4) 2233648; fax (4) 360793; e-mail omsca@abissnet.al; fiction; Dir LUAN PENGILI.

Onufri: Rruga Sulejman Pasha, Tirana; tel. (4) 2270399; e-mail info@onufri.com; literary; Dir BUJAR HUDHRI.

Shtëpia Botuese e Librit Shkollor: Rruga Mine Peza 1/1, Tirana; tel. and fax (4) 2223633; e-mail info@shblsh.com; internet www.shblsh.com; f. 1967; educational books; Dir SHPËTIM BOZDO.

Shtëpia Botuese Naim Frashëri: Tirana; tel. (4) 2227906; f. 1950; fiction, poetry, drama, criticism, children's literature, translations; Dir GAQO BUSHAKA.

Skanderbeg Books: Rruga H. H. Dalliu, Pallat 184/9, Tirana; tel. and fax (4) 2260945; e-mail flutura@skanderbegbooks.com; internet www.skanderbegbooks.com; literary fiction and non-fiction in translation; Dir FLUTURA AÇKA.

Toena: Rruga Muhamet Gjollesha, POB 1420, Tirana; tel. (4) 2240116; fax (4) 2240117; e-mail toena@toena.com.al; internet www.toena.com.al; history, social sciences, humanities, fiction, linguistics; Pres. FATMIR TOÇI.

Uegen: Rruga Vaso Pasha, pall. Fratari kat. 3; tel. and fax (4) 2272858; e-mail uegen@pronet.com.al; internet www.uegen.com; f. 1992; fiction, history, psychology, philosophy, etc.; Dir XHEVAIR LLESHI.

PUBLISHERS' ASSOCIATION

Albanian Publishers' Asscn: Rruga Dervish Hima 32, Tirana; tel. (4) 2240116; fax (4) 2240117; e-mail toena@icc.al.org; f. 1992; Dir. PETRIT YMERI.

Broadcasting and Communications

TELECOMMUNICATIONS

At January 2011 there were six main telecommunications operators in Albania.

Albanian Mobile Communications (AMC): Rruga Gjergi Legisi, Laprakë, Tirana; tel. (4) 2275000; fax (4) 2275243; e-mail contact_us@amc.al; internet www.amc.al; f. 1996; 85% owned by Cosmote (Greece/Norway); operates mobile telephone network; Man. Dir DIMITRIS BLATSIOS.

Albtelecom: Rruga Myslym Shyri 42, Tirana; tel. (4) 2232169; fax (4) 2233323; e-mail corporatesales@albtelecom.al; internet www.albtelecom.al; 80% stake owned by consortium of Turk Telekom and Calik Enerji (both of Turkey); Chief Exec. ILIRIAN KUKA.

Eagle Mobile: Rruga Murat Toptani, Qendra e Biznesit 12 Katëshe, Kati 9-10, Tirana; tel. (4) 2290100; fax (4) 2290190; e-mail info@eaglemobile.al; internet www.eaglemobile.al; f. 2008; Dir-Gen. ALI TASKIN.

PLUS Communication: Rruga Dëshmorët e Shkurtit 4, Tirana; tel. (4) 4501500; fax (4) 44501538; e-mail info@plus.al; internet www.plus.al; f. 2009; mobile cellular telecommunications; CEO MONI BUCHNIK.

Vodafone Albania: Autostrada Tiranë-Durrës, Rruga Pavarësia 61, Kashar, Tirana; tel. (4) 2283072; fax (4) 2283333; e-mail info.al@vodafone.com; internet www.vodafone.al; f. 2001; mobile cellular telecommunications; Gen. Dir THOMAS PAPASPYROU.

BROADCASTING

In 1991 state broadcasting was removed from political control and made subordinate to the Parliamentary Commission for the Media. In addition to the public national broadcasting service, in 2010 there were two national television stations, two satellite television channels, 71 local television stations, 83 cable television channels, two national radio stations and 46 local radio stations licensed by the National Council of Radio and Television.

Regulatory Authority

National Council of Radio and Television (NCRT) (Këshilli Kombëtar i Radios dhe Televizionit—KKRT): Rruga Abdi Toptani, Ish Hotel Drini, Tirana; tel. (4) 233599; fax (4) 226288; e-mail kkrt@kkrt.gov.al; internet www.kkrt.gov.al; f. 1999; Chair. ENDIRA BUSHATI.

Radio

Radio Televizioni Shqiptar: Rruga Ismail Qemali 11, Tirana; tel. and fax (4) 2222481; e-mail dushiulp@yahoo.com; internet www.rtsh.al; f. 1938 as Radio Tirana; two channels of domestic services (19 and five hours daily) and a third channel covering international broadcasting (two services in Albanian and seven in foreign languages); several local channels; 65% state-funded; 35% funded through commercial advertising and fees; Chair. KASTRIST CAUSBI; Dir-Gen. EDUARD MAZI; Dir of Radio MARTIN LEKA.

Plus 2 Radio: Rruga Aleksandër Moisiu Nr 76/1, Tirana; tel. (4) 4301016; e-mail info@plus2radio.com.al; internet www.plus2radio.com.al; f. 1998; popular music.

Top Albania Radio: Qendra Ndërkombëtare e Kulturës, Bulevardi Dëshmorët e Kombit, Tirana; tel. (4) 2247492; fax (4) 2247493; e-mail contact@topalbaniaradio.com; internet www.topalbaniaradio.com; Dir ENKELEJD JOTI.

Television

Radio Televizioni Shqiptar: Rruga Ismail Qemali 11, Tirana; tel. (4) 2256056; fax (4) 2256058; e-mail dushiulp@yahoo.com; internet www.rtsh.al; f. 1960; broadcasts range of television programmes; 65% state-funded; 35% funded through commercial advertising and fees; Chair. KASTRIST CAUSBI; Dir-Gen. EDUARD MAZI; Dir of Television VENA ISAK.

Albanian Satellite Television (ALSAT TV): Rruga Siri Kodra, Tirana; tel. and fax (4) 271738; e-mail info@alsat.tv; internet www.alsat.tv; news satellite broadcasting in Albanian; from mid-2003 programmes also broadcast by local TV stations in Albania, the former Yugoslav republic of Macedonia and Kosovo.

Shijak TV: Rruga Kavajes, Sheshi Ataturk 5, Tirana; tel. (4) 2247135; fax (4) 2252619; e-mail shijaktv01@albaniaonline.net; internet www.shijaktv.com; f. 1995; local station; Pres. GËZIM ISMAILI.

Top Channel TV: Qendra Ndërkombëtare e Kulturës, Bulevardi Dëshmorët e Kombit, Tirana; tel. (4) 2253177; fax (4) 2253178; e-mail info@top-channel.tv; internet www.top-channel.tv; f. 2001; Dir ENKELEJD JOTI.

TVA—Televizioni Arbëria: Pall. i Kulturës, Kati III, Tirana; tel. (4) 2243932; fax (4) 8301466; e-mail tva@telearberia.tv; internet www.telearberia.tv; Dir ESTELA DASHI.

TV Klan: Rruga Aleksander Moisiu 97, Ish-Kinostudio, Tirana; tel. (4) 2347805; fax (4) 2347808; e-mail info@tvklan.tv; internet www.tvklan.tv; Dir-Gen. ALEKSANDER FRANGAJ.

Finance

(cap. = capital; res = reserves; dep. = deposits; m. = million; brs = branches; amounts in lekë, unless otherwise stated)

BANKING

The Savings Bank of Albania, which accounted for more than 50% of activity in the banking sector, was sold to Raiffeisen Bank (of Austria) at the beginning of 2004. At mid-2009 there were 16 commercial banks operating in the country.

Central Bank

Bank of Albania (Banka e Shqipërisë): Sheshi Avni Rustemi, nr. 24 Tirana; tel. (4) 2419301; fax (4) 2419408; e-mail public@bankofalbania.org; internet www.bankofalbania.org; f. 1992; cap. 2,500m., res 30,048m., dep. 82,709m. (Dec. 2009); Gov. ARDIAN FULLANI; 5 brs.

Other Banks

Banka Credins: Rruga Ismail Qemali 21, Tirana; tel. (4) 2234096; fax (4) 2222916; e-mail info@bankacredins.com; internet www.bankacredins.com; f. 2003; cap. 2,404.7m., res 801.6m., dep. 44,242.8m. (Dec. 2009); Gen. Man. and Exec. Dir ARTAN SANTO.

Emporiki Bank-Albania: Tirana Tower, Rruga e Kavajës 59, Tirana; tel. (4) 2258755; fax (4) 2258752; e-mail headoffice@emporiki.com.al; internet www.emporiki.com.al; f. 1999 as Intercommercial Bank; name changed as above 2004; owned by Emporiki Bank of Greece; cap. 4,649.7m., res 56.9m., dep. 24,271.5m. (Dec. 2009); Dir CHRISTOS KATSANIS; CEO GEORGE CARACOSTAS.

Intesa Sanpaolo Bank Albania (Banka Amerikanë e Shqipërisë): Rruga Ismail Qemali 27, POB 8319, Tirana; tel. (4) 2276000; fax (4) 2248762; e-mail info@intesasanpaolobank.al; internet www.intesasanpaolobank.al; f. 1998; owned by Intesa Sanpaolo Group; fmrly American Bank of Albania; name changed Oct. 2008, following merger with Banca Italo-Albanese; cap. 5,562.5m., res 2,663.2m., dep. 1,011,982.2m. (2009); Chair. MASSIMO PIERDICCHI; Pres. and CEO STEFANO FARABBI.

National Commercial Bank of Albania (Banka Kombëtare Tregtare ShA): Bulevardi Zhan D'Ark, Tirana; tel. (4) 2250955; fax (4) 2250956; e-mail info@bkt.com.al; internet www.bkt.com.al; f. 1993 by merger; privatized in 2000; cap. US $78.2m., res $–0.1m., dep $1,236.7m. (Dec. 2009); Chair. MEHMET USTA; 55 brs.

ProCredit Bank (Albania) (Banka ProCredit): Rruga Sami Frasheri, POB 2395, Tirana; tel. (4) 2271272; fax (4) 2271276; e-mail info@procreditbank.com.al; internet www.procreditbank.com.al; f. 1995 as Foundation for Enterprise Finance and Development; name changed to Fedad Bank ShA in 1999, and as above in 2003; cap. 2,025.9m., res 533.3m., dep. 33,892.7m. (Dec. 2009); Chair. C. P. ZEITINGER; CEO BORISLAV KOSTADINOV; 9 brs.

Raiffeisen Bank: European Trade Centre, 6th Floor, Tirana; tel. (4) 2381381; fax (4) 2275599; e-mail info@raiffeisen.al; internet www.raiffeisen.al; f. 1991 as Savings Bank of Albania; acquired by Raiffeisen Zentralbank Österreich AG (Austria) in Jan. 2004; cap. 4,348.2m., res 2,819.7m., dep. 227,770.2m. (Dec. 2008); CEO CHRISTIAN CANACARIS; 37 brs.

Société Générale Albania: Bulevardi Dëshmorët e Kombit, Twin Towers, Tower 1, 9th Floor, Tirana; tel. (4) 2280442; fax (4) 2280441; e-mail sgalb.info@socgen.com; internet www.societegenerale.al; f. 2004 as Banka Popullore; renamed in 2010 following acquisition by Société Générale, France; cap. 4,449.4m., res –7.7m., dep. 34,274.5m. (Dec. 2009); Chair. EDVIN LIBOHOVA; Man. ENTELA GJOKA.

Tirana Bank: Rruga Dëshmorët 4 Shkurtit, POB 2400/1, Tirana; tel. (4) 2277700; fax (4) 2277691; e-mail managingdirector@tiranabank.net; internet www.tiranabank.al; f. 1996; cap. 6,938.1m., res 2,749.8m., dep. 72,620.5m. (Dec. 2009); Man. Dir DIMITRIS SANTIXIS; 56 brs.

United Bank of Albania: Rruga e Durrësit (Zogu i zi), 14th Floor, POB 128, Tirana; tel. and fax (4) 2228460; e-mail info@ubaal.com; f. 1994; cap. US $12.6m., res $0.7m., dep. $40.0m. (Dec. 2008); fmrly Arab-Albanian Islamic Bank, present name adopted 2003; Chair. Sheikh SOLAIMAN ELKHEREIJI; Gen. Man. HIKMET GULER; 6 brs.

STOCK EXCHANGE

Tirana Stock Exchange (Bursa e Tiranes): Rruga Dora D'Istria, Kutia Postare 274/1, Tirana; tel. (4) 2265058; fax (4) 2265058; e-mail tseinfo@abcom-al.com; internet www.tse.com.al; f. 1996; CEO ANILA FURERAJ.

INSURANCE

Agjensia Shqiptare e Garancisë (ASHG): Rruga Ismail Qemali Pall 34/1/2, Tirana; tel. (4) 2247048; fax (4) 2247047; e-mail aga@aga-al.com.

Atlantik: Rruga Themistokli Gërmenji 3/1, Tirana; tel. and fax (4) 2235088; e-mail info@atlantik.com.al; internet www.atlantik.com.al; f. 2001; Gen. Dir DRITAN ÇELAJ.

Health Insurance Institute (Instituti i Sigurimeve të Kujdesit Shëndetsor): Rruga Sami Frashëri 8, Tirana; tel. (4) 2230984; fax (4) 2274953; e-mail ehana@isksh.com.al; internet www.isksh.com.al; Dir ELVANA HANA.

Insurance Institute of Albania (INSIG) (Instituti i Sigurimeve të Shqipërisë): Rruga e Dibrës 91, Tirana; tel. (4) 234170; fax (4) 223838; e-mail info@insig.com.al; internet www.insig.com.al; f. 1991; 61% owned by American Reserve Life Insurance (USA); European Bank for Reconstruction and Development (United Kingdom) and the International Finance Corpn each acquired 19.5% stake in 2004; all types of insurance; Gen. Dir SAIMIR ZËMBLAKU; 12 brs.

INTERSIG: Rruga e Durrësit, Tirana; tel. and fax (4) 2270577; e-mail info@intersig.com.al; internet www.intersig.al; f. 2001; non-life insurance; CEO FITNETE SULAJ.

Sigal: Bulevardi Zogu I 1, Tirana; tel. (4) 2233308; fax (4) 2250220; e-mail info@sigal.com.al; internet www.sigal.com.al; f. 1999; property, engineering, motor, marine, aviation, liability, accidents, banking, agriculture, credit, surety; Gen. Dir AVNI PONARI; 12 brs, 260 agencies (2005).

SIGMA: Rruga Komuna e Parisit, Pall. Lura, POB 1714, Tirana; tel. (4) 2258254; fax (4) 258253; e-mail info@sigma-al.com; internet www.sigma-al.com; Gen. Dir QEMAL DISHA.

INSURERS' ASSOCIATION

Association of Albanian Insurers (Shoqata e Siguruesve të Shqipërisë): Rruga Gjergj Fishta, Pall. Edil–Al–It, Kati II, Tirana;

tel. (4) 2254033; fax (4) 2267221; e-mail bshs@insurers-al.org; internet www.insurers-al.org; f. 2003; Exec. Dir ANTONETA ÇELA.

Trade and Industry

PRIVATIZATION AGENCY

National Agency for Privatization (NAP) (Agjencia Kombetare e Privatizimit): Bulevardi Dëshmorët e Kombit, Tirana; tel. (4) 2257457; fax (4) 2227933; f. 1991; govt agency under the control of the Council of Ministers; prepares and proposes the legal framework concerning privatization procedures and implementation; Gen. Dir KOZETA FINO.

SUPERVISORY ORGANIZATIONS

Albkontroll: Rruga Skënderbej 45, Durrës; tel. (52) 223377; fax (52) 222791; f. 1962; brs throughout Albania; independent control body for inspection of goods for import and export, means of transport, etc.; Gen. Man. DILAVER MEZINI; 15 brs.

State Supreme Audit Control (Kontrolli i Larte i Shtetit): Bulevardi Dëshmorët e Kombit 3, Tirana; tel. (4) 2247294; fax (4) 2232491; e-mail klsh@klsh.org.al; internet www.klsh.org.al; Pres. BUJAR LESKAJ.

DEVELOPMENT ORGANIZATIONS

Albanian Business and Investment Agency (Albinvest): Bulevardi Gjergj Fishta, Pall. Shallvare, Tirana 1000; tel. (4) 2252886; fax (4) 2222341; e-mail info@albinvest.gov.al; internet www.albinvest.gov.al; Exec. Dir VIOLA PUCI.

Albanian Development Fund (Fondi Shqiptar i Zhvillimit): Rruga Sami Frashëri 10, Tirana; tel. (4) 2235597; fax (4) 2234885; e-mail adf@albaniandf.org; internet www.albaniandf.org; Exec. Dir BENET BECI.

Albanian Economic Development Agency (AEDA): Bulevardi Zhan D'Ark, Tirana 1000; tel. (4) 2230133; fax (4) 2228439; e-mail aeda@albnet.net; f. 1993; fmrly Albanian Centre for Foreign Investments Promotion; govt agency to promote foreign investment in Albania and to provide practical support to foreign investors; publ. *Ekonomia*; Chair. SELAMI XHEPA.

CHAMBERS OF COMMERCE

Union of Chambers of Commerce and Industry of Albania (Bashkimi i Dhomave të Tregtisë dhe Industrisë të Shqipërisë): Blvd Zhan D'Ark 23, Tirana; tel. and fax (4) 2247105; e-mail ilir.zhilla@uccial.al; internet www.uccial.al; f. 1958; Chair. ILIR ZHILLA; 14 mems (2010).

Dibër Chamber of Commerce and Industry: Bulevardi Elez Isufi, Peshkopi, Dibër; tel. and fax (218) 22645; e-mail ccidiber@gmail.com; Chair. ILIR BULKU.

Durrës Chamber of Commerce and Industry: Lagjja 11, Rruga A. Goga, POB 220, Durrës; tel. (52) 224440; fax (52) 222199; e-mail info@ccidr.al; internet www.ccidr.al; f. 1995; Chair. ANDREA XHAVARA.

Elbasan Chamber of Commerce and Industry (Dhoma e Tregtisë dhe ë Industrisë Elbasan): Godina e Prefekturës Elbasan, Kati 1, Elbasan; tel. (54) 255490; e-mail cciel@albmail.com; Chair. VELI KAZAZI.

Shkodër Chamber of Commerce and Industry (Dhoma ë Tregtisë dhe e Industrisë Shkodër): Shkodër; tel. (224) 22460; fax (224) 23656; e-mail ccish@abissnet.com.al; Chair. ANTON LEKA.

Tirana Chamber of Commerce and Industry (Dhoma e Tregtisë dhe ë Industrisë Tirane): Pallati i Kulturës, Sheshi Skenderbej, Tirana; tel. (4) 2230877; fax (4) 2227997; e-mail info@cci.al; internet www.cci.al; f. 1926; Chair. NIKOLIN JAKA.

Vlorë Chamber of Commerce and Industry (Dhoma e Tregtisë dhe Industrisë Vlorë): Pall. i Kulturës Liberia, Kati 1, Vlorë; tel. (33) 222111; fax (33) 225737; e-mail info@ccivlora.org; f. 1985; Chair. EDMOND LEKA; 1,800 mems.

There are also chambers of commerce in Berat, Fier, Gjirokastër, Korçë, Kukës and Lezhë.

UTILITIES

Electricity

State Electricity Corporation of Albania (KESH) (Korporata Elektroenergjetikë Shqiptarë): Biloky Vasil Shanto, Tirana; tel. (4) 2262947; fax (4) 2232046; e-mail mail@kesh.com.al; internet www.kesh.com.al; state corpn for the generation, transmission, distribution and export of electrical energy; govt-controlled; scheduled for transfer to private ownership; fmr distribution subsidiary OSSH was privatized in March 2009; Dir ENGJËLL ZEQO.

TRADE UNIONS

During 1991 independent trade unions were established. The most important of these was the Union of Independent Trade Unions of Albania. Other unions were established for workers in various sectors of the economy.

Alliance of Independent Trade Unions of Albania (Bashkimi i Sindikatave të Pavarura të Shqipërisë—BSPSh): Rruga Zogu i zi, Pall. i Kulturës Ali Kelmendi, Tirana; tel. and fax (4) 2232157; e-mail bspsh@albmail.com; f. 1991; Chair. GËZIM KALAJA; 85,000 mems (2010).

Confederation of Trade Unions of Albania (Konfederata e Sindikatave të Shqipërisë—KSSH): Sheshi Garibaldi 3, Pallati Tekstilisti, Kombinat, 1027 Tirana; tel. and fax (4) 2477284; e-mail kssh@icc-al.org; internet www.kssh.org; f. 1991; includes 12 sectoral trade union federations; Chair. KOL NIKOLLAJ; 105,000 mems (2007).

Transport

RAILWAYS

In 2009 there were 423 km of railway track in Albania.

Albanian Railways (Hekurudha Shqiptare): Rruga Skënderbej, Durrës; tel. and fax (52) 222037; CEO SOKOL KAPIDANI.

ROADS

In 2002 the road network comprised an estimated 18,000 km of classified roads, including 3,220 km of main roads and 4,300 km of secondary roads; 39% of the total network was paved. In December 2002 a 23.5-km road linking Greece with southern Albania was opened. In 2003 the Albanian Government secured financing from the World Bank, the European Investment Bank and the European Bank for Reconstruction and Development for a number of road-maintenance projects. As part of the European Union's Transport Corridor Europe–Central Asia (TRACECA) programme, the construction of a west–east highway (Corridor VIII) from the port of Durrës to the Black Sea, via the former Yugoslav republic of Macedonia and Bulgaria, has been undertaken. Corridor X, another TRACECA project, runs north–south from Hani Hotit, at the border with Montenegro, to Tri Urat on the Greek frontier. A highway linking Tirana and Vlorë was completed in 2006. The construction of a major highway linking Durrës with Kosovo was completed in 2010.

SHIPPING

At December 2009 Albania's merchant fleet had 71 vessels, with a total displacement of 67,212 grt. The chief ports are those in Durrës, Vlorë, Sarandë and Shëngjin. Ferry services have been established between Durrës and three Italian ports (Trieste, Bari and Ancona) and between Sarandë and the Greek island of Corfu. Services also connect Vlorë with the Italian ports of Bari and Brindisi. The World Bank, the European Union and the Organization of the Petroleum Exporting Countries Fund For International Development have financed projects to improve existing port facilities.

Adetare Shipping Agency: 1 Rruga Taulantia, Durrës; tel. (52) 226191; fax (52) 232614; e-mail adeag@albmail.com; f. 1991; Dir ARMANT GJERGJI.

Albanian State Shipping Enterprise: Durrës; tel. (52) 222233; fax (52) 229111.

Durrës Port Authority: Lagija 1, Rruga Tregtare, Durrës; tel. (52) 228636; fax (52) 223115; e-mail apd@apdurres.com.al; internet www.apdurres.com.al; state-owned; Gen. Dir EDUARD NDREU.

CIVIL AVIATION

There is a small international airport at Rinas, 17 km from Tirana. Reconstruction of the airport was undertaken in the late 1990s, and it was privatized in April 2005. A civil and military airport was constructed at Pish Poro, 29 km from Vlorë, under an agreement between Albania and Italy. The construction of a second international airport (Zayed International Airport) at the north-eastern town of Kukës, with funding from the Government of the United Arab Emirates, was completed in November 2005.

General Directorate of Civil Aviation: Rruga e Kavajes, Përballë Xhamise, POB 205, Tirana; tel. and fax (4) 2223969; e-mail dpac2@albanet.net; CEO AGRON DIBRA.

Tourism

In 2008 there were some 1,419,191 international tourist arrivals, including same-day visitors. In that year receipts from tourism totalled US $1,849m., compared with $1,055m. in 2007. The main tourist centres include Tirana, Durrës, Sarandë, Shkodër and

Pogradec. The Roman amphitheatre at Durrës is one of the largest in Europe. The ancient towns of Gjirokastër and Butrint are important archaeological sites, and there are many other towns of historic interest. However, expansion of tourism has been limited by the inadequacy of Albania's infrastructure and by a lack of foreign investment in the development of new facilities.

Albturist: Bulevardi Dëshmorët e Kombit 8, Hotel Dhajti, Tirana; tel. (4) 2251849; fax (4) 2234359; e-mail albturist@yahoo.com; brs in main towns and all tourist centres; 28 hotels throughout the country; Dir-Gen. BESNIK PELLUMBI.

Committee for Development and Tourism: Bulevardi Dëshmorët e Kombit 8, Tirana; tel. (4) 2258323; fax (4) 2258322; e-mail arskenderi@albaniaonline.com; govt body.

Defence

As assessed at November 2011, the total strength of the Albanian armed forces was about 14,245, including a Joint Force Command of 8,150 and a Support Command of 4,300. There is a 500-member paramilitary force. From September 1999 a 2,400-member contingent, known as Communications Zone West (COMMZ-W), was deployed in Albania to maintain civil order and to support North Atlantic Treaty Organization (NATO) forces in neighbouring Kosovo. In June 2002 COMMZ-W was officially dissolved, and a NATO headquarters was established at Tirana. Under legislation adopted in August 2008, compulsory military service of 12 months ended officially at the end of 2010. NATO member states completed the process of ratifying Albania's accession protocol in February 2009; the country joined the Alliance on 1 April.

Defence Expenditure: Budgeted at 13,800m. lekë in 2011.

Chief of the General Staff: Brig.-Gen. XHEMAL GJUNKSHI.

Education

Education in Albania is free and compulsory for children between the ages of six and 14 years. Enrolment at pre-primary schools included 55% of children in the relevant age-group (males 56%; females 54%) in 2008/09. In that year enrolment at primary schools included 85% of children in the relevant age-group (males 86%; females 84%), while, according to UNESCO estimates, secondary education enrolment was equivalent to 72% of children in the appropriate age-group (males 72%; females 73%). In 2008/09 a total of 116,292 students were enrolled at Albania's institutions of higher education. Spending on education accounted for some 10.6% of government expenditure in 2004 (equivalent to some 3.0% of GDP).

ALGERIA

Introductory Survey

LOCATION, CLIMATE, LANGUAGE, RELIGION, FLAG, CAPITAL

The People's Democratic Republic of Algeria lies in northern Africa, with the Mediterranean Sea to the north, Mali and Niger to the south, Tunisia and Libya to the east, and Morocco and Mauritania to the west. The climate on the Mediterranean coast is temperate, becoming more extreme in the Atlas mountains immediately to the south. Further south is part of the Sahara, a hot and arid desert. Temperatures in Algiers, on the coast, are generally between 9°C (48°F) and 29°C (84°F), while in the interior they may exceed 50°C (122°F). Arabic is the official language, but French is widely used. Tamazight, the principal language of Algeria's Berber community, was granted 'national' status in 2002. Islam is the state religion, and almost all Algerians are Muslims. The national flag (proportions 2 by 3) has two equal vertical stripes, of green and white, with a red crescent moon and a five-pointed red star superimposed in the centre. The capital is Algiers (el-Djezaïr).

CONTEMPORARY POLITICAL HISTORY

Historical Context

Algeria was conquered by French forces in the 1830s and annexed by France in 1842. The territory was colonized with French settlers, and many French citizens became permanent residents. Unlike most of France's overseas possessions, Algeria was not formally a colony but was 'attached' to metropolitan France. However, the indigenous Muslim majority were denied equal rights, and political and economic power within Algeria was largely held by the settler minority.

On 1 November 1954 the principal Algerian nationalist movement, the Front de libération nationale (FLN), began a war for national independence, in the course of which about 1m. Muslims were killed or wounded. The French Government agreed to a cease-fire in March 1962, and independence was declared on 3 July. In August the Algerian provisional Government transferred its functions to the Political Bureau of the FLN, and in September a National Constituent Assembly was elected (from a single list of FLN candidates) and a Republic proclaimed. A new Government was formed, with Ahmed Ben Bella, founder of the FLN, as Prime Minister.

A draft Constitution, providing for a presidential regime with the FLN as the sole party, was approved by popular referendum in September 1963. Ben Bella was elected President, although real power remained with the bureaucracy and the army. In June 1965 the Minister of Defence, Col Houari Boumedienne, deposed Ben Bella in a bloodless coup and took control of the country as President of a Council of the Revolution, composed chiefly of army officers. In 1975 Boumedienne announced a series of measures to consolidate the regime and enhance his personal power, including the holding of elections for a President and National People's Assembly. A newly drafted National Charter, which enshrined both the creation of a socialist system and the maintenance of Islam as the state religion, and Constitution were approved at referendums held in June and November 1976, respectively, and in December Boumedienne was elected President unopposed. The new formal structure of power was completed in February 1977 by the election of FLN members to the National People's Assembly.

President Boumedienne died in December 1978, and the Council of the Revolution took over the Government. In January 1979 the FLN adopted a new party structure, electing a Central Committee that was envisaged as the highest policy-making body both of the party and of the nation as a whole. The Committee's choice of Col Ben Djedid Chadli, commander of Oran military district and new party Secretary-General, as the sole presidential candidate was endorsed by a referendum in February. Chadli appointed a Prime Minister, Col Muhammad Abd al-Ghani, anticipating constitutional changes approved by the National People's Assembly in June, which included the obligatory appointment of a premier. In mid-1980 the FLN authorized Chadli to form a smaller Political Bureau, with more limited responsibilities, thereby increasing the power of the President. Chadli was re-elected to the presidency in January 1984, and subsequently appointed Abd al-Hamid Brahimi as Prime Minister. Following a public debate on Boumedienne's National Charter in 1985, a revised Charter—which emphasized a state ideology based on the twin principles of socialism and Islam while encouraging the development of private enterprise—was approved by a referendum in January 1986.

During the second half of the 1980s opposition to the Government was increasingly manifest. In 1985 22 Berber cultural and human rights activists were imprisoned after being convicted of belonging to illegal organizations. In 1987 several leading activists of an Islamist group were killed by security forces, and some 200 of the group's members were imprisoned. From mid-1988 severe unemployment, high consumer prices and shortages of essential supplies provoked a series of strikes, and in October rioting in the capital, Algiers, spread to Oran and Annaba. In November constitutional amendments allowing non-FLN candidates to participate in elections and making the Prime Minister answerable to the National People's Assembly (rather than to the President) were approved in a referendum. In December Chadli was elected President for a third term of office.

In February 1989 a new Constitution, signifying the end of the one-party socialist state, was approved by referendum. The executive, legislative and judicial functions of the state were separated and made subject to the supervision of a Constitutional Council. In July legislation permitting the formation of political associations outside the FLN entered force: by mid-1991 a total of 47 political parties had been licensed by the Government, including a radical Islamist group, the Front islamique du salut (FIS), the Mouvement pour la démocratie en Algérie (MDA), which had been founded by Ben Bella in 1984, the Parti d'avant-garde socialiste (renamed Ettahaddi in 1993), the Parti social-démocrate (PSD) and the Berber Rassemblement pour la culture et la démocratie (RCD). Other legislation adopted in July 1989 further reduced state control of the economy, allowed the expansion of foreign investment and ended the state monopoly of the press (although the principal newspapers remained under FLN control). In September President Chadli appointed Mouloud Hamrouche as Prime Minister.

At local elections held in June 1990 the FIS received some 55% of total votes cast, while the FLN obtained about 32%. In July, following internal disagreement concerning the pace of economic and political reform, Hamrouche and four other ministers resigned from the FLN's Political Bureau. In December the National People's Assembly adopted a law whereby, from 1997, Arabic would be Algeria's only official language and the use of French and the Berber language, Tamazight, in schools and in official transactions would be punishable offences; more than 100,000 people subsequently demonstrated in Algiers against political and religious intolerance.

Domestic Political Affairs

In April 1991 President Chadli declared that Algeria's first multi-party general election would take place in late June. The FIS argued that a presidential election should be held simultaneously with, or shortly after, the general election, and in May organized an indefinite general strike and demonstrations to demand Chadli's resignation and changes in the electoral laws. Violent confrontations in June between Islamist activists and the security forces prompted Chadli to declare a state of emergency and postpone the general election; he also announced that he had accepted the resignation of the Prime Minister and his Government. Sid-Ahmad Ghozali was appointed premier, and he duly nominated a Council of Ministers consisting mainly of political independents.

Meanwhile, the FLN and the FIS reached a compromise whereby the strike was abandoned, and legislative and presidential elections were to be held before the end of 1991. In July, however, army units arrested some 700 Islamists and occupied the headquarters of the FIS. Among those arrested were the party's President, Abbassi Madani, who had threatened to launch a *jihad* ('holy war') if the state of emergency was not ended, and Vice-President, Ali Belhadj; both were charged with armed conspiracy against the state. The state of emergency was revoked in September.

Following revisions to the electoral code, the first round of the multi-party general election to the newly enlarged 430-seat legislature was held on 26 December 1991, with a second, run-off ballot scheduled for 16 January 1992. In all, 231 seats were won outright at the first round: the FIS took 188 seats (with 47.5% of the votes cast), the Front des forces socialistes (FFS) 25, the FLN just 15 and independents three. The FLN alleged widespread intimidation and electoral malpractice on the part of the FIS. On 11 January Chadli resigned as President, announcing that he had (one week earlier) dissolved the National People's Assembly. The following day the High Security Council (comprising the Prime Minister, three generals and two senior ministers) cancelled the second round of legislative voting, at which the FIS had been expected to consolidate its first-round victory.

On 14 January 1992 a five-member High Council of State (HCS) was appointed to act as a collegiate presidency until, at the latest, the expiry of Chadli's term of office in 1993; however, its constitutional legality was disputed by all the political parties. The HCS was chaired by Muhammad Boudiaf, a veteran of the war of independence, but its most influential figure was believed to be Maj.-Gen. Khaled Nezzar, the Minister of Defence. The HCS declared a 12-month state of emergency in February 1992, and detention centres were opened in the Sahara. The FIS, which was officially dissolved by the Government in March, claimed that 150 people had been killed, and as many as 30,000 detained, since the military-sponsored takeover. In April Boudiaf announced the creation of a 60-member National Consultative Council (NCC), which was to meet each month in the building of the suspended Assembly, although it was to have no legislative powers. In June Boudiaf promised a constitutional review, the dissolution of the FLN and a presidential election. Moreover, despite continuing violence, he ordered the release from detention of 2,000 FIS militants.

Boudiaf was assassinated on 29 June 1992, while making a speech in Annaba; the FIS denied all responsibility for his murder. Ali Kafi (President of the war veterans' association, the Organisation nationale des moudjahidine) succeeded Boudiaf as Chairman of the HCS, and Redha Malek, the Chairman of the NCC, was appointed as a new member of the HCS. In early July Ghozali resigned in order to enable Kafi to appoint his own Prime Minister. He was replaced by Belaid Abd el-Salam, who appointed a new Council of Ministers later that month.

In July 1992 Madani and Belhadj were sentenced to 12 years' imprisonment for conspiracy against the state. Violent protests erupted in Algiers and quickly spread to other cities. As political manoeuvring and attempts at reconciliation continued against a background of escalating violence, in February 1993 the state of emergency was renewed for an indefinite period. In June the HCS announced that it would dissolve itself in December, asserting that a modern democracy and free market economy would be created within three years of that date.

The presidency of Liamine Zéroual

In July 1993 a retired general, Liamine Zéroual, succeeded Maj.-Gen. Nezzar as Minister of Defence. In August another member of the HCS, Redha Malek, replaced Abd el-Salam as Prime Minister and appointed a new Council of Ministers the following month. In October the HCS appointed a National Dialogue Commission (NDC), which was charged with the preparation of a political conference to organize the transition to an elected and democratic form of government. In December it was announced that the HCS would not be disbanded until a new presidential body had been elected at the NDC conference in January 1994. However, all the main political parties (with the exception of the moderate Islamist Hamas) boycotted the conference. Zéroual (who retained the defence portfolio in the Council of Ministers) was inaugurated as President on 31 January for a three-year term.

An attack by Islamist militants on the high-security Tazoult prison, near Batna, in March 1994 resulted in the release of more than 1,000 political prisoners. Certain towns were virtually controlled by Islamist activists, and the deaths of a number of foreign nationals led several countries to advise their citizens to leave Algeria. In response to the rise in violence, the security forces intensified their campaign against armed Islamist groups, resorting to air attacks, punitive raids, torture and psychological warfare, and the killing of thousands of militants.

Malek resigned as Prime Minister in April 1994, and was replaced by Mokdad Sifi. In May the President inaugurated a National Transition Council (NTC), an interim legislature of 200 appointed members, the aim of which was to provide a forum for debate pending legislative elections. With the exception of Hamas, most of the 21 parties that agreed to participate in the NTC were virtually unknown, and the 22 seats that were allocated to other major parties remained vacant.

In August 1994 members of the FLN, the Parti du renouveau algérien (PRA), the MDA, Al-Nahda and Hamas engaged in a national dialogue with the Government; the meetings were boycotted by Ettahaddi, the FFS and the RCD. At further negotiations held in early September discussion focused on two letters sent to the President by Abbassi Madani, purportedly offering a 'truce'. Madani and Belhadj were released from prison in mid-September and placed under house arrest; however, the FIS did not participate in the next round of national dialogue later that month, declaring that negotiations could take place only after the granting of a general amnesty, the rehabilitation of the FIS and the repeal of the state of emergency. The most prominent and radical Islamist militant group, the Groupe islamique armé (GIA), threatened reprisals if the FIS entered into dialogue with the regime, and intensified its campaign of violence against secular society by targeting educational institutions.

In November 1994 representatives of several major Algerian parties, including the FIS, the FLN, the FFS and the MDA, attended a two-day conference in Rome, Italy, organized by the Sant' Egidio Roman Catholic community to foster discussion about the crisis in Algeria. The ensuing Sant' Egidio pact, endorsed by all the participants at a meeting in Rome in January 1995, rejected the use of violence to achieve or maintain power, and urged the Algerian regime to repeal the state of emergency and thereby facilitate negotiations between all parties. However, the pact was dismissed as a 'non-event' by the Government.

Some 40 candidates announced their intention to contest the presidential election, the first round of which was scheduled for 16 November 1995, but only four were confirmed as having attained the required 75,000 signatures from at least 25 of 48 provinces in order to qualify. Despite an appeal by the FLN, the FFS and the FIS for voters to boycott the election, official figures showed that some 75% of the electorate participated in the poll, in which Zéroual secured an outright victory, with 61.0% of the valid votes cast. Zéroual was inaugurated for a five-year term on 27 November. Shortly afterwards the Government announced the closure of the last of seven detention centres opened since 1992, thereby releasing some 650 (mainly pro-Islamist) prisoners. In December 1995 Ahmed Ouyahia, a career diplomat, replaced Sifi as Prime Minister. Ouyahia's Government, named in January 1996, included two members of Hamas and a dissident leader of the FIS.

In May 1996 Zéroual announced his intention to hold legislative elections in early 1997. In addition, he proposed that a referendum be held, prior to the elections, on amendments to the Constitution: these included measures to increase the powers of the President while limiting his tenure to a maximum of two consecutive mandates; the creation of a second parliamentary chamber, the Council of the Nation (with one-third of members chosen by the President); the establishment of a State Council and a High State Court; and, significantly, a ban on political parties that were based on religion, language, gender or regional differences. The proposed constitutional amendments were promulgated in December, having been approved by some 86% of the voters at a referendum held in November.

In January 1997 the Secretary-General of the FLN-affiliated Union Générale des Travailleurs Algériens (UGTA), Abd al-Hak Benhamouda, was shot dead in Algiers. Although an Islamist group claimed responsibility for the assassination, there was speculation that it may have been perpetrated by opponents within the regime. In February the NTC adopted restrictive legislation concerning political parties in accordance with the amended Constitution; new electoral legislation replacing the majority system with proportional representation was also adopted. Later that month Abdelkader Bensalah, the President of the NTC, formed a centrist grouping, the Rassemblement national démocratique (RND), which received support from a wide range of organizations, including trade unions and anti-Islamist groups, and was closely linked with Zéroual and the Government. Several other political parties subsequently emerged, while certain existing parties changed their names to comply with the new legislation: notably, Hamas became the Mouvement de la société pour la paix (MSP).

Some 39 political parties contested the elections to the National People's Assembly, held on 5 June 1997, although the FIS and Ettahaddi urged a boycott of the polls. According to official results, the RND won 156 of the Assembly's 380 seats, followed by the MSP (69) and the FLN (62); Al-Nahda took 34 seats, the FFS 20 and the RCD 19. Opposition leaders complained of irregularities during the electoral process, and accused officials of manipulating the results in favour of the RND. International observers also commented that the rate of voter participation (officially estimated at 65.5% of the electorate) seemed unrealistically high. President Zéroual asked Ahmed Ouyahia to form a new Government, and later in June Ouyahia announced a new Council of Ministers, comprising members of the RND, the FLN and the MSP.

In September 1998 President Zéroual announced that a presidential election would be held in early 1999, nearly two years ahead of schedule. There was considerable speculation that the announcement had been prompted primarily by a power struggle within the regime between the faction loyal to the President and figures close to Lt-Gen. Muhammad Lamari, the Chief of Staff of the Army. In December 1998 Ouyahia resigned; he was replaced as premier by Smaïl Hamdani.

The presidential election of 1999

A total of 47 candidates registered to contest the presidential election scheduled for 15 April 1999; however, the Constitutional Council declared only seven eligible to stand. Although the senior generals had decided not to nominate a member of the armed forces for the presidency, Abdelaziz Bouteflika was believed to have the support of the military establishment, as well as that of the four main political parties and the UGTA. On the eve of the election Bouteflika's six rivals withdrew their candidacies after Zéroual refused to postpone the poll following allegations of massive electoral fraud in favour of Bouteflika. Voting papers were, nevertheless, distributed for all seven candidates, and no official boycott of the election was organized. The credibility of the poll was, however, seriously diminished, and Bouteflika announced that he would accept the presidency only if there were both a high rate of voter participation and a large majority in his favour. According to official results, Bouteflika won 73.8% of the votes cast (his closest rival, Ahmed Taleb Ibrahimi, a former Minister of Foreign Affairs who was now supported by the outlawed FIS, secured 12.5%). However, Bouteflika's overwhelming victory, together with the estimated official turn-out of more than 60%, was immediately disputed by his opponents, who maintained that only 23.3% of the registered electorate had participated, and that Bouteflika had received only 28% of the votes cast, compared with 20% for Ibrahimi. At his inauguration, on 27 April, Bouteflika emphasized the need for national reconciliation to end the civil conflict in Algeria, but pledged to continue the military campaign against terrorists.

Following clandestine negotiations between the Government and representatives of the FIS, in June 1999 the Armée islamique du salut (AIS, the armed wing of the FIS) announced the permanent cessation of its armed struggle against the Government. President Bouteflika's plans for a national reconciliation initiative were incorporated in a Law on Civil Concord, promulgated in July, whereby there was to be an amnesty for members of armed Islamist groups who surrendered within a six-month deadline and who were not implicated in mass killings, rape or bomb attacks on public places. The legislation was approved by 98.6% of those who voted in a national referendum in September. Meanwhile, Bouteflika exhibited unprecedented candour, admitting in August that the civil conflict of the past seven years had resulted in the deaths of at least 100,000 people (hitherto the authorities had put the number of deaths at 30,000). Bouteflika finally named his Council of Ministers in December, led by Ahmed Benbitour and comprising members of the FLN, the MSP, Al-Nahda, the RCD, the Alliance nationale républicaine (ANR), the RND and the PRA.

In early January 2000 the Government, army and the AIS reached an agreement whereby the AIS pledged to disband in return for the restoration of full civil and political rights to its former members. It was estimated that some 1,500–3,000 rebels were to be granted a full pardon under the agreement, some of whom were to be temporarily enlisted in an auxiliary unit to assist the security forces in apprehending members of the GIA and of a breakaway group from the GIA, the Groupe salafiste pour la prédication et le combat (GSPC, or Da'wa wal Djihad). In mid-January, following the expiry of the amnesty period specified under the Law on Civil Concord, the armed forces launched a concerted assault on rebel strongholds in the north-east and south-west of the country, in an attempt to eliminate remaining anti-Government factions. It was officially stated at this time that 80% of members of armed groups had surrendered. Following visits to Algeria in mid-2000, the human rights organizations Amnesty International and the Fédération internationale des ligues des droits de l'homme reported that there had been a significant decline in violence and a clear improvement in the country's human rights situation, although concern was expressed about the fate of an estimated 22,000 missing persons who had disappeared since 1992. Moreover, more than 1,300 deaths were reported as a result of continuing attacks involving armed Islamist groups between late 2000 and the holy month of Ramadan in 2001. Meanwhile, in August 2000 Benbitour resigned the premiership and was replaced by Ali Benflis, a former Minister of Justice who had directed Bouteflika's presidential campaign.

A total of 23 parties contested elections to the newly enlarged National People's Assembly held on 30 May 2002, although the polls were boycotted by the FFS and the RCD. According to official results, the FLN won 199 of the 389 available seats, while the RND suffered a significant loss of support, with its parliamentary representation reduced to just 47. Sheikh Abdallah Djaballah's Mouvement El Islah took 43 seats, the MSP 38 and the Parti des travailleurs (PT) 21. Independent candidates secured 30 seats. The overall credibility of the election was undermined, however, by the fact that only 46.2% of eligible voters cast their ballot; participation rates in Béjaïa and Tizi Ouzou, in the north-eastern region of Kabylia, were recorded at just 2.6% and 1.8%, respectively. The FFS and the RCD demanded an annulment of the results, claiming that real voter turn-out had reached no more than 15%–20%. Bouteflika subsequently reappointed Ali Benflis as Prime Minister, and in June Benflis named a new coalition Government.

However, at the FLN party congress held in March 2003, evidence of a serious rift between the two men emerged when Benflis announced his opposition to a number of Bouteflika's economic policies and withdrew the party's support for the President. Furthermore, it was rumoured that Benflis intended to stand as a candidate in the presidential election scheduled for April 2004. Benflis, who was re-elected Secretary-General of the FLN for a further five-year term, was also granted considerably increased powers, including the right to appoint senior party officials and to call extraordinary party congresses. In May 2003 Bouteflika dismissed Benflis as Prime Minister, reportedly owing to 'far-reaching divergencies'. The former premier, Ahmed Ouyahia, was subsequently appointed to succeed Benflis, and he announced a new coalition Government shortly afterwards. In September Bouteflika reorganized the Council of Ministers, dismissing a number of FLN ministers who had indicated their support for Benflis's presidential campaign. In October the remaining pro-Benflis FLN ministers withdrew from the Government. The following day, at an extraordinary congress of the FLN, 1,375 of the 1,500 members present approved Benflis's candidature, thus confirming him as the party's representative at the 2004 presidential election.

The two leaders of the proscribed FIS, Abbassi Madani and Ali Belhadj, were released in July 2003, after having completed their 12-year sentences. However, upon their release, both men were issued with court orders prohibiting them from: engaging in any political activity; holding meetings; establishing a political, cultural, charitable or religious association; and voting or standing as candidates in any election. (Belhadj was rearrested in July 2005, after a statement broadcast by the Qatar-based satellite television channel Al Jazeera in support of the insurgency in Iraq.) Despite an escalation of violence in January 2003, after some 60 people (including at least 43 soldiers) were killed in an ambush by GSPC fighters near Batna, violent incidents in Algeria declined markedly during 2003; according to official figures, fewer than 900 people were killed as a result of violence involving Islamists and the security forces in that year, compared with some 1,400 in 2002 and almost 1,900 in 2001. The Government attributed this to the increased efficiency of the security forces, who had successfully dismantled many of the terrorists' support networks, and to divisions within the Islamist groups. It was claimed that the GIA, the leader of which, Rachid Abou Tourab, was apparently captured in November 2003, had been reduced to just 30 members, while three separate factions of the GSPC were reportedly operating in the country.

In December 2003 the administrative chamber of the Algiers Court suspended all activities of the FLN after the pro-Bouteflika faction of the party lodged a complaint maintaining that the party congress in March had been held illegally and that the results of the congress were 'null and void'. The decision was condemned by Benflis, and in January 2004 he and 10 other leading politicians (including four other former heads of government) signed a statement calling for the formation of an interim government ahead of the presidential election—citing the lack of impartiality in the current Government—and an independent body to oversee the polls. Prime Minister Ouyahia (whose party, the RND, had already declared its support for President Bouteflika were he to stand for re-election) responded to the communiqué by affirming that he had no intention of stepping down and pledging that the Government would organize a free and fair presidential election in the early part of the year.

Meanwhile, indirect elections took place on 30 December 2003 to renew 46 members of the Council of the Nation. The RND won 17 seats, while the (pro-Benflis) FLN obtained 11 seats, the Corrective Movement of the FLN 10, the MSP four, and El Islah and independents secured two seats each. One-half of the presidential appointees to the Council were also replaced on 8 January 2004. However, these elections and appointments were incomplete, principally owing to unrest in Kabylia. By-elections for five seats in the Council were held on 23 February 2006.

President Bouteflika's second term of office

In advance of the 2004 presidential election, Bouteflika declared that a committee would be established to ensure the fairness and transparency of the ballot, and invited representatives of international organizations to observe the electoral process. Although more than 40 candidates applied to contest the poll, only six obtained the requisite 75,000 signatures from more than one-half of the country's 48 provinces. Bouteflika was joined in the presidential race by Benflis; Sheikh Abdallah Djaballah, leader of the Islamist El Islah; Saïd Saâdi, President of the RCD; Louisa Hanoune, head of the PT; and Ali Fawzi Rebaïne, Secretary-General of the small nationalist party Ahd 54. Prior to the election Bouteflika dismissed claims that he was monopolizing state media and using state funds to set his re-election campaign in motion before the electoral race had officially begun.

Bouteflika was decisively re-elected for a second term of office on 8 April 2004. He received 85.0% of the valid votes cast, while his nearest rival, Benflis, took 6.4%. Djaballah secured 5.0%, Saâdi 1.9%, Hanoune 1.0% and Rebaïne 0.6%. The rate of turn-out by eligible voters was reported to be 58.1%, although it was estimated to be as low as 18% in Kabylia. Bouteflika's rivals immediately accused the President of electoral malpractice; however, international observers declared the election to have been representative of popular will and free from any vote-rigging. The authorities responded to criticism by Algerian newspapers of Bouteflika's overwhelming victory by imposing tighter restrictions on both the domestic and international media. Both Benflis and Saâdi boycotted Bouteflika's inauguration ceremony on 19 April, at which he vowed to resolve the Berber crisis, to improve the rights of women by readdressing the controversial family code of 1984, and to continue his campaign for 'true national reconciliation'. On 26 April 2004, having been reappointed as Prime Minister, Ouyahia named his new Council of Ministers; this consisted principally of FLN members and non-partisan supporters of Bouteflika, with some RND and MSP representation. Meanwhile, Benflis resigned as Secretary-General of the FLN. At a party congress held in January 2005 the Minister of State for Foreign Affairs, Abdelaziz Belkhadem, was elected to the post, while Bouteflika was elected honorary President of the FLN.

Meanwhile, violence between the GSPC and the Algerian military began to escalate, particularly in Kabylia. In March 2004 it was reported that fighting had occurred between the Chadian military and a faction of the GSPC led by the group's second-in-command, Amari Saifi, resulting in the deaths of more than 40 militants. Saifi was wanted in Algeria and abroad for various crimes, including the kidnapping in 2003 of 32 European tourists, and the killing of 43 Algerian soldiers. It was announced in October 2004 that Saifi had been taken into Algerian custody, having been intercepted by Libyan authorities on the Chadian–Libyan border. Meanwhile, in June 2004 Nabil Sahraoui, the GSPC's leader since October 2003, was reportedly killed by the Algerian military in Kabylia during a gun battle that also killed four of his senior aides, including his likely successor, Abdi Abdelaziz. The army subsequently announced that it had 'completely neutralized' the leadership of the GSPC and had seized many of its weapons and documents. In September 2004 Sahraoui was replaced as leader of the GSPC by Abdelmalek Droukdal (also known as Abu Musab Abd al-Wadud).

In January 2005 the Ministry of the Interior and Local Authorities announced that the GIA had been virtually destroyed following a military campaign during the latter part of 2004, in which they had arrested the group's leader, Noureddine Boudiafi, and later killed his replacement, Chabaâne Younès. The Ministry also confirmed that, despite reports to the contrary, former GIA leader Tourab had been killed by members of his own group in July 2004. In April 2005 14 civilians were killed by suspected GIA militants in a roadside ambush in the Blida region; later that month the group's 'emir', Boulenouar Oukil, was arrested on suspicion of having planned the attack. In June the GSPC's Amari Saifi was sentenced *in absentia* to life imprisonment, having been found guilty of forming a terrorist group and of 'propagating terror'.

In August 2005 Bouteflika announced that a referendum to decide whether to grant a partial amnesty to Islamist rebels who had surrendered their weapons after the January 2000 deadline would take place in the following month. The FFS and the RCD appealed for a boycott of the referendum on the grounds that an amnesty would 'consecrate impunity' for the crimes committed by the security forces during Algeria's civil war. In the run-up to the vote, there was an increase in violence on the part of armed Islamists in Algiers, where some 44 people were killed in attacks during September. A reported 79.8% of the electorate participated in the referendum on 29 September, with 97.4% of voters approving the partial amnesty. However, the result was marred by reports of violence in Kabylia, with turn-out in Tizi Ouzou registered at just 11.4%. Amnesty International criticized the Charter for Peace and National Reconciliation, stating that it would simply 'obliterate crimes of the past'.

The Government revealed the exact details of the partial amnesty in February 2006: those Islamist rebels who had not been involved in mass killings, rape or bomb attacks on public places would have six months to surrender to the authorities, while more than 2,000 armed Islamists imprisoned during the civil conflict would be pardoned and released by mid-March; a small number of detainees would have their sentences reduced. The release of the first group of prisoners, which included Belhadj and Abdelhak Layada, second-in-command of the GIA, took place in early March. Nevertheless, the threat of Islamist terrorism continued, and attacks attributed to militants of the GSPC resulted in the deaths of a number of Algerian security officials in April. By the time that the six-month amnesty expired, in August, the Minister of State for the Interior and Local Authorities, Noureddine Yazid Zerhouni, stated that only some 250–300 militants had given up their weapons; it was estimated that up to 800 Islamist fighters, mostly of the GSPC, remained at large.

Meanwhile, in May 2006 Ouyahia resigned as Prime Minister. President Bouteflika subsequently appointed Abdelaziz Belkhadem, the FLN Secretary-General and, since May 2005, Minister of State and Special Representative of the President, to succeed him. Ouyahia had been strongly criticized for a perceived reluctance to use increased revenues from hydrocarbons exports to effect social reform, and a disagreement with Belkhadem over proposed constitutional reforms had precipitated rumours of a rift within the presidential alliance.

The emergence of the 'al-Qa'ida Organization in the Land of the Islamic Maghreb'

It was reported in January 2007 that the GSPC had restyled itself as the 'al-Qa'ida Organization in the Land of the Islamic Maghreb' (AQIM), having apparently joined the international al-Qa'ida organization led by the Saudi-born Islamist Osama bin Laden. There were widespread fears that an intensification of Islamist violence across North Africa was being co-ordinated by militant groups with an al-Qa'ida connection. Days after the GSPC had announced its name change, 15 people were killed in clashes between Algerian security forces and Islamist militants in Batna. In March seven police officers were killed in a militant attack in Tizi Ouzou, while four pipeline construction workers (from Russia and Ukraine), together with three Algerians, died in a further attack in Aïn Defla, south-west of the capital; AQIM claimed responsibility for both incidents. The same group declared that it had carried out car bomb attacks targeted at sites in Algiers in early April, in which 33 people were killed and more than 200 wounded; one of the bombs exploded close to the Prime Minister's office and was widely believed to be the country's first suicide bombing. Later that month Algerian military officials announced that the second-in-command of AQIM, Samir Saioud (also known as Samir Moussaâb), had been shot dead during fighting to the east of the capital.

The Government announced in February 2007 that Algeria's electoral lists were to be revised in preparation for elections to the National People's Assembly scheduled for May. The FFS declared in March that it intended to boycott the elections, as had been the case in 2002, citing its lack of confidence in the country's parliamentary system as a means of bringing about real political change. The FLN retained its dominance of the legislature following the 17 May 2007 polls, winning 136 of the 389 seats and thus an overall majority (although the party had previously been represented by 199 deputies). The RND again held the second highest number of seats, with 62 (compared with 48 in 2002), while the MSP and the PT also increased their representation, taking 51 and 26 seats, respectively (compared with 38 and 21). The RCD, which had boycotted the 2002 elections, secured 19 seats. In contrast, El Islah, which had been the principal opposition movement in the outgoing legislature, won only three seats. Independent candidates secured 33 seats. Although the rate of voter participation was reported to be a mere 36%, Zerhouni asserted that similar rates were not unusual in some Western democracies and denied that the new legislature would lack credibility. In June 2007 President Bouteflika appointed a new Council of Ministers, with Abdelaziz Belkhadem retaining the premiership and the Minister of Finance, Mourad Medelci, being appointed Minister of Foreign Affairs.

Two suicide bombings apparently carried out by AQIM in Batna and Algiers in September 2007 claimed up to 60 lives. These bomb attacks, the first of which was intended to assassinate President Bouteflika, resulted in an anti-violence demonstration in the capital by thousands of Algerians. In October security forces claimed to have killed the deputy leader of AQIM, Hareg Zoheir (or Sofiane Abu Fasila), in Tizi Ouzou. Nevertheless, the violence being perpetrated by militant Islamists continued, with two suicide car bombings in Algiers in December resulting in a large number of fatalities. Official estimates put the death toll at 26, while local medics assessed it to be around 70. According to independent sources, an estimated 491 people were believed to have died as a result of political violence by the end of 2007.

In January 2008 a car bomb attack against a police station and an ambush on a military convoy, both in the Algiers region, resulted in the deaths of four police officers and five soldiers, respectively. The authorities responded to this renewed violence, for which AQIM claimed responsibility, by arresting many suspected Islamist militants and further tightening their security measures. Eight Algerian gendarmes were killed in a suspected ambush by AQIM extremists in the south-eastern province of el-Oued in February. In June 19 people reportedly died, including several members of the security forces, in a series of bomb attacks to the east of Algiers. AQIM was blamed for these attacks, and for renewed suicide bombings to the east of the capital in August. In one of the deadliest attacks in Algeria in recent years, on 19 August 43 people were reportedly killed when a car bomb exploded at a gendarmerie academy; the majority of those killed were prospective recruits who were queuing up to register for the entry exam to the academy.

President Bouteflika effected an unexpected reorganization of the Council of Ministers in June 2008, in which the most notable appointment was that of Ahmed Ouyahia to succeed Abdelaziz Belkhadem as Prime Minister. Ouyahia—who had previously served in the post from 1995–98, and again from 2003–06—was known for his firm stance against Islamist militants, and his appointment was understood, in part, as a reaction to the recent increase in Islamist violence. In spite of concerns expressed by opposition parties, on 12 November 2008 both parliamentary chambers approved an amendment to the Constitution—which stipulated that a President could only renew his term of office once—in order to allow Bouteflika to seek a third term at the presidential election subsequently scheduled to take place in April 2009. The amending legislation also formally established the post of Prime Minister to replace that of Head of Government, allowed for the President to appoint several deputy prime ministers and guaranteed a greater representation of women at all levels of Algerian politics.

Recent developments: challenges confronting President Bouteflika in his third term

The candidates standing against Bouteflika in the presidential election of 9 April 2009 were: Hanoune; Rebaïne; Moussa Touati, President of the FNA; Muhammad Djahid Younsi, Secretary-General of El Islah; and Mohand Oussaïd Belaïd, a moderate Islamist independent. The incumbent President invited representatives from international organizations, including the League of Arab States (the Arab League, see p. 364), to observe the electoral process in an effort to appease demands by opposition parties for greater impartiality and transparency in the ballot. However, as in the previous presidential election, in the weeks leading up to the poll opposition parties claimed that Bouteflika wielded excessive control over state media and had allocated state funds in favour of his re-election campaign. The President consistently dismissed these allegations.

Bouteflika was re-elected for a third term of office, having received 90.2% of the valid votes cast. His closest challenger, Hanoune, secured 4.5%, Touati 2.0%, Younsi 1.5%, and Belaïd and Rebaïne both took 0.9%. The rate of participation by eligible voters was reported to be 74.6%, although opposition parties disputed this figure. Indeed, several of Bouteflika's rivals questioned the legitimacy of the poll: both Hanoune (who intended to contest the results through the Constitutional Council) and Rebaïne boycotted the President's inauguration ceremony on 19 April. However, the Minister of State and Minister of the Interior and Local Authorities, Zerhouni, firmly denied any allegations of electoral malpractice. On 27 April Bouteflika reappointed Prime Minister Ouyahia and the entire Council of Ministers, with the exception of the Minister of State, Soltani Boudjerra, who left the Government at his own request.

In August 2009 Algeria hosted a summit attended by senior army personnel from Mali, Mauritania and Niger to discuss enhanced border security and the co-ordination of security policies in an attempt to contain and prevent terrorist actions in the region. In November it was announced that an additional 3,000 Algerian troops would be deployed on the country's southern borders, in addition to the 15,000 troops currently patrolling those areas. It was further announced that these areas would become designated military zones, within which civilian movement was to be subject to a permit system and crossings into Algeria restricted to eight patrolled locations. In April 2010 the same four Saharan countries opened a joint military command and control centre in Tamanrasset, in southern Algeria; it was hoped that, once the centre was operational, it would tackle the combined threats to the region of Islamist violence, kidnapping, and both weapons- and drugs-trafficking.

Islamist violence also persisted inside Algeria's borders in 2009 and early 2010, although the security forces continued to issue reports of successful action against militants, particularly those belonging to AQIM. In June 2009 there were three separate attacks, including an ambush on a police convoy which resulted in the deaths of at least 18 gendarmes. In July at least 14 soldiers were killed in a roadside ambush in the north of the country. Responsibility for all these attacks was subsequently claimed by AQIM. It was reported in mid-2009 that, further to the recent increase in violence, support was growing within the Algerian establishment for a new amnesty for Islamist militants, to include even the most senior AQIM members in the region. In October it was revealed that several militants had surrendered to the Algerian security forces in previous months, notably including the group's leader in the Zemmouri region, Nabil Touati. However, two soldiers were killed in separate attacks in December, and in January 2010 two military personnel, including the commander of the Béjaïa district, were killed during a clash with militants in northern Algeria.

Meanwhile, on 29 December 2009 indirect elections took place to renew one-half of the 96 elected members of the Council of the Nation. The FLN won 22 seats, while the RND took 20. The MSP and the FNA each received two seats, and the RCD one; the remaining seat was won by a FLN-aligned independent candidate. The overall outcome of the election was to increase the representation of the presidential alliance (comprising the FLN, the RND and the MSP), the constituent parties having secured 45 of the 48 seats available. In January 2010 the partial renewal was completed when President Bouteflika nominated 16 members to replace the outgoing presidential appointees.

In May 2010 Bouteflika effected a limited reorganization of the Council of Ministers, with Ouyahia remaining as Prime Minister. The most high-profile change was the replacement of Chakib Khelil, the Minister of Energy and Mining since 1999, by Youcef Yousfi (who had previously held both the energy and foreign affairs portfolios). The decision to replace Khelil was believed to be linked to an ongoing investigation into allegations of corruption among senior officials of the state-owned oil and gas company, Sonatrach, with whom the former minister was reported to have been closely associated. Although the President and Director-General of Sonatrach, Muhammad Meziane, was dismissed and later imprisoned for his role in the scandal, Khelil (himself a former head of Sonatrach) was not formally questioned by police. Another notable appointment to the Government was that of Dahou Ould Kablia as Minister of the Interior and Local Authorities, replacing Noureddine Yazid Zerhouni, who assumed the newly created post of Vice-Prime Minister. The issue of corruption was the subject of much debate in Algeria during 2010, since Bouteflika had pledged a significant anti-corruption drive following his re-election; measures taken by the authorities included the creation in August of an anti-corruption agency, the Office central de répression de la corruption.

Despite an increase in security co-operation between Algeria and other Saharan countries, Islamist militants continued to wage a violent campaign against representatives of the Algerian defence establishment and other targets. In June 2010 AQIM claimed responsibility for the deaths of 11 paramilitary gendarmes in Tinzaoutine, close to the border with Mali. The Algerian military again offered militants the opportunity to surrender their weapons and renounce violence under the terms of the 2005 Charter for Peace and National Reconciliation, or be eliminated. President Bouteflika declared at this time that the groups carrying out terrorist attacks had increasingly close links with transnational criminal networks, which were engaged in the smuggling of illegal goods such as drugs and arms, and the seizing of hostages for ransom. In July 2010 four soldiers were killed when three underground bombs exploded in the east of the country, close to Tizi Ouzou. In early October five soldiers were killed in an ambush by AQIM in Tizi Ouzou, and later that month a local director of public works and four businessmen died in an explosion at Oum el-Kamakem. According to various newspaper reports, on 9 December the Algerian army launched what was said to be the largest military offensive against AQIM in recent years in the Kabylia region, where the organization's 'northern command' (including its leader, Abdelmalek Droukdal) was thought to be based. The massive ground and air assault was ordered after the Government reportedly received intelligence claiming that a meeting of the AQIM leadership was imminent. By 30 December up to 50 suspected AQIM fighters were reported to have been killed, and military officials claimed that a significant plot to bomb the towns of Tizi Ouzou, Boumerdès and Bouira had been uncovered. Rumours that Droukdal had been killed in a military operation in the Tizi Ouzou region on 10 December proved to be unfounded. Indeed, in January 2011 a court in Boumerdès handed down a death sentence, *in absentia*, to Droukdal and 15 other militants. During the large-scale protests that were taking place across North Africa in that month, the AQIM leader urged Algerian and Tunisian protesters to seize the opportunity to overthrow their Governments and install Islamic states in both countries.

Following a series of strikes and protests during 2009–10, in early January 2011 significant demonstrations were held in Algiers in protest against a sharp increase in the price of basic food items (such as sugar, wheat and cooking oil), high levels of unemployment among young Algerians, inadequate housing and generally poor living standards. Two protesters were reported to have died during a confrontation with security forces in the Tipaza and M'Sila provinces, while other youths set fire to themselves as unrest spread across the country. In response, the authorities temporarily reduced taxes on certain foodstuffs, and President Bouteflika asked the Government to expand the provision of projects that would ease 'social distress', including improved housing. However, in late January several people were reportedly injured when riot police intervened to halt a renewed demonstration by protesters in Algiers who were demanding greater political rights. It appeared that disillusioned Algerians, who were now looting government buildings and private businesses, had been emboldened by recent developments in neighbouring Tunisia—where escalating protests had resulted in President Zine al-Abidine Ben Ali being forced into exile in Saudi Arabia. Government sources reported in late January that five people had been killed in the unrest earlier that month, 800 injured (most of whom were police officers) and some 1,100 arrests made by security forces. In an apparent attempt to placate the protesters, some of whom had begun to demand the ouster of President Bouteflika (following the removal from office of Egypt's President Hosni Mubarak) in late February Bouteflika repealed the state of emergency originally imposed in 1992. However, new anti-terrorism laws were introduced, under which the army retained significant powers, and public demonstrations remained illegal in the capital.

In mid-April 2011, amid ongoing unrest, Bouteflika made a televised address, in which he promised to introduce constitutional reforms, as well as amendments to the country's electoral law, prior to the legislative elections scheduled for May 2012. According to the President, these reforms—including changes to legislation concerning political parties and the media—would 'reinforce' democracy in Algeria. In late May 2011 the Commission nationale de consultation sur les réformes politiques (CNCRP) was formally established under the chairmanship of Abdelkader Bensalah (President of the Council of the Nation), and asked to draft proposed amendments to the Constitution, to be submitted to a parliamentary vote or a referendum. The commission presented its final report to Bouteflika in late July, although no precise details were disclosed. The political dialogue had been opposed by many leading political figures, and several groups—such as the opposition FFS, RCD and Ahd 54—had declined to participate, claiming that the President's reforms did not go far enough and that a change of leadership was needed. In September Bouteflika announced that a new information law to be submitted to parliament would allow the establishment of private radio and television stations, create a new regulatory commission for the print media, and end the practice of imprisoning journalists convicted of libel.

As President Bouteflika was unveiling his proposed constitutional reforms in April 2011, suspected AQIM militants attacked a military post near Tizi Ouzou, killing 13 soldiers. In early June four police officers died when a bomb exploded in Naciria, to the east of Algiers. Following further militant attacks in June–July, which led to the deaths of at least four soldiers and the killing or arrest by security forces of a number of would-be perpetrators, in late August two suicide bombers detonated their explosives at a military academy west of the capital. A reported 16 soldiers and two civilians were killed in the large-scale attack, which was again blamed on AQIM. Algerian security forces launched further operations to capture or kill suspected AQIM operatives, some of whom were believed to be benefiting from the state of civil war in neighbouring Libya. In late October two Spanish and one Italian aid worker were kidnapped from a camp for Western Sahara refugees near Tindouf in western Algeria. Nevertheless, despite the continuing violence, in early January 2012 the Minister of the Interior and Local Authorities, Dahou Ould Kablia, declared that the security situation in Algeria was improving. Reports at the end of December 2011 had indicated that one Mauritania-based militant group previously under the wing of AQIM, the Jamat Tawhid wal Jihad fi Garbi Afriqqiya (Movement for Unity and Jihad in West Africa), had chosen to break away from AQIM. The group claimed earlier in that month that it had been responsible for the abduction of the three European aid workers in October.

At the start of January 2012 the MSP announced that it was withdrawing from the presidential alliance (which also comprised the FLN and the RND), in advance of the May legislative elections. Leaders of the moderate Islamist party—which had four cabinet ministers and 51 parliamentary seats—cited differences with its former partners over the extent of the reforms proposed by Bouteflika in response to the serious rioting which had taken place in 2011. Furthermore, the MSP urged the President to appoint a government of technocrats to oversee the forthcoming polls. Renewed protests were reported at the start of 2012, as many Algerians complained that local authorities had not fulfilled pledges made in the aftermath of the previous year's unrest. In February Bouteflika announced that the legislative elections would take place on 10 May.

The Campaign for Cultural and Language Rights in Kabylia

In addition to the upheaval caused by Islamist violence in the mid-1990s, a campaign for enhanced cultural and language rights by Berber activists in Kabylia intensified in the wake of the Government's policy of 'Arabization'. In late 1994 the Berber RCD urged a boycott of the start of the school year, and a general strike was organized, in protest at the exclusion of the Berber language, Tamazight, from the syllabus and at the prospect of the FIS entering the national dialogue. In May 1995 the RCD welcomed the establishment of a government body to oversee the teaching of Tamazight in schools and universities from October, and to promote its use in the official media. Violent protests erupted in Kabylia in June 1998, following the assassination of Lounès Matoub, a popular Berber singer and outspoken critic of both the Government and the fundamentalist Islamist movement. There were further protests in July, when controversial legislation on the compulsory use of the Arabic language in public life came into effect; Berber activists demanded the recognition of Tamazight as an official language.

In April 2001 clashes broke out between protesters and security forces in several villages in Kabylia following the death of a secondary school student (who had been apprehended for allegedly committing an assault during a robbery) in police custody at Beni Douala near the regional capital, Tizi Ouzou. Thousands of local inhabitants joined demonstrations, demanding a full inquiry into the incident and the withdrawal of paramilitary gendarmes from Kabylia. The situation was further inflamed when three young Kabyles were assaulted by gendarmes near Béjaïa. The incidents coincided with demonstrations traditionally held to mark the anniversary of the so-called 'Berber Spring' protests of 1980, when Berber activism had first taken form, and although the two major political parties in Kabylia—the FFS and the RCD—appealed for calm, violence rapidly escalated throughout the area; as many as 80 people had reportedly died by the end of the month. In a televised address, President Abdelaziz Bouteflika announced the creation of a national commission of inquiry, to be headed by Mohand Issad, a lawyer originating from Kabylia, to investigate recent events in the region. Bouteflika also indicated that he planned revisions to the Constitution that would address the status of Tamazight, and revealed his intention to adopt a proposal making instruction in the Berber language compulsory in Tamazight-speaking areas. Furthermore, he accused unnamed groups both inside and outside the country of inciting extremism. Bouteflika's speech was strongly criticized by the main political groupings in Kabylia, and the RCD withdrew from the coalition Government. Increasingly violent demonstrations by Berbers took place during May and June 2001; in mid-June all protests in Algiers were prohibited.

By the end of June 2001 unrest had spread beyond Kabylia to the Aurès region, as well as to Annaba and Biskra. Official reports stated that 56 people had been killed, and 1,300 injured, since the violence first erupted. Despite repeated demands in the independent press for his resignation, Bouteflika declared that he would not relinquish the presidency and again urged rioters not to participate in what he termed an external plot to undermine security in Algeria. In July the Issad commission issued its preliminary report into the events in Kabylia, in which it blamed the gendarmerie for the rioting, since gendarmes had adopted a 'shoot-to-kill' policy and had acted in an illegal manner. However, the report failed to name those responsible for ordering the gendarmes' actions, and the commission complained of attempts, apparently on the part of vested interests within the security forces, to obstruct its investigations.

Security forces blocked roads in August 2001, in order to prevent a large number of Berbers from marching on the capital, where they intended to present a list of 15 demands at the presidential palace. This 'El-Kseur platform' (named after the Kabyle town in which it had been drawn up) notably requested: the granting of official status to Tamazight without the holding of a referendum; the removal of all paramilitary gendarmes from Kabylia; the annulment of legal proceedings against demonstrators; and the trial by civilian courts of all those who had ordered or perpetrated crimes and their dismissal from the security forces or the civil service.

In September 2001 President Bouteflika formally invited Berber community and tribal leaders, known as the *Aarouch*, to present their demands for social and political change, and designated Prime Minister Ali Benflis to act as interlocutor between the authorities and the Berbers. Although some Berber leaders were unwilling to enter into negotiations with the Government, a meeting reportedly took place in October between Benflis and moderate *Aarouch*, at which Benflis informed them that the President had decided to grant Tamazight the status of a national language in a forthcoming constitutional amendment. In January 2002 a series of resolutions were adopted, including proposals for the establishment of a special ministerial council to implement the creation of decentralized government councils in Kabylia at *wilaya* (department) level. The more radical *Aarouch* voiced their disapproval of the resolutions, stating that the El-Kseur platform was non-negotiable, and again insisted that the gendarmerie be withdrawn from Kabylia. However, this demand was consistently dismissed by Bouteflika as 'inconceivable'. In December the final report of the Issad commission was published, confirming the initial findings that the gendarmerie had been to blame for the repression in Kabylia, and also expressing deep pessimism about the immediate future of the region. Emphasizing the increasing authority of the military throughout the country since 1992, the report stated that the responsibilities of the civil and military authorities had become blurred and denounced the subtle slide from 'a state of emergency to a state of siege'.

In a televised address in March 2002, Bouteflika officially announced that Tamazight would be recognized as a national language without the issue being put to a referendum. Accordingly, on 8 April the National People's Assembly voted almost unanimously in favour of amending the Constitution to grant Tamazight this status. Nevertheless, Kabyle leaders urged a boycott of the legislative elections scheduled for May (see Domestic Political Affairs), and the region was brought to a standstill by a series of strikes. Prior to local elections in October, the persistence of divisions within the Berber movement was highlighted when the RCD, supported by the Coordination des aârchs, daïras et communes (CADC—also known as the Coordination des comités de villages Kabyles), announced that it would again boycott the polls. This was in direct contrast to the FFS, which was to present candidates in 40 of the country's 48 *wilayat*, maintaining that these would provide ordinary Kabyles with the possibility of attaining some form of political representation. At the elections the FLN won 668 of the 1,541 communes and thus secured control of 43 *wilayat*, although there were violent clashes in Kabylia, where demonstrators attempted to prevent voting from taking place.

The Government announced in July 2003 that it had agreed to reintroduce the use of Tamazight into Algeria's educational system, thereby fulfilling one of the demands of the El-Kseur platform. Moreover, in August the Government granted more than €23m. in 'overdue' development aid to Kabylia. In early January 2004 lengthy negotiations took place between the *Aarouch* and the Government, following which the authorities pledged to acquiesce to five of the six points deemed by the *Aarouch* to be 'prerequisites' to any further talks relating to the El-Kseur platform; these included the release of all remaining prisoners and the annulment of legal proceedings against demonstrators detained during the riots of April 2001. The sixth point, regarding the dissolution of municipal and regional councils elected in Kabylia in October 2002, was settled in late January 2004, when the Government agreed to remove any councillors who had been elected illegally in the contested polls. Days later the Algerian authorities released five Berber leaders who had been imprisoned for their role in the rioting, and Ouyahia stated that the meetings had provided a 'fundamental turning point' in the process between the two sides. However, the negotiations collapsed following the Government's assertion that the status of Tamazight should be decided in a national referendum, and further unrest ensued in Kabylia, while the FFS declared that it would not participate in the forthcoming presidential election. In January 2005, following a new round of talks, the Government and the *Aarouch* reached an agreement regarding implementation of the El-Kseur platform; two joint committees were established to implement and monitor the agreement.

In June 2010 the founder and leader of the separatist Mouvement pour l'autonomie de la Kabylie, Ferhat Mehenni, announced that his movement had established a provisional 'government-in-exile' in Paris, France, with Mehenni leading a cabinet of nine ministers which would seek directly to challenge the Algerian leadership and to represent the Kabylia region at the international level. Although the formation of the Gouvernement Provisoire Kabyle was dismissed as insignificant by Ouyahia, there were reports that an arrest warrant had been issued for Mehenni.

Foreign Affairs

Relations with France

The Algerian military takeover in January 1992 was welcomed by the French Government, and French economic and political support for the Algerian regime increased in early 1993, following the appointment of Edouard Balladur as Prime Minister of France. Alleged Islamist militants residing in France continued to be prosecuted, and in August 1994, following the killing of five French embassy employees in Algiers, 26 suspected Algerian extremists were interned in northern France; 20 of them were subsequently expelled to Burkina Faso. In September the French embassy in Algiers confirmed that entry visas would be issued to Algerians only in exceptional cases. By November the number of French nationals killed by Islamist militants in Algeria had reached 21 and the French Government urged its citizens to leave Algeria. An Air France aircraft was hijacked at Algiers airport in December by members of the GIA, resulting in the deaths of three passengers and, later, in the killing of the hijackers by French security forces when the aircraft landed in France. The GIA claimed responsibility for numerous bomb attacks across France between July and November 1995, in which seven people were killed and more than 160 injured. In August 1996 the success of a visit to Algeria by Hervé de Charette, the French Minister of Foreign Affairs, was marred by the assassination of the French Roman Catholic Bishop of Oran only hours after meeting de Charette. In December four people were killed as a result of a bomb explosion on a passenger train in Paris, prompting speculation that the GIA had resumed its campaign of violence in France. In early 1998 a French court sentenced 36 Islamist militants to terms of imprisonment of up to 10 years for providing logistical support for the bomb attacks in France in 1995. A further 138 people stood trial in France in September 1998, accused of criminal association with Algerian terrorists.

In June 1999 the French National Assembly voted unanimously to abandon the official claim that the struggle between Algerian nationalists and French troops during 1954–62 had been no more than 'an operation for keeping order', and thus admitted that France had indeed fought in the Algerian war of independence. An apparent improvement in bilateral relations was further signalled by a meeting in September 1999 between Bouteflika and the French President, Jacques Chirac, in New York, USA (the first meeting between the leaders of the two countries since 1992). In June 2000 Bouteflika made a full state visit to France—the first of its kind by an Algerian head of state.

Algeria's relations with France were placed under strain from late 2000 by a series of much-publicized revelations, mainly regarding occurrences during the war of independence. In November Gen. Jacques Massu, who had commanded French troops during the Battle of Algiers in 1957, asserted in an interview with the French daily *Le Monde* that France should admit and condemn the use of torture by its forces during the conflict. Moreover, a book published in May 2001 by a retired French general, Paul Aussarresses, contained allegations of Algerian army involvement in the torture and massacre of civilians since 1992. In August 2001 eight 'harkis'—Algerian Muslims who had served in the French army prior to independence—filed a formal complaint against the French Government for crimes and complicity in crimes against humanity. As many as 130,000 harkis were estimated to have been murdered by FLN troops following France's withdrawal from Algeria in 1962. In September 2001 President Chirac unveiled a plaque in Paris to commemorate those who were killed, and acknowledged his country's failure to halt the reprisals against the harkis. In November 2003 it was announced that Pierre Messmer, the French Minister of the Armed Forces during the latter stages of the war of independence, would face charges of committing 'crimes against humanity' for his role in the decision not to allow the harkis to settle in France.

Following a marked improvement in relations during 2002, in March 2003 Jacques Chirac became the first French President to make a full state visit to Algeria since 1962. Bouteflika and Chirac signed the 'Declaration of Algiers', whereby both countries pledged to rebuild bilateral relations by holding annual meetings of their heads of state as well as twice-yearly talks between their respective ministers responsible for foreign affairs. In June 2003 Air France resumed flights to Algeria, which had been suspended since the hijacking of one of its aircraft in December 1994. Furthermore, in August 2004 Bouteflika visited France to mark the 60th anniversary of the Algerian landings in Provence, which had opened up a new front against the Nazi German occupiers. However, in May 2005 Bouteflika again urged France to acknowledge that Algerians had been tortured and killed during French colonial rule and, specifically, to admit to the massacre of 45,000 Algerian protesters who were demanding independence at the end of the Second World War in May 1945. In May 2006 Bouteflika announced that the proposed treaty of friendship would remain on hold until France issued an apology to the Algerian people for 'crimes' committed under colonialism.

Shortly after his election to the French presidency, in July 2007 Nicolas Sarkozy visited Algeria and Tunisia, apparently to demonstrate the intention of his administration to forge even closer ties with the countries of the Maghreb. President Sarkozy undertook a further visit to Algiers in December, at which his failure to offer an explicit apology on behalf of the French nation for the era of colonial rule again angered some Algerian officials. Nevertheless, the French President did acknowledge that France's colonization of Algeria had been 'profoundly unfair', and the two countries signed several important bilateral agreements in the fields of petroleum, gas and nuclear energy. Moreover, the French Government announced subsequently that it was to offer financial compensation to thousands of harkis. At the end of a two-day visit by the French Prime Minister, François Fillon, to Algiers in June 2008, further agreements were signed concerning civil nuclear collaboration, military co-operation and bilateral financial matters. In May 2009 a visit to France by President Bouteflika scheduled for June was postponed indefinitely. The official reason given was a lack of sufficient time, although some commentators cited as possible reasons Algeria's displeasure at the French media's criticism of the conduct of the April 2009 presidential election and France's failure to provide a formal apology for its period of colonial rule. Algerians were also angered when, in January 2010, their country was named on a list of those whose citizens were perceived to threaten France's national security. In July, after a French aid worker was kidnapped by militant Islamists in Niger and subsequently murdered by his captors, Fillon declared his country to be 'at war' with AQIM across North Africa. France was expected to provide further assistance to the countries of the Sahel-Sahara region in training their armies to fight the militant group. In 2010 several leading French politicians visited Algeria in an effort to settle outstanding disagreements, and the Algerian President travelled to the French city of Nice in May to attend the 25th Africa-France Summit. However, the onset of civil war in Libya in early 2011 placed a further strain on relations between France and Algeria. The Algerian authorities opposed the North Atlantic Treaty Organization (NATO)-led intervention in the Libyan conflict from March onwards, while the French Government—which played a leading role in the NATO military action—accused Algeria of supporting the Qaddafi regime.

Regional relations

During the 1980s Algeria attempted to achieve a closer relationship with the other countries of the Maghreb region (Libya, Mauritania, Morocco and Tunisia). The Maghreb Fraternity and Co-operation Treaty, signed by Algeria and Tunisia in March 1983 and by Mauritania in December, established a basis for the creation of the long-discussed 'Great Arab Maghreb'. Although bilateral relations continued to be affected by the dispute over Western Sahara (see the chapter on Morocco), in May 1988 Algeria and Morocco restored diplomatic relations (severed in 1976) at ambassadorial level. Meeting in Algiers in June, the five heads of state of the Maghreb countries announced the formation of a Maghreb commission to examine areas of regional integration. In February 1989 the leaders signed a treaty establishing the Union du Maghreb arabe (UMA, see p. 452), with the aim of encouraging economic co-operation and eventually establishing a full customs union. The Algerian army's intervention in January 1992 to prevent victory by the FIS in the general election provoked relief in Tunisia and Morocco that the establishment of a neighbouring fundamentalist state had been pre-empted.

Morocco imposed entry visas on Algerian nationals in August 1994, following the murder of two Spanish tourists in Morocco, allegedly by Algerian Islamist extremists. Algeria reciprocated by closing the border between the two countries and imposing entry visas on Moroccan nationals. Although in September Algeria announced the appointment of a new ambassador to Morocco, in December King Hassan II of Morocco expressed his disapproval at Algeria's alleged continuing support for the independence of Western Sahara, and demanded that UMA activities be suspended. A UMA summit meeting, scheduled for later that month, was subsequently postponed. Following his accession to the presidency in April 1999, Bouteflika initially attempted further to improve bilateral relations during a visit to the Moroccan capital to attend the funeral of King Hassan. However, the rapprochement was halted in August, on the day when the imminent reopening of the common border was announced, by the massacre by the GIA of 29 civilians in the border region of Béchar. Bouteflika's public allegation that Morocco was providing sanctuary for the perpetrators of the attack extended to accusations of drugs-trafficking and arms-dealing on the Algerian border. In September Bouteflika accused both Morocco and Tunisia of acting against the interests of the UMA by negotiating separate agreements with the European Union (EU, see p. 276).

In April 2000 Bouteflika met with the new Moroccan ruler, King Muhammad VI, at the Africa-EU summit held in Cairo,

Egypt. The two leaders agreed to establish joint committees in an attempt to reduce the number of violent incidents on their mutual border, and joint military security operations began in May. In March 2001 a meeting in Algiers of the UMA's council of ministers responsible for foreign affairs ended acrimoniously following disagreements between Moroccan and Algerian delegations. Relations were further strained after Algeria announced its opposition to UN proposals for a settlement to the Western Sahara issue, believing that the plans unduly favoured Morocco and would inevitably lead to the formal integration of the disputed territory into Morocco. In July 2004 talks on the future of Western Sahara between the Moroccan Minister of the Interior, Al Mustapha Sahel, and the Algerian Minister of State for the Interior and Local Authorities, Noureddine Yazid Zerhouni, recommenced in Algeria; senior French and Spanish representatives were also in attendance. However, Morocco remained opposed to the UN proposals, stating that they jeopardized its sovereignty, and Morocco's ongoing dispute with Algeria over Western Sahara led to the eventual breakdown of the talks. A UMA summit meeting due to take place in Tripoli, Libya, in May 2005 was postponed indefinitely after King Muhammad announced that he would not be attending. In September, however, Sahel announced that the Moroccan Government was committed to improving relations with Algeria and negotiating a political end to the conflict.

A summit meeting of UMA foreign ministers took place in Tripoli in December 2009. Measures were put in place to facilitate the creation of the Maghreb Bank for Investment and Foreign Trade, which was intended to encourage the circulation of capital in the region and fund common agricultural and industrial projects. It was subsequently announced that Algeria would hold the chairmanship of the bank's board of directors for the first three years of operation. There were signs of an improvement in Algerian-Moroccan relations in early 2011, particularly as far as economic co-operation was concerned. Amid this rapprochement, reports emerged in May that the reopening of the countries' joint border, which had been closed since 1994, was imminent. However, at the end of May 2011 Algeria's Prime Minister, Ahmed Ouyahia, clarified the situation, asserting that his Government had no immediate plans to reopen the frontier owing to the current political climate between Algeria and Morocco. In late January 2012 Morocco's newly appointed Prime Minister, Abdelilah Benkirane, stated his Government's intention to seek rapprochement with fellow Maghreb countries. On 23 January the Moroccan Minister of Foreign Affairs and Co-operation, Saadeddine el-Othmani, began a two-day official visit to Algeria, the first such visit since 2003.

Algeria's relationship with Tunisia remained stable after President Zine al-Abidine was forced from office by Tunisian demonstrators in January 2011 (see Domestic Political Affairs). In early July the Algerian and Tunisian Governments signed an accord finalizing the demarcation of their maritime borders.

The long-standing rivalry between Algeria and Egypt descended into violence in November 2009, after the two countries' national teams contested qualification matches for the football World Cup. Prior to the first match in Cairo, three members of the Algerian squad were injured when rocks were thrown at the team bus. In the aftermath of Egypt's victory in that contest, some 20 Algerian nationals were reported to have been injured, while in Algiers several Egyptian businesses were attacked by Algerian supporters. Following the deciding match in Khartoum, Sudan, which was won by Algeria, the Egyptian authorities claimed that 21 of its citizens had been assaulted. Egyptian businesses in Algiers were again attacked, and fighting broke out between Egyptians and Algerians resident in Marseille, France. The Egyptian Government subsequently recalled its ambassador to Algeria for consultations, while Algeria's ambassador to Egypt was summoned to the Egyptian Ministry of Foreign Affairs to discuss the attacks on Egyptian interests in Algiers. In late November 2009 it was announced that, following requests by the Arab League, the Libyan leader Col Muammar al-Qaddafi had agreed to mediate between the two countries. The Algerian ambassador was returned to Cairo in January 2010 and the Egyptian envoy to Algiers in February, while a short visit to Algeria in July by Egypt's President Hosni Mubarak to offer his condolences to President Bouteflika on the death of his brother signalled a willingness on both sides to improve bilateral relations.

In late August 2011, following the fall of Tripoli to forces loyal to Libya's opposition National Transitional Council, it was revealed that the wife, daughter and two sons of Col Qaddafi had fled to Algeria. The authorities asserted that the fugitives had been permitted to enter Algeria 'on humanitarian grounds'. The Council demanded that the Algerian Government hand over Qaddafi's relatives to the interim Libyan authorities, and the country was the subject of considerable international criticism for harbouring them. Nevertheless, in late September Algeria formally recognized the Council as 'the legitimate representatives of the Libyan people'. The Algerian authorities expressed concerns during 2011 that weapons employed during the Libyan civil war might be recovered by AQIM militants and used in future terrorist attacks in Algeria and other parts of the Sahel-Sahara region.

Other external relations

In December 1996 the EU and Algeria began negotiations on Algeria's participation in a Euro-Mediterranean free trade zone. In January 2001 the President of the European Commission, Romano Prodi, visited Algeria, where he signed the financing protocols for a number of joint projects. In December negotiations for the EU-Algeria Euro-Mediterranean Association Agreement were concluded, and both parties formally signed the agreement in April 2002. Following ratification by the European Parliament and requisite EU member states, it entered into effect on 1 September 2005.

In 2007 Nicolas Sarkozy proposed the idea of a Mediterranean Union as part of his election campaign for the French presidency. The initiative, which was intended to foster economic, political and cultural links between Mediterranean states, was described by Sarkozy as building upon the Barcelona Process launched by Euro-Mediterranean foreign ministers in November 1995. By the beginning of 2008 the project had been modified to encompass not just those nations bordering the Mediterranean Sea, but all EU member states. Despite expressing reservations about the project—namely that it would undermine the work of the Arab League and represent something of a return to colonial rule—Bouteflika was among the many heads of state of the 43 EU and Mediterranean member nations to be in attendance when the Union for the Mediterranean (as it had been renamed) was officially inaugurated at a summit meeting in Paris on 13 July. At the fifth meeting of the EU-Algeria Association Council in Luxembourg in June 2010, the Algerian Minister of Foreign Affairs, Mourad Medelci, urged member states to increase the level of direct EU investment in Algeria's economy. It was agreed to establish a sub-committee through which issues such as security and human rights could be discussed, while preparations for the creation of a free trade area in 2017 were also discussed. At the sixth meeting of the Association Council in mid-June 2011, Medelci again asked for financial assistance from the EU in order to support Algeria's ongoing economic reform programme.

The Algerian Government was swift to condemn the suicide attacks on New York and Washington, DC, on 11 September 2001, for which the USA held the international al-Qa'ida network responsible, and to offer assistance for the USA's proposed 'coalition against terror'. Later that month the Algerian authorities handed the US authorities a list containing the profiles of some 350 Islamist militants it believed had links to bin Laden and al-Qa'ida. In September 2002 Algerian security forces killed a senior al-Qa'ida operative, who was alleged to be liaising with the GSPC, in a raid near Batna. In December the US Administration announced that it had for the first time agreed to sell weaponry and other military equipment to Algeria as part of the USA's policy of intensifying bilateral security co-operation. In December 2003 the US Secretary of State, Colin Powell, visited Algeria for talks with President Bouteflika, at which he praised Algeria's assistance in the 'war on terror'. In November 2010 the two countries concluded a three-year co-operation accord concerning the training of military personnel, holding of military exercises and sharing of vital technology in their joint struggle against terrorism in North Africa. Co-operation between Algeria and the USA on regional and international counter-terrorism efforts was increased during 2011. Medelci visited Washington, DC, in early May for talks with senior US officials, including the Secretary of State, Hillary Clinton. Besides the fight against Islamist terrorism, topics under discussion included Algerian political and economic reforms, and regional developments such as the Libyan conflict and recent change of government in Tunisia.

In March 2003 four Algerians were given prison terms by a court in Frankfurt am Main, Germany, after being convicted of conspiracy to commit murder and of weapons violations. It was alleged that the men had been plotting to detonate a series of bombs in Strasbourg, France, prior to their arrest in December 2000. During the early part of 2003 several Algerians were arrested in the United Kingdom and charged with terrorist offences, including the production of a chemical weapon; others were imprisoned by the British authorities for funding terrorism. In June 2006 Algeria and the United Kingdom signed a memorandum of understanding on the extradition of Algerian citizens suspected of involvement in terrorist activity. Two such alleged Islamist militants were deported to Algeria in that month and another five reportedly agreed to be extradited in January 2007. In December 2009 an EU delegation visited Algiers to discuss security in the Sahel-Sahara region and agree on a joint strategy to fight terrorism following the increased threat of attacks from AQIM outside the country's borders.

Algeria has generally enjoyed strong bilateral relations with Russia since the era of the USSR, and in recent years Russia has provided the Bouteflika regime with both military and technical assistance. Following a visit by Russian President Vladimir Putin in March 2006, Russia pledged to forgive Soviet-era debt in exchange for Algeria's agreement to import a range of Russian products. In August the two countries' state-owned gas companies, Sonatrach and Gazprom, signed a memorandum of understanding according to which the Russian firm would assist in the development of Algeria's natural gas reserves. During a visit by President Dmitrii Medvedev to Algiers in October 2010, it was agreed that regular meetings at both presidential and ministerial level would be convened in order to strengthen bilateral co-operation, particularly in the fields of energy and transport.

CONSTITUTION AND GOVERNMENT

A new Constitution for the People's Democratic Republic of Algeria, approved by popular referendum, was promulgated on 22 November 1976. The Constitution was amended by the National People's Assembly on 30 June 1979 and, by referendum, on 3 November 1988, 23 February 1989 and 28 November 1996. On 8 April 2002 the Assembly approved an amendment that granted Tamazight, the principal language spoken by Algeria's Berber population, the status of a national language. On 12 November 2008 the Assembly endorsed an amendment to abolish the limit on the number of terms a President may serve.

Under the terms of the Constitution, Algeria is a multi-party state, with parties subject to approval by the Ministry of the Interior and Local Authorities. The head of state is the President of the Republic, who is elected by universal adult suffrage for a five-year term; there is no limit on the number of terms he may serve. The President presides over a Council of Ministers and a High Security Council. The President must appoint a Prime Minister as Head of Government, who appoints a Council of Ministers. The bicameral legislature consists of the 389-member National People's Assembly and the 144-member Council of the Nation. The members of the National People's Assembly are elected by universal, direct, secret suffrage for a five-year term. Two-thirds of the members of the Council of the Nation are elected by indirect, secret suffrage from regional and municipal authorities; the remainder are appointed by the President of the Republic. The Council's term of office is six years; one-half of its members are replaced every three years. Both the Head of Government and the parliamentary chambers may initiate legislation, which must be deliberated upon by the National People's Assembly and the Council of the Nation, respectively, before promulgation. The country is divided into 48 departments (*wilayat*), which are, in turn, sub-divided into communes. Each *wilaya* and commune has an elected assembly.

REGIONAL AND INTERNATIONAL CO-OPERATION

Algeria is a member of the Union of the Arab Maghreb (UMA, see p. 452), which aims to promote economic integration of member states. It is also a member of the African Union (AU, see p. 189) and the League of Arab States (the Arab League, see p. 364). A Euro-Mediterranean Association Agreement between Algeria and the European Union, signed in April 2002, entered into effect on 1 September 2005.

Having gained independence from France in May 1962, Algeria became a member of the UN on 8 October of that year. Algeria also participates in the Organization of the Petroleum Exporting Countries (OPEC, see p. 408) and the Group of 77 developing countries (G77, see p. 450). Negotiations concerning Algeria's accession to the World Trade Organization (WTO, see p. 433), which commenced in 1987, were still ongoing in early 2012.

ECONOMIC AFFAIRS

In 2010, according to estimates by the World Bank, Algeria's gross national income (GNI), measured at average 2008–10 prices, was US $157,939m., equivalent to $4,450 per head (or $8,120 on an international purchasing-power parity basis). During 2001–10, it was estimated, the population increased at an average annual rate of 1.5%, while gross domestic product (GDP) per head increased, in real terms, by an average of 2.3% per year. Overall GDP increased, in real terms, at an average annual rate of 3.8% in 2001–10; it grew by 3.0% in 2010.

According to the African Development Bank, agriculture (including forestry and fishing) contributed 9.8% of GDP in 2009. According to official estimates, the sector employed 11.7% of the labour force in 2010. Domestic production of food crops is insufficient to meet the country's requirements. The principal crops are wheat, barley, potatoes and tomatoes. Dates are Algeria's principal non-hydrocarbon export; onions, citrus fruits, watermelons and grapes are also grown, and wine has been an important export since the French colonial era. According to the World Bank, during 2001–09 agricultural GDP increased at an average annual rate of 3.5%; sectoral growth was 2.0% in 2009.

Industry (including mining, manufacturing, construction and power) contributed 50.4% of GDP in 2009, according to the African Development Bank. The sector, according to official estimates, engaged 33.1% of the employed population in 2010. According to the World Bank, during 2001–09 industrial GDP increased at an average annual rate of 3.4%; it expanded by 2.6% in 2009.

The mining sector provides almost all of Algeria's export earnings, although it engaged only 1.7% of the employed population in 2004. According to the African Development Bank, the sector contributed 32.9% of GDP in 2009, including petroleum and gas, which are overwhelmingly Algeria's principal exports (providing 98.3% of total export earnings in 2010). Algeria's proven reserves of petroleum were 12,200m. barrels at the end of 2010, sufficient to maintain output at that year's levels—which averaged 1.8m. barrels per day (b/d)—for 18.5 years. As a member of the Organization of the Petroleum Exporting Countries (OPEC), Algeria is subject to production quotas agreed by the Organization's Conference. Proven reserves of natural gas at the end of 2010 totalled 4,504,000m. cu m, sustainable at that year's production level (totalling 80,412m. cu m) for more than 56 years. Algeria currently transports natural gas through two pipelines—one (the Pedro Duran Farrell pipeline—formerly Maghreb–Europe Gas) to Spain and Portugal via Morocco, and the other (the Enrico Mattei pipeline—formerly Transmediterranean or Transmed) to Italy via Tunisia. A further pipeline (Medgaz) enabling gas to be exported to Spain and thereafter France was inaugurated in March 2011. Plans to construct a second pipeline (GALSI) linking Algeria to Italy via the island of Sardinia were also under way, although the project has experienced numerous delays and construction was not scheduled to begin until at least 2012. Substantial reserves of iron ore, phosphates, barite (barytes), lead, zinc, mercury, salt, marble and industrial minerals are also mined, and the exploitation of gold reserves commenced in 2001. The GDP of the hydrocarbons sector increased by 6.1% in 1999 and by an estimated 4.9% in 2000, while that of other mining activities declined by 3.0% in 1999 but expanded by some 6.5% in 2000.

Manufacturing provided 4.9% of GDP in 2009, according to the African Development Bank, and engaged 10.9% of the employed population in 2004, according to official estimates. Measured by gross value of output, the principal branches of manufacturing are: food products, beverages and tobacco; metals, metal products, machinery and transport and scientific equipment; non-metallic mineral products; chemical, petroleum, coal, rubber and plastic products; wood, paper and products; and textiles and clothing. According to the World Bank, during 2001–09 the GDP of the manufacturing sector increased at an average annual rate of 3.0%; manufacturing GDP grew by 6.4% in 2009.

According to the African Development Bank, the construction sector contributed 11.5% of GDP in 2009. The sector engaged 19.4% of the employed labour force in 2010.

Energy is derived principally from natural gas (which contributed 97.3% of total electricity output in 2008). Algeria is a net exporter of fuels, with imports of energy products comprising only an estimated 1.1% of the value of merchandise imports in 2009.

According to the African Development Bank, services provided 39.9% of GDP in 2009. The sector engaged 55.2% of the employed labour force in 2010, according to official estimates. According to the World Bank, during 2001–09 the combined GDP of the service sectors increased at an average annual rate of 5.3%; services GDP increased by 9.3% in 2008 and again, by 2.4%, in 2009.

In 2009 Algeria recorded a visible trade surplus of US $7,800m., while there was a surplus of $300m. on the current account of the balance of payments. France was the principal source of imports in 2009 (providing 15.7% of the total); other important suppliers were the People's Republic of China, Italy, Spain, Germany and the USA. The USA was the principal market for exports (22.9%) in that year; other major purchasers were Italy, Spain, France, the Netherlands and Canada. The principal exports in 2009 were, overwhelmingly, mineral fuels and lubricants. The principal imports in that year were machinery and transport equipment, basic manufactures, and food and live animals.

In 2010, according to the IMF, Algeria recorded an overall budget deficit of AD 119,900m., equivalent to 1.0% of GDP. Algeria's general government gross debt was AD 1,049.6m in 2009, equivalent to 10.4% of GDP. The country's total external debt at the end of 2009 amounted to US $5,345m., of which almost $2,871m. was public and publicly guaranteed debt. The annual rate of inflation averaged 3.9% in 2001–10. Consumer prices increased by an average of.4.1% in 2010. According to an official labour force survey conducted in December 2010, some 10.0% of the labour force were unemployed.

Algeria's economy remains reliant on hydrocarbons, which accounted for 98.3% of exports in 2010. In that year the country was the world's seventh largest exporter of liquefied natural gas, supplying about 6.5% of world demand and exporting chiefly to Europe. By early 2010 it was apparent that Algeria had fared better than many other countries as far as the impact of the global economic slowdown from late 2008 was concerned. This was partly owing to a good grain harvest and strong performance in those parts of the economy targeted for increased public investment; the authorities had also introduced legislation in 2009 limiting foreign direct investment to investments where at least 51% of the shares remained in Algerian ownership. In July 2010 President Bouteflika ratified a five-year investment plan worth US $286,000m., in an effort to reduce over-reliance on the hydrocarbons sector and to create some 3m. jobs by 2014. Although the official rate of unemployment had declined considerably from 29.8% of the labour force in 2000 to 10.0% in 2010, the rates for young people and women remained significantly higher, at 21% and 19%, respectively. Following GDP growth of 3.0% in 2010 (with the non-hydrocarbons sector performing well), the IMF in October 2011 predicted that GDP would increase by 2.5% in 2011 and by 3.0% in 2012. Large-scale demonstrations were held in January 2011, initially attributed to popular discontent over significant increases in the price of basic foodstuffs, the poor quality of housing, and high levels of unemployment and poverty. The Government attempted to prevent further unrest by using its considerable revenues from petroleum exports to subsidize some essential food items and accelerate measures to stimulate investment, reduce unemployment and improve housing provision. This 25% increase in public expenditure, as part of a draft supplementary 2011 budget announced in May, led to a fiscal deficit of almost 34% of GDP. In July renewed unrest was evident when employees of the national airline, Air Algérie, staged strikes to demand salary increases. Meanwhile, in that month the world's first ever hybrid (gas-solar) power plant was inaugurated near Hassi R'Mel, as part of the Government's strategy to promote the development of renewable energy sources. In another positive development, the long-anticipated Algiers metro system—a project initiated in 1982—opened in November 2011. Discussions between Algeria and the EU concerning energy co-operation were reported to be at an advanced stage in January 2012.

PUBLIC HOLIDAYS

2013: 1 January (New Year), 23 January* (Mouloud, Birth of Muhammad), 1 May (Labour Day), 5 June* (Leilat al-Meiraj, Ascension of Muhammad), 19 June (Ben Bella's Overthrow), 5 July (Independence Day), 8 July* (Ramadan begins), 7 August* (Id al-Fitr, end of Ramadan), 14 October* (Id al-Adha, Feast of the Sacrifice), 1 November (Anniversary of the Revolution), 4 November* (Muharram, Islamic New Year), 13 November* (Ashoura).

* These holidays are dependent on the Islamic lunar calendar and may differ by one or two days from the dates given.

Statistical Survey

Source (unless otherwise stated): Office National des Statistiques, 8 rue des Moussebilines, BP 202, Ferhat Boussad, Algiers; tel. (21) 63-99-74; fax (21) 63-79-55; e-mail ons@ons.dz; internet www.ons.dz.

Area and Population

AREA, POPULATION AND DENSITY

Area (sq km)	2,381,741*
Population (census results)	
25 June 1998	29,100,867
16 April 2008	
Males	17,232,747
Females	16,847,283
Total	34,080,030
Population (official estimates at 1 January)	
2009	35,100,000
2010	35,600,000
2011	36,300,000
Density (per sq km) at 1 January 2011	15.2

* 919,595 sq miles.

POPULATION BY AGE AND SEX

(UN estimates at mid-2011)

	Males	Females	Total
0–14	4,933,015	4,711,724	9,644,739
15–64	12,483,234	12,184,233	24,667,467
65 and over	742,432	925,560	1,667,992
Total	18,158,681	17,821,517	35,980,198

Source: UN, *World Population Prospects: The 2010 Revision*.

POPULATION BY WILAYA (ADMINISTRATIVE DISTRICT)

(2008 census)

	Area (sq km)	Population	Density (per sq km)
Adrar	439,700	399,714	0.9
Aïn Defla	4,897	766,013	156.4
Aïn Témouchent	2,379	371,239	156.0
Algiers (el-Djezaïr)	273	2,988,145	10,945.6
Annaba	1,439	609,499	423.6
Batna	12,192	1,119,791	91.8
el-Bayadh	78,870	228,624	2.9
Béchar	162,200	270,061	1.7
Béjaïa	3,268	912,577	279.2
Biskra (Beskra)	20,986	721,356	34.4
Blida (el-Boulaïda)	1,696	1,002,937	591.4
Borj Bou Arreridj	4,115	628,475	152.7
Bouira	4,439	695,583	156.7
Boumerdès	1,591	802,083	504.1
Chlef (el-Cheliff)	4,795	1,002,088	209.0
Constantine (Qacentina)	2,187	938,475	429.1
Djelfa	66,415	1,092,184	16.4
Ghardaïa	86,105	363,598	4.2
Guelma	4,101	482,430	117.6
Illizi	285,000	52,333	0.2
Jijel	2,577	636,948	247.2
Khenchela	9,811	386,683	39.4
Laghouat	25,057	455,602	18.2
Mascara (Mouaskar)	5,941	784,073	132.0
Médéa (Lemdiyya)	8,866	819,932	92.5
Mila	9,375	766,886	81.8

—*continued*	Area (sq km)	Population	Density (per sq km)
Mostaganem	2,175	737,118	338.9
M'Sila	18,718	990,591	52.9
Naâma	29,950	192,891	6.4
Oran (Ouahran)	2,121	1,454,078	685.6
Ouargla	211,980	558,558	2.6
el-Oued	54,573	647,548	11.9
Oum el-Bouaghi	6,768	621,612	91.8
Relizane (Ghilizane)	4,870	726,180	149.1
Saïda	6,764	330,641	48.9
Sétif (Stif)	6,504	1,489,979	229.1
Sidi-bel-Abbès	9,096	604,744	66.5
Skikda	4,026	898,680	223.2
Souk Ahras	4,541	438,127	96.5
Tamanrasset (Tamanghest)	556,200	176,637	0.3
el-Tarf	3,339	408,414	122.3
Tébessa (Tbessa)	14,227	648,703	45.6
Tiaret (Tihert)	20,673	846,823	41.0
Tindouf	159,000	49,149	0.3
Tipaza	2,166	591,010	272.9
Tissemsilt	3,152	294,476	93.4
Tizi Ouzou	3,568	1,127,607	316.0
Tlemcen	9,061	949,135	104.7
Total	2,381,741	34,080,030	14.3

PRINCIPAL TOWNS

(population at 1998 census)

Algiers (el-Djezaïr, capital)	1,519,570	Tébessa (Tbessa)	153,246
Oran (Ouahran)	655,852	Blida (el-Boulaïda)	153,083
Constantine (Qacentina)	462,187	Skikda	152,335
Batna	242,514	Béjaïa	147,076
Annaba	215,083	Tiaret (Tihert)	145,332
Sétif (Stif)	211,859	Chlef (el-Cheliff)	133,874
Sidi-bel-Abbès	180,260	el-Buni	133,471
Biskra (Beskra)	170,956	Béchar	131,010
Djelfa	154,265		

Mid-2010 ('000, incl. suburbs, UN estimates): Algiers 2,799.6; Oran 769.6 (Source: UN, *World Urbanization Prospects: The 2009 Revision*).

BIRTHS, MARRIAGES AND DEATHS*

	Registered live births†		Registered marriages		Registered deaths†	
	Number	Rate (per 1,000)	Number	Rate (per 1,000)	Number	Rate (per 1,000)
2003	649,000	20.4	240,463	7.6	145,000	4.6
2004	669,000	20.7	267,633	8.3	141,000	4.4
2005	703,000	21.4	279,548	8.5	147,000	4.5
2006	739,000	22.1	295,295	8.8	144,000	4.3
2007	783,000	23.0	325,485	9.6	149,000	4.4
2008	817,000	23.6	331,190	9.6	153,000	4.4
2009	849,000	24.1	341,321	9.7	159,000	4.5
2010	888,000	24.7	344,819	9.6	157,000	4.4

* Figures refer to the Algerian population only, and include adjustment for underenumeration.

† Excluding live-born infants dying before registration of birth.

Life expectancy (years at birth, WHO estimates): 72 (males 71; females 74) in 2009 (Source: WHO, *World Health Statistics*).

ECONOMICALLY ACTIVE POPULATION

('000 persons aged 15 years and over at September)

	2003	2004
Agriculture, hunting, forestry and fishing	1,411.8	1,616.2
Mining and quarrying	82.9	135.1
Manufacturing	616.7	846.7
Electricity, gas and water	104.6	79.1
Construction	799.9	967.6
Trade; repair of motor vehicles, motorcycles and personal household goods	880.9	1,174.4
Hotels and restaurants	102.5	164.8
Transport, storage and communications	405.4	435.9
Financial intermediation	67.6	68.8
Real estate, renting and business activities	68.0	72.4
Public administration and defence; compulsory social security	1,071.2	1,104.1
Education	627.7	634.0
Health and social work	245.0	235.5
Other community, social and personal service activities	183.4	208.9
Households with employed persons	12.2	34.9
Extra-territorial organizations and bodies	2.9	3.9
Sub-total	6,682.7	7,782.2
Activities not adequately defined	1.4	16.2
Total employed	6,684.1	7,798.4
Unemployed	2,078.0	1,671.5
Total labour force	8,762.1	9,469.9

Source: ILO.

2010 (sample survey at December, '000 persons aged 15 years and over): Agriculture 1,136; Industry 3,223 (Construction 1,886); Services 5,377; *Total employed* 9,735 (males 8,261, females 1,474); Unemployed 1,076 (males 728, females 348); *Total labour force* 10,811 (males 8,989, females 1,822).

Health and Welfare

KEY INDICATORS

Total fertility rate (children per woman, 2009)	2.3
Under-5 mortality rate (per 1,000 live births, 2009)	32
HIV/AIDS (% of persons aged 15–49, 2009)	0.1
Physicians (per 1,000 head, 2002)	1.1
Hospital beds (per 1,000 head, 2004)	1.7
Health expenditure (2008): US $ per head (PPP)	437
Health expenditure (2008): % of GDP	5.4
Health expenditure (2008): public (% of total)	86.1
Access to water (% of persons, 2008)	83
Access to sanitation (% of persons, 2008)	95
Total carbon dioxide emissions ('000 metric tons, 2007)	140,005.1
Carbon dioxide emissions per head (metric tons, 2007)	4.1
Human Development Index (2011): ranking	96
Human Development Index (2011): value	0.698

For sources and definitions, see explanatory note on p. vi.

Agriculture

PRINCIPAL CROPS

('000 metric tons)

	2008	2009	2010
Wheat	1,111	2,953	3,100*
Barley	396	2,203	1,500*
Oats	27	96	85†
Potatoes	2,171	2,636	3,290*
Broad beans, dry	24	36	36†
Chick-peas	11	18	21†
Almonds	40	47	44†
Olives	254	475	555†
Rapeseed†	35	36	43
Cabbages	37	47	45†
Artichokes	34	40	39†
Tomatoes	559	641	579†
Cauliflowers and broccoli	68	82	81†
Pumpkins, squash and gourds	151	190	195†

—continued	2008	2009	2010
Cucumbers and gherkins	89	102	119†
Aubergines (Eggplants)	54	76	74†
Chillies and peppers, green	280	319	318†
Onions, dry	759	980	1,111†
Garlic	56	60	71†
Beans, green	40	45	48†
Peas, green	83	103	97†
Carrots and turnips	254	271	263†
Oranges	503	626	740†
Tangerines, mandarins, clementines and satsumas	150	157	186†
Lemons and limes	43	60	71†
Apples	261	267	316†
Pears	177	160	189†
Apricots	172	203	240†
Peaches and nectarines	119	147	174†
Plums and sloes	59	74	88†
Grapes	402	493	582†
Watermelons	845	1,035	946†
Figs	79	84	99†
Dates	553	601	710*
Tobacco, unmanufactured	6	8	8†

* Unofficial figure.
† FAO estimate(s).

Aggregate production ('000 metric tons, may include official, semi-official or estimated data): Total cereals 1,536 in 2008, 5,253 in 2009, 4,686 in 2010; Total roots and tubers 2,171 in 2008, 2,636 in 2009, 3,290 in 2010; Total vegetables (incl. melons) 3,787 in 2008, 4,543 in 2009, 4,536 in 2010; Total fruits (excl. melons) 2,620 in 2008, 2,992 in 2009, 3,536 in 2010.

Source: FAO.

LIVESTOCK
('000 head, year ending September, unless otherwise indicated)

	2008	2009*	2010*
Sheep	19,946	20,000	20,000
Goats	3,751	3,800	3,800
Cattle	1,641	1,650	1,650
Horses	45	45	45
Asses	147	150	150
Mules	38†	40	40
Camels	295	295	290
Chickens (million)	125*	125	125

* FAO estimate(s).
† Unofficial figure.

Source: FAO.

LIVESTOCK PRODUCTS
('000 metric tons)

	2008	2009	2010
Cattle meat*	125	127	133
Goat meat*	14	14	14
Chicken meat*	254	254	254
Rabbit meat*	7	7	7
Sheep meat*	175	178	180
Cows' milk	1,500*	1,750	1,811*
Sheep's milk*	255	260	231
Goats' milk*	230	221	248
Hen eggs	184	185*	189*
Honey	3	3*	3*
Wool, greasy*	25	26	26

* FAO estimate(s).

Source: FAO.

Forestry

ROUNDWOOD REMOVALS
('000 cubic metres, excl. bark)

	2007	2008	2009
Pulpwood	51	51*	51*
Other industrial wood*	52	52	52
Fuel wood*	7,867	7,968	8,072
Total*	7,970	8,071	8,175

* FAO estimate(s).

2010: Production assumed to be unchanged from 2009 (FAO estimates).

Sawnwood production ('000 cubic metres, incl. railway sleepers, FAO estimates): 13 per year in 1975–2010.

Source: FAO.

Fishing

('000 metric tons, live weight)

	2007	2008	2009
Capture	147.4	138.9	127.9
Bogue	5.0	7.7	6.6
Jack and horse mackerels	27.6	32.0	18.5
Sardinellas	16.9	22.8	16.2
European pilchard (sardine)	73.7	40.0	55.3
European anchovy	1.4	2.2	3.2
Aquaculture	0.4	2.8*	2.2*
Total catch	147.8	141.6*	130.1*

* FAO estimate.

Source: FAO.

Mining

('000 metric tons unless otherwise indicated)

	2007	2008	2009
Crude petroleum*	86,500	85,600	77,900
Natural gas (million cu m)†	198,200	201,200	196,900
Iron ore (gross weight)	1,982	2,077	1,307
Phosphate rock§	1,800	1,805	1,017
Barite (Barytes)	63	60	38
Salt (unrefined)	183	202	269
Gypsum (crude)	1,198	1,672	1,757

* Source: BP, *Statistical Review of World Energy*.
† Figures refer to gross volume. Production on a dry basis (in million cu m) was: 84,800 in 2007; 85,800 in 2008; 81,400 in 2009.
§ Figures refer to gross weight. The estimated phosphoric acid content (in '000 metric tons, estimated) was 536 in 2007; 542 in 2008; 305 in 2009.

Mercury (kilograms): 73,451 in 2005.

Source (unless otherwise indicated): US Geological Survey.

Crude petroleum ('000 metric tons): 77,700 in 2010 (Source: BP, *Statistical Review of World Energy*).

Natural gas (dry basis, million cu m): 80,400 in 2010 (Source: BP, *Statistical Review of World Energy*).

Industry

SELECTED PRODUCTS

('000 metric tons unless otherwise indicated)

	2006	2007	2008
Olive oil (crude)	32	22	28
Naphthas	3,274	3,698	3,641
Motor spirit (petrol)	2,320	2,100	2,780
Jet fuel	855	1,034	988
Gas-diesel (distillate fuel) oils	6,385	6,388	7,403
Residual fuel oils	5,337	5,518	6,009
Lubricating oils	148	143	89
Petroleum bitumen (asphalt)	269	331	315
Liquefied petroleum gas:			
from natural gas plants	8,252	8,627	8,724
from petroleum refineries	495	556	516
Pig-iron for steel-making	1,093	1,193	690
Crude steel (ingots)	1,158	1,278	646
Electric energy (million kWh)	35,226	37,196	40,236

2004 ('000 metric tons, unless otherwise indicated): Refined sugar 135; Beer ('000 hectolitres) 124; Zinc—unwrought 28.8; Cement 9,543; Refrigerators for household use ('000) 215; Television receivers 205,800.

Source: UN Industrial Commodities Statistics Database.

Finance

CURRENCY AND EXCHANGE RATES

Monetary Units

100 centimes = 1 Algerian dinar (AD).

Sterling, Dollar and Euro Equivalents (30 November 2011)

£1 sterling = 118.709 dinars;
US $1 = 76.056 dinars;
€1 = 102.052 dinars;
1,000 Algerian dinars = £8.42 = $13.15 = €9.80.

Average Exchange Rate (dinars per US $)

2008 64.583
2009 72.647
2010 74.386

GOVERNMENT FINANCE

(central government operations, '000 million AD)

Summary of Balances

	2007	2008	2009
Revenue and grants	3,687.9	5,190.6	3,672.9
Less Expenditure	3,114.2	4,191.2	4,224.8
Budget balance	573.6	999.4	–551.9
Special accounts balance	–18.9	–31.2	–7.3
Less Net lending by Treasury	141.3	123.8	134.6
Overall balance	413.4	844.4	–693.8

Revenue and Grants

	2007	2008	2009
Hydrocarbon revenue	2,796.8	4,088.6	2,412.7
Sonatrach dividends	85.0	85.0	85.0
Other revenue	890.9	1,101.9	1,259.4
Tax revenue	766.8	965.3	1,144.5
Taxes on income and profits	258.1	331.5	460.8
Wage income taxes	124.9	125.9	182.7
Taxes on goods and services	347.4	435.2	479.0
Customs duties	133.1	164.9	169.1
Registration and stamps	28.1	33.6	35.6
Non-tax revenue	124.1	136.7	114.9
Grants	0.2	0.1	0.8
Total	3,687.9	5,190.6	3,672.9

Expenditure

Expenditure by economic type	2007	2008	2009
Current expenditure	1,672.0	2,218.0	2,299.0
Personnel expenditure	628.7	826.6	879.9
War veterans' pensions	101.6	103.0	130.7
Material and supplies	93.8	111.7	112.5
Current transfers	762.8	1,115.2	1,138.5
Interest payments	85.0	61.4	37.4
Capital expenditure	1,442.3	1,973.3	1,925.8
Total	3,114.2	4,191.2	4,224.8

Sectoral allocation of capital expenditure*	2007	2008	2009
Agriculture and fishery	15.1	15.4	25.8
Irrigation and waterworks	183.9	217.1	256.6
Industry and energy	0.2	0.01	0.1
Economic infrastructure	380.4	522.6	398.5
Housing	184.7	177.9	230.8
Education and professional training	126.1	122.1	144.9
Social infrastructure	41.8	49.0	68.5
Administrative infrastructure	54.4	66.6	85.7
Urban development	79.4	57.1	77.6
Unallocated	111.6	97.1	136.7
Total	1,177.7	1,325.0	1,425.5

* Commitment basis.

Source: IMF, *Algeria: Statistical Appendix* (February 2011).

2010 (central government operations, '000 million AD, projections): *Revenue and Grants:* Hydrocarbons revenue 3,006; Other revenue 1,497 (Tax revenue 1,331, Non-tax revenue 166); Grants 0; Total 4,503. *Expenditure:* Current expenditure 3,013 (Personnel expenditure 1,330, War veterans' pensions 147, Material and supplies 159, Current transfers 1,339, Interest payments 38); Capital expenditure 1,943; Total 4,956 (Source: IMF, *Algeria: 2010 Article IV Consultation—Staff Report; Public Information Notice on the Executive Board Discussion; and Statement by the Executive Director for Algeria*—February 2011).

CENTRAL BANK RESERVES

(US $ million at 31 December)

	2008	2009	2010
Gold*	301	306	301
IMF special drawing rights	10	1,686	1,653
Reserve position in IMF	131	133	394
Foreign exchange	143,102	147,221	160,568
Total	143,544	149,346	162,916

* National valuation.

Source: IMF, *International Financial Statistics*.

MONEY SUPPLY

('000 million AD at 31 December)

	2008	2009	2010
Currency outside depository corporations	1,539.97	1,829.35	2,098.63
Transferable deposits	2,795.43	2,541.94	2,804.41
Other deposits	2,160.77	2,228.89	2,524.28
Broad money	6,496.18	6,600.18	7,427.32

Source: IMF, *International Financial Statistics*.

COST OF LIVING

(Consumer Price Index; base: 2000 = 100)

	2005	2006	2007
Food	116.6	119.3	126.7
Clothing	113.5	113.7	114.2
Rent (incl. fuel and light)	121.6	125.9	126.1
All items (incl. others)	116.7	118.8	123.5

2008: Food 134.6; All items (incl. others) 128.9.

2009: Food 150.7; All items (incl. others) 140.1.

2010: Food 157.1; All items (incl. others) 145.9.

Source: ILO.

NATIONAL ACCOUNTS

('000 million AD at current prices)

Expenditure on the Gross Domestic Product

	2007	2008	2009
Government final consumption expenditure	1,089.0	1,458.8	1,643.0
Private final consumption expenditure	2,963.8	3,338.8	3,748.1
Gross fixed capital formation	2,462.1	3,228.3	3,811.4
Changes in inventories	771.6	915.9	874.4
Total domestic expenditure	7,286.5	8,941.8	10,076.9
Exports of goods and services	4,402.2	5,298.0	3,524.4
Less Imports of goods and services	2,326.1	3,170.8	3,583.8
GDP at purchasers' values	9,362.7	11,069.0	10,017.5

Gross Domestic Product by Economic Activity

	2007	2008	2009
Agriculture	704.2	711.8	926.4
Mining and quarrying	4,099.8	5,014.5	3,125.1
Manufacturing	381.6	408.9	465.8
Electricity, gas and water	87.7	93.7	91.2
Construction	825.1	956.7	1,094.8
Wholesale and retail trade, restaurants and hotels	944.0	1,094.4	1,257.1
Finance, insurance and real estate	328.9	372.8	416.7
Transport and communications	822.4	863.6	914.4
Public administration and defence	777.1	1,057.4	1,193.9
Sub-total	8,970.8	10,573.8	9,485.4
Less Imputed bank service charge	140.5	158.6	179.0
GDP at factor cost	8,830.2	10,415.1	9,306.4
Taxes on products (net)	532.5	653.9	711.1
GDP at purchasers' values	9,362.7	11,069.0	10,017.5

Source: African Development Bank.

BALANCE OF PAYMENTS

(US $ '000 million)

	2007	2008	2009
Exports of goods f.o.b.	60.6	78.6	45.2
Imports of goods f.o.b.	–26.4	–38.0	–37.4
Trade balance	34.2	40.6	7.8
Exports of services	2.9	3.5	3.0
Imports of services	–6.9	–11.1	–11.7
Balance on goods and services	30.2	33.0	–0.9
Other income received	3.8	5.1	4.7
Other income paid	–5.6	–6.5	–6.1
Balance on goods, services and income	28.4	31.6	–2.3
Transfers (net)	2.2	2.8	2.6
Current balance	30.6	34.5	0.3
Direct investment (net)	1.4	2.3	2.5
Official capital (net)	–0.8	–0.4	1.3
Short-term capital and net errors and omissions	–1.7	0.6	–0.4
Overall balance	29.6	37.0	3.9

Source: IMF, *Algeria: Statistical Appendix* (February 2011).

External Trade

Note: Data exclude military goods. Exports include stores and bunkers for foreign ships and aircraft.

PRINCIPAL COMMODITIES

(distribution by HS, US $ million)

Imports c.i.f.	2007	2008	2009
Dairy products, eggs, honey, edible animal products, etc.	1,063.9	1,275.7	862.6
Milk and cream (concentrated or sweetened)	978.5	1,164.6	799.7
Cereals	1,958.2	4,016.0	2,313.6
Wheat and meslin	1,394.3	3,174.2	1,830.3
Pharmaceutical products	1,447.6	1,849.9	1,743.0
Medicament mixtures	1,309.6	1,656.2	1,509.4
Plastics and plastic products	889.6	1,180.8	1,188.7
Iron and steel	1,664.3	3,355.9	2,524.1
Bars of iron, etc.	1,003.4	2,152.1	1,487.2
Iron or steel products	2,431.6	3,545.8	4,979.8
Tubes, pipes and related products	1,148.7	1,510.6	1,982.4
Machinery, nuclear reactors, boilers, etc.	4,481.1	6,042.5	7,361.1
Electrical and electronic equipment	2,145.1	3,229.2	3,335.7
Vehicles (other than railway and tramway)	3,571.3	4,815.0	4,797.6
Cars and station wagons	1,491.2	2,029.0	1,524.0
Trucks, motor vehicles for the transport of goods	960.7	1,385.2	1,465.6
Total (incl. others)	27,631.2	39,474.7	39,258.3

Exports f.o.b.	2007	2008	2009
Mineral fuels, lubricants, etc.	59,187.6	77,822.5	44,443.0
Crude petroleum oils, etc.	33,799.1	41,649.3	21,284.5
Petroleum gases	19,474.2	28,990.0	17,855.4
Petroleum oils, other than crude oil	5,558.0	6,722.9	4,976.5
Total (incl. others)	60,163.2	79,297.6	45,193.9

Source: Trade Map-Trade Competitiveness Map, International Trade Centre, www.intracen.org/marketanalysis.

PRINCIPAL TRADING PARTNERS

(US $ million)

Imports c.i.f.	2007	2008	2009
Argentina	922.4	1,263.2	807.3
Austria	359.1	311.6	266.4
Belgium	717.5	862.0	777.6
Brazil	603.6	736.1	883.7
Canada	497.6	968.9	418.8
China, People's Republic	2,389.4	4,066.9	4,750.6
Egypt	254.8	195.6	502.9
France (incl. Monaco)	4,613.6	6,503.8	6,159.9
Germany	1,788.2	2,411.4	2,765.4
India	444.4	749.4	805.4
Italy	2,406.9	4,308.8	3,659.8
Japan	1,064.6	1,416.7	1,193.8
Korea, Republic	809.6	961.1	1,119.7
Mexico	169.2	616.2	221.5
Netherlands	340.2	461.0	394.1
Spain	1,587.9	2,914.8	2,971.5
Sweden	372.5	440.9	420.6
Switzerland	347.3	355.6	504.8
Turkey	921.4	1,345.8	1,746.3
United Kingdom	551.6	641.1	725.6
Ukraine	474.1	374.7	291.2
USA	2,134.8	2,197.6	2,013.7
Total (incl. others)	27,631.2	39,474.7	39,258.3

Exports f.o.b.	2007	2008	2009
Belgium	1,202.8	2,059.3	1,135.9
Brazil	1,824.3	2,638.5	1,465.9
Canada	4,666.2	5,423.6	2,438.9
China, People's Republic	1,106.3	503.3	874.4
Egypt	429.4	606.9	472.8
France (incl. Monaco)	4,099.7	6,370.4	4,424.3
India	1,550.5	1,166.2	506.9
Italy	7,967.2	12,293.9	5,701.6
Japan	257.5	856.7	220.9
Korea, Republic	800.5	1,498.2	1,459.8
Morocco	612.8	712.7	392.2
Netherlands	4,527.7	6,111.2	3,265.2
Portugal	948.0	2,045.1	960.3
Spain	5,338.4	9,093.3	5,402.4
Tunisia	85.7	859.1	451.0
Turkey	2,043.2	2,919.7	2,002.3
United Kingdom	1,576.8	2,241.4	1,141.8
USA	18,090.6	18,952.5	10,365.2
Total (incl. others)	60,163.2	79,297.6	45,193.9

Source: Trade Map-Trade Competitiveness Map, International Trade Centre, www.intracen.org/marketanalysis.

Transport

RAILWAYS
(traffic)

	1999	2000	2001
Passengers carried ('000)	32,027	n.a.	n.a.
Freight carried ('000 metric tons)	7,842	n.a.	n.a.
Passenger-km (million)	1,069	1,142	981
Freight ton-km (million)	2,033	1,980	1,990

Source: mostly UN, *Statistical Yearbook*.

2001 ('000 passenger journeys): 28,800 (Source: Railway Gazette).

2005 (million): Passengers carried 27.3; Freight carried (metric tons) 8.3; Passenger-km 929; Freight ton-km 1,471 (Source: World Bank, World Development Indicators database).

ROAD TRAFFIC
(motor vehicles in use at 31 December)

	2000	2001	2002
Passenger cars	1,692,148	1,708,373	1,739,286
Lorries	296,145	298,125	300,171
Vans	609,617	612,523	615,663
Buses and coaches	42,791	44,323	46,136
Motorcycles	9,198	9,245	9,258

2006 (motor vehicles in use at 31 December): Passenger cars 2,042,824; Lorries and vans 1,166,231; Buses and coaches 54,769; Motorcycles and mopeds 9,507 (Source: IRF, World Road Statistics).

2008 (motor vehicles in use at 31 December): Passenger cars 2,462,003; Lorries and vans 1,313,475; Buses and coaches 67,311; Motorcycles and mopeds 10,434 (Source: IRF, World Road Statistics).

SHIPPING

Merchant Fleet
(registered at 31 December)

	2007	2008	2009
Number of vessels	128	129	130
Total displacement ('000 grt)	736.2	747.7	767.9

Source: IHS Fairplay, *World Fleet Statistics*.

International Sea-borne Freight Traffic
('000 metric tons)

	1997	1998	1999
Goods loaded	74,300	75,500	77,900
Goods unloaded	15,200	16,000	16,600

Note: Figures are rounded to the nearest 100,000 metric tons.

CIVIL AVIATION
(traffic on scheduled services)

	2007	2008	2009
Kilometres flown (million)	46	53	53
Passengers carried ('000)	2,813	4,428	4,371
Passenger-km (million)	2,941	3,962	3,814
Total ton-km (million)	281	394	382

Source: UN, *Statistical Yearbook*.

Tourism

FOREIGN TOURIST ARRIVALS BY COUNTRY OF ORIGIN*

	2006	2007	2008
France	161,090	170,233	170,538
Germany	14,771	10,177	10,961
Italy	15,055	16,554	15,477
Libya	13,353	13,523	13,940
Mali	13,703	15,354	18,100
Morocco	13,213	15,101	14,852
Spain	17,427	19,748	20,000
Tunisia	120,478	108,879	148,157
United Kingdom	8,164	10,837	8,703
Total (incl. others)	478,358	511,188	556,697

* Excluding arrivals of Algerian nationals resident abroad: 1,159,224 in 2006; 1,231,896 in 2007; 1,215,052 in 2008.

Tourism receipts (US $ million, incl. passenger transport): 215 in 2006; 219 in 2007; 325 in 2008.

Source: World Tourism Organization.

Communications Media

	2008	2009	2010
Telephones ('000 main lines in use)	3,069.1	2,576.2	2,922.7
Mobile cellular telephones ('000 subscribers)	27,032.0	32,730.0	32,780.2
Internet users ('000)	3,500	4,700	n.a.
Broadband subscribers ('000)	485	818	900

Personal computers: 350,000 (10.7 per 1,000 persons) in 2005.

Book production (titles, excl. pamphlets): 133 in 1999.

Television receivers ('000 in use): 3,500 in 2001.

Daily newspapers: 17 in 2004.

1998: Daily newspapers 24 (average circulation 796,440 copies); Non-daily newspapers 82 (average circulation 908,751 copies); Periodicals 106.

Sources: UNESCO, *Statistical Yearbook*; UN, *Statistical Yearbook*; International Telecommunication Union.

Education

(2009/10 unless otherwise indicated)

	Institutions	Teachers	Pupils
Pre-primary	n.a.	5,464*	137,803*
Primary	17,041†	141,994	3,312,440
Secondary	5,267†	176,375‡	4,585,189§
Tertiary	n.a.	39,782	1,144,271

* 2007/08.
† 2004/05.
‡ 2003/04.
§ 2008/09.

Sources: UNESCO, Institute for Statistics, and Ministère de l'Education nationale.

1998/99 (Pre-primary and primary): 15,729 institutions; 170,562 teachers; 4,843,313 pupils.

Pupil-teacher ratio (primary education, UNESCO estimate): 23.3 in 2009/10 (Source: UNESCO Institute for Statistics).

Adult literacy rate (UNESCO estimates): 75.4% (males 84.3%; females 66.4%) in 2007 (Source: UNESCO Institute for Statistics).

Directory

The Government

HEAD OF STATE

President and Minister of National Defence: ABDELAZIZ BOUTEFLIKA (inaugurated 27 April 1999; re-elected 8 April 2004 and 9 April 2009).

COUNCIL OF MINISTERS

(May 2012)

Prime Minister: AHMED OUYAHIA.

Vice-Prime Minister: NOUREDDINE YAZID ZERHOUNI.

Minister of State and Personal Representative to the Head of State: ABDELAZIZ BELKHADEM.

Minister of the Interior and Local Authorities: DAHOU OULD KABLIA.

Minister of Foreign Affairs: MOURAD MEDELCI.

Minister of Finance: KARIM DJOUDI.

Minister of Commerce: MUSTAPHA BENBADA.

Minister of Energy and Mining: YOUCEF YOUSFI.

Minister of Water Resources: ABDELMALEK SELLAL.

Minister of Future Planning and Statistics: ABDELHAMID TEMMAR.

Minister of Religious Affairs and Awqaf (Religious Endowments): Prof. BOUABDELLAH GHLAMALLAH.

Minister of War Veterans: MUHAMMAD CHÉRIF ABBAS.

Minister of Territorial Planning and the Environment: Dr CHÉRIF RAHMANI.

Minister of Transport: AMAR TOU.

Minister of Youth and Sports: HACHEMI DJIAR.

Minister of Agriculture and Rural Development: Dr RACHID BENAÏSSA.

Minister of Public Works: Dr AMAR GHOUL.

Minister of National Solidarity and the Family: Dr SAÏD BARKAT.

Minister of Culture: KHALIDA TOUMI.

Minister of Industry, Small and Medium-sized Enterprises and Investment Promotion: MUHAMMAD BENMERADI.

Minister of National Education: Prof. BOUBAKEUR BENBOUZID.

Minister of Higher Education and Scientific Research: RACHID HARROUBIA.

Minister of Postal Services and Information and Communication Technologies: MOUSSA BENHAMMADI.

Minister of Training and Vocational Education: Dr EL-HADI KHALDI.

Minister of Housing and Urban Development: NOUREDDINE MOUSSA.

Minister of Labour, Employment and Social Security: TAYEB LOUH.

Minister of Health, Population and Hospital Reform: DJAMEL OULD ABBÈS.

Minister of Tourism and Handicrafts: SMAÏL MIMOUNE.

Minister of Relations with Parliament: MAHMOUD KHEDRI.

Minister of Fisheries and Marine Resources: ABDALLAH KHANAFOU.

Minister of Information: NACER MEHAL.

Minister-delegate to the Minister of Foreign Affairs, in charge of Maghreb and African Affairs: ABDELKADER MESSAHEL.

Minister-delegate to the Minister of National Solidarity, Family and National Community Abroad, in charge of Family and Women's Affairs: NOUARA SAÂDIA DJAFFAR.

Minister-delegate to the Minister of National Defence: Gen. (retd) ABDELMALEK GUENAÏZIA.

Minister-delegate to the Minister of Higher Education and Scientific Research, in charge of Scientific Research: SOUAD BENDJABALLAH.

Secretary of State to the Minister of Future Planning and Statistics, in charge of Statistics: ALI BOUKRAMI.

Secretary of State to the Minister of Foreign Affairs, responsible for the Algerian Expatriate Community: HALIM BENATALLAH.

Interim Minister of Justice and Attorney-General, and Secretary General to the Government: AHMED NOUI.

MINISTRIES

Office of the President: Présidence de la République, el-Mouradia, Algiers; tel. (21) 69-15-15; fax (21) 69-15-95; e-mail president@el-mouradia.dz; internet www.el-mouradia.dz.

Office of the Prime Minister: rue Docteur Saâdane, Algiers; tel. (21) 73-23-40; fax (21) 71-79-29; internet www.cg.gov.dz.

Ministry of Agriculture and Rural Development: 12 blvd Col Amirouche, Algiers; tel. (21) 71-17-12; fax (21) 74-51-29; internet www.minagri.dz.

Ministry of Commerce: Cité Zerhouni Mokhtar les El Mohamadia, Algiers; tel. (21) 89-00-74; fax (21) 89-00-34; e-mail info@mincommerce.gov.dz; internet www.mincommerce.gov.dz.

Ministry of Culture: BP 100, Palais de la Culture 'Moufdi Zakaria', Plateau des Annassers, Kouba, Algiers; tel. (21) 29-10-10; fax (21) 29-20-89; e-mail contact@m-culture.gov.dz; internet www.m-culture.gov.dz.

Ministry of Defence: Les Tagarins, el-Biar, Algiers; tel. (21) 71-15-15; fax (21) 64-67-26.

Ministry of Energy and Mining: BP 677, Tower A, Val d'Hydra, Alger-Gare, Algiers; tel. (21) 48-85-26; fax (21) 48-85-57; e-mail info@memalgeria.org; internet www.mem-algeria.org.

Ministry of Finance: Immeuble Ahmed Francis, Ben Aknoun, Algiers; tel. (21) 59-51-51; e-mail mfmail@mf.gov.dz; internet www.mf.gov.dz.

Ministry of Fisheries and Marine Resources: route des Quatre Canons, Algiers; tel. (21) 43-31-74; fax (21) 43-31-68; e-mail info@mpeche.gov.dz; internet www.mpeche.gov.dz.

Ministry of Foreign Affairs: place Mohamed Seddik Benyahia, el-Mouradia, Algiers; tel. (21) 29-12-12; fax (21) 50-43-63; internet www.mae.dz.

Ministry of Future Planning and Statistics: Algiers.

Ministry of Health, Population and Hospital Reform: 125 rue Abderrahmane Laâla, el-Madania, Algiers; tel. (21) 67-53-15; fax (21) 65-36-46; internet www.sante.gov.dz.

Ministry of Higher Education and Scientific Research: 11 chemin Doudou Mokhtar, Ben Aknoun, Algiers; tel. (21) 91-23-23; e-mail webmaster@mesrs.dz; internet www.mesrs.dz.

Ministry of Housing and Urban Development: 135 rue Mourad Didouche, Algiers; tel. (21) 74-07-22; e-mail mhabitat@wissal.dz; internet www.mhu.gov.dz.

Ministry of Industry and Investment Promotion: Immeuble de la Colisée, 2 rue Ahmed Bey, el-Biar, Algiers; tel. (21) 23-91-43; fax (21) 23-94-88; internet www.mipi.dz.

Ministry of the Interior and Local Authorities: 18 rue Docteur Saâdane, Algiers; tel. (21) 73-76-81; fax (21) 73-61-54.

Ministry of Justice: 8 place Bir Hakem, el-Biar, Algiers; tel. (21) 92-41-83; fax (21) 92-17-01; e-mail contact@mjustice.dz; internet www.mjustice.dz.

Ministry of Labour, Employment and Social Security: 44 rue Muhammad Belouizdad, 16600 Algiers; tel. and fax (21) 65-99-99; e-mail informa@mtess.gov.dz; internet www.mtess.gov.dz.

Ministry of National Education: 8 rue de Pékin, el-Mouradia, Algiers; tel. (21) 60-55-60; fax (21) 60-67-02; e-mail education@men.dz.

Ministry of Postal Services and Information and Communication Technologies: 4 blvd Krim Belkacem, Algiers 16027; tel. (21) 71-12-20; fax (21) 73-00-47; e-mail contact@mptic.dz; internet www.mptic.dz.

Ministry of Public Works: 6 rue Moustafa Khalef, Ben Aknoun, Algiers; tel. (21) 91-49-47; fax (21) 91-35-85; e-mail info@mtp-dz.com; internet www.mtp.gov.dz.

Ministry of Religious Affairs and Awqaf (Religious Endowments): 4 rue de Timgad, Hydra, Algiers; tel. (21) 76-18-60; fax (21) 69-15-69; e-mail redaction@marwakf-dz.org; internet www.marwakf-dz.org.

Ministry of Small and Medium-sized Enterprises and Handicrafts: 119 rue Didouche Mourad, Algiers; tel. (21) 71-34-34; fax (21) 71-49-65; e-mail info@pmeart-dz.org; internet www.pmeart-dz.org.

Ministry of Social Action and National Solidarity: BP 31, route nationale no 1, Les Vergers, Bir Khadem, Algiers; tel. (21) 44-99-46; fax (21) 44-97-26; e-mail cellulemassn@massn.gov.dz; internet www.massn.gov.dz.

Ministry of Territorial Planning, the Environment and Tourism: rue des Quatre Canons, Bab-el-Oued, Algiers; tel. (21) 43-28-01; fax (21) 43-28-55; e-mail deeai@ifrance.com; internet www.matet.dz.

Ministry of Training and Vocational Education: rue des frères Aïssou, Ben Aknoun, Algiers; tel. (21) 91-15-03; fax (21) 91-22-66; e-mail contacts@mfep.gov.dz; internet www.mfep.gov.dz.

Ministry of Transport: 1 chemin ibn Badis el-Mouiz (ex Poirson), el-Biar, 16300 Algiers; tel. (21) 92-98-85; fax (21) 92-98-94; internet www.ministere-transports.gov.dz.

Ministry of War Veterans: 2 ave du Lt Muhammad Benarfa, el-Biar, Algiers; tel. (21) 92-23-55; fax (21) 92-35-16; e-mail sinformatique@m-moudjahidine.dz; internet www.m-moudjahidine.dz.

Ministry of Water Resources: 3 rue du Caire, Kouba, Algiers; tel. (21) 28-39-01; e-mail deah@mre.gov.dz; internet www.mre.gov.dz.

Ministry of Youth and Sports: 3 rue Muhammad Belouizdad, Algiers; tel. (21) 68-33-50; fax (21) 65-77-78; e-mail contact@mjs.dz; internet www.mjs.dz.

President and Legislature

PRESIDENT

Presidential Election, 9 April 2009

Candidate	Votes	% of votes
Abdelaziz Bouteflika	13,019,787	90.23
Louisa Hanoune	649,632	4.50
Moussa Touati	294,411	2.04
Muhammad Djahid Younsi	208,549	1.45
Mohand Oussaïd Belaïd	133,315	0.92
Ali Fawzi Rebaïne	124,559	0.86
Total	14,430,253*	100.00

* Excluding 925,711 invalid votes.

LEGISLATURE

National People's Assembly

18 blvd Zighout Youcef, 16000 Algiers; tel. (21) 73-86-00; internet www.apn-dz.org.

President: ABDELAZIZ ZIARI.

General Election, 17 May 2007

	Votes	% of votes	Seats
Front de libération nationale (FLN)	1,314,494	22.95	136
Rassemblement national démocratique (RND)	597,712	10.44	62
Mouvement de la société pour la paix (MSP)	556,401	9.71	51
Parti des travailleurs (PT)	291,395	5.09	26
Rassemblement pour la culture et la démocratie (RCD)	185,616	3.24	19
Front national algérien (FNA)	241,594	4.22	15
Mouvement national pour la nature et le développement (MNND)	115,075	2.01	7
Al-Nahda	193,908	3.39	5
Mouvement pour la jeunesse et la démocratie (MJD)	130,992	2.29	5
Alliance nationale républicaine (ANR)	125,862	2.20	4
Mouvement de l'entente nationale (MEN)	121,961	2.13	4
Parti du renouveau algérien (PRA)	103,356	1.80	4
Infitah	150,423	2.63	3
Mouvement El Islah	146,528	2.56	3
Front national des indépendants pour la concorde (FNIC)	112,263	1.96	3
Ahd 54	129,865	2.27	2
Mouvement national de l'espérance (MNE)	98,604	1.72	2
Rassemblement patriotique républicain (RPR)	84,497	1.48	2
Rassemblement algérien (RA)	100,391	1.75	1
Front national démocratique (FND)	78,596	1.37	1
Mouvement démocratique et social (MDS)	50,879	0.89	1
Independents	564,169	9.85	33
Others	233,246	4.07	—
Total	5,727,827*	100.00	389

* Excluding 965,064 invalid votes.

Council of the Nation

7 blvd Zighout Youcef, 16000 Algiers; tel. (21) 74-60-85; fax (21) 74-60-79; e-mail hamrani@majliselouma.dz; internet www.majliselouma.dz.

President: ABDELKADER BENSALAH.

Elections, 28 December 2006 and 29 December 2009*

	Seats
Front de libération nationale (FLN)	54
Rassemblement national démocratique (RND)	32
Mouvement de la société pour la paix (MSP)	5
Front national algérien (FNA)	2
Rassemblement pour la culture et la démocratie (RCD)	1
Independents	2
Appointed by the President†	48
Total	144

* Deputies of the 144-member Council of the Nation serve a six-year term; one-half of its members are replaced every three years. Elected representatives are selected by indirect, secret suffrage from regional and municipal authorities.

† 24 members were appointed by the President on 10 January 2010.

Political Organizations

Until 1989 the FLN was the only legal party in Algeria. Amendments to the Constitution in February of that year permitted the formation of other political associations, with some restrictions. The right to establish political parties was guaranteed by constitutional amendments in November 1996; however, political associations based on differences in religion, language, race, gender or region were proscribed. Some 24 political parties contested the legislative elections of May 2007. The most prominent political organizations are listed below.

Ahd 54 (Oath 54): 53 rue Larbi Ben M'Hedi, Algiers; tel. (21) 73-00-83; fax (21) 73-00-82; e-mail info@ahd54.com; internet www.ahd54.com; f. 1991; small nationalist party; Pres. ALI FAWZI REBAÏNE.

Alliance nationale républicaine (ANR): 202 blvd Bougara, el-Biar, Algiers; tel. (21) 91-69-30; fax (21) 91-48-34; e-mail contact@anr.dz; f. 1995; anti-Islamist; Leader REDHA MALEK.

Front des forces socialistes (FFS): 56 ave Souidani Boudjemaâ, el-Mouradia, 16000 Algiers; tel. (21) 69-41-41; fax (21) 48-45-54; internet www.ffs-dz.com; f. 1963; revived 1989; seeks greater autonomy for Berber-dominated regions and official recognition of the Berber language; Leader HOCINE AÏT AHMED; Sec.-Gen. ALI LASKRI.

Front de libération nationale (FLN): 7 rue du Stade, 16405 Hydra, Algiers; tel. (21) 69-42-81; fax (21) 69-47-07; e-mail contact@pfln.dz; internet www.pfln.dz; f. 1954; sole legal party until 1989; socialist in outlook, the party is organized into a Secretariat, a National Council, an Executive Committee, Federations, Kasmas and cells; under the aegis of the FLN are various mass political orgs, incl. the Union Nationale de la Jeunesse Algérienne and the Union Nationale des Femmes Algériennes; Pres. ABDELAZIZ BOUTEFLIKA; Sec.-Gen. ABDELAZIZ BELKHADEM.

Front national algérien (FNA): 18 rue Chaib Ahmed, 16100 Algiers; tel. (21) 73-07-88; fax (21) 73-30-96; e-mail touatimoussa@yahoo.fr; internet www.fna.dz; f. 1999; advocates eradication of poverty and supports the Govt's peace initiative; Pres. MOUSSA TOUATI.

Mouvement pour l'autonomie de la Kabylie (MAK): Tizi Ouzou; e-mail info@makabylie.info; internet mak.makabylie.info; f. 2001; advocates autonomy for the north-eastern region of Kabylia within a federal Algerian state; Leader FERHAT MEHENNI.

Mouvement démocratique et social (MDS): 67 blvd Krim Belkacem, 16200 Algiers; tel. (21) 63-86-05; fax (21) 63-89-12; e-mail mds-algerie@orange.fr; f. 1998 by fmr mems of Ettahaddi; left-wing party; 4,000 mems; Sec.-Gen. AHMED MELIANI.

Mouvement El Islah (MRN) (Mouvement de la réforme nationale): Algiers; internet www.elislah.net; f. 1998; radical Islamist party; Sec.-Gen. HAMLAOUI AKOUCHI.

Mouvement pour la jeunesse et la démocratie (MJD): tel. (21) 39-49-30; advocates sexual equality; Pres. CHALABIA MAHDJOUBIA.

Mouvement de la renaissance islamique (Al-Nahda) (Harakat al-Nahda al-Islamiyya): blvd des Martyrs, 16100 Algiers; tel. (21) 74-85-14; fundamentalist Islamist group; Leader FATEH REBAI.

Mouvement de la société pour la paix (MSP) (Harakat Mujtamaa al-Silm): 63 rue Ali Haddad, Algiers; e-mail hms@hmsalgeria.net; internet hmsalgeria.net; fmrly known as Hamas; adopted current name in 1997; moderate Islamist party, favouring the gradual introduction of an Islamic state; Pres. BOUDJERRA SOLTANI.

Parti national pour la solidarité et le développement (PNSD): BP 110, Staouéli, Algiers; tel. and fax (21) 39-40-42; e-mail cherif_taleb@yahoo.fr; f. 1989 as Parti social démocrate; Leader MOHAMED CHERIF TALEB.

Parti du renouveau algérien (PRA): 8 ave de Pékin, 16209 el-Mouradia, Algiers; tel. (21) 59-43-00; Sec.-Gen. KAMEL BENSALEM; Leader NOUREDDINE BOUKROUH.

Parti des travailleurs (PT): 2 rue Belkheir Hassan Badi, el-Harrach, 16000 Algiers; tel. (21) 52-62-45; fax (21) 52-89-90; internet www.ptalgerie.com; workers' party; Leader LOUISA HANOUNE.

Rassemblement pour la culture et la démocratie (RCD): 40 rue Muhammad Chabane, el-Biar, Algiers; tel. (21) 92-50-76; fax (21) 92-51-01; e-mail info@rcd-algerie.org; internet www.rcd-algerie.org; f. 1989; social democratic and secular party; advocates inclusion of Berber traditions into the Algerian identity; Pres. MOHCINE BELABBAS.

Rassemblement national démocratique (RND): BP 10, Cité des Asphodèles, Ben Aknoun, Algiers; tel. (21) 91-64-10; fax (21) 91-47-40; e-mail contact@rnd-dz.com; internet www.rnd-dz.com; f. 1997; centrist party; Sec.-Gen. AHMED OUYAHIA.

Wafa wa al-Adl (Wafa): Algiers; f. 1999; unauthorized; Leader AHMED TALEB IBRAHIMI.

The following groups are in armed conflict with the Government:

Al-Qa'ida Organization in the Land of the Islamic Maghreb (AQIM): f. 1998 as the Groupe salafiste pour la prédication et le combat (GSPC), a breakaway faction from the Groupe islamique armé; adopted current name in Jan. 2007, when it aligned itself with the militant Islamist al-Qa'ida network led by Osama bin Laden; particularly active to the east of Algiers and in Kabylia; as the GSPC, traditionally responded to preaching by Ali Belhadj, the second most prominent member of the proscribed Front islamique du salut; Leader ABDELMALEK DROUKDAL (also known as ABU MUSAB ABD AL-WADUD).

Groupe islamique armé (GIA): f. 1992; was the most prominent and radical Islamist militant group in the mid-1990s, but has reportedly split into several factions that do not all adhere to one leader; Leader BOULENOUAR OUKIL.

Diplomatic Representation

EMBASSIES IN ALGERIA

Angola: 12 rue Mohamed Khoudi, el-Biar, Algiers; tel. (21) 92-21-43; fax (21) 92-04-18; e-mail ngolamd@wissal.dz; Chargé d'affaires a.i. CELESTINO CARLOS FERNANDES.

Argentina: Villa 68, Derb el-Feth, el-Biar, 16030 Algiers; tel. (21) 92-31-18; fax (21) 92-31-08; e-mail earge@mrecic.gov.ar; Ambassador BIBIANA LUCÍA JONES.

Austria: 17 chemin Abd al-Kader Gadouche, 16035 Hydra, Algiers; tel. (21) 69-10-86; fax (21) 69-12-32; e-mail algier-ob@bmeia.gv.at; Ambassador ALOISIA WÖRGETTER.

Belgium: BP 341, 16030 el-Biar, Algiers; tel. (21) 92-26-20; fax (21) 92-50-36; e-mail algiers@diplobel.be; internet www.diplomatie.be/algiersfr; Ambassador CHRISTIAAN VAN DRIESSCHE.

Benin: BP 103, 16 Lot du Stade Birkhadem, Algiers; tel. (21) 56-52-71; Ambassador LEONARD ADJIN.

Brazil: 55 Bis, chemin Cheikh Bachir el-Ibrahimi, el-Biar, Algiers; tel. (21) 92-44-37; fax (21) 92-41-25; e-mail brasemb.argel@itamaraty.gov.br; internet argel.itamaraty.gov.br; Ambassador HENRIQUÉ SARDINHA PINTO.

Bulgaria: 13 blvd Col Bougara, Algiers; tel. (21) 23-00-14; fax (21) 23-05-33; e-mail alger_ambassade_bg@abv.bg; Ambassador DIMITAR DIMITROV.

Burkina Faso: BP 212, 23 Lot el-Feth, chemin ibn Badis el-Mouiz (ex Poirson), el-Biar, Didouche Mourad, Algiers; tel. (21) 92-33-39; fax (21) 92-73-90; e-mail abfalger@yahoo.fr; Ambassador MAMADOU SERME.

Cameroon: 26 chemin Cheikh Bachir el-Ibrahimi, 16011 el-Biar, Algiers; tel. (21) 92-11-24; fax (21) 92-11-25; e-mail ambacam_alger@yahoo.fr; Chargé d'affaires JEAN MISSOUP.

Canada: BP 464, 18 rue Mustapha Khalef, Ben Aknoun, 16306 Algiers; tel. (770) 08-30-00; fax (770) 08-30-40; e-mail alger@international.gc.ca; internet www.international.gc.ca/world/embassies/algeria; Ambassador GENEVIÈVE DES RIVIÈRES.

Chad: Villa 18, Cité DNC, chemin Ahmed Kara, Hydra, Algiers; tel. (21) 69-26-62; fax (21) 69-26-63; Ambassador El-Hadj MAHAMOUD ADJI.

Chile: 8 rue F. les Crêtes, Hydra, Algiers; tel. (21) 48-31-63; fax (21) 60-71-85; e-mail embachileargelia@gmail.com; Ambassador PABLO MUÑOZ ROMERO.

China, People's Republic: 34 blvd des Martyrs, Algiers; tel. (21) 69-27-24; fax (21) 69-30-56; e-mail chinaemb_dz@mfa.gov.cn; internet dz.chineseembassy.org; Ambassador LIU YUHE.

Congo, Republic: 13 rue Rabah Noel, Algiers; tel. (21) 58-06-13; Ambassador JEAN-BAPTISTE DZANGUÉ.

Côte d'Ivoire: BP 260, Immeuble 'Le Bosquet', Parc Paradou, Hydra, Algiers; tel. (21) 69-23-78; fax (21) 69-28-28; Ambassador AMON SYLVESTRE AKA.

Croatia: 12 rue Ismail Chaâlal, el-Mouradia, Algiers; tel. (21) 69-67-63; fax (21) 48-48-98; e-mail croemb.algeria@mvpei.hr; Ambassador MIRKO BOLFEK.

Cuba: 22 rue Larbi Allik, Hydra, Algiers; tel. (21) 69-21-48; fax (21) 69-32-81; e-mail embacubargelia@assila.net; Ambassador EUMELIO CABALLERO RODRÍGUEZ.

Czech Republic: BP 358, Villa Koudia, 3 chemin Ziryab, Alger-Gare, Algiers; tel. (21) 23-00-56; fax (21) 23-01-03; e-mail algiers@embassy.mzv.cz; internet www.mzv.cz/algiers; Ambassador PAVEL KLUCKÝ.

Egypt: BP 297, 8 chemin Abd al-Kader Gadouche, 16300 Hydra, Algiers; tel. (21) 69-16-73; fax (21) 69-29-52; Ambassador EZZ EL-DIN FAHMI MAHMOUD.

Finland: 10 rue des Cèdres, el-Mouradia, Algiers; tel. (21) 69-29-25; fax (21) 69-16-37; e-mail sanomat.alg@formin.fi; internet www.finlandalgeria.org; Ambassador HANNELE VOIONMAA.

France: 25 chemin Abd al-Kader Gadouche, 16035 Hydra, Algiers; tel. (21) 98-17-17; fax (21) 98-17-09; e-mail contact@ambafrance-dz.org; internet www.ambafrance-dz.org; Ambassador XAVIER DRIENCOURT.

Gabon: BP 125, Rostomia, 21 rue Hadj Ahmed Mohamed, Hydra, Algiers; tel. (21) 69-24-00; fax (21) 60-25-46; Ambassador YVES ONGOLLO.

Germany: BP 664, 165 chemin Sfindja, Alger-Gare, 16000 Algiers; tel. (21) 74-19-56; fax (21) 74-05-21; e-mail zreg@algi.diplo.de; internet www.algier.diplo.de; Ambassador JUTTA WOLKE.

Ghana: 62 rue des Frères Benali Abdellah, Hydra, Algiers; tel. (21) 60-64-44; fax (21) 69-28-56; Ambassador ADOLPHUS KINGSLEY ARTHUR.

Greece: 60 blvd Col Bougara, 16030 el-Biar, Algiers; tel. (21) 92-34-91; fax (21) 92-34-90; e-mail gremb.alg@mfa.gr; internet www.mfa.gr/algiers; Ambassador VASILIOS MOUTSOGLOU.

Guinea: 43 blvd Central Saïd Hamdine, Hydra, Algiers; tel. (21) 69-36-11; fax (21) 69-34-68; e-mail ambaga49@yahoo.fr; Ambassador ANSOUMANE CAMARA.

Guinea-Bissau: BP 32, 17 rue Ahmad Kara, Colonne Volrol, Hydra, Algiers; tel. (21) 60-01-51; fax (21) 60-97-25; Ambassador JOSÉ PEREIRA BATISTA.

Holy See: 1 rue Noureddine Mekiri, 16021 Bologhine, Algiers (Apostolic Nunciature); tel. (21) 95-45-20; fax (21) 95-40-95; e-mail nuntiusalger2@yahoo.fr; Apostolic Nuncio Most Rev. THOMAS YEH SHENG-NAN (Titular Archbishop of Leptis Magna).

Hungary: BP 68, 18 ave des Fréres Oughlis, el-Mouradia, Algiers; tel. (21) 69-79-75; fax (21) 69-81-86; e-mail alg.missions@kum.hu; Ambassador JÓZSEF HAJGATÓ.

India: BP 108, 14 rue des Abassides, 16030 el-Biar, Algiers; tel. (21) 92-32-88; fax (21) 92-40-11; e-mail indembalg_com@hotmail.com; internet www.indianalg.org; Ambassador Dr KULDEEP SINGH BHARDWAJ.

Indonesia: BP 62, 17 chemin Abd al-Kader Gadouche, 16070 el-Mouradia, Algiers; tel. (21) 69-49-15; fax (21) 69-49-10; e-mail kbrialger@indonesia-dz.org; internet www.indonesia-dz.org; Ambassador AHMAD NI'AM SALIM.

Iraq: 4 rue Abri Arezki, Hydra, Algiers; tel. (21) 69-31-25; fax (21) 69-10-97; e-mail algemb@iraqmofamail.net; Ambassador UDAY AL-KHAIRALLAH.

Italy: 18 rue Muhammad Ouidir Amellal, 16030 el-Biar, Algiers; tel. (21) 92-23-30; fax (21) 92-59-86; e-mail segretaria.algeri@esteri.it; internet www.ambalgeri.esteri.it; Ambassador GIAMPAOLO CANTINI.

Japan: BP 80, 1 chemin el-Bakri (ex Macklay), Ben Aknoun, Algiers; tel. (21) 91-20-04; fax (21) 91-20-46; internet www.dz.emb-japan.go.jp; Ambassador TSUKASA KAWADA.

Jordan: 47 rue Ammani Belkalem, Hydra, Algiers; tel. (21) 69-20-31; fax (21) 69-15-54; e-mail jordan@wissal.dz; Ambassador TURKI HADITHA AL-KHRAISHA.

Korea, Democratic People's Republic: Algiers; tel. (21) 62-39-27; Ambassador PAK HO IL.

Korea, Republic: BP 92, 39 ave Mohamed Khoudi, el-Biar, Algiers; tel. (21) 79-34-00; fax (21) 79-34-04; e-mail koemal@mofat.go.kr; internet dza.mofat.go.kr/kor/af/dza/main/index.jsp; Ambassador CHOI SUNG-JOO.

Kuwait: chemin Abd al-Kader Gadouche, Hydra, Algiers; tel. (21) 59-31-57; Ambassador SAUD FAISAL SAUD AL-DAWEESH.

Lebanon: 9 rue Kaïd Ahmad, el-Biar, Algiers; tel. (21) 78-20-94; Ambassador BASSAM ALI TARABAH.

Libya: 15 chemin Cheikh Bachir el-Ibrahimi, Algiers; tel. (21) 92-15-02; fax (21) 92-46-87; Ambassador ABD AL-MOULA EL-GHADHBANE.

Madagascar: BP 65, 22 rue Abd al-Kader Aouis, 16090 Bologhine, Algiers; tel. (21) 95-03-74; fax (21) 95-17-76; e-mail ambamadalg@yahoo.fr; Ambassador VOLA DIEUDONNÉ RAZAFINDRALAMBO.

Mali: Villa 15, Cité DNC/ANP, chemin Ahmed Kara, Hydra, Algiers; tel. (21) 69-13-51; fax (21) 69-20-82; Ambassador BOUBACAR KARAMOKO COULIBALY (designate).

Mauritania: 107 Lot Baranès, Aire de France, Bouzaréah, Algiers; tel. (21) 79-21-39; fax (21) 78-42-74; Ambassador BOULAH OULD MOGUEYE.

Mexico: BP 329, 25 chemin El-Bakri, Ben Aknoun, 16306 Algiers; tel. (21) 91-46-00; fax (21) 91-46-01; e-mail embamexargelia@gmail.com; internet www.sre.gob.mx/argelia; Ambassador EDUARDO ROLDÁN ACOSTA.

Morocco: 8 rue Abd al-Kader Azil, el-Mouradia, Algiers; tel. (21) 60-57-07; fax (21) 60-50-47; e-mail ambmaroc-alg@maec.gov.ma; Ambassador ABDELLAH BELKEZIZ.

Netherlands: BP 72, 23 chemin Cheikh Bachir el-Ibrahimi, el-Biar, Algiers; tel. (21) 92-28-28; fax (21) 92-29-47; e-mail alg@minbuza.nl; internet alger.nlambassade.org; Ambassador FRANS BIJVOET.

Niger: 54 rue Vercors Rostamia, Bouzaréah, Algiers; tel. (21) 78-89-21; fax (21) 78-97-13; Ambassador MOUSSA SANGARE.

Nigeria: BP 629, 27 bis rue Blaise Pascal, Algiers; tel. (21) 69-18-49; fax (21) 69-11-75; Ambassador JEREMIAH HASSAN.

Norway: 7 chemin Doudou Mokhtar, Ben Aknoun, 16035 Algiers; tel. (21) 94-65-65; fax (21) 94-64-65; e-mail emb.alger@mfa.no; internet www.norvege-algerie.org; Ambassador ARILD RETVEDT ØYEN.

Oman: BP 201, 52 rue Djamel Eddine, el-Afghani, Bouzaréah, Algiers; tel. (21) 91-28-35; fax (21) 91-47-37; e-mail algeria@mofa.gov.om; Ambassador ALI ABDULLAH AL-ALAWI.

Pakistan: Villa no 18, rue des Idrissides, el-Biar, Algiers; tel. (21) 79-37-56; fax (21) 79-37-58; e-mail pakembagiers@yahoo.com; Ambassador MUHAMMAD ASLAM.

Peru: 20 ave Franklin Roosevelt, 1er étage, 16006 Algiers; tel. (21) 68-15-95; fax (21) 68-16-96; e-mail amb.perou@eepad.dz; Ambassador JOSÉ RAFAEL EDUARDO BERAÚN ARANÍBAR.

Poland: 104 Hay el-Binaa, Dely Ibrahim, 16302 Algiers; tel. (21) 91-77-82; fax (21) 91-78-12; e-mail ambalgier@yahoo.pl; internet www.algier.polemb.net; Ambassador MICHAŁ RADLICKI.

Portugal: 4 rue Mohamed Khoudi, el-Biar, Algiers; tel. (21) 92-53-14; fax (21) 92-53-13; e-mail embportdz@yahoo.fr; internet www.embaixadaportugalargel.com; Ambassador Dr JOSÉ FERNANDO MOREIRA DA CUNHA.

Qatar: BP 348, 7 chemin Doudou Mokhtar, Algiers; tel. (21) 91-20-09; fax (21) 91-20-11; e-mail algeria@mofa.gov.qa; Ambassador ABDULLAH NASSER ABDULLAH AL-HUMAIDI.

Romania: 24 rue Abri Arezki, Hydra, Algiers; tel. (21) 60-08-71; fax (21) 69-36-42; e-mail amroalg@gmail.com; Ambassador VICTOR MIRCEA.

Russia: 7 chemin du Prince d'Annam, el-Biar, Algiers; tel. (21) 92-31-39; fax (21) 92-28-82; e-mail ambrussie@yandex.ru; internet www.ambrussie.gov.dz; Ambassador ALEKSANDR EGOROV.

Saudi Arabia: 62 rue Med. Drafini, chemin de la Madeleine, Hydra, Algiers; tel. (21) 60-35-18; e-mail dzemb@mofa.gov.sa; Ambassador Dr SAMI BIN ABDULLAH BIN OTHMAN AL-SALIH.

Senegal: BP 720, 350 Parc Ben Omar Kouba, Alger-Gare, Algiers; tel. (21) 54-90-90; fax (21) 54-90-94; e-mail senegal@wissal.dz; Ambassador PAPA OUSMANE SEYE.

Serbia: BP 366, 7 rue des Frères Ben-hafid, Hydra, Algiers; tel. (21) 69-12-18; fax (21) 69-34-72; e-mail ambasada@ambserbie-alger.com; internet www.ambserbie-alger.com; Chargé d'affaires a.i. NEBOJŠA JERKOVIĆ.

South Africa: 21 rue du Stade, Hydra, Algiers; tel. (21) 48-44-18; fax (21) 48-44-19; e-mail teffahim@foreign.gov.za; internet www.saealgiers.com; Ambassador JOSEPH KOTANE.

Spain: BP 142, 46 bis, rue Muhammad Chabane, el-Biar, Algiers; tel. (21) 92-27-13; fax (21) 92-27-19; e-mail emb.argel@mae.es; Ambassador GABRIEL BUSQUETS APARICIO.

Sudan: Algiers; tel. (21) 56-66-23; fax (21) 69-30-19; Ambassador AHMED HAMAD AL-FAKI HAMAD.

Sweden: BP 263, rue Olof Palme, Nouveau Paradou, Hydra, Algiers; tel. (21) 54-83-33; fax (21) 54-83-34; e-mail ambassaden.alger@foreign.ministry.se; internet www.swedenabroad.se/algersv; Ambassador EVA EMNÉUS.

Switzerland: Villa 5, rue no 4, Parc du Paradou, 16035 Hydra, Algiers; tel. (21) 60-04-22; fax (21) 60-98-54; e-mail alg.vertretung@eda.admin.ch; internet www.eda.admin.ch/alger; Ambassador JEAN-CLAUDE RICHARD.

Syria: Domaine Tamzali, 11 chemin Abd al-Kader Gadouche, Hydra, Algiers; tel. (21) 91-20-26; fax (21) 91-20-30; Ambassador NAMIR WAHIB GHANEM.

Tunisia: 5 rue du Bois, Hydra, 16405 Algiers; tel. (21) 60-13-88; fax (21) 69-23-16; e-mail ambassade@ambtunisie-dz.com; Ambassador MUHAMMAD EL-FADHAL KHALIL.

Turkey: Villa Dar el-Ouard, chemin de la Rochelle, blvd Col Bougara, Algiers; tel. (21) 23-00-04; fax (21) 23-01-12; e-mail cezayir.be@mfa.gov.tr; internet algiers.emb.mfa.gov.tr; Ambassador AHMET BIGALI.

Ukraine: 19 rue des Frères Benhafid, Hydra, Algiers; tel. (21) 69-13-87; fax (21) 69-48-87; e-mail emb_dz@mfa.gov.ua; Ambassador VALERIY KIRDODA.

United Arab Emirates: BP 165, Alger-Gare, 14 rue Muhammad Drarini, Hydra, Algiers; tel. (21) 69-25-74; fax (21) 69-37-70; Ambassador MUHAMMAD ALI NASSER AL-WALI AL-MAZROUEI.

United Kingdom: 3 chemin Capitaine Hocine Slimane, Hydra, Algiers; tel. (770) 08-50-00; fax (770) 08-50-99; e-mail britishembassy.algiers@fco.gov.uk; internet ukinalgeria.fco.gov.uk; Ambassador MARTYN ROPER.

USA: BP 549, 5 chemin Cheikh Bachir el-Ibrahimi, el-Biar, 16030 Algiers; tel. (770) 08-20-00; fax (21) 60-73-35; e-mail algiers_webmaster@state.gov; internet algiers.usembassy.gov; Ambassador HENRY S. ENSHER.

Venezuela: BP 297, 3 impasse Ahmed Kara, Hydra, Algiers; tel. (21) 54-74-14; fax (21) 54-73-96; e-mail hector.mujica@mre.gob.ve; internet www.embaveneargelia.com; Ambassador HECTOR MICHEL MUJICA.

Viet Nam: 30 rue de Chenoua, Hydra, Algiers; tel. (21) 60-88-43; fax (21) 69-37-78; e-mail sqvnalgerie@yahoo.com.vn; internet www.vietnamembassy-algerie.org; Ambassador TRONG CUONG DO.

Yemen: 18 chemin Mahmoud Drarnine, Hydra, Algiers; tel. (21) 54-89-50; fax (21) 54-87-40; Ambassador JAMAL AWADH NASSER.

Judicial System

The highest court of justice is the Supreme Court (Cour suprême) in Algiers, established in 1963, which is served by 150 judges. Justice is exercised through 183 courts (tribunaux) and 31 appeal courts (cours d'appel), grouped on a regional basis. New legislation, promulgated in March 1997, provided for the eventual establishment of 214 courts and 48 appeal courts. The Court of Accounts (Cour des comptes) was established in 1979. Algeria adopted a penal code in 1966, retaining the death penalty. In February 1993 three special courts were established to try suspects accused of terrorist offences; however, the courts were abolished in February 1995. Constitutional amendments introduced in November 1996 provided for the establishment of a High State Court (empowered to judge the President of the Republic in cases of high treason, and the Head of Government for crimes and offences), and a State Council to regulate the administrative judiciary. In addition, a Conflicts Tribunal has been established to adjudicate in disputes between the Supreme Court and the State Council.

Supreme Court

rue du 11 décembre 1960, Ben Aknoun, Algiers; tel. (21) 92-58-57; fax (21) 92-96-44; e-mail sg_coursupreme@mjustice.dz; internet www.coursupreme.dz.

President of Supreme Court: KADDOUR BERRADJA.

Attorney-General: AHMED NOUI (ad interim).

Religion

ISLAM

Islam is the official religion, and the vast majority of Algerians are Muslims.

High Islamic Council

16 rue du 11 décembre 1960, Ben Aknoun, 16030 Algiers; tel. (21) 91-54-10; fax (21) 91-54-09; e-mail hci@hci.dz; internet www.hci.dz.

President of the High Islamic Council: Dr CHEIKH BOUAMRANE.

CHRISTIANITY

The majority of the European inhabitants, and a few Arabs, are Christians.

The Roman Catholic Church

Algeria comprises one archdiocese and three dioceses (including one directly responsible to the Holy See). In December 2006 there were an estimated 4,700 adherents in the country. The Bishops' Conference of North Africa (Conférence des Evêques de la Région Nord de l'Afrique—CERNA) moved from Algiers to Tunis, Tunisia, in 2004.

Archbishop of Algiers: Most Rev. GHALEB ABDULLAH MOUSSA, 22 chemin d'Hydra, 16030 el-Biar, Algiers; tel. (21) 92-56-67; fax (21) 92-55-76; e-mail evechealger@yahoo.fr.

Protestant Church

Eglise Réformée d'Alger: 31 rue Reda Houhou, 16110 Alger-HBB, Algiers; tel. and fax (21) 71-62-38; e-mail protestants_alger@yahoo.com; 38 parishes; 7,000 mems; Pres. MOUSTAFA KRIM.

The Press

In 2008 there were an estimated 290 newspapers in circulation, including more than 60 dailies.

DAILIES

El Acil: 1 rue Kamel Ben Djelit, Constantine; tel. and fax (31) 92-46-13; e-mail elacilquotidien@yahoo.fr; f. 1993; French; Dir GHALIB DJABBOUR.

Akher Sâa: Intersection Bougandoura Miloud et Sakhri Abdelhamid, Annaba; tel. (38) 86-02-41; fax (38) 86-47-19; e-mail saidbel@hotmail.com; internet www.akhersaa-dz.com; Arabic; Dir SAÏD BELHADJOUDJA.

L'Authentique: 4 rue Abane Ramdane, Algiers; tel. (17) 06-13-80; fax (21) 74-27-15; e-mail lauthentiqueredaction@yahoo.fr; French; Editorial Dir NADJIB STAMBOULI.

Ech-Cha'ab (The People): 1 ave Pasteur, 16000 Algiers; tel. (21) 60-70-40; fax (21) 60-67-93; e-mail webmaster@ech-chaab.com; internet www.ech-chaab.com; f. 1962; Arabic; journal of the Front de libération nationale; Dir AZZEDINE BOUKERDOUSSE; circ. 24,000.

Echorouk El-Youmi: Maison de la presse Abdelkader Safir, Kouba, Algiers; tel. and fax (21) 29-89-41; e-mail contact@echoroukonline.com; internet www.echoroukonline.com; f. 2000; Arabic; Dir ALI FOUDIL.

Le Courier d'Algérie: Maison de la presse Abdelkader Kouba, Algiers; tel. (21) 46-25-12; fax (21) 46-25-13; e-mail redactioncourrier@yahoo.fr; internet www.lecourrier-dalgerie.com; f. 2003; French; Dir AHMED TOUMIAT.

La Dépêche de Kabylie: Maison de la presse Tahar Djaout, place du 1er mai, 16016 Algiers; tel. (21) 66-38-05; fax (21) 66-37-87; e-mail info@depechedekabylie.com; internet www.depechedekabylie.com; f. 2001; Dir IDIR BENYOUNÈS.

Djazair News: Maison de la presse Tahar Djaout, place du 1er mai, 16016 Algiers; tel. (21) 66-36-93; fax (21) 66-36-93; e-mail djazairnews@gmail.com; internet www.djazairnews.info; f. 2003; Arabic; Man. Dir HMIDA AYACHI.

L'Expression: Maison de la presse Abdelkader Safir, Kouba, Algiers; tel. (21) 68-94-55; fax (21) 28-02-29; e-mail laredaction@lexpressiondz.com; internet www.lexpressiondz.com; f. 2000; French; Editor AHMED FATTANI; circ. 70,000.

Al-Fedjr: Maison de la presse Tahar Djaout, place du 1er mai, 16016 Algiers; tel. and fax (21) 65-76-60; e-mail fadjr@al-fadjr.com; internet www.al-fadjr.com; f. 2000; Arabic; Dir ABDA HADDA HAZEM.

Horizons: 20 rue de la Liberté, Algiers; tel. (21) 73-67-24; fax (21) 73-61-34; e-mail administration@horizons-dz.com; internet www.horizons-dz.com; f. 1985; evening; French; Dir NAÂMA ABBAS; circ. 35,000.

Le Jeune Indépendant: Maison de la presse Tahar Djaout, 1 rue Bachir Attar, place du 1er mai, 16016 Algiers; tel. (21) 67-07-48; fax (21) 67-07-46; e-mail redaction@jeune-independant.net; internet www.jeune-independant.net; f. 1990; French; Man. Dir ALI MECHERI; Editor NAÏMA NEFLA; circ. 60,000.

El-Joumhouria (The Republic): 6 rue Bensenouci Hamida, Oran; tel. (41) 39-04-97; fax (41) 39-10-39; e-mail djoumhouria@yahoo.fr; internet www.eldjoumhouria.dz; f. 1963; Arabic; Editor BENAMEUR BOUKHALFA; circ. 20,000.

El Khabar: 32 rue El Feth Ibn Khlakane, Hydra, Algiers; tel. (21) 48-44-37; fax (21) 48-44-31; e-mail admin@elkhabar.com; internet www.elkhabar.com; f. 1990; Arabic; Dir-Gen. CHERIF REZKI; circ. 500,000.

Liberté: BP 178, 37 rue Larbi Ben M'Hidi, Alger-Gare, Algiers; tel. (21) 64-34-25; fax (21) 64-34-29; e-mail infos@liberte-algerie.com; internet www.liberte-algerie.com; f. 1992; French; independent; Dir ALI OUAFEK; Editors SALIM TAMANI, AMAR OUALI; circ. 20,000.

El-Massa: Maison de la presse Abdelkader Safir, Kouba, 16000 Algiers; tel. (21) 74-57-99; fax (21) 74-57-90; e-mail info@el-massa.com; internet www.el-massa.com; f. 1977; evening; Arabic; Dir ABDERRAHMANE TIGANE; circ. 45,000.

Le Matin: Maison de la Presse Tahar Djaout, 1 rue Bachir Attar, place du 1er mai, 16016 Algiers; tel. (21) 66-07-08; fax (21) 66-20-97; e-mail redactionlematin@gmail.com; internet www.lematindz.net; French; Dir MUHAMMAD BENCHICOU.

El-Moudjahid (The Fighter): 20 rue de la Liberté, Algiers; tel. (21) 73-70-81; fax (21) 73-56-70; e-mail elmoudja@elmoudjahid.com; internet www.elmoudjahid.com; f. 1965; govt journal in French and Arabic; Dir ABDELMADJID CHERBAL; circ. 392,000.

An-Nasr (The Victory): BP 388, Zone Industrielle, La Palma, Constantine; tel. (31) 66-82-61; fax (31) 66-81-45; e-mail contact@annasronline.com; internet www.annasronline.com; f. 1963; Arabic; Dir LARBI OUANOUGHI; circ. 340,000.

La Nouvelle République: Maison de la presse Tahar Djaout, 1 rue Bachir Attar, place du 1er mai, 16016 Algiers; tel. (21) 67-10-44; fax (21) 67-10-75; e-mail inr98@yahoo.fr; internet www.lanouvellerepublique.com; French; Dir ABDELWAHAB DJAKOUNE; Editor MEHENNA HAMADOUCHE.

Ouest Tribune: 13 Cité Djamel, 31007 Oran; tel. (41) 45-31-30; fax (41) 45-34-62; e-mail redaction@ouestribune-dz.com; internet www.ouestribune-dz.com; French; Dir ABDELMADJID BLIDI.

Le Quotidien d'Oran: BP 110, 63 ave de l'ANP, 1 rue Laid Ould Tayeb, Oran; tel. (41) 32-63-09; fax (41) 32-51-36; e-mail infos@lequotidien-oran.com; internet www.lequotidien-oran.com; French; Dir-Gen. MUHAMMAD ABDOU BENABBOU.

Sawt al-Ahrar: 6 ave Pasteur, Algiers; tel. (21) 73-47-76; fax (21) 73-47-65; e-mail sawtalahrar@hotmail.com; internet www.sawt-alahrar.net; Arabic; Dir MUHAMMAD NADIR BOULAGROUNE.

Le Soir d'Algérie: Maison de la presse Tahar Djaout, 1 rue Bachir Attar, place du 1er mai, 16016 Algiers; tel. (21) 67-06-58; fax (21) 67-06-76; e-mail info@lesoirdalgerie.com; internet www.lesoirdalgerie.com; f. 1990; evening; independent information journal in French; Dir FOUAD BOUGHANEM; Editor NACER BELHADJOUDJA; circ. 80,000.

La Tribune: Maison de la presse Tahar Djaout, 1 rue Bachir Attar, place du 1er mai, 16016 Algiers; tel. (21) 68-54-21; fax (21) 68-54-22; e-mail latribun@latribune-online.com; internet www.latribune-online.com; f. 1994; current affairs journal in French; Dir HASSAN BACHIR-CHERIF; Editorial Dir ABDELKRIM GHEZALI.

La Voix de l'Oranie: 3 rue Rouis Rayah, Haï Oussama, 31000 Oran; tel. (41) 32-22-18; fax (41) 35-18-01; e-mail contact@voix-oranie.com; internet www.voix-oranie.com; French; Dir RAFIK CHARRAK.

El Watan: Maison de la presse, 1 rue Bachir Attar, place du 1er mai, 16016 Algiers; tel. (21) 68-21-83; fax (21) 68-21-87; e-mail admin@elwatan.com; internet www.elwatan.com; f. 1990; French; Dir OMAR BELHOUCHET; circ. 140,000.

El-Youm: Maison de la presse Tahar Djaout, 1 rue Bachir Attar, place du 1er mai, 16016 Algiers; tel. (21) 66-70-82; fax (21) 67-57-05; e-mail pubelyoum@yahoo.fr; internet www.elyawm.com; Arabic; Dirs MAHFOUD HADJI, AMINA HADJI; Editor KHALED LAKHDARI; circ. 54,000.

WEEKLIES

Les Débats: 2 blvd Muhammad V, Algiers; tel. (21) 63-73-05; fax (21) 63-70-05; e-mail lesdebats@hotmail.com; internet www.lesdebats.com; French; Dir AÏSSA KHELLADI.

Al-Mohakik Assiri (The Secret Enquirer): 2 ave Nafaâ Hafaf, Algiers; tel. (21) 71-05-58; e-mail almohakik@yahoo.fr; internet www.almohakik.com; f. 2006; Arabic; Dir HABET HANNACHI.

La Nation: 33 rue Larbi Ben M'hidi, Algiers; tel. (21) 43-21-76; f. 1992; French; Dir ATTIA OMAR; Editor SALIMA GHEZALI; circ. 35,000.

Révolution Africaine: Algiers; tel. (21) 59-77-91; fax (21) 59-77-92; current affairs journal in French; socialist; Dir FERRAH ABDELLALI; circ. 50,000.

OTHER PERIODICALS

Al-Acala: 4 rue Timgad, Hydra, Algiers; tel. (21) 60-85-55; fax (21) 60-09-36; f. 1970; publ. by the Ministry of Religious Affairs and Awqaf (Religious Endowments); fortnightly; Arabic; Editor MUHAMMAD AL-MAHDI.

Algérie Médicale: Algiers; f. 1964; publ. of the Union médicale algérienne; 2 a year; French; circ. 3,000.

Alouan (Colours): 119 rue Didouche Mourad, Algiers; f. 1973; cultural review; monthly; Arabic.

L'Auto Marché: 139 blvd Krim Belkacem; tel. (21) 74-44-59; fax (21) 74-14-63; e-mail contact@lautomarche.com; internet www.lautomarche.com; f. 1998; fortnightly; French; motoring; Dir MOURAD CHEBOUB.

Bibliographie de l'Algérie: Bibliothèque Nationale d'Algérie, BP 127, Hamma el-Annasser, 16000 Algiers; tel. (21) 67-57-81; fax (21) 67-23-00; e-mail contact@biblionat.dz; internet www.biblionat.dz;

f. 1963; lists books, theses, pamphlets and periodicals publ. in Algeria; bi-annual; Arabic and French; Dir-Gen. MUHAMMAD AÏSSA OUMOUSSA.

Le Buteur: Maison de la presse Tahar Djaout, 1 rue Bachir Attar, place du 1er mai, 16016 Algiers; tel. (21) 73-25-76; fax (21) 73-99-71; e-mail contact@lebuteur.com; internet www.lebuteur.com; Mon., Thur. and Sat.; French; sports; Dir BOUSAÂD KAHEL.

Al-Cha'ab al-Thakafi (Cultural People): Algiers; f. 1972; cultural monthly; Arabic.

Al-Chabab (Youth): Algiers; journal of the Union Nationale de la Jeunesse Algérienne; bi-monthly; Arabic and French.

Al-Djeich (The Army): Office de l'Armée Nationale Populaire, Algiers; f. 1963; monthly; Arabic and French; Algerian army review; circ. 10,000.

IT Mag: BP 849, CyberParc de Sidi Abdellah, CA-E1-15, Rahmania, Algiers; tel. (21) 66-29-92; fax (21) 65-03-28; e-mail info@itmag-dz.com; internet www.itmag.dz; f. 2002; French; telecommunications and IT in North Africa; Dir ABDERRAFIQ KHENIFSA.

Journal Officiel de la République Algérienne Démocratique et Populaire: pl. Seddik Ben Yahia, el-Mouradia, Algiers; tel. (21) 68-65-50; internet www.joradp.dz; f. 1962; Arabic and French.

Révolution et Travail: Maison du Peuple, 1 rue Abdelkader Benbarek, place du 1er mai, Algiers; tel. (21) 66-73-53; journal of the Union Générale des Travailleurs Algériens (central trade union) with Arabic and French edns; monthly; Editor-in-Chief RACHIB AÏT ALI.

Revue Algérienne du Travail: 28 rue Hassiba Bouali, Algiers; f. 1964; labour publ; quarterly; French; Dir A. DJAMAL.

Al-Thakafa (Culture): 2 place Cheikh Ben Badis, Algiers; tel. (21) 62-20-73; f. 1971; every 2 months; cultural review; Editor-in-Chief CHEBOUB OTHMANE; circ. 10,000.

NEWS AGENCIES

Agence Algérienne d'Information (AAI): Maison de la presse Tahar Djaout, 1 rue Bachir Attar, place du 1er mai, 16016 Algiers; tel. (21) 67-07-44; fax (21) 67-07-32; e-mail aai@aai-online.com; f. 1999; Dir HOURIA AÏT KACI.

Algérie Presse Service (APS): BP 444, 58 ave des Frères Bouadou, Bir Mourad Raïs, 16300 Algiers; tel. (21) 56-44-44; fax (21) 44-03-12; e-mail aps@aps.dz; internet www.aps.dz; f. 1961; provides news reports in Arabic, English and French.

Publishers

BERTI Editions: Lot el-Nadjah no 24, 16320 Dely Ibrahim, Algiers; tel. (21) 37-16-87; fax (21) 36-83-08; e-mail bertieditions@yahoo.com; internet www.berti-editions.com; f. 1995; publishes books on medicine, law, finance and IT; Dir MUHAMMAD GACI.

Casbah Editions: Lot Saïd Hamdine, Hydra, 16012 Algiers; tel. (21) 54-79-10; fax (21) 54-72-77; f. 1995; literature, essays, memoirs, textbooks and children's literature; Dir-Gen. SMAÏN AMZIANE.

CHIHAB Diffusion (CHIDIF): BP 74/4, Zone industriel de Reghaia, 16000 Algiers; tel. (21) 84-87-02; fax (21) 85-83-25; e-mail chidif@chihab.com; internet www.chihab.com; f. 1989; publishes educational textbooks.

Editions Bouchène: 4 rue de l'oasis, Algiers; tel. (21) 59-69-23; e-mail edbouchene@wanadoo.fr; internet www.bouchene.com; f. 1998; publishes books on the Maghreb region.

Editions Dahlab: 108 rue de Tripoli, Hussein Dey, Algiers; tel. (21) 49-67-39; fax (21) 64-31-75; e-mail editiondahlab@yahoo.fr; history, social sciences, economics; Dir ABDELLAH CHEGHNANE.

Editions du Tell: 3 rue des Frères Yacoub Torki, 09000 Blida; tel. (25) 31-10-35; fax (25) 31-10-36; e-mail contact@editions-du-tell.com; internet www.editions-du-tell.com; f. 2002; publishes books on literature, history, economics and social sciences.

Entreprise Nationale des Arts Graphiques (ENAG): BP 75, Zone industriel de Réghaia, Algiers; tel. (21) 84-86-11; fax (21) 84-80-08; e-mail edition@enag.dz; internet www.enag.dz; f. 1983; art, literature, social sciences, economics, science, religion, lifestyle and textbooks; Dir-Gen. HAMIDOU MESSAOUDI.

Maison d'Édition El Amel: Cité 600, Logement EPLF 53, 15000 Tizi Ouzou; tel. (26) 21-96-55; fax (26) 21-07-21; law and political science publishers.

Office des Publications Universitaires (OPU): 1 place Centrale de Ben Aknoun, 16306 Algiers; tel. (21) 91-23-14; fax (21) 91-21-81; e-mail info@opu-dz.com; internet www.opu-dz.com; publishes university textbooks; Dir-Gen. NOUREDDINE LACHEB.

Sedia: Cité les Mandariniers, Lot 293, al-Mohammadia, 16211 Algiers; tel. (21) 60-14-82; fax (21) 21-90-16; e-mail sedia@sedia-dz.com; internet www.sedia-dz.com; f. 2000; part of the Hachette Livre group (France); literature and educational textbooks; Pres. and Dir-Gen. BRAHIM DJELMAMI-HANI.

Broadcasting and Communications

TELECOMMUNICATIONS

New legislation approved by the National People's Assembly in August 2000 removed the state's monopoly over the telecommunications sector and redefined its role to that of a supervisory authority. Under the legislation, an independent regulator for the sector was created, and both the fixed-line and mobile sectors were opened to foreign competition.

Regulatory Authority

Autorité de Régulation de la Poste et des Télécommunications (ARPT): 1 rue Kaddour Rahim, Hussein Dey, 16008 Algiers; tel. (21) 47-02-05; fax (21) 47-01-97; e-mail info@arpt.dz; internet www.arpt.dz; f. 2001; Pres. DERDOURI ZOHRA; Dir-Gen. YACINE ABDELHAK.

Principal Operators

Algérie Télécom: route Nationale 5, Cinq Maisons, Mohammadia, 16130 Algiers; tel. (21) 82-38-38; fax (21) 82-38-39; e-mail contact@algerietelecom.dz; internet www.algerietelecom.dz; f. 2001 to manage and develop telecommunications infrastructure; Pres. and Dir-Gen. MOUSSA BENHAMADI.

Mobilis: Site Sider, 7 rue Belkacem Amani, Paradou, Hydra, Algiers; tel. (21) 54-71-63; fax (21) 54-72-72; e-mail commercial@mobilis.dz; internet www.mobilis.dz; f. 2003; subsidiary of Algérie Télécom; Pres. and Dir-Gen. BERTRAND DE TALHOUËT.

Djezzy GSM: Orascom Telecom Algérie, rue Mouloud Feraoun, Lot no. 8A, el-Beida, Algiers; tel. (70) 85-00-00; fax (70) 85-70-85; e-mail djezzy.entreprises@otalgerie.com; internet www.otalgerie.com; f. 2002; operates mobile cellular telephone network; some 14m. subscribers (May 2008); Pres. and Dir-Gen. NAGUIB SAWIRIS; Dir-Gen., Algeria TAMER EL-MAHDI.

Wataniya Telecom Algérie (Nedjma): BP 74, Algiers; e-mail mtouati@wta.dz; internet www.nedjma.dz; f. 2004; owned by Nat. Mobile Telecommunications Co KSC (Kuwait); offers mobile cellular telecommunications services under brand name *Nedjma*; Dir-Gen. JOSEPH GED.

BROADCASTING

Radio

Radiodiffusion Algérienne (ENRS): 21 blvd des Martyrs, Algiers; tel. (21) 48-37-90; fax (21) 23-08-23; e-mail info@algerian-radio.dz; internet www.radioalgerie.dz; govt-controlled; operates 30 local radio stations; Dir-Gen. AZZEDINE MIHOUBI.

Arabic Network: transmitters at Adrar, Aïn Beïda, Algiers, Béchar, Béni Abbès, Djanet, El Goléa, Ghardaïa, Hassi Messaoud, In Aménas, In Salah, Laghouat, Les Trembles, Ouargla, Reggane, Tamanrasset, Timimoun, Tindouf.

French Network: transmitters at Algiers, Constantine, Oran and Tipaza.

Kabyle Network: transmitter at Algiers.

Television

The principal transmitters are at Algiers, Batna, Sidi-Bel-Abbès, Constantine, Souk-Ahras and Tlemcen. Television plays a major role in the national education programme.

Télévision Algérienne (ENTV): BP 16070, 21 blvd des Martyrs, Algiers; tel. (21) 60-23-00; fax (21) 60-19-22; e-mail alger-contact@entv.dz; internet www.entv.dz; f. 1986; govt-controlled; Dir-Gen. ABDELKADER LALMI.

Finance

(cap. = capital; res = reserves; dep. = deposits; brs = branches; m. = million; amounts in Algerian dinars)

BANKING

Central Bank

Banque d'Algérie: Immeuble Joly, 38 ave Franklin Roosevelt, 16000 Algiers; tel. (21) 23-00-23; fax (21) 23-03-71; e-mail ba@bank-of-algeria.dz; internet www.bank-of-algeria.dz; f. 1962 as Banque Centrale d'Algérie; present name adopted 1990; bank of issue; cap. 40m., res 74,367.5m. (March 2006); Gov. MUHAMMAD LAKSACI; 48 brs.

Nationalized Banks

Banque Al-Baraka d'Algérie: Haï Bouteldja Houidef, Villa 1, Ben Aknoun, Algiers; tel. (21) 91-64-50; fax (21) 91-64-57; e-mail info@albaraka-bank.com; internet www.albaraka-bank.com; f. 1991; Algeria's first Islamic financial institution; owned by the Saudi Arabia-based Al-Baraka Investment and Devt Co (56%) and the local Banque de l'Agriculture et du Développement Rural (44%); cap. 10,000m., res 1,011m., dep. 76,554m. (Dec. 2009); Chair. ADNANE AHMAD YOUCEF; Gen. Man. HAFID MUHAMMAD SEDDIK; 8 brs.

Banque Extérieure d'Algérie (BEA): 48 rue des Trois Frères Bouadou, Bir Mourad Raïs, Algiers; tel. (21) 44-90-25; fax (21) 56-17-40; e-mail dircom@bea.dz; internet www.bea.dz; f. 1967; chiefly concerned with energy and maritime transport sectors; cap. 24,500m., res 44,744m., dep. 2,169,098m. (Dec. 2008); Pres. and Dir-Gen. MUHAMMAD LOUKAL; 80 domestic brs, 1 abroad.

Banque du Maghreb Arabe pour l'Investissement et le Commerce (BAMIC): 7 rue Dubois, Hydra, Algiers; tel. (21) 69-45-43; fax (21) 60-19-54; e-mail bamic@bamic-dz.com; internet www.bamic-dz.com; f. 1988; owned by Libyan Arab Foreign Bank (50%) and by Banque Extérieure d'Algérie, Banque Nationale d'Algérie, Banque de l'Agriculture et du Développement Rural and Crédit Populaire d'Algérie (12.5% each); cap. 50m., res 16.2m. (Dec. 2005); Pres. MUHAMMAD DJELLAB; Dir-Gen. IBRAHIM AL-BISHARY.

Crédit Populaire d'Algérie (CPA): BP 411, 2 blvd Col Amirouche, 16000 Algiers; tel. (21) 63-57-05; fax (21) 63-57-13; e-mail info@cpa-bank.com; internet www.cpa-bank.dz; f. 1966; specializes in light industry, construction and tourism; cap. and res 28,002m., total assets 367,847m. (Dec. 2002); Pres. and Dir-Gen. MUHAMMAD DJELLAB; 128 brs.

Development Banks

Banque de l'Agriculture et du Développement Rural (BADR): BP 484, 17 blvd Col Amirouche, 16000 Algiers; tel. (21) 63-49-22; fax (21) 63-51-46; e-mail dcm@badr-bank.net; internet www.badr-bank.net; f. 1982; wholly state-owned; finance for the agricultural sector; cap. 33,000m., res 1,995m., dep. 470,386m. (Dec. 2004); Pres. and Dir-Gen. BOUALEM DJEBBAR; 270 brs.

Banque Algérienne de Développement (BAD): 21 blvd Zighout Youcef, Algiers; tel. (21) 73-99-04; e-mail bad@ist.cerist.dz; f. 1963; a public establishment with fiscal sovereignty; aims to contribute to Algerian economic devt through long-term investment programmes; cap. and res 7,125.4m., total assets 132,842.3m. (Dec. 2003); Dir-Gen. SADEK ALILAT; 4 brs.

Banque de Développement Local (BDL): 5 rue Gaci Amar, Staouéli, 16000 Algiers; tel. (21) 39-28-58; fax (21) 39-37-57; e-mail clientele@bdl.dz; internet www.bdl.dz; f. 1985; regional devt bank; cap. 15,800m., res 11,026m., dep. 231,417m. (Dec. 2009); CEO MUHAMMAD ARSLANE BACHTARZI; 15 brs.

Caisse Nationale d'Epargne et de Prévoyance (CNEP-Banque): 42 rue Khélifa Boukhalfa, Algiers; tel. (21) 71-33-53; fax (21) 71-70-22; e-mail infos@cnepbanque.dz; internet www.cnepbanque.dz; f. 1964; savings and housing bank; cap. and res 22.6m., total assets 443,239.6m. (Dec. 2001); Pres. and Dir-Gen. DJAMEL BESSA.

Private Banks

Algeria Gulf Bank: BP 26, route de Chérage, Dély Ibrahim, Algiers; tel. (21) 91-00-31; fax (21) 91-02-37; e-mail agbank_dz@hotmail.com; internet www.ag-bank.com; f. 2004; owned by United Gulf Bank, Bahrain (60%), Tunis Int. Bank (30%) and Jordan Kuwait Bank (10%); Pres. ABDELKRIM AL-KABARITY; Man. Dir MUHAMMAD LOUAB.

Arab Banking Corporation (Algeria): BP 367, 54 ave des Trois Frères Bouadou, Algiers; tel. (21) 54-15-37; fax (21) 54-16-04; e-mail abc.general_management@arabbanking.com.dz; internet www.arabbanking.dz; f. 1998; cap. 2,670m., res 1,391m., dep. 21,737m. (Dec. 2008); Chair. Dr SHOKRI MUHAMMAD ABDEL SALAM; Dir-Gen. AHMED REDHA KARA-TERK.

Arab Leasing Corpn: BP 74, chemin Ahmed Ouaked, Dély Brahim, Algiers; tel. (21) 91-77-72; fax (21) 91-76-72; e-mail aleasinggroup@yahoo.fr; internet www.arableasing-dz.com; f. 2001; owned by Arab Banking Corpn (34%), The Arab Investment Co (25%), CNEP (20%) and other small shareholders; cap. and res 758m., total assets 801.6m. (Dec. 2002); Dir-Gen. ABDERREZAK TRABELSI.

BNP Paribas El-Djazair: 8 rue de Cirta, 16405 Hydra, Algiers; tel. (21) 60-39-42; fax (21) 60-39-29; e-mail mounir.belaidene@bnpparibas.com; internet www.algerie.bnpparibas.com; f. 2001; cap. and res 2,125.1m., total assets 22,090.3m. (Dec. 2004); Chair. MICHEL PEBEREAU; Man. Dir LAURENT DUPUCH.

Trust Bank Algeria: 70 chemin Larbi Allik, Hydra, Algiers; tel. (21) 54-97-55; fax (21) 54-97-50; e-mail direction@trust-bank-algeria.com; internet www.trust-bank-algeria.com; f. 2002; Dir-Gen. REIDH SLIMANE TALEB; 3 brs.

Banking Association

Association des banques et des établissements financiers (ABEF): 03 chemin Romain, Val d'Hydra, el-Biar, Algiers; tel. (21) 91-55-77; fax (21) 91-56-08; e-mail abenkhalfa@gmail.com; f. 1995; serves and promotes the interests of banks and financial institutions in Algeria; Del.-Gen. ABDERRAHMANE BENKHALFA.

STOCK EXCHANGE

Bourse d'Alger (Algiers Stock Exchange): 27 blvd Col Amirouche, 16000 Algiers; tel. and fax (21) 63-47-99; e-mail sgbv-email@sgbv.dz; internet www.sgbv.dz; f. 1999; Pres. MILOUD GHOLLAM; Dir-Gen. MUSTAPHA FERFERA.

Commission d'Organisation et de Surveillance des Opérations de Bourse (COSOB): 17 Campagne Chkiken, 16045 Hydra, Algiers; tel. and fax (21) 59-10-13; e-mail contact@cosob.org; internet www.cosob.org; f. 1993; Pres. ALI SADMI.

INSURANCE

The insurance sector is dominated by the state; however, in 1997 regulations were drafted to permit private companies to enter the Algerian insurance market.

L'Algérienne des Assurances (2a): 1 rue de Tripoli, Hussein-Dey, Algiers; tel. (21) 47-68-72; fax (21) 47-65-78; e-mail info@assurances-2a.com; internet www.assurances-2a.com; f. 1999; general; Pres. ABDELWAHAB RAHIM; Dir-Gen. TAHAR BALA.

Caisse Nationale de Mutualité Agricole (CNMA): 24 blvd Victor Hugo, Algiers; tel. (21) 74-33-28; fax (21) 73-34-79; e-mail cnma@cnma.dz; internet www.cnma.dz; f. 1972; Dir-Gen. KAMEL ARBA; 62 brs.

Cie Algérienne d'Assurances (CAAT): 52 rue des Frères Bouaddou, Bir Mourad Raïs, Algiers; tel. (21) 44-90-75; fax (21) 44-92-03; e-mail info@caat.dz; internet www.caat.dz; f. 1985; general; majority state ownership; Pres. and Dir-Gen. ABDELKRIM DJAFRI.

Cie Algérienne d'Assurance et de Réassurance (CAAR): 48 rue Didouche Mourad, 16000 Algiers; tel. (21) 63-20-72; fax (21) 63-13-77; e-mail caaralg@caar.com.dz; internet www.caar.com.dz; f. 1963 as a public corpn; partial privatization pending; Pres. and Dir-Gen. BRAHIM DJAMEL KASSALI.

Cie Centrale de Réassurance (CCR): Lot Saïd Hamdine, Bir Mourad Raïs, 16012 Algiers; tel. (21) 54-70-33; fax (21) 54-75-06; e-mail contact@ccr.dz; internet www.ccr.dz; f. 1973; general; Pres. and Dir-Gen. HADJ MUHAMMAD SEBA.

Société Nationale d'Assurances (SAA): 5 blvd Ernesto Ché Guévara, Algiers; tel. (21) 71-47-60; fax (21) 71-22-16; internet www.saa.dz; f. 1963; state-sponsored co; Pres. and Dir-Gen. AMARA LATROUS.

Trust Algeria Assurances-Réassurance: 70 chemin Larbi Allik, 16405 Hydra, Algiers; tel. (21) 54-88-00; fax (21) 54-71-36; e-mail secretariat@trustalgerians.com; f. 1987; 60% owned by Trust Insurance Co (Bahrain), 17.5% owned by CAAR; Pres. and Dir-Gen. ABD AL-SALAM ABU NAHL.

Trade and Industry

GOVERNMENT AGENCIES AND DEVELOPMENT ORGANIZATIONS

Agence Algérienne de Promotion du Commerce Extérieur (ALGEX): 5 rue Nationale, Algiers; tel. (21) 52-12-10; fax (21) 52-11-26; e-mail info@algex.dz; internet www.algex.dz; f. 2004; Dir-Gen. MUHAMMAD BENNINI.

Agence Nationale de l'Aménagement du Territoire (ANAT): 30 ave Muhammad Fellah, Kouba, Algiers; tel. (21) 68-78-16; fax (21) 68-85-03; e-mail anat@anat.dz; f. 1980; Dir-Gen. MUHAMMAD MEKKAOUI.

Agence Nationale de Développement de l'Investissement (ANDI): 27 rue Muhammad Merbouche, Hussein-Dey, Algiers; tel. (21) 77-32-62; fax (21) 77-32-57; e-mail dg@andi.dz; internet www.andi.dz; Dir-Gen. ABDELKARIM MANSOURI.

Institut National de la Productivité et du Développement Industriel (INPED): 35000 Boumerdès; tel. (24) 81-77-50; fax (24) 81-59-14; e-mail dg@inped.edu.dz; internet www.inped.edu.dz; f. 1967; Dir-Gen. ABDERRAHMANE MOUFEK.

Office National de Recherche Géologique et Minière (ORGM): BP 102, Cité Ibn Khaldoun, 35000 Boumerdès; tel. (24) 81-75-99; fax (24) 81-83-79; e-mail orgm-dg@orgm.com.dz; f. 1992; mining, cartography, geophysical exploration; Dir-Gen. ESSAID AOULI.

CHAMBERS OF COMMERCE

Chambre Algérienne de Commerce et d'Industrie (CACI): BP 100, Palais Consulaire, 6 blvd Amilcar Cabral, place des Martyres, 16003 Algiers; tel. (21) 96-77-77; fax (21) 96-70-70; e-mail infos@caci.dz; internet www.caci.dz; f. 1980; Pres. TAHER KELLIL; Dir-Gen. YAHIA SAHRAOUI.

Chambre Française de Commerce et d'Industrie en Algérie (CFCIA): Villa Clarac, 3 rue des Cèdres, 16070 el-Mouradia, Algiers; tel. (21) 48-08-00; fax (21) 60-95-09; e-mail jf.heugas@cfcia.org; internet www.cfcia.org; f. 1975; c. 24,500 mems; Pres. JEAN MARIE PINEL.

INDUSTRIAL ASSOCIATIONS

Centre d'Etudes et de Services Technologiques de l'Industrie des Matériaux de Construction (CETIM): BP 93, Cité Ibn Khaldoun, 35000 Boumerdès; tel. (24) 81-99-72; fax (24) 81-72-97; e-mail contact@cetim-dz.com; f. 1982; CEO ABDENNOUR ADJTOUTAH.

Institut National Algérien de la Propriété Industrielle (INAPI): 42 rue Larbi Ben M'hidi, 16000 Algiers; tel. (21) 73-01-42; fax (21) 73-55-81; e-mail info@inapi.org; internet www.inapi.org; f. 1973; Dir-Gen. NABILA KADRI.

Institut National des Industries Manufacturières (INIM): 35000 Boumerdès; tel. (21) 81-62-71; fax (21) 82-56-62; f. 1973; Dir-Gen. YOUSUF OUSLIMANI.

STATE TRADING ORGANIZATIONS

Since 1970 all international trading has been carried out by state organizations, of which the following are the most important:

Entreprise Nationale d'Approvisionnement en Outillage et Produits de Quincaillerie Générale (ENAOQ): 5 rue Amar Semaous, Hussein-Dey, Algiers; tel. (21) 23-31-83; fax (21) 47-83-33; tools and general hardware; Dir-Gen. SMATI BAHIDJ FARID.

Entreprise Nationale de Produits Alimentaires (ENAPAL): 29 rue Larbi Ben M'hidi, Algiers; tel. (21) 76-10-11; f. 1983; monopoly of import, export and bulk trade in basic foodstuffs; brs in more than 40 towns; Chair. LAÏD SABRI; Man. Dir BRAHIM DOUAOURI.

Office Algérien Interprofessionnel des Céréales (OAIC): 5 rue Ferhat-Boussaad, Algiers; tel. (21) 23-73-04; fax (21) 23-70-83; e-mail oaic@ist.cerist.dz; f. 1962; responsible for the regulation, distribution and control of the national market and the importation of cereals and vegetables; Dir-Gen. MUHAMMAD KACEM.

Office National de Commercialisation des Produits Viti-Vinicoles (ONCV): 112 Quai Sud, Algiers; tel. (21) 73-82-59; fax (21) 73-72-97; e-mail info@oncv-dz.com; internet www.oncv-groupe.com; f. 1968; monopoly of importing and exporting products of the wine industry; Man. Dir MAJID AMZIANI.

Société des Emballages Fer Blanc et Fûts (EMB-FBF): BP 245, Kouba, route de Baraki, Gué de Constantine, Algiers; tel. (21) 83-94-23; fax (21) 83-05-29; e-mail info@emb-fbf.com; internet www.emb-fbf.com; Dir-Gen. HAMID ZITOUN.

UTILITIES

Regulatory Authority

Commission de Régulation de l'Electricité et du Gaz (CREG): Immeuble du Ministère de l'Energie et des Mines, Tour B, Val d'Hydra, Algiers; tel. (21) 48-81-48; fax (21) 48-84-00; e-mail contact@creg.mem.gov.dz; internet www.creg.gov.dz; f. 2005; Pres. NADJIB OTMANE.

Electricity and Gas

Linde Gas Algérie SpA (GI): BP 247, 23 ave de l'ALN, Hussein-Dey, Kouba, Algiers; tel. (21) 49-85-99; fax (21) 49-71-94; internet www.gaz-industriels.com.dz; f. 1972 as Entreprise Nationale des Gaz Industriels; production, distribution and commercialization of industrial and medical gas; Pres. and Dir-Gen. LAHOCINE BOUCHERIT.

Société Algérienne de l'Electricité et du Gaz (Sonelgaz SpA): 2 blvd Col Krim Belkacem, Algiers; tel. (21) 72-31-00; fax (21) 71-26-90; e-mail n.boutarfa@sonelgaz.dz; internet www.sonelgaz.dz; f. 1969; production, distribution and transportation of electricity and transportation and distribution of natural gas; Chair. and CEO NOUREDDINE BOUTARFA.

Société de Travaux d'Electrification (KAHRIF): Villa Nour, Aïn d'Heb, Médéa; tel. (25) 58-51-67; fax (25) 61-31-14; e-mail hadjeb.mohamed@kahrif.com; internet www.kahrif.com; f. 1982; planning and maintenance of electrical infrastructure; Pres. and Dir-Gen. MUHAMMAD HADJEB.

Water

L'Algérienne des Eaux (ADE): BP 548, 3 rue du Caire, Kouba, 16016 Algiers; tel. (21) 28-28-07; fax (21) 28-10-06; internet www.ade.dz; f. 1985 as Agence Nationale de l'Eau Potable et Industrielle et de l'Assainissement; state-owned co; Dir-Gen. ABDELKRIM MECHIA.

STATE HYDROCARBONS AGENCIES AND COMPANIES

Agence Nationale pour la Valorisation des Ressources en Hydrocarbures (Alnaft): Ministère de l'Energie et des Mines, Tour B, Val d'Hydra, Algiers; tel. (21) 48-82-67; fax (21) 48-82-76; e-mail firstender-alnaft@alnaft.mem.gov.dz; f. 2005; Dir SID ALI BETATA.

Autorité de Régulation des Hydrocarbures (ARH): Ministère de l'Energie et des Mines, Tour B, Val d'Hydra, Algiers; tel. (21) 48-81-67; fax (21) 48-83-15; e-mail arh@arh.mem.gov.dz; internet www.arh.gov.dz; f. 2005; Dir NOUREDDINE CHEROUATI.

Société Nationale pour la Recherche, la Production, le Transport, la Transformation et la Commercialisation des Hydrocarbures (Sonatrach): Djenane el-Malik, Hydra, Algiers; tel. (21) 54-70-00; fax (21) 54-77-00; e-mail sonatrach@sonatrach.dz; internet www.sonatrach-dz.com; f. 1963; exploration, exploitation, transport and marketing of petroleum, natural gas and their products; Pres. and Dir-Gen. ABDELHAMID ZERGUINE; Gen. Sec. ABDELMALEK ZITOUNI.

The following companies are wholly owned subsidiaries of Sonatrach:

Entreprise Nationale de Canalisation (ENAC): 132 rue Tripoli, Algiers; tel. (21) 77-04-63; fax (21) 53-85-53; internet www.enac-dz.com; piping; Vice-Pres. HOCINE CHEKIRED.

Entreprise Nationale de Forage (ENAFOR): BP 211, Hassi Messaoud, W. Ouargla; tel. (29) 73-81-85; fax (29) 73-21-70; e-mail zoubir@enafor.dz; internet www.enafor.dz; f. 1981; drilling; CEO ABDELKADER ZOUBIRI.

Entreprise Nationale de Géophysique (ENAGEO): BP 140, 30500 Hassi Messaoud, Ouargla; tel. (29) 73-77-00; fax (29) 73-72-12; e-mail engeoh1@wissal.dz; internet www.enageo.com; f. 1981; seismic acquisition, geophysics; Dir-Gen. RÉDA RAHAL.

Entreprise Nationale des Grands Travaux Pétroliers (ENGTP): BP 09, Zone Industrielle, Reghaïa, Boumerdès; tel. (21) 84-86-26; fax (21) 84-80-34; e-mail engtpcommunication@engtp.com; internet www.engtp.com; f. 1980; major industrial projects; Dir-Gen. MUHAMMAD SEGHIR LAOUISSI.

Société Nationale de la Pétrochimie (ENIP): BP 215, Zone industrielle, 21000 Skikda; tel. (38) 74-52-94; fax (38) 74-52-80; e-mail inr@enip-dz.com; internet www.enip-dz.com; f. 1984; design and construction for petroleum-processing industry; Dir-Gen. N. KOURDACHE.

Entreprise Nationale des Services aux Puits (ENSP): BP 83, 30500 Hassi Messaoud, Ouargla; tel. (29) 73-73-33; e-mail info@enspgroup.com; internet www.enspgroup.com; f. 1981; oil-well services; Pres. and Dir-Gen. ABDELWAHAB OUBIRA.

Entreprise Nationale des Travaux aux Puits (ENTP): BP 206–207, Base du 20 août 1955, 30500 Hassi Messaoud, Ouargla; tel. (29) 73-88-50; fax (29) 73-84-06; e-mail contact@entp-dz.com; internet www.entp-dz.com; f. 1981; oil-well construction; Pres. and Dir-Gen. BACHIR BEN AMOR.

Société Nationale de Commercialisation et de Distribution des Produits Pétroliers (NAFTAL, SpA): BP 73, route des Dûnes, Chéraga, Algiers; tel. (21) 38-13-13; fax (21) 38-19-19; e-mail webmaster@naftal.dz; internet www.naftal.dz; f. 1987; international marketing and distribution of petroleum products; Pres. and Dir-Gen. SAÏD AKRETCHE.

Société Nationale de Génie Civil et Bâtiment (GCB, SpA): BP 110, blvd de l'ALN, Boumerdès-Ville; tel. (24) 41-41-50; fax (24) 81-38-80; e-mail contact@gcb.dz; internet www.gcb.dz; civil engineering.

TRADE UNIONS

Syndicat National des Journalistes (Algerian Journalists' Union): Maison de la presse Tahar Djaout, 1 rue Bachir Attar, place du 1er mai, 16016 Algiers; tel. and fax (21) 67-36-61; e-mail snjalgerie2006@yahoo.fr; f. 2001; Sec.-Gen. KAMEL AMARNI.

Union Générale des Entrepreneurs Algériens (UGEA): Villa 28, Quartier Aïn Soltane, les Oliviers, Birkhadem, Algiers; tel. and fax (21) 54-10-82; fax (21) 54–02–99; e-mail ugea_algerie@yahoo.fr; Pres. Dr ABDELMADJID DENNOUNI.

Union Générale des Travailleurs Algériens (UGTA): Maison du Peuple, place du 1er mai, Algiers; tel. (21) 65-07-36; e-mail sgeneral@ugta.dz; internet www.ugta.dz; f. 1956; there are 10 national 'professional sectors' affiliated to the UGTA; Sec.-Gen. ABDELMADJID SIDI SAÏD.

Union Nationale des Paysans Algériens (UNPA): f. 1973; 700,000 mems; Sec.-Gen. KAMEL ALIOUI.

Transport

RAILWAYS

Entreprise du Métro d'Alger (EMA): 170 rue Hassiba Ben Bouali, Algiers; tel. (21) 66-17-47; fax (21) 66-17-57; e-mail contact@metroalger-dz.com; internet metroalger-dz.com; initial 9-km section (10 stations) commenced operations Nov. 2011; construction of a second line currently underway, as well as extensions to line 1; Pres. and Dir-Gen. OMAR HADBI.

Infrafer (Entreprise Publique Economique de Réalisation des Infrastructures Ferroviaires): BP 208, 15 rue Col Amirouche, 35300 Rouiba; tel. (21) 85-67-02; fax (21) 85-49-62; e-mail info@infrafer.com; internet www.infrafer.com; f. 1986; responsible for construction and maintenance of track; Dir-Gen. ABDERAHMANE AKTOUF.

Société Nationale des Transports Ferroviaires (SNTF): 21–23 blvd Muhammad V, Algiers; tel. (21) 71-15-10; fax (21) 63-32-98; e-mail dg-sntf@sntf.dz; internet www.sntf.dz; f. 1976 to replace Société Nationale des Chemins de Fer Algériens; 5,090 km of track, of which 289 km are electrified; daily passenger services from Algiers to the principal provincial cities and services to Tunisia and Morocco; Dir-Gen. OMAR BENAMEUR.

ROADS

In 2008 there were an estimated 111,261 km of roads and tracks; some 73.5% of the road network was paved. The French administration built a good road system (partly for military purposes), which, since independence, has been allowed to deteriorate in places. New roads have been built linking the Sahara oilfields with the coast, and the Trans-Sahara highway is a major project. Construction of the 1,216-km East–West motorway, linking el-Tarf with Tlemcen, at an estimated cost of more than US $11,000m., was scheduled for completion by the end of 2010. Progress was subsequently delayed. By early 2012 around 1,000 km of the route was open to traffic, although it was reported that the remaining sections would not open until 2013.

Agence Nationale des Autoroutes (ANA): BP 72M Mohammadia, El Harrach, Algiers; tel. (21) 53-09-63; fax (21) 53-09-62; e-mail dgana@ana.org.dz; internet www.ana.org.dz; f. 2005 to manage the construction and maintenance of the motorway network; Dir-Gen. MUHAMMAD ZIANI.

Société Nationale des Transports Routiers (SNTR): 27 rue des Trois Frères Bouadou, Bir Mourad Raïs, Algiers; tel. (21) 54-06-00; fax (21) 54-05-35; e-mail dg-sntr@sntr-groupe.com; internet www.sntr-groupe.com; f. 1967; goods transport by road; maintainance of industrial vehicles; Pres. and Dir-Gen. ABDELLAH BENMAÂROUF.

Société Nationale des Transports des Voyageurs (SNTV): Algiers; tel. (21) 66-00-52; f. 1967; long-distance passenger transport by road; Man. Dir MUHAMMAD DIB.

SHIPPING

Algiers is the main port, with anchorage of between 23 m and 29 m in the Bay of Algiers, and anchorage for the largest vessels in Agha Bay. The port has a total quay length of 8,380 m. In November 2008 United Arab Emirates-based DP World signed a 30-year contract with the Algerian Government to manage and redevelop the ports at Algiers and Djen-Djen. The proposed redevelopment at Algiers port included an expansion of capacity from 500,000 20-ft equivalent units (TEUs) to 800,000 TEUs. DP World officially commenced operations at Algiers in March 2009 and at Djen-Djen in June. There are also important ports at Annaba, Arzew, Béjaïa, Djidjelli, Ghazaouet, Mostaganem, Oran, Skikda and Ténès. Petroleum and liquefied gas are exported through Arzew, Béjaïa and Skikda. Algerian crude petroleum is also exported through the Tunisian port of La Skhirra. In December 2009 Algeria's merchant fleet totalled 130 vessels, with an aggregate displacement of 767,939 grt.

Port Authorities

Entreprise Portuaire d'Alger (EPAL): BP 259, 2 rue d'Angkor, Alger-Gare, Algiers; tel. (21) 42-36-14; fax (21) 42-36-03; e-mail epal@portalger.com.dz; internet www.portalger.com.dz; f. 1982; responsible for management and growth of port facilities and sea pilotage; Dir-Gen. ABDELAZIZ GUERRAH.

Entreprise Portuaire d'Annaba (EPAN): BP 1232, Môle Cigogne, quai Nord, 23000 Annaba; tel. (38) 86-31-31; fax (38) 86-54-15; e-mail epan@annaba-port.com; internet www.annaba-port.com; Pres. and Dir-Gen. DJILANI SALHI.

Entreprise Portuaire d'Arzew (EPA): BP 46, 7 rue Larbi Tebessi, 31200 Arzew; tel. and fax (41) 47-21-27; e-mail contact@arzew-ports.com; internet www.arzewports.com; Pres. and Dir-Gen. NOUREDDINE HADJIOUI.

Entreprise Portuaire de Béjaïa (EPB): BP 94, 13 ave des frères Amrani, 06000 Béjaïa; tel. (34) 21-18-07; fax (34) 20-14-88; e-mail portbj@portdebejaia.dz; internet www.portdebejaia.dz; Dir-Gen. DJELLOUL ACHOUR.

Entreprise Portuaire de Djen-Djen (EPJ): BP 87, El Achouat Taher-Wilaya de JIJEL, 18000 Jijel; tel. (34) 44-21-64; fax (34) 44-21-60; e-mail contact@djendjen-port.com; internet www.djendjen-port.com; f. 1984; Pres. and Dir-Gen. ABDERREZAK SELLAMI.

Entreprise Portuaire de Ghazaouet (EPG): BP 217, Wilaya de Tlemcen, 13400 Ghazaouet; tel. (43) 32-32-37; fax (43) 32-32-55; e-mail contact@portdeghazaouet.com; internet www.portdeghazaouet.com; f. 1982; Pres. and Dir-Gen. BRAHIM ABDELMALEK.

Entreprise Portuaire de Mostaganem (EPM): BP 131, quai du Maghreb, 27000 Mostaganem; tel. (45) 21-14-11; fax (45) 21-78-05; e-mail epm@port-mostaganem.dz; internet www.port-mostaganem.dz; Pres. and Dir-Gen. MOKHTAR CHERIF.

Entreprise Portuaire d'Oran (EPO): 1 rue du 20 août, 31000 Oran; tel. (41) 33-24-49; fax (41) 33-24-98; e-mail pdg@port-oran.dz; internet www.port-oran.dz; Dir-Gen. MUHAMMAD BOUTOUIL (acting).

Entreprise Portuaire de Skikda (EPS): BP 65, 46 ave Rezki Rahal, 21000 Skikda; tel. (38) 75-68-50; fax (38) 75-20-15; e-mail epskikda@skikda-port.com; internet www.skikda-port.com; Man. Dir LAÏDI LEMRABET.

Entreprise Portuaire de Ténès (EPT): BP 18, Wilaya de Chlef, 02200 Ténès; tel. (27) 76-61-96; fax (27) 76-61-77; e-mail porttenes@yahoo.fr; Man. Dir ALI ASSENOUNI.

Principal Shipping Companies

Cie Algéro-Libyenne de Transport Maritime (CALTRAM): 19 rue des Trois Frères Bouadou, Bir Mourad Raïs, Algiers; tel. (21) 54-17-00; fax (21) 54-21-04; e-mail caltram@wissal.dz; f. 1974; Man. Dir A. KERAMANE.

Cie Nationale de Navigation (CNAN Group): BP 280, 2 quai no 9, Nouvelle Gare Maritime, Algiers; tel. (21) 42-33-89; fax (21) 42-31-28; f. 2003 as part of restructuring of the Société Nationale de Transports Maritimes/Compagnie Nationale Algérienne de Navigation (SNTM/CNAN); state-owned; fleet of 12 freight ships; includes CNAN Maghreb Lines; rep. offices in Marseille (France) and La Spezia (Italy), and rep. agencies in Antwerp (Belgium), Barcelona (Spain), Hamburg (Germany) and the principal ports in many other countries; Dir-Gen. ALI BOUMBAR.

Entreprise Nationale de Réparation Navale (ERENAV): quai no 12, Algiers; tel. (21) 42-37-83; fax (21) 42-30-39; e-mail azzedine.bourouga@erenav.com; f. 1987; ship repairs; Pres. and Dir-Gen. A. BOUROUGA.

Entreprise Nationale de Transport Maritime de Voyageurs—Algérie Ferries (ENTMV): BP 467, 5–6 rue Jawharlal Nehru, 16001 Algiers; tel. (21) 42-46-50; fax (21) 42-98-74; e-mail entmv@algerieferries.com; internet www.algerieferries.com; f. 1987 as part of restructuring of SNTM-CNAN; responsible for passenger transport; operates car ferry services between Algiers, Annaba, Skikda, Alicante (Spain), Marseille (France) and Oran; Dir-Gen. AHCÈNE GRAÏRIA.

HYPROC Shipping Co (HYPROC SC): BP 7200, Zone des Sièges 'ZHUN-USTO', el-Seddikia, 31025 Oran; tel. (41) 42-62-62; fax (41) 42-32-75; e-mail hyproc@hyproc.com; internet www.hyproc.com; f. 1982 as Société Nationale de Transports Maritimes des Hydrocarbures et des Produits Chimiques; name changed as above in 2003; wholly owned subsidiary of Sonatrach; Pres. and Dir-Gen. MOSTEFA MUHAMMADI.

Société Générale Maritime (GEMA): BP 368, 2 rue Jawharlal Nehru, 16100 Algiers; tel. (21) 74-73-00; fax (21) 74-76-73; e-mail gemadg@gema-groupe.com; internet www.gema-groupe.com; f. 1987 as part of restructuring of SNTM/CNAN; shipping, ship-handling and forwarding; Pres. and Dir-Gen. ALI LARBI CHÉRIF.

CIVIL AVIATION

Algeria's principal international airport, Houari Boumedienne, is situated 20 km from Algiers. Other international airports are situated at Constantine, Annaba, Tlemcen and Oran. There are, in addition, 65 aerodromes, of which 20 are public, and a further 135 airstrips connected with the petroleum industry.

Air Algérie (Entreprise Nationale d'Exploitation des Services Aériens): BP 858, 1 place Maurice Audin, Immeuble el-Djazair, Algiers; tel. (21) 74-24-28; fax (21) 61-05-53; e-mail contacts@airalgerie.dz; internet www.airalgerie.dz; f. 1953 by merger; state-owned from 1972; privatization pending; internal services and extensive services to Europe, North and West Africa, and the Middle East; flies to more than 70 destinations; Dir-Gen. and CEO MUHAMMAD SALAH BOULTIF.

Tassili Airlines: BP 301, blvd Mustapha Ben Boulaïd, 30500 Hassi Messaoud; tel. (29) 73-80-25; fax (29) 73-84-24; internet www.tassiliairlines.dz; f. 1997; wholly owned by Sonatrach; domestic passenger services; Chair. and Man. Dir FAIÇAL KHELIL.

Tourism

Algeria's tourist attractions include the Mediterranean coast, the Atlas mountains and the Sahara desert. In 2008 there were a total of 1,771,749 visitors to Algeria (including 1,215,052 Algerian nationals resident abroad). Receipts from tourism totalled US $325m. in 2008. It was announced in early 2007 that the Government was investing some $1,000m. in the tourism sector; the construction of 42 new resorts was scheduled to be completed by 2015.

Agence Nationale de Développement Touristique (ANDT): BP 78, Sidi Fredj Staoueli, Algiers; tourism promotion; Dir-Gen. NOUREDDINE NEDRI.

Office National du Tourisme (ONT): 2 rue Ismail Kerrar, 16000 Algiers; tel. (21) 43-80-60; fax (21) 43-80-59; e-mail ont@ont-dz.org; internet www.ont-dz.org; f. 1988; state institution; oversees tourism promotion policy; Dir-Gen. HADJ SAÏD MUHAMMAD AMINE.

ONAT (Entreprise Nationale Algérienne de Tourisme): 126 bis A, rue Didouche Mourad, 16000 Algiers; tel. (21) 74-44-48; fax (21) 74-32-14; e-mail direction-marketing@onat-dz.com; internet www.onatalgerie.com; f. 1983; Pres. and Dir-Gen. SELATNIA MUHAMMAD CHÉRIF.

Touring Club d'Algérie (TCA): 30 rue Hassène Benaâmane, Les Vergers, Bir Mourad Raïs, Algiers; tel. (21) 54-13-13; fax (21) 54-15-11; e-mail sg_touring@algeriatouring.dz; internet www.algeriatouring.dz; f. 1963; Pres. ABDERRAHMANE ABDEDAÏM.

Touring Voyages Algérie: Centre commercial 'el-Hammadia', Bouzaréah, Algiers; tel. (21) 54-13-13; fax (21) 94-26-87; e-mail contact@touring-algerie.com; internet www.touringvoyagesalgerie.dz; f. 1995 to manage the commercial activities of Touring Club d'Algérie; 89% owned by Touring Club d'Algérie; Pres. and Dir-Gen. TAHAR SAHRI.

Defence

Chief of Staff of the People's National Army: Lt-Gen. AHMED GAID SALAH.

Commander of the Land Force: Maj.-Gen. AHCÈNE TAFER.

Commander of the Air Force: Maj.-Gen. ABDELKADER LOUNES.

Commander of the Naval Forces: Maj.-Gen. MALEK NECIB.

Commander of the Territory Air Defence Forces: Maj.-Gen. AMAR AMRANI.

Commander of the National Gendarmerie: Maj.-Gen. AHMED BOUSTEILA.

Commander of the Republican Guard: Maj.-Gen. AHMED MOULAY MILIANI.

Defence Budget (2011): AD 631,000m.

Military Service: 18 months (army only).

Total Armed Forces (as assessed at November 2011): 130,000: army 110,000 (75,000 conscripts); navy est. 6,000; air force 14,000. Reserves 150,000.

Paramilitary Forces (as assessed at November 2011): est. 187,200 (National Security Forces 16,000; Republican Guards 1,200; an est. 150,000 self-defence militia and communal guards and a gendarmerie of 20,000).

Education

Education, in the national language (Arabic), is officially compulsory for a period of nine years, for children between six and 15 years of age. Primary education begins at the age of six and lasts for five years. Secondary education begins at 11 years of age and lasts for up to seven years, comprising first cycle of four years and a second of three years. In 2008/09 the total enrolment at primary schools included 94% of children in the relevant age-group. The comparable ratio for secondary enrolment in 2008/09 was equivalent to 96% of students in the relevant age-group. In 2007 10.7% of capital expenditure (some AD 126,100m.) was allocated to education and professional training by the central Government.

There were some 137,803 pupils at pre-primary schools in 2007/08, while in 2009/10 3,312,440 pupils attended primary schools (compared with about 800,000 in 1962). In 2008/09 some 4,585,189 pupils attended secondary schools. Most education at primary level is in Arabic, but at higher levels French is still widely used. In mid-2003 the Government agreed to permit the use of the Berber language, Tamazight, as a language of instruction in Algerian schools. The majority of foreign teachers in Algeria come from Egypt, Syria, Tunisia and other Arab countries.

In 2008/09 the number of students receiving higher education (including post-graduate) was 1,149,666. In addition to the 27 main universities, there are 16 other *centres universitaires* and a number of technical colleges. Several thousand students go abroad to study. Efforts have been made to combat adult illiteracy by means of a large-scale campaign in which instruction is sometimes given by young people who have only recently left school, and in which the broadcasting services are widely used.

ANDORRA

Introductory Survey

LOCATION, CLIMATE, LANGUAGE, RELIGION, FLAG, CAPITAL

The Principality of Andorra lies in the eastern Pyrenees, bounded by France and Spain, and is situated roughly midway between Barcelona and Toulouse. The climate is alpine, with frequent snow in winter and a warm summer. The average minimum temperature is −2°C (28°F), while the average maximum temperature is 24°C (76°F), although temperatures vary significantly between low-lying and mountainous regions. Average annual precipitation is between 700 mm and 1,100 mm. The official language is Catalan, but French and Spanish are also widely spoken. Most of the inhabitants profess Christianity and more than 90% are Roman Catholics. The civil flag (proportions 2 by 3) has three equal vertical stripes, of blue, yellow and red. The state flag has, in addition, the state coat of arms (a quartered shield above the motto *Virtus unita fortior*) in the centre of the yellow stripe. The capital is Andorra la Vella.

CONTEMPORARY POLITICAL HISTORY

Historical Context

Andorra effectively gained its independence in 1278, when the Spanish Bishop of Urgell and the French Count of Foix settled their territorial dispute by agreeing to become joint overlords, or Co-Princes (Coprínceps). Sovereignty eventually passed from the Count of Foix to the King of France and, subsequently, to the President of the French Republic, but the system of government remained largely unchanged until 1993. Owing to the lack of distinction between the authority of the Co-Princes and the General Council (Consell General), founded in 1419, the Andorrans encountered many difficulties in their attempts to gain international status for their country and control over its essential services.

Until 1970 the franchise was granted only to third-generation Andorran males who were more than 25 years of age. Thereafter, women, persons aged between 21 and 25 years, and second-generation Andorrans were allowed to vote in elections to the General Council. In 1977 the franchise was extended to include all first-generation Andorrans of foreign parentage who were aged 28 years and over. The electorate remained small, however, when compared with the size of the population, and Andorra's foreign residents increased their demands for political and nationality rights.

Prior to 1993 political parties were not directly represented in the General Council, but there were loose groupings with liberal and conservative sympathies. The country's only political organization, the Partit Democràtic d'Andorra (PDA—Andorran Democratic Party), was technically illegal and in the 1981 elections to the General Council the party urged its supporters to cast blank votes.

Domestic Political Affairs

In 1980, during discussions on institutional reform, representatives of the Co-Princes and the General Council agreed that an executive council should be formed and that a referendum should be held on changes to the electoral system. In early 1981 the Co-Princes formally requested the General Council to prepare plans for reform, in accordance with these proposals. Following the December elections to the General Council, in January 1982 the new legislature elected Oscar Ribas Reig as Head of Government (Cap de Govern). Ribas appointed an executive of six ministers, who expressed their determination to provide Andorra with a written constitution. The formation of the Government (Govern) constituted the separation of powers between an executive and a legislature.

An economic downturn led to the introduction of income tax in August 1983, in an effort to alleviate Andorra's budgetary deficit and to provide the Government with extra revenue for development projects. Subsequent government proposals for indirect taxation encountered strong opposition from financial and tourism concerns, and prompted the Government's resignation in April 1984. Josep Pintat Solans, a local business executive, was elected unopposed by the General Council as Head of Government in May. At the December 1985 elections to the General Council the electorate was increased by about 27%, as a result of the newly introduced lower minimum voting age of 18 years. The Council re-elected Pintat as Head of Government in January 1986, when he won the support of 27 of its 28 members.

Further proposals for institutional reforms were approved by the General Council in October 1987. The transfer to the Andorran Government of responsibility for such matters as public order was proposed, while the authority of the Co-Princes in the administration of justice was recognized. The drafting of a constitution for Andorra was also envisaged. The implementation of the reforms was, however, dependent on the agreement of the Co-Princes. In April 1988 Andorra enacted legislation recognizing the Universal Declaration of Human Rights, adopted by the UN General Assembly in 1948.

Elections to the General Council took place in December 1989, following which the reformist Ribas was elected as Head of Government. In June the Council voted unanimously to establish a special commission to draft a constitution. The proposed document was to promulgate popular sovereignty and to limit the role of the Co-Princes. In April 1991 representatives of the Co-Princes agreed to recognize popular sovereignty in Andorra and to permit the drafting of a constitution, which would be subject to approval by referendum. In September, however, Ribas was threatened with a vote of no confidence by traditionalist members of the Council, who were opposed to the proposed constitution, which would effectively legalize political parties and trade unions. There followed a period of political impasse, during which no official budget was authorized for the principality. In January 1992, following small, but unprecedented, public demonstrations in protest against the political deadlock, Ribas and the General Council resigned. The result of a general election, which took place in April, was inconclusive, necessitating a second round of voting one week later, following which supporters of Ribas secured a narrow majority of the 28 seats. Accordingly, Ribas was re-elected as Head of Government.

At a referendum held in March 1993, in which 75.7% of the electorate participated, 74.2% of those who voted approved the draft Constitution. The document was signed by the Co-Princes in April, and was promulgated on 4 May. Under its provisions, the Co-Princes remained as Heads of State, but with greatly reduced powers, while Andorran nationals were afforded full sovereignty and (together with foreigners who had lived in Andorra for at least 20 years) were authorized to form and to join political parties and trade unions. The Constitution provided for the establishment of an independent judiciary and permitted the principality to formulate its own foreign policy and to join international organizations. The Co-Princes were to retain a right of veto over treaties with France and Spain that affected Andorra's borders or security.

The first general election under the terms of the new Constitution took place on 12 December 1993. One of the constitutional provisions was the implementation of a new system of partial proportional representation—one-half of the General Council's 28 members were directly elected from a single national constituency by a system of proportional representation, the remainder being elected by Andorra's seven parishes (two for each parish). Ribas's Agrupament Nacional Democràtic (AND—National Democratic Grouping), the successor to the PDA, won the largest number of seats, and in January 1994 Ribas was re-elected Head of Government. However, opposition to Ribas's proposed budget and tax legislation led in November to the adoption of a motion of no confidence in the Government. Ribas immediately submitted his resignation; Marc Forné Molné, the leader of the Unió Liberal (UL), was subsequently elected Head of Government.

Forné's Government lacked an overall majority in the General Council; however, the support of councillors from regional political organizations enabled the Government to adopt more than 30 bills between December 1994 and July 1996—including controversial legislation allowing certain foreign nationals to become 'nominal residents', for the purpose of avoiding taxation, on payment of an annual levy. After being censured twice in one year by the General Council, Forné was obliged to announce an early general election, which took place in February 1997. The UL won an overall majority, securing 18 seats, and in April Forné announced the formation of a new, expanded Government. The UL was subsequently renamed the Partit Liberal d'Andorra (PLA—Andorran Liberal Party). In 2000 the AND split into two parties—the Partit Socialdemòcrata (PS—Social Democratic Party) and the Partit Demòcrata (PD—Democratic Party).

Elections to the General Council took place in March 2001, when 81.6% of the registered electorate participated; however, the number of citizens eligible to vote represented only 20.7% of Andorra's total population. The PLA won 15 of the 28 seats, six seats were secured by the PS, the PD took five seats and the two remaining seats went to independent candidates. Forné was re-elected Head of Government by the General Council.

In May 2003 Joan Enric Vives i Sicília succeeded Joan Martí Alanis as the Bishop of Urgell and therefore as ex officio Episcopal Co-Prince of Andorra. In September 2004 the PLA selected the former Minister of Foreign Affairs, Albert Pintat Santolària, as its candidate for Head of Government in the forthcoming general election, following Forné's decision not to seek a new term of office. The PS signed a co-operation agreement in December 2004 with two other opposition parties, Renovació Democràtica (RD—Democratic Renewal) and the Grup d'Unió Parroquial Independents (GUPI—Group of United Parish Independents), to contest the forthcoming elections. Elections to the General Council took place on 24 April 2005; 80.4% of the electorate participated. The PLA won 14 seats, the PS secured 11, a coalition of two smaller centrist parties, the Centre Demòcrata Andorrà (CDA—Andorran Democratic Centre, the successor to the PD) and Segle 21 (21st Century) took two seats and the RD secured one seat. Albert Pintat, whose candidacy was supported by the PLA and one of the CDA/Segle 21 councillors, was elected Head of Government on 27 May. Since no party had won an absolute majority, the PLA began negotiations with the CDA/Segle 21 coalition on the formation of a government. However, as no agreement on the division of portfolios was reached, CDA/Segle 21 agreed to support only part of the PLA's programme.

As a result of the global financial crisis in 2008–09, international resolve to prevent tax evasion in the 'offshore' banking sector was strengthened. Many jurisdictions, including Andorra, which was listed by the Organisation for Economic Co-operation and Development (OECD, see p. 379) as an 'unco-operative tax haven', were subject to pressure from world leaders prior to the meeting of the Group of 20 leading industrialized and developing nations (G20) in London, United Kingdom, in April 2009. In March Andorra agreed to amend its secrecy laws to allow for greater transparency and to comply with OECD rules on the sharing of bank data to combat tax evasion. As a result, in May Andorra was removed from the OECD's list of 'unco-operative tax havens' (along with Liechtenstein and Monaco, the only two remaining countries listed).

At elections to the General Council held on 26 April 2009, the PS won 14 of the 28 seats, thus ending 14 years of dominance in the legislature by the PLA. The newly formed Coalició Reformista (Reformist Coalition), which was led by the PLA, won 11 seats and Andorra pel Canvi (ApC—Andorra for Change), which was supported by the RD, secured three; 75.3% of the electorate participated. The leader of the PS, Jaume Bartumeu Cassany, was elected Head of Government by the General Council in June. Bartumeu appointed a Government of six ministers (three fewer than the previous administration), which included Pere López Agràs as Minister of the Economy and Finance and Xavier Espot Miró, a politically independent diplomat, as Minister of Foreign Affairs and Institutional Relations. The new Government expressed its commitment to introducing new forms of taxation, and to accelerating the introduction of legislation to address banking secrecy. Accordingly, in September the General Council approved legislation allowing for the exchange of financial information with foreign jurisdictions, providing bilateral agreements for this purpose were in place. By November 2010 a total of 18 bilateral agreements had been concluded, and seven more were being negotiated.

In December 2009 the Government failed to gain the support of the ApC members of the General Council for the proposed budget for 2010, and was therefore obliged to operate using the equivalent of one-twelfth of the previous year's budgeted expenditure for each month. In October it was announced that, once again, the PS had not reached agreement with the ApC members of the legislature on adopting a budget for 2011: Bartumeu stated that, if no agreement could be reached on the budget, an early general election would take place in 2011, as the Constitution does not allow a Government to operate with an unapproved budget for two consecutive years. Also in October 2010 a new political party, the Partit Reformista d'Andorra (PRA—Reform Party of Andorra) was formed. In December the General Council adopted legislation introducing three new forms of direct taxation, comprising income tax for non-residents, a corporate tax and a tax on economic activities. Negotiations on a monetary agreement with the EU (which had begun in 2004, but came to a halt in 2006) were resumed in 2010, and an agreement was concluded on 10 February 2011 and signed on 30 June of that year. Under the agreement the euro was officially to become Andorra's currency and the country was to be permitted to mint its own coins from 2013.

The Government's failure, once again, to agree the budget, led Bartumeu, on 15 February 2011, to dissolve the General Council and to announce that elections would take place on 3 April 2011. A major cause of disagreement within the General Council had been the proposal by the PS to introduce income tax for residents, a policy which was opposed by every other major political group in Andorra. The opposition formed a centre-right alliance styled Demòcrates per Andorra (DA—Democrats for Andorra), replacing the former electoral alliance the Reformist Coalition, in order to contest the election. The DA led by Antoni Martí Petit, a former mayor of Escaldes, won a decisive victory at the election with 20 of the 28 seats in the legislature, while the PS took only six seats. The Unió Laurediana, a local conservative grouping allied to the DA, only contested one parish constituency, Sant Julià de Lòria, but secured both its seats. Some 74.1% of eligible voters participated in the election. Martí was inaugurated as Head of Government on 12 May. Prominent members of his executive council included Gilbert Saboya Sunyé, named as Minister of Foreign Affairs, Jordi Cinca Mateos as Minister of Finance and Public Service and Jordi Alcobé Font as Minister of Economy and Planning.

Foreign Affairs

Following the referendum of March 1993, Andorra formally applied for membership of the Council of Europe (see p. 256), gaining entry in October 1994. In June 1993 the Andorran Government signed a treaty of co-operation with France and Spain, which explicitly recognized the sovereignty of Andorra. In the following month Andorra became the 184th member of the UN. Andorra enjoys 'most favoured nation' status with the European Union (EU, see p. 276). In 2003 Forné announced plans for Andorra to join the EU within 15 years. In June 2004 the Charter of Fundamental Social Rights of Workers (commonly known as the Social Charter) of the EU was ratified by the General Council; however, certain articles of the Charter, relating to employment rights, were omitted. A co-operation agreement with the EU was signed in November and came into effect on 1 July 2005, together with an agreement on the taxation of savings income. A monetary agreement with the EU was concluded in February 2011 and signed on 30 June of that year.

CONSTITUTION AND GOVERNMENT

According to the Constitution promulgated in May 1993, Andorra is a parliamentary co-principality, in which the Co-Princes—the President of the French Republic and the Spanish Bishop of Urgell—serve jointly as head of state.

The General Council (Consell General) currently comprises 28 councillors (although the number can be between 28 and 42), who are elected by universal suffrage for a four-year period. Two councillors are directly elected by each of the seven parishes of Andorra, and the remainder are elected from a single national constituency by a system of proportional representation. At its opening session the Council elects as its head the Speaker (Síndic General) and the Deputy Speaker (Subsíndic General), who cease to be members of the Council on their election. The General Council elects the Head of Government (Cap de Govern), who, in turn, appoints ministers to the executive body, the Govern.

Andorra is divided into seven parishes, each of which is administered by a communal council. Communal councillors are elected for a four-year term by direct universal suffrage. At its opening session each communal council elects two consuls, who preside over it.

REGIONAL AND INTERNATIONAL CO-OPERATION

In 1990 Andorra approved a trade agreement with the European Community (EC, now the European Union—EU), which was effective from July 1991, allowing for the establishment of a customs union with the EC and enabling Andorran companies to sell non-agricultural goods to the EU market without being subject to the external tariffs levied on third countries. Andorra benefits from duty free transit for goods imported via EU countries. A monetary agreement with the EU was signed in June 2011. Andorra was admitted to the Council of Europe (see p. 256) in 1994, and is also a member of the Organization for Security and Co-operation in Europe (OSCE).

Andorra joined the UN in 1993, following the country's accession to full sovereignty. Andorra is an observer at the World Trade Organization (WTO, see p. 433).

ECONOMIC AFFAIRS

In 2008, according to World Bank estimates, Andorra's gross national income (GNI), measured at average 2007–09 prices, US $3,447m., equivalent to $41,750 per head. During 2001–10 the population grew at an estimated average rate of 2.8% per year, while gross domestic product (GDP) per head increased, in real terms, by an average of 2.0% per year during 2001–08. Overall GDP increased, in real terms, at an average annual rate of 5.2% in 2001–08; growth in 2008 was 3.6%.

Agricultural land accounts for only 4% of the total area of Andorra. Andorra's principal crop is tobacco; livestock-rearing, particularly sheep and cattle, is also of importance. The agricultural sector (including forestry and hunting) accounted for only 0.4% of total employment (excluding unclassified occupations) in 2010 and Andorra is dependent on imports of foodstuffs to satisfy domestic requirements.

Industry in Andorra includes the production of foodstuffs and beverages, wood products, graphic arts and the manufacture of cigars and cigarettes. In addition to forested timber, natural resources include iron, lead, alum and stone. Including manufacturing, construction and the production and distribution of electricity, industry provided 17.1% of total employment (excluding unclassified occupations) in 2010. Construction alone provided 12.2% of the total employment in that year.

The country's hydroelectric power plant supplied 16.4% of domestic needs in 2010, and Andorra is dependent on imports of electricity and other fuels from France and Spain. In 2010 fuel imports accounted for 10.3% of total merchandise imports. In 2006 a project to extend the production capacity of the hydroelectric plant commenced as part of a government strategic energy plan for 2006–15. The generation of electricity from the combustion of urban waste also began in 2006 and contributed 2.1% of Andorra's electricity supply in 2010. Andorra's total electricity consumption in 2010 amounted to 610.6 GWh.

The services sector accounted for 82.5% of total employment (excluding unclassified occupations) in 2010. Tourism and tourist-related commerce are the principal contributors to GDP. Andorra attracts visitors owing to its well-developed facilities for winter sports and also the availability of low-duty consumer items. A total of 1.8m. tourists and 6.7m. excursionists (mostly from Spain and France) visited Andorra in 2010. The hotel industry provided 13.2% of total employment (excluding unclassified occupations) in 2010. The absence of income tax, inheritance tax or capital transfer tax, in addition to the laws on secrecy governing the country's banks, favoured the development of Andorra as a tax haven. The banking and insurance sectors make a significant contribution to the economy.

Andorra's external trade is dominated by the import of consumer goods destined for sale, with low rates of duty, to visitors. In 2010 imports were valued at €1,142.8m. and exports at only €40.8m. Spain and France are Andorra's principal trading partners, respectively providing 60.4% and 17.7% of imports and taking 63.0% and 20.6% of exports in 2010. The European Union (EU, see p. 276) as a whole provided 90.9% of imports and received 96.3% of exports in 2006.

In 2009, according to official figures, there was a marginal budget surplus of €0.1m., and liabilities on the revenue account of the budget decreased to €0.03m from €47m in 2006. In the absence of direct taxation (although a capital gains tax was introduced in 2007), the Government derives its revenue from levies on imports and on financial institutions, indirect taxes on petrol and other items, stamp duty and the sale of postage stamps. Total general government debt was equivalent to an estimated 18% of GDP in 2007. There is no recorded unemployment in Andorra: the restricted size of the indigenous labour force necessitates high levels of immigration. Consumer prices increased by an annual average of 2.7% in 2001–10. The annual rate of inflation was negligible in 2009, but prices grew by 1.5% in 2010.

Andorra has a small, open, prosperous economy, which is narrowly focused on the services sector, principally tourism, tourism-related commerce and banking. It is thus vulnerable to economic conditions in France and Spain. In 2010, despite recent economic difficulties and an increase in unemployment, GDP per head in Andorra was estimated at US $45,157, representing one of the highest per capita incomes in the world. Economic growth during most of the 2000s was robust, however, GDP contracted by 2.9% in 2009, by 1.2% in 2010 and by an estimated 0.2% in 2011, partly owing to a decline in tourist arrivals (which suffered from increased competition from ski resorts in central Europe), but predominantly as a result of the global economic crisis, which had a severe impact on Spain in particular. In an attempt to increase foreign investment and encourage economic diversification, in November 2008 the Government introduced reforms increasing the maximum investment for non-Andorrans from 33% to 49% of a business in key areas, such as ski resorts and property, and to 100% in other industries. The principality's favourable tax regime and banking secrecy have fostered the development of a large financial sector, although increased scrutiny of tax evasion by the Organisation for Economic Co-operation and Development (OECD, see p. 379) and individual national governments led to the withdrawal of some foreign funds from 'offshore' accounts. Under international pressure, Andorra agreed to amend banking secrecy laws ensuring greater transparency and compliance with OECD rules and by November 2010 Andorra had signed bilateral agreements to share financial data with 18 jurisdictions. Although from 2002 its de facto currency was the euro, Andorra had no formal monetary agreement with the EU until such an agreement was finally concluded in June 2011. In 2010 government spending was constrained by the failure of the legislature to reach agreement on a budget for the year, so that monthly expenditure was limited to one-twelfth of the previous year's total. The budget for 2011, which envisaged expenditure of €381.6m., a deficit of €82.6m., and, crucially, the introduction of income tax for residents, similarly failed to gain approval in the legislature, resulting in the dissolution of the General Council and early elections. The emphatic victory of the centre-right Demòcrates per Andorra (DA—Democrats for Andorra) alliance in the election promised a period of political stability and the introduction of a range of measures aimed at strengthening the important tourism sector and increasing employment in the country.

PUBLIC HOLIDAYS

2013: 1 January (New Year's Day), 6 January (Epiphany), 11 February (Carnival), 14 March (Constitution Day), 29 March (Good Friday), 1 April (Easter Monday), 1 May (Labour Day), 20 May (Whit Monday), 15 August (Assumption), 8 September (National Day), 1 November (All Saints' Day), 8 December (Immaculate Conception), 25 December (Christmas Day), 26 December (St Stephen's Day).

Each parish also holds its own annual festival, which is taken as a public holiday, usually lasting for three days, in July, August or September.

Statistical Survey

Source (unless otherwise stated): Servei d'Estudis, Ministeri de Finances, Carrer Prat de la Creu 62–64, Andorra la Vella AD500; tel. 865714; fax 829218; e-mail servest@andorra.ad; internet www.estadistica.ad.

AREA AND POPULATION

Area: 467.8 sq km (180.6 sq miles).

Population: 65,844 (males 34,268, females 31,576) at census of 31 December 2000; 85,015, comprising: Andorrans 32,962, Spanish 26,688, Portuguese 11,849, French 5,087 and others 8,429 at 31 December 2010. Source: partly UN, *Population and Vital Statistics Report*.

Density (31 December 2010): 181.7 per sq km.

Population by Age and Sex (persons at 31 December 2010): *0–14:* 12,229 (males 6,329, females 5,900); *15–64:* 61,463 (males 32,217, females 29,246); *65 and over:* 11,323 (males 5,651, females 5,672); *Total* 85,015 (males 44,197, females 40,818).

Parishes (population at 31 December 2010): Andorra la Vella (capital) 23,505; Escaldes-Engordany 16,920; Encamp 14,357; La Massana 9,937; Sant Julià de Lòria 9,706; Canillo 6,194; Ordino 4,396.

Births, Marriages and Deaths (2010): Registered live births 828 (birth rate 9.7 per 1,000); Registered marriages 287 (marriage rate 3.4 per 1,000); Registered deaths 239 (death rate 2.8 per 1,000).

Life Expectancy (years at birth, WHO estimates): 82 (males 79; females 85) in 2009. Source: WHO, *World Health Statistics*.

Employment (2010): Agriculture, forestry and hunting 148; Mining 3; Construction 4,491; Manufacturing 1,664; Production and distribution of electricity 158; Repair and sale of motor vehicles 9,732; Hotels 4,862; Real estate 4,078; Administration 4,355; Finance and insurance 1,661; Transport and storage 1,154; Education 563; Other services 4,067; *Sub-total* 36,936; Unclassified occupations 1,616; *Total* 38,552 (males 20,098, females 18,454).

HEALTH AND WELFARE

Key Indicators

Total Fertility Rate (children per woman, 2009): 1.3.

Under-5 Mortality Rate (per 1,000 live births, 2009): 4.

Physicians (per 1,000 head, 2006): 3.6.

Hospital Beds (per 1,000 head, 2006): 2.6.

Health Expenditure (2008): US $ per head (PPP): 3,128.

Health Expenditure (2008): % of GDP: 7.5.

Health Expenditure (2008): public (% of total): 69.9.

Human Development Index (2011): ranking: 32.

Human Development Index (2011): value: 0.838.

For sources and definitions, see explanatory note on p. vi.

AGRICULTURE

Principal Crop (metric tons, 2010): Tobacco 237.5.

Livestock (head, 2010): Cattle 1,565; Sheep 2,364; Horses 896; Goats 553.

FINANCE

Currency and Exchange Rates: 100 cent = 1 euro (€). *Sterling and Dollar Equivalents* (30 December 2011): £1 sterling = €1.195; US $1 = €0.773; €10 = £8.37 = US $12.94. *Average Exchange Rate* (euros per US dollar): 0.7198 in 2009; 0.7550 in 2010; 0.7194 in 2011. Note: French and Spanish currencies were formerly in use. From the introduction of the euro, with French and Spanish participation, on 1 January 1999, fixed exchange rates of €1 = 6.55957 francs and €1 = 166.386 pesetas were in operation. Euro notes and coins were introduced on 1 January 2002. The euro and local currencies circulated alongside each other until 17 February (francs) and 28 February (pesetas), after which the euro became the sole legal tender.

Budget (€ million, 2009): *Revenue:* Direct taxes 6.3; Indirect taxes 312.4; Property income 14.2; Other taxes and income 24.8; Current transfers 0.0; Assets 0.1; Liabilities 260.0; Total 618.0. *Expenditure:* Current expenditure 242.7 (Personnel emoluments 92.7, Goods and services 45.6, Interest payments 29.2, Current transfers 75.3); Capital expenditure 114.9 (Fixed capital investment 50.2, Capital transfers 64.7); Assets 0.2; Liabilities 260.1; Total 617.9.

Cost of Living (Consumer Price Index at December; base: 2001 = 100): All items 125.3 in 2008; 125.3 in 2009; 127.2 in 2010.

Gross Domestic Product (€ million at current prices, UN estimates): 2,371.2 in 2007; 2,534.1 in 2008; 2,694.1 in 2009. Source: UN National Accounts Main Aggregates Database.

EXTERNAL TRADE

Principal Commodities (€ million, 2010): *Imports:* Live animals and animal products 58.9; Sugars and sugar-based substances 7.9; Alcoholic drinks and vinegars 59.5; Tobacco and tobacco substitutes 31.5; Flammable minerals, oils, petroleum 117.4; Pharmaceutical products 27.2; Essential oils, perfume and toiletries 85.3; Plastics and articles thereof 13.1; Clothes and clothing accessories, knitted 33.4; Clothes and clothing accessories, not knitted 72.9; Shoes and boots 30.5; Cast products in iron or steel 18.1; Nuclear reactors, boilers and mechanical engines 52.6; Electric machines, tools and materials 86.5; Automobile vehicles, tractors, motorcycles 84.4; Optical instruments 21.9; Toys, games and sports articles 28.7; Total (incl. others) 1,142.8. *Exports:* Essential oils, perfumes and toiletries 1.9; Press products 1.2; Clothes and clothing accessories, not knitted 2.1; Cast products in iron or steel 0.6; Nuclear reactors, boilers and mechanical engines 2.7; Electric machines, tools and materials 5.4; Automobile vehicles, tractors, motorcycles 9.2; Optical instruments 0.4; Art objects, collection or antiques 0.5; Total (incl. others) 40.8.

Principal Trading Partners (€ million, 2010): *Imports c.i.f.:* China, People's Republic 47.7; France 202.1; Germany 51.0; Italy 31.7; Japan 10.6; Spain 690.7; Switzerland 11.4; United Kingdom 15.6; Total (incl. others) 1,142.8. *Exports f.o.b.:* Belgium 0.2; France 8.4; Germany 0.3; Italy 0.4; Spain 25.7; Total (incl. others) 40.8.

TRANSPORT

Road Traffic (registered motor vehicles, 2010): Passenger cars 52,336; Buses and coaches 208; Trucks (lorries) and vans 5,279; Tractors 358; Motorcycles 10,225.

TOURISM

Tourist Arrivals (country of residence, 2010): Spain 1,414,298; France 310,800; Total (incl. others) 1,808,001. Note: Figures exclude excursionists, numbering 6,743,263 in 2010.

COMMUNICATIONS MEDIA

Radio Receivers (1997): 16,000 in use.

Television Receivers (2000): 36,000 in use (Source: UNESCO.

Daily Newspapers (2005): 2 titles published.

Telephones (main lines in use, 2010): 38,200.

Mobile Cellular Telephones (subscribers, 2010): 65,500.

Internet Subscribers ('000, 2009): 32.0.

Broadband Subscribers ('000, 2010): 24.5.

Source: partly International Telecommunication Union and Servei de Telecomunicacions d'Andorra.

EDUCATION

Pre-primary Enrolment (2006/07 unless otherwise indicated): 2,558 (Andorran schools 1,015, French schools 832, Spanish schools* 711). *2010/11:* 2,380.

Primary Enrolment (2006/07 unless otherwise indicated): 4,427 (Andorran schools 1,689, French schools 1,293, Spanish schools* 1,445). *2010/11:* 4,263.

Secondary Enrolment (2006/07 unless otherwise indicated): Andorran schools 1,028; French schools 1,267; Spanish schools* 1,445. *2010/11:* Total secondary basic 2,900; Total secondary superior 889.

Non-university Higher Education Enrolment (2006/07 unless otherwise indicated): 245 (Andorran institutions 68, French institutions 166, Spanish institutions 11). *2010/11:* 370.

University Enrolment (2005/06): Andorra 431 (males 205, females 226); France 131 (males 53, females 78); Spain 503 (males 204, females 299); Total (incl. others) 1,066 (males 462, females 604).

* Including congregational schools.

Pupil-teacher Ratio (primary education, UNESCO estimate): 9.6 in 2009/10 (Source: UNESCO Institute for Statistics).

Directory

The Government

HEAD OF STATE

Episcopal Co-Prince: JOAN ENRIC VIVES I SICÍLIA (Bishop of Urgell).

French Co-Prince: NICOLAS SARKOZY (President of the French Republic).

Note: François Hollande was elected President of France on 6 May 2012 and was expected to take office on 15 May.

GOVERN
(May 2012)

The executive is formed by the Demòcrates per Andorra (Democrats for Andorra).

Head of Government (Cap de Govern): ANTONI MARTÍ PETIT.

Minister of Finance and Public Service: JORDI CINCA MATEOS.

Minister of Economy and Planning: JORDI ALCOBÉ FONT.

Minister of Foreign Affairs: GILBERT SABOYA SUNYÉ.

Minister of Justice and the Interior: MARC VILA AMIGÓ.

Minister of Education, Youth and Sport: ROSER SUÑÉ PASCUET.

Minister of Health and Welfare: CRISTINA RODRÍGUEZ GALAN.

Minister of Tourism and the Environment: FRANCESC CAMP TORRES.

Minister of Culture: ALBERT ESTEVE GARCIA.

MINISTRIES

Office of the Head of Government: Govern d'Andorra, Carrer Prat de la Creu 62–64, Edif. Administratiu, Andorra la Vella AD500; tel. 875700; e-mail portal@govern.ad; internet www.govern.ad.

Ministry of Culture: Carrer Prat de la Creu 62–64, Edif. Administratiu, Andorra la Vella AD500; tel. 875700; fax 826707.

Ministry of Economy and Planning: Carrer Prat de la Creu 62–64, Edif. Administratiu, Andorra la Vella AD500; tel. 875701; fax 875757; e-mail muot@andorra.ad.

Ministry of Education, Youth and Sport: Prada Casadet, Andorra la Vella AD500; tel. 829456; fax 743310; internet www.educacio.ad; www.joventut.ad; www.esports.ad.

Ministry of Finance and Public Service: Carrer Prat de la Creu 62–64, Edif. Administratiu, Andorra la Vella AD500; tel. 875700; fax 860962; e-mail finances.gov@andorra.ad; internet www.finances.ad.

Ministry of Foreign Affairs: Carrer Prat de la Creu 62–64, Edif. Administratiu, Andorra la Vella AD500; tel. 875704; fax 869559; e-mail exteriors.gov@andorra.ad; internet www.mae.ad.

Ministry of Health and Welfare: Avinguda Príncep Benlloch 26, Edif. Clara Rabassa, Planta 4, Andorra la Vella AD500; tel. 860345; fax 829347; e-mail iolanda_latorre@govern.ad; internet www.salutibenestar.ad.

Ministry of Justice and the Interior: Carretera de l'OBAC, Edif. Administratiu de l'OBAC, Escaldes-Engordany AD700; tel. 872080; fax 869250.

Ministry of Tourism and the Environment: Camí de la Grau, Edifici Prat del Rull, Andorra la Vella AD500; tel. 875702; fax 860184; internet www.turisme.ad; www.mediambient.ad.

Legislature

GENERAL COUNCIL
(Consell General)

General Council (Consell General): Casa de la Vall, Andorra la Vella AD500; tel. 877877; fax 869863; e-mail consell_general@parlament.ad; internet www.consell.ad.

Speaker (Síndic General): VICENÇ MATEU ZAMORA.

Deputy Speaker (Subsíndica General): MÒNICA BONELL TUSET.

General Election, 3 April 2011

Party	Votes cast*	% of votes*	Seats†
Demòcrates per Andorra	8,553	55.15	20
Partit Socialdemòcrata	5,397	34.80	6
Andorra pel Canvi	1,040	6.71	—
Els Verds d'Andorra	520	3.35	—
Unió Laurediana	—	—	2
Total	15,510	100.00	28

* Figures refer to votes cast in the national constituency, from which 14 candidates were elected by proportional representation. In addition, two candidates were elected from each of the seven parishes.

† Figures refer to both the national and parochial lists. The Unió Laurediana only contested one parish constituency, Sant Julià de Lòria.

Election Commission

Junta Electoral: Carrer Prat de la Creu 62–64, Edif. Administratiu, Andorra la Vella AD500; tel. 875700; e-mail portal@govern.ad; internet www.eleccions.ad; govt agency; Pres. DAVID MOYNAT ROSSELL.

Political Organizations

The establishment of political parties was sanctioned under the Constitution that was promulgated in May 1993.

Andorra pel Canvi (ApC) (Andorra for Change): Baixada del Molí 3-5, Edif. Molí Parc, Andorra la Vella AD500; f. 2008; Parliamentary Leader EUSEBI NOMEN.

Demòcrates per Andorra (DA) (Democrats for Andorra): Avinguda del Fener 15, Andorra la Vella AD500; tel. 805777; internet www.democratesperandorra.ad; f. February 2011 to contest the election in April; alliance, including the PLA, the PRA and Nou Centre; Leader ANTONI MARTÍ PETIT.

Nou Centre (New Centre): Andorra la Vella AD500; f. 2005 by the merger of Segle 21 and the Centre Demòcrata Andorrà; contested the 2009 general election as part of the Coalició Reformista.

Partit Liberal d'Andorra (PLA) (Andorran Liberal Party): Carrer Babot Camp 13, 2°, Andorra la Vella AD500; tel. 807715; fax 869728; f. 1992 as Unió Liberal; contested 2009 election as part of the Coalició Reformista; Pres. ENRIC PUJAL ARENY; Sec.-Gen. JORDI GALLARDO.

Partit Reformista d'Andorra (PRA) (Reform Party of Andorra): Andorra; f. 2010; Spokesman GILBERT SABOYA.

Partit Socialdemòcrata (PS) (Social Democratic Party): Carrer Verge del Pilar 5, 3°, Andorra la Vella AD500; tel. 805260; fax 821740; e-mail psdandorra@gmail.com; internet www.psa.ad; f. 2000; Pres. VICTOR NAUDI ZAMORA; First Sec. JUDITH SALAZAR.

Renovació Democràtica (RD) (Democratic Renewal): Avinguda Carlemany 67, 5° 2A, Escaldes-Engordany AD700; tel. 801770; fax 821775; e-mail renovaciodemocratica@renovaciodemocratica.ad; internet www.renovaciodemocratica.ad; formed alliance with ApC to contest 2009 elections; Pres. RICARD DE HARO JIMÉNEZ.

Unió Nacional de Progrés (UNP) (National Union for Progress): Avinguda Carlemany 36, Hotel Eureka, Escaldes-Engordany AD700; tel. and fax 821149; e-mail unp@unionacionaldeprogres.com; internet www.unionacionaldeprogres.com; f. 2007; Parliamentary Leader TOMAS PASCUAL CASABOSCH.

Els Verds d'Andorra (The Andorran Greens): Carrer Ciutat de Consuegra 10, 1° 3A, Edif. Orio, Andorra la Vella AD500; tel. 363797; e-mail verds@verds.ad; internet www.verds.ad; f. 2004; Pres. ANTÒNIA ESCODA.

Other parties exist at the parish level: these include Acció Comunal d'Ordino, the Grup d'Unió Parroquial Independents (GUPI—Ordino), the Unió Laurediana (Sant Julià de Lòria) and the Unió del Poble (Escaldes-Engordany).

Diplomatic Representation

EMBASSIES IN ANDORRA

France: Carrer les Canals 38–40, POB 155, Andorra la Vella AD500; tel. 736700; fax 736701; e-mail info@ambafrance-ad.org; internet www.ambafrance-ad.org; Ambassador JEAN-PIERRE BERÇOT.

Portugal: Carrer Prat de la Creu 59–65, 4°, Andorra la Vella AD500; tel. 805308; fax 869555; e-mail mail@andorra.dgaccp.pt; internet www.portugalandorra.com; Ambassador MÁRIO FERNANDO DAMAS NUNES.

Spain: Carrer Prat de la Creu 34, Andorra la Vella AD500; tel. 800030; fax 868500; e-mail embaspad@correo.mae.es; internet www.maec.es/embajadas/andorra; Ambassador ALBERTO MORENO.

Judicial System

Judicial power is vested, in the first instance, in the Magistrates' Courts (Batllia) and in the Judges' Tribunal (Tribunal de Batlles), the criminal law courts (Tribunal de Corts) and the Higher Court of Justice (Tribunal Superior de la Justícia). The judiciary is represented, directed and administered by the Higher Council of Justice (Consell Superior de la Justícia), whose five members are appointed for single terms of six years. Final jurisdiction, in constitutional matters, is vested in the Constitutional Court (Tribunal Constitucional), whose four members hold office for no more than two consecutive eight-year terms.

The 1993 Constitution guarantees the independence of the judiciary.

Higher Council of Justice (Consell Superior de la Justícia): Carrer Prat de la Creu 8, Andorra la Vella AD500; tel. 808390; fax 868778; e-mail con.sup.justicia@andorra.ad; internet www.justicia.ad.

President of the Higher Council of Justice: ENRIC CASADEVALL MEDRANO.

Religion

More than 90% of the population of Andorra are Roman Catholic. Andorra forms part of the Spanish diocese of Urgell.

The Press

7 DIES: Carrer Bonaventura Riberaygua 39, 5°, Andorra la Vella AD500; tel. 877477; e-mail 7dies@7dies.com; f. 1994; weekly; free; local issues, advertising; Dir-Gen. IGNASI DE PLANELL; Dir ROBERT PASTOR; circ. 30,500.

Bondia: Carrer Maria Pla 28, Primera Planta, Andorra la Vella AD500; tel. 808888; fax 828888; e-mail bondia@bondia.ad; internet www.bondia.ad; f. 2004; daily; distributed free of charge; edn in Lleida, Spain; Dir MARC SEGALÉS.

Butlletí Oficial del Principat d'Andorra: Carrer Dr Vilanova 15, Andorra la Vella AD500; tel. 729410; fax 724300; e-mail atencio.public.bopa@govern.ad; internet www.bopa.ad; official govt gazette; weekly.

Diari d'Andorra: Carrer Bonaventura Riberaygua 39, Andorra la Vella AD500; tel. 877477; fax 863800; e-mail info@diariandorra.ad; internet www.diariandorra.ad; f. 1991; daily; local issues; Pres. MARC VILA AMIGÓ; Dir-Gen. IGNASI DE PLANELL; circ. 17,165.

El Periòdic d'Andorra: Fiter i Rossell 4, Escaldes-Engordany AD700; tel. 736200; fax 736210; e-mail redaccio@elperiodicdandorra.ad; internet www.elperiodicdandorra.ad; daily; local issues; Propr Grupo Zeta, SA (Spain); Dir JOAN RAMON BAIGES; Editor-in-Chief EVA ARASA.

Broadcasting and Communications

TELECOMMUNICATIONS

Andorra Telecom: Carrer Mossen Lluis Pujol 8–14, Santa Coloma AD500; tel. 875105; fax 725003; internet www.andorratelecom.ad; f. 1975 as Servei de Telecomunicacions d'Andorra; provides national and international telecommunications and internet services under the SOM brand; manages the radio and television broadcasting infrastructure; Dir-Gen. JAUME SALVAT FONT.

BROADCASTING

In 2007 there were five radio stations in Andorra. In 2010 one television station was active in Andorra; it was possible to receive broadcasts from television stations in neighbouring countries. Digital television broadcasts began in October 2004 and analogue broadcasting was phased out entirely in late September 2007.

Radio

Ràdio i Televisió d'Andorra, SA—Ràdio Nacional Andorra (RTVA): Baixada del Molí 24, Andorra la Vella AD500; tel. 873777; fax 863242; e-mail rtva@rtva.ad; internet www.rtva.ad; f. 1990 as an Andorran-owned commercial public broadcasting service; adopted present name in 2000; Ràdio Nacional Andorra (RNA) is the national radio station; Dir-Gen. JORDI MARTICELLA CANELA.

AD Ràdio: Avinguda Riberaygua 39, Andorra la Vella AD500; tel. 877477; fax 863800; internet www.adradio.ad.

R7P Ràdio: Avinguda Príncep Benlloch 24, Encamp AD200; tel. 732000; fax 731517; e-mail info@cadenapirenaica.com; internet www.cadenapirenaica.com; commercial broadcasting service, aimed at people aged 25–45 years; owned by Cadena Pirenaica de Ràdio i Televisió; Man. Dir EDUARD NAVARRO ISCLA.

Ràdio Valira: Avinguda Príncep Benlloch 24, Encamp AD200; tel. 732000; fax 834831; e-mail info@cadenapirenaica.com; internet www.cadenapirenaica.com; f. 1986; commercial broadcasting service, aimed at people aged 40–65 years; owned by Cadena Pirenaica de Ràdio i Televisió; Man. Dir EDUARD NAVARRO ISCLA.

Television

Ràdio i Televisió d'Andorra, SA—Andorra Televisió (RTVA): Baixada del Molí 24, Andorra la Vella AD500; tel. 873777; fax 864232; e-mail rtva@rtva.ad; internet www.rtvasa.ad; f. 1995 as an Andorran-owned commercial public broadcasting service; Andorra Televisió (ATV) is the national television channel; Dir-Gen. JORDI MARTICELLA CANELA.

Finance

(cap. = capital; res = reserves; dep. = deposits; m. = million; brs = branches; amounts in euros)

REGULATORY AUTHORITY

Institut Nacional Andorrà de Finances (INAF): Carrer Bonaventura Armengol, Edif. Montclar 10, bloc 2, Planta 4A, Andorra la Vella AD500; tel. 808898; fax 865977; e-mail inaf.sc@inaf.ad; internet www.inaf.ad; f. 1993; Chair. RAÜL GONZÁLEZ FERNÁNDEZ; CEO MARIA COSAN CANUT.

BANKS

In 2010 five banking groups were operating in Andorra.

Andbanc: Carrer Manuel Cerqueda i Escaler 6, Escaldes-Engordany AD700; tel. 873333; fax 873353; e-mail corporate@andbanc.com; internet www.andbanc.com; f. 2001 as Andorra Banc Agrícol Reig by merger of Banca Reig and Banc Agrícol i Comercial d'Andorra; cap. 78.1m., res 296.7m., dep. 2,513.9m. (Dec. 2010); Chair. MANEL CERQUERDA DONADEU; Gen. Man. JORDI COMAS PLANAS; 12 brs.

BIBM: Avinguda Meritxell 96, Andorra la Vella AD500; tel. 884488; fax 884499; e-mail bibm@bibm.ad; internet www.bibm.ad; f. 1958 as Banc International; merged with Banca Mora in 1976; cap. 42.4m., res 162.3m., dep. 1,917.7m. (Dec. 2010); Chair. FRANCESC MORA SAGUÉS; Chief Exec. JOAN QUERA FONT; 11 brs.

BPA (Banca Privada d'Andorra SA): Avinguda Carlemany 119, POB 25, Escaldes-Engordany AD700; tel. 873501; fax 873515; e-mail bpa@bpa.ad; internet www.bpa.ad; f. 1962 as Banca Cassany SA; name changed to Banca Privada d'Andorra in 1994; cap. 70.0m., res 125.9m., dep. 1,415.7m. (Dec. 2010); Pres HIGINI CIERCO NOGUER, RAMON CIERCO NOGUER; Gen. Man. JOAN PAU MIQUEL PRATS; 7 brs.

BancSabadell d'Andorra: Avinguda del Fener 7, Andorra la Vella AD500; tel. 735600; fax 735601; e-mail bsa@bsa.ad; internet www.bsandorra.com; cap. 30.1m., res 15.0m., dep. 487.6m. (Dec. 2010); Chair. ROBERT CASSANY I VILA; Gen. Man. MIQUEL ALABERN I COMAS; 6 brs.

Crèdit Andorrà: Avinguda Meritxell 80, Andorra la Vella AD500; tel. 888600; fax 888601; e-mail comunicacio@creditandorra.ad; internet www.creditandorra.ad; f. 1949; merged with CaixaBank SA in 2007; cap. 70.0m., res 369.5m., dep. 4,393.1m. (Dec. 2010); Chair. ANTONI PINTAT; CEO JOSEP PERALBA; 21 brs.

Banking Association

Associació de Bancs Andorrans (Association of Andorran Banks—ABA): Carrer Ciutat de Consuegra 16, Edif. L'Illa, Escala A-2°, Andorra la Vella AD500; tel. 807110; fax 866847; e-mail aba@aba.ad; internet www.aba.ad; f. 1960; Dir ANTONI ARMENGOL.

INSURANCE

In 2007 there were 16 Andorran insurance companies registered, while a further 18 foreign companies were also authorized to operate in Andorra.

Assegurances Generals Andorra, SA: Carrer Sant Salvador 7, Edif. Rosella, Andorra la Vella AD500; tel. 877677; fax 860093; e-mail aga@andorra.ad; internet www.assegurancesgenerals.com; Pres. AMADEU CALVÓ CASAL.

BPA Assegurances, SA: Avinguda Carlemany 119, Escalades-Engordany AD700; tel. 873501; fax 873515; e-mail bpa@bpa.ad; internet www.bpa.ad; savings, life and health; insurance division of Banca Privada d'Andorra.

Companyia Andorrana d'Assegurances, SA: Avinguda Meritxell 88, Andorra la Vella AD500; tel. 806806; fax 824605; e-mail sinistres.caa@andorra.ad.

Financera d'Assegurances, SA: Carrer Babot Camp 11, Andorra la Vella AD500; tel. 890300; fax 864717; e-mail info@e-financera.com; internet www.e-financera.com; non-life.

Previsió i Futur, SA: Avinguda Meritxell 9, Andorra la Vella AD500; tel. 800333; fax 860237; e-mail info@previsioifutur.com; internet www.previsioifutur.com; f. 2000; life.

Trade and Industry

GOVERNMENT AGENCY

Andorra Desenvolupament i Inversió (ADI) (Andorra Development and Investment): Carrer Prat de la Creu 59–65, Andorra la Vella AD500; tel. 812020; fax 812021; e-mail info@adi.ad; internet www.adi.ad; f. 2009; fmrly Oficina d'Innovació Empresarial; promotes economic development and foreign investment; Dir CARLES ALEIX.

CHAMBER OF COMMERCE

Cambra de Comerç, Indústria i Serveis d'Andorra (Chamber of Commerce, Industry and Services of Andorra): Carrer Prat de la Creu 8, Edif. Le Mans, Andorra la Vella AD500; tel. 809292; fax 809293; e-mail ccis@andorra.ad; internet www.ccis.ad; Pres. MARC PANTEBRE PALMITJAVILA; Dir PILAR ESCALER PENELLA.

UTILITIES

Electricity

The Forces Elèctriques d'Andorra (FEDA) distributes 69% of energy used in Andorra, while four smaller companies, supplied by FEDA, distribute the rest of the electricity used.

Forces Elèctriques d'Andorra (FEDA): Avinguda de la Barta s/n, Encamp AD200; tel. 739100; fax 739118; e-mail feda@feda.ad; internet www.feda.ad; f. 1988; state-owned; imports, generates and distributes electricity; Pres. PERE LÓPEZ AGRÀS (Minister of the Economy and Finance); Dir-Gen. ALBERT MOLES BETRIU.

EMPLOYERS' ORGANIZATIONS

Associació Empresa Familiar Andorrana (EFA): Edif. OCCESA, Carrer Bonaventura Armengol 15, 6è, Andorra la Vella AD500; tel. 808136; fax 826174; e-mail efa@andorra.ad; internet www.efa.ad; f. 2002; family-owned businesses; c. 50 mems.

Associació de la Micro, Petita i Mitjana Empresa d'Andorra (PIME): Avda Doctor Mitjavila 36, 1er, Andorra la Vella AD500; tel. 824344; fax 855750; e-mail info@pimeandorra.com; internet www.pimeandorra.com; f. 2005; small and medium-sized enterprises; Pres. MARC ALEIX TUGÁS; c. 150 mems.

Club de Marketing d'Andorra: Avinguda Meritxell 105 5é, Andorra La Vella AD500; tel. 327757; fax 863737; e-mail retroferran@gmail.com; internet www.clubmarketingandorra.com; Pres. MONTSERRAT RONCHERA.

Confederació Empresarial Andorrana (CEA): Carrer Prat de la Creu 59-65, Escala B, 2on, Andorra la Vella AD500; tel. 800020; fax 800024; e-mail info@cea.ad; internet www.cea.ad; f. 2006; Pres. XAVIER ALTIMIR PLANES.

TRADE UNIONS

Sindicat Andorrà de Treballadors (SAT): Carretera de l'Adosa, Edif. Busquets, Anyós, La Massana; tel. 826085; Sec.-Gen. GUILLEM FORNIELES.

Sindicat de l'Ensenyament Públic (SEP): Carrer de les Escoles 3, La Massana AD400; tel. 379630; e-mail contacte@sep.ad; internet www.sep.ad; f. 2007; Sec.-Gen. SANTI RODRÍGUEZ.

Unió Sindical d'Andorra (USdA): Carrer de les Boïgues s/n, Edif. Pic Blanc, Andorra la Vella AD500; tel. 356270; fax 826770; e-mail usda@andorra.ad; internet www.usda.ad; Sec.-Gen. GABRIEL UBACH.

Transport

RAILWAYS

There are no railways in Andorra. The nearest stations are Ax-les-Thermes, L'Hospitalet and La Tour de Carol, in France (with trains from Toulouse and Perpignan), and Puigcerdà, in Spain, on the line from Barcelona. There is a connecting bus service from all four stations to Andorra.

ROADS

A good road connects the Spanish and French frontiers, passing through Andorra la Vella. The Envalira tunnel, between Andorra and France, was opened in September 2002. Work began on the Dos Valires tunnel to link Encamp and La Massana in late 2005. The tunnel was scheduled to open in 2012. Two companies, Cooperativa Interurbana Andorrana and Hispano Andorrana, operate bus services within Andorra.

CIVIL AVIATION

The Pirineus-La Seu airport at La Seu d'Urgell, located in Spanish territory 10 km from the border with Andorra, reopened in June 2010 following a redevelopment programme financed jointly by the Andorran, Spanish and Catalan administrations.

Tourism

Andorra has attractive mountain scenery, and winter sports facilities are available at five skiing centres. Tourists are also attracted by Andorra's duty-free shopping facilities. A total of 1.8m. tourists visited Andorra in 2010, as well as 6.7m. excursionists, mainly from Spain and France. In 2004 the valley of Madriu was declared a UNESCO World Heritage Site.

Andorra Turisme, SAU: Carrer Dr Vilanova, Edif. Davi 13B, Andorra la Vella AD500; tel. 820214; fax 825823; e-mail info@andorra.ad; internet www.andorra.ad; f. 2008; Man. ALEXANDRE ANDRÉS.

Ski Andorra: Avinguda Tarragona 58-70, Despatx 14, Andorra la Vella AD500; tel. 805200; fax 865910; e-mail skiandorra@skiandorra.ad; internet www.skiandorra.ad; association of ski stations; Dir MARTA ROTÉS.

Unió Hotelera d'Andorra (Hotel Association of Andorra): Antic Carrer Major 18, Andorra la Vella AD500; tel. 820602; fax 861539; e-mail uhotelera@uha.ad; internet www.uha.ad; f. 1961; Pres. ALEX ARMENGOL; Sec.-Gen. ELISABETH ROSSELL; 200 mems.

Each parish has its own tourist office.

Defence

Andorra has no defence budget.

Education

Education is compulsory for children of between six and 16 years of age, and is provided free of charge by Catalan-, French- and Spanish-language schools. (Children educated under the French or Spanish state systems are required to study some Catalan.) Six years of primary education are followed by four years of secondary schooling. University education is undertaken either at the University of Andorra or abroad, mostly in Spain and France. The University of Andorra offers degrees in business administration, education science, nursing and computer science. In 2005/06 86.4% of the relevant age-group were enrolled in pre-primary education, 82.9% in primary education and 73.9% in secondary education. In 2006/07 there were a total of 10,804 pupils attending Andorra's schools (of whom 2,558 pupils were enrolled at pre-primary schools, 4,427 at primary schools, 3,574 at secondary schools and 245 at institutions providing non-university higher education). Of these, 3,800 were under the Andorran education system (where Catalan is the teaching medium), 3,570 were attending French-speaking schools and 3,434 were being educated under the Spanish system (secular and congregational). In 2005/06 1,066 students were in higher education; 431 students were studying in Andorra, 131 in France and 503 in Spain. A new baccalaureate examination, which was intended to facilitate direct access for students in the Andorran education system to universities in other European countries, was introduced in 2008. The 2008 budget allocated €73.6m. (17.0% of total projected expenditure) to education.

ANGOLA

Introductory Survey

LOCATION, CLIMATE, LANGUAGE, RELIGION, FLAG, CAPITAL

The Republic of Angola lies on the west coast of Africa. The province of Cabinda is separated from the rest of the country by the estuary of the River Congo and territory of the Democratic Republic of the Congo (DRC—formerly Zaire), with the Republic of the Congo lying to its north. Angola is bordered by the DRC to the north, Zambia to the east and Namibia to the south. The climate is tropical, locally tempered by altitude. There are two distinct seasons (wet and dry) but little seasonal variation in temperature. It is very hot and rainy in the coastal lowlands but temperatures are lower inland. The official language is Portuguese, but African languages (the most widely spoken being Umbundu, Lunda, Kikongo, Chokwe and Kwanyama) are also in common use. Much of the population follows traditional African beliefs, although a majority profess to be Christians, mainly Roman Catholics. The flag (proportions 2 by 3) has two equal horizontal stripes, of red and black; superimposed in the centre, in gold, are a five-pointed star, half a cog-wheel and a machete. The capital is Luanda.

CONTEMPORARY POLITICAL HISTORY

Historical Context

Formerly a Portuguese colony, Angola became an overseas province in 1951. African nationalist groups began to form in the 1950s and 1960s, including the Movimento Popular de Libertação de Angola (MPLA) in 1956, the Frente Nacional de Libertação de Angola (FNLA) in 1962 and the União Nacional para a Independência Total de Angola (UNITA) in 1966. Severe repression followed an unsuccessful nationalist rebellion in 1961, but, after a new wave of fighting in 1966, nationalist guerrilla groups were able to establish military and political control in large parts of eastern Angola and to press westward. Following the April 1974 *coup d'état* in Portugal, Angola's right to independence was recognized.

In January 1975 a transitional Government was established, comprising representatives of the MPLA, the FNLA, UNITA and the Portuguese Government. However, following violent clashes between the MPLA and the FNLA, by the second half of 1975 control of Angola was effectively divided between the three major nationalist groups, each aided by foreign powers. The MPLA (which held the capital) was supported by the USSR and Cuba, the FNLA by Zaire and Western powers (including the USA), while UNITA was backed by South African forces. The FNLA and UNITA formed a united front to fight the MPLA.

The Portuguese Government proclaimed Angola independent from 11 November 1975, transferring sovereignty to 'the Angolan people' rather than to any of the liberation movements. The MPLA proclaimed the People's Republic of Angola in Luanda under the presidency of Dr Agostinho Neto. The FNLA and UNITA proclaimed the Democratic People's Republic of Angola, based in Nova Lisboa (renamed Huambo). By the end of February 1976, however, the MPLA, aided by Cuban technical and military expertise, had effectively gained control of the whole country.

Domestic Political Affairs

Neto died in September 1979, and José Eduardo dos Santos, hitherto the Minister of Planning, was elected party leader and President by the Central Committee of the Movimento Popular de Libertação de Angola—Partido do Trabalho (MPLA—PT, as the MPLA had been renamed in December 1977). Elections to the Assembleia Popular Nacional (National People's Assembly), which replaced the Conselho da Revolução (Council of the Revolution), were first held in 1980.

The MPLA—PT Government's recovery programme was continually hindered by security problems and UNITA conducted sustained and disruptive guerrilla activities, mainly in southern and central Angola, throughout the 1980s. In addition, forces from South Africa, which was providing UNITA with considerable military aid, made numerous armed incursions over the Angolan border with Namibia, ostensibly in pursuit of guerrilla forces belonging to the South West Africa People's Organisation (SWAPO), which was supported by the Angolan Government. UNITA was excluded from a series of major peace negotiations, between Angola, Cuba and South Africa (with the unofficial mediation of the USA), which commenced in May 1988. By July the participants had agreed to a document containing the principles for a peace settlement that provided for independence for Namibia, the discontinuation of South African military support for UNITA and the withdrawal of Cuban troops from Angola. Following the conclusion of the New York accords on Angola and Namibia in December, the UN Security Council established the UN Angola Verification Mission (UNAVEM) to verify the phased withdrawal of Cuban troops from Angola, which was completed in May 1991.

In October 1990 the Central Committee of the MPLA—PT proposed a general programme of reform, including the replacement of the party's official Marxist-Leninist ideology with a commitment to 'democratic socialism', the legalization of political parties, the transformation of the army from a party institution to a state institution, the introduction of a market economy, a revision of the Constitution and the holding of multi-party elections in 1994, following a population census. In March 1991 the Assembleia Popular approved legislation permitting the formation of political parties.

On 1 May 1991 the Government and UNITA concluded a peace agreement in Estoril, Portugal, which provided for a cease-fire from 15 May and a new national army of 50,000 men was to be established, comprising equal numbers of government and UNITA soldiers. Free and democratic elections were to be held by the end of 1992. On 31 May the Government and UNITA signed a formal agreement in Lisbon, Portugal, ratifying the Estoril agreement. The UN Security Council agreed to establish UNAVEM II, with a mandate to ensure implementation of the peace accord.

Representatives of the Government and 26 political parties met in Luanda in January 1992 to discuss the transition to multi-party democracy. It was agreed in February that the elections, which were to take place in September, would be conducted on the basis of proportional representation, with the President elected for a five-year term, renewable for a maximum of three terms. The legislature would be a national assembly, elected for a four-year term. In April the Assembleia Popular adopted electoral legislation incorporating these decisions and providing for the creation of an Assembleia Nacional (National Assembly) comprising 223 members (90 to be elected in 18 provincial constituencies and the remainder from national lists).

In April 1992 the Tribunal da Relação (Supreme Court) approved UNITA's registration as a political party. In May the MPLA—PT voted to enlarge the membership of the Central Committee to include prominent dissidents who had returned to the party and removed the suffix Partido do Trabalho from the organization's official name. In August the legislature approved a further revision of the Constitution, removing the remnants of the country's former Marxist ideology, and deleting the words 'People's' and 'Popular' from the Constitution and from the names of official institutions. The name of the country was changed from the People's Republic of Angola to the Republic of Angola.

In early September 1992 in Cabinda province, the enclave that provides most of Angola's petroleum revenue, secessionist groups, notably the Frente para a Libertação do Enclave de Cabinda (FLEC), intensified attacks on government troops. Later that month the government Forças Armadas Populares de Libertação de Angola (FAPLA) and the UNITA forces were formally disbanded, and the new national army, the Forças Armadas de Angola (FAA), was established.

Presidential and legislative elections were held, as scheduled, on 29 and 30 September 1992. When preliminary results indicated victory for the MPLA in the elections to the new Assembleia Nacional, the leader of UNITA, Dr Jonas Savimbi, accused the Government of electoral fraud, withdrew his troops from the FAA, and demanded the suspension of the official announcement of the election results until an inquiry into the alleged irregularities had been conducted. A second round of the presidential election was required to be held between dos Santos and Savimbi, as neither candidate had secured 50% of the votes cast in the first round. Savimbi agreed to participate in this second round on the condition that it be conducted by the UN, while the Government insisted that the election should not take place until UNITA had satisfied the conditions of the Estoril peace agreement by transferring its troops to assembly points or to the FAA.

Post-election conflict

By the end of October 1992, following the release of the official election results, hostilities had spread throughout Angola, with the majority of UNITA's demobilized soldiers returning to arms. In November Savimbi agreed to abide by the results of the September elections, although he maintained that the ballot had been fraudulent. Subsequently dos Santos announced that the Assembleia Nacional would be inaugurated on 26 November. On that day delegations from the Government and UNITA issued a joint communiqué, declaring full acceptance of the validity of the Estoril peace agreement and the intention to implement immediately a nation-wide cease-fire. However, UNITA's 70 elected deputies failed to attend the inauguration of the Assembleia. On 27 November 1992 dos Santos announced the appointment of Marcolino José Carlos Moco, the Secretary-General of the MPLA, as Prime Minister. At the end of November, however, hostilities broke out in the north of the country.

In December 1993 an agreement was reportedly reached between UNITA and the Government on issues concerning the demobilization and confinement of UNITA troops, the surrender of UNITA weapons to the UN, and the integration of UNITA generals into the FAA, prompting the UN to postpone additional sanctions against the rebels. An agreement was also reached in Lusaka, Zambia, on the formation, under UN supervision, of a national police force of 26,700 members, of which UNITA was to provide 5,500, while in June 1994 an 18-point document on national reconciliation was signed and acceptance of the September 1992 election results by both sides was reaffirmed.

In September 1994, following successive extensions, the UN Security Council further extended the mandate of UNAVEM II until 31 October. Talks continued throughout October, concentrating on the issue of Savimbi's security and the replacement of the joint political and military commission with a new joint commission, which was to be chaired by the UN Secretary-General's special representative and was to comprise representatives of the Government and UNITA and observers from the USA, Russia and Portugal. A peace accord was finally initialled on 31 October and formally signed on 20 November. However, hostilities continued beyond 22 November, when a permanent cease-fire was to have come into force, notably in Huambo and in Bié province. In February 1995 the UN Security Council adopted a resolution creating UNAVEM III, but deployment of the new peace-keeping mission remained conditional on the cessation of hostilities and the disengagement of government and UNITA forces.

In May 1995 dos Santos and Savimbi met in Lusaka for direct talks, which concluded with the ratification of the Lusaka peace accord. Savimbi recognized the status of dos Santos as President of Angola and pledged his full co-operation in the reconstruction of the nation. The two leaders agreed to accelerate the consolidation of the cease-fire, to create conditions for the deployment of UNAVEM III, to expedite the integration of UNITA troops into the FAA, and to establish a government of unity based on the provisions of the Lusaka accord (subsequent to the demobilization of the UNITA forces). Dos Santos requested that Savimbi immediately nominate the UNITA appointees to the new Government.

In July 1995 the Assembleia approved the creation of two new vice-presidential positions, of which one was to be offered to Savimbi, conditional upon the prior disbanding of UNITA forces. The other post was to be assumed by Fernando José França van-Dúnem, the President of the Assembleia Nacional. Savimbi, who had publicly expressed his intention to accept the vice-presidency, had in June declared the war in Angola to be at an end and appealed to neighbouring nations to prevent the traffic of arms to the country. In July the UN announced that the deployment of UNAVEM III personnel would be completed by the end of August.

In March 1996 discussions between dos Santos and Savimbi, conducted in Libreville, Gabon, resulted in agreement on the establishment of a government of national unity, in accordance with the provisions of the Lusaka accord. Savimbi proposed the UNITA governmental nominees, while dos Santos formally invited Savimbi to assume the vice-presidency. Agreement was also reached in Libreville on the formation of a unified national army, which, it was envisaged, would be concluded in June. In May agreement was reached on a programme to integrate UNITA troops into the FAA. Also in May the Government and a Cabinda secessionist faction, FLEC—Forças Armadas Cabindesas (FLEC—FAC), signed an agreement outlining the principles of a cease-fire. However, following renewed fighting later that month between government troops and the secessionists, the leader of FLEC—FAC, N'zita Henriques Tiago, declared that a definitive cease-fire would only follow the withdrawal of the FAA from Cabinda. A separate cease-fire had been signed with FLEC—Renovada (FLEC—R) in September 1995.

In November 1996 the Assembleia Nacional adopted a constitutional revision extending its mandate, which was due to expire that month, for a period of between two and four years, pending the establishment of suitable conditions for the conduct of free and fair elections. In April 1997 an agreement was reached to accord Savimbi the special status of official 'leader of the opposition'. Following the arrival of the full contingent of UNITA deputies and government nominees in Luanda, on 11 April the new Government of National Unity and Reconciliation was inaugurated. As envisaged, UNITA assumed a number of ministerial and deputy ministerial portfolios.

On 30 June 1997 the UN Security Council unanimously approved the discontinuation of UNAVEM III and its replacement by a scaled-down observer mission, the UN Observer Mission in Angola (MONUA), with a seven-month mandate to oversee the implementation of the remaining provisions of the Lusaka accord. In late July the UN condemned UNITA's failure to adhere to the Lusaka accord and threatened to impose further sanctions on the movement if it did not take irreversible steps towards fulfilling its obligations.

Protracted peace attempts

On 31 October 1997, as a result of UNITA's continued failure to meet its obligations under the peace accord, the UN Security Council finally ordered the implementation of additional sanctions against the movement. In November UNITA expressed its intention to continue to pursue a peaceful settlement, and during the ensuing months ceded further territory to state administration, including the important Cuango valley diamond mines in Lunda-Norte province.

In January 1998 a new schedule was agreed for the implementation of the Lusaka protocol. In early March UNITA announced the disbandment of its remaining forces, following which it received official recognition as a legally constituted party. However, allegations persisted of preparations by UNITA for a resumption of hostilities. By June fighting had spread to 14 of the country's 18 provinces, displacing some 150,000 people. In August UNITA accused the observer countries in the joint commission of bias in the Government's favour and declared that it would no longer negotiate with them. On 31 August the Government suspended UNITA's government and parliamentary representatives from office.

In September 1998 a group of five UNITA moderates issued a manifesto declaring the suspension of Savimbi and the introduction of an interim UNITA leadership, pending a general congress of the party. Although the group, which styled itself UNITA—Renovada (UNITA—R), commanded very limited support among UNITA's leaders in Luanda, the Government welcomed the development, recognizing UNITA—R as the sole and legitimate representative of UNITA in negotiations concerning the implementation of the Lusaka peace process. The UN Security Council continued to seek a dialogue between dos Santos and Savimbi as the only solution to the conflict. In late September the Government revoked the suspension of UNITA's representatives in the Government and legislature and in October the Assembleia Nacional revoked Savimbi's special status. In that month UNITA—R failed to impose its candidate to lead the UNITA parliamentary group when Abel Chivukuvuku was overwhelmingly re-elected as its Chairman. Chivukuvuku, while no longer claiming allegiance to Savimbi, was opposed to UNITA—R and subsequently formed his own wing of UNITA.

Following increasingly frequent outbreaks of fighting, in January 1999, in an effort to address the prevailing military and economic crisis, dos Santos assumed the role of Prime Minister. In the same month UNITA—R conducted its first congress in Luanda, at which Eugénio N'Golo 'Manuvakola' was elected leader of the faction. In February the UN Security Council voted unanimously to end MONUA's mandate and withdraw its operatives by 20 March, on the grounds that conditions had deteriorated to such an extent that UN personnel were no longer able to function. In October the UN and the Government formally agreed on the establishment of a 30-member 'follow-up' mission, the UN Office in Angola (UNOA), which was to focus on issues concerning humanitarian assistance and human rights.

During 1999 the UN increased its efforts to impose sanctions on UNITA, with the appointment of Canada's ambassador to the UN, Robert Fowler, as Chairman of the UN Sanctions Committee. A UN report published in June disclosed the contravention of UN sanctions by a number of African heads of state, who were apparently involved in the trading of arms for UNITA-mined diamonds. In October 1999 the South African diamond company De Beers, which controls the majority of the international trade in diamonds, announced that it had placed a world-wide embargo on the purchase of all diamonds from Angola, except those whose acquisition was already under contract. The Angolan Government also attempted to stem the flow of illegal diamonds by introducing a strict regime of stone certification. In early 2000 the Angolan Government announced the establishment of a state-owned company, which was to be responsible for centralizing and regulating the country's diamond trade. All marketing was transferred to the newly created Angolan Selling Corporation. In December the UN Angola Sanctions Committee issued a further report on the smuggling of UNITA diamonds, which confirmed that sanctions had failed to prevent the movement's involvement in the diamond trade, and accused several countries of supporting the illegal trade.

In February 2002 Savimbi was killed during an ambush by FAA soldiers in Moxico province. In March the Government halted military offensives against UNITA, and at the end of that month, following talks between the Government and UNITA's Chief-of-Staff, Gen. Abreu 'Kamorteiro' Muengo, both parties signed a memorandum of understanding, aimed at ending the civil war. On 4 April a cease-fire agreement was ratified, in which UNITA accepted the Lusaka protocol and agreed to the cantonment of its soldiers. Some 5,000 UNITA soldiers were to be integrated into the FAA, and UNITA representatives were to take up positions in central, provincial and local government.

By the end of July 2002 some 85,000 UNITA soldiers and an estimated 300,000 family members had registered in quartering camps, and in early August UNITA announced that its military wing had been disbanded, following the integration of its soldiers into the FAA. Also in August, the UN Security Council established the UN Mission in Angola (UNMA) to succeed UNOA until 15 February 2003. On 23 August 2002 the Government and UNITA set a 45-day deadline for the full implementation of the Lusaka protocol, which was to be monitored by a UN-led joint commission, comprising representatives of the Government, UNITA and observer countries (Portugal, Russia and the USA). In October the inauguration of a new national political commission for UNITA, including former members of UNITA—R, marked the official reunification of the party; Gen. Paulo Lukamba 'Gato' was confirmed as interim leader of the party, pending a full congress.

The FAA maintained forces in Cabinda throughout 2003, and by the middle of that year it was believed that, with the exception of some pockets of resistance in the north, the province had been pacified. In September 2004 the merger was announced of FLEC—FAC and FLEC—R. The new grouping, which adopted the name FLEC, was led by Tiago, while António Bento Bembe, previously the President of FLEC—R, became Secretary-General of the movement. A political wing, styling itself FLEC—Conselho Superior Alargado (FLEC—CSA), with the stated aim of achieving independence through political means, was subsequently established under the leadership of Liberal Nuno.

Towards constitutional reform

In early December 2002 Fernando (Nando) da Piedade Dias dos Santos, hitherto Minister of the Interior, was appointed as Prime Minister, a post that President dos Santos had held since January 1999. The Council of Ministers was subsequently reorganized, with the inclusion of the four UNITA representatives. Shortly afterwards the UN Security Council voted to lift all remaining sanctions on UNITA, having previously removed travel restrictions on officials of the former rebel group. Meanwhile, a Constitutional Commission (which had been established by the Assembleia Nacional in 1998) was considering proposals for a new draft constitution. Agreement was reached on a major point of contention in January 2003, when the Commission decided that the President of the Republic would remain Head of Government, as favoured by MPLA deputies; UNITA had advocated the devolvement of executive power to the Prime Minister. In February UNMA withdrew from Angola, as scheduled. The demobilization of former UNITA soldiers continued throughout 2003. The Government closed the 35 quartering camps in June, and by November around 80,000 soldiers, along with their families, had been demobilized.

In January 2004 the Constitutional Commission was presented with a draft constitution and in mid-2004 the Government, which had identified 14 'key tasks' it wished to accomplish before calling concurrent legislative and presidential elections—including constitutional reform and the compiling of an electoral register—stated that polls would not take place until late 2006. A government report recommended that a minimum period of one year be allowed in order to prepare for the elections; however, several opposition parties, including UNITA, insisted that elections could take place in 2005 without constitutional reform and withdrew from the Commission in May 2004 in protest against the perceived lack of progress towards elections. In November the Commission was dissolved, after a draft constitutional bill had been presented to the Assembleia Nacional. In July 2005 the Tribunal da Relação ruled that President dos Santos was eligible to stand for re-election, and in August, following approval by the that body, dos Santos signed into law legislation providing for the creation of a Comissão Nacional Eleitoral (CNE—National Electoral Commission).

In August 2006 a peace agreement was signed with FLEC, recognizing Cabinda as part of Angola but granting it special status, with a greater degree of autonomy than other provinces. Human rights organizations alleged that this deal had been imposed by force, and members of the Fórum Cabindês para o Diálogo (FCD) claimed that Bembe, with whom the agreement had been reached, was not a valid spokesman (as did members of FLEC). In August 2007 President dos Santos announced further steps to consolidate peace, including the appointment of a number of FCD members to positions in government; most notably, Bembe was sworn in as Minister without Portfolio, while the FLEC military chief Maurício Amado Zulo was appointed Deputy Chief of General Staff of the Armed Forces.

At a UNITA party Congress, which was held in July 2007, Isaías Samakuva was re-elected to the presidency of the party, after comfortably defeating the sole challenger Chivukuvuku. In September the Government announced that the voter registration process had been completed and that some 8m. Angolans would be eligible to vote in the legislative elections.

The 2008 legislative elections

A total of 14 political parties contested the first legislative elections to take place in Angola for 16 years, which were held on 5–6 September 2008. Official results released by the CNE on 16 September indicated that some 7.2m. Angolans (representing 87.4% of those eligible to vote) had participated in the polls, at which the ruling MPLA secured 81.6% of the valid votes cast, equating to 191 of the 220 seats in the Assembleia Nacional. UNITA became the second largest party in the legislature, taking 10.4% of the total votes cast and winning 16 seats. The remaining seats were taken by the Partido de Renovação Social (eight), the FNLA (three) and the Nova Democracia—União Eleitoral (two). Observers from the European Union (EU, see p. 276) noted organizational problems and declared that owing to state control of the media the election fell short of international standards. None the less, the head of the EU mission stated that the election still marked an 'advance for democracy'. In late September António Paulo Kassoma, a member of the MPLA politburo and hitherto the Governor of Huambo province, was appointed Prime Minister, and early the following month a new 35-member Government, which included 17 new ministers, was named. The two most senior members of the outgoing administration, the Minister of National Defence, Gen. Kundi Paihama, and the Minister of the Interior, Gen. Roberto Leal Monteiro, retained their posts.

A new Constitution

In October 2009 three different draft versions of the proposed text of the new constitution were made available for a public consultation process. While opposition parties favoured the insertion of a clause providing for the direct popular election of the President, the ruling MPLA was expected to be able to secure its preferred constitutional document (which advocated the selection of the President by the largest party in the legislature) owing to the overwhelming majority of its members in both the Assembleia Nacional and the Tribunal Constitucional (Constitutional Court).

In late January 2010 the Assembleia Nacional approved the text of the new constitution and, after minor amendments were made by the Tribunal Constitucional, on 5 February President dos Santos officially promulgated the new basic law. According to the Constitution, the presidency was henceforth to be assumed by the leader of the political party, or coalition of political parties, obtaining the majority of votes in legislative elections, and the President, who was to be both Head of State and Head of Government, was eligible to serve a maximum of two five-year terms. The 223 members of the Assembleia Nacional were also to serve five-year terms concurrent with that of the President (hitherto they had served four-year terms that had run to a different schedule). The position of Prime Minister was abolished and a Vice-President (the deputy leader of the ruling party) was to be appointed. The new Constitution also outlawed the death penalty and was widely welcomed by most sections of society. On 6 February dos Santos announced the formation of a new Government, in accordance with the provisions of the new Constitution. Former Prime Minister Nando dos Santos (hitherto the President of the Assembleia Nacional) became Vice-President. Monteiro and the ministers responsible for the economy and foreign affairs portfolios in the outgoing administration were all reappointed; however, Cândido Pereira dos Santos Van-Dúnem replaced Gen. Paihama as Minister of National Defence. Later in February outgoing Prime Minister Kassoma was selected as the new President of the Assembleia Nacional.

In September 2010, less than one year after being appointed Minister of the Interior, Gen. Roberto Leal Ramos Monteiro (Ngongo) was dismissed from his post amid claims that the ministry had illegally detained and extradited a Portuguese citizen resident in São Tomé and Príncipe; Jorge Manuel dos Santos Oliveira was to be tried in Angola for fraud against an Angolan company. Sebastião José António Martins was subsequently named as Ramos Monteiro's replacement. Further ministerial changes were effected in November; most notably, George Rebelo Chicoty, hitherto Secretary of State for Foreign Affairs, was appointed Minister of Foreign Affairs, replacing Assunção Afonso dos Anjos.

Recent developments: anti-Government protests

Inspired by the pro-democracy demonstrations that had erupted across the Middle East and North Africa during early 2011, a small group of online activists attempted to stage its own anti-Government rally in Luanda in March to demand the resignation of the dos Santos regime. However, the authorities pre-emptively disbanded the march and briefly detained 15 demonstrators and journalists, attracting criticism from human rights organizations. The Government had earlier organized multiple pro-MPLA rallies, attended by some 20,000 people, and had issued threats against potential protesters. Further arrests were made in May, when a small-scale protest against poverty was dispersed by the Luandan police, and in September, following violent clashes in the capital between police and demonstrators. As a result of the latter incident, 18 anti-regime protesters received short gaol sentences (which were subsequently rescinded by the Tribunal da Relação) and demonstrations in central Luanda were proscribed. Another small, youth-led demonstration was halted by the police in late September, and several journalists were reportedly attacked by unknown assailants. The MPLA repeatedly accused UNITA of orchestrating the protests, a charge denied by the opposition party.

It was unclear whether President dos Santos, shaken by this unprecedented popular challenge to his authority, would lead the MPLA in the upcoming legislative elections, which were scheduled to be held by the end of 2012. There was media speculation in late 2011 that Manuel Vicente, CEO of the government-owned oil concern Sociedade Nacional de Combustíveis de Angola, would succeed dos Santos. Similar uncertainty also affected UNITA, although Samakuva was re-elected as party President in December.

Refugees

Between late 2002 and late 2003 the Angolan Government and the office of the UN High Commissioner for Refugees (UNHCR) established separate tripartite commissions with Zambia, the DRC, Namibia, Botswana, the Republic of the Congo and South Africa, with the aim of facilitating the repatriation of Angolan refugees from these countries. In 2010 there were an estimated 118,157 Angolan refugees in the region, including 79,617 in the DRC and 25,265 in Zambia. This was a significant reduction from figures from early 2003, at which time UNHCR had estimated that there were some 470,000 Angolan refugees in the region. UNHCR's budget for Angola was significantly increased in 2010 to accommodate plans to resume repatriation of the remaining Angolan refugees. UNHCR also continued to seek co-operation from governments in the country of asylum in finding alternative solutions for refugees, including naturalization or local integration with permanent residency. In mid-2010 UNHCR stated that from the end of 2011 Angolans living in the DRC, Zambia or other countries would no longer be considered refugees as options for repatriation were available. UNHCR resumed its Angolan refugee repatriation scheme in November 2011.

Foreign Affairs

Regional relations

Following the internal uprising in August 1998 against the regime of Laurent-Désiré Kabila in the DRC, the Angolan Government moved swiftly to provide Kabila with military support against the rebels. In October, as the conflict escalated in the east of the DRC, Angola, in alliance with Namibia and Zimbabwe, stated that it would continue supporting Kabila until the rebels were defeated. Following the assassination of Kabila in January 2001, the Angolan Government announced its intention to allow its troops stationed in the DRC to remain there until further notice; moreover, several thousand additional Angolan troops were moved into that country later in January. However, by the end of October 2002 Angola, Namibia and Zimbabwe had completed the withdrawal of their troops from the DRC. Between December 2003 and August 2004 the Angolan authorities were reported to have expelled an estimated 120,000 illegal diamond workers, mostly DRC nationals, from northern Angola. During 2008 and 2009 the Angolan and Congolese authorities engaged in mutual expulsions of refugees from their respective territories. In 2009 it was estimated that some 160,000 Congolese had been expelled from Angola, while at least 30,000 Angolans had been forcibly removed from the DRC. Although the two countries had agreed in October 2009 to cease these activities, during 2010–11 Angola continued to expel large numbers of DRC nationals, many of whom were reportedly beaten, tortured or sexually assaulted. It was widely believed that the forced repatriations (which often affected illegal diamond miners from the DRC) reflected bilateral tensions over the control of natural resources in the proximity of their shared border, the delineation of which was in dispute. Recurrent Angolan incursions into the DRC, ostensibly to monitor FLEC rebels, were also a source of discord.

In November 2008 President dos Santos was appointed Chairman of the Gulf of Guinea Commission, a regional dialogue bloc founded in 1999 to foster the co-operation and development of member countries, and to facilitate the prevention and resolution of conflicts in the region. The organization's headquarters had been established in Luanda in 2006, giving Angola a central role in the working of the Commission. The other members of the Commission are the DRC, Nigeria, São Tomé and Príncipe, Gabon, Cameroon and Equatorial Guinea.

Other external relations

In 2000 a French judicial inquiry was instigated into alleged arms-trafficking to Angola by a French company, Brenco International, and a French businessman, Pierre Falcone. The company, along with a number of prominent French politicians, was alleged to have engaged in money-laundering and the unauthorized sales of arms worth some US $600m. to the dos Santos Government in 1993–94. Falcone was placed under provisional detention in France in December 2000, but was released after one year, the maximum term allowed for temporary detention. French investigations into the sale of weapons to Angola, as well as the settlement of the country's debt to Russia, continued during 2005. Meanwhile, Falcone's appointment, in June 2003, as a plenipotentiary minister at the Angolan permanent delegation to UNESCO, entitling him to diplomatic immunity, provoked considerable international controversy and condemnation from Angolan opposition parties and civil society organizations. None the less, in April 2007 it was reported that 42 people, including Falcone and the Russian-Israeli businessman Arkadi Gaydamak (who remained in Israel and was therefore to be tried *in absentia*), would face charges ranging from arms-trafficking to tax evasion. Other notable defendants in the trial, which began in Paris in October 2008, were former French Minister of the Interior Charles Pasqua, and Jean-Christophe Mitterrand, son of former French President François Mitterrand. Of the 42 charged none were Angolan nationals, although prosecutors claimed that many officials in that country, including dos Santos, had received tens of millions of dollars in illegal payments. In

October 2009 guilty verdicts were handed down to Gaydamak and Falcone, who were each sentenced to six years' imprisonment. Pasqua was jailed for three years, two of which were suspended, and was fined €100,000, while Jean-Christophe Mitterrand was given a two-year suspended prison sentence and fined €375,000. Gaydamak had returned to Russia in early 2009, owing to the existence of an extradition treaty between Israel and France. (No such treaty applied to Russia and France.) Following an appeal, in April 2011 a French court acquitted Pasqua and reduced the prison sentences imposed upon Falcone and Gaydamak to two-and-a-half years and three years, respectively.

In July 1996 Angola was among the five lusophone African countries that, together with Portugal and Brazil, formed the Comunidade dos Países de Língua Portuguesa (see p. 463), a Portuguese-speaking commonwealth seeking to achieve collective benefits from co-operation in technical, cultural and social matters. In 2004 Angola joined the African Peer Review Mechanism, a group designed to monitor economic and political development. In May 2007 the Governments of Angola and Mozambique signed an agreement on employment and social security, pledging to increase efforts in the fight against poverty and to provide better working conditions for their people. In May 2010 Angola and Portugal reached an agreement on military co-operation, including military training. Some 3,000 Angolan military personnel had been trained in academies in Portugal since the 1990s it was reported. Discussions on defence were also carried out in early 2010 with Namibia and Guinea-Bissau, and with Brazil in August.

The Vice-President of the People's Republic of China, Xi Jinping, met with officials from Angola in November 2010 to discuss co-operation between the two countries. The delegations agreed that the two nations were strategic partners and pledged to improve dialogue, realign their institutional mechanisms and raise the level of trade and economic co-operation. This joint declaration was regarded as an attempt to build on the foundations established in 2008 when the Angolan and Chinese Governments signed a Framework Agreement on Co-operation.

CONSTITUTION AND GOVERNMENT

According to the Constitution promulgated on 5 February 2010, legislative power is vested in the Assembleia Nacional (National Assembly), with 223 members elected for five years on the basis of proportional representation. Executive power is held by the President, who serves a term of five years (renewable for a maximum of two terms). The leader of the political party, or coalition of political parties, obtaining the majority of votes in legislative elections shall be named President of the Republic and shall be assisted by a Vice-President; the position of Vice-President shall be filled by the deputy leader of the ruling party. As Head of State and Commander-in-Chief of the armed forces, the President governs with the assistance of an appointed Council of Ministers.

For the purposes of local government, the country is divided into 18 provinces, each administered by an appointed Governor.

REGIONAL AND INTERNATIONAL CO-OPERATION

Angola is a member of the African Union (see p. 189), of the Common Market for Eastern and Southern Africa (COMESA, see p. 237), of the Southern African Development Community (SADC, see p. 423), and of the Gulf of Guinea Commission (see p. 463).

Angola became a member of the UN in 1976, and was admitted to the World Trade Organization (WTO, see p. 433) in 1996. Angola participates in the Group of 77 (G77, see p. 450) developing countries. In 2007 Angola joined the Organization of the Petroleum Exporting Countries (see p. 408). Angola is also a member of the Comunidade dos Países de Língua Portuguesa (see p. 463).

ECONOMIC AFFAIRS

In 2010, according to estimates by the World Bank, Angola's gross national income (GNI), measured at average 2008–10 prices, was US $75,150m., equivalent to $3,940 per head (or $5,400 per head on an international purchasing-power parity basis). During 2001–10, it was estimated, Angola's population increased at an average annual rate of 3.2%, while gross domestic product (GDP) per head increased, in real terms, by an average of 8.4% per year. Overall GDP increased, in real terms, at an average annual rate of 11.9% in 2001–10; growth in 2010 was 2.3%.

According to the World Bank, agriculture contributed an estimated 10.0% of GDP in 2010. An estimated 68.1% of the total working population were employed in the agricultural sector in 2012, according to FAO figures. Coffee is the principal cash crop. The main subsistence crops are cassava, sweet potatoes, maize, potatoes, bananas and sugar cane. The widespread presence of unexploded anti-personnel mines continued to be an obstacle to the successful redevelopment of the agricultural sector. From 2005 the Government commenced a programme of investment in the formerly flourishing fisheries sector, which held much potential for redevelopment. During 2001–10, according to the World Bank, agricultural GDP increased at an average annual rate of 14.1%, increasing by 12.0% in 2010.

Industry (including mining, manufacturing, construction and power) provided an estimated 62.9% of GDP in 2010, according to the World Bank, and employed an estimated 10.5% of the labour force in 1991. The economic recovery in the country, as well as increased petroleum production and earnings, and Chinese sponsorship, led to strong expansion in the construction sector from 2005, with investment in the redevelopment of infrastructure. Industrial GDP increased, in real terms, at an average annual rate of 11.7% in 2001–10; growth in industrial GDP was 5.6% in 2010.

Mining contributed an estimated 69.1% of GDP in 2009, according to the African Development Bank (AfDB). Petroleum production (including liquefied petroleum gas) accounted for an estimated 58.5% of GDP in 2006. Angola's principal mineral exports are petroleum and diamonds. In addition, there are reserves of iron ore, copper, lead, zinc, gold, manganese, phosphates, salt and uranium. At the end of 2010 Angola had estimated petroleum reserves of 13,500m. barrels, sufficient to sustain production at current levels for some 20 years. As a member of the Organization of the Petroleum Exporting Countries (OPEC, see p. 408), Angola is subject to production quotas agreed by the Organization's Conference.

The manufacturing sector provided an estimated 5.8% of GDP in 2010, according to the World Bank. The principal branch of manufacturing is petroleum refining. Other manufacturing activities include food-processing, brewing, textiles and construction materials. The GDP of the manufacturing sector increased at an average annual rate of 17.5% in 2001–10; growth in manufacturing GDP was 9.0% in 2010.

Construction provided 0.9% of GDP in 2009, according to the AfDB. The GDP of the construction sector grew by 13.5% in 2008, but declined by 0.1% in 2009.

Energy is derived mainly from hydroelectric power, which, according to the World Bank, provided 96.3% of Angola's electricity production in 2008, while petroleum accounted for 3.7%. Angola's power potential exceeds its requirements; however, power supply is erratic and the country lacks a national grid.

According to the World Bank, services accounted for an estimated 27.1% of GDP in 2010, and engaged an estimated 20.1% of the labour force in 1991. In real terms, the GDP of the services sector increased at an average annual rate of 11.3% in 2001–10. However, services GDP decreased by 1.8% in 2009 and by 10.0% in 2010.

In 2009 Angola recorded an estimated visible trade surplus of US $18,168m., while there was a deficit of $7,572m. on the current account of the balance of payments. In 2009 the principal source of imports was Portugal (19.6%); other major suppliers were the People's Republic of China, the USA, Brazil and France. The principal market for exports in 2009 was China (37.0%); the USA and France were also significant purchasers of Angola's exports. The principal export in 2008 was crude petroleum, accounting for an estimated 96.5% of total export earnings, while diamonds contributed 1.9%. In 2007 it was estimated that Angola was the largest supplier of crude petroleum to China.

According to IMF estimates, in 2009 there was a budget deficit, on an accrual basis, of 515.5m. kwanza, equivalent to 8.6% of GDP in that year. (For 2010 the IMF projected a budget deficit of 581.0m. kwanza, equivalent to 7.5% of GDP.) Angola's general government gross debt was 2,654.5m. kwanza in 2010, equivalent to 35.0% of GDP. Angola's total external debt at the end of 2008 was US $16,715m., of which $13,722m. was public and publicly guaranteed debt. In that year the cost of servicing long-term public and publicly guaranteed debt and repayments to the IMF was equivalent to 8.4% of the value of exports of goods, services and income (excluding workers' remittances). In 2010 a Public Debt Management Unit was established to improve the mechanisms in place for monitoring and controlling the country's debt. In 2000–10 the average annual rate of inflation was

42.4%, according to the International Labour Organization. Consumer prices increased by an average of 14.5% in 2010.

Following the ratification of a cease-fire agreement in April 2002 that brought an end to the civil war, Angola experienced dramatic economic growth, led largely by developments in the petroleum sector. By 2010, according to the BP Statistical Review of World Energy, total national output of crude petroleum had reached 1.9m. barrels per day, and Angola was the second largest oil producer in Africa behind Nigeria. In 2008 Angola became the second largest supplier of petroleum to China, and in so doing secured some US $13,000m. in financial assistance. However, opposition parties and international observers maintained that the benefits of the investment (most notably in infrastructure projects) had not filtered through to the Angolan people; some two-thirds of the population continued to subsist on less than $1 per day, while the rate of unemployment stood at around 65% in the late 2000s. This was partly a result of the migration of vast numbers of agricultural workers to Luanda during the civil war, leaving just 10% of productive land cultivated in 2008. The global financial crisis and the resultant decrease in international oil prices precipitated a deceleration in real GDP growth to 2.4% in 2009 (from 13.8% in 2008) and left the country unable to service its debts. Hence, in November 2009 the IMF approved a 27-month Stand-By Arrangement totalling $1,320m., and the Government, in return, agreed to implement a fiscal reform programme, which involved significantly decreasing public expenditure. As a result of these measures and a subsequent rise in the price of oil, by late 2011 Angola's financial position had improved markedly. According to the IMF, real GDP expanded by 3.4% in 2010, while growth of 3.7% was expected in 2011. The Government had anticipated higher growth rates, but technical issues negatively affected oil output during 2010–11. Nevertheless, with the production problems resolved, the IMF projected real GDP growth of 10.8% in 2012, although this was dependent upon stable oil prices. The diamond sector also benefited from a rebound in global prices, with output and exports forecast to rise during 2011 and several new diamond-mining operations expected to enter production in the near future.

PUBLIC HOLIDAYS

2013: 1 January (New Year's Day), 4 January (Martyrs' Day), 4 February (Anniversary of the outbreak of the armed struggle against Portuguese colonialism), 12 February (Carnival Day and International Women's Day), 27 March (Victory Day)*, 29 March (Good Friday), 4 April (Peace and National Reconciliation Day), 14 April (Youth Day)*, 1 May (Workers' Day), 25 May (Africa Day), 1 June (International Children's Day), 1 August (Armed Forces' Day)*, 17 September (National Hero's Day, birthday of Dr Agostinho Neto), 2 November (All Souls' Day), 11 November (Independence Day), 1 December (Pioneers' Day)*, 10 December (Foundation of the MPLA Day)*, 25 December (Christmas Day and Family Day).

* Although not officially recognized as public holidays, these days are popularly treated as such.

Statistical Survey

Sources (unless otherwise stated): Instituto Nacional de Estatística, Av. Ho Chi Minh, CP 1215, Luanda; tel. 222322776; e-mail ine@angonet.gn.apc.org; Ministério do Planeamento, Largo do Palácio do Povo, Rua 17 de Setembro, Luanda; tel. 222390188; fax 222339586; e-mail geral@minplan.gov.ao; internet www.minplan.gov.ao.

Area and Population

AREA, POPULATION AND DENSITY

Area (sq km)	1,246,700*
Population (census results)	
30 December 1960	4,480,719
15 December 1970	
Males	2,943,974
Females	2,702,192
Total	5,646,166
Population (UN estimates at mid-year)†	
2010	19,081,912
2011	19,618,432
2012	20,162,518
Density (per sq km) at mid-2012	16.2

* 481,354 sq miles.

† Source: UN, *World Population Prospects: The 2010 Revision*.

POPULATION BY AGE AND SEX
(UN estimates at mid-2012)

	Males	Females	Total
0–14	4,644,934	4,610,293	9,255,227
15–64	5,121,760	5,284,176	10,405,936
65 and over	223,739	277,616	501,355
Total	9,990,433	10,172,085	20,162,518

Source: UN, *World Population Prospects: The 2010 Revision*.

PROVINCES
(population estimates, 2002)

	Area (sq km)	Population	Density (per sq km)
Luanda	2,418	2,700,421	1,116.8
Huambo	34,274	1,454,352	42.4
Bié	70,314	997,860	14.2
Malanje	87,246	784,820	9.0
Huíla	75,002	1,161,410	15.5
Uíge	58,698	929,120	15.8
Benguela	31,788	1,595,193	50.2
Kwanza-Sul	55,660	744,235	13.4
Kwanza-Norte	24,110	375,316	15.6
Moxico	223,023	369,290	1.7
Lunda-Norte	102,783	386,036	3.8
Zaire	40,130	290,400	7.2
Cunene	88,342	397,750	4.5
Cabinda	7,270	192,454	26.5
Bengo	31,371	424,856	13.5
Lunda-Sul	56,985	470,072	8.2
Kuando Kubango	199,049	391,670	2.0
Namibe	58,137	281,745	4.8
Total	1,246,600	13,947,000	11.2

PRINCIPAL TOWNS
(population at 1970 census)

Luanda (capital)	480,613	Benguela	40,996
Huambo (Nova Lisboa)	61,885	Lubango (Sá da Bandeira)	31,674
Lobito	59,258	Malange	31,559

Source: Direcção dos Serviços de Estatística.

Mid-2010 ('000, incl. suburbs, UN estimates): Huambo 1,034; Luanda 4,772 (Source: UN, *World Urbanization Prospects: The 2009 Revision*).

BIRTHS AND DEATHS
(annual averages, UN estimates)

	1995–2000	2000–05	2005–10
Birth rate (per 1,000)	51.0	49.0	43.5
Death rate (per 1,000)	21.1	17.6	15.3

Source: UN, *World Population Prospects: The 2010 Revision*.

Life expectancy (years at birth, WHO estimates): 52 (males 51; females 53) in 2009 (Source: WHO, *World Health Statistics*).

ECONOMICALLY ACTIVE POPULATION
('000 persons, 1991, estimates)

	Males	Females	Total
Agriculture, etc.	1,518	1,374	2,892
Industry	405	33	438
Services	644	192	836
Total labour force	2,567	1,599	4,166

Source: UN Economic Commission for Africa, *African Statistical Yearbook*.

Mid-2012 (estimates in '000): Agriculture, etc. 6,193; Total (incl. others) 9,011 (Source: FAO).

Health and Welfare

KEY INDICATORS

Total fertility rate (children per woman, 2009)	5.6
Under-5 mortality rate (per 1,000 live births, 2009)	161
HIV/AIDS (% of persons aged 15–49, 2009)	2.0
Physicians (per 1,000 head, 2004)	0.08
Hospital beds (per 1,000 head, 2005)	0.1
Health expenditure (2008): US $ per head (PPP)	183
Health expenditure (2008): % of GDP	3.3
Health expenditure (2008): public (% of total)	85.0
Access to water (% of persons, 2008)	50
Access to sanitation (% of persons, 2008)	57
Total carbon dioxide emissions ('000 metric tons, 2007)	24,743.0
Carbon dioxide emissions per head (metric tons, 2007)	1.4
Human Development Index (2011): ranking	148
Human Development Index (2011): value	0.486

For sources and definitions, see explanatory note on p. vi.

Agriculture

PRINCIPAL CROPS
('000 metric tons)

	2008	2009	2010
Wheat*	4	5	5
Rice, paddy	8	14	14*
Maize	702	970	970*
Millet	27	40	41*
Potatoes	402	823	827*
Sweet potatoes	820	983	997*
Cassava (Manioc)	10,057	12,828	12,867*
Sugar cane*	360	360	360
Beans, dry	124	247	250*
Groundnuts, with shell	92	111	109*
Palm oil†	46	55	57
Sunflower seed*	12	11	24
Oil palm fruit*	250	280	280
Cottonseed*	1	1	1
Tomatoes*	15	15	16
—continued	**2008**	**2009**	**2010**
Onions and shallots, green*	19	19	17
Bananas*	430	432	433
Citrus fruit*	96	97	100
Pineapples*	42	42	44
Coffee, green†	3	1	2

* FAO estimate(s).

† Unofficial figures.

Aggregate production ('000 metric tons, may include official, semi-official or estimated data): Total cereals 742 in 2008, 1,030 in 2009, 1,030 in 2010; Total roots and tubers 11,279 in 2008, 14,633 in 2009, 14,690 in 2010; Total vegetables (incl. melons) 291 in 2008, 297 in 2009, 275 in 2010; Total fruits (excl. melons) 607 in 2008, 602 in 2009, 608 in 2010.

Source: FAO.

LIVESTOCK
('000 head, year ending September, FAO estimates)

	2008	2009	2010*
Cattle	4,921	5,031	5,143
Pigs*	785	788	791
Sheep*	345	350	355
Goats	2,478	2,524*	2,571
Chickens*	7,000	7,100	7,200

* FAO estimate(s).

Source: FAO.

LIVESTOCK PRODUCTS
('000 metric tons, FAO estimates)

	2008	2009	2010
Cattle meat	100.3	104.4	105.5
Goat meat	11.2	11.4	11.4
Pig meat	28.0	28.2	32.5
Chicken meat	8.0	8.1	8.1
Game meat	7.3	7.8	8.9
Sheep meat	1.3	1.3	1.3
Cows' milk	195.5	158.4	183.8
Hen eggs	4.9	4.5	4.5
Honey	26.6	25.6	22.9

Source: FAO.

Forestry

ROUNDWOOD REMOVALS
('000 cubic metres, excluding bark, FAO estimates)

	2007	2008	2009
Sawlogs, veneer logs and logs for sleepers	46	46	46
Other industrial wood	1,050	1,050	1,050
Fuel wood	3,741	3,828	3,917
Total	4,837	4,924	5,013

2010: Production assumed to be unchanged from 2009 (FAO estimates).

Source: FAO.

SAWNWOOD PRODUCTION
('000 cubic metres, including railway sleepers, FAO estimates)

	1983	1984	1985
Total	6	2	5

1986–2010: Annual production as in 1985 (FAO estimates).

Source: FAO.

Fishing

('000 metric tons, live weight)

	2007	2008	2009
Capture	306.4*	305.8*	272.3
Freshwater fishes	9.0*	7.5*	5.8
West coast sole	10.2	0.9	0.8
West African croakers	15.3	21.9	19.1
Dentex	22.1	26.2	33.8
Cunene horse mackerel	31.7	44.4	13.8
Pilchards and sardinellas	80.6	70.4	74.2
Chub mackerel	6.4	7.6	10.1
Aquaculture*	0.2	0.2	0.2
Total catch (incl. others)*	306.6	306.0	272.5

* FAO estimate(s).

Source: FAO.

Mining

('000 metric tons, unless otherwise indicated)

	2008	2009	2010*
Crude petroleum ('000 42-gallon barrels)	684,375	651,000	676,000
Salt (unrefined)	35	35	45
Diamonds ('000 carats)†	8,907	13,828	13,000

* Estimates.

† Reported figures, based on estimates of 10% of production at industrial grade.

Source: US Geological Survey.

Industry

SELECTED PRODUCTS

('000 metric tons, unless otherwise indicated)

	2001	2002	2003
Frozen fish	57.8	43.9	36.2
Wheat flour	20.3	21.0	38.2
Bread	313.7	n.a.	264.0
Beer ('000 hl)	82.0	80.0	192.0
Non-alcoholic beverages ('000 hl)	82.0	56.0	88.8
Jet fuels	330.9	352.5	324.8
Motor spirit (petrol)	107.2	104.6	95.9
Kerosene	31.2	36.9	43.9
Distillate fuel oils	501.7	461.0	407.5
Residual fuel oils	552.8	590.7	639.3
Butane gas	31.5	34.3	30.0

Source: IMF, *Angola: Selected Issues and Statistical Appendix* (April 2005).

2004 ('000 metric tons): Jet fuels 302; Motor gasoline 96; Naphthas 85; Kerosene 41; Distillate fuel oils 669; Residual fuel oils 604; Cement 250 (Source: UN Industrial Commodity Statistics Database).

2005 ('000 metric tons): Jet fuels 290; Motor gasoline 134; Naphthas 79; Kerosene 31; Distillate fuel oils 675; Residual fuel oils 609 (Source: UN Industrial Commodity Statistics Database).

2006 ('000 metric tons): Jet fuels 313; Motor gasoline 98; Naphthas 155; Kerosene 5; Distillate fuel oils 681; Residual fuel oils 587 (Source: UN Industrial Commodity Statistics Database).

2007 ('000 metric tons): Jet fuels 351; Motor gasoline 56; Naphthas 140; Kerosene 0.5; Distillate fuel oils 513; Residual fuel oils 601 (Source: UN Industrial Commodity Statistics Database).

2008 ('000 metric tons): Jet fuels 325; Motor gasoline 68; Naphthas 118; Kerosene 1; Distillate fuel oils 527; Residual fuel oils 680 (Source: UN Industrial Commodity Statistics Database).

Cement ('000 metric tons): 1,400 in 2007; 1,780 in 2008; 1,800 in 2009; 1,500 in 2010 (estimate) (Source: US Geological Survey).

Finance

CURRENCY AND EXCHANGE RATES

Monetary Units

100 lwei = 1 kwanza.

Sterling, Dollar and Euro Equivalents (30 December 2011)

£1 sterling = 147.300 kwanza;
US $1 = 95.272 kwanza;
€1 = 123.272 kwanza;
1,000 kwanza = £6.79 = $10.50 = €8.11.

Average Exchange Rate (kwanza per US $)

2009 79.328
2010 91.906
2011 93.740

Note: In April 1994 the introduction of a new method of setting exchange rates resulted in an effective devaluation of the new kwanza, to US $1 = 68,297 new kwanza, and provided for an end to the system of multiple exchange rates. Further substantial devaluations followed, and in July 1995 a 'readjusted' kwanza, equivalent to 1,000 new kwanza, was introduced. The currency, however, continued to depreciate. Between July 1997 and June 1998 a fixed official rate of US $1 = 262,376 readjusted kwanza was in operation. In May 1999 the Central Bank announced its decision to abolish the existing dual currency exchange rate system. In December 1999 the readjusted kwanza was replaced by a new currency, the kwanza, equivalent to 1m. readjusted kwanza.

BUDGET

('000 million kwanza)

Revenue	2005	2006	2007
Tax revenue	1,050.3	1,589.5	2,052.8
Petroleum	862.1	1,350.6	1,722.0
Income tax	62.2	82.5	120.3
Tax on goods and services	54.9	67.0	91.5
Taxes on foreign trade	47.0	58.2	78.8
Other taxes	24.1	31.2	40.2
Contributions to social welfare	21.0	63.7	48.2
Grants	6.4	—	2.3
Other revenue	8.2	31.8	21.4
Total	1,085.8	1,685.0	2,124.7

Expenditure	2005	2006	2007
Current	725.0	852.4	1,068.2
Personnel*	246.7	311.3	364.5
Goods and services	245.1	308.4	343.9
Interest payments	53.5	53.3	50.9
Transfers	179.7	179.3	308.9
Capital	134.7	436.0	531.3
Total	859.7	1,288.4	1,599.5

* Including wages and salaries of defence and public order personnel.

Source: Ministry of Finance, Luanda.

2008 ('000 million kwanza, estimates): *Revenue:* Tax revenue 3,070.2 (Petroleum 2,601.9, Non-petroleum 468.3); Non-tax revenue 145.3; Total 3,215.5 (excl. grants 1.9). *Expenditure:* Current 1,761.2 (Personnel 543.0, Goods and services 539.1, Interest payments due 93.9, Transfers 585.2); Capital expenditure 892.6; Total 2,653.8 (Source: IMF, *Angola: Second and Third Reviews Under the Stand-By Arrangement and Request for Waivers of Nonobservance of Two Performance Criteria*—September 2010).

2009 ('000 million kwanza, estimates): *Revenue:* Tax revenue 1,703.7 (Petroleum 1,164.8, Non-petroleum 539.0); Non-tax revenue 142.9; Total 1,846.6 (excl. grants 1.3). *Expenditure:* Current 1,620.1 (Personnel 660.2, Goods and services 383.3, Interest payments due 130.0, Transfers 446.6); Capital expenditure 743.3; Total 2,363.4 (Source: IMF, *Angola: Second and Third Reviews Under the Stand-By Arrangement and Request for Waivers of Nonobservance of Two Performance Criteria*—September 2010).

2010 ('000 million kwanza, projections): *Revenue:* Tax revenue 3,109 (Petroleum 2,476, Non-petroleum 632); Non-tax revenue 160; Total 3,269 (excl. grants 2). *Expenditure:* Current 2,095 (Personnel 779, Goods and services 586, Interest payments due 163, Transfers 567); Capital expenditure 595; Total 2,690 (Source: IMF, *Angola: Fourth Review Under the Stand-By Arrangement, Request for Waivers of Nonobservance of Performance Criteria, Request for Waivers of Applicability of Performance Criteria, and Request for Modification of Performance Criteria*—February 2011).

INTERNATIONAL RESERVES
(US $ million at 31 December)

	2008	2009	2010
IMF special drawing rights	0.26	425.65	410.13
Foreign exchange	17,869.15	13,238.45	19,339.35
Total	17,869.41	13,664.10	19,749.47

Source: IMF, *International Financial Statistics*.

MONEY SUPPLY
(million kwanza at 31 December)

	2008	2009	2010
Currency outside banks	126,079	169,748	173,387
Demand deposits at banking institutions	508,789	607,017	677,489
Total (incl. others)	634,872	776,770	855,284

Source: IMF, *International Financial Statistics*.

COST OF LIVING
(Consumer Price Index for Luanda at December; base: 1994 average = 100)

	1999	2000	2001
Food	3,551.1	11,211.2	22,494.2
Clothing	5,189.4	21,449.2	45,733.9
Rent, fuel and light	28,392.7	157,756.4	434,224.6
All items (incl. others)	5,083.6	18,723.6	40,456.1

Source: IMF, *Angola: Selected Issues and Statistical Appendix* (September 2003).

All items (Consumer Price Index for Luanda; base: 2000 = 100): 2,347.7 in 2007; 2,640.5 in 2008; 3,003.0 in 2009; 3,437.5 in 2010 (Source: ILO).

NATIONAL ACCOUNTS
(million kwanza at current prices)

Expenditure on the Gross Domestic Product

	2007	2008	2009
Government final consumption expenditure	1,017,251	1,667,255	1,442,455
Private final consumption expenditure	1,480,719	2,111,973	2,481,784
Gross fixed capital formation	604,638	959,465	918,327
Increase in stocks	31,613	50,163	48,014
Total domestic expenditure	3,134,221	4,788,856	4,890,580
Exports of goods and services	3,429,315	4,820,382	2,933,215
Less Imports of goods and services	2,017,677	3,235,538	2,294,924
GDP in purchasers' values	4,545,860	6,373,700	5,528,871

Gross Domestic Product by Economic Activity

	2007	2008	2009
Agriculture, forestry and fishing	424,070	488,112	477,014
Mining and quarrying	3,185,046	4,435,571	3,830,608
Manufacturing	41,313	51,907	48,228
Construction	26,707	97,001	49,499
Wholesale and retail trade; restaurants and hotels	476,741	720,507	583,229
Other services	457,252	674,856	554,704
GDP at factor cost	4,611,130	6,467,955	5,543,281
Less Imputed bank service charge*	65,270	94,255	14,410
GDP in purchasers' values	4,545,860	6,373,700	5,528,871

* Figures obtained as residuals.

Source: African Development Bank.

BALANCE OF PAYMENTS
(US $ million)

	2007	2008	2009
Exports of goods f.o.b.	44,396.2	63,913.9	40,827.9
Imports of goods f.o.b.	–13,661.5	–20,982.2	–22,659.9
Trade balance	30,734.7	42,931.8	18,168.0
Exports of services	310.7	329.5	623.1
Imports of services	–12,643.2	–22,139.3	–19,169.4
Balance on goods and services	18,402.2	21,121.9	–378.2
Other income received	622.6	422.3	131.3
Other income paid	–8,211.6	–14,139.8	–6,954.5
Balance on goods, services and income	10,803.2	7,404.3	–7,201.3
Current transfers received	45.7	154.5	56.8
Current transfers paid	–267.6	–364.5	–427.1
Current balance	10,581.3	7,194.2	–7,571.7
Capital account (net)	6.9	6.5	4.1
Direct investment abroad	–911.8	–2,569.6	–6.8
Direct investment from abroad	–893.3	1,679.0	2,205.3
Portfolio investment assets	–2,015.4	–1,757.5	–558.1
Portfolio investment liabilities	—	—	68.0
Other investment assets	–4,854.9	–2,709.2	–1,369.0
Other investment liabilities	2,833.3	6,576.1	1,784.1
Net errors and omissions	–1,641.0	–1,235.9	454.7
Overall balance	3,105.0	7,183.5	–4,989.3

Source: IMF, *International Financial Statistics*.

External Trade

SELECTED COMMODITIES

Imports (million kwanza)	1983	1984	1985
Animal products	1,315	1,226	1,084
Vegetable products	2,158	3,099	2,284
Fats and oils	946	1,006	1,196
Food and beverages	2,400	1,949	1,892
Industrial chemical products	1,859	1,419	1,702
Plastic materials	431	704	454
Textiles	1,612	1,816	1,451
Base metals	1,985	3,730	2,385
Electrical equipment	3,296	2,879	2,571
Transport equipment	2,762	2,240	3,123
Total (incl. others)	20,197	21,370	19,694

Exports (US $ million)	2006	2007	2008
Crude petroleum	29,928.6	42,351.8	61,665.7
Refined petroleum products	294.6	323.8	400.1
Gas (per barrel)	259.8	327.9	391.6
Diamonds	1,154.6	1,182.0	1,209.8
Total (incl. others)	31,862.2	44,396.2	63,913.9

* Estimates.

Total imports (US $ million): 8,777.6 in 2006; 13,661.4 in 2007; 20,982.1 in 2008.

Sources: Banco Nacional de Angola; African Development Bank; IMF, *Angola: Selected Issues and Statistical Appendix* (October 2007).

PRINCIPAL TRADING PARTNERS
(US $ million)*

Imports c.i.f.	2007	2008	2009
Brazil	1,218.1	1,974.6	1,333.0
China, People's Republic	1,234.5	2,942.5	2,386.0
France	742.0	745.3	752.7
Italy	267.2	334.0	714.4
Portugal	2,302.2	3,339.1	3,126.7
Korea, Republic	173.7	1,266.3	325.3
South Africa	772.2	897.8	682.0
USA	1,280.2	2,117.0	1,422.9
Total (incl. others)	12,317.1	20,296.9	15,918.8

Exports f.o.b.	2007	2008	2009
Canada	1,117.8	2,607.3	1,207.2
China, People's Republic	12,888.7	22,382.5	14,675.8
France	2,370.5	4,010.3	3,270.5
Germany	196.0	701.3	343.4
Portugal	507.1	601.5	211.2
South Africa	1,645.8	2,686.5	1,370.6
Sweden	—	148.6	553.5
Taiwan	2,121.5	2,012.7	1,058.6
USA	12,926.0	19,497.7	9,703.1
Total (incl. others)	40,222.6	67,504.1	39,620.3

* Data are compiled on the basis of reporting by Angola's trading partners, and totals may differ to those for trade recorded by commodity as a result.

Source: Trade Map-Trade Competitiveness Map, International Trade Centre, www.intracen.org/marketanalysis.

Transport

GOODS TRANSPORT
(million metric tons)

	2002	2003	2004
Air	646.4	248.6	21,745.0
Road	7,505.7	4,635.5	19,031.0
Railway	253.6	129.3	54.0
Water	3,523.8	4,259.7	1,189.0

Source: Portais Governo de Angola.

PASSENGER TRANSPORT
(million passenger-km)

	2002	2003	2004
Air	804.9	978.4	21,229.0
Road	235,208.0	1,112,272.0	1,188,063.0
Railway	2,975.2	3,708.4	192.0
Water	—	—	1,522.0

Source: Portais Governo de Angola.

ROAD TRAFFIC
(motor vehicles in use at 31 December, estimates)

	1997	1998	1999
Passenger cars	103,400	107,100	117,200
Lorries and vans	107,600	110,500	118,300
Total	211,000	217,600	235,500

2000–02: data assumed to be unchanged from 1999 (estimates).

Source: UN, *Statistical Yearbook*.

2007 (motor vehicles in use at 31 December): Total 671,060 (Source: IRF, *World Road Statistics*).

SHIPPING

Merchant Fleet
(registered at 31 December)

	2007	2008	2009
Number of vessels	130	134	153
Total displacement (grt)	56,770	59,433	63,098

Source: IHS Fairplay, *World Fleet Statistics*.

International Sea-borne Freight Traffic
(estimates, '000 metric tons)

	1989	1990	1991
Goods loaded	19,980	21,102	23,288
Goods unloaded	1,235	1,242	1,261

Source: UN Economic Commission for Africa, *African Statistical Yearbook*.

CIVIL AVIATION
(traffic on scheduled services)

	2007	2008	2009
Kilometres flown (million)	7	7	7
Passengers carried ('000)	277	284	275
Passenger-km (million)	691	706	680
Total ton-km (million)	140	135	126

Source: UN, *Statistical Yearbook*.

Tourism

FOREIGN TOURIST ARRIVALS

Country of origin	2006	2007	2008
Belgium	1,016	1,469	1,654
Brazil	10,589	21,749	35,231
France	10,103	13,305	26,649
Germany	1,161	1,790	2,551
Italy	1,747	2,308	3,324
Philippines	2,143	3,488	7,043
Portugal	25,984	37,905	53,568
Russia	1,634	2,241	2,477
South Africa	9,648	13,328	15,476
Spain	1,605	2,044	2,593
United Kingdom	10,737	15,440	20,425
USA	6,967	10,593	14,319
Total (incl. others)	121,426	194,730	294,258

Tourist arrivals ('000): 366 in 2009; 425 in 2010 (provisional).

Tourism receipts (US $ million, incl. passenger transport, unless otherwise indicated): 91 in 2006; 236 in 2007; 293 in 2008; 534 in 2009 (excl. passenger transport).

Source: World Tourism Organization.

Communications Media

	2008	2009	2010
Telephones ('000 main lines in use)	114.3	303.2	303.2
Mobile cellular telephones ('000 subscribers)	6,773.4	8,109.4	8,909.2
Internet subscribers ('000)	107	320	n.a.
Broadband subscribers ('000)	15.9	20.0	20.0

Personal computers: 110,614 (6.5 per 1,000 persons) in 2006.

Source: International Telecommunication Union.

Radio receivers ('000 in use, 1999): 840 (Source: UN, *Statistical Yearbook*).

Daily newspapers (2004): 1 (average circulation 35,0000 copies) (Source: UNESCO Institute for Statistics).

Book production (1995): 22 titles (all books) (Source: UNESCO, *Statistical Yearbook*).

Education

(2009/10)

	Teachers	Students		
		Males	Females	Total
Pre-primary	18,032	332,182	336,176	668,358
Primary	93,379	2,361,331	1,911,675	4,273,006
Secondary:				
general	13,694	261,906	225,623	487,529
vocational	8,294	219,144	141,651	360,795
Higher	2,407	36,172	30,079	66,251

Source: mainly UNESCO Institute for Statistics.

Pupil-teacher ratio (primary education, UNESCO estimate): 45.8 in 2009/10 (Source: UNESCO Institute for Statistics).

Adult literacy rate (UNESCO estimates): 70.0% (males 82.9%; females 57.6%) in 2009 (Source: UNESCO Institute for Statistics).

Directory

The Government

HEAD OF STATE

President: JOSÉ EDUARDO DOS SANTOS.

Vice-President: FERNANDO DA PIEDADE DIAS DOS SANTOS.

COUNCIL OF MINISTERS
(May 2012)

President: JOSÉ EDUARDO DOS SANTOS.

Vice-President: FERNANDO DA PIEDADE DIAS DOS SANTOS.

Minister of State and Head of Civil Staff: CARLOS MARIA DA SILVA FEIJÓ.

Minister of State and Head of Military Staff: Gen. MANUEL HÉLDER VIEIRA DIAS, Jr.

Minister of the Economy: ABRAHÃO PIO DOS SANTOS GOURGEL.

Minister of Foreign Affairs: GEORGE REBELO CHICOTY.

Secretary of State for Foreign Affairs: DOMINGOS MANUEL AUGUSTO.

Secretary of State for Foreign Affairs, responsible for Administrative Organization: RUI JORGE CARNEIRO MANGUEIRA.

Secretary of State for Co-operation: EXALGINA RENÉE OLAVO GAMBÔA.

Minister of National Defence: Gen. CÂNDIDO PEREIRA DOS SANTOS VAN-DÚNEM.

Minister of the Interior: SEBASTIÃO JOSÉ ANTÓNIO MARTINS.

Minister of Parliamentary Affairs: NORBERTO FERNANDO DOS SANTOS.

Minister of Territorial Administration: BORNITO DE SOUSA BALTAZAR DIOGO.

Minister of Justice: GUILHERMINA CONTREIRAS DA COSTA PRATA.

Minister of Public Administration, Labour and Social Security: Dr ANTÓNIO DOMINGOS PITRA DA COSTA NETO.

Minister of Social Communication: CAROLINA CERQUEIRA.

Minister of Youth and Sports: GONÇALVES MANUEL MUANDUMBA.

Minister of Planning: ANA AFONSO DIAS LOURENÇO.

Minister of Finance: CARLOS ALBERTO LOPES.

Secretary of State for Finance: VALENTINA MATIAS DE SOUSA FILIPE.

Secretary of State for the Budget: ALCIDES SAFECA.

Secretary of State for the Treasury: MANUEL NETO COSTA.

Minister of Commerce: MARIA IDALINA DE OLIVEIRA VALENTE.

Secretary of State for Commerce: AUGUSTO ARCHER DE SOUSA MANGUEIRA.

Minister of Hotels and Tourism: PEDRO MUTINDI.

Minister of Agriculture, Rural Development and Fisheries: AFONSO PEDRO CANGA.

Secretary of State for Agriculture: JOSÉ AMARO TATI.

Secretary of State for Rural Development: MARIA FILOMENA DE FÁTIMA LOBÃO TELO CANGA.

Secretary of State for Fisheries: VITÓRIA FRANCISCO LAPAS CRISTÓVÃO DE BARROS NETO.

Minister of Geology, Mines and Industry: JOAQUIM DUARTE DA COSTA DAVID.

Secretary of State for Geology and Mines: MANKENDA AMBROISE.

Secretary of State for Industry: KIALA NGONE GABRIEL.

Minister of Petroleum: JOSÉ MARIA BOTELHO DE VASCONCELOS.

Minister of the Environment: MARIA DE FÁTIMA MONTEIRO JARDIM.

Minister of Town Planning and Construction: FERNANDO ALBERTO SOARES DA FONSECA DE LEMOS.

Secretary of State for Town Planning and Housing: JOAQUIM SILVESTRE ANTÓNIO.

Secretary of State for Construction: JOSÉ JOANES ANDRÉ.

Minister of Transport: AUGUSTO DA SILVA TOMÁS.

Minister of Telecommunications and Information Technology: JOSÉ CARVALHO DA ROCHA.

Minister of Energy and Water: JOÃO BAPTISTA BORGES.

Secretary of State for Energy: JOÃO BAPTISTA BORGES.

Secretary of State for Water: LUÍS FILIPE DA SILVA.

Minister of Health: JOSÉ VIERA DIAS VAN-DÚNEM.

Minister of Education: M'PINDA SIMÃO.

Minister of Higher Education, Science and Technology: MARIA CÂNDIDA PEREIRA TEIXEIRA.

Secretary of State for Higher Education: ADÃO GASPAR FERREIRA DO NASCIMENTO.

Secretary of State for Science and Technology: JOÃO SEBASTIÃO TETA.

Minister of Culture: ROSA MARIA MARTINS DA CRUZ E SILVA.

Minister of Social Assistance and Reintegration: JOÃO BAPTISTA KUSSUMUA.

Minister of Family and the Promotion of Women: GENOVEVA DA CONCEIÇÃO LINO.

Minister of Former Combatants and War Veterans: KUNDI PAIHAMA.

Secretary of State for Human Rights: ANTÓNIO BENTO BEMBE.

In addition there were 30 Deputy Ministers.

MINISTRIES

Office of the President: Rua 17 de Setembro, Palácio do Povo, Luanda; tel. 222332939; fax 222339855; internet www.pr.ao.

Office of the Vice-President: Largo 17 de Setembro, Luanda; tel. 222396501; fax 222397071; internet www.vicepresidencia.gov.ao.

Ministry of Agriculture, Rural Development and Fisheries: Largo António Jacinto, CP 527, Luanda; tel. 222322377; fax 222320553; e-mail geral@minagri.gov.ao; internet www.minagri.gov.ao.

Ministry of Commerce: Palácio de Vidro, Largo 4 de Fevereiro 3, CP 1242, Luanda; tel. 222311191; fax 222310335; e-mail gamaarte63@yahoo.com.br; internet www.minco.gov.ao.

Ministry of Culture: Edif. Ministerial, 1° andar, Largo António Jacinto, Luanda; tel. and fax 222322070; e-mail geral@mincult.gov.ao; internet www.mincult.gov.ao.

Ministry of the Economy: Luanda; e-mail geral@minec.gov.ao; internet www.minec.gov.ao.

Ministry of Education: Largo António Jacinto, CP 1281, Luanda; tel. 222321236; fax 222321592; e-mail geral@med.gov.ao; internet www.med.gov.ao.

Ministry of Energy and Water: Rua Cónego Manuel das Neves 234, CP 2229, Luanda; tel. 222393681; fax 222393684; e-mail geral@minen.gov.ao; internet www.minerg.gov.ao.

Ministry of the Environment: Rua Frederico Engels 94, 8° andar, Luanda; tel. 222334761; fax 222394758; e-mail geral@minam.gov.ao; internet www.minam.gov.ao.

Ministry of Family and the Promotion of Women: Palácio de Vidro, 2° andar, Largo 4 de Fevereiro, Luanda; tel. and fax 222311728; e-mail geral@minfamu.gov.ao; internet www.minfamu.gov.ao.

Ministry of Finance: Largo da Mutamba, Luanda; tel. and fax 222338548; e-mail geral@minfin.gov.ao; internet www.minfin.gv.ao.

Ministry of Foreign Affairs: Rua Major Kanhangulo, Luanda; tel. 222394827; fax 222393246; e-mail geral@mirex.gov.ao; internet www.mirex.gov.ao.

Ministry of Former Combatants and War Veterans: Av. Comandante Gika 2, CP 3828, Luanda; tel. 222321648; fax 222320876; e-mail geral@macvg.gov.ao; internet www.macvg.gov.ao.

Ministry of Geology, Mines and Industry: Av. Comandante Gika, CP 1260, Luanda; tel. 222322905; fax 222321655; e-mail geral@mgm.gov.ao; internet www.mgm.gov.ao.

Ministry of Health: Rua 17 de Setembro, CP 1201, Luanda; tel. and fax 222391641; e-mail geral@minsa.gov.ao; internet www.minsa.gov.ao.

Ministry of Higher Education, Science and Technology: Av. Lenine 106/108, Maianga, Luanda; tel. 222330218; fax 222338210; e-mail geral@mct.gov.ao; internet www.mct.gov.ao.

Ministry of Hotels and Tourism: Luanda.

Ministry of the Interior: Largo do Palácio de Vidro, Rua 25 de Abril 1 R/C, CP 2723, Luanda; tel. 222335976; fax 222395133; e-mail geral@minint.gov.ao; internet www.minint.gov.ao.

Ministry of Justice: Rua 17 de Setembro, CP 2250, Luanda; tel. and fax 222336045; e-mail geral@minjus.gov.ao; internet www.minjus.gov.ao.

Ministry of National Defence: Rua 17 de Setembro, Luanda; tel. 222330354; fax 222334276; e-mail geral@minden.gov.ao; internet www.minden.gov.ao.

Ministry of Petroleum: Av. 4 de Fevereiro 105, CP 1279, Luanda; tel. and fax 222385847; e-mail geral@minpet.gov.ao; internet www.minpet.gov.ao.

Ministry of Planning: Largo do Palácio do Povo, Rua 17 de Setembro, Luanda; tel. 222390188; fax 222339586; e-mail geral@minplan.gov.ao; internet www.minplan.gov.ao.

Ministry of Public Administration, Labour and Social Security: Rua do 1° Congresso do MPLA 5, Luanda; tel. 222399506; fax 222399507; e-mail geral@mapess.gov.ao; internet www.mapess.gov.ao.

Ministry of Social Assistance and Reintegration: Av. Hoji Ya Henda 117, CP 102, Luanda; tel. 222440370; fax 222342988; e-mail geral@minars.gov.ao; internet www.minars.gov.ao.

Ministry of Social Communication: Av. Comandante Valódia 206, 1° e 2° andares, CP 2608, Luanda; tel. and fax 222443495; e-mail geral@mcs.gov.ao; internet www.mcs.gov.ao.

Ministry of Telecommunications and Information Technology: Av. 4 de Fevereiro, Rua das Alfândegas 10, Luanda; tel. and fax 222390895; e-mail geral@mtti.gov.ao; internet www.mtti.gov.ao.

Ministry of Territorial Administration: Av. Comandante Gika 8, Luanda; tel. 222321072; fax 222323272; internet www.mat.gov.ao.

Ministry of Town Planning and Construction: Av. 4 de Fevereiro, Luanda; tel. 222334429; e-mail geral@minuh.gov.ao; internet www.minuh.gov.ao.

Ministry of Transport: Av. 4 de Fevereiro 42, CP 1250-C, Luanda; tel. 222311303; fax 222311582; e-mail geral@mintrans.gov.ao; internet www.mintrans.gov.ao.

Ministry of Youth and Sports: Av. Comandante Valódia 299, 4° andar, Luanda; tel. and fax 222443521; e-mail geral@minjud.gov.ao; internet www.minjud.gov.ao.

PROVINCIAL GOVERNORS

(May 2012)

All Provincial Governors are ex officio members of the Government.

Bengo: João Bernardo de Miranda.

Benguela: Armando da Cruz Neto.

Bié: Álvaro Manuel de Boavida Neto.

Cabinda: Mawete João Baptista.

Cunene: António Didalelwa.

Huambo: Fernando Faustino Muteka.

Huíla: Isaac Francisco Maria dos Anjos.

Kuando Kubango: Eusébio de Brito Teixeira.

Kwanza-Norte: Henrique André Júnior.

Kwanza-Sul: Serafim Maria do Prado.

Luanda: Bento Sebastião Francisco Bento.

Lunda-Norte: Ernesto Muangala.

Lunda-Sul: Cândida Maria Guilherme Narciso.

Malanje: Boaventura Cardoso.

Moxico: João Ernesto dos Santos.

Namibe: Cândida Celeste da Silva.

Uíge: Paulo Pombolo.

Zaire: Pedro Sebastião.

President and Legislature

PRESIDENT*

Presidential Election, 29–30 September 1992

Candidate	Votes	% of votes
José Eduardo dos Santos (MPLA)	1,953,335	49.57
Dr Jonas Malheiro Savimbi (UNITA)	1,579,298	40.07
António Alberto Neto (PDA)	85,249	2.16
Holden Roberto (FNLA)	83,135	2.11
Honorato Lando (PDLA)	75,789	1.92
Luís dos Passos (PRD)	59,121	1.47
Others	105,957	2.69
Total	3,940,884	100.00

* Under the terms of the electoral law, a second round of the presidential election was required to take place in order to determine which of the two leading candidates from the first round would be elected. A resumption of hostilities between UNITA and government forces prevented a second round from taking place. The electoral process was to resume only when the provisions of the Estoril peace agreement, concluded in May 1991, had been fulfilled. However, provision in the Lusaka peace accord of November 1994 for the second round of the presidential election was not pursued.

LEGISLATURE

Assembleia Nacional: CP 1204, Luanda; tel. 222334021; fax 222331118; e-mail assembleianacional@parlamento.ebonet.net; internet www.parlamento.ao.

President: António Paulo Kassoma.

General Election, 5–6 September 2008

Party	% of votes	Seats
MPLA	81.64	191
UNITA	10.39	16
PRS	3.17	8
ND	1.20	2
FNLA	1.11	3
Others	2.49	—
Total	100.00*	220

* The total number of votes cast was 7,213,281, while the number of valid votes cast was 6,450,407.

Election Commission

Comissão Nacional Eleitoral (CNE): Av. Amílcar Cabral, 30–31, Luanda; tel. 222393825; internet www.cne.ao; f. 2005; govt agency; Pres. Dr Suzana António da Conceição Nicolau Inglês.

Political Organizations

In June 2010 there were 77 legally recognized political parties in Angola.

Angola Democrática—Coligação (AD): e-mail info@ad-coligacao.org; internet www.ad-coligacao.org; Pres. Kengele Jorge (acting).

Bloco Democrático: 4º andar, 74 C, Av. de Portugal, Luanda; tel. 222397482; fax 222440556; Pres. Justino Pinto de Andrade; Sec.-Gen. Dr Filomeno Vieira Lopes.

Fórum Fraternal Angolano Coligação (FOFAC): Luanda; f. 1997; Leader Artur Quixona Finda.

Frente Nacional de Libertação de Angola (FNLA): Av. Hoji Va Henda (ex Av. do Brasil) 91/306, CP 151, Luanda; e-mail contact@fnla.net; internet www.fnla.net; f. 1962; Pres. Lucas Ngonda; Sec.-Gen. Benjamim Manuel da Silva.

Movimento Popular de Libertação de Angola (MPLA) (People's Movement for the Liberation of Angola): Luanda; e-mail sede@mpla-angola.org; internet www.mpla-angola.org; f. 1956; in 1961–74 conducted guerrilla operations against Portuguese rule; governing party since 1975; known as Movimento Popular de Libertação de Angola—Partido do Trabalho (MPLA—PT) (People's Movement for the Liberation of Angola—Workers' Party) 1977–92; in Dec. 1990 replaced Marxist-Leninist ideology with commitment to 'democratic socialism'; absorbed the Fórum Democrático Angolano (FDA) in 2002; Chair. José Eduardo dos Santos; Sec.-Gen. Julião Mateus Paulo.

Nova Democracia—União Eleitoral: f. 2006; a splinter group from the Partidos de Oposição Civil comprising the Frente Unida para Liberdade Democratica (FULD), the Movimento para Democracia de Angola (MPDA), the Partido Angolano Republicano (PAR), the Partido Social Independente de Angola (PSIA), the Partido Socialista Liberal (PSL) and the União Nacional para Democracia (UND); Sec.-Gen. Quintino de Moreira.

Partido Democrático para o Progresso de Aliança Nacional Angolana (PDP—ANA): Rua n° 6, Casa n° 73, Quarterão 6, Bairro Palanca, Municipio de Kilamba Kiaxi; tel. 926013905; e-mail pdpana@pdp-ana.org; internet www.pdp-ana.org; f. 1991; Pres. Sediangani Mbimbi.

Partido Democrático de Renovação Social: Luanda; f. 2009; Leader Lindo Bernardo Tito.

Partido de Renovação Social (PRS): Rua nº1, Martires de Kifangondo n° 33D; tel. 222326293; fax 222323037; e-mail sede@prs-angola.com; internet www.prs-angola.com; Pres. Eduardo Kwangana; Sec.-Gen. João Baptista Ngandajina.

Partido Renovador Democrático (PRD): internet prd-angola.org; Leader Luís da Silva dos Passos.

Plataforma Política Eleitoral (PPE): nine-party coalition; Leader José Manuel.

União Nacional para a Independência Total de Angola (UNITA): Rua 28 de Maio, 1A Travessa 2, Maianga, Luanda; tel. and fax 222331215; e-mail info@unitaangola.org; internet www.unitaangola.com; f. 1966 to secure independence from Portugal; later received Portuguese support to oppose the MPLA; UNITA and the Frente Nacional de Libertação de Angola conducted guerrilla campaign against the MPLA Govt with aid from some Western countries, 1975–76; supported by South Africa until 1984 and in 1987–88, and by USA after 1986; obtained legal status in March 1998, but hostilities between govt and UNITA forces resumed later that year; signed cease-fire agreement with the MPLA Govt in April 2002; joined the Govt in Dec. 2002; support drawn mainly from Ovimbundu ethnic group; Pres. ISAÍAS SAMAKUVA.

Other major parties include:

Forças de Libertação do Estado de Cabinda/Posição Militar (FLEC/PM): f. 2003; a breakaway faction of FLEC seeking the secession of Cabinda province; Sec.-Gen. RODRIGUES MINGAS.

Frente para a Libertação do Enclave de Cabinda (FLEC): f. 1963; comprises several factions, claiming total forces of c. 5,000 guerrillas, seeking the secession of Cabinda province; in Sept. 2004 the Frente para a Libertação do Enclave de Cabinda—Forças Armadas Cabindesas (FLEC—FAC) and the Frente para a Libertação do Enclave de Cabinda—Renovada (FLEC—R) merged under the above name; Leader N'ZITA HENRIQUES TIAGO; Sec.-Gen. ANTÓNIO BENTO BEMBE.

Frente para a Libertação do Enclave de Cabinda—Conselho Superior Alargado (FLEC—CSA): f. 2004; political wing of FLEC; supports Cabindan independence through negotiation.

The **Fórum Cabindês para o Diálogo (FCD)** was formed in 2004 to provide a united platform for Cabindan separatists and civil-society leaders with which to negotiate with the Government. Its leader was ANTÓNIO BENTO BEMBE.

Diplomatic Representation

EMBASSIES IN ANGOLA

Algeria: Edif. Siccal, Rua Rainha Ginga, CP 1389, Luanda; tel. 222332881; fax 222334785; e-mail ambalg@netangola.com; Ambassador KAMEL BOUGHABA.

Argentina: Rua Comandante Nicolau Gomes Spencer 62, Bairro Maculusso, Luanda; tel. 222325098; fax 222324095; JUAN AGUSTÍN CABALLERO.

Belgium: Av. 4 de Fevereiro 93, 3° andar, CP 1203, Luanda; tel. 222336437; fax 222336438; e-mail luanda@diplobel.fed.be; internet www.diplomatie.be/luanda; Ambassador CHARLES DELOGNE.

Brazil: Rua Houari Boumedienne 132, Miramar, CP 5428, Luanda; tel. 222441307; fax 222444913; e-mail bras.secretariado@netcabo.co.ao; Ambassador ANA LUCY GENTIL CABRAL PETERSEN.

Cape Verde: Rua Oliveira Martins 3, Luanda; tel. 222321765; fax 222320832; Ambassador DOMINGOS PEREIRA MAGALHÃES.

China, People's Republic: Rua Houari Boumedienne 196, Miramar, CP 52, Luanda; tel. 222441683; fax 222444185; internet ao.chineseembassy.org; Ambassador GAO KOTIANG.

Congo, Democratic Republic: Rua Cesário Verde 24, Luanda; tel. 222361953; Ambassador ERIC PALUKU KAMUVU.

Congo, Republic: Av. 4 de Fevereiro 3, Luanda; tel. 222310293; Ambassador CHRISTIAN GILBERT BEMBET.

Côte d'Ivoire: Rua Eng. Armindo de Andrade 75, Miramar, CP 432, Luanda; tel. 222440878; fax 222440907; e-mail aciao@ambaci-angola.org; internet www.ambaci-angola.org; Ambassador ASSAMOI B. DÉSIRÉ.

Cuba: Rua Che Guevara 42, Ingombotas, Luanda; tel. 222339171; fax 222339165; e-mail embcuba.ang@supernet.ao; internet emba.cubaminrex.cu/angola; Ambassador PEDRO ROSS LEAL.

Egypt: Rua Comandante Stona 247, Alvalade, CP 3704, Luanda; tel. 222321591; fax 222323285; e-mail embegipto@ebonet.net; Ambassador GAMAL ABDEL METWALY.

Equatorial Guinea: Luanda; Ambassador JOSE MICHA AKENG.

France: Rua Reverendo Pedro Agostinho Neto 31–33, CP 584, Luanda; tel. 222334841; fax 222391949; e-mail cad.luanda-amba@diplomatie.gouv.fr; internet www.ambafrance-ao.org; Ambassador PHILIPPE GARNIER.

Gabon: Av. 4 de Fevereiro 95, Luanda; tel. 222372614; Ambassador FRANÇOIS MOUELY-KOUMBA.

Germany: Av. 4 de Fevereiro 120, CP 1295, Luanda; tel. 222334516; fax 222372551; e-mail info@luanda.diplo.de; internet www.luanda.diplo.de; Ambassador JORG-WERNER WOLFGANG MARQUARDT.

Ghana: Rua Cirilo da Conceição E Silva 5, 1A, CP 1012, Luanda; tel. 222338239; fax 222338235; e-mail embassyghana@ebonet.net; Ambassador MARTIN ACHIAMPONG QUANSAH.

Holy See: Rua Luther King 123, CP 1030, Luanda; tel. 222330532; fax 222332378; Apostolic Nuncio Most Rev. NOVATUS RUGAMBWA.

India: Rua Marquês das Minas 18A, Macalusso, CP 6040, Luanda; tel. 222392281; fax 222371094; e-mail indembluanda@netcabo.co.ao; internet www.indembangola.org; Ambassador SHIRI PRADHN.

Israel: Edif. Siccal, 11° andar, Rua Rainha Ginga 34, Luanda; tel. 222331501; fax 222397331; e-mail info@luanda.mfa.gov.il; internet luanda.mfa.gov.il; Ambassador IRIT WAIDERGORN.

Italy: Rua Américo Boavida 51, Ingombotas, CP 6220, Luanda; tel. 222331245; fax 222333743; e-mail segreteria.luanda@esteri.it; internet www.ambluanda.esteri.it; Ambassador GUISEPPE MISTRELLA.

Japan: Rua Armindo de Andrade 183–185, Miramar, Luanda; tel. 222442007; fax 222449888; internet www.angola.emb-japan.go.jp; Ambassador RYOZO MYOI.

Mali: Rua Alfredo Felner 5, Nelito Souares 11, Luanda; e-mail ambamali@netangola.com; Ambassador FAROUK CAMARA.

Morocco: Edif. Siccal, 10° andar, Rua Rainha Ginga, CP 20, Luanda; tel. 222393708; fax 222338847; e-mail aluanda@supernet.ao; Ambassador EL GHALLAOUI SIDATI.

Mozambique: Rua Salvador Alende 55, Luanda; tel. and fax 222334871; e-mail embamoc.angola@minec.gov.mz; Ambassador DOMINGOS FERNANDES.

Namibia: Rua dos Coqueiros 37, CP 953, Luanda; tel. 222395483; fax 222339234; e-mail embnam@netangola.com; Ambassador CLAUDIA NDADALEKA USHONA.

Netherlands: Edif. Secil, 6°, Av. 4 de Fevereiro 42, CP 3624, Luanda; tel. 222310686; fax 222310966; e-mail lua@minbuza.nl; internet www.mfa.nl/lua-en; Ambassador Dr COR VAN HONK.

Nigeria: Rua Houari Boumedienne 120, Miramar, CP 479, Luanda; tel. and fax 222340089; Ambassador FOLORUNSO OLUKAYODE OTUKOYA.

Norway: Rua de Benguela 17, Bairro Patrice Lumumba, CP 3835, Luanda; tel. 222449936; fax 222446248; e-mail emb.luanda@mfa.no; internet www.noruega.ao; Ambassador JON VEA.

Poland: Rua Comandante N'zagi 21–23, Alvalade, CP 1340, Luanda; tel. 222323088; fax 222323086; e-mail luanda.amb.sekretariat@msz.gov.pl; internet www.luanda.polemb.net; Ambassador MAREK ROHR-GARZTECKI.

Portugal: Av. de Portugal 50, CP 1346, Luanda; tel. 222333027; fax 222390392; e-mail embaixada.portugal@netcabo.co.ao; internet www.embaixadadeportugal-luanda.com.pt; Ambassador FRANCISCO MARIA DE SOUSA RIBEIRO TELLES.

Romania: Rua Ramalho Ortigão 30, Alvalade, Luanda; tel. and fax 222321076; e-mail ambromania@ebonet.net; Chargé d'affaires a.i. IACOB PRADA.

Russia: Rua Houari Boumedienne 170, CP 3141, Luanda; tel. 222445028; fax 222445320; e-mail rusemb@netangola.com; Ambassador SERGUEY NENÁCHEV.

São Tomé and Príncipe: Rua Armindo de Andrade 173–175, Luanda; tel. 222345677; Ambassador ARMINDO BRITO FERNANDES.

Serbia: Rua Comandante N'zagi 25–27, Alvalade, CP 3278, Luanda; tel. 222321421; fax 222321724; e-mail serbiaemb@snet.co.ao; Ambassador DANILO MILIC.

South Africa: Edif. Maianga, 1° e 2° andares, Rua Kwamme Nkrumah 31, Largo da Maianga, CP 6212, Luanda; tel. 222334187; fax 222398730; e-mail saemb.ang@netangola.com; internet www.sambangola.info; Ambassador GODFREY NGWENYA.

Spain: Av. 4 de Fevereiro 95, 1° andar, CP 3061, Luanda; tel. 222391166; fax 222332884; e-mail emb.luanda@maec.es; Ambassador JOSÉ MARÍA CASTROVIEJO Y BOLIBAR.

Sweden: Rua Garcia Neto 9, CP 1130, Miramar, Luanda; tel. 222440706; fax 222443460; e-mail ambassaden.luanda@foreign.ministry.se; internet www.swedenabroad.com/luanda; Ambassador BO EMTHÉN.

Turkey: Hotel Colinas do Sol, Talatona, Luanda; tel. 914522800 (mobile); fax 222393330; e-mail embassy.luanda@mfa.gov.tr; Ambassador HAMIT OSMAR.

Ukraine: Rua Companhia de Jesus 35, Miramar, Luanda; tel. 222447492; fax 222448467; e-mail emb_ao@mfa.gov.ua; Chargé d'affaires VOLODYMYR BOGOLIUBOV.

United Kingdom: Rua Diogo Cão 4, CP 1244, Luanda; tel. 222334582; fax 222333331; e-mail ppa.luanda@fco.gov.uk; internet ukinangola.fco.gov.uk; Ambassador RICHARD WILDASH.

USA: Rua Houari Boumedienne 32, Miramar, CP 6468, Luanda; tel. 222641000; fax 222641232; e-mail ConsularLuanda@state.gov; internet angola.usembassy.gov; Ambassador CHRISTOPHER J. MCMULLEN.

Viet Nam: Rua Alexandre Peres 4, Maianga, CP 1774, Luanda; tel. 222390684; fax 222390369; e-mail dsqvnangola@netangola.com; internet www.vietnamembassy-angola.org; Ambassador PHAM TIEN NHIEN.

Zambia: Rua Rei Katyavala 106–108, CP 1496, Luanda; tel. 222331145; Ambassador RAPHAEL CHISHETA.

Zimbabwe: Edif. Secil, Av. 4 de Fevereiro 42, CP 428, Luanda; tel. and fax 222311528; e-mail embzimbabwe@ebonet.net; Ambassador (vacant).

Judicial System

The country's highest judicial body is the Tribunal Constitucional (Constitutional Court), while there is also a Tribunal da Relação (Supreme Court) and a Court of Appeal. There are also civil, criminal and military courts.

Tribunal Constitucional (Constitutional Court): Luanda; internet www.tribunalconstitucional.ao; f. 2008; 7 judges; Pres. Dr RUI CONSTANTINO DA CRUZ FERREIRA.

Tribunal da Relação (Supreme Court): Rua 17 de Setembro, Luanda; fax 222335411; Pres. Dr CRISTIANO ANDRÉ.

Office of the Attorney-General: Rua 17 de Setembro, Luanda; tel. 222333171; fax 222333172; Attorney-General JOÃO MARIA DE SOUSA.

Religion

In 1998 it was estimated that 47% of the population followed indigenous beliefs, with 53% professing to be Christians, mainly Roman Catholic. There is a small Muslim community, which comprises less than 1% of the population.

CHRISTIANITY

In early 2005 some 85 Christian denominations were registered in Angola.

Conselho de Igrejas Cristãs em Angola (CICA) (Council of Christian Churches in Angola): Rua 15 24, Bairro Cassenda, CP 1301/1659, Luanda; tel. 222354838; fax 222356144; e-mail info@cicaangola.org; f. 1977 as Conselho Angolano de Igrejas Evangélicas; 14 mem. churches; 5 assoc. mems; 1 observer; Pres. Rev. ALVARO RODRIGUES; Gen. Sec. Rev. LUÍS NGUIMBI.

Protestant Churches

Evangelical Congregational Church in Angola (Igreja Evangélica Congregacional em Angola—IECA): CP 1552, Luanda; tel. 222355108; fax 222350868; e-mail iecageral@snet.co.ao; f. 1880; 750,000 mems; Gen. Sec. Rev. AUGUSTO CHIPESSE.

Evangelical Lutheran Church of Angola: CP 222, Lubango; tel. 22228428; e-mail iela_lubango@yahoo.com.br; 40,000 mems (2010); Pres. Rev. TOMÀS NDAWANAPO.

Evangelical Pentecostal Church of Angola (Missão Evangélica Pentecostal de Angola): CP 219, Porto Amboim; 13,600 mems; Sec. Rev. JOSÉ DOMINGOS CAETANO.

United Evangelical Church of Angola (Igreja Evangélica Unida de Angola): CP 122, Uíge; 11,000 mems; Gen. Sec. Rev. A. L. DOMINGOS.

Other active denominations include the African Apostolic Church, the Church of Apostolic Faith in Angola, the Church of Our Lord Jesus Christ in the World, the Evangelical Baptist Church, the Evangelical Church in Angola, the Evangelical Church of the Apostles of Jerusalem, the Evangelical Reformed Church of Angola, the Kimbanguist Church in Angola, the Maná Church and the United Methodist Church.

The Roman Catholic Church

Angola comprises five archdioceses and 14 dioceses. An estimated 52% of the population were Roman Catholics.

Bishops' Conference

Conferência Episcopal de Angola e São Tomé (CEAST), CP 3579, Luanda; tel. 222443686; fax 222445504; e-mail ceast@snet.co.ao.

f. 1967; Pres. Most Rev. GABRIEL MBILINGI (Archbishop of Lubango).

Archbishop of Huambo: Most Rev. JOSÉ DE QUEIRÓS ALVES, Arcebispado, CP 10, Huambo; tel. 241220130; fax 241220133; e-mail bispado.huambo@asat.signis.net.

Archbishop of Luanda: Most Rev. DAMIÃO ANTÓNIO FRANKLIN, Arcebispado, Largo do Palácio 9, CP 87, 1230-C, Luanda; tel. 222331481; fax 222334433; e-mail spastoral@snet.com.ao.

Archbishop of Lubango: Most Rev. GABRIEL MBILINGI, Arcebispado, CP 231, Lubango; tel. and fax 261230140; e-mail arquidiocese.lubango@netangola.com.

Archbishop of Malanje: Most Rev. LUIS MARÍA PÉREZ DE ONRAITA AGUIRRE, CP 192, Malanje; tel. 2038421708.

Archbishop of Saurimo: Most Rev. JOSÉ MANUEL IMBAMBA, CP 52, Saurimo; tel. 761572551 (mobile); fax 761572553 (mobile).

The Press

A free press was reinstituted in 1991, after 15 years of government control. In 2004 there were seven privately owned newspapers in Angola.

DAILIES

Diário da República: CP 1306, Luanda; tel. 217810870; fax 213945750; e-mail dre@incm.pt; internet www.dre.pt; official govt bulletin.

O Jornal de Angola: Rua Rainha Ginga 18–24, CP 1312, Luanda; tel. 222335531; fax 222333342; e-mail jornaldeangola@nexus.ao; internet jornaldeangola.sapo.ao; f. 1975; state-owned; Dir JOSÉ RIBEIRO; mornings and Sun.; circ. 41,000.

PERIODICALS

Actual: Rua Fernando Pessoa 103, Vila Alice, CP 6959, Luanda; tel. and fax 222332116; e-mail actuals@hotmail.com; f. 2003; weekly; Editor JOAQUIM ALVES.

Angolense: Rua Cónego Manuel das Neves 83B, Luanda; tel. 222445753; fax 222340549; e-mail angolense@netangola.com; internet www.jornalangolense.com; f. 1998; weekly; Dir AMÉRICO GONÇALVES; Editor-in-Chief SUZANA MENDES.

O Apostolado: Rua Comandante Bula 118, São Paulo, CP 3579, Luanda; tel. 222432641; fax 222440628; e-mail redaccao@apostolado-angola.org; internet www.apostolado-angola.org; f. 1935; current and religious affairs; Dir MAURÍCIO AGOSTINHO CAMUTO.

A Capital: Rua Canego Manuel das Neves, Prédio 5, 1° andar, Luanda; tel. 222440549; e-mail info@semanarioacapital.com; internet semanarioacapital.com; f. 2003; weekly; Dir TANDALA FRANCISCO.

Chocolate: Rua Augusto Tadeu de Bastos 52, Maianga, Luanda; tel. 222398565; e-mail revistachocolate@visao.co.ao; internet www.revistachocolate.com; publ. by Media Nova; monthly; lifestyle; circ. 10,000.

Comércio Actualidade: Rua da Missão 81, CP 6375, Luanda; tel. 222334060; fax 222392216; e-mail actualidade@ebonet.net; f. 1993; weekly; Editor VICTOR ALEIXO.

Eme: Luanda; tel. 222321130; f. 1996; fortnightly; MPLA publ.; Dir FERNANDO FATI.

EXAME Angola: Zona Residencial ZR6-B, Lote 32, Sector de Talatona, Luanda Sul; tel. 222003275; fax 222003289; e-mail info@exameangola.com; internet www.exameangola.com; publ. by Media Nova; Editor CARLOS ROSADO DE CARVALHO.

Folha 8: Rua Conselheiro Júlio de Vilhena 24, 5° andar, CP 6527, Luanda; tel. 222391943; fax 222392289; e-mail folha8@ebonet.net; internet folha8online.com; f. 1994; two a week; Editor WILLIAM TONET.

Jornal dos Desportos: Rua Rainha Ginga 18–24, CP 1312, Luanda; tel. 222335531; fax 222335481; e-mail jornaldosdesportos@hotmail.com; internet jornaldosdesportos.sapo.ao; f. 1994; bi-weekly; Dir MATIAS ADRIANO; Editorial Dir POLICARPO DA ROSA; circ. 5,000.

Lavra & Oficina: CP 2767-C, Luanda; tel. 222322421; fax 222323205; e-mail uea@uea-angola.org; internet www.uea-angola.org; f. 1975; journal of the União dos Escritores Angolanos (Union of Angolan Writers); monthly; circ. 5,000.

O País: Casa Amarela, Lote 32, Sector de Talatona, Zona Residencial 6-B, Luanda; tel. 222003275; fax 222003289; e-mail info@opais.co.ao; internet www.opais.net; f. 2008; publ. by Media Nova; weekly; Editor-in-Chief JOSÉ KALIENGUE.

Semanário Angolense: Rua António Feliciano de Castilho 103, Luanda; tel. 222264915; fax 222263506; e-mail info@semanarioangolense.net; internet www.semanarioangolense.net; f. 2003; independent; current affairs; Dir FELIZBERTO GRAÇA CAMPOS; weekly.

Semanário Económico: Luanda; f. 2009; publ. by Media Nova; weekly; Editor PEDRO NARCISO.

Tempos Novos: Av. Combatentes 244, 2° andar, CP 16088, Luanda; tel. and fax 222349534; f. 1995.

Vida: Casa Amarela, Lote 32, Sector de Talatona, Zona Residencial 6-B, Luanda; tel. 222003275; fax 222003289; e-mail info@opais.co.ao; publ. by Media Nova; Dir-Gen. LUÍS FERNANDO.

NEWS AGENCIES

In early 2006 legislation was passed by the Assembléia Nacional ending the governmental monopoly over news agencies.

Agência Angola Press (ANGOP): Rua Rei Katyavala 120, CP 2181, Luanda; tel. 222447343; fax 222447342; e-mail angop@netangola.com; internet www.angolapress-angop.ao; f. 1975; Dir-Gen. MANUEL DA CONCEIÇÃO.

Centro de Imprensa Anibal de Melo (CIAM): Rua Cerqueira Lukoki 124, CP 2805, Luanda; tel. 222393341; fax 222393445; govt press centre; Dir Dr OLYMPIO DE SOUSA E SILVA.

Publishers

Chá de Caxinde: Av. do 1° Congresso do MPLA 20–24, CP 5958, Luanda; tel. 222336020; fax 222332876; e-mail chacaxinde@ebonet.net; f. 1999; Dir JAQUES ARLINDO DOS SANTOS.

Editorial Kilombelombe: Luanda; Dir MATEUS VOLÓDIA.

Editorial Nzila: Rua Comandante Valódia 1, ao Largo do Kinaxixi, Luanda; tel. 222447137; e-mail edinzila@hotmail.com.

Plural Editores: Rua Lucrécia Paim 16A, Bairro do Maculusso, Luanda; tel. 924351990; fax 222339107; e-mail plural@pluraleditores.co.ao; internet www.pluraleditores.co.ao; f. 2005; 100% owned by Porto Editora (Portugal); technical and educational; CEO ALEXANDRE ALVES.

Ponto Um Indústria Gráfica: Rua Sebastião Desta Vez 55, Luanda; tel. 222448315; fax 222449424.

União dos Escritores Angolanos (UEA): Luanda; tel. and fax 222323205; e-mail uea@uea-angola.org; internet www.uea-angola.org.

GOVERNMENT PUBLISHING HOUSE

Imprensa Nacional, UEE: CP 1306, Luanda; f. 1845; Gen. Man. ANA MARÍA SOUSA E SILVA.

Broadcasting and Communications

TELECOMMUNICATIONS

Angola Telecom (AT): Rua das Quipacas 186, CP 625, Luanda; tel. 222395990; fax 222391688; internet www.angolatelecom.com; state telecommunications co; Pres. FELICIANO ANTÓNIO.

Movicel Telecomunicações, Lda: Rua Mãe Isabel 1, Luanda; tel. 222692000; fax 222692090; internet www.movicel.co.ao; f. 2002; mobile cellular telephone operator; Chair. MANUEL AVELINO; Exec. Dir CARLOS BRITO.

Mundo StarTel: Rua Ndunduma 188, São Paulo, Município de Sambizanga, Luanda; tel. 222432417; fax 222446972; e-mail sede@startel.co.ao; internet www.startel.co.ao; f. 2004; 44% owned by Telecom Namibia; Dir-Gen. PAULO ANTÓNIO DA MOTTA GARCIA.

Nexus Telecomunicações e Serviços SARL: Rua dos Enganos 1, 1° andar, Luanda; tel. 228740041; fax 228740741; e-mail nexus@nexus.ao; internet www.nexus.ao; began operations mid-2004; fixed-line operator.

Unitel SARL: Talatona Sector 22, Via C3, Luanda Sul; tel. 923192222 (mobile); fax 222013624; e-mail unitel@unitel.co.ao; internet www.unitel.ao; f. 1998; 25% owned by Portugal Telecom; private mobile telephone operator; Dir-Gen. MIGUEL F. VEIGA MARTINS; 5.7m. subscribers.

Regulatory Authority

Instituto Angolano das Comunicações (INACOM): Av. de Portugal 92, 7° andar, CP 1459, Luanda; tel. 222338352; fax 222339356; e-mail inacom.dg@netangola.com; internet www.inacom.og.ao; f. 1999; monitoring and regulatory authority; Dir-Gen. DOMINGOS PEDRO ANTÓNIO.

BROADCASTING

Radio

A decree on the regulation of radio broadcasting was approved in 1997. Since that time private operators had reportedly experienced difficulty in gaining permission to broadcast, although several private stations were operating in Luanda in the mid-2000s.

Rádio Nacional de Angola: Av. Comandante Gika, CP 1329, Luanda; tel. 222320192; fax 222324647; e-mail dgeral@rna.ao; internet www.rna.ao; state-controlled; operates Canal A, Radio 5, Radio FM Estério, Radio Luanda and Radio N'gola Yetu; broadcasts in Portuguese, English, French, Spanish and vernacular languages (Chokwe, Kikongo, Kimbundu, Kwanyama, Fiote, Ngangela, Luvale, Songu, Umbundu); Dir-Gen. ALBERTO DE SOUSA.

Luanda Antena Comercial (LAC): Rua Luther King 5, CP 3521, Luanda; tel. 222394989; fax 222396229; e-mail lac@ebonet.net; internet www.nexus.ao/lac; popular music.

Radio CEFOJOR: Rua Luther King 123/4, Luanda; tel. 222336140; f. 2003; commercial station, provides journalistic training; Dir-Gen. JOAQUIM PAULO DA CONCEIÇÃO.

Rádio Ecclésia—Emissora Católica de Angola: Rua Comandante Bula 118, São Paulo, CP 3579, Luanda; tel. 222447153; fax 222446346; e-mail info@radioecclesia.org; internet www.radioecclesia.org; f. 1955; broadcasts mainly restricted to Luanda; coverage of politics and current affairs; Dir-Gen. MUANAMOSSI MATUMONA.

Radio Escola: Rua Luther King 123/124, Luanda; tel. 222337409; fax 222446346; educational.

Rádio Mais: Edifício Laranja, Projecto Nova Vida, Rua 40, Luanda; tel. 928818316; e-mail info@radiomais.co.ao; internet www.radiomais.co.ao; Dir-Gen. JOSÉ MARQUES VIEIRA.

Rádio Morena Comercial, Lda: Rua Comandante Kassanji, CP 537, Benguela; tel. 272232525; fax 272234242.

The Voice of America (internet www.ebonet.net/voa) also broadcasts from Luanda.

Television

In early 2006 legislation was passed by the Assembléia Nacional ending the Government's monopoly over television and simplifying the radio licensing process. A digital television system, TV Cabo Angola, began broadcasting in early 2006.

Televisão Pública de Angola (TPA): Av. Ho Chi Minh, CP 2604, Luanda; tel. 222320026; fax 222323027; e-mail gabinetedg@tpa.ao; internet www.tpa.ao; f. 1976; state-controlled; 2 channels; Co-ordinator of the Executive Committee HÉLDER BÁRBER.

TV Zimbo: Av. do Talatona, Luanda Sul; tel. 222004201; e-mail info@tvzimbo.co.ao; internet www.tvzimbo.net; Dir-Gen. FILIPE CORREIA DE SÁ.

Finance

(cap. = capital; res = reserves; dep. = deposits; m. = million; brs = branches; amounts in kwanza (equivalent to 1m. readjusted kwanza), unless otherwise indicated)

BANKING

All banks were nationalized in 1975. In 1995 the Government authorized the formation of private banks. In 2011 there were 23 banks licensed to operate in Angola.

Central Bank

Banco Nacional de Angola: Av. 4 de Fevereiro 151, CP 1298, Luanda; tel. and fax 222333717; e-mail bna.cri@ebonet.net; internet www.bna.ao; f. 1976; bank of issue; cap. 5m., res –39,106m., dep. 1,291,174m. (Dec. 2008); Gov. JOSÉ DE LIMA MASSANO; 6 brs.

Commercial Banks

Banco Angolano de Negócios e Comércios SA: 126 Rua Amilcar Cabral, Luanda; tel. 222339285; fax 222394972; e-mail servicosgerais@banc.ws; internet www.banc.ws; f. 2007; cap. 930m., res 539m., dep. 6,664m. (Dec. 2009); Chair. SÉRGIO FILIPE DE SOUSA.

Banco BIC SA: Rua Major Kanhangulo 212, Luanda; tel. 222371227; fax 222395099; e-mail bancobic@bancobic.ao; internet www.bancobic.ao; f. 2005; 25% owned by Fidel Kiluange Assis Araujo; 20% owned by Fernando Mendes Teles; cap. 2,414.5m., res 25,413.2m., dep. 334,646.0m. (Dec. 2009); Chair. FERNANDO MENDES TELES.

Banco Comercial Angolano SARL (BCA): Av. Comandante Valódia 83A, CP 6900, Luanda; tel. 222449548; fax 222449516; internet www.bca.co.ao; f. 1997; 50% owned by Absa; cap. 0.9m., res 347.4m., dep. 1,799.3m. (Dec. 2002); Pres. FRANCISCO DA SILVA CRISTOVÃO; CEO MATEUS FILIPE MARTINS; 4 brs (2005).

Banco de Fomento Angola—BFA: Rua Amílcar Cabral 58, Maianga, Luanda; tel. 222638900; fax 222638925; internet www.bfa.ao; f. 1993 as Banco Fomento Exterior; name changed to above in 2001; 50.1% owned by Banco BPI, SA, Portugal; cap. 3,522.0m., res 26,183.2m., dep. 463,411.7m. (Dec. 2009); CEO EMIDIO PINHEIRO; 38 brs (2005).

Banco Millennium Angola SA: 59 Av. Lenine, Luanda; tel. 222632100; fax 222632494; e-mail comunicacao@millenniumangola.ao; internet www.millenniumangola.ao; f. 2006; 52.7% owned by Banco Comercial Português SA, 31.5% owned by Sonangol, 15.8% owned by Banco Privado Atlântico; cap. 3,809.3m., res 8,684.6m., dep. 79,727.0m. (Dec. 2009); Pres. and CEO Eng. JOSÉ REINO DA COSTA.

Banco de Poupança e Crédito SARL (BPC): Largo Saydi Mingas, CP 1343, Luanda; tel. and fax 222372529; e-mail bpc@bpc.ao; internet www.bpc.ao; f. 1956 as Banco Comercial de Angola; 99%

state-owned, 1% owned by the Instituto Nacional de Segurança Social; cap. 7,507.4m., res 28,252.4m., dep. 390,946.7m. (Dec. 2009); Chair. PAIXÃO ANTÓNIO JÚNIOR.

Banco Regional do Keve SARL: Edif. Robert Hudson, Rua Rainha Ginga 77, CP 1804, Luanda; tel. 222394100; fax 222395101; e-mail sedecentral@bancokeve.ao; internet www.bancokeve.ao; f. 2003; cap. 4,000.0m., res 1,781.3m., dep. 29,681.3m. (Dec. 2009); Pres. AMILCAR AZEVEDO DA SILVA.

Banco Sol: Rua Rei Katyavala 110–112, Maculusso, Zona 8, Ingombotas, CP 814, Luanda; tel. 222394717; fax 222440226; e-mail banco.sol@ebonet.net; internet www.bancosol.ao; f. 2000; 55% owned by SANSUL; cap. 1,377.5m., res 1,914.8m., dep. 93,189.0m. (Dec. 2009); Pres. SEBASTIÃO BASTOS LAVRADOR.

Development Banks

Banco de Comércio e Indústria SARL: Rua Rainha Ginga, Largo do Atlético 73–83, POB 1395, Luanda; tel. 222330209; fax 222334924; e-mail falfredo@bci.ebonet.net; internet www.bci.ao; f. 1991; 91% state-owned; privatization pending; provides loans to businesses in all sectors; cap. 2,531.9m., res 5,078.3m., dep. 58,865.6m. (Dec. 2008); Chair. ADRIANO RAFAEL PASCOAL; 5 brs.

Banco de Desenvolvimento de Angola (BDA): Av. 4 de Fevereiro 113, Luanda; tel. 222692800; fax 222396901; e-mail bancobda@bda.ao; internet www.bda.ao; f. 2006; Pres. FRANCO PAIXÃO.

Investment Bank

Banco Angolano de Investimentos SARL (BAI): Rua Major Kanhangulo 34, CP 6022, Luanda; tel. 222693800; fax 222335486; e-mail baised@bancobai.co.ao; internet www.bancobai.co.ao; f. 1997; fmrly Banco Africano de Investimentos SARL; name changed as above in 2011; 8.95% owned by BAI Treasury Stock; 8.5% owned by SONANGOL; cap. 14,786.7m., res 21,371.7m., dep. 652,032.6m. (Dec. 2009); Chair. Dr JOSÉ CARLOS DE CASTRO PAIVA; 45 brs.

Foreign Banks

Banco Comercial Português—Atlântico SA: Rua Rainha Ginga 83, CP 5726, Luanda; tel. 222397922; fax 222397397; Gen. Man. MARIA NAZARÉ FRANCISCO DANG.

Banco Espírito Santo Angola SARL (BESA): Rua 1, Congresso No. 27, Ingombotas, Luanda; tel. 222693600; fax 222693697; internet www.besa.ao; f. 2002; 79.96% owned by Banco Espírito Santo SA (Portugal); cap. US $162.9m., res $24.4m., dep. $5,958.6m. (Dec. 2009); Pres. and Chair. ALVARO DE OLIVEIRA MADALENO SOBRINAO.

Banco Totta de Angola SARL: Av. 4 de Fevereiro 99, CP 1231, Luanda; tel. 222332729; fax 222333233; e-mail tottango@ebonet.net; 99.98% owned by Banco Santander Totta; cap. €15.5m. (Dec. 2003); Man. Dir Dr MÁRIO NELSON MAXIMINO; 7 brs.

NovoBanco: Rua Ndunduma 253/257, Bairro Miramar, Município Sambizanga, Luanda; tel. 222430040; fax 222430074; e-mail secretariado@novobanco.ao; internet www.novobanco.net; f. 2004; Pres. MARIO A. BARBER.

STOCK EXCHANGE

Bolsa de Valores e Derivativos do Angola (BVDA): Mutamba, Luanda; f. 2006; Pres. JOSÉ PEDRO DE MORAIS.

INSURANCE

AAA Seguros SA: Rua Lenine 58, Luanda; tel. 222691331; fax 222691342; e-mail saovicente@aaa.co.ao; f. 2000; life and non-life; Pres. Dr CARLOS MANUEL DE SÃO VICENTE.

ENSA Seguros de Angola (Empresa Nacional de Seguros e Resseguros de Angola, UEE): Av. 4 de Fevereiro 93, CP 5778, Luanda; tel. 222332990; fax 222332946; e-mail geral@ensa.co.ao; f. 1978; state-owned; to be privatized; Chair. MANUEL JOAQUIM GONÇALVES; Pres. and Dir-Gen. ALEIXO AUGUSTO.

GA Angola Seguros (Global Alliance Insurance Angola): Av. 4 de Fevereiro 79, 1° andar, Luanda; tel. 222330368; fax 222398815; e-mail blara@globalalliance.co.ao; internet www.globalalliance.co.ao; f. 2005; owned by Global Alliance Group (United Kingdom); Gen. Man BRIAN LARA.

Nova Sociedade de Seguros de Angola S.A. (Nossa Seguros): Av. 4 de Fevereiro 111, Luanda; tel. 222399909; fax 222399153; e-mail info@nossaseguros.com; internet www.nossaseguros.com.

Trade and Industry

GOVERNMENT AGENCIES

Agência Nacional para o Investimento Privado (ANIP): Rua Cerqueira Lukoki No. 25, Edificio do Ministerio da Industria, 9º andar, Luanda; tel. 222391434; fax 222332965; e-mail info@investinangola.com; internet www.anip.co.ao; f. 2003; Co-ordinator Dr AGUINALDO JAIME.

Gabinete de Obras Especiais: Luanda; Dir MANUEL FERREIRA CLEMENTE JÚNIOR.

Gabinete de Reconstrução Nacional: Luanda; f. 2004; monitors economic and social reconstruction programmes; Dir ANTÓNIO TEIXEIRA FLOR.

Gabinete de Redimensionamento Empresarial: Rua Cerqueira Lukoki 25, 9° andar, CP 594, Luanda; tel. 222390496; fax 222392987; internet www.gare-minfin.org; privatization agency.

Instituto Angolano da Propriedade Industrial: Rua Cerqueira Lukoki 25, 6º andar, CP 3840, Luanda; tel. 222004991; fax 222336428; e-mail prudencia.iapi@hotmail.com; Dir BARROS BEBIANO JOSÉ LICENÇA.

Instituto de Desenvolvimento Agrário: Rua Comandante Gika, CP 2109, Luanda; tel. and fax 222323651; e-mail ida.canga@netangola.com; promotes agricultural devt; Dir MARCOS NHUNGA.

Instituto de Desenvolvimento Industrial de Angola (IDIA): Rua Cerqueira Lukoki 25, 8° andar, CP 594, Luanda; tel. and fax 222338492; e-mail idiadg@netangola.com; f. 1995; promotes industrial devt; Dir BENJAMIM DO ROSÁRIO DOMBOLO.

Instituto de Investimento Estrangeiro (IIE): Rua Cerqueira Lukoki 25, 9º andar, CP 594, Luanda; tel. 222392620; fax 222393381; foreign investment agency.

Instituto Nacional de Cereais (INCER): Av. 4 de Fevereiro 101, CP 1105, Luanda; tel. and fax 222331611; promotes cereal crops; Dir-Gen. BENJAMIM ALVARO CASTELO.

CHAMBER OF COMMERCE

Câmara de Comércio e Indústria de Angola (CCIA) (Angolan Chamber of Commerce and Industry): Largo do Kinaxixi 14, 1° andar, CP 92, Luanda; tel. 222444506; fax 222444629; e-mail ccira@ebonet.net; internet www.ccia.ebonet.net; Pres. ANTÓNIO JOÃO DOS SANTOS; Sec.-Gen. ANTÓNIO TIAGO GOMES.

INDUSTRIAL AND TRADE ASSOCIATIONS

Associação Comercial de Benguela: Rua Sacadura Cabral 104, CP 347, Benguela; tel. 272232441; fax 272233022; e-mail acbenguela@netangola.com; internet www.netangola.com/acb; f. 1907; Pres. AIRES PIRES ROQUE.

Associação Comercial e Industrial da Ilha de Luanda (ACIL): Largo do Kinaxixi 9, Luanda; tel. 222341866; fax 222349677; Pres. PEDRO GODHINO DOMINGOS.

Associação Comercial e Industrial de Luanda (ACOMIL): Largo do Kinaxixi 14–30, Luanda; tel. 222335728; Pres. JOÃO ADÃO ANTÓNIO TIGRE.

Associação Comercial de Luanda (ASCANGOLA): Edif. Palácio de Comércio, 1° andar, CP 1275, Luanda; tel. 222332453.

Associação Industrial de Angola (AIA): Rua Manuel Fernando Caldeira 6, CP 61227, Luanda; tel. 222330624; fax 222338650; e-mail contactos@aiangola.net; internet aiangola.net; Pres. JOSÉ SEVERINO.

Associação de Mulheres Empresárias: Largo do Kinaxixi 14, 3° andar, Luanda; tel. 222346742; fax 222343088; f. 1990; asscn of business women; Sec.-Gen. HENRIQUETA DE CARVALHO.

Rede Angolana do Sector Micro-Empresarial (RASME): Luanda; asscn of small businesses; Exec.-Co-ordinator BAY KANGUDI.

STATE TRADING ORGANIZATIONS

Angolan Selling Corporation (ASCORP): Edif. Soleil B, Rua Tipografia Mama Tita, Ingombotas, CP 3978, Luanda; tel. 222396465; fax 222397615; e-mail ascorpadmin@ebonet.net; f. 1999; 51% state-owned diamond-trading co; Pres. NOE BALTAZAR.

Direcção dos Serviços de Comércio (DNCI) (Dept of Trade): Palácio de Vidro, 3° andar, Largo 4 de Fevereiro 7, CP 1337, Luanda; tel. and fax 222310658; e-mail minco.dnci.gc@netangola.com; internet www.dnci.net; f. 1970; brs throughout Angola; Dir GOMES CARDOSO.

Exportang, UEE (Empresa de Exportações de Angola): Rua dos Enganos 1A, CP 1000, Luanda; tel. 222332363; co-ordinates exports.

Importang, UEE (Empresa de Importações de Angola): Calçada do Município 10, CP 1003, Luanda; tel. 222337994; f. 1977; co-ordinates majority of imports; Dir-Gen. SIMÃO DIOGO DA CRUZ.

Nova Angomédica, UEE: Rua do Sanatório, Bairro Palanca, CP 2698, Luanda; tel. 222261366; fax 222260010; f. 1981; production and distribution of pharmaceutical goods; Gen. Dir JOSÉ LUÍS PASCOAL.

Sociedade de Comercialização de Diamantes de Angola SARL (SODIAM): Edif. Endiama/De Beers, Rua Rainha Ginga 87, CP 1072, Luanda; tel. 222370217; fax 222370423; e-mail sodiamadmin@ebonet.net; f. 2000; part of the ENDIAMA group; diamond-trading org.; Man. Dir MANUEL ARNALDO DE SOUSA CALADO.

STATE INDUSTRIAL ENTERPRISES

Bricomil: Rua Massano Amorim 79, Chicala, Luanda; tel. 222343895; fax 222342533; f. 1986; 55% state-owned; privatization planned; civil construction; 650 employees.

Companhia do Açúcar de Angola: Rua Direita 77, Luanda; production of sugar.

Empresa de Construção de Edificações, UEE (CONSTROI): Rua Amílcar Cabral 167, 1° andar, Luanda; tel. 222333930; construction.

Empresa de Obras Especiais (EMPROE): Rua Ngola Kiluange 183–185, Luanda; tel. 222382142; fax 222382143; building and civil engineering; Dir-Gen. SILVA NETO.

Empresa de Rebenefício e Exportação do Café de Angola, UEE (CAFANGOL): Rua Robert Shields 4–6, CP 342, Luanda; tel. 222337916; fax 222332840; e-mail cafangol@nexus.ao; f. 1983; nat. coffee-processing and trade org.; Dir-Gen. ISAIAS DOMINGOS DE MENEZES.

Empresa dos Tabacos de Angola: Rua Major Kanyangulu, 220, CP 1238, Luanda; tel. 222332760; fax 222331091; e-mail eta@nexus.ao; manufacture of tobacco products; Gen. Man. K. BITTENCOURT.

Empresa Nacional de Cimento, UEE (ENCIME): CP 157, Lobito; tel. 272212325; cement production.

Empresa Nacional de Diamantes de Angola (ENDIAMA), UEE: Rua Major Kanhangulo 100, CP 1247, Luanda; tel. and fax 222332718; fax 222337216; internet www.endiama.co.ao; f. 1981; commenced operations 1986; diamond mining; a number of subsidiary cos undergoing privatization; Pres. Dr MANUEL ARNALDO DE SOUSA CALADO.

Empresa Nacional de Ferro de Angola (FERRANGOL): Rua João de Barros 26, CP 2692, Luanda; tel. 222373800; iron production; Chair. DIAMANTINO PEDRO DE AZEVEDO; Dir ARMANDO DE SOUSA.

Empresa Nacional de Manutenção, UEE (MANUTECNICA): Rua 7, Av. do Cazenga 10, CP 3508, Luanda; tel. 222383646; assembly of machines and specialized equipment for industry.

Geotécnica Unidad Económica Estatal: Rua Angola Kilmanse 389–393, Luanda; tel. 222381795; fax 222382730; f. 1978; surveying and excavation; Man. P. M. M. ELVINO, Jr.

Siderurgia Nacional, UEE: Rua Farol Lagostas, Luanda; tel. 222383587; f. 1963; nationalized 1980; scheduled for privatization; steelworks and rolling mill plant.

Sociedade Nacional de Combustíveis de Angola (SONANGOL): Rua Rainha Ginga 22, CP 1316, Luanda; tel. 226643342; fax 2223919782; e-mail hld.gci@sonangol.co.ao; internet www.sonangol.co.ao; f. 1976; exploration, production and refining of crude petroleum, and marketing and distribution of petroleum products; sole concessionary in Angola, supervises on- and offshore operations of foreign petroleum cos; 11 subsidiaries, incl. shipping cos; holds majority interest in jt ventures with Cabinda Gulf Oil Co (CABGOC), Fina Petróleos de Angola and Texaco Petróleos de Angola; CEO MANUEL VICENTE; c. 7,000 employees.

Sonangalp, Lda: Rua Manuel Fernando Caldeira 25, 1725 Luanda; tel. 222334527; fax 222339802; e-mail geral@sonangalp.co.ao; internet www.sonangalp.co.ao/v1; f. 1994; 51% owned by SONANGOL, 49% owned by Petrogal Angola (Portugal); fuel distribution; Pres. ANTÓNIO SILVESTRE.

UTILITIES

Electricity

Empresa Nacional de Construções Eléctricas, UEE (ENCEL): Rua Comandante Che Guevara 185–187, CP 5230, Luanda; tel. 222446712; fax 222446759; e-mail encel@encel.co.ao; internet www.encel.co.ao; f. 1982; supplier of electromechanical equipment; Dir-Gen. DANIEL SIMAS.

Empresa Nacional de Electricidade, EP (ENE): Edif. Geominas 6°–7° andar, CP 772, Luanda; tel. 222321499; fax 222323382; e-mail enepdg@netangola.com; internet www.ene.co.ao; f. 1980; production and distribution of electricity; Pres. and Dir-Gen. Eng. FERNANDO BARROS C. GONGA.

Water

Empresa Provincial de Água de Luanda (EPAL): Rua Frederich Engels 3, CP 1387, Luanda; tel. 222335001; fax 222330380; e-mail epalsdg@snet.co.ao; state-owned; Pres. LEONÍDIO GUSTAVO FERREIRA DE CEITA.

TRADE UNIONS

Sindicato dos Jornalistas Angolanos (SJA): CP 2805, Luanda; tel. 222334888; fax 222393445; f. by fmr mems of the União dos Jornalistas Angolanos; Sec.-Gen. Dr LUÍSA ROGÉRIO.

Sindicato Nacional de Professores (Sinprof): Rua da Missão 71, 4° andar, Luanda; tel. 222371780; e-mail sinprof@sinprof.org; teachers' union; Pres. GUILHERME SILVA; Sec.-Gen. GRAÇA MANUEL.

União dos Jornalistas Angolanos (UJA): Rua Francisco Távora 8, 1° andar, CP 2140, Luanda; tel. 222338972; fax 222332420; f. 1992; Pres. AVELINO MIGUEL; Gen. Sec. LUISA ROGÉRIO; 1,253 mems in 2003.

União Nacional das Associações de Camponeses Angolanos (UNACA): Rua Major Kanhangulo 146, 1° andar, CP 2465, Luanda; e-mail secretaria@unaca.org; peasants' asscn; Gen. Sec. PAULO UIME.

União Nacional dos Trabalhadores Angolanos (UNTA) (National Union of Angolan Workers): Av. 4 de Fevereiro 210, CP 28, Luanda; tel. 222334670; fax 222393590; e-mail untadis@netangola.com; f. 1960; Sec.-Gen. MANUEL AUGUSTO VIAGE; c. 160,000 mems (2007).

Transport

The transport infrastructure was severely dislocated by the civil war that ended in 2002. Subsequently, major rebuilding and upgrading projects were undertaken.

RAILWAYS

There are three main railway lines in Angola, the Benguela railway, which runs from the coast to the Zambian border, the Luanda–Malange line, and the Moçâmedes line, which connects Namibe and Kuando Kubango. In 2004 only 850 km out of a total of almost 3,000 km of track were operational. A plan introduced in late 2004 to rehabilitate and extend the rail network was expected to take 11 years and to cost US $4,000m. In mid-2005 a project for rebuilding and upgrading the railway system was approved by the Southern African Development Community (SADC). Some 190 km of the 424-km Luanda–Malange line became operational in 2010 when goods transport started between Luanda and Dondo. The Benguela line—a significant export route—was scheduled to reopen in mid-2013, following demining and reconstruction work by Chinese workers. The Moçamedes line was scheduled to reopen in 2012.

Direcção Nacional dos Caminhos de Ferro: Rua Major Kanhangulo, CP 1250, Luanda; tel. 222370091; f. 1975; nat. network operating 4 fmrly independent systems covering 2,952 track-km; Dir JULIO BANGO.

Benguela Railway (Caminho de Ferro de Benguela—Empresa Pública): Praça 11 Novembro 3, CP 32, Lobito, Benguela; tel. 272222645; fax 272225133; e-mail cfbeng@ebonet.net; owned by Govt of Angola; line carrying passenger and freight traffic from the port of Lobito across Angola, via Huambo and Luena, to the border of the Democratic Republic of the Congo (DRC, fmrly Zaire); 1,301 track-km; in 2004 a consortium from China (People's Republic) agreed to rehabilitate the line to the DRC; CEO JOSÉ CARLOS GOMES; 1,700 employees.

Caminho de Ferro de Moçâmedes (CFM): CP 130, Lubango; tel. 261221752; fax 261224442; e-mail gab.dir.cfm@netangola.com; f. 1905; main line from Namibe to Menongue, via Lubango; br. lines to Chibia and iron ore mines at Cassinga; 838 track-km; Chair. DANIEL KIPAXE; CEO JÚLIO BANGO JOAQUIM.

Luanda Railway (Empresa de Caminho de Ferro de Luanda, UEE): CP 1250-C, Luanda; tel. 222370061; f. 1886; serves an iron-, cotton- and sisal-producing region between Luanda and Malange; 536 track-km; CEO OSVALDO LOBO DO NASCIMENTO.

ROADS

In 2001 Angola had 51,429 km of roads, of which 7,944 km were main roads and 13,278 km were secondary roads. About 10.4% of roads were paved. It was estimated that 80% of the country's road network was in disrepair. In 2005–06 contracts were awarded to various foreign companies to upgrade the road network, including the main north–south coastal road. A government programme to rebuild some 14,000 km of the road network by 2011 was underway.

Direcção Nacional dos Transportes Rodoviárias: Rua Rainha Ginga 74, 1° andar, Luanda; tel. 222339390; fax 222334427.

Instituto Nacional de Estradas de Angola (INEA): Rua Amílcar Cabral 35, 3° andar, CP 5667, Luanda; tel. 222332828; fax 222335754; Dir-Gen. JOAQUIM SEBASTIÃO.

SHIPPING

The main harbours are at Lobito, Luanda and Namibe. The first phase of a 10-year SADCC (now SADC) programme to develop the 'Lobito corridor', for which funds were pledged in January 1989, was to include the rehabilitation of the ports of Lobito and Benguela. In January 2007 the Japanese authorities pledged US $9m. for the rehabilitation of the quays of Namibe and Lobito ports. The port of Luanda was due to be upgraded by the end of 2010. In December 2009

Angola's registered merchant fleet comprised 153 vessels, totalling 63,098 grt.

Instituto Marítimo e Portuário de Angola (IMPA): Rua Rainha Ginga 74, 4° andar, Luanda; tel. and fax 222390034; Dir-Gen. VICTOR DE CARVALHO.

Agenang, UEE: Rua Engracia Fragoso 47–49, CP 485, Luanda; tel. 222393988; fax 222391444; state shipping co; scheduled for privatization.

Cabotang—Cabotagem Nacional Angolana, UEE: Av. 4 de Fevereiro 83A, Luanda; tel. 222373133; operates off the coasts of Angola and Mozambique; Dir-Gen. JOÃO OCTAVIO VAN-DÚNEM.

Empresa Portuária do Lobito, UEE: Av. da Independência 16, Lobito, Benguela; tel. 272222645; fax 272222865; e-mail dop@portodolobito.com; long-distance sea transport; CEO BENTO PAIXÃO DOS SANTOS.

Empresa Portuária de Luanda: Av. 4 de Fevereiro, CP 1229, Porto de Luanda; tel. 222311753; fax 222311178; e-mail geral@portoluanda.co.ao; internet www.portoluanda.co.ao; CEO FRANCISCO VENÂNCIO.

Empresa Portuária de Moçâmedes—Namibe, UEE: Rua Pedro Benje 10A e C, CP 49, Namibe; tel. 264260643; long-distance sea transport; CEO JOAQUIM DOMINGOS NETO.

Orey Angola, Lda: Largo 4 de Fevereiro 3, 3° andar, CP 583, Luanda; tel. 222311454; fax 222310882; e-mail orey@oreylad.ebonet.net; internet www.orey-angola.com; int. shipping, especially to Portugal; Dir JOÃO TEIGA.

Sécil Marítima SARL, UEE: Edif. Secil, Av. 4 de Fevereiro 42, 1° andar, CP 5910, Luanda; tel. 222311334; fax 222311784; e-mail secilmaritima@msn.com; operates ports at Lobito, Luanda and Namibe; Gen. Man. MARIA AMÉLIA RITA.

CIVIL AVIATION

Angola's airport system is well developed, but suffered some damage in the later years of the civil war. The 4 de Fevereiro international airport in Luanda underwent modernization in the late 2000s, while a new international airport, at Huíla was opened in January 2010. During the late 2000s airports at Luanda, Lobito, Soyo, Namibe, Saurimo, Uíge, Huambo and Bié also underwent rehabilitation. In 2009 it was announced that two further international airports were to be built in Luanda and Benguela.

Direcção Nacional da Aviação Civil: Rua Frederich Engels 92, 6° andar, CP 569, Luanda; tel. 222339412.

Instituto Nacional da Aviação Civil: Rua Miguel de Melo 96, 6° andar, Luanda; tel. 222335936; fax 222390529; internet www.inavic.gv.ao; Dir-Gen. Dr GASPAR FRANCISCO DOS SANTOS.

Empresa Nacional de Aeroportos e Navegação Aerea (ENANA): Av. Amílcar Cabral 110, CP 841, Luanda; tel. and fax 222351267; e-mail cai_enana@snet.co.ao; administers airports; Chair. MANUEL FERREIRA DE CEITA.

Air Nacoia: Rua Comandante Che Guevara 67, 1° andar, Luanda; tel. and fax 222395477; f. 1993; Pres. SALVADOR SILVA.

SONAIR SARL: Aeroporto Internacional 4 de Fevereiro, Luanda; tel. 222633502; fax 222321572; e-mail commercial.sonair@sonangol.co.ao; internet www.sonairsarl.com; f. 1998; subsidiary of SONANGOL; operates direct flights between Luanda and Houston, USA; Chair. MANUEL D. VICENTE; CEO JOÃO ALVES ANDRADE.

TAAG—Linhas Aéreas de Angola: Rua da Missão 123, CP 79, Luanda; tel. 222332338; fax 222390396; e-mail gci_taag@ebonet.net; internet www.nexus.ao/taag; f. 1938; internal scheduled passenger and cargo services, and services from Luanda to destinations within Africa and to Europe and South America; Chair. Dr ANTÓNIO LUIS PIMENTEL DE ARAÚJO.

Angola Air Charter: Aeroporto Internacional 4 de Fevereiro, CP 3010, Luanda; tel. 222321290; fax 222320105; e-mail aacharter@independente.net; f. 1992; subsidiary of TAAG; CEO A. DE MATOS.

Transafrik International Ltd: Aeroporto Internacional 4 de Fevereiro, Luanda; tel. 222353714; fax 222354183; e-mail info@transafrik.com; internet www.transafrik.com; f. 1986; operates int. contract cargo services; CEO BJÖRN NÄF; Chief Financial Officer STEPHAN BRANDT.

Tourism

Angola's tourism industry is undeveloped as a result of the years of civil war, although its potential for development is great. Tourist arrivals totalled 425,000 in 2010 and receipts from tourism in 2009 amounted to US $534m.

National Tourist Agency: Palácio de Vidro, Largo 4 de Fevereiro, CP 1240, Luanda; tel. 222372750.

Defence

In accordance with the peace agreement concluded by the Government and the União Nacional para a Independência Total de Angola (UNITA) in May 1991, a new 50,000-strong national army, the Forças Armadas de Angola (FAA), was established, comprising equal numbers of government forces, the Forças Armadas Populares de Libertação de Angola (FAPLA), and UNITA soldiers. After elections in 1992, UNITA withdrew its troops from the FAA and hostilities resumed. Following the signing of the Lusaka Accord in November 1994, the integration of the UNITA contingent into the FAA resumed. In 1995 agreement was reached between the Government and UNITA on the enlargement of the FAA to comprise a total of 90,000 troops, and discussions began concerning the potential formation of a fourth, non-combatant branch of the FAA, which would engage in public works projects. In mid-1997 the Government estimated that UNITA maintained a residual force numbering some 25,000–30,000 troops, while UNITA claimed to have a force of only 2,963 'police'. In March 1998 UNITA issued a declaration announcing the complete demobilization of its forces and by May some 11,000 UNITA soldiers had been integrated into the FAA. However, the integration process was abandoned following the resumption of hostilities between the Government and UNITA in December 1998. Following the ratification of a cease-fire in April 2002, only 5,000 UNITA fighters were integrated into the FAA; it was estimated that 80,000 had been reintegrated into civilian life by November 2003. As assessed at November 2011, the FAA had an estimated total strength of 107,000: army 100,000, navy 1,000 and air force 6,000. In addition, there was a paramilitary force numbering an estimated 10,000.

Defence Expenditure: Budgeted at 352,000m. kwanza for 2012.

Chief of General Staff of the Armed Forces: Gen. GERALDO SACHIPENGO NUNDA.

Chief of General Staff of the Army: Gen. JORGE BARROS NGUTÓ.

Chief of General Staff of the National Air Force: Gen. FRANCISCO GONÇALVES AFONSO.

Chief of General Staff of the Navy: Adm. AUGUSTO DA SILVA CUNHA.

Education

Education is officially compulsory for eight years, between seven and 15 years of age, and is provided free of charge by the Government. Primary education begins at seven years of age and lasts for six years. Secondary education, beginning at the age of 11, lasts for up to six years, comprising two cycles of three years each. As a proportion of the school-age population, the total enrolment at primary and secondary schools was equivalent to 83% in 2009/10. According to UNESCO estimates, enrolment at primary schools in 2009/10 included 86% of children in the relevant age-group (boys 93%; girls 78%), while secondary enrolment in 2009/10 included 12% of children in the relevant age-group (boys 12%; girls 13%). In 2009/10 a total of 66,251 students were enrolled in tertiary education. In November 2002 the Government announced plans for the construction of seven provincial universities, five science and technology institutes, three medical schools and a nutrition research centre. There are also four private universities. Much education is now conducted in vernacular languages rather than Portuguese. In 2004 the Government recruited 29,000 new teachers, to be trained by the UN Children's Fund (UNICEF). The 2006 budget allocated an estimated 83,500m. kwanza to education.

ANTARCTICA

INTRODUCTION

The continent of Antarctica is estimated to cover 13,661,000 sq km. There are no indigenous inhabitants, but a number of permanent research stations have been established. W. S. Bruce, of the Scottish National Antarctic Expedition (1902–04), established a meteorological station on Laurie Island, South Orkney Islands, in 1903. After the expedition, this was transferred to the Argentine authorities (the British Government having declined to operate the station), who have maintained the observatory since 1904 (see Orcadas, below). The next permanent stations were established in 1944 by the United Kingdom, and then subsequently by other countries.

RESEARCH

Scientific Committee on Antarctic Research (SCAR): Secretariat: Scott Polar Research Institute, Lensfield Rd, Cambridge, CB2 1ER, United Kingdom; tel. (1223) 336550; fax (1223) 336549; e-mail info@scar.org; internet www.scar.org; f. 1958 to initiate, promote and co-ordinate scientific research in the Antarctic, and to provide scientific advice to the Antarctic Treaty System; an inter-disciplinary cttee of the International Council for Science (ICSU); 31 Full Mems; 9 ICSU Scientific Unions Mems; 5 Assoc. Mems.

President: Prof. MAHLON C. KENNICUTT, II (USA).

Vice-Presidents: Prof. Dr SERGIO A. MARENSSI (Argentina), Dr AD H. L. HUISKES (Netherlands), Dr RASIK RAVINDRA (India), Dr YEADONG KIM (Republic of Korea).

Executive Director: Dr MIKE SPARROW.

WINTERING STATIONS

(The following list includes wintering stations south of latitude 60° occupied during austral winter 2012)

	Latitude	Longitude
ARGENTINA		
Belgrano II, Bertrab Nunatak, Luitpold Coast	77° 53' S	34° 38 'W
Esperanza, Hope Bay	63° 24' S	57° 00' W
Jubany, King George Island	62° 14' S	58° 40' W
Marambio, Seymour Island	64° 15' S	56° 39' W
Orcadas, Laurie Island	60° 44' S	44° 44' W
San Martín, Barry Island	68° 08' S	67° 06' W
AUSTRALIA		
Casey, Vincennes Bay, Budd Coast	66° 17' S	110° 31' E
Davis, Ingrid Christensen Coast	68° 35' S	77° 58' E
Mawson, Mac. Robertson Land	67° 36' S	62° 52' E
BRAZIL		
Comandante Ferraz, King George Island*	62° 05' S	58° 23' W
CHILE		
Eduardo Frei, King George Island	62° 12' S	58° 58' W
Bernardo O'Higgins, Cape Legoupil	63° 19' S	57° 54' W
Arturo Prat, Greenwich Island	62° 29' S	59° 40' W
PEOPLE'S REPUBLIC OF CHINA		
Chang Cheng (Great Wall), King George Island	62° 13' S	58° 58' W
Zhongshan, Princess Elizabeth Land	69° 22' S	76° 22' E
FRANCE		
Dumont d'Urville, Terre Adélie	66° 40' S	140° 00' E
FRANCE-ITALY†		
Concordia, Dome C	75° 06' S	123° 24' E
GERMANY		
Neumayer, Ekstrømisen	70° 38' S	08° 16' W
INDIA		
Maitri, Schirmacheroasen	70° 46' S	11° 44' E
JAPAN		
Syowa, Ongul	69° 00' S	39° 35' E
REPUBLIC OF KOREA		
King Sejong, King George Island	62° 13' S	58° 47' W
NEW ZEALAND		
Scott Base, Ross Island	77° 51' S	166° 46' E
NORWAY		
Troll	72° 00' S	02° 32' E
POLAND		
Arctowski, King George Island	62° 10' S	58° 28' W
RUSSIA		
Bellingshausen, King George Island	62° 12' S	58° 58' W
Mirny, Queen Mary Land	66° 33' S	93° 01' E
Novolazarevskaya, Prinsesse Astrid Kyst	70° 46' S	11° 52' E
Progress 2, Princess Elizabeth Land	69° 23' S	76° 23' E
Vostok, East Antarctica	78° 28' S	106° 48' E
SOUTH AFRICA		
SANAE IV, Vesleskarvet	71° 40' S	02° 50' W
UKRAINE		
Vernadsky, Argentine Islands	65° 15' S	64° 15' W
UNITED KINGDOM		
Halley, Brunt Ice Shelf, Caird Coast	75° 35' S	26° 32' W
Rothera, Adelaide Island	67° 34' S	68° 07' W
USA		
McMurdo, Ross Island	77° 51' S	166° 40' E
Palmer, Anvers Island	64° 47' S	64° 03' W
Amundsen-Scott	South Pole‡	
URUGUAY		
Artigas, King George Island	62° 11' S	58° 54' W

* The station was destroyed by fire in 2011 and would remain closed for the 2012 season; rebuilding work was scheduled to begin in 2013.

† The Concordia research station is a joint venture between France and Italy.

‡ The precise co-ordinates of the location of this station are: 89° 59' 51″ S, 139° 16' 22″ E.

TERRITORIAL CLAIMS

Territory	Claimant State
Antártida Argentina	Argentina
Australian Antarctic Territory	Australia
British Antarctic Territory	United Kingdom
Dronning Maud Land	Norway
Ross Dependency	New Zealand
Terre Adélie	France
Territorio Chileno Antártico	Chile

These claims are not recognized by the USA or Russia. No claims in the sector of the Antarctic continent between 90° W and 150° W have been defined by governments. However, Peter I Øy (68° 47'S, 90° 35'W) is claimed as Norwegian territory.

Article 4, Clause 2 of the Antarctic Treaty (see below) states that, 'No acts or activities taking place while the present Treaty is in force shall constitute a basis for asserting, supporting or denying a claim to territorial sovereignty in Antarctica or create any rights of sovereignty in Antarctica. No new claim, or enlargement of an existing claim, to territorial sovereignty in Antarctica shall be asserted while the present Treaty is in force.

THE ANTARCTIC TREATY

The Antarctic Treaty was signed in Washington, DC, on 1 December 1959 by the 12 nations co-operating in the Antarctic during the International Geophysical Year (1957–58), and entered into force on 23 June 1961. The Treaty made provision for a review of its terms 30 years after ratification; however, no signatory to the Treaty has requested such a review.

The full original text of the Antarctic Treaty is reproduced by the Antarctic Treaty Secretariat at www.ats.aq/documents/ats/treaty_original.pdf.

Signatories

The Original Signatories to the Antarctic Treaty are Argentina, Australia, Belgium, Chile, France, Japan, New Zealand, Norway, Russia (as successor to the former USSR), South Africa, the United Kingdom and the USA. Each holds the status of Consultative Party.

By virtue of their scientific activity in Antarctica, Brazil, Bulgaria, the People's Republic of China, Ecuador, Finland, Germany, India, Italy, the Republic of Korea, the Netherlands, Peru, Poland, Spain, Sweden, Ukraine and Uruguay have the status of Consultative Party under the Treaty. Austria, Belarus, Canada, Colombia, Cuba, the Czech Republic, Denmark, Estonia, Greece, Guatemala, Hungary, the Democratic People's Republic of Korea, Malaysia, Monaco, Papua New Guinea, Portugal, Romania, Slovakia, Switzerland, Turkey and Venezuela are Acceding States but do not have Consultative Party status.

Antarctic Treaty Secretariat: Maipú 757, 4°, C1006ACI Buenos Aires; tel. (11) 4320-4250; fax (11) 4320-4253; e-mail ats@ats.aq; internet www.ats.aq; f. 2004; Exec. Sec. Dr MANFRED REINKE.

Antarctic Treaty Consultative Meetings

Meetings of representatives of the original signatory nations of the Antarctic Treaty and acceding nations accorded consultative status are held annually to discuss scientific, environmental and political matters. The 35th meeting was scheduled to take place in Hobart, Australia, in June 2012.

Among the numerous measures that have been agreed and implemented by the Consultative Parties are several designed to protect the Antarctic environment and wildlife. These include the designation of Specially Protected Areas and Sites of Special Scientific Interest, a Convention for the Conservation of Antarctic Seals, and a Convention on the Conservation of Antarctic Marine Living Resources.

The Protocol on Environmental Protection to the Antarctic Treaty was adopted by the original signatory nations in October 1991. It entered into force in January 1998, having been ratified by all 26 of the then Consultative Parties. Under Article 7, any activity relating to mineral resources, other than scientific research, is prohibited. Article 25, on modification or amendment, states that a conference shall be held as soon as practicable if, after the expiration of 50 years from the date of entry into force of the Protocol, any of the Antarctic Treaty Consultative Parties so requests; it further specifies that, in respect of Article 7, any proposed modification to the prohibition on mining activity shall be considered only if a regulatory regime is in place. The first four annexes to the Protocol, providing for environmental impact assessment, conservation of fauna and flora, waste disposal, and monitoring of marine pollution, entered into force with the Protocol; a fifth annex, on area protection and management, entered effect in May 2002. A sixth annex, on liability arising from environmental emergencies, was adopted in June 2005, and was to take effect upon ratification by all Consultative Parties to the Protocol. The Protocol effectively superseded the provisions of the 1964 Agreed Measures for the Conservation of Antarctic Fauna and Flora, including area protection in Antarctica. A Committee for Environmental Protection (CEP) was established in 1998, under the provisions of the Protocol on Environmental Protection. The CEP meets at the location of the annual Antarctic Treaty Consultative Meeting.

Committee for Environmental Protection (CEP): e-mail cep@cep.aq; internet www.cep.aq; f. 1998; Chair. Dr YVES FRENOT.

RECENT DEVELOPMENTS

The World Meteorological Organization (WMO) reported that the hole in the ozone layer formed over Antarctica in 2006 was the most serious on record. Having reached 29.5m. sq km at its maximum point, the area of the hole marginally exceeded that recorded in 2000 (29.4m. sq km), hitherto the largest recorded. Furthermore, according to WMO, there had been the greatest recorded mass deficit in 2006—of 40.8m. metric tons, compared with 39.6m. tons in 2000—with the effect that the mass of ozone over Antarctica was lower than that ever previously recorded. WMO data for 2007 showed that the ozone hole area, at a maximum of 25m. sq km, was somewhat weaker, as was the mass deficit, which reached 28m. tons. WMO stated that the relatively smaller size of the ozone hole was not a sign of recovery, but was instead related to mild temperatures in the Antarctic stratosphere during the 2007 austral winter. In 2008 the ozone hole area reached 27m. sq km, and the mass deficit 35m. tons: each was the fourth largest recorded since 1999 (having been surpassed only in 2000, 2003 and 2006). The daily maximum ozone hole area in 2009 was 24.0m. sq km. For 2010 the ozone hole reached a peak daily maximum of 22.6m. sq km in late September. The relatively shallow ozone hole in 2010, and a slow start to its formation, was attributed to the impact of warmer than usual stratospheric temperatures in reducing the volume of stratospheric clouds early in the season. In 2011 the daily maximum ozone hole area reached 26.0m. sq km in September. The mass deficit increased faster in 2011 than in 2008 or 2010, and in October was close to an all time maximum, reaching 36.8m. tons early in the month.

A comprehensive study of glaciers in the Antarctic Pensinsula, published by researchers of the British Antarctic Survey in April 2005 (and conducted as part of a project by the US Geological Survey to map changes to Antarctica's coastline) showed that 87% of glaciers there were retreating, and that the rate of retreat had increased markedly since 2000. The survey's analysis of data back to the 1950s identified that an increasing number of glaciers had been retreating in recent decades compared to the situation in the 1950s, when a majority of glaciers were stable or advancing. Research published in March 2006, led by the University of Colorado, USA, gave evidence of the significant decline of the total mass balance of the Antarctic ice sheet. Satellite data indicated that the volume of ice being lost was raising global sea levels by some 0.4 mm per year. As much as 152 cu km was being lost annually from the ice sheet, with the bulk of the loss being from the West Antarctic sheet. Research published by an international team of scientists in January 2008 estimated that 132,000m. metric tons of ice had been lost from West Antarctica in 2006, compared with 83,000m. tons in 1996. Loss of ice from the Antarctic Peninsula was estimated at 60,000m. tons, compared with 25,000m. tons 10 years earlier. Loss was concentrated at narrow glacier outlets with accelerating ice flow, suggesting that the mass balance of the entire ice sheet had been altered by glacier flow. (Previous simulation had suggested that the ice mass would increase in response to future climate change during the 21st century, owing to increased snowfall.) While recorded loss to the East Antarctic ice sheet was near zero in 1996–2006, the thinning of maritime sectors suggested to the researchers that this may change in the near future. Analysis published in November 2009 by scientists at the University of Texas at Austin, USA, of satellite data gathered in 2002–09 from the NASA Gravity Recovery and Climate Experiment suggested that the East Antarctic ice sheet was losing mass, mainly in coastal areas, at an estimated rate of some 57,000m. tons annually: it was thought that this loss may have begun as early as 2006. The same study confirmed annual ice loss from West Antarctica of 132,000m. tons. A study of changes in polar ice mass and trends in acceleration in polar ice loss, published in the journal *Geophysical Research Letters* in March 2011, based on analysis of data from 1992–2009, found that loss from the Antarctic ice sheet was increasing by an average of 14,500m. metric tons per year. The authors concluded that continuation in this rapid acceleration in loss, cumulatively with accelerated loss, also shown by the study, from the Greenland ice sheet, could contribute 150 mm to average global sea level by 2050. At present trends, according to the study, the overall rise in average sea level was likely to be higher than that predicted by the 2007 *Fourth Assessment Report* of the Intergovernmental Panel on Climate Change. Meanwhile, a study, led by US academics, of trends in Antarctic surface temperatures during 1957–2006, results of which were released in January 2009, suggested that the continent was warming by an average of about 0.1°C per decade, with the strongest warming trends being in winter and spring and over West Antarctica (where the rate of warming was faster than the world average). The report's authors concluded that while natural climatic cycles probably influenced the warming, it was difficult to explain the warming trend without considering the near-certain impact of increased concentrations of greenhouse gases.

Research published in July 2008 by the British Antarctic Survey, based on studies of the West Antarctic Peninsula seabed, suggested that the frequency of disturbance of the seabed by icebergs, known as scouring, was likely to increase as winter sea ice (which restricts the movement of icebergs in coastal waters) diminishes in extent and duration. This increased disturbance could, according to the report's authors, bring about unpredictable changes in near-shore marine ecosystems. An ice bridge linking the Wilkins ice shelf to the Charcot and Latady islands collapsed in April 2009. It had been reported in March 2008 that the Wilkins shelf was retreating more rapidly than had previously been anticipated, with the disintegration, at the end of the austral summer, of an area of ice of some 414 sq km. The collapse of the ice bridge would allow a mass of broken ice and icebergs to drift into the Southern Ocean. In February 2010 an iceberg measuring some 2,550 sq km was dislodged from the Mertz Glacier Tongue, East Antarctica, by an older berg which had begun to drift in 2009.

TOURISM AND MARITIME SAFETY

Tourism is promoted by the International Association of Antarctica Tour Operators (IAATO). The number of tourists visiting Antarctica in 2010/11 totalled 33,824 (compared with 4,700 in 1990/91), including 19,445 landed passengers. The rate of increase in tourist numbers led to expressions of concern by the early 2000s regarding the environmental impact of the industry on the region. In April 2009 signatories to the Antarctic Treaty agreed, subject to ratification, to prevent vessels carrying more than 500 passengers from landing in Antarctica, and to allow no more than 100 passengers on permitted vessels to land at any one time. A mandatory safety code for vessels operating in the Antarctic region was also adopted. At its November 2009 Assembly the International Maritime Organization (IMO) adopted guidelines for ships operating in polar waters; the guidelines formed the basis of a planned mandatory Polar Code, intended to address the risks specific to shipping operations in polar waters, taking into account the extreme environmental conditions and remoteness of operation, as well as comprehensively to address the possible impact on the environment of shipping activity. Under amendments to the IMO International Convention for the Prevention of Pollution from Ships (MARPOL), the use of heavy fuel oils by passenger and cargo ships in Antarctic waters was prohibited with effect from 1 August 2011.

ANTIGUA AND BARBUDA

Introductory Survey

LOCATION, CLIMATE, LANGUAGE, RELIGION, FLAG, CAPITAL

The country comprises three islands: Antigua (280 sq km—108 sq miles), Barbuda (161 sq km—62 sq miles) and the uninhabited rocky islet of Redonda (1.6 sq km—0.6 sq mile). They lie along the outer edge of the Leeward Islands chain in the West Indies. Barbuda is the most northerly (40 km—25 miles north of Antigua), and Redonda is 40 km south-west of Antigua. The French island of Guadeloupe lies to the south of the country, the United Kingdom Overseas Territory of Montserrat to the south-west and Saint Christopher and Nevis to the west. The climate is tropical, although tempered by constant sea breezes and the trade winds, and the mean annual rainfall of 1,000 mm (40 ins) is slight for the region. The temperature averages 27°C (81°F), but can rise to 33°C (93°F) during the hot season between May and October. English is the official language, but an English patois is commonly used. The majority of the inhabitants profess Christianity, and are mainly adherents of the Anglican Communion. The national flag consists of an inverted triangle centred on a red field; the triangle is divided horizontally into three unequal bands, of black, blue and white, with the black stripe bearing a symbol of the rising sun in gold. The capital is St John's, on Antigua.

CONTEMPORARY POLITICAL HISTORY

Historical Context

The British colonized Antigua in the 17th century. The island of Barbuda, formerly a slave stud farm for the Codrington family, was annexed to the territory in 1860. Until December 1959 Antigua and other nearby British territories were administered, under a federal system, as the Leeward Islands. The first elections under universal adult suffrage were held in 1951. The colony participated in the West Indies Federation, which was formed in January 1958 but dissolved in May 1962.

Attempts to form a smaller East Caribbean Federation failed, and most of the eligible colonies subsequently became Associated States in an arrangement that gave them full internal self-government while the United Kingdom retained responsibility for defence and foreign affairs. Antigua attained associated status in February 1967. A House of Representatives replaced the Legislative Council, the Administrator became Governor and the Chief Minister was restyled Premier.

Domestic Political Affairs

In the first general election under associated status, held in February 1971, the Progressive Labour Movement (PLM) ousted the Antigua Labour Party (ALP), which had held power since 1946. George Walter, leader of the PLM, replaced Vere C. Bird, Sr, as Premier. However, a general election in February 1976 was won by the ALP. Vere Bird, the ALP's leader, again became Premier, while Lester Bird, one of his sons, became Deputy Premier.

In 1975 the Associated States agreed to seek independence separately. In the 1976 elections the PLM campaigned for early independence while the ALP opposed it. In September 1978, however, the ALP Government declared that the economic foundation for independence had been laid, and a premature general election was held in April 1980, when the ALP was re-elected. There was strong opposition in Barbuda to gaining independence as part of Antigua, and at local elections in March 1981 the Barbuda People's Movement (BPM), which continued to campaign for secession from Antigua, won all the seats on the Barbuda Council. However, the territory finally became independent, as Antigua and Barbuda, on 1 November 1981, remaining within the Commonwealth. The grievances of the Barbudans concerning control of land and devolution of power were unresolved, although the ALP Government had conceded a certain degree of internal autonomy to the Barbuda Council. The Governor, Sir Wilfred Jacobs, became Governor-General, while the Premier, Vere Bird, Sr, became the country's first Prime Minister.

Following disagreements within the opposition PLM, George Walter formed his own political party, the United People's Movement (UPM), in 1982. In April 1984, at the first general election since independence, divisions within the opposition allowed the ALP to win all of the 16 seats that it contested. The remaining seat, representing Barbuda, was retained by an unopposed independent.

In November 1986 controversy surrounding a rehabilitation scheme at the international airport on Antigua led to an official inquiry, which concluded that Vere Bird, Jr (a senior minister and the eldest son of the Prime Minister), had acted inappropriately by awarding part of the contract to a company with which he was personally involved. The affair divided the ALP, with eight ministers (including Lester Bird, the Deputy Prime Minister) demanding the resignation of Vere Bird, Jr, and Prime Minister Bird refusing to dismiss him. The ALP remained the ruling party at a general election in March 1989.

In April 1990 the Government of Antigua and Barbuda received a diplomatic note of protest from the Government of Colombia regarding the sale of weapons to the Medellín cartel of drugs-traffickers in Colombia. The weapons had originally been sold by Israel to Antigua and Barbuda, but, contrary to regulation, were then immediately shipped on to Colombia in April 1989. The communication from the Colombian Government implicated Vere Bird, Jr, and the Prime Minister eventually agreed to establish a judicial inquiry. In October 1990 the Chamber of Commerce recommended the resignation of the Government, and in November the Government dismissed Vere Bird, Jr, and banned him for life from holding office in the Government. The head of the defence force, Col Clyde Walker, was also dismissed.

Discontent within the ALP (including dissatisfaction with the leadership of Vere Bird, Sr) provoked a serious political crisis in early 1991. The Minister of Finance, John St Luce, resigned in February after claiming that the Prime Minister ignored his proposals for a restructuring of government. A subsequent cabinet reorganization (in which Lester Bird lost his deputy premiership) provoked the immediate resignation of three ministers. In September, however, Bird and St Luce accepted invitations from the Prime Minister to rejoin the Cabinet.

In 1992 further reports of corruption involving Vere Bird, Sr, provoked public unrest and demands for his resignation. In April the Antigua Caribbean Liberation Movement, the PLM and the United National Democratic Party (formed by the merger in 1986 of the UPM with the National Democratic Party) consolidated their opposition to the Government by merging to form the United Progressive Party (UPP). In August further controversy arose when proposed anti-corruption legislation was withdrawn as a result of legal intervention by the Prime Minister.

The Government of Lester Bird, 1994–2004

At a general election in March 1994 the ALP remained the ruling party, although with a reduced majority. Following the election, Lester Bird assumed the premiership.

In February 1995 an ALP activist, Leonard Aaron, was charged with threatening to murder Tim Hector, editor of an opposition newspaper, *The Outlet*. It was reported that Hector's house had been burgled on several occasions, when material containing allegedly incriminating information relating to members of the Government had been stolen. Aaron was subsequently released following the intervention of the Prime Minister. In May the Prime Minister's brother, Ivor Bird, was arrested following an incident in which he collected luggage at V. C. Bird International Airport, from a Barbadian citizen from Venezuela, that contained 12 kg of cocaine. *The Outlet* claimed that such an exchange had occurred on at least three previous occasions. Ivor Bird's subsequent release from police custody, upon payment of a fine of EC $200,000, attracted considerable criticism. A report published by the US Government in early 1998 found Antigua and Barbuda to be 'of primary concern' with regard to drugs-trafficking and money-laundering.

In May 1996 Vere Bird, Jr, who had been declared unfit for public office in 1990, was controversially appointed to the post of

Special Adviser to the Prime Minister. In September Molwyn Joseph resigned as Minister of Finance over allegations of corruption. A demonstration took place at the end of the month at which some 10,000 people demanded a full inquiry into the affair and an early general election. In early December 1997, however, Joseph was reinstated in the Cabinet, an appointment that was vehemently condemned by the opposition.

In March 1997 the opposition BPM defeated the ALP's ally, the New Barbuda Development Movement, in elections to the Barbuda Council, winning all five of the contested seats and thus gaining control of all the seats in the nine-member Council. In the same month the High Court upheld a constitutional motion presented by UPP leader Baldwin Spencer seeking the right of expression for the opposition on state-owned radio and television (denied during the electoral campaign in March 1994). In May and June the UPP boycotted sittings of the House of Representatives (the first legislative boycotts in the country's history) during a parliamentary debate on a proposed US $300m. tourism development on Guiana Island, claiming that the initiative had not been adequately publicized and would be detrimental to the island's ecology. The project was subsequently endorsed by the legislature, but continued to provoke controversy.

Meanwhile, in August 1997 *The Outlet* published further allegations regarding government-supported drugs-trafficking, including a claim that a Colombian drugs cartel had contributed US $1m. to the ALP's election campaign in 1994. In response, Prime Minister Lester Bird obtained a High Court injunction in early September prohibiting the newspaper from publishing further material relating to the allegations. In November the printing presses of *The Outlet* were destroyed by fire, two days after Tim Hector had publicly alleged that a large consignment of 'sophisticated' weaponry had entered Antigua. The Government denied allegations that it was responsible for the fire, and stated that a shipment of 'basic' arms had been imported for police use.

At a general election held on 9 March 1999, the ALP increased its representation in the 17-seat House of Representatives from 11 to 12, at the expense of the UPP, which secured four seats; the BPM retained its single seat. Lester Bird was reappointed Prime Minister, and a new Cabinet was duly appointed, which again controversially included Vere Bird, Jr. Independent observers declared the election to have been free, although they expressed reservations concerning its fairness, owing to the ALP's large-scale expenditure and use of the media during its electoral campaign.

Also in March 1999 the US Government published a report that claimed that recent Antiguan financial legislation had weakened regulations concerning money-laundering and increased the secrecy surrounding 'offshore' banks. It also advised US banks to scrutinize all financial dealings with Antigua and Barbuda, which was described as a potential 'haven for money-laundering activities'. In April the United Kingdom issued a similar financial advisory to its banks. In response, in July Antigua and Barbuda became the first Eastern Caribbean country to bring into force a treaty with the USA on extradition and mutual legal assistance and in September established an independent body, the International Financial Sector Regulatory Authority, to regulate 'offshore' banking. Although in 2000 Antigua and Barbuda's financial system was criticized by the Organisation for Economic Co-operation and Development (OECD, see p. 379) and by the Financial Action Task Force (FATF, see p. 454), in 2001 the FATF recognized the state as a 'fully co-operative jurisdiction against money-laundering'. The USA and the United Kingdom also both withdrew their financial advisory notices. In December the Government signed a tax information exchange agreement with the USA. In 2003 the Government strongly criticized OECD and the FATF for protecting the financial regimes of powerful states at the expense of smaller nations.

In January 2000 the Government established a commission to review the Constitution. The commission's recommendations, reported in February 2002, included the replacement of the Queen as head of state with a President chosen by the majority party in Parliament, and amalgamation of the Senate and House of Representatives into a unicameral legislature.

In November 2003 a UPP request for a motion of no confidence in two government ministers, Molwyn Joseph and Gaston Brown, was denied by the Speaker; the opposition party alleged that both men received substantial sums of money from Allen Stanford, a US businessman and Chairman of the Bank of Antigua, during the negotiation of a real-estate transaction between the Government and the bank.

The Governments of Baldwin Spencer, 2004–

At a general election on 23 March 2004 the opposition UPP, led by Baldwin Spencer, secured 12 out of the 17 parliamentary seats, thereby removing from government the ALP, which had held power since 1976. The ALP, which had been weakened by personal allegations surrounding Lester Bird and by a damaging contraction in the crucial tourism sector, secured only four seats. An extremely high rate of participation—91.2% of the electorate—was interpreted as a strong indication of public resentment towards the Bird regime. The BPM narrowly retained its seat. In advance of the general election a completely new electoral register was, with the assistance of the Electoral Office of Jamaica, prepared for the first time since 1975. Elimination of deceased and non-resident names reduced the list by more than one-fifth, while voters were issued with identity cards. Spencer was sworn in as Prime Minister on 24 March.

In November 2005 the Government dismissed the board of the Antigua Public Utilities Authority (APUA), which had been appointed by Spencer in July 2004, following reports of financial irregularities and conflicts of interest, particularly regarding the proposed sale of APUA's digital mobile cellular telephone network to an Irish-owned multinational company, Digicel. Spencer transferred responsibility for APUA to the Office of the Prime Minister as part of a cabinet reorganization in December 2006. APUA filed a lawsuit against five ex-cabinet ministers, including Bird, in June 2007, seeking to recover an estimated US $34m. allegedly misappropriated from the company and used to finance several projects around the country.

In July 2007 Louise Lake-Tack was sworn in as Governor-General, becoming the first woman in the country's history to assume the role.

At a general election on 12 March 2009 the incumbent UPP secured 50.9% of the vote, winning nine of the 17 seats, while the ALP gained 47.2% of total votes and seven seats. The BPM secured one seat. Some 79.9% of eligible voters participated in the poll. Spencer subsequently announced a reorganization of his Cabinet and a reduction in the number of ministries. Errol Cort, the previous Minister of Finance, who had lost his parliamentary seat in the election, returned in the newly created post of Minister of National Security, while Spencer himself assumed responsibility for foreign affairs and utilities.

Following complaints by the ALP regarding the conduct of the general election, in March 2010 the High Court of Justice invalidated the election of Spencer and two members of his Cabinet owing to delays in the opening of polling stations in their constituencies, necessitating by-elections or another general election. The Government initiated an appeal against the decision with the Eastern Caribbean Court of Appeal (ECCA), and in October the ECCA overturned the High Court's ruling, arguing that it was highly unlikely that the late opening times had distorted the election results. Lester Bird criticized the ECCA judgment, accusing the Court of 'political decision-making', while Spencer denounced the ALP for generating a climate of uncertainty that discouraged foreign investment. In a related development, in June the Speaker of the House of Representatives controversially suspended ALP deputy Gaston Browne for the remainder of the parliamentary session for initiating a disruptive protest in the legislature, in which he demanded that the Prime Minister resign and new elections be held.

The replacement of Sir Gerald Watt as Chairman of the Antigua and Barbuda Electoral Commission (ABEC) with Juno Samuel in January 2011 prompted further controversy. Watt had been suspended in July 2010 along with two other electoral commissioners over alleged breaches of electoral procedure in the 2009 election, including the delays in opening certain polling stations. A tribunal in December 2010 had cleared Watt and Deputy Chairman Nathaniel James of any wrongdoing. The ALP condemned the appointment as politically motivated while Watt appealed to the High Court. (A judicial review into Watt's dismissal was ongoing in late 2011.) In November 2011 Lester Bird and several other ALP deputies walked out of the House of Representatives in protest during a debate over controversial legislation to restructure the ABEC. Nevertheless, the amendments, which transferred some of the powers of the Chief Elections Officer to an expanded body of commissioners, were approved later that month. The Government argued that a larger, more decentralized commission would hinder potential attempts to interfere in its operations and eliminate the procedural problems experienced in the 2009 poll. However, the ALP and Watt contended that these measures were in contravention of the Constitution and that the commissioners would be appointed by the Government, thereby jeopardizing the independence of the ABEC.

Meanwhile, in April 2011 Hilroy Humphreys, a former ALP Minister of Agriculture, was fined after being convicted of defrauding the Medical Benefits Scheme. Humphreys appealed against a further conviction in September, following a court ruling that declared him guilty of involvement in a fraudulent land deal.

Crime

The number of violent crimes in the country increased rapidly from the mid-2000s: reported murders totalled 19 in 2007, 14 in 2008 and 16 in 2009 (compared with just three in 2005). The trend was attributed to an increase in the number of criminal deportees from the USA being repatriated to a region that lacked the necessary facilities to manage the situation, and in 2007 the Government undertook a series of discussions with the US Department of Homeland Security, aimed at increasing co-operation between the two countries on this matter.

Antigua's worsening crime problem received international attention in July 2008 after a British couple was murdered on their honeymoon. The affair cost the country, according to a statement by the Minister of Tourism, Civil Aviation, Culture and the Environment, Harold Lovell, in excess of US $1m. in lost tourism revenue. In December Minister of Finance and the Economy Errol Cort announced that the police force was to be strengthened by 120 new officers, as well as outlining a 23% budget increase to improve the force's criminal database and forensic capabilities. The number of murders declined sharply in 2010, to just six.

In July 2010 the authorities seized 900 kg of cocaine, valued at approximately US $47m., from a vessel arriving in the country from Venezuela. The drugs seizure represented 'the largest in the history of Antigua and Barbuda', according to the Office of National Drug and Money Laundering Control Policy.

Recent developments: the Stanford affair

Parliament, which had been suspended in early February 2009 in preparation for a general election in the following month, was hastily reconvened on 26 February, following a crisis that threatened the economic stability of the islands and made them the focus of international attention. Revelations concerning the business practices of Sir Allen Stanford (as he had become) led to the US Securities and Exchange Commission (SEC) issuing charges of fraud against him totalling some US $8,000m. Companies owned by Stanford were Antigua's second largest employer after the civil service. Parliament approved the compulsory acquisition of land owned by Stanford and his extensive assets, both in Antigua and Barbuda and throughout the region, were frozen by the US authorities, pending further investigation. The revelations came only months after Antigua's Financial Services Regulatory Commission (FSRC, as the International Financial Sector Regulatory Authority had become) had declared Stanford International Bank to be operating satisfactorily. In June, following the issuing of criminal charges against Stanford, the millionaire businessman surrendered to US authorities. Stanford's trial commenced in January 2012 and in March he was convicted of 13 of the 14 charges of fraud against him. Also in June 2011, and following an extradition request from the USA, the Chairman of the FSRC, Leroy King, was dismissed from his post. King had been charged by the SEC with accepting bribes in return for ignoring alleged fraudulent practices by Stanford-owned companies. At the end of April 2010 Antigua's Chief Magistrate ruled in favour of King's extradition to the USA. In April 2012 King was still appealing against this decision.

Foreign Affairs

Regional relations

In foreign relations Antigua and Barbuda has traditionally followed a policy of non-alignment, although it has strong links with the USA. In November 2006 the Antiguan Government received US $7.5m. under the Bolivarian Alternative for the Americas (Alternativa Bolivariana para las Américas—ALBA) initiative, introduced by the Government of Venezuela to facilitate infrastructure and development programmes across the Caribbean region.

In 2003 the Government challenged US restrictions on 'offshore' internet gambling, a significant industry in Antigua and Barbuda, through the structures of the WTO, and in April 2005 received a ruling that was interpreted as partly in its favour. However, the dispute continued unabated throughout 2006, aggravated by the successful passage of an 'Unlawful Internet Gambling Enforcement Act' in the US Congress on 30 September. In March 2007 the WTO Dispute Settlement Body ruled that the US ban was illegal, and in May the USA announced that it would withdraw from any commitments relating to gambling under the General Agreement on Trade in Services (GATS). In June the Government of Antigua and Barbuda filed formal trade sanctions against the USA, demanding US $3,400m. in compensation; however, the USA contended that the terms it had originally negotiated under the Agreement did not explicitly refer to internet gambling, thus rendering it exempt from the payment of such compensation. WTO arbitrators ruled in December 2007 that Antigua be awarded the right to levy $21m. per year in sanctions from the USA, although the Government declined to exercise this option, preferring instead to continue to seek a negotiated settlement. However, with the issue still unresolved, in July 2010 Spencer, speaking at a CARICOM Heads of Government meeting in Jamaica, threatened to impose these sanctions upon the USA. CARICOM supported this position and expressed its concern that an agreement had yet to be concluded despite the efforts of the Antiguan Government. In April 2011 the Government strongly criticized US legal action against an Antiguan gambling website used by, *inter alias*, US citizens. Harold Lovell, the Minister of Finance, Economy and Public Administration declared that the prosecution of non-US internet gambling companies was 'in clear contravention of international law'. In 2011 and 2012 the Antiguan Government signed co-operation agreements with Guadeloupe and Martinique, respectively.

Other external relations

At the annual meeting of the International Whaling Commission in June 2006, Antigua and Barbuda voted, along with other members of the Organisation of Eastern Caribbean States (OECS, see p. 465), in favour of an end to a 20-year commercial whaling moratorium. The Government's apparent pro-whaling stance provoked allegations that Japanese financial assistance had amounted to bribery (Japan was in favour of ending the ban). At the May 2007 meeting of the Commission Antigua and Barbuda was among several OECS countries to confirm their concurrence with a request, issued by Saint Vincent and the Grenadines, for an increase to those islands' commercial whaling quotas. An appeal for the protection of the indigenous and coastal population's rights to preserve their traditional fishing practices—and for acknowledgement of earlier recommendations, by Saint Christopher and Nevis, that a policy of appropriate management of marine resources be adopted as opposed to a complete ban—was presented to the Commission.

In November 2003 the People's Republic of China granted Antigua a US $12m. loan, a large part of which was to fund the construction of a new sports stadium for the 2007 International Cricket Council Cricket World Cup. Spencer held discussions with a delegation of visiting Chinese officials in January 2011, and several trade and technology accords were concluded. Furthermore, an agreement was signed regarding the construction of an additional terminal at V. C. Bird International Airport, to be financed by a $45m. Chinese loan.

In September 2001 the Government established diplomatic relations with Libya, after that country announced a US $1m. aid package to Antigua. The Government of Libya announced further financial assistance for Antigua in 2007, for the development of transport infrastructure. The signing of a joint communiqué between Antigua and Barbuda and Qatar in October 2006, and subsequently with Bahrain in October, signalled the commencement of a hitherto unprecedented diplomatic foray into the Middle East by the Caribbean state; a similar agreement was signed in December with Singapore, and the Government established diplomatic relations with Egypt in July 2010.

CONSTITUTION AND GOVERNMENT

Antigua and Barbuda is a constitutional monarchy. The Consitution came into force at independence, on 1 November 1981. Executive power is vested in the British sovereign, as Head of State, and exercised by the Governor-General, who represents the sovereign locally and is appointed on the advice of the Antiguan Prime Minister. Legislative power is vested in Parliament, comprising the sovereign, a 17-member Senate and a 17-member House of Representatives. Members of the House are elected from single-member constituencies for up to five years by universal adult suffrage. The Senate is composed of 11 members (of whom one must be an inhabitant of Barbuda) appointed on the advice of the Prime Minister, four appointed on the advice of the Leader of the Opposition, one appointed at the discretion of the Governor-General and one appointed on the advice of the Barbuda Council. Government is effectively by the Cabinet. The Governor-General appoints the Prime Minister and, on the latter's recommendation, selects the other ministers. The Prime Minister must be able to command the support of a majority of the House, to which the Cabinet is responsible. The Barbuda Council has nine seats, with partial elections held every two years.

REGIONAL AND INTERNATIONAL CO-OPERATION

Antigua and Barbuda is a member of the Caribbean Community (CARICOM, see p. 227), the Association of Caribbean States (see p. 448), the Organisation of Eastern Caribbean States (OECS, see p. 465), the Organization of American States (see p. 394), and of the Community of Latin American and Caribbean States (see p. 462), which was formally inaugurated in December 2011. Antigua and Barbuda is also a member of the Eastern Caribbean Central Bank (see p. 453) and the Eastern Caribbean Securities Exchange (both based in Saint Christopher and Nevis). On 18 June 2010 Antigua and Barbuda was a signatory to the Revised Treaty of Basseterre, establishing an Economic Union among member states. The Economic Union, which involved the removal of barriers to trade and the movement of labour as a step towards a single financial and economic market, came into effect on 21 January 2011. Freedom of movement between the signatory states was granted to OECS nationals on 1 August, and a regional tourism plan was in the development stages in late 2011. In July 2007 the country joined the single market component of CARICOM's Single Market and Economy, full implementation of which was expected by 2015.

Antigua and Barbuda became a member of the UN upon independence in 1981. As a contracting party to the General Agreement on Tariffs and Trade, Antigua and Barbuda joined the World Trade Organization (see p. 433) on its establishment in 1995. The country is a member of the Commonwealth (see p. 239) and is a signatory of the Cotonou Agreement (the successor agreement to the Lomé Conventions) with the European Union (EU, see p. 276) and is a member of the Group of 77 (see p. 450) organization of developing states. In May 2006 the country was admitted to the Non-aligned Movement (see p. 464). Antigua became a member of the International Organization for Migration (see p. 347) in December 2011.

ECONOMIC AFFAIRS

In 2010, according to estimates by the World Bank, Antigua and Barbuda's gross national income (GNI), measured at average 2008–10 prices, was US $939m., equivalent to $10,590 per head (or $15,350 per head on an international purchasing-power parity basis). During 2001–10, it was estimated, the population increased at an average rate of 1.3% per year while gross domestic product (GDP) per head increased, in real terms, by an average of 0.8% per year. Overall GDP increased, in real terms, at an average annual rate of 2.1% in 2001–10; real GDP decreased by 8.9% in 2010.

Agriculture (including forestry and fishing) engaged an estimated 2.8% of the active labour force in 2008. According to Eastern Caribbean Central Bank (ECCB) estimates, the sector contributed 2.1% of GDP in 2010. Agricultural GDP increased, in real terms, at an average rate of 5.8% per year in 2001 and 2010. The sector's GDP increased by 0.5% in 2009, but decreased by 5.7% in 2010. The principal crops are cucumbers, pumpkins, sweet potatoes, mangoes, coconuts, limes, melons and the speciality 'Antigua Black' pineapple. Lobster, shrimp and crab farms are also in operation.

Industry (comprising mining, manufacturing, construction and utilities) employed an estimated 15.6% of the active labour force in 2008. According to ECCB estimates, the sector provided 21.9% of GDP in 2010. Industrial GDP increased, in real terms, at an average rate of 6.3% per year during 2001–10; the sector contracted by 12.8% in 2010.

Mining and quarrying employed only some 0.3% of the active labour force in 2008. According to ECCB estimates, the sector contributed 0.8% of GDP in 2010. The real GDP of the mining sector increased at an average rate of 1.4% per year during 2001–10. The sector decreased by 25.3% in 2010.

The manufacturing sector consists of some light industries producing garments, paper, paint, furniture and food and beverage products, and the assembly of household appliances and electrical components for export. Manufacturing contributed 2.2% of GDP in 2010, and employed an estimated 4.6% of the active labour force in 2008. In real terms, the GDP of the manufacturing sector increased at an average rate of 2.7% per year during 2001–10. Manufacturing GDP increased by 10.6% in 2009, but decreased by 12.4% in 2010.

The construction sector contributed 14.7% to GDP in 2010, and employed an estimated 9.2% of the employed labour force in 2008. In real terms, the GDP of the construction sector increased at an average rate of 8.1% per year in 2001–10. Construction GDP decreased by 15.3% in 2010.

Most of the country's energy production is derived from imported fuel. Imports of mineral fuels, lubricants and related materials accounted for 6.3% of total imports in 2008. In 2005 the Government became one of 13 Caribbean administrations to sign the PetroCaribe accord, under which Antigua and Barbuda would be allowed to purchase petroleum from Venezuela at reduced prices. In September 2011 a new 30-MW power plant on Antigua came into operation. The plant, commissioned to combat the worsening power shortages on the islands, was financed by a US $47m. loan from the Export and Import Bank of China (China Exim Bank).

Services provided 81.6% of employment in 2008 and 76.0% of GDP in 2010. The combined GDP of the service sectors increased, in real terms, at an average rate of 1.2% per year during 2001–10. The sector contracted by 8.2% in 2010. The islands' economy is heavily dependent on the tourism industry, which is particularly vulnerable to external factors, such as the behaviour of the world economy and the movement of tropical storms. Visitor arrivals fluctuated throughout the 2000s. Numbers fell to 888,801 in 2008, increasing to 965,431 in 2009, before falling again to 812,859 in 2010. Receipts from the sector also oscillated in the same period, reaching EC $912.2m. in 2007, but fell thereafter, to EC $803.9m. in 2010. Construction of a new terminal at V. C. Bird International Airport, also financed by a China Exim Bank loan, commenced in late 2011. A significant number (35.5% in 2010) of stop-over tourists are from the USA, followed by the United Kingdom (29.0% in 2010). The real GDP of the hotels and restaurants sector increased in 2010, by 1.0%, when its contribution to GDP stood at 12.6%.

Antigua and Barbuda recorded a visible trade deficit in 2010 of EC $1,097.8m. and a deficit of $512.8m. on the current account of the balance of payments. The country's principal trading partners are the other members of the Caribbean Community and Common Market (CARICOM, see p. 227), the USA, the United Kingdom and Canada. In 2007 the USA provided 58.1% of total imports and was also an important market for exports (mainly re-exports).

In 2010, according to provisional estimates, there was a budgetary deficit of EC $81.7m., equivalent to 2.6% of GDP. Antigua and Barbuda's general government gross debt was EC $2,339m. in 2010, equivalent to 69.6% of GDP. By the end of 2009, according to IMF estimates, total public external debt amounted to EC $1,352m., and the cost of servicing long-term public and publicly guaranteed debt and repayments to the IMF was equivalent to 3.9% of the value of exports of goods, services and income (excluding workers' remittances). According to ECCB estimates, the annual average rate of inflation was 2.3% in 2001–10. Consumer prices rose by 2.9% in 2010. The rate of unemployment in 2001 was reported to be 8.1% of the labour force.

Despite some efforts at diversification, for example, the development of 'offshore' financial services, the economy of Antigua and Barbuda is dominated by tourism. The World Travel and Tourism Council (WTTC) estimated that in 2011 the tourism industry directly provided 18.0% of total employment and 17.8% of GDP. The number of tourist arrivals was forecast to rise by 8.8% in 2011, according to the WTTC, following a decrease of 15.8% in 2010. The economy contracted by 8.9% in 2010, largely owing to the impact of the global economic and financial crisis on the tourism and construction sectors. In June 2010 the IMF concluded a stand-by arrangement for Antigua and Barbuda, worth SDR 81m. over three years, the first tranche of which was disbursed in October. Under the terms of the arrangement, the Government would reduce public spending, implement measures to increase tax revenues and discuss debt-restructuring with its creditors. The IMF reported 'notable success' in the Government's efforts, with the 'Paris Club' of creditors agreeing to reschedule US $117m. of Antiguan debt in September and a further restructuring plan finalized with the OPEC Fund for International Development in the following month. In mid-2011 the Government concluded debt-rescheduling arrangements with France and Japan, restructuring arrears totalling some $34m. and $33m., respectively. Meanwhile, in November 2010 the Government was allocated a €9m. vulnerability assistance scheme grant from the European Union, while in August the Caribbean Development Bank released the first disbursement of a $30m. policy-based loan. The IMF forecast modest growth of 2.0% in 2011 and 2.5% in 2012, driven by a nascent recovery in tourist arrivals. The construction industry remained depressed in 2011, although the Government anticipated that the building, with Chinese funding, of a new airport terminal (expected to be completed by 2013) would revive the sector and, in turn, the broader economy.

PUBLIC HOLIDAYS

2013: 1 January (New Year's Day), 29 March (Good Friday), 1 April (Easter Monday), 6 May (Labour Day), 20 May (Whit Monday), 5 August (Carnival Monday—J'Ouvert), 6 August (Carnival Tuesday—Last Lap), 1 November (Independence Day), 9 December (National Heroes' Day), 25–26 December (Christmas).

Statistical Survey

Source (unless otherwise stated): Ministry of Information, Broadcasting, Telecommunications, Science & Technology, Coolidge Business Complex, Sir George Walter Highway, St John's; tel. 468-4600; e-mail minfinance@antigua.gov.ag; internet www.ab.gov.ag.

AREA AND POPULATION

Area: 441.6 sq km (170.5 sq miles).

Population: 62,922 at census of 28 May 1991; 76,886 (males 36,107, females 40,779) at census of 28 May 2001. *Mid-2011* (projected estimate): 92,495 (Source: Eastern Caribbean Central Bank).

Density (mid-2011): 209.5 per sq km.

Population by Age and Sex (2007): *0–14:* 24,276 (males 12,098, females 12,178); *15–64:* 55,721 (males 25,668, females 30,053); *65 and over:* 5,906 (males 2,576, females 3,330); *Total* 85,903 (males 40,342, females 45,561).

Principal Town: St John's (capital), population 24,451 at 2001 census. *Mid-2009* (UN estimate, incl. suburbs): St John's 26,580 (Source: UN, *World Urbanization Prospects: The 2009 Revision*).

Births, Marriages and Deaths (2007 unless otherwise indicated): Live births 1,240 (birth rate 14.44 per 1,000); Marriages 1,863; Deaths 504 (death rate 5.87 per 1,000). *2008:* Birth rate 16.8 per 1,000; Death rate 6.1 per 1,000. *2010:* Birth rate 16.4 per 1,000; Death rate 5.8 per 1,000 (Source: Pan American Health Organization).

Life Expectancy (years at birth, WHO estimates): 74 (males 73; females 76) in 2009. Source: WHO, *World Health Statistics*.

Employment (persons aged 15 years and over, official estimates, 2008): Agriculture, hunting and forestry 789; Fishing 290; Mining and quarrying 121; Manufacturing 1,754; Electricity, gas and water supply 585; Construction 3,557; Wholesale and retail trade 5,516; Hotels and restaurants 5,783; Transport, storage and communications 3,203; Financial intermediation 1,195; Real estate, renting and business activities 1,665; Public administration and defence 4,986; Education 1,956; Health and social work 1,955; Other community, social and personal service activities 3,057; Households with employed persons 1,485; Extra-territorial organizations and bodies 572; Total employed 38,470 (males 19,321, females 19,149). Source: ILO.

HEALTH AND WELFARE

Key Indicators

Total Fertility Rate (children per woman, 2009): 2.1.

Under-5 Mortality Rate (per 1,000 live births, 2009): 12.

Physicians (per 1,000 head, 1999): 0.2.

Hospital Beds (per 1,000 head, 2009): 2.2.

Health Expenditure (2008): US $ per head (PPP): 958.

Health Expenditure (2008): % of GDP: 4.7.

Health Expenditure (2008): public (% of total): 68.6.

Access to Water (% of persons, 2004): 96.

Access to Sanitation (% of persons, 2004): 91.

Total Carbon Dioxide Emissions ('000 metric tons, 2006): 425.0.

Total Carbon Dioxide Emissions Per Head (metric tons, 2006): 5.0.

Human Development Index (2011): ranking: 60.

Human Development Index (2011): value: 0.764.

For sources and definitions, see explanatory note on p. vi.

AGRICULTURE, ETC.

Principal Crops ('000 metric tons, 2010, FAO estimates): Cantaloupes and other melons 0.8; Vegetables (incl. melons) 2.8; Guavas, mangoes and mangosteens 1.3; Fruits (excl. melons) 8.6.

Livestock ('000 head, 2010, FAO estimates): Asses 1.7; Cattle 14.6; Pigs 3.0; Sheep 20.0; Goats 37.0; Poultry 110.0.

Livestock Products ('000 metric tons, 2010, FAO estimates): Cattle meat 0.6; Cows' milk 5.7; Hen eggs 0.4.

Fishing (metric tons, live weight, 2009): Groupers and seabasses 301; Snappers and jobfishes 291; Grunts and sweetlips 177; Parrotfishes 271; Surgeonfishes 189; Triggerfishes and durgons 82; Caribbean spiny lobster 103; Stromboid conchs 758; Total catch (incl. others) 2,490.

Source: FAO.

INDUSTRY

Production (1988 estimates unless otherwise indicated): Rum 4,000 hectolitres; Wines and vodka 2,000 hectolitres; Electric energy (2008) 118m. kWh. Source: partly UN Industrial Commodity Statistics Database and Yearbook.

FINANCE

Currency and Exchange Rates: 100 cents = 1 Eastern Caribbean dollar (EC $). *Sterling, US Dollar and Euro Equivalents* (30 December 2011): £1 sterling = EC $4.174; US $1 = EC $2.700; €1 = EC $3.494; EC $100 = £24.00 = US $37.04 = €28.62. *Exchange rate:* Fixed at US $1 = EC $2.700 since July 1976.

Budget (EC $ million, 2010, provisional): *Revenue:* Tax revenue 576.5; Other current revenue 63.1; Capital revenue 14.8; Total 654.4. *Expenditure:* Current expenditure 682.5 (Wages and salaries 272.6, Goods and services 125.5, Interest payments 78.9, Pensions 70.0, Transfers and subsidies 135.5); Capital expenditure 53.6; Total 736.1. Source: Eastern Caribbean Central Bank.

International Reserves (US $ million at 31 December 2010): IMF special drawing rights 0.47; Foreign exchange 136.08; Total 136.55. Source: IMF, *International Financial Statistics*.

Money Supply (EC $ million at 31 December 2010): Currency outside depository corporations 137.74; Transferable deposits 1,021.87; Other deposits 2,040.57; *Broad money* 3,200.18. Source: IMF, *International Financial Statistics*.

Cost of Living (Consumer Price Index; base: January 2001 = 100): 117.5 in 2008; 120.4 in 2009; 123.9 in 2010. Source: Eastern Caribbean Central Bank.

Expenditure on the Gross Domestic Product (EC $ million at current prices, 2010, preliminary): Government final consumption expenditure 532.10; Private final consumption expenditure 1,874.55; Gross capital formation 1,130.49; *Total domestic expenditure* 3,537.14; Exports of goods and services 1,414.39; *Less* Imports of goods and services 1,836.30; *GDP at market prices* 3,115.23. Source: Eastern Caribbean Central Bank.

Gross Domestic Product by Economic Activity (EC $ million at current prices, 2010, preliminary): Agriculture, hunting, forestry and fishing 57.76; Mining and quarrying 23.24; Manufacturing 61.06; Electricity and water 115.98; Construction 403.60; Trade 338.09; Restaurants and hotels 336.08; Transport and communications 350.82; Finance, insurance, real estate and business services 577.37; Government services 227.38; Education 133.20; Other community, social and personal service activities 127.68; *Sub-total*

2,752.26; *Less* Financial intermediation services indirectly measured 80.32; *Gross value added in basic prices* 2,671.93; Taxes, less subsidies, on products 443.30; *GDP in market prices* 3,115.23. Source: Eastern Caribbean Central Bank.

Balance of Payments (EC $ million, 2010): Goods (net) –1,265.65; Services (net) 760.30; *Balance on goods and services* –505.35; Income (net) –84.69; *Balance on goods, services and income* –590.04; Current transfers (net) 77.27; *Current balance* –512.77; Capital account (net) 10.02; Direct investment (net) 283.61; Portfolio investment (net) 3.51; Other investments (net) 167.30; Net errors and omissions 5.87; *Overall balance* –42.47. Source: Eastern Caribbean Central Bank.

EXTERNAL TRADE

Total Trade (EC $ million): *Imports f.o.b.:* 1,758.8 in 2008; 1,397.3 in 2009; 1,159.8 in 2010. *Exports f.o.b.:* 72.9 in 2008; 63.6 in 2009; 62.0 in 2010. Source: Eastern Caribbean Central Bank.

Principal Commodities (US $ million, 2007): *Imports:* Food and live animals 85.7 (Meat and meat preparations 18.7; Vegetables and fruit 18.4); Beverages and tobacco 27.7 (Beverages 25.6); Crude materials (inedible) except fuels 15.3; Mineral fuels, lubricants, etc. 36.3 (Refined petroleum products 35.5); Chemicals and related products 43.3; Basic manufactures 93.5; Machinery and transport equipment 163.5 (Telecommunications and sound equipment 29.6; Road vehicles 46.7); Miscellaneous manufactured articles 106.4; Total (incl. others) 573.1. *Exports:* Beverages and tobacco 2.1 (Beverages 2.0); Crude materials (inedible) except fuels 0.6; Chemicals and related products 1.2 (Pigments, paints, varnishes, etc. 0.8); Basic manufactures 9.4 (Textiles, yarn, fabrics, made-up articles, etc. 3.2; Iron and steel 1.3); Machinery and transport equipment 19.7 (General industrial machinery and equipment 1.0; Telecommunications and sound equipment 8.1; Road vehicles 1.7); Miscellaneous manufactured articles 8.5; Total (incl. others) 98.6. Source: UN, *International Trade Statistics Yearbook*.

Principal Trading Partners (US $ million, 2007): *Imports:* Barbados 7.5; Brazil 5.2; Canada 13.4; China, People's Republic 7.6; Dominica 5.1; Dominican Republic 7.0; France (incl. Monaco) 5.3; Italy 15.9; Jamaica 5.0; Japan 24.6; Netherlands Antilles 23.8; Switzerland (incl. Liechtenstein) 7.9; Trinidad and Tobago 22.3; United Kingdom 36.8; USA 333.3; Total (incl. others) 573.1. *Exports:* Anguilla 2.8; Barbados 8.1; Dominica 6.0; France (incl. Monaco) 3.1; Germany 1.2; Jamaica 1.4; Netherlands Antilles 30.5; Nicaragua 3.9; Saint Christopher and Nevis 3.9; Saint Lucia 1.6; Saudi Arabia 1.6; United Kingdom 4.1; USA 23.2; Total (incl. others) 98.6. Source: UN, *International Trade Statistics Yearbook*.

TRANSPORT

Road Traffic (registered vehicles, 1998): Passenger motor cars and commercial vehicles 24,000. Source: UN, *Statistical Yearbook*.

Shipping (international freight traffic, '000 metric tons, 1990): Goods loaded 28; Goods unloaded 113 (Source: UN, *Monthly Bulletin of Statistics*). *Merchant Fleet* (registered at 31 December): 1,237 vessels (total displacement 9,992,950 grt) in 2009 (Source: IHS Fairplay, *World Fleet Statistics*).

Civil Aviation (traffic on scheduled services, 2009): Kilometres flown (million) 6; Passengers carried ('000) 748; Passenger-km (million) 123; Total ton-km (million) 11. Source: UN, *Statistical Yearbook*.

TOURISM

Visitor Arrivals: 888,992 (265,955 stop-over visitors, 25,913 yacht passengers, 597,124 cruise ship passengers) in 2008; 965,431 (234,410 stop-over visitors, 21,226 yacht passengers, 709,795 cruise ship passengers) in 2009; 812,859 (229,943 stop-over visitors, 25,886 yacht passengers, 557,030 cruise ship passengers) in 2010.

Tourism Receipts (EC $ million): 901.7 in 2008; 823.8 in 2009; 803.9 in 2010.

Source: Eastern Caribbean Central Bank.

COMMUNICATIONS MEDIA

Radio Receivers (1997): 36,000 in use*.

Television Receivers (1999): 33,000 in use*.

Telephones (2010): 36,300 main lines in use†.

Mobile Cellular Telephones (2010): 168,000 subscribers†.

Internet Subscribers (2010): 14,600†.

Broadband Subscribers (2010): 7,100†.

Personal Computers: 17,500 (206.9 per 1,000 persons) in 2006†.

Daily Newspapers (2004): 2.

Non-daily Newspapers (1996): 4*.

* Source: UNESCO, *Statistical Yearbook*.

† Source: International Telecommunication Union.

EDUCATION

Pre-primary (2009/10 unless otherwise indicated): 21 schools (1983); 267 teachers (all females); 2,512 pupils (males 1,287, females 1,225). Source: UNESCO Institute for Statistics.

Primary (2009/10 unless otherwise indicated): 55 schools (2000/01); 747 teachers (males 42, females 705); 11,254 students (males 5,927, females 5,327). Source: UNESCO Institute for Statistics.

Secondary (2009/10 unless otherwise indicated): 14 schools (2000/01); 694 teachers (males 196, females 498); 8,436 students (males 4,118, females 4,318). Source: UNESCO Institute for Statistics.

Special (2000/01): 2 schools; 15 teachers; 61 students.

Tertiary (2009/10 unless otherwise indicated): 2 colleges (1986); 173 teachers (males 66, females 107); 1,170 students (males 309, females 861). Source: UNESCO Institute for Statistics.

Pupil-teacher ratio (primary education, UNESCO estimate): 15.1 in 2009/10. Source: UNESCO Institute for Statistics.

Adult Literacy Rate: 99.0% in 2009 (males 98.4, females 99.4). Source: UNESCO Institute for Statistics.

Directory

The Government

HEAD OF STATE

Queen: HM Queen ELIZABETH II.

Governor-General: LOUISE LAKE-TACK (took office on 17 July 2007).

CABINET
(May 2012)

The Cabinet comprised members of the United Progressive Party.

Prime Minister and Minister of Foreign Affairs: WINSTON BALDWIN SPENCER.

Minister of Health, Social Transformation and Consumer Affairs: WILMOTH STAFFORD DANIEL.

Minister of National Security: Sen. Dr ERROL CORT.

Minister of Agriculture, Lands, Housing and the Environment: HILSON BAPTISTE.

Minister of Tourism, Civil Aviation and Culture: JOHN HERBERT MAGINLEY.

Minister of Finance, Economy and Public Administration: HAROLD E. E. LOVELL.

Minister of Works and Transport: TREVOR MYKE WALKER.

Minister of Education, Sports, Youth and Gender Affairs: Dr JACQUI QUINN-LEANDRO.

Attorney-General and Minister of Legal Affairs: JUSTIN L. SIMON.

Minister of State in the Ministry of Legal Affairs: Sen. JOANNE MAUREEN MASSIAH.

Minister of State in the Ministry of Education, Sports, Youth and Gender Affairs: WINSTON VINCENT WILLIAMS.

Minister of State in the Ministry of Tourism, Civil Aviation and Culture: ELESTON MONTGOMERY ADAMS.

Minister of State in the Office of the Prime Minister: Sen. Dr EDMOND MANSOOR.

Minister of State in the Ministry of Agriculture, Lands, Housing and the Environment: CHANLAH CODRINGTON.

Minister of State in the Ministry of Works and Transport: ELMORE CHARLES.

Minister of State in the Ministry of National Security: COLIN V. A. DERRICK.

MINISTRIES

Office of the Prime Minister: Queen Elizabeth Hwy, St John's; tel. 462-4956; fax 462-3225; internet www.antigua.gov.ag.

Ministry of Agriculture, Lands, Housing and the Environment: Queen Elizabeth Hwy, St John's; tel. 462-1543; fax 462-6104.

Ministry of Education, Sports, Youth and Gender Affairs: Govt Office Complex, Queen Elizabeth Hwy, St John's; tel. 462-4959; fax 462-4970; e-mail doristeen.etinoff@ab.gov.ag.

Ministry of Finance, Economy and Public Administration: Govt Office Complex, Parliament Dr., St John's; tel. 462-5015; fax 462-4860; e-mail minfinance@antigua.gov.ag.

Ministry of Foreign Affairs: Queen Elizabeth Hwy, St John's; tel. 462-1052; fax 462-2482; e-mail foreignaffairs@ab.gov.ag; internet www.foreignaffairs.gov.ag.

Ministry of Health, Social Transformation and Consumer Affairs: St John's.

Ministry of Legal Affairs: Government Complex, Queen Elizabeth Hwy, St John's; tel. 462-0017; fax 462-2465; e-mail legalaffairs@ab.gov.ag.

Ministry of National Security: Govt Office Complex, Parliament Dr., St John's.

Ministry of Tourism, Civil Aviation and Culture: Government Office Complex, Bldg 1, Queen Elizabeth Hwy, St John's; tel. 462-0480; fax 462-2483; e-mail mblackman@tourism.gov.ag.

Ministry of Works and Transport: St John's.

Legislature

PARLIAMENT

Senate

President: HAZELYN FRANCIS.

There are 17 nominated members.

House of Representatives

Speaker: D. GISELLE ISAAC-ARRINDELL.

Ex Officio Member: The Attorney-General.

Clerk: SYLVIA WALKER.

General Election, 12 March 2009

Party	Votes cast	%	Seats
United Progressive Party	21,205	51.1	9
Antigua Labour Party	19,460	47.0	7
Barbuda People's Movement	474	1.1	1
Independents	194	0.5	—
Organisation for National Development	119	0.3	—
Total	41,452	100.0	17

Election Commission

Antigua and Barbuda Electoral Commission (ABEC): Queen Elizabeth Hwy, POB 664, St John's; tel. 562-4196; fax 562-4331; e-mail eleccom@candw.ag; internet www.abec.gov.ag; f. 2001; Chair. Sir GERALD WATT (removed in Jan. 2010, reinstated in Jan. 2012 following high court ruling); Chief Elections Officer LORNA SIMON.

Political Organizations

Antigua Labour Party (ALP): Upper Nevis St, St John's; tel. 562-7405; e-mail alpelection@hotmail.com; f. 1946; Leader LESTER BRYANT BIRD; Chair. and Dep. Leader GASTON BROWNE.

Barbuda People's Movement (BPM): Codrington; campaigns for separate status for Barbuda; allied to United Progressive Party; Parliamentary Leader THOMAS HILBOURNE FRANK; Chair. FABIAN JONES.

Barbuda People's Movement for Change (BPMC): Codrington; f. 2004; effectively replaced Organisation for National Reconstruction, which was f. 1983 and re-f. 1988 as Barbuda Independence Movt; advocates self-govt for Barbuda; supports the Antigua Labour Party; Pres. ARTHUR SHABAZZ-NIBBS.

Barbudans for a Better Barbuda: Codrington; f. 2004 by fmr Gen. Sec. of Barbuda People's Movement for Change; Leader ORDRICK SAMUEL.

National Movement for Change (NMC): St John's; f. 2003; Leader ALISTAIR THOMAS.

Organisation for National Development: Upper St Mary's St, St John's; f. 2003 by breakaway faction of the United Progressive Party; Leader MELFORD NICHOLAS.

United Progressive Party (UPP): UPP Headquarters Bldg, Upper Nevis St, POB 2379, St John's; tel. 481-3888; fax 481-3877; e-mail info@uppantigua.com; internet www.uppantigua.com; f. 1992 by merger of the Antigua Caribbean Liberation Movt (f. 1979), the Progressive Labour Movt (f. 1970) and the United National Democratic Party (f. 1986); Leader BALDWIN SPENCER; Deputy Leader HAROLD E. E. LOVELL; Chair. LEON (CHAKU) SYMISTER.

Diplomatic Representation

EMBASSIES IN ANTIGUA AND BARBUDA

Brazil: Price Water House Bldg, Old Parham Rd, St. John's; tel. 562-7532; fax 562-7537; e-mail michael.neele@itamaraty.gov.br; Ambassador RAUL CAMPOS E CASTRO.

China, People's Republic: Cedar Valley, POB 1446, St John's; tel. 462-1125; fax 462-6425; e-mail chinaemb_ag@mfa.gov.cn; internet ag.chineseembassy.org/eng; Ambassador LIU HANMING.

Cuba: Friar's Hill, St John's; tel. 562-5864; fax 562-5867; e-mail cubanembassy@candw.ag; Ambassador JOSÉ MANUEL INCLÁN EMBADE.

Venezuela: Jasmine Court, Friar's Hill Rd, POB 1201, St John's; tel. 462-1574; fax 462-1570; e-mail embaveneantigua@yahoo.es; Ambassador JAVIER FLORENCIO LÓPEZ MORILLO.

Judicial System

Justice is administered by the Eastern Caribbean Supreme Court (ECSC), based in Saint Lucia, which consists of a High Court of Justice and a Court of Appeal. Three of the Court's High Court Judges are resident in and responsible for Antigua and Barbuda, and preside over the Court of Summary Jurisdiction on the islands. One of two ECSC Masters, chiefly responsible for procedural and interlocutory matters, is also resident in Antigua. Magistrates' Courts in the territory administer lesser cases.

High Court Judges: MARIO MICHEL, JENNIFER REMY, RICHARD G. FLOYD.

Master: CHERYL MATHURIN.

Registrar: CHARLESWORTH TABOR.

Religion

The majority of the inhabitants profess Christianity, and the largest denomination is the Church in the Province of the West Indies (Anglican Communion).

CHRISTIANITY

Antigua Christian Council: POB 863, St Mary's St, St John's; tel. 461-1135; fax 462-2383; f. 1964; five mem. churches; Pres. Archdeacon PETER DALEY; Treas. MARY-ROSE KNIGHT.

The Anglican Communion

Anglicans in Antigua and Barbuda are adherents of the Church in the Province of the West Indies. The diocese of the North Eastern Caribbean and Aruba comprises 12 islands: Antigua, St Kitts, Nevis, Anguilla, Barbuda, Montserrat, Dominica, Saba, St Martin/St Maarten, Aruba, St Bartholomew and St Eustatius. The See City is St John's, Antigua. According to the latest census (2001), some 26% of the population are Anglicans.

Bishop of the North Eastern Caribbean and Aruba: Rt Rev. LEROY ERROL BROOKS, Bishop's Lodge, POB 23, St John's; tel. 462-0151; fax 462-2090; e-mail dioceseneca@candw.ag.

The Roman Catholic Church

The diocese of St John's-Basseterre, suffragan to the archdiocese of Castries (Saint Lucia), includes Anguilla, Antigua and Barbuda, the British Virgin Islands, Montserrat and Saint Christopher and Nevis. The Bishop participates in the Antilles Episcopal Conference (whose Secretariat is based in Trinidad and Tobago). Some 10% of the population are Roman Catholics, according to the 2001 census.

Bishop of St John's-Basseterre: Mgr KENNETH DAVID OSWIN RICHARDS, Chancery Offices, POB 863, St John's; tel. 461-1135; fax 462-2383; e-mail djr@candw.ag.

Other Christian Churches

According to the 2001 census, some 12% of the population are Seventh-day Adventists, 11% are Pentecostalists, 10% are Moravians, 8% are Methodists and 5% are Baptists.

East Caribbean Baptist Mission: POB 2678, St John's; tel. 462-2894; fax 462-6029; e-mail admin@baptistantigua.org; internet www.baptistantigua.org; f. 1991; mem. congregation of the Baptist Circuit of Churches in the East Caribbean Baptist Mission; Presiding Elder Dr HENSWORTH W. C. JONAS.

Methodist Church: Methodist Manse, Hodges Bay, POB 69, St John's; tel. 764-5998; fax 560-5922; e-mail methodis@candw.ag; internet www.lidmethodist.org; Supt Rev. NOVELLE C. JOSIAH.

St John's Church of Christ: Golden Grove, Main Rd, St John's; tel. and fax 461-6732; e-mail stjcoc@candw.ag; Contact Evangelist CORNELIUS GEORGE.

St John's Evangelical Lutheran Church: Woods Centre, POB W77, St John's; tel. and fax 462-2896; e-mail sjluther@candw.ag; Principal ANDREW JOHNSTON; Pastors Rev. ANDREW JOHNSTON, Rev. JOSHUA STERNHAGEN, Rev. JASON RICHARDS, Rev. PAUL WORKENTINE.

The Press

Daily Observer: LIAT Rd, Coolidge, POB 1318, St John's; tel. 480-1750; fax 480-1757; e-mail dailyobserver@candw.ag; internet www.antiguaobserver.com; ind.; Publr WINSTON A. DERRICK; Editor MICKEL BRANN; circ. 5,000.

The Worker's Voice: Emancipation Hall, 46 North St, POB 3, St John's; tel. 462-0090; f. 1943; 2 a week; official organ of the Antigua Labour Party and the Antigua Trades and Labour Union; Editor NOEL THOMAS; circ. 6,000.

Publishers

Antigua Printing and Publishing Ltd: Factory Rd, POB 670, St John's; tel. 462-1265; fax 462-6200.

Caribbean Publishing Co Ltd: Ryan's Pl., Suite 1B, High St, POB 1451, St John's; tel. 462-2215; fax 462-0962.

Treasure Island Publishing Ltd: Anchorage Dockyard Dr., POB W283, Wood Centre, St John's; tel. and fax 463-7414; e-mail colettif@candw.ag; internet www.thetreasureislands.com; Publr and Editor FRANCESCA COLETTI.

West Indies Publishing Ltd: 3 Jasmine Court, Friar's Hill Rd, POB W883, St John's; tel. 461-0565; fax 461-9750; e-mail wip@candw.ag; internet www.westindiespublishing.com; f. 1992.

Broadcasting and Communications

TELECOMMUNICATIONS

Regulatory Body

Antigua Public Utilities Authority (APUA): see Trade and Industry—Utilities; a new regulatory authority was scheduled to be established in 2012.

Major Operators

Digicel Antigua and Barbuda: Antigua Wireless Ventures Ltd, POB W32, St John's; tel. 480-2050; fax 480-2060; e-mail customercareantiguaandbarbuda@digicelgroup.com; internet www.digicelantiguaandbarbuda.com; acquired Cingular Wireless' Caribbean operations and licences in 2005; owned by an Irish consortium; Chair. DENIS O'BRIEN; Eastern Caribbean CEO JOHN DELVES.

I-Mobile: Cassada Gardens, POB 416, St John's; tel. 480-7000; fax 480-7476; internet www.apua.ag; f. 2000 as PCS, relaunched in July 2011 under present name; owned by Antigua Public Utilities Authority (see Trade and Industry—Utilities); digital mobile cellular telephone network; controls less than 20% of market; Gen. Man. ALLAN WILLIAMS.

LIME: Cable & Wireless, Wireless Rd, Clare Hall, St John's; tel. 480-4000; e-mail talk2us@candw.ag; internet www.time4lime.com/ag; fmrly Cable & Wireless (Antigua and Barbuda) Ltd; name changed as above in 2008; contact centres in Jamaica and Saint Lucia; CEO DAVID SHAW.

BROADCASTING

Radio

ABS Radio: POB 590, St John's; tel. 462-3602; e-mail alex@hotmail.com; internet www.cmatt.com/abs.htm; f. 1956; subsidiary of Antigua and Barbuda Broadcasting Service (see Television); Programme Man. KENNY NIBBS.

Abundant Life Radio: Codrington Village, Barbuda; tel. 562-4821; e-mail afternoonpraise@gmail.com; internet www.abundantliferadio.com; f. 2001; began broadcasting in Antigua in 2003; Christian station; daily, 24-hour broadcasts; Man. Dir Rt Rev. CLIFTON FRANCOIS.

Caribbean Radio Lighthouse: POB 1057, St John's; tel. 462-1454; fax 462-7420; e-mail info@radiolighthouse.org; internet www.radiolighthouse.org; f. 1975; religious broadcasts in Spanish and English; operated by Baptist Int. Mission Inc (USA); Gen. Man. CURT WAITE.

Crusader Radio: Redcliffe St, POB 2379, St John's; tel. 562-4610; fax 481-3892; e-mail crusaderradio@candw.ag; internet www.crusaderradio.com; f. 2003; Crusader Publishing & Broadcasting Ltd; official station of the UPP; Station Man. CONRAD POLE.

Gem Radio Network: Tristan's Crescent Cedar Valley, POB W939, St John's; tel. 744-7768; fax 720-7017; e-mail gemfmstereo@gmail.com.

Observer Radio: tel. 460-0911; e-mail voice@antiguaobserver.com; internet www.antiguaobserver.com; f. 2001; independently owned station; Gen. Man. WINSTON A. DERRICK.

ZDK Liberty Radio International (Radio ZDK): Grenville Radio Ltd, Bryant Pasture, Bird Rd, Ottos, POB 1100, St John's; tel. 462-1100; fax 462-1116; e-mail mail@radiozdk.com; internet www.radiozdk.com; f. 1970; commercial; also operates SUN Radio; Man. Dir IVOR GRENVILLE BIRD; CEO E. PHILIP.

Television

Antigua and Barbuda Broadcasting Service (ABS): Directorate of Broadcasting and Public Information, POB 590, St John's; tel. 462-0010; fax 462-4442; scheduled for privatization; Dir-Gen. HOLLIS HENRY; CEO DENIS LEANDRO.

ABS Television: POB 1280, St John's; tel. 462-0010; fax 462-1622; f. 1964; Programme Man. JAMES TANNY ROSE.

CTV Entertainment Systems: 25 Long St, St John's; tel. 462-0346; fax 462-4211; cable television co; transmits 33 channels of US television 24 hours per day to subscribers; Programme Dir K. BIRD.

Finance

(cap. = capital; res = reserves; dep. = deposits; m. = millions; brs = branches)

BANKING

The Eastern Caribbean Central Bank, based in Saint Christopher, is the central issuing and monetary authority for Antigua and Barbuda.

ABI Bank Ltd (ABIB): ABI Financial Center, 156 Redcliffe St, POB 1679, St John's; tel. 480-2700; fax 480-2750; e-mail abib@abifinancial.com; internet www.abifinancial.com/ABIB; f. 1990 as Antigua Barbuda Investment Bank Ltd; part of the ABI Financial Group; Govt intervened in operations in 2012; cap. EC $21.2m., res EC $38.0m., dep. EC $997.7m. (Sept. 2008); Chair. SYLVIA O'MARD; Country Man. EVERETT CHRISTIAN; 3 brs.

Antigua and Barbuda Development Bank: 27 St Mary's St, POB 1279, St John's; tel. 462-0838; fax 462-0839; f. 1974; Gen. Man. DON CHARLES.

Antigua Commercial Bank: St Mary's and Thames Sts, POB 95, Loans, St John's; tel. 481-4200; fax 481-4229; e-mail acb@acbonline.com; internet www.acbonline.com; f. 1955; auth. cap. EC $5m.; Chair. DAVIDSON CHARLES; Man. GLADSTON S. JOSEPH; 2 brs.

Bank of Nova Scotia: High and Market Sts, POB 342, St John's; tel. 480-1500; fax 480-1554; e-mail bns.antigua@soctiabank.com; internet www.antigua.scotiabank.com; f. 1961; subsidiary of Bank of Nova Scotia, Canada; Country Man. MARLON RAWLINS; 2 brs.

Caribbean Union Bank Ltd: Friar's Hill Rd, POB W2010, St John's; tel. 481-8278; fax 481-8290; e-mail customerservice@caribbeanunionbank.com; internet www.caribbeanunionbank.com; f. 2005; total assets US $42.4m. (Sept. 2007); Chair. LUDOLPH BROWN; Man. Dir VERE I. HILL; 2 brs.

Eastern Caribbean Amalgamated Bank (ECAB): 1000 Airport Blvd, Pavilion Dr., POB 315, Coolidge; tel. 480-5300; fax 480-5433; e-mail info@ecab.com; internet www.ecab.com; f. 1981 as Bank of Antigua; name changed in 2010 following purchase by Eastern Caribbean Amalgamated Financial Co Ltd in 2009; total assets EC $560m. (Dec. 2007); Chair. Sir EDMUND W. LAWRENCE; Gen. Man. HENRY HAZEL; 3 brs.

FirstCaribbean International Bank (Barbados) Ltd: High and Market Sts, POB 225, St John's; tel. 480-5000; fax 462-4910; internet www.firstcaribbeanbank.com; adopted present name in 2002 following merger of Caribbean operations of CIBC and Barclays Bank PLC; Barclays relinquished its stake in 2006; Exec. Chair. MICHAEL MANSOOR; CEO JOHN D. ORR; 2 brs.

Global Bank of Commerce Ltd (GBC): Global Commerce Centre, Old Parham Rd, POB W1803, St John's; tel. 480-2240; fax 462-1831; e-mail customer.service@gbc.ag; internet www.globalbank.ag; f. 1983; int. financial services operator; total assets US $74.4m.; shareholder equity US $8.1m.; Chair. and CEO BRIAN STUART-YOUNG; Gen. Man. WINSTON ST AGATHE; 1 br.

RBTT Bank Caribbean Ltd: 45 High St, POB 1324, St John's; tel. 462-4217; fax 462-5040; e-mail info@ag.rbtt.com; internet www.rbtt.com; total assets TTD $53.5m.; shareholder equity TTD $5m. (March 2008); Chair. JIM WESTLAKE; Br. Man. BERNARD LEONCE.

In 2010 there were 15 registered 'offshore' banks in Antigua and Barbuda.

Regulatory Body

Financial Services Regulatory Commission (FSRC): Royal Palm Pl., Friar's Hill Rd, POB 2674, St John's; tel. 481-3300; fax 463-0422; e-mail anuifsa@candw.ag; internet www.fsrc.gov.ag; fmrly known as International Financial Sector Regulatory Authority, adopted current name in 2002; Chair. ALTHEA CRICK; Administrator and CEO JOHN BENJAMIN.

STOCK EXCHANGE

Eastern Caribbean Securities Exchange: tel. (869) 466-7192; fax (869) 465-3798; e-mail info@ecseonline.com; internet www.ecseonline.com; based in Basseterre, Saint Christopher and Nevis; f. 2001; regional securities market designed to facilitate the buying and selling of financial products for the eight mem. territories—Anguilla, Antigua and Barbuda, Dominica, Grenada, Montserrat, St Kitts and Nevis, St Lucia and St Vincent and the Grenadines; Chair. and Man. Dir Sir K. DWIGHT VENNER; Gen. Man. TREVOR E. BLAKE.

INSURANCE

Several foreign companies have offices in Antigua. Local insurance companies include the following:

ABI Insurance Co Ltd (ABII): ABI Financial Center, 156 Redcliffe St, POB 2386, St John's; tel. 480-2825; fax 480-2834; e-mail abii@abifinancial.com; internet www.abifinancial.com/abii; f. 1999; subsidiary of the ABI Financial Group; Chair. BRADLEY LEWIS.

Antigua Insurance Co Ltd (ANICOL): Long St, POB 511, St John's; tel. 480-9000; fax 480-9035; e-mail anicol@candw.ag; internet www.anicolinsurance.com.

General Insurance Co Ltd: Upper Redcliffe St, POB 340, St John's; tel. 462-2346; fax 462-4482; Man. Dir PETER BLANCHARD.

Sagicor Life Inc: Sagicor Financial Centre, 9 Factory Rd, St. John's; tel. 480-5500; fax 480-5520; e-mail info_antigua@sagicor.com; internet www.sagicorlife.com; f. 1863; Man. Dr TREVOR VIGO.

Selkridge Insurance Agency Ltd: 7 Woods Centre, Friar's Hill Rd, POB W306, St John's; tel. 462-2042; fax 462-2466; e-mail selkins@candw.ag; internet www.selkridgeinsuranceantigua.com; f. 1961; agents for American Life Insurance Co (ALICO) and Island Heritage Insurance Co; Man. CHARLENE SELKRIDGE.

State Insurance Co Ltd: Redcliffe St, POB 290, St John's; tel. 481-7804; fax 481-7860; e-mail stateins@candw.ag; f. 1977; fmrly State Insurance Corpn; privatized in March 2011; Chair. Dr VINCENT RICHARDS; Gen. Man. LYNDELL BUTLER.

Trade and Industry

DEVELOPMENT ORGANIZATIONS

Antigua and Barbuda Investment Authority: Sagicor Financial Centre, POB 80, St John's; tel. 481-1000; fax 481-1020; e-mail abia@antigua.gov.ag; internet www.investantiguabarbuda.org; f. 2007; Exec. Dir LESTROY SAMUEL.

Barbuda Development Agency: St John's; economic devt projects for Barbuda.

Development Control Authority: Cecil Charles Bldg, 1st Floor, Cross St, POB 895, St John's; tel. 462-6427; fax 462-1919; developing lands, regulating construction; Chair. SYLVESTER BROWN.

St John's Development Corpn: Thames St, POB 1473, St John's; tel. 462-3925; fax 462-3931; e-mail info@stjohnsdevelopment.com; internet www.stjohnsdevelopment.com; f. 1986; manages the Heritage Quay Duty Free Shopping Complex, Vendors' Mall, Public Market and Cultural and Exhibition Complex; Chair. LENWORTH JOHNSON; Exec. Dir Sen. ANTHONY STUART.

CHAMBER OF COMMERCE

Antigua and Barbuda Chamber of Commerce and Industry Ltd: Cnr of North and Popeshead Sts, POB 774, St John's; tel. 462-0743; fax 462-4575; e-mail chamcom@candw.ag; f. 1944 as Antigua Chamber of Commerce Ltd; name changed as above in 1991; Pres. ERROL SAMUEL; Exec. Dir HOLLY PETERS.

INDUSTRIAL AND TRADE ASSOCIATIONS

Antigua and Barbuda Manufacturers' Association (ABMA): POB 115, St John's; tel. 462-1536; fax 462-1912.

Antigua and Barbuda Marine Association (ABMA): English Harbour, St John's; tel. 562-5085; e-mail info@abma.ag; internet www.abma.ag; protection and improvement of marine industry; Pres. FRANKLYN BRAITHWAITE.

EMPLOYERS' ORGANIZATIONS

Antigua and Barbuda Employers' Federation: Upper High St, POB 298, St John's; tel. and fax 462-0449; e-mail aempfed@candw.ag; internet abef-anu.org; f. 1950; affiliated to the International Organization of Employers and the Caribbean Employers' Confederation; 135 mems; Chair. ACRES STOWE; Exec. Sec. J. ARLENE MARTIN.

Antigua and Barbuda Small Business Association Ltd (ABSBA): Cross and Tanner Sts, POB 1401, St John's; tel. and fax 461-5741; Pres. LAWRENCE KING.

UTILITIES

Antigua Public Utilities Authority (APUA): Cassada Gardens, POB 416, St John's; tel. 480-7000; fax 480-7042; e-mail support@apua.ag; internet www.apua.ag; f. 1973; state-owned; generation, transmission and distribution of electricity; telecommunications; colln, treatment, storage and distribution of water; Gen. Man. ESWORTH MARTIN.

Antigua Power Co Limited: Old Parham Rd, POB 10, St John's; tel. 460-9461; fax 460-9462; e-mail cmills@candw.ag; electricity provider; Gen. Man. CALID HASSAD.

TRADE UNIONS

Antigua and Barbuda Meteorological Officers' Association: c/o V. C. Bird Int. Airport, Gabatco, POB 1051, St John's; tel. and fax 462-4606; Pres. CICELY CHARLES.

Antigua and Barbuda Nurses Association (ABNA): Nurses HQ, Queen Elizabeth Hwy, St John's; tel. 462-0251; fax 462-5003; Pres. HENRIETTA JAMES; Sec. ELAINE EDWARDS.

Antigua and Barbuda Public Service Association (ABPSA): Popeshead St, POB 1285, St John's; tel. 461-5821; fax 562-4571; e-mail abpsa_tradeunion@yahoo.com; Pres. JANNELLE WEHNER; Gen. Sec. EMILE FLOYD; 365 mems.

Antigua and Barbuda Trades Union Congress (ABTUC): c/o Antigua and Barbuda Workers' Union, Freedom Hall, Newgate St, POB 940, St John's; tel. 462-0442; fax 462-5220; e-mail awu@candw.ag; Pres. KIM BURDON; Gen. Sec. NATASHA MUSSINGTON.

Antigua and Barbuda Union of Teachers: Factory Rd and Teachers' Lane, POB 553, St John's; tel. and fax 462-3750; e-mail teachersunion@candw.ag; internet www.abut.edu.ag; f. 1926; Pres. VERNEST MACK; Gen. Sec. ASHWORTH AZILLE.

Antigua and Barbuda Workers' Union (ABWU): Freedom Hall, Newgate St, POB 940, St John's; tel. 462-2005; fax 462-5220; e-mail awu@candw.ag; f. 1967 following split with ATLU; not affiliated to any party; Pres. ESROME ROBERTS; Gen. Sec. Sen. DAVID MASSIAH; 10,000 mems.

Antigua Trades and Labour Union (ATLU): 46 North St, POB 3, St John's; tel. 462-0090; fax 462-4056; e-mail atandlu@hotmail.com; f. 1939; affiliated to the Antigua Labour Party; Pres. WIGLEY GEORGE; Gen. Sec. ALRICK DANIEL; about 10,000 mems.

Leeward Islands Pilots Association (LIALPA): POB 2313, St John's; tel. 463-0439; fax 462-0929; Chair. (vacant).

Transport

ROADS

There are 384 km (239 miles) of main roads and 781 km (485 miles) of secondary dry-weather roads. Of the total 1,165 km (724 miles) of roads, only 33% are paved.

SHIPPING

The port of St John's has three operating harbours. The Deep Water Harbour handles cargo and is the main commercial pier. The other two harbours, Nevis Pier and Heritage Quay, are used by cruise ships and a number of foreign shipping lines. There are regular cargo and passenger services internationally and regionally. The other harbours in Antigua include Falmouth, English and Jolly on the south-eastern and southern parts of the island. These harbours are used by yachts and private pleasure craft.

Antigua and Barbuda Port Authority: Terminal Bldg, Deep Water Harbour, POB 1052, St John's; tel. 484-3400; fax 462-4243; e-mail abpa@port.gov.ag; internet www.port.gov.ag; f. 1968; responsible to Ministry of Works, Transportation and the Environment; Chair. GREGG WALTER; Port Man. AGATHA C. DUBLIN.

Barbuda Express: POB 958, St. John's; tel. 560-7989; fax 460-0059; e-mail info@barbudaexpress.com; internet www.antiguaferries.com; f. 2004; ferry services between the islands of Antigua and Barbuda; Owner GREG URLWIN; Man. NATHALIE NEDD.

Brysons Shipping: Friar's Hill Rd, POB 162, St Johns; tel. 480-1240; fax 462-0170; e-mail bryship@candw.ag; internet www.brysonsantigua.com; f. 1835; all shipping services; represents major cruise line; local agent for CMA-CGM Group; Gen. Man. NATHAN DUNDAS.

Consolidated Maritime Services: CMS Enterprise Complex, Old Parham Rd, POB 2478, St John's; tel. 462-1224; fax 462-1227; e-mail Caribms@candw.ag; shipping agents for Crowley Corpn and Navivan Corpn; liner and freight services; Gen. Man. TERRENCE D'ORNELLAS.

Geest Line: Francis Trading Agency Ltd, High St, POB 194, St John's; tel. 462-0854; fax 462-0849; e-mail ftaship@candw.ag; internet www.geestline.com; operates between Europe and the Windward and Leeward islands; Man. Dir Sir EUSTACE FRANCIS.

Tropical Shipping: Antigua Maritime Agencies Ltd, Milburn House, Old Parham Rd, POB W1310, St John's; tel. 562-2934; fax 562-2935; internet www.tropical.com; f. 1992; operates between Canada, USA and the Caribbean; Pres. MIKE PELLICCI.

Vernon Edwards Shipping Co: Thames St, POB 82, St John's; tel. 462-2034; fax 462-2035; e-mail vedwards@candw.ag; cargo service to and from San Juan, Puerto Rico; Man. Dir VERNON G. EDWARDS, Jr.

CIVIL AVIATION

Antigua's V. C. Bird (formerly Coolidge) International Airport, 9 km (5.6 miles) north-east of St John's, is modern and accommodates jet-engined aircraft. There is a small airstrip at Codrington on Barbuda. Antigua and Barbuda Airlines, a nominal company, controls international routes, but services to Europe and North America are operated by foreign airlines. Antigua and Barbuda is a shareholder in, and the headquarters of, the regional airline LIAT. Other regional services are operated by Caribbean Airlines (Trinidad and Tobago) and Air BVI (British Virgin Islands). In November 2011 construction of a new airport terminal at the V. C. Bird International Airport began, with Chinese financing of some US $45m. The new terminal was scheduled to open in late 2013.

LIAT Airlines: V. C. Bird Int. Airport, POB 819, St John's; tel. 480-5713; fax 480-5717; e-mail customerrelations@liatairline.com; internet www.liatairline.com; f. 1956 as Leeward Islands Air Transport Services; privatized in 1995; shares are held by the Govts of Antigua and Barbuda, Montserrat, Grenada, Barbados, Trinidad and Tobago, Jamaica, Guyana, Dominica, Saint Lucia, Saint Vincent and the Grenadines and Saint Christopher and Nevis (30.8%), Caribbean Airlines (29.2%), LIAT employees (13.3%) and private investors (26.7%); acquired Caribbean Star Airlines in Mar. 2007; scheduled passenger and cargo services to 19 destinations in the Caribbean; charter flights are also undertaken; Chair. Dr JEAN HOLDER; CEO BRIAN CHALLENGER (acting).

Tourism

Tourism is the country's main industry. Antigua offers a reputed 365 beaches, an annual international sailing regatta and Carnival week, and the historic Nelson's Dockyard in English Harbour (a national park since 1985). Barbuda is less developed, but is noted for its beauty, wildlife and beaches of pink sand. In 2010 there were some 229,943 stop-over visitors and 557,030 cruise ship passengers. Tourism receipts totalled EC $803.9m. in 2010.

Antigua & Barbuda Cruise Tourism Association (ABCTA): POB 2208, St John's; tel. 480-1244; fax 462-0170; e-mail abcta@candw.ag; f. 1995; Pres. NATHAN DUNDAS; 42 mems.

Antigua and Barbuda Department of Tourism: c/o Ministry of Tourism, Civil Aviation and Culture, Govt Complex, Queen Elizabeth Hwy, POB 363, St John's; tel. 462-0480; fax 462-2483; e-mail deptourism@antigua.gov.ag; internet www.antigua-barbuda.org; Dir-Gen. CORTHWRIGHT MARSHALL.

Antigua Hotels and Tourist Association (AHTA): Island House, Newgate St, POB 454, St John's; tel. 462-0374; fax 462-3702; e-mail ahta@candw.ag; internet www.antiguahotels.org; Exec. Dir NEIL FORRESTER.

Defence

There is a small defence force of 170 men (army 125, navy 45). There were also joint reserves numbering 75. The US Government leases two military bases on Antigua. Antigua and Barbuda participates in the US-sponsored Regional Security System. The defence budget in 2011 was estimated at EC $16m.

Education

Education is compulsory for 11 years between five and 16 years of age. Primary education begins at the age of five and normally lasts for seven years. Secondary education, beginning at 12 years of age, lasts for five years, comprising a first cycle of three years and a second cycle of two years. In 2009/10 there were 63 primary and 20 secondary schools; the majority of schools are administered by the Government. According to UNESCO estimates, in 2008/09 enrolment at both primary and secondary schools included 88% of pupils in their relevant age-groups. An estimated 61% of children in the appropriate age-group were enrolled in pre-primary education in 2008. Teacher training and technical training are available at the Antigua State College in St John's. An extra-mural department of the University of the West Indies offers several foundation courses leading to higher study at branches elsewhere. In addition, 11 other tertiary educational institutes are registered with the Ministry of Education. Government expenditure on education in 2012 was projected at EC $76.3m.

ARGENTINA

Introductory Survey

LOCATION, CLIMATE, LANGUAGE, RELIGION, FLAG, CAPITAL

The Argentine Republic occupies almost the whole of South America south of the Tropic of Capricorn and east of the Andes. It has a long Atlantic coastline stretching from Uruguay and the River Plate to Tierra del Fuego. To the west lie Chile and the Andes mountains, while to the north are Bolivia, Paraguay and Brazil. Argentina also claims the Falkland Islands (known in Argentina as the Islas Malvinas), South Georgia, the South Sandwich Islands and part of Antarctica. The climate varies from sub-tropical in the Chaco region of the north to sub-arctic in Patagonia, generally with moderate summer rainfall. Temperatures in Buenos Aires are usually between 5°C (41°F) and 29°C (84°F). The language is Spanish. The great majority of the population profess Christianity: about 90% are Roman Catholics and about 2% Protestants. The national flag (proportions 14 by 9) has three equal horizontal stripes, of light blue (celeste), above white, above light blue. The state flag (proportions 1 by 2) has the same design with, in addition, a gold 'Sun of May' in the centre of the white stripe. The capital is Buenos Aires.

CONTEMPORARY POLITICAL HISTORY

Historical Context

During the greater part of the 20th century, government in Argentina tended to alternate between military and civilian rule. In 1930 Hipólito Yrigoyen, a member of the reformist Unión Cívica Radical (UCR), who in 1916 had become Argentina's first President to be freely elected by popular vote, was overthrown by an army coup, and the country's first military regime was established. Civilian rule was restored in 1932, only to be supplanted by further military intervention in 1943. A leading figure in the new military regime, Col (later Lt-Gen.) Juan Domingo Perón Sosa, won a presidential election in 1946. He established the Peronista party in 1948 and pursued a policy of extreme nationalism and social improvement, aided by his second wife, Eva ('Evita') Duarte de Perón, whose popularity greatly enhanced his position and contributed to his re-election as President in 1951. In 1954, however, his promotion of secularization and the legalization of divorce brought him into conflict with the Roman Catholic Church. In September 1955 President Perón was deposed by a revolt of the armed forces. He went into exile, eventually settling in Spain, from where he continued to direct the Peronist movement.

Following the overthrow of Perón, Argentina entered another lengthy period of political instability. Political control continued to pass between civilian (mainly Radical) and military regimes during the late 1950s and the 1960s. Congressional and presidential elections were conducted in March 1973. The Frente Justicialista de Liberación, a Peronist coalition, secured control of the Congreso Nacional (National Congress), while the presidential election was won by the party's candidate, Dr Héctor Cámpora. However, Cámpora resigned in July, to enable Gen. Perón, who had returned to Argentina, to contest a fresh presidential election. In September Perón was returned to power, with more than 60% of the votes.

Domestic Political Affairs

Military rule

Gen. Perón died in July 1974 and was succeeded as President by his widow, María Estela ('Isabelita') Martínez de Perón, hitherto Vice-President. The Government's economic austerity programme and the soaring rate of inflation led to widespread strike action and demands for the President's resignation. In March 1976 the armed forces, led by Gen. Jorge Videla, overthrew the President and installed a three-man junta: Gen. Videla was sworn in as head of state. The junta substantially altered the Constitution, dissolved the Congreso Nacional, suspended political and trade union activity and removed most government officials from their posts. Several hundred people were arrested, while 'Isabelita' Perón was detained and later went into exile. The military regime launched a ferocious offensive against left-wing guerrillas and opposition forces. The imprisonment, torture and murder of suspected left-wing activists by the armed forces provoked domestic and international protests. Repression eased in 1978, after all armed opposition had been eliminated.

In March 1981 Gen. Roberto Viola, a former junta member, succeeded President Videla and made known his intention to extend dialogue with political parties as a prelude to an eventual return to democracy. Owing to ill health, he was replaced in December by Lt-Gen. Leopoldo Galtieri, the Commander-in-Chief of the Army, who attempted to cultivate popular support by continuing this process of political liberalization.

In April 1982, in order to distract attention from an increasingly unstable domestic situation, and following unsuccessful negotiations with the United Kingdom in February over Argentina's long-standing sovereignty claim, President Galtieri ordered the invasion of the Falkland Islands (Islas Malvinas—see chapter on the Falkland Islands). The United Kingdom recovered the islands after a short conflict, in the course of which about 750 Argentine lives were lost. Argentine forces surrendered in June 1982, but no formal cessation of hostilities was declared until October 1989. Humiliated by the defeat, Galtieri was forced to resign, and the members of the junta were replaced. The army, under the control of Lt-Gen. Cristino Nicolaides, installed a retired general, Reynaldo Bignone, as President in July 1982. The armed forces were held responsible for the disastrous economic situation, and the transfer of power to a civilian government was accelerated. Moreover, in 1983 a Military Commission of Inquiry into the Falklands conflict concluded in its report that the main responsibility for Argentina's defeat lay with members of the former junta. Galtieri was sentenced to imprisonment, while several other officers were put on trial for corruption, murder and insulting the honour of the armed forces. In the same year the regime approved the Ley de Pacificación Nacional, an amnesty law which granted retrospective immunity to the police, the armed forces and others for political crimes that had been committed over the previous 10 years.

Civilian rule

General and presidential elections were held in October 1983, in which the UCR defeated the Peronist Partido Justicialista (PJ), attracting the votes of many former Peronist supporters. Dr Raúl Alfonsín, the UCR candidate, took office as President on 10 December. He promptly announced a radical reform of the armed forces, which led to the immediate retirement of more than one-half of the military high command. In addition, he repealed the Ley de Pacificación Nacional and ordered the court martial of the first three military juntas to rule Argentina after the 1976 coup, for offences including abduction, torture and murder. Public opposition to the former military regime was reinforced by the discovery and exhumation of hundreds of bodies from unmarked graves throughout the country. (It was believed that 15,000–30,000 people 'disappeared' during the so-called 'dirty war' between the former military regime and its opponents in 1976–83.) President Alfonsín also announced the formation of the National Commission on the Disappearance of Persons to investigate the events of the 'dirty war'. The trial of the former leaders began in April 1985. Several hundred prosecution witnesses gave testimonies which revealed the systematic atrocities and the campaign of terror perpetrated by the former military leaders. In December four of the accused were acquitted, but sentences were imposed on five others, including sentences of life imprisonment for Gen. Videla and Adm. Eduardo Massera (they were released in late 1990). In May 1986 all three members of the junta that had held power during the Falklands conflict were found guilty of negligence and received prison sentences, including a term of 12 years for Galtieri.

In December 1986 the Congreso Nacional approved the Punto Final ('Full Stop') law, whereby civil and military courts were to begin new judicial proceedings against members of the armed forces accused of violations of human rights, within a 60-day period ending on 22 February 1987. However, in May 1987, following a series of minor rebellions at army garrisons, the Government announced new legislation, known as the Obediencia Debida ('Due Obedience') law, whereby an amnesty was to be declared for all but senior ranks of the police and armed forces. Therefore, of the 350–370 officers hitherto due to be prosecuted for alleged violations of human rights, only 30–50 senior officers were now to be tried.

A return to Peronismo

In the campaign for the May 1989 elections, Carlos Saúl Menem headed the Frente Justicialista de Unidad Popular (FREJUPO) electoral alliance, comprising his own PJ grouping, the Partido Demócrata Cristiano (PDC) and the Partido Intransigente (PI). On 14 May the FREJUPO alliance secured 49% of the votes cast in the presidential election and 310 of the 600 seats in the electoral college. The Peronists were also victorious in the election for 127 seats (one-half of the total) in the Cámara de Diputados (Chamber of Deputies). The failure of attempts by the retiring and incoming administrations to collaborate left the nation in a political vacuum. Although Menem was scheduled to take office as President in December, the worsening economic situation compelled Alfonsín to resign five months early, and Menem assumed the presidency on 8 July.

In early 1990 the Government introduced a radical economic readjustment plan, incorporating the expansion of existing plans for the transfer to private ownership of many state-owned companies and the restructuring of the nation's financial systems. In August the Minister of the Economy, Antonio Erman González, appointed himself head of the Central Bank and assumed almost total control of the country's financial structure. Public disaffection with the Government's economic policy was widespread. Failure to contain the threat of hyperinflation led to a loss in purchasing power, and unrest became more frequent. In January 1991 Erman González was forced to resign as Minister of the Economy following a sudden spectacular decline in the value of the austral in relation to the US dollar. He was succeeded by Domingo Cavallo.

In October 1989 the Government pardoned 210 officers and soldiers who had been involved in the 'dirty war', as well as the governing junta during the Falklands conflict (including Gen. Galtieri) and leaders of three recent military uprisings (including Lt-Col Rico and Col Seineldín). Widespread public concern at the apparent impunity of military personnel further increased after a second round of presidential pardons in late 1990.

In gubernatorial and congressional elections, held throughout 1991, the Peronists performed well. Their success was widely attributed to the popularity of Domingo Cavallo, who abolished index-linked wage increases and implemented the 'Convertibility Plan', which linked the austral to the US dollar, at a fixed rate of exchange. This Plan achieved considerable success in reducing inflation, and impressed international finance organizations sufficiently to secure the negotiation of substantial loan agreements. In October the President ordered the removal of almost all of the remaining bureaucratic apparatus of state regulation of the economy, and in November the Government announced plans to accelerate the transfer to private ownership of the remaining public sector concerns. Continuing economic success in 1992 helped to secure agreements for the renegotiation of repayment of outstanding debts with the Government's leading creditor banks and with the 'Paris Club' of Western creditor governments. The October 1993 elections to renew 127 seats in the Cámara de Diputados were won convincingly by the PJ.

Former President Alfonsín returned to political prominence in November 1993, amid fears that the UCR would be excluded from negotiations on constitutional reform, which was to be voted on at a national referendum scheduled for late that year. Consequently, Alfonsín entered into a dialogue with the President, resulting in a declaration that a framework for constitutional reform had been negotiated, apparently in return for Menem's postponement of the referendum and acceptance of modified reform proposals. In December the UCR national convention endorsed the terms of the agreement, which included the possibility of re-election of the President for one consecutive term, a reduction in the presidential term (to four years), the abolition of the presidential electoral college, the delegation of some presidential powers to a Chief of Cabinet, an increase in the number of seats in the Senado (Senate) and a reduction in the length of the mandate of all senators, a reform of the procedure for judicial appointments, the removal of religious stipulations from the terms of eligibility for presidential candidates, and the abolition of the President's power to appoint the mayor of the federal capital. The need for constitutional reform was approved by the Congreso later in the month. Following the convening of a Constituent Assembly in May 1994, a new Constitution was promulgated in August.

Menem's campaign for re-election in 1995 concentrated on the economic success of his previous administration and, despite the increasingly precarious condition of the economy, he secured 50% of the votes at the presidential election in May, thereby avoiding a second ballot. José Octavio Bordón, the candidate of the Frente del País Solidario (Frepaso—a centre-left alliance of socialist, communist, Christian Democrat and dissident Peronist groups), was second with 29% of the votes, ahead of the UCR candidate, Horacio Massaccesi, who received 17%. However, Frepaso won the largest share of the 130 contested seats in the Cámara de Diputados at concurrent legislative elections and significantly increased its representation in the Senado (as did the Peronists), largely at the expense of the UCR.

Meanwhile, the Government's ongoing programme of economic austerity continued to provoke violent opposition, particularly from the public sector. In March 1995 the Government presented an economic consolidation programme aimed at protecting the Argentine currency against devaluation and supporting the ailing banking sector, which had been adversely affected by the financial crisis in Mexico in late 1994 (the so-called 'tequila effect').

In 1996 public disaffection with the Government was reflected in the PJ's poor performance in the first direct elections for the Head of Government of the Autonomous City of Buenos Aires, as well as in concurrent elections to the 60-member Constituent Assembly (which was charged with drafting a constitution for the newly autonomous capital). In July Cavallo was dismissed as Minister of the Economy following months of bitter dispute with the President and other cabinet members. Roque Fernández, hitherto President of the Central Bank, assumed the economy portfolio. Cavallo became increasingly vociferous in his attacks against the integrity of certain cabinet members, and in October, as Menem launched a well-publicized campaign against corruption after the discovery of wide-scale malpractice within the customs service, he accused the Government of having links with organized crime.

Industrial and social unrest increased in 1996–97, owing to widespread discontent with proposed labour reforms, as well as reductions in public expenditure and high levels of unemployment. General strikes, organized by the Confederación General de Trabajo (CGT), the Congreso de los Trabajadores Argentinos (CTA) and the Movimiento de Trabajadores Argentinos (MTA), received widespread support in August and September 1996. In October relations between the Government and the trade unions deteriorated following the submission to the Congreso of controversial labour reform legislation. In December Menem introduced part of the reforms by decree, although a court declared the decrees to be unconstitutional in the following month. In May 1997 police clashed with thousands of anti-Government demonstrators who had occupied government buildings and blockaded roads and bridges. In July some 30,000 people demonstrated in the capital to protest at the high level of unemployment, then estimated at more than 17%. A general strike in August, organized by the MTA and the CTA, was only partially observed, however.

At the mid-term congressional elections in October 1997 the UCR and Frepaso (united in the Alianza por el Trabajo, la Justicia y la Educación—ATJE) increased their representation to 110 lower-house seats. The PJ lost its overall majority in the Cámara de Diputados, its total number of seats being reduced to 118, and received only 41% of the votes in the critical constituency of the Province of Buenos Aires, compared with the ATJE's 48%.

Economic crisis

A presidential election was held on 24 October 1999. The ATJE candidate, Fernando de la Rúa, ended 10 years of Peronist rule, winning 49% of the votes cast. The ATJE also performed well in concurrent congressional elections. De la Rúa took office as President on 10 December. Later that month the new Congreso Nacional approved an austerity budget that reduced public expenditure by US $1,400m., as well as a major tax-reform programme and a federal revenue-sharing scheme.

In April 2000 the Senado approved a controversial revision of employment law. The legislation led to mass demonstrations by public sector workers and, subsequently, to two 24-hour national strikes organized by the CGT. Later that year the Government came under intense pressure after it was alleged that some senators had received bribes from government officials to approve the employment legislation. In September the Senado voted to end the immunity that protected law-makers, judges and government ministers from criminal investigation in order to allow an inquiry into the corruption allegations. The political crisis intensified on 6 October when Carlos Alvarez resigned as Vice-President, one day after a cabinet reorganization in which two ministers implicated in the bribery scandal were not removed. One of these, former labour minister Alberto Flamarique, who was appointed presidential Chief of Staff in the reshuffle, resigned later the same day. The other, Fernando de Santibáñez, head of the state intelligence service, resigned in late October. Earlier that month the President of the Senado, José Genoud, also resigned after he too was implicated in the bribery allegations.

The economic situation continued to deteriorate in 2000–01. In November 2000 thousands of unemployed workers blocked roads throughout the country in protest at the worsening economic conditions and a 36-hour national strike was organized in response to the Government's proposed introduction of an IMF-backed economic recovery package that included a five-year freeze on federal and provincial spending, a reform of the pension system and an increase in the female retirement age. In December the Congreso approved the reforms and, later in the month, the IMF agreed a package, worth an estimated US $20,000m., to meet Argentina's external debt obligations for 2001.

The resignation of the Minister of the Economy, José Luis Machinea, precipitated another political crisis in March 2001. The announcement by his successor, Ricardo López Murphy, of major reductions in public expenditure resulted in several cabinet resignations. As a consequence, in late March a second reshuffle occurred, in which Domingo Cavallo was reappointed Minister of the Economy. In June Cavallo announced a series of measures designed to ease the country's financial situation. The most controversial of these was the introduction of a complex trade tariff system that created multiple exchange rates (based on the average of a euro and a US dollar); this was, in effect, a devaluation of the peso for external trade, although the dollar peg remained in operation for domestic transactions. As Argentina's debt crisis intensified and fears of a default increased, a further emergency package, the seventh in 19 months, was implemented in July. A policy of 'zero deficit' was announced, whereby neither the federal Government nor any province would be allowed to spend more than it collected in taxes. In order to achieve this, state salaries and pensions were to be reduced by 13%. Despite mass protests and a one-day national strike, the measures were approved by the Congreso at the end of July. In the legislative elections of October 2001 the PJ won control of the Cámara de Diputados and increased its majority in the Senado.

In December 2001, as the economic situation deteriorated and the possibility of a default on the country's debt increased considerably, owing to the IMF's refusal to disburse more funds to Argentina, the Government introduced restrictions on bank account withdrawals and appropriated private pension funds. These measures provoked two days of rioting and demonstrations nation-wide, in which at least 27 people died. On 20 December Cavallo resigned as Minister of the Economy and de la Rúa stepped down as President. Because Alvarez had resigned as Vice-President in the previous year, the newly appointed head of the Senado, Ramón Puerta, became acting President, but was succeeded two days later by the Peronist Adolfo Rodríguez Saá. He, in turn, resigned one week later after protests against his proposed economic reforms (including the introduction of a new currency and the suspension of debt repayments) resulted in further unrest. (Due to Puerta's resignation as President of the Senado, Eduardo Camaño, the head of the Cámara de Diputados, briefly became acting President.) On 1 January 2002 the former Peronist presidential candidate and recently elected Senator for the Province of Buenos Aires, Eduardo Alberto Duhalde, was elected President by the Congreso. On 3 January Argentina officially defaulted on its loan repayments, reportedly the largest ever debt default, and three days later the Senado authorized the Government to set the exchange rate, thus officially ending the 10-year-old parity between the US dollar and the peso. In the following month the Government initiated the compulsory conversion to pesos of US dollar bank deposits in order to prevent capital flight. This process of 'pesofication' led to many lawsuits (*amparos*) being brought by depositors against financial institutions in an attempt to recover their losses. However, in October 2004 the Supreme Court ruled that the 'pesofication' was not unconstitutional, thereby effectively ruling against future *amparos*.

Nevertheless, in February 2002 the Supreme Court ruled that the restrictions imposed on bank withdrawals (the *corralito*) were unconstitutional. In order to forestall the complete collapse of the financial system, the Government imposed a six-month ban on legal challenges to the remainder of the bank withdrawal regime. Numerous bank holidays were also decreed to prevent another run on the banks and a further devaluation of the currency. Later that month the Government signed a new tax-sharing pact with the provincial Governors, linking the monthly amount distributed to the provinces to tax collections, as recommended by the IMF. However, in April Jorge Remes Lenicov resigned as Minister of the Economy following the Senado's refusal to support an emergency plan to exchange frozen bank deposits for government bonds. He was replaced by Roberto Lavagna.

The economy achieved mixed progress during 2002. While the number of deposits in Argentine banks increased, Argentina still defaulted on a US $805m. loan instalment to the World Bank in November, thus jeopardizing the country's last remaining source of external finance. Public anger against the Government and at the state of the economy did not subside.

Kirchnerismo

At a presidential election on 27 April 2003 Menem, one of three Peronist candidates, obtained the largest share of the popular vote, with 24% of the votes cast, followed by Néstor Carlos Kirchner (representing the Frente para la Victoria—FPV—faction of the PJ), with 22% of the ballot. Ricardo López Murphy of the centre-right Movimiento Federal para Recrear el Crecimiento alliance came third, with 16% of the ballot. As no candidate had secured a majority of votes, a run-off ballot between the two leading candidates was scheduled for 18 May. However, faced with the very likely possibility of a decisive protest vote against him, Menem withdrew his candidacy. Kirchner was thus elected by default. He was sworn in as President on 25 May.

Upon taking office, the new President sought to strengthen his relatively weak popular mandate. Having pledged to put the needs of the Argentine people before the demands of the IMF, Kirchner immediately announced a series of popular measures, including the replacement of several high-ranking military and police commanders, the opening of an investigation into allegedly corrupt practices by several Supreme Court Justices (which prompted the resignation of the President of the Supreme Court in June) and increases in pensions and minimum wages. He also announced a programme of investment in infrastructure, particularly housing, intended to lower the high unemployment rate.

President Kirchner's increasing popularity translated into significant gains for the PJ in the legislative elections that were held during the latter half of 2003, which resulted in a working majority for the PJ and its allies in both the Cámara de Diputados and the Senado. Moreover, the corruption inquiry within the Supreme Court resulted in the removal of four Justices considered to be hostile to Kirchner. Nevertheless, frequent demonstrations against high levels of crime and unemployment continued to cause disruption. Loosely organized groups of protesters, known as *piqueteros*, became increasingly radical, erecting roadblocks and occupying both private and public institutions to demand jobs, redistribution of money and an end to a perceived culture of impunity.

At mid-term elections to the Congreso, held in October 2005, President Kirchner's FPV faction of the PJ secured a resounding victory over the faction of the party led by former President Duhalde, Peronismo Federal. Following the ballot, the FPV controlled 118 of the 257 seats in the Cámara de Diputados, compared with 31 held by Peronismo Federal, while the PJ bloc as a whole had 33 of the 72 senatorial seats. The UCR controlled 36 seats in the lower house and 11 in the Senado. The two PJ factions were bitterly divided throughout the electoral campaign, a division most evident in the hostile campaigning of Duhalde's wife, Hilda Beatriz González, and Kirchner's wife, Cristina Elisabet Fernández de Kirchner, who were both elected as Senators for the Province of Buenos Aires. President Kirchner effected a major cabinet reorganization in November. Notably, Lavagna resigned as Minister of Economy and Production and was replaced by Felisa Miceli; the ministers for foreign affairs and defence were also replaced by ministers believed to be more closely aligned with Kirchner's policies for regional integration.

Election of Cristina Fernández de Kirchner

Factional division in both the PJ and the UCR characterized the elections of October 2007. Following several months of speculation concerning President Kirchner's intention to seek re-election, in July it was announced that his wife, Cristina Fernández, would instead stand as the FPV candidate in the presidential election. Her bid was supported by a significant section of the UCR, known as the 'K Radicals', whereas another faction of that party—the so-called 'L Radicals'—endorsed the candidacy of Lavagna, who also received support from Peronists opposed to President Kirchner's policies. Alberto Rodríguez Saá (brother of Adolfo Rodríguez Saá) entered the contest representing another anti-Kirchner faction of the PJ. Fernández's campaign was damaged to some extent by a number of allegations of corruption that affected the Government in 2007, including Miceli's resignation as Minister of Economy and Production in July following judicial investigations into the discovery of a large quantity of cash in her office. (She was replaced by Miguel Peirano.) In the following month a scandal surrounded the discovery of nearly US $800,000 in cash in the suitcase of Guido Antonini Wilson, a Venezuelan businessman who was travelling from Venezuela to Argentina on an aircraft chartered by a state-owned company. Opposition parties accused the Government of illegally importing the money in order to fund Fernández's election campaign.

In spite of these obstacles, Fernández won a decisive victory in the presidential election held on 28 October 2007, securing 41.8% of the votes cast. No candidate succeeded in unifying the opposition: Elisa M. A. Carrió of the Afirmación para una República Igualitaria, who stood as part of the Coalición Cívica alliance, obtained 21.3% of the vote, while Lavagna received 15.6% of votes cast and Rodríguez Saá took just 7.1%. Fernández's margin of victory was thus considerably in excess of the 10 percentage points below which a run-off ballot would have been required. The participation rate was 76.2%. Following the concurrent partial elections to the Congreso the FPV legislative bloc emerged with 120 seats in the Cámara de Diputados and 42 seats in the Senado, thereby gaining an overall majority in the upper chamber, while the UCR's representation was reduced to 24 and eight seats, respectively. President Fernández was sworn in on 10 December. Her Cabinet retained seven members of the outgoing administration.

In mid-March 2008 the four main agricultural unions began strike action and erected roadblocks in protest at sharp increases in tariffs on the export of soybeans, sunflower products and other foodstuffs. Despite causing serious food shortages, the protests attracted widespread popular support. The Government defended the tax rises as necessary to control inflation resulting from substantial rises in grain prices on international markets, as well as to guarantee domestic supplies. A 30-day truce was called by the unions in April to allow for negotiations with the Government; however, strikes resumed in May after talks failed. Meanwhile, a rally in Rosario organized by the farming unions in late May was attended by an estimated 200,000 people, while further large-scale demonstrations took place in mid-June in protest at the Government's increasingly uncompromising attitude towards the unions' demands. Shortly afterwards, and in response to the public exhortation of Vice-President Julio César Cleto Cobos, President Fernández agreed to allow the Congreso to ratify the tariff increases. (The farmers' fourth and final strike ended two days later.) The ensuing draft legislation was narrowly approved by the Cámara de Diputados, but was defeated in the Senado in mid-July by the casting vote of Cobos, the chamber's President. The decree that had introduced the tariff increases was subsequently revoked. The Government's defeat in the legislature, which occurred despite the FPV's dominance of both chambers, resulted in the resignation of the Cabinet Chief, Alberto Fernández. He was replaced by Sergio Massa.

In October 2008 the Government announced plans to assume state control of Argentina's 10 private pension funds (Administradoras de Fondos de Jubilaciones y Pensiones—AFJPs). President Fernández declared that nationalization would protect workers' investments from the decline in the value of the funds caused by turmoil in world-wide financial markets, but the opposition claimed that the Government intended to use the AFJPs' assets (worth some US $30,000m.) to meet its rising debt-servicing obligations. None the less, the take-over received congressional approval in November and took effect in January 2009.

Mid-term congressional elections due in October 2009 were held four months early, on 28 June. Critics of the Government alleged that the move was an attempt to lessen the electoral damage that the FPV might have suffered later in the year as a result of the worsening economic situation. In spite of the rescheduling, the Government performed badly in the mid-term elections, losing its majority in both legislative houses. Following the ballot, the FPV's representation was reduced from 116 to 87 in the 257-seat lower house and from 38 to 30 in the Senado. Notably, the list of candidates headed by former President Kirchner in the Province of Buenos Aires secured fewer seats in the Cámara de Diputados than that led by Francisco de Narváez of the centre-right Unión PRO alliance; immediately after the ballot Kirchner resigned as President of the PJ (although the party leadership committee voted to reject his resignation in November, and he reassumed the PJ presidency in March 2010). Nevertheless, the fragmented nature of the opposition meant that the FPV remained the largest congressional bloc. The UCR held 43 of the seats in the Cámara de Diputados, although it was allied to the Partido Socialista (PS) and the Coalición Cívica, among others, bringing its total support to around 70. The Unión PRO, comprising the Propuesta Republicana (PRO) and various dissident Peronist factions, could count on the support of some 47 deputies in the lower house.

Following the elections both Carlos Fernández, the Minister of Economy and Public Finance, and the Cabinet Chief, Sergio Massa, resigned. Amado Boudou was appointed to the public finance ministry, while Aníbal Domingo Fernández, hitherto justice and security minister, became Cabinet Chief. Boudou had presided over the nationalization of the AFJPs in 2008 and his appointment was a signal that the Fernández Government intended to continue with its economic policies despite its seeming unpopularity with the electorate. In August 2009 the Congreso approved a further year's extension to the temporary law allowing certain legislative powers to be delegated to the executive. The original legislation, which notably allowed the Government to set the agricultural export tariffs, the raising of which had prompted the ongoing dispute with the farming unions, had been approved during the 2001–02 financial crisis. In the same month Fernández used her presidential veto to overturn another law temporarily suspending grain export duties and granting emergency aid to the agricultural sector. The Government claimed that income from the tariffs would fund anti-poverty initiatives, launched in the wake of criticism by the head of the Roman Catholic Church, Pope Benedict, who referred to the 'scandal of poverty and social inequality' prevalent in Argentina. In November, moreover, the Senado approved the extension until the end of 2011 of further executive 'super powers', first granted in January 2002, which allowed the Government to regulate prices, renegotiate public utility contracts and restructure public debt without congressional approval; these powers were further extended, until the end of 2013, in December 2011.

The Government succeeded in gaining legislative approval for a controversial reform of the media in October 2009. The new law provided for a reduction in the number of television or radio licences that broadcasting companies were allowed to own, from 24 to 10, and the establishment of a federal body to oversee the broadcast media. Critics of the legislation claimed that it gave the Government too much control over the sector and that President Fernández's supporters had rushed through adoption of the proposals before they lost control of the Congreso in December. In December the Government also secured congressional approval for major political reforms, forcing political parties to hold simultaneous open primaries to select their presidential candidates, banning the private financing of radio and television advertising in electoral campaigns, reducing the length of political campaigns and establishing a minimum level of membership for parties. A legal challenge against the media law, initiated by the Clarín group, had some success in October 2010, when the Supreme Court upheld an earlier ruling by a lower court that, pending a final verdict on the constitutionality of the legislation, suspended the requirement that companies with more than 10 licences should sell off their excess operations within one year of the law's enactment.

A presidential decree providing for the use of some US $6,600m. of central bank reserves to guarantee debt payments provoked significant tensions between the Government and other state institutions in early 2010. Opposition figures maintained that the use of the reserves required congressional authorization, while the refusal of the Governor of the Central Bank, Martín Redrado, to disburse the funds led to his dismissal by President Fernández on 7 January. Redrado insisted that only the legislature was empowered to remove him from office, a stance supported on the following day by a federal court judge, who reinstated Redrado to his post and suspended the decree on the proposed use of federal reserves. However, Redrado announced his resignation in late January, a few days before a specially convened congressional commission voted in support of his dismissal. Some concern was expressed that the appointment of a strong ally of Fernández, Mercedes Marcó de Pont, hitherto President of the state-owned Banco de la Nación Argentina, as Redrado's successor could weaken the Central Bank's autonomy. The congressional commission also recommended the continued suspension of the decree on the use of the reserves, pending the consideration of its legitimacy by the Congreso. When the Congreso returned from recess at the beginning of March, however, Fernández announced the annulment of this decree and the introduction of two new ones establishing funds to which central bank reserves would be transferred: the first, amounting to $2,190m., was destined to service debt payments to multilateral lending institutions, and the second, amounting to $4,380m., was for the repayment of private creditors. Subsequent attempts by opposition leaders to challenge the new decrees ultimately failed.

Héctor Timerman, ambassador to the USA, was appointed as Minister of Foreign Affairs, International Trade and Worship in June 2010, following the resignation of the incumbent Jorge Taiana, reportedly over policy differences and alleged leaks to the media regarding efforts to resolve the pulp mill dispute between Argentina and Uruguay (see Foreign Affairs). In December the illegal occupation of land in the Parque Indoamericano, in the south of Buenos Aires, by thousands of people demanding housing and social assistance led to violence in which at least three squatters were killed. The creation of a new Ministry of Security in response to the unrest was interpreted as a rebuke to the Cabinet Chief, Aníbal Fernández, whose delay in deploying federal police to the Parque Indoamericano had allowed confrontations between the squatters and local residents to escalate. Nilda Garré, hitherto Minister of Defence, was appointed as Minister of Security, being replaced at the Ministry of Defence by Arturo Puricelli. The Parque Indoamericano was eventually cleared after the federal and city Governments agreed to fund a joint housing plan. Members of the four main agricultural unions halted the sale of wheat and other cereals for one week in January 2011 in a renewed protest against the system of export tariffs and quotas (see above), although the strike action received less support than in 2008.

Recent developments: a second term for Fernández

Speculation regarding the presidential election due in October 2011 intensified following the sudden death, in October 2010, of former President Kirchner, who had been widely expected to be the FPV candidate. President Fernández did not confirm her intention to seek re-election until a few days before the deadline for registration in June 2011, her popularity having risen in the preceding months, according to opinion polls, amid public sympathy following her husband's death and robust economic growth. Opposition to Fernández was largely divided. The UCR, the PS and the Coalición Cívica did not renew their alliance from the 2009 mid-term elections, the first two instead joining with more minor parties to form new coalitions, namely the Unión para el Desarrollo Social (Udeso) and the Frente Amplio Progresista (FAP). Ricardo Alfonsín, son of former President Raúl Alfonsín, became the presidential candidate of the UCR-led Udeso, while Hermes Binner, the outgoing Governor of Santa Fe, represented the centre-left FAP (having earlier been mooted as Alfonsín's vice-presidential candidate), and Elisa Carrió, the leader of the Coalición Cívica, was to stand for a third time. Following a failed attempt by the Peronismo Federal faction of the PJ to select a presidential candidate in a primary election conducted earlier in the year, the two main challengers for the nomination, former President Duhalde and Alberto Rodríguez Saá, the outgoing Governor of San Luis, opted to contest the presidency separately, for two newly formed Peronist coalitions: the Frente Popular and the Alianza Compromiso Federal, respectively.

In accordance with the political reforms adopted in December 2009, mandatory primary elections to select presidential candidates took place for the first time on 14 August 2011. However, with all political parties and alliances having chosen to field single candidates, the poll was effectively a dry run for the actual contest in October. Of the 10 candidates in the primary election, Fernández received by far the strongest support, obtaining 50.2% of the vote nation-wide and winning in every province with the exception of San Luis, where Governor Rodríguez Saá was favoured. Rodríguez Saá was placed fifth overall, however, with 8.2% of the vote, after Alfonsín (12.2%), Duhalde (12.1%) and Binner (10.2%). Only two other candidates exceeded the 1.5% share of the vote required to proceed to the general election on 23 October: Carrió and Jorge Altamira, representing the Alianza Frente de Izquierda y de los Trabajadores.

As expected, Fernández achieved an outright and convincing victory in the presidential election on 23 October 2011, securing re-election with a provisional 53.96% of the valid votes cast, the most emphatic win since the return to civilian rule in 1983. The opposition vote remained split, although Binner improved on his performance in the primary elections, to come second with 16.87% of the vote, followed by Alfonsín, with 11.15%, Rodríguez Saá, with 7.98%, and Duhalde, with 5.89%. A participation rate of 78.9% was recorded. In addition to achieving a third consecutive term in presidential office for the PJ, the FPV and its allies also regained control of both legislative chambers in the concurrent partial congressional elections, increasing their combined representation to some 134 seats in the Cámara de Diputados (of which the FPV itself held 115) and to 38 seats in the Senado. The UCR retained its position as the largest opposition party, with 38 and 14 seats in the lower and upper chambers, respectively.

Only four days after Fernández's re-election in late October 2011, the Government implemented a series of economic measures aimed at stabilizing the exchange rate of the peso and at curbing capital flight, amid rising demand for US dollars resulting from fears of a devaluation of the national currency (see Economic Affairs). However, the Government's actions prompted concerns regarding the country's balance of payments position. Meanwhile, long-running tensions between the Government and trade union leaders, particularly Hugo Moyano, the Secretary-General of the CGT, continued, with Fernández stating her opposition to a bill advocated by Moyano that would require companies to share their profits with employees. Forthcoming discussions on salary increases were also expected to be difficult owing to the wide disparity between official inflation figures and private estimates.

President Fernández was sworn in to serve her second term of office on 10 December 2011. Her Cabinet was largely unchanged, only the three ministers who had left office to contest seats in the general election in October being replaced. Hernán Lorenzino, who as Secretary of Finance had managed the second phase of negotiations to restructure Argentina's debt in 2009–10, succeeded Amado Boudou, the new Vice-President, as Minister of Economy and Public Finance. The other two new appointees were Juan Manuel Abal Medina, who was designated Cabinet Chief, following Aníbal Fernández's election to the Senate, and Norberto Yahuar, who became Minister of Agriculture, Livestock and Fisheries, replacing Julián Domínguez, who had secured a seat in the Cámara de Diputados (of which he was later elected President).

With its congressional majority restored, the Government moved swiftly to secure approval of several bills in a number of special legislative sessions in December 2011. Most controversial was legislation that, deeming the production, sale and distribution of newsprint to be of national interest, granted the Government the power to determine the price of newsprint and the operating capacity of the country's sole newsprint producer, Papel Prensa. The Clarín and La Nación media groups, which together owned a majority stake in Papel Prensa, strongly opposed the new law, which would allow the Government to seize control of the company if it failed to meet production targets.

Human Rights and the 'Dirty War'

Despite public expressions of regret (in 1995 and 2004) by the heads of the navy, the army and the air force for crimes committed by the armed forces during 1976–83, issues concerning the 'dirty war' remained politically sensitive in the early 21st century. In July 2001 Alfredo Astiz, a notorious former naval captain, was arrested at the request of an Italian court on the grounds of his involvement in the murder of three Italian citizens during the dictatorship. He was released the following month. In July 2003 President Kirchner revoked a decree, issued by President de la Rúa in 2001, that had prevented the extradition of Argentine citizens suspected of human rights violations. Courts in Spain, France, Germany and Sweden all subsequently sought the extradition of former Argentine military personnel for crimes committed against their citizens. Astiz was the subject of extradition requests by the Italian, French and Swedish Governments. In April 2010 an Argentine court refused a French extradition request for Astiz, who was standing trial in Buenos Aires (see below). (In 1990 Astiz had been convicted in France, *in absentia*, and sentenced to life imprisonment for murder, and in

2007 he was convicted of the same crime, again *in absentia*, in an Italian court.) In February 1998 the Swiss authorities revealed that they had discovered a number of Swiss bank accounts belonging to former Argentine military officials, including Astiz and Antonio Domingo Bussi, then Governor of Tucumán. It was rumoured that the accounts contained funds stolen by the military regime from Argentines who had been detained or 'disappeared'. In April 2000 a mass grave was discovered in Lomas de Zamora, containing the remains of about 90 victims of the 'dirty war'. In September 2001 Videla was ordered to stand trial for the abduction of 72 foreigners under 'Plan Condor', an alleged scheme among right-wing dictators in Argentina, Chile, Uruguay and Bolivia to eradicate leftist political opponents living in exile during the 1970s. In July 2002 former dictator Gen. Galtieri was arrested, along with at least 30 others, on charges relating to the torture and murder of 20 members of the left-wing Montoneros guerrilla group in 1980. In September 2002 he was imprisoned, along with 24 other former military officers, pending trial. (Galtieri remained under house arrest until his death in January 2003.)

In August 2003 the Senado approved legislation that would allow the annulment of the Punto Final and Obediencia Debida laws (adopted in 1986 and 1987, respectively), and ratified a UN Convention that ostensibly removed all constitutional limitations on human rights prosecutions. In August 2004 the Supreme Court ruled, in reference to the assassination in Buenos Aires in 1974 of Carlos Prats (the former head of the Chilean army) and his wife, that crimes against humanity have no statutory limitations. In June 2005 the Supreme Court voted to annul the Punto Final and Obediencia Debida laws.

In September 2006 Miguel Etchecolatz, a former senior police officer, was sentenced to life imprisonment after being convicted on charges of murder, torture and kidnapping during the 'dirty war'. However, the day before he was sentenced, an important witness in the case, Jorge Julio López, went missing, prompting fears that López's disappearance was linked to his testimony, and was intended to deter others from giving evidence in future cases. In April 2010 Bignone and six other former officials and military officers were convicted of charges related to the abduction, torture and killing of 56 government opponents during the 'dirty war'; Bignone was sentenced to 25 years' imprisonment. In December, moreover, after a five-month trial in Córdoba, Videla and several co-defendants received life sentences for their involvement in the murder in 1976 of 31 political prisoners. Bignone and Videla, who were both to serve their sentences in civilian prisons, rather than in military institutions or under house arrest, stood trial accused of further human rights abuses in 2011. Their trial, together with former navy chief Vice-Adm. Rubén Oscar Franco and five other defendants, on charges related to the abduction and illegal adoption of some 30 children whose parents had died or disappeared during the dictatorship, commenced in February, while Bignone received a life sentence for murder in a separate case in April. As many as 300 infants born in special holding centres during the 'dirty war' were believed to have been abducted by the military and police, and in November 2009 the Congreso had approved a law compelling those thought to have been illegally adopted to undergo DNA tests in order to establish their true parentage. In October 2011, following a 22-month trial, Alfredo Aziz was among 12 former military officials sentenced to life imprisonment after being found guilty of perpetrating torture, murder and forced disappearance at a naval school that was used as a secret detention facility during the dictatorship; four other defendants received prison sentences ranging from 18 to 25 years, while two were acquitted.

In 1996 a criminal investigation was begun in Spain regarding the torture, disappearance and killing of several hundred Spanish citizens in Argentina during 1976–83. A parallel investigation was initiated into the abduction of 54 children of Spanish victims during this period. In October 1997 Adolfo Scilingo, a former Argentine military official, was arrested in Madrid after admitting to his involvement in the 'dirty war'. Although he later retracted his confession, claiming it was given under duress, in April 2005 Scilingo was convicted of crimes against humanity, including the torture and murder of 30 prisoners; he was sentenced to 640 years' imprisonment. The Argentine Government expressed its approval of the verdict. During 1997 a Spanish High Court judge issued international arrest warrants for several other Argentine officers, including Adm. Massera and Gen. Galtieri. Following further investigations, in November 1999 international arrest warrants on charges of genocide, terrorism and torture were issued for 98 of those accused. In December the Spanish magistrate Baltasar Garzón issued international arrest warrants for 49 people, including former military presidents Videla and Galtieri, effectively confining them to Argentine territory. However, in January 2000 a federal judge refused to extradite them. In October 2004 the Supreme Court ruled that the state should pay compensation to Susana Yofre de Vaca Nervaja, who fled Argentina after her husband and son were killed by military personnel during the 'dirty war', as exile of this nature was equivalent to illegal detention. This ruling was widely expected to set a precedent for claims for compensation to be brought by others, thought to number between 10,000 and 50,000, who also fled Argentina during the years of military rule.

Foreign Affairs

Regional relations

In August 1991 Argentina and Chile reached a settlement regarding claims to territory in the Antarctic region; however, the sovereignty of the territory remained under dispute, necessitating the signing of an additional protocol in late 1996. In December 1998 the Presidents of the two countries signed a new agreement on the border demarcation of the contested 'continental glaciers' territory in the Antarctic region (despite the 1991 treaty); the accord became effective in June 1999 following ratification by the Argentine and Chilean legislatures. In February 1999 President Carlos Saúl Menem and the Chilean President, Eduardo Frei Ruiz-Tagle, signed a significant defence agreement and issued a joint declaration on both countries' commitment to the consolidation of their friendship. Relations between the two countries were strained in mid-2004, however, following President Néstor Carlos Kirchner's decision to reduce exports of gas to Chile by some 25% in order to meet a critical shortfall in stocks for domestic consumption. Following the election of Michelle Bachelet Jeria to the Chilean presidency in January 2006, a bilateral group was established to resolve more effectively any future disagreements over energy matters. Nevertheless, in July the Government of Chile reacted angrily to Argentina's decision to introduce a surcharge on motor fuel sold to vehicles with foreign licence plates. In spite of this, in December the two countries announced the formation of a joint military force, the 'Cruz del Sur', which would participate in UN peacekeeping operations. Bilateral relations were strained by the decision, in September 2010, of Argentina's national refugee commission to grant political asylum to Sergio Galvarino Apablaza Guerra, a former Chilean guerrilla leader whose extradition was sought by the Chilean authorities to answer murder and kidnapping charges.

Argentina was a founder member of the Southern Common Market, Mercosur (Mercado Común del Sur, see p. 428), which came into effect on 1 January 1995. Mercosur, comprising Argentina, Brazil, Paraguay and Uruguay, removed customs barriers on 80%–85% of mutually exchanged goods, and was intended to lead to the eventual introduction of a common external tariff. Following a series of trade disputes within Mercosur, particularly between Argentina and Brazil, the two largest members, a document, known as the 'Buenos Aires Consensus', was signed in 2003 by President Carlos Néstor Kirchner and his Brazilian counterpart, Luiz Inácio Lula da Silva. The agreement was to study the creation of common institutions for resolving trade disputes, in addition to the eventual establishment of a Mercosur legislature. A tribunal responsible for ruling on disputes duly commenced operations in mid-2004, while the Mercosur parliament, Parlasur, was inaugurated in 2007. Mercosur heads of state agreed on a new common customs code at a summit meeting held in San Juan, in August 2010.

From 2005 relations between Argentina and Uruguay were strained owing to the latter's decision to allow the construction of two pulp mills on the Uruguayan side of the River Uruguay by Botnia of Finland and Ence of Spain. The Argentine Government opposed the project on environmental grounds, although a World Bank study released in April 2006 concluded that the mills posed no threat to the environment. Argentina, however, demanded an independent assessment (the mills were partly financed by the World Bank) and ecological groups from Argentina erected roadblocks across bridges spanning the river. Following the failure of bilateral negotiations in April, Argentina filed a complaint with the International Court of Justice (ICJ) in The Hague, Netherlands, claiming that the mills violated the Statute of the River Uruguay signed by both countries in 1975. An initial finding by the ICJ in July 2006 dismissed Argentina's demand that the construction be halted, ruling that it would not cause irreversible damage to the environment. In September, however, the ongoing dispute prompted Ence to cancel its plans for a mill, although construction of the Botnia plant continued. Also in September, a three-member arbitration panel appointed by Mercosur ruled that Argentina had failed to adhere to the trade agreement's free trade clauses by not preventing the ongoing roadblocks, although it also ruled that it had not done so intentionally. A final ruling by the World Bank, concurring with Uruguayan claims that the project met all international environmental standards, was dismissed by Argentina in October, and prompted further roadblocks across the bridges. The inauguration of the Botnia mill in September 2007 provoked large-scale demonstrations by Argentine protesters, and the Argentine roadblocks remained in place following the start of operations at the plant in November. The ICJ issued its ruling on the dispute in April 2010, concluding that Uruguay had breached its procedural obligations under the Statute of the River Uruguay by failing to inform Argentina of its plans for the construction of the mills, but had not violated its environmental obligations. The Court rejected Argentina's request for the dismantling of the plant in operation (now owned by UPM of Finland) and for compensation for alleged damage to its economy. In July President Cristina Fernández de Kirchner and Uruguayan President José Mujica, who had sought to improve relations with Argentina since taking office in March, signed an agreement on the establishment of a bilateral scientific committee to monitor the environmental impact of all industrial and agricultural operations on the banks of the River Uruguay. A further technical agreement, on the details of the joint monitoring programme, was signed by the two Governments in November. At a meeting in Buenos Aires in August 2011, Fernández and Mujica signed a series of bilateral agreements aimed at strengthening relations in a number of areas, including transport infrastructure and the business sector.

Other external relations

Full diplomatic relations were restored with the United Kingdom in February 1990, following senior-level negotiations in Madrid, Spain. The improvement in relations between Argentina and the United Kingdom prompted the European Community (now European Union, EU, see p. 276) to sign a new five-year trade and co-operation agreement with Argentina in April. In November Argentina and the United Kingdom concluded an agreement for the joint administration of a comprehensive protection programme for the lucrative South Atlantic fishing region. Subsequent agreements to regulate fishing in the area were made in 1992 and 1993. The question of sovereignty over the disputed islands was not resolved. The results of seismic investigations in late 1993, which indicated rich petroleum deposits in the region, further complicated the issue. In 1998 relations with the United Kingdom were strained by the presentation of draft legislation to the Congreso on the imposition of sanctions on petroleum companies and fishing vessels operating in Falkland Island waters without Argentine authorization. Although a comprehensive agreement on exploration was signed by both countries in September 1995, negotiations on fishing rights in the region remained tense. Relations between Argentina and the United Kingdom improved in January 1997 when the two countries agreed to resume negotiations on a long-term fisheries accord. Moreover, in October 1998 President Menem made an official visit to the United Kingdom, during which he held talks with the British Prime Minister, Tony Blair, on issues including the arms embargo, defence, trade and investment. In late 1998 the United Kingdom partially lifted its arms embargo against Argentina. In July 1999 an agreement was reached providing for an end to the ban on Argentine citizens visiting the Falkland Islands and for the restoration of air links between the islands and South America, with stop-overs in Argentina to be introduced from October. In September Argentine and British government officials reached an understanding on co-operation against illegal fishing in the South Atlantic, and naval forces from both countries held joint exercises in the region in November. Tensions between the two countries were exacerbated in March 2007, when Argentina withdrew from the 1995 agreement on petroleum exploration, and again in May 2008, when the Argentine Government accused the United Kingdom of 'illegitimately' issuing licences for hydrocarbon exploration and extraction activities around the Falkland Islands. In February 2010, as oil companies prepared to commence drilling in the waters around the Islands, President Cristina Fernández de Kirchner decreed that ships entering Argentine waters en route to the Falklands would be required to obtain prior permission. One week later, after the drilling operations proceeded as planned, the Minister of Foreign Affairs, International Trade and Worship, Jorge Taiana, formally requested the UN to initiate negotiations with the United Kingdom over the sovereignty of the islands. The United Kingdom's announcement in October that it was to conduct military exercises, including the firing of missiles off the coast of the Falklands provoked strong protests from the Argentine Government, although the British Government insisted that the manoeuvres were 'routine'. Meanwhile, Argentina's Mercosur partners demonstrated their support for Argentine sovereignty over the Falklands, with Uruguay and Brazil refusing to allow British naval vessels to refuel at their ports en route to the islands in September 2010 and January 2011, respectively. In December 2011, moreover, at a summit held in Montevideo, Uruguay, Mercosur heads of state decided to prevent vessels flying the flag of the Falkland Islands from entering their ports. Fernández reiterated demands that the British Government agree to engage in talks on the status of the islands.

CONSTITUTION AND GOVERNMENT

A new Constitution was introduced in 1994. Executive power is vested in the President, who is elected directly for a four-year term, renewable only once. Legislative power is vested in the bicameral Congress (Congreso): the Chamber of Deputies (Cámara de Diputados) has 257 members, elected by universal adult suffrage for a term of four years (with approximately one-half of the seats renewable every two years); the Senate (Senado) has 72 members, with three members drawn from each of the 23 provinces and the City of Buenos Aires. Senators are elected for a six-year term (with one-third of the seats renewable every two years). The President is directly elected for a four-year term, renewable once. Each province has its own elected Governor and legislature, concerned with all matters not delegated to the federal Government. Judicial power is exercised by the Supreme Court and all other competent tribunals.

For administrative purposes Argentina comprises 23 provinces together with the Autonomous City (formerly the Federal District) of Buenos Aires. The provinces are generally subdivided into departments and municipalities.

REGIONAL AND INTERNATIONAL CO-OPERATION

Argentina is a member of the Organization of American States (see p. 394), the Inter-American Development Bank (see p. 334), the Latin American Integration Association (ALADI, see p. 362) and of Mercosur (Mercado Común del Sur, see p. 428). In December 2004 Argentina was one of 12 countries that were signatories to the agreement, signed in Cusco, Peru, creating the South American Community of Nations (Comunidad Sudamericana de Naciones, which was renamed the Union of South American Nations—Unión de Naciones Suramericanas, UNASUR, see p. 466, in April 2007), intended to promote greater regional economic integration. The country was also a member of the Community of Latin American and Caribbean States (see p. 462), which was formally inaugurated in December 2011

Argentina was a founder member of the UN in 1945. As a contracting party to the General Agreement on Tariffs and Trade, Argentina joined the World Trade Organization (see p. 433) on its establishment in 1995. The country is a member of the Group of 15 (G15, see p. 450), of the Group of 20 (G20, see p. 454), and of the Group of 77 (see p. 450) organization of developing states.

ECONOMIC AFFAIRS

In 2010, according to estimates by the World Bank, Argentina's gross national income (GNI), measured at average 2008–10 prices, was US $343,636m., equivalent to $8,500 per head (or $15,250 on an international purchasing-power parity basis). During 2001–10, it was estimated, Argentina's population increased at an average rate of 0.9% per year, while gross domestic product (GDP) per head increased, in real terms, by an average of 4.4% per year. According to official estimates, overall GDP increased, in real terms, at an average annual rate of 5.4% in 2001–10; growth was just 0.9% in 2009, but real GDP grew by 9.2% in 2010.

Agriculture (including forestry and fishing) contributed 10.0% of GDP in 2010. The sector engaged 7.1% of the total labour force in mid-2012, according to FAO estimates. The principal cash crops are wheat, maize, sugar cane and soybeans. Beef production is also important. During 2001–10, according to official estimates, agricultural GDP increased at an average annual rate of 3.4%; the GDP of the sector declined by 15.7% in 2009, owing to the worst drought in 100 years, but it grew by 28.5% in 2010.

Industry (including mining, manufacturing, construction and power) engaged 23.7% of the employed labour force in 2006 and contributed an estimated 30.9% of GDP in 2010. During 2001–10, according to official estimates, industrial GDP increased, in real terms, at an average annual rate of 5.6%; sectoral GDP declined by 1.2% in 2009, but increased by 7.8% in 2010.

Mining contributed an estimated 3.6% of GDP in 2010, and engaged 0.4% of the employed labour force in 2006. Although Argentina used to possess substantial deposits of petroleum and natural gas, as well as steam coal and lignite, few hydrocarbon deposits have been discovered since the mid-1990s. According to official estimates, the GDP of the mining sector remained constant during 2001–10; the sector's GDP decreased by 1.5% in 2010.

Manufacturing contributed an estimated 20.5% of GDP in 2010, and employed 14.0% of the working population in 2006. During 2001–10, according to official estimates, manufacturing GDP increased, in real terms, at an average annual rate of 5.8%; manufacturing GDP decreased by 0.5% in 2009, but increased by 9.8% in 2010.

The construction sector contributed 5.6% of GDP in 2010, and engaged 8.8% of the employed labour force in 2006. During 2001–10, according to official estimates, the GDP of the sector increased at an average annual rate of 7.4%; construction GDP decreased by 3.8% in 2009, but increased by 5.2% in 2010.

Energy is derived principally from thermal power (largely fuelled by natural gas), responsible for the production of 65.3% of net national production in 2008. Hydroelectricity accounted for 24.9% of Argentina's total energy production in the same year, while the country's two nuclear power stations produced 6.0%. In 2010 imports of mineral fuels comprised an estimated 7.4% of the country's total imports.

Services engaged 75.2% of the employed labour force in 2006 and accounted for an estimated 59.1% of GDP in 2010. According to official estimates, the combined GDP of the service sectors increased, in real terms, at an average rate of 5.0% per year during 2001–09; sectoral GDP increased by 7.6% in 2010.

In 2010 Argentina recorded a visible trade surplus of US $14,266m., and there was a surplus of $3,016m. on the current account of the balance of payments. In 2010, according to provisional figures, the principal source of imports was Brazil (31.3%), followed by the People's Republic of China, the USA, and Germany. Brazil was also the principal recipient of exports, accounting for 21.2% of total exports in that year, followed by the People's Republic of China, Chile and the USA. The principal exports in 2010, according to provisional figures, were vehicles (11.7% of the total value) followed by mineral fuels and lubricants. The principal imports were vehicles (17.9% of the total value) and machines and mechanical appliances.

In 2010 a consolidated central government budgetary surplus of 12,905m. new pesos was recorded. Argentina's general government gross debt was 707,848m. new pesos in 2010, equivalent to 49.1% of GDP. Argentina's total external debt in 2009 was US $120,183m., of which $72,923m. was public and publicly guaranteed debt. The cost of servicing long-term public and publicly guaranteed debt and repayments to the IMF was equivalent to 7.1% of the value of exports of goods, services and income (excluding workers' remittances). The annual rate of inflation averaged 10.7% in 2001–10; consumer prices increased by 9.8% in 2010. According to labour force survey figures, the national unemployment rate was 7.4% in the first quarter of 2011.

The country recovered well from its major default on sovereign debt to the IMF in 2002. None the less, fears of a second default on its sovereign debt in late 2008 led to significant outflows of domestically and internationally held capital, while the exchange rate declined sharply as investors converted their peso holdings into dollars. The Government of Cristina Fernández de Kirchner announced a series of measures intended to alleviate the impact of economic downturn, including a major programme of public works, various tax incentives, the extension of full employment status to workers in the informal sector, and a plan to improve access to credit. The risk of default receded in 2009, following the rise in the price of soybeans, one of Argentina's principal commodities, and in 2010 the Government announced that it had successfully restructured 66% of the $18,300m. of outstanding defaulted debt that Argentina owed to creditors. A strong performance by the agricultural sector, in addition to increasing consumption and investment, as well as growing demand from Brazil and China, Argentina's principal trading partners, resulted in rapid economic growth, of 9.2%, in 2010. GDP growth slowed to an estimated 8.3% in 2011, and a further deceleration, to 5.1%, was forecast for 2012. Rising inflationary pressures continued to be of concern, as did the risk of further capital flight, amid fears of a rapid devaluation of the peso. In October 2011 the Government implemented economic measures aimed at stabilizing the exchange rate and at curbing the outflow of capital, imposing restrictions on foreign exchange transactions and forcing mining and energy companies to repatriate their export revenues. The announcement, in April 2012, that the Fernández administration was to expropriate the majority of shares in the formerly state-run oil company Repsol YPF prompted disquiet among the international community and was expected to lead to a decline in foreign investment.

PUBLIC HOLIDAYS

2013: 1 January (New Year's Day), 24 March (Truth and Justice Memorial Day), 29 March (Good Friday), 2 April (Veterans' Day and Tribute to the Fallen of the Falklands (Malvinas) War), 1 May (Labour Day), 25 May (Anniversary of the 1810 Revolution), 17 June (Death of Gen. Manuel Belgrano), 9 July (Independence Day), 19 August (Death of Gen. José de San Martín), 14 October (for Columbus Day), 8 December (Immaculate Conception), 25 December (Christmas).

Statistical Survey

Sources (unless otherwise stated): Instituto Nacional de Estadística y Censos, Avda Julio A. Roca 609, C1067AAB Buenos Aires; tel. (11) 4349-9200; fax (11) 4349-9601; e-mail ces@indec.mecon.gov.ar; internet www.indec.mecon.ar; Banco Central de la República Argentina, Reconquista 266, C1003ABF Buenos Aires; tel. (11) 4348-3500; fax (11) 4348-3955; e-mail sistema@bcra.gov.ar; internet www.bcra.gov.ar.

Area and Population

AREA, POPULATION AND DENSITY

Area (sq km)	2,780,403*
Population (census results)†	
17–18 November 2001	36,260,130
27 October 2010	
Males	19,523,766
Females	20,593,330
Total	40,117,096
Population (official estimates at mid-year)	
2011	40,900,496
2012	41,281,631
Density (per sq km) at mid-2012	14.8

* 1,073,519 sq miles. The figure excludes the Falkland Islands (Islas Malvinas) and Antarctic territory claimed by Argentina.

† Figures exclude adjustment for underenumeration.

POPULATION BY AGE AND SEX

(at 2010 census)

	Males	Females	Total
0–14	5,195,096	5,027,221	10,222,317
15–64	12,654,528	13,135,603	25,790,131
65 and over	1,674,142	2,430,506	4,104,648
Total	19,523,766	20,593,330	40,117,096

ADMINISTRATIVE DIVISIONS

(official estimates at mid-2012)

	Area (sq km)	Population	Density (per sq km)	Capital
Buenos Aires—City	203	3,072,426	15,135.1	—
Buenos Aires—Province	307,571	15,571,686	50.6	La Plata
Catamarca	102,602	420,314	4.1	San Fernando del Valle de Catamarca
Chaco	99,633	1,090,451	10.9	Resistencia
Chubut	224,686	480,592	2.1	Rawson
Córdoba	165,321	3,451,910	20.9	Córdoba
Corrientes	88,199	1,058,161	12.0	Corrientes
Entre Ríos	78,781	1,307,740	16.6	Paraná
Formosa	72,066	572,060	7.9	Formosa
Jujuy	53,219	716,978	13.5	San Salvador de Jujuy
La Pampa	143,440	349,240	2.4	Santa Rosa
La Rioja	89,680	369,727	4.1	La Rioja
Mendoza	148,827	1,800,895	12.1	Mendoza
Misiones	29,801	1,145,600	38.4	Posadas
Neuquén	94,078	582,560	6.2	Neuquén
Río Negro	203,013	609,553	3.0	Viedma
Salta	155,488	1,311,499	8.4	Salta
San Juan	89,651	734,301	8.2	San Juan
San Luis	76,748	476,191	6.2	San Luis
Santa Cruz	243,943	242,275	1.0	Río Gallegos
Santa Fe	133,007	3,326,511	25.0	Santa Fe
Santiago del Estero	136,351	902,063	6.6	Santiago del Estero
Tierra del Fuego	21,571	141,303	6.6	Ushuaia
Tucumán	22,524	1,547,595	68.7	San Miguel de Tucumán
Total	2,780,403	41,281,631	14.8	—

PRINCIPAL TOWNS

(population at 2001 census)*

Buenos Aires (capital)	2,776,138	Malvinas Argentinas†	290,691
Córdoba	1,267,521	Berazategui†	287,913
La Matanza†	1,255,288	Bahía Blanca†	284,776
Rosario	908,163	Resistencia	274,490
Lomas de Zamora†	591,345	Vicente López†	274,082
La Plata†	574,369	San Miguel†	253,086
General Pueyrredón†	564,056	Posadas	252,981
San Miguel de Tucumán	527,150	Esteban Echeverría†	243,974
Quilmes†	518,788	Paraná	235,967
Almirante Brown†	515,556	Pilar†	232,463
Merlo†	469,985	San Salvador de Jujuy	231,229
Salta	462,051	Santiago del Estero	230,614
Lanús†	453,082	José C. Paz†	230,208
General San Martín†	403,107	Guaymallén	223,365
Moreno†	380,503	Neuquén	201,868
Santa Fe	368,668	Formosa	198,074
Florencio Varela†	348,970	Godoy Cruz	182,563
Tres de Febrero†	336,467	Escobar†	178,155
Avellaneda†	328,980	Hurlingham†	172,245
Corrientes	314,546	Las Heras	169,248
Morón†	309,380	Ituzaingó	158,121
Tigre†	301,223	San Luis	153,322
San Isidro†	291,505	San Fernando†	151,131

* In each case, the figure refers to the city proper. At the 2001 census the population of the Buenos Aires agglomeration was 12,045,921.

† Settlement within the Province of Buenos Aires.

2010 census (population of capital and settlements within the Province of Buenos Aires at 27 October): Buenos Aires (capital) 2,890,151; La Matanza 1,775,816; La Plata 654,324; General Pueyrredón 618,989; Lomas de Zamora 616,279; Quilmes 582,943; Almirante Brown 552,902; Merlo 528,494; Lanús 459,263; Moreno 452,505; Florencio Varela 426,005; General San Martín 414,196; Tigre 376,381; Avellaneda 342,677; Tres de Febrero 340,071; Berazategui 324,244; Malvinas Argentinas 322,375; Morón 321,109; Bahía Blanca 301,572; Esteban Echeverría 300,959; Pilar 299,077; San Isidro 292,878; San Miguel 276,190; Vicente López 269,420; José C. Paz 268,981; Escobar 213,619; Hurlingham 181,241; San Fernando 163,240.

BIRTHS, MARRIAGES AND DEATHS

	Registered live births		Marriages		Registered deaths	
	Number	Rate (per 1,000)	Number	Rate (per 1,000)	Number	Rate (per 1,000)
2002	694,684	18.3	122,343	3.3	291,190	7.7
2003	697,952	18.4	129,049	3.4	302,064	8.0
2004	736,261	19.3	128,212	3.4	294,051	7.7
2005	712,220	18.5	132,720	3.4	293,529	7.6
2006	696,451	17.9	134,496	3.5	292,313	7.5
2007	700,792	17.8	136,437	3.5	315,852	8.0
2008	746,460	18.8	133,060	3.3	302,133	7.6
2009	745,336	18.6	126,081	3.1	304,525	7.6

Sources: Dirección de Estadísticas e Información en Salud (DEIS) and UN, *Demographic Yearbook* and *Population and Vital Statistics Report*.

Life expectancy (years at birth, WHO estimates): 75 (males 72; females 79) in 2009 (Source: WHO, *World Health Statistics*).

ECONOMICALLY ACTIVE POPULATION

(labour force survey of 31 urban agglomerations, persons aged 10 years and over, 2006)

	Males	Females	Total
Agriculture, hunting and forestry	59,242	13,640	72,882
Fishing	8,215	821	9,036
Mining and quarrying	34,127	5,687	39,814
Manufacturing	988,343	422,321	1,410,664
Electricity, gas and water	38,066	5,991	44,057
Construction	854,764	29,917	884,681
Wholesale and retail trade; repair of motor vehicles, motorcycles and personal and household goods	1,263,477	755,160	2,018,637
Hotels and restaurants	213,854	166,975	380,829
Transport, storage and communications	557,431	86,613	644,044
Financial intermediation	95,938	93,497	189,435
Real estate, renting and business activities	528,349	281,460	809,809
Public administration and defence; compulsory social security	444,379	324,337	768,716
Education	185,900	620,900	806,800
Health and social work	163,470	426,735	590,205
Other community, social and personal services	317,127	229,607	546,734
Private households with employed persons	18,151	778,801	796,952
Extra-territorial organizations and bodies	2,031	164	2,195
Sub-total	5,772,864	4,242,626	10,015,490
Activities not adequately described	13,854	11,161	25,015
Total employed	5,786,718	4,253,787	10,040,505
Unemployed	488,935	560,263	1,049,198
Total labour force	6,275,653	4,814,050	11,089,703

2007 (labour force survey of 31 urban agglomerations at January–March, '000 persons aged 10 years and over): Total employed 10,052; Unemployed 1,095; Total labour force 11,147.

2008 (labour force survey of 31 agglomerations at January–March, '000 persons aged 10 years and over): Total employed 10,216; Unemployed 938; Total labour force 11,154.

2009 (labour force survey of 31 agglomerations at January–March, '000 persons aged 10 years and over): Total employed 10,370; Unemployed 948; Total labour force 11,318.

2010 (labour force survey of 31 agglomerations at January–March, '000 persons aged 10 years and over): Total employed 10,467; Unemployed 944; Total labour force 11,411.

2011 (labour force survey of 31 agglomerations at January–March, '000 persons aged 10 years and over): Total employed 10,605; Unemployed 846; Total labour force 11,451.

Health and Welfare

KEY INDICATORS

Total fertility rate (children per woman, 2009)	2.2
Under-5 mortality rate (per 1,000 live births, 2009)	15
HIV (% of persons aged 15–49, 2009)	0.5
Physicians (per 1,000 head, 1998)	3.0
Hospital beds (per 1,000 head, 2000)	4.1
Health expenditure (2008): US $ per head (PPP)	1,062
Health expenditure (2008): % of GDP	7.4
Health expenditure (2008): public (% of total)	71.3
Access to water (% of persons, 2008)	97
Access to sanitation (% of persons, 2008)	90
Total carbon dioxide emissions ('000 metric tons, 2007)	183,577.4
Carbon dioxide emissions per head (metric tons, 2007)	4.6
Human Development Index (2011): ranking	45
Human Development Index (2011): value	0.797

For sources and definitions, see explanatory note on p. vi.

Agriculture

PRINCIPAL CROPS

('000 metric tons)

	2008	2009	2010
Wheat	8,508	8,851	14,915
Rice, paddy	1,246	1,334	1,241
Barley	1,690	1,365	2,983
Maize	22,017	13,121	22,677
Rye	34	25	44
Oats	291	182	660
Sorghum	2,937	1,471	3,629
Potatoes*	1,900	1,950	2,001
Sweet potatoes*	347	340	341
Cassava (Manioc)*	163	180	181
Sugar cane*	30,000	29,000	29,000
Beans, dry	337	313	338
Soybeans (Soya beans)	46,238	30,993	52,677
Groundnuts, with shell	625	605	611
Olives*	150	160	165
Sunflower seed	4,650	2,483	2,221
Artichokes*	91	90	85
Tomatoes*	701	708	698
Pumpkins, squash and gourds*	285	333	327
Chillies and peppers, green*	139	140	145
Onions, dry*	678	650	695
Garlic*	125	120	129
Carrots and turnips*	241	235	224
Watermelons*	128	121	127
Cantaloupes and other melons*	76	75	76
Bananas*	180	170	171
Oranges	943	899	833
Tangerines, mandarins, clementines and satsumas	411	402	424
Lemons and limes	1,362	1,426	1,113
Grapefruit and pomelos	244	237	189
Apples*	950	1,027	851
Pears	740*	700	704*
Peaches and nectarines*	309	291	318
Plums and sloes*	136	155	150
Grapes	2,822	2,182	2,617
Tea	80	72	88
Mate	238	228	250
Tobacco, unmanufactured	130	136	123*

* FAO estimate(s).

Aggregate production ('000 metric tons, may include official, semi-official or estimated data): Total cereals 36,760 in 2008, 26,382 in 2009, 46,204 in 2010; Total roots and tubers 2,410 in 2008, 2,470 in 2009, 2,523 in 2010; Total vegetables (incl. melons) 3,200 in 2008, 3,154 in 2009, 3,215 in 2010; Total fruits (excl. melons) 8,170 in 2008, 7,567 in 2009, 7,446 in 2010.

Source: FAO.

LIVESTOCK

('000 head, year ending September)

	2008	2009	2010
Horses*	3,680	3,680	3,680
Asses*	98	98	98
Mules*	185	185	185
Cattle	57,583	54,464	48,950
Pigs*	2,270	2,270	2,270
Sheep*	15,700	15,800	15,800
Goats*	4,250	4,250	4,250
Chickens*	96,000	96,000	96,000
Ducks*	2,450	2,450	2,450
Geese*	150	150	150
Turkeys	2,950	2,950	2,950

* FAO estimates.

Source: FAO.

LIVESTOCK PRODUCTS
('000 metric tons)

	2008	2009	2010
Cattle meat	3,134	3,378	2,630
Sheep meat*	46	47	46
Pig meat	274	289	281
Horse meat	40	38	30
Chicken meat	1,400	1,501	1,598
Cows' milk	10,320	10,366	10,502
Butter and ghee*	58	51	51
Cheese*	491	508	580
Hen eggs	495†	507†	505*
Honey	72	62	59
Wool, greasy	65	65	54

* FAO estimate(s).
† Unofficial figure.

Source: FAO.

Forestry

ROUNDWOOD REMOVALS
('000 cubic metres, excl. bark)

	2006	2007	2008
Sawlogs, veneer logs and logs for sleepers	3,486	2,920	1,889
Pulpwood	5,514	5,744	6,428
Other industrial wood	499	590	567
Fuel wood	4,372	4,297	4,652
Total	13,871	13,551	13,536

2009–10: Production assumed to be unchanged from 2008 (FAO estimates).

Source: FAO.

SAWNWOOD PRODUCTION
('000 cubic metres, incl. railway sleepers)

	2006	2007	2008
Coniferous (softwood)	1,078	822	470
Broadleaved (hardwood)	1,025	694	485
Total	2,103	1,516	955

2009–10: Production assumed to be unchanged from 2008 (FAO estimates).

Source: FAO.

Fishing

('000 metric tons, live weight)

	2007	2008	2009
Capture	985.4	995.1	859.9
Southern blue whiting	19.0	19.8	21.7
Argentine hake	301.7	263.3	280.7
Patagonian grenadier	98.8	110.3	110.7
Argentine red shrimp	47.6	47.4	53.6
Patagonian scallop	53.7	58.7	80.8
Argentine shortfin squid	233.1	255.5	71.4
Aquaculture	3.0	2.7*	2.6*
Total catch	988.4	997.8*	862.5*

* FAO estimate.

Note: The data exclude aquatic animals, recorded by number rather than by weight. The number of minke whales caught was 1 in 2008. The number of dolphins and toothed whales caught was 1 in 2007; 27 in 2008; 112 in 2009. The number of broad-nosed and spectacled caimans caught was 7,208 in 2007; 4,838 in 2008; 10,831 in 2009.

Source: FAO.

Mining

('000 metric tons unless otherwise indicated)

	2005	2006	2007
Crude petroleum ('000 cu metres)	38,323	38,249	37,175
Natural gas (million cu metres)	48,738	51,665	50,891
Lead ore*	10.7	12.1†	17.0†
Zinc ore*	30.2	29.8†	27.0†
Lithium‡	5.9	6.3	6.7
Silver ore (kg)*	263,766	245,124†	255,567†
Copper ore*	187.3	180.1†	180.2†
Gold ore (kg)*§	27,904	44,131	42,021
Boron	632.8	533.5†	669.6†
Gypsum (crude)	1,073.3	1,202.8†	1,226.5†
Clay (common)	6,373.7	6,832.2†	8,429.9†
Salt	1,845.6	1,917.7†	2,357.7†
Sand:			
for construction§	20,194.1	21,143.5	28,381.3
Silica (glass) sand	461.2	446.2†	456.2†
Limestone	12,267.0	12,993.4†	16,152.3†
Stone (various crushed)§	11,533.5	12,692.4	22,586.5
Rhodochrosite (kg)	118,200	78,832†	50,593†
Gemstones (kg)	80,579	53,355†	12,745†

* Figures refer to the metal content of ores and concentrates.
† Provisional.
‡ Lithium oxide (Li_2O) content.
§ Estimates.

2008: Crude petroleum 36,523,000 cu m; Natural gas 50,271 million cu m.
2009: Crude petroleum 36,032,000 cu m; Natural gas 48,417 million cu m.

Industry

SELECTED PRODUCTS
('000 metric tons unless otherwise indicated)

	2008	2009	2010
Wheat flour	4,781	4,704	4,895*
Beer (sales, '000 hectolitres)†	18,190	18,640	19,860
Wine (sales, '000 hectolitres)	10,677	10,342	9,753
Cigarettes (sales, million packets)	2,173	2,120	2,102
Paper (excl. newspaper)	1,549	1,557	1,614
Aluminium	394	413	417
Iron (primary)	4,428	2,849	4,098
Crude steel	5,541	4,013	5,138
Rubber tyres for motor vehicles ('000, excl. tractors)	10,977	n.a.	n.a.
Portland cement	9,703	9,385	10,423
Refined petroleum ('000 cu metres)*	35,226	33,572	35,877
Ethylene	682	738	640
Urea	882	1,118	942
Ammonia	572	690	590
Washing machines ('000 units)	765	908	1,103
Home refrigerators ('000 units)	451	642	750
Air conditioning units (domestic, '000)	1,374	571	1,138
Motor vehicles ('000)	399	380	508

* Provisional figure(s).
† Estimates.

Electric energy (million kWh): 115,197 in 2006; 115,428 in 2007; 123,422 in 2008 (Source: UN Industrial Commodity Statistics database).

Finance

CURRENCY AND EXCHANGE RATES

Monetary Units

100 centavos = 1 nuevo peso argentino (new Argentine peso).

Sterling, Dollar and Euro Equivalents (30 December 2011)

£1 sterling = 6.623 new pesos;
US $1 = 4.284 new pesos;
€1 = 5.543 new pesos;
100 new pesos = £15.10 = $23.34 = €18.04.

Average Exchange Rate (new pesos per US $)

2009 3.710
2010 3.896
2011 4.110

Note: From April 1996 to December 2001 the official exchange rate was fixed at US $1 = 99.95 centavos. In January 2002 the Government abandoned this exchange rate and devalued the peso: initially there was a fixed official exchange rate of US $1 = 1.40 new pesos for trade and financial transactions, while a free market rate was applicable to other transactions. In February, however, a unified 'floating' exchange rate system, with the rate to be determined by market conditions, was introduced.

CENTRAL GOVERNMENT BUDGET

(million new pesos)

Revenue	2008	2009	2010
Current revenue	212,740.9	267,203.8	326,242.2
Tax revenue	153,297.4	173,143.3	198,264.8
Social security contributions	46,379.1	64,735.3	88,558.8
Sale of public goods and services	1,024.0	1,220.4	6,186.6
Property income	6,587.9	12,506.0	1,574.9
Other non-tax revenue	3,925.2	4,415.8	29,672.6
Current transfers	1,527.2	11,182.8	1,984.5
Capital revenue	1,382.2	2,289.7	2,596.4
Total	214,123.1	269,493.5	328,838.6

Expenditure	2008	2009	2010
Current expenditure	179,091.4	230,827.8	294,948.7
Consumption expenditure	29,046.6	40,112.3	54,576.7
Remuneration	20,127.3	27,658.1	37,607.9
Goods and services	8,917.5	12,452.0	16,960.0
Other	1.7	2.2	8.8
Property income	22,686.8	28,356.9	26,409.2
Interest	22,684.1	28,350.4	26,401.8
Other income	2.7	6.4	7.4
Social security benefits	65,053.7	85,429.5	106,352.5
Other current expenditure	8.8	7.8	15.4
Current transfers	62,295.6	76,921.3	107,594.9
Private sector	38,899.1	43,949.5	61,948.3
Public sector	22,958.4	32,469.0	45,099.0
External sector	438.1	502.9	547.7
Capital expenditure	26,644.0	33,582.4	46,794.9
Real direct investment	10,092.7	11,298.4	12,883.1
Capital transfers	15,262.5	20,977.5	32,573.0
Financial investment	1,288.8	1,306.5	1,338.7
Total	205,735.4	264,410.3	341,743.6

Note: Budget figures refer to the consolidated accounts of the central Government only.

Source: Oficina Nacional de Presupuesto, Secretaría de Hacienda, Ministerio de Economía, Buenos Aires.

INTERNATIONAL RESERVES

(US $ million at 31 December)

	2008	2009	2010
Gold (national valuation)	1,514	1,932	2,497
IMF special drawing rights	494	3,170	3,114
Foreign exchange	44,360	42,922	46,619
Total	46,368	48,024	52,230

Source: IMF, *International Financial Statistics*.

MONEY SUPPLY

(million new pesos at 31 December)

	2008	2009	2010
Currency outside banks	74,099	86,073	113,554
Demand deposits at commercial banks	37,604	44,996	59,253
Total money	111,703	131,069	172,807

Source: IMF, *International Financial Statistics*.

COST OF LIVING

(Consumer Price Index for Buenos Aires metropolitan area; annual averages; base: April 2008 = 100)

	2008	2009	2010
Food and beverages	100.1	102.9	116.9
Housing and basic services	101.0	104.8	109.7
Clothing	103.2	116.2	131.5
Transport and communications	101.0	112.1	118.2
All items (incl. others)	101.1	107.5	118.0

NATIONAL ACCOUNTS

(million new pesos at current prices, preliminary)

Expenditure on the Gross Domestic Product

	2008	2009	2010
Government final consumption expenditure	138,827	174,002	215,278
Private final consumption expenditure	595,012	667,375	826,794
Increase in stocks*	18,931	3,176	35,468
Gross fixed capital formation	240,486	239,637	317,417
Total domestic expenditure	993,256	1,084,190	1,394,957
Exports of goods and services	252,772	244,569	313,150
Less Imports of goods and services	213,269	183,300	265,451
Gross domestic product (GDP) in market prices	1,032,758	1,145,458	1,442,655
GDP at constant 1993 prices	383,444	386,704	422,130

* Including statistical discrepancy.

Gross Domestic Product by Economic Activity

	2008	2009	2010
Agriculture, forestry and hunting	90,780	77,208	129,882
Fishing	2,399	2,155	2,484
Mining and quarrying	35,688	38,512	47,727
Manufacturing	201,175	224,188	271,665
Electricity, gas and water supply	12,321	13,459	15,716
Construction	56,554	60,158	74,212
Wholesale and retail trade	112,481	128,767	161,325
Hotels and restaurants	25,083	27,349	33,543
Transport, storage and communications	80,279	86,695	107,326
Financial intermediation	48,648	59,845	76,646
Real estate, renting and business activities	104,244	121,024	140,273
Public administration and defence*	58,186	73,170	91,606
Education, health and social work	81,027	97,229	115,803
Other community, social and personal service activities†	38,343	47,884	54,991
Sub-total	947,208	1,057,643	1,323,199
Value-added tax	84,265	90,843	120,152
Import duties	8,988	7,700	11,428
Less Financial intermediation services indirectly measured	7,702	10,728	12,124
GDP in market prices	1,032,758	1,145,458	1,442,655

* Including extra-territorial organizations and bodies.

† Including private households with employed persons.

BALANCE OF PAYMENTS

(US $ million)

	2008	2009	2010
Exports of goods f.o.b.	70,019	55,672	68,134
Imports of goods f.o.b.	–54,596	–37,146	–53,868
Trade balance	15,423	18,526	14,266
Exports of services	12,156	11,038	13,112
Imports of services	–13,440	–12,229	–14,074
Balance on goods and services	14,138	17,335	13,304
Other income received (net)	–7,552	–8,956	–9,942
Balance on goods, services and income	6,586	8,379	3,362
Current transfers (net)	170	2,706	–346
Current balance	6,756	11,085	3,016
Capital account (net)	181	74	78
Net investment in banking sector	1,733	–986	–2,566
Net investment in public sector	–517	–732	2,243
Net investment in private sector	–9,206	–7,685	4,103
Net errors and omissions	1,062	–409	–2,717
Overall balance	9	1,346	4,157

External Trade

PRINCIPAL COMMODITIES

(US $ million)

Imports c.i.f.	2008	2009	2010*
Mineral fuels, lubricants and related products	4,133	2,436	4,188
Paper and cardboard	975	742	1,010
Rubber and manufactures of rubber	1,078	705	1,183
Organic chemicals and related products	3,114	2,030	2,660
Pharmaceutical products	1,141	1,208	1,566
Plastic and manufactures of laminate	2,226	1,750	2,428
Metalliferous ore	1,692	725	1,423
Electrical machinery	6,526	4,972	6,980
Vehicles	9,367	5,778	10,125
Nuclear reactors, boilers, machines and mechanical appliances	9,066	6,086	8,540
Optical instruments and apparatus, etc.	1,090	989	1,227
Total (incl. others)	57,462	38,786	56,502

* Provisional figures.

Exports f.o.b.	2008	2009	2010*
Meat and meat products	1,926	2,066	1,694
Milk and milk products	1,015	810	1,057
Skins and leathers	897	663	1,001
Fish	1,256	1,086	1,306
Fats and oils	7,059	4,479	5,192
Cereals	6,773	3,215	4,621
Oil seeds and oleaginous fruits	4,887	1,981	5,338
Mineral fuels, lubricants and related materials	6,562	5,660	5,386
Mineral by-products	1,235	1,278	1,815
Metalliferous ore	1,856	1,288	1,201
Plastic and manufactures of laminate	1,479	1,225	1,346
Vehicles	6,492	5,376	7,971
Nuclear reactors, boilers and mechanical appliances	1,824	1,539	1,689
Total (incl. others)	70,019	55,672	68,134

* Provisional figures.

PRINCIPAL TRADING PARTNERS

(US $ million)*

Imports c.i.f.	2008	2009	2010†
Brazil‡	17,687	11,819	17,658
Chile‡	952	665	885
China, People's Republic§	7,143	4,823	7,678
France (incl. Monaco)	1,483	811	1,529
Germany	2,534	1,994	3,215
Italy	1,205	850	1,297
Japan	1,378	909	1,191
Mexico	1,595	1,164	1,817
Paraguay	1,783	699	436
Spain	1,054	788	1,024
United Kingdom	545	376	487
USA	7,023	5,183	6,125
Uruguay‡	527	348	587
Total (incl. others)	57,462	38,786	56,502

Exports f.o.b.	2008	2009	2010†
Belgium	543	457	349
Bolivia	607	581	608
Brazil‡	13,272	11,379	14,420
Canada	471	467	1,402
Chile‡	4,713	4,387	4,490
China, People's Republic§	6,562	3,948	6,117
Colombia	810	874	1,302
France (incl. Monaco)	914	446	527
Germany	1,508	1,391	1,832
Italy	1,688	1,501	1,586
Japan	519	493	855
Mexico	1,337	935	1,227
Netherlands	2,962	2,392	2,367
Paraguay	1,088	845	1,154
Peru	1,313	795	1,121
South Africa	1,010	666	879
Spain	2,768	1,852	2,242
United Kingdom	814	762	756
USA	5,402	3,681	3,656
Uruguay‡	1,763	1,608	1,552
Venezuela	1,420	1,043	1,424
Total (incl. others)	70,019	55,672	68,134

* Imports by country of origin; exports by country of destination.
† Provisional figures.
‡ Including free trade zones.
§ Including Hong Kong and Macao.

Transport

RAILWAYS

(traffic)

	2007	2008	2009
Passengers carried ('000)	425,760	450,914	433,420
Freight carried ('000 tons)	24,927	23,619	20,731
Passenger-km (million)	8,248	9,053	8,810
Freight ton-km (million)	12,871	12,025	10,649

ROAD TRAFFIC

('000 motor vehicles in use)

	2003	2004	2005
Passenger cars	4,668	4,926	5,230
Commercial vehicles	1,198	1,684	1,775

Source: UN, *Statistical Yearbook*.

2007 ('000 motor vehicles in use at 31 December): Total vehicles 12,399.9 (Source: IRF, *World Road Statistics*).

SHIPPING

Merchant Fleet
(registered at 31 December)

	2007	2008	2009
Number of vessels	569	576	583
Total displacement ('000 grt)	838.0	785.3	743.4

Source: IHS Fairplay, *World Fleet Statistics*.

International Sea-borne Freight Traffic
('000 metric tons)

	1996	1997	1998
Goods loaded	52,068	58,512	69,372
Goods unloaded	16,728	19,116	19,536

Goods unloaded: 22,992 in 2007; 25,836 in 2008; 16,044 in 2009; 23,736 in 2010.

Source: UN, *Monthly Bulletin of Statistics*.

Total maritime freight handled ('000 metric tons): 152,921 in 2005; 152,074 in 2006; 168,260 in 2007; 169,421 in 2008; 133,001 in 2009 (Source: Dirección Nacional de Puertos).

CIVIL AVIATION

	2007	2008	2009
Kilometres flown (million)	178	186	190
Passengers carried ('000)	14,735	15,105	15,508
Passenger-km (million)	19,537	20,038	21,286
Total freight carried ('000 metric tons)	389	306	219

Tourism

TOURIST ARRIVALS BY REGION

('000 arrivals at Ezeiza International Airport)

	2007	2008	2009
Europe	563.3	614.5	550.0
North America	340.0	346.5	300.4
South America	1,247.1	1,232.7	1,015.8
Brazil	497.7	600.6	456.2
Chile	270.6	190.0	160.6
Total (incl. others)	2,298.1	2,327.2	1,999.5

Tourism receipts (US $ million): 3,045 in 2007; 3,370 in 2008; 2,623 in 2009.

Communications Media

	2008	2009	2010
Telephones ('000 main lines in use)	9,742.8	9,768.1	10,000.0
Mobile cellular telephones ('000 handsets in use)	46,508.8	52,482.8	57,300.0
Internet subscribers ('000)	3,737.4	4,695.9	n.a.
Broadband subscribers ('000)	3,185.3	3,474.1	3,862.4

Personal computers: 3,500,000 (90.4 per 1,000 persons) in 2005.

Television receivers ('000 in use): 11,800 in 2001.

Radio receivers ('000 in use): 24,300 in 1997.

Book production: 13,148 titles in 2001.

Daily newspapers: 184 in 2004 (average circulation 1,363,000).

Sources: mainly UNESCO Institute for Statistics and *Statistical Yearbook*, and International Telecommunication Union.

Education

(2010 unless otherwise indicated)

	Institutions	Teachers	Students
Pre-primary	17,726	112,653	1,553,418
Primary	22,227	334,350	4,637,463
Secondary	21,281*	141,389*	3,679,628
Basic	14,155*	44,210*	2,276,041
Specialized	7,126*	97,179*	1,403,587
Higher			
University†	37	n.a.	1,273,156
Non-university	2,129	20,049	691,007

* 2007.

† 2004.

Source: partly Red Federal de Información Educativa, *Relevamiento 2004* and *Relevamiento 2007*.

Pupil-teacher ratio (primary education, UNESCO estimate): 16.3 in 2007/08 (Source: UNESCO Institute for Statistics).

Adult literacy rate (UNESCO estimates): 97.7% (males 97.7%; females 97.7%) in 2009 (Source: UNESCO Institute for Statistics).

Directory

The Government

HEAD OF STATE

President of the Nation: CRISTINA ELISABET FERNÁNDEZ DE KIRCHNER (took office 10 December 2007, re-elected 23 October 2011).

Vice-President: AMADO BOUDOU.

CABINET
(May 2012)

The Cabinet is composed of members of the Frente para la Victoria-Partido Justicialista alliance.

Cabinet Chief: JUAN MANUEL ABAL MEDINA.

Minister of the Interior: ANÍBAL FLORENCIO RANDAZZO.

Minister of Foreign Affairs, International Trade and Worship: HÉCTOR MARCOS TIMERMAN.

Minister of Defence: ARTURO ANTONIO PURICELLI.

Minister of Economy and Public Finance: HERNÁN LORENZINO.

Minister of Industry: DÉBORA ADRIANA GIORGI.

Minister of Tourism: CARLOS ENRIQUE MEYER.

Minister of Education: ALBERTO ESTANISLAO SILEONI.

Minister of Science, Technology and Productive Innovation: LINO BARAÑAO.

Minister of Labour, Employment and Social Security: CARLOS ALFONSO TOMADA.

Minister of Federal Planning, Public Investment and Services: JULIO MIGUEL DE VIDO.

Minister of Health: JUAN LUIS MANZUR.

Minister of Security: NILDA GARRÉ.

Minister of Justice and Human Rights: JULIO CÉSAR ALAK.

Minister of Social Development: ALICIA MARGARITA KIRCHNER.

Minister of Agriculture, Livestock and Fisheries: NORBERTO YAHUAR.

MINISTRIES

General Secretariat to the Presidency: Balcarce 50, C1064AAB Buenos Aires; tel. and fax (11) 4344-3600; e-mail dgi@presidencia.gov.ar; internet www.secretariageneral.gov.ar.

Office of the Cabinet Chief: Avda Julio Argentino Roca 782, C1067ABP Buenos Aires; tel. (11) 4344-3768; e-mail prensa@jgm.gov.ar; internet www.jgm.gov.ar.

Ministry of Agriculture, Livestock and Fisheries: Avda Paseo Colón 982, C1063ACW Buenos Aires; tel. (11) 4349-2000; fax (11) 4349-2589; internet www.minagri.gob.ar.

Ministry of Defence: Azopardo 250, C1328ADB Buenos Aires; tel. (11) 4346-8800; e-mail mindef@mindef.gov.ar; internet www.mindef.gov.ar.

Ministry of Economy and Public Finance: Hipólito Yrigoyen 250, C1086AAB Buenos Aires; tel. (11) 4349-5000; e-mail ciudadano@mecon.gov.ar; internet www.mecon.gov.ar.

Ministry of Education: Pizzurno 935, C1020ACA Buenos Aires; tel. (11) 4129-1000; e-mail info@me.gov.ar; internet www.me.gov.ar.

Ministry of Federal Planning, Public Investment and Services: Hipólito Yrigoyen 250, 11°, Of. 1112, C1086AAB Buenos Aires; tel. (11) 4349-5000; internet www.minplan.gov.ar.

Ministry of Foreign Affairs, International Trade and Worship: Esmeralda 1212, C1007ABR Buenos Aires; tel. (11) 4819-7000; e-mail webmaster@mrecic.gov.ar; internet www.cancilleria.gov.ar.

Ministry of Health: 9 de Julio 1925, C1073ABA Buenos Aires; tel. (11) 4379-9000; fax (11) 4381-2182; e-mail consultas@msal.gov.ar; internet www.msal.gov.ar.

Ministry of Industry: Hipólito Yrigoyen 250, C1086AAB Buenos Aires; tel. (11) 4349-3000; e-mail prensa@industria.gob.ar; internet www.minprod.gob.ar.

Ministry of the Interior: 25 de Mayo 101/145, C1002ABC Buenos Aires; tel. (11) 4339-0800; fax (11) 4331-6376; e-mail info@mininterior.gov.ar; internet www.mininterior.gov.ar.

Ministry of Justice and Human Rights: Sarmiento 329, C1041AAG Buenos Aires; tel. (11) 5300-4000; e-mail prensa@jus.gov.ar; internet www.jus.gov.ar.

Ministry of Labour, Employment and Social Security: Avda Leandro N. Alem 650, C1001AAO Buenos Aires; tel. (11) 4311-2913; fax (11) 4312-7860; e-mail consultas@trabajo.gov.ar; internet www.trabajo.gov.ar.

Ministry of Science, Technology and Productive Innovation: Avda Córdoba 831, C1054AAH Buenos Aires; tel. (11) 4891-8300; fax (11) 4312-8364; e-mail contacto@mincyt.gov.ar; internet www.mincyt.gov.ar.

Ministry of Security: Gelly y Obes 2289, C1425EMA Buenos Aires; internet www.minseg.gob.ar.

Ministry of Social Development: 9 de Julio 1925, 14°, C1073ABA Buenos Aires; tel. (11) 4379-3648; e-mail privadaministro@desarrollosocial.gov.ar; internet www.desarrollosocial.gov.ar.

Ministry of Tourism: Buenos Aires; e-mail info@turismo.gov.ar; internet www.turismo.gov.ar.

President and Legislature

PRESIDENT

Election, 23 October 2011, official preliminary results

Candidates	Votes	% of valid votes cast
Cristina E. Fernández de Kirchner (Frente para la Victoria)	11,593,023	53.96
Hermes Juan Binner (Frente Amplio Progresista)	3,624,518	16.87
Ricardo Luis Alfonsín (Unión para el Desarrollo Social)	2,395,056	11.15
Alberto J. Rodríguez Saá (Alianza Compromiso Federal)	1,714,385	7.98
Eduardo Duhalde (Frente Popular)	1,264,609	5.89
Jorge Altamira (Alianza Frente de Izquierda y de los Trabajadores)	497,082	2.31
Elisa M. A. Carrió (Coalición Cívica Afirmación para una República Igualitaria)	396,171	1.84
Total valid votes*	21,484,844	100.00

* In addition, there were 678,724 blank and 206,030 spoiled ballots. There were also a further 23,921 contested votes.

CONGRESO

Cámara de Diputados
(Chamber of Deputies)

President: JULIÁN DOMÍNGUEZ.

The Cámara has 257 members, who hold office for a four-year term, with approximately one-half of the seats renewable every two years. The last election was held on 23 October 2011.

Distribution of Seats by Legislative Bloc, December 2011

	Seats
Frente para la Victoria—Partido Justicialista	115
Unión Cívica Radical (UCR)	38
Frente Peronista	21
Propuesta Republicana (PRO)	11
Frente Cívico por Santiago*	7
Coalición Cívica†	6
Partido Socialista	6
Frente Cívico—Córdoba‡	5
Generación para un Encuentro Nacional	5
Unidad Popular	5
Nuevo Encuentro Popular y Solidario	5
Unión Peronista§	3
Proyecto Sur	3
Movimiento Popular Neuquino	3
Partido Justicialista La Pampa	2
Córdoba Federal‖	2
Demócrata de Mendoza	2
Frente Cívico y Social de Catamarca	2
Others	16
Total	257

* Comprising mainly members of the Frente para la Victoria and the UCR.
† Supported by the Coalición Cívica Afirmación para una República Igualitaria.
‡ Comprising members of the Partido Nuevo Contra la Corrupción, por la Honestidad y la Transparencia.
§ Dissident members of the Partido Justicialista who split from the Frente para la Victoria.
‖ Comprising members of the Unión por Córdoba.

Following the 2011 elections the following blocs were also represented in the Cámara de Diputados: Libres del Sur, Renovador de Salta, Corriente de Pensamiento Federal, Frente Peronista Federal, Partido Federal Fueguino, Salta Somos Todos, Demócrata Progresista, Democracia Igualitaria y Participativa, Movimiento Popular Fueguino, Socialista del Mijd, Unidad para el Desarollo Social y la Equalidad, Unión por Todos and Unión por San Juan.

Senado
(Senate)

President: AMADO BOUDOU.

The Senate has 72 directly elected members, three from each province. One-third of these seats are renewable every two years. The last election was held on 23 October 2011.

Distribution of Seats by Legislative Bloc, December 2011

	Seats
Frente para la Victoria—Partido Justicialista	31
Unión Cívica Radical (UCR)	14
Federalismo y Liberación	2
Frente Cívico de la Provincia de Córdoba	2
Frente Cívico y Social de Catamarca	2
Justicialista San Luis	2
Justicialista 8 de Octubre	2
Nuevo Encuentro	2
Partido Justicialista La Pampa	2
Partido Socialista	2
Others	11
Total	72

Provincial Administrators

(May 2012)

Head of Government of the Autonomous City of Buenos Aires: MAURICIO MACRI (PRO).

Governor of the Province of Buenos Aires: DANIEL OSVALDO SCIOLI (FPV).

Governor of the Province of Catamarca: LUCÍA CORPACCI (FPV).

Governor of the Province of Chaco: JORGE MILTON CAPITANICH (PJ).

Governor of the Province of Chubut: MARTÍN BUZZI (Modelo Chubut).

Governor of the Province of Córdoba: JOSÉ MANUEL DE LA SOTA (PJ).

Governor of the Province of Corrientes: RICARDO COLOMBI (UCR).

Governor of the Province of Entre Ríos: SERGIO DANIEL URRIBARRI (PJ).

Governor of the Province of Formosa: Dr GILDO INSFRÁN (PJ).

Governor of the Province of Jujuy: EDUARDO FELLNER (PJ).

Governor of the Province of La Pampa: OSCAR MARIO JORGE (PJ).

Governor of the Province of La Rioja: LUIS BEDER HERRERA-TERESITA LUNA (PJ).

Governor of the Province of Mendoza: FRANCISCO PÉREZ (FPV).

Governor of the Province of Misiones: MAURICE FABIÁN CLOSS (Frente Renovador de la Concordia).

Governor of the Province of Neuquén: JORGE AUGUSTO SAPAG (MPN).

Governor of the Province of Río Negro: ALBERTO WERETILNECK (FPV).

Governor of the Province of Salta: JUAN MANUEL URTUBEY (PJ).

Governor of the Province of San Juan: Dr JOSÉ LUIS GIOJA (FPV).

Governor of the Province of San Luis: CLAUDIO POGGI (Compromiso Federal).

Governor of the Province of Santa Cruz: DANIEL ROMAN PERALTA (FPV).

Governor of the Province of Santa Fe: ANTONIO BONFATTI (PS).

Governor of the Province of Santiago del Estero: Dr GERARDO ZAMORA (UCR).

Governor of the Province of Tierra del Fuego: MARÍA FABIANA RÍOS (ARI).

Governor of the Province of Tucumán: JOSÉ JORGE ALPEROVICH (PJ).

Election Commissions

Cámara Nacional Electoral (CNE): Avda 25 de Mayo 245, C1002ABE Buenos Aires; tel. (11) 4331-8421; internet www.pjn.gov.ar; f. 1971; Pres. RODOLFO MUNNÉ.

Dirección Nacional Electoral: 25 de Mayo 101, 3°, Of. 346, C1002ABC Buenos Aires; tel. (11) 4346-1683; fax (11) 4346-1634; e-mail dineprivada@mininterior.gov.ar; part of the Ministry of the Interior; Dir ALEJANDRO TULLIO.

Political Organizations

Alianza Compromiso Federal: Humberto I 2087, C1229AAE Buenos Aires; tel. (11) 4942-4134; fax (11) 3527-5795; internet www.unirargentina.com.ar; f. 2011; Presidential Candidate ALBERTO JOSÉ RODRÍGUEZ SAÁ; coalition formed to contest the 2011 presidential election with Es Posible, Movimiento Independiente de Jubiados y Desocupados and the following parties:

Política Abierta para la Integridad Social (PAIS): Avda Corrientes 2141, Oficina 10, C1043AAL Buenos Aires; tel. (11) 4383-6350; e-mail info@partidopais.com.ar; internet www.partidopais.com.ar; f. 1994; following split with the PJ; Pres. FÉLIX MARIANO ACEVEDO.

Unión del Centro Democrático (UCeDé): Hipólito Yrigoyen 636, 6° B Buenos Aires; tel. (11) 4381-3763; internet ucedenacional.blogspot.com; f. 1980; Pres. JORGE PEREYRA DE OLAZÁBAL; Sec. Gen. HUGO EDUARDO BONTEMPO; 77,000 mems.

Alianza Frente de Izquierda y de los Trabajadores: La Rioja 853, C1221ACG Buenos Aires; tel. (11) 4932-9297; e-mail laverdadobrera@pts.org.ar; internet www.frentedeizquierda.org; f. 2011 to contest the elections of that year; left-wing; Pres. JORGE ALTAMIRA; comprises the following parties:

Partido Izquierda Socialista: Hipólito Yrigoyen 1115, C1086AAS Buenos Aires; tel. (11) 4381-4240; e-mail opinaellector@izquierdasocialista.org.ar; internet www.izquierdasocialista.org.ar; f. 2006; Pres. CARLOS ALBERTOS RODRIGUEZ.

Partido Obrero: Ayacucho 444/8, C1026AAB Buenos Aires; tel. (11) 4953-3824; fax (11) 4954-5829; e-mail secprensa@po.org.ar; internet www.po.org.ar; f. 1982; Trotskyist; Pres. NÉSTOR PITROLA; Vice-Pres. GABRIELA ARROYO; 26,000 mems.

Partido de los Trabajadores Socialistas (PTS): La Rioja 853, C1221ACG Buenos Aires; tel. (11) 4932-9297; e-mail pts@pts.org.ar; internet www.pts.org.ar; f. 1988 as a schism of Movimiento al Socialismo; Trotskyist; Pres. GUILLERMO ERMILI.

Alianza Proyecto Sur: Buenos Aires; tel. 1565186265 (mobile); internet www.proyecto-sur.org; f. 2001; contested the 2009 elections as part of the Movimiento Proyecto Sur alliance; Presidential Candidate FERNANDO 'PINO' SOLANAS; coalition formed to contest the 2011 presidential election with the following parties:

Movimiento Proyecto Sur: Sarandí 56, C1088AAI Buenos Aires; tel. (11) 4952-3103; e-mail sur@proyecto-sur.com.ar; internet www.proyecto-sur.com.ar; f. 2001 as an alliance comprising Partido Socialista Auténtico, Partido Proyecto Sur and Buenos Aires para Todos; Pres. FERNANDO 'PINO' SOLANAS.

Movimiento Socialista de los Trabajadores (MST): San Nicolas, Peru 439, Buenos Aires; tel. (11) 4342-7520; e-mail webmaster@mst.org.ar; internet www.mst.org.ar; f. 1944; Sec.-Gen. ALEJANDRO BODART.

Partido Socialista Auténtico: Sarandí 56, C1081ACB Buenos Aires; tel. and fax (11) 4952-3103; e-mail consultas@psa.org.ar; internet www.psa.org.ar; contested the 2009 elections as part of the Movimiento Proyecto Sur alliance; Sec.-Gen. MARIO MAZZITELLI; 13,000 mems.

Coalición Cívica Afirmación para una República Igualitaria (CCARI): Callao 143, C1022AAB Buenos Aires; tel. (11) 4384-1268; e-mail arinacional@ari.org.ar; internet www.ccari.org.ar; f. 2001 as Alternativa por una República de Iguales; progressive party; contested the 2009 elections as part of the Acuerdo Cívico y Social alliance; Pres. ELISA M. A. CARRIÓ; Sec.-Gen. CARLOS LÓPEZ IGLESIAS; 48,000 mems.

Frente Amplio Progresista (FAP): f. 2011; Presidential Candidate HERMES JUAN BINNER; coalition formed to contest the 2011 presidential election with Partido Nuevo and the following parties:

Corriente Nacional por la Unidad Popular: Rivadavia 2515, C1034ACE Buenos Aires; tel. (11) 2055-7778; e-mail info@corrienteup.org; internet corrienteup.org; comprises the Unidad Popular, Unión de los Neuquinos (UNE), Buenos Aires para Todos, Participación, Ética y Solidaridad (PARES) and Cruzada Renovadora de San Juan; Leader LILIANA PARADA.

Generación para un Encuentro Nacional (GEN): Riobamba 67, 1°, C1025ABA Buenos Aires; tel. (11) 4951-9503; e-mail gen@partidogen.com.ar; internet www.partidogen.com.ar; f. 2007; contested the 2009 elections as part of the Acuerdo Cívica y Social alliance; Leader MARGARITA ROSA STOLBIZER; Sec.-Gen. JUAN CARLOS JUÁREZ.

Libres del Sur: Humberto I 542, San Telmo, C1103ACL Buenos Aires; tel. (11) 4307-3724; e-mail contacto@libresdelsur.org.ar; internet www.libresdelsur.org.ar; Leader CECILIA MERCHÁN; Sec.-Gen. HUMBERTO TUMINI.

Partido Socialista (PS): Entre Ríos 488, 2°, Buenos Aires; tel. (11) 4383-2395; e-mail pscen@ar.inter.net; internet www.partidosocialista.org.ar; f. 2002 following merger of the Partido Socialista Democrático and the Partido Socialista Popular; contested the 2009 elections as part of the Acuerdo Cívica y Social alliance; Pres. RUBÉN HÉCTOR GIUSTINIANI; Sec.-Gen. CARLOS ROBERTO; 115,000 mems.

Frente Popular: Buenos Aires; f. 2011; Presidential Candidate EDUARDO DUHALDE; coalition formed to contest the 2011 presidential election with the following parties:

Partido Autonomista: Parana 755, 2° A y B, Buenos Aires; contested the 2009 elections as part of the F.R.A.L. alliance; Leader JOSÉ ANTONIO ROMERO FERIS.

Movimiento de Integración y Desarrollo (MID): Ayacucho 49, C1025AAA Buenos Aires; tel. (11) 4954-0817; e-mail midinterior@mid.org.ar; internet www.mid.org.ar; f. 1963; Leader CARLOS ZAFFORE; Gen. Sec. EFRAÍN GUSTAVO PUYÓ PEÑA; 51,000 mems.

Partido Demócrata Cristiano (PDC): Combate de los Pozos 1055, C1222AAK Buenos Aires; tel. (11) 4305-1229; fax (11) 4306-8242; e-mail pdcblog@fibertel.com.ar; internet democracia-cristiana.blogspot.com; f. 1954; Pres. Dr CARLOS LIONEL TRABOULSI; Sec.-Gen. CARLOS PÉREZ; 51,000 mems.

Unión Popular: Calcena 518, 4°, Buenos Aires; Pres. OLGA OVANESOFF; Vice-Pres. JOSÉ FERNANDO HERRERA; 16,000 mems.

Frente para la Victoria (FPV): e-mail webmaster@diarioelsol.com.ar; internet www.frenteparalavictoria.org; f. 2003 as faction of the PJ supporting presidential campaign of Néstor Carlos Kirchner; centre-left electoral alliance; Presidential Candidate CRISTINA FERNÁNDEZ DE KIRCHNER; coalition formed to contest the 2011 presidential elections with the following parties:

Partido Conservador Popular: Rivadavia 1645, (Entre Piso C), C1033AAG Buenos Aires; f. 1958; Pres. MARCO AURELIO MICHELLI.

Partido Frente Grande: Avda de Mayo, 1480, 2° der, C1085ABR Buenos Aires; e-mail info@frentegrande.org.ar; internet www.frentegrande.org.ar; f. 1993 as an electoral front; contested the 2009 elections as part of the Frente para la Victoria alliance; Pres. EDUARDO SIGAL; Sec.-Gen. DANIEL SAN CRISTOBAL.

Partido Humanista: Avda San Juan 1828, Buenos Aires; tel. (11) 6176-4132; e-mail info@partidohumanista.deargentina.org; internet www.partidohumanista.deargentina.org; f. 1984; contested the 2009 elections as part of the Frente Amplio Hacia la Unidad Latinoamericana alliance; Gen. Sec. BERNARDITA ZALISÑAK.

Partido Intransigente: Riobamba 482, C1025ABJ Buenos Aires; tel. (11) 4954-2283; e-mail nacional@pi.org.ar; internet www.pi.org.ar; f. 1957; left-wing; contested the 2009 elections as part of the Frente para la Victoria alliance; Pres. Dr ENRIQUE GUSTAVO CARDESA; Sec. AMERICO PARODI; 57,000 mems.

Partido Justicialista (PJ): Domingo Matheu 128/130, C1082ABD Buenos Aires; tel. (11) 4954-2450; fax (11) 4954-2421; e-mail contacto@pj.org.ar; internet www.pj.org.ar; f. 1945; Peronist party; contested the 2009 elections as part of the Frente para la Victoria alliance; Pres. JOSÉ CÁCERES; 3.6m. mems.

Movimiento por la Dignidad y la Independencia (Modin): Yrigoyen 820, 2°G, C1086AAN Buenos Aires; e-mail modin@funescoop.com.ar; internet www.modin.org.ar; f. 1991; nationalist; Pres. JOSÉ ALEJANDRO BONACCI; 7,000 mems.

Movimiento Popular Neuquino (MPN): Neuquén; internet www.mpn.org.ar; f. 1961; provincial party; Pres. JORGE OMAR SOBISCH; 112,000 mems.

Nuevo Encuentro: Buenos Aires; f. 2009; centre-left; forms the Nuevo Encuentro Popular y Solidario bloc in the Congreso; Leader MARTÍN SABBATELLA.

Partido Comunista de Argentina: Entre Ríos 1039, C1080ABQ Buenos Aires; tel. and fax (11) 4304-0066; e-mail info@pca.org.ar; internet www.pca.org.ar; f. 1918; Leader PATRICIO ECHEGARAY.

Partido Demócrata Progresista (PDP): Chile 1934, C1227AAD Buenos Aires; tel. (11) 4942-9930; e-mail info@demoprogresista.org.ar; internet www.demoprogresista.org.ar; f. 1914; contested the 2009 elections as part of the PRO alliance; Pres. JOSÉ EDUARDO DE CARA; Gen. Sec. OSCAR MOSCARIELLO; 36,000 mems.

Partido Nacional Contra la Corrupción, por la Honestidad y la Transparencia: Córdoba; e-mail info@partidonuevocordoba.com.ar; internet www.partidonuevocordoba.com.ar; Pres. LUIS ALFREDO JUEZ; Sec.-Gen. RUBÉN ALBERTO BORELLO.

Partido Recrear para el Crecimiento (RECREAR): Avda de Mayo 605, 9°, Buenos Aires; tel. (11) 4342-2400; e-mail juntanacional@recrear.org.ar; internet recrear.org.ar; f. 2002; forms part of the PRO bloc in the Congreso; Pres. ESTEBAN BULLRICH; Sec. JAVIER PRIDA; 59,000 mems.

Propuesta Republicana (PRO): Alsina 1325, C1088AAI Buenos Aires; e-mail info@pro.com.ar; internet www.pro.com.ar; f. 2005; part of the Unión PRO alliance; Leader MAURICIO MACRI.

Solidaridad e Igualdad (SI): Buenos Aires; internet www.espaciosi.org; f. 2008 as breakaway grouping from ARI; centre-left; forms the Sí por la Unidad Popular bloc in the Congreso; Leader EDUARDO MACALUSE.

Unión para el Desarrollo Social (Udeso): f. 2011; Presidential Candidate RICARDO LUIS ALFONSÍN; coalition formed to contest the 2011 presidential elections with the following parties:

Unión Celeste y Blanco: tel. (11) 4779-6418; e-mail denarvaezprensa@denarvaez.com; Leader FRANCISCO DE NARVÁEZ.

Unión Cívica Radical (UCR): Alsina 1786, C1088AAR Buenos Aires; tel. and fax (11) 5199-0600; e-mail webmaster@ucr.org.ar; internet www.ucr.org.ar; f. 1890; moderate; contested the 2009 elections as part of the Acuerdo Cívica y Social alliance; Pres. ANGEL ROZAS; Gen. Sec. JESÚS RODRÍGUEZ; 2.5m. mems.

Unión por Córdoba: Córdoba; internet www.unionporcordoba.com; forms the Córdoba Federal bloc in the Congreso; Leader FRANCISCO J. FORTUNA.

OTHER ORGANIZATIONS

Asociación Madres de Plaza de Mayo: Hipólito Yrigoyen 1584, C1089AAD Buenos Aires; tel. (11) 4383-0377; fax (11) 4954-0381; e-mail madres@madres.org; internet www.madres.org; f. 1979; formed by mothers of those who 'disappeared' during the years of military rule, it has since become a broad-based anti-poverty grouping with socialist aims; Pres. ESTELA DE CARLOTTO; Founder and Leader HEBE MARÍA PASTOR DE BONAFINI.

Corriente Clasista y Combativa (CCC): e-mail info@cccargentina.org.ar; internet www.cccargentina.org.ar; radical grouping; Leader JUAN CARLOS ALDERETE.

Movimiento Barrios de Pie: e-mail correos@barriosdepie.org.ar; internet www.barriosdepie.org.ar; f. 2001; moderate grouping; Leader JORGE CEBALLOS.

Movimiento Libres del Sur: Humberto I 542, Buenos Aires; tel. (11) 4307-3724; e-mail contacto@libresdelsur.org.ar; internet libresdelsur.org.ar; f. 2006; alliance of pro-President Kirchner *piquetero* groups; Leader HUMBERTO TUMINI.

Numerous other *piquetero* groupings also exist.

Diplomatic Representation

EMBASSIES IN ARGENTINA

Albania: Juez Tedín 3036, 4°, C1425CWH Buenos Aires; tel. (11) 48093574; fax (11) 48078767; e-mail embassy.buenosaires@mfa.gov.al; Ambassador REZAR BREGU.

Algeria: Montevideo 1889, C1021AAE Buenos Aires; tel. (11) 4815-1271; fax (11) 4815-8837; e-mail argeliae@interserver.com.ar; Ambassador BENAOUDA HAMEL.

Angola: La Pampa 3452–56, C1430BXD Buenos Aires; tel. (11) 4554-8383; fax (11) 4554-8998; Ambassador HERMÍNIO JOAQUIM ESCÓRCIO.

Armenia: José Andrés Pacheco de Melo 1922, C1126AAD Buenos Aires; tel. (11) 4816-8710; fax (11) 4812-2803; e-mail armenia@fibertel.com.ar; Ambassador VAHAGN MELIKYAN.

Australia: Villanueva 1400, C1426BMJ Buenos Aires; tel. (11) 4779-3500; fax (11) 4779-3581; e-mail info.ba.general@dfat.gov.au; internet www.argentina.embassy.gov.au; Ambassador PATRICIA ANN HOLMES.

Austria: French 3671, C1425AXC Buenos Aires; tel. (11) 4807-9185; fax (11) 4805-4016; e-mail buenos-aires-ob@bmeia.gv.at; internet www.austria.org.ar; Ambassador Dr ROBERT ZISCHG.

Azerbaijan: Gorostiaga 2176, C1426BMC Buenos Aires; tel. (11) 4777-3655; fax (11) 4777-8928; e-mail buenosaires@azembassy.com.ar; internet www.azembassy.com.ar; Ambassador MAMMAD AHAMDZADA.

Belarus: Cazadores 2166, C1428 Capital Federal, Buenos Aires; tel. (11) 4788-9394; fax (11) 4788-2322; e-mail argentina@belembassy.org; internet www.argentina.belembassy.org; Chargé d'affaires a.i. GEORGY KISLYAK.

Belgium: Defensa 113, 8°, C1065AAA Buenos Aires; tel. (11) 4331-0066; fax (11) 4331-0814; e-mail BuenosAires@diplobel.fed.be; internet www.diplomatie.be/buenosaires; Ambassador THOMAS ANTOINE.

Bolivia: Corrientes 545, 2°, C1043AAF Buenos Aires; tel. (11) 4394-1463; fax (11) 4394-0460; e-mail embolivia-baires@ree.gov.bo; internet www.embajadadebolivia.com.ar; Ambassador MARÍA LEONOR ARAUCO LEMAITRE.

Brazil: Cerrito 1350, C1010ABB Buenos Aires; tel. (11) 4515-2400; fax (11) 4515-2401; e-mail info@embrasil.org.ar; internet www.brasil.org.ar; Ambassador ENIO CORDEIRO.

Bulgaria: Mariscal A. J. de Sucre 1568, C1428DUT Buenos Aires; tel. (11) 4781-8644; fax (11) 4781-1214; e-mail embular@uolsinectis.com.ar; internet www.mfa.bg/buenos-aires; Chargé d'affaires a.i. VALENTIN MODEV.

Canada: Tagle 2828, C1425EEH Buenos Aires; tel. (11) 4808-1000; fax (11) 4808-1111; e-mail bairs-webmail@international.gc.ca; internet www.canadainternational.gc.ca/argentina-argentine; Ambassador GWYNETH A. KUTZ.

Chile: Tagle 2762, C1425EEF Buenos Aires; tel. (11) 4808-8600; fax (11) 4804-5927; e-mail data@embajadadechile.com.ar; Ambassador MIGUEL ADOLFO GERARDO ZALDÍVAR LARRAÍN.

China, People's Republic: Crisólogo Larralde 5349, C1431APM Buenos Aires; tel. (11) 4547-8100; fax (11) 4545-1141; e-mail chinaemb_ar@mfa.gov.cn; internet ar.chineseembassy.org/esp; Ambassador YIN HENGMIN.

Colombia: Carlos Pellegrini 1363, 3°, C1011AAA Buenos Aires; tel. (11) 4325-0258; fax (11) 4322-9370; e-mail ebaires@cancilleria.gov.co; internet www.embajadaenargentina.gov.co; Ambassador CARLOS ENRIQUE RODADO NORIEGA.

Congo, Democratic Republic: Arcos 2340, 2°, Depto G, C1428EON Buenos Aires; tel. (11) 4896-4963; e-mail rdcbuenos@hotmail.com; Chargé d'affaires a.i. YEMBA LOHAKA.

Costa Rica: Pacheco de Melo 1833, 5°, C1126AAD Buenos Aires; tel. (11) 4802-6297; fax (11) 4801-3222; e-mail embarica@fibertel.com.ar; Ambassador CARLOS VILLALOBOS SZUSTER.

Croatia: Gorostiaga 2104, C1426CTN Buenos Aires; tel. (11) 4777-6409; fax (11) 4777-9159; e-mail croemb.ar@mvpei.hr; Chargé d'affaires a.i. DUSKA PARAVIC.

Cuba: Virrey del Pino 1810, Belgrano, C1426EGF Buenos Aires; tel. (11) 4782-9049; fax (11) 4786-7713; e-mail info@ar.embacuba.cu; internet www.embacuba.com.ar; Ambassador JORGE NÉSTOR LAMADRID MASCARÓ.

Czech Republic: Junín 1461, C1113AAM Buenos Aires; tel. (11) 4807-3107; fax (11) 4800-1088; e-mail buenosaires@embassy.mzv.cz; internet www.mzv.cz/buenosaires; Ambassador ŠTĚPÁN ZAJAC.

Denmark: Avda Leandro N. Alem 1074, 9°, C1001AAS Buenos Aires; tel. (11) 4312-6901; fax (11) 4312-7857; e-mail bueamb@um

.dk; internet www.buenosaires.um.dk; Ambassador Ole Henrik Frijs-Madsen.

Dominican Republic: Santa Fe 830, 7°, C1059ABP Buenos Aires; tel. (11) 4312-9378; fax (11) 4894-2078; e-mail consuldo@hotmail .com; Ambassador Guillermo Eduardo Piña-Contreras.

Ecuador: Quintana 585, 9°, C1129ABB Buenos Aires; tel. (11) 4804-0073; fax (11) 4804-0074; e-mail embecuador@embecuador.com.ar; Ambassador Gonzalo Eduardo Wellington Sandoval Córdova.

Egypt: Virrey del Pino 3140, C1426EHF Buenos Aires; tel. (11) 4553-3311; fax (11) 4553-0067; e-mail embegypt@fibertel.com.ar; Ambassador Soha Elfar.

El Salvador: Rodriguez Peña 1625, C1011ACD Buenos Aires; tel. (11) 4813-2525; fax (11) 4811-8236; e-mail elsalvador@fibertel.com .ar; internet www.embajadaelsalvador.com.ar; Ambassador Oscar Ernesto Menjibar Chávez.

Finland: Santa Fe 846, 5°, C1059ABP Buenos Aires; tel. (11) 4312-0600; fax (11) 4312-0670; e-mail sanomat.bue@formin.fi; internet www.finlandia.org.ar; Ambassador Jukka Pietikäinen.

France: Cerrito 1399, C1010ABA Buenos Aires; tel. (11) 4515-2930; fax (11) 4515-0120; e-mail ambafr@abaconet.com.ar; internet www .embafrancia-argentina.org; Ambassador Jean-Pierre Asvazadourian.

Germany: Villanueva 1055, C1426BMC Buenos Aires; tel. (11) 4778-2500; fax (11) 4778-2550; e-mail info@buenos-aires.diplo.de; internet www.buenos-aires.diplo.de; Ambassador Günter Kniess.

Greece: Arenales 1658, C1061AAT Buenos Aires; tel. (11) 4811-4811; fax (11) 4816-2600; e-mail gremb.bay@mfa.gr; Ambassador Eleni Leivaditou.

Guatemala: Juncal 802, 3° h, C1062ABF Buenos Aires; tel. (11) 4313-9160; fax (11) 4313-9181; e-mail embagua@ciudad.com.ar; Ambassador Rosa María Mérida de Mora.

Haiti: Avda Figueroa Alcorta 3297, C1425CKL Buenos Aires; tel. (11) 4802-0211; fax (11) 4802-3984; e-mail embajadahaiti@fibertel .com.ar; Chargé d'affaires a.i. Jean Ceradieu Augustave.

Holy See: Marcelo T. de Alvear 1605, C1014AAD Buenos Aires; tel. (11) 4813-9697; fax (11) 4815-4097; e-mail nunciaturaapostolica@ speedy.com.ar; Apostolic Nuncio Most Rev. Emil Paul Tscherrig (Titular Archbishop of Voli).

Honduras: Avda Callao 1564, 2°, C1024AAO Buenos Aires; tel. (11) 4806-9914; fax (11) 4806-9880; e-mail embajadadehonduras@fibertel .com.ar; Ambassador Juan José Cueva Membreño.

Hungary: Plaza 1726, C1430DGF Buenos Aires; tel. (11) 4553-4646; fax (11) 4555-6859; e-mail mission.bue@kum.hu; internet www.mfa .gov.hu/emb/buenosaires; Ambassador Pál Varga Koritár.

India: Torre Madero, 19°, Avda Eduardo Madero 942, C1106ACW Buenos Aires; tel. (11) 4393-4001; fax (11) 4393-4063; e-mail indemb@indembarg.org.ar; internet www.indembarg.org.ar; Ambassador Rengaraj Viswanathan.

Indonesia: Mariscal Ramón Castilla 2901, C1425DZE Buenos Aires; tel. (11) 4807-2211; fax (11) 4802-4448; e-mail emindo@ tournet.com.ar; internet www.indonesianembassy.org.ar; Ambassador Nurmala Kartini Pandjaitan Sjahrir.

Iran: Avda Figueroa Alcorta 3229, C1425CKL Buenos Aires; tel. (11) 4802-1470; fax (11) 4805-4409; e-mail embajadairan@fibertel.com .ar; Chargé d'affaires a.i. Seyed Ali Pakdaman.

Ireland: Avda del Libertador 1068, Edif. Bluesky, 6°, Recoleta, C1112ABN Buenos Aires; tel. (11) 5787-0801; fax (11) 5787-0802; e-mail info@irlanda.org.ar; internet www.embassyofireland.org.ar; Ambassador James McIntyre.

Israel: Avda de Mayo 701, 10°, C1084AAC Buenos Aires; tel. (11) 4338-2500; fax (11) 4338-2624; e-mail info@buenosaires.mfa.gov.il; internet buenosaires.mfa.gov.il; Ambassador Daniel Gazit.

Italy: Billinghurst 2577, C1425DTY Buenos Aires; tel. (11) 4011-2100; fax (11) 4011-2159; e-mail segreteria.buenosaires@esteri.it; internet www.ambbuenosaires.esteri.it; Ambassador Guido Walter La Tella.

Japan: Bouchard 547, 17°, C1106ABG Buenos Aires; tel. (11) 4318-8200; fax (11) 4318-8210; e-mail taishikan@japan.org.ar; internet www.ar.emb-japan.go.jp; Ambassador Masashi Mizukami.

Korea, Republic: Avda del Libertador 2395, C1425AAJ Buenos Aires; tel. (11) 4802-9665; fax (11) 4803-6993; e-mail argentina@ mofat.go.kr; internet www.embcorea.org.ar; Ambassador Han Byung-kil.

Kuwait: Uruguay 739, C1015ABO Buenos Aires; tel. (11) 4374-7202; fax (11) 4374-8718; e-mail info@embajadadekuwait.com.ar; internet www.embajadadekuwait.com.ar; Ambassador Saud Abd al-Aziz al-Roomi.

Lebanon: Avda del Libertador 2354, C1425AAW Buenos Aires; tel. (11) 4802-0466; fax (11) 4802-0929; e-mail embajada@ellibano.com .ar; internet www.ellibano.com.ar; Ambassador Dr Hicham Salim Hamdan.

Libya: Virrey del Pino 3432, C1426EHL Buenos Aires; tel. (11) 4553-4669; fax (11) 4551-6187; e-mail oficinapopularlibia@hotmail.com; Chargé d'affaires a.i. Mustafa M. S. Eshwin.

Lithuania: Mendoza 1018, C1428DJN, Buenos Aires; tel. (11) 4788-2153; fax (11) 4785-7915; e-mail embajada@lituania.org.ar; internet ar.mfa.lt; Ambassador Vaclovas Šalkauskas.

Malaysia: Villanueva 1040, C1426BMD Buenos Aires; tel. (11) 4776-2553; fax (11) 4776-0604; e-mail mwbaires@fibertel.com.ar; Ambassador Dato' Zulkifli bin Yaacob.

Mexico: Arcos 1650, C1426BGL Buenos Aires; tel. (11) 4118-8800; fax (11) 4118-8837; e-mail embamexarg@interlink.com.ar; internet www.embamex.int.ar; Ambassador Francisco Eduardo del Río López.

Morocco: Castex 3461, C1425CDG Buenos Aires; tel. (11) 4801-8154; fax (11) 4802-0136; e-mail sifamarruecos@fibertel.com.ar; Ambassador Fouad Yazough.

Netherlands: Edif. Porteño II, Olga Cossettini 831, 3°, C1107BVA Buenos Aires; tel. (11) 4338-0050; fax (11) 4338-0060; e-mail bue@ minbuza.nl; internet www.embajadaholanda.int.ar; Ambassador Hein de Vries.

New Zealand: Carlos Pellegrini 1427, 5°, C1011AAC Buenos Aires; tel. (11) 4328-0747; fax (11) 4328-0757; e-mail kiwiarg@speedy.com .ar; internet www.nzembassy.com/buenosaires; Ambassador Darryl Dunn.

Nicaragua: Santa Fe 1845, 7°, Of. b, C1123AAA Buenos Aires; tel. (11) 4811-0973; fax (11) 4816-6315; e-mail zmasis@cancilleria.gob.ni; Ambassador Zoraya Faviola Masis Mayorga.

Nigeria: Juez Estrada 2746, Palermo, C1425CPD Buenos Aires; tel. (11) 4808-9245; fax (11) 4807-1782; e-mail info@nigerianembassy .org; internet www.nigerianembassy.org.ar; Ambassador Empire Nduka Kanu.

Norway: Carlos Pelegrini 1427, 2°, C1011AAC Buenos Aires; tel. (11) 4328-8717; fax (11) 4328-9048; e-mail emb.buenosaires@mfa.no; internet www.noruega.org.ar; Ambassador Nils Haugstveit.

Pakistan: Gorostiaga 2176, C1426CTN Buenos Aires; tel. (11) 4775-1294; fax (11) 4776-1186; e-mail parepbaires@fibertel.com.ar; internet www.embassypakistan.com.ar; Ambassador Naela Chohan.

Panama: Santa Fe 1461, 1°, C1060ABA Buenos Aires; tel. (11) 4811-1254; fax (11) 4814-0450; e-mail epar@fibertel.com.ar; internet www .embajadadepanama.com.ar; Ambassador Mario Boyd Galindo.

Paraguay: Las Heras 2545, C1425ASC Buenos Aires; tel. (11) 4802-3826; fax (11) 4807-7600; e-mail embaparba@fibertel.com.ar; Ambassador Gabriel Manuel Enciso López.

Peru: Avda del Libertador 1720, C1425AAQ Buenos Aires; tel. (11) 4802-2000; fax (11) 4802-5887; e-mail contacto@embajadadelperu .com.ar; internet www.embajadadelperu.com.ar; Ambassador Nicolás Lynch Gamero.

Philippines: Blvd Lidoro Quinteros 1386, C1428BXR Buenos Aires; tel. (11) 4782-4752; fax (11) 4788-9692; e-mail pheba@fibertel.com .ar; internet www.buenosairespe.com.ar; Ambassador Rey A. Carandang.

Poland: Alejandro María de Aguado 2870, C1425CEB Buenos Aires; tel. (11) 4808-1700; fax (11) 4808-1701; e-mail emb@buenosaires .polemb.net; internet www.buenosaires.polemb.net; Ambassador Jacek Bazański.

Portugal: Maipú 942, 17°, C1006ACN Buenos Aires; tel. (11) 4312-3524; fax (11) 4311-2586; e-mail embpor@buenosaires.dgaccp.pt; internet www.embaixadaportugal.com.ar; Ambassador Henrique Silveira Borges.

Romania: Arroyo 962–970, C1007AAD Buenos Aires; tel. (11) 4326-5888; fax (11) 4322-2630; e-mail embarombue@rumania.org.ar; internet www.rumania.org.ar; Ambassador Manuela Vulpe.

Russia: Rodríguez Peña 1741, C1021ABK Buenos Aires; tel. (11) 4813-1552; fax (11) 4815-6293; e-mail embrusia@fibertel.com.ar; internet www.argentina.mid.ru; Ambassador Victor Koronelli.

Saudi Arabia: Alejandro María de Aguado 2881, C1425CEA Buenos Aires; tel. (11) 4802-0760; fax (11) 4806-1581; e-mail aremb@mofa .gov.sa; Ambassador Turki M. A. al-Madi.

Serbia: Marcelo T. de Alvear 1705, C1060AAG Buenos Aires; tel. (11) 4812-9133; fax (11) 4812-1070; e-mail serbembaires@ciudad.com .ar; Ambassador Gordana Vidović.

Slovakia: Figueroa Alcorta 3240, C1425CKY Buenos Aires; tel. (11) 4801-3917; fax (11) 4801-4654; e-mail emb.buenosaires@mzv.sk; Ambassador Pavel Šípka.

Slovenia: Santa Fe 846, 6°, C1059ABP Buenos Aires; tel. (11) 4894-0621; fax (11) 4312-8410; e-mail vba@gov.si; internet www .buenosaires.veleposlanistvo.si; Ambassador Tomaž Mencin.

South Africa: Marcelo T. de Alvear 590, 8°, C1058AAF Buenos Aires; tel. (11) 4317-2900; fax (11) 4317-2963; e-mail embajador

.argentina@foreign.gov.za; internet www.sudafrica.org.ar; Ambassador ANTHONY LEON.

Spain: Mariscal Ramón Castilla 2720, C1425DZA Buenos Aires; tel. (11) 4802-6031; fax (11) 4802-0719; e-mail emb.buenosaires@maec.es; internet www.embajadaenargentina.es; Ambassador ROMÁN OYARSZUN MARCHESI.

Sweden: Tacuari 147, 6°, C1071AAC Buenos Aires; tel. (11) 4329-0800; fax (11) 4342-1697; e-mail ambassaden.buenos-aires@foreign.ministery.se; internet www.swedenabroad.com/buenosaires; Ambassador BRITT CHARLOTTE WRANGBERG.

Switzerland: Santa Fe 846, 12°, C1059ABP Buenos Aires; tel. (11) 4311-6491; fax (11) 4313-2998; e-mail bue.vertretung@eda.admin.ch; internet www.eda.admin.ch/buenosaires; Ambassador JOHANN STEPHAN MATYASSY.

Syria: Callao 956, C1023AAP Buenos Aires; tel. (11) 4813-2113; fax (11) 4814-3211; Chargé d'affaires a.i. ADNAN ASAAD.

Thailand: Vuelta de Obligado 1947, 12°, C1428ADC Buenos Aires; tel. (11) 4780-0555; fax (11) 4782-1616; e-mail thaiembargen@fibertel.com.ar; internet www.thaiembargen.org; Ambassador MEDHA PROMTHEP.

Tunisia: Ciudad de la Paz 3086, C1429ACD Buenos Aires; tel. (11) 4544-2618; fax (11) 4545-6369; e-mail atbuenosaires@infovia.com.ar; Chargé d'affaires a.i. MOUNIR FOURATI.

Turkey: 11 de Septiembre 1382, C1426BKN Buenos Aires; tel. (11) 4788-3239; fax (11) 4784-9179; e-mail turquia@fibertel.com.ar; internet buenosaires.be.mfa.gov.tr; Ambassador METIN HÜSREV ÜNLER BÜYÜKELÇI.

Ukraine: Conde 1763, C1426AZI Buenos Aires; tel. (11) 4552-0657; fax (11) 4552-6771; e-mail embucra@embucra.com.ar; internet www.mfa.gov.ua/argentina; Ambassador OLEKSANDR TARANENKO.

United Arab Emirates: Olleros 2021, C1426BRK Buenos Aires; tel. (11) 4771-9716; fax (11) 4772-5169; Ambassador MOHAMMED ISA AL-QATTAM AL-ZA'ABI.

United Kingdom: Dr Luis Agote 2412, C1425EOF Buenos Aires; tel. (11) 4808-2200; fax (11) 4808-2274; e-mail askinformation.baires@fco.gov.uk; internet ukinargentina.fco.gov.uk; Ambassador SHAN MORGAN.

USA: Avda Colombia 4300, C1425GMN Buenos Aires; tel. (11) 5777-4533; fax (11) 5777-4240; internet argentina.usembassy.gov; Ambassador VILMA S. MARTINEZ.

Uruguay: Las Heras 1907, C1127AAB Buenos Aires; tel. (11) 4807-3040; fax (11) 4807-3050; e-mail urubaires@embajadadeluruguay.com.ar; internet www.embajadadeluruguay.com.ar; Ambassador GUILLERMO JOSÉ POMI BARRIOLA.

Venezuela: Virrey Loreto 2035, C1426DXK Buenos Aires; tel. (11) 4788-4944; fax (11) 4784-4311; e-mail embaven@arnet.com.ar; Ambassador CARLOS EDUARDO MARTÍNEZ MENDOZA.

Viet Nam: 11 de Septiembre 1442, C1426BKP Buenos Aires; tel. (11) 4783-1802; fax (11) 4782-0078; e-mail sqvnartn@fibertel.com.ar; Ambassador DAO VAN NGUYEN.

Judicial System

SUPREME COURT

Corte Suprema

Talcahuano 550, 4°, C1013AAL Buenos Aires; tel. (11) 4370-4600; fax (11) 4340-2270; e-mail consultas@cjsn.gov.ar; internet www.csjn.gov.ar.

The members of the Supreme Court are appointed by the President, with the agreement of at least two-thirds of the Senate. Members can be dismissed by impeachment. In December 2006 the Congreso approved legislation reducing the number of judges from nine to five.

President: RICARDO LUIS LORENZETTI.

Vice-President: ELENA I. HIGHTON DE NOLASCO.

Justices: EUGENIO RAÚL ZAFFARONI, ENRIQUE SANTIAGO PETRACCHI, JUAN CARLOS MAQUEDA, CARLOS S. FAYT, CARMEN MARÍA ARGIBAY.

OTHER COURTS

Judges of the lower, national or further lower courts are appointed by the President, with the agreement of the Senate, and can be dismissed by impeachment. From 1999, however, judges were to retire on reaching 75 years of age.

The Federal Court of Appeal in Buenos Aires has three courts: civil and commercial, criminal, and administrative. There are six other courts of appeal in Buenos Aires: civil, commercial, criminal, peace, labour, and penal-economic. There are also federal appeal courts in La Plata, Bahía Blanca, Paraná, Rosario, Córdoba, Mendoza, Tucumán and Resistencia. In 1994, following constitutional amendments, the Office of the Attorney-General was established as an independent entity and a Council of Magistrates was envisaged. In 1997 the Senate adopted legislation to create the Council.

The provincial courts each have their own Supreme Court and a system of subsidiary courts. They deal with cases originating within and confined to the provinces.

Attorney-General: Dr ESTEBAN RIGHI.

Religion

CHRISTIANITY

The Roman Catholic Church

Some 76% of the population are Roman Catholics.

Argentina comprises 14 archdioceses, 51 dioceses (including one each for Uniate Catholics of the Ukrainian rite, of the Maronite rite and of the Armenian rite), four territorial prelatures and an apostolic exarchate for Catholics of the Melkite rite. The Bishop of San Gregorio de Narek en Buenos Aires is also the Apostolic Exarch of Latin America and Mexico for Catholics of the Armenian rite, and the Archbishop of Buenos Aires is also the Ordinary for Catholics of other Oriental rites.

Bishops' Conference: Suipacha 1034, C1008AAV Buenos Aires; tel. (11) 4328-0993; fax (11) 4328-9570; e-mail seccea@cea.org.ar; internet www.cea.org.ar; f. 1959; Pres. Cardinal JORGE MARIO BERGOGLIO (Archbishop of Buenos Aires).

Armenian Rite

Bishop of San Gregorio de Narek en Buenos Aires: VARTÁN WALDIR BOGHOSSIAN, Charcas 3529, C1425BMU Buenos Aires; tel. (11) 4824-1613; fax (11) 4827-1975; e-mail exarmal@pcn.net.

Latin Rite

Archbishop of Bahía Blanca: GUILLERMO JOSÉ GARLATTI, Avda Colón 164, B8000FTO Bahía Blanca; tel. (291) 455-0707; fax (291) 452-2070; e-mail arzobis@arzobispadobahia.org.ar.

Archbishop of Buenos Aires: Cardinal JORGE MARIO BERGOGLIO, Rivadavia 415, C1002AAC Buenos Aires; tel. (11) 4343-0812; fax (11) 4334-8373; e-mail arzobispado@arzbaires.org.ar; internet www.arzbaires.org.ar.

Archbishop of Córdoba: CARLOS JOSÉ ÑÁÑEZ, Hipólito Irigoyen 98, X5000JHN Córdoba; tel. and fax (351) 422-1015; e-mail info@arzobispado.org.ar; internet www.arzobispadocba.org.ar.

Archbishop of Corrientes: ANDRÉS STANOVNIK, 9 de Julio 1543, W3400AZA Corrientes; tel. and fax (3783) 422436; e-mail info@corrientes.arzobispado.net; internet corrientes.arzobispado.net.

Archbishop of La Plata: HÉCTOR RUBÉN AGUER, Calle 14 Centro 1009, B1900DVQ La Plata; tel. (221) 425-1656; e-mail arzobispadodelaplata@speedy.com.ar; internet www.arzolap.org.ar.

Archbishop of Mendoza: JOSÉ MARÍA ARANCIBIA, Catamarca 98, M5500CKB Mendoza; tel. (261) 423-3862; fax (261) 429-5415; e-mail arzobispadomza@supernet.com.ar.

Archbishop of Mercedes-Luján: AGUSTÍN ROBERTO RADRIZZANI, Calle 22 745, B6600HDU Mercedes; tel. (2324) 432-412; fax (2324) 432-104; e-mail arzomerce@yahoo.com.ar; internet www.basilicadelujan.org.

Archbishop of Paraná: JUAN ALBERTO PUIGGARI, Monte Caseros 77, E3100ACA Paraná; tel. (343) 431-1440; fax (343) 423-0372; e-mail arzparan@arzparan.org.ar.

Archbishop of Resistencia: FABRICIANO SIGAMPA, Bartolomé Mitre 363, Casilla 35, H3500BLG Resistencia; tel. and fax (3722) 441908; e-mail arzobrcia@arnet.com.ar.

Archbishop of Rosario: JOSÉ LUIS MOLLAGHAN, Córdoba 1677, S2000AWY Rosario; tel. (341) 425-1298; fax (341) 425-1207; e-mail arzobros@uolsinectis.com.ar; internet www.delrosario.org.ar.

Archbishop of Salta: MARIO ANTONIO CARGNELLO, España 596, A4400ANL Salta; tel. (387) 421-4306; fax (387) 421-3101; e-mail arzobispadosalta@arnet.com.ar; internet www.arquidiocesissalta.org.ar.

Archbishop of San Juan de Cuyo: ALFONSO ROGELIO DELGADO EVERS, Bartolomé Mitre 250 Oeste, J5402CXF San Juan; tel. (264) 422-2578; fax (264) 427-3530; e-mail arzobispadosanjuan@infovia.com.ar.

Archbishop of Santa Fe de la Vera Cruz: JOSÉ MARÍA ARANCEDO, Avda Brig.-Gen. E. López 2720, S3000DCJ Santa Fe; tel. (342) 459-1780; fax (342) 459-4491; e-mail curia@arquisantafe.org.ar; internet www.arquisantafe.org.ar.

Archbishop of Tucumán: ALFREDO ZECCA, Avda Sarmiento 895, T4000GTI San Miguel de Tucumán; tel. (381) 431-0617; e-mail arztuc@arnet.com.ar; internet www.arztucuman.org.ar.

Maronite Rite

Bishop of San Charbel en Buenos Aires: CHARBEL GEORGES MERHI, Eparquía Maronita, Paraguay 834, C1057AAL Buenos Aires; tel. (11) 4311-7299; fax (11) 4312-8348; e-mail mcharbel@hotmail .com.

Melkite Rite

Apostolic Exarch: ABDO ARBACH, Exarcado Apostólico Greco-Melquita, Corrientes 276, X5000ANF Córdoba; tel. (351) 421-0625.

Ukrainian Rite

Bishop of Santa María del Patrocinio en Buenos Aires: Rt Rev. MIGUEL MYKYCEJ, Ramón L. Falcón 3950, Casilla 28, C1407GSN Buenos Aires; tel. (11) 4671-4192; fax (11) 4671-7265; e-mail pokrov@ ciudad.com.ar.

The Anglican Communion

The Iglesia Anglicana del Cono Sur de América (Anglican Church of the Southern Cone of America) was formally inaugurated in Buenos Aires in April 1983. The Church comprises seven dioceses: Argentina, Northern Argentina, Chile, Paraguay, Peru, Bolivia and Uruguay. The Primate is the Bishop of Argentina.

Bishop of Argentina: Rt Rev. GREGORY J. VENABLES, 25 de Mayo 282, C1002ABF Buenos Aires; tel. (11) 4342-4618; fax (11) 4331-0234; e-mail diocesisanglibue@fibertel.com.ar; internet www .anglicanaargentina.org.ar.

Bishop of Northern Argentina: (vacant), Casilla 187, A4400ANL Salta; tel. (387) 431-1718; fax (387) 431-2622; e-mail sinclair@salnet .com.ar; jurisdiction extends to Jujuy, Salta, Tucumán, Catamarca, Santiago del Estero, Formosa and Chaco.

Other Christian Churches

Federación Argentina de Iglesias Evangélicas (Argentine Federation of Evangelical Churches): Condarco 321, C1604AFE Buenos Aires; tel. and fax (11) 4611-1437; e-mail presidencia@faie.org.ar; internet www.faie.org.ar; f. 1938; 21 mem. churches; Pres. KARIN KRUG; Sec. Dr ALBERTO ROLDÁN.

Convención Evangélica Bautista Argentina (Baptist Evangelical Convention): Virrey Liniers 42, C1174ACB Buenos Aires; tel. and fax (11) 4864-2711; e-mail ceba@sion.com; internet www.ceba .sion.com; f. 1908; Pres. NÉSTOR GOLLUSCIO.

Iglesia Evangélica Luterana Argentina (Evangelical Lutheran Church of Argentina): Ing. Silveyra 1639-41, B1607BQM Villa Adelina, Buenos Aires; tel. (11) 4735-4155; fax (11) 4766-7948; e-mail ielapresidente@arnet.com.ar; internet www.iela.org.ar; f. 1905; 30,000 mems; Pres. EDGARDO ELSESER.

Iglesia Evangélica Luterana Unida (United Evangelical Lutheran Church): Marcos Sastre 2891, C1417FYE Buenos Aires; tel. (11) 4501-3925; fax 4504-7358; e-mail ielu@ielu.org; internet www.ielu.org; 11,000 mems; Pres. Rev. ALAN ELDRID.

Iglesia Evangélica Metodista Argentina (Methodist Church of Argentina): Rivadavia 4044, 3°, C1205AAN Buenos Aires; tel. (11) 4982-3712; fax (11) 4981-0885; e-mail secretariaadministracion@ iglesiametodista.org.ar; internet www.iglesiametodista.org.ar; f. 1836; Bishop NELLIE RITCHIE.

Iglesia Evangélica del Río de la Plata (Evangelical Church of the Plate River): Mariscal Sucre 2855, C1428DVY Buenos Aires; tel. (11) 4787-0436; fax (11) 4787-0335; e-mail presidente@ierp.org.ar; internet www.iglesiaevangelica.org; f. 1899; 27,500 mems; Pres. FEDERICO HUGO SCHÄFER; Gen. Sec. JUAN ABELARDO SCHVINDT.

JUDAISM

There are about 230,000 Jews in Argentina, mostly in Buenos Aires.

Delegación de Asociaciones Israelitas Argentinas (DAIA) (Delegation of Argentine Jewish Associations): Pasteur 633, 7°, C1028AAM Buenos Aires; tel. and fax (11) 4378-3200; e-mail daia@daia.org.ar; internet www.daia.org.ar; f. 1935; Pres. ALDO DONZIS; Exec. Dir JORGE ELBAUM.

The Press

PRINCIPAL DAILIES

Buenos Aires

Ambito Financiero: Paseo Colón 1196, C1063ACY Buenos Aires; tel. (11) 4349-1500; fax (11) 4349-1505; e-mail mensajesaleditor@ ambito.com.ar; internet www.ambito.com.ar; f. 1976; morning (Mon.–Fri.); business; Pres. ORLANDO MARIO VIGNATTI; Dir GUSTAVO ISAACK; circ. 115,000.

Boletín Oficial de la República Argentina: Suipacha 767, C1008AAO Buenos Aires; tel. and fax (11) 4322-4055; e-mail dnro@boletinoficial.gov.ar; internet www.boletinoficial.gov.ar; f. 1893; morning (Mon.–Fri.); official records publ; Dir Dr JORGE EDUARDO FEIJOÓ; circ. 15,000.

Buenos Aires Herald: Avda San Juan 141, C1064AEB Buenos Aires; tel. and fax (11) 4349-1524; e-mail info@buenosairesherald .com; internet www.buenosairesherald.com; f. 1876; English; morning; independent; Dir ORLANDO VIGNETTI; circ. 20,000.

Clarín: Piedras 1743, C1140ABK Buenos Aires; tel. (11) 4309-7500; fax (11) 4309-7559; e-mail cartas@claringlobal.com.ar; internet www .clarin.com; f. 1945; morning; independent; Dir ERNESTINA HERRERA DE NOBLE; circ. 342,749 (daily), 686,287 (Sun.).

Crónica: Juan de Garay 40, C1063ABN Buenos Aires; tel. (11) 5550-8608; fax (11) 4361-4237; e-mail gerenciacomercial@cronica.com.ar; internet www.cronica.com.ar; f. 1963; morning and evening; Dirs MARIO ALBERTO FERNÁNDEZ (morning), RICARDO GANGEME (evening); circ. 330,000 (morning), 190,000 (evening), 450,000 (Sun.).

El Cronista Comercial: Paseo Colón 740/6, 1°, C1063ACU Buenos Aires; tel. (11) 4121-9300; fax (11) 4121-9301; e-mail info@cronista .com; internet www.cronista.com; f. 1908; morning; Dir FERNANDO GONZÁLEZ; circ. 65,000.

La Nación: Bouchard 551, C1106ABG Buenos Aires; tel. (11) 4319-1600; fax (11) 4319-1969; e-mail cescribano@lanacion.com.ar; internet www.lanacion.com.ar; f. 1870; morning; independent; Pres. JULIO SAGUIER; circ. 150,000.

Página 12: Solís 1525, C1134ADG Buenos Aires; tel. (11) 6772-4444; fax (11) 6772-4428; e-mail publicidad@pagina12.com.ar; internet www.pagina12.com.ar; f. 1987; morning; independent; Dir ERNESTO TIFFENBERG; Pres. FERNANDO SOKOLOWICZ; circ. 280,000.

La Prensa: Azopardo 715, C1107ADK Buenos Aires; tel. (11) 4349-1000; e-mail informaciongeneral@laprensa.com.ar; internet www .laprensa.com.ar; f. 1869; morning; independent; Dir FLORENCIO ALDREY IGLESIAS; circ. 100,000.

La Razón: Río Cuarto 1242, C1168AFF Buenos Aires; tel. and fax (11) 4309-6000; e-mail lectores@larazon.com.ar; internet www .larazon.com.ar; f. 1992; evening; Dir OSCAR MAGDALENA; circ. 62,000.

PRINCIPAL PROVINCIAL DAILIES

Catamarca

El Ancasti: Sarmiento 526, 1°, K4700EML Catamarca; tel. (3833) 431385; fax (3833) 453995; e-mail lector@elancasti.net.ar; internet www.elancasti.com.ar; f. 1988; morning; Dir MARCELO SOSA; circ. 9,000.

Chaco

Norte: Carlos Pellegrini 744, H3500CDP Resistencia; tel. (3722) 428204; fax (3722) 426047; internet www.diarionorte.com; f. 1968; Dir MIGUEL ANGEL FERNÁNDEZ; circ. 16,500.

Chubut

Crónica: Namuncurá 122, U9000BVD Comodoro Rivadavia; tel. (297) 447-1200; fax (297) 447-1780; internet www.diariocronica.com .ar; f. 1962; morning; Dir DANIEL CÉSAR ZAMIT; circ. 15,000.

Córdoba

Comercio y Justicia: Félix Paz 310, Alto Alberdi, X5002IGQ Córdoba; tel. and fax (351) 488-0088; e-mail redaccion@ comercioyjusticia.info; internet www.comercioyjusticia.com.ar; f. 1939; morning; economic and legal news with periodic supplements on architecture and administration; Pres. EDUARDO POGROBINKI; Dir JAVIER ALBERTO DE PASCUALE; circ. 5,800.

La Voz del Interior: Monseñor P. Cabrera 6080, X5008HKJ Córdoba; tel. (351) 475-7000; fax (351) 475-7282; e-mail lavoz@ lavozdelinterior.com.ar; internet www.lavozdelinterior.com.ar; f. 1904; morning; independent; Dir Dr CARLOS HUGO JORNET; circ. 57,000.

Corrientes

El Litoral: Hipólito Yrigoyen 990, W3400AST Corrientes; tel. and fax (3783) 411524; e-mail redaccion@el-litoral.com.ar; internet www .el-litoral.com.ar; f. 1960; morning; Dir CARLOS A. ROMERO FERIS; circ. 25,000.

Entre Ríos

El Diario: Buenos Aires y Urquiza, E2823XBC Paraná; tel. (343) 423-1000; fax (343) 431-9104; e-mail info@eldiarioentrerios.com.ar; internet www.eldiario.com.ar; f. 1914; morning; Dir Dr LUIS F. ETCHEVEHERE; circ. 7,100.

El Heraldo: Quintana 42, E3200XAE Concordia; tel. (345) 421-5304; fax (345) 421-1397; e-mail admin@elheraldo.com.ar; internet www

.elheraldo.com.ar; f. 1915; evening; Editor Dr CARLOS LIEBERMANN; circ. 10,000.

Mendoza

Los Andes: San Martín 1049, M5500AAK Mendoza; tel. (261) 449-1200; fax (261) 420-2011; e-mail aguardiola@losandes.com.ar; internet www.losandes.com.ar; f. 1982; morning; Chair. RAÚL FLAMARIQUE; Pres. ARTURO GUARDIOLA; circ. 30,400.

Misiones

El Territorio: Quaranta No 4307, N3301GAC Posadas; tel. and fax (3752) 451844; internet www.territoriodigital.com.ar; f. 1925; Dir GONZALO PELTZER; circ. 4,800.

Provincia de Buenos Aires

El Atlántico: Bolívar 2975, B7600GDO Mar del Plata; e-mail info@diarioelatlantico.com; internet www.diarioelatlantico.com; f. 1938; morning; Dir OSCAR ORTIZ; circ. 20,000.

La Capital: Champagnat 2551, B7604GXA Mar del Plata; tel. (223) 478-8490; fax (223) 478-1038; e-mail diario@lacapitalnet.com.ar; internet www.lacapitalnet.com.ar; f. 1905; Dir FLORENCIO ALDREY IGLESIAS; circ. 32,000.

El Día: Avda A, Diagonal 80 815, B1900CCI La Plata; tel. (221) 425-0101; fax (221) 423-2996; e-mail lectores@eldia.com; internet www.eldia.com; f. 1884; morning; independent; Dir RAÚL E. KRAISELBURD; circ. 54,868.

Ecos Diarios: Calle 62, No. 2486, B7630XAF Necochea; tel. and fax (2262) 430754; e-mail ecosdiar@satlink.com; internet www.ecosdiarios.com; f. 1921; morning; independent; Dir GUILLERMO A. IGNACIO; circ. 2,300.

La Nueva Provincia: Rodríguez 55, B8000HSA Bahía Blanca; tel. (291) 459-0000; fax (291) 459-0001; e-mail redaccionweb@lanueva.com.ar; internet www.lanueva.com.ar; f. 1898; morning; independent; Dir DIANA JULIO DE MASSOT; circ. 14,000.

El Nuevo Cronista: 5 Calle 619, B8000XAV Mercedes; tel. (11) 2324-4001; internet www.nuevocronista.com.ar; Dir JAVIER GUEVARA.

El Popular: Vicente López 2626, B7400CRH Olavarría; tel. and fax (22) 8442-0502; e-mail redaccion@elpopular.com.ar; internet www.diarioelpopular.com.ar; f. 1899; morning; Dir JORGE GABRIEL BOTTA; circ. 6,100.

El Sol: Hipólito Yrigoyen 122, B1878FND Quilmes; tel. and fax (11) 4257-6325; e-mail elsol@elsolquilmes.com.ar; internet www.elsolquilmes.com.ar; f. 1927; Dir RODRIGO GHISANI; circ. 25,000.

La Voz del Pueblo: San Martín 991, B7500IKJ Tres Arroyos; tel. (2983) 430680; fax (2938) 430682; e-mail vecinos@lavozdelpueblo.com.ar; internet www.lavozdelpueblo.com.ar; f. 1902; morning; independent; Dir ALBERTO JORGE MACIEL; circ. 3,400.

Río Negro

Río Negro: 9 de Julio 733, R8332AAO General Roca; tel. (2941) 439300; fax (2941) 439638; e-mail compras@rionegro.com.ar; internet www.rionegro.com.ar; f. 1912; morning; Dir JULIO RAJNERI; Co-Dir NÉLIDA RAJNERI DE GAMBA; circ. 30,000.

Salta

El Tribuno: Avda Ex Combatientes de Malvinas 3890, A4412BYA Salta; tel. (387) 424-6200; fax (387) 424-6240; e-mail redaccion@eltribuno.com.ar; internet www.eltribuno.com.ar; f. 1949; morning; Dir ROBERTO E. ROMERO; circ. 20,000.

San Juan

Diario de Cuyo: Mendoza 380 Sur, J5402GUH San Juan; tel. (264) 429-0038; fax (264) 429-0063; e-mail comercialdc@diariodecuyo.com.ar; internet www.diariodecuyo.com.ar; f. 1947; morning; independent; Dir FRANCISCO B. MONTES; circ. 14,450.

San Luis

El Diario de La República: Lafinur 924, D5700ASO San Luis; tel. and fax (2623) 422037; e-mail redaccion@eldiariodelarepublica.com; internet www.eldiariodelarepublica.com; f. 1966; Dir FELICIANA RODRIGUEZ SAÁ; circ. 7,650.

Santa Fe

La Capital: Sarmiento 763, S2000CMK Rosario; tel. (341) 420-1100; fax (341) 420-1114; internet www.lacapital.com.ar; f. 1867; morning; independent; Dirs ORLANDO MARIO VIGNATTI, DANIEL EDUARDO VILA; circ. 40,000.

El Litoral: 25 de Mayo 3536, S3002DPJ Santa Fe; tel. (342) 450-2500; fax (342) 450-2530; e-mail litoral@litoral.com.ar; internet www.litoral.com.ar; f. 1918; morning; independent; Dir GUSTAVO VÍTTORI; circ. 16,500.

Santiago del Estero

El Liberal: Libertad 263, G4200CZC Santiago del Estero; tel. (385) 422-4400; fax (385) 422-4538; e-mail redaccion@elliberal.com.ar; internet www.elliberal.com.ar; f. 1898; morning; Dir ANTONIO ENRIQUE CASTIGLIONE; circ. 30,000.

Tucumán

La Gaceta: Mendoza 654, T4000DAN San Miguel de Tucumán; tel. (381) 484-2200; fax (381) 431-1597; e-mail redaccion@lagaceta.com.ar; internet www.lagaceta.com.ar; f. 1912; morning; independent; Dir DANIEL DESSEIN; circ. 54,000.

WEEKLY NEWSPAPER

Diario Perfil: Chacabuco 271, 8°, C1069AAE Buenos Aires; tel. (11) 4341-9000; fax (11) 4341-8988; e-mail perfilcom@perfil.com.ar; internet www.diarioperfil.com.ar; f. 2005; Saturday and Sunday; Dir JORGE FONTEVECCHIA; circ. 38,600.

PERIODICALS

Aeroespacio: Dorrego 4019, C1425GBE Buenos Aires; tel. and fax (11) 4514-1561; e-mail info@aerospacio.com.ar; internet www.aeroespacio.com.ar; f. 1940; every 2 months; aeronautics; Dir DANIEL M. RUSSO; circ. 24,000.

Billiken: Azopardo 565, C1307ADG Buenos Aires; tel. (11) 4346-0107; fax (11) 4343-7040; e-mail billiken@atlantida.com.ar; internet www.billiken.com.ar; f. 1919; weekly; children's magazine; Dir JUAN CARLOS PORRAS; circ. 54,000.

Caras: Chacabuco 271, C1069AAE Buenos Aires; tel. (11) 4341-9000; fax (11) 4341-8988; e-mail correocaras@perfil.com.ar; internet www.revista-caras.com.ar; f. 1992; weekly; celebrities; Dir LILIANA CASTAÑO; circ. 41,000.

Chacra: The New Farm Company, SA, Paseo Colón 728, 7°B, C1063ACU Buenos Aires; tel. (11) 4342-4390; e-mail agritotal@agritotal.com; internet www.agritotal.com; f. 1930; monthly; farm and country magazine; Dir RUBÉN BARTOLOMÉ; circ. 12,000.

El Economista: Córdoba 632, 2°, C1054AAS Buenos Aires; tel. (11) 4322-7360; fax (11) 4322-8157; e-mail redaccion@eleconomista.com.ar; internet www.eleconomista.com.ar; f. 1951; weekly; financial; Dir Dr D. RADONJIC; circ. 37,800.

El Federal: Tucumán 1, 19° y 20°, C1049AAA Buenos Aires; tel. (11) 4318-7700; e-mail comercial@infomedia.com.ar; weekly; farming and countryside; Dir FABIÁN CASAS; circ. 18,900.

Fortuna: Chacabuco 271, C1069AAE Buenos Aires; tel. (11) 4341-9000; fax (11) 4341-8988; e-mail correofortuna@perfil.com.ar; internet www.revista-fortuna.com.ar; f. 2003; weekly; economics and business; Editor JUAN PABLO DE SANTIS; circ. 4,700.

Gente: Azopardo 565, C1307ADG Buenos Aires; tel. (11) 4346-0240; e-mail genteonline@atlantida.com.ar; internet www.gente.com.ar; f. 1965; weekly; general; Dir JORGE DE LUJÁN GUTIÉRREZ; circ. 45,000.

El Gráfico: Balcarce 510, 1064 Buenos Aires; tel. (11) 5235-5100; e-mail elgrafico@elgrafico.com.ar; internet www.elgrafico.com.ar; f. 1919; monthly; sport; Editor MARTIN MAZUR; circ. 40,000.

Mercado: Peru 263, 2°, CP, C1067AAE Buenos Aires; tel. (11) 5166-9400; fax (11) 4343-7880; e-mail info@mercado.com.ar; internet www.mercado.com.ar; f. 1969; monthly; business; Dir MIGUEL ANGEL DIEZ; circ. 28,000.

Mundo Israelita, SA: Corrientes 4006, 4°, Of. 35, C1194ABS Buenos Aires; tel. (11) 4861-2224; fax (11) 4861-8434; e-mail mundoeditor@hotmail.com; internet www.mundoisraelita.com.ar; f. 1923; owned by Mundo Editor, SA; fortnightly; Jewish interest; Editor-Dir Dr CORINA SCHVARTZAPEL; circ. 2,000.

Noticias de la Semana: Chacabuco 271, C1069AAE Buenos Aires; tel. (11) 4341-9000; fax (11) 4341-8988; e-mail correonoticias@perfil.com.ar; internet www.revista-noticias.com.ar; f. 1977; weekly; news and current affairs; Editor GUSTAVO GONZÁLEZ; circ. 63,000.

Para Ti: Azopardo 565, C1107ADG Buenos Aires; tel. (11) 4331-4591; fax (11) 4331-3272; e-mail parati@atlantida.com.ar; internet www.parati.com.ar; f. 1922; weekly; women's interest; Dir JUAN CARLOS PORRAS; circ. 35,000.

La Prensa Médica Argentina: Junín 917, 2°D, C1113AAA Buenos Aires; tel. and fax (11) 4961-9213; e-mail presmedarg@hotmail.com; internet www.prensamedica.com.ar; f. 1914; monthly; medical; Editor Dr PABLO A. LÓPEZ; circ. 8,000.

Prensa Obrera: Ayacucho 444, C1026AAB Buenos Aires; tel. (11) 4953-3824; fax (11) 4953-7164; e-mail prensaobrera@po.org.ar; internet www.po.org.ar; f. 1982; weekly; publ. of Partido Obrero; circ. 16,000.

Saber Vivir: Magallanes 1315, C1288ABA Buenos Aires; tel. (11) 4303-2305; e-mail sabervivir@gentille.biz; f. 1999; fortnightly; health; Dir Ricardo Gentille; circ. 81,000.

Veintitrés: Serrano 1139, C1414DEW Buenos Aires; tel. (11) 4775-0300; e-mail lectores@veintitres.com; internet www.elargentino.com/medios-120-Veintitres.html; f. 1998; weekly; political and cultural; Dir Roberto Caballero; circ. 35,000.

NEWS AGENCIES

Diarios y Noticias (DYN): Julio A. Roca 636, 8°, C1067ABO Buenos Aires; tel. (11) 4342-3040; fax (11) 4342-3043; e-mail editor@dyn.com.ar; internet www.dyn.com.ar; f. 1982; Chair. José Pochat; Dir Hugo E. Grimaldi.

Noticias Argentinas, SA (NA): Dr Mariano Moreno 769, 3°, C1091AAO Buenos Aires; tel. and fax (11) 4331-3850; e-mail infogral@noticiasargentinas.com; internet www.noticiasargentinas.com; f. 1973; Pres. Fernando Cuello; Dir Guillermo Vucetich.

Télam, SE: Bolívar 531, C1066AAK Buenos Aires; tel. (11) 4339-0330; fax (11) 4339-0353; e-mail telam@telam.com.ar; internet www.telam.com.ar; f. 1945; state-owned; Pres. (vacant).

PRESS ASSOCIATION

Asociación de Entidades Periodísticas Argentinas (ADEPA): Chacabuco 314, 3°, C1069AAH Buenos Aires; tel. and fax (11) 4331-1500; e-mail adepa@adepa.org.ar; internet www.adepa.org.ar; f. 1962; Pres. Gustavo Vittori; Sec.-Gen. Carlos Rago.

Publishers

Aguilar, Altea, Alfaguara, Taurus, SA de Ediciones: Leandro N. Alem 720, C1001AAP Buenos Aires; tel. (11) 4119-5000; fax (11) 4119-5021; e-mail info@alfaguara.com.ar; internet www.alfaguara.com.ar; f. 1946; part of Grupo Editorial Santillana Argentina; general, literature, children's books; Pres. Emiliano Martinez; Dir-Gen. David Delgado de Robles.

Aique Grupo Editor, SA: Francisco Acuña de Figueroa 352, C1180AAF Buenos Aires; tel. (11) 4867-7000; e-mail centrodocente@aique.com.ar; internet www.aique.com.ar; f. 1976; educational; Dir-Gen. María Pía Gagliardi.

Amorrortu Editores, SA: Paraguay 1225, 7°, C1057AAS Buenos Aires; tel. (11) 4816-5812; fax (11) 4816-3321; e-mail info@amorrortueditores.com; internet www.amorrortueditores.com; f. 1967; academic, social sciences and humanities; Man. Dir Horacio de Amorrortu.

a-Z Editora, SA: Paraguay 2351, C1121ABK Buenos Aires; tel. (11) 4961-4036; fax (11) 4961-0089; e-mail contacto@az.com.ar; internet www.az.com.ar; f. 1976; educational, children's, literature, social sciences, medicine, law; Pres. Ramiro Villalba Garibaldi.

Biblioteca Nacional de Maestros: c/o Ministerio de Educación, Pizzurno 935, planta baja, C1020ACA Buenos Aires; tel. (11) 4129-1272; fax (11) 4129-1268; e-mail bnminfo@me.gov.ar; internet www.bnm.me.gov.ar; f. 1884; Dir Graciela Teresa Perrone.

Cosmopolita, SRL: Piedras 744, C1070AAP Buenos Aires; tel. (11) 4361-8925; fax (11) 4361-8049; e-mail editorialcosmopolita@fullzero.com.ar; internet www.ed-cosmopolita.com.ar; f. 1940; science and technology; Man. Dir Ruth F. de Rapp.

Crecer Creando Editorial: Viamonte 2052, C1056ABF Buenos Aires; tel. (11) 4372-4165; fax (11) 4371-9351; e-mail info@crecercreando.com.ar; internet www.crecercreando.com.ar; educational; Pres. Carlos Rivera.

De Los Cuatro Vientos Editorial: Venezuela 726, C1096ABD Buenos Aires; tel. and fax (11) 4331-4542; e-mail info@deloscuatrovientos.com.ar; internet www.deloscuatrovientos.com.ar; f. 2000; Dir Pablo Gabriel Albornoz; Editor Mariela Fernanda Aquilano.

Distribuidora Lumen, SRL: Viamonte 1674, C1055ABF, Buenos Aires; tel. (11) 4373-1414; fax (11) 4375-0453; e-mail ventas@lumen.com.ar; internet www.lumen.com.ar; f. 1958; imprints include Lumen (religion, spirituality, etc.), Magisterio (educational), Lumen-Hvmanitas (social sciences) and Lohlé-Lumen (politics, philosophy, literature); Man. Basilio Makar.

Ediciones de la Flor SRL: Gorriti 3695, C1172ACE Buenos Aires; tel. (11) 4963-7950; fax (11) 4963-5616; e-mail edic-flor@datamarkets.com.ar; internet www.edicionesdelaflor.com.ar; f. 1966; fiction, poetry, theatre, juvenile, humour and scholarly; Co-Dirs Ana María Miler, Daniel Divinsky.

Ediciones Gránica: Lavalle 1634, 3° G, C1048AAN Buenos Aires; tel. (11) 4374-1456; fax (11) 4373-0669; e-mail granica.ar@granicaeditor.com; internet www.granicaeditor.com; management, reference.

Ediciones Macchi, SA: Pacheco 3190, C1431FJN Buenos Aires; tel. and fax (11) 4542-7835; e-mail info@macchi.com; internet www.macchi.com; f. 1946; economic sciences; Pres. Raúl Luis Macchi.

Ediciones Manantial, SRL: Avda de Mayo 1365, 6°, Of. 28, C1085ABD Buenos Aires; tel. (11) 4383-6059; fax (11) 4383-7350; e-mail info@emanantial.com.ar; internet www.emanantial.com.ar; f. 1984; social science, education and psychoanalysis; Gen. Man. Carlos A. de Santos.

Ediciones Nueva Visión, SAIC: Tucumán 3748, C1189AAV Buenos Aires; tel. (11) 4864-5050; fax (11) 4863-5980; e-mail ednuevavision@ciudad.com.ar; f. 1954; psychology, education, social sciences, linguistics; Man. Dir Haydée P. de Giacone.

Ediciones del Signo: Julián Alvarez 2844, 1° A, C1425DHT Buenos Aires; tel. (11) 4804-4147; fax (11) 4782-1836; e-mail edicionesdelsigno@arnet.com.ar; internet www.edicionesdelsigno.com.ar; f. 1995; philosophy, psychoanalysis, politics and scholarly; Man. Beatriz Gercman.

Editorial Albatros, SACI: Torre Las Plazas, J. Salguero 2745, 5°, Of. 51, C1425DEL Buenos Aires; tel. (11) 4807-2030; fax (11) 4807-2010; e-mail info@albatros.com.ar; internet www.albatros.com.ar; f. 1945; technical, non-fiction, social sciences, sport, children's books, medicine and agriculture; Pres. Andrea Inés Canevaro.

Editorial Argenta Sarlep, SA: Avda Corrientes 1250, 3°, Of. F, C1043AAZ Buenos Aires; tel. (11) 4382-9085; fax (11) 4381-6100; e-mail info@editorialargenta.com; internet www.editorialargenta.com; f. 1970; literature, poetry, theatre and reference; Man. Alexander Ernst Rennes.

Editorial Bonum, SACI: Avda Corrientes 6687, C1427BPE Buenos Aires; tel. and fax (11) 4554-1414; e-mail ventas@editorialbonum.com.ar; internet www.editorialbonum.com.ar; f. 1960; religious, educational and self-help; Pres. Martín Gremmelspacher.

Editorial Catálogos, SRL: Avda Independencia 1860, C1225AAN Buenos Aires; tel. and fax (11) 4381-5708; e-mail catalogos@ciudad.com.ar; internet www.catalogossrl.com.ar; religion, literature, academic, general interest and self-help; Co-Dirs Horacio García, Leonardo Pérez.

Editorial Claretiana: Lima 1360, C1138ACD Buenos Aires; tel. (11) 4305-9597; fax (11) 4305-6552; e-mail editorial@editorialclaretiana.com.ar; internet www.editorialclaretiana.com.ar; f. 1956; Catholicism; Man. Dir P. Gustavo M. Larrazábal.

Editorial Claridad, SA (Editorial Heliasta, SRL): Juncal 3451, C1425AYT Buenos Aires; tel. and fax (11) 4804-0472; e-mail editorial@heliasta.com.ar; internet www.heliasta.com.ar; f. 1922; literature, biographies, social science, politics, reference, dictionaries; Co-Dirs Dra Ana María Cabanellas de las Cuevas, Guillermo Cabanellas de las Cuevas.

Editorial Don Bosco (edebé): Don Bosco 4069, C1206ABM Buenos Aires; tel. (11) 4883-0111; fax (11) 4883-0115; e-mail comercial@edb.com.ar; internet www.edb.com.ar; f. 1993; religious and educational; Pres. P. Roque Sella; Editorial Dir Juan L. Rodríguez.

Editorial Errepar: Paraná 725, C1017AAO Buenos Aires; tel. (11) 4370-2002; fax (11) 4383-2202; e-mail clientes@errepar.com; internet www.errepar.com; encyclopaedias, technical and legal texts; Pres. Ricardo Parada; Dir Francisco Cañada.

Editorial Grupo Cero: Mansilla 2686, planta baja 1 y 2, C1425BPD Buenos Aires; tel. (11) 4966-1710; fax (11) 4966-1713; e-mail pedidos@editorialgrupocero.com; internet www.editorialgrupocero.com; fiction, poetry and psychoanalysis; Dir María Norma Menassa.

Editorial Guadalupe: Mansilla 3865, C1425BQA Buenos Aires; tel. and fax (11) 4826-8587; e-mail gerencia@editorialguadalupe.com.ar; internet www.editorialguadalupe.com.ar; f. 1895; social sciences, religion, anthropology, children's books and pedagogy; Man. Dir P. Luis O. Liberti; Man. Editor Liliana Ferreirós.

Editorial Hispano-Americana, SA (HASA): Rincón 686, C1227ACD Buenos Aires; tel. (11) 4943-7111; fax (11) 4943-7061; e-mail info@hasa.com.ar; internet www.hasa.com.ar; f. 1934; science and technology; Pres. Prof. Héctor Alberto Algarra.

Editorial Inter-Médica, SAICI: Junín 917, 1° A, C1113AAC Buenos Aires; tel. (11) 4961-9234; fax (11) 4961-5572; e-mail info@inter-medica.com.ar; internet www.inter-medica.com.ar; f. 1959; medicine and veterinary; Pres. Jorge Modyeievsky.

Editorial Juris: Moreno 1580, S2000DLF Rosario, Santa Fe; tel. (341) 426-7301; e-mail editorial@editorialjuris.com; internet www.editorialjuris.com; f. 1952; legal texts; Dir Luis Maesano.

Editorial Kier, SACIFI: Avda Santa Fe 1260, C1059ABT Buenos Aires; tel. (11) 4811-0507; fax (11) 4811-3395; e-mail info@kier.com.ar; internet www.kier.com.ar; f. 1907; Eastern doctrines and religions, astrology, parapsychology, tarot, I Ching, occultism, cabbala, freemasonry and natural medicine; Pres. Héctor S. Pibernus; Dirs Cristina Grigna, Osvaldo Pibernus.

Editorial Losada, SA: Avda Corrientes 1551, C1042AAB Buenos Aires; tel. (11) 4375-5001; fax (11) 4373-4006; e-mail losada@

editoriallosada.com; internet www.editoriallosada.com; f. 1938; general; Pres. JOSÉ JUAN FERNÁNDEZ REGUERA; Editor GONZALO LOSADA.

Editorial Médica Panamericana, SA: Marcelo T. de Alvear 2145, C1122AAG Buenos Aires; tel. (11) 4821-5520; fax (11) 4825-1214; e-mail info@medicapanamericana.com; internet www.medicapanamericana.com.ar; f. 1962; medicine and health sciences; Pres. HUGO BRIK.

Editorial Mercosur: Dean Funes 923, C1231ABI Buenos Aires; tel. (11) 4956-2297; e-mail info@editorialmercosur.com; internet www.editorialmercosur.com; self-help and general interest.

Editorial del Nuevo Extremo: Angel J. Carranza 1852, C1414COV Buenos Aires; tel. (11) 4773-3228; fax (11) 4773-8445; e-mail info@delnuevoextremo.com; internet www.delnuevoextremo.com; general interest; Pres. MIGUEL ANGEL LAMBRÉ; Dir TOMÁS LAMBRÉ.

Editorial Sigmar, SACI: Avda Belgrano 1580, 7°, C1093AAQ Buenos Aires; tel. (11) 4381-2510; fax (11) 4383-5633; e-mail editorial@sigmar.com.ar; internet www.sigmar.com.ar; f. 1941; children's books; Man. Dir ROBERTO CHWAT.

Editorial Stella: Viamonte 1984, C1056ABD Buenos Aires; tel. (11) 4374-0346; fax (11) 4374-8719; e-mail ventas@editorialstella.com.ar; internet www.editorialstella.com.ar; f. 1941; general non-fiction and textbooks; owned by Asociación Educacionista Argentina; Dir TELMO MEIRONE; Editor ADOLFO GARCÍA SÁEZ.

Editorial Sudamericana Random House Mondadori: Humberto Primo 545, 1°, C1103ACK Buenos Aires; tel. (11) 5235-4400; fax (11) 4362-7364; e-mail info@edsudamericana.com.ar; internet www.edsudamericana.com.ar; f. 1939; general fiction and non-fiction; Gen. Man. OLAF HANTEL.

Editorial Troquel, SA: Olleros 1818, 4° I, C1426CRH Buenos Aires; tel. and fax (11) 4779-9444; e-mail editorial@troguel.com.ar; internet www.troquel.com.ar; f. 1954; general literature, religion, philosophy and education; Pres. GUSTAVO A. RESSIA.

Editorial Zeus, SRL: Balcarce 730, S2000DNP Rosario, Santa Fe; tel. (341) 449-5585; fax (341) 425-4259; e-mail zeus@zeus.com.ar; internet www.zeus.com.ar; legal texts; Editor and Dir GUSTAVO L. CAVIGLIA.

Emecé Editores, SA: Avda Independencia 1668, C1100ABQ Buenos Aires; tel. (11) 4124-9100; fax (11) 4124-9190; e-mail info@planeta.com.ar; internet www.editorialplaneta.com.ar; f. 1939; fiction, non-fiction, biographies, history, art, essays; subsidiary of Grupo Planeta, Spain; Editorial Dir ALBERTO DÍAZ.

EUDEBA (Editorial Universitaria de Buenos Aires): Avda Rivadavia 1573, C1033AAF Buenos Aires; tel. (11) 4383-8025; fax (11) 4383-2202; e-mail info@eudeba.com.ar; internet www.eudeba.com.ar; f. 1958; university textbooks and general interest publs; Pres. GONZALO ALVAREZ; Gen. Man. LUIS QUEVEDO.

Galerna: Lambaré 893, C1185ABA Buenos Aires; tel. (11) 4867-1661; fax (11) 4862-5031; e-mail contacto@galerna.net; internet www.galernalibros.com; fiction, theatre, poetry and scholarly; Man. HUGO LEVÍN.

Gram Editora: Cochabamba 1652, C1148ABF Buenos Aires; tel. (11) 4304-4833; fax (11) 4304-5692; e-mail grameditora@infovia.com.ar; internet www.grameditora.com.ar; f. 1990; education; Man. MANUEL HERRERO MONTES.

Grupo Santillana Argentina: Avda Leandro N. Alem 720, C1001AAP Buenos Aires; tel. (11) 4119-5000; e-mail info@santillana.com.ar; internet www.santillana.com.ar; f. 1963; part of Grupo Editorial Santillana (Spain); education; Dir-Gen. DAVID DELGADO DE ROBLES.

Kapelusz Editora, SA: San José 831, C1076AAQ Buenos Aires; tel. (11) 5236-5000; fax (11) 5236-5005; e-mail jvergara@kapelusz.com.ar; internet www.kapelusz.com.ar; f. 1905; textbooks, psychology, pedagogy, children's books; Vice-Pres. RAFAEL PASCUAL ROBLES.

LexisNexis Argentina: Carlos Pellegrini 887, 3°, C1013AAQ Buenos Aires; tel. (11) 5236-8800; fax (11) 5236-8811; e-mail info@lexisnexis.com.ar; internet www.lexisnexis.com.ar; f. 1999 upon acquisition of Depalma and Abeledo-Perrot; periodicals and books covering law, politics, sociology, philosophy, history and economics; Gen. Man. CAROLINA TRONGE.

Siglo Veintiuno Editores: Guatemala 4824, C1425BUP Buenos Aires; tel. and fax (11) 4770-9090; e-mail info@sigloxxieditores.com.ar; internet www.sigloxxieditores.com.ar; social science, history, economics, art; Editorial Dir CARLOS E. DIEZ.

PUBLISHERS' ASSOCIATIONS

Cámara Argentina del Libro: Avda Belgrano 1580, 4°, C1093AAQ Buenos Aires; tel. (11) 4381-8383; fax (11) 4381-9253; e-mail cal@editores.org.ar; internet www.editores.org.ar; f. 1938; Pres. CARLOS DE SANTOS; Sec. GRACIELA ROSENBERG.

Cámara Argentina de Publicaciones: Lavalle 437, 5°, Of. A, C1047AAI Buenos Aires; tel. (11) 5218-9707; e-mail info@publicaciones.org.ar; internet www.publicaciones.org.ar; f. 1970; Pres. HÉCTOR DI MARCO; Sec. MARÍA PÍA GAGLIARDI.

Broadcasting and Communications

TELECOMMUNICATIONS

Regulatory Bodies

Cámara de Informática y Comunicaciones de la República Argentina (CICOMRA): Avda Córdoba 744, 2° D, C1054AAT Buenos Aires; tel. (11) 4325-8839; fax (11) 4325-9604; e-mail gerente@cicomra.org.ar; internet www.cicomra.org.ar; f. 1985; represents enterprises in the communications sector; Pres. NORBERTO CAPELLÁN; Exec. Dir ALFREDO BALLARINO.

Comisión Nacional de Comunicaciones (CNC): Perú 103, 1°, C1067AAC Buenos Aires; tel. (11) 4347-9501; fax (11) 4347-9897; internet www.cnc.gov.ar; f. 1996; Insp. CEFERINO NAMUNCURÁ.

Major Operators

AT&T Argentina: Alicia Moreau de Justo 400, C1107AAH Buenos Aires; tel. (11) 4310-8700; fax (11) 4310-8706; e-mail info_Argentina@cla.att.com; internet www.att.com; Vice-Pres. (Canada, Caribbean and Latin America) MARY E. LIVINGSTON; Country Pres. ALEJANDRO ROSSI.

Cía Ericsson, SACI: Güemes 676, 1°, Vicente López PCIA, B1638CJF Buenos Aires; tel. (11) 4319-5500; fax (11) 4315-0629; e-mail infocom@cea.ericsson.se; internet www.ericsson.com; Head (Latin America) SERGIO QUIROGA DA CUNHA; Exec. Vice-Pres. (Argentina) DANIEL CARUSO.

Claro Argentina, SA (AMX Argentina, SA): Edif. Corporativo, Avda de Mayo 878, C1084AAQ Buenos Aires; tel. (11) 4109-8888; e-mail nscocimarro@claro.com.ar; internet argentina.claro.com.ar; f. 1994 as CTI Móvil; wholly owned subsidiary of América Móvil, SA de CV (Mexico) since 2003; mobile cellular telephone services; Dir-Gen. ROGELIO VIESCA.

Movistar: Avda Corrientes 655, 3º, C1043AAG Buenos Aires; tel. (11) 5321-0000; fax (11) 5321-1604; internet www.movistar.com.ar; 98% owned by Telefónicas Móviles, SA (Spain); operates mobile telephone network; Dir (Products and Services) LEANDRO MUSCIANO.

Nextel Communications Argentina, SRL: Olga Cossettini 363, Dique 4, C1107CCG Buenos Aires; tel. (11) 5359-0000; e-mail prensa@nextel.com.ar; internet www.nextel.com.ar; f. 1998; Pres. RUBEN BUTVILOFSKY.

Telcosur, SA: Don Bosco 3672, 5°, C1206ABF Buenos Aires; tel. (11) 4865-9060; e-mail telcosur@telcosur.com.ar; internet www.telcosur.com.ar; f. 1998; 99% owned by Transportador de Gas del Sur (TGS); Operations Man. EDUARDO VIGILANTE; Commercial Man. EDUARDO MARTÍN.

Telecom Argentina, SA: Alicia Moreau de Justo 50, 10°, C1107AAB Buenos Aires; tel. (11) 4968-4000; fax (11) 4968-1420; e-mail contactos@telecompersonal.com.ar; internet www.telecom.com.ar; provision of telecommunication services in the north of Argentina; provides wireless services under the brand *Telecom Personal*; Pres. ENRIQUE GARRIDO; Exec. Dir FRANCO BERTONE.

BROADCASTING

Regulatory Bodies

Autoridad Federal de Servicios de Comunicación Audiovisual (COMFER): Suipacha 765, 9°, C1008AAO Buenos Aires; tel. (11) 4320-4900; fax (11) 4394-6866; e-mail prensa@afsca.gob.ar; internet www.afsca.gov.ar; f. 1972 as Comisión Nacional de Radio y Televisión (CONART); name changed to Comité Federal de Radiodifusión (COMFER) in 1981; reorg. as a decentralized regulatory authority and adopted present name in 2009; controls various technical aspects of broadcasting and transmission of programmes; Pres. JUAN GABRIEL MARIOTTO.

Secretaría de Comunicaciones: Sarmiento 151, 4°, C1041AAC Buenos Aires; tel. (11) 4318-9410; fax (11) 4318-9432; internet www.secom.gov.ar; co-ordinates 30 stations and the international service; Sec. CARLOS LISANDRO SALAS.

Radio

Radio Nacional Argentina (RNA): Maipú 555, C1006ACE Buenos Aires; tel. (11) 4325-9100; fax (11) 4325-4313; e-mail direccionlra1@radionacional.gov.ar; internet www.radionacional.gov.ar; f. 1937; five national radio stations: Nacional; Nacional Folklórica; Nacional Clásica; Nacional Rock 93.7; and RAE (q.v.); 39 provincial stations; Exec. Dir MARÍA SEOANE.

Radiodifusión Argentina al Exterior (RAE): Maipú 555, C1006ACE Buenos Aires; tel. (11) 4325-6368; fax (11) 4325-9433; e-mail rae@radionacional.gov.ar; f. 1958; broadcasts in seven languages to all areas of the world; Dir LUIS MARÍA BARASSI (acting).

Asociación de Radiodifusoras Privadas Argentinas (ARPA): Juan D. Perón 1561, 3°, C1037ACC Buenos Aires; tel. (11) 4371-5999; fax 4382-4483; e-mail arpaorg@arpa.org.ar; internet www.arpa.org.ar; f. 1958; asscn of privately owned commercial stations; Pres. Cdre CARLOS MARIA MOLINA; Exec. Dir HECTOR J. PARREIRA.

Television

The national television network is regulated by the Comité Federal de Radiodifusión (see above). The following are some of the more important television stations in Argentina: Argentina Televisora Color LS82 Canal 7, LS83 (Canal 9 Libertad), LV80 Telenueva, LU81 Teledifusora Bahiense SA, LV81 Canal 12 Telecor SACI, Dicor Difusión Córdoba, LV80 TV Canal 10 Universidad Nacional Córdoba, and LU82 TV Mar del Plata SA.

The Argentine Government holds a 20% stake in the regional television channel Telesur, which began operations in May 2005 and is based in Caracas, Venezuela.

América TV: Fitzroy 1650, C1414CHX Buenos Aires; tel. (11) 5032-2222; e-mail americanoticias@america2.com.ar; internet www.america2.com.ar; Pres. DANIEL VILA; CEO GUSTAVO CAPUA.

Canal 9 (Telearte, SA): Dorrego 1782, C1414CKZ Buenos Aires; tel. (11) 3220-9999; e-mail webmaster@canal9.com.ar; internet www.canal9.com.ar; f. 1960; private channel; Pres. CARLOS E. LOREFICE LYNCH; Dir-Gen. ENRIQUE TABOADA.

Canal 13: Lima 1261, C1138ACA Buenos Aires; tel. (11) 4305-0013; fax (11) 4331-8573; e-mail eltrecetv@artear.com; internet www.eltrecetv.com.ar; f. 1989; part of Arte Radiotelevisivo Argentino, SA; leased to a private concession in 1992; Gen. Man. DANIEL ZANARDI; Programme Man. PABLO CODEVILLA.

LS82 TV Canal 7 (TV Pública): Avda Figueroa Alcorta 2977, C1425CKI Buenos Aires; tel. (11) 4808-2500; e-mail contacto@tvpublica.com.ar; internet www.tvpublica.com.ar; state-controlled; Pres. TRISTÁN BAUER; Exec. Dir MARTÍN BONAVETTI.

Telefé (Canal 11): Pavón 2444, C1248AAT Buenos Aires; tel. (11) 4941-9549; fax (11) 4942-6773; e-mail prensa@telefe.com.ar; internet www.telefe.com.ar; private channel; Programme Man. CLAUDIO VILLARRUEL.

Asociación de Teleradiodifusoras Argentinas (ATA): Avda Córdoba 323, 6°, C1054AAC Buenos Aires; tel. (11) 4312-4208; fax (11) 4315-4681; e-mail info@ata.org.ar; internet www.ata.org.ar; f. 1959; asscn of 23 private television channels; Pres. PABLO CASEY; Exec. Dir CARLOS MOLINERO.

Finance

(cap. = capital; res = reserves; dep. = deposits; m. = million; brs = branches; amounts in nuevos pesos argentinos, unless otherwise stated)

BANKING

Central Bank

Banco Central de la República Argentina: Reconquista 266, C1003ABF Buenos Aires; tel. (11) 4348-3500; fax (11) 4348-3955; e-mail sistema@bcra.gov.ar; internet www.bcra.gov.ar; f. 1935 as a central reserve bank; bank of issue; all capital is held by the state; cap. 14,604.7m., res 34,972.1m., dep. 108,855.3m. (Dec. 2009); Pres. MERCEDES MARCO DEL PONT.

Government-owned Commercial Banks

Banco del Chubut: Rivadavia 615, Rawson, U9103ANG Chubut; tel. (2965) 482505; fax (2965) 484196; internet www.bancochubut.com.ar; cap. and res 124.5m., dep. 1,476.2m. (June 2009); Pres. Dr CARLOS ALBERTO GARCÍA LOREA.

Banco de la Ciudad de Buenos Aires: Sarmiento 630, C1005AAH Buenos Aires; tel. (11) 4329-8600; fax (11) 4329-8729; e-mail bcdad39@sminter.com.ar; internet www.bancociudad.com.ar; municipal bank; f. 1878; cap. 985.7m., res 598.7m., dep. 14,459.5m. (Dec. 2010); Chair. and Pres. FEDERICO STURZENEGGER; 65 brs.

Banco de Inversión y Comercio Exterior, SA (BICE): 25 de Mayo 526/32, C1002ABL Buenos Aires; tel. (11) 4317-6900; fax (11) 4311-5596; e-mail informatica@bice.com.ar; internet www.bice.com.ar; f. 1991; cap. and res 1,130.4m. (Dec. 2009); Pres. MAURO ALEM; Gen. Man. JORGE GIACOMOTTI.

Banco de la Nación Argentina: Bartolomé Mitre 326, Capital Federal Of. 235, C1036AAF Buenos Aires; tel. (11) 4347-6000; fax (11) 4347-6316; e-mail mbravo@bna.com.ar; internet www.bna.com.ar; f. 1891; national bank; cap. 5,799.1m., res 1,993.5m., dep. 68,600.9m. (Dec. 2009); Pres. JUAN CARLOS FÁBREGA; Gen. Man. RUBÉN DARIO NOCERA; 645 brs.

Banco de la Pampa SEM: Carlos Pellegrini 255, L6300DRE Santa Rosa; tel. (295) 451-0000; e-mail cexterior@blp.com.ar; internet www.blp.com.ar; f. 1958; cap. 128.5m., res 59.8m., dep. 1,910.7m. (Dec. 2009); Chair. LAURA AZUCENA GALLUCCIO; Gen. Man. CARLOS DESINANO; 51 brs.

Banco de la Provincia de Buenos Aires: Calle 7, 726, B1900TFS La Plata, Buenos Aires; tel. (11) 4347-0238; fax (11) 4348-9496; e-mail delriom@bpba.com.ar; internet www.bapro.com.ar; f. 1822; provincial govt-owned bank; cap. 2,162.7m., dep. 32,301.2m. (Dec. 2010), res 1,760m. (Dec. 2009); Pres. GUILLERMO FRANCOS; Gen. Man. EDUARDO ORDÓÑEZ; 343 brs.

Banco de la Provincia de Córdoba: San Jerónimo 231/235, X5000AGD Córdoba; tel. (351) 420-7507; fax (351) 420-7492; internet www.bancor.com.ar; f. 1873; provincial bank; cap. 210.2m., res 16.8m., dep. 4,775.9m. (Dec. 2009); Pres. MARIO CUNEO; Gen. Man. PABLO VIERA; 143 brs.

Banco Provincia del Neuquén: Avda Argentina 41, 1°, Q8300AYA Neuquén; tel. (299) 449-6618; fax (299) 449-6622; internet www.bpn.com.ar; f. 1960; cap. and res 145.4m., dep. 1,357.4m. (Dec. 2009); Pres. OMAR GUTIÉRREZ; Gen. Man. ADRIANA VELASCO; 22 brs.

Banco de Tierra del Fuego: Maipú 897, V9410BJQ Ushuaia; tel. (2901) 441600; fax (2901) 441601; e-mail info@bancotdf.com.ar; internet www.bancotdf.com.ar; national bank; cap. and res 173.9m., dep. 536m. (Dec. 2009); Pres. RICARDO IGLESIAS; Gen. Man. JORGE CERROTA; 8 brs.

Nuevo Banco de la Rioja, SA: Rivadavia 702, F5300ACU La Rioja; tel. (3822) 430575; fax (3822) 430618; e-mail nblrsa@nblr.com.ar; internet www.nblr.com.ar; f. 1994; provincial bank; cap. and res 52.5m., dep. 299.3m. (Dec. 2009); Pres. ELIAS SAHAD; Gen. Man. CLAUDIA L. DE BRIGIDO; 13 brs.

Nuevo Banco de Santa Fe, SA: 25 de Mayo 2499, S3000FTS Santa Fe; tel. (342) 450-4700; e-mail contactobc@bancobsf.com.ar; internet www.bancobsf.com.ar; f. 1847 as Banco Provincial de Santa Fe, adopted current name in 1998; provincial bank; cap. 91.1m., res 690.1m., dep. 9,202.7m. (Dec. 2010); Chair. ENRIQUE ESKINAZI; Exec. Dir MARCELO BUIL; 105 brs.

Private Commercial Banks

Banco BI Creditanstalt, SA: Bouchard 547, 24° y 25°, C1106ABG Buenos Aires; tel. (11) 4319-8400; fax (11) 4319-8230; e-mail info@bicreditanstalt.com.ar; internet www.bicreditanstalt.com.ar; f. 1971 as Banco Interfinanzas; adopted current name 1997; cap. and res 444.8m., dep. 8.6m. (Dec. 2009); Pres. Dr MIGUEL ANGEL ANGELINO; Gen. Man. RICARDO RIVERO HAEDO.

Banco CMF, SA: Macacha Güemes 150, Puerto Madero, C1106BKD Buenos Aires; tel. (11) 4318-6800; fax (11) 4318-6859; e-mail info@bancocmf.com.ar; internet www.bancocmf.com.ar; f. 1978 as Corporación Metropolitana de Finanzas, SA; adopted current name in 1999; cap. 275.3m., dep. 1,283.7m. (Dec. 2010), res 47.8m. (Dec. 2009); Pres. and Chair. JOSÉ ALBERTO BENEGAS LYNCH; Gen. Man. MARCOS PRIETO.

Banco COMAFI: Roque S. Peña 660, C1035AAO Buenos Aires; tel. (11) 4347-0400; fax (11) 4347-0404; e-mail contactenos@comafi.com.ar; internet www.comafi.com.ar; f. 1984; assumed control of 65% of Scotiabank Quilmes in April 2002; cap. 36.7m., res 88.5m., dep. 2,797.2m. (June 2010); Pres. GUILLERMO CERVIÑO; Vice-Pres. EDUARDO MASCHWITZ; 56 brs.

Banco de Corrientes: 9 de Julio 1002, esq. San Juan, W3400AYQ Corrientes; tel. (3783) 479300; fax (3783) 479372; e-mail bcteservicios@bcoctes.com.ar; internet www.bancodecorrientes.com.ar; f. 1951; est. as Banco de la República de Corrientes; adopted current name in 1993, after transfer to private ownership; cap. and res 119.4m., dep. 870.4m. (Dec. 2009); Pres. Dr ALEJANDRO ABRAHAN; Gen. Man. CARLOS GUSTAVO MACORATTI; 33 brs.

Banco Finansur, SA: Sarmiento 700, esq. Maipú, Buenos Aires; tel. (11) 4324-3400; fax (11) 4322-4687; e-mail bafin@bancofinansur.com.ar; internet www.bancofinansur.com.ar; f. 1973; est. as Finansur Compañía Financiera, SA; adopted current name in 1993; cap. 32.7m., res 9.2m., dep. 490.7m. (Dec. 2010); Pres. JORGE SÁNCHEZ CÓRDOVA; 4 brs.

Banco de Galicia y Buenos Aires, SA: Juan D. Perón 407, Casilla 86, C1038AAI Buenos Aires; tel. (11) 6329-0000; fax (11) 6329-6100; e-mail bancogalicia@bancogalicia.com.ar; internet www.bancogalicia.com.ar; f. 1905; cap. 562.3m., res 1,193.3m., dep. 14,008.8m. (Dec. 2008); Chair. ANTONIO R. GARCÉS; 236 brs.

Banco Industrial: San Martin 549, Azul 7300, Buenos Aires; tel. (2281) 431779; e-mail sucazul@bancoindustrial.com.ar; internet www.bancoindustrial.com.ar; f. 1971; cap. 116.5m., res 102.5m., dep. 2,064.2m. (Dec. 2010); Pres. CARLOTA EVELINA DURST; Gen. Man. LUIS LARA; 30 brs.

Banco Itaú Buen Ayre, SA: 25 de Mayo 476, 2°, C1002ABJ Buenos Aires; tel. (11) 4378-8400; fax (11) 4394-1057; e-mail contactenos@itau.com.ar; internet www.itau.com.ar; fmrly Banco Itaú Argentina,

SA; renamed as above following purchase of Banco del Buen Ayre, SA, in 1998; subsidiary of Banco Itaú, SA (Brazil); 117 brs.

Banco Macro, SA: Sarmiento 447, 4°, C1041AAI Buenos Aires; tel. (11) 5222-6500; fax (11) 5222-6624; e-mail relacionesinstitucionales@macro.com.ar; internet www.macro.com .ar; f. 1995 as Banco Bansud by merger; merged with Banco Macro in 2002; adopted current name 2006; cap. 594.5m., res 1,369.5m., dep. 29,167.1m. (Dec. 2011); Pres. JORGE HORACIO BRITO; 400 brs.

Banco Mariva, SA: Sarmiento 500, C1041AAJ Buenos Aires; tel. (11) 4321-2200; fax (11) 4321-2292; e-mail info@mariva.com.ar; internet www.mariva.com.ar; f. 1980; cap. and res 92.8m., dep. 583.2m. (Dec. 2009); Pres. JOSÉ LUIS PARDO.

Banco Patagonia, SA: Juan D. Perón 500, C1038AAJ Buenos Aires; tel. (11) 4132-6300; fax (11) 4132-6059; e-mail international@bancopatagonia.com.ar; internet www .bancopatagonia.com.ar; f. 1912; fmrly Banco Sudameris; adopted current name in 2004 following merger with Banco Patagonia; cap. 748.1m., res 457.5m., dep. 6,522.3m. (Dec. 2009); Chair. JORGE GUILLERMO STUART MILNE.

Banco de San Juan: Ignacio de la Roza 85, J5402DCA San Juan; tel. (264) 429-1000; fax (264) 421-4126; internet www.bancosanjuan .com; f. 1943; 20% owned by provincial govt of San Juan; 80% privately owned; cap. and res 266.7m., dep. 1,294m. (Dec. 2009); Pres. ENRIQUE ESKENAZI; Gen. Man. MARIA SILVINA BELLANTIG TARDIO; 8 brs.

Banco Santander Río, SA: Bartolomé Mitre 480, C1036AAH Buenos Aires; tel. (11) 4341-1000; fax (11) 4341-1020; internet www.santanderrio.com.ar; f. 1908 as Banco Río de la Plata; adopted current name 2007; owned by Banco Santander (Spain); cap. and res 1,465.6m., dep. 19,398.5m. (Dec. 2009); Pres. JOSÉ LUIS ENRIQUE CRISTOFANI; 276 brs.

Banco Santiago del Estero: Belgrano 529/37 Sur, G4200AAF Santiago del Estero; tel. (385) 450-2300; fax (385) 450-2316; e-mail info@bse.com.ar; internet www.bse.com.ar; Pres. NÉSTOR CARLOS ICK; Gen. Man. ALDO RENÉ MAZZOLENI.

Banco Supervielle, SA: Bartolomé Mitre 434, C1036AAH Buenos Aires; tel. (11) 4324-8000; fax (11) 4324-8090; internet www .supervielle.com.ar; f. 1887; owned by Grupo Supervielle; took over Banco Regional de Cuyo in Oct. 2010; cap. 154.7m., res 1,392.1m. (Dec. 2010); Pres. JUAN CARLOS NOUGUES; Gen. Man. JOSE LUIS PANERO; 165 brs.

Banco de Valores, SA: Sarmiento 310, C1041AAH Buenos Aires; tel. (11) 4323-6900; fax (11) 4323-6942; e-mail info@banval.sba.com .ar; internet www.bancodevalores.com; f. 1978; cap. 75m., res 99.5m., dep. 912.1m. (Dec. 2010); Pres. HÉCTOR JORGE BACQUÉ; 1 br.

BBVA Banco Francés, SA: Reconquista 199, C1003ABC Buenos Aires; tel. (11) 4346-4000; fax (11) 4346-4320; internet www .bancofrances.com; f. 1886 as Banco Francés del Río de la Plata, SA; changed name to Banco Francés, SA, in 1998 following merger with Banco de Crédito Argentino; adopted current name in 2000; cap. 536.3m., res 1,378.6m., dep. 22,461.3m. (Dec. 2010); Pres. JORGE C. BLEDEL; Dir RICARDO MORENO; 308 brs.

HSBC Bank Argentina, SA: Florida 229, C1005AAE Buenos Aires; tel. (11) 4320-2800; fax (11) 4132-2409; internet www.hsbc.com.ar; f. 1978 as Banco Roberts, SA; name changed to HSBC Banco Roberts, SA, in 1998; adopted current name in 1999; cap. 1,244.1m., res 148.7m., dep. 11,496.2m. (June 2009); Pres. ANTONIO M. LOSADA; 68 brs.

Nuevo Banco de Entre Ríos, SA: Monte Caseros 128, E3100ACD Paraná; tel. (343) 423-1200; fax (343) 421-1221; e-mail info@ nuevobersa.com.ar; internet www.nuevobersa.com.ar; f. 1935; provincial bank; transferred to private ownership in 1995; cap. 20.4m., dep. 624.5m. (Dec. 2002); Pres. ENRIQUE ESKENAZI; Gen. Man. LUIS NÚÑEZ; 73 brs.

Standard Bank Argentina: Della Paolera 265, 13°, C1001ABA Buenos Aires; tel. (11) 4820-9200; fax (11) 4820-2050; e-mail standardbank.argentina@standardbank.com; internet www .standardbank.com.ar; f. 2005; cap. 847.1m., res 61.8m., dep. 9,865.1m. (Dec. 2010); CEO EDUARDO SPANGENBERG; 98 brs.

Co-operative Bank

Banco Credicoop Cooperativo Ltdo: Reconquista 484, C1003ABJ Buenos Aires; tel. (11) 4320-5000; fax (11) 4324-5891; e-mail credicoop@bancocredicoop.coop; internet www .bancocredicoop.coop; f. 1979; cap. 848,000 (June 2008), res 983.4m., dep. 12,252.8m. (June 2010); Chair., Pres. and CEO CARLOS HELLER; Gen. Man. GERARDO GALMÉS; 249 brs.

Bankers' Associations

Asociación de Bancos Argentinos (ADEBA): Juan D. Perón 564, 6°, C1038AAL Buenos Aires; tel. and fax (11) 5238-7790; e-mail info@ adebaargentina.com.ar; internet www.adebaargentina.com.ar; f. 1972; Pres. JORGE HORACIO BRITO; 28 mems.

Asociación de Bancos de la Argentina (ABA): San Martín 229, 10°, 1004 Buenos Aires; tel. (11) 4394-1836; fax (11) 4394-6340; e-mail webmaster@aba-argentina.com; internet www .aba-argentina.com; f. 1999 by merger of Asociación de Bancos de la República Argentina (f. 1919) and Asociación de Bancos Argentinos (f. 1972); Pres. CLAUDIO CESARIO; 27 mems.

Asociación de Bancos Públicos y Privados de la República Argentina (ABAPPRA): Florida 470, 1°, C1005AAJ Buenos Aires; tel. and fax (11) 4322-5342; e-mail info@abappra.com.ar; internet www.abappra.com; f. 1959; Pres. JUAN CARLOS FABREGA; Exec. Dir DEMETRIO BRAVO AGUILAR; 31 mems.

STOCK EXCHANGE

Mercado de Valores de Buenos Aires, SA: 25 de Mayo 367, 8°–10°, C1002ABG Buenos Aires; tel. and fax (11) 4316-6000; e-mail merval@merval.sba.com.ar; internet www.merval.sba.com.ar; f. 1929; Pres. PABLO ALDAZABAL.

There are also stock exchanges at Córdoba, Rosario, Mendoza and La Plata.

Supervisory Authority

Comisión Nacional de Valores (CNV): 25 de Mayo 175, C1002ABC Buenos Aires; tel. (11) 4329-4600; fax (11) 4331-0639; e-mail webadm@cnv.gov.ar; internet www.cnv.gob.ar; monitors capital markets; Pres. ALEJANDRO VANOLI.

INSURANCE

There were 180 insurance companies operating in Argentina in 2011, of which 100 were general insurance companies. The following is a list of those offering all classes or a specialized service.

Supervisory Authority

Superintendencia de Seguros de la Nación: Julio A. Roca 721, 5°, C1067ABC Buenos Aires; tel. (11) 4338-4000; fax (11) 4331-9821; e-mail consultasydenuncias@ssn.gov.ar; internet www.ssn.gov.ar; f. 1938; Supt JUAN A. BONTEMPO.

Major Companies

Allianz Argentina, Cía de Seguros, SA: Avda Corrientes 299, C1043AAC, Buenos Aires; tel. 4222-3443; fax 4320-7143; e-mail atencionalcliente@allianz.com.ar; internet www.allianz.com.ar; f. 1988; fmrly AGF Allianz Argentina; changed name as above 2007; CEO EDWARD HENRY LANGE.

Aseguradora de Créditos y Garantías, SA (ACG): Maipú 71, 4°, C1084ABA Buenos Aires; tel. (11) 4320-7200; fax (11) 4320-7277; e-mail infoacg@bristolgroup.com.ar; internet www.bristolgroup.com .ar/ACG; f. 1965; part of the Bristol Group; Pres. HORACIO G. SCAPPARONE.

Aseguradores de Cauciones, SA: Paraguay 580, C1057AAF Buenos Aires; tel. (11) 5235-3700; fax (11) 5235-3784; e-mail consultas@caucion.com.ar; internet www.caucion.com.ar; f. 1968; all classes; Pres. JOSÉ DE VEDIA.

Berkley International Argentina, SA: Avda Carlos Pellegrini 1023, 1009, Buenos Aires; tel. 4378-8100; e-mail comercial@berkley .com.ar; internet www.berkley.com.ar; f. 1908; part of Berkley International Latinoamérica; Pres. EDUARDO I. LLOBET.

Caja de Seguros, SA: Fitz Roy 957, C1414CHI Buenos Aires; tel. (11) 4857-8118; fax (11) 4857-8001; e-mail suc_villacrespo@lacaja .com.ar; internet www.lacaja.com.ar; f. 1992; Pres. GERARDO WERTHEIN.

CESCE Argentina—Seguro de Crédito y Garantías, SA: Corrientes 345, 7°, C1043AAD Buenos Aires; tel. (11) 4313-4303; fax (11) 4313-2919; e-mail info@casce.com.ar; internet www.casce.com.ar; f. 1967 as Cía Argentina de Seguros de Créditos a la Exportación; part of Grupo CESCE Internacional; covers credit and extraordinary and political risks for Argentine exports; Pres. EDUARDO ANGEL FORNS; Gen. Man. LUIS IMEDIO SERRANO.

Chiltington Internacional, SA: Reconquista 559, 8°, C1003ABK Buenos Aires; tel. (11) 4312-8600; fax (11) 4312-8884; e-mail msmith@chiltington.com.ar; internet chiltington.com; f. 1982; Regional Head MARTIN SMITH.

Cía. de Seguros La Mercantil Andina, SA: Avda Eduardo Madero 942, 18°, C1106ACW Buenos Aires; tel. 4310-5400; internet www .mercantilandina.com.ar; f. 1923; part of Grupo Pescarmona since 1978; Gen. Man. PEDRO MIRANTE.

El Comercio Seguros, SA: Maipú 71, baja, C1084ABA Buenos Aires; tel. (11) 4324-1300; fax (11) 4393-1311; e-mail gguerrero@ bristolgroup.com.ar; internet www.bristolgroup.com.ar/ec; f. 1889; all classes; part of the Bristol Group; Exec. Dirs CLAUDIO LANDA, JORGE DURBANO.

Generali Argentina, Cía de Seguros, SA: Reconquista 458, 3°, C1003ABJ, Buenos Aires; tel. 4857-7942; fax 4857-7946; e-mail infogenerali@generali.com.ar; internet www.generali.com.ar; f. 1948 as Assicurazioni Generali; changed name as above 1998; Gen. Man. CLAUDIO MELE.

Mapfre Argentina: Juana Manso 205, C1107CBE Buenos Aires; tel. (11) 4320-9439; fax (11) 4320-9444; e-mail comunicacion@mapfre.com.ar; internet www.mapfre.com.ar; all classes; Exec. Pres. DIEGO SERGIO SOBRINI.

Liberty Seguros Argentina, SA: Avda Paseo Colón 357, C1063ACD Buenos Aires; tel. 4104-0000; fax 4346-0400; e-mail centrodecontacto@libertyseguros.com.ar; internet www.libertyseguros.com.ar; f. 1995; Pres. SUSANA AUGUSTÍN.

Prudential Seguros, SA: Avda Leandro N. Alem 855, 5°, C1001AAD Buenos Aires; tel. (11) 4891-5000; fax 4314-3435; e-mail atencionalcliente@prudential.com; internet www.prudentialseguros.com.ar; f. 2000; Pres. MAURICIO ZANATTA.

RSA Argentina (United Kingdom): Lima 653, Buenos Aires; tel. (11) 4339-0000; fax (11) 4331-1453; e-mail atencion.cliente@rsagroup.com; internet www.rsagroup.com.ar; fmrly known as Royal & Sun Alliance Seguros; life and general; Pres. FERRARO ROBERTO PASCUAL.

L'UNION de Paris Compañía Argentina de Seguros, SAC: Tte Gral D. Perón 650, 5°, C1038AAN Buenos Aires; tel. (11) 5300-3300; fax (11) 5811–0744; e-mail lunion@lunion.com.ar; internet www.lunion.com.ar; f. 1897 as L'Union IARD; present name adopted 2004; part of HDI Seguros group from April 2011; general; Pres. MATTHIAS MAAK.

Victoria Seguros, SA: Florida 556, C1005AAL Buenos Aires; tel. (11) 4322-1100; fax (11) 4325-9016; e-mail seguros@victoria.com.ar; internet www.victoria.com.ar; f. 1921; Pres. SEBASTIÁN BAGÓ; Vice-Pres. and Exec. Dir DANIEL RICARDO SALAZAR.

Zurich Argentina Cía de Seguros, SA: Cerrito 1010, C1010AAV Buenos Aires; tel. (11) 4819-1010; e-mail servicioalcliente@zurich.com; internet www.zurich.com.ar; f. 1947; all classes; Pres. JOSÉ MARÍA ORLANDO POTT.

Insurance Association

Asociación Argentina de Cías de Seguros (AACS): 25 de Mayo 565, 2°, C1002ABK Buenos Aires; tel. (11) 4312-7790; fax (11) 4312-6300; e-mail info@aacs.org.ar; internet www.aacs.org.ar; f. 1894; 27 mems; Pres. FRANCISCO ASTELARRA; Sec. LUCAS PESCARMONA.

Trade and Industry

GOVERNMENT AGENCIES

Agencia Nacional de Desarrollo de Inversiones (ProsperAr): Florida 375, 8°B, C1005AAG Buenos Aires; tel. (11) 4328-9510; e-mail info@prosperar.gov.ar; internet www.prosperar.gov.ar; promotion of investment in Argentina; Dir Dra BEATRIZ NOFAL.

Consejo Federal de Inversiones: San Martín 871, C1004AAQ Buenos Aires; tel. (11) 4317-0700; fax (11) 4315-1238; e-mail administrator@cfired.org.ar; internet www.cfired.org.ar; f. 1959; federal board to co-ordinate domestic and foreign investment and provide technological aid for the provinces; Sec.-Gen. JUAN JOSÉ CIÁCERA.

Dirección de Forestación (DF): Paseo Colón 982, Anexo Jardín, C1063ACW Buenos Aires; tel. (11) 4349-2124; fax (11) 4349-2102; e-mail bfores@minagri.gob.ar; internet www.forestacion.gov.ar; assumed the responsibilities of the national forestry commission (Instituto Forestal Nacional—IFONA) in 1991, following its dissolution; supervised by the Secretaría de Agricultura, Ganadería, Pesca y Alimentos; maintains the Centro de Documentación e Información Forestal; Dir GUSTAVO CORTÉS.

Instituto de Desarrollo Económico y Social (IDES): Aráoz 2838, C1425DGT Buenos Aires; tel. (11) 4804-4949; fax (11) 4804-5856; e-mail ides@ides.org.ar; internet www.ides.org.ar; f. 1960; investigation into social sciences and promotion of social and economic devt; 1,100 mems; Pres. MARIANO PLOTKIN.

Oficina Nacional de Control Comercial Agropecuario (ONCCA): Paseo Colón 922, C1063ACW Buenos Aires; tel. (11) 4349-2492; fax (11) 4349-2005; e-mail infooncca@mecon.gov.ar; internet www.oncca.gov.ar; oversees the agricultural sector; supervised by the Secretaría de Agricultura, Ganadería, Pesca y Alimentos; Pres. JUAN MANUEL CAMPILLO.

Organismo Nacional de Administración de Bienes (ONABE): José Ramos Mejía 1302, 3°, Of. 300, C1104AJN Buenos Aires; tel. (11) 4318-3658; e-mail sistemas@onabe.gov.ar; internet www.onabe.gov.ar; f. 2000; responsible for administration of state property; supervised by the Ministry of Federal Planning, Public Investment and Services; Dir JOSÉ FRANCISCO LÓPEZ; Exec. Dir FERNANDO MIGUEL SUÁREZ.

DEVELOPMENT ORGANIZATIONS

Instituto Argentino del Petróleo y Gas: Maipú 639, C1006ACG Buenos Aires; tel. (11) 4325-8008; fax (11) 4393-5494; e-mail informa@iapg.org.ar; internet www.iapg.org.ar; f. 1957; promotes the devt of petroleum exploration and research; Pres. ERNESTO LÓPEZ ANADÓN.

Instituto para el Desarrollo Social Argentino (IDESA): Montevideo 451, 3°, Of. 33, C1019ABI Buenos Aires; tel. (11) 4371-1177; internet www.idesa.org; centre for research in public policies related to social devt; Pres. OSVALDO GIORDANO; Exec. Dir ALEJANDRA TORRES.

Sociedad Rural Argentina: Florida 460, C1005AAJ Buenos Aires; tel. (11) 4324-4700; e-mail prensa@sra.org.ar; internet www.sra.org.ar; f. 1866; private org. to promote the devt of agriculture; Pres. Dr HUGO LUIS BIOLCATI; 9,400 mems.

CHAMBERS OF COMMERCE

Cámara Argentina de Comercio: Avda Leandro N. Alem 36, C1003AAN Buenos Aires; tel. (11) 5300-9000; fax (11) 5300-9058; e-mail difusion2@cac.com.ar; internet www.cac.com.ar; f. 1927; Pres. CARLOS RAÚL DE LA VEGA; Sec. ALBERTO O. DRAGOTTO.

Cámara de Comercio de los Estados Unidos en la República Argentina (AMCHAM): Viamonte 1133, 8º, C1053ABW Buenos Aires; tel. (11) 4371-4500; fax (11) 4371-8400; e-mail amcham@amchamar.com.ar; internet www.amchamar.com.ar; f. 1918; US Chamber of Commerce; CEO ALEJANDRO DÍAZ.

Cámara de Comercio Exterior de Rosario: Córdoba 1868, Rosario, S2000AXD Santa Fe; tel. and fax (341) 425-7147; e-mail consultas@commerce.com.ar; internet www.commerce.com.ar; f. 1958; deals with imports and exports; Pres. JUAN CARLOS RETAMERO; Vice-Pres. GUILLERMO BECCANI; 150 mems.

Cámara de Comercio, Industria y Producción de la República Argentina: Florida 1, 4°, C1005AAA Buenos Aires; tel. (11) 4331-0813; fax (11) 4331-9116; e-mail cacipra@fibertel.com.ar; internet www.cacipra.org.ar; f. 1913; Pres. Dr CAYETANO NINO ROTA; 1,500 mems.

Cámara de Comercio Italiana de Rosario: Córdoba 1868, 1°, S2000AXD, Rosario; tel. and fax (341) 426-68789; e-mail ngonzalez@italrosario.com; internet www.ccir.com.ar; f. 1985; promotes Argentine–Italian trade; Dir GUSTAVO MICATROTTA.

Cámara de Exportadores de la República Argentina: Roque Sáenz Peña 740, 1°, C1035AAP Buenos Aires; tel. and fax (11) 4394-4482; e-mail contacto@cera.org.ar; internet www.cera.org.ar; f. 1943; export promotion; 700 mems; Pres. Dr ENRIQUE S. MANTILLA.

Similar chambers are located in most of the larger centres, and there are many other foreign chambers of commerce.

INDUSTRIAL AND TRADE ASSOCIATIONS

Asociación Argentina de Productores Porcinos: Florida 520, C1005AAL Buenos Aires; internet www.porcinos.org.ar; f. 1922; promotion of pork products; Pres. JUAN LUIS UCCELLI.

Asociación Argentina de Químicos y Coloristas Textiles: Simbrón 5756, C1408BHJ Buenos Aires; tel. (11) 4644-3996; fax (11) 4644-7520; e-mail aaqct@aaqct.org.ar; internet www.aaqct.org.ar; f. 1954; textile industry; Pres. GUILLERMO CEVASCO.

Asociación de Importadores y Exportadores de la República Argentina: Manuel Belgrano 124, 1°, C1092AAO Buenos Aires; tel. (11) 4342-0010; fax (11) 4342-1312; e-mail aiera@aiera.org.ar; internet www.aiera.org; f. 1966; Pres. HORACIO CONSOLO; Man. ADRIANO A. DE FINA.

Bodegas de Argentina: Thames 2334, 16A, C1425FIH Buenos Aires; tel. (11) 5786-1220; fax (11) 5786-1266; e-mail info@bodegasdeargentinaac.com; internet www.bodegasdeargentina.org; f. 2001 following merger between Centro de Bodegueros de Mendoza and Asociación Vitivinícola Argentina; wine industry; Pres. ÁNGEL VESPA.

Cámara de la Industria Aceitera de la República Argentina—Centro de Exportadores de Cereales: Bouchard 454, 7°, C1106ABS Buenos Aires; tel. (11) 4311-4477; fax (11) 4311-3899; internet www.ciaracec.com.ar; f. 1980; vegetable oil producers and grain exporters; Pres. RAÚL PADILLA.

Cámara de Sociedades Anónimas: Libertad 1340, C1016ABB Buenos Aires; tel. and fax (11) 4000-7399; fax (11) 4000-7703; e-mail camsocanon@camsocanon.com; internet www.camsocanon.com; Pres. HORACIO DE LAS CARRERAS; Man. EDUARDO BACQUÉ.

Confederación Argentina de la Mediana Empresa (CAME): Florida 15, 3°, C1005AAA Buenos Aires; tel. (11) 5556-5556; fax (11) 5556-5502; e-mail info@came.org.ar; internet www.came.org.ar; f. 1956; fmrly Coordinadora de Actividades Mercantiles Empresarias; adopted current name 2006; small and medium enterprises; Pres. OSVALDO CORNIDE.

Confederación Intercooperativa Agropecuaria Ltda (CONINAGRO): Lavalle 348, 4°, C1047AAH Buenos Aires; tel. (11) 4311-4664; fax (11) 4311-0623; internet www.coninagro.org.ar; f. 1958; farming co-operative; Pres. CARLOS ALBERTO GARETTO.

Confederaciones Rurales Argentinas (CRA): México 628, 2°, C1097AAN Buenos Aires; tel. (11) 4300-4451; internet www.cra.org.ar; f. 1943; promotion and devt of agricultural activities; 14 federations comprising over 300 mem. orgs, representing 109,000 farmers; Pres. MARIO LLAMBÍAS.

Consorcio de Exportadores de Carnes Argentinas (ABC): San Martín 575, 5°B, C1004AAK Buenos Aires; tel. (11) 4394-9734; fax (11) 4394-9658; e-mail gerencia@abc consorcio.com.ar; internet www.abc-consorcio.com.ar; f. 2002 following the merger between the Asociación de Industrias Argentinas de Carnes and several meat exporters; meat industry; refrigerated and canned beef and mutton; Pres. MARIO DARÍO RAVETTINO.

Federación Agraria Argentina (FAA): Alfonsina Storni 745, S2000DYA Rosario, Santa Fe; tel. (341) 512-2000; fax (341) 512-2001; e-mail comunicacion@faa.com.ar; internet www.faa.com.ar; f. 1912; oversees the interests of small and medium-sized grain producers; Pres. EDUARDO BUZZI.

Federación Lanera Argentina: 25 de Mayo 516, 4°, C1002ABL Buenos Aires; tel. (11) 4878-8800; fax (11) 4878-8804; e-mail info@flasite.com; internet www.flasite.com; f. 1929; wool industry; Pres. RAÚL ERNESTO ZAMBONI; Sec. JUAN PABLO LEFEBVRE; 40 mems.

EMPLOYERS' ORGANIZATION

Unión Industrial Argentina (UIA): Avda de Mayo 1147/57, C1085ABB Buenos Aires; tel. (11) 4124-2300; fax (11) 4124-2301; e-mail uia@uia.org.ar; internet www.uia.org.ar; f. 1887; re-established in 1974 with the fusion of the Confederación Industrial Argentina (CINA) and the Confederación General de la Industria; following the dissolution of the CINA in 1977, the UIA was formed in 1979; asscn of manufacturers, representing industrial corpns; Pres. HÉCTOR MÉNDEZ; Sec. Dr JOSÉ IGNACIO DE MENDIGUREN.

UTILITIES

Regulatory Authorities

Compañía Administradora del Mercado Mayorista Eléctrico, SA (CAMMESA): Avda Madero 942, 1°, C1106ACW Buenos Aires; tel. (11) 4319-3700; e-mail agentes@cammesa.com.ar; internet portalweb.cammesa.com; f. 1992; responsible for administering the wholesale electricity market; 20% state-owned, 80% by electricity companies; Pres. JULIO MIGUEL DE VIDO (Minister of Federal Planning, Public Investment and Services).

Ente Nacional Regulador de la Electricidad (ENRE): Avda Eduardo Madero 1020, 10°, C1106ACX Buenos Aires; tel. (11) 4510-4600; fax (11) 4510-4210; internet www.enre.gov.ar; f. 1993; agency for regulation and control of electricity generation, transmission and distribution; Pres. MARIO DE CASAS.

Ente Nacional Regulador del Gas (ENARGAS): Suipacha 636, 10°, C1008AAN Buenos Aires; tel. (11) 4325-2500; fax (11) 4348-0550; internet www.enargas.gov.ar; regulates and monitors gas utilities; Insp. ANTONIO LUIS PRONSATO.

Electricity

Central Puerto, SA (CEPU): Tomás Edison 2701, C1104BAB Buenos Aires; tel. (11) 4317-5000; fax (11) 4317-5099; e-mail info@centralpuerto.com; internet www.centralpuerto.com; electricity generating co; Pres. BERNARDO VELAR DE IRIGOYEN.

Comisión Nacional de Energía Atómica (CNEA): Avda del Libertador 8250, C1429BNP Buenos Aires; tel. (11) 4704-1000; fax (11) 4704-1154; e-mail comunicacion@cnea.gov.ar; internet www.cnea.gov.ar; f. 1950; nuclear energy science and technology; operates three nuclear power stations for research purposes; Pres. NORMA LUISA BOERO.

Comisión Técnica Mixta de Salto Grande (CTMSG): Avda Leandro N. Alem 449, C1003AAE Buenos Aires; tel. (11) 5554-3400; fax (11) 5554-3402; e-mail ctmsgda@sion.com; internet www.saltogrande.org; operates Salto Grande hydroelectric station, which has an installed capacity of 650 MW; jt Argentine-Uruguayan project; Pres., Argentine delegation ENRIQUE TOPOLANSKY; Gen. Mans CARLOS MASCINO (Argentina), HUGO MAQUEIRA (Uruguay).

Dirección Provincial de Energía: Calle 55, 629, e/7 y 8, La Plata, B1900BGY Buenos Aires; tel. and fax (221) 427-1185; e-mail dpe@dpe.mosp.gba.gov.ar; internet www.dpe.mosp.gba.gov.ar; f. 1957 as Dirección de Energía de la Provincia de Buenos Aires; name changed as above in 2000; electricity co for province of Buenos Aires; Dir NÉSTOR CALLEGARI.

Empresa Distribuidora y Comercializadora Norte, SA (EDENOR): Azopardo 1025, 16° y 17°, C1107ADQ Buenos Aires; tel. (11) 4348-2121; fax (11) 4334-0805; e-mail ofitel@edenor.com.ar; internet www.edenor.com.ar; f. 1992; distribution of electricity; Pres. ALEJANDRO MACFARLANE.

Empresa Distribuidora Sur, SA (EDESUR): San José 140, C1076AAD Buenos Aires; tel. (11) 4381-8981; fax (11) 4383-3699; e-mail prensa@edesur.com.ar; internet www.edesur.com.ar; f. 1992; distribution of electricity; Gen. Man. JOSÉ MARÍA HIDALGO.

Endesa Costanera, SA (CECCO): España 3301, C1107ANA Buenos Aires; tel. (11) 4307-3040; fax (11) 4300-4168; e-mail comercialweb@ccostanera.com.ar; internet www.endesacostanera.com; subsidiary of Endesa (Spain); generation, transmission, distribution and sale of thermal electric energy; Pres. JOSEPH M. HIDALGO MARTÍN-MATEOS; Gen. Man. JOSÉ MIGUEL GRANGED BRUÑEN.

Energía Argentina, SA (ENARSA): Avda Libertador 1068, 2°, C1112ABN Buenos Aires; tel. and fax (11) 4801-9325; e-mail contacto@enarsa.com.ar; internet www.enarsa.com.ar; f. 2004; state-owned; generation and distribution of electricity, especially from renewable sources; exploration, extraction and distribution of natural gas and petroleum; Pres. JOSÉ GRANERO.

Entidad Binacional Yacyretá: Eduardo Madero 942, 21°, C1106ACW Buenos Aires; tel. (11) 4510-7500; e-mail rrpp@eby.org.ar; internet www.eby.org.ar; operates the hydroelectric dam at Yacyretá on the Paraná river; owned jtly by Argentina and Paraguay; completed in 1998, it is one of the world's largest hydroelectric complexes, consisting of 20 generators with a total generating capacity of 3,200 MW; 14,673 GWh of electricity produced in 2007; Exec. Dir OSCAR ALFREDO THOMAS.

Hidronor Ingeniería y Servicios, SA (HISSA): Hipólito Yrigoyen 1530, 6°B, C1089AAD Buenos Aires; tel. and fax (11) 4382-6316; fax (11) 4382-5111; e-mail hidronor@ciudad.com.ar; internet www.hidronor.com; f. 1967; fmrly HIDRONOR, SA, the largest producer of electricity in Argentina; responsible for developing the hydroelectric potential of the Limay and neighbouring rivers; Pres. CARLOS ALBERTO ROCCA; transferred to private ownership in 1992 and divided into the following companies.

Central Hidroeléctrica Alicurá, SA: Avda Leandro N. Alem 712, 7°, C1001AAP Buenos Aires.

Central Hidroeléctrica Cerros Colorados, SA: Avda Leandro N. Alem 690, 12°, C1001AAO Buenos Aires.

Central Hidroeléctrica El Chocón, SA: Suipacha 268, 9°, Of. A, C1008AAF Buenos Aires.

Hidroeléctrica Piedra del Aguila, SA: Tomás Edison 1251, C1104AYL Buenos Aires; tel. and fax (11) 4311-3296; Pres. Dr JÉRÔME FERRIER; Gen. Man. HORACIO TURRI.

Transener, SA: Paseo Colón 728, 6°, C1063ACU Buenos Aires; tel. (11) 4342-6925; fax (11) 4342-7147; e-mail info-trans@transx.com.ar; internet www.transener.com.ar; energy transmission co; Gen. Man. CARLOS A. GONZÁLEZ.

Petrobrás Energía, SA: Maipú 1, 22°, C1084ABA Buenos Aires; tel. (11) 4344-6000; fax (11) 4344-6315; internet www.petrobras.com.ar; f. 1946 as Pérez Companc, SA; petroleum interests acquired by Petrobrás of Brazil in 2003; operates the hydroelectric dam at Pichi Picún Leufu; Exec. Dir DÉCIO FABRICIO ODDONE DA COSTA.

Gas

Asociación de Distribuidores de Gas (ADIGAS): Diagonal Norte 740, 5° B, C1035AAP Buenos Aires; tel. (11) 4393-8294; e-mail consultas@adigas.com.ar; internet www.adigas.com.ar; f. 1993 to represent newly privatized gas companies; Gen. Man. CARLOS ALBERTO ALFARO.

Distribuidora de Gas del Centro, SA: Ituzaingó 774, Córdoba; tel. (351) 468-8108; fax (351) 468-1568; e-mail clientescentro@ecogas.com.ar; internet www.ecogas.com.ar/appweb/leo/centro/centro.php; state-owned co; distributes natural gas in Córdoba, Catamarca and La Rioja; Pres. EDUARDO A. HURTADO.

Distribuidora de Gas Cuyana, SA: Ituzaingó 774, Córdoba; tel. (351) 468-8108; fax (351) 468-1568; e-mail clientescuyo@ecogas.com.ar; internet www.ecogas.com.ar/appweb/leo/cuyo/cuyo.php; state-owned co; distributes natural gas in Mendoza, San Juan, San Luis; Pres. EDUARDO A. HURTADO.

Energía Argentina, SA (ENARSA): see Electricity.

Gas Natural Ban, SA: Isabel la Católica 939, C1268ACS Buenos Aires; tel. (11) 4754-1137; e-mail comercial@gasnaturalban.com.ar; internet www.gasnaturalban.com.ar; f. 1992; distribution of natural gas; Gen. Man. HORACIO CRISTIANI.

Metrogás, SA: Gregorio Aráoz de Lamadrid 1360, C1267AAB Buenos Aires; tel. (11) 4309-1000; fax (11) 4309-1025; e-mail atencionclientes@metrogas.com.ar; internet www.metrogas.com.ar; f. 1992; gas distribution; Dir. Gen. ANDRÉS CORDERO.

Transportadora de Gas del Norte, SA: Don Bosco 3672, 3°, C1206ABF Buenos Aires; tel. (11) 4008-2000; fax (11) 4008-2242; internet www.tgn.com.ar; f. 1992; distributes natural gas; Gen. Man. FREDDY CAMEO.

Transportadora de Gas del Sur, SA (TGS): Don Bosco 3672, 6°, C1206ABF Buenos Aires; tel. (11) 4865-9050; fax (11) 4865-9059; e-mail totgs@tgs.com.ar; internet www.tgs.com.ar; f. 1992; processing and transport of natural gas; Gen. Dir CARLOS SEIJO.

Water

Agua y Saneamientos Argentinos, SA (AySA): Tucumán 752, C1049APP Buenos Aires; tel. (11) 6319-0000; fax (11) 6139-2460; e-mail prensa@aysa.com.ar; internet www.aysa.com.ar; f. 2006; 90% state-owned; distribution of water in the Buenos Aires metropolitan area; Pres. Dr CARLOS HUMBERTO BEN.

TRADE UNIONS

Central de Trabajadores de la Argentinos (CTA): Piedras 1065, C1070AAU Buenos Aires; tel. (11) 4307-3829; fax (11) 4300-1015; e-mail prensacentral@cta.org.ar; internet www.cta.org.ar; f. 1992; dissident trade union confederation; Gen. Sec. HUGO YASKY.

Confederación General del Trabajo (CGT) (General Confederation of Labour): Azopardo 802, C1107ADN Buenos Aires; tel. (11) 4334-0596; fax (11) 4334-0599; e-mail secgral@cgtra.org.ar; internet www.cgtra.org.ar; f. 1930; Peronist; represents approx. 90% of Argentina's 1,100 trade unions; Sec.-Gen. HUGO ANTONIO MOYANO.

Federación Argentina de Trabajadores de Luz y Fuerza (FATLYF): Lima 163, C1073AAC, Buenos Aires, DF; tel. (11) 4383-4541; e-mail secretariageneral@fatlyf.org; internet www.fatlyf.org; f. 1948; Sec.-Gen. JULIO CÉSAR IERACII.

Unión Ferroviaria (UF): Avda Independencia 2880, C1225AAX Buenos Aires; tel. (11) 4957-4921; fax 4957-4928; e-mail info@unionferroviaria.org.ar; internet www.unionferroviaria.org.ar; f. 1922; train workers' union; part of the CGT; Sec.-Gen. JOSÉ ANGEL PEDRAZA.

CGT Azul y Blanca: Avda Belgrano 1280, C1093AAN Buenos Aires; f. 2008 by dissident faction of CGT comprising c. 60 unions; Sec.-Gen. LUIS BARRIONUEVO.

Unión Argentina de Trabajadores Rurales y Estibadores (UATRE) (Argentine Union of Rural Workers and Stevedores): Reconquista 630, 4º y 5º, C1003ABN, Buenos Aires; tel. (11) 4312-2500; e-mail igualdadygenero@uatre.org.ar; internet www.uatre.org.ar; Gen. Sec. GERÓNIMO (MOMO) VENEGAS.

Transport

Comisión Nacional de Regulación del Transporte (CNRT): Maipú 88, Apdo 129, C1000WAB Buenos Aires; tel. (11) 4819-3000; e-mail cnrt@miv.gov.ar; internet www.cnrt.gov.ar; f. 1996; regulates domestic and international transport services; Pres. EDUARDO SÍCARO.

Secretaría de Transporte de la Nación: Hipólito Yrigoyen 250, 12°, C1086AAB Buenos Aires; tel. (11) 4349-7254; fax (11) 4349-7201; e-mail transporte@minplan.gov.ar; internet www.transporte.gov.ar; Sec. JUAN PABLO SCHIAVI.

RAILWAYS

There are direct rail links with the Bolivian Railways network to Santa Cruz de la Sierra and La Paz; with Chile, through the Las Cuevas–Caracoles tunnel (across the Andes) and between Salta and Antofagasta; with Brazil, across the Paso de los Libres and Uruguayana bridge; with Paraguay (between Posadas and Encarnación by ferry-boat); and with Uruguay (between Concordia and Salto). In 2009 there were 25,023 km of tracks.

Following a privatization programme in the early 1990s the state-run Ferrocarriles Argentinos was replaced by Ente Nacional de Administración de Bienes Ferroviarios (ENABIEF), which assumed responsibility for railway infrastructure and the rolling stock not already sold off. The Buenos Aires commuter system was divided into eight concerns (one of which incorporates the underground railway system) and was offered for sale to private operators as 10- or 20-year (subsidized) concessions. ENABIEF was subsumed by the Organismo Nacional de Administración de Bienes (see Trade and Industry—Govt Agencies) in 2000. The railway network is regulated by the Comisión Nacional de Regulación del Transporte (CNRT—see above). Construction of a 710-km high-speed railway linking Buenos Aires, Rosario and Córdoba was planned, although by 2012 the project remained stalled.

ALL Mesopotámica: Santa Fe 4636, 3°, C1425BHV Buenos Aires; tel. (11) 4778-2425; fax (11) 4778-2493; internet www.rrdc.com/op_argentina_all_meso.html; f. 1993 as Ferrocarril Mesopotámico; bought by Brazil's América Latina Logística, SA, in 1999; operates freight services on the Urquiza lines; Exec. Dir ALEXANDRE SANTORO; 2,704 km of track.

Cámara de Industriales Ferroviarios: Alsina 1609, 1°, C1088AAO Buenos Aires; tel. (11) 4382-0598; e-mail cifra@argentina.com; private org. to promote the devt of Argentine railway industries; Pres. ANA MARÍA GHIBAUDI.

Ferrobaires: Gen. Hornos 11, 4°, C1154ACA Buenos Aires; tel. (11) 4305-5174; fax (11) 4305-5933; e-mail calidadservicio@ferrobaires.gba.gov.ar; internet www.ferrobaires.gba.gov.ar; f. 1993; owned by the govt of the Province of Buenos Aires; local services; Gen. Man. Dr JOSÉ PUCCIARELLI.

Ferroexpreso Pampeano, SA (FEPSA): Conesa 1073, C1426AQU Buenos Aires; tel. (11) 4510-4900; e-mail feppau@fepsa.com.ar; operates services on the Rosario–Bahía Blanca grain lines; 5,094 km of track; Man. PABLO AUTILLO.

Ferrosur Roca (FR): Bouchard 680, 8°, C1106ABJ Buenos Aires; tel. (11) 4319-3900; fax (11) 4319-3901; e-mail ferrosur@elsitio.net; internet www.ferrosur.com.ar; f. 1993; operator of freight services on the Roca lines; Gen. Man. PABLO TERRADAS; 3,000 km of track.

Ferrovías: Avda Dr Ramos Mejía 1430, C1104AJO Buenos Aires; tel. (11) 4314-1444; fax (11) 3311-1181; internet www.ferrovias.com.ar; f. 1994; operates northern commuter line (Belgrano Norte) in Buenos Aires; Pres. GABRIEL ROMERO.

Metrovías (MV): Bartolomé Mitre 3342, C1201AAL Buenos Aires; tel. (11) 4959-6800; fax (11) 4866-3037; e-mail info@metrovias.com.ar; internet www.metrovias.com.ar; f. 1994; operates subway (Subterráneos de Buenos Aires—Subte, q.v.), a light rail line (Premetro) and Urquiza commuter line; Pres. ALDO ROGGIO.

Nuevo Central Argentino, SA (NCA): Avda Alberdi 50, Rosario; tel. (3411) 437-6561; e-mail sac@nca.com.ar; internet www.nca.com.ar; f. 1993; operates freight services on the Bartolomé Mitre lines; Pres. MIGUEL ALBERTO ACEVEDO; Gen. Man. HORACIO DÍAZ HERMELO; 5,011 km of track.

Subterráneos de Buenos Aires (Subte): Bartolomé Mitre 3342, C1201AAL Buenos Aires; tel. (11) 4862-6844; fax (11) 4864-0633; internet www.sbase.com.ar; f. 1913; completely state-owned in 1951–93, responsibility for operations was transferred in 1993 to a private consortium, Metrovías (q.v.), with control returned to the Municipalidad de la Ciudad de Buenos Aires (from the federal authorities) from 2012; six underground lines totalling 53.7 km, 74 stations, and a 7.4 km light rail line (Premetro) with 17 stations; three additional lines planned; Pres. JUAN PABLO PICCARDO.

Trenes de Buenos Aires, SA (TBA): Avda Ramos Mejía 1358, C1104AJN Buenos Aires; tel. (11) 4317-4400; fax (11) 4317-4409; e-mail prensa@tbanet.com.ar; internet www.tbanet.com.ar; took over operations of the Mitre and Sarmiento commuter lines from state in 1995; 400 km of track; Pres. CARLO MICHELE FERRARI; Vice-Pres. JORGE DE LOS REYES.

Unidad de Gestión Operativa Ferroviaria de Emergencia, SA (UGOFE): internet www.ugofe.com.ar; f. 2005; Pres. ROBERTO LATTANZI; consortium of Ferrovías, Metrovías and TBA formed to assume control of three lines (Belgrano Sur, Roca and San Martín) following termination of concession held by Metropolitano (f. 1995); 304-km network.

ROADS

In 2007 the intercity road network comprised 230,125 km of roads, of which 31% were paved. Of the total, 38,313 km were under the national road network and 191,812 km formed the provincial road network. In the national network, 87% roads are paved, whereas only 20% of provincial roads are paved. Four branches of the Pan-American highway run from Buenos Aires to the borders of Chile, Bolivia, Paraguay and Brazil. In 2006 the Inter-American Development Bank (IDB) agreed to finance the road network development project in the Norte Grande region with US $1,200m. and covering approximately 1,470 km of the road network. In 2012 the IDB approved a further US $300m. for the second phase of road network development project.

Asociación Argentina de Empresarios Transporte Automotor (AAETA): Bernardo de Irigoyen 330, 6°, C1072AAH Buenos Aires; tel. (11) 4334-3254; fax (11) 4334-6513; e-mail info@aaeta.org.ar; internet www.aaeta.org.ar; f. 1941; Pres. Dr JUAN ZUNINO; Gen. Man. MARCELO GONZALVEZ.

Dirección Nacional de Vialidad: Julio A. Roca 783, C1067ABC Buenos Aires; tel. (11) 4343-8520; internet www.vialidad.gov.ar; controlled by the Secretaría de Transportes; Gen. Man. NELSON GUILLERMO PERIOTTI.

Federación Argentina de Entidades Empresarias de Autotransporte de Cargas (FADEEAC): Sánchez de Bustamante 54, C1173AAB Buenos Aires; tel. (11) 4860-7700; fax (11) 4383-7870; e-mail fadeeac@fadeeac.org.ar; internet www.fadeeac.org.ar; Pres. LUIS A. MORALES.

There are several international passenger and freight services, including:

Autobuses Sudamericanos, SA: Tres Arroyos 287, C1414EAC Buenos Aires; tel. (11) 4857-3065; fax (11) 4307-1956; f. 1928; international bus services; car and bus rentals; charter bus services; Pres. ARMANDO SCHLECKER HIRSCH; Gen. Man. MIGUEL ANGEL RUGGIERO.

INLAND WATERWAYS

There is considerable traffic in coastal and river shipping, mainly carrying petroleum and its derivatives.

Dirección Nacional de Vías Navegables: Avda España 221, 4°, Buenos Aires; tel. (11) 4361-5964; e-mail amparadela@yahoo.com.ar; internet www.sspyvn.gov.ar; part of the Ministry of Federal Planning, Public Investment and Services, Transport Secretariat; responsible for the maintenance and improvement of waterways and dredging operations; Dir Dr JOSÉ BENI.

SHIPPING

There are more than 100 ports, of which the most important are Buenos Aires, Quequén and Bahía Blanca. There are specialized terminals at Ensenada, Comodoro Rivadavia, San Lorenzo and Campana (petroleum); Bahía Blanca, Rosario, Santa Fe, Villa Concepción, Mar del Plata and Quequén (cereals); and San Nicolás and San Fernando (raw and construction materials). In 2010 Argentina's merchant fleet totalled 981 vessels.

Administración General de Puertos: Avda Ing. Huergo 431, 1°, C1107AOE Buenos Aires; tel. (11) 4342-1727; fax (11) 4342-6836; e-mail institucionales@puertobuenosaires.gov.ar; internet www.puertobuenosaires.gov.ar; f. 1956 as a state enterprise for administration of all national sea- and river-ports; following privatization of much of its activity in mid-1990s, operates the port of Buenos Aires; Gen. Man. Dr JORGE FRANCISCO CHOLVIS.

Consorcio de Gestión del Puerto de Bahía Blanca: Dr Mario M. Guido s/n, 8103 Provincia de Buenos Aires; internet www.puertobahiablanca.com; Pres. HUGO ANTONIO BORELLI; Gen. Man. VALENTÍN D. MORAN.

Terminales Río de la Plata: Avda Ramón Castillo y Avda Cdre Py, Puerto Nuevo, Buenos Aires; tel. (11) 4319-9500; e-mail info@trp.com.ar; internet www.trp.com.ar; operates one of five cargo and container terminals in the port of Buenos Aires; Gen. Man. GUSTAVO FIGUEROLA.

CIVIL AVIATION

Argentina has 10 international airports (Aeroparque Jorge Newbery, Córdoba, Corrientes, El Plumerillo, Ezeiza, Jujuy, Resistencia, Río Gallegos, Salta and San Carlos de Bariloche). Ezeiza, 22 km from Buenos Aires, is one of the most important air terminals in Latin America.

Aerolíneas Argentinas: Bouchard 547, 9°, C1106ABG Buenos Aires; tel. (11) 4317-3000; fax (11) 4320-2116; internet www.aerolineas.com.ar; f. 1950; bought by Grupo Marsans (Spain) in 2001; renationalized in 2008; services to North and Central America, Europe, the Far East, New Zealand, South Africa and destinations throughout South America; the internal network covers the whole country; passengers, mail and freight are carried; Gen. Man. MARIANO RECALDE.

Austral Líneas Aéreas: Corrientes 485, 9°, C1043AAE Buenos Aires; tel. (11) 4317-3600; fax (11) 4317-3777; internet www.austral.com.ar; f. 1971; domestic flights.

LAN Argentina: Avda Cerrito 866, C1010AR Buenos Aires; tel. (11) 4378-2200; fax (11) 4378-2298; internet www.lan.com; subsidiary of LAN Airlines, SA (Chile); services between airports in Argentina, Chile and the USA.

Líneas Aéreas del Estado (LADE): Perú 710, C1068AAF Buenos Aires; tel. (11) 5353-2387; fax (11) 4362-4899; e-mail director@lade.com.ar; internet www.lade.com.ar; f. 1940.

Sol Líneas Aéreas: Aeropuerto Internacional Rosario, entre Ríos 986, S2000CRR Rosario; tel. (11) 6091-0032; e-mail contacto@sol.com.ar; internet www.sol.com.ar; f. 2005; services between destinations in Argentina and Uruguay.

Tourism

Argentina's superb tourist attractions include the Andes mountains, the lake district centred on Bariloche (where there is a National Park), Patagonia, the Atlantic beaches and Mar del Plata, the Iguazú falls, the Pampas and Tierra del Fuego. Arrivals at Ezeiza International Airport in 2009 totalled some 2.0m. In 2009 tourism receipts amounted to US $2,623m.

Asociación Argentina de Agencias de Viajes y Turismo (AAAVYT): Viamonte 640, 10°, B6015XAA Buenos Aires; tel. (11) 4325-4691; fax (11) 4322-9641; e-mail secretaria@aaavyt.org.ar; internet www.aaavyt.org.ar; f. 1951; Pres. FABRICIO DI GIAMBATTISTA; Exec. Dir GERARDO BELIO.

Instituto Nacional de Promoción Turística (INPROTUR): Paraguay 866, 8°, C1057AAL Buenos Aires; tel. (11) 4850-1400; fax (11) 4313-6834; e-mail inprotur@turismo.gov.ar; internet www.argentina.travel; f. 2005; Pres. ENRIQUE MEYER; Exec. Sec. LEONARDO BOTO.

Defence

As assessed at November 2011, Argentina's Armed Forces numbered an estimated 73,100: Army 38,500, Navy 20,000 (including Naval Air Force), Air Force 14,600. There were also paramilitary forces numbering 31,240. In 1995 conscription was ended and a professional (voluntary) military service was created in its place.

Defence Budget: An estimated 12,500m. new pesos in 2012.

Chair. of the Joint Chiefs of Staff: Brig.-Gen. JORGE ALBERTO CHEVALIER.

Chief of Staff (Army): Lt-Gen. LUIS ALBERTO POZZI.

Chief of Staff (Navy): Adm. CARLOS ALBERTO PAZ.

Chief of Staff (Air Force): Brig.-Gen. NORMANDO CONSTANTINO.

Education

Education from pre-school to university level is available free of charge. Education is officially compulsory for all children at primary level, between the ages of six and 14 years. Secondary education lasts for between five and six years, depending on the type of course: the normal certificate of education (bachillerato) takes five years, a course leading to a commercial bachillerato lasts five years, and one leading to a technical or agricultural bachillerato takes six years. Technical education is supervised by the Consejo Nacional de Educación Técnica. Non-university higher education, usually leading to a teaching qualification, is for three or four years, while university courses last for four years or more. There were 37 state universities and some 48 private universities in 2004. Enrolment at primary schools in 2005 included 99% of the relevant age-group, while enrolment at secondary schools in 2008 included 80% of pupils in the relevant age-group.Government expenditure on education and culture for 2010 was 22,205.4m. new pesos.

ARMENIA

Introductory Survey

LOCATION, CLIMATE, LANGUAGE, RELIGION, FLAG, CAPITAL

The Republic of Armenia is situated in the western South Caucasus. It borders Turkey to the south-west, Iran to the south, Azerbaijan to the east, and Georgia to the north. Naxçıvan, an exclave of Azerbaijan, is situated to the south. The climate is typically continental: dry, with wide temperature variations. The average January temperature in Yerevan is −3°C (26°F), while August temperatures average 25°C (77°F), although high altitude moderates the heat in much of the country. The official language is Armenian, the sole member of a distinct Indo-European language group, written in the Armenian script. Most of the population are adherents of Christianity, the largest denomination being the Armenian Apostolic Church. There are also Islamic and Yazidi communities. The national flag (approximate proportions 2 by 3) consists of three equal horizontal stripes, of red, blue and orange. The capital is Yerevan.

CONTEMPORARY POLITICAL HISTORY

Historical Context

Although Armenia was an important power in ancient times, and formed the first Christian state, around AD 300, for much of its history it was ruled by foreign powers. In 1639 Armenia was partitioned, with the larger, western part being annexed by the Osmanlı (Ottoman) Empire and the eastern region becoming part of the Persian Empire. In 1828 eastern Armenia was ceded to the Russian Empire. At the beginning of the 20th century Armenians living in western, or Anatolian, Armenia, under Ottoman rule, were subject to severe persecution by the Turks. As a result of brutal massacres and deportations (particularly in 1915), the Anatolian lands were largely emptied of their Armenian population, and it was estimated that during 1915–23 some 1.5m. Armenians perished. After the collapse of Russian imperial power in 1917, Caucasian Armenia joined the anti-Bolshevik Transcaucasian Federation, alongside Georgia and Azerbaijan. This collapsed when threatened by Turkish forces, and on 28 May 1918 Armenia was proclaimed an independent state. The newly formed republic was forced to cede territory to the Turks. Armenia was recognized as an independent state by the Allied Powers and by Turkey in the Treaty of Sèvres, signed on 10 August 1920. However, the new Turkish regime led by Mustafa Kemal rejected the treaty and in September attacked Armenia, but was prevented from establishing control over the territory by a Bolshevik invasion, and the founding, on 29 November, of a Soviet Republic of Armenia. In December 1922 the republic was absorbed into the Transcaucasian Soviet Federative Socialist Republic (TSFSR) as a constituent republic of the USSR. In 1936 the TSFSR was dissolved, and the Armenian Soviet Socialist Republic (SSR) was formed.

The Soviet authorities implemented a policy of agricultural collectivization and industrialization. Thousands of Armenians were deported, executed or imprisoned during the 1930s. During the Second World War (1939–45), Armenia provided an essential source of labour for the Soviet economy, and an estimated 350,000 Armenians were killed while serving in the Soviet military. In the late 1940s an estimated 150,000 Armenians of the diaspora returned to the republic.

The reformist policies of Soviet leader Mikhail Gorbachev (1985–91) had little initial impact in Armenia. The most significant of the historical and ethnic concerns discussed from late 1987 was the status of the largely Armenian-populated Nagornyi Karabakh autonomous oblast (region) within neighbouring Azerbaijan (See the section on Nagornyi Karabakh in the Azerbaijan chapter, p. 767). In February 1988 some 1m. people took part in demonstrations in Yerevan, the Armenian capital, led by the outlawed Karabakh Committee, in support of demands from inhabitants of Nagornyi Karabakh for the incorporation of the territory into Armenia. As ethnic tensions intensified, Azeris began to leave Armenia, while anti-Armenian riots in Sumqayıt, Azerbaijan, in late February, resulted in the deaths of 26 Armenians. The ruling of the Presidium of the USSR's Supreme Soviet (legislature) that Nagornyi Karabakh should remain under Azerbaijani jurisdiction provoked further Armenian anger. In May, as unrest continued, the First Secretary of the ruling Communist Party of Armenia (CPA) was dismissed. Inter-ethnic violence resulted in the killing of numerous Azeris in and near Gugark, in northern Armenia, in late November. In December, however, the question of Nagornyi Karabakh was temporarily subordinated to the problem of overcoming the effects of a severe earthquake, which had struck northern Armenia, killing some 25,000 people. Following the earthquake, members of the Karabakh Committee were arrested, ostensibly for interfering in relief work. Following huge demonstrations, they were released in May 1989. Meanwhile, in January a Special Administration Committee (SAC) of the USSR Council of Ministers was formed to preside over Nagornyi Karabakh, which was to remain under Azerbaijani jurisdiction. In September Azerbaijan announced the closure of its borders with Armenia, seriously affecting the post-earthquake reconstruction. In November the SAC was disbanded. The USSR Supreme Soviet ruled a subsequent pronouncement of Armenian Supreme Soviet that Nagornyi Karabakh formed part of a 'unified Armenian Republic' to be unconstitutional.

The Pan-Armenian National Movement (PANM), the successor to the Karabakh Committee, won some 35% of the seats at elections held to the Armenian Supreme Soviet, in May–July 1990. Levon Ter-Petrossian of the PANM was elected to the chairmanship of the Supreme Soviet. Another PANM leader, Vazgen Manukian, was appointed Prime Minister. On 23 August the legislature adopted a declaration of sovereignty, and demanded international recognition of the Turkish massacres of Armenians in 1915 as an act of genocide.

The Armenian Government refused to enter into negotiations on a new treaty of union between Soviet republics, and boycotted the referendum on the renewal of the USSR, which was held in March 1991 in nine republics. Instead, the legislature resolved to schedule a referendum on secession from the USSR for September.

Domestic Political Affairs

The attempted coup by conservative communists in the Soviet and Russian capital, Moscow, in August 1991, further strengthened the position of those, in Armenia, demanding independence. According to the official results of the referendum held on 21 September, 99.3% of those participating (some 94.4% of the electorate) supported Armenia's reconstitution as an independent, democratic state. On 23 September the Supreme Soviet declared Armenia to be a fully independent state, and a congress of the CPA voted to dissolve the party. Six candidates contested an election to the post of republican President held on 16 October; Ter-Petrossian won, with some 87% of the votes cast. Armenia joined the Commonwealth of Independent States (CIS, see p. 246), signing the founding Almaty (Alma-Ata) Declaration on 21 December. In early 1992 the country was admitted to the Conference on Security and Co-operation in Europe (CSCE—now the Organization for Security and Co-operation in Europe—OSCE, see p. 388) and the UN.

In 1992 economic conditions deteriorated, and the situation was exacerbated by the influx of refugees resulting from the continuing conflict in Nagornyi Karabakh (see below), the closure of borders with Azerbaijan and fighting in neighbouring Georgia (which impeded supplies to Armenia). Substantial public dissatisfaction with the Ter-Petrossian administration ensued, including the staging of mass rallies in Yerevan to demand the President's resignation. In February Ter-Petrossian dismissed the Prime Minister, Khosrov Haroutunian, and a new Council of Ministers was subsequently announced, headed by Hrant Bagratian. The assassination in December of a former mayor of Yerevan prompted the Government to effect a number of measures that it described as aimed at eliminating terrorism, including the suspension of the leading opposition party, the radical nationalist Armenian Revolutionary Federation (ARF, Dashnaktsutiun, or Dashnaks).

Armenia's first post-Soviet legislative elections were held in July 1995. Some 13 parties and organizations contested elections to the new 190-member Azgayin Zhoghov (National Assembly), while nine parties were barred from participation. The Republican bloc—an alliance of six groups led by the PANM—won 119 seats, and 45 independent candidates were elected. In late July Ter-Petrossian appointed a new Government, again led by Bagratian. In a referendum held concurrently with the general election, 68% of those who voted (56% of the electorate) endorsed a new national Constitution, which granted wide-ranging executive authority to the President and provided for a smaller, 131-member Azgayin Zhoghov.

A presidential election was held on 22 September 1996. Ter-Petrossian was the candidate of the Republican bloc, while five opposition parties united to support Manukian, now the Chairman of the National Democratic Union (NDU). Although preliminary results indicated that Ter-Petrossian had been re-elected, the opposition made allegations of widespread electoral malpractice (seemingly confirmed by international observers), and staged protest rallies in Yerevan. On 25 September supporters of Manukian stormed the Azgayin Zhoghov, injuring, among others, the Chairman and his deputy. According to the final results, Ter-Petrossian received 51.8% of the votes cast, and Manukian secured 41.3%. Bagratian resigned as Prime Minister in November; he was replaced by Armen Sarkissian. The latter resigned in March 1997 on grounds of ill health. In what was regarded as an attempt to appease opposition nationalist groups, Ter-Petrossian appointed as Sarkissian's successor Robert Kocharian, hitherto the self-styled President of the unrecognized 'Republic of Nagornyi Karabakh'.

The presidency of Robert Kocharian 1998–2008

President Ter-Petrossian resigned on 3 February 1998, after his support for an OSCE plan concerning the status of Nagornyi Karabakh (see below), had generated accusations that Ter-Petrossian was insufficiently protective of Armenian interests. Kocharian, who campaigned on a nationalist platform, was elected as President in a second round of voting on 30 March, defeating the former CPA leader, Karen Demirchian, and obtaining 59.5% of the votes cast. Kocharian was inaugurated as President on 9 April. On the following day he appointed Armen Darbinian as Prime Minister. In May the ARF was legalized, and two members of the party were appointed to the Government.

In the elections to the Azgayin Zhoghov held on 30 May 1999, the Unity bloc, an alliance of the Republican Party of Armenia (RPA) and the People's Party of Armenia (PPA), won 55 of 131 elective seats; 32 independent candidates were elected. The CPA (which had been permitted to reform) secured 11 seats and the ARF obtained nine. On 11 June Darbinian (who became Minister of the Economy) was replaced as Prime Minister by Vazgen Sarkissian, the unofficial leader of the RPA and hitherto Minister of Defence. Meanwhile, Demirchian, the leader of the PPA, was elected as legislative Chairman.

On 27 October 1999 five gunmen staged an attack in the Azgayin Zhoghov, killing eight people, including Prime Minister Sarkissian, Demirchian and his two deputies, and a cabinet minister. The gunmen, who claimed no political affiliation, announced that they were seeking revenge against the 'corrupt political élite'. On their surrender the assailants were charged with murder and terrorist offences. In the aftermath of the attack, the Ministers of the Interior and of National Security tendered their resignations. In November Armen Khachatrian of the PPA was elected parliamentary Chairman. (Demirchian's son, Stepan, replaced him as leader of the PPA.) Aram Sarkissian, the younger brother of the murdered premier, was subsequently appointed Prime Minister. In May 2000 Kocharian appointed Andranik Markarian, the leader of the RPA, as Prime Minister, prior to a government reorganization.

In October 2001 the PPA (which had left the Unity bloc in the previous month), together with the recently formed Republic grouping and the National Unity Party, organized a rally to demand the impeachment of President Kocharian, whom they accused of precipitating an economic crisis, acting in contravention of the Constitution and condoning terrorism. In April 2002 thousands of people participated in protests against the closure of the independent television station, A1+. In the same month legislation was adopted abolishing the death penalty, although the new law was not to apply retroactively to those found guilty of perpetrating terrorist offences. However, the Council of Europe (see p. 256) threatened to expel Armenia from membership, unless it abolished capital punishment fully and unconditionally; in September 2003 the Government finally did so.

Nine candidates participated in the presidential election held on 19 February 2003. In the second round of voting, held on 5 March, Kocharian was re-elected President with 67.5% of the votes cast, defeating Stepan Demirchian. Monitors from the OSCE and the Council of Europe recorded irregularities in electoral procedure, and thousands of people took part in protests against the results, which were, none the less, endorsed by the Constitutional Court.

At legislative elections, held on 25 May 2003, the RPA won 32 seats, the Law-Governed Country Party of Armenia (LCPA) 18 seats, the Justice bloc (led by Demirchian) 15 and the ARF 11. International observers and opposition parties again reported incidences of electoral malpractice. A concurrent referendum on proposed constitutional amendments failed to win the approval of the requisite one-third of registered voters. On 11 June the RPA, the LCPA and the ARF formed a coalition Government, again led by Markarian. The Chairman of the LCPA, Artur Baghdasarian, was appointed Chairman of the Azgayin Zhoghov. Members of the Justice bloc boycotted parliamentary sessions until September, in protest at the results of the election.

In November 2003 Armen Sarkissian, brother of the former premiers Vazgen and Aram Sarkissian, was sentenced to 15 years' imprisonment, after being found guilty of organizing the killing of the Chairman of the Board of Armenian Public Television and Radio, Tigran Naghdalian, in December 2002. Sarkissian denied the charge, which he claimed had been politically motivated. In December 2003 six men were sentenced to life imprisonment for their involvement in the attack on the Azgayin Zhoghov in October 1999 (one other defendant was imprisoned for 14 years).

The Justice bloc resumed its legislative boycott in February 2004, after the Azgayin Zhoghov refused to debate proposed constitutional amendments permitting a referendum of confidence in the President (the boycott continued on a selective basis for the following two years). In mid-2004 demonstrations organized by those parties boycotting the legislature began in Yerevan, urging Kocharian's resignation. Two of the three ministerial representatives of the LCPA left office during 2004.

The issue of proposed constitutional reform (in relation to which the Government had pledged, in negotiations with the Council of Europe, to hold a referendum) remained a topic of contention. The Azgayin Zhoghov finally approved draft constitutional amendments that would limit the powers of the President and enhance those of the judiciary in September 2005. In the constitutional referendum, held on 27 November, with the participation of 65.3% of the electorate, some 94.5% of the valid votes were in favour of the proposed amendments. In December Markarian acknowledged that some electoral violations had taken place, and in January 2006 the Parliamentary Assembly of the Council of Europe (PACE) issued a statement condemning elements of the conduct of the polls. Meanwhile, in December 2005 a prominent businessman and member of the legislature, Gagik Tsarukian, founded a new party, Prosperous Armenia (PA).

In May 2006 Baghdasarian resigned the chairmanship of the Azgayin Zhogov and withdrew the LCPA from the governing coalition; he had begun to position himself in opposition to the Government, declaring support for a foreign policy stance more supportive of the North Atlantic Treaty Organization (NATO, see p. 370). Some members of the party defected to other political blocs in response to Baghdasarian's actions. The United Labour Party agreed to co-operate with the remaining members of the coalition and was allocated one ministerial portfolio and other senior official posts. Tigran Torossian of the RPA was elected Chairman of the Azgayin Zhogov in June. In July the Minister of Defence, Serge Sarkissian, joined the ruling RPA and was appointed to a senior position in the party.

On 25 March 2007 Prime Minister Markarian died, having suffered a heart attack; he was succeeded as premier, on 4 April, by Sarkissian, who had also been appointed as acting President of the RPA. Sarkissian was succeeded as Minister of Defence by the hitherto Armed Forces Chief of General Staff, Col-Gen. Mikhail Haroutunian. At legislative elections, conducted on 12 May 2007, the RPA obtained 64 seats, with 33.9% of the votes cast, while its allies, PA and the ARF, were placed second and third, with 25 seats (15.1% of the ballot) and 16 seats (13.2%), respectively. Two opposition parties obtained the minimum 5% threshold of votes required to secure parliamentary representation: the LCPA, with nine seats (7.1% of the votes cast), and the Heritage Party, with seven seats (6.0%). A joint group of OSCE and Council of Europe observers assessed that the elections were conducted largely in accordance with international standards, but observed numerous irregularities. The RPA and three other opposition parties unsuccessfully filed appeals with the Constitutional Court and demanded the holding of fresh elections.

Despite having secured an outright parliamentary majority, the RPA agreed to form a coalition administration with PA and the ARF; the three parties together controlled 105 of the 131 legislative seats. Sarkissian was reappointed Prime Minister, and in the new Government, announced in June 2007, 11 portfolios were allocated to the RPA, and three each to PA and the ARF. The RPA's decision to enter into a coalition was widely perceived to reflect the wish of Sarkissian to broaden his base of support prior to the next presidential election. By November, when it was announced that the poll was to be held on 19 February 2008, former President Ter-Petrossian had established himself as the principal challenger to Sarkissian.

The presidency of Serge Sarkissian

The presidential poll was conducted, as scheduled, on 19 February 2008; according to official results, Serge Sarkissian secured 52.8% of the votes cast and Ter-Petrossian 21.5%. Ter-Petrossian (and other opposition candidates) immediately attributed the results to widespread falsification and demanded that the ballot be repeated, prompting his followers to stage mass protests. On 1 March at least eight demonstrators were killed and some 200 people injured in Yerevan during the violent suppression of opposition protests by special police units and interior ministry forces, following which President Kocharian announced the imposition of a state of emergency for a period of 20 days. More than 100 associates of Ter-Petrossian and opposition members were subsequently arrested on charges of instigating the violence. On 8 March the Constitutional Court upheld the final official election results, rejecting an appeal by Ter-Petrossian. Sarkissian was officially inaugurated as President on the following day; he immediately nominated Tigran Sarkissian, hitherto the Governor of the Central Bank of Armenia, as Prime Minister. Later that month a new administration, in which 10 of the incumbent ministers were retained, was formed.

In April 2008 PACE adopted a resolution that demanded the conduct of an independent inquiry into the violence of 1 March, the immediate release of opposition supporters detained in its aftermath, and the annulment of restrictions on the right to stage public rallies and demonstrations. On 11 June the Azgayin Zhoghov voted in favour of lifting the restrictions. An opposition demonstration in support of Ter-Petrossian, who demanded that Kocharian stand trial for crimes against the Armenian people, was conducted in Yerevan in June. In August, at a further rally in Yerevan, Ter-Petrossian officially announced the establishment of an opposition alliance, the Armenian National Congress (ANC), comprising 16 parties and public organizations. In September Torossian tendered his resignation as Chairman of the Azgayin Zhoghov, following pressure from the RPA leadership to cede the post to Hovik Abrahamian, a long-term supporter of both Kocharian and President Sarkissian; Torossian subsequently left the RPA. Abrahamian was elected as the new parliamentary Chairman later in September.

In October 2008 Ter-Petrossian announced the suspension of the post-election campaign of rallies and demonstrations by his supporters, citing the necessity of supporting the Government in discussions with the Azerbaijani authorities over Nagornyi Karabakh (see Foreign Affairs). In December the trial began of seven prominent opposition members, including a former Minister of Foreign Affairs, Alexander Arzumanian, and three parliamentary deputies, who were accused of attempting to overthrow the Government during the post-election protests; at that time it was reported that some 70 of those arrested after the disturbances remained in detention, of whom most had been tried and received custodial sentences. In the same month the PACE Monitoring Committee criticized the trial of opposition members, whom it described as political prisoners, and recommended the imposition of sanctions against Armenia, in response to the failure of the authorities to comply with its April resolution. However, after the Government pledged to amend two articles of the criminal code that allowed the trial of the opposition supporters, PACE, convening in late January 2009, significantly amended the resolution of the Monitoring Committee and extended the stipulated date for the authorities' adherence to democratic standards until April of that year. Meanwhile, the trial of the seven opposition activists was repeatedly adjourned. In February the ANC announced the resumption of demonstrations in support of Ter-Petrossian. The ANC organized a rally in Yerevan on 1 March to mark the anniversary of the violently suppressed demonstrations of 2008.

In May 2009 the ARF announced its withdrawal from the governing coalition, expressing discontent at the Government's continuing policy of rapprochement with Turkey (see Foreign Affairs). Three new ministers, one from each of the remaining coalition partners, were appointed to replace the former ARF office-holders. On 31 May municipal elections were held in Yerevan, representing the first occasion on which, in accordance with constitutional amendments adopted in 2005, the Mayor of the capital city (hitherto a presidential appointment) was elected by the 65-member city assembly. At the elections to the assembly, the RPA were the most successful party, obtaining 47.4% of the votes cast and 35 representatives, ahead of PA, with 22.7% of the votes cast and 17 representatives and the ANC (which had nominated Ter-Petrossian as its mayoral candidate), with 17.6% of the votes cast and 13 representatives. Therefore, the RPA nominee, Gagik Baglarian, who had been appointed Mayor by President Sarkissian in early March, was effectively confirmed in office.

In June 2009 the Government granted a general amnesty covering those detained during the 2008 protest, resulting in the release of numerous imprisoned activists, including Arzumanian and two parliamentary deputies who had been sentenced in June in connection with the post-election protests. However, this amnesty was accompanied by the cessation of operations of the commission investigating the deaths resulting from clashes between police and protesters. A prominent opposition journalist (and supporter of Ter-Petrossian), Nikol Pashinian, the editor of the daily newspaper *Haikakan Zhamanak*, who had been in hiding since March 2008, surrendered himself to police under the terms of this amnesty. (Pashinian's trial, on charges of inciting and organizing mass disorder during the post-election protests, commenced in October; he was sentenced to seven years' imprisonment in January 2010.)

In March 2010 Baghdasarian announced that he was to replace two of the three LCPA government ministers, and subsequently appointed two close associates to the Government, both of whom joined the party shortly before assuming ministerial office. In June the Azgayin Zhoghov approved legislation allowing private foreign-language schools to operate, despite widespread public opposition. A civic pressure group that had been formed to campaign against the legislation (which was regarded as providing for greater use of the Russian language in the education sector) received the support of the main opposition parties and prominent pro-establishment politicians. A defence agreement signed with Russia in August, under which the lease of a Russian military base in the northern town of Gyumri was to be extended until 2044 and its mission upgraded, was strenuously criticized by opposition parties as compromising national sovereignty. In September the ANC resumed the organization of regular protests in Yerevan, led by Ter-Petrossian, who reiterated demands for the immediate release of ANC members remaining in detention, Sarkissian's resignation and the organization of early elections.

Anti-Government protests

In early December 2010 Beglarian was obliged to tender his resignation as Mayor of Yerevan, after physically assaulting a presidential aide. Shortly afterwards, the Minister of Justice was dismissed from the Government, after failing to discipline the head of a ministry agency for allegedly assaulting an employee. Later that month the Minister of the Economy, Nerses Yetitsian, was also dismissed, and succeeded by Tigran Davtian (hitherto Minister of Finance), while severe food shortages and sharp price increases prompted the replacement of the Minister of Agriculture, amid public discontent at increasing economic hardship. On 17 December Karen Karapetian, hitherto head of the Armenian-Russian natural gas producer ArmRosGazProm, who had been nominated by Sarkissian as the RPA candidate, was elected as the new Mayor of Yerevan. Also in December the Azgayin Zhoghov rejected a motion proposed by the Heritage Party providing for recognition of the independence of Nagornyi Karabakh, because of concerns that this would undermine the negotiating process. In February 2011 the head of the National Security Service opposed draft amendments to state legislation regulating the right to public assembly, including the powers granted to law enforcement bodies, which had been proposed by the newly appointed Minister of Justice, Hrair Tovmasian, in compliance with Council of Europe standards. Also in early 2011 an announcement by Sarkissian of proposals to create a second chamber in the Armenian legislature, in which elected representatives of the diaspora would participate, prompted public controversy, although Abrahamian subsequently announced that the required constitutional amendments would not be considered until after the elections to the Azgayin Zhoghov due to be held in 2012. In February, under pressure from Sarkissian, the PA, together with the LCPA, signed a joint declaration with the RPA pledging to support Sarkissian's candidacy in the 2013 presidential election.

Meanwhile, the ANC increased its campaign of anti-Government protests and on 1 March 2011, to mark the anniversary of the violent suppression of the March 2008 demonstrations, convened a large-scale opposition rally in Yerevan, when Ter-Petrossian issued an ultimatum for the Government to accede to his political and economic demands, including the holding of new parliamentary and presidential elections. Despite an official prohibition of the holding of protests in a central piazza in Yerevan, Liberty Square, imposed after the violence of 2008, on 15 March 2011 the Chairman of the Heritage Party, Raffi Hovannisian, began a hunger strike in the Square in support of a number of demands, including an end to official corruption, the recission of the accords with Turkey (which remained unratified), and the recognition of the statehood of the 'Republic of Nagornyi Karabakh'. On 17 March police officers permitted an estimated 10,000 demonstrators (who were attending an authorized protest march led by the ANC) to enter the Square and conduct a rally. Later in the month several parliamentary deputies of the Heritage Party, gathering in Liberty Square, also demanded that early elections be held, and reforms to the electoral code be adopted.

In early April 2011, despite the continuing official ban, some 12,000 people attended a further ANC rally, at which Ter-Petrossian made a speech, in Liberty Square. The prohibition on demonstrating in Liberty Square was formally rescinded shortly before a further large opposition demonstration, which was staged, as planned, on 28 April, with protesters officially permitted to gather in the Square. On 26 May the Azgayin Zhoghov adopted legislation acceding to several of the demands of the ANC, including the release of some 396 prisoners (among them Pashinian and a number of other opposition activists convicted of involvement in the violent protests of 2008), and the reduction in sentences of 379 others, while the investigation into the deaths that occurred during the clashes was to be reopened. Nevertheless, at the end of May, and in subsequent months, the ANC organized mass rallies demanding early presidential and parliamentary elections. In October the ANC announced the establishment of a new grouping, the Civic Forum, which was to organize its campaign of anti-Government protests.

Recent developments: preparations for legislative elections

In late October 2011 Yerevan Mayor Karen Karapetian unexpectedly resigned from office, prompting speculation that Sarkissian had been displeased at protests staged by vendors in Yerevan in response to a ban on street trading ordered by Karapetian. In November Abrahamian announced his resignation as Chairman of the Azgayin Zhoghov in order to lead the RPA campaign for the legislative elections scheduled to take place in May 2012; he was succeeded by Samvel Nikoian. Also in November 2011 Mikael Minasian, President Sarkissian's son-in-law, was dismissed as deputy chief of presidential staff, while police chief Alik Sarkissian was also removed. The removal of these senior officials by President Sarkissian was attributed by many observers to their connections with former President Kocharian, who in a media interview in September had indicated that he envisaged a return to political life. Following Kocharian's declaration, his associate, PA leader Tsarukian, had refused to reaffirm support for Sarkissian's candidacy in the 2013 presidential election. In January 2012 the ARF and the Heritage Party submitted proposals in the Azgayin Zhoghov for the amendment of the electoral system so that all 131 parliamentary seats would be contested on a party-list basis in the forthcoming elections; the ANC announced that it would organize further demonstrations in support of these demands.

Foreign Affairs

Regional relations

In September 1991 the disputed territory of Nagornyi Karabakh (in Azerbaijan, but with a predominately ethnically Armenian population) declared itself an independent republic. (Political developments within the territory are covered in greater detail in the chapter on Azerbaijan.) Violence intensified following the dissolution of the USSR in December. International efforts to negotiate a peace settlement foundered, owing to Azerbaijan's insistence that the conflict was a domestic problem. In May 1992 the Nagornyi Karabakh 'self-defence forces' (which the Armenian Government continued to claim were operating without its military support) captured Şuşha, gaining complete control of the territory. With the capture of the Laçin valley, the ethnic Armenian militia succeeded in opening a 'corridor' linking Nagornyi Karabakh with Armenia. Following an Azerbaijani counter-offensive in August, a state defence committee, in close alignment with the Ter-Petrossian administration of Armenia, replaced the Government of Nagornyi Karabakh. With the capture of the Kelbacar district in April 1993, a second corridor linking the territory with Armenia was formed, and by June ethnic Armenian forces had secured full control of Nagornyi Karabakh. The seizure of Azerbaijani territory outside the oblast prompted international condemnation. UN Security Council Resolutions 822 and 853, which demanded the withdrawal of occupying and local Armenian forces from Azerbaijan, went unheeded; hostilities intensified further, and more than 20% of Azerbaijan's total territory was reported to have been captured by the Nagornyi Karabakh forces; Azerbaijani forces recaptured some territory in a counter-offensive launched in December. In February 1994 it was reported that as many as 18,000 people had been killed since 1988, with a further 25,000 wounded. More than 500,000 Azeris were believed to have been displaced.

In May 1994 a new cease-fire agreement was signed by the Ministers of Defence of Armenia and Azerbaijan and representatives of Nagornyi Karabakh. The agreement was formalized in July. Ter-Petrossian held talks with the President of Azerbaijan, Heydär Äliyev, in Moscow, in September, but Äliyev stated that his willingness to negotiate a peace accord depended on the unconditional withdrawal of Armenian forces from Azerbaijani territory. Negotiations were held at regular intervals throughout 1995, under the aegis of the OSCE's 11-nation Minsk Group, although only limited progress towards a political settlement was made. In May the three sides carried out a large-scale exchange of prisoners of war. Direct discussions between Armenia and Azerbaijan were initiated in December.

Elections to the post of 'President' of Nagornyi Karabakh, held in November 1996, and at which the incumbent, Robert Kocharian, was re-elected, were criticized by the Minsk Group as a hindrance to the peace process. In December Ter-Petrossian and Äliyev attended an OSCE summit meeting in Lisbon, Portugal. Following the submission of demands by Azerbaijan, the OSCE Chairman issued a statement recommending three principles that would form the basis of a future settlement: the territorial integrity of Armenia and Azerbaijan; the legal status of Nagornyi Karabakh as a broadly autonomous region within Azerbaijan; and security guarantees for the population of Nagornyi Karabakh. Armenia, however, refused to accept the terms of the statement.

In late 1997 the newly elected 'President' of Nagornyi Karabakh, Arkadii Ghukassian, rejected the proposed OSCE peace settlement on the grounds that the proposals presupposed Azerbaijan's sovereignty over the territory. A subsequent statement by President Ter-Petrossian that Nagornyi Karabakh could hope neither to gain full independence, nor to be united with Armenia, appeared to indicate a significant change in policy, but the President's moderate approach to the crisis, which provoked widespread disapproval in Armenia, led to his resignation in February 1998 and his subsequent replacement by Kocharian. Several meetings between the Armenian and Azerbaijani Presidents in 1999–2002, produced no substantive progress towards a resolution of the dispute. After İlham Äliyev succeeded his father as President of Azerbaijan in late 2003, negotiations resumed. In January 2005 PACE approved a resolution, expressing concern at large-scale ethnic expulsions resulting from the Nagornyi Karabakh conflict. In July 2006 the Minsk Group publicized for the first time the details of its fundamental criteria for an agreement between the two countries. On 10 December the territory held an internationally unrecognized referendum, which affirmed the population's desire for independence from Azerbaijan. In July 2007 Bako Sahakian, a former head of Nagornyi Karabakh's security service, was elected as 'President' of the territory.

In March 2008, after several people had been killed in renewed clashes in Nagornyi Karabakh, a non-binding resolution, submitted by Azerbaijan, reaffirming its territorial integrity and demanding the withdrawal of all occupying forces, was adopted by the UN General Assembly, by 39 votes in favour and seven opposing (and 100 abstentions); in addition to Armenia, countries that rejected the resolution included France, Russia and the USA. In June Sarkissian met President Äliyev of Azerbaijan for discussions on the occasion of a CIS summit meeting in St Petersburg, Russia.

Meeting near the Russian capital, Moscow, on 2 November 2008, Sarkissian and Äliyev, together with Russian President Dmitrii Medvedev, in the capacity of mediator, signed a joint declaration reaffirming their commitment to reach a political resolution to the Nagornyi Karabakh conflict. Three further such trilateral meetings took place during 2009. In April 2010 the head of the Armenian Apostolic Church, Supreme Patriarch Karekin II, made his first official visit to Azerbaijan, attending a international gathering of religious leaders in the capital, Baku, where he urged a resolution to the conflict. President Medvedev convened meetings between Sarkissian and Äliyev in Sochi, Russia, in January and during the St Petersburg Economic Forum in June. However, shortly afterwards in June, one Azerbaijani and four Armenian soldiers were killed in what Armenia claimed was an attack by Azerbaijani forces at the cease-fire line in Nagornyi Karabakh. Later that month the Presidents of Russia, the USA and France (the states co-chairing the OSCE Minsk Group) issued a joint statement urging the Armenian and Azerbaijani Governments to finalize the drafting of a peace agreement. In September three Armenian and two Azerbaijani soldiers were killed in a further clash at the border of the enclave. Further discussions between Sarkissian and Äliyev, convened by Medvedev in Astrakhan, Russia, in October, resulted in a formal agreement on a mutual exchange of prisoners of war and the return of the remains of those killed in clashes, but no significant concessions. However, on the occasion of an OSCE summit, held in Astana, Kazakhstan, in December, a planned meeting between Sarkissian and Äliyev failed to take place (reflecting a deadlock in negotiations). Discussions between Sarkissian, Äliyev and Medvedev, convened in Sochi in March 2011, resulted only in a joint declaration urging the full implementation of the agreement reached the previous October. Further trilateral discussions took place in the Russian city of Kazan in June 2011, and in Sochi in January 2012; on the latter occasion the Armenian and Azerbaijani Presidents issued a statement affirming their commitment to accelerating the process of reaching agreement on the main principles of a settlement. Hopes that planned Armenian participation in the annual European festival of popular music, the Eurovision Song Contest, which was to be held in Baku in May 2012, would serve as a demonstration of improved relations (and provide a rare opportunity on which Armenian citizens would be permitted to visit Azerbaijan) were thwarted when, in early March, it was announced that Armenia would not, in fact, participate, despite Azerbaijan having agreed to provide security guarantees to Armenian citizens visiting Azerbaijan. The withdrawal was precipitated by an incident in which an Armenian conscript soldier had been killed in late February, as a result of which a nationalist campaign against Armenian participation in the contest was intensified, although initial reports that the death had been attributed to Azerbaijani sniper fire were withdrawn after it became apparent that the shooting had actually been perpetrated by another Armenian soldier.

In 1997 the Armenian legislature ratified a 1995 treaty that allowed Russia to maintain military bases in Armenia for a period of 25 years, and several bilateral agreements were concluded in 2000. A further, 10-year economic co-operation agreement was signed in 2001. On 20 August 2010, during a visit by Medvedev to Yerevan, a bilateral defence agreement amending the 1995 treaty was signed, allowing Russia's military presence in the country to be extended until 2044 and the mission of some 4,000 Russian troops based in the northern town of Gyumri (hitherto confined to protecting Russian interests) to be upgraded to defending Armenia's security in co-operation with the Armenian army. Russia was also committed to supplying Armenia with modern armaments under the agreement. During a visit to Azerbaijan in September, however, President Medvedev assured Äliyev that the new agreement would not affect the balance of power in the region. In February 2011 President Sarkissian met Medvedev for discussions in St Petersburg, Russia.

Armenia's relations with Georgia were generally relatively cordial in the post-Soviet period, although concerns were expressed regarding the condition or treatment of historic Armenian sites within Georgia on several occasions, including, notably, the construction of a major Georgian Orthodox cathedral complex on the site of a former Armenian cemetery in Tbilisi. The Armenian Government reacted with caution to Russian military operations in Georgia, taken in support of separatists in South Ossetia (see the chapter on Georgia), in early August 2008. The conflict in Georgia (Armenia's major supply route from abroad) inflicted considerable temporary damage to the Armenian economy, including severe shortages of fuel and food. Presidents Sarkissian and Medvedev met in Sochi, Russia, on 2 September to discuss the situation in Georgia and proposed new, large-scale, bilateral co-operation projects between Russia and Armenia. On the following day, when the committee of the chiefs of the security councils convened in Yerevan, Russia sought the recognition of South Ossetian and Abkhazian independence by Armenia and other member states of the Collective Security Treaty Organization (CSTO). (Sarkissian subsequently declared that his country would not recognize the independence of South Ossetia and Abkhazia while the status of Nagornyi Karabakh remained unresolved.) Armenia officially assumed the presidency of the CSTO at a summit meeting in early September. In January 2009 the arrest in Georgia, in the region of Samtskhe-Javakheti, predominately inhabited by ethnic Armenians, of two ethnic Armenians on charges of espionage and of attempting to establish a paramilitary grouping prompted public outrage in Armenia. In March the two men were released on bail, having pleaded guilty to espionage.

Meanwhile, relations with Turkey (which controlled large areas of historic Armenia, including Mount Ararat, regarded as a national symbol by many Armenians) remained uneasy, particularly after Turkey closed its borders with Armenia in 1993, as an expression of support for Azerbaijan in the conflict over Nagornyi Karabakh. In December 2004, following an appeal from President Kocharian, the European Parliament issued a statement that Turkey should recognize that the killings of Armenians in 1915 constituted an act of genocide, and open its borders; in September 2005 the European Parliament issued a further non-binding resolution, which indicated that Turkey's refusal to recognize the killings as genocide could adversely affect its efforts to secure membership of the European Union (EU, see p. 276). Both Armenia's campaign to secure recognition by other states of the killings as genocide and its continuing conflict with Azerbaijan remained serious obstacles to the development of closer relations with Turkey. The murder of a prominent ethnic-Armenian Turkish journalist in Turkey in January 2007 further heightened the sensitivity of relations between the two countries.

In October 2007 the US House of Representatives' Foreign Affairs Committee approved a non-binding resolution that would officially characterize the Turkish massacre of Armenians in 1915 as an act of genocide, provoking outrage from Turkey. However, following strong opposition to the resolution from the US Administration, which expressed concern that it would cause considerable damage to US-Turkish relations, a vote on the issue in the House was subsequently postponed. Hopes of a rapprochement between Armenia and Turkey, after President Sarkissian's installation in April 2008, increased significantly when Turkish President Abdullah Gül accepted an invitation from President Sarkissian to attend the first football match between the national teams in Yerevan on 6 September (the first visit by a Turkish Head of State to Armenia). The Armenian Government additionally waived visa requirements to allow Turkish football fans to travel to Armenia. The announcement followed confirmation by Turkish foreign ministry officials in July of speculation in the Turkish media that Turkish and Armenian delegations had met in Switzerland for informal discussions on bilateral relations. Turkey had proposed the creation of a 'Caucasus Stability and Co-operation Platform' as a regional framework for negotiations, after the outbreak of hostilities between Russia and Georgia in early August. In late September the Ministers of Foreign Affairs of Turkey, Armenia and Azerbaijan met in New York, USA, to conduct discussions on the issue of Nagornyi Karabakh. At the end of January 2009 Sarkissian met Turkish Prime Minister Recep Tayyip Erdoğan on the occasion of the Davos World Economic Forum, and conducted discussions with the Turkish Minister of Foreign Affairs at the Munich Security Conference, in Germany, in early February. In April the ministries of foreign affairs of the two countries announced that further Swiss-brokered discussions had resulted in the drawing-up of a comprehensive framework for normalization of relations. In late August the two ministries issued a joint statement announcing that they had agreed to conduct internal political consultations over a period of six weeks on two protocols, one establishing diplomatic relations and the other developing bilateral ties, which would then be signed and submitted to their respective legislatures for ratification. On 10 October the Ministers of Foreign Affairs of Turkey and Armenia, meeting in Geneva, Switzerland, signed an agreement providing for the normalization of relations between their two countries, which would take effect following its ratification by the legislature of each country.

Progress towards ratification of the treaty subsequently halted, however. A ruling by the Armenian Constitutional Court, on 12 January 2010, that the treaty was constitutionally legitimate, precipitated controversy among some Turkish nationalists, who alleged that the ruling also drew into question the status of the existing border between the two countries. Moreover, the approval, on 25 February, by the Armenian legislature of a Law on International Treaties, which provided for a relatively easy process by which the Government could suspend or rescind international agreements, presented a potential threat to the process of normalization of relations with Turkey. Turkish–Armenian tensions increased again, in March, when the US House of Representatives' Foreign Affairs Committee again voted to recognize the killings of Armenians in 1915 as genocide, as did the legislature of Sweden, although the Armenian and Turkish leadership continued to express support for the rapprochement of their two countries. However, in April President Sarkissian suspended ratification of the Armenian-Turkish treaty, after Turkey made ratification conditional on progress towards a resolution of the Nagornyi Karabakh conflict. In September some 1,000 Armenian Christians travelled to the Turkish island of Akhtamar, in Lake Van in eastern Anatolia, to attend the first religious services to be held in a 10th-century Armenian church since 1915, after the Turkish Government had restored the church and had agreed, as part of efforts to demonstrate goodwill, that an act of worship could be held there once a year. However, the Armenian Government criticized the failure of the Turkish authorities to place a cross on the church prior to the service, an omission which was reported to have discouraged many diaspora Armenians and religious officials from attending. In early October an extreme nationalist Turkish party organized an Islamic religious ceremony, with official permission, in an 11th century Armenian church in the abandoned historic town (and former Armenian capital) of Ani, in Anatolia; the ceremony was strongly condemned by the Armenian Apostolic Church and representatives of the Armenian diaspora. In August 2011 Sarkissian reiterated warnings that Armenia would withdraw from the treaty with Turkey unless the Turkish Government unconditionally ratified the protocols. In January 2012 Turkey's diplomatic relations with France were severely strained, after the upper chamber of the French legislature, the Sénat (Senate) voted to approve legislation criminalizing the denial of killings determined by French law to constitute genocide, including the 1915 Turkish massacres of Armenians.

Armenia generally enjoyed cordial relations with Iran, with a permanent bridge between the two countries being opened in 1995. In September 2004 President Muhammad Khatami of Iran made a long-postponed official visit to Armenia, signing seven bilateral agreements with President Kocharian, which, *inter alia*, were to promote enhanced co-operation in energy and transport. Bilateral relations subsequently strengthened (amid Iran's increasing international isolation). In May 2009 Armenia began to import natural gas from Iran through a new pipeline (which had been completed in late 2008). In July 2010 it was announced that construction of a new Armenian-Iranian power transmission line was to begin, prior to planned exports of Armenian electricity to Iran. A bilateral agreement, approved by the Armenian Government in September, provided for the construction of two large hydroelectric plants near the border with Iran and an oil pipeline linking the two countries. Work on the pipeline was scheduled to commence in 2012 (although an intensified US and EU embargo against Iran prompted concerns early that year that its Government would be unable to finance the bilateral projects).

Other external relations

In June 2000 PACE voted to admit both Armenia and Azerbaijan to the Council of Europe; they became full members in January 2001. In June 2004 Armenia, Azerbaijan and Georgia were included in the EU's new European Neighbourhood Policy and in November 2006 a five-year action plan for co-operation was adopted, focusing on eight areas of priority. With the aim of strengthening relations and addressing integration aspirations, in December 2008 the European Commission presented an Eastern Partnership proposal for Armenia, Azerbaijan, and Georgia, together with Ukraine, Moldova and Belarus; the new programme, offering further economic integration and envisaging enhanced free trade and visa arrangements, was officially established at an EU summit meeting in May 2009. On 19 July 2010 Armenia and the EU began negotiations on the signature of an Association Agreement within the framework of the Eastern Partnership. The Armenian Government presented to the European Commission a plan of further political and economic reforms, including in the areas of human rights protection, judicial reform, tax and customs administration, in September 2011, and subsequently expressed hopes that discussions on the creation of the envisaged free trade area would begin in 2012.

CONSTITUTION AND GOVERNMENT

Under the Constitution of 1995, the President of the Republic is Head of State and Supreme Commander-in-Chief of the armed forces, but also holds broad executive powers. The President is directly elected for a term of five years (and for no more than two consecutive terms of office). The President appoints the Prime Minister (upon the approval of the majority of members of the Azgayin Zhoghov—National Assembly) and, on the Prime Minister's recommendation, the members of the Government. Legislative power is vested in the 131-member Azgayin Zhoghov, which is elected by universal adult suffrage for a term of five years. Judicial power is exercised by the Court of Cassation, the members of which are appointed by the President, for life, and appellate courts. For administrative purposes, Armenia is divided into 11 regions (*marzer*), including the capital, Yerevan.

REGIONAL AND INTERNATIONAL CO-OPERATION

Armenia is a founder member of the Commonwealth of Independent States (CIS, see p. 246) and was admitted to the Conference on Security and Co-operation in Europe (CSCE—now the Organization for Security and Co-operation in Europe—OSCE, see p. 388) in 1992. It is also a member of the Organization of the Black Sea Economic Co-operation (BSEC, see p. 402).

Armenia joined the UN in 1992 and was admitted to the World Trade Organization (WTO, see p. 433) in 2003.

ECONOMIC AFFAIRS

In 2010, according to estimates by the World Bank, Armenia's gross national income (GNI), measured at average 2008–10 prices, was US \$9,556m., equivalent to \$3,090 per head (or \$5,450 on an international purchasing-power parity basis). In 2001–10, it was estimated, the population increased by an annual average of 0.1%, while gross domestic product (GDP) per head increased, in real terms, by an annual average of 7.5%. In 2001–10 Armenia's overall GDP increased, in real terms, by an annual average rate of 7.6%. Real GDP declined by 14.3% in 2009 and by 0.9% in 2010.

According to official figures, agriculture, hunting, forestry and fishing contributed 19.3% of GDP and employed 45.4% of the working population in 2010. (However, the FAO estimated the proportion of the working population employed in agriculture at just 9.1% in 2011 and 8.9% in 2012.) The principal crops are potatoes and other vegetables, cereals and fruit, primarily grapes. In 2001–10, according to estimates by the World Bank, agricultural GDP increased, in real terms, at an average annual rate of 5.0%. The GDP of the sector declined by 1.0% in 2009 but increased by 1.7% in 2010, according to the World Bank.

According to official figures, industry (including mining, manufacturing, construction and power) contributed 35.4% of GDP and employed 15.1% of the working population in 2010. World Bank estimates indicated that in 2001–10 real industrial GDP increased at an annual average rate of 6.8%. According to World Bank figures, the GDP of the sector declined substantially, by some 33.8% in 2009, partly because of a downturn in construction activity, in 2009; it decreased further, by 0.1%, in 2010.

The mining sector has not been extensively developed. Copper, molybdenum, gold, silver and iron are extracted on a small scale, and there are reserves of lead and zinc. There are also substantial, but largely unexploited, reserves of mineral salt, calcium oxide and carbon. Gold production increased in the early 2000s, from 600 kg of gold ore in 2000 to 2,100 kg in 2004, although output declined to 1,400 kg in 2005. According to official figures, production in the mining sector increased by an annual average rate of 8.0% in 2000–08. In 2009 the sector accounted for 0.7% of total industrial production; in 2010 it contributed 2.8% of GDP.

In 2010, according to official figures, the manufacturing sector provided 10.5% of GDP and employed 7.0% of the working population. According to the World Bank, in 2001–10 the GDP of the manufacturing sector increased, in real terms, at an average annual rate of 3.9%. Real sectoral GDP declined by 7.4% in 2009 but increased by 3.1% in 2010.

In 2010, according to official figures, the construction sector provided 19.0% of GDP and employed 5.1% of the working population. According to the Asian Development Bank (ADB, see p. 210), in 2001–10 the GDP of the sector increased, in real terms, at an average annual rate of 20.6%. Real sectoral GDP decreased by 38.6% in 2009 but increased by 20.6% in 2010.

Armenia is heavily dependent on imported energy, much of which is supplied by Russia (petroleum and derivatives) and Turkmenistan (natural gas). In March 2007 a 141-km natural gas pipeline connecting the pipeline networks of Armenia and Iran, to provide Armenia with supplies of natural gas from Iran (although this was likely to be sourced from Turkmenistan) was inaugurated. By July 1999 Armenia had a surplus of electricity, some of which was exported to Georgia; a new high-voltage electricity line opened between the two countries in December 2000, and two high-voltage lines were subsequently opened to permit exports of electric energy to Iran. In 2005 Armenia, Georgia and Iran pursued plans to integrate their electricity networks. In November 2007 the Government approved a plan for the closure of Armenia's sole nuclear power station, at Medzamor, although no specific date for the closure was given. In late 2009 the Government decided that a new nuclear power station would be constructed in Armenia, with Russian assistance. Although it had initially been anticipated that construction would commence in 2011, the project was significantly delayed. The construction of some 15 small hydroelectric power stations was initiated in 2004, and the construction of two joint Armenian-Iranian hydroelectric plants on the River Araks was expected to commence in 2010. In 2008 nuclear power contributed 42.6% of the country's electricity output, natural gas produced 26.2% and hydroelectric power provided 31.1% of the total. Imports of mineral fuels comprised 15.5% of the value of merchandise imports in 2009. Armenia produced a total of 5,672m. kWh of electric energy in 2009, of which of which 336m. kWh was exported. Imports of electric energy amounted to 291m. kWh in that year. In 2010 Armenia produced a total of 6,491m. kWh of electric energy.

According to official figures, the services sector contributed 45.4% of GDP and engaged 39.5% of the employed labour force in 2010. According to the World Bank, in 2001–10 the GDP of the sector increased by an average annual rate of 9.1%, in real terms. Real sectoral GDP increased by 7.2% in 2008 but declined by 5.4% in 2009.

In 2010 Armenia recorded a visible trade deficit of US $2,032.5m., while the deficit on the current account of the balance of payments was $1,373.2m. In 2010 the principal sources of imports were Russia (which supplied 22.3% of total imports), the People's Republic of China, Ukraine, Germany, Turkey and Iran. Armenia's principal export partner in that year was Russia (taking 15.4% of total exports). Other important purchasers were Bulgaria, Germany, Netherlands, Iran, the USA and Belgium. The principal exports in 2009 were manufactured goods (which contributed 45.1% of the total exports and included non-ferrous metals, ferro alloys, non-metallic mineral manufactures and diamonds), metalliferous ore and metal scrap, and beverages. The principal imports in that year were machinery and transport equipment (accounting for 23.8% of imports), manufactured goods, mineral fuels and food and live animals.

In 2010 there was a budgetary deficit of 173,159m. drams (equivalent to 4.9% of GDP). Armenia's general government gross debt was 1,371,990m. drams in 2010, equivalent to 39.2% of GDP. At the end of 2009 Armenia's gross external debt was US $4,935m., of which $2,376m. were external debt stocks, public and publicly-guaranteed. In that year, the cost of debt-servicing long-term public and publicly guaranteed debt and repayments to the IMF was equivalent to 3.5% of the value of exports of goods, services and income (excluding workers' remittances). According to the International Labour Organization (ILO), consumer prices increased at an average annual rate of 4.6% in 2001–10. Consumer prices increased by 8.2% in 2010. The rate of unemployment was 7.0% in 2010, according to official figures.

The critical economic situation in Armenia in the early 1990s was exacerbated by the conflict in Nagornyi Karabakh and the ensuing closure by Azerbaijan and Turkey of their borders with Armenia, in addition to the challenges of post-Soviet transition. An extensive programme of market-based reforms was initiated, and after 2001 steady GDP growth was recorded. An agreement was reached with the IMF on a fourth Poverty Reduction and Growth Facility (PRGF) arrangement in November 2008. In response to the international financial crisis, which resulted in a sharp contraction in GDP in 2009, the Government implemented numerous measures, providing support to banks and making available credits and guarantees to the private sector. In June 2010 the IMF confirmed Armenia's recovery from the downturn, and approved a new three-year Extended Fund Facility (EFF) and Extended Credit Facility (ECF) arrangement worth US $395m. In July Armenia and the EU began negotiations on the signature of an Association Agreement in the framework of the EU's Eastern Partnership, which envisaged the eventual establishment of a free trade area. In December 2010 the IMF concluded Armenia's first programme review under the EFF/ECF arrangement, allowing a disbursement of about $54m. In June and December 2011 the IMF conducted further favourable performance reviews, extending tranches of around $113.9m in total; the planned adoption of comprehensive tax reforms in 2012 was particularly commended. The Fund projected GDP growth of around 4.6% in both 2011 and 2012; however, Armenia's sustained recovery was considered to be dependent on continued growth in Russia and on economic recovery in Europe. Armenia was to benefit from increased EU bilateral assistance during 2011–13, and the Government expressed the hope that discussions on the proposed free trade area would commence in 2012. In October 2011 Armenia and seven other member states of the Commonwealth of Independent States (CIS, see p. 246) (but not Azerbaijan, Turkmenistan or Uzbekistan) signed a free trade agreement, which was expected to enter into effect in 2012. Both the Armenian Government and the regional representative of the European Commission stated that Armenia's participation in this free trade agreement would not inhibit the commencement of discussions on the proposed Deep and Comprehensive Free Trade Area between Armenia and the EU.

PUBLIC HOLIDAYS

2013: 1–2 January (New Year), 6 January (Christmas), 28 January (Army Day), 8 March (Women's Day), 24 April (Armenian Genocide Commemoration Day), 1 May (Labour Day), 3–5 May (Easter), 9 May (Victory and Peace Day), 28 May (Declaration of the First Armenian Republic Day), 5 July (Constitution Day), 21 September (Independence Day).

Statistical Survey

Principal source: National Statistical Service of the Republic of Armenia, 0010 Yerevan, Republic Sq., Government House 3; tel. (10) 52-42-13; fax (10) 52-19-21; e-mail info@armstat.am; internet www.armstat.am.

Area and Population

AREA, POPULATION AND DENSITY

Area (sq km)	29,743*
Population (census results)†	
12 January 1989	3,287,677
10 October 2001	
Males	1,407,220
Females	1,595,374
Total	3,002,594
Population (official estimates at 1 January)‡	
2009	3,238,000
2010	3,249,500
2011	3,262,600
Density (per sq km) at 1 January 2011	109.7

* 11,484 sq miles (including inland water, totalling 1,278 sq km).

† Figures refer to de facto populations, although the methodology for calculating the relationship between *de jure* and de facto populations was amended for the 2001 census, and later figures are, therefore, not strictly comparable with those for 1989; the *de jure* total population for 2001 was 3,213,011.

‡ Figures include persons temporarily absent.

POPULATION BY AGE AND SEX

('000, official estimates at 1 January 2011)

	Males	Females	Total
0–14	315.9	276.6	592.5
15–64	1,143.3	1,207.6	2,350.9
65 and over	124.3	194.9	319.2
Total	1,583.5	1,679.1	3,262.6

POPULATION BY ETHNIC GROUP*

(permanent inhabitants, 2001 census)

	Number	%
Armenian	3,145,354	97.89
Yazidi	40,620	1.26
Others	27,037	0.84
Total	3,213,011	100.00

* According to official declaration of nationality; figures refer to *de jure* population.

MARZER (PROVINCES)

(1 January 2011)

Marz (Province)	Area (sq km)	Estimated population	Density (per sq km)	Capital
Yerevan City	227	1,121,900	4,942.3	Yerevan
Aragatsotn	2,753	142,400	51.7	Ashtarak
Ararat	2,096	280,400	133.8	Artashat
Armavir	1,242	285,800	230.1	Armavir
Gegharkunik	5,348	242,400	45.3	Gavar
Kotayk	2,089	282,100	135.0	Hrazdan
Lori	3,789	282,100	74.5	Vanadzor
Shirak	2,681	282,000	105.2	Gyumri
Syunik	4,506	152,900	33.9	Kapan
Tavush	2,704	134,600	49.8	Ijevan
Vayots Dzor	2,308	56,000	24.3	Yeghegnadzor
Total	29,743	3,262,600	109.7	—

PRINCIPAL TOWNS

(estimated population at 1 January 2011)

Yerevan (capital)	1,121,900	Etchmiadzin	57,600
Gyumri	146,100	Hrazdan	53,400
Vanadzor	105,000	Kapan	45,500

BIRTHS, MARRIAGES AND DEATHS

	Registered live births		Registered marriages		Registered deaths	
	Number	Rate (per 1,000)	Number	Rate (per 1,000)	Number	Rate (per 1,000)
2003	35,793	11.2	15,463	4.8	26,014	8.1
2004	37,520	11.7	16,975	5.3	25,679	8.0
2005	37,499	11.7	16,624	5.2	26,379	8.2
2006	37,639	11.7	16,887	5.2	27,202	8.5
2007	40,105	12.4	18,145	5.6	26,830	8.3
2008	41,185	12.7	18,465	5.7	27,412	8.5
2009	44,413	13.7	18,773	5.8	27,528	8.5
2010	44,825	13.8	17,984	5.5	27,921	8.6

Life expectancy (years at birth, WHO estimates): 70 (males 66; females 74) in 2009 (Source: WHO, *World Health Statistics*).

ECONOMICALLY ACTIVE POPULATION

(annual averages, '000 persons)

	2008	2009	2010
Agriculture, hunting and forestry	493.0	496.2	500.7
Fishing	0.5	0.3	0.6
Mining and quarrying	8.3	7.3	7.6
Manufacturing	94.8	83.9	77.8
Electricity, gas and water supply	24.5	23.9	25.3
Construction	60.4	49.5	56.3
Wholesale and retail trade; repair of motor vehicles, motorcycles and personal household goods	113.2	104.2	106.3
Hotels and restaurants	12.4	12.5	14.3
Transport, storage and communications	51.6	53.8	54.1
Financial intermediation	10.6	11.0	11.7
Real estate, renting and business activities	26.7	26.6	27.0
Public administration and defence; compulsory social security	39.7	40.4	43.9
Education	100.9	100.6	103.2
Health and social work	44.5	45.7	43.0
Other community, social and personal service activities	36.3	33.5	33.1
Total employed	1,117.6	1,089.4	1,104.8
Registered unemployed	74.9	81.4	83.3
Total labour force	1,192.5	1,170.8	1,188.1
Males	589.7	575.2	589.8
Females	602.8	595.6	598.3

Health and Welfare

KEY INDICATORS

Total fertility rate (children per woman, 2009)	1.7
Under-five mortality rate (per 1,000 live births, 2009)	22
HIV (% of persons aged 15–49, 2009)	0.1
Physicians (per 1,000 head, 2008)	3.7
Hospital beds (per 1,000 head, 2006)	4.4
Health expenditure (2008): US $ per head (PPP)	224
Health expenditure (2008): % of GDP	3.8
Health expenditure (2008): public (% of total)	44.5
Access to water (% of persons, 2008)	96
Access to sanitation (% of persons, 2008)	90
Total carbon dioxide emissions ('000 metric tons, 2007)	5,052.7
Carbon dioxide emissions per head (metric tons, 2007)	1.6
Human Development Index (2011): ranking	86
Human Development Index (2011): value	0.716

For sources and definitions, see explanatory note on p. vi.

Agriculture

PRINCIPAL CROPS
('000 metric tons)

	2008	2009	2010
Wheat	236.4	206.5	183.5
Barley	149.1	145.1	118.6
Maize	21.2	15.2	12.8
Potatoes	648.6	593.6	482.0
Cabbages and brassicas	122.7	115.9	114.3
Tomatoes	293.8	278.6	251.9
Cauliflowers and broccoli	6.8	9.2	9.9
Cucumbers and gherkins	81.8	80.9	63.3
Onions, dry	61.4	50.4	38.3
Garlic	9.2	9.3	8.8
Carrots and turnips	27.0	23.4	21.4
Watermelons	182.2	216.1	132.5
Apples*	110.0	110.0	57.3
Pears*	45.1	46.0	24.0
Apricots*	24.0	27.0	6.6
Peaches and nectarines*	51.0	55.0	13.4
Plums and sloes*	50.0	52.0	12.7
Grapes	185.8	208.6	222.9

* Unofficial figures.

Aggregate production ('000 metric tons, may include official, semi-official or estimated data): Total cereals 419.9 in 2008, 377.5 in 2009, 324.9 in 2010; Total roots and tubers 648.6 in 2008, 593.5 in 2009, 482.0 in 2010; Total pulses 6.2 in 2008, 5.8 in 2009, 4.7 in 2010; Total vegetables (incl. melons) 1,007.5 in 2008, 1,035.9 in 2009, 841.1 in 2010; Total fruits (excl. melons) 503.7 in 2008, 540.7 in 2009, 351.4 in 2010.

Source: FAO.

LIVESTOCK
('000 head, year ending September)

	2008	2009	2010
Horses	12	11	11
Asses*	6	6	6
Mules	0.3	0.3	0.3
Cattle	629	585	577
Pigs	87	85	113
Sheep	598	527	511
Goats	39	33	27
Chickens	3,793†	3,950†	4,000*
Turkeys	225†	238†	200*

* FAO estimate(s).
† Unofficial figure.

Source: FAO.

LIVESTOCK PRODUCTS
('000 metric tons)

	2008	2009	2010
Cattle meat	49	50	49
Sheep meat	7	7	7
Pig meat	8	9	9
Chicken meat	7	5	5
Cows' milk	619	574	557
Sheep's milk	39	39	40
Hen eggs*	32	35	39
Wool: greasy	1	1	1

* Unofficial figures.

Source: FAO.

Forestry

ROUNDWOOD REMOVALS
('000 cubic metres, excluding bark)

	2006	2007	2008
Sawlogs, veneer logs and logs for sleepers	5	6*	2*
Fuel wood*	63	40	40
Total	68	44	42

* Unofficial figure(s).

2009–10: Production assumed to be unchanged from 2008 (FAO estimates).

Source: FAO.

SAWNWOOD PRODUCTION
('000 cu m, incl. railway sleepers)

	2006	2007	2008
Total (all broadleaved)	2.3	0.9	0.2

2009–10: Production assumed to be unchanged from 2008 (FAO estimates).

Source: FAO.

Fishing

(metric tons, live weight, FAO estimates)

	2007	2008	2009
Capture	1,065	601	619
Common carp	49	56	58
Crucian carp	73	83	85
Other freshwater fishes	73	69	71
Trouts	91	78	80
Whitefishes	50	43	44
Danube crayfish	717	258	266
Aquaculture	3,650	5,100	5,240
Common carp	430	600	620
Crucian carp	90	120	120
Silver carp	460	580	600
Trouts	2,305	3,326	3,400
Total catch	4,715	5,701	5,859

Source: FAO.

Mining

	2007	2008	2009
Copper concentrates (metric tons)*	17,600	18,800	19,000
Molybdenum concentrates (metric tons)*	4,080	4,250	4,100
Silver ores (kg)*†	4,000	4,000	4,000
Gold ores (kg)*†	1,400	1,400	1,400
Salt ('000 metric tons)	35	37	35

* Figures refer to the metal content of ores and concentrates.
† Estimates.

Source: US Geological Survey.

Industry

SELECTED PRODUCTS

('000 metric tons unless otherwise indicated)

	2008	2009	2010
Wheat flour	128	131	n.a.
Wine ('000 hectolitres)	33	43	51
Beer ('000 hectolitres)	105	108	154
Soft drinks ('000 hectolitres)	442	376	383
Cigarettes (million)	3,117	3,310	4,127
Wool yarn—pure and mixed (metric tons)	16	n.a.	n.a.
Cotton fabrics ('000 sq metres)	77	10	14
Carpets ('000 sq metres)	19	24	14
Cement	770	467	488
Electric energy (million kWh)	6,114	5,672	6,491

Woollen fabrics ('000 sq metres): 2 in 2006.

Finance

CURRENCY AND EXCHANGE RATES

Monetary Units

100 louma = 1 dram.

Sterling, Dollar and Euro Equivalents (30 December 2011)

£1 sterling = 596.439 drams;
US $1 = 385.770 drams;
€1 = 499.148 drams;
1,000 drams = £1.68 = $2.59 = €2.00.

Average Exchange Rate (drams per US $)

2009 363.283
2010 373.660
2011 372.501

Note: The dram was introduced on 22 November 1993, replacing the Russian (formerly Soviet) rouble at a conversion rate of 1 dram = 200 roubles. The initial exchange rate was set at US $1 = 14.3 drams, but by the end of the year the rate was $1 = 75 drams. After the introduction of the dram, Russian currency continued to circulate in Armenia. The rouble had been withdrawn from circulation by March 1994.

STATE BUDGET

(million drams)

Revenue	2009	2010
Tax revenue	503,328.8	574,066.8
Value-added tax	254,158.1	301,730.5
Enterprise profits tax	97,272.0	98,912.9
Income tax	60,204.7	73,939.8
Excises	42,767.1	48,140.5
Customs duties	25,111.3	29,366.7
Fixed payments	23,815.6	21,976.4
Financial duties	19,033.5	20,034.6
Compulsory social security contributions	102,903.1	105,335.9
Transfers	8,127.8	6,056.2
Other revenue	43,022.9	50,339.6
Total	676,416.0	755,833.0

Expense by economic type	2009	2010
Current expenditure	709,493.8	750,570.5
Wages	70,798.5	73,141.9
Compulsory social security payments	5,258.1	5,281.2
Purchase of goods and services	152,683.5	160,018.8
Interest	16,187.4	30,190.0
Grants	19,032.2	17,854.5
Current transfers	79,692.8	94,481.4
Social benefits and pensions	240,209.4	244,039.7
Other current expenditure	125,631.9	125,562.9
Capital expenditure	115,221.5	106,248.0
Additional expenditure	102,901.7	72,173.2
Total	927,617.1	928,991.7

Outlays by function of government	2009	2010
General public services	111,843.8	141,795.7
Defence	130,594.2	147,585.5
Public order, security and justice	66,758.0	65,172.5
Economic affairs	50,271.8	38,886.6
Environmental protection	2,637.9	2,388.7
Housing and community services	10,602.1	31,180.1
Health	52,540.0	52,694.6
Recreation, culture and religion	16,305.9	16,030.4
Education	105,769.4	95,262.8
Social protection	243,428.5	244,063.5
Other expenditures (incl. reserve funds)	33,963.8	21,758.2
Total	824,715.4	856,818.5

INTERNATIONAL RESERVES

(US $ million at 31 December)

	2008	2009	2010
IMF special drawing rights	2.91	124.64	33.48
Foreign exchange	1,403.89	1,878.98	1,832.34
Total	1,406.80	2,003.62	1,865.82

Source: IMF, *International Financial Statistics*.

MONEY SUPPLY

(million drams at 31 December)

	2008	2009	2010
Currency outside depository corporations	316,053	282,674	304,543
Transferable deposits	169,244	221,379	246,884
Other deposits	222,925	319,968	359,776
Broad money	708,222	824,021	911,203

Source: IMF, *International Financial Statistics*.

COST OF LIVING

(Consumer Price Index; base: 2000 = 100)

	2006	2007	2008
Food (incl. non-alcoholic beverages)	132.0	140.9	156.5
Electricity, gas and other fuels	107.6	106.3	114.3
Clothing (incl. footwear)	102.2	105.9	113.0
Rent	147.2	156.4	158.2
All items (incl. others)	121.1	126.5	137.8

2009: Food (incl. non-alcoholic beverages) 155.1; All items (incl. others) 142.5.

2010: Food (incl. non-alcoholic beverages) 169.7; All items (incl. others) 154.2.

Source: ILO.

NATIONAL ACCOUNTS

('000 million drams at current prices)

Expenditure on the Gross Domestic Product

	2008	2009	2010
Government final consumption expenditure	365.0	419.0	460.1
Private final consumption expenditure	2,553.8	2,525.0	2,833.1
Increase in stocks	39.6	–54.6	10.5
Gross fixed capital formation	1,418.8	1,143.8	1,157.9
Total domestic expenditure	4,377.2	4,033.2	4,461.6
Exports of goods and services	536.9	486.2	720.8
Less Imports of goods and services	1,450.7	1,351.0	1,568.1
Statistical discrepancy*	104.8	–26.6	–112.6
GDP in market prices	3,568.2	3,141.7	3,501.6

* Referring to the difference between the sum of the expenditure components and official estimates of GDP, compiled from the production approach.

Gross Domestic Product by Economic Activity

	2008	2009	2010
Agriculture, hunting and forestry	574.8	524.5	601.1
Fishing	7.1	6.8	8.3
Construction	903.0	584.4	600.3
Manufacturing	315.5	273.1	331.9
Mining and quarrying	55.5	52.3	87.9
Electricity, gas and water supply	103.3	96.0	99.2
Wholesale and retail trade; repair of motor vehicles, motorcycles and personal and household goods; hotels and restaurants	428.1	419.8	480.5
Transport, storage and communications	242.3	226.0	237.4
Financial intermediation; real estate, renting and business activities; public administration and defence; other community, social and personal service activities	588.2	676.7	719.1
Sub-total	3,218.0	2,859.7	3,165.7
Less Financial intermediation services indirectly measured	55.0	50.6	53.1
Gross value added in basic prices	3,162.9	2,809.1	3,112.6
Taxes, *less* subsidies on products	405.3	332.6	389.0
GDP in market prices	3,568.2	3,141.7	3,501.6

Note: Totals may not be equal to the sum of components, owing to rounding.

BALANCE OF PAYMENTS
(US $ million)

	2008	2009	2010
Exports of goods f.o.b.	1,112.0	748.9	1,175.4
Imports of goods f.o.b.	–3,775.6	–2,830.1	–3,208.0
Trade balance	–2,663.5	–2,081.3	–2,032.5
Exports of services	645.0	589.5	761.5
Imports of services	–973.1	–857.6	–1,003.8
Balance on goods and services	–2,991.7	–2,349.4	–2,274.8
Other income received	994.4	715.2	959.8
Other income paid	–523.2	–549.2	–621.1
Balance on goods, services and income	–2,520.5	–2,183.4	–1,936.1
Current transfers received	1,239.5	894.8	783.7
Current transfers paid	–101.8	–80.9	–220.8
Current balance	–1,382.9	–1,369.5	–1,373.2
Capital account (net)	148.9	89.1	107.9
Direct investment abroad	–10.2	–52.7	–8.3
Direct investment from abroad	935.4	777.5	570.1
Portfolio investment assets	2.6	–10.6	–1.5
Portfolio investment liabilities	5.7	6.7	12.2
Other investment assets	–580.6	–478.0	–245.6
Other investment liabilities	653.3	1,182.9	647.2
Net errors and omissions	13.7	20.1	17.6
Overall balance	–214.0	165.5	–273.5

Source: IMF, *International Financial Statistics*.

External Trade

PRINCIPAL COMMODITIES
(distribution by SITC, US $ million)

Imports c.i.f.	2007	2008	2009
Food and live animals	378.7	531.1	448.3
Cereals and cereal preparations	127.3	146.3	129.5
Beverages and tobacco	113.8	148.4	107.0
Mineral fuels, etc.	482.7	640.4	491.5
Petroleum and petroleum products	238.8	383.5	254.1
Petroleum oils, etc.	226.4	369.4	238.1
Gas, natural and manufactured	231.1	252.6	235.2
Natural gas	226.0	248.0	231.1
Chemicals and related products	296.3	365.5	325.8
Manufactured goods classified chiefly by material	704.7	874.8	667.1
Non-metallic mineral manufactures	235.0	255.6	137.7
Diamonds	163.4	144.9	65.4
Iron and steel	205.9	216.2	130.0
Machinery and transport equipment	648.1	920.2	756.9
Telecommunications, sound recording and reproducing equipment	119.5	152.9	85.6
Road vehicles	174.5	260.4	94.2
Miscellaneous manufactured articles	203.9	323.0	236.9
Commodities and transactions not classified elsewhere	130.9	156.1	39.4
Gold (non-monetary, unwrought, in powder or semi-manufactured)	129.8	153.1	38.2
Total (incl. others)	3,052.6	4,101.2	3,174.6

Exports f.o.b.	2007	2008	2009
Food and live animals	38.7	43.4	38.1
Beverages and tobacco	130.3	161.1	88.7
Beverages	126.1	153.3	80.1
Alcoholic beverages	120.6	146.8	75.5
Spirits distilled from grape wine or grape marc	115.4	141.4	71.3
Crude materials (inedible) except fuels	172.1	156.7	137.0
Metalliferous ore and metal scrap	144.9	140.6	129.2
Copper ores and concentrates	88.1	101.6	98.8
Manufactured goods classified chiefly by material	598.6	548.6	308.4
Non-metallic mineral manufactures	215.1	198.8	81.8
Diamonds	160.6	145.6	59.7
Iron and steel	240.2	210.5	87.4
Ferro alloys	235.7	208.8	86.5
Non-ferrous metals	129.6	121.1	128.6
Copper	67.3	64.2	60.8
Unrefined copper	66.7	63.3	60.5
Total (incl. others)	1,121.2	1,055.0	684.0

Source: UN, *International Trade Statistics Yearbook*.

PRINCIPAL TRADING PARTNERS
(US $ million)

Imports c.i.f.	2008	2009	2010
Austria	161.6	57.3	56.6
Belgium	94.6	58.5	71.4
Bulgaria	118.6	86.3	112.4
China, People's Republic	382.2	284.6	404.0
France (incl. Monaco)	127.4	73.5	76.7
Georgia	49.4	40.9	54.3
Germany	255.2	176.0	210.7
Greece	38.9	30.8	50.9
Iran	203.0	162.4	199.9
Israel	28.2	10.5	14.0
Italy	157.2	113.7	122.2

Imports c.i.f.—*continued*	2008	2009	2010
Kazakhstan	18.5	3.2	11.9
Korea, Republic	82.0	89.1	72.8
Netherlands	22.6	26.7	23.5
Romania	100.2	72.8	85.7
Russia	851.2	792.2	835.3
Switzerland-Liechtenstein	19.7	123.0	69.4
Turkey	268.2	177.6	210.4
Turkmenistan	38.0	14.3	25.8
Ukraine	314.8	201.9	229.9
United Arab Emirates	32.3	30.8	37.3
United Kingdom	44.8	30.4	37.8
USA	218.8	120.8	110.8
Total (incl. others)	4,426.1	3,321.1	3,749.0

Exports f.o.b.	2008	2009	2010
Belgium	89.6	46.8	72.5
Bulgaria	59.6	60.0	156.6
Canada	15.9	34.1	29.6
Georgia	81.8	52.8	49.0
Germany	183.7	115.0	132.6
Iran	25.1	33.0	84.8
Israel	5.0	0.4	4.2
Italy	27.6	6.9	4.8
Netherlands	130.9	52.2	98.6
Poland	31.4	33.9	30.3
Russia	208.2	107.4	160.5
Spain	11.2	7.6	15.2
Switzerland-Liechtenstein	12.1	25.2	16.9
Ukraine	21.9	12.6	12.1
United Arab Emirates	10.4	5.3	8.2
USA	52.8	67.0	82.7
Total (incl. others)	1,057.2	710.2	1,041.1

Transport

RAILWAYS
(traffic)

	2008	2009	2010
Passenger journeys ('000)	679.8	756.6	844.4
Passenger-km (million)	26.6	34.5	50.1
Freight carried ('000 metric tons)	2,755.1	2,942.6	3,063.3
Freight ton-km (million)	705.0	717.9	743.2

CIVIL AVIATION
(traffic)

	2008	2009	2010
Passengers carried ('000)	1,507.0	1,469.3	1,664.4
Passengers-km (million)	1,127.1	1,151.3	1,278.6
Freight carried ('000 metric tons)	10.8	8.4	8.8
Cargo ton-kilometres ('000)	13.1	9.5	9.7

Tourism

ARRIVALS BY NATIONALITY

	2007	2008	2009
Argentina	25,654	26,450	26,600
Brazil	9,490	10,110	10,500
Canada	28,969	32,110	30,200
CIS countries*	182,587	202,650	208,328
France	22,210	23,500	24,100
Germany	16,120	18,780	18,970
Iran	37,450	40,699	55,243
Japan	10,150	11,110	11,900
Lebanon	19,790	22,200	23,100
Syria	19,890	20,210	21,000
United Kingdom	8,665	9,450	8,100
USA	59,232	62,250	63,100
Total (incl. others)	510,622	558,443	575,284

* Comprising Azerbaijan, Belarus, Georgia, Kazakhstan, Kyrgyzstan, Moldova, Russia, Tajikistan, Turkmenistan, Ukraine and Uzbekistan.

Tourism receipts (US $ million, incl. passenger transport): 343 in 2007; 377 in 2008; 374 in 2009.

Source: World Tourism Organization.

Communications Media

	2008	2009	2010
Telephones ('000 main lines in use)	626.6	599.9	592.3
Mobile cellular telephones ('000 subscribers)	1,442.0	2,191.5	3,865.4
Internet subscribers ('000)	77.6	79.4	96.6
Broadband subscribers	11,100	31,300	85,200

Television receivers ('000 in use): 860 in 2000.

Personal computers: 297,000 (96.9 per 1,000 persons) in 2005.

Book production (including brochures): 1,025 (titles) and 660,000 (copies) in 2003; 970 (titles) and 427,000 (copies) in 2004; 991 (titles) and 796,000 (copies) in 2005.

Newspapers: 120 (titles) and 325,000 (total circulation) in 2003; 170 (titles) and 600,000 (total circulation) in 2004; 177 (titles) and 553,000 (total circulation) in 2005.

Periodicals: 77 (titles) and 309,000 (total circulation) in 2003; 112 (titles) and 412,000 (total circulation) in 2004; 120 (titles) and 401,000 (total circulation) in 2005.

Source: International Telecommunication Union; and UNESCO Institute for Statistics.

Education

(2010/11 unless otherwise indicated, public institutions)

	Institutions	Teachers	Students
Pre-primary	639	7,585*	58,300
General	1,450	41,400	370,900
Gymnasia and lyceums	44†	313‡	10,400†
Specialized secondary schools	101	2,961	29,600
Higher schools (incl. universities)	74	8,843	111,000

* 1998/99.
† 2008/09.
‡ 2004/05.

Pupil-teacher ratio (primary education, UNESCO estimate): 19.3 in 2006/07 (Source: UNESCO Institute for Statistics).

Adult literacy rate (UNESCO estimates): 99.5% (males 99.7%; females 99.4%) in 2009 (Source: UNESCO Institute for Statistics).

Directory

The Government

HEAD OF STATE

President: SERGE SARKISSIAN (elected 19 February 2008, inaugurated 9 April 2008).

GOVERNMENT

(May 2012)

A coalition of the Republican Party of Armenia (RPA), Prosperous Armenia (PA) and the Law-Governed Country Party of Armenia (LCPA).

Prime Minister: TIGRAN SARKISSIAN (RPA).

Deputy Prime Minister and Minister of Territorial Administration: ARMEN GEVORGIAN (Independent).

Minister of Foreign Affairs: EDVARD NALBANDIAN (Independent).

Minister of Defence: SEYRAN OHANIAN (Independent).

Minister of Finance: VACHE GABRIELIAN (RPA).

Minister of Justice: HRAIR TOVMASIAN (RPA).

Minister of Energy and Natural Resources: ARMEN MOVSISSIAN (RPA).

Minister of Labour and Social Affairs: ARTUR GRIGORIAN (PA).

Minister of Health: HARUTYUN KUSHKIAN (PA).

Minister of Agriculture: SERGO KARAPETIAN (LCPA).

Minister of Environmental Protection: ARAM HAROUTUNIAN (RPA).

Minister of the Economy: TIGRAN DAVTIAN (RPA).

Minister of Education and Science: ARMEN ASHOTIAN (RPA).

Minister of Culture: HASMIK POGHOSSIAN (Independent).

Minister of Sport and Youth Affairs: ARTUR PETROSSIAN (PA).

Minister of Transport and Communications: MANUK VARDANIAN (LCPA).

Minister of Urban Development: VARDAN VARDANIAN (PA).

Minister of Emergency Situations: ARMEN YERETSIAN (LCPA).

Minister of Diaspora Affairs: HRANUSH HACOBIAN (RPA).

Government Chief of Staff: DAVID SARKISSIAN (RPA).

MINISTRIES

Office of the President: 0077 Yerevan, Marshal Baghramian Ave 26; tel. and fax (10) 52-23-64; e-mail press@president.am; internet www.president.am.

Office of the Prime Minister: 0010 Yerevan, Republic Sq., Govt Bldg 1; tel. (10) 51-57-21; fax (10) 15-10-35; internet www.gov.am.

Ministry of Agriculture: 0010 Yerevan, Republic Sq., Govt Bldg 3; tel. and fax (10) 52-46-41; e-mail agro@minagro.am; internet www.minagro.am.

Ministry of Culture: 0010 Yerevan, Republic Sq., Govt Bldg 3; tel. (10) 54-40-27; fax (10) 52-39-22; e-mail info@mincult.am; internet www.mincult.am.

Ministry of Defence: 0044 Yerevan, Bagrevand St 5; tel. (10) 29-46-99; fax (10) 29-45-31; e-mail press@mil.am; internet www.mil.am.

Ministry of Diaspora Affairs: 0010 Yerevan, Vazgen Sarkissian St 26/1; tel. (10) 58-56-01; fax (10) 58-56-02; e-mail contact@mindiaspora.am; internet www.mindiaspora.am.

Ministry of the Economy: 0010 Yerevan, M. Mkrtchian St 5; tel. (10) 56-61-85; fax (10) 52-65-77; e-mail secretariat@mineconomy.am; internet www.mineconomy.am.

Ministry of Education and Science: 0010 Yerevan, Republic Sq., Govt Bldg 3; tel. and fax (10) 52-66-02; fax (41) 52-73-43; e-mail info@edu.am; internet www.edu.am.

Ministry of Emergency Situations: 0054 Yerevan, Mikoian St 109/8; tel. (10) 36-20-15; fax (10) 36-34-50; e-mail mes@ema.am; internet www.mes.am.

Ministry of Energy and Natural Resources: 0010 Yerevan, Republic Sq., Govt Bldg 2; tel. (10) 52-19-64; fax (10) 52-63-65; e-mail minenergy@minenergy.am; internet www.minenergy.am.

Ministry of Environmental Protection: 0079 Yerevan, Republic Sq., Govt Bldg 3; tel. (10) 52-10-99; fax (10) 54-08-57; e-mail min_ecology@mnp.am; internet www.mnp.am.

Ministry of Finance: 0010 Yerevan, Melik-Adamian St 1; tel. (10) 59-53-62; fax (10) 52-42-82; e-mail press@minfin.am; internet www.minfin.am.

Ministry of Foreign Affairs: 0010 Yerevan, Republic Sq., Govt Bldg 2; tel. (10) 54-40-41; fax (10) 54-39-25; e-mail info@mfa.am; internet www.mfa.am.

Ministry of Health: 0010 Yerevan, Republic Sq., Govt Bldg 3; tel. (10) 58-24-13; fax (10) 15-10-97; e-mail info@moh.am; internet www.moh.am.

Ministry of Justice: 0079 Yerevan, Halabian St 41 A; tel. and fax (10) 31-90-96; e-mail info@moj.am; internet www.moj.am.

Ministry of Labour and Social Affairs: 0010 Yerevan, Republic Sq., Govt Bldg 3; tel. and fax (10) 52-08-30; e-mail hasmik.khachatryan@mss.am; internet www.mss.am.

Ministry of Sport and Youth Affairs: 0001 Yerevan, Abovian 9; tel. (10) 54-69-33; fax (10) 52-65-29; e-mail info@msy.am; internet www.minsportyouth.am.

Ministry of Territorial Administration: 0010 Yerevan, Republic Sq., Govt Bldg 2; tel. (10) 51-13-02; fax (10) 51-13-32; e-mail info@mta.gov.am; internet www.mta.gov.am.

Ministry of Transport and Communications: 0010 Yerevan, Nalbandian St 28; tel. (10) 59-00-17; e-mail info@mtc.am; internet www.mtc.am.

Ministry of Urban Development: 0010 Yerevan, Republic Sq., Govt Bldg 3; tel. (10) 58-90-80; fax (10) 52-32-00; e-mail info@mud.am; internet www.mud.am.

President

Presidential Election, 19 February 2008

Candidates	Votes	% of votes
Serge Sarkissian	862,369	52.82
Levon Ter-Petrossian	351,222	21.51
Artur Baghdasarian	272,427	16.69
Vahan Hovannisian	100,966	6.18
Others	45,682	2.80
Total	1,632,666	100.00

Legislature

Azgayin Zhoghov
(National Assembly)

0095 Yerevan, Marshal Baghramian St 19; tel. (10) 58-82-25; fax (10) 52-98-26; e-mail abrahamyan@parliament.am; internet www.parliament.am.

Chairman: SAMVEL NIKOIAN.

General Election, 12 May 2007

		Seats		
Parties	%*	A†	B†	Total
Republican Party of Armenia	33.91	41	23	64
Prosperous Armenia	15.13	18	7	25
Armenian Revolutionary Federation—Dashnaktsutyun	13.16	16	—	16
Law-Governed Country Party of Armenia	7.05	8	1	9
Heritage Party	6.00	7	—	7
Alliance	2.44	—	1	1
Independents	—	—	9	9
Others	22.31	—	—	—
Total	100.00	90	41	131

* Percentage refers to the share of the vote cast for seats awarded on the basis of party lists.

† Of the 131 seats in the Azgayin Zhoghov, 90 (A) are awarded according to proportional representation on the basis of party lists, and 41 (B) are elected in single-member districts.

Election Commission

Central Electoral Commission (CEC): 0009 Yerevan, G. Kochar St 21A; tel. and fax (10) 54-35-23; e-mail cec@elections.am; internet www.elections.am; Chair. TIGRAN MUKUCHIAN.

Political Organizations

At February 2010 there were 74 registered political parties.

Armenian Christian Democratic Union (HDQM): 0010 Yerevan, Vardanants St 8A; tel. and fax (10) 54-11-33; e-mail info@acdu.am; internet www.acdu.am; f. 1990; Chair. KHOSROV HAROUTUNIAN.

Armenian Democratic Party (Hayastani Demokratakan Kusaktsutyun): 0009 Yerevan, Koriun St 14; tel. and fax (10) 53-90-24; e-mail democracy@armenia.com; f. 1992 by elements of Communist Party of Armenia; Chair. ARAM SARKISSIAN.

Armenian Liberal Democratic Party (Ramgavar Azatagan—HRAK): Yerevan, ul. Agaronyana, dom 2; tel. and fax (77) 00-22-11; e-mail ramgavar@gmail.com; internet www.ramgavar.org; f. 1991; centre-right; merged with Alliance (Dashink) Nov. 2007; Chair. MIKE KHARABIAN.

Armenian National Congress (ANC): 0010 Yerevan, Koryun St 19A; tel. (10) 52-09-74; e-mail info@anc.am; internet www.anc.am; f. 2008; coalition of movements opposed to regime of Pres. Sarkissian; Pres. LEVON TER-PETROSSIAN.

Armenian Revolutionary Federation—Dashnaktsutyun (ARF) (Hai Heghapokhakan Dashnaktsutiun): 0010 Yerevan, Mher Mkrtchian St 30, POB 123; tel. (10) 52-18-90; fax (10) 52-14-53; e-mail intsec@arf.am; internet www.arfd.am; f. 1890; formed the ruling party in independent Armenia, 1918–20; prohibited under Soviet rule, but continued its activities in other countries; permitted to operate legally in Armenia from 1991; suspended in December 1994; legally reinstated 1998; Chair. HRANT MARKARIAN.

Heritage Party (Zharangutyun): 0002 Yerevan, Moscovian St 31; tel. (10) 53-69-13; fax (10) 53-26-97; e-mail info@heritage.am; internet www.heritage.am; f. 2002; liberal nationalist party; Chair. RAFFI HOVANNISIAN.

Law-Governed Country Party of Armenia (LCPA) (Orinats Yerkir—OY): 0009 Yerevan, Abovian St 43; tel. (10) 56-65-05; fax (10) 56-99-69; e-mail info@oek.am; internet www.oek.am; f. 1998; centrist; Head ARTUR BAGHDASARIAN.

Mighty Fatherland (Hzor Hayrenik): 0010 Yerevan, Tigran Mets Ave 9; tel. (10) 52-92-15; fax (10) 52-25-45; e-mail hzor_hayrenik@xter.net; f. 1997; Chair. VARDAN VARDAPETIAN.

National Democratic Party (AZhK): 0015 Yerevan, Paronian St 11/4; tel. and fax (10) 56-21-50; e-mail ajk_info@web.am; internet www.ajk.am; f. 2001 following the division of the National Democratic Union; contested the 2003 parliamentary elections as part of the Justice (Artarutiun) bloc, but withdrew from the bloc in Dec. 2005; Leader SHAVARSH KOCHARIAN.

National Democratic Union (Azgayin Zhoghovrdavarakan Miutyun): 0001 Yerevan, Abovian St 12; tel. (10) 52-34-12; fax (10) 56-31-88; e-mail ajmndu@netsys.am; f. 1991; Chair. VAZGEN M. MANUKIAN; 2,600 mems (Jan. 2011).

National Unity Party (Azgayin Miabanutyun—MAK): 0002 Yerevan, Moscovian St 33A; tel. (10) 53-36-32; fax (10) 53-03-31; e-mail amiab@yandex.ru; internet www.amiab.am; f. 1998; Chair. ARTASHES GEGHAMIAN.

New Times Party (Nor Zhamanakner): 0001 Yerevan, Mamikoniants St 58; tel. (10) 56-83-17; fax (10) 56-83-39; e-mail nor_jamanakner@yahoo.com; f. 2003; Chair. ARAM KARAPETIAN.

People's Party of Armenia (PPA) (Hayastani Zhoghovrdakan Kusaktsutyun—HzhK): 0002 Yerevan, Ghazar Parpeci St; tel. (10) 53-15-01; fax (10) 53-77-01; f. 1998; Chair. STEPAN DEMIRCHIAN.

Prosperous Armenia (PA) (Bargavach Hayastan Kusaktsutyun—BHK): Yerevan, David Anhaght St 12; tel. (10) 24-82-96; e-mail info@bhk.am; internet www.bhk.am; f. 2004; Pres. GAGIK TSARUKIAN.

Republic (Hanrapetutiun): 0002 Yerevan, Mashtots Ave 37/30; tel. (10) 53-86-34; e-mail republic@arminco.com; f. 2001 by members of the Yerkrapah Union of Volunteers and fmr members of the Republican Party of Armenia; Chair. ARAM SARKISSIAN.

Republican Party of Armenia (Haiastani Hanrapetakan Kusaktsutiun—RPA) (HHK): 0010 Yerevan, Melik-Adamian St 2; tel. (10) 58-00-31; fax (10) 50-12-59; e-mail hhk@hhk.am; internet www.hhk.am; f. 1990; national conservative party; Chair. SERGE SARKISSIAN; 140,000 mems (2011).

United Communist Party of Armenia (Hayastani Miatsial Komunistakan Kusaktsutyun—HMKK): Yerevan, Pushkin St 46/4; tel. and fax (10) 53-12-14; f. 2003 by the merger of seven pro-communist parties, including the Renewed Communist Party of Armenia, the Party of Intellectuals, the Communist Party of the Working People and the United Progressive Communist Party; First Sec. YURI MANUKIAN.

Diplomatic Representation

EMBASSIES IN ARMENIA

Argentina: Yerevan, Aygestan St 12/6; tel. (10) 57-64-52; fax (10) 57-64-51; e-mail earme@mrecic.gov.ar; Ambassador MIGUEL ANGEL CUNEO.

Belarus: 0028 Yerevan, N. Duman St 12–14; tel. (10) 22-02-69; fax (10) 26-03-84; e-mail armenia@belembassy.org; internet www.armenia-new.belembassy.org; Ambassador STEPAN SUKHORENKO.

Brazil: 0010 Yerevan, S. Yerevantsi St. 57; tel. (10) 50-02-10; fax (10) 50-02-11; e-mail embassy@brasil.am; internet www.brasil.am; Ambassador MARCELA M. NICODEMOS.

Bulgaria: Yerevan, Nor Aresh, Sofia St 16; tel. (10) 45-82-33; fax (10) 45-46-02; e-mail embassy.yerevan.mfa.bg; internet www.mfa.bg/bg/15/; Ambassador GEORGI KARASTAMATOV.

China, People's Republic: 0019 Yerevan, Marshal Baghramian St 12; tel. (10) 56-00-67; fax (10) 54-57-61; e-mail chinaemb-am@mfa.gov.cn; internet am.chineseembassy.org; Ambassador TIAN CHANGCHUN.

Egypt: 0028 Yerevan, Sepuhi St 6A; tel. (10) 22-01-17; fax (10) 22-64-25; e-mail egyemb@arminco.com; Ambassador MUHAMMAD ALA ELDIN SAAD EL LEIS.

France: 0015 Yerevan, Grigor Lusavorich St 8; tel. (10) 59-19-50; fax (10) 59-19-70; e-mail admin@ambafran.am; internet www.ambafrance-am.org; Ambassador HENRI REYNAUD.

Georgia: 0010 Yerevan, Arami St 42; tel. (10) 58-55-11; fax (10) 56-41-83; e-mail yerevan.emb@mfa.gov.ge; internet www.armenia.mfa.gov.ge; Ambassador TENGIZ SHARMANASHVILI.

Germany: 0025 Yerevan, Charents St 29; tel. (10) 52-32-79; fax (10) 52-47-81; e-mail info@eriw.diplo.de; internet www.eriwan.diplo.de; Ambassador HANS-JOCHEN SCHMIDT.

Greece: 0002 Yerevan, Demirchian St 6; tel. (10) 53-00-51; fax (10) 53-00-49; e-mail gremb.ere@mfa.gr; internet www.greekembassy.am; Ambassador (vacant).

India: 0019 Yerevan, Dzorapi St 50/2; tel. (10) 53-91-73; fax (10) 53-39-84; e-mail ambassador@embassyofindia.am; internet www.indianembassy.am; Ambassador ACHAL KUMAR MALHOTRA.

Iran: Yerevan, Budaghian St 1; tel. (10) 28-04-57; fax (10) 23-00-52; e-mail info@iranembassy.am; internet www.iranembassy.am; Ambassador SEYED ALI SAGHAEYAN.

Italy: 0010 Yerevan, Italia St 5; tel. (10) 54-23-35; fax (10) 54-23-41; e-mail ambitaly@arminco.com; internet www.ambjerevan.esteri.it; Ambassador BRUNO SCAPINI.

Kazakhstan: 0019 Yerevan, Aygedzor St 66; tel. (10) 21-13-33; fax (10) 27-41-70; e-mail kazembassy@web.am; internet www.kazembassy.am; Ambassador AIYMDOS YE. BOZZHIGITOV (resident in Almatı, Kazakhstan).

Kuwait: Yerevan; Ambassador BASSAM MUHAMMAD ALQABANDI.

Lebanon: 0010 Yerevan, Dzoragyugh St 13/14; tel. (10) 50-13-03; fax (10) 50-13-01; e-mail libarm@arminco.com; Chargé d'affaires ZIAD ATALLAH.

Lithuania: 0037 Yerevan, Babaian St 2/13; tel. (10) 29-76-80; fax (10) 29-76-81; e-mail amb.am@urm.lt; Ambassador GIEDRIUS APUOKAS.

Poland: 0010 Yerevan, Hanrapetutiun St 44A; tel. (10) 54-24-93; fax (10) 54-24-98; e-mail erewan.amb.sekretariat@msz.gov.pl; internet www.erewan.polemb.net; Ambassador ZDZISŁAW RACZYŃSKI.

Romania: Yerevan, Barbusse St 15; tel. (10) 27-53-32; fax (10) 22-75-47; e-mail ambrom@netsys.am; Ambassador RODICA CRINA PRUNARIU.

Russia: 0015 Yerevan, Grigor Lusavorich St 13A; tel. (10) 56-74-27; fax (10) 56-71-97; e-mail info@rusembassy.am; internet www.armenia.mid.ru; Ambassador VYACHESLAV YE. KOVALENKO.

Syria: 0019 Yerevan, Marshal Baghramian Ave 14; tel. (10) 52-40-36; fax (10) 54-52-19; e-mail syrem_ar@intertel.am; Chargé d'affaires a.i. MAMUN HARIRI.

Turkmenistan: 0033 Yerevan, Yerznkian St 52; tel. (10) 22-10-29; fax (10) 22-66-56; e-mail tmembassy@netsys.am; internet www.turkmenistanembassy.am; Ambassador ATA SERDAROV.

Ukraine: 0037 Yerevan, Arabkir 29/5/1; tel. (10) 22-97-27; fax (10) 27-12-14; e-mail ukremb@cornet.am; internet www.mfa.gov.ua/armenia; Ambassador IVAN KUKHTA.

United Kingdom: 0019 Yerevan, Marshal Baghramian Ave 34; tel. (10) 26-43-01; fax (10) 26-43-18; e-mail enquiries.yerevan@fco.gov.uk; internet www.ukinarmenia.fco.gov.uk; Ambassador JONATHAN AVES, KATHERINE LEACH.

USA: 0082 Yerevan, American Ave 1; tel. (10) 46-47-00; fax (10) 46-47-42; e-mail usinfo@usa.am; internet yerevan.usembassy.gov; Ambassador JOHN HEFFERN.

Judicial System

A new judicial and legal system came into force in January 1999. Members of the Court of Cassation, the highest court of appeal, were appointed by the President, for life. A constitutional referendum, held in November 2005, provided for the President to cede the chairmanship of the Council of Justice to the Chairman of the Court of Cassation; the Azgayin Zhoghov (National Assembly) was henceforth to appoint the Prosecutor-General; and the Council of Justice was to nominate the chairmen of all courts (including the Court of Cassation) and to draw up a list of proposed judges for approval by the President.

Constitutional Court: 0019 Yerevan, Marshal Baghramian St 10; tel. (10) 58-81-30; fax (10) 52-99-91; e-mail armlaw@concourt.am; internet www.concourt.am; f. 1996; Chair. GAGIK HAROUTUNIAN.

Court of Cassation: 0010 Yerevan, Vazgen Sarkissian St 5; tel. (10) 51-17-45; fax (10) 56-31-73; internet www.court.am; Chair. ARMAN MKRTUMIAN.

Office of the Prosecutor-General: 0010 Yerevan, V. Sarkissian St 5; tel. (10) 51-16-50; e-mail info@genpro.am; internet www.genproc.am; Prosecutor-General AGHVAN HOVSEPPIAN.

Religion

The major religion is Christianity. The Armenian Apostolic Church is the leading denomination and was widely identified with the movement for national independence. There are also Russian Orthodox and Islamic communities, although the latter lost adherents as a result of the departure of large numbers of Muslim Azeris from the republic. Most Kurds are also adherents of Islam, although some are Yazidis. In 2006 10 religious organizations were registered in Armenia. (The Jehovah's Witness community was estimated to number 12,000, but failed to qualify for registration as its statutes were deemed to be in contravention of the Constitution.)

ADVISORY COUNCIL

Religious Council: Yerevan, c/o Department for National Minorities and Religious Affairs; tel. (10) 58-16-63; f. 2002 as a consultative council to advise the Government on religious affairs; was to comprise representatives of the Government, the Office of the Prosecutor-General, the Armenian Apostolic Church, and the Catholic and Protestant Churches.

CHRISTIANITY

Armenian Apostolic Church: 1101 Etchmiadzin, Monastery of St Etchmiadzin; tel. (10) 51-71-10; fax (10) 51-73-01; e-mail divanatun@etchmiadzin.am; internet www.armenianchurch.org; eight dioceses in Armenia, 22 dioceses and bishoprics in the rest of the world; Supreme Patriarch KAREKIN II (Catholicos of All Armenians).

The Roman Catholic Church

Armenian Rite

Armenian Catholics in Eastern Europe are under the jurisdiction of an Ordinary. At 31 December 2007 there were an estimated 540,000 adherents within this jurisdiction.

Ordinary of Eastern Europe of Catholics of the Armenian Rite: Most Rev. RAPHAËL FRANÇOIS MINASSIAN (Titular Archbishop of Cesarea di Cappadocia of the Armenian Rite), Yerevan, Tbilisi St 1/3; e-mail ordiarm@mail.ru.

Latin Rite

The Apostolic Administrator of Latin Rite Catholics of the Caucasus is resident in Tbilisi, Georgia (q.v.).

JUDAISM

In the early 2000s the Jewish community numbered around 1,000, and was located principally in Yerevan.

Mordechay Navi Jewish Religious Community of Armenia: 0018 Yerevan, Nar-Dosi St 23; tel. (10) 57-19-68; fax (10) 55-41-32; e-mail mordechay@netsys.am; internet www.yehudim.am; f. 1992; Chief Rabbi of Armenia GERSH MEIR BURSHTEIN; Chair. of the Jewish Community in Armenia RIMMA VARJAPETYAN.

The Press

PRINCIPAL NEWSPAPERS

In 2005 177 newspaper titles were published in Armenia. Those listed below are in Armenian except where otherwise stated.

168 zham (168 Hours): 0010 Yerevan, Pushkin St 3A, 2nd Floor; tel. (10) 58-48-31; fax (10) 52-29-58; e-mail info@168.am; internet www.168.am; f. 1994; 3 a week; opposition; news; also online edn in Armenian and English; Editor-in-Chief SATIK SEIRANIAN.

Aravot (The Morning): 0023 Yerevan, Arshakuniats Ave 2, 15th Floor; tel. (10) 56-89-68; fax (10) 52-87-52; e-mail news@aravot.am; internet www.aravot.am; f. 1994; daily; Editor ARAM ABRAMIAN; circ. 5,000.

Azg (The Nation): 0010 Yerevan, Hanrapetutiun St 47; tel. (10) 52-93-53; fax (10) 56-28-63; e-mail azg@azg.am; internet www.azg.am; f. 1991; daily; also daily online edition in Armenian, Russian, Turkish and English; Editor-in-Chief HAGOP AVETIKIAN; circ. 3,000 (2009).

Delovoi Ekspress (Business Express): 0005 Yerevan, Tigran Mets Ave 67A; tel. (10) 57-33-05; fax (10) 57-31-25; e-mail delovoy@express.am; internet www.express.am; f. 1992; weekly; economic; in Russian; Editor EDUARD NAGDALIAN.

Golos Armenii (The Voice of Armenia): 0023 Yerevan, Arshakuniats Ave 2, 7th Floor; tel. (10) 52-77-23; fax (10) 52-89-08; e-mail info@golosarmenii.am; internet www.golos.am; f. 1934 as *Kommunist*; current name adopted in 1991; 3 a week; in Russian; Chief Editor FLORA NAKHSHKARIAN.

Grakan Tert (Literary Paper): 0019 Yerevan, Marshal Baghramian St 3; tel. (10) 52-05-94; e-mail gr_tert@free.am; f. 1932; weekly; organ of the Union of Writers; Editor SAMUEL KOSIAN.

Haiastani Hanrapetutiun (Republic of Armenia): 0023 Yerevan, Arshakuniats Ave 2; tel. (10) 52-69-74; fax (10) 54-86-11; e-mail hh@press.aic.net; internet www.hhpress.am; f. 1990; daily; Editor-in-Chief TIGRAN FARMANIAN; circ. 6,000.

Haikakan Zhamanak (Armenian Times): 0016 Yerevan, Israelian St 37; tel. (10) 58-11-75; e-mail editor@armtimes.com; internet www.armtimes.com; f. 1999; daily; Editor-in-Chief NIKOL PASHINIAN; circ. 6,000.

Haiots Ashkhar (Armenian World): 0001 Yerevan, Tumanian St 38; tel. (10) 53-88-65; fax (10) 53-32-21; e-mail hayashkh@arminco.com; internet www.armworld.am; f. 1997; daily; Editor GAGIK MKRTCHIAN; circ. 3,500.

Iravunk (Right): 0002 Yerevan, Yeznik Koghbatsu St 50A; tel. (10) 53-27-30; fax (10) 53-41-92; e-mail iskakan@mail.ru; internet www.iravunk.com; f. 1989; twice weekly; opposition newspaper; Editor HOVHANNES GALAJIAN; circ. 17,000.

Lusantsk: 0023 Yerevan, Arshakuniats Ave 2/13; tel. (10) 52-38-75; e-mail lusantsk@list.ru; f. 2007; weekly; Editor-in-Chief SUREN GEKAMIAN.

Novoye Vremya (New Times): 0023 Yerevan, Arshakuniats Ave 2, 3rd Floor; tel. (10) 52-29-61; fax (10) 52-73-97; e-mail nv@nv.am; internet www.nv.am; f. 1992; 3 a week; in Russian; Editor RUBEN SATIAN; circ. 5,000 (2009).

Respublika Armenia (Republic of Armenia): 0023 Yerevan, Arshakuniats Ave 2, 9th Floor; tel. and fax (10) 54-57-00; e-mail ra@arminco.com; internet www.ra.am; f. 1990; state-owned; twice weekly; in Russian; Editor YELENA KURDIYAN; circ. 3,000.

Taregir: 0025 Yerevan, Tigran Mets 49; tel. (10) 57-39-03; e-mail taregir@hotmail.com; internet www.taregir.am; f. 2007; two a week; politics and current affairs; in Armenian; Editor-in-Chief VASAK DARBINIAN.

Yeter: 0025 Yerevan, A. Manukian St 5; tel. (10) 55-34-13; fax (10) 55-17-13; e-mail editor@eter.am; internet www.eter.am; weekly; independent; television and radio programming information; in Armenian with Russian supplement; Editor GOR KAZARIAN.

Zhamanak Yerevan (The Yerevan Times): 0010 Yerevan, Hanrapetutiun St 76/3; tel. (10) 52-04-60; e-mail zhamanakyerevan@gmail.com; internet www.zhamanak.com; in Armenian; also online edn in English; daily; Editor-in-Chief ARMAN BABAZHANIAN.

Zhamanaki Mitk (Thoughts of The Times): Yerevan; tel. and fax (10) 35-73-54; weekly; Editor-in-Chief SIMON SARKISSIAN; circ. 3,000.

PRINCIPAL PERIODICALS

In 2005 120 periodicals were published.

Agrogitutiun/ Agronauka (Agricultural Science): 0010 Yerevan, Republic Sq., Govt Bldg 3; tel. (10) 23-20-17; fax (10) 232441; e-mail agrpress@arminco.com; every two months; agriculture and forestry; in Armenian and Russian; publ. by Ministry of Agriculture; Editor ARMEN KHOJOIAN; circ. 500 (2009).

Armenia: Finance and Economy: 0023 Yerevan, Arshakuniats Ave 2A, 10th Floor; tel. (10) 54-48-97; e-mail armef@arminco.com; f. 1999; Editor-in-Chief MHER DAVOIAN.

Armenia Now: 0002 Yerevan, Parpetsi St 26/9; tel. (10) 53-24-22; e-mail info@armenianow.com; internet www.armenianow.com; f. 2002; online only; weekly; in Armenian, Russian and English; Editor-in-Chief JOHN HUGHES.

Aroghchapoutiun (Health): 0036 Yerevan, Halabian St 46; tel. (10) 39-65-36; e-mail mharut@dmc.am; f. 1956; quarterly; theoretical, scientific-methodological, organizational and practical journal of the Ministry of Health; Editor M. A. MURADIAN; circ. 2,000–5,000.

Bazis (Basis): 1000 Yerevan; tel. (10) 50-10-48; e-mail basis@anfas .am; 10 a year; economics; in Russian; Chief Editor ASHOT ARAMIAN.

De Facto: 0010 Yerevan, Amirian St 3/20; tel. (10) 56-43-64; fax (10) 54-77-80; e-mail spdefacto@yahoo.com; internet www.hayastan .com/defacto; politics and society; in Armenian; monthly; Editor-in-Chief MENUA HARUTYUNIAN.

EL Style (Elite Life Style): 0010 Yerevan, Vardants St 15/29; tel. (10) 54-88-91; e-mail editor@el.am; internet www.el.am; fashion, culture, travel; f. 2004; 10 a year; Editor MAYA POGHOSSIAN.

Garun (Spring): 0015 Yerevan, Grigor Lusavorich St 15; tel. (10) 56-29-56; fax (10) 56-29-06; e-mail garinfo@freenet.am; f. 1967; monthly; independent; fiction, poetry and socio-political issues; Editor V. S. AYVAZIAN; circ. 1,500.

Gitutiun ev Tekhnika (Science and Technology): 0048 Yerevan, Komitas Ave 49/3; tel. (10) 23-37-27; e-mail giteknik@rambler.ru; f. 1963; monthly; journal of the Research Institute of Scientific-Technical Information and of Technological and Economic Research; Dir S. AGAJANIAN; Editor H. R. KHACHATRIAN; circ. 1,000.

Literaturnaya Armeniya (Literary Armenia): 0019 Yerevan, Marshal Baghramian St 3; tel. (10) 56-35-57; fax (10) 56-36-66; f. 1958; quarterly; journal of the Union of Writers; fiction; in Russian; Editor ALBERT NALBANDIAN.

Sobesednik Armenii (Armenian Interlocutor): Yerevan, Moskovyan St 31; tel. (10) 53-65-09; fax (10) 53-65-89; e-mail info@ sobesednik.am; internet www.sobesednik.am; f. 2007; weekly; in Russian; politics, society, the arts; Editor-in-Chief GENOFIA MARTIROSIAN.

TV-Mol/ TV-Man: 0037 Yerevan, shosse Yegvardi 1; tel. (10) 36-83-31; e-mail best@tvmall.am; f. 2004; Armenian and Russian edns; weekly; Editor-in-Chief ARTASHES KHACHATRIAN; total circ. 45,000.

Yerkir (The Country): 0010 Yerevan, Hanrapetutiun St 30; tel. (10) 52-15-01; fax (10) 52-04-26; e-mail news@yerkir.am; internet www .yerkir.am; f. 1991; weekly; organ of the ARF; also published in Lebanon; Editor-in-Chief SPARTAK SEYRANIAN; circ. 2,500.

NEWS AGENCIES

Arka News Agency: 0010 Yerevan, Pavstos Byuzand St 1/3; tel. (10) 52-21-52; fax (10) 52-40-80; e-mail arka@arminco.com; internet www .arka.am; f. 1996; economic, financial and political news; Russian and English; Dir KONSTANTIN PETROSSOV.

Armenia Today: Yerevan; tel. (91) 40-35-56; e-mail editor@ armtoday.info; internet www.armtoday.info; f. 2007; Editor ARGISHTI KIVIRIAN.

Armenpress (Armenian News Agency): 0009 Yerevan, Isaahakian St 28, 4th Floor; tel. (10) 52-67-02; fax (10) 52-67-82; e-mail info@ armenpress.am; internet www.armenpress.am; f. 1918 as state information agency, transformed into state joint-stock company in 1997; Armenian, English and Russian; Dir HRAYR ZORIAN.

Arminfo: 0009 Yerevan, Isaahakian St 28, 2nd Floor; tel. (10) 54-31-74; fax (10) 54-31-72; e-mail news@arminfo.am; internet www .arminfo.info; f. 1991; Dir EMMANUIL MKRTCHIAN.

De Facto: 0023 Yerevan, Arshakuniats Ave 2A, 9th Floor; tel. (10) 54-57-99; fax (10) 54-53-89; e-mail info@defacto.am; internet www .defacto.am; f. 2000; Chair. KAREN ZAKHARIAN.

Noyan Tapan (Noah's Ark): 0009 Yerevan, Isaahakian St 28, 3rd Floor; tel. (10) 56-59-65; fax (10) 52-42-79; e-mail info@nt.am; internet www.nt.am; f. 1991; Dir TIGRAN HAROUTUNIAN.

Panarmenian.net: 0025 Yerevan, Aleq Manukian St 5; tel. (10) 55-36-23; e-mail editorial@panarmenian.net; internet www .panarmenian.net; f. 2000; Dir ARMEN AZARIAN.

Panorama: 0018 Yerevan, Khorenatsi St 34B; tel. (10) 54-72-75; e-mail info@panorama.am; internet www.panorama.am; f. 2005; Exec. Dir TAMARA AVANESOVA.

Tert.am: 0023 Yerevan, Arshakuniats St 2; tel. (10) 52–17–75; e-mail editor@tert.am; internet www.tert.am; f. 2008; Dir NARINE HOVHANNISIAN.

Publishers

Academy of Sciences Publishing House: 0019 Yerevan, Marshal Baghramian St 24G; tel. (10) 52-70-31; fax (10) 56-92-81; Dir KH. H. BARSEGHIAN.

Arevik Publishing House: 0009 Yerevan, Terian St 91; tel. (10) 52-45-61; fax (10) 52-05-36; e-mail smbatg@mail.ru; internet www .arevik.am; f. 1986; political, scientific, fiction for children, textbooks; Pres. DAVID HOVHANNES; Dir ASTGHIK STEPANIAN.

Haikakan Hanragitaran Hratarakchutioun (Armenian Encyclopedia Publishing House): 1015 Yerevan, Grigor Lusavorich St 15; tel. (10) 52-13-50; fax (10) 52-43-41; e-mail encyclop@sci.am; internet www.encyclopedia.am; f. 1967; encyclopedias and other reference books; Editor-in-Chief HOVHANNES M. AIVAZIAN.

Hayastan (Armenia Publishing House): 0009 Yerevan, Isaahakian St 28; tel. (10) 52-85-20; fax (10) 52-57-62; f. 1921; science, social sciences, fiction and children's books; Dir VAHAGN SARKISSIAN.

Louys Publishing Co: 0009 Yerevan, Isaahakian St 28; tel. (10) 52-53-13; fax (10) 56-55-07; e-mail louys@arminco.com; f. 1955; textbooks; Dir HOVHANNES Z. HAROUTUNIAN.

Tigran Mets (Tigran the Great) Publishing House: 0023 Yerevan, Arshakuniats St 2; tel. (10) 52-17-75; e-mail info@tigran-mets .am; internet www.tigran-mets.am; fiction, poetry, science and children's books; Dir VREJ MARKOSSIAN.

Yerevan State University Publishing House: 0025 Yerevan, A. Manukian St 1; tel. (10) 55-52-40; fax (10) 55-46-41; e-mail pr-int@ ysu.am; internet www.ysu.am; f. 1919; textbooks and reference books, history, literary criticism, science and fiction; Dir PERCH STEPANIAN.

Zangak-97: 0051 Yerevan, Komitas St 49/2; tel. (10) 23-25-28; fax (10) 54-06-07; e-mail info@zangak.am; internet www.zangak.am; f. 2000; scientific works, school teaching manuals, literature for children, translations of foreign authors; Pres. SOKRAT MKRTCHIAN.

PUBLISHERS' ASSOCIATION

National Union of Armenian Publishers: 0009 Yerevan, G. Lusavorich St 15; tel. (10) 58-21-72; fax (10) 22-34-34; e-mail armnpa@netsys.am; f. 1999; Pres. VAHAN KHACHATRIAN.

Broadcasting and Communications

TELECOMMUNICATIONS

Modernization of Armenia's telecommunications sector started about in the mid-2000s, and by 2011 the sector was 100% privately owned. In the first quarter of that year there were 650,000 fixed telephone lines and 3.8m. subscriptions to mobile telephone services in Armenia.

Armenia Telephone Co (ArmenTel): 0037 Yerevan, Azatutiun Ave 24; tel. (10) 54-91-00; fax (10) 28-98-88; e-mail pr@beeline.am; internet www.beeline.am; f. 1995; 100% owned by VimpelCom (Russia); fixed line and mobile communications operator; Dir-Gen. IGOR KLIMKO.

Orange Armenia: 0010 Yerevan, Vazgen Sarkissian St 26/1; tel. (10) 51-35-51; fax (10) 56-06-19; e-mail contact-centre@ orangearmenia.am; internet www.orangearmenia.am; f. 2009; mobile telecommunications and internet service provider; subsidiary of France Telecom (q.v.); Dir BRUNO DUTOIS.

VivaCell: 0015 Yerevan, Argishti St 4/1; tel. (10) 56-87-77; fax (10) 56-92-22; e-mail info@mts.am; internet www.vivacell.am; f. 2004; mobile telecommunications provider; operated by K Telecom CJSC; Man. Dir RALPH YERIKIAN.

BROADCASTING

In addition to the publicly owned national broadcast network, Armenia Public Radio, and the two public television stations, the country has 20 major private radio stations and 40 major private local to near national television stations.

National Commission for Television and Radio (NCTR) (HRAH): 0002 Yerevan, Isahakian St 28; tel. (10) 52-83-70; fax (10) 53-90-34; e-mail nctr@tvradio.am; internet www.tvradio.am; Dir GRIGOR AMALIAN.

Radio

Armenian Public Radio: 0025 Yerevan, A. Manukian St 5; tel. (10) 55-11-43; fax (10) 55-46-00; e-mail aa@arradio.am; internet www .armradio.am; domestic broadcasts in Armenian, Russian and Kurdish; external broadcasts in Armenian, Russian, Kurdish, Azerbaijani, Arabic, English, French, German, Spanish and Farsi; Dir-Gen. ARMEN AMIRIAN.

Television

Armenian Public Television—First Channel: 0047 Yerevan, Hovsepian St 26; tel. (10) 65-00-15; fax (10) 65-05-23; e-mail support@ armtv.com; internet www.1tv.am; state jt-stock co; Chair. of Council ALEKSAN HAROUTUNIAN; Exec. Dir GAGIK BUNIATIAN.

Armenia TV: 0054 Yerevan, Yeghvard Ave 1; tel. (10) 36-93-44; fax (10) 36-68-52; e-mail info@armeniatv.am; internet www.armeniatv .am; f. 1999; largest private television company in Armenia;

transmits programming terrestrially, by cable and by satellite; Dir BAGRAT SARKISSIAN.

H2 (Armenian Second TV Channel): 0088 Yerevan, Ajapniak, Nazarbekian Distr., G. 3, Bl. 3/1; tel. (10) 39-88-31; fax (10) 39-25-36; e-mail h2@tv.am; internet www.tv.am; f. 1998; present name adopted 2005; Dir SAMVEL A. MAYRAPETIAN.

Hrazdan TV: 2301 Kotayk Marz, Hrazdan; tel. (223) 20-292; e-mail hrazdantv@mail.ru; internet www.hrazdantv.am; f. 1990; privately owned; Exec. Dir MNATSAKAN HARUTYUNIAN.

Shant TV: 0028 Yerevan, Kievian St 16, 10th Floor; tel. (10) 27-76-68; fax (10) 26-16-88; e-mail info@shanttv.am; internet www.shant-tv.com; f. 1994; private, independent; Pres. ARTHUR A. YEZEKIAN.

Finance

(cap. = capital; res = reserves; dep. = deposits; m. = million; brs = branches; amounts in drams, unless otherwise stated)

BANKING

Central Bank

Central Bank of the Republic of Armenia: 0010 Yerevan, Vazgen Sarkissian St 6; tel. (10) 58-38-41; fax (10) 52-38-52; e-mail mcba@cba.am; internet www.cba.am; f. 1993; state-owned; cap. 100.0m., res 95,641.7m., dep. 382,380.9m. (Dec. 2009); Chair. KONSTANTIN R. SAROIAN.

Selected Banks

At the end of June 2010 there were 21 commercial banks, with total assets amounting to 1,329,200m. drams, in operation in Armenia.

ACBA-Credit Agricole Bank CJSC: 0009 Yerevan, Byron St 1; tel. (10) 56-58-58; fax (10) 54-34-85; e-mail acba@acba.am; internet www.acba.am; f. 1996 as Agricultural Co-operative Bank of Armenia; name changed as above Sept. 2006; cap. 10,000.0m., res 11,180.0m., dep. 51,983.6m. (Dec. 2010); Gen. Man. STEPAN GISHIAN.

Ameriabank: 0015 Yerevan, G. Lusavorich St 9; tel. (10) 56-11-11; fax (10) 51-31-33; e-mail office@ameriabank.am; internet www.ameriabank.am; f. 2008; cap. 25,447.6m., res 47.7m., dep. 74,222.3m. (Dec. 2010); Gen. Dir ARTAK HANESIAN; 5 brs.

Ardshininvestbank (ASHIB) (Bank for Industry, Construction and Investment): 0015 Yerevan, Grigor Lusavorich St 13; tel. (10) 59-05-01; fax (10) 56-74-86; e-mail office@ashib.am; internet www.ashib.am; f. 2003 with acquisition of banking business of Ardshinbank and partially acquired the assets of Armagrobank; 87% owned by Business Investments Centre Ltd, 10% owned by International Finance Corpn (USA); cap. 13,802.4m., res 4,403.6m., dep. 72,009.0m. (Dec. 2010); Chair. of Man. Bd KARAPET GEVORGIAN; 55 brs.

Armbusinessbank (ABB): 0010 Yerevan, Nalbandian St 48; tel. (10) 59-20-00; fax (10) 54-58-35; e-mail info@armbusinessbank.am; internet www.armbusinessbank.am; f. 1991; owned by Chrystie Management Inc; cap. 13,450.0m., res 212.0m., dep. 54,693.4m. (Dec. 2010); Chair. of Bd ARA KIRAKOSSIAN.

Armenian Development Bank: 0015 Yerevan, Paronian St 21/1; tel. (10) 59-14-00; fax (10) 59-14-05; e-mail info@armdb.com; internet www.armdb.com; f. 1990; cap. 4,526.0m., res 431.1m., dep. 11,277.6m. (Dec. 2010); Chief Exec. KAREN SARKISSIAN.

Armenian Economy Development Bank (Armeconombank) (AEB): 0002 Yerevan, Amirian St 23/1; tel. (10) 51-09-10; fax (10) 53-89-04; e-mail bank@aeb.am; internet www.aeb.am; f. 1988; jt-stock co; corporate banking; cap. 2,333.3m., res 5,464.8m., dep. 25,649.6m. (Dec. 2010); 25% owned by the European Bank for Reconstruction and Development (United Kingdom); Chair. of Bd SARIBEK SUKIASSIAN; CEO ARMEN NALZHIAN; 39 brs.

Artsakhbank: 0028 Yerevan, Kievian St 3; tel. (10) 27-77-19; fax (10) 27-77-49; e-mail artsakhbank@ktsurf.net; internet www.artsakhbank.am; f. 1996; cap. 6,561.2m., res 678.0m., dep. 33,350.1m. (Dec. 2010); Chair. of Bd of Dirs HRATCH KAPRIELIAN; Chair. of Bd KAMO NERSISSIAN; 12 brs.

Converse Bank: 0010 Yerevan, Vazgen Sarkissian St 26/1; tel. (10) 51-12-00; fax (10) 51-12-12; e-mail post@conversebank.am; internet www.conversebank.am; f. 1993; 95% owned by Advanced Global Investments (USA); cap. 1,233.1m., profits and res 2,761.8m., dep. 66,056.2m. (Dec. 2009); Exec. Dir TIGRAN DAVTIAN; 16 brs (2008).

HSBC Bank Armenia: 0009 Yerevan, Terian St 66; tel. (10) 51-50-00; fax (10) 51-50-01; e-mail hsbc.armenia@hsbc.com; internet www.hsbc.am; f. 1996; 70% owned by HSBC Europe BV (Netherlands), 30% by Wings Establishment (Liechtenstein); cap. 10,439.0m., res 145.8m., dep. 107,444.4m. (Dec. 2010); Pres. WATCHE MANOUKIAN; Chief Exec. ASTRID CLIFFORD; 4 brs.

InecoBank: 0001 Yerevan, Tumanian St 17; tel. (10) 51-05-10; fax (10) 51-05-73; e-mail inecobank@inecobank.am; internet www.inecobank.am; f. 1996; cap. 3,463.2m., res 3,132.8m., dep. 20,354.7m. (Dec. 2010); Chair. ASHOT AVETISSIAN.

Mellat Bank: 0010 Yerevan, Amirian St 6, POB 24; tel. (10) 58-17-91; fax (10) 54-08-85; e-mail mellat@mellatbank.am; internet www.mellatbank.am; f. 1995; wholly owned by Bank Mellat (Iran); cap. 6,850.0m. (Dec. 2009); Chair. and Gen. Dir MOHAMMAD BAGHER BAGHERI.

Prometey Bank: 0010 Yerevan, Hanrapetutiun St 44/2; tel. (10) 56-20-36; fax (10) 54-57-19; e-mail info@prometeybank.am; internet www.prometeybank.am; f. 1990; present name adopted 2001; cap. 7,200.0m., res 67.7m., dep. 11,996.3m. (Dec. 2010); Chair. of Bd EMIL SOGHOMONIAN.

VTB Bank (Armenia): 0010 Yerevan, Nalbandian St 46; tel. (10) 58-04-51; fax (10) 56-55-78; e-mail info@vtb.ru; internet www.vtb.am; f. 1923 under the name Armsavingsbank; present name adopted 2006; owned by Bank VTB (Russia); cap. 13,775.7m., res 3,522.6m., dep. 73,614.7m. (Dec. 2010); Chair. VALERY V. OVSYANNIKOV; 81 brs.

Banking Union

Union of Banks of Armenia: 0009 Yerevan, Koriun St 19A; tel. and fax (10) 52-77-31; e-mail uba@uba.am; internet www.uba.am; f. 1995; oversees banking activity; Chair. ASHOT OSIPIAN; Exec. Dir SEYRAN SARGSYAN.

COMMODITY AND STOCK EXCHANGES

NASDAQ OMX Armenia: 0010 Yerevan, Mher Mkrtchian St 5B, 3rd & 4th Floors; tel. (10) 54-33-21; fax (10) 54-33-24; e-mail info@nasdaqomx.am; internet www.nasdaqomx.am; f. 1997 as Armenian Securities Market Members Asscn; renamed as Armenian Stock Exchange in Nov. 2000, and as above in Jan. 2009; CEO ARMEN G. MELIKYAN.

Yerevan Adamand Commodity and Raw Materials Exchange: 0010 Yerevan, Agatangeghos St 6/1; tel. and fax (10) 56-52-28; e-mail info@yercomex.am; internet www.yercomex.am; f. 1990; Dir GRIGOR VARDIKIAN.

INSURANCE

In 2010 there were nine licensed insurance companies in Armenia.

AHA Royal Insurance: 0010 Yerevan, Hanrapetutiun St 62/98; tel. (10) 52-67-30; fax (10) 52-67-40; e-mail aharoyal@insurer.am; internet www.insurer.am; f. 2004; insurance and reinsurance; Gen. Dir HRACHA I. KARAPETIAN.

Cascade Insurance (CIN): 0033 Yerevan, Hrachya Kochari St 5/1; tel. (10) 22-21-11; fax (10) 27-82-21; e-mail info@cin.am; internet www.cascadeinsurance.am; f. 2004; 35% owned by the European Bank for Reconstruction and Development; CEO GARNIK TONOYAN.

Garant-Limence Insurance: Yerevan, Shirvan St 17; tel. (10) 23-60-68; fax (10) 23-03-81; e-mail info@glinsurance.am; internet glinsurance.am; f. 2000; all types of insurance; Exec. Dir ARTAK MARTIROSIAN.

Ingo Armenia: 0010 Yerevan, Tpagrichneri St 8; tel. (10) 54-31-34; fax (10) 54-75-06; e-mail info@ingoarmenia.am; internet www.ingoarmenia.am; f. 1997; Exec. Dir LEVON ALTUNIAN.

ISG Insurance: Yerevan, Belyakov St 5/4; tel. (10) 54-68-60; fax (10) 56-03-92; e-mail isg@isg.am; internet www.isg.am; f. 2007; general insurance; Chair. NAVASARD KHACHATRIAN.

Nairi Insurance: 1101 Yerevan, Vazgen Sarkissian St 10/110; tel. (10) 54-35-91; fax (10) 54-35-94; e-mail nairi@nairi-insurance.am; internet www.nairi-insurance.am; f. 1996; non-life insurance; Chair. VAHAN GABRIELIAN.

RESO Insurance: 0010 Yerevan, Vardanants St 1/1 16; tel. and fax (10) 56-05-50; e-mail info@reso.am; internet www.reso.am; f. 2008; as UniRESO; renamed as above in Oct. 2009; life and general insurance; Gen-Man. SAMVEL GRIGORIAN.

Sil Insurance Co: 0018 Yerevan, Tigran Mets Ave 39; tel. (10) 53-52-90; fax (10) 56-52-34; e-mail silinsurance@netsys.am; internet www.silinsurance.am; f. 2000; Exec. Dir HAYK BAGHRAMIAN.

State Insurance Armenia (Gosstrakh-Armenia): 0001 Yerevan, Hanrapetutiun St 76/3; tel. and fax (10) 56-06-89; f. 2001; Russian-Armenian joint venture; insurance and reinsurance; Man. Dir VAHAN H. AVETISSIAN.

Trade and Industry

GOVERNMENT AGENCY

Armenian Development Agency (ADA): 0010 Yerevan, M. Mkrtchian St 5; tel. and fax (10) 57-01-70; e-mail info@ada.am;

internet www.ada.am; f. 1998; foreign investment and export development; Gen. Dir Dr ROBERT HARUTIUNIAN.

CHAMBER OF COMMERCE

Chamber of Commerce and Industry of the Republic of Armenia: 0010 Yerevan, Khanjian St 11; tel. (10) 56-01-84; fax (10) 58-78-71; e-mail armcci@arminco.com; internet www.armcci.am; f. 1959; Chair. MARTIN G. SARKISSIAN.

EMPLOYERS' ORGANIZATION

Armenian Union of Manufacturers and Businessmen (Employers) of Armenia—UMB(E)A: 0018 Yerevan, Tigran Mets Ave 20/2, 2nd Floor; tel. and fax (10) 54-07-15; e-mail umba@arminco.com; internet www.umba.info.am; f. 1996; Chair. ARSEN KHAZARIAN.

TRADE ASSOCIATION

Union of Merchants of Armenia: 0037 Yerevan, Azatutioun Ave 1/1; tel. (10) 25-28-54; fax (10) 25-91-76; e-mail merchants@netsys.am; f. 1993; reorganized 1999; Pres. TSOLVARD GEVORGIAN.

UTILITIES

Public Services Regulatory Commission of Armenia (PSRC): 0002 Yerevan, Sarian St 22; tel. (10) 52-25-22; fax (10) 52-55-63; e-mail psrc@psrc.am; internet www.psrc.am; f. 1997; fmrly Energy Commission of Armenia; Chair. ROBERT NAZARIAN.

Electricity

Armenian Energy Power Operator: 0009 Yerevan, Abovian St 27; tel. (10) 52-47-25; fax (10) 54-73-17; e-mail office@energyoperator.am; internet www.energyoperator.am; f. 2003; assumed part of the function of former state monopoly Armenergo; Dir-Gen. MNACAKAN MNACAKANIAN.

Electricity Networks of Armenia (ArmElNet—ENA): 0047 Yerevan, Armenakian St 127; tel. (10) 59-12-27; fax (10) 65-16-64; e-mail office@ena.am; internet www.ena.am; f. 2002; owned by Inter RAO (Russia); national electricity distributor comprising the four former regional electricity networks; Gen. Dir EVGENII A. BIBIN; 12 brs.

Gas

ArmRosGazProm—ARG: 0091 Yerevan, Tbilisi Highway 43; tel. (10) 29-49-33; fax (10) 29-47-28; e-mail inbox@armrusgasprom.am; internet www.armrusgasprom.am; f. 1997; Armenian-Russian joint-stock co; 26% state-owned, 68% owned by Gazprom (Russia) (q.v.); sole natural gas producer in Armenia; Exec. Dir VARDAN R. ARUTIUNIAN.

Water

Yerevan Djur—Veolia Armenia (YD): 0025 Yerevan, Abovian St 66A; tel. (10) 56-13-26; fax (10) 56-93-57; e-mail office@yerevandjur.am; internet www.veoliadjur.am; f. 2005; contracted to provide water and sewerage services to Yerevan municipality for the period 2006–16; subsidiary of Veolia Environnement (France); Gen. Man. GOR GRIGORIAN; 1,450 employees (2011).

TRADE UNIONS

At 1 January 2006 some 743 trade union organizations were registered with the Ministry of Justice.

Confederation of Trade Unions of Armenia: 0010 Yerevan, Vazgen Sarkissian St 26/3; tel. (10) 54-52-37; fax (10) 58-34-66; e-mail hamk@xar.am; internet www.hamk.am; Chair. EDWARD TUMASIAN; 24 mem. unions.

Transport

RAILWAYS

In 2010 there were 725 km of railway track in Armenia. There are international lines to Iran and Georgia.

Armenia Railways: 0005 Yerevan, Tigran Mets Ave 50; tel. (10) 52-04-28; fax (10) 57-36-30; e-mail arway@mbox.amilink.net; f. 1998; managed by Russian Railways (q.v.); Pres. ARARAT KHRIMIAN.

Yerevan Metro: 0033 Yerevan, Marshal Baghramian St 78; tel. and fax (10) 27-30-81; e-mail mmetro.arm@gmail.com; f. 1981; govt-owned; 12.1 km, with 10 stations (2005); Dir PAILAK YAILOIAN.

ROADS

In 2008 the total length of the road network was estimated at 7,704 km, of which 90.52% was paved. As a result of the closure of Azerbaijan's and Turkey's borders with Armenia, the Kajaran highway linking Armenia with Iran is Armenia's most important international road connection.

CIVIL AVIATION

Zvartnots International Airport, 15 km west of Yerevan, is the main national airport; there are also international airports in Gyumri and Yerebuni.

Civil Aviation Department: 0042 Yerevan, Zvartnots Airport; tel. (10) 59-30-03; fax (10) 28-53-45; e-mail artiom.movsesyan@aviation.am; internet www.aviation.am; f. 1933; Dir Gen. ARTYOM MOVSESIAN.

Armavia: 0042 Yerevan, Zvartnots Airport; tel. (60) 37-42-70; fax (60) 37-44-10; e-mail info@u8.am; internet www.u8.am; f. 1996; operates flights to destinations in Europe and Asia; Gen. Dir NORAIR BELLUIAN; 480 employees.

Tourism

According to the World Tourism Organization, tourism receipts (including passenger transport) amounted to US $374m. in 2009. In that year Armenia received 575,284 tourist arrivals. The major tourist attractions include Yerevan, the capital; an early trading centre on the 'Silk Road', Artashat; and medieval monasteries.

Armenian Tourism Development Agency (ATDA): 0010 Yerevan, Nalbandian St 3; tel. (10) 54-23-03; fax (10) 54-47-92; e-mail help@armeniainfo.am; internet www.armeniainfo.am; f. 2001; Dir NINA HOVNANIAN.

Defence

Following the dissolution of the USSR in December 1991, Armenia became a member of the Commonwealth of Independent States and its collective security system, which was formally transformed into a regional defence organization, the Collective Security Treaty Organization (CSTO), in April 2003. The country also began to establish its own armed forces. The armed forces numbered 48,834, as assessed at November 2011, including an army of 45,846 (including 25,880 conscripts) and air defence forces of 2,988. There was also a paramilitary force of 6,694. Military service is compulsory and lasts for two years (a law adopted in 2002 provided for a 42-month alternative civilian service). There were approximately 3,303 Russian troops on Armenian territory at November 2011. In 1994 Armenia joined the North Atlantic Treaty Organization's 'Partnership for Peace' programme of military co-operation. In December 2005 Armenia's 'individual partnership action plan' with that body was approved, envisaging large-scale military reforms.

Defence Expenditure: Budgeted at 155,000m. drams in 2011.

Chief of General Staff of the Armed Forces: Col-Gen. YURI G. KHACHATUROV.

Education

Education is free and compulsory at primary and secondary levels. Until the early 1990s the general education system conformed to that of the centralized Soviet system. Extensive changes were subsequently made, with greater emphasis placed on Armenian history and culture. Armenia adopted an 11-year system of schooling in 2001/02. In 2006 it was announced that this would be extended to 12 years. In 2007 total enrolment at pre-school establishments was equivalent to 37% of the relevant age-group. Both primary and secondary enrolment in 2007 included 85% of children in the relevant age-group. Most instruction is in Armenian, although Russian is widely learnt as a second language. In 2007/08 some 98.6% of students in general education schools were taught in Armenian, while for 1.2% Russian was the main language of instruction. In 2009/10 114,600 students were enrolled at 77 higher schools (including universities). State expenditure on education was 105,769.4m. drams in 2009 (12.8% of total state expenditure).

AUSTRALIA

Introductory Survey

LOCATION, CLIMATE, LANGUAGE, RELIGION, FLAG, CAPITAL

The Commonwealth of Australia occupies the whole of the island continent of Australia, lying between the Indian and Pacific Oceans, and its offshore islands, principally Tasmania to the south-east. Australia's nearest neighbours are Timor-Leste (formerly East Timor) and Papua New Guinea, to the north. In the summer (November–February) there are tropical monsoons in the northern part of the continent (except for the Queensland coast), but the winters (July–August) are dry. Both the north-west and north-east coasts are liable to experience tropical cyclones between December and April. In the southern half of the country, winter is the wet season; rainfall decreases rapidly inland. Very high temperatures, sometimes exceeding 50°C (122°F), are experienced during the summer months over the arid interior and for some distance to the south, as well as during the pre-monsoon months in the north. The official language is English; 170 indigenous languages are spoken by Aboriginal and Torres Strait Islander peoples, who comprise 2.3% of the population according to the census of August 2006. The majority of the population profess Christianity (of whom 25.8% were Roman Catholic and 18.7% Anglican at the 2006 census). The national flag (proportions 1 by 2) is blue, with a representation of the United Kingdom flag in the upper hoist, a large seven-pointed white star in the lower hoist and five smaller white stars, in the form of the Southern Cross constellation, in the fly. The capital, Canberra, lies in one of two enclaves of federal territory known as the Australian Capital Territory (ACT).

CONTEMPORARY POLITICAL HISTORY

Historical Context

The Commonwealth of Australia was established in 1901, having been colonized by European settlers, who originally included many convicts transported from the United Kingdom. The abolition of the 'White Australia' policy after 1945 resulted in the arrival of large numbers of non-European immigrants. After the signing of a security treaty in 1951 and the establishment of ANZUS (see p. 462), Australia co-operated more closely with the USA. Australia subsequently began to acknowledge the strategic importance of the Asia-Pacific region, strengthening its relations with Indonesia, Japan and the People's Republic of China.

Domestic Political Affairs

At the election of December 1949 the ruling Australian Labor Party (ALP) was defeated by the recently established Liberal Party, in coalition with the Country Party. In January 1966 Sir Robert Menzies resigned after 16 years as Prime Minister, and was succeeded by Harold Holt, who was returned to office at elections in December of that year. However, Holt died in December 1967. His successor, Senator John Gorton, took office in January 1968 but resigned, after losing a parliamentary vote of confidence, in March 1971. William McMahon was Prime Minister from March 1971 until December 1972, when, after 23 years in office, the Liberal-Country Party coalition was defeated at a general election. The ALP, led by Gough Whitlam, won 67 of the 125 seats in the House of Representatives. Following conflict between the Whitlam Government and the Senate, both Houses of Parliament were dissolved in April 1974, and a general election was held in May. The ALP was returned to power, although with a reduced majority in the House of Representatives. However, the Government failed to secure a majority in the Senate, and in October 1975 the Opposition in the Senate obstructed approval of budget proposals. The Government was not willing to consent to a general election over the issue, but in November the Governor-General, Sir John Kerr, intervened and took the unprecedented action of dismissing the Government. An interim administration was installed under Malcolm Fraser, the Liberal leader, who formed a coalition Government with the Country Party. This coalition secured large majorities in both Houses of Parliament at a general election in December 1975, but the majorities were progressively reduced at elections in December 1977 and October 1980.

Fraser's coalition Government was defeated by the ALP at a general election in March 1983. Bob Hawke, the Labor leader, became the new Prime Minister and immediately organized a meeting of representatives of government, employers and trade unions to reach agreement on a prices and incomes policy (the 'Accord') that would allow economic recovery. At an early general election held in December 1984, the ALP was returned to power with a reduced majority in the House of Representatives. The opposition coalition between the Liberal Party and the National Party (formerly the Country Party) disintegrated in April 1987, when 12 National Party MPs withdrew from the agreement and formed the New National Party (led by the right-wing Sir Johannes Bjelke-Petersen, the Premier of Queensland); the remaining 14 National Party MPs continued to support their leader, Ian Sinclair, who wished to remain within the alliance. At an early general election held in July, the ALP was returned to office with an increased majority, securing 86 of the 148 seats in the House of Representatives. The Liberal and National Parties renewed their opposition alliance in August. Four months later Bjelke-Petersen was forced to resign as Premier of Queensland, under pressure from National Party officials.

During 1988 the Hawke Government suffered several defeats at by-elections, seemingly as a result of its unpopular policy of wage restraint. The ALP narrowly retained power at state elections in Victoria, but was defeated in New South Wales, where it had held power for 12 years. In May 1989 the leader of the Liberal Party, John Howard, was replaced by Andrew Peacock, and Charles Blunt succeeded Ian Sinclair as leader of the National Party. In July a commission of inquiry into alleged corruption in Queensland published its findings. The report documented several instances of official corruption and electoral malpractice by the Queensland Government, particularly during the administration of Bjelke-Petersen. In December the ALP defeated the National Party in the state election. By the end of 1991 four former members of the Queensland Cabinet and the former chief of the state's police force had received custodial sentences for corruption. The trial of Bjelke-Petersen, initially on charges of perjury and corruption but subsequently of perjury alone, resulted in dismissal of the case, when the jury failed to reach a verdict. Meanwhile, the Government's position was further strengthened by the removal of an unpopular Labor leadership in Western Australia and its replacement by the country's first female state Premier, Dr Carmen Lawrence, who took office in February 1990.

Parliamentary elections were held in March 1990. Although the opposition parties won the majority of the first-preference votes in the election for the House of Representatives, the endorsement of environmental groups delivered a block of second-preference votes to the ALP, which was thus returned to power, albeit with a reduced majority, securing 78 of the 148 seats. Peacock immediately resigned as leader of the Liberal Party and was replaced by Dr John Hewson, a former professor of economics. Blunt lost his seat in the election and was succeeded as leader of the National Party by Timothy Fischer.

In September 1990 senior ALP members endorsed government proposals to initiate a controversial programme of privatization, effectively ending almost 100 years of the ALP's stance against private ownership. Plans for constitutional and structural reform envisaged the creation of national standards in regulations and services, and measures to alleviate the financial dependence of the states and territories on the Federal Government. Despite strong opposition from sections of the public services, the trade unions and the business community, in July 1991 the leaders of the federal and state Governments finally agreed to reforms in the country's systems of marketing, transport, trade and taxation.

In June 1991 Hawke narrowly defeated a challenge to his leadership from Paul Keating, the Deputy Prime Minister and Treasurer, who then resigned. In December 1991 Hawke dismissed John Kerin, Keating's replacement as Treasurer, following a series of political and economic crises. Hawke called another leadership election, but this time he was defeated by

Keating, who accordingly became Prime Minister. A major reorganization of the Cabinet was implemented.

Following the ALP's defeat in state elections in Tasmania, the party encountered further embarrassment in April 1992, when a by-election in Melbourne to fill the parliamentary seat vacated by Bob Hawke was won by a local football club coach, standing as an independent candidate. Meanwhile, Brian Burke, the former Labor Premier of Western Australia, was arrested, after it was alleged that, during his term of office, he had misused a parliamentary expense account. In October 1992 the conclusions of the inquiry into the ALP's alleged involvement in corrupt practices in Western Australia were released. The Royal Commission was highly critical of the improper transactions between successive governments of Western Australia and business entrepreneurs. In July 1994 Burke received a prison sentence of two years upon conviction on four charges of fraud; he was released in February 1995, but was sentenced to three years' imprisonment in February 1997 for theft from ALP funds. In February 1995, furthermore, Ray O'Connor, Premier of Western Australia between 1982 and 1983, received a short prison sentence, having been found guilty of the theft in 1984 of a donation to the Liberal Party.

In September 1992 John Bannon, the ALP Premier of South Australia, became the seventh state Premier since 1982 to leave office in disgrace. His resignation was due to a scandal relating to attempts to offset the heavy financial losses incurred by the State Bank of South Australia. At state elections in Queensland in mid-September, the ALP administration of Wayne Goss was returned to power. In the following month, however, the ruling ALP was defeated in state elections in Victoria. Furthermore, in November a new financial scandal emerged: the federal Treasurer was alleged to have suppressed information pertaining to the former ALP Government of Victoria, which, in a clandestine manner prior to the state elections, was believed to have exceeded its borrowing limits. At state elections in Western Australia in February 1993, the incumbent Labor Government was defeated. Dr Carmen Lawrence was replaced as Premier by Richard Court of the Liberal-National coalition.

At the general election held in March 1993 the ALP was unexpectedly returned to office for a fifth consecutive term, having secured 80 of the 147 seats in the House of Representatives. In early 1994 two ministers resigned in connection with separate financial scandals. In May Dr John Hewson was replaced as leader of the Liberal Party by Alexander Downer, a supporter of the monarchy. In January 1995, however, Downer resigned and was replaced by John Howard, also a monarchist.

At state elections in New South Wales in March 1995 the ALP defeated the ruling Liberal-National coalition. Robert (Bob) Carr was appointed Premier. However, at a federal by-election in Canberra the ALP suffered a serious reverse when, for the first time in 15 years, the seat was taken by the Liberal Party. In July, at state elections in Queensland, the ALP Government of Wayne Goss was narrowly returned to office, only to be ousted following a by-election defeat in February 1996. In June 1995, meanwhile, the Deputy Prime Minister, Brian Howe, announced his resignation from the Cabinet. He was replaced by the Minister for Finance, Kim Beazley.

The Howard administration, 1996–2007

At the general election held in March 1996 the Liberal-National coalition achieved a decisive victory, securing a total of 94 of the 148 seats in the House of Representatives. The ALP won only 49 seats. In the Senate the minor parties and independent members retained the balance of power. John Howard of the Liberal Party became Prime Minister, and immediately promised to give priority to the issues of industrial relations, the transfer to partial private ownership of the state telecommunications company, Telstra, and to expanding relations with Asia. The leader of the National Party, Tim Fischer, was appointed Deputy Prime Minister and Minister for Trade. Paul Keating was replaced as leader of the ALP by Kim Beazley.

Meanwhile, fears for Australia's tradition of racial tolerance continued to grow. In October 1996 Pauline Hanson, a newly elected independent member of the House of Representatives, aroused much controversy when, in a speech envisaging 'civil war', she reiterated her demands for the ending of immigration from Asia and for the elimination of special funding for Aboriginal people. The Prime Minister drew criticism for his initial failure to issue a direct denunciation of the views of Hanson, a former member of the Liberal Party. In March 1997 Hanson established the One Nation party, which rapidly attracted support. In subsequent months, however, large protests against her policies took place. In August the Government issued a document on foreign policy, in which Hanson's views were strongly repudiated and in which Australia's commitment to racial equality was reiterated. In December the New One Nation Party was established by former supporters of Hanson who had become disillusioned with her autocratic style of leadership. In June 1998, at state elections in Queensland, One Nation won 23% of first-preference votes, thus securing 11 of the 89 seats in the legislature and arousing renewed concern among tourism and business leaders.

At the early federal election held in October 1998, the Liberal-National coalition was narrowly returned to office, winning a total of 80 of the 148 seats in the House of Representatives. The ALP increased its representation to 67 seats. Contrary to expectations, the One Nation party failed to win any representation in the lower house, the controversial Pauline Hanson losing her Queensland seat, and secured one seat in the Senate. In a referendum held on the same day, the electorate of the Northern Territory unexpectedly rejected a proposal for the territory's elevation to full statehood.

In February 1999 Pauline Hanson was re-elected leader of One Nation, despite a series of defections, including the departure from the party of several of the 11 One Nation members of the Queensland legislature. At state elections in New South Wales in March, at which the ALP was returned to power, One Nation won two seats in the 42-member upper chamber. In January 2000 police officers in Queensland and New South Wales seized hundreds of documents from party premises. In April the Queensland Electoral Commission ruled that the party had been fraudulently registered, owing to the falsification of significant sections of its 200-name membership list. As the sole signatory on the registration papers, Hanson found herself personally responsible for the repayment of $A0.5m. of public funding to the party. Hanson repaid the funds after a successful appeal for public donations, and she re-registered the One Nation party in January 2001 to contest the forthcoming Queensland state elections (see below). Following state elections in Victoria in September 1999, meanwhile, the Liberal-National Premier, Jeffrey Kennett, was replaced by Stephen Bracks of the ALP.

A marked increase in the number of asylum-seekers attempting to enter Australia by sea prompted the introduction of new legislation empowering Australian police to board vessels in international waters. In 1999 almost 2,000 asylum-seekers were intercepted by the authorities and transferred to detention centres in Australia, while many others were believed to have died at sea. The issue of alleged maltreatment of asylum-seekers detained in Australia was highlighted by a series of protests at a privately managed detention centre in Woomera, South Australia. Moreover, in November the Government ordered an inquiry into allegations that children at the centre had been subjected to systematic sexual abuse. Campaigners claimed that the Government had suppressed evidence of abuse at Woomera and other detention centres.

Australia's handling of immigration issues provoked international condemnation in August 2001 when the Prime Minister refused to admit 433 refugees, stranded on a Norwegian cargo ship off Christmas Island, onto the Australian mainland. The Government swiftly enacted new legislation empowering the navy to prevent migrants coming ashore and excluding remote Australian island territories from the definition of official landfall. The situation was eventually resolved when New Zealand, Nauru and Papua New Guinea agreed to accommodate the asylum-seekers while their applications for asylum were processed. In the interim, however, traffic in asylum-seekers attempting to reach Australia's outlying territories (the majority via Indonesia) continued to increase. The Government proposed a 'Pacific solution', whereby neighbouring South Pacific nations could agree to host asylum-seekers during their processing in exchange for substantial aid. Nauru signed an agreement to take up to 1,200 refugees at any one time. Concerns about Australia's immigration policy again focused on the Woomera detention centre in January 2002, when 259 detainees began a hunger strike in protest at poor living conditions and at the long delays in the processing of their applications. In February the Australian Government announced that a representative of the UN High Commissioner for Human Rights and other observers would be permitted to inspect the camp.

A state election in Western Australia in February 2001 resulted in defeat for the governing Liberal-National coalition and the replacement of Premier Richard Court by the state's Labor leader, Geoffrey Gallop. Ongoing anxieties regarding illegal immigration were reflected in the unexpected success of One Nation, which secured almost 10% of votes at the poll. At the state election in Queensland in the same month, the ALP Government, led by Peter Beattie, was decisively re-elected. One Nation garnered 9% of the total votes.

A federal election took place in November 2001. The Liberal-National coalition won 82 of the 150 seats in the House of Representatives, thereby narrowly securing a third consecutive term of office. Despite its successes at state and territorial elections in Western Australia and the Northern Territory earlier in the year, the ALP won 65 seats, two fewer than at the previous federal election. Many political commentators attributed the coalition's apparent recovery to Howard's stance on immigration. Kim Beazley resigned as leader of the ALP and was replaced by Simon Crean. One Nation won no seats in either the House of Representatives or the Senate. (In December Pauline Hanson resigned as leader of the party to concentrate on contesting charges of electoral fraud brought against her in July 2001.)

John Howard announced the composition of his third Government in late November 2001, appointing six new cabinet ministers. Changes included the incorporation of the Department of Reconciliation and Aboriginal and Torres Strait Islander Affairs into the new portfolio of Immigration and Multicultural and Indigenous Affairs. At a state election in South Australia in February 2002 the ruling Liberal-National coalition was defeated. Mike Rann of the ALP was appointed Premier.

In February 2002, after it emerged that government claims that refugees in a ship intercepted by the Australian navy had thrown their children into the sea were false, John Howard withstood a parliamentary motion of censure. In November the ruling ALP, led by Stephen Bracks, won a state election in Victoria. The Labor Government in New South Wales was re-elected in March 2003 for an unprecedented third term; Bob Carr was reappointed Premier. Meanwhile, in February the Senate approved a motion of no confidence in Howard over the Government's decision to deploy troops to the Middle East in preparation for the likelihood of a US-led military campaign to remove the regime of Saddam Hussain in Iraq. Public demonstrations against Australia's anticipated involvement in the campaign followed. Public support for Howard rose substantially from May, largely owing to the apparent swift end to the immediate conflict in Iraq and the absence of Australian casualties. In July, however, a former UN weapons inspector, Richard Butler, claimed that the Government had misled the public about Iraq's programme to develop weapons of mass destruction. A former senior intelligence analyst, who had resigned in protest over Australia's involvement in Iraq, informed a parliamentary inquiry in August that the Government had exaggerated and fabricated intelligence used to justify the case for war. Meanwhile, in July Australia committed 870 troops to assist in the rehabilitation of Iraq. In February 2005 the Government announced that it would send 450 additional troops to Iraq.

Protesters against the Government's mandatory detention of all asylum-seekers stormed the Woomera detention centre in March 2002. Most of the approximately 50 asylum-seekers who managed to escape were recaptured. In April riots occurred at detention centres in Curtin and Port Hedland, Western Australia. The Government offered financial incentives to Afghan asylum-seekers to return to their homeland, but by mid-July only 76 out of 1,000 Afghans had accepted the offer. In June concerns about the alleged maltreatment of asylum-seekers were raised again after supporters helped 34 detainees to escape from the Woomera detention centre. More than 120 inmates began a hunger strike to protest against their living conditions and processing delays. In December the Minister for Immigration and Multicultural and Indigenous Affairs, Philip Ruddock, announced plans to expand a programme to allow women and children asylum-seekers to live in the community rather than in the detention camps. The authorities strengthened security measures at detention centres following riots at Woomera, Baxter (near Port Augusta), Port Hedland and on Christmas Island in late December.

In March 2003 Ruddock announced that the Woomera detention centre was to be closed down, for reasons of cost. Families risked being separated after it was revealed that fathers and husbands would be moved to the Baxter detention centre, while women and children would continue to live in the community in Woomera. It was then announced that the Christmas Island detention centre would also be closed. In April the Federal Court issued a ruling that the Government had no right to detain asylum-seekers indefinitely prior to deportation, even if the asylum-seeker had been refused permission to enter another country. The Government lodged an appeal at the High Court, which in August 2003 upheld the ruling and rebuked the Government. The Family Court ordered the Government to release from custody five children who had been detained as illegal immigrants since January 2002. The Government came under heavy criticism again in November 2003 when, in response to the arrival of an Indonesian boat carrying 14 Turkish Kurdish asylum-seekers at Melville Island, the Government immediately separated the island and 4,000 other small islands from the Australian migration zone. It then ordered an Australian warship to tow the boat to the Indonesian island of Yamdena. The UN High Commissioner for Refugees stated that Australia's exclusion of the islands was 'meaningless', since its obligations as a signatory to the UN refugee convention applied to its entire territory. The Indonesian Government insisted that its agreement to the Kurds' expulsion had neither been requested nor given. In May 2004 Australia's Human Rights and Equal Opportunities Commission issued a report describing the country's immigration detention system as 'cruel, inhumane and degrading', and urged the Government to release all child detainees within a month. In July it was announced that 9,500 asylum-seekers who had been released from detention centres since 1999 on temporary protection visas (renewable every three years) would be entitled to apply for permanent settlement in Australia.

In June 2003 John Howard ended months of speculation by announcing that he intended to seek a fourth term of office. Although the leader of the opposition ALP, Simon Crean, won a leadership challenge mounted against him by his predecessor, Kim Beazley, he subsequently failed to reunite the party and resigned as leader in November. In December the republican Mark Latham was elected ALP leader, defeating Beazley. Meanwhile, in August Richard Butler was appointed Governor of Tasmania, replacing Sir Guy Green. In the same month Pauline Hanson was convicted of electoral fraud and sentenced to a three-year prison term; however, her conviction was overruled by a court of appeal in November. In September the Cabinet was reorganized. Changes included the transfer of the controversial Minister for Immigration and Multicultural and Indigenous Affairs, Philip Ruddock, to the post of Attorney-General; Senator Amanda Vanstone was allocated the immigration portfolio. At a state election in Queensland in February 2004, the ruling ALP was re-elected for a third term; Peter Beattie was reappointed Premier. In mid-February riots broke out in the predominantly Aboriginal district of Redfern in Sydney in protest against the death of an Aboriginal youth in an apparent cycling accident while, it was claimed, being pursued by police. More than 30 police officers were injured during Sydney's worst violence in many years; three separate inquiries into the death of the youth and into the riots were instigated. In August the New South Wales state coroner deemed the youth's death to have been an accident.

In March 2004 the parliamentary committee on intelligence on Iraq's weapons of mass destruction published its report, largely exonerating the Government from claims that it had manipulated the intelligence used to justify Australia's involvement in the military campaign in Iraq. In July an independent inquiry into the performance of the intelligence agencies concluded that there had been an overall serious failure of intelligence relating to Iraq's alleged weapons of mass destruction, but that the Australian agencies' assessment of the available material had been more measured than that of their counterparts in the United Kingdom and the USA.

In August 2004 the Governor of Tasmania, Richard Butler, stood down after four senior members of his staff tendered their resignations; he was replaced by William Cox, hitherto Chief Justice of Tasmania. Meanwhile, an issue that had caused controversy at the federal election of 2001 re-emerged, when Mike Scrafton, a former government adviser, revealed that he had informed Prime Minister Howard, prior to the election, that government claims that refugees in a ship intercepted by the Australian navy had thrown their children overboard (see above) were unsubstantiated. In December 2004 a senate inquiry into Scrafton's allegations concluded that his evidence was credible and implied that the Prime Minister had misled the public.

Meanwhile, the Liberal-National coalition increased its majority in the House of Representatives at the federal election on 9 October 2004, securing 86 of the 150 seats, and gained an outright majority in the Senate. Prime Minister John Howard was thus returned to office for a fourth consecutive term. The

ALP won 60 seats in the lower chamber, five fewer than at the 2001 election, surprising many political analysts, who had predicted a much closer result. The coalition's victory was widely attributed to the continued strong performance of the economy.

In January 2005 Mark Latham, leader of the ALP, announced his resignation from both the party leadership and the legislature, for health reasons. Kim Beazley was elected to succeed him as ALP leader later in that month, thus resuming the position. In March Australia's asylum policy came to the fore once again, following a ruling by the High Court that the country was obliged to accept refugees fleeing persecution in their homeland. It was subsequently announced that a small number of detainees, who had been refused refugee status but were unable to return to their homelands, were to be released and granted visas. In May the Minister for Immigration, Amanda Vanstone, announced that 201 cases of possible wrongful detention of immigrants were to be reviewed. In June the Deputy Prime Minister and Minister for Transport and Regional Services, John Anderson, resigned from both the Cabinet and the leadership of the National Party, citing health reasons. In the following month a minor cabinet reorganization took place; Mark Vaile succeeded Anderson as both Deputy Prime Minister and National Party leader. Meanwhile, at elections to the 25-seat Northern Territory legislature in June, the ALP increased its majority, winning 19 seats. In July Bob Carr, long-serving Premier of New South Wales, announced his resignation; he was succeeded in August by Morris Iemma.

Racially motivated rioting, believed to have been co-ordinated by right-wing extremists, broke out in the Sydney suburb of Cronulla in December 2005. As the disturbances continued, the New South Wales legislature approved emergency legislation to prevent civil unrest.

In January 2006 the Premier of Western Australia, Geoffrey Gallop, resigned on the grounds of ill health. He was replaced by Alan Carpenter. In the same month Dr Ken Michael succeeded Lt-Gen. John Murray Sanderson as Governor of the state. Also in January Robert Hill resigned as federal Minister for Defence, prompting a minor cabinet reorganization, in which he was succeeded by Dr Brendan Nelson, hitherto Minister for Education, Science and Training. In April Prof. David de Kretser was sworn in as Governor of Victoria. Federal cabinet members Mark Vaile and Warren Truss exchanged portfolios in September 2006: Mark Vaile remained Deputy Prime Minister but also assumed responsibility for the transport and regional services portfolio, while Warren Truss became Minister for Trade. In December Kevin Rudd, the foreign affairs spokesman of the ALP, mounted a successful leadership challenge against Kim Beazley to become the federal Leader of the Opposition. Prime Minister Howard effected a ministerial reorganization in January 2007: among the appointees were Malcolm Turnbull as Minister for the Environment and Water Resources and Kevin Andrews as Minister for Immigration and Citizenship.

In March 2006, meanwhile, the ALP was returned to power at state elections in both South Australia and Tasmania. In September Peter Beattie of the ALP gained a fourth consecutive term as Premier of Queensland at state elections. The ALP's dominance of state politics continued with its victory at elections in Victoria in November, thus ensuring a third term for Premier Stephen Bracks; however, Bracks resigned in July 2007 and was replaced by John Brumby. The ALP also prevailed at elections in New South Wales in March 2007, returning Premier Morris Iemma to office. In September Queensland Premier Peter Beattie resigned and was succeeded by Anna Bligh, who was returned to the post at state elections in March 2009.

The findings of the so-called Cole Inquiry were published in November 2006. Led by retired judge Terence Cole, the inquiry had been established at the end of 2005 in order to investigate allegations of misconduct or unlawful actions by Australian companies in connection with the UN's oil-for-food programme in Iraq (whereby the Government of Saddam Hussain had been permitted to use revenue from oil exports to purchase food and medicines). The inquiry found that, in contravention of UN regulations, between 1999 and 2003 irregular payments totalling $A300m. had been made by the Australian Wheat Board (AWB) to the Government of Iraq in order to secure lucrative contracts under the oil-for-food programme. The Cole report exonerated the Australian Government, but recommended that 11 former AWB executives answer charges of corruption.

The Rudd administration, 2007–10

At the federal election held on 24 November 2007, the ALP garnered enough public support to secure a majority in the House of Representatives, winning 83 of the 150 seats. The Liberal Party won only 55 seats, while the National Party, its coalition partner, took 10 seats. The Liberal-National coalition also lost its majority in the upper chamber, although the newly elected Senators were not scheduled to take office until mid-2008. Prime Minister Howard suffered a humiliating personal defeat in his long-held constituency of Bennelong. He was succeeded as Federal Parliamentary Leader of the Liberal Party by the erstwhile Minister of Defence, Dr Brendan Nelson. Kevin Rudd was sworn in as Prime Minister in early December, along with a Cabinet that included Julia Gillard as Deputy Prime Minister, Stephen Smith as Minister for Foreign Affairs and Wayne Swan as Treasurer. Fulfilling his election pledge, Rudd's first undertaking as Prime Minister was to ratify the Kyoto Protocol (negotiated in Japan in 1997), thereby committing Australia to reducing its emissions of carbon dioxide and other greenhouse gases. Among other commitments, he reiterated his intention to withdraw Australian troops from Iraq and to reverse the previous Government's position on a formal apology to the Aboriginal peoples (see Other Aboriginal Issues).

In April 2008 Prime Minister Rudd hosted the so-called Australia 2020 Summit. More than 1,000 invited delegates, including representatives of the business community, academics and opposition politicians, participated in discussions on 10 long-term national policy challenges. A final report outlined the principal recommendations submitted during the conference, which included constitutional reform (see below), formal legal recognition for Aboriginal and Torres Strait Islander people, the promotion of sustainable energy and a revision of the taxation system.

In May 2008 the Labor Premier of Tasmania, Paul Lennon, whose administration had been marred by various scandals and who had recently been criticized for his support of plans for the construction of a controversial timber pulp mill, announced his resignation and departure from politics. He was succeeded by the Deputy Premier, David Bartlett.

The Northern Territory election of August 2008 presented the ruling ALP with its first electoral test since the federal polls of late 2007. The incumbent Labor Chief Minister, Paul Henderson, was returned to office by only a narrow margin, after a substantial transfer of support to the Liberal Party. In September Morris Iemma, the Labor Premier of New South Wales, unexpectedly resigned, following a revolt by party members who had refused to endorse his proposed removal of several cabinet ministers, precipitated by the resignation of the state's Deputy Premier. Nathan Rees was selected as Iemma's successor. Also in September the ALP lost its parliamentary majority at state elections in Western Australia. Colin Barnett of the Liberal Party replaced Alan Carpenter as the state's Premier, heading a Liberal-National administration.

In September 2008 the Liberal Party elected Malcolm Turnbull, a former leader of the Australian Republican Movement and erstwhile Minister for the Environment and Water Resources, as Federal Parliamentary Leader, in place of Dr Brendan Nelson, who had served as Leader of the Opposition for less than 10 months.

In December 2008 the Prime Minister announced various new measures intended to curb Australia's greenhouse gas emissions. Describing the initiatives as the most important structural reforms of the country's economy for a generation, Rudd pledged to reduce emissions by at least 5% by 2020 in comparison with the levels of 2000, and by as much as 15% in the 'unlikely' event of international agreement on such a percentage decrease being reached by developed nations. A carbon trading scheme, applicable to 75% of Australia's emissions, was to be introduced by 2010. However, environmentalists immediately denounced these targets as inadequate. In May 2009, under pressure from the business sector, the Government postponed the introduction of the emissions trading scheme to July 2011, citing deteriorating global economic conditions. Having been endorsed by the House of Representatives, the legislation failed to secure approval in the opposition-controlled Senate in August 2009. Attempts to reach a compromise with the Liberal-National coalition prior to the next vote in the Senate in November dismayed environmental groups and exposed divisions within the opposition, with a number of senior party members emerging as strongly opposed to the scheme. In December Malcolm Turnbull, a supporter of carbon emissions trading, was narrowly defeated in a ballot for the Liberal Party leadership by Tony Abbott, a 'climate change sceptic' and erstwhile Minister for Health. The new Leader of the Opposition immediately stated his intention to oppose the Government's emissions trading legislation. The previously agreed compromise was thus abandoned. The proposed legislation was once again rejected by the Senate, leading to speculation that the Prime Minister might not be able to secure the passage of the legislation in its current form in the upper chamber.

From late 2008 the number of boats carrying asylum-seekers to Australia began to increase rapidly, partly as a result of the worsening conflicts in Sri Lanka and Afghanistan. The Government was therefore obliged to review its policy with regard to the use of the Christmas Island detention centre, which had been commissioned by the Howard administration but remained unused. In December, therefore, the new facility received the first asylum-seekers (see the chapter on Christmas Island).

In April 2009 a boat carrying 47 Afghan asylum-seekers, which was being towed to Christmas Island by the Australian Navy, exploded near Ashmore Reef in Australian territorial waters, killing five of the Afghans on board. The surviving asylum-seekers were later granted permanent protection visas. Two Indonesians were subsequently convicted of illegally bringing asylum-seekers to Australia and sentenced to five years' imprisonment. In March 2010 a coroner's inquest into the incident concluded that the boat had been deliberately set on fire by three of the asylum-seekers, in an effort to avoid being returned to Indonesia, the starting point of their voyage. An amendment to the Migration Act, which sought to end the much-criticized policy of charging asylum-seekers for the cost of their detention, was approved by the House of Representatives in June 2009 and by the Senate in September. Between 2006 and 2008 detainees had received bills totalling $A54m., of which only $2m. had been recovered.

Also in June 2009 the Minister for Defence, Joel Fitzgibbon, resigned following reports of a number of discrepancies in his declarations of interest and a meeting between his brother, head of a health insurance fund, and defence officials regarding potential business opportunities. Following this resignation, the Prime Minister reorganized his Cabinet: *inter alia*, Senator John Faulkner became the new Minister for Defence; Greg Combet, parliamentary secretary for climate change, entered the Government as Minister for Defence Personnel, Materiel and Science, and Minister Assisting the Minister for Climate Change; and Senator Mark Arbib became Minister for Employment Participation. In a major set-back for the Government's energy-saving programme in February 2010, the responsibilities of the Minister for the Environment, Heritage and the Arts, Peter Garrett, were downgraded, following the revelation that defects in the installation of home insulation materials had caused several electrocutions and numerous house fires. In the ensuing reorganization of the Government, the Department of Climate Change became the Department of Climate Change and Energy Efficiency.

In state politics, in December 2009 the Labor Premier of New South Wales, Nathan Rees, was defeated in a party leadership ballot by the state's Minister for Planning, Kristina Keneally, amid reports of factional divisions. Keneally promptly reorganized the Cabinet, which had undergone numerous changes in the previous 12 months. At state elections in South Australia in March 2010 Labor Premier Mike Rann was returned to office for a third consecutive term. However, some controversy followed state elections in Tasmania, where neither of the two main political parties secured a majority. Although his party had received fewer votes than the Liberal Party, the incumbent Labor Premier, David Bartlett, was invited by the Tasmanian Governor, Peter Underwood (who had replaced William Cox in April 2008), to form a minority government. The Labor administration was thus reinstalled, in coalition with the Greens.

In April 2010 the newly created federal post of Minister for Population was given to Tony Burke, in addition to his responsibilities for agriculture, fisheries and forestry. In the same month the Government announced that the processing of applications for visas for asylum-seekers from Afghanistan and Sri Lanka was to be suspended with immediate effect: those arriving by boat would still be taken to the Christmas Island detention centre, but would not be permitted to apply for asylum in Australia. Also in April, Rudd announced that the introduction of the emissions trading scheme was to be further postponed, until after the expiry in 2012 of the Kyoto Protocol (see above): he thereby incurred criticism for having apparently abandoned an important principle. In May 2010 the Government announced the imposition of a tax of 40% on the profits of mining companies, to be known as the Resource Super Profits Tax, on the grounds that royalties paid by mining companies to the state administrations had not increased in proportion to the industry's considerable profits over the past 10 years. Rudd argued that, since the mining companies were often partly or largely foreign-owned, an unfair share of the country's wealth was being transferred overseas. The mining companies, in response, claimed that their contribution to the economy had helped Australia to avoid the recession that had affected most other developed countries in 2008/09, and argued that the new tax would deter investment, reduce the competitiveness of the Australian mining industry and create unemployment.

Controversy over the postponement of the emissions trading scheme and the debate regarding the proposed mining tax appeared to lead to a rapid decline in popular support for the Prime Minister in May 2010. In addition, there was reportedly criticism within the ALP of his abrasive style of leadership. In June Rudd was challenged for the leadership of the party by the Deputy Prime Minister, Julia Gillard. Acknowledging his likely defeat, Rudd resigned before the proposed party ballot. On 24 June Gillard became the Federal Parliamentary Leader of the ALP and was sworn in as the country's first female Prime Minister. Wayne Swan, the federal Treasurer, was elected unopposed as deputy party leader and assumed the post of Deputy Prime Minister.

Recent developments: the Gillard administration 2010–

Upon taking office in June 2010 Julia Gillard made few initial ministerial changes: the portfolios previously held by Gillard, namely education, employment, workplace relations and social inclusion, were given to Simon Crean; the latter's former post of Minister for Trade was allocated to Stephen Smith, who remained Minister for Foreign Affairs. In July the new Government announced that the controversial additional resource tax on mines, proposed by its predecessor, would apply to coal and iron ore mines only, and would exclude those companies earning annual profits of less than $A50m., while the rate of taxation was to be reduced from 40% to 30% of the profits.

The general election that had been due to take place before the end of 2010 was brought forward to 21 August, when the ALP narrowly avoided being ejected from office, winning 72 seats in the 150-member House of Representatives, while the Liberal-National coalition also won 72 (with one member of the National Party of Western Australia declaring himself an independent); the Greens won a federal seat for the first time. It was announced on 7 September that the ALP would form a minority Government (the first since 1940), relying on the support of the single Greens representative and of three independents. In simultaneous elections to 40 of the 76 seats in the Senate, the Greens won six seats in addition to the three that they already held, thus acquiring a powerful position in the upper house (with effect from 1 July 2011, when most of the new senators were to assume their seats). Julia Gillard's new administration included the previous Prime Minister, Kevin Rudd, as Minister for Foreign Affairs, while Stephen Smith became Minister for Defence and Wayne Swan remained as Deputy Prime Minister and Treasurer.

In July 2010 Gillard had proposed that a regional processing centre for asylum-seekers be established in Timor-Leste, but this was rejected by the legislature of that country. In October the Government announced that two new detention centres for asylum-seekers were to be established within Australia, while family groups were to be given community-based accommodation so as to avoid confining children in detention. In November legislation was approved on the creation of a high-speed national broadband network to improve telecommunications, particularly in rural areas; the promised introduction of the network had been a major factor in securing the support of independent members of the House of Representatives for the ALP (the opposition favoured a less expensive but less technically advanced network).

In December 2010 and January 2011 heavy rains, believed to be caused by the recurrent weather phenomenon known as La Niña, resulted in severe flooding in Queensland, and to a lesser extent in Victoria. At least 35 people lost their lives, and there was extensive damage to property, crops, infrastructure and the region's important coal mines. In January Gillard announced the imposition of a new tax to help meet the cost of reconstruction, which was initially estimated to require $A5,600m. in federal spending: the levy was to be imposed for 12 months, with effect from 1 July, on individuals earning more than $A50,000 per year. Reductions in previously planned expenditure were also announced (including infrastructure projects and several environmental measures intended to reduce carbon emissions) in order to finance reconstruction projects. In early February further serious damage was caused in northern Queensland by Cyclone Yasi.

At state elections in Victoria in November 2010 the ruling Labor administration was defeated by the Liberal-National coalition after 11 years in office, and Ted Baillieu replaced John Brumby as Premier. In January 2011 the Labor Premier of Tasmania, David Bartlett, resigned, citing the needs of his family, and was replaced by Lara Giddings, who retained her previous posts as state Treasurer and Minister for the Arts. At state elections in New South Wales in March, the Labor administration of Kristina Keneally was heavily defeated. Barry O'Farrell of the Liberal Party was subsequently appointed as the state's Premier. In April Alex Chernov, Chancellor of the University of Melbourne, replaced Prof. David de Kretser as Governor of Victoria. In October Sally Thomas became Administrator of the Northern Territory, replacing Tom Pauling.

In July 2011 the federal Government announced the introduction of a Clean Energy Bill, which would impose a 'carbon price' on some 500 Australian companies that were causing the most pollution in the form of carbon dioxide emissions: according to the proposed legislation, such companies were to pay $A23 per metric ton of emissions over a three-year period, with effect from July 2012, and from July 2015 this arrangement would be replaced by a market-based carbon emissions trading scheme. Despite the inclusion of measures to compensate households for resultant higher electricity costs, and to assist industries to adopt the use of less polluting energy sources, the plan encountered vociferous opposition, particularly since, before the 2010 election, Gillard had undertaken not to introduce such a tax (she had been obliged to reverse this undertaking by her Government's dependence on the Greens for support). The legislation was adopted by a small majority in the House of Representatives in October 2011, and by the Senate in November. The controversial tax on mining companies (see above) was also approved by the lower house in November, and by the Senate in March 2012.

The Government attempted to respond to domestic concerns about border security in July 2011 by concluding an agreement with the Malaysian Government that was intended to deter asylum-seekers from arriving by boat, often under dangerous conditions, and to prevent their exploitation by people-smugglers. These so-called 'irregular maritime arrivals' (IMAs) were reported to number 6,535 in 2010 and 2,183 in the first eight months of 2011; in late August 2011 there were about 4,400 IMAs in detention on the mainland, and some 800 more on Christmas Island. According to the agreement, over a four-year period Australia would dispatch 800 asylum-seekers to Malaysia for processing, while Malaysia would send to Australia 4,000 refugees whose status had been approved. In August, however, the Australian High Court declared the agreement unlawful, because Malaysia was not a signatory to the UN Convention relating to the Status of Refugees and therefore did not provide adequate legal protection for asylum-seekers. An agreement concluded earlier in that month to reopen an assessment centre in Papua New Guinea for asylum-seekers arriving in Australia was brought into question by the same ruling. In October the Government's attempt to amend legislation in order to reverse the High Court's judgment was defeated. In November the Government began to allocate 'bridging visas' to some asylum-seekers whose refugee status had not yet been determined, thus ending the policy of mandatory detention for all arriving without visas.

The ALP administration's precarious status in the House of Representatives improved slightly in November 2011 when the Speaker, Harry Jenkins, an ALP member, unexpectedly resigned from his post, citing a desire to return to party politics, and was thus enabled to vote in the legislature; he was replaced by Peter Slipper, a reportedly disaffected member of the Liberal Party, which thus lost one of its voting members. Slipper's appointment was criticized as underhand by the opposition.

A ministerial reorganization was effected in December 2011. Among other changes, Nicola Roxon, hitherto Minister for Health and Ageing, was appointed as Attorney-General, replacing Robert McClelland, who became Minister for Housing, for Homelessness and for Emergency Management. Three existing Ministers were promoted to an expanded Cabinet: Tanya Plibersek as Minister for Health, Bill Shorten as Minister for Employment and Workplace Relations and for Financial Services and Superannuation, and Mark Butler as Minister for Mental Health and Ageing, and for Social Inclusion.

In January 2012 an independent member of the House of Representatives threatened to withdraw his support from the Government if it failed to introduce legislation on gambling machines ('pokies'), which would allow limits on losses to be preset by the user; the proposal was vehemently opposed by the gambling industry. Gillard conceded the need for measures to combat excessive gambling, but stated that there was not enough support in the legislature for the measure to be adopted.

Kevin Rudd announced his resignation as Minister for Foreign Affairs on 22 February 2012, during a visit to Washington, DC, USA, amid speculation that he and his supporters intended to force a leadership election. On 27 February, following a bitter campaign that exposed the deep divisions within the party, Gillard defeated Rudd in a ballot for the ALP leadership, which she had organized, by 71 votes to 31. As part of a ministerial reorganization announced on 2 March, the former Premier of New South Wales, Bob Carr, was appointed as Minister for Foreign Affairs and allocated a seat in the Senate, while Robert McClelland, an ally of Rudd, left the Government. McLelland's portfolios were divided between Brendan O'Connor, hitherto Minister for Human Services and Minister Assisting for School Education, who joined the Cabinet as Minister for Small Business, for Housing and for Homelessness, and Nicola Roxon, the Attorney-General, who assumed additional responsibility for emergency management. The ALP was heavily defeated by the Liberal National Party at state elections in Queensland later in March; Campbell Newman replaced Anna Bligh as Premier.

Aboriginal Land Rights

The sensitive issue of Aboriginal land rights was addressed by the Government in August 1985, when it formulated proposals for legislation that would give Aboriginal people inalienable freehold title to national parks, vacant Crown land and former Aboriginal reserves, in spite of widespread opposition from state governments (which had previously been responsible for their own land policies), from mining companies and from the Aboriginal people themselves, who were angered by the Government's withdrawal of its earlier support for the Aboriginal right to veto mineral exploitation. In October Uluru (also known as Ayers Rock, the main tourist attraction of the Northern Territory) was officially transferred to the Mutijulu Aboriginal community, on condition that continuing access to the site be guaranteed. In 1986, however, the Government abandoned its pledge to impose such federal legislation on unwilling state governments, and this led to further protests from Aboriginal leaders. In June 1991 the Government imposed a permanent ban on mining at a traditional Aboriginal site in the Northern Territory.

An important precedent was established in June 1992, when the High Court overruled the concept of *terra nullius* (unoccupied land) by recognizing the existence of land titles that predated European settlement in 1788 in cases where a close association with the land in question had been continued; however, land titles legally acquired since 1788 were to remain intact. As a result of the 'Mabo' decision of 1992 (named after the Aboriginal claimant, Eddie Mabo), in December 1993 Parliament approved the Native Title Act, historic legislation granting Aboriginal people the right to claim title to their traditional lands. The legislation aroused much controversy, particularly in Western Australia (vast areas of the state being vacant Crown land), where rival legislation to replace native title rights with lesser rights to traditional land usage, such as access for ceremonial purposes only, had been enacted. In March 1995 the High Court declared the Native Title Act to be valid, rejecting as unconstitutional Western Australia's own legislation.

In October 1996, following protracted delays in the development of a valuable zinc mine in Queensland owing to Aboriginal land claims, the Howard Government announced proposals to amend the Native Title Act to permit federal ministers to overrule Aboriginal concerns if a project of 'major economic benefit' to Australia were threatened. In December the Larrakia people of the Northern Territory presented a claim under the Native Title Act, the first such claim to encompass a provincial capital, namely Darwin. Meanwhile, in October the federal High Court upheld an appeal by two Aboriginal communities in Queensland (including the Wik people of Cape York) against an earlier ruling that prevented them from submitting a claim to land leased by the state government to cattle and sheep farmers. The Court's decision, known as the Wik judgment, was expected to encourage similar challenges to 'pastoral' leases.

In April 1997 the first native title deed to be granted on mainland Australia was awarded to the Dunghutti people of New South Wales. In the same month the Prime Minister announced the introduction of legislation to clarify the issue of land tenure; a 10-point plan was to be drawn up in consultation with state governments and with representatives of the Aboriginal community. In September the Government introduced the Wik Native Title Bill, which was subsequently approved by the House of Representatives. In November, however, the Senate questioned the constitutional validity of the proposed legislation, whereby pastoralists' rights and activities would prevail over, but not extinguish (as had been assumed), the Aboriginal people's rights to native title. In December the Government refused to accept the Senate's proposed amendments to the legislation, and in April 1998 the Senate rejected the legislation for a second time. Finally, in July, following a protracted and acrimonious debate, the Senate narrowly approved the Native Title Amendment Bill, thereby restricting the Aboriginal people's rights to claim access to Crown land leased to farmers. The approval of the controversial legislation was immediately denounced by Aboriginal leaders. In the same month, however, at a session in Darwin the Federal Court granted communal (but not exclusive or commercial) native title to the waters and seabed around Croker Island in the Northern Territory to five Aboriginal groups. With about 140 similar claims over Australian waters pending, the historic ruling represented the first recognition of native title rights over the sea. However, the area's traditional owners launched an appeal against the decision, insisting on the commercial right to negotiate on fishing and pearling activities. In March 1999, in a conciliatory gesture that settled a land claim case outstanding since 1845, the Tasmanian Government relinquished the site of a mission station at Wybellena, where 200 Aboriginal people had been forcibly resettled; most had subsequently died of disease and maltreatment.

In August 2002 the High Court in Canberra rejected a claim by the Miriuwung-Gajerrong people to territory in Western Australia and the Northern Territory that contained the Argyle diamond mine, owned by the Anglo-Australian mining company Rio Tinto. In September, however, Rio Tinto offered to close the Jabiluka uranium mine in the Northern Territory, following opposition to the project from the indigenous Mirrar people (the owners of the land) and environmental groups. The Mirrar people welcomed the proposal; the Government of the Northern Territory approved a plan to fill in the mine in August 2003. Meanwhile, in September 2002 the state Government of Western Australia agreed to return about 13.7m. ha of land to the Martu people. In December the Australian High Court rejected the Aboriginal Yorta Yorta people's claim to territory along the River Murray on the border of Victoria and New South Wales. A federal court ruling in September 2006 granted the Noongar Aboriginal people native title over more than 6,000 sq km of land in Western Australia, around and including Perth. The Government of Western Australia announced that it would appeal against the ruling. In the following month the Australian Attorney-General stated that the federal Government intended to contest the ruling in order to clarify questions arising from the decision, including the issue of public access to vacant Crown land. In April 2007 the federal and state Governments' appeal was lodged at the Federal Court. In April 2008 parts of the appeal were upheld. Efforts to reach an out-of-court settlement of the matter were subsequently undertaken.

In December 2008, citing a lack of due process, the Federal Court ruled against Xstrata, an Anglo-Swiss mining corporation, which in 2006 had been permitted by the Government to proceed with the expansion of a controversial zinc mine in the Northern Territory. Also opposed by environmentalists owing to the risk of pollution, the project had involved the diversion of a river, which Aboriginal leaders now demanded be restored to its original course. The ruling was regarded as a major set-back for the country's mining industry.

In July 2010 a court in Queensland awarded native title rights over 40,000 sq km of sea to the Torres Strait Islanders, who had first submitted the claim in 2001: this represented the largest maritime claim so far made. In June 2011 Rio Tinto announced that it had concluded agreements with five Aboriginal groups in the Pilbara region of Western Australia, allowing the company to expand its iron mining operations on their land over a period of 40 years, in return for a share of the profits and an undertaking by the company to ensure that at least 14% of its employees would comprise Aboriginal workers.

Other Aboriginal Issues

In November 1987 an official commission of inquiry into the cause of the high death rate among Aboriginal prisoners recommended immediate government action. In August 1988 a UN report accused Australia of violating international human rights in its treatment of Aboriginal people. In November the Government announced an inquiry into its Aboriginal Affairs Department, following accusations by the opposition coalition of nepotism and misuse of funds. The commission of inquiry published its first official report in February 1989, following which the Government announced the creation of a $A10m. programme to combat the high death rate among Aboriginal prisoners. In October an unofficial study indicated that Aboriginal people, although accounting for only 1% of the total population of Australia, comprised more than 20% of persons in prison. In May 1991 the report of the Royal Commission into Aboriginal Deaths in Custody was published: it gave evidence of racial prejudice in the police force and included more than 300 recommendations for changes in policies relating to Aboriginal people. In June Parliament established a Council for Aboriginal Reconciliation. In March 1992 radical plans for judicial, economic and social reforms, with the objective of improving the lives of Aboriginal people, were announced. The Government made an immediate allocation of $A150m.; a total of $A500m. was to be made available over the next 10 years. In February 1993 the human rights organization Amnesty International issued a highly critical report on the prison conditions of Aboriginal people, and in March 1996 it claimed that Australia had made little progress with regard to its treatment of Aboriginal prisoners. In March 2000 the UN Committee on Elimination of Racial Discrimination issued a report denouncing Australia's treatment of its indigenous people. The report was particularly critical of the mandatory prison sentences for minor property offences in force in the Northern Territory and Western Australia, which appeared to target juvenile Aboriginal people. In July a legal case was initiated against the Australian Government accusing it of breaching the human rights of Aboriginal people with these harsh mandatory sentencing laws. In November 2004 the death of an Aboriginal man in police custody prompted rioting by some 300 people on Palm Island, off the coast of Queensland, one of the country's largest Aboriginal communities; in 2007 the police officer accused of causing the victim's death was acquitted of manslaughter.

In July 1996 the Roman Catholic Church issued an apology for its role in the forcible removal from their parents of tens of thousands of Aboriginal and part-Aboriginal children, in a controversial practice of placement in institutions and white foster homes, where many were abused. Some received little or no education, with girls being employed as domestic servants and boys as stockmen. This policy of so-called assimilation had continued until the late 1960s. In May 1997 the publication of the findings of a two-year inquiry into the removal of as many as 100,000 Aboriginal children from their families had profound political repercussions. At a conference on reconciliation at the end of the month, the Prime Minister made an unexpected personal apology to the 'stolen generation'. However, the Government repudiated the commission's assertion that the policy of assimilation had been tantamount to genocide and rejected recommendations that compensation be paid to victims. In December the Howard Government reaffirmed that it would not issue a formal apology to the 'stolen generation'. However, a $A63m. programme to help reunite divided Aboriginal families was announced. In February 1998 the Anglican Church apologized unreservedly for its part in the removal of Aboriginal children from their families. In May 2000 250,000 supporters of reconciliation between white and Aboriginal Australia took part in a march across Sydney Harbour Bridge.

Two separate UN reports, released in March and July 2000, were highly critical of Australia's treatment of the Aboriginal population; their findings were strongly rejected by the Australian Government. In August, at the conclusion of a test case brought in the Northern Territory by two members of the 'stolen generation' who hoped to win compensation for the trauma occasioned by their removal from their families, the Federal Court ruled that the Government was not obliged to pay punitive damages to the two Aboriginal claimants, on the grounds of insufficient evidence. As many as 30,000 similar cases had been pending. In December some 300,000 people took part in demonstrations in Melbourne and Perth in support of reconciliation between the white and indigenous communities. The Government rejected a Senate committee's recommendations for the issue of an apology to the 'stolen generation' and for the establishment of a reparations tribunal to deal with compensation claims. In August 2001, at a human rights conference in Sydney, various indigenous and legal groups finalized a new proposal for a reparations tribunal; again the Government rejected it, insisting that its own $A60m. programme of 'practical' assistance was sufficient.

In November 2001 Pope John Paul II apologized to Australia's Aboriginal community for what he called the 'shameful injustices' of the past, asking for forgiveness for the Roman Catholic Church's role in forcibly removing Aboriginal children from their families. In October 2006 the Premier of Tasmania, Paul Lennon, announced that funds from a $A5m. compensation scheme would be made available to the state's Aboriginal victims of the 'stolen generation' or their descendants. In January 2008 compensation was awarded to 84 members of the 'stolen generation' and to the offspring of 22 deceased victims, the applications of 45 other claimants having been dismissed. Meanwhile, hitherto only one individual claim, instigated in South Australia in 1998 by Bruce Trevorrow, an Aboriginal who as a baby had been forcibly removed from his family and, he successfully argued, deprived of his cultural identity, had resulted in a payment of compensation: in an unusually well-documented case, Trevorrow was awarded $A525,000 in August 2007.

In April 2004 Prime Minister Howard announced controversial plans to abolish the elected Aboriginal and Torres Strait Islander Commission (ATSIC), claiming that it had failed to improve conditions for the indigenous community since commencing operations in 1990. In response, the first national party for Aboriginal people, Your Voice, was launched in May 2004. Legislation to dismantle ATSIC was approved by the House of Representatives in June, and in December a new government-appointed advisory body on Aboriginal affairs, the 14-member National Indigenous Council, held its first meeting. In March 2005, following a senate committee report, legislation to abolish ATSIC was approved.

In June 2007 the Howard Government announced plans to ban alcohol and the most offensive types of pornography in Aboriginal communities in the Northern Territory, along with other federal measures formulated in response to reports of widespread child abuse and the prevalence of poor health and social conditions in the area. Amid much controversy, the House of Representatives approved the relevant legislation in August. In order to permit the implementation of the intervention measures in the Northern Territory, the Racial Discrimination Act of 1975 was suspended.

In February 2008 the new Prime Minister, Kevin Rudd, issued a long-awaited formal apology for the 'profound grief, suffering and loss' inflicted upon indigenous people by successive governments, in particular the mistreatment of the 'stolen generation'. The motion received unanimous parliamentary approval, although some Liberal members were reported to have boycotted the historic opening session. Although they remained unrepresented in the legislature, the ceremony was attended by 100 delegates from the Aboriginal community and members of the 'stolen generation'. While Rudd's initiative was generally welcomed, his decision not to grant federal compensation to those affected by the policies of previous governments drew some criticism; instead, the Government reiterated its intention to give priority to the improvement of health and educational services in Aboriginal areas. Rudd declared his commitment to raising Aboriginal life expectancy to a level comparable to that of other Australians within a generation and also his intention to halve the indigenous infant mortality rate within a decade. In July funding of $A550m., to be provided for various projects over a five-year period, was agreed. In April 2009, in a reversal of the previous Government's policy, the Rudd administration adopted the UN Declaration on the Rights of Indigenous Peoples.

In July 2009 a national report into Aboriginal disadvantage found little improvement in social and economic conditions among indigenous communities. In August the UN Special Rapporteur on human rights and indigenous peoples, James Anaya, visited Aboriginal communities to investigate the situation. Anaya described the Australian Government's controversial intervention in the Northern Territory (see above) as a discriminatory act that infringed upon Aboriginal people's rights and self-determination. He expressed particular concern with regard to the suspension of the Racial Discrimination Act. The federal minister responsible for indigenous affairs, Jenny Macklin, defended the intervention as necessary to protect the rights of indigenous people; however, a number of national and international human rights groups continued to protest against the Government's action. The process of income management, whereby one-half of welfare payments to indigenous people was 'quarantined' for food and other necessities, was regarded as a particular source of humiliation for Aboriginal people. In June 2010 the Racial Discrimination Act was reinstated, and the policy of income management was extended to non-indigenous recipients of welfare payments.

A new representative body, the National Congress of Australia's First Peoples, was formed in May 2010: it was to comprise 120 members elected by Aboriginal people and Torres Strait Islanders.

At the general election in August 2010 an Aboriginal member of the Liberal Party was elected to the House of Representatives: this was the first time that the indigenous community had been represented in the lower house of the legislature (although there had previously been two Aboriginal senators). In November the Government established a panel of experts to prepare for a referendum, to be conducted within the next three years, on an amendment to the Constitution that would explicitly recognize Aboriginal people and Torres Strait Islanders. In December it was announced that a new Aboriginal grouping, First Nations Political Party, led by Maurie Japarta Ryan, had applied for registration with the Australian Electoral Commission; this was duly granted in early 2011.

International Terrorism

In 2002 Australia was for the first time obliged directly to address the issue of international terrorism. On 12 October 88 Australians were among the 202 killed in a bomb explosion in a nightclub on the Indonesian island of Bali. The Islamist militant group Jemaah Islamiah (JI) was held principally responsible for the attack. The Australian Government proscribed the organization, which was suspected of having links with the al-Qa'ida network, and successfully led a campaign to have JI listed as a terrorist organization by the UN. In March 2003 the Attorney-General announced a ban, effective immediately, on the Iraqi Kurdish Sunni Islamist fundamentalist group Ansar al-Islam. It was announced in April that the Government had banned six more militant Islamist groups. In May the Government decided to create a new counter-terrorist unit from the country's volunteer military reserve force. One month later the Senate approved anti-terrorism legislation giving significant new powers to the Australian Security Intelligence Organisation, including the power to detain suspects for up to seven days without charge. In February 2004 Australia and Indonesia co-hosted a counter-terrorism conference held on Bali. A bomb exploded outside the Australian embassy in the Indonesian capital of Jakarta in September, killing at least nine people, mostly Indonesians, and injuring more than 180 others. JI was suspected of being responsible for the attack. In October 2005 four Australian citizens were among 20 people killed in three suicide bombings on Bali.

In September 2005 Prime Minister John Howard announced a series of proposals intended to strengthen Australia's anti-terrorism laws, including plans to make the incitement of terrorist acts a criminal offence and to detain suspects for up to 14 days without charge. In November it was reported that Australian police had averted a potential terrorist attack by Islamist extremists upon an unspecified target in the country, arresting a number of suspects in operations in Sydney and Melbourne. Meanwhile, the Senate had approved amendments to existing anti-terrorism legislation, enabling police to intervene at any stage of terrorist planning, and to charge suspects without evidence of a specific terrorist act. Following the arrests, the new counter-terrorism proposals that Howard had announced in September were introduced into Parliament.

The Government's handling of a case involving suspected terrorist David Hicks, an Australian national also known as Muhammed Dawood, continued to arouse public concern. Hicks had been detained without trial by the US authorities since early 2002, having reportedly trained with supporters of al-Qa'ida and served with the ruling Taliban in Afghanistan, prior to his capture and detention at Guantánamo Bay in Cuba. Formal charges against him were filed in 2004 but later abandoned. Hicks was subsequently found guilty of providing 'material support for terrorism' by a US military commission, thus becoming the first detainee held at Guantánamo Bay to be processed in this way. He was returned to Australia to serve the remainder of a seven-year sentence at a labour prison in Adelaide, during which time any contact with the media was forbidden. Hicks obtained his release in December 2007, but he remained subject to a federal control order restricting his movements.

In September 2008 the Supreme Court of Victoria convicted Abdul Nacer Benbrika, a Muslim cleric of Algerian origin, and six of his followers on charges of membership of a terrorist organization, which in 2005 had plotted attacks against sporting events in Melbourne in an attempt to effect the withdrawal of Australian troops from Iraq. The convictions were the culmination of Australia's largest and most protracted trial on terrorism-related charges to date, with the proceedings representing a significant test case in the so-called 'war on terror' (see below). In February 2009 Benbrika was sentenced to a prison term of 15 years.

In Melbourne in August 2009 five men were arrested in a counter-terrorism operation by the police and charged with planning a suicide attack on an army barracks in Sydney, apparently motivated by opposition to Australia's military involvement in Iraq and Afghanistan. Three of the accused were found guilty in December 2010, and in December 2011 they were sentenced to 18 years' imprisonment. In another terrorism-related trial in Sydney five Islamists, who had been arrested in September 2005 but who could not be named for legal reasons, were convicted in October 2009 of conspiring to commit a terrorist act. In February 2010 the men received maximum sentences, ranging from 23 to 28 years' imprisonment.

Issues with the United Kingdom

In March 1986 Australia's constitutional links with the United Kingdom were reduced by the Australia Act, which abolished the British Parliament's residual legislative, executive and judicial controls over Australian state law. In February 1992, shortly after a visit by Queen Elizabeth II, Prime Minister Keating caused a furore by accusing the United Kingdom of abandoning Australia to the Japanese threat during the Second World War. Following a visit to the United Kingdom in September 1993, Keating announced that, subject to approval by referendum, Australia was to become a republic by 2001. Although John Howard personally favoured the retention of the monarchy, in 1996 the new Prime Minister announced plans for a constitutional convention, which met in February 1998. The Constitutional Convention endorsed proposals to adopt a republican system and to replace the British monarch as head of state; however, delegates were divided over the method of election of a future head of state. At the subsequent referendum on the issue, conducted in November 1999, 55% of voters supported the retention of the monarchy. Moreover, 61% of voters expressed opposition to a proposal to include a preamble to the Constitution, recognizing Aboriginals as 'the nation's first people'. Many observers interpreted the referendum result as a rejection of the particular form of republicanism offered, opinion polls having indicated that more than two-thirds of Australians would support the introduction of a republican system of government if the President were to be directly elected.

In June 2001 the Anglican Archbishop of Brisbane, Peter Hollingworth, was sworn in as Governor-General, succeeding Sir William Deane. In February 2002, as the Queen commenced a visit to Australia to celebrate her Golden Jubilee, Hollingworth refused to yield to pressure to resign over claims that he had deliberately concealed alleged cases of child abuse by the clergy in Queensland. The Prime Minister rejected demands for the dismissal of the Governor-General. In May 2003 Hollingworth temporarily relinquished his post, pending the investigation of rape allegations against him. Sir Guy Green, the Governor of Tasmania, was appointed acting Governor-General. Hollingworth strongly denied the charge against him, which dated back to the 1960s. The woman accusing him of rape committed suicide in April 2003, and the case was subsequently dismissed at the request of her family. Although the Prime Minister continued to show support for Hollingworth, the Governor-General resigned in May. The former Governor of Western Australia, Maj.-Gen. Michael Jeffery, was sworn in as the country's new Governor-General in August.

In December 2003 the High Court ruled that long-term British residents without Australian citizenship who committed a crime in Australia could be deported to the United Kingdom. The judgment overruled the special status held by British residents, according to which they did not have to take Australian citizenship, and declared that any non-citizen who had arrived in the country after 26 January 1949 would henceforth be considered a foreign alien for immigration purposes. In March 2006 the Queen visited Australia. During her stay she made a speech upon the theme of the maturing of Australia as a nation, which was perceived by many commentators as an acknowledgement that the country might ultimately make the transition towards a republican system of government.

In June 1993, following a joint operation to ascertain the extent of plutonium contamination resulting from British nuclear weapons testing at Maralinga in South Australia between 1956 and 1963, Australia announced its acceptance of $A45m. in compensation from the British Government for the cost of decontamination. In December 1994 the local Aboriginal people, the Maralinga Tjarutja, who had been displaced by the testing and had pressed for compensation and the return of their lands, reached an agreement with the Federal Government on a settlement of $A13.5m. The payment was to be spent on health, employment and infrastructural projects. Despite the completion of the decontamination programme, involving the removal of 300,000 cu m of plutonium-contaminated topsoil, the Australian Government issued a report in May 2000 stating that some 120 sq km of the territory were still considered too contaminated for permanent habitation, permitting only limited access. In December 2009, following another decontamination operation, the remaining lands were finally returned to the Maralinga Tjarutja people at a formal ceremony.

At the Australia 2020 Summit convened in April 2008 (see above) proposals for a popular consultation on the establishment of a republic were renewed, with a further referendum on the issue being envisaged. On 5 September Quentin Bryce was formally inaugurated as Governor-General, replacing Maj.-Gen. Michael Jeffery. Bryce, who had previously served as Governor of Queensland, was the first woman to occupy the post since its inception in 1901. Debate over whether Australia should become a republic was revived in January 2010 with the visit of Prince William, second-in-line to the British throne, to Australia. In October 2011 Queen Elizabeth paid an 11-day visit to Australia, the 16th of her reign, during which she opened a meeting of Commonwealth heads of government in Perth.

In February 2010, following the issue of an apology to the 'forgotten Australians' by the Australian Prime Minister in November of the previous year, the United Kingdom formally apologized for its role in the dispatch of thousands of children to Australia under the Child Migrants Programme, a policy of white emigration that had operated until the late 1960s. Taken from British orphanages or poor families, many children were subjected to mental and physical abuse in Australian institutions, often being deprived of adequate education.

Foreign Affairs

From the 1980s Australia placed increasing emphasis on its relations with Asia. The Australian Government initiated the creation of Asia-Pacific Economic Cooperation (APEC, see p. 204), a forum to facilitate the exchange of services, tourism and direct foreign investment in the region. The inaugural APEC conference took place in Canberra in November 1989.

Relations with South-East Asia

In November 2004 it was announced that Australia, New Zealand and the members of the Association of Southeast Asian Nations (ASEAN, see p. 214) were to commence negotiations on a free trade agreement. In December, however, Australia provoked tensions with South-East Asia when it proposed the creation of a coastal security zone extending five times as far as its territorial waters. Under this counter-terrorist measure, which took effect in March 2005, all ships entering the 1,000-nautical mile zone would be monitored, with Australian naval and customs ships given powers to intercept and board all vessels suspected of constituting a terrorist threat. Nevertheless, in December 2005 Australia acceded to ASEAN's Treaty of Amity and Co-operation; the free trade agreement was signed in February 2009.

Australian relations with Indonesia, which had been strained since the Indonesian annexation of the former Portuguese colony of East Timor in 1976, improved in August 1985, when Prime Minister Hawke made a statement recognizing Indonesian sovereignty over the territory. In December 1989 Australia and Indonesia signed an accord regarding joint exploration for petroleum and gas reserves in the Timor Gap (an area of sea forming a disputed boundary between the two countries). In April 1992 Paul Keating's visit to Indonesia, the new Prime Minister's first official overseas trip, aroused controversy, owing to the repercussions of the massacre of unarmed civilians in Dili, East Timor, by Indonesian troops in November 1991. In July 1995, as a result of strong opposition in Australia, Indonesia was obliged to withdraw the appointment as ambassador to Canberra of Lt-Gen. (retd) Herman Mantiri, a former Chief of the General Staff of the Armed Forces. Nevertheless, in December Australia and Indonesia unexpectedly signed a joint security treaty. In March 1997 the two countries signed a treaty defining their seabed and 'economic zone' boundaries.

Meanwhile, the investigation into the deaths of six Australia-based journalists in East Timor in 1975 had been reopened, and in June 1996 a government report concluded that they had been murdered by Indonesian soldiers. In August 1998 the International Commission of Jurists, the Geneva-based human rights organization, reported that five of the six journalists had been murdered in an East Timorese village in October 1975 in an attempt to conceal the invasion of the territory, while the sixth man was killed in Dili in December of that year. Furthermore, it was claimed that the Australian embassy in Jakarta had been aware of the forthcoming invasion of East Timor but had failed to give adequate warning to the journalists. In late 1998, as newly emerging evidence continued to suggest that the truth had been suppressed, Australia announced that its judicial inquiry was to be reopened. Government documents declassified in late 2000 proved conclusively that Australian officials had prior knowledge of Indonesia's plans to invade East Timor. In September 2009 the Australian police opened a war crimes investigation into the killings of the five journalists in 1975.

In January 1999, in a significant shift in its policy, Australia announced that henceforth it would support eventual self-determination for East Timor. A rapid escalation of violence followed a referendum held in August, when the territory's people voted overwhelmingly in favour of independence. Thousands of refugees were airlifted to safety in northern Australia. With a commitment of 4,500 troops in its largest operation since the Viet Nam War, Australia took a leading role in the deployment of a multinational peace-keeping force in East Timor. In November 2000 the Australian Government agreed to help create an East Timor defence force, contributing some US $26m. over five years and providing training for police officers and border guards.

In December 2002 Timor-Leste's Parliament ratified a treaty with Australia on production, profit-sharing and royalty and tax distribution from oil and gas reserves. In August 2003 the two countries signed a memorandum of understanding to collaborate in combating terrorism. However, Australia's relations with Timor-Leste were made difficult by disagreements over the maritime boundaries in the Timor Sea. In January 2005, in the absence of any agreement, Woodside Petroleum, the Australian company involved in the gas project, confirmed that it was halting development. In January 2006 the two countries finally signed an agreement to share the revenue from the Greater Sunrise oil and gas field equally between them. However, the accord was criticized for including a condition that a final decision regarding the disputed maritime boundaries be postponed for at least 50 years. In October the two Governments agreed to ensure bilateral co-operation in security operations in the Joint Petroleum Development Area.

In May 2006, following looting and violence in Dili, Australia responded to a request for assistance from the Timorese Government by leading a multinational security force comprising approximately 2,500 troops, drawn from Australia (its contingent numbering 1,800), New Zealand, Malaysia and Portugal. The instability continued, and in August the United Nations Integrated Mission in Timor-Leste (UNMIT) was established. Also in August, the Australian Government announced the expansion of its army and police force in order to deal with security issues in South-East Asia and the Pacific region.

In June 2010 the President of Timor-Leste, José Ramos Horta, visited Australia to open a new Timor-Leste embassy in Canberra; during his visit he expressed concern at the safety implications of a proposal by the consortium developing the shared oil and gas field to build a floating platform to process gas, a technique that had not previously been used anywhere else.

Relations with Indonesia continued to improve. Abdurrahman Wahid made a long-postponed official visit to Australia in June 2001, the first Indonesian President to do so in 26 years. John Howard was the first foreign leader to meet the next President of Indonesia, Megawati Sukarnoputri, when he visited the country in August. In April 2005 President Susilo Bambang Yudhoyono of Indonesia paid an official visit to Australia. Meanwhile, the increasing numbers of asylum-seekers attempting to enter Australia by boat via Indonesia became a contentious issue. Senior-level discussions between Australian and Indonesian officials took place in the latter part of 2001. At an international forum on the issue of people-smuggling in February 2002, delegates agreed to pursue a 12-month programme, which included imposing stricter law enforcement and better information and intelligence-sharing, to combat smuggling and illegal immigration. Officials from Australia, Indonesia and Timor-Leste (formerly East Timor) held the first trilateral discussions on future co-operation issues on the Indonesian island of Bali. In September three Indonesians were convicted of attempting to smuggle illegal immigrants into Australia in October 2001; they were sentenced to five years' imprisonment. Relations between Australia and Indonesia were strained as a result of Australia's treatment of Indonesian-born Muslims suspected of having links with the banned Islamist militant organization JI in the aftermath of the bomb attack on Bali in October 2002 (see above).

In March 2006 a diplomatic dispute developed between the two countries following the Australian Government's decision to grant temporary visas to several Indonesian asylum-seekers from the province of Papua. In November the Australian Minister for Foreign Affairs, Alexander Downer, and his Indonesian counterpart signed a treaty informally known as the Lombok Agreement, providing for the strengthening of bilateral relations and increased co-operation in the field of security. The Lombok Treaty succeeded the bilateral defence pact of 1995 and entered into force in February 2008. In June 2008 Prime Minister Kevin Rudd undertook his first state visit to Indonesia, meeting President Yudhoyono for discussions on bilateral and regional co-operation, following which the two leaders signed an agreement to address the issue of climate change. Australia was to support Indonesia in its efforts to reduce its substantial levels of greenhouse gas emissions, arising mainly from the continued deforestation of the country.

In 2009, as the number of asylum-seekers entering Australian waters via Indonesia continued to increase, discussions between the two countries took place on how best to co-operate in apprehending people-smugglers. Relations were tested in October when a group of Tamil asylum-seekers from Sri Lanka was rescued from a sinking vessel in Indonesian waters by an Australian ship and taken to the Indonesian island of Bintan, where they refused to disembark, demanding to be taken to Australia for processing. After four weeks of stalemate, the Tamils finally agreed to be transferred to an Indonesian detention centre. All 78 asylum-seekers were subsequently found to be genuine refugees, and were resettled in Australia and elsewhere. The Indonesian President made a state visit to Australia in March 2010, during which he undertook to introduce legislation in Indonesia that would make people-trafficking a criminal offence. In April 2010, however, the Australian Government announced that the processing of all new asylum claims by Sri Lankan and Afghan nationals was to be suspended with immediate effect. In December some 50 asylum-seekers died when their ship was wrecked off Christmas Island. In January 2011 three Indonesian members of the ship's crew were charged in Australia with illegally transporting people to Australia, and later in that month an Australian citizen, suspected of organizing the voyage, was arrested in Indonesia.

In November 2010 the recently appointed Australian Prime Minister, Julia Gillard, paid a visit to Indonesia, during which she undertook to provide $A500m. for education in Indonesia over the next five years, and the two Governments agreed to begin negotiations on an economic partnership agreement, to cover trade, economic co-operation and investment. In January 2012 the agreement on free trade between ASEAN members, Australia and New Zealand (see above) entered into force for Indonesia: under the accord, 92% of Australian exports to Indonesia and 99% of Indonesian exports to Australia would eventually be tariff-free.

A crisis in Australia's relations with Malaysia arose in late 1993, when Paul Keating described the Malaysian Prime Minister as a 'recalcitrant' for his failure to attend the APEC summit meeting in the USA in November. However, relations subsequently improved, and in January 1996 Keating undertook the first official visit to Malaysia by an Australian Prime Minister since 1984. A bilateral trade and investment agreement took effect in January 1998. During 1999 Australia was critical of the continued detention and the trials of Anwar Ibrahim, the former Deputy Prime Minister and Minister of Finance. After Prime Minister Howard stated in December 2002 that he would be prepared to conduct pre-emptive strikes on militant organizations in neighbouring countries suspected of planning terrorist attacks on Australia, Malaysia warned that any incursion into its territory would be considered as an act of war. Relations with Malaysia appeared to improve following the succession of Abdullah Ahmad Badawi to the premiership of that country in October. In June 2004, during a visit to Malaysia by the Australian Minister for Foreign Affairs, agreement was reached to hold formal annual talks with his Malaysian counterpart. In April 2005 Prime Minister Abdullah Badawi visited Australia, the first visit to the country by a Malaysian leader in more than 20 years, and the two Governments agreed to begin negotiations on a bilateral free trade agreement. Australia's increasing involvement in regional affairs was emphasized by its attendance at the inaugural East Asia Summit meeting, held in Kuala Lumpur, Malaysia, in December. After attending the fifth East Asia Summit meeting in Hanoi, Viet Nam, in October 2010, Julia Gillard visited Malaysia, where the principal topics of discussion were the possible establishment of a regional processing centre for asylum-seekers, and the bilateral free trade agreement. During a visit to Australia by the Malaysian Prime Minister, Najib Tun Razak, in March 2011, the two heads of government declared their commitment to concluding the agreement within one year. A bilateral agreement concluded in July, under which Australia would send asylum-seekers to Malaysia for processing in return for accepting refugees from Malaysia, provoked considerable controversy and was ruled unlawful by the Australian High Court in August (see Recent developments: the Gillard administration 2010–).

Relations with Myanmar continued to be dominated by issues of human rights. In October 2002 the Australian Minister for Foreign Affairs met Myanma government officials and opposition leader Aung Sang Suu Kyi for discussions, during the first visit to Myanmar by an Australian minister for nearly 20 years. In October 2009 the Australian chargé d'affaires in Myanmar, along with diplomats from the United Kingdom and the USA, was able to have substantive discussions with Suu Kyi in Yangon, Myanmar, in the first such meeting between an Australian representative and the opposition leader since February 2003. The Australian Government expressed serious reservations about the circumstances that surrounded the holding of elections in Myanmar in November 2010.

Relations with East Asia

By the early 21st century China had become one of Australia's most important trading partners. However, in the 1990s relations were strained by the issue of China's nuclear-testing programme, and deteriorated further in September 1996 when the Dalai Lama, the exiled spiritual leader of Tibet, was received in Sydney by the Prime Minister. In March 1997 the Australian Prime Minister embarked upon an official visit to China, where he had discussions with Premier Li Peng. In July 1999, during a visit to Beijing by the Australian Minister for Foreign Affairs, Australia endorsed China's application for membership of the World Trade Organization (WTO). The two countries also signed a bilateral trade pact. In September, however, President Jiang Zemin's visit to Australia was disrupted by pro-Tibet and Taiwan activists. During President Hu Jintao's visit to Australia in October 2003 Australia agreed to supply China with liquefied natural gas for a period of 25 years. In April 2005 Australia and China agreed to begin negotiations on a free trade agreement. In June Chen Yonglin, a senior diplomatic official who had defected from the Chinese consulate in Sydney, claimed that China maintained a significant espionage network in Australia. His allegations were supported by at least two other Chinese defectors. Chen and his family were subsequently granted permanent residency by the Australian authorities. In June 2007 the Australian Prime Minister, John Howard, held a meeting with the Dalai Lama in Sydney.

In April 2008, in the final stage of an 18-day international tour that also incorporated the USA, Prime Minister Kevin Rudd visited China. In fluent Mandarin he addressed students at Beijing University. In a live televised press conference, Prime Minister Rudd referred to 'significant human rights problems' in Tibet, but declared his willingness to discuss the issue with President Hu Jintao and Prime Minister Wen Jiabao. The Australian and Chinese Prime Ministers agreed to increase joint co-operation to combat climate change. In July 2009 Stern Hu, an employee of the Anglo-Australian mining company Rio Tinto and a naturalized Australian citizen, was arrested in China on charges of bribery and industrial espionage; three Chinese employees of the company were also arrested. Diplomats failed to reach agreement on the handling of the charges against Stern Hu, and in February 2010 the case was formally transferred to a court in the Chinese city of Shanghai. In the following month Stern Hu and his colleagues were found guilty. Stern Hu was sentenced to 10 years' imprisonment, while the other defendants also received unexpectedly long prison terms. The Australian Prime Minister expressed serious misgivings with regard to the conduct of the case, which had partly been heard in secret. The granting of an Australian visa for a visit in August 2009 by the exiled separatist Uygur leader, Rebiya Kadeer, also caused bilateral tensions. None the less, in the same month a major agreement providing for China's purchase of liquefied natural gas, to the value of $A50,000m. over a 20-year period, was signed in Beijing. In June 2010 the Chinese Vice-President, Xi Jinping, paid an official visit to Australia, during which agreements were concluded on Chinese investment in major Australian mining projects, and Xi reaffirmed China's commitment to the future conclusion of a free trade agreement with Australia. During a visit to Beijing in April 2011 Prime Minister Gillard held discussions with the Chinese leadership. The Chinese Government gave a guarded response to the announcement in November that US military personnel were to be stationed in northern Australia (see below), declaring that their deployment might not be 'appropriate'.

Australia's relations with Japan were strained in the late 1990s by a fishing dispute relating to the latter's failure to curb its catches of the endangered southern bluefin tuna, as agreed in a treaty of 1993, to which New Zealand was also a signatory. In August 1999, however, an international tribunal ruled in favour of Australia and New Zealand. Another cause of contention was Japan's continued hunting of whales in the Southern Ocean, ostensibly for scientific purposes, as permitted by an agreement imposing a moratorium on commercial whaling, which had been concluded by the members of the International Whaling Commission (IWC) in 1982. In March 2007 Prime Minister Howard and his Japanese counterpart, Shinzo Abe, signed an agreement on security in order to further bilateral co-operation, particularly in the areas of counter-terrorism and disaster relief. Negotiations on a free trade agreement between the two countries began in April. In June 2008 Prime Minister Kevin Rudd visited Japan for discussions with Prime Minister Yasuo Fukuda. The two leaders agreed to the establishment of an international commission on nuclear disarmament but were unable to reach a common position on whaling; however, they maintained that disagreement on the latter issue would not undermine bilateral relations. A serious confrontation in Australian territorial waters between an anti-whaling organization, Sea Shepherd, and the Japanese whaling fleet occurred in January 2010, when Japanese whaling officials denied accusations that a speedboat belonging to Sea Shepherd had been deliberately rammed by a patrol vessel. At a meeting of the IWC in June the Australian delegation successfully argued against a proposal to reverse the ban on commercial whaling, and the Australian Government announced that it would apply to the International Court of Justice to prevent Japan from hunting whales for the purposes of scientific research. In February 2011 the Australian Government welcomed Japan's decision to withdraw its whaling vessels from the Southern Ocean for the remainder of the current whaling season, and reiterated its demand for an end to Japanese whaling. In the same month negotiations on a free trade agreement recommenced: the discussions had been delayed by Japan's reluctance to remove protection for its agricultural producers. As part of an official visit to East Asia in April, Prime Minister Gillard had discussions with her Japanese counterpart, Naoto Kan, on the issues of trade, investment and defence co-operation. In October Rudd (now Minister for Foreign Affairs) deplored Japan's decision to proceed with its whale-hunting activities in the forthcoming season. In January 2012 Japan protested to Australia after three Australian anti-whaling activists boarded a Japanese patrol boat that was escorting the whaling fleet; the three were released without charge. Gillard declared that the activists' action was unacceptable, and that the judicial proceedings initiated by Australia provided the best way of bringing an end to commercial whaling.

In May 2000 diplomatic relations between Australia and the Democratic People's Republic of Korea (North Korea), which had been severed in 1975, were restored. Discussions between the two nations, initiated by the North Korean Government in April 1999, had been dominated by the International Atomic Energy Agency's concerns over nuclear facilities and long-range missile testing. The Australian Minister for Foreign Affairs paid an official two-day visit to Pyongyang in November 2000, and an Australian trade mission visited North Korea in December. Australia and North Korea agreed to establish, within two years, embassies in their respective capitals when North Korea's Minister of Foreign Affairs paid Australia a reciprocal visit in June 2001, and a memorandum of understanding was signed to facilitate co-operation between Australian and North Korean scientists in agricultural research. Plans to open an embassy in North Korea were deferred in late 2002, however, owing to North Korea's efforts to reactivate its nuclear weapons programme, and in early 2008 the North Korean embassy in Canberra was closed down, apparently for financial reasons. In October 2006, meanwhile, North Korea's announcement that it had conducted its first test of a nuclear weapon prompted Australia to ban North Korean ships from its ports. During her official visit to East Asia in April 2011, Prime Minister Gillard's discussions with the South Korean leadership emphasized the importance of a bilateral free trade agreement, which was expected to be concluded by early 2012.

Relations with the Pacific islands

Australia's relations with neighbouring Pacific island states have been intermittently strained. At a meeting of the South Pacific Forum (now Pacific Islands Forum, see p. 416) in September 1997, the member countries failed to reach agreement on a common policy regarding mandatory targets for the reduction of emissions of greenhouse gases. The low-lying nation of Tuvalu was particularly critical of Australia's refusal to compromise, the Australian Prime Minister declaring that the Pacific islands' concerns over rising sea levels were exaggerated. In July 2001 Australia declined Tuvalu's request to take in more Tuvaluan nationals.

Australia's relations with Papua New Guinea were strained in early 1997 as a result of the latter's decision to engage the services of a group of foreign mercenaries in the Government's operations against secessionists on the island of Bougainville. In early 1998 a permanent cease-fire agreement between the Papua New Guinea Government and the Bougainville secessionists was signed in New Zealand. Australia reaffirmed its commitment to the provision of a peace-monitoring force. Since 1998 both Canberra and Townsville, in Queensland, had provided a neutral venue for negotiations regarding the Bougainville issue, and in August 2001 the Minister for Foreign Affairs, Alexander Downer, signed the Bougainville Peace Agreement as a witness. In October the Government concluded an agreement with Papua New Guinea for that country to accommodate 223 asylum-seekers in exchange for $A1m. In December 2003 the Australian Government announced its intention to send around 300 police officers and civil servants to Papua New Guinea as part of a five-year operation to counter crime and corruption. In July 2004 the National Parliament of Papua New Guinea approved legislation allowing the deployment of the Australian police officers and officials; the first contingent of police officers arrived in Bougainville in September. However, in May 2005, following a ruling by the Papua New Guinea Supreme Court that the deployment violated the Constitution, the police officers were withdrawn from the country. Tensions mounted between Australia and Papua New Guinea in October 2006 over the former's extradition request for an Australian lawyer, Julian Moti, to answer criminal charges. Moti had been arrested in Port Moresby, but had escaped from Papua New Guinea to Solomon Islands, where he had previously been appointed Attorney-General (see below).

In March 2008 Kevin Rudd visited Papua New Guinea for discussions with Sir Michael Somare. The two Prime Ministers committed themselves to a partnership to reduce carbon emissions resulting from deforestation. The Australian Prime Minister announced a $A38m. increase in aid to Papua New Guinea (in addition to the annual allocation of more than $A355m.). Rudd also announced a new policy for the development of the Pacific islands, embodied in the Port Moresby Declaration. This manifesto of 20 objectives confirmed the Australian Government's commitment to developing partnerships in the region and its assistance in addressing the challenges confronting the Pacific islands in areas such as governance, public services, economic development and climate change.

Australia played a leading role in the aftermath of a coup in Solomon Islands in June 2000. The Australian navy dispatched a warship to assist in the evacuation of Australian and other nationals from the islands, while a similar ship anchored off shore served as a venue for negotiations between the two warring ethnic militias. The Australian Minister for Foreign Affairs led an international delegation with the aim of facilitating discussions between the factions. In October a peace agreement was signed in Townsville, which ended the two-year conflict; it was qualified and complemented by the Marau Peace Agreement, signed in February 2001. The Australian Government subsequently led an International Peace Monitoring Team. Australia provided financial and technical support for democratic elections held in December 2001. In July 2003 an Australian-led regional peace-keeping force was deployed in Solomon Islands to restore law and order. The Regional Assistance Mission to Solomon Islands (RAMSI) was welcomed by the islanders, and at the end of the year the operation was judged to have been a success. However, following the dispute arising from the Moti affair in October 2006 (see above), Prime Minister Manasseh Sogavare of Solomon Islands warned Australia that repeated extradition requests might lead to the expulsion of Australian peace-keepers from the country. Relations deteriorated further when Australian peace-keepers forcibly entered Sogavare's office in search of evidence relating to the Moti affair. At the Pacific Islands Forum meeting soon afterwards, Sogavare acted to diminish Australia's role in RAMSI; the Forum decided instead to establish a task force to evaluate its operations. In September 2007 Australia's extradition request for Julian Moti was formally rejected by the Solomon Islands Government. However, following Sogavare's removal from office in December and his replacement by Derek Sikua, Julian Moti was dismissed as Attorney-General, and the extradition request was subsequently granted. In September 2008 Moti consented to stand trial on sexual abuse charges in a Brisbane court. In October 2009 the Brisbane Supreme Court heard an application by Moti to have the charges dismissed, on the grounds that Solomon Islands officials had acted illegally in extraditing him to Australia. In December the Court found that the Australian Federal Police prosecution was an abuse of process and granted a permanent stay of the proceedings.

In March 2008 Prime Minister Rudd visited Solomon Islands and expressed gratitude for Prime Minister Sikua's continued support for the RAMSI peace-keeping force, announcing additional Australian aid of $A14m. for the purposes of rural development. Sikua welcomed the Australian Prime Minister's announcement of the Port Moresby Declaration on his recent visit to Papua New Guinea (see above). In August 2010 Australia provided a group of observers, under the auspices of the Pacific Islands Forum, to monitor the general election in Solomon Islands. In February 2011 the Australian Government firmly denied allegations made by the office of the recently appointed Prime Minister of Solomon Islands, Danny Philip, that Australia had supported efforts by the country's opposition to eject him from his post.

In November 2006 pro-democracy protests in the Tongan capital, Nuku'alofa, led to serious rioting and the destruction of numerous buildings; several people were killed in the violence. In response to an appeal from the Tongan Government, Australian and New Zealand security forces, including 50 soldiers and 35 police officers from Australia, were deployed in Tonga to restore stability.

The Australian Government responded to the military coup in Fiji in December 2006 by suspending military co-operation with the country and by banning those associated with the leader of the coup, Cdre Frank Bainimarama, from travelling to and via Australia. The Government's sanctions against Fiji were extended to incorporate a suspension of aid to several sectors, excluding health and education. Following the abrogation of the Constitution by the Fijian President in April 2009, Australia demonstrated support for the country's suspension from the Commonwealth. In November 2009 Fiji expelled the envoys of Australia and New Zealand; in response, their Fijian counterparts were also expelled. The Australian Government expressed deep disappointment at Fiji's actions. In July 2010 Fiji expelled Australia's acting high commissioner, claiming that Australia had used its influence to persuade Vanuatu to cancel a meeting of the Melanesian Spearhead Group, at which Bainimarama had been expected to assume the chair of the regional organization.

In October 2010 the newly elected Australian Government, led by Julia Gillard, affirmed its commitment to the liberalization of regional trade through the Pacific Agreement on Closer Economic Relations (PACER Plus), currently being negotiated by members of the Pacific Islands Forum.

Other external relations

The viability of the ANZUS military pact, which was signed in 1951, linking Australia, New Zealand and the USA, was disputed by the US Government following the New Zealand Government's declaration in July 1984 that vessels believed to be powered by nuclear energy, or to be carrying nuclear weapons, would be barred from the country's ports. Prime Minister Hawke did not support the New Zealand initiative, and Australia continued to participate with the USA in joint military exercises from which New Zealand had been excluded. However, the Hawke Government declined directly to endorse the US action against New Zealand, and in 1986 stated that Australia regarded its 'obligations to New Zealand as constant and undiminishing'. In September 1990 Australia and New Zealand signed an agreement to establish a joint venture to construct as many as 12 naval frigates to patrol the South Pacific. In February 1994 the USA announced its decision to resume senior-level contacts with New Zealand. In July 1996 Australia and the USA upgraded their defence alliance. In July 2000 the US Secretary of Defense made an official visit to Australia, following which he re-emphasized the importance of bilateral defence co-operation. Prime Minister John Howard condemned the terrorist attacks against the USA in September 2001 and subsequently expressed his support for the USA's 'war on terror'. In early 2003 some 2,000 Australian troops were deployed to the Middle East in preparation for the US-led military campaign to oust the regime of Saddam Hussain in Iraq. During a visit to Australia by US President George W. Bush in October, the US leader commended Australia for its support. Relations between Australia and the USA were further strengthened with the conclusion of a free trade agreement, which entered into force in January 2005.

In March 2008 Kevin Rudd's major international tour began with a visit to the USA. President George W. Bush expressed his understanding of the new Australian administration's decision to withdraw combat troops from Iraq. Rudd announced that Australia would campaign to secure a two-year term on the UN Security Council from 2013, by which time it would be more than 25 years since the country had last held a non-permanent seat.

In accordance with the Prime Minister's electoral pledge, 500 Australian combat troops were duly withdrawn from southern Iraq on 1 June 2008, when they were replaced by US forces; however, more than 300 military personnel remained in the country in non-combat roles, which included guarding the Australian embassy in Baghdad. Australia's full, formal withdrawal from Iraq took place at the end of July 2009. The Australian military involvement in Afghanistan continued, with 1,550 personnel deployed there in January 2012, including task forces for mentoring and reconstruction.

During 2010 Bush's successor as US President, Barack Obama, was twice obliged to postpone a planned visit to Australia (in March and again in June), owing to domestic political crises. In November, however, the US Secretary of State, Hillary Clinton, paid a visit to Australia, during which she praised Australia's role in maintaining stability in the Asia-Pacific region; discussions were held on, among other topics, increased access to Australian ports and facilities by US military forces, and on the possible establishment in Australia of a joint centre for monitoring space traffic in the southern hemisphere. Prime Minister Gillard undertook her first official visit to the USA in March 2011. The situation in Libya, the continuing conflict in Afghanistan, climate change and trade matters were among the issues discussed. President Obama paid a visit to Australia in November, when the two leaders celebrated the 60th anniversary of the ANZUS pact and announced that 2,500 US military personnel were to be permanently stationed in Darwin, in the Northern Territory, as part of the expansion of the USA's role as a 'Pacific power'.

Owing to Australian opposition to French testing of nuclear weapons at Mururoa Atoll (French Polynesia) in the South Pacific Ocean, a ban on uranium sales to France was introduced in 1983. However, in August 1986 the Government announced its decision to resume uranium exports. In December Australia ratified a treaty declaring the South Pacific area a nuclear-free zone. France's decision, in April 1992, to suspend its nuclear-testing programme was welcomed by Australia. In June 1995, however, the French President's announcement that the programme was to be resumed provoked outrage throughout the Pacific region. The Australian ambassador to France was recalled, and the French consulate in Perth was destroyed in an arson attack. Further widespread protests followed the first of the new series of tests in September. Australia's relations with the United Kingdom were strained by the British Government's refusal to join the condemnation of France's policy. The final test was conducted in January 1996. On an official visit to Paris in September, the Australian Minister for Foreign Affairs adopted a conciliatory stance (which drew much criticism from anti-nuclear groups). A ban on new contracts for the supply of uranium to France, imposed in September 1995, was removed in October 1996. Meanwhile, Australia remained committed to achieving the elimination of all nuclear testing. In August, following a veto of the draft text by India and Iran at the UN Conference on Disarmament in Geneva, Switzerland, Australia took the initiative in leading an international effort to secure the passage of the Comprehensive Test Ban Treaty. In an unusual procedure, the Treaty was referred to the UN General Assembly, which voted overwhelmingly in its favour in September.

In January 2008 the new Australian Government reinstated the ban on sales of uranium to India, owing to that country's continued refusal to sign the Treaty on the Non-Proliferation of Nuclear Weapons (NPT). Australia's long-standing ban had been removed by the Howard administration in August of the previous year. Nevertheless, in September 2008 Australia was one of 45 supplier nations that, reportedly under pressure from the USA, agreed to a unique provision granting India the right to conduct trade in civilian nuclear fuel and technology. In December 2011 the Australian Government agreed to remove the ban on uranium exports to India on the grounds that, although not a signatory of the NPT, India had undertaken to observe limits on the use of nuclear power similar to those imposed by the treaty. Meanwhile, the Indian Government criticized the Rudd administration for what it perceived as an inadequate response to numerous apparently racist attacks on Indian students in Australia in 2009, and the fatal stabbing of an Indian student in Melbourne in January 2010 further exacerbated relations.

In July 2008 Pope Benedict XVI embarked upon a 10-day visit to Australia. The Pope participated with more than 400,000 pilgrims in World Youth Day celebrations in Sydney, culminating in an open-air papal mass. A major focus of the visit was Benedict XVI's public apology for the sexual abuse perpetrated by Catholic clergy in Australia and his affirmation that offenders should be brought to justice.

CONSTITUTION AND GOVERNMENT

Australia comprises six states and three territories. Executive power is vested in the British monarch and exercised by the monarch's appointed representative, the Governor-General, who normally acts on the advice of the Federal Executive Council (the Ministry), led by the Prime Minister. The Governor-General officially appoints the Prime Minister and, on the latter's recommendation, other Ministers.

Legislative power is vested in the Federal Parliament. This consists of the monarch, represented by the Governor-General, and two chambers elected by universal adult suffrage (voting is compulsory). The Senate has 76 members (12 from each state and two each from the Northern Territory and the Australian Capital Territory), who are elected by a system of proportional representation for six years when representing a state, with half the seats renewable every three years, and for a term of three years when representing a territory. The House of Representatives has 150 members, elected for three years (subject to dissolution) from single-member constituencies. The Federal Executive Council is responsible to Parliament.

Each state has a Governor, representing the monarch, and its own legislative, executive and judicial system. The state governments are essentially autonomous, but certain powers are placed under the jurisdiction of the Federal Government. All states except Queensland have an upper house (the Legislative Council) and a lower house (the Legislative Assembly or House of Assembly). The chief ministers of the states are known as Premiers, as distinct from the Federal Prime Minister. The Northern Territory (self-governing since 1978) and the Australian Capital Territory (self-governing since 1988) have unicameral legislatures, and each has a government led by a Chief Minister. The Jervis Bay Territory is not self-governing.

REGIONAL AND INTERNATIONAL CO-OPERATION

Australia is a member of the Asian Development Bank (ADB, see p. 210), the Pacific Islands Forum (see p. 416), the Pacific Community (see p. 413) and the Colombo Plan (see p. 449). In 1989 Australia played a major role in the creation of Asia-Pacific Economic Cooperation (APEC, see p. 204), a grouping that aimed to promote economic development in the region. Australia is a member of the UN's Economic and Social Commission for Asia and the Pacific (ESCAP, see p. 40).

Australia was a founder member of the UN in 1945. As a contracting party to the General Agreement on Tariffs and Trade, Australia joined the World Trade Organization (WTO, see p. 433) on its establishment in 1995. The country participates in the Group of 20 (G20) industrial nations and in the Group of 77 (G77, see p. 450) developing countries. Australia is also a member of the Organisation for Economic Co-operation and Development (OECD, see p. 379), the Cairns Group (see p. 504) of agricultural exporters and the International Grains Council (see p. 446).

ECONOMIC AFFAIRS

In 2009, according to estimates by the World Bank, Australia's gross national income (GNI), measured at average 2007–09 prices, was US $956,912m., equivalent to US $43,590 per head (or US $38,380 per head on an international purchasing-power parity basis). During 2001–10, it was estimated, the population increased at an average annual rate of 1.6%, while gross domestic product (GDP) per head increased, in real terms, by an average of 1.7% during 2001–09. Overall GDP increased, in real terms, at an average annual rate of 3.2% in 2001–09. GDP increased by 1.3% in 2009.

Agriculture (including forestry, hunting and fishing) contributed 2.8% of GDP in 2010/11. The sector engaged 3.2% of the employed labour force (excluding undefined activities) in 2008. In the first decade of the 21st century agricultural production was severely affected by drought conditions, although rainfall in most of the country was significantly above average in 2010–11, with flooding causing damage to crops. The principal crops are wheat, fruit, sugar and cotton. Wheat production reached 22.1m. metric tons in 2010. Australia is the world's leading producer of wool. Export earnings from wool and sheepskins totalled $A3,427m. in 2010/11. Australia has become one of the world's largest exporters of wine. The value of wine exports was $A2,167m. in the 12 months to June 2010. Meat production is also important; beef is Australia's leading meat export. According to World Bank estimates, agricultural GDP decreased at an average annual rate of 0.7% in 2001–08, although the sector's GDP increased by an estimated 6.9% in 2008.

Industry (comprising mining, manufacturing, construction and utilities) employed 21.6% of the working population (excluding activities not defined) in 2008, and provided 27.8% of GDP in 2010/11. Industrial GDP increased at an average rate of 3.0% per year between 2001 and 2008, according to World Bank estimates, rising by 3.6% in 2008.

The mining sector employed 1.2% of the working population (excluding activities not defined) in 2008, and contributed 9.5% of GDP in 2010/11. Australia is one of the world's leading exporters of coal. Production of black coal reached 471m. metric tons in 2009/10. Earnings from coal, coke and briquettes in 2010/11 reached $A44,042m., accounting for 17.9% of total export receipts in that year. Other principal minerals extracted are iron ore, gold, silver and magnesite. Bauxite, zinc, copper, titanium, nickel, tin, lead, zirconium and diamonds are also mined. Production of crude petroleum reached 25,572m. litres in 2009/10. The Gorgon gas project, off the north-western coast, is being developed in collaboration with various overseas companies. Upon completion, the liquefied natural gas (LNG) plant was expected to reach an annual production capacity of 15m. tons of LNG. Between 2001 and 2010, according to the UN, the GDP of the mining sector combined with that of utilities increased at an average annual rate of 2.2%.

Manufacturing contributed 8.3% of GDP in 2010/11. The sector employed 10.3% of the working population (excluding undefined activities) in 2008. The principal branches of manufacturing include food, beverages and tobacco, equipment and machinery, chemical products and metal products. According to World Bank estimates, the manufacturing sector's GDP grew at an average annual rate of 1.4% between 2001 and 2008; manufacturing GDP increased by 3.3% in 2008.

Construction contributed 7.7% of GDP in 2010/11. The sector employed 9.2% of the working population (excluding undefined activities) in 2008. Between 2001 and 2010, according to the UN, the GDP of the construction sector increased at an average annual rate of 5.8%.

Energy is derived principally from coal and natural gas. Coal accounted for 76.9% and natural gas for 15.0% of electricity production in 2008. Imports of fuels accounted for 13.7% of total import costs in 2010.

The services sector provided 69.4% of GDP in 2010/11, and engaged 75.1% of the employed labour force (excluding activities not defined) in 2008. The tourism industry has become a major source of foreign exchange earnings. The number of visitor arrivals was estimated to have declined by 0.2% in 2011, to 5,875,300. Receipts from international tourism reached an estimated $A23,681m. in 2010/11. According to World Bank estimates, the GDP of the services sector increased at an average annual rate of 3.8% between 2001 and 2008, rising by 4.0% in 2008.

In 2010 Australia recorded a visible trade surplus of US $18,180m., while there was a deficit of US $31,990m. on the current account of the balance of payments. In 2010 the People's Republic of China remained the principal source of imports, supplying 18.7%, followed by the USA, Japan, Thailand and Singapore. China was also the principal market for exports in 2010 (purchasing 25.3%). Other major export markets were Japan, the Republic of Korea, India, the USA, Taiwan, the United Kingdom and New Zealand. The principal exports in 2010 included iron ore, coal, petroleum gases and crude petroleum oils, and non-monetary gold. The principal imports included crude petroleum oils and cars.

For the fourth consecutive year a budgetary shortfall was projected for 2011/12, when the deficit was expected to amount to $A15,856m. A return to surplus was forecast for 2012/13, with projected expenditure of $A380,500m. and revenue of $A383,100m. General government gross debt totalled $A276,144m. in 2010, equivalent to 20.5% of GDP. At the end of September 2011 Australia's net foreign debt stood at $A740,504m. (equivalent to 52.1% of GDP), some 75% of which was incurred by the private sector. The rate of unemployment was estimated at 5.2% of the labour force in December 2011. According to ILO estimates, the annual rate of inflation averaged 2.8% in 2001–10. Consumer prices rose by 2.8% in 2010.

Although the Australian economy contracted in the final quarter of 2008, thereafter it proved able to withstand the effects of the global financial crisis and avoid recession. A significant factor was sustained demand from China, a major purchaser of Australian mineral commodities, particularly coal and iron ore. Australia's resilience was also attributed to the Government's fiscal stimulus programmes in 2008 and 2009, providing support for lower-income families and investment in infrastructure. From October 2009, as the Australian economy strengthened, the Reserve Bank of Australia, the central bank, implemented several increases in the official interest rate, in order to curb inflation, and by November 2010 the rate stood at 4.75% (a high level compared with that of most developed economies), at which it remained for most of 2011. Damage caused in early 2011 to the agricultural and mining sectors by severe flooding and by Cyclone Yasi resulted in a temporary contraction in GDP, but for the year as a whole GDP was forecast to increase by 2%, according to the IMF. Australia's unprecedented mining 'boom' contrasted with less favourable conditions for manufacturing and agriculture. These sectors were disadvantaged by the strength of the Australian dollar, which made exports less competitive and also adversely affected tourism by making the country a more expensive destination. The Reserve Bank reduced the official interest rate to 4.5% in November 2011 and to 4.25% in December, with the aim of stimulating economic growth by encouraging domestic spending, while limiting inflation to a level of 2%–3% in 2012 and 2013. During 2011 unemployment remained relatively low, at 5.2% in December, and a shortage of skilled labour exerted pressure on wage costs. The federal budget for 2011/12 included extra support for training workers and investment in infrastructure, while making reductions in other areas of expenditure with the aim of returning the budget to surplus by 2012/13. An increase of 3.5% in GDP was predicted by the IMF for 2012. Australia remained vulnerable, however, to any reduction in growth among the Asian countries that formed the principal market for its mineral exports, and was also likely to be affected by any slowing in global recovery caused by the sovereign debt crisis in Europe and other unpredictable external factors.

PUBLIC HOLIDAYS*

2013: 1 January (New Year's Day), 28 January (for Australia Day), 29 March–1 April (Easter), 25 April (Anzac Day), 10 June (Queen's Official Birthday, except Western Australia), 25–26 December (Christmas).

* National holidays only. Some states observe these holidays on different days. There are also numerous individual state holidays.

Statistical Survey

Source (unless otherwise stated): Australian Bureau of Statistics, POB 10, Belconnen, ACT 2616; tel. (2) 6252-7983; fax (2) 6251-6009; internet www.abs.gov.au.

Area and Population

AREA, POPULATION AND DENSITY

Area (sq km)	7,692,024*
Population (census results)†	
7 August 2001	18,769,249
8 August 2006	
Males	9,799,252
Females	10,056,036
Total	19,855,288
Population (official estimate at 31 December)‡	
2008	21,730,585
2009§	22,151,909
2010§	22,477,378
Density (per sq km) at 31 December 2010§	2.9

* 2,969,907 sq miles; including Jervis Bay Territory.

† Population is *de jure*.

‡ Including Jervis Bay Territory, Christmas Island and the Cocos (Keeling) Islands.

§ Preliminary.

POPULATION BY AGE AND SEX

(estimated population at 30 June 2010, preliminary)

	Males	Females	Total
0–14	2,164,335	2,054,089	4,218,424
15–64	7,562,087	7,513,295	15,075,382
65 and over	1,375,224	1,630,745	3,005,969
Total	11,101,646	11,198,129	22,299,775

STATES AND TERRITORIES

(estimated population at 31 December 2010, preliminary)

	Area (sq km)	Population	Density (per sq km)
New South Wales (NSW)	800,642	7,272,158	9.1
Victoria	227,416	5,585,566	24.6
Queensland	1,730,648	4,548,661	2.6
South Australia	983,482	1,650,377	1.7
Western Australia	2,529,875	2,317,064	0.9
Tasmania	68,401	509,292	7.4
Northern Territory	1,349,129	229,874	0.2
Australian Capital Territory (ACT)	2,358	361,914	153.5
Other territories*	73	2,472	—
Total	7,692,024	22,477,378	2.9

* Area refers to Jervis Bay Territory only, but population also includes data for Christmas Island and the Cocos (Keeling) Islands.

PRINCIPAL TOWNS

(estimated population at 30 June 2010, preliminary)*

Sydney (capital of NSW)	4,575,532	Wollongong	292,190
Melbourne (capital of Victoria)	4,077,036	Sunshine Coast	251,081
Brisbane (capital of Queensland)	2,043,185	Hobart (capital of Tasmania)	214,705
Perth (capital of W Australia)	1,696,065	Geelong	178,650
Adelaide (capital of S Australia)	1,203,186	Townsville	172,316
Gold Coast-Tweed	591,473	Cairns	150,920
Newcastle	546,788	Toowoomba	131,258
Canberra (national capital)	358,222	Darwin (capital of N Territory)	127,532

* Figures refer to metropolitan areas, each of which normally comprises a municipality and contiguous urban areas.

BIRTHS, MARRIAGES AND DEATHS*

	Registered live births		Registered marriages		Registered deaths	
	Number	Rate (per 1,000)	Number	Rate (per 1,000)	Number	Rate (per 1,000)
2003	251,161	12.6	106,394	5.3	132,292	6.5
2004	254,246	12.6	110,958	5.5	132,508	6.3
2005	259,791	12.7	109,323	5.4	130,714	6.0
2006	265,949	12.8	114,222	5.5	133,739	6.0
2007	285,213	13.6	116,322	5.5	137,854	6.0
2008	296,621	13.8	118,756	5.5	143,946	6.1
2009	295,738	13.5	120,118	5.5	140,760	5.8
2010	297,903	13.4	121,176	5.4	143,473	5.7

* Data are tabulated by year of registration rather than by year of occurrence.

Life expectancy (years at birth, WHO estimates): 82 (males 80; females 84) in 2009 (Source: WHO, *World Health Statistics*).

IMMIGRATION AND EMIGRATION

(year ending 30 June)*

	2007/08	2008/09	2009/10
Permanent immigrants	149,365	158,021	140,610
Permanent emigrants	76,923	81,018	86,277

* Figures refer to persons intending to settle in Australia, or Australian residents intending to settle abroad.

ECONOMICALLY ACTIVE POPULATION

(annual averages, '000 persons aged 15 years and over, excluding armed forces)

	2006	2007	2008
Agriculture, hunting and forestry	340.2	339.7	343.5
Fishing	10.1	11.4	11.2
Mining and quarrying	116.7	119.0	133.0
Manufacturing	1,074.3	1,092.2	1,102.1
Electricity, gas and water	85.3	86.2	98.5
Construction	914.4	946.3	987.0
Wholesale and retail trade; repair of motor vehicles, motorcycles and personal and household goods	1,785.3	1,823.4	1,847.1
Hotels and restaurants	667.0	704.4	708.3
Transport, storage and communications	641.2	678.6	695.6
Financial intermediation	387.1	407.1	401.5
Real estate, renting and business activities	1,279.6	1,291.8	1,326.3
Public administration and defence; compulsory social security	626.0	641.6	644.5
Education	741.7	771.0	807.5
Health and social work	1,078.1	1,097.6	1,129.6
Other community, social and personal service activities	470.7	500.1	502.5
Private households with employed persons	0.5	1.8	2.1
Total employed	10,218.3	10,512.3	10,740.5
Unemployed	517.7	487.5	470.9
Total labour force	10,736.0	10,999.8	11,211.4
Males	5,883.1	6,015.6	6,116.1
Females	4,852.9	4,984.1	5,095.3

Source: ILO.

Health and Welfare

KEY INDICATORS

Total fertility rate (children per woman, 2009)	1.8
Under-5 mortality rate (per 1,000 live births, 2009)	5
HIV/AIDS (% of persons aged 15–49, 2009)	0.1
Physicians (per 1,000 head, 2001)	2.5
Hospital beds (per 1,000 head, 2005)	4.0
Health expenditure (2008): US $ per head (PPP)	3,365
Health expenditure (2008): % of GDP	8.5
Health expenditure (2008): public (% of total)	65.4
Total carbon dioxide emissions ('000 metric tons, 2007)	373,739.0
Carbon dioxide emissions per head (metric tons, 2007)	17.7
Human Development Index (2011): ranking	2
Human Development Index (2011): value	0.929

For sources and definitions, see explanatory note on p. vi.

Agriculture

PRINCIPAL CROPS
('000 metric tons)

	2008	2009	2010
Wheat	21,420.2	21,656.0	22,138.0
Rice, paddy	176.0	652.0	206.0
Barley	7,996.5	7,909.0	7,294.0
Maize	387.0	375.7	328.0
Oats	1,160.0	1,180.0	1,374.0
Millet	37.0*	38.0†	36.9†
Sorghum	3,789.9	2,691.8	1,598.0
Triticale (wheat-rye hybrid)	362.8	545.0	502.0
Potatoes	1,400.2	1,178.5	1,278.1
Sugar cane	32,621.1	30,284.0	31,457.0
Beans, dry	45.5	50.6	43.5
Broad beans, dry	217.0	192.0	202.3†
Peas, dry	238.1	356.0	280.0
Chick-peas	442.5	445.0	602.0
Lentils	64.2	143.0	140.0
Lupins	708.0	614.0	629.0
Soybeans (Soya beans)	35.0	80.1	59.6
Sunflower seed	73.0	55.3	41.0
Rapeseed	1,844.2	1,920.0	2,180.6†
Seed cotton	320.6	795.0	939.0
Lettuce and chicory	168.7	164.5	166.1†
Tomatoes	381.8	440.1	471.9
Cauliflower and broccoli	64.3	70.3	70.9†
Pumpkins, squash and gourds	114.4	103.7	104.7†
Onions, dry	254.4	283.8	256.0
Peas, green	39.3	41.5	41.9†
Carrots and turnips	272.6	263.5	267.4
Watermelons	152.1	131.1	132.3†
Cantaloupes and other melons	66.9	75.6	76.3†
Bananas	207.1	270.4	302.2
Oranges	409.3	347.7	391.3
Tangerines, mandarins, clementines and satsumas	94.4	90.3	91.0
Apples	265.5	295.1	264.4
Pears	130.5	120.4	95.1
Peaches and nectarines	128.0†	117.2	113.7†
Grapes	1,956.8	1,797.0	1,684.4
Pineapples	162.0†	157.7	153.0†

* Unofficial figure.
† FAO estimate.

Aggregate production ('000 metric tons, may include official, semi-official or estimated data): Total cereals 35,211.1 in 2008, 34,500.6 in 2009, 33,515.0 in 2010; Total roots and tubers 1,438.6 in 2008, 1,221.0 in 2009, 1,324.1 in 2010; Total vegetables (incl. melons) 1,880.8 in 2008, 1,924.4 in 2009, 1,943.2 in 2010; Total fruits (excl. melons) 3,591.5 in 2008, 3,413.1 in 2009, 3,312.7 in 2010.

Source: FAO.

LIVESTOCK
('000 head at 30 June)

	2008	2009	2010
Horses	260.0*	256.4	256.4*
Cattle	27,321.0	27,906.8	26,733.0
Pigs	2,411.5	2,301.7	2,289.3
Sheep	79,937.6	72,739.7	68,085.5
Goats*	3,200.0	4,500.0	4,500.0
Chickens	88,629	95,409	83,024
Ducks	1,200*	1,473	1,473*
Turkeys	1,500*	1,203	1,950*

* FAO estimate(s).

Source: FAO.

LIVESTOCK PRODUCTS
('000 metric tons)

	2008	2009	2010
Cattle meat	2,131.9	2,124.0	2,108.3
Sheep meat	659.5	653.1	555.6
Goat meat*	17.5	25.0	25.0
Pig meat	360.3	321.2	335.8
Horse meat*	25.8	25.8	25.8
Chicken meat	800.2	831.3	881.0
Duck meat*	14.9	18.5	19.6
Turkey meat*	23.5	22.3	22.4
Cows' milk	9,223.0	9,388.0	9,023.0
Hen eggs	160.0*	159.3	174.0
Honey*	17.1	16.6	16.2
Wool, greasy	458.7	420.3	382.3

* FAO estimate(s).

Note: Figures for meat and milk refer to the 12 months ending 30 June of the year stated.

Source: FAO.

Forestry

ROUNDWOOD REMOVALS
('000 cubic metres, excl. bark)

	2007	2008	2009
Sawlogs, veneer logs and logs for sleepers	12,530	12,654	11,195
Pulpwood	13,815	14,908	13,549
Other industrial wood	738	648	560
Fuel wood	5,181	5,059	4,828
Total	32,264	33,269	30,132

2010: Production assumed to be unchanged from 2009 (FAO estimates).

Source: FAO.

SAWNWOOD PRODUCTION
('000 cubic metres, incl. railway sleepers)

	2007	2008	2009
Coniferous (softwood)	3,929	4,263	3,740
Broadleaved (hardwood)	1,135	1,109	990
Total	5,064	5,372	4,730

2010: Production assumed to be unchanged from 2009 (FAO estimates).

Source: FAO.

Fishing

('000 metric tons, live weight, year ending 30 June)

	2006/07	2007/08	2008/09
Capture	188.1	181.8	172.8
Blue grenadier	3.9	3.6	2.3
Clupeoids	33.0	33.6	31.5
Australian spiny lobster	8.7	9.0	7.6
Penaeus shrimps	9.2	10.2	10.0
Scallops	10.6	10.3	7.5
Aquaculture*	55.8	58.9	64.5
Atlantic salmon	25.3	25.7	29.6
Total catch*	243.9	240.7	237.3

* FAO estimates.

Note: Figures exclude aquatic plants ('000 metric tons, capture only): 2.2 in 2006/07; 1.9 in 2007/08; 1.9 in 2008/09 (FAO estimate). Also excluded are crocodiles, recorded by number rather than by weight. The number of estuarine crocodiles caught was: 21,314 in 2006/07; 28,626 in 2007/08; 26,990 in 2008/09. Also excluded are whales, recorded by number rather than weight. The number of Baleen whales caught was: 1 in 2006/07; 2 in 2007/08–2008/09. The number of toothed whales (incl. dolphins) caught was: 66 in 2006/07; 45 in 2007/08; 33 in 2008/09. Also excluded are pearl oyster shells (metric tons, estimates): 200 each year in 2006/07–2008/09.

Source: FAO.

Mining

(year ending 30 June, '000 metric tons, unless otherwise indicated)

	2007/08	2008/09	2009/10
Black coal	421,181	446,174	471,089
Brown coal*	66,000	68,000	69,000
Crude petroleum (million litres)	25,789	26,950	25,572
Natural gas (million cu metres)	39,283	41,499	43,767
Iron ore: gross weight*	324,693	353,163	423,393
Copper ore*†	863	890	819
Nickel ore*†	190	185	160
Bauxite: gross weight	63,463	64,055	67,810
Bauxite: alumina content	19,359	19,597	20,057
Lead ore*†	641	596	617
Zinc ore*†	1,571	1,411	1,362
Tin ore (metric tons)*†	1,631	4,045	19,829
Manganese ore (metallurgical): gross weight*	5,412	3,730	5,795
Ilmenite*	2,208	1,932	1,394
Leucoxene*	157	117	123
Rutile*	327	285	361
Zirconium concentrates*	562	485	408
Silver (metric tons)*†	1,867	1,764	1,809
Uranium (metric tons)†	10,114	10,311	7,156
Gold (metric tons)*†	230	218	240
Salt (unrefined)*†‡	11,243	11,311	11,745
Diamonds ('000 carats, unsorted)	16,528	15,169	11,138

* Estimated production.

† Figures refer to the metal content of ores and concentrates.

‡ Excludes production in Victoria.

Source: Australian Bureau of Agricultural and Resource Economics, *Australian Mineral Statistics* and *Australian Commodity Statistics*.

Industry

SELECTED PRODUCTS

(year ending 30 June, '000 metric tons, unless otherwise indicated)

	2007/08	2008/09	2009/10
Raw steel	8,151	5,568	6,886
Aluminium—unwrought*	1,964	1,974	1,920
Copper—unwrought*	444	499	395
Lead—unwrought*	203	213	189
Zinc—unwrought*	507	506	515
Automotive gasoline (million litres)	17,079	17,159	16,771
Fuel oil (million litres)	979	872	846
Diesel-automotive oil (million litres)	12,177	12,231	11,720
Aviation turbine fuel (million litres)	5,182	5,494	5,341

* Primary refined metal only.

Pig Iron ('000 metric tons): 6,765 in 2005/06.

Tin (unwrought, '000 metric tons): 321 in 2006/07.

Sources: mainly Australian Bureau of Agricultural and Resource Economics, *Australian Mineral Statistics*, *Australian Commodity Statistics* and *Energy in Australia*.

Finance

CURRENCY AND EXCHANGE RATES

Monetary Units

100 cents = 1 Australian dollar ($A).

Sterling, US Dollar and Euro Equivalents (30 December 2011)

£1 sterling = $A1.522;
US $1 = $A0.985;
€1 = $A1.274;
$A100 = £65.69 = US $101.6 = €78.49.

Average Exchange Rate (Australian dollars per US $)

2009 1.2822
2010 1.0902
2011 0.9718

COMMONWEALTH GOVERNMENT BUDGET

($A million, year ending 30 June)

Revenue	2009/10	2010/11*	2011/12*
Tax revenue	268,000	290,298	329,247
Income taxes	187,016	206,040	240,630
Individuals	122,820	136,330	150,890
Taxes on fringe benefits	3,523	3,670	3,760
Superannuation taxation	6,182	7,220	9,330
Companies	53,193	57,880	74,600
Petroleum resource rent tax	1,297	940	2,050
Sales taxes	47,800	49,400	51,900
Excise and customs	30,295	32,100	33,850
Excise duty revenue	24,547	26,060	26,330
Other taxes	2,889	2,758	2,867
Non-tax revenue	24,767	20,480	20,714
Total	292,767	310,779	349,961

Expenditure	2009/10	2010/11*	2011/12*
Defence	20,150	20,136	21,277
Education	34,889	32,555	29,938
Health	51,426	57,240	59,858
Social security and welfare	109,197	116,739	121,907
Other services	44,090	38,204	40,009
General purpose inter-governmental transactions	47,157	48,919	51,152
General public services	19,203	21,239	20,887
Public-debt interest	6,303	9,286	11,632
Total (incl. others)	339,239	350,803	365,817

* Budget estimates.

Source: Government of Australia.

OFFICIAL RESERVES
(US $ million at 31 December)

	2008	2009	2010
Gold (national valuation)	2,233	2,792	3,608
IMF special drawing rights	174	4,856	4,764
Reserve position in IMF	649	1,092	1,102
Foreign exchange	29,867	33,002	32,793
Total	32,923	41,742	42,267

Source: IMF, *International Financial Statistics.*

MONEY SUPPLY
($A million at 31 December)

	2008	2009	2010
Currency outside banks	45,063	46,056	47,901
Demand deposits at trading and savings banks	312,367	326,830	367,023
Total money (incl. others)	357,864	372,907	414,973

Source: IMF, *International Financial Statistics.*

COST OF LIVING
(Consumer Price Index*; base 2000 = 100)

	2006	2007	2008
Food	129.2	132.3	138.5
Clothing	98.9	99.8	100.0
Rent†	116.5	122.9	132.4
Electricity, gas and other fuels	129.4	135.4	148.2
All items (incl. others)	120.2	123.1	128.3

* Weighted average of eight capital cities.

† Including expenditure on maintenance and repairs of dwellings; excluding mortgage interest charges and including house purchase and utilities.

2009: Food 143.6; All items (incl. others) 130.7.

2010: Food 145.8; All items (incl. others) 134.4.

Source: ILO.

NATIONAL ACCOUNTS
($A million, current prices, year ending 30 June)

National Income and Product

	2008/09	2009/10	2010/11
Compensation of employees	596,098	618,137	665,951
Gross operating surplus	435,943	443,829	486,180
Gross mixed income	100,966	103,549	109,944
Total factor incomes	1,133,007	1,165,515	1,262,075
Taxes, less subsidies, on production and imports	119,211	127,865	134,699
Statistical discrepancy	—	—	4,394
GDP in market prices	1,252,218	1,293,380	1,401,168
Net primary incomes from abroad	–46,078	–47,816	–52,437
Statistical discrepancy	—	—	–4,394
Gross national income	1,206,140	1,245,564	1,344,337
Current taxes on income, wealth, etc.	1,485	1,216	1,310
Other current transfers (net)	–2,850	–3,172	–3,321
Gross disposable income	1,204,775	1,243,608	1,342,326

Expenditure on the Gross Domestic Product

	2008/09	2009/10	2010/11
Government final consumption expenditure	220,597	233,697	248,997
Private final consumption expenditure	676,214	712,181	756,144
Gross fixed capital formation	351,111	356,033	371,420
Change in inventories	–3,058	–3,913	5,465
Total domestic expenditure	1,244,864	1,298,000	1,382,026
Exports of goods and services	284,571	253,762	297,507
Less Imports of goods and services	277,218	258,383	276,631
Statistical discrepancy	—	—	–1,733
GDP in market prices	1,252,218	1,293,380	1,401,168

Gross Domestic Product by Economic Activity

	2008/09	2009/10	2010/11
Agriculture, hunting, forestry and fishing	29,043	28,764	35,803
Mining and quarrying	114,382	96,105	122,919
Manufacturing	109,117	107,707	107,965
Electricity, gas and water	27,154	28,623	30,786
Construction	89,641	95,804	99,553
Wholesale and retail trade	110,196	113,386	117,309
Hotels and restaurants	28,254	29,474	31,421
Transport, storage and communications	102,289	107,215	114,193
Finance and insurance	121,272	125,399	137,187
Rental, hiring and real estate services	25,719	27,260	29,707
Professional, scientific and technical services	74,344	81,043	86,302
Ownership of dwellings	93,475	103,271	109,606
Public administration and defence	60,608	64,117	68,008
Education	53,286	57,546	61,069
Health and community services	68,012	72,627	79,980
Cultural and recreational services	10,448	10,911	11,253
Administrative and support services	29,010	30,246	32,317
Personal and other services	22,625	23,548	23,906
Gross value added at basic prices	1,168,875	1,203,046	1,299,285
Taxes, less subsidies, on products	83,343	90,334	97,488
Statistical discrepancy	—	—	4,395
GDP in market prices	1,252,218	1,293,380	1,401,168

BALANCE OF PAYMENTS
(US $ million)

	2008	2009	2010
Exports of goods f.o.b.	189,057	154,788	212,850
Imports of goods f.o.b.	–193,972	–159,003	–194,670
Trade balance	–4,915	–4,215	18,180
Exports of services	45,240	41,589	48,490
Imports of services	–48,338	–42,121	–51,470
Balance on goods and services	–8,013	–4,747	15,200
Other income received	37,320	27,923	38,587
Other income paid	–76,719	–65,998	–84,390
Balance on goods, services and income	–47,412	–42,822	–30,603
Current transfers received	4,431	5,069	6,063
Current transfers paid	–4,805	–6,138	–7,451
Current balance	–47,786	–43,891	–31,990
Capital account (net)	1,994	–313	–213
Direct investment abroad	–38,110	–15,721	–24,526
Direct investment from abroad	47,281	27,246	30,576
Portfolio investment assets	3,035	–70,990	–42,407
Portfolio investment liabilities	30,397	145,696	109,561
Financial derivatives assets	2,289	39,021	28,039
Financial derivatives liabilities	–2,167	–45,407	–27,723
Other investment assets	–55,611	–27,787	–13,544
Other investment liabilities	62,000	2,122	–27,035
Net errors and omissions	370	–1,426	–303
Overall balance	3,692	8,550	434

Source: IMF, *International Financial Statistics.*

External Trade

PRINCIPAL COMMODITIES
(distribution by HS, US $ million)

Imports c.i.f.	2008	2009	2010
Mineral fuels, oils, distillation products, etc.	30,098	20,136	25,926
Crude petroleum oils	15,146	9,760	14,576
Petroleum oils, not crude	12,756	8,142	8,962
Pharmaceutical products	6,726	7,089	8,280
Pearls, precious stones, metals, coins, etc.	9,942	8,839	8,043
Gold, unwrought, or in semi-manufactured forms	8,252	7,286	6,330
Nuclear reactors, boilers, machinery, etc.	27,864	24,977	28,104
Automatic data processing machines; optical readers, etc.	4,933	4,429	5,862
Electrical, electronic equipment	19,032	17,754	20,265
Vehicles other than railway, tramway	22,979	16,471	24,028
Cars (incl. station wagons)	12,507	9,253	14,300
Trucks, motor vehicles for the transport of goods	5,317	3,392	5,352
Optical, photo, technical, medical, etc. apparatus	6,116	5,733	6,557
Total (incl. others)	191,584	158,941	188,741

Exports f.o.b.	2008	2009	2010
Meat and edible meat offal	5,986	5,141	5,958
Ores, slag and ash	35,264	31,195	55,840
Iron ores and concentrates; including roasted iron pyrites	25,379	23,573	44,290
Mineral fuels, oils, distillation products, etc.	59,868	45,372	59,753
Coal; briquettes, ovoids and similar solid fuels manufactured from coal	39,253	30,942	38,572
Crude petroleum oils	8,709	5,629	9,385
Petroleum gases	8,783	6,771	9,452
Inorganic chemicals, precious metal compounds, isotopes	5,910	4,064	5,067
Aluminium oxide (incl. artificial corundum); aluminium hydroxide	5,373	3,732	4,687
Pearls, precious stones, metals, coins, etc.	12,965	12,667	13,909
Gold, unwrought, or in semi-manufactured forms	12,030	11,760	12,816
Aluminium and articles thereof	5,221	3,465	4,367
Unwrought aluminium	4,415	2,881	3,750
Nuclear reactors, boilers, machinery, etc.	5,019	4,233	5,044
Total (incl. others)	186,853	153,767	206,705

Source: Trade Map-Trade Competitiveness Map, International Trade Centre, www.intracen.org/marketanalysis.

PRINCIPAL TRADING PARTNERS
(US $ million)

Imports c.i.f.	2008	2009	2010
Canada	2,203	1,478	1,561
China, People's Republic	29,896	28,351	35,261
France	4,241	3,239	3,434
Germany	9,624	8,411	9,424
India	1,553	1,609	1,767
Indonesia	4,449	3,612	4,773
Ireland	1,895	1,852	2,075
Italy	4,523	3,873	4,395
Japan	17,155	13,223	16,327
Korea, Republic	5,450	5,252	6,416
Malaysia	7,595	5,985	8,196
New Zealand	6,447	5,201	6,469
Papua New Guinea	2,478	2,313	2,711
Singapore	13,721	8,853	9,597
Sweden	2,204	1,698	1,967
Switzerland	1,920	1,952	1,978
Taiwan	3,746	2,633	3,252
Thailand	8,608	9,213	9,887
United Arab Emirates	1,964	1,701	2,003
United Kingdom	8,441	4,908	5,213
USA	23,014	18,005	20,947
Viet Nam	4,399	2,471	2,808
Total (incl. others)	191,584	158,941	188,741

Exports f.o.b.	2008	2009	2010
China, People's Republic	27,225	33,360	52,314
Hong Kong	2,528	2,255	2,824
India	11,380	11,354	14,694
Indonesia	3,587	3,247	4,021
Japan	42,732	29,988	39,137
Korea, Republic	15,486	12,271	18,329
Malaysia	3,362	2,455	3,263
Netherlands	3,051	1,580	2,343
New Zealand	7,867	6,216	7,179
Saudi Arabia	2,099	1,353	1,404
Singapore	5,154	4,199	4,331
South Africa	2,061	1,174	1,615
Taiwan	6,947	5,089	7,501
Thailand	4,489	3,323	5,250
United Arab Emirates	3,291	1,649	1,913
United Kingdom	7,844	7,071	7,456
USA	10,184	7,461	8,232
Total (incl. others)	186,853	153,767	206,705

Source: Trade Map-Trade Competitiveness Map, International Trade Centre, www.intracen.org/marketanalysis.

Transport

RAILWAYS
(traffic)*

	1997/98	1998/99	1999/2000
Passengers carried (million)	587.7	595.2	629.2
Freight carried (million metric tons)	487.5	492.0	508.0
Freight ton-km ('000 million)	125.2	127.4	134.2

* Traffic on government railways only.

Passengers carried (million): 610 in 2003/04; 616 in 2004/05.

Freight carried (million metric tons): 557.3 in 2001/02; 589.1 in 2002/03.

Freight ton-km ('000 million): 150.7 in 2001/02; 161.8 in 2002/03.

ROAD TRAFFIC
('000 vehicles, registered at 31 March, unless otherwise indicated)

	2009	2010	2011*
Passenger vehicles	12,023	12,269	12,474
Light commercial vehicles	2,371	2,461	2,531
Trucks†	572	585	597
Buses	84	86	88
Motorcycles	624	660	679

* Beginning in 2011, traffic census data at 31 January.

† Including camper vans, previously classified as passenger vehicles.

SHIPPING

Merchant Fleet
(registered at 31 December)

	2007	2008	2009
Number of vessels	696	693	719
Total displacement ('000 grt)	1,911.2	1,828.2	1,836.5

Source: IHS Fairplay, *World Fleet Statistics*.

International Sea-borne Traffic
('000 metric tons, year ending 30 June)

	2000/01	2001/02	2002/03
Goods loaded	496,204	506,317	540,570
Goods unloaded	54,579	58,041	62,459

CIVIL AVIATION
(traffic)*

	2006	2007	2008
International services ('000):			
Passenger arrivals	10,835.7	n.a.	11,881.1
Passenger departures	10,644.3	n.a.	11,584.1
Domestic services:			
Passengers carried ('000)	43,674	46,745	49,857
Passenger-km (million)	46,933	50,315	54,132

* Includes estimates for regional airline data.

1999 (metric tons): International freight carried 680,458; International mail carried 25,316; Domestic freight and mail carried 192,326.

Tourism

VISITOR ARRIVALS BY COUNTRY OF ORIGIN
('000)*

	2006	2007	2008
Canada	109.7	114.6	124.6
China, People's Republic	308.5	357.6	356.4
Germany	148.3	151.6	160.7
Hong Kong	154.6	147.0	144.0
Japan	651.0	573.0	457.3
Korea, Republic	260.8	253.3	218.3
Malaysia	150.3	159.4	171.0
New Zealand	1,075.8	1,138.0	1,113.3
Singapore	253.4	263.8	270.9
Taiwan	93.8	92.7	77.6
United Kingdom	732.6	687.7	670.9
USA	456.1	459.7	454.4
Total (incl. others)	5,532.4	5,644.1	5,585.8

* Visitors intending to stay for less than one year.

Total visitor arrivals ('000): 5,584 in 2009; 5,885 in 2010 (provisional).

Receipts from tourism (US $ million, excl. passenger transport): 24,755 in 2008; 25,384 in 2009; 30,103 in 2010 (provisional).

Source: World Tourism Organization.

Communications Media

	2008	2009	2010
Telephones ('000 main lines in use)	9,370	9,020	8,660
Mobile cellular telephones ('000 subscribers)	22,120	22,200	22,500
Internet subscribers ('000)	6,450	6,100	n.a.
Broadband subscribers ('000)	5,150	5,092	5,165

Personal computers: 13,720,000 in 2005.

Television receivers ('000 in use): 14,168 in 2001.

Source: International Telecommunication Union.

Radio receivers ('000 in use): 25,500 in 1997 (Source: UNESCO, *Statistical Yearbook*).

Book production (1994): 10,835 titles (Source: UNESCO, *Statistical Yearbook*).

Newspapers (2004): 49 dailies (estimated combined circulation 3,114,000); 435 non-dailies (circulation 433,000) (Source: UNESCO, *Statistical Yearbook*).

Education

(August 2010 unless otherwise indicated)

	Institutions	Teaching staff*	Students
Government schools	6,743	163,698	2,282,357†
Non-government schools	2,725	87,724	1,204,522†
Universities‡	39	86,624	1,066,095

* Full-time teaching staff and full-time equivalent of part-time teaching staff.

† Primary and secondary students. In 2010 the total at both government and non-government schools comprised 2,010,327 primary and 1,476,552 secondary students.

‡ 2008 (Source: Department of Education, Science and Training).

Directory

The Government

Queen: HM Queen ELIZABETH II (succeeded to the throne 6 February 1952).

Governor-General: QUENTIN BRYCE (assumed office 5 September 2008).

THE MINISTRY
(May 2012)

The Government is formed by the Australian Labor Party.

Cabinet Ministers

Prime Minister: JULIA GILLARD.

Deputy Prime Minister and Treasurer: WAYNE SWAN.

Minister for Foreign Affairs: Senator ROBERT JOHN CARR.

Minister for Trade and Competitiveness: CRAIG EMERSON.

Minister for Defence: STEPHEN SMITH.

Minister for Agriculture, Fisheries and Forestry, and Minister Assisting on Queensland Floods Recovery: Senator JOE LUDWIG.

Minister for Regional Australia, Regional Development and Local Government, and for the Arts: SIMON CREAN.

Minister for Broadband, Communications and the Digital Economy, and Minister Assisting the Prime Minister on Digital Productivity: Senator STEPHEN CONROY.

Minister for Finance and Deregulation: Senator PENNY WONG.

Minister for Tertiary Education, Skills and Science and Research: Senator CHRIS EVANS.

Minister for Health: TANYA PLIBERSEK.

Minister for Families, Community Services and Indigenous Affairs, and for Disability Reform: JENNY MACKLIN.

Minister for School Education, Early Childhood and Youth: PETER GARRETT.

Minister for Infrastructure and Transport: ANTHONY ALBANESE.

Minister for Small Business, for Housing, and for Homelessness: BRENDAN O'CONNOR.

Minister for Climate Change and Energy Efficiency, and for Industry and Innovation: GREG COMBET.

Minister for Immigration and Citizenship: CHRIS BOWEN.

Minister for Sustainability, Environment, Water, Population and Communities and Vice-President of the Executive Council: TONY BURKE.

Minister for Resources and Energy, and for Tourism: MARTIN FERGUSON.

Minister for Employment and Workplace Relations, and for Financial Services and Superannuation: BILL SHORTEN.

Minister for Mental Health and Ageing, and for Social Inclusion: MARK BUTLER.

Attorney-General and Minister for Emergency Management: NICOLA ROXON.

Other Ministers

Minister for Human Services, and Minister Assisting for School Education: Senator KIM CARR.

Minister for Community Services, for Indigenous Employment and Economic Development, and for the Status of Women: JULIE COLLINS.

Minister for Home Affairs, for Justice, and for Defence Material: JASON CLARE.

Minister for Veterans' Affairs, for Defence Science and Personnel, and for Indigenous Health: WARREN SNOWDON.

Special Minister of State and Minister for the Public Service and Integrity: GARY GRAY.

Minister for Employment Participation, and for Early Childhood and Childcare: KATE ELLIS.

Minister for Sport and for Multicultural Affairs and Minister Assisting for Industry and Innovation: Senator KATE LUNDY.

Assistant Treasurer and Minister Assisting for Deregulation: DAVID BRADBURY.

DEPARTMENTS

Department of the Prime Minister and Cabinet: 1 National Circuit, Canberra, ACT 2600; tel. (2) 6271-5111; fax (2) 6271-5414; internet www.dpmc.gov.au.

Department of Agriculture, Fisheries and Forestry: GPOB 858, Canberra, ACT 2601; tel. (2) 6272-3933; internet www.daff.gov.au.

Attorney-General's Department: Central Office, 3–5 National Circuit, Barton, ACT 2600; tel. (2) 6141-6666; internet www.ag.gov.au.

Department of Broadband, Communications and the Digital Economy: GPOB 2154, Canberra, ACT 2601; tel. (2) 6271-1000; fax (2) 6271-1901; e-mail patricia.scott@dbcde.gov.au; internet www.dbcde.gov.au.

Department of Climate Change and Energy Efficiency: GPOB 854, Canberra, ACT 2600; tel. (2) 6159-7000; e-mail communications@climatechange.gov.au; internet www.climatechange.gov.au.

Department of Defence: Russell Offices, Russell Dr., Campbell, Canberra, ACT 2600; tel. (2) 6265-9111; e-mail public.enquiries@defence.gov.au; internet www.defence.gov.au.

Department of Education, Employment and Workplace Relations: GPOB 9880, Canberra, ACT 2601; tel. (2) 6240-8111; fax (2) 6240-8571; e-mail feedback@deewr.gov.au; internet www.deewr.gov.au.

Department of Families, Housing, Community Services and Indigenous Affairs: POB 7576, Canberra Business Centre, ACT 2610; tel. (2) 6244-6385; e-mail enquiries@fahcsia.gov.au; internet www.fahcsia.gov.au.

Department of Finance and Deregulation: John Gorton Bldg, King Edward Tce, Parkes, ACT 2600; tel. (2) 6215-2222; fax (2) 6273-3021; e-mail feedback@finance.gov.au; internet www.finance.gov.au.

Department of Foreign Affairs and Trade: R. G. Casey Bldg, John McEwen Cres., Barton, ACT 0221; tel. (2) 6261-1111; fax (2) 6261-3111; internet www.dfat.gov.au.

Department of Health and Ageing: GPOB 9848, Canberra, ACT 2601; tel. (2) 6289-1555; e-mail enquiries@health.gov.au; internet www.health.gov.au.

Department of Human Services: POB 3959, Manuka, ACT 2603; tel. (2) 6223-4000; fax (2) 6223-4499; e-mail enquiries@humanservices.gov.au; internet www.humanservices.gov.au.

Department of Immigration and Citizenship: POB 25, Belconnen, ACT 2616; tel. (2) 6264-1111; fax (2) 6225-6970; internet www.immi.gov.au.

Department of Industry, Innovation, Science, Research and Tertiary Education: GPOB 9839, Canberra, ACT 2601; tel. (2) 6213-6000; fax (2) 6213-7000.

Department of Infrastructure and Transport: GPOB 594, Canberra, ACT 2601; tel. (2) 6274-7111; fax (2) 6257-2505; e-mail publicaffairs@infrastructure.gov.au; internet www.infrastructure.gov.au.

Department of Regional Australia, Local Government, Arts and Sport: GPOB 803, Canberra, ACT 2601; tel. (2) 6274-7977; fax (2) 6257-2505; e-mail enquiries@regional.gov.au; internet www.regional.gov.au.

Department of Resources, Energy and Tourism: GPOB 1564, Canberra, ACT 2601; tel. (2) 6276-1000; fax (2) 6243-7037; e-mail ret@ret.gov.au; internet www.ret.gov.au.

Department of Sustainability, Environment, Water, Population and Communities: GPOB 787, Canberra, ACT 2601; tel. (2) 6274-1111; fax (2) 6274-1666; internet www.environment.gov.au.

Department of the Treasury: Langton Cres., Parkes, ACT 2600; tel. (2) 6263-2111; fax (2) 6273-2614; e-mail department@treasury.gov.au; internet www.treasury.gov.au.

Department of Veterans' Affairs: POB 21, Woden, ACT 2606; tel. (2) 6289-6736; fax (2) 6289-6257; e-mail generalenquiries@dva.gov.au; internet www.dva.gov.au.

Legislature

FEDERAL PARLIAMENT

Senate

President: JOHN HOGG.

Distribution of seats following election, 21 August 2010

Party	Seats*
Liberal-National Coalition	34
Australian Labor Party	31
Australian Greens	9
Others	2
Total	76

* The election was for 36 of the 72 seats held by state senators, who serve a six-year term, and for the two senators representing the Northern Territory and the two representing the Australian Capital Territory. The newly elected senators took office 1 July 2011, with the exception of the four Territory representatives, whose three-year term of office commenced on election.

House of Representatives

Speaker: ANNA BURKE (acting).

Distribution of seats following election, 21 August 2010

Party	Seats
Australian Labor Party	72
Liberal Party of Australia	44
Liberal National Party of Queensland	21
National Party of Australia	7
Australian Greens	1
Country Liberals	1
Independents	4
Total	150

State and Territory Governments

(May 2012)

NEW SOUTH WALES

Governor: Prof. MARIE BASHIR, Level 3, Chief Secretary's Bldg, 121 Macquarie St, Sydney, NSW 2000; tel. (2) 9242-4200; fax (2) 9242-4266; internet www.nsw.gov.au.

Premier: BARRY O'FARRELL (Liberal), GPOB 5341, Sydney, NSW 2001; tel. (2) 9228-5239; fax (2) 9228-3935; e-mail office@premier.nsw.gov.au; internet www.premier.nsw.gov.au.

VICTORIA

Governor: ALEX CHERNOV, Government House, Melbourne, Vic 3004; tel. (3) 9655-4211; fax (3) 9650-9050; internet www.governor.vic.gov.au.

Premier: EDWARD (TED) BAILLIEU (Liberal), 1 Treasury Place, Melbourne, Vic 3002; tel. (3) 9651-5000; fax (3) 9651-5054; e-mail premier@dpc.vic.gov.au; internet www.premier.vic.gov.au.

QUEENSLAND

Governor: PENELOPE WENSLEY, GPOB 434, Brisbane, Qld 4001; tel. (7) 3858-5700; fax (7) 3858-5701; e-mail govhouse@govhouse.qld.gov.au; internet www.govhouse.qld.gov.au.

Premier: CAMPBELL NEWMAN (LNP), POB 15185, City East, Qld 4002; tel. (7) 3224-4500; fax (7) 3229-2900; e-mail thepremier@premiers.qld.gov.au; internet www.thepremier.qld.gov.au.

SOUTH AUSTRALIA

Governor: Rear Adm. KEVIN SCARCE, GPOB 2373, Adelaide, SA 5001; tel. (8) 8203-9800; fax (8) 8203-9899; e-mail governors.office@sa.gov.au; internet www.governor.sa.gov.au.

Premier: JAY WEATHERILL (Labor), GPOB 2343, Adelaide, SA 5001; tel. (8) 8463-3166; fax (8) 8463-3168; e-mail premier@dpc.sa.gov.au; internet www.premier.sa.gov.au.

WESTERN AUSTRALIA

Governor: MALCOLM MCCUSKER, Government House, St George's Terrace, Perth, WA 6000; tel. (8) 9429-9199; fax (8) 9325-4476; e-mail enquiries@govhouse.wa.gov.au; internet www.govhouse.wa.gov.au.

Premier: COLIN BARNETT (Liberal), 24th Floor, Gov. Stirling Tower, 197 St George's Terrace, Perth, WA 6000; tel. (8) 6552-5000; fax (8) 6552-5001; e-mail wa-government@dpc.wa.gov.au; internet www.premier.wa.gov.au.

TASMANIA

Governor: PETER UNDERWOOD, Government House, Lower Domain Rd, Hobart, Tas 7000; tel. (3) 6234-2611; fax (3) 6234-2556; e-mail admin@govhouse.tas.gov.au; internet www.govhouse.tas.gov.au.

Premier: LARA GIDDINGS (Labor), Executive Bldg, Level 11, 15 Murray St, Hobart, Tas 7000; tel. (3) 6233-3464; fax (3) 6234-1572; e-mail lara.giddings@dpac.tas.gov.au; internet www.premier.tas.gov.au.

NORTHERN TERRITORY

Administrator: SALLY THOMAS, GPOB 497, Darwin, NT 0801; tel. (8) 8999-7103; fax (8) 8999-5521; e-mail governmenthouse.darwin@nt.gov.au; internet www.nt.gov.au/administrator.

Chief Minister: PAUL HENDERSON (Labor), GPOB 3146, Darwin, NT 0801; tel. (8) 8901-4000; fax (8) 8901-4099; e-mail chiefminister@nt.gov.au; internet chiefminister.nt.gov.au.

AUSTRALIAN CAPITAL TERRITORY

Chief Minister: KATY GALLAGHER (Labor), GPOB 1020, Canberra, ACT 2601; tel. (2) 6205-0840; fax (2) 6205-3030; e-mail gallagher@act.gov.au; internet www.cmd.act.gov.au.

Election Commission

Australian Electoral Commission (AEC): West Block Offices, Queen Victoria Terrace, Parkes, ACT 2600; POB 6172, Kingston, ACT 2604; tel. (2) 6271-4411; fax (2) 6271-4558; e-mail info@aec.gov.au; internet www.aec.gov.au; f. 1984; statutory body; administers federal elections and referendums; Chair. PETER HEEREY; Electoral Commr ED KILLESTEYN.

Political Organizations

Australians for Constitutional Monarchy (ACM): GPOB 9841, Sydney, NSW 2001; tel. (2) 9251-2500; fax (2) 9261-5033; e-mail acmhq@norepublic.com.au; internet www.norepublic.com.au; f. 1992; also known as No Republic; Nat. Convener Prof. DAVID FLINT.

Australian Democrats Party: 711 South Rd, Black Forest, SA 5035; tel. (8) 8371-1441; e-mail inquiries@democrats.org.au; internet www.democrats.org.au; f. 1977; comprises the fmr Liberal Movement and the Australia Party; Nat. Pres. JULIA MELLAND; Nat. Exec. BRUCE CARNWELL.

Australian Greens: GPOB 1108, Canberra, ACT 2601; tel. (2) 6140-3217; fax (2) 6247-6455; e-mail greens@greens.org.au; internet www.greens.org.au; f. 1992; Parl. Leader Senator CHRISTINE MILNE; Nat. Convener ADAM BANDT.

Australian Labor Party (ALP): POB 6222, Kingston, ACT 2604; tel. (2) 6120-0800; fax (2) 6120-0801; e-mail info@cbr.alp.org.au; internet www.alp.org.au; f. 1891; advocates social democracy; trade unions form part of its structure; Fed. Parl. Leader JULIA GILLARD; Nat. Pres. JENNY MCALLISTER; Nat. Sec. KARL BITAR.

Australian Republican Movement (ARM): GPOB 611, Canberra, ACT 2601; tel. (2) 6257-3705; fax (2) 6257-3670; e-mail republic@republic.org.au; internet www.republic.org.au; f. 1991; Chair. MICHAEL KEATING.

Communist Party of Australia: 74 Buckingham St, Surry Hills, NSW 2010; tel. (2) 9699-8844; fax (2) 9699-9833; e-mail cpa@cpa.org.au; internet www.cpa.org.au; f. 1971; fmrly Socialist Party; advocates public ownership of the means of production, working-class political power; Pres. Dr VINNIE MOLINA; Gen. Sec. HANNAH MIDDLETON.

First Nations Political Party (FNPP): e-mail firstnationspoliticalparty@hotmail.com; internet www.firstnationspoliticalparty.org; f. 2010; represents interests of Aboriginal people; Leader MAURIE JAPARTA RYAN.

Liberal National Party of Queensland (LNP): POB 5156, West End, Qld 4101; tel. (7) 3844-0666; fax (7) 3844 0388; e-mail info@lnp.org.au; internet lnp.org.au; f. 2008; est. by merger of Qld Liberals and Qld Nationals; aims to provide prosperity and security for Queensland; Pres. BRUCE MCIVER; Vice-Pres. GARY SPENCE.

Liberal Party of Australia: POB 6004, Kingston, ACT 2604; tel. (2) 6273-2564; fax (2) 6273-1534; e-mail libadm@liberal.org.au; internet www.liberal.org.au; f. 1944; advocates private enterprise, social justice, individual liberty and initiative; committed to national devt, prosperity and security; Fed. Dir BRIAN LOUGHNANE; Fed. Parl. Leader TONY ABBOTT; Fed. Pres. ALAN STOCKDALE.

National Party of Australia: POB 6190, Kingston, ACT 2604; tel. (2) 6273-3822; fax (2) 6273-1745; e-mail federal.nationals@nationals.org.au; internet www.nationals.org.au; f. 1916 as the Country Party of Australia; adopted present name in 1982; advocates balanced national devt based on free enterprise, with special emphasis on the needs of people outside the major metropolitan areas; Fed. Pres. JOHN TANNER; Fed. Parl. Leader WARREN TRUSS; Fed. Dir BRAD HENDERSON.

Diplomatic Representation

EMBASSIES AND HIGH COMMISSIONS IN AUSTRALIA

Afghanistan: POB 155, Deakin West, ACT 2600; tel. (2) 6282-7311; fax (2) 6282-7322; e-mail ambassador@afghanembassy.net; internet www.afghanembassy.net; Ambassador NASIR AHMAD ANDISHA.

Algeria: 9 Terrigal Cres., O'Malley, ACT 2606; tel. (2) 6286-7355; fax (2) 6286-7037; e-mail info@algeriaemb.org.au; internet www.algeriaemb.org.au; Ambassador HADI BROURI.

Argentina: POB 4835, Kingston, ACT 2604; tel. (2) 6273-9111; fax (2) 6273-0500; e-mail info@argentina.org.au; internet www.argentina.org.au; Ambassador PEDRO VILLAGRA DELGADO.

Austria: POB 3375, Manuka, ACT 2603; tel. (2) 6295-1533; fax (2) 6239-6751; e-mail canberra-ob@bmeia.gv.at; internet www.austria.org.au; Ambassador Dr HANNES PORIAS.

Bangladesh: 57 Culgoa Circuit, O'Malley, ACT 2606; tel. (2) 6290-0511; fax (2) 6290-0544; e-mail hoc@bhcanberra.com; internet www.bhcanberra.com; High Commissioner Lt-Gen. MASUD UDDIN CHOWDHURY.

Belgium: 19 Arkana St, Yarralumla, ACT 2600; tel. (2) 6273-2501; fax (2) 6273-3392; e-mail canberra@diplobel.fed.be; internet www.diplomatie.be/canberra; Ambassador PATRICK RENAULT.

Bosnia and Herzegovina: 5 Beale Cres., Deakin, ACT 2600; tel. (2) 6232-4646; fax (2) 6232-5554; e-mail embassy@bih.org.au; internet www.bih.org.au; Ambassador DAMIR ARNAUT.

Botswana: POB 3812, Manuka, ACT 2603; tel. (2) 6234-7500; fax (2) 6282-4140; e-mail botaus-info@gov.bw; internet www.botswanahighcom.org.au; High Commissioner MOLOSIWA SELEPENG.

Brazil: GPOB 1540, Canberra, ACT 2601; tel. (2) 6273-2372; fax (2) 6273-2375; e-mail brazilemb@brazil.org.au; internet www.brazil.org.au; Ambassador RUBEM CORRÊA BARBOSA.

Brunei: POB109, Curtin, ACT 2605; tel. (2) 6285-4500; fax (2) 6285-4545; e-mail canberra.australia@mfa.gov.bn; internet brunei.org.au; High Commissioner ADNAN JAAFAR.

Bulgaria: POB 6096, Mawson, ACT 2607; tel. (2) 6286-9711; fax (2) 6286-9600; e-mail embassy@bulgaria.org.au; internet www.bulgaria.org.au; Ambassador KRASSIMIR STEFANOV.

Cambodia: 5 Canterbury Cres., Deakin, ACT 2600; tel. (2) 6273-1259; fax (2) 6273-1053; e-mail cambodianembassy@ozemail.com.au;

internet www.embassyofcambodia.org.nz/au.htm; Ambassador CHUM SOUNRY.

Canada: Commonwealth Ave, Canberra, ACT 2600; tel. (2) 6270-4000; fax (2) 6270-4081; e-mail cnbra@international.gc.ca; internet www.canadainternational.gc.ca/australia-australie; High Commissioner MICHAEL SMALL.

Chile: POB 5023, Garran, ACT 2605; tel. (2) 6286-2430; fax (2) 6286-1289; e-mail echileau@embachile-australia.com; internet chileabroad.gov.cl/australia/en/; Ambassador PEDRO PABLO DÍAZ HERRERA.

China, People's Republic: 15 Coronation Dr., Yarralumla, ACT 2600; tel. (2) 6273-4780; fax (2) 6273-5848; e-mail chinaemb_au@mfa.gov.cn; internet au.china-embassy.org/eng; Ambassador CHEN YUMING.

Colombia: POB 227, Civic Sq., ACT 2608; tel. (2) 6230-4203; fax (2) 6230-4209; e-mail embassyofcolombia@bigpond.com; internet www.cancilleria.gov.co/wps/portal/embajada_australia; Ambassador DIEGO BETANCUR.

Croatia: 14 Jindalee Cres., O'Malley, ACT 2600; tel. (2) 6286-6988; fax (2) 6286-3544; e-mail croemb.canberra@mvpei.hr; Ambassador VICENCIJE BIUK.

Cuba: 1 Gerogery Place, O'Malley, ACT 2606; tel. (2) 6290-2151; fax (2) 6286-9354; e-mail embajada@cubaus.net; internet embacuba.cubaminrex.cu/australiaing; Ambassador PEDRO MONZÓN BARATA.

Cyprus: 30 Beale Cres., Deakin, ACT 2600; tel. (2) 6281-0832; fax (2) 6281-0860; e-mail info@cyprus.org.au; internet www.cyprus.org.au; High Commissioner YANNIS IACOVOU.

Czech Republic: 8 Culgoa Circuit, O'Malley, ACT 2606; tel. (2) 6290-1386; fax (2) 6290-0006; e-mail canberra@embassy.mzv.cz; internet www.mzv.cz/canberra; Ambassador Dr HYNEK KMONICEK.

Denmark: 15 Hunter St, Yarralumla, ACT 2600; tel. (2) 6270-5333; fax (2) 6270-5324; e-mail cbramb@um.dk; internet www.oceanien.um.dk; Ambassador SUSANNE HOFFMANN SHINE.

Ecuador: 6 Pindari Cres., O'Malley, ACT 2606; tel. (2) 6286-4021; fax (2) 6286-1231; e-mail embassy@ecuador-au.org; Ambassador RAÚL GANGOTENA RIVADENEIRA.

Egypt: 1 Darwin Ave, Yarralumla, ACT 2600; tel. (2) 6273-4437; fax (2) 6273-4279; e-mail egyembassy@bigpond.com; Ambassador OMAR MUHAMMAD T. METWALLY.

Fiji: POB 159, Deakin West, ACT 2600; tel. (2) 6260-5115; fax (2) 6260-5105; e-mail admin@aus-fhc.org; internet www.fijihighcom.com; High Commissioner CHERYL BROWN-IRAVA (acting).

Finland: 12 Darwin Ave, Yarralumla, ACT 2600; tel. (2) 6273-3800; fax (2) 6273-3603; e-mail sanomat.can@formin.fi; internet www.finland.org.au; Ambassador MAIJA LÄHTEENMÄKI.

France: 6 Perth Ave, Yarralumla, ACT 2600; tel. (2) 6216-0100; fax (2) 6216-0127; e-mail info@ambafrance-au.org; internet www.ambafrance-au.org; Ambassador STÉPHANE ROMATET.

Germany: 119 Empire Circuit, Yarralumla, ACT 2600; tel. (2) 6270-1911; fax (2) 6270-1951; e-mail info@canberra.diplo.de; internet www.canberra.diplo.de; Ambassador CHRISTOPH MUELLER.

Ghana: 13 Numeralla St, O'Malley, ACT 2606; tel. (2) 6290-2110; fax (2) 6290-2115; e-mail gh57391@bigpond.net.au; internet www.ghanahighcom.org.au; High Commissioner PAUL YAW ESSEL.

Greece: 9 Turrana St, Yarralumla, ACT 2600; tel. (2) 6273-3011; fax (2) 6273-2620; e-mail gremb.can@mfa.gr; Ambassador ALEXIOS CHRISTOPOULOS.

Holy See: POB 3633, Manuka, ACT 2603 (Apostolic Nunciature); tel. (2) 6295-3876; fax (2) 6295-3690; e-mail nuntius@cyberone.com.au; Apostolic Nuncio Most Rev. GIUSEPPE LAZZAROTTO (Titular Archbishop of Numana).

Hungary: 17 Beale Cres., Deakin, ACT 2600; tel. (2) 6282-3226; fax (2) 6285-3012; e-mail mission.cbr@mfa.gov.hu; internet www.mfa.gov.hu/kulkepviselet/au; Ambassador ANNA SIKÓ.

India: 3–5 Moonah Pl., Yarralumla, ACT 2600; tel. (2) 6273-3999; fax (2) 6273-1308; e-mail hco@hcindia-au.org; internet www.hcindia-au.org; High Commissioner SUJATHA SINGH.

Indonesia: 8 Darwin Ave, Yarralumla, ACT 2600; tel. (2) 6250-8600; fax (2) 6273-6017; e-mail indonemb@kbri-canberra.org.au; internet www.kemlu.go.id/canberra; Ambassador PRIMO ALUI JOELIANTO.

Iran: POB 705, Mawson, ACT 2607; tel. (2) 6290-2430; fax (2) 6290-2825; e-mail amb.office@iranembassy.org.au; internet www.iranembassy.org.au; Ambassador MAHMOUD BABAEE.

Iraq: 48 Culgoa Circuit, O'Malley, ACT 2606; tel. (2) 6286-2744; fax (2) 6286-8744; e-mail iraqembcnb@hotmail.com; internet www.iraqembassyaustralia.org; Ambassador MOUAYED SALEH.

Ireland: 20 Arkana St, Yarralumla, ACT 2600; tel. (2) 6214-0000; fax (2) 6273-3741; e-mail canberraembassy@dfa.ie; internet www.embassyofireland.au.com; Ambassador NOEL WHITE.

Israel: 6 Turrana St, Yarralumla, ACT 2600; tel. (2) 6215-4500; fax (2) 6215-4555; e-mail info@canberra.mfa.gov.il; internet canberra.mfa.gov.il; Ambassador YUVAL ROTEM.

Italy: 12 Grey St, Deakin, ACT 2600; tel. (2) 6273-3333; fax (2) 6273-4223; e-mail ambasciata.canberra@esteri.it; internet www.ambcanberra.esteri.it; Ambassador GIAN LUDOVICO DE MARTINO DI MONTEGIORDANO.

Japan: 112 Empire Circuit, Yarralumla, ACT 2600; tel. (2) 6273-3244; fax (2) 6273-1848; e-mail cultural@japan.org.au; internet www.au.emb-japan.go.jp; Ambassador SHIGEKAZU SATO.

Jordan: 20 Roebuck St, Red Hill, ACT 2603; tel. (2) 6295-9951; fax (2) 6239-7236; e-mail jordan@jordanembassy.org.au; internet www.jordanembassy.org.au; Ambassador RIMA AHMAD ALAADEEN.

Kenya: GPOB 1990, Canberra, ACT 2601; tel. (2) 6247-4788; fax (2) 6257-6613; e-mail khc-canberra@kenya.asn.au; internet www.kenya.asn.au; High Commissioner STEPHEN K. TARUS.

Korea, Republic: 113 Empire Circuit, Yarralumla, ACT 2600; tel. (2) 6270-4100; fax (2) 6273-4839; e-mail info@korea.org.au; internet www.korea.org.au; Ambassador CHO TAE-YONG.

Kuwait: POB 26, Woden, ACT 2606; tel. (2) 6286-7777; fax (2) 6286-3733; e-mail Kuwaitcan_2002@yahoo.com.au; internet www.kuwaitemb-australia.com; Ambassador KHALED AL-SHAIBANI.

Laos: 1 Dalman Cres., O'Malley, ACT 2606; tel. (2) 6286-4595; fax (2) 6290-1910; e-mail laoemb@bigpond.net.au; internet www.laosembassy.net; Ambassador RANGSY KONGSAYSY.

Lebanon: 27 Endeavour St, Red Hill, ACT 2603; tel. (2) 6295-7378; fax (2) 6239-7024; e-mail lebanemb@tpg.com.au; internet www.lebanemb.org.au; Ambassador JEAN DANIEL.

Libya: 50 Culgoa Circuit, O'Malley, ACT 2606; tel. (2) 6290-7900; fax (2) 6286-4522; Ambassador a.i. MUSBAH A. A. ALLAFI.

Macedonia, former Yugoslav republic: POB 1890, Canberra, ACT 2601; tel. (2) 6282-6220; fax (2) 6282-6229; e-mail info@macedonianemb.org.au; internet www.missions.gov.mk/canberra; Ambassador PERO STOJANOVSKI.

Malaysia: 7 Perth Ave, Yarralumla, ACT 2600; tel. (2) 6120-0300; fax (2) 6273-2496; e-mail malcanberra@malaysia.org.au; internet www.malaysia.org.au; High Commissioner SALMAN AHMAD.

Malta: 38 Culgoa Circuit, O'Malley, ACT 2606; tel. (2) 6290-1724; fax (2) 6290-2453; e-mail highcommission.canberra@gov.mt; internet www.foreign.gov.mt/australia; High Commissioner FRANCIS TABONE.

Mauritius: 2 Beale Cres., Deakin, ACT 2600; tel. (2) 6281-1203; fax (2) 6282-3235; e-mail mhccan@cyberone.com.au; High Commissioner MARIE FRANCE LISIANNE MIRELLA CHAUVIN.

Mexico: 14 Perth Ave, Yarralumla, ACT 2600; tel. (2) 6273-3963; fax (2) 6273-1190; e-mail embamex@mexico.org.au; internet www.mexico.org.au; Ambassador MARÍA LUISA BEATRIZ LÓPEZ GARGALLO.

Mongolia: 1/44 Dalman Cres., O'Malley, ACT 2606; tel. (2) 6286-2947; fax (2) 6286-6381; e-mail mngemb@bigpond.com; internet www.canberra.mfat.gov.mn; Ambassador RAVDANGIIN BOLD.

Morocco: POB 3531, Manuka, ACT 2603; tel. (2) 6290-0755; fax (2) 6290-0744; e-mail sifmacan@moroccoembassy.org.au; internet www.moroccoembassy.org.au; Ambassador MOHAMED MAEL-AININ.

Myanmar: 22 Arkana St, Yarralumla, ACT 2600; tel. (2) 6273-3811; fax (2) 6273-3181; e-mail mecanberra@bigpond.com; internet www.myanmarembassycanberra.com; Ambassador PAW LWIN SEIN.

Nepal: Suite 2.02, AAPT Bldg, 24 Marcus Clarke St, Canberra, ACT 2601; tel. (2) 6162-1554; fax (2) 6162-1557; e-mail info@necan.gov.np; internet www.necan.gov.np; Ambassador YOGENDRA DHAKAL.

Netherlands: 120 Empire Circuit, Yarralumla, ACT 2600; tel. (2) 6220-9400; fax (2) 6273-3206; e-mail can@minbuza.nl; internet australie.nlambassade.org; Ambassador WILLEM ANDREAE.

New Zealand: Commonwealth Ave, Canberra, ACT 2600; tel. (2) 6270-4211; fax (2) 6273-3194; e-mail nzhccba@bigpond.net.au; internet www.nzembassy.com/australia; High Commissioner Maj.-Gen. (retd) MARTYN DUNNE.

Nigeria: POB 241, Civic Sq., ACT 2608; tel. 0424757698 (mobile); fax (2) 6282-8471; e-mail chancery@nigeria-can.org.au; internet www.nigeria-can.org.au; High Commissioner AYOOLA LAWRENCE OLUKANNI.

Norway: 17 Hunter St, Yarralumla, ACT 2600; tel. (2) 6273-3444; fax (2) 6273-3669; e-mail emb.canberra@mfa.no; internet www.norway.org.au; Ambassador SIREN GJERME ERIKSEN.

Pakistan: POB 684, Mawson, ACT 2607; tel. (2) 6290-1676; fax (2) 6290-1073; e-mail parepcanberra@internode.on.net; internet www.pakistan.org.au; High Commissioner ABDUL MALIK ABDULLAH.

Papua New Guinea: POB E6317, Kingston, ACT 2604; tel. (2) 6273-3322; fax (2) 6273-3732; e-mail kunducbr@netspeed.com.au; internet www.pngcanberra.org; High Commissioner CHRIS HAIVETA.

Peru: Level 2, 40 Brisbane Ave, Barton, ACT 2600; tel. (2) 6273-7351; fax (2) 6273-7354; e-mail embassy@embaperu.org.au; internet www.embaperu.org.au; Ambassador LUIS FELIPE QUESADA INCHAUSTEGUI.

Philippines: 1 Moonah Place, Yarralumla, ACT 2600; tel. (2) 6273-2535; fax (2) 6273-3984; e-mail cbrpe@philembassy.org.au; internet www.philembassy.org.au; Ambassador BELEN F. ANOTA.

Poland: 7 Turrana St, Yarralumla, ACT 2600; tel. (2) 6272-1000; fax (2) 6273-3184; e-mail canberra.amb.sekretariat@msz.gov.pl; internet www.canberra.polemb.net; Ambassador ANDRZEJ JAROSZYŃSKI.

Portugal: 23 Culgoa Circuit, O'Malley, ACT 2606; tel. (2) 6290-1733; fax (2) 6290-1957; e-mail embportcanb@internode.on.net; Ambassador RUI QUARTÍN SANTOS.

Qatar: Rm 309, The Hyatt Hotel, Canberra, ACT 2600; tel. (2) 6269-8309; fax (2) 6269-8387; e-mail majaber@mofa.gov.qa; Ambassador YOUSEF ALI AL-KHATER.

Romania: 4 Dalman Cres., O'Malley, ACT 2606; tel. (2) 6286-2343; fax (2) 6286-2433; e-mail embassy@roemb.com.au; internet www.canberra.mae.ro; Ambassador Dr MIHAI STEFAN STUPARU.

Russia: 78 Canberra Ave, Griffith, ACT 2603; tel. (2) 6295-9033; fax (2) 6295-1847; e-mail rusembassy.australia@rambler.ru; internet www.australia.mid.ru; Ambassador VLADIMIR MOROZOV.

Samoa: POB 3274, Manuka, ACT 2603; tel. (2) 6286-5505; fax (2) 6286-5678; e-mail samoahcaussi@netspeed.com.au; High Commissioner LEMALU TATE SIMI.

Saudi Arabia: POB 9162, Deakin, ACT 2600; tel. (2) 6250-7000; fax (2) 6282-8911; e-mail amb.auemb@mofa.gov.sa; internet www.saudiembassy.org.au; Ambassador HASSAN TALAT NAZER.

Serbia: POB 728, Mawson, ACT 2607; tel. (2) 6290-2630; fax (2) 6290-2631; e-mail serbembau@optusnet.com.au; Ambassador NEDA MALETIĆ.

Singapore: 17 Forster Cres., Yarralumla, ACT 2600; tel. (2) 6271-2000; fax (2) 6273-9823; e-mail singhc_cbr@sgmfa.gov.sg; internet www.mfa.gov.sg/canberra; High Commissioner MICHAEL TEO.

Slovakia: 47 Culgoa Circuit, O'Malley, ACT 2606; tel. (2) 6290-1516; fax (2) 6290-1755; e-mail emb.canberra@mzv.sk; internet www.mzv.sk/canberra; Ambassador EVA PONOMARENKOVÁ.

Slovenia: 26 Akame Circuit, O'Malley, ACT 2606; tel. (2) 6290-0000; fax (2) 6290-0619; e-mail vca@gov.si; internet canberra.veleposlanistvo.si; Ambassador MILAN BALAŽIC.

Solomon Islands: POB 256, Deakin West, ACT 2600; tel. (2) 6282-7030; fax (2) 6282-7040; e-mail info@solomonemb.org.au; High Commissioner BERAKI JINO.

South Africa: cnr State Circle and Rhodes Place, Yarralumla, ACT 2600; tel. (2) 6272-7300; fax (2) 6273-3203; e-mail info.canberra@foreign.gov.za; internet www.sahc.org.au; High Commissioner KOLEKA ANITA MQULWANA.

Spain: 15 Arkana St, Yarralumla, ACT 2600; tel. (2) 6273-3555; fax (2) 6273-3918; e-mail emb.canberra@maec.es; internet www.maec.es/embajadas/canberra; Ambassador ENRIQUE VIGUERA RUBIO.

Sri Lanka: 35 Empire Circuit, Forrest, ACT 2603; tel. (2) 6239-7041; fax (2) 6239-6166; e-mail admin@slhcaust.org; internet www.slhcaust.org; High Commissioner Adm. (retd) THISARA SAMARASINGHE.

Sweden: 5 Turrana St, Yarralumla, ACT 2600; tel. (2) 6270-2700; fax (2) 6270-2755; e-mail sweden@iimetro.com.au; internet www.swedenabroad.com/canberra; Ambassador SVEN-OLOF PETERSSON.

Switzerland: 7 Melbourne Ave, Forrest, ACT 2603; tel. (2) 6162-8400; fax (2) 6273-3428; e-mail can.vertretung@eda.admin.ch; internet www.eda.admin.ch/australia; Ambassador MARCEL STUTZ.

Syria: 41 Culgoa Circuit, O'Malley, ACT 2606; tel. (2) 6218-5200; fax (2) 6218-5250; e-mail info@syrianembassy.org.au; internet www.syrianembassy.org.au; Ambassador MOHAMMED KHADDOUR.

Thailand: 111 Empire Circuit, Yarralumla, ACT 2600; tel. (2) 6206-0100; fax (2) 6206-0123; e-mail thaican@mfa.go.th; internet canberra.thaiembassy.org; Ambassador MARIS SANGIAMPONGSA.

Timor-Leste: 7 Beale Cres., Deakin, ACT 2600; tel. (2) 6260-4833; fax (2) 6232-4075; e-mail timor.embassy@bigpond.com; Ambassador ABEL GUTERRES.

Tonga: 7 Newdegate St, Deakin, ACT 2600; tel. (2) 6232-4806; fax (2) 6232-4807; e-mail info@tongahighcom.com.au; High Commissioner (vacant).

Tunisia: POB 229, Civic Sq., ACT 2608; tel. (2) 6162-0534; fax (2) 6246-0300; e-mail canberra@embassytunisia.com; Ambassador RAOUF CHATTY.

Turkey: 6 Moonah Place, Yarralumla, ACT 2600; tel. (2) 6234-0000; fax (2) 6273-4402; e-mail embassy.canberra@mfa.gov.tr; internet kanberra.be.mfa.gov.tr; Ambassador OĞUZ ÖZGE.

Uganda: POB 34, Woden, ACT 2606; tel. (2) 6286-1234; fax (2) 6286-1243; e-mail ugandahc@velocitynet.com.au; High Commissioner ENOCH NKURUHO (acting).

Ukraine: Level 12, St George Centre, 60 Marcus Clarke St, Canberra, ACT 2601; tel. (2) 6230-5789; fax (2) 6230-7298; e-mail ukremb@bigpond.com; internet www.mfa.gov.ua/australia; Ambassador VALENTYN ADOMAYTIS.

United Arab Emirates: POB 5173, Garran, ACT 2605; tel. (2) 6286-8802; fax (2) 6286-8804; e-mail uaeembassy@bigpond.com; internet www.uaeembassy.org.au; Ambassador ALI NASSER AL-NUAIMI.

United Kingdom: Commonwealth Ave, Canberra, ACT 2600; tel. (2) 6270-6666; fax (2) 6273-3236; e-mail PPA.Canberra@fco.gov.uk; internet ukinaustralia.fco.gov.uk; High Commissioner PAUL MADDEN.

Uruguay: POB 5058, Kingston, ACT 2604; tel. (2) 6273-9100; fax (2) 6273-9099; e-mail urucan@iimetro.com.au; Ambassador ALBERTO L. FAJARDO KLAPPENBACH.

USA: Moonah Place, Yarralumla, ACT 2600; tel. (2) 6214-5600; fax (2) 6214-5970; e-mail usrsaustralia@state.gov; internet canberra.usembassy.gov; Ambassador JEFFREY L. BLEICH.

Vanuatu: Canberra; High Commissioner KALVAU KALORIS.

Venezuela: POB 37, Woden, ACT 2606; tel. (2) 6290-2968; fax (2) 6290-2911; e-mail embaustralia@venezuela-emb-org.au; internet www.venezuela-emb.org.au; Ambassador NELSÓN DÁVILA-LAMEDA.

Viet Nam: 6 Timbarra Cres., O'Malley, ACT 2606; tel. (2) 6286-6059; fax (2) 6286-4534; e-mail vembassy@webone.com.au; internet www.vietnamembassy.org.au; Ambassador HOANG VINH THANH.

Zimbabwe: 7 Timbarra Cres., O'Malley, ACT 2606; tel. (2) 6286-2700; fax (2) 6290-1680; e-mail zimbabwe1@iimetro.com.au; Ambassador JACQUELINE NOMHLE ZWAMBILA.

Judicial System

The judicial power of the Commonwealth of Australia is vested in the High Court of Australia, in such other Federal Courts as the Federal Parliament creates, and in such other courts as it invests with Federal jurisdiction.

In March 1986 all remaining categories of appeal from Australian courts to the Queen's Privy Council in the United Kingdom were abolished by the Australia Act.

HIGH COURT OF AUSTRALIA

The High Court consists of a Chief Justice and six other Justices, each of whom is appointed by the Governor-General in Council, and has both original and appellate jurisdiction.

The High Court's original jurisdiction extends to all matters arising under any treaty, affecting representatives of other countries, in which the Commonwealth of Australia or its representative is a party, between states or between residents of different states or between a state and a resident of another state, and in which a writ of mandamus, or prohibition, or an injunction is sought against an officer of the Commonwealth of Australia. It also extends to matters arising under the Australian Constitution or involving its interpretation, and to many matters arising under Commonwealth laws.

The High Court's appellate jurisdiction has, since June 1984, been discretionary. Appeals from the Federal Court, the Family Court and the Supreme Courts of the states and of the territories may now be brought only if special leave is granted, in the event of a legal question that is of general public importance being involved, or of there being differences of opinion between intermediate appellate courts as to the state of the law.

Chief Justice: ROBERT S. FRENCH, POB 6309, Kingston, Canberra, ACT 2604; tel. (2) 6270-6811; fax (2) 6270-6868; e-mail enquiries@hcourt.gov.au; internet www.hcourt.gov.au.

Justices: WILLIAM MONTAGUE CHARLES GUMMOW, KENNETH MADISON HAYNE, JOHN DYSON HEYDON, SUSAN MAREE CRENNAN, SUSAN MARY KIEFEL, VIRGINIA MARGARET BELL.

FEDERAL COURT OF AUSTRALIA

Chief Justice: PATRICK ANTHONY KEANE, Law Courts Bldg, Level 17, Queens Sq., NSW 2000; tel. (2) 9230-8535; fax (2) 9230-8295; e-mail query@fedcourt.gov.au; internet www.fedcourt.gov.au.

In 2012 there were 43 other judges.

FAMILY COURT OF AUSTRALIA

Chief Justice: DIANA BRYANT, GPOB 9991, Parramatta, NSW 2150; tel. (2) 8892-8578; fax (2) 8892-8585; e-mail enquiries@familylawcourts.gov.au; internet www.familycourt.gov.au.

In 2012 there were 35 other judges.

STATE SUPREME COURTS

Chief Justices: JAMES JACOB SPIGELMAN (New South Wales), MARILYN WARREN (Victoria), PAUL DE JERSEY (Queensland), JOHN JEREMY DOYLE (South Australia), WAYNE MARTIN (Western Australia), EWAN CRAWFORD (Tasmania), TERENCE JOHN HIGGINS (Australian Capital Territory), TREVOR JOHN RILEY (Northern Territory).

Religion

CHRISTIANITY

According to the provisional results of the population census of August 2006, Christians numbered 12,685,834.

National Council of Churches in Australia: Locked Bag 199, Sydney, NSW 1230; tel. (2) 9299-2215; fax (2) 9262-4514; e-mail secretariat@ncca.org.au; internet www.ncca.org.au; f. 1946; est. as Australian Council of Churches; assumed present name in 1994; 19 mem. churches; Pres. Most Rev. MICHAEL PUTNEY; Gen. Sec. Rev. TARA CURLEWIS.

The Anglican Communion

The constitution of the Church of England in Australia, which rendered the church an autonomous member of the Anglican Communion, came into force in January 1962. The body was renamed the Anglican Church of Australia in August 1981. The Church comprises five provinces (together containing 22 dioceses) and the extra-provincial diocese of Tasmania. According to the 2006 population census there were 3,718,248 adherents.

Anglican Church of Australia—General Synod Office: Suite 2, Level 9, 51 Druitt St, Sydney, NSW 2000; tel. (2) 8267-2700; fax (2) 8267-2727; e-mail reception@anglican.org.au; internet www.anglican.org.au; Primate Most Rev. Dr PHILLIP ASPINALL; Gen. Sec. MARTIN DREVIKOVSKY.

Archbishop of Adelaide and Metropolitan of South Australia: Most Rev. JEFFREY DRIVER, 18 King William Rd, North Adelaide, SA 5006; tel. (8) 8305-9350; fax (8) 8305-9399; e-mail diocesanoffice@adelaide.anglican.com.au; internet www.adelaide.anglican.com.au.

Archbishop of Brisbane and Metropolitan of Queensland, Primate of Australia: Most Rev. Dr PHILLIP JOHN ASPINALL, Bishopsbourne, GPOB 421, Brisbane, Qld 4001; tel. (7) 3835-2222; fax (7) 3832-5030; e-mail info@anglicanbrisbane.org.au; internet www.anglicanbrisbane.org.au.

Archbishop of Melbourne and Metropolitan of Victoria: Most Rev. Dr PHILIP FREIER, The Anglican Centre, 209 Flinders Lane, Melbourne, Vic 3000; tel. (3) 9653-4220; fax (3) 9653-4268; e-mail archbishop@melbourne.anglican.com.au; internet www.melbourne.anglican.com.au.

Archbishop of Perth and Metropolitan of Western Australia: Most Rev. ROGER ADRIAN HERFT, GPOB W2067, Perth, WA 6846; tel. (8) 9325-7455; fax (8) 9221-4118; e-mail diocese@perth.anglican.org; internet www.perth.anglican.org; also has jurisdiction over Christmas Island and the Cocos (Keeling) Islands.

Archbishop of Sydney and Metropolitan of New South Wales: Most Rev. Dr PETER F. JENSEN, POB Q190, QVB PO, Sydney, NSW 1230; tel. (2) 9265-1555; fax (2) 9261-4485; e-mail reception@sydney.anglican.asn.au; internet www.sydneyanglicans.net.

The Roman Catholic Church

Australia comprises five metropolitan archdioceses, two archdioceses directly responsible to the Holy See and 24 dioceses, including one diocese each for Catholics of the Maronite and Melkite rites, and one military ordinariate. At 31 December 2007 there were an estimated 5,340,466 adherents in the country.

Australian Catholic Bishops' Conference: GPOB 368, Canberra, ACT 2601; tel. (2) 6201-9845; fax (2) 6247-6083; e-mail gensec@catholic.org.au; internet www.acbc.catholic.org.au; f. 1979; Pres. Most Rev. PHILIP WILSON (Archbishop of Adelaide); Sec. Rev. BRIAN LUCAS.

Archbishop of Adelaide: Most Rev. PHILIP WILSON, GPOB 1364, Adelaide, SA 5001; tel. (8) 8210-8108; fax (8) 8223-2307; e-mail archbishop3@adelaide.catholic.org.au; internet www.adelaide.catholic.org.au.

Archbishop of Brisbane: Most Rev. MARK BENEDICT COLERIDGE, 790 Brunswick St, New Farm, Brisbane, Qld 4005; tel. (7) 3336-9361; fax (7) 3358-1357; e-mail archbishop@bne.catholic.net.au; internet www.bne.catholic.net.au.

Archbishop of Canberra and Goulburn: Most Rev. MARK BENEDICT COLERIDGE, GPOB 3089, Canberra, ACT 2601; tel. (2) 6201-9800; fax (2) 6257-7410; e-mail archbishop@cg.catholic.org.au; internet www.cg.catholic.org.au.

Archbishop of Hobart: Most Rev. ADRIAN DOYLE, GPOB 62, Hobart, Tas 7001; tel. (3) 6208-6222; fax (3) 6208-6292; e-mail vicar.general@aohtas.org.au; internet www.hobart.catholic.org.au.

Archbishop of Melbourne: Most Rev. DENIS JAMES HART, POB 146, East Melbourne, Vic 3002; tel. (3) 9926-5677; fax (3) 9926-5617; e-mail info@cam.org.au; internet www.cam.org.au.

Archbishop of Perth: Most Rev. TIMOTHY COSTELLOE, Catholic Church Office, 25 Victoria Ave, Perth, WA 6000; tel. (8) 9223-1351; fax (8) 9221-1716; e-mail enquiries@perthcatholic.org.au; internet www.perthcatholic.org.au.

Archbishop of Sydney: Cardinal GEORGE PELL, Polding Centre, 133 Liverpool St, Sydney, NSW 2000; tel. (2) 9390-5100; fax (2) 9261-8312; e-mail chancery@sydneycatholic.org; internet www.sydney.catholic.org.au.

Orthodox Churches

Greek Orthodox Archdiocese of Australia: 242 Cleveland St, Redfern, Sydney, NSW 2016; tel. (2) 9690-6100; fax (2) 9698-5368; e-mail webmaster@greekorthodox.org.au; internet www.greekorthodox.org.au; f. 1924; 700,000 mems; Primate Archbishop STYLIANOS HARKIANAKIS.

The Antiochian, Coptic, Romanian, Serbian and Syrian Orthodox Churches are also represented.

Other Christian Churches

Baptist Union of Australia: 1 Francis Ave, Broadview, SA 5083; tel. (8) 8261-1844; e-mail bua@baptist.org.au; internet www.baptist.org.au; f. 1926; 61,409 mems; 868 churches; Nat. Dir Rev. Dr JOHN BEASY.

Churches of Christ in Australia: 1st Floor, 582 Heidelberg Rd, Fairfield, Vic 3078; tel. (3) 9488-8800; fax (3) 9481-8543; e-mail eo.nc@churchesofchrist.org.au; internet cofcaustralia.org; 40,000 mems; Chair. ANDREW BALL; Fed. Coordinator CRAIG BROWN.

Lutheran Church of Australia: National Office, 197 Archer St, North Adelaide, SA 5006; tel. (8) 8267-7300; fax (8) 8267-7310; e-mail president@lca.org.au; internet www.lca.org.au; f. 1966; 70,000 mems; Pres. Rev. Dr M. P. SEMMLER.

United Pentecostal Church of Australia: POB 60, Woden, ACT 2606; tel. (2) 6291-7885; fax (2) 6281-2330; e-mail contact@upca.org.au; internet www.upca.org.au; f. 1952; over 3,000 adherents in 2008; associated with United Pentecostal Church Int. in North America; Gen. Superintendent JOHN DOWNS.

Uniting Church in Australia: POB A2266, Sydney South, NSW 1235; tel. (2) 8267-4428; fax (2) 8267-4222; e-mail enquiries@nat.uca.org.au; internet uca.org.au; f. 1977; est. as a union of Methodist, Presbyterian and Congregational Churches; 300,000 mems; Pres. Rev. ALISTAIR MACRAE; Gen. Sec. Rev. TERENCE CORKIN.

ISLAM

At the census of August 2006, the Muslim community was estimated to number 340,390.

The Australian Federation of Islamic Councils: 932 Bourke St, Zetland, Sydney, NSW 2017; tel. (2) 9319-6733; fax (2) 9319-0159; e-mail admin@afic.com.au; internet www.afic.com.au; Pres. IKEBAL PATEL; Vice-Pres. HAFEZ KASSEM.

JUDAISM

The Jewish community numbered 88,826 at the census of August 2006.

Great Synagogue: 166 Castlereagh St, Sydney, NSW; tel. (2) 9267-2477; fax (2) 9264-8871; e-mail admin@greatsynagogue.org.au; internet www.greatsynagogue.org.au; f. 1878; Sr Rabbi JEREMY LAWRENCE; Pres. MICHAEL GOLD.

OTHER FAITHS

According to the August 2006 census, Buddhists numbered 418,757 and Hindus 148,127.

The Press

The total circulation of Australia's daily newspapers is relatively high, but in the remoter parts of the country weekly papers are even more popular. Most of Australia's newspapers are published in sparsely populated rural areas where the demand for local news is strong.

ACP Publishing Pty Ltd: 54–58 Park St, Sydney, NSW 2000; tel. (2) 9282-8000; fax (2) 9267-4361; internet www.acp.com.au; publishes 60 magazines, incl. *Australian Women's Weekly*, *Cleo*, *Cosmopolitan*, *Woman's Day*, *Dolly*, *Ralph* and *Wheels*; Man. Dir PHIL SCOTT.

APN News and Media Ltd: Level 4, 100 William St, Sydney, NSW 2011; tel. (2) 9333-4999; fax (2) 9333-4900; e-mail info@apn.com.au; internet www.apn.com.au; publishes 14 daily newspapers, incl. *The Chronicle*, *Daily Mercury*, *Northern Star* and over 75 community publs; Chair. TED HARRIS (acting); Chief Exec. BRENDAN M. A. HOPKINS.

Fairfax Media: GPO 506, Sydney, NSW 2001; tel. (2) 9282-2833; fax (2) 9282-3133; internet www.fxj.com.au; f. 1987; fmrly known as John Fairfax Holdings Ltd; merged with Rural Press Ltd 2007; Chair. ROGER CORBETT; Chief Exec. GREG HYWOOD; publs include *The Sydney Morning Herald*, *The Australian Financial Review* and *Sun-Herald* (NSW), *The Age* and *BRW Publications* (Victoria), and *The Canberra Times*; also provides online and interactive services.

News Ltd: Level 23, 175 Liverpool St, Sydney, NSW 2001; tel. (2) 9288-3000; fax (2) 9288-2300; e-mail newsroom@news.com.au; internet www.news.com.au; Australian subsidiary of US News Corpn; Chair. and CEO JOHN HARTIGAN; controls *The Australian* and *The Weekend Australian* (national), *Daily Telegraph*, *Sunday Telegraph* (NSW), *The Herald Sun* and *Sunday Herald Sun* (Victoria), *Northern Territory News* (Darwin), *Sunday Times* (WA), *Townsville Bulletin*, *Courier Mail*, *Sunday Mail* (Queensland), *The Mercury* (Tasmania), *The Advertiser*, *Sunday Mail* (South Australia).

West Australian Newspapers Holdings Ltd: Newspaper House, 50 Hasler Rd, Osborne Park, WA 6017; tel. (8) 9482-9047; fax (8) 9482-9051; e-mail westinfo@wanews.com.au; internet www.thewest.com.au; Chair. KERRY STOKES; CEO CHRIS WHARTON.

NEWSPAPERS

Australian Capital Territory

The Canberra Times: POB 7155, Canberra Mail Centre, ACT 2610; tel. (2) 6280-2122; fax (2) 6280-2282; e-mail letters.editor@canberratimes.com.au; internet www.canberratimes.com.au; f. 1926; daily and Sun.; morning; Editor-in-Chief JACK WATERFORD; Editor ROD QUINN; circ. 32,116 (Mon.–Fri.), 53,051 (Sat.), 33,439 (Sun.).

New South Wales

Dailies

The Australian: POB 4245, Sydney, NSW 2001; tel. (2) 9288-3000; fax (2) 9288-2250; e-mail letters@theaustralian.com.au; internet www.theaustralian.com.au; f. 1964; distributed nationally; edited in Sydney, simultaneous edns in Sydney, Melbourne, Perth, Townsville, Adelaide and Brisbane; Editor-in-Chief CHRIS MITCHELL; Editor PAUL WHITTAKER; circ. 136,268 (Mon.–Fri.); *The Weekend Australian* (Sat.) 300,079.

Australian Financial Review: GPOB 55, Melbourne, Vic 3001; tel. (2) 9282-1547; e-mail afreditor@afr.com.au; internet www.afr.com; f. 1951; distributed nationally; Publr/Editor-in-Chief MICHAEL GILL; Editor GLENN BURGE; circ. 75,339 (Mon.–Fri.), 72,898 (Sat.).

The Daily Telegraph: News Ltd, 2 Holt St, Surry Hills, NSW 2010; tel. (2) 9288-3000; fax (2) 9288-2300; e-mail news@dailytelegraph.com.au; internet www.dailytelegraph.com.au; f. 1879; merged in 1990 with *Daily Mirror* (f. 1941); 24-hour tabloid; Editor GARRY LINNELL; circ. 363,399 (Mon.–Fri.), 325,000 (Sat.).

The Manly Daily: 26 Sydney Rd, Manly, NSW 2095; tel. (2) 9976-1909; fax (2) 9977-1203; e-mail editor@manlydaily.com.au; internet www.manlydaily.com.au; f. 1906; Tue.–Sat.; Editor LUKE MCILVEEN; circ. 91,816.

The Newcastle Herald: 28–30 Bolton St, Newcastle, NSW 2300; tel. (2) 4979-5000; fax (2) 4979-5588; e-mail news@theherald.com.au; internet www.theherald.com.au; f. 1858; morning; 6 a week; Editor ROGER BROCK; Gen. Man. JULIE AINSWORTH; circ. 48,000.

The Sydney Morning Herald: GPOB 506, Sydney, NSW 2001; tel. (2) 9282-2833; fax (2) 9282-3253; e-mail newsdesk@smh.com.au; internet www.smh.com.au; f. 1831; morning; Editor-in-Chief PETER FRAY; circ. 204,421 (Mon.–Fri.), 332,066 (Sat.).

Weeklies

Bankstown Canterbury Torch: 47 Allingham St, Condell Park, NSW 2200; tel. (2) 9795-0000; fax (2) 9795-0096; e-mail torch@torchpublishing.com.au; internet www.torchpublishing.com.au; f. 1920; Wed.; owned by Torch Publishing Co Pty Ltd; Editor MARK KIRKLAND; circ. 91,335 (Oct. 2009).

Northern District Times: Suite 2, 3 Carlingford Rd, Epping, NSW 2121; tel. (2) 9024-8716; fax (2) 9024-8788; e-mail editor@northerndistricttimes.com.au; internet www.northerndistricttimes.com.au; f. 1921; Wed.; Editor COLIN KERR; circ. 58,450.

The Parramatta Advertiser: 142–154 Macquarie St, Parramatta, NSW 2150; tel. (2) 9689-5323; fax (2) 9689-5388; e-mail editor@parramattaadvertiser.com.au; internet www.parramattaadvertiser.com.au; f. 1933; Wed.; Editor RICK ALLEN; circ. 82,677.

St George and Sutherland Shire Leader: 13A, Montgomery St, Kogarah, NSW 2217; tel. (2) 9588-8888; fax (2) 9588-8887; e-mail leaderenquiries@fairfaxmedia.com.au; internet www.theleader.com.au; f. 1960; Tue. and Thur.; Editor ALBERT MARTINEZ; circ. 148,713.

Sun-Herald: GPOB 506, Sydney, NSW 2001; tel. (2) 9282-2833; fax (2) 9282-2151; e-mail newsdesk@smh.com.au; internet www.smh.com.au; f. 1953; Sun.; Editor RICK FENELEY; circ. 429,199.

Sunday Telegraph: 2 Holt St, Surry Hills, NSW 2010; tel. (2) 9288-3000; fax (2) 9288-2300; e-mail letters@sundaytelegraph.com.au; f. 1938; Editor NEIL BREEN; circ. 635,269.

Northern Territory

Daily

Northern Territory News: Printers Place, GPOB 1300, Darwin, NT 0801; tel. (8) 8944-9900; fax (8) 8981-6045; e-mail ntnmail@ntnews.com.au; internet www.ntnews.com.au; f. 1952; morning; Editor-in-Chief JULIAN RICCI; Gen. Man. EVAN HANNAH; circ. 22,989 (Mon.–Sat.); *The Sunday Territorian*, circ. 22,624.

Weekly

Centralian Advocate: 2 Gap Rd, Alice Springs, NT 0871; tel. (8) 8950-9777; fax (8) 8950-9740; e-mail ceneditorial@aliceadvocate.com.au; f. 1947; Tue. and Thur.; Editor DALLAS FRAKKING; circ. 6,992 (Sept. 2009).

Queensland

Dailies

The Courier-Mail: Cnr Mayne Rd and Campbell St, Bowen Hills, Qld 4001; tel. (7) 3666-6775; fax (7) 3666-6696; e-mail crutcherm@gnp.newsltd.com.au; internet www.thecouriermail.com.au; f. 1933; morning; Editor MICHAEL CRUTCHER; Man. Editor ANNA REYNOLDS; circ. 206,110 (Mon.–Fri.), 278,982 (Sat.).

Gold Coast Bulletin: 385 Southport Nerang Rd, Molendinar, Qld 4214; tel. (7) 5584–2000; internet www.goldcoast.com.au; f. 1885; 6 a week; Editor DEAN GOULD; circ. 39,128 (Mon.–Fri.), 64,915 (Sat.).

Weekly

The Sunday Mail: cnr Mayne Rd and Campbell St, Bowen Hills, Qld 4006; tel. (7) 3666-6276; fax (7) 3666-6767; e-mail mcanenya@qnp.newsltd.com.au; internet www.thesundaymail.com.au; f. 1923; Editor SCOTT THOMPSON; circ. 1,115,000.

South Australia

Daily

The Advertiser: 31 Waymouth St, Adelaide, SA 5000; tel. (8) 8206-2000; fax (8) 8206-3669; e-mail tiser@adv.newsltd.com.au; internet www.adelaidenow.com.au; f. 1858; morning; Editor MELVIN MANSELL; circ. 180,807 (Mon.–Fri.), 242,903 (Sat.).

Weekly

Sunday Mail: Level 2, 31 Waymouth St, GPOB 339, Adelaide, SA 5000; tel. (8) 8206-2000; fax (8) 8206-3646; e-mail mailedit@sundaymail.com.au; internet www.adelaidenow.com.au; f. 1912; Editor MEGAN LLOYD; circ. 294,930.

Tasmania

Dailies

The Advocate: POB 63, Burnie, Tas 7320; tel. (3) 6440-7409; fax (3) 6440-7340; e-mail news@theadvocate.com.au; internet www.theadvocate.com.au; f. 1890; morning; Editor JASON PURDIE; circ. 22,786.

Examiner: 71–75 Paterson St, POB 99, Launceston, Tas 7250; tel. (3) 6336-7111; fax (3) 6334-7328; e-mail admin@examiner.com.au; internet www.examiner.com.au; f. 1842; 6 a week; Editor MARTIN GILMOUR; Gen. Man. PHIL LEERSEN; circ. 31,144.

Mercury: 93 Macquarie St, Hobart, Tas 7000; tel. (3) 6230-0622; fax (3) 6230-0711; e-mail mercury.news@dbl.newsltd.com.au; internet www.themercury.com.au; f. 1854; morning; Man. Dir REX GARDNER; Editor GARRY BAILEY; circ. 44,221 (Mon.–Fri.), 60,082 (Sat.); *Sunday Tasmanian*, circ. 57,868.

Weekly

Sunday Examiner: 71–75 Paterson St, Launceston, Tas 7250; tel. (3) 6336-7111; fax (3) 6334-7328; e-mail mail@examiner.com.au; internet www.examiner.com.au; f. 1924; Editor MARTIN GILMOUR; circ. 38,826.

Victoria

Dailies

The Age: 655 Collins St, Docklands, Melbourne, Vic 3008; tel. (3) 8667-2250; e-mail newsdesk@theage.com.au; internet www.theage.com.au; f. 1854; morning; Editor-in-Chief PAUL RAMADGE; Chief Exec. DON CHURCHILL; circ. 190,100 (Mon.–Fri.), 273,700 (Sat.).

Geelong Advertiser: 191–195 Ryrie St, Geelong, Vic 3220; tel. (3) 5227-4300; fax (3) 5227-4330; internet www.geelongadvertiser.com.au; f. 1840; morning; Editor STEELE TALLON; circ. 25,586 (Mon.–Fri.), 44,319 (Sat.).

Herald Sun: HWT Tower, 40 City Rd, Southbank, Vic 3006; tel. (3) 9292-2000; fax (3) 9292-2112; e-mail news@heraldsun.com.au; internet www.heraldsun.com.au; f. 1840; Editor-in-Chief PETER BLUNDEN; Editor SIMON PRISTEL; circ. 500,800 (Mon.–Fri.), 495,600 (Sat.).

Weeklies

The Sunday Age: 655 Collins St, Docklands, Melbourne, Vic 3008; tel. (3) 8667-2250; e-mail newsdesk@theage.com.au; internet www.theage.com.au; f. 1989; Editor GAY ALCORN; circ. 226,700.

Sunday Herald Sun: HWT Tower, 40 City Rd, Southbank, Vic 3006; tel. (3) 9292-2963; fax (3) 9292-2080; e-mail sundayhs@heraldsun.com.au; internet www.heraldsun.com.au; f. 1991; Editor SIMON PRISTEL; circ. 593,700.

Western Australia

Daily

The West Australian: GPOB D162, Perth, WA 6840; tel. (8) 9482-3111; fax (8) 9482-9080; internet www.thewest.com.au; f. 1833; morning; Editor BRETT MCCARTHY; circ. 192,230 (Mon.–Fri.), 316,062 (Sat.).

Weekly

Sunday Times: 34 Stirling St, Perth, WA 6000; tel. (8) 9326-8326; fax (8) 9221-1121; e-mail editorial@sundaytimes.newsltd.com.au; internet www.perthnow.com.au; f. 1897; Man. Dir DAVID MAGUIRE; Editor SAM WEIR; circ. 293,136.

PRINCIPAL PERIODICALS

Weeklies and Fortnightlies

Business Review Weekly (BRW): GPOB 55, Melbourne, Vic 3001; tel. (2) 9282-1111; fax (2) 9282-1779; e-mail brweditor@brw.fairfax.com.au; internet www.brw.com.au; f. 1981; Editor-in-Chief SEAN AYLMER; Editor KATE MILLS; circ. 45,467.

Computerworld Australia: Level 22, 8–20 Napier St, North Sydney, NSW 2060; tel. (2) 9902-2700; fax (2) 9439-5512; e-mail editor@idg.com.au; internet www.computerworld.com.au; weekly; information technology news; Editor MATT RODGERS.

The Countryman: GPOB D162, Perth, WA 6840; tel. (8) 9482-3327; fax (8) 9482-3314; e-mail countryman@wanews.com.au; internet countryman.thewest.com.au; f. 1885; Thur.; farming; Editor CAMERON MORSE; circ. 10,500.

The Medical Journal of Australia: Locked Bag 3030, Strawberry Hills, NSW 2012; tel. (2) 9562-6666; fax (2) 9562-6699; e-mail medjaust@ampco.com.au; internet www.mja.com.au; f. 1914; fortnightly; Editor Dr MARTIN VAN DER WEYDEN; circ. 27,532.

New Idea: 35–51 Mitchell St, McMahons Point, NSW 2060; tel. (2) 9464-3200; fax (2) 9464-3203; e-mail letters@newidea.com.au; internet www.newidea.com.au; weekly; women's; Editor KIM WILSON; Publr SUZANNE MONKS; circ. 327,649.

News Weekly: 35 Whitehorse Rd, POB 251, Balwyn, Vic 3103; tel. (3) 9816-0800; fax (3) 9816-0899; e-mail nw@newsweekly.com.au; internet www.newsweekly.com.au; f. 1943; publ. by Nat. Civic Council; fortnightly; Sat.; political, social, educational and trade union affairs; Editor PETER WESTMORE; circ. 9,000.

NW: 54 Park St, Sydney, NSW 2000; tel. (2) 9282-2000; e-mail nw@acp.com.au; internet www.nwonline.com.au; weekly; entertainment news; Editor LISA SINCLAIR; circ. 143,302.

People: Level 18, 66–68 Goulburn St, Sydney, NSW 2000; tel. (2) 9282-8388; fax (2) 9283-7923; e-mail mvine@acpmagazines.com.au; internet www.acpmagazines.com.au/people.htm; weekly; men's interest; Editor SHANE CUBIS; circ. 40,045.

Picture: GPOB 5201, Sydney, NSW 2001; tel. (2) 9288-9686; fax (2) 9267-4372; e-mail picture@acp.com.au; internet www.acp.com.au/the_picture.htm; weekly; men's interest; Editor SHAYNE BUGDEN; circ. 56,559.

Queensland Country Life: cnr Finucane Rd and Delancey St, Ormiston, Qld 4160; tel. (7) 3826-8200; fax (7) 3821-1226; e-mail editorialsec.qcl@ruralpress.com; internet qcl.farmonline.com.au; f. 1935; Thur.; Editor MARK PHELPS; Gen. Man. JOHN WARLTERS; circ. 31,770.

Stock and Land: Unit 6, 99–101 Western Ave, Tullamarine, Vic 3043; tel. (3) 9344-9999; fax (3) 9338-1044; e-mail stockandland@ruralpress.com; internet www.stockandland.com; f. 1914; weekly; agricultural and rural news; Editor ALISHA FOGDEN; circ. 8,820 (2011).

Take 5: 54–58 Park St, Sydney, NSW 2000; tel. (2) 9282-8000; fax (2) 9267-4361; e-mail take5@acpmagazines.com.au; internet www.take5mag.com.au; weekly; Editor BELINDA WALLIS; circ. 221,033.

That's Life!: 35–51 Mitchell St, McMahons Point, NSW 2060; tel. (2) 9464-3300; fax (2) 9464-3480; e-mail thatslife@pacificmags.com.au; internet www.thatslife.com.au; f. 1994; weekly; features; Editor LINDA SMITH; circ. 305,607.

Time South Pacific: Level 10, 32 Walker St, North Sydney, NSW 2060; tel. (2) 9925-2500; fax (2) 9954-0828; e-mail letters@time.com; internet www.time.com/time/magazine/pacific; weekly; current affairs; Editor STEVE WATERSON; circ. 76,514.

TV Week: 54 Park St, Sydney, NSW 2000; tel. (2) 9288-9611; fax (2) 9283-4849; e-mail tvweek@acp.com.au; internet www.tvweek.ninemsn.com.au; f. 1957; Wed.; colour national; Editor EMMA NOLAN; circ. 226,832.

The Weekly Times: POB 14999, Melbourne, Vic 8001; tel. (3) 9292-2672; fax (3) 9292-2697; e-mail wtimes@theweeklytimes.com.au; internet www.weeklytimesnow.com.au; f. 1869; farming, regional issues, country life; Wed.; Editor ED GANNON; circ. 78,900.

Woman's Day: POB 5245, Sydney, NSW 2001; tel. (2) 9282-8000; fax (2) 9267-4360; e-mail womansday@acp.com.au; internet womansday.ninemsn.com.au; weekly; circulates throughout Australia and NZ; Editor FIONA CONNOLLY; circ. 406,825.

Monthlies and Others

Architectural Product News: Architecture Media Pty Ltd, Level 6, 163 Eastern Rd, South Melbourne, Vic 3205; tel. (3) 8699-1000; fax (3) 9696-2617; e-mail apn@archmedia.com.au; internet www.architecturemedia.com; 6 a year; Editorial Dir CAMERON BRUHN; Editor PETER DAVIES; circ. 24,584.

Australian Geographic: 54 Park St, Sydney, NSW 2000; tel. (2) 9263-9813; fax (2) 9263-9810; e-mail editorial@ausgeo.com.au; internet www.australiangeographic.com.au; f. 1986; every 3 months; Man. Dir RORY SCOTT; Editor IAN CONNELLAN; circ. 140,724.

Australian Good Taste: Locked Bag 5030, Alexandria, NSW 2015; tel. (2) 9353-6666; fax (2) 9353-6699; e-mail goodtaste@newsmagazines.com.au; internet www.taste.com.au/good+taste; monthly; food and lifestyle; Editor BRODEE MYERS-COOKE; circ. 134,003.

Australian Gourmet Traveller: GPOB 4088, Sydney, NSW 2001; tel. (2) 9282-8758; fax (2) 9264-3621; e-mail gourmet@acpmagazines.com.au; internet gourmettraveller.com.au; monthly; food and travel; Editor ANTHEA LOUCAS; circ. 74,292.

Australian Home Beautiful: 35–51 Mitchell St, McMahons Point, NSW 2060; tel. (2) 9464-3218; fax (2) 9464-3263; e-mail homebeautiful@pacificmags.com.au; internet www.homebeautiful.com.au; f. 1925; monthly; Editor WENDY MOORE; circ. 70,480.

Australian House and Garden: 54 Park St, Sydney, NSW 2000; tel. (2) 9282-8456; fax (2) 9267-4912; internet www.houseandgarden.com.au; f. 1948; monthly; design, decorating, renovating, gardens, food, travel, health and beauty; Editor-in-Chief LISA GREEN; circ. 96,554.

Australian Journal of Mining: Informa Australia Pty Ltd, Level 2, 120 Sussex St, Sydney, NSW 2000; tel. (2) 9080-4443; e-mail charles.macdonald@informa.com.au; internet www.theajmonline.com; f. 1986; bi-monthly; mining and exploration throughout Australia and South Pacific; Editor CHARLES MACDONALD; circ. 5,875.

Australian Journal of Pharmacy: Level 5, 8 Thomas St, Chatswood, NSW 2067; tel. (2) 8117-9500; fax (2) 8117-9511; e-mail david.weston@appco.com.au; internet www.ajp.com.au; f. 1886; monthly; journal for pharmacists and pharmaceutical industry; Publishing Dir DAVID WESTON; Editor MATTHEW ETON; circ. 16,260.

Australian Law Journal: 100 Harris St, Pyrmont, NSW 2009; tel. (2) 8587-7000; fax (2) 8587-7104; e-mail lta.alj@thomsonreuters.com; internet www.thomsonreuters.com.au; f. 1927; monthly; Gen. Editor Justice P. W. YOUNG; circ 4,500.

Australian Photography: 17–21 Bellevue St, Surry Hills, NSW 2010; tel. (2) 9281-2333; fax (2) 9281-2750; e-mail robertkeeley@yaffa.com.au; f. 1950; monthly; Editor ROBERT KEELEY; circ. 9,099.

The Australian Women's Weekly: 54–58 Park St, Sydney, NSW 2000; tel. (2) 9282-8000; fax (2) 9267-4459; e-mail womensweekly@acpmagazines.com.au; internet www.aww.ninemsn.com.au; f. 1933; monthly; Editor-in-Chief HELEN MCCABE; circ. 493,301.

Belle: 54 Park St, Sydney, NSW 2000; tel. (2) 9282-8000; fax (2) 9267-8037; e-mail belle@acp.com.au; internet www.acpmagazines.com.au/belle.htm; f. 1975; every 2 months; interior design and architecture; Editor-in-Chief NEALE WHITAKER; circ. 35,190.

Better Homes and Gardens: 35–51 Mitchell St, McMahon's Point, NSW 2060; e-mail bhgmagenquiries@pacificmags.com.au; internet au.lifestyle.yahoo.com/better-homes-gardens; f. 1978; 13 a year; Editor JULIA ZAETTA; circ. 370,000.

Cleo: 54 Park St, Sydney, NSW 2000; tel. (2) 9282-8617; fax (2) 9267-4368; internet www.cleo.com.au; f. 1972; women's monthly; Editor NATALIE POOL; circ. 134,286.

Cosmopolitan: 54 Park St, Sydney, NSW 2000; tel. (2) 9282-8039; fax (2) 9267-4457; e-mail cosmo@acp.com.au; internet www.cosmopolitan.com.au; f. 1973; monthly; women's lifestyle; Editor BRONWYN MCCAHON; circ. 166,208.

Delicious: Locked Bag 5030, Alexandria, NSW 2015; tel. (2) 9353-6666; fax (2) 9353-6699; e-mail delicious@newsmagazines.com.au; internet www.taste.com.au/delicious; 11 a year; food and lifestyle; Editor TRUDI JENKINS; circ. 129,626.

Dolly: 54–58 Park St, Sydney, NSW 2000; tel. (2) 9282-8437; fax (2) 9126-3715; internet dolly.ninemsn.com.au/dolly; f. 1970; monthly; for young women; Editor TIFFANY DUNK; circ. 103,131.

Family Circle: Pacific Magazines, Media City, 8 Central Ave, Eveleigh, NSW 2015; tel. (2) 9394-2866; fax (2) 9394-2481; internet www.pacificmagazines.com.au; 2 a year; Editor-in-Chief JULIA ZAETTA; circ. 87,301.

FHM: EMAP Australia, Level 6, 187 Thomas St, Haymarket, Sydney, NSW 2000; tel. (2) 9581-9400; fax (2) 9581-9570; e-mail incoming@emap.com.au; internet www.fhm.com.au; monthly; men's interest; Editor GUY MOSEL; circ. 51,063.

Financial Review Smart Investor: 201 Sussex St, GPOB 506, Sydney, NSW 2000; tel. (2) 9282-2822; fax (2) 9603-3137; e-mail smartinvestor@afr.com.au; internet www.afrsmartinvestor.com; monthly; Editor NICOLE PEDERSEN-MCKINNON.

Gardening Australia: POB 199, Alexandria, NSW 1435; tel. (2) 9353-6666; fax (2) 9317-4615; e-mail ga@newsmagazines.com.au; internet www.gardeningaustralia.com.au; f. 1991; monthly; Editor JENNIFER STACKHOUSE; circ. 94,868.

Girlfriend: Media City, 8 Central Ave, Eveleigh, NSW 2015; tel. (2) 9464-3300; fax (2) 9464-3483; e-mail girlfriend@pacificmags.com.au; internet www.girlfriend.com.au; monthly; for teenage girls; Editor SARAH TARCA; circ. 108,119.

Good Health and Medicine: 54 Park St, Sydney, NSW 2000; tel. (2) 9282-8000; fax (2) 9267-4361; internet health.ninemsn.com.au/goodmedicine/goodmedicine.aspx; monthly; fmrly Good Medicine; health and beauty; Editor CATHERINE MARSHALL; circ. 66,115.

Houses: Architecture Media Pty Ltd, Level 6, 163 Eastern Rd, South Melbourne, Vic 3205; tel. (3) 8699-1000; fax (3) 9696-2617; e-mail houses@archmedia.com.au; internet www.architecturemedia.com/houses; f. 1989; 6 a year; Publisher/Editorial Dir SUE HARRIS; Editoral Dir CAMERON BRUHN; circ. 19,877.

K-Zone: Media City, 8 Central Ave, Eveleigh, NSW 2015; tel. (2) 9394-2760; fax (2) 9464-3483; e-mail kzone@pacificmags.com.au; internet www.kzone.com.au; monthly; gaming and entertainment; Editor DANIEL FINDLAY; circ. 50,272.

Marie Claire: Media City, 8 Central Ave, Eveleigh, NSW 2015; tel. (2) 9394-2372; e-mail marieclaire@pacificmags.com.au; internet www.marieclaire.com.au; f. 1995; owned by Pacific Magazines Pty Ltd; monthly; fashion and lifestyle; Editor and Publr JACKIE FRANK; circ. 100,128 (2011).

Motor: POB 4088, Sydney, NSW 2001; tel. (2) 9288-9172; fax (2) 9263-9777; e-mail motor@acpmagazines.com.au; f. 1954; monthly; Editor ANDREW MACLEAN; circ. 50,085.

Open Road: NRMA Publishing, Level 1, 9 George St, North Strathfield, NSW 2137; tel. (2) 8741-6675; fax (2) 8741-6697; e-mail open.road@mynrma.com.au; internet www.openroad.com.au; f. 1927; every 2 months; journal of Nat. Roads and Motorists' Asscn (NRMA); Publr BERNADETTE BRENNAN; Editor-in-Chief SUZANNE MONKS; circ. 1,555,917.

Ralph: 54–58 Park St, Sydney, NSW 2000; tel. (2) 9282-8000; fax (2) 9267-4361; internet ralph.ninemsn.com.au; monthly; men's lifestyle; Editor SANTI PINTADO; circ. 68,061.

Reader's Digest: GPOB 5030, Sydney, NSW 2001; tel. (2) 9690-6111; fax (2) 9690-6211; e-mail editors.au@readersdigest.com; internet www.readersdigest.au.com; monthly; Editor-in-Chief SUE CARNEY; circ. 325,028.

Street Machine: Locked Bag 756, Epping, NSW 2121; tel. (2) 9868-4832; fax (2) 9869-7390; e-mail streetmachine@acpaction.com.au; internet www.acpmagazines.com.au/street_machine.htm; monthly; motoring magazine; Editor GEOFF SEDDON; circ. 50,840.

Super Food Ideas: Locked Bag 5030, Alexandria, NSW 2015; tel. (2) 9353-6666; fax (2) 9353-6699; e-mail superfoodideas@newsmagazines.com.au; internet www.taste.com.au/super+food+ideas; 11 a year; Editor REBECCA COX; circ. 271,376.

TV Soap: Level 5, 55 Chandos St, St Leonards, NSW 2065; tel. (2) 9901-6132; fax (2) 9901-6116; e-mail tvsoap@next.com.au; internet www.tvsoap.com.au; f. 1983; monthly; Editor VESNA PETROPOULOS; circ. 103,000.

Vogue Australia: 180 Bourke Rd, Alexandria, NSW 2015; tel. (2) 9353-6666; fax (2) 9353-0935; e-mail vogue@vogue.com.au; internet www.vogue.com.au; f. 1959; monthly; fashion; Editor KIRSTIE CLEMENTS; circ. 50,752.

Wheels: GPOB 4088, Sydney, NSW 2001; tel. (2) 9263-9732; fax (2) 9263-9702; e-mail wheels@acp.com.au; internet motoring.ninemsn.com.au/wheelsmag; f. 1953; monthly; international motoring magazine; Editor GED BULMER; circ. 55,338.

Your Garden: Media City 8, Cen. Ave, Eveleigh, NSW 2015; tel. (2) 9394-2381; fax (2) 9394-4206; e-mail yg@pacificmags.com.au; internet pacificmagazines.com.au/Pages/Magazines; f. 1947; every three months; owned by Pacific Magazines; Editor GEOFFREY BURNIE; circ. 53,824.

NEWS AGENCY

AAP: 3 Rider Blvd, Rhodes Waterside, Rhodes, NSW 2138; tel. (2) 9322-8000; fax (2) 9322-8888; e-mail customerservice@aap.com.au; internet www.aap.com.au; f. 1983; owned by major daily newspapers of Australia; Chair. MICHAEL GILL; CEO BRUCE DAVIDSON.

PRESS ASSOCIATIONS

Australian Press Council: Suite 10.02, 117 York St, Sydney, NSW 2000; tel. (2) 9261-1930; fax (2) 9267-6826; e-mail info@presscouncil.org.au; internet www.presscouncil.org.au; Chair. Prof. JULIAN DISNEY.

Community Newspapers of Australia Pty Ltd: POB 234, Auburn, NSW 1835; tel. (2) 8789-7362; fax (2) 8789-7387; e-mail kim@cna.org.au; internet www.cna.org.au; Fed. Pres. GENE SWINSTEAD; Exec. Sec. ROBYN BAKER.

Country Press Association of SA Inc: 198 Greenhill Rd, Eastwood, SA 5063; tel. (8) 8373-6533; fax (8) 8373-6544; e-mail countrypsa@bigpond.com; internet www.sacountrypress.com.au; f. 1912; represents South Australian country newspapers; Pres. T. MCAULIFFE; Admin. Officer MARILYN MCAULIFFE.

Country Press Australia: 163 Epsom Rd, Flemington, Vic 3031; tel. (3) 8387-5580; fax (3) 9372-2427; internet www.countrypress.net.au; f. 1906; 420 mems.

Queensland Country Press Association: POB 229, Kelvin Grove DC, Qld 4059; tel. (7) 3356-0033; fax (7) 3356-0027; e-mail nmclary@qcpa.com.au; internet www.qcpa.com.au; Pres. DAVID RICHARDSON; Exec. Dir NEAL MCLARY; 26 mems.

Tasmanian Press Association Pty Ltd: 71–75 Paterson St, Launceston, Tas 7250; tel. (3) 6336-7111; Sec. TOM O'MEARA.

Victorian Country Press Association Ltd: 1st Floor, 163 Epsom Rd, Flemington, Vic 3031; tel. (3) 8387-5500; fax (3) 9371-2792; internet www.vcpa.com.au; f. 1910; Pres. KEN JENKINS; Exec. Dir J. E. RAY; 110 mems.

Publishers

Allen and Unwin Pty Ltd: 83 Alexander St, Crows Nest, NSW 2065; tel. (2) 8425-0100; fax (2) 9906-2218; e-mail info@allenandunwin.com; internet www.allenandunwin.com; fiction, trade, academic, children's; Exec. Chair. and Publishing Dir PATRICK A. GALLAGHER; Man. Dir PAUL DONOVAN.

Australasian Medical Publishing Co Pty Ltd: AMPCo House, 277 Clarence St, Sydney, NSW 2000; tel. (2) 9562-6666; fax (2) 9562-6699; e-mail ampco@ampco.com.au; internet www.ampco.com.au; f. 1913; scientific, medical and educational; Gen. Man. JACKIE GAMBRELL.

Black Inc: 37–39 Langridge St, Collingwood, Vic 3066; tel. (3) 9654-0288; fax (3) 9654-0244; e-mail enquiries@blackincbooks.com; internet www.blackincbooks.com; f. 2000; literary fiction and non-fiction; an imprint of Schwartz Publishing; Man. Dir SOPHY WILLIAMS.

Cambridge University Press (Australia): 477 Williamstown Rd, PB 31, Port Melbourne, Vic 3207; tel. (3) 8671-1411; fax (3) 9676-9966; e-mail enquiries@cambridge.edu.au; internet www.cambridge.org/aus; scholarly and educational; Chief Exec. STEPHEN BOURNE.

Cengage Learning Australia Pty Ltd: Level 7, 80 Dorcas St, South Melbourne, Vic 3205; tel. (3) 9685-4111; fax (3) 9685-4199; e-mail anz.customerservice@cengage.com; internet www.cengage.com.au; fmrly Thomson Learning Australia, name changed as above 2007; educational; Gen. Man. PAUL PETRULIS.

Commonwealth Scientific and Industrial Research Organisation (CSIRO Publishing): 150 Oxford St, POB 1139, Collingwood, Vic 3066; tel. (3) 9662-7500; fax (3) 9662-7595; e-mail publishing@csiro.au; internet www.publish.csiro.au; f. 1926; scientific and technical journals, books, magazines, videos, CD-ROMs; Gen. Man. P. W. REEKIE.

Elsevier Australia: Level 12, Tower 1, 475 Victoria Ave, Chatswood, NSW 2067; tel. (2) 9422-8500; fax (2) 9422-8501; e-mail customerserviceau@elsevier.com; internet www.elsevier.com.au; a division of Reed Int. Books Australia Pty Ltd; health sciences, science and medicine; Man. Dir ROB KOLKMAN.

Encyclopaedia Britannica Australia Ltd: POB 5608, Chatswood West, NSW 1515; tel. (2) 9915-8800; fax (2) 9419-5247; e-mail feedback@britannica.com.au; internet www.britannica.com.au; reference, education, art, science and commerce; Man. Dir JAMES BUCKLE.

Harlequin Enterprises (Australia) Pty Ltd: Locked Bag 7002, Chatswood, NSW 2067; tel. (2) 9415-9200; fax (2) 9415-9292; internet www.eHarlequin.com.au; Man. Dir MICHELLE LAFOREST.

Hyland House Publishing Pty Ltd: POB 1116, Carlton, Vic 3053; tel. (3) 9818-5700; fax (3) 9818-5044; e-mail info@hylandhouse.com.au; internet www.hylandhouse.com.au; f. 1977; Aboriginal and children's literature, gardening, pet care; Rep. MICHAEL SCHOO.

Lansdowne Publishing: POB 1669, Crows Nest, NSW 1585; tel. and fax (2) 9436-2974; e-mail info@lansdownepublishing.com.au; internet www.lansdownepublishing.com.au; cookery, new age, interior design, gardening, health, history, spirituality; Chief Exec. STEVEN MORRIS.

LexisNexis: Tower 2, 475–495 Victoria Ave, Chatswood, NSW 2067; tel. (2) 9422-2174; fax (2) 9422-2405; e-mail customer.relations@lexisnexis.com.au; internet www.lexisnexis.com.au; f. 1910; div. of Reed Elsevier; legal and commercial; CEO T. J. VILJOEN.

McGraw-Hill Australia Pty Ltd: Level 2, The Everglade Bldg, 82 Waterloo Rd, North Ryde, NSW 2113; tel. (2) 9900-1800; fax (2) 9900-1980; e-mail cservice_sydney@mcgraw-hill.com; internet www.mcgraw-hill.com.au; f. 1964; educational, professional and technical; Man. Dir MURRAY ST LEGER.

Melbourne University Publishing Ltd: 187 Grattan St, Carlton, Vic 3053; tel. (3) 9342-0300; fax (3) 9342-0399; e-mail mup-info@unimelb.edu.au; internet www.mup.com.au; f. 1922; scholarly non-fiction, Australian history and biography; CEO LOUISE ADLER.

Murdoch Books: GPOB 4115, Sydney, NSW 2001; tel. (2) 8220-2000; fax (2) 8220-2558; e-mail inquiry@murdochbooks.com.au; internet www.murdochbooks.com.au; cooking, gardening, DIY, craft, gift, general leisure and lifestyle, narrative, history, non-fiction, travel memoirs and business; CEO MATT HANDBURY; Publishing Dir CHRIS RENNIE.

National Library of Australia: Parkes Place, Canberra, ACT 2600; tel. (2) 6262-1111; fax (2) 6257-1703; e-mail media@nla.gov.au; internet www.nla.gov.au; f. 1968; produces trade and library-related publs; Chair. JAMES J. SPIGELMAN.

Oxford University Press: 253 Normanby Rd, South Melbourne, Vic 3205; tel. (3) 9934-9123; fax (3) 9934-9100; e-mail cs.au@oup.com; internet www.oup.com.au; f. 1908; general non-fiction and educational; Man. Dir MAREK PALKA.

Pan Macmillan Australia Pty Ltd: Level 25, BT Tower, 1 Market St, Sydney NSW 2000; tel. (2) 9285-9100; fax (2) 9285-9190; e-mail pansyd@macmillan.com.au; internet www.panmacmillan.com.au; general, reference, children's, fiction, non-fiction; Chair. R. GIBB.

Pearson Education Australia Pty Ltd: Unit 4, Level 3, 14 Aquatic Dr., Frenchs Forest, NSW 2086; tel. (2) 9454-2200; fax (2) 9453-0089; e-mail customer.service@pearson.com.au; internet www.pearson.com.au; f. 1957; mainly educational, academic, computer, some general; CEO MARJORIE SCARDINO.

Penguin Group (Australia): POB 701, Hawthorn, Vic 3122; tel. (3) 9811-2400; fax (3) 9811-2620; internet www.penguin.com.au; f. 1946; general; Man. Dir GABRIELLE COYNE; Publishing Dir ROBERT SESSIONS.

Random House Australia Pty Ltd: Level 3, 100 Pacific Highway, North Sydney, NSW 2060; tel. (2) 9954-9966; fax (2) 9954-4562; e-mail random@randomhouse.com.au; internet www.randomhouse.com.au; fiction, non-fiction and children's; Man. Dir MARGARET SEALE.

Reader's Digest (Australia) Pty Ltd: GPOB 5030, Sydney, NSW 2001; tel. (2) 9018-6000; fax (2) 9018-7000; e-mail customerservice.au@readersdigest.com; internet www.readersdigest.com.au; general; Man. Dir PAUL HEATH.

Scholastic Australia Pty Ltd: 76–80 Railway Cres., Lisarow, NSW 2250; tel. (2) 4328-3555; fax (2) 4323-3827; e-mail customer_service@scholastic.com.au; internet www.scholastic.com.au; f. 1968; educational and children's; Man. Dir DAVID PEAGRAM.

Schwartz Publishing (Victoria) Pty Ltd: 37–39 Langridge St, Melbourne, Vic 3000; tel. (3) 9486-0288; fax (3) 9486-0244; e-mail admin@blackincbooks.com; internet www.blackincbooks.com; non-fiction; Dir MORRY SCHWARTZ.

Simon and Schuster (Australia) Pty Ltd: Suite 19A, Level 1, Bldg C, 450 Miller St, Cammeray, NSW 2062; tel. (2) 9983-6600; fax (2) 9988-4232; e-mail cservice@simonandschuster.com.au; internet www.simonandschuster.com.au; non-fiction incl. anthropology, cooking, gardening, house and home, craft, parenting, health, history, travel, biography, motivation and management; Man. Dir LOU JOHNSON.

Thames and Hudson Australia Pty Ltd: 11 Central Boulevard, Portside Business Park, Fishermans Bend, Vic 3207; tel. (3) 9646-7788; fax (3) 9646-8790; e-mail enquiries@thaust.com.au; internet www.thamesandhudson.com.au; art, history, archaeology, architecture, photography, design, fashion, textiles, lifestyle; Man. Dir JAMIE CAMPLIN.

Thomson Reuters Australia Ltd: Level 5, 100 Harris St, Pyrmont, NSW 2009; tel. (2) 8587-7980; fax (2) 8587-7981; e-mail LTA.Service@thomsonreuters.com; internet www.thomsonreuters.com.au; legal, professional, tax and accounting; CEO TONY KINNEAR.

Thorpe-Bowker: Level 1, 607 St Kilda Rd, Melbourne, Vic 3004; tel. (3) 8517-8333; fax (3) 8517-8399; e-mail yoursay@thorpe.com.au; internet www.thorpe.com.au; bibliographic, library and book trade reference; Gen. Man. GARY PENGELLY.

UNSW Press Ltd: University of New South Wales, Sydney, NSW 2052; tel. (2) 9664-0900; fax (2) 9664-5420; e-mail enquiries@newsouthpublishing.com.au; internet www.unswpress.com.au; f. 1962; scholarly, general and tertiary texts; Chief Exec. KATHY BAIL.

University of Queensland Press: POB 6042, St Lucia, Qld 4067; tel. (7) 3365-7244; fax (7) 3365-7579; e-mail uqp@uqp.uq.edu.au; internet www.uqp.uq.edu.au; f. 1948; scholarly and general cultural interest, incl. Black Australian writers, adult and children's fiction; Gen. Man. GREG BAIN.

University of Western Australia Press: 35 Stirling Highway, Crawley, WA 6009; tel. (8) 6488-3670; fax (8) 6488-1027; e-mail admin-uwap@uwa.edu.au; internet uwap.uwa.edu.au; f. 1935; literary fiction, natural history, history, literary studies, Australiana, general non-fiction; Dir Assoc. Prof. TERRI-ANN WHITE.

John Wiley & Sons Australia, Ltd: POB 3065, Stafford BC, Qld 4053; tel. (7) 3859-9755; fax (7) 3859-9715; e-mail brisbane@wiley.com; internet au.wiley.com; f. 1954; educational, reference and trade; Pres. and CEO STEPHEN SMITH.

PUBLISHERS' ASSOCIATION

Australian Publishers Association Ltd: 60/89 Jones St, Ultimo, NSW 2007; tel. (2) 9281-9788; fax (2) 9281-1073; e-mail apa@publishers.asn.au; internet www.publishers.asn.au; f. 1948; over 210 mems; Pres. STEPHEN MAY; Chief Exec. MAREE MCCASKILL.

Broadcasting and Communications

TELECOMMUNICATIONS

In 2012 189 licensed telecommunications carriers were in operation.

AAPT Ltd: 680 George St, Sydney, NSW 2000; tel. (2) 9009-9009; fax (2) 9009-9999; internet www.aapt.com.au; f. 1991; part of Telecom New Zealand Group; long-distance telecommunications carrier; CEO DAVID YUILE.

Hutchison Telecoms Australia: Level 7, 40 Mount St, NSW 2060; tel. (2) 8579-8888; fax (2) 8904-0457; e-mail investors@hutchison.com.au; internet www.hutchison.com.au; f. 2003; mobile services; owns 50% share in Vodafone Hutchison Australia; Chair. CANNING FOK KIN-NING.

Optus Ltd: POB 1, North Sydney, NSW 2059; tel. (2) 9342-7800; fax (2) 9342-7100; internet www.optus.com.au; f. 1992; division of Singapore Telecommunications Ltd; general and mobile telecommunications, data and internet services, pay-TV; Chair. Sir RALPH ROBINS; Chief Exec. PAUL O'SULLIVAN.

Telstra Corpn Ltd: Level 41, 242 Exhibition St, Melbourne, Vic 3000; tel. (3) 9634-6400; e-mail companysecretary@team.telstra.com; internet www.telstra.com.au; general and mobile telecommunication services; Chair. CATHERINE LIVINGSTONE; CEO DAVID THODEY.

Vodafone Hutchison Australia: Level 7, 40 Mount St, NSW 2060; tel. (2) 8579-8888; fax (2) 8904-0457; internet www.three.com.au; third generation (3G) mobile services; est. following merger between Hutchison Whampoa and Vodafone Australia Ltd in 2009; CEO NIGEL DEWS.

Regulatory Authority

Australian Communications and Media Authority (ACMA): POB 13112, Law Courts, Melbourne, Vic 8010; tel. (3) 9963-6800; fax (3) 9963-6899; e-mail candinfo@acma.gov.au; internet www.acma.gov.au; f. 2005; Commonwealth regulator for telecommunications, broadcasting, internet and radiocommunications; Chair. CHRIS CHAPMAN.

BROADCASTING

Many programmes are provided by the non-commercial statutory corporation, the Australian Broadcasting Corporation (ABC). Commercial radio and television services are provided by stations operated by companies under licences granted and renewed by the Australian Communications and Media Authority (ACMA). They rely for their income on the broadcasting of advertisements. In late 2011 there were about 273 commercial radio stations in operation, and 69 commercial television stations.

Australian Broadcasting Corporation (ABC): 700 Harris St, Ultimo, POB 9994, Sydney, NSW 2001; tel. (2) 8333-1500; fax (2) 8333-5344; internet www.abc.net.au; f. 1932; est. as Australian Broadcasting Comm; became corpn in 1983; one national television network operating on about 961 transmitters, one international television service broadcasting via satellite to Asia and the Pacific and nine radio networks operating on more than 6,000 transmitters; Chair. JAMES SPIGELMAN; Man. Dir MARK SCOTT.

Radio Australia: GPOB 428, Melbourne 3001; tel. (3) 9626-1500; fax (3) 9626-1899; internet www.radioaustralia.net.au; international service broadcast by short wave and satellite in English, Burmese, French, Indonesian, Standard Chinese, Khmer, Tok Pisin and Vietnamese; CEO MIKE MCCLUSKEY.

Radio

Digital radio services were introduced in Adelaide, Brisbane, Melbourne, Perth and Sydney in 2009.

Commercial Radio Australia Ltd: Level 5, 88 Foveaux St, Surry Hills, NSW 2010; tel. (2) 9281-6577; fax (2) 9281-6599; e-mail mail@commercialradio.com.au; internet www.commercialradio.com.au; f. 1930; represents the interests of Australia's commercial radio broadcasters; CEO JOAN WARNER.

Major Commercial Broadcasting Station Licensees

Associated Communications Enterprises (ACE) Radio Broadcasters Pty Ltd: Level 8C, 18 Albert Rd, South Melbourne, Vic 3205; tel. (3) 9645-9877; fax (3) 9645-9866; e-mail headoffice@aceradio.com.au; internet www.aceradio.com.au; operates six stations; Chair. ROWLY PATERSON; Man. Dir S. EVERETT.

Austereo Pty Ltd: Ground Level, 180 St Kilda Rd, St Kilda, Vic 3182; tel. (3) 9230-1051; fax (3) 9593-9007; e-mail guy.dobson@austereo.com.au; internet www.austereo.com.au; operates 15 stations; CEO GUY POBSON.

Australian Radio Network Pty Ltd: 3 Byfield St, North Ryde, NSW 2113; tel. (2) 8899-9999; fax (2) 8899-9811; e-mail webmaster@arn.com.au; internet www.arn.com.au; operates 12 stations; jt venture between APN News & Media and Clear Channel Communications Inc, Texas; CEO CIARAN DAVIS.

Capital Radio Network: POB 1206, Mitchell, ACT 2911; tel. (2) 6452-1521; fax (2) 6452-1006; operates seven stations; Man. Dir KEVIN BLYTON.

DMG Radio Australia: Level 5, 75 Hindmarsh St, Adelaide, SA 5000; tel. (8) 8419-5000; fax (8) 8419-5062; e-mail enquiries@dmgradio.com.au; internet www.dmgradio.com.au; operates 11 stations; Chair. LACHLAN MURDOCH; CEO CATHY O'CONNOR.

Grant Broadcasting Pty Ltd: Suite 303, 10–12 Clarke St, Crows Nest, NSW 2065; tel. (2) 9437-8888; fax (2) 9437-8881; e-mail corporate@grantbroadcasters.com.au; internet www.grantbroadcasters.com.au; operates 31 stations; Man. Dir JANET CAMERON.

Greater Cairns Radio Ltd: Virginia House, Abbott St, Cairns, Qld 4870; tel. (7) 4050-0800; fax (7) 4051-8060; e-mail cnssales@dmgradio.com.au; Gen. Man. ROD COUTTS.

Macquarie Radio Network: Level 1, Bldg C, 33–35 Saunders St, Pyrmont, NSW 2009; tel. (2) 8570-0000; fax (2) 8570-0219; internet www.mrn.com.au; operates two stations; Chair. RUSSELL TATE.

Prime Radio: N. A. B. Bldg, 17 Carnaby St, Maroochydore, Qld 4558; tel. (7) 5475-1911; fax (7) 5475-1961; e-mail info@primeradio.com.au; internet www.primeradio.com.au; operates 10 stations; Group Gen. Man. BRYCE NIELSEN.

Regional Broadcasters (Australia) Pty: McDowal St, Roma, Qld 4455; tel. (7) 4622-1800; fax (7) 4622-3697; Chair. G. MCVEAN.

Rural Press Ltd: 159 Bells Line of Rd, North Richmond, NSW 2754; tel. (2) 4570-4444; fax (2) 4570-4663; internet www.ruralpress.com; f. 1911; operates six stations; Man. Dir and CEO B. K. MCCARTHY.

Southern Cross Media Pty Ltd: Level 2, 257 Clarendon St, South Melbourne, Vic 3205; tel. (3) 9252-1019; fax (3) 9252-1270; e-mail corporate@scmedia.com.au; internet www.scmediagroup.com.au; operates 68 stations; Exec. Chair. MAX MOORE-WILTON; CEO RHYS HOLLERAN.

RadioWest: 89 Egan St, Kalgoorlie, WA 6430; tel. (8) 9021-2666; fax (8) 9091-2209; e-mail rhutchinson@radiowest.com.au; internet theradio.com.au; f. 1931; operates 10 stations along with HOT FM in Western Australia.

SEA FM Pty Ltd: Level 2, Oracle East, 3 Oracle Blvd, Broadbeach, Qld 4218; tel. (7) 5591-5000; fax (7) 5591-6080; e-mail paul.bartlett@sca.com.au; internet www.seafm.com.au; operates 28 stations.

Super Radio Network: POB 1269, Pyrmont, NSW 2009; owned by Broadcast Operations Pty Ltd; operates 33 stations; Chair. BILL CARALIS.

Radio 2SM Gold 1269: Level 3, 8 Jones Bay Rd, Pyrmont, NSW 2009; tel. (2) 9660-1269; fax (2) 9552-2979; e-mail admin@2sm.com.au; internet www.2sm.com.au; f. 1931.

Tamworth Radio Development Company Pty Ltd: POB 497, Tamworth, NSW 2340; tel. (2) 6765-7055; fax (2) 6762-0008; e-mail traffic@2tn.com.au; operates two stations; acquired by Super Radio Network in 1993; Man. W. A. MORRISON.

Tasmanian Broadcasting Network (TBN): POB 665G, Launceston, Tas 7250; tel. (3) 6431-2555; fax (3) 6431-3188; operates three stations; Chair. K. FINDLAY.

Tasmanian Radio Network: 109 York St, Launceston, Tas 7250; tel. (3) 6331-4844; fax (3) 6334-5858; internet www.bestmusicmix.com.au; operates six radio stations and part of Macquarie Regional Radioworks; Man. MATT RUSSELL.

Television

Free TV Australia: 44 Avenue Rd, Mosman, NSW 2088; tel. (2) 8968-7100; fax (2) 9969-3520; e-mail contact@freetv.com.au; internet www.freetv.com.au; f. 1960; fmrly Commercial Television Australia; represents all commercial free-to-air broadcasters in Australia; CEO JULIE FLYNN.

Commercial Television Station Licensees

Channel 9 South Australia Pty Ltd: 202 Tynte St, North Adelaide, SA 5006; tel. (8) 8267-0111; fax (8) 8267-3996; e-mail news@nws9.com.au; internet www.nws9.com.au; f. 1959; Gen. Man. GRAEME GILBERTSON.

General Television Corporation Pty Ltd: 22–46 Bendigo St, POB 100, Richmond, Vic 3121; tel. (3) 9429-0201; fax (3) 9429-3670; e-mail customer.service@ninemsn.com.au; internet www.ninemsn.com.au; f. 1957; operates one station; Man. Dir GRAEME YARWOOD.

Golden West Network Pty Ltd: Roberts Cres., Bunbury, WA 6230; tel. (8) 9721-4466; fax (8) 9792-2932; e-mail gwn.bunbury@gwn.com.au; internet www.gwn.com.au; f. 1967; subsidiary of Prime Television Ltd; operates three stations (SSW10, VEW and WAW); CEO W. FENWICK.

Imparja Television Pty Ltd: POB 52, Alice Springs, NT 0871; tel. (8) 8950-1411; fax (8) 8950-1422; e-mail imparja@imparja.com.au; internet www.imparja.com; CEO ALISTAIR FEEHAN.

NBN Television Ltd: 11–17 Mosbri Cres., Newcastle, NSW 2300; tel. (2) 4929-2933; fax (2) 4926-2936; internet www.nbntv.com.au; f. 1962; operates one station; Man. Dir DENIS LEDBURY.

Network Ten Ltd: GPOB 10, Sydney, NSW 2000; tel. (2) 9650-1010; fax (2) 9650-1111; e-mail tenwebsite@ten.com.au; internet www.ten.com.au; f. 1964; operates Australian TV network and commercial stations in Sydney, Melbourne, Brisbane, Perth and Adelaide; Exec. Chair. BRIAN LONG; CEO JAMES WARBURTON.

Nine Network Australia Pty Ltd: Level 7, Tower Bldg, Australia Sq., 264–278 George St, Sydney, NSW 2000; tel. (2) 9383-6000; fax (2) 9383-6100; e-mail customer.service@ninemsn.com.au; internet www.ninemsn.com.au; f. 1956; division of Publishing and Broadcasting Ltd; operates three stations: TCN Channel Nine Pty Ltd (Sydney), Queensland Television Ltd (Brisbane) and General Television Corpn Ltd (Melbourne); CEO MARK BRITT.

Prime Television (Holdings) Pty Ltd: POB 878, Dickson, ACT 2602; tel. (2) 6242-3700; fax (2) 6242-3889; e-mail primetv@primetv.com.au; internet www.primemedia.com.au; part of Prime Media Group Ltd; Chair. PAUL RAMSAY; CEO IAN AUDSLEY.

Queensland Television Ltd: GPOB 72, Brisbane, Qld 4001; tel. (7) 3214-9999; fax (7) 3369-3512; f. 1959; operated by Nine Network Australia Pty Ltd; Gen. Man. CHRIS TAYLOR.

Seven Network Ltd: 38-42 Pirrama Rd, Pyrmont, NSW 2009; tel. (2) 8777-7777; internet www.sevencorporate.com.au; owns Amalgamated Television Services Pty Ltd (Sydney), Brisbane TV Ltd (Brisbane), HSV Channel 7 Pty Ltd (Melbourne), South Australian Telecasters Ltd (Adelaide) and TVW Enterprises Ltd (Perth); Exec. Chair. KERRY STOKES; CEO DAVID JOHN LECKIE.

Channel Seven Adelaide Pty Ltd: 40 Port Rd, Hindmarsh, SA 5007; tel. (8) 8342-7777; fax (8) 8342-7717; f. 1965; mem. of Seven Network; Man. Dir TONY DAVISON.

Channel Seven Brisbane Pty Ltd: Sir Samuel Griffith Dr., Mt Coot-tha, Qld 4006; tel. (7) 3369-7777; fax (7) 3368-7410; f. 1959; operates one station; mem. of Seven Network; Man. Dir MAX WALTERS.

Channel Seven Melbourne Pty Ltd: 160 Harbour Esplanade, Docklands Melbourne, Vic 3008; tel. (3) 9697-7777; fax (3) 9697-7747; e-mail daspinall@seven.com.au; f. 1956; operates one station; Gen. Man. LEWIS MARTIN.

Channel Seven Perth Pty Ltd: POB 77, Tuart Hill, WA 6939; tel. (8) 9344-0777; fax (8) 9344-0670; e-mail traffic@7perth.com.au; internet www.7perth.com.au; f. 1959; Man. Dir MARIO D'ORAZIO.

Channel Seven Queensland Pty Ltd: 140–142 Horton Parade, Maroochydore, Qld 4558; tel. (7) 5430-1777; fax (7) 5430-1760; f. 1965; fmrly Sunshine Television Network Ltd.

Southern Cross Media Pty Ltd: (see above) operates two stations: Southern Cross Ten and Southern Cross Television.

Special Broadcasting Service (SBS): Locked Bag 028, Crows Nest, NSW 1585; tel. (2) 9430-2828; fax (2) 9430-3047; e-mail comments@sbs.com.au; internet www.sbs.com.au; f. 1980; national multi-cultural broadcaster of TV and radio; Chair. JOSEPH SKRZYNSKI; Man. Dir MICHAEL EBEID.

Spencer Gulf Telecasters Ltd: 76 Wandearah Rd, Port Pirie, SA 5540; tel. (8) 8632-2555; fax (8) 8633-0984; e-mail dweston@centralonline.com.au; f. 1968; operates two stations; Chair. P. M. STURROCK.

Swan Television & Radio Broadcasters Pty Ltd: POB 99, Tuart Hill, WA 6939; tel. (8) 9449-9999; fax (8) 9449-9900; Gen. Man. P. BOWEN.

Territory Television Pty Ltd: POB 1764, Darwin, NT 0801; tel. (8) 8981-8888; fax (8) 8981-6802; f. 1971; operates one station; Gen. Man. A. G. BRUYN.

WIN Corpn Pty Ltd: Television Ave, Mt St Thomas, NSW 2500; tel. (2) 4227-3682; fax (2) 4223-4199; internet www.wintv.com.au; f. 1962; Owner BRUCE GORDON.

Satellite, Cable and Digital Television

Digital television became available in metropolitan areas in January 2001 and was available in all major regional areas by 2004.

Austar United Communications Ltd: Locked Mailbag A3940, Sydney South, NSW 1235; tel. (2) 9251-6999; fax (2) 9251-0134; e-mail corporate@austar.com.au; internet www.austarunited.com.au; began operations in 1995; 750,000 subscribers (2011); Chair. MICHAEL T. FRIES; CEO JOHN C. PORTER.

Australia Network: GPOB 9994, Sydney, NSW 2001; tel. (2) 8333-5598; fax (2) 8333-1558; internet australianetwork.com; f. 2001; international satellite service; broadcasts to countries and territories in Asia and the Pacific; owned by Australian Broadcasting Corpn; Chief Exec. BRUCE DOVER.

Foxtel: 5 Thomas Holt Dr., North Ryde, NSW 2113; tel. (2) 9813-6000; fax (2) 9813-7303; e-mail corporateaffairs@foxtel.com.au; internet www.foxtel.com.au; owned by News Corpn, Telstra Corpn and Consolidated Media Holdings Ltd; over 1,630,000 subscribers; Chair. BRUCE AKHURST; CEO RICHARD FRUEDENSTEIN.

Optus Television: Tower B, Level 15, 16 Zenith Centre, 821–841 Pacific Highway, Chatswood, NSW 2067; provides Foxtel cable television under the Optus brand as part of its broader services.

Finance

(cap. = capital; p.u. = paid up; res = reserves; dep. = deposits; m. = million; brs = branches; amounts in Australian dollars)

Australian Prudential Regulation Authority (APRA): GPOB 9836, Sydney, NSW 2001; tel. (2) 9210-3000; fax (2) 9210-3411; internet www.apra.gov.au; f. 1998; responsible for regulation of banks, insurance cos, superannuation funds, credit unions, building societies and friendly societies; Chair. Dr JOHN LAKER.

BANKING

Central Bank

Reserve Bank of Australia: 65 Martin Place, Sydney, NSW 2000; tel. (2) 9551-8111; fax (2) 9551-8000; e-mail rbainfo@rba.gov.au; internet www.rba.gov.au; f. 1911; est. as Commonwealth Bank of Australia; assumed functions of central bank in 1959; responsible for monetary policy, financial system stability, payment system development; cap. 40m., res 10,154m., dep. 20,987m., total assets 85,652m. (June 2010); Gov. GLENN STEVENS.

Development Bank

Rabobank Australia Ltd: GPOB 4577, Sydney, NSW 2001; tel. (2) 8115-4000; e-mail sydney.webmaster@rabobank.com; internet www.rabobank.com.au; f. 1978 as Primary Industry Bank of Australia Ltd; name changed as above 2003; Chair. WILLIAM P. GURRY; CEO THEODORUS GIESKES; 219 brs.

Trading Banks

Arab Bank Australia Ltd: Suite 1A, 200 George St, Sydney, NSW 2000; tel. (2) 9377-8917; fax (2) 9221-5428; e-mail service@arabbank.com.au; internet www.arabbank.com.au; cap. 55.0m., res 8.0m., dep. 1,051.7m. (Dec. 2009); Chair. SAMIR KAWAR; Man. Dir JAMES WAKIM.

Australia and New Zealand Banking Group Ltd: ANZ Centre, 833 Collins St, Docklands, Vic 3008; tel. (3) 8654-7682; fax (3) 8654-9977; e-mail investor.relations@anz.com; internet www.anz.com; f. 1835; present name adopted in 1970; cap. 20,757m., res –2,587m., dep. 369,210m. (Sept. 2010); Chair. JOHN MORSCHEL; CEO PHILIP CHRONICAN; 748 domestic brs, 204 overseas brs.

Bank of America Merrill Lynch Australia Ltd: Level 63, MLC Centre, 19–29 Martin Place, Sydney, NSW 2000; tel. (2) 9931-4200; fax (2) 9221-1023; f. 1964; Man. Dir JOHN LILES.

Bank of Queensland Ltd: 229 Elizabeth St, POB 898, Brisbane, Qld 4001; tel. (7) 3212-3463; fax (7) 3212-3399; internet www.boq.com.au; f. 1874; cap. 2,057m., res 86.6m., dep. 28,415.8m. (Aug. 2010); Chair. NEIL SUMMERSON; Man. Dir DAVID P. LIDDY; 162 brs.

Bank of Tokyo-Mitsubishi UFJ Ltd: Level 25, Gateway, 1 Macquarie Place, Sydney, NSW 2000; tel. (2) 9296-1111; fax (2) 9247-4266; f. 1985; Gen. Man. K. TSUSHIMA.

Bank of Western Australia Ltd (BankWest): Level 47, BankWest Tower, 108 St George's Terrace, Perth, WA 6000; tel. (8) 9449-2840; fax (8) 9449-2570; internet www.bankwest.com.au; f. 1895 as Agricultural Bank of Western Australia, est. 1945 as Rural and Industries Bank of Western Australia; present name adopted in 1994; 100% owned by HBOS Australia; cap. 872.3m., res 300,000, dep. 16,436.9m. (Dec. 2002); Chair. HARVEY COLLINS; Man. Dir ROB DE LUCA; 87 brs.

Bankers' Trust Financial Group: 275 Kent St, Sydney, NSW 2000; tel. (2) 8253-2999; fax (2) 9274-5786; internet www.btfg.com.au; f. 1986; wealth management division of Westpac Banking Corpn; CEO BRAD COOPER.

Bendigo and Adelaide Bank Ltd: The Bendigo Centre, Bendigo, Vic 3550; tel. (3) 5485-7873; fax (3) 5485-7660; e-mail oncall@bendigobank.com.au; internet www.bendigobank.com.au; f. 1995; cap. 3,522.5m., res 29.5m., dep. 33,918.8m. (June 2010); Chair. ROBERT N. JOHANSON; Man. Dir MIKE HIRST; 373 brs.

Citigroup Pty Ltd: GPOB 40, Sydney, NSW 2001; tel. (2) 8225-0615; fax (2) 8225-5306; internet www.citibank.com.au; f. 1954; fmrly Citibank Pty Ltd, name changed as above in 2005; cap. 460.0m, res 387.0m., dep. 12,978m. (Dec. 2009); CEO STEPHEN ROBERTS; 6 brs.

Commonwealth Bank of Australia: Ground Floor, Tower 1, 201 Sussex St, Sydney, NSW 2000; tel. (2) 9378-2000; fax (2) 9118-7192; internet www.commbank.com.au; f. 1912; merged with Colonial Ltd in 2000; cap. 24,020m., res 1,089.0m., dep. 427,497.0m. (June 2010); Chair. DAVID TURNER; CEO and Man. Dir RALPH NORRIS; more than 1,200 brs world-wide.

HSBC Bank Australia Ltd: Level 32, HSBC Centre, 580 George St, Sydney, NSW 2000; tel. (2) 9006-5888; fax (2) 9255-2647; e-mail pr@hsbc.com.au; internet www.hsbc.com.au; f. 1985; fmrly Hongkong Bank of Australia; cap. 811.0m., res 1.0m., dep. 15,921.0m. (Dec. 2009); Chair GRAHAM BRADLEY; CEO PAULO MAIA; 35 brs.

ING DIRECT (Australia) Ltd: 140 Sussex St, Sydney, NSW 2001; tel. (2) 9028-4077; fax (2) 9028-4708; internet www.ingdirect.com.au; f. 1994; fmrly known as ING Bank; name changed as above 2007; cap. 1,334m., res 40.5m., dep. 43,644.6m. (Dec. 2009); CEO DON KOCH.

Investec Bank (Australia) Ltd: Level 31, Chifley Tower, 2 Chifley Sq., Phillip St, Sydney, NSW 2000; tel. (2) 9323-2000; fax (2) 9323-2002; e-mail australia@investec.com.au; internet www.investec.com.au; fmrly N. M Rothschild & Sons; acquired by Investec Bank in July 2006; Chair. DAVID GONSKI; CEO DAVID CLARKE; 3 brs.

JPMorgan Australia: Level 32, Grosvenor Place, 225 George St, Sydney, NSW 2000; tel. (2) 9250-4111; internet www.jpmorgan.com/australia; formed through merger of Ord Minnett, Chase Manhattan Bank, JPMorgan and Bank One; Head (Asia-Pacific) GABY ABDELNOUR.

Macquarie Group Ltd: 1 Martin Place, Sydney, NSW 2000; tel. (2) 8232-3333; fax (2) 8232-3350; internet www.macquarie.com.au; f. 1969 as Hill Samuel Australia Ltd; present name adopted in 1985; cap. 6,990m., res –26.0m., dep. 109,653m. (March 2010); Chair. DAVID S. CLARKE; Man. Dir NICHOLAS MOORE; 4 brs.

National Australia Bank Ltd (NAB): 800 Bourke St, Melbourne, Vic 3008; tel. (3) 8641-9083; fax (3) 8641-4912; e-mail feedback@nab.com.au; internet www.nab.com.au; f. 1858; cap. 23,551m., res –639m., dep. 509,618m. (Sept. 2010); Chair. MICHAEL CHANEY; Group CEO CAMERON CLYNE; 2,349 brs.

RBS Group (Australia) Pty Ltd: RBS Tower, 88 Phillip St, Sydney, NSW 2000; tel. (2) 8259-5000; fax (2) 8259-5444; e-mail mailbox.au@rbs.com; internet www.rbs.com.au; f. 1971; fmrly ABN AMRO Australia Pty Ltd, rebranded as above in 2009; CEO STEPHEN WILLIAMS.

SG Australia Ltd: Level 23, 400 George St, Sydney, NSW 2000; tel. (2) 9210-8000; fax (2) 9231-2196; internet www.sgcib.com.au; f. 1981; fmrly Société Générale Australia Ltd; Chief Officer ANDRE GOURRET.

St George Bank Ltd: Locked Bag 1, St George House, 4–16 Montgomery St, Kogarah, NSW 2217; tel. (2) 9553-5173; fax (2) 9952-1000; internet www.stgeorge.com.au; f. 1937 as building society; purchased by Westpac Group in Dec. 2008; Chair. JOHN CURTIS; CEO GEORGE FRAZIS; 409 brs.

Standard Chartered Bank Australia Ltd: Level 1, 345 George St, Sydney, NSW 2000; tel. (2) 9232-9333; fax (2) 9232-9334; internet www.standardchartered.com/au; f. 1986; Chair. JOHN PEACE; CEO (Asia) JASPAL SINGH BINDRA.

Westpac Banking Corporation: 275 Kent St, Sydney, NSW 2000; tel. (2) 9293-9270; fax (2) 8253-4128; internet www.westpac.com.au; f. 1817; merged with St George Bank Ltd in Dec. 2008; cap. 24,496m., res –57m., dep. 545,508m. (Sept. 2010); Chair. TED EVANS; CEO GAIL KELLY; 825 domestic brs, 197 brs in New Zealand, 48 other brs.

STOCK EXCHANGES

Australian Securities Exchange (ASX): Level 7, 20 Bridge St, Sydney, NSW 2000; tel. (2) 9227-0000; fax (2) 9347-0005; e-mail info@asx.com.au; internet www.asx.com.au; Australian Stock Exchange f. 1987 by merger of the stock exchanges in Sydney, Adelaide, Brisbane, Hobart, Melbourne and Perth, to replace the fmr Australian Associated Stock Exchanges; demutualized and listed Oct. 1998; Australian Securities Exchange formed through merger of Australian Stock Exchange and Sydney Futures Exchange July 2006; ASX group operates under the brand Australian Securities Exchange; spans markets for corporate control, capital formation and price discovery; operator, supervisor, central counter-party clearer and payments system facilitator; Chair. RODERIC HOLLIDAY-SMITH; Man. Dir and CEO ELMER FUNKE KUPPER.

Chi-X: Level 23, Gov. Phillip Tower, 1 Farrer Pl., Sydney, NSW 2000; tel. (2) 8078-1701; e-mail support-cxa@chi-x.com; internet www.chi-x.com/australia; f. 2011; wholly owned subsidiary of Chi-X Global Inc; COO PETER FOWLER.

Supervisory Body

Australian Securities and Investments Commission (ASIC): GPOB 9827, Sydney, NSW 2001; tel. (2) 9911-2000; fax (2) 9911-2414; internet www.asic.gov.au; f. 1990; corpns and financial products regulator; Chair. TODO D'ALOISIO.

PRINCIPAL INSURANCE COMPANIES

Allianz Australia Ltd: GPOB 4049, Sydney, NSW 2001; tel. (7) 3023-9322; e-mail corporate_communications@allianz.com.au; internet www.allianz.com.au; f. 1914; workers' compensation; fire, general accident, motor and marine; Chair. J. S. CURTIS; Man. Dir T. TOWELL.

AMP Ltd: AMP Bldg, Level 24, 33 Alfred St, Sydney, NSW 2000; tel. (2) 9257-5000; fax (2) 9257-7178; internet www.amp.com.au; f. 1849; fmrly Australian Mutual Provident Society; life insurance; Chair. PETER MASON; CEO and Man. Dir CRAIG DUNN.

AXA Asia Pacific Holdings Ltd: 750 Collins St, Melbourne, Vic 3008; tel. (3) 8688-3911; fax (3) 9614-2240; e-mail investor.relations@axa.com.au; internet www.axaasiapacific.com.au; f. 1869; fmrly The Nat. Mutual Life Asscn of Australasia Ltd; financial advice, funds management, superannuation, retirement and savings products, life and trauma insurance, income protection; Chair. R. H. ALLERT; CEO ANDREW PENN.

Calliden Insurance Ltd: Level 7, 100 Arthur St, North Sydney, NSW 2060; tel. (2) 9551-1111; fax (2) 9551-1155; e-mail feedback@calliden.com.au; internet www.calliden.com.au; general insurance products; CEO NICHOLAS KIRK.

Catholic Church Insurances Ltd: Level 8, 485 La Trobe St, Melbourne, Vic 3001; tel. (3) 9934-3000; fax (3) 9934-3464; e-mail info@ccinsurances.com.au; internet ww1.ccinsurances.com.au; f. 1911; Chair. PAUL A. GALLAGHER; CEO PETER RUSH.

General Reinsurance Australia Ltd: Level 24, 123 Pitt St, Sydney, NSW 2000; tel. (2) 8236-6100; fax (2) 9222-1540; e-mail lifesydney@genre.com; f. 1961; reinsurance, life and health, fire, accident, marine; Chair. F. A. MCDONALD; Man. Dir C. J. CROWDER.

GIO Australia Holdings Ltd: GPOB 1453, Brisbane, Qld 4001; tel. (3) 8650-4196; fax (3) 8650-4552; e-mail emailus@gio.com.au; internet www.gio.com.au; f. 1926; CEO PETER CORRIGAN.

Guild Insurance Ltd: 5 Burwood Rd, Hawthorn, Vic 3122; tel. (3) 9810-9820; fax (3) 9810-9810; internet www.guildinsurance.com.au; f. 1963; Chair. JOHN BARRINGTON; CEO MARIO J. PIRONE.

Insurance Australia Group Ltd: Level 26, 388 George St, Sydney, NSW 2000; tel. (2) 9292-9222; fax (2) 9292-8485; e-mail investor.relations@iag.com.au; internet www.iag.com.au; f. 1926; fmrly NRMA Insurance Ltd; name changed as above 2002; Chair. BRIAN SCHWARTZ; CEO MIKE WILKINS.

Lumley General Insurance Ltd: Level 9, Lumley House, 309 Kent St, Sydney, NSW 2000; tel. (2) 9248-1111; fax (2) 9248-1122; e-mail general@lumley.com.au; internet www.lumley.com.au; owned by Wesfarmers General Insurance Ltd; Man. Dir ROBERT SCOTT.

MLC Wealth Management Ltd: POB 200, North Sydney, NSW 2059; tel. (3) 8634-4721; fax (3) 9964-3334; e-mail contactmlc@mlc.com.au; internet www.mlc.com.au; f. 2000; est. as CGNU following merger of CGU and Norwich Union, renamed as Aviva Australia Holdings Ltd in 2003; renamed as above after acquisition by National Australia Bank in 2009; CEO STEVE TUCKER.

QBE Insurance Group Ltd: Level 2, 82 Pitt St, Sydney, NSW 2000; tel. (2) 9375-4193; fax (2) 9231-6104; e-mail corporate@qbe.com; internet www.qbe.com; f. 1886; general insurance; Chair. BELINDA HUTCHINSON; CEO JOHN NEAL.

RAC Insurance Pty Ltd: 228 Adelaide Terrace, Perth, WA 6000; tel. (8) 9436-4444; fax (8) 9421-4593; internet rac.com.au; f. 1947; Chair. ALDEN HALSE.

RACQ Insurance: POB 4, Springwood, Qld 4127; tel. (7) 3361-2444; fax (7) 3361-2140; e-mail racq@racq.com.au; internet www.racq.com.au; f. 1971; Chair. RICHARD PIETSCH; CEO IAN GILLESPIE.

Suncorp Ltd: Level 18, 36 Wickham Tce, Brisbane, Qld 4000; tel. (7) 3362-1222; fax (7) 3836-1190; e-mail direct@suncorp.co.au; internet www.suncorp.com.au; f. 1996; Chair. JOHN STORY; CEO PATRICK SNOWBALL.

Swiss Reinsurance Co Ltd: Level 29, 363 George St, Sydney, NSW 2000; tel. (2) 8295-9500; fax (2) 8295-9600; internet www.swissre.com; f. 1956; Head of Australia and New Zealand operations MARK SENKEVICS.

Vero Insurance Ltd: GPOB 3999, Sydney, NSW 2001; tel. (8) 8205-5878; e-mail veroinformation@vero.com.au; internet www.vero.com.au; fmrly RSA Insurance Australia Ltd; name changed as above 2003; CEO ANTHONY DAY.

Wesfarmers Insurance Ltd (WFI): 184 Railway Parade, Bassendean, WA 6054; tel. (8) 9273-5333; fax (8) 9378-2172; e-mail info@wfi.com.au; internet www.wfi.com.au; Man. Dir ROBERT SCOTT.

Westpac Life Insurance Services Ltd: 275 Kent St, Sydney, NSW 2000; tel. (2) 9293-9270; fax (2) 8253-4128; e-mail online@westpac.com.au; internet www.westpac.com.au; f. 1986; CEO GAIL KELLY.

Zurich Financial Services Australia Ltd: 5 Blue St, North Sydney, NSW 2060; tel. (2) 9995-1111; fax (2) 9995-3797; e-mail client.service@zurich.com.au; internet www.zurich.com.au; Chair. TERENCE JOHN PARADINE; CEO DAVID SMITH.

Insurance Associations

Australian and New Zealand Institute of Insurance and Finance: Level 8, 600 Bourke St, Melbourne, Vic 3000; tel. (3) 9613-72080; fax (3) 9642-4166; e-mail customerservice@theinstitute.com.au; internet www.theinstitute.com.au; f. 1884; provider of education, training, and professional devt courses across the region; 15,000 mems; 8,500 students; Pres. and Chair. of the Bd DUNCAN WEST; CEO JOAN FITZPATRICK.

Financial Services Council (FSC): Level 24, 44 Market St, Sydney, NSW 2000; tel. (2) 9299-3022; fax (2) 9299-3198; e-mail info@fsc.org.au; internet www.fsc.org.au; f. 1997; est. following merger of Australian Investment Managers' Asscn, Investment Funds Asscn and Life, Investment and Superannuation Asscn of Australia Inc; fmrly Investment and Financial Services Association (IFSA); non-profit org.; Chair. PETER MAHER; CEO JOHN BROGDEN.

Insurance Council of Australia Ltd: Level 4, 56 Pitt St, Sydney, NSW 2000; tel. (2) 9253-5100; fax (2) 9253-5111; e-mail comms@insurancecouncil.com.au; internet www.insurancecouncil.com.au; f. 1975; Pres. T. R. TOWELL; CEO R. W. WHELAN.

Trade and Industry

GOVERNMENT AGENCY

Austrade: Level 23, Aon Tower, 201 Kent St, Sydney, NSW 2000; tel. (2) 9390-2000; fax (2) 9390-2024; e-mail info@austrade.gov.au; internet www.austrade.gov.au; f. 1931; export promotion agency; CEO PETER GREY.

CHAMBERS OF COMMERCE

Australian Chamber of Commerce and Industry (ACCI): POB 6005, Kingston, ACT 2604; tel. (2) 6273-2311; fax (2) 6273-3286; e-mail info@acci.asn.au; internet www.acci.asn.au; Pres. DAVID MICHAELIS; CEO PETER ANDERSON.

Chamber of Commerce and Industry of Western Australia (CCIWA): POB 6209, East Perth, WA 6892; tel. (8) 9365-7627; fax (8) 9365-7550; e-mail info@cciwa.com; internet www.cciwa.com; f. 1890; 5,200 mems; Chief Exec. PETER HOOD; Pres. Dr PENNY FLETT.

Commerce Queensland: Industry House, 375 Wickham Terrace, Brisbane, Qld 4000; tel. (7) 3842-2244; fax (7) 3832-3195; e-mail contact@cciq.com.au; internet www.cciq.com.au; f. 1868; operates World Trade Centre, Brisbane; 5,500 mems; Pres. DAVID GOODWIN; Gen. Man. NICK WILLIS.

South Australian Employers' Chamber of Commerce and Industry Inc: Enterprise House, 136 Greenhill Rd, Unley, SA

5061; tel. (8) 8300-0103; fax (8) 8300-0204; e-mail enquiries@business-sa.com; internet www.business-sa.com; f. 1839; 4,700 mems; Pres. VINCENT TREMAINE; CEO PETER VAUGHAN.

Sydney Chamber of Commerce: Level 12, 83 Clarence St, Sydney, NSW 2000; tel. (2) 9350-8100; fax (2) 9350-8199; e-mail enquiries@thechamber.com.au; internet www.thechamber.com.au; f. 1825; offers advice to and represents over 70,000 businesses; Pres. ROGER HOOD; Exec. Dir PATRICIA FORSYTHE.

Tasmanian Chamber of Commerce and Industry: GPOB 793, Hobart, Tas 7001; tel. (3) 6236-3600; fax (3) 6231-1278; e-mail admin@tcci.com.au; internet www.tcci.com.au; Chair. TROY HARPER; CEO ROBERT WALLACE.

Victorian Employers' Chamber of Commerce and Industry: Industry House, 486 Albert St, Melbourne, Vic 3002; tel. (3) 8662-5333; fax (3) 8662-5462; e-mail vecci@vecci.org.au; internet www.vecci.org.au; f. 1851; Pres. PETER MCMULLIN; CEO WAYNE KAYLER-THOMSON.

AGRICULTURAL, INDUSTRIAL AND TRADE ASSOCIATIONS

Australian Business Ltd: Locked Bag 938, North Sydney, NSW 2059; tel. (2) 9458-7500; fax (2) 9923-1166; e-mail customerservice@australianbusiness.com.au; internet www.australianbusiness.com.au; f. 1885; fmrly Chamber of Manufactures of NSW; Man. Dir and CEO KEVIN MACDONALD.

Australian Coal Association: POB 9115, Deakin, ACT 2600; tel. (2) 6120-0200; fax (2) 6120-0222; e-mail info@australiancoal.com.au; internet www.australiancoal.com.au; mems include coal producers and processors; Chair. JOHN PEGLER; CEO Dr NIKKI WILLIAMS.

Australian Manufacturers' Export Council: POB E14, Queen Victoria Terrace, ACT 2600; tel. (2) 6273-2311; fax (2) 6273-3196; f. 1955; Exec. Dir G. CHALKER.

Australian Wine and Brandy Corporation (AWBC): POB 2733, Kent Town Business Centre, Kent Town, SA 5071; tel. (8) 8228-2000; fax (8) 8228-2022; e-mail awbc@awbc.com.au; internet www.wineaustralia.com; f. 1981; Chair. JAMES DOMINGUEZ; Chief Exec. ANDREW CHEESMAN.

Australian Wool Innovation Ltd: Level 30, HSBC Centre, 580 George St, Sydney, NSW 2000; tel. (2) 8295-3100; fax (2) 8295-4100; e-mail info@wool.com; internet www.wool.com; f. 2001; est. following privatization of Australian Wool Research and Promotion Org; owner of The Woolmark Co; Chair. WALTER B. MERRIMAN; CEO STUART MCCULLOGH.

Business Council of Australia (BCA): GPOB 1472, Melbourne, Vic 3001; tel. (3) 8664-2664; fax (3) 8664-2666; e-mail info@bca.com.au; internet www.bca.com.au; public policy research and advocacy; governing council comprises chief execs of Australia's major cos; Pres. GRAHAM BRADLEY; Chief Exec. KATIE LAHEY.

Cotton Australia: 247 Coward St, Suite 4.01, Mascot, NSW 2020; tel. (2) 9669-5222; fax (2) 9669-5511; e-mail talktous@cottonaustralia.com.au; internet www.cottonaustralia.com.au; Chair. ANDREW WATSON; CEO ADAM KAY.

Meat and Livestock Australia: Level 1, 165 Walker St, North Sydney, NSW 2060; tel. (2) 9463-9333; fax (2) 9463-9393; e-mail info@mla.com.au; internet www.mla.com.au; producer-owned co; represents, promotes, protects and furthers interests of industry in both the marketing of meat and livestock and industry-based research and devt activities; Chair. ARTHUR (DON) HEATLEY; Man. Dir DAVID PALMER.

National Farmers' Federation: POB E10, Kingston, ACT 2604; tel. (2) 6273-3855; fax (2) 6273-2331; e-mail nff@nff.org.au; internet www.nff.org.au; Pres. JOCK LAURIE; CEO MATT LINNEGAR.

Natural Resource Management Ministerial Council (NRMMC): NRMMC Secretariat, GPOB 858, Canberra, ACT 2601; tel. (2) 6272-3076; fax (2) 6272-4772; e-mail nrmmc@daff.gov.au; internet www.mincos.gov.au; f. 2002; replaced the Agricultural and Resource Management Council of Australia and New Zealand; promotes the conservation and sustainable use of Australia's natural resources; mems comprising the Commonwealth/state/territory and New Zealand ministers responsible for environment, water and natural resources.

Primary Industries Ministerial Council (PIMC): Dept of Agriculture, Fisheries and Forestry, GPOB 858, Canberra, ACT 2601; tel. (2) 6272-5216; fax (2) 6272-4772; e-mail pimc@daff.gov.au; internet www.mincos.gov.au; f. 2002; develops and promotes sustainable, innovative and profitable agriculture, fisheries, food and forestry industries; mems comprising the state/territory and New Zealand ministers responsible for agriculture, fisheries, food and forestry.

Winemakers' Federation of Australia (WFA): National Wine Centre, Botanic Rd, POB 2414, Kent Town, SA 5071; tel. (8) 8222-9255; fax (8) 8222-9250; e-mail wfa@wfa.org.au; internet www.wfa.org.au; f. 1990; Pres. TONY D'ALOISIO; Chief Exec. STEPHEN STRACHAN.

WoolProducers Australia: POB E10, Kingston, Canberra, ACT 2604; tel. (2) 6273-2531; fax (2) 6273-1120; e-mail woolproducers@nff.org.au; internet www.woolproducers.com.au; f. 2001; fmrly Wool Council Australia; represents wool-growers in dealings with the Federal Govt and industry; Pres. DONALD HAMBLIN.

EMPLOYERS' ORGANIZATIONS

Australian Industry Group: 51 Walker St, North Sydney, NSW 2060; tel. (2) 9466-5566; fax (2) 9466-5599; e-mail helpdesk@aigroup.asn.au; internet www.aigroup.asn.au; f. 1998 through merger of Metal Trades Industry Association and Australian Chamber of Manufacturers; 11,500 mems; Nat. Pres. LUCIO DI BARTOLOMEO; CEO HEATHER RIDOUT.

Australian Meat Industry Council: POB 1208, Crows Nest, NSW 1585; tel. (2) 9086-2200; fax (2) 9086-2201; e-mail admin@amic.org.au; internet www.amic.org.au; f. 1928; represents meat retailers, processors and small goods mfrs; Chair. TERRY NOLAN; CEO KEVIN COTTRILL.

NSW Farmers' Association: GPOB 1068, Sydney, NSW 2001; tel. (2) 8251-1700; fax (2) 8251-1750; e-mail emailus@nswfarmers.org.au; internet www.nswfarmers.org.au; f. 1978; Pres. CHARLES ARMSTRONG; CEO MATT BRAND.

UTILITIES

Australian Institute of Energy: POB 193, Surry Hills, Vic 3127; fax (3) 9898-0249; e-mail aie@aie.org.au; internet www.aie.org.au; f. 1977; Pres. TONY VASSALLO.

Australian Water Association: POB 222, St Leonards, NSW 1590; tel. (2) 9436-0055; fax (2) 9436-0155; e-mail info@awa.asn.au; internet www.awa.asn.au; f. 1962; c. 5,500 mems; Pres. PETER ROBINSON; CEO TOM MOLLENKOPF.

Energy Supply Association of Australia: GPOB 1823, Melbourne, Vic 3001; tel. (3) 9670-0188; fax (3) 9670-1069; e-mail info@esaa.com.au; internet www.esaa.com.au; Chair. TONY CONCANNON; CEO BRAD PAGE.

Electricity Companies

Country Energy: POB 718, Queanbeyan, NSW 2620; tel. (2) 6338-3628; fax (2) 6589-8695; internet www.countryenergy.com.au; f. 2001; est. following merger of Advance Energy, Great Southern Energy and NorthPower; state-owned; electricity and gas distributor; Chair. BARBARA WARD; Man. Dir TERRY BENSON.

Delta Electricity: Level 20, 175 Liverpool St, Sydney, NSW 2000; tel. (2) 9285-2700; fax (2) 9285-2777; e-mail raymond.madden@de.com.au; internet www.de.com.au; f. 1996; Chief Exec. GREGORY EVERETT.

ENERGEX: GPOB 1461, Brisbane, Qld 4001; tel. (7) 3664-4000; fax (7) 3025-8301; e-mail enquiries@energex.com.au; internet www.energex.com.au; spans Queensland and New South Wales; Chair. JOHN DEMPSEY; Gen. Man. MICHAEL RUSSELL.

EnergyAustralia: GPOB 4009, Sydney, NSW 2001; tel. (2) 9269-4200; fax (2) 9269-2830; internet www.energyaustralia.com.au; supplies customers in NSW; Chair. JOHN CONDE; Man. Dir GEORGE MALTABAROW.

Ergon Energy: POB 1090, Townsville, Qld 4810; tel. (7) 4921-6001; fax (7) 3228-8118; e-mail customerservice@ergon.com.au; internet www.ergon.com.au; national retailer of electricity; Chair. RALPH CRAVEN; Chief Exec. IAN MCLEOD.

Power and Water Corpn: Mitchell Centre, Level 2, 55 Mitchell St, Darwin, NT 0800; tel. (8) 8923-4681; fax (8) 8924-7730; e-mail customerservice@powerwater.com.au; internet www.powerwater.com.au; state-owned; supplier of electricity, water and sewerage services in NT; Chair. JUDITH KING; Man. Dir ANDREW MACRIDES.

Powercor Australia Ltd: Locked Bag 14-090, Melbourne, Vic 8001; fax (3) 9683-4499; e-mail info@powercor.com.au; internet www.powercor.com.au; Chair. PETER TULLOCH; CEO SHANE BREHENY.

Snowy Hydro Ltd: AMP Centre, Level 37, 50 Bridge St, Sydney, NSW 2000; tel. (2) 9278-1888; fax (2) 9278-1879; e-mail info@snowyhydro.com.au; internet www.snowyhydro.com.au; Chair. RICK HOLLIDAY-SMITH; Man. Dir TERRY V. CHARLTON.

United Energy Ltd: Locked Bag 7000, Mount Waverley, Vic 3149; tel. (3) 8544-9000; internet www.ue.com.au; f. 1994; est. following division of State Electricity Comm. of Victoria; transferred to private sector; distributor of electricity and gas; CEO HUGH GLEESON.

Western Power Corpn: 363 Wellington St, Perth, WA 6000; tel. (8) 9326-4911; fax (8) 9326-4595; e-mail info@westernpower.com.au; internet www.westernpower.com.au; f. 1995; principal supplier of electricity in WA; Chair. MARK BARNABA; CEO DOUG ABERLE.

Gas Companies

APA Group: HSBC Bldg, Level 19, 580 George St, Sydney, NSW 2000; tel. (2) 9693-0000; fax (2) 9693-0093; e-mail feedback@pipelinetrust.com.au; internet www.apa.com.au; f. 2000; Chair. LEONARD BLEASEL; CEO MICHAEL MCCORMACK.

Australian Gas Light Co: AGL Centre, Level 22, 101 Miller St, North Sydney, NSW 2060; tel. (2) 9921-2999; fax (2) 9957-3671; e-mail aglmail@agl.com.au; internet www.agl.com.au; f. 1837; Chair. JEREMY MAYCOCK; Man. Dir and CEO MICHAEL FRASER.

Envestra: 10th Floor, 81 Flinders St, Adelaide, SA 5000; tel. (8) 8227-1500; fax (8) 8277-1511; e-mail envestra@envestra.com.au; internet www.envestra.com.au; f. 1997; est. by merger of South Australian Gas Co, Gas Corpn of Queensland and Centre Gas Pty Ltd; purchased Victorian Gas Network in 1999; Chair. JOHN GEOFFREY ALLPASS; Man. Dir IAN BRUCE LITTLE.

Epic Energy: Level 8, 60 Collins St, Melbourne, Vic 3000; tel. (3) 8626-8400; fax (3) 8626-8454; internet www.epicenergy.com.au; f. 1996; privately owned gas transmission co; Chair. BRUCE MCKAY; Man. Dir and CEO STEVE BANNING.

Origin Energy: Level 45, Australia Sq., 264–278 George St, Sydney, NSW 2000; tel. (2) 8345-5000; fax (2) 9252-9244; e-mail enquiry@originenergy.com.au; internet www.originenergy.com.au; Chair. H. KEVIN MCCANN; Man. Dir GRANT KING.

TRUenergy: Locked Bag 14060, Melbourne Mail Centre, Vic 8001; tel. (3) 8628-1000; fax (3) 9299-2777; internet www.truenergy.com.au; formed through merger of TXU, Yallourn Energy and Auspower; owned by CLP Power Asia; Man. Dir RICHARD MCINDOE.

WestNet Infrastructure Group: GPOB W2030, Perth, WA 6846; tel. (8) 6213-7000; e-mail info@wng.com.au; internet www.wng.com.au; fmrly AlintaGas; acquired in 2007 by consortium comprising Singapore Power Int., Babcock & Brown Infrastructure and Babcock & Brown Power; CEO JOHN CLELAND.

Water Companies

Melbourne Water Corpn: POB 4342, Melbourne, Vic 3001; tel. (3) 9235-7100; fax (3) 9235-7200; internet www.melbournewater.com.au; state-owned; Chair. ELEANOR UNDERWOOD; Man. Dir ROB SKINNER.

Power and Water Corpn: see Electricity, above.

South Australian Water Corpn: SA Water House, Ground Floor, 250 Victoria Sq., Adelaide, SA 5000; tel. (8) 8204-1000; fax (8) 7003-3329; e-mail customerservice@sawater.com.au; internet www.sawater.com.au; state-owned; Chair. PHILIP PLEDGE; Chief Exec. JOHN RINGHAM.

South East Water Ltd: Locked Bag 1, Moorabbin, Vic 3189; tel. (3) 9552-3000; fax (3) 9552-3001; e-mail info@sewl.com.au; internet www.southeastwater.com.au; f. 1995; state-owned; Chair. DOUG SHIRREFS; Man. Dir SHAUN COX.

Sydney Water Corpn: POB 399, Parramatta, NSW 2124; internet www.sydneywater.com.au; state-owned; Chair. Dr THOMAS PARRY; Man. Dir Dr KERRY SCHOTT.

Water Corpn: 629 Newcastle St, Leederville, WA 6007; tel. (8) 9420-2420; fax (8) 9423-7722; e-mail customer@watercorporation.com.au; internet www.watercorporation.com.au; state-owned; Chair. PATRICK O'CONNOR; CEO SUE MURPHY.

Yarra Valley Water Ltd: Private Bag 1, Mitcham, Vic 3132; tel. (3) 9874-2122; fax (3) 9872-1353; e-mail enquiry@yvw.com.au; internet www.yvw.com.au; f. 1995; state-owned; Chair. PETER WILSON; Man. Dir TONY KELLY.

TRADE UNIONS

Australian Council of Trade Unions (ACTU): Level 6, 365 Queen St, Melbourne, Vic 3000; tel. (3) 9664-7333; fax (3) 9600-0050; e-mail help@actu.org.au; internet www.actu.org.au; f. 1927; br. in each state, generally known as a Trades and Labour Council; 45 affiliated trade unions; Pres. GED KEARNEY; Sec. JEFF LAWRENCE.

Principal Affiliated Unions

Association of Professional Engineers, Scientists & Managers, Australia (APESMA): GPOB 1272, Melbourne, Vic 8060; tel. (3) 9695-8800; fax (3) 9695-8902; e-mail info@apesma.asn.au; internet www.apesma.asn.au; Nat. Pres. DARIO TOMAT; Nat. Sec. ROBYN PORTER; 25,000 mems.

Australasian Meat Industry Employees' Union (AMIEU): Level 1, 39 Lytton Rd, East Brisbane, Qld 4169; tel. (7) 3217-3766; fax (7) 3217-4462; e-mail federal@amieuqld.asn.au; internet amieu.net; Fed. Pres. GRANT COURTNEY; Fed. Sec. BRIAN CRAWFORD; 20,484 mems.

Australian Education Union (AEU): Ground Floor, 120 Clarendon St, Southbank, Vic 3006; tel. (3) 9693-1800; fax (3) 9693-1805; e-mail aeu@aeufederal.org.au; internet www.aeufederal.org.au; f. 1984; Fed. Pres. ANGELO GAVRIELATOS; Fed. Sec. SUSAN HOPGOOD; 175,000 mems.

Australian Manufacturing Workers' Union (AMWU): POB 160, Granville, NSW 2142; tel. (2) 9897-9133; fax (2) 9897-9274; e-mail info@amwu.asn.au; internet www.amwu.org.au; Nat. Pres. PAUL BASTIAN; Nat. Sec. DAVE OLIVER; 170,000 mems.

Australian Services Union (ASU): Ground Floor, 116–124 Queensberry St, Carlton South, Vic 3053; tel. (3) 9342-1400; fax (3) 9342-1499; e-mail info@asu.asn.au; internet www.asu.asn.au; f. 1885; amalgamated in present form in 1993; Nat. Sec. PAUL SLAPE; 125,000 mems.

Australian Workers' Union (AWU): Level 10, 377-383 Sussex St, Sydney, NSW 2000; tel. (3) 8005-3333; fax (3) 8005-3300; e-mail members@nat.awu.net.au; internet www.awu.net.au; f. 1886; Nat. Pres. BILL LUDWIG; Nat. Sec. PAUL HOWES; 135,000 mems.

Communications, Electrical and Plumbing Union of Australia (CEPU): Suite 701, Level 7, 5–13 Rosebery Ave, Rosebery, NSW 2018; tel. (2) 9663-3699; fax (2) 9663-5599; e-mail edno@nat.cepu.asn.au; internet www.cepu.asn.au; Nat Pres. ED HUSIC; Nat. Sec. PETER TIGHE; 180,000 mems.

Community and Public Sector Union (CPSU): Level 5, 191–199 Thomas St, Haymarket, NSW 2000; tel. (2) 9334-9200; fax (2) 8204-6902; e-mail members@cpsu.org.au; internet www.cpsu.org.au; Nat. Pres. MICHAEL TULL; Nat. Sec. NADINE FLOOD; 200,000 mems.

Construction, Forestry, Mining and Energy Union (CFMEU): Box Q235, QVB PO, Sydney, NSW 1230; tel. (2) 8524-5850; fax (2) 8524-5851; e-mail queries@fed.cfmeu.asn.au; internet www.cfmeu.net.au; f. 1992 by amalgamation; Nat. Pres. TONY MAHER; Nat. Sec. JOHN SUTTON; 120,000 mems.

Finance Sector Union of Australia (FSU): GPOB 9893, 341 Queen St, Melbourne, Vic 3001; tel. 1300-366378; fax 1300-307943; e-mail fsuinfo@fsunion.org.au; internet www.fsunion.org.au; f. 1991; Nat. Pres. CAROL GORDON; Nat. Sec. LEON CARTER; 50,000 mems.

Health Services Union (HSU): 208-212 Park St, South Melbourne, Vic 3205; tel. (3) 9341-3328; fax (3) 9341-3329; e-mail hsu@hsu.net.au; internet www.hsu.net.au; Nat. Pres. MICHAEL WILLIAMSON; Nat. Sec. KATHY JACKSON; 90,000 mems.

Independent Education Union of Australia (IEU): POB 177, Deakin West, ACT 2600; tel. (3) 6273-3107; fax (3) 6273-3710; e-mail ieu@ieu.org.au; internet www.ieu.org.au; Fed. Sec. CHRIS WATT; Fed. Pres. RICHARD SHEARMAN; 63,000 mems.

Maritime Union of Australia (MUA): 2nd Floor, 365–367 Sussex St, Sydney, NSW 2000; tel. (2) 9267-9134; fax (2) 9261-3481; e-mail muano@mua.org.au; internet www.mua.org.au; f. 1993; Nat. Sec. PADDY CRUMLIN; 10,012 mems.

Media, Entertainment & Arts Alliance (MEAA): POB 723, Strawberry Hills, NSW 2012; tel. (2) 9333-0999; fax (2) 9333-0933; e-mail mail@alliance.org.au; internet www.alliance.org.au; Pres. PATRICIA AMPHLETT; Fed. Sec. CHRISTOPHER WARREN; 17,235 mems.

National Union of Workers (NUW): POB 343, North Melbourne, Vic 3051; tel. (3) 9287-1850; fax (3) 9287-1818; e-mail nuwnat@nuw.org.au; internet www.nuw.org.au; Gen. Sec. CHARLES DONNELLY; Gen. Pres. DOUG STEVENS; 100,000 mems.

Rail, Tram and Bus Union (RTBU): 83–89 Renwick St, Redfern, NSW 2016; tel. (2) 9310-3966; fax (2) 9319-2096; e-mail rtbu@rtbu-nat.abn.au; internet www.rtbu-nat.asn.au; Nat. Pres. KEN MASON; Nat. Sec. ALLEN BARDEN; 35,000 mems.

Shop, Distributive & Allied Employees Association (SDA): 6th Floor, 53 Queen St, Melbourne, Vic 3000; tel. (3) 8611-7000; fax (3) 8611-7099; e-mail general@sda.org.au; internet www.sda.org.au; f. 1908; Nat. Pres. GERARD DWYER; Nat. Sec. JOE DE BRUYN; 214,029 mems.

Textile, Clothing and Footwear Union of Australia (TCFUA): 359 Exhibition St, Melbourne, Vic 3000; tel. (2) 9639-2955; fax (2) 9639-2944; e-mail nationaloffice@tcfvic.org.au; f. 1919; Pres. BARRY TUBNER; Nat. Sec. MICHELE O'NEIL; 21,354 mems.

Transport Workers' Union of Australia (TWU): POB 47, Parramatta, NSW 2124; tel. (2) 8114-6500; fax (2) 8114-6515; e-mail twu@twu.com.au; internet www.twu.com.au; Nat. Pres. WAYNE MADER; Nat. Sec. TONY SHELDON; 82,000 mems.

United Voice: Locked Bag 9, Haymarket, NSW 1240; tel. (2) 8204-3000; fax (2) 9281-4480; e-mail info@unitedvoice.org.au; internet www.unitedvoice.org.au; f. 1915; Nat. Pres. BRIAN DALEY; Nat. Sec. LOUISE TARRANT; 126,916 mems.

Transport

Australian Transport Council: POB 594, Canberra, ACT 2601; tel. (2) 6274-7462; fax (2) 6274-8090; e-mail atc@infrastructure.gov.au; internet www.atcouncil.gov.au; f. 1993; mems include Australian and New Zealand ministers responsible for transport; Sec. TONY MAZZER.

Adelaide Metro: Dept of Transport, Energy and Infrastructure, Public Transport Div., POB 1, Walkerville, SA 5081; fax (8) 8303-0849; e-mail dtei-ptd@saugov.sa.gov.au; internet www.adelaidemetro.com.au; f. 1999; operates metropolitan bus, train and tram services; CEO BOB STOBBE.

State Transit Authority of New South Wales: 219–241 Cleveland St, Strawberry Hills, NSW 2010; tel. (2) 9245-5777; e-mail info@sydneybuses.nsw.gov.au; internet www.sydneybuses.info; operates government buses and ferries in Sydney and Newcastle metropolitan areas; Chair. BARRLE UNSWORTH; CEO PETER ROWLEY.

RAILWAYS

In June 2011 there were 43,063 km of railways in Australia. In 2003 the construction of a 1,400-km railway between Alice Springs and Darwin was completed. The rail link was to be used principally for transporting freight. The development of a high-speed network for the country's east coast was under consideration in 2011–12.

Pacific National: Level 6, 15 Blue St, North Sydney, NSW 2060; tel. (2) 8484-8000; fax (2) 8484-8151; e-mail communication@pacificnational.com.au; internet www.pacificnational.com.au; freight; fmrly Nat. Rail Corpn Ltd; CEO MARK ROWSTHORN.

QR (Queensland Rail): GPOB 1429, Brisbane, Qld 4001; tel. (7) 3235-2180; fax (7) 3235-1373; internet www.queenslandrail.com.au; f. 1863; passenger commuter and long-distance services, freight and logistic services, track access and rail-specific expert services; Chair. JOHN B. PRESCOTT; CEO LANCE HOCKRIDGE.

RailCorp: POB K349, Haymarket, NSW 1238; tel. (2) 8202-2000; fax (2) 8202-2111; internet www.railcorp.info; f. 1980; responsible for passenger rail and associated coach services in NSW; Chair. ELIZABETH CROUCH; CEO ROB MASON.

Victorian Rail Track (VicTrack): Level 8, 1010 LaTrobe St, Docklands, Vic 3008; tel. (3) 9619-1111; fax (3) 9619-8851; e-mail victrack@victrack.com.au; internet www.victrack.com.au; f. 1997; Chair. BRUCE COHEN; Chief Exec. JOHN SUTTON.

ROADS

In 2007 there were 815,074 km of roads open for general traffic. This included 18,773 km of highways and national roads, 122,082 km of regional roads and 672,118 km of other roads.

Austroads: Suite 2, Level 9, 287 Elizabeth St, Sydney, NSW 2000; tel. (2) 9264-7088; fax (2) 9264-1657; e-mail austroads@austroads.com.au; internet www.austroads.com.au; f. 1989; assen of road transport and traffic authorities; Chair. ALAN TESCH; Chief Exec. MURRAY KIDNIE.

SHIPPING

In December 2009 the Australian merchant fleet comprised 719 vessels, with a total displacement of 1,836,500 grt.

ANL Ltd (Australian National Line): GPOB 2238, Melbourne, Vic 3001; tel. (3) 8842-5555; fax (3) 9257-0619; e-mail webmaster@anl.com.au; internet www.anl.com.au; f. 1998; shipping agents; coastal and overseas container shipping and coastal bulk shipping; container management services; overseas container services to Asia; extensive transshipment services; Chair. JACQUES SAADE; Man. Dir JOHN LINES.

Svitzer Australasia: Level 23, 201 Elizabeth St, Sydney, NSW 2000; tel. (2) 9369-9200; fax (2) 9369-9277; e-mail ausydinfo@svitzer.com; internet www.svitzer.com; f. 1875; fmrly Adelaide Steamship Co; later known as Adsteam Marine Ltd, until acquisition by Svitzer (Denmark); Man. Dir ANDERS EGEHUS.

CIVIL AVIATION

Jetstar Airways Pty Ltd: GPOB 4713, Melbourne, Vic 3001; tel. (3) 9347-0091; internet www.jetstar.com.au; f. 2004; owned by Qantas Airways Ltd; low-cost domestic passenger services and flights to New Zealand, Fiji, Singapore, Indonesia, Japan and other Asia-Pacific destinations; Chief Exec. BRUCE BUCHANAN.

National Jet Systems: National Dr., Adelaide Airport, SA 5950; tel. (8) 8154-7000; fax (8) 8154-7019; internet www.nationaljet.com.au; f. 1989; chartered flights; CEO PETER NOTTAGE; Group Gen. Man. MATTHEW LANG.

Qantas Airways Ltd: Qantas Centre, 203 Coward St, Mascot, NSW 2020; tel. (2) 9691-3636; fax (2) 9691-3339; internet www.qantas.com; f. 1920; est. as Queensland and Northern Territory Aerial Services; Australian Govt became sole owner in 1947; merged with Australian Airlines in Sept. 1992; British Airways purchased 25% in March 1993; remaining 75% transferred to private sector in 1995; services throughout Australia and to 36 countries, including destinations in Europe, Africa, the USA, Canada, South America, Asia, the Pacific and New Zealand; subsidiary QantasLink operates regional services; Chair. LEIGH CLIFFORD; CEO ALAN JOYCE.

Strategic Airlines Pty Ltd: 34 Navigator Pl., Hendra, QLD 4011; tel. (7) 3169-3900; fax (7) 3169-3901; e-mail info@airaustralia.com; internet www.airaustralia.com; trading name Air Australia Airways; low-cost international and domestic services; CEO MICHAEL JAMES.

Virgin Blue: 56 Edmondstone Rd, Bowen Hills, QLD 4006; tel. (7) 3295-3000; e-mail corporatecommunications@virginaustralia.com; internet www.virginaustralia.com; f. 2000 as Virgin Blue; renamed as above in 2011; domestic and international services; CEO JOHN BORGHETTI.

Tourism

The main attractions are the cosmopolitan cities, the Great Barrier Reef, the Blue Mountains, water sports and also winter sports in the Australian Alps, notably the Snowy Mountains. The town of Alice Springs, the Aboriginal culture and the sandstone monolith of Uluru (also known as Ayers Rock) are among the attractions of the desert interior. Much of Australia's wildlife is unique to the country. Australia received nearly 5.9m. foreign visitors in 2011, a decline of 0.2% in comparison with 2010, when an increase of 5.4% had been recorded. New Zealand, the United Kingdom, the People's Republic of China, the USA, Japan and Singapore are the principal sources of visitors. Receipts from international tourism totalled an estimated $A23,681m. in 2010/11. Tourist accommodation facilities comprised 225,974 rooms in September 2011.

Tourism Australia: GPOB 2721, Sydney, NSW 1006; tel. (2) 9360-1111; fax (2) 9331-6469; e-mail corpaffairs@tourism.australia.com; internet www.tourism.australia.com; f. 2004; govt authority responsible for marketing of international and domestic tourism; Chair. GEOFF DIXON.

Defence

As assessed at November 2011, Australia's active armed forces numbered 56,552: army 28,246, navy 14,250, air force 14,056. There were also reserve forces of 20,440. Military service is voluntary. All restrictions on the deployment of women in combat roles were ended in September 2011. Australia is a member of the ANZUS Security Treaty (with New Zealand and the USA), and of the Five Power Defence Arrangements (with Singapore, Malaysia, the United Kingdom and New Zealand). In November 2011, in support of peacekeeping efforts, 1,550 Australian troops were stationed in Afghanistan, with 35 personnel remaining in Iraq. A total of 380 Australian military personnel were present in Timor-Leste, while 80 remained in Solomon Islands.

Defence Expenditure: Estimated at $A26,500m. for 2012.

Chief of the Defence Force: Gen. DAVID HURLEY.

Chief of Navy: Vice-Adm. RAY GRIGGS.

Chief of Army: Lt-Gen. DAVID MORRISON.

Chief of Air Force: Air Marshal GEOFFREY BROWN.

Education

Education is the responsibility of each of the states and the Federal Government. It is free of charge and compulsory for all children from the ages of six to at least 16 years (in most states) or 17 if not going into training. Primary education generally begins with a preparatory year commencing at five years of age, followed by six or seven years of schooling. Secondary education, beginning at the age of 12, usually lasts for five or six years. In 2008/09 enrolment at primary schools included 97% of pupils in the relevant age-group, while enrolment at secondary schools included 85% of pupils (males 84%; females 86%) in the relevant age-group. In August 2010 there were 2,010,327 children enrolled in primary schools (including those attending non-government schools, the majority being Catholic institutions) and 1,476,552 in secondary schools. A total of 1,066,095 students were attending 39 universities in 2008. Public expenditure on education under the federal budget for the financial year 2011/12 was projected at $A29,938m.

AUSTRALIAN EXTERNAL TERRITORIES

CHRISTMAS ISLAND

Introductory Survey

LOCATION, CLIMATE, LANGUAGE, RELIGION, FLAG, CAPITAL

Christmas Island lies 360 km south of Java Head (Indonesia) in the Indian Ocean. The nearest point on the Australian coast is North West Cape, 1,408 km to the south-east. Christmas Island has no indigenous population. The climate is equable, with temperatures varying between 26°C (79°F) and 28°C (83°F), and rainfall of 2,000 mm per year. A variety of languages are spoken (more than 60% of the population spoke a language other than English in 2001), but English is the official language. The Christmas Island flag (proportions 1 by 2) is divided diagonally from the upper hoist to the lower fly: the upper portion displays a Golden Bosun bird in silhouette on a green background, the lower portion has five white five-pointed stars, in the form of the Southern Cross constellation, on a blue background, and in the centre is a golden circle containing the shape of the island in green. The predominant religious affiliation is Buddhist (30% in 2006). The principal settlement and only anchorage is Flying Fish Cove.

CONTEMPORARY POLITICAL HISTORY

Historical Context

Following annexation by the United Kingdom in 1888, Christmas Island was incorporated for administrative purposes with the Straits Settlements (now Singapore and part of Malaysia) in 1900. Japanese forces occupied the island from March 1942 until the end of the Second World War, and in 1946 Christmas Island became a dependency of Singapore. Administration was transferred to the United Kingdom on 1 January 1958, pending final transfer to Australia, effected on 1 October 1958. The Australian Government appointed Official Representatives to the Territory until 1968, when new legislation provided for an Administrator, appointed by the Governor-General. Responsibility for the island's administration lies with the Minister for Regional Australia, Regional Development and Local Government. In 1980 an Advisory Council was established for the Administrator to consult. In 1984 the Christmas Island Services Corporation was created to perform those functions that are normally the responsibility of municipal government. This body was placed under the direction of the Christmas Island Assembly, the first elections to which took place in September 1985. Nine members were elected for one-year terms. In November 1987 the Assembly was dissolved, and the Administrator empowered to perform its functions. The Corporation was superseded by the Christmas Island Shire Council in 1992.

Domestic Political Affairs

In May 1994 an unofficial referendum on the island's status was held concurrently with local government elections. At the poll, sponsored by the Union of Christmas Island Workers, the islanders rejected an option to secede from Australia, but more than 85% of voters favoured increased local government control. The referendum was prompted, in part, by the Australian Government's plans to abolish the island's duty-free status (which had become a considerable source of revenue).

Since 1981 all residents of the island have been eligible to acquire Australian citizenship. In 1984 the Australian Government extended social security, health and education benefits to the island, and enfranchised Australian citizens resident there. Full income-tax liability was introduced in the late 1980s. The Territories Law Reform Act 2010 (see Norfolk Island) included provision for the comprehensive application of the laws of Western Australia to Christmas Island.

Asylum-seekers and Detention Arrangements

During the late 1990s an increasing number of illegal immigrants travelling to Australia landed on Christmas Island. In January 2001 Australian government officials denied claims by Christmas Islanders that some 86 illegal immigrants who had arrived at the island from the Middle East via Indonesia were being detained in inhumane conditions. Local people claimed that the detainees were sleeping on concrete floors and were being denied adequate food and medical care.

International attention was focused on Christmas Island in August 2001 when the *MV Tampa*, a Norwegian container ship carrying 433 refugees whom it had rescued from a sinking Indonesian fishing boat, was refused permission to land on the island. As the humanitarian crisis escalated, the Australian Government's steadfast refusal to admit the mostly Afghan refugees prompted international condemnation and led to a serious diplomatic dispute between Australia and Norway. The office of the UN High Commissioner for Refugees (UNHCR) and the International Organization for Migration (IOM) expressed grave concern at the situation. Hundreds of Christmas Island residents attended a rally urging the Australian Government to reconsider its uncompromising stance. In September the refugees were transferred (via Papua New Guinea and New Zealand) to Nauru, where their applications for asylum were to be processed. In the same month the Senate in Canberra approved new legislation, which excised Christmas Island and other outlying territories from Australia's official migration zone. The new legislation also imposed stricter criteria for the processing of asylum-seekers and the removal of their right to recourse to the Australian court system. Meanwhile, increasing numbers of asylum-seekers continued to attempt to reach Christmas Island via Indonesia. Among the many controversial incidents that occurred in the waters of Christmas Island in late 2001 was that involving 186 Iraqis who jumped into the sea when ordered to leave Australian waters in October. They were temporarily held on Christmas Island before being transferred to Nauru.

In March 2002 the Government announced plans to establish a permanent detention centre on the island, at a projected cost of more than $A150m., in order to accommodate an anticipated total of 18,000 asylum-seekers who were expected to arrive at Christmas Island during 2002–06. However, plans to scale down the project were announced in February 2003. In July of that year a boat carrying 53 asylum-seekers from Viet Nam was intercepted in Australian waters (the first such vessel to be found in the region since 2001), and its passengers were transferred to Christmas Island. In mid-2005 a total of 32 asylum-seekers remained in the Territory. Some 42 Indonesian refugees from Papua province arrived at Christmas Island in January 2006. They were granted temporary visas in March, while awaiting transfer to the Australian city of Melbourne. The construction of the 800-bed detention centre began in February 2005; some 100 construction workers were engaged on the project. Speculation among some observers that the Australian Government intended to use the completed centre as a military base for US forces was dismissed by official sources. However, the islanders became increasingly suspicious of the Government's intentions, particularly when unofficial information began to circulate that the building specifications of the project were similar to those implemented in high-security military facilities, such as those used to detain terrorists. The Australian Immigration Department would confirm only that it would be a modern detention facility. By late 2007 the estimated cost had reportedly increased to $A396m. Although the centre was completed in early 2008, it was unused, in accordance with the new Australian Government's policy of opposition to its construction. Meanwhile, in February 2007 more than 80 Sri Lankan refugees, en route from Indonesia, were intercepted by a ship of the Australian navy and detained on Christmas Island, prior to being transferred to Nauru.

The new Government of Kevin Rudd relaxed Australia's policy on the treatment of refugees in July 2008, when it announced that the automatic incarceration of asylum-seekers upon arrival was to be ended. However, in December the Government announced that a group of suspected asylum-seekers found in a boat off the north-west coast of Australia was to be taken to the Christmas Island detention centre; a total of 172 people had arrived in Australian waters seeking asylum since September. In January 2009 28 refugees from Afghanistan and Iran, who had been intercepted off Western Australia in the latter part of 2008 and detained on Christmas Island, were granted permanent residency in Australia. The members of this group, which included 10 children, were thus the first beneficiaries of the Labor Government's 'more humane' approach to the issue. In 2009 the number of asylum-seekers arriving in Australian waters increased dramatically, reportedly owing to the deteriorating security situation in countries such as Afghanistan and Sri Lanka. These asylum-seekers were taken to Christmas Island for processing, and in October the Government announced plans to increase the detention centre's capacity beyond 1,400, in order to accommodate the growing numbers. Representatives of Amnesty International were permitted to visit the detention centre in August 2008 and again in December 2009, when the human rights organization reiterated its concerns with regard to the facilities and described the Australian Government's policy as 'unviable and inhumane'. By January 2010, according to the Australian Department of Immigration, the detention centre held a total of 1,628 asylum-seekers. In February, with numbers at the centre again approaching capacity, the Government announced plans for a further extension of the facility, to hold 2,200 inmates. In June, in an attempt to ease the overcrowding, the authorities commenced the transfer of dozens of asylum-seekers from the centre to a disused mining camp on the mainland, located at Leonora in Western Australia. Meanwhile, asylum-seekers on Christmas Island continued to be processed and resettled in mainland Australia. In April, however, the Government imposed moratoriums of six and of three months respectively on applicants who had travelled from Afghanistan and from Sri Lanka, in response to 'changing conditions' in those countries.

In November 2010, in a unanimous ruling that was expected to have extensive implications for government policy, the Australian High Court found in favour of two unsuccessful Sri Lankan seekers of asylum. The two Tamil migrants had been detained on Christmas Island and had argued that legislation that prevented them from appealing against the rejection of their asylum claims was unfair. The dispute centred on the official distinction made between asylum-seekers who arrived by sea and those who had travelled by air: the latter category was not subject to automatic detention and had the right of appeal in the event of the rejection of a claim for asylum.

In a major incident in rough seas in December 2010 some 50 asylum-seekers, mainly from Iraq and Iran, perished when their wooden vessel disintegrated on rocks off Christmas Island. In January 2011 three Indonesian members of the ship's crew were indicted on charges of illegally transporting people to Australia. Also, an Australian citizen of Iranian descent was arrested in Indonesia in connection with various allegations of immigration offences, including arrangements for the dispatch of the boat that had foundered off Christmas Island in the previous month. In May, following his deportation from Indonesia, the suspect appeared in court in the Australian city of Sydney, whereupon he was charged with people-smuggling. In November, in a court in Perth, Western Australia, he pleaded not guilty to 14 counts of aggravated people-smuggling. Meanwhile, a parliamentary inquiry into the disaster held in Australia concluded in June that the response of the authorities to the disaster had been as effective as possible under the prevailing weather conditions.

In March 2011 about 170 asylum-seekers were recaptured following a mass escape from the detention centre. Furthermore, in a protest against the slow processing of their applications for asylum, detainees were reported to have set fire to the facility and to have assaulted security personnel. The authorities resorted to the use of tear gas to quell the disturbances. In June riot police were drafted in to curb further protests, and there was renewed unrest in July when as many as 100 inmates were involved in a confrontation during which medical records were destroyed. At 31 January 2012 there were 832 people in immigration detention on Christmas Island.

ECONOMIC AFFAIRS

Despite its auspicious climate, Christmas Island does not possess a significant agricultural sector. The predominance of tropical forest (much of which has been granted national park status) has discouraged commercial farming activities and the territory relies, for the most part, on food imports from mainland Australia. Abundant marine resources exist in the island's surrounding waters, although without proper regulation opportunities for commercial fishing have remained limited. Islanders who participate in subsistence and recreational fishing activities do so without licences, and therefore no official data exist relating to the volume of activity in this sector.

The recovery of phosphates has been the principal economic activity on Christmas Island. In November 1987 the Australian Government announced the closure of the phosphate mine, owing to industrial unrest, and mining activity ceased in December of that year. However, in 1990 the Government allowed private operators to recommence phosphate extraction, subject to certain conditions. A new 21-year lease, drawn up by the Government and the owner of the mine, Phosphate Resources Ltd, took effect in February 1998. The agreement incorporated environmental safeguards and provided for a conservation levy, based on the tonnage of phosphate shipped, which was to finance a programme of rainforest rehabilitation. At the census of 2006, 14.8% of Christmas Island's employed population were engaged in the mining sector.

The services sector engaged 63.2% of the employed labour force at the census of 2006. Efforts have been made to develop the island's considerable potential for tourism. In 1989, in an attempt to protect the natural environment and many rare species of flora and fauna (including the Abbott's Booby and the Christmas frigate bird), the National Park was extended to cover some 70% of the island. A large hotel and casino complex was opened in November 1993, and revenue from the development totalled $A500m. in 1994. In April 1998, however, the complex was closed down, and some 350 employees were made redundant. In 2003 receipts from Christmas Island's tourism, hospitality and retail sector were estimated at between $A3m. and $A5m.

Between 1992 and 1999 the Australian Government invested an estimated $A110m. in the development of Christmas Island's infrastructure as part of the Christmas Island Rebuilding Programme. The main areas of expenditure under this programme were a new hospital, the upgrading of port facilities, school extensions, the construction of housing, power, water supply and sewerage, and the repair and construction of roads. In 2000 further improvements to marine facilities and water supply were carried out, in addition to the construction of new housing to relocate islanders away from a major rockfall risk area. In 2001 the Australian Government pledged a total of more than $A50m. for further developments including improvements to the airport and the road network, as well as an alternative port. The proposed additional port was to be constructed on the east coast of the island, allowing for the handling of sea freight and the launching of emergency vessels at times when the existing port at Flying Fish Cove is closed owing to north-west swells. These closures, which most commonly occur between December and March, had resulted in inflated costs for shipping companies and inconvenience for Christmas Islanders. The Australian Government announced in April 2004 that it would provide $A2.5m. to fund a new mobile telephone network for the Territory.

The cost of the island's imports from Australia decreased from $A17m. in 1999/2000 to $A5m. in 2006/07, when the Territory's exports to that country earned $A26m. Exports to New Zealand in 2006/07 were worth $NZ9m. The 2010/11 budget envisaged operating revenue of $A10.1m. and operating expenditure of nearly $A9.0m. Capital expenditure was almost $A1.7m. The 2006 census recorded 5.0% of the total labour force as being unemployed.

The closure of the casino resort in 1998 had serious economic and social repercussions for Christmas Island. A project to develop a communications satellite launching facility on the island received government approval in 2000, but the scheme was subsequently postponed indefinitely. A major issue for the local population has been the substantial rise in the cost of living on the island, largely owing to the presence of 2,800 mainland personnel, including immigration officials, security guards and medical staff. Furthermore, prospects for the development of eco-tourism have been curtailed by the negative publicity surrounding the detention centre. Christmas Island possesses more than 20 species of crab. These include the robber (or coconut) crab, the largest land invertebrate in the world. In 2010, however, local reports suggested that increasing numbers of this protected native species were being killed by road vehicles driven at undue speed by personnel from the mainland.

PUBLIC HOLIDAYS

2013: 1 January (New Year's Day), 28 January (for Australia Day), 11–12 February (Chinese New Year), 18 March (Labour Day), 29 March (Good Friday), 25 April (Anzac Day), 7 August (Hari Raya Puasa), 7 October (Territory Day), 14 October (Hari Raya Haji), 25–26 December (Christmas).

Statistical Survey

AREA AND POPULATION

Area: 136.7 sq km (52.8 sq miles).

Population: 1,508 at census of 7 August 2001; 1,347 (males 765, females 582) at census of 8 August 2006. *2007* (estimate): 1,400 (Source: Commonwealth Secretariat).

Density (2007): 10.2 per sq km.

Population by Age and Sex (2006 census): *0–14:* 314 (males 152, females 162); *15–64:* 967 (males 570, females 397); *65 and over:* 66 (males 43, females 23); *Total* 1,347 (males 765, females 582).

Country of Birth (2006 census): Australia 609; Malaysia 412; United Kingdom 41; Singapore 39; Indonesia 21; New Zealand 20.

Births and Deaths (1985): Registered live births 36 (birth rate 15.8 per 1,000); Registered deaths 2.

Economically Active Population (persons aged 15 years and over, excl. overseas visitors, 2006 census): Agriculture, forestry and fishing 4; Mining 96; Manufacturing 23; Electricity, gas and water 14; Construction 101; Wholesale and retail trade, restaurants and hotels 91; Transport, storage and communications 41; Financing, insurance, real estate and business services 16; Government administration and defence 96; Community, social and personal services 165; Activities not stated or not adequately defined 34; *Total employed* 681 (males 442, females 239); Unemployed 36 (males 20, females 16); *Total labour force* 717 (males 462, females 255).

MINING

Natural Phosphates ('000 metric tons, official estimates): 285 in 1994; 220 in 1995. Note: By 2007 it was estimated that 600,000 metric tons of phosphates were being mined each year.

FINANCE

Currency and Exchange Rates: Australian currency is used.

Budget ($A, year ending 30 June 2011): Operating revenue 10,102,249 (General purpose funding 4,573,132; Welfare 235,215; Community amenities 1,215,431; Recreation and culture 1,379,485; Transport 2,489,946); Operating expenditure 8,987,719 (Governance 500,441; Law and order and public safety 164,869; Health 105,292; Welfare 491,889; Housing 148,194; Community amenities 1,231,064; Recreation and culture 2,251,135; Transport 3,808,906); Capital expenditure 1,667,261 (Community amenities 365,094; Recreation and culture 222,502; Transport 942,777).

EXTERNAL TRADE

Exports: An estimated 600,000 metric tons of phosphates are exported each year to mainland Australia and markets in South-East Asia.

Principal Trading Partners (phosphate exports, '000 metric tons, year ending 30 June 1984): Australia 463; New Zealand 332; Total (incl. others) 1,136.

2006/07 ($A million): *Imports:* Australia 5. *Exports:* Australia 26. Source: Australian Bureau of Statistics, *Year Book Australia*.

2006/07 ($NZ million): *Exports:* New Zealand 9. Source: Ministry of Foreign Affairs and Trade, New Zealand.

TRANSPORT

International Sea-borne Shipping (estimated freight traffic, '000 metric tons, 1990): Goods loaded 1,290; Goods unloaded 68. Source: UN, *Monthly Bulletin of Statistics*.

TOURISM

Visitor Arrivals and Departures by Air: 2,712 in 1998. Source: *Year Book Australia*.

COMMUNICATIONS MEDIA

Radio Receivers (1997): 1,000 in use.

Personal Computers (home users, 2001 census): 506.

Internet Users (2006 census): 480.

EDUCATION

Pre-primary (August 2008): 38 pupils.

Primary (August 2008): 124 pupils.

Secondary (August 2007): 88 pupils.

Source: Education Department of Western Australia.

Directory

The Government

The Administrator, appointed by the Governor-General of Australia and responsible to the Minister for Regional Australia, Regional Development and Local Government, is the senior government representative on the island.

Administrator: Brian James Lacy.

Office of the Administrator: POB 868, Christmas Island 6798, Indian Ocean; tel. (8) 9164-7960; fax (8) 9164-7961.

Shire of Christmas Island: George Fam Centre, POB 863, Christmas Island 6798, Indian Ocean; tel. (8) 9164-8300; fax (8) 9164-8304; e-mail kelvin@shire.gov.cx; internet www.christmas.shire.gov.cx; CEO Kelvin Matthews; Pres. Foo Kee Heng.

Judicial System

Judicial services on Christmas Island are provided through the Western Australian Department of the Attorney-General. Western Australian Court Services provides a Magistrate's Court, District Court, Supreme Court, Family Court, Children's Court and Coroner's Court.

Managing Registrar: Jeffrey Low, c/o Dept of Regional Australia, Regional Development and Local Government, POB 868, Christmas Island 6798, Indian Ocean; tel. (8) 9164-7901; fax (8) 9164-8530; e-mail jeffrey.low@dotars.gov.cx.

Religion

According to the census of 2006, a total of 407 Christmas Island residents were Buddhists (about 30%), 266 (20%) were Muslims and 238 (18%) were Christians, of whom 157 were Roman Catholics and 81 were Anglicans. Within the Christian churches, Christmas Island lies in the jurisdiction of both the Anglican and Roman Catholic Archbishops of Perth, in Western Australia.

The Press

The Islander: Shire of Christmas Island, George Fam Centre, POB 863, Christmas Island 6798, Indian Ocean; tel. (8) 9164-8300; fax (8) 9164-8304; e-mail chong@shire.gov.cx; newsletter; fortnightly; Editor Kelvin Matthews.

Broadcasting and Communications

BROADCASTING

Radio

Christmas Island Community Radio Service: f. 1967; operated by the Administration since 1991; daily broadcasting service by Radio VLU-2 on 1422 KHz and 102 MHz FM, in English, Malay, Cantonese and Mandarin; Station Man. William Taylor.

Christmas Island Radio VLU2–FM: POB 474, Christmas Island 6798, Indian Ocean; tel. (8) 9164-8316; fax (8) 9164-8315; daily broadcasts on 102.1FM and 105.3FM in English, Malay, Cantonese and Mandarin; Chair. and Station Man. Tony Smith.

Television

Christmas Island Television: POB AAA, Christmas Island 6798, Indian Ocean.

Finance

BANKING

Commercial Bank

Westpac Banking Corpn (Australia): Flying Fish Cove, Christmas Island, Indian Ocean; tel. (8) 9164-8221; fax (8) 9164-8241.

Trade and Industry

Administration of Christmas Island: POB 868, Christmas Island 6798, Indian Ocean; tel. (8) 9164-7901; fax (8) 9164-8245; operates power, public housing, local courts; Dir of Finance Jeffery Tan.

Christmas Island Chamber of Commerce: POB 510, Christmas Island 6798, Indian Ocean; tel. (8) 9164-8856; fax (8) 9164-8322; e-mail info@cicommerce.org.cx; Pres. John Richardson; Vice-Pres. Phillip Oakley.

Shire of Christmas Island: see The Government.

Union of Christmas Island Workers (UCIW): Poon Saan Rd, POB 84, Christmas Island 6798, Indian Ocean; tel. (8) 9164-8471; fax (8) 9164-8470; e-mail uciw@pulau.cx; fmrly represented phosphate workers; Pres. Foo Kee Heng; Gen. Sec. Gordon Thomson.

Transport

There are good roads in the developed areas. National Jet Systems operates a twice-weekly flight from Perth, via the Cocos (Keeling) Islands, and a private Christmas Island-based charter company operates services to Jakarta, Indonesia. The Australian National Line (ANL) operates ships to the Australian mainland. Cargo vessels from Fremantle deliver regular supplies to the island. The Joint Island Supply System, established in 1989, provides a shipping service for Christmas Island and the Cocos Islands. The only anchorage is at Flying Fish Cove.

Tourism

Tourism has the potential to be an important sector of the island's economy. Much of the unique flora and fauna is found in the national park, which covers about 70% of the island and contains large tracts of rainforest. Other attractions are the waterfalls, beaches, coves and excellent conditions for scuba-diving and game-fishing.

Christmas Island Tourism Association/Christmas Island Visitor Information Centre: POB 63, Christmas Island 6798, Indian Ocean; tel. (8) 9164-8382; fax (8) 9164-8080; e-mail cita@christmas.net.au; internet www.christmas.net.au.

Christmas Island Travel: Christmas Island 6798, Indian Ocean; tel. (8) 9164-7168; fax (8) 9164-7169; e-mail xch@citravel.com.au; internet www.citravel.com.au; Dir TAN SIM KIAT.

Island Bound Holidays: tel. (8) 9381-3644; fax (8) 9381-2030; e-mail info@islandbound.com.au.

Parks Australia: POB 867, Christmas Island 6798, Indian Ocean; tel. (8) 9164-8700; fax (8) 9164-8755; internet www.environment.gov.au/parks/christmas/index.html.

Education

The Christmas Island District High School, operated by the Western Australia Ministry of Education, provides education from pre-school level up to Australian 'Year 12'. In August 2008 enrolment totalled 38 in pre-primary and 124 in primary institutions. Secondary pupils totalled 88 in August 2007.

COCOS (KEELING) ISLANDS

Introductory Survey

LOCATION, CLIMATE, LANGUAGE, RELIGION, FLAG, CAPITAL

The Cocos (Keeling) Islands are 27 in number and lie 2,768 km north-west of Perth, in the Indian Ocean. The islands, with a combined area of 14 sq km (5.4 sq miles), form two low-lying coral atolls, densely covered with coconut palms. The climate is equable, with temperatures varying from 21°C (69°F) to 32°C (88°F), and rainfall of 2,000 mm per year. English is the official language, but Cocos Malay and Malay are also widely spoken. Most of the inhabitants are Muslims (75% in 2006). The flag of the Cocos Islands (proportions 1 by 2) is green, with a palm tree on a gold disc in the upper hoist, a gold crescent in the centre and five gold five-pointed stars, in the form of the Southern Cross constellation, in the fly. The Cocos Malay community is based on Home Island. The only other inhabited island is West Island, where most of the European community lives and where the administration is based.

CONTEMPORARY POLITICAL HISTORY

Historical Context

The Cocos Islands were declared a British possession in 1857 and came successively under the authority of the Governors of Ceylon (now Sri Lanka), from 1878, and the Straits Settlements (now Singapore and part of Malaysia), from 1886. In 1946, when the islands became a dependency of the Colony of Singapore, a resident administrator, responsible to the Governor of Singapore, was appointed. Administration of the islands was transferred to the Commonwealth of Australia on 23 November 1955. The agent of the Australian Government was known as the Official Representative until 1975, when an Administrator was appointed. The Minister for Regional Australia, Regional Development and Local Government is responsible for the governance of the islands. The Territory is part of the Northern Territory Electoral District.

Domestic Political Affairs

In June 1977 the Australian Government announced new policies concerning the islands, which resulted in its purchase from land-owner John Clunies-Ross of the whole of his interests in the islands, with the exception of his residence and associated buildings. Although in 1886 the Clunies-Ross family had been granted all land above the high-water mark in perpetuity by the British Crown, the Australian Government's purchase for $A6.5m. took effect on 1 September 1978. An attempt by the Australian Government to acquire Clunies-Ross' remaining property was deemed by the Australian High Court in October 1984 to be unconstitutional.

In July 1979 the Cocos (Keeling) Islands Council was established, with a wide range of functions in the Home Island village area (which the Government transferred to the Council on trust for the benefit of the Cocos Malay community) and, from September 1984, in most of the rest of the Territory.

On 6 April 1984 a referendum to decide the future political status of the islands was held by the Australian Government, with UN observers present. A large majority voted in favour of integration with Australia. As a result, the islanders were to acquire the rights, privileges and obligations of all Australian citizens. In July 1992 the Cocos (Keeling) Islands Council was replaced by the Cocos (Keeling) Islands Shire Council, composed of seven members and modelled on the local government and state law of Western Australia. The first Shire Council was elected in 1993. The Clunies-Ross family was declared bankrupt in mid-1993, following unsuccessful investment in a shipping venture, and the Australian Government took possession of its property.

In September 2001, following an increase in the numbers of illegal immigrants reaching Australian waters (see Christmas Island), legislation was enacted removing the Cocos Islands and other territories from Australia's official migration zone. In October of that year the Australian Government sent contingency supplies to the islands as a precaution, should it be necessary to accommodate more asylum-seekers. This development provoked concern among many Cocos residents that the former quarantine station used as a detention centre might become a permanent asylum-processing facility under the order of the Australian Government. In December 123 Sri Lankan and Vietnamese asylum-seekers were housed at the station, which was built to accommodate only 40. They were transferred to Christmas Island in February 2002.

In July 2009 an edict reportedly issued by the Shire Council banning employees and students from speaking Cocos Malay caused considerable consternation among the Malay residents. Those found speaking languages other than English in the workplace or at school were liable to penalties. The ban exacerbated the growing tensions between the majority Cocos Malay population and Australian public servants, deployed from the mainland, with regard to pay claims and cultural attitudes.

The Territories Law Reform Act 2010 (see Norfolk Island) included provision for the comprehensive application of the laws of Western Australia to the Cocos Islands.

ECONOMIC AFFAIRS

The Cocos Islands possess substantial marine resources, and opportunities for local fishing are plentiful. In 2006 the Australian Department of Fisheries introduced a basic regulatory framework for recreational fishing in the Territory, with the aim of fostering greater sustainability. A clam farm, established in 2000, was one of the first commercial ventures on the islands. Coconuts, grown throughout the islands, are the sole cash crop: total output was an estimated 7,600 metric tons in 2006, with copra production being estimated at 1,000 tons. Although some livestock is kept, and domestic gardens provide vegetables, bananas and papayas (pawpaws), the Islands are not self-sufficient, and foodstuffs are imported from mainland Australia. According to the 2006 census, agriculture, together with forestry and fishing, provided 1.6% of the employed population with work.

Industrial activity remains limited on the islands, the majority of those working in this area being engaged in the utilities sector. Activities related to the production of electricity, gas and water accounted for 7.9% of the employed labour force in 2006.

The islands have a small tourism industry. During August, September and October 2003, for example, there were a total of 76 non-resident arrivals, of whom 28 were travelling on business and 19 were visiting relatives. In 1995 a national park was designated on North Keeling Island. Some controversy arose in July 2004 when it was revealed that the Australian Government had drawn up plans to develop a resort on the Cocos Islands without having undertaken any consultation with the islanders. A Cocos postal service (including a philatelic bureau) came into operation in September 1979, and revenue from the service is used for the benefit of the community. In early 2000 the islands' internet domain name suffix, '.cc', was sold to Clear Channel, a US radio group, thus providing additional revenue. According to census data, the services sector engaged 81.5% of the employed population in 2006.

The cost of the islands' imports from Australia decreased from $A11m. in 2000/01 to $A6m. in 2006/07. Exports to Australia totalled $A2m. in 1996/97, but by 2002 the Cocos Islands had ceased to export any goods or produce. The Grants Commission estimated that the Australian Government's net funding of the Territory amounted to some $A18m. in 1999. In 2000/01 the Cocos Administration expended approximately $A9m. An estimated 19% of the total labour force were unemployed in 2001, 60% of whom were under the age of 30. The Shire Council and the Co-operative Society were the principal employers.

PUBLIC HOLIDAYS

2013 (provisional): 1 January (New Year's Day), 23 January (Hari Maulad Nabi), 28 January (for Australia Day), 29 March (Good Friday), 1 April (Easter Monday), 5 April (for Act of Self Determination Day), 25 April (Anzac Day), 7 August (Hari Raya Puasa), 14 October (Hari Raya Haji), 5 November (Islamic New Year), 25–26 December (Christmas).

Statistical Survey

AREA AND POPULATION

Area: 14.1 sq km (5.4 sq miles).

Population: 621 at census of 7 August 2001; 572 (males 274, females 298) at census of 8 August 2006. *2007* (estimate): 600 (Source: Commonwealth Secretariat).

Density (2007): 42.6 per sq km.

Country of Birth (2006 census): Australia (incl. Cocos Islands) 512; Malaysia 22; Singapore 11; Kenya 3; Netherlands 3.

Births and Deaths (1986): Registered live births 12 (birth rate 19.8 per 1,000); Registered deaths 2.

Economically Active Population (persons aged 15 years and over, excl. overseas visitors, 2006 census): Agriculture, forestry and fishing 3; Manufacturing 4; Electricity, gas and water 15; Construction 13; Wholesale and retail trade, restaurants and hotels 29; Transport, storage and communications 25; Government administration and defence 39; Community, social and personal services 61; Activities not stated or not adequately defined 21; *Total employed* 210 (males 133, females 77).

AGRICULTURE

Production (metric tons, 2006, FAO estimate): Coconuts 7,600. Source: FAO.

INDUSTRY

Production (metric tons, 2006, FAO estimates): Copra 1,000; Coconut (copra) oil 650. Source: FAO.

FINANCE

Currency and Exchange Rates: Australian currency is used.

EXTERNAL TRADE

Principal Commodities (metric tons, year ending 30 June 1985): *Exports:* Coconuts 202. *Imports:* Most requirements come from Australia. The trade deficit is offset by philatelic sales and Australian federal grants and subsidies. *2006/07* ($A '000, imports from Australia): 6,000.

Source: *Year Book Australia*.

COMMUNICATIONS MEDIA

Radio Receivers (1992): 300 in use.

Personal Computers (home users, 2001 census): 142.

Internet Users (2001 census): 171.

EDUCATION

Pre-primary (August 2008): 15 pupils.

Primary (August 2008): 83 pupils.

Secondary (August 2008): 31 pupils.

Teaching Staff (2004): 17 (10 primary, 7 secondary).

Source: Education Department of Western Australia.

Directory

The Government

The Administrator, appointed by the Governor-General of Australia and responsible to the Minister for Regional Australia, Regional Development and Local Government, is the senior government representative in the islands.

Administrator: BRIAN JAMES LACY (non-resident).

Administrative Offices: Administration Bldg, Morea Close, Cocos (Keeling) Islands 6799, Indian Ocean; tel. (8) 9162-6600; fax (8) 9162-6691; e-mail cocosadmin@afp.gov.au.

Cocos (Keeling) Islands Shire Council: POB 1094, Home Island, Cocos (Keeling) Islands 6799, Indian Ocean; tel. (8) 9162-6649; fax (8) 9162-6668; e-mail info@cocos.wa.gov.au; internet www.shire.cc; f. 1992 by Territories Law Reform Act; Pres. AINDIL MINKOM; CEO PETER CLARKE.

Judicial System

Judicial services in Cocos (Keeling) Islands are provided through the Western Australian Department of the Attorney-General. Western Australian Court Services provide a Magistrates Court, District Court, Supreme Court, Family Court, Children's Court and Coroner's Court.

Court Services: c/o Australian Federal Police, Cocos (Keeling) Islands 6799, Indian Ocean; tel. (8) 9162-6600; fax (8) 9162-6691; e-mail cocosadmin@afp.gov.au.

Religion

According to the census of 2006, of the 572 residents, 431 (some 75%) were Muslims and 73 (13%) Christians. The majority of Muslims live on Home Island, while most Christians are West Island residents. The Cocos Islands lie within both the Anglican and the Roman Catholic archdioceses of Perth (Western Australia).

Broadcasting and Communications

BROADCASTING

Radio

As well as a local radio station, Radio 6CKI (see below), the Cocos (Keeling) Islands receive daily broadcasts from ABC regional radio and the Western Australian station Red FM.

Radio 6CKI Voice of the Cocos (Keeling) Islands: POB 1084, Cocos (Keeling) Islands 6799, Indian Ocean; tel. and fax (8) 9162-6666; e-mail 6cki@cki.cc; non-commercial, run by volunteers; daily broadcasting service in Cocos Malay and English; Chair. KELLY EDWARDS.

Television

Four television stations, ABC, SBS, WIN and GWN, are broadcast from Western Australia via satellite.

Industry

Cocos (Keeling) Islands Co-operative Society Ltd: POB 1058, Home Island, Cocos (Keeling) Islands 6799, Indian Ocean; tel. (8) 9162-6708; fax (8) 9162-6764; e-mail admin@CocosCoOp.com; internet www.cocoscoop.com; f. 1979; conducts the business enterprises of the Cocos Islanders; activities include boat construction and repairs, copra and coconut production, sail-making, stevedoring and airport operation; owns and operates a supermarket and tourist accommodation; Chair. MOHAMMED SAID CHONGKIN; Gen. Man. RONALD TAYLOR.

Transport

An airport is located on West Island. Virgin Blue Airlines operates a twice-weekly service from Perth (Western Australia), via Christmas Island, for passengers to and from the airport on West Island. Cargo vessels from Singapore and Perth deliver regular supplies. The islands have a total of 10 km of sealed and 12 km of unsealed roads.

Zentner Shipping Pty Ltd: tel. (8) 9337-5911; e-mail zentner1@iinet.au; operates sea freight service from Fremantle (WA) every 4–6 weeks.

Tourism

Tourism is relatively undeveloped. However, the Cocos Islands possess unique flora and fauna, along with pristine beaches and coral reefs that offer excellent opportunities for scuba-diving and snorkelling. In 2009 there was one 28-room hotel on West Island, as well as several self-catering villas.

Cocos Island Tourism Association: Admiralty House, POB 1030, Cocos (Keeling) Islands 6799, Indian Ocean; tel. (8) 9162-6790; fax (8) 9162-7708; e-mail info@cocoskeelingislands.com.au; internet www.cocoskeelingislands.com.au.

Parks Australia: POB 1043, Cocos (Keeling) Islands 6798, Indian Ocean; tel. (8) 9162-6678; fax (8) 9162-6680; internet www.environment.gov.au/parks/cocos/index.html.

Education

Pre-primary and primary education is provided at the schools on Home and West Islands. Secondary education is provided to the age of 16 years on West Island. In August 2008 pre-primary pupils totalled 15. Primary pupils numbered 83, and there were 31 secondary students. A bursary scheme enables Cocos Malay children to continue their education on the Australian mainland.

NORFOLK ISLAND

Introductory Survey

LOCATION, CLIMATE, LANGUAGE, RELIGION, FLAG, CAPITAL

Norfolk Island lies off the eastern coast of Australia, about 1,400 km east of Brisbane, to the south of New Caledonia and 640 km north of New Zealand. The Territory also comprises the uninhabited Phillip Island and Nepean Island, 7 km and 1 km south of the main island respectively. Norfolk Island is hilly and fertile, with a coastline of cliffs and an area of 34.6 sq km (13.3 sq miles). It is about 8 km long and 4.8 km wide. The climate is mild and subtropical, with temperatures varying between 18°C (64°F) and 25°C (77°F), and the average annual rainfall is 1,350 mm, most of which occurs between May and August. English and Norfuk, which combines elements of a local Polynesian dialect (related to Pitcairnese) and 18th-century English, are the official languages. Most of the population (67% at the 2001 census) adhere to the Christian religion. The island's flag (proportions 1 by 2) has three vertical stripes (proportions 7:9:7) of green, white and green, with a Norfolk Island pine in green silhouette on the centre stripe. The capital of the Territory is Kingston.

CONTEMPORARY POLITICAL HISTORY

Historical Context

The island was uninhabited when discovered in 1774 by a British expedition, led by Capt. James Cook. Norfolk Island was used as a penal settlement from 1788 to 1814 and again from 1825 to 1855, when it was abandoned. In 1856 it was resettled by 194 emigrants from Pitcairn Island, which had become overpopulated. Norfolk Island was administered as a separate colony until 1897, when it became a dependency of New South Wales. In 1913 control was transferred to the Australian Government. However, disagreement with the Federal Government concerning Norfolk Island's status as a territory of the Commonwealth of Australia and issues relating to the island's system of governance remained unresolved in the early 21st century.

Domestic Political Affairs

Under the Commonwealth Norfolk Island Act 1979, Norfolk Island was to progress to responsible legislative and executive government, enabling the Territory to administer its own affairs to the greatest practicable extent. Wide powers were to be exercised henceforth by the nine-member Legislative Assembly and by the Executive Council, comprising the executive members of the Legislative Assembly who were given ministerial-type responsibilities. The Act preserved the Australian Government's responsibility for Norfolk Island as a territory under its authority, with the Minister for Infrastructure, Transport, Regional Development and Local Government designated as the responsible minister. The Act indicated that consideration would be given within five years to an extension of the powers of the Legislative Assembly and the political and administrative institutions of Norfolk Island. In 1985 legislative and executive responsibility was assumed by the Norfolk Island Government for public works and services, civil defence, betting and gaming, territorial archives and matters relating to the exercise of executive authority. In 1988 further amendments empowered the Legislative Assembly to select a Norfolk Island government auditor (territorial accounts were previously audited by the Commonwealth Auditor-General). The office of Chief Minister was replaced by that of the President of the Legislative Assembly. David Buffett was reappointed to this post following the May 1992 general election.

A lack of consensus among members of the Executive Council on several major issues prompted early legislative elections in April 1994. The newly elected Legislative Assembly was notable for its inclusion of three female members. Following elections in April 1997, in which 22 candidates contested the nine seats, George Smith was appointed President (subsequently reverting to the title of Chief Minister) of the Legislative Assembly. At legislative elections in February 2000 three new members were elected to the Assembly, and Ronald Nobbs was subsequently appointed Chief Minister. Geoffrey Gardner, hitherto Minister for Health, replaced Nobbs as Chief Minister following the elections of November 2001. The incoming Assembly included four new members. In late 1997 the Legislative Assembly debated the issue of increased self-determination for the island.

In August 1998 a referendum proposing that the Norfolk Island electoral system be integrated more closely with that of mainland Australia (initiated in Canberra by the Minister for Regional Development, Territories and Local Government) was rejected by 78% of the Territory's electorate. A similar referendum in May 1999 was opposed by 73% of voters. Frustration with the Australian Government's perceived reluctance to facilitate the transfer of greater powers to the Territory (as outlined in the Norfolk Island Act of 1979, see above) led the island's Legislative Assembly in mid-1999 to vote in favour of full internal self-government. Negotiations regarding the administration of crown land on the island, which continued in 2000, were seen as indicative of the islanders' determination to pursue greater independence from Australia.

Legislation was approved in March 2003 to amend the requirements for voting in Norfolk Island elections. Under the new system Australian, New Zealand and British citizens were to be allowed to vote after a residency period of 12 months (reduced from 900 days). The amendments, which followed a series of occasionally acrimonious discussions with the Australian Government, provoked concern among islanders who feared that succumbing to Australian pressure to reform the Norfolk Island Act would result in the effective removal of authority over electoral matters from island control. Moreover, a report by an Australian parliamentary committee published in July 2003 was critical of Norfolk Island's Government and public services. Many residents believed that the report constituted a further attempt by Australia to undermine their autonomy. The Chief Minister rejected the committee's claims. A further report by the Australian Government published later in the year alleged that officials on the island used intimidation to achieve political and financial gain and recommended that Norfolk Island's elections, government and financial matters be overseen by the federal authorities.

The inhabitants of Norfolk Island were profoundly shocked when the Deputy Chief Minister and long-serving politician, Ivens Buffett, was shot dead in his office in July 2004. A local man was arrested at the scene of the crime, and it was subsequently revealed that the suspect was the politician's son. Leith Buffett, the politician's son, was arrested but, owing to severe mental illness, was found to be incompetent to stand trial.

A total of 14 candidates contested the legislative election held on 20 October 2004. Geoffrey Gardner, the Chief Minister, retained his seat in the nine-member Legislative Assembly, as did Speaker David Buffett. However, two long-serving members were defeated in the poll.

In early 2005 the Legislative Assembly declared Norfuk, the local creole spoken by around one-half of the island's population and described as a hybrid of Tahitian and 18th-century English, as an official language alongside English. The legislature's action was prompted by reports of a decline in the use of the language among islanders. Norfuk was subsequently introduced into the school curriculum on Norfolk Island, its usage having previously been forbidden in schools. In August 2007 the UN placed Norfuk on its list of endangered languages.

In February 2006 the Australian Government unexpectedly announced that it was to resume responsibility for matters such as immigration, customs and quarantine, claiming that the existing arrangements under the Norfolk Island Act of 1979 had become too complex and costly for a community of the island's size to sustain. Two main alternative options were to be considered: a form of modified self-government that would allow greater powers for involvement by the Australian Government; and a model of local government whereby Australia might assume responsibility for state-type functions. Other options under consideration included the possibility of an island territory government with the power to legislate on local responsibilities. The island's revenue-raising capacities were also to be reviewed, along with the provision of basic services such as health and education. In December 2006, however, following the conclusion of this comprehensive review, it was declared that no restructuring of the system of governance was necessary, an announcement that brought mixed reactions from the people of Norfolk Island. While many in the Territory wished to retain a degree of autonomy, concerns remained over the future sustainability of the island's economy.

In November 2006 a group of Norfolk Islanders challenged the introduction of new electoral laws requiring voters to be citizens of Australia. The group claimed that this did not take into consideration the fact that a proportion of Norfolk Island's adult population did not have Australian citizenship. However, lawyers for the Australian Government dismissed the argument. The group's claim that Norfolk Islanders represented a distinct community, and thus should be considered separately from Australia, was also dismissed as unfounded.

Following the legislative election of 21 March 2007, Andre Nobbs replaced David Buffett as the island's Chief Minister. Neville Christian was replaced as Speaker of the Legislative Assembly by Lisle Snell, but remained as Minister for Finance. Christopher Magri was appointed to the new post of Minister for Commerce and Industry. In October 2007, following Grant Tambling's departure from the post, Owen Walsh was appointed Administrator.

In August 2008 the Government of Norfolk Island issued its response to an Australian Senate Committee inquiry into the financial management of the island. The local Government claimed that the existing arrangements remained viable, reiterating its commitment to the continued improvement of the delivery of services on the island. The Government expressed particular concern in relation to its repeated obligation to divert the island's scarce human and financial resources to the task of responding to what was perceived to be constant scrutiny by external committees and consultants, often with regard to issues that it believed to have been adequately addressed on previous occasions. In October Bob Debus, the Australian Minister for Home Affairs (whose remit included responsibility for Australian territories) warned that Norfolk Island was in danger of becoming a 'failed state'. The Minister subsequently visited Norfolk Island, where he had discussions with Chief Minister Andre Nobbs. In December the island's Government submitted its formal response to the concerns raised by Debus, in which it disputed the Minister's claims that the current governance arrangements were operating 'to the disadvantage of many on Norfolk Island'. The local Government reiterated the view that, while the island might benefit from minor modifications to the legislation of 1979, the implementation of radical changes was unnecessary. Meanwhile, the Government had commissioned an independent review of the Norfolk Island Act of 1979, following which detailed proposals for the simplification and modernization of the prevailing legislation were presented to Debus. The retention of the role of Administrator was envisaged. Throughout 2009 Norfolk Island government officials had discussions about governance reforms with Debus and, following his retirement, the new Minister for Home Affairs, Brendan O'Connor. By the end of 2009 no substantive progress had been achieved, although it had been agreed that more regular meetings to discuss self-governing arrangements, particularly financial matters and accountability, would take place.

Elections to the Legislative Assembly were held on 17 March 2010 and were contested by a total of 28 candidates. David Buffett was appointed to the post of Chief Minister, replacing Andre Nobbs, who became Minister for Tourism, Industry and Development. The other portfolios were similarly rearranged: Craig Anderson was appointed as Attorney-General and Minister for Finance, and Timothy Sheridan was allocated the portfolio of community services. The incoming Legislative Assembly included several new members. Robin Adams replaced Lisle Snell as Speaker, the latter becoming Deputy Speaker.

On the same day as the island's legislative election the Territories Law Reform Bill 2010 was introduced into the House of Representatives in Canberra. While the Norfolk Island Government again acknowledged the need for reform, it regarded the draft legislation as inappropriate and raised numerous concerns, particularly in relation to the proposed reduction in local powers. The parliamentary debate was subsequently adjourned. The Australian Senate referred the draft law to the Joint Standing Committee on the National Capital and External Territories, which was required to conduct an inquiry and compile its report by May. In that month the Committee concluded that the proposed reforms would lead to improvements in the accountability and transparency of Norfolk Island's governance, recommending that the changes be adopted. It was envisaged that the Governor-General of Australia and the federal minister responsible for Norfolk Island would play a more active role in the drafting and enactment of legislation. The radical reforms were to include provision for the removal of the Chief Minister by the island's Administrator in 'exceptional circumstances'.

In October 2010 it was reported that, in collaboration with an Australian university, the world's first trial of a personal carbon trading programme was to commence on Norfolk Island in 2011. In addition to reducing greenhouse gas emissions, it was hoped that the three-year trial would reduce obesity and improve the health of islanders. Residents and visitors to the island were to be offered a carbon credit card, to be used initially when purchasing petrol or power. Frugal users would be able to exchange the remaining units of their annual quota for cash. Researchers hoped to add foodstuffs to the scheme in 2012, ranking products in terms of health as well as carbon costs.

In November 2010, as the island's financial situation continued to deteriorate, it was announced that, in exchange for federal funding and access to welfare facilities and other services, the local Government had agreed in principle to the implementation of the Territories Law Reform Bill. The Bill was duly enacted as the Territories Law Reform Act 2010 in December, following its approval by the Australian legislature. The stringent conditions attached to the Australian Government's provision of emergency funding included the introduction of federal law in areas such as privacy and freedom of information. Under an initial funding agreement concluded in December, the federal Government was to provide $A3.8m. in emergency financial support for Norfolk Island for the remainder of the 2010/11 financial year; the provision of a further $A1.8m. for that year was agreed in April 2011. Meanwhile, in March the federal and local Governments published a roadmap outlining a five-year plan for wide-ranging reforms in Norfolk Island aimed at strengthening governance, the economy, social cohesion, and heritage and environment. Also that month Craig Anderson resigned as Attorney-General and Minister for Finance, although he remained a member of the Legislative Assembly. His ministerial duties were redistributed between the remaining three members of the Executive Council, with Chief Minister David Buffett notably assuming responsibility for most financial matters and justice. In September a funding agreement for 2011/12 was signed: in return for federal funding of up to $A2.9m., the local Government was to implement further reforms, including the gradual removal of immigration restrictions on Australian citizens moving to Norfolk Island and the reduction of barriers to competition for businesses.

Neil Pope was sworn in as Administrator, replacing Owen Walsh, on 21 March 2012.

ECONOMIC AFFAIRS

Despite Norfolk Island's natural fertility, agriculture is no longer the principal economic activity. Agriculture and quarrying accounted for only 5.7% of all paid employment in 2006. About 400 ha of land are arable. The main crops are Kentia palm seed, cereals, vegetables and fruit. Cattle and pigs are farmed for domestic consumption. Development of a fisheries industry is restricted by the lack of a harbour. Some flowers and plants are grown commercially. The administration is increasing the area devoted to Norfolk Island pine and hardwoods. Seed and seedlings of the Norfolk Island pine are exported. Potential oil- and gas-bearing sites in the island's waters may provide a possible future source of revenue.

The Government is the most important employer, and there were 67 public sector workers in 2006. Tourism is the island's main industry. In the mid-1980s the Governments of Australia and Norfolk Island jointly established the 465-ha Norfolk Island National Park. In 2006 some 26.3% of the employed labour force were engaged in tourism and recreation. A re-export industry has been developed to serve the island's tourism industry. The resurfacing of the island's main runway in mid-2005 allowed the airport to accommodate larger aircraft and would, it was hoped, improve the potential for an increase in tourist arrivals. However, the cessation of operations by Norfolk Jet Express, the airline linking Norfolk Island with Australia, in June 2005 and the initial uncertainty surrounding the establishment of a replacement service illustrated the island's reliance on overseas airlines for the success of its tourist industry. Tourist arrivals declined by 16% in 2005/06, to 28,219, as a result of the failure of Norfolk Jet Express, but recovered to reach 34,318 in 2006/07, following the establishment of Norfolk Air by the Government. However, the global economic crisis depressed the tourism sector in 2008/09, causing a sharp decrease in arrivals, to 29,639, followed by further declines, to 26,339 in 2009/10 and to 24,268 in 2010/11. Reviving the tourism industry was a principal aim of the roadmap of reforms developed by the federal and local Governments in early 2011 (see Contemporary Political History); efforts to improve access to the island, to reduce the costs of travel and to facilitate visits by cruise ships were planned. The government-operated Norfolk Air was to cease operations in February 2012, with Air New Zealand to operate flights between Norfolk Island and the Australian mainland, in addition to its existing service to New Zealand.

In 2005/06 the cost of the island's imports, purchased mainly from Australia and New Zealand, reached almost $A32.1m., compared with $A41.3m. in 2000/01. Imports from New Zealand totalled $NZ7.8m. and exports to that country earned only $NZ25,000 in 2006/07. The authorities receive revenue from customs duties (projected at $A1.1m., equivalent to 11.5% of total revenue, in 2008/09), departure taxes (also projected at $A1.1m. in 2008/09), mail order services and the sale of postage stamps. In December 2005, in order to raise funds for road projects and health services, the Norfolk Sustainability Levy (NSL), a 1% tax on goods and services, was implemented for an initial six-month trial period, which was subsequently extended. In April 2007 it was announced that the NSL, along with various other taxes such as the accommodation levy, was to be replaced by a broader tax on goods and services, which was to be imposed at a rate of 9% with effect from January 2007. Following a major review (see Contemporary Political History), in December 2006 it was confirmed that Norfolk Island was to remain exempt from federal income taxes. Although the Territory would thus retain its attraction as a tax haven for wealthy individuals, many islanders expressed disappointment at the decision, as they had hoped that this potential source of government revenue might provide support in meeting the high costs of education and health care.

The 2009/10 budget envisaged revenue of almost $A11.4m., of which a projected $A7.5m. was to be derived from receipts from the goods-and-services tax, and expenditure of nearly $A13.8m., of which an estimated $A6.0m. was to be allocated to the payment of wages and salaries.

In 2006, as part of its contribution to the inquiry into the system of governance on Norfolk Island, the local Government commissioned its own report into the island's financial position. This independent report concluded that the Government's net operating cash flow over the next five years would be insufficient to meet the island's investment requirements. A revised report was released in February 2009. This took account of recent changes in taxation, notably the introduction of the goods-and-services tax, and of the projected growth in tourist arrivals. An average annual budget surplus of $A0.3m. was envisaged for the three years to 2011/12. In late 2008, in a report submitted in response to renewed concerns regarding the economic viability of the island (see Contemporary Political History), the Government declared that it would welcome assistance in the area of internal auditing.

The global economic downturn of 2008/09 had a significant impact on Norfolk Island, particularly in terms of tourism revenue. In November 2009 the Government reported a decrease in its revenue of $A3.9m. in 2008/09, in comparison with the previous financial year. This decline was attributed to a 15% reduction in tourist arrivals and to an increase in public expenditure of $A1.1m., which was due mainly to a general wage increase awarded by the Norfolk Island Public Sector Remuneration Tribunal. Government measures to alleviate the economic situation included, *inter alia*, the sale of surplus government assets and land, a freeze on discretionary spending and tax increases. The Australian Government deferred Norfolk Island's repayments on an interest-free loan of $A12m., used in 2005–06 for the purposes of upgrading the airport. Norfolk Air recorded a loss of more than $A1m. in the first three months of the 2009/10 financial year. An audit conducted at mid-2010 revealed that the island's reserves stood at only $A220,000. Bills were no longer being paid by the Government, and creditors were being deferred. Furthermore, 11 retail outlets were reported to have closed, with attendant job losses, while other businesses began to retrench. Although the goods-and-services tax was levied at 12%, islanders had remained exempt from income tax. However, following the approval of the Territories Law Reform Act in late 2010 (see Contemporary Political History), the integration of Norfolk Island into the federal taxation system from 2013/14 was envisaged, while federal health and social security benefits would be extended to residents of the island. Barriers to business investment were also to be removed. Meanwhile, the Australian Government agreed to provide financial support for the provision of essential services in 2010/11 and 2011/12, pending the negotiation of longer-term arrangements with Norfolk Island.

PUBLIC HOLIDAYS

2013: 1 January (New Year's Day), 28 January (for Australia Day), 6 March (Foundation Day), 29 March (Good Friday), 1 April (Easter Monday), 25 April (Anzac Day), 8 June (Bounty Day), 10 June (Queen's Official Birthday), 28 November (Thanksgiving), 25–26 December (Christmas).

Statistical Survey

Source: The Administration of Norfolk Island, Administration Offices, Kingston, Norfolk Island 2899; tel. 22001; fax 23177; internet www.norfolk.gov.nf.

AREA AND POPULATION

Area: 34.6 sq km (13.3 sq miles).

Population: 2,601 (males 1,257, females 1,344), including 564 visitors, at census of 7 August 2001; 2,523 (males 1,218, females 1,305), comprising 1,863 'ordinarily resident' and 660 visitors, at census of 8 August 2006.

Density (2006 census): 72.9 per sq km.

Population by Age and Sex (2006 census): *0–14:* 359 (males 185, females 174); *15–64:* 1,587 (males 763, females 824); *65 and over:* 561 (males 263, females 298); *Total* 2,523* (males 1,218, females 1,305).

* Including 16 persons (males 7, females 9) of unknown age.

Births, Marriages and Deaths (2005/06 unless otherwise indicated): Live births 22; Marriages 35 (2002/03); Deaths 13.

Employment (ordinarily resident population aged 15 years and over, 2006 census): Agriculture, forestry and fishing 53; Mining and quarrying 13; Manufacturing 30; Electricity, gas and water 37; Construction 104; Wholesale and retail trade 280; Transport and storage 41; Communication 40; Finance, property and business services 49; Public administration and defence 67; Health 59; Education, museum and library services 48; Other community services 28; Restaurants, hotels, accommodation and clubs 206; Other recreational and personal services 97; *Sub-total* 1,152; Activities not stated or not adequately described 31; *Total* 1,183 (males 604, females 579).

FINANCE

Currency and Exchange Rates: Australian currency is used.

Budget (year ending 30 June 2009): Revenue $A26,167,730; Expenditure $A28,039,551.

Cost of Living (Retail Price Index, average of quarterly figures; base: October–December 1990 = 100): All items 159.7 in 2004; 168.6 in 2005; 181.1 in 2006.

EXTERNAL TRADE

2005/06 (year ending 30 June): *Imports:* $A32,065,392, mainly from Australia and New Zealand.

Trade with Australia ($A million, 2006/07): *Imports* 10.

Trade with New Zealand ($NZ '000, 2006/07): *Imports* 7,801. *Exports* 25.

TOURISM

Visitors (year ending 30 June): 29,639 in 2008/09; 26,339 in 2009/10; 24,268 in 2010/11.

COMMUNICATIONS MEDIA

Radio Receivers (1996): 2,500 in use.

Television Receivers (1996): 1,200 in use.

Telephones (2002/03): 2,374 main lines in use.

Internet Users (2002/03): 494.

Non-daily Newspaper (2002): 1 (estimated circulation 1,400).

EDUCATION

Institution (2003): 1 state school incorporating infant, primary and secondary levels.

Teachers (2004/05): Primary 8; Secondary 12.

Students (1999/2000): Infants 79; Primary 116; Secondary 119.

Directory

The Government

The Administrator, who is the senior representative of the Commonwealth Government, is appointed by the Governor-General of Australia and is accountable to a minister of the federal Cabinet. A form of responsible legislative and executive government was extended to the island in 1979.

Administrator: NEIL POPE.

EXECUTIVE COUNCIL

(May 2012)

Chief Minister: DAVID E. BUFFETT.

Minister for Tourism, Industry and Development: ANDRE N. NOBBS.

Minister for Community Services: TIMOTHY J. SHERIDAN.

MINISTRIES

All Ministries are located at:

Old Military Barracks, Quality Row, Kingston, Norfolk Island 2899; tel. 22003; fax 22624; e-mail executives@assembly.gov.nf; internet www.norfolk.gov.nf.

GOVERNMENT OFFICES

Office of the Administrator: POB 201, New Military Barracks, Norfolk Island 2899; tel. 22152; fax 22681.

Administration of Norfolk Island: Administration Offices, Kingston, Norfolk Island 2899; tel. 22001; fax 23177; e-mail records@admin.gov.nf; internet www.norfolkislandgovernment.com; all govt depts; CEO BRUCE TAYLOR (acting).

Legislature

LEGISLATIVE ASSEMBLY

Nine candidates are elected for not more than three years. The most recent general election was held on 17 March 2010.

Speaker: ROBIN E. ADAMS.

Deputy Speaker: LISLE D. SNELL.

Other Members: TIMOTHY J. SHERIDAN, CRAIG M. ANDERSON, ANDRE N. NOBBS, DAVID E. BUFFETT, MELISSA WARD, MICHAEL W. KING, RHONDA E. GRIFFITHS.

Judicial System

Supreme Court of Norfolk Island: Kingston; appeals lie to the Federal Court of Australia.

Chief Magistrate: WARREN DONALD.

Judges: PETER JACOBSEN (Chief Justice), GARY KEITH DOWNES, BRUCE THOMAS LANDER.

Religion

The majority of the population professes Christianity (66.6%, according to the census of 2001), with the principal denominations being the Church of England (34.9%), the Roman Catholic Church (11.7%) and the Uniting Church (11.2%).

The Press

Norfolk Island Government Gazette: Kingston, Norfolk Island 2899; tel. 22001; fax 23177; internet www.info.gov.nf; weekly.

Norfolk Islander: Greenways Press, POB 248, Norfolk Island 2899; tel. 22159; fax 22948; e-mail news@islander.nf; internet www.norfolkislander.com; f. 1965; weekly; Co-Editors TOM LLOYD, JONATHAN SNELL; circ. 1,350.

Broadcasting and Communications

TELECOMMUNICATIONS

Norfolk Telecom: New Cascade Rd, POB 469, Kingston; tel. 322244; fax 322499; e-mail webmaster@ni.net.nf; internet www.ni.net.nf; mobile services introduced in 2007; Man. KIM DAVIES.

BROADCASTING

Radio

Norfolk Island Broadcasting Service: New Cascade Rd, POB 456, Norfolk Island 2899; tel. 22137; fax 23298; e-mail manager@radio.gov.nf; internet www.radio.gov.nf; govt-owned; non-commercial; broadcasts seven days per week; relays television and radio programmes from Australia and New Zealand; Broadcast Man. GEORGE SMITH.

Radio Norfolk: New Cascade Rd, POB 456, Norfolk Island 2899; tel. 22137; fax 23298; e-mail manager@radio.gov.nf; internet www.radio.gov.nf; f. 1950s; govt-owned; Man. GEORGE SMITH.

Television

Norfolk Island Broadcasting Service: see Radio.

Norfolk Island Television Service: f. 1987; govt-owned; relays programmes of Australian Broadcasting Corpn, Special Broadcasting Service Corpn and Central Seven TV by satellite.

TV Norfolk (TVN): locally operated service featuring programmes of local events and information for tourists.

Finance

BANKING

Commonwealth Bank of Australia (Australia): Taylors Rd, Norfolk Island 2899; tel. 22144; fax 22805.

Westpac Banking Corpn Savings Bank Ltd (Australia): Burnt Pine, Norfolk Island 2899; tel. 22120; fax 22808.

Trade

Norfolk Island Chamber of Commerce Inc: POB 370, Norfolk Island 2899; tel. 22317; fax 23221; e-mail photopress@ni.net.nf; f. 1966; affiliated to the Australian Chamber of Commerce and Industry; 60 mems; Pres. GARY ROBERTSON; Sec. MARK MCGUIRE.

Norfolk Island Gaming Authority: POB 882, Norfolk Island 2899; tel. 22002; fax 22499; e-mail secgameauth@norfolk.net.nf; internet www.gamingauthority.nlk.nf; Dir RODERICK MCALPINE.

Transport

ROADS

There are some 53 km of paved roads and 27 km of unpaved roads.

SHIPPING

Norfolk Island is served by three shipping lines, Neptune Shipping, Pacific Direct Line and Roslyndale Shipping Company Pty Ltd. A small tanker from Nouméa (New Caledonia) delivers petroleum products to the island and another from Australia delivers liquid propane gas.

CIVIL AVIATION

Norfolk Island's airport has two runways and is capable of taking jet-engined aircraft. Work to resurface the main runway, in order to accommodate larger aircraft, was completed in 2006. Norfolk Air, which was operated by the Norfolk Island Government and provided services to the Australian cities of Brisbane, Sydney, Melbourne and Newcastle, ceased operations in February 2012. Air New Zealand, which already provided a service from Auckland, began to operate flights between Norfolk Island and the Australian mainland from March, with twice-weekly services to Brisbane and Sydney.

Tourism

Visitor arrivals totalled 24,268 in 2010/11, the majority of whom came from Australia. In 2002/03 tourist accommodation totalled 1,551 beds.

Norfolk Island Tourism: Taylors Rd, Burnt Pine, POB 211, Norfolk Island 2899; tel. 22147; fax 23109; e-mail info@nigtb.gov.nf; internet www.norfolkisland.com.au; Chair. WALLY BEADMAN; Gen. Man. NICOLE MOORE.

Education

Education is free and compulsory for all children between the ages of six and at least 15. Pupils attend the one government school from infant to secondary level. In 2002/03 a total of 187 pupils were enrolled at infant and primary levels and 118 at secondary levels. Students wishing to follow higher education in Australia are eligible for bursaries and scholarships. The budgetary allocation for education was more than $A2.4m. in 2006/07.

Other Australian Territories

Ashmore and Cartier Islands

The Ashmore Islands (known as West, Middle and East Islands) and Cartier Island are situated in the Timor Sea, about 850 km and 790 km west of Darwin respectively. The Ashmore Islands cover some 93 ha of land and Cartier Island covers 0.4 ha. The islands are small and uninhabited, consisting of sand and coral, surrounded by shoals and reefs. Grass is the main vegetation. Maximum elevation is about 2.5 m above sea-level. The islands abound in birdlife, sea-cucumbers (*bêches-de-mer*) and, seasonally, turtles.

The United Kingdom took formal possession of the Ashmore Islands in 1878, and Cartier Island was annexed in 1909. The islands were placed under the authority of the Commonwealth of Australia in 1931. They were annexed to, and deemed to form part of, the Northern Territory of Australia in 1938. On 1 July 1978 the Australian Government assumed direct responsibility for the administration of the islands; this rests with a parliamentary secretary appointed by the Minister for Regional Australia, Regional Development and Local Government. Periodic visits are made to the islands by the Royal Australian Navy and aircraft of the Royal Australian Air Force, and the Civil Coastal Surveillance Service makes aerial surveys of the islands and neighbouring waters. The oilfields of Jabiru and Challis are located in waters adjacent to the Territory.

In August 1983 Ashmore Reef was declared a national nature reserve. An agreement between Australia and Indonesia permits Indonesian traditional fishermen to continue fishing in the territorial waters and to land on West Island to obtain supplies of fresh water. In 1985 the Australian Government extended the laws of the Northern Territory to apply in Ashmore and Cartier, and decided to contract a vessel to be stationed at Ashmore Reef during the Indonesian fishing season (March–November) to monitor the fishermen.

From 2000 increasing numbers of refugees and asylum-seekers attempted to land at Ashmore Reef, hoping to gain residency in Australia. The majority had travelled from the Middle East via Indonesia, where the illegal transport of people was widespread. Consequently, in late 2000 a vessel with the capacity to transport up to 150 people was chartered to ferry unauthorized arrivals to the Australian mainland. In September 2001 the Australian Government introduced legislation to Parliament excising Ashmore Reef and other outlying territories from Australia's migration zone. However, in March 2004 a group of nine women and six men, believed to be seeking asylum in Australia, was discovered on Ashmore Reef. A government spokesperson reiterated the Territory's exclusion from Australia's migration zone, stating that this would preclude the group from seeking any form of residency in the country. In December 2008 it was reported that a vessel carrying suspected asylum-seekers had been apprehended by the Australian authorities in the vicinity of the Ashmore Islands. A total of 35 passengers and five crew members were taken into custody, pending the processing of their claims. Such interceptions by the authorities continued in 2009. Suspected asylum-seekers continued to be transferred to Christmas Island for processing. In a major incident off Ashmore Reef in April 2009, a boat carrying 47 asylum-seekers, which had been intercepted by the Australian Navy, caught fire and sank following an explosion. Five of the asylum-seekers were killed in the incident, and the survivors were taken to Darwin for medical treatment.

In April 2005 the Australian Government invited petroleum exploration companies to bid for a number of leases which it had made available in an area covering some 920 sq km near the islands. In mid-2006 two permits were granted for exploration to take place in the territory's Bonaparte Basin. Two more offshore petroleum exploration permits were issued in April 2007, with further permits being granted subsequently.

Australian Antarctic Territory

The Australian Antarctic Territory was established by Order in Council in February 1933 and proclaimed in August 1936, subsequent to the Australian Antarctic Territory Acceptance Act (1933). It consists of the portion of Antarctica (divided by the French territory of Terre Adélie) lying between 45°E and 136°E, and between 142°E and 160°E. The Australian Antarctic Division (AAD) of the Department of the Environment, Sport and Territories (subsequently renamed the Department of the Environment and Water Resources and currently the Department of Sustainability, Environment, Water, Population and Communities) was established in 1948 as a permanent agency, and to administer and provide support for the Australian National Antarctic Research Expeditions (ANARE), which maintains three permanent scientific stations (Mawson, Davis and Casey) in the Territory. The area of the Territory is estimated to be 5,896,500 sq km (2,276,650 sq miles), and there are no permanent inhabitants, although there is a permanent presence of scientific personnel, which increases from around 70 in winter to some 200 in summer. Environmentalists expressed alarm at proposals in the late 1990s to encourage tourism in the Territory, which, they claimed, could damage the area's sensitive ecology. In November 2001 an international team of scientists commenced Australia's largest ever scientific expedition, to gather data on the influence of the Southern Ocean on the world's climate and the global carbon cycle. In January 2002 Australia attempted to expel Japanese whaling ships from the 200-nautical-mile exclusive economic zone it claimed to be under the jurisdiction of the Australian Antarctic Territory. However, the Government was severely criticized in mid-2005 for its failure to protect whales in its Antarctic territorial waters. Its reluctance to intercept Japanese whaling vessels in its territorial waters for 'diplomatic reasons' was blamed for the slaughter of more than 400 whales since 2000, when a whale sanctuary had been established in these waters. Australia is a signatory to the Antarctic Treaty (see p. 615). As part of the Australian Government's commitment to the establishment of regular flights to the Territory, a trial runway was constructed in the 2005/06 Antarctic summer season at the Wilkins Aerodrome, located 75 km from Casey. A full runway was opened in December 2007, with regular flights between the Tasmanian capital of Hobart and Antarctica becoming operational during the 2007/08 Antarctic summer season. In the 2009/10 financial year the Government allocated $A36.9m. to the Antarctic Division over a two-year period, with an additional $A25.2m. to be invested in Antarctic activities over the same period. The 2011/12 budget allocated $A28.3m. to Antarctic research.

Coral Sea Islands Territory

The Coral Sea Islands became a Territory of the Commonwealth of Australia under the Coral Sea Islands Act of 1969. The Territory lies east of Queensland, between the Great Barrier Reef and longitude 156° 06'E, and between latitude 12°S and 24°S, and comprises several islands and reefs. The islands are composed largely of sand and coral, and have no permanent fresh water supply, but some have a cover of grass and scrub. The area has been a notorious hazard to shipping since the 19th century, the danger of the reefs being compounded by shifting sand cays and occasional tropical cyclones. The Coral Sea Islands have been acquired by Australia by numerous acts of sovereignty since the early years of the 20th century.

Extending over a sea area of approximately 780,000 sq km (300,000 sq miles), all the islands and reefs in the Territory are very small, totalling only a few sq km of land area. They include Cato Island, Chilcott Islet in the Coringa Group, and the Willis Group. In 1997 the Coral Sea Islands Act was amended to include Elizabeth and Middleton Reefs. A meteorological station, operated by the Commonwealth Bureau of Meteorology and with a staff of four, has provided a service on one of the Willis Group since 1921. The other islands are uninhabited. There are eight automatic weather stations (on Cato Island, Flinders Reef, Frederick Reef, Holmes Reef, Lihou Reef, Creal Reef, Marion Reef and Gannet Cay) and several navigation aids distributed throughout the Territory.

The Act constituting the Territory did not establish an administration on the islands, but provides means of controlling the activities of those who visit them. The Lihou Reef and Coringa-Herald National Nature Reserves were established in 1982 to provide protection for the wide variety of terrestrial and marine wildlife, which include rare species of birds and sea turtles (one of which is the largest, and among the most endangered, of the world's species of sea turtle). The Australian Government has concluded agreements for the protection of endangered and migratory birds with Japan and the People's Republic of China. The Governor-General of Australia is empowered to make ordinances for the peace, order and good government of the Territory and, by ordinance, the laws of the Australian Capital Territory apply. The Supreme Court and Court of Petty Sessions of Norfolk Island have jurisdiction in the Territory. The Territory is administered by a parliamentary secretary, who is appointed by the Minister for Regional Australia, Regional Development and Local Government. The area is visited regularly by the Royal Australian Navy. In late November 2011 the Government announced plans for the creation of a marine reserve over a large area of the Coral Sea, initiating a three-month public consultation on the proposals, which would restrict fishing in the area and outlaw exploration for petroleum and gas.

Heard Island and the McDonald Islands

These islands are situated about 4,000 km (2,500 miles) south-west of Perth, Western Australia. The Territory, consisting of Heard Island, Shag Island (8 km north of Heard) and the McDonald Islands, is almost entirely covered in ice and has a total area of 369 sq km (142 sq miles). Sovereignty was transferred from the United Kingdom to the Commonwealth of Australia on 26 December 1947, following the establishment of a scientific research station on Heard Island (which functioned until March 1955). The islands are administered by the Antarctic Division of the Australian Department of Sustainability, Environment, Water, Population and Communities. There are no permanent inhabitants. However, in 1991 evidence emerged of a Polynesian community on Heard Island some 700 years before the territory's discovery by European explorers. The island is of considerable scientific interest, as it is believed to be one of the few Antarctic habitats uncontaminated by introduced organisms. Heard Island is about 44 km long and 20 km wide and possesses an active volcano, named Big Ben. In January 1991 an international team of scientists travelled to Heard Island to conduct research involving the transmission of sound waves, beneath the surface of the ocean, in order to monitor any evidence of the greenhouse effect (melting of polar ice and the rise in sea-level as a consequence of pollution). The pulses of sound, which travel at a speed largely influenced by temperature, were to be received at various places around the world, with international co-operation. Heard Island was chosen for the experiment because of its unique location, from which direct paths to the five principal oceans extend. The McDonald Islands, with an area of about 1 sq km (0.4 sq miles), lie some 42 km west of Heard Island. Only two successful landings by boat have been recorded since the discovery of the McDonald Islands in the late 19th century. In late 1997 Heard Island and the McDonald Islands were accorded World Heritage status by UNESCO in recognition of their outstanding universal significance as a natural landmark.

In 1999 concern was expressed that stocks of the Patagonian toothfish in the waters around the islands were becoming depleted as a result of over-exploitation, mainly by illegal operators. (The popularity of the fish in Japan and the USA, where it is known as Chilean sea bass, increased significantly during the early 21st century.) This problem was highlighted in August 2003 when a Uruguayan fishing vessel was seized, following a 20-day pursuit over 7,400 km by Australian, South African and British patrol boats. The trawler had been fishing illegally in waters near Heard and McDonald and had a full cargo of Patagonian toothfish worth some US $1.5m. Experts feared that, if poaching continued at current rates, the species would become extinct by 2007. In response to this situation, the Australian Government announced in December 2003 that it was to send an ice-breaking patrol vessel with deck-mounted machine guns to police the waters around Heard and McDonald Islands. It was hoped that this action might serve to deter illegal fishing activity in the area, much of which was believed to involve international criminal organizations. However, it was reported that many vessels continued fishing in protected waters, including operations on the Banzare Bank, a plateau in the Southern Ocean, which in February 2005 was closed to fishing by the Convention for the Conservation of Arctic Marine Living Resources Commission. (An anomaly of international law meant that vessels flying flags of non-member countries of the Commission could not be evicted by Australian forces.) In August the Australian customs department announced that it was to train commandos to patrol the protected waters around Heard and McDonald for vessels fishing illegally. In September 2006 conservation groups petitioned the USA, a major importer of Patagonian toothfish, urging the Government to impose sanctions on Spain for failing to comply with laws governing fishing activities in the region.

In 2001 the Australian Government's Antarctic Division conducted a five-month scientific expedition to Heard Island. It claimed that glacial cover had retreated by 12% since 1947 as a result of global warming. In October 2002 the Australian Government declared the establishment of the Heard Island and McDonald Islands Marine Reserve. Covering 6.5m. ha, the marine reserve was to be one of the largest in the world, strengthening existing conservation measures and imposing an official ban on all fishing and petroleum and mineral exploitation. Among the many species of plant, bird and mammal to be protected by the reserve were the southern elephant seal, the sub-Antarctic fur seal and two species of albatross. Limited scientific research and environmental monitoring were to be allowed in the Marine Reserve. The Marine Reserve draft management plan, announced in 2005, proposed measures further to restrict human activity on the islands, in an attempt to protect their unique flora and fauna from damage and from introduced organisms. The islands remained the only unmodified example of a sub-Antarctic island ecosystem in the world.

AUSTRIA

Introductory Survey

LOCATION, CLIMATE, LANGUAGE, RELIGION, FLAG, CAPITAL

The Republic of Austria lies in central Europe, bordered by Germany and the Czech Republic to the north, by Slovakia and Hungary to the east, by Italy and Slovenia to the south and by Switzerland and Liechtenstein to the west. The mean annual temperature lies between 7°C and 9°C (45°F and 48°F). The population is 99% German-speaking, with small Croat- and Slovene-speaking minorities. The majority of the inhabitants profess Christianity: more than two-thirds are Roman Catholics and about 5% are Protestants. The national flag (proportions 2 by 3) consists of three equal horizontal stripes, of red, white and red. The state flag has, in addition, the coat of arms (a small shield, with horizontal stripes of red separated by a white stripe, superimposed on a black eagle, wearing a golden crown and holding a sickle and a hammer in its feet, with a broken chain between its legs) in the centre. The capital is Vienna (Wien).

CONTEMPORARY POLITICAL HISTORY

Historical Context

Austria was formerly the centre of the Austrian (later Austro-Hungarian) Empire, which comprised a large part of central Europe. The Empire, under the Habsburg dynasty, was dissolved in 1918, at the end of the First World War, and Austria proper became a republic. The first post-war Council of Ministers was a coalition led by Dr Karl Renner, who remained Chancellor until 1920, when a new Constitution introduced a federal form of government. Many of Austria's inhabitants favoured union with Germany, but this was forbidden by the post-war peace treaties. In March 1938, however, Austria was occupied by Nazi Germany's armed forces and incorporated into the German Reich, led by the Austrian-born Adolf Hitler.

After Hitler's defeat in Austria, a provisional Government, under Renner, was established in April 1945. In July, following Germany's surrender to the Allied forces, Austria was divided into four zones, occupied respectively by forces of the USA, the USSR, the United Kingdom and France. At the first post-war elections to the 165-seat National Council (Nationalrat), held in November 1945, the conservative Österreichische Volkspartei (ÖVP—Austrian People's Party) won 85 seats and the Sozialistische Partei Österreichs (SPÖ—Socialist Party of Austria) secured 76. The two parties formed a coalition Government. In December Renner became the first Federal President of the second Austrian Republic, holding office until his death in December 1950. However, it was not until May 1955 that the four powers signed a State Treaty with Austria, recognizing Austrian independence, effective from 27 July; occupation forces left in October.

Domestic Political Affairs

More than 20 years of coalition government came to an end in April 1966 with the formation of a Council of Ministers by the ÖVP alone, under Dr Josef Klaus, the Federal Chancellor since April 1964. The SPÖ won a plurality of seats in the March 1970 general election and formed a minority Government, with Dr Bruno Kreisky as Chancellor. In April 1971 the incumbent President, Franz Jonas of the SPÖ, was re-elected, defeating the ÖVP candidate, Dr Kurt Waldheim (who subsequently served two five-year terms as UN Secretary-General, beginning in January 1972). The SPÖ won an absolute majority of seats in the National Council at a general election in October 1971 (when the number of seats was increased to 183) and October 1975. President Jonas died in April 1974, and the subsequent presidential election, held in June, was won by Dr Rudolf Kirchschläger, who had been the Minister of Foreign Affairs since 1970. He was re-elected for a second six-year term in 1980.

At the general election in May 1979 the SPÖ increased its majority in the National Council. The general election of April 1983, however, marked the end of the 13-year era of one-party government: the SPÖ lost its absolute majority in the National Council and Kreisky, unwilling to participate in a coalition, resigned as Chancellor. Kreisky's successor, Dr Fred Sinowatz (the former Vice-Chancellor and Federal Minister of Education), took office in May, leading a coalition of the SPÖ and the right-of-centre Freiheitliche Partei Österreichs (FPÖ—Freedom Party of Austria).

The presidential election held in May 1986 was won by Waldheim, who stood independently, although with the support of the ÖVP. The campaign was dominated by allegations that Waldheim, a former officer in the army of Nazi Germany, had been implicated in atrocities committed by the Nazis in the Balkans during 1942–45. The defeat of the SPÖ presidential candidate, Dr Kurt Steyrer (the Federal Minister of Health and Environment), led Chancellor Sinowatz and four of his ministers to resign. Dr Franz Vranitzky, hitherto Federal Minister of Finance, became the new Chancellor.

Waldheim's election to the presidency was controversial both domestically and internationally, and Austria's relations with Israel and the USA, in particular, were severely strained. In February 1988 a specially appointed international commission of historians concluded that Waldheim must have been aware of the atrocities that had been committed. Waldheim refused to resign, but in June 1991 he announced that he would not seek a second presidential term.

In September 1986 the FPÖ elected a controversial new leader, Dr Jörg Haider, who represented the far-right wing of his party. This precipitated the end of the governing coalition, and the general election for the National Council was brought forward to November 1986. No party won an absolute majority: the SPÖ won 80 seats, the ÖVP 77, the FPÖ 18 and an alliance of three environmentalist parties eight.

SPÖ-ÖVP 'grand coalitions': 1987–2000

Following several weeks of negotiations, a 'grand coalition' of the SPÖ and the ÖVP, with Vranitzky as Chancellor, was formed in January 1987. The coalition presided over a period of economic expansion from 1988. However, it was beset by numerous political scandals, including large-scale tax evasion by senior SPÖ officials and revelations from a parliamentary inquiry established to investigate sinking in 1977 of a freighter, the *Lucona*, in which six crew members died. Two SPÖ ministers who were implicated by the inquiry in hindering investigations into the incident, which had formed part of a fraudulent insurance claim, were forced to resign in January 1989.

At the general election held in October 1990 the SPÖ increased its number of seats to 81, while the ÖVP obtained only 60; the FPÖ's representation rose to 33 seats. The FPÖ's success was attributed, in large part, to its support for restrictions on immigration, especially from Eastern Europe. The Grüne Alternative Liste (GAL, Green Alternative List), an informal electoral alliance comprising Die Grüne Alternative (The Green Alternative) and the Vereinte Grüne Österreichs (United Green Party of Austria), increased the representation of environmentalist parties to nine. In December the SPÖ and the ÖVP again formed a coalition government under Vranitzky.

A congress of the SPÖ held in June 1991 voted to revert to the party's original name, the Sozialdemokratische Partei Österreichs (SPÖ—Social Democratic Party of Austria). In the same month Haider was dismissed as Governor of Carinthia (Kärnten) after publicly praising Hitler's employment policies. In December the National Council approved government legislation whereby Austria became the only country in Europe able to reject asylum requests from individuals without identity papers. Following the imprisonment in January 1992 of a prominent right-wing activist for demanding the restoration of the Nazi party, and the subsequent fire-bombing of a refugee hostel by neo-Nazis in northern Austria, the National Council voted unanimously in February to amend anti-Nazi legislation. The minimum prison sentence for Nazi agitation was reduced from five years to one year (in order to increase the number of successful prosecutions) and denial of the Nazi Holocaust was made a criminal offence.

At the presidential election held in April 1992 the two main candidates were Dr Rudolf Streicher for the SPÖ (hitherto the Federal Minister of Public Economy and Transport) and Dr

Thomas Klestil (a former ambassador to the USA), representing the ÖVP. In a run-off ballot, held in May, Klestil received almost 57% of the votes cast; he assumed the presidency in July.

In January 1993 the FPÖ organized a national petition seeking to require the National Council to debate the introduction of legislation that would halt immigration into Austria and impose stricter controls on foreign residents in the country. Some 417,000 people signed the petition (the constitutional requirement to force parliamentary debate was 100,000). The initiative was strongly opposed by a broad coalition of politicians, church leaders and intellectuals. In February five FPÖ deputies in the National Council (including the party's Vice-President) left the party and formed the Liberales Forum (LiF, Liberal Forum).

At the general election held in October 1994 the ruling coalition lost its two-thirds' majority in the National Council. The SPÖ won 66 seats, the ÖVP 52 and the FPÖ 42. Die Grünen (the Greens) and the LiF also made gains, winning 13 and 10 seats, respectively. The success of the FPÖ's populist campaign, which had concentrated on countering corruption and immigration and had advocated referendum-based rather than parliamentary-based governance, unsettled the Austrian political establishment after years of relative consensus. At the end of November the SPÖ and ÖVP finally agreed to form a new coalition Government, with Vranitzky remaining as Chancellor.

The new SPÖ-ÖVP coalition was beleaguered by disagreements, mainly concerning differences in approach to the urgent need to reduce the budget deficit, in compliance with Austria's commitment, following its accession to the European Union (EU) in January 1995, to future Economic and Monetary Union (EMU, see p. 312). In early 1995 five ministers, including the Vice-Chancellor, Dr Erhard Busek, resigned. Busek was replaced as Chairman of the ÖVP by Dr Wolfgang Schüssel. In October a rift between the SPÖ and ÖVP regarding the means of curtailing the budget deficit precipitated the collapse of the coalition. At a general election held in December the SPÖ won 71 seats, the ÖVP 53, the FPÖ 40, the LiF 10 and the Greens nine. In March 1996, following lengthy negotiations, the SPÖ and ÖVP agreed an economic programme and formed a new coalition Government, again under Vranitzky. However, in January 1997 Vranitzky unexpectedly resigned from the chancellorship. Viktor Klima, hitherto the Federal Minister of Finance, replaced Vranitzky as Chancellor and as Chairman of the SPÖ.

At the presidential election held in April 1998 Klestil was re-elected, winning 63.5% of the votes cast. The FPÖ made significant gains at regional elections in March 1999, becoming the dominant party in Carinthia; Haider was subsequently elected Governor of Carinthia (having been dismissed from that post in 1991—see above). The general election held in October 1999 resulted in unprecedented success for the FPÖ, which narrowly took second place ahead of the ÖVP. The SPÖ won 65 seats, while the FPÖ and ÖVP both secured 52 and the Greens 14. The FPÖ had campaigned on a programme that included a halt to immigration, the obstruction of EU expansion, the radical deregulation of the business sector and the introduction of a uniform low rate of income tax and of hugely increased child allowances for Austrian citizens. During the election campaign Haider allegedly revived nationalist terminology previously employed by the Nazi regime; nevertheless, he consistently denied embracing neo-Nazi ideology. The election result was widely regarded as a protest against the 'grand coalition', which had acquired a reputation for unwieldy bureaucracy and for sanctioning politically motivated appointments to public companies.

During the late 1990s a number of lawsuits were filed by US interests against several Austrian banks, which were accused of having profited during the Second World War from handling stolen Jewish assets. In November 1999 Bank Austria AG agreed to pay US $33m. as compensation to Holocaust survivors and to establish a humanitarian fund to assist survivors resident in Austria. Similar lawsuits were also filed against the Government. In July 2000 the legislature approved the establishment of a €438m. fund, which was to be financed by unspecified contributions from the Government and from Austrian businesses that had profited from slave labour, to compensate an estimated 150,000 concentration camp inmates, who had been forced into slave labour by the Nazis. In January 2001 Austria signed an agreement with the USA to pay $500m. to compensate Jews for property lost when the Nazis took power.

ÖVP-FPÖ coalition Government: 2000–02

Following the failure of negotiations aimed at renewing the outgoing coalition, in February 2000 President Klestil reluctantly presided over the inauguration of an ÖVP-FPÖ coalition Government, with Schüssel as Chancellor. Haider elected not to participate directly in the new administration, which included an FPÖ Vice-Chancellor, Dr Susanne Riess-Passer, and five FPÖ ministers. Although the new coalition had adopted a relatively moderate political programme, the FPÖ's participation in government provoked strong opposition both within Austria and abroad. Israel and the USA immediately recalled their ambassadors from Vienna, while Austria's fellow EU member states each suspended bilateral political co-operation, maintaining diplomatic relations at a 'technical' level, pending the removal of the FPÖ from the coalition. In late February Haider announced that he was to resign as FPÖ leader, while remaining Governor of Carinthia; few people, however, doubted that he would retain significant influence within the party.

In February 2000 Klima was succeeded as Chairman of the SPÖ by Dr Alfred Gusenbauer. In April Gusenbauer apologized on behalf of his party for decades of political opportunism and for its recruitment of former Nazis after the Second World War. He later established a commission of independent historians to investigate the matter. The commission reported in January 2005 that the SPÖ had actively recruited former Nazis in order to help them reintegrate into society, as had the ÖVP. Meanwhile, an EU delegation that visited Austria in July 2000 recommended in its subsequent report that the diplomatic sanctions be lifted. While criticizing the FPÖ, the report confirmed that Austria's treatment of minorities was superior to that of some other EU member states. The EU lifted its sanctions in September, but warned that it would continue to monitor closely the influence of the FPÖ, and Haider, upon government policies.

By the end of 2000 the FPÖ's influence and popularity was in decline. The party fared badly in two provincial elections and, in November, the Federal Minister for Science and Transport, Michael Schmid, became the third FPÖ minister to resign since the formation of the Government, citing the FPÖ's poor electoral performance. Schmid subsequently resigned from the FPÖ. Poor electoral results, instability and repeated indiscretions linking the party with Nazism were, however, overshadowed by the emergence of a major political scandal. In October a number of senior members of the FPÖ (including the Federal Minister for Justice, Dr Dieter Böhmdorfer) were accused of using illicitly obtained police files to discredit opponents. Böhmdorfer survived a third vote of no confidence against him in October. By November the number of FPÖ members under investigation had risen to 67.

In September 2001, purportedly as part of a plan to combat international terrorism following the devastating suicide attacks in the USA, Haider asserted that refugees from continents other than Europe seeking asylum within the EU should no longer be granted residence in Europe while their requests were being processed. The FPÖ also suggested the introduction of 'biometric' identification methods, a fortnightly 'control' of all asylum seekers and the immediate expulsion of any foreigners suspected of being involved in criminal activities. Furthermore, the FPÖ proposed the introduction of a so-called *Integrationsvertrag* (integration contract) for immigrant workers and their families, including those who were already living in the country. Under this contract, immigrants would be obliged to attend courses and pass tests on both the German language and citizenship; those who did not comply within four years would have their social security benefits gradually reduced, and, in extreme cases, would face expulsion from the country. The proposals provoked fierce criticism both within Austria and throughout the EU. Despite initial reservations, in October the ÖVP endorsed the FPÖ's recommendations regarding asylum seekers and immigrants (with the exception of the proposal to deny those seeking asylum the right of temporary residence). The proposed measures were approved by the legislature and came into force on 1 January 2003.

An internal power struggle within the FPÖ led to the resignation in September 2002 of a number of moderate FPÖ ministers, including Vice-Chancellor Riess-Passer. Hitherto, Schüssel's strategy of persuading these ministers to eschew the more extremist elements of their party's credo, while himself adopting some of the FPÖ's more reasonable policies, had contributed to a loss of support for the FPÖ. In late September the instability within the junior coalition partner led Schlüssel to dissolve the legislature. At an early general election held on 24 November the ÖVP received 42.3% of the votes cast (the party's largest single share of the votes in more than 30 years), securing 79 seats, mainly at the expense of the FPÖ, which obtained only 10.0% of the votes cast (18 seats), compared with 26.9% in 1999.

Second ÖVP-FPÖ coalition Government: 2003–06

In February 2003, following the reluctance of the SPÖ and the Greens to enter into coalition talks, Schüssel invited the FPÖ, now led by Herbert Haupt, to form another coalition administration with the ÖVP. The new Government included only three ministers from the FPÖ.

The FPÖ suffered heavy losses in regional elections held in September 2003. The following month Haupt resigned as Vice-Chancellor, but retained his ministerial position. He remained as the nominal leader of the FPÖ pending party elections in 2004, but under the supervision of the party's new Managing Chairwoman, Haider's sister, Ursula Haubner. Many observers viewed the latter's appointment as evidence that Haider had again assumed control of the FPÖ. In March 2004 local elections were held in Carinthia; forecasts of an SPÖ victory were confounded when the FPÖ won 42.4% of the votes cast, compared with 38.4% for the SPÖ and only 11.6% for the ÖVP. Haider, therefore, retained the governorship of his home province.

In October 2003 the National Council approved amendments to Austria's asylum legislation that were intended to accelerate the asylum process; the office of the UN High Commissioner for Refugees, however, described the amendments as 'among the most restrictive pieces of legislation' within the EU, while other critics claimed that the revised legislation was in breach of the Geneva Convention and the Austrian Constitution. The changes included measures such as deporting some asylum seekers while their appeals were under review, demanding full statements from asylum seekers within 72 hours of their arrival in Austria, and medically certifying cases involving traumatized people.

A presidential election was held on 25 April 2004, at which Dr Heinz Fischer of the SPÖ defeated Dr Benita Ferrero-Waldner of the ÖVP with 52.4% of the votes cast. On 5 July, just three days before the end of his term of office, President Klestil suffered a heart attack: he died the following day. Chancellor Schüssel assumed charge of Klestil's duties until 8 July, when Fischer was sworn in as the new President.

As a result of the continuing decline in support for the FPÖ, Haider split from the party in early April 2005 to form Bündnis Zukunft Österreich (BZÖ—Alliance for the Future of Austria). The FPÖ government ministers, several FPÖ members of Parliament (Parlament) and the party Chairwoman, Haubner (who had been elected unopposed in July 2004), all defected to the BZÖ. The party replaced the FPÖ in the ruling coalition and the ministers retained their posts in the Government. Haider was elected as leader of the BZÖ, while Heinz-Christian Strache was elected to the chairmanship of the FPÖ. In mid-April Siegfried Kampl, a BZÖ member from Carinthia, who was due to assume the rotating presidency of the Federal Council (Bundesrat) in July, provoked considerable controversy when he denounced deserters from Austria's Nazi-era armed forces and deplored what he called the 'brutal persecution' of Austrian Nazis following the Second World War. Amid the ensuing furore, he resigned from the BZÖ but stated his intention to take up the presidency of the Federal Council as planned. However, a constitutional amendment adopted in June with the support of all parties allowed Carinthia to withdraw Kampl's nomination and to designate Peter Mitterer as President of the Federal Council for the last six months of 2005.

The SPÖ performed well at elections held in three provinces in October 2005. In Styria the party defeated the ÖVP, which had previously held the governorship of the province for some 60 years without interruption. The FPÖ and the BZÖ failed to win any seats in the provincial assembly. The SPÖ increased its dominance in Burgenland, where it secured an absolute majority, and in Vienna, where only one-fifth of the votes were cast in favour of one of the government parties, the BZÖ taking only 1.2%. As a result of the provincial elections, the ruling ÖVP-BZÖ coalition lost its majority in the Federal Council. In May 2006 Haider resigned as leader of the BZÖ; Peter Westenthaler was elected as his replacement in June.

Political activity in 2006 was dominated by a financial scandal surrounding the Bank für Arbeit und Wirtschaft AG PSK (BAWAG PSK), which was owned by the Österreichischer Gewerkschaftsbund (ÖGB—Austrian Trade Union Federation) and had links to the SPÖ. BAWAG was revealed to have accumulated huge debts and to have used the ÖGB strike fund to conceal the losses. The federal Government intervened to prevent the collapse of the bank, which was sold to a US-based company in December. At the general election held on 1 October 2006 the SPÖ won 68 seats in the legislature (one fewer than in 2002), while the ÖVP won 66 seats, compared with 79 in 2002. The Greens and the FPÖ won 21 seats apiece, while the BZÖ won seven seats.

Return to 'grand coalition': Gusenbauer 2007–08

Following the 2006 election, the SPÖ began talks with the ÖVP over the formation of a 'grand coalition'. Negotiations were hindered after the SPÖ allied itself at the first meeting of the new National Council with the Greens and the FPÖ to initiate a parliamentary inquiry into a controversial purchase agreement entered into by the Government in 2002 for 18 Eurofighter aircraft. The SPÖ also instigated a parliamentary inquiry into banking sector reforms undertaken by the previous Government.

On 8 January 2007 the SPÖ and ÖVP finally formed a 'grand coalition', giving the Government control of 134 of the 183 seats in the National Council. The new Council of Ministers, comprising seven ministers each from the SPÖ and ÖVP, was sworn in on 11 January. Gusenbauer became Chancellor and Wilhelm Molterer of the ÖVP was appointed Vice-Chancellor and Federal Minister for Finance. Gusenbauer was subsequently accused of reneging on election promises in order to reach an agreement with the ÖVP. He was also criticized for conceding control of the key ministries of finance, foreign affairs and economy to the ÖVP. The new coalition's programme comprised austerity measures aimed at eradicating the budget deficit by 2010, with savings to be achieved largely by administrative reform, but also included increases in spending on education and social issues and a rise in personal contributions to the health system. Molterer was officially elected as ÖVP Chairman at the party congress in Salzburg in April 2007, while Schüssel, who had resigned in the light of the party's poor electoral performance, assumed the leadership of the ÖVP parliamentary group.

Relations between the coalition partners were strained in June 2007 by an announcement from the SPÖ Federal Minister for Defence, Norbert Darabos, that he had signed a new contract with the manufacturers of the Eurofighter jets, reducing the number of aircraft involved from 18 to 15, before the parliamentary inquiry into the purchase had published its findings. The committee closed its inquiry in July, concluding that although evidence of wrongdoing in the circumstances surrounding the awarding of the contract potentially justified a complete withdrawal, the probability of exposure to lengthy judicial proceedings, owing to a lack of conclusive proof of bribery, made such a course inadvisable.

Relations between the two governing parties became increasingly acrimonious in March 2008, following the SPÖ's decision to support an opposition motion in the National Council to establish a parliamentary commission of inquiry into abuses of office in the Federal Ministry of the Interior under the control of the ÖVP. The inquiry was prompted by accusations by a former federal police chief, Herwig Haidinger: that errors in a child kidnapping case in 1998 had been suppressed in 2006 by the Federal Minister for the Interior in order to avoid a political scandal shortly before the general election in October, and that in the same year the Ministry of the Interior had instructed Haidinger to pass findings from investigations into the BAWAG scandal to the ÖVP in an attempt to find information to discredit the SPÖ during the election campaign.

By mid-2008 relations between the coalition parties had deteriorated significantly. In early June leading figures from both the ÖVP and the SPÖ, including the Federal Minister for Agriculture, Forestry, the Environment and Water Management, Josef Pröll of the ÖVP, and former Chancellor Vranitzky, issued public statements criticizing Gusenbauer's leadership. The SPÖ's poor performance in provincial elections held in Tyrol on 8 June, at which it received just 15.6% of the vote, provoked further discontent within the party. Later that month Gusenbauer was replaced as Chairman of the SPÖ on an interim basis by the Federal Minister for Transport, Innovation and Technology, Werner Faymann.

Following the accession of Faymann to the leadership of the SPÖ, the party sought to recover its standing in the opinion polls by adopting a more populist policy with regard to the EU. In July 2008 the influential Eurosceptic daily newspaper the *Kronen Zeitung* published an open letter co-authored by Faymann and Gusenbauer, in which they indicated that any future EU treaties or amendments to treaties requiring ratification, as well as any decision on Turkish accession to the union, would be submitted to a referendum. The change in policy on the part of the SPÖ led to the withdrawal of the largely pro-EU ÖVP from the 'grand coalition', the dissolution of the legislature and the scheduling of an early general election. Gusenbauer subsequently nominated Faymann as the SPÖ's candidate for the role of Chancellor. Faymann was elected as Chairman of the SPÖ in August. Later that month Haider was re-elected as leader of the BZÖ, replacing Westenthaler, following the latter's conviction for perjury during a trial in which his bodyguard was accused of assault.

At the general election, which took place on 28 September 2008, the SPÖ retained its position as the largest party in the legislature, winning 57 seats, while the ÖVP lost support, securing just 51 seats. By contrast, large gains were made by the two right-wing populist parties: the FPÖ won 34 seats, while the BZÖ tripled its representation, securing 21 seats. The Greens lost support, winning just 20 seats. In accordance with reforms promulgated in June 2007, the parliamentary term was extended to five years following the election; voter participation was recorded at 78.8%. The following day Molterer resigned as Chairman of the ÖVP. Pröll was appointed as his successor on an interim basis. Despite the electoral success of the FPÖ and the BZÖ, both the SPÖ and the ÖVP ruled out forming a coalition with the two right-wing parties and subsequently began talks over the formation of a new 'grand coalition' government.

Recent developments: 'grand coalition' under Faymann

In late November 2008 the SPÖ and the ÖVP agreed to form a new 'grand coalition'. Ursula Plassnik of the ÖVP, hitherto the Federal Minister for European and International Affairs, announced that she would not accept a position in the new Council of Ministers owing to Faymann's refusal to include in the terms of the coalition agreement a guarantee that future EU treaties or amendments to treaties would be ratified through Parliament, rather than by referendum. The new Council of Ministers was sworn in at the beginning of December. Faymann was appointed Chancellor, while Pröll replaced Molterer as Vice-Chancellor and Federal Minister for Finance.

Meanwhile, in October 2008 Haider was killed in a road traffic accident near Klagenfurt, while driving under the influence of alcohol. His deputy, Stefan Petzner, was nominated to succeed him as leader of the BZÖ, while Gerhard Dörfler, hitherto the Deputy Governor of Carinthia, replaced him as Governor of that province. However, Petzner's suitability to lead the party was questioned, following an emotional radio interview in which he made indiscreet remarks regarding his personal relationship with Haider. In mid-November Petzner resigned as interim party leader and was replaced by a former FPÖ Minister of Defence, Herbert Scheibner.

At provincial elections on 1 March 2009 in Carinthia and Salzburg the BZÖ and the FPÖ both made gains at the expense of the SPÖ. In Carinthia, with a campaign that emphasized the legacy of Haider, the BZÖ won 45.5% of the vote, the SPÖ 28.8% and the ÖVP 16.8%. The Greens won 5.1% of the votes cast, but the FPÖ only 3.8%, thus failing to gain representation in the provincial parliament. Dörfler retained the post of Governor of Carinthia. In Salzburg the SPÖ managed to maintain a small plurality, winning 39.5% of the votes cast. The ÖVP won 36.5% of votes, the FPÖ increased its share of the vote to 13.0%, the Greens won 7.3% and the BZÖ 3.7%. The SPÖ and the ÖVP formed another coalition Government.

At regional elections in Vorarlberg in September 2009 the incumbent ÖVP won a majority of 50.8% of votes and formed a one-party Government, the first in the region's history. The SPÖ's fortunes continued to decline. The party won only 10.1% of the votes cast, while the FPÖ secured 25.3%, and the Greens 10.4%. The following week, in provincial elections in Upper Austria (Oberösterreich), the ÖVP won 46.8% of the votes cast and formed a coalition Government with the Greens, who won 9.2%. The SPÖ won 24.9% of the votes cast and the FPÖ 15.3%. The BZÖ, which, at national level, had in April elected its Parliamentary Spokesman, Josef Bucher, to serve concurrently as party leader, failed to gain representation in the provincial parliament.

At the elections to the European Parliament on 7 June 2009, the ÖVP won the most votes (30.0% of the total), although this represented a slight decline from the 32.7% it took in 2004. The SPÖ performed poorly, winning only 23.7% of the votes cast, compared with 33.3% in 2004, and the Greens won 9.9%, down from 12.9%. The Liste Dr Hans-Peter Martin—für Demokratie, Kontrolle, Gerechtigkeit (the Hans-Peter Martin List for Democracy, Control and Justice), won 17.7% of the votes cast, compared with 14.0% in 2004. The FPÖ's controversial campaign centred around warnings of a growing 'Islamization' of Austria and Europe and used images of a cross and the slogan 'The West in Christian hands'. Advertisements also warned of the possibility of Israel and Turkey entering the EU. The campaign was condemned by church leaders, politicians and Islamic and Jewish groups; none the less, at the polls the FPÖ gained 12.7% of votes, compared with 6.3% in 2004. The ÖVP was allocated six seats in the European Parliament, the SPÖ four (down from seven), the Liste Dr Hans-Peter Martin three, the Greens two and the FPÖ two.

In November 2009 the ÖVP Minister of Science and Research, Johannes Hahn, was nominated for the post of EU Commissioner for Regional Policy. In January 2010 Beatrix Karl, the General Secretary of the Österreichischer Arbeitnehmerinnen und Arbeitnehmer Bund (ÖAAB—the Austrian Workers' Association), replaced Hahn as Minister of Science and Research. The role included responsibility for universities, and her appointment prompted protests by students against her reported intention to reimpose university fees, which were partially abolished in September 2008, and place limits on university student numbers.

President Fischer was re-elected to a second and final term of office at a presidential election held on 25 April 2010, securing 79.3% of the votes cast, with the support of the Greens, as well as his own party, the SPÖ. His closest rival, Barbara Rosenkranz of the FPÖ, won 15.2% of the votes. Rosenkranz's candidacy attracted substantial media attention during the electoral campaign: following considerable controversy surrounding her vague responses in interviews to questions regarding her views on the Holocaust, she signed a public statement pledging never to contest anti-Nazi legislation. An historically low turn-out of 53.6% was attributed, in part, to the decision of the ÖVP neither to nominate nor to endorse a candidate.

The SPÖ lost its absolute majority in the provincial assembly in Burgenland at elections in May 2010, receiving 48.3% of the votes (compared with 52.2% in 2005), although it retained the governorship, with support for the ÖVP also declining. The FPÖ increased its share of the votes to 9.0% (from 5.8%), while the Greens and the Liste Burgenland (Burgenland List, led by former FPÖ officials) also narrowly secured representation in the assembly.

In mid-2010 it was reported that prosecutors investigating the near collapse, in December 2009, of Carinthian-based banking group Hypo Group Alpe Adria had discovered several secret bank accounts in Liechtenstein in which the late Jörg Haider had allegedly deposited up to US $45m.; it was also claimed that Haider had accepted donations for the FPÖ from the Libyan leader, Muammar al-Qaddafi, and the late Iraqi President, Saddam Hussain, both of whom he had visited while leader of the party.

As in Burgenland in May 2010, the FPÖ performed well in two provincial elections held in September and October. In Styria, on 26 September, the party increased its share of the vote to 10.7% (from only 4.6% in the 2005 polls), securing six seats in the provincial assembly and a guaranteed post in the provincial government, despite having provoked widespread condemnation during the electoral campaign by launching a (subsequently banned) online video game, entitled 'Bye Bye Mosque', in which players attempted to shoot down mosques and minarets. The SPÖ narrowly retained its position as the largest party in the Styrian assembly, receiving 38.3% of the votes, compared with the ÖVP's 37.2%, with both parties' share of the votes again declining. In the elections in Vienna, held on 10 October, the FPÖ made substantial gains, increasing its share of the votes to 25.8%, and replacing the ÖVP, which recorded its poorest ever result in Vienna, as the second largest party in the provincial assembly. The results were also disappointing for the ÖVP's federal coalition partner, the SPÖ, which lost its absolute majority in the assembly, securing only 44.3% of the votes. The SPÖ later formed a coalition Government in Vienna with the Greens, who had won 12.6% of the votes. Christine Marek, the ÖVP's leader in Vienna, resigned as State Secretary in the Federal Ministry of Economy, Family and Youth in November; she was replaced by Verena Remler.

In April 2011 a new Federal Government was sworn in following changes necessitated by the resignation of Pröll as Vice-Chancellor and Minister of Finance, on the grounds of ill health. Pröll also resigned as the leader of the ÖVP; he was replaced as party leader and thus as Vice-Chancellor, by Dr Michael Spindelegger, who retained his position as the Federal Minister for European and International Affairs. Among other notable changes to ÖVP portfolios, Dr Maria Fekter was allocated the finance portfolio, Dr Beatrix Karl took over the Ministry of Justice, Johanna Mikl-Leitner became Minister of the Interior, and Karlheinz Töchterle assumed responsibility for the science and research portfolio.

Austrian politicians were subject to a series of corruption allegations in 2011. Two ÖVP members of the European Parliament, Ernst Strasser and Hella Ranner, resigned from office in March, following accusations, which both refuted, that the former had accepted bribes in return for proposing amendments to European legislation and that the latter had intended to use her parliamentary expense account to repay a business debt. In August, moreover, Uwe Scheuch, the Deputy Governor of Carinthia and Chairman of Die Freiheitlichen in Kärnten (FPK, Freedom Party in Carinthia), was sentenced to 18 months' imprisonment (including 12 suspended), after being found guilty of offering, in 2009, to assist a Russian entrepreneur to gain Austrian citizenship in return for a donation to the BZÖ, the party to which he then belonged; Scheuch appealed against the verdict. (The FPK was formerly the Carinthian branch of the BZÖ; in 2010 it disassociated from the federal BZÖ to co-operate with the FPÖ at federal level.) Meanwhile, further scandals emerged in which several former government ministers from the ÖVP-FPÖ/BZÖ coalition administrations in office in 2000–07 were implicated. Strasser, who had served as Minister of the Interior in 2000–04, and two former FPÖ ministers, Hubert Gorbach and Mathias Reichhold, were accused of receiving illicit payments from Telekom Austria or lobbyists co-operating with the partially state-owned telecommunications provider, while former managers of the company were alleged to have paid a broker to manipulate its share price in 2004 in order to secure large bonuses. In addition, the role of the former Minister of Finance, Karl-Heinz Grasser, in the controversial privatization of the real estate company Die Bauen und Wohnen GmbH (BUWOG) was under investigation, as was alleged impropriety by the former Minister of Defence, Herbert Scheibner, in relation to the purchase of Eurofighter aircraft. Although he had not personally been accused of corruption, former Chancellor Schüssel resigned as a member of Parliament in early September, claiming that he was retiring from politics in order to facilitate the investigations into his former ministers. Later that month Parliament agreed to establish a committee of inquiry to probe the various corruption allegations.

Economic concerns came to the fore from late 2011. In the context of the sovereign debt crisis affecting the wider euro area, the Government sought to avert a threatened downgrading of the 'AAA' credit status assigned to Austria's debt by rating agencies, amid fears that the heavy exposure of the Austrian banking sector to financially stricken Central and Eastern European economies, particularly Hungary, had made it vulnerable. (In July Österreichische Volksbanken-AG had been among eight European banks, of 91 examined, to fail a 'stress test' designed to assess their resilience to potential shocks such as the sharp contraction in credit markets that occurred in 2008.) In November 2011 the Government pledged to accelerate reductions in public expenditure and to introduce a constitutional amendment that would commit the Government to lowering the ratio of public debt to gross domestic product to 60% by 2020 (from some 72% in 2011). However, differences of opinion between the governing SPÖ and the ÖVP on what austerity measures to implement made subsequent negotiations difficult, while the support of at least one opposition party was required to achieve the two-thirds' parliamentary majority needed to revise the Constitution. In early December the opposition parties refused to support the coalition Government's draft constitutional amendment on the debt limit, prompting the SPÖ and the ÖVP to adopt the proposal as a regular law with a simple majority. Later that month the Government announced its intention to reduce expenditure by some €2,000m. per year by 2017; a detailed plan on achieving this target remained under consideration in early 2012. In January 2012, none the less, the credit rating agency Standard & Poor's downgraded Austria's credit rating, to AA+; however, the two other major rating agencies, Moody's and Fitch, had recently confirmed Austria's AAA rating.

Foreign Affairs

Regional relations

Austria was formally admitted to the European Union (EU, see p. 276) on 1 January 1995, following a national referendum in June 1994, at which 66.4% of those who voted supported Austria's accession to the Union. Austria participated in the introduction of the European single currency, the euro, on 1 January 1999. In May 2005 the Austrian Parliament ratified the EU's Treaty establishing a Constitution for Europe. However, the treaty was rejected at referendums held in France and the Netherlands. In April 2008 Parliament ratified the Treaty of Lisbon, which replaced the rejected constitutional treaty and which came into effect in December 2009. During 2010–11 the Austrian Government supported EU efforts to improve the financial stability of the euro area, including agreements on the establishment of the European Financial Stability Facility in June 2010, on the European Stability Mechanism in October of that year and on new, stricter fiscal arrangements in December 2011.

In October 2005 a demand by Austria that a 'privileged partnership' with the EU be offered to Turkey rather than full membership threatened to delay the official launch of accession talks with that country. Austria was finally persuaded to withdraw this demand, and negotiations commenced. Observers suggested that Austria's concession on Turkey was linked to the decision to proceed with previously suspended talks with Croatia, whose bid for membership of the EU the Austrian Government supported. Relations with Turkey were again strained prior to the European Parliament elections in June 2009, with both the ÖVP and the FPÖ campaigning on a platform of opposition to full EU membership for Turkey. Criticism of Austria's treatment of immigrants from Turkey made by the Turkish ambassador to Austria, Kadri Ecvet Tezcan, in a newspaper interview provoked further diplomatic tensions in November 2010; Tezcan was replaced as ambassador a year later. Meanwhile, in May 2011 Turkey's President, Abdullah Gül, sought to strengthen bilateral relations, particularly economic ties, during the first Turkish presidential visit to Austria for 13 years. During the visit, however, Chancellor Faymann reiterated his position that Austria would conduct a national referendum on Turkey's membership of the EU, whatever the outcome of negotiations between the EU and the Turkish Government on Turkish accession. In June, moreover, tensions arose when Turkey vetoed an application by the former Austrian Minister for European and International Affairs, Ursula Plassnik, for the position of Secretary-General of the Organization for Security and Co-operation in Europe owing to her opposition to Turkish membership of the EU.

The activation in October 2000 of a Soviet-designed nuclear power installation at Temelín in the Czech Republic, 48 km from the border with Austria, prompted protests from environmental activists and claims by both Austria and Germany that the plant was dangerously flawed: Austria subsequently suspended imports of Czech electricity. Following negotiations between the Austrian and Czech authorities, an agreement was signed by the two countries in December under which the plant was not to operate at commercial capacity until a full evaluation of its safety and environmental impact had been completed by a joint Austro-Czech safety body under the supervision of the European Commission. In August 2001 the Czech authorities reconnected the plant with the national power network, citing the findings of a report by the European Commission; however, the Austrian and German Governments continued to express concern over the safety of the plant. Later that year Chancellor Schüssel threatened to veto the Czech Republic's accession to the EU unless the matter were satisfactorily resolved. Further safety issues were subsequently agreed, however, and in April 2003 the Temelín installation commenced production at full capacity for an 18-month trial period, prior to entering into commercial operations by the end of 2004. Relations between Austria and the Czech Republic were further marred by the latter's refusal to abolish the so-called Beneš Decrees—legislation enacted at the end of the Second World War, providing for the expulsion of about 2.5m. ethnic Sudeten Germans from the Czech Republic without recourse to compensation. Austria repeatedly threatened to block the Czech Republic's anticipated accession to the EU in 2004 unless the Decrees were annulled; the EU authorities, however, did not regard their abolition as a prerequisite for entry, and Austria did not carry out its threats. Following the Czech Republic's accession to the EU in May 2004, relations between the two countries improved. None the less, the Czech Republic's plan to commence construction of an additional two nuclear rectors at its Temelín installation in 2013 was opposed by the Austrian Government, which advocated that European countries abandon the production and use of nuclear energy.

The heads of government of Austria, Hungary and Slovakia met on several occasions during the late 1990s in order to pursue co-operation on security and economic issues. In September

1999, however, Austria threatened to hinder Slovakia's entry into the EU, in protest at the alleged inadequacy of that country's nuclear safety standards. Following diplomatic pressure from Austria, the terms of Slovakia's accession treaty included a commitment to decommission two Soviet-era nuclear reactors at Jaslovské Bohunice, some 40 km from the border with Austria, by the end of 2008; the first reactor was duly disconnected in late 2006 and the second on 31 December 2008. Meanwhile, however, work on the expansion of Slovakia's Mochovce nuclear power station proceeded in 2008, despite Austrian opposition, with completion envisaged for 2013.

The implementation in December 2007 of the Schengen Agreement on border controls by nine Central and Eastern European countries included four countries that share a border with Austria. In order to assuage public fears of mass migration, the Government promised to mount a guard on its borders, provoking anger in the Czech Republic and Hungary. Relations with Hungary were already strained following an attempt by the Austrian oil and gas company OMV to take over its Hungarian counterpart, MOL. The border patrols were initially scheduled to end in 2009; however, in December the SPÖ Federal Minister of Defence and Sports, Norbert Darabos, announced that the patrols would continue. Meanwhile, in October 2009 the Minister of the Interior, Dr Maria Fekter, expressed the Austrian Government's support for Bulgaria and Romania's entry into the Schengen Agreement in 2011, although their entry was delayed in the event, owing to Finnish and Dutch concerns regarding corruption and organized crime in the two countries. From May 2011 Austria and Germany opened their labour markets to citizens of the eight Central and Eastern European countries that joined the EU in May 2004 (the Czech Republic, Estonia, Hungary, Latvia, Lithuania, Poland, Slovenia and Slovakia), having imposed the longest period of restrictions on workers from these countries of the 15 longer-standing EU members.

Austria's relations with Lithuania were severely strained in July 2011, after Austrian prosecutors released a former officer of the Soviet state security service (KGB) accused by the Lithuanian Government of orchestrating the violent seizure of a broadcasting centre in the Lithuanian capital, Vilnius, in January 1991 in which 13 people died. The Austrian Government denied suggestions that it had bowed to Russian pressure not to extradite the former KGB officer to Lithuania, insisting that Austrian prosecutors had taken the decision to release him, after one day in detention, because Lithuania's European arrest warrant was not sufficiently detailed. The Lithuanian Government recalled its ambassador from Vienna for talks, while the foreign ministers of Lithuania, Estonia and Latvia referred the matter to Viviane Reding, the European Commissioner responsible for Justice, Fundamental Rights and Citizenship, who subsequently concluded that Austria had not contravened any law.

Other external relations

In March 1998, following months of debate, the Government announced that Austria would not apply to join the North Atlantic Treaty Organization (NATO, see p. 370), and would thereby preserve its traditional neutrality. Nevertheless, in April 1999 Austria, in conjunction with the three other officially neutral EU member countries, signed an EU declaration stating that the ongoing bombing of Serbia by NATO forces was, although regrettable, 'both necessary and warranted'. During the 1990s, in its capacity as a participant of NATO's Partnership for Peace programme (which it had joined in 1995), Austria took an active role in the aftermath of the wars and ethnic conflicts in the Balkans, participating in UN-authorized peace-keeping operations in Bosnia and Herzegovina and providing substantial humanitarian aid.

Austria's relationship with the USA was, on the whole, free from tension, notwithstanding the strain caused by the election of Dr Kurt Waldheim in 1986, and the formation of the coalition Government between the ÖVP and FPÖ in 2000. The Austrian Government deployed 93 troops on a three-month mission to Afghanistan to assist in stabilizing the country prior to elections in 2005, although under their mandate of neutrality the troops did not engage in combat. In 2009 the US President, Barack Obama, sought more international assistance in the ongoing campaign against the Taliban in Afghanistan. However, in December of that year the Federal Minister of Defence and Sports, Norbert Darabos, reportedly stated that, despite pressure from the USA and also the United Kingdom, Austria would not commit more troops.

Austria's reliance on natural gas supplies from Russia left the nation vulnerable to ongoing disputes over prices and supply between Russia and Ukraine, a key transit country. According to figures from the European Council on Foreign Relations, Russia supplied more than 60% of Austria's gas supplies in 2006; securing another source was thus a major issue for the nation. In 2002 Austria participated in discussions with Bulgaria, Hungary, Romania and Turkey regarding the construction of a gas pipeline. The impetus to reach agreement on an alternative gas supply route was intensified, following an incident in January 2009 when Russia shut down its main pipeline to Europe for two weeks in a price dispute with Ukraine, leaving houses and businesses throughout Europe without energy. An agreement to build the 'Nabucco' pipeline was signed by the countries' respective leaders at a ceremony in July 2009. The pipeline, which was to run from Erzurum, Turkey, through Romania, Bulgaria and Hungary to Baumgarten an der March, Austria, had formal backing from the EU and USA. None the less, Austria was also involved in the Russian-led 'South Stream' pipeline project, which was to carry Russian gas under the Black Sea to Baumgarten an der March via Bulgaria, Serbia and Hungary. Austria's participation in 'South Stream' was confirmed in April 2010, during a visit to Vienna by the Russian Prime Minister, Vladimir Putin, with the signature of an agreement on the construction of the Austrian section of the pipeline.

Controversy arose in November 2007 after the National Council approved the deployment of up to 160 Austrian troops to Chad as part of the EU Force (EUFOR) peace-keeping mission in the east of that country, despite vociferous opposition from the Greens, the FPÖ and the BZÖ. A limited deployment of Austrian troops took place in January 2008. However, in early February an assault on the Chadian capital, N'Djamena, by forces opposed to President Idriss Deby forced the postponement of further troop arrivals. Despite calls by the opposition for Austria to withdraw from the mission, the deployment was completed in April. The Austrian troops remained in Chad when a UN force replaced EUFOR in March 2009, but almost all of them had been withdrawn by the end of that year, with the remainder returning to Austria in early 2010.

CONSTITUTION AND GOVERNMENT

The Austrian Constitution of 1920, as amended in 1929, was restored on 1 May 1945. Austria is a federal republic, divided into nine provinces, each with its own provincial assembly and government. The head of state, the Federal President (Bundespräsident), is elected by popular vote for a six-year term. The President is eligible for re-election only once in succession. Legislative power is held by the bicameral Parliament (Parlament). The first chamber, the National Council (Nationalrat), has 183 members, elected by universal, direct adult suffrage for four years (subject to dissolution) on the basis of proportional representation. In 2007 the National Council approved legislation extending the maximum parliamentary term from four to five years. The reform entered into effect following the early legislative election on 28 September 2008. The second chamber, the Federal Council (Bundesrat), has 62 members, elected for varying terms by the provincial assemblies. The Federal Assembly (Bundesversammlung—a joint meeting of the National Council and the Federal Council) is convened for certain matters of special importance, for example to witness the swearing-in of the Federal President. The Federal Government consists of the Federal Chancellor, the Vice-Chancellor and the other ministers and state secretaries, who may vary in number. The Chancellor is chosen by the President, usually from the party with the strongest representation in the newly elected National Council, and the other ministers are then selected by the President on the advice of the Chancellor. The Federal President normally acts on the advice of the Council of Ministers, which is responsible to the National Council.

REGIONAL AND INTERNATIONAL CO-OPERATION

Austria joined the European Union (EU, see p. 276) in January 1995 and participated in the introduction of the European single currency, the euro, on 1 January 1999. Austria is also a member of the Council of Europe (see p. 256) and the Central European Initiative (see p. 462). The Secretariat of the Organization for Security and Co-operation in Europe (OSCE, see p. 388), in which Austria participates, is based in Vienna.

Austria joined the UN in 1955 and hosts the third headquarters of the organization. As a contracting party to the General Agreement on Tariffs and Trade, Austria joined the World Trade Organization (WTO, see p. 433) on its establishment in 1995. The country is also a member of the Organisation for Economic Co-operation and Development (OECD, see p. 379). Austria participates in the Partnership for Peace framework of the North Atlantic Treaty Organization (NATO, see p. 370). Austria hosts the International Atomic Energy Agency (IAEA, see p. 122) and the Organization of Petroleum Exporting Countries (OPEC, see p. 408).

ECONOMIC AFFAIRS

In 2010, according to estimates by the World Bank, Austria's gross national income (GNI), measured at average 2008–10 prices, was US $391,511m., equivalent to $46,690 per head (or $39,390 per head on an international purchasing-power parity basis). During 2001–10 the population grew at an estimated average rate of only 0.5% per year, while gross domestic product (GDP) per head increased, in real terms, at an average annual rate of 1.2%. According to the UN, overall GDP grew, in real terms, at an average annual rate of 1.6% in 2001–10; GDP declined by 3.8% in 2009 but increased by 2.3% in 2010.

The contribution of agriculture (including hunting, forestry and fishing) to GDP was 1.5% in 2010. In 2008, according to the International Labour Organization (ILO), 5.6% of the employed labour force were engaged in the agricultural sector. Austrian farms produce more than 90% of the country's food requirements, and surplus dairy products are exported. The principal crops are sugar beet, maize, wheat and barley. According to UN estimates, the GDP of the agricultural sector increased at an average annual rate of 1.1% in 2001–10; agricultural GDP declined by 4.3% in 2009 but increased, by a meagre 0.1%, in 2010.

Industry (including mining and quarrying, manufacturing, construction and power) contributed 28.2% of GDP in 2010; according to the ILO, the sector engaged 26.0% of the employed labour force in 2008. According to UN estimates, industrial GDP increased, in real terms, at an average annual rate of 1.7% in 2001–10; it declined by 12.1% in 2009 but increased by 4.5% in 2010.

In 2009 mining and quarrying contributed 0.4% of GDP. According to the ILO, the sector employed 0.3% of the employed labour force in 2008. The most important indigenous mineral resource is iron ore (2.0m. metric tons were mined in 2006). Austria also has deposits of petroleum, natural gas, magnesite and tungsten. Austria is one of the world's leading producers of sand and gravel. According to UN estimates, the GDP of the mining sector increased, in real terms, at an average annual rate of 1.1% in 2001–10, it increased by 7.9% in 2009, while it declined by 1.5% in 2010.

Manufacturing (including mining and quarrying) contributed 18.0% of GDP in 2010 and, according to the ILO, the sector engaged 17.0% of the employed labour force in 2008. Measured by the gross value of output, the principal branches of manufacturing in 2004 were metals and metal products (accounting for 16.6% of the total), non-electrical machinery (12.5%), electrical machinery and telecommunications equipment (10.1%), food products (9.4%), wood and paper products (8.6%), road vehicles and parts (6.9%) and chemicals and chemical products (6.2%). According to UN estimates, the GDP of the manufacturing sector increased, in real terms, at an average annual rate of 2.0% during 2001–10; it declined by 14.3% in 2009 but expanded by 6.7% in 2010.

Construction contributed 6.9% of GDP in 2010. According to the ILO, the sector engaged 8.1% of the employed labour force in 2008. According to UN estimates, the GDP of the construction sector decreased, in real terms, at an average annual rate of 0.2% in 2001–10; it declined by 6.4% in 2010.

Hydroelectric power resources provide the major domestic source of energy, accounting for 59.0% of total electricity production in 2008, followed by gas (17.4%), coal (10.7%) and petroleum (1.9%). Austria is heavily dependent on imports of energy, mainly from Eastern Europe. Crude materials and mineral fuel imports accounted for 15.8% of the total cost of imports in 2010.

The services sector contributed 70.3% of GDP in 2010. In 2008, according to the ILO, the sector engaged 68.4% of the employed labour force. Tourism has traditionally been a leading source of revenue, providing receipts of US $18,663m. in 2010 (excluding passenger transport). Real estate and business services accounted for 18.5% of GDP in 2010, while wholesale and retail trade contributed 13.6%. According to UN estimates, the GDP of the services sector increased, in real terms, at an average annual rate of 1.9% in 2001–10; it fell by 1.6% in 2009 but grew by 2.2% in 2010.

In 2010, according to the IMF, Austria recorded a visible trade deficit of US $4,303m., while there was a surplus of $10,555m. on the current account of the balance of payments. According to official figures, in 2010 the principal source of imports was Germany (39.5%); other major suppliers were Italy (6.8%) and Switzerland (including Liechtenstein, 5.2%). Principal markets for exports were Germany (31.6%) and Italy (7.8%). The principal exports in 2010 were machinery and transport equipment (37.8%), basic manufactures (23.0%), chemicals and related products (13.0%), miscellaneous manufactured articles (11.8%) and food and live animals (5.2%). In the same year, the principal imports were machinery and transport equipment (32.5%), basic manufactures (15.9%), miscellaneous manufactured articles (14.5%), chemicals and related products (12.7%), mineral fuels (10.7%), food and live animals (5.9%) and crude materials (5.1%).

In 2010 there was a general government deficit of €12,536m., equivalent to 4.4% of GDP. Austria's general government gross debt was €205,212m. in 2010, equivalent to 72.2% of GDP. In 2008 the central Government's debt was €176,575m., equivalent to 62.6% of GDP. The average annual rate of inflation was 1.8% in 2001–10. Consumer prices increased by 1.9% in 2010. In 2009 7.2% of the labour force were unemployed.

Austria is a small, wealthy country with an open economy, which is largely dependent on the export of manufactured products. GDP growth led by exports and investment was strong in 2004–07, following the successful implementation of much-needed structural reforms. From late 2008, however, Austria's economic performance was adversely affected by the global economic crisis. Although Austrian banks were not directly affected by the global financial crisis, since they had little involvement in the US market in low-income mortgages, they were affected by the lack of availability of credit and their exposure to the economies of Central and Eastern Europe, where the impact of the international downturn had been particularly severe, and two banks were nationalized. The Government introduced large fiscal stimulus measures to promote growth and provided funding to stabilize the financial markets and encourage interbank lending. Nevertheless, GDP contracted by 3.8% in 2009, representing the economy's worst performance since the Second World War, largely owing to a decline in exports. The fiscal measures had a severely detrimental effect on the state finances. The budget deficit, which had been equivalent to 0.9% of GDP in 2008, increased to 4.1% in 2009, while public debt, which had declined to 60.2% of GDP in 2007, close to the limit of 60% set by the EU Stability and Growth Pact, rose to 63.8% in 2008 and to 69.5% in 2009. The Austrian economy returned to growth in 2010, of 2.3%, primarily owing to a significant increase in exports. However, public debt and the budget deficit rose further, to 71.8% and 4.4% of GDP, respectively. Following the introduction of a series of austerity measures, including a 'solidarity tax' on banks' assets, the budget deficit narrowed in 2011, to an estimated 3.6% of GDP, but public debt increased again, to an estimated 72.0% of GDP. Moreover, having remained strong in the first two quarters of 2011, GDP growth slowed in the third, owing to weaker external demand; GDP growth of 2.9% was forecast for the year as a whole, followed by only 0.9% in 2012. In November 2011 the Government pledged to lower public debt to 60% of GDP by 2020, and commenced discussions on measures to reduce expenditure by some €2,000m. per year by 2017 (see Domestic Political Affairs), while the central bank announced stricter capital requirements for banks and a limit on the loan to deposit ratio of 110% for lending in Central and Eastern Europe. Nevertheless, in January 2012, amid continued concerns regarding the sovereign debt crisis in the euro area, Austria was among several countries to suffer a downgrading of its credit rating by the rating agency Standard & Poor's.

PUBLIC HOLIDAYS

2013: 1 January (New Year's Day), 6 January (Epiphany), 1 April (Easter Monday), 1 May (Labour Day), 9 May (Ascension Day), 20 May (Whit Monday), 30 May (Corpus Christi), 15 August (Assumption), 26 October (National Holiday), 1 November (All Saints' Day), 8 December (Immaculate Conception), 25 December (Christmas Day), 26 December (St Stephen's Day).

Statistical Survey

Sources (unless otherwise stated): Statistik Austria, Hintere Zollamtsstr. 2B, 1033 Vienna; tel. (1) 711-28-76-55; fax (1) 711-28-77-28; e-mail info@statistik.gv.at; internet www.statistik.at; Austrian National Bank, Postfach 61, Otto-Wagner-Pl. 3, 1090 Vienna; tel. (1) 404-20-0; fax (1) 404-20-66-96; e-mail oenb.info@oenb.co.at; internet www.oenb.at.

Area and Population

AREA, POPULATION AND DENSITY

Area (sq km)	83,871*
Population (census results)†	
15 May 1991	7,795,786
15 May 2001	
Males	3,889,189
Females	4,143,737
Total	8,032,926
Population at 1 January	
2009	8,355,260
2010	8,375,290
2011	8,404,252
Density (per sq km) at 1 January 2011	100.2

* 32,383 sq miles.

† Figures include all foreign workers.

POPULATION BY AGE AND SEX

(at 1 January 2010)

	Males	Females	Total
0–14	637,877	606,993	1,244,870
15–64	2,829,150	2,825,349	5,654,499
65 and over	612,066	863,855	1,475,921
Total	4,079,093	4,296,197	8,375,290

PROVINCES

(official estimates at 1 January 2010)

	Area (sq km)	Population	Density (per sq km)	Capital (with population)*
Burgenland	3,965.5	283,965	71.6	Eisenstadt (12,562)
Kärnten (Carinthia)	9,536.0	559,315	58.7	Klagenfurt (92,807)
Niederösterreich (Lower Austria)	19,177.8	1,607,976	83.8	Sankt Pölten (51,518)
Oberösterreich (Upper Austria)	11,981.9	1,411,238	117.8	Linz (189,069)
Salzburg	7,154.2	529,861	74.1	Salzburg (149,201)
Steiermark (Styria)	16,391.9	1,208,372	73.7	Graz (250,653)
Tirol (Tyrol)	12,647.7	706,873	55.9	Innsbruck (118,362)
Vorarlberg	2,601.5	368,868	141.8	Bregenz (125,484)
Wien (Vienna)	414.7	1,698,822	4,096.5	—
Total	83,871.1	8,375,290	99.9	—

* At census of 15 May 2001.

PRINCIPAL TOWNS

(population at 1 January 2010)

Wien (Vienna, the capital)	1,698,822	Klagenfurt	93,949
Graz	257,328	Villach	59,089
Linz	189,311	Wels	58,574
Salzburg	147,571	Sankt Pölten	51,688
Innsbruck	119,249	Dornbirn	45,261

BIRTHS, MARRIAGES AND DEATHS

	Registered live births		Registered marriages		Registered deaths	
	Number	Rate (per 1,000)	Number	Rate (per 1,000)	Number	Rate (per 1,000)
2003	76,944	9.5	37,195	4.6	77,209	9.5
2004	78,968	9.7	38,528	4.7	74,292	9.1
2005	78,190	9.5	39,153	4.8	75,189	9.1
2006	77,914	9.4	36,923	4.5	74,295	9.0
2007	76,250	9.2	35,996	4.3	74,625	9.0
2008	77,752	9.3	35,223	4.2	75,083	9.0
2009	76,344	9.1	35,469	4.2	77,381	9.3
2010	78,742	9.4	37,545	4.5	77,199	9.2

Life expectancy (years at birth, WHO estimates): 80 (males 78; females 83) in 2009 (Source: WHO, *World Health Statistics*).

IMMIGRATION AND EMIGRATION

Immigrants from:	2007	2008	2009
Europe	79,559	82,733	79,143
Bosnia and Herzegovina	3,126	3,060	2,532
Croatia	2,146	1,880	1,795
Germany	20,414	21,906	19,954
Hungary	4,615	5,307	5,958
Poland	5,398	4,463	3,944
Romania	9,223	9,217	9,262
Russia	2,242	2,943	2,414
Serbia and Montenegro*	6,484	6,299	6,361
Slovakia	3,658	5,005	4,091
Turkey	5,412	5,198	5,061
Africa	3,575	3,598	3,827
Americas	4,336	4,392	4,247
Asia	10,080	10,034	11,095
China, People's Republic	1,229	1,235	1,408
Iran	n.a.	1,754	1,930
Oceania	427	487	444
Stateless, undeclared or unknown	8,928	8,830	9,029
Total	106,905	110,074	107,785

Emigrants to:	2007	2008	2009
Europe	50,041	52,787	61,039
Bosnia and Herzegovina	2,255	2,135	2,129
Croatia	1,973	1,800	1,914
Germany	10,305	11,946	13,626
Hungary	2,858	3,242	4,081
Poland	3,403	3,425	3,806
Romania	3,627	4,705	6,020
Serbia and Montenegro*	5,585	4,809	5,692
Slovakia	2,455	2,845	3,123
Turkey	3,375	3,269	3,379
Africa	2,862	2,803	3,154
Americas	4,181	4,511	4,803
Asia	5,675	5,796	6,909
Oceania	416	427	534
Stateless, undeclared or unknown	11,016	9,314	10,750
Total	74,191	75,638	87,189

* Although the federation of Serbia and Montenegro was dissolved in 2006, official reporting of Austrian immigration and emigration data with the successor states has continued to be aggregated.

Note: Totals for immigration include Austrian nationals returning from permanent residence abroad: 14,955 in 2007; 15,313 in 2008; 15,967 in 2009.

ECONOMICALLY ACTIVE POPULATION
('000 persons aged 15 years and over)

	2006	2007	2008
Agriculture, hunting and forestry	216.7	230.7	227.3
Fishing	0.2	0.6	0.9
Mining and quarrying	9.8	8.8	10.6
Manufacturing	741.5	730.5	694.8
Electricity, gas and water supply	31.3	30.1	25.6
Construction	323.7	329.1	332.0
Wholesale and retail trade; repair of motor vehicles, motorcycles and personal and household goods	610.8	645.6	663.8
Hotels and restaurants	242.6	258.6	251.1
Transport, storage and communications	241.8	243.2	244.9
Financial intermediation	133.1	135.1	142.5
Real estate, renting and business activities	350.7	363.3	398.4
Public administration and defence; compulsory social security	253.0	275.4	278.3
Education	222.2	211.6	229.5
Health and social work	347.8	347.3	364.9
Other community, social and personal service activities	186.9	202.9	206.6
Private households with employed persons	10.0	8.8	11.7
Extra-territorial organizations and bodies	6.1	6.3	7.2
Total employed	3,928.3	4,027.9	4,090.0
Unemployed	195.6	185.6	162.3
Total labour force	4,123.9	4,213.5	4,252.3
Males	2,244.6	2,298.2	2,303.9
Females	1,879.2	1,915.2	1,948.4

Source: ILO.

Health and Welfare

KEY INDICATORS

Total fertility rate (children per woman, 2009)	1.4
Under-5 mortality rate (per 1,000 live births, 2009)	5
HIV/AIDS (% of persons aged 15–49, 2009)	0.3
Physicians (per 1,000 head, 2006)	3.70
Hospital beds (per 1,000 head, 2006)	7.6
Health expenditure (2008): US $ per head (PPP)	4,150
Health expenditure (2008): % of GDP	10.5
Health expenditure (2008): public (% of total)	73.7
Total carbon dioxide emissions ('000 metric tons, 2007)	68,674.4
Carbon dioxide emissions per head (metric tons, 2007)	8.3
Human Development Index (2011): ranking	19
Human Development Index (2011): value	0.885

For sources and definitions, see explanatory note on p. vi.

Agriculture

PRINCIPAL CROPS
('000 metric tons)

	2008	2009	2010
Wheat	1,689.7	1,523.4	1,517.8
Barley	967.9	835.1	778.0
Maize	2,147.2	1,890.5	2,168.8
Rye	218.5	183.6	163.6
Oats	108.1	109.4	97.9
Triticale (wheat-rye hybrid)	250.7	254.5	230.5
Potatoes	756.9	722.1	671.7
Sugar beet	3,091.4	3,083.1	3,131.7
Peas, dry	45.4	34.7	32.8
Sunflower seed	79.7	71.0	66.5
Rapeseed	174.6	171.1	170.6
Cabbages and other brassicas	91.9	94.2	94.6*
Lettuce	57.5	55.2	47.6
Onions, dry	122.6	139.4	154.1
Carrots and turnips	80.8	83.6	85.6
Apples	551.4	485.6	332.0
Pears	84.7	168.7	48.4
Plums	63.4	71.7	33.2
Grapes	399.2	313.6	231.7

* Unofficial figure.

Aggregate production ('000 metric tons, may include official, semi-official or estimated data): Total cereals 5,748.1 in 2008, 5,144.2 in 2009, 5,330.0 in 2010; Total roots and tubers 756.9 in 2008, 722.1 in 2009, 671.7 in 2010; Total vegetables (incl. melons) 580.4 in 2008, 594.6 in 2009, 593.2 in 2010; Total fruits (excl. melons) 1,204.1 in 2008, 1,156.0 in 2009, 735 in 2010.

Source: FAO.

LIVESTOCK
('000 head at December)

	2008	2009	2010
Horses*	85.0	85.0	85.0
Cattle	1,997.2	2,026.3	2,013.3
Pigs	3,286.3	3,064.2	3,134.0
Sheep	351.3	333.2	358.0
Goats	60.5	62.5	71.8
Chickens*	14,000	14,500	15,500
Ducks*	58	60	63
Geese*	25	25	25
Turkeys*	750	750	750

* FAO estimates.

LIVESTOCK PRODUCTS
('000 metric tons)

	2008	2009	2010
Cattle meat	224.2	218.2	224.8
Sheep meat	7.3	6.5	7.2
Pig meat	532.9	540.3	542.1
Chicken meat	97.1	101.0	96.6
Cows' milk	3,196.0	3,229.8	3,258.0
Sheep's milk	8.0	9.2	9.5
Goats' milk	17.2	17.9	18.7
Hen eggs	96.2	92.0	93.0
Honey	5.3	5.6	6.1*

* FAO estimate.

Source: FAO.

Forestry

ROUNDWOOD REMOVALS
('000 cubic metres, excl. bark)

	2008	2009	2010
Sawlogs, veneer logs and logs for sleepers	13,162	9,105	10,167.4
Pitprops (mine timber), pulpwood, and other industrial wood	3,609	3,039	3,114.1
Fuel wood	5,024	4,584	4,549.5
Total	21,795	16,727	17,831.0

Source: FAO.

SAWNWOOD PRODUCTION
('000 cubic metres, incl. railway sleepers)

	2008	2009	2010
Coniferous (softwood)	10,595	8,295	9,445
Broadleaved (hardwood)	240	160	158
Total	10,835	8,455	9,603

Source: FAO.

Fishing

(metric tons, live weight)

	2007	2008	2009
Capture	350	350	350
Freshwater fishes	350	350	350
Aquaculture	2,539	2,087	2,141
Common carp	377	362	345
Rainbow trout	1,633	1,204	1,246
Brook trout	253	257	244
Total catch	2,889	2,437	2,491

Source: FAO.

Mining

('000 metric tons unless otherwise indicated)

	2007	2008	2009*
Crude petroleum ('000 barrels)	6,009	6,066	6,000
Iron ore:			
gross weight	2,153	2,033	1,500
Magnesite (crude)	812	837	750
Tungsten, concentrate (metric tons)†	435	434	350
Gypsum and anhydrite (crude)	1,006	1,023	900
Kaolin (crude)	57	50	40
Basalt	1,902	1,795	1,500
Dolomite	4,296	4,435	4,000
Limestone and marble	23,462	24,620	23,000
Quartz and quartzite	306	322	250
Natural gas (million cu metres)	1,835	1,544	1,500

* Estimates.

† Figures refer to metal content.

Source: US Geological Survey.

Industry

SELECTED PRODUCTS

('000 metric tons, unless otherwise indicated)

	2005	2006	2007
Wheat flour	326	338	342
Mechanical wood pulp	414	388	392
Chemical and semi-chemical wood pulp	1,277	1,290	1,333
Newsprint	416	424	418
Other printing and writing paper	2,509	2,620	2,591
Other paper and paperboard	2,025	2,169	2,190
Motor spirit (petrol)	1,798	1,615	1,702
Jet fuel	592	526	604
Distillate fuel oils	3,894	3,685	3,461
Residual fuel oils	1,009	915	880
Cement*	4,560	4,852	5,203
Crude steel*	7,031	7,129	7,578
Refined copper—unwrought:			
secondary*	72	73	81
Passenger motor cars (number)	230,505	248,059	199,969
Electric energy (million kWh)	65,681	63,445	63,357

* Data from the US Geological Survey.

Sources: FAO; UN Industrial Commodity Statistics Database; International Road Federation, *World Road Statistics*.

2008 ('000 metric tons): Mechanical wood pulp 380; Chemical and semi-chemical wood pulp 1,335; Newsprint 420; Other printing and writing paper 2,648; Other paper and paperboard 2,085; Cement 5,309; Crude steel 7,594; Refined copper—unwrought: secondary 107.0 (Source: FAO and US Geological Survey).

2009 ('000 metric tons): Mechanical wood pulp 303; Chemical and semi-chemical wood pulp 1,235; Newsprint 299; Other printing and writing paper 2,248; Other paper and paperboard 2,074; Cement 4,600 (estimate); Crude steel 5,662; Refined copper—unwrought: secondary 96.2 (Source: FAO).

Finance

CURRENCY AND EXCHANGE RATES

Monetary Units

100 cent = 1 euro (€).

Sterling and Dollar Equivalents (30 December 2011)

£1 sterling = 1.195euros;
US $1 = 0.773 euros;
€10 = £8.37 = $12.94.

Average Exchange Rate (euros per US $)

2009 0.7198
2010 0.7550
2011 0.7194

Note: The national currency was formerly the Schilling. From the introduction of the euro, with Austrian participation, on 1 January 1999, a fixed exchange rate of €1 = 13.7603 Schilling was in operation. Euro notes and coins were introduced on 1 January 2002. The euro and local currency circulated alongside each other until 28 February, after which the euro became the sole legal tender.

GOVERNMENT FINANCE

(general government transactions, non-cash basis, € '000 million)

Summary of Balances

	2007	2008	2009*
Revenue	130,346	136,572	133,858
Less Expense	132,114	138,448	143,779
Net operating balance	–1,768	–1,876	–9,921
Less Net acquisition of non-financial assets	–255	–345	–253
Net lending/borrowing	–1,512	–1,531	–9,668

Revenue

	2007	2008	2009*
Taxes	74,855	79,564	75,660
Taxes on income, profits and capital gains	34,795	37,714	33,295
Taxes on goods and services	31,985	33,199	33,508
Social contributions	42,959	44,899	45,644
Grants	615	297	333
Other revenue	11,917	11,811	12,221
Total	130,346	136,572	133,858

Expense/Outlays

Expense by economic type	2007	2008	2009*
Compensation of employees	24,783	25,970	27,174
Use of goods and services	11,592	12,814	12,790
Consumption of fixed capital	3,151	3,263	3,335
Interest	7,787	7,381	7,455
Subsidies	8,917	9,882	10,291
Grants	2,529	2,073	2,221
Social benefits	63,476	66,588	70,075
Other expense	9,879	10,477	10,438
Total	132,114	138,448	143,779

Outlays by function of government†	2007	2008	2009*
General public services	18,524	18,086	18,830
Defence	2,324	2,823	2,237
Public order and safety	3,884	4,138	4,303
Economic affairs	12,528	13,833	13,579
Environmental protection	1,254	1,247	1,466
Housing and community amenities	1,675	1,702	1,954
Health	20,598	21,900	22,522
Recreation, culture and religion	2,940	2,860	2,925
Education	14,063	15,088	15,898
Social protection	54,070	56,426	59,814
Total	131,859	138,103	143,527

* Preliminary figures.

† Including net acquisition of non-financial assets.

Source: IMF, *Government Finance Statistics Yearbook*.

2010 (€ million): Total Revenue 137,792; Total expenditure 150,328.

INTERNATIONAL RESERVES
(US $ million at 31 December)

	2008	2009	2010
Gold*	7,787	9,938	12,695
IMF special drawing rights	306	2,744	2,691
Reserve position in IMF	362	589	723
Foreign exchange	8,244	4,781	6,175
Total	16,699	18,052	22,284

* Eurosystem valuation.

Source: IMF, *International Financial Statistics*.

MONEY SUPPLY
(incl. shares, depository corporations, national residency criteria, € '000 million at 31 December)

	2008	2009	2010
Currency issued	21.35	21.81	22.76
Oesterreichische Nationalbank	7.79	4.90	–2.16
Demand deposits	88.36	104.87	105.78
Other deposits	182.72	171.56	171.49
Securities other than shares	265.33	259.43	252.06
Money market fund shares	3.48	2.61	2.34
Other items (net)	30.59	46.35	55.68
Total	591.8	606.62	610.11

Source: IMF, *International Financial Statistics*.

COST OF LIVING
(Consumer Price Index; base: 2005 = 100)

	2008	2009	2010
Food and non-alcoholic beverages	112.8	113.0	113.6
Alcoholic beverages, tobacco	107.6	108.9	111.1
Housing, water, energy	112.1	114.1	117.1
Communication	87.0	86.1	87.7
Household goods/furnishings and operations	104.5	106.9	108.2
Clothing and footwear	103.4	105.0	106.2
Recreation and culture	98.7	99.3	100.1
Health	104.6	106.8	108.5
Education	110.8	98.0	93.4
Restaurants and hotels	108.7	111.2	112.4
Transport	108.6	103.9	107.4
Other goods and services	107.1	110.7	113.8
All items	107.0	107.5	109.5

NATIONAL ACCOUNTS
(€ '000 million at current prices)

National Income and Product

	2008	2009	2010
Compensation of employees	138.47	139.67	143.00
Gross operating surplus and mixed income	114.59	105.26	112.30
Gross domestic product (GDP) at factor cost	253.06	244.93	255.30
Taxes, less subsidies, on production and imports	29.69	29.88	30.90
GDP in market prices	282.75	274.82	286.20
Net primary incomes from abroad	–0.56	–1.81	–1.52
Gross national income (GNI)	282.19	273.01	284.68
Less Consumption of fixed capital	43.39	44.49	46.01
Net national income	238.79	228.51	238.67
Net current transfers from abroad	–1.97	–2.37	–2.63
Net national disposable income	236.83	226.14	236.04

Expenditure on the Gross Domestic Product

	2008	2009	2010
Private final consumption expenditure	149.26	149.71	156.12
Government final consumption expenditure	52.76	54.51	55.44
Gross capital formation	64.46	57.79	61.94
Total domestic expenditure	266.48	262.01	273.50
Exports of goods and services	167.57	138.56	154.46
Less Imports of goods and services	151.30	125.51	142.13
Statistical discrepancy	0.00	–0.24	0.37
GDP in market prices	282.75	274.82	286.20

Gross Domestic Product by Economic Activity

	2008	2009	2010
Agriculture, hunting, forestry and fishing	4.05	3.41	3.80
Mining and quarrying and manufacturing	50.13	44.02	46.57
Electricity, gas and water	8.12	8.45	8.76
Construction	18.31	17.91	17.72
Wholesale and retail trade; repair of motor vehicles, motorcycles and personal and household goods	32.95	32.40	35.14
Restaurants and hotels	12.08	12.32	12.65
Transport, storage and communications	20.62	20.13	20.18
Finance and insurance	13.92	11.89	12.79
Real estate and business services*	45.79	45.78	47.77
Public administration and defence	14.47	15.08	15.33
Other services	35.76	36.91	37.95
Sub-total	256.19	248.28	258.65
Taxes, less subsidies, on products	26.55	26.53	27.55
GDP in market prices	282.75	274.82	286.20

* Including imputed rents of owner-occupied dwellings.

BALANCE OF PAYMENTS
(US $ million)

	2008	2009	2010
Exports of goods f.o.b.	179,201	135,289	147,464
Imports of goods f.o.b.	–179,794	–138,546	–151,767
Trade balance	–592	–3,258	–4,303
Exports of services	63,728	54,710	54,749
Imports of services	–42,894	–37,013	–36,794
Balance on goods and services	20,241	14,440	13,651
Other income received	44,478	35,002	35,525
Other income paid	–42,093	–36,150	–35,890
Balance on goods, services and income	22,627	13,292	13,286
Current transfers received	5,411	4,928	4,504
Current transfers paid	–7,911	–7,224	–7,235
Current balance	20,127	10,995	10,555
Capital account (net)	–70	328	506
Direct investment abroad	–29,536	–5,434	21,372
Direct investment from abroad	6,602	8,714	–26,605
Portfolio investment assets	11,996	–4,762	–8,805
Portfolio investment liabilities	25,298	–5,373	–1,992
Financial derivatives (net)	635	835	337
Other investment assets	–58,927	35,788	19,551
Other investment liabilities	21,141	–36,715	–7,795
Net errors and omissions	1,895	–5,426	–5,689
Overall balance	–840	–1,050	1,435

Source: IMF, *International Financial Statistics*.

External Trade

Note: Austria's customs territory excludes Mittelberg im Kleinen Walsertal (in Vorarlberg) and Jungholz (in Tyrol). The figures also exclude trade in silver specie and monetary gold.

SELECTED COMMODITIES
(distribution by SITC, € million)

Imports c.i.f.	2008	2009	2010
Food and live animals	6,717	6,329	6,679
Fruit and vegetables	1,698	1,531	1,740
Beverages and tobacco	642	714	866
Crude materials (inedible) except fuels	5,307	3,935	5,811
Cork and wood	1,061	1,054	1,218
Mineral fuels, lubricants, etc.	14,340	9,845	12,167
Crude petroleum and bituminous oils	9,069	5,804	7,716
Gas, natural and manufactured	2,998	2,254	2,923
Chemicals and related products	13,353	12,227	14,441
Medicinal and pharmaceutical products	4,252	4,904	5,476
Basic manufactures	20,144	14,892	18,060
Metal manufactures	3,468	2,085	3,238
Machinery and transport equipment	41,064	32,238	36,958
General industrial machinery and equipment	6,492	5,130	5,923
Road vehicles	11,677	9,120	10,761
Miscellaneous manufactured articles	16,145	14,974	16,499
Total (incl. others)	119,568	97,574	113,652

Exports f.o.b.	2008	2009	2010
Food and live animals	5,758	5,222	5,671
Dairy products and birds' eggs	963	868	933
Beverages and tobacco	1,708	1,516	1,614
Crude materials (inedible) except fuels	3,676	2,962	3,692
Cork and wood	1,599	1,250	1,492
Mineral fuels, lubricants, etc.	4,048	2,982	3,511
Crude petroleum and bituminous oils	1,688	1,091	1,395
Electricity	1,017	1,154	1,289
Chemicals and related products	12,904	12,116	14,167
Medicinal and pharmaceutical products	5,020	5,549	6,207
Basic manufactures	28,626	21,085	25,162
Iron and steel	8,088	4,941	6,083
Metal manufactures	6,214	4,569	5,443
Machinery and transport equipment	46,638	35,292	41,365
General industrial machinery and equipment	7,298	4,944	5,651
Electrical machinery, apparatus and appliances, etc.	7,996	6,244	7,967
Road vehicles	11,282	7,242	8,711
Miscellaneous manufactured articles	13,387	11,858	12,924
Total (incl. others)	117,525	93,739	109,373

PRINCIPAL TRADING PARTNERS
(€ million)*

Imports c.i.f.	2008	2009	2010
Belgium-Luxembourg	2,138	1,694	2,017
China, People's Republic	4,975	4,482	5,428
Czech Republic	4,237	3,382	4,186
Finland	648	459	444
France	3,712	2,973	3,234
Germany	48,490	39,827	44,851
Hungary	3,228	2,337	3,132
Italy	8,274	6,627	7,690
Japan	1,884	1,514	1,777
Netherlands	3,369	2,767	3,231
Poland	2,145	1,560	1,896
Russia	2,497	1,703	2,317
Slovakia	2,388	1,948	2,630
Spain	1,700	1,556	1,772
Sweden	1,476	1,082	1,247
Switzerland-Liechtenstein	5,021	5,620	5,941
United Kingdom	2,104	1,606	1,728
USA	3,405	2,562	3,261
Total (incl. others)	119,568	97,574	113,652

Exports f.o.b.	2008	2009	2010
Belgium-Luxembourg	1,849	1,512	1,632
China, People's Republic	1,875	2,017	2,807
Croatia	1,527	473	1,130
Czech Republic	4,402	3,382	4,145
France	4,423	2,973	4,557
Germany	35,010	39,827	34,530
Hungary	4,214	2,337	3,345
Italy	10,085	6,627	8,576
Japan	1,002	772	1,023
Netherlands	2,067	2,767	1,719
Poland	3,271	1,560	2,745
Russia	2,972	1,703	2,547
Slovakia	2,383	1,948	2,276
Slovenia	2,551	994	2,221
Spain	2,816	1,556	2,003
Sweden	1,308	1,082	1,191
Switzerland-Liechtenstein	4,468	5,620	5,199
United Kingdom	3,686	1,606	3,319
USA	5,202	4,035	4,958
Total (incl. others)	117,525	93,739	109,373

* Imports by country of production; exports by country of consumption.

Transport

RAILWAYS
(traffic, Federal Railways only)

	2008	2009	2010
Number of passengers carried ('000)	238,900	239,700	242,100
Passenger-km (millions)	10,837	10,653	10,737
Domestic freight gross ton-km (millions)	21,915	17,767	19,833
Freight tons carried ('000)	121,579	98,887	107,670

ROAD TRAFFIC
(motor vehicles in use at 31 December)

	2008	2009	2010
Passenger cars	4,284,919	4,359,944	4,441,027
Buses and coaches	9,368	9,599	9,648
Goods vehicles	362,990	370,907	379,965
Motorcycles	372,112	389,574	406,822
Mopeds and motor scooters	319,131	322,518	321,030

SHIPPING

Merchant Fleet
(registered at 31 December)

	2007	2008	2009
Number of vessels	4	4	2
Total displacement ('000 grt)	14.0	14.0	9.9

Source: IHS Fairplay, *World Fleet Statistics*.

International Freight Traffic on the Danube
('000 metric tons, excl. transit traffic)

	2008	2009	2010
Goods loaded	2,166.4	1,581.4	1,667.8
Goods unloaded	5,730.6	4,945.3	6,199.9

CIVIL AVIATION
(Austrian Airlines, '000)

	2000	2001	2002
Kilometres flown	70,411	66,316	129,649
Passenger ton-km	914,870	846,385	1,434,582
Cargo ton-km	284,533	252,406	396,021
Mail ton-km	11,635	12,539	28,099

2003 (traffic, millions): Kilometres flown 130; Passengers carried 6.9; Passenger-km 14,558; Total ton-km 1,983 (Source: UN, *Statistical Yearbook*).

2004 (traffic, millions): Kilometres flown 149; Passengers carried 7.6; Passenger-km 17,530; Total ton-km 2,366 (Source: UN, *Statistical Yearbook*).

2005 (traffic, millions): Kilometres flown 159; Passengers carried 8.0; Passenger-km 18,835; Total ton-km 2,542 (Source: UN, *Statistical Yearbook*).

2006 (traffic, millions): Kilometres flown 170; Passengers carried 8.8; Passenger-km 19,921; Total ton-km 2,696 (Source: UN, *Statistical Yearbook*).

2007 (traffic, millions): Kilometres flown 160; Passengers carried 9.1; Passenger-km 17,408; Total ton-km 2,291 (Source: UN, *Statistical Yearbook*).

2008 (traffic, millions): Kilometres flown 159; Passengers carried 9.1; Passenger-km 16,465; Total ton-km 2,155 (Source: UN, *Statistical Yearbook*).

2009 (traffic, millions): Kilometres flown 145; Passengers carried 8.5; Passenger-km 14,775; Total ton-km 1,893 (Source: UN, *Statistical Yearbook*).

Tourism

FOREIGN TOURIST ARRIVALS
(by country of origin, '000)*

	2008	2009	2010
Belgium	462.8	461.3	461.8
France (incl. Monaco)	473.2	478.7	499.9
Germany	10,709.3	10,622.8	10,706.2
Italy	1,033.3	1,056.5	1,067.7
Netherlands	1,650.1	1,655.0	1,617.7
Switzerland-Liechtenstein	960.4	994.6	1,053.6
United Kingdom	825.3	701.2	731.4
USA	483.6	441.8	505.4
Total (incl. others)	21,935.4	21,355.4	22,004.3

* Arrivals at accommodation establishments.

Tourism receipts (US $ million, excl. passenger transport): 21,587 in 2008; 19,404 in 2009; 18,663 in 2010 (provisional) (Source: World Tourism Organization).

Communications Media

	2008	2009	2010
Radio licences issued	3,337,961	3,395,000	3,440,000
Television licences issued	3,218,301	3,239,000	3,252,000
Telephones ('000 main lines in use)	3,285	3,253	3,245
Mobile cellular telephones ('000 subscribers)	10,816	11,434	12,241
Internet subscribers ('000)	2,047*	2,149*	n.a.
Broadband subscribers ('000)	1,729	1,846	2,002*
Daily newspapers:			
copies	31	31	n.a.
circulation ('000)	5,117	5,299	5,231
Weekly newspapers	207	n.a.	n.a.
Other periodicals	2,850	n.a.	n.a.

* Estimated figure.

Personal computers: 4,996,000 (606.8 per 1,000 persons) in 2005.

Source: partly International Telecommunication Union.

Education

(2008/09 unless otherwise indicated)

	Institutions	Staff	Students
Pre-primary*	7,950	43,696†	299,036
General primary and secondary	6,221	123,148	1,189,586
Compulsory vocational	160	5,090	140,373
Secondary technical and vocational	1,037	23,038	212,504
Teacher training:			
second level	38	1,498	12,668
third level‡	28	2,799	11,535
Universities §	21	13,944	223,562
Tertiary vocational‡§	205	3,942	28,426

* Including crèches.
† Including non-teaching staff.
‡ 2006/07 figures.
§ Excluding private institutions.

Pupil-teacher ratio (primary education, UNESCO estimate): 11.4 in 2008/09 (Source: UNESCO Institute for Statistics).

Directory

The Government

HEAD OF STATE

Federal President: Dr Heinz Fischer (sworn in 8 July 2004; re-elected 25 April 2010).

FEDERAL GOVERNMENT
(May 2012)

A coalition of the Sozialdemokratische Partei Österreichs (SPÖ—Social Democratic Party of Austria) and the Österreichische Volkspartei (ÖVP—Austrian People's Party).

Federal Chancellor: Werner Faymann (SPÖ).

Vice-Chancellor and Federal Minister for European and International Affairs: Dr Michael Spindelegger (ÖVP).

Federal Minister of Finance: Dr Maria Fekter (ÖVP).

Federal Minister of Health: Alois Stöger (SPÖ).

Federal Minister of Justice: Dr Beatrix Karl (ÖVP).

Federal Minister of the Interior: Johanna Mikl-Leitner (ÖVP).

Federal Minister for Agriculture, Forestry, Environment and Water Management: Nikolaus (Niki) Berlakovich (ÖVP).

Federal Minister of Defence and Sports: NORBERT DARABOS (SPÖ).

Federal Minister of Labour, Social Affairs and Consumer Protection: RUDOLF HUNDSTORFER (SPÖ).

Federal Minister for Education, Arts and Culture: Dr CLAUDIA SCHMIED (SPÖ).

Federal Minister for Transport, Innovation and Technology: DORIS BURES (SPÖ).

Federal Minister of Economy, Family and Youth: Dr REINHOLD MITTERLEHNER (ÖVP).

Federal Minister of Science and Research: KARLHEINZ TÖCHTERLE (ÖVP).

Federal Minister for Women and Public Administration: GABRIELE HEINISCH-HOSEK (SPÖ).

State Secretary in the Federal Chancellery: Dr JOSEF OSTERMAYER (SPÖ).

Secretary of State in the Federal Ministry of European and International Affairs: WOLFGANG WALDNER (ÖVP).

State Secretary in the Federal Ministry of Finance: ANDREAS SCHEIDER (SPÖ).

State Secretary in the Federal Ministry of the Interior: SEBASTIAN KURZ (ÖVP).

MINISTRIES

Office of the Federal President: Hofburg, Leopoldinischer Trakt, 1014 Vienna; tel. (1) 534-22; fax (1) 535-65-12; e-mail heinz.fischer@hofburg.at; internet www.hofburg.at.

Office of the Federal Chancellor: Ballhauspl. 2, 1014 Vienna; tel. (1) 531-15-0; fax (1) 535-03-38-0; e-mail post@bka.gv.at; internet www.bka.gv.at.

Federal Ministry of Agriculture, Forestry, Environment and Water Management: Stubenring 1, 1012 Vienna; tel. (1) 711-00-0; fax (1) 711-00-21-40; e-mail office@lebensministerium.at; internet www.lebensministerium.at.

Federal Ministry of Defence: Rossauer Lände 1, 1090 Vienna; tel. (1) 502-01-0; fax (1) 502-01-10-17-041; e-mail presse@bmlvs.gv.at; internet www.bmlv.gv.at.

Federal Ministry of Economy, Family and Youth: Stubenring 1, 1011 Vienna; tel. (1) 711-00-0; fax (1) 710-85-73; e-mail service@bmwfj.gv.at; internet www.bmwfj.gv.at.

Federal Ministry of Education, Arts and Culture: Minoritenpl. 5, 1014 Vienna; tel. (1) 531-20-0; fax (1) 531-20-30-99; e-mail ministerium@bmukk.gv.at; internet www.bmukk.gv.at.

Federal Ministry of European and International Affairs: Minoritenpl. 8, 1014 Vienna; tel. (5) 011-50-0; fax (5) 011-59-0; e-mail post@bmeia.gv.at; internet www.bmeia.gv.at.

Federal Ministry of Finance: Hintere Zollamtstr. 2B, 1030 Vienna; tel. (1) 514-33-0; fax (1) 514-33-50-70-87; e-mail buergerservice@bmf.gv.at; internet www.bmf.gv.at.

Federal Ministry of Health: Radetzkystr. 2, 1030 Vienna; tel. (1) 711-00-0; fax (1) 711-00-14-30-0; e-mail buergerservice@bmg.gv.at; internet www.bmg.gv.at.

Federal Ministry of the Interior: Herrengasse 7, Postfach 100, 1014 Vienna; tel. (1) 531-26-0; fax (1) 531-26-10-86-13; e-mail oeffentlichkeitsarbeit@bmi.gv.at; internet www.bmi.gv.at.

Federal Ministry of Justice: Museumstr. 7, 1070 Vienna; tel. (1) 521-52-0; fax (1) 521-52-27-30; internet www.bmj.gv.at.

Federal Ministry of Labour, Social Affairs and Consumer Protection: Stubenring 1, 1010 Vienna; tel. (1) 711-00-0; fax (1) 711-00-14-26-6; e-mail briefkasten@bmask.gv.at; internet www.bmask.gv.at.

Federal Ministry of Science and Research: Minoritenpl. 5, 1014 Vienna; tel. (1) 531-20-0; fax (1) 531-20-90-99; e-mail infoservice@bmwf.gv.at; internet www.bmwf.gv.at.

Federal Ministry of Transport, Innovation and Technology: Radetzkystr. 2, Postfach 3000, 1030 Vienna; tel. (1) 711-62-65-0; fax (1) 711-62-65-74-98; e-mail info@bmvit.gv.at; internet www.bmvit.gv.at.

Federal Ministry of Women and Public Administration: Bundeskanzleramt Österreich, Sektion Frauenangelegenheiten und Gleichstellung, Minoritenpl. 3, 1014 Vienna; tel. (1) 531-15-0; fax (1) 531-15-75-05; internet www.frauen.bka.gv.at.

President and Legislature

PRESIDENT

Presidential Election, 25 April 2010

Candidates	Votes	% of votes
Dr Heinz Fischer	2,508,373	79.33
Barbara Rosenkranz	481,923	15.24
Dr Rudolf Gehring	171,668	5.43
Total	3,161,964	100.00

PARLIAMENT

(Parlament)

Dr. Karl Renner-Ring 3, 1017 Vienna; tel. and fax (1) 401-10-0; e-mail services@parlament.gv.at; internet www.parliament.gv.at

National Council

(Nationalrat)

President of the National Council: BARBARA PRAMMER (SPÖ).

General Election, 28 September 2008

Party	Votes	% of votes	Seats
Sozialdemokratische Partei Österreichs (SPÖ)	1,430,202	29.26	57
Österreichische Volkspartei (ÖVP)	1,269,655	25.98	51
Freiheitliche Partei Österreichs (FPÖ)	857,028	17.54	34
Bündnis Zukunft Österreich (BZÖ)	522,933	10.70	21
Die Grünen	509,937	10.43	20
Liberales Forum (LiF)	102,249	2.09	—
Bürgerforum Österreich—Liste Fritz Dinkhauser	86,194	1.76	—
Others	109,106	2.23	—
Total	4,887,304	100.00	183

Federal Council

(Bundesrat)

(May 2012)

President of the Federal Council: GREGOR HAMMERL (ÖVP) (Jan.–June. 2012).

Provinces	ÖVP	SPÖ	FPÖ	Other	Total seats
Burgenland	1	2	—	—	3
Carinthia (Kärnten)	1	1	1	1	4
Lower Austria (Niederösterreich)	7	3	1	1	12
Upper Austria (Oberösterreich)	6	3	1	1	11
Salzburg	2	2	—	—	4
Styria (Steiermark)	4	4	1	—	9
Tyrol (Tirol)	3	1	—	1	5
Vorarlberg	2	—	1	—	3
Vienna (Wien)	1	6	3	1	11
Total	27	22	8	5	62

Governments of the Federal Provinces

BURGENLAND

Governor: HANS NIESSL (SPÖ).

President of the Provincial Assembly (Landtag): GERHARD STEIER (SPÖ).

Burgenländischer Landtag: Europapl. 1, 7000 Eisenstadt; tel. (57) 600-20-00; fax 600-20-50; e-mail post@bgld-landtag.at; internet www.bgld.gv.at/politik-verwaltung/landtag.

Election, 30 May 2010

Party	Seats
SPÖ	18
ÖVP	13
FPÖ	3
Die Grünen	1
Liste Burgenland	1
Total	36

CARINTHIA (KÄRNTEN)

Governor: GERHARD DÖRFLER (FPK).

President of the Provincial Assembly (Landtag): JOSEF LOBNIG (FPK).

Kärntner Landtag: Landhaus, 9020 Klagenfurt; tel. (463) 577-57-20-1; fax (463) 577-57-20-0; e-mail post.landtagsamt@ktn.gv.at; internet www.kaerntner-landtag.ktn.gv.at.

Election, 1 March 2009

Party	Seats
BZÖ*	18
SPÖ	11
ÖVP	7
Total	36

* The provincial branch of the BZÖ seceded from the federal party in January 2010 and was renamed Die Freiheitlichen in Kärnten (FPK).

LOWER AUSTRIA (NIEDERÖSTERREICH)

Governor: Dr ERWIN PRÖLL (ÖVP).

President of the Provincial Assembly (Landtag): HANS PENZ (ÖVP).

Landtag Niederösterreich: Landhauspl. 1, 3109 St. Pölten; tel. (2742) 900-51-24-31; fax (2742) 900-51-34-30; e-mail post.landtagsdirektion@noel.gv.at; internet www.landtag-noe.at.

Election, 9 March 2008

Party	Seats
ÖVP	31
SPÖ	15
FPÖ	6
Die Grünen	4
Total	56

SALZBURG

Governor: GABI BURGSTALLER (SPÖ).

President of the Provincial Assembly (Landtag): GUDRUN MOSLER-TÖRNSTRÖM (SPÖ).

Salzburger Landtag: Chiemseehof, 5010 Salzburg; tel. (662) 804-22-23-8; fax (662) 804-22-91-0; internet www.salzburg.gv.at/pol/landtag.

Election, 1 March 2009

Party	Seats
SPÖ	15
ÖVP	14
FPÖ	5
Die Grünen	2
Total	36

STYRIA (STEIERMARK)

Governor: FRANZ VOVES (SPÖ).

President of the Provincial Assembly (Landtag): MANFRED WEGSCHEIDER (SPÖ).

Landtag Steiermark: Herrengasse 16, 8010 Graz; tel. (316) 877-22-16; fax (316) 877-21-98; e-mail ltd@stmk.gv.at; internet www.landtag.steiermark.at.

Election, 26 September 2010

Party	Seats
SPÖ	23
ÖVP	22
FPÖ	6
Die Grünen	3
KPÖ	2
Total	56

TYROL (TIROL)

Governor: GÜNTHER PLATTER (ÖVP).

President of the Provincial Assembly (Landtag): Prof. Dr HERWIG VAN STAA (ÖVP).

Tiroler Landtag: Eduard-Wallnöfer-Pl. 3, 6020 Innsbruck; tel. (512) 508-30-12; fax (512) 508-30-05; e-mail landtag.direktion@tirol.gv.at; internet www.tirol.gv.at/landtag.

Election, 8 June 2008

Party	Seats
ÖVP	16
Liste Fritz Dinkhauser—Bürgerforum Tirol	7
SPÖ	5
FPÖ	4
Die Grünen	4
Total	36

UPPER AUSTRIA (OBERÖSTERREICH)

Governor: Dr JOSEF PÜHRINGER (ÖVP).

President of the Provincial Assembly (Landtag): FRIEDRICH BERNHOFER (ÖVP).

Oberösterreichischer Landtag: Klosterstr. 7, 4021 Linz; tel. (732) 772-01-11-71; fax (732) 772-01-17-13; e-mail ltdion.post@ooe.gv.at; internet www.ooe.gv.at.

Election, 27 September 2009

Party	Seats
ÖVP	28
SPÖ	14
FPÖ	9
Die Grünen	5
Total	56

VIENNA (WIEN)

Bürgermeister (Mayor) and Governor: Dr MICHAEL HÄUPL (SPÖ).

President of the Provincial Assembly (Landtag): Prof. HARRY KOPIETZ (SPÖ).

Wiener Landtag: Rathaus, 1082 Vienna; e-mail post-ltg@mdgb.wien.gv.at; internet www.wien.gv.at/politik/landtag.

Election, 10 October 2010

Party	Seats
SPÖ	49
FPÖ	27
ÖVP	13
Die Grünen	11
Total	100

VORARLBERG

Governor: MARKUS WALLNER (ÖVP).

President of the Provincial Assembly (Landtag): Dr BERNADETTE MENNEL (ÖVP).

Vorarlberger Landtag: Landhaus, 6901 Bregenz; tel. (5574) 511-30-00-5; fax (5574) 511-30-09-5; e-mail landtag@vorarlberg.at; internet www.vorarlberg.at/landtag.

Election, 20 September 2009

Party	Seats
ÖVP	20
FPÖ	9
Die Grünen	4
SPÖ	3
Total	36

Election Commission

Bundeswahlbehörde (Federal Election Board): Bundesministerium für Inneres, Abteilung III/6, Postfach 100, 1014 Vienna; tel. (1) 53126-2464; fax (1) 53126-2110; e-mail wahl@bmi.gv.at; internet www.bmi.gv.at/cms/bmi_wahlen/bundeswahlbehoe; comprises 17 *Beisitzer* (assessors); 15 of the assessors are nominated by the political orgs represented in the Nationalrat; the remaining 2 are members of the judiciary; Chair. JOHANNA MIKL-LEITNER (Minister for the Interior).

Political Organizations

Bündnis Zukunft Österreich (BZÖ) (Alliance for the Future of Austria): Volksgartenstr. 3/5, 1010 Vienna; tel. (1) 513-28-38; fax (1) 513-28-38-9; e-mail office@bzoe.at; internet www.bzoe.at; f. 2005 by split from Freiheitliche Partei Österreichs (FPÖ); proponent of social market economy, controlled immigration and protection of Austria's cultural identity; Leader and Parliamentary Spokesman JOSEF BUCHER.

Die Freiheitlichen in Kärnten (FPK) (Freedom Party in Carinthia): Karfreitstr. 4, 9020 Klagenfurt; tel. (463) 564-04-0; fax (463) 564–04-24; e-mail office@freiheitliche-ktn.at; internet freiheitliche-ktn.at; f. 2010 by Carinthian branch of the Bündnis Zukunft Österreich (BZÖ) after it disassociated from the federal party; co-operates with the Freiheitliche Partei Österreichs (FPÖ) at federal level; Chair. UWE SCHEUCH.

Freiheitliche Partei Österreichs (FPÖ/Die Freiheitlichen) (Freedom Party of Austria): Friedrich Schmidt-Pl. 4/3A, 1080 Vienna; tel. and fax (1) 512-35-35-0; e-mail bgst@fpoe.at; internet www.fpoe.at; f. 1955; partially succeeded the Verband der Unabhängigen (League of Independents, f. 1949); popularly known as Die Freiheitlichen; populist right-wing party advocating the participation of workers in management, stricter immigration controls and deregulation in the business sector; opposes Austria's membership of the EU; Chair. and Parliamentary Spokesperson HEINZ-CHRISTIAN STRACHE.

Die Grünen (Greens): Rooseveltpl. 4–5, 1090 Vienna; tel. (1) 236-39-98-0; fax (1) 526-91-10; e-mail bundesbuero@gruene.at; internet www.gruene.at; f. 1986; campaigns for environmental protection, peace and social justice; Chair. and Parliamentary Spokesperson Dr EVA GLAWISCHNIG-PIESCZEK.

Kommunistische Partei Österreichs (KPÖ) (Communist Party of Austria): Drechslergasse 42, 1140 Vienna; tel. (1) 503-65-80-0; fax (1) 503-65-80-49-9; e-mail bundesvorstand@kpoe.at; internet www.kpoe.at; f. 1918; strongest in the industrial centres and trade unions; advocates a policy of strict neutrality; mem. party of European Left; Chairs and Parliamentary Spokespersons MELINA KLAUS, Dr MIRKO MESSNER.

Liberales Forum (LiF) (Liberal Forum): Canovagasse 7/2, 1010 Vienna; tel. (676) 646-56-10; e-mail office@liberale.at; internet www.liberale.at; f. 1993; Leader and Parliamentary Spokesperson Dr ANGELIKA MLINAR.

Liste Fritz Dinkhauser—Bürgerforum Tirol (Fritz Dinkhauser List—Tyrol Residents' Forum): Maximilianstr. 2, 6020 Innsbruck; tel. (512) 561-16-60; fax (512) 561-16-688; e-mail office@liste-fritz.at; internet www.listefritz.at; f. 2008 to contest elections to the Tyrol provincial parliament; contested Sept. 2008 federal election as Bürgerforum Österreich—Liste Fritz Dinkhauser; campaigns for political and economic reform; Chair. FRITZ DINKHAUSER.

Österreichische Volkspartei (ÖVP) (Austrian People's Party): Lichtenfelsgasse 7, 1010 Vienna; tel. (1) 401-26-0; fax (1) 401-26-10-9; e-mail email@oevp.at; internet www.oevp.at; f. 1945; Christian Democratic party; advocates an ecologically orientated social market economy; Chair. MICHAEL SPINDELEGGER; Parliamentary Spokesman KARLHEINZ KOPF; Sec.-Gen. HANNES RAUCH.

Sozialdemokratische Partei Österreichs (SPÖ) (Social Democratic Party of Austria): Löwelstr. 18, 1014 Vienna; tel. (1) 534-27; fax (1) 535-96-83; e-mail direkt@spoe.at; internet www.spoe.at; f. as the Social Democratic Party in 1889, subsequently renamed the Socialist Party, reverted to its original name in 1991; advocates democratic socialism and Austria's permanent neutrality; Chair. WERNER FAYMANN; Parliamentary Spokesperson Dr JOSEF CAP; Secs LAURA RUDAS, Dr GÜNTHER KRÄUTER.

Diplomatic Representation

EMBASSIES IN AUSTRIA

Afghanistan: Lackierergasse 9, 1090 Vienna; tel. (1) 524-78-06; fax (1) 406-02-19; e-mail afg.emb.vie@chello.at; Ambassador ABDUL MOHAMMAD SHOOGUFAN.

Albania: Prinz-Eugen-Str. 18/1/5, 1040 Vienna; tel. (1) 328-86-56; fax (1) 328-86-58; e-mail embassy.vienna@mfa.gov.al; Ambassador Dr VILI MINAROLLI.

Algeria: Rudolfinergasse 18, 1190 Vienna; tel. (1) 369-88-53; fax (1) 369-88-56; e-mail office@algerische-botschaft.at; internet www.algerische-botschaft.at; Ambassador TAOUS FEROUKHI.

Andorra: Kärntner Ring 2A/13, 1010 Vienna; tel. (1) 961-09-09; fax (1) 961-09-09-50; e-mail office@ambaixada-andorra.at; Chargé d'affaires a.i. GEMMA CANÓ BERNE.

Angola: Seilerstätte 15/10, 1010 Vienna; tel. (1) 718-74-88; fax (1) 718-74-86; e-mail embangola.viena@embangola.at; internet www.embangola.at; Ambassador Dr FIDELINO LOY DE JESUS FIGUEIREDO.

Argentina: Goldschmiedgasse 2/1, 1010 Vienna; tel. (1) 533-84-63; fax (1) 533-87-97; e-mail embajada@embargviena.at; Ambassador EUGENIO MARIA CURIA.

Armenia: Hadikgasse 28, 1140 Vienna; tel. (1) 522-74-79; fax (1) 522-74-81; e-mail armenia@armembassy.at; Ambassador ARMAN KIRAKOSSIAN.

Australia: Mattiellistr. 2–4, 1040 Vienna; tel. (1) 506-74-0; fax (1) 504-11-78; e-mail austemb@aon.at; internet www.australian-embassy.at; Ambassador MICHAEL POTTS.

Azerbaijan: Hügelgasse 2, 1130 Vienna; tel. (1) 403-13-22; fax (1) 403-13-23; e-mail vienna@mission.mfa.gov.az; Ambassador GALIB M. ISRAFILOV.

Belarus: Hüttelbergstr. 6, 1140 Vienna; tel. (1) 419-96-30-11; fax (1) 416-96-30-30; e-mail austria@belembassy.org; internet austria.mfa.gov.by; Ambassador Dr VALERY VORONETSKY.

Belgium: Wohllebengasse 6, 1040 Vienna; tel. (1) 502-07-0; fax (1) 502-07-22; e-mail vienna@diplobel.fed.be; internet www.diplomatie.be/vienna; Ambassador FRANK RECKER.

Belize: Franz Josefs Kai 13/5/16, Postfach 982, 1011 Vienna; tel. (1) 533-76-63; fax (1) 533-81-14; e-mail belizeembassy@utanet.at; Ambassador ALEXANDER PILETSKY.

Bolivia: Waaggasse 10/4, 1040 Vienna; tel. (1) 587-46-75; fax (1) 586-68-80; e-mail embolaustria@of-viena.at; Chargé d'affaires a.i. Dr RICARDO JAVIER MARTÍNEZ COVARRUBIAS.

Bosnia and Herzegovina: Tivoligasse 54, 1120 Vienna; tel. (1) 811-85-55; fax (1) 811-85-69; e-mail bhbotschaft@bhbotschaft.at; internet www.bhbotschaft.at; Ambassador TANJA MILAŠINOVIĆ MARTINOVIĆ.

Brazil: Pestalozzigasse 4, 1010 Vienna; tel. (1) 512-06-31; fax (1) 513-83-74; e-mail mail@brasilemb.at; internet www.brasilemb.at; Ambassador JULIO CEZAR ZELNER GONÇALVES.

Bulgaria: Schwindgasse 8, 1040 Vienna; tel. (1) 505-31-13; fax (1) 505-14-23; e-mail embassy.vienna@mfa.bg; Ambassador RADI NAIDENOV.

Burkina Faso: Strohgasse 14C, 1030 Vienna; tel. (1) 503-82-64-0; fax (1) 503-82-64-20; e-mail s.r@abfvienne.at; internet www.abfvienne.at; Ambassador Dr SALIF DIALLO.

Canada: Laurenzerberg 2, 3rd Floor, 1010 Vienna; tel. (1) 531-38-30-00; fax (1) 531-38-33-21; e-mail vienn@international.gc.ca; internet www.canadainternational.gc.ca/austria-autriche; Ambassador JOHN BARRETT.

Chile: Lugeck 1/3/10, 1010 Vienna; tel. (1) 512-92-08; fax (1) 512-92-08-33; e-mail echileat1@chello.at; internet www.chileabroad.gov.cl/austria; Ambassador ALFREDO LABBÉ VILLA.

China, People's Republic: Metternichgasse 4, 1030 Vienna; tel. (1) 714-31-49; fax (1) 713-68-16; e-mail chinaemb_at@mfa.gov.cn; internet www.chinaembassy.at; Ambassador SHI MINGDE.

Colombia: Stadiongasse 6–8/15, 1010 Vienna; tel. (1) 405-42-49; fax (1) 408-83-03; e-mail embcolviena@aon.at; internet www.embcol.or.at; Ambassador FREDDY PADILLA DE LEÓN.

Costa Rica: Wagramerstr. 23/1/1 Top 2 and 3, 1220 Vienna; tel. (1) 263-38-24; fax (1) 263-38-24-5; e-mail embajadaaustria_costa.rica@chello.at; Ambassador ANA TERESA DENGO BENAVIDES.

Côte d'Ivoire: Neulinggasse 26/6/20, 1030 Vienna; tel. (1) 581-00-76; fax (1) 581-00-76-31; Chargé d'affaires a.i. MARC AUBIN YAO ZADJEHI BANNY.

Croatia: Heuberggasse 10, 1170 Vienna; tel. (1) 485-95-24; fax (1) 480-29-42; e-mail croemb.bec@mvep.hr; internet at.mfa.hr; Ambassador GORDAN BAKOTA.

Cuba: Kaiserstr. 84/1/1, 1070 Vienna; tel. (1) 877-81-98; fax (1) 877-81-98-20; e-mail secembajador@ecuaustria.at; internet www.cubadiplomatica.cu/austria; Ambassador NJUAN CARLOS MARSAN AGUILERA.

Cyprus: Parkring 20, 1010 Vienna; tel. (1) 513-06-30; fax (1) 513-06-32; e-mail office@cyprusembassy.at; Ambassador COSTAS A. PAPADEMAS.

Czech Republic: Penzingerstr. 11-13, 1140 Vienna; tel. (1) 899-58-111; fax (1) 894-12-00; e-mail vienna@embassy.mzv.cz; internet www.mzv.cz/vienna; Ambassador Dr JAN KOUKAL.

Denmark: Führichgasse 6, Postfach 19, 1015 Vienna; tel. (1) 512-79-04; fax (1) 513-81-20; e-mail vieamb@um.dk; internet www.ambwien.um.dk; Ambassador TORBEN BRYLLE.

Dominican Republic: Prinz-Eugen-Str. 18, 1040 Vienna; tel. (1) 505-85-55; fax (1) 505-85-55-20; e-mail mprdoiv@yahoo.com; Ambassador RAMÓN ANDRÉS QUIÑONES RODRÍGUEZ.

Ecuador: Goldschmiedgasse 10/2/205, 1010 Vienna; tel. (1) 535-32-08; fax (1) 535-08-97; e-mail mecaustria@chello.at; Ambassador JUAN DIEGO STACEY MORENO.

Egypt: Hohe Warte 50–54, 1190 Vienna; tel. (1) 370-81-04; fax (1) 370-81-04-27; e-mail egyptembassyvienna@egyptembassyvienna.at; internet www.egyptembassyvienna.at; Ambassador KHALED ABD AL-RAHMAN ABD AL-LATIF SHAMAA.

El Salvador: Prinz-Eugen-Str. 72/2/1, 1040 Vienna; tel. (1) 505-38-74; fax (1) 505-38-76; e-mail elsalvador@embasal.at; Ambassador MARIO ANTONIO RIVERA MORA.

Estonia: Wohllebengasse 9/13, 1040 Vienna; tel. (1) 503-77-61; fax (1) 503-77-61-20; e-mail embassy@estwien.at; internet www.estemb.at; Ambassador EVE-KÜLLI KALA.

Ethiopia: Wagramerstr. 14/1/2, 1220 Vienna; tel. (1) 710-21-68; fax (1) 710-21-71; e-mail office@ethiopianembassy.at; Ambassador MINELIK ALEMU GETAHUN.

Finland: Gonzagagasse 16, 1010 Vienna; tel. (1) 531-59-0; fax (1) 535-57-03; e-mail sanomat.wie@formin.fi; internet www.finnland.at; Ambassador MARJATTA RASI.

France: Technikerstr. 2, 1040 Vienna; tel. (1) 502-75-0; fax (1) 502-75-16-8; e-mail contact@ambafrance-at.org; internet www.ambafrance-at.org; Ambassador STÉPHANE GOMPERTZ.

Georgia: Doblhoffgasse 5/5, 1010 Vienna; tel. (1) 403-98-48; fax (1) 403-98-48-20; e-mail vienna@geomission.at; internet www.austria.mfa.gov.ge; Ambassador PAATA GAPRINDASHVILI.

Germany: Metternichgasse 3, 1030 Vienna; tel. (1) 711-54-0; fax (1) 713-83-66; e-mail info@wien.diplo.de; internet www.wien.diplo.de; Ambassador HANS HENNING BLOMEYER-BARTENSTEIN.

Greece: Argentinierstr. 14, 1040 Vienna; tel. (1) 506-15; fax (1) 505-62-17; e-mail gremb@griechischebotschaft.at; internet www.griechische-botschaft.at; Ambassador THEMISTOKLIS DIMIDIS.

Guatemala: Landstr. Hauptstr. 21/Top 9, 1030 Vienna; tel. (1) 714-35-70; fax (1) 714-35-70-15; e-mail embajada@embaguate.co.at; Ambassador CARLA MARÍA RODRÍGUEZ MANCIA.

Holy See: Theresianumgasse 31, 1040 Vienna; tel. (1) 505-13-27; fax (1) 505-61-40; e-mail nuntius@nuntiatur.at; internet www.nuntiatur.at; Apostolic Nuncio Most Rev. PETER STEPHAN ZURBRIGGEN (Titular Archbishop of Glastonia).

Hungary: Bankgasse 4–6, 1010 Vienna; tel. (1) 537-80-30-0; fax (1) 535-99-40; e-mail kom@kum.hu; internet www.mfa.gov.hu/emb/vienna; Ambassador VINCE SZALAY-BOBROVNICZKY.

Iceland: Naglergasse 2/3/8, 1010 Vienna; tel. (1) 533-27-71; fax (1) 533-27-74; e-mail emb.vienna@mfa.is; internet www.iceland.org/at; Ambassador STEFÁN SKJALDARSON.

India: Kärntner Ring 2, 2nd Floor, 1010 Vienna; tel. (1) 505-86-66; fax (1) 505-92-19; e-mail indemb@eoivien.vienna.at; internet www.indianembassy.at; Ambassador DINKAR KHULLAR.

Indonesia: Gustav-Tschermak-Gasse 5–7, 1180 Vienna; tel. (1) 476-23-0; fax (1) 479-05-57; e-mail unitkom@kbriwina.at; internet www.kbriwina.at; Ambassador I GUSTI AGUNG WESAKA PUJA.

Iran: Jaurèsgasse 9, 1030 Vienna; tel. (1) 712-26-57; fax (1) 713-57-33; e-mail public@iranembassy-wien.at; internet www.iranembassy-wien.at; Ambassador EBRAHIM SHEIBANY.

Iraq: Laurenzerbergstraße 2, 1A, Postfach 599, 1010 Vienna; tel. (1) 713-81-95; fax (1) 713-67-20; e-mail office@iraqembassy.at; Chargé d'affaires a.i. SUROOD R. NAJIB NAJIB.

Ireland: Rotenturmstr. 16–18, 5th Floor, 1010 Vienna; tel. (1) 715-42-46; fax (1) 713-60-04; e-mail vienna@dfa.ie; internet www.embassyofireland.at; Ambassador JAMES BRENNAN.

Israel: Anton-Frank-Gasse 20, 1180 Vienna; tel. (1) 476-46-0; fax (1) 476-46-55-5; e-mail ambassador-assist@vienna.mfa.gov.il; internet vienna.mfa.gov.il; Ambassador AVIV AHARON SHIR-ON.

Italy: Rennweg 27, 1030 Vienna; tel. (1) 712-51-21; fax (1) 713-97-19; e-mail ambasciata.vienna@esteri.it; internet www.ambvienna.esteri.it; Ambassador EUGENIO D'AURIA.

Japan: Hessgasse 6, 1010 Vienna; tel. (1) 531-92-0; fax (1) 532-05-90; e-mail info@embjp.at; internet www.at.emb-japan.go.jp; Ambassador SHIGEO IWATANI.

Jordan: Rennweg 17/4, 1030 Vienna; tel. (1) 405-10-25; fax (1) 405-10-31; e-mail info@jordanembassy.at; internet www.jordanembassy.at; Ambassador MAKRAM QUEISI.

Kazakhstan: Felix-Mottl-Str. 23, 1190 Vienna; tel. (1) 367-66-57-11; fax (1) 367-66-57-20; e-mail embassy@kazakhstan.at; internet www.kazakhstan.at; Ambassador KAIRAT ABDRAKHMANOV.

Kenya: Neulinggasse 29/8, 1030 Vienna; tel. (1) 712-39-19; fax (1) 712-39-22; e-mail kenyarep-vienna@aon.at; Ambassador UKUR KANACHO YATANI.

Korea, Democratic People's Republic: Beckmanngasse 10–12, 1140 Vienna; tel. (1) 894-23-13; fax (1) 894-31-74; e-mail d.v.r.korea.botschaft@chello.at; Ambassador KIM GWANG SOP.

Korea, Republic: Gregor-Mendel-Str. 25, 1180 Vienna; tel. (1) 478-19-91; fax (1) 478-10-13; e-mail mail@koreaemb.at; internet aut.mofat.go.kr; Ambassador CHO HYUN.

Kosovo: Goldeggasse 2/13, 1040 Vienna; tel. (664) 415-17-65; e-mail embassy.austria@ks-gov.net; Ambassador SABRI KIQMARI.

Kuwait: Strassergasse 32, 1190 Vienna; tel. (1) 405-56-46; fax (1) 405-56-46-13; e-mail kuwait.embassy.vienna@speed.at; Ambassador MUHAMMAD SAAD OUDAH AL-SALLAL.

Kyrgyzstan: Invalidenstr. 3/8, 1030 Vienna; tel. (1) 535-03-79; fax (1) 535-03-79-13; e-mail kyremb@inode.at; internet www.kyremb.at; Ambassador LYDIA IMANALIEVA.

Latvia: Stefan-Esders-Pl. 4, 1190 Vienna; tel. (1) 403-31-12; fax (1) 403-31-12-27; e-mail embassy.austria@mfa.gov.lv; Ambassador INDULIS BĒRZIŅŠ.

Lebanon: Oppolzergasse 6/3, 1010 Vienna; tel. (1) 533-88-21; fax (1) 533-49-84; e-mail embassy.lebanon@inode.at; Ambassador ISHAYA AL-KHOURY.

Liberia: Kärntner Ring 5–7, 1010 Vienna; tel. (1) 205-11-60-10-31; Chargé d'affaires a.i. ANDREW W. KRONYANH.

Libya: Blaasstr. 33, 1190 Vienna; tel. (1) 367-76-39; fax (1) 367-76-01; e-mail office@libyanembassyvienna.at; Sec. of the People's Bureau AHMED M. A. MENESI.

Liechtenstein: Löwelstr. 8/7, 1010 Vienna; tel. (1) 535-92-11; fax (1) 535-92-11-4; e-mail info@vie.llv.li; internet www.liechtenstein.li/fl-aussenstelle-wien; Ambassador Princess MARIA-PIA KOTHBAUER of Liechtenstein.

Lithuania: Löwengasse 47/4, 1030 Vienna; tel. (1) 718-54-67; fax (1) 718-54-69; e-mail amb.at@urm.lt; internet at.mfa.lt; Chargé d'affaires a.i. MINDAUGAS RUKSTELE.

Luxembourg: Sternwartestr. 81, 1180 Vienna; tel. (1) 478-21-42; fax (1) 478-21-44; e-mail vienne.amb@mae.etat.lu; internet vienne.mae.lu/ge; Ambassador HUBERT WURTH.

Macedonia, former Yugoslav republic: Kinderspitalgasse 5, 1090 Vienna; tel. (1) 524-87-56; fax (1) 524-87-53; e-mail botschaft@makedonien.co.at; Ambassador Prof. Dr GJORGJI FILIPOV.

Malaysia: Floridsdorfer Hauptstr. 1–7, Florido Tower, 24th Floor, 1210 Vienna; tel. (1) 505-10-42-0; fax (1) 505-79-42; e-mail embassy@embassymalaysia.at; Ambassador MUHAMMAD SHAHRUL IKRAM BIN YAAKOB.

Malta: Opernring 5/1, 1010 Vienna; tel. (1) 586-50-10; fax (1) 586-50-10-9; e-mail maltaembassy.vienna@gov.mt; Ambassador COLIN SCICLUNA.

Mexico: Operngasse 21/10, 1040 Vienna; tel. (1) 310-73-83; fax (1) 310-73-87; e-mail embamex@embamex.or.at; internet www.sre.gob.mx/austria; Ambassador ALEJANDRO DÍAZ Y PÉREZ DUARTE.

Moldova: Löwengasse 47/10, 1030 Vienna; tel. (1) 961-10-30; fax (1) 961-10-30-34; e-mail viena@mfo.md; Ambassador VALERIU CHIVERI.

Mongolia: Fasangartengasse 45, 1130 Vienna; tel. (1) 535-28-07-12; fax (1) 535-28-07-20; e-mail office@embassymon.at; internet www.embassymon.at; Ambassador Dr JARGALSAIKHAN ENKHSAIKHAN.

Montenegro: Nibelungengasse 13/II, 1010 Vienna; tel. (1) 715-31-02; fax (1) 715-31-02-20; e-mail diplomat-mn@me-austria.eu; Ambassador DRAGANA RADULOVIĆ.

Morocco: Opernring 3–5, 1010 Vienna; tel. (1) 586-66-50; fax (1) 586-76-67; e-mail emb-pmissionvienna@morocco.at; Ambassador ALI EL MHAMDI.

Namibia: Zuckerkandlgasse 2, 1190 Vienna; tel. (1) 402-93-71; fax (1) 402-93-70; e-mail nam.emb.vienna@speed.at; internet www.embnamibia.at; Ambassador RAPHAEL DINYANDO.

Netherlands: Opernring 5, 7th Floor, 1010 Vienna; tel. (1) 589-39; fax (1) 589-39-26-5; e-mail wen-public@minbuza.nl; internet www.mfa.nl/wen; Ambassador ALPHONS CLEMENS MARIA HAMER.

New Zealand: Mattiellistr. 2–4/3, 1040 Vienna; tel. (1) 505-30-21; fax (1) 505-30-20; e-mail nzpm@aon.at; internet www.nzembassy.com/austria; Ambassador PHILIP GRIFFITHS.

Nicaragua: Ebendorferstr. 10/3/12, 1010 Vienna; tel. (1) 403-18-38; fax (1) 403-27-52; e-mail embanic-viena@aon.at; Chargé d'affaires a.i. ISOLDA ALICIA FRIXIONE MIRANDA.

Nigeria: Rennweg 25, 1030 Vienna; tel. (1) 712-66-85; fax (1) 714-14-02; e-mail info@nigeriaembassyvienna.com; internet www.nigeriaembassyvienna.com; Ambassador MARIA O. LAOSE.

Norway: Reisnerstr. 55–57, 1030 Vienna; tel. (1) 715-66-92; fax (1) 712-65-52; e-mail emb.vienna@mfa.no; internet www.norwegen.or.at; Ambassador JAN PETERSEN.

Oman: Währingerstr. 2–4/24–25, 1090 Vienna; tel. (1) 310-86-43; fax (1) 310-72-68; e-mail embassy.oman@chello.at; Ambassador Dr BADR BIN MUHAMMAD ZAHIR AL-HINAI.

Pakistan: Hofzeile 13, 1190 Vienna; tel. (1) 368-73-81; fax (1) 368-73-76; e-mail parepvienna@gmail.com; internet www.mofa.gov.pk/austria; Ambassador KHURSHID ANWAR.

Panama: Elisabethstr. 4/5/4/10, 1010 Vienna; tel. (1) 587-23-47; fax (1) 586-30-80; e-mail mail@empanvienna.co.at; Ambassador RICARDO VALLARINO PEREZ.

Paraguay: Prinz-Eugen-Str. 18/1/2/7, 1040 Vienna; tel. (1) 505-46-74; fax (1) 941-98-98; e-mail embaparviena@chello.at; Ambassador Dr HORACIO NOGUÉS ZUBIZARRETA.

Peru: Mahlerstrasse 7/22, 2nd Floor, 1010, Vienna; tel. (1) 713-43-77; fax (1) 712-77-04; Ambassador ANTONIO JAVIER ALEJANDRO GARCÍA REVILLA.

Philippines: Laurenzerberg 2, 1010 Vienna; tel. (1) 533-24-01; fax (1) 533-24-01-24; e-mail office@philippine-embassy.at; internet www.philippine-embassy.at; Ambassador LOURDES O. YPARRAGUIRRE.

Poland: Hietzinger Hauptstr. 42C, 1130 Vienna; tel. (1) 870-15-10-0; fax (1) 870-15-22-2; e-mail wieden.amb.sekretariat@msz.gov.pl; internet www.wien.polemb.net; Ambassador JERZY MARGAŃSKI.

Portugal: Opernring 3, 1010 Vienna; tel. (1) 586-75-36-0; fax (1) 586-75-36-99; e-mail portugal@portembassy.at; Ambassador ANA MARIA MARQUES MARTINHO.

Romania: Prinz-Eugen-Str. 60, 1040 Vienna; tel. (1) 505-32-27; fax (1) 504-14-62; e-mail ambromvienna@ambrom.at; internet viena.mae.ro; Ambassador SILVIA DAVIDOIU.

Russia: Reisnerstr. 45–47, 1030 Vienna; tel. (1) 712-12-29; fax (1) 712-33-88; e-mail info@rusemb.at; internet www.austria.mid.ru; Ambassador SERGEI YU. NECHAYEV.

San Marino: Prinz-Eugen-Str. 16/1/5A, 1040 Vienna; tel. (1) 941-59-69; fax (1) 941-59-75; e-mail emolaroni@gmail.com; Ambassador Dr ELENA MOLARONI BERGUIDO.

Saudi Arabia: Formanekgasse 38, 1190 Vienna; tel. (1) 367-25-31; fax (1) 367-25-40; e-mail emb.saudiarabia.vienna@aon.at; Ambassador Prince MANSOUR BIN KHALID AL SA'UD.

Serbia: Rennweg 3, 1030 Vienna; tel. (1) 713-25-95; fax (1) 713-25-97; e-mail ambasada@amb.srbije.net; internet www.vienna.mfa.gov.rs; Ambassador MILOVAN BOŽINOVIĆ.

Slovakia: Armbrustergasse 24, 1190 Vienna; tel. (1) 318-90-55-20-0; fax (1) 318-90-55-20-8; e-mail slovakembassy@vienna.mfa.sk; internet www.vienna.mfa.sk; Ambassador Dr JURAJ MACHÁČ.

Slovenia: Kolingasse 12, 1090 Vienna; tel. (1) 319-11-60; fax (1) 586-12-65; e-mail vdu@gov.si; internet www.vienna.embassy.si; Ambassador ALEKSANDER GERŽINA.

South Africa: Sandgasse 33, 1190 Vienna; tel. (1) 320-64-93; fax (1) 320-64-93-51; e-mail vienna.ambassador@foreign.gov.za; internet www.saembvie.at; Ambassador XOLISA MFUNDISO MABHONGO.

Spain: Argentinierstr. 34, 1040 Vienna; tel. (1) 505-57-88; fax (1) 505-57-88-125; e-mail emb.viena@maec.es; internet www.maec.es/embajadas/viena/es; Ambassador YAGO PICO DE COAÑA Y DE VALICOURT.

Sri Lanka: Weyringergasse 33–35, 4th Floor, 1040 Vienna; tel. (1) 503-79-88; fax (1) 503-79-93; e-mail embassy@srilankaembassy.at; internet www.srilankaembassy.at; Ambassador A. L. ABDUL AZEEZ.

Sudan: Reisnerstr. 29/5, 1030 Vienna; tel. (1) 710-23-43; fax (1) 710-23-46; e-mail sudanivienna@prioritytelecom.biz; Ambassador MAHMOUD HASSAN AL-AMIN.

Sweden: Obere Donaustr. 49–51, Postfach 18, 1020 Vienna; tel. (1) 217-53-0; fax (1) 217-53-370; e-mail ambassaden.wien@foreign.ministry.se; internet www.swedenabroad.com/wien; Ambassador NILS DAAG.

Switzerland: Prinz-Eugen-Str. 7, 1030 Vienna; tel. (1) 795-05; fax (1) 795-05-21; e-mail vie.vertretung@eda.admin.ch; internet www.eda.admin.ch/wien; Ambassador Dr URS BREITER.

Syria: Daffingerstr. 4, 1030 Vienna; tel. (1) 533-46-33; fax (1) 533-46-32; e-mail vienna_embassy@syrianembassy.jet2web.at; Ambassador BASSAM SABBAGH.

Tajikistan: Universitätsstr. 8/1A, 1090 Vienna; tel. and fax (1) 409-82-66; fax (1) 409-82-66-14; e-mail tajikembassy@chello.at; internet www.tajikembassy.org; Ambassador NURIDDIN T. SHAMSOV.

Thailand: Cottagegasse 48, 1180 Vienna; tel. (1) 478-33-35; fax (1) 478-29-07; e-mail embassy@thaivienna.at; internet www.thaiembassy.at; Ambassador NONGNUTH PHETCHARATANA.

Tunisia: Sieveringerstr. 187, 1190 Vienna; tel. (1) 581-52-81; fax (1) 581-55-92; e-mail at.vienne@aon.at; Ambassador MUHAMMAD SAMIR KOUBAA.

Turkey: Prinz-Eugen-Str. 40, 1040 Vienna; tel. (1) 505-73-38-0; fax (1) 505-36-60; e-mail tuerkische-botschaft@chello.at; Ambassador AYSE SEZGIN.

Turkmenistan: Argentinierstr. 22/II/EG, 1040 Vienna; tel. (1) 503-64-70; fax (1) 503-64-73; e-mail info@botschaft-turkmenistan.at; internet www.botschaft-turkmenistan.at; Ambassador SILAPBERDI NURBERDIEV.

Ukraine: Naaffgasse 23, 1180 Vienna; tel. (1) 479-71-72-11; fax (1) 479-71-72-47; e-mail info@ukremb.at; internet www.mfa.gov.ua/austria; Ambassador ANDRIY BEREZNYI.

United Arab Emirates: Peter-Jordan-Str. 66, 1190 Vienna; tel. (1) 368-14-55; fax (1) 368-44-85; e-mail emirates@aon.at; Ambassador MUHAMMAD HAMAD ABDULLAH OMRAN AL-SHAMSI.

United Kingdom: Jaurèsgasse 12, 1030 Vienna; tel. (1) 716-13-0; fax (1) 716-13-29-99; e-mail press@britishembassy.at; internet ukinaustria.fco.gov.uk; Ambassador SIMON SMITH.

USA: Boltzmanngasse 16, 1090 Vienna; tel. (1) 313-39-0; fax (1) 310-06-82; e-mail embassy@usembassy.at; internet austria.usembassy.gov; Ambassador WILLIAM C. EACHO, III.

Uruguay: Palais Esterhazy, Wallnerstr. 4/3/17, 1010 Vienna; tel. (1) 535-66-36; fax (1) 535-66-18; e-mail uruvien@embuy.at; Ambassador CARLOS ALEJANDRO BARROS OREIRO.

Uzbekistan: Poetzleinsdorferstr. 49, 1180 Vienna; tel. (1) 315-39-94; fax (1) 315-39-93; e-mail info@usbekistan.at; internet www.usbekistan.at; Chargé d'affaires a.i. RAVSHENBAK DUSCHANOV.

Venezuela: Prinz-Eugen-Str. 72/1.OG/Steige 1/Top1.1, 1040 Vienna; tel. (1) 712-26-38; fax (1) 715-32-19; e-mail embajada@austria.gob.ve; internet www.austria.gob.ve; Ambassador ALÍ DE JESÚS UZCATEGUI DUQUE.

Viet Nam: Félix-Mottl-Str. 20, 1190 Vienna; tel. (1) 368-07-55; fax (1) 368-07-54; e-mail office@vietnamembassy.at; internet www.vietnamembassy.at; Ambassador THIEP NGUYEN.

Yemen: Reisnerstr. 18–20, 1st Floor, Top 3–4, 1030 Vienna; tel. (1) 503-29-30; fax (1) 505-31-59; e-mail yemenembassy.vienna@aon.at; Ambassador Dr ABD AL-HAKIM ABD AL-RAHMAN YAHYA AL-ERYANI.

Zimbabwe: Strozzigasse 10/15, 1080 Vienna; tel. (1) 407-92-36; fax (1) 407-92-38; e-mail z.vien@chello.at; internet www.zimbabweembassyvienna.at; Ambassador GRACE TSITSI MUTANDIRO.

Judicial System

The Austrian legal system is based on the principle of a division between legislative, administrative and judicial power. There are three supreme courts (Verfassungsgerichtshof, Verwaltungsgerichtshof and Oberster Gerichtshof). The judicial courts are organized into 141 local courts (Bezirksgerichte), 20 provincial and district courts (Landesgerichte), and four higher provincial courts (Oberlandesgerichte) in Vienna, Graz, Innsbruck and Linz.

SUPREME ADMINISTRATIVE COURTS

Verfassungsgerichtshof (Constitutional Court): Judenpl. 11, 1010 Vienna; tel. (1) 531-22-0; fax (1) 531-22-49-9; e-mail vfgh@vfgh.gv.at; internet www.vfgh.gv.at; f. 1919; deals with matters affecting the Constitution, examines the constitutionality of legislation and administration; Pres. Dr GERHART HOLZINGER; Vice-Pres. Dr BRIGITTE BIERLEIN.

Justices: Dr HERBERT HALLER, Dr LISBETH LASS, Dr WILLIBALD LIEHR, Dr HANS GEORG RUPPE, Dr PETER OBERNDORFER, Dr RUDOLF MÜLLER, Dr HELMUT HÖRTENHUBER, Dr ELEONORE BERCHTOLD-OSTERMANN, Dr CLAUDIA KAHR, Dr JOHANNES SCHNIZER, Dr SIEGLINDE GAHLEITNER, Dr CHRISTOPH GRABENWARTER.

Verwaltungsgerichtshof (Administrative Court): Judenpl. 11, Postfach 73, 1014 Vienna; tel. (1) 531-11-0; fax (1) 531-11-50-8; internet www.vwgh.gv.at; deals with matters affecting the legality of administration; Pres. Prof. Dr CLEMENS JABLONER; Vice-Pres. Prof. Dr RUDOLF THIENEL.

Presidents of the Senate: Dr FRANZ HÖSZ, Dr JOHANNES WOLFGANG STEINER, Dr GUNTHER GRUBER, Dr RUDOLF MÜLLER, Dr PETER NOVAK,

Dr GERHART MIZNER, Dr LEOPOLD BUMBERGER, Dr KARL HÖFINGER, HERBERT HEINZL, Dr HEINZ KAIL, Dr MARIANNE HÄNDSCHKE, Dr ERNST GALL, Dr JOSEF SULYOK.

SUPREME JUDICIAL COURT

Oberster Gerichtshof: Schmerlingpl. 11, 1016 Vienna; tel. (1) 521-52-0; fax (1) 521-52-37-10; e-mail ogh.praesidium@justiz.gv.at; internet www.ogh.gv.at; Pres. Prof. Dr ECKART RATZ; Vice-Pres. Dr RONALD ROHRER (civil matters), Prof. Dr KURT KIRSCBACHER (criminal matters).

Presidents of the Senate: Dr PETER SCHINKO, Dr ILSE HUBER, Dr GÜNTER HOLZWEBER, Dr HELGE SCHMUCKER, Prof. Dr HERBERT PIMMER, Dr PETER BAUMANN, Dr GERHARD PRÜCKNER, Prof. Dr KARL-HEINZ DANZL, Dr BRIGITTE SCHENK, Dr FRANZ ZEHETNER, Dr ANTON SPENLING, Prof. Dr ECKART RATZ, Dr THOMAS PHILIPP.

Religion

At the 2001 census, professed membership in major religions was as follows: Roman Catholic Church 74.0% of the population; Lutheran and Presbyterian churches (Evangelical Church, Augsburg and Helvetic confessions) 4.7%; Islam 4.2%; Judaism 0.1%; Eastern Orthodox (Russian, Greek, Serbian, Romanian and Bulgarian) 2.2%; other Christian churches 0.9%; other non-Christian religious groups 0.2%. Atheists accounted for 12% of respondents, while 2% did not indicate a religious affiliation. The vast majority of groups termed 'sects' by the Government are small organizations with fewer than 100 members. Among the larger groups are the Church of Scientology, with between 5,000 and 6,000 members, and the Unification Church, with approximately 700 adherents.

CHRISTIANITY

Ökumenischer Rat der Kirchen in Österreich (Ecumenical Council of Churches in Austria): Severin-Schreiber-Gasse 3, 1180 Vienna; tel. (1) 479-15-23-30-0; fax (1) 479-15-23-33-0; e-mail oerkoe@kirchen.at; internet www.kirchen.at; f. 1948; 14 mem. Churches, 10 observers; Pres. Bischofsvikar Dr NICOLAE DURA (Romanian Orthodox Church); Vice-Pres Bishop Dr MICHAEL BÜNKER (Roman Catholic Church), Dr MANFRED SCHEUER (Roman Catholic Church); Sec. Mag. ERIKA TUPPY (Protestant Church of the Helvetic Confession).

The Roman Catholic Church

Austria comprises two archdioceses, seven dioceses and the territorial abbacy of Wettingen-Mehrerau (directly responsible to the Holy See). The Archbishop of Vienna is also the Ordinary for Catholics of the Byzantine rite in Austria (totalling an estimated 8,000).

Bishops' Conference

Österreichische Bischofskonferenz, Rotenturmstr. 2, 1010 Vienna; tel. (1) 516-11-0; fax (1) 516-11-34-36; e-mail sekretariat@bischofskonferenz.at; internet www.bischofskonferenz.at.

f. 1849; Pres. Cardinal CHRISTOPH SCHÖNBORN (Archbishop of Vienna); Gen. Sec. Mgr ÄGIDIUS ZSIFKOVICS.

Archbishop of Salzburg: Most Rev. Dr ALOIS KOTHGASSER, Kapitelpl. 2, 5020 Salzburg; tel. (662) 80-47; fax (662) 80-47-20-29; e-mail office@kommunikation.kirchen.net; internet www.kirchen.net.

Archbishop of Vienna: Cardinal CHRISTOPH SCHÖNBORN, Wollzeile 2, 1010 Vienna; tel. (1) 515-52-0; fax (1) 515-52-37-28; internet stephanscom.at.

The Anglican Communion

Within the Church of England, Austria forms part of the diocese of Gibraltar in Europe. The Bishop is resident in London, United Kingdom.

Archdeacon of the Eastern Archdeaconry: Ven. PATRICK CURRAN, Christ Church, Jaurèsgasse 12, 1030 Vienna; tel. and fax (1) 714-89-00; e-mail office@christchurchvienna.org; internet www.christchurchvienna.org.

Protestant Churches

Bund der Baptistengemeinden in Österreich (Fed. of Baptist Communities): Krummgasse 7/4, 1030 Vienna; tel. (1) 713-68-28; fax (1) 713-68-28-11; e-mail bund@baptisten.at; internet www.baptisten.at; Gen. Sec. WALTER KLIMT.

Evangelische Kirche Augsburgischen Bekenntnisses in Österreich (Protestant Church of the Augsburg Confession): Severin-Schreiber-Gasse 3, 1180 Vienna; tel. (1) 479-15-23-10-0; fax (1) 479-15-23-11-0; e-mail bischof@evang.at; internet www.evang.at; 311,548 mems (2010); Bishop Dr MICHAEL BÜNKER.

Evangelische Kirche HB (Helvetischen Bekenntnisses) (Protestant Church of the Helvetic Confession): Dorotheergasse 16, 1010 Vienna; tel. (1) 513-65-64; fax (1) 512-44-90; e-mail kirche-hb@evang.at; internet www.reformiertekirche.at; 13,784 mems (2010); Landessuperintendent Pfarrer THOMAS HENNEFELD.

Evangelisch-methodistische Kirche (United Methodist Church): Sechshauserstr. 56, 1150 Vienna; tel. (1) 604-53-47; fax (1) 89-75-87-6; e-mail lother.poell@emk.at; internet www.emk.at; Superintendent Pastor LOTHAR PÖLL.

Orthodox Churches

The Armenian Apostolic Church and the Bulgarian, Coptic, Greek, Romanian, Russian, Serbian and Syrian Orthodox Churches are active in Austria.

Other Christian Churches

Altkatholische Kirche Österreichs (Old Catholic Church in Austria): Schottenring 17/1/3/12, 1010 Vienna; tel. (1) 317-83-94; fax (1) 317-83-94-9; e-mail kilei@altkatholiken.at; internet www.altkatholiken.at; c. 18,000 mems; Bishop JOHN OKORO.

ISLAM

In 2001 there were 338,988 Muslims in Austria.

Islamische Glaubensgemeinschaft in Österreich (Official Islamic Religious Community in Austria—IGGIÖ): Bernardgasse 5, 1070 Vienna; tel. (1) 526-31-22; fax (1) 526-31-22-4; e-mail info@derislam.at; internet www.derislam.at; Pres. Dr FUAT SANAC.

JUDAISM

There are five Jewish communities in Austria, the largest of which is in Vienna. At the end of 2004 there were 6,890 Jews in Vienna, and a combined total of 400 in Graz, Innsbruck, Linz and Salzburg.

Israelitische Kultusgemeinde Graz (Jewish Community in Graz): David-Herzog-Pl. 1, 8020 Graz; tel. (316) 712-46-8; fax (316) 720-43-3; e-mail office@ikg-graz.at; internet www.ikg-graz.at; Pres. GÉRARD SONNENSCHEIN.

Israelitische Kultusgemeinde Salzburg (Jewish Community in Salzburg): Lasserstr. 8, 5020 Salzburg; tel. (662) 872-22-8; e-mail office@ikg-salzburg.at; internet www.ikg-salzburg.at.

Israelitische Kultusgemeinde für Tirol und Vorarlberg (Jewish Community in Tyrol and Vorarlberg): Sillgasse 15, 6020 Innsbruck; tel. and fax (512) 586-89-2; e-mail office@ikg-innsbruck.at; internet www.ikg-innsbruck.at; Pres. Dr ESTHER FRITSCH.

Israelitische Kultusgemeinde Wien (Jewish Community in Vienna): Seitenstettengasse 4, 1010 Vienna; tel. (1) 531-04-10-3; fax (1) 531-04-10-8; e-mail office@ikg-wien.at; internet www.ikg-wien.at; Pres. OSKAR DEUTSCH; Gen. Sec. RAIMUND FASTENBAUER.

The Press

Austria's first newspaper was published in 1605. *Wiener Zeitung*, founded in 1703, is one of the world's oldest daily newspapers still in circulation. Restrictions on press freedom are permissible only within the framework of Article 10 (2) of the European Convention on Human Rights.

Vienna is the focus of newspaper and periodical publishing, although there is also a strong press in some provinces.

In 2009 there were 31 daily newspapers, three of which were distributed without charge.

PRINCIPAL DAILIES

(Average net circulation figures, for January–June 2011, unless otherwise stated)

Bregenz

NEUE Vorarlberger Tageszeitung: Gutenbergstr. 1, 6858 Schwarzach; tel. (5572) 501-850; fax (5572) 501-860; e-mail neue-redaktion@neue.vol.at; internet www.neue.vol.at; f. 1972; morning, Tues.–Sun.; independent; Editor-in-Chief FRANK ANDRES; circ. 12,318.

Vorarlberger Nachrichten: Gutenbergstr. 1, 6858 Schwarzach; tel. (5572) 501-993; fax (5572) 501-227; e-mail redaktion@vn.vol.at; internet www.vn.vol.at; morning; Editor-in-Chief Dr CHRISTIAN ORTNER; circ. Mon.–Sat. 68,780.

Graz

Kleine Zeitung: Schönaugasse 64, 8010 Graz; tel. (316) 875-0; fax (316) 875-40-34; e-mail redaktion@kleinezeitung.at; internet www.kleinezeitung.at; f. 1904; independent; Editor-in-Chief HUBERT PATTERER; circ. Mon.–Sat. 208,731.

Innsbruck

Tiroler Tageszeitung: Ing.-Etzel-Str. 30, 6020 Innsbruck; tel. (512) 53-54-0; fax (512) 53-54-38-99; e-mail redaktion@tt.com; internet www.tt.com; morning; independent; Editors-in-Chief ALOIS VAHRNER, MARIO ZENHÄUSERN; circ. Mon.–Sat. 106,427.

Klagenfurt

Kärntner Tageszeitung: Viktringer Ring 28, 9010 Klagenfurt; tel. (463) 51-20-00; fax (463) 38-15-0; e-mail redaktion@ktz.at; internet www.ktz.at; f. 1946; morning except Mon.; socialist; Editor-in-Chief RALF MOSSER; circ. 32,000 (2007).

Kleine Zeitung: Funderstr. 1A, 9020 Klagenfurt; tel. (463) 58-00-0; fax (463) 58-00-31-3; e-mail redaktion@kleinezeitung.at; internet www.kleinezeitung.at; independent; Editor-in-Chief REINHOLD DOTTOLO; circ. Mon.–Sat. 102,621.

Linz

Neues Volksblatt: Hafenstr. 1–3, 4010 Linz; tel. (732) 76-06-78-2; fax (732) 76-06-70-7; e-mail verlagsleitung@volksblatt.at; internet www.volksblatt.at; f. 1869; organ of Austrian People's Party; Editor-in-Chief Dr WERNER ROHRHOFER.

Oberösterreichische Nachrichten: Promenade 23, 4010 Linz; tel. (732) 78-05-0; fax (732) 78-05-73-1; e-mail redaktion@nachrichten.at; internet www.nachrichten.at; f. 1865; morning; independent; Editor-in-Chief GERALD MANDLBAUER; circ. Mon.–Sat. 133,354.

Salzburg

Salzburger Nachrichten: Karolingerstr. 40, 5021 Salzburg; tel. (662) 83-73-0; fax (662) 83-73-39-9; e-mail redakt@salzburg.com; internet www.salzburg.com; f. 1945; morning; independent; Editor-in-Chief MANFRED PERTERER; circ. Mon.–Sat. 88,963.

Salzburger Volkszeitung: Schrannengasse 6, 5020 Salzburg; tel. (662) 87-94-91; fax (662) 87-94-91-13; e-mail redaktion@svz.at; internet www.svz.at; f. 1945; fmrly organ of the Austrian People's Party; acquired by Aistenleitner Holding in 2005; Editor-in-Chief KONNIE AISTLEITNER; circ. weekdays 12,030 (2007).

Wien
(Vienna)

Heute: Heiligenstädter Lände 29/Top 6, 1190 Vienna; tel. (50) 950-12-20-0; fax (50) 950-12-22-2; e-mail redaktion@heute.at; internet www.heute.at; distributed free of charge; Editor-in-Chief WOLFGANG AINETTER; circ. weekdays 396,171.

Kronen Zeitung: Muthgasse 2, 1190 Vienna; tel. (1) 360-11-0; fax (1) 369-83-85; e-mail lokales@kronenzeitung.at; internet www.krone.at; f. 1900; independent; Editor and Publr HANS DICHAND; circ. weekdays 894,493 (2009), Sun. 1,346,712 (2009).

Kurier: Lindengasse 48–52, 1070 Vienna; tel. (1) 521-00-0; fax (1) 521-00-22-57; e-mail leser@kurier.at; internet www.kurier.at; f. 1954; independent; Editor-in-Chief CHRISTOPH KOTANKO; circ. weekdays 208,276 (2009), Sun. 417,370 (2009).

Die Presse: Hainburgerstr. 33, 1030 Vienna; tel. (1) 514-14-0; fax (1) 514-14-71; e-mail chefredaktion@diepresse.com; internet www.diepresse.com; f. 1848; morning; independent; Editor-in-Chief MANUEL REINARTZ; circ. Mon.–Sat. 96,189.

Der Standard: Wallnerstr. 8, 1010 Vienna; tel. (1) 531-70-70-0; fax (1) 531-70-13-1; e-mail redaktion@derstandard.at; internet derstandard.at; f. 1988; independent; Editor-in-Chief ALEXANDRA FÖDERL-SCHMID; circ. Mon.–Sat. 109,932.

Wiener Zeitung: Wiedner Gürtel 10, 1040 Vienna; tel. and fax (1) 206-99-0; fax (1) 206-99-10-0; e-mail redaktion@wienerzeitung.at; internet www.wienerzeitung.at; f. 1703; morning; official govt paper; Editor-in-Chief REINHARD GÖWEIL; circ. 20,020 (2006).

WirtschaftsBlatt: Hainburgerstr. 33, 1030 Vienna; tel. (1) 601-17-0; fax (1) 601-17-25-9; e-mail redaktion@wirtschaftsblatt.at; internet www.wirtschaftsblatt.at; Mon.–Fri.; business and economics; independent; Editor-in-Chief Dr WOLFGANG UNTERHUBER; circ. weekdays 34,084.

PRINCIPAL WEEKLIES

(Average net circulation figures, for January–June 2011, unless otherwise stated)

Die Furche: Lobkowitzpl. 1, 1010 Vienna; tel. (1) 512-52-61-0; fax (1) 512-82-15; e-mail furche@furche.at; internet www.furche.at; f. 1945; Editor-in-Chief CLAUS REITAN; circ. 18,694.

Kärntner Nachrichten: Kohldorferstr. 98, 1st Floor, 9020 Klagenfurt; tel. (463) 51-15-15; fax (463) 51-15-15-51; e-mail office@abc-werbeagentur.at; internet www.abc-werbeagentur.at; f. 1954; Weds.; Editor Dr HELMUT PRASCH.

KirchenZeitung Diözese Linz: Kapuzinerstr. 84, 4020 Linz; tel. (732) 761-03-94-4; fax (732) 761-03-93-9; e-mail office@kirchenzeitung.at; internet www.kirchenzeitung.at; f. 1945; publ. by Diocese of Linz; Editor-in-Chief MATTHÄUS FELLINGER; circ. 37,439.

Neue Wochenschau: J. N. Bergerstr. 2, 7210 Mattersburg; tel. and fax (2622) 67-47-3; e-mail redaktion@wochenschau.at; internet www.wochenschau.at; f. 1908; Publr and Editor-in-Chief HELMUT WALTER.

NFZ (Neue Freie Zeitung): Friedrich-Schmidt-Pl. 4, 1080 Vienna; tel. (1) 512-35-35-0; fax (1) 512-35-35-9; internet www.fpoe.at; f. 1949; organ of Freedom Party; Man. Editor ANDREAS RUTTINGER.

Niederösterreichische Nachrichten: Gutenbergstr. 12, 3100 St Pölten; tel. (2742) 802-13-18; fax (2742) 802-14-80; e-mail chefredaktion@noen.at; internet www.noen.at; Editor-in-Chief HARALD KNABL; circ. 132,078 (2007).

Oberösterreichische Rundschau: Hafenstr. 1–3, 4020 Linz; tel. (732) 76-16-0; fax (732) 76-16-30-2; e-mail linz@bezirksrundschau.com; internet www.rundschau.co.at; Editor-in-Chief Dr THOMAS WINKLER.

Österreichische Bauernzeitung: Brucknerstr. 6, 1040 Vienna; tel. (1) 533-14-48; fax (1) 533-14-48-33; e-mail demuth@bauernzeitung.at; internet www.bauernzeitung.at; Thurs.; f. 2001; publ. by Österreichischer Bauernbund; Editorial Coordinator CHRISTINE DEMUTH.

Rupertusblatt: Kaigasse 8, 5020 Salzburg; tel. (662) 87-22-23-0; fax (662) 87-22-23-13; e-mail rupertusblatt@kommunikation.kirchen.net; internet www.kirchen.net/rupertusblatt; publ. by Archdiocese of Salzburg; Editor-in-Chief KARL ROITHINGER; circ. 14,490(.

Der Sonntag: Stephanspl. 4/VI/DG, Postfach 152, 1014 Vienna; tel. (1) 512-60-63-39-71; fax (1) 512-60-63-39-70; e-mail redaktion@dersonntag.at; internet www.dersonntag.at; f. 1848 as the *Wiener Kirchenzeitung*; present name adopted in 2004; publ. by the Archdiocese of Vienna; Editor-in-Chief ELVIRA GROISS; circ. 23,000.

POPULAR PERIODICALS

Alles Auto: Beckgasse 24, 1130 Vienna; tel. (1) 877-97-11; fax (1) 877-97-114; e-mail redaktion@allesauto.at; internet www.allesauto.at; 10 a year; motoring; Publr GÜNTHER EFFENBERGER; Editor-in-Chief ENRICO FALCHETTO; circ. 30.791 (Jan.–June 2010).

Austria-Ski: Olympiastr. 10, 6010 Innsbruck; tel. (512) 335-01-0; fax (512) 361-99-8; e-mail schmid@oesv.at; internet www.oesv.at; 7 a year; official journal of Austrian Skiing Asscn; Editor JOSEF SCHMID.

Auto Touring: ÖAMTC Verlag GmbH, Tauchnergasse 5, 3400 Klosterneuburg; tel. (2243) 404-27-01; fax (2243) 404-27-21; e-mail autotouring.redaktion@oeamtc.at; internet www.autotouring.at; monthly; official journal of the Austrian Automobile Organization; Editor-in-Chief PETER PISECKER; circ. 1,376,814.

Format: Taborstr. 1–3, 1020 Vienna; tel. (1) 217-55-0; e-mail redaktion@news.at; internet www.format.at; f. 1998; weekly, Fri.; business; independent; Editor-in-Chief ANDREAS LAMPL; circ. 27,780 (Jan.–June 2010).

Die Ganze Woche: Heiligenstädter Str. 121, 1190 Vienna; tel. (1) 290-97-30; fax (1) 290-97-30-30; e-mail redaktion@dgw.at; internet www.ganzewoche.at; f. 1985; circ. 326,971 (Jan.–June 2010).

Gewinn: Stiftgasse 31, 1071 Vienna; tel. (1) 521-24-0; fax 521-24-40; e-mail gewinn@gewinn.com; internet www.gewinn.com; monthly; business, economics, personal finances; Editor-in-Chief Prof. Dr GEORG WAILAND; circ. 46,392 (Jan.–June 2010).

Gusto: Ferdinandstr. 4, 1020 Vienna; tel. (1) 863-31-53-01; fax (1) 863-31-56-10; e-mail redaktion@gusto.at; internet www.gusto.at; f. 1983; monthly; food and drink; Editor-in-Chief WOLFGANG SCHLÜTER; circ. 43,466 (Jan.–June 2010).

Maxima: IZ NÖ Süd, Str. 3, Objekt 16, 2351 Wiener Neudorf; tel. (2236) 600-67-30; fax (2236) 600-67-70; e-mail redaktion@maxima.co.at; internet www.maxima.at; f. 1996; 10 a year; women's magazine; Editor-in-Chief BRIGITTE B. FUCHS; circ. 75,822 (Jan.–June 2010).

NEWS: Taborrstr. 1–3, 1020 Vienna; tel. (1) 213-12-0; fax (1) 213-12-666-1; e-mail redaktion@news.at; internet www.news.at; f. 1992; weekly, Thurs.; illustrated; Editor-in-Chief PETER PELINKA; circ. 121,097 (Jan.–June 2010).

ORF nachlese: Würzburggasse 30, 1136 Vienna; tel. (1) 870-77-14-50-0; fax (1) 870-77-14-82-4; e-mail nachlese@orf.at; internet www.enterprise.orf.at; f. 1979; monthly; programme guide to television and radio broadcasts; Editor-in-Chief KATJA ZINGGL-POKORNY; circ. 59,953 (Jan.–June 2010).

Profil: Taborstr. 1-3, 1020 Vienna; tel. (1) 534-70-35-02; fax (1) 534-70-35-00; e-mail redaktion@profil.at; internet www.profil.at; f. 1970; weekly, Mon.; political, general; independent; Editor-in-Chief and Publr Dr CHRISTIAN RAINER; circ. 63,140 (Jan.–June 2010).

Seitenblicke: Heinrich-Collin Str. 1/Top 1, 1140 Vienna; tel. (1) 90-220-0; fax (1) 90-220-990; e-mail redaktion@seitenblicke.at; internet www.seitenblicke.at; fortnightly; lifestyle, celebrity news; Editor-in-Chief ANDREAS WOLLINGER; circ. 28,052 (Jan.–June 2010).

Sportzeitung: Ringstr. 44, 3500 Krems; tel. (2732) 820-00; fax (2732) 820-00-82; e-mail sportzeitung@lwmedia.at; internet www.sportzeitung.at; f. 1949; weekly sports illustrated; Editors-in-Chief HORST HÖTSCH, GERHARD WEBER; circ. 11,146 (Jan.–June 2010).

TOPIC: Königsklostergasse 7/15, 1060 Vienna; tel. (1) 535-57-83; e-mail topic@topmedia.at; internet www.mytopic.at; 11 a year; politics, economics and culture for young people; publ. by Austrian Youth Red Cross and Austrian Youth Book Club; Dir Dr EVA LINGENS; circ. 147,250 (Jan.–June 2010).

Trend: Taborstr. 1–3, 1020 Vienna; tel. (1) 213-12-0; fax (1) 213-12-06-66-1; e-mail redaktion@trend.at; internet www.trend.at; monthly; economics; Editor-in-Chief ANDREAS LAMPL; circ. 32,570 (Jan.–June 2010).

TV-Media: Taborstr. 1–3, 1020 Vienna; tel. (1) 213-12-0; fax (1) 213-12-06-66-1; e-mail redaktion@tv-media.at; internet www.tv-media.at; f. 1995; weekly, Weds.; illustrated; Editor-in-Chief HADUBRAND SCHREIBERSHOFEN; circ. 215,752 (Jan.–June 2009).

Welt der Frau: Lustenauerstr. 21, 4020 Linz; tel. (732) 77-00-01-11; fax (732) 77-00-01-24; e-mail info@welt-der-frau.at; internet www.welt-der-frau.at; women's monthly; Editor-in-Chief Dr CHRISTINE HAIDEN; circ. 41,047 (Jan.–June 2010).

Wienerin: Geiselbergstr. 15, 1100 Vienna; tel. (1) 601-17-963; fax (1) 601-17-967; e-mail wienerin@wienerin.at; internet www.wienerin.at; monthly; women's interest; Editor-in-Chief SYLVIA MARGRET STEINITZ; circ. 44,031 (Jan.–June 2010).

Woman: Taborstr. 1-3, 1020 Vienna; tel. (1) 213-12-0; fax (1) 213-12-66-61; e-mail kindl.gabriele@woman.at; internet www.woman.at; fortnightly; women's interest; Editor-in-Chief EUKE FRANK; circ. 140,113 (Jan.–June 2010).

SPECIALIST PERIODICALS

FSG Direkt: Verlag des ÖGB GmbH, Johann-Böhm-Pl. 1, 1020 Vienna; tel. (1) 662-32-96-0; fax (1) 662-32-96-39-79-3; e-mail karin.stieber@oegbverlag.at; internet www.fsg.or.at; monthly; organ of the Fraktion Sozialdemokratischer GewerkschafterInnen (FSG—Social Democratic movement within the Austrian Trade Union Fed.); Editor-in-Chief CHRISTOPH HÖLLRIEGL; circ 47,500.

ITM praktiker: Apollogasse 22, Postfach 36, 1072 Vienna; tel. (1) 526-46-68-0; fax (1) 546-80-01-17; e-mail redaktion@praktiker.at; internet www.praktiker.at; f. 1945; technical hobbies, photography; Editor-in-Chief FELIX WESSELY; circ. 10,500.

Juristische Blätter (mit Beilage 'Wirtschaftsrechtliche Blätter'): Springer Verlag, Sachsenpl. 4, Postfach 89, 1201 Vienna; tel. (1) 330-24-15-0; fax (1) 330-24-26; internet www.springer.at/jbl; f. 1872; monthly; law; Editor M. LUKAS; circ. 6,500.

Die Landwirtschaft: Wiener Str. 64, 3100 St Pölten; tel. (2742) 259-93-00; fax 259-95-93-00; e-mail presse@lk-noe.at; internet www.lk-noe.at; f. 1922; monthly; Editor-in-Chief ULRIKE RASER; circ. 42,000.

Literatur und Kritik: Otto-Müller-Verlag, Ernest-Thun-Str. 11, 5020 Salzburg; tel. (662) 88-19-74; fax (662) 87-23-87; e-mail info@omvs.at; internet www.omvs.at; f. 1966; 5 a year; Austrian and European literature and criticism; Editor KARL-MARKUS GAUSS.

MEDIZIN Populär: Nibelungengasse 13, 1010 Vienna; tel. (1) 512-44-86-0; fax (1) 512-44-86-24; e-mail k.kirschbichler@aerzteverlagshaus.at; internet www.medizinpopulaer.at; monthly; health and fitness; Editor-in-Chief KARIN KIRSCHBICHLER; circ. 25,380 (Jan.–June 2010).

Öffentliche Sicherheit: Postfach 100, Herrengasse 7, 1014 Vienna; tel. (1) 531-26-24-88; fax (1) 531-26-27-01; e-mail oeffentlichkeitsarbeit@bmi.gv.at; internet www.bmi.gv.at/oeffentlsicherheit; 6 a year; published by the Federal Ministry of the Interior; Editor-in-Chief WERNER SABITZER; circ. 15,000.

onrail: Leberstr. 122, 1110 Vienna; tel. (1) 740-95-53-5; fax (1) 740-95-53-8; e-mail redaktion@onrail.at; internet www.onrail.at; every 2 months; travel; Editor-in-Chief CHRISTINA DANY; circ. 85,000.

Österreichische Ärztezeitung: Nibelungengasse 13, 1010 Vienna; tel. (1) 512-44-86; fax (1) 512-44-86-64; e-mail a.muehlgassner@aerzteverlagshaus.at; internet www.aerztezeitung.at; f. 1945; 20 a year; organ of the Austrian Medical Board; Editor-in-Chief Dr AGNES M. MÜHLGASSNER; circ. 39,811 (Jan.–June 2010).

Österreichische Ingenieur- und Architekten-Zeitschrift (ÖIAZ): Eschenbachgasse 9, 1010 Vienna; tel. (1) 587-35-36; fax (1) 370-58-06-33-3; e-mail office@oiav.at; internet www.oiav.at; f. 1849; 6 a year; Editor PETER REICHEL; circ. 2,200.

Österreichische Monatshefte: Rathausstr. 10, 1010 Vienna; tel. (1) 409-55-37-26-1; fax (1) 409-55-37-26-9; e-mail redaktion.omh@alpha-medien.at; internet www.alpha-medien.at; f. 1945; 6 a year; organ of Österreichische Volkspartei; Editor-in-Chief ANDREAS KRATSCHMAR.

Österreichische Musikzeitschrift: Hegelgasse 1/3/3/6, 1010 Vienna; tel. (1) 664-186-386-8; e-mail redaktion@oemz.at; internet www.oemz.at; f. 1946; bi-monthly; music; Editor Dr DANIEL ENDER; circ. 5,000.

Reichsbund-Aktuell mit SPORT: Laudongasse 16, 1080 Vienna; tel. and fax (1) 729-19-55; e-mail info@amateurfussball.at; internet www.amateurfussball.at; f. 1917; monthly; Catholic; organ of Reichsbund, Bewegung für christliche Gesellschaftspolitik und Sport; Editor WALTER RAMING; circ. 12,000.

SPÖ-Aktuell: Löwelstr. 18, 1014 Vienna; tel. (1) 534-27-27-5; fax (1) 534-27-28-2; e-mail spoe.aktuell@spoe.at; internet aktuell.spoe.at; weekly; organ of Social Democratic Party; Dir UTE PICHLER.

Wiener Klinische Wochenschrift: Sachsenpl. 4–6, 1201 Vienna; tel. (1) 330-24-15; fax (1) 330-24-26; e-mail journals@springer.at; internet www.springer.at/wkw; f. 1888; medical bi-weekly; Editor-in-Chief M. KÖLLER.

NEWS AGENCY

APA (Austria Presse Agentur): Laimgrubengasse 10, 1060 Vienna; tel. (1) 360-60-0; fax (1) 360-60-30-99; e-mail apa@apa.at; internet www.apa.at; f. 1946; co-operative agency of the Austrian Newspapers and Broadcasting Co (private co, incl. 15 daily newspapers and Österreichische Rundfunk); CEO PETER KROPSCH; Editor-in-Chief MICHAEL LANG.

PRESS ASSOCIATIONS

Österreichischer Zeitschriften- und Fachmedien-Verband (Austrian Magazine Publishers Asscn): Renngasse 12/6, 1010 Vienna; tel. and fax (1) 319-70-01; e-mail oezv@oezv.or.at; internet www.oezv.or.at; f. 1946; 149 mems; Man. Dir Dr WOLFGANG BRANDSTETTER.

Verband Österreichischer Zeitungen (Austrian Newspaper Asscn): Wipplingerstr. 15, Postfach 144, 1013 Vienna; tel. (1) 533-79-79-0; fax (1) 533-79-79-42-2; e-mail office@voez.at; internet www.voez.at; f. 1946; 64 mems; mems include 16 daily newspapers and 48 other newspapers and periodicals; Pres. Dr HANS GASSER; Dir GERALD GRÜNBERGER.

Publishers

Akademische Druck- und Verlagsanstalt (ADEVA): Radetzkystr. 6, 8010 Graz; tel. (316) 36-44; fax (316) 36-44-24; e-mail info@adeva.com; internet www.adeva.com; f. 1949; scholarly reprints and new works, facsimile editions of codices, fine art facsimile editions, music books and facsimile editions; Man. Dr HUBERT CHRISTIAN KONRAD.

Amalthea Signum Verlag: Am Heumarkt 19, 1030 Vienna; tel. (1) 712-35-60; fax (1) 713-89-95; e-mail verlag@amalthea.at; internet www.amalthea.at; f. 2002 by merger of Amalthea Verlag (f. 1917) and Buchverlags Signum (f. 1978); politics, economics; Man. Dir Dr HERBERT FLEISSNER.

Böhlau Verlag GmbH & Co KG: Wiesingerstr. 1, 1010 Vienna; tel. (1) 330-24-27-0; fax (1) 330-24-32; e-mail boehlau@boehlau.at; internet www.boehlau.at; f. 1947; history, law, philology, the arts, sociology, social sciences; Dir Dr PETER RAUCH.

Verlag Brüder Hollinek und Co GmbH: Luisenstr. 20, 3002 Purkersdorf; tel. and fax (2231) 673-65; fax (2231) 673-65-24; e-mail office@hollinek.at; internet www.hollinek.at; f. 1872; science, law and administration, printing, reference works, dictionaries; Dir RICHARD HOLLINEK.

Christian Brandstätter Verlag GmbH & Co KG: Wickenburggasse 26, 1080 Vienna; tel. (1) 512-15-43-0; fax (1) 512-15-43-23-1; e-mail info@cbv.at; internet www.cbv.at; f. 1982; the arts, lifestyle; Chair. Dr CHRISTIAN BRANDSTÄTTER.

Wilhelm Braumüller Universitäts Verlagsbuchhandlung GmbH: Servitengasse 5, 1090 Vienna; tel. (1) 319-11-59; fax (1) 310-28-05; e-mail office@braumueller.at; internet www.braumueller.at; f. 1783; politics, law, ethnology, literature and theatre, linguistics, history, journalism, sociology, philosophy, psychology, communications; university publrs; Dirs BERNHARD BOROVANSKY, KONSTANZE BOROVANSKY.

Czernin Verlags GmbH: Kupkagasse 4, 1080 Vienna; tel. (1) 403-35-63; fax (1) 403-35-63-15; e-mail office@czernin-verlag.com; internet www.czernin-verlag.com; f. 1999; philosophy, politics, literature, the arts; Dir BENEDICT FÖGER.

Edition und Atelier Koenigstein: Anzengrubergasse 50, 3400 Klosterneuburg; tel. (2243) 26-04-6; e-mail office@koenigsteinkunst.com; internet www.koenigsteinkunst.com; f. 1987; stories, fairy tales, poetry; Publr GEORG KOENIGSTEIN.

Facultas Verlags- und Buchhandels AG: Berggasse 5, 1090 Vienna; tel. (1) 310-53-56; fax (1) 319-70-50; e-mail office@facultas

.at; internet www.facultas.at; f. 2001 by merger of WUV Universitätsverlags GmbH and Servicebetriebe GmbH an der Wirtschaftsuniversität Wien; imprint: facultas.wuv; science, medicine, law, social sciences; Dir THOMAS STAUFFER.

Folio Verlagsgesellschaft mbH: Schönbrunner Str. 31, 1050 Vienna; tel. (1) 581-37-08-0; fax (1) 581-37-08-20; literature, contemporary art, non-fiction; Dirs LUDWIG PAULMICHL, HERMANN GUMMERER.

Freytag-Berndt u. Artaria KG: Brunnerstr. 69, 1230 Vienna; tel. (1) 869-90-90-0; fax (1) 869-90-90-61; e-mail office@freytagberndt.at; internet www.freytagberndt.at; f. 1879; cartography, geography, atlases, maps, guides, geographical data; Dir Dr CHRISTIAN HALBWACHS.

Haymon Verlag GesmbH: Erlerstr. 10, 6020 Innsbruck; tel. (512) 57-63-00; fax (512) 57-63-00-14; e-mail office@haymonverlag.at; internet www.haymonverlag.at; f. 1982; fiction, non-fiction; Dir MARKUS HATZER.

Jugend and Volk GmbH: Universitätsstr. 11, 1016 Vienna; tel. (1) 407-27-07; fax (1) 407-27-07-22; e-mail verlag@jugendvolk.at; internet www.jugendvolk.at; f. 1921; pedagogics, textbooks; Dir IRIS BLATTERER.

Verlag Kremayr & Scheriau KG: Währinger Str. 76/8, 1090 Vienna; tel. (1) 713-87-70-0; fax (1) 713-87-70-20; e-mail office@kremayr-scheriau.at; internet www.kremayr-scheriau.at; f. 1951; non-fiction, history, lifestyle; Dir MARTIN SCHERIAU.

Kunstverlag Wolfrum: Augustinerstr. 10, 1010 Vienna; tel. (1) 512-53-98-0; fax (1) 512-53-98-57; e-mail wolfrum@wolfrum.at; internet www.wolfrum.at; f. 1919; art; Publr HUBERT WOLFRUM.

Leykam Buchverlagsgesellschaft mbH Nfg & Co KG: Karlauergürtel 1, 8020 Graz; tel. (501) 09-65-30; fax (501) 09-65-39; e-mail verlag@leykam.com; internet www.leykamverlag.at; f. 1585; art, literature, academic, law; Dirs Dr WOLFGANG HÖLZL, KLAUS BRUNNER.

LexisNexis Verlag ARD ORAC GmbH & Co KG: Marxergasse 25, 1030 Vienna; tel. (1) 534-52-0; fax (1) 534-52-14-1; e-mail verlag@lexisnexis.at; internet www.lexisnexis.at; f. 1946; legal books, periodicals and online databases; subsidiary of Reed Elsevier Group PLC (UK); CEO PETER J. DAVIES; Dir Dr GERIT KANDUTSCH.

Linde Verlag Wien GmbH: Scheydgasse 24, 1211 Vienna; tel. (1) 246-30-0; fax (1) 246-30-23; e-mail office@lindeverlag.at; internet www.lindeverlag.at; f. 1925; business, economics, law; Dirs ANDREAS JENTZSCH, Dr ELEONORE BREITEGGER, Dr OSKAR MENNEL.

Literaturverlag Droschl GmbH: Stenggstr. 33, 8043 Graz; tel. (316) 32-64-04; fax (316) 32-40-71; e-mail office@droschl.com; internet www.droschl.com; f. 1978; contemporary literature.

MANZ'sche Verlags- und Universitätsbuchhandlung GmbH: Johannesgasse 23, 1010 Vienna; tel. (1) 531-61-0; fax (1) 531-61-18-1; e-mail verlag@manz.at; internet www.manz.at; f. 1849; law, tax and economic sciences; textbooks and school books; Man. Dir SUSANNE STEIN-DICHTL; Publr Dr WOLFGANG PICHLER.

Wilhelm Maudrich KG: Spitalgasse 21A, 1090 Vienna; tel. (1) 402-47-12; fax (1) 408-50-80; e-mail maudrich@maudrich.com; internet www.maudrich.com; f. 1909; medical.

Musikverlag Doblinger: Dorotheergasse 10, 1010 Vienna; tel. (1) 515-03-0; fax (1) 515-03-51; e-mail music@doblinger.at; internet www.doblinger.at; f. 1876; music; Dir PETER PANY.

Niederösterreichisches Pressehaus Druck- und Verlagsgesellschaft mbH (Residenz Verlag): Gutenbergstr. 12, 3100 St Pölten; tel. (2742) 802-14-15; fax (2742) 802-14-31; e-mail info@residenzverlag.at; internet www.residenzverlag.at; f. 1956; literature, children's, non-fiction; Dir CLAUDIA ROMEDER.

Otto Müller Verlag: Ernest-Thun-Str. 11, 5020 Salzburg; tel. (662) 88-19-74-0; fax (662) 87-23-87; e-mail info@omvs.at; internet www.omvs.at; f. 1937; general; Man. ARNO KLEIBEL.

Verlag Österreich GmbH: Bäckerstr. 1, 1010 Vienna; tel. (1) 610-77-0; fax (1) 610-77-41-9; e-mail office@verlagoesterreich.at; internet www.verlagoesterreich.at; f. 1804; fmrly state-owned; acquired by Wissenschaftlichen Verlags GmbH (Germany) in 2008; law, CD-ROMs; Dirs ANDRÉ CARO.

Österreichischer Bundesverlag Schulbuch GmbH & Co KG: Frankgasse 4, 1090 Vienna; tel. (1) 401-36-0; fax (1) 401-36-18-5; e-mail office@oebv.at; internet www.oebv.at; educational books, dictionaries; Dir Dr RAINER STAHL.

Picus Verlag GmbH: Friedrich-Schmidt-Pl. 4, 1080 Vienna; tel. (1) 408-18-21; fax (1) 408-18-21-6; e-mail info@picus.at; internet www.picus.at; f. 1984; children's books, literature, travel; Dirs DOROTHEA LÖCKER, Dr ALEXANDER POTYKA.

Springer-Verlag GmbH: Sachsenpl. 4–6, 1201 Vienna; tel. (1) 330-24-15-55-0; fax (1) 330-24-26-65; e-mail stephen.soehnlen@springer.at; internet www.springer.at; f. 1924; medicine, natural sciences, technology, law, sociology, economics, architecture, art, periodicals; Man. Dir KATHARINA OPPITZ.

Leopold Stocker Verlag GmbH: Hofgasse 5, 8011 Graz; tel. (316) 82-16-36; fax (316) 83-56-12; e-mail stocker-verlag@stocker-verlag.com; internet www.stocker-verlag.com; f. 1917; history, nature, hunting, fiction, agriculture, textbooks; Dir WOLFGANG DVORAK-STOCKER.

Verlagsgruppe Styria GmbH & Co KG: Lobkowitzpl. 1, 1010 Vienna; tel. (1) 512-88-08-0; fax (1) 512-88-08-75; e-mail office@styriabooks.at; internet www.verlagsgruppestyria.at; f. 2003 by merger of Styria Verlag and Pichler Verlag; biographies, theology, religion, philosophy; imprints: Styria Verlag, Pichler Verlag, Molden Verlag, Verlag Carinthia and Edition Oberösterreich; Man. Dir GERDA SCHAFFELHOFER.

Tyrolia Buchverlag: Postfach 220, Exlgasse 20, 6020 Innsbruck; tel. (512) 223-32-02; fax (512) 223-32-06; e-mail buchverlag@tyrolia.at; internet www.tyrolia-verlag.at; f. 1888; subsidiary of Verlagsanstalt Tyrolia GmbH; geography, history, science, children's, religion, fiction; Chair. Dr GOTTFRIED KOMPATSCHER.

Verlag Carl Ueberreuter GmbH: Alserstr. 24, 1090 Vienna; tel. (1) 404-44-0; fax (1) 404-44-5; e-mail office@ueberreuter.at; internet www.ueberreuter.at; f. 1946; non-fiction, children's, literature; imprints: Annette Betz and Tosa; Man. Dir Dr SILVIA DE SORDI.

Universal Edition AG: Karlspl. 6, 1010 Vienna; tel. (1) 337-23-0; fax (1) 337-23-40-0; e-mail office@universaledition.com; internet www.universaledition.com; f. 1901; music; Dirs JOHANN JURANEK, ASTRID KOBLANCK, STEFAN RAGG.

VERITAS Verlags- und Buchhandelsgesellschaft mbH & Co OHG: Hafenstr. 2A, 4010 Linz; tel. (732) 77-64-51-0; fax (732) 77-64-51-22-39; e-mail kundenberatung@veritas.at; internet www.veritas.at; f. 1945; acquired Oldenbourg Schulbuch-Verlag in 2006; training materials, educational books; Dir MANFRED MERANER.

Paul Zsolnay Verlag Deuticke GmbH: Prinz-Eugen-Str. 30, 1041 Vienna; tel. (1) 505-76-61-0; fax (1) 505-76-61-10; e-mail info@zsolnay.at; internet www.zsolnay.at; f. 1923; fiction, non-fiction; incl. Deuticke Verlag; Dir MICHAEL KRÜGER.

PUBLISHERS' ASSOCIATION

Hauptverband des Österreichischen Buchhandels (Asscn of Austrian Publrs and Booksellers): Grünangergasse 4, 1010 Vienna; tel. (1) 512-15-35; fax (1) 512-84-82; e-mail sekretariat@hvb.at; internet www.buecher.at; f. 1859; Pres. Dr GERALD SCHANTIN; Man. Dir Dr INGE KRALUPPER; 530 mems.

Broadcasting and Communications

REGULATORY BODIES

Rundfunk und Telekom Regulierungs GmbH (Austrian Regulatory Authority for Broadcasting and Telecommunications—RTR): Mariahilfer Str. 77–79, 1060 Vienna; tel. (1) 580-58-0; fax (1) 580-58-91-91; e-mail rtr@rtr.at; internet www.rtr.at; f. 2001; comprises 2 divisions: broadcasting and telecommunications; provides operational support to KommAustria and Telekom-Control Kommission; CEO Telecommunications Dr GEORG SERENTSCHY; CEO Broadcasting Dr ALFRED GRINSCHGL.

Kommunikationsbehörde Austria (KommAustria) (Austrian Communications Authority): Mariahilferstr. 77–79, 1060 Vienna; tel. (1) 580-58-0; fax (1) 580-58-91-91; e-mail rtr@rtr.at; internet www.rtr.at/de/rtr/organekommaustria; f. 2001; regulatory authority for the Austrian broadcasting industry (responsible for activities such as issuing licenses to private television and radio stations, managing broadcasting frequencies, handling the legal supervision of private broadcasters, as well as preparing and launching digital broadcasting in Austria); Chair. MICHAEL OGRIS.

Telekom-Control-Kommission (TKK): Mariahilferstr. 77–79, 1060 Vienna; tel. (1) 580-58-0; fax (1) 580-58-91-91; e-mail rtr@rtr.at; internet www.rtr.at/en/rtr/OrganeTKK; f. 1997; regulates competition in the telecommunications market, as well as postal services; Chair. Dr ELFRIEDE SOLÉ.

TELECOMMUNICATIONS

A1 Telekom Austria: Postfach 1001, 1011 Vienna; tel. 506-64-0; e-mail kundenservice@telekom.at; internet www.a1telekom.at; f. 2010 following the merger of Telekom Austria AG and mobilkom austria; fixed-line telecommunications and broadband internet access; part of Telekom Austria Group; CEO Dr HANNES AMETSREITER.

Hutchison 3G Austria GmbH (3 AT): Gasometer C, Guglgasse 12/10/3, 1110 Vienna; tel. (5) 066-00; fax (5) 066-30-30-31; e-mail 3serviceteam@drei.at; internet www.drei.at; f. 2002; mobile cellular telecommunications; subsidiary of Hutchison Whampoa Ltd (Hong Kong); CEO JAN TRIONOW.

Orange Austria Telecommunication GmbH: Brünner Str. 52, 1210 Vienna; tel. (1) 277-28-0; fax (0) 699-70-77-0; e-mail info@orange.co.at; internet www.orange.at; f. 1998; fmrly ONE GmbH; present name adopted 2008; mobile cellular telecommunications; acquired by Hutchison 3G Austria GmbH in 2012; CEO MICHAEL KRAMMER.

Tele2 Telecommunication GmbH: Donau-City-Str. 11, 1220 Vienna; tel. (5) 050-0; fax (5) 050-03-79-4; e-mail kundenservice@at.tele2.com; internet www.tele2.at; f. 1998; owned by Tele2 AB (Sweden); fixed-line telecommunications and broadband internet access; Man. Dir Dr ALFRED PUFITSCH.

tele.ring: Rennweg 97–99, Postfach 1012, 1030 Vienna; tel. (1) 795-85-60-30; fax (1) 795-85-65-86; e-mail info@telering.co.at; internet www.telering.at; mobile cellular telecommunications; wholly owned by T-Mobile Austria GmbH; Chair. ROBERT CHVÁTAL.

T-Mobile Austria GmbH: Rennweg 97–99, 1030 Vienna; tel. (1) 795-85-0; fax (1) 795-85-65-86; e-mail presse@t-mobile.at; internet www.t-mobile.at; f. 1996 as max.mobil; present name adopted 2002; subsidiary of T-Mobile International AG & Co KG (Germany); CEO ROBERT CHVÁTAL.

UPC Austria GmbH: Wolfganggasse 58-60, 1120 Vienna; tel. (1) 960-60-60-0; fax (1) 960-60-96-0; e-mail info.wien@upc.at; internet www.upc.at; fixed-line telecommunications, broadband internet access (under brand name Chello), and digital cable television; also owns internet service provider, Inode; owned by Liberty Global, Inc. (USA); Man. Dir THOMAS HINTZE.

BROADCASTING

Radio

The state-owned Österreichischer Rundfunk (ORF) provides three national and nine regional radio channels, as well as an overseas service. The provision of radio services was liberalized in 1998.

Österreichischer Rundfunk (ORF) (Austrian Broadcasting Company): Würzburggasse 30, 1136 Vienna; tel. (1) 870-70-30; fax (1) 878-70-33-0; e-mail kundendienst@orf.at; internet zukunft.orf.at; f. 1924; state-owned; operates 3 national radio stations: Ö1, Hitradio Ö3 and FM4; 9 regional radio stations (Ö2): Radio Burgenland, Radio Kärnten, Radio Niederösterreich, Radio Oberösterreich, Radio Salzburg, Radio Steiermark, Radio Tirol, Radio Vorarlberg, Radio Wien; 1 foreign-language radio station: Slovenski spored; 1 international radio station: Radio Österreich 1 International; 1 internet-based radio station: oe1campus; 4 television channels: ORF1, ORF2, ORF Sport Plus and TW1; operates satellite television channel, 3 Sat, in conjunction with ARD (Germany), SRG (Switzerland) and ZDF (Germany); also distributes content via teletext and internet; Dir-Gen. Dr ALEXANDER WRABETZ; Dirs KARL AMON (Radio), KATHRIN ZECHNER (Television), THOMAS PRANTNER (Online and New Media).

Private and Commercial Radio Operators

Antenne Kärnten Regionalradio GmbH & Co KG: Hasnerstr. 2, 9020 Klagenfurt; tel. (463) 458-88-0; fax (463) 458-88-90-9; e-mail servicektn@antenne.net; internet www.antennekaernten.at; one FM station, Antenne Kärnten; broadcasts in Carinthia; Mans GOTTFRIED BICHLER, RUDOLF KUZMICKI, Dr KLAUS SCHWEIGHOFER.

Antenne Oberösterreich GmbH: Durisolstr. 7/Top22A, 4600 Wels; tel. and fax (7242) 351-29-9; e-mail info@antennewels.at; internet www.antennewels.at; one FM station, Antenne Wels 98.3; broadcasts in Oberösterreich; Man. Dr CHRISTOPH LEON.

Antenne Österreich GmbH (Niederlassung Salzburg): Friedensstr. 14A, 5020 Salzburg; tel. (662) 40-80-0; fax (662) 40-80-70; e-mail info@antennesalzburg.at; internet www.antennesalzburg.at; one FM station, Antenne Salzburg; broadcasts in Salzburg and Lienz; Dir SYLVIA BUCHHAMMER; Station Man. MATTHIAS NIESWANDT.

Antenne Österreich GmbH (Niederlassung Tirol): Maria-Theresien-Str. 8, 6020 Innsbruck; tel. (512) 574-12-72-3; fax (512) 574-12-75-0; e-mail info@antennetirol.at; internet www.antennetirol.at; two FM stations, Antenne Tirol (Innsbruck) and Antenne Tirol (Unterland); broadcasts in Tyrol; Dir SYLVIA BUCHHAMMER; Station Man. MATTHIAS NIESWANDT.

Antenne Österreich GmbH (Niederlassung Wien): Makartgasse 3, 1010 Vienna; tel. (1) 217-00-0; fax (1) 217-00-77-09; e-mail office@antennewien.at; internet www.antennewien.at; one FM station, Antenne Wien 102.5; broadcasts in Vienna; Dir SYLVIA BUCHHAMMER.

Antenne Steiermark Regionalradio GmbH & Co KG: Am Sendergrund 15, 8143 Dobl; tel. (3136) 505-0; fax (3136) 505-11-1; e-mail info@antenne.net; internet www.antenne.net; one FM station, Antenne Steiermark; broadcasts in Styria; Mans GOTTFRIED BICHLER, RUDOLF KUZMICKI, Dr KLAUS SCHWEIGHOFER.

KRONEHIT: KRONEHIT Radiobetriebs GmbH, Daumegasse 1, 1100 Vienna; tel. (1) 600-61-00; e-mail office@kronehit.at; internet www.kronehit.at; Austria's sole national, private radio operator; popular music; Man. Dr ERNST SWOBODA.

Radio Arabella GmbH: Alser Str. 4, Hof 1, Altes AKH, 1090 Vienna; tel. (1) 492-99-29-20-2; fax (1) 492-99-29-20-1; e-mail office@radioarabella.at; internet www.radioarabella.at; 5 radio stations in Austria: Radio Arabella Mostviertel-St. Pölten, Radio Arabella Oberösterreich, Radio Arabella Salzburg, Radio Arabella Tulln-Krems and Radio Arabella Wien; sister station broadcasts in Munich, Germany; Man. Dir WOLFGANG STRUBER.

88.6—wir spielen was wir wollen: Radio Eins Privatradio GmbH, Heiligenstädter Lände 29, 1190 Vienna; tel. (1) 360-88-0; fax (1) 360-88-30-9; e-mail webmaster@radio886.at; internet www.radio886.at; broadcasts in Vienna, Burgenland and Lower Austria; popular music; Mans OLIVER BÖHM, HOLGER WILLOH.

Television

The state-owned Österreichischer Rundfunk (ORF) retained a monopoly over television broadcasting in Austria until 2001. It operates two terrestrial television channels and a satellite station in conjunction with German and Swiss companies. Digital television services, comprising three television channels, ORF1, ORF2 and a commercial service, ATV, were launched in October 2006. Analogue broadcasting began to be phased out in favour of digital broadcasting in March 2007 and was discontinued in 2011.

Österreichischer Rundfunk: see Radio.

Private and Commercial Television Operators

ATV Privat TV GmbH & Co KG: Aspernbrückengasse 2, 1020 Vienna; tel. (1) 213-64-0; fax (1) 213-64-99-9; e-mail atv@atv.at; internet www.atv.at; f. 2003; CEO LUDWIG BAUER.

Austria 9 TV GmbH: Rosenhügel Filmstudios, Speisinger Str. 121–127, 1230 Vienna; tel. (1) 888-04-03; fax (1) 888-04-03-99; e-mail office@austria9.at; internet www.austria9.at; f. 2007; free-to-air digital satellite and cable channel; owned by Hubert Burda Media AG & Co KG (Germany); Man. Dir Dr CONRAD HEBERLING.

Puls4 TV GmbH & Co KG: Mariahilfer Str. 2, 1070 Vienna; tel. (1) 999-88-0; fax (1) 999-88-88-88; e-mail office@puls4.com; internet www.puls4.com; f. 2004 as Puls TV; commercial channel (Puls4), broadcast via digital satellite and cable; acquired by ProSiebenSat1. Media AG (Germany) in 2007; Man. Dir MARKUS BREITENECKER.

Sky Österreich GmbH: Schönbrunne Str. 297/2, 1120 Vienna; tel. (1) 166-20-0; e-mail service@sky.at; internet www.sky.at; f. 2003 as Premiere Fernsehen GmbH; adopted current name in 2009; satellite operator offering films, sport and adult programming; wholly owned by Sky Deutschland AG; Man. Dirs CARSTEN SCHMIDT, KAI MITTERLECHNER.

Finance

(cap. = capital; res = reserves; dep. = deposits; m. = million; brs = branches; amounts in euros)

BANKS

Banks in Austria, apart from the National Bank, belong to one of five categories: banks that are organized as corporations (i.e. joint-stock and private banks), and special-purpose credit institutions; savings banks; and co-operative banks. Co-operative banks include rural credit co-operatives (*Raiffeisenbanken*) and industrial credit co-operatives (*Volksbanken*). The remaining two categories comprise the mortgage banks of the various Austrian federal provinces, and the building societies. The majority of Austrian banks (with the exception of the building societies) operate on the basis of universal banking, although certain categories have specialized. Banking operations are governed by the Banking Act of 1993 *Bankwesengesetz*.

At the end of 2009 there were 855 banks and credit organizations in Austria.

Central Bank

Oesterreichische Nationalbank (Austrian National Bank): Otto-Wagner-Pl. 3, 1090 Vienna; tel. (1) 404-20; fax (1) 404-23-99; e-mail oenb.info@oenb.co.at; internet www.oenb.at; f. 1922; 100% state owned; cap. 12m., res 4,136.6m., dep. 35,168.6m. (Dec. 2009); Pres. KLAUS J. RAIDL; Gov. Prof. Dr EWALD NOWOTNY; brs in Graz, Innsbruck and Linz.

Commercial Banks

Adria Bank AG: Gonzagagasse 16, 1010 Vienna; tel. (1) 514-09-0; fax (1) 514-09-43; e-mail headoffice@adriabank.at; internet www.adriabank.at; f. 1980; 50.54% owned by Nova Kreditna Banka Maribor and 28.46% by Nova Ljubljanska Banka (both Slovenia), 21% by Beogradska Banka (Serbia); cap. 9.4m., res 20.9m., dep. 187.9m. (Dec. 2009); Chair. MATJAZ KOVACIC.

Alpenbank AG: Kaiserjägerstr. 9, 6020 Innsbruck; tel. (512) 599-77; fax (512) 562-01-5; e-mail private-banking@alpenbank.com; internet www.alpenbank.at; f. 1983 as Save Rössler Bank AG; name changed as above in 1991; cap. 10.2m., res 4.4m., dep. 204.8m. (Dec. 2009); Gen. Mans MARTIN STERZINGER, Dr HEIDI VEROCAI-DÖNZ.

Bank Gutmann AG: Schwarzenbergpl. 16, 1010 Vienna; tel. (1) 502-20-0; fax (1) 502-202-249; e-mail mail@gutmann.at; internet www.gutmann.at; f. 1970 as Bank Gebrüd AG; present name adopted 1995; 83% owned by Gutmann Holding AG, 17% owned by partners; cap. 12.2m., res 20.2m., dep. 624.2m. (Dec. 2009); Chair. Dr FRANK W. LIPPITT.

Bank Vontobel Österreich AG: Rathauspl. 4, 5024 Salzburg; tel. (662) 810-40; fax (662) 810-47; e-mail austria@vontobel.com; internet www.vontobel.at; f. 1885 as Bankhaus Berger & Co AG; name changed to Vontobel Bank AG 1998; present name adopted 2000; 99.95% owned by Vontobel Holding AG (Switzerland); cap. 9.6m., res 22.5m., dep. 296.7m. (Dec. 2009); CEO Dr ZENO STAUB.

Bank Winter & Co AG: Singerstr. 10, 1010 Vienna; tel. (1) 515-04-0; fax (1) 515-04-20-0; e-mail contact@bankwinter.com; internet www.bankwinter.com; f. 1892; re-established 1959; present name adopted 1986; dep. 977.1m., total assets 1,140.8m. (June 2010); Chair. and CEO THOMAS MOSKOVICS.

Bankhaus Carl Spängler und Co AG: Postfach 41, 5024 Salzburg; Schwarzstr. 1, 5020 Salzburg; tel. (662) 86-86-0; fax (662) 86-86-15-8; e-mail bankhaus@spaengler.at; internet www.spaengler.at; f. 1828; cap. 15m., res 41.3m., dep. 1,003.8m. (Dec. 2009); Chair., Management Bd HELMUT GERLICH; 9 brs.

Bankhaus Krentschker und Co AG: Am Eisernen Tor 3, 8010 Graz; tel. (316) 80-30-0; fax (316) 80-30-86-90; e-mail mail@krentschker.at; internet www.krentschker.at; f. 1924; 92.58% owned by Steiermärkische Bank und Sparkassen AG, 7.34% by Kärntner Sparkasse AG, and 0.08% by private shareholders; cap. 13.8m., res 44.6m., dep. 931.7m. (Dec. 2009); Chair., Management Bd Dr GEORG WOLF-SCHÖNACH; 3 brs.

Bankhaus Schelhammer & Schattera AG: Postfach 618, 1011 Vienna; Goldschmiedgasse 3, 1010 Vienna; tel. (1) 534-34-0; fax (1) 534-34-80-65; e-mail bank.office@schelhammer.at; internet www.schelhammer.at; f. 1832; cap. 50m., res 17.7m., dep. 656m. (Dec. 2009); Chair. MICHAEL MARTINEK; 1 br.

BAWAG PSK Bank für Arbeit und Wirtschaft und Österreichische Postsparkasse AG (BAWAG PSK): Georg-Coch-Pl. 2, 1018 Vienna; tel. (1) 599-05; fax (1) 534-53-22-84-0; e-mail kundenservice@bawagpsk.com; internet www.bawag.com; f. 1922 as Bank für Arbeit und Wirtschaft AG; acquired by Cerberus Capital Management (USA) in 2006; cap. 250m., res 1,821.5m., dep. 25,166m. (Dec. 2010); Chair., Management Bd BYRON HAYNES; 150 brs.

Capital Bank-Grawe Gruppe AG: Burgring 16, 8010 Graz; tel. (316) 807-20; fax (316) 807-23-90; e-mail office.graz@capitalbank.at; internet www.capitalbank.at; f. 1922 as Gewerbe- und Handelsbank; present name adopted 2001; wholly owned by Hypo-Bank Burgenland AG (Austria); cap. 10m., res 106.6m., dep. 482.7m. (Dec. 2009); CEO CHRISTIAN JAUK.

DenizBank AG: Thomas-Klestil-Pl. 1, 1030 Vienna; tel. (1) 505-10-52-02-0; fax (1) 505-10-52-02-9; e-mail service@denizbank.at; internet www.denizbank.at; f. 1996 as ESBANK AG; present name adopted 2003; 64.06% owned by DenizBank AS (Turkey), 35.93% by Deniz Leasing AS (Turkey); cap. 27.8m., res 48.5m., dep. 1,519.1m. (Dec. 2009); Chair., Supervisory Bd HAKAN ATES.

Investkredit Bank AG: Renngasse 10, 1010 Vienna; tel. (1) 531-35-0; fax (1) 531-35-98-3; e-mail invest@investkredit.at; internet www.volksbank.com/investkredit; f. 1957; owned by Österreichische Volksbanken AG; cap. 46m., res 336.8m., dep. 6,360.4m. (Dec. 2010); Pres. FRANZ PINKL; Chair. GERALD WENZEL.

Kathrein und Co Privatgeschäftsbank AG: Postfach 174, Wipplingerstr. 25, 1013 Vienna; tel. (1) 534-51-26-9; fax (1) 534-51-23-3; e-mail anita.ilic@kathrein.at; internet www.kathrein.at; f. 1924 as Kathrein & Co. Bank AG; present name adopted in 1998; owned by Raiffeisen Zentralbank Österreich AG; cap. 20m., res 7.1m., dep. 508m. (Dec. 2010); Chair. Dr CHRISTOPH KRAUS.

Meinl Bank AG: Postfach 99, Bauernmarkt 2, 1010 Vienna; tel. (1) 531-88-0; fax (1) 531-88-44-0; e-mail servicecenter@meinlbank.com; internet www.meinlbank.com; f. 1923; cap. 9m., res 60.1m., dep. 352.9m. (Dec. 2009); Chair., Management Bd Dr ROBERT KOFLER; 2 brs.

Österreichische Verkehrskreditbank AG: Auerspergstr. 17, 1080 Vienna; tel. (1) 93-11-09-0; fax (1) 93-11-09-18; e-mail vst-sekretariat@verkehrskreditbank.at; internet www.verkehrskreditbank.at; f. 1969; owned by BAWAG PSK Bank für Arbeit und Wirtschaft PSK; cap. 3.7m., res 9.4m., dep. 63.1m. (Dec. 2009); Pres. STEPHAN KOREN; Chair., Management Bd and CEO MANFRED SOOS.

Schoellerbank AG: Palais Rothschild, Renngasse 3, 1010 Vienna; tel. (1) 534-71-0; fax (1) 534-71-655; e-mail info@schoellerbank.at; internet www.schoellerbank.at; f. 1998 by merger of Schoellerbank AG (f. 1833) and Salzburger Kredit- und Wechsel-Bank AG (f. 1922); owned by UniCredit Bank Austria AG; cap. 20m., res 61.7m., dep. 1,649.2m. (Dec. 2009); Chair. ROBERT ZADRAZIL.

Unicredit Bank Austria AG: Schottengasse 6–8, 1010 Vienna; tel. (0) 505–05-25; fax (0) 505-05-56155; e-mail info@unicreditgroup.at; internet www.bankaustria.at; f. 1991; name changed as above in 2008; 96.3% owned by UniCredito Italiano, SpA; cap. 1,681m., res 5,128m., dep. 116,558m.(Dec. 2010); Group Chair. FEDERICO GHIZZONI; CEO WILLI CERNKO; 297 brs.

VakifBank International AG: Kärntner Ring 18, 1010 Vienna; tel. (1) 512-35-20; fax (1) 512-35-20-20; e-mail info@vakifbank.at; internet www.vakifbank.at; f. 1999 as Vakifbank International (Wien) AG; present name adopted 2002; 90% owned by Türkiye Vakifar Bankası TAO, 10% owned by Pension Fund of Türkiye Vakifar Bankası TAO; cap. 16m., res 29.7m., dep. 396.3m. (Dec. 2009); Chair. SÜLEYMAN KALKAN; Dep. Chair. VEDAT PAKDIL; 3 brs in Austria.

Valartis Bank (Austria) AG: Postfach 306, Rathausstr. 20, 1011 Vienna; tel. (0) 577-89-0; fax (0) 577-89-200; internet www.valartis.at; f. 1890 as Bankhaus Rosenfeld; present name adopted 2009; 80.1% owned by Valartis (Austria) GmbH, 19.9% by Valartis (Wien) GmbH; cap. 6.6m., res 71.6m., dep. 741.8m. (Dec. 2009); Man. Dirs GERALD DIGLAS, FRANZ WILHELM.

VTB Bank (Austria) AG: Postfach 560, Parkring 6, 1011 Vienna; tel. (1) 515-35; fax (1) 515-35-29-7; e-mail general@vtb-bank.at; internet www.vtb-bank.at; f. 1974 as Donau-Bank AG; present name adopted 2006; owned by Bank for Foreign Trade (Russia); cap. 212.7m., res 265m., dep. 1,892m. (Dec. 2009); CEO IGOR STREHL.

Regional Banks

Allgemeine Sparkasse Oberösterreich Bank AG (Sparkasse Oberösterreich): Postfach 92, Promenade 11–13, 4041 Linz; tel. (0) 50100-40000; fax (0) 50100-940000; e-mail info@sparkasse-ooe.at; internet www.sparkasse.at/oberoesterreich; f. 1849 as Allgemeine Sparkasse; present name adopted 1991; cap. 56.9m., res 43.8m., dep. 8,880.7m. (Dec. 2010); CEO and Chair. Dr MARKUS LIMBERGER; 140 brs.

Bank für Tirol und Vorarlberg AG (BTV): Postfach 573, Stadtforum, 6020 Innsbruck; tel. (512) 53-33-0; fax (512) 533-31-14-08; e-mail btv@btv.at; internet www.btv.at; f. 1904; mem. of 3 Banken Gruppe; cap. 50m., res 78.1m., dep. 6,903.6m. (Dec. 2010); Chair. Dr FRANZ GASSELSBERGER; 37 brs.

BKS Bank AG: St. Veiter Ring 43, 9020 Klagenfurt; tel. (463) 58-58-0; fax (463) 58-58-32-9; e-mail bks@bks.at; internet www.bks.at; f. 1922; fmrly Bank für Kärnten und Steiermark AG, present name adopted 2005; mem. of 3 Banken Gruppe; cap. 65.5m., res 97.9m., dep. 4,807.7m. (Dec. 2010); Dir-Gen. Dr HEIMO PENKER; 51 brs.

Hypo Alpe-Adria-Bank AG: Postfach 517, Alpen-Adria-Pl. 1, 9020 Klagenfurt; tel. (0) 502-02-0; fax (0) 502-02-30-00; e-mail austria@hypo-alpe-adria.com; internet www.hypo-alpe-adria.com; f. 1896 as Kärntner Landes- und Hypothekenbank AG; present name adopted 1999; 100% state-owned following the nationalization of Hypo Group Alpe Adria in Dec. 2009; cap. 30m., res 119.3m., dep. 5,564.8m. (Dec. 2010); Chair., Exec. Bd Dr GOTTWALD KRANEBITTER; 21 brs.

Hypo Alpe-Adria-Bank International AG: Alpen-Adria-Pl. 1, 9020 Klagenfurt; tel. (0) 502-02-0; fax (0) 502-02-3000; e-mail international@hypo-alpe-adria.com; internet www.hypo-alpe-adria.com; f. 1896 as Kaerntner Landes-und Hypothekenbank AG; reorganized structure in 2004 to form above; operates in 11 other European countries; 100% state-owned following the nationalization of Hypo Group Alpe Adria in Dec. 2009; cap. 1,623.2m., res -135.4m., dep. 34,786.2m. (Dec. 2010); Chair., Supervisory Bd Dr JOHANNES DITZ; Chair., Management Bd Dr GOTTWALD KRANEBITTER.

HYPO NOE Gruppe Bank AG: Kremsergasse 20, 3100 St Pölten; tel. (2742) 49-20-0; e-mail office@hypoinvest.at; internet www.hypoinvest.at; f. 1888 as Landes-Hypothekenbank Niederösterreich; present name adopted 2010; cap. 52m., res 144.8m, dep. 4,950.9m. (Dec. 2010); Pres. and Chair. HERBERT FICHTA; Gen. Man. Dr PETER HAROLD; 26 brs.

Hypo Tirol Bank AG: Meranerstr. 8, 6020 Innsbruck; tel. (512) 50-70-0; fax (512) 50-70-04-10-00; e-mail office@hypotirol.com; internet www.hypotirol.at; f. 1901 as Landes-Hypothekenbank Tirol AG; present name adopted 2000; owned by federal province of Tyrol; cap. 108.8m., res 83.2m., dep. 4,219.1m. (Dec. 2010); CEO Dr MARKUS JOCHUM; 20 brs in Austria.

Oberbank AG: Untere Donaulände 28, 4020 Linz; tel. (732) 78-02-0; fax (732) 78-02-21-40; e-mail office@oberbank.at; internet www.oberbank.at; f. 1869 as Bank für Oberösterreich und Salzburg; present name adopted 1998; mem. of 3 Banken Gruppe; cap. 86.3m., res 220.5m., dep. 13,018.5m. (Dec. 2010); Pres. and CEO Dr FRANZ GASSELSBERGER; 140 brs and sub-brs.

Oberösterreichische Landesbank AG (Hypo Oberösterreich): Landstr. 38, 4010 Linz; tel. (70) 76-39-0; fax (70) 76-39-37-3; e-mail vorstand@hypo-ooe.at; internet www.hypo.at; f. 1891 as Oberösterreichische Landes-Hypothekenanstalt; present name adopted 1988; 50.57 % owned by federal province of Upper Austria, 48.59% by Hypo Holding GmbH, 0.84% by employees; cap. 14m., res -14.9m., dep. 2,982.3m. (Dec. 2010); Pres. Dr WOLFGANG STAMPFL; Chair. and Gen. Man. Dr ANDREAS MITTERLEHNER; 18 brs.

Salzburger Landes-Hypothekenbank AG: Postfach 136, Residenzpl. 7, 5020 Salzburg; tel. (662) 804-6; fax (662) 804-64-64-6; e-mail office@hyposalzburg.at; internet www.hyposalzburg.at; f. 1909 as bank of the Government of Salzburg; present name adopted 1992; 50.03% owned by Hypo Holding GmbH, 25% owned by Oberösterreichische Landesbank AG, 14.97% owned by Raiffeisenlandesbank Oberösterreich AG, 10% owned by Salzburger Landesholding; dep. 4,661.1m., total assets 4,991.8m. (Dec. 2009); Gen. Man. Dr REINHARD SALHOFER; 25 brs.

Steiermärkische Bank und Sparkassen AG (Steiermärkische Sparkasse): Postfach 844, Am Sparkassenpl. 4, 8010 Graz; tel. (0) 50100-36000; fax (0) 50100-936000; e-mail international@steiermaerkische.com; internet www.sparkasse.at/steiermaerkische; f. 1825 as Steiermärkischer Sparkasse Graz; present name adopted 1992 following merger; 73% owned by Steiermärkische Verwaltungssparkasse, 25% by Erste Bank der oesterreichischen Sparkassen AG, 2% by employees; cap. 55.5m., res 122.5m., dep. 10,957.5m. (Dec. 2010); CEO Dr GERHARD FABISCH; 188 brs.

Tiroler Sparkasse Bankaktiengesellschaft Innsbruck (Tiroler Sparkasse): Postfach 245, Sparkassenpl. 1, 6020 Innsbruck; tel. (512) 59-10-07-00-00; fax (512) 50-10-09-70-00-0; e-mail sparkasse@tirolersparkasse.at; internet www.sparkasse.at/tirolersparkasse; f. 1822 as Sparkasse der Stadt Innsbruck; present name adopted 1990, following merger in 1975; 97.6% owned by AVS Beteiligungs GmbH, 1.8% owned by Erste Bank der oesterreichischen Sparkassen AG; cap. 66m., res 131.4m., dep. 3,514.1m. (Dec. 2009); Dirs WOLFGANG HECHENBERGER, HANS UNTERDORFER, KARL OBERNOSTERER; 49 brs.

Volkskreditbank AG (VKB Bank): Postfach 116, Rudigierstr. 5–7, 4010 Linz; tel. (732) 76-37-0; fax (732) 76-37-39-2; e-mail international@vkb-bank.at; internet www.vkb-bank.at; f. 1872; wholly owned by Volkskredit Verwaltungsgenossenschaft; cap. 5.6m., res 0.018m., dep. 2,274.6m. (Dec. 2010); Chair., Supervisory Bd KURT RUPP; CEO Dr ALBERT WAGNER; 40 brs.

Vorarlberger Landes- und Hypothekenbank AG: Hypo-Passage 1, 6900 Bregenz; tel. (50) 414-10-00; fax (50) 414-10-50; e-mail info@hypovbg.at; internet www.hypovbg.at; f. 1899 as Hypothekenbank des Landes Vorarlberg; name changed to Vorarlberger Landes- und Hypothekenbank 1990; status changed as above 1996; dep. 12,302m., total assets 13,159m. (Dec. 2008); Chair. Dr KURT RUPP; Chair., Management Bd Dr JODOK SIMMA; 25 brs.

Specialized Banks

European American Investment Bank AG (Euram Bank): Palais Esterházy, Wallnerstr. 4, 1010 Vienna; tel. (1) 512-38-80-0; fax (1) 512-388-08-88; e-mail office@eurambank.com; internet www.eurambank.com; f. 1999; cap. 10m., res 4.6m., dep. 711.7m. (June 2010); CEO VIKTOR POPOVIC.

Kommunalkredit Austria AG: Türkenstr. 9, 1092 Vienna; tel. (1) 316-31-0; fax (1) 316-31-105; e-mail kommunal@kommunalkredit.at; internet www.kommunalkredit.at; f. 1958; 99.78% stake acquired by federal Govt in Nov. 2008; cap. 225.3m., res 116.8m., dep. 2,670.6m. (Dec. 2010); Chair., Supervisory Bd Dr KLAUS LIEBSCHER; CEO and Chair., Exec. Bd ALOIS STEINBICHLER.

Oesterreichische Clearingbank AG (OeCAG): Am Hof 4, 1010 Vienna; tel. (1) 531-27-29-83; fax (1) 531-27-59-59; e-mail office@clearingbank.at; internet www.clearingbank.at; f. Oct. 2008 to facilitate provision of credit and loans within the banking sector; owned by 16 Austrian credit institutions; cap. 120m., res 20m. (Feb. 2009); Man. Dirs Dr JOHANN KERNBAUER, PETER NOWAK.

Oesterreichische Kontrollbank AG (OeKB): Postfach 70, Am Hof 4 & Strauchgasse 1–3, 1011 Vienna; tel. (1) 531-27-24-41; fax (1) 531-27-56-98; e-mail public.relations@oekb.at; internet www.oekb.at; f. 1946; administration of guarantees, export financing, stock exchange clearing, organization and administration of domestic bond issues, central depository for securities and settlement of off-floor transactions, money market operations; cap. 130m., res 3.3m., dep. 11,809.6m. (Dec. 2010); Mans Dr JOHANNES ATTEMS, Dr RUDOLF SCHOLTEN.

Zürcher Kantonalbank Österreich AG: Griesgasse 11, 5020 Salzburg; tel. (662) 80-48-0; fax (662) 80-48-33-3; e-mail info@zkb-oe.at; internet www.zkb-oe.at; f. 1885 as Bankhaus Daghofer & Co AG; present name adopted 2011; 100% owned by Zürcher Kantonalbank, Switzerland; cap. 6m., res 0.6m., dep. and bonds 129m. (Dec. 2009); Man. Dirs ADRIAN KOHLER, HERMANN WONNEBAUER, MICHAEL WALTERSPIEL; 2 brs.

Savings Banks

Dornbirner Sparkasse Bank AG: Postfach 199, Bahnhofstr. 2, 6850 Dornbirn; tel. (50100) 740-00; fax (50100) 741-80; e-mail service@dornbirn.sparkasse.at; internet www.sparkasse.at/dornbirn; f. 1867 as Dornbirner Sparkasse; name changed as above in 2002; 74% owned by Dornbirner Anteilsverwaltungssparkasse, 26% owned by DOSPA Aktienverwaltung GmbH; cap. 10m., res 198.4m., dep. 2,353.7m. (Dec. 2010); Gen. Man. WERNER BÖHLER; 15 brs.

Erste Bank der oesterreichischen Sparkassen AG (Erste Bank): Postfach 162, Graben 21, 1010 Vienna; tel. (1) 501-00-0; fax (1) 501-00-9; e-mail service.center@erstebank.at; internet www.sparkasse.at/erstebank; f. 1819; present name adopted 1997; cap. 2,513m., res 5,662.3m., dep. 142,692.3m. (Dec. 2010); Chair. ANDREAS TREICHL; Pres. HEINZ KESSLER; 1,043 brs in Austria.

Kärntner Sparkasse AG: Neuer Pl. 14, 9020 Klagenfurt; tel. (0) 50100-20706; fax (0) 50100-30000; e-mail info@kaerntnersparkasse.co.at; internet www.sparkasse.at/kaernten; f. 1835; 75% owned by private foundation Die Kärntner Sparkasse AG, 25% owned by Erste Group Bank AG; dep. 4,172.9m., total assets 4,598.5m. (Dec. 2009); Pres. HEINZ WOLSCHNER; Chair. and Gen. Man. ALOIS HOCHEGGER; 61 brs.

Salzburger Sparkasse Bank AG: Postfach 180, Alter Markt 3, 5021 Salzburg; tel. (0) 50100-20404; fax (0) 50100-941000; e-mail info@salzburg.sparkasse.at; internet www.sparkasse.at/salzburg; f. 1855 as Salzburger Sparkasse; present name adopted 1991; absorbed ALPHA-Beteiligungs GmbH in 1997; 95.7% owned by Erste Group Bank AG; cap. 34m., res 146.5m., dep. 3,856.9m. (Dec. 2009); Chair. PETER BOSEK; 79 brs.

Co-operative Banks

Österreichische Volksbanken-AG (VBAG): Kolingasse 19, 1090 Vienna; tel. (1) 504-00-40; fax (1) 504-004-36-83; e-mail mail@volksbank.com; internet www.volksbank.com; f. 1922 as Österreichische Zentralgenossenschaftskasse rGmbH; present name adopted 1974; cap.,339.2m., res -226m., dep. 24,597.8m., total assets 52,924m. (Dec. 2010); Chair. and CEO GERALD WENZEL.

Raiffeisen Centrobank AG: Tegetthoffstr. 1, 1015 Vienna; tel. (1) 515-20-0; fax (1) 513-43-96; e-mail office@rcb.at; internet www.rcb.at; f. 1973 as Centro International Handelsbank; present name adopted 2001; 99.99% owned by RZB IB Beteiligungs GmbH, 0.01% owned by Raiffeisen-Invest-Gesellschaft mbH; cap. 47.6m., res 6.7m., dep. 167m. (Dec. 2010); Chair. Dr EVA MARCHART.

Raiffeisen-Landesbank Steiermark AG: Kaiserfeldgasse 5–7, 8010 Graz; tel. (316) 80-36-0; fax (316) 80-36-24-37; e-mail info@rlb-stmk.raiffeisen.at; internet www.rlbstmk.at; f. 1927; cap. 135.3m., res 423.8m., dep. 5,794.8m. (Dec. 2010); Chair., Management Bd MARKUS MAIR; 89 mem. banks, with 339 brs.

Raiffeisen-Landesbank Tirol AG (RLB Tirol AG): Adamgasse 1–7, 6020 Innsbruck; tel. (512) 530-50; fax (512) 530-05-35-49; e-mail andrea.zankl@rlb-tirol.at; internet www.rlb-tirol.at; f. 1894; cap. 85m., res 259m., dep. 6,808.3m. (Dec. 2009); Chair. JOSEF GRABER; 82 mem. banks, with 272 brs.

Raiffeisenlandesbank Kärnten-Rechenzentrum und Revisionsverband rGmbH: Raiffeisenpl. 1, 9020 Klagenfurt; tel. (463) 99300-0; fax (463) 99300-30; e-mail rlb-ktn@rbgk.raiffeisen.at; internet www.raiffeisen.at/ktn; f. 1900 as Spar- und Darlehensverband Kärnten; present name adopted 1996; cap. 7m., res 171.6m., dep. 2,358.2m. (Dec. 2010); Chair. Dr HANS MALLIGA; Man. Dir PETER GAUPER.

Raiffeisenlandesbank Niederösterreich-Wien AG: Friedrich-Wilhelm-Raiffeisen-Pl. 1, Raiffeisenhaus, 1020 Vienna; tel. (1) 517-00-90-0; e-mail info@raiffeisenbank.at; internet www.raiffeisenbank.at; f. 1898; cap. 291m., res 432.7m., dep. 22,388.8m. (Dec. 2010); Chair., Supervisory Bd Dr JOHANNES SCHUSTER; Chair., Management Bd and CEO Dr MICHAEL KLAR, WALTER MÖSENBACHER, ELFRIEDE MARIA SCHIEFERMAIR.

Raiffeisenlandesbank Oberösterreich AG: Postfach 455, Europapl. 1A, 4020 Linz; tel. (732) 65-96-0; fax (732) 65-96-27-39; e-mail internet@rlbooe.at; internet www.rlbooe.at; f. 1900 as Oberösterreichische Raiffeisen-Zentralkasse rGmbH; name changed as above in 2004; cap. 253m., res 996.6m., dep. 12,778m. (Dec. 2010); Chair. Dr LUDWIG SCHARINGER; 100 mem. banks, with 451 brs.

Raiffeisenlandesbank Vorarlberg Waren-und Revisions Verband rGmbH: Rheinstr. 11, 6900 Bregenz; tel. (5574) 40-50; fax (5574) 40-53-31; e-mail info@raiba.at; internet www.raiba.at; f. 1895 as Verband der Spar-und Darlehenskassenvereine; name changed as above in 1995; cap. 28.4m., res 166.2m., dep. 6,129.5m. (Dec. 2009); Chair., Management Bd WILFRIED HOPFNER; 24 mem. banks, with 99 brs.

Raiffeisenverband Salzburg rGmbH: Postfach 6, Schwarzstr. 13–15, 5024 Salzburg; tel. (662) 88-86-0; fax (662) 88-86-13-80-9; e-mail friedrich.buchmueller@rvs.at; internet ww.rvs.at; f. 1905 as Salzburgische Genossenschafts-Zentralkasse; present name adopted 1949; cap. 54.2m., res 310.6m., dep. 6,249.6m. (Dec. 2010); Chair., Management Bd Dr GÜNTHER REIBERSDORFER; 67 mem. banks, with 150 brs.

Raiffeisen Zentralbank Österreich AG (RZB-Austria): Am Stadtpark 9, 1030 Vienna; tel. (1) 717-07-0; fax (1) 717-07-17-15; internet www.rzb.at; f. 1927; cap. 693.7m., res 1,050.6m., dep. 91,758.4m. (Dec. 2010); central institute of the Austrian Raiffeisen banking group; Chair., Supervisory Bd Dr CHRISTIAN KONRAD; Chair., Management Bd Dr WALTER ROTHENSTEINER.

Volksbank Linz-Wels-Mühlviertel AG: Postfach 234, Pfarrgasse 5, 4601 Wels; tel. (7242) 495-0; fax (7242) 495-97; e-mail office@volksbank-wels.at; internet www.volksbank-wels.at; f. 1912 as Welser Handels- und Gewerbekasse rGmhH; present name adopted 2010 following merger with Volksbank Linz-Mühlviertel rGmbH; cap. 3.3m., res 21m., dep. 306,9m. (Dec. 2009); Gen. Mans ANDREAS PIRKLBAUER, CHRISTIAN MAYR; 19 brs.

Bankers' Organization

Verband Österreichischer Banken und Bankiers (Austrian Bankers' Asscn): Börsegasse 11, 1010 Vienna; tel. (1) 535-17-71-0; fax (1) 535-17-71-38; e-mail bv@bankenverband.at; internet www.bankenverband.at; f. 1946; Pres. WILLIBALD CERNKO; CEO and Chair. Dr FRANZ GASSELSBERGER; Gen. Sec. MARIA GEYER; 64 mems and 17 extraordinary mems (Jan. 2010).

STOCK EXCHANGE

Wiener Börse (Vienna Stock Exchange): Wallnerstr. 8, 1014 Vienna; tel. (1) 531-65-0; fax (1) 532-97-40; e-mail info@wienerborse.at; internet www.wienerborse.at; f. 1771; 2 sections: Stock Exchange, Commodity Exchange; absorbed equity and futures exchanges in 1997; CEO Dr HEINRICH SCHALLER, Dr MICHAEL BUHL.

INSURANCE COMPANIES

In 2008 there were 60 insurance companies in Austria, with total assets of €92,580m.

Allianz Elementar Lebensversicherung-AG: Hietzinger Kai 101–105, 1130 Vienna; tel. (5) 900-90; fax (5) 900-970-000; e-mail feedback@allianz.at; internet www.allianz.at; life insurance; Chair., Supervisory Bd Dr WERNER ZEDELIUS; Chair., Management Bd Dr WOLFRAM LITTICH.

Allianz Elementar Versicherungs-AG: Hietzinger Kai 101–105, 1130 Vienna; tel. (5) 900-90; fax (5) 900-970-000; e-mail feedback@allianz.at; internet www.allianz.at; f. 1860; owned by Allianz SE; all classes except life insurance; Chair., Supervisory Bd Dr WERNER ZEDELIUS; Chair., Management Bd Dr WOLFRAM LITTICH.

Bank Austria Versicherung: Modecenterstr. 17, 1011 Vienna; tel. (1) 313-83-0; fax (1) 313-83-60-30; e-mail office@ba-v.at; internet www.ba-versicherung.at; f. 1911; life insurance; Dir. Gen. JOSEF ADELMANN.

Donau Versicherung AG: Argentinierstr. 22, 1040 Vienna; tel. (0) 503-307-01-10; fax (0) 503-309-970-110; e-mail wien@donauversicherung.at; internet www.donauversicherung.at; f. 1867; all classes; mem. of Vienna Insurance Group; Gen. Dir FRANZ KOSYNA.

FinanceLife Lebensversicherung AG: Postfach 150, Untere Donaustr. 21, 1029 Vienna; tel. (1) 214-54-01; fax (1) 214-54-01-37-80; e-mail service@financelife.com; internet www.financelife.com; life insurance; fmrly MLP-Lebensversicherung AG Wien; mem. of UNIQA Group; Chair., Management Bd HARTWIG LÖGER.

Generali Versicherung AG: Landskrongasse 1–3, 1011 Vienna; tel. (1) 534-01-0; fax (1) 532 09-49-11-011; e-mail headoffice@generali.at; internet www.generali.at; f. 1882 as Erste Österreichische Allgemeine Unfall-Versicherungs-Gesellschaft; Gen. Man. LUCIANO CIRINÀ.

Grazer Wechselseitige Versicherung AG (GRAWE): Herrengasse 18–20, 8011 Graz; tel. (316) 80-37-62-22; fax (316) 80-37-64-90; e-mail service@grawe.at; internet www.grawe.at; f. 1828; all classes; Gen. Dir Dr OTHMAR EDERER.

Oberösterreichische: Gruberstr. 32, 4020 Linz; tel. (0) 578-910; fax (0) 578-917-15-66; e-mail office@ooev.at; internet www.keinesorgen.at; f. 1811; life and non-life; Exec. Dir OTHMAR NAGL.

Raiffeisen-Versicherung AG: Untere Donaustr. 21, 1029 Vienna; tel. (1) 202-55-88; fax (1) 211-19-14-19; e-mail service@raiffeisen-versicherung.at; internet www.raiffeisen-versicherung.at; f. 1970; mem. of UNIQA Group; life and non-life; CEO Dr KLAUS PEKAREK.

Sparkassen Versicherung AG: Wipplingerstr. 36–38, 1011 Vienna; tel. (501) 007-54-00; fax (501) 009-754-00; e-mail sag@s-versicherung.co.at; internet www.s-versicherung.co.at; f. 1985; mem. of VIG; all classes; Dirs ERWIN HAMMERBACHER, MANFRED RAPF, HEINZ SCHUSTER.

UNIQA Versicherungen AG: Untere Donaustr. 21, 1029 Vienna; tel. (1) 211-75-0; fax (1) 214-33-36; e-mail info@uniqa.at; internet www.uniqagroup.com; f. 1999; CEO Dr ANDREAS BRANDSTETTER.

VIG (Vienna Insurance Group): Schottenring 30, 1010 Vienna; tel. (0) 503-502-00-00; fax (0) 503-509-920-000; e-mail info@vig.com; internet www.vig.com; f. 1824; life and non-life; CEO GÜNTER GEYER.

Wiener Städtische Versicherung AG: Schottenring 30, Ringturm, 1010 Vienna; tel. (0) 503-502-00-00; fax (0) 503-509-920-000; e-mail kundenservice@staedtische.co.at; internet www.wienerstaedtische.at; f. 1824; all classes; mem. of VIG; Dir-Gen. ROBERT LASSHOFER.

Wüstenrot Versicherungs-AG: Alpenstr. 61, 5033 Salzburg; tel. (570) 701-00; fax (570) 701-09; e-mail versicherung@wuestenrot.at; internet www.wuestenrot.at; life and non-life; Dirs Dr SUSANNE RIESS, Prof. ANDREAS GRÜNBICHLER.

Zürich Versicherungs AG: Schwarzenbergpl. 15, 1010 Vienna; tel. (1) 800-080-80-80; fax (1) 800-080-80-81; e-mail service@at.zurich.com; internet www.zurich.at; f. 1876; all classes; Chair. and CEO GERHARD MATSCHNIG.

Insurance Organization

Verband der Versicherungsunternehmen Österreichs (Asscn of Austrian Insurance Cos): Schwarzenbergpl. 7, 1030 Vienna; tel. (1) 711-56-0; fax (1) 711-56-27-0; e-mail vvo@vvo.at; internet www.vvo.at; f. 1945; Pres. WOLFRAM LITTICH; 143 mems.

Trade and Industry

GOVERNMENT AGENCIES

ABA—Invest in Austria: Opernring 3, 1010 Vienna; tel. (1) 588-58-0; fax (1) 586-86-59; e-mail office@aba.gv.at; internet www.aba.gv.at; f. 1982; promotes foreign investment in Austria; state-owned; Man. Dir RENÉ SIEGL.

Österreichische Industrieholding AG (ÖIAG): Dresdner Str. 87, 1201 Vienna; tel. (1) 711-14-0; fax (1) 711-14-24-5; e-mail kommunikation@oiag.at; internet www.oiag.at; f. 1946; Chair., Supervisory Bd Dr PETER MITTERBAUER; Man. Dir Dr PETER MICHAELIS.

CHAMBERS OF COMMERCE

All Austrian enterprises must by law be members of the Economic Chambers. The Federal Economic Chamber promotes international contacts and represents the economic interests of trade and industry at a federal level.

Wirtschaftskammer Österreich (Austrian Federal Economic Chamber): Wiedner Hauptstr. 63, 1045 Vienna; tel. (0) 590-90-0; fax (0) 590-90-02-50; e-mail office@wko.at; internet www.wko.at; f. 1946; 7 divisions: Banking and Insurance, Commerce, Crafts and Trades, Industry, Information and Consulting, Tourism and Leisure, Transport and Communications; these divisions are subdivided into branch asscns; Regional Economic Chambers with divisions and branch asscns in each of the 9 federal provinces; Pres. Dr CHRISTOPH LEITL; Sec.-Gen. ANNA-MARIA HOCHHAUSER; c. 370,000 mems.

INDUSTRIAL AND TRADE ASSOCIATIONS

Wirtschaftskammer Österreich—Bundessparte Industrie: Wiedner Hauptstr. 63, 1045 Vienna; tel. (0) 590900-3417; fax (0) 590900-273; internet www.wko.at/industrie; f. 1896 as Zentralverband der Industrie Österreichs (Central Fed. of Austrian Industry), merged into present org. 1947; Pres. CHRISTOPH LEITL; Sec.-Gen. ANNA MARIA HOCHHAUSER; comprises the following industrial feds:

Fachverband der Audiovisions- und Filmindustrie Österreichs (Film): Postfach 327, Wiedner Hauptstr. 63, 1045 Vienna; tel. (0) 590900-3010; fax (0) 590900-276; e-mail mueller@fafo.at; internet www.fafo.at; Pres. DANIEL KRAUSZ; Man. Dir Dr WERNER MÜLLER; 2,878 mem. cos (2006).

Fachverband der Bauindustrie (Building): Schaumburgergasse 20/8, 1040 Vienna; tel. (1) 718-37-37-0; fax (1) 718-37-37-22; e-mail office@bau.or.at; internet bau.or.at; Pres. HANS PETER HASELSTEINER; Gen. Dir MANFRED KATZENSCHLAGER; 150 mems.

Fachverband Bergwerke und Stahl (Mining and Steel Production): Wiedner Haupstr. 63, 1045 Vienna; tel. (1) 590900-3311; e-mail office@bergbaustahl.at; internet www.bergbaustahl.at; Pres. HEIMO STIX; Gen. Dir ROMAN STIFTNER; 35 mems.

Fachverband der Chemischen Industrie (Chemicals): Wiedner Hauptstr. 63, 1045 Vienna; tel. (0) 590900-3340; fax (0) 590900-

280; e-mail office@fcio.wko.at; internet www.fcio.at; Pres. PETER UNTERSPERGER; Gen. Dir Dr WOLFGANG EICKHOFF; 530 mems.

Fachverband der Elektro- und Elektronikindustrie—FEEI (Electrical): Mariahilfer Str. 37–39, 1060 Vienna; tel. (1) 588-39-0; fax (1) 586-69-71; e-mail info@feei.at; internet www.feei.at; Pres. ALBERT HOCHLEITNER; Man. Dir Dr LOTHAR ROITNER; c. 300 mems.

Fachverband der Fahrzeugindustrie (Vehicles): Wiedner Hauptstr. 63, 1045 Vienna; tel. (0) 590900-4800; fax (0) 590900-289; e-mail kfz@wko.at; internet www.fahrzeugindustrie.at; Pres. BRUNO KRAINZ; Gen. Sec. WALTER LINSZBAUER; c. 200 mems.

Fachverband der Gas- und Wärmeversorgungsunternehmungen (Gas and Heating): Schubertring 14, 1010 Vienna; tel. (1) 513-15-88-0; fax (1) 513-15-88-25; e-mail office@gaswaerme.at; internet www.gaswaerme.at; f. 1947; Pres. HELMUT MIKSITS; Gen. Dir MICHAEL MOCK; c. 500 mems.

Fachverband der Giessereiindustrie (Foundries): Postfach 339, Wiedner Hauptstr. 63, 1045 Vienna; tel. (0) 590900-3463; fax (0) 590900-279; e-mail giesserei@wko.at; internet www.diegiesserei.at; Pres. PETER MAIWALD; Dir ADOLF KERBL; 47 mems.

Fachverband der Glasindustrie (Glass): Wiedner Hauptstr. 63, 1045 Vienna; tel. (0) 590-900-3448; fax (0) 590-900-281; e-mail office@fvglas.at; internet www.fvglas.at; Dir ALEXANDER KRISSMANEK; 66 mems.

Fachverband der Holzindustrie (Wood): Postfach 123, Schwarzenbergpl. 4, 1037 Vienna; tel. (1) 712-26-01; fax (1) 713-03-09; e-mail office@holzindustrie.at; internet www.holzindustrie.at; f. 1947 as Fachverband der Sägeindustrie Österreichs; present name adopted 2000; Pres. Dr ERICH WIESNER; Dir Dr CLAUDIUS KOLLMANN; c. 1,500 mems.

Fachverband der Ledererzeugenden Industrie (Leather Production): Postfach 312, Wiedner Hauptstr. 63, 1045 Vienna; tel. (0) 590900-3453; fax (0) 590900-278; e-mail fvleder@wko.at; internet www.leather-industry.at; f. 1945; Pres. ULRICH SCHMIDT; Dir REGINA MICHELITSCH; 7 mems.

Fachverband Maschinen & Metallwaren Industrie (Machinery and Metalware Industries): Wiedner Hauptstr. 63, 1045 Vienna; tel. (0) 590900-3482; fax (0) 150-51-02-0; e-mail office@fmmi.at; internet www.fmmi.at; Pres. Dr CLEMENS MALINA-ALTZINGER; Man. Dir Dr BERNDT-THOMAS KRAFFT.

Fachverband der NE-Metallindustrie Österreichs (Austrian Non-Ferrous Metals Federation): Wiedner Hauptstr. 63, 1045 Vienna; tel. (0) 590900-3310; fax (0) 590900-3378; e-mail office@nemetall.at; internet www.nemetall.at; f. 1946; Pres. GERHARD GRILLER; Man. Dir ROMAN STIFTNER; 59 mems.

Fachverband der Mineralölindustrie (Petroleum): Wiedner Hauptstr. 63, 1045 Vienna; tel. (0) 590900-4892; fax (0) 590900-4895; e-mail office@oil-gas.at; internet www.oil-gas.at; f. 1947; Pres. GERHARD ROISS; Gen. Dir Dr CHRISTOPH CAPEK; 22 mems (2011).

Fachverband der Nahrungs- und Genussmittelindustrie (Provisions): Zaunergasse 1–3, 1030 Vienna; tel. (1) 712-21-21; fax (1) 712-21-21-35; e-mail fiaa@dielebensmittel.at; internet dielebensmittel.at; Pres. JOHANN MARIHART; Dir Dr MICHAEL BLASS; 422 mems.

Fachverband der Papier und Pappe verarbeitenden Industrie (Paper and Board Processing): Brucknerstr. 8, 1041 Vienna; tel. (1) 505-53-82-0; fax (1) 505-90-18; e-mail ppv@ppv.at; internet www.ppv.at; Pres. GEORG DIETER FISCHER; Gen. Dir MARTIN WILDERMANN; 98 mems.

Fachverband der Papierindustrie (Paper): Gumpendorferstr. 6, 1061 Vienna; tel. (1) 588-86-20-5; fax (1) 588-86-22-2; e-mail austropapier@austropapier.at; internet www.austropapier.at; Pres. THOMAS M. SALZER; Dir MARK LUNABBA; 27 mems.

Fachverband der Stein- und keramischen Industrie (Stone and Ceramics): Postfach 329, Wiedner Hauptstr. 63, 1045 Vienna; tel. (0) 590900-3531; fax (1) 505-62-40; e-mail steine@wko.at; internet www.baustoffindustrie.at; f. 1947; Pres. Dr ERHARD SCHASCHL; Gen. Dir Dr CARL HENNRICH; 400 mems.

Fachverband der Textil-, Bekleidungs-, Schuh- und Lederindustrie (Clothing, Shoe and Leather): Wiedner Hauptstr. 63, 1045 Vienna; tel. (0) 590900-4903; fax (0) 590900-4908; e-mail tbsl@wko.at; internet www.tbsl.at; Pres. REINHARD BACKHAUSEN; Man. Dir Dr FRANZ JOSEF PITNIK; 550 mems.

UTILITIES

Electricity

Burgenländische Elektrizitätswirtschafts-AG (BEWAG): Kasernenstr. 9, 7000 Eisenstadt; tel. (2682) 900-0; fax (2682) 900-01-90-0; e-mail info@bewag.at; internet www.bewag.at; f. 1958; owned by federal province of Burgenland (51%) and Burgenland Holding AG (49%); Chair., Management Bd HANS LUKITS.

Energie AG Oberösterreich: Postfach 298, Böhmerwaldstr. 3, 4021 Linz; tel. (732) 9000-0; fax (800) 8180-01; e-mail service@energieag.at; internet www.energieag.at; fmrly Oberösterreichische Kraftwerke AG; subsidiaries active in Germany, the Czech Republic, Hungary and Slovakia; 51% owned by federal province of Upper Austria; Chair. and Man. Dir Dr LEOPOLD WINDTNER.

Energie Steiermark AG: Leonhardstr. 59, 8010 Graz; tel. (316) 900-0; fax (316) 900-05-91-9; e-mail office@e-steiermark.com; internet www.estag.com; f. 1996 as holding co. for Steirische Wasserkraft- und Elektrizitäts-AG, Steirische Fernwärme and Steirische Ferngas; 75% owned by federal province of Steiermark; Chair. Dr OSWIN KOIS.

Energie-Versorgung-Niederösterreich AG (EVN): EVN Pl., 2344 Maria Enzersdorf; tel. (2236) 200-0; fax (2236) 200-20-30; e-mail info@evn.at; internet www.evn.at; Chair., Supervisory Bd GILBERT FRIZBERG.

Kärntner Elektrizitäts-AG (KELAG): Postfach 176, Arnulfpl. 2, 9010 Klagenfurt; tel. (463) 525-0; fax (463) 525-15-96; e-mail office@kelag.at; internet www.kelag.at; f. 1923; 51% owned by Kärntner Energieholding, 49% owned by RWE Energy AG; Pres Dr HERMANN EGGER, ARMIN WIERSMA, HARALD KOGLAR.

Österreichische Elektrizitätswirtschafts-AG (Verbund): Am Hof 6A, 1010 Vienna; tel. (1) 503-13-0; fax (1) 503-13-54-19-1; e-mail info@verbund.at; internet www.verbund.at; f. 1947; federal electricity authority; operates national grid, sells electricity wholesale to the 9 regional operators; Chair., Supervisory Bd Dr GILBERT FRIZBERG; Chair., Management Bd WOLFGANG ANZENGRUBER.

Salzburg AG für Energie, Verkehr und Telekommunikation: Bayerhamerstr. 16, 5020 Salzburg; tel. (662) 88-84-0; fax (662) 88-84-17-0; e-mail office@salzburg-ag.at; internet www.salzburg-ag.at; f. 2000 by merger of SAFE and Salzburger Stadtwerke; 42.56% owned by federal province of Salzburg, 31.31% by city of Salzburg and 26.13% by Energie Oberösterreich Service- und Beteiligungsverwaltungs-GmbH; Chair., Supervisory Bd DAVID BRENNER; Mans Dr ARNO GASTEIGER, AUGUST HIRSCH BICHLER.

Tiroler Wasserkraftwerke AG (TIWAG): Eduard-Wallnöfer-Pl. 2, 6020 Innsbruck; tel. 50607-27060; fax 50607-27050; e-mail office@tiwag.at; internet www.tiwag.at; f. 1924; Chair., Management Bd Dr BRUNO WALLNÖFER.

Vorarlberger Kraftwerke AG (VKW): Weidachstr. 6, 6900 Bregenz; tel. (5574) 601-0; fax (5574) 601-78-50-6; e-mail unternehmen@vkw.at; internet www.vkw.at; f. 1901; Chair. Dr LUDWIG SUMMER.

Wien Energie GmbH: Schottenring 30, 1011 Vienna; tel. (1) 531-23-0; e-mail office@wienenergie.at; internet www.wienenergie.at; Mans ROBERT GRÜNEIS, Dr ERICH HAIDER, FRIEDRICH PINK.

Gas

BEGAS (Burgenländische Erdgasversorgungs AG): Kasernenstr. 10, 7000 Eisenstadt; tel. (2682) 709-0; fax (2682) 709-174; e-mail marketing@begas.at; internet www.begas.at; Exec. Dirs RUDOLF SIMANDL (Commercial), REINHARD SCHWEIFER (Technical).

Oberösterreichische Ferngas-AG: Postfach 1, Neubauzeile 99, 4030 Linz; tel. (732) 38-83-0; fax (732) 38-83-93-00; e-mail ferngas@ooefg.co.at; internet www.ooeferngas.at; Chair. Dr JOHANN GRÜNBERGER.

Steirische Gas-Wärme GmbH: Gaslaternenweg 4, 8041 Graz; tel. (316) 900-0; fax (316) 900-02-80-00; e-mail gaswaerme@e-steiermark.com; internet www.e-steiermark.com; f. 2003 by merger of Steirische Fernwärme GmbH with Steirische Ferngas GmbH; part of Energie Steiermark AG; Man. Dir OLAF KIESER.

Water

Water is supplied to 90% of the population by municipalities, either directly or through private companies in which they retain a majority stake. The remaining 10% of the population accesses water from private wells or small facilities organized as co-operative societies.

Österreichischer Wasser- und Abfallwirtschaftsverband (ÖWAV) (Austrian Water and Waste Management Assen): Marc-Aurel-Str. 5, 1010 Vienna; tel. (1) 535-57-20; fax (1) 535-40-64; e-mail buero@oewav.at; internet www.oewav.at; f. 1909; Man. Dir MANFRED ASSMANN.

Association

Österreichische Vereinigung für das Gas- und Wasserfach (ÖVGW) (Austrian Association for Gas and Water): Schubertring 14, 1010 Vienna; tel. (1) 513-15-88-0; fax (1)513-15-88-25; e-mail office@ovgw.at; internet www.ovgw.at; f. 1881; independent, non-profit-making body, representing the technical, scientific and economic interests of gas and water; Man. MICHAEL MOCK.

TRADE UNIONS

National Federation

Österreichischer Gewerkschaftsbund (ÖGB) (Austrian Trade Union Fed.): Johann-Böhm-Pl 1, 1020 Vienna; tel. (1) 534-44-39-10-0; fax (1) 534-44-20-4; e-mail oegb@oegb.at; internet www.oegb.at; f. 1945; non-party union org. with voluntary membership; affiliated with ITUC and the ETUC; 8 affiliated unions; Pres. ERICH FOGLAR; 1,247,795 mems (Dec. 2007).

Affiliated Unions

Gewerkschaft Bau-Holz (Building Workers and Woodworkers): Ebendorferstr. 7, 1010 Vienna; tel. (1) 401-47; fax (1) 401-47-258; e-mail bau-holz@gbh.at; internet www.bau-holz.at; Pres. JOHANN HOLPER; 150,000 mems (2006).

Gewerkschaft der Gemeindebediensteten—Kunst, Medien, Sport, freie Berufe (Municipal Employees—Arts, Media, Sports and the Professions): Maria-Theresien-Str. 11, 1090 Vienna; tel. (1) 313-16-83-69-0; fax (1) 313-16-83-89-0; e-mail internationales.eu@gdg-kmsfb.at; internet www.gdg-kmsfb.at; Pres. CHRISTIAN MEIDLINGER; c. 155,000 mems.

Gewerkschaft Öffentlicher Dienst (Public Employees): Teinfaltstr. 7, 1010 Vienna; tel. (1) 534-54-0; fax (1) 534-54-207; e-mail goed@goed.at; internet www.goed.at; f. 1945; Pres. FRITZ NEUGEBAUER; c. 230,000 mems.

Gewerkschaft der Post- und Fernmeldebediensteten (Postal and Telecommunications Workers): Postfach 343, Biberstr. 5, 1010 Vienna; tel. (1) 512-55-11-0; fax (1) 512-55-11-52; e-mail gpf@gpf.at; internet www.gpf.at; f. 1945; Pres. GERHARD FRITZ; 59,618 mems (2006).

Gewerkschaft der Privatangestellten Druck, Journalismus und Papier (GPA—djp) (Commercial, Clerical and Technical Employees, Printing, Journalism and Paper Trade Workers): Alfred-Dallinger-Pl. 1, 1034 Vienna; tel. (1) 503-01-301; fax (1) 503-01-300; e-mail service@gpa-djp.at; internet www.gpa-djp.at; f. 2006 by merger of Gewerkschaft der Privatangestellten (f. 1945) and Gewerkschaft Druck, Journalismus und Papier (f. 1842); Pres. WOLFGANG KATZIAN.

Gewerkschaft vida: Margaretenstr. 166, 1050 Vienna; tel. (1) 546-41-0; fax (1) 534-44-10-21-00; e-mail info@vida.at; internet www.vida.at; f. 2006 by merger of Gewerkschaft der Eisenbahner, Gewerkschaft Handel, Transport, Verkehr and Gewerkschaft Hotel, Gastgewerbe, Persönlicher Dienst; Pres. RUDOLF KASKE; Sec.-Gen. NORBERT BACHER-LAGLER; c. 155,000 mems.

PRO-GE: Plösgasse 15, 1041 Vienna; tel. (1) 501-46; fax (1) 534-44-10-33-00; e-mail office@proge.at; internet www.proge.at; f. 2009 by the merger of Gewerkschaft der Chemiearbeiter (GdC)and Gewerkschaft Metall-Textil-Nahrung (GMTN); Pres. RAINER WIMMER.

Transport

RAILWAYS

ÖBB-Konzern (Austrian Federal Railways) operates more than 90% of all the railway routes in Austria. At December 2010 the total length of operated railway lines stood at 5,818 km, of which 1,824 km of single-track lines and 2,044 km of double-track lines were electrified. There are also several private railway companies.

ÖBB-Konzern (Austrian Federal Railways): Wienerbergstr. 11, 1100 Vienna; tel. (1) 930-00-0; fax (1) 930-00-25010; e-mail holding@oebb.at; internet www.oebb.at; f. 2004 following reorg. of Östereichische Bundesbahnen (ÖBB) in 2003; Chair., Management Bd CHRISTIAN KERN; consists of ÖBB Holding AG (management) and the following orgs:

ÖBB-Infrastruktur AG: Vivenotgasse 10, 1120 Vienna; tel. (1) 930-00-0; e-mail info@bau.oebb.at; internet www.oebb.at/infrastruktur; responsible for construction and maintenance of the rail infrastructure; provides power and telecommunications for the network; Chair., Management Bd ANDREAS MATTHÄ.

ÖBB-Personenverkehr AG: Wagramer Str. 17–19, 1220 Vienna; tel. (1) 930-00-0; e-mail service@pv.oebb.at; internet www.oebb.at/pv; passenger transport; jointly responsible, with Rail Cargo Austria AG (q.v.), for ÖBB-Produktion GmbH (locomotives) and ÖBB-Technische Services GmbH (technical services); subsidiary: ÖBB-Postbus GmbH; Chair., Management Bd GABRIELE LUTTER.

Rail Cargo Austria AG: Erdberger Lände 40–48, 1030 Vienna; tel. (1) 577-50; fax (1) 577-50-70-0; e-mail info@railcargo.at; internet www.railcargo.at; freight and logistics; jointly responsible, with ÖBB-Personenverkehr AG (q.v.), for ÖBB-Produktion GmbH (locomotives) and ÖBB-Technische Services GmbH (technical services); Chair., Management Bd FRIEDRICH MACHER.

ROADS

In 2008 Austria had some 107,262 km of classified roads, of which 2,133 km were motorways and 1,677 km were expressways. There are 145 tunnels with a total length of 340 km. The Autobahnen- und Schnellstrassen-Finanzierungs-Aktiengesellschaft (AFSINAG) regulates the planning, financing and maintaining of expressways and other roads.

Autobahnen- und Schnellstrassen-Finanzierungs-Aktiengesellschaft (AFSINAG): Rotenturmstr. 5–9, Postfach 983, 1011 Vienna; tel. (50) 108-0; e-mail office@asfinag.at; internet www.asfinag.at; f. 1982; planning, financing and maintaining of expressways and other roads; wholly owned by the Austrian Government; Chair. Dr KLAUS SCHIERHACKL.

INLAND WATERWAYS

The Danube (Donau) is Austria's only navigable river. It enters Austria from Germany at Passau and flows into Slovakia near Hainburg. The length of the Austrian section of the river is 350 km. Danube barges carry up to 1,800 metric tons, but loading depends on the water level, which varies considerably throughout the year. Cargoes are chiefly petroleum and derivatives, coal, coke, iron ore, iron, steel, timber and grain. The Rhine–Main–Danube Canal opened in 1992. A passenger service is maintained on the Upper Danube and between Vienna and the Black Sea. Passenger services are also provided on Bodensee (Lake Constance) and Wolfgangsee by Austrian Federal Railways, and on all the larger Austrian lakes.

CIVIL AVIATION

Civil aviation is regulated by the Federal Ministry of Transport, Innovation and Technology, as well as Austro Control GmbH (Austrian air traffic control), Österreichischer Aeroclub (the Austrian Aeroclub), provincial governors and district administrative authorities. The main international airport is located at Schwechat, near Vienna. There are also international flights from Graz, Innsbruck, Klagenfurt, Linz and Salzburg, and internal flights between these cities.

Principal Airlines

Austrian Airlines Group (Österreichische Luftverkehrs AG): Office Park 2, Postfach 100, 1300 Vienna Airport; tel. (1) 517-66; fax (1) 688-55-05; e-mail public.relations@austrian.com; internet www.aua.com; f. 1957; 95.4% owned by Deutsche Lufthansa AG, following a takeover in 2009; serves 130 cities in 66 countries worldwide; Chair., Supervisory Bd STEFAN LAUER; CEO JAAN ALBRECHT.

Austrian Arrows: Postfach 98, Fürstenweg 176, 6026 Innsbruck; tel. (512) 22-22-0; fax (512) 28-66-46; e-mail pressestelle@tyrolean.at; internet www.tyrolean.at; f. 1978 as Aircraft Innsbruck; renamed Tiroler Luftfahrt GmbH 1980; present name adopted 2003; brand name of Tyrolean Airlines; operates scheduled services and charter flights within Austria and to other European countries; Man. Dir CHRISTIAN FITZ.

Lauda Air Luftfahrt GmbH: Office Park 2, Postfach 56, 1300 Vienna-Schwechat; tel. (517) 667-38-00; fax (517) 667-90-05; e-mail info@laudaair.com; internet www.laudaair.com; f. 1979; became a scheduled carrier 1987; wholly owned by Austrian Airlines Group; operates scheduled passenger services and charter flights to Europe, Australia, the Far East and the USA; Chair. THOMAS SURITSCH.

Tourism

Tourism plays an important part in the Austrian economy. In 2010 Austria received 22.0m. foreign visitors at accommodation establishments. Receipts from the tourism sector were provisionally estimated at US $18,663m. in 2010. The country's mountain scenery attracts visitors in both summer and winter, while Vienna and Salzburg, hosts to a number of internationally renowned arts festivals, are important cultural centres.

Österreich Werbung (Austrian National Tourist Office): Margaretenstr. 1, 1040 Vienna; tel. (1) 588-66-0; fax (1) 588-66-40; e-mail b2b_info@austria.info; internet www.austriatourism.com; f. 1955; Pres. Dr REINHOLD MITTERLEHNER (Federal Minister of Economy, Family and Youth); CEO Dr PETRA STOLBA.

Defence

After the ratification of the State Treaty in 1955, Austria declared its permanent neutrality. To protect its independence, the armed forces were instituted. In 1995 Austria joined the Partnership for Peace programme of the North Atlantic Treaty Organization (NATO), but reaffirmed its neutrality in March 1998, having evaluated and discounted the possibility of becoming a full member of NATO. Military service is compulsory for male citizens and normally consists of six months' initial training, after which men remain liable for conscription until 50 years of age (65 years for officers, non-commissioned officers and specialists). As assessed at November 2011, the total armed forces numbered some 25,758. The air force (numbering 2,239), is an integral part of the armed forces. Total reserves in November 2011 numbered 187,886. In November 2004 the European Union (EU) ministers responsible for defence agreed to create a number of 'battlegroups' (each numbering about 1,500 men), which could be deployed at short notice to crisis areas around the world. The EU battlegroups, two of which were to be ready for deployment at any one time, following a rotational schedule, reached full operational capacity from 1 January 2007. Austria was committed to contributing troops to a battlegroup with the Netherlands, Germany and Finland in 2011. It was also to contribute troops to a battlegroup with Germany and the Czech Republic in 2012.

Defence Expenditure: Budgeted at €2,080m. for 2012.

Commander-in-Chief of the Armed Forces: Federal President Dr HEINZ FISCHER.

Chief of the Defence Staff: Gen. EDMUND ENTACHER.

Education

The central controlling body is the Federal Ministry of Education, Arts and Culture. Provincial boards (*Landesschulräte*) supervise school education in each of the nine federal provinces. According to preliminary figures, expenditure on education in 2008 was €15,042m. (equivalent to 10.9% of total spending).

Education is free and compulsory for nine years between the ages of six and 15 years. Pre-primary education at a *Kindergarten* between the ages of three to six years is optional. Primary education at a *Volksschule* lasts for four years between the ages of six and 10 years. For the first four years of secondary education, most students attend a *Hauptschule* (general secondary school) or an *Allgemeinbildende höhere Schule* (academic secondary school). After four years the *Hauptschule* may be followed by one of a variety of schools offering technical, vocational and other specialized training. The *Allgemeinbildende höhere Schule*, to which admission is gained through achievement at primary level or by entrance examination, provides an eight-year general education, divided into two four-year cycles, covering a wide range of subjects. After the lower secondary cycle the student may remain at the *Allgemeinbildende höhere Schule* or enrol at a *Berufsbildende höhere Schule* (higher technical and vocational college). Both these routes culminate in the *Reifeprüfung* or *Matura* (school-leaving certificate), which gives access to Austrian universities. A new comprehensive system of *Neue Mittelschulen* (New Secondary Schools) to cater for all children aged between 10 and 14 years was introduced on a trial basis in five provinces from September 2008. There were 244 of these schools in 2008/09.

Enrolment at pre-primary level included 86.5% of all children aged three to five years in 2008/09. Enrolment at primary level was equivalent to 97.4% of children in the relevant age-group (males 96.8%; females 98.0%). In 2007/08, according to the European Commission, approximately 80% of pupils aged 15 to 19 years were in education. About 91% of students attended public educational institutions in 2007/08, with the remaining 9% attending private institutions, which are mostly maintained by the Roman Catholic Church.

At tertiary level there are universities, *Fachhochschulen* (universities of applied sciences), private universities and colleges of teacher education, as well as vocational institutions. Institutes of adult education, *Volkshochschulen*, of which there were 207 in 2007, are found in all provinces, as are other centres operated by public authorities, church organizations and the Austrian Trade Union Federation. In addition, all Austrian citizens over the age of 24 years, and with professional experience, may attend certain university courses in connection with their professional career or trade. In 2005/06 enrolment at tertiary level was equivalent to 50% of those in the relevant age-group (males 46%; females 55%).

AZERBAIJAN

Introductory Survey

LOCATION, CLIMATE, LANGUAGE, RELIGION, FLAG, CAPITAL

The Republic of Azerbaijan is situated in the eastern South Caucasus, on the western coast of the Caspian Sea. To the south it borders Iran, to the west Armenia, to the north-west Georgia, and to the north the Republic of Dagestan, in Russia. The Autonomous Republic of Naxçıvan is part of Azerbaijan, although it is separated from the rest of Azerbaijan by Armenian territory. Azerbaijan also includes the territory of the self-proclaimed 'Republic of Nagornyi Karabakh' (Dağlik Karabağ), which is largely populated by Armenians. The Kura plain has a dry, temperate climate with an average July temperature of 27°C (80°F) and an average January temperature of 1°C (34°F). Average annual rainfall on the lowlands is 200 mm–300 mm, but the Lankaran plain normally receives between 1,000 mm and 1,750 mm. The official language is Azerbaijani, a South Turkic language. Religious adherence corresponds largely to ethnic origins: almost all ethnic Azerbaijanis (Azeris) are Muslims, some 70% being Shi'ite and 30% Sunni. There are also Christian communities, mainly representatives of the Russian Orthodox and Armenian Apostolic denominations. The national flag (proportions 1 by 2) consists of three equal horizontal stripes, of pale blue, red and green, with a white crescent moon framing a white eight-pointed star on the central red stripe. The capital is Baku (Bakı).

CONTEMPORARY POLITICAL HISTORY

Historical Context

An independent state in ancient times, Azerbaijan was dominated for much of its subsequent history by foreign powers. Under the Treaty of Turkmanchai of 1828, Azerbaijan was divided between Persia (now Iran) and Russia. During the latter half of the 19th century petroleum was discovered in Azerbaijan, and by 1900 the region had become one of the world's leading petroleum producers. Immigrant Slavs began to dominate Baku and other urban areas.

After the October Revolution of 1917 in Russia, there was a short period of pro-Bolshevik rule in Baku before a nationalist Government took power and established an independent state on 28 May 1918, with Gäncä (formerly Elisavetpol, but renamed Kirovabad in 1935–89) as the capital. Independent Azerbaijan was occupied by troops of both the Allied and Central Powers; after their withdrawal, it was invaded by the Red Army, and on 28 April 1920 a Soviet Republic of Azerbaijan was established. In December 1922 the republic became a member of the Transcaucasian Soviet Federative Socialist Republic (TSFSR), within the newly formed Union of Soviet Socialist Republics (USSR). The TSFSR was disbanded in 1936, and the Azerbaijani Soviet Socialist Republic (SSR) was formed.

Following the Soviet seizure of power in 1920, many nationalist and Islamic activists were killed. In 1930–31 forced collectivization of agriculture led to peasant uprisings, which were suppressed by Soviet troops. The purges of 1937–38, under the Soviet leader, Stalin (Iosif V. Dzhugashvili), involved the execution or imprisonment of many prominent members of the Communist Party of Azerbaijan (CPA). In 1945 the Soviet Government attempted to unite the Azeri population of northern Iran with the Azerbaijan SSR, by providing military support for a local 'puppet' government in Iran; Soviet troops were forced to withdraw from Iran in the following year by US-British opposition.

In 1982 Heydär Äliyev, First Secretary of the CPA since 1969, was promoted to First Deputy Chairman of the USSR Council of Ministers, while retaining his republican office; he remained influential at all-Union level until his dismissal from the Politburo in October 1987.

Domestic Political Affairs

From 1988, a principal focus of political debate concerned the status of Nagornyi Karabakh (a nominally autonomous oblast, or region, within Azerbaijan, which had a majority of ethnic Armenians among its population—see the separate section on this territory). In February the Soviet and Azerbaijani authorities rejected a request by the Nagornyi Karabakh regional soviet (council) for the transfer of the territory to Armenia. Amid rising inter-ethnic tensions, Azeris began leaving Armenia, and reports that refugees had been attacked led to three days of anti-Armenian violence in the Azerbaijani town of Sumqayıt. According to official figures, 32 people died, 26 of whom were Armenians. Disturbances continued, leading to a large-scale migration of refugees from both Armenia and Azerbaijan. In January 1989 the Soviet Government suspended the activities of the Nagornyi Karabakh authorities and established a Special Administration Committee (SAC), responsible to the USSR Council of Ministers. The dispatch of some 5,000 Soviet troops failed to reduce tensions within Nagornyi Karabakh.

In 1989 the nationalist Azerbaijan Popular Front Party (APFP) was established. The party organized a national strike in September and demanded discussion on the issues of sovereignty, Nagornyi Karabakh, the release of political prisoners and official recognition of the party. The Azerbaijan Supreme Soviet (Supreme Mäclis) agreed concessions to the APFP, including official recognition, and on 23 September adopted a 'Constitutional Law on the Sovereignty of the Azerbaijan SSR'. Azerbaijan closed its borders and prohibited all trade with Armenia. In November the Soviet Government transferred control of Nagornyi Karabakh from the SAC to an Organizing Committee, dominated by Azeris. The Armenian Supreme Soviet denounced this decision and declared Nagornyi Karabakh to be part of a 'unified Armenian republic', prompting further outbreaks of violence in Nagornyi Karabakh and along the Armenian–Azerbaijani border, while growing unrest within Azerbaijan was exacerbated by the influx of refugees from Armenia.

In January 1990 radical members of the APFP led assaults on CPA and government buildings in Baku. Border posts were attacked on the Soviet–Iranian border, and nationalist activists seized CPA buildings in Naxçıvan. Following renewed violence against Armenians, with some 60 people killed in rioting in Baku, the remaining non-Azeris were evacuated from the city. On 19 January a state of emergency was declared in Azerbaijan, and Soviet troops were ordered into Baku, where the APFP was in control. According to official reports, 131 people were killed during the Soviet intervention. The inability of the CPA to ensure stability led to the dismissal of Abdul Vezirov as First Secretary of the party; he was replaced by Ayaz Mutalibov.

Continuing unrest caused the scheduled elections to the republic's Supreme Soviet to be postponed until September–October 1990, and the continuing state of emergency severely disrupted campaigning by the opposition. When the new Supreme Soviet convened in February 1991, some 80% of its deputies were members of the CPA. The small group of opposition deputies united as the Democratic Bloc of Azerbaijan.

Unlike the other Caucasian republics (Armenia and Georgia), Azerbaijan declared a willingness to sign a new Union Treaty and participated in the all-Union referendum on the preservation of the USSR, which took place in March 1991. Official results of the referendum demonstrated qualified support for the preservation of the USSR, with 75.1% of the electorate participating, of whom 93.3% voted for a 'renewed federation'. In the exclave of Naxçıvan (separated from metropolitan Azerbaijan by Armenia), however, only 20% of voters supported the proposal.

In August 1991, following the attempted seizure of power in Moscow, the Russian and Soviet capital, by the conservative communist 'State Committee for the State of Emergency', Mutalibov issued a statement that appeared to demonstrate support for the coup. Large demonstrations took place, demanding his resignation; the declaration of Azerbaijan's independence; the repeal of the state of emergency; and the postponement of the presidential election, scheduled for 8 September. The opposition was supported by Heydär Äliyev, now Chairman of the Supreme Soviet of Naxçıvan. Mutalibov responded by ending the state of emergency and resigning as First Secretary of the CPA; on 30 August the Azerbaijani Supreme Soviet voted to 'restore the independent status of Azerbaijan'. The election to the presidency proceeded, although it was boycotted by the opposition, with the result that Mutalibov was the only candidate. According to official results, he won 84% of the total votes cast. At a congress of the CPA, held later in September, it was agreed to dissolve the party.

Independence

Independence was formally declared on 18 October 1991. On 21 December Azerbaijan joined the Commonwealth of Independent States (CIS, see p. 246), signing the Almaty (Alma-Ata) Declaration. Following the dissolution of the USSR, hostilities intensified in Nagornyi Karabakh. In March 1992 Mutalibov resigned as President, owing to military reverses. He was replaced, on an interim basis, by Yagub Mamedov, the Chairman of the Milli Mäclis, or National Assembly (which had replaced the Supreme Soviet following its suspension in late 1991), pending a presidential election in June. However, following further military reverses, the Mäclis reinstated Mutalibov as President in May. His immediate declaration of a state of emergency and the cancellation of the forthcoming presidential election outraged the APFP, which organized a large protest rally in Baku. Demonstrators occupied both the Mäclis building and the presidential palace, and succeeded in deposing Mutalibov, who took refuge in Russia. In June the leader of the APFP, Abulfaz Elchibey, was elected President of Azerbaijan in a popular vote, defeating four other candidates by a substantial margin.

The military defeats and continuing economic decline severely undermined the Government and led to divisions within the APFP in 1993. In June a rebel army, led by Col Surat Husseinov (the former Azerbaijani military commander in Nagornyi Karabakh), seized the city of Gäncä and advanced towards Baku, with the apparent intention of deposing Elchibey. In an attempt to bolster his leadership, Elchibey summoned Heydär Äliyev to the capital, and in mid-June Äliyev was elected Chairman of the Milli Mäclis. Following Elchibey's subsequent flight from Baku, in late June virtually all presidential powers were transferred, on an acting basis, to Äliyev by the Milli Mäclis (which had voted to impeach Elchibey), and Husseinov was appointed Prime Minister, with control over the security services. A referendum of confidence in Elchibey (who had taken refuge in Naxçıvan and still laid claim to the presidency) was held in late August 1993; of the 92% of the electorate that participated, 97.5% voted against him. The Milli Mäclis endorsed the result and announced a direct presidential election, which took place on 3 October. Äliyev was duly elected President, with 98.8% of the votes cast. The APFP boycotted the election.

The domestic political situation remained tense during 1994. Opponents of President Äliyev and his New Azerbaijan Party (NAP) were subject to increasing harassment. The signature, in May, of a cease-fire agreement in Nagornyi Karabakh led to further unrest, and large anti-Government demonstrations were organized by the APFP in Baku in May and September. In September the Deputy Chairman of the Milli Mäclis and Äliyev's security chief were assassinated; three members of the special militia, OPON, attached to the Ministry of Internal Affairs were subsequently arrested. In early October 100 OPON troops, led by Col Rövşän Cavadov, stormed the office of the Procurator-General, taking him and his officials hostage and securing the release of the three OPON members in custody. Äliyev described the incident as an attempted coup and declared a state of emergency in Baku and Gäncä. In the immediate aftermath of these events, other forces mutinied in Baku and elsewhere in Azerbaijan. In Gäncä, rebel forces occupied government and strategic buildings, although troops loyal to Äliyev quickly re-established control. Husseinov was dismissed as Prime Minister, and replaced, on an acting basis, by Fuad Quliyev. However, Äliyev stated that he would head the Government for the immediate future, and initiated a series of dismissals of senior members of the Government and the armed forces. In October the Milli Mäclis voted unanimously to remove Husseinov's parliamentary immunity from prosecution (he was, however, believed to have fled to Russia).

Further political turmoil arose in March 1995, following a decree by the Government to disband OPON. In response, OPON forces seized government and police buildings in Baku and in north-western regions, and many casualties were reported, as government forces clashed with the OPON units. The rebellion was crushed when government troops stormed the OPON headquarters near Baku; Cavadov and many of his men were killed, and some 160 rebels were arrested. Äliyev accused Elchibey and Husseinov of collusion in the attempted coup. The APFP was also accused of involvement, and the party was banned. In April Äliyev extended the state of emergency in Baku until June, although that in Gäncä was lifted. In May Quliyev was confirmed as Prime Minister.

Elections to the new, 125-member Milli Mäclis took place on 12 November 1995. Of Azerbaijan's 31 officially registered parties, only eight were permitted to participate; of these, only two were opposition parties—the APFP (recently relegalized) and the Azerbaijan National Independence Party (ANIP). Almost 600 nominally independent candidates were barred from participation. The elections were held under a mixed system of voting: 25 seats were to be filled by proportional representation on the basis of party lists and the remaining 100 by majority voting in single-member constituencies. These included the constituencies within Nagornyi Karabakh and the other territories occupied by ethnic Armenian forces (refugees from those regions voted in areas under Azerbaijani control). The results demonstrated widespread support for Äliyev's NAP, which won 19 of the 25 party-list seats (with the APFP and the ANIP receiving three seats each). The NAP and independent candidates supporting Äliyev won most of the single-constituency seats. Of the remaining 28 seats in the Mäclis, 27 were filled at subsequent 'run-off' elections, and one seat remained vacant. Some international observers declared that serious electoral violations had taken place. Concurrently with the election of the Milli Mäclis, Azerbaijan's new Constitution, which granted extensive executive powers to the President, was approved by 91.9% of the electorate in a national referendum.

In early 1996 supporters of Husseinov and Elchibey received lengthy custodial sentences for their involvement in the coup attempts of 1994 and 1995. In February 1996 two former government members were sentenced to death on charges of treason and several others were sentenced to death on conspiracy charges in the following months. Mutalibov, whom Äliyev had accused of conspiring with Cavadov, was arrested in Russia in April, although the Russian authorities refused to extradite him. Repressive measures against the opposition continued. In July Fuad Quliyev resigned as Prime Minister; he was succeeded by Artur Rasizadä, hitherto First Deputy Prime Minister. In September the Chairman of the Milli Mäclis, Räsul Quliyev, resigned. Murtuz Aleskerov, a staunch supporter of Äliyev, was elected in his place. In January 1997 the authorities released details of an abortive coup in October 1996, which had reportedly been organized by, among others, Mutalibov and Husseinov. Charges were subsequently brought against some 40 alleged conspirators, and in early 1997 many people received prison sentences for their part in the attempted coups of October 1994 and March 1995. Husseinov was extradited from Russia in March 1997 and was sentenced to life imprisonment in February 1999. (He received a presidential pardon in March 2004.) In January 1998 the Azerbaijani authorities accused Quliyev (who was now resident in the USA) of organizing a conspiracy to depose President Äliyev. In April Quliyev, who denied the accusations, was charged *in absentia* with alleged abuses of power while Chairman of the Milli Mäclis. (Further charges were brought against him in October 2000.)

Heydär Äliyev re-elected as President

A law regarding presidential elections, which required candidates to collect 50,000 signatures in order to stand, was approved in June 1998; the initially announced minimum level of voter participation of 50% was reduced to 25% in July. The opposition protested that the law favoured Äliyev's re-election, and launched a series of demonstrations to demand the cancellation of the election scheduled to be held in October. In September police and demonstrators clashed violently in Baku.

The presidential election was held, as planned, on 11 October 1998. According to official results, Äliyev was re-elected with 77.6% of the votes cast. Five other candidates contested the election, which was criticized by the Organization for Security and Co-operation in Europe (OSCE, see p. 388) and the Council of Europe (see p. 256) for failing to meet democratic standards. In late October the majority of government ministers, including the Prime Minister, were reconfirmed in their positions by President Äliyev. In December the Milli Mäclis approved a revised Constitution for Naxçıvan, which defined the exclave as an 'autonomous state' within Azerbaijan.

In April 2000 a large demonstration was organized by the Democratic Congress (including members of the APFP and the Civic Solidarity Party—CSP), which demanded the introduction of measures to ensure that the legislative elections due to be held in November would be free and fair. (Widespread electoral violations had been observed in the country's first municipal elections, held in December 1999.) Many arrests were made, and the security forces were accused of using excessive force. The death, in August, of Elchibey prompted the division of the APFP into traditionalist and reformist factions; the Central Electoral Commission (CEC) recognized only the reformist wing, led by Ali Kerimli. In September the CEC refused to register eight opposition parties. Although the CEC's decision was revoked, following strong criticism from the US Administration, a number of political parties decided to boycott the legislative elections, which they condemned as undemocratic.

The legislative elections, held, as scheduled, on 5 November 2000, were condemned by the OSCE for the falsification of results and intimidatory practices, and country-wide protests followed. Of the 25 seats filled by proportional representation, 17 were obtained by the NAP and four by the APFP, while the CPA and the CSP each secured two seats. Of the 99 seats contested in single-mandate constituencies, 62 were obtained by the NAP and 26 by independent candidates. The election results were invalidated in 11 constituencies, where polls were repeated on 7 January 2001. Although divisions within the NAP became increasingly evident during 2001, the ruling élite consolidated their control at a party congress in November, at which Äliyev was re-elected as Chairman and his son İlham (the Vice-Chairman of the State Oil Company of the Azerbaijan Republic—SOCAR) was elected First Deputy Chairman.

On 24 August 2002 a referendum was held on numerous constitutional amendments, including the transfer of executive power to the (presidentially appointed) Prime Minister from the Chairman of the Milli Mäclis in the event of the President's inability to govern; and for the outcome of the presidential election to be determined by a majority of the votes cast, rather than the existing prerequisite of two-thirds. According to official figures, 96% of votes (cast by 84% of the electorate) approved the constitutional amendments, although demonstrations followed, after reports by opposition parties and observers from the OSCE and the USA of fraud and procedural violations. Protest rallies and demonstrations to demand the President's resignation continued into the first half of 2003.

In April 2003 President Äliyev collapsed while delivering a televised speech, and in subsequent months he reportedly travelled abroad for medical treatment. On 4 August an emergency session of the Milli Mäclis approved İlham Äliyev's appointment as Prime Minister. Two days later Rasizadä assumed the premiership, on an acting basis, to allow İlham Äliyev to campaign for the presidential election, scheduled to take place in October. In early October it was announced that Heydär Äliyev was formally to withdraw his candidacy, in favour of his son.

The Presidency of İlham Äliyev

İlham Äliyev secured 79.5% of the votes cast in the presidential election, held on 15 October 2003. The second-placed candidate, the Chairman of the Equality Party (Müsavat), İsa Qämbär, obtained 12.1% of the votes cast, according to official results. Following reports of widespread electoral malpractice, the opposition refused to recognize the validity of the results and opposition protests were violently repressed by the authorities; there were reports of a number of deaths. İlham Äliyev was inaugurated as President in late October. The Milli Mäclis approved the nomination of Rasizadä as premier on 4 November, and the majority of ministers in the previous administration were subsequently reappointed. Heydär Äliyev's death was announced in mid-December. In April 2004 İlham Äliyev appointed a new Minister of Foreign Affairs, Elmar Mämmädyarov, and in July dismissed the long-standing Minister of National Security, Namiq Abbasov. By January 2005 some 50 people had received custodial sentences for their involvement in the protests that followed the 2003 presidential election.

Municipal elections were held on 17 December 2004, in which the NAP won 64.7% of seats and independent candidates received 31.1%. The elections failed to meet democratic norms, according to the OSCE. Three of the four largest opposition parties boycotted the elections in protest at pressure exerted by the authorities prior to the ballot, and the ANIP was the only major opposition party to participate; Etibar Mamedov resigned as Chairman of the ANIP shortly after the elections.

In advance of the legislative elections scheduled for late 2005, the only groups to submit a sufficient number of candidates to be entitled to campaign by way of the broadcast media were the ruling NAP, the Azerbaijan Liberal Party, the Freedom bloc (Azadlıq—comprising the Equality Party, the APFP and the Azerbaijan Democratic Party—ADP) and the New Policy bloc, which included the ANIP. These legislative elections were to be the first to be contested on a basis of single-mandate seats, rather than with the mixed system of voting previously in place. Another innovation was the emergence of several opposition youth groups, of which New Thinking was the most prominent. In August 2005 the leader of New Thinking was detained on conspiracy charges. None the less, several opposition leaders, detained on charges of inciting violence following the 2003 election, were released, under amnesty, in March 2005, and public demonstrations in Baku, prohibited since October 2003, were once again authorized.

In mid-October 2005 Räsul Quliyev, now in exile as leader of the ADP, was detained in Simferopol, Ukraine, after his aircraft was prevented from landing in Baku, where he had been intending to return in order to participate in the elections. Allegations emerged that a former Minister of Finance, Fikret Yusifov, had facilitated the transfer of large amounts of money from Quliyev to the prominent, reformist, Minister of Economic Development, Farhad Äliyev, in order to finance a coup attempt. In late October Farhad Äliyev and the Minister of Public Health, Ali Insanov, were dismissed from their government posts and arrested. Heydär Babayev, the erstwhile head of the State Securities Commission, was appointed as Minister of Economic Development in place of Farhad Äliyev. (In October 2007 Farhad Äliyev was sentenced to 10 years' imprisonment on charges of corruption and abuse of power, together with his brother, Rafiq, previously President of the Azpetrol Group, who received a term of nine years; four former senior ministry officials were also sentenced to custodial terms, while 13 were acquitted.)

The legislative elections were held on 6 November 2005. Observers from the OSCE and the Council of Europe stated that the polls again failed to meet democratic standards, and opposition parties subsequently held a number of large-scale protests. In late November the security forces violently dispersed a demonstration organized by the Freedom bloc, and further rallies were prohibited. Following the elections, İlham Äliyev dismissed several regional governors, whom he accused of having failed to prevent electoral irregularities. On 1 December the Constitutional Court endorsed the results of the elections in 115 of the 125 constituencies, but annulled the results in the remainder (including two constituencies in which opposition candidates, including Ali Kerimli of the APFP, had been elected). In total, the NAP won 56 seats, non-party candidates obtained 43 seats and the Freedom bloc received six seats; a number of other parties also obtained representation. Elections were repeated on 13 May 2006 in those constituencies in which the initial results had been annulled; subsequently, the NAP held a total of 61 seats, and there were 46 independent deputies.

The newly elected Milli Mäclis convened for the first time on 2 December 2005, and Oktai Äsädov of the NAP replaced Aleskerov as its Chairman. Following the elections President Äliyev effected numerous personnel changes, including the appointment in early December of Natiq Äliyev, hitherto the President of SOCAR, as Minister of Industry and Energy, the appointment in February 2006 of Col-Gen. Kämaläddin Heydärov as Minister of Emergency Situations, and the dismissal in April of the long-standing Minister of Finance, Avaz Alekperov. In May Abbas Abbasov, who had served as First Deputy Prime Minister for some 14 years, tendered his resignation. A new ministerial portfolio of Defence Industries was additionally created.

Following the elections, the opposition again fragmented, largely owing to a lack of consensus among the opposition parties over whether their deputies should participate in the Milli Mäclis. In November 2005 the ADP and the reformist wing of the APFP announced their intention to boycott both the new legislature and the forthcoming repeat elections. In February 2006 the Equality Party confirmed that it intended to participate in the work of the Milli Mäclis and announced its withdrawal from the Freedom bloc; the party had won four of the six legislative seats hitherto controlled by the bloc. Meanwhile, in January the ANIP divided into two rival factions, one supporting the party's Chairman, Ali Äliyev, and the other supporting the founder of the party, honorary party leader Etibar Mamedov, after Äliyev proposed withdrawing the ANIP from the New Policy bloc and aligning it with the Freedom bloc.

Serious irregularities were again observed during the municipal elections held on 6 October 2006. Meanwhile, the repression of independent media intensified, with frequent severe attacks and imprisonment, on what were widely regarded as fabricated charges, of journalists, particularly those employed by the *Azadlıq* (Freedom) newspaper (which, together with associated organizations, was evicted from its premises in November). In

January 2007 the European Court of Human Rights (ECHR) ruled in favour of Sardar Jalaloğlu of the ADP, who stated that his treatment by the authorities following the presidential election of 2003 constituted torture. In April 2007 a prominent journalist critical of the Government, Eynulla Fatullayev, was imprisoned for two-and-a-half years, on charges of libel relating to an internet article that suggested that both Azerbaijanis and Armenian forces were responsible for a massacre of hundreds of Azeri civilians during the conflict in Nagornyi Karabakh; in October he was sentenced to eight-and-a-half years' imprisonment on charges, widely considered to have been politically motivated, of terrorism, inciting ethnic hatred and tax evasion. In March 2008 a further attack against an *Azadlıq* journalist, allegedly connected with an article that he had written about the fraudulent sale of land by government officials, prompted strong international criticism and protests from local media organizations.

In response to the approval, in June 2008, by the Milli Mäclis of amendments to the electoral code, the main opposition parties, which regarded these as further benefiting the authorities, announced a boycott of the forthcoming presidential election in October; nevertheless, six minor opposition leaders registered to contest the poll. On 15 October İlham Äliyev was overwhelmingly elected to a second term of office, obtaining 88.7% of the votes cast, according to official results. Although international observers had reported a general lack of public interest during the campaign, reflecting a perceived lack of genuine competition resulting from the boycott, voter turn-out was officially recorded at 75.6%. While opposition parties complained of malpractice perpetrated by the authorities, an International Election Observation Mission stated that there had been significant improvements in the conduct of the election, but that it had failed to meet international standards in democratic pluralism, particularly with regard to bias in media coverage during the campaign. The US Administration issued a statement welcoming perceived progress in the organization of the election. On 24 October Äliyev was inaugurated for a second presidential term.

The abolition of presidential term limits

In October 2008 the Government announced a decision to prohibit broadcasts by international radio stations on national frequencies; the ban, which entered into effect in January 2009, attracted strong criticism from the Council of Europe. In March the Milli Mäclis adopted a number of controversial amendments to legislation on the media, notably allowing the suspension of media outlets for 'abuse of power'.

Meanwhile, shortly after İlham Äliyev's re-election in October 2008, the Executive Secretary of the NAP, Ali Ahmedov, proposed that the constitutional stipulation restricting the President to two terms of office be removed. In December the Milli Mäclis voted overwhelmingly in favour of conducting a national referendum on proposed legislation (strongly contested by opposition parties and civil society groups) to amend the Constitution accordingly. The Constitutional Court ruled in favour of the legality of the referendum, although opposition leaders urged a boycott of the plebiscite. The referendum, held as scheduled on 18 March 2009, resulted in the overwhelming approval of amendments to 29 articles of the Constitution; in addition to removing the limit on presidential terms, the amendments made provision for indefinite extension of the presidential and parliamentary mandates in the event of a state of war. Opposition parties disputed the official results and the official rate of participation of 70.8%, while the Council of Europe stated that adoption of the constitutional amendments violated government commitments to democratic principles. On 2 April Äliyev signed a decree officially incorporating the new amendments into the Constitution. An appeal submitted by opposition campaign groups against the final results was rejected by the Baku Appeals Court in early April. In June the Milli Mäclis adopted legislation placing new restrictions on the operations of non-governmental organizations (NGOs). In November a court in Baku convicted and sentenced to terms of imprisonment two authors of an online journal on charges of minor assault; their journal had hosted a satirical video appearing to mock Azerbaijani politicians and media. In March 2010 President Äliyev granted pardons to 72 prisoners, among them the editor-in-chief of *Azadlıq*. In November the ECHR upheld an appeal brought by former Minister of Economic Development Farhad Äliyev against the Azerbaijani authorities on the grounds that his sentence in October 2007 was in breach of his human rights; nevertheless, Farhad Äliyev and his brother, Rafiq, remained in detention.

The 2010 legislative elections

At the elections to the Milli Mäclis, held on 7 November 2010, the NAP secured 72 of the 125 seats, while two electoral alliances formed by parties regarded as loyal to the Government, the Democratic Bloc and Reform Bloc, took four and three seats, respectively; nominally independent candidates received 41 seats. Although all the opposition parties contested the elections (despite the registration of more than one-half of their nominated candidates having been rejected), the main opposition alliance, the APFP-Equality Bloc, failed to win any mandates. International observers suggested that the low voter turn-out, of only about 50.1%, reflected public disaffection following the failure of many prospective electoral candidates to secure registration. The Government rejected opposition demands that the legislative elections be repeated; however, findings by OSCE, the Parliamentary Assembly of the Council of Europe and European Parliament observers upheld allegations that the conduct of the elections had not been sufficiently democratic, citing a deficient candidate registration process, a restrictive political environment, biased media coverage and severe irregularities during the poll.

The resignation of the Chairman of the Supreme Council of the Equality Party from the opposition movement in December 2010, following differences with the party Chairman, and those of a number of senior and other members in early 2011, were widely attributed to discontent at its performance in the elections. Meanwhile, a government ban on the wearing of the *hijab* (headscarf) by female students in state educational institutions, which had been announced by the Minister of Education in November, prompted protests by Muslim activists in the following month. In January 2011 the leader of the proscribed Azerbaijan Islamic Party (AIP), Movsum Samadov, was arrested on charges of conspiring to overthrow the Government, after a video of a speech he had made denouncing President Äliyev was released on the internet. Later that month the Government announced the intensification of efforts to suppress corruption in the country. A number of local corruption investigations were subsequently initiated, and public sector employees removed and arrested.

Recent developments: anti-Government protests

In February 2011 a revived opposition grouping known as Public Chamber urged a campaign of anti-Government demonstrations. In early March about 50 people were detained during ensuing unauthorized anti-Government protests in Baku, which were led by youth groups and co-ordinated through social networking websites. A subsequent demonstration organized by opposition parties was violently dispersed by police forces. (Several prominent activists had also been arrested in the weeks prior to the demonstrations.) On 2 April some 200 arrests were reported during a large and unauthorized opposition demonstration termed a 'day of rage' in Baku; the OSCE condemned the violent measures employed by the security forces against the protesters. Further anti-Government demonstrations were organized by Public Chamber in central Baku during May and June, and were again accompanied by the arrest of large numbers of participants. In late May Fatullayev (whose continued detention had been condemned in 2010 by the ECHR) was released from prison under an amnesty announced by President Äliyev. However, later that year a number of opposition leaders arrested during the demonstrations received custodial terms, notably six prominent members of the Public Chamber grouping, who in August were sentenced to some three years' imprisonment for participation in the unauthorized 2 April protest; later in August a three-year sentence was imposed on a human rights activist, Vidadi Iskandarov, for alleged offences committed during the 2010 parliamentary election campaign.

In July 2011 the AIP, which had organized a number of protests against the ban on the *hijab* concurrently with the Public Chamber campaign, was refused authorization by the authorities to conduct a rally in Baku. The party's Deputy Chairman, Arif Qaniyev, and two other prominent members were arrested by the security services in August, following suspicions that they had engaged in subversive activities in collaboration with the Iranian authorities. In early October Samadov was convicted and sentenced to 12 years' imprisonment on charges of possession of armaments, planning to seize power and preparing a terrorist act; six other prominent AIP members received custodial terms of between 10 and 12 years. Also in October a further seven opposition activists were sentenced to terms of between two and three years for participation in the

2 April demonstration. In November the Milli Mäclis adopted legislation imposing severe penalties for the distribution of unsanctioned religious literature, enforcing participation in religious activity and the performance of religious ceremonies without governmental permission by individuals educated abroad. The introduction of the measures coincided with the publication of a report by the international human rights NGO Amnesty International criticizing a campaign of repression by the Azerbaijani authorities against opposition members and the independent media. In January 2012 the Ministry of National Security announced that it had discovered a conspiracy by an Iranian-sponsored group of terrorists to assassinate a number of public figures in Baku, including the Israeli ambassador to Azerbaijan. On 1 March riots broke out in the north-eastern town of Quba, and the house of the regional governor (whose resignation was demanded by the rioters, in response to derogatory remarks he had made about the residents of the region) was set alight, before the protesters were forcibly dispersed. One day later President Äliyev dismissed the governor. Later in the month four TV journalists were arrested on charges related to the riots. In mid-March a Azerbaijani journalist working for Radio Free Europe/Radio Liberty, Khadija Ismayilova, who had investigated incidents of corruption alleged to have been carried out by the family and entourage of the President, announced that she had received threats that a video of her engaging in sexual activity would be published online if she did not cease publishing the results of her investigations. After she made news of the threat public, the video was indeed published; the human rights organization Amnesty International stated that the video appeared to have been made with official complicity. In mid-April another prominent journalist, Idrak Abbasov, was hospitalized, after he was beaten by security guards working for SOCAR as he attempted to film the demolition of houses on behalf of the company on the outskirts of Baku.

Foreign Affairs

Regional relations

Although Azerbaijan signed the Almaty Declaration that established the CIS in December 1991, in October 1992 the Milli Mäclis voted that the country not participate in the organization. With the overthrow of the APFP Government and the accession to power of Heydär Äliyev, the country's stance was reversed, and in September 1993 Azerbaijan was formally admitted to full membership of the body. Azerbaijan did not renew its membership of the CIS Collective Security Treaty in 1999, because of the continued occupation of Nagornyi Karabakh by ethnic Armenian troops, and in protest against Russia's supply of armaments to Armenia. A visit to Azerbaijan by Russian President Vladimir Putin in January 2001, and the signature of a number of co-operation agreements, appeared to signal a new stage in relations between the two countries. President Heydär Äliyev undertook a reciprocal visit to Russia in January 2002, when a 10-year economic co-operation plan between the two countries was agreed. Furthermore, in September a bilateral agreement was signed on the delimitation of the Caspian Sea, according to which the seabed would be divided into national sectors, and the surface be used in common. A similar agreement had already been reached with Kazakhstan, and a trilateral agreement was signed in May 2003. In February 2004 the newly elected President of Azerbaijan, İlham Äliyev, undertook an official visit to Russia, during which the so-called Moscow Declaration was signed, reaffirming bilateral agreements signed in 1997 and 2001; a further visit followed in 2005. However, in December 2006 the Russian state-controlled natural gas monopoly Gazprom sharply increased the price of natural gas exports to Azerbaijan, prompting Azerbaijan to cease importing gas from Russia. Relations were further adversely affected by the rapprochement between Russia and Armenia in 2006.

Relations with Russia improved (amid rival Russian and European Union—EU, see p. 276) plans for prospective gas pipeline networks to supply fuel from the Caspian region to Europe); in June 2009 SOCAR and Gazprom signed an agreement during a visit to Azerbaijan by Russian President Dmitrii Medvedev, whereby Russia was to purchase 500m. cu m of natural gas annually from Azerbaijan, with effect from 2010. Following a defence co-operation agreement signed between Russia and Armenia in August 2010 that included Russian guarantees to protect Armenian security, in early September Medvedev made an official visit to Azerbaijan, where he provided assurances to İlham Äliyev that Russia's stated neutrality with regard to Nagornyi Karabakh remained unchanged. While Armenia had also announced plans in August to modernize its armed forces with supplies from Russia, reports (which were denied by Russian officials) emerged that Russia had sold air-defence missile systems to Azerbaijan. During Medvedev's visit to Baku an agreement was signed, under which the volume of natural gas exported to Russia by Azerbaijan was to increase significantly from 2011; an accord relating to the Samur river border between the two countries was also finalized.

The strengthening of relations with Turkey, which had been cultivated by successive leaderships following independence in 1991, continued throughout the 1990s and 2000s. Turkey supported Azerbaijan in the conflict over Nagornyi Karabakh, providing humanitarian and other aid and reinforcing Armenia's international isolation by closing its borders and prohibiting trade with that country. An intergovernmental agreement in support of the construction of a pipeline to connect the Azerbaijani petroleum fields near Baku with the Turkish port of Ceyhan, via Tbilisi, Georgia, was signed in October 1998 (see Economic Affairs). The BTC pipeline, as it was known, was inaugurated in 2005 and became fully operational in the following year. From 2005 plans to complete a rail transport connection between Turkey, Georgia and Azerbaijan (Kars–Akhalkalaki–Tbilisi–Baku) were revived, despite criticism from the USA, which objected to the project's exclusion of Armenia; construction officially began in November 2007. Also in November the recently elected Turkish President, Abdullah Gül, made an official visit to Azerbaijan. Following a significant improvement in relations between Turkey and Armenia (see the chapter on Armenia), in late September 2008 the ministers of foreign affairs of Azerbaijan, Armenia and Turkey met during the occasion of the UN General Assembly in New York, USA, to discuss the status of Nagornyi Karabakh. The measures taken by Armenia and Turkey from 2008 towards the normalization of relations between their countries was a source of concern within Azerbaijan. In May 2009 the Turkish Prime Minister, Reçep Tayyip Erdoğan, visited Baku, where he gave assurances that the Turkish–Armenian border would not be reopened until a resolution of the dispute over Nagornyi Karabakh had been reached. In October Turkey and Armenia signed an agreement on the normalization of relations; however, continued pressure from the Azerbaijani Government was instrumental in the Turkish legislature's subsequent failure to ratify the agreement and the formal suspension of the process by Armenia in April 2010. In May Azerbaijan and Turkey established a Strategic Partnership Council, which was intended to strengthen political, economic and cultural links. At the 10th summit meeting of Turkic-speaking countries in İstanbul, Turkey, in September, the Heads of State of Turkey, Azerbaijan, Kyrgyzstan, Kazakhstan and Turkmenistan finalized the formation of a Co-operation Council of Turkic-Speaking Countries.

In October 2011, at a ceremony in İzmir, Turkey, attended by President Äliyev and Prime Minister Erdoğan, agreements establishing the terms for gas transit from Azerbaijan to Europe via Turkey, and for Azerbaijani gas supplies to Turkey, were signed. On 26 December Azerbaijan and Turkey signed a memorandum of understanding in Ankara, Turkey, for the construction of a Trans-Anatolia gas pipeline to Europe, of which the consortium would be 80% owned by SOCAR; construction work was scheduled to begin in 2012 and to reach completion in 2017 (when the Şah Deniz gas field in the Caspian Sea was expected to enter into production).

The large Azeri minority in neighbouring Iran (numbering an estimated 20m.) was regarded as a potential source of tension. Nevertheless, official relations between Iran and Azerbaijan remained amicable. However, tensions arose over the status of the Caspian Sea, together with Azerbaijan's increasing involvement with international petroleum companies. In July 2001 an Iranian military patrol boat ordered Azerbaijani survey vessels leased by the company BP (of the United Kingdom) to leave a disputed area of the sea. In May 2002 President Heydär Äliyev paid an official visit to Iran, signing a number of accords on bilateral co-operation. A further agreement on economic co-operation was signed in October, which included plans for the construction of a pipeline to carry natural gas from Iran to Naxçıvan. In August 2004 President Muhammad Khatami of Iran visited Azerbaijan, signing 10 bilateral accords. President İlham Äliyev made a reciprocal visit to Iran in January 2005, where he signed further agreements. In December Presidents Äliyev and Khatami attended a ceremony in Naxçıvan to inaugurate a new natural gas pipeline, and a memorandum of understanding on further co-operation in the energy sector was signed.

During his first official visit to Baku in August 2007, Iranian President Mahmoud Ahmadinejad held talks with President Äliyev; five co-operation agreements, including one on energy matters, were signed. In November the Presidents of the Caspian littoral states of Azerbaijan, Iran, Kazakhstan, Russia and Turkmenistan signed a security co-operation agreement at a Caspian summit meeting in Baku. At a further meeting in Astana, Kazakhstan, in November 2011, however, representatives of the five littoral states failed to reach a settlement on issues of division of the Caspian Sea. In late 2011 the Azerbaijani Government accused the Iranian authorities of supporting subversive activities by militant Islamists within Azerbaijan and in January 2012 claimed that it had thwarted an Iranian conspiracy to assassinate the Israeli ambassador in Baku. In February Azerbaijan, in turn, strongly denied that it was assisting Israeli intelligence agents operating against Iranian targets on Azerbaijani territory, following a formal protest from the Iranian Government, although it was reported later in the month that Azerbaijan had purchased some US $1,600m. worth of advanced military equipment from an Israeli state-owned company, despite international concerns at the rapid increases in military expenditure in both Azerbaijan and Armenia in recent years. In March, as speculation mounted that Israel was planning to launch an attack on Iran, the Azerbaijani Ministry of Defence denied reports that it had permitted the Israeli military air force access to air bases near the Iranian border.

Other external relations

US-Azerbaijani relations improved significantly in the mid-1990s, and in 1997 President Heydär Äliyev visited the USA. A bilateral agreement on military co-operation was signed, and four contracts between SOCAR and US petroleum companies to develop offshore oilfields in the Caspian Sea were also concluded. New contracts for the development of the petroleum industry, worth US $10m., were signed during a visit to Washington, DC, USA, by Äliyev in 1999, and a financial agreement on the construction of the BTC pipeline was signed in Washington in 2000. In 2001 the USA agreed to halt the provision of financial assistance to separatists in Nagornyi Karabakh and commit funds to Azerbaijan, through the temporary suspension of Amendment 907 to the Freedom Support Act of 1992 (establishing a foreign assistance programme to the countries of the former USSR), which prevented the donation of aid to Azerbaijan while that country's closure of the Armenian border remained in place. The waiver was renewed annually. In 2005 Azerbaijan confirmed that two new, US-funded radar stations were under construction close to the Iranian and Russian borders, respectively. In October of that year Azerbaijan and the USA co-hosted the second annual Black Sea and Caspian Sea Maritime Non-proliferation Conference in Baku. In April 2006 President Ilham Äliyev made his first official visit to the USA. From 2008 Azerbaijan's relations with the USA were adversely affected by US support for the rapprochement between Armenia and Turkey. In July 2010 US Secretary of State Hillary Clinton met Äliyev for discussions in Baku during a regional tour. In September two members of the US Senate, at the instigation of a US-based Armenian advocacy group, indefinitely blocked the nomination of Matthew Bryza as the new US ambassador to Azerbaijan (a post that had remained vacant since July 2009), apparently as a result of the Turkish origins and connections of Bryza's wife. In December 2010 the Azerbaijani Government welcomed a decision by President Obama to appoint Bryza directly as ambassador on an interim basis. At the end of December 2011, however, Bryza left the post, following the continued failure of the Senate to confirm his appointment.

Following the outbreak of conflict involving Russia in Georgia in early August 2008 (see the chapter on Georgia), US Vice-President Dick Cheney visited Azerbaijan in the first part of a regional tour in early September. Later that month Äliyev visited Moscow to discuss the impact of the conflict in Georgia with his Russian counterpart, President Dmitrii Medvedev. In January 2009 Russia's suspension of gas supplies to Europe following a dispute with the Ukrainian Government over payment arrears, rendering the diversification of gas supply a main priority for the EU, further reinforced Azerbaijan's importance as an alternative source of energy to the Union. In that month the Government agreed to begin exports of gas to Greece and Bulgaria (pending transit agreements); Italy was also expected to become a purchaser of Azerbaijani gas.

By 2009 it appeared that Azerbaijan was seeking to diversify further the markets to which it would sell gas. In May President Äliyev, along with Presidents Mikheil Saakashvili of Georgia and Abdullah Gül of Turkey, and the Egyptian Minister of Petroleum, signed an agreement with the EU intended to result in the establishment of a 'Southern Corridor' of gas supplies from the Caspian to the Mediterranean region. In July 2010 Azerbaijan and the EU began negotiations on the signature of an Association Agreement in the framework of the Eastern Partnership established in the previous year. During a meeting in September in Baku, Presidents Äliyev, Saakashvili of Georgia, and Traian Băsescu of Romania, together with Prime Minister Viktor Orbán of Hungary, announced the launching of a liquefied natural gas project (the Azerbaijan–Georgia–Romania Interconnector) which was to import natural gas from Azerbaijan to Romania and then to Hungary. The Azerbaijani Government's commitment to providing large volumes of gas for the EU's planned Nabucco project (which would supply gas from the Caspian region to Western and Central Europe) continued to be widely regarded as essential for construction of the pipeline to proceed. In January 2011 Äliyev and European Commission President José Manuel Barroso signed a declaration on development of the 'Southern Corridor' to Europe, which was believed to be preparatory to investment decisions for the second phase of production at the Şah Deniz gas field in the Caspian Sea, and for construction of the Nabucco pipeline within the 'Southern Corridor' to Europe. Despite an unresolved dispute over the Azerbaijani–Turkmenistani maritime boundary in the Caspian Sea, the President of Turkmenistan, Gurbanguly Berdymuhamedov, subsequently declared his support for plans to transport Turkmenistani gas across the Caspian Sea to Azerbaijan and through the 'Southern Corridor' to Europe (also see Regional relations).

CONSTITUTION AND GOVERNMENT

Under the Constitution of November 1995, the President of the Republic of Azerbaijan is Head of State and Commander-in-Chief of the armed forces. The President, who is directly elected for a five-year term of office, holds supreme executive authority in conjunction with the Cabinet of Ministers, which is appointed by the President and is headed by the Prime Minister. Supreme legislative power is vested in the 125-member Milli Mäclis (National Assembly), which is directly elected for a five-year term. Judicial power is exercised by the Supreme Court, the Economic Court, the Court on Grave Crimes, the Court of Appeal and local courts. Naxçıvan has its own Supreme Court. Azerbaijan is divided into 74 administrative districts (rayons), of which eight are located within the Autonomous Republic of Naxçıvan, which forms an exclave to the west of metropolitan Azerbaijan, separated from the rest of the country by Armenian territory. The former autonomous oblast (region) of Nagornyi Karabakh and seven rayons located between Nagornyi Karabakh and Armenia are governed by internationally unrecognized authorities.

REGIONAL AND INTERNATIONAL CO-OPERATION

Azerbaijan is a member of the Commonwealth of Independent States (CIS, see p. 246) and the Organization for Security and Co-operation in Europe (OSCE, see p. 388). It is also a member of the Council of Europe (see p. 256), the Economic Co-operation Organization (ECO, see p. 269), the Organization of the Black Sea Economic Co-operation (see p. 402) and the Organization for Democracy and Economic Development (GUAM, see p. 465).

Azerbaijan joined the UN in 1992. The country joined the 'Partnership for Peace' programme of the North Atlantic Treaty Organization (NATO, see p. 373) in May 1994, and was awarded observer status at the Alliance in June 1999.

ECONOMIC AFFAIRS

In 2010, according to World Bank estimates, Azerbaijan's gross national income (GNI), measured at average 2008–10 prices, was US $45,983m., equivalent to $5,080 per head (or $9,050 per head on an international purchasing-power parity basis). During 2001–10, it was estimated, the population increased at an average rate of 1.2% per year, while gross domestic product (GDP) per head increased, in real terms, at an average annual rate of 14.1%. Overall GDP increased, in real terms, at an average annual rate of 15.5% in 2001–10. Real GDP increased by 5.0% in 2010.

According to the Asian Development Bank (ADB), agriculture (including fishing) contributed 5.7% of GDP in 2010, when some 38.2% of the working population were employed in the sector, according to official figures. The principal crops are grain, potatoes, barley, tomatoes, watermelons, apples and sugar beet. By 2001 all collective farms had been privatized. During 2001–10, according to World Bank estimates, agricultural GDP increased, in real terms, at an average annual rate of 5.2%. Agricultural GDP increased by 5.0% in 2010.

According to the ADB, industry (including mining, manufacturing, construction and power) contributed 64.0% of GDP in 2010. In that year 13.7% of the working population were employed in the sector, according to official sources. According to the World Bank, during 2001–10 industrial GDP increased, in real terms, at an average annual rate of 18.9%. Real sectoral GDP increased by 3.2% in 2010. Growth was driven principally by the mining sector.

Mining accounted for 49.0% of GDP in 2010 according to the ADB, while the sector employed just 1.0% of the working population, according to official figures. Azerbaijan is richly endowed with mineral resources, the most important of which is petroleum. The country's proven reserves of petroleum were estimated to total 1,000m. metric tons at the end of 2010, mainly located in offshore fields in the Caspian Sea, and production in that year was estimated at 50.9m. tons. In September 1994 the Azerbaijani Government and a consortium of international petroleum companies, the Azerbaijan International Operating Company (AIOC), concluded an agreement to develop the offshore oilfields, despite an unresolved dispute over the delineation of the maritime border with Turkmenistan. By 2000 the Azerbaijani state-owned oil company SOCAR had signed more than 20 production-sharing agreements with international partners. In October 2000 the Government of Azerbaijan signed an agreement with SOCAR and a consortium of petroleum companies on the construction of a pipeline from Baku, via Tbilisi (Georgia), to Ceyhan in Turkey. Construction work on what became known as the BTC pipeline began in 2003 and deliveries through the pipeline commenced in 2006. Although Azerbaijan has substantial reserves of natural gas (mostly off-shore), a lack of suitable infrastructure has meant that the country has been a net importer of gas. In 1999 a gas field was discovered at Şah Deniz in the Caspian Sea, with reserves estimated at 1,000,000m. cu m, and a pipeline was constructed to transport gas to Erzurum (Turkey), via Tbilisi, running parallel with the BTC pipeline. This new BTE or South Caucasus Pipeline commenced operations in 2006. Output of natural gas in 2010 amounted to 15,091m. cu m. Other minerals extracted include gold, silver, iron ore, copper concentrates, alunite (alum-stone), iron pyrites, barytes, cobalt and molybdenum.

According to the ADB, manufacturing accounted for some 5.8% of GDP in 2010, when it employed 4.8% of the population, according to official figures. The GDP of the sector rose, in real terms, at an average annual rate of 10.7% in 2001–08, according to the World Bank. Sectoral growth was 7.1% in 2008.

In 2010 the construction sector provided 8.0% of GDP, according to the ADB, and employed 6.6% of the working population, according to official figures. During 2001–10, according to UN figures, the GDP of the sector increased at an average annual rate of 29.4%. Construction GDP decreased by 8.8% in 2009 but increased by 22.7% in 2010.

In 2008 only 6.6% of Azerbaijan's supply of primary energy was provided by petroleum and petroleum products, compared with 72.0% in 2000. Natural gas accounted for 84.1% of production in 2008, compared with 19.8% in 2000. From 2006 the Russian gas supplier Gazprom significantly increased the prices charged to several of the states of the former USSR, prompting Azerbaijan to reduce drastically its imports of Russian gas later in that year and to suspend SOCAR's petroleum exports via the Baku–Novorossiisk pipeline in early 2007, in order to fuel domestic thermal power stations. In November 2006 a memorandum on energy co-operation was signed between Azerbaijan and the European Union (EU, see p. 276). Mineral fuels accounted for only 3.2% of merchandise imports in 2010.

In 2010 the services sector provided 30.4% of GDP, according to the ADB, and accounted for 48.1% of employment, according to official figures. During 2001–10 the GDP of the services sector increased, in real terms, at an average annual rate of 9.5%; growth of 4.5% was recorded in 2010, according to the World Bank.

In 2010 Azerbaijan recorded a visible trade surplus of US $19,730.4m., and there was a surplus of $15,040.4m. on the current account of the balance of payments. In that year the principal source of imports was Russia (supplying 17.3% of the total). Other major sources of imports were Turkey, Germany, the People's Republic of China and Ukraine. Italy was the largest export market in 2010, accounting for 33.0% of total exports. Other important purchasers were France and the USA. The principal exports in 2010 were mineral products, which accounted for 94.2% of all exports. The principal imports were machinery and electrical equipment (28.8% of all exports), base metals, vehicles and transportation equipment, prepared foodstuffs, chemical products and vegetable products.

Azerbaijan's budgetary surplus for 2010 was some 5,935.0m. manats. Azerbaijan's general government gross debt was 4,734m. manats in 2010, equivalent to 10.8% of GDP. At the end of 2009 the country's total external debt was US $4,865m., of which $3,403m. was public and publicly guaranteed debt. In that year, the cost of servicing long-term public and publicly guaranteed debt and repayments to the IMF was equivalent to 1.2% of the value of exports of goods, services and income (excluding workers' remittances). According to the International Labour Organization (ILO), consumer price inflation increased at an annual average rate of 8.1% during 2001–10. Consumer prices increased by 5.7% in 2010. According to official figures, 5.6% of the total labour force were registered as unemployed in 2010.

Despite economic disruption following the dissolution of the USSR, the economic prospects of Azerbaijan remained favourable, owing to its substantial mineral wealth and its strategic location between Russia, Central Asia and Southern Europe. In 1999 the State Oil Fund of Azerbaijan (SOFAZ) was established to manage petroleum- and gas-related revenue. Extremely rapid economic growth was recorded in 2005–07, following ithe operational launch of the BTC pipeline, while state revenue increased, partly owing to the expiry of the preferential tax arrangements hitherto enjoyed by foreign petroleum companies developing the Caspian oilfields. In 2010 lower international prices for oil and gas, combined with a downturn in export demand, resulted in considerably lower growth. Nevertheless, Azerbaijan's economic prospects continued to improve, owing in part to the increased gas dependency of the EU. In July 2010 Azerbaijan and the EU began negotiations on the signature of an Association Agreement in the framework of the Eastern Partnership established in May 2009, with objectives including the eventual establishment of a free trade area. Among major gas agreements reached by Azerbaijan, in January 2011 the Government and the President of the European Commission signed a declaration on developing a 'Southern Corridor' of gas supplies to Europe, within which, it was envisaged, a pipeline, known as Nabucco, would be constructed. (However, in March 2012 several of the companies involved in the project proposed that the envisaged Nabucco pipeline be reduced substantially in length and capacity.) In September the Azerbaijani authorities announced the discovery of significant new natural gas reserves at an off-shore field, near the Abşeron peninsula, increasing estimated reserves to 350,000m. cu m of gas. In December Azerbaijan and Turkey signed a memorandum of understanding for the construction of a Trans-Anatolia gas pipeline to Europe, by means of a consortium in which SOCAR was to hold an 80% share. By 2011, nevertheless, the Government, in accordance with IMF recommendations, increasingly favoured economic diversification, with development projects largely focused on non-energy-related sectors; modest overall economic growth in that year, anticipated at less than 4%, was largely generated by the non-oil sector.

PUBLIC HOLIDAYS

2013: 1 January (New Year), 8 March (International Women's Day), 20–21 March (Novruz Bayramy, Spring Holiday), 9 May (Victory Day), 28 May (Republic Day), 15 June (Gayidish, Day of Liberation of the Azerbaijani People), 26 June (Day of the Foundation of the Army), 7 August* (Ramazan Bayramy, end of Ramadan), 14 October* (Kurban Bayramy, Feast of the Sacrifice), 18 October (Day of Statehood), 12 November (Constitution Day), 17 November (Day of National Revival), 31 December (Day of Azerbaijani Solidarity World-wide).

* These holidays are dependent on the Islamic lunar calendar and may vary by one or two days from the dates given.

Statistical Survey

Source (unless otherwise stated): State Statistical Committee of the Republic of Azerbaijan, 1136 Baku, İnşaatçılar pr.; tel. (12) 438-64-98; fax (12) 438-24-42; e-mail sc@azstat.org; internet www.azstat.org.

Area and Population

AREA, POPULATION AND DENSITY

Area (sq km)	86,600*
Population (census results)†	
27 January 1999	7,953,438
13 April 2009 (rounded figure, preliminary)	
Total	8,922,300
Population (official estimate at 1 January)	
2011	9,111,100
Density (per sq km) at 1 January 2011	105.2

* 33,400 sq miles.
† Figures refer to *de jure* population.

POPULATION BY AGE AND SEX

(UN estimates at mid-2012)

	Males	Females	Total
0–14	1,078,907	927,261	2,006,168
15–64	3,346,728	3,475,265	6,821,993
65 and over	242,467	350,607	593,074
Total	4,668,102	4,753,133	9,421,235

Source: UN, *World Population Prospects: The 2010 Revision*.

Population by Age ('000, official estimates at 1 January 2011): *0–14:* 2,056.6; *15–64:* 6,512.8; *65 and over:* 541.7; *Total* 9,111.1.

ETHNIC GROUPS

(permanent inhabitants, 1999 census)

	Number ('000)	%
Azeri	7,205.5	90.6
Lazs (Lezghi)	178.0	2.2
Russian	141.7	1.8
Armenian	120.7	1.5
Talish	76.8	1.0
Others	230.7	2.9
Total	7,953.4	100.0

ECONOMIC REGIONS

(estimated population at 2009 census, preliminary)

	Area ('000 sq km)	Population (rounded)	Population density (per sq km)
Bakı şahari (Baku city)	2.13	2,046,100	960.6
Abşeron	3.29	514,200	156.3
Gäncä-Qazax	12.48	1,172,200	93.9
Şäki-Zaqatala	8.96	565,900	63.2
Länkäran	6.07	823,900	135.7
Quba-Xaçmaz	6.96	488,300	70.2
Aran	21.43	1,797,300	83.9
Yuxarı Qarabağ	7.25	607,500	83.8
Kälbäcär-Laçın	6.40	227,300	35.5
Dağlıq Şirvan	6.06	281,200	46.4
Naxçıvan*	5.50	398,400	72.4
Total	86.60	8,922,300	103.0

* Autonomous republic.

Note: The secessionist 'Republic of Nagornyi Karabakh', estimated to occupy some 11,458 sq km of the territory of the Republic of Azerbaijan, reported a total population of 137,747 at 1 January 2007.

PRINCIPAL TOWNS

(preliminary population results of 2009 census, unless otherwise indicated)

Bakı (Baku, the capital)	2,046,100	Naxçıvan	73,900
Gäncä*	313,300	Yevlax	55,100‡
Sumqayıt	309,700	Xankändi (Stepanakert)	55,000
Mingäçevir	96,400	Länkäran	48,500‡
Şirvan†	77,300	Ağdam	39,900‡

* Known as Kirovabad between 1935 and 1989.
† Known as Äli-Bayramlı between 1938 and 2008.
‡ Estimated population at 1 January 2008.

BIRTHS, MARRIAGES AND DEATHS

	Registered live births		Registered marriages		Registered deaths	
	Number	Rate (per 1,000)	Number	Rate (per 1,000)	Number	Rate (per 1,000)
2003	113,467	14.0	56,091	6.9	49,001	6.0
2004	131,609	16.1	62,177	7.6	49,568	6.1
2005	141,901	17.2	71,643	8.7	51,962	6.3
2006	148,946	17.8	79,443	9.5	52,248	6.2
2007	151,963	18.0	81,758	9.7	53,655	6.3
2008	152,086	17.8	79,964	9.3	52,710	6.2
2009	152,139	17.2	78,072	8.8	52,514	5.9
2010	165,643	18.5	79,172	8.9	53,580	6.0

Life expectancy (years at birth, official estimates): 73.6 (males 70.9; females 76.2) in 2010.

ECONOMICALLY ACTIVE POPULATION

(ISIC major divisions, annual average, '000 persons)

	2008	2009	2010
Agriculture, hunting, forestry and fishing	1,571.4	1,569.7	1,655.0
Mining and quarrying	43.1	41.2	41.5
Manufacturing	206.2	206.5	208.9
Electricity, gas and water supply	69.1	65.9	55.8
Construction	220.4	220.8	287.5
Wholesale and retail trade; repair of motor vehicles, motorcycles and household goods	653.4	654.5	626.7
Hotels and restaurants	25.4	25.4	46.9
Transport, storage and communications	209.4	209.8	234.9
Financial intermediation	21.0	21.0	24.4
Real estate, renting and business activities	151.8	152.0	161.7
Public administration and defence; compulsory social security	259.7	260.1	279.1
Education	346.4	348.0	349.8
Health and social work	187.6	194.6	170.3
Other community, social and personal service activities	146.4	148.5	186.6
Total employed	4,111.3	4,118.0	4,329.1
Unemployed	262.2	260.2	258.3
Total labour force	4,373.5	4,378.2	4,587.4

Health and Welfare

KEY INDICATORS

Total fertility rate (children per woman, 2009)	2.2
Under-five mortality rate (per 1,000 live births, 2009)	33
HIV (% of persons aged 15–49, 2007)	0.2
Physicians (per 1,000 head, 2006)	3.6
Hospital beds (per 1,000 head, 2006)	8.1
Health expenditure (2008): US $ per head (PPP)	395
Health expenditure (2008): % of GDP	4.3
Health expenditure (2008): public (% of total)	19.3
Access to water (% of persons, 2008)	80
Access to sanitation (% of persons, 2008)	45
Total carbon dioxide emissions ('000 metric tons, 2007)	31,748.6
Carbon dioxide emissions per head (metric tons, 2007)	3.7
Human Development Index (2011): ranking	91
Human Development Index (2011): value	0.700

For sources and definitions, see explanatory note on p. vi.

Agriculture

PRINCIPAL CROPS

('000 metric tons)

	2008	2009	2010
Wheat	1,645.8	2,096.2	1,272.3
Rice, paddy	3.7	4.4	3.9
Barley	605.5	643.7	513.3
Maize	158.6	151.2	134.7
Potatoes	1,077.1	983.0	953.7
Sugar beet	190.7	188.7	251.9
Hazelnuts	27.7	30.4	29.2
Cotton seed*	36.6	21.1	25.2
Cabbages and other brassicas	101.2	95.5	94.1
Tomatoes	468.0	424.8	434.0
Cucumbers and gherkins	207.6	209.6	217.0
Onions, dry	184.7	168.8	171.6
Garlic	21.5	22.7	21.1
Watermelons	299.1	300.7	328.8
Oranges	12.6	7.6	8.0*
Apples	205.0	204.2	211.7
Pears	37.2	36.2	35.5
Apricots	21.5	20.2	19.2
Peaches and nectarines	19.3	19.3	16.7
Plums	20.5	20.7	20.4
Grapes	115.8	129.2	129.5
Tobacco (leaves)	2.5	2.6	3.2
Cotton (lint)*	18.3	10.5	12.6

* Unofficial figure(s).

Aggregate production ('000 metric tons, may include official, semi-official or estimated data): Total cereals 2,419.9 in 2008, 2,903.4 in 2009, 1,927.4 in 2010; Total nuts 40.1 in 2008, 43.3 in 2009, 41.8 in 2010; Total pulses 26.2 in 2008, 23.2 in 2009, 21.8 in 2010; Total roots and tubers 1,077.1 in 2008, 983.0 in 2009, 953.7 in 2010; Total vegetables (incl. melons) 1,637.4 in 2008, 1,587.9 in 2009, 1,624.4 in 2010; Total fruits (excl. melons) 865.4 in 2008, 878.5 in 2009, 891.0 in 2010.

Source: FAO.

LIVESTOCK

('000 head, year ending September)

	2008	2009	2010
Horses	72	73	74
Asses	47	46	46
Cattle	2,213	2,281	2,328
Buffaloes	299	289	283
Pigs	19	10	5
Sheep	7,523	7,685	7,802
Goats	587	591	608
Chickens*	19,900	21,450	21,150
Turkeys*	854	903	800

* Unofficial figures.

Source: FAO.

LIVESTOCK PRODUCTS

('000 metric tons)

	2008	2009	2010
Cattle meat	77.0	102.5	114.2
Sheep meat	46.4	66.8	74.3
Pig meat	0.8	0.8	0.8
Chicken meat	51.6	67.0	64.5
Cows' milk	1,354.9	1,460.1	1,500.4
Hen eggs	60.8	72.4*	70.6*
Wool, greasy	14.8	15.3	15.6

* Unofficial figure.

Source: FAO.

Forestry

ROUNDWOOD REMOVALS

('000 cu m, excl. bark)

	2001	2002	2003
Total	13,500*	52,800†	6,500†

* FAO estimate.
† Unofficial figure.

2004–10: Total production assumed to be unchanged from 2003 (FAO estimates).

Source: FAO.

Fishing

(metric tons, live weight)

	2007	2008	2009
Capture	2,943	1,517	1,202
Azov sea sprat	2,450	1,020	839
Aquaculture	113	89	101
Total catch	3,056	1,606	1,303

Source: FAO.

Mining

	2008	2009	2010
Crude petroleum ('000 metric tons)	44,749	50,629	50,880
Natural gas (million cu m)	14,784	14,772	15,091

Source: BP, *Statistical Review of World Energy*.

Industry

SELECTED PRODUCTS

('000 metric tons, unless otherwise indicated)

	2006	2007	2008
Wheat flour	1,402	1,421	1,313
Wine ('000 hectolitres)	53	64	86
Beer ('000 hectolitres)	309	328	325
Mineral water ('000 hectolitres)	539	1,122	765
Soft drinks ('000 hectolitres)	1,899	2,182	2,235
Cigarettes (million units)	6,224	3,789	2,773
Cotton yarn—pure and mixed (metric tons)	360	377	382
Woven cotton fabrics ('000 sq m)	2,113	1,690	1,052
Footwear, excluding rubber ('000 pairs)	311	302	360
Cement	1,639	1,687	1,587
Caustic soda (Sodium hydroxide)	31	17	30
Jet fuels	693	761	731
Motor spirit (petrol)	1,043	1,129	1,320
Kerosene	44	32	41
Gas-diesel (distillate fuel) oil	2,095	2,109	2,525
Lubricants	77	55	66
Residual fuel oil (Mazout)	2,899	2,340	1,276
Electric energy (million kWh)	24,542	21,847	21,643

Bricks (million): 53 in 2005.

Source: UN Industrial Commodity Statistics Database.

2008 ('000 metric tons, unless otherwise indicated): Cement 1,595; Motor spirit (petrol) 1,320; Kerosene 771; Gas-diesel (distillate fuel) oil 2,526; Residual fuel oil (Mazout) 1,163; Finished cotton fabrics ('000 sq m) 768; Electric energy ('000 million kWh) 20.4.

2009 ('000 metric tons, unless otherwise indicated): Cement 1,286; Motor spirit (petrol) 1,235; Kerosene 610; Gas-diesel (distillate fuel) oil 2,367; Residual fuel oil (Mazout) 273; Finished cotton fabrics ('000 sq m) 807; Electric energy ('000 million kWh) 17.8.

2010 ('000 metric tons, unless otherwise indicated): Cement 1,277; Motor spirit (petrol) 1,250; Kerosene 601; Gas-diesel (distillate fuel) oil 2,488; Residual fuel oil (Mazout) 217; Finished cotton fabrics ('000 sq m) 1,103; Electric energy ('000 million kWh) 17.8.

Finance

CURRENCY AND EXCHANGE RATES

Monetary Units

100 gopik = 1 new Azerbaijani manat.

Sterling, Dollar and Euro Equivalents (30 December 2011)

£1 sterling = 1.216 new manats;
US $1 = 0.787 new manats;
€1 = 1.018 new manats;
10 new manats = £8.22 = $12.71 = €9.83.

Average Exchange Rate (Azerbaijani manats per US $)

2009 0.8038
2010 0.8027
2011 0.7897

Note: The Azerbaijani manat was introduced in August 1992, initially to circulate alongside the Russian (formerly Soviet) rouble, with an exchange rate of 1 manat = 10 roubles. In December 1993 Azerbaijan left the rouble zone, and the manat became the country's sole currency. The manat was redenominated from 1 January 2006, with 1 new unit of currency (new manat) equivalent to 5,000 of the old currency. Figures in this survey are given in terms of the new manat, where possible. In 1993 the Armenian dram was introduced as the prevailing currency in the self-declared 'Republic of Nagornyi Karabakh'.

STATE BUDGET

(million new manats)

Revenue*	2009	2010†	2011‡
Tax revenue	5,591	5,834	7,318
Value-added tax	2,013	2,082	2,451
Excises	485	515	495
Taxes on income	1,911	2,020	2,727
Taxes on international trade	421	292	651
Social security contributions	582	697	705
Other	179	227	289
Non-tax revenue	8,777	13,549	13,609
Total	14,368	19,383	20,927

Expenditure	2009	2010†	2011‡
Current expenditure	7,649	8,157	9,594
Wages and salaries	1,825	1,884	2,433
Goods and services	3,105	3,540	3,586
Transfers to households	2,287	2,328	3,001
Subsidies	289	239	214
Oil fund operating expenditures	10	14	15
Other purposes	97	114	173
Interest	36	39	172
Investment expenditure and net lending	4,378	5,294	7,632
Total	12,027	13,451	17,226

* Excluding grants received (million new manats): 0 in 2009; 3 in 2010 (preliminary); 0 in 2011 (projection).

† Preliminary figures.

‡ Projected figures.

Source: IMF, *Republic of Azerbaijan: Staff Report for the 2011 Article IV Consultation* (January 2012).

INTERNATIONAL RESERVES

(excl. gold, US $ million at 31 December)

	2008	2009	2010
IMF special drawing rights	1.61	237.84	236.59
Reserve position in IMF	0.12	0.21	0.21
Foreign exchange	6,465.51	5,125.73	6,172.17
Total	6,467.24	5,363.78	6,408.97

Source: IMF, *International Financial Statistics*.

MONEY SUPPLY

(million new manats at 31 December)

	2008	2009	2010
Currency outside depository corporations	4,145.67	4,174.77	5,455.78
Transferable deposits	1,552.17	1,492.60	1,825.50
Other deposits	2,707.18	2,764.27	3,227.28
Securities other than shares	89.20	37.55	18.92
Broad money	8,494.23	8,469.18	10,527.49

Source: IMF, *International Financial Statistics*.

COST OF LIVING

(Consumer Price Index; base: 2000 = 100)

	2007	2008	2009
Food (incl. tobacco)	174.6	224.4	221.0
Fuel	434.4	435.9	505.6
Clothing	160.4	266.9	394.6
All items (incl. others)	157.7	190.6	193.4

2010: Food (incl. tobacco) 237.0; All items (incl. others) 204.4.

Source: ILO.

NATIONAL ACCOUNTS

(million new manats at current prices)

Expenditure on the Gross Domestic Product

	2008	2009	2010
Government final consumption expenditure	3,409.7	3,960.1	3,994.5
Private final consumption expenditure	13,420.1	15,222.0	18,247.4
Changes in stocks	46.1	46.0	45.0
Gross fixed capital formation	7,457.0	6,700.0	7,035.0
Total domestic expenditure	24,332.9	25,928.1	29,321.9
Exports of goods and services	26,400.7	18,383.1	22,907.0
Less Imports of goods and services	9,418.9	8,226.9	8,772.2
Statistical discrepancy	–1,177.5	–482.8	–1,882.1
GDP in purchasers' values	40,137.2	35,601.5	41,574.6

Gross Domestic Product by Economic Activity

	2008	2009	2010
Agriculture and fishing	2,236.0	2,179.5	2,221.1
Mining	21,164.5	15,090.4	19,131.6
Manufacturing	1,888.7	1,967.3	2,255.9
Electricity, gas and water	443.8	418.1	465.0
Construction	2,800.3	2,554.3	3,134.3
Transport and communications	2,693.8	3,117.2	3,281.6
Trade	2,534.3	2,729.6	3,182.8
Finance	709.3	760.4	785.3
Public administration	599.2	764.9	783.5
Other services	2,959.4	3,778.7	3,823.4
Sub-total	38,029.3	33,360.4	39,064.5
Less Financial intermediation services indirectly measured	580.7	568.9	456.8
Indirect taxes *less* subsidies	2,688.6	2,810.0	2,967.0
GDP in purchasers' values	40,137.2	35,601.5	41,574.6

Source: Asian Development Bank.

BALANCE OF PAYMENTS

(US $ million)

	2008	2009	2010
Exports of goods f.o.b.	30,586.3	21,096.8	26,476.0
Imports of goods f.o.b.	–7,574.7	–6,513.9	–6,745.6
Trade balance	23,011.7	14,582.9	19,730.4
Exports of services	1,547.9	1,778.9	2,113.9
Imports of services	–3,891.2	–3,389.5	–3,846.0
Balance on goods and services	20,668.4	12,972.3	17,998.4
Other income received	595.1	551.4	675.5
Other income paid	–5,861.2	–4,070.6	–4,142.6
Balance on goods, services and income	15,402.4	9,453.2	14,531.3
Current transfers received	1,500.1	1,292.4	1,420.4
Current transfers paid	–449.7	–570.7	–911.3
Current balance	16,452.8	10,174.9	15,040.4
Capital account (net)	10.6	5.4	14.3
Direct investment abroad	–555.6	–326.1	–232.0
Direct investment from abroad	14.8	473.3	563.1
Portfolio investment assets	–320.8	–84.3	–163.3
Portfolio investment liabilities	–26.6	–54.5	24.5
Other investment assets	–13,197.5	–9,326.4	–14,698.0
Other investment liabilities	926.9	–364.0	1,810.6
Net errors and omissions	–845.1	–1,461.2	–989.7
Overall balance	2,459.5	–963.0	1,370.0

Source: IMF, *International Financial Statistics*.

External Trade

PRINCIPAL COMMODITIES

(US $ million)

Imports c.i.f.	2008	2009	2010
Vegetable products	519.5	313.9	437.4
Prepared foodstuffs, beverages, spirits and vinegar; tobacco and manufactured substitutes	486.0	519.6	616.4
Mineral products	336.8	172.2	208.2
Products of chemical or allied industries	438.0	402.4	437.9
Base metals and articles thereof	764.2	663.7	925.2
Machinery and mechanical appliances; electrical equipment; sound and television apparatus	2,208.3	2,132.3	1,903.2
Vehicles, aircraft, vessels and associated transportation equipment*	1,218.7	776.7	796.9
Miscellaneous manufactured articles	109.0	68.5	94.2
Total (incl. others)	7,170.0	6,123.1	6,600.6

Exports f.o.b.	2008	2009	2010
Vegetable products	252.1	227.6	190.3
Mineral products	46,369.5	13,644.2	20,119.9
Products of the chemical industry	107.6	33.7	47.9
Base metals and articles thereof	363.6	121.2	126.2
Vehicles, aircraft, vessels and associated transportation equipment*	130.5	171.4	181.1
Total (incl. others)	47,756.0	14,701.4	21,360.2

* Excluding railway or tramway rolling stock, ships and air transport facilities.

PRINCIPAL TRADING PARTNERS

(US $ million)

Imports c.i.f.	2008	2009	2010
China, People's Republic	478.8	485.2	587.6
France	132.8	142.2	136.1
Georgia	51.5	59.9	50.4
Germany	598.6	554.2	607.1
India	110.4	54.7	35.8
Iran	97.2	78.7	118.2
Italy	190.6	127.7	118.3
Japan	241.6	146.3	146.3
Kazakhstan	200.1	63.6	293.6
Netherlands	80.3	54.9	46.4
Russia	1,350.4	1,072.1	1,145.0
Sweden	22.6	118.1	42.7
Turkey	807.2	906.9	771.4
Turkmenistan	51.6	26.2	13.9
Ukraine	567.2	511.7	465.6
United Kingdom	386.0	274.7	302.8
USA	267.0	260.6	206.3
Total (incl. others)	7,170.0	6,123.1	6,600.6

Exports f.o.b.	2008	2009	2010
China, People's Republic	499.0	129.9	338.9
Croatia	542.7	193.7	787.2
France	2,322.7	1,326.1	1,856.5
Georgia	490.7	395.0	411.0
Germany	205.5	86.7	9.9
Greece	290.9	179.7	255.0
Iran	355.6	90.1	125.0
Israel	3,605.8	123.6	174.5
Italy	19,220.0	3,788.4	7,044.2
Russia	582.9	746.4	773.6
Spain	1,497.7	316.6	178.5
Turkey	626.2	107.6	170.9
USA	6,014.3	1,746.8	1,623.0
Total (incl. others)	47,756.0	14,701.4	21,360.2

Transport

RAILWAYS

	2008	2009	2010
Passengers carried ('000)	6,394	6,389	4,865
Passenger-km (million)	1,049	1,024	926
Freight carried (million metric tons)	27.4	20.8	22.2
Freight ton-km (million)	10,021	7,592	8,223

ROAD TRAFFIC
(vehicles in use at 31 December)

	2008	2009	2010
Passenger cars	700,080	759,203	815,683
Buses	29,340	29,985	29,569
Lorries and vans	113,088	117,378	118,460
Motorcycles	2,330	1,969	1,643

SHIPPING

Merchant Fleet
(registered at 31 December)

	2007	2008	2009
Number of vessels	302	301	305
Total displacement ('000 grt)	708.4	725.9	743.0

Source: IHS Fairplay, *World Fleet Statistics*.

International Sea-borne Freight Traffic
('000 metric tons)

	2009	2010	2011
Goods loaded	5,124	10,764	11,880
Goods unloaded	24	60	72

Source: UN, *Monthly Bulletin of Statistics*.

CIVIL AVIATION
(traffic on scheduled services)

	2008	2009	2010
Passengers carried ('000)	1,396	941	1,017
Passenger-km (million)	2,002	1,488	1,613
Freight carried ('000 metric tons)	43	32	40
Total ton-km (million)	129	110	138

Tourism

FOREIGN TOURIST ARRIVALS

Country of residence	2007	2008	2009
Georgia	403,677	607,875	529,613
Iran	201,109	308,650	329,913
Russia	497,876	630,860	598,894
Turkey	101,537	157,827	177,308
Total (incl. others)	1,332,701	1,898,936	1,830,367

Tourism receipts (incl. passenger transport unless otherwise indicated, US $ million): 454 in 2008; 456 in 2009; 621 in 2010 (excl. passenger transport, provisional).

Source: World Tourism Organization.

Communications Media

	2008	2009	2010
Telephones ('000 main lines in use)	1,310.5	1,401.1	1,506.6
Mobile cellular telephones ('000 subscribers)	6,548.0	7,757.1	9,100.1
Internet subscribers ('000)	410.0	521.5	870.6
Broadband subscribers ('000)	60.0	100.0	460.0

1999: Daily newspapers (number) 15; Daily newspapers (circulation) 80,000; Non-daily newspapers (number) 329; Non-daily newspapers (circulation) 122,000.

2000: Television receivers ('000 in use) 2,000; Book production (titles, incl. pamphlets) 400.

2005: Newspapers and magazines sent by post 17.3m.

Personal computers: 698,424 (80.5 per 1,000 persons) in 2008.

Sources: UN, *Statistical Yearbook*; UNESCO, *Statistical Yearbook*; and International Telecommunication Union.

Education

(2010/11 unless otherwise indicated)

	Institutions	Teachers	Students
Pre-primary	1,638	10,947*	112,892
General (primary and secondary)	4,532	173,123†	1,324,564
Specialized secondary education institutions	62	7,165†	53,451
Higher	51‡	14,933†	140,241

* State institutions only, 2004/05.
† 2009/10.
‡ Including specialized higher educational schools.

Pupil-teacher ratio (primary education, UNESCO estimate): 11.0 in 2009/10 (Source: UNESCO Institute for Statistics).

Adult literacy rate (UNESCO estimates): 99.5% (males 99.8%; females 99.2%) in 2007 (Source: UNESCO Institute for Statistics).

Directory

The Government

HEAD OF STATE

President: İLHAM ÄLIYEV (elected 15 October 2003, inaugurated 31 October; re-elected 15 October 2008, inaugurated 24 October).

CABINET OF MINISTERS
(May 2012)

Prime Minister: ARTUR RASIZADÄ.

First Deputy Prime Minister: YAQUB EYYUBOV.

Deputy Prime Minister: ELÇIN ÄFÄNDIYEV.

Deputy Prime Minister, responsible for Refugees and Displaced Persons: ÄLI HÄSÄNOV.

Deputy Prime Minister: ABID ŞÄRIFOV.

Minister of Foreign Affairs: ELMAR MÄMMÄDYAROV.

Minister of Internal Affairs: Col RAMIL USUBOV.

Minister of National Security: Lt-Gen. ELDAR MAHMUDOV.

Minister of Defence: Col-Gen. SÄFÄR ÄBIYEV.

Minister of Justice: FIKRÄT MÄMMÄDOV.

Minister of Defence Industries: YAVÄR CAMALOV.

Minister of Finance: SAMIR ŞÄRIFOV.

Minister of Taxation: FAZIL MÄMMÄDOV.

Minister of Economic Development: ŞAHIN MUSTAFAYEV.

Minister of Emergency Situations: Col-Gen. KÄMALÄDDIN HEYDÄROV.

Minister of Labour and Social Protection: FÜZULI ÄLÄKBÄROV.

Minister of Agriculture: İSMÄT ABASOV.

Minister of Culture and Tourism: ÄBÜLFÄZ QARAYEV.

Minister of Education: MISIR MÄRDANOV.

Minister of Health: OQTAY ŞIRÄLIYEV.

Minister of Communications and Information Technology: ÄLI ABBASOV.

Minister of Industry and Energy: NATIQ ÄLIYEV.

Minister of Youth and Sport: AZAD RÄHIMOV.

Minister of Ecology and Natural Resources: HÜSEYNQULU BAĞIROV.

Minister of Transport: ZIYA MÄMMÄDOV.

Note: The Chairmen of State Committees and Agencies are also members of the Cabinet of Ministers.

MINISTRIES

Office of the President: 1066 Baku, İstiqlaliyyät küç. 19; tel. (12) 492-53-81; fax (12) 492-35-43; e-mail office@pa.gov.az; internet www.president.az.

Office of the Prime Minister: 1066 Baku, Lermontov küç. 68; tel. (12) 492-84-19; fax (12) 492-91-79; e-mail nk@cabmin.gov.az; internet www.cabmin.gov.az.

Ministry of Agriculture: 1000 Baku, U. Hacıbayov küç., 40 Hökümat House; tel. and fax (12) 498-64-49; e-mail agro@azerin.com; internet agro.gov.az.

Ministry of Communications and Information Technology: 1000 Baku, Zarifa Äliyeva küç. 33; tel. (12) 498-58-38; fax (12) 498-79-12; e-mail mincom@mincom.gov.az; internet www.mincom.gov.az.

Ministry of Culture and Tourism: 1000 Baku, Azadlıq meydanı 1, 3rd Floor; tel. (12) 493-43-98; fax (12) 493-56-05; e-mail tourism_azerbaijan@yahoo.com; internet www.mct.gov.az.

Ministry of Defence: 1139 Baku, Azärbaycan pr.; tel. (12) 439-41-89; fax (12) 492-92-50.

Ministry of Defence Industries: 1141 Baku, Matbuät pr. 40; tel. (12) 539-24-53; fax (12) 510-63-47; e-mail info@mdi.gov.az; internet www.mdi.gov.az.

Ministry of Ecology and Natural Resources: 1073 Baku, Bahram Ağayev küç. 100A; tel. (12) 538-04-81; fax (12) 592-59-07; e-mail ekologiya.nazirliyi@gmail.com; internet eco.gov.az.

Ministry of Economic Development: 1016 Baku, Uzeyir Hajibeyov küç. 40, Government House; tel. (12) 493-88-67; fax (12) 492-58-95; e-mail office@economy.gov.az; internet www.economy.gov.az.

Ministry of Education: 1008 Baku, Xatai pr. 49; tel. (12) 496-06-47; fax (12) 496-34-83; e-mail office@edu.gov.az; internet edu.gov.az.

Ministry of Emergency Situations: 1073 Baku, M. Müşfiq küç. 501; tel. (12) 512-00-61; fax (12) 512-00-46; e-mail info@fhn.gov.az; internet www.fhn.gov.az.

Ministry of Finance: 1022 Baku, Samed Vurghun küç. 83; tel. (12) 404-47-46; fax (12) 493-05-62; e-mail info@maliyye.gov.az; internet maliyye.gov.az.

Ministry of Foreign Affairs: 1009 Baku, S. Qurbanov küç. 4; tel. (12) 596-90-00; fax (12) 596-90-01; e-mail katiblik@mfa.gov.az; internet www.mfa.gov.az.

Ministry of Health: 1022 Baku, M. Mirqasımov küç. 1A; tel. (12) 598-50-94; fax (12) 493-06-95; e-mail office@health.gov.az; internet sehiyye.gov.az.

Ministry of Industry and Energy: 1000 Baku, U. Hacibeyov küç. 40, Hökumat House; tel. (12) 598-16-75; fax (12) 598-16-78; e-mail azer.mensimli@mie.gov.az; internet www.mie.gov.az.

Ministry of Internal Affairs: 1005 Baku, Azerbaycan pr. 7; tel. (12) 590-92-22; fax (12) 492-45-90; e-mail info@mia.gov.az; internet mia.gov.az.

Ministry of Justice: 1000 Baku, İnşaatçılar pr. 1; tel. and fax (12) 430-09-77; e-mail contact@justice.gov.az; internet www.justice.gov.az.

Ministry of Labour and Social Protection: 1009 Baku, S. Asgarov küç. 85; tel. (12) 596-50-03; fax (12) 596-50-22; e-mail mlspp@mlspp.gov.az; internet www.mlspp.gov.az.

Ministry of National Security: 1006 Baku, Parlement pr. 2; tel. and fax (12) 493-76-22; e-mail cpr@mns.gov.az; internet mns.gov.az.

Ministry of Taxation: 1073 Baku, Landau küç. 16; tel. (12) 403-89-70; fax (12) 403-89-71; e-mail office@taxes.gov.az; internet www.taxes.gov.az.

Ministry of Transport: 1122 Baku, Tbilisi pr. 1054; tel. (12) 430-99-41; fax (12) 430-99-42; e-mail ziyamamedov@mintrans.az; internet mot.gov.az.

Ministry of Youth and Sport: 1072 Baku, Olimpiya küç. 4; tel. (12) 465-64-42; fax (12) 465-64-38; e-mail mys@mys.gov.az; internet mys.gov.az.

President

Presidential Election, 15 October 2008

Candidates	Votes	% of votes
İlham Äliyev (New Azerbaijan Party)	3,232,259	88.73
İqbal Ağazadä (Azerbaijan Hope Party)	104,279	2.86
Fazıl Mustafayev (Great Creation Party)	89,985	2.47
Qüdrät Häsänquliyev (United Azerbaijan Popular Front Party)	83,037	2.28
Qulamhüseyn Surxay Älibayli (Independent)	81,120	2.23
Others	52,194	1.43
Total	3,642,874	100.00

Legislature

Milli Mäclis (National Assembly)

1152 Baku, Parlament pr. 1; tel. (12) 437-21-27; fax (12) 493-49-43; e-mail azmm@meclis.gov.az; internet www.meclis.gov.az.

Chairman: OKTAY ÄSÄDOV.

General Election, 7 November 2010

Parties and blocs	Seats
New Azerbaijan Party	72*
Democratic Bloc	4†
Reform Bloc	3‡
Fatherland Party	2
Karabakh Bloc	1§
Azerbaijan Social Welfare Party	1
Civic Unity Party	1
Others	41¶
Total	125

* Including one party member who contested the elections as an independent candidate.

† Comprising three members of the Civic Solidarity Party and one member of the Azerbaijan Democratic Reforms Party.

‡ Comprising one member of the United Azerbaijan Popular Front Party, one member of the Great Creation Party and one member of the Justice Party.

§ Comprising one member of the Azerbaijan Hope Party.

¶ Comprising 35 independent candidates, three members of non-partisan initiative groups and three candidates who did not state any party membership.

Election Commission

Central Electoral Commission: 1000 Baku, Rasul Rza küç. 3; tel. (12) 493-60-08; fax (12) 562-70-09; e-mail office@cec.gov.az; internet www.cec.gov.az; f. 1998; Chair. MAZAHIR PANAHOV.

Political Organizations

Azerbaijan Democratic Party (Azärbaycan Demokrat Partiyası): 1000 Baku, Sabail rayonu, Acad. A. Älizadä küç. 13; tel. (12) 496-07-22; fax (12) 496-18-61; e-mail adp2005@mail.ru; f. 1991; formed part of the Freedom bloc at legislative elections in 2005; Chair. SARDAR MÄMMÄDOV.

Azerbaijan Democratic Reforms Party (Azärbaycan Demokratik İslahatlar Partiyası): 1078 Baku, Bünyat Sardarov 17/2; tel. (12) 437-15-76; fax (12) 437-15-77; e-mail demreforms@party.az; internet www.demreforms.org; f. 2005; contested 2010 legislative elections as mem. of the Democratic Bloc; Chair. ASIM MOLLAZADÄ.

Azerbaijan Hope Party (Azärbaycan Ümid Partiyası): 1000 Baku, Qanub küç. 19/29; tel. and fax (12) 496-65-48; e-mail umid_info@mail.ru; f. 1993; contested 2010 legislative elections as mem. of the Karabakh Bloc; Chair. İQBAL AĞAZADÄ.

Azerbaijan Islamic Party (Azärbaycan İslam Partiyası—AİP): 1000 Baku; tel. (12) 491-86-45; fax (12) 491-83-88; e-mail AIP@

azer.net; f. 1992; officially proscribed since 1995; forms part of the Union of Pro-Azerbaijanist Forces; Chair. MOVSUM SAMADOV.

Azerbaijan National Independence Party (ANIP) (Azärbaycan Milli İstiqlal Partiyası—AMIP): 1000 Baku, Näsimi rayonu, Mirqasımov küç. 4; tel. (12) 441-53-09; e-mail nipa@azeri.com; f. 1992; centre-right; supports liberalization of the economy and strengthening of democratic institutions; opposed to admin. of Pres. İlham Äliyev; formed part of the New Policy bloc in 2005; Chair. YUSIF BAGIRADZE.

Azerbaijan Popular Front Party (APFP) (Azärbaycan Xalq Cabhasi Partiyası—AXCP): 1152 Baku, Milli Mäclis, Mehti Hussein küç. 2; tel. (12) 498-07-94; e-mail faiq73@mail.ru; internet www.axcp.az; f. 1989; formed part of the Freedom bloc in advance of 2005 legislative elections, and formed electoral bloc with Equality Party (q.v.) in advance of 2010 legislative elections; Chair. ÄLI KERIMLI.

Azerbaijan Social Welfare Party (CPA) (Azärbaycan Sosial Rifah Partiyası—ASRP): 1000 Baku, A. Täbriz küç. 92; tel. (12) 496-34-43; fax (12) 567-07-58; internet www.asrp.az; Chair. XANHÜSEYN KAZIMLI.

Civic Solidarity Party (CSP) (Vätändaş Hämräylıyı Partiyası): 1000 Baku, Sabail rayonu, Abdülkarim Älizada küç. 9; tel. (12) 490-66-22; fax (12) 493-71-45; e-mail vhp.1992@gmail.com; internet www.vhp.az; f. 1992; contested 2010 legislative elections as mem. of the Democratic Bloc; Chair. SABIR RÜSTAMXANLI.

Civic Unity Party (Vätändaş Birliyi Partiyası—VBP): Baku; f. 1999; Leader SABIR HACIYEV.

Equality Party (Müsavat) (Müsavat Partiyası): 1025 Baku, Därnägül qäsäbäsi 30/97; tel. (12) 448-23-82; fax (12) 448-23-84; e-mail info@musavat.org; internet www.musavat.com; f. 1992 as revival of party founded in 1911 and in exile from 1920; withdrew from the Freedom bloc (est. in advance of legislative elections in 2005) in Feb. 2006; formed electoral bloc with Azerbaijan Popular Front Party in advance of 2010 legislative elections; Chair. İSA QÄMBÄR; Gen. Sec. VURGUN EYYUB.

Fatherland Party (Ana Vätän Partiyası—AVP): 1000 Baku, Aziz Äliyev küç. 3; tel. (12) 493-82-92; f. 1992; supports administration of Pres. İlham Äliyev; represents interests of Naxçıvan Autonomous Republic in Azerbaijan; Leader FAZAIL AGAMÄLIYEV.

Great Creation Party (Böyük Quruluş Partiyası): Baku, Şövkät Mämmädova küç. 3; tel. and fax (12) 490-39-59; e-mail info@bqp.az; internet www.bqp.az; f. 2003; nationalist; contested 2010 legislative elections as mem. of the Reform Bloc; Leader FAZIL MUSTAFA.

Justice Party (Ädalät) (Adalat Partiyası): 1000 Baku, Näsimi rayonu, Ceyhun Hacıbäyli küç. 2; tel. (12) 440-85-23; e-mail adalat@azinternet.com; f. 2001; mem. of the Democratic Azerbaijan alliance; contested 2010 legislative elections as mem. of the Reform Bloc; Leader İLYAS İSMAYILOV; 21,000 mems.

New Azerbaijan Party (NAP) (Yeni Azärbaycan Partiyası—YAP): 1000 Baku, Bül-Bül pr. 13; tel. (12) 493-84-25; fax (12) 498-59-71; e-mail secretariat@yap.org.az; internet www.yap.org.az; f. 1992; Chair. İLHAM ÄLIYEV; 557,805 mems (2011).

United Azerbaijan Popular Front Party (Bütöv Azärbaycan Xalq Cabhasi Partiyası—BAXCP): 1000 Baku, 12-ci Aşırım küç. 70A; tel. (12) 492-96-23; fax (12) 461-29-42; e-mail qudrat@hasanquliyev.com; internet www.xalqcebhesi.az; f. 2003 by fmr mems of reformist wing of Azerbaijan Popular Front Party (q.v.); contested 2010 legislative elections as mem. of the Reform Bloc; Leader QÜDRÄT HÄSÄNQULIYEV.

Diplomatic Representation

Austria: 1010 Baku, Nizami küç. 90A, 7th Floor; tel. (12) 465-99-33; fax (12) 465-99-94; e-mail baku-ob@bmeia.gv.at; internet www.bmeia.gv.at/baku; Ambassador SYLVIA MEIER-KAJBIC.

Belarus: 1069 Baku, Gänclik, Kral Huseyn küç. 64; tel. (12) 436-46-38; fax (12) 436-46-37; e-mail azerbaijan@mfa.gov.by; internet www.azerbaijan.belembassy.org; Ambassador NIKOLAI Y. PATSKEVICH.

Belgium: 1073 Baku, S. Dadaşev küç. 19; tel. (12) 437-37-70; fax (12) 437-37-71; e-mail embassy.baku@diplobel.fed.be; Ambassador LUC TROJEN.

Brazil: 1069 Baku, Haci Murad küç. 23A; tel. (12) 598-20-46; fax (12) 598-2-03; e-mail bakubrasemb@gmail.com; Ambassador (vacant).

Bulgaria: 1069 Baku, Gänclik, Oqtai Karimov küç. 34; tel. (12) 441-43-81; fax (12) 440-81-82; e-mail embassy.baku@mfa.bg; internet www.mfa.bg/bg/114/; Ambassador VASIL KALINOV.

China, People's Republic: 1010 Baku, Xaqani küç. 67; tel. (12) 498-62-57; fax (12) 498-00-10; e-mail chinaemb_az@mfa.gov.cn; internet az.china-embassy.org; Ambassador HONG JIUYIN.

Cuba: 1000 Baku, Jafar Xandan 10C; tel. (12) 596-24-74; fax (12) 568-07-21; e-mail embajada@az.embacuba.cu; internet www.cubadiplomatica.cu/azerbaijan; Ambassador MARCELO CABALLERO TORRES.

Czech Republic: 1065 Baku, C. Cabbarlı küç. 44, Caspian Plaza, 16th floor; tel. (12) 436-85-55; fax (12) 436-85-57; e-mail baku@embassy.mzv.cz; internet www.mzv.cz/baku; Ambassador RADEK MATULA.

Egypt: 1000 Baku, H. Äliyev küç. 7; tel. (12) 498-79-06; fax (12) 498-79-54; e-mail emb.egypt@azeuro.net; Ambassador SABER ABD AL-KADER MANSUR.

France: 1000 Baku, Rasul Rza küç. 7, POB 36; tel. (12) 490-81-00; fax (12) 490-81-01; e-mail presse.bakou-amba@diplomatie.gouv.fr; internet www.ambafrance-az.org; Ambassador GABRIEL KELLER.

Georgia: 1069 Baku, Yaşar Huseynov küç. 15; tel. (12) 497-45-60; fax (12) 497-45-61; e-mail baku@geoemb.az; internet www.azerbaijan.mfa.gov.ge; Ambassador TEIMURAZ SHARASHENIDZE.

Germany: 1005 Baku, Nizami küç. 69, ISR Plaza; tel. (12) 465-41-00; fax (12) 465-41-28; e-mail info@baku.diplo.de; internet www.baku.diplo.de; Ambassador HERBERT QUELLE.

Greece: 1065 Baku, C. Cabbarlı küç. 44, Caspian Plaza, 9th floor; tel. (12) 492-01-19; fax (12) 492-48-35; e-mail gremb.bak@mfa.gr; internet www.mfa.gr/baku; Ambassador IOANNIS METAKSAS.

Hungary: 1004 Baku, Mirza Mansur küç. 72; tel. (12) 492-8626; fax (12) 492-1273; e-mail mission.bku@kum.hu; internet www.mfa.gov.hu/emb/baku; Ambassador ZSOLT CHUTORA.

India: 1069 Baku, Gänclik, Oqtay Karimov küç. 31/39; tel. (12) 447-25-62; fax (12) 447-25-72; e-mail amb.baku@indianembassybaku.org; internet www.indianembassybaku.org; Ambassador DEBNAT SHAW.

Iran: 1000 Baku, B. Sardarov küç. 4; tel. (12) 492-19-64; fax (12) 498-07-33; e-mail press@iranembassyaz.org; internet www.iranembassy.az; Ambassador MUHAMMAD BAGIR BAHRAMI.

Iraq: 1000 Baku, Jeyhun Hajibeyli küç.2; tel. (12) 564-76-14; fax (12) 564-76-11; e-mail bakemb@iraqmofamail.net; Ambassador HEYDAR SHIYA GUBEYSHI AL-BERRAKI.

Israel: 1065 Baku, İzmir küç. 1033, Hyatt Tower III, 7th Floor; tel. (12) 490-78-81; fax (12) 490-78-92; e-mail info@baku.mfa.gov.il; internet baku.mfa.gov.il; Ambassador MICHAEL LAVON-LOTEM.

Italy: 1004 Baku, İçeri Şahar, Kiçik Qala küç. 44; tel. (12) 497-51-33; fax (12) 497-52-02; e-mail ambasciata.baku@esteri.it; internet www.ambbaku.esteri.it; Ambassador MARIO GIORGIO STEFANO BALDI.

Japan: 1065 Baku, İzmir küç. 1033, Hyatt Tower III, 6th Floor; tel. (12) 490-78-18; fax (12) 490-78-20; e-mail info@bk.mofa.go.jp; internet www.az.emb-japan.go.jp; Ambassador SHUSUKE WATANABE.

Jordan: 1065 Baku, Jafar Jabarli küç. 44; tel. (12) 437-31-21; fax (12) 437-31-23; e-mail baku@fm.gov.jo; Ambassador ADEL ADEILEH.

Kazakhstan: 1078 Baku, X. Äliyev küç. 882/82; tel. (12) 465-62-48; fax (12) 465-62-49; e-mail embassyk@azdata.net; Ambassador SERIK D. PRIMBETOV.

Korea, Republic: 1078 Baku, X. Äliyev küç 1/12; tel. (12) 596-79-01; fax (12) 596-79-04; e-mail azeremb@mofat.go.kr; internet aze.mofat.go.kr; Ambassador JIHA LEE.

Kuwait: 1000 Baku, C. Cabbarlı küç. 44, Caspian Plaza 2, 15th Floor; tel. (12) 596-81-72; fax (12) 596-81-75; e-mail baku@mofa.gov.kw; Ambassador GHASSAN ABD AL-BARI AL-ZAWAWI.

Latvia: 1065 Baku, C. Cabbarlı küç. 44; tel. (12) 436-67-78; fax (12) 436-67-79; e-mail embassy.azerbaijan@mfa.gov.lv; Ambassador HARDIJS BAUMANIS.

Lithuania: 1073 Baku, S. Dadaşev küç. 35/523; tel. (12) 537-04-07; fax (12) 510-86-88; e-mail amb.az@urm.lt; internet www.az.mfa.lt; Ambassador KĘSTUTIS KUDZMANAS.

Moldova: 1073 Baku, H. Cavid pr. 520/12; tel. (12) 510-15-38; fax (12) 403-52-91; e-mail baku@mfa.md; Ambassador IGOR BODYU.

Morocco: 1078 Baku, H. Äliyev küç. 2; tel. (12) 596-51-30; fax (12) 480-25-42; Ambassador HASSAN HAMI.

Netherlands: 1010 Baku, Nizami küç 96, Landmark Bldg I/3; tel. (12) 465-99-22; fax (12) 465-99-72; e-mail bak@minbuza.nl; internet azerbaijan.nlembassy.org; Ambassador ARJEN UYTERLINDE.

Norway: 1000 Baku, Nizami küç. 340, ISR Plaza, 11th floor; tel. (12) 497-43-25; fax (12) 497-37-98; e-mail emb.baku@mfa.no; internet www.norway.az; Ambassador ERLING SKJØNSBERG.

Pakistan: 1000 Baku, Atatürk pr. 30; tel. (12) 436-08-39; fax (12) 436-08-41; e-mail parepbaku@yahoo.com; internet www.mofa.gov.pk/azerbaijan; Ambassador INAYATULLAH KAKAR.

Poland: 1000 Baku, Içari Şahar, Kiçik Qala küç. 2; tel. (12) 492-01-14; fax (12) 492-02-14; e-mail baku.amb.sekretariat@msz.gov.pl; internet www.baku.polemb.net; Ambassador MICHAŁ ŁABENDA.

Qatar: 1000 Baku, Temyur Äliyev küç. 70; tel. (12) 564-58-24; fax (12) 564-58-25; Ambassador MUBARAK BIN FAHD AL THANI.

Romania: 1000 Baku, Gänclik, Häsän Äliyev küç. 125A; tel. (12) 465-63-78; fax (12) 456-60-76; e-mail rom_amb_baku@azdata.net; Ambassador DANIEL CRISTIAN CIOBANU.

Russia: 1022 Baku, Bakıxanov küç. 17; tel. (12) 597-08-70; fax (12) 597-16-73; e-mail embrus@embrus-az.com; internet www.embrus-az.com; Ambassador VLADIMIR DOROKHIN.

Saudi Arabia: 1073 Baku, S. Dadaşev küç. 44/2; tel. (12) 497-23-05; fax (12) 497-23-02; e-mail azemb@mofa.gov.sa; Ambassador FAHD BIN ALI AL-DUSARI.

Serbia: 1004 Baku, Gesr side küç. 1; tel. (12) 492-50-80; fax (12) 492-51-72; e-mail serbianembassy.baku@azeurotel.com; internet www.serbianembassy-baku.org; Ambassador ZORAN VAJOVIĆ.

Switzerland: 1004 Baku, Böyük Qala küç. 9; tel. (12) 437-38-50; fax (12) 437-38-51; e-mail baku.vertretung@eda.admin.ch; internet www.eda.admin.ch/baku; Ambassador SABINE ULMANN SHABAN.

Tajikistan: 1000 Baku, Badamdar, Baghlar küç. 20; tel. and fax (12) 502-14-32; e-mail embassy.rtra@gmail.com; Ambassador ZOKIR VAZIROV.

Turkey: 1000 Baku, Samad Vurghun küç. 94; tel. (12) 444-73-20; fax (12) 444-73-55; e-mail embassy.baku@mfa.gov.tr; internet www.baku.emb.mfa.gov.tr; Ambassador HULUSI KILIÇ.

Turkmenistan: 1000 Baku, Ş. Rähimov küç. 14; tel. and fax (12) 465-48-76; Ambassador TOYLI KOMEKOV.

Ukraine: 1069 Baku, Yusif Vazirov küç. 49; tel. (12) 449-40-95; fax (12) 449-40-96; e-mail ukremb@azeurotel.com; internet www.mfa.gov.ua/azerbaijan; Ambassador OLEKSANDR P. MISHCHENKO.

United Arab Emirates: Baku; Ambassador SALEM KHALIFA AL GHAFLI.

United Kingdom: 1010 Baku, Xaqani küç. 45; tel. (12) 497-51-88; fax (12) 492-27-39; e-mail generalenquiries.baku@fco.gov.uk; internet ukinazerbaijan.fco.gov.uk; Ambassador PETER BATEMAN.

USA: 1007 Baku, Azadlıq pr. 83; tel. (12) 498-03-36; fax (12) 465-66-71; internet azerbaijan.usembassy.gov; Chargé d'affaires ADAM STERLING.

Uzbekistan: 1021 Baku, Patamdart, 1 şosse, 9 dönga, 437; tel. (12) 497-25-49; fax (12) 497-25-48; e-mail office@uzembassy.az; Ambassador (vacant).

Judicial System

The judicial system in Azerbaijan is implemented by the following courts: regional (municipal) courts; the Court on Grave Crimes; the Military Court on Grave Crimes; local economic courts; the Economic Court on Disputes arising from International Agreements; the Supreme Court of Naxçıvan Autonomous Republic; the Court of Appeal; the Economic Court; the Supreme Court.

Supreme Court (Azärbaycan Respublikası Ali Mähkämäsi)

1193 Baku, Yusif Säfärov küç. 14; tel. (12) 493-18-37; e-mail contact@supremecourt.gov.az; internet www.supremecourt.gov.az.

The highest judicial body in civil, criminal, administrative and other cases, referring to the activity of the general courts; judges are nominated by the President of the Republic and confirmed in office by the Milli Mäclis.

President: RAMIZ RZAYEV.

Office of the Prosecutor-General (Baş Prokurorluğu): 1001 Baku, Nigar Räfibäyli küç. 7; tel. (12) 492-97-03; e-mail info@genprosecutor.gov.az; internet www.genprosecutor.gov.az; Prosecutor-General ZAKIR QARALOV.

Constitutional Court (Azärbaycan Repub1ıkasi Konstıtusıya Mähkamäsı)

1005 Baku, Gänclär meydanı 1; tel. (12) 492-96-68; fax (12) 492-36-78; e-mail inter.dept@constcourt.gov.az; internet www.constcourt.gov.az.

f. 1998; comprises a Chairman and eight judges, who are nominated by the President and confirmed in office by the Milli Mäclis for a term of office of 15 years. Only the President, the Milli Mäclis, the Cabinet of Ministers, the Procurator-General, the Supreme Court and the legislature of the Naxçıvan Autonomous Republic are permitted to submit cases to the Constitutional Court.

Chairman: FARHAD ABDULLAYEV.

Religion

ISLAM

The majority (some 70%) of Azerbaijanis are Shi'ite Muslims; most of the remainder are Sunni (Hanafi school). In 1944 the Soviet authorities established a Spiritual Board of Muslims of the Caucasus, with spiritual jurisdiction over the Muslims of Armenia, Georgia and Azerbaijan. (A separate Muslim Affairs Department, with jurisdiction over Georgia, was established in 2011.) The Chairman of the Board, which is based in Baku, is normally a Shi'ite, while the Deputy Chairman is usually a Sunni.

Spiritual Board of Muslims of the Caucasus: 1000 Baku; Chair. Sheikh ul-Islam Haci ALLAŞUKUR PASHEZADÄ.

CHRISTIANITY

The Roman Catholic Church

A Mission was established in October 2000, and the first Roman Catholic Church in Azerbaijan was consecrated in March 2008, in Baku. There were an estimated 320 adherents at 31 December 2007.

Superior: Fr VLADIMIR FEKETE, 1069 Baku, Teimur Äliyev küç. 69B/1; tel. (12) 562-22-55; fax (12) 436-09-43; e-mail admin@catholic.az; internet www.catholic.az.

The Russian Orthodox Church (Moscow Patriarchate)

Bishop of Baku and the Caspian Region: ALEKSANDR, 1010 Baku, Ş. Azizbekova küç. 205; tel. (12) 440-43-52; fax (12) 440-04-43; e-mail baku@eparchia.ru.

The Press

PRINCIPAL NEWSPAPERS AND PERIODICALS

In Azerbaijani, except where otherwise stated.

525-ci Qazet: 1033 Baku, Ş. Mustafayev küç. 27/121; tel. (12) 466-67-98; fax (12) 466-25-20; e-mail info@525.az; internet www.525.az; f. 1992; 5 a week; in Azerbaijani, also online edns in English and Russian; Editor-in-Chief RASHAD MAJID.

Adabiyyat qazeti (Literary Gazette): 1146 Baku, Matbuät pr. 529; tel. (12) 439-50-37; internet www.edebiyyatqazeti.com; f. 1934; every two weeks; organ of the Union of Writers of Azerbaijan; Chief Editor AYAZ VAFALI.

Ädalät (Justice): Baku; tel. (12) 438-51-49; fax (12) 465-10-64; e-mail aqilabbas@rambler.ru; internet www.adalet-az.com; f. 1990; 5 a week; publ. of Office of the Prosecutor-General; Editor AGIL ABBAS.

Ayna/ Zerkalo (Mirror): 1138 Baku, Sharifzadeh küç. 1; tel. (12) 497-51-68; fax (12) 497-71-23; e-mail gazeta@zerkalo.az; internet www.ayna.az; internet www.zerkalo.az; f. 1990; daily; independent; Azerbaijani and Russian edns; Editor-in-Chief ELCIN SIXLINSKI; circ. 4,500 (daily).

Azadlıq (Freedom): 1000 Baku, Xaqani küç. 33; tel. (12) 498-90-81; fax (12) 498-78-18; e-mail mail@azadliq.com; internet www.azadliq.info; f. 1989; weekly; independent; organ of the Azerbaijan Popular Front; Editor-in-Chief GANIMAT ZAKHIDOV.

Azärbaycan (Azerbaijan): 1073 Baku, Matbuät pr. 529/4; tel. (12) 438-20-87; fax (12) 439-43-23; e-mail azerbaijan_newspaper@azeronline.com; internet www.azerbaijan-news.az; f. 1991; 5 a week; publ. by the Milli Mäclis; Editor-in-Chief BAKHTIYAR SADIGOV.

Azernews: 1130 Baku, Darnagul seher 3097, 4th Floor; tel. (12) 561-01-42; fax (12) 562-06-45; e-mail azernews@azeurotel.com; internet www.azernews.net; f. 1997; weekly; in Azerbaijani, Russian and English; Editor-in-Chief FAZIL ABBASOV; circ. 5,000–6,000.

Bakı Xäbär (Baku News): 1000 Baku, Matbuät pr. 529; tel. (12) 510-87-40; internet www.baki-xeber.com; f. 2003; newspaper of the Azerbaijan Democratic Party; 6 a week; Editor-in-Chief AYDIN QULIYEV; circ. 5,000 (2007).

Bakinskii Rabochii (The Baku Worker): 1073 Baku, Matbuät pr. 529; tel. (12) 438-00-29; fax (12) 438-78-49; e-mail bakrab1906@gmail.com; internet www.br.az; f. 1906; 5 a week; govt newspaper; in Russian; Chief Editor AGABEK ASKEROV.

Bizim Yol (Our Way): Baku, H.Z. Tağıyev küç. 15/3; tel. (12) 418-91-79; e-mail info@bizimyol.az; internet bizimyol.az; f. 2003; independent; weekly; associated with the Popular Front Party of Azerbaijan; Editor-in-Chief BAHADDIN HAZIYEV.

Day: 1000 Baku; e-mail editor@day.az; internet www.day.az; online only; in Russian and English.

Ekho (Echo): 1138 Baku, Sharifzadeh küç. 1; tel. (12) 497-50-31; fax (12) 447-41-50; e-mail gazeta@echo-az.com; internet www.echo-az.com; daily; in Russian; Editor-in-Chief RAUF TALISHINSKYI; circ. 10,000.

Ekspress (The Express): 1000 Baku, Xaqani küç. 20B/43; tel. (12) 498-08-63; internet www.ekspress.az; Editor QAZANFAR BAYRAMOV.

İki Sahil: 1025 Baku, Zardabi 88A; tel. (12) 530-26-46; fax (21) 430-87-47; e-mail ikisahil@azdata.net; internet www.ikisahil.com; f. 1965; 5 a week; organ of SOCAR; Editor-in-Chief VUQAR RAHIMZADEH; circ. 7,500.

İstiqlal (Independence): 1014 Baku, 28 May küç. 3–11; tel. (12) 493-33-78; fax (12) 498-75-55; e-mail istiklal@ngonet.baku.az; 4 a month; organ of the Azerbaijan Social Democratic Party; Editor ZARDUSHT ÄLIZÄDE; circ. 5,000.

Respublıka (Republic): 1146 Baku, Matbuät pr. 529; tel. (12) 493-59-08; fax (12) 493-50-87; e-mail resp@azdata.net; internet www.respublica-news.az; f. 1996; daily; govt newspaper; Editor-in-Chief T. ÄHMÄDOV; circ. 5,500.

Şarq (The East): 1000 Baku, Matbuät pr. 529; tel. (12) 447-37-80; fax (12) 447-37-80; e-mail sharq@azerin.com; internet www.sherg.az; Editor AKIF ISHIGLI.

Vyshka—Oil (Oil Derrick): 1073 Baku, Matbuät pr. 529; tel. and fax (12) 439-96-97; e-mail medina@vyshka.com; internet vyshka.com; f. 1928; weekly; independent; in Russian; Editor MEDINA HÄSÄNOV.

Xalq Cäbhäsi (Popular Front): Baku; internet www.xalqcebhesi.az; 5 a week.

Xalq Qazetı (Popular Gazette): 1000 Baku, Bül-Bül pr. 18; tel. (12) 493-59-03; fax (12) 493-02-80; e-mail info@xalqqazeti.com; internet www.xalqqazeti.com; f. 1919; fmrly *Kommunist*; 6 a week; in Azerbaijani; also online edns in Russian and English; organ of the Office of the President; Editor HÄSÄN HÄSÄNOV.

Yeni Azärbaycan (A New Azerbaijan): 1095 Baku, Uzeyir Hajibeyov küç. 32; tel. (12) 498-81-24; fax (12) 497-53-04; e-mail yeniazerbaycan@azdata.net; internet www.yeniazerbaycan.com; f. 1993; 5 a week; organ of the New Azerbaijan Party; Editor ALGYSH MUSAYEV; circ. 2,493.

Yeni Müsavat (A New Equality): 1000 Baku; tel. (12) 498-00-61; e-mail ymusavat@azeronline.com; internet www.musavat.com; independent; pro-opposition; Chief Editor RAUF ARIFOĞLU.

NEWS AGENCIES

Azadinform Information Agency: 1146 Baku, Matbuät pr. 529; tel. (12) 510-70-43; fax (12) 498-47-60; e-mail info@azadinform.az; internet azadinform.az; f. 1998; independent information agency; Chief Editor ASAF HAJIYEV.

AzarTAc—Azärbaycan Dövlat Teleqraf Agentlıyı (Azerbaijan State Telegraph Agency—AzerTAg): 1000 Baku, Bül-Bül pr. 18; tel. (12) 493-59-29; fax (12) 493-62-65; e-mail azertac@azdata.net; internet www.azertag.gov.az; f. 1920; provides information in Azerbaijani, Russian and English; Dir-Gen. ASLAN ASLANOV.

Azeri Press Agency (APA): 1000 Baku, Zarifa Äliyeva küç. 27; tel. (12) 596-33-57; fax (12) 596-31-94; e-mail apa@azeurotel.com; internet www.apa.az; f. 2004; in Azerbaijani, Russian and English; Dir-Gen. VUSALA MAHIRGIZI.

Trend Information-Analytical Agency: 1141 Baku, Firudin Agayev küç. 14; tel. (12) 497-31-72; fax (12) 497-30-89; e-mail agency@trendaz.com; internet trend.az; f. 1995; in Azerbaijani, Russian, Farsi, Arabic and English; Dir-Gen. ILGAR HUSEYNOV.

Turan İnformasıya Agentlıyı: 1000 Baku, Xaqani küç. 20/56; tel. (12) 498-42-26; fax (12) 498-38-17; e-mail agency@turan.az; internet www.turan.az; f. 1990; independent news agency; in Azerbaijani, Russian and English; Dir MEHMAN ÄLIYEV.

PRESS ASSOCIATION

Azerbaijan Press Council (Azärbaycan Metbuät Şurası): 1010 Baku, Zarifa Äliyeva küç. 27; tel. and fax (12) 596-33-57; fax (12) 596-31-94; e-mail apa@azeurotel.com; internet www.az.apa.az; f. 2004; mediates disputes between the media and the authorities; acts as a self-regulatory body for the print media; Dir-Gen. VUSALA MAHIRGIZI.

Publishers

Azärbaycan Ensiklopediyasi (Azerbaijan Encyclopedia): 1004 Baku, Böyük Qala küç. 41; tel. (12) 492-87-11; fax (12) 492-77-83; e-mail azenciklop@ctc.net.az; f. 1965; encyclopedias and dictionaries; Gen. Dir I. O. VELIYEV.

Azarneshr State Publishing House: 1005 Baku, Gusi Haciyev küç. 4; tel. (12) 492-50-15; f. 1924; Dir A. MUSTAFAZADE; Dir AGABEK ASKEROV.

Elm Azerbaijani Academy of Sciences Publishing House: 1141 Baku, F. Agayev küç. 9; scientific books and journals.

Khazar University Press (KUP): 1096 Baku, Mehseti küç. 11; tel. (12) 421-79-27; fax (12) 498-93-79; e-mail contact@khazar.org; internet www.khazar.org/general/publication.htm; f. 1995; autonomous division of Khazar University; textbooks, reference books and journals.

Broadcasting and Communications

TELECOMMUNICATIONS

Azerbaijan's fixed-line telephone sector is dominated by the state operator, and in 2011 there were four providers of mobile cellular communications services. In 2010 there were 1.5m. subscriptions to fixed-line telephone services and 9.1m. subscriptions to mobile telephone services.

Azercell Telecom: 1139 Baku, Tbilisi pr. 61A; tel. (12) 496-70-07; fax (12) 430-05-68; e-mail customercare@azercell.com; internet www.azercell.com; f. 1996; jt venture between the Ministry of Communications and Information Technology and Fintur Holdings B.V. (Netherlands); CEO ALI AĞAN.

Azerfon: 1025 Baku, Nobel pr. 1240/20C; tel. (12) 444-07-30; fax (12) 444-07-31; e-mail corpcom@azerfon.az; internet www.narmobile.az; f. 2007; provides mobile cellular communications under the Narmobile brand name; CEO JÜRGEN PEETZ.

AzTelecom Production Asscn: 1122 Baku, Tbilisi pr. 3166; tel. (12) 431-51-94; fax (12) 493-17-87; e-mail aztelekom@aztelekom.net; internet www.aztelekom.net; national monopoly fixed-line telecommunications operator; f. 1992; owned by the Ministry of Communications and Information Technology; privatization pending; Dir MUHAMMAD MAMEDOV.

Bakcell: 1010 Baku, Neftchilar pr. 153; tel. (12) 498-94-44; fax (12) 464-04-00; e-mail info@bakcell.com; internet www.bakcell.com; f. 1994; mobile telecommunications service provider; wholly owned by GTIB (Israel); CEO RICHARD SHEARER.

RADIO AND TELEVISION

Regulatory Authority

National Television and Radio Council (Milli Televiziya vä Radio Şurası): 1000 Baku, Nizami küç. 105; tel. (12) 598-36-59; fax (12) 498-76-68; e-mail office@ntrc.gov.az; internet www.ntrc.gov.az; f. 2002; regulatory body, comprising nine mems, six of whom are presidential appointees; Chair. NUSHIRAVAN MAGERRAMLI.

Broadcasters

ANS Independent Broadcasting and Media Co (Azerbaijan News Service): 1073 Baku, Matbuät pr. 28/11; tel. (12) 497-72-67; fax (12) 498-94-98; e-mail ans@ans.az; f. 1999; independent; broadcasts ANS-TV (f. 1990) and NAS-CHM Radio (f. 1994); Pres. VAHID MUSTAFAYEV.

Azerbaijan Television and Radio Broadcasting Co: 1011 Baku, Mehti Hussein küç. 1; tel. (12) 492-38-07; fax (12) 497-20-20; e-mail webmaster@aztv.az; internet www.aztv.az; f. 1956; closed jt-stock co.; Chair. ARIF ALIŞANOV.

Lider TV and Radio: 1141 Baku, A. Alekperov küç. 83/23; tel. (12) 497-88-99; fax (12) 497-87-77; e-mail mail@media-az.com; internet www.lidertv.com; f. 2000.

Public Television and Radio Broadcasting Co (İctimiai Televizya va Radiyo Yayımları Şirkati—ITV): 1012 Baku, Sherifzadch küç. 241; tel. (12) 430-22-64; fax (12) 430-23-04; e-mail info@itv.az; internet www.itv.az; f. 2005; created from the second channel of the state broadcasting co (AzTV2); broadcasts in Azerbaijani and Armenian; Gen. Dir ISMAYIL OMAROV.

Radio Antenn: 1130 Baku, Azadlıq pr. 189; tel. (12) 565-31-01; e-mail info@antenn.az; internet www.antenn.az; f. 1998.

Regional Television Network of Azerbaijan (RTNA): Sumqayıt, Qarabağ Cinema, c/o Dunya TV; f. 2005; includes seven regional channels: Alternativ TV in Gäncä; Mingäçevir TV; Xayal TV in Quba; Dunya TV in Sumqayıt; Länkäran TV; Simurq TV in Tovuz; and Aygun TV in Zaqatala.

Finance

(cap. = capital; res = reserves; dep. = deposits; m. = million; brs = branches; amounts in new manats, unless otherwise stated)

BANKING

The banking sector in Azerbaijan is dominated by the state-owned International Bank of Azerbaijan, which accounts for around one-half of all banking assets in the country.

Central Bank

Central Bank of the Republic of Azerbaijan: 1014 Baku, R. Behbutov küç. 32; tel. (12) 493-11-22; fax (12) 493-55-41; internet www.cbar.az; f. 1992 as National Bank of Azerbaijan; renamed as above in 2009; central bank and supervisory authority; cap. 10.0m., res 209.5m., dep. 1,382.0m. (Dec. 2009); Chair. Dr ELMAN RUSTAMOV.

State-owned Bank

International Bank of Azerbaijan (Azärbaycan Beynälxalq Banki): 1005 Baku, Nizami küç. 67; tel. (12) 493-00-91; fax (12) 493-40-91; e-mail ibar@ibar.az; internet www.ibar.az; f. 1992 to succeed br. of USSR Vneshekonombank; 50.2% owned by the Ministry of Finance (q.v.), 11.2% by other state entities; f. 1992; provides all banking services; cap. 240.0m., res 19.2m., dep. 2,941.8m. (Dec. 2009); Chair. of Bd JAHANGIR F. HAJIYEV; 36 brs.

Other Banks

In 2010 there were a total of 46 commercial banks operating in Azerbaijan, 23 of which included foreign capital.

Amrahbank: 1025 Baku, Y. Säfärov küç. 10; tel. (12) 497-88-60; fax (12) 497-88-63; e-mail info@amrahbank.com; internet www.amrahbank.com; f. 1993; 49% owned by International Investment Bank (Bahrain); cap. 12.8m., res 5.1m., dep. 72.8m. (Dec. 2009); Pres. YUNUS ILDIRIMZADEH; Chair. EMIL MÄMMÄDOV.

AtaBank: 1010 Baku, Ş. Badalbäyli küç. 102; tel. (12) 497-87-00; fax (12) 498-74-47; e-mail atabank@atabank.com; internet www.atabank.com; f. 1994; cap. 15.0m., res 3.8m., dep. 169.4m., (Dec. 2009); Exec. Chair. ILTIFAT AGAYEV.

Azärbaycan Sänaye Banki (ASB) (Azerbaijan Industry Bank): 1005 Baku, Zarifa Äliyeva küç. 3; tel. (12) 493-14-16; fax (12) 493-84-50; e-mail info@asb.az; internet www.asb.az; f. 1996; fmrly Capital Investment Bank; present name adopted Nov. 2006; 97% owned by Anadolu Investment Kompani; cap. 21.5m., dep. 41.5m., total assets 128.6m. (Dec. 2010); Pres. ZEYNAB KONYAR; Chair. of Bd of Dirs AHMET YEMAN; 6 brs.

Azerigazbank: 1073 Baku, Landau küç. 16; tel. (12) 497-50-17; fax (12) 498-96-15; e-mail agbank@agbank.az; internet www.azerigazbank.com; f. 1992; jt stock investment bank; cap. 18.6m., res 8.6m., dep. 179.6m. (Dec. 2010); Chair. AZER F. MOVSUMOV; 5 brs.

Bank of Baku: 1069 Baku, Atatürk pr. 40/42; tel. (12) 447-00-55; fax (12) 498-82-78; e-mail fsalizade@bankofbaku.com; internet www.bankofbaku.com; f. 1994; merged with Ilkbank in Feb. 2005; 40% owned by NAB DIS Ticarat (Turkey); 28.9% owned by Azpetrol Holding; cap. 12.9m., res 4.8m., dep. 175.2m. (Dec. 2010); Chair. of Bd FARID ALIZADA; 16 brs.

Bank Respublika: 1095 Baku, Xaqani küç. 21; tel. (12) 598-08-00; fax (12) 598-08-80; e-mail info@bankrespublika.az; internet www.bankrespublika.az; f. 1992; cap. 37.5m., res 6.0m., dep. 119.0m. (Dec. 2010); Chair. of Exec. Bd KHADIJA HÄSÄNOVA.

Bank Standard: 1005 Baku, Azärbaycan pr. 4; tel. (12) 497-10-71; fax (12) 497-20-94; e-mail bank@bankstandard.com; internet www.bankstandard.com; f. 1995; present name adopted 2004; cap. 75.0m., res 6.3m., dep. 340.9m. (Dec. 2010); Chief Exec. SALIM KRIMAN.

DämirBank (DemirBank): 1008 Baku, Qarabağ küç. 31; tel. (12) 444-71-71; fax (12) 441-19-76; e-mail info@demirbank.az; internet www.demirbank.az; f. 1992 as Azärdämiryolbank; renamed as above in 2009; 25% plus one share owned by European Bank for Reconstruction and Development (United Kingdom), 10% by Netherlands Development Finance Company (The Netherlands); cap. 20.0m., res 8.7m., dep. 164.9m. (Dec. 2010); Chair. of Bd ROMAN AMIRJANOV; 30 brs.

Kapital Bank: 1014 Baku, Fizuli küç. 71; tel. (12) 598-12-95; fax (12) 493-79-05; e-mail office@kapitalbank.az; internet www.kapitalbank.az; f. 2000 by merger; present name adopted 2005; 99.75% owned by Pasha Holding; cap. 24.0m., res 46.2m., dep. 425.7m. (Dec. 2009); Chair. ELMAR MÄMMÄDOV; 87 brs.

Rabitäbank: 1010 Baku, Ü. Hacıbayov küç. 33/35; tel. (12) 492-57-61; fax (12) 497-11-01; e-mail rb@rabitabank.com; internet www.rabitabank.com; f. 1993; jt stock commercial bank; operates mainly in telecommunications sector; cap. 10.1m., res 4.2m., dep. 74.1m. (Dec. 2010); Exec. Chair. ELDAR AGAYEV; 9 brs.

Royal Bank of Baku (RoyalBank): 1073 Baku, H. Cavid pr. 5; tel. (12) 510-78-37; fax (12) 510-78-35; e-mail info@royalbank.az; internet www.royalbank.az; f. 1993 as Ozbank; cap. 22.3m., dep. 118.4m., total assets 163.1m. (Dec. 2010); Chair. SAMIR AKBAROV; 32 brs.

Unibank Commercial Bank: 1022 Baku, Raşid Behbudov küç. 55; tel. (12) 498-22-44; fax (12) 498-09-53; e-mail bank@unibank.az; internet www.unibank.az; f. 2002 by merger; cap. 44.9m., res 0.5m., dep. 196.1m. (Dec. 2010); Chair. FAIG HUSEYNOV; 24 brs.

Association

Association of Banks of Azerbaijan (Azerbaycan Banklar Assosiasiyası): 1073 Baku, Dadashov küç. 29; tel. (12) 497-61-69; fax (12) 497-15-15; e-mail aba@aba.az; internet www.aba.az; f. 1990; co-ordinates banking activity; Pres. ELDAR ISMAYLOV; 47 mems.

STOCK EXCHANGE

Baku Stock Exchange (Bakı Fond Birjasi): 1000 Baku, Bül-Bül pr. 19; tel. (12) 498-98-20; fax (12) 493-77-93; e-mail info@bse.az; internet www.bse.az; f. 2000; Pres. ANAR AKHUNDOV.

INSURANCE

At January 2005 there were 30 insurance companies operating in Azerbaijan.

Atäşgah Insurance Co: Baku, Sabir küç. 3; tel. and fax (12) 497-81-82; e-mail ateshgah@ateshgah.com; internet www.ateshgah.com; f. 1996; 30% owned by State Oil Co of Azerbaijan, 30% owned by Atlantic Reinsurance Co, 19% owned by Lukoil Azerbaijan; Man. ROBERT BRUNDRETT.

AXA MBASK Insurance Co: 1095 Baku, Azi Aslanov küç. 90/9; tel. (12) 498-91-90; fax (12) 498-10-62; e-mail office@mbask.com; internet www.axambask.az; f. 1992; fmrly MBASK Insurance Co, renamed as above after AXA Group (France) acquired controlling stake in Dec. 2010; 30% owned by the European Bank for Reconstruction and Development (United Kingdom); 7 brs; Chair. of Bd of Dirs JAMIL MALIKOV.

Azärqarant Sigorta (Azergarant Sigorta): 1072 Baku, May küç. 28; tel. (12) 498-68-42; fax (12) 493-85-38; e-mail azergarant@rambler.ru; internet www.azergarant.az; f. 1993; Pres. Dr ALEKPER MAMEDOV; Gen. Dir FAIG HUSSEINOV.

Azersiğorta: 1014 Baku, Fäzuli 69; tel. (12) 495-95-64; fax (12) 495-94-69; e-mail azersigorta@azeuro.net; Dir MÄMMÄD MÄMMÄDOV.

AzSığorta: 1073 Baku, Qutqaşınlı küç. 99/1; tel. (12) 497-34-30; fax (12) 497-89-59; e-mail info@azinsurance.eu; internet www.azinsurance.eu; f. 2007; Chair. ABBAS BABAYEV.

Beynälxalq Sığorta Şirkäti (International Insurance Co—IIC): 1065 Baku, C. Cabbarlı küç. 40C, IIC Bldg; tel. (12) 596-22-02; fax (12) 596-22-12; e-mail iic@iic.az; internet www.iic.az; f. 2002; universal insurance co; wholly owned subsidiary of the International Bank of Azerbaijan; Chair. of Bd MÄMMÄD SADIX MÄMMÄDOV.

Paşa Sığorta: 1000 Baku, Tolstoy küç. 170; tel. (12) 598-18-03; fax (12) 598-18-07; e-mail office@pasha-insurance.az; internet www.pasha-insurance.az; f. 2006; Man. Dir MIR JAMAL PASHAYEV.

Qala Heyat Sığorta: 1000 Baku, Araza küç. 7; tel. (12) 537-07-23; fax (12) 537-08-23; f. 2010; life.

Standard Insurance: 1014 Baku, Şämsi Bädälbäyli küç. 94; tel. (12) 497-37-60; fax (12) 598-37-60; e-mail office@standardinsurance.az; internet www.standardinsurance.az; f. 2002; Chair. KAMAL İBRAHIMOV.

Trade and Industry

GOVERNMENT AGENCY

Azerbaijan Export and Investment Promotion Foundation: 1001 Baku, Häsän Abdullayev küç. 11; tel. (12) 598-01-47; fax (12) 598-01-52; e-mail office@azpromo.org; internet www.azpromo.org; internet www.azerinvest.az; f. 2003 under the Ministry of Economic Development; Pres. ADIL MÄMMÄDOV.

CHAMBER OF COMMERCE

Chamber of Commerce and Industry: 1001 Baku, İstiqlaliyyät küç. 31/33; tel. (12) 492-89-12; fax (12) 497-19-97; e-mail expo@chamber.baku.az; Pres. SULEYMAN TATLIYEV.

INDUSTRIAL AND TRADE ASSOCIATIONS

National Confederation of Entrepreneurs' (Employers') Organizations of Azerbaijan (Azärbaycan Respublikasi Sahibkarlar—İşägötüränlär—Täşkilatları Milli Konfederasiyası—ASK): 1110 Baku, Häsän Äliyev küç. 57; tel. (12) 465-72-42; fax (12) 465-72-43; e-mail office@ask.org.az; internet www.ask.org.az; f. 1999; Pres. MAMMAD MUSAYEV.

UTILITIES

Electricity

Azärenerji: 1005 Baku, A. Älizäde küç. 10; tel. (12) 492-31-09; fax (12) 492-63-55; e-mail azerenerji@azerenerji.com; internet www.azerenerji.gov.az; f. 1962; state-owned jt stock co; power generation and transmission company; Pres. ETIBAR S. PIRVERDIYEV.

Bakı Electrikşebeke (Baku Electricity Network): 1065 Baku, Bakikhanov 13; tel. (12) 440-39-93; fax (12) 565-05-72; e-mail info@bes.az; internet www.bes.az; f. 2001.

Bayva-Enerji: 2000 Gäncä, Ruzigar Qasimov küç. 10; tel. and fax (22) 56-97-40; e-mail bayva-qerbenerji@mail.ru; f. 2002 as Gäncä-elektrikşebeke; comprising the Azerbaijani electricity distribution network's western zone; managed by Bakı Yüksakgarginlikli

Elektroavadanliq (BYGEA—Baku High Voltage Electrical Equipment Co); Gen. Dir RAMIZ AGAMÄLIYEV.

Gas

Azäriqaz (AzeriGaz): 1025 Baku, Yusif Säfärov küç. 23; tel. (12) 490-43-34; fax (12) 490-42-92; e-mail info@azerigaz.com; f. 1992; transport, distribution, sale, compression and storage of natural gas; acquired by State Oil Co of the Azerbaijan Republic (SOCAR) (q.v.) in 2010; Chair. AKBAR HAJIYEV; 13,000 employees.

TRADE UNIONS

Confederation of Azerbaijan Trade Unions (AHIK): 1000 Baku, Gänclär meydanı 3; tel. (12) 492-66-59; fax (12) 492-72-68; e-mail ahik@azerin.com; internet www.ahik.org; Chair. SATTAR MEHBÄLIYEV; 1.3m. mems.

Trade Union of Oil and Gas Industry Workers: 1033 Baku, Aga Neymatulla küç. 39; tel. and fax (12) 564-88-20; e-mail oilunion@online.az; f. 1906; 161 local orgs in the petroleum and gas sectors; 67,900 mems (2003); Chair. JAHANGIR ÄLIYEV.

Transport

RAILWAYS

In 2010 there were 2,079 km of railway track, of which 1,241 km were electrified. Services on the railway between metropolitan Azerbaijan and Naxçıvan, and on that to Armenia have been suspended, owing to Azerbaijan's economic blockade of Armenia. An international line links Naxçıvan with Tabriz (Iran). In late 2007 construction began on a new 258-km railway line, linking Kars, in north-eastern Turkey, with Tbilisi (via Akhalkalaki, Georgia) and Baku; the project was scheduled for completion in 2012. There is an underground railway in Baku.

Azerbaijani Railways (ADDY): 1010 Baku, Dilara Äliyeva küç. 230; tel. (12) 499-44-99; fax (12) 499-49-38; e-mail info@addy.gov.az; internet addy.gov.az; f. 1992; Chair. ARIF ASKEROV.

Baku Metro (Bakı Metropoliteni): 1073 Baku, H. Cavid pr. 33A; tel. (12) 490-00-00; fax (12) 497-53-96; e-mail akhmedov_tagi@metro.gov.az; internet www.metro.gov.az; f. 1967; 20 stations on two lines (30 km); Gen. Man. TAGI M. AKHMEDOV.

ROADS

In 2006 the total length of roads in Azerbaijan was 52,942 km, of which 50.60% were paved.

SHIPPING

At 31 December 2009 the Azerbaijani merchant fleet comprised 305 vessels, with a combined displacement of 743,000 grt.

Baku International Sea Trade Port: 1010 Baku, U. Hacibeyov küç. 72; tel. (12) 493-02-68; fax (12) 493-36-72; e-mail office@bakuseaport.az; internet www.bakuseaport.az; Gen. Dir ELÇIN MIRZAYEV.

Shipowning Company

Azerbaijani Caspian Shipping Co (ADXDG) (Azärbaycan Dövlat Xazar Daniz Gamiçiliyi): 1005 Baku, M. Rasulzade küç. 5; tel. (12) 493-20-58; fax (12) 493-53-39; e-mail adxdg@caspar.az; internet www.caspar.baku.az; transports crude petroleum and petroleum products; operates cargo and passenger ferries; fleet of 80 vessels; Pres. AYDIN BASHIROV.

CIVIL AVIATION

There are five airports in Azerbaijan, of which Heydär Äliyev Airport at Baku is the largest.

State Civil Aviation Administration: 1095 Baku, Azadlıq pr. 11; tel. and fax (12) 598-51-91; e-mail hq@caa.gov.az; internet www.caa.gov.az; f. 2006; Dir ARIF MÄMMÄDOV.

Azerbaijan Airlines (AZAL) (Azärbaycan Hava Yollari): 1010 Baku, Nizami küç. 84; tel. (12) 598-88-80; fax (12) 437-40-87; e-mail info@swtravel.az; internet azal.az; f. 1992; state airline operating scheduled and charter passenger and cargo services domestically and internationally; Gen. Dir JAHANGIR ASKEROV.

Turan Air: 1044 Baku, Heydär Äliyev Airport; tel. (12) 437-40-94; fax (12) 437-40-92; e-mail root@turan-air.com; internet www.turan-air.com; f. 1994; operates international scheduled and charter passenger and cargo services; Gen. Dir VAGIF ISKENDEROV.

Tourism

Tourism is not widely developed. There were 1,830,367 tourist arrivals in 2009. In 2010 receipts from tourism totalled US $621m.

Dept of Tourism of the Ministry of Culture and Tourism: 1004 Baku, Neftchilar pr. 65; tel. (12) 492-87-13; fax (12) 492-98-41; e-mail tourism@myst.co-az.net; Head TEYMUR MEHDIYEV.

Defence

As assessed at November 2011 the Azerbaijani military numbered 66,940: an army of 56,840, a navy of 2,200 and an air force of 7,900. Reserves number some 300,000. The country has a share of the former Soviet Caspian Flotilla. Military service is for 17 months (but may be extended for ground forces). The Ministry of Internal Affairs controls a militia of some 10,000 and a border guard of an estimated 5,000. In May 1994 Azerbaijan joined the North Atlantic Treaty Organization's 'Partnership for Peace' programme.

Defence Expenditure: Budgeted at 1,330m. new manats in 2011.

Chief of the General Staff: Col-Gen. NÄCMÄDDIN SADIQOV.

Education

Education is compulsory between the ages of six and 17 years. Primary education begins at the age of six years. Secondary education, comprising a first cycle of five years and a second cycle of two years, begins at the age of 10. In 2006/07 an estimated 24% of children of the relevant age attended pre-primary schools. In the same year estimated total net enrolment at primary schools was 95% of the relevant age-group; the comparable ratio for secondary enrolment was 83%. The main language of instruction is Azerbaijani. In 2010/11 there were 51 institutions of higher education and 140,241 students in higher education. Government expenditure on education was estimated at 723m. new manats in 2007, representing 12.1% of total state spending.

AZERBAIJANI SECESSIONIST TERRITORY

The self-proclaimed 'Republic of Nagornyi Karabakh', which has a predominately ethnically Armenian population, is located in the south-west of Azerbaijan, and borders Armenia to the south-west. The regional assembly of the Nagorno-Karabakh Autonomous Oblast (which comprised a smaller territory, and did not share a border with Armenia) proclaimed a 'Republic of Nagornyi Karabakh' on 2 September 1991. Following the dissolution of the USSR at the end of that year, the territory declared its independence from Azerbaijan on 6 January 1992. All such pronouncements were declared invalid by the Azerbaijani authorities, and military conflict ensued, in which the separatists obtained control of other areas of Azerbaijan, until a cease-fire entered into effect in May 1994. Although a political solution remained elusive, local forces secured a de facto independence. While the separatist authorities have enjoyed de facto political and military support from Armenia, the self-proclaimed 'Republic' is not formally recognized by any state.

NAGORNYI KARABAKH

Introductory Survey

LOCATION, CLIMATE, LANGUAGE, RELIGION, FLAG, CAPITAL

Nagornyi Karabakh, Upper or Mountainous Karabakh (Dağlıq Qarabağ in Azerbaijani, Artsakh in Armenian), is on the north-eastern slopes of the Lesser Caucasus. The region lies in the south-west of Azerbaijan and the territory claimed by the 'Republic of Nagornyi Karabakh' (unlike the Soviet-era Autonomous Oblast) has a south-western border with Armenia. The climate is mild and mostly subtropical. Average temperatures range from −1°C (30°F) in January to 22°C (72°F) in July, although the climate in lowland areas is markedly warmer than in the mountain ranges. Precipitation averages 410 mm–480 mm per year in the lowlands, but in the highlands amounts to 560 mm–840mm. The population principally speak Armenian, the sole member of a distinct Indo-European language group, written in the Armenian script. Most of the population are adherents of Christianity, the largest denomination being the Armenian Apostolic Church. The separatist authorities use a flag (proportions 1 by 2) based upon that of Armenia, comprising three equal horizontal stripes, of red, blue and orange, with each stripe being divided, towards the fly, by a white zig-zag chevron. The principal city and capital of the self-proclaimed 'Republic' is Stepanakert (known in Azerbaijani as Xankändi).

CONTEMPORARY POLITICAL HISTORY

Historical Context

After the collapse of the Russian Empire in 1917, and the subsequent proclamation of independent Armenian and Azerbaijani republics, Nagornyi Karabakh was disputed by both states. Following the Soviet conquest of the region, in June 1921 the Bolshevik Bureau for Caucasian Affairs (Kavburo) voted to unite Nagornyi Karabakh with Armenia. However, following intervention by Stalin, the decision was reversed, and in 1923 the territory was declared an autonomous oblast within Azerbaijan.

The policies of glasnost (openness) promoted by the Soviet leader Mikhail Gorbachev in the late 1980s encouraged a revival of nationalism. In February 1988 the Soviet and Azerbaijani authorities rejected a request by the Nagornyi Karabakh regional soviet (council) for the transfer of the territory to Armenia, provoking huge demonstrations by Armenians in both Nagornyi Karabakh and Yerevan, the capital of Armenia, while outbreaks of inter-ethnic violence, and, on occasion, killings, in both Armenia and Azerbaijan (most notably against Armenians in Sumqayıt, Azerbaijan, in February, and against Azeris in and around Gugark, Armenia, in November), brought about a large-scale migration of refugees between both countries. In November 10 days of demonstrations by Azeris opposed to any change in the status of Nagornyi Karabakh took place in Baku.

In January 1989 the Soviet Government suspended the activities of the Nagornyi Karabakh authorities and established a Special Administration Committee (SAC), responsible to the USSR Council of Ministers. The dispatch of some 5,000 Soviet troops failed to reduce tensions within Nagornyi Karabakh. In November the SAC was disbanded. The USSR Supreme Soviet ruled a subsequent pronouncement of the Armenian Supreme Soviet that Nagornyi Karabakh formed part of a 'unified Armenian Republic' to be unconstitutional.

Upon the USSR's disintegration in 1991, the leadership of Nagornyi Karabakh declared the enclave to be an independent republic. In January 1992 the President of Azerbaijan, Ayaz Mutalibov, placed the region under direct presidential rule; in the same month Azerbaijani forces surrounded and attacked Stepanakert (Xankändi), the capital of Nagornyi Karabakh, while Armenian forces laid siege to Shushi (Şuşha), a town with a mainly Azeri population. In May the Nagornyi Karabakh 'self-defence forces' (which the Armenian Government continued to claim were operating without its military support) captured Shushi, gaining complete control of the territory and ending the bombardment of Stepanakert. With the capture of the Laçin valley, the ethnic Armenian militia succeeded in opening a 'corridor' linking Nagornyi Karabakh with Armenia. In June Azerbaijani forces launched a sustained counter-offensive in Nagornyi Karabakh, displacing several thousand inhabitants. In August Azerbaijani forces resumed the bombardment of Stepanakert. In response, a state defence committee, in close alignment with the Armenian administration of President Levon Ter-Petrossian, replaced the Government of Nagornyi Karabakh. The UN Security Council subsequently adopted a series of resolutions demanding an immediate cease-fire and the withdrawal of all occupying units from Azerbaijan. In December Azerbaijani forces launched a new counter-offensive. Meanwhile, international efforts to halt the conflict continued, led by the 11-nation Minsk Group of the Conference on Security and Co-operation in Europe (CSCE—later Organization for Security and Co-operation in Europe—OSCE, see p. 388). In April 1993 ethnic Armenian forces had formed a second corridor linking Nagornyi Karabakh with Armenia, by capturing the Kelbacar district, and by June they had secured full control of Nagornyi Karabakh. The seizure of Azerbaijani territory outside the oblast prompted international condemnation. UN Security Council Resolutions 822 and 853, which demanded the withdrawal of occupying and local Armenian forces from Azerbaijan, went unheeded; hostilities intensified further, and more than 20% of Azerbaijan's total territory was captured by the Nagornyi Karabakh forces, although Azerbaijani forces recaptured some territory in a counter-offensive launched in December. In February 1994 it was reported that as many as 18,000 people had been killed since 1988, with a further 25,000 wounded. More than 500,000 Azeris were believed to have been displaced.

In May 1994 Azerbaijan signed the so-called Bishkek Protocol, which had been adopted by the Inter-Parliamentary Assembly of the Commonwealth of Independent States (CIS), with the approval of representatives of both Armenia and the self-styled 'Republic of Nagornyi Karabakh'. On 8 May the Nagornyi Karabakh leadership ordered its forces to cease hostilities, in accordance with the Protocol. Although isolated violations were subsequently reported, the cease-fire remained in force. In the latter half of the year efforts were made to co-ordinate the peace proposals of the CSCE Minsk Group and of Russia. However, Azerbaijan refused either to negotiate a peace settlement or to discuss the future status of Nagornyi Karabakh until ethnic Armenian forces were withdrawn entirely from Azerbaijani territory and Azeri refugees had returned to their homes.

Domestic Political Affairs

In December 1994 Robert Kocharian, hitherto Chairman of the State Defence Committee and premier, was elected by the Nagornyi Karabakh Supreme Soviet as the (internationally unrecognized) 'President' of Nagornyi Karabakh. In April–June a new, 33-seat legislature, the Azgayin Zhoghov (National Assembly)was elected in Nagornyi Karabakh—replacing the 81-member Supreme Soviet. In November 1996 Kocharian was re-elected as 'President' by popular vote, with more than 86% of the votes cast. In December President Heydär Äliyev and his Armenian counterpart, Ter-Petrossian, attended a summit meeting of the OSCE, in Lisbon, Portugal. Following demands by Azerbaijan, a statement was released by the OSCE Chairman, recommending three principles that would form the basis of a political settlement to the conflict: the territorial integrity of Armenia and Azerbaijan; legal status for Nagornyi Karabakh, which would be granted self-government within Azerbaijan; and security guarantees for the population of Nagornyi Karabakh. However, Armenia refused to accept the terms of the statement.

The appointment of Kocharian as Prime Minister of Armenia in March 1997, and the consequent proposed presidential election in Nagornyi Karabakh, were severely criticized by Äliyev. The election of Arkadii Ghukassian as 'President' of Nagornyi Karabakh in September threatened to hamper further progress on reaching a settlement, owing to his rejection of the OSCE proposals; later in that month, however, both Azerbaijan and Armenia were reported to have accepted a revised plan drawn up by the Minsk Group. In an apparently significant change in Armenian policy, Ter-Petrossian publicly admitted that Nagornyi Karabakh could expect neither to gain full independence, nor to be united with Armenia. Ter-Petrossian's approach to the Nagornyi Karabakh crisis provoked much disapproval in Armenia and led to his resignation in February 1998; he was replaced by Kocharian. In November the Armenian Government announced that, despite some reservations, it officially accepted the latest proposals put forward by the Minsk Group, which were based on the principle of a 'common state' (comprising Azerbaijan and Nagornyi Karabakh). The Azerbaijani Government, however, rejected the proposals, claiming that they threatened the country's territorial integrity.

Following an assassination attempt against Ghukassian in March 2000, the former 'Minister of Defence' of Nagornyi Karabakh, Samuel Babaian, was charged with organizing the attack, as part of a purported coup. (He was sentenced to 14 years' imprisonment in February 2001, but was released in September 2004.) Legislative elections were held in Nagornyi Karabakh on 18 June 2000. On 11 August 2002 Ghukassian was re-elected 'President', receiving 88.4% of the votes cast. Meanwhile, direct negotiations between the Armenian and Azerbaijani Presidents continued in 1999–2002, but little progress was made towards reaching a final solution to the dispute. Negotiations resumed in 2004, under the administration of the new Azerbaijani President, İlham Äliyev.

In January 2005 the OSCE agreed to a request by Azerbaijan that it monitor settlements in the region, in which Azerbaijan claimed some 23,000 ethnic Armenians had been settled by the Armenian authorities, and report on its findings. On 25 January the Parliamentary Assembly of the Council of Europe adopted a resolution describing the occupation of Azerbaijani territory by ethnic Armenian forces as a 'grave violation' and stating that aspects of the conflict resembled 'ethnic cleansing'. The resolution also urged Azerbaijani leaders to establish contacts with the secessionist leaders (which they had hitherto refused to do) and refrain from the use of force. Legislative elections, held in Nagornyi Karabakh in June 2006, were not recognized by Azerbaijan or the international community. A referendum was held on 10 December, in which some 84% of eligible voters participated; a constitution defining the territory as an independent and sovereign state was approved by some 98.6% of the votes cast. At an election to the 'Presidency' of Nagornyi Karabakh, which was conducted on 19 July 2007, Bako Sahakian, a former head of the territory's security service, secured a decisive victory, with 85.1% of the votes cast. Sahakian was installed on 7 September. His nomination of nominated Arayik Harutiunian, the leader of the Free Motherland party, as 'Prime Minister' was approved on 3 September, and a new 'Government' was formed later that month. In late November the Azerbaijani and Armenian foreign ministers met with the Co-Chairmen of the Minsk Group, who presented a draft of 10 basic principles for resolving the conflict.

In March 2008 clashes between ethnic Armenian forces and Azerbaijani military units erupted in Nagornyi Karabakh; five members of the Azerbaijani armed forces were confirmed to have been killed, while Azerbaijan claimed that a number of Armenian soldiers had also died. On 14 March a non-binding resolution, submitted by Azerbaijan, reaffirming its territorial integrity and demanding the withdrawal of all Armenian forces, was adopted by the UN General Assembly, with 39 votes in favour and seven opposing (with 100 abstentions); in addition to Armenia, countries that rejected the resolution included France, Russia and the USA. In June Äliyev met the recently installed Armenian President, Serge Sarkissian (who had previously played a senior role in organizing the Nagornyi Karabakh military forces, and who, like his predecessor, was a native of Stepanakert) for discussions in St Petersburg, Russia; the two heads of state agreed that negotiations on the situation in Nagornyi Karabakh continue on the basis of the 2007 proposals submitted by the OSCE Minsk Group. Meeting near the Russian capital, Moscow, on 2 November 2008, Äliyev, Sarkissian and Russian President Dmitrii Medvedev, in the capacity of mediator, signed a joint declaration reaffirming their commitment to reach a resolution to the conflict by diplomatic means. Negotiations, under the auspices of the Minsk Group, continued throughout 2009, with three trilateral meetings between Äliyev, Sarkissian and Medvedev.

Azerbaijan condemned the organization of legislative elections in Nagornyi Karabakh on 23 May 2010. Free Motherland emerged as the largest party in the new Azgayin Zhoghov, with 14 of the 33 seats. The Democratic Party of Artsakh obtained seven seats, while the local branch of the Armenian Revolutionary Federation—Dashnaktsutyun (Dashnaks) obtained six seats. Six independent candidates were elected. Meanwhile, President Medvedev convened further meetings between Sarkissian and Äliyev in January and in June. However, shortly afterwards in June one Azerbaijani and four Armenian soldiers were killed in what Armenia claimed was an attack by Azerbaijani forces at the cease-fire line in Nagornyi Karabakh. In September it was reported that three Armenian and two Azerbaijani soldiers had been killed in a further clash at the border of the enclave. Further discussions between Sarkissian and Äliyev, convened by Medvedev in the Russian city of Astrakhan on 27 October, resulted in an agreement on a mutual exchange of prisoners of war and the return of the remains of those killed in clashes, but no significant concessions. A planned meeting between Sarkissian and Äliyev during an OSCE summit meeting in Astana, Kazakhstan, in December failed to take place, reflecting the impasse in negotiations. Further discussions between Sarkissian, Äliyev and Medvedev, convened in Sochi in March 2011, resulted only in a joint declaration urging the full implementation of the agreement reached the previous October, and further trilateral negotiations were held in Kazan, Russia, in June.

Recent developments: proposals for construction of a wall

In September 2011 it was announced that, with the approval of the Azerbaijani Government, work had commenced on the construction of a wall, which was officially described as constituting 'protection from Armenian snipers', to separate Azerbaijani-inhabited centres of population from territory controlled by the Nagornyi Karabakh authorities. Following further discussions between Sarkissian, Äliyev and Medvedev in Sochi in January 2012, the Armenian and Azerbaijani Presidents issued a statement affirming their commitment to accelerating the process of reaching agreement on the main principles of a settlement. Azerbaijan's election, in October 2011, as a non-permanent member of the UN Security Council was expected to strengthen the state's international standing.

PUBLIC HOLIDAYS

2013: 1–2 January (New Year), 6 January (Christmas), 8 March (Women's Day), 24 April (Armenian Genocide Commemoration Day), 1 May (Labour Day), 9 May (Victory Day and Liberation of Shushi Day), 28 May (Declaration of the First Armenian Republic Day), 2 September (Independence Day), 31 December (New Year's Eve).

Directory

The Government of the 'Republic of Nagornyi Karabakh'

Note: the territories that constitute the territories proclaimed as, or administered by, the 'Republic of Nagornyi Karabakh' officially form part of the following districts (rayons) of Azerbaijan: Cäbrayıl; Füzuli; Kälbäcär; Laçın; Qubadlı; Şuşa; Xankändi; Xocalı; Xocavänd; and Zängilan.

President: Bako Sahakian.

COUNCIL OF MINISTERS
(May 2012)

Prime Minister: Arayik Harutiunian.

Deputy Prime Minister, Minister of Finance: Spartak Tevosian.

Minister of Health: Sergey Movsesian.

Minister of Justice: Narine Narimanian.

Minister of Productive Infrastructure: Karlen Petrosian.

Minister of Foreign Affairs: Vasily Atajanian (acting).

Minister of Agriculture: Andranik Khachtrian.

Minister, Head of the Government Apparatus: Armen Abagian.

Minister of Education and Science: Vladik Khachatrian.

Minister of Defence: Movses Hakobian.

Minister of Social Welfare: Narine Astsatrian.

Minister of Culture and Youth Affairs: Narine Aghabalian.

Minister of Urban Planning: Karen Shahramanian.

Minister of Economic Development: Karen Yesaian.

MINISTRIES

Office of the President: 374430 Stepanakert, 20 February St 3; tel. and fax (47) 94-52-22; e-mail ps@president.nkr.am; internet www.president.nkr.am.

Office of the Prime Minister: 374430 Stepanakert; tel. and fax (47) 94-22-86; e-mail info@karabakh.net; internet www.karabakh.net.

Ministry of Agriculture: 374430 Stepanakert; tel. and fax (47) 94-22-86; internet www.karabakh.net/?section=resources/index&type=3&subtype=10.

Ministry of Culture and Youth Affairs: 374430 Stepanakert; tel. and fax (47) 94-22-86; e-mail mcartsakh@rambler.ru; internet www.mc.am.

Ministry of Defence: 374430 Stepanakert; tel. and fax (47) 94-22-86; e-mail info@nkrmil.am; internet www.nkrmil.am.

Ministry of Economic Development: 374430 Stepanakert, 20 February St 1; tel. and fax (47) 94-09-16; e-mail econom@mineconomy.nk.am; internet www.mineconomy.nk.am.

Ministry of Education and Science: 374430 Stepanakert; tel. and fax (47) 94-22-86; internet www.karabakh.net/?section=resources/index&type=3&subtype=12.

Ministry of Finance: 374430 Stepanakert; tel. and fax (47) 94-22-86; internet www.minfin.nkr.am.

Ministry of Foreign Affairs: 374430 Stepanakert, Azatmartikneri St 28; tel. (47) 94-40-87; fax (47) 97-15-51; internet www.nkr.am.

Ministry of Health: 374430 Stepanakert; tel. and fax (47) 94-22-86; internet www.karabakh.net/?section=resources/index&type=3&subtype=7.

Ministry of Justice: 374430 Stepanakert; tel. and fax (47) 94-22-86; internet www.karabakh.net/?section=resources/index&type=3&subtype=8.

Ministry of Productive Infrastructure: 374430 Stepanakert; tel. and fax (47) 94-22-86; internet www.karabakh.net/?section=resources/index&type=3&subtype=21.

Ministry of Social Welfare: 374430 Stepanakert, Azatmartikneri St 54; tel. and fax (47) 94-22-86; e-mail info@mdd.nkr.am; internet www.mss.nkr.am.

Ministry of Urban Planning: 374430 Stepanakert; tel. and fax (47) 94-22-86; internet www.karabakh.net/?section=resources/index&type=3&subtype=16.

President

Presidential Election, 19 July 2007

Candidates	Votes	% of votes
Bako Sahakian	59,326	85.12
Masis Mailian	8,734	12.53
Armen Abgarian	867	1.24
Hrant Melkumian	554	0.79
Vanya Avanesian	212	0.30
Total	69,693	100.00

Legislature

Azgayin Zhoghov (National Assembly)

374430 Stepanakert; e-mail parlpress@ktsurf.net; internet www.nkrusa.org/country_profile/national_assembly.shtml.

Chairman: Ashot Ghulian.

General Election, 23 May 2010

Parties and blocs	Seats		
	A*	B*	Total
Free Motherland	8	6	14
Democratic Party of Artsakh	5	2	7
Armenian Revolutionary Federation—Dashnaktsutyun	4	2	6
Independents	—	6	6
Total	17	16	33

* Of the 33 seats in the Azgayin Zhoghov, 17 (A) are awarded according to proportional representation on the basis of party lists, and 16 (B) are elected in single-mandate constituencies.

Political Organizations

The following are among the principal political parties operating in the 'Republic of Nagornyi Karabakh'.

Armenian Revolutionary Federation—Dashnaktsutyun (ARF) (Hai Heghapokhakan Dashnaktsutiun): c/o 374430 Stepanakert, National Assembly; local branch of ARF, headquartered in Yerevan, Armenia (q.v.).

Communist Party of Artsakh (Artsakhi Komunistakan Kusaktsutyun): Stepanakert; Chair. Hrant Melkumian.

Democratic Party of Artsakh (Artsakhi Demokratakan Kusaktsutyun): c/o 374430 Stepanakert, National Assembly; fmrly Democratic Artsakh Union; Chair. Ashot Ghulian.

Free Motherland (Azat Hayrenik): c/o 374430 Stepanakert, National Assembly; Chair. Arayik Harutiunian.

THE BAHAMAS

Introductory Survey

LOCATION, CLIMATE, LANGUAGE, RELIGION, FLAG, CAPITAL

The Commonwealth of the Bahamas consists of about 700 islands and more than 2,000 cays and rocks, extending from east of the Florida coast of the USA to just north of Cuba and Haiti, in the West Indies. The main islands are New Providence, Grand Bahama, Andros, Eleuthera and Great Abaco. Almost 70% of the population reside on the island of New Providence. The remaining members of the group are known as the 'Family Islands'. A total of 29 of the islands are inhabited. The climate is mild and sub-tropical, with average temperatures of about 30°C (86°F) in summer and 20°C (68°F) in winter. The average annual rainfall is about 1,000 mm (39 ins). The official language is English. Most of the inhabitants profess Christianity, the largest denominations being the Anglican, Baptist, Roman Catholic and Methodist Churches. The national flag (proportions 1 by 2) comprises three equal horizontal stripes, of blue, gold and blue, with a black triangle at the hoist, extending across one-half of the width. The capital is Nassau, on the island of New Providence.

CONTEMPORARY POLITICAL HISTORY

Historical Context

A former British colonial territory, the Bahamas attained internal self-government in January 1964, although the parliamentary system dates back to 1729. The first elections under universal adult suffrage were held in January 1967 for an enlarged House of Assembly. The Progressive Liberal Party (PLP), supported mainly by Bahamians of African origin and led by Lynden (later Sir Lynden) Pindling, formed a Government and Pindling became Premier. At the next elections, in April 1968, the PLP increased its majority at the expense of the United Bahamian Party (UBP), dominated by those of European origin.

In the elections of September 1972, which were dominated by the issue of independence, the PLP maintained its majority. Following a constitutional conference in December 1972, the Bahamas became an independent nation, within the Commonwealth, on 10 July 1973.

Domestic Political Affairs

The PLP increased its majority in the elections of July 1977 and was again returned to power in the June 1982 elections, with 32 of the 43 seats in the enlarged House of Assembly. The remaining 11 seats were won by the Free National Movement (FNM), which had reunited for the elections after splitting into several factions over the previous five years.

Trading in illicit drugs, mainly for the US market, became a major problem for the country, since many of the small islands and cays were used by drugs-traffickers in their smuggling activities. In 1983 allegations of widespread corruption, and the abuse of Bahamian bank secrecy laws by drugs-traffickers and US tax evaders, led Pindling to appoint a Royal Commission to investigate thoroughly the drugs trade in the Bahamas. The Commission's hearings revealed the extent to which money deriving from this trade had permeated Bahamian social and economic affairs. Evidence presented to the Commission led to the resignation, in October 1984, of two cabinet ministers, and by November 1985 a total of 51 suspects had been indicted, including the assistant police commissioner. The Commission also revealed that Pindling had received several million dollars in gifts and loans from business executives, although it found no evidence of a link to the drugs trade. Despite this, the PLP was returned to power for a fifth consecutive term in June 1987.

Despite predictions of a PLP victory, the FNM won the August 1992 general election. Hubert Ingraham, the FNM leader, replaced Pindling as Prime Minister, and announced a programme of measures aimed at increasing the accountability of government ministers, combating corruption and revitalizing the economy.

A marked increase in violent crime in parts of New Providence led the Government to announce the creation, in March 1995, of a special police unit to address the problem. Meanwhile, the trade in illegal drugs remained widespread in the country. In October of that year the Prime Minister introduced further legislation that aimed to prevent the abuse of Bahamian banks by drugs-traffickers, and thus improve the reputation of the country's financial sector, particularly in the USA.

At a general election held in March 1997 the FNM won an overwhelming victory. Its win was attributed both to the Prime Minister's success in reversing the economic decline and the involvement of the PLP in various financial scandals. Most notably, Pindling was implicated in February in the findings of a public inquiry to investigate alleged corruption and misappropriation of funds in the three principal state corporations. Following the election, Pindling resigned as leader of the PLP and was replaced by Perry Christie.

Violent crime continued to be of major concern to Bahamians. In April 1998 the Government signed a convention drawn up by the Organization of American States (OAS, see p. 394) to ban illegal guns, amid a disturbing increase in gun-related crime. In September, following the murders of several tourists, the Prime Minister increased security in tourist areas, and announced plans to limit the right of appeal against death sentences. The hanging in October of two convicted murderers caused controversy, despite growing public demand for execution as a deterrent against crime. The Government had rejected a last-minute plea for clemency from the European Union, on the grounds that both men had appeals pending at the Inter-American Court of Human Rights (IACHR, see p. 395). In August 1999 the Bahamian authorities were strongly criticized by human rights groups after they announced their intention to execute another two convicted murderers who had also submitted petitions to the IACHR. In March 2006 the Privy Council in the United Kingdom banned the mandatory death penalty for murder. Despite attempts to reduce levels of crime, the murder rate continued to rise (see below).

The PLP takes power

At the general election held in May 2002 the PLP unexpectedly secured an overwhelming victory over the FNM, winning 29 of the 40 seats in the House of Assembly. The FNM retained seven seats (with 41.1% of the ballot). Independent candidates won the remaining four seats.

Significant disruption was caused within the Bahamas' judicial system in November 2006 when a supreme court ruling concluded that the Cabinet had acted illegally in failing to appoint a commission to review judicial salaries and, consequently, had compromised the independence of the judiciary. Despite the furore over judicial pay, on 18 December a contingent of Law Lords from the Privy Council sat in the Court of Appeal in Nassau, the first instance of the country's final appellate court operating outside the United Kingdom. The Bahamas retained the Privy Council as its ultimate court of appeal, in contrast to several other Caribbean countries that had accepted the jurisdiction of the Caribbean Court of Justice following its inauguration in April 2005.

In December 2006 a National Health Insurance Act was approved by the House of Assembly. The new legislation allowed private sector participation in the national health care system in an effort to improve the quality of public health care. Doctors, employers and trade unions opposed the reform on the grounds that the scheme, which was to cost an estimated US $235m. per year, was not financially viable.

Recent developments: the return of the FNM

The PLP was defeated at the general election of 2 May 2007, retaining 18 seats in the 41-seat House of Assembly, while the FNM won 23 seats. The rate of participation by the electorate was high, with some 91.3% of eligible voters participating in the poll. The FNM formed a new Government, with party leader Hubert Ingraham sworn in as Prime Minister. Ingraham also assumed the portfolio for finance, and Tommy Turnquest, who had regained his seat in the House of Assembly, became Minister of National Security and Immigration. Ingraham declared that his immediate areas of concern were security issues at Lynden Pindling International Airport, illegal immigration and land policy matters. The FNM had its majority in the House of Assembly increased to seven seats in January 2009 when the former opposition deputy Kenyatta Gibson joined the party.

In July 2008 Ingraham reorganized his Cabinet following the resignation of Sidney Collie as Minister of Lands and Local Government after widespread criticism regarding his failure to act within electoral law in the recent local government elections. Two new ministries were created, one for youth, sports and culture and the other for the environment. Dr Earl Deveaux, hitherto Minister of Public Works and Transport, was appointed head of the latter. Deveaux's previous responsibilities were given to Neko Grant, who was in turn succeeded as Minister of Tourism and Aviation by Vincent Vanderpool-Wallace.

In August 2009 the Minister of Legal Affairs and Attorney-General, Michael Barnett, resigned from his post in order to be sworn in as the Bahamas' new Chief Justice. The appointment of Barnett was criticized by members of the newly formed National Development Party for overtly politicizing the judiciary. Meanwhile, Sir Arthur Foulkes, one of the founders of the FNM, was inaugurated as Governor-General on 14 April 2010.

Following the announcement in early December 2010 by Cable & Wireless Communications of the United Kingdom that it had reached agreement with the Government to purchase a majority stake in the Bahamas Telecommunications Corporation, public sector trade unions threatened a nation-wide strike in protest against the privatization. Tensions increased after a violent demonstration on 15 December in which union supporters clashed with police officers. The opposition PLP also raised objections to the sale. In January 2011 several communications workers unions lodged an appeal against the sale with the Supreme Court, but it was turned down in early February. Further clashes between protesters and police occurred later that month in front of the House of Assembly, which, nevertheless, adopted legislation in March approving the privatization. The Government claimed that the divestment was 'essential for the advancement of the Bahamian economy'.

A record 87 murders were committed in the Bahamas in 2009, and this figure was surpassed in 2010, when 94 murders were recorded, raising fears of a violent crime epidemic. Ingraham stated that the illegal drugs trade was a major factor in the rising murder rate and argued that inadequacies in the judicial system were contributing to the problem. Detection rates also remained low. A special court was established in January 2011 to expedite cases involving firearms offences, a particular concern given the high proportion of murders committed with such weapons (73% in 2010). To complement this initiative, an illegal firearms task force was created at the same time, and earlier that month the police had announced the commencement of Operation Rapid Strike, which was to target violent crime. Other measures included the installation of security cameras in high crime areas and the introduction of an electronic system to monitor individuals granted bail. In May structural reforms within the judicial system were implemented in an attempt to streamline criminal trials. However, Minister of National Security Orville Turnquest generated controversy in September, when he accused the judiciary of excessive leniency when authorizing bail, prompting criticism from the opposition and a strong rebuttal from the Chief Justice.

In spite of the authorities' efforts, compared with the same period in 2010, official data indicated that between January and October 2011 crime levels rose by 10%, with violent crime increasing by 15%. The murder rate surged by over 40% during this period, and by late October the number of reported murders had reached a record 105. Anti-crime legislation under consideration in late 2011 included new bail restrictions for those accused of violent crimes and increased sentences for those convicted, and the expanded use of the death penalty.

The Government defended legislation, approved in November 2011 in preparation for legislative elections due to be held by mid-2012, that reduced the number of constituencies in the country. The PLP claimed that this restructuring of electoral boundaries amounted to gerrymandering, although proponents maintained that the process had been unprejudiced and had been implemented to rebalance the number of voters in each constituency and to reduce public expenditure. Meanwhile, parliamentary deputy Branville McCartney resigned from the FNM in March 2011 and shortly thereafter founded a new party, the Democratic National Alliance, to challenge the FNM and the PLP in the upcoming elections. In April 2012 Ingraham announced that the general election was to be held on 7 May.

Foreign Affairs

Regional relations

The Bahamas' traditionally close relationship with the USA has been strained in recent years by the increasingly uncompromising attitude of the US authorities towards bank secrecy laws and drugs-smuggling in the islands. There was a fall in the rate of suspected drugs-transshipment detection in the Bahamas in the early 2000s, reportedly in part owing to the withdrawal of some US detection and monitoring aircraft following the terrorist attacks on the USA in September 2001. Relations with the USA, however, improved in July 2004 after the Bahamian Government amended the country's extradition laws to give the state increased rights of appeal against the release of a suspect by the courts. These rights were exercised in September 2006 when leading drugs-trafficker Samuel Knowles was extradited to the USA. In July 2008, as part of the implementation of the USA's Proliferation Security Initiative, an agreement was signed that would allow US officials to board and inspect Bahamian-registered ships if they were suspected of carrying weapons of mass destruction.

Meanwhile, relations with the Bahamas' other neighbours, Haiti and Cuba, were strained by the influx of large numbers of illegal immigrants from both countries. In 1995–2003 more than 35,000 Haitian illegal migrants and refugees were deported from the Bahamas. In November 2003 the human rights organization Amnesty International released a report that accused the Bahamas of mistreating asylum-seekers from Cuba and Haiti; the Christie Government countered that the report was 'unbalanced'. A report published in 2005 found the Haitian population in the Bahamas to total between 30,000 and 60,000. In June 2007 the Narcotics Joint Task Force, comprising government representatives from the Bahamas, Turks and Caicos Islands and the USA, identified increased cocaine traffic from Hispaniola as an immediate threat and resolved to work towards a more comprehensive integration of their respective law enforcement agencies' efforts to combat the illegal transshipment of migrants and drugs in the region. In June 2008 the country was again criticized in a report by Amnesty International for beatings and unlawful killings allegedly carried out by security forces, as well as for the continued deportation and reported ill-treatment of migrants. Following the earthquake that devastated Haiti in January 2010, the Government of the Bahamas suspended the deportation of Haitian refugees on humanitarian grounds. However, repatriation proceedings resumed in September after the authorities reported 'a noticeable increase' in the number of Haitians attempting to enter the Bahamas illegally. Following many years of discussions, in October 2011 the Bahamas and Cuba finally delimited their shared border. The agreement was expected to precipitate petroleum exploration operations in Bahamian waters.

The Government in 2005 rejected the opportunity to join the Caribbean Single Market and Economy (CSME), which was launched on 1 January 2006 under the auspices of the Caribbean Community and Common Market (CARICOM, see p. 227). The Government argued that the CSME, which enshrined monetary union and the free movement of people among its signatory states, would place too great an economic and social burden on the Bahamas, one of the wealthier countries in the region.

Other external relations

Relations with China were strengthened in February 2009 by the signing of an agricultural agreement, which would see the Bahamas benefit from Chinese production and farming technology. These ties were reinforced by the visit of Wu Bangguo, Chairman of the Standing Committee of the National People's Congress of the People's Republic of China, to the Bahamas in September. As a result of the visit, a 20-year concessionary loan for the construction of a new four-lane highway and a grant for the National Stadium were agreed. Further co-operation agreements were signed in 2011, pledging Chinese assistance in the construction and funding of various infrastructural schemes on the islands.

In 2000 the Bahamas was listed by the Financial Action Task Force (FATF, see p. 454) as a 'non-co-operative' jurisdiction, and by the Organisation for Economic Co-operation and Development (OECD, see p. 379) as a tax haven. The Bahamas also remained classified as a 'Country of Primary Concern' in the US International Narcotics Control Strategy Report, partly because of its banking secrecy laws and the size of its 'offshore' financial sector. The Government responded by establishing a Financial Intelligence Unit and by adopting legislation intended to encourage transparency in the sector. As a result, in August 2001 the FATF removed the Bahamas from its 'black list'. In January 2002 an agreement to share information on tax matters with the USA was signed, while in March OECD accepted the Bahamas' commitment to improve the transparency of its financial sector. However, in 2005 a US Department of State report on global money-laundering and drugs-trafficking listed the Bahamas as a 'major money laundering country'. In April 2009 OECD placed the Bahamas on its 'grey list' of nations that had failed to sign a sufficient number of tax information exchange agreements with other states. The country was removed from the list in March 2010, after signing 18 such agreements, and received a positive assessment from the organization in April 2011.

CONSTITUTION AND GOVERNMENT

Although a representative House of Assembly was first established in 1729, universal adult suffrage was not introduced until 1962. A new Constitution for the Commonwealth of the Bahamas came into force at independence, in 1973. Legislative power is vested in the bicameral Parliament. The Senate has 16 members, of whom nine are appointed by the Governor-General on the advice of the Prime Minister, four by the Leader of the Opposition and three after consultation with the Prime Minister. The House of Assembly has 41 members, elected for five years (subject to dissolution) by universal adult suffrage. Executive power is vested in the British monarch, represented by a Governor-General, who is appointed on the Prime Minister's recommendation and who acts, in almost all matters, on the advice of the Cabinet. The Governor-General appoints the Prime Minister and, on the latter's recommendation, selects the other ministers. The Cabinet is responsible to the House of Assembly. The Constitution provides for a Supreme Court and a Court of Appeal.

REGIONAL AND INTERNATIONAL CO-OPERATION

The Bahamas is a member of the Caribbean Community (CARICOM—although it is not a member of CARICOM's Common Market, see p. 227), of the Organization of American States (OAS, see p. 394), of the Inter-American Development Bank (IDB, see p. 334), of the Association of Caribbean States (see p. 448), and of the Community of Latin American and Caribbean States (see p. 462), which was formally inaugurated in December 2011. The Bahamas became a member of the UN following independence, in 1973. The Government applied for membership of the World Trade Organization (see p. 433) in 2001, and initial accession talks began in September 2010. Accession to full membership would take at least three years to achieve. The Bahamas is a member of the Commonwealth (see p. 239) and is a signatory of the Cotonou Agreement (see p. 328) with the European Union (see p. 276). The country is a member of the Group of 77 (see p. 450) organization of developing states.

ECONOMIC AFFAIRS

In 2009, according to estimates by the World Bank, the Bahamas' gross national income (GNI), measured at average 2008–10 prices, was US $6,973m., equivalent to US $20,610 per head. During 2001–10 it was estimated that the population increased at an average annual rate of 1.4%. According to official estimates, in 2001–10 gross domestic product (GDP) per head decreased, in real terms, at an average annual rate of 0.3%. Overall GDP increased, in real terms, by 0.4% in 2009, but decreased by 23.5% in 2010.

Agriculture, hunting, forestry and fishing together accounted for only 1.9% of GDP in 2009 and engaged an estimated 2.9% of the employed labour force in 2009. Crops grown for export included cucumbers, tomatoes, pineapples, papayas, avocados, mangoes, limes and other citrus fruits. The development of commercial fishing has concentrated on conchs and crustaceans. In 2007 exports of Caribbean spiny lobster (crawfish) provided 21.5% of domestic export earnings, and in 2008 accounted for 62.5% of the fishing total. There is also some exploitation of pine forests in the northern Bahamas. According to official estimates, in 2001–10 agricultural GDP decreased at an average annual rate of 1.7%; sectoral GDP for agriculture declined by an estimated 6.7% in 2010.

Industry (comprising mining, manufacturing, construction and utilities) employed an estimated 16.0% of the working population in 2009 and provided 13.6% of GDP in the same year. According to official estimates, in 2001–10 industrial GDP increased at an average annual rate of 2.8%; sectoral GDP increased by an estimated 3.0% in 2010.

Mining and quarrying contributed only 1.3% of GDP in 2009. The sector (including utilities) provided an estimated 1.6% of employment in the same year. The islands' principal mineral resource is salt. Minerals provided 25.7% of total export earnings in 2010. According to official estimates, in 2001–10 mining GDP increased at an average annual rate of 5.1%; sectoral GDP increased by an estimated 1.9% in 2010.

The manufacturing sector contributed some 4.0% of GDP and employed 3.4% of the working population in 2009. According to official estimates, in 2001–10 manufacturing GDP increased at an average annual rate of 2.1%; sectoral GDP declined by an estimated 0.9% in 2010. The principal branches of manufacturing were beverages, chemicals, and printing and publishing. Exports of rum accounted for 5.1% of export earnings in 2007.

Construction contributed some 6.6% to the GDP and employed 9.6% of the employed labour force in 2009. The construction sector experienced much activity in the early 21st century, owing to the construction of hotels, tourist complexes and harbour developments. According to official estimates, in 2001–10 construction GDP decreased at an average annual rate of 0.3%; however, sectoral GDP declined by an estimated 23.5% in 2010.

Most of the energy requirements of the Bahamas are fulfilled by the petroleum that Venezuela and Mexico provide. In 2005 the Bahamas signed the PetroCaribe agreement with Venezuela, under which the Bahamas was allowed to purchase petroleum at reduced prices. Imports of mineral products accounted for 24.0% of the total value of imports in 2010.

Service industries constitute the principal sectors of the economy, providing some 84.5% of GDP and about 80.8% of total employment in 2009. According to official estimates, in 2001–10 services GDP increased at an average annual rate of 0.5%; sectoral GDP increased by an estimated 1.8% in 2010. At the end of 2009 a total of 1,426 vessels were registered under the Bahamian flag. With a combined displacement of 48.1m. grt, the fleet is among the largest in the world. Banking is the second most important economic activity in the Bahamas, and there is a large 'offshore' financial sector. In 2000 a stock exchange, where it was planned to develop trading in global depository receipts for overseas companies, became operational; it was trading the shares of 21 local companies in June 2011. Tourism is the predominant sector of the economy, directly and indirectly accounting for almost one-half of GDP and employing about one-third of the working population. The majority of stop-over visitors come from the USA (some 80.5% in 2008), although attempts are being made to attract visitors from other countries following amendments in 2007 to the Western Hemisphere Travel Initiative requiring all US citizens travelling to and from the Caribbean to hold a valid passport. Visitor arrivals increased from 4.65m. in 2009 to 5.25m. in 2010. Receipts from tourism fell slightly to B $1,929m. in 2009, from $2,144 in 2008, mainly owing to the global economic downturn, particularly in the USA, but it increased to $2,059m. in 2010. The Bahamas receives more cruise ship arrivals annually than any other Caribbean destination.

According to preliminary official figures, in 2010 the Bahamas recorded a visible trade deficit of B $1,888.2m., and there was a deficit of $887.8m. on the current account of the balance of payments. The USA is the principal trading partner of the Bahamas, providing 94.5% of non-petroleum imports and taking 66.6% of non-petroleum exports in 2009. The principal imports in 2010 were mineral products (24.0% of total imports), machinery and transport equipment (17.3%), food and live animals (14.9%), products of chemical or allied industries (11.4%) and manufactured goods classified chiefly by materials (11.2%). In that year the principal exports were products of chemical or allied industries (34.9% of total exports), mineral products (25.7%), and machinery and transport equipment (11.9%).

According to preliminary official figures, in 2011/12 there was a budgetary deficit of B $359.4m. The Bahamas' general government gross debt was B $3,520m. in 2010, equivalent to 45.4% of GDP. At 31 December 2005 the external debt of the central Government was some $286.5m. In that year, the cost of servicing long-term debt and repayments to the IMF was equivalent to 3.3% of the value of exports of goods, services and income (excluding workers' remittances). The annual rate of inflation averaged 2.4% in 2004–10; consumer prices increased by 1.3% in 2010. The rate of unemployment stood at some 14.2% of the labour force in 2009.

The Bahamian economy is heavily reliant upon tourism and the financial services industry, particularly the 'offshore' banking sector. In an effort to improve the country's reputation and to comply with its obligations to the Organisation for Economic Co-operation and Development (OECD, see p. 379) to improve the transparency of its banking system, by late 2011 the Bahamas had signed tax information sharing agreements with 27 other states. OECD issued a report in April 2011 commending the Bahamian authorities for increasing the transparency of the country's financial sector and for concluding an acceptable number of tax agreements. Meanwhile, the tourism sector continued to expand with the construction of tourist resorts on Grand Bahama, Eleuthera and New Providence Island. In February 2011 construction began of a US $2,600m. resort on Nassau, the Baha Mar, to be financed, in part, by the Export-Import Bank of China. The project had been criticized for its recruitment of foreign, mostly Chinese, workers, rather than utilizing Bahamians, although proponents argued that up to 7,000 full-time jobs would be created for local workers once the resort was built. By mid-2011 work on the resort had reportedly generated nearly 900 domestic jobs, with another 3,000 expected to be created throughout the construction period. According to the IMF, in 2009 the global economic crisis led to a 10% decrease in tourism numbers, a contraction in real GDP of 5.4% and a sharp decline in foreign direct investment. The IMF reported that modest growth of 1.0% had been achieved in 2010, led by a recovery in the tourism sector and an upsurge in foreign investment. However, the fiscal deficit rose in 2010/11, and debt levels also increased. None the less, real GDP was forecast by the IMF to expand by 2.0% in 2011, driven by increasing tourist arrivals and the commencement of work on the Baha Mar resort, although further growth would be dependent upon an improvement in the global economic climate. With the conclusion of boundary delimitation negotiations with Cuba in October 2011, petroleum exploration operations were expected to commence in 2012 following the approval of new environmental regulations (which were still under consideration in 2012).

PUBLIC HOLIDAYS

2013: 2 January (for New Year's Day), 29 March (Good Friday), 1 April (Easter Monday), 20 May (Whit Monday), 1 June (Labour Day), 10 July (Independence Day), 6 August (Emancipation Day), 12 October (Discovery Day/Columbus Day/National Heroes Day), 25–26 December (Christmas).

Statistical Survey

Source (unless otherwise stated): Department of Statistics, Clarence A. Bain Bldg, Thompson Blvd, POB N-3904, Nassau; tel. 302-2400; fax 325-5149; e-mail dpsdp@bahamas.gov.bs; internet statistics.bahamas.gov.bs/index.php; The Central Bank of the Bahamas, Frederick St, POB N-4868, Nassau; tel. 322-2193; fax 322-4321; e-mail cbob@centralbankbahamas.com; internet www.centralbankbahamas.com.

AREA AND POPULATION

Area: 13,939 sq km (5,382 sq miles).

Population: 303,611 at census of 1 May 2000; 353,658 (males 170,926, females 182,732) at census of 3 May 2010 (preliminary); 355,200 at mid-2012 (official estimate). *By Island* (census of 2010, preliminary): New Providence 248,948; Grand Bahama 51,756; Eleuthera 7,826; Andros 7,386; Others 37,742.

Density (at mid-2012): 25.5 per sq km.

Population by Age and Sex ('000, official estimates at mid-2012): *0–14:* 86.6 (males 44.4, females 42.2); *15–64:* 246.0 (males 119.6, females 126.4); *65 and over:* 22.6 (males 9.5, females 13.1); *Total* 355.2 (males 173.5, females 181.7).

Principal Town (incl. suburbs, UN estimate): Nassau (capital) 247,659 in mid-2009. Source: UN, *World Urbanization Prospects: The 2009 Revision*.

Births, Marriages and Deaths (2006): Registered live births 4,594 (birth rate 13.9 per 1,000); Registered deaths 1,751 (death rate 5.3 per 1,000); Registered marriages 5,375 (marriage rate 16.3 per 1,000). *2008:* Registered deaths 1,863 (death rate 5.5 per 1,000). *2009:* Registered live births 5,027 (Source: partly UN, *Population and Vital Statistics Report*).

Life Expectancy (years at birth, WHO estimates): 76 (males 72; females 78) in 2009. Source: WHO, *World Health Statistics*.

Economically Active Population (persons aged 15 years and over, excl. armed forces, 2009): Agriculture, hunting, forestry and fishing 4,530; Mining, quarrying, electricity, gas and water 2,595; Manufacturing 5,315; Construction 17,345; Wholesale and retail trade 22,185; Hotels and restaurants 24,315; Transport, storage and communications 10,985; Finance, insurance, real estate and other business services 19,405; Community, social and personal services 50,550; *Sub-total* 157,225; Activities not adequately defined 580; *Total employed* 157,805 (males 80,335, females 77,470); Unemployed 26,215 (males 13,565, females 12,650); *Total labour force* 184,020 (males 93,900, females 90,120).

HEALTH AND WELFARE
Key Indicators

Total Fertility Rate (children per woman, 2009): 2.0.

Under-5 Mortality Rate (per 1,000 live births, 2009): 12.

HIV/AIDS (estimated % of persons aged 15–49, 2009): 3.1.

Physicians (per 1,000 head, 1998): 1.1.

Hospital Beds (per 1,000 head, 2006): 3.2.

Health Expenditure (2008): US $ per head (PPP): 1,737.

Health Expenditure (2008): % of GDP: 7.2.

Health Expenditure (2008): public (% of total): 47.7.

Access to Water (% of persons, 2004): 97.

Total Carbon Dioxide Emissions ('000 metric tons, 2007): 2,147.1.

Total Carbon Dioxide Emissions Per Head (metric tons, 2007): 6.4.

Human Development Index (2011): ranking: 53.

Human Development Index (2011): value: 0.771.

For sources and definitions, see explanatory note on p. vi.

AGRICULTURE, ETC.

Principal Crops ('000 metric tons, 2010, FAO estimates): Sweet potatoes 0.9; Sugar cane 57.5; Bananas 4.3; Lemons and limes 10.2; Grapefruit and pomelos 19.1; Vegetables (incl. melons) 22.5; Fruits (excl. melons) 37.0.

Livestock ('000 head, year ending September 2010, FAO estimates): Cattle 0.8; Pigs 5.0; Sheep 6.5; Goats 14.5; Poultry 3,000.

Livestock Products ('000 metric tons, 2010, FAO estimates): Chicken meat 6.7; Cows' milk 1.0; Goat's milk 1.8; Hen eggs 1.3.

Forestry ('000 cubic metres, 2010, FAO estimates): *Roundwood Removals (excl. bark):* Sawlogs and veneer logs 17 (output assumed to be unchanged since 1992); *Sawnwood Production (incl. railway sleepers):* Coniferous (softwood) 1.4 (output assumed to be unchanged since 1970).

Fishing (metric tons, live weight, 2009): Capture 9,020 (Nassau grouper 199; Snappers 596; Caribbean spiny lobster 7,138; Stromboid conchs 724); Aquaculture 2 (Whiteleg shrimp 2); *Total catch* 9,022.

Source: FAO.

MINING

Production ('000 metric tons, 2009, estimates): Unrefined salt 1,000.0; Aragonite 1.1. Source: US Geological Survey.

INDUSTRY

Production (million kWh, 2009): Electric energy 2,068.7.

FINANCE

Currency and Exchange Rates: 100 cents = 1 Bahamian dollar (B $). *Sterling, US Dollar and Euro Equivalents* (30 December 2011): £1 sterling = B $1.546; US $1 = B $1.000; €1 = B $1.294; B $100 = £64.68 = US $100.00 = €77.29. *Exchange Rate:* Since February 1970 the official exchange rate, applicable to most transactions, has been US $1 = B $1, i.e. the Bahamian dollar has been at par with the US dollar. There is also an investment currency rate, applicable to certain capital transactions between residents and non-residents and to direct investments outside the Bahamas. Since 1987 this exchange rate has been fixed at US $1 = B $1.225.

General Budget (B $ million, 2011/12, budget, preliminary): *Revenue:* Taxation 1,385.2 (Taxes on international trade and transactions 717.9; Taxes on property 116.8; Taxes on companies 125.2); Other current revenue 110.5; Capital revenue 17.0; Grants 7.6; Total 1,520.2. *Expenditure:* Current expenditure 1,598.0 (Wages and salaries 610.8; Goods and services 360.6; Interest payments 218.8; Subsidies and transfers 407.8); Capital expenditure and net lending 281.6; Total 1,879.6.

International Reserves (B $ million at 31 December 2010): IMF special drawing rights 175.8; Reserve position in IMF 9.6; Foreign exchange 858.7; Total 1,044.2. Source: IMF, *International Financial Statistics*.

Money Supply (B $ million at 31 December 2009): Currency outside banks 208; Demand deposits at deposit money banks 1,038; Total money (incl. others) 1,252. Source: IMF, *International Financial Statistics*.

Cost of Living (Consumer Price Index; base: 2005 = 100): All items 109.7 in 2008; 111.9 in 2009; 113.4 in 2010. Source: IMF, *International Financial Statistics*.

Gross Domestic Product (B $ million at current prices): 8,240.2 in 2008; 7,806.8 in 2009; 7,701.6 in 2010 (preliminary).

Expenditure on the Gross Domestic Product (B $ million at current prices, 2010, preliminary): Government final consumption expenditure 1,143.8; Private final consumption expenditure 5,595.1; Change in stocks 93.7; Gross fixed capital formation 1,578.6; *Total domestic expenditure* 8,411.2; Exports of goods and services 3,236.3; *Less* Imports of goods and services 3,945.9; *GDP in purchasers' values* 7,701.6.

Gross Domestic Product by Economic Activity (B $ million at current prices, 2009, provisional): Agriculture, hunting, forestry and fishing 143.9; Mining and quarrying 98.2; Manufacturing 310.0; Electricity and water 135.3; Construction 509.3; Wholesale and retail trade 900.1; Restaurants and hotels 837.7; Transport, storage and communications 711.4; Finance, insurance, real estate and business services 2,450.2; Government services 440.4; Education 335.7; Health 311.7; Other community, social and personal services 529.2; *Sub-total* 7,713.2; *Less* Financial intermediation services indirectly measured 423.8; *Gross value added in basic prices* 7,289.4; Net indirect taxes 517.4; *GDP in purchasers' values* 7,806.8.

Balance of Payments (B $ million, 2010, preliminary): Exports of goods f.o.b. 702.4; Imports of goods f.o.b. –2,590.6; *Trade balance* –1,888.2; Services (net) 1,223.4; *Balance on goods and services* –664.8; Other income (net) –220.4; *Balance on goods, services and income* –885.2; Current transfers (net) –2.6; *Current balance* –887.8; Capital account (net) –3.6; Financial account (net) 1,132.6; Net errors and omissions –196.7; *Overall balance* 44.5.

EXTERNAL TRADE

Principal Commodities (B $ million, 2010, distribution according to HS): *Imports c.i.f.:* Food and live animals 426.6; Beverages and tobacco 67.3; Crude materials, inedible, excl. fuels 63.9; Mineral products 687.1; Products of chemical or allied industries 326.7; Manufactured goods classified chiefly by material 377.0; Machinery and transport equipment 493.9; Miscellaneous manufactured articles 321.7; Total (incl. others) 2,862.8. *Exports (incl. re-exports) f.o.b.:* Food and live animals 75.3; Mineral products 159.7; Products of chemical or allied industries 216.5; Machinery and transport equipment 73.8; Total (incl. others) 620.2.

Principal Trading Partners (non-petroleum transactions, B $ million, 2010): *Imports c.i.f.:* United Kingdom 12.9; USA 1,982.6; Total (incl. others) 2,175.7. *Exports f.o.b.:* United Kingdom 30.8; USA 315.9; Total (incl. others) 460.5.

TRANSPORT

Road Traffic (vehicles in use, '000): Passenger cars 90 (2002); Commercial vehicles 25 (2001); Total 27,058 (2007). Sources: IRF, *World Road Statistics*; Auto and Truck International (Illinois), *World Automotive Market Report*.

Shipping: *Merchant Fleet* (vessels registered at 31 December 2009): Number 1,426; Displacement ('000 grt) 48,119 (Source: IHS Fairplay, *World Fleet Statistics*). *International Sea-borne Freight Traffic* (estimates, '000 metric tons, 1990): Goods loaded 5,920; Goods unloaded 5,705 (Source: UN, *Monthly Bulletin of Statistics*).

Civil Aviation (2009): Kilometres flown (million) 8; Passengers carried ('000) 979; Passenger-km (million) 276; Total ton-km of freight (million) 25. Source: UN, *Statistical Yearbook*.

TOURISM

Visitor Arrivals ('000): 4,394 (1,393 by air, 3,001 by sea) in 2008; 4,645 (1,252 by air, 3,393 by sea) in 2009; 5,248 (1,295 by air, 3,953 by sea) in 2010.

Tourism Receipts (B $ million, excl. passenger transport): 2,144 in 2008; 1,929 in 2009; 2,059 in 2010 (preliminary) (Source: partly World Tourism Organization).

COMMUNICATIONS MEDIA

Radio Receivers: 215,000 in use in 1997.

Television Receivers: 73,000 in use in 1999.

Personal Computers: 40,000 (122.9 per 1,000 persons) in 2005.

Telephones: 129,300 main lines in use in 2010.

Mobile Cellular Telephones: 428,400 subscribers in 2010.

Internet Subscribers: 24,700 in 2010.

Broadband Subscribers: 24,700 in 2010.

Daily Newspapers (1996, unless otherwise indicated): 3 titles (total circulation 28,000 copies); 4 titles in 2004.

Sources: UN, *Statistical Yearbook*; UNESCO, *Statistical Yearbook*; International Telecommunication Union.

EDUCATION

Pre-primary (2002/03, unless otherwise indicated): 20 schools (1996/97); 338 teachers (all females); 3,771 pupils (males 1,931, females 1,840).

Primary (2008/09 unless otherwise indicated): 113 schools (1996/97); 2,683 teachers (males 427, females 2,256); 34,865 pupils (males 17,492 females 17,373).

Secondary (2008/09 unless otherwise indicated): 37 junior/senior high schools (1990); 2,780 teachers (males 829, females 1,951); 34,274 students (males 17,103, females 17,171).

Tertiary (1987): 249 teachers; 5,305 students. In 2002 there were 3,463 students registered at the College of the Bahamas.

Pupil-teacher Ratio (primary education, UNESCO estimate): 13.0 in 2008/09.

Sources: UNESCO, *Statistical Yearbook*; UN, Economic Commission for Latin America and the Caribbean, *Statistical Yearbook*; Caribbean Development Bank, *Social and Economic Indicators 2001*.

Adult Literacy Rate (UNESCO estimates): 95.0% (males 95.0%; females 95.0%) in 2003. Source: UN Development Programme, *Human Development Report*.

Directory

The Government

HEAD OF STATE

Queen: HM Queen ELIZABETH II.

Governor-General: Sir ARTHUR FOULKES (took office 14 April 2010).

THE CABINET
(May 2012)

The Cabinet is formed by the Free National Movement.

Prime Minister and Minister of Finance: HUBERT ALEXANDER INGRAHAM.

Deputy Prime Minister and Minister of Foreign Affairs: THEODORE BRENT SYMONETTE.

Minister of National Security: ORVILLE (TOMMY) TURNQUEST.

Minister of Tourism and Aviation: VINCENT VANDERPOOL-WALLACE.

Minister of Agriculture and Marine Resources: LAWRENCE (LARRY) CARTWRIGHT.

Minister of Education: T. DESMOND BANNISTER.

Minister of Health: Dr HUBERT MINNIS.

Minister of Public Works and Transport: NEKO C. GRANT.

Minister of the Environment: Dr EARL D. DEVEAUX.

Attorney-General and Minister of Legal Affairs: JOHN K. F. DELANEY.

Minister of Labour and Social Development: DION FOULKES.

Minister of Housing: (vacant).

Minister of Youth, Sports and Culture: CHARLES T. MAYNARD.

Minister of State for Lands and Local Government: BYRAN WOODSIDE.

Minister of State for Immigration: W. A. BRANVILLE MCCARTNEY.

Minister of State in the Ministry of the Environment: PHENTON NEYMOUR.

Minister of State for Finance: ZHIVARGO LAING.

Minister of State for Social Development: LORETTA BUTLER-TURNER.

MINISTRIES

Attorney-General's Office and Ministry of Legal Affairs: Post Office Bldg, 7th Floor, East Hill St, POB N-3007, Nassau; tel. 502-0400; fax 322-2255.

Office of the Prime Minister: Sir Cecil Wallace Whitfield Centre, West Bay St, POB CB-10980, Nassau; tel. 327-5826; fax 327-5806; e-mail info@opm.gov.bs.

Office of the Deputy Prime Minister: Goodman's Corporate Bay Centre, POB N-3746, Nassau; tel. 322-7624; fax 328-8212; e-mail brentsymonette@bahamas.gov.bs.

Ministry of Agriculture and Marine Resources: Levy Bldg, East Bay St, POB N-3028, Nassau; tel. 325-7502; fax 322-1767; e-mail nathanieladderley@bahamas.gov.bs.

Ministry of Education: Thompson Blvd, POB N-3913, Nassau; tel. 502-2700; fax 322-8491; e-mail info@bahamaseducation.com; internet www.bahamaseducation.com.

Ministry of the Environment: Dockendale House, 3rd Floor, West Bay St, POB N-3040, Nassau; tel. 328-2701; e-mail earldeveaux@bahamas.gov.bs.

Ministry of Finance: Cecil Wallace-Whitfield Centre, West Bay St, POB N-3017, Nassau; tel. 327-1530; fax 327-1618; e-mail mofgeneral@bahamas.gov.bs; internet www.bahamas.gov.bs/finance.

Ministry of Foreign Affairs: Goodman's Bay Corporate Centre, West Bay St, POB N-3746, Nassau; tel. 322-7624; fax 328-8212; e-mail mofa@bahamas.gov.bs.

Ministry of Health: Meeting St, POB N-3730, Nassau; tel. 502-4700; fax 325-5421; internet www.bahamas.gov.bs/health.

Ministry of Housing: Claughton House, Frederick St, POB N-4849, Nassau; tel. 322-6027; fax 322-6064.

Ministry of Labour and Social Development: Post Office Bldg, 2nd Floor, East Hill St, POB N-3008, Nassau; tel. 323-7814; fax 325-1920.

Ministry of National Security: East Hill St, POB N-3746, Nassau; tel. 322-7624; fax 328-8212.

Ministry of Public Works and Transport: John F. Kennedy Dr., POB N-8156, Nassau; tel. 322-4830; fax 326-6629; e-mail admin@mowt.bs; internet www.bahamas.gov.bs/publicworks.

Ministry of Tourism and Aviation: Bolam House, George St, POB N-3701, Nassau; tel. 302-2000; fax 302-2098.

Ministry of Youth, Sports and Culture: POB 3913, Nassau; tel. 502-0600; internet myscems.bahamas.gov.bs.

Legislature

PARLIAMENT

Senate

President: LYNN HOLOWESKO.

There are 16 nominated members.

House of Assembly

Speaker: ALVIN SMITH.

The House has 41 members.

General Election, 2 May 2007

Party	Seats
Free National Movement (FNM)	23
Progressive Liberal Party (PLP)	18
Total	41

Election Commission

Office of the Parliamentary Commissioner: c/o Ministry of National Security, Farrington Rd, POB N-1653, Nassau; tel. 325-2888; fax 322-1637; e-mail errolbethel@hotmail.com; internet www.bahamas.gov.bs/parliamentary; Chair. ERROL W. BETHEL.

Political Organizations

Democratic National Alliance (DNA): Prince Charles Dr. Shopping Center (Above KFC), Prince Charles Dr., POB AP59217, Nassau; tel. 326-9362; e-mail headquarters@mydnaparty.org; internet www.mydnaparty.org; f. 2011; Leader BRANVILLE MCCARTNEY.

Free National Movement (FNM): 144 Mackey St, POB N-10713, Nassau; tel. 393-7853; fax 393-7914; e-mail info@freenationalmovement.org; internet www.freenationalmovement.org; f. 1972; incorporated Bahamas Democratic Movt (f. 2000) in 2011; Leader HUBERT ALEXANDER INGRAHAM; Deputy Leader BRENT T. SYMONETTE.

Progressive Liberal Party (PLP): Sir Lynden Pindling Centre, PLP House, Farrington Rd, POB N-547, Nassau; tel. 326-9688; fax 328-0808; internet www.myplp.com; f. 1953; centrist party; Leader PERRY G. CHRISTIE; Deputy Leader PHILIP (BRAVE) DAVIS.

Workers Party: Black Village, POB N-9288, Nassau; tel. 322-8654; Leader RODNEY MONCUR.

Diplomatic Representation

EMBASSIES IN THE BAHAMAS

Brazil: Gilingam House, 2nd Floor, East Bay St, Montague, POB SS-6252, Nassau; tel. 393-3410; fax 393-3007; e-mail brasembnassau@yahoo.com.br; Ambassador REANALDO DE CAMPOS VERAS.

China, People's Republic: 3 Orchard Terrace, Village Rd, POB SS-6389, Nassau; tel. 393-1415; fax 393-0733; e-mail chinaemb_bs@mfa.gov.cn; internet bs.china-embassy.org; Ambassador HU SHAN.

Cuba: 61 Miller House, Collins Ave, POB EE-15679, Nassau; tel. 356-3473; fax 356-3472; e-mail cubanembassy@coralwave.com; internet embacu.cubaminrex.cu/bahamas; Ambassador ENERSTO SOBERÓN GUZMÁN.

Haiti: Sears House, Shirley St and Sears Rd, POB N-3036, Nassau; tel. 326-0325; fax 322-7712; Ambassador ANTONIO RODRIGUE.

San Marino: 291, The Office of the Old Fort Bay, Bldg 2, Western Rd, POB N-7776, Nassau; tel. 362-4382; fax 362-4669; Ambassador GIULIA GHIRARDI BORGHESE.

USA: Mosmar Bldg, Queen St, POB N-8197, Nassau; tel. 322-1181; fax 328-7838; e-mail embassynassau@state.gov; internet nassau.usembassy.gov; Charge d'affaires a.i. JOHN DINKELMAN.

Judicial System

The Judicial Committee of the Privy Council (based in the United Kingdom), the Bahamas Court of Appeal, the Supreme Court and the Magistrates' Courts are the main courts of the Bahamian judicial system.

All courts have both a criminal and civil jurisdiction. The Magistrates' Courts are presided over by professionally qualified Stipendiary and Circuit Magistrates in New Providence and Grand Bahama, and by Island Administrators sitting as Magistrates in the Family Islands.

Whereas all magistrates are empowered to try offences that may be tried summarily, a Stipendiary and Circuit Magistrate may, with the consent of the accused, also try certain less serious indictable offences. In 2006 the Bahamas' sole coroner's court was disbanded and magistrates endowed with the power to hear inquests. The jurisdiction of magistrates is, however, limited by law.

The Supreme Court consists of the Chief Justice, two Senior Justices and six Justices. The Supreme Court also sits in Freeport, with two Justices.

Appeals in almost all matters lie from the Supreme Court to the Court of Appeal, with further appeal in certain instances to the Judicial Committee of the Privy Council.

Supreme Court of the Bahamas

Bank Lane, POB N-167, Nassau; tel. 322-3315; fax 323-6463; internet www.bahamassupremecourt.gov.bs; Chief Justice HARTMAN LONGLEY (acting).

Registrar of the Supreme Court: DONNA NEWTON, The Registry, Ansbacher House, 3rd Floor, East St and Bank Lane, POB N-167, Nassau; tel. 322-4348; fax 325-6895; e-mail registrar@courts.gov.bs.

Court of Appeal: Claughton House, 3rd Floor, POB N-3209, Nassau; tel. 328-5400; fax 323-4659; e-mail info@courtofappeal.org .bs; internet www.courtofappeal.org.bs; Pres. ANITA ALLEN.

Magistrates' Courts: POB N-421, Nassau; tel. 325-4573; fax 323-1446; 15 magistrates and a circuit magistrate.

Office of the Attorney-General: Post Office Bldg, 3rd Floor, East Hill St, POB N-3007, Nassau; tel. 502-0400; fax 322-7111; e-mail administrationoag@bahamas.gov.bs; internet www.bahamas.gov .bs/attorneygeneral; Dir of Legal Affairs DEBORAH FRASER; Dir of Public Prosecutions VINETTE GRAHAM ALLEN.

Registrar-General: SHANE MILLER (acting), Shirley House, 50 Shirley St, POB N-532, Nassau; tel. 322-3316; fax 322-5553; e-mail registrargeneral@bahamas.gov.bs; internet www.bahamas .gov.bs/rgd.

Religion

Most of the population profess Christianity, but there are also small communities of Jews and Muslims.

CHRISTIANITY

Bahamas Christian Council: POB N-3103, Nassau; tel. 326-7114; f. 1948; 27 mem. churches; Pres. Rev. PATRICK PAUL.

The Baptist Church

According to the latest available census figures (2000), some 35% of the population are Baptists.

Bahamas National Baptist Missionary and Education Convention: Blue Hill Rd, Nassau; tel. 325-0729; fax 326-5473; mem. of the Baptist World Alliance; 270 churches and c. 75,000 mems; Pres. Dr ANTHONY CARROLL.

The Roman Catholic Church

The Bahamas comprises the single archdiocese of Nassau. According to the latest available census figures (2000), some 14% of the population are Roman Catholics. The Archbishop participates in the Antilles Episcopal Conference (whose Secretariat is based in Port of Spain, Trinidad). The Turks and Caicos Islands are also under the jurisdiction of the Archbishop of Nassau.

Archbishop of Nassau: Most Rev. PATRICK PINDER, Archdiocesan Pastoral Centre, West St North, POB N-8187, Nassau; tel. 322-8919; fax 322-2599; e-mail rcchancery@batelnet.bs; internet www .archdioceseofnassau.org.

The Anglican Communion

Anglicans in the Bahamas, who account for some 15% of the population, according to the 2000 census, are adherents of the Church in the Province of the West Indies. The diocese also includes the Turks and Caicos Islands.

Archbishop of the West Indies, and Bishop of Nassau and the Bahamas: Rt Rev. LAISH BOYD, Bishop's Lodge, Sands Rd, POB N-656, Nassau; tel. 322-3015; fax 322-7943; e-mail media@ bahamasanglicans.org; internet www.bahamas.anglican.org.

Other Christian Churches

According to the latest available census figures (2000), 8% of the population are Pentecostalists, 5% belong to the Church of God, 4% are Methodists and 4% are Seventh-day Adventists.

Bahamas Conference of the Methodist Church: Baltic Ave, Off Mackey St, POB SS-5103, Nassau; tel. 393-3726; fax 393-8135; e-mail bcmc@bahamasmethodist.org; internet bahamasmethodist .org; 34 mem. churches; Pres. WILLIAM HIGGS.

Bahamas Conference of Seventh-day Adventists: Tonique Williams-Darling Hwy, POB N-356, Nassau; tel. 341-4021; fax 341-4088; e-mail info@bahamasconference.org; internet www .bahamasconference.org; Pres. PAUL A. SCAVELLA.

Greek Orthodox Church: Church of the Annunciation, West St, POB N-823, Nassau; tel. 326-0850; fax 326-0851; e-mail parishpresident@annunciation.bs.goarch.org; internet www .annunciation.bs.goarch.org; f. 1928; part of the Archdiocese of North and South America, based in New York (USA); Priest Rev. THEDORE ROUPAS.

Other denominations include African Methodist Episcopal, the Assemblies of Brethren, Christian Science, the Jehovah's Witnesses, the Salvation Army, Presbyterian and Lutheran churches.

OTHER RELIGIONS

Bahá'í Faith

Bahá'í National Spiritual Assembly: POB N-7105, Nassau; tel. 326-0607; e-mail nsabaha@mail.com; internet www.bs.bahai.org.

Islam

There is a small community of Muslims, numbering 292 at the 2000 census.

Islamic Centre: Carmichael Rd, POB N-10711, Nassau; tel. 341-6612; fax 364-6233; e-mail jamaa.ahlussunnah@gmail.com; internet www.jamaa-ahlussunnah-bahamas.com; fmrly Jamaat Ul-Islam of the Commonwealth of the Bahamas.

Judaism

Most of the Bahamian Jewish community, numbering 228 at the 2000 census, are based on Grand Bahama.

Bahamas Jewish Congregation Synagogue: Luis de Torres Synagogue, POB F-41786, Freeport; tel. 373-9457; fax 373-2130; e-mail jberlind@coralwave.com; internet www .grandbahamasynagogue.org; Pres. TONY GEE; Sec. JEAN BERLIND.

The Press

NEWSPAPERS

The Abaconian: Marsh Harbour, POB AB-20551, Abaco; tel. 367-2677; fax 367-3677; e-mail davralph@batelnet.bs; internet abaconian .com; f. 1993; privately owned; local news; Editor and Publr DAVE RALPH.

The Bahama Journal: Media House, East St North, POB N-8610, Nassau; tel. 325-3082; fax 325-3996; internet www.jonesbahamas .com; f. 1987; daily; circ. 5,000.

Bahamas Press: Nassau; e-mail media@bahamaspress.com; internet bahamaspress.com; online newspaper; f. 2007; Editor ALEXANDER JAMES.

The Eleutheran: Cupid's Cay, POB EL-25166, Governor's Harbour, Eleuthera; tel. 422-9350; fax 364-1275; e-mail editor@theeleutheran .com; internet www.eleutheranews.com; Man. Editor ELIZABETH BRYAN.

The Freeport News: Cedar St, POB F-40007, Freeport; tel. 352-8321; fax 351-3449; e-mail oswald@nasguard.com; internet freeport .nassauguardian.net; f. 1961; owned by *The Nassau Guardian*; daily; Gen. Man. DORLAN COLLIE; Editor OSWALD T. BROWN; circ. 5,000.

The Nassau Guardian: 4 Carter St, Oakes Field, POB N-3011, Nassau; tel. 302-2300; fax 328-8943; e-mail editor@nasguard.com; internet www.thenassauguardian.com; f. 1844; daily; Pres. ANTHONY FERGUSON; Man. Editor ERICA WELLS; circ. 15,000.

The Tribune: Shirley St, POB N-3207, Nassau; tel. 322-1986; fax 328-2398; e-mail tips@tribunemedia.net; internet www.tribune242 .com; f. 1903; daily; Publr EILEEN CARRON; Man. Editor JOHN FLEET; circ. 15,000.

PERIODICALS

The Bahamas Financial Digest: Miramar House, 2nd Floor, Bay and Christie Sts, POB N-4824, Nassau; tel. 322-5030; fax 326-2849; e-mail bfd@bahamas.net.bs; internet bfd-financial.com/Digest/ digest.html; f. 1973; 4 a year; business and investment; Publr and Editor MICHAEL A. SYMONETTE; circ. 15,890.

Bahamas Tourist News: Fred Ramsay Bldg, Shirley Park St, Nassau; tel. 322-3724; fax 322-4527; e-mail starpub@batelnet.bs; f. 1962; monthly; Editor BOBBY BOWER; circ. 371,000 (annually).

Ca Mari: POB N-3672, Nassau; tel. 565-9069; e-mail camari@ camariinc.com; internet www.camariinc.com; lifestyle magazine for women; Editor-in-Chief CAMILLE KENNY.

Insitu Arch: West Bay St, SP-60785, Nassau; tel. 376-4600; fax 327-8931; e-mail info@insitumag.com; internet www.insitumag.com; architechture; quarterly; CEO MARCUS LAING.

Nu Woman: Freddie Munnings Manor, Harbour Bay, CB-13236, Nassau; tel. 424-9879; fax 479-2318; e-mail nuwomanbs@gmail.com; internet www.nuwomanbs.com; f. 2008; lifestyle magazine for women; Publr and Editor-in-Chief ERICA MEUS-SAUNDERS.

Official Gazette: Government Publications, c/o Cabinet Office, POB N-7147, Nassau; tel. 322-2805; weekly; publ. by the Cabinet Office.

What's On Bahamas: Woodes Rogers Wharf, POB CB-11713, Nassau; tel. 323-2323; fax 322-3428; e-mail info@whatsonbahamas .com; internet www.whatsonbahamas.com; monthly; Publr NEIL ABERLE.

Publishers

Aberland Publications Ltd: Woodes Rodger's Wharf, CB-11713, Nassau; tel. 323-2323; fax 322-3428; e-mail submissions@whatsonbahamas.com; internet www.whatsonbahamas.com; Publr ANDREW BERLANDA.

Dupuch Publications Ltd: 51 Hawthorne Rd, Oakes Field, POB N-7513, Nassau; tel. 323-5665; fax 323-5728; e-mail info@dupuch.com; internet www.dupuch.com; f. 1959; publishes *Bahamas Handbook*, *Trailblazer* maps, *What To Do* magazines, *Welcome Bahamas* and *Dining and Entertainment Guide*; Publr ETIENNE DUPUCH, Jr.

Guanima Press Ltd: East Bay St, POB CB-13151, Nassau; e-mail guanimapressltd@yahoo.com; internet www.guanimapress.com; tel. and fax 393-3221; Owner P. MEICHOLAS.

Media Enterprises Ltd: 31 Shirley Park Ave, POB N-9240, Nassau; tel. 325-8210; fax 325-8065; e-mail info@bahamasmedia.com; internet www.bahamasmedia.com; f. 1984; educational and other non-fiction books; Pres. and Gen. Man. LARRY A. SMITH; Publishing Dir NEIL E. SEALEY.

Star Publishers Ltd: Fred Ramsay Bldg, Shirley Park St, Nassau; tel. 322-3724; fax 322-4527; e-mail starpub@bahamas.net.bs; CEO BOB BOWER.

Broadcasting and Communications

Utilities Regulation and Competition Authority (URCA): UBS Annex Bldg, East Bay St, POB N-4860, Nassau; tel. 393-0234; fax 393-0153; e-mail info@urcabahamas.bs; internet www.urcabahamas.bs; f. 2009; replaced both the Public Utilities Commission and the Television Regulatory Authority; regulatory authority for electronic communications and broadcasting (including cable television); Chair. WAYNE ARANHA; CEO (vacant).

TELECOMMUNICATIONS

Bahamas Telecommunications Co (BTC): John F. Kennedy Dr., POB N-3048, Nassau; tel. 302-7008; fax 326-8423; internet www.btcbahamas.com; f. 1966, fmrly known as BaTelCo; 51% stake acquired by Cable and Wireless (United Kingdom) in April 2011; Exec. Chair. JULIAN FRANCIS; Acting Pres. and CEO KIRK GRIFFIN.

Cable Bahamas Ltd: Robinson Rd at Marathon, POB CB-13050, Nassau; tel. 356-8940; fax 356-8997; e-mail info@cablebahamas.com; internet www.cablebahamas.com; f. 1995; provides cable television and internet services; Chair. PHILIP KEEPING; Pres. and CEO ANTHONY BUTLER.

BROADCASTING

Radio

Broadcasting Corporation of the Bahamas: Harcourt 'Rusty' Bethel Dr., 3rd Terrace, Centreville, POB N-1347, Nassau; tel. 502-3800; fax 322-6598; e-mail yourcomments@znsbahamas.com; internet www.znsbahamas.com; f. 1936; govt-owned; operates the ZNS radio and television network; Chair. MICHAEL MOSS; Gen. Man. EDWIN LIGHTBOURNE.

Radio ZNS Bahamas: internet www.znsbahamas.com; f. 1936; broadcasts 24 hours per day on 4 stations: the main Radio Bahamas ZNS1, Radio New Providence ZNS2, which are both based in Nassau, Radio Power 104.5 FM, and the Northern Service (ZNS3—Freeport); Station Man. ANTHONY FORSTER.

Cool 96 FM: Yellow Pine St, POB F-40773, Freeport, Grand Bahama; tel. 351-2665; fax 352-8709; e-mail cool96@coralwave.com; internet cool96fm.com; f. 1995; opened office in Nassau in Jan. 2005; Pres. and Gen. Man. ANDREA GOTTLIEB.

Gems Radio: 51 Sears Hill, POB SS-6094, Nassau; tel. 326-4381; fax 326-4371; e-mail shenac@gemsbahamas.com; internet gemsbahamas.com; f. 2006; subsidiary of Bartlett-McWeeney Communications Ltd; Programming Dir SHENA CARROL.

Island FM: EdMark House, Dowdeswell St, POB N-1807, Nassau; tel. 322-8826; fax 356-4515; internet www.islandfmonline.com; Owner EDDIE CARTER.

Love 97 FM: Bahamas Media House, East St North, POB N-3909, Nassau; tel. 356-2555; fax 356-7256; e-mail twilliams@jonescommunications.com; internet www.jonesbahamas.com; operated by Jones Communications Ltd.

More 94 FM: Carmichael Rd, POB CR-54245, Nassau; tel. 361-2447; fax 361-2448; e-mail media@more94fm.com; internet www.more94fm.com.

One Hundred JAMZ: Shirley and Deveaux St, POB N-3207, Nassau; tel. 677-0950; fax 356-5343; e-mail michelle@100jamz.com; internet www.100jamz.com; operated by *The Tribune* newspaper; Gen. Man. STEPHEN HAUGHEY; Programme Dir ERIC WARD.

Television

Broadcasting Corporation of the Bahamas: see Radio.

Bahamas Television: f. 1977; broadcasts for Nassau, New Providence and the Central Bahamas; transmitting power of 50,000 watts; full colour; Programme Man. CARL BETHEL.

US television programmes and some satellite programmes can be received. Most islands have a cable television service.

Finance

The Bahamas developed into one of the world's foremost financial centres (there are no corporation, income, capital gains or withholding taxes or estate duty), and finance has become a significant feature of the economy. In December 2010 there were 110 'offshore' banks and trust companies in operation in the islands, with a further 150 on restricted licences. In 2010 there were 162,872 registered International Business Companies, of which only 42,745 were active.

BANKING

(cap. = capital; res = reserves; dep. = deposits; m. = million; brs = branches)

Central Bank

The Central Bank of the Bahamas: Frederick St, POB N-4868, Nassau; tel. 302-2600; fax 322-4321; e-mail cbob@centralbankbahamas.com; internet www.centralbankbahamas.com; f. 1974; bank of issue; cap. B $3.0m., res B $127.1m., dep. B $411.4m. (Dec. 2009); Gov. and Chair. WENDY M. CRAIGG.

Development Bank

The Bahamas Development Bank: Cable Beach, West Bay St, POB N-3034, Nassau; tel. 702-5700; fax 327-5047; internet bahamasdevelopmentbank.com; f. 1978 to fund approved projects and channel funds into appropriate investments; total assets B $58.3m. (Dec. 2004); Chair. DARRON B. CASH; Man. Dir ANTHONY WOODSIDE; 1 br.

Principal Banks

Bank of the Bahamas Ltd (Bank of the Bahamas International): Claughton House, Shirley and Charlotte Sts, POB N-7118, Nassau; tel. 326-2560; fax 325-2762; e-mail info.bob@bankbahamas.com; internet www.bankbahamasonline.com; f. 1970; est. as Bank of Montreal (Bahamas and Caribbean); name changed as above in 2002; 50% owned by Govt, 50% owned by c. 4,000 Bahamian shareholders; cap. B $50.0m., res B $32.6m., dep. B $602.9m. (June 2010); Chair. MACGREGOR ROBERTSON; Man. Dir PAUL MCWEENEY; 13 brs.

Banque Privée Edmond de Rothschild Ltd (Switzerland): Lyford Financial Centre, Lyford Cay #2, West Bay St, POB SP-63948, Nassau; tel. 702-8000; fax 702-8008; e-mail dswaby@bper.ch; internet www.groupedr.bs; f. 1997; owned by Banque Privée Edmond de Rothschild SA (Switzerland); cap. 15.0m. Swiss francs, res 20.0m. Swiss francs, dep. 336.6m. Swiss francs (Dec. 2009); Chair. BENJAMIN DE ROTHSCHILD; CEO CLAUDE MESSULAM.

BSI Overseas (Bahamas) Ltd (Italy): Goodman's Bay Corporate Centre, West Bay St, Sea View Dr., POB N-7130, Nassau; tel. 502-2200; fax 502-2230; e-mail info@bsibank.com; internet www.bs.bsibank.com; f. 1969 as Banca della Svizzera Italiana (Overseas) Ltd; name changed as above 1990; wholly owned subsidiary of BSI SA Lugano; cap. US $10.0m., res US $18.2m., dep. US $3,857.8m. (Dec. 2010); Chair. GIORGIO GHIRINGHELLI; CEO ALFREDO GYSI.

Canadian Imperial Bank of Commerce (CIBC) (Canada): Goodman's Bay Corporate Centre, West Bay St, POB 3933, Nassau; tel. 356-1800; fax 322-3692; e-mail privatebanking@cibc.com; internet www.cibc.com; Pres. GERALD T. MCCAUGHEY; Area Man. TERRY HILTS; 9 brs.

Citibank NA (USA): Citibank Bldg, 4th Floor, Thompson Blvd, Oakes Field, POB N-8158, Nassau; tel. 302-8500; fax 323-3088; internet www.citibank.com; CEO RAUL ANAYA; 2 brs.

Commonwealth Bank Ltd: The Plaza, Mackey St, POB SS 5541, Nassau; tel. 502-6200; fax 394-5807; e-mail cbinquiry@combankltd.com; internet www.combankltd.com; f. 1960; total assets B $1,179.2m. (Dec. 2007); Chair. WILLIAM BATEMAN SANDS, Jr; Pres. IAN ANDREW JENNINGS; 11 brs.

Crédit Agricole Suisse Bank & Trust (Bahamas) Ltd: Goodman's Bay Corporate Centre, Ground Floor, POB N-3015, Nassau; tel. 502-8100; fax 502-8166; internet www.ca-suisse.bs; f. 1978; 100% owned by Crédit Agricole (Suisse) SA, Geneva; fmrly National Bank of Canada (International) Ltd; name changed as above 2008; cap. US $20.0m., dep. US $175.6m., total assets US $498.9m. (Oct. 2006); Pres. JEAN-MARIE SANDER; Dir-Gen. JEAN-PAUL CHIFFLET.

Crédit Suisse (Bahamas) Ltd (Switzerland): Bahamas Financial Centre, 4th Floor, Shirley and Charlotte Sts, POB N-4928, Nassau; tel. 356-8100; fax 326-6589; internet www.credit-suisse.com/bs; f. 1968; subsidiary of Crédit Suisse Zurich; portfolio and asset management, 'offshore' company management, trustee services, foreign exchange; cap. US $12.0m., res US $20.0m., dep. US $579.2m. (Dec. 2004); CEO BRADY W. DOUGAN.

FirstCaribbean International Bank Ltd: Bahamas International Banking Centre, Shirley St, POB N-8350, Nassau; tel. 322-8455; fax 326-6552; internet www.firstcaribbeanbank.com; f. 2002 following merger of Caribbean operations of Barclays Bank PLC and CIBC; Barclays Bank relinquished its stake to CIBC in 2006; cap. B $12.0m., res B $430.4m., dep. B $2,767.3m. (Oct. 2010); Exec. Chair. MICHAEL MANSOOR; CEO JOHN ORR; 16 brs.

Guaranty Trust Bank Ltd: Lyford Manor Ltd, Lyford Cay, POB N-4918, Nassau; tel. 362-7200; fax 362-7210; e-mail info@guarantybahamas.com; internet www.guarantybahamas.com; f. 1962; cap. US $18.0m., res US $0.3m., dep. US $59.8m. (Dec. 2009); Chair. Sir WILLIAM C. ALLEN; Man. Dir JAMES P. COYLE.

HSBC Private Banking (Bahamas) Ltd (Switzerland): Centre of Commerce, 3rd Floor, Suite 306, 1 Bay St, POB N-4917, Nassau; tel. 502-2555; fax 502-2566; e-mail hfccfint@bahamas.net.bs; internet www.hsbcprivatebank.com/offices/bahamas.html; f. 1971 as Handelsfina Int.; name changed as above in 2002; cap. US $5.0m., res US $15.5m., dep. US $581.3m. (Dec. 1999); Chair. DOUGLAS FLINT; CEO STEPHEN GULLIVER.

Pictet Bank and Trust Ltd (Switzerland): Bldg No. 1, Bayside Executive Park, West Bay St and Blake Rd, POB N-4837, Nassau; tel. 302-2222; fax 327-6610; e-mail pbtbah@bahamas.net.bs; internet www.pictet.com; f. 1978; cap. US $1.0m., res US $10.0m., dep. US $126.2m. (Dec. 1995); Chair. FRANCIS HODGSON; Pres. and Man. Dir YVES LOURDIN.

Private Investment Bank Ltd: Devonshire House, Queen St, POB N-3918, Nassau; tel. 302-5950; fax 302-5970; e-mail pibbank@pib.bs; f. 1984; est. as Bank Worms and Co International Ltd; renamed in 1990, 1996 and 1998; in 2000 merged with Geneva Private Bank and Trust (Bahamas) Ltd; wholly owned by Banque de Patrimoines Privés Genève BPG SA (Switzerland); cap. US $3.0m., res US $12.0m., dep. US $163.6m. (Dec. 2009); Chair. and Dir JEAN-FRANÇOIS FURRER.

Royal Bank of Canada Ltd (Canada): 323 Bay St, POB N-7549, Nassau; tel. 322-8700; fax 328-7145; e-mail banks@rbc.com; internet www.rbc.com; f. 1869; Chair. DAVID P. O'BRIEN; Pres. and CEO GORDON M. NIXON; 25 brs.

Scotiabank (Bahamas) Ltd (Canada): Scotiabank Bldg, Rawson Sq., POB N-7518, Nassau; tel. 356-1697; fax 356-1689; e-mail scotiabank.bs@scotiabank.com; internet www.bahamas.scotiabank.com; Chair. ANTHONY C. ALLEN; Man. Dir KEVIN TESLYK; 20 brs.

SG Hambros Bank and Trust (Bahamas) Ltd (United Kingdom): SG Hambros Bldg, West Bay St, POB N-7788, Nassau; tel. 302-5000; fax 326-6709; e-mail renaud.vielfaure@socgen.com; internet www.privatebanking.societegenerale.com; f. 1936; above name adopted in 1998; cap. B $2.0m., res –B $3.2m., dep. B $435.2m. (Dec. 2008); Chair. WARWICK NEWBURY.

UBS (Bahamas) Ltd (Switzerland): UBS House, East Bay St, POB N-7757, Nassau; tel. 394-9300; fax 394-9333; internet www.ubs.com/bahamas; f. 1968; est. as Swiss Bank Corpn (Overseas) Ltd, name changed as above 1998; wholly owned by UBS AG (Switzerland); cap. US $4.0m., dep. US $420.2m. (Dec. 1997); Chair. KASPAR VILLIGER; CEO OSWALD J. GRÜBEL.

Principal Bahamian Trust Companies

Ansbacher (Bahamas) Ltd: 308 East Bay St, POB N-7768, Nassau; tel. 322-1161; fax 326-5020; e-mail info@ansbacher.bs; internet www.ansbacher.bs; f. 1957; offers bank and trust services; total assets US $128m. (2012); Man. Dir CARLTON MORTIER.

Bank of Nova Scotia Trust Co (Bahamas) Ltd: Scotia House, 404 East Bay St, POB N-3016, Nassau; tel. 502-5700; fax 393-0582; e-mail scotiatrust@coralwave.com; internet www.bahamas.scotiabank.com; wholly owned by the Bank of Nova Scotia; Vice-Pres. and Head JAMES STOOKE.

Winterbotham Trust Co Ltd: Winterbotham Pl., Marlborough and Queen Sts, POB N-3026, Nassau; tel. 356-5454; fax 356-9432; e-mail adavidson@winterbotham.com; internet www.winterbotham.com; total assets US $14.1m. (Dec. 2007); Pres. and Man. Dir GEOFFREY HOOPER; CEO ALAN MCLEOD DAVIDSON; 2 brs.

Bankers' Organizations

Association of International Banks and Trust Companies in the Bahamas: Goodman's Bay Corporate Centre, West Bay St, POB N-7880, Nassau; tel. 356-3898; fax 328-4663; e-mail info@aibt-bahamas.com; internet www.aibt-bahamas.com; f. 1976; Chair. JEAN-MARC FELLAY.

Bahamas Financial Services Board (BFSB): Goodman's Bay Corporate Centre, 1st Floor, West Bay St, POB N-1764, Nassau; tel. 326-7001; fax 326-7007; e-mail info@bsfb-bahamas.com; internet www.bfsb-bahamas.com; f. 1998; jt govt/private initiative responsible for overseas marketing of financial services; CEO and Exec. Dir ALIYA ALLEN; Chair. PAUL WINDER.

Bahamas Institute of Financial Services (BIFS): Verandah House, Market St and Trinity Pl., POB N-3202, Nassau; tel. 325-4921; fax 325-5674; e-mail info@bifs-bahamas.com; internet www.bifs-bahamas.com; f. 1974 as Bahamas Institute of Bankers, name changed as above 2003; Pres. TANYA MCCARTNEY; Exec. Dir KIM W. BODIE.

STOCK EXCHANGE

Bahamas International Securities Exchange (BISX): Fort Nassau Centre, 2nd Floor, British Colonial Hilton, Bay St, POB EE-15672, Nassau; tel. 323-2330; fax 323-2320; e-mail info@bisxbahamas.com; internet www.bisxbahamas.com; f. 1999; 25 primary listings and 20 mutual funds in Dec. 2011; Chair. IAN FAIR; CEO KEITH DAVIES.

INSURANCE

The leading British and a number of US, Canadian and Caribbean companies have agents in Nassau and Freeport. Local insurance companies include the following:

BAF Financial: Independence Dr., POB N-4815, Nassau; tel. 461-1000; fax 361-2524; e-mail info@mybafsolutions.com; internet bahamas.mybafsolutions.com; f. 1920; est. as British American Insurance Co; name changed to British American Financial in 2007 when comprehensive range of financial services added; rebranded as above in 2010; wholly owned by local consortium, BAB Holdings Ltd, since Feb. 2007; Chair. BASIL L. SANDS; Pres. and CEO CHESTER COOPER.

Bahamas First General Insurance Co Ltd: Bahamas First Centre, 32 Collins Ave, POB SS-6238, Nassau; tel. 302-3900; fax 302-3901; e-mail info@bahamasfirst.com; internet www.bahamasfirst.com; f. 1983; Pres. and CEO PATRICK G. W. WARD.

ColinaImperial Insurance Ltd: 308 Bay St, POB N-4728, Nassau; tel. 396-2100; fax 396-2188; e-mail info@colinaimperial.com; internet www.colinaimperial.com; Colina Insurance Co merged with Global Life Assurance Bahamas in July 2002; operates under above name; fully owned subsidiary of Colina Holdings Bahamas Ltd; Chair. TERENCE HILTS; Exec. Vice-Chair. and CEO EMANUEL M. ALEXIOU.

Family Guardian Insurance Co Ltd (FamGuard): East Bay & Shirley St, POB SS-6232, Nassau; tel. 396-4000; fax 393-1100; e-mail info@familyguardian.com; internet www.familyguardian.com; f. 1965; life and health; fully owned subsidiary of FamGuard Corpn Ltd; Pres. and CEO PATRICIA A. HERMANNS.

Summit Insurance Co Ltd: Island Traders Bldg, East Bay St, POB SS-19028, Nassau; tel. 394-2351; fax 394-2353; e-mail info@summitbah.com; internet www.summitbahamas.com; f. 1994; Chair. CEDRIC A. SAUNDERS; Gen. Man. and Dir TIMOTHY N. INGRAHAM.

Association

Bahamas General Insurance Association (BGIA): Royal Palm Mall, Unit 8, Mackey St, POB N-860, Nassau; tel. 394-6625; fax 394-6626; e-mail bgia@coralwave.com; internet www.bahamasinsurance.org; Chair. VENENTIA (TINA) CAMBRIDGE; Co-ordinator ROBIN B. HARDY; 18 mems.

Trade and Industry

DEVELOPMENT ORGANIZATIONS

Bahamas Agricultural and Industrial Corpn (BAIC): Levy Bldg, East Bay St, POB N-4940, Nassau; tel. 322-3740; fax 322-2123; e-mail nasoffice@baic.gov.bs; internet www.bahamas.gov.bs/baic; f. 1981; an amalgamation of Bahamas Development Corpn and Bahamas Agricultural Corpn for the promotion of greater co-operation between tourism and other sectors of the economy through the development of small and medium-sized enterprises; Chair. EDISON KEY; Gen. Man. BENJAMIN RAHMING.

Bahamas Financial Services Board (BFSB): see Finance—Bankers' Organizations.

Bahamas Investment Authority: Cecil V. Wallace-Whitfield Centre, West Bay St, POB CB-10980, Nassau; tel. 327-5826; fax 327-5806; e-mail bia@bahamas.gov.bs; govt-owned; operates from the Office of the Prime Minister; Dir of Investments JOY JIBRILU.

Nassau Paradise Island Promotion Board: Hotel Center, S. G. Hambros Bldg, West Bay St, Nassau; tel. 322-8381; fax 326-5346; e-mail rknowles@bahamashotels.org; internet www

.nassauparadiseisland.com; f. 1970; Chair. GEORGE R. MYERS; Sec. MICHAEL C. RECKLEY; 30 mems.

CHAMBERS OF COMMERCE

Bahamas Chamber of Commerce: Shirley St and Collins Ave, POB N-665, Nassau; tel. 322-2145; fax 322-4649; e-mail info@thebahamaschamber.com; internet www.thebahamaschamber.com; f. 1935 to promote, foster and protect trade, industry and commerce; Pres. KHAALIS ROLLE; over 700 mems.

Grand Bahama Chamber of Commerce: 5 Mall Dr., POB F-40808, Freeport, Grand Bahama; tel. 352-8329; fax 352-3280; e-mail gbchamber@batelnet.bs; internet www.gbchamber.com; Pres. PETER TURNQUEST; Exec. Dir MERCYNTH FERGUSON; 264 mems.

EMPLOYERS' ASSOCIATIONS

Bahamian Contractors' Association: POB N-9286, Nassau; tel. 322-2145; fax 322-4649; e-mail info@bahamiancontractors.org; internet www.bahamascontractors.com; f. 1959; Pres. STEPHEN WRINKLE; Sec. ROBIN OGILVIE.

Bahamas Employers' Confederation (BECon): Bahamas Chamber of Commerce Bldg, Collins Ave and Shirley St, POB N-166, Nassau; tel. 328-5719; fax 322-4649; e-mail becon@bahamasemployers.org; internet www.bahamasemployers.org; f. 1966; Pres. and Dir BRIAN NUTT.

Bahamas Hotel Employers' Association: SG Hambros Bldg, West Bay, POB N-7799, Nassau; tel. 322-2262; fax 502-4221; e-mail bhea4mcr@hotmail.com; f. 1958; Pres. J. BARRIE FARRINGTON; Exec. Vice-Pres. MICHAEL C. RECKLEY; 16 mems.

Bahamas Institute of Chartered Accountants: Maritima House, 2nd Floor, Frederick St, POB N-7037, Nassau; tel. 326-6619; fax 326-6618; e-mail secbica@batelnet.bs; internet www.bica.bs; f. 1971; Pres. REECE CHIPMAN.

Bahamas Motor Dealers' Association (BMDA): POB SS-6213, Nassau; tel. 302-1030; internet www.bmda.bs; 17 mem. cos.

Bahamas Real Estate Association: Dowdeswell St, POB N-8860, Nassau; tel. 356-4578; fax 356-4501; e-mail info@bahamasrealestateassociation.com; internet www.bahamasrealestateassociation.com; f. 1959; Pres. PATRICIA BIRCH; Sec. JAMES NEWBOLD; more than 600 mems.

Professional Engineers Board (PEB): 3 21st Century Rd, POB N-3817, Nassau; tel. 328-3574; e-mail info@pebahamas.org; internet www.pebahamas.org; f. 2004; Chair. MICHAEL MOSS.

UTILITIES

Electricity

Bahamas Electricity Corpn (BEC): Big Pond and Tucker Rds, POB N-7509, Nassau; tel. 302-1000; fax 323-6852; e-mail customercare@bahamaselectricity.com; internet www.bahamaselectricity.com; f. 1956; state-owned, scheduled for privatization; provides electricity to approx. 96,000 customers; Exec. Chair. MICHAEL MOSS; Gen. Man. KEVIN A. BASDEN.

Grand Bahama Power Co (GBPC): POB F-40888, Freeport; tel. 350-9000; fax 352-8449; e-mail evismissick@gb-power.com; internet www.gb-power.com; f. 1962 as Freeport Power Co Ltd; 80% owned by Emera (Canada); Vice-Pres. and CFO ANTHONY LOPEZ.

Gas

Tropigas: Gladstone Rd, POB SS-5833, Nassau; tel. 361-2695; fax 341-4875.

Water

Bahamas Water and Sewerage Corpn (WSC): 87 Thompson Blvd, POB N-3905, Nassau; tel. 302-5500; fax 302-5080; e-mail wcinfo@wsc.com.bs; internet www.wsc.com.bs; f. 1976; state-run; Chair. ANTON A. SAUNDERS; Gen. Man. GLEN LAVILLE.

TRADE UNIONS

All Bahamian unions are members of one of the following:

Commonwealth of the Bahamas Trade Union Congress: 3 Warwick St, POB N-3399, Nassau; tel. 394-6301; fax 394-7401; e-mail tuc@bahamas.net.bs; Pres. OBIE FERGUSON, Jr; Gen.-Sec. TIMOTHY MOORE; 12,500 mems.

National Congress of Trade Unions (NCTUB): Horseshoe Dr., POB GT-2887, Nassau; tel. 356-7459; fax 356-7457; e-mail office@nctu-bahamas.org; internet nctu-bahamas.org; Pres. JENNIFER ISAACS-DOTSON; Gen. Sec. MARIO CURRY; 20,000 mems.

The main unions are as follows:

Airport, Airline and Allied Workers' Union: Workers' House, Harold Rd, POB N-3364, Nassau; tel. 323-5030; fax 326-8763; e-mail aaawu@batelnet.com; f. 1958; Acting Pres. and Gen. Sec. ANTHONY BAIN.

Bahamas Communications and Public Officers' Union: Farrington Rd, POB N-3190, Nassau; tel. 322-1537; fax 323-8719; e-mail union@bcpou.com; internet bcpou.org; f. 1973; Pres. BERNARD EVANS; Gen. Sec. DENISE WILSON; 2,100 mems.

Bahamas Doctors' Union: School Lane, Nassau; tel. 326-4166; Pres. FRANCIS WILLIAMS; Gen. Sec. GEORGE SHERMAN.

Bahamas Electrical Workers' Union: 52 Poinciana Dr., POB GT-2535, Nassau; tel. 322-4289; fax 322-4711; e-mail bewupresident2002@hotmail.com; Pres. DENNISE WILLIAMS; Gen. Sec. STEPHANO GREENE.

Bahamas Gaming and Allied Workers' Union: Taxi Union Bldg, Old Airport Rd, POB F-43070, Freeport; tel. 375-9804; fax 352-8837; e-mail bgawu@hotmail.com; internet bgaworkersunion.tripod.com; Pres. DENNIS BRITTON; Gen. Sec. TIFFANY MARTIN.

Bahamas Hotel, Catering and Allied Workers' Union: Harold Rd, POB GT-2514, Nassau; tel. 325-0807; fax 325-6546; e-mail bhcawu@batelnet.com; f. 1958; Pres. NICOLE MARTIN; Gen. Sec. DARRIN WOODS; 6,500 mems.

Bahamas Musicians' and Entertainers' Union: Horseshoe Dr., POB N-880, Nassau; tel. 322-3734; fax 323-3537; f. 1958; Pres. PERCIVAL SWEETING; Gen. Sec. PORTIA NOTTAGE; 410 mems.

Bahamas Nurses' Union: Centreville, Eighth Terrace, POB N-11530, Nassau; tel. and fax 325-3008; e-mail bnu_17199@hotmail.com; Pres. CLEOLA HAMILTON; Gen. Sec. ANEKA JOHNSON.

Bahamas Public Services Union: Wulff Rd, POB N-4692, Nassau; tel. 325-0038; fax 323-5287; e-mail bpsu@batelnet.bs; f. 1959; Pres. JOHN PINDER; Sec.-Gen. STEVEN J. MILLER; 4,247 mems.

Bahamas Taxi-Cab Union: Nassau St, POB N-1077, Nassau; tel. 323-5818; fax 323-6919; e-mail btcunion@coralwave.com; internet www.bahamastaxicabunion.com; Pres. LEON GRIFFIN; Gen. Sec. ROSCOE WEECH.

Bahamas Union of Teachers (BUT): Teachers' National Secretariat, 104 Bethel Ave, Stapledon Gardens, POB N-3482, Nassau; tel. 323-4491; fax 323-7086; e-mail idatp@hotmail.com; internet teachersvoicebahamas.com; f. 1945; Pres. BELINDA WILSON; Sec.-Gen. STEPHEN MCPHEE; 4,000 mems.

Eastside Stevedores' Union: Wulff Rd, POB GT-2813, Nassau; tel. 322-4069; fax 323-7566; f. 1972; Pres. DAVID BETHEL; Gen. Sec. HAROLDINE STUBBS, Jr.

Transport

ROADS

There are about 1,600 km (994 miles) of roads in New Providence and 1,368 km (850 miles) in the Family Islands, mainly on Grand Bahama, Cat Island, Eleuthera, Exuma and Long Island. In 2001 57.4% of roads were paved.

SHIPPING

The principal seaport is at Nassau (New Providence), which can accommodate the very largest cruise ships. Passenger arrivals exceed 2m. annually. The other main ports are at Freeport (Grand Bahama), where a container terminal opened in 1997, and Matthew Town (Inagua). There are also modern berthing facilities for cruise ships at Potters Cay (New Providence), Governor's Harbour (Eleuthera), Morgan's Bluff (North Andros) and George Town (Exuma). In 2012 plans were approved for construction of a new port in northern Abaco, financed by the Export-Import Bank of China at the cost of US $33m. The 35-acre project was expected to be completed by 2013.

The Bahamas converted to free-flag status in 1976. The fleet's aggregate displacement was 48,119,081 grt in December 2009 (the third largest national fleet in the world).

There is a weekly cargo and passenger service to all the Family Islands.

Bahamas Maritime Authority: Manx Corporate Centre, 3rd Floor East, West Bay St, POB N-4679, Nassau; tel. 356-5772; fax 356-5889; e-mail nassau@bahamasmaritime.com; internet www.bahamasmaritime.com; f. 1995; promotes ship registration and co-ordinates maritime administration; state-owned; CEO and Dir Cdre DAVY F. ROLLE.

Freeport Harbour Co Ltd: POB F-42465, Freeport; tel. 350-8000; fax 350-8044; internet www.freeportcontainerport.com; owned by Hutchison Port Holdings (HPH), Hong Kong; CEO GARY GILBERT; Dir ORLANDO FORBES.

Grand Bahama Port Authority (GBPA): Pioneer's Way and East Mall Dr., POB F-42666, Freeport; tel. 350-9002; fax 352-6184; e-mail fstubbs@gbpa.com; internet www.gbpa.com; f. 1955; receivers were appointed to operate co in Nov. 2006 pending outcome of contested ownership trial, which was resolved in 2010; Chair. HANNES BABAK; Pres. IAN ROLLE.

Principal Shipping Companies

Bahamas Ferries: Potters Cay West, Nassau; tel. 323-2166; fax 393-7451; e-mail customerservice@bahamasferries.com; internet www.bahamasferries.com; f. 1999; services Spanish Wells, Harbour Island, Current Island and Governors Harbour in Eleuthera, Morgan's Bluff and Fresh Creek in Andros, Sandy Point in Abaco and George Town in Exuma; Gen. Man. ALAN BAX.

Dean's Shipping Co: 11 Parkgate, POB EE17318, Nassau; tel. 394-0245; fax 394-0253; e-mail deansshippingco@gmail.com; internet www.deanshipping.com; Man. TWEED DEAN.

Dockendale Shipping Co Ltd: Dockendale House, 3rd Floor, West Bay St, POB N-3033, Nassau; tel. 325-0448; fax 328-1542; e-mail dscopr@dockendale.com; internet www.dockendale.com; f. 1973; ship management; Man. Dirs LESLIE J. FERNANDES, KAMMANA VALLURI.

Freeport Ship Services: 8 Logwood Rd, POB F-40423, Freeport; tel. 351-4343; fax 351-4332; e-mail info@freeportshipservices.com; internet www.freeportshipservices.com; f. 2003; privately owned co; affiliated to United Shipping Co Ltd; agents, customs brokers, logistics providers, chandlers; Pres. JEREMY CAFFERATA; Gen. Man. JOHN LANE.

Tropical Shipping Co Ltd: Container Terminals Ltd, John Alfred Dock, Bay St, POB N-8183, Nassau; tel. 322-1012; fax 323-7566; internet www.tropical.com; Pres. MIKE PELLICCI.

United Shipping Co (Nassau) Ltd: Centreville House, 5th Floor, Terrace 2, West Centreville, POB N-4005, Nassau; tel. 322-1341; fax 323-8779; e-mail operations@unitedshippingnassau.com; internet www.uscbahamas.com; sister co of Freeport Ship Services; Chair. TERRY MUNDAY.

United Abaco Shipping Co Ltd: Marsh Harbour, POB AB-20737, Abaco; tel. 367-2091; fax 367-2235; e-mail unitedabacoshippingco@coralwave.com; internet www.unitedabacoshipping.com; Man. SIDNEY ALBURY.

CIVIL AVIATION

Lynden Pindling International Airport (formerly Nassau International Airport) (15 km—9 miles—outside the capital), Freeport International Airport (5 km—3 miles—outside the city, on Grand Bahama) and Marsh Harbour International Airport (on Abaco Island) are the main terminals for international and internal services. There are also important airports at West End (Grand Bahama) and Rock Sound (Eleuthera) and some 50 smaller airports and landing strips throughout the islands. An estimated US $200m. development of Lynden Pindling International Airport was scheduled to be completed by late 2013.

Bahamasair Holdings Ltd: Windsor Field, POB N-4881, Nassau; tel. 702-4100; fax 702-4180; e-mail astuart@bahamasair.com; internet bahamasair.com; f. 1973; state-owned, proposed privatization plans shelved indefinitely by 2009; scheduled services between Nassau, Freeport, Cuba, Jamaica, Dominican Republic, Turks and Caicos Islands, destinations within the USA and 20 locations within the Family Islands; Chair. J. BARRIE FARRINGTON; Man. Dir HENRY WOODS.

Western Air Limited: San Andros International Airport, POB AP 532900, North Andros, Nassau; tel. 329-4000; fax 329-4013; e-mail westernairltd@gmail.com; internet www.westernairbahamas.com; f. 2001; private, wholly Bahamian-owned company; scheduled services between Nassau, Freeport, San Andros and Bimini, and on-demand charter flights throughout the Bahamas, the Caribbean and Central and South America; Pres. and CEO REX ROLLE.

Tourism

The mild climate and beautiful beaches attract many tourists. In 2010 tourist arrivals totalled some 5,248,000, including 3,953,000 visitors by sea. The majority of stop-over arrivals (82.7% in 2007) were from the USA. Receipts from the tourism industry stood at B $2,059m. in 2010.

Bahamas Hotel Association: Bahamas Tourism Centre, 3rd Floor, J. F. K. Dr., POB N-7799, Nassau; tel. 322-8381; fax 502-4246; e-mail bha@bahamashotels.org; internet www.bhahotels.com; Pres. STUART BOWE; Exec. Vice-Pres. FRANK COMITO.

Hotel Corporation of the Bahamas: Marlborough St and Navy Lion Rd, POB N-9520, Nassau; tel. 356-4571; fax 356-4846; operates from Office of the Prime Minister; Chair. MICHAEL SCOTT.

Nassau Tourism Development Board: POB N-4740, Nassau; tel. 326-0992; fax 323-2998; e-mail linkages@batelnet.bs; f. 1995; Chair. CHARLES KLONARIS.

Defence

The Royal Bahamian Defence Force, a paramilitary coastguard, is the only security force in the Bahamas, and numbered 860, as assessed at November 2011. Increasing concerns over rising crime levels in the Caribbean region prompted the recruitment of an additional 100 personnel to the Royal Bahamas Defence Force and 200 officers to the Royal Bahamas Police Force in 2007.

Defence Budget: an estimated B $56m. in 2012.

Commodore: RODERICK BOWE.

Education

Education is compulsory between the ages of five and 16 years, and is provided free of charge in government schools. There are several private and denominational schools. Primary education begins at five years of age and lasts for six years. Secondary education, beginning at the age of 11, also lasts for six years and is divided into two equal cycles. In 2007/08 91% of children in the relevant age-group were enrolled at primary level, while 85% of children in the relevant age-group were enrolled at secondary level. The University of the West Indies has an extra-mural department in Nassau, offering degree courses in hotel management and tourism. Ross University School of Medicine, which has a 126-acre campus on Grand Bahama for overseas medical students, began initial teaching activities in 2009. Technical, teacher-training and professional qualifications can be obtained at the two campuses of the College of the Bahamas.

In 2011/12 the estimated capital expenditure on education was B $14.1m.

BAHRAIN

Introductory Survey

LOCATION, CLIMATE, LANGUAGE, RELIGION, FLAG, CAPITAL

The Kingdom of Bahrain consists of a group of some 36 islands, situated midway along the Persian (Arabian) Gulf, approximately 24 km (15 miles) from the east coast of Saudi Arabia (to which it is linked by a causeway), and 28 km from the west coast of Qatar. There are six principal islands in the archipelago, the largest of these being Bahrain itself, which is about 50 km long, and between 13 km and 25 km wide. To the north-east of Bahrain island, and linked to it by a causeway and road, lies Muharraq island, which is approximately 6 km long. Another causeway links Bahrain island with Sitra island. The climate is temperate from December to the end of March, with temperatures ranging from 19°C to 25°C, but becomes very hot and humid during the summer months. In August and September temperatures can rise to 40°C. The official language is Arabic, but English is also widely spoken. More than 80% of Bahraini citizens are Muslims, divided into two sects: Shi'ites (almost 60%) and Sunnis (more than 40%). Non-Bahrainis comprised an estimated 54.0% of the total population, according to preliminary results of the April 2010 census. The national flag (proportions 3 by 5) is red, with a vertical white stripe at the hoist, the two colours being separated by a serrated line forming five white triangles. The capital is Manama, on Bahrain island.

CONTEMPORARY POLITICAL HISTORY

Historical Context

Bahrain, a traditional Arab monarchy, became a British Protected State in the 19th century. Under this arrangement, government was shared between the ruling Sheikh and his British adviser. Following a series of territorial disputes in the 19th century, Persia (renamed Iran in 1935) made renewed claims to Bahrain in 1928. This disagreement remained unresolved until May 1970, when Iran accepted the findings of a UN-commissioned report showing that the inhabitants of Bahrain overwhelmingly favoured complete independence, rather than union with Iran.

Sheikh Sulman bin Hamad Al Khalifa, who became ruler of Bahrain in 1942, was succeeded upon his death in November 1961 by his eldest son, Sheikh Isa bin Sulman Al Khalifa. Extensive administrative and political reforms were implemented in January 1970, when a supreme executive authority, the 12-member Council of State, was established, representing the first formal derogation of the ruler's powers. Sheikh Khalifa bin Sulman Al Khalifa, the ruler's eldest brother, was appointed President of the Council.

Meanwhile, in January 1968 the United Kingdom had announced its intention to withdraw British military forces from the area by 1971. Plans to create a fully independent, federal state to be comprised of Bahrain, Qatar and the Trucial States (now United Arab Emirates—UAE) proved unworkable, and Bahrain became a separate independent state on 15 August 1971. Sheikh Isa took the title of Amir, while the Council of State became the Cabinet, with Sheikh Khalifa as Prime Minister. A Constituent Assembly, convened in December 1972, formulated a new Constitution, which came into force on 6 December 1973. Elections to a new National Assembly, comprised of 14 cabinet ministers and 30 elected members, were conducted the following day. In the absence of political parties, candidates sought election as independents. However, in August 1975 the Assembly was dissolved by Amiri decree, following complaints from the Prime Minister that its members were obstructing the Government's legislative programme. New elections were to be held following minor changes to the Constitution and the electoral law, but the National Assembly was not reconvened; thus, the ruling family continued to exercise near-absolute power.

On 16 January 1993 a 30-member Majlis al-Shura (Consultative Council)—appointed by the ruling authorities and comprising a large number of business executives and some members of the old National Assembly—held its inaugural meeting. The Council was to act in a purely advisory capacity, with no legislative powers.

Domestic Political Affairs

For many years there have been indications of tension between Shi'ite Muslims, who form a slender majority in Bahrain (and many of whom are of Iranian descent), and the dominant Sunni Muslims, to which sect the ruling family belongs. During the 1980s two plots to overthrow the Government, one of which was alleged to have Iranian support, were uncovered, as was a plan to sabotage Bahrain's petroleum installations, in which Iran was also alleged to be implicated. In December 1993 the human rights organization Amnesty International published a report criticizing the Bahraini Government's treatment of Shi'ite Muslims, some of whom had been forcibly exiled. In March 1994 the Amir issued a decree pardoning 64 Bahrainis who had been in exile since the 1980s and permitting them to return to Bahrain. In December 1994, however, Sheikh Ali Salman Ahmad Salman, a Muslim cleric, was arrested following his criticism of the Government and his public appeal for reform, particularly the restoration of the National Assembly. Widespread rioting ensued throughout Bahrain, especially in Shi'ite districts, and large-scale demonstrations were held in Manama in support of Sheikh Salman's demands and to petition for his release. Civil unrest continued despite the Amir's pledge to extend the powers of the Consultative Council; 12 people died and some 2,500 demonstrators were arrested in clashes with the security forces during December and January 1995. Sheikh Salman was deported and sought asylum in the United Kingdom (a request that was finally granted in July 1998). The unprecedented scale of the protests was widely attributed to a marked deterioration in socio-economic conditions in Bahrain, and in particular to a high level of unemployment.

There were further anti-Government demonstrations in Shi'ite districts in March and April 1995, following a police search of the property of an influential Shi'ite cleric, Sheikh Abd al-Amir al-Jamri, who was subsequently placed under house arrest and later imprisoned. In June, in an apparent attempt to appease Shi'ite opposition leaders, the Prime Minister announced the first major government reorganization for 20 years; the new Cabinet included five Shi'ite ministers, although many strategic portfolios remained unchanged.

In August 1995 the Government initiated talks with Shi'ite opposition leaders in an effort to foster reconciliation, while the Amir pardoned 150 people detained since the unrest. However, a report issued by Amnesty International in September indicated that as many as 1,500 demonstrators remained in detention, and that two prisoners had died in police custody following torture. The talks collapsed in mid-September, although more than 40 political prisoners, among them Sheikh al-Jamri, were released later in the month. In October al-Jamri and six other opposition figures began a hunger strike in protest at the Government's refusal to concede to their demands, which included the release of all political prisoners and the restoration of the National Assembly. Following a large demonstration to mark the end of the hunger strike, the Government announced in November that it would take 'necessary action' to prevent future 'illegal' gatherings. In December the Amir declared an amnesty for nearly 150 prisoners, most of whom had been arrested during the recent disturbances. There were large-scale demonstrations in December and January 1996, in protest at the heavy deployment of security forces in Shi'ite districts and at the closure of two mosques. In mid-January eight opposition leaders, including Sheikh al-Jamri, were arrested on charges of inciting unrest. In February Ahmad al-Shamlan, a noted lawyer and writer, became the first prominent Sunni to be detained in connection with the disturbances, after he accused the Government of authoritarianism. A number of bomb explosions in February and March culminated in an arson attack on a restaurant in Sitra, in which seven Bangladeshi workers died. Also in March jurisdiction with regard to a number of criminal offences was transferred from ordinary courts to the High Court of Appeal, acting in the capacity of State Security Court. This move effectively accelerated the pace of court proceedings, while removing the right of appeal and limiting the role of the defence. In late March Isa Ahmad Hassan Qambar was executed by firing squad, having been condemned to death for killing a police officer during the unrest of March 1995. The execution—the first to take place in Bahrain since 1977—provoked mass protests by Bahrainis, while international human rights organizations challenged the validity of Qambar's confession and trial.

Civil tensions were exacerbated by the Government's announcement, in April 1996, of the creation of a Higher Council of Islamic Affairs (to be appointed by the Prime Minister and headed by the Minister of Justice and Islamic Affairs) to supervise all religious activity (including that of the Shi'ite community) in Bahrain. In June, however, the Amir sought to appease the demands of opposition reformers by announcing the future expansion of the Consultative Council from 30 to 40 members: a new 40-member Council was duly appointed by the Amir in September. Meanwhile, in July the State Security Court imposed death sentences on three of the eight Bahrainis convicted of the arson attack in Sitra, while four men were sentenced to life imprisonment. The death sentences were commuted to life imprisonment in December 2000.

In January 1997 a National Guard was created, to provide support for the Bahrain Defence Force (BDF) and the security forces of the Ministry of the Interior. The Amir's son, Hamad, was appointed to command the new force, prompting speculation that its primary duty would be to protect the ruling family. In March a week of anti-Government protests marked the first anniversary of the execution of Isa Qambar. It was reported that since the outbreak of civil unrest at the end of 1994 some 28 people had been killed and 220 imprisoned in connection with the protests. In November 1997 the trial *in absentia* of eight prominent exiled activists (including Sheikh Ali Salman) on charges including the attempted overthrow of the regime resulted in the imposition of prison sentences of between five and 15 years. Although the activists claimed not to have been summoned to stand trial, their sentences were considered lenient in view of the severity of their alleged offences. Furthermore, during 1997 publishing restrictions were relaxed, and in December the Amir announced plans to allow greater media coverage of the activities of the Consultative Council.

The accession of Sheikh Hamad and constitutional change

Sheikh Isa died on 6 March 1999. He was succeeded as Amir by his son, Crown Prince Sheikh Hamad bin Isa Al Khalifa; Sheikh Hamad's eldest son, Sheikh Salman bin Hamad Al Khalifa, became Crown Prince and also assumed his father's military command. Initially, opposition groups welcomed Sheikh Hamad's accession, which raised expectations of political change. In his first months in office Sheikh Hamad permitted Shi'ites to join the armed forces, allowed an investigation by Amnesty International into alleged brutality by the security forces and released more than 300 Shi'ite prisoners being held on security-related charges. However, the opposition claimed that 1,200–1,500 political prisoners remained in detention, and Sheikh Hamad was regarded as having failed to initiate prompt negotiations to end political unrest. In July Sheikh al-Jamri, who was brought to trial in February, having been detained since 1996 under the terms of the 1974 Decree Law on State Security Measures, was sentenced to 10 years' imprisonment for espionage and inciting anti-Government unrest; a substantial fine was also imposed. Following intense international pressure, Sheikh Hamad granted al-Jamri an official pardon the following day, although he remained effectively under house arrest. In August 1999 Bahrain's longest serving political prisoner, Al-Sayed Jafar al-Alawi, was released from detention, having served 18 years of a 25-year prison sentence imposed in 1981 for plotting against the Government. In November–December 1999 the Amir ordered the release of some 345 detainees. In October, meanwhile, Sheikh Hamad issued a decree ordering the Consultative Council to establish a human rights committee. None the less, Amnesty International asserted in November 2000 that, while the human rights situation in Bahrain had improved, the mechanisms that had facilitated past violations remained in place.

In May 2000 the Prime Minister stated that municipal elections, on the basis of universal suffrage, would be held in early 2001 and that parliamentary elections would take place in 2004. In September 2000 four women, as well as a number of non-Muslims, were appointed for the first time to the Consultative Council. The Amir announced in November that a 46-member Supreme National Committee (SNC) had been formed to prepare a National Action Charter (NAC), which would outline the further evolution of Bahrain's political system. Among the SNC's recommendations, submitted in December, were that there should be a transition from an emirate to a constitutional monarchy, comprising a directly elected bicameral parliament (with women permitted both to vote and to seek election), a consultative chamber that would be appointed by the Government from all sections of society and an independent judiciary. Critics of the Bahrain regime dismissed the proposed transition to a monarchy as a pretext for the continuation of autocratic rule.

The new Charter was submitted for approval in a national referendum held on 14–15 February 2001 (at which Bahraini women were permitted to vote for the first time), and was duly endorsed by 98.4% of participating voters. Two committees were formed by Sheikh Hamad later that month. The tasks of the first committee, the Committee for the Activation of the National Charter, headed by the Crown Prince, were to implement the NAC and to define the respective roles of the legislature and the monarchy. The second committee, chaired by the Minister of Justice and Islamic Affairs, was required to oversee amendments to the Constitution. The Decree Law on State Security Measures and the State Security Court were both abolished. Prior to the referendum all political prisoners, including Sheikh al-Jamri, were reportedly released by the Amir. Moreover, following the removal of travel restrictions for members of the opposition, by March 2001 at least 100 political exiles had returned to Bahrain, among them Sheikh Ali Salman. In the same month the Government granted a licence to the independent Bahrain Human Rights Society (BHRS).

On 14 February 2002 Sheikh Hamad announced the establishment of a constitutional monarchy in Bahrain, proclaiming himself King. The new monarch approved the amendments to the Constitution outlined in the NAC and dissolved the Consultative Council. Municipal elections were held on 9 May (with run-off voting one week later); however, female candidates—for the first time permitted to stand for public office—failed to win any seats on the five new regional councils.

The 2002 and 2006 legislative elections

In early 2002 it was announced that Bahrain's first legislative election for 27 years would take place on 24 October. Draft electoral legislation approved by the Government in June was criticized by opposition groups on the grounds that it barred all trade unions and overtly political organizations from participating in the ballot; in September, however, King Hamad removed restrictions on campaigning by political groups. Opposition activists expressed strong concern, furthermore, that the unelected Consultative Council would have the same rights as the elected Majlis al-Nuab (Council of Representatives) in the bicameral parliament, and stated that they would boycott the polls. Meanwhile, in July the King ordered the establishment of an independent financial auditing court, with far-reaching powers to monitor state spending. The creation of a Constitutional Court was also approved by the Government: this became operational in April 2005.

At the election, held on 24 October 2002, 21 of the 40 seats were won by independents and 'moderate' Sunni candidates, with the remaining 19 seats taken by more radical Islamists. The rate of participation by voters was recorded as 53.2% of the registered electorate. Reformists expressed their view that the newly elected legislature did not reflect the structure of Bahraini society, since a large proportion of the Shi'ite majority had boycotted the elections and female candidates had failed to win any seats (there had been eight women among a total of 174 candidates). Opposition groups, both leftist and Islamist, also complained that international human rights groups had not been permitted to monitor the elections. Moreover, there was considerable criticism of the policy of political naturalization adopted by the King (whereby Sunnis from the Eastern Province of Saudi Arabia were granted full voting rights), which was interpreted as a deliberate attempt to reduce the size of the Shi'ite majority. On 17 November the new Consultative Council was sworn in by the King; the number of women appointed to the Council remained unchanged at four. Earlier in November King Hamad named an expanded Cabinet: the changes included the appointment of two Shi'ites, Dr Majid bin Hassan al-Alawi and Sheikh Jawad bin Salem al-Oraid, as Minister of Labour and Social Affairs and Minister of Justice, respectively. Meanwhile, legislation permitting the establishment of independent trade unions was ratified in November.

In April 2004 Dr Nada Haffadh was appointed as Minister of Health, thereby becoming the first woman to attain cabinet rank in Bahrain. In May King Hamad dismissed the long-serving Minister of the Interior, Sheikh Muhammad bin Khalifa Al

Khalifa, following clashes between Bahraini police and mainly Shi'ite protesters who were demonstrating against US military operations in two Shi'ite holy cities in Iraq. Lt-Gen. Sheikh Rashid bin Abdullah bin Ahmad Al Khalifa was named as his successor. In a government reorganization in September 2005, Sheikh Khalid bin Ahmad Al Khalifa, the former Bahraini ambassador to the United Kingdom, was appointed as Minister of Foreign Affairs, replacing Sheikh Muhammad bin Mubarak Al Khalifa, who remained one of three Deputy Prime Ministers and assumed additional responsibility for ministerial committees. Another notable change was the dissolution of the Ministry of Oil, the functions of which were transferred to a newly established National Oil and Gas Authority.

In preparation for legislative elections scheduled for October 2006, in late 2005 the King's reform strategy was tested by the progress of the draft political societies law that would oblige political groupings to agree to certain conditions, such as a pledge to work within the existing Constitution and the refusal of funding from foreign benefactors, in order to receive a licence (in effect granting a group political party status) from the Ministry of Justice. Al-Wefaq National Islamic Society (or the Islamic National Accord Association), the largest Shi'ite group, which had boycotted the 2002 parliamentary election, agreed to register under the proposed regulations. The group, however, was reported to have split into two factions over the issue; as anticipated, the smaller of the two groups—now called Al-Haq (Movement for Liberty and Democracy)—did not compete in the 2006 election, for which a date of 25 November had since been designated.

During the months preceding the legislative polls, allegations of unscrupulous campaign tactics, coupled with the Government's veto on international election monitors, provoked tensions between the opposing Sunni and Shi'ite political assemblies and increased fears of an undemocratic ballot. In an effort to minimize such concerns, and to preserve the political neutrality of the military sector, the Ministry of the Interior prohibited military staff from participating in election campaigns and appointed the BHRS as an independent election monitor. However, a report compiled by Dr Salah al-Bandar, Chancellor of Strategic Planning in the Ministry of Cabinet Affairs, and released in September 2006, accused several government officials of deliberately exacerbating sectarianism and of contriving unfairly to influence the elections. Dr al-Bandar, a Sudanese-born British citizen, was deported to the United Kingdom, and Bahrain's Higher Criminal Court issued an edict prohibiting any press coverage or comment relating to the affair. The ensuing censorship of over 20 discussion and news websites precipitated considerable unease among international human rights observers. The Government's policy of incremental naturalization also provoked protests, amid allegations of politically motivated citizenship awards; such claims were strenuously denied by the Minister of the Interior. It was feared by opposition groups that changes to electoral boundaries since 2002 and exploitation of new naturalization legislation were altering the population balance, to Shi'ite disadvantage; the announcement that 5,000 non-Bahraini citizens of other Cooperation Council for the Arab States of the Gulf (or Gulf Cooperation Council—GCC, see p. 250) states would be permitted voting rights was also interpreted as an effort to increase the number of Sunni voters. A large demonstration staged one day prior to the elections demanded an investigation into an alleged plot to marginalize the Shi'ite population and appealed for the resignation of the Prime Minister.

The initial round of elections to the Council of Representatives on 25 November 2006 attracted a strong turn-out, estimated at 73% of eligible voters. A run-off ballot was subsequently held on 2 December to determine the distribution of the remaining 11 contested seats. In the second round the Shi'ite opposition Al-Wefaq National Islamic Society, led by Sheikh Ali Salman, secured a further seat, increasing its total representation to 17, and the mandate of an additional aligned independent effectively brought its overall presence in the Council to 18; however, Sunni candidates—comprising 12 Sunni Islamists and 10 independent Sunnis—achieved a majority, winning 22 seats. (Only one seat was attained by a liberal candidate.) Of 18 women among the 209 participating in the elections, only one attained a position on the Council: Latifa al-Qouood became the first female parliamentarian in the Gulf states when her constituency seat remained unopposed. Overall participation of registered voters in both polls was reported as 71%. The election results were contentious, however, as opposition organizations made applications to the Court of Cassation challenging several appointments on the grounds of illegal campaign practices perpetrated by Sunni Islamist groups. Meanwhile, municipal elections were held concurrently with the legislative polls.

On 5 December 2006 King Hamad announced the appointment of the new Consultative Council, the composition of which contrasted markedly with that of the newly elected Council of Representatives, and with the previous Consultative Council, since it included 10 female members and just two religious personalities (compared with 30 elected to the lower house); the selection was widely regarded as a counterbalancing measure to achieve a more representative parliament. Sheikh Khalifa presented his new 24-member Cabinet on 11 December, notably appointing a Shi'ite, Jawad bin Salem al-Arrayed, as one of three Deputy Prime Ministers for the first time in the kingdom's history. The Cabinet instituted one new portfolio pertaining to Oil and Gas Affairs, which was awarded to the head of the National Oil and Gas Authority, Dr Abd al-Hussain bin Ali Mirza, and also introduced the post of Minister of State for Defence Affairs, to which Dr Sheikh Muhammad bin Abdullah Al Khalifa was appointed. Members of Al-Wefaq boycotted parliament's inauguration on 15 December, protesting that the composition of the new Cabinet effectively marginalized the Shi'ite majority. In the absence of Shi'ite participation from the first two working sessions of the new parliament, Sunnis were appointed to the speakership and deputy speakerships: Khalifa al-Dhahrani was re-elected as Speaker, while Ghanem Fadhel al-Buainain and Dr Salah Ali Abd al-Rahman secured the latter positions. The boycott ended in early January 2007 with the presentation of the 2007–10 economic development plan.

Civil unrest

In May 2007 the US-based Human Rights Watch submitted a letter to King Hamad, urging the holding of a full and independent investigation into allegations of torture suffered by two men detained in police custody, who were among those arrested following clashes between anti-riot police and opposition activists earlier that month. Hundreds of demonstrators were reportedly injured in sporadic riots in Shi'ite villages during subsequent months. The unrest appeared to indicate an intensification of sectarian tensions between the kingdom's Sunni and Shi'ite populations. In mid-December, when Shi'ite demonstrators gathered in the streets of the capital to commemorate those killed in the riots of December 1994 and to protest against human rights violations, police were reported to have used tear-gas and rubber bullets to disperse the crowds, injuring dozens of people, while one man was reported to have been killed. Although the authorities maintained that the man's death was due to natural causes, the protesters claimed that he had died as a result of inhaling tear-gas, and clashes between the demonstrators and police intensified in subsequent days. Dozens of people were arrested, a number of whom claimed to have been tortured while in police custody; this prompted the independent BHRS to apply to the authorities in late December 2007 for permission to visit the inmates. An official at the Ministry of the Interior stated in January 2008 that medical tests carried out on the relevant prisoners 'proved' that no form of torture had been committed. However, the BHRS continued to be denied access with independent doctors to examine them. The trial of 15 of the detainees took place in July, with 11 receiving sentences of between one and seven years and four being acquitted owing to insufficient evidence. The perceived harshness of the sentences led to sporadic outbreaks of violent unrest in Shi'ite areas throughout 2008. A report published by Human Rights Watch in February 2010, and based on interviews with detainees as well as medical and court records, concluded that, since late 2007, security forces in Bahrain had resumed the use of torture against detainees. The Minister of Foreign Affairs, Sheikh Khalid, subsequently announced that the Government would conduct an internal inquiry into the allegations and pledged to co-operate fully with the human rights organization.

Meanwhile, in a development that was widely seen as an attempt to strengthen royal control over the military, King Hamad announced by royal decree, in January 2008, the disbandment of the Ministry of Defence and the appointment of Crown Prince Sheikh Salman bin Hamad Al Khalifa as Deputy Commander-in-Chief of the BDF. The outgoing Minister of Defence, Maj.-Gen. Sheikh Khalifa bin Ahmad Al Khalifa, was appointed to the position of Commander-in-Chief of the BDF, and the administration of matters pertaining to the military was henceforth to be managed by the Minister of State for Defence Affairs. The transfer of military authority from a government ministry to the direct control of the King, in his capacity as Supreme Commander of the BDF, rendered the military, according to the terms of the Constitution, immune to scrutiny by the legislature. At a time when the condition of King Hamad's health was reported to be a source of some concern, the changes were also regarded as a means of preparing for the eventual handover of power to the Crown Prince. In mid-January Sheikh Salman identified disunity within the Government and a lack of co-ordinated endeavour as the principal reasons for the slow pace of economic reform; his comments, made in a letter written to the King, were generally interpreted as public criticism of Prime Minister Sheikh Khalifa and as further evidence of the increasing power and influence enjoyed by the future heir to the throne.

In mid-December 2008 security forces made a number of arrests in Shi'a villages outside Manama. The authorities announced that they had uncovered a plot to launch a series of co-ordinated terrorist attacks on police, government and commercial targets in Manama to coincide with Bahrain's National Day, 16 December. At least 14 suspects were detained, and on 28 December Bahrain Television broadcast a series of alleged confessions, in which prisoners apparently admitted to having received directions from two Bahraini nationals resident in the United Kingdom, and to having travelled to Syria to obtain training in the use of weapons and explosives. In January 2009 lawyers for the accused claimed that they had thus far been unable to meet their clients without the police being present, and claimed that some detainees showed signs of physical mistreatment. Human rights activists also protested that the public broadcasting of extra-judicial confessions contravened both international and Bahraini law. In late January police arrested a further three Shi'ite political activists in connection with the National Day plot. Hassan Mesheima, Secretary-General of Al-Haq movement, Dr Abd al-Jalil al-Singace, an Al-Haq spokesperson, and Muhammad al-Moqdad, a Shi'ite cleric, were charged variously with aiding and financing a terrorist organization and plotting to overthrow the Government; all three denied the charges. Al-Singace was released shortly thereafter, whereas the other two activists remained in custody. The arrests provoked clashes between protesters and police in various Shi'ite areas, such as Jidd Hafs, Karzakan and Sanabis. In March a Pakistani national was killed during a firebomb attack in Ma'ameer village. Following intensive pressure from international human rights organizations, a royal pardon was granted to 178 political prisoners, including Mesheima and al-Moqdad, in April. The detainees held in connection with the incident in Ma'ameer, as well as those accused of the murder of a police officer in Karzakan in April 2008, were excluded from the pardon. However, in October 2009 19 men accused of involvement in the police officer's death were acquitted, following the publication of a medical report which concluded that the death had been accidental. In May 2010 two Bahrainis were convicted of plotting to attack foreign interests in Bahrain and were both sentenced to five years' imprisonment; the men had been arrested in April 2009 having allegedly smuggled weapons and ammunition into Bahrain following contact with a militant group.

The 2009/10 budget and labour market reforms

Following a protracted impasse concerning the 2009/10 budget, with points of contention including measures to mitigate the effects of rising inflation, as well as the perceived high level of defence spending in the kingdom, in early March 2009 the Council of Representatives voted to reject the budget; however, it was finally approved by parliament later that month following the intervention of King Hamad, who instructed the Government to allocate an additional BD 100m. to fund a monthly anti-inflation subsidy for poorer families. None the less, the relationship between the legislature and the executive remained tense into 2010. In May 2009 members of parliament rejected the closing budget statements for 2006 and 2007 because the Government had withheld some details of spending on defence and on the Royal Court. The closing budget statement for 2008 was rejected on the same grounds in January 2010. Also that month the Council of Representatives established committees to investigate allegations of financial irregularities at the state-owned companies Gulf Air, Mumtalakat and the Bahrain Real Estate Investment Co (Edamah), despite opposition from some senior government officials.

Meanwhile, in April 2009 the Minister of Labour, Majid bin Hassan al-Alawi, announced the introduction of a Labour Market Reform Law, which guaranteed freedom of movement in the labour market for expatriate workers, thus ending the controversial sponsorship system that gave employers complete control over foreign workers. Under the new legislation, which came into effect on 1 August, expatriates could apply for government-issued work permits and would be entitled to seek new employment without the permission of their current employer. A limited system of unemployment benefits for Bahraini citizens was also introduced. The legislation, which was intended to reduce the exploitation of foreign workers, end the illegal trade in work permits and increase competition, drew widespread praise from international labour and human rights organizations but met with considerable opposition from Bahraini employers, who claimed that the reforms would have a detrimental effect on their operations.

In March 2010 the legislature approved the introduction of a voluntary pension scheme, while the authorities tightened restrictions on visas for expatriates in an attempt to reduce the number of visitors to Bahrain remaining in the country beyond the authorized duration of their stay. In the same month it was announced that Minister of State Mansoor bin Rajab had been removed from the Cabinet by the King, following his arrest by Bahraini police in connection with allegations of money-laundering; bin Rajab denied the claims.

The 2010 legislative elections

The third direct elections to the Council of Representatives since Bahrain became a constitutional monarchy took place on 23 October 2010 (with run-off elections subsequently held in nine districts on 30 October). The elections were held against a backdrop of escalating tensions between the country's Shi'ite and Sunni communities, following the detention of a number of Shi'ite opposition figures and political activists, including the re-arrest in August of Mesheima and al-Singace of the Al-Haq movement (see Civil unrest); Mesheima and al-Singace were among 23 people charged in September with 'conducting a wide-ranging propaganda campaign against the Kingdom and seeking to overthrow the regime by force'. Later that month a bomb explosion in a residential district of Manama damaged four cars belonging to security officials, and the authorities subsequently claimed to have foiled a much larger plot. Minister of Foreign Affairs Sheikh Khalid bin Ahmad Al Khalifa insisted that the spate of arrests was related exclusively to security concerns and was in no way connected to the forthcoming elections. None the less, several opposition alliances, including Al-Haq and the Islamic Action Society, boycotted the elections in protest both against the arrests and against claims that the Government had manipulated electoral boundaries in order to prevent the Shi'ite opposition from securing a parliamentary majority. Critics of the Government and international human rights organizations—including Amnesty International and Human Rights Watch—cited numerous examples of alleged government repression of Shi'ites in advance of the polls, while the Government's continued refusal to allow foreign observers to monitor elections elicited further criticism.

Despite the elevated tensions, the poll passed off without major incident, and voter turn-out was reported at about 67% of the registered electorate. Following both rounds of voting, Shi'ite opposition group Al-Wefaq had secured 18 seats, representing an increase of one from the 2006 election, while five seats were won by Sunni Islamist candidates (three from Al-Asala Islamic Society, two from Al-Menbar Islamic Society); the remaining 17 seats were won by pro-government Sunni independents, affording supporters of the Government a narrow majority in the 40-seat lower chamber. A new 40-seat Consultative Council was appointed by King Hamad on 25 November 2010, and included 10 new members. A minor government reorganization had been announced earlier that month, in which former Minister of Justice and Islamic Affairs Sheikh Khalid bin Abdullah Al Khalifa was appointed as a fourth Deputy Prime Minister. Meanwhile, in March Al-Wefaq had called for the cabinet to be selected by the Council of Representatives, rather than being appointed directly by the King, adding that the power-sharing arrangement envisaged in Bahrain's 2002 amended Constitution had not yet been satisfactorily implemented.

Anti-Government protests of 2011

In mid-February 2011 a number of demonstrations by protesters demanding democratic reforms—including greater powers for parliament and anti-corruption measures—and the release of Shi'ite activists from custody took place in villages surrounding Manama, and in the capital itself. These were seemingly inspired by the anti-Government protests which had erupted in Tunisia and Egypt in early 2011 and which led to the removal from office of both countries' Presidents. On 15 February large crowds gathered to begin protests at the Pearl roundabout in central Manama. During 14–15 February two protesters were shot dead in the capital during clashes with the police; following the deaths, King Hamad gave a televised address, in which he expressed condolences to the families of those killed and apologized for the conduct of the police. However, on 17 February security forces entered the area surrounding the roundabout in an attempt to disperse protesters who had been camping there, allegedly firing tear-gas and rubber bullets into the encampment; four people were reported to have been killed during the raid. The crackdown prompted vehement criticism from opposition politicians, including the leadership of Al-Wefaq, while the US Secretary of State, Hillary Clinton, and other foreign government officials expressed concern over the deaths of protesters and urged the Bahraini authorities to exercise restraint in their response to the demonstrations.

Nevertheless, violent confrontations continued in the capital until 21 February 2011, when the armed forces withdrew from the Pearl roundabout, thus allowing protesters to reoccupy the area. In a concession to one of the protesters' key demands, on 23 February some 50 people—including the Shi'ite political activists charged in September 2010—were released from gaol, while Mesheima and al-Singace were granted official pardons by King Hamad. Prior to those activists' release, opponents of the Government had been urged to participate in a 'National Dialogue', to be led by Crown Prince Sheikh Salman bin Hamad Al Khalifa. Despite these concessions, opposition activists remained critical of the Government and on 27 February 2011 Al-Wefaq announced that its 18 parliamentarians had submitted letters of resignation in protest against the deaths of seven anti-Government demonstrators earlier that month (11 of which were accepted by the Council on 29 March, and the remaining seven on 17 May). Meanwhile, on 26 February the King issued a decree reallocating several cabinet portfolios. Among the most notable appointments were those of Dr Majjid bin Mohsen al-Alawi as Minister of Housing, in place of Sheikh Ibrahim bin Khalifa al-Khalifa, and of Jamil Humaidan as Minister of Labour. Furthermore, a new Ministry of Energy was created: Dr Abd al-Hussein bin Ali Mirza (hitherto Minister of Oil and Gas Affairs) assumed responsibility for the expanded portfolio. Other initiatives announced in the decree included a reduction in housing costs and an acceleration of existing housing construction projects. However, these measures were some way short of the demands of the protesters for the removal from office of Prime Minister Sheikh Khalifa bin Sulman Al Khalifa and for the replacement of the Cabinet with a government elected by the Council of Representatives. Indeed, in early March the protests spread to other strategic locations in Manama, including the parliament building and the Prime Minister's office.

On 13 March 2011 anti-Government demonstrators asserted control of parts of the capital, including its Financial Harbour district, following clashes with police. The following day around 1,500 troops and police officers from Saudi Arabia, the UAE and Qatar arrived in Bahrain as part of a GCC 'Peninsula Shield' force, ostensibly to assist the Bahraini security forces in protecting strategic buildings and facilities; their entry into the country was denounced by members of Al-Wefaq as an 'overt occupation'. (The GCC had earlier that week agreed to provide some US $10,000m. of aid to the Bahraini Government in support of the National Dialogue process.) Later the same day at least five people were reported to have been killed amid attempts by government forces to disperse protesters gathered at locations in central Manama, including the Pearl roundabout and the Salmaniya hospital, bringing the total number of deaths since the protests began to 12. Reports that security forces had attacked medical staff who were attempting to treat wounded protesters provoked widespread local anger and international condemnation. On 15 March King Hamad issued a decree announcing a three-month state of 'national safety', under the terms of which the BDF implemented curfews in parts of the capital previously occupied by protesters. Fears of a sectarian conflict increased thereafter, as the Bahraini authorities accused the Iranian Government and the Lebanese Shi'ite militant organization Hezbollah of fomenting sectarian unrest, while it was reported that Bahrain's security forces had launched a series of attacks against predominantly Shi'a suburbs of Manama and villages outside the capital. On 17 March six people, including Mesheima, al-Singace and Ibrahim Sharif (of the secular Al-Waad party), were arrested on charges including 'communicating with foreign countries' and 'inciting murder and the destruction of property'; by early April it was estimated that up to 400 people had been arrested in connection with the protests. On 8 May Mesheima, al-Singace and Sharif were among 21 opposition activists charged with attempting to overthrow the monarchy with the aid of a foreign terrorist organization. On 22 June, having been convicted of the charges, Mesheima, al-Singace and six other leading Shi'a campaigners were sentenced to life imprisonment. The remaining 13 defendants were given gaol terms of up to 15 years, including Sharif, who received a five-year term; seven of these were sentenced *in absentia*. Meanwhile, on 18 March the statue at the Pearl roundabout, which had become a focal point for anti-Government protesters, was destroyed by the authorities and the area renamed Al-Farooq Junction. A further cabinet reorganization was announced in late March, following the resignations of the recently appointed Ministers of Health and of Housing in protest against the Government's response to the demonstrations. In mid-June a new Ministry of Human Rights and Social Development was created.

The authorities continued to use repressive measures in response to pro-democracy protests during April 2011, and hundreds of demonstrators, opposition politicians, human rights campaigners and lawyers, doctors and nurses were arrested and subsequently put on trial for their involvement in the demonstrations. Human rights groups claimed that some of those in detention were being tortured, and four protesters died in police custody in early April. In mid-April it was reported that at least 100 public sector workers had been dismissed from their posts for participating in the demonstrations. (In July the General Federation of Bahrain Trade Unions claimed that some 2,500 workers had been removed, although some of these had later been allowed to return to work.) There were also reports of Bahraini security forces, assisted by Saudi Arabian troops, having destroyed a number of Shi'ite mosques and other holy shrines, with officials claiming that some had been built illegally. However, many in the protest movement accused the Bahraini Government of seeking to exaggerate the sectarian nature of the unrest, stating that their grievances were against the monarchy and not against members of the Sunni community. In mid-April the Government declared that it was seeking legal authority to dissolve Al-Wefaq and the Islamic Action Society because, it claimed, the Shi'a parties had 'violated' the Constitution and damaged 'social peace and national unity'; however, after receiving criticism from the US Administration, the authorities agreed to delay the imposition of such a ban until after the events surrounding the political unrest had been investigated. At the end of April four Shi'a protesters were sentenced to death by a military court in Manama, while three others were sentenced to life imprisonment, having been convicted of the murder of two police officers during recent clashes.

On 3 May 2011 the Ministry of Justice and Islamic Affairs charged 47 Shi'a medical workers (23 doctors and 24 nurses) who had treated wounded anti-Government demonstrators with crimes including acting against the state and failing to treat injured Sunnis during the recent protests; their trial began on 6 June. By mid-2011 more than 32 people were reported to have died as a result of the political violence of February–March. However, amid an apparent restoration of calm, on 1 June—two weeks earlier than originally stipulated—King Hamad declared an end to the three-month state of national safety. At the end of the month a partial withdrawal of the GCC troops was announced, although heightened security measures continued to be employed, particularly in Shi'a villages. Nevertheless, in mid-June the ban imposed on the Al-Waad party in April was lifted, in preparation for the country's National Dialogue. On 29 June King Hamad issued a decree establishing the Bahrain Independent Commission of Inquiry (BICI)—an independent, international commission of judicial and human rights experts—to investigate both the causes of the recent unrest and allegations of human rights violations arising from the state of national safety. These were to include any violent acts perpetrated by the police, demonstrators or foreign forces deployed in Bahrain. The five-member commission, led by former UN human rights lawyer Prof. Cherif Bassiouni, was asked to report its findings by the end of October.

The King's National Dialogue process was inaugurated in Manama on 2 July 2011, under the chairmanship of parliamentary Speaker Khalifa al-Dhahrani. Some 300 representatives of Bahrain's political parties, civil society and expatriate groups, human rights organizations and other leading figures participated in discussions concerning political, legal, social and economic issues affecting the country's future. However, although

Al-Wefaq agreed to participate in the dialogue, in mid-July the party reportedly declined to attend the meetings concerning economic and social issues, citing excessive government control of the talks. Meanwhile, opponents of the National Dialogue process staged protests in the capital, resulting in violent clashes with police. The discussions ended on 25 July, and three days later King Hamad unveiled plans to expand the legislative and monitoring powers of the Council of Representatives and henceforth to stipulate that cabinet members would require parliamentary approval prior to assuming their posts. However, representatives of Al-Wefaq strongly criticized the National Dialogue process and the King's intended reforms, demanding the resignation of the entire Cabinet. On 12 August the party joined Al-Waad in declaring a boycott of the parliamentary by-elections scheduled to take place in September to choose deputies to fill the 18 seats that had been vacated by Al-Wefaq in February. The King did grant a number of concessions to opposition parties in August, such as lifting the charges against some of those arrested since the recent unrest, instituting labour market and pensions reforms, and raising food subsidies.

Parliamentary by-elections were held on 24 September 2011 to elect representatives in 14 of the 18 vacant seats, with candidates in the remaining four being returned unopposed. A run-off ballot was held on 1 October for nine seats where no candidate had secured 50% of the vote. Turn-out during the first round of voting was reported at only 17% of eligible voters, owing to the widespread opposition boycott; however, a higher rate was reported at the second round. The majority of those elected were said to be pro-Government, although some described themselves as independents. Two female candidates were elected to the Council of Representatives in the second round of voting, bringing the total number of women in the chamber to four. On 29 September eight doctors and 12 other medical personnel—all Shi'as who worked at the Salmaniya hospital—were found guilty by a military court in Manama of 'incitement to overthrow the Government' during the recent protests; they were convicted of refusing to treat wounded Sunnis and using ambulances to supply weapons to the protesters, and were sentenced to prison terms of between five and 15 years. A number of the medical practitioners alleged that they had been tortured by security forces while in detention. The verdicts were met with international condemnation, notably from Bahrain's allies such as the USA and the United Kingdom, and in late October, following an intervention by King Hamad, the Government announced that all 20 defendants would be retried in a civilian court. (The trial proceedings were adjourned in late November, and again in early January 2012. Despite reports to the contrary, it was announced in March that proceedings would recommence against all 20 defendants.)

Recent developments: publication of the BICI report

The Government admitted on 21 November, prior to the release of the BICI's report, that its security forces had been guilty of 'excessive force and mistreatment of detainees', and affirmed that 20 security officials would face criminal proceedings as a result of such violations. On 23 November—the date that the commission officially published its findings—the BICI found that a 'culture of impunity' had developed among Bahrain's security forces, and that they had been involved in the illegal detention and systematic torture of detained protesters. Of the 35 deaths recorded during the period under investigation by the BICI (14 February–15 April), security forces were found to have been responsible for 19 protesters' deaths; five of these were as a result of torture. Five of those 35 people killed were members of Bahrain's security forces, while the remainder were civilians. A total of 46 deaths (mostly of protesters) were linked to the political unrest between February and October. It was also noted that Sunnis had been attacked by members of the majority Shi'a population. The report found 'no discernible evidence' of Iranian involvement in the protests and no evidence that any GCC troops had committed human rights abuses.

King Hamad announced his acceptance of the Commission's findings, although he continued to insist that Iran had been responsible for provoking sectarian tensions. The King declared that a National Commission would be established (including Sunni and Shi'a representatives) to oversee implementation of the BICI's recommendations and to suggest possible legislative reforms by February 2012, and that civilians would no longer be tried by military courts. However, there were renewed clashes between police and protesters after 23 November 2011, as opposition parties demanded the Government's resignation; Al-Wefaq and Al-Waad declared that they would boycott further reconciliation talks. On 29 November Sheikh Khalifa bin Abdullah Al Khalifa, head of the National Security Agency (NSA), which—together with the Ministry of the Interior—was accused of having tortured protesters, was replaced in an acting capacity by Adel bin Khalifa al-Fadhel. Sheikh Khalifa was appointed as Secretary-General of the Supreme Defence Council and an adviser to the King. As the BICI had recommended, the NSA had its powers to arrest suspects withdrawn. In late December opposition spokesmen claimed that the authorities had not improved their record, despite expressions of regret from some leading officials, after a teenage protester in a mainly Shi'a village died after reportedly having been hit by a police tear-gas canister. Official sources denied such claims, stating that the boy had been wounded while throwing a petrol bomb at police, and announced an investigation into the incident.

It was announced on 1 January 2012 that some 300 leading members of Bahrain's Sunni and Shi'ite communities had drawn up a joint action plan in an effort to ease the sectarian tensions exacerbated by the political unrest of the previous year. On the same day the Chairman of the Consultative Council, Ali bin Saleh al-Saleh, resigned as Chairman of the National Commission, after he was accused of 'irregularities' concerning the reinstatement of four Council members. On 2 January the Supreme Judicial Council announced that a new judicial body would be established to review some of the verdicts handed down to civilians by military tribunals following the anti-Government protests; however, this would exclude those found to have incited violence. Also in early January the Government reported continued instances of violence being perpetrated against members of the security forces; the harsh response by Bahraini police and security officials to further sporadic protests against its leadership led to criticism from the US Administration in that month. On 10 January thousands of demonstrators held a peaceful protest outside the UN offices in Manama, demanding the removal from office of Prime Minister Sheikh Khalifa. On 15 January King Hamad announced a series of constitutional reforms that granted additional powers to the Council of Representatives to scrutinize the Government and question ministers suspected of wrongdoing; the King pledged to issue decrees detailing the proposed reforms later in 2012. The Government also pledged to rebuild Shi'a mosques that had been destroyed by the authorities. In late April three parliamentarians were appointed to the Government by King Hamad. Ganem al-Buainain, hitherto a member of the Council of Representatives, assumed the vacant post of Minister of State for Foreign Affairs. Two members of the Consultative Council also assumed new roles: Sameera Rajab was appointed as Minister of State for Information Affairs and Salah Ali as Minister of State for Human Rights Affairs.

Foreign Affairs

Regional relations

Although relations between Bahrain and Iran were upgraded to ambassadorial level in late 1990, the situation between the two countries began to deteriorate in the mid-1990s. While there was sufficient evidence to suggest largely domestic motivation for the recent increase in popular disaffection, the Bahraini authorities continued to imply that the disturbances were fomented by Iranian-backed militant Shi'ite fundamentalists seeking to destabilize the country. These allegations were frequently dismissed by Iran. In June 1996 the Bahraini Government announced that it had uncovered details of a plot, initiated in 1993 with support from fundamentalist Shi'ite groups in Iran, to oust the Government and ruling family in Bahrain and replace them with a pro-Iranian administration. It was claimed that a previously unknown Shi'ite group, Hezbollah Bahrain, had been established and financed by Iran's Islamic Revolutionary Guards Corps. Young Bahraini Shi'ites were alleged to have received military training in Iran and at guerrilla bases in Lebanon, in preparation for a terrorist offensive in Bahrain, which had culminated in the unrest of the previous 18 months. Within days of the Government's announcement more than 50 Bahrainis had been arrested in connection with the alleged plot, many of whom admitted membership of Hezbollah Bahrain. The Iranian authorities denied any involvement in the planned insurrection, but bilateral relations were severely undermined; the two countries' respective ambassadors were withdrawn, and diplomatic relations were downgraded. During 1996 and early 1997 more than 60 Bahrainis received prison sentences of between one and 15 years from the State Security Court for offences connected to the disturbances.

There was a period of *détente* in relations between most countries of the GCC and Iran following the election of Muhammad Khatami to the Iranian presidency in May 1997, and in December 1999 relations at ambassadorial level were formally restored between Bahrain and Iran. However, relations deteriorated in 2005, following the publication in the Bahraini daily *Al-Ayam* of a cartoon that Iranians considered insulting to their Supreme Leader, Ayatollah Ali Khamenei. Moreover, Bahrain took umbrage at the display of pictures of Iranian religious leaders during the country's own Ashoura festival. By mid-2006 Bahrain and Iran had taken steps to repair ties, with reciprocal visits of the two countries' ministers responsible for foreign affairs.

In July 2007 an editorial published in a conservative Iranian newspaper, in which its author revived claims that Bahrain was rightfully an Iranian province, provoked protests outside the Iranian embassy in Manama. Distancing itself from the comments, the Iranian Government dispatched the Minister of Foreign Affairs, Manouchehr Mottaki, to meet with his counterpart in Manama and convey a public message of 'peace and friendship' to the Bahraini Government, while an official at the Iranian embassy stated that the editor's views did not represent Iran's official position. Sheikh Khalid asserted that the editorial had not compromised bilateral relations, which, he insisted, remained strong. Iranian President Mahmoud Ahmadinejad (who had assumed office in August 2005) made an official visit to Manama in November 2007, where he held discussions with King Hamad. During his visit a memorandum of understanding (MOU) pertaining to oil and gas was signed. In March 2008 the Prime Minister publicly endorsed Iran's right to develop nuclear technology for peaceful purposes, and a framework agreement concerning the import of large quantities of Iranian gas was signed by the two countries in October. Sheikh Khalid, Bahrain's Minister of Foreign Affairs, visited Tehran in December, holding talks with his counterpart, Mottaki, and with President Ahmadinejad, which led to the signing of an extended security agreement, covering drugs-trafficking and counter-terrorism, as well as plans for the establishment of a joint security committee.

The positive trend in relations with Iran was jeopardized in mid-February 2009, following reports that Ali Akbar Nateq Nouri, a senior political figure and current member of the Council to Determine the Expediency of the Islamic Order, had described Bahrain as a former province of Iran, in a speech marking the 30th anniversary of the establishment of the Islamic Republic. The remark, which was interpreted by many as an attack on Bahrain's sovereignty, provoked vociferous condemnation from numerous regional and international leaders. Negotiations over the planned gas import agreement were suspended as a result of the controversy. However, the Iranian authorities acted quickly to defuse the crisis, issuing several statements affirming their respect for Bahrain's sovereignty and describing the incident as a misunderstanding caused by the media. Sadeq Mahsouli, Iran's Minister of the Interior, visited Manama in late February and, following a visit by Sheikh Khalid to Tehran in early March, the diplomatic row was officially ended and trade negotiations were resumed; the gas import negotiations, nevertheless, remained suspended. The sensitive nature of relations with Iran was illustrated again in June by the Bahraini Ministry of Culture and Information's decision to suspend publication of a prominent daily newspaper, *Akhbar al-Khaleej*, following its inclusion of an article written by a member of the Consultative Council, Sameera Rajab, in which she criticized the Iranian authorities and the conduct of the disputed presidential election in Iran. In October Dr Abd al-Hussain bin Ali Mirza, the Minister for Oil and Gas Affairs, announced Bahrain's readiness to resume the gas import negotiations, and in September 2010 Iran's Deputy Minister of Petroleum, Javad Oji, announced that Iranian and Bahraini officials had met in Tehran to discuss proposals to construct a natural gas pipeline under the waters of the Gulf, which would transfer some 1,000m. cu m of Iranian gas to Bahrain, and to establish a joint commission intended to increase co-operation in the natural gas sector.

Meanwhile, in January 2010 a high-level Bahraini delegation led by the Speaker of the Council of Representatives, Khalifa bin Ahmad al-Dhahrani, travelled to Tehran. During the visit President Ahmadinejad declared that relations between the two countries were based on mutual respect and recognition of sovereignty, and invited King Hamad to visit Tehran. In August Sheikh Khalid insisted that Bahrain would not allow the USA to launch an attack on Iran from its military bases in Bahrain, stating that Bahrain's military agreements with the USA were purely for defence. However, relations with Iran were compromised following the publication by the WikiLeaks organization of a series of classified US diplomatic cables in late 2010; in one such communiqué, King Hamad was reported to have identified Iran as the cause of the ongoing violence in Iraq and Afghanistan (q.v.) and to have argued vehemently in favour of forceful action to terminate Iran's nuclear programme. Ongoing contention between the USA (among other countries) and Iran over the latter's nuclear programme was regarded by some observers as a potential threat to Bahrain's security: in the event of conflict, the US Fifth Fleet military base in Manama was considered a likely priority target for Iranian military action. In early 2011 relations deteriorated again after the Bahraini authorities accused Iran of influencing anti-Government demonstrations which erupted in Manama from mid-February. Bilateral tensions were further exacerbated following the arrival in Bahrain in mid-March of the (Saudi-led) GCC Peninsula Shield force to assist the authorities in quelling the unrest. In late March the Iranian chargé d'affaires in Manama was expelled from the country, owing to alleged links to Bahraini opposition groups; a diplomat at Bahrain's embassy in Tehran was later ordered to leave Iran in retaliation. In a further diplomatic incident in late November, the Iranian authorities protested to Bahrain's chargé d'affaires after the Bahraini Government claimed to have uncovered a terrorist cell in the kingdom which it claimed had links to Iran's Revolutionary Guards.

In common with other Gulf states, Bahrain consistently expressed support for Iraq at the time of the Iran–Iraq War (1980–88). However, following the Iraqi invasion of Kuwait in August 1990, the Government firmly supported the implementation of UN economic sanctions against Iraq and permitted the stationing of US troops and combat aircraft in Bahrain. (Military co-operation with the USA had been close for many years.) In June 1991, following the liberation of Kuwait in February, it was confirmed that Bahrain would remain a regional support base for the USA, and later in the year the two countries signed a defence co-operation agreement. In January 1994 Bahrain signed further accords of military co-operation with the USA and the United Kingdom. Relations with Iraq remained strained, and in October hopes of improved relations receded when Iraqi forces were again deployed in the Iraq–Kuwait border area. In response, Bahrain deployed combat aircraft and naval units to join GCC and US forces in the defence of Kuwait. However, in February 1998 Bahrain strongly advocated a diplomatic solution to the ongoing dispute between Iraq and the UN weapons inspectors, and refused to allow US military aircraft to launch attacks on Iraq from Bahraini bases. In June, as part of a wider US effort to reduce its military presence in the region, US military aircraft were withdrawn from Bahrain. A further US-led military campaign against Iraq centred in Manama in December was supported by the Bahraini authorities, although Bahrain refrained from any public endorsement of the air-strikes.

Bahrain joined the other GCC states in condemning the suicide attacks on New York and Washington, DC, on 11 September 2001, and pledged to co-operate with the USA's attempts to forge an international 'coalition against terror', notably by freezing the financial assets of individuals or organizations allegedly linked to the militant Islamist al-Qa'ida network of Osama bin Laden, held by the USA to be principally responsible for the attacks. Nevertheless, as the momentum grew towards a US-led military campaign to oust the regime of Saddam Hussain in Iraq, anti-war riots became increasingly frequent in Bahrain, and in February 2003 police opened fire on a 2,000-strong violent demonstration outside the US embassy in Manama. Although King Hamad expressed hope that a diplomatic solution to the crisis might be found, Bahrain announced that it would contribute a frigate and an unspecified number of troops to the defence of Kuwait from possible Iraqi retaliation should the US-led campaign proceed.

Following the commencement, later in March 2003, of US-led military action in Iraq, in April Bahrain ordered the expulsion of an Iraqi diplomat who was alleged to be linked to an explosion outside the Fifth Fleet base. Sporadic violent incidents and threats, believed to be related to the continued presence of the US military in Bahrain, continued throughout 2003–04. The bombing of the al-Askari Mosque (or Golden Mosque) in Samarra, one of the holiest Shi'ite shrines in Iraq, by insurgents in February 2006 prompted the largest demonstration in Bahrain for many years. In an effort to combat terrorism, King Hamad presented a 'Protecting Society from Terrorist

Acts' bill to parliament in July; despite protestations of human rights contravention by the UN and Amnesty International (among others), the legislation was ratified in August. In October 2007 three Bahraini nationals became the first people to go on trial under the remit of the controversial new legislation after they were charged with belonging to a terrorist cell plotting attacks on US interests in Manama, and of supporting insurgents loyal to the deposed Taliban regime in Afghanistan; a fourth Bahraini man and a Qatari citizen were tried *in absentia*. In January 2008 all five were convicted and sentenced to six months' imprisonment; despite the verdict, the leniency of the sentences was a source of intense irritation to the US Administration.

After more than three years without a senior diplomatic representative in Iraq, Bahrain appointed an ambassador to that country, Salah al-Maliki, in October 2008—the chargé d'affaires, Hassan Ansari, had been withdrawn after narrowly escaping an assassination attempt in 2005. Minister of Foreign Affairs Sheikh Khalid visited Baghdad in October 2008, declaring his country's support for the Iraqi Government. Following the formation of a new cabinet in Iraq in November 2010, Sheikh Khalid reiterated Bahrain's support for the steps being taken by Iraq to regain its former position in Arab and regional affairs, while his Iraqi counterpart, Hoshyar al-Zibari, asserted his country's desire to foster closer bilateral relations with Bahrain at all levels. Following the intervention of GCC troops in the unrest in Bahrain of early 2011, Iraqi Prime Minister Nuri al-Maliki warned that the intervention of foreign forces might lead to renewed sectarian conflict across the Middle East.

In April 1986 Qatari military forces raided the island of Fasht al-Dibal, which had been artificially constructed on a coral reef (submerged at high tide), situated midway between Bahrain and Qatar; both countries claimed sovereignty over the island. Following GCC mediation, in May the two Governments agreed to destroy the island. Other areas of dispute between the two states were Zubarah (which was part of Bahraini territory until the early 20th century), in mainland Qatar, and the Hawar islands, which were believed to contain potentially valuable reserves of petroleum and natural gas. In July 1991 Qatar instituted proceedings at the International Court of Justice (ICJ) in The Hague, Netherlands, regarding the islands (in 1939 a British judgment had awarded them to Bahrain), Fasht al-Dibal and Qit'at Jaradah (over which the British Government had recognized Bahrain's 'sovereign rights' in 1947), together with the delimitation of the maritime border between Qatar and Bahrain. The question of sovereignty was further confused in April 1992, when the Government of Qatar issued a decree redefining its maritime borders to include territorial waters claimed by Bahrain, and tensions were exacerbated by Qatar's unilateral application to the ICJ, despite Bahrain's insistence that the two countries should seek joint recourse to the Court. Moreover, Bahrain had reportedly attempted to widen the issue to include its claim to the Zubarah region. In December 1996 Bahrain boycotted the GCC annual summit convened in Doha, Qatar, at which it was decided to establish a quadripartite committee (comprising those GCC members not involved in the dispute) to facilitate a solution. The committee reportedly made some progress, and following senior-level ministerial meetings between Bahrain and Qatar in London, United Kingdom, and in Manama in early 1997, it was announced that diplomatic relations at ambassadorial level were to be established between the two countries. Qatar, however, was alone in nominating its diplomatic representative shortly afterwards.

At the end of 1999 the Amir of Qatar made his first official visit to Manama, during which it was agreed that a joint committee, headed by the Crown Princes of Bahrain and Qatar, would be established to encourage bilateral co-operation. Qatar also agreed to withdraw its petition from the ICJ in the event of the joint committee's reaching a solution to the territorial disputes. In January 2000 the new Amir of Bahrain, Sheikh Hamad, visited Qatar, and the two countries agreed to hasten the opening of embassies in Manama and Doha. In February, following the first meeting of the Bahrain-Qatar Supreme Joint Committee, it was announced that the possibility of constructing a causeway (to be named the Friendship Bridge) to link the two states was to be investigated; Qatar officially named its ambassador to Bahrain on the same day. In May, however, Bahrain unilaterally suspended the Supreme Joint Committee pending the ruling of the ICJ. A verdict was issued in March 2001, whereby Bahrain was found to have sovereignty over the Hawar islands and Qit'at Jaradah, while Qatar held sovereignty over Zubarah, Janan island and the low-tide elevation of Fasht al-Dibal; the Court drew a single maritime boundary between the two states. Both Bahrain and Qatar accepted the ICJ ruling. Later in March, following a high-profile visit by Sheikh Hamad to Doha, the two sides announced that meetings of the Supreme Joint Committee would resume.

From early 2002 international oil companies were invited to submit bids to drill for petroleum and gas off the Hawar islands, which the newly enthroned King Hamad intended to transform into a major tourist resort. Approval for the construction of the causeway linking Bahrain to Qatar was finally given in May 2004, and a public commission to oversee the project was appointed in February 2005. After protracted discussions and numerous delays, in May 2008 the contract to design and build the causeway, at a total cost of some US $4,000m., was awarded to a French-led consortium. Construction was expected to begin in 2010 and to be completed in 2014–15. However, in early 2011 the project appeared to have stalled amid heightened bilateral tensions. Relations had been damaged in May 2010 when a Bahraini fisherman was seriously injured by Qatari coastguards in a 'naval incident', which had resulted in a resumption of hostilities over ownership of the Hawar islands. Tensions were further exacerbated later that month following the airing by the Qatar-based satellite broadcaster Al Jazeera of a television programme on poverty and the treatment of foreign labourers in Bahrain; the programme was widely interpreted as a criticism of the Bahraini Government, which promptly announced a suspension of the local operations of Al Jazeera, citing a 'breach of press and publishing regulations'. Work on the causeway had yet to commence by early 2012.

As part of the negotiations concerning a free trade agreement with the USA, in September 2005 Bahrain became the first GCC member to lift its ban on Israeli imports; however, Sheikh Muhammad bin Mubarak Al Khalifa, the Deputy Prime Minister and Minister of Foreign Affairs at the time, strongly denied that this represented the first step towards the establishment of diplomatic relations between Bahrain and Israel. Israel's military offensive against Islamic Resistance Movement (Hamas) targets in the Gaza Strip, launched in late December 2008, provoked vociferous condemnation from various leading elements of Bahraini society. King Hamad attended an emergency GCC summit in Riyadh, Saudi Arabia, in mid-January 2009 to discuss the crisis in Gaza and attempt to forge a unified response. Meanwhile, on 13 January the Council of Representatives released a statement denouncing the Israeli operation and appealing to all Arab nations to cease all forms of co-operation with Israel. In October draft legislation criminalizing all contact with Israel—economic, diplomatic or private—was approved by the Council of Representatives. It had been proposed in response to the perception that unofficial contacts between the two countries were increasing. Several senior members of the Bahraini Government criticized the bill, claiming that it would impede the kingdom's participation in the Middle East peace process. However, the legislation required approval by the Consultative Council, and this had not occurred by early 2012.

Other external relations

Following an unusually short period of negotiations, in September 2004 Bahrain signed a free trade agreement with the USA. In response, the Saudi Government, which claimed that the accord contravened the GCC's external tariff agreement (a view disputed by Bahrain), threatened to impose customs duties on foreign goods imported duty-free through GCC countries, a move that would affect US goods imported to Bahrain under the bilateral agreement. In December Crown Prince Abdullah of Saudi Arabia declined to attend the GCC annual summit in Manama, a decision that appeared to demonstrate the seriousness of the dispute over the free trade accord. In what was interpreted as a punitive measure, Saudi Arabia reduced petroleum transfers by withdrawing the extra output resulting from the doubling of capacity at the jointly owned Abu Saafa oilfield. Nevertheless, in May 2005 GCC ministers responsible for finance reportedly decided to allow bilateral commercial accords between individual member states and the USA, and the Bahraini-US agreement was duly implemented following US congressional approval in December (although it did not become effective until August 2006).

George W. Bush became the first US President to embark upon an official visit to Bahrain when he travelled to the Gulf state in January 2008 during a wider regional tour. King Hamad welcomed President Bush's visit as a reflection of the burgeoning relationship enjoyed by the two allies, and proposed further bilateral military co-operation, while Bush was unreserved in his praise of King Hamad and the Bahraini Government's efforts to create significant political change in the Gulf state. In March the King paid an official visit to the USA, during which he signed an MOU on civil nuclear co-operation with the US Administration. In May Houda Nonoo, a female member of the Consultative Council, was appointed as Bahrain's ambassador to the USA, thereby becoming the first Jewish envoy from the Arab world to occupy such a post.

Despite maintaining extremely close ties with the kingdom, the US Administration under President Barack Obama expressed concern at the Bahraini Government's crackdown on pro-democracy protesters in early 2011, and affirmed the validity of many of the protesters' demands for reform. In mid-May President Obama urged the Government to improve its human rights record and to release imprisoned opposition leaders, and in mid-June Bahrain was listed among a group of countries which the USA considered should be placed under the scrutiny of the UN Human Rights Council.

In December 2008 King Hamad paid his first ever official visit to Russia, during which he held talks with Russian President Dmitrii Medvedev. During the summit the King voiced his support for Russia's involvement in the Middle East peace process. The two countries also signed an MOU on civil nuclear co-operation. In February 2009 French President Nicolas Sarkozy paid an official visit to Bahrain, during which both a military co-operation agreement and a joint declaration on civil nuclear energy projects were signed. Although the European Union joined the USA in criticizing the Bahraini authorities for their harsh response to the anti-Government demonstrations from early 2011, France continued to enjoy largely favourable relations with the kingdom. In mid-2011 Crown Prince Salman and other senior Bahraini officials visited a number of Bahrain's traditional allies, including the USA, the United Kingdom and France, to seek to reinforce relations and to secure those countries' support for the newly instituted National Dialogue process (see Domestic Political Affairs). In early December a small bomb explosion was reported in the vicinity of the British embassy in Manama; however, no casualties or damage resulted from the blast.

CONSTITUTION AND GOVERNMENT

The 108-article Constitution that came into force on 6 December 1973 stated that 'all citizens shall be equal before the law' and guaranteed freedom of speech, of the press, of conscience and of religious beliefs. Other provisions included compulsory free primary education and free medical care. The Constitution also provided for a National Assembly, composed of 14 members of the Cabinet and 30 members elected by popular vote, although this was dissolved in August 1975. A National Action Charter, drafted in late 2000 by a Supreme National Committee and approved in a national referendum held in February 2001, recommended the transition from an emirate to a constitutional monarchy. The Amir proclaimed himself King in February 2002, when the amended Constitution was promulgated. Subsequently, a bicameral legislature, comprising a directly elected legislative body and a royally appointed consultative chamber, was instituted; each body was to serve a four-year term. Elections to a 40-member Majlis al-Nuab (Council of Representatives) took place in October 2002, and a new Majlis al-Shura (Consultative Council), comprising 40 appointed members, was sworn in by the King in November. Further legislative polls held in November 2006 resulted in a narrow Sunni Islamist parliamentary majority, a majority that was maintained following Bahrain's third direct legislative elections in October 2010.

REGIONAL AND INTERNATIONAL CO-OPERATION

Bahrain is a member of the Cooperation Council for the Arab States of the Gulf (or Gulf Cooperation Council—GCC, see p. 250), the six members of which established a unified regional customs tariff in 2003. The economic convergence criteria for the proposed introduction of a single market and currency were agreed at a heads of state meeting in Abu Dhabi, the UAE, in 2005, and in January 2008 the GCC launched its common market. A monetary union agreement, signed by four member states including Bahrain, in Riyadh, Saudi Arabia, in June 2009, defined the characteristics of the planned unified currency and monetary institutions. In addition, Bahrain is a participant in the League of Arab States (Arab League, see p. 364) and the Organization of Arab Petroleum Exporting Countries (OAPEC, see p. 401).

Bahrain became a member of the UN in 1971 and, as a contracting party to the General Agreement on Tariffs and Trade, joined the World Trade Organization (WTO, see p. 433) on its establishment in 1995. The country also participates in the Organization of Islamic Cooperation (OIC, see p. 404).

ECONOMIC AFFAIRS

In 2008, according to estimates by the World Bank, Bahrain's gross national income (GNI), measured at average 2006–08 prices, was US $19,714m., equivalent to $18,730 per head (or $24,710 per head on an international purchasing-power parity basis). During 2001–10, it was estimated, the population increased at an average annual rate of 7.8%, while gross domestic product (GDP) per head declined, in real terms, by an average of 0.5% per year in 2001–08. According to provisional official figures, overall GDP increased, in real terms, at an average annual rate of 6.1% per year in 2001–10; growth was 3.1% in 2009 and 4.5% in 2010.

According to FAO, agriculture (including hunting, forestry and fishing) engaged 0.6% of the labour force in mid-2012. According to provisional official figures, the sector contributed 0.4% of GDP in 2010. The principal crops are dates, tomatoes, and lemons and limes. Livestock production is also important. Agricultural GDP increased by an average annual rate of 2.9% in 2001–10; the GDP of the sector increased by an estimated 3.0% in 2009, but declined by 3.3% in 2010.

Industry (comprising mining, manufacturing, construction and utilities) engaged 28.0% of the employed labour force in 2001, and provided 43.3% of GDP in 2010, according to provisional figures. During 2001–10 industrial GDP increased by an average of 4.3% per year; the sector declined by 4.4% in 2009, before increasing by some 6.7% in 2010.

Mining and quarrying engaged 1.0% of the employed labour force in 2001, and, according to provisional figures, contributed 23.7% of GDP in 2010. The major mining activities are the exploitation of petroleum and natural gas, production of which accounted for 22.3% of GDP in that year. At the beginning of 2011 Bahrain's proven published reserves of crude petroleum were estimated at just 125m. barrels. Including output from the Abu Saafa oilfield (situated between Bahrain and Saudi Arabia), all revenue from which was, until the field was expanded in 2004, allocated to Bahrain, total crude oil production for 2010 was recorded at 66.4m. barrels. Excluding output from Abu Saafa, Bahrain produced an estimated 11.6m. barrels of crude oil in the same year.Bahrain's reserves of natural gas at the end of 2010 were put at 200,000m. cu m, sufficient to maintain production (at 2010 levels) for just under 17 years. According to provisional official figures, mining GDP declined at an average annual rate of 1.3% in 2001–10; the sector's GDP declined by 1.6% in 2009, but increased by 2.6% in 2010.

In 2001 manufacturing engaged 17.2% of the employed labour force, and the sector provided 14.4% of GDP in 2010, according to provisional figures. Important industries include the petroleum refinery at Sitra, aluminium (Bahrain is the region's largest producer) and aluminium-related enterprises, shipbuilding, iron and steel, and chemicals. Since the mid-1980s the Government has encouraged the development of light industry. During 2001–10 manufacturing GDP increased at an average annual rate of 9.6%; the sector's GDP decreased by 1.0% in 2009, before increasing by some 11.4% in 2010.

The construction sector engaged 9.1% of the employed labour force in 2001. According to provisional official figures, the sector contributed 3.9% of GDP in 2010. During 2001–10 the GDP of the sector increased at an average annual rate of 10.1%; the sector contracted by 19.5% in 2009, but expanded by 3.4% in 2010.

Industrial expansion has resulted in energy demand that threatens to exceed the country's 2,319-MW total installed generating capacity, particularly as not all of the installed capacity is operational. (Fuel imports amounted to 52.0% of total merchandise imports in 2007.) The largely state-owned Aluminium Bahrain (ALBA) smelter plant was supplementing domestic power generation in an attempt to accommodate the energy deficit. By 2008 the Al-Ezzal independent power project provided some 30% of the country's generating capacity. As part of the Electricity and Water Authority's strategic plan for the electricity sector up to 2020, several new power stations were to be built during 2007–11 in order to extend Bahrain's distribution network. The initial phase of a US $1,100m. regional electricity 'inter-exchange' grid, connecting members of the Cooperation Council for the Arab States of the Gulf (or Gulf Cooperation Council—GCC, see p. 250) (linking Qatar, Bahrain, Saudi Arabia and Kuwait) was completed in July 2009, and formally launched in December. Interconnection with the United Arab Emirates (UAE) was achieved in April 2011, and the network was ultimately to achieve regional self-sufficiency in electricity generation to 2058.

The services sector engaged 70.4% of the employed labour force in 2001, and contributed 56.4% of GDP in 2010, according to provisional figures. The financial services industry, notably the operation of 'offshore' banking units (OBUs), is a major source of Bahrain's prosperity. Bahrain has also developed as a principal centre for Islamic banking and finance. The first International Islamic Financial Market, with a liquidity management centre and Islamic ratings agency based in Bahrain, was inaugurated in August 2002. The Bahrain Financial Harbour project was completed in 2009: this redeveloped the Manama port area to provide a home for the 'offshore' financial sector and protect Bahrain's status as a leading financial centre in the Gulf. The Bahrain Chamber of Dispute Resolution was launched in January 2010 with the aim of becoming a regional centre for the provision of internationally recognized arbitration for commercial and financial disputes. According to provisional official figures, during 2001–10 the services sector showed an average GDP increase of 7.5% per year; the GDP of the sector increased by 0.1% in 2009 and by 4.5% in 2010.

In 2010 Bahrain recorded a visible trade surplus of US $2,642.8m., and there was a surplus of some $770.1m. on the current account of the balance of payments. According to provisional figures, in 2008 the principal source of imports was Saudi Arabia (accounting for 73.9% of the total). Saudi Arabia also provided most of Bahrain's petroleum imports. Among the member states of the GCC, the UAE (32.8% of the total) and Saudi Arabia (26.9% of the total) were the principal customers for Bahrain's non-petroleum exports in that year. The principal exports are mineral products and base metals. Sales of mineral products provided an estimated 80.5% of total export earnings in 2008, according to provisional figures. The principal import is crude petroleum (for domestic refining), which accounted for about 67.2% of total imports in 2008. The main category of non-petroleum imports is machinery and mechanical appliances, and electrical equipment.

According to provisional figures, a budgetary deficit of BD 459.8m. (equivalent to 5.6% of GDP) was recorded in 2010. Bahrain's general government gross debt was BD 2,730m. in 2010, equivalent to 32.0% of GDP. According to ILO, the annual rate of inflation averaged 2.2% in 2001–10; according to central bank figures, consumer prices increased by an annual average of 2.0% in 2010. Some 75.8% of the employed labour force were non-Bahrainis in 2008. The official rate of unemployment was 5.5% in 2001, but unofficial sources estimated unemployment to be at around 20% in 2005. According to figures published by the Ministry of Labour, by the end of 2010 the unemployment rate had declined to 3.6%, although some observers contended that the actual figure remained significantly higher, a perception that was thought to have contributed to the eruption of anti-Government protests in early 2011.

In recognition of the fact that Bahrain's reserves of petroleum and natural gas are nearing exhaustion, the Government has introduced measures both to diversify the country's industrial base and to attract greater foreign investment. The latter objective was aided by moves towards political liberalization and the Government's gradual privatization of state enterprises (excluding the petroleum sector). However, it has been hindered by the recent political instability resulting from the anti-Government protests that began in February 2011; among the protesters' economic grievances were unemployment, the chronic shortage of housing and poor social security provision. In 2008 King Hamad launched the 'Economic Vision 2030', a new directive formulated by the Economic Development Board, in order to further the process of economic diversification. Substantial investment in infrastructure was one of the key measures identified in the document. The new Khalifa Bin Salman port complex opened in April 2009, while construction of a new US $7,900m. public transport network and expansion of the King Fahd Causeway, connecting Bahrain and Saudi Arabia, were both planned. However, a long-anticipated $4,000m. project to build a road and rail causeway linking Bahrain with Qatar, construction of which had been expected to commence in 2010, stalled in early 2011 and by the following year remained suspended. Expansion of Bahrain's energy supplies and the upgrade of existing facilities was also regarded as vital for future industrial growth. Bahrain's predominance in the field of Islamic banking provided some institutions with insurance in the midst of the global financial crisis from late 2008, since operations adhering to this method resulted in a lower accumulation of debt. However, there was evidence by late 2011 that financial institutions were being forced to adapt in response to lenders' fears regarding the country's stability; in August Bahrain Islamic Bank and Al Salam Bank Bahrain announced that they intended to merge. Evidence of the damage caused to Bahrain's international reputation by the political unrest was demonstrated by the decision of the International Automobile Federation (Fédération Internationale de l'Automobile—FIA) to cancel the Formula One motor-racing Grand Prix, which had originally been scheduled to take place in Bahrain in March 2011, for security reasons; the Government was thought to have lost revenues of $500m. as a result of the decision. In an effort to restore public confidence, in February 2011 King Hamad announced economic measures including a one-time grant for families, improved food subsidies and the construction of 50,000 new homes; in June the King endorsed an expansionary budget for 2011–12. After Bahrain's sovereign credit rating was downgraded by three international ratings agencies in early 2011, there were fears that, if calm was not restored across the kingdom, investors would favour neighbouring territories such as Qatar and Dubai (UAE); analysts also predicted an increase in debt restructuring in 2012. Nevertheless, in November 2011 the Government successfully issued a $750m. sovereign bond. Following the pro-democracy protests, in mid-2011 the Government halved its projection for GDP growth in that year to 2%–3%, compared with 4.5% in 2010; however, some external sources predicted a far lower rate of growth.

PUBLIC HOLIDAYS

2013: 1 January (New Year's Day), 23 January* (Mouloud, Birth of the Prophet), 1 May (Labour Day), 7 August* (Id al-Fitr, end of Ramadan), 14 October* (Id al-Adha, Feast of the Sacrifice), 4 November* (Muharram, Islamic New Year), 13 November* (Ashoura), 16 December (National Day).

* These holidays are dependent on the Islamic lunar calendar and may vary by one or two days from the dates given.

Statistical Survey

Sources (unless otherwise stated): Central Informatics Organization (formerly Central Statistics Organization), POB 33305, Manama; tel. 17727722; e-mail ciohelpdesk@cio.gov.bh; internet www.cio.gov.bh; Central Bank of Bahrain, POB 27, Bldg 96, Block 317, Rd 1702, Manama; tel. 17547777; fax 17530399; e-mail info@cbb.gov.bh; internet www.cbb.gov.bh; Ministry of Finance, POB 333, Diplomatic Area, Manama; tel. 17575000; fax 17532713; e-mail mofne@batelco.com.bh; internet www.mofne.gov.bh.

Area and Population

AREA, POPULATION AND DENSITY

Area (sq km)	757.5*
Population (census results)	
7 April 2001	650,604
27 April 2010	
Males	768,414
Females	466,157
Total	1,234,571
Bahrainis	568,399
Non-Bahrainis	666,172
Density (per sq km) at 2010 census	1,629.8

* 292.5 sq miles.

POPULATION BY AGE AND SEX

(population at 2010 census)

	Males	Females	Total
0–14	126,693	120,910	247,603
15–64	628,816	331,918	960,734
65 and over	12,905	13,329	26,234
Total	768,414	466,157	1,234,571

REGIONS

(population at 2001 census)

	Area (sq km)	Population	Density (per sq km)
Hidd	17.1	11,637	731.9
Muharraq	39.0	91,939	3,024.3
Manama	31.2	153,395	5,096.2
Jidd Hafs	25.0	52,450	2,098.8
Northern	45.6	43,691	995.2
Sitra	31.0	43,910	1,435.0
Central	35.5	49,969	1,407.6
Isa Town	12.4	36,833	2,963.2
Rifa'a	297.9	79,985	271.1
Western	157.6	26,149	166.1
Hawar	52.1	3,875	74.4
Hamad Town	13.1	52,718	4,018.1
Total*	757.5	650,604	877.5

* Area as at 2008; total population includes 4,053 nationals residing abroad.

PRINCIPAL TOWNS

(at 2001 census)

Manama (capital)	153,395	Hamad Town	52,718
Muharraq	91,939	Jidd Hafs	52,450
Rifa'a	79,985		

Mid-2009 (incl. suburbs, UN estimate): Manama 163,000 (Source: UN, *World Urbanization Prospects: The 2009 Revision*).

BIRTHS, MARRIAGES AND DEATHS

	Registered live births		Registered marriages		Registered deaths	
	Number	Rate (per 1,000)	Number	Rate (per 1,000)	Number	Rate (per 1,000)
2001	13,468	20.6	4,504	6.9	1,979	3.0
2002	13,576	19.1	4,909	7.3	2,035	2.9
2003	14,560	19.0	5,373	7.8	2,114	2.8
2004	14,968	18.2	4,929	7.0	2,215	2.7
2005	15,198	17.1	4,669	6.4	2,222	2.5
2006	15,053	15.7	4,724	6.4	2,317	2.4
2007	16,062	15.4	4,981	4.8	2,270	2.2
2008	17,022	15.4	n.a.	n.a.	2,390	2.2

Life expectancy (years at birth, WHO estimates): 74 (males 73; females 76) in 2009 (Source: WHO, *World Health Statistics*).

ECONOMICALLY ACTIVE POPULATION

(persons aged 15 years and over, at 2001 census)

	Males	Females	Total
Agriculture and animal husbandry	2,193	76	2,269
Fishing	2,176	38	2,214
Mining and quarrying	2,583	197	2,780
Manufacturing	42,733	7,246	49,979
Electricity, gas and water	2,421	94	2,515
Construction	25,969	447	26,416
Trade and repair	31,127	3,350	34,477
Restaurants and hotels	11,201	1,892	13,093
Transport, storage and communications	11,621	2,148	13,769
Banks, insurance and finance	4,601	1,874	6,475
Real estate and business	14,659	1,554	16,213
Government, defence, social affairs and security	48,133	4,255	52,388
Education	5,732	7,825	13,557
Health	3,179	4,393	7,572
Community, social and personal services	8,775	1,769	10,544
Households with employed persons	7,662	21,921	29,583
Regional and international organizations	1,611	496	2,107
Sub-total	226,376	59,575	285,951
Workers abroad and activities not adequately defined	5,148	279	5,427
Total employed	231,524	59,854	291,378
Unemployed	9,953	7,012	16,965
Total labour force	241,477	66,866	308,343

2008 (annual averages, employed persons aged 15 years and over): Bahraini 140,096 (males 95,396, females 44,700); Non-Bahraini 438,211 (males 371,720, females 66,491); Total employed 578,307 (public sector 59,067, private sector 519,240).

Mid-2012 (estimates in '000): Agriculture and animal husbandry 4; Total labour force 675 (Source: FAO).

Health and Welfare

KEY INDICATORS

Total fertility rate (children per woman, 2009)	2.2
Under-5 mortality rate (per 1,000 live births, 2009)	12
HIV/AIDS (% of persons aged 15–49, 2003)	0.2
Physicians (per 1,000 head, 2005)	2.7
Hospital beds (per 1,000 head, 2006)	2.7
Health expenditure (2008): US $ per head (PPP)	1,282
Health expenditure (2008): % of GDP	3.7
Health expenditure (2008): public (% of total)	69.9
Total carbon dioxide emissions ('000 metric tons, 2007)	22,445.7
Carbon dioxide emissions per head (metric tons, 2007)	29.6
Human Development Index (2011): ranking	42
Human Development Index (2011): value	0.806

For sources and definitions, see explanatory note on p. vi.

Agriculture

PRINCIPAL CROPS
('000 metric tons)

	2008	2009	2010*
Lettuce	0.7	0.7	0.7
Tomatoes	4.3	4.2	3.8
Onions, dry	0.8	0.7	0.7
Bananas	0.9*	1.0*	0.9
Lemons and limes	0.9*	1.1*	1.1
Dates	13.2	12.9	14.0

* FAO estimate(s).

Aggregate production ('000 metric tons, may include official, semi-official or estimated data): Total vegetables (incl. melons) 15.9 in 2008, 16.3 in 2009, 16.4 in 2010; Total fruits (excl. melons) 19.9 in 2008, 20.6 in 2009, 22.1 in 2010.

Source: FAO.

LIVESTOCK
('000 head, year ending September)

	2008	2009	2010*
Cattle	7	7	10
Sheep	40	41	41
Goats	19	19	19
Chickens	520*	525*	530

* FAO estimate(s).

Source: FAO.

LIVESTOCK PRODUCTS
('000 metric tons)

	2008	2009	2010*
Cattle meat	1.0*	1.0*	1.0
Sheep meat	13.1*	13.1*	13.1
Goat meat	0.2*	0.2*	0.2
Chicken meat	6.1	6.2	6.3
Cows' milk	9.2	9.0	9.3

* FAO estimate(s).

Source: FAO.

Fishing

('000 metric tons, live weight)

	2007	2008	2009
Capture	15.0	14.2	16.4
Spangled emperor	0.8	0.6	0.5
Spinefeet (Rabbitfishes)	1.7	1.6	1.4
Blue swimming crab	3.2	4.7	4.1
Green tiger prawn	2.8	2.4	3.4
Aquaculture	0.0	0.0	0.0
Total catch	15.0	14.2	16.4

Source: FAO.

Mining

	2008	2009	2010
Crude petroleum ('000 barrels)*	66,864.0	66,510.0	66,376.0
Natural gas ('000 million cu ft)	538.2	543.4	556.6

* Including a share of production from the Abu Saafa offshore oilfield, shared with Saudi Arabia (54,837,000 barrels in 2008, 54,760,000 barrels in 2009 and 54,741,000 barrels in 2010).

Industry

SELECTED PRODUCTS
('000 barrels unless otherwise indicated)

	2007	2008	2009
Liquefied petroleum gas	950	1,095	1,132
Butane	896	920	907
Propane	944	949	953
Naptha	1,663	1,699	1,730
Motor spirit (petrol)	6,350	7,300	7,600
Kerosene and jet fuel	21,936	21,557	21,827
Distillate fuel oil	35,332	32,850	32,886
Residual fuel oil*	15,768	15,002	14,856
Aluminium (unwrought, metric tons)	865,048	871,658	847,738
Electric energy (million kWh)	10,689	11,657	12,120

* Estimates.

2010: Electric energy (million kWh) 13,757.

Source: mainly US Geological Survey.

Finance

CURRENCY AND EXCHANGE RATES

Monetary Units
1,000 fils = 1 Bahraini dinar (BD).

Sterling, Dollar and Euro Equivalents (30 December 2011)
£1 sterling = 581 fils;
US $1 = 376 fils;
€1 = 487 fils;
10 Bahraini dinars = £17.20 = $26.60= €20.55.

Average Exchange Rate

Note: This has been fixed at US $1 = 376 fils (BD 1 = $2.6596) since November 1980.

BUDGET
(BD million)

Revenue	2008	2009	2010
Petroleum and gas	2,284.5	1,417.8	1,852.1
Taxation and fees	183.0	159.3	179.0
Government goods and services	137.3	44.7	52.0
Investments and government properties	25.6	23.9	19.4
Grants	29.5	28.4	28.6
Sale of capital assets	0.8	0.9	0.4
Fines, penalties and miscellaneous	16.9	33.1	44.1
Total	2,677.6	1,708.2	2,175.6

Expenditure	2008	2009	2010
Recurrent expenditure	1,552.0	1,692.3	1,868.0
Manpower	822.1	833.9	868.1
Services	114.5	129.7	130.5
Consumption	177.0	78.2	79.7
Assets	19.3	21.1	20.8
Maintenance	44.3	47.4	44.4
Transfers	212.8	444.1	529.4
Grants and subsidies	162.0	137.8	195.1
Projects	508.3	389.9	767.4
Total	2,060.3	2,082.2	2,635.4

2011: Total revenue 2,287.9 (Net oil revenue 1,997.9, Other 252.4, Grants 37.6); Total expenditure 3,123.6 (Recurrent expenditure 2,488.6, Projects 635.0).

2012: Total revenue 2,348.0 (Net oil revenue 2,058.0, Other 252.4, Grants 37.6); Total expenditure 3,075.0 (Recurrent expenditure 2,375.0, Projects 700.0).

INTERNATIONAL RESERVES

(US $ million at 31 December)

	2008	2009	2010
Gold (national valuation)	6.6	6.6	6.6
IMF special drawing rights	14.0	200.0	196.8
Reserve position in IMF	109.7	111.6	109.7
Foreign exchange (central bank)*	3,796.8	3,533.5	4,782.2
Total*	3,927.1	3,851.7	5,095.3

* Excluding foreign exchange reserves held by government.

Source: IMF, *International Financial Statistics*.

MONEY SUPPLY

(BD million at 31 December)

	2008	2009	2010
Currency outside banks	304.2	323.0	349.6
Demand deposits at commercial banks	1,594.5	1,835.3	1,954.3
Total money	1,898.7	2,158.3	2,303.9

Source: IMF, *International Financial Statistics*.

COST OF LIVING

(Consumer Price Index; base: 2006 = 100)

	2005	2007	2008
Food, beverages and tobacco	98.0	104.5	115.9
Clothing	100.7	102.1	104.1
House-related expenses, water, electricity, gas and other fuels	96.4	104.1	107.1
Goods for home service	100.6	94.3	106.0
Transport	98.8	102.6	101.6
Education	98.8	100.6	102.4
Health	96.8	104.1	101.6
Culture, entertainment and recreation	101.2	100.2	101.0
Communication	100.0	100.0	100.0
Other goods and services	91.9	102.3	107.7
All items	98.0	103.3	106.9

2009: All items 109.9.

2010: All items 112.1.

NATIONAL ACCOUNTS

(BD million at current prices)

National Income and Product

	2006	2007	2008*
Compensation of employees	1,728.8	2,150.5	2,502.4
Operating surplus	3,694.1	4,133.8	4,994.0
Domestic factor incomes	5,422.9	6,284.3	7,496.4
Consumption of fixed capital	363.1	481.6	527.0
Gross domestic product (GDP) at factor cost	5,786.0	6,765.9	8,023.4
Indirect taxes, less subsidies	174.3	179.7	211.9
GDP in purchasers' values	5,960.3	6,945.7	8,235.3
Primary income (net)	–145.1	–112.3	–347.3
Gross national income	5,815.2	6,833.4	7,888.0
Less Consumption of fixed capital	363.1	481.6	527.0
Net national income	5,452.1	6,351.8	7,361.0
Current transfers (net)	–575.6	–557.5	–667.2
Net national disposable income	4,876.5	5,794.3	6,693.8

* Provisional figures.

Expenditure on the Gross Domestic Product

	2008	2009	2010*
Government final consumption expenditure	1,106.3	1,189.6	1,233.8
Private final consumption expenditure	2,533.9	2,528.4	2,818.5
Gross fixed capital formation	2,726.1	1,950.0	2,316.3
Change in stocks	99.4	73.3	78.0
Total domestic expenditure	6,465.7	5,741.3	6,446.6
Exports of goods and services	7,983.0	5,905.0	6,723.0
Less Imports of goods and services	6,119.9	4,269.1	4,924.5
GDP in purchasers' values	8,328.8	7,377.1	8,245.1
GDP at constant 2001 prices	4,734.9	4,880.5	5,100.2

* Provisional figures.

Gross Domestic Product by Economic Activity

	2008	2009	2010*
Agriculture and fishing	27.2	31.7	31.0
Mining	2,420.7	1,717.4	2,100.2
Petroleum and gas	2,361.7	1,666.6	2,041.9
Manufacturing	1346.6	1,056.5	1,273.0
Electricity and water	84.0	104.7	113.2
Construction	429.3	334.7	346.7
Transport and communications	479.0	516.9	563.7
Trade	655.9	554.2	597.6
Hotels and restaurants	163.3	178.9	194.9
Real estate and business activities	556.8	513.9	529.6
Finance and insurance	1,678.3	1,605.0	1,698.6
Government services	914.1	962.1	998.2
Education	111.2	146.2	157.3
Health	46.1	58.5	64.1
Other social and personal services	100.2	111.8	118.2
Private non-profit institutions serving households	6.0	6.8	7.7
Households with employed persons	44.7	52.7	62.7
Sub-total	9,063.4	7,952.0	8,856.7
Less Financial intermediation services indirectly measured	833.2	657.8	709.3
GDP at factor cost	8,230.2	7,294.2	8,147.4
Import duties	98.7	83.3	98.2
GDP in purchasers' values	8,328.8	7,377.5	8,245.6

* Provisional figures.

BALANCE OF PAYMENTS
(US $ million)

	2008	2009	2010
Exports of goods f.o.b.	17,491.2	12,051.9	13,833.2
Imports of goods f.o.b.	–14,246.3	–9,613.0	–11,190.4
Trade balance	3,244.9	2,438.8	2,642.8
Exports of services	3,740.2	3,652.9	4,047.1
Imports of services	–2,030.1	–1,741.0	–1,905.1
Balance on goods and services	4,955.1	4,350.8	4,784.8
Other income received	7,088.0	1,680.1	1,467.6
Other income paid	–8,011.7	–4,080.0	–3,840.6
Balance on goods, services and income	4,031.4	1,950.9	2,411.8
Current transfers (net)	–1,774.5	–1,391.0	–1,641.8
Current balance	2,256.9	560.0	770.1
Capital account (net)	50.0	50.0	50.0
Direct investment abroad	–1,620.5	1,791.5	–334.0
Direct investment from abroad	1,794.0	257.1	155.8
Portfolio investment assets	6,286.8	6,710.1	2,051.6
Portfolio investment liabilities	2,990.1	1,565.5	2,704.2
Other investment assets	–3,264.6	18,123.8	2,739.7
Other investment liabilities	–8,756.6	–28,926.4	–6,964.8
Net errors and omissions	–30.3	–250.0	107.1
Overall balance	–294.2	–118.5	1,279.5

Source: IMF, *International Financial Statistics*.

External Trade

PRINCIPAL COMMODITIES
(BD million)

Imports	2006	2007*	2008*
Live animals and animal products	79.7	85.4	45.1
Vegetables and vegetable products	60.6	67.1	34.5
Prepared foodstuffs, beverages and tobacco	115.6	117.7	75.1
Mineral products	1,988.5	2,369.5	2,770.8
Petroleum	1,843.0	2,205.0	2,708.8
Products of chemical and allied industries	382.0	436.5	131.3
Plastic and rubber articles	65.5	82.5	55.2
Textiles and textile articles	86.2	77.6	43.1
Base metals and articles thereof	259.1	318.7	205.8
Machinery and appliances, electrical equipment	547.6	588.4	299.3
Transport equipment	401.1	531.4	192.7
Total (incl. others)	4,253.3	4,956.1	4,028.9

Exports f.o.b.	2006	2007*	2008*
Live animals and animal products	9.7	12.2	48.1
Prepared foodstuffs, beverages and tobacco	13.2	14.5	36.0
Mineral products	3,571.8	4,185.2	5,240.0
Petroleum	3,465.8	4,059.2	5,184.6
Products of chemical and allied industries	110.9	222.5	199.6
Textiles and textile articles	41.4	47.0	40.0
Base metals and articles thereof	721.2	642.3	658.7
Machinery and appliances, electrical equipment	42.6	71.3	104.3
Transport equipment	86.5	123.6	82.0
Total (incl. others)	4,665.2	5,398.0	6,510.6

* Provisional figures.

PRINCIPAL TRADING PARTNERS
(BD million)

Imports	2006	2007*	2008*
Australia	244.2	318.6	70.4
China, People's Republic	181.7	227.4	90.7
France	73.1	95.3	42.0
Germany	171.8	169.7	72.1
India	74.5	82.4	44.7
Japan	263.0	275.2	86.9
Saudi Arabia	2,038.9	2,446.9	2,976.7
United Kingdom	128.3	117.0	54.2
USA	169.7	238.1	83.6
Total (incl. others)	4,253.3	4,954.2	4,029.0

Non-Oil Exports†	2006	2007	2008
Australia	18.6	44.0*	58.7*
India	67.4	61.2*	30.4*
Japan	41.9	10.5*	11.2*
Kuwait	30.6	31.6	56.6
Oman	11.4	46.1	52.4
Qatar	65.7	154.4	191.8
Saudi Arabia	206.6	301.9	356.7
United Arab Emirates	247.5	225.9	434.5
USA	98.9	142.2*	106.8*
Total (incl. re-exports and others)	1,199.4	1,338.8	1,326.0

* Provisional figure.

† Only data for trade with countries of the Cooperation Council for the Arab States of the Gulf (or Gulf Cooperation Council—GCC) and selected other trading partners were available; total exports (incl. petroleum) were recorded as (BD million): 4,665.2 in 2006; 5,398.0 in 2007 (provisional); 6,510.6 in 2008 (provisional).

Transport

ROAD TRAFFIC
(motor vehicles in use at 31 December, estimates)

	2008	2009	2010
Passenger cars	296,238	315,265	328,536
Buses and coaches	7,924	9,460	10,134
Lorries and vans	52,737	55,850	58,622
Motorcycles and mopeds	5,140	6,086	7,136

SHIPPING

Merchant Fleet
(vessels registered at 31 December)

	2007	2008	2009
Number of vessels	182	193	209
Total displacement ('000 grt)	325.1	498.4	517.6

Source: IHS Fairplay, *World Fleet Statistics*.

International Sea-borne Freight Traffic ('000 metric tons, 1990): *Goods loaded:* Dry cargo 1,145; Petroleum products 12,140. *Goods unloaded:* Dry cargo 3,380; Petroleum products 132 (Source: UN, *Monthly Bulletin of Statistics*).

CIVIL AVIATION
(traffic on scheduled services)

	2007	2008	2009
Kilometres flown (million)	79	100	105
Passengers carried ('000)	4,451	5,643	5,668
Passenger-km (million)	10,505	13,656	13,949
Total ton-km (million)	1,504	1,837	1,849

Source: UN, *Statistical Yearbook*.

Tourism

FOREIGN TOURIST ARRIVALS BY NATIONALITY
('000)

	2005	2006	2007
India	466.8	590.2	718.4
Kuwait	239.5	298.6	309.3
Philippines	143.6	198.3	225.6
Saudi Arabia	3,864.6	4,225.6	4,366.6
United Kingdom	210.1	245.1	263.7
USA	137.3	168.4	187.2
Total (incl. others)	6,313.2	7,288.7	7,833.6

Receipts from tourism (US $ million, incl. passenger transport, unless otherwise indicated): 1,786 in 2006; 1,854 in 2007; 1,927 in 2008; 1,118 in 2009 (provisional, excl. passenger transport).

Source: World Tourism Organization.

Communications Media

	2008	2009	2010
Telephones ('000 main lines in use)	220.4	238.0	228.0
Mobile cellular telephones ('000 subscribers)	1,440.8	1,402.0	1,567.0
Internet subscribers ('000)	10.9	79.4	n.a.
Broadband subscribers ('000)	76.6	75.9	154.0

Personal computers: 547,200 (745.8 per 1,000 persons) in 2008.

Radio receivers ('000 in use): 338 in 1997.

Book production (titles): 40 in 1996, n.a. in 1997, 92 in 1998.

Daily newspapers: 6 in 2004.

Non-daily newspapers: 5 (average circulation 17,000) in 1993.

Other periodicals (titles): 26 in 1993 (average circulation 73,000).

Television receivers ('000 in use): 275 in 2000.

Sources: UNESCO, *Statistical Yearbook*; UNESCO Institute for Statistics; UN, *Statistical Yearbook*; and International Telecommunication Union.

Education

(state schools only, 2009/10 unless otherwise indicated)

	Institutions	Teachers	Students
Primary	109	4,788	54,433
Primary/Intermediate	21	1,165	13,429
Intermediate	36	2,141	24,496
Intermediate/Secondary	2	218	2,306
Secondary	30	3,385	29,059
Religious institutes	3	167	1,880
University level*	16	1,240	29,678

* 2005/06 figures.

Private education (2009/10): *Pre-primary:* 143 schools; 1,084 teachers; 16,593 infants. *Other:* 65 schools; 3,768 teachers; 56,078 students.

Pupil-teacher ratio (primary education, UNESCO estimate): 16.4 in 2001/02 (Source: UNESCO Institute for Statistics).

Adult literacy rate (UNESCO estimates): 91.4% (males 92.2%; females 90.2%) in 2009 (Source: UNESCO Institute for Statistics).

Directory

The Government

HEAD OF STATE

King and Supreme Commander of the Bahrain Defence Force: HM Sheikh HAMAD BIN ISA AL KHALIFA (acceded as Amir 6 March 1999; proclaimed King 14 February 2002).

CABINET
(May 2012)

Prime Minister: Sheikh KHALIFA BIN SULMAN AL KHALIFA.

Deputy Prime Ministers: Sheikh MUHAMMAD BIN MUBARAK AL KHALIFA, Sheikh ALI BIN KHALIFA AL KHALIFA, Sheikh KHALID BIN ABDULLAH AL KHALIFA, JAWAD BIN SALEM AL-ARRAYED.

Minister of Foreign Affairs: Sheikh KHALID BIN AHMAD AL KHALIFA.

Minister of the Interior: Lt-Gen. Sheikh RASHID BIN ABDULLAH BIN AHMAD AL KHALIFA.

Minister of Justice and Islamic Affairs: Sheikh KHALID BIN ALI AL KHALIFA.

Minister of Municipal Affairs and Urban Planning: Dr JUMA AL-KA'ABI.

Minister of Energy: Dr ABD AL-HUSSAIN BIN ALI MIRZA.

Minister of Works: ISAM BIN ABDULLAH KHALAF.

Minister of Housing: BASSEM BIN YACOUB AL-HAMER.

Minister of Finance: Sheikh AHMAD BIN MUHAMMAD AL KHALIFA.

Minister of Culture: SHEIKA MAI BINT MUHAMMAD AL KHALIFA.

Minister of Industry and Commerce: Dr HASSAN BIN ABDULLAH FAKHRO.

Minister of Education: Dr MAJID BIN ALI AL-NO'AIMI.

Minister of Labour: JAMIL HUMAIDAN.

Minister of Human Rights and Social Development: Dr FATIMA MUHAMMAD AL-BLUSHI.

Minister of Health: SADIQ BIN ABD AL-KARIM AL-SHEHABI.

Minister of Transportation: KAMAL BIN AHMAD MUHAMMAD.

Minister of Shura Council and Parliament Affairs: ABD AL-AZIZ BIN MUHAMMAD AL-FADHIL.

Minister of State for Foreign Affairs: GANEM AL-BUAINAIN.

Minister of State for Human Rights Affairs: SALAH ALI.

Minister of State for Information Affairs: SAMEERA RAJAB.

Minister of State for Defence Affairs: Dr SHEIKH MUHAMMAD BIN ABDULLAH AL KHALIFA.

Minister of State for Follow-up Affairs: MUHAMMAD BIN IBRAHIM AL-MUTAWA.

MINISTRIES

Royal Court: POB 555, Riffa Palace, Manama; tel. 17666666; fax 17663070.

Prime Minister's Court: POB 1000, Government House, Government Rd, Manama; tel. 17253361; fax 17533033.

Ministry of Cabinet Affairs: POB 26613, Manama; tel. 17223366; fax 17225202.

Ministry of Culture: POB 253, Manama; tel. 17871111; fax 17682777; e-mail webmaster@info.gov.bh; internet www.moci.gov.bh.

Ministry of Defence: POB 245, West Rifa'a; tel. 17653333; fax 17663923.

Ministry of Education: POB 43, Manama; tel. 17278727; fax 17273656; e-mail moe@moe.gov.bh; internet www.education.gov.bh.

Ministry of Energy: Manama.

Ministry of Finance: POB 333, Diplomatic Area, Manama; tel. 17575000; fax 17532713; e-mail mofne@batelco.com.bh; internet www.mofne.gov.bh.

Ministry of Foreign Affairs: POB 547, Government House, Government Rd, Manama; tel. 17227555; fax 17212603; e-mail info@mofa.gov.bh; internet www.mofa.gov.bh.

Ministry of Health: POB 12, Bldg 1228, Rd 4025, Juffair 340, Manama; tel. 17288888; fax 17286691; e-mail webmaster@health.gov.bh; internet www.moh.gov.bh.

Ministry of Housing: Manama; tel. 17533000; fax 17534115; internet www.housing.gov.bh.

Ministry of Human Rights and Social Development: POB 32868, Isa Town; tel. 17873999; fax 17682248; e-mail info@social.gov.bh; internet www.social.gov.bh.

Ministry of Industry and Commerce: POB 5479, Diplomatic Area, Manama; tel. 17574777; fax 17530151; e-mail info@moic.gov.bh; internet www.moic.gov.bh.

Ministry of the Interior: POB 13, Police Fort Compound, Manama; tel. 17254699; fax 17233482; internet www.interior.gov.bh.

Ministry of Justice and Islamic Affairs: POB 450, Diplomatic Area, Manama; tel. 175313000; fax 17536343; internet www.moj.gov.bh.

Ministry of Labour: POB 32333, Isa Town; tel. 17873777; fax 17686954; e-mail web.contain@mol.gov.bh; internet www.mol.gov.bh.

Ministry of Municipal Affairs and Urban Planning: POB 53, Manama; tel. 17501565; fax 17293694; e-mail helpdesk@mun.gov.bh; internet www.mun.gov.bh.

Ministry of Transportation: POB 10325, Diplomatic Area, Manama; tel. 17534534; fax 17534041; internet www.transportation.gov.bh.

Ministry of Works: POB 5, Manama; tel. 17545555; fax 17545608; e-mail info@works.gov.bh; internet www.works.gov.bh.

Legislature

Majlis al-Shura (Consultative Council)

POB 2991, Manama; tel. 17748888; fax 17717377; e-mail info@shura.gov.bh; internet www.shura.bh.

The new 40-seat Consultative Council was appointed by King Hamad on 25 November 2010.

Chairman: ALI BIN SALEH AL-SALEH.

Majlis al-Nuab (Council of Representatives)

POB 54040, Manama; tel. 17748444; fax 17748491; e-mail info@nuwab.gov.bh; internet www.nuwab.gov.bh

Speaker: KHALIFA BIN AHMAD AL-DHAHRANI.

Election, 23 and 30 October 2010

Groups	Seats
Al-Wefaq National Islamic Society	18
Al-Asala Islamic Society	3
Al-Menbar Islamic Society	2
Independents	17
Total	40

Political Organizations

Political parties are still prohibited in Bahrain. However, several political and civic societies (many of which were previously in exile) are now active in the country, and a number of new groups have been established since 2001. Restrictions on campaigning by political groups were revoked prior to the first elections to the new Majlis al-Nuab (Council of Representatives), held in October 2002. By mid-2009 it was reported that there were 18 political alliances or blocs functioning in Bahrain. Organizations currently represented in the Majlis include:

Al-Asala Islamic Society: Manama; Sunni Islamist; promotes the implementation of strict Salafi principles in society and law; Pres. GHANEM FADHEL AL-BUAINAIN.

Al-Menbar Islamic Society (Islamic National Tribune Society): Bldg 30, Sheikh Salman St, Muharraq; tel. 17324996; fax 17324997; e-mail info@almenbar.org; internet www.almenber.org; Sunni Islamist; political wing of the al-Islah Soc., affiliated with the Muslim Brotherhood; Sec.-Gen. SHEIKH ABDUL LATIF.

Al-Wefaq National Islamic Society (Islamic National Accord Association): POB 1553, Manama; tel. 17254440; fax 17244099; e-mail info@alwefaq.org; internet www.alwefaq.org; Shi'a Islamist; mems of the soc. won 18 out of 40 seats in the 2010 elections; Sec.-Gen. SHEIKH ALI SALMAN AHMAD SALMAN.

Other prominent groups include Al-Adala (National Justice Movement—a secular, liberal society established in 2006), Al-Haq (Movement for Liberty and Democracy—a radical breakaway faction of Al-Wefaq, opposed to participation in parliamentary politics), the Islamic Action Society (Shi'a Islamist), Al-Meethaq (liberal, pro-democracy) and Al-Waad (National Democratic Action—secular, left-wing).

Diplomatic Representation

EMBASSIES IN BAHRAIN

Algeria: POB 26402, Villa 579, Rd 3622, Adliya, Manama; tel. 17713669; fax 17713662; e-mail abdemyh@hotmail.com; Ambassador NADJIB SENOUSSI.

Bangladesh: House 674, Rd 3213, Area 332, Mahooz, Manama; tel. 17741976; fax 17741927; e-mail bangla@batelco.com.bh; internet www.banglaembassy.com.bh; Ambassador MUHAMMAD ALI AKBAR.

Brunei: POB 15700, House 892, Rd 3218, Area 332, Mahooz, Manama; tel. 17720222; fax 17741757; e-mail kbbhhom@batelco.com.bh; Chargé d'affaires Haji AHMAD Haji JUMAAT.

China, People's Republic: POB 3150, Bldg 158, Rd 4156, Juffair Ave, Area 341, Manama; tel. 17723800; fax 17727304; e-mail chinaemb_bh@mfa.gov.cn; internet bh.china-embassy.org; Ambassador YANG WEIGUO.

Egypt: Villa 18, Rd 33, Block 332, Mahooz, Manama; tel. 17720005; fax 17721518; e-mail egyembbh@batelco.com.bh; Ambassador MUHAMMAD ASHRAF HARB SALAMAH.

France: POB 11134, Bldg 51A, Rd 1901, Area 319, Diplomatic Area, Manama; tel. 17298660; fax 17298607; e-mail chancellerie.manama-amba@diplomatie.gouv.fr; internet www.ambafrance-bh.org; Ambassador CHRISTIAN TESTOT.

Germany: POB 10306, Al-Hasan Bldg, 1st Floor, Sheikh Hamad Causeway, Area 317, Manama; tel. 17530210; fax 17536282; e-mail info@manama.diplo.de; internet www.manama.diplo.de; Ambassador SABINE TAUFMANN.

India: POB 26106, Bldg 182, Rd 2608, Area 326, Adliya, Manama; tel. 17712785; fax 17715527; e-mail indemb@batelco.com.bh; internet indianembassybahrain.com; Ambassador MOHAN KUMAR.

Iran: POB 26365, Bldg 1034, Rd 3221, Area 332, Mahooz, Manama; tel. 17722880; fax 17722101; e-mail iranemb@batelco.com.bh; Ambassador MEHDI AGA JAFFARI.

Iraq: al-Mahawez, Bldg 396, Rd 3207, Manama; tel. 17741472; fax 17720756; e-mail bhremb@iraqmofamail.net; Chargé d'affaires SAWSAN MUWAFQ IBRAHIM.

Italy: POB 397, Villa 1554, Rd 5647, Area 356, Manama; tel. 17252424; fax 17277060; e-mail ambasciata.manama@esteri.it; internet www.ambmanama.esteri.it; Ambassador ENRICO PADULA.

Japan: POB 23720, 55 Salmaniya Ave, Salmaniya 327, Manama; tel. 17716565; fax 17715059; e-mail jpembbh@batelco.com.bh; internet www.bh.emb-japan.go.jp; Ambassador SHIGEKI SUMI.

Jordan: POB 5242, Villa 43, Rd 1901, Area 319, Manama; tel. 17291109; fax 17291980; e-mail jordemb@batelco.com.bh; Ambassador MUHAMMED ALI ABD AL-HAMID SIRAJ.

Kuwait: POB 786, Rd 1703, Diplomatic Area, Manama; tel. 17534040; fax 17530278; e-mail almanama@mofa.gov.kw; Ambassador Sheikh AZZAM MUBARAK AL-SABAH.

Lebanon: Villa 1556, Rd 5647, Area 356, Manama; tel. 17579001; fax 17232535; e-mail lebem@batelco.com.bh; Chargé d'affaires a.i. SAMI HADDAD.

Libya: POB 26015, Villa 787, Rd 3315, Manama 333; tel. 17722252; fax 17722611; Ambassador MABRUK E. O. AL-BUAISHI.

Malaysia: POB 18292, Bldg 2771, Rd 2835, Area 428, al-Seef District, Manama; tel. 17564551; fax 17564552; e-mail malmnama@kln.gov.my; internet www.kln.gov.my/perwakilan/manama; Ambassador AHMAD SHAHIZAN.

Morocco: POB 26229, Villa 415, Rd 3207, Area 332, Mahooz, Manama; tel. 17740566; fax 17740178; e-mail sifamana@batelco.com; Ambassador AHMAD RASHID KHATTABI.

Oman: POB 26414, Bldg 37, Rd 1901, Diplomatic Area, Manama; tel. 17293663; fax 17293540; e-mail oman@batelco.com.bh; Ambassador ABDULLAH BIN MUHAMMAD BIN SULAIMAN AL-AMRI.

Pakistan: Bldg 35, Rd 1901, Blk 319, Manama; tel. 17244113; fax 17255960; e-mail parepbah@batelco.com.bh; internet www.mofa.gov.pk/bahrain; Ambassador JUAHER SALEEM.

Philippines: POB 26681, Villa 992, Rd 3119, Area 331, Manama; tel. 17250990; fax 17258583; e-mail manamape@batelco.com.bh; internet philembassy-bahrain.com; Ambassador CORAZON YAP-BAHJIN.

Qatar: POB 15105, Villa 814, Rd 3315, Area 333, Mahooz, Manama; tel. 17722922; fax 17740662; Ambassador Sheikh ABDULLAH BIN THAMIR AL THANI.

Russia: POB 26612, Manama; tel. 17725222; fax 17725921; e-mail rusemb@zain.com.bh; internet www.bahrain.mid.ru; Ambassador VICTOR YU. SMIRNOV.

Saudi Arabia: POB 1085, Bldg 82, Rd 1702, Block 317, Diplomatic Area, Manama; tel. 17537722; fax 17533261; Ambassador Dr ABD AL-MOHSEN FAHAD AL-MARQ.

Senegal: Villa 25, Rd 33, Area 333, Mahooz, Manama; tel. 17821060; fax 17721650; Ambassador ABDOU LAHAT SOURANG.

Sudan: Villa 423, Rd 3614, Area 336, Manama; tel. 17717959; fax 17710113; e-mail sudanimanama@hotmail.com; Ambassador ABDULLAH AHMED OTHMAN MUHAMMAD SALEH.

Syria: POB 11585, Villa 867, Rd 3315, Area 333, Mahooz, Manama; tel. 17722484; fax 17740380; e-mail syremb@batelco.com.bh; Chargé d'affaires a.i. FAYZEH ISKANDAR AHMAD.

Thailand: POB 26475, Bldg 132, Rd 66, Area 360, Zinj Area, Manama; tel. 17246242; fax 17272714; e-mail thaimnm@mfa.go.th; internet www.mfa.go.th/web/1444.php?depid=269; Ambassador VICHAI VARASIRIKUL.

Tunisia: POB 26911, House 54, Rd 3601, Area 336, Manama; tel. 17714149; fax 17715702; e-mail atmanama@batelco.bh; Ambassador ZINE EL-ABIDINE EL-TERRAS.

Turkey: POB 10821, Suhail Centre, 5th Floor, Bldg 81, Rd 1702, Area 317, Manama; tel. 17533448; fax 17536557; e-mail tcbahrbe@batelco.com.bh; internet www.manama.emb.mfa.gov.tr; Ambassador AHMET ÜLKER.

United Arab Emirates: Bldg 270, Rd 2510, Area 325, Manama; tel. 17748333; fax 17717724; e-mail uaeembassybahrain@hotmail.com; Ambassador ABD AL-AZIZ BIN HADEF AL-SHAMSI.

United Kingdom: POB 114, 21 Govt Ave, Area 306, Manama; tel. 17574100; fax 17574161; e-mail british.embassy@batelco.com.bh; internet ukinbahrain.fco.gov.uk; Ambassador IAIN LINDSAY.

USA: POB 26431, Bldg 979, Rd 3119, Area 331, Zinj, Manama; tel. 17242700; fax 17272594; e-mail manamaconsular@state.gov; internet bahrain.usembassy.gov; Ambassador THOMAS C. KRAJESKI.

Yemen: Bldg 80, Rd 2802, Area 328, Umm al-Hassam, Manama; tel. 17822110; fax 17822078; Ambassador Dr ALI MANSOUR BIN SAFA'A.

Judicial System

Since the termination of British legal jurisdiction in 1971, intensive work has been undertaken on the legislative requirements of Bahrain. All nationalities are subject to the jurisdiction of the Bahraini courts, which guarantee equality before the law irrespective of nationality or creed. The 1974 Decree Law on State Security Measures and the State Security Court were both abolished in February 2001. The adoption of the amended Constitution in 2002 provided for the establishment of an independent judiciary; however, all judges are appointed by royal decree. The Criminal Law is at present contained in various Codes, Ordinances and Regulations; a new Code of Criminal Procedure was introduced in 2002.

SUPERIOR COURT

Constitutional Court: POB 18380, Manama; tel. 17578181; fax 17224475; e-mail info@constitutional-court.bh; internet www.constitutional-court.org.bh; f. 2005 to undertake review of, and to settle disputes concerning, the constitutionality of laws and regulations; consists of seven members appointed by the King.

Chairman: SALEM MUHAMMAD SALEM AL-KUWARI.

CIVIL AND CRIMINAL COURTS

Court of Cassation: f. 1990; serves as the final court of appeal for all civil and criminal cases.

President: Sheikh KHALIFA BIN RASHID AL KHALIFA.

Civil Law Courts: All civil and commercial cases, including disputes relating to the personal affairs of non-Muslims, are settled in the Civil Law Courts, which comprise the Higher Civil Appeals Court, Higher Civil Court and Lesser Civil Courts.

Criminal Law Courts: Higher Criminal Court, presided over by three judges, rules on felonies; Lower Criminal Courts, presided over by one judge, rule on misdemeanours.

Prosecutor-General: ALI BIN FADHUL AL-BUAINAIN.

RELIGIOUS COURTS

Shari'a Judiciary Courts operate according to Islamic principles of jurisprudence and have jurisdiction in all disputes relating to the personal affairs of Muslims, including marriage contracts and inheritances. They are structured according to the following hierarchy: Higher *Shari'a* Appeals Court, Greater *Shari'a* Court, Lesser *Shari'a* Court; each court has separate Sunni and Shi'a departments.

SUPREME JUDICIAL COUNCIL

Founded in 2000, and further regulated by law decree in 2002, the Supreme Judicial Council, headed by the King, is made up of the most senior figures from each branch of the judiciary. The Council supervises the performance of the courts and recommends candidates for judicial appointments and promotions.

Religion

At the April 2001 census the population was 650,604, distributed as follows: Muslims 528,393; Christians 58,315; others 63,896.

ISLAM

Muslims are divided between the Sunni and Shi'ite sects. The ruling family is Sunni, although the majority of the Muslim population (estimated at almost 60% in 2010) are Shi'ite.

CHRISTIANITY

The Anglican Communion

Within the Episcopal Church in Jerusalem and the Middle East, Bahrain forms part of the diocese of Cyprus and the Gulf. There are two Anglican churches in Bahrain: St Christopher's Cathedral in Manama and the Community Church in Awali. The congregations are entirely expatriate. The Dean of St Christopher's Cathedral is the Archdeacon in the Gulf, while the Bishop in Cyprus and the Gulf is resident in Cyprus.

Archdeacon in the Gulf: Very Rev. ALAN HAYDAY, St Christopher's Cathedral, POB 36, al-Mutanabi Ave, Manama; tel. 17253866; fax 17246436; e-mail cathedra@batelco.com.bh; internet www.stchcathedral.org.bh.

Roman Catholic Church

A small number of adherents, mainly expatriates, form part of the Apostolic Vicariate of Northern Arabia. The Vicar Apostolic is resident in Kuwait.

The Press

DAILIES

Akhbar al-Khaleej (Gulf News): POB 5300, Manama; tel. 17620111; fax 17621566; e-mail editor@aaknews.com; internet www.aaknews.com; f. 1976; Arabic; Chair. and Editor-in-Chief ANWAR ABD AL-RAHMAN; circ. 32,000.

Al-Ayam (The Days): POB 3232, Manama; tel. 17617777; fax 17617111; e-mail alayam@batelco.com.bh; internet www.alayam.com; f. 1989; Arabic; publ. by Al-Ayam Establishment for Press and Publications; Editor-in-Chief ISA AL-SHAIJI; circ. 36,000.

Bahrain Tribune: POB 3232, Manama; tel. 17827111; fax 17827222; e-mail tribune@batelco.com.bh; internet www.bahraintribune.com; f. 1997; English; Editor-in-Chief JALIL OMAR; circ. 13,000.

Gulf Daily News: POB 5300, Manama; tel. 17620222; fax 17622141; e-mail gdn1@batelco.com.bh; internet www.gulf-daily-news.com; f. 1978; English; publ. by Al-Hilal Publishing and Marketing Group; Chair. ANWAR ABD AL-RAHMAN; Editor-in-Chief GEORGE WILLIAMS; circ. 11,000.

Khaleej Times: POB 26707, City Centre Bldg, Suite 403, 4th Floor, Government Ave, Manama; tel. 17213911; fax 17211819; e-mail ktimesbn@batelco.com.bh; internet www.khaleejtimes.com; f. 1978; English; based in Dubai (United Arab Emirates); circ. 72,565.

Al-Meethaq: Manama; tel. 17877777; fax 17784118; f. 2004; Arabic; supports the Govt's reform programme; publ. by Al-Meethaq Media and Publishing House; Editor-in-Chief MUHAMMAD HASSAN AL-SATRI; circ. 35,000.

Al-Wasat: Dar al-Wasat for Publishing and Distribution, POB 31110, Manama; tel. 17596999; fax 17596900; e-mail news@alwasatnews.com; internet www.alwasatnews.com; Editor-in-Chief MANSOOR AL-JAMRI.

Al-Watan: Rifa'a; tel. 17496666; fax 17496667; e-mail malaradi@alwatannews.net; internet www.alwatannews.net; f. 2005; Arabic; Man. Editor AHMAD ABU ZEITOUN.

WEEKLIES

Al-Adhwaa' (Lights): POB 250, Old Exhibition Rd, Manama; tel. 17290942; fax 17293166; f. 1965; Arabic; publ. by Arab Printing and Publishing House; Chair. RAID MAHMOUD AL-MARDI; Editor-in-Chief MUHAMMAD QASSIM SHIRAWI; circ. 7,000.

The Gulf: POB 224, Manama; tel. 17293131; fax 17293400; e-mail editorial@thegulfonline.com; internet www.thegulfonline.com; f. 2008; English; business and current affairs; publ. by Al-Hilal Publishing and Marketing Group; Editor DIGBY LIDSTONE; circ. 7,500.

Gulf Weekly: POB 5300, Manama; tel. 17293131; fax 17293400; e-mail editor@gulfweekly.com; internet www.gulfweekly.com; f. 2002; English; publ. by Al-Hilal Publishing and Marketing Group; Editor STAN SZECOWKA; circ. 13,000.

Huna al-Bahrain (Here is Bahrain): POB 26005, Isa Town; tel. 17870166; fax 17686600; e-mail bahrainmag@info.gov.bh; internet www.moci.gov.bh/en/PressandPublications/; f. 1957; Arabic; publ. by the Ministry of Culture and Information; Editor ABD AL-QADER AQIL; circ. 3,000.

Al-Mawakif (Attitudes): POB 1083, Manama; tel. 17231231; fax 17271720; e-mail mwmradhi@batelco.com.bh; f. 1973; Arabic; general interest; Editor-in-Chief MANSOOR M. RADHI; circ. 6,000.

Oil and Gas News: POB 224, Bldg 149, Exhibition Ave, Manama; tel. 17293131; fax 17293400; e-mail editor@oilandgasnewsworldwide.com; internet www.oilandgasnewsworldwide.com; f. 1983; English; publ. by Al-Hilal Publishing and Marketing Group; Editor-in-Chief CLIVE JACQUES; circ. 5,000.

Sada al-Usbou (Weekly Echo): POB 549, Manama; tel. 17291234; fax 17290507; f. 1969; Arabic; Owner and Editor-in-Chief ALI ABDULLAH SAYYAR; circ. 40,000 (in various Gulf states).

OTHER PERIODICALS

Arab Agriculture: POB 10131, Bahrain Tower, 8th Floor, Manama; tel. 17213900; fax 17211765; e-mail fanar@batelco.com.bh; f. 1984; annually; English and Arabic; publ. by Fanar Publishing WLL; Editor-in-Chief ABD AL-WAHED ALWANI; circ. 13,000.

Arab World Agribusiness: POB 10131, Bahrain Tower, 8th Floor, Manama; tel. 17213900; fax 17211765; e-mail fanar@batelco.com.bh; internet www.fanarpublishing.com; f. 1985; 9 per year; English and Arabic; publ. by Fanar Publishing WLL; Editor-in-Chief ABD AL-WAHED ALWANI; circ. 18,000.

Bahrain Telegraph: POB 55055, Manama; tel. 17530535; fax 17530353; e-mail info@bahraintelegraph.com; internet www.bahraintelegraph.com; f. 2009; monthly; English; news, business and politics; Editor-in-Chief SOMAN BABY.

Al-Bahrain ath-Thaqafia: POB 2199, Manama; tel. 17290210; fax 17292678; e-mail zahraam@info.gov.bh; internet www.moci.gov.bh; quarterly; Arabic; publ. by the Ministry of Culture and Information; Editor ABD AL-QADER AQIL.

Bahrain This Month: POB 20461, Manama; tel. 17813777; fax 17813700; e-mail redhouse@batelco.com.bh; internet www.bahrainthismonth.com; f. 1997; monthly; English; publ. by Red House Marketing; Publr and Man. Dir GEORGE F. MIDDLETON; circ. 10,000.

Gulf Construction: POB 224, Exhibition Ave, Manama; tel. 17293131; fax 17293400; e-mail editor@gulfconstructionworldwide.com; internet www.gulfconstructionworldwide.com; f. 1980; monthly; English; publ. by Al-Hilal Publishing and Marketing Group; Editor BINA PRABHU GOVEAS; circ. 26,539.

Gulf Industry: POB 224, Manama; tel. 17293131; fax 17293400; e-mail editor@gulfindustryworldwide.com; internet www.gulfindustryworldwide.com; English; industry and transport; publ. by Al-Hilal Publishing and Marketing Group; Editor SALVADOR ALMEIDA; circ. 10,924.

Al-Hayat at-Tijariya (Commerce Review): POB 248, Manama; tel. 17229555; fax 17224985; e-mail bcci@bcci.bh; monthly; English and Arabic; publ. by Bahrain Chamber of Commerce and Industry; Editor KHALIL YOUSUF; circ. 7,500.

Al-Hidayah (Guidance): POB 450, Manama; tel. 17727100; fax 17729819; f. 1978; monthly; Arabic; publ. by Ministry of Islamic Affairs; Editor-in-Chief ABD AL-RAHMAN BIN MUHAMMAD RASHID AL KHALIFA; circ. 5,000.

Al-Mohandis (The Engineer): POB 835, Manama; tel. 17727100; fax 17729819; e-mail mohandis@batelco.com.bh; internet www.mohandis.org; f. 1972; quarterly; Arabic and English; publ. by Bahrain Society of Engineers; Editor Dr OSAMA AL-BAHARNA.

Al-Musafir al-Arabi (Arab Traveller): POB 10131, Bahrain Tower, 8th Floor, Manama; tel. 17213900; fax 17211765; e-mail fanar@batelco.com.bh; internet www.fanarpublishing.com; f. 1985; 6 per year; Arabic; publ. by Fanar Publishing WLL; Editor-in-Chief ABD AL-WAHED ALWANI; circ. 36,000.

Al-Quwwa (The Force): POB 245, Manama; tel. 17291331; fax 17659596; e-mail dgcdf@gmail.com; internet www.bdf.gov.bh; f. 1977; monthly; Arabic; publ. by Bahrain Defence Force; Editor-in-Chief Maj. AHMAD MAHMOUD AL-SUWAIDI.

Travel and Tourism News Middle East: POB 224, Exhibition Ave, Manama; tel. 17293131; fax 17293400; e-mail editor@ttnworldwide.com; internet www.ttnworldwide.com; f. 1983; monthly; English; travel trade; publ. by Al-Hilal Publishing and Marketing Group; Publishing Dir KIM THOMPSON; circ. 12,370.

Woman This Month: POB 20461, Manama; tel. 17813777; fax 17813700; e-mail editor@womanthismonth.com; internet www.womanthismonth.com; f. 2003; English; monthly; publ. by Red House Marketing; Editor KIRSTY EDWARDS-HARRIS; Publr and Man. Dir GEORGE F. MIDDLETON.

NEWS AGENCY

Bahrain News Agency (BNA): Ministry of Culture and Information, POB 572, Manama; tel. 17689044; fax 17683825; e-mail bna@brtc.gov.bh; internet www.bna.bh; f. 2001 to cover local and foreign news; replaced Gulf News Agency as national news agency.

PRESS ASSOCIATION

Bahrain Journalists' Association (BJA): 2057, Rd 4156, Block 0341, Juffair, Manama 332; tel. 17811770; e-mail bja@batelco.com.bh; internet www.bja-bh.org; f. 2000; Chair. ISA AL-SHAIJI; Sec.-Gen. JAWAD ABD AL-WAHAB; 250 mems.

Publishers

Arabian Magazines Group: POB 26810, Manama; tel. 17822388; fax 17721722; e-mail info@arabianmagazines.com; internet www.arabianmagazines.com; f. 2001; publs include *Confidential*, *Areej*, *Gulf Financial Insider*, *Car Bahrain*; CEO NICHOLAS COOKSEY.

Fanar Publishing WLL: POB 10131, Manama; tel. 17213900; fax 17211765; e-mail fanar@batelco.com.bh; internet www.fanarpublishing.com; f. 1985; Editor-in-Chief ABD AL-WAHID ALWANI.

Al-Hilal Publishing and Marketing Group: POB 224, Exhibition Ave, Manama; tel. 17293131; fax 17293400; e-mail hilalad@tradearabia.net; internet www.alhilalgroup.com; f. 1978; specialist magazines, newspapers and websites of commercial interest, incl. *Gulf Daily News*, *Gulf Weekly*, *Gulf Construction* and *Trade Arabia.com*; Chair. A. M. ABD AL-RAHMAN; Man. Dir RONNIE MIDDLETON.

Manama Publishing Co WLL: POB 1013, Manama; tel. 17295578; fax 17295579; e-mail mecon@batelco.com.bh.

Al-Masirah Journalism, Printing and Publishing House: POB 5981, Manama; tel. 17258882; fax 17276178; e-mail almasera@batelco.com.bh.

Primedia International BSC: POB 2738, Manama; tel. 17490000; fax 17490001; e-mail info@primediaintl.com; internet www.primedia.com.bh; f. 1977; fmrly Tele-Gulf Directory Publications WLL; publrs of, *inter alia*, annual *Gulf Directory* and *Arab Banking and Finance*, as well as *Bahrain Telephone Directory with Yellow PagesQatar Telephone Directory with Yellow Pages* and *Banks in Bahrain*; CEO MIKE ORLOV.

Red House Marketing: POB 20461, Manama; tel. 17813777; fax 17813700; e-mail redhouse@batelco.com.bh; internet www.redhousemarketing.com; British-owned; publs include *Bahrain This Month*, *Woman This Month*, *Bahrain Hotel & Restaurant Guide*, maps, tourist guides and various specialist trade publs; Man. Editor GEORGE F. MIDDLETON.

GOVERNMENT PUBLISHING HOUSE

Directorate of Press and Publications: POB 253, Manama; tel. 17717525; e-mail jamaldawood@hotmail.com; internet www.info.gov.bh/en/PressandPublications; Dir JAMAL DAWOOD AL-JLAHMA.

Broadcasting and Communications

TELECOMMUNICATIONS

The telecommunications sector in Bahrain was fully opened to private sector competition in 2002. Since liberalization of the sector Bahrain has been at the forefront of the development of new infrastructure and technologies in the region. Several companies provide fixed-line services. Three providers have been awarded mobile telecommunications licences; the third mobile licence was awarded to Saudi Telecom (STC) in January 2009.

Regulatory Authority

Telecommunications Regulatory Authority (TRA): POB 10353, Taib Tower, 7th Floor, Diplomatic Area, Manama; tel. 17520000; fax 17532125; e-mail contact@tra.org.bh; internet www.tra.org.bh; f. 2002; Chair. Dr MUHAMMAD AHMAD AL-AMER; Gen. Dir MUHAMMAD HAMAD BUBSHAIT.

Principal Operators

Bahrain Telecommunications Co BSC (BATELCO): POB 14, Manama; tel. 17881881; fax 17311120; e-mail batelco@btc.com.bh; internet www.batelco.com.bh; f. 1981; cap. BD 120m.; 100% owned by Govt of Bahrain, financial institutions and public of Bahrain; launched mobile cellular telecommunications service, Sim Sim, in 1999; provides fixed-line and mobile telephone services, broadband internet and data services; Chair. Sheikh HAMAD BIN ABDULLAH BIN MUHAMMAD AL KHALIFA; CEO PETER KALIAROPOULOS.

Nuetel Communications: POB 50960, Amwaj Islands; tel. 16033000; fax 16033001; e-mail info@nue-tel.com; internet www.nue-tel.com; f. 2006; provides fixed-line telephone, broadband internet, internet telephony and data services; CEO MARK NIXON.

Saudi Telecommunications Co—Saudi Telecom (STC): POB 87912, Riyadh 11652, Saudi Arabia; tel. (1) 215-3030; fax (1) 215-2734; e-mail contactus@stc.com.sa; internet www.stc.com.sa; f. 1998; mobile telephone services; Chair. Dr MUHAMMAD BIN SULIMAN AL-JASER; Pres. Eng. SA'UD BIN MAJID AL-DAWEESH.

2Connect Bahrain WLL: POB 18057, 12th Floor, NBB Tower, Government Ave, Manama; tel. 16500110; fax 16500109; e-mail info@2connectbahrain.com; internet www.2connectbahrain.com; f. 2004; provides fixed-line telephone, broadband internet and data-hosting services; Man. Dir FAHAD SHIRAWI.

Zain Bahrain: POB 266, Manama; tel. 36107107; e-mail customercare@bh.zain.com; internet www.bh.zain.com; f. 2003 under the name MTC Vodafone Bahrain; present name adopted 2007; acquired Celtel International (Netherlands) in 2005; 60% owned by Mobile Telecommunications Co (Kuwait), 40% by Bahraini Govt; provides mobile telephone services; Group CEO Dr SAAD AL-BARRAK; CEO (Middle East) MAHMOUD HASHISH; Gen. Man. MUHAMMAD ZAIN AL-ABDEEN.

BROADCASTING

Radio

Bahrain Radio and Television Corpn: POB 702, Manama; tel. 17871405; fax 17681622; e-mail ceobrtc@batelco.com.bh; internet www.bahraintv.com; f. 1955; state-owned; two 10-kW transmitters; programmes are in Arabic and English, and include news, drama and discussions; CEO Sheikh RASHID BIN ABD AL-RAHMAN AL KHALIFA.

Radio Bahrain: POB 702, Manama; tel. 17871585; fax 17780911; e-mail info@radiobahrain.fm; internet www.radiobahrain.fm; f. 1977; English-language commercial radio station; Head of Station SALAH KHALID.

Television

Bahrain Radio and Television Corpn: POB 1075, Manama; tel. 17686000; fax 17681544; e-mail ceobrtc@batelco.bh; internet www.bahraintv.com; commenced colour broadcasting in 1973; broadcasts on 5 channels, of which the main Arabic and the main English channel accept advertising; offers a 24-hour Arabic news and documentary channel; covers Bahrain, eastern Saudi Arabia, Qatar and the United Arab Emirates; an Amiri decree in early 1993 established the independence of the Corpn, which was to be controlled by a committee; CEO Sheikh RASHID BIN ABD AL-RAHMAN AL KHALIFA.

Finance

(cap. = capital; res = reserves; dep. = deposits; m. = million; br.(s) = branch(es); amounts in Bahraini dinars unless otherwise stated)

BANKING

Central Bank

Central Bank of Bahrain (CBB): POB 27, Bldg 96, Block 317, Rd 1702, Diplomatic Area, Manama; tel. 17547777; fax 17530399; e-mail info@cbb.gov.bh; internet www.cbb.gov.bh; f. 1973 as Bahrain Monetary Agency; in operation from Jan. 1975; name changed as above Sept. 2006; controls issue of currency, regulates exchange control and credit policy, organization and control of banking and insurance systems, bank credit and stock exchange; cap. 200m., res 276m., dep. 1,156m. (Dec. 2009); Chair. QASSIM MUHAMMAD FAKHRO; Gov. RASHID MUHAMMAD AL-MARAJ.

Locally incorporated Commercial Banks

Ahli United Bank BSC (AUB): POB 2424, Bldg 2495, Rd 2832, al-Seef District 428, Manama; tel. 17585858; fax 17580549; e-mail info@ahliunited.com; internet www.ahliunited.com; f. 2001 by merger of Al-Ahli Commercial Bank and Commercial Bank of Bahrain; cap. US $1,199m., res $1,013m., dep. $19,740m. (Dec. 2009); Chair. FAHAD AL-RAJAAN; Group CEO and Man. Dir ADEL EL-LABBAN; 130 brs.

Awal Bank BSC: POB 1735, Manama; tel. 17203333; fax 17203355; e-mail info@awal-bank.com; internet www.awal-bank.com; f. 2004; owned by Saad Group (Saudi Arabia); placed into administration July 2009; cap. US $2,000m., res $72.2m., dep. $4,861.2m. (Dec. 2008); Chair. MAAN A. AL-SANEA; CEO and Dir ALISTAIR MACLEOD (acting).

Bahrain Islamic Bank BSC: POB 5240, Al-Salam Tower, Diplomatic Area, Manama; tel. 17546111; fax 17535808; e-mail info@bisbonline.com; internet www.bisbonline.com; f. 1979; cap. 72m., res 67m., dep. 760m. (Dec. 2009); Chair. KHALID ABDULLAH AL-BASSAM; CEO MUHAMMAD EBRAHIM MUHAMMAD; 13 brs.

Bahraini Saudi Bank BSC (BSB): POB 1159, Al-Saddah Bldg, Government Ave, Manama; tel. 17578999; fax 17210989; e-mail info@bsb.com.bh; internet www.bsb.com.bh; f. 1983; acquired by Al-Salam Bank Bahrain BSC in 2009; cap. 50m., res 1m., dep. 120m. (Dec. 2009); Chair. Dr ANWAR KHALIFA AL-SADAH; CEO AHMAD SWALEH ABD AL-SHEIKH (acting); 10 brs.

BBK BSC: POB 579, 43 Government Ave, Area 305, Manama; tel. 17207777; fax 17225109; e-mail abeer.swar@bbkonline.com; internet www.bbkonline.com; f. 1971 as Bank of Bahrain and Kuwait BSC; name changed as above 2005; cap. 64.0m., res 80.2m. (Dec. 2006), dep. 1,756.4m. (Dec. 2009); Chair. MURAD ALI MURAD; Chief Exec. ABD AL-KARIM AHMAD BUCHEERY; 20 brs.

Future Bank BSC: POB 785, Government Rd, Manama; tel. 17505000; fax 17224402; e-mail info@futurebank.com.bh; internet www.futurebank.com.bh; f. 2004; owned by Ahli United Bank BSC, Bank Melli Iran and Bank Saderat Iran; cap. US $120m., dep. $1,151.3m., total assets $1,321.2m. (Dec. 2007); Chair. Dr HAMID BORHANI; CEO GHOLAM SOURI; 3 brs.

Ithmaar Bank BSC: POB 2820, 10th Floor, Addax Tower, Manama; e-mail info@ithmaarbank.com; internet www.ithmaarbank.com; f. 1984 as Faisal Investment Bank of Bahrain EC, a wholly owned subsidiary of Shamil Bank of Bahrain BSC; acquired by Dar al-Maal al-Islami and assumed name as above in 2003; merged with Shamil Bank of Bahrain in April 2010; cap. US $568m., res. $142m., dep. $3,664m. (Dec 2009); Chair. Prince AMR MUHAMMAD AL-FAISAL; CEO MUHAMMAD ABD AL-RAHMAN BUCHEEREI; 11 brs.

National Bank of Bahrain BSC (NBB): POB 106, Government Ave, Manama; tel. 17228800; fax 17228998; e-mail nbb@nbbonline.com; internet www.nbbonline.com; f. 1957; 49% govt-owned; cap. 206m., res 435m., dep. 4,962m. (Dec. 2009); Chair. FAROUK YOUSUF AL-MOAYYED; CEO and Dir ABD AL-RAZAK A. HASSAN AL-QASSIM; 25 brs.

Al-Salam Bank Bahrain BSC: POB 18282, Bldg 22, Ave 58, al-Seef District, Manama; tel. 17560000; fax 17560003; internet www.alsalambahrain.com; f. 2006; acquired Bahraini Saudi Bank in July 2009; Islamic bank; cap. 142m., res 55m., dep. 439m. (Dec 2009); Chair. MUHAMMAD ALI AL-ABBAR; CEO and Dir YOUSUF ABDULLAH TAQI; 2 brs.

Specialized Financial Institutions

Bahrain Development Bank (BDB): POB 20501, Manama; tel. 17511111; fax 17534005; e-mail info@bdb-bh.com; internet www.bdb-bh.com; f. 1992; invests in manufacturing, agribusiness and services; cap. 50m., res 1m., dep. 50m. (Dec. 2009); Chair. Sheikh MUHAMMAD BIN ISSA BIN MUHAMMAD AL KHALIFA; CEO NEDHAL S. AL-AUJAN.

First Energy Bank BSC: POB 209, Manama; tel. 17100001; fax 17100002; internet www.1stenergybank.com; f. 2008; owned by Gulf Finance House BSC and other Gulf shareholders; Islamic wholesale bank providing investment and advice for energy projects; cap. US $1,000m., res. $4m., dep. $171m. (Dec. 2009); CEO MUHAMMAD SHUKRI GHANEM (acting); Chair. KHADEM ABDULLAH AL-QUBAISI.

'Offshore' Banking Units

Bahrain has been encouraging the establishment of 'offshore' banking units (OBUs) since 1975. An OBU is not permitted to provide local banking services, but is allowed to accept deposits from governments and large financial organizations in the area and make medium-term loans for local and regional capital projects. In late 2006 there were 49 OBUs in operation in Bahrain.

ABC Islamic Bank EC: POB 2808, ABC Tower, Diplomatic Area, Manama; tel. 17543000; fax 17536379; e-mail webmaster@arabbanking.com; internet www.arabbanking.com; f. 1987 as ABC Investment and Services Co (EC); name changed as above in 1998 when converted into Islamic bank; 100% owned by Arab Banking

Corpn BSC; cap. US $132m., res $44m., dep. $1,133m. (Dec. 2009); Pres. and Chief Exec. Hassan Ali Juma; Chair. Saddek el-Kaber.

Allied Banking Corpn (Allied Bank); Philippines: POB 20493, Bahrain Tower, 11th Floor, Government Ave, Manama; tel. 17224707; fax 17210506; e-mail ally3540@batelco.com.bh; internet www.alliedbank.com.ph; f. 1980; Chair. Domingo T. Chua; Pres. Anthony Q. Chua.

Alubaf Arab International Bank BSC: POB 11529, Sheraton Tower 13F, Manama; tel. 17517722; fax 17540094; e-mail info@alubafbank.com; internet www.alubafbank.com; f. 1982; 95.1% owned by Libyan Arab Foreign Bank; cap. US $100m., res $4m., dep. $619m. (Dec. 2009); Chair. Dr Muhammad Abdullah Bait Elmal; Gen. Man. Ahmad Imhamad Rajab.

Arab Bank PLC (Jordan): POB 813, Manama; tel. 17549000; fax 17541116; e-mail arabbank@batelco.com.bh; internet www.arabbank.bh; f. 1930; Chair. Abd al-Hamid Shoman.

Arab Banking Corpn BSC: POB 5698, ABC Tower, Diplomatic Area, Manama; tel. 17543000; fax 17533062; e-mail webmaster@arabbanking.com; internet www.arabbanking.com; f. 1980; cap. US $2,000m., res $191m., dep. $20,246m. (Dec. 2009); Chair. Muhammad Husain Layas; Pres. and Chief Exec. Hassan Ali Juma.

Arab Investment Co SAA (Saudi Arabia): POB 5559, Bldg 2309, Rd 2830, al-Seef District 428, Manama; tel. 17588888; fax 17588885; e-mail taic@taicobu.com; internet www.taic.com; f. 1974; cap. US $600m., res $80.7m., dep. $2,712.8m. (Dec. 2008); Chair. Yousef bin Ibrahim al-Bassam; Chief Exec. Dr Saleh al-Humaidan.

BNP Paribas (France): POB 5253, Bahrain Financial Harbour, West Tower, Manama; tel. 17866223; fax 17866601; e-mail jean-christophe.durand@mideastbnpparibas.com; internet www.bahrain.bnpparibas.com; f. 1975; Regional Man. Jean-Christophe Durand.

Gulf International Bank BSC (GIB): POB 1017, Al-Duwali Bldg, 3 Palace Ave, Area 317, Manama; tel. 17534000; fax 17522633; e-mail info@gibbah.com; internet www.gibonline.com; f. 1975; cap. US $2,500m., res $230m., dep. $10,614m. (Dec. 2009); Chair. Sheikh Jammaz bin Abdullah al-Suhaimi; CEO Yahya al-Yahya.

Korea Exchange Bank (Repub. of Korea): POB 5767, Yateem Centre Bldg, 5th Floor, Manama; tel. 17229333; fax 17225327; e-mail bahrain@keb.co.kr; internet www.keb.co.kr; f. 1977; Chair. and CEO Larry A. Klane.

MCB Bank Ltd (MCB) (Pakistan): POB 10164, Diplomatic Area, Manama; tel. 17533306; fax 17533308; e-mail mcbobubh@batelco.com.bh; internet www.mcb.com.pk; f. 1947 as Muslim Commercial Bank Ltd, name changed as above in 2005; Chair. Muhammad Mansha.

National Bank of Abu Dhabi (UAE): POB 5886, Manama 304; tel. 17214450; fax 17210086; e-mail Hassan.Bahzad@nbad.com; internet www.nbad.com; f. 1977; Regional Man. Hassan Behzad.

National Bank of Kuwait SAK: POB 5290, Bahrain BMB Centre, Diplomatic Area, Manama; tel. 17532225; fax 17530658; e-mail nbkbah@batelco.com.bh; f. 1977; Gen. Man. Ali Y. Fardan.

Standard Chartered Bank (United Kingdom): POB 29, Manama; tel. 17223636; fax 17225001; internet www.standardchartered.com/bh; f. 1976; CEO Jonathan Morris.

State Bank of India: POB 5466, Bahrain Tower, Government Ave, Manama; tel. 17224956; fax 17224692; e-mail sbibah@batelco.com.bh; internet www.sbibahrain.com; f. 1977; CEO Sanjeev Nautiyal.

Yapi ve Kredi Bankasi AS (Turkey): POB 10615, c/o Bahrain Development Bank, Diplomatic Area, Manama; tel. 17530313; fax 17530311; internet www.yapikredi.com; f. 1982; Chair. Tayfun Bayazit.

Investment Banks

Al-Baraka Islamic Bank BSC (EC): POB 1882, Diplomatic Area, Manama; tel. 17535300; fax 17533993; e-mail baraka@batelco.com.bh; internet www.barakaonline.com; f. 1984 as Al-Baraka Islamic Investment Bank BSC (EC); current name adopted 1998; owned by Al-Baraka Banking Group BSC; cap. 46m., res 9m., dep. 44m. (Dec. 2009); Chair. Khalid Rashid al-Zayani; CEO Muhammad al-Mutaweh; 240 brs.

Arcapita Bank BSC: POB 1406, Manama; tel. 17218333; fax 17217555; internet www.arcapita.com; f. 1997; cap. US $1,077m., res –$17m., dep. $2,360m. (June. 2010); Chair. Muhammad Abd al-Aziz al-Jomaih; CEO Atif A. Abd al-Malik; 1 domestic br., 3 abroad.

Bahrain Middle East Bank BSC (BMB Investment Bank): POB 797, BMB Centre, Diplomatic Area, Manama; tel. 17532345; fax 17530526; e-mail requests@bmb.com.bh; internet www.bmb.com.bh; f. 1982; fmrly Bahrain Middle East Bank EC; cap. US $54m., res –$31m., dep. $23m. (Dec. 2009); Chair. Wilson S. Benjamin; CEO Akbar A. Habib; 1 br.

Capital Management House (CMH): POB 1001, Manama; tel. 17540454; fax 17540464; e-mail info@capitalmh.com; internet www.capitalmh.com; f. 2006; cap. US $47.7m.; Islamic investment co licensed with the powers of an investment bank; Chair. Khalid Abdullah al-Bassam; Man. Dir and CEO Khalid Muhammad Najibi.

First Investment Bank: 7th Floor, Euro Tower, al-Seef District, POB 10016, Manama; tel. 17389089; fax 17556621; e-mail info@first-ibank.com; internet www.first-ibank.com; f. 2007; Islamic investment bank; jt venture between 8 Gulf investors; cap. US $200m.; Chair. Muhammad A. al-Alloush; Dep. CEO Yousif al-Thawadi.

Global Banking Corpn (GBCORP): POB 1486, GBCORP Tower, Bahrain Financial Harbour, Manama; tel. 17200200; fax 17200300; e-mail info@gbcorponline.com; internet www.gbcorponline.com; f. 2007; Islamic investment bank; cap. p.u. US $250m; Chair. Saleh al-Ali al-Rashed; Vice-Chair. and Man. Dir Abd al-Rahman Muhammad al-Jasmi.

Gulf Finance House BSC: POB 10006, Bahrain Financial Harbour, Manama; tel. 17538538; fax 17540006; e-mail info@gfh.com; internet www.gfhouse.com; f. 1999 as Gulf Finance House EC, name changed as above in 2004; cap. US $604m., res $261m., dep. $459m. (Dec. 2009); Chair. Esam Y. Janahi; CEO Ted Pretty.

INVESTCORP Bank BSC: POB 5340, Investcorp House, Diplomatic Area, Manama; tel. 17532000; fax 17530816; e-mail info@investcorp.com; internet www.investcorp.com; f. 1982 as Arabian Investment Banking Corpn (Investcorp) EC, current name adopted in 1990; cap. US $708m., res $220m., dep. $365m. (June 2010); Pres. and CEO Nemir A. Kirdar; Exec. Chair. and CEO Nemir A. Kirdar.

Nomura Investment Banking (Middle East) EC: POB 26893, BMB Centre, 7th Floor, Diplomatic Area, Manama; tel. 17530531; fax 17530365; f. 1982; cap. US $25.0m., res $46.3m., dep. $0.3m. (Dec. 2007); Chair. Takuya Furuya.

TAIB Bank BSC: POB 20485, TAIB Tower, 79 Rd 1702, Diplomatic Area, Manama 317; tel. 17549494; fax 17533174; e-mail taibprivatebank@taib.com; internet www.taibdirect.com; f. 1979 as Trans-Arabian Investment Bank EC, renamed TAIB Bank EC in 1994, current name adopted in 2004; cap. US $112.3m., res –$9.3m., dep. $218.4m. (Dec. 2009); Chair. Abd al-Razaq Muhammad Abdullah Ali al-Jassim; Vice-Chair Abd al-Aziz Rashed A. al-Rashed.

United Gulf Bank BSC: POB 5964, UGB Tower, Diplomatic Area, Manama; tel. 17533233; fax 17533137; e-mail info@ugbbah.com; internet www.ugbbah.com; f. 1980; cap. US $207m., res $179m., dep. $1,255m. (Dec. 2009); Chair. Masaud M. J. Hayat; CEO Muhammad Haroon (acting).

Venture Capital Bank BSC: POB 11755, Manama; tel. 17518888; fax 17518880; e-mail info@vc-bank.com; internet www.vc-bank.com; f. 2005; Islamic investment bank; cap. US $158m., res $94m. (Dec. 2009); Chair. Dr Ghassan Ahmed al-Sulaiman; CEO Abd al-Latif Muhammad Janahi al-Sulaiman.

Other investment banks operating in Bahrain include Al-Amin Bank, Amex (Middle East) EC, Capital Union EC, Daiwa Securities SMBC Europe Ltd (Middle East), Global Banking Corpn BSC, Investors Bank EC, Al-Khaleej Islamic Investment Bank (BSC) EC and Merrill Lynch Int. Bank Ltd.

STOCK EXCHANGES

Bahrain Bourse: POB 3203, Manama; tel. 17261260; fax 17256362; e-mail info@bahrainbourse.com.bh; internet www.bahrainbourse.com.bh; f. 1989; 51 listed cos at Dec. 2008; scheduled for privatization; Chair. Yousuf Abdulla Humood; Dir Fouad A. Rahman Rashid.

Bahrain Financial Exchange (BFX): POB 1936, 12th Floor, East Tower, Bahrain Financial Harbour, Manama; tel. 16511511; fax 16511599; e-mail info@bfx.bh; internet www.bfx.bh; f. 2009; trading in securities, derivatives, commodities, foreign exchange and *Shari'a*-compliant financial products; owned by Financial Technologies Group (India); Chair. Jignesh Shah; Man. Dir and CEO Arshad Khan.

INSURANCE

In 2009 there were 25 locally incorporated insurance firms operating in Bahrain, including:

Al-Ahlia Insurance Co BSC: POB 5282, Chamber of Commerce Bldg, 4th Floor, King Faisal Rd, Manama; tel. 17225860; fax 17224870; e-mail alahlia@alahlia.com; internet www.alahlia.com; f. 1976; Chair. Hussain Ali Sajwani; Gen. Man. Tawfiq Shehab.

Arab Insurance Group BSC (ARIG): POB 26992, Arig House, Diplomatic Area, Manama; tel. 17544444; fax 17531155; e-mail info@arig.com.bh; internet www.arig.com.bh; f. 1980; owned by Govts of Kuwait, Libya and the United Arab Emirates (49.5%), and other shareholders; reinsurance and insurance; Chair. Khalid Ali al-Bustani; CEO Yassir Albaharna.

Bahrain Kuwait Insurance Co BSC: POB 10166, Diplomatic Area, Manama; tel. 17542222; fax 17530799; e-mail info@bkic.com;

internet www.bkic.com; f. 1975; CEO IBRAHIM SHARIF AL-RAYES; Chair. ABDULLAH HASSAN BUHINDI.

Bahrain National Holding Co BSC (BNH): POB 843, BNH Tower, al-Seef District; tel. 17587300; fax 17583099; e-mail bnh@bnhgroup.com; internet www.bnhgroup.com; f. 1999 by merger of Bahrain Insurance Co and Nat. Insurance Co; all classes incl. life insurance; Chair. FAROUK Y. AL-MOAYYED; Chief Exec. MAHMOUD AL-SOUFI.

Gulf Union Insurance and Reinsurance Co: POB 10949, Manama Centre, Ground Floor, Manama; tel. 17215622; fax 17215421; e-mail guirco@batelco.com.bh; internet www.thyra.com/Sites/gulfunion; Chair. Sheikh IBRAHIM BIN HAMAD AL KHALIFA.

Solidarity Insurance Co: POB 18668, Seef Tower, 11th Floor, al-Seef District, Manama; tel. 17585222; fax 17585200; e-mail mail@solidarity.cc; internet www.solidarity.cc; f. 2004 by Qatar Islamic Bank; Chair. KHALID ABDULLAH JANAHI; CEO ASHRAF BSEISU.

Takaful International Co: POB 3230, B680 R2811, al-Seef District 428, Manama; tel. 17565656; fax 17582688; internet www.takafulweb.com; f. 1989 as Bahrain Islamic Insurance Co; restructured and renamed as above in 1998; Chair. BARA'A ABD AL-AZIZ AL-QENAEI; CEO YOUNIS J. AL-SAYED.

Insurance Association

Bahrain Insurance Association (BIA): POB 2851, Manama; tel. 17532555; fax 17536006; e-mail biabah@batelco.com.bh; internet www.bia-bh.com; f. 1993; 43 mems; Chair. YOUNIS JAMAL AL-SAYED.

Trade and Industry

GOVERNMENT AGENCIES

Economic Development Board (EDB): POB 11299, Manama; tel. 17589999; fax 17589900; e-mail info@bahrainedb.com; internet www.bahrainedb.com; f. 2000; assumed duties of Bahrain Promotions and Marketing Board (f. 1993) and Supreme Council for Economic Devt (f. 2000) in 2001; provides national focus for Bahraini marketing initiatives; attracts inward investment; encourages devt and expansion of Bahraini exports; Chair. Sheikh SALMAN BIN HAMAD AL KHALIFA; CEO Sheikh MUHAMMAD BIN ISSA AL KHALIFA.

National Oil and Gas Authority (NOGA): POB 1435, Manama; tel. 17312644; fax 17293007; e-mail info@noga.gov.bh; internet www.noga.gov.bh; f. 2005 for the regulation and devt of oil- and gas-related industries in the kingdom; Chair. Dr ABD AL-HUSSAIN BIN ALI MIRZA.

CHAMBER OF COMMERCE

Bahrain Chamber of Commerce and Industry: POB 248, Bldg 122, Rd 1605, Block 216, Manama; tel. 17576666; fax 17576600; e-mail bcci@bcci.bh; internet www.bcci.bh; f. 1939; 12,023 mems (Jan. 2007); Chair. Dr ESSAM ABDULLAH YOUSUF FAKHRO; CEO IBRAHIM AHMAD AL-LANGAWI (acting).

STATE HYDROCARBONS COMPANIES

Bahrain National Gas Co BSC (BANAGAS): POB 29099, Rifa'a; tel. 17756222; fax 17756991; e-mail bng@banagas.com.bh; internet www.banagas.com.bh; f. 1979; responsible for extraction, processing and sale of hydrocarbon liquids from associated gas derived from onshore Bahraini fields; 75% owned by Govt of Bahrain, 12.5% by Caltex and 12.5% by Boubyan Petrochemical Co; produces approx. 2,900 barrels per day (b/d) of propane, 2,700 b/d of butane and 5,200 b/d of naphtha; Chair. ALI BIN MUHAMMAD AL-JALAHMA; Chief Exec. Dr Sheikh MUHAMMAD BIN KHALIFA AL KHALIFA.

Bahrain Petroleum Co BSC (BAPCO): POB 25555, Awali; tel. 17704040; fax 17704070; e-mail info@bapco.net; internet www.bapco.com.bh; f. 1999 by merger of Bahrain Nat. Oil Co (f. 1976) and Bahrain Petroleum Co (f. 1980); 100% govt-owned; fully integrated co responsible for exploration, drilling and production of oil and gas; supply of gas to power-generating plants and industries, refining crude petroleum, international marketing of crude petroleum and refined petroleum products, supply and sale of aviation fuel at Bahrain International Airport, and local distribution and marketing of petroleum products; Chair. Dr ABD AL-HUSSAIN BIN ALI MIRZA (Minister of Energy); CEO FAISAL MUHAMMAD AL-MAHROOS.

Gulf Petrochemical Industries Co BSC (GPIC): POB 26730, Manama; tel. 17731777; fax 17731047; e-mail gpic@gpic.com; internet www.gpic.com; f. 1979 as jt venture between the Govts of Bahrain, Kuwait and Saudi Arabia, each with one-third equity participation; a petrochemical complex at Sitra, inaugurated in 1981; produces 1,200 metric tons of both methanol and ammonia per day; Chair. Sheikh ISA BIN ALI AL KHALIFA; Gen. Man. A. RAHMAN A. HUSSEIN JAWAHERI.

UTILITIES

Electricity and Water Authority: POB 2, King Faisal Rd, Manama; tel. 17546767; fax 17541182; e-mail publicrelations@ewa.bh; internet www.mew.gov.bh; f. 2007; privatization of electricity production was approved in December 2003; CEO Sheikh NAWAF BIN IBRAHIM AL KHALIFA.

TRADE UNIONS

In November 2002 legislation was ratified to permit the establishment of independent trade unions. There were reported to be more than 50 trade unions operating within Bahrain by early 2007. Only one trade union is allowed at each work-place, and all unions must belong to the General Federation of Bahrain Trade Unions.

General Federation of Bahrain Trade Unions (GFBTU): Manama; tel. 17727333; fax 17729599; f. 2002; Sec.-Gen. SALMAN JAFFAR AL-MAHFOUD.

Transport

RAILWAYS

There are no railways in Bahrain. In early 2011 a detailed feasibility study began into plans for a 184-km domestic rail network, to be constructed in three phases by 2030. Construction work on the project was expected to begin by late 2012. The Bahraini project was expected to form part of a planned regional rail network, connecting Bahrain with member countries of the Cooperation Council for the Arab States of the Gulf (or Gulf Cooperation Council—GCC).

ROADS

In 2010 Bahrain had 4,122 km of roads, including 576 km of highways, main or national roads, 579 km of secondary or regional roads and 2,237 km of other roads; 82.3% of roads were paved. The King Fahd Causeway, a 25-km causeway link with Saudi Arabia, was opened in 1986. A three-lane dual carriageway links the causeway to Manama. Other causeways link Bahrain with Muharraq island and with Sitra island. The Strategic Roads Masterplan 2021, launched by the Ministry of Works in 2005, outlined plans for the modernization of Bahrain's road network in anticipation of significant increases in road traffic volume. Approval for the construction of a causeway linking Askar in eastern Bahrain with Ras Ishairij in Qatar (the Friendship Bridge) was given in 2004. The project was to be supervised by a committee established in February 2005 by the Governments of both countries. After protracted discussions and numerous delays, in May 2008 the contract to design and build the causeway, at a cost of some US $3,000m., was awarded to a France-based consortium. The decision, in late 2008, to incorporate a dual railway line into the project necessitated substantial design revisions that were expected to add up to $1,000m. to the cost of the causeway. Construction work had been expected to begin in early 2009, with a projected completion date of 2013; however, following further delays as a result of financial difficulties, by early 2012 construction work had yet to commence.

Responsibility for the management and development of Bahrain's roads is divided between the Ministry of Works (Roads Projects and Maintenance Directorate, and Roads, Planning and Design Directorate) and the Ministry of Interior (Directorate of Traffic).

SHIPPING

Numerous shipping services link Bahrain and the Gulf with Europe, the USA, Pakistan, India, the Far East and Australia.

The deep-water harbour of Mina Salman was opened in 1962. However, following the opening of Khalifa bin Salman port in 2009 (see below), commercial operations at Mina Salman were phased out and plans for an expanded US Navy base at the port were under discussion.

In 1999 work began on the construction of a new port and industrial zone at Hidd, on Muharraq island. Incorporating the Bahrain Gateway Terminal, the new port, Khalifa bin Salman, which became operational in April 2009 (at an estimated cost of over US $350m.), has an annual handling capacity of 1.1m. 20-foot equivalent units (TEUs). The port, which has 1,800 m of quayside walls and a quayside depth of 12.8 m (due to be increased to 15 m), includes a general cargo berth and two container berths with roll-on roll-off facilities. Khalifa bin Salman is managed and operated by APM Terminals Bahrain, under the terms of a 25-year contract awarded in 2007. In December 2009 Bahrain's merchant fleet totalled 209 vessels, with an aggregate displacement of 517,600 grt.

Port and Regulatory Authorities

APM Terminals Bahrain BSC: PO Box 50490, Khalifa bin Salman Port, Hidd; tel. 17365500; fax 17365505; e-mail bahapmtcom@apmterminals.com; internet www.apmterminals.com/africa-mideast/bahrain; f. 2006; 80% owned by APM Terminals Management BV, 20% by Yusuf bin Ahmad Kanoo Holdings; management and operation of Bahrain's commercial port; Man. Dir STEEN DAVIDSEN.

General Organization of Sea Ports: POB 75315, Manama; tel. 17359595; fax 17359359; e-mail info@gop.gov.bh; internet www.gop.bh; responsible for regulation, devt and promotion of maritime and logistics zones; Chair. Sheikh DAIJ BIN SALMAN BIN DAIJ AL KHALIFA; Dir-Gen. HASSAN ALI AL-MAJID.

Principal Shipping Companies

Alsharif Group WLL: POB 1322, Manama; tel. 17515055; fax 17537637; e-mail alsharif@batelco.com.bh; internet www.alsharifbahrain.com; f. 1957; shipping agency; Man. Dir ALI ABD AL-RASOOL AL-SHARIF; Gen. Man. BALAJI ARDHANARI.

Arab Shipbuilding and Repair Yard Co (ASRY): POB 50110, Hidd; tel. 17671111; fax 17670236; e-mail asryco@batelco.com.bh; internet www.asry.net; f. 1974 by OAPEC mems; 500,000-ton dry dock opened 1977; 2 floating docks in operation since 1992; new twin slipway completed 2008; repaired 139 ships in 2006; Chair. Sheikh DAIJ BIN SALMAN BIN DAIJ AL KHALIFA; Chief Exec. CHRIS POTTER.

The Gulf Agency Co (Bahrain) WLL: POB 412, Rd 20, 224 Muharraq Area, GLS Premises, Manama; tel. 17339777; fax 17320498; e-mail bahrain@gac.com; internet www.gacworld.com/bahrain; f. 1957; shipping agency; operates at Sitra, Mina Salman and Hidd ports; Man. Dir MIKAEL LEIJONBERG.

Al-Jazeera Shipping Co WLL: POB 302, Mina Salman Industrial Area, Manama; tel. 17728837; fax 17728217; e-mail almelaha@batelco.com.bh; internet www.ajsco.com; operates a fleet of tugboats and barges; Man. Dir ALI HASSAN MAHMOUD.

Kanoo Shipping: POB 45, Al Khalifa Ave, Manama; tel. 17220220; fax 17229122; e-mail kanoomgt@batelco.com.bh; internet www.ybakanoo.com; f. 1890; owned by Yusuf bin Ahmad Kanoo Group; air and shipping cargo services, commercial and holiday services; Chair. (vacant); Shipping Man. DON BANNERMAN.

Nass Marine Services: POB 669, Manama; tel. 17467722; fax 17467773; e-mail nassmarine@batelco.com.bh; internet www.nassgroup.com; f. 2006; part of Nass Group; shipbuilding and ship-repair; Chair. ABDULLAH AHMAD NASS.

UCO Marine Contracting WLL: POB 1074, Manama; tel. 17730816; fax 17732131; e-mail ucomarin@batelco.com.bh; owns and operates a fleet of bulk carriers, tugboats, barges and dredgers; Man. Dirs BADER AHMAD KAIKSOW, HASSAN SABAH AL-BINALI, ALI AL-MUSALAM.

CIVIL AVIATION

Bahrain International Airport (BIA) has a first-class runway, capable of taking the largest aircraft in use. In 2010 BIA handled some 8.9m. passengers. Plans for a two-phase project to expand the airport's capacity through the construction of a two new passenger terminals, at an estimated total cost of US $4,700m., were finalized in late 2009. However, in mid-2011 it was announced that plans for a second passenger terminal had been abandoned. The project to expand the existing terminal to accommodate up to 13.5m. passengers per year was to continue and was due to be completed by 2015.

Department of Civil Aviation Affairs: POB 586, Manama; tel. 17321110; fax 17339066; e-mail prelation@caa.gov.bh; internet www.caa.gov.bh; Under-Sec. Capt. ABD AL-RAHMAN MUHAMMAD AL-GAOUD.

Bahrain Air: POB 23736, Muhammad Centre, Bldg 44, Rd 151, Area 243, Muharraq; tel. 17463330; fax 17463331; e-mail info@bahrainair.net; internet www.bahrainair.net; f. 2007; Bahrain's first privately owned budget carrier, providing services to 17 destinations in the Middle East, Africa and South Asia; Man. Dir Capt. IBRAHIM ABDULLAH AL-HAMER; CEO RICHARD NUTTALL.

Gulf Air: POB 138, Manama; tel. 17339339; fax 17224494; e-mail gfpr@batelco.com.bh; internet www.gulfairco.com; f. 1950 as Gulf Aviation Co; name changed 1974; wholly owned by the Govt of Bahrain; services to the Middle East, South-East Asia, the Far East, Australia, Africa and Europe; Chair. TALAL AL-ZAIN; CEO SAMER MAJALI.

Tourism

There are several archaeological sites of importance in Bahrain, which is the site of the ancient trading civilization of Dilmun. Qal'at al-Bahrain, the ancient capital of Dilmun, was designated a UNESCO World Heritage Site in 2005. In early 2012 major hotel and resort developments were ongoing at Bahrain Bay, City Centre Mall, Al-Areen, the Amwaj Islands and Durrat al-Bahrain. The Government is currently promoting Bahrain as a destination for sports and leisure activities. The Bahrain Grand Prix, held annually since 2004, was the first Formula One event to be held in the Middle East. In 2011 the event was cancelled owing to unrest in the country, but in 2012 the Grand Prix took place as scheduled, despite continued protests within Bahrain and international criticism. In 2007 Bahrain received 7.8m. foreign visitors. Income from tourism totalled US $1,118m. in 2009, according to provisional figures.

Bahrain Exhibition and Convention Authority: POB 11644, Manama; tel. 17558800; fax 17555513; e-mail info@bahrainexhibitions.com; internet www.bahrainexhibitions.com; Chair. Dr HASSAN BIN ABDULLAH FAKHRO (Minister of Industry and Commerce); CEO DEBBIE STANFORD-KRISTIANSEN (acting).

Bahrain Tourism Co (BTC): POB 5831, Manama; tel. 17530530; fax 17530867; e-mail btc@alseyaha.com; internet www.alseyaha.com; f. 1974; Chair. QASSIM MUHAMMAD FAKHROO; CEO ABD AL-NABI DAYLAMI.

Tourism Affairs: Ministry of Culture and Information, POB 26613, Manama; tel. 17201215; fax 17229757; e-mail btour@bahraintourism.com; internet www.bahraintourism.com; Asst Under-Sec. for Tourism Dr KADHIM RAJAB.

Defence

Supreme Commander of the Bahrain Defence Force: HM Sheikh HAMAD BIN ISA AL KHALIFA.

Commander-in-Chief of the Bahrain Defence Force: Field Marshal Sheikh KHALIFA BIN AHMAD AL KHALIFA.

Chief of Staff of the Bahrain Defence Force: Maj.-Gen. Sheikh DUAIJ BIN SALMAN BIN AHMAD AL KHALIFA.

Defence Budget (2012): BD 358m.

Military Service: voluntary.

Total Armed Forces (as assessed at November 2011): 8,200 (army 6,000; navy 700; air force 1,500).

Paramilitary Forces (as assessed at November 2011): est. 11,260 (police 9,000; national guard est. 2,000; coastguard some 260).

Education

Although education is not compulsory, it is provided free of charge up to the secondary level. Basic education, from the ages of six to 14, is divided into two levels: children attend primary school from six to 11 years of age and intermediate school from 12 to 14. Secondary education, beginning at the age of 15, lasts for three years; students choose to follow a general (science or literary), commercial, technical or vocational curriculum. In 1996 enrolment at primary, intermediate and secondary levels was 97.8%, 96.0% and 95.0% of the relevant age-groups, respectively. According to UNESCO, in 2008/09 the total enrolment at primary schools included 97% of children in the relevant age-group, while the comparable ratio for secondary enrolment in 2008/09 was 89%. Private and religious education are also available. In 2010 expenditure by the Ministry of Education totalled BD 222.7m. (equivalent to 11.9% of total recurrent government expenditure).

The University of Bahrain, established by Amiri decree in 1986, comprises nine Colleges: of Engineering, Arts, Science, Information Technology, Law, Applied Studies, Business Administration, Bahrain Teachers College and the Academy of Physical Education and Physiotherapy. Some 12,709 students were enrolled at the University in 2010/11. Higher education is also provided by the College of Health Sciences. The Arabian Gulf University (AGU), funded by seven Arab Governments, also provides higher education. The AGU comprises the College of Medicine and Medical Sciences, and the College of Graduate Studies. The Royal College of Surgeons in Ireland Medical University of Bahrain was founded in 2004, and construction of a new campus at Muharraq was completed in 2008, at an estimated cost of US $78.9m. In addition, ambitious plans to establish a Higher Education City, at a projected cost of $1,000m., were finalized in December 2006; the development was to include a full branch of a leading US university, an international research centre and a specialist academy.

BANGLADESH

Introductory Survey

LOCATION, CLIMATE, LANGUAGE, RELIGION, FLAG, CAPITAL

The People's Republic of Bangladesh lies in southern Asia, surrounded by Indian territory except for a short south-eastern frontier with Myanmar (formerly Burma) and a southern coast fronting the Bay of Bengal. The country has a tropical monsoon climate and suffers from periodic cyclones. The average temperature is 19°C (67°F) from October to March, rising to 29°C (84°F) between May and September. The average annual rainfall in Dhaka is 188 cm (74 ins), of which about three-quarters occurs between June and September. About 95% of the population speak Bengali, the state language, while the remainder mostly use tribal dialects. More than 85% of the people are Muslims, Islam being the state religion, and there are small minorities of Hindus, Buddhists and Christians. The national flag (proportions 3 by 5) is dark green, with a red disc slightly off-centre towards the hoist. The capital is Dhaka (Dacca).

CONTEMPORARY POLITICAL HISTORY

Historical Context

Present-day Bangladesh was formerly East Pakistan, one of the five provinces into which Pakistan was divided at its initial creation, when Britain's former Indian Empire was partitioned in August 1947. East Pakistan and the four western provinces were separated by about 1,000 miles (1,600 km) of Indian territory. East Pakistan was created from the former Indian province of East Bengal and the Sylhet district of Assam. Although the East was more populous, government was based in West Pakistan. Dissatisfaction in East Pakistan at its dependence on a remote central government flared up in 1952, when Urdu was declared Pakistan's official language. Bengali, the main language of East Pakistan, was finally admitted as the joint official language in 1954, and in 1955 Pakistan was reorganized into two wings, east and west, with equal representation in the central legislative assembly. However, discontent continued in the eastern wing, particularly as the region was under-represented in the administration and armed forces, and received a disproportionately small share of Pakistan's development expenditure. The leading political party in East Pakistan was the Awami League (AL), led by Sheikh Mujibur (Mujib) Rahman, who demanded autonomy for the East. A general election in December 1970 gave the AL an overwhelming victory in the East, and thus a majority in Pakistan's National Assembly. Sheikh Mujib should therefore have been appointed Prime Minister, but Pakistan's President, Gen. Yahya Khan, would not accept this, and negotiations on a possible constitutional compromise broke down. The convening of the new National Assembly was postponed indefinitely in March 1971, leading to violent protests in East Pakistan. The AL decided that the province should unilaterally secede from Pakistan, and on 26 March Sheikh Mujib proclaimed the independence of the People's Republic of Bangladesh ('Bengal Nation').

Civil war immediately broke out. President Yahya Khan outlawed the AL and arrested its leaders. By April 1971 the Pakistan army dominated the eastern province. In August Sheikh Mujib was secretly put on trial in West Pakistan. However, resistance continued from the Liberation Army of East Bengal (the Mukhti Bahini), which launched a major offensive in November. As a result of the conflict, an estimated 9.5m. refugees crossed into India. On 4 December India declared war on Pakistan, with Indian forces intervening in support of the Mukhti Bahini. Pakistan surrendered on 16 December, and Bangladesh became independent. Pakistan was thus confined to its former western wing. In January 1972 Sheikh Mujib was freed by Pakistan's new President, Zulfiqar Ali Bhutto, and became Prime Minister of Bangladesh. Under a provisional Constitution, Bangladesh was declared to be a secular state and a parliamentary democracy. The new nation quickly achieved international recognition, causing Pakistan to withdraw from the Commonwealth in January 1972. Bangladesh joined the Commonwealth in April. The members who had been elected from the former East Pakistan for the Pakistan National Assembly and the Provincial Assembly in December 1970 formed the Bangladesh Constituent Assembly. A new Constitution was approved by this Assembly in November 1972 and came into effect in December. A general election for the country's first Jatiya Sangsad (Parliament) was held in March 1973. The AL received 73% of the total votes and won 292 of the 300 directly elective seats in the legislature. Bangladesh was finally recognized by Pakistan in February 1974. Internal stability, however, was threatened by opposition groups that resorted to terrorism and included extremists such as Islamist fundamentalists and Maoists. In December a state of emergency was declared and constitutional rights were suspended. In January 1975 parliamentary government was replaced by a presidential form of government. Sheikh Mujib became President, assuming absolute power, and created the Bangladesh Peasants' and Workers' Awami League. In February Bangladesh became a one-party state.

Domestic Political Affairs

Gen. Zia in power (1975–81)

In August 1975 Sheikh Mujib and his family were assassinated in a right-wing coup, led by a group of Islamist army officers. Khandakar Mushtaq Ahmed, the former Minister of Commerce, was installed as President; martial law was declared, and political parties were banned. A counter-coup on 3 November brought to power Brig. Khalid Musharaf, the pro-Indian commander of the Dhaka garrison, who was appointed Chief of Army Staff; on 7 November a third coup overthrew Brig. Musharaf's brief regime, and power was assumed jointly by the three service chiefs, under a non-political President, Abusadet Mohammed Sayem, the Chief Justice of the Supreme Court. A neutral non-party Government was formed, in which the reinstated Chief of Army Staff, Major-Gen. Ziaur Rahman (Gen. Zia), took precedence over his colleagues. Political parties were legalized again in July 1976.

An early return to representative government was promised, but in November 1976 elections were postponed indefinitely and, in a major shift of power, Gen. Zia took over the role of Chief Martial Law Administrator from President Sayem, assuming the presidency also in April 1977. He amended the Constitution, making Islam, instead of secularism, its first basic principle. In a national referendum held in May 99% of voters affirmed their confidence in President Zia's policies, and in June 1978 the country's first direct presidential election resulted in a clear victory for Zia, who formed a Council of Ministers to replace his Council of Advisers. Parliamentary elections followed in February 1979: in an attempt to persuade opposition parties to participate in the elections, Zia met some of their demands by repealing 'all undemocratic provisions' of the 1974 constitutional amendment, releasing political prisoners and withdrawing press censorship. Consequently, 29 parties contested the elections, in which Zia's Bangladesh Jatiyatabadi Dal (Bangladesh Nationalist Party—BNP) received 49% of the total votes and won 207 of the 300 contested seats in the Jatiya Sangsad. In April 1979 a new Prime Minister was appointed, and martial law was repealed. The state of emergency was revoked in November.

Political instability recurred, however, when Gen. Zia was assassinated on 30 May 1981 during an attempted military coup, allegedly led by Maj.-Gen. Mohammad Abdul Manzur, an army divisional commander who was himself later killed in unclear circumstances. The Vice-President, Justice Abdus Sattar, assumed the role of acting President, prior to securing an overwhelming victory at the presidential election held in November. President Sattar announced his intention of continuing the policies of the late Gen. Zia.

Ershad in power (1982–90)

President Sattar found it increasingly difficult to retain civilian control over the country, and in January 1982 formed a National Security Council, which included military personnel, led by the Chief of Army Staff, Lt-Gen. Hossain Mohammad Ershad. On 24 March Lt-Gen. Ershad seized power in a bloodless coup, claiming that political corruption and economic mismanagement had become intolerable. The country was placed under martial law, with Ershad as Chief Martial Law Administrator (redesignated Prime Minister in October), aided by a mainly military Council of Advisers. Ershad nominated a retired judge, Justice Abul Chowdhury, as President. Political activities were banned, and several former ministers were later tried and imprisoned on charges of corruption.

Although the Government's economic policies achieved some success and gained a measure of popular support for Ershad, there were increasing demands in 1983 for a return to democratic government. The two principal opposition groups that emerged were an eight-party alliance headed by the AL under Sheikh Hasina Wajed (daughter of the late Sheikh Mujib), and a seven-party group led by the BNP under former President Sattar (who died in 1985) and Begum Khaleda Zia (widow of Gen. Zia). In September 1983 the two groups formed an alliance, the Movement for the Restoration of Democracy (MRD), and jointly issued demands for an end to martial law, for the release of political prisoners and for the holding of parliamentary elections before any other polls. In November the resumption of political activity was permitted, and it was announced that a series of local elections between December 1983 and March 1984 were to precede a presidential election and parliamentary elections later in the year. A new political party, the Jana Dal (People's Party), was formed in November 1983 to support Ershad as a presidential candidate. Following demonstrations demanding civilian government, the ban on political activity was reimposed at the beginning of December, only two weeks after it had been rescinded, and leading political figures were detained. On 11 December Ershad declared himself President.

Strikes and political demonstrations occurred frequently during 1984. Local elections, planned for March, were postponed, as the opposition objected to their taking place prior to the presidential and parliamentary elections, on the grounds that Ershad was trying to strengthen his power base. The presidential and parliamentary elections, scheduled for May, were also postponed until December, in response to persistent opposition demands for the repeal of martial law and for the formation of an interim neutral government to oversee a fair election. In October an offer by Ershad to repeal martial law if the opposition would participate in the elections was met with an appeal for a campaign of civil disobedience, which led to the indefinite postponement of the elections.

In January 1985 it was announced that parliamentary elections would be held in April, to be preceded by a partial relaxation of martial law: the Constitution was to be fully restored after the elections. The announcement was followed by the formation of a new Council of Ministers, composed entirely of military officers and excluding all members of the Jana Dal, in response to demands by the opposition parties for a neutral government during the pre-election period. Once more, the opposition threatened to boycott the elections, as President Ershad would not relinquish power to an interim government, and in March the elections were abandoned and political activity was again banned. This was immediately followed by a referendum, held in support of the presidency, in which Ershad reportedly received 94% of the total votes. Local elections were held in May, without the participation of the opposition, following which Ershad claimed that 85% of the elected council chairmen were his supporters, although not necessarily members of his party. In September a new five-party political alliance, the National Front (comprising the Jana Dal, the United People's Party, the Gonotantrik Party, the Bangladesh Muslim League and a breakaway section of the BNP), was established to promote government policies.

In January 1986 the 10-month ban on political activity was ended. The five components of the National Front formally became a single pro-Government entity, named the Jatiya Party (National Party). In March President Ershad announced that parliamentary elections were to be held (under martial law) at the end of April. However, he relaxed martial law by removing all army commanders from important civil posts and by abolishing more than 150 military courts and the martial law offices. These concessions fulfilled some of the opposition's demands, and candidates from the AL alliance (including Sheikh Hasina herself), the Islamist Jamaat-e-Islami Bangladesh and other smaller opposition parties consequently participated in the parliamentary elections—which eventually proceeded in May. However, the BNP alliance, led by Khaleda Zia, boycotted the polls, which were characterized by allegations of extensive fraud, violence and intimidation. The Jatiya Party won 153 of the 300 directly elective seats in the Jatiya Sangsad. In addition, 30 seats reserved for women were filled by nominees of the Jatiya Party. In July a predominantly civilian Council of Ministers was sworn in. Mizanur Rahman Chowdhury, former General Secretary of the Jatiya Party, was appointed Prime Minister.

In order to be eligible to stand as a candidate in the forthcoming presidential election, Ershad retired as Chief of Army Staff in August 1986, while remaining Chief Martial Law Administrator and Commander-in-Chief of the Armed Forces. In September Ershad officially joined the Jatiya Party, whereupon he was elected as Chairman of the party and nominated as its presidential candidate. The presidential election, held in October, was boycotted by both the BNP and the AL, and resulted in an overwhelming victory for Ershad over his 11 opponents.

In November 1986 the Jatiya Sangsad approved indemnity legislation, effectively legitimizing the military regime's actions since March 1982. Ershad repealed martial law and restored the 1972 Constitution. The opposition alliances criticized the indemnity law, stating that they would continue to campaign for the dissolution of the Jatiya Sangsad and the overthrow of the Ershad Government. In December 1986, in an attempt to curb increasing dissent, President Ershad formed a new Council of Ministers, including four AL members of the legislature. The Minister of Justice, Justice A. K. M. Nurul Islam, was appointed Vice-President.

Opposition groups continued to organize anti-Government strikes and demonstrations during 1987, often with the support of trade unions and student groups. In July the Jatiya Sangsad approved a bill enabling army representatives to participate alongside elected representatives in the district councils. The adoption of this controversial legislation provoked widespread and often violent strikes and demonstrations, organized by the opposition groups, which perceived the measure as an attempt by the President to entrench military involvement in the governing of the country despite the ending of martial law in November 1986. Owing to the intensity of public opposition, President Ershad was forced to withdraw the legislation in August 1987 and return it to the Jatiya Sangsad for reconsideration. In November, in a renewed effort to oust President Ershad, opposition groups combined forces and organized further protests. Thousands of activists were detained, but demonstrations and strikes continued. In an attempt to forestall another general strike, President Ershad declared a nation-wide state of emergency on 27 November, suspending political activity and civil rights and banning all anti-Government protests. Disturbances persisted, despite the imposition of curfews on the main towns. In December, as about 6,000 activists remained in detention, opposition parties in the Jatiya Sangsad announced that their representatives intended to resign their seats. After 12 opposition members had withdrawn and the 73 AL members had agreed to do likewise, President Ershad dissolved the Jatiya Sangsad. In January 1988 the President announced that parliamentary elections would be held on 28 February, but leaders of the main opposition parties declared their intention to boycott the proposed poll while Ershad remained in office. Local elections, held throughout Bangladesh in February, were not boycotted by the opposition but were marred by serious outbreaks of violence. The parliamentary elections (postponed until 3 March) were also characterized by widespread violence, as well as by alleged fraud and malpractice. The opposition's appeal for a boycott of the polls was widely heeded, with the actual level of participation by the electorate appearing to have been considerably lower than the Government's estimate of 50%. As expected, the Jatiya Party won a large majority of the seats.

A radical reorganization of the Council of Ministers later in March 1988 included the appointment of a new Prime Minister, Moudud Ahmed, a long-time political ally of Ershad and hitherto the Minister of Industry and a Deputy Prime Minister, in place of Mizanur Rahman Chowdhury. In response to an abatement in the opposition's anti-Government campaign, Ershad repealed the state of emergency in April. Despite strong condemnation by the political opposition and sections of the public, a constitutional amendment establishing Islam as Bangladesh's state religion was approved by an overall majority in the Jatiya Sangsad in June.

In July 1989 the Jatiya Sangsad approved legislation limiting the tenure of the presidency to two electoral terms of five years each and creating the post of a directly elected Vice-President. (However, in the event of the vice-presidency being vacated, the President could make a new appointment with the prior approval of the Jatiya Sangsad.) In August Ershad appointed Moudud

Ahmed as Vice-President to replace Justice A. K. M. Nurul Islam, who was dismissed following charges of inefficiency. Kazi Zafar Ahmed, formerly the Minister of Information and a Deputy Prime Minister, was in turn promoted to the post of Prime Minister. Local elections held in March 1990 were officially boycotted by the opposition parties, although many members participated on an individual basis.

Opposition groups, with the support of thousands of students, co-operated to intensify their anti-Government campaign in late 1990. On 27 November President Ershad proclaimed a nation-wide state of emergency for the second time in three years, suspending civil rights, imposing strict press censorship and enforcing an indefinite curfew throughout the country. On the following day, however, army units were summoned to impose order in the capital as thousands of protesters defied the curfew and attacked police. Under increasing pressure from the opposition groups, Ershad resigned on 4 December and declared that parliamentary elections would be held before the presidential election scheduled for mid-1991; the state of emergency was revoked, and the Jatiya Sangsad was dissolved. Following his nomination by the opposition, Justice Shahabuddin Ahmed, the Chief Justice of the Supreme Court, was appointed Vice-President. He assumed the responsibilities of acting President and was appointed to lead a neutral interim Government pending fresh parliamentary elections. Shahabuddin Ahmed undertook a comprehensive reorganization of personnel in financial institutions, local government and the civil service in an effort to remove Ershad's appointees from important posts. The opposition parties welcomed these developments and abandoned their protest campaigns. They also demanded that Ershad be tried for alleged corruption and abuse of power. Ershad was placed under house arrest, and was later sentenced to 20 years' imprisonment for illegal possession of firearms and other offences.

The end of presidential rule: Khaleda Zia and the Bangladesh Nationalist Party in power (1991–96)

The BNP alliance won an overall majority at parliamentary elections held in February 1991. Following discussions with Jamaat-e-Islami, as a result of which the BNP was ensured a small working majority in the Jatiya Sangsad, Khaleda Zia assumed office as Prime Minister. In August the Jatiya Sangsad approved a constitutional amendment ending 16 years of presidential rule and restoring the Prime Minister as executive leader (under the previous system, both the Prime Minister and the Council of Ministers had been responsible to the President). The amendment, which was approved by national referendum in the following month, reduced the role of the President, who was now to be elected by the Jatiya Sangsad for a five-year term, to that of a titular head of state. Accordingly, a new President was elected by the Jatiya Sangsad in October. The successful candidate was the BNP nominee, former Speaker of the Jatiya Sangsad Abdur Rahman Biswas. In September the BNP had secured an absolute majority in the Jatiya Sangsad as a result of the party's success in a number of by-elections.

The opposition initiated a boycott of parliamentary proceedings in February 1994, and organized mass anti-Government demonstrations from late 1993, culminating in the resignation of all the opposition members from the Jatiya Sangsad in December 1994. In response to an intensification of the anti-Government campaign, and in an attempt to break the political impasse caused by the refusal of the opposition parties to take part in forthcoming by-elections, the Jatiya Sangsad was dissolved in November 1995 at the request of the Prime Minister, pending the holding of a general election in early 1996. Despite opposition demands for a neutral interim government to oversee the election, the President requested that Khaleda Zia's administration continue in office in an acting capacity. All of the main opposition parties boycotted the general election, which was held in mid-February, and independent monitors estimated the turn-out at only about 10%–15% of the registered electorate. Of the 207 legislative seats declared by the end of February, the BNP had won 205 (a partial repoll had been ordered in most of the 93 remaining constituencies where violence had disrupted the electoral process). The opposition refused to recognize the legitimacy of the polls, and announced the launch of a 'non-co-operation' movement against the Government. Renewed street protests rendered the country virtually ungovernable, and Khaleda Zia eventually agreed to the holding of fresh elections under neutral auspices. The Prime Minister and her Government duly resigned on 30 March, and the Jatiya Sangsad was dissolved. President Biswas appointed former Chief Justice Muhammad Habibur Rahman as acting Prime Minister, and requested that a fresh general election be held, under the auspices of an interim neutral government, within three months.

The Awami League takes power under Sheikh Hasina (1996–2001)

At the general election, held on 12 June 1996, the AL won 146 of the 300 elective seats in the Jatiya Sangsad, the BNP 116, the Jatiya Party 32 and Jamaat-e-Islami three. An understanding was rapidly reached between the AL and the Jatiya Party, the latter's major interest being the release of Ershad, who had secured a legislative seat from within prison. (The former President was released on bail in January 1997.) Sheikh Hasina was sworn in as Prime Minister on 23 June 1996. On 23 July the AL's presidential nominee, retired Chief Justice and former acting President Shahabuddin Ahmed, was elected unopposed as Bangladesh's head of state. In September the AL won eight of the 15 seats contested in by-elections; this result gave the AL, which was also allocated 27 of the 30 nominated women's parliamentary seats in July, an absolute majority in the Jatiya Sangsad.

On assuming power, Sheikh Hasina had vowed to bring to justice those responsible for the assassination of her father, Sheikh Mujibur Rahman, in 1975. In November 1996 the Jatiya Sangsad voted unanimously to repeal the indemnity law enacted in 1975 to protect the perpetrators of the military coup in that year; the BNP and Jamaat-e-Islami, however, boycotted the vote. The trial of 19 people accused of direct involvement in Sheikh Mujib's assassination began in March 1997, with 14 of the defendants being tried *in absentia*. (In November 2009 the Supreme Court rejected the appeals against the convictions and death sentences imposed on five former army officers in November 1998 for the murder of Sheikh Mujib, and the convicted men were executed in January 2010.)

Sheikh Hasina's tenure was marred by persistent civil and political instability. In addition to the disruption caused by a series of strikes and demonstrations organized by the BNP in conjunction with Islamist and right-wing groups (which frequently led to violent clashes between demonstrators and police), the efficacy of the Jatiya Sangsad was undermined by several boycotts of parliamentary proceedings organized by BNP deputies. The BNP's foremost demand was the holding of fresh elections, replicating the AL's earlier campaign. However, the AL strengthened its position through a series of by-election victories, and the departure of the Jatiya Party from the coalition in March 1998 had little effect on the ruling party's hold on power. In June and August the opposition leader, Khaleda Zia, was charged with corruption and abuse of power, allegedly perpetrated during her tenure as Prime Minister (the charges were later dismissed as politically motivated).

The announcement in February 2000 of the introduction of the controversial Public Safety Act, which permitted detention without trial for up to 90 days, provoked a three-day nationwide strike. Following accusations that the Government was conspiring to amend the Constitution, opposition members instigated another parliamentary boycott. In September Khaleda Zia was accused by the anti-corruption unit of financial irregularities.

In June 2001 Sheikh Hasina became the first Prime Minister in the history of Bangladesh to complete a five-year term of office. In July the Government resigned, and the Jatiya Sangsad was dissolved in order to allow an interim neutral administration to prepare for a general election, to be held within three months (in accordance with Bangladesh's unique electoral system). The interim administration was established shortly afterwards under the leadership of former Chief Justice Latifur Rehman. The election campaign was reportedly the most violent in the country's history, and Rehman ordered the deployment of more than 50,000 troops to curb the unrest.

The BNP returns to power (2001–06)

The general election proceeded on 1 October 2001, although voting was postponed in several constituencies owing to violent incidents. The AL claimed that voting had been manipulated as it became clear that the opposition alliance, led by the BNP, had won an overwhelming majority of the 300 directly elective seats in the Jatiya Sangsad; however, international monitors declared the poll to be free and fair. Following elections on 9 October in 15 of those constituencies where voting had been delayed, the BNP-led alliance controlled a total of 214 of the directly elective seats, the AL 62 and the Jatiya Party 14. On 10 October Khaleda Zia was sworn in as Prime Minister. At the end of October newly elected members of Parliament representing the AL took the oath of office, but refused to join the opening session of the Jatiya Sangsad, in continuing protest against what they considered a rigged election; the opposition party also demanded that the Government demonstrate a greater commitment to curbing the violence allegedly perpetrated by the BNP-led alliance and its supporters against AL members and religious minority groups. Reports of attacks, particularly against the Hindu minority, increased markedly after the victory of the BNP-led coalition. Many Hindus either sought refuge in AL offices or fled the country to neighbouring India. Although dismissing reports of widespread attacks as overstated, the Government announced that an investigation would be conducted into alleged violent acts against religious minorities and women, and into reports that Hindus had left the country.

In November 2001 Prof. A. Q. M. Badruddoza Chowdhury, a former Minister of Foreign Affairs, was declared President after his sole nominated opponent, Mohammad Rowshan Ali, withdrew his candidacy. Prof. Chowdhury immediately resigned from the BNP, and was sworn into office two days later. The AL (which had refused to participate in the presidential election) boycotted the oath-taking ceremony. In December the Jatiya Sangsad repealed the Father of the Nation Family Security Act. The Security Act, which had been approved in June under the AL administration, guaranteed lifelong security for Sheikh Hasina and her sister, the daughters of Sheikh Mujib (the 'father of the nation' according to the AL), because several convicted assassins of the latter remained at large; however, the Act was strongly criticized by the BNP, which considered its own founder, Gen. Zia, to be the 'father of the nation'.

AL members of Parliament continued their boycott of the Jatiya Sangsad until June 2002. The party also refused to take part in civic elections in April and carried out a policy of agitation, organizing a series of strikes in protest against higher taxes, crime and rises in fuel prices. In response to the opposition's campaign, the Government filed two corruption charges against Sheikh Hasina and other AL members in December 2001, in relation to a weapons contract with Russia signed in 1999.

In June 2002 the President yielded to pressure from the BNP to resign from office after he failed to visit Gen. Zia's grave on the anniversary of the latter's assassination. The resignation was considered unconstitutional by many observers. Some two days later Khaleda Zia appointed her son, Tarique Rahman, to the post of Secretary-General of the BNP, prompting claims that the Prime Minister intended eventually to relinquish power to Rahman. In September the BNP candidate, Iajuddin Ahmed, was declared President by the Election Commission after it was established that the nomination papers of the two other candidates were invalid.

In September 2002 bomb explosions in the south-western town of Satkhira were reported to have killed at least 10 people and seriously injured 150. Islamist militant groups were suspected of having carried out the attack, although none claimed responsibility. In October the Government launched a campaign to curb crime; some 40,000 members of the armed forces had been enlisted to assist the police. The AL claimed that the Government was using this campaign as a guise for the harassment of opposition members. By the end of the month almost 3,500 people had been arrested, including two former AL ministers. Concerns were raised over the unusually high number of people who had died in army custody. In January 2003 the Government approved a law granting the armed forces legal immunity for any actions carried out during the three-month operation against crime. Meanwhile, in December 2002 bomb explosions at four cinemas in the town of Mymensingh were reported to have killed at least 18 people and injured some 300. The Prime Minister rejected suggestions that the Islamist militant al-Qa'ida organization was involved in the attack. However, it was claimed that Bangladeshi Islamist militant groups had collaborated with South-East Asian Islamist groups connected with al-Qa'ida since 1999.

A report published by the Bureau of Human Rights Bangladesh in September 2003 stated that nearly 3,000 people had been killed in separate violent occurrences throughout Bangladesh between January and September. In January 2004 a bomb explosion at the Muslim Hazrat Shah Jalal shrine in Sylhet killed five people. In May a grenade attack at the shrine resulted in the deaths of three people and injuries to at least a further 100, including the British High Commissioner to Bangladesh, Anwar Chowdhury. By the end of that month more than 100 people had been arrested in connection with the attack. Also in May Ahsanullah Master, an AL legislator, was shot dead in his constituency. While the AL accused the Government of having ordered the attack, the Government blamed factional fighting within the AL.

In May 2004 the Jatiya Sangsad approved a bill of constitutional amendments (comprising the 14th Amendment to the Constitution) that made provision for the existing 300-member legislature to be enlarged to 345 members—45 seats were to be reserved for women (the constitutional provision for women to hold 30 seats in the legislature had lapsed in 2001). The AL and most other opposition parties boycotted the vote, on the grounds that the seats for women would be awarded on a proportional representation basis, rather than by direct election. (The 14th Amendment was formally introduced in December 2004.) In June the AL announced the end of the parliamentary boycott that it had initiated one year previously, following the return of several AL legislators to the Jatiya Sangsad in the previous month as a tribute to the deceased Ahsanullah Master.

In August 2004 another grenade attack on an AL rally in Dhaka resulted in the deaths of 20 people, including the President of the AL women's wing, Ivy Rahman. AL leader Sheikh Hasina was slightly injured. Widespread rioting subsequently took place in Dhaka and other towns in Bangladesh, and the AL called a series of general strikes in protest. Later in that month a previously unknown group, Hikmatul Zihad, claimed responsibility for the attack. In January 2005 an explosion at an AL rally in Habiganj, in the north-east of the country, killed five party activists, including Shah Kibria, a former Minister of Finance. The worsening security situation in Bangladesh provoked increasing international disquiet, owing largely to the Government's ongoing failure to bring to justice the perpetrators of many of the violent incidents.

In February 2005 the Government acknowledged, for the first time, that fundamentalist Islamist groups were operating in the country and officially banned two such organizations, Jamatul Mujahideen Bangladesh (JMB) and Jagrata Muslim Janata Bangladesh (JMJB), which were believed to have been responsible for several bomb attacks on the offices of aid agencies. In March 10 people were charged with involvement in the January grenade attack that had resulted in the death of Shah Kibria. It was reported that eight of those accused were district officials or members of the ruling BNP, lending credence to opposition accusations that the BNP, acting through its coalition partner, Jamaat-e-Islami Bangladesh, was covertly encouraging the activities of Islamist militant groups in the country. On 17 August approximately 500 small bombs exploded virtually simultaneously at around 300 locations across Bangladesh, killing two people. The JMB claimed responsibility for the attacks, and the AL alleged that the BNP had, once again, been complicit. Several arrests were subsequently made in connection with the bombings; however, the leaders of both banned organizations, who were suspected of having planned the attacks, evaded capture. In October another Islamist militant group, Harakat-ul-Jihad-i-Islami (HJI), was outlawed by the Government. Media reports suggested that the HJI had 'merged' with other militant groups in the country, including the JMB and the JMJB, in order to conduct a concerted terrorist campaign intended to effect the transformation of Bangladesh into an Islamic state. In November two bomb attacks on courthouses in Gazipur and Chittagong, which were believed to be the country's first suicide bombings, resulted in the deaths of nine people. A spate of attacks in the area followed. Approximately 800 alleged members of the JMB had been arrested by the end of 2005, as the Government attempted to bring the deteriorating security situation under control. In January 2006 a member of the JMB became the first Islamist militant to be convicted of explosives offences in Bangladesh; he was sentenced to a 15-year prison term. In February 21 people received death sentences for carrying out six bomb attacks in Jhenidah district in August 2005 (part of the large-scale bombing campaign mentioned above). In March 2006 Siddiqul Islam and Abdur Rahman, who were alleged to be senior figures in the JMB, were sentenced to death, along with five others, on murder charges arising from the November 2005 courthouse bombings. In August 2006 Ataur Rahman, who was reported to be the leader of the JMB's military wing, and two others were sentenced to death for their role in bomb attacks that took place in August and October 2005. It was reported in March 2007 that six militants, including Islam and Abdur Rahman, had been executed.

Meanwhile, in January 2006 the opposition, led by the AL, called a general strike, claiming that the Government was attempting to manipulate the electoral list in advance of the general election, which was due to be held in January 2007. In February 2006 the AL ended the parliamentary boycott that it had instigated one year previously, while continuing to co-ordinate a campaign of civil disobedience against the Government. Political and civil unrest continued throughout 2006, a year characterized by regular strikes, growing discontent over electricity shortages, demonstrations, and clashes between government and opposition supporters. In May protests by garment workers demanding increased wages and a reduction in working hours erupted into violence. In August at least six people were killed in demonstrations against plans for the development of an open-cast coal mine in Phulbari. The controversial project, which would have necessitated the relocation of around 50,000 people, was subsequently cancelled by the Government. In October several members of the BNP defected to form a new party, the Liberal Democratic Party, with former President Prof. A. Q. M. Badruddoza Chowdhury and Col (retd) Oli Ahmed as its leaders.

Bangladesh under a caretaker government (2006–08)

Tensions mounted with the approach of the 2007 election, as increasingly vociferous demands for electoral reform were made by the AL and its coalition, including the installation of a non-partisan caretaker government and election officials, and a revision of the electoral roll. Prime Minister Khaleda Zia and her Government duly stepped down at the end of their term in office in October 2006, but confusion about their successors remained and the transition was marked by widespread protests and sporadic violence. The original nominee for Chief Adviser (the head of the caretaker government that was to oversee the election process), K. M. Hasan, declined the post following the AL's assertion that it would not contest the election should he take office, in view of his alleged support for the BNP. Shortly afterwards President Iajuddin Ahmed announced that he himself would assume the additional role of Chief Adviser in an attempt to curb the unrest. A team of advisers was also appointed, including Fazlul Haq and Akbar Ali Khan, but President Ahmed took charge of the key portfolios of defence, foreign affairs and home affairs. In November transport blockades called by the opposition coalition caused widespread disruption. Later in November the scheduled date of 22 January 2007 for the general election, set by the Bangladesh Election Commission, was rejected by the AL-led coalition, which argued that it did not allow sufficient time for the necessary reforms to be enacted. In December 2006 it was reported that the former President and the Chairman of the Jatiya Party, Lt-Gen. Ershad, who earlier in the year had been acquitted of several corruption charges dating back to the previous decade, had decided to join the opposition coalition. President Ahmed's deployment of army troops to control opposition protests prompted four members of his team of advisers to resign in December 2006; four new advisers were promptly appointed and the President placed the troops on standby rather than on active service.

On 3 January 2007 the AL coalition announced a boycott of the elections and appealed for another transport blockade. The interim Government stood firm, stressing that, according to constitutional stipulations, it was required to hold elections within 90 days of assuming power. Thousands of protesters took to the streets in Dhaka as the nation-wide transport blockade was implemented. On 11 January both the European Union (EU, see p. 276) and the UN suspended their election observer missions in Bangladesh. On the same day President Ahmed stepped down as Chief Adviser, postponed the elections and declared a state of emergency; nine of the 10 advisers also resigned. Dr Fakhruddin Ahmed was sworn in as Chief Adviser on 12 January, and 10 new advisers were subsequently appointed. On 21 January Justice M. A. Aziz, who in November 2006 had begun a three-month leave of absence, permanently stepped down as Chief Election Commissioner, followed by five other election commissioners. Under emergency rules, a ban on political activity came into effect, along with curbs on certain media reports. The electoral roll that had been released prior to the postponed elections was subsequently invalidated by the High Court.

The interim Government embarked on a large-scale campaign against corruption, apparently as part of a wider attempt to overhaul the political system and prepare the country for free and fair elections to be held by the end of 2008. A new Chairman, former Chief of Army Staff Lt-Gen. (retd) Hasan Mashhud Chowdhury, was appointed to head the reconstituted Anti-Corruption Commission (ACC). Large numbers of prominent politicians, from the BNP and the AL, and businessmen were detained, and several (including a number of former government ministers) were subsequently charged and convicted of corruption or other crimes. Most noteworthy were the arrests of the two dominant figures in Bangladeshi politics: Sheikh Hasina was detained in July 2007 on charges of extortion, and her erstwhile rival Khaleda Zia was arrested in September on corruption charges. Both were denied bail. Meanwhile, there was growing discontent in certain quarters over the perceived severity of the emergency measures and the curtailment of civil rights, including the reported maintenance of media restrictions. In August clashes between students and security forces at universities in Dhaka, Chittagong, Sylhet and three other cities prompted the imposition of temporary curfews. The Government announced a partial suspension of its ban on political activity in the following month, while upholding restrictions on outdoor rallies and functions. Iajuddin Ahmed's term as President, which duly expired in September, was extended in light of the delayed legislative elections. In November the lengthy process of transferring power over the judiciary away from the executive arm of government appeared to be complete, with the announcement that judges and magistrates would henceforth be selected by the Supreme Court.

In May 2008 it was announced that legislative elections would be held in December. However, the AL and the BNP expressed reluctance to participate in preparatory negotiations with the interim Government, citing the continuing detention of their respective leaders, Sheikh Hasina and Khaleda Zia. In the same month the Chairman of Jamaat-e-Islami Bangladesh, Motiur Rahman Nizami, was arrested and charged with corruption; he was released on bail in July, but was detained again in November. (In October the Islamist party amended its constitution to comply with Election Commission regulations, recognizing Bangladesh's Constitution, sovereignty and the 1971 war of liberation; the party was officially renamed Bangladesh Jamaat-e-Islami.) Owing to poor health, Sheikh Hasina was released on parole in order to travel abroad in June. (She returned to Bangladesh in September.) In the same month thousands were arrested as part of a major government 'clean-up' campaign; although the arrests were carried out ostensibly to ensure free and fair elections, political organizations claimed that many of the detainees were from their ranks. It was reported in July that a 'Truth and Accountability Commission' had been established in order to pursue the interim Government's objective of tackling corruption. In the same month the Bangladesh Election Commission announced that it had completed the revision of the electoral register, reducing the number of voter names by approximately 13m., to 80m. Electoral reforms came into effect, including the limiting of constituencies to three per candidate and an increase in the maximum permitted amount of campaign funding. Local elections were held in August, with candidates supported by the AL securing the majority of positions. In November the Bangladesh Election Commission set a new date of 29 December for the election. Campaigning began in mid-December, with the interim Government lifting the state of emergency shortly afterwards.

The Awami League returns to power (2008–)

The AL secured a decisive victory over the BNP in the legislative election held on 29 December 2008, winning 230 of the 300 elective parliamentary seats. The BNP secured a mere 29 seats, but, after initially accusing the AL of electoral fraud, eventually accepted the results as valid. Turn-out was high, at an estimated 70% of the electorate, and the election process was generally deemed to have been free and fair. Sheikh Hasina was sworn in as Prime Minister in January 2009, assuming responsibility for the defence portfolio and heading a new Council of Ministers that included Dipu Moni as Minister of Foreign Affairs and Sahara Khatun as Minister of Home Affairs. On 11 February the AL's candidate, Zillur Rahman, was elected unopposed as President.

In February 2009 a revolt by a unit of the Bangladesh Rifles (BDR—paramilitary forces responsible for patrolling the border) led to violent clashes in Dhaka and elsewhere. Members of the BDR, whose demands for increased salaries, improved conditions and other changes had been rejected by the army, seized their headquarters in Pilkhana, in the Dhaka district, taking hostages and fighting with army troops in the capital and at bases around the country. The mutiny resulted in some 74 deaths (mostly senior army officers, including the commandant). Government investigators claimed to have found evidence of potential links between a number of the mutineers and the banned Islamist extremist group the JMB. In December 2010 the BDR was renamed the Border Guard Bangladesh (BGB), its command structure was reorganized and mutiny was rendered a crime punishable by the death penalty. However, the trials of those accused of mutinying who had not also participated in more serious offences were to be held under the old, comparatively lenient, BDR laws, under which the maximum punishment for mutiny was seven years' imprisonment; six special military courts had been established to this end in November 2009, while those charged with murder, rape, arson, looting and other serious offences were to be tried in civilian courts.

The first trial of those accused of mutiny at the Pilkhana headquarters opened in Dhaka in February 2010, the trials in the four special courts outside the capital having commenced earlier. In October the six special courts were reorganized into 10 new tribunals, five of which were in Dhaka and the remainder were to operate outside the capital. Meanwhile, the first verdict among the special courts was announced in April 2010, by the special court responsible for mutinies in the Dinajpur and Rangpur sectors of the BDR: all 29 defendants in that trial were convicted of rebellion; 13 were handed down the maximum seven years' gaol term, with the remaining 16 given prison terms ranging between four months and six years. The first verdict in the trials of those charged with involvement in the revolt at Pilkhana was handed down at the beginning of February 2011: 111 soldiers were convicted of rebellion and were handed down gaol terms ranging between 30 months and seven years, of which 45 received the maximum prison sentence. By the end of June about 3,000 soldiers had been sentenced to prison terms ranging from four months to the maximum seven years, and each had been fined 100 taka, having been convicted of involvement in the mutiny. Human Rights Watch expressed concern following the mass trial in June of 666 soldiers, in which all but nine were convicted of the charges against them, stating: 'It is impossible to try hundreds of people at the same time and expect anything resembling a fair trial'. The legitimacy of the trials was further undermined by allegations of the use of torture to extract confessions and witness testimony, and by the summary nature of the judicial process. While the torture allegations were adamantly denied by the authorities, the Government did acknowledge that more than 50 soldiers had died in police custody following their arrest for alleged involvement in the revolt. By the end of July 800 soldiers had been indicted by civilian courts on charges of murder, rape, arson, looting and other serious offences.

Meanwhile, in May 2010 the corruption charges against Sheikh Hasina were dismissed by the High Court, which ruled that the ACC had not followed the due legal process when filing charges against her and that the accusations did not constitute a criminal offence. In July the High Court outlawed punishments handed down by Islamic *fatwas*, ruling that anyone issuing or executing 'such an extrajudicial penalty' should themselves face criminal prosecution. (In May 2011 the Supreme Court rescinded the ban on the issuing of *fatwas*, but ruled that it remained illegal to enforce such edicts or to punish anyone for contravening them.) Also in July 2010 the Supreme Court repealed the majority of the constitutional amendments introduced in 1979; *inter alia*, the Court's ruling stated that henceforth Islamist parties would not be able to use religion in politics, and declared the 1975–90 period of military rule to have been illegal. The discovery of a large weapons and explosives cache, together with Islamic literature, in a residential property in Dhaka in late July 2010, which the authorities stated had been intended for use in a large-scale terrorist attack in the capital, prompted an escalation in efforts to apprehend suspected Islamist militants. In August five JMB members were sentenced to life imprisonment, following their conviction of involvement in a series of bombings in the northern Bogra district that had injured several people in 2005.

In March 2010 the Government established an International Crimes Tribunal (ICT) to prosecute those accused of committing war crimes (including collaborating with Pakistan) during Bangladesh's war of independence in 1971. In July 2010 Motiur Rahman Nizami and Ali Ahsan Mohammad Mojaheed, Chairman and Secretary-General, respectively, of Bangladesh Jamaat-e-Islami, and three other senior leaders of the Islamist party, Delawar Hossain Sayedee, Mohammad Kamaruzzaman and Abdul Kader Mollah, were detained on suspicion of committing mass atrocities during the conflict. Travel bans were imposed on approximately 40 other suspects. In December Salauddin Quader Chowdhury, a prominent member of the BNP, was detained on suspicion of crimes against humanity. It was claimed by some human rights organizations, including Amnesty International, that Chowdhury had been tortured during his five-day interrogation by the police. The claims were repudiated by the Bangladeshi authorities. In March 2011 Mohd Abdul Alim, a former BNP legislator, was detained on suspicion of crimes against humanity, having allegedly been involved in the killing of more than 10,000 innocent people, including a local AL leader, in 1971. Alim was subsequently granted conditional bail.

Delawar Hossain Sayedee became the first person to be formally charged by the ICT, in October 2011, when he was charged with, *inter alia*, genocide, rape, torture and religious persecution. Sayedee pleaded not guilty to all of the charges against him. His trial—the tribunal's first—opened in late November 2011. Meanwhile, similar charges were formally submitted against Salauddin Quader Chowdhury in mid-November. Nizami, Mojaheed and Kamaruzzaman were formally charged in December, together with Ghulam Azam, who had been Chairman of Jamaat-e-Islami Bangladesh during 1969–2000; an arrest warrant was issued for Azam, who was subsequently detained in January 2012. All of those charged denied the allegations against them, declaring them to be politically motivated. In order to address irregularities in the original submission, charges against Mojaheed were resubmitted by the prosecution in mid-January and included 34 separate alleged atrocities.

Meanwhile, in mid-November 2010 supporters of Khaleda Zia and the BNP clashed with the authorities in Dhaka, following the eviction from her home of the former Prime Minister in October; the house had been allocated to her on humanitarian grounds following the assassination of her husband Gen. Zia in the 1981 abortive military coup. The BNP and its supporters staged a general strike in protest at Zia's treatment, with hundreds of people gathering in Dhaka and other major cities around the country. Although no major violence was reported, the crowds in the capital were dispersed by the police using batons, tear gas and rubber bullets, and several protesters were reported to have been injured. A bomb explosion at the private residence of an AL legislator in south-western Bangladesh on the previous day claimed the lives of three people and injured two others; the legislator was unharmed. A second general strike was staged by the BNP in protest against perceived government misrule and 'harassment' of the opposition, with BNP Secretary-General Khandaker Delwar Hossain claiming that the police had arrested some 1,300 opposition supporters in the previous few days. (Following a period of illness, Hossain died in March 2011; he was replaced as BNP Secretary-General on an interim basis by Mirza Fakhrul Islam Alamgir.) A further general strike was staged by the opposition in February 2011, in response to controversial plans announced by the Government for a new international airport (which was denounced by the BNP as a waste of public funds), escalating food prices and sharp reductions in the general indexes of the two trading bourses since the turn of the year. Minor clashes were reported in a number of towns across the country, and about 15 protesters were arrested in the north-western town of Rajshahi, following angry confrontations between protesters and the authorities. An additional 8,500 police officers were dispatched to tighten security in Dhaka.

Meanwhile, December 2010 brought further unrest, with textile workers staging protests in Dhaka, Chittagong and the northern district of Gazipur, demanding improved working conditions and the immediate implementation of a promised increase in the minimum monthly wage, from US $23 (at which level it had remained since 2006) to $43; the increase had been scheduled to be introduced across the country by 1 December, but many companies had failed to meet the deadline. Several thousand workers picketed factories and blocked roads, with some protesters attacking factories and vehicles in Chittagong. Three people were reported to have been killed during the protests, with dozens more injured, as police again dispersed the crowds with tear gas and rubber bullets.

In a firm indication of the ruling party's declining popularity, BNP-backed candidates performed strongly in local elections held in January 2011, overturning the AL's majority to secure 33 of the 72 mayoral positions and 95 of the 243 urban municipalities; candidates supported by the AL won 18 and 93 seats, respectively. Later that month a report published by Human Rights Watch claimed that the Bangladeshi Government had not ended 'systematic human rights abuses', including torture and extrajudicial killings by the security forces, and urged the Government to establish an impartial inquiry into each killing and hold to account those found to be responsible. The report also contended that many Bangladeshis who had crossed the border into India in pursuit of employment opportunities had been killed by the Indian border security forces, and appealed to the Bangladeshi Government to be more forceful in its efforts to encourage the Indian authorities to restrain its border forces.

In March 2011 the Council of Ministers approved a new National Women's Development Policy (NWDP), which set out the Government's commitment to safeguarding and promoting equal rights for women with regard to employment, education, health, inheritance and ownership of property. The policy was subject to strong opposition from several Islamist groups, who claimed that legislation based on the NWDP would violate Koranic principles, notably the granting of equal inheritance rights to women; hitherto, inheritance in Bangladesh has been governed by *Shari'a* principles, under which female heirs normally receive only half as much as their male counterparts. Islamist groups staged protests against the NWDP; a protestor was killed during clashes with the security forces on 3 April in Jessore, while major disruption to schools, businesses and transport occurred in major cities on the following day during a general strike called by the Islami Oikya Jote, an alliance of hardline Islamist groups.

Recent developments: the 15th Amendment to the Constitution

In June 2011 the Jatiya Sangsad approved a bill of constitutional amendments (comprising the 15th Amendment to the Constitution) by 291 votes to one, in a motion that was boycotted by the BNP. The Amendment restored secularism as one of the four fundamental principles of the State, while retaining Islam as the state religion and rescinding the ban on religion-based politics. It also provided for the abolition of the existing electoral system (introduced in 1996) whereby, upon completion of a government's term, legislative power was transferred to an interim neutral administration, which was responsible for overseeing new parliamentary elections, to be held within 90 days. (In May 2011 the Supreme Court had ruled that the interim system of government was illegal—overturning a previous decision by the High Court, which had upheld the constitutionality of the provision in 2004—but had decreed that the system could remain in place for the next two parliamentary terms, for the sake of national stability. Later in May 2011 the Supreme Court upheld a previous High Court ruling outlawing the Truth and Accountability Commission established by the interim Government in 2008.) The BNP was vehemently opposed to the abolition of the interim government system, arguing that without it incumbent governments could manipulate the staging of future elections, and boycotted parliamentary sessions from May in protest at the proposal.

The 15th Amendment also provided for a number of other changes to the charter, including an increase in the number of parliamentary seats reserved for women, from 45 to 50. Another provision decreed that rulings issued by the ICT could not be appealed in any court, thereby rendering the tribunal as the highest judicial authority for charges pertaining to atrocities allegedly committed during Bangladesh's 1971 war of independence.

Twelve Islamic political parties staged a 30-hour nation-wide strike in early July 2011 in protest at the restoration of secularism within the Constitution. A few days later the BNP, together with Bangladesh Jamaat-e-Islami, the Jatiya Party, Islami Oikya Jote, Khelafat Majlish and a number of smaller parties, staged a 48-hour, nation-wide general strike—the seventh general strike to be called by the BNP since the 2008 parliamentary elections—in protest at the abolition of the caretaker government system, insisting that elections overseen by the incumbent Government would be neither free nor fair. The BNP demanded the resignation of Minister of Home Affairs Sahara Khatun after police officers allegedly attacked its chief whip, Zainul Abdin Farooque, during the strike. The opposition party claimed that nearly 550 people were injured in police action and more than 400 protesters were arrested. Further strikes were called by the BNP in September in response to the Government increasing fuel prices by 19% earlier in the month. In October the BNP and its allies staged a 'road march' from the party's headquarters in Dhaka towards Sylhet, and in November a second 'road march' towards Khulna was held, to underscore the opposition's demands for the reintroduction of the caretaker government system.

Responsibility for a series of minor bomb explosions in Dhaka, which killed one person and injured another, on 17–19 December 2011 was attributed by the authorities to supporters of the BNP. Four bombs exploded on 17 December in Jessore district along the border with West Bengal, India, during a demonstration staged by the BNP in protest at the killing of a local party leader, Mazmul Islam, who was found dead on 16 December, having been abducted by unidentified assailants on the previous day. Several bomb explosions occurred in downtown Dhaka during clashes between BNP supporters and police officers on 18 December. A further eight bombs were detonated on 19 December, near the BNP headquarters. More than 200 BNP members were reported to have been arrested in the aftermath of the explosions, which prompted further violent protests by the opposition.

In mid-January 2012 the Bangladeshi army announced that it had foiled a conspiracy intended to overthrow the Sheikh Hasina Government. A military spokesperson claimed that the alleged coup plot had involved a group of up to 16 Islamist military officers, some of whom had been in active service, and had been orchestrated by expatriate Bangladeshi nationals. Some of those alleged to have been involved had already been apprehended, and were to appear before a military court, but others remained at large. Some observers suggested that the increasing secularization of the Bangladeshi state, as a result of the 2011 constitutional amendments, was a primary motivating factor behind the alleged coup plot.

Meanwhile, the perceived persecution by the authorities of former premier Khaleda Zia—see The Awami League returns to power (2008–)—appeared to intensify from mid-2011. In June Zia's younger son, Arafat Rahman, was convicted *in absentia*, together with Ismail Hossain Saimon, of money-laundering, having been found to have siphoned off around US $1m. through bank accounts in Singapore during Zia's tenure as Prime Minister. Both men were imprisoned for six years and fined $5.2m. In July a warrant was issued for the arrest of Zia's elder son, Tarique Rahman, who was accused of orchestrating the grenade attack on an AL rally in Dhaka that had resulted in the deaths of 20 people in August 2004—see The BNP returns to power (2001–06). Tarique Rahman was reported to have been living in exile in the United Kingdom since 2008 and at early 2012 it remained unclear whether he would return to Bangladesh to face trial. Arrest warrants were issued for 18 others, primarily BNP members, who were also accused of involvement in the attack. Tarique Rahman was also charged by the ACC in August 2011, accused of laundering $2.7m. in bribes into a foreign bank account. Khaleda Zia herself was charged with abuse of power by the ACC in January 2012; the agency claimed to have found evidence of funding irregularities in a land purchase deal in 2005 on behalf of a charitable trust established by Zia and three others. The BNP adamantly denied all of the allegations against Khaleda Zia and her sons, insisting that the charges were politically motivated.

Meanwhile, in separate reports published in May and August 2011, respectively, Human Rights Watch and Amnesty International both accused Bangladesh's special police force, the Rapid Action Battalion (RAB), of extrajudicial killings and other human rights violations. Amnesty claimed that the RAB had been implicated in the unlawful killing of more than 700 people since its establishment in 2004, and urged the Government to honour previous pledges to end extrajudicial killings. The RAB denied any wrongdoing, claiming that such killings were either accidental or the result of police officers defending themselves against violent attacks by detainees. Amnesty's report also alleged that prisoners were frequently subjected to torture in custody.

An investigation was initiated in September 2011 into corruption allegations pertaining to a US $2,900m. project to build a bridge over the Padma river, which was intended to connect the north-west of Bangladesh with Dhaka and Chittagong Port. The probe, launched by the Canadian authorities, was to investigate the bidding process for the project—construction of which had been provisionally scheduled to commence before the end of 2011—following allegations that Bangladeshi officials, including the Minister of Communications, Syed Abul Hossain, had been offered bribes by employees of Canada's SNC-Lavalin Group. The corruption allegations prompted the World Bank to withdraw pledged funding of $1,200m. that had been earmarked for the bridge project. Hossain, who had previously attracted criticism for his ministry's failure adequately to maintain and repair the national road system, was dismissed from the communications portfolio in a government reorganization effected in early December in an apparent bid to salvage the bridge project. Hossain was transferred to the newly created Ministry of Information and Communication Technology, and was replaced as Minister of Communications by Obaidul Quader. Other notable appointments included that of Suranjit Sengupta, who was named as head of the newly created Ministry of Railways. A few days after his appointment, Quader held discussions with the World Bank with a view to securing a resumption of funding for the bridge project; a decision remained pending at early 2012. In April the Government was undermined by a further corruption scandal, following the discovery of a large quantity of cash in a vehicle carrying officials from the Ministry of Railways and Bangladesh Railway. Investigations into the incident were launched by both the ministry and the ACC. Despite denying any involvement in the alleged corruption, Sengupta resigned from his post in mid-April. (Quader was assigned responsibility for the railways portfolio on interim basis.)

The BNP-led opposition continued to mount a high-profile campaign for the restoration of the caretaker government system throughout early 2012, culminating in a major rally in Dhaka on 12 March, which was the largest event of its kind since the 2008 elections. In her address to the rally, which passed off peacefully, Khaleda Zia issued the Government with a 90-day ultimatum to accede to the opposition's demands regarding the caretaker government, or be faced with an intensified campaign of strikes and protests. In mid-April, in a further effort to bolster the opposition movement, Khaleda Zia announced the formation of an 18-party opposition alliance, comprising the BNP, Bangladesh Jamaat-e-Islami and 16 much smaller parties. In the same week, the disappearance of a BNP official from Sylhet provoked allegations by the opposition that agents of the Government had abducted the official. The opposition initiated a series of general strikes throughout the country and violent confrontations between police and opposition supporters were reported in Sylhet and Dhaka. Meanwhile, with the BNP maintaining its practice of regularly boycotting parliamentary sessions, and with growing opposition threats to boycott the forthcoming parliamentary elections, scheduled for early 2013, further political tension during 2012 appeared inevitable.

The Chittagong Hill Tracts

In 1989 the Government attempted to suppress the insurgency in the Chittagong Hill Tracts, in south-eastern Bangladesh, where Buddhist tribal rebels, the Shanti Bahini, had waged a lengthy guerrilla campaign against the Bangladeshi police and Bengali settlers, by introducing concessions providing limited autonomy to the region in the form of three new semi-autonomous hill districts. Voting to elect councils for the districts took place relatively peacefully in June, despite attempts at disruption by the Shanti Bahini, who continued to demand total autonomy for the Chakma tribals. The powers vested in the councils were designed to give the tribals sufficient authority to regulate any further influx of Bengali settlers to the districts (the chief complaint of the tribals since Bengalis were settled in the Chittagong Hill Tracts, as plantation workers and clerks, by the British administration in the 19th century). Despite these concessions, violence continued unabated, and Chakma refugees continued to flee across the border into India (the number of refugees living in camps in the Indian state of Tripura reached about 56,000). Following successful negotiations between Bangladesh and India, a process of phased repatriation of the refugees commenced in early 1994. In December 1997 the Bangladeshi Government signed a peace agreement with the political wing of the Shanti Bahini. The treaty offered the rebels a general amnesty in return for the surrender of their weapons and gave the tribal people greater powers of self-governance through the establishment of three new elected district councils (to control the area's land management and policing) and a regional council (the chairman of which was to enjoy the rank of a state minister). The peace agreement, which was strongly criticized by the opposition for representing a 'sell-out' of the area to India and a threat to Bangladesh's sovereignty, served to accelerate the process of repatriating the remaining refugees from Tripura (who totalled about 31,000 at the end of 1997). By the end of 2000 most of the Chakma refugees had been repatriated, the district and regional councils were in operation, and a land commission had been established. However, rioting in the Chittagong area in mid-2001 and the accession to power of the BNP-led alliance in October of that year prompted thousands of members of Buddhist, Christian and Hindu minorities to flee to Tripura. In December 2003 and January 2004 protesters in the south-eastern Hill Tracts succeeded in cutting off the region from the rest of the country as they demanded the full implementation of the 1997 peace agreement. In December 2005 the Government and the United Nations Development Programme (UNDP) announced investment of US $50m. in the Hill Tracts, in order to assist with implementation of the 1997 agreement by strengthening the local economy. In July 2009 the Government announced plans to carry out a large-scale withdrawal of troops from the Hill Tracts over the following few months (the most substantive withdrawal since the signing of the peace agreement in 1997). However, in February 2010 violence again erupted in the Hill Tracts with a series of clashes between Bengali settlers and tribal people. A number of buildings, including two Buddhist temples, were burnt down, allegedly by Bengali settlers, and the severity of the incidents (with several people reportedly being killed) necessitated the redeployment of troops to the region.

Foreign Affairs

Regional relations

In foreign affairs, Bangladesh has traditionally maintained a policy of non-alignment. Relations with Pakistan improved in 1976: ambassadors were exchanged, and trade, postal and telecommunication links were resumed. In September 1991 Pakistan finally agreed to initiate a process of phased repatriation and rehabilitation of some 250,000 Urdu-speaking Bihari Muslims (who openly supported Pakistan in Bangladesh's war of liberation in 1971) still remaining in refugee camps in Bangladesh. The first group of Bihari refugees returned to Pakistan from Bangladesh in January 1993, but the implementation of the repatriation process has been very slow. In May 2008 the Dhaka High Court concluded that approximately 150,000 Biharis (those who had been minors in 1971 or who had been born in the intervening years) could become citizens of Bangladesh. Meanwhile, a diplomatic row arose in September 2000 over who was responsible for the events during Bangladesh's war of liberation, culminating in the withdrawal of the Pakistani Deputy High Commissioner to Bangladesh. However, in July 2002 Pakistani President Pervez Musharraf paid a visit to Bangladesh, during which he expressed regret for the atrocities committed by Pakistani troops during the 1971 war. In February 2006 Prime Minister Khaleda Zia visited Pakistan to hold talks with her Pakistani counterpart, Shaukat Aziz; the latter hailed the visit, during which the two sides signed four memoranda of understanding on trade, agriculture, tourism, and standardization and quality control, as a turning point in bilateral relations. A fifth round of Bangladesh-Pakistan bilateral consultations was held, after a three-year hiatus, in the Pakistani capital, Islamabad, in November 2010, during which the Bangladeshi delegation requested a formal apology from Pakistan for the war of liberation; other issues discussed were reported to include repatriation of those Pakistanis in refugee camps in Bangladesh and the division of state assets pertaining to the pre-separation period. The Bangladeshi delegation also formally raised the issue of war reparations for the first time. While Pakistani officials affirmed their willingness 'to continue discussion on these [issues] at all levels', no tangible progress towards resolution of the chief issues was reported.

Relations with India have been strained over the questions of cross-border terrorism (especially around the area of the Chittagong Hill Tracts—q.v.) and of the Farakka barrage, which was constructed by India on the Ganges (Ganga) river in 1975, so depriving Bangladesh of water for irrigation and river transport during the dry season. In December 1996, however, Indo-Bangladeshi relations were given a major boost following the signing of an historic 30-year water-sharing agreement; the agreement also allowed for India to have transit rights over Bangladeshi territory in order to reach parts of its remote north-eastern states more easily. In January 1997 Indian Prime Minister H. D. Deve Gowda paid an official visit to Bangladesh, the first Indian premier to do so for 20 years. In June 1999, during a visit to Dhaka by Indian Prime Minister Atal Bihari Vajpayee to celebrate the inauguration of the first direct passenger bus service between Bangladesh and India, Vajpayee promised Bangladesh greater access to Indian markets and announced that India would give its neighbour substantial financial aid to help develop its transport and industrial infrastructure.

In June 1992 the Indian Government, under the provisions of an accord signed with Bangladesh in 1974, formally leased the Tin Bigha Corridor (a small strip of land covering an area of only 1.5 ha) to Bangladesh for 999 years. India maintained sovereignty over the corridor, but the lease gave Bangladesh access to its enclaves of Dahagram and Angarpota. In September 1997 India granted Nepal a transit route through a 60-km corridor in the Indian territory joining Nepal and Bangladesh, thus facilitating trade between those two countries. Despite the 1992 border agreement between Bangladesh and India, the issue of territorial rights to pockets of land or enclaves along the irregular border remained a source of dispute, and occasional efforts to resolve this problem failed to prevent intermittent clashes between border guards. The worst fighting between the two countries since 1976 took place in April 2001 on the Bangladeshi border with the Indian state of Meghalaya. Three members of the BDR and 16 members of the Indian Border Security Forces (BSF) were killed. The situation was brought under control, and following bilateral border negotiations in June and July, two joint working groups were established to review the undemarcated section of the border.

During negotiations between senior Bangladeshi and Indian officials in Dhaka in September 2004, some progress was made in resolving the issue of water-sharing between the two countries, and an agreement was reached to co-ordinate border patrols. However, relations continued to be strained, with clashes between the two countries' border patrols occurring in October and again in March 2005. Talks were held later in the latter month in an attempt to resolve the ongoing problems, which had been exacerbated by India's continued construction of a fence along the border, in contravention of its obligations under a 1974 treaty. The Indian Government claimed that the fence was intended to prevent illegal immigrants and insurgents from crossing the border. Several further clashes occurred in the following months, as relations remained tense.

In March 2006 Prime Minister Khaleda Zia, during her first official visit to India since her term in office began in 2001, held talks with the Indian Prime Minister, Dr Manmohan Singh, and other senior officials. The two countries signed agreements on trade and anti-drugs-trafficking measures, and stressed their commitment to working together on security issues. Security, however, remained a point of contention between Bangladesh and India throughout 2006. The Bangladeshi Government vehemently denied reports in the Indian media that the explosives used in the Mumbai bomb attacks in July (see the chapter on India) originated in Bangladesh. In August the Indian BSF gave a list of more than 100 militants, including several Assamese rebel leaders, to the BDR, requesting that they be handed over. The BSF had also appealed for separatist camps on Bangladeshi soil to be dismantled. However, the existence of such bases in Bangladesh was denied by the BDR. In January 2007, as violence in the Indian state of Assam (Asom) escalated, the BSF again accused Bangladesh of harbouring leaders of the United Liberation Front of Assam (ULFA). In the following month, after a series of high-level bilateral talks in Dhaka, the two countries agreed to increase co-operation in their respective fights against terrorism. Military officials from Bangladesh and India held talks in Dhaka in October to work towards a resolution of border issues, with the two sides agreeing to provide each other with information and assistance in order to combat militant and criminal activity in border areas. A direct train link between Dhaka and Kolkata (Calcutta), India, began operating in April 2008. Relations between the two neighbouring countries were improved by the arrest and transfer into Indian custody by the Bangladeshi authorities of several ULFA leaders, and, in October 2010, of Rajkumar Meghen, the leader of the United National Liberation Front, a prominent separatist group in the north-eastern Indian state of Manipur.

Following a visit to New Delhi made by the Bangladeshi Prime Minister, Sheikh Hasina, in January 2010, it was reported that Bangladesh and India aimed to remove all barriers to mutual trade in an effort to improve bilateral economic co-operation. In August the two countries announced an agreement providing for a US $1,000m. Indian loan to fund infrastructural development and improve road and rail connectivity in Bangladesh. Border talks resumed in November, following a five-year hiatus, which was interpreted by some observers as a tacit acknowledgement from India of the importance of ensuring continued growth and development in Bangladesh in order to safeguard the development and security of India's north-eastern states. A joint border survey of disputed frontier areas commenced in December and was concluded in early 2011. In August 2011 Bangladesh and India began the process of approving border maps, officially recognizing their 4,156-km frontier; however, a 6.5-km stretch of the border had yet to be demarcated and remained disputed. Meanwhile, following discussions between the Bangladeshi and Indian ministers responsible for water resources in New Delhi in June, the two countries were reported to be close to concluding an interim bilateral agreement on the sharing of waters from the Teesta river, which is crucial to agricultural production in north-western Bangladesh.

The water-sharing agreement was one of several significant deals that had been expected to be finalized during Indian Prime Minister Manmohan Singh's first official visit to Dhaka—the first state visit to Bangladesh by an Indian premier in 12 years—which took place in September 2011. In a sign of the growing importance of India's relations with Bangladesh, Singh was to have been accompanied on his visit by the Chief Ministers of Assam, Meghalaya, Mizoram, Tripura and West Bengal. However, in the event, Mamata Banerjee, the Chief Minister of West Bengal, refused to join the delegation, owing to her anger over the proposed water-sharing agreement, which would have provided for a 50:50 share of the waters from the Teesta river; Banerjee argued that this was too great a share for India to cede to Bangladesh and would have been to the detriment of farmers in her state, who also depended on the river's water supply. Reportedly owing to Banerjee's objections, Singh withdrew the deal during his two-day visit. The two countries also failed to reach agreement on a land transit accord that would have granted India overland access to its landlocked north-eastern states through Bangladeshi territory. (Bangladesh had insisted that the latter agreement was dependent upon a successful conclusion to the water-sharing deal.) Nevertheless, a land border agreement, resolving demarcation of the remaining 6.5-km stretch on the bilateral frontier, and an agreement providing for the exchange of 111 Indian enclaves within Bangladesh and 51 Bangladeshi enclaves within India, were signed, formally concluding a dispute dating back to 1947. Under the terms of the latter agreement, residents within the enclaves would have the right to determine whether they wanted to become Indian or Bangladeshi citizens. Other agreements signed included a comprehensive framework agreement on bilateral co-operation, a memorandum of understanding providing for enhanced co-operation within the field of renewable energy and an agreement to expand trade links, including the granting of tax concessions by India on Bangladeshi textile exports, which was seen as another step towards the conclusion of a bilateral free trade agreement, discussions on which had been reported in mid-2011 to have been well advanced, although the stated objective of concluding the pact by the end of 2011 was not fulfilled. Meanwhile, both countries' respective Governments hailed Singh's visit as a success and pledged to continue discussions on all remaining bilateral issues; they also expressed confidence that a resolution to the water-sharing dispute would soon be achieved. During a two-day visit to Tripura, India, in January 2012, Prime Minister Sheikh Hasina urged the Indian Government to be more flexible in order to facilitate the resolution of outstanding bilateral issues, including the issue of water-sharing, a view that was reiterated by the Tripura Chief Minister, Manik Sarkar.

The question of settlers has been the prevalent issue in Bangladesh's relations with its eastern neighbour Myanmar. While the 320-km border itself was finally demarcated in 1985, in accordance with a 1979 agreement, during 1991–92 about 270,000 Rohingya Muslims, a Myanma ethnic minority who live in the western Arakan region, crossed into Bangladesh, claiming persecution by the Myanma authorities. In 1992 an agreement was signed between the Governments of Bangladesh and Myanmar to allow for voluntary repatriation. The official deadline for the repatriation of the Rohingya refugees expired in August 1997, by which time about 230,000 refugees were reported to have returned to Myanmar. Smaller-scale repatriations resumed in late 1998 following intervention by the office of the UN High Commissioner for Refugees (UNHCR). According to UNHCR data, 16,000 of the Rohingyas remaining in Bangladesh were considered by the Government of Myanmar to be ineligible for repatriation, since they had not been authorized for return prior to August 1997, and 5,000 were unwilling to return owing to protection concerns; however, the Bangladeshi Government continued to favour repatriation of the refugees.

In January 2001 Bangladeshi and Myanma border guards exchanged fire, amid rising tension over a controversial dam project on the Naaf river, which Bangladesh claimed would cause flooding in its territory. In February, following border negotiations between the two countries, Myanmar agreed permanently to halt construction of the dam. The official visit of the Myanma ruler, Gen. Than Shwe, to Bangladesh in December 2002 indicated an apparent improvement in relations despite the ongoing Rohingya issue. In December 2009 it was announced that Myanmar had agreed to repatriate about 9,000 Rohingyas living in Bangladeshi camps following a meeting between the two countries' respective ministers responsible for foreign affairs.

An escalation in military activity on the Myanma side of the border from late 2009 (as preparations for legislative elections in 2010 got underway) prompted the Bangladeshi authorities to place their border troops on alert and to deploy additional army personnel. At early 2012 an estimated 28,000 Rohingyas with official refugee status remained in the two camps run by UNHCR, the rate of repatriation having slowed considerably; in addition, there were an estimated 200,000 stateless Rohingyas living in squalid unregistered camps around Cox's Bazar (already one of the most impoverished areas of Bangladesh).

Meanwhile, a long-running dispute concerning the shared maritime boundary of Bangladesh and Myanmar was aggravated in late 2008 when several vessels, under licence from Myanmar and accompanied by a Myanma naval escort, began conducting hydrocarbon survey work in a disputed area close to Bangladesh's St Martin's Island (which is located in the Bay of Bengal, less than 10 km from both Bangladeshi and Myanma territory). Tensions were heightened following the dispatch of a Bangladeshi naval patrol to interrupt the survey. However, following an intervention by the authorities of the People's Republic of China and the Republic of Korea (South Korea), both of whom had hydrocarbon interests in the area, a temporary cessation of the exploration activities was agreed. In December 2009 Bangladesh initiated proceedings with the UN International Tribunal for the Law of the Sea (ITLOS) concerning delimitation of the maritime boundary with Myanmar. The verdict issued in mid-March 2012 by ITLOS, which was the Tribunal's first ever ruling on a maritime boundary dispute, was broadly interpreted as a vindication of Bangladesh's claims. ITLOS upheld Bangladesh's claim to a full 200-nautical-mile exclusive economic zone in the Bay of Bengal and awarded Bangladesh control of a 12-nautical-mile zone surrounding St Martin's Island. Moreover, the Tribunal recognized Bangladesh's right to a proportional share of the outer continental shelf, beyond the 200-nautical-mile zone. It was anticipated that the settlement would enable significant development of Bangladesh's offshore hydrocarbon projects.

Bangladesh is a member of the South Asian Association for Regional Cooperation (SAARC, see p. 420), formally constituted in 1985, with Bhutan, India, the Maldives, Nepal, Pakistan and Sri Lanka. Included in SAARC's charter are pledges of non-interference by members in each other's internal affairs and a joint effort to avoid 'contentious' issues whenever the association meets. The SAARC Preferential Trading Arrangement (SAPTA) was signed in April 1993 and came into effect in December 1995. At the 12th SAARC summit meeting held in Islamabad, Pakistan, in January 2004, members signed an agreement providing for the establishment of a South Asian Free Trade Area (SAFTA—which came into force on 1 January 2006, although its phased implementation was not due to be fully effected until 2016). An additional protocol on terrorism was also signed. Bangladesh hosted the 13th SAARC summit meeting in December 2005, at which the gathered heads of state reiterated their commitment to enduring regional co-operation as a means of facilitating peace, progress and stability in the South Asian region. At a SAFTA Working Group meeting in September 2011, the Bangladeshi Government announced that, pending approval by the Bangladeshi Council of Ministers, it was to eliminate import tariffs on 248 products from India, Pakistan and Sri Lanka, and 246 products from Afghanistan, Bhutan, the Maldives and Nepal, in exchange for similar measures by the seven other SAFTA signatories. It was hoped that the tariff concessions would help to boost interregional trade.

Other external relations

Relations with China had uncertain beginnings, with China initially refusing to recognize Bangladesh's sovereignty upon the latter's accession to independence in 1971. However, following the establishment of bilateral relations in 1975, they have steadily gained in importance in recent years, with the East Asian country increasingly establishing itself as a significant challenger for India's position as the main trading superpower within the South Asian region. During a visit to the Chinese capital, Beijing, by Prime Minister Sheikh Hasina in March 2010, the two countries signed a series of agreements, including, most notably, a Closer Comprehensive Partnership of Co-operation, which formalized the signatories commitment to expanding mutually beneficial co-operation; a memorandum of understanding providing for enhanced bilateral co-operation in the oil and gas sector was also signed. The Chinese Vice-President, Xi Jinping, made a state visit to Dhaka in June, during which the two countries signed an economic co-operation agreement providing for substantial Chinese investment in Bangladeshi infrastructure and industrial projects. In the following month, in a development that was thought likely to have caused intense irritation to the Indian Government, China announced the elimination of tariffs on exports from Bangladesh and Nepal, effective from the start of that month. An agreement signed between Bangladesh and the Export and Import Bank of China in June 2011 provided for a Chinese loan of US $211m., to be disbursed on the upgrading of Bangladesh's telecommunications network. During a visit to Beijing in September, Bangladesh's Chief of Army Staff, Gen. Mohammed Abdul Mubeenin, held discussions with the Chinese Minister of National Defence, Liang Guanglie, during which they agreed to enhance bilateral military co-operation and underscored the importance of Bangladeshi-Chinese relations to the Governments of both countries.

In March 2000 the US President, Bill Clinton, visited Bangladesh as part of a tour of South Asia. This constituted the first ever state visit by a US President to Bangladesh. In September 2001 Bangladesh's interim administration agreed, with the support of the AL and BNP, to offer the USA use of Bangladeshi airspace and ports in the event of military action against Afghanistan, where the Taliban leadership was believed to be harbouring Osama bin Laden and other members of al-Qa'ida—held principally responsible by the USA for that month's suicide attacks against New York and Washington, DC. However, the US-led military campaign to oust the regime of Saddam Hussain in Iraq from March 2003 provoked anti-US and anti-British demonstrations in Dhaka. In June 2004 US Secretary of Defense Donald Rumsfeld visited Bangladesh and held talks with Prime Minister Khaleda Zia. There were protests against his visit, as it was believed that he intended to request that Bangladesh contribute troops to assist the US-led coalition in Iraq. Although Bangladesh had been a regular contributor of personnel to UN peace-keeping operations throughout the world, the Bangladeshi Minister of Foreign Affairs stressed that no troops would be sent to Iraq without a UN mandate. As of November 2009 over 10,000 Bangladeshi military personnel were deployed overseas on peace-keeping operations. Positive relations between Bangladesh and the USA were reaffirmed during a visit by the Bangladeshi Minister of Foreign Affairs, Dipu Moni, to Washington, DC, in October 2011, during which he met with US Secretary of State Hillary Clinton, and the US Assistant Secretary of State for South and Central Asian Affairs, Robert Blake; the latter US official hailed Bangladesh as a 'strong partner' of the USA but urged its Government to ensure safeguards on the freedom of expression of the media and non-governmental organizations operating within Bangladesh. In April 2012 Bangladeshi officials participated in the inaugural US-Bangladeshi Dialogue on Security Issues in Washington, DC. The forum aimed to promote bilateral co-operation on a range of military and security initiatives, including joint military exercises, peacekeeping missions and maritime security.

CONSTITUTION AND GOVERNMENT

The members who were returned from East Pakistan (now Bangladesh) for the Pakistan National Assembly and the Provincial Assembly in the December 1970 elections formed the Bangladesh Constituent Assembly. A new Constitution for the People's Republic of Bangladesh was approved by this Assembly on 4 November 1972 and came into effect on 16 December 1972. Following the military coup of 24 March 1982, the Constitution was suspended, and the country was placed under martial law. On 10 November 1986 martial law was repealed and the suspended Constitution was revived. The Constitution was initially based on the fundamental principles of nationalism, socialism, democracy and secularism, but in 1977 an amendment replaced secularism with Islam. A further amendment in 1988 established Islam as the state religion. Under the 15th Amendment to the Constitution of 2011, secularism was restored as a fundamental principle of the state, while Islam was retained as the state religion.

The role of the President, who is elected by the Jatiya Sangsad (Parliament) for a five-year term, is essentially that of a titular head of state. Executive power is held by the Prime Minister, who heads the Council of Ministers. The President appoints the Prime Minister and, on the latter's recommendation, other ministers. The Jatiya Sangsad comprises 345 members, 300 of whom are elected by universal suffrage: an additional 45 female members are appointed by the elective members on the basis of proportional representation. The Jatiya Sangsad serves a five-year term, subject to dissolution.

For purposes of local government, the country is divided into seven administrative divisions (each named after their respective divisional headquarters), which are themselves subdivided into 64 administrative districts— *zila* (each of which is further subdivided into subdistricts— *upazila*).

REGIONAL AND INTERNATIONAL CO-OPERATION

Bangladesh is a member of the Asian Development Bank (ADB, see p. 210), of the South Asian Association for Regional Cooperation (SAARC, see p. 420) (see Regional relations) and of the Colombo Plan (see p. 449). Having joined the UN in 1974, Bangladesh is a member of the UN Economic and Social Commission for Asia and the Pacific (ESCAP, see p. 40).

As a contracting party to the General Agreement on Tariffs and Trade (GATT), Bangladesh became a member of the World Trade Organization (WTO) on its establishment in 1995. In addition, Bangladesh is a member of the International Jute Study Group (see p. 446) (formerly the International Jute Organization), which is based in Dhaka. In 1997 eight of the world's major Muslim states, including Bangladesh, established the Developing Eight (D-8), with a view to furthering economic and political co-operation among the member countries.

ECONOMIC AFFAIRS

In 2010, according to estimates by the World Bank, Bangladesh's gross national income (GNI), measured at average 2008–10 prices, was US $104,478m., equivalent to $700 per head (or $1,800 per head on an international purchasing-power parity basis). During 2001–10, it was estimated, the population increased at an average annual rate of 1.3%, while gross domestic product (GDP) per head increased, in real terms, by an average of 4.5% per year. Overall GDP increased at an average annual rate of 5.9% in 2001–10. According to the Asian Development Bank (ADB), GDP grew by 5.7% in 2009, by 6.1% in 2010 and by 6.7% in 2011.

Agriculture (including hunting, forestry and fishing) contributed an estimated 18.4% of total GDP in 2010/11, according to provisional figures. In 2006 48.1% of the total employed labour force was engaged in that sector. The principal sources of revenue in the agricultural sector are jute, tea, shrimps and fish. Raw jute and jute goods accounted for 4.5% of total export earnings in 2009/10. Despite severe flooding in 2000, Bangladesh achieved self-sufficiency in basic foods for the first time in 2000/01, mainly owing to increased rice production. According to the ADB, the GDP of the agricultural sector increased by 5.0% in 2010/11. Agricultural GDP expanded at an average annual rate of 3.4% in 2001–10.

Industry (including mining, manufacturing, power and construction) employed 14.6% of the working population in 2006. The industrial sector contributed an estimated 28.6% of total GDP in 2010/11. During 2001–10, according to the ADB, industrial GDP increased at an average annual rate of 7.4%; growth in the industrial sector was 6.5% in 2009/10 and 8.2% in 2010/11.

Recent discoveries of huge reserves of natural gas appeared to offer opportunities both in terms of domestic fuel self-sufficiency and, in the longer term, export potential. Bangladesh's proven reserves of natural gas totalled 400,000m. cu m at the end of 2010. According to the US Geological Survey, production of natural gas increased from 17,014m. cu m in 2006/07 to 19,000m. cu m in 2008/09. In November 2004 the US company Unocal signed an agreement with the state-owned Petrobangla corporation to develop the country's most extensive gas field, at Bibiyana. Bangladesh possesses substantial deposits of coal (estimated at more than 1,000m. metric tons, although difficulties of exploitation continue to make coal imports necessary) and petroleum.

Manufacturing contributed an estimated 18.2% of GDP in 2010/11, according to official figures. The sector employed 11.0% of the working population in 2006. The principal branches of the manufacturing sector include textiles, food products, garments and chemicals. During 2001–10, according to the ADB, manufacturing GDP increased at an average annual rate of 7.5%; the GDP of the manufacturing sector grew by 5.7% in 2009/10.

The construction sector contributed 8.2% of GDP in 2010/11, and engaged 3.2% of the employed labour force in 2006. During 2001–10, according to the ADB, the GDP of the sector increased at an average annual rate of 7.3%; sectoral GDP grew by 5.8% in 2009/10.

Energy is derived principally from natural gas (which contributed 89.0% of total electricity output in 2008). Imports of petroleum products comprised 8.5% of the cost of total imports in 2009/10, according to official provisional figures. In March 2010 it was reported that, owing to under-investment in new electrical-generating capacity, Bangladesh produced only about 3,800 MW of electricity per day against peak demand of approximately 6,000 MW. In early 2012 the Bangladesh Power Development Board signed a joint venture agreement with the National Thermal Power Corporation of India for the construction of a 1,320-MW coal-fired power plant, at an estimated cost of US $1,500m.

The services sector accounted for an estimated 53.0% of total GDP in 2010/11. In 2006 37.3% of the employed labour force was engaged in the sector. According to the ADB, the GDP of the services sector increased at an average annual rate of 6.1% during 2001–10; the sector's GDP expanded by 6.6% in 2010/11.

In 2010, according to the IMF, Bangladesh recorded a visible trade deficit of US $5,484.6m., while there was a surplus of $2,502.4m. on the current account of the balance of payments. In 2010, according to the ADB, the principal sources of imports were the People's Republic of China (which contributed 22.3% of the total) and India (contributing 11.8%), while the USA was the principal market for exports (accounting for 22.1% of the total). Other major trading partners were Japan, Singapore, Germany and the United Kingdom. The principal exports in 2009/10 were knitwear, hosiery products and ready-made garments (together accounting for an estimated 77.1% of total export revenue), frozen shrimp and fish, and raw jute and jute goods. The principal imports were petroleum products, textiles, capital machinery, and iron and steel.

In 2009/10, according to the ADB, the overall fiscal deficit of the central Government amounted to the equivalent of 3.9% of GDP, compared with 3.7% in the previous year. According to ADB figures, Bangladesh's total external debt was US $21,792m. at the end of 2010. In that year, the cost of debt-servicing long-term public and publicly guaranteed debt and repayments to the IMF was equivalent to 3.0% of the value of goods, services and income (excluding workers' remittances). The annual rate of inflation averaged 6.8% in 2001–10, according to the International Labour Organization. According to the Bangladesh Bank, consumer prices increased by an average of 6.7% in 2008/09 and 7.3% in 2009/10. According to the ADB, about 4.2% of the total labour force was unemployed in 2006.

The problems confronting developing Bangladesh include widespread poverty, severe infrastructural deficiencies and the economy's heavy dependence on foreign aid. Limited success in diversifying the national export base has been achieved, particularly within the information and communications technology industry. Government expenditure of some 611,000m. taka was allocated to the power and energy sectors in 2010/11. A series of loans granted by the ADB in 2010 and 2011 were also expected to assist efforts to address Bangladesh's infrastructural deficiencies. In October 2010 the ADB announced a US $100m. loan for the establishment of a cross-border electricity transmission grid between Bangladesh and India, which would provide for the import to Bangladesh of 500 MW of Indian electricity. In the following month the ADB agreed to an additional loan, of $108m., to be disbursed on improving Bangladesh's urban planning and infrastructure, and a separate loan, of $615m., to fund construction of a bridge over the Padma river, which would constitute Bangladesh's first fixed river-crossing for road traffic and was to link south-western Bangladesh with the northern and eastern regions. (The World Bank approved a loan of $1,200m. for the Padma bridge project in April 2011, but suspended funding in October owing to corruption allegations—see Contemporary Political History.) In August 2011 the ADB extended a further $300m. loan for construction of an energy-efficient, combined-cycle, natural gas power plant, which was intended to address the country's ongoing power shortages. A new Country Partnership Strategy for Bangladesh covering the period 2011–15 was approved by the ADB in October 2011, and included a $4,500m. investment programme intended to address, *inter alia*, infrastructural deficits, a shortage of skilled labour and the effects of rapid urbanization; the programme was to prioritize agriculture, education, energy, finance, transport and urban development. Meanwhile, the failure of the Bangladeshi Government to meet a number of stipulated tax and banking regulations caused discussions to stall with the IMF on a new three-year Extended Credit Facility (ECF) worth $991m., which had been approved in principle in December 2010 and was intended to elevate Bangladesh to a higher growth trajectory, in order to accelerate poverty reduction and achieve the status of a middle-income country by the 2020s. Following a visit to Dhaka by an IMF delegation in late 2011, during which discussions regarding a possible resumption of the ECF were held, the IMF noted the need for a strong policy response to macroeconomic and structural challenges posed by the recent weakening in the global economic environment and rising oil imports and subsidy costs, and for further efforts to tighten monetary and fiscal policy. However, it was hoped that a new ECF agreement might be concluded during 2012. Meanwhile, growth in foreign remittances declined from a peak of 32.4% in 2007/08 to 6.1% in 2010/11, primarily owing to an ongoing decline in labour migration rates. According to the ADB, GDP growth increased from 6.1% in 2010 to 6.7% in 2011, bolstered by robust export performance; growth was forecast to increase further to 7.0% in 2012. However, inflation remained high, at 8.8% in 2011, and was forecast to rise to 11.0% in 2012.

PUBLIC HOLIDAYS

2013: 23 January* (Eid-i-Milad-un-Nabi, Birth of the Prophet), 21 February (Shaheed Day and International Mother Language Day), 17 March (Birth of the Father of the Nation), 26 March (Independence Day), 14 April (Bengali New Year), 1 May (May Day), 25 May* (Buddha Purnima), 23 June* (Shab-i Bharat), 1 July (Bank Holiday), 2 August* (Jumatul Wida), 3 August* (Shab-i Qadr), 7 August* (Id al-Fitr, end of Ramadan), 15 August (National Mourning Day), 28 August* (Janmashtami), 14 October* (Id al-Adha, Feast of the Sacrifice; Durga Puja), 13 November* (Ashoura), 16 December (Victory Day), 25 December (Christmas Day), 31 December (Bank Holiday).

* Dates of certain religious holidays are subject to the sighting of the moon, and there are also optional holidays for different religious groups.

Statistical Survey

Source (unless otherwise stated): Bangladesh Bureau of Statistics, Statistics Division, Ministry of Planning, E-27/A, Agargaon, Sher-e-bangla Nagar, Dhaka 1207; tel. (2) 9118045; fax (2) 9111064; e-mail ndbp@bangla.net; internet www.bbs.gov.bd.

Area and Population

AREA, POPULATION AND DENSITY

Area (sq km)	143,998*
Population (census results)†	
22 January 2001	124,355,263
15 March 2011 (preliminary)	
Males	71,255,000
Females	71,064,000
Total	142,319,000
Density (per sq km) at 2011 census	988.3

* 55,598 sq miles.

† Including adjustment for underenumeration, estimated to have been 4.95% in 2001.

POPULATION BY AGE AND SEX

(UN estimates at mid-2012)

	Males	Females	Total
0–14	23,428,692	22,358,807	45,787,499
15–64	50,162,127	49,364,277	99,526,404
65 and over	3,503,869	3,591,000	7,094,869
Total	77,094,688	75,314,084	152,408,772

Note: Estimates not adjusted to take account of 2011 census.

Source: UN, *World Population Prospects: The 2010 Revision*.

ADMINISTRATIVE DIVISIONS

('000 population at 2011 census, preliminary)

Division	Area (sq km)	Population	Density (per sq km)
Barisal	13,297	8,147	612.7
Chittagong	33,771	28,079	831.5
Dhaka	31,120	46,729	1,501.6
Khulna	22,272	15,563	698.8
Rajshahi	18,197	18,329	531.1
Rangpur*	16,317	15,665	960.0
Sylhet	12,596	9,807	778.6
Total	147,570	142,319	988.3

* Officially designated an administrative division in 2010, formerly part of Rajshahi division.

PRINCIPAL TOWNS

(population at 1991 census)*

Dhaka (capital)	3,612,850	Comilla	135,313
Chittagong	1,392,860	Nawabganj	130,577
Khulna	663,340	Dinajpur	127,815
Rajshahi	294,056	Bogra	120,170
Narayanganj	276,549	Sylhet	114,300
Sitakunda	274,903	Brahmanbaria	109,032
Rangpur	191,398	Tangail	106,004
Mymensingh (Nasirabad)	188,713	Jamalpur	103,556
Barisal (Bakerganj)	170,232	Pabna	103,277
Tongi (Tungi)	168,702	Naogaon	101,266
Jessore	139,710	Sirajganj	99,669

* Figures in each case refer to the city proper. The population of the largest urban agglomerations at the 1991 census was: Dhaka 6,487,459 (including Narayanganj and Tongi); Chittagong 2,079,968 (including Sitakunda); Khulna 921,365; Rajshahi 507,435; Mymensingh 273,350; Sylhet 225,541; Comilla 225,259; Rangpur 208,294; Barisal 202,746; Jessore 169,349; Bogra 161,155.

Mid-2008 (official estimates): *City Corporations:* Dhaka 7,000,940; Chittagong 2,579,107; Khulna 855,650; Rajshahi 472,775; Sylhet 463,198; Barisal 210,374. *Statistical Metropolitan Areas (SMA):* Dhaka 12,797,394; Chittagong 3,858,093; Khulna 1,388,425; Rajshahi 775,495.

Mid-2010 (incl. suburbs, UN estimates): Dhaka 14,648,354; Chittagong 4,961,826; Khulna 1,682,330; Rajshahi 878,038 (Source: UN, *World Urbanization Prospects: The 2009 Revision*).

BIRTHS, MARRIAGES AND DEATHS*

(crude rates per 1,000 persons)

	Live births	Marriages	Deaths
2001	18.9	8.9	4.8
2002	20.1	9.5	5.1
2003	20.9	10.4	5.9
2004	20.8	12.4	5.8
2005	20.7	n.a.	5.8
2006	20.6	12.5	5.6
2007	20.9	12.5	6.2
2008	20.5	11.6	6.0

* Estimates based on sample vital registration system (SVRS). According to UN estimates, the average annual rates per 1,000 for births and deaths were: Births 29.1 in 1995–2000, 25.4 in 2000–05, 21.5 in 2005–10; Deaths 8.0 in 1995–2000, 6.9 in 2000–05, 6.3 in 2005–10 (Source: UN, *World Population Prospects: The 2010 Revision*).

1997 (provisional): Registered live births 3,057,000 (birth rate 24.6 per 1,000); Registered deaths 958,000 (death rate 7.7 per 1,000) (Source: UN, *Population and Vital Statistics Report*).

Marriages: 1,181,000 in 1997 (Source: UN, *Demographic Yearbook*).

Life expectancy (years at birth, WHO estimates): 65 (males 64; females 66) in 2009 (Source: WHO, *World Health Statistics*).

ECONOMICALLY ACTIVE POPULATION*
(sample survey, '000 persons aged 15 years and over, year ending June 2000)

	Males	Females	Total
Agriculture, hunting, forestry and fishing	17,256	14,914	32,171
Mining and quarrying	107	188	295
Manufacturing	2,346	1,436	3,783
Electricity, gas and water	116	18	134
Construction	999	100	1,099
Trade, restaurants and hotels	5,769	506	6,275
Transport, storage and communications	2,432	77	2,509
Financing, insurance, real estate and business services	357	46	403
Community, social and personal services	1,243	1,726	2,969
Sub-total	30,625	19,011	49,638
Activities not adequately defined	1,744	384	2,126
Total employed	32,369	19,395	51,764
Unemployed	1,083	666	1,750
Total labour force	33,452	20,061	53,514

* Figures exclude members of the armed forces.

Note: Totals may not be equal to sum of components, owing to rounding.

Source: ILO.

2006 (labour force survey, million persons aged 15 years and over, year ending 30 June): Agriculture, forestry and fishing 22.8; Mining and quarrying 0.1; Manufacturing 5.2; Electricity, gas and water 0.1; Construction 1.5; Trade, hotels and restaurants 7.8; Transport, storage and communications 4.0; Finance, real estate and business services 0.7; Health, education, public administration and defence 2.6; Community and personal services 2.6; *Total employed* 47.4; Unemployed 2.1; *Total labour force* 49.5.

Health and Welfare

KEY INDICATORS

Total fertility rate (children per woman, 2009)	2.3
Under-five mortality rate (per 1,000 live births, 2009)	54
HIV/AIDS (% of persons aged 15–49, 2009)	<0.1
Physicians (per 1,000 head, 2005)	0.3
Hospital beds (per 1,000 head, 2001)	0.3
Health expenditure (2008): US $ per head (PPP)	44
Health expenditure (2008): % of GDP	3.3
Health expenditure (2008): public (% of total)	31.4
Access to water (% of persons, 2008)	80
Access to sanitation (% of persons, 2008)	53
Total carbon dioxide emissions ('000 metric tons, 2007)	43,715.2
Carbon dioxide emissions per head (metric tons, 2007)	0.3
Human Development Index (2011): ranking	146
Human Development Index (2011): value	0.500

For sources and definitions, see explanatory note on p. vi.

Agriculture

PRINCIPAL CROPS
('000 metric tons, year ending 30 June)

	2007/08	2008/09	2009/10
Wheat	844	849	901
Maize	1,346	730	887
Rice, paddy	46,742	47,724	49,355*
Millet	13	12	24*
Potatoes	6,648	5,268	7,930
Sweet potatoes	307	305	307
Sugar cane	4,984	5,233	5,304
Other sugar crops	302	313	315
Beans, dry	40	49	53†
Lentils	72	61	71
Groundnuts, with shell	44	47	53
Areca nuts (betel)	98	105	92
Coconuts	88*	77*	90†
Rapeseed	228	203	222
Sesame seed	28	32	45*
Linseed	8	7	7
Seed cotton*	39	36	47
Cabbages and other brassicas	211	206	220
Lettuce and chicory	34	33	35
Spinach	44	43	45
Tomatoes	143	151	190
Cauliflowers and broccoli	156	161	160
Pumpkins, squash and gourds	316	340	352
Onions, dry	889	735	872
Garlic	145	155	164
Beans, green	83	88	89
Cantaloupes and other melons	205	200	189
Guavas, mangoes and mangosteens	803	828	1,048
Pineapples	210	229	234
Bananas	877	836	818
Papayas	104	130	113
Tea	59	60	60
Tobacco, unmanufactured	40	40	55
Ginger	77	73	75
Jute	849	924	1,201†

* Unofficial figure(s).
† FAO estimate.

Aggregate production ('000 metric tons, may include official, semi-official or estimated data): Total cereals 48,947 in 2007/08, 49,316 in 2008/09, 51,169 in 2009/10; Total roots and tubers 6,955 in 2007/08, 5,573 in 2008/09, 8,237 in 2009/10; Total vegetables (incl. melons) 3,473 in 2007/08, 3,421 in 2008/09, 3,763 in 2009/10; Total pulses 202 in 2007/08, 205 in 2008/09, 225 in 2009/10; Total fruits (excl. melons) 3,558 in 2007/08, 3,632 in 2008/09, 3,955 in 2009/10.

Source: FAO.

LIVESTOCK
('000 head, year ending September)

	2008	2009	2010
Cattle	22,900	22,976	23,051
Buffaloes	1,260	1,304	1,349
Sheep*	1,644	1,730	1,820
Goats*	56,400	60,600	65,000
Chickens	212,470	221,394	228,035
Ducks*	23,000	24,000	25,000

* FAO estimates.

Source: FAO.

LIVESTOCK PRODUCTS
('000 metric tons, FAO estimates)

	2008	2009	2010
Cattle meat	187	188	189
Buffalo meat	5.6	5.8	6.0
Sheep meat	3.5	3.7	3.9
Goat meat	210	225	242
Chicken meat	151	157	162
Duck meat	23.0	23.0	25.0
Cows' milk	825	827	830
Buffalo milk	34	35	36
Sheep's milk	32.8	34.5	36.4
Goats' milk	2,168	2,328	2,496
Hen eggs (in shell)	186	154	188
Other poultry eggs (in shell)	79.2	65.7	67.7

Source: FAO.

Forestry

ROUNDWOOD REMOVALS
('000 cubic metres, excl. bark)

	2007	2008	2009
Sawlogs, veneer logs and logs for sleepers*	174	174	174
Pulpwood†	18	18	18
Other industrial wood†	90	90	90
Fuel wood†	27,508	27,433	27,359
Total	27,790	27,715	27,641

* Annual output assumed to be unchanged since 1996.
† FAO estimates.

2010: Production assumed to be unchanged from 2009.

Source: FAO.

SAWNWOOD PRODUCTION
('000 cubic metres, incl. railway sleepers)

	2001	2002	2003
Total (all broadleaved)	79*	255	388

* FAO estimate.

2004–10: Production assumed to be unchanged from 2003 (FAO estimates).

Source: FAO.

Fishing

('000 metric tons, live weight)

	2007	2008	2009
Capture	1,494.2	1,557.8	1,821.6
Freshwater fishes	924.3	891.0	1,028.1
Hilsa shad	279.2	290.0	298.9
Marine fishes	236.5	179.4	259.5
Aquaculture	945.8	1,005.5	1,064.3
Roho labeo	183.2	203.2	227.0
Catla	155.2	151.7	178.9
Silver carp	168.0	165.0	172.5
Penaeus shrimps	63.6	67.2	8.1
Total catch	2,440.0	2,563.3	2,885.9

Source: FAO.

Mining

(million cubic metres, year ending 30 June)

	2006/07	2007/08	2008/09
Natural gas	17,014	18,516	19,000

Source: US Geological Survey.

Industry

SELECTED PRODUCTS
('000 metric tons, unless otherwise indicated; year ending 30 June)

	2007/08	2008/09	2009/10
Refined sugar	163.8	79.9	62.2
Cigarettes (million)	24,180	23,641	23,679
Cotton yarn ('000 bales)*	951	981	1,006
Woven cotton fabrics ('000 metres)	46,079	50,566	52,975
Jute goods	295.3	n.a.	n.a.
Paper	24.1	24.2	18.7
Fertilizers	1,581.4	1,342.0	1,138.6

* 1 bale = 180 kg.

Cement ('000 metric tons): 2,195.6 in 2005/06.

Electric energy (million kWh): 22,741 in 2005/06.

Source: Bangladesh Bank.

Finance

CURRENCY AND EXCHANGE RATES

Monetary Units:
100 poisha = 1 taka.

Sterling, Dollar and Euro Equivalents (30 December 2011):
£1 sterling = 126.553 taka;
US $1 = 81.853 taka;
€1 = 105.909 taka;
1,000 taka = £7.90 = $12.22 = €9.44.

Average Exchange Rate (taka per US $):
2009 69.039
2010 69.649
2011 74.152

BUDGET
(million taka, year ending 30 June)

Revenue*	2008/09	2009/10†	2010/11‡
Taxation	528,660	639,560	760,420
Import duties	84,400	104,300	108,850
Income and profit taxes	134,330	165,600	210,050
Excise duties	2,830	2,610	2,750
Value-added tax	191,180	227,950	270,920
Other revenue	112,310	155,280	168,050
Total	640,970	794,840	928,470

Expenditure§	2008/09	2009/10†	2010/11‡
General public services	63,770	127,140	160,420
Local government and rural development	14,890	16,320	18,660
Defence	61,770	77,430	89,480
Public order and safety	52,940	61,900	65,010
Education and technology	90,060	117,960	133,140
Health	31,690	40,030	46,560
Social security and welfare	62,730	64,610	75,720
Housing	6,440	7,130	7,930
Recreation, culture and religious affairs	7,050	7,230	9,120
Fuel and energy	300	370	400
Agriculture, forestry and fishing	77,420	81,090	82,200
Industrial and economic services	3,680	3,950	3,980
Transport and communications	23,590	29,700	33,120
Interest payments	151,800	146,460	147,090
Gross current expenditure	648,190	781,380	872,840

* Excluding grants, loans and food account transactions.
† Revised figures.
‡ Forecasts.
§ Non-development expenditure, excluding loans and advances, domestic and foreign debt, food account operations and structural adjustment.

Note: Totals may not be equivalent to the sum of components, owing to rounding.

Source: Ministry of Finance (Finance Division).

PUBLIC-SECTOR DEVELOPMENT EXPENDITURE
(departmental allocation, million taka, year ending 30 June)

	2007/08	2008/09*	2009/10†
Agriculture	19,760	20,040	23,750
Local government and rural development	55,460	58,250	71,510
Industrial and economic services	3,290	5,360	5,240
Fuel and energy	35,560	28,760	42,780
Transport and communications	27,450	25,540	47,990
Housing	1,840	7,120	5,650
Education and technology	29,960	32,050	41,050
Health	23,630	26,150	30,750
Social security and welfare	10,690	15,980	16,940

—continued	2007/08	2008/09*	2009/10†
Public order and safety	3,930	5,080	7,220
Defence	1,750	980	2,610
Recreation, culture and religious affairs	2,760	2,700	3,400
Public services	16,950	14,320	17,500
Total development expenditure‡	233,040	242,340	316,390

* Revised figures.

† Forecasts.

‡ Including transfers (million taka): 8,040 in 2007/08; 12,340 in 2008/09; 11,390 in 2009/10.

Note: Totals may not be equal to the sum of components, owing to rounding.

Source: Ministry of Finance (Economic Relations Division).

INTERNATIONAL RESERVES

(US $ million at 31 December)

	2008	2009	2010
Gold*	99.3	124.4	613.2
IMF special drawing rights	2.1	718.5	659.6
Reserve position in IMF	0.5	0.5	0.6
Foreign exchange	5,686.7	9,499.9	9,904.1
Total	5,788.6	10,343.3	11,177.5

* Valued at market-related prices.

Source: IMF, *International Financial Statistics*.

MONEY SUPPLY

(million taka at 31 December)

	2008	2009	2010
Currency outside depository corporations	370,820	409,163	523,528
Transferable deposits	269,689	336,851	466,526
Other deposits	2,143,498	2,621,705	3,115,468
Securities other than shares	429,396	496,861	574,059
Broad money	3,213,403	3,864,580	4,679,581

Source: IMF, *International Financial Statistics*.

COST OF LIVING

(Consumer Price Index, year ending 30 June; base: 1995/96 = 100)

	2007/08	2008/09	2009/10
Food, beverages and tobacco	206.8	221.6	240.6
Rent, fuel and lighting	174.7	184.5	191.5
Household requisites	178.6	194.8	215.0
Clothing and footwear	164.5	173.1	181.3
Transport and communications	211.0	222.1	214.4
All items (incl. others)	193.5	206.4	221.5

Source: Bangladesh Bank.

NATIONAL ACCOUNTS

('000 million taka at current prices, year ending 30 June)

Expenditure on the Gross Domestic Product

	2007/08	2008/09	2009/10
Government final consumption expenditure	288.3	319.0	374.6
Private final consumption expenditure	4,061.4	4,589.4	5,234.2
Gross capital formation	1,321.3	1,488.4	1,728.3
Statistical discrepancy	246.3	189.2	29.4
Total domestic expenditure	5,917.3	6,586.0	7,366.5
Exports of goods and services	1,110.2	1,194.4	1,283.1
Less Imports of goods and services	1,569.3	1,632.4	1,725.8
GDP in purchasers' values	5,458.2	6,148.0	6,923.8
GDP at constant 1995/96 prices	3,217.3	3,402.0	3,600.5

Source: mostly IMF, *International Financial Statistics*.

Gross Domestic Product by Economic Activity

	2008/09	2009/10	2010/11*
Agriculture and forestry	894.3	1,005.9	1,133.9
Fishing	218.1	242.3	269.9
Mining and quarrying	70.9	81.1	90.2
Manufacturing	1,064.5	1,201.1	1,384.3
Electricity, gas and water	65.4	72.0	77.1
Construction	501.3	556.6	623.3
Wholesale and retail trade	882.8	1,003.0	1,139.0
Hotels and restaurants	44.6	51.5	59.7
Transport, storage and communications	642.8	718.8	840.2
Finance and insurance	102.5	123.0	144.6
Real estate, renting and business services	416.2	456.8	498.9
Public administration and defence	163.6	187.6	219.8
Education	154.9	179.1	209.6
Health and social work	133.9	151.4	175.5
Other community, social and personal services	583.6	684.7	750.6
Sub-total	5,939.2	6,714.7	7,616.6
Import duties	208.7	228.6	258.4
GDP in purchasers' values	6,148.0	6,943.2	7,875.0

* Provisional figures.

Source: Bangladesh Bank.

BALANCE OF PAYMENTS

(US $ million)

	2008	2009	2010
Exports of goods f.o.b.	15,501.8	15,072.6	19,238.7
Imports of goods f.o.b.	−21,505.9	−19,677.7	−24,723.4
Trade balance	−6,004.1	−4,605.1	−5,484.6
Exports of services	1,995.9	1,976.1	2,414.2
Imports of services	−3,664.4	−3,396.3	−4,352.5
Balance on goods and services	−7,672.6	−6,025.3	−7,422.9
Other income received	192.3	49.1	112.5
Other income paid	−1,211.2	−1,448.4	−1,518.9
Balance on goods, services and income	−8,691.6	−7,424.6	−8,829.3
Current transfers received	9,768.0	11,246.7	11,702.5
Current transfers paid	−150.3	−265.9	−370.7
Current balance	926.2	3,556.1	2,502.4
Capital account (net)	490.5	474.9	470.9
Direct investment from abroad	1,009.6	713.4	967.6
Portfolio investment assets	−57.6	−11.7	−778.6
Portfolio investment liabilities	19.2	43.3	165.9
Other investment assets	−2,188.1	−1,336.1	−2,657.4
Other investment liabilities	948.6	1,542.4	676.3
Net errors and omissions	−129.6	−647.8	−395.5
Overall balance	1,018.8	4,334.6	951.5

Source: IMF, *International Financial Statistics*.

FOREIGN AID DISBURSEMENTS

(US $ million, year ending 30 June)

	2003/04	2004/05	2005/06
Bilateral donors	495	440	406
Canada	21	8	62
China, People's Republic	—	19	33
Denmark	20	5	14
France	7	—	—
Germany	26	24	15
Japan	79	45	31
Kuwait	7	5	9
Netherlands	41	5	13
Norway	6	4	11
Sweden	11	—	—
United Kingdom	94	85	157
USA	12	8	4

—continued	2003/04	2004/05	2005/06
Multilateral donors	538	1,049	1,162
Asian Development Bank	172	208	265
International Development Association	225	696	635
European Union	21	8	73
International Fund for Agricultural Development	15	9	14
UN Development Programme	36	—	111
UNICEF	30	26	18
Islamic Development Bank	17	70	25
Total aid disbursements	1,033	1,488	1,568

Source: IMF, *Bangladesh: Statistical Appendix* (July 2007).

External Trade

PRINCIPAL COMMODITIES
(US $ million, year ending 30 June)

Imports c.i.f.	2007/08	2008/09	2009/10
Food grains	1,410	882	837
Edible oil	1,006	865	1,050
Petroleum products	2,058	1,997	2,021
Chemicals	890	960	972
Plastics, rubber and articles thereof	808	840	966
Cotton	1,212	1,291	1,439
Yarn	691	792	718
Textiles	1,892	2,099	1,986
Iron and steel	1,179	1,502	1,453
Machinery	1,664	1,420	1,595
Total (incl. others)*	21,629	22,507	23,738

* Figures include imports from Economic Processing Zone (EPZ): 1,294 in 2007/08; 1,302 in 2008/09; 1,413 in 2009/10.

Exports f.o.b.	2007/08	2008/09	2009/10
Raw jute	165	148	196
Jute goods (excl. carpets)	318	269	540
Leather and leather products	284	177	231
Frozen shrimp and fish	534	455	437
Ready-made garments	5,167	5,919	6,013
Knitwear and hosiery products	5,533	6,429	6,483
Total (incl. others)*	14,111	15,565	16,205

* Figures include exports from Economic Processing Zone (EPZ): 1,730 in 2007/08; 1,900 in 2008/09; 2,150 in 2009/10.

Source: Bangladesh Bank.

PRINCIPAL TRADING PARTNERS
(US $ million)

Imports c.i.f.	2008	2009	2010
China, People's Republic	3,511	3,524	6,133
Hong Kong	858	783	921
India	3,498	2,749	3,253
Indonesia	496	584	981
Japan	975	1,010	1,147
Korea, Republic	796	805	849
Kuwait	1,797	374	599
Malaysia	621	973	1,249
Singapore	1,682	1,646	1,796
Thailand	508	585	866
Total (incl. others)	23,821	21,803	27,487

Exports f.o.b.	2008	2009	2010
Belgium	386	311	454
Canada	435	502	753
France	864	931	981
Germany	1,804	1,833	2,144
India	319	268	307
Italy	528	531	619
Netherlands	647	848	764
Spain	489	495	645
United Kingdom	1,169	1,242	1,375
USA	2,823	2,910	3,946
Total (incl. others)	13,628	14,378	17,879

Note: Data reflect the IMF's direction of trade methodology, and, as a result, the totals may not be equal to those presented for trade in commodities.

Source: Asian Development Bank.

Transport

RAILWAYS
(traffic, year ending 30 June)

	2007/08	2008/09	2009/10
Passengers ('000)	53,816	65,029	65,627
Passenger-km (million)	5,609	6,801	7,305
Freight ('000 metric tons)	3,282	3,010	2,450
Freight ton-km (million)	870	800	641

Source: Bangladesh Railway.

ROAD TRAFFIC
(motor vehicles in use at 31 December)

	2006	2007	2008
Passenger cars	195,861	158,109	177,638
Buses and coaches	66,604	31,622	71,264
Lorries and vans	57,330	168,649	138,512
Motorcycles and mopeds	389,514	653,515	768,121

Source: IRF, *World Road Statistics*.

SHIPPING

Merchant Fleet
(registered at 31 December)

	2007	2008	2009
Number of vessels	320	322	329
Total displacement ('000 grt)	440.5	440.2	644.6

Source: IHS Fairplay, *World Fleet Statistics*.

International Sea-borne Freight Traffic
('000 metric tons, year ending 30 June)

	2008	2009	2010
Total goods loaded	924	4,056	4,656
Total goods unloaded	18,012	31,944	38,604

Source: UN, *Monthly Bulletin of Statistics*.

CIVIL AVIATION
(traffic on scheduled services)

	2007	2008	2009
Kilometres flown (million)	23	26	24
Passengers carried ('000)	1,287	1,516	1,301
Passenger-km (million)	4,186	4,741	4,344
Total ton-km (million)	588	474	433

Source: UN, *Statistical Yearbook*.

Tourism

TOURIST ARRIVALS BY COUNTRY OF NATIONALITY

	2005	2006	2007
Canada	4,519	5,085	10,573
China, People's Republic	6,892	6,955	11,825
India	86,231	60,516	78,568
Japan	6,269	4,370	5,851
Korea, Republic	5,332	4,135	6,020
Malaysia	1,045	2,671	6,408
Nepal	3,378	3,422	4,537
Pakistan	5,671	6,680	12,224
United Kingdom	27,292	37,136	51,314
USA	13,422	16,516	34,638
Total (incl. others)	207,662	200,311	289,110

Tourism receipts (US $ million, incl. passenger transport): 79 in 2005; 80 in 2006; 76 in 2007; 91 in 2008.

Source: World Tourism Organization.

Communications Media

	2008	2009	2010
Telephones ('000 main lines in use)	1,344.5	1,522.9	900.0
Mobile cellular telephones ('000 subscribers)	44,640.0	52,430.0	68,650.0
Internet users ('000)	556.0	617.3	n.a.
Broadband subscribers ('000)	50.0	55.0	60.0

Personal computers: 3,500,000 (22.5 per 1,000 persons) in 2006.

Radio receivers ('000 in use): 6,150 in 1997.

Television receivers ('000 in use): 2,200 in 2001.

Newspapers (provisional, 1998): *Daily:* 233 titles with average circulation of 6.7m. *Non-daily incl. periodicals:* 509 titles with average circulation of 9.3m.

Books published: 483 titles in 1998.

Sources: mainly UNESCO, *Statistical Yearbook*; UN, *Statistical Yearbook*; International Telecommunication Union.

Education

(2009/10)

	Institutions	Teachers	Students
Primary schools†	82,981	344,789*	16,539,000
Secondary schools‡	21,015	264,863	7,699,565
Universities (government)*	24	6,852	115,929

* 2004/05.

† 2008/09.

‡ Estimates.

Technical and vocational institutes (2004/05): 2,728 institutions, 18,185 teachers, 241,336 students.

Source: Ministry of Education.

Pupil-teacher ratio (primary education, UNESCO estimate): 45.8 in 2008/09 (Source: UNESCO Institute for Statistics).

Adult literacy rate (UNESCO estimates): 55.9% (males 60.7%; females 51.0%) in 2009 (Source: UNESCO Institute for Statistics).

Directory

The Government

HEAD OF STATE

President: ZILLUR RAHMAN (took office 12 February 2009).

COUNCIL OF MINISTERS

(May 2012)

The Government is formed by the Bangladesh Awami League.

Prime Minister and Minister of the Armed Forces Division, the Cabinet Division, Defence, and Public Administration: Sheikh HASINA WAJED.

Minister of Foreign Affairs: Dr DIPU MONI.

Minister of Finance: A. M. A. MUHITH.

Minister of Law, Justice and Parliamentary Affairs: SHAFIQ AHMED.

Minister of Home Affairs: SAHARA KHATUN.

Minister of Planning: Air Vice Marshal (retd) A. K. KHANDAKER.

Minister of Post and Telecommunications: RAZIUDDIN AHMED RAJU.

Minister of Agriculture: MATIA CHOWDHURY.

Minister of Textiles and Jute: ABDUL LATIF SIDDIQUI.

Minister of Local Government, Rural Development and Co-operatives: SYED ASHRAFUL ISLAM.

Minister of Labour and Employment, and Expatriates' Welfare and Overseas Employment: KHANDAKER MOSHARRAF HOSSAIN.

Minister of Land: REZAUL KARIM HIRA.

Minister of Information and Cultural Affairs: ABUL KALAM AZAD.

Minister of Information and Communication Technology: SYED ABUL HOSSAIN.

Minister of Social Welfare: ENAMUL HAQ MOSTAFA SHAHID.

Minister of Industries: DILIP BARUA.

Minister of Water Resources: ROMESH CHANDRA SEN.

Minister of Civil Aviation and Tourism: Lt-Col (retd) MD FARUK KHAN.

Minister of Commerce: G. M. QUADER.

Minister of Communications and Acting Minister of Railways: OBAIDUL QUADER.

Minister of Food and Disaster Management: Dr ABDUR RAZZAK.

Minister of Primary and Mass Education: Dr MOHAMMAD AFSARUL AMIN.

Minister of Shipping: SHAHJAHAN KHAN.

Minister of Health and Family Welfare: Prof. A. F. M. RUHUL HAQUE.

Minister of Education: NURUL ISLAM NAHID.

Minister of Environment and Forests: HASAN MAHMUD.

Minister of Fisheries and Livestock: ABDUL LATIF BISWAS.

In addition, there were 18 Ministers of State.

MINISTRIES

Prime Minister's Office: Old Sangsad Bhaban, Tejgaon, Dhaka 1215; tel. (2) 8151159; fax (2) 8113244; e-mail info@pmo.gov.bd; internet www.pmo.gov.bd.

Ministry of Agriculture: Bangladesh Secretariat, Bhaban 4, Dhaka 1000; tel. (2) 832137; internet www.moa.gov.bd.

Ministry of Chittagong Hill Tracts Affairs: Bangladesh Secretariat, Bhaban 4, Dhaka 1000; tel. (2) 7161774; e-mail nazma@mochta.gov.bd; internet www.mochta.gov.bd.

Ministry of Civil Aviation and Tourism: Bangladesh Secretariat, Bhaban 6, 19th Floor, Dhaka 1000; tel. (2) 7163835; fax (2) 7169206; e-mail info@mocat.gov.bd; internet www.mocat.gov.bd.

Ministry of Commerce: Bangladesh Secretariat, Bhaban 3, Dhaka 1000; tel. (2) 7169687; e-mail mincom@intechworld.net; internet www.mincom.gov.bd.

Ministry of Communications: Bangladesh Secretariat, Bhaban 7, 8th Floor, Dhaka 1000; tel. (2) 7168943; e-mail jsadmin@moc.gov.bd; internet www.moc.gov.bd.

Ministry of Cultural Affairs: Bangladesh Secretariat, Bhaban 6, Dhaka 1000; tel. (2) 9570667; fax (2) 7169008; e-mail sas-moca@mailcity.com; internet www.moca.gov.bd.

Ministry of Defence: Gonobhaban Complex, Sher-i-Bangla Nagar, Dhaka 1207; tel. (2) 8116955; e-mail modgob@bttb.net.bd; internet www.mod.gov.bd.

Ministry of Education: Bangladesh Secretariat, Bhaban 6, 17th–18th Floors, Dhaka 1000; tel. (2) 7168711; fax (2) 7167577; e-mail info@moedu.gov.bd; internet www.moedu.gov.bd.

Ministry of Environment and Forests: Bangladesh Secretariat, Bhaban 6, 13th Floor, Chamber 1307, Dhaka 1000; tel. (2) 7167240; fax (2) 7169210; e-mail dsadmin@moef.gov.bd; internet www.moef.gov.bd.

Ministry of Establishment: Bangladesh Secretariat, Bhaban 1, Dhaka 1000; e-mail info@moestab.gov.bd; internet www.moestab.gov.bd.

Ministry of Expatriates' Welfare and Overseas Employment: Bangladesh Secretariat, Bhaban 7, 4th Floor, Dhaka 1000; tel. (2) 9570086; fax (2) 7171622; e-mail js@probashi.gov.bd; internet probashi.gov.bd.

Ministry of Finance: Bangladesh Secretariat, Bhaban 7, 3rd Floor, Dhaka 1000; tel. (2) 8690202; fax (2) 865581; internet www.mof.gov.bd.

Ministry of Fisheries and Livestock: Bangladesh Secretariat, Bhaban 6, 5th and 14th Floors, Dhaka 1000; tel. (2) 7164700; fax (2) 7161117; e-mail jslmofl@accesstel.net; internet www.mofl.gov.bd.

Ministry of Food and Disaster Management: Bangladesh Secretariat, Bhaban 4, Dhaka 1000; tel. (2) 7160762; e-mail info@food.gov.bd; internet www.mofdm.gov.bd.

Ministry of Foreign Affairs: Segunbagicha, Dhaka 1000; tel. (2) 9562862; fax (2) 9555283; e-mail info@mofabd.org; internet www.mofa.gov.bd.

Ministry of Health and Family Welfare: Bangladesh Secretariat, Bhaban 3, Dhaka; tel. (2) 7160204; fax (2) 9559216; e-mail dsadmin@mohfw.gov.bd; internet www.mohfw.gov.bd.

Ministry of Home Affairs: Bangladesh Secretariat, Bhaban 8, Dhaka; tel. (2) 7169076; fax (2) 7164788; e-mail info@mha.gov.bd; internet www.mha.gov.bd.

Ministry of Housing and Public Works: Bangladesh Secretariat, Bhaban 5, Dhaka 1000; tel. (2) 7164854; fax (2) 7167125; e-mail jsamohpw@bangla.net; internet www.mohpw.gov.bd.

Ministry of Industries: Shilpa Bhaban, 91 Motijheel C/A, Dhaka 1000; tel. (2) 9567024; fax (2) 860588; e-mail indsecy@bttb.net.bd; internet www.moind.gov.bd.

Ministry of Information: Bangladesh Secretariat, Bhaban 4, 8th Floor, Dhaka; tel. (2) 7168555; fax (2) 7167236; e-mail moisecretary@yahoo.com; internet www.moi.gov.bd.

Ministry of Information and Communication Technology: Dhaka.

Ministry of Labour and Employment: Bangladesh Secretariat, Bhaban 7, 5th Floor, Dhaka; tel. (2) 7169215; fax (2) 7168660; e-mail sas@mole.gov.bd; internet www.mole.gov.bd.

Ministry of Land: Bangladesh Secretariat, Bhaban 4, 3rd Floor, Dhaka 1000; tel. (2) 7164131; e-mail info@minland.gov.bd; internet www.minland.gov.bd.

Ministry of Law, Justice and Parliamentary Affairs: Bangladesh Secretariat, Bhaban 4, 7th Floor, Dhaka 1000; tel. (2) 7164693; e-mail info@minlaw.gov.bd; internet www.minlaw.gov.bd.

Ministry of Liberation War Affairs: Transport Pool Bhaban, Secretariat Link Rd, Dhaka; tel. (2) 9550149; e-mail info.molwa@yahoo.com; internet www.molwa.gov.bd.

Ministry of Local Government, Rural Development and Co-operatives: Bangladesh Secretariat, Bhaban 7, Dhaka 1000; tel. (2) 7169179; e-mail info@lgd.gov.bd; internet www.lgd.gov.bd.

Ministry of Planning: Block No. 7, Sher-e-Bangla Nagar, Dhaka; tel. (2) 815142; fax (2) 822210.

Ministry of Post and Telecommunications: Bangladesh Secretariat, Bhaban 7, Dhaka 1000; tel. (2) 7168689; fax (2) 7166670; e-mail info@mopt.gov.bd; internet www.mopt.gov.bd.

Ministry of Power, Energy and Mineral Resources: Bangladesh Secretariat, Bhaban 6, 1st Floor, Dhaka 1000; tel. (2) 9559928; internet www.powerdivision.gov.bd.

Ministry of Primary and Mass Education: Dhaka; tel. (2) 7165167; fax (2) 7168871; e-mail jsadmn@mopme.gov.bd; internet www.mopme.gov.bd.

Ministry of Public Administration: Bangladesh Secretariat, Bhaban 1, Dhaka 1000; tel. (2) 7164080; fax (2) 7169584; e-mail info@mopa.gov.bd; internet www.mopa.gov.bd.

Ministry of Railways: Dhaka.

Ministry of Religious Affairs: Bangladesh Secretariat, Bhaban 8, Dhaka 1000; tel. (2) 7165800; fax (2) 7165040.

Ministry of Science and Technology: Bangladesh Secretariat, Bhaban 6, 9th Floor, Dhaka 1000; tel. (2) 7170840; fax (2) 7169606; e-mail section16@mail.mosict.gov.bd; internet www.mosict.gov.bd.

Ministry of Shipping: Bangladesh Secretariat, Bhaban 6, 8th Floor, Dhaka 1000; tel. (2) 7168033; fax (2) 7160311; internet www.mos.gov.bd.

Ministry of Social Welfare: Bangladesh Secretariat, Bhaban 6, Dhaka 1000; tel. (2) 7160452; fax (2) 7168969; e-mail secsw@bttb.net.bd; internet www.msw.gov.bd.

Ministry of Textiles and Jute: Bangladesh Secretariat, Bhaban 6, 7th and 11th Floors, Dhaka 1000; tel. (2) 7167266; fax (2) 9515536; e-mail sectext@gmail.com; internet www.motj.gov.bd.

Ministry of Water Resources: Bangladesh Secretariat, Bhaban 7, Dhaka 1000; tel. (2) 9514202; e-mail sayfullah77@gmail.com; internet www.mowr.gov.bd.

Ministry of Women and Children's Affairs: Bangladesh Secretariat, Bhaban 6, 3rd Floor, Dhaka 1000; tel. (2) 7163639; fax (2) 7162892; internet mowca.gov.bd.

Ministry of Youth and Sports: Bangladesh Secretariat, Bhaban 7, Dhaka 1000; tel. (2) 7164299; fax (2) 7160683; e-mail pstostateminister@moysports.gov.bd; internet www.moysports.gov.bd.

President and Legislature

PRESIDENT

On 11 February 2009 the Awami League's presidential candidate, ZILLUR RAHMAN, was declared elected unopposed by the Jatiya Sangsad as Bangladesh's new Head of State; he was sworn in on the following day.

JATIYA SANGSAD
(Parliament)

Speaker: ABDUL HAMID.

Deputy Speaker: SHAWKAT ALI.

General Election, 29 December 2008 (unofficial results)

	Seats*
Bangladesh Awami League (AL)†	230
Bangladesh Jatiyatabadi Dal (Bangladesh Nationalist Party—BNP)‡	29
Jatiya Party	27
Jatiya Samajtantrik Dal (Inu)	3
Jamaat-e-Islami Bangladesh	2
Workers' Party of Bangladesh	2
Bangladesh Jatiya Party (BJP)	1
Liberal Democratic Party	1
Independents	4
Vacant	1
Total	300

* In addition to the 300 directly elected members, a further 45 seats are reserved for women members.

† Leader of Grand Alliance.

‡ Leader of Four-Party Alliance.

Election Commission

Bangladesh Election Commission: Block 5/6, Election Commission Secretariat, Sher-e-Bangla Nagar, Dhaka 1207; tel. (2) 8113601; fax (2) 8119819; e-mail ecs@bol-online.com; internet becs.info@gmail.com; f. 1972; independent; commrs appointed by the President; Chief Election Commr KAZI RAKIBUDDIN AHMAD.

Political Organizations

Bangladesh Awami League (AL): 23 Bangabandhu Ave, Dhaka; tel. (2) 9677881; fax (2) 8621155; e-mail info@albd.org; internet www.albd.org; f. 1949; supports parliamentary democracy; advocates socialist economy, but with a private sector, and a secular state; pro-Indian; 28-member central executive committee, 15-member central advisory committee and a 13-member presidium; Pres. Sheikh HASINA WAJED; Gen. Sec. SYED ASHRAFUL ISLAM; c. 1,025,000 mems.

Bangladesh Biplobi Workers' Party (Revolutionary Workers' Party of Bangladesh): 27/8A Topkhana Rd, 3rd Floor, Segun Bagicha, Dhaka 1000; tel. (2) 8121659; fax (2) 9122130; e-mail rwpb2004@gmail.com; Pres. KHANDAKAR ALI ABBAS; Gen. Sec. SAIFUL HAQUE.

Bangladesh Islami Front: 62/1, North Kamalapur, 2nd Floor, Motijheel, Dhaka 1217; fax (2) 9355737; Chair. Allama al-Haj M. A. MANNAN; Gen. Sec. al-Haj M. A. MATIN.

Bangladesh Jamaat-e-Islami: 505 Elephant Rd, Bara Maghbazar, Dhaka 1217; tel. (2) 9331581; fax (2) 8321212; e-mail info@jamaat-e-islami.org; internet www.jamaat-e-islami.org; f. 1941; fmrly known as Jamaat-e-Islami Bangladesh; renamed as above in 2008; Islamist party striving to establish an Islamic state through the democratic process; mem. of the BNP-led four-party alliance; Chair. MAQBUL AHMAD (acting); Sec.-Gen. Dr SHAFIQUR RAHMAN (acting).

Bangladesh Jatiya Party (BJP): 50 DIT Extension Rd, Easternview, 5th Floor, Naya Paltan, Dhaka 1000; tel. (2) 8317634; fax (2) 8319694; f. 1999 as breakaway faction of Jatiya Party; Chair. ANDALIB RAHMAN PARTHO; Gen. Sec. SHAMIM AL MAMUN.

Bangladesh Jatiyatabadi Dal (Bangladesh Nationalist Party—BNP): 28/1 Naya Paltan, VIP Rd, Dhaka 1000; tel. (2) 8351929; fax (2) 8318678; e-mail bnpbd@e-fsbd.net; internet www.bnp-bd.com; f. 1978 by merger of groups supporting Ziaur Rahman, including Jatiyatabadi Gonotantrik Dal (Jagodal—Nationalist Democratic Party); right of centre; favours multi-party democracy and parliamentary system of govt; Chair. Begum KHALEDA ZIA; Sr Vice-Chair. TARIQUE RAHMAN; Sec.-Gen. MIRZA FAKHRUL ISLAM ALAMGIR (acting).

Bangladesh Kalyan Dal (Bangladesh Welfare Party): Siddiq Mansion, 4th Floor, Purana Paltan, Dhaka 1000; tel. (2) 9555864; e-mail info@bkp-bd.org; internet www.bkp-bd.org; f. 2007; Chair. Maj.-Gen. (retd) SYED MUHAMMAD IBRAHIM.

Bangladesh Khelafat Andolon (Bangladesh Caliphate Movement): 314/2 J. N. Saha Rd, Lalbagh Kellar Morr, Dhaka 1211; tel. (2) 8612465; fax (2) 8653249; e-mail khelafat@dhaka.net; internet bangladeshkhelafatandolan.blogspot.com; f. 1981; Supreme Leader Maulana SHAH AHMADULLAH ASHRAF IBN HAFEZZEE HUZUR; Sec.-Gen. Maulana MUHAMMAD ZAFRULLAH KHAN.

Bangladesh Khelafat Majlis: 59/3/3 Purana Paltan, 5th Floor, Dhaka 1000; tel. (2) 9553693; fax (2) 9569002; e-mail info@bangladeshkhelafatmajlis.org; internet www.bangladeshkhelafatmajlis.org; f. 1989; movement for an Islamic state of Bangladesh; Ameer HABIBUR RAHMAN; Gen. Sec. Maulana NIZAMUDDIN.

Bangladesh Muslim League: 15 Outer Circular Rd, Motijheel C/A, Dhaka 1217; tel. (2) 9362375; Pres. Alhaj A. N. M. YUSUF; Sec. Gen. Kazi ABDUL KHAYER.

Bangladesh Samajtantrik Dal (Socialist Party of Bangladesh—SPB): 23/2 Topkhana Rd, 3rd Floor, Shahbagh, Dhaka 1000; tel. (2) 7169830; fax (2) 9554772; e-mail mail@spb.org.bd; internet www.spb.org.bd; f. 1980; Gen. Sec. Comrade KHALEQUZZAMAN.

Bangladesh Tariqat Federation: 1/4, Block A, Section 1, Protishthanik Elaka, Mirpur Housing Estate, Dhaka 1212; tel. (2) 8362622; fax (2) 9349134; e-mail tariqatfederation@yahoo.com; f. 2005; Chair. al-Haj SYED NAJIBUL BASHAR MAIZBHANDARI; Gen. Sec. SYED REZAUL HAQUE CHANDPURI.

Bikalpa Dhara Bangladesh (BDB): House 19, Rd 12, Block K, Baridhara, Dhaka 1212; tel. (2) 8855252; fax (2) 9890978; e-mail bchowdhury@dbn-bd.net; f. 2004; Pres. Prof. A. Q. M. BADRUDDOZA CHOWDHURY; Sec.-Gen. Major (retd) ABDUL MANNAN.

Communist Party of Bangladesh (CPB): 'Mukti Bhaban', 2 Comrade Moni Singh Rd, Purana Paltan, Dhaka 1000; tel. (2) 9558612; fax (2) 9552333; e-mail info@cpb.org.bd; internet www.cpb.org.bd; f. 1968 following split from Communist Party of Pakistan; Pres. MANZURUL AHASAN KHAN; Gen. Sec. MUJAHIDUL ISLAM SELIM; c. 22,000 mems.

Freedom Party: 47 Naseer Uddin Sarkar Lane, Nichtala, Dholaikhal, Sutrapur, Dhaka 1000; tel. (2) 8860474; f. 1987; Islamic; Chair. SYED TAREQ RAHMAN (acting); Gen. Sec. M. A. SATTAR NAZLI.

Gono Forum (People's Forum): Eden Complex, 2/1A Arambagh, Dhaka 1000; tel. (2) 7102899; fax (2) 7101991; f. 1993; Pres. Dr KAMAL HOSSEIN; Gen. Sec. SUBROTO CHOWDHURY (acting).

Gono Front: 24/1/A, Topkhana Rd, Dhaka 1000; tel. (2) 9551332; fax (2) 9567757; f. 1979; Chair. A. K. M. RAFIQULLAH CHOWDHURY; Gen. Sec. AHMED ALI SHEIKH.

Gonotantri Party: 79, Kakryle, Mayakanan, 3rd Floor, Dhaka 1000; tel. (2) 9111275; fax (2) 8114820; e-mail gonotantri@gmail.com; Pres. MOHAMMAD AFZAL; Gen. Sec. NURUR RAHMAN SELIM.

Islami Andolan Bangladesh (IAB): 55B Purana Paltan, 3rd Floor, Dhaka 1000; tel. (2) 9567130; internet www.islamiandolanbd.org; Ameer Maulana Mufti SYED MOHAMMAD REZAUL KARIM; Gen. Sec. HAFEZ MAULANA YOUSUF AHMAD.

Islami Oikya Jote (Islamic Unity Front—IOJ): 57 Kazi Riyazuddin Rd, Lalbagh, Dhaka 1211; tel. (2) 8631490; mem. of the BNP-led alliance; Chair. Mufti FAZLUL HAQUE AMINI; Gen. Sec. Maulana MOHAMMAD ABDUL LATIF NEZAMI.

Islamic Front Bangladesh: 60A Purana Paltan, 4th Floor, Dhaka 1000; tel. (2) 9565524; e-mail islamicfront@gmail.com; Chair. SYED BAHADUR SHAH MUJADDEDI; Gen. Sec. ABUL BASHAR MOHAMMAD ZAINUL ABEDIN (ZUBAIR).

Jamiat-e-Ulema-e-Islam Bangladesh: 116/2 Naya Paltan, 4th Floor, Culvert Rd, Dhaka 1000; Chair. Hazrat Maulana SHEIKH ABDUL MOMIN; Gen. Sec. Maulana Mufti MUHAMMAD WAKKAS.

Jatiya Gonotantrik Party: Rd 1, House 2, Asad Gate Rd, Mohammad, Dhaka 1207; tel. (2) 1717310456; Leader SHAFIUL ALAM PRADHAN; Gen. Sec. KHANDKAR LUTFAR REHMAN.

Jatiya Party (National Party): 27/8/A Topkhana Rd, Dhaka 1000; tel. (2) 9571658; fax (2) 8813433; e-mail ershad@dhaka.agni.com; f. 1983 as Jana Dal; reorg. 1986, when the National Front (f. 1985), a five-party alliance of the Jana Dal, the United People's Party, the Gonotantrik Dal, the Bangladesh Muslim League and a breakaway section of the Bangladesh Nationalist Party, formally converted itself into a single pro-Ershad grouping; advocates nationalism, democracy, Islamic ideals and progress; Chair. Lt-Gen. HOSSAIN MOHAMMAD ERSHAD; Gen. Sec. A. B. M. RUHUL AMIN HAWLADER.

Jatiya Samajtantrik Dal (JASOD): 35–36 Bangobondhu Ave, Dhaka 1000; tel. (2) 9559972; e-mail jsd@dhaka.net; f. 1972; Pres. HASANUL HAQ INU; Gen. Sec. SHARIF NURUL AMBIA.

Jatiya Samajtantrik Dal (Rab): 65 Bangobondhu Ave, 4th Floor, Dhaka 1000; tel. (2) 9560300; fax (2) 9562668; e-mail amr.reforms@yahoo.com; f. 2002; Pres. NUR ALAM ZIKU; Gen. Sec. ABDUL MALEK RATAN.

Khelafat Majlish: 116 Naya Paltan, Zaman Mansion, 4th Floor, Culvert Rd, Dhaka 1000; tel. (2) 9349907; fax (2) 8314747; internet www.khelafatmajlis.org; Ameer Maulana MOHAMMAD IS-HAQUE; Gen. Sec. AHMAD ABDUL KADER.

Krishak Sramik Janata League (KSJL) (Peasants' and Workers' People's Party): 80 Motijheel Banijyik Elaka, Dhaka; tel. (2) 8114393; fax (2) 8114761; f. 1999; Pres. Bangabir KADER SIDDIQUI; Gen. Sec. HABIBUR RAHMAN TALUKDAR.

Liberal Democratic Party (LDP): 63/A Bara Magbazaar, Ramana, Dhaka; tel. (2) 9338903; f. 2006; comprises several former members of BNP; split into two factions June 2007; Pres. Col (retd) OLI AHMAD; Sec.-Gen. Begum JAHANARA.

National Awami Party—Bangladesh (NAP): House 118, Rd 15, Block C, Banani, Dhaka 1213; tel. (2) 8836271; fax (2) 8836273; e-mail bd_nap@yahoo.com; f. 1957; Maoist; Pres. JEBEL RAHMAN GANI; Gen. Sec. M. GULAM MOSTAFA BHUIYAN.

National Awami Party—Muzaffar (NAP—M): 20–21 Dhanmandi Hawkers' Market, 2nd Floor, Dhaka 1205; tel. (2) 9669948; f. 1957; reorg. 1967; Pres. MUZAFFAR AHMED; Sec.-Gen. ENAMUL HAQUE; c. 500,000 mems.

National People's Party (NPP): Dhaka; tel. (2) 9361174; f. 2007; Chair. Sheikh SHAWKAT HOSSAIN NILU; Gen. Sec. FARIDDUZAMAN FARHAD.

Oikyobaddha Nagorik Andolan (United Citizens' Movement—UCM): House 9/3, Lane 1, Block B, Mirpur-6, Dhaka 1216; e-mail nagorikandolan@yahoo.com; Pres. Kazi FAROOQ AHMED; Gen. Sec. ABDUS SAMAD PINTU.

Progotisheel Gonotantrik Dal (Progressive Democratic Party—PDP): 8/4A Topkhana Rd, Segun Bagicha, Dhaka 1000; tel. (2) 7162855; fax (2) 7161340; e-mail info@pdpbangladesh.com; internet www.pdpbangladesh.com; f. 2007; Chair. Dr FERDOUS AHMAD QURESHI; Gen. Sec. NUR MOHAMMAD KHAN.

Samyabadi Dal (ML): 27/11/1, Topkhana Rd, Dhaka 1000; tel. (2) 8313409; Marxist-Leninist; Gen. Sec. DILIP BARUA.

Workers' Party of Bangladesh: 31 Topkhana Rd, Dhaka 1000; tel. (2) 9567975; fax (2) 9558545; e-mail wpartybd@bangla.net; f. 1980; Pres. RASHID KHAN MENON; Gen. Sec. BIMAL BISWAS.

Zaker Party: House 19, Rd 3, Block I, Banani, Gulshan, Dhaka 1213; tel. (2) 9895510; fax (2) 9895478; f. 1989; supports sovereignty and the introduction of an Islamic state system; Chair. Peerzada Alhaj MOSTAFA AMIR FAISAL MUJADDEDI; Gen. Sec. MUNSI ABDUL LATIF.

Diplomatic Representation

EMBASSIES AND HIGH COMMISSIONS IN BANGLADESH

Afghanistan: House CWN(C) 2A, 24 Gulshan Ave, Gulshan Model Town, Dhaka 1212; tel. (2) 9895994; fax (2) 9884767; e-mail afghanembassydhaka@yahoo.com; Ambassador ABDUL RAHIM QRAZ.

Australia: 184 Gulshan Ave, Gulshan 2, Dhaka 1212; tel. (2) 8813105; fax (2) 8811125; e-mail ahc.dhaka@dfat.gov.au; internet www.bangladesh.embassy.gov.au; High Commissioner JUSTIN LEE.

Bhutan: House 12, Rd 107, Gulshan 2, Dhaka 1212; tel. (2) 8826863; fax (2) 8823939; e-mail bhtemb@bdmail.net; Ambassador Dasho BAP KESANG.

Brunei: House 26, Rd 6, Baridhara, Dhaka 1212; tel. (2) 8819552; fax (2) 8819551; e-mail dhaka.bangladesh@mfa.gov.bn; High Commissioner Haji ABDUL RAZAK BIN Haji MOHD HUSSAINI.

Canada: United Nations Rd, Baridhara, Dhaka 1212; tel. (2) 9887091; fax (2) 8823043; e-mail dhaka@international.gc.ca; internet www.international.gc.ca/bangladesh; High Commissioner HEATHER CRUDEN.

China, People's Republic: Plots 2 and 4, Embassy Rd, Block 1, Baridhara, Dhaka; tel. (2) 8824164; fax (2) 8823004; e-mail chinaemb_bd@mfa.gov.cn; internet bd.china-embassy.org; Ambassador LI JUN (designate).

Denmark: House 1, Rd 51, Gulshan Model Town, POB 2056, Dhaka 1212; tel. (2) 8821799; fax (2) 8823638; e-mail dacamb@um.dk; internet www.ambdhaka.um.dk; Ambassador SVEND OLLING.

Egypt: House 9, Rd 90, Gulshan 2, Dhaka; tel. (2) 8858738; fax (2) 8858747; e-mail egypt.emb.dhaka@mfa.gov.eg; internet www.mfa.gov.eg/dhaka_emb; Ambassador MAHMOUD EZZAT.

France: House 18, Rd 108, Gulshan, Dhaka; tel. (2) 8813811; fax (2) 8813612; e-mail webmestre.dacca-amba@diplomatie.gouv.fr; internet www.ambafrance-bd.org; Ambassador MICHEL TRINQUIER.

Germany: 178 Gulshan Ave, Gulshan 2, POB 6126, Dhaka 1212; tel. (2) 8853521; fax (2) 8853260; internet www.dhaka.diplo.de; Ambassador HOLGER MICHAEL.

Holy See: United Nations Rd 2, Diplomatic Enclave, Baridhara Model Town, Gulshan, POB 6003, Dhaka 1212; tel. (2) 8822018; fax (2) 8823574; e-mail nuntius@dhaka.net; Apostolic Nuncio JOSEPH MARINO.

India: House 2, Rd 142, Gulshan-I, Dhaka; tel. (2) 9889339; fax (2) 9893050; e-mail hc@hcidhaka.org; internet www.hcidhaka.org; High Commissioner PANKAJ SARAN (designate).

Indonesia: Plot No. 14, Rd 53, Gulshan 2, Dhaka 1212; tel. (2) 8812260; fax (2) 8825391; e-mail Pensosbud@jakarta-dhaka.com; internet www.jakarta-dhaka.com; Ambassador ZET MIRZAL ZAINUDDIN.

Iran: House No. 7, Rd 6, Baridhara Model Town, Dhaka; tel. (2) 8825896; fax (2) 8828780; e-mail iranembassydhaka@persiabd.com; Ambassador HOSSEIN AMINIAN JOUSI.

Italy: Plot 2/3, Rd 74/79, Gulshan 2, POB 6062, Dhaka 1212; tel. (2) 8822781; fax (2) 8822578; e-mail consolare.dhaka@esteri.it; internet www.ambdhaka.esteri.it; Ambassador GIORGIO GUGLIELMINO.

Japan: 5 and 7, Dutabash Rd, Baridhara, Dhaka 1212; tel. (2) 8810087; fax (2) 8826737; e-mail information@embjp.accesstel.net; internet www.bd.emb-japan.go.jp; Ambassador SHIRO SADOSHIMA.

Korea, Democratic People's Republic: House 5A, Rd 54, Gulshan 2, Dhaka; tel. (2) 8811893; fax (2) 8810813; Ambassador SIN HONG CHOL.

Korea, Republic: 4 Madani Ave, Diplomatic Enclave, Baridhara, Dhaka 1212; tel. (2) 8812088; fax (2) 8823871; e-mail embdhaka@embdhaka.org; internet bgd.mofat.go.kr; Ambassador CHO YOUNG TAI.

Kuwait: Plot 39, Rd 23, Block J, Banani, Dhaka 1213; tel. (2) 8822700; fax (2) 8823753; e-mail dhaka@mofa.gov.kw; Ambassador AHMAD IBRAHIM AL-DHUFAIRI.

Libya: NE(D), 3A Gulshan Ave (N), Gulshan Model Town, Dhaka 1212; tel. (2) 600141; Ambassador (vacant).

Malaysia: House 19, Rd 6, Baridhara Diplomatic Enclave, Dhaka 1212; tel. (2) 8827759; fax (2) 8823115; e-mail mwdhaka@citech-bd.com; internet www.kln.gov.my/perwakilan/dhaka; High Commissioner JAMALUDDIN BIN SABEH.

Maldives: House 45, United Nations Rd, Baridhara, Dhaka 1212; tel. (2) 2651179; fax (2) 2581200; High Commissioner AHMED SAREER.

Morocco: House 44, United Nations Rd, POB 6112, Baridhara, Dhaka 1212; tel. (2) 8823176; fax (2) 8810018; e-mail sifmadac@citech-bd.net; Ambassador MOHAMMED HOURORO.

Myanmar: House 3, Block NE(L), Rd 84, Gulshan 2, Dhaka 1212; tel. (2) 9888903; fax (2) 8823740; e-mail mynembdk@dhaka.net; Ambassador MIN LWIN.

Nepal: United Nations Rd, Rd 2, Diplomatic Enclave, Baridhara, Dhaka; tel. (2) 9892490; fax (2) 8826401; e-mail eondhaka@dhaka.net; internet www.nepembassy-dhaka.org; Ambassador HARI KUMAR SHRESHTHA.

Netherlands: House 49, Rd 90, Gulshan 2, POB 166, Dhaka; tel. (2) 8822715; fax (2) 8823326; e-mail dha@minbuza.nl; internet www.netherlandsembassydhaka.org; Ambassador ALPHONS JEAN ANTOINE JOSEPH MARIE GERTRUDE HENNEKENS.

Norway: House 9, Rd 111, Gulshan, Dhaka 1212; tel. (2) 8816276; fax (2) 8823661; e-mail emb.dhaka@mfa.no; internet www.norway.org.bd; Ambassador RAGNE BIRTE LUND.

Pakistan: House NE(C) 2, Rd 71, Gulshan 2, Dhaka 1212; tel. (2) 8825388; fax (2) 8850673; e-mail parepdka@agni.com; internet phc-dhaka.com; High Commissioner AFRASIAB MEHDI HASHMI.

Philippines: House 17, Rd 7, Baridhara, Dhaka 1212; tel. (2) 9881590; fax (2) 8823686; e-mail philemb2@aknetbd.com; internet www.philembassydhaka.org; Ambassador BAHNARIM GUINOMLA.

Qatar: House 1, Rd 79/81, Gulshan 2, Dhaka 1212; tel. (2) 8823346; fax (2) 9896071; e-mail dhaka@mofa.gov.qa; Ambassador ABDUL RAHMAN YOUSIF AL-MULLA.

Russia: NE(J) 9, Rd 79, Gulshan 2, Dhaka 1212; tel. (2) 9884847; fax (2) 9863285; e-mail rusembbd@gmail.com; internet www.bangladesh.mid.ru; Ambassador ALEXANDER NIKOLAEV.

Saudi Arabia: House 12, Rd 92, Gulshan (North), Dhaka 1212; tel. (2) 889124; fax (2) 883616; Ambassador ABDULLAH BIN NASSER AL-BUSSAIRI.

Sri Lanka: House 4A, Rd 113, Gulshan Model Town, Dhaka 1212; tel. (2) 9896353; fax (2) 8823971; e-mail slhc@citec-bd.com; internet www.slhcdhaka.org; High Commissioner W. A. SARATH K. WERAGODA.

Sweden: House 1, Rd 51, Gulshan, Dhaka 1212; tel. (2) 8833144; fax (2) 8823948; e-mail ambassaden.dhaka@foreign.ministry.se; internet www.swedenabroad.com/dhaka; Ambassador ANNELI LINDAHL KENNY.

Switzerland: Bir Bikram Major Hafiz Sarak, House 31B, Rd 18, Banani, Dhaka 1213; tel. (2) 8812874; fax (2) 8823872; e-mail dha.vertretung@eda.admin.ch; internet www.eda.admin.ch/dhaka; Ambassador Dr URS HERREN.

Thailand: 18 & 20, Madani Ave, Baridhara, Dhaka 1212; tel. (2) 8812795; fax (2) 8854280; e-mail thaidac@mfa.go.th; internet www.thaidac.com; Ambassador (vacant).

Turkey: House 7, Rd 2, Baridhara, Dhaka 1212; tel. (2) 8822198; fax (2) 8823873; e-mail turkemb.dhaka@mfa.gov.tr; internet dhaka.emb.mfa.gov.tr; Ambassador M. VAKUR ERKUL.

United Arab Emirates: POB 6014, Dhaka 1212; tel. (2) 9882244; fax (2) 8823225; e-mail info@uaeembassydhaka.com; Ambassador KHALFAN BATTAL AL-MANSOURI.

United Kingdom: United Nations Rd, Baridhara, POB 6079, Dhaka 1212; tel. (2) 8822705; fax (2) 8823437; e-mail Dhaka.Chancery@fco.gov.uk; internet ukinbangladesh.fco.gov.uk; High Commissioner ROBERT WINNINGTON GIBSON (designate).

USA: Madani Ave, Baridhara, POB 323, Dhaka 1212; tel. (2) 8855500; fax (2) 8823744; e-mail DhakaPA@state.gov; internet dhaka.usembassy.gov; Ambassador DAN W. MOZENA.

Viet Nam: Vintage Bldg, Plot 7, Rd 104, Gulshan 2, Dhaka 1212; tel. (2) 8854052; fax (2) 8854051; e-mail dhaka@mofa.gov.vn; internet www.vietnamembassy-bangladesh.org; Ambassador NGUYEN VAN THAT.

Judicial System

A judiciary, comprising a Supreme Court with a High Court and an Appellate Division, is in operation (see under Constitution). On 1 November 2007 the Government announced the formal separation of the judiciary from the executive.

Supreme Court

Ramna, Dhaka 1000; tel. (2) 433585; fax (2) 9565058; e-mail supremec@bdcom.com; internet www.supremecourt.gov.bd.

Chief Justice: MUZAMMEL HOSSAIN.

Attorney-General: MAHBUBEY ALAM.

Deputy Attorney-General: RAJIK AL-JALIL.

Religion

The results of the 2004 census classified 89.5% of the population as Muslims (the majority of whom were of the Sunni sect), 9.6% as caste Hindus and scheduled castes, and the remainder as Buddhists, Christians, animists and others.

Freedom of religious worship is guaranteed under the Constitution, but, under the 1977 amendment to the Constitution, Islam was declared to be one of the nation's guiding principles and, under the 1988 amendment, Islam was established as the state religion. However, in 2011 a constitutional amendment restored secularism as a fundamental principle of the nation, while Islam was retained as the state religion.

ISLAM

Islamic Foundation Bangladesh: Agargaon, Sher-e-Bangla Nagar, Dhaka 1207; tel. (2) 9115010; fax (2) 9144235; e-mail islamicfoundationbd@yahoo.com; internet www.islamicfoundation.org.bd; f. 1975; under supervision of Ministry of Religious Affairs; Dir-Gen. SHAMIM MOHAMMAD AFZAL.

BUDDHISM

World Fellowship of Buddhists Regional Centre: Dharmarajik Buddhist Monastery, Atish Dipanker Sarak, Basabo, Dhaka 1214; tel. (2) 7205665; fax (2) 7202503; f. 1962; Pres. Ven. SUDDHANANDA MAHATHERO; Sec.-Gen. P. K. BARUYA.

CHRISTIANITY

Jatiyo Church Parishad (National Council of Churches): POB 220, Dhaka 1000; tel. (2) 9332869; fax (2) 8312996; e-mail nccb@bangla.net; f. 1949 as East Pakistan Christian Council; four mem. churches; Pres. PAUL S. SARKER; Gen. Sec. DAVID A. DAS.

Church of Bangladesh—United Church

After Bangladesh achieved independence, the Diocese of Dacca (Dhaka) of the Church of Pakistan (f. 1970 by the union of Anglicans, Methodists, Presbyterians and Lutherans) became the autonomous Church of Bangladesh. In 2001 the Church had an estimated 14,000 members. In 1990 a second diocese, the Diocese of Kushtia, was established.

Bishop of Dhaka: Rt Rev. PAUL SARKAR, 54/1 Barobag, Mirpur 2, Dhaka 1216; tel. (2) 8053729; fax (2) 7118218; e-mail cbdacdio@bangla.net.

Bishop of Kushtia: Rt Rev. PAUL SHISHIR SARKAR, Church of Bangladesh, 94 N. S. Rd, Thanapara, Kushtia; tel. (71) 54618; fax (71) 54618.

The Roman Catholic Church

For ecclesiastical purposes, Bangladesh comprises one archdiocese and five dioceses. At 31 December 2007 there were an estimated 318,603 adherents in the country.

Catholic Bishops' Conference of Bangladesh (CBCB): 24C Asad Avenue, Mohammadpur, Dhaka 1207; tel. (2) 9123108; fax (2) 9127339; e-mail cbcbsec@dhaka.net; internet www.cbcbsec.org; f. 1971; Pres. Most Rev. PATRICK COSTA D'ROZARIO (Archbishop of Dhaka).

Secretariat: CBCB Centre, 24C Asad Ave, Mohammadpur, Dhaka 1207; tel. and fax (2) 9127339; e-mail cbcbsg@bdonline.com; Sec.-Gen. Rt Rev. THEOTONIUS GOMES (Titular Bishop of Zucchabar).

Archbishop of Dhaka: Most Rev. PATRICK D'ROZARIO, Archbishop's House, 1 Kakrail Rd, Ramna, POB 3, Dhaka 1000; tel. (2) 9358247; e-mail abpcosta@bangla.net.

Other Christian Churches

Bangladesh Baptist Sangha: 33 Senpara Parbatta, POB 8018, Mirpur 10, Dhaka 1216; tel. (2) 8012967; fax (2) 803556; e-mail bbsangha@bdmail.net; f. 1922; 35,150 mems (2004); Pres. Dr JOYANTO ADHIKARI; Gen. Sec. MILTON BISWAS.

Bangladesh Evangelical Lutheran Church: POB 6, Lutheran Mission, Auliapur, Dinajpur 5200; e-mail bnelc_din@yahoo.com.

Bangladesh Lutheran Church: Jogdal Mission, Birganj, Dist. Dinjapur 5220; tel. (531) 89152; e-mail blcmiss@btcl.net.bd; Moderator Rev. AROBINDU BORMON.

In early 2002 there were about 51 denominational churches active in the country, including the Bogra Christian Church, the Evangelical Christian Church, the Garo Baptist Union, the Reformed Church of Bangladesh and the Sylhet Presbyterian Synod. The Baptist Sangha was the largest Protestant Church.

The Press

PRINCIPAL DAILIES

Bengali

Bangladesh Protidin: 371A, Block D, Basundhara Residential Area, Baridhara, Dhaka; tel. (2) 8402361; fax (2) 8402364; e-mail ibdpratidin@gmail.com; internet www.bd-pratidin.com; Editor NAEEM NIZAM.

Daily Inqilab: 2/1 Ramkrishna Mission Rd, Dhaka 1203; tel. (2) 7122771; fax (2) 9552881; e-mail inqilab08@dhaka.net; internet www.dailyinqilab.com; Editor A. M. M. BAHAUDDIN; circ. 180,025.

Daily Jugantor: 12/7, North Kamalpur, Dhaka 1217; tel. (2) 8419211; fax (2) 8419218; e-mail info@jugantor.com; internet www.jugantor.com; Editor SALMA ISLAM.

Daily Kaler Kantho: Basundhara R/A, Plot 371/A, Block D, Baridhara, Dhaka 1229; tel. (2) 8402372; fax (2) 8402368; e-mail info@kalerkantho.com; internet www.dailykalerkantho.com; f. 2010; current affairs, sports and entertainment; Editor IMDADUL HAQ MILON (acting).

Daily Naya Diganta: 167/2E, Inner Circular Rd, Motijheel, Dhaka 1000; tel. (2) 7191017; fax (2) 7101877; e-mail info@dailynayadiganta.com; internet www.dailynayadiganta.com; f. 2004; Editor ALAMGIR MOHIUDDIN.

Daily Sangbad: 36 Purana Paltan, Dhaka 1000; tel. (2) 9567557; fax (2) 9558900; e-mail sangbaddesk@gmail.com; internet www.sangbad.com.bd; Editor ALTAMASH KABIR; circ. 77,109.

Dainik Azadi: 9 CDA. C/A, Momin Rd, Chittagong; tel. (31) 612380; e-mail info@dainikazadi.net; internet www.dainikazadi.org; f. 1960; Editor M. A. MALEK; circ. 13,000.

Dainik Bhorer Kagoj: Karnaphuli Media Point, 3rd Floor, 70 Shahid Sangbadik Selina Parveen Sarak (New Circular Rd, Malibagh), Dhaka 1217; tel. (2) 9360285; fax (2) 9362734; e-mail info@bhorerkagoj.net; internet www.bhorerkagoj.net; Editor SHYAMAL DUTTA; circ. 50,000.

Dainik Ittefaq: 40 Kawran Bazar, Dhaka 1215; tel. (2) 7122660; fax (2) 7554974; e-mail dailyittefaq@yahoo.com; internet new.ittefaq.com.bd; f. 1953; Editor ANWAR HOSSAIN; circ. 200,000.

Dainik Jahan: 3/B Shehra Rd, Mymensingh; f. 1980; Chief Editor HABIBUR RAHMAN SHEIKH; circ. 4,000.

Dainik Janakantha (Daily People's Voice): Janakantha Bhaban, 24/A New Eskaton Rd, POB 3380, Dhaka 1000; tel. (2) 9347780; fax (2) 9351317; e-mail news@dailyjanakantha.com; internet www.dailyjanakantha.com; f. 1993; Editor MD ATIKULLAH KHAN MASUD; circ. 100,000.

Dainik Janata: Khalil Mansion, 3rd, 5th and 6th Floors, 149/A DIT Extension Ave, Dhaka 1000; tel. (2) 8311068; fax (2) 8314174; e-mail info@dailyjanatabd.com; internet www.dailyjanatabd.com; Editor AHSAN ULLAH.

Dainik Karatoa: Chalkjadu Rd, Bogra 5800; tel. (51) 63660; fax (51) 60422; e-mail dkaratoa@yahoo.com; internet www.karatoa.com.bd; f. 1976; Editor MOZAMMEL HAQUE LALU; circ. 44,000.

Dainik Khabar: 260/C Tejgaon I/A, Dhaka 1208; e-mail khabar@dekko.net.bd; f. 1985; Editor MIZANUR RAHMAN MIZAN; circ. 18,000.

Dainik Purbanchal: Purbanchal House, 38 Iqbal Nagar, Mosque Lane, Khulna 9100; tel. (41) 722251; fax (41) 721013; e-mail liakat@purbanchal.com; internet www.purbanchal.com; f. 1974; Man. Editor FERDOUSI ALI; Editor Alhaj LIAKAT ALI; circ. 46,000.

Dainik Sangram: 423 Elephant Rd, Magh Bazar, Dhaka 1217; tel. (2) 9346448; fax (2) 9337127; e-mail dsangram@gmail.com; internet www.dailysangram.com; f. 1970; Chair. ALI AHSAN MUHAMMAD MUJAHID; Editor ABUL ASAD; circ. 50,000.

Jaijaidin: Jaijaidin Mediaplex, Love Rd, Tejgaon Industrial Area, Dhaka 1208; tel. (2) 8832222; fax (2) 8832233; e-mail admin@jjdbd.com; internet www.jjdin.com; f. 1984; Chief Editor SAID HUSSAIN CHOWDHURY; circ. 100,000.

Jugabheri: Sylhet; f. 1931; Editor FAHMEEDA RASHEED CHOWDHURY; circ. 6,000.

Manab Zamin (Human Land): 149 Tejgaon Industrial Area, Dhaka 1208; tel. (2) 8189160; fax (2) 8128313; internet www.mzamin.com; f. 1998; tabloid; Editor MEHBOOBA CHOUDHURY.

Prothom Alo: C. A. Bhaban, 100 Kazi Nazrul Islam Ave, Karwan Bazar, Dhaka 1215; tel. (2) 8110081; fax (2) 9130496; e-mail info@prothom-alo.com; internet www.prothom-alo.com; f. 1998; publ. by MediaStar Ltd; Editor MATIUR RAHMAN.

Shamokal: 136 Tejgaon Industrial Area, Dhaka 1208; tel. (2) 8870179; fax (2) 8870191; e-mail info@samakal.com.bd; internet www.shamokal.com; Editor GOLAM SARWAR.

English

The Bangladesh Today: Concord Royal Court, 4th Floor, Plot No. 275G, Dhanmondi R/A, Dhaka 1209; tel. (2) 9118807; fax (2) 9127103; e-mail editor@thebangladeshtoday.com; internet www.thebangladeshtoday.com; Editor SYED SAJJAD AHMED.

Daily Star: 64–65 Kazi Nazrul Islam Ave, POB 3257, Dhaka 1215; tel. (2) 9102973; fax (2) 8125155; e-mail editor@thedailystar.net; internet www.thedailystar.net; f. 1991; Publr and Editor MAHFUZ ANAM; circ. 40,000 (weekdays), 60,000 (weekends).

Daily Sun: East West Media Group Ltd, 371/A, Block D, Bashundhara R/A, Dhaka 1229; tel. (2) 8402046; fax (2) 8402096; e-mail editor@daily-sun.com; internet www.daily-sun.com; f. 2010; owned by the Bashundhara Group; Editor Dr SYED ANWAR HUSAIN.

Daily Tribune: 38 Iqbal Nagar Mosque Lane, Khulna 9100; tel. (41) 721944; fax (41) 721013; e-mail ferdousi@purbanchal.com; f. 1978; morning; Editor FERDOUSI ALI; circ. 24,000.

Financial Express: Tropicana Tower, 4th Floor, 45 Topkhana Road, POB 2526, Dhaka 1000; tel. (2) 9568154; fax (2) 9567049; e-mail editor@thefinancialexpress-bd.com; internet www.thefinancialexpress-bd.com; f. 1993; Editor MOAZZEM HOSSAIN.

The Independent: BEL Tower, 5th and 6th Floors, 19 Dhanmondi, Rd No. 1, Dhaka 1205; tel. (2) 9672091; fax (2) 8629785; e-mail editor@bol-online.com; internet www.theindependent-bd.com; f. 1995; Editor MAHBUBUL ALAM.

New Age: Holiday Bldg, 30 Tejgaon Industrial Area, Dhaka 1208; tel. (2) 8153034; fax (2) 8153033; e-mail newagebd@global-bd.net; internet newagebd.com/newspaper1; f. 2003; Editor NURUL KABIR.

New Nation: 1 Ramkrishna Mission Rd, Dhaka 1203; tel. (2) 7122654; fax (2) 7122650; e-mail n_editor@bangla.net; internet thenewnationbd.com; f. 1981; privately owned; Editor MOSTAFA KAMAL MAJUMDER; circ. 15,000.

The News Today: Shah Ali Tower, 3rd Floor, 33 Karwan Bazar, Dhaka 1215; tel. (2) 9111395; fax (2) 9140721; e-mail newstoday@dhaka.net; internet www.newstoday.com.bd; Editor REAZUDDIN AHMED.

People's View: 253 Nazir Ahmed Chowdhury Rd, Chittagong; tel. (31) 2854333; fax (31) 2854577; e-mail editor@peoples-view.net; internet www.peoples-view.net; f. 1969; Chief Editor NAZIMUDDIN MOSTAN; circ. 3,000.

PERIODICALS

Bengali

Ajker Surjodoy: 212 Shahid Syed Najrul Islam Sarani, 2nd Floor, Bijoy Nagar, Dhaka; tel. (2) 9557360; fax (2) 9567757; f. 1991; weekly; news; Editor KHANDAKER MOZAMMEL HAQUE.

Amod: Chowdhury Para, Comilla 3500; tel. (81) 65193; e-mail bakin_302002@yahoo.com; internet www.weeklyamod.com; f. 1955; weekly; Editor SHAMSUN NAHAR RABBI; circ. 10,000.

Bank Parikrama: Bangladesh Institute of Bank Management, Plot 4, Main Road 1 (South), Mirpur 2, Dhaka 1216; fax (2) 9006756; e-mail office@bibm.org.bd; internet www.bibm-bd.org; banking and finance; quarterly.

Bartaman Sanglap: Jyoti Bhavan, Section 6, Block C, Rd 13, Plot 5, Pallabi, Mirpur, Dhaka 1216; tel. (2) 9002663; e-mail sanglap@bartamansanglap.com; internet www.bartamansanglap.com; weekly; news and culture; Editor SHEIKH ABDUL HANIF.

Begum: 66 Loyal St, Dhaka 1; tel. (2) 7390681; f. 1947; women's illustrated weekly; Editor NURJAHAN BEGUM; circ. 25,000.

Computer Jagat: House 29, Rd 6, Dhanmondi, Dhaka 1205; tel. (2) 8610445; fax (2) 9664723; e-mail jagat@comjagat.com; internet www.comjagat.com; monthly; computers and IT; Editor GOLAP MUNIR.

Fashal: 28J Toyenbee Circular Rd, Motijheel C/A, Dhaka 1000; tel. (2) 9136044; f. 1965; agricultural weekly; Chief Editor ERSHAD MAZUMDAR; circ. 8,000.

Kali O Kalam: Bengal Center, Plot No. 2, New Airport Rd, Khilkhet, Dhaka 1229; e-mail mail@kaliokalam.com; internet www.kaliokalam.com; f. 1927; monthly; focus on literature and arts; Editor ABUL HASNAT.

Muktibani: 28 A/3, Toyenbee Circular Rd, Motijheel C/A, Dhaka 1000; tel. (2) 9553522; e-mail muktibani@yahoo.com; f. 1972; Editor NIZAM UDDIN AHMED; circ. 35,000.

Natun Katha: 31E Topkhana Rd, Dhaka; weekly; Editor HAJERA SULTANA; circ. 4,000.

Nipun: 520 Peyarabag, Magbazar, Dhaka 11007; monthly; Editor SHAJAHAN CHOWDHURY.

Parjatan Bichitra: M. R. Centre, 7th Floor, House 49, Rd 17, Banani C/A, Dhaka 1213; tel. (2) 8829692; fax (2) 8829809; e-mail info@parjatanbichitra.com; internet www.parjatanbichitra.com; monthly; tourism, wildlife and travel magazine; Editor MOHIUDDIN HELAL.

Protirodh: Ansar and VDP Headquarters, Khilgaon, Dhaka 1219; tel. (2) 7214937; e-mail editor_protirod@ansarvdp.gov.bd; internet www.ansarvdp.gov.bd; f. 1977; fortnightly; publ. of the Bangladesh Ansar and Village Defence Party; circ. 20,000.

Robbar: 1 Ramkrishna Mission Rd, Dhaka; tel. and fax (2) 7122660; f. 1978; weekly; Exec. Editor KAMAL HOSSAIN BABLU; circ. 25,000.

Sachitra Bangladesh: 112 Circuit House Rd, Dhaka 1000; tel. (2) 9333149; internet www.dfp.gov.bd; f. 1979; weekly publ. of the Dept of Films and Publs, Ministry of Information; fortnightly; Editor ROKASANA AKTER.

Sachitra Sandhani: Dhaka; f. 1978; weekly; Editor GAZI SHAHABUDDIN MAHMUD; circ. 13,000.

Shaptahik 2000: 52 Motijheel C/A, Dhaka 1000; tel. (2) 9350951; internet www.shaptahik-2000.com; f. 1998; weekly; entertainment and news; Editor MOINUL AHSAN SABER.

Shaptahik Ekhon: Dhaka; internet www.weeklyekhon.com; weekly; Editor ATAUS SAMAD.

Shishu: Bangladesh Shishu Academy, Old High Court Compound, Dhaka 1000; tel. (2) 9564128; e-mail shishubsa@yahoo.com; internet www.shishuacademy.gov.bd/pub_bok_mn.htm; f. 1977; children's monthly; Exec. Editor SHUJAN BIKASH BARUA; circ. 5,000.

Sonar Bangla: 423 Elephant Rd, Magh Bazar, Dhaka 1217; tel. (2) 8319065; fax (2) 8315571; e-mail weeklysonarbangla@yahoo.com; internet www.weeklysonarbangla.net; f. 1961; Editor MUHAMMED QAMARUZZAMAN; circ. 25,000.

Tarokalok: 622 Boro Mogbazar, Romna, Dhaka; tel. (2) 9668326; fax (2) 8614330; e-mail tarokalok_bd@yahoo.com; fortnightly; Editor IBRAHIM KHALIL KHOKON.

Weekly Ekota: Dhaka; e-mail info@cpb.org.bd; internet www.cpb.org.bd/Ekota.htm; f. 1970; weekly; organ of the Communist Party of Bangladesh; Editor AFROZA NAHAR.

English

The Bangladesh Monitor: City Heart, 9th Floor, 67 Naya Paltan, Dhaka 1000; tel. (2) 8351148; fax (2) 8314306; e-mail info@bangladeshmonitor.net; internet www.bangladeshmonitor.net; f. 1991; fortnightly; aviation and tourism; Editor KAZI WAHIDUL ALAM.

Bangladesh Quarterly: Department of Films and Publications, 112 Circuit House Rd, Dhaka 1000; internet www.dfp.gov.bd; current affairs and history; Chief Editor KAMRUN NAHAR.

Bangladesh Gazette: Bangladesh Government Press, Tejgaon, Dhaka; tel. (2) 9117415; e-mail info@bgpress.gov.bd; internet www.bgpress.gov.bd; f. 1947; name changed 1972; weekly; official notices; Editor MASUM KHAN.

Bangladesh Illustrated Weekly: Dhaka; Editor ATIQUZZAMAN KHAN; circ. 3,000.

Detective: Polwell Bhaban, Naya Paltan, Dhaka 1000; tel. (2) 9357451; e-mail detective.bd@gmail.com; f. 1960; monthly; also publ. in Bengali; Editor-in-Chief N. B. K. TRIPURA; circ. 5,000.

Dhaka Courier: Cosmos Centre, 69/1 New Circular Rd, Malibagh, Dhaka 1217; e-mail info@dhakacourier.com.bd; internet www.dhakacourier.com.bd; f. 1984; weekly; Editor ENAYETULLAH KHAN.

Holiday: Holiday Bldg, 30 Tejgaon Industrial Area, Dhaka 1208; tel. (2) 9122950; fax (2) 9127927; e-mail holiday@bangla.net; internet www.weeklyholiday.net; f. 1965; weekly; independent; Editor SAYED KAMALUDDIN; circ. 18,000.

Weekly Blitz: Eastern Commercial Complex, 3rd Floor, Suite 308, 73 Kakrail, Dhaka 1000; tel. (11) 91350884; e-mail ediblitz@yahoo.com; internet www.weeklyblitz.net; f. 2003; weekly (Wednesdays); Publr and Editor SALAH UDDIN SHOAIB CHOUDHURY; circ. 39,000.

NEWS AGENCIES

Bangladesh Sangbad Sangstha (BSS) (Bangladesh News Agency): 68/2 Purana Paltan, Dhaka 1000; tel. (2) 9555036; fax (2) 9568970; e-mail bssadmin@bssnews.org; internet www.bssnews.net; f. 1972; Man. Dir and Chief Editor IHSANUL KARIM HELAL; Man. Editor AZIZUL ISLAM BHUIYAN.

United News of Bangladesh (UNB): Cosmos Centre, 69/1 New Circular Rd, Malibagh, Dhaka 1217; tel. (2) 9345543; fax (2) 9344556; e-mail unb_news@yahoo.com; internet www.unbnews.org; f. 1988; independent; Chair. AMANULLAH KHAN.

PRESS ASSOCIATIONS

Bangladesh Press Council: 40 Topkhana Rd, Dhaka 1000; tel. and fax (2) 7172049; e-mail info@presscouncilbd.com; internet presscouncil.gov.bd; f. 1974; established under an act of Parliament to preserve the freedom of the press and maintain and develop standards of newspapers and news agencies; Chair. Justice B. K. DAS.

Bangladesh Sangbadpatra Press Sramik Federation (Newspaper Press Workers' Federation): 1 Ramkrishna Mission Rd, Dhaka

1203; f. 1960; Pres. M. ABDUL KARIM; Sec.-Gen. BOZLUR RAHMAN MILON.

Dhaka Union of Journalists: National Press Club, Dhaka 1000; f. 1947.

Newspaper Owners' Association of Bangladesh (NOAB): c/o The Independent, Beximco Media Complex, 32 Kazi Nazrul Islam Ave, Karwan Bazar, Dhaka 1215; tel. (2) 9672091; f. 2002; promotes interests of the newspaper industry; Pres. MAHBUBUL ALAM.

Overseas Correspondents' Association of Bangladesh (OCAB): 18 Topkhana Rd, Dhaka 1000; tel. (2) 7215388; e-mail naweed@bdonline.com; f. 1979; Pres. ZAHIDUZZMAN FARUQUE; Gen. Sec. SHAMIM AHMED; 60 mems.

Press Institute of Bangladesh: 3 Circuit House Rd, Dhaka 1000; tel. (2) 9330081; fax (2) 8317458; e-mail dgpib@yahoo.com; internet www.pib.gov.bd; f. 1976; trains journalists, conducts research, operates a newspaper library and data bank; Chair. HABIBUR RAHMAN MILON.

Publishers

Academic Press and Publishing Library (APPL): 70/1 Prantik Apts, Rd 6, Dhanmondi 1209; tel. (2) 8125394; fax (2) 8117277; e-mail appl@dhaka.net; internet www.applbooks.com; f. 1982; social sciences and sociology; Chair. Dr MIZANUR RAHMAN SHELLEY.

Agamee Prakashani: 36 Bangla Bazar, Dhaka 1100; tel. (2) 7111332; fax (2) 7110021; e-mail info@agameeprakashani-bd.com; f. 1986; fiction and academic; CEO and Proprietor OSMAN GANI.

Ahmed Publishing House: 7 Zindabahar 1st Lane, Dhaka; tel. (2) 36492; f. 1942; literature, history, science, religion, children's, maps and charts; Man. Dir KAMALUDDIN AHMED; Man. MESBAHUDDIN AHMED.

Ankur Prakashani: 40/1 Purana Paltan, Dhaka 1000; tel. (2) 9564799; fax (2) 7410986; e-mail info@ankur-prakashani.com; internet www.ankur-prakashani.com; f. 1984; academic and general; Dir MESBAHUDDIN AHMED.

Ashrafia Library: 4 Hakim Habibur Rahman Rd, Chawk Bazar, Dhaka 1000; Islamic religious books, texts, and reference works of Islamic institutions.

Asiatic Society of Bangladesh: 5 Old Secretariat Rd, Nimtali, Ramna, Dhaka 1000; tel. (2) 7168940; fax (2) 7168853; e-mail info@asiaticsociety.org.bd; internet www.asiaticsociety.org.bd; f. 1952; periodicals on science, Bangla and humanities; Pres. Prof. SIRAJUL ISLAM.

Bangla Academy (National Academy of Arts and Letters of Bangladesh): Burdwan House, 3 Kazi Nazrul Islam Ave, Dhaka 1000; tel. (2) 8619577; fax (2) 8612352; e-mail bacademy@citechco.net; internet www.banglaacademy.org.bd; f. 1955; higher education textbooks in Bengali, books on language, literature and culture, language planning, popular science, drama, encyclopaedias, translations of world classics, dictionaries; Dir-Gen. Prof. SHAMSUZZAMAN KHAN.

Bangladesh Books International Ltd: Ittefaq Bhaban, 1 Ramkrishna Mission Rd, POB 377, Dhaka; tel. (2) 256071; f. 1975; reference, academic, research, literary, children's in Bengali and English; Chair. MOINUL HOSSEIN; Man. Dir ABDUL HAFIZ.

Gatidhara: 38/2-Ka Bangla Bazar, POB 2723, Dhaka 1000; tel. (2) 7117515; fax (2) 7123472; e-mail gatidara@gmail.com; internet www.gatidhara.com; f. 1992; academic, general and fiction; Publr and Chief Exec. SIKDER ABUL BASHAR.

Gono Prakashani: House 14/E, Rd 6, Dhanmondhi R/A, Dhaka 1205; tel. (2) 8617208; fax (2) 8613567; e-mail gk@citechco.net; f. 1978; science and medicine; Man. Dir SHAFIQ KHAN; Editor BAZLUR RAHIM.

Muktadhara: 74 Farashganj, Dhaka 1100; tel. (2) 7111374; e-mail muktadhara1971@yahoo.com; f. 1971; educational and literary; Bengali and English; Dir JAHAR LAL SAHA; Man. Dir BIJALI PRAVA SAHA.

Mullick Brothers: 160–161 Dhaka New Market, Dhaka; tel. (2) 8619125; fax (2) 8610562; educational; Man. Dir KAMRUL HASAN MULLICK.

Shahitya Prakash: 42 Topkhana Rd, Dhaka 1000; tel. (2) 281327; fax (2) 863797; f. 1970; Prin. Officer MOFIDUL HOQUE.

Somoy Prokashon: 38/2-Ka Bangla Bazar, Dhaka 1100; tel. (2) 7121652; e-mail somoy@somoy.com; internet www.somoy.com; publr of fiction, history and studies on arts and sciences; Dir FARID AHMED.

University Press Ltd: Red Crescent House, 61 Motijheel C/A, POB 2611, Dhaka 1000; tel. (2) 9565444; fax (2) 9565443; e-mail upl@btcl.net.bd; internet www.uplbooks.com.bd; f. 1975; educational, academic and general; Man. Dir MOHIUDDIN AHMED.

GOVERNMENT PUBLISHING HOUSES

Bangladesh Bureau of Statistics: Parishankhan Bhaban, E-27/A, Agargaon, Sher-e-Bangla Nagar, Dhaka 1207; tel. (2) 9112589; fax (2) 9111064; e-mail dg@bbs.gov.bd; internet www.bbs.gov.bd; f. 1971; statistical year book and pocket book, censuses, surveys, agricultural year book, special reports, etc.; Dir-Gen. MOHAMMAD SHAHJAHAN ALI MOLLAH.

Bangladesh Government Press: Tejgaon, Dhaka 1209; tel. (2) 9117415; fax (2) 8891250; e-mail info@bgpress.gov.bd; internet www.bgpress.gov.bd; f. 1972; Dir Gen. A. L. M. ABDUR RAHMAN.

Department of Films and Publications: 112 Circuit House Rd, Dhaka 1000; tel. (2) 8331034; fax (2) 8331030; e-mail dfp_bd@yahoo.com; internet www.dfp.gov.bd; Dir-Gen. Dr MOHAMMAD JAHANGIR HOSSAIN.

Press Information Department: Bhaban 6, Bangladesh Secretariat, Dhaka 1000; tel. (2) 7161091; fax (2) 7165942; e-mail pid_1@bangla.net; internet www.bdpressinform.org; Prin. Information Officer HARUN UR-RASHID.

PUBLISHERS' ASSOCIATIONS

Bangladesh Publishers' and Booksellers' Association: 3 Liaquat Ave, 3rd Floor, Dhaka 1100; tel. (2) 7111666; f. 1972; Pres. ABU TAHER; 2,500 mems.

National Book Center of Bangladesh: 5c Bangabandhu Ave, Dhaka 1000; tel. (2) 9555745; e-mail info@nbc.org.bd; internet www.nbc.org.bd; f. 1963; est. to promote the cause of 'more, better and cheaper books'; organizes book fairs, publishes monthly journal; Dir RAFIQ AZAD.

Broadcasting and Communications

TELECOMMUNICATIONS

According to the Bangladesh Telecommunication Regulatory Commission, in January 2011 there were some 70.3m. active mobile cellular telephone subscriptions.

Bangladesh Telecommunication Regulatory Commission (BTRC): IEB Bhaban, 5th, 6th and 7th Floors, Ramna, Dhaka 1000; tel. (2) 7162277; fax (2) 9556677; e-mail btrc@btrc.gov.bd; internet www.btrc.gov.bd; f. 2002; regulates the telecommunications sector; Chair. Maj.-Gen. (retd) ZIA AHMED; Sec. MUHAMMAD MAHBOOB AHMED.

Bangladesh Telecommunications Co Ltd (BTCL): Central Office, Telejogajog Bhaban, 37/E Eskaton Garden, Dhaka 1000; tel. (2) 8311500; fax (2) 832577; e-mail md@btcl.net.bd; internet www.btcl.gov.bd; formed through division of Bangladesh Telegraph and Telephone Board in 2008; govt-owned provider of fixed-line telephone and internet services; Chair. SUNIL KANTI BOSE; Man. Dir ASHRAFUL ALIM.

GrameenPhone Ltd: GP House, Basundhara, Baridhara, Dhaka 1229; tel. (2) 9882990; fax (2) 9882970; e-mail info@grameenphone.com; internet www.grameenphone.com; f. 1996 by Grameen Bank to expand cellular telephone service in rural areas; 55.8% owned by Telenor (Norway), 34.2% by Grameen Telecom Corpn and 10% by general retail and institutional investors; the leading telecommunications service provider in Bangladesh with more than 30m. subscribers (Feb. 2011); CEO TORE JOHNSEN.

Orascom Telecom Bangladesh Ltd (Banglalink): 4 Gulshan Ave, Gulshan Model Town, Dhaka 1212; tel. (2) 9885770; fax (2) 8827265; e-mail info@banglalinkgsm.com; internet www.banglalinkgsm.com; f. 1998; provides mobile cellular telephone services; Man. Dir and CEO AHMED ABOU DOMA.

Pacific Bangladesh Telecom Ltd (Citycell): Pacific Centre, 14 Mohakhali C/A, Dhaka 1212; tel. (2) 8822186; fax (2) 8823575; e-mail customerservice@citycell.com; internet www.citycell.com; CEO MEHBOOB CHOWDHURY.

Robi Axiata Ltd (Robi): 53 Gulshan Ave, Dhaka 1212; tel. (2) 9887146; fax (2) 9885463; e-mail info@axiata.com; internet www.robi.com.bd; f. 1996; jt venture between Axiata Group Berhad, Malaysia (70%) and NTT DoCoMo Inc, Japan (30%); mobile cellular telephone services; Man. Dir and CEO MICHAEL KUEHNER.

Teletalk Bangladesh Ltd: 41 Rd 27, Blk A, Banani, Dhaka 1213; tel. (2) 8851060; fax (2) 9882828; e-mail info@teletalk.com.bd; internet www.teletalk.com.bd; f. 2004; govt-owned provider of mobile cellular telephone services; affiliated to Bangladesh Telecommunications Co; Man. Dir MUHAMMAD MUJIBUR RAHMAN.

Warid Telecom International: POB 3016, Dhaka; fax (2) 8951786; e-mail customerservice@bd.airtel.com; internet www.waridtel.com.bd; awarded licence to provide mobile cellular telephone services in 2005; service commenced in 2007; fmrly a subsidiary of Abu Dhabi Group of United Arab Emirates; 70% stake acquired by Bharti Airtel Ltd, India in Jan. 2010; CEO CHRIS TOBIT.

BROADCASTING

Radio

ABC Radio: Dhaka Trade Centre, 3rd Floor, 99 Kazi Nazrul Islam Ave, Karwan Bazar, Dhaka 1215; tel. (2) 8142038; fax (2) 9128141; e-mail program@abcradiobd.fm; internet abcradiobd.fm; f. 2007; regular news bulletins, documentaries and talk shows; Bangla and English; CEO MOHAMMAD SANAULLAH.

Bangladesh Betar: 121 Kazi Nazrul Islam Ave, Shahabag, Dhaka 1000; tel. (2) 8651083; fax (2) 9662600; e-mail dgbetar@btcl.net.bd; internet www.betar.org.bd; f. 1939; govt-controlled; 12 regional stations broadcast a total of approximately 255 hours daily; external service broadcasts 8 transmissions daily in Arabic, Bengali, English, Hindi, Nepalese and Urdu; Dir-Gen. A. K. M. SHAMEEM CHOWDHURI.

Radio Aamar: Uniwave Broadcasting Co Ltd, Silver Tower, 12th Floor, 52 Gulshan Ave, Dhaka 1212; tel. (2) 9886800; internet www.radioaamar.com; f. 2007; bilingual news and Bangla music.

Radio Foorti: 10 Kazi Nazrul Islam Ave, 5th Floor, Jahangir Tower, Karwan Bazar, Dhaka 1215; tel. (2) 9125792; e-mail info@radiofoorti.fm; internet www.radiofoorti.fm; f. 2006; Bangla music; CEO DANIEL AFZALUR RAHMAN.

Radio Today: 34 Kamal Ataturk Ave, 13th and 19th Floors, Awal Centre, Banani, Dhaka 1213; tel. (2) 8829293; e-mail info@radiotodaybd.fm; internet www.radiotodaybd.fm; f. 2006; owned by Radio Broadcasting FM (Bangladesh) Co Ltd; contemporary music; Chair. MOHAMMAD MOZAMMEL HAQUE; Man. Dir. MOHAMMAD RAFIQUL HAQUE.

Television

Bangladesh Television (BTV): Television House, Rampura, Dhaka 1219; tel. (2) 9330131; fax (2) 8312927; e-mail news@btt.net.bd; internet www.btv.gov.bd; f. 1964; govt-controlled; daily broadcasts on one channel from Dhaka station for 12 hours; transmissions also from nation-wide network of 15 relay stations; Dir-Gen. KAZI ABU ZAFAR MOHAMMAD HASSAN SIDDIQUI; Gen. Man. MUHAMMAD MONWARUL ISLAM.

ATN Bangla: WASA Bhaban, 1st Floor, 98 Kazi Nazrul Islam Ave, Karwan Bazar, Dhaka 1215; tel. (2) 8111207; fax (2) 8111876; e-mail atn@dhaka.agni.com; internet www.atnbangla.tv; f. 1997; private satellite channel; broadcasts in Bengali; Chair. and Man. Dir MAHFUZUR RAHMAN.

Banglavision: Bir Uttam C. R. Dutta Rd, Dhaka 1205; tel. (2) 8653175; e-mail info@banglavision.tv; internet www.banglavision.tv; owned by Shamol Bangla Media Ltd; Chair. ABDUL HAQUE; Man. Dir AMINUL HUQ.

Desh Television Ltd: 70 Shaheed Sangbadik Selina Parveen Sarak Malibagh, Dhaka 1217; tel. (2) 8332958; fax (2) 8332981; e-mail web@desh.tv; internet www.desh.tv; f. 2009; private satellite channel; broadcasts in Bengali.

Ekushey Television: Jahangir Tower, 10 Karwan Bazar, Dhaka 1215; tel. (2) 8126535; fax (2) 8121270; e-mail info@ekushey-tv.com; internet www.ekushey-tv.com; private entertainment channel; broadcasts in Bengali; Chair. and CEO ABDUS SALAM.

Islamic TV: 34/1 Paribag, 3rd Floor, Sonargaon Rd, Hatirpul, Dhaka 1000; tel. (2) 8610769; fax (2) 8610866; e-mail info@islamictv.com.bd; internet www.islamictv.com.bd; f. 2007; programmes on Islamic doctrine, culture and news.

NTV Bangladesh: BSEC Bhaban, 6th Floor, 102 Kazi Nazrul Islam Ave, Karwan Bazar, Dhaka 1215; tel. (2) 9143381; fax (2) 9143386; e-mail info@ntvbd.com; internet www.ntvbd.com; f. 2003; private satellite channel; Chair. AL-HAJ MUHAMMAD MOSADDAK ALI.

Sangsad Bangladesh Television: 121 Kazi Nazrul Islam Ave, Dhaka 1000; tel. (2) 9330131; fax (2) 8312927; f. 2011; currently under the supervision of the Development Channel of Bangladesh Television (BTV); broadcasts foreign parliamentary proceedings and documentaries on legislative systems in other countries.

Finance

(cap. = capital; res = reserves; dep. = deposits; m. = million; brs = branches; amounts in taka)

BANKING

Central Bank

Bangladesh Bank: Motijheel C/A, POB 325, Dhaka 1000; tel. (2) 7126101; fax (2) 9566212; e-mail governor@bangla.net; internet www.bangladesh-bank.org; f. 1971; cap. 30m., res 93,546m., dep. 331,680m. (June 2009); Gov. ATIUR RAHMAN; 9 brs.

Nationalized Commercial Banks

Agrani Bank Ltd: 9D Dilkusha C/A, Dhaka 1000; tel. (2) 9566160; fax (2) 9562346; e-mail agrani@agranibank.org; internet www.agranibank.org; f. 1972; 100% state-owned; cap. 5,465m., res 5,758m., dep. 202,325m. (Dec. 2010); Chair. Dr KHONDOKER BAZLUL HOQUE; Man. Dir and CEO SYED ABDUL HAMID; 867 brs.

Janata Bank Ltd: 110 Motijheel C/A, POB 468, Dhaka 1000; tel. (2) 9552078; fax (2) 9564644; e-mail id-obd@janatabank-bd.com; internet www.janatabank-bd.com; f. 1972; 100% state-owned; cap. 5,000m., res 10,247m., dep. 283,287m. (Dec. 2010); CEO and Man. Dir S. M. AMINUR RAHMAN; 856 brs in Bangladesh, 4 brs in the UAE.

Rupali Bank Ltd: Rupali Bhaban, 34 Dilkusha C/A, POB 719, Dhaka 1000; tel. (2) 9551525; fax (2) 9564148; e-mail rblhocom@bdcom.com; internet www.rupalibank.org; f. 1972; cap. 1,250m., res 1,821.8m., dep. 72,476.2m. (Dec. 2007); scheduled for privatization; Chair. Dr AHMED AL-KABIR; Man. Dir M. FARID UDDIN; 492 brs.

Sonali Bank Ltd: 35–44 Motijheel C/A, POB 3130, Dhaka 1000; tel. (2) 9550426; fax (2) 9561410; e-mail sbhoid@bdmail.net; internet www.sonalibank.com.bd; f. 1972; 100% state-owned; cap. 9,000.0m., res 23,604m., dep. 469,490m. (Dec. 2010); Chair. QUAZI BAHARUL ISLAM; CEO and Man. Dir HUMAYUN KABIR; 1,189 brs incl. 2 overseas brs.

Private Commercial Banks

AB Bank Ltd: Head Office, BCIC Bhaban, 30–31 Dilkusha C/A, POB 3522, Dhaka 1000; tel. (2) 9560312; fax (2) 9564122; e-mail info@abbank.com.bd; internet www.abbank.com.bd; f. 1981; fmrly known as Arab Bangladesh Bank Ltd; name changed as above in 2007; 99.3% owned by Bangladesh nationals and 0.7% by Bangladesh Govt; cap. 3,686m., res 5,955m., dep. 125,271m. (Dec. 2011); Chair. M. WAHIDUL HAQUE; Pres. and Man. Dir M. FAZLUR RAHMAN; 81 brs, 1 br. in India.

Al-Arafah Islami Bank Ltd: 6th–9th Floors, 36 Dilkusha C/A, Dhaka 1000; tel. (2) 7123255; fax (2) 9569351; e-mail aibl@al-arafahbank.com; internet www.al-arafahbank.com; f. 1995; 100% owned by 23 sponsors; cap. 4,677m., res 1,746m., dep. 52,161m. (Dec. 2010); Chair. BADIUR RAHMAN; Man. Dir EKRAMUL HOQUE; 53 brs.

The City Bank Ltd: 136 Gulshan Ave, Gulshan-2, Dhaka 1212; tel. (2) 8813483; fax (2) 9884446; e-mail mail@thecitybank.com; internet www.thecitybank.com; f. 1983; 50% owned by sponsors and 50% by public; cap. 3,888m., res 6,192m., dep. 66,763m. (Dec. 2010); Chair. RUBEL AZIZ; Man. Dir and CEO K. MAHMOOD SATTAR; 88 brs.

Dhaka Bank Ltd: 1st Floor, Biman Bhaban, 100 Motijheel C/A, Dhaka 1000; tel. (2) 9554514; e-mail info@dhakabank.com.bd; internet www.dhakabankltd.com; f. 1995; cap. 3,590m., res 4,191m., dep. 84,177m. (Dec. 2011); Chair. RESHADUR RAHMAN; Man. Dir KHONDKER FAZLE RASHID; 55 brs.

Dutch-Bangla Bank Ltd: 4th Floor, Sena Kalyan Bhaban, 195 Motijheel C/A, Dhaka 1000; tel. (2) 7176390; fax (2) 9561889; internet www.dbbl.com.bd; f. 1996; cap. 2,000m., res 5,201m., dep. 99,601m. (Dec. 2011); Chair. ZAHEED HOSSAIN KHAN; Man. Dir SHAMSHI TABREZ; 96 brs.

Eastern Bank Ltd: Jiban Bima Bhaban, 10 Dilkusha C/A, Dhaka; tel. (2) 9556360; fax (2) 9558392; internet www.ebl.com.bd; f. 1992; appropriated assets and liabilities of fmr Bank of Credit and Commerce International (Overseas) Ltd; 83% owned by public, 17% owned by govt and private commercial banks; cap. 4,527m., res 8,144m., dep. 74,389m. (Dec. 2011); Chair. MOHD. NOOR ALI; Man. Dir and CEO ALI REZA IFTEKHAR; 49 brs.

ICB Islamic Bank Ltd: T. K. Bhaban, 15th Floor, 13 Kazi Nazrul Islam Ave, Karwan Bazar, Dhaka 1215; tel. (2) 9143361; fax (2) 9111994; e-mail enquiry@icbislamic-bd.com; internet www.icbislamic-bd.com; f. 1987 on Islamic banking principles; fmrly Al-Baraka Bank Bangladesh Ltd, later Oriental Bank Ltd; cap. 6,647m., res 632.7m., dep. 13,449m. (Dec. 2010); Chair. Tan Sri Dr HADENAN BIN ABDUL JALIL; Man. Dir MAMOON MAHMOOD SHAH; 33 brs.

International Finance Investment and Commerce Bank Ltd (IFICB): BSB Bldg, 8th–10th & 16th–19th Floors, 8 Rajuk Ave, POB 2229, Dhaka 1000; tel. (2) 9563020; fax (2) 9562015; e-mail info@ificbankbd.com; internet www.ificbankbd.com; f. 1983; 58.63% owned by public, 32.75% owned by Govt and 8.62% owned by private industry; cap. 2,179m., res 2,266m., dep. 54,709m. (Dec. 2010); Chair. SALMAN F. RAHMAN; Man. Dir MOHAMMAD ABDULLAH; 87 brs.

Islami Bank Bangladesh Ltd (IBBL): Islami Bank Tower, 40 Dilkusha C/A, POB 233, Dhaka 1000; tel. (2) 9563040; fax (2) 9564532; e-mail info@islamibankbd.com; internet www.islamibankbd.com; f. 1983 on Islamic banking principles; cap. 7,413m., res 13,486m., dep. 288,956m. (Dec. 2010); Chair. Prof. ABU NASSER MUHAMMED ABDUZ ZAHER; Man. Dir MOHAMMAD ABDUL MANNAN; 251 brs.

Mercantile Bank Ltd: 61 Dilkusha C/A, Dhaka 1000; tel. (2) 9559333; fax (2) 9561213; e-mail mbl@bol-online.com; internet www.mblbd.com; f. 1999; cap. 4,968m., res 3,513m., dep. 92,946m.

(Dec. 2011); Chair. MOHAMMED ABDUL JALIL; Man. Dir and CEO A. K. M. SHAHIDUL HAQUE; 65 brs.

National Bank Ltd: 18 Dilkusha C/A, Dhaka 1000; tel. (2) 9563081; fax (2) 9563953; e-mail nblho@nblbd.com; internet www.nblbd.com; f. 1983; 50% owned by sponsors and 50% by general public; cap. 8,603m., res 7,802.9m., dep. 125,457m. (Dec.2011); Chair. ZAINUL HAQUE SIKDER; Man. Dir NEAZ AHMED; 130 brs.

National Credit and Commerce Bank Ltd (NCC Bank): 7–8 Motijheel C/A, Dhaka 1000; tel. (2) 9561902; fax (2) 9566290; e-mail nccbl@bdmail.net; internet www.nccbank.com.bd; f. 1993; 50% owned by sponsors, 50% by general public; cap. 5,941m., res 3,784m., dep. 79,371.9m. (Dec. 2011); Chair. NURUN NEWAZ; Man. Dir and CEO MUHAMMAD NURUL AMIN; 80 brs.

ONE Bank Ltd: HRC Bhaban, 46 Kawaran Bazar C/A, Dhaka 1215; tel. (2) 9118161; fax (2) 9134794; e-mail obl@onebankbd.com; internet www.onebankbd.com; f. 1999; cap. 3,188.6m., res 1,931m., dep. 56,577m. (Dec. 2011); Chair. ZAHUR ULLAH; Man. Dir FARMAN R. CHOWDHURY.

Prime Bank Ltd: Adamjee Court, Annex Bldg No. 2, 119–120 Motijheel C/A, Dhaka 1000; tel. (2) 9567265; fax (2) 9567230; e-mail info@primebank.com; internet www.primebank.com.bd; f. 1995; cap. 7,798m., res 8,538m., dep. 156,835m. (Dec. 2011); Chair. MOHD SHIRAJUL ISLAM MOLLAH; Man. Dir M. EHSANUL HAQUE; 94 brs.

Pubali Bank Ltd: 26 Dilkusha C/A, POB 853, Dhaka 1000; tel. (2) 9551614; fax (2) 9564009; e-mail mailbox@pubalibankbd.com; internet www.pubalibangla.com; f. 1959 as Eastern Mercantile Bank Ltd; name changed to Pubali Bank in 1972; privately owned; cap. 4,968m., res 7,070m., dep. 96,358m. (Dec. 2010); Chair. HAFIZ AHMED MAJUMDER; Man. Dir and CEO HELAL AHMED CHOWDHURY; 399 brs.

Social Islami Bank Ltd: 15 Dilkusha C/A, Dhaka 1000; tel. (2) 9559014; fax (2) 9568098; e-mail info@sibl-bd.com; internet www.siblbd.com; f. 1995 as Social Investment Bank; renamed as above in 2009; cap. 2,987.8m., res 788m., dep. 44,233m. (Dec. 2010); Chair. MD ANISUL HOQUE; Man. Dir MUHAMMAD ALI; 64 brs.

Southeast Bank Ltd: Eunoos Trade Center, 2nd, 3rd, 4th and 16th Floors, 52–53 Dilkusha C/A, Dhaka 1000; tel. (2) 9571115; fax (2) 9550093; e-mail info@southeastbank.com.bd; internet www.sebankbd.com; f. 1995; cap. 8,317m., res 8,991m., dep. 125,660m. (Dec. 2011); Chair. ALAMGIR KABIR; Man. Dir MAHBUBUL ALAM; 65 brs.

Trust Bank Ltd: 2nd, 16th and 17th Floors, Peoples Insurance Bhaban, 36 Dilkusha C/A, Dhaka 1000; tel. (2) 9570261; fax (2) 9572315; e-mail info@trustbanklimited.com; internet www.trustbank.com.bd; f. 1999; cap. 2,217m., res. 1,684m., dep. 49,701.8m. (Dec. 2010); Chair. Gen. ABDUL MUBEEN; Man. Dir M. SHAH ALAM SARWAR; 45 brs.

United Commercial Bank Ltd: Plot CWS(A) 1, Rd 34, Gulshan Ave, Dhaka 1212; tel. and fax (2) 8852500; e-mail info@ucbl.com; internet www.ucbl.com; f. 1983; 54.17% owned by sponsors and 45.83% by general public; cap. 2,909.9m., res 3,451m., dep. 110,427.9m. (Dec. 2010); Chair. AKHTARUZZAMAN CHOWDHURY; Man. Dir M. SHAJAHAN BHUIYAN; 107 brs.

Uttara Bank Ltd: Uttara Bank Bhaban, 47, Bir Uttom Shahid Ashfaq us-Samad Rd, 90 Motijheel C/A, POB 217 and 818, Dhaka 1000; tel. (2) 9551162; fax (2) 7168376; e-mail uttara@citechco.net; internet www.uttarabank-bd.com; f. 1965 as Eastern Banking Corpn Ltd; name changed to Uttara Bank in 1972 and to Uttara Bank Ltd in 1983; 100% publicly owned; cap. 2,395.9m., res 5,224m., dep. 64,175.7m. (Dec. 2010); Chair. AZHARUL ISLAM; Man. Dir SHAMSUDDIN AHMED; 211 brs.

Development Finance Organizations

Bangladesh Development Bank Ltd (BDBL): 8 Rajuk Ave, Dhaka; tel. (2) 9563476; fax (2) 9562061; e-mail md@bdbl.com.bd; internet www.bdbl.com.bd; f. 2010 as result of merger of Bangladesh Shilpa Bank and Bangladesh Shilpa Rin Sangstha; 100% state-owned; auth. cap. 4,000m., res. 11,465m., dep. 3,234m. (Dec. 2010); Chair. NAZEM AHMED CHOWDHURY; Man. Dir MOHAMMAD MIZANUR RAHMAN; 17 brs.

Bangladesh House Building Finance Corpn (BHBFC): 22 Purana Paltan, Dhaka 1000; tel. (2) 9561315; fax (2) 9561324; e-mail bhbfc@bangla.net; internet bhbfc.gov.bd; f. 1952; provides low-interest credit for residential house-building; 100% state-owned; Chair. M. JANIBUL HAQUE; Man. Dir KAZI FAQURUL ISLAM; 9 zonal offices, 13 regional offices and 2 camp offices.

Bangladesh Krishi Bank (BKB): Krishi Bank Bhaban, 83–85 Motijheel C/A, Dhaka 1000; tel. (2) 9560021; fax (2) 9561211; e-mail info@krishibank.org.bd; internet www.krishibank.org.bd; f. 1961; fmrly the Agricultural Development Bank of Pakistan, name changed as above in 1973; provides credit for agricultural and rural devt; also performs all kinds of banking; 100% state-owned; cap. 9,000m., res 2,059.9m., dep. 110,874m. (June 2010); Chair. KHONDKAR IBRAHIM KHALED; Man. Dir MUKTER HUSSAIN; 954 brs.

BASIC Bank Ltd: Bana Sena Kalyan Bhaban, 5th Floor, 195 Motijheel C/A, Dhaka 1000; tel. (2) 9568190; fax (2) 9564829; e-mail basicho@citechco.net; internet www.basicbanklimited.com; f. 1988 as Bangladesh Small Industries and Commerce Bank Ltd; renamed as above in 2001; 100% state-owned; cap. 1,964m., res 2,079m., dep. 48,662m. (Dec. 2010); Chair. SHEIKH ABDUL HYE BACCHU; Man. Dir SK. MONZUR MORSHED; 34 brs.

Export-Import Bank of Bangladesh Ltd: Plot SE(F) 9, Rd 142, Gulshan Ave, Dhaka 1212; tel. (2) 9889363; fax (2) 8828962; e-mail itd@eximbankbd.com; internet www.eximbankbd.com; f. 1999; cap. 6,832m., res 3,217m., dep. 93,796.9m. (Dec. 2010); Chair. NAZRUL ISLAM MAZUMDER; Man. Dir MD FARIDUDDIN AHMED; 59 brs.

Grameen Bank: Grameen Bank Bhavan, Mirpur 2, Dhaka 1216; tel. (2) 8011138; fax (2) 8013559; e-mail grameen.bank@grameen.net; internet www.grameen.com; f. 1976; provides credit for the landless rural poor; 10% owned by Govt; Chair. MUZAMMEL HUQ; Man. Dir MOHAMMAD SHAHJAHAN (acting); 2,565 brs.

Infrastructure Development Co Ltd (IDCOL): UTC Bldg, 16th Floor, 8 Panthapath, Karwan Bazar, Dhaka 1215; tel. (2) 9102171; fax (2) 8116663; e-mail contact@idcol.org; internet www.idcol.org; f. 1997; state-owned; Chair. M. MUSHARRAF HOSSAIN BHUIYAN; Exec. Dir and CEO ISLAM SHARIF.

Investment Corpn of Bangladesh (ICB): BDBL Bldg, 12th–15th Floors, 8 Rajuk Ave, Dhaka 1000; tel. (2) 9563455; fax (2) 9563313; e-mail icb@agni.com; internet www.icb.gov.bd; f. 1976; provides investment banking services; 27% owned by Govt; cap. 500.0m., res 1,646.1m. (June 2008); Chair. Dr M. KHAIRUL HOSSAIN; Man. Dir MOHAMMAD FAYEKUZZAMAN; 7 brs.

Rajshahi Krishi Unnayan Bank: Kazihata, Rajshahi 6000; tel. (721) 775008; fax (721) 775947; e-mail info@rakub.org.bd; internet www.rakub.org.bd; f. 1987; 100% state-owned; Chair. Dr M. SHAH NOWAZ ALI; Man. Dir PRADIP KUMAR DUTTA; 365 brs.

Banking Association

Bangladesh Association of Banks: Jabbar Tower, 16th Floor, Rd 135, 42 Gulshan Ave, Gulshan-1, Dhaka 1212; tel. (2) 8859885; fax (2) 8851015; e-mail admin@bab.com.bd; internet www.bab.com.bd; f. 1993; Chair. MD NUZRUL ISLAM MAZUMDER.

STOCK EXCHANGES

Chittagong Stock Exchange: CSE Bldg, 1080 Sheikh Mujib Rd, Agrabad, Chittagong; tel. (31) 714632; fax (31) 714101; e-mail info@cse.com.bd; internet www.cse.com.bd; f. 1995; Pres. AL MARUF KHAN; CEO and Dir SYED SAJID HUSAIN.

Dhaka Stock Exchange Ltd: Stock Exchange Bldg, 9F Motijheel C/A, Dhaka 1000; tel. (2) 9564601; fax (2) 9564727; e-mail dse@bol-online.com; internet www.dsebd.org; f. 1954; 284 listed cos; Pres. MD SHAKIL RIZVI; CEO SATIPATI MOITRA.

Regulatory Authority

Bangladesh Securities and Exchange Commission: Jiban Bima Tower, 15th, 16th and 20th Floors, 10 Dilkusha C/A, Dhaka 1000; tel. (2) 9568101; fax (2) 9563721; e-mail secbd@bdmail.net; internet www.secbd.org; f. 1993; Chair. M. KHAIRUL HOSSAIN.

INSURANCE

Bangladesh General Insurance Co Ltd (BGIC): 42 Dilkusha C/A, Dhaka 1000; tel. (2) 9555073; fax (2) 9564212; e-mail bgic@citechco.net; internet www.bgicinsure.com; f. 1985; Chair. TOWHID SAMAD; Man. Dir A. K. AZIZUL HUQ CHAUDHURI.

Bangladesh Insurance Association: Rupali Bima Bhaban, 7th Floor, 7 Rajuk Ave, Dhaka 1000; tel. (2) 9557330; fax (2) 9562345; e-mail bia@bdcom.com; Chair. A. K. M. RAFIQUL ISLAM.

Eastern Insurance Co Ltd: 2nd Floor, 44 Dilkusha C/A, Dhaka 1000; tel. (2) 9563033; fax (2) 9569735; e-mail eicl@dhaka.net; f. 1986; Chair. MUJIBUR RAHMAN; Man. Dir MOHAMMAD HAROON PATWARY.

Jiban Bima Corpn (JBC): 24 Motijheel C/A, Dhaka 1000; tel. (2) 9551414; e-mail mds@jbc.gov.bd; internet www.jbc.gov.bd; state-owned; life insurance; Chair.and Dir MOHAMMED SOHRAB UDDIN; Man. Dir PARIKSHIT DATTA CHOUDHURY.

Pioneer Insurance Co Ltd: Symphony, 5th Floor, SE(F)9, Rd 142, South Ave, Gulshan, Dhaka 1212; tel. (2) 8817512; fax (2) 8817234; e-mail piclho@pioneerinsurance.com.bd; internet www.pioneerinsurance.com.bd; f. 1996; Chair. TAPAN CHOWDHURY; Man. Dir Q. A. F. M. SERAJUL ISLAM.

Pragati Insurance Ltd: Pragati Rhone–Poulence Centre, 6th Floor, 20–21 Kawran Bazar, Dhaka 1215; tel. (2) 8189184; fax (2) 9124024; e-mail info@pragatilife.com; internet www.pragatilife.com; Chair. KHALILUR RAHMAN; Man. Dir ZAFAR HALIM.

Reliance Insurance Ltd: Shanta Western Tower, Level 5, 186 Tejgaon I/A, Dhaka 1208; tel. (2) 8878836; fax (2) 8878831; e-mail info@reliance-bd.com; internet www.reliance.com.bd; f. 1988; Chair. RAJIV PRASAD SHAHA; Man. Dir and CEO AKHTAR AHMED.

Sadharan Bima Corpn: Sadharan Bima Bhaban, 33 Dilkusha C/A, Dhaka 1000; e-mail head-office@sbc.org.bd; internet www.sbc.gov.bd; state-owned; general insurance; Chair. M. SHAMSUL ALAM; Man. Dir MD REZAUL KARIM.

Regulatory Authority

Insurance Development and Regulatory Authority (IDRA): Dhaka; f. 2011, to replace the office of the Chief Controller of Insurance; Chair. SHEFAQ AHMED.

Trade and Industry

GOVERNMENT AGENCIES

Board of Investment: Jiban Bima Tower, 19th Floor, 10 Dilkusha C/A, Dhaka 1000; tel. (2) 7169580; fax (2) 9562312; e-mail service@boi.gov.bd; internet boi.gov.bd; f. 1989; Exec. Chair. Dr S. A. SAMAD.

Export Promotion Bureau: TCB Bhaban, 2nd and 4th Floors, 1 Karwan Bazar, Dhaka 1215; tel. (2) 9144821; fax (2) 9119531; e-mail info@epb.gov.bd; internet www.epb.gov.bd; f. 1972; semi-autonomous govt org., chaired by Minister of Commerce; regional offices in Chittagong, Khulna, Rajshahi; br. offices in Narayanganj, Comilla and Sylhet; Vice-Chair. SHUBHASHISH BOSE.

Planning Commission: Planning Commission Secretariat, Sher-e-Bangla Nagar, Dhaka 1207; e-mail masuddhk@gmail.com; internet www.plancomm.gov.bd; f. 1972; chaired by Prime Minister, with Minister of Planning serving as Vice-Chair.; responsible for all aspects of economic planning and development including the preparation of the five-year plans and annual development programmes (in conjunction with appropriate govt ministries), promotion of savings and investment, compilation of statistics, and evaluation of development schemes and projects; Planning Division Sec. BHUIYAN SHAFIQUL ISLAM.

Privatization Commission: Transport Pool Bldg, Levels 8, 9 & 10, Secretariat Link Rd, Dhaka 1000; tel. (2) 9551986; fax (2) 9556433; e-mail pc@intechworld.net; internet www.pc.gov.bd; f. 1993; Chair. Dr MIRZA ABDUL JALIL.

Tariff Commission: Ministry of Commerce, 9th Floor, Govt Office Bldg, Segunbagicha, Dhaka 1000; tel. (2) 9335930; fax (2) 8315685; e-mail btariff@intechworld.net; internet www.bdtariffcom.org; f. 1973; advises the govt on trade and fiscal policies, regional and multilateral trade negotiations and issues facing indigenous industries; Chair. Dr MOHAMMAD MOZIBUR RAHMAN.

Trading Corpn of Bangladesh: 2nd Floor, TCB Bhaban, 1 Kawran Bazar, Dhaka 1215; tel. (2) 8141827; fax (2) 8120853; e-mail tcb@tcb.gov.bd; f. 1972; national trade org. of the Ministry of Commerce; imports, exports and markets goods through appointed dealers and agents; Chair. Brig.-Gen. SARWAR JAHAN TALUKDER; Dir ABU SYED MOHAMMAD HASHIM.

DEVELOPMENT ORGANIZATIONS

Bangladesh Chemical Industries Corpn (BCIC): BCIC Bhaban, 30–31 Dilkusha C/A, Dhaka 1000; tel. (2) 9562140; fax (2) 9564120; e-mail bcic.info@gmail.com; internet www.bcic.gov.bd; f. 1976; state-owned; est. to promote industrial and socio-economic development and food self-sufficiency; manages 13 enterprises incl. Chhatak Cement Co, Chittagong Urea Fertilizer Co, Karnaphuli Paper Mills Ltd, Urea Fertilizer Factory Ltd, Natural Gas Fertilizer Factory Ltd; Chair. MD GOLAM RABBANI.

Bangladesh Export Processing Zones Authority (BEPZA): BEPZA Complex, House 19/D, Rd 6, Dhanmondi R/A, Dhaka 1000; tel. (2) 9670530; fax (2) 8650060; e-mail chairman@bepza.org; internet www.epzbangladesh.org.bd; f. 1983 to plan, develop, operate and manage export processing zones (EPZs) in Bangladesh; Exec. Chair. Maj.-Gen. A. T. M. SHAHIDUL ISLAM; Sec. MD SHAWKAT NABI.

Bangladesh Fisheries Development Corpn (BFDC): 24–25 Dilkusha C/A, Dhaka 1000; tel. (2) 9553975; fax (2) 9563990; e-mail bfdc_64@yahoo.com; internet bfdc-gov.org; f. 1964; under Ministry of Fisheries and Livestock; development and commercial activities; Chair. KHURSHIDA KHATUN.

Bangladesh Forest Industries Development Corpn (BFIDC): Bana Shilpa Bhaban, 73 Motijheel C/A, Dhaka 1000; tel. (2) 9560086; fax (2) 9563035; e-mail cm.bfidc@gmail.com; internet bfidc.info; f. 1959; state-owned; Chair. MOHAMMAD FARHAD UDDIN.

Bangladesh Small and Cottage Industries Corpn (BSCIC): 137–138 Motijheel C/A, Dhaka 1000; tel. (2) 9556191; fax (2) 9550704; e-mail info@bscic.gov.bd; internet www.bscic.gov.bd; f. 1957; Chair. MOHAMMAD FAKRUL ISLAM.

Bangladesh Steel and Engineering Corpn (BSEC): BSEC Bhaban, 102 Kazi Nazrul Islam Ave, Dhaka 1215; tel. (2) 9115144; fax (2) 8189642; e-mail bsecheadoffice@gmail.com; internet www.bsec.gov.bd; f. 1976; 9 industrial units; Chair. MOHAMMAD ABU HAFIZ; 2,710 employees.

Bangladesh Sugar and Food Industries Corpn (BSFIC): Chini Shilpa Bhaban, 3 Dilkusha C/A, Dhaka 1000; tel. (2) 9565869; fax (2) 9550481; e-mail chinikal@btcl.net.bd; internet www.bsfic.gov.bd; f. 1976; Chair. MAHMUDUL HAQUE BHUIYAN.

Bangladesh Tea Board: 171–172 Baizid Bostami Rd, Nasirabad, Chittagong; tel. (31) 682903; fax (31) 682863; e-mail secretary@teaboard.gov.bd; internet www.teaboard.gov.bd; f. 1951; regulates, controls and promotes the cultivation and marketing of tea, both in Bangladesh and abroad; Chair. Maj.-Gen. MOHAMMAD MAHBUBUL HASAN.

CHAMBERS OF COMMERCE

Federation of Bangladesh Chambers of Commerce and Industry (FBCCI): Federation Bhaban, 60 Motijheel C/A, Dhaka 1000; tel. (2) 9560102; fax (2) 7176030; e-mail fbcci@bol-online.com; internet www.fbcci-bd.org; f. 1973; comprises 259 trade asscns and 81 chambers of commerce and industry; Pres. A. K. AZAD; Sec.-Gen. MIR SHAHABUDDIN MOHAMMAD.

Barisal Chamber of Commerce and Industry: Chamber Bhaban, Nasir Pool, Shaw Rd, POB 30, Barisal; tel. (431) 52020; Pres. Sheikh ABDUR RAHIM.

Chittagong Chamber of Commerce and Industry: Chamber House, 38 Agrabad C/A, POB 481, Chittagong; tel. (31) 713366; fax (31) 710183; e-mail info@chittagongchamber.com; internet www.chittagongchamber.com; f. 1959; more than 5,000 mems; Pres. M. A. LATIF; Sec. OSMAN GANI CHOWDHURY.

Dhaka Chamber of Commerce and Industry: Dhaka Chamber Bldg, 65–66 Motijheel C/A, POB 2641, Dhaka 1000; tel. (2) 9552562; fax (2) 9560830; e-mail info@dhakachamber.com; internet www.dhakachamber.com; f. 1958; more than 4,500 mems; Pres. ASIF IBRAHIM.

Foreign Investors' Chamber of Commerce and Industry: L. R. Villa, 1st Floor, Apt 1A2, House 9, Rd 113, Gulshan 2, Dhaka 1212; tel. (2) 9893049; fax (2) 9893058; e-mail ficci@bdcom.net; internet www.ficci.org.bd; f. 1963 as Agrabad Chamber of Commerce and Industry, name changed as above in 1987; Pres. SYED ERSHAD AHMED; Exec. Dir M. A. MATIN.

Khulna Chamber of Commerce and Industry: Chamber Mansion, 5 KDA C/A, Khulna 9100; tel. (41) 721695; fax (41) 725365; e-mail khulnachamber@gmail.com; internet www.khulnachamber.com; f. 1934; Pres. KAZI AMINUL HAQUE.

Metropolitan Chamber of Commerce and Industry: Chamber Bldg, 4th Floor, 122–124 Motijheel C/A, Dhaka 1000; tel. (2) 9565208; fax (2) 9565211; e-mail info@mccibd.org; internet www.mccibd.org; f. 1904; Pres. Maj.-Gen. AMJAD KHAN CHOUDHURY; Sec.-Gen. FAROOQ AHMED.

Rajshahi Chamber of Commerce and Industry: Chamber Bhaban, Station Rd, PO Ghoramara, Rajshahi 6100; tel. (721) 812122; fax (721) 812133; e-mail rcci_raj@yahoo.com; internet rajshahichamber.org; f. 1951; Pres. Alhaj MD ABU BAKKER ALI.

Sylhet Chamber of Commerce and Industry: Chamber Bldg, Jail Rd, POB 97, Sylhet 3100; tel. (821) 714403; fax (821) 715210; e-mail scci@btsnet.net; internet www.sylhetchamber.org; f. 1966; Pres. FARUQUE AHMED MISBAH.

INDUSTRIAL AND TRADE ASSOCIATIONS

Bangladesh Frozen Foods Exporters' Association: Skylark Point, 10th Floor, 24/A Bijoynagar, North South Rd, Dhaka 1000; tel. (2) 8316882; fax (2) 8317531; e-mail bffea@dhaka.net; internet www.bffea.net; f. 1984; Pres. KAZI SHANEWAZ.

Bangladesh Garment Manufacturers and Exporters Association (BGMEA): BGMEA Complex, 23/1 Panthapath Link Rd, Karwan Bazar, Dhaka 1215; tel. (2) 9144552; fax (2) 8113951; e-mail info@bgmea.com; internet www.bgmea.com.bd; Pres. MD SHAFIUL ISLAM.

Bangladesh Jute Association: BJA Bldg, 77 Motijheel C/A, Dhaka; tel. (2) 9552916; fax (2) 9561122; e-mail bjute@bangla.net; Chair. MAHFUZUL HAQUE.

Bangladesh Jute Mills Association: Adamjee Court, 4th Floor, 115–120 Motijheel C/A, Dhaka 1000; tel. (2) 9560071; fax (2) 9566472; e-mail info@bjma-bd.org; Chair. NAZMUL HAQUE.

Bangladesh Jute Spinners Association (BJSA): 55A Purana Paltan, 3rd Floor, Dhaka 1000; tel. (2) 9551317; fax (2) 9562772; e-mail bjsa_bd@yahoo.com; internet www.juteyarn-bjsa.org; f. 1979; 86 mems; Chair. MUHAMMAD SHAMS-UZ-ZOHA; Sec. SHAHIDUL KARIM.

Bangladesh Knitwear Manufacturers and Exporters Association (BKMEA): Planners Tower, 12th Floor, 13/A Sonagargaon Rd,

Banglamotor, Dhaka; tel. (2) 9670498; fax (2) 9673337; e-mail info@bkmea.com; internet www.bkmea.com; f. 1996; Pres. A. K. M. SALIM OSMAN.

Bangladesh Marine Fisheries Association (BMFA): 13/A Center Point Concord, Dhaka 1215; tel. (2) 9120234; e-mail info@bmfabd.com; internet www.bmfabd.com; f. 1980; asscn of 18 trawler companies; exports frozen shrimp and sea water fish; Chair. A. K. SHAMSUDDIN KHAN.

Bangladesh Textile Mills Association (BTMA): Unique Trade Centre, 8th Floor, 8 Panthapath, Karwan Bazar, Dhaka 1215; tel. (2) 9143461; fax (2) 9125338; e-mail btmasg@gmail.com; internet www.btmadhaka.com; Pres. JAHANGIR ALAMIN.

Bangladeshiyo Cha Sangsad (Tea Planters Association of Bangladesh): 'Progressive Tower', 4th Floor, 1837 Sheikh Mujib Rd (Badamtali), Agrabad, Chittagong 4100; tel. (31) 716407; f. 1952; Chair. MOHAMMAD SAFWAN CHOUDHURY; Sec. G. S. DHAR.

UTILITIES

Electricity

Bangladesh Atomic Energy Commission (BAEC): Paramanu Bhaban, E-12/A Agargaon, Sher-e-Bangla Nagar, Dhaka 1207; tel. (2) 8130469; fax (2) 8130102; e-mail baec@agni.com; internet www.baec.org.bd; f. 1964 as Atomic Energy Centre of the fmr Pakistan Atomic Energy Comm. in East Pakistan; reorg. 1973; operates atomic energy research establishments and a 3-MW research nuclear reactor (inaugurated in January 1987) at Savar, an atomic energy centre at Dhaka; Chair. ABU SAYEED MOHAMMAD FIROZ.

Bangladesh Energy Regulatory Commission (BERC): TCB Bhaban, 3rd Floor, 1 Karwan Bazar, Dhaka 1215; tel. (2) 9140125; fax (2) 8155743; internet www.berc.org.bd; f. 2004; regulates activities of gas, electricity and petroleum sectors; Chair. SYED YUSUF HOSSAIN.

Bangladesh Power Development Board (BPDB): WAPDA Bldg, 1st Floor, Motijheel C/A, Dhaka; tel. (2) 9562154; fax (2) 9564765; e-mail chbpdb@bol-online.com; internet www.bpdb.gov.bd; f. 1972; under Ministry of Power, Energy and Mineral Resources; generation, transmission and distribution of electricity; installed capacity 5,202 MW (2008); Chair. A. S. M. ALAMGIR KABIR.

Dhaka Electric Supply Co Ltd (DESCO): House 3, Rd 24, Block K, Banani Model Town, Dhaka 1213; tel. (2) 8859642; fax (2) 8854648; e-mail info@desco.org.bd; internet www.desco.org.bd; f. 1997; Chair. SHAHJAHAN SIDDIQUI; Man. Dir MD MONZUR RAHMAN.

Dhaka Power Distribution Co Ltd (DPDC): Biddut Bhaban, 1 Abdul Gani Rd, Dhaka 1000; e-mail md@dpdc.org; internet www.dpdc.org.bd; f. 2005 to replace Dhaka Electric Supply Authority; under Ministry of Power, Energy and Mineral Resources; Chair. TAPOS KUMAR ROY; Man. Dir MD ABDUS SOBHAN.

Power Grid Company of Bangladesh Ltd (PGCB): IEB Bldg, 3rd and 4th Floors, Ramna, Dhaka 1000; tel. (2) 9553663; fax (2) 7171833; e-mail info@pgcb.org.bd; internet www.pgcb.org.bd; f. 1996; responsible for power transmission throughout Bangladesh; Chair. MD ABUL KALAM AZAD; Sec. MOHAMMAD ASHRAF HOSSAIN.

Rural Electrification Board: House 3, Rd 12, Nikunja-2, Khilkhet, Dhaka 1229; tel. (2) 8916424; fax (2) 8916400; e-mail seict@reb.gov.bd; internet www.reb.gov.bd; under Ministry of Power, Energy and Mineral Resources; Chair. Brig.-Gen. MOIN UDDIN.

Water

Bangladesh Water Development Board (BWDB): WAPDA Bldg, Motijheel C/A, Dhaka 1000; tel. (2) 9552194; fax (2) 9564763; e-mail cm-bwdb@bangla.net; internet www.bwdb.gov.bd; f. 1972; fmrly part of East Pakistan Water and Power Development Authority; water resources management and development; Dir-Gen. ABUL KALAM MOHD AZAD.

Chittagong Water Supply and Sewerage Authority: WASA Bhaban, Dampara, Chittagong; tel. (31) 621606; internet cwasa.org; f. 1963; govt corpn; Chair. SULTAN MAHMUD CHOWDHURY.

Dhaka Water Supply and Sewerage Authority: 98 Kazi Nazrul Islam Ave, Karwan Bazar, Dhaka 1215; tel. (2) 8116792; fax (2) 8112109; e-mail secretary@dwasa.org.bd; internet www.dwasa.org.bd; f. 1963; govt corpn; Man. Dir TAQSEM A. KHAN.

Water Resources Planning Organization (WARPO): House 103, Rd 1, Banani, Dhaka 1213; tel. (2) 8814217; fax (2) 9883456; e-mail dg@warpo.gov.bd; internet www.warpo.gov.bd; f. 1992; fmrly Master Plan Organization; macro-level planning org. for integrated water resources management; Dir-Gen. MD SHAHIDUR RAHMAN.

TRADE UNIONS

Bangladesh Free Trade Union Congress (BFTUC): 6A 1/19 Mirpur, Dhaka 1216; tel. (2) 8017001; fax (2) 8015919; e-mail bftuc@agni.com; f. 1983; Gen. Sec. M. R. CHOWDHURY; 95,000 mems.

Bangladesh Jatiyatabadi Sramik Dal: 28/1 Naya Paltan, 4th Floor, VIP Rd, Dhaka 1000; tel. (2) 418214; fax (2) 869723; e-mail bils@agni.com; f. 1979; Sec.-Gen. MD ZAFRUL HASAN.

Bangladesh Labour Federation: Sadharan Bima Sadan, 8th Floor, 24-25 Dilkusha C/A, POB 2514, Dhaka 1000; tel. (2) 9560104; fax (2) 7171335; e-mail mdhk_blf@yahoo.com; Pres. SHAH MOHAMMAD ABU ZAFAR.

Bangladesh Mukto Sramik Federation: House 86, Rd No. 11A, Dhanmondhi, Dhaka; tel. 1713007814 (mobile); e-mail mojiburbhuiyan1950@yahoo.com; f. 1973; Gen. Sec. MUHAMMAD MOJIBUR RAHMAN BHUIYAN; 20,050 mems.

Bangladesh Sanjukta Sramik Federation: 2/2 Purana Paltan, 2nd Floor, Dhaka 1000; tel. (2) 7174065; fax (2) 9125078; e-mail bssfhq@intechworld.net; f. 1978.

Jatio Sramik League (JSL): 23 Bangabandhu Ave, POB 2730, Dhaka 1000; tel. (2) 9554499; fax (2) 7162222; e-mail jsl@mail.aitlbd.net; f. 1969; Pres. ABDUL MATIN MASTER; 62,000 mems.

Transport

RAILWAYS

Plans to modernize and extend the railway network through an Asian Development Bank (ADB)-funded Railway Sector Investment Programme were finalized in 2008. Plans to establish direct rail links with Nepal and Bhutan via India were also under consideration. In late 2011 a new Ministry of Railways was created to govern the railways sector.

Bangladesh Railway: Rail Bhaban, 16 Abdul Ghani Rd, Dhaka 1000; tel. (2) 9561200; fax (2) 9563413; e-mail dg@railway.gov.bd; internet www.railway.gov.bd; f. 1862; supervised by the Ministry of Railways; divided into East and West Zones, with East Zone HQ at Chittagong (tel. (31) 843200; fax (31) 843215) and West Zone HQ at Rajshahi (tel. (721) 761576; fax (721) 761982); total length of 2,835 route km (2009); 440 stations (2009); Dir-Gen. MOHAMMAD ABU TAHER; Gen. Man. (East Zone) (vacant); Gen. Man. (West Zone) AMJAD HOSSAIN.

ROADS

In 2007 the total length of roads in use was 271,401 km (including 7,839 km of national and regional highways), of which 23.47% were paved. The 4.8-km Bangabandhu Jamuna Multipurpose Bridge, which linked the east and the west of the country with a railway and road network, was officially opened in June 1998. Funding arrangements for the 6.1-km, combined road and rail Padma Bridge, the country's largest-ever infrastructure project, were finalized in mid-2011; the project was expected to cost an estimated US $2,900m., to be financed mainly by the World Bank, the Asian Development Bank and the Japan International Cooperation Agency. However, the project, which would connect Dhaka with the less-developed south-west of the country, was subsequently postponed, owing to alleged irregularities in the tendering process.

Bangladesh Road Transport Corpn: Paribahan Bhaban, 21 Rajuk Ave, Dhaka; tel. (2) 9555786; fax (2) 9555788; e-mail info@brtc.gov.bd; internet www.brtc.gov.bd; f. 1961; state-owned; operates transport services, incl. truck division; transports govt food grain; Chair. Major (retd) M. M. IQBAL.

INLAND WATERWAYS

In Bangladesh there are some 8,433 km of navigable waterways, which transport 70% of total domestic and foreign cargo traffic and on which are located the main river ports of Dhaka, Narayanganj, Chandpur, Barisal and Khulna.

Bangladesh Inland Water Transport Corpn: 5 Dilkusha C/A, Dhaka 1000; tel. (2) 9555031; fax (2) 9563653; e-mail info@biwtc.gov.bd; internet www.biwtc.gov.bd; f. 1972; Chair. GOLAM MOSTAFA KAMAL; 608 vessels.

SHIPPING

In 2010 the Government launched a major programme to expand and develop the country's ports. Chittagong, comprising two container terminals, is the chief port and handles more than 90% of seaborne traffic; in 2009 the port handled 1.1m. 20-ft equivalent units (TEUs) and 30.5m. tons of cargo. The port at Mongla, situated some 100 km upstream on the Pasur River, also receives seagoing vessels. Mongla handled some 2.7m. tons of cargo in 2010/11.

Chittagong Port Authority: POB 2013, Chittagong 4100; tel. (31) 2522200; fax (31) 2510889; e-mail info@cpa.gov.bd; internet www.cpa.gov.bd; f. 1887; management and development of Chittagong Port, and provision of bunkering, ship repair, towage and lighterage facilities; Chair. Cdre MOHAMMAD ANWARUL ISLAM.

Mongla Port Authority: Mongla, Bagerhat 9351; tel. (4662) 75200; fax (2) 75224; e-mail cech@mpa.gov.bd; internet www.mpa.gov.bd; govt-owned; Chair. Cdre M. FAROOQ.

Atlas Shipping Lines Ltd: 142 Sir Iqbal Rd, 3rd Floor, Khulna; tel. and fax (4) 1732669; e-mail atlas@khulna.bangla.net; Man. Dir S. U. CHOWDHURY; Gen. Man. MUHAMMAD ABU RASEL.

Bangladesh Shipping Corpn: BSC Bhaban, Saltgola Rd, POB 641, Chittagong 4100; tel. (31) 2521162; fax (31) 710506; e-mail md@bsc.gov.bd; internet www.bsc.gov.bd; f. 1972; maritime shipping; 13 vessels; state-owned; Chair. SHAHJAHAN KHAN (Minister of Shipping); Man. Dir Cdre MOQSUMUL QUADER.

Bengal Shipping Line Ltd: Palm View, 100A Agrabad C/A, Chittagong 4100; tel. (31) 500692; fax (31) 710488; e-mail bsl@mkrgroup.com; Chair. MOHAMMED ABDUL AWWAL; Man. Dir MOHAMMED ABDUL MALEK.

Brave Royal Shipping Ltd: Kabir Manzil, Sheikh Mujib Rd, Agrabad C/A, Chittagong 4100; tel. (31) 715222; internet brsml.com; manufactures and operates bulk carrier vessels; Man. Dir MOHAMMAD SHAHJAHAN; Gen. Man. MEHERUL KARIM.

Continental Liner Agencies: Facy Bldg, 3rd Floor, 87 Agrabad C/A, Chittagong; tel. (31) 721572; fax (31) 710965; Chair. SHAH ALAM; Dir (Technical and Operations) Capt. MAHFUZUL ISLAM.

Nishan Shipping Lines Ltd: Monzoor Bldg, 1st Floor, 67 Agrabad C/A, Chittagong; tel. (31) 710855; fax (31) 710044; Dir Capt. A. K. M. ALAMGIR.

CIVIL AVIATION

There is an international airport at Dhaka (Shahjalal International Airport—as Zia International Airport was renamed in early 2010), situated at Kurmitola, with the capacity to handle 5m. passengers annually. There are two further international airports at Chittagong and Sylhet. The main domestic airports are located at Barisal, Cox's Bazar, Jessore, Rajshahi and Saidpur.

Best Air: 43 Rd 1/A, Blk J, Baridhara Diplomatic Area, Dhaka 1212; tel. (2) 9888780; fax (2) 8860248; e-mail info@bestairbd.com; internet www.bestairbd.com; f. 1999; est. as helicopter operator, later freight airline; currently operates one domestic passenger service; international services to India, Thailand and China; 80% shares purchased by Destiny Group in late 2010; Man. Dir M. HAIDER UZZAMAN; Chair. MOHAMMAD RAFIQUL AMIN.

Biman Bangladesh Airlines: Head Office, Balaka, Kurmitola, Dhaka 1229; tel. (2) 8917400; fax (2) 8913005; e-mail dgmpr@bdbiman.com; internet www.biman-airlines.com; f. 1972; fmrly state-owned; transferred to private ownership in 2007; domestic services to four major towns; international services to 18 destinations in the Middle East, the Far East, Europe and North America; Chair. Air Marshal (retd) JAMAL UDDIN AHMED; CEO and Man. Dir Air Cdre (retd) MUHAMMAD ZAKIUL ISLAM.

GMG Airlines: Plot Nos 1 and 3, Rd 21, Nikunja 2, Dhaka 1229; tel. (2) 8900460; fax (2) 8924390; e-mail info@gmgairlines.com; internet www.gmgairlines.com; f. 1997; private, domestic airline; Man. Dir SHAHAB SATTAR.

Regent Airways: Plot No. 15, Dhaka Mymensingh Rd, Sector 3, Uttara Model Town, Dhaka 1230; tel. (2) 8953003; e-mail info@flyregent.com; internet www.flyregent.com; f. 2010; fully-owned subsidiary of Habib Group; domestic flights to 5 destinations; CEO IMRAN ASIF.

United Airways (BD) Ltd: 1 Jasimuddin Ave, Uttara Tower, 5th Floor, Uttara, Dhaka 1230 ; tel. (2) 8931712; fax (2) 8932339; e-mail info@uabdl.com; internet www.uabdl.com; privately-owned domestic airline; gained permit for international flights 2008; Chair. and CEO Capt. TASBIRUL AHMED CHOUDHURY.

Tourism

Tourist attractions include the cities of Dhaka and Chittagong, Cox's Bazar—which has the world's longest beach (120 km)—on the Bay of Bengal, and Teknaf, at the southernmost point of Bangladesh. In 2008 there was an estimated 21% rise in the number of tourist arrivals to reach a total of 349,837, and receipts from tourism amounted to around US $91m.

Bangladesh Parjatan Corpn (Govt Tourism Organization): Setu Bhaban, 5th Floor, New Airport Rd, Banani, Dhaka 1212; tel. (2) 8833229; fax (2) 8833900; e-mail info@bangladeshtourism.gov.bd; internet www.parjatan.gov.bd; f. 1973; in addition to the one in Dhaka, there are tourist information centres in Bogra, Chittagong, Cox's Bazar, Dinajpur, Khulna, Kuakata, Mongla, Rangamati, Rangpur, Rajshahi, Sylhet, Teknaf and Tungi Para; Chair. HEMAYET UDDIN TALUKDER.

Defence

As assessed at November 2011, the total active armed forces numbered 157,053: the army had a total strength of 126,153, the navy 16,900 and the air force 14,000. The paramilitary forces, which totalled 63,900, comprised an armed police reserve of 5,000, a coast guard of 900, a 20,000-strong security guard and the Bangladesh Rifles (or Border Guard Bangladesh), numbering 38,000. Military service is voluntary.

Defence Budget: Estimated at 89,480m. taka for 2010/11 (equivalent to 10.2% of total projected budgetary expenditure).

Chief of Army Staff: Gen. MOHAMMED ABDUL MUBEEN.

Chief of Naval Staff: Vice-Adm. ZAHIR UDDIN AHMED.

Chief of Air Staff: Air Marshal SHAH MOHAMMAD ZIAUR RAHMAN.

Dir-Gen. of Border Guard Bangladesh: Maj.-Gen. ANWAR HUSSAIN.

Education

The Government provides free schooling for children of both sexes for eight years. Primary education, which is compulsory, begins at six years of age and lasts for five years. Secondary education, beginning at the age of 11, lasts for up to seven years, comprising a first cycle of three years, a second cycle of two years and a third cycle of two further years. In the late 1980s the Government laid great emphasis on the improvement of the primary education system in an attempt to raise the rate of literacy. A scheme was, therefore, undertaken to establish one primary school for every 2,000 people in Bangladesh. In 2008/09 an estimated 92% of children (88% of boys; 97% of girls) in the relevant age group were enrolled at primary schools, while the enrolment ratio at secondary schools was 46% (44% of boys; 48% of girls) in the same year. In 2008/09 there were 82,981 primary schools; there were an estimated 21,015 secondary schools in 2009/10. Secondary schools and colleges in the private sector vastly outnumber government institutions. Educational reform is designed to assist in satisfying the manpower needs of the country, and the greatest importance is given to primary, technical and vocational education. In 2007/08 there were 31 state universities, including one for agriculture and one for engineering and technology, and an Islamic university. In the same year there were 3,116 technical colleges, vocational institutes and colleges offering general education. The Government launched an Open University Project in 1992. The 2009/10 budget allocated 117,960m. taka to education and technology (equivalent to 15.1% of total projected government expenditure).

BARBADOS

Introductory Survey

LOCATION, CLIMATE, LANGUAGE, RELIGION, FLAG, CAPITAL

Barbados is the most easterly of the Caribbean islands, lying about 320 km (200 miles) north-east of Trinidad. The island has a total area of 430 sq km (166 sq miles). There is a rainy season from July to November and the climate is tropical, tempered by constant sea winds, during the rest of the year. The mean annual temperature is about 26°C (78°F). Average annual rainfall varies from 1,250 mm (49 ins) on the coast, to 1,875 mm (74 ins) in the interior. The official language is English. Almost all of the inhabitants profess Christianity, but there are small groups of Hindus, Muslims and Jews. The largest denomination is the Anglican church, but about 90 other Christian sects are represented. The national flag (proportions 2 by 3) has three equal vertical stripes, of blue, gold and blue; superimposed on the centre of the gold band is the head of a black trident. The capital is Bridgetown.

CONTEMPORARY POLITICAL HISTORY

Historical Context

Barbados was formerly a British colony. The Barbados Labour Party (BLP) won a general election in 1951, when universal adult suffrage was introduced, and held office until 1961. Although the parliamentary system dates from 1639, ministerial government was not established until 1954, when the BLP's leader, Sir Grantley Adams, became the island's first Premier. He was subsequently Prime Minister of the West Indies Federation from January 1958 until its dissolution in May 1962.

Domestic Political Affairs

Barbados achieved full internal self-government in October 1961. The Democratic Labour Party (DLP), formed in 1955 by dissident members of the BLP, won an election in December. The DLP's leader, Errol Barrow, became Premier, succeeding Dr Hugh Cummins of the BLP. When Barbados achieved independence on 30 November 1966, Barrow became the island's first Prime Minister, following another electoral victory by his party earlier in the month.

The DLP retained power in 1971, but in the 1976 general election the BLP, led by J. M. G. M. (Tom) Adams (Sir Grantley's son), ended Barrow's 15-year rule. The BLP was returned to office at a general election in 1981. Adams died in March 1985 and was succeeded as Prime Minister by his deputy, Bernard St John, a former leader of the BLP.

At a general election in 1986 the DLP won a decisive victory, and Errol Barrow returned as Prime Minister. However, in June 1987 Barrow died suddenly. He was succeeded by L. Erskine Sandiford (hitherto the Deputy Prime Minister), who pledged to continue Barrow's economic and social policies. In September, however, the Minister of Finance, Richie Haynes, resigned, accusing Sandiford of failing to consult him over financial appointments. Sandiford assumed the finance portfolio, but acrimony over government policy continued to trouble the DLP. In February 1989 Haynes and three other members of Parliament resigned from the DLP and announced the formation of the National Democratic Party. Haynes was subsequently appointed as leader of the parliamentary opposition.

At a general election in January 1991 the DLP won 18 of the 28 seats in the enlarged House of Assembly, while the BLP secured the remaining 10. The creation of a Ministry of Justice and Public Safety by the new Government and the reintroduction of flogging for convicted criminals reflected widespread concern over increased levels of violent crime on the island. Moreover, as a result of serious economic problems, a series of austerity measures was proposed, resulting in public unrest. The increasing unpopularity of Sandiford's premiership provoked continued demands for his resignation, culminating, in June 1994, in his narrow defeat in a parliamentary motion of confidence. At a general election in September the BLP won a decisive victory and Owen Arthur was subsequently appointed Prime Minister.

The BLP in power

In May 1995 Arthur announced the formation of a commission to advise the Government on possible reforms of the country's Constitution and political institutions. The commission was asked to consider, in particular, the continuing role of the British monarch as Head of State in Barbados. The commission's report, published in December 1998, recommended, as expected, the replacement of the British monarch with a ceremonial President. It also proposed changes in the composition of the Senate and the substitution of a jointly administered regional court for the existing highest judicial body, the Privy Council in the United Kingdom; in February 2001 Caribbean leaders agreed to establish such a court (see below).

In November 1998, owing to a recent significant increase in the number of violent crimes, stricter penalties for unlawful possession of firearms were introduced. Amid fears that the escalation in gun crime might affect the country's tourism industry, it was announced in October 1999 that an anti-firearms unit was to be established in the police force. In 2002 the Government established a National Commission on Law and Order to help develop a plan of action to combat the rising crime rate. By 2006 the annual murder rate of 13 people per 100,000 was among the lowest in the Caribbean, but still double the level of the mid-1990s. In October 2007 plans were announced to reform the prison system following a riot in 2005 in which Glendairy prison was burnt down: the replacement facility incorporated the classified separation of prisoners and a parole system.

The BLP won an overwhelming victory at the general election held in January 1999. The heavy defeat for the DLP was largely attributed to the Government's recent successes in reviving the Barbadian economy, particularly in reducing unemployment. The Prime Minister announced an expanded 14-member Cabinet, including the new post of Minister of Social Transformation, whose major concern was to be poverty alleviation.

In August 2000 Arthur announced that there would be a referendum on the replacement of the monarchy with a republic, a move that had the support of all political parties. New constitutional legislation was drafted in 2002; however, the only change made was an amendment approved in September to override human rights judgments by the Privy Council, making it easier to make use of the death penalty.

Owen Arthur's BLP secured a third successive victory at the general election of 21 May 2003, attracting 56% of the votes cast, and securing 23 of the 30 seats in the enlarged House of Assembly. The DLP did, however, increase its share of the popular vote to 44% (from 35% in 1999) and its parliamentary strength to seven, while the BLP retained four of its seats only by narrow margins. Clyde Mascoll, a former Central Bank economist, was appointed DLP and opposition leader. Arthur, meanwhile, appointed Mia Mottley, the Attorney-General and Minister of Home Affairs, as Deputy Prime Minister.

In June 2003 the Governor-General announced that the Government intended to transform Barbados into a republic. In February 2005 Arthur stated that a referendum on the issue would be held by the end of the year; however, owing to legislative obstacles, the referendum was delayed. By late 2011 no official date had been set for the plebiscite.

In November 2005 the former DLP leader and President of the party, David Thompson, was again elected to lead the party, replacing Mascoll. In January 2006 Mascoll defected from the DLP to join the BLP, and was rapidly appointed to the Cabinet as Minister of State in the Ministry of Finance. Among several other ministerial changes effected by Arthur, the most significant was the transfer of Deputy Prime Minister Mottley to the new Ministry of Economic Affairs and Development. Dale Marshall, hitherto Minister of Industry and International Business, replaced Mottley as Attorney-General and Minister of Home Affairs.

A DLP Government

The opposition DLP won a majority in the general election held on 15 January 2008, securing 52.7% of the votes cast and 20 seats in the House of Assembly. The BLP won the remaining 10 seats. Thompson was sworn in as Prime Minister on the following day, when a new Cabinet was also installed. Following his party's defeat, Arthur announced his retirement from politics after three consecutive terms in office; Mottley replaced him as BLP leader.

Thompson effected a major reorganization of his Cabinet in November 2008, which included the removal of Christopher Sinckler as Minister of Foreign Affairs, Foreign Trade and International Business and the appointment of the Attorney-General and Minister of Home Affairs, Freundel Stuart, as Deputy Prime Minister in addition to his existing portfolios. Maxine McClean assumed responsibility for foreign affairs and foreign trade, and George Hutson was appointed to head the new Ministry of International Business and International Transport. Another cabinet reorganization was carried out in March 2010, although the main portfolios were left unaltered.

In March 2009 Thompson survived an opposition-led motion of no confidence in the House of Assembly over his handling of the financial instability that was precipitated by the collapse of CLICO Holdings, an insurance company based in Trinidad and the largest in the region. He was accused by the BLP of failing in his duty to safeguard Barbadian jobs, pensions and policy-holders' interests. The Government announced a new immigration policy in May: to avoid deportation, Caribbean Community and Common Market (CARICOM, see p. 227) nationals living illegally in Barbados would have until the end of the year to prove they had lived in Barbados for at least eight years prior to 2005, pass a security background check and produce evidence of their employment. This policy was expected to impact mostly on nationals from Guyana, who comprised the majority of the estimated 20,000 illegal immigrants in the country, and seemed to be supported by Barbadians as a response to the increasingly grave economic situation and rising levels of unemployment.

Recent developments: Stuart's premiership

Thompson went on leave from 1 July 2010 to receive medical treatment in the USA, with Stuart serving as acting Prime Minister during his absence. Although Thompson returned to work at the end of August, it was announced in September that he had been diagnosed with pancreatic cancer, but he cwould remain as Prime Minister. On 4 October Thompson reallocated a number of his portfolios (notably promoting Sinckler to Minister of Finance and Economic Affairs). Thompson died on 23 October. Stuart was sworn in as Prime Minister and Minister of National Security later the same day, while Adriel Brathwaite took over the new premier's previous responsibilities, becoming Deputy Prime Minister, Minister of Home Affairs and Attorney-General. Thompson's vacant legislative seat was won by his widow, Mara, in a by-election held in January 2011. Stuart implemented a cabinet reorganization in June, with most of the changes affecting the economic portfolios, underlining the Government's priorities. A new Ministry of Industry, Small Business and Rural Development was created.

Meanwhile, Mottley, after losing the support of some of her colleagues, was replaced by Arthur as BLP leader in October 2010, creating divisions within the party. Aware of the need for unity prior to the upcoming general election (the date of which was due to be announced by mid-2012), in April 2011 Arthur made efforts to reconcile with Mottley. However, despite subsequent proclamations of rapprochement, tensions within the BLP remained in late 2011, amid concerns that the ruling party would be defeated in the next general election under his stewardship.

The Caribbean Court of Justice

In April 2005, following many delays, the Caribbean Court of Justice (CCJ—see above), which replaced the United Kingdom-based Privy Council, was inaugurated in Trinidad and Tobago; however, by late 2011 only Barbados, Guyana and Belize had instituted the Court as their supreme appellate body. The CCJ issued its first seminal ruling in November 2006, endorsing a decision of the Appeal Court of Barbados to reduce to life imprisonment the death penalties requested against two convicted murderers, and thus demonstrating the CCJ's disinclination to reinstate capital punishment (1984 saw the last execution in Barbados).

Foreign Affairs

The Governments of Barbados and Trinidad and Tobago agreed in 1999 to draft a boundary delimitation treaty and to establish a negotiating mechanism to resolve trade disputes. The issue of boundary delimitation, however, remained unresolved, and in 2004 the Prime Minister of Trinidad and Tobago indicated that he would refer the matter to CARICOM (see p. 227). Relations between the two countries worsened after several Barbadian fishermen were arrested in Trinidad and Tobago's waters; in response, the Government imposed sanctions against Trinidad and Tobago manufacturers. Later that month Barbados referred the dispute for arbitration under the UN Convention on the Law of the Sea. In 2005 the Barbados Government formed a committee to investigate whether a significant natural gas discovery off east Trinidad fell within Barbadian maritime territory. The Government of Trinidad and Tobago insisted the discovery was within its jurisdiction. Hearings on the boundary dispute commenced in October at the International Dispute Resolution Centre, and in April 2006 a tribunal ruling established a boundary between the two states. This gave Barbados a large area to the south-east of the island, which had been claimed by Trinidad and Tobago, and was thought to have potential for deep-water oil and gas exploration. The tribunal rejected the Barbadian claim to a large area to the north of Tobago, but instructed the two countries to negotiate a fishing agreement for this area 'in good faith'. However, despite initial progress, by 2011 talks to establish an agreement had stalled. Moreover, 10 Barbadians were briefly detained by the Trinidad and Tobago authorities in December after they were discovered fishing illegally in waters near Tobago. This incident prompted the Prime Minister to approach his Trinidadian counterpart, Kamla Persad-Bissessar, regarding the resumption of negotiations, and fresh talks were expected to commence during 2012. Meanwhile, the Permanent Court of Arbitration's ruling conferred security on these new demarcations of jurisdiction, enabling Barbados to begin auctioning oil-exploration rights to leading hydrocarbon companies. In July 2008 Venezuela claimed that two of the blocks allocated for exploration violated its maritime border; however, the Barbadian Government maintained that all of the blocks were located within its exclusive economic zone.

In October 2009 Barbados signed an agreement with France on the delimitation of the maritime boundary between Barbados, Martinique and Guadeloupe. Barbados opened an embassy in the People's Republic of China in July 2010. In particular, the Government hoped to strengthen investment, tourism, energy and education ties. Two months later the Government also inaugurated an embassy in Cuba, in part to enhance trade and investment links with its Caribbean neighbour. Some Bds $16m. was secured from the Chinese Government in September 2011 to finance a number of sporting and educational projects on the island, which had been agreed in June when Prime Minister Stuart had travelled to China for discussions with Chinese Premier Wen Jiabao.

In 1996 Barbados signed an agreement with the USA to co-operate with a regional initiative to combat the illegal drugs trade. The Government signed a similar agreement with the Organization of American States (OAS) in January 2005. The US Department of the Treasury froze the assets of a Barbados-registered 'offshore' company, Kattus Corporation, in December 2006 after it was implicated in the operations of a Colombian drugs cartel. In June 2000 Barbados officially declared its acceptance of the compulsory jurisdiction of the Inter-American Court of Human Rights (see p. 395), an institution of the OAS. Meanwhile, Barbados joined CARICOM's Caribbean Single Market and Economy (CSME), which was established on 1 January 2006. The CSME was intended to enshrine the free movement of goods, services and labour throughout the CARICOM region, although only six of the organization's 15 members were signatories to the new project from its inauguration. The CSME had originally been expected to be fully operational by 2015, but Stuart, in his role as Lead Head of Government with Responsibility for the CSME, announced in mid-2011 that this target would not be attained.

CONSTITUTION AND GOVERNMENT

Executive power is vested in the British monarch, represented by a Governor-General, who acts on the advice of the Cabinet. The Governor-General appoints the Prime Minister and, on the latter's recommendation, other members of the Cabinet. Legislative power is vested in the bicameral Parliament, comprising a Senate of 21 members, appointed by the Governor-General, and a House of Assembly with 30 members, elected by universal adult suffrage for five years (subject to dissolution) from single-member constituencies. The Cabinet is responsible to Parliament.

The island is divided into 11 parishes, all of which are administered by the central Government.

REGIONAL AND INTERNATIONAL CO-OPERATION

Barbados is a member of the Caribbean Community and Common Market (CARICOM, see p. 227) and of CARICOM's Caribbean Single Market and Economy, which was launched on 1 January 2006 (see Foreign Affairs), the Inter-American Development Bank (see p. 334), the Latin American Economic System (see p. 451), the Association of Caribbean States (see p. 448), and of the Community of Latin American and Caribbean States (see p. 462), which was formally inaugurated in December 2011.

Barbados acceded to the UN in 1966, upon independence. As a contracting party to the General Agreement on Tariffs and Trade, Barbados joined the World Trade Organization (see p. 433) on its establishment in 1995. The country became a member of the Commonwealth (see p. 239) upon independence. Barbados is a member of the Group of 77 (see p. 450) organization of developing states.

ECONOMIC AFFAIRS

In 2009, according to estimates by the World Bank, the island's gross national income (GNI), measured at average 2007–09 prices, was US $3,454m., equivalent to US $12,660 per head (or US $18,830 on an international purchasing-power parity basis in 2009). Between 2001 and 2010 the population increased at an average rate of 0.2% per year. Barbados' gross domestic product (GDP) per head, decreased, in real terms, at an average rate of 0.3% per year during 2001–09. Overall GDP increased, in real terms, at an average annual rate of 2.1% in 2000–06, according to estimates by the Central Bank of Barbados. Real GDP increased by 0.2% in 2008, according to the World Bank, but contracted by 5.3% in 2009.

Agriculture (including hunting, forestry and fishing) contributed an estimated 3.0% of GDP in 2009, according to the World Bank, while the sector engaged an estimated 3.4% of the employed labour force in the second quarter of 2011. Sugar, traditionally the main commodity export, was in decline, and in 2005 rum superseded sugar as the principal domestic export commodity, yielding Bds $50.7m. in that year, compared with $44.4m. for sugar. The other principal crops, primarily for local consumption, are sweet potatoes, carrots, yams, and other vegetables and fruit. Fishing was also developed in the late 20th century. The GDP of the agricultural sector declined, in real terms, at an average rate of 3.9% per year during 2000–06. According to central bank estimates, agricultural GDP expanded by 8.0% in 2005, but decreased by an estimated 5.7% in 2006.

In 2009 industry accounted for an estimated 23.2% of GDP, according to the World Bank, and 19.1% of the working population were employed in all industrial activities (manufacturing, construction, quarrying and utilities) in the second quarter of 2011. In real terms, industrial GDP increased at an average rate of 3.0% annually in 2000–06, according to estimates by the Central Bank. Real industrial GDP increased by an estimated 5.2% in 2006.

Mining contributed a preliminary 1.0% of GDP in 2006. The mining and construction sector employed 10.5% of the working population in the second quarter of 2011. The sector decreased by an average annual rate of 1.3% in 2000–06. Mining GDP contracted by an estimated 3.0% in 2006.

In 2006 manufacturing contributed a preliminary 6.6% of GDP and employed 6.4% of the working population in the second quarter of 2011. Excluding sugar factories and refineries, the principal branches of manufacturing were chemical, petroleum, rubber and plastic products, food products and beverages, and tobacco. According to central bank estimates, manufacturing GDP decreased, in real terms, at an average rate of 0.9% per year during 2000–06; it increased, however, by an estimated 1.1% in 2006.

The construction sector contributed a preliminary 6.7% of GDP in 2006 and employed 10.5% (including mining) of the working population in the second quarter of 2011. During 2000–06 the GDP of the sector increased at an average annual rate of 6.3%, according to central bank estimates. Construction GDP increased by an estimated 6.9% in 2006.

Production of natural gas decreased from 46.9m. cu m in 1998 to an estimated 15.4m. cu m in 2008. Imports of mineral fuels accounted for an estimated 13.4% of total imports in 2009. Owing to fluctuations in international prices, the production of crude petroleum declined substantially from its peak in 1985, to 328,000 barrels in 1997. As a result of an onshore drilling programme begun in 1997, production increased markedly, reaching 708,500 barrels in 1999; however, production fell thereafter and stood at a provisional 289,692 barrels in 2008.

Service industries are the main sector of the economy, accounting for 73.8% of GDP in 2009, according to World Bank estimates, and 77.6% of employment in the second quarter of 2011. The combined GDP of the services sector increased, in real terms, at an average rate of 2.3% per year during 2000–06, according to the Central Bank. The sector expanded by an estimated 4.1% in 2006. Business and financial services contributed 17.5% of GDP in 2006. The Government has encouraged the growth of 'offshore' financial facilities, particularly through the negotiation of double taxation agreements with other countries. In April 2011 there were 45 'offshore' banks registered. Barbados has an active anti-money-laundering regime. In January 2002 Barbados was removed from the Organisation for Economic Co-operation and Development (OECD)'s (see p. 379) list of tax havens. Tourism made a direct contribution of an estimated 11.4% to GDP in 2006, and it employed 10.7% of the working population in the second quarter of 2011. Receipts from the tourism industry totalled US $1,105m. in 2010. In 2009 the number of stop-over tourist arrivals stood a provisional 518,600, a fall of 8.7% on the previous year's total. Cruise ship passenger numbers increased in 2009, however, to a provisional 635,700 (from a recorded 597,500 in the previous year). Receipts from tourism increased from US $1,068m. in 2009 to a provisional $1,105m. in 2010. The contraction in stop-over numbers in recent years was mainly attributed to the global economic downturn, as well as amendments to the Western Hemisphere Travel Initiative in 2007 requiring all US citizens travelling to and from the Caribbean to hold a valid passport. Barbados was exploring promotion of its tourism facilities beyond the US market, particularly focusing on the United Kingdom and the rest of the Caribbean.

In 2009 Barbados recorded a visible trade deficit of US $1,825.6m., while there was a deficit of $511.7m. on the current account of the balance of payments. In 2008 the USA was both the principal source of imports (36.5%) and the largest single recipient of exports (25.7%). CARICOM countries were the second most important trading partner in 2008, accounting for 25.4% of imports and 43.2% of exports. The principal exports in 2008 were miscellaneous manufactured articles (24.5%), chemicals (16.4%), food and live animals (15.7%) and beverages and tobacco (12.9%). The principal imports were machinery and transport equipment (22.5%), and mineral fuels and lubricants, etc. 17.8%).

For the financial year ending 31 March 2010 there was an estimated total budgetary deficit of Bds $714.4m., equivalent to 8.8% of GDP. Barbados's general government gross debt was Bds $9,073m. in 2009, equivalent to 114.9% of GDP. In 2006 the total external debt of Barbados was some Bds $2,946m. In that year, the cost of servicing long-term public and publicly guaranteed debt and repayments to the IMF, at Bds $253.2m., was equivalent to 6.3% of the value of exports of goods, services and income (excluding workers' remittances). The average annual rate of inflation was 4.2% in 2001–10. Consumer prices rose by an average of 5.8% in 2010. In the second quarter of 2011 the unemployment rate was 12.1%.

Political stability and consensus have contributed to the economic strengths of Barbados. Tourism dominates the economy but 'offshore' banking and sugar and rum production are also important. The declining sugar industry, however, has come under increased pressure to reform in recent years, particularly as further liberalization of international trade has made the export less competitive. In June 2011 the Government announced plans for a US $100m. initiative to support the industry in expanding the range of sugars produced on the island. The economy declined by 4.2% in 2009 as the global economic crisis led to a sharp decline in tourism revenues, exports and foreign direct investment. Activity in the main sectors of the Barbadian economy—tourism, financial services and housing—remained slow in 2010, resulting in rising rates of unemployment and government debt, and real GDP grew by just 0.2% in that year, according to the IMF. An austerity budget was announced in November 2010 in an attempt to constrain the fiscal deficit. Among the unpopular measures were a temporary 2.5% rise in value-added tax, an increase in public sector transportation prices and the withdrawal of a range of tax breaks. Although the number of tourist arrivals rose during 2011, other sectors of the economy remained depressed and the unemployment rate reached 12% by the middle of the year. According to the

Central Bank, the economy expanded by 0.5% in 2011. Inflation also increased in that year—the result of rising food and fuel prices on international markets—and levels of public debt were still unsustainably high. The IMF expected real GDP to expand by 1.2% in 2012, with further growth largely contingent upon economic developments within the United Kingdom and the USA, the countries of origin of most of the island's tourists.

PUBLIC HOLIDAYS

2013: 1 January (New Year's Day), 21 January (Errol Barrow Day), 29 March (Good Friday), 1 April (Easter Monday), 29 April (National Heroes' Day), 1 May (Labour Day), 20 May (Whit Monday), 1 August (Emancipation Day), 5 August (Kadooment Day), 30 November (Independence Day), 25–26 December (Christmas).

Statistical Survey

Sources (unless otherwise stated): Barbados Statistical Service, National Insurance Bldg, 3rd Floor, Fairchild St, Bridgetown; tel. 427-7841; fax 435-2198; e-mail barstats@caribsurf.com; internet www.barstats.gov.bb; Central Bank of Barbados, Tom Adams Financial Centre, Spry St, POB 1016, Bridgetown; tel. 436-6870; fax 427-9559; e-mail cbb.libr@caribsurf.com; internet www.centralbank.org.bb.

AREA AND POPULATION

Area: 430 sq km (166 sq miles).

Population: 257,082 (provisional) at census of 2 May 1990; 250,010 (males 119,926, females 130,084) (provisional) at census of 1 May 2000; 274,532 at mid-2012 (Source: UN, *World Population Prospects: The 2010 Revision*).

Density (at mid-2012): 638.4 per sq km.

Population by Age and Sex (UN estimates at mid-2012): *0–14:* 45,659 (males 23,346, females 22,313); *15–64:* 196,495 (males 99,795, females 96,700); *65 and over:* 32,378 (males 13,071, females 19,307); *Total* 274,532 (males 136,212, females 138,320) (Source: UN, *World Population Prospects: The 2010 Revision*).

Ethnic Groups (*de jure* population, excl. persons resident in institutions, 1990 census): Black 228,683; White 8,022; Mixed race 5,886; Total (incl. others) 247,288.

Parishes (population at 2000 census, preliminary): Christ Church 49,498; St Andrew 5,254; St George 17,868; St James 22,741; St John 8,873; St Joseph 6,805; St Lucy 9,328; St Michael 83,684; St Peter 10,699; St Philip 22,864; St Thomas 12,397; *Total* 250,010.

Principal Towns (population at 2000 census, preliminary): Bridgetown (capital) 5,996; Speightstown 2,604; Holetown 1,087; Oistins 1,203. *Mid-2009* (population in '000, incl. suburbs): Bridgetown 112 (Source: UN, *World Urbanization Prospects: The 2009 Revision)*.

Births, Marriages and Deaths (2007, unless otherwise indicated): Live births 3,537 (birth rate 12.9 per 1,000); Marriages (2000) 3,518 (marriage rate 13.1 per 1,000); Deaths 2,213 (death rate 8.1 per 1,000). Source: partly UN, *Population and Vital Statistics Report*.

Life Expectancy (years at birth, WHO estimates): 76 (males 73; females 80) in 2009. Source: WHO, *World Health Statistics*.

Economically Active Population (labour force sample survey, '000 persons aged 15 years and over, excl. armed forces, April–June 2011): Agriculture, forestry and fishing 4.3; Manufacturing 8.1; Electricity, gas and water 2.8; Construction and quarrying 13.4; Wholesale and retail trade 20.2; Tourism 13.6; Transport, storage and communications 9.0; Finance and insurance 6.1; Professional, scientific and technical services 4.1; Administrative and support services 8.5; Public administration and defence 9.4; Education 6.6; Health and social welfare 6.8; Household employees 4.7; Other services 9.8; *Sub-total* 127.4; Not classified 0.5; *Total employed* 127.9 (males 65.7, females 62.2); Unemployed 17.6 (males 8.4, females 9.2); *Total labour force* 145.5 (males 74.1, females 71.4).

HEALTH AND WELFARE

Key Indicators

Total Fertility Rate (children per woman, 2009): 1.5.

Under-5 Mortality Rate (per 1,000 live births, 2009): 11.

HIV/AIDS (% of persons aged 15–49, 2009, estimate): 1.4.

Physicians (per 1,000 head, 1999): 1.2.

Hospital Beds (per 1,000 head, 2005): 6.7.

Health Expenditure (2008): US $ per head (PPP): 1,498.

Health Expenditure (2008): % of GDP: 6.7.

Health Expenditure (2008): public (% of total): 63.8.

Total Carbon Dioxide Emissions ('000 metric tons, 2007): 1,344.7.

Total Carbon Dioxide Emissions Per Head (metric tons, 2007): 5.3.

Human Development Index (2011): ranking: 47.

Human Development Index (2011): value: 0.793.

For sources and definitions, see explanatory note on p. vi.

AGRICULTURE, ETC.

Principal Crops ('000 metric tons, 2010, FAO estimates): Sweet potatoes 2.2; Yams 1.3; Avocados 0.6; Pulses 1.0; Coconuts 1.7; Tomatoes 1.1; Cucumbers 1.0; Chillies and peppers, green 0.7; Onions, dry 0.5; String beans 1.1; Carrots and turnips 0.6; Okra 0.8; Maize, green 0.7; Bananas 0.9.

Livestock ('000 head, year ending September 2010, FAO estimates): Horses 1.3; Asses 2.3; Mules 2.0; Cattle 11.0; Pigs 20.0; Sheep 11.5; Goats 5.2; Poultry 3,658.

Livestock Products ('000 metric tons, 2010, FAO estimates): Cattle meat 0.2; Pig meat 2.6; Chicken meat 14.3; Cows' milk 7.6; Hen eggs 2.4.

Forestry ('000 cubic metres, 2010, FAO estimates): Roundwood removals 11.0.

Fishing (metric tons, live weight, 2009): Total catch 3,496 (Yellowfin tuna 79; Flying fishes 2,292; Common dolphinfish 870).

Source: FAO.

MINING

Production (2008, provisional, unless otherwise indicated): Natural gas 20.9m. cu m (2007); Crude petroleum 289,692 barrels; Cement 301,427,000 metric tons.

INDUSTRY

Selected Products (2007, unless otherwise indicated): Raw sugar 34,000 metric tons (2008); Rum 11,000,000 litres (2003); Beer 8,500,000 litres; Cigarettes 65m. (1995); Batteries 17,165 (official estimate, 1998); Electric energy 948.0m. kWh (2008). Sources: partly UN Industrial Commodity Statistics Database, and IMF, *Barbados: Statistical Appendix* (May 2004).

FINANCE

Currency and Exchange Rates: 100 cents = 1 Barbados dollar (Bds $). *Sterling, US Dollar and Euro Equivalents* (30 December 2011): £1 sterling = Bds $3.092; US $1 = Bds $2.000; €1 = Bds $2.588; Bds $100 = £32.34 = US $50.00 = €38.64. *Exchange Rate*: Fixed at US $1 = Bds $2.000 since 1986.

Budget (Bds $ million, year ending 31 March 2010, provisional): *Revenue:* Tax revenue 2,135.6 (Direct taxes 880.2, Indirect taxes 1,255.4); Non-tax revenue and grants 162.7; Total 2,298.3. *Expenditure:* Current 2,831.1 (Wages and salaries 851.5, Other goods and services 380.7, Interest payments 471.0, Transfers and subsidies 1,127.8); Capital (incl. net lending) 181.6; Total 3,012.7.

International Reserves (US $ million at 31 December 2010): IMF special drawing rights 86.75; Reserve position in IMF 8.94; Foreign exchange 737.85; Total 833.54. Source: IMF, *International Financial Statistics*.

Money Supply (Bds $ million at 31 December 2009): Currency outside depository corporations 494.0; Transferable deposits 3,098.2; Other deposits 7,355.6; *Broad money* 10,947.8. Source: IMF, *International Financial Statistics*.

Cost of Living (Consumer Price Index; base: 2005 = 100): All items 120.7 in 2008; 125.1 in 2009; 132.4 in 2010. Source: IMF, *International Financial Statistics*.

Gross Domestic Product (Bds $ million at constant 1974 prices): 1,023.6 in 2004; 1,065.3 in 2005; 1,106.4 in 2006 (preliminary).

Expenditure on the Gross Domestic Product (Bds $ million at current prices, 2006, preliminary): Government final consumption expenditure 1,360.3; Private final consumption expenditure 3,706.7; Increase in stocks 876.3; Gross fixed capital formation 839.7; *Total domestic expenditure* 6,783.0; Exports of goods and services 4,142.6; *Less* Imports of goods and services 4,442.6; Statistical discrepancy 18.1; *GDP in purchasers' values* 6,501.1.

Gross Domestic Product by Economic Activity (estimates, Bds $ million at current prices, 2006, preliminary): Agriculture, hunting, forestry and fishing 175.1; Mining and quarrying 53.0; Manufacturing 357.1; Electricity, gas and water 197.3; Construction 361.1; Wholesale and retail trade 893.8; Hotels and restaurants 612.9; Transport, storage and communications 330.2; Finance, insurance, real estate and business services 1,165.5; Government services 854.2; Other community, social and personal services 383.5; *GDP at factor cost* 5,383.7; Indirect taxes, *less* subsidies 1,117.4; *GDP in purchasers' values* 6,501.1.

Balance of Payments (Bds $ million, 2009): Exports of goods f.o.b. 762.1; Imports of goods f.o.b. –2,587.7; *Trade balance* –1,825.6; Exports of services 2,944.6; Imports of services –1,503.2; *Balance on goods and services* –384.2; Other income received 455.7; Other income paid –640.8; *Balance on goods, services and income* –569.3; Current transfers received 204.2; Current transfers paid –146.5; *Current balance* –511.7; Capital and financial accounts (net) 643.8; Net errors and omissions –54.0; *Overall balance* 78.1.

EXTERNAL TRADE

Principal Commodities (excl. petroleum, Bds $ million, 2008, provisional): *Imports c.i.f.:* Food and live animals 489.3; Beverages and tobacco 107.3; Crude materials (inedible) except fuels 102.4; Mineral fuels, lubricants, etc. 622.5; Animal and vegetable oils and fats 32.0; Chemicals 374.5; Manufactured goods classified chiefly by material 494.8; Machinery and transport equipment 785.9; Miscellaneous manufactured articles 462.3; Miscellaneous transactions and commodities 22.0; Total 3,493.0. *Exports f.o.b.:* Food and live animals 114.5; Beverages and tobacco 94.3; Crude materials (inedible) except fuels 15.3; Mineral fuels, lubricants, etc. 49.3; Animal and vegetable oils and fats 11.8; Chemicals 119.7; Manufactured goods classified chiefly by material 86.9; Machinery and transport equipment 53.8; Miscellaneous manufactured articles 179.0; Miscellaneous transactions and commodities 5.4; Total 730.1 (incl. re-exports 203.8).

Principal Trading Partners (excluding petroleum, Bds $ million, 2008, provisional): *Imports c.i.f.:* Canada 121.4; CARICOM 885.5; Germany 56.3; Japan 126.4; United Kingdom 185.0; USA 1,274.4; Total (incl. others) 3,493.0. *Exports f.o.b.:* Canada 20.7; CARICOM 315.1; United Kingdom 82.3; USA 187.4; Total (incl. others) 730.1 (incl. re-exports 203.8).

TRANSPORT

Road Traffic (motor vehicles in use, 2007): Passenger cars 103,535; Buses and coaches 631; Lorries and vans 15,151; Motorcycles and mopeds 2,525. Source: IRF, *World Road Statistics*.

Shipping (estimated freight traffic, '000 metric tons, 1990): Goods loaded 206; Goods unloaded 538 (Source: UN, *Monthly Bulletin of Statistics*). *Total Goods Handled* ('000 metric tons, 2009): 1,082 (Source: Barbados Port Authority). *Merchant Fleet* (vessels registered at 31 December 2009): Number of vessels 130; Total displacement 824,310 grt (Source: IHS Fairplay, *World Fleet Statistics*).

Civil Aviation (1994): Aircraft movements 36,100; Freight loaded 5,052.3 metric tons; Freight unloaded 8,548.3 metric tons.

TOURISM

Tourist Arrivals ('000 persons): *Stop-overs:* 573.9 in 2007; 567.6 in 2008; 518.6 in 2009 (provisional). *Cruise-ship passengers:* 616.4 in 2007; 597.5 in 2008; 635.7 in 2009 (provisional).

Tourist Arrivals by Country ('000 persons, 2009, provisional): Canada 63.8; Germany 7.0; Trinidad and Tobago 26.3; Other CARICOM 62.5; United Kingdom 190.6; USA 122.3; Total (incl. others) 518.6.

Tourism Receipts (US $ million, excl. passenger transport): 1,189 in 2007; 1,194 in 2008; 1,068 in 2009; 1,105 in 2010 (provisional) (Source: World Tourism Organization).

COMMUNICATIONS MEDIA

Radio Receivers (1999): 175,000 in use.

Television Receivers (2000): 83,000 in use.

Telephones (2010): 137,500 main lines in use.

Mobile Cellular Telephones (2010): 350,100 subscribers.

Personal Computers: 40,000 (157.9 per 1,000 persons) in 2005.

Internet Subscribers (2009): 61,000.

Broadband Subscribers (2010): 56,200.

Newspapers: *Daily* (1996): 2 (circulation 53,000); (2004): 2 titles. *Non-daily* (1990): 4 (estimated circulation 95,000).

Sources: partly UNESCO, *Statistical Yearbook*, UN, *Statistical Yearbook*, and International Telecommunication Union.

EDUCATION

Pre-primary (20/09/10 unless otherwise indicated): 84 schools (1995/96); 359 teachers (males 11, females 348); 5,814 pupils (males 2,902, females 2,912).

Primary (2009/10 unless otherwise indicated): 109 schools (2005/06); 1,742 teachers (males 375, females 1,367); 22,659 pupils (males 11,522, females 11,137).

Secondary (2005/06 unless otherwise indicated): 32 schools; 1,430 teachers (males 589, females 841); 19,497 pupils (males 9,834, females 9,663) (2009/10).

Tertiary (2008/09 unless otherwise indicated): 4 schools (2002); 786 teachers (males 403, females 383) (2006/07); 14,324 students (males 4,490, females 9,834).

Sources: Ministry of Education, Youth Affairs and Sport and UNESCO Institute for Statistics.

Pupil-teacher Ratio (primary education, UNESCO estimate): 13.0 in 2009/10 (Source: UNESCO Institute for Statistics).

Adult Literacy Rate (UN estimates): 99.7% (males 99.7%; females 99.7%) in 2003. Source: UN Development Programme, *Human Development Report*.

Directory

The Government

HEAD OF STATE

Queen: HM Queen ELIZABETH II.

Acting Governor-General: ELLIOT BELGRAVE (appointed 1 November 2011).

THE CABINET

(May 2012)

The Cabinet is formed by the Democratic Labour Party.

Prime Minister and Minister of Civil Service, National Security and Urban Development: FREUNDEL STUART.

Attorney General and Minister of Home Affairs: ADRIEL BRATHWAITE.

Minister of Finance and Economic Affairs: CHRISTOPHER SINCKLER.

Minister of Education and Human Resource Development: RONALD JONES.

Minister of Housing and Lands: MICHAEL LASHLEY.

Minister of Tourism: RICHARD SEALY.

Minister of Social Care, Constituency Empowerment and Community Development: STEVEN BLACKETT.

Minister of Transport and Works: JOHN BOYCE.

Minister of Family, Culture, Sports and Youth: STEPHEN LASHLEY.

Minister of International Business and International Transport: GEORGE HUTSON.

Minister of Drainage and the Environment: DENIS LOWE.

Minister of Agriculture, Food, Fisheries and Water Resource Management: DAVID ESTWICK.

Minister of Health: DONVILLE INNISS.

Minister of Foreign Affairs and Foreign Trade: MAXINE MCCLEAN.

Minister of Commerce and Trade: HAYNESLEY BENN.

Minister of Labour and Social Security: Dr ESTHER BYER SUCKOO.

Minister of Industry, Small Business and Rural Development: DENIS KELLMAN.

Minister of State, Ministry of Housing and Lands: PATRICK TODD.

Minister in the Prime Minister's Office (Energy, Telecommunications, Immigration and Investment): DARCY BOYCE.

MINISTRIES

Office of the Prime Minister: Government HQ, Bay St, St Michael; tel. 436-6435; fax 436-9280; e-mail info@primeminister.gov.bb; internet www.primeminister.gov.bb.

Ministry of Agriculture, Food, Fisheries and Water Resource Management: Graeme Hall, POB 505, Christ Church; tel. 434-5000; fax 420-8444; e-mail info@agriculture.gov.bb; internet www.agriculture.gov.bb.

Ministry of the Civil Service and Urban Development: E. Humphrey Walcott Bldg, Culloden Rd, St Michael; tel. 426-4617.

Ministry of Commerce and Trade: Pelican Industrial Estate, Fontabelle, St Michael; tel. 426-4452; fax 431-0056.

Ministry of Drainage and the Environment: S. P. Musson Bldg, Hinks St, St Michael; tel. 467-5700; fax 437-8859.

Ministry of Education and Human Resource Development: Elsie Payne Complex, Constitution Rd, St Michael; tel. 430-2705; fax 436-2411; e-mail mined1@caribsurf.com; internet www.mes.gov.bb.

Ministry of Family, Culture, Sports and Youth: Mall Internationale, Haggatt Hall, St Michael; tel. 621-2700; fax 228-0180.

Ministry of Finance and Economic Affairs: Government HQ, Bay St, St Michael; tel. 426-3179; fax 436-9280.

Ministry of Foreign Affairs and Foreign Trade: 1 Culloden Rd, St Michael; tel. 431-2200; fax 429-6652; e-mail barbados@foreign.gov.bb; internet www.foreign.gov.bb.

Ministry of Health: Jemmott's Lane, St Michael; tel. 426-5570; fax 426-4669.

Ministry of Home Affairs: General Post Office Bldg, Level 5, Cheapside, St Michael; tel. 228-8950; fax 437-3794; e-mail mha@caribsurf.com.

Ministry of Housing and Lands: National Housing Corpn Bldg, 'The Garden', Country Rd, St Michael; tel. 467-7801; fax 435-0174.

Ministry of Industry Small Business and Rural Development: British American Insurance Bldg, 2nd Floor, Magazine Lane, Bridgetown, St Michael; tel. 417-3120; fax 271-6155.

Ministry of International Business and International Transport: The Warrens Office Complex, 3rd Floor, Warrens, St Michael; tel. 310-2200; fax 424-2533.

Ministry of Labour and Social Security: The Warrens Office Complex, 3rd Floor West, Warrens, St Michael; tel. 310-1400; fax 425-0266; e-mail mol@labour.gov.bb; internet labour.caribyte.com/index.

Ministry of National Security: St Michael.

Ministry of Social Care, Constituency Empowerment and Community Development: The Warrens Office Complex, 4th Floor, Warrens, St Michael; tel. 310-1604; fax 424-2908; e-mail info@socialtransformation.gov.bb; internet www.socialcare.gov.bb.

Ministry of Tourism: Sherbourne Conference Centre, Two Mile Hill, St Michael; tel. 430-7504; fax 436-4828; e-mail barmot@sunbeach.net; internet www.barmot.gov.bb.

Ministry of Transport and Works: Pine East-West Blvd, St Michael; tel. 429-2191; fax 437-8133; e-mail info@mtw.gov.bb; internet www.mtw.gov.bb.

Office of the Attorney-General: Cedar Court, Wildey Business Park, Wildey Rd, St Michael; tel. 431-7700; fax 228-5433; e-mail attygen@caribsurf.com.bb.

Legislature

PARLIAMENT

Senate

President: BRANFORD M. TAITT.

There are 21 members.

House of Assembly

Speaker: ISHMAEL ROETT.

General Election, 15 January 2008

Party	% of total	Seats
Democratic Labour Party (DLP)	52.66	20
Barbados Labour Party (BLP)	47.14	10
Total (incl. others)	100.00	30

Election Commission

Electoral and Boundaries Commission: National Insurance Bldg, Ground Floor, Fairchild St, Bridgetown BB11122; tel. 227-5817; fax 437-8229; e-mail electoral@barbados.gov.bb; Chief Electoral Officer ANGELA TAYLOR.

Political Organizations

Barbados Labour Party (BLP): Grantley Adams House, 111 Roebuck St, Bridgetown; tel. 429-1990; fax 427-8792; e-mail will99@caribsurf.com; internet www.blp.org.bb; f. 1938 as Barbados Progressive League, name changed as above 1946; moderate social democrat; Leader OWEN ARTHUR; Gen. Sec. GEORGE PAYNE.

Clement Payne Movement (CPM): Crumpton St, Bridgetown; tel. 435-2334; fax 437-8216; e-mail cpmbarbados2@yahoo.com; f. 1988 in honour of national hero; non-electoral founding assoc. of the PEP; links to the Pan-Caribbean Congress and promotes international Pan-Africanism; Pres. DAVID A. COMISSIONG; Gen. Sec. BOBBY CLARKE.

People's Empowerment Party (PEP): Clement Payne Cultural Centre, Crumpton St, Bridgetown; tel. 423-6089; fax 437-8216; e-mail pepbarbados@gmx.com; internet pepbarbados.blogspot.com; f. 2006 by the Clement Payne Movt; left-of-centre; Leader DAVID COMISSIONG.

Democratic Labour Party (DLP): 'Kennington', George St, Belleville, St Michael; tel. 429-3104; fax 427-0548; internet www.dlpbarbados.org; f. 1955; Pres. and Leader DAVID J. H. THOMPSON; Gen. Sec. CHRISTOPHER SINCKLER.

Diplomatic Representation

EMBASSIES AND HIGH COMMISSIONS IN BARBADOS

Brazil: The Courtyard, Hastings, POB BB15156, Christ Church; tel. 427-1735; fax 427-1744; e-mail brasemb@caribsurf.com; internet www.brazilbb.org; Ambassador APPIO CLAUDIO MUNIZ ACQUARONE.

Canada: Bishops Court Hill, Pine Rd, POB 404, Bridgetown; tel. 429-3550; fax 429-3780; e-mail bdgtn@international.gc.ca; internet www.canadainternational.gc.ca/barbados-barbade; High Commissioner RUTH ARCHIBALD.

China, People's Republic: 17 Golf View Terrace, Golf Club Rd, POB 428, Rockley, Christ Church; tel. 435-6890; fax 435-8300; e-mail chineseembbds@caribsurf.com; internet bb.chineseembassy.org; Ambassador (vacant).

Cuba: Palm View, Erdiston Dr., Pine Rd, St Michael; tel. 435-2769; fax 435-2534; e-mail embajadadecuba@sunbeach.net; Ambassador LISSETTE BÁRBARA PÉREZ PÉREZ.

United Kingdom: Lower Collymore Rock, POB 676, Bridgetown; tel. 430-7800; fax 430-7860; e-mail britishhcb@sunbeach.net; internet www.britishhighcommission.gov.uk/barbados; High Commissioner PAUL BRUMMELL.

USA: Wildey Business Park, Wildey, POB 302, Bridgetown BB14006; tel. 227-4000; fax 227-4088; e-mail BridgetownPublicAffairs@state.gov; internet bridgetown.usembassy.gov; Ambassador LARRY LEON PALMER.

Venezuela: Hastings, Main Rd, Christ Church; tel. 435-7619; fax 435-7830; e-mail embaven@sunbeach.net; Ambassador JOSÉ GÓMEZ FEBRES.

Judicial System

Justice is administered by the Supreme Court of Judicature, which consists of a High Court and a Court of Appeal. Final appeal lies with the Caribbean Court of Justice (CCJ), which was inaugurated in Port of Spain, Trinidad and Tobago, on 16 April 2005; previously, final appeals were administered by the Judicial Committee of the Privy Council in the United Kingdom. There are Magistrates' Courts for lesser offences, with appeal to the Court of Appeal.

Supreme Court: Judiciary Office, Coleridge St, Bridgetown; tel. 426-3461; fax 246-2405; internet www.lawcourts.gov.bb.

Chief Justice: MARSTON GIBSON.

Justices of Appeal: SANDRA MASON; PETER A. WILLIAMS; KAYE GOODRIDGE (acting); SHERMAN MOORE.

Judges of the High Court: ELNETH KENTISH; WILLIAM CHANDLER; MARGARET REIFER; RANDALL WORRELL; JACQUELINE CORNELIUS; SONIA RICHARDS; MAUREEN CRANE-SCOTT.

Registrar of the Supreme Court: MARVA CLARKE.

Office of the Attorney-General: Jones Bldg, Wildey Business Park, Wildey, St Michael; tel. 621-0110; fax 228-5433; e-mail attygen@caribsurf.com.

Attorney-General: ADRIEL BRATHWAITE.

Solicitor-General: JENNIFER C. EDWARDS.

Religion

More than 100 religious denominations and sects are represented in Barbados, but the vast majority of the population profess Christianity.

CHRISTIANITY

Barbados Christian Council

Caribbean Conference of Churches Bldg, George St and Collymore Rock, St Michael; tel. 426-6014; Chair. Rt Rev. JOHN WALDER DUNLOP HOLDER.

The Anglican Communion

According to the latest available census figures (2000), some 28% of the population are Anglicans. Anglicans in Barbados are adherents of the Church in the Province of the West Indies, comprising eight dioceses. The Archbishop of the Province is the Bishop of Nassau and the Bahamas, resident in Nassau, the Bahamas. In Barbados there is a Provincial Office (St George's Church, St George) and an Anglican Theological College (Codrington College, St John).

Bishop of Barbados: Rt Rev. JOHN WALDER DUNLOP HOLDER, Anglican Diocese of Barbados, Mandeville House, Henry's Lane, Collymore Rock, St Michael; tel. 426-2761; fax 426-0871; e-mail mandeville@sunbeach.com; internet www.anglican.bb.

The Roman Catholic Church

According to the 2000 census, some 4% of the population are Roman Catholics. Barbados comprises a single diocese (formed in 1990, after the diocese of Bridgetown-Kingstown was divided), which is suffragan to the archdiocese of Port of Spain (Trinidad and Tobago). The Bishop participates in the Antilles Episcopal Conference (currently based in Port of Spain, Trinidad and Tobago).

Bishop of Bridgetown: CHARLES JASON GORDON, Bishop's House, Ladymeade Gardens, St Michael, POB 1223, Bridgetown; tel. 426-3510; fax 429-6198; e-mail rcbishopbgl@caribsurf.com.

Other Churches

According to the 2000 census, other significant denominations in terms of number of adherents include Pentecostal (19% of the population), Adventist (5%), Methodist (5%), Church of God (2%), Jehovah's Witnesses (2%) and Baptist (2%).

Baptist Churches of Barbados: Emmanuel Baptist Church, President Kennedy Dr., Bridgetown; tel. 426-2697; e-mail emmbaptc@caribsurf.com.

Church of God: Chapman St, POB 1, St Michael; tel. 426-5327; e-mail generalassemblychog@caribsurf.com; internet chogbarbados.org; Pres. Rev. LIONEL GIBSON.

Church of Jesus Christ of Latter-Day Saints (Mormons)—West Indies Mission: 14 Walkers Terrace, St George; tel. 429-1385; fax 435-6486.

Church of the Nazarene: District Office, Eagle Hall, St Michael; tel. 425-1067; fax 435-6486.

Methodist Church: Bethel Church Office, Bay St, Bridgetown; tel. and fax 426-2223; e-mail methodist@caribsurf.com.

Moravian Church: Calvary Office, Roebuck St, St Michael; tel. 426-2337; fax 228-4381; e-mail calvarymoravian@sunbeach.net; Supt Rev. ERROL CONNOR.

Seventh-day Adventists (East Caribbean Conference): Brydens Ave, Brittons Hill, POB 22, St Michael; tel. 429-7234; fax 429-8055; e-mail info@eastcarib.org; internet eastcarib.org; Pres. DAVID BECKLES.

Wesleyan Holiness Church: General Headquarters, Whitepark Rd, Bank Hall; tel. 429-4888; internet www.carringtonwesleyan.org; District Supt Rev. C. WILLIAMS.

Other denominations include the Abundant Life Assembly, the African Orthodox Church, the Apostolic Church, the Assemblies of Brethren, the Berean Bible Brethren, the Bethel Evangelical Church, Christ is the Answer Family Church, the Church of God the Prophecy, the Ethiopian Orthodox Church, the Full Gospel Assembly, Love Gospel Assembly, the New Testament Church of God, the Pentecostal Assemblies of the West Indies, the People's Cathedral, the Salvation Army, Presbyterian congregations, the African Methodist Episcopal Church and the Mt Olive United Holy Church of America.

ISLAM

According to the 2000 census, around 1% of the population are Muslims.

Islamic Teaching Centre: Harts Gap, Hastings, Bridgetown; tel. 427-0120.

JUDAISM

According to the 2000 census, there are 96 Jews on the island (less than 1% of the population).

Jewish Community: Shaare Tzedek Synagogue, Rockley New Rd, Christ Church; Nidhe Israel Synagogue, Synagogue Lane, POB 651, Bridgetown; tel. 437-0907; fax 437-0829; Pres. JACOB HASSID; Sec. SHARON ORAN.

HINDUISM

According to the census of 2000, there are 840 Hindus on the island (less than 1% of the population).

Hindu Community: Hindu Temple, Roberts Complex, Government Hill, St Michael BB11066; tel. 434-4638.

The Press

Barbados Advocate: POB 230, St Michael; tel. 467-2000; fax 434-1000; e-mail news@barbadosadvocate.com; internet www.barbadosadvocate.com; f. 1895; daily; Exec. Editor GILLIAN MARSHALL; circ. 11,413.

The Broad Street Journal: Boarded Hall House, Boarded Hall, St. George; tel. 230-5687; e-mail bsjbarbados@gmail.com; internet www.broadstreetjournalbarbados.com; f. 1993; online; business; Publr and Editor PATRICK R. HOYOS.

The Nation: Nation House, Fontabelle, POB 1203, St Michael BB11000; tel. 430-5400; fax 427-6968; e-mail roxannegibbs@nationnews.com; internet www.nationnews.com; f. 1973; daily; also publishes *The Midweek Nation*, *The Weekend Nation*, *The Sun on Saturday*, *The Sunday Sun* (q.v.) and *The Visitor* (a free publ. for tourists); owned by One Caribbean Media Ltd; Publr VIVIAN-ANNE GITTENS; Exec. Editor ROXANNE GIBBS; circ. 31,533 (Daily), 51,440 (Sun.).

Sunday Advocate: POB 230, St Michael; tel. 467-2000; fax 434-1000; e-mail news@sunbeach.net; internet www.barbadosadvocate.com; f. 1895; Editor REUDON EVERSLEY; Exec. Editor GILLIAN MARSHALL; circ. 17,490.

The Sunday Sun: Nation House, Fontabelle, POB 1203, St Michael BB11000; tel. 430-5400; fax 427-6968; e-mail roxannegibbs@nationnews.com; internet www.nationnews.com; f. 1977; owned by One Caribbean Media Ltd; Publr VIVIAN-ANNE GITTENS; Exec. Editor ROXANNE GIBBS; circ. 48,824.

NEWS AGENCY

Caribbean Media Corporation (CMC): Harbour Industrial Estate, Unit 1B, Bldg 6A, St Michael BB11145; tel. 467-1037; fax 429-4355; e-mail admin@cmccaribbean.com; internet www.cananews.net; f. 2000; formed by merger of Caribbean News Agency (CANA) and Caribbean Broadcasting Union; Dir PATRICK COZIER.

Publishers

Advocate Publishers (2000) Inc: POB 230, Fontabelle, St Michael; tel. 467-2000; fax 434-2020; e-mail news@barbadosadvocate.com; Dir HENRY MOULTON.

Miller Publishing Co: Edgehill, St Thomas; tel. 421-6700; fax 421-6707; e-mail info@barbadosbooks.com; internet www.barbadosbooks.com; f. 1983; publishes general interest books, tourism and business guides; Jt Man. Dirs KEITH MILLER, SALLY MILLER.

Nation Publishing Co Ltd: Nation House, POB 1203, Fontabelle, St Michael; tel. 430-5400; fax 427-6968; internet www.nationpublishing.com; f. 1973; owned by One Caribbean Media Ltd; Publr and CEO VIVIAN-ANNE GITTENS; Exec. Editor ROXANNE GIBBS.

National Cultural Foundation of Barbados: West Terrace, St James; tel. 424-0909; fax 424-0916; internet www.ncf.bb; Chair. KENNETH D. KNIGHT; CEO DEVERE BROWNE.

Broadcasting and Communications

TELECOMMUNICATIONS

Digicel Barbados Ltd: The Courtyard, Hastings, Christ Church; tel. 434-3444; fax 426-3444; e-mail BDS_CustomerCare_External@digicelgroup.com; internet www.digicelbarbados.com; f. 2001; awarded licence to operate cellular telephone services in 2003; approval granted in 2006 for the acquisition of Cingular Wireless' operation in Barbados; owned by an Irish consortium; CEO BARRY O'BRIEN.

LIME: Carlisle House, Hincks St, Bridgetown, St Michael; tel. 292-5050; e-mail CallCenterSupport@time4lime.com; internet www.time4lime.com; f. 1984; fmrly Cable & Wireless (Barbados) Ltd; Barbados External Telecommunications Ltd became Cable & Wireless BET Ltd; name changed as above in 2008; provides international telecommunications services; contact centres in Jamaica and Saint Lucia; owned by Cable & Wireless PLC (United Kingdom); CEO DAVID SHAW.

Sunbeach Communications: 'San Remo', Belmont Rd, St Michael; tel. 430-1569; fax 228-6330; e-mail customerservice@sunbeach.net; internet www.sunbeach.net; f. 1995 as an internet service provider; licence to operate cellular telephone services obtained in 2003; launch of cellular operations postponed indefinitely in 2007; Vtel (Saint Lucia) acquired controlling 52.9% share in Dec. 2006; CEO MARWAN ZAWAYDEH.

TeleBarbados Inc: CGI Tower, 6th Floor, Warrens, St Michael; tel. 620-1000; fax 620-1010; e-mail info@telebarbados.com; internet www.telebarbados.com; f. 2005; internet and private telecommunications network provider; awarded licence to operate fixed-line service in 2005; Pres. BRIAN HARVEY; Vice-Pres. PATRICK HINKSON.

BROADCASTING

Radio

Barbados Broadcasting Service Ltd: Astoria, St George, Bridgetown; tel. 437-9550; fax 437-9203; e-mail action@sunbeach.net; f. 1981; operates BBS FM and Faith 102.1 FM (religious broadcasting); Man. Dir GAIL S. PADMORE.

Caribbean Broadcasting Corporation (CBC): The Pine, POB 900, Wildey, St Michael; tel. 467-5400; fax 429-4795; e-mail customerservices@cbc.bb; internet www.cbc.bb; f. 1963; state-owned; operates 3 radio stations; Gen. Man. LARS SÖDERSTRÖM.

CBC Radio 900 AM: Caribbean Broadcasting Corpn, The Pine, St Michael; tel. 434-1900; fax 429-4795; f. 1963; spoken word and news.

Quality 100.7 FM: Caribbean Broadcasting Corpn, The Pine, St Michael; tel. 434-1007; fax 429-4795; e-mail dsthill@cbc.bb; internet www.cbc.bb/index.pl/radio3; international and regional music, incl. folk, classical, etc.

The One 98.1 FM: Caribbean Broadcasting Corpn, The Pine, St Michael; tel. 434-1981; fax 429-4795; internet www.981fm.net; f. 1984; popular music.

Starcom Network Inc: River Rd, POB 1267, Bridgetown; tel. 430-7300; fax 426-5377; internet www.starcomnetwork.net; f. 1935 as Radio Distribution; owned by One Caribbean Media Ltd; operates 4 radio stations: Gospel 790 AM, Hott 95.3 FM, LOVE FM 104, VOB 92.9 FM; Man. Dir VICTOR FERNANDES.

Television

CBC-TV 8: The Pine, POB 900, Wildey, St Michael; tel. 467-5400; fax 429-4795; e-mail news@cbc.bb; internet www.cbc.bb; f. 1964; part of the Caribbean Broadcasting Corpn (q.v.); Channel Eight is the main national service, broadcasting 24 hours daily; a maximum of 115 digital subscription channels will be available through Multi-Choice Television; Dir of Television CECILY CLARKE-RICHMOND.

DIRECTV: Nation House, Roebuck St, Bridgetown, St Michael; tel. 435-7362; fax 228-5553; e-mail cscbds@directvtt.com; digital satellite television service; owned by the Starcom Network; Administrator M. OWANA SKEETE.

Finance

In August 2010 there were 53 'offshore' banks registered in Barbados and in December 2008 there were approximately 3,334 International Business Companies.

REGULATORY AUTHORITY

Financial Services Commission: Cotton Park Bldg, 1st Floor, Walrond St, Bridgetown BB11127; tel. 437-3924; fax 437-3931; e-mail seccom@caribsurf.com; f. 2011 to regulate and supervise the operations of the non-banking financial sector.

BANKING

(cap. = capital; res = reserves; dep. = deposits; brs = branches; m. = million; amounts in Barbados dollars unless otherwise indicated)

Central Bank

Central Bank of Barbados: Tom Adams Financial Centre, Spry St, POB 1016, Bridgetown BB11126; tel. 436-6870; fax 427-9559; e-mail info@centralbank.org.bb; internet www.centralbank.org.bb; f. 1972; bank of issue; cap. 2.0m., res 6.5m., dep. 712.3m. (Dec. 2009); Gov. R. DELISLE WORRELL.

Commercial Banks

Barbados National Bank Inc. (BNB): Independence Sq., POB 1002, Bridgetown; tel. 431-5700; fax 228-3287; e-mail info@bnbbarbados.com; internet www.bnbbarbados.com; f. 1978 by merger; privatized in 2003; 65% of shares owned by Republic Bank Ltd (Trinidad and Tobago); cap. 48.0m., res 146.6m., dep. 1,754.2m. (Sept. 2010); Chair. RONALD F. D. HARFORD; Man. Dir and CEO ROBERT LE HUNTE; 9 brs.

Butterfield Bank (Barbados) Ltd: Carlisle House, 1st Floor, Hincks St, POB 1256, Bridgetown; tel. 431-4500; fax 430-0222; e-mail info@bb.butterfieldgroup.com; internet www.bb.butterfieldgroup.com; f. 2003; fmrly The Mutual Bank of the Caribbean; owned by The Bank of NT Butterfield & Son Ltd, Bermuda; cap. 36.9m., res 11.2m. dep. 481.5m. (Dec. 2010); Man. Dir LLOYD WIGGAN.

FirstCaribbean International Bank Ltd: Warrens, POB 503, St Michael; tel. 367-2300; fax 424-8977; e-mail firstcaribbeanbank@firstcaribbeanbank.com; internet www.firstcaribbeanbank.com; f. 2002; previously known as CIBC West Indies Holdings, adopted present name following merger of CIBC West Indies and Caribbean operations of Barclays Bank PLC; Barclays relinquished its stake to CIBC in June 2006; cap. US $1,117.3m., res US $–234.5m., dep. US $7,971.6m. (Oct. 2010); Chair. MICHAEL K. MANSOOR; CEO JOHN ORR; 9 brs.

RBC Royal Bank Barbados: Broad St, POB 68, Bridgetown BB11000; tel. 467-4000; fax 427-8393; internet www.rbcroyalbank.com/caribbean/barbados; f. 1911; subsidiary of RBC Financial Group, Canada; Pres. and Country Head HORACE COBHAM.

RBTT Bank Barbados Ltd: Lower Broad St, POB 1007C, Bridgetown; tel. 431-2500; fax 431-2530; internet www.rbtt.com/bb/personal; f. 1984; est. as Caribbean Commercial Bank Ltd; purchased by RBTT Financial Holdings, Trinidad and Tobago in 2004 when current name adopted; acquired by Royal Bank of Canada in 2008; cap. 25.0m., res 6.0m., dep. 258.5m. (Dec. 2002); Chair. GORDON M. NIXON; CEO SURESH SOOKOO; 4 brs.

Regional Development Bank

Caribbean Development Bank: Wildey, POB 408, St Michael BB11000; tel. 431-1600; fax 426-7269; e-mail info@caribank.org; internet www.caribank.org; f. 1970; cap. US $157.4m., res US $365.7m., total assets US $1,287.9m. (Dec. 2009); Pres. Dr WARREN SMITH.

Trust Companies

Bayshore Bank and Trust (Barbados) Corpn: Lauriston House, Lower Collymore Rock, POB 1132, Bridgetown, St Michael BB11000; tel. 430-8650; fax 430-5335; e-mail info@bayshorecapital.com; internet www.bayshorebank.com; chartered bank with affiliates in the Cayman Islands and Toronto, Canada; acquired by J&T Bank and Trust Inc in 2008; Chair. and CEO JOHN BUJOUVES.

Clico Mortgage & Finance Corporation: Clico Corporate Centre, Walrond St, Bridgetown; tel. 431-4716; fax 426-6168; e-mail info@clicomortgage.com; internet www.clicomortgage.com; f. 1984; incorporated as the Caribbean Commercial Trust Co Ltd; name changed as above in 1998; subsidiary of the C. L. Financial Group, based in Trinidad and Tobago; sale to Barbados Public Workers' Cooperative Credit Union approved in Oct. 2009; Chair. LEROY C. PARRIS; Pres. and CEO ANDREW N. ST JOHN.

Concorde Bank Ltd: The Corporate Centre, Bush Hill, Bay St, POB 1161, St Michael; tel. 430-5320; fax 429-7996; e-mail concorde@concordebb.com; f. 1987; cap. US $2.0m., res US $2.0m., dep. US $7.6m. (June 2008); Pres. and Chair. GERARD LUSSAN; Man. MARINA CORBIN.

FirstCaribbean International Trust and Merchant Bank (Barbados) Ltd: Warrens, POB 503, St Michael; tel. 367-2300; fax 424-8977; internet www.firstcaribbeanbank.com; known as

CIBC Trust and Merchant Bank until 2002; Exec. Chair. MICHAEL MANSOOR; CEO JOHN D. ORR.

Globe Finance Inc: Rendezvous Court, Suite 6, Rendezvous Main Rd, Christ Church BB15112; tel. 426-4755; fax 426-4772; e-mail info@globefinanceinc.com; internet www.globefinanceinc.com; f. 1998; offers loans and hire-purchasing financial services; Man. Dir RONALD DAVIS.

Royal Bank of Canada Financial Corporation: Bldg 2, 2nd Floor, Chelston Park, Collymore Rock, POB 986, St Michael; tel. 467-4300; fax 429-3800; internet www.rbcroyalbank.com; Pres. and CEO GORDON M. NIXON; Man. N. L. (ROY) SMITH.

St Michael Trust Corpn: Braemar Court, Deighton Rd, St Michael BB14017; tel. 467-6677; fax 467-6678; e-mail info@stmichael.bb; internet www.stmichaeltrust.com; f. 1987; Pres. IAN HUTCHISON.

STOCK EXCHANGE

Barbados Stock Exchange (BSE): Eighth Ave, Belleville, St Michael BB11114; tel. 436-9871; fax 429-8942; e-mail marlon.yarde@bse.com.bb; internet www.bse.com.bb; f. 1987 as the Securities Exchange of Barbados; in 1989 the Govts of Barbados, Trinidad and Tobago and Jamaica agreed to link exchanges; cross-trading began in April 1991; reincorporated in 2001; Gen. Man. MARLON YARDE.

INSURANCE

The leading British and a number of US and Canadian companies have agents in Barbados. In December 2008 there were 228 exempt and qualified exempt insurance companies registered in the country. Local insurance companies include the following:

Insurance Corporation of Barbados Ltd (ICBL): Roebuck St, POB 11000, Bridgetown; tel. 434-6000; fax 426-3393; e-mail icb@icb.com.bb; internet www.icb.com.bb; f. 1978; 51% owned by BF&M Ltd of Bermuda; cap. Bds $39m.; Chair. R. JOHN WIGHT; Man. Dir WISMAR A. GREAVES; Gen. Man. DENIS A. BRADSHAW.

McLarens Young International: Warrens Complex, 106 Warrens Terrace East, Suite 3, POB 5004, St Michael BB28000; tel. 438-9231; e-mail barbados@mclarensyoung.com; internet www.mclarensyoung.com; Dir GERRY DOWNES.

Sagicor: Sagicor Financial Centre, Lower Collymore Rock, St Michael; tel. 467-7500; fax 436-8829; e-mail info@sagicor.com; internet www.sagicor.com; f. 1840 as Barbados Mutual Life Assurance Society (BMLAS); changed name as above in 2002 after acquiring majority ownership of Life of Barbados (LOB) Ltd; Chair. STEPHEN MCNAMARA; Pres. and CEO DODRIDGE D. MILLER.

United Insurance Co Ltd: United Insurance Centre, Lower Broad St, POB 1215, Bridgetown; tel. 430-1900; fax 436-7573; e-mail mail@unitedinsure.com; internet unitedinsure.com; f. 1976; Man. Dir HOWARD HALL; Regional Man. CECILE COX.

Association

Insurance Association of the Caribbean Inc: The Thomas Pierce Bldg, Lower Collymore Rock, St Michael BB11115; tel. 427-5608; fax 427-7277; e-mail info@iac-caribbean.com; internet www.iac-caribbean.com; regional asscn; Pres. DOUGLAS CAMACHO; Country Dir DAVIS BROWNE.

Trade and Industry

GOVERNMENT AGENCY

Barbados Agricultural Management Co Ltd (BAMC): Warrens, POB 719C, St Michael; tel. 425-0010; fax 421-7879; internet agriculture.gov.bb; f. 1993; Gen. Man. LESLIE PARRIS.

DEVELOPMENT ORGANIZATIONS

Barbados Agriculture Development and Marketing Corpn (BADMC): Fairy Valley, Christ Church; tel. 428-0250; fax 428-0152; e-mail andrew.skeete@badmc.org; internet agriculture.gov.bb; f. 1993 by merger; programme of diversification and land reforms; CEO ANDREW SKEETE.

Barbados Investment and Development Corpn (BIDC): Pelican House, Princess Alice Hwy, POB 1250, Bridgetown BB11000; tel. 427-5350; fax 426-7802; e-mail bidc@bidc.org; internet www.bidc.com; f. 1992 by merger; facilitates the devt of the industrial sector, especially in the areas of manufacturing, information technology and financial services; offers free consultancy to investors; provides factory space for lease or rent; administers the Fiscal Incentives Legislation; Chair. DON MARSHALL; CEO WILBUR T. 'BASIL' LAVINE (acting).

Barbados Small Business Association: 1 Pelican Industrial Park, Bridgetown; tel. 228-0162; fax 228-0163; e-mail theoffice@sba.org.bb; internet www.sba.org.bb; f. 1982; non-profit org. representing interests of small businesses; Pres. LYNETTE P. HOLDER.

CHAMBER OF COMMERCE

Barbados Chamber of Commerce and Industry: Braemar Court, Deighton Rd, St Michael; tel. 620-4750; fax 620-2907; e-mail bcci@bdscham.com; internet www.barbadoschamberofcommerce.com; f. 1825; 220 mem. firms; some 345 reps; Exec. Dir LISA GALE.

INDUSTRIAL AND TRADE ASSOCIATIONS

Barbados Agricultural Society: The Grotto, Beckles Rd, St Michael; tel. 436-6683; fax 435-0651; e-mail bdosagriculturalsociety@caribsurf.com; internet www.basonevoice.org; Pres. TYRONE POWER.

Barbados Association of Professional Engineers: Christie Bldg, Garrison Hill, St Michael BB14038; tel. 429-6105; fax 434-6673; e-mail engineers@caribsurf.com; internet www.bape.org; f. 1964; Pres. ANTONIO ELCOCK; Hon. Sec. D. ANDRE ALLEYNE; 213 mems.

Barbados International Business Association (BIBA): 19 Pine Rd, Belleville, St Michael; tel. 436-2422; fax 434-2423; e-mail biba@biba.bb; internet www.biba.bb; f. 1993 as Barbados Asscn of International Business Cos and Offshore Banks (BAIBCOB); changed name as above in 1997; org. comprising cos engaged in int. business; Pres. CONNIE SMITH; Exec. Dir HENDERSON HOLMES; 170 mem. cos.

Barbados Manufacturers' Association: Suite 201, Bldg 8, Harbour Industrial Park, St Michael; tel. 426-4474; fax 436-5182; e-mail info@bma.bb; internet www.bma.org.bb; f. 1964; Pres. DAVID FOSTER; Exec. Dir BOBBI MCKAY; 110 mem. firms.

Barbados Sugar Industry Ltd (BSIL): Bridgetown; Chair Dr ATLEE BRATHWAITE.

EMPLOYERS' ORGANIZATION

Barbados Employers' Confederation (BEC): Braemar Court, Deighton Rd, POB 33B, Brittons Hill, St Michael; tel. 435-4753; fax 435-2907; e-mail becon@barbadosemployers.com; internet barbadosemployers.com; f. 1956; Pres. IAN GOODING-EDGHILL; Exec. Dir ANTHONY WALCOTT; 235 mems (incl. assoc. mems).

UTILITIES

Electricity

Barbados Light and Power Co (BL & P): POB 142, Garrison Hill, St Michael; tel. 430-4300; fax 228-1396; internet www.blpc.com.bb; f. 1911; 80% owned by Emera (Canada); electricity generator and distributor; operates 3 stations with a combined capacity of 209,500 kW; Chair. IAN CUMMING; Man. Dir PETER WILLIAMS.

Gas

Barbados National Oil Co Ltd (BNOCL): POB 175, Woodbourne, St Philip; tel. 420-1800; fax 420-1818; e-mail ronhewitt@bnocl.com; internet www.bnocl.com; f. 1982; exploration and extraction of petroleum and natural gas; state-owned; Gen. Man. RONALD HEWITT; 88 employees.

National Petroleum Corporation (NPC): Wildey, POB 175, St Michael; tel. 430-4020; fax 426-4326; e-mail customerserv@npc.com.bb; internet npc.com.bb; gas production and distribution; Chair. HARCOURT LEWIS; Gen. Man. JAMES BROWNE.

Water

Barbados Water Authority: Pine East-West Blvd, The Pine, St Michael; tel. 427-3990; fax 426-4507; e-mail bwa@caribsurf.com; internet www.bwa.bb; f. 1980; Exec. Chair. ARNI WALTERS; Gen. Man. DENIS YEARWOOD.

TRADE UNIONS

Barbados Police Association: Speightstown, St Peter; tel. 432-0447; e-mail rpba@caribsurf.com; Pres. Sgt MICHAEL SOBERS; Gen. Sec. SAMUEL HINDS.

Barbados Registered Nurses Association: Gibson House, Lower Collymore Rock, St. Michael, POB 120C, Bridgetown; tel. 427-5627; fax 436-6279; e-mail brna@sunbeach.net; Pres. BLONDELLE MULLIN.

Barbados Secondary Teachers' Union: The Patrick Frost Centre, Eighth Ave, Belleville, St Michael; tel. and fax 429-7676; e-mail bstu_org@yahoo.com; internet www.bstu.org; f. 1946 as Asscn of Asst Teachers in Secondary Schools; present name adopted 1970; Pres. MARY-ANN REDMAN; Gen. Sec. MONA ROBINSON; 440 mems.

Barbados Union of Teachers: Merry Hill, Welches, POB 58, St Michael; tel. 436-6139; fax 426-9890; e-mail but@hotmail.com;

internet butbarbados.org; f. 1974; Pres. KAREN BEST; Gen. Sec. HERBERT GITTENS; 1,800 mems.

Barbados Workers' Union (BWU): 'Solidarity' House, Harmony Hall, POB 172, St Michael; tel. 426-3492; fax 436-6496; e-mail bwu@caribsurf.com; internet www.bwu-bb.org; f. 1941; operates a Labour College; Pres.-Gen. LINDA BROOKS; Gen. Sec. Sir ROY TROTMAN; 25,000 mems.

National Union of Public Workers: Dalkeith Rd, POB 174, St Michael; tel. 426-1764; fax 436-1795; e-mail nupwbarbados@sunbeach.net; internet www.nupwbarbados.com; f. 1944 as the Barbados Civil Service Asscn; present name adopted in 1971; Pres. WALTER MALONEY; Gen. Sec. DENNIS L. CLARKE; c. 8,000 mems.

Transport

ROADS

In 2004 the total length of roads was 1,600 km.

Ministry of Transport and Works: Pine East-West Blvd, St Michael; tel. 429-2191; fax 437-8133; e-mail info@mtw.gov.bb; internet mtw.gov.bb; maintains a network of 1,600 km (994 miles) of paved roads; Permanent Sec. LIONEL NURSE.

Barbados Transport Board: Weymouth, Roebuck St, St Michael BB11083; tel. 310-3500; fax 310-3573; e-mail customerservice@transportboard.com; internet www.transportboard.com; f. 1955; Gen. Man. SANDRA FORDE.

SHIPPING

Bridgetown harbour has berths for eight ships and simultaneous bunkering facilities for five. A new cruise ship pier was built in the mid-2000s. A further joint-venture expansion project along with reformation of cruise facilities was planned, with construction expected to begin in 2012. A new regional ferry service operating from Trinidad and Tobago to Barbados, Grenada, Saint Vincent and the Grenadines and Saint Lucia, was scheduled to begin in 2012.

Barbados Port Inc: University Row, Princess Alice Hwy, Bridgetown; tel. 430-6100; fax 429-5348; e-mail administrator@barbadosport.com; internet www.barbadosport.com; f. 1979 as the Barbados Port Authority and was incorporated in 2003; Chair. LARRY TATEM; Man. Dir and CEO EVERTON WALTERS.

The Shipping Association of Barbados: Trident House, 2nd Floor, Broad St, Bridgetown; tel. 427-9860; fax 426-8392; e-mail info@shippingbarbados.com; internet www.shippingbarbados.com; f. 1981; Pres. MARC SAMPSON; Exec. Vice-Pres. ROVEL MORRIS.

Principal Shipping Companies

Barbados Shipping and Trading Co Ltd (B. S. & T.): The Auto Dome, 1st Floor, Warrens, St Michael; tel. 417-5110; fax 417-5116; e-mail info@bsandtco.com; internet www.bsandtco.com; f. 1920; acquired by energy and industrial asscn Neal & Massy (Trinidad and Tobago) in 2008; CEO ANTHONY KING.

Bernuth Agencies: T. Geddes Grant White Park Rd, Bridgetown; tel. 431-3343; e-mail info@bernuth.com; internet www.bernuth.com; Pres. Capt. JORDAN MONOCANDILOS; Port Co-ordinator YAILEEN RODRIGUEZ.

Booth Steamship Co (Barbados) Ltd: Prescod Blvd, St Michael BB11124; tel. 436-6094; fax 426-0484; e-mail info@boothsteamship.com; internet www.boothsteamship.com; f. 1961; represents Crowley Liner Services, Mediterranean Shipping Co (MSC), Inchcape Shipping Services; Chair. RANDALL I. BANFIELD; Gen. Man. NOEL M. NURSE.

DaCosta Mannings Inc (DMI): Brandons, POB 103, St Michael; tel. 430-4800; fax 431-0051; e-mail sales@dmishipping.com; internet www.dmishipping.com; f. 1995 following merger of DaCosta Ltd and Manning, Wilkinson & Challenor Ltd; shipping and retail company; acquired the shipping lines of of T. Geddes Grant Bros in 2002; agent for P & O Nedlloyd, Princess Cruises, Bernuth Agencies, Columbus/Hamburg Sud and K Line; Exec. Dir MARK SEALY; Gen. Man. GLYNE ST HILL.

Hassell, Eric and Son Ltd: Carlisle House, Hincks St, Bridgetown; tel. 436-6102; fax 429-3416; e-mail info@erichassell.com.bb; internet www.erichassell.com.bb; f. 1969; shipping agent, stevedoring contractor and cargo fowarder; represents Seaboard Marine; Man. Dir ERICA LUKE; Operations Man. MITCHELL FORDE.

Seaboard International Shipping Company Ltd, Barbados: St James House, Second St, St James; tel. 432-4000; fax 432-4004; e-mail melb@seaboardintl.com; internet www.seaboardintl.com; f. 1936; parent co in Vancouver, Canada; Rep. MEL BJORNDAL.

Sea Freight Agencies (Barbados) Ltd: Atlantis Bldg, Shallow Draught, Bridgetown Port, Bridgetown; tel. 429-9688; fax 429-5107; e-mail operations@seafrt.com; internet www.seafrt.com; f. 1988; ship agent and stevedoring contractor; represents the Geest Line and Europe Caribbean Line; Chair. and CEO DAVID HARDING; Man. (Operations) GLADSTONE WHARTON.

Tropical Shipping: Goddards Shipping & Tours Ltd, Goddards Complex, Fontabelle Rd, POB 1283, St Michael; tel. 426-9918; fax 426-7322; e-mail gst_shipagent@goddent.com; internet www.tropical.com; Pres. MIKE PELLICCI; Gen. Man. ROVEL MORRIS.

CIVIL AVIATION

The principal airport is Grantley Adams International Airport, at Seawell, 18 km (11 miles) from Bridgetown. Construction of a new arrivals terminal was completed in 2006. Barbados is served by a number of regional and international airlines, including Air Jamaica, LIAT Airlines (see Antigua and Barbuda), Air Canada and British Airways. An inter-island service, operating flights between Saint Lucia and Barbados (three days a week), was launched by the US-based American Eagle carrier in 2007. The first low-fare airline servicing the Caribbean region, Redjet, suspended operations in 2012.

Barbados Civil Aviation Department: Grantley Adams Industrial Park, Bldg 4, Christ Church BB17089; tel. 428-0930; fax 428-2539; e-mail civilav@sunbeach.net; internet www.bcad.gov.bb; Ministry of International Business and International Transport departments operating as internal regulator of air transport; Dir E. ANTHONY ARCHER.

Tourism

The natural attractions of the island consist chiefly of the warm climate and varied scenery. In addition, there are many facilities for outdoor sports of all kinds. In 2009 the number of stop-over tourist arrivals was an estimated 518,600, while the number of visiting cruise ship passengers was an estimated 635,700. Tourism receipts (excluding passenger transport) totalled US $1,105m. in 2010.

Barbados Hotel and Tourism Association (BHTA): Fourth Ave, Belleville, St Michael; tel. 426-5041; fax 429-2845; e-mail info@bhta.org; internet www.bhta.org; f. 1952 as the Barbados Hotel Asscn; adopted present name in 1994; non-profit trade asscn; Pres. WAYNE CAPALDI.

Barbados Tourism Authority: Harbour Rd, POB 242, Bridgetown; tel. 427-2623; fax 426-4080; e-mail btainfo@visitbarbados.org; internet www.visitbarbados.org; f. 1993 to replace Barbados Board of Tourism; offices in Europe, South America and the USA; Chair. ADRIAN ELCOCK; Pres. and CEO DAVID RICE.

Defence

The Barbados Defence Force is divided into regular defence units and a coastguard service with armed patrol boats. The total strength of the armed forces, as assessed at November 2011, was an estimated 610, comprising an army of 500 members and a navy (coastguard) of 110. There was also a reserve force of 430 members.

Defence Budget: an estimated Bds $57m. (US $28m.) in 2011.

Chief of Staff: Col ALVIN QUINTYNE.

Education

Education is compulsory for 12 years, between five and 16 years of age. Primary education begins at the age of five and lasts for seven years. Secondary education, beginning at 12 years of age, lasts for six years. In 2009/10 22,659 pupils were enrolled at primary schools, while there were 19,497 pupils at secondary schools. Tuition at all government schools is free. There were 14,324 students in higher education in 2008/09. Degree courses in arts, law, education, natural sciences and social sciences are offered at the Cave Hill campus of the University of the West Indies; three higher education training establishments, although remaining administratively discrete, were to be consolidated to form the University College of Barbados. A two-year clinical-training programme for medical students is conducted by the School of Clinic Medicine and Research of the University, while an in-service training programme for teachers is provided by the School of Education. Approved government expenditure on education for 2011/12 was Bds $435.6m.

BELARUS

Introductory Survey

LOCATION, CLIMATE, LANGUAGE, RELIGION, FLAG, CAPITAL

The Republic of Belarus is a landlocked state in north-eastern Europe. It is bounded by Lithuania and Latvia to the north-west, by Ukraine to the south, by Russia to the east, and by Poland to the west. The climate is of a continental type, with an average January temperature, in Minsk, of −5°C (23°F) and an average for July of 19°C (67°F). Average annual precipitation is between 560 mm and 660 mm. The official languages of the Republic are Belarusian and Russian. The major religion is Eastern Orthodox Christianity. The national flag (proportions 1 by 2) consists of two unequal horizontal stripes, of red over light green, with a red-outlined white vertical stripe at the hoist, bearing in red a traditional embroidery pattern. The capital is Minsk (Miensk).

CONTEMPORARY POLITICAL HISTORY

Historical Context

Following periods of Lithuanian and Polish rule, Belarus became a part of the Russian Empire in the late 18th century. During the 19th century there was a growth of national consciousness in Belarus, industrialization and urbanization. After the February Revolution of 1917 in Russia, Belarusian nationalists and socialists formed a rada (council), which sought a degree of autonomy from the Provisional Government in Petrograd (St Petersburg). In November, after the Bolsheviks had seized power in Petrograd, Red Army troops were dispatched to Minsk, and the rada was dissolved. However, the Bolsheviks were forced to withdraw by the invasion of the German army. The Treaty of Brest-Litovsk, signed in March 1918, assigned most of Belarus to Germany. On 25 March Belarusian nationalists convened to proclaim a Belarusian National Republic (BNR), but it achieved only limited autonomy. After the Germans had withdrawn, the Bolsheviks reoccupied Minsk. A Belarusian Soviet Socialist Republic (SSR) was declared on 1 January 1919, but this was merged with Lithuania in February, as 'Litbel'. In April Polish armed forces entered Litbel, which was declared part of Poland. In July 1920 the Bolsheviks recaptured Minsk, and in August the Belarusian SSR was re-established; Lithuania became an independent state. However, the Belarusian SSR comprised only the eastern regions of the lands populated by Belarusians. Western territories were granted to Poland by the Treaty of Rīga, signed on 18 March 1921. The Treaty assigned Belarus's easternmost regions to the Russian Federation, but they were returned to Belarus in 1924 and 1926. Meanwhile, Belarus, with Ukraine and the Transcaucasian Federation (Armenia, Azerbaijan and Georgia), had joined with Russia to establish the Union of Soviet Socialist Republics (USSR) in December 1922. Following the emergence of Stalin (Iosif V. Dzhugashvili) as the dominant figure in the USSR, by 1929, a campaign to collectivize agriculture was strongly resisted by the peasantry, and a series of purges, which initially targeted nationalists and intellectuals, by 1936–38 had widened to include all sectors of the population.

After the invasion of Poland by German and Soviet forces in September 1939, Belarus was enlarged by the inclusion of the lands that it had lost to Poland and Lithuania in 1921. Between 1941 and 1944 Belarus was occupied by Nazi German forces; an estimated 2.2m. people were killed in the Republic. At the Yalta conference, in February 1945, the Allies agreed to recognize the 'Curzon line' as the basis for the western border of the USSR, thus endorsing the unification of western and eastern Belarus. The requirements of the post-war reconstruction programme and the local labour shortage led to an increase in Russian immigration and an ensuing process of 'russification'.

The relative prosperity of the Republic effectively permitted the ruling Communist Party of Belarus (CPB) to resist implementing the economic and political reforms supported by the Soviet leader, Mikhail Gorbachev, from 1985. Although there was some support for campaigns for the greater use of the Belarusian language, and for the release of information about the consequences of the explosion of April 1986 at the Chornobyl (Chernobyl) nuclear power station in Ukraine, which had affected large areas of southern Belarus, there remained little opportunity for overt political opposition. A Belarusian Popular Front (BPF), established in October 1988, enjoyed some success at elections to the all-Union Congress of People's Deputies, held in March 1989. In January 1990 Belarusian was declared to be the state language of the Republic, with effect from September.

The BPF was not officially permitted to participate in elections to the Belarusian Supreme Soviet (Supreme Council) in March 1990. Instead, its members joined other pro-reform groups in the Belarusian Democratic Bloc, which secured about one-quarter of the 310 seats that were decided by popular election; most of the remainder were won by CPB members. The opposition won most seats in the large cities, notably Gomel (Homiel) and Minsk, where Zyanon Paznyak, the leader of the BPF, was elected. On 27 July the Belarusian Supreme Soviet unanimously adopted a Declaration of State Sovereignty. None the less, the Belarusian Government took part in the negotiation of a new Treaty of Union in late 1990–early 1991. The all-Union referendum on the preservation of the USSR took place in the Belarusian SSR on 17 March 1991; of the 83% of the electorate who participated, 83% voted in favour of Gorbachev's proposals for a renewed federation.

On 10 April 1991 a general strike took place, and an estimated 100,000 people demonstrated in Minsk. The Government agreed to economic concessions, including wage increases, but the strikers' political demands, including the resignation of the Belarusian Government and the depoliticization of republican institutions, were rejected. Some 200,000 workers took part in a second general strike on 23 April, in protest at the legislature's refusal to reconvene. When the Belarusian Supreme Soviet was convened in May, the authority of the CPB was threatened by internal dissent. In June 33 deputies joined an opposition 'Communists for Democracy' faction, led by Alyaksandr Lukashenka, the director of a state farm.

The Belarusian leadership did not strongly oppose the attempted coup, led by conservative communists, in Moscow, the Russian and Soviet capital, in August 1991. The Presidium of the Supreme Soviet released a neutral statement on the last day of the coup, but the Central Committee of the CPB declared its unequivocal support. Following the failure of the coup, Mikalay Dzemyantsei, the Chairman of the Belarusian Supreme Soviet (republican head of state), was forced to resign; he was replaced in an interim capacity by Stanislau Shushkevich. The Supreme Soviet agreed to nationalize CPB property and to suspend the party's operations. On 25 August the legislature voted to grant constitutional status to the July 1990 Declaration of State Sovereignty.

Domestic Political Affairs

On 19 September 1991 the Belarusian Supreme Soviet voted to rename the Belarusian SSR the Republic of Belarus, and also elected Shushkevich as its Chairman. On 8 December Shushkevich, with the Russian and Ukrainian Presidents, signed the Minsk Agreement, establishing a Commonwealth of Independent States (CIS, see p. 246), which was to have its headquarters in Minsk, effectively signalling the dissolution of the USSR. On 21 December the leaders of 11 Soviet republics confirmed this decision by the Almaty (Alma-Ata) Declaration.

In March 1993 the CPB and 17 other groups supportive of reunification with Russia formed an informal coalition, the Popular Movement of Belarus. Despite the opposition of Shushkevich and the BPF to the proposals, a new Constitution, providing for a presidential system of government, was adopted in March 1994. A further point of dispute was whether Belarus should adopt closer relations with Russia and the CIS (as advocated by the Supreme Council). Although Shushkevich and the BPF opposed signing the Collective Security Treaty concluded by six other CIS states in May 1992, on the grounds that this would contravene the Declaration of State Sovereignty, which defined Belarus as a neutral state, in April 1993 the Supreme Council voted to authorize the signature of the Treaty. Shushkevich delayed doing so, and in July the legislature approved a vote of no confidence in him; Shushkevich remained in office until his failure to win a vote of confidence, held in January 1994—by which time he had signed the Treaty—resulted in his dismissal. He was replaced by Mechislau Gryb. Meanwhile, in February 1993 the suspension on the CPB was lifted, and the party was re-established.

Lukashenka elected as President

Allegations of corruption against the premier, Vyacheslau Kebich, and leading members of the Council of Ministers, coupled with the worsening economic situation, culminated in a BPF-led general strike in Minsk in February 1994, as a consequence of which Gryb announced an early presidential election. Six candidates contested the election, including Kebich, Shushkevich, Paznyak and Lukashenka, head of the Supreme Council's anti-corruption committee. In the first round of voting, held in June, no candidate secured an overall majority, although Lukashenka, with 47% of the valid votes cast, led by a considerable margin. In the second round, held on 10 July, Lukashenka received 85% of the votes cast, defeating Kebich, and he was inaugurated as the first President of Belarus on 20 July. Mikhail Chigir, an economic reformist, became Chairman of a new Council of Ministers (Prime Minister).

In early 1995 there were repeated confrontations between Lukashenka and the Supreme Council over constitutional issues. In January the Council voted for a second time to adopt legislation that would permit the removal of the President by a two-thirds' quorum of the Council. In March Lukashenka announced that a referendum would be held on four questions in May, concurrently with scheduled legislative elections. In April, following the Council's rejection of all but one of the proposed questions (on closer integration with Russia), Lukashenka threatened to dissolve the legislature. A number of opposition deputies (including Paznyak) were forcibly evicted from the legislative building, where they had declared a hunger strike in protest at the referendum. Shortly afterwards, deputies voted to include the three remaining questions in text of the referendum: on granting Russian equal status with Belarusian as an official language; on the abandonment of the state insignia and flag of independent Belarus in favour of a modified version of those of the Belarusian SSR; and on the amendment of the Constitution to empower the President to suspend the Supreme Council in the event of unconstitutional acts. Some 65% of the electorate participated in the referendum, held on 14 May, at which all four questions were approved.

On the same day, at Belarus's first post-Soviet legislative elections, only 18 of the 260 seats in the Supreme Council were filled. A further 101 deputies were elected at 'run-off' elections held on 28 May 1995, but the necessary two-thirds' quorum was only achieved after two further rounds of voting, held on 29 November and 10 December, brought the total membership of the Supreme Council to 198. The CPB emerged with the largest number of seats in the new legislature (42), followed by the Belarusian Agrarian Party (BAP, with 33) and the United Civic Party (UCP, with nine); 95 independent candidates were elected. The BPF failed to win representation in the Council, as the 62 seats remaining vacant, largely owing to low electoral participation, were mostly in areas where the BPF commanded its strongest support. The Supreme Council held its inaugural session in January 1996. Syamyon Sharetski, the leader of the BAP, was appointed Chairman of the Council.

Despite substantial opposition, President Lukashenka and the Russian President, Boris Yeltsin, signed the Treaty on the Formation of a Community of Sovereign Republics in Moscow on 2 April 1996, which provided for extensive military, economic and political co-operation between the two countries. Following the Treaty's endorsement, confrontation between Lukashenka and the opposition parties intensified. A warrant was issued in April for the arrest of Paznyak, who was accused of organizing the anti-Union demonstrations; he fled the country and later applied for political asylum in the USA.

Lukashenka scheduled another national referendum for 24 November 1996 (with polling stations to be open from 9 November for those unable to vote on the later date). The revocation by presidential decree, in November, of a ruling of the Constitutional Court that any constitutional amendments agreed by referendum would not be legally binding provoked fierce criticism. The referendum ballot papers contained seven questions, four of which were proposed by Lukashenka: that amendments be made to the Constitution to extend the President's term of office from 1999 until 2001, to enable the President to issue decrees that would carry legal force, and to grant him extensive powers of appointment both to the judiciary and to an envisaged bicameral legislature; that Belarusian Independence Day be moved from 27 July (the anniversary of the Declaration of State Sovereignty) to 3 July (the anniversary of the liberation from the Nazis); that there be an unrestricted right to purchase and sell land; and that the death penalty be abolished. The remaining questions were submitted by the Supreme Council, and proposed that there be a significant reduction in the powers of the President. After the Chairman of the central electoral commission, Viktar Hanchar, stated that he would not approve the results of the voting, owing to electoral violations, Lukashenka dismissed him. In November 1996 Chigir resigned as Chairman of the Council of Ministers, urging that the referendum be cancelled; he was replaced by Syarhey Ling. Some 10,000 people attended an anti-Government rally in Minsk, protesting at the restrictions on freedom of expression. The Council of Europe (see p. 256) declared that the draft of the amended Constitution did not comply with European standards. Meanwhile, 75 deputies in the Supreme Council submitted a motion to the Constitutional Court to begin impeachment proceedings against the President; although the Court had already found 17 decrees issued by Lukashenka to be unconstitutional, it was forced to abandon the motion, as deputies retracted their support.

The referendum results revealed considerable support for the President, but their accuracy was disputed. According to official figures, some 84% of the electorate took part; none of the proposals of the Supreme Council were approved, while two of the President's proposals—on the date on which national independence would be celebrated, and on constitutional amendments—obtained the requisite majority of votes; the other two proposals—on the right to buy and sell land and on the abolition of the death penalty—were overwhelmingly rejected. The amended Constitution was published on 27 November 1996 and took effect immediately.

Following the referendum, the Supreme Council divided into two factions. More than 100 deputies declared their support for Lukashenka, establishing a 110-member Palata Predstaviteley (House of Representatives), which was to be the lower chamber of the new bicameral Natsionalnoye Sobraniye (National Assembly), to replace the Supreme Council. Some 50 other deputies denounced the referendum as invalid, declaring themselves to be the legitimate legislature. The Palata Predstaviteley convened shortly afterwards and elected Anatol Malafeyeu as its Chairman. Deputies were granted a four-year mandate, while the term of office of those opposed to the new legislature was curtailed to two months. Deputies elected in the by-elections held simultaneously with the referendum were denied registration. Legislation governing the formation of the new upper house of the legislature, the 64-member Soviet Respubliki (Council of the Republic), was approved by Lukashenka in December 1996: eight members were to be appointed by the President and the remaining 56 elected by regional councils. The Soviet Respubliki convened in January 1997. Meanwhile, in protest at the constitutional amendments, the Chairman of the Constitutional Court and several judges announced their resignations.

In January 1997 a 'shadow' cabinet comprising politicians opposed to the new arrangements, calling itself the Public Coalition Government-National Economic Council (PCG-NEC), was formed, chaired by Genadz Karpenka. Meanwhile, international organizations expressed doubts as to the legitimacy of the referendum; the Council of Europe suspended Belarus's 'guest status', while the Permanent Council of the Parliamentary Assembly of the Organization for Security and Co-operation in Europe (OSCE, see p. 388) recognized a delegation from the former Supreme Council, rather than from the Palata Predstaviteley, as official Belarusian representatives.

Treaty of Union with Russia

The signing with Russia of the Treaty of Union, and initialling of the Charter of the Union on 2 April 1997, by Presidents Lukashenka and Yeltsin (see Foreign Affairs) prompted a protest demonstration in Minsk, which was suppressed by the police. Nevertheless, support for the treaty appeared to be widespread, and some 15,000 people participated in a pro-Union rally in Minsk in mid-May. The Charter of the Union was signed in Moscow on 23 May. The Treaty and Charter were ratified shortly afterwards by the respective legislatures, and came into effect in mid-June.

Negotiations mediated by the Council of Europe and the European Union (EU, see p. 276) to end the confrontation between the former Supreme Council and the new legislature, in June–July 1997, were unsuccessful. In November the opposition launched a campaign for the next presidential election to be held in 1999, as required by the 1994 Constitution. A number of senior BPF members and other demonstrators were arrested in April 1998 during protest rallies. In June legislation was approved that rendered defamation of the President an offence punishable by up to five years' imprisonment. In November Lukashenka decreed the formation of a special economic committee, which was to supersede the Council of Ministers in economic policy. A new law on local elections was approved by the Palata Predstaviteley in December, effectively banning those with a police record or fine from standing in the local elections that were to be held in April 1999. In the event, the opposition organized an electoral boycott, and the majority of the seats in the elections were each contested by a single candidate.

Meanwhile, in January 1999 the Central Electoral Commission of the former Supreme Council scheduled a 'shadow presidential election' for 16 May. In March the Commission's Chairman, Hanchar, was arrested, but was released after a 10-day hunger strike. Chigir was registered as a candidate for the election in March, but was arrested and detained in April. (In May 2000 he was convicted of abuse of office and received a three-year, suspended sentence.) Following the death of Karpenka in April 1999, Gryb was elected Chairman of the PCG-NEC in November. In the event, it proved impossible to organize fixed polling stations for the poll, which was not recognized by the Government or by the international community. The election results were declared invalid later in the month, owing to irregularities; the rate of participation was reported as 53%. In July Sharetski fled to Lithuania to avoid arrest after the Supreme Council designated him 'acting President' of Belarus.

In January 1999 Lukashenka had decreed that political parties, trade unions and other organizations were required to re-register by 1 July; those failing to do so were to be dissolved. By September 17 of the 28 existing official parties had been re-registered. In October Vintsuk Vyachorka was elected Chairman of the BPF, which was renamed Revival—BPF in December. (Supporters of Paznyak had formed a breakaway party in the previous month.) OSCE-mediated negotiations between the Government and the opposition, concerning the legislative elections to be held in 2000, which commenced in September 1999, proved fruitless. Subsequently, a number of critics of the President disappeared in unexplained circumstances, including Hanchar and a former Minister of the Interior, Yuriy Zakharenka. In October 15,000 people were estimated to have taken part in an anti-Government 'Freedom March' in Minsk.

In February 2000 Ling resigned as Chairman of the Council of Ministers; he was replaced by Uladzimir Yermoshin. In that month opposition parties agreed to boycott the parliamentary elections due to take place in October. This decision appeared to prompt increased repression of both the unofficial media and the opposition. The staging, in March, of a second 'Freedom March' was followed by the prohibition of demonstrations in central Minsk. A further demonstration later in the month, to commemorate the creation of the BNR in 1918 was suppressed by the security forces and resulted in hundreds of arrests. In the following month the Minister of Internal Affairs, Yuriy Sivakow, resigned, ostensibly for health reasons.

A large-scale rally by opposition activists preceded the elections to the Natsionalnoye Sobraniye, which were held in two rounds on 15 and 29 October 2000. The OSCE described the elections as neither free nor fair, and the international community refused to recognize the validity of the elections, in which nominally independent candidates obtained the majority of seats. In March 2001 President Lukashenka signed a decree imposing severe restrictions on the use of foreign financial assistance by both individuals and national organizations. In May the five main opposition leaders announced their intention to nominate a single candidate to contest the presidential election scheduled for September.

In June 2001 two former investigators at the Office of the Prosecutor-General, who had been granted asylum in the USA, claimed that senior government officials had organized the assassinations of political opponents to Lukashenka's regime, and alleged them to be responsible for the deaths of Hanchar and Zakharenka, as well as Dmitrii Zavadski, a cameraman for a Russian television channel, whose location had been unknown since July 2000. The allegations were supported by the Chairman of the Federation of Trade Unions of Belarus, Uladzimir Hancharyk, who in July 2001 revealed documents that apparently linked the Prosecutor-General, Viktar Sheyman, and former Minister of Internal Affairs Sivakow with the disappearance and presumed murder of Hanchar and Zakharenka. In July the opposition selected Hancharyk as its candidate for the presidency. In August two state security agents released to the media a recorded testimony, in which they supported claims that Hanchar, together with a business associate, had been kidnapped and killed in September 1999 by a special police unit.

An increase in repression

The presidential election was held, as scheduled, on 9 September 2001, although a constitutional provision had permitted some voting to begin on 4 September. Lukashenka was re-elected with 75.7% of the valid votes cast. Hancharyk received 15.7% of the votes, and the only other candidate, the leader of the Liberal Democratic Party of Belarus (LDPB), Syarhey Haydukevich, received just 2.5%. The election was described as flawed by the OSCE, and Hancharyk urged the public to protest against Lukashenka's victory, to little effect. Following Lukashenka's inauguration on 20 September, Yermoshin tendered the resignation of his Government. Lukashenka subsequently reorganized the Council of Ministers. On 10 October the Palata Predstaviteley approved the nomination of former Deputy Prime Minister Genadz Navitsky as premier. In late 2001 and early 2002 a number of state officials and managers of state enterprises were arrested (several were subsequently imprisoned) as part of an ostensible anti-corruption campaign.

In March 2002 two former police officers were sentenced to life imprisonment, having been found guilty of kidnapping Zavadski. However, there were claims that the charges had been fabricated to divert attention from the involvement of more senior government officials in the abduction. In July 2002 Chigir was given a three-year, suspended prison sentence, following his conviction for tax evasion. In September the editor of an independent newspaper was sentenced to two years' corrective labour, after he accused the President of having profited from illicit arms sales. The Government also began to reduce the diffusion in Belarus of Russian broadcast media, which were often critical of Lukashenka, imposing new registration requirements on radio and television companies.

Local elections were held in March 2003, amid opposition allegations of electoral irregularities. In July the President dismissed premier Genadz Navitsky, Deputy Prime Minister Alyaksandr Papkow and the Minister of Agriculture and Food, Mikhail Rusy. The First Deputy Prime Minister, Syarhey Sidorsky, was appointed acting premier. In the same month Navitsky was elected Chairman of the Soviet Respubliki. In December Sidorsky was confirmed as Prime Minister, and a further reorganization of the Council of Ministers took place.

State repression continued in 2003–04, with the closure of several non-governmental organizations (NGOs), efforts to prevent the publication of several independent newspapers, and the imposition of further restrictions on access to Russian media. In November 2003 the Belarusian Party of Labour, the Belarusian Social Democratic Hramada (Assembly), Revival—BPF, the Party of Communists of Belarus (PCB) and the UCP announced the formation of an opposition alliance, the 'Five Plus' Popular Coalition. Restrictions on political parties increased, and in August 2004 the Supreme Court proscribed the Belarusian Party of Labour. Meanwhile, a prominent opponent of the Government, Mikhail Marinich, was arrested in April, on charges of theft and embezzlement, prompting a widely observed strike in June and other incidents of unrest. (In December Marinich was sentenced to five years' imprisonment, although the sentence was subsequently halved.) At the time of the legislative elections, which took place on 17 October, the opposition comprised three broad groupings: Five Plus; the 'Free Belarus' European Coalition, which included the Belarusian Social Democratic Assembly, and favoured EU membership rather than federation with Russia; and a youth bloc, the Young Belarusians. No opposition candidates won seats in the elections, in which 96 nominally independent candidates were elected, the CPB obtained eight mandates, the BAP three, and the LDPB one. According to official results of a constitutional referendum, held concurrently with the elections, 77.3% of those participating voted to approve an amendment that would permit Lukashenka to contest a third presidential term. The official rate of participation was almost 90%.

Meanwhile, in January 2004 the Parliamentary Assembly of the Council of Europe (PACE) published a preliminary report on the disappearances of Zakharenka, Hanchar, Zavadski and an associate of Hanchar, Anatol Krasouski. The report concluded that senior government officials may have been involved, and urged member states of the Council of Europe to exert political pressure on the Belarusian Government to prompt an independent investigation into the alleged murders. In August Sivakow was banned by EU member states from entering Greece (he had been appointed as Minister of Sports and Tourism in January 2003, and planned to visit the summer Olympic Games), in a further attempt to persuade the Government to authorize an investigation.

In March 2005 a demonstration of up to 1,500 people demanding the resignation of Lukashenka was forcibly dispersed by the police. A smaller opposition rally took place in April. In that month Assembly and the Belarusian Social Democratic Party (National Hramada) merged to form the Assembly (Hramada)—Belarusian Social-Democratic Party (BSDP); Alyaksandr Kazulin was elected as the party's Chairman in July. In May the opposition activist Syarhey Skryabets was detained and sentenced on what were widely alleged to be politically motivated charges. On 31 May the President decreed that NGOs and independent media organizations were no longer permitted to include the words 'Belarusian' or 'national' in their names, and that, if necessary, they would have to re-register under new designations. In June two opposition leaders were sentenced to terms of corrective labour for having organized a series of unauthorized demonstrations. In the same month the organizer of the demonstration held in March 2005 was imprisoned for 18 months.

In October 2005 a congress of opposition groups nominated civil society activist Alyaksandr Milinkevich as its candidate in the presidential election due to take place in 2006. In December 2005 the Soviet Respubliki approved legislative amendments to the criminal code, which included measures to penalize citizens for activities deemed to threaten personal or public security, or to discredit Belarus internationally; the measures were widely interpreted as forming part of efforts to curb opposition activity in advance of the presidential election, which was subsequently scheduled for 19 March 2006.

Lukashenka elected to a third term

In January 2006 PACE urged member states to support the broadcast from abroad of independent media to Belarus. Meanwhile, the European Commission awarded €2m. to a German-led consortium for the initiation of foreign broadcasts to the country prior to the presidential election. In the days preceding the election many opposition politicians and supporters were detained by the authorities. Early results of the election, conducted on 19 March, indicated that Lukashenka had been returned to office by a significant majority, and on the same day some 20,000 opposition supporters gathered to protest at alleged electoral malpractice. Further demonstrations took place in the week following the election. Meanwhile, the OSCE declared that the election had failed to meet democratic standards, and Milinkevich demanded that the poll be repeated. According to the final results, Lukashenka received 83.0% of the votes cast, and Milinkevich was placed second, with 6.1%, ahead of Haydukevich and Kazulin. Kazulin was arrested on 25 March, prompting international protests. Both the USA and the EU imposed visa bans and financial sanctions on Belarusian officials allegedly involved in electoral malpractice. Lukashenka was inaugurated as President on 8 April, and Sidorsky was subsequently reappointed as Prime Minister. PACE urged the Belarusian authorities to hold a new presidential election in accordance with the demands of the opposition. Later in April Milinkevich was detained and sentenced to 15 days' imprisonment, having been found guilty of participating in an unauthorized demonstration. In July Kazulin was convicted on charges of disorderly conduct, and was sentenced to a prison term of five-and-a-half years.

Meanwhile, in May 2006 Lukashenka effected a government reorganization, appointing Viktar Bura, hitherto Deputy Chairman of the Minsk City Executive Committee, Deputy Prime Minister, and naming five new ministers. In October the Palata Predstaviteley voted to amend Belarus's electoral legislation, prior to local elections that were scheduled to take place in January 2007. In the local elections, conducted on 14 January, the opposition secured only two seats on local councils, despite presenting 300 candidates. The USA and the EU declared that the conduct of the elections had failed to meet democratic standards.

In March 2007 an authorized opposition demonstration was staged in Minsk, to mark the anniversary of the creation of the BNR in 1918; opposition leaders declared that up to 10,000 supporters had attended the rally, of whom 100 had been detained. A series of arrests of youth opposition leaders in August and September prompted the EU to suspend its participation in a proposed second round of negotiations with Belarus on energy security. The most prominent of those arrested, Zmitser Dashkevich, received an 18-month term of imprisonment in November, on charges of engaging in activities for an unregistered political organization. Meanwhile, the Ministry of Justice continued to reject applications for official registration by new opposition parties, including Milinkevich's For Freedom Movement. In October an opposition rally of some 5,000 people was staged in Minsk to demand that the Government implement various policy measures stipulated by the European Commission as prerequisites for Belarus's access to greater aid and trade co-operation. In November a new public association supportive of Lukashenka, White Rus, chaired by Minister of Education Alyaksandr Radzkow, was established. In January 2008 special police violently dispersed an unauthorized demonstration of about 3,000 people in Minsk, which had been organized in protest at a presidential decree restricting small-business activities. Dashkevich and another youth opposition leader were granted an early release in January, following protests by the EU and USA. In February Andrey Klimau, another opponent of Lukashenka who had been been imprisoned for 'inciting revolution' was also released before he had served his full two years' sentence.

In June 2008 the Soviet Respubliki imposed additional restrictions on media outlets. On 4 July a bomb exploded at a concert held in Minsk to commemorate Independence Day, injuring 54 people. A number of opposition activists were subsequently arrested, including former members of a banned nationalist organization, the Belarusian Union of Military Personnel. Several days later Lukashenka dismissed the State Secretary of the Security Council and the head of the presidential administration, criticizing them for failing to prevent the bomb attack. In August, shortly after Kazulin was temporarily released from gaol to attend the funeral of his father-in-law, Lukashenka granted him a pardon. Kazulin subsequently declared that he accepted his release but not the pardon extended, and demanded compensation from the state. Although he had been replaced as Chairman of the BSDP earlier in August and subsequently resigned from the party, Kazulin confirmed that he would remain in political life. European Commission and other international officials welcomed Lukashenka's decision and urged the release of the remaining political prisoners.

The 2008 legislative elections

Elections to the Palata Predstaviteley, which some 500 OSCE observers were invited to monitor by the Belarusian authorities, were conducted on 28 September 2008. While some 70 opposition candidates were permitted to participate in the poll, none obtained representation; it was reported that all of the 110 elected deputies were pro-Government, although 103 were nominally independent. Some 800 opposition supporters staged a protest against the conduct of the election on the same day. A preliminary OSCE report stated that the election process had again failed to meet international democratic standards. Following the election of 56 senators by regional councils on 3–10 October (and appointment of the remaining eight deputies by Lukashenka), a new Soviet Respubliki was installed at the end of that month. In December, to conform with EU demands, the Ministry of Justice registered Milinkevich's For Freedom Movement as a political party. The annual opposition rally organized in Minsk in February 2009 was violently dispersed by police.

On 6 April 2009 Uladzimir Naumau, Minister of Internal Affairs since 2000, resigned. He was succeeded, initially in an acting capacity, by Anatoly Kulyashou. In early June, in a minor governmental reorganization, the hitherto Minister of Labour and Social Protection, Uladzimir Patupchyk, was appointed as a Deputy Prime Minister. A further governmental reshuffle was implemented later in the month. In September police in Minsk detained the leaders of the UCP and the PCB as they attempted to distribute publicity material for a protest against the Government's economic policies. In late October the Palata Predstaviteley voted to amend the electoral code. A more substantial reorganization of the Government was implemented on 4 December, as part of measures that were reportedly intended to address popular dissatisfaction with the economic downturn. Notably, Yuri Zhadobin, the hitherto Secretary of the Security Council, succeeded Leanid Maltsaw as Minister of Defence (who was appointed to Zhadobin's former position), Maryana Shchotkina was appointed as Minister of Labour and Social Protection, Mikalay Snapkou replaced Mikalay Zaychanka as Minister of the Economy, and Aleh Pralyaskouski, who had advocated the imposition of stricter restrictions on the operations of media organs, was appointed as Minister of Information. In March 2010 the offices of a pro-democracy group, Charter 97, in Minsk, were raided by police, several journalists beaten, and a number of computers confiscated, apparently in response to the publication of a report on the group's website to the effect that Andrey Sannikau, the leader of an unregistered opposition group, European Belarus, was intending to contest the presidential election due in 2011.

In early September 2010 the body of a prominent journalist and opposition activist, Oleh Bebenin, the founder and director of a leading opposition website, *Charter97.org*, was found hanged. Opposition figures, including Sannikau, expressed doubt at the official attribution of the cause of Bebenin's death to suicide, and the OSCE urged that a credible and independent inquiry into the death be held. On 14 September an extraordinary session of the Palata Predstaviteley voted to schedule a presidential election for 19 December, several months earlier than had been anticipated or was required by the Constitution. Lukashenka subsequently confirmed his intention of seeking re-election, and by the end of September some 17 candidates had been registered. Although seven of these subsequently withdrew from the contest, or were unable to gather the requisite 100,000 signatures, several of the opposition candidates were, unprecedentedly, allowed a limited degree of access to state media to campaign, while an opposition protest rally, held in Minsk in early December, was attended by around 3,000 people. However, the principal opposition leaders, including Kazulin and Milinkevich declined to contest the election.

The 2010 presidential election

The presidential election, held on 19 December 2010, was contested by 10 candidates. According to the official results, Lukashenka was overwhelmingly re-elected to a further term of office, receiving 79.7% of the votes cast. His nearest rival was Sannikau, with only 2.4%; about 6.5% of the votes cast were 'against all candidates'. According to official figures, around 84% of the electorate participated. The announcement of the preliminary results of the elections, several hours after the polls closed, precipitated demonstrations of some 10,000 people outside the parliamentary buildings in central Minsk, who protested against alleged electoral improprieties. Lukashenka harshly condemned the demonstrators, and riot police forcibly dispersed the crowds. Seven of the nine opposition candidates, including Sannikau, together with his wife, journalist Irina Khalip, were among several hundred people who were arrested, and at least one candidate, Uladzimer Nyaklyaeu, was beaten by police. In total, around 600 demonstrators were detained. Observers from the OSCE criticized the conduct of the election, stating that the counting of votes lacked transparency, although an observer mission from the CIS described the poll as being both 'free and fair'. On the following day police officers beat and arrested members of numerous human rights organizations. By the end of the month four of the opposition candidates had been charged with organizing riots, while three other candidates remained under judicial investigation. During the second half of December the homes and offices of several independent journalists were raided by law-enforcement or security officials. The harsh treatment of the opposition, as well as the conduct of the election, was criticized by Western Governments, the OSCE and the EU. At the end of the month the OSCE closed its mission in Minsk, in response to the demands of the Belarusian authorities, which claimed that the organization had fulfilled its mandate in the country. In January 2011 the Vice-President of the European Commission and High Representative of the EU for Foreign Affairs and Security Policy, Catherine Ashton, urged Belarus to release from detention all those held on political grounds and to desist from the official harassment of opposition activists. In late January Nyaklyaeu and Khalip were released from detention. At the end of the month, however, the EU sanctions against Belarusian officials, which had been suspended in 2008, were reinstated (see Regional relations).

Meanwhile, on 28 December 2010 Mikhail Myasnikovich, who had served as Head of the Presidential Administration in 1995–2001, was appointed Prime Minister, replacing Sidorsky. Several new ministerial appointments, including those of three new deputy premiers, were made shortly afterwards. On 21 January 2011 Lukashenka was formally inaugurated to a new presidential term. In February Dzmitry Katsyarynich, hitherto the Chairman of a state-owned manufacturing company, Belshina, was appointed Minister of Industry, succeeding Alyaksandr Radzevich.

On 11 April 2011 a bomb exploded at a station on the Minsk Metro, killing 15 people and injuring almost 400. In May Sannikau was sentenced to five years' imprisonment on charges of organizing mass protests after the December 2010 election. (During his trial he claimed that he had been subject to physical torture while in detention.) Khalip subsequently received a suspended prison sentence, having been found guilty of similar charges.

Recent developments: economic crisis and popular protests

From late May 2011 unauthorized demonstrations, many organized through social networking websites, were staged on a weekly basis in Minsk and other cities, to protest at the deteriorating economic situation in the country; some 400 people were reported to have been detained during June. On 29 June, when a further unauthorized anti-Government demonstration took place in central Minsk, protesters (instead of assembling in silence as before) clapped their hands in unison; police subsequently dispersed the demonstration, detaining around 50 people. On 3 July, the occasion of Independence Day, an estimated 3,000 people participated in a further 'clapping protest' in Minsk, and many demonstrators were arrested. Lukashenka, addressing a military parade, referred to such demonstrations as an attempt to incite revolution. Similar demonstrations continued to take place in Minsk and across the country. By the end of July it was reported that around 2,000 people had been detained during the protests, and some 500 had received short prison sentences, while the Government published draft legislation, intended to prevent the 'silent' and 'clapping' protests, by prohibiting groups of people from assembling to take part in any expression of 'action or inaction'. In early August a prominent human rights activist was arrested and formally charged with tax evasion (owing to his use of personal bank accounts in Lithuania and Poland to receive funding from international donors); in November he was sentenced to four-and-a-half years' imprisonment.

On 4 October 2011 Lukashenka dismissed Viktar Halavanau as Minister of Justice, following the appointment of a new Prosecutor-General in the previous month. On 3 November Lukashenka declared that the Chairmen of the Executive Committees of Minsk and the six oblasts (regions) would be granted the military rank of Major-General, and that they would have additional responsibilities pertaining to territorial defence. In the same month Lukashenka announced the formation of a territorial army numbering 120,000, and established an advisory body, the Council for the Development of an Informational Society, headed by himself, with his son Viktar as deputy. At the end of November two Belarusian nationals were convicted and sentenced to death for organizing the metro bomb attack in April, as well as those at the 2008 Independence Day concert in Minsk and in the north-eastern city of Vitebsk in 2005, after they pleaded guilty to the charges against them (although one of them withdrew his confession). Domestic and international human rights groups cast doubt on the evidence against the two men and petitioned the Government to commute the death sentence against them, while the Council of Europe urged an immediate moratorium on capital punishment in Belarus. None the less, both men were executed in March 2012. In December 2011 it was reported that a Deputy Minister of Internal Affairs, who had been largely responsible for the violent police response to the post-election and later protests, had been arrested. In mid-April 2012 Lukashenka dismissed Valery Ivanou as a Deputy Prime Minister, appointing Rusy in his place. Also in mid-April President Lukashenka announced that he had granted a presidential pardon to Sannikau and to an associate of Sannikau, Zmitser Bandarenka (who had been serving a two-year prison sentence on charges of participating in the unrest after the 2010 election), both of whom were thereby released from gaol with immediate effect. The EU (the member states of which had withdrawn their ambassadors from Belarus in late February—see Regional relations) demanded the release of all other political prisoners in Belarus.

Foreign Affairs

Regional relations

Following the dissolution of the USSR, Belarus's closest relations continued to be with member states of the CIS, particularly Russia. Belarus signed the CIS Collective Security Treaty in December 1993, and accords on closer economic co-operation with CIS states followed. With the dissolution of the USSR,

Belarus effectively became a nuclear power, with approximately 80 intercontinental ballistic missiles stationed on its territory. However, the Government described Belarus as a neutral and non-nuclear state, and in May 1992 Belarus signed the Lisbon Protocol to the Treaty on the Non-Proliferation of Nuclear Weapons (see p. 125), under which it pledged to transfer all nuclear missiles to Russia. The USA pledged financial and technical aid to Belarus to help the dismantling of its nuclear arsenal, and the country's final nuclear warhead was transported to Russia in 1996.

In April 1994 Belarus and Russia concluded an agreement on eventual monetary union, and in April 1996 concluded a Treaty on the Formation of a Community of Sovereign Republics, providing for closer economic, political and military integration. On 2 April 1997 a further Treaty of Union, providing for the 'voluntary unification of the member states', was signed by Presidents Yeltsin and Lukashenka. The Union's Parliamentary Assembly (which had convened in March) was to comprise 36 members from the legislature of each country. A Charter detailing the process of integration was signed in Moscow on 23 May. The respective legislatures ratified the documents in June, before the first official session of the Parliamentary Assembly. In November 1998 the Parliamentary Assembly of the Russia-Belarus Union voted for the creation of a unified, bicameral parliament. (However, establishment of the proposed unified legislature was held in abeyance.) In December 1998 Presidents Lukashenka and Yeltsin signed an outline union accord. The signature of a treaty creating a more formal union structure, the Union State of Russia and Belarus, took place in Moscow on 8 December. The treaty was ratified and took effect in January 2000, when Lukashenka was appointed Chairman of the Supreme State Council of the Union State (comprising the Presidents, Prime Ministers and the heads of each of the parliamentary chambers in both countries). An agreement (in accordance with which the Russian rouble was to be adopted as the union currency from 2005, prior to the adoption of a new currency in 2008) on the introduction of a single currency was signed on 30 November; it was ratified by the Natsionalnoye Sobraniye in April 2001.

During 2002 disagreements over the nature of the planned union arose. Although Belarus and Russia reached agreement on the harmonization of customs and tax laws and the removal of trade barriers, in June Vladimir Putin, who had succeeded Yeltsin as President of Russia in 2000, publicly criticized Lukashenka's proposals for union, and in August presented Lukashenka with a new unification plan, providing for the absorption of the seven administrative regions of Belarus (rather than Belarus as a country) into the Russian Federation; Lukashenka denounced the plan as an insult to Belarus's sovereignty. Detailed negotiations on monetary union commenced in 2003. However, the two countries' failure to sign a final agreement on a single currency delayed its planned introduction indefinitely. In October 2005 a draft constitutional act was drawn up; it was envisaged that it would be submitted for approval at referendums to be held in both countries, although by early 2012 no date for a referendum had been announced by either Belarus or Russia.

Bilateral relations were strained in 2003–04 by inconclusive negotiations over the settlement of Belarusian fuel arrears, which led to the repeated suspension of gas supplies by the Russian state-controlled energy supplier Gazprom in early 2004. An agreement was reached in June 2004, whereupon Gazprom resumed supplies to Belarus; a further agreement was signed in December 2005. In January 2007 Belarus imposed a retaliatory levy on Russian oil passing through its territory, after Gazprom more than doubled the price of gas supplied to Belarus and Russia introduced an oil export duty. Russia subsequently accused Belarus of abstracting almost 80,000 metric tons of Russian crude oil in transit through the country, and in response ceased the transit of oil through Belarus. The situation was resolved three days later, when Belarus agreed to lift the transit duty and Russia in turn reduced its duty on oil exports.

In May 2008 Lukashenka (in his capacity as Chairman of the Supreme State Council of the Union State of Russia and Belarus) announced that he had appointed Putin, who had become the Russian Chairman of the Government (premier) following the election of Dmitrii Medvedev to the presidency, Prime Minister of the Union State. Lukashenka expressed support for the military action taken by Russia in Georgia in early August to assist separatists in the South Ossetia region (see the chapter on Georgia), and in November he announced that Belarus would extend formal recognition to the Georgian separatist regions of South Ossetia and Abkhazia as independent states, as Russia had done in August. (However, he subsequently failed to adhere to this pledge.) Russia granted Belarus a loan of some US $2,000m. toward energy supplies in November and later agreed concessionary prices in the payment of natural gas, following the deteriorating financial position in Belarus (see Economic Affairs). In February 2009 it was announced that Belarus and Russia had signed an official treaty providing for the creation of a joint air defence system. The Belarusian Ministry of Defence reported that the two countries had commenced joint training operations, although Belarus subsequently expressed reluctance to participate in a proposed rapid-response unit that the Collective Security Treaty Organization (CSTO, see p. 462) was intending to establish. Relations with Russia deteriorated somewhat during 2009–10, partly in response to the development of warmer relations between Belarus and the EU (see below). In May 2009 Russia announced that it was to delay the release of a tranche worth US $500m. of a loan agreed in late 2008, and in June 2009 it imposed a ban on the import of many items of dairy produce from Belarus, ostensibly because they failed to meet Russian packaging requirements. In protest at this development, Lukashenka boycotted a meeting of the CSTO held in Moscow in mid-June, at which Belarus had been due to assume the rotational chairmanship of the Organization. (Russia instead assumed this position on a temporary basis.) In March 2010 Putin visited Belarus, where he met Belarusian Prime Minister Sidorsky and chaired a meeting, in Brest, of the Council of Ministers of the Union State. However, at apparently short notice, on the day of Putin's visit Lukashenka had undertaken a visit to Venezuela, where he met President Hugo Chávez. It was reported that Belarus had offered military assistance to Venezuela, and that Venezuela was to supply petroleum to Belarus. Relations deteriorated further when a state-controlled TV channel in Russia broadcast a series of documentary programmes that were particularly critical of Lukashenka, and which criticised abuses of human rights in Belarus. Moreover, in early October President Medvedev made a speech in which he strongly denounced Lukashenka's personal behaviour, particularly with regard to Belarus's failure to recognize Abkhazia and South Ossetia, and expressed disapproval at human rights and judicial abuses in the country. Earlier in the month Lukashenka had accused Russian companies of funding the campaigns of opposition candidates in the forthcoming presidential election. However, in the event, the Russian authorities did not support any of the opposition candidates at the presidential election, and in early December, shortly before the poll, terms were agreed on a reduction in the duties paid by Belarus on imports of Russian petroleum, and for Belarus to pay to Russia all the duties that it received from re-exporting Russian petroleum products. The conduct of the election, and the ensuing arrest and detention of opposition leaders and human rights activists had the effect of degrading Belarus's relations with many Western countries, and concomitantly strengthening its relations with Russia.

In March 2011 Belarus reached an agreement with Russia on the construction of the country's first nuclear power station, for which Russia would provide a US $9,400m. loan over 25 years. In June, amid an increasing economic crisis (see Economic Affairs), Russian electricity exporting company Inter RAO temporarily suspended electricity supplies to Belarus, as a result of unpaid debts. In November Putin announced that the Russian Government had granted a substantial discount in the price of natural gas supplied by Russia from the beginning of 2012, with the aim that Belarus would pay the price charged to neighbouring regions of Russia from 2014. In exchange, the Russian state-owned corporation Gazprom acquired the remaining 50% of Belarus's gas transport network Beltransgaz, thereby obtaining total control of the network. The agreement increased Western concerns about Russia's dominant influence in Belarus (in August 2011 Putin had, again, publicly suggested that Belarus become part of Russia).

In March 1996 Belarus, Kazakhstan, Kyrgyzstan and Russia signed the Quadripartite Treaty, which envisaged a common market and a customs union between the four countries, as well as joint transport, energy and communications systems (Tajikistan signed the Treaty in 1998). In April 2003 Armenia, Belarus, Kazakhstan, Kyrgyzstan, Russia and Tajikistan had formally inaugurated a new regional defence structure as the successor to the CIS Collective Security Treaty, the CSTO. Belarus was, together with Kazakhstan, Kyrgyzstan, Russia and Tajikistan, a founding member of the Eurasian Economic Community (EUR-

ASEC, see p. 449), the formal establishment of which took place in 2001; Armenia, Moldova and Ukraine were subsequently granted observer status, and Uzbekistan acceded to full membership in 2006. In October 2007 EURASEC leaders approved the legal basis for the establishment of a new customs union that was initially to comprise Belarus, Kazakhstan and Russia, with Kyrgyzstan, Tajikistan and Uzbekistan initially expected to join later. In November 2009 Belarus, Kazakhstan and Russia formalized their agreement on the customs union, which, following the unification of customs tariffs on 1 January 2010, entered into effect from 1 July. Meanwhile, in April Lukashenka announced that Belarus had granted asylum to the recently deposed President of Kyrgyzstan, Kurmanbek Bakiyev, and declined the request of the new Kyrgyzstani authorities for his extradition. In November 2011 Lukashenka, Medvedev and President Nursultan Nazarbaev of Kazakhstan signed an accord in Moscow that provided for the creation of a body to regulate their countries' closer economic integration, with the stated aim of establishing a 'Eurasian economic union' by 2015.

Although the parliamentary elections of October 2008 were judged to have failed to meet democratic standards, EU officials increasingly favoured dialogue with the Belarusian Government, a policy that was supported by principal opposition leaders Kazulin and Milinkevich. At a summit meeting on 13 October EU ministers of foreign affairs suspended for an initial period of six months the entry visa ban imposed against Lukashenka and a number of other senior officials, in recognition of improvements in the authorities' observance of human rights. (The suspension of the entry visa ban was subsequently extended until January 2011.) However, visa restrictions remained in place against a number of officials, notably the Chairman of the central electoral commission. The EU continued to insist that the Belarusian authorities release designated political prisoners, end restrictions on independent newspapers and media, and allow the freedom of assembly of political associations before it would normalize relations. In January 2009 EU officials expressed support for commitments made by the Government towards reform and in March confirmed the inclusion of Belarus in the EU's proposed Eastern Partnership programme, which envisaged enhanced free trade and visa arrangements with a number of countries (Armenia, Azerbaijan, Georgia, Moldova and Ukraine, in addition to Belarus). The EU Commissioner, responsible for External Relations and European Neighbourhood Policy visited Belarus in April, and in the same month invited Belarus to participate in a summit on the Eastern Partnership to be held in Prague, Czech Republic, in May. In late April President Lukashenka visited Italy and Vatican City, where he met Italian premier Silvio Berlusconi and Pope Benedict XVI. In late November Berlusconi undertook a reciprocal visit to Belarus, becoming the first senior leader of an EU state to visit the country for more than a decade. None the less, in November a meeting of EU foreign affairs ministers voted to maintain the sanctions against various members of the Government (while extending the suspension of certain of these sanctions). Following the presidential election of December 2010, and an escalation in human rights abuses in Belarus, relations with the EU deteriorated sharply, and in January 2011 the EU reinstated the sanctions that it had suspended in 2008, while the number of officials subject to restrictions, including an asset freeze and a prohibition on entering the EU, increased from around 40 to 158. In September Belarus refused to participate in an Eastern Partnership summit meeting in Warsaw, Poland, denouncing perceived discrimination against its Government, after the Polish EU Presidency invited the Belarusian Minister of Foreign Affairs, rather than Lukashenka, to attend. In January 2012 the EU noted a further worsening in the human rights situation in Belarus, and announced that it intended to expand its list of banned officials (then numbering 210). In response to the expansion of sanctions to cover a further 21 senior police and judicial officials, on 28 February the Belarusian authorities demanded the immediate expulsion from the country of the ambassadors of the EU and Poland. On the following day, all EU member states withdrew their ambassadors from Belarus, in protest at these expulsions. The Swedish ambassador returned to Minsk in late April, and the ambassadors of the other EU states were expected to return shortly afterwards.

Other external relations

In October 2004 the US Congress approved the Belarus Democracy Act of 2004, which authorized financial assistance to organizations campaigning for democracy within Belarus and also prohibited US government agencies from providing non-humanitarian aid to the Belarusian Government. In January 2005 the US Secretary of State, Condoleezza Rice, described Belarus as an 'outpost of tyranny', and in April she urged that the presidential election due to take place in March 2006 be free and fair. Following the election, relations with the USA deteriorated further, as the USA imposed visa bans and financial sanctions on prominent Belarusian officials (see Domestic Political Affairs). In December the US House of Representatives approved an extension to the Belarus Democracy Act until 2008. In the same month the Canadian Government imposed economic sanctions on Belarus. The USA subsequently implemented additional financial sanctions, freezing assets belonging to Belarus's largest petrochemical company, Belneftekhim. The US Administration announced that it intended to impose similar measures against other Belarusian enterprises unless the authorities released political prisoners. In February 2008 Lukashenka authorized the establishment of a European Commission office in Minsk. In March the USA extended sanctions to include all Belarusian petrochemical companies in which the state's share was 50% or more. Belarus responded by recalling its ambassador in the USA for consultations; the USA subsequently complied with Belarus's request that the US ambassador leave the country. In May Belarus expelled a further 10 US diplomats from the country. In September, in response to the release of Kazulin and other political prisoners, the US Administration announced the suspension of sanctions against two of the main subsidiaries of Belneftekhim, initially for a period of six months; the suspension was subsequently extended on a further three occasions. In common with the EU, in response to the mass arrests of opposition supporters after the December presidential election, in January 2011 the USA announced additional travel restrictions and the reimposition of sanctions against the two Belneftekhim subsidiaries (with a further four subject to sanctions from August). In January 2012 the US Administration, reaffirming its demands for fresh presidential and parliamentary elections conducted in accordance with OSCE standards and for the release of all political prisoners, extended its visa restrictions and financial sanctions to those involved in the post-election violence.

CONSTITUTION AND GOVERNMENT

Under the Constitution of March 1994, which was amended in November 1996, legislative power is vested in the bicameral Natsionalnoye Sobraniye (National Assembly). The lower chamber, the 110-member Palata Predstaviteley (House of Representatives), is elected by universal adult suffrage for a term of four years. The upper chamber, the Soviet Respubliki (Council of the Republic), comprises 64 members: 56 members elected by organs of local administration, and eight members appointed by the President. The President is the Head of State, and is elected by popular vote for five years. Executive authority is exercised by the Council of Ministers, which is led by the Chairman (Prime Minister) and is responsible to the Natsionalnoye Sobraniye. Judicial authority is exercised by the Supreme Court, the Supreme Economic Court and regional courts. For administrative purposes, Belarus is divided into six regions (oblasts) and the capital city of Minsk; the regions are divided into districts (rayons).

REGIONAL AND INTERNATIONAL CO-OPERATION

Belarus is a founder member of the Commonwealth of Independent States (CIS, see p. 246), the headquarters of which are located in the Belarusian capital city, Minsk. Belarus is also a member of the Eurasian Economic Community (EURASEC, see p. 449) and the Collective Security Treaty Organization (CSTO, see p. 462) and participates in the CIS Customs Union (comprising Belarus, Kazakhstan and Russia) established in January 2010.

Belarus was, as the Belarusian Soviet Socialist Republic, a founder member of the UN. Prior to the dissolution of the USSR in 1991, both Belarus and Ukraine had formally separate UN membership from that of the USSR, despite both republics forming integral parts of the Union. Belarus is a permanent member of the Non-aligned Movement (see p. 464).

ECONOMIC AFFAIRS

In 2010, according to estimates by the World Bank, Belarus's gross national income (GNI), measured at average 2008–10 prices, was US $58,169m., equivalent to $6,130 per head. In terms of purchasing-power parity, GNI in 2010 was equivalent to $14,250 per head. During 2001–10 the population declined at an average annual rate of 0.5%, while gross domestic product (GDP) per head increased at an average annual rate of 8.4%, in real terms. During 2001–10, overall GDP increased, in real terms, by an average of 7.8% annually. Real GDP increased by 0.2% in 2009 and by 7.6% in 2010.

Agriculture (including forestry) contributed 9.2% of GDP in 2010. In 2006 13.5% of the employed labour force were engaged in the sector, according to IMF figures. The principal crops are potatoes, grain and sugar beet. Large areas of arable land (some 1.6m. ha) remain unused after being contaminated in 1986, following the accident at the Chornobyl nuclear power station in Ukraine. The Belarusian authorities have largely opposed private farming, and by 1999 collective and state farms still accounted for some 83% of agricultural land. However, private farms produced the majority of Belarus's potatoes, fruit and vegetables, as well as a significant proportion of total livestock-product output. In 1998, according to the IMF, 49.8% of total crop output was produced by the private sector. During 2001–10, according to World Bank estimates, real agricultural GDP increased at an average annual rate of 4.6%. However, in 2010 agricultural output remained constant.

Industry (comprising mining, manufacturing, construction and power) provided 43.4% of GDP in 2010. The sector engaged 35.1% of the employed labour force in 2006, according to IMF figures. According to the World Bank, industrial GDP increased, in real terms, at an average annual rate of 10.4% during 2001–10. Real industrial GDP remained constant in 2010.

Belarus has relatively few mineral resources, although there are small deposits of petroleum and natural gas, and important peat reserves. Peat extraction, however, was severely affected by the disaster at Chornobyl, since contaminated peat could not be burned. Some 2.2m. metric tons of peat for fuel were mined in 2009, according to the US Geological Survey. Belarus produced 50% of the former USSR's output of potash; annual output of around 4.4m. metric tons was reported in 2004. Less than 0.5% of the labour force were engaged in mining and quarrying in 2001.

According to the World Bank, the manufacturing sector contributed an estimated 27.4% of GDP in 2010, and employed 26.5% of the labour force in 1994. Machine-building, power generation and chemicals are the principal branches of the sector. During 2001–10 manufacturing GDP increased, in real terms, at an average annual rate of 8.7%, according to World Bank estimates. Overall sectoral GDP remained constant in 2010.

The construction sector contributed 12.7% of GDP in 2010, and, according to IMF figures, engaged 7.6% of the employed labour force in 2006. During 2001–10, according to UN figures, the GDP of the sector increased at an average annual rate of 17.0%. Construction GDP increased by 16.9% in 2010.

In 2008 much of Belarus's supply of energy was provided by natural gas (96.9%), with petroleum and petroleum products accounting for almost all of the remainder. In 2005, according to IMF figures, the country imported 98.2% of its crude-oil consumption, 99.9% of its natural gas consumption and 28.1% of its electricity consumption. Energy products comprised 39.6% of the total value of imports in 2009. There are two large petroleum refineries, at Novopolotsk and Mozyr.

The services sector provided 47.4% of GDP in 2010 and, according to the IMF, accounted for 51.4% of total employment in 2006. The sector is led by transport and communications, and trade and catering, which accounted, respectively, for 10.9% and 12.8% of GDP in 2010. According to World Bank estimates, during 2001–10 the GDP of the services sector increased, in real terms, at an average annual rate of 8.2%. The rapid growth in the services sector in 2010 was in large part attributable to the effects of an enhancement in trade relations with Russia and Kazakhstan. Sectoral GDP increased by 8.1% in 2009 and by 32.2% in 2010.

In 2010 Belarus recorded a visible trade deficit of US $9,077.6m., and there was a deficit of $8,316.8m. on the current account of the balance of payments. Trading partners within the Commonwealth of Independent States (CIS, see p. 246) accounted for 58.4% of Belarus's imports and 53.1% of its exports in 2010. In 2010 Russia was Belarus's principal supplier of imports, providing 51.3% of the total. Germany and Ukraine were also major sources of imports. Russia was also Belarus's principal export partner, receiving 38.5% of total exports. Netherlands and Ukraine were also major recipients of exports. In 2010 the principal exports were mineral fuels and lubricants, machinery and transport equipment, basic manufactures, chemicals and related products, food and live animals, and miscellaneous manufactured articles. The principal imports were petroleum and gas, machinery and transport equipment, basic manufactures, chemicals and related products, and foodstuffs. According to IMF forecasts, in 2010 the consolidated republican and local government budgets, including the social protection fund, recorded a deficit of 2,900,000m. roubles. Belarus's general government gross debt was 43,244,920m. roubles in 2010, equivalent to 46.3% of GDP. Belarus's total external debt was US $17,158m. at the end of 2009. In 2009 public and publicly guaranteed debt stood at $4,758m. In that year, the cost of servicing long-term public and publicly guaranteed debt and repayments to the IMF was equivalent to 1.0% of the value of exports of goods, services and income (excluding workers' remittances). During 2001–10 consumer prices increased at an average rate of 16.2% per year. The annual average rate of inflation was 7.7% in 2010. In 2010 the rate of unemployment was 0.7%. However, the true rate of unemployment was believed to be far higher, as many people were unwilling to register, owing to the low level of official benefits.

Following the dissolution of the USSR, Belarus was slow to adopt liberalization measures, and the state continued to play a prominent economic role in 2012. Robust growth was recorded in 2004–08. The international financial crisis, as well as sharply reducing foreign investment, resulted in a widening of the current account deficit, which was equivalent to around 16% of GDP in 2010. In January 2009 the IMF approved a 15-month stand-by arrangement totalling US $2,460m. With the aim of diversifying energy suppliers, arrangements to import oil from Venezuela were agreed in early 2010. The establishment, in that year, of a Customs Union with Russia and Kazakhstan was expected to facilitate greater integration with the economies of those countries. In early 2011, amid a sharp deterioration in the country's financial situation, the Government sought emergency financing from the IMF and Russia. The IMF strongly criticized government policies, including large public-sector pay rises in the previous year and higher foreign-currency borrowing by the National Bank; the Fund demanded the implementation of substantial reforms before it would agree any new financial arrangement. In March the National Bank devalued the currency by 10% against the US dollar (a previous 20% devaluation having been undertaken in January 2009). In June 2011 Russian electricity exporting company Inter RAO suspended electricity supplies to Belarus as a result of unpaid debts, while a series of popular protests were staged in response to the Government's sharp increase of fuel prices. Also in June Belarus was granted a loan of US $3,000m. over a period of three years from the crisis fund of the Eurasian Economic Community (EURASEC, see p. 449), and an initial tranche of $800m. was disbursed. In October the National Bank announced the decision to restore a single exchange rate (thereby again substantially devaluing the rouble). In November the Russian Government agreed to grant Belarus a substantial discount on the price of natural gas that it supplied Belarus, with effect from 2012. The IMF projected GDP growth at 5.5% in 2011, with an average rise in consumer prices of 38% forecast in that year; the current account deficit was forecast to fall slightly to 14.7% of GDP.

PUBLIC HOLIDAYS

2013: 1 January (New Year's Day), 7 January (Orthodox Christmas), 8 March (International Women's Day), 15 March (Constitution Day), 31 March (Catholic Easter), 1 May (Labour Day), 5 May (Orthodox Easter), 9 May (Victory Day), 14 May (Radunitsa, Remembrance Day), 3 July (Independence Day), 7 November (October Revolution Day), 25 December (Catholic Christmas).

Statistical Survey

Source: mainly National Statistical Committee of the Republic of Belarus, 220070 Minsk, pr. Partizanski 12; tel. (17) 249-42-78; fax (17) 249-22-04; e-mail minstat@mail.belpak.by; internet www.belstat.gov.by.

Area and Population

AREA, POPULATION AND DENSITY

Area (sq km)	207,595*
Population (census results)	
16 February 1999†	10,045,237
14–24 October 2009	
Males	4,420,039
Females	5,083,768
Total	9,503,807
Population (official estimates at 1 January)	
2010	9,499,972
2011	9,481,193
2012‡	9,465,400
Density (per sq km) at 1 January 2012	45.6

* 80,153 sq miles.

† Figure refers to the *de jure* population.

‡ Figure rounded to the nearest 100 persons.

POPULATION BY AGE AND SEX

(official estimates at 1 January 2011)

	Males	Females	Total
0–14	726,383	686,786	1,413,169
15–64	3,266,949	3,494,205	6,761,154
65 and over	414,827	892,043	1,306,870
Total	4,408,159	5,073,034	9,481,193

POPULATION BY ETHNIC GROUP

(2009 census, % of total population)

Belarusian	84
Russian	8
Polish	3
Ukrainian	2
Others	3
Total	100

ADMINISTRATIVE DIVISIONS*

(official population estimates at 1 January 2012)

Oblasts (Regions)	
Brest (Bieraścіe)	1,391,500
Gomel (Homiel)	1,429,800
Grodno (Horadnia)	1,061,300
Minsk (Miensk)	1,403,500
Mogilev (Mahiloŭ)	1,080,100
Vitebsk (Viciebsk)	1,214,100
Capital City	
Minsk (Miensk)	1,885,100
Total	9,465,400

* The Belarusian names are given in parentheses after the more widely used Russian names.

Note: Figures are rounded to the nearest 100 persons.

PRINCIPAL TOWNS

(estimated population at 1 January 2011)*

Minsk (Miensk, capital)	1,864,000	Borisov (Barysau)	146,000
Gomel (Homiel)	501,000	Orsha (Vorsha)	133,000
Vitebsk (Viciebsk)	362,000	Pinsk	132,000
Mogilev (Mahiloŭ)	361,000	Mozyr (Mazyr)	110,000
Grodno (Horadnia)	338,000	Novopolotsk	105,000
Brest (Bieraście)	316,000	Soligorsk	103,000
Bobruysk (Babrujsk)	216,000	Lida	98,000
Baranovichi (Baranavichy)	169,000	Molodechno	94,000

* The Belarusian names are given in parentheses after the more widely used Russian names, where they differ.

Note: Figures are rounded to the nearest 100 persons.

BIRTHS, MARRIAGES AND DEATHS

	Registered live births		Registered marriages		Registered deaths	
	Number	Rate (per 1,000)	Number	Rate (per 1,000)	Number	Rate (per 1,000)
2004	88,943	9.1	60,265	6.1	140,064	14.3
2005	90,508	9.3	73,333	7.5	141,857	14.5
2006	96,721	9.9	78,979	8.1	138,426	14.2
2007	103,626	10.7	90,444	9.3	132,993	13.7
2008	107,876	11.1	77,201	8.0	133,879	13.8
2009	109,263	11.5	78,800	8.3	135,097	14.2
2010	108,050	11.4	76,978	8.1	137,132	14.4
2011	109,364	11.5	86,785	9.2	135,099	14.3

Life expectancy (years at birth, WHO estimates): 70 (males 64; females 76) in 2009 (Source: WHO, *World Health Statistics*).

EMPLOYMENT

(monthly averages, '000 persons)*

	2004	2005	2006
Agriculture	473	458	444
Forestry	32	33	32
Industry†	976	974	969
Construction	237	261	267
Transport and communications	268	268	265
Trade and related services‡	251	260	263
Communal services	177	184	187
Health and social services	304	308	310
Education, culture and science	561	560	566
Banks and insurance	57	59	60
Administration	84	86	86
Other activities	74	74	71
Total employed	3,494	3,525	3,520
Unemployed	83	68	52
Total labour force	3,577	3,593	3,572

* Excluding small non-state enterprises.

† Comprising manufacturing (except printing and publishing), mining and quarrying, electricity, gas, logging, and fishing.

‡ Including material and technical supply and procurement.

Source: IMF, *Republic of Belarus: Statistical Appendix* (September 2007).

2007 ('000 persons): Total employed 4,518; Unemployed 44; Total labour force 4,562.

2008 ('000 persons): Total employed 4,611; Unemployed 37; Total labour force 4,648.

2009 ('000 persons): Total employed 4,644; Unemployed 40; Total labour force 4,684.

2010 ('000 persons): Total employed 4,666; Unemployed 33; Total labour force 4,699.

Health and Welfare

KEY INDICATORS

Total fertility rate (children per woman, 2009)	1.3
Under-5 mortality rate (per 1,000 live births, 2009)	12
HIV/AIDS (% of persons aged 15–49, 2009)	0.3
Physicians (per 1,000 head, 2006)	4.8
Hospital beds (per 1,000 head, 2006)	11.2
Health expenditure (2008): US $ per head (PPP)	688
Health expenditure (2008): % of GDP	5.6
Health expenditure (2008): public (% of total)	72.2
Access to sanitation (% of persons, 2008)	93
Total carbon dioxide emissions ('000 metric tons, 2007)	66,747.1
Carbon dioxide emissions per head (metric tons, 2007)	6.9
Human Development Index (2011): ranking	65
Human Development Index (2011): value	0.756

For sources and definitions, see explanatory note on p. vi.

Agriculture

PRINCIPAL CROPS

('000 metric tons)

	2008	2009	2010
Wheat	2,045.2	1,979.0	1,740.5
Barley	2,211.9	2,123.4	1,966.5
Maize	494.7	448.7	550.6
Rye	1,491.9	1,226.8	735.4
Oats	605.4	552.4	442.6
Buckwheat	18.0	19.4	18.4
Triticale (wheat-rye hybrid)	1,818.7	1,788.3	1,254.5
Potatoes	8,748.6	7,125.0	7,831.1
Sugar beet	4,030.4	3,973.0	3,770.0
Beans, dry	132.5	173.9	150.4
Peas, dry	38.8	48.8	36.0
Walnuts, with shell*	12.8	13.6	13.5
Sunflower seed†	22.0	23.0	22.0
Rapeseed	514.0	611.0	374.6
Linseed	19.5	10.0	10.4
Cabbages and other brassicas	589.4	593.2	580.9
Tomatoes	274.6	287.0	310.2
Cucumbers and gherkins	306.2	318.2	325.1
Onions, dry	212.4	191.7	183.2
Carrots and turnips	363.6	361.1	358.1
Apples	379.8	431.6	525.6
Pears	52.5	60.9	73.3
Plums and sloes	62.3	80.9	77.7
Sour (Morello) cherries	44.6	54.7	51.1
Flax fibre and tow	60.9	46.9	45.8

* FAO estimates.

† Unofficial figures.

Aggregate production ('000 metric tons, may include official, semi-official or estimated data): Total cereals 8,712.7 in 2008, 8,153.5 in 2009, 6,729.5 in 2010; Total roots and tubers 8,748.6 in 2008, 7,125.0 in 2009, 7,831.1 in 2010; Total pulses 300.4 in 2008, 356.9 in 2009, 264.8 in 2010; Total vegetables (incl. melons) 2,303.0 in 2008, 2,315.3 in 2009, 2,341.2 in 2010; Total fruits (excl. melons) 594.7 in 2008, 691.7 in 2009, 790.1 in 2010.

Source: FAO.

LIVESTOCK

('000 head at 1 January)

	2008	2009	2010
Horses	147	137	126
Cattle	4,007	4,131	4,151
Pigs	3,598	3,704	3,782
Sheep	53	53	53
Goats	72	73	75
Chickens*	27,500	29,200	32,000

* Unofficial figures.

Source: FAO.

LIVESTOCK PRODUCTS

('000 metric tons)

	2008	2009	2010
Cattle meat	268.9	307.9	308.9
Sheep meat	1.2	1.3	1.4
Pig meat	376.0	388.2	398.4
Chicken meat*	191.5	218.8	258.0
Cows' milk	6,195.3	6,547.0	6,597.9
Hen eggs*	183.7	190.3	196.0

* Unofficial figures.

Source: FAO.

Forestry

ROUNDWOOD REMOVALS

('000 cubic metres, excl. bark)

	2008*	2009	2010
Sawlogs, veneer logs and logs for sleepers	3,703	3,223	3,486
Pulpwood	1,861	1,353	2,067
Other industrial wood	1,847	2,142	2,521
Fuel wood	1,345	2,094†	2,292†
Total	8,756	8,812	10,364

* FAO estimates.

† Unofficial figure.

Source: FAO.

SAWNWOOD PRODUCTION

('000 cubic metres, incl. railway sleepers, FAO estimates)

	2008	2009	2010
Coniferous (softwood)	1,945	2,102	2,300
Broadleaved (hardwood)	514	277	271
Total	2,458	2,379	2,571

Source: FAO.

Fishing

(metric tons, live weight)

	2003	2004	2005*
Capture	6,925	890	900
Freshwater bream	393	164	160
Common carp	4,953	26	30
Crucian carp	497	188	190
Northern pike	336	125	130
Aquaculture	5,393	4,150	4,150
Common carp	3,386	3,207	3,207
Crucian carp	1,608	721	721
Total catch	12,318	5,040	5,050

* FAO estimates.

2006–09: Catch assumed to be unchanged from 2005 (FAO estimates).

Source: FAO.

Mining

('000 metric tons unless otherwise indicated)

	2007	2008	2009
Crude petroleum	1,760	1,740	1,720
Natural gas (million cu metres)	201	203	205
Peat: for fuel	2,502	2,361	2,213

Source: US Geological Survey.

Industry

SELECTED PRODUCTS

('000 metric tons unless otherwise indicated)

	2006	2007	2008
Refined sugar	814	657	708
Wheat flour	576	649	665
Ethyl alcohol ('000 hectolitres)	741	860	956
Spirits, liqueurs and other spirituous beverages ('000 hectolitres)	1,082	1,275	1,466
Beer ('000 hectolitres)	3,322	3,556	3,544
Mineral water ('000 hectolitres)	1,935	2,014	1,916
Soft drinks ('000 hectolitres)	3,381	3,638	3,543
Cigarettes (million)	15,650	18,699	19,499
Bed linen, articles ('000)	7,003	8,082	8,514
Blouses, women's and girls' ('000)	1,359	1,474	1,526
Skirts, slacks and shorts for women and girls ('000)	3,505	3,135	3,142

—continued	2006	2007	2008
Shirts, men's and boys' ('000)	2,470	2,736	2,772
Blankets ('000)	248	357	328
Carpets, tufted ('000 sq metres)	5,069	5,035	5,127
Footwear (excluding rubber, '000 pairs)	10,864	11,184	n.a.
Plywood ('000 cu metres)	159	169	161
Paper and paperboard*	285.0	285.0	285.0
Nitrogenous fertilizers (a)*†	711.5	749.5	728.0
Phosphate fertilizers (b)*†	148.8	152.4	173.4
Potash fertilizers (c)*†	4,565.1	5,097.4	5,066.1
Soap	7.0	6.0	6.0
Rubber tyres: for agricultural and other off-road vehicles ('000)	341	466	522
Rubber tyres: for road motor vehicles ('000)	2,482	3,406	3,484
Rubber footwear ('000 pairs)	6,605	6,695	5,715
Quicklime	853	925	900
Cement	3,495	3,821	4,219
Domestic refrigerators ('000)	1,050	1,072	1,106
Radio receivers ('000)	8	5	9
Motorcycles ('000)	10	11	6
Bicycles ('000)	458	374	250
Watches ('000)	785	448	429
Electric energy (million kWh)	31,811	31,829	35,048

* Source: FAO.

† Production in terms of (a) nitrogen (N); (b) phosphorous pentoxide (P_2O_5); or (c) potassium oxide (K_2O).

Source (unless otherwise indicated): UN Industrial Commodity Statistics Database.

2008 (figures are rounded): Sausages ('000 metric tons) 307; Footwear ('000 pairs) 11,000; Particle board ('000 cu metres) 443; Paper ('000 metric tons) 56; Tyres for automobiles and agricultural machinery 5,068,000; Cement ('000 metric tons) 4,219; Tractors 65,100 units; Refrigerators and freezers 1,106,000 units; Television receivers 717,000 units; Bicycles (excl. children's) 250,000; Electric energy (million kWh) 35,100.

2009 (figures are rounded): Sausages ('000 metric tons) 295; Footwear ('000 pairs) 11,000; Particle board ('000 cu metres) 308; Paper ('000 metric tons) 70; Tyres for automobiles and agricultural machinery 5,073,000; Cement ('000 metric tons) 4,350; Tractors 45,300 units; Refrigerators and freezers 1,007,000 units; Television receivers 352,000 units; Bicycles (excl. children's) 130,000; Electric energy (million kWh) 30,400.

2010 (figures are rounded): Sausages ('000 metric tons) 317; Footwear ('000 pairs) 13,100; Particle board ('000 cu metres) 300; Paper ('000 metric tons) 103; Tyres for automobiles and agricultural machinery 4,818,000; Cement ('000 metric tons) 4,531; Tractors 44,400 units; Refrigerators and freezers 1,106,000 units; Television receivers 446,000 units; Bicycles (excl. children's) 133,000; Electric energy (million kWh) 34,900.

2011 (figures are rounded): Sausages ('000 metric tons) 285; Footwear ('000 pairs) 13,700; Particle board ('000 cu metres) 239; Paper ('000 metric tons) 111; Tyres for automobiles and agricultural machinery 5,164,000; Cement ('000 metric tons) 4,625; Tractors 59,100 units; Refrigerators and freezers 1,197,000 units; Television receivers 404,000 units; Bicycles (excl. children's) 170,000; Electric energy (million kWh) 32,200.

Finance

CURRENCY AND EXCHANGE RATES

Monetary Units

100 kopeks = 1 readjusted Belarusian rouble (rubel).

Sterling, Dollar and Euro Equivalents (30 December 2011)

£1 sterling = 12,909.94 readjusted roubles;
US $1 = 8,350.00 readjusted roubles;
€1 = 10,804.07 readjusted roubles;
10,000 readjusted Belarusian roubles = £0.77 = $1.20 = €0.93.

Average Exchange Rate (readjusted Belarusian roubles per US $)

2009	2,793.05
2010	2,978.51
2011	4,974.63

Note: The Belarusian rouble was introduced in May 1992, initially as a coupon currency, to circulate alongside (and at par with) the Russian (formerly Soviet) rouble. The parity between Belarusian and Russian currencies was subsequently ended, and the Belarusian rouble was devalued. In August 1994 a new Belarusian rouble, equivalent to 10 old roubles, was introduced. On 1 January 1995 the Belarusian rouble became the sole national currency, while the circulation of Russian roubles ceased. On 1 January 2000 a readjusted Belarusian rouble, equivalent to 1,000 of the former units, was introduced.

GOVERNMENT FINANCE

(general government transactions, non-cash basis, '000 million roubles)

Summary of Balances

	2007	2008	2009
Revenue	49,343.7	67,495.4	64,924.1
Less Expense	42,125.9	55,423.0	58,722.9
Net operating balance	7,217.8	12,072.4	6,201.3
Less Net cash outflow from investments in non-financial assets	6,069.7	7,485.5	6,637.2
Net lending/borrowing	1,148.1	4,586.9	–435.9

Revenue

	2007	2008	2009
Taxes	34,235.6	48,881.6	41,304.7
Taxes on income, profits and capital gains	7,464.7	11,176.3	9,630.7
Taxes on goods and services	17,035.3	20,756.1	20,167.4
Social contributions	11,256.7	14,496.5	15,799.4
Other revenue	3,851.4	4,117.3	7,820.0
Total	49,343.7	67,495.4	64,924.1

Expense/Outlays

Expense by economic type	2007	2008	2009
Compensation of employees	10,029.8	11,627.6	12,443.6
Use of goods and services	9,526.1	11,935.2	10,710.9
Interest	386.8	742.1	1,069.3
Subsidies	7,441.8	11,765.6	12,166.8
Grants	125.0	137.8	179.4
Social benefits	12,553.9	15,466.7	17,861.3
Other expense	2,062.6	3,748.1	4,291.6
Total	42,125.9	55,423.0	58,722.9

Outlays by functions of government*	2007	2008	2009
General public services	3,266.7	4,033.2	4,779.8
Defence	1,213.0	1,432.7	1,369.0
Public order and safety	2,257.5	2,625.3	2,769.7
Economic affairs	11,690.2	17,354.7	15,802.6
Environmental protection	537.8	555.1	410.6
Housing and community amenities	3,371.2	5,058.6	5,039.8
Health	4,905.4	5,717.5	6,156.7
Recreation, culture and religion	1,852.3	2,560.7	2,657.7
Education	6,350.0	7,665.6	7,995.4
Social protection	13,060.1	16,218.6	18,663.1
Total	48,504.1	63,222.1	65,644.4

* Including net acquisition of non-financial assets.

Source: IMF, *Government Finance Statistics Yearbook*.

2010 (general government transactions, '000 million roubles, rounded figures, preliminary): *Revenue:* Personal income tax 5,400; Profit tax 5,600; Value-added tax 16,200; Excise taxes 4,400; Property tax 1,900; Customs duties 5,800; Other income 6,700; Revenue of budgetary funds 2,900; Total 48,800. *Expenditure (incl. changes in expenditure arrears):* Wages and salaries 11,500; Social protection fund contributions 3,100; Goods and services 10,000; Interest 1,100; Subsidies and transfers 13,700; Capital expenditures 13,600; Net lending 100; Total 53,000. Note: Expenditure figures exclude the accounts of the social protection fund (revenue 19,700; expenditure 18,400). (Source: IMF, *The Republic of Belarus: First Post-Program Monitoring Discussions*—September 2011).

2011 (general government transactions, '000 million roubles, rounded figures, projections): *Revenue:* Personal income tax 7,400; Profit tax 6,400; Value-added tax 22,800; Excise taxes 5,700; Property tax 2,300; Customs duties 12,200; Other income 7,300; Revenue of budgetary funds 2,400; Total 66,500. *Expenditure (incl. changes in expenditure arrears):* Wages and salaries 16,900; Social protection fund contributions 4,600; Goods and services 12,700; Interest 3,000; Subsidies and transfers 21,600; Capital expenditures 12,900; Net lending 400; Total 72,100. Note: Expenditure figures exclude the accounts of the social protection fund (revenue 26,600; expenditure 24,600). (Source: IMF, *The Republic of Belarus: First Post-Program Monitoring Discussions*—September 2011).

INTERNATIONAL RESERVES
(US $ million at 31 December)

	2008	2009	2010
IMF special drawing rights	0.97	578.40	567.73
Reserve position in IMF	0.03	0.03	0.03
Foreign exchange	2,685.99	4,252.95	2,863.27
Total	2,686.99	4,831.38	3,431.03

Source: IMF, *International Financial Statistics*.

MONEY SUPPLY
(million roubles at 31 December)

	2008	2009	2010
Currency outside depository corporations	3,836.24	3,647.23	4,493.90
Transferable deposits	10,284.32	11,238.36	14,220.91
Other deposits	15,923.55	21,527.05	28,822.14
Securities other than shares	916.99	1,694.44	2,723.22
Broad money	30,961.00	38,107.07	50,260.17

Source: IMF, *International Financial Statistics*.

COST OF LIVING
(Consumer Price Index; base: 2000 = 100)

	2006	2007	2008
Food (incl. beverages)	380.1	417.4	491.1
Fuel and light	1,810.1	1,999.3	2,825.4
Clothing (incl. footwear)	223.0	227.5	233.6
Rent	4,097.7	4,313.3	4,917.1
All items (incl. others)	411.2	445.9	512.0

2009: Food (incl. beverages) 559.8; All items (incl. others) 578.3.

2010: Food (incl. beverages) 595.7; All items (incl. others) 622.9.

Source: ILO.

NATIONAL ACCOUNTS
('000 million roubles at current prices)

Expenditure on the Gross Domestic Product

	2008	2009	2010
Final consumption expenditure	88,883.6	99,346.4	116,949.4
Households	66,244.4	74,997.4	89,242.4
Non-profit institutions serving households	1,191.3	1,164.3	1,413.5
Government	21,447.9	23,184.7	26,293.5
Gross capital formation	48,855.4	51,230.6	66,211.1
Gross fixed capital formation	43,225.2	49,345.6	63,085.2
Changes in inventories	5,630.2	1,885.0	3,125.9
Total domestic expenditure	137,739.0	150,577.0	183,160.5
Exports of goods and services	79,091.6	69,449.2	89,016.6
Less Imports of goods and services	89,116.6	84,912.6	111,351.1
Statistical discrepancy	2,076.8	2,328.6	2,137.6
GDP in market prices	129,790.8	137,442.2	162,963.6

Gross Domestic Product by Economic Activity

	2008	2009	2010
Agriculture and forestry	10,846.2	11,145.8	13,103.9
Industry*	36,398.5	35,122.5	43,622.2
Construction	12,052.7	14,095.6	17,997.6
Transport and communications	11,340.3	13,348.3	15,507.0
Trade and catering	13,937.7	14,608.8	18,163.4
Material supply and procurement	424.7	531.4	460.5
Housing and public utilities	3,900.2	4,685.6	5,048.0
Health care	4,087.4	4,303.1	5,121.4
Education, culture and science	6,519.8	7,166.2	8,320.0
Other	11,440.2	13,130.3	14,709.8
GDP at factor cost	110,947.7	118,137.6	142,053.8
Taxes, less subsidies, on products	18,843.1	19,304.6	20,909.8
GDP in market prices	129,790.8	137,442.2	162,963.6

* Principally mining, manufacturing, electricity, gas and water.

BALANCE OF PAYMENTS
(US $ million)

	2008	2009	2010
Exports of goods f.o.b.	32,804.7	21,360.7	25,405.1
Imports of goods f.o.b.	−39,041.5	−28,317.7	−34,482.7
Trade balance	−6,236.8	−6,957.0	−9,077.6
Exports of services	4,258.0	3,504.3	4,504.0
Imports of services	−2,629.5	−2,115.8	−2,884.5
Balance on goods and services	−4,608.3	−5,568.5	−7,458.1
Other income received	633.6	476.3	491.3
Other income paid	−1,184.2	−1,359.2	−1,654.1
Balance on goods, services and income	−5,158.9	−6,451.9	−8,620.9
Current transfers received	400.6	505.5	951.0
Current transfers paid	−229.8	−231.4	−646.9
Current balance	−4,988.1	−6,177.8	−8,316.8
Capital account (net)	137.0	159.8	144.9
Direct investment abroad	−30.6	−102.2	−50.4
Direct investment from abroad	2,180.6	1,884.4	1,402.8
Portfolio investment assets	4.8	16.5	−59.4
Portfolio investment liabilities	0.5	2.3	1,245.0
Other investment assets	−477.0	−507.7	−1,178.4
Other investment liabilities	2,347.6	3,965.7	4,780.6
Net errors and omissions	−300.4	300.3	593.9
Overall balance	−1,125.6	−458.7	−1,437.8

Source: IMF, *International Financial Statistics*.

External Trade

PRINCIPAL COMMODITIES
(distribution by SITC, US $ million)

Imports c.i.f.	2008	2009	2010
Food and live animals	1,644.7	1,776.0	2,241.9
Crude materials (inedible) except fuels	1,519.6	836.8	1,271.6
Mineral fuels, lubricants, etc.	15,775.6	11,293.3	12,033.2
Petroleum, petroleum products and related materials	11,241.2	8,396.0	7,670.6
Gas, natural and manufactured	4,151.7	2,676.3	4,188.0
Chemicals and related products	3,873.6	2,789.3	3,608.4
Basic manufactures	5,696.3	3,699.2	5,270.8
Textile yarn, fabrics, etc.	567.2	421.3	525.8
Iron and steel	2,333.6	1,279.3	2,110.0
Machinery and transport equipment	6,615.7	5,590.2	6,753.7
Machinery specialized for particular industries	1,048.9	986.8	1,225.3
General industrial machinery and equipment	1,580.5	1,299.5	1,588.6
Electric machinery, apparatus and appliances, etc.	1,018.3	850.4	1,200.5
Road vehicles	1,085.0	994.2	756.8
Miscellaneous manufactured articles	1,490.8	1,150.2	1,411.8
Total (incl. others)	37,499.6	28,563.6	34,868.2

Exports f.o.b.	2008	2009	2010
Food and live animals	3,334.4	2,128.3	3,074.1
Crude materials (inedible) except fuels	651.7	463.3	633.3
Mineral fuels, lubricants, etc.	13,255.3	7,970.9	7,098.2
Petroleum, petroleum products, etc.	12,910.7	7,829.1	6,847.7
Refined petroleum products	11,606.0	7,005.1	6,751.7
Chemicals and related products	6,147.0	2,949.9	3,730.9
Fertilizers, manufactured	3,421.3	1,570.7	2,445.8
Potassium chloride	2,881.8	1,357.9	2,225.6
Basic manufactures	4,536.0	2,869.7	3,782.0
Textile yarn, fabrics, etc.	617.3	454.0	614.5
Iron and steel	1,362.9	823.3	1,102.7
Other metal manufactures	798.0	538.9	689.2
Machinery and transport equipment	5,932.5	3,086.6	4,331.0
Machinery specialized for particular industries	1,567.8	929.3	1,125.0
Electrical machinery, apparatus and appliances, etc.	1,015.0	707.9	909.0
Road vehicles	2,282.5	844.5	1,487.3
Lorries and special purpose motor vehicles	1,285.1	446.1	7,256857.8
Miscellaneous manufactured articles	1,772.8	1,279.0	1,585.7
Clothing and accessories (excl. footwear)	464.3	338.8	443.4
Total (incl. others)	36,250.8	21,282.2	25,225.9

Source: UN, *International Trade Statistics Yearbook*.

PRINCIPAL TRADING PARTNERS
(US $ million)

Imports c.i.f.	2008	2009	2010
Brazil	86.5	118.4	157.1
China, People's Republic	2,099.5	1,081.4	1,639.9
Czech Republic	259.2	238.2	316.2
France	409.3	392.9	371.9
Germany	2,394.6	2,215.8	2,383.8
Italy	678.5	708.4	769.0
Japan	226.5	205.5	181.8
Lithuania	253.7	194.8	247.2
Netherlands	345.4	232.1	317.7
Poland	1,094.4	786.9	1,075.8
Russia	21,650.2	16,717.1	17,878.9
Sweden	105.7	150.7	175.2
Ukraine	1,871.6	1,289.4	1,873.2
United Kingdom	380.3	256.4	312.0
USA	376.5	431.6	402.0
Total (incl. others)	37,499.6	28,563.6	34,868.2

Exports f.o.b.	2008	2009	2010
Brazil	1,215.8	449.8	705.5
China, People's Republic	775.9	173.9	469.4
Estonia	1,144.2	119.6	150.1
France	62.9	67.5	57.6
Germany	1,607.7	986.9	440.0
India	155.9	487.8	327.4
Italy	513.1	187.0	189.9
Kazakhstan	790.2	313.4	462.7
Latvia	2,583.9	1,658.5	930.6
Lithuania	735.9	370.8	450.8
Netherlands	4,109.6	3,680.3	2,773.1
Poland	1,092.0	823.4	885.5
Russia	11,797.9	6,713.9	9,702.4
Sweden	79.2	72.7	73.6
Ukraine	5,085.2	1,693.1	2,560.0
United Kingdom	360.3	799.4	984.0
USA	110.4	41.3	72.7
Total (incl. others)	36,250.8	21,282.2	25,225.9

Source: UN, *International Trade Statistics Yearbook*.

Transport

RAILWAYS
(traffic)

	2008	2009	2010
Passengers carried ('000)	88,000	83,500	83,600
Passenger-km (million)	8,188	7,401	7,578
Freight carried ('000 tons)	147,200	134,000	139,900
Freight ton-km (million)	48,994	42,742	46,224

ROAD TRAFFIC
(motor vehicles in use at 31 December)

	2005	2006	2007
Passenger cars	1,775,167	1,970,022	2,329,243
Buses and coaches	7,784	7,769	31,476
Motorcycles and mopeds	444,540	427,892	377,715

Source: IRF, *World Road Statistics*.

CIVIL AVIATION
(traffic on scheduled services)

	2008	2009	2010
Passenger carried ('000)	800	800	1,000
Passenger-km (million)	1,280	1,284	1,571
Total ton-km (million)	56	50	44

Tourism

FOREIGN TOURIST ARRIVALS

Country of nationality	2007	2008	2009
Estonia	4,288	1,166	690
Germany	7,826	3,027	2,568
Israel	4,333	491	956
Italy	4,183	2,672	2,531
Latvia	3,855	1,425	1,550
Lithuania	9,309	2,600	2,979
Poland	3,337	2,832	3,729
Russia	36,492	50,444	56,547
Turkey	4,064	6,087	4,680
United Kingdom	4,413	7,674	4,962
USA	5,268	1,168	864
Total (incl. others)	104,890	91,232	94,719

Tourism receipts (US $ million, incl. passenger transport): 479 in 2007; 582 in 2008; 562 in 2009.

Source: World Tourism Organization.

Communications Media

	2008	2009	2010
Telephones ('000 main lines in use)	3,718.1	3,983.2	4,138.6
Mobile cellular telephones ('000 subscribers)	8,128.0	9,686.2	10,332.9
Internet subscribers ('000)	1,597.9	1,630.5	2,044.1
Broadband subscribers ('000)	477.8	1,092.3	1,665.9
Book production (incl. pamphlets):			
titles	13,210	12,885	11,040
copies ('000)	55,400	52,800	43,100
Newspapers (daily and non-daily):			
number	689	700	713
average circulation ('000)	10,000	8,700	8,100
Other periodicals:			
number	777	884	885
annual circulation ('000)	41,500	54,000	59,100

Radio receivers ('000 in use): 3,020 in 1997.

Television receivers ('000 in use): 3,500 in 2000.

Personal computers: 79,016 (8.1 per 1,000 persons) in 2005.

Daily newspapers (number of titles): 15 in 2002, 21 in 2003, 13 in 2004; Total average circulation ('000): 1,401 in 2002, 814 in 2003, 800 in 2004.

Non-daily newspapers (number of titles): 654 in 2002, 690 in 2003, 709 in 2004; Total average circulation ('000): 9,852 in 2002, 10,592 in 2003, 10,120 in 2004.

Sources: partly International Telecommunication Union; UNESCO, *Statistical Yearbook*.

Education

(2011/12 unless otherwise indicated)

	Institutions	Teachers	Students
Pre-primary	4,099*	52,524†	384,000*
Primary (Grades 1–4) / Secondary (Grades 5–11)	3,707	133,100*	938,100
Vocational and technical	219*	14,772†	106,000*
Specialized secondary	220	12,748†	162,900
Higher	55	21,684†	445,600
Institutions offering post-graduate studies†	377	9,000	570,000

* 2010/11.

† 2001/02.

Source: partly Ministry of Education, Minsk.

Pupil-teacher ratio (primary education, UNESCO estimate): 15.0 in 2009/10 (Source: UNESCO Institute for Statistics).

Adult literacy rate (UNESCO estimates): 99.7% (males 99.8%; females 99.7%) in 2009 (Source: UNESCO Institute for Statistics).

Directory

The Government

HEAD OF STATE

President: ALYAKSANDR R. LUKASHENKA (elected 10 July 1994; inaugurated 20 July; re-elected 9 September 2001; re-elected 19 March 2006; re-elected 19 December 2010).

COUNCIL OF MINISTERS
(May 2012)

Prime Minister: MIKHAIL U. MYASNIKOVICH.

First Deputy Prime Minister: ULADZIMIR I. SEMASHKA.

Deputy Prime Minister: MIKHAIL I. RUSY.

Deputy Prime Minister: ANATOL M. KALININ.

Deputy Prime Minister: SYARHEY M. RUMAS.

Deputy Prime Minister: ANATOL A. TOZIK.

Minister of Agriculture and Food: LEONID A. MARINICH (acting).

Minister of Architecture and Construction: ANATOL I. NICHKASAU.

Minister of Communications and Information Technologies: MIKALAY P. PANTSYALEY.

Minister of Culture: PAVEL P. LATUSHKA.

Minister of Defence: YURI V. ZHADOBIN.

Minister of the Economy: MIKALAY H. SNAPKOU.

Minister of Education: SYARHEY A. MASKEVICH.

Minister of Emergency Situations: ULADZIMIR A. VASHCHANKA.

Minister of Energy: ALYAKSANDR U. AZYARETS.

Minister of Finance: ANDREY M. KHARKAVETS.

Minister of Foreign Affairs: SYARHEY M. MARTYNAU.

Minister of Forestry: MIKHAIL M. AMELYANOVICH.

Minister of Health: VASIL I. ZHARKO.

Minister of Housing and Municipal Services: ANDREY V. SHORATS.

Minister of Industry: DZMITRY S. KATSYARYNICH.

Minister of Information: ALEH V. PRALYASKOUSKI.

Minister of Internal Affairs: ANATOLY N. KULYASHOU.

Minister of Justice: ALEH L. SLIZHEUSKI.

Minister of Labour and Social Protection: MARYANA A. SHCHOTKINA.

Minister of Natural Resources and Environmental Protection: ULADZIMIR H. TSALKO.

Minister of Sports and Tourism: ALEH L. KACHAN.

Minister of Taxes and Duties: ULADZIMIR M. PALUYAN.

Minister of Trade: VALYANTSIN S. CHAKANAU.

Minister of Transport and Communications: IVAN I. SHCHERBO.

MINISTRIES

Office of the President: 220016 Minsk, vul. K. Marksa 38, Dom Urada; tel. (17) 222-35-03; fax (17) 222-30-20; e-mail press@president.gov.by; internet president.gov.by.

Office of the Council of Ministers: 220010 Minsk, vul. Savetskaya 11; tel. (17) 222-69-05; fax (17) 222-66-65; e-mail contact@government.by; internet government.by.

Ministry of Agriculture and Food: 220050 Minsk, vul. Kirava 15; tel. (17) 227-37-51; fax (17) 227-42-96; e-mail kanc@mshp.minsk.by; internet mshp.minsk.by.

Ministry of Architecture and Construction: 220048 Minsk, vul. Myasnikova 39; tel. (17) 227-26-42; fax (17) 220-74-24; e-mail mas@mas.by; internet mas.by.

Ministry of Communications and Information Technologies: 220050 Minsk, pr. Nezavisimosti 10; tel. (17) 227-38-61; fax (17) 227-21-57; e-mail mpt@mpt.gov.by; internet mpt.gov.by.

Ministry of Culture: 220004 Minsk, pr. Pobeditelei 11; tel. (17) 203-75-74; fax (17) 223-90-45; e-mail ministerstvo@kultura.by; internet kultura.by.

Ministry of Defence: 220034 Minsk, vul. Kamunistychnaya 1; tel. (17) 297-12-12; fax (17) 297-15-36; e-mail mod@mod.mil.by; internet mod.mil.by.

Ministry of the Economy: 220050 Minsk, vul. Bersona 14; tel. (17) 222-60-48; fax (17) 200-37-77; e-mail minec@economy.gov.by; internet www.economy.gov.by.

Ministry of Education: 220010 Minsk, vul. Savetskaya 9; tel. (17) 227-47-36; fax (17) 200-84-83; e-mail root@minedu.unibel.by; internet minedu.unibel.by.

Ministry of Emergency Situations: 220050 Minsk, vul. Revolutsionnaya 5; tel. (17) 203-94-28; fax (17) 203-77-81; e-mail mcs@infonet.by; internet rescue01.gov.by.

Ministry of Energy: 220030 Minsk, vul. K. Marksa 14; tel. (17) 218-21-02; fax (17) 218-24-68; e-mail info@min.energo.net.by; internet minenergo.gov.by.

Ministry of Finance: 220010 Minsk, vul. Savetskaya 7; tel. (17) 222-61-37; fax (17) 222-45-93; e-mail minfin@minfin.gov.by; internet minfin.gov.by.

Ministry of Foreign Affairs: 220030 Minsk, vul. Lenina 19; tel. (17) 327-29-22; fax (17) 327-45-21; e-mail mail@mfa.gov.by; internet mfa.gov.by.

Ministry of Forestry: 220048 Minsk, vul. Myastnikov 39; tel. (17) 200-46-01; fax (17) 200-44-97; e-mail mlh@mlh.by; internet www.mlh.by.

Ministry of Health: 220048 Minsk, vul. Myasnikova 39; tel. (17) 222-60-33; fax (17) 222-47-09; e-mail mzrb@belcmt.by; internet minzdrav.gov.by.

Ministry of Housing and Municipal Services: 220030 Minsk, vul. Bersona 16; tel. (17) 220-15-45; fax (17) 220-87-08; e-mail info@mjkx.gov.by; internet mjkx.gov.by.

Ministry of Industry: 220033 Minsk, pr. Partizansky 2; tel. (17) 224-95-95; fax (17) 224-87-84; e-mail minprom4@minprom.gov.by; internet minprom.gov.by.

Ministry of Information: 220004 Minsk, pr. Pobeditelei 11; tel. (17) 203-92-31; fax (17) 203-34-35; e-mail info@mininform.gov.by; internet mininform.gov.by.

Ministry of Internal Affairs: 220050 Minsk, vul. Gorodskoy Val 2; tel. (17) 218-79-89; fax (17) 218-70-35; e-mail miapress@mia.by; internet mvd.gov.by.

Ministry of Justice: 220004 Minsk, vul. Kalektarnaya 10; tel. (17) 200-86-87; fax (17) 200-97-55; e-mail kanc@minjust.by; internet minjust.by.

Ministry of Labour and Social Protection: 220004 Minsk, pr. Pobeditelei 23, kor. 2; tel. (17) 306-38-84; fax (17) 222-49-30; e-mail mail@mintrud.gov.by; internet mintrud.gov.by.

Ministry of Natural Resources and Environmental Protection: 220048 Minsk, vul. Kalektarnaya 10; tel. (17) 200-66-91; fax (17) 200-52-63; e-mail minproos@mail.belpak.by; internet www.minpriroda.gov.by.

Ministry of Sports and Tourism: 220000 Minsk, vul. Kirava 8, kor. 2; tel. (17) 227-72-37; fax (17) 227-76-22; e-mail foreign@mst.gov.by; internet mst.by.

Ministry of Taxes and Duties: 220010 Minsk, vul. Savetskaya 9; tel. (17) 229-79-11; fax (17) 222-64-50; e-mail gnk@mail.belpak.by; internet nalog.by.

Ministry of Trade: 220030 Minsk, vul. Kirava 8, kor. 1; tel. and fax (17) 227-24-80; e-mail mintorgrb@mail.belpak.by; internet mintorg.gov.by.

Ministry of Transport and Communications: 220029 Minsk, vul. Chicherina 21; tel. (17) 334-11-52; fax (17) 239-42-26; e-mail mail@mintrans.mtk.by; internet www.mintrans.by.

President

Presidential Election, 19 December 2010

Candidates	Votes	%
Alyaksandr Lukashenka	5,130,557	79.65
Andrey Sannikau	156,419	2.43
Yaraslau Ramanchuk	127,281	1.98
Ryhor Kastusyou	126,999	1.97
Uladzimer Nyaklyaeu	114,581	1.78
Viktar Tsyareshchanka	76,764	1.19
Vital Rymasheuski	70,515	1.09
Mikalay Statkevich	67,583	1.05
Ales Mikhalevich	65,748	0.78
Dzmitry Vus	25,117	0.39
Against all candidates	416,925	6.47
Total*	6,441,031	100.00

* Including 62,542 invalid votes (0.97% of the total).

Legislature

NATSIONALNOYE SOBRANIYE
(National Assembly)

Soviet Respubliki (Council of the Republic)
220016 Minsk, vul. Krasnoarmeiskaya 4; tel. (17) 227-46-74; fax (17) 227-23-18; e-mail cr@sovrep.gov.by; internet www.sovrep.gov.by.

Chairman: BARYS V. BATURA.

The Soviet Respubliki is the upper chamber of the legislature and comprises 64 deputies. Of the total, 56 deputies are elected by regional councils (eight each from the six oblasts and the city of Minsk) and eight deputies are appointed by the President of the Republic.

Palata Predstaviteley (House of Representatives)
220010 Minsk, vul. Savetskaya 11; tel. (17) 227-25-14; fax (17) 222-31-78; e-mail admin@gov.house.by; internet house.gov.by.

Chairman: ULADZIMIR P. ANDREYCHENKO.

General Election, 28 September 2008

Parties or groups	Seats
Independents	103
Communist Party of Belarus	6
Belarusian Agrarian Party	1
Total	110

Election Commission

Central Commission of the Republic of Belarus for Elections and Referendums: 220010 Minsk, vul. Savetskaya 11, Dom Pravitelstva; tel. and fax (17) 227-19-03; e-mail centrizb@pmrb.gov.by; internet www.rec.gov.by; f. 1989; Chair. LYDIA M. YERMOSHINA.

Political Organizations

In late 2008 there were 15 officially registered political parties operating in Belarus, of which the most important are listed below.

Belarusian Agrarian Party (BAP) (Belaruskaya Agrarnaya Partya): 220073 Minsk, vul. Zakharava 31; tel. (17) 220-38-29; fax (17) 249-50-18; f. 1992; Leader MIKHAIL V. SHYMANSKI.

Belarusian Fair World Party of the United Left (Belaruskaya partya ab'yadnanykh levykh 'Spravyadlivy svet'): 220012 Minsk, POB 373, per. Kalinina 12-312; tel. and fax (17) 292-25-73; e-mail ck_smir@tut.by; f. 1991; Chair. SYARHEY KALYAKIN.

Belarusian Party of Greens (Belaruskaya Partya Zyaleny): 220029 Minsk, pr. Masherova, 9/109; tel. 334-0827; e-mail info@belgreens.org; internet belgreens.org; f. 1994; Leader ALEH NOVIKAU.

Belarusian Social-Democratic Party (Hramada) (Belaruskaya Satsyal-demakratychnaya Partya 'Hramada'—BSDP): 220095 Minsk, pr. Rakowskaga 52/1, POB 241A; tel. and fax (17) 246-86-94; e-mail bsdpps@tut.by; internet www.bsdp.org; f. 2005; the Belarusian Social Democratic Party (National Hramada), f. 1991, and the Belarusian Social-Democratic Hramada (f. 1998) merged in April 2005, although a dissenting faction of the Belarusian Social-Democratic Hramada remained; Chair. IHAR MASLOUSKI (acting).

Communist Party of Belarus (CPB) (Kamunistychnaya Partya Belarusi): 220029 Minsk, vul. Chicherina 412; tel. (17) 293-48-88; fax (17) 222-43-79; e-mail karpenko@house.gov.by; internet www.comparty.by; f. 1996 as revival of Soviet-era party; Chair. TATSYANA H. HOLUBEVA.

Conservative Christian Party of the 'Revival' Belarusian Popular Front (CCP-BPF) (Kanservatyuna-Khrystsiyanskaya Partiya—BNF—Belaruski Narodny Front 'Adradzhennye'): 220005 Minsk, pr. Masherova 8; tel. (17) 285-34-70; internet www.narodnaja-partyja.org; f. 1999; political and legal successor of the political movement, Belarusian Popular Front (f. 1988); Chair. ZYANON S. PAZNYAK; 3,500 mems.

For Freedom Movement (Rukh 'Za Svabodu'): 220005 Minsk; tel. and fax (17) 280-88-63; e-mail info@pyx.by; internet www.pyx.by; f. 2006; officially registered Dec. 2008; Chair. ALYAKSANDR U. MILINKEVICH.

Liberal Democratic Party of Belarus (Liberalna-Demakratychnaya Partya Belarusi): 223000 Minsk, vul. Chernyshevskogo 10A; tel. and fax (17) 385-62-13; e-mail minsk_ldpb@mail.ru; internet www.ldpb.net; f. 1994; advocates continued independence of Belarus, increased co-operation with other European countries and eventual membership of the European Union, and expansion of the private sector; Leader SYARHEY V. HAYDUKEVICH; approx. 40,000 mems (2010).

Revival—Belarusian National Front (Belaruski Narodny Front 'Adradzhennye'): 220005 Minsk, pr. Masherova 8; tel. and fax (17) 284-50-12; e-mail pbnf@pbnf.org; f. 1988; fmrly the Belarusian National Front, name changed as above Dec. 1999; anti-communist movement campaigning for democracy, genuine independence for Belarus, and national and cultural revival; Chair. AYLAKSEY YANUKEVICH.

United Civic Party (UCP) (Abyadnanaya Hramadzyanskaya Partya): 220123 Minsk, vul. Khoruzhey 22/1701; tel. and fax (17)

289-50-09; e-mail info@ucpb.org; internet www.ucpb.org; f. 1995; liberal-conservative; Chair. ANATOL U. LYABEDZKA.

Diplomatic Representation

EMBASSIES IN BELARUS

Armenia: 220050 Minsk, vul. Kirava 17; tel. and fax (17) 227-51-53; e-mail armbelarusembassy@mfa.am; Ambassador ARMEN KHACHATRIAN.

Azerbaijan: 220113 Minsk, vul. Vostochnaya 133/167; tel. (17) 293-33-99; fax (17) 293-34-99; e-mail minsk@mission.mfa.gov.az; internet www.azembassy.by; Ambassador ISFANDIYAR VAHABZADÄ.

Brazil: 220030 Minsk, vul. Engelsa 34A; Chargé d'affaires a.i. JOSE EDUARDO GIRAUDO.

Bulgaria: 220034 Minsk, pl. Svoboda 11; tel. (17) 328-65-58; fax (17) 328-65-59; e-mail embassy.minsk@mfa.bg; internet www.mfa.bg/bg/17/; Chargé d'affaires IVAILO IVANOV.

China, People's Republic: 220071 Minsk, vul. Brestyanskaya 22; tel. (17) 285-36-82; fax (17) 285-36-81; e-mail chinaemb_by@mfa.gov.cn; internet by.china-embassy.org; Ambassador GONG JIANWEI.

Cuba: 220005 Minsk, vul. Krasnozvezdnaya 13; tel. (17) 200-03-83; fax (17) 200-23-45; e-mail embacuba@bn.by; internet www.cubadiplomatica.cu/belarus; Ambassador ALFREDO NIEVES PORTUONDO.

Czech Republic: 220030 Minsk, Muzychny zav. 1/2; tel. (17) 226-52-44; fax (17) 211-01-37; e-mail minsk@embassy.mzv.cz; internet www.mzv.cz/minsk; Ambassador JIŘÍ KARAS.

Estonia: 220034 Minsk, Platonova 1B; tel. (17) 217-70-60; fax (17) 217-70-69; e-mail embassy.minsk@mfa.ee; internet www.estemb.by; Ambassador JAAK LENSMENT.

France: 220030 Minsk, pl. Svabody 11; tel. (17) 229-18-00; e-mail webmestreby@diplomatie.fr; internet www.ambafrance-by.org; Ambassador MICHEL RAINERI.

Georgia: 220030 Minsk, pl. Svabody 4; tel. (17) 227-61-93; fax (17) 227-62-19; e-mail minsk.emb@mfa.gov.ge; internet www.belarus.mfa.gov.ge; Ambassador GIORGI CHKHEIDZE.

Germany: 220034 Minsk, vul. Zakharava 26; tel. (17) 217-59-00; fax (17) 294-85-52; e-mail info@minsk.diplo.de; internet www.minsk.diplo.de; Ambassador Dr CHRISTOF WEIL.

Holy See: 220050 Minsk, vul. Valadarskaga 6; tel. (17) 289-15-84; fax (17) 289-15-17; e-mail nuntius@catholic.by; internet nunciature.catholic.by; Apostolic Nuncio CLAUDIO GUGEROTTI (Titular Archbishop of Rebellum).

Hungary: 222034 Minsk, vul. Platonova 1 B; tel. (17) 233-91-68; fax (17) 233-91-69; e-mail mission.msk@kum.hu; internet www.mfa.gov.hu/emb/minsk; Ambassador FERENC KONTRA.

India: 220040 Minsk, vul. Sobinova 63; tel. (17) 262-93-99; fax (17) 288-47-99; e-mail amb@indemb.bn.by; internet www.indembminsk.org; Ambassador MANOJ KUMAR BHARTI.

Iran: 220012 Minsk, vul. Kalinina 7B; tel. (17) 385-60-00; fax (17) 237-79-53; e-mail info@iranembassy.by; Ambassador SEYED ABDULLAH HOSSEINI.

Israel: 220033 Minsk, pr. Partizansky 6A; tel. (17) 211-44-31; fax (17) 298-44-03; e-mail ambass-sec@minsk.mfa.gov.il; Ambassador YOSEF SHAGAL.

Italy: 220004 Minsk, vul. Rakovskaya 16B; tel. (17) 220-29-69; fax (17) 306-20-37; e-mail ambasciata.minsk@esteri.it; internet www.ambminsk.esteri.it; Ambassador ARNALDO ABETI.

Japan: 220004 Minsk, pr. Pobeditelei 23/1, 8th Floor; tel. (17) 223-62-33; fax (17) 210-21-69; Chargé d'affaires a.i. NAOTAKE YAMASHITA.

Kazakhstan: 220029 Minsk, vul. Kuibysheva 12; tel. (17) 288-10-26; fax (17) 334-96-50; e-mail kazemb@nsys.by; internet www.kazembassy.by; Ambassador YERGALI B. BULEGENOV.

Korea, Republic: 220035 Minsk, pr. Pobeditelei 59, 5th Floor; tel. (17) 306-01-47; fax (17) 306-01-60; e-mail belemb@mofat.go.kr; internet blr.mofat.go.kr; Ambassador KANG WEON-SIK.

Kyrgyzstan: 220002 Minsk, vul. Starovilenskaya 57; tel. (17) 334-91-17; fax (17) 334-16-02; e-mail manas@nsys.by; internet kgembassy.by; Ambassador ERIK A. ASANALIEV.

Latvia: 220013 Minsk, vul. Doroshevicha 6A; tel. (17) 211-30-33; fax (17) 284-74-94; e-mail embassy.belarus@mfa.gov.lv; internet www.am.gov.lv/belarus; Ambassador MIHAILS POPKOVS.

Libya: 220000 Minsk, vul. Belaruskaya 4; tel. (17) 328-39-92; fax (17) 328-39-97; Ambassador ABDALLAH AL-MAGRAVI.

Lithuania: 220088 Minsk, vul. Zakharava 68; tel. (17) 217-64-91; fax (17) 285-33-37; e-mail amb.by@urm.lt; internet by.mfa.lt; Ambassador EDMINAS BAGDONAS.

Moldova: 220030 Minsk, vul. Belaruskaya 2; tel. (17) 289-14-41; fax (17) 289-11-47; e-mail minsk@mfa.md; internet www.belarus.mfa.md; Ambassador GHEORGHE HIOARĂ.

Poland: 220034 Minsk, vul. Rumyantsava 6; tel. (17) 288-21-14; fax (17) 233-97-50; e-mail ambasada@minsk.polemb.net; internet www.minsk.polemb.net; Ambassador LESZEK SZEREPKA.

Romania: 220012 Minsk, Kaliningradskii per. 12; tel. (17) 292-73-99; fax (17) 292-73-83; e-mail romania@mail.belpak.by; Chargé d'affaires a.i. CONSTANTIN EREMIA.

Russia: 220053 Minsk, vul. Novovilenskaya 1A; tel. (17) 233-35-90; fax (17) 233-35-97; e-mail rusemb-minsk@yandex.ru; internet www.belarus.mid.ru; Ambassador ALEKSANDR A. SURIKOV.

Serbia: 220034 Minsk, vul. Rumyantseva 4; tel. (17) 284-29-84; fax (17) 233-92-26; e-mail embassy.minsk@mfa.rs; internet www.ambasadasrbije.info; Ambassador Dr STOJAN JEVTIĆ.

Slovakia: 220034 Minsk, vul. Volodarskogo 6; tel. (17) 285-29-99; fax (17) 283-68-48; e-mail emb.minsk@mzv.sk; internet www.mzv.sk/minsk; Ambassador MARIÁN SERVÁTKA.

Sweden: 222030 Minsk, vul. Revalyutsyynaya 15; tel. (17) 226-55-40; fax (17) 226-55-43; e-mail ambassaden.minsk@foreign.ministry.se; internet www.swedenabroad.com/minsk; Ambassador STEFAN ERIKSSON.

Syria: 220049 Minsk, vul. Suvorova 2; tel. (17) 280-37-08; fax (17) 280-72-00; e-mail syrembmin@yahoo.com; Ambassador Dr FAROUK TAHA.

Tajikistan: 223033 Minsk, vul. Zelenaya 42; tel. and fax (17) 549-01-83; e-mail tajemb-belarus@mail.ru; internet www.tajembassy.by; Ambassador KOZIDAVLAT KOIMDODOV.

Turkey: 220050 Minsk, vul. Valadarskaya 6; tel. (17) 227-13-83; fax (17) 227-27-46; e-mail trembassy@mail.bn.by; internet minsk.emb.mfa.gov.tr; Ambassador CEVAT NEZIHI ÖZKAYA.

Turkmenistan: 220050 Minsk, vul. Kirava 17; tel. (17) 335-24-51; Ambassador ATA GUNDOGDIYEV.

Ukraine: 220002 Minsk, vul. Staravilenskaya 51; tel. (17) 283-19-89; fax (17) 283-19-80; e-mail emb_by@mfa.gov.ua; internet www.belarus.mfa.gov.ua; Ambassador VIKTOR TIKHONOV.

United Arab Emirates: 220018 Minsk, vul. Privabnaya 6/8; tel. (17) 313-26-01; fax (17) 313-26-04; internet uaeembassy.by; Ambassador (vacant).

United Kingdom: 220030 Minsk, vul. K. Marksa 37; tel. (17) 229-82-00; fax (17) 220-23-06; e-mail britinfo@nsys.by; internet ukinbelarus.fco.gov.uk; Ambassador ROSEMARY THOMAS.

USA: 220002 Minsk, vul. Starovilenskaya 46; tel. (17) 210-12-83; fax (17) 234-78-53; e-mail webmaster@usembassy.minsk.by; internet minsk.usembassy.gov; Chargé d'affaires a.i. MICHAEL SCANLAN.

Venezuela: 220029 Minsk, vul. Kuibysheva 14; tel. (17) 284-50-99; fax (17) 284-93-47; e-mail info@embavenez.by; internet www.embavenez.by; Ambassador AMÉRICO DÍAZ NUÑEZ.

Viet Nam: 222040 Minsk, vul. Mozhaiskogo 3; tel. and fax (17) 293-15-38; e-mail dsqvn.belarus@mofa.gov.vn; internet www.vietnamembassy-belarus.org; Ambassador DANG HUY TRAN.

Judicial System

Supreme Court: 220030 Minsk, vul. Lenina 28; tel. (17) 226-12-06; fax (17) 227-12-25; e-mail scjustrb@pmrb.gov.by; internet www.supcourt.by; f. 1923; Chair. VALENTIN O. SUKALO.

Supreme Economic Court: 220050 Minsk, vul. Valadarskaya 8; tel. (17) 220-23-27; fax (17) 227-76-01; e-mail bxc@court.by; internet www.court.by; Chair. VIKTAR S. KAMYANKOV.

Office of the Prosecutor-General: 220088 Minsk, vul. Zaharova 76; tel. and fax (17) 294-38-08; e-mail npc@prokuratura.gov.by; internet www.prokuratura.gov.by; Prosecutor-General ALYAKSANDR U. KONYUK.

Constitutional Court: 220016 Minsk, vul. K. Marksa 32; tel. (17) 227-80-12; e-mail ksrb@kc.gov.by; internet www.kc.gov.by; f. 1994; 12 mem. judges; Chair. PYOTR MIKLASHEVICH.

Religion

CHRISTIANITY

The major grouping is the Eastern Orthodox Church, but there are also an estimated 1.4m. adherents of the Roman Catholic Church. Of these, some 25% are ethnic Poles, while there are a significant number of Catholics of the Eastern (Byzantine) Rites.

The Eastern Orthodox Church

In 1990 Belarus was designated an exarchate of the Russian Orthodox Church (Moscow Patriarchate), known as the Belarusian Orthodox Church.

Belarusian Orthodox Church (Moscow Patriarchate): 220004 Minsk, vul. Osvobozhdeniya 10; tel. (17) 203-46-01; e-mail press-service@church.by; internet www.church.by; 1,277 parishes (2006); Metropolitan of Minsk and Slutsk, Patriarchal Exarch of All Belarus FILARET (VAKHROMEYEV).

The Roman Catholic Church

Belarus comprises one archdiocese and three dioceses. In 1989 an apostolic administration to Belarus was established, and in April 1991 an archbishop was appointed to the recently formed Archdiocese of Minsk-Mogilev (Mahiloŭ). At 31 December 2007 the Catholic Church had an estimated 1,402,605 adherents in Belarus (about 18.8% of the population).

Archdiocese of Minsk and Mogilev: 220030 Minsk, ul. Revolutsionna 1A; tel. (17) 203-68-44; fax (17) 226-90-92; e-mail archdioces@catholic.by; internet catholic.by; Archbishop Mgr TADEUSZ KONDRUSIEWICZ.

Protestant Church

Union of Evangelical Christian Baptists in the Republic of Belarus: 220107 Minsk, POB 25; tel. and fax (17) 295-67-84; e-mail office@baptist.by; internet www.baptist.by; f. 1989; Pres. NIKOLAY SINKOVETS.

The Press

PRINCIPAL DAILIES

In Russian, except where otherwise stated. The Russian-based newspapers *Argumenty i Fakty* and *Komosomolskaya Pravda* (in a special edition, *Komsomolskaya Pravda v Belorusii*) also maintain a high rate of circulation in the country.

BDG Delovaya Gazeta (BDG Business Newspaper): 220039 Minsk, vul. Chekalova 12; tel. (17) 216 25 83; fax (17) 216-25-85; e-mail bdginfo@gmail.com; internet www.bdg.by; f. 1992; 2 a week; business affairs; suspended for three months in May 2003; subsequently printed in Smolensk, Russia; independent; present name adopted 2005; Editor-in-Chief (vacant).

Belaruskaya Niva (Belarusian Cornfield): 220013 Minsk, vul. B. Hmyalnitskaga 10A; tel. (17) 287-16-20; fax (17) 232-39-62; e-mail info@belniva.by; internet belniva.by; f. 1921; 5 a week; organ of the Council of Ministers; in Belarusian and Russian; Editor E. SEMASHKO; circ. 34,021 (Aug. 2004).

Narodnaya Hazeta (The People's Newspaper): 220013 Minsk, vul. B. Hmyalnitskaga 10A; tel. and fax (17) 287-18-70; e-mail veche@ng.by; internet www.ng.by; f. 1990; 5 a week; official publication; in Belarusian and Russian; Editor-in-Chief VLADIMIR V. ANDREYVICH.

Narodnaya Volya (People's Will): 220030 Minsk, vul. Engelsa 34A; tel. and fax (17) 328-68-71; e-mail nv@promedia.by; internet www.nv-online.info; f. 1995; daily; independent; 5 a week; in Belarusian and Russian; Editor-in-Chief IOSIF R. SYAREDZICH; circ. 27,000.

Respublika (Republic): 220013 Minsk, vul. B. Hmyalnitskaga 10A; tel. (17) 287-16-15; fax (17) 287-16-12; e-mail info@respublika.info; internet www.respublika.info; 5 a week; publ. of Council of Ministers; in Belarusian and Russian; Editor ANATOLII I. LEMIASHENOK; circ. 101,000 (2005).

Sovetskaya Belorussiya (Soviet Belarus): 220013 Minsk, vul. B. Hmyalnitskaga 10A; tel. and fax (17) 292-51-01; e-mail admin@sb.by; internet www.sb.by; 5 a week; Editor-in-Chief PAVEL I. YAKUBOVICH; circ. 400,000 (2004).

Znamya Yunosti (Banner of Youth): 220013 Minsk, vul. B. Hmyalnitskaga 10A; tel. and fax (17) 292-02-63; e-mail zn@zn.by; internet www.zn.by; f. 1938; 5 a week; organ of the Ministry of Education; Editor-in-Chief EUGENE K. MELESHKO; circ. 32,000 (2007).

Zvyazda (Star): 220013 Minsk, vul. B. Hmyalnitskaga 10A; tel. and fax (17) 287-19-19; e-mail info@zvyazda.minsk.by; internet www.zviazda.by; f. 1917; 5 a week; publ. by the National Assembly and the Council of Ministers; in Belarusian; Editor-in-Chief ALEKSANDR M. KARLYUKEVICH; circ. 30,000 (2012).

PRINCIPAL PERIODICALS

In Belarusian, except where otherwise stated.

7 Dnei (7 Days): 222030 Minsk, vul. Engelsa 30; tel. (17) 227-86-22; internet 7days.belta.by; f. 1990; weekly; in Russian; domestic and international affairs, culture, general; Chief Editor VIKTOR V. CHIKIN; circ. 40,000 (2011).

Agropanorama: 220013 Minsk, vul. B. Hmyalnitskaga 10A; 6 a year; in Belarusian and Russian; agriculture and agricultural technology.

Alesya (Rabotnitsa i Sialianka) (Alesya—Working Woman and Peasant Woman): 220013 Minsk, pr. Nezavisimosti 77; tel. and fax (17) 292-43-03; e-mail magalesya@mail.ru; f. 1924; monthly; Editor TAMARA BUNTO; circ. 6,500.

Belaruska Dumka (Belarusian Thought): 222030 Minsk, vul. Engelsa 30; tel. (17) 227-55-33; fax (17) 289-19-55; e-mail beldumka@belta.by; internet www.beldumka.belta.by; f. 1991; monthly; publ. of the Presidential Administration; socio-political and popular science; Chief Editor VADZIM HIHIN.

Detekivnaya Gazeta (Detective Magazine): 220014 Minsk, vul. M. Lynkova 15B/2; tel. (17) 250-36-05; monthly; crime stories; Chief Editor VLADIMIR KHACHIRASHVILI.

Holas Radzimy (Voice of the Motherland): 220005 Minsk, pr. Nezavisimosti 44; tel. and fax (17) 288-12-80; e-mail mail@golas.by; internet www.golas.by; f. 1955; weekly; articles of interest to Belarusians in other countries; Editor-in-Chief VIKTAR KHARKOŬ.

Kultura (Culture): 220013 Minsk, pr. Nezavisimosti 77; tel. (17) 290-22-50; fax (17) 334-57-41; e-mail kultura@tut.by; internet www.kimpress.by; f. 1991; weekly; colour illustrated; incorporates *Mastatstva* (Arts); Editor-in-Chief LUDMILA KRUSHINSKAYA; circ. 9,000 (2012).

Litaratura i Mastatstva (Literature and Arts): 220034 Minsk, vul. Zakharava 19; tel. (17) 284-79-85; fax (17) 284-66-73; e-mail main_lim@mail.ru; internet www.main.lim.by; f. 1932; weekly; Editor ALES KARLYUKEVICH; circ. 3,428 (2007).

Maladosts (Youth): 220005 Minsk, pr. Nezalezhnastsi 39; tel. (17) 284-85-24; e-mail maladost@bk.ru; f. 1953; monthly; publ. by the state media holding, Litaratura i Mastatstva; novels, short stories, essays, translations, etc., for young people; Editor-in-Chief RAISA A. BARAVIKOVA.

Narodnaya Asveta (People's Education): 220023 Minsk, vul. Makayenka 12; tel. (17) 267-64-69; fax (17) 267-62-68; e-mail info@n-asveta.com; internet www.n-asveta.na.by; f. 1924; publ. by the Ministry of Education; Editor-in-Chief ALLA V. MASLAVA.

Nasha Niva (Our Field): 220050 Minsk, POB 537; tel. (17) 284-73-29; e-mail nn@nn.by; internet www.nn.by; f. 1991 as revival of publication originally founded in 1906; independent; weekly; Editor-in-Chief ANDREY SKURKO; circ. 10,500 (2009).

Tsarkovnae Slova (Words of the Church): 222004 Minsk, vul. Rakovskaya 4; tel. (017) 203-33-44; e-mail tsar.sl@open.by; internet www.sppsobor.by; f. 1992; publ. of the Belarusian Orthodox Church (Moscow Patriarchate); in Russian and Belarusian; Chief Editor ANDREI KHARITONOV; circ. 9,000 (2010).

PRESS ASSOCIATIONS

Belarusian Association of Journalists (Belaruskaya Asatsyyatsyya Zhurnalistau): 220030 Minsk, pl. Svabody 17/304; tel. (17) 203-63-66; fax (17) 226-70-98; e-mail baj@baj.by; internet www.baj.by; f. 1995; Chair. ZHANNA LITVINA.

Belarusian Union of Journalists: 220034 Minsk, vul. Rumyantsava 3; tel. and fax (17) 294-51-95; internet www.buj.by; 3,000 mems; Chair. ANATOLY LEMESHENOK.

NEWS AGENCIES

BelaPAN: 222012 Minsk, vul. Akademecheskaya 17/3; tel. (17) 292-55-01; fax (17) 292-56-57; e-mail redactor@belapan.com; internet www.belapan.com; f. 1991; in Belarusian, English and Russian; independent, commercial information company; Dir ALES LIPAY.

Belta—Belarusian Telegraph Agency: 220030 Minsk, vul. Kirava 26; tel. (17) 227-19-92; fax (17) 227-13-46; e-mail oper@belta.by; internet www.belta.by; f. 1918; Gen. Dir DMITRIY A. ZHUK.

Interfaks Zapad (Interfax-West): 222013 Minsk, vul. Brovki 3/2; tel. (17) 284-05-71; fax (17) 284-05-76; e-mail info@interfax.by; internet www.interfax.by; f. 1994; affiliated with Interfaks (Russia); regional bureau in Mogilev; online political and business news; publs *Belarus Business Daily*, *Belarus News Wire*; Dir-Gen. VYACHESLAV ZENKOVICH.

Publishers

Aversev: 220090 Minsk, vul. Oleshva 1; tel. (17) 268-09-79; e-mail info@aversev.by; internet www.aversev.by; f. 1994; teaching and methodical literature.

Belaruskaya Navuka (Belarusian Science): 220141 Minsk, Staroborisovsky trakt 40; tel. and fax (17) 263-76-18; e-mail belnauka@infonet.by; internet www.belnauka.by; f. 1924; scientific, technical, reference books, educational literature and fiction in Belarusian and Russian; Dir ALYAKSANDR STASHKEVICH.

Belarusky Dom Druku (Belarusian Printing House): 220013 Minsk, pr. Nezavisimosti 79; tel. (17) 292-81-28; fax (17) 331-91-15; e-mail lan@domdruku.by; internet www.domdruku.by; f. 1917; social, political, children's and fiction in Belarusian, Russian and other European languages, newspapers and magazines; Gen. Dir ROMAN OLEINIK.

Belblankavyd: 220038 Minsk, vul. Botanicheska 6A; tel. (17) 375-29-49; fax (17) 294-91-16; reference books in Belarusian and Russian; Dir VALENTINA MILOVANOVA.

Litaratura i Mastatstva (Literary Fiction and Fine Arts): 220034 Minsk, vul. Zakharava 19; tel. (17) 288-12-94; fax (17) 284-84-61; e-mail main_lim@main.ru; internet www.lim.by; f. 2002; fiction in Belarusian and Russian; Dir ALES M. KARLYUKEVICH.

Mastatskaya Litaratura (Fine Arts Literature): 220004 Minsk, pr. Pobeditelei 11; tel. (17) 203-83-63; fax (17) 203-58-09; e-mail director@mastlit.by; internet www.mastlit.by; f. 1972; state-owned; Dir VLADISLAV A. MACHULSKY.

Narodnaya Asveta (People's Education): 220004 Minsk, pr. Pobeditelei 11; tel. (17) 203-61-84; fax (17) 203-89-25; e-mail director@narasveta.by; internet www.narasveta.by; f. 1951; scientific, educational, reference literature and fiction in Belarusian, Russian and other European languages; Dir LARISA MINKO.

Petrus Brovka Belarusian Encyclopedia Publishing House (Belaruskaya Entsiklopediya): 220072 Minsk, vul. Akademicheska 15A; tel. and fax (17) 284-17-67; e-mail belen@mail.belpak.by; f. 1967; encyclopedias, dictionaries, directories and scientific books; Editor-in-Chief T. V. BELOVA.

Vysheyshaya Shkola (Higher School): 220048 Minsk, pr. Pobeditelei 11; tel. (17) 223-54-15; fax (17) 203-70-08; e-mail info@vshph.by; internet www.vshph.com; f. 1954; textbooks and science books for higher educational institutions; in Belarusian, Russian and other European languages; absorbed the Universitetskaye publishing house in 2002; Dir ANATOL A. ZHADAN; Editor-in-Chief TETYANA K. MAIBORODA.

Broadcasting and Communications

TELECOMMUNICATIONS

Belarus is behind its neighbours in upgrading telecommunications infrastructure. The state-owned company, Beltelecom, dominates the provision of fixed-line telephones, while the mobile communications market consists of four major service providers. In 2010 there were 4.1m. fixed telephone lines and 10.3m. subscriptions to mobile telephone services in Belarus.

BelCel: 22005 Minsk, vul. Zolotaya Gorka 5; tel. (17) 282-02-82; fax (17) 476-11-11; e-mail belcel@belcel.by; internet www.belcel.by; f. 1993; jtly owned by SIV BV (Netherlands) and Beltelecom; mobile telecommunications services; Gen. Dir ANDREY A. SOBOROV.

Beltelecom: 220030 Minsk, vul. Engelsa 6; tel. (17) 217-10-05; fax (17) 227-44-22; e-mail info@main.beltelecom.by; internet www.beltelecom.by; f. 1995; national telecommunications operator; Dir-Gen. SYARHEY POPKOV.

Best: 220030 Minsk, vul. Chervonoarmeiska 24; tel. (17) 295-99-99; fax (17) 328-58-86; e-mail info@life.com.by; internet www.life.com.by; f. 2008; mem. of Turkcell Group (Turkey); provides mobile cellular telecommunications services; Dir-Gen. ISMET YAZICI.

MTS Belarus: 222043 Minsk, pr. Nezavisimosti 95; tel. (17) 237-98-98; e-mail info@mts.by; internet company.mts.by; f. 2002; mobile cellular communications; 49% owned by Mobile TeleSystems (Russia); Dir-Gen. VLADIMIR S. KARPOVICH.

Velcom: 220002 Minsk, vul. Masherova 19; tel. (17) 222-49-01; fax (17) 206-62-52; e-mail pr@velcom.by; internet www.velcom.by; f. 1999; mobile cellular telecommunications; 4.5m. subscribers (2011); Gen. Dir MIKHAIL A. BATRANETS.

BROADCASTING

National State Television and Radio Company of Belarus (Belteleradiocompany): 220807 Minsk, vul. A. Makayenka 9; tel. (17) 267-75-95; fax (17) 267-81-82; e-mail pr@tvr.by; internet www.tvr.by; f. 1925; parent co of Belarusian Radio (q.v.) and Belarusian Television (q.v.); Chair. GENNADY B. DAVIDKO.

Radio

Belarusian Radio: 220807 Minsk, vul. Chyrvonaya 4; tel. (17) 284-84-24; fax (17) 290-62-42; e-mail radio1@tvr.by; internet www.tvr.by; f. 1925; stations include Culture Channel, First National Channel (news), Radio Stalitsa (Capital Radio) and Radio Belarus (foreign service in Belarusian, Russian, German and English); Dir ANTON B. VASYUKEVICH.

Television

Belarusian Television: 220807 Minsk, vul. A. Makayenka 9; tel. (17) 269-97-72; fax (17) 263-21-78; e-mail pr@tvr.by; internet www.tvr.by; f. 1956; Dir ULADZIMIR V. ISAT.

Belarus-TV: 220807 Minsk, vul. A. Makayenka 9; tel. (17) 389-61-46; fax (17) 267-84-32; e-mail belarus-tv@tvr.by; internet www.tvr.by; f. 2005; international satellite channel; Dir VALERII A. RADUTSKI.

First National Channel: 220807 Minsk, vul. A. Makayenka 9; tel. (17) 389-63-12; fax (17) 264-81-82; main state news channel; also shows entertainment, sport, films, etc.; Dir ANTON VASYUKEVICH.

LAD Telekanal: 220807 Minsk, vul. A. Makayenka 9; tel. (17) 389-63-12; fax (17) 267-81-82; e-mail lad@tvr.by; internet www.lad.tvr.by; f. 2003; family channel; Gen. Dir SYARHEY A. KUKHTO.

Belsat TV: 220013 Minsk, POB 383; tel. 22 547-69-07; e-mail info@belsat.eu; internet www.belsat.eu; f. 2007; also broadcasts to Warsaw, Poland; owned by Telewizja Polska (Poland); Dir AGNIESZKA ROMASZEWSKA-GUZY.

ONT—Obshchenatsionalnoye Televideniye (Nation-wide TV): 220029 Minsk, ul. Kommunisticheskaya 6; tel. (17) 290-66-72; e-mail reklama@ont.by; internet www.ont.by; f. 2002; 51% state-owned; broadcasts nation-wide; Chair. GRIGORIY L. KISEL.

TVS—Televizionnaya Veshchatelnaya Set (TBN—Television Broadcasting Network): 220072 Minsk, pr. Nezavisimosti 15A; tel. (17) 284-09-13; fax (17) 284-10-86; e-mail tbn@promedia.by; f. 1995; comprises 16 private television cos in Belarus's largest cities and an advertising co.

Finance

(cap. = capital; res = reserves; dep. = deposits; m. = million; brs = branches; amounts in readjusted Belarusian roubles, unless otherwise indicated)

BANKING

In August 2010 there were 30 commercial banks registered in Belarus.

Central Bank

National Bank of the Republic of Belarus: 220008 Minsk, pr. Nezavisimosti 20; tel. (17) 328-59-13; fax (17) 227-48-79; e-mail email@nbrb.by; internet www.nbrb.by; f. 1990; cap. 250,000.0m., res 198,547.4m., dep. 20,353,567.3m. (Dec. 2009); Chair. NADEZHDA A. ERMAKOVA.

Commercial Banks

Alfa-Bank: 220030 Minsk, vul. Savetskaya 12; tel. (17) 200-68-80; fax (17) 200-17-00; e-mail office@alfa-bank.by; internet www.alfa-bank.by; f. 1999; 93.8% owned by ABH Belarus Ltd (Cyprus); fmrly ITI Bank—International Trade and Investment Bank; present name adopted 2008; cap. 76,205m., res –7m., dep. 424,528m. (Dec. 2009); Chair. of Bd DENIS A. KALIMOV; 5 brs.

Bank Moskva-Minsk (Moscow-Minsk Bank): 220002 Minsk, vul. Kamunistychnaya 49; tel. (17) 288-63-01; fax (17) 288-63-02; e-mail mmb@mmbank.by; internet www.mmbank.by; f. 2000; wholly owned by Bank of Moscow (Russia); cap. US $22.9m., res –$13.3m., dep. $399.9m. (Dec. 2009); Gen. Dir Dr ALEKSANDR RAKOVETS; 5 brs.

Bank Torgovyi Kapital (Trade Capital Bank): 220035 Minsk, vul. Timirazeva 65A; tel. (17) 312-10-12; fax (17) 312-10-08; e-mail info@tcbank.by; internet www.tcbank.by; f. 2008; Chair. ANDREY B. VERETELNIKOV.

Belagroprombank: 220036 Minsk, pr. Zhukov 3; tel. (17) 218-57-77; fax (17) 218-57-14; e-mail info@belapb.by; internet www.belapb.by; f. 1991; 70% state-owned; cap. 4,438,544m., res –11,168m., dep. 14,518,269m. (Dec. 2009); Chair. VLADIMIR I. PODKOVIROV (acting); 90 brs.

Belarusbank: 220050 Minsk, vul. Myasnikova 32; tel. (17) 200-18-31; fax (17) 226-47-50; e-mail info@belarus-bank.by; internet www.belarus-bank.by; f. 1995 following merger with Sberbank (Savings Bank; f. 1922); cap. 1,980,923m., res –35,226m., dep. 29,684,290m. (Dec. 2009); Chair. NADEZHDA A. YERMAKOVA; 106 brs.

Belgazprombank: 220121 Minsk, vul. Pritytsky 60/2; tel. (17) 259-40-24; fax (17) 259-45-25; e-mail bank@bgpb.by; internet www.belgazprombank.by; f. 1990; present name adopted 1997; 49% owned by Gazprombank (Russia), 49% owned by OAO Gazprom (Russia); cap. 434,316m., res –75m., dep. 1,521,475m. (Dec. 2009); Chair. of Bd VIKTAR D. BABARIKO; 8 brs.

Belinvestbank—Belarusian Bank for Development and Reconstruction: 220002 Minsk, pr. Masherova 29; tel. (17) 289-

28-99; fax (17) 289-35-22; e-mail corr@belinvestbank.by; internet www.belinvestbank.by; f. 2001 by merger; 85.8% owned by the State Committee for Property; 6.5% owned by National Bank of the Republic of Belarus (q.v.); universal bank; cap. 447,182m., res 22,081m., dep. 4,341,793m. (Dec. 2009); Chair. of Bd ALYAKSANDR E. RUTKOVSKY; 11 brs.

Belvneshekonombank (Belarusian Bank for Foreign Economic Affairs): 220050 Minsk, vul. Myasnikova 32; tel. (17) 238-12-15; fax (17) 226-48-09; e-mail office@bveb.minsk.by; internet www.bveb.by; f. 1991; 97.4% owned by Vneshekonombank (Bank for Foreign Economic Affairs—Russia); cap. 807,806m., res 667m., dep. 1,184,235m. (Dec. 2009); Chair. of Bd PAVEL V. KALLAUR; 24 brs.

BPS-Sberbank: 220005 Minsk, Blvd Muliavin 6; tel. (17) 289-41-48; fax (17) 210-03-42; e-mail inbox@bpsb.by; internet www.bps-sberbank.by; f. 1923; fmrly Belpromstroibank; 97.9% owned by Sberbank—Russia; cap. 633,345m., res 186,488m., dep. 4,983,841m. (Dec. 2010); Dir-Gen. VASILII S. MATUSHEVSKII; 175 brs.

BTA Bank: 220123 Minsk, vul. V. Khoruzhey 20; tel. (17) 289-58-00; fax (17) 289-58-22; e-mail info@btabank.by; internet www.btabank.by; f. 2002 as Astanaekssimbank; present name adopted 2008; 99.7% owned by BTA Bank, Almatı (Kazakhstan); cap. 57,508m., dep. 145,606m., total assets 253,330m. (Dec. 2009); Chair. of Bd SULTAN T. MARENOV.

Minski Tranzitnyi Bank (Minsk Transit Bank): 220033 Minsk, pr. Partizansky 6A; tel. (17) 213-29-00; fax (17) 213-29-09; e-mail ycor@mtbank.by; internet www.mtbank.by; f. 1994; 98% owned by MTB Investments Holdings Ltd; cap. US $49.2m., res $5.9m., dep. $101.0m. (July 2010); Chair. of Bd ANDREY K. ZHISHKEVICH; 6 brs.

Onerbank (Honorbank): 220004 Minsk, vul. Tsetkin 51; tel. and fax (17) 306-25-91; f. 2009; Chair. TALEBI GELIN GESHALGI.

Paritetbank: 220090 Minsk, vul. Gamarnika 9/4; tel. (17) 288-32-50; fax (17) 228-38-37; e-mail info@paritetbank.by; internet www.paritetbank.by; f. 1992; present name adopted 2004; 98.7% owned by the National Bank of the Republic of Belarus (q.v.); cap. 166,860m., res 10,923m., dep. 219,993m. (Dec. 2009); Chair. of Bd SERGEI L. PANKOVETS.

Priorbank: 220002 Minsk, vul. V. Khoruzhey 31A; tel. (17) 289-90-90; fax (17) 289-91-91; e-mail info@priorbank.by; internet www.priorbank.by; f. 1989, present name since 1991; 87.7% owned by Raiffeisen International Bank-Holding AG (Austria); cap. 412,279m., res 5,488m., dep. 4,178,027m. (Dec. 2009); Chair. of Bd SERGEY A. KOSTYUCHENKO.

Trustbank: 220035 Minsk, vul. Ignatenka 11; tel. and fax (17) 250-43-88; e-mail cbis@trustbank.by; internet www.trustbank.by; f. 1994; jt-stock co; fmrly Infobank, present name adopted Feb. 2005; cap. 82,378m., dep. 241,729m., total assets 343,292m. (Dec. 2009); Chair. YURII M. KASHTANOV.

VTB Bank (Belarus): 220004 Minsk, vul. Tsetkin 51; tel. (17) 306-26-36; fax (17) 306-26-37; e-mail info@vtb-bank.by; internet www.vtb-bank.by; f. 1996 as Slavneftebank; name changed as above 2007; 71.4% owned by VTB Bank (Russia); cap. 107,802m., res 34,215m., dep. 1,350,345m. (Dec. 2009); Chair. of Bd ULADZIMIR V. IVANOV; 6 brs.

BANKING ASSOCIATION

Association of Belarusian Banks: 220005 Minsk, vul. Smolyachkova 9; tel. (17) 227-78-90; fax (17) 227-58-41; e-mail mail@abbanks.by; Chair. FELIX CHERNYAVSKY.

COMMODITY AND STOCK EXCHANGES

Belarusian Currency and Stock Exchange (Belorusskaya Valyutno-Fondovaya Birzha): 220013 Minsk, vul. Surganova 48 A; tel. (17) 209-41-03; fax (17) 209-41-10; e-mail bcse@bcse.by; internet www.bcse.by; f. 1998; currency and securities exchange trading organization, depository, clearing and information activities; value of trade US $8,934.5m. (2004); Gen. Dir PAVEL TSEKHANOVICH.

Belarusian Universal Commodity Exchange (BUTB): 220099 Minsk, vul. Kazintsa 2/200; tel. (17) 224-48-25; e-mail info@butb.by; internet www.butb.by; f. 2004; jt-stock co; trades in timber, metal and agricultural produce; Pres. ARKADII S. SALIKOV.

INSURANCE

B & B Insurance Co: 220013 Minsk, ul. Kolas 38; tel. (17) 285-76-22; internet www.bbinsurance.by; f. 1995; life and non-life.

Beleksimgarant: 220004 Minsk, 2 Melnicate st; tel. (17) 209-40-67; fax (17) 209-40-28; e-mail info@eximgarant.by; internet eximgarant.by; f. 2001; state-owned; Gen. Dir GENNADY MITSKEVICH.

Belgosstrakh Belarusian Republican Unitary Insurance Co: 220036 Minsk, vul. K. Libknekht 70; tel. (17) 269-26-00; fax (17) 213-08-05; e-mail bgs@info.by; internet www.belgosstrakh.by; f. 1921; state-owned; Dir-Gen. ANATOLIY SVERZH; 145 brs.

Belingosstrakh: 220050 Minsk, pr. Myasnikov 40; tel. (17) 203-58-78; fax (17) 217-84-19; e-mail office@belingo.by; internet belingo.by; f. 1992; non-life, property, vehicle and cargo insurance; Dir-Gen. ALYAKSANDR KHAMYAKOU.

Belkoopstrah: 220004 Minsk, pr. Pobeditelei 17; tel. (17) 226-80-64; e-mail office@belkoopstrah.by; internet www.belkoopstrah.by; f. 1992; life and non-life.

Belneftestrakh: 220004 Minsk, pr. Pobeditelei 23/1; tel. (17) 203-24-55; fax (17) 226-78-88; e-mail insurance@bns.by; internet www.bns.by; f. 1996; life and non-life; Dir Gen. YURIY NESMASHNY; 10 brs.

Belrosstrahe: 220034 Minsk, vul. Ulyanovsk 31; tel. (17) 222-47-48; fax (17) 210-46-33; e-mail info@belrosstrakh.by; internet www.belrosstrakh.by; f. 1991; Belarusian-German jt-stock co; renamed as above after merging with Brolly in March 2009; Dir-Gen. SERGEI KOVALEV.

Kupala: 220004 Minsk, vul. Nemiga 40; tel. (17) 200-80-71; fax (17) 200-80-13; e-mail office@kupala.by; internet www.kupala.by; f. 1993; affiliate of Wiener Städtische Allgemeine Versicherung AG (Austria); Dir-Gen. VIKTOR S. NOVIK.

Promtransinvest: 220039 Minsk, vul. Voronyanskogo 7A; tel. (17) 228-12-48; fax (17) 297-04-35; e-mail insurance@promtransinvest.by; internet promtransinvest.by; f. 1993; life and non-life.

TASK: 220005 Minsk, pr. Nezavisimosti 58/9; tel. (17) 225-11-24; fax (17) 296-68-35; e-mail info@task.by; internet www.task.by; f. 1991; partly state-owned; all forms of insurance; Gen. Dir I. I. VOLKOV.

INSURANCE ASSOCIATION

Belarusian Insurance Union (BIU) (Belaruskii Strakhovoi Soyuz): 220114 Minsk, pr. Nezavisimosti 169/905; tel. (29) 650-08-91; fax (17) 218-14-65; e-mail info@biu.by; internet www.biu.by; f. 1992; 56 mems; Pres. VIKTAR HOMYARCHUK.

Trade and Industry

GOVERNMENT AGENCIES

Belarusian Foreign Investment Promotion Agency (BFIPA): 220004 Minsk, pr. Pobeditelei 7; tel. (17) 226-81-02; fax (17) 203-07-78; e-mail ncm@export.by; internet www.export.by; Dir BORIS SMOLKIN.

Belarusian Fund for the Financial Support of Entrepreneurs (BFFSE): 220048 Minsk, vul. Myasnikova 39; e-mail fund@belpak.minsk.by; f. 1996.

CHAMBER OF COMMERCE

Belarusian Chamber of Commerce and Industry (Belorusskaya Torgovo-promyshlennaya Palata): 220029 Minsk, vul. Kammunisticheska 11; tel. (17) 290-72-49; fax (17) 290-72-48; e-mail mbox@cci.by; internet www.cci.by; f. 1952; brs in Brest, Gomel, Grodno, Mogilev and Vitebsk; Pres. MIKHAIL M. MYATLIKOV.

EMPLOYERS' ORGANIZATION

Business Union of Entrepreneurs and Employers (Biznes Soyuz Predprinimatelei i Nanimatelei): 220033 Minsk, vul. Fabrichnaya 22; tel. (17) 298-11-49; fax (17) 298-27-92; e-mail bspn-org@nsys.by; internet www2.bspn.nsys.by; f. 1990; Pres. GEORGY BADEY.

UTILITIES

Electricity

Belenergo/Belenerha (Belarusian Energy Co): 220030 Minsk, vul. K. Marksa 14; tel. (17) 218-23-59; fax (17) 218-26-39; e-mail info@min.energo.by; internet www.energo.by; f. 1995; generation, transmission and distribution of electric power; Dir-Gen. ALEKSEI R. SHIRMA.

Gas

Beltopgaz: 220002 Minsk, vul. V. Khoruzhey 3; tel. (17) 288-23-93; fax (17) 284-37-86; e-mail mail@topgas.by; internet www.topgas.by; f. 1992; distributes natural gas to end-users; Dir-Gen. LEONID I. RUDINSKII.

Beltransgaz: 220040 Minsk, vul. Nekrasov 9; tel. (17) 280-01-01; fax (17) 285-63-36; e-mail mail@btg.by; internet www.btg.by; 100% owned by Gazprom (Russia); natural gas transportation and supply; underground gas storage; Dir VLADIMIR MAYAROU.

TRADE UNIONS

Automobile and Agricultural Machinery Workers' Union: 220126 Minsk, pr. Pobeditelei 21/1103; tel. and fax (17) 203-84-27; e-mail acmbel7@mail.belpak.by; f. 1990; Leader VALERY KUZMICH.

Belarusian Congress of Democratic Trade Unions (BKDP): 220095 Minsk, vul. Yakubova 80/80, etazh 15/2; tel. (17) 214-89-05; fax (17) 214-89-06; e-mail bcdtu@mail.ru; internet www.bkdp.org;

f. 1993; alliance of four independent trade unions; Pres. ALYAKSANDR YARASHUK; International Sec. OLEG PODOLINSKI; 10,000 mems (2010).

Belarusian Peasants' Union (Syalansky Sayuz): 220199 Minsk, vul. Brestskaya 64/327; tel. (17) 277-99-93; Chair. KASTUS YARMOLENKA.

Federation of Trade Unions of Belarus (FPB): 220126 Minsk, pr. Pobeditelei 21; tel. (17) 203-90-31; fax (17) 210-43-37; e-mail press@fpb.by; internet www.fpb.by; f. 1990; Chair. LEANID P. KOZIK.

Transport

RAILWAYS

In 2010 the total length of railway lines in use was around 5,502 km, of which 898 km were electrified. There is an underground railway in Minsk.

Belarusian State Railways (Belorusskaya Zheleznaya Doroga): 220745 Minsk, vul. Lenina 17; tel. (17) 225-49-46; fax (17) 227-56-48; e-mail ns@rw.by; internet www.rw.by; f. 1992; Dir ANATOLIY A. SIVAK.

Minsk Metro: 220007 Minsk, pr. Kooperativny 12; tel. (17) 219-86-01; fax (17) 222-94-84; e-mail info@minsktrans.by; internet www.minsktrans.by; f. 1984; two lines (30.3 km) with 25 stations (2007); Gen. Dir LEONTIY T. PAPENOK.

ROADS

In 2005 the total length of roads in Belarus was 94,797 km (comprising 15,432 km of main roads and 70,265 km of secondary roads). Some 88.64% of the total network was hard-surfaced.

CIVIL AVIATION

Minsk has two airports.

State Committee for Aviation: 220007 Minsk, vul. Aerodromnaya 4; tel. (17) 222-53-93; fax (17) 222-77-28; e-mail gka@ivcavia.com; internet www.avia.by; Chair. VADZIM H. MELNIK.

Belavia Belarusian Airlines: 220004 Minsk, vul. Nemiga 14; tel. (17) 220-25-55; fax (17) 220-23-83; e-mail info@belavia.by; internet www.belavia.by; f. 1996; state carrier; operates services in Europe and to the CIS and the Middle East; Dir-Gen. ANATOLIY GUSAROV.

Tourism

Tourism is not developed, although the Government has sought to promote Belarus as a destination for those interested in hunting a variety of animals and birds, and for those who wish to visit sites associated with the Second World War. According to the World Tourism Organization, there were 94,719 tourist arrivals in 2009, when receipts from tourism (including passenger transport) amounted to US $562m.

Belintourist: 220004 Minsk, pr. Pobeditelei 19; tel. (17) 226-98-40; fax (17) 203-11-43; e-mail out@belintourist.by; internet www.belintourist.by; f. 1992; national tour operator; Dir MARIA I. FILIPOVICH.

Defence

As assessed at November 2010, the total strength of Belarus's armed forces was 72,940, comprising ground forces of 29,600 and an air force of 18,170, as well as 25,170 in centrally controlled units and Ministry of Defence staff. Reserves totalled 289,500. There are also paramilitary forces, controlled by the Ministry of Internal Affairs, which number 110,000, including a border guard of 12,000 and a militia of 87,000. Military service is compulsory and lasts for between nine and 12 months. The formation of a new territorial defence force, in which regional governors were to play a leading role, was announced in 2011. Belarus joined the North Atlantic Treaty Organization's 'Partnership for Peace' programme of military co-operation in January 1995.

Defence Expenditure: Budgeted at 2,100,000m. readjusted roubles in 2011.

Chief of the General Staff: Maj.-Gen. PYOTR TIKHONOVSKY.

Commander of the Army: Maj.-Gen. ALYAKANSDR NIKITIN.

Commander of the Air Force and Air Defence: DMITRIY PAHMELKIN.

Education

In 2001/02 27.7% of all pupils were taught in Belarusian, and 72.2% were taught in Russian (0.1% were taught in Polish). In 2006/07 the total enrolment at pre-primary level was equivalent to 90.2% of children in the relevant age-group. In that year enrolment at primary level included 90.7% of pupils in the relevant age-group. Education is compulsory for nine years, but usually lasts for 11 years, between the ages of six and 17 years. Secondary education comprises a first cycle of five years and a second of two years. In 2006/07 secondary enrolment included 86.9% of pupils in the relevant age-group. At early 2007 there were 43 state-owned and 12 private higher education institutions, including 29 universities. In 2010/11 some 442,900 students were enrolled in higher education. General government expenditure on education was 7,358,100m. roubles (equivalent to 11.6% of total spending) in 2008.

BELGIUM

Introductory Survey

LOCATION, CLIMATE, LANGUAGE, RELIGION, FLAG, CAPITAL

The Kingdom of Belgium lies in north-western Europe, bounded to the north by the Netherlands, to the east by Luxembourg and Germany, to the south by France, and to the west by the North Sea. The climate is temperate. Temperatures in the capital, Brussels, are generally between 0°C (32°F) and 23°C (73°F). Dutch (also known as Flemish), spoken in the north (Flanders), and French, spoken in the south (Wallonia), are the two main official languages. Brussels (which is situated in Flanders) has bilingual status. Nearly 60% of the population are Dutch-speaking and about 40% are French-speaking. There is a small German-speaking community, comprising less than 1% of the population, in eastern Wallonia. The majority of the inhabitants profess Christianity, and about three-quarters of the population are Roman Catholics. The national flag (proportions 13 by 15) consists of three equal vertical stripes, of black, yellow and red.

CONTEMPORARY POLITICAL HISTORY

Historical Context

In the latter half of the 20th century Belgium's linguistic divisions were exacerbated by the political and economic polarization of Dutch-speaking Flanders in the north and francophone Wallonia in the south. The faster-growing and relatively prosperous population of Flanders traditionally supported the conservative Flemish Christelijke Volkspartij (CVP—Christian People's Party) and the nationalist Volksunie—Vlaamse Vrije Democraten (VU, People's Union—Flemish Free Democrats), while Wallonia was a stronghold of socialist political sympathies. Moderate constitutional reforms, introduced in 1971, were followed by further concessions to regional and cultural sensitivities: in 1972 the German-speaking Community gained representation in the Council of Ministers for the first time, and in 1973 linguistic parity was assured in central government. Provisional legislation, adopted in 1974, established separate Regional Councils and Ministerial Committees. The administrative status of Brussels remained contentious: the majority of the city's inhabitants are francophone, but the Flemish parties were, until the late 1980s, unwilling to grant the capital equal status with the other two regional bodies.

Domestic Political Affairs

In June 1977 the Prime Minister, Leo Tindemans (who had held office since 1974), formed a coalition composed of the CVP and the francophone Parti Social Chrétien (PSC—Christian Social Party), which were collectively known as the Christian Democrats, together with the Flemish and French-speaking Socialist parties, the Front Démocratique des Francophones (FDF—Francophone Democratic Front) and the VU. The Council of Ministers, in what became known as the Egmont Pact, proposed the abolition of the virtually defunct nine-province administration, and devolution of power from the central Government to create a federal Belgium, comprising three political and economic regions (Flanders, Wallonia and Brussels) and two linguistic communities. However, these proposals were not implemented. Tindemans resigned in October 1978 and the Minister of Defence, Paul Vanden Boeynants, was appointed Prime Minister in a transitional Government. Legislative elections in December caused little change to the distribution of seats in the Chamber of Representatives. Four successive prime ministerial nominees failed to form a new government, the main obstacle being the future status of Brussels. The six-month crisis was finally resolved when a new coalition Government was formed in April 1979 under Dr Wilfried Martens, the President of the CVP.

During 1980 the linguistic conflict worsened, sometimes involving violent incidents. Legislation was formulated, under the terms of which Flanders and Wallonia were to be administered by regional assemblies, with control of cultural matters, public health, roads, urban projects and 10% of the national budget, while Brussels was to retain its three-member executive. Belgium suffered severe economic difficulties during the late 1970s and early 1980s, and internal disagreement over Martens' proposals for their resolution resulted in the formation of four successive coalition Governments between April 1979 and October 1980. Proposed austerity measures provoked demonstrations and lost Martens the support of the Socialist parties. Martens also encountered widespread criticism over plans to install North Atlantic Treaty Organization (NATO, see p. 370) nuclear missiles in Belgium. In April 1981 a new Government was formed, comprising a coalition of the Christian Democrats and the Socialist parties and led by Mark Eyskens (of the CVP), hitherto Minister of Finance. However, lack of parliamentary support for his policies led to Eyskens' resignation in September. In December Martens formed a new centre-right Government, comprising the Christian Democrats and the two Liberal parties. In 1982 Parliament granted special powers for the implementation of economic austerity measures; these were effective until 1984 and similar powers were approved in March 1986. Opposition to reductions in public spending was vigorous, with public sector trade unions undertaking damaging strike action throughout the 1980s.

In July 1985 six Liberal government ministers resigned in connection with a riot at the Heysel football stadium in Brussels in May during which 39 people died. This led to the collapse of the governing coalition. Martens offered the resignation of his Government, but this was suspended by King Baudouin pending a general election, which was called for October. Meanwhile, however, controversy regarding educational reform provoked a dispute between the two main linguistic groups and caused the final dissolution of Parliament in September. The general election returned the Christian Democrat-Liberal alliance to power, and in November Martens formed his sixth Council of Ministers.

The Government collapsed in October 1987, as a result of continuing division between the French- and Dutch-speaking parties of the coalition. At the ensuing general election in December, no party won a clear mandate for power, and negotiations for a new coalition lasted 146 days. During this time Martens assumed a caretaker role, while a series of mediators, appointed by the King, attempted to reach a compromise. In May 1988 Martens was sworn in at the head of his eighth administration, after agreement was finally reached by the French- and Dutch-speaking wings of both the Christian Democrats and Socialists and by the VU.

Constitutional reform

The five-party coalition agreement committed the new Government to a programme of further austerity measures, together with tax reforms and increased federalization. In August 1988 Parliament approved the first phase of the federalization plan, whereby increased autonomy would be granted to the country's language communities and regions in several areas of jurisdiction, including education and socio-economic policy. It was also agreed that Brussels would have its own regional council, with an executive responsible to it, giving the city equal status with Flanders and Wallonia. In January 1989 Parliament approved the second phase of the federalization programme, allocating the public funds necessary to give effect to the regional autonomy that had been approved in principle in August 1988. The relevant constitutional amendments formally came into effect in July 1989.

A brief constitutional crisis in 1990 provoked widespread demands for a review of the powers of the monarch, as defined by the Constitution. In March proposals for the legalization of abortion (in strictly controlled circumstances) received parliamentary approval. However, King Baudouin had previously stated that his religious convictions would render him unable to give royal assent to any such legislation. A compromise solution was reached in April, whereby Article 82 of the Constitution, which makes provision for the monarch's 'incapacity to rule', was invoked. Baudouin thus abdicated for 36 hours, during which time the new legislation was promulgated. A joint session of Parliament was then convened to declare the resumption of Baudouin's reign. However, the incident prompted considerable alarm within Belgium: it was widely perceived as setting a dangerous precedent for the reinterpretation of the Constitution.

The Government was weakened by the resignation of both VU ministers in September 1991 and by the resultant loss of its two-thirds' parliamentary majority, necessary for the implementation of the third stage of the federalization programme. Further linguistic conflict between the remaining coalition partners led to Martens' resignation as Prime Minister in October and the subsequent collapse of the Government. The results of a general election in November reflected a significant decline in popular support for all five parties represented in the outgoing Government. In March 1992 the Christian Democrats and the Socialists (which together controlled 120 seats in the 212-member Chamber of Representatives) agreed to form a new four-party administration; Jean-Luc Dehaene of the CVP was appointed Prime Minister. The new Government committed itself to the completion of the constitutional reforms that had been initiated under Martens' premiership.

In February 1993 Parliament voted to amend the Constitution to create a federal state of Belgium, comprising the largely autonomous Flemish, Walloon and Brussels-Capital Regions. The three regions, and the country's three linguistic groups, were to be represented by the following directly elected administrations: a combined administration for the Flemish Region and Community; regional administrations for Wallonia and Brussels; and separate administrations for French- and German-speakers. The regional administrations were to assume sole responsibility for the environment, housing, transport and public works, while the language community administrations were to supervise education policy and culture. Legislation to implement the reforms was enacted in July.

The second coalition under Dehaene

At a general election held in May 1995 the ruling centre-left coalition retained significant support, securing a total of 82 seats in the Chamber of Representatives (membership of which had been reduced to 150). Elections to the regional assemblies were held concurrently. The Christian Democrat-Socialist coalition was re-formed shortly after the election and in June a new Council of Ministers was appointed, under Dehaene. The Government introduced several strict economic austerity measures in late 1995; public sector trade unions organized strike action in response. In May 1996 Parliament granted the Dehaene administration special emergency powers to implement economic austerity measures by decree.

The latter half of 1996 was dominated by extreme public concern over allegations of endemic official corruption, following the discovery, in August, of an international paedophile network based in Belgium, and subsequent widespread speculation (fuelled by the arrests in September of several police officers) that this had received protection from the police force and from the judicial and political establishment. During September King Albert II promised a thorough investigation of the network and, in an unprecedented gesture, demanded a review of the judicial system. In October, however, allegations of a conspiracy to impede the progress of the investigation were prompted by the removal from the case of Jean-Marc Connerotte, a widely respected senior investigating judge. In April 1997 a parliamentary committee investigating allegations of official corruption and mismanagement issued a report that claimed that rivalry between the country's various police and judicial divisions often prevented their effective co-operation; it recommended the establishment of a single integrated national police force. However, the committee found little evidence that paedophile networks had received official protection. In February 1998 the Government announced that, in place of the recommended integrated national police force, efforts would be made to facilitate 'voluntary co-operation contracts' between the various law enforcement services. In April Marc Dutroux, a convicted paedophile whose arrest in August 1996 on charges of child kidnapping and murder had prompted the review of judicial institutions, briefly escaped from police custody. The incident incited renewed public anger and precipitated the resignations of several high-ranking figures, including the commander of the national gendarmerie and the Ministers of the Interior and Justice. A proposed vote of no confidence in the Government, also ensuing from Dutroux's escape, was defeated in the Chamber of Representatives. Dehaene immediately reaffirmed his commitment to restructuring the police and judiciary.

In June 1999 two ministers resigned following the revelation that farms throughout Belgium had been supplied with animal feed contaminated with industrial oil containing dioxin (a carcinogenic chemical). At a general election later in June, the Christian Democrats suffered heavy losses, mainly at the hands of the Liberals and the ecologist parties. The Vlaamse Liberalen en Demokraten—Partij van de Burger (VLD, Flemish Liberals and Democrats—Citizens' Party) emerged as the largest single party in the 150-member Chamber of Representatives, with 23 seats, while the extreme right-wing Vlaams Blok (Flemish Bloc) became the fifth largest party, with 15 seats. The electoral defeat of the outgoing coalition was largely attributed to public dissatisfaction with the authorities' response to the dioxin crisis, compounded by general disquiet over the earlier scandals.

The Verhofstadt Governments

On 12 July 1999 a new six-party coalition Government was sworn in, led by the President of the VLD, Guy Verhofstadt, and comprising the VLD, the francophone Parti Réformateur Libéral (PRL—Reformist Liberal Party), the two Socialist parties and the two ecologist parties, Anders Gaan Leven (Agalev) and Ecolo (the Ecologistes Confédérés pour l'Organisation des Luttes Originales). The new administration was the first Belgian Government in 40 years not to include the Christian Democrats, the first to include the ecologist parties and the first to be headed by a Liberal Prime Minister since 1884.

During 2001–02 several political parties underwent significant change and reform. In 2001 the CVP changed its name to the Christen Democratisch en Vlaams (CD&V—Christian Democratic and Flemish), emphasizing its commitment to Flemish issues, while the Flemish Socialist party, which had moved towards a more centrist ideological position, adopted the name SP.A (formally, the Socialistische Partij Anders—Socialist Party Otherwise). In late 2001 the VU disbanded and split into two parties: Spirit, which adopted a social-liberal stance and later formed an alliance with the SP.A, and a Flemish nationalist grouping, the Nieuw-Vlaamse Alliantie (N-VA—New Flemish Alliance). Finally, in 2002 the PSC adopted a new statute, ceased to espouse an explicitly Christian Democratic philosophy and was renamed the Centre Démocrate Humaniste (CDH).

At the general election on 18 May 2003 the outgoing centre-left coalition was returned to power. The ecologist parties suffered heavy losses, while the controversial Vlaams Blok achieved the best result in its 25-year history, gaining 18% of the Flemish vote and winning 18 seats. The VLD won 25 seats in the Chamber of Representatives, as did the francophone Parti Socialiste (PS). The Mouvement Réformateur (MR) coalition, which included the PRL, obtained 24 seats, while the SP.A-Spirit alliance won 23 seats and the CD&V secured 21. The ecologist parties Ecolo and Agalev (later renamed Groen!), which had together won 20 seats in the 1999 election, were reduced to four representatives. Following negotiations between the Liberal and Socialist parties, a new coalition Government, led by Verhofstadt and comprising the VLD, the MR, the PS, the SP.A and Spirit, took office in July. The Government pledged to reduce personal income tax, to increase expenditure on health and justice, and to create 200,000 new jobs by 2007.

In the European and regional elections concurrently held on 10 June 2004, the Vlaams Blok increased its representation in the European Parliament to three of Belgium's 24 seats and it became the second largest party in the Flemish Parliament (while the VLD was only the fourth largest). In November the Court of Cassation found the Vlaams Blok guilty of promoting racial discrimination and ruled that freedom of speech should be curtailed in the interests of national security and to protect the rights of other people. The Vlaams Blok was fined and lost access both to state funding and to television exposure, thus effectively forcing it to disband. However, the organization consequently changed its statutes and renamed itself Vlaams Belang (Flemish Interest).

In October 2005 government proposals to reform the pension and social security systems prompted the first general strike in 12 years. The reforms, designed to expand the work-force by increasing employment among younger and older workers and, most controversially, by raising the minimum retirement age, were severely criticized by employers' organizations and trade unions. Later in the same month some 80,000 protesters participated in a demonstration in Brussels against the reforms. Following the Government's introduction of a number of minor amendments, employers' groups agreed to the reforms. However, the trade unions remained dissatisfied and organized further industrial action.

In municipal elections held on 8 October 2006 Vlaams Belang, which had campaigned against immigration and in favour of independence for Flanders, expanded its influence beyond its traditional base in Antwerp, winning more than 20% of the vote in the 308 municipal councils in Flanders. In Antwerp, however, although Vlaams Belang won 33.5% of the vote, the SP.A-Spirit alliance won the largest representation with 35.5%. The VLD and other members of the governing coalition performed poorly in the municipal elections, largely reflecting voter dissatisfaction with federal policies, notably attempts at economic reform.

The 2007 general election

At the general election of 10 June 2007 the CD&V made significant gains in Flanders, mainly at the expense of the VLD, which contested the election as Open Vld in alliance with two smaller Flemish liberal parties, Liberaal Appèl Plus and Vivant. The MR replaced the PS as the leading francophone party, while an alliance of the CD&V and the nationalist N-VA emerged as the largest group in the Chamber of Representatives, winning 30 seats of the 150 seats, while the MR won 23 seats. The PS won 20 seats, and the Open Vld 18 seats. A collapse in support for the SP.A-Spirit alliance, which won just 14 seats, allowed Vlaams Belang to become the fifth largest party in the Chamber of Representatives, despite a reduction in its own representation to 17 seats. The CDH won 10 seats. In response to the poor electoral performance of the main coalition parties, Verhofstadt announced the resignation of the Council of Ministers, although the Government was to remain in office until the successful conclusion of negotiations over a new coalition agreement.

In July 2007 the Chairman of the CD&V, Yves Leterme, was charged with forming a new government, and duly initiated formal discussions regarding a coalition agreement between the Christian Democrats and the Liberals. However, divisions quickly emerged between the Flemish and French-speaking parties over proposals to devolve further powers to the regional and community administrations and to divide the electoral constituency of Brussels-Halle-Vilvoorde. (This comprised the Brussels-Capital Region together with 35 districts surrounding the capital but located in the Flemish Region, some of which contained a majority of French-speaking inhabitants. Voters in these districts were thus able to vote for francophone parties at federal and European elections, an anomaly that had been ruled unconstitutional by the Court of Arbitration in May 2003.) In mid-August 2007 the talks were suspended by King Albert, who requested the newly appointed President of the Chamber of Representatives, Herman Van Rompuy of the CD&V, to assess the willingness of the main political parties to recommence talks over a coalition agreement. Following the completion of Van Rompuy's mission in September, the King again asked Leterme to lead attempts to form a government. On 1 December Leterme resigned as *formateur* (prime ministerial nominee), having failed to broker an agreement owing to disagreement over the issues of devolution and boundary changes. Two days later King Albert asked Verhofstadt to preside over negotiations to form an interim administration, which would have the power to adopt a budget. On 21 December an interim coalition Government, comprising the CD&V, the MR, Open Vld, the PS and the CDH, was sworn in. Verhofstadt remained as Prime Minister, while Leterme was appointed Deputy Prime Minister and Minister for the Budget and Structural Reform.

By mid-March 2008 the five parties of the interim coalition had agreed a programme for government and on 20 March Verhofstadt resigned as Prime Minister. As had been envisaged under the interim coalition agreement, Leterme was sworn in as Prime Minister by King Albert. Didier Reynders, the leader of the MR, was appointed as one of five Deputy Prime Ministers and retained the role of Minister of Finance. The agreed government programme focused principally on economic issues, including increasing pension benefits and reducing taxation, while the prospects for devolution continued to be considered by a group of senior politicians. A deadline of mid-July was established for agreement on constitutional reform.

Having failed to secure an agreement on constitutional reform by the self-imposed deadline, on 14 July 2008 Leterme submitted his resignation as Prime Minister. However, this was rejected by King Albert. In an attempt to break the impasse, the King announced the appointment of a commission comprising two prominent francophone politicians, François-Xavier de Donnea and Raymond Langendries, and the Minister-President of the German Community, Karl-Heinz Lambertz, to explore possible solutions to the ongoing crisis. The commission published its report in September, defining the basis for negotiations and recommending that a partial agreement be reached prior to the next regional elections in June 2009. However, the report was criticized by some politicians from both linguistic communities for its moderation. The N-VA withdrew its parliamentary support for the federal Government, citing the lack of progress on constitutional reform, while the party's sole member of the Flemish regional Government, Geert Bourgeois, resigned from his post.

Leterme's resignation and return

In early December 2008 the Brussels Court of Appeal ordered the suspension of the proposed sale of a 75% stake in Fortis Bank, which had been nationalized in October, following a successful court case brought by the bank's former shareholders. It was subsequently alleged that government officials had sought to influence the court's decision, although Yves Leterme and his ministers denied any wrongdoing. However, the President of the Court of Cassation, Ghislain Londers, wrote in an open letter to the President of the Chamber of Representatives that, while no admissible evidence existed to confirm any impropriety on the part of government officials, there remained 'significant indications' of interference. On 19 December Jo Vandeurzen of the CD&V resigned as Deputy Prime Minister and Minister of Justice and of Institutional Reform, claiming that suspicion of improper conduct impeded him from effectively carrying out his duties. Later that day Leterme announced the resignation of the entire Council of Ministers. King Albert requested Leterme's Government to remain in office in an interim capacity and requested former Prime Minister Wilfried Martens to seek a solution through negotiations with the leaders of the main political parties. Following the completion of those discussions, the King appointed the President of the Chamber of Representatives, Van Rompuy of the CD&V (who had served as Deputy Prime Minister in 1993–99), as Prime Minister at the head of a similarly constituted five-party coalition Government.

In July 2009 the Deputy Prime Minister and Minister of Foreign Affairs, Karel De Gucht of Open Vld, was appointed to the European Commission and duly resigned from his cabinet post. In the ensuing cabinet reorganization, Leterme was brought back into the Government to replace De Gucht as Minister of Foreign Affairs, while Guy Vanhengel of Open Vld was appointed Deputy Prime Minister and Minister of the Budget. In November, at a meeting of the European Council in Brussels, Van Rompuy was nominated to be the first permanent President of the European Council following the entry into force of the Treaty of Lisbon in December. King Albert asked Martens to lead negotiations towards finding a new Prime Minister. On 25 November the King appointed Leterme (who had reportedly been exonerated from involvement in the Fortis Bank affair) as Prime Minister for a second time. Steven Vanackere, also of the CD&V, succeeded Leterme as Minister of Foreign Affairs and Institutional Reform, while remaining one of the five Deputy Prime Ministers. The King asked former Prime Minister Jean-Luc Dehaene to mediate between the political parties in order to find a solution to the dispute over constitutional reform, including the Brussels-Halle-Vilvoorde question, before mid-April 2010. As no negotiated settlement was reached by the agreed deadline, Open Vld withdrew from the ruling coalition on 22 April. Leterme submitted the resignation of the Government, which was accepted by the King on 26 April. The Government continued in office in an interim capacity, pending the formation of a new administration following a general election.

The 2010 general election and continued political stalemate

At the general election, which was held on 13 June 2010, the Flemish separatist N-VA, led by Bart De Wever, won the largest number of seats in the Chamber of Representatives, with 27 of the 150 seats, closely followed by the French-speaking PS of Elio Di Rupo, which increased its representation to 26 seats. The other major parties all suffered a loss of support: the MR secured 18 seats in the lower chamber, while the CD&V obtained 17, the SP.A and Open Vld 13 each, Vlaams Belang 12 and the CDH nine. The strong performance of the N-VA, which advocated a gradual move towards independence for Flanders, inevitably intensified uncertainty about Belgium's future. On 17 June King Albert designated De Wever as *informateur*, charged with exploring the possibilities for the formation of a new coalition government. De Wever submitted his report to the King on 8 July, suggesting that the differences between the parties were still too substantial to be able to form a government, and was relieved of his mission. On the following day King Albert appointed Di Rupo as *préformateur*, in which role he was to lead negotiations between the parties with a view to establishing the basis for a stable coalition. However, Di Rupo was unable to broker a coalition agreement. The King accepted Di Rupo's resignation as *préformateur* in early September, subsequently asking the Presidents of the two legislative chambers to mediate between the parties with the aim of reviving the coalition talks. Negotiations collapsed in early October, after the N-VA withdrew, citing the unwillingness of the francophone parties to devolve greater responsibility for financial affairs to the regions and communities. On 8 October the King set De Wever a 10-day deadline to attempt to resolve the political stalemate, but on 18 October the francophone parties rejected the N-VA leader's proposals on constitutional reform, notably his suggestion that tax-raising powers should be transferred from the federal authorities to the regional administrations. Three days later the King appointed Johan Vande Lanotte, a former leader of the SP.A, to mediate between the seven parties hitherto involved in the negotiations—the Flemish N-VA, CD&V, SP.A and Groen!, and the French-speaking PS, CDH and Ecolo.

In early January 2011 Lanotte presented a compromise plan for government to the leaders of the seven parties, but it was rejected by the N-VA and the CD&V, prompting Lanotte to tender his resignation as mediator on 6 January. Five days later, at King Albert's request, Lanotte agreed to resume his role, but on 26 January, declaring that it had been impossible to overcome the impasse between the parties, he again submitted his resignation, which was accepted this time. In an indication of public frustration with the continued uncertainty, a few days earlier at least 34,000 people had participated in a march in Brussels in support of demands for national unity and the formation of a permanent government. Meanwhile, amid increasing concern in the financial markets regarding Belgium's mounting government debt, the King asked Leterme's interim Government, which was operating with only limited powers, to prepare an austerity budget for 2011. The budget was finally approved in May.

Didier Reynders of the MR, the Deputy Prime Minister and Minister of Finance and of Institutional Reform, was appointed *informateur* by the King at the beginning of February 2011. His unsuccessful attempts to resolve the impasse ended a month later. The role of royal mediator was subsequently taken by Wouter Beke of the CD&V, who expanded the negotiations to include nine parties, with the additional participation of the Liberal MR and Open Vld. However, Beke resigned as mediator in mid-May, following the failure of these talks, and King Albert appointed Di Rupo as *formateur*. Relations between the linguistic communities deteriorated further later that month, when the parliament of the French Community voted in favour of renaming the Community as the Wallonia-Brussels Federation, noting the strong alliance between francophones in Wallonia and Brussels. The Minister-President of the Flemish Region and Community, Kris Peeters, denounced this move as unconstitutional, refusing to recognize the Federation as an official body. However, it appeared that the new name would be used as an additional name and not in official documents in which the constitutional name of the French Community would be required.

Legislation outlawing the wearing in public of face-covering veils, which prescribed penalties on conviction of a maximum fine of €137.50 and a prison sentence of up to seven days, came into force in July 2011, following its approval by an overwhelming majority in the Chamber of Representatives in April 2010. Two Muslim women who wore burkas launched an immediate challenge at the Constitutional Court against the law, which followed the introduction of a similar ban in France in April, on the grounds that it violated fundamental rights, including freedom of expression and religion.

Meanwhile, Di Rupo tendered his resignation as *formateur* on 9 July 2011, following the rejection of his draft programme for government by De Wever, who claimed that the institutional reforms proposed would provide insufficient autonomy for the regions. However, King Albert refused to accept Di Rupo's resignation, and later that month hopes of a resolution of the protracted political crisis were raised when the CD&V agreed to continue coalition negotiations without the N-VA's participation, on which it had hitherto insisted. Talks on Di Rupo's proposals, now involving eight parties, subsequently resumed.

Di Rupo presented a revised programme for government in early September 2011. Efforts to reach a compromise intensified in mid-September, after it emerged that acting Prime Minister Leterme was to take up a senior post at the Organisation for Economic Co-operation and Development before the end of the year, and shortly afterwards it was announced that the eight negotiating parties had reached an agreement on the division of the Brussels-Halle-Vilvoorde electoral constituency, thereby removing one of the principal obstacles to the formation of a new government. In October, moreover, the eight parties concluded an accord on wide-ranging institutional reforms, which, *inter alia*, provided for the devolution of further powers from the federal Government to the regional and community authorities, including some tax-raising powers and responsibility for public expenditure amounting to some €17,000m. (around 4% of national income), notably in the areas of health care and social welfare; and, with effect from 2014, an increase in the term of office of the Chamber of Representatives to five years and the transformation of the Senate into a non-permanent assembly of 50 representatives of the three linguistic communities. Shortly afterwards Di Rupo announced that discussions would continue in the absence of the two ecologist parties (other negotiating parties having urged a reduction in the number of coalition partners), and would focus on budgetary and socio-economic issues. Meanwhile, pressure from the financial markets to form a new government with a mandate to introduce much-needed austerity measures and structural reforms was mounting, with the announcement that Dexia Bank Belgium was to be nationalized prompting heightened concerns regarding the country's rising public debt.

Recent developments: new government formed

Di Rupo again submitted his resignation as *formateur* on 21 November 2011, after the two Liberal parties rejected his proposed budget for 2012, but King Albert asked him to reconsider. Finally, on 26 November, a day after the credit rating agency Standard and Poor's downgraded Belgium's sovereign debt rating, a budget was agreed, followed by a comprehensive programme for government a few days later. A new coalition Government, comprising the Dutch and French-speaking Socialists, Christian Democrats and Liberals (which held a total of 96 of the 150 seats in the Chamber of Representatives), was sworn in on 6 December, 541 days after the general election, with Di Rupo becoming the first francophone Prime Minister in more than 30 years. With five of the six coalition partners having participated in the outgoing administration (the SP.A being the only new addition), 13 of the 19 ministers and secretaries of state appointed to the new Council of Ministers had also served in Leterme's Government. Didier Reynders and Steven Vanackere notably exchanged portfolios, the former becoming Deputy Prime Minister and Minister of Foreign Affairs, Foreign Trade and European Affairs and the latter Deputy Prime Minister and Minister of Finance and of Sustainable Development. The N-VA questioned the Government's legitimacy on the grounds that it did not represent a majority of Flemish members of Parliament, while trade unions expressed concern regarding the potential impact of the planned austerity measures, organizing a general strike in protest in late December.

Foreign Affairs

Regional Relations

Since the Second World War, Belgium has promoted international co-operation in Europe. It was a founder member of many important international organizations, including the North Atlantic Treaty Organization (NATO, see p. 370), the European Community, now the European Union (EU, see p. 276), the Council of Europe (see p. 256) and the Benelux Economic Union (see p. 448). In July 2008 Belgium completed the parliamentary ratification of the EU's Treaty of Lisbon, which was designed to reform the institutions of the EU to improve decision-making following the enlargement of the Union to 27 members. The Treaty of Lisbon had replaced the controversial Treaty establishing a Constitution for Europe, which had been rejected in referendums by France and the Netherlands in 2005. The treaty entered into force in December 2009, following its ratification by all 27 member states. Belgium exercised the rotating Presidency of the Council of the EU during the second half of 2010 (for the 12th time).

At a summit meeting held in The Hague, Netherlands, in June 2008 the heads of government of Belgium, the Netherlands and Luxembourg signed a new Benelux Treaty on political and economic co-operation. The document expanded the scope of the previous treaty, signed in 1958, to provide for greater co-operation between the three Governments on justice and home affairs, as well as customs and cross-border trade. In recognition of this, the official title was to change from the Benelux Economic Union to the Benelux Union. The new treaty entered into force on 1 January 2012, following its ratification by the national legislatures of the three countries and by the parliaments of the German-speaking Community, the Flemish Region and Community, the Brussels-Capital Region in Belgium, the Walloon Region and the French Community.

Other external relations

From the late 1980s Belgium's hitherto cordial relations with its former colonies underwent considerable strain. Proposals made by Prime Minister Wilfried Martens in November 1988 regarding the relief of debts owed to Belgium by Zaire (formerly the Belgian Congo, renamed the Democratic Republic of the Congo—DRC—in 1997) provoked allegations in the Belgian press of corruption within the Zairean Government and of the misappropriation of development aid. President Mobutu Sese Seko of Zaire responded by ordering the withdrawal of all Zairean state-owned businesses from Belgium and by demanding that all Zairean nationals resident in Belgium remove their assets from, and leave, their host country. Following the collapse of public order in Zaire in September 1991, the Belgian Government dispatched 1,000 troops to Zaire for the protection of the estimated 11,000 Belgian nationals resident there. By the end of 1991 all the troops had been withdrawn and about 8,000 Belgian nationals had been evacuated. Prospects for the normalization of relations improved following the establishment of a transitional Government in Zaire in July 1992 and the removal of Zairean sanctions against Belgium. Relations deteriorated again, however, in January 1993, when, in response to rioting by troops loyal to President Mobutu, Belgium dispatched 520 troops to evacuate the remaining 3,000 Belgian nationals in Zaire. In August 1997, following the deposition of Mobutu's regime in May by the forces of Laurent-Désiré Kabila, it was announced that normal relations between Belgium and the DRC (as Zaire was now renamed) would be gradually restored.

The election of a new Government in Belgium in June 1999 led to an improvement in relations with the DRC. The new Belgian Minister of Foreign Affairs, Louis Michel, was determined to develop a new strategy towards the central African countries with which Belgium had historical ties. Following the assassination of Kabila in January 2001, the Belgian Government intensified its attempts to relaunch the peace initiative in the region. During a visit to Belgium by the new DRC President, Kabila's son, Joseph, the Belgian Prime Minister urged Kabila to commit to peace negotiations under the auspices of the UN. Michel also aimed to add an 'ethical' dimension to Belgian foreign policy. Initiatives that reflected this new approach included an apology made by Belgium in February 2002 for its role in the murder of the Belgian Congo's first Prime Minister, Patrice Lumumba, in 1961. Following a peace accord formalized in April 2003 and the installation in June of Joseph Kabila as leader of an interim DRC Government, in October the Belgian Government announced its intention to double its aid to the DRC to €82m. in 2004. In October 2004, however, the Government of the DRC recalled its ambassador from Brussels, in protest at remarks made by the Belgian Minister of Foreign Affairs, Karel De Gucht, criticizing the DRC authorities for their alleged continuing corrupt practices and lack of democracy. In May 2008 the DRC again recalled its ambassador from Brussels, in protest at further remarks made by De Gucht regarding corruption in the DRC. By 2010 cordial relations had been restored, and in June King Albert visited the DRC, at Kabila's invitation, to attend the celebration of the 50th anniversary of the country's independence.

In October 1990 the Martens Government dispatched 600 troops to protect some 1,600 Belgian nationals resident in Rwanda (part of the former Belgian territory of Ruanda-Urundi), when exiled opponents of the incumbent regime invaded that country. In late October a cease-fire agreement came into effect, and in November Belgian forces were withdrawn from Rwanda. Nevertheless, the conflict in Rwanda continued during 1991–94. Following the signing of a peace accord in August 1993, some 420 Belgian troops were redeployed as part of a UN peace-keeping force; this was, however, unable to prevent an outbreak of extreme violence, beginning in April 1994, which resulted in the deaths of many hundreds of thousands of people. Following the execution of 10 Belgian troops in April, the Belgian Government withdrew its peace-keeping contingent. It also dispatched some 800 paratroopers to Rwanda to co-ordinate the evacuation of the estimated 1,500 Belgian expatriates remaining in the country, as well as other foreign nationals. The Belgian Ministries of Foreign Affairs and Defence rejected allegations, published in November 2003, of racist, aggressive and undisciplined behaviour by Belgian UN troops at the start of Rwanda's 1994 genocide. In September 2010 a civil trial commenced in Brussels in a case filed against the Belgian state and three former Belgian army officers by survivors of a massacre of more than 2,000 refugees in Rwanda in April 1994. The defendants, who were accused of failing to act to prevent or put an end to violations of international human rights, maintained that they had been acting on the orders of the UN when they had evacuated 92 Belgian UN troops from a school in which the refugees had sought sanctuary and were subsequently killed. In an interim judgment in December 2010, however, the court ruled that the decision to withdraw the troops from the school had been taken by the Belgian authorities rather than the UN; the case was ongoing in early 2012.

Legislation introduced in 1993 endowed Belgian courts with universal jurisdiction in human rights cases. In June 2001, in the first case to be successfully conducted under the new law, four Rwandan nationals were convicted of war crimes for their role in the ethnic violence in Rwanda in 1994. In February 2002, however, the International Criminal Court ruled that Belgium did not have the right to try suspects who were protected by diplomatic immunity. Moreover, in June judges ruled that a case against the Israeli Prime Minister, Ariel Sharon, for war crimes allegedly committed against Palestinian refugees in Lebanon in 1982 (when he was Minister of Defence), could not be brought to trial since, according to the Belgian criminal code, alleged crimes committed outside the country required subjects to be on Belgian territory to be investigated and tried. Another human rights case, against President Laurent Gbagbo of Côte d'Ivoire, was similarly dismissed. In February 2003 the Court of Cassation reversed the earlier ruling regarding Sharon, but recognized his diplomatic immunity so that proceedings against him were inadmissible while he remained the Israeli premier.

The 1993 law also jeopardized relations with the USA, particularly in the wake of the US-led invasion of Iraq in March 2003 (which was opposed by the Belgian Government). In May Gen. Tommy Franks, the retiring US commander in Iraq, was indicted under the legislation by a Belgian lawyer representing 19 Iraqis. Despite the fact that the case was ended the following week under new procedures introduced in April to prevent the legislation being used for politically motivated litigation, the US Government demanded the repeal of the legislation. The USA warned that its officials would be unable to attend meetings of NATO and threatened to withdraw US funding for a new NATO headquarters in Belgium. In July 2003 cases were initiated (and dismissed) against several other prominent US politicians, including President George W. Bush, as well as against the British Prime Minister, Tony Blair, for their roles in the military action in Afghanistan and Iraq. Legislation was passed in August that repealed the 1993 law and established a procedure for nullifying pending cases; it limited the jurisdiction of the law to cases involving Belgian citizens and long-term residents, and granted automatic legal immunity to all officials attending meetings at NATO and the EU.

Since March 2002 Belgium has contributed troops to the International Security Assistance Force (ISAF) in Afghanistan, which was established following the US-led military campaign against the Taliban and al-Qa'ida militants in 2001 and was placed under the command of NATO in August 2003; some 520 Belgian troops were participating in ISAF in early 2012. Following the outbreak of civil conflict in Libya in early 2011, and the UN Security Council's adoption in March of Resolution 1973, permitting UN member states to take 'all necessary measures' (short of military occupation) to protect civilians in that country, Belgian military forces participated in the enforcement of an air exclusion zone over Libya and a naval blockade of that country. NATO military action in Libya ended in October, following the death of the Libyan leader, Col Muammar al-Qaddafi.

CONSTITUTION AND GOVERNMENT

The Belgian Constitution, originally promulgated in 1831, was revised and consolidated in 1993 to provide for a federal structure of government. It has been subsequently amended on a number of occasions. Belgium is a constitutional and hereditary monarchy, consisting of a federation of the largely autonomous regions of Brussels, Flanders and Wallonia and of the Dutch-, French- and German-speaking language communities. The central legislature consists of a bicameral Parliament (the Chamber of Representatives and the Senate). The Chamber has 150 members, all directly elected for a term of four years by universal adult suffrage, on the basis of proportional representation. The Senate has 71 normal members, of whom 40 are directly elected at intervals of four years, also by universal suffrage on the basis of proportional representation, 21 are appointed by the legislative bodies of the three language communities, and 10 are co-opted by the elected members. In addition, children of the King are entitled to honorary membership of the Senate from 18 years of age and acquire voting rights at the age of 21. Executive power, nominally vested in the King, is exercised by the Council of Ministers. The King appoints the Prime Minister and, on the latter's advice, other ministers. The Council of Ministers is responsible to the Chamber of Representatives. The three regions and three linguistic communities are represented by the following directly elected legislative administrations: a combined administration for the Flemish Region and Community; administrations for the Walloon and Brussels-Capital Regions; and separate administrations for the French and German communities. The regional administrations have sole responsibility for the environment, housing, transport and public works, while the language community administrations supervise education policy and culture. Under a constitutional amendment approved by the Chamber of Representatives in June 2001, the regions were also granted greater autonomy over taxation and public expenditure, agriculture, and policies regarding foreign aid and trade. The coalition Government that took office in December 2011 proposed the introduction of a number of constitutional reforms, including the devolution of further powers to the regions and communities, an increase in the term of office of the Chamber of Representatives to five years and the transformation of the Senate, from 2014, into a non-permanent body, comprising 50 indirectly elected members representing the three linguistic communities and 10 co-opted members.

REGIONAL AND INTERNATIONAL CO-OPERATION

Belgium was a founder member of the European Community, now the European Union (EU, see p. 276), the principal institutions of which are based in Brussels. Belgium uses the European single currency, the euro. Belgium was also a founder member of the Benelux Economic Union (see p. 448), the Council of Europe (see p. 256) and the Organization for Security and Co-operation in Europe (OSCE, see p. 388).

Belgium was a founder member of the UN in 1945. As a contracting party to the General Agreement on Tariffs and Trade, Belgium joined the World Trade Organization (WTO, see p. 433) on its establishment in 1995. Belgium was also a founder member of the North Atlantic Treaty Organization (NATO, see p. 370), which has its headquarters in Brussels, and the Organisation for Economic Co-operation and Development (OECD, see p. 379).

ECONOMIC AFFAIRS

In 2010, according to estimates by the World Bank, Belgium's gross national income (GNI), measured at average 2008–10 prices, was US $493,526m., equivalent to $45,360 per head (or $37,800 per head on an international purchasing-power parity basis). During 2001–10, it was estimated, the population increased at an average annual rate of 0.6%, while gross domestic product (GDP) per head increased, in real terms, by an average of 0.8% per year. Overall GDP increased, in real terms, at an average annual rate of 1.4% during 2001–10; GDP contracted by 2.8% in 2009, but increased by 2.2% in 2010.

Agriculture (including hunting, forestry and fishing) contributed 0.7% of GDP in 2010 and engaged 1.8% of the employed labour force in 2008. The principal agricultural products are sugar beet, cereals and potatoes. Pig meat, beef and dairy products are also important. Exports of food and live animals accounted for 8.1% of Belgium's total export revenue in 2010. According to estimates by the World Bank, agricultural GDP declined, in real terms, at an average annual rate of 0.6% in 2001–09; it declined by 1.9% in 2008 and by 0.4% in 2009.

Industry (including mining and quarrying, manufacturing, power and construction) contributed 22.3% of GDP in 2010 and engaged 24.6% of the employed labour force in 2008. According to estimates by the World Bank, although real industrial GDP remained constant with a negligible growth in 2001–09, it decreased by 6.7% in 2009.

Belgium has few mineral resources and the country's last coal mine closed in 1992. Extractive activities accounted for only 0.1% of GDP in 2010 and engaged only 0.1% of the employed labour force in 2008. Belgium is, however, an important producer of copper, zinc and aluminium, smelted from imported ores. The sector's GDP declined at an average rate of 3.3% per year during 2001–07; it increased by 10.2% in 2006, and by 5.0% in 2007.

Manufacturing contributed 13.6% of GDP in 2010 and engaged 16.4% of the employed labour force in 2008. In 2010 the main branches of manufacturing, in terms of value added, were chemicals, chemical products and man-made fibres (accounting for 14.4% of the total), basic metals and fabricated metal products (14.5%) and food products, beverages and tobacco (16.0%). According to estimates by the World Bank, during 2000–07 manufacturing GDP increased at an average annual rate of 1.1%; it rose by 2.6% in 2007.

Construction contributed 5.7% of GDP in 2010 and engaged 7.2% of the employed labour force in 2008.

Belgium's seven nuclear reactors accounted for 54.5% of total electricity generation in 2008. In 2008 29.5% was produced by natural gas power stations and 8.7% by coal-fired stations. The country's dependence on imported petroleum and natural gas has increased since 1988, following the announcement by the Government in that year of the indefinite suspension of its nuclear programme and of the construction of a gas-powered generator. In 2003 legislation was enacted to phase out the use of nuclear power by 2025, with the first nuclear power station scheduled to be closed in 2015. In October 2009 the Government agreed to postpone closure until 2025. However, legislation to this effect was not adopted by the legislature, owing to a change of government in April 2010. The coalition Government that took office in December 2011 stated its intention to phase out the use of nuclear power, but did not immediately set a date to do so. Fuel imports comprised an estimated 11.8% of the value of Belgium's total imports in 2009.

The services sector contributed 77.0% of GDP in 2010 and engaged 73.5% of the employed labour force in 2008. Financial services and the insurance sector provide significant contributions to GDP. The presence in Belgium of the offices of many international organizations and businesses is a significant source of revenue. Tourism is an expanding industry in Belgium, and in 2010 an estimated 7.2m. foreign tourists visited the country. According to provisional figures, tourism receipts totalled US $10,287m. in 2010 and the tourism sector contributed about 3.3% to the GDP in that year. According to estimates by the World Bank, the GDP of the services sector increased at an average annual rate of 1.8% in 2001–09; it increased by 2.0% in 2008 but decreased by 1.5% in 2009.

In 2010 Belgium recorded a visible trade deficit of US $2,331m., but there was a surplus of $4,481m. on the current account of the balance of payments. Belgium's principal source of imports in 2010 was the Netherlands (providing 23.3% of the total); other major suppliers were Germany (16.2%), France (12.5%) and the United Kingdom (6.3%). The principal markets for exports in that year were Germany (accounting for 16.44% of the total) and France (accounting for 16.42%); other major purchasers were the Netherlands (13.2%) and the United Kingdom (6.5%). The principal exports in 2010 were chemicals and related products (16.9%), machinery and equipment, transport equipment (including road vehicles), and mineral fuels, lubricants and related products. The principal imports in that year were mineral fuels, lubricants and related products (18.2%), machinery and equipment, chemicals and related products, and transport equipment.

In 2010 there was a budget deficit of €14,839m., equivalent to 4.2% of GDP. Belgium's general government gross debt was €340,803m. in 2010, equivalent to 96.7% of GDP. The country's total public debt was equivalent to 89.8% of GDP in 2008. The annual rate of inflation averaged 2.0% in 2001–10. Inflation was 0.1% in 2009, but consumer prices increased by 2.2% in 2010. In 2010 the unemployment rate was 8.4%.

Belgium is a small, open economy, which, as it is reliant on exports and benefits from high levels of foreign investment, was adversely affected by the global economic downturn in 2008–09. Having recorded a modest trade surplus throughout the 2000s, Belgium recorded visible trade deficits in 2008–10. The Belgian authorities acted swiftly in late 2008 to secure the positions of several financial institutions that had been weakened by the financial crisis, and were forced to nationalize Dexia Bank Belgium in 2011, after it suffered difficulties resulting from the sovereign debt crisis in the euro zone. Having contracted by 2.8% in 2009, according to official figures, real GDP rose by 2.2% in 2010, driven by strong export growth. However, the interventions in financial institutions and the costs of the recovery plan had a detrimental effect on the already high debt-to-GDP ratio. Having increased from 84.1% of GDP in 2007 (already significantly above the 60% stipulated in the EU's Stability and Growth Pact) to 96.2% by 2010, general government gross debt was forecast to rise to 97.7% of GDP in 2011. However, the introduction of reforms needed to restore long-term fiscal sustainability was hindered by disagreements between the main political parties, culminating in their failure to form a new government following inconclusive elections in June 2010. The political deadlock during 2011 prompted increasing concern within the financial markets regarding Belgium's ability to service the mounting public debt and to meet its commitment to lower the budget deficit from 4.2% of GDP in 2010 to 2.8% of GDP by 2012, and the country's sovereign debt rating was downgraded by two rating agencies in late 2011. The coalition Government that finally took office in December 2011 planned to reduce expenditure by €11,300m. in 2012 and to achieve a balanced budget by 2015. However, under newly agreed arrangements according the EU enhanced powers to enforce fiscal discipline, in January 2012 the European Commission required the Government to make further cuts that year, estimating that the deficit would otherwise reach some 3.25% of GDP. Growth decelerated during 2011, partly owing to weaker external demand, with the National Bank forecasting growth of 2.0% for that year and of only 0.5% for 2012.

PUBLIC HOLIDAYS

2013: 1 January (New Year's Day), 1 April (Easter Monday), 1 May (Labour Day), 9 May (Ascension Day), 20 May (Whit Monday), 11 July (Flemish Community), 21 July (Independence Day), 15 August (Assumption), 27 September (French Community), 1 November (All Saints' Day), 11 November (Armistice Day), 15 November (German-speaking Community), 25 December (Christmas Day).

Statistical Survey

Sources (unless otherwise stated): Direction générale Statistique et Information économique, 30 blvd Simon Bolivar, 1000 Brussels; tel. (2) 277-70-76; e-mail info .stat@economie.fgov.be; internet www.statbel.fgov.be; National Bank of Belgium, 14 blvd de Berlaimont, 1000 Brussels; tel. (2) 221-21-11; fax (2) 221-31-00; e-mail info@nbb.be; internet www.nbb.be.

Area and Population

AREA, POPULATION AND DENSITY

Area (sq km)	30,528*
Population (census results)‡	
1 March 1991	9,848,647
1 October 2001†	
Males	5,035,446
Females	5,260,904
Total	10,296,350
Population (official estimates at 1 January)‡	
2009	10,730,029
2010	10,807,396
2011	10,886,032
Density (per sq km) at 1 January 2011	356.6

* 11,787 sq miles.

† Refers to the General Socio-Economic Survey, which replaced the methodology of previous censuses.

‡ Population is *de jure*.

POPULATION BY AGE AND SEX

(official estimates at 1 January 2011)

	Males	Females	Total
0–14	941,499	900,866	1,842,365
15–64	3,596,466	3,569,333	7,165,799
65 and over	788,647	1,089,221	1,877,868
Total	5,326,612	5,559,420	10,886,032

REGIONS AND PROVINCES

(official estimates at 1 January 2011)

	Area (sq km)	Population	Density (per sq km)	Capital
Flemish Region	13,521	6,270,418	463.8	
Antwerpen (Antwerp)	2,867	1,749,786	610.3	Antwerpen
Limburg	2,422	842,589	347.9	Hasselt
Oost-Vlaanderen (East Flanders)	2,982	1,433,045	480.6	Gent
Vlaams-Brabant (Flemish Brabant)	2,106	1,085,852	515.6	Leuven
West-Vlaanderen (West Flanders)	3,144	1,159,146	368.7	Brugge
Walloon Region	16,845	3,529,256	209.5	
Brabant Wallon (Walloon Brabant)	1,091	385,135	353.0	Wavre
Hainaut	3,786	1,321,044	348.9	Mons
Liège	3,862	1,076,526	278.7	Liège
Luxembourg	4,440	270,944	61.0	Arlon
Namur	3,666	475,607	129.7	Namur
Brussels-Capital Region	162	1,086,358	6,705.9	Brussels
Total	30,528	10,886,032	356.6	

PRINCIPAL TOWNS

(population of city proper at 1 January 2010)

Antwerpen (Antwerp)	483,505*	Mons	91,759
Gent (Ghent)	243,666	Mechelen	80,940
Charleroi	202,598	Aalst	80,043
Liège	192,504	La Louvière	78,071
Bruxelles/Brussel (Brussels—capital)	157,673	Kortrijk	74,911
Brugge (Bruges)	116,741	Hasselt	73,067
Namur	108,950	Sint-Niklaas	71,806
Leuven	95,463		

* Including Deurne and other suburbs.

BIRTHS, MARRIAGES AND DEATHS

	Registered live births		Registered marriages*		Registered deaths†	
	Number	Rate (per 1,000)	Number	Rate (per 1,000)	Number	Rate (per 1,000)
2001	114,172	11.1	42,110	4.1	103,447	10.1
2002	111,225	10.8	40,434	3.9	105,642	10.2
2003	112,149	10.8	41,777	4.0	107,039	10.3
2004	115,618	11.1	43,296	4.2	101,946	9.8
2005	118,002	11.3	43,141	4.1	103,278	9.9
2006	121,382	11.5	44,813	4.3	101,587	9.7
2007	120,663	11.4	45,561	4.3	100,658	9.5
2008	128,049	12.0	45,613	4.3	n.a.	n.a.

* Including marriages among Belgian armed forces stationed outside the country and alien armed forces in Belgium, unless performed by local foreign authority.

† Including Belgian armed forces stationed outside the country, but excluding alien armed forces stationed in Belgium.

Registered marriages: 43,303 (4.0 per 1,000 persons) in 2009.

Life expectancy (years at birth, WHO estimates): 80 (males 77; females 83) in 2009 (Source: WHO, *World Health Statistics*).

ECONOMICALLY ACTIVE POPULATION*
('000 persons aged 15 and over)

	2006	2007	2008
Agriculture, hunting and forestry	82.9	80.2	79.4
Fishing	0.4	1.1	1.0
Mining and quarrying	9.4	9.1	6.2
Manufacturing	715.2	724.6	727.5
Electricity, gas and water supply	35.1	34.3	40.4
Construction	292.9	302.1	321.8
Wholesale and retail trade	559.4	589.0	571.0
Hotels and restaurants	140.1	150.8	141.9
Transport, storage and communications	320.0	316.1	331.8
Financial intermediation	155.6	162.6	175.7
Real estate, renting and business activities	404.4	414.0	417.9
Public administration and defence	422.1	431.7	436.9
Education	375.6	378.5	375.6
Health and social work	528.9	534.7	564.1
Other community, social and personal service activities	172.0	185.1	181.8
Private households with employed persons	23.7	33.9	42.1
Extra-territorial organizations and bodies	24.8	32.7	30.7
Total employed	4,262.8	4,380.3	4,445.9
Unemployed	383.2	353.0	333.7
Total labour force	4,646.0	4,733.3	4,779.6
Males	2,582.0	2,618.1	2,631.2
Females	2,063.7	2,115.2	2,148.4

* Includes professional armed forces, but excludes compulsory military service.

Source: ILO.

2009 ('000, annual averages): Total employed 4,522; Unemployed 555; Total labour force 5,077.

Health and Welfare

KEY INDICATORS

Total fertility rate (children per woman, 2009)	1.8
Under-5 mortality rate (per 1,000 live births, 2009)	5
HIV/AIDS (% of persons aged 15–49, 2009)	0.2
Physicians (per 1,000 head, 2006)	4.2
Hospital beds (per 1,000 head, 2006)	5.3
Health expenditure (2008): US $ per head (PPP)	4,096
Health expenditure (2008): % of GDP	11.1
Health expenditure (2008): public (% of total)	66.8
Total carbon dioxide emissions ('000 metric tons, 2007)	102,951.1
Carbon dioxide emissions per head (metric tons, 2007)	9.7
Human Development Index (2011): ranking	18
Human Development Index (2011): value	0.886

For sources and definitions, see explanatory note on p. vi.

Agriculture

PRINCIPAL CROPS
('000 metric tons)

	2008	2009	2010
Wheat	1,850	1,910	1,850
Barley	329	453	373
Maize	859	808	746
Oats	31	35	25
Triticale (wheat-rye hybrid)	41	45	44
Potatoes	2,943	3,296	3,456
Sugar beet	4,714	5,186	4,465
Rapeseed	33	42	42
Cabbages and other brassicas	117	102	97*
Lettuce and chicory	76	69	64*
Spinach	81	87	84*
Tomatoes	226	232	263*
Cauliflowers and broccoli	93	88	86*
Leeks and other alliaceous vegetables	159	165	165*
Beans, green	102	123	117*
Peas, green	54	67	42*
Carrots and turnips	289	326	301*
Mushrooms and truffles*	40	42	41
Chicory roots	425	474	492*
Apples	335	311	269*
Pears	171	281	260*
Strawberries	37	33	33*

* FAO estimate(s).

Aggregate production ('000 metric tons, may include official, semi-official or estimated data): Total cereals 3,113 in 2008, 3,256 in 2009, 3,042 in 2010; Total roots and tubers 2,943 in 2008, 3,296 in 2009, 3,456 in 2010; Total vegetables (incl. melons) 1,859 in 2008, 1,962 in 2009, 1,966 in 2010; Total fruits (excl. melons) 551 in 2008, 635 in 2009, 572 in 2010.

Source: FAO.

LIVESTOCK
('000 head, year ending September)

	2008	2009	2010
Horses	33	37	37
Cattle	2,606	2,600	2,593
Pigs	6,282	6,321	6,430
Sheep	132	126	120
Goats	31	32	22
Chickens	32,493	33,240	34,375
Turkeys	190	205	210*

* FAO estimate.

Source: FAO.

LIVESTOCK PRODUCTS
('000 metric tons)

	2008	2009	2010
Cattle meat	267	255	263
Sheep meat*	3	2	3
Pig meat	1,056	1,082	1,124
Horse meat	2*	2*	2†
Chicken meat	450†	460	461†
Turkey meat†	5	5	5
Cows' milk	2,849	2,954	3,067
Hen eggs	194	200	189†

* Unofficial figure(s).
† FAO estimate(s).

Source: FAO.

Forestry

ROUNDWOOD REMOVALS
('000 cubic metres, excluding bark)

	2008	2009*	2010*
Sawlogs, veneer logs and logs for sleepers	2,520	2,320	2,601
Pulpwood	1,320	1,200	1,345
Other industrial wood	160	150	168
Fuel wood	700	725	713
Total	4,700	4,395	4,827

* Unofficial figures.

Source: FAO.

SAWNWOOD PRODUCTION
('000 cubic metres, including railway sleepers)

	2008	2009*	2010*
Coniferous (softwood)	1,200	1,075	1,142
Broadleaved (hardwood)	200	180	190
Total	1,400	1,255	1,332

* Unofficial figures.

Source: FAO.

Fishing

('000 metric tons, live weight)

	2007	2008	2009
Capture	24.5	22.6	21.7
European plaice	5.7	5.2	5.0
Lemon sole	0.9	0.9	0.7
Common sole	3.9	3.8	4.0
Atlantic cod	1.3	1.1	1.1
Monkfishes (Angler)	1.4	1.0	0.9
Rays	1.9	0.6	0.6
Aquaculture	0.1	0.1	0.6
Total catch	24.7	22.7	22.3

Source: FAO.

Mining

('000 metric tons, unless otherwise indicated)

	2007	2008	2009
Barite (Barytes)*	28	28	28
Lime and dead-burned dolomite, quicklime*	2,400	2,400	2,400
Clay, kaolin*	460	460	460
Copper (primary and secondary, refined)	394	396	395*
Distillate fuel oil ('000 barrels)	95,815	96,425	96,400*

* Estimated production.

Source: US Geological Survey.

Industry

SELECTED PRODUCTS

('000 metric tons unless otherwise indicated)

	2006	2007	2008
Wheat flour	1,195	1,195	1,185
Mechanical wood pulp*	163	163†	159‡
Newsprint*	265†	265†	299‡
Other paper and paperboard*	513	547	566
Jet fuels	1,744	1,751	1,878
Motor spirit (petrol)	5,357	5,041	4,338
Kerosene	42	32	31
Distillate fuel oils	12,660	12,737	12,959
Residual fuel oil	7,128	7,391	7,268
Petroleum bitumen (asphalt)	1,406	1,425	1,300
Liquefied petroleum gas (from refineries)	403	464	524
Coke-oven coke	2,895	2,607	2,309
Cement§	8,192	9,571	9,500†
Pig iron ('000 metric tons)§	7,516	6,576	7,125
Crude steel§	11,238	10,692	10,700†
Refined copper—unwrought§	383	394	396
Refined lead—unwrought§	62	63	81
Zinc—unwrought§	260	281	279†
Tin—unwrought (metric tons)§	7,600	8,400	9,200†
Electric energy (million kWh)	85,617	88,820	84,930

* Source: FAO.

† Estimate.

‡ Unofficial figure.

§ Source: US Geological Survey.

2009: Mechanical wood pulp ('000 metric tons, FAO estimate) 159; Newsprint ('000 metric tons, FAO estimate) 299; Other paper and paperboard ('000 metric tons) 540; Cement ('000 metric tons, estimate) 9,500; Pig iron ('000 metric tons) 3,087; Crude steel ('000 metric tons) 5,635; Refined copper—unwrought ('000 metric tons, estimate) 395; Refined lead—unwrought ('000 metric tons, estimate) 81; Zinc—unwrought ('000 metric tons, estimate) 279; Tin—unwrought (metric tons, estimate) 9,200.

2010: Mechanical wood pulp ('000 metric tons, unofficial figure) 1,084; Newsprint ('000 metric tons, unofficial figure) 259; Other paper and paperboard ('000 metric tons) 532.

Sources: UN Industrial Commodity Statistics Database and UN, *Industrial Commodity Statistics Yearbook*; FAO; US Geological Survey.

Finance

CURRENCY AND EXCHANGE RATES

Monetary Units
100 cent = 1 euro (€).

Sterling and Dollar Equivalents (30 December 2011)
£1 sterling = 1.195 euros;
US $1 = 0.773 euros;
€10 = £8.37 = $12.94.

Average Exchange Rate (euros per US $)
2009 0.7198
2010 0.7550
2011 0.7194

Note: The national currency was formerly the Belgian franc. From the introduction of the euro, with Belgian participation, on 1 January 1999, a fixed exchange rate of €1 = 40.3399 Belgian francs was in operation. Euro notes and coins were introduced on 1 January 2002. The euro and local currency circulated alongside each other until 28 February, after which the euro became the sole legal tender.

GENERAL GOVERNMENT BUDGET

(€ million)

Revenue	2008	2009	2010
Fiscal and parafiscal receipts	150,502	145,450	153,267
Direct taxes	56,842	51,577	55,098
Individuals	44,609	42,400	44,804
Companies	12,089	9,006	10,126
Indirect taxes	43,208	42,552	45,472
Actual social contributions	48,082	49,087	50,208
Taxes on capital	2,370	2,234	2,490
Non-fiscal and non-parafiscal receipts	17,721	17,864	19,510
Total	168,222	163,314	172,777

Expenditure	2008	2009	2010
Current expenditure excluding interest charges	149,957	159,158	165,250
Compensation of employees	41,640	43,256	44,512
Intermediate consumption and paid taxes	12,792	13,429	13,676
Subsidies to companies	7,235	7,466	8,875
Social benefits	80,495	86,334	89,090
Current transfers to the rest of the world	3,610	4,065	4,057
Other current transfers	4,185	4,608	5,041
Interest charges	13,257	12,565	12,307
Capital expenditure	9,504	11,506	10,058
Gross capital formation	5,510	5,756	5,840
Other capital expenditure	3,995	5,750	4,218
Total	172,718	183,229	187,616

INTERNATIONAL RESERVES

(US $ million at 31 December)

	2008	2009	2010
Gold (Eurosystem valuation)	6,327	8,076	10,315
IMF special drawing rights	570	6,907	6,789
Reserve position in IMF	982	1,199	1,831
Foreign exchange	7,767	7,801	7,880
Total	15,646	23,983	26,815

Source: IMF, *International Financial Statistics*.

MONEY SUPPLY
(incl. shares, depository corporations, national residency criteria, € million at 31 December)

	2008	2009	2010
Currency issued	26,047	27,059	28,229
Banque Nationale de Belgique	3,249	8,331	9,769
Demand deposits	86,859	101,227	102,658
Other deposits	260,136	256,984	278,502
Securities other than shares	72,068	94,865	75,260
Money market fund shares	4,475	1,546	1,524
Shares and other equity	62,330	63,487	66,546
Other items (net)	16,461	7,682	5,299
Total	528,373	552,851	558,018

Source: IMF, *International Financial Statistics*.

COST OF LIVING
(Consumer Price Index; base: 2000 = 100)

	2006	2007	2008
Food	115.0	119.1	126.1
Electricity, gas and other fuels	123.0	122.5	154.6
Clothing	106.5	105.2	106.3
Rent	114.9	116.9	119.2
All items (incl. others)	113.0	115.1	120.3

2009: Food 127.4; All items (incl. others) 120.2.

2010: Food 129.4; All items (incl. others) 122.8.

Source: ILO.

NATIONAL ACCOUNTS
(€ million at current prices)

National Income and Product

	2008	2009	2010
Compensation of employees	177,060.3	178,409.7	182,417.3
Gross operating surplus and mixed income	131,687.5	125,941.5	134,325.7
Taxes, less subsidies, on production and imports	37,382.3	36,046.4	37,634.5
GDP in market prices	346,130.1	340,397.6	354,377.5
Primary incomes (net)	4,966.5	−2,101.3	6,243.1
Gross national income (GNI)	351,096.6	338,296.3	360,620.6

Expenditure on the Gross Domestic Product

	2008	2009	2010
Private final consumption expenditure	185,683.6	176,192.9	187,450.3
Government final consumption expenditure	80,088.3	83,740.7	85,766.8
Gross fixed capital formation	71,698.6	74,676.2	71,614.1
Increase in stocks	5,696.5	−3,503.7	−25.7
Total domestic expenditure	343,167.0	331,106.1	344,805.5
Exports of goods and services	292,765.8	246,334.5	283,533.0
Less Imports of goods and services	289,802.7	237,043.0	273,961.0
GDP in market prices	346,130.1	340,397.6	354,377.5

Gross Domestic Product by Economic Activity

	2008	2009	2010
Agriculture, forestry and fishing	2,077.4	2,043.8	2,318.5
Mining and quarrying	339.2	311.3	307.5
Manufacturing	46,314.8	40,696.5	42,890.5
Electricity, gas and water supply	8,715.6	9,032.7	9,293.0
Construction	17,996.2	17,749.6	17,999.4
Wholesale and retail trade; repair of motor vehicles, motorcycles and personal and household goods	39,326.2	37,870.8	40,150.4
Hotels and restaurants	5,077.2	4,987.5	5,242.7
Transport, storage and communications	25,052.5	24,054.7	23,964.4
Financial intermediation	16,382.1	18,649.3	20,574.1
Real estate, renting and business activities	73,679.2	71,949.4	73,320.0
Public administration and defence; compulsory social security	22,384.6	23,134.8	23,685.6
Education	20,521.3	21,267.3	22,080.1
Health and social work	21,913.6	23,009.1	23,995.2
Other community, social and personal service activities	9,055.8	9,161.6	9,478.2
Private households with employed persons	518.6	522.1	524.1
Gross value added in basic prices	309,354.3	304,440.5	315,823.8
Taxes on products	39,223.3	37,921.8	40,730.0
Less Subsidies on products	2,447.5	1,964.7	2,176.3
GDP at market prices	346,130.1	340,397.6	354,377.5

BALANCE OF PAYMENTS
(US $ million)

	2008	2009	2010
Exports of goods f.o.b.	332,372	249,818	282,297
Imports of goods f.o.b.	−348,507	−256,429	−284,628
Trade balance	−16,135	−6,611	−2,331
Exports of services	87,952	83,903	86,001
Imports of services	−83,088	−73,944	−79,072
Balance on goods and services	−11,271	3,349	4,598
Other income received	107,751	70,555	61,651
Other income paid	−94,974	−63,883	−54,571
Balance on goods, services and income	1,507	10,021	11,678
Current transfers received	10,682	10,726	11,717
Current transfers paid	−20,221	−19,029	−18,914
Current balance	−8,032	1,718	4,481
Capital account (net)	−2,850	−1,805	244
Direct investment abroad	−160,878	16,740	−37,068
Direct investment from abroad	136,568	25,307	62,811
Portfolio investment assets	−295	18,624	7,879
Portfolio investment liabilities	48,102	21,625	−9,025
Financial derivatives (net)	5,747	728	1,772
Other investment assets	71,264	116,743	10,525
Other investment liabilities	−89,131	−194,912	−42,611
Net errors and omissions	−1,811	2,200	1,809
Overall balance	−1,316	6,968	819

Source: IMF, *International Financial Statistics*.

External Trade

PRINCIPAL COMMODITIES
(distribution by HS, € million)

Imports c.i.f.	2008	2009	2010
Prepared foodstuffs, tobacco and beverages, etc.	8,623.9	8,512.9	8,828.2
Mineral products	47,496.2	28,373.6	38,763.2
Mineral fuels, oils and products of their distillation	44,533.8	26,878.8	36,062.1
Chemicals and related products	28,396.9	25,366.8	27,623.7
Organic chemicals	10,792.2	7,631.4	9,809.2
Pharmaceutical products	6,713.1	8,606.6	7,885.7
Plastics and rubber and related materials	12,119.9	9,810.6	11,557.9
Plastics and related materials	9,236.1	7,581.3	8,758.3
Textiles and textile products	6,872.6	6,137.5	6,387.9
Natural or cultured pearls, precious or semi-precious stones	11,882.9	8,206.9	12,850.3
Base metals and related products	21,805.0	14,211.1	18,322.4
Iron and steel	9,834.2	5,403.4	7,558.4

Imports c.i.f.—*continued*	2008	2009	2010
Machinery and mechanical appliances and electrical equipment, etc.	33,392.9	27,222.0	29,515.8
Nuclear reactors, boilers, general industrial machinery, equipment and parts	21,338.1	16,397.9	17,762.6
Electrical machinery, apparatus, etc.	12,054.9	10,824.0	11,753.2
Transport equipment	28,212.1	22,823.5	24,619.3
Road vehicles (incl. air cushion vehicles) and parts	26,242.0	21,142.7	23,277.0
Total (incl. others)	234,770.9	182,877.3	213,302.5

Exports f.o.b.	2008	2009	2010
Live animals and animal products	5,631.8	5,287.4	5,708.3
Prepared foodstuffs, tobacco and beverages, etc.	10,673.9	10,613.5	11,259.6
Mineral products	26,919.1	16,939.9	23,255.0
Mineral fuels, oils and products of their distillation	25,709.2	15,878.1	22,115.0
Chemicals and related products	31,660.0	30,586.5	35,430.9
Organic chemicals	10,040.3	8,397.8	10,287.7
Pharmaceutical products	7,620.9	10,695.1	11,305.1
Plastics and rubber and related materials	19,762.6	16,052.3	19,987.8
Plastics and related materials	17,178.6	13,754.7	17,258.8
Textiles and textile articles	7,541.5	6,428.8	6,785.1
Natural or cultured pearls, precious or semi-precious stones	12,884.5	9,767.0	14,813.3
Base metals and related products	25,786.2	16,475.1	21,137.8
Iron and steel	15,159.1	8,977.0	11,668.3
Machinery and mechanical appliances and electrical equipment, etc.	27,137.2	20,376.7	22,936.4
Nuclear reactors, boilers, general industrial machinery, equipment and parts	17,455.4	12,697.9	14,558.4
Electrical machinery, apparatus, etc.	9,681.8	7,678.7	8,378.0
Transport equipment	27,415.1	20,314.8	21,845.3
Road vehicles (incl. air cushion vehicles) and parts	25,854.8	18,936.5	20,608.7
Total (incl. others)	223,739.3	177,583.2	209,413.4

PRINCIPAL TRADING PARTNERS
(€ million)*

Imports c.i.f.	2008	2009	2010
China, People's Republic	5,806.0	5,014.4	6,102.1
France†	28,294.5	24,183.4	26,588.9
Germany	37,860.9	30,747.0	34,479.6
India	2,668.8	1,992.9	2,860.8
Ireland	2,560.8	2,858.9	2,588.9
Italy	7,436.3	6,359.2	6,508.4
Japan	5,660.9	5,102.2	5,074.8
Netherlands	57,334.6	41,667.0	49,743.5
Norway	4,061.9	2,291.8	2,937.6
Poland	2,445.4	2,143.3	2,937.6
Russia	4,759.0	3,552.6	5,587.3
Spain	5,277.4	4,469.3	5,290.5
Sweden	5,195.6	3,169.3	4,065.7
United Kingdom	14,594.9	10,444.9	13,385.3
USA	9,955.0	8,017.7	8,611.0
Total (incl. others)	234,770.9	182,877.3	213,302.5

Exports f.o.b.	2008	2009	2010
Austria	2,309.6	1,976.9	2,149.0
China, People's Republic	2,788.4	3,382.2	4,248.0
France†	38,931.9	31,601.4	34,394.4
Germany	38,302.6	29,933.4	34,427.6
India	4,756.0	4,250.5	6,483.8
Israel	2,033.4	1,137.6	1,849.6
Italy	9,818.4	7,573.1	8,856.0
Japan	1,187.5	1,058.5	1,425.0
Luxembourg	5,479.6	4,126.5	4,912.0
Netherlands	30,339.9	24,573.4	27,618.5
Poland	3,958.6	3,103.4	3,733.4
Spain	7,064.9	5,488.0	5,872.6
Sweden	3,332.1	2,420.8	3,016.9
Switzerland	3,307.8	2,305.8	3,106.7
Turkey	2,388.2	1,983.7	2,850.7
United Kingdom	15,676.1	12,805.6	13,637.0
USA	8,567.8	7,588.8	9,562.6
Total (incl. others)	223,739.3	177,583.2	209,413.4

* Imports by country of production; exports by country of last consignment.
† Including trade with Overseas Departments (French Guiana, Guadeloupe, Martinique and Réunion).

Transport

RAILWAYS
(domestic and international traffic)

	2008	2009	2010
Passenger journeys (million)	216.7	219.8	224.0
Passenger-km (million)	10,403	10,427	10,564
Freight carried ('000 metric tons)	57,328	36,521	n.a.

Freight ton-km: (million): 7,293 in 2003; 7,691 in 2004; 8,130 in 2005.

ROAD TRAFFIC
(motor vehicles in use at 1 August)

	2009	2010	2011
Passenger cars	5,192,566	5,276,283	5,407,015
Buses and coaches	16,061	16,226	16,100
Lorries and vans	676,644	690,837	714,370
Road tractors	47,418	46,673	46,844
Motorcycles and mopeds	403,940	418,915	433,958

SHIPPING

Merchant Fleet
(registered at 31 December)

	2007	2008	2009
Number of vessels	243	243	246
Displacement ('000 grt)	4,091.3	4,241.8	4,301.0

Source: IHS Fairplay, *World Fleet Statistics*.

International Sea-borne Freight Traffic
('000 metric tons, estimates)

	2001	2002	2003
Goods loaded	422,700	439,900	419,400
Goods unloaded	436,900	447,100	427,000

Source: UN, *Monthly Bulletin of Statistics*.

CIVIL AVIATION
(traffic)

	2007	2008	2009
Kilometres flown (million)	163	154	144
Passengers carried ('000)	5,614	5,288	4,859
Passenger-km (million)	7,859	7,690	7,158
Total ton-km (million)	1,695	1,763	1,543

Source: UN, *Statistical Yearbook*.

Tourism

TOURIST ARRIVALS BY COUNTRY OF ORIGIN
('000 persons)*

Country of residence	2008	2009	2010
China, People's Rep.	75	75	80
France	1,080	1,096	1,154
Germany	775	770	815
Italy	236	237	258
Japan	101	80	81
Netherlands	1,839	1,839	1,934
Spain	298	296	342
United Kingdom	1,036	859	870
USA	275	264	293
Total (incl. others)	7,165	6,815	7,189

* Non-residents staying in accommodation establishments.

Tourism receipts (US $ million, excl. passenger transport): 11,762 in 2008; 9,970 in 2009; 10,287 in 2010 (provisional) (Source: World Tourism Organization).

Communications Media

	2008	2009	2010
Telephones ('000 main lines in use)	4,734.5	4,636.0	4,639.8
Mobile cellular telephones ('000 subscribers)	11,341.7	11,775.2	12,154.0
Internet subscribers ('000)	3,055.7	3,205.1	n.a.
Broadband subscribers ('000)	2,962.5	3,134.1	3,373.1

Personal computers: 3,954,000 (377.3 per 1,000 persons) in 2005.

Radio receivers ('000 in use): 8,000 in 1995; 8,050 in 1996; 8,075 in 1997.

Television receivers ('000 in use): 5,400 in 1999; 5,500 in 2000; 5,600 in 2001.

Daily newspapers: 29 in 2004 (circulation 1,706,000).

Sources: International Telecommunication Union, UN, *Statistical Yearbook*; UNESCO, *Statistical Yearbook*.

Education

(2010/11 unless otherwise indicated)

	Institutions		Students	
	French*	Flemish	French†	Flemish
Pre-primary	1,861‡	2,257	179,393	259,399
Primary	1,960‡	2,356	322,178	410,208
Secondary	645	1,071	365,894	444,307
Non-university higher education	329	22	84,875	123,629
University level	9	7	73,249	79,575

* 2004/05.
† 2008/09.
‡ Figure includes 1,640 joint pre-primary and primary institutions.

Teachers: *French (2004/05):* Pre-primary and primary 30,645; Secondary 36,038; Special education (pre-primary, primary and secondary) 6,450; Non-university higher education 10,055; University level 1,822. *Flemish (2010/11 unless otherwise indicated):* Pre-primary and primary 52,919; Secondary 61,929; Non-university higher education 7,812; University level 11,268 (2007/08).

Sources: Entreprise des Technologies Nouvelles de l'Information et de la Communication, *Short statistical overview of full-time and social promotion education*; Vlaams Ministerie van Onderwijs en Vorming, *Vlaams onderwijs in beeld*.

German-speaking communities (2010/11 unless otherwise indicated): Students 14,576 (pre-primary 2,322, primary 5,123, secondary 5,381, part-time 38, higher 183, special 302, training 1,227); teachers (at May 2009) 2,047 (Source: Ministerium der Deutschsprachigen Gemeinschaft, Eupen).

Pupil-teacher ratio (primary education, UNESCO estimate): 11.1 in 2008/09 (Source: UNESCO Institute for Statistics).

Directory

The Government

HEAD OF STATE

King of the Belgians: HM King ALBERT II (succeeded to the throne 9 August 1993).

THE COUNCIL OF MINISTERS
(April 2012)

A coalition of Parti Socialiste (PS), Christen-Democratisch en Vlaams (CD&V), Mouvement Réformateur (MR), Centre Démocrate Humaniste (CDH), Socialistische Partij Anders—Socialist Party (SP.A) and Open Vld.

Prime Minister: ELIO DI RUPO (PS).

Deputy Prime Minister and Minister of Finance and of Sustainable Development, in charge of Civil Service: STEVEN VANACKERE (CD&V).

Deputy Prime Minister and Minister of Foreign Affairs, Foreign Trade and European Affairs: DIDIER REYNDERS (MR).

Deputy Prime Minister and Minister of Economy, Consumer Affairs and the North Sea: JOHAN LANOTTE (SP.A).

Deputy Prime Minister and Minister of Pensions: VINCENT VAN QUICKENBORNE (Open Vld).

Deputy Prime Minister and Minister of the Interior and Equal Opportunities: JOËLLE MILQUET (CDH).

Deputy Prime Minister and Minister of Social Affairs and Health, in charge of Beliris and Federal Cultural Institutions: LAURETTE ONKELINX (PS).

Minister of Small and Medium-sized Enterprises, the Self-employed and Agriculture: SABINE LARUELLE (MR).

Minister of Defence: PIETER DE CREM (CD&V).

Minister of Public Enterprise, Science Policy and Development, in charge of Larger Towns: PAUL MAGNETTE (PS).

Minister of Justice: ANNEMIE TURTELBOOM (Open Vld).

Minister of the Budget and Administrative Simplification: OLIVIER CHASTEL (MR).

Minister of Employment: MONICA DE CONINCK (SP.A).

There are six Secretaries of State.

FEDERAL PUBLIC SERVICES AND MINISTRIES

Federal Public Service Chancellery of the Prime Minister: 16 rue de la Loi, 1000 Brussels; tel. (2) 501-02-11; fax (2) 217-33-28; e-mail info@premier.fed.be; internet www.premier.be.

Federal Public Service of the Budget and Management Control: 138/2 rue Royale, 1000 Brussels; tel. (2) 212-37-11; fax (2) 212-39-35; e-mail jean-pierre.meunier@budget.fed.be; internet www.budgetfederal.be.

Ministry of Defence: 8 rue Lambermont, 1000 Brussels; tel. (2) 550-28-11; fax (2) 550-29-19; e-mail cabinet@mod.mil.be; internet www.mil.be.

Federal Public Service of the Economy, Small and Medium-sized Enterprises, the Middle Classes and Energy: 50 rue de Progrès, 1210 Brussels; tel. (2) 277-51-11; fax (2) 277-51-07; e-mail info.eco@economie.fgov.be; internet www.economie.fgov.be.

Federal Public Service of Employment, Labour and Social Dialogue: 1 rue Ernest Blerot, 1070 Brussels; tel. (2) 233-41-11; fax (2) 233-44-88; e-mail information@employment.belgium.be; internet www.emploi.belgique.be.

Federal Public Service of Finance: 33 blvd du Roi Albert II, BP 70, 1030 Brussels; tel. (2) 572-57-57; e-mail info.tax@minfin.fed.be; internet www.minfin.fgov.be.

Federal Public Service of Foreign Affairs, Foreign Trade and Development Co-operation: 15 rue des Petits Carmes, 1000 Brussels; tel. (2) 501-81-11; fax (2) 501-81-70; e-mail contact@diplobel.fed.be; internet www.diplomatie.be.

Federal Public Service of Health, Food Chain Security and the Environment: Eurostation II, 40 place Victor Horta, BP 10, 1060 Brussels; tel. (2) 524-94-94; fax (2) 524-95-27; e-mail info@health.fgov.be; internet www.health.fgov.be.

Federal Public Service of Information and Communication Technology: 1/3 rue Marie-Thérèse, 1000 Brussels; tel. (2) 212-96-00; fax (2) 212-96-99; e-mail info@fedict.belgique.be; internet www.fedict.belgium.be.

Federal Public Service of the Interior: 1 rue de Louvain, 1000 Brussels; tel. (2) 500-21-11; fax (2) 500-20-39; e-mail info@ibz.fgov.be; internet www.ibz.be.

Federal Public Service of Justice: 115 blvd de Waterloo, 1000 Brussels; tel. (2) 542-65-11; fax (2) 542-70-39; e-mail info@just.fgov.be; internet www.just.fgov.be.

Federal Public Service of Mobility and Transport: 56 rue du Progrès, 1210 Brussels; tel. (2) 277-31-11; fax (2) 277-40-05; e-mail info@mobilit.fgov.be; internet www.mobilit.fgov.be.

Federal Public Service of Personnel and Organization: 51 rue de la Loi, 1040 Brussels; tel. (2) 790-58-00; fax (2) 790-58-99; e-mail info@p-o.belgium.be; internet www.fedweb.belgium.be.

Federal Public Service of Social Security: Eurostation II, 40 place Victor Horta, BP 20, 1060 Brussels; tel. (2) 528-60-11; fax (2) 528-69-53; e-mail social.security@minsoc.fed.be; internet socialsecurity.fgov.be.

Legislature

Chambre des Représentants/Kamer van Volksvertegenwoordigers (Chamber of Representatives)

Palais de la Nation, 1008 Brussels; tel. (2) 549-81-11; e-mail pri@lachambre.be; internet www.lachambre.be.

President: André Flahaut (PS).

General Election, 13 June 2010

Party	Votes cast	% of votes	Seats
N-VA	1,135,617	17.40	27
PS	894,543	13.70	26
MR	605,617	9.28	18
CD&V	707,986	10.85	17
SP.A	602,867	9.24	13
Open Vld	563,873	8.64	13
Vlaams Belang	506,697	7.76	12
CDH	360,441	5.52	9
Ecolo	313,047	4.80	8
Groen!	285,989	4.38	5
Lijst Dedecker	150,577	2.31	1
Parti Populaire	84,005	1.29	1
Total (incl. others)	6,527,367	100.00	150

Sénat/Senaat (Senate)

Palais de la Nation, 1009 Brussels; tel. (2) 501-70-70; internet www.senate.be.

President: Sabine De Bethune (CD&V).

General Election, 13 June 2010

Party	Votes cast	% of votes	Seats
N-VA	1,268,780	19.61	9
PS	880,828	13.62	7
CD&V	646,375	9.99	4
SP.A	613,079	9.48	4
MR	599,618	9.27	4
Open Vld	533,124	8.24	4
Vlaams Belang	491,547	7.60	3
Ecolo	353,111	5.46	2
CDH	331,870	5.13	2
Groen!	251,546	3.89	1
Total (incl. others)	6,469,103	100.00	40

In addition, the Senate has 21 members appointed by and from within the legislative bodies of the three language communities and 10 members co-opted by the elected and appointed members. Children of the monarch are entitled to honorary membership of the Senate from 18 years of age and acquire voting rights at the age of 21, although they do not exercise their voting rights in practice.

Advisory Councils

Conseil Central de l'Economie/Centrale Raad voor het Bedrijfsleven: 17–21 ave de la Joyeuse entrée, 1040 Brussels; tel. (2) 233-88-11; fax (2) 233-89-12; e-mail luden@ccecrb.fgov.be; internet www.ccecrb.fgov.be; f. 1948; representative and consultative body; advises the authorities on economic issues; 54 mems; Pres. Baron Robert Tollet.

Conseil d'Etat/Raad van State: 33 rue de la Science, 1040 Brussels; tel. (2) 234-96-11; e-mail info@raadvst-consetat.be; internet www.raadvst-consetat.be; f. 1946; advisory body on legislative and regulatory matters; supreme administrative court; hears complaints against the actions of the legislature; 44 mems; First Pres. Robert Andersen.

Regional and Community Administrations

Belgium is a federal state, and considerable power has been devolved to the regional administrations for Brussels, Wallonia and Flanders, and to the Flemish, French and German-speaking Communities. The regional authorities have sole responsibility for the environment, housing, transport and public works and for certain aspects of social welfare, while the community administrations are primarily responsible for cultural affairs and education. In addition, in June 2001 Parliament granted the regions greater responsibility for taxation and public expenditure, agriculture and matters relating to foreign aid and trade. The Flemish Region and the Flemish Community share a combined administration.

FLEMISH REGION AND COMMUNITY

Minister-President: Kris Peeters (CD&V).

Vlaamse Regering (Flemish Government): Boudewijnlaan 30, 1000 Brussels; tel. (2) 553-29-11; fax (2) 553-29-05; e-mail voorlichtingsambtenaar@vlaanderen.be; internet www.vlaamseregering.be; 10 mems.

Vlaams Parlement (Flemish Parliament): Leuvensweg 86, 1011 Brussels; tel. (2) 552-11-11; fax (2) 552-11-22; e-mail algemeen@vlaamsparlement.be; internet www.vlaamsparlement.be/pi; f. 1972

President of the Parliament: Jan Peumans (N-VA).

Election, 7 June 2009

Party	Seats
CD&V	31
Vlaams Belang	21
Open Vld	21
SP.A	19
N-VA	16
Lijst Dedecker	8
Groen!	7
Union des Francophones	1
Total	124

WALLOON REGION

Minister-President: Rudy Demotte (PS).

Gouvernement Wallon (Walloon Government): 1 place de la Wallonie, Bât 2, 5100 Namur; tel. (81) 33-31-60; fax (81) 33-31-66; e-mail vancau@gov.wallonie.be; internet gov.wallonie.be; 9 mems.

Parlement Wallon (Walloon Parliament): 24 rue Saint-Nicolas, 5000 Namur; tel. (81) 23-10-36; fax (81) 23-12-20; e-mail presse@parlement-wallon.be; internet www.parlement-wallon.be; elects Walloon Govt.

President of the Parliament: Emily Hoyos (Ecolo).

Election, 7 June 2009

Party	Seats
PS	29
MR	19
Ecolo	14
CDH	13
Total	75

BRUSSELS-CAPITAL REGION

Minister-President: Charles Picqué (PS).

Gouvernement de la Région de Bruxelles-Capitale/Brussels Hoofdstedelijke Regering (Government of Brussels-Capital): 7–9 rue Ducale, 1000 Brussels; tel. (2) 506-32-11; fax (2) 514-40-22; internet www.bruxelles.irisnet.be; 8 mems.

Parlement de la Région de Bruxelles-Capitale/Brussels Hoofdstedelijk Parlement (Parliament of the Region of Brussels-Capital): 22 rue du Chêne, 1005 Brussels; tel. (2) 549-62-11; fax (2) 549-62-12; e-mail greffe@parlbru.irisnet.be; internet www.parlbru.irisnet.be.

President of the Parliament: FRANÇOISE DUPUIS (PS).

Election, 7 June 2009

Party	Seats
French-speaking group	
MR	24
PS	21
Ecolo	16
CDH	11
N-VA	1
Dutch-speaking group	
SP.A	4
Open Vld	4
Vlaams Belang	3
CD&V	3
Groen!	2
Total (incl. both groups)	89

FRENCH COMMUNITY

Minister-President: RUDY DEMOTTE (PS).

Gouvernement de la Communauté française Wallonie-Bruxelles (Government of the French Community): 15–17 pl. Surlet de Chokier, 1000 Brussels; tel. (2) 227-32-11; fax (2) 227-33-53; internet www.gouvernement-francophone.be; 7 mems.

Parlement de la Communauté française de Belgique (Parliament of the French Community): 6 rue de la Loi, 1000 Brussels; tel. (2) 506-38-11; fax (2) 506-38-08; e-mail cellule-internet@pcf.be; internet www.pcf.be; 94 mems, comprising the 75 mems of the Walloon Parliament and 19 French-speaking mems of the Council of the Region of Brussels-Capital.

President of the Parliament: JEAN-CHARLES LUPERTO (PS).

GERMAN-SPEAKING COMMUNITY

Minister-President: KARL-HEINZ LAMBERTZ (SP).

Regierung der Deutschsprachigen Gemeinschaft Belgiens (Government of the German-speaking Community): Klötzerbahn 32, 4700 Eupen; tel. (87) 59-64-00; fax (87) 74-02-58; e-mail regierung@dgov.be; internet www.dglive.be; 4 mems.

Parlament der Deutschsprachigen Gemeinschaft in Belgien (Parliament of the German-speaking Community): Kaperberg 8, 4700 Eupen; tel. (87) 59-07-20; fax (87) 59-07-30; e-mail stephan.thomas@dgparlament.be; internet www.dgparlament.be.

President of the Parliament: FERDEL SCHRÖDER (PFF).

Election, 7 June 2009

Party	Seats
CSP	7
SP	5
PFF	4
ProDG	4
Ecolo	3
Vivant	2
Total	25

Election Commission

Direction des Elections/Directie van de Verkiezingen: Parc Atrium, 11 rue des Colonies, 1000 Brussels; tel. (2) 518-21-81; fax (2) 518-21-19; e-mail marina.devos@rrn.ibz.fgov.be; internet www.ibz.rrn.fgov.be; part of the General Directorate of Institutions and Population, a department of the Federal Public Service of the Interior; Dir-Gen. LUC VANNESTE.

Political Organizations

DUTCH-SPEAKING PARTIES

Christen-Democratisch en Vlaams (CD&V) (Christian Democratic and Flemish): Wetstraat 89, 1040 Brussels; tel. (2) 238-38-11; fax (2) 238-38-11; e-mail info@cdenv.be; internet www.cdenv.be; f. 1945 as Parti Social Chrétien/Christelijke Volkspartij (PSC/CVP); CVP separated from PSC by 1972 and adopted current name in 2001; Chair. WOUTER BEKE.

Groen! (Green!): Sergeant De Bruynestraat 78–82, 1070 Anderlecht; tel. (2) 219-19-19; fax (2) 223-10-90; e-mail info@groen.be; internet www.groen.be; f. 1982 as Anders Gaan Leven (Agalev); adopted current name in 2003; absorbed the Sociaal-Liberaal Partij in 2009; ecologist; Chair. WOUTER VAN BESIEN; Vice-Chair. BJÖRN RZOSKA.

Lijst Dedecker: Bellevue 5, 9050 Ghent; tel. (9) 210-03-80; fax (9) 210-03-89; e-mail info@lijstdedecker.com; internet www.lijstdedecker.com; f. 2007; advocates economic liberalism and greater independence for Flanders; Leader JEAN-MARIE DEDECKER.

Nieuw-Vlaamse Alliantie (N-VA) (New-Flemish Alliance): Koningsstraat 47, Postbus 6, 1000 Brussels; tel. (2) 219-49-30; fax (2) 217-35-10; e-mail info@n-va.be; internet www.n-va.be; f. 2001 following disintegration of the Volksunie (VU, f. 1954); Flemish nationalist party advocating an independent Flemish state within a federal Europe; Chair. BART DE WEVER; 11,000 mems.

Open Vld: Melsensstraat 34, 1000 Brussels; tel. (2) 549-00-20; fax (2) 512-60-25; e-mail contact@openvld.be; internet www.openvld.be; f. 1846 as Liberale Partij; name changed to Vlaamse Liberalen en Demokraten (VLD—Flemish Liberals and Democrats) in 1992; adopted the name Open Vld in 2007 to contest the general election in alliance with 2 minor parties, Liberaal Appèl Plus and Vivant; Pres. ALEXANDER DE CROO; c. 70,000 mems.

SP.A (Socialistische Partij Anders—Socialist Party): Grasmarkt 105/37, 1000 Brussels; tel. (2) 552-02-00; fax (2) 552-02-55; e-mail info@s-p-a.be; internet www.s-p-a.be; f. 1885; fmrly Socialistische Partij; adopted current name in 2001; Chair. BRUNO TOBBACK; Sec. ALAIN ANDRÉ.

Vlaams Belang (Flemish Interest): Madouplein 8, Postbus 9, 1210 Brussels; tel. (2) 219-60-09; fax (2) 219-50-47; e-mail info@vlaamsbelang.org; internet www.vlaamsbelang.org; f. 2004 as the successor to the Vlaams Blok (f. 1979), which had been forced to disband; advocates Flemish separatism and is anti-immigration; Chair. BRUNO VALKENIERS.

FRENCH-SPEAKING PARTIES

Centre Démocrate Humaniste (CDH) (Humanist Democrats): 41 rue des Deux-Eglises, 1000 Brussels; tel. (2) 238-01-11; fax (2) 238-01-29; e-mail info@lecdh.be; internet www.lecdh.be; f. 1945 as Parti Social Chrétien/Christelijke Volkspartij (PSC/CVP); PSC separated from CVP by 1972 and adopted current name in 2002; Pres. BENOÎT LUTGEN.

Ecolo (Ecologistes Confédérés pour l'Organisation des Luttes Originales): 52 ave de Marlagne, 5000 Namur; tel. (81) 22-78-71; fax (81) 23-06-03; e-mail info.sf@ecolo.be; internet www.ecolo.be; ecologist; Co-Pres EMILY HOYOS, OLIVIER DELEUZE.

Fédéralistes Démocrates Francophones (FDF) (Francophone Federalist Democrats): 127 chaussée de Charleroi, 1060 Brussels; tel. (2) 538-83-20; fax (2) 539-36-50; e-mail fdf@fdf.be; internet www.fdf.be; f. 1964 as Front Démocratique des Francophones; adopted current name in Jan. 2010; aims to preserve the French character of Brussels; Pres. OLIVIER MAINGAIN.

Front National (FN): 6 Drève des Tumuli, BP 2, 1170 Watermael-Boitsfort; tel. (2) 503-06-91; fax (2) 503-16-92; e-mail secretariat@fn.be; f. 1985; extreme right-wing nationalist party; Pres. DANIEL HUYGENS.

Mouvement Réformateur (MR) (Reformist Movement): 84–86 ave de la Toison d'Or, 1060 Brussels; tel. (2) 500-35-11; fax (2) 500-35-00; e-mail mr@mr.be; internet www.mr.be; f. 2002; Pres. CHARLES MICHEL; 5,900 mems.

Association of the following parties:

Mouvement des Citoyens pour le Changement (MCC): 50 rue de la Vallée, 1000 Brussels; tel. (2) 642-29-99; fax (2) 642-29-90; e-mail info@lemcc.be; internet www.lemcc.be; Pres. GÉRARD DEPREZ.

Parti Réformateur Libéral (PRL) (Reformist Liberal Party): 84–86 ave de la Toison d'Or, 1060 Brussels; tel. (2) 500-35-11; fax (2) 500-35-00.

Parti Socialiste (PS) (Socialist Party): Maison du PS, 13 blvd de l'Empereur, 1000 Brussels; tel. (2) 548-32-11; fax (2) 548-33-80; e-mail secretariat@ps.be; internet www.ps.be; f. 1885 as the Parti Ouvrier Belge; split from the Socialistische Partij in 1978; Pres. THIERRY GIET (acting); Sec.-Gen. GILLES MAHIEU.

GERMAN-SPEAKING PARTIES

Christlich Soziale Partei (CSP) (Christian Social Party): Kaperberg 6, 4700 Eupen; tel. (87) 55-59-86; fax (87) 55-59-82; e-mail csp-fraktion@dgparlament.be; internet www.csp-dg.be; Pres. MATHIEU GROSCH.

Partei für Freiheit und Fortschritt (PFF): Kaperberg 6, 4700 Eupen; tel. (87) 55-59-88; fax (87) 55-59-83; e-mail info@pff.be; internet www.pff.be; German-speaking wing of the Parti Réformateur Libéral (see French-speaking Parties); Pres. KATTRIN JADIN.

ProDG (Pro Deutsche Gemeinschaft) (Pro German-speaking Community): Kaperberg 6, 4700 Eupen; tel. (87) 55-59-87; fax (87) 55-59-84; e-mail info@prodg.be; internet www.prodg.be; f. 2008; comprises fmr members of Partei der Deutschsprachigen Belgier (PJU-PDB, f. 1971); promotes equality for the German-speaking minority; Chair. GUIDO BREUER; Parliamentary Leader GERHARD PALM.

Sozialistische Partei (SP): Klötzerbahn 8, 4700 Eupen; tel. (87) 55-77-43; e-mail info@buergerbuero.be; internet www.sp-dg.be; German-speaking section of the Parti Socialiste (see French-speaking Parties); Pres. ANTONIOS ANTONIADIS; Sec. BERNI SCHMITZ.

OTHER PARTIES

Partij van de Arbeid van België/Parti du Travail de Belgique (PvdA/PTB) (Workers' Party of Belgium): 171 blvd M. Lemonnier, BP 2, 1000 Brussels; tel. (2) 504-01-10; fax (2) 513-98-31; e-mail wpb@wpb.be; internet www.ptb.be; f. 1979; Marxist; publ. *Solidaire/Solidair* (weekly); Pres. PETER MERTENS.

Parti Populaire/Personenpartij (People's Party): 42 ave du Houx, 1170 Brussels; tel. (2) 830-30-14; fax (2) 830-30-15; e-mail info@partipopulaire.be; internet www.partipopulaire.be; f. 2009; advocates economic liberalism, administrative simplification and greater emphasis on justice and security; Pres. MISCHAËL MODRIKAMEN.

Vivant (Voor Individuele Vrijheid en Arbeid in een Nieuwe Toekomst): Zuidlaan 25-27, 1000 Brussels; tel. (2) 160-06-65-2; fax (2) 502-01-07; e-mail info@vivant.org; internet www.vivant.org; liberal; contested the 2007 legislative elections as part of Open Vld alliance; Chair. ROLAND DUCHÂTELET.

Diplomatic Representation

EMBASSIES IN BELGIUM

Afghanistan: 61 ave de Wolvendael, 1180 Uccle; tel. (2) 761-31-66; fax (2) 761-31-67; e-mail ambassade.afghanistan@skynet.be; Ambassador HUMAYUN TANDAR.

Albania: 30 rue Tenbosch, 1000 Brussels; tel. (2) 640-14-22; fax (2) 640-28-58; e-mail amb.brx@skynet.be; Ambassador ILIR TEPELENA.

Algeria: 207 ave Molière, 1050 Brussels; tel. (2) 343-50-78; fax (2) 343-51-68; e-mail info@algerian-embassy.be; internet www.algerian-embassy.be; Ambassador AMAR BENDJAMA.

Andorra: 10 rue de la Montagne, 1000 Brussels; tel. (2) 513-28-06; fax (2) 513-07-41; Ambassador EVA DESCARREGA GARCIA.

Angola: 182 rue Franz Merjay, 1050 Brussels; tel. (2) 346-87-48; fax (2) 344-08-94; e-mail angola.embassy.belgium@skynet.be; Ambassador MARIA ELIZABETH A. SIMBRÃO DE CARVALHO.

Argentina: 225 ave Louise, 3e étage, 1050 Brussels; tel. (2) 647-78-12; fax (2) 647-93-19; e-mail ebelg@mrecic.gov.ar; Ambassador JOSÉ MARIA VASQUEZ OCAMPO.

Armenia: 28 rue Montoyer, 1000 Brussels; tel. (2) 348-44-00; fax (2) 348-44-01; e-mail armembel@skynet.be; internet www.armembassy.be; Ambassador AVET ADONTS.

Australia: 6–8 rue Guimard, 1040 Brussels; tel. (2) 286-05-00; fax (2) 230-07-88; e-mail austemb.brussels@dfat.gov.au; internet www.eu.mission.gov.au; Ambassador Dr BRENDAN NELSON.

Austria: 5 place du Champ de Mars, BP 5, 1050 Brussels; tel. (2) 289-07-00; fax (2) 513-66-41; e-mail bruessel-ob@bmeia.gv.at; internet www.bmeia.gv.at/botschaft/bruessel; Ambassador KARL SCHRAMEK.

Azerbaijan: 464 ave Molière, 1050 Brussels; tel. (2) 345-26-60; fax (2) 345-91-58; e-mail office@azembassy.be; internet www.azembassy.be; Ambassador EMIN EYYUBOV.

Bahrain: 250 ave Louise, 1050 Brussels; tel. (2) 627-00-32; fax (2) 647-22-74; e-mail brussels.mission@mofa.gov.bh; Ambassador AHMED MUHAMMAD YOUSUF AL-DOSERI.

Bangladesh: 29–31 rue Jacques Jordaens, 1000 Brussels; tel. (2) 640-55-00; fax (2) 646-59-98; e-mail bdootbrussels@skynet.be; internet www.bangladeshembassy.be; Ambassador ISMAT JAHAN.

Barbados: 100 ave F. D. Roosevelt, 1050 Brussels; tel. (2) 732-17-37; fax (2) 732-32-66; e-mail brussels@foreign.gov.bb; Ambassador SAMUEL JEFFERSON CHANDLER.

Belarus: 192 ave Molière, 1050 Brussels; tel. (2) 340-02-70; fax (2) 340-02-87; e-mail embbel@skynet.be; internet www.belembassy.org/belgium; Ambassador ANDREI YEUDACHENKA.

Belize: 136 blvd Brand Witlock, 1200 Brussels; tel. (2) 732-62-04; fax (2) 732-62-46; e-mail embelize@skynet.be; Ambassador AUDREY ANN JOY GRANT.

Benin: 5 ave de l'Observatoire, 1180 Brussels; tel. (2) 374-91-92; fax (2) 375-83-26; e-mail ambabenin_benelux@yahoo.fr; Ambassador CHARLES BORROMÉE TODJINOU.

Bhutan: 70 ave Jules César, 1150 Brussels; tel. (2) 761-95-70; fax (2) 761-95-77; Ambassador SONAM TSHONG.

Bolivia: 176 ave Louise, 1050 Brussels; tel. (2) 627-00-10; fax (2) 647-47-82; e-mail embajada.bolivia@embolbrus.be; Ambassador RENÉ ERNESTO FERNANDEZ REVOLLO.

Bosnia and Herzegovina: 15–17 rue Belliard, 1040 Brussels; tel. (2) 502-01-88; fax (2) 644-32-54; e-mail info@bhembassy.be; Ambassador BRANIMIR JUKIĆ.

Botswana: 169 ave de Tervueren, 1150 Brussels; tel. (2) 735-20-70; fax (2) 735-63-18; e-mail botswana@brutele.be; Ambassador SAMUEL OTSILE OUTLULE.

Brazil: 350 ave Louise, 6e étage, 1050 Brussels; tel. (2) 640-20-15; fax (2) 640-81-34; e-mail brasbruxelas@beon.be; internet www.brasbruxelas.be; Ambassador ANDRÉ MATTOSO MAIA AMADO.

Brunei: 238 ave F. D. Roosevelt, 1050 Brussels; tel. (2) 675-08-78; fax (2) 672-93-58; e-mail kedutaan-brunei.brussels@skynet.be; Ambassador Dato' Paduka SERBINI bin Haji ALI.

Bulgaria: 58 ave Hamoir, 1180 Brussels; tel. (2) 374-59-63; fax (2) 375-84-94; e-mail embassy@bulgaria.be; internet www.bulgaria.be; Ambassador HRISTO GEORGIEV.

Burkina Faso: 16 place Guy d'Arezzo, 1180 Brussels; tel. (2) 345-99-12; fax (2) 345-06-12; e-mail ambassade.burkina@skynet.be; internet www.ambassadeduburkina.be; Ambassador KADRÉ DÉSIRÉ OUEDRAOGO.

Burundi: 46 square Marie-Louise, 1000 Brussels; tel. (2) 230-45-35; fax (2) 230-78-83; e-mail ambassade.burundi@skynet.be; internet www.ambassade-burundi.be; Ambassador BALTHAZAR BIGIRIMANA.

Cambodia: 264A ave de Tervueren, 1150 Brussels; tel. (2) 772-03-72; fax (2) 772-89-99; e-mail amcambel@skynet.be; Ambassador HEM SAEM.

Cameroon: 131 ave Brugmann, 1190 Brussels; tel. (2) 345-18-70; fax (2) 344-57-35; e-mail embassy@cameroon.be; internet www.cameroon.be; Ambassador DANIEL EVINA ABÉE.

Canada: 2 ave de Tervueren, 1040 Brussels; tel. (2) 741-06-11; fax (2) 741-06-43; e-mail bru@international.gc.ca; internet www.ambassade-canada.be; Ambassador LOUIS DE LORIMIER.

Cape Verde: 29 ave Jeanne, 1050 Brussels; tel. (2) 643-62-70; fax (2) 646-33-85; e-mail emb.caboverde@skynet.be; Ambassador MARIA DE JESUS VEIGA MIRANDA MASCARENHAS.

Central African Republic: 416 blvd Lambermont, 1030 Brussels; tel. (2) 242-28-80; fax (2) 705-56-02; e-mail ambassade.rca.be@hotmail.com; Chargé d'affaires a.i. ABEL SABONO.

Chad: 52 blvd Lambermont, 1030 Brussels; tel. (2) 215-19-75; fax (2) 216-35-26; e-mail ambassade.tchad@chello.be; Ambassador AHMAT AWAD SAKINE.

Chile: 106 rue des Aduatiques, 1040 Brussels; tel. (2) 743-36-60; fax (2) 736-49-94; e-mail embachile@embachile.be; internet www.embachile.be; Ambassador CARLOS APPELGREN BALBONTÍN.

China, People's Republic: 443–445 ave de Tervueren, 1150 Brussels; tel. (2) 771-14-97; fax (2) 779-28-95; e-mail chinaemb_be@mfa.gov.cn; internet www.chinaembassy-org.be; Ambassador LIAO LIQIANG.

Colombia: 96A ave F. D. Roosevelt, 1050 Brussels; tel. (2) 649-56-79; fax (2) 646-54-91; e-mail embcolombia@emcolbru.org; internet www.emcolbru.org; Ambassador JOSÉ RODRIGO RIVERA SALAZAR.

Comoros: 63 rue Berthelot, 1190 Brussels; tel. and fax (2) 779-58-38; e-mail ambacom.bxl@skynet.be; Ambassador SULTAN CHOUZOUR.

Congo, Democratic Republic: 30 rue Marie de Bourgogne, 1000 Brussels; tel. (2) 213-49-81; fax (2) 213-49-95; e-mail secretariat@ambardc.be; internet www.ambardc.be; Ambassador HENRI MOVA SAKANYI.

Congo, Republic: 16–18 ave F. D. Roosevelt, 1050 Brussels; tel. (2) 648-38-56; fax (2) 646-22-20; e-mail contact@ambacobrazza.eu; internet www.ambacobrazza.eu; Ambassador ROGER JULIEN MENGA.

Costa Rica: 489 ave Louise, 1050 Brussels; tel. (2) 640-55-41; fax (2) 648-31-92; e-mail info@costaricaembassy.be; internet www.costaricaembassy.be; Ambassador FRANCISCO TOMÁS DUEÑAS LEIVA.

Côte d'Ivoire: 234 ave F. D. Roosevelt, 1050 Brussels; tel. (2) 672-23-57; fax (2) 672-04-91; e-mail mailbox@ambcibnl.be; internet www.ambacibnl.be; Ambassador JEAN VINCENT ZINSOU.

Croatia: 425 ave Louise, 1050 Brussels; tel. (2) 639-20-36; fax (2) 512-03-38; e-mail croemb.bruxelles@mvp.hr; internet be.mvp.hr; Ambassador BORIS GRIGIĆ.

Cuba: 80 ave Brugmann, 1190 Brussels; tel. (2) 343-00-20; fax (2) 344-96-91; e-mail mision@embacuba.be; internet www.embacuba.be; Ambassador MIRTHA MARÍA HORMILLA CASTRO.

Cyprus: 61 ave de Cortenbergh, 1000 Brussels; tel. (2) 650-06-10; fax (2) 650-06-20; e-mail ambassade.cyprus@skynet.be; internet www.mfa.gov.cy/embassybrussels; Ambassador ATHENA MAVRONICOLA-DROUSHIOTIS.

Czech Republic: Czech House, 60 rue du Trône, 7e étage, 1050 Brussels; tel. (2) 213-94-01; fax (2) 213-94-02; e-mail brussels@embassy.mzv.cz; internet www.mzv.cz/brussels; Ambassador IVO SRAMEK.

Denmark: 73 rue d'Arlon, 1040 Brussels; tel. (2) 233-09-00; fax (2) 233-09-32; e-mail bruamb@um.dk; internet www.ambbruxelles.um.dk; Ambassador POUL SKYTT CHRISTOFFERSEN.

Djibouti: 204 ave F. D. Roosevelt, 1050 Brussels; tel. (2) 347-69-67; fax (2) 347-69-63; e-mail amb_djib@yahoo.fr; Ambassador BADRI ALI BOGOREH.

Dominican Republic: 130A ave Louise, 3e étage, 1050 Brussels; tel. (2) 346-49-35; fax (2) 346-51-52; e-mail embajadombxl@gmail.com; Ambassador ALEJANDRO GONZÁLEZ PONS.

Eastern Caribbean States (Dominica, Saint Christopher and Nevis, Saint Lucia, Saint Vincent and the Grenadines): 42 rue de Livourne, 1000 Brussels; tel. (2) 534-26-11; fax (2) 539-40-09; e-mail ecs.embassies@skynet.be; Ambassador SHIRLEY SKERRITT-ANDREW.

Ecuador: 363 ave Louise, 9e étage, 1050 Brussels; tel. (2) 644-32-58; fax (2) 644-28-13; e-mail amb.equateur@skynet.be; internet www.ecuador.be; Ambassador FERNANDO YÉPEZ LASSO.

Egypt: 19 ave de l'Uruguay, 1000 Brussels; tel. (2) 663-58-00; fax (2) 675-58-88; e-mail eg.sec.be@hotmail.com; Ambassador FATMA AL-ZAHRA ETMAN.

El Salvador: 171 ave de Tervueren, 1150 Brussels; tel. (2) 733-04-85; fax (2) 735-02-11; e-mail embajadabruselas@rree.gob.sv; Ambassador EDGAR HERNAN VARELA ALAS.

Equatorial Guinea: 6 place Guy Arezzo, 1180 Brussels; tel. (2) 346-25-09; fax (2) 346-33-09; Ambassador CARMELO NVONO NCA.

Eritrea: 15–17 ave Wolvendael, 1180 Brussels; tel. (2) 374-44-34; fax (2) 372-07-30; Ambassador MOHAMMED SULIEMAN AHMED.

Estonia: 11–13, rue Guimard, 1040 Brussels; tel. (2) 779-07-55; fax (2) 779-28-17; e-mail embassy.brussels@mfa.ee; internet www.estemb.be; Ambassador (vacant).

Ethiopia: 231 ave de Tervueren, 1150 Brussels; tel. (2) 771-32-94; fax (2) 771-49-14; e-mail etebru@brutele.be; Ambassador KASSU YILALA ASHAME.

Fiji: 92–94 square Eugène Plasky, 5e étage, 1030 Brussels; tel. (2) 736-90-50; fax (2) 736-14-58; e-mail info@fijiembassy.be; internet www.fijiembassy.be; Ambassador PECELI VUNIWAQA VOCEA.

Finland: 58 ave des Arts, 5e étage, 1000 Brussels; tel. (2) 287-12-12; fax (2) 287-12-00; e-mail sanomat.bry@formin.fi; internet www.finlande.be; Ambassador PER-MIKAEL ENGBERG.

France: 65 rue Ducale, 1000 Brussels; tel. (2) 548-87-11; fax (2) 548-87-32; e-mail ambafr@ambafrance-be.org; internet www.ambafrance-be.org; Ambassador MICHÈLE BOCCOZ.

Gabon: 112 ave Winston Churchill, 1180 Brussels; tel. (2) 340-62-10; fax (2) 346-46-69; e-mail ambassadedugabon@brutele.be; Ambassador FÉLICITÉ ONGOUORI NGOUBILI.

Gambia: 126 ave F. D. Roosevelt, 1050 Brussels; tel. (2) 640-10-49; fax (2) 646-32-77; e-mail info@gambiaembassy.be; internet www.gambiaembassy.be; Ambassador MAMOUR A. JAGNE.

Georgia: 62 ave de Tervueren, 1040 Brussels; tel. (2) 761-11-90; fax (2) 761-11-99; e-mail info@georgia-embassy.be; internet www.belgium.mfa.gov.ge; Ambassador SALOME SAMADASHVILI.

Germany: 8–14 rue Jacques de Lalaing, 1040 Brussels; tel. (2) 787-18-00; fax (2) 787-28-00; e-mail info@bruessel.diplo.de; internet www.bruessel.diplo.de; Ambassador Dr ECKART CUNTZ.

Ghana: 7 blvd Général Wahis, 1030 Brussels; tel. (2) 705-82-20; fax (2) 705-66-53; e-mail ghanaemb@chello.be; internet www.ghanaembassy.be; Ambassador KONADU YIADOM.

Greece: 10 rue des Petits Carmes, 1000 Brussels; tel. (2) 545-55-00; fax (2) 545-55-85; e-mail ambagre@skynet.be; Ambassador PLATON ALEXIS HADZIMICHALIS.

Grenada: 24 ave de la Toison d'Or, 1050 Brussels; tel. (2) 223-73-03; fax (2) 223-73-09; e-mail office@embassyofgrenadabxl.net; Ambassador STEPHEN FLETCHER.

Guatemala: 185 ave Winston Churchill, 1180 Brussels; tel. (2) 345-90-58; fax (2) 344-64-99; e-mail guatemala@skynet.be; Chargé d'affaires a.i. CARLOS JOSE ESCOBEDO MENENDEZ.

Guinea: 108 blvd Auguste Reyers, 1030 Brussels; tel. (2) 771-01-26; fax (2) 762-60-36; Ambassador AHMED TIDIANE SAKHO.

Guinea-Bissau: 70 ave F. D. Roosevelt, 1050 Brussels; tel. (2) 290-51-81; fax (2) 290-51-56; Ambassador ALFREDO LOPES CABRAL.

Guyana: 12 ave du Brésil, 1000 Brussels; tel. (2) 672-62-16; fax (2) 675-55-98; Ambassador PATRICK IGNASIUS GOMES.

Haiti: 139 chaussée de Charleroi, 1060 Brussels; tel. (2) 649-73-81; fax (2) 640-60-80; e-mail ambassade@amb-haiti.be; Ambassador RAYMOND MAGLOIRE.

Holy See: 9 ave des Franciscains, 1150 Brussels; tel. (2) 762-20-05; fax (2) 762-20-32; internet www.vatican.va; Apostolic Nuncio Most Rev. GIACINTO BERLOCO (Titular Archbishop of Fidenae).

Honduras: 3 ave des Gaulois, 5e étage, 1040 Brussels; tel. (2) 734-00-00; fax (2) 735-26-26; e-mail ambassade.honduras@chello.be; Ambassador RAMÓN CUSTODIO ESPINOZA.

Hungary: 44 ave du Vert Chasseur, 1180 Brussels; tel. (2) 348-18-00; fax (2) 347-60-28; e-mail mission.bxl@mfa.gov.hu; internet www.mfa.gov.hu/emb/bxl; Ambassador ZOLTÁN HERNYES.

Iceland: 11 rond point Robert Schuman, 1040 Brussels; tel. (2) 238-50-00; fax (2) 230-69-38; e-mail emb.brussels@mfa.is; internet www.iceland.org/be; Ambassador THORIR IBSEN.

India: 217 chaussée de Vleurgat, 1050 Brussels; tel. (2) 640-91-40; fax (2) 648-96-38; e-mail info@indembassy.be; internet www.indembassy.be; Ambassador (vacant).

Indonesia: 38 blvd de la Woluwe, 1200 Brussels; tel. (2) 775-01-20; fax (2) 772-82-10; e-mail primebxl@skynet.be; internet www.embassyofindonesia.eu; Ambassador ARIF HAVAS OEGROSENO.

Iran: 15 ave F. D. Roosevelt, 1050 Brussels; tel. (2) 627-03-50; fax (2) 762-39-15; e-mail secretariat@iranembassy.be; internet www.iranembassy.be; Ambassador (vacant).

Iraq: 115 ave F. D. Roosevelt, 1050 Brussels; tel. (2) 374-59-92; fax (2) 374-76-15; e-mail ambassade.irak@skynet.be; Ambassador MOHAMMED ABDULLAH AL-HUMAIMIDI.

Ireland: 180 chaussée d'Etterbeek, 1040 Brussels; tel. (2) 235-66-76; fax (2) 235-66-71; e-mail embassybrussels@dfa.ie; internet www.embassyofireland.be; Ambassador EAMONN MAC AODHA.

Israel: 40 ave de l'Observatoire, 1180 Brussels; tel. (2) 373-55-00; fax (2) 373-56-17; e-mail info@brussels.mfa.gov.il; internet brussels.mfa.gov.il; Ambassador YAACOV JACQUES REVAH.

Italy: 28 rue Emile Claus, 1050 Brussels; tel. (2) 643-38-50; fax (2) 648-54-85; e-mail ambbruxelles@esteri.it; internet www.ambbruxelles.esteri.it; Ambassador ROBERTO BETTARINI.

Jamaica: 77 ave Hansen-Soulie, 1000 Brussels; tel. (2) 230-11-70; fax (2) 234-69-69; e-mail emb.jam.brussels@skynet.be; Ambassador MARCIA YVETTE GILBERT-ROBERTS.

Japan: 58 ave des Arts, 6e étage, 1000 Brussels; tel. (2) 513-23-40; fax (2) 513-15-56; e-mail info.embjapan@skynet.be; internet www.be.emb-japan.go.jp; Ambassador JUN YOKOTA.

Jordan: 104 ave F. D. Roosevelt, 1050 Brussels; tel. (2) 640-77-55; fax (2) 640-27-96; e-mail jordan.embassy@skynet.be; internet www.jordanembassy.be; Ambassador Dr MONTASER OKLAH AL-ZOU'BI.

Kazakhstan: 30 ave Van Bever, 1180 Brussels; tel. (2) 373-38-90; fax (2) 374-50-91; e-mail kazakhstan.embassy@swing.be; internet www.kazakhstanembassy.be; Ambassador ERIK UTEMBAYEV.

Kenya: 208 ave Winston Churchill, 1180 Brussels; tel. (2) 340-10-40; fax (2) 340-10-50; e-mail info@kenyabrussels.com; internet www.kenyabrussels.com; Ambassador JAMES KEMBI-GITURA.

Korea, Republic: 175 chaussée de la Hulpe, 1170 Brussels; tel. (2) 662-57-77; fax (2) 675-52-21; e-mail eukorea@mofat.go.kr; Ambassador KIM SEUNG-HO.

Kosovo: 6 rond point Robert Schuman, BP 5, 1040 Brussels; tel. (2) 234-77-88; fax (2) 234-78-00; e-mail embassy.belgium@ks-gov.net; Ambassador ILIR DUGOLLI.

Kuwait: 43 ave F. D. Roosevelt, 1050 Brussels; tel. (2) 647-79-50; fax (2) 646-12-98; e-mail embassy.kwt@skynet.be; Ambassador NABEELA ABDULLA AL-MULLA.

Kyrgyzstan: 47 rue de l'Abbaye, 1050 Brussels; tel. (2) 640-18-68; fax (2) 640-01-31; e-mail kyrgyz.embassy@skynet.be; Ambassador JYRGALBEK K. AZYLOV.

Laos: 19–21 ave de la Brabançonne, 1000 Brussels; tel. (2) 740-09-50; fax (2) 734-16-66; e-mail laoembassy@ambalao.be; internet www.ambalao.be; Ambassador SOUTHAM SAKONHNINHOM.

Latvia: 23 ave des Arts, 1000 Brussels; tel. (2) 238-32-36; fax (2) 238-32-54; e-mail embassy.belgium@mfa.gov.lv; internet www.mfa.gov.lv/belgium; Ambassador LELDE LĪCE-LĪCĪTE.

Lebanon: 2 rue Guillaume Stocq, 1050 Brussels; tel. (2) 645-77-65; fax (2) 645-77-69; e-mail ambassade.liban@brutele.be; Ambassador (vacant).

Lesotho: 45 blvd Général Wahis, 1030 Brussels; tel. (2) 705-39-76; fax (2) 705-67-79; e-mail lesothobrussels@hotmail.com; Ambassador MAMORUTI TIHELI.

Liberia: 50 ave du Château, 1081 Brussels; tel. (2) 411-01-12; fax (2) 411-09-12; e-mail info@embassyofliberia.be; internet www.embassyofliberia.be; Chargé d'affaires a.i. COMFORT SWENGBE.

Libya: 28 ave Victoria, 1000 Brussels; tel. (2) 647-37-37; fax (2) 640-90-76; e-mail libyan_bureau_br@yahoo.com; Sec. of the People's Bureau (vacant).

Liechtenstein: 1 place du Congrès, 1000 Brussels; tel. (2) 229-39-00; fax (2) 219-35-45; e-mail ambassade.liechtenstein@bru.llv.li; Ambassador KURT JÄGER.

Lithuania: 48 rue Maurice Liétart, 1150 Brussels; tel. (2) 772-27-50; fax (2) 772-17-01; e-mail info@lt-embassy.be; internet be.mfa.lt; Chargé d'affaires a.i. DANGUOLĖ VINCIŪNIENĖ.

Luxembourg: 75 ave de Cortenbergh, 1000 Brussels; tel. (2) 737-57-00; fax (2) 737-57-10; e-mail bruxelles.amb@mae.etat.lu; internet bruxelles.mae.lu; Ambassador JEAN-JAQUES WELFRING.

Macedonia, former Yugoslav republic: 20 rue Vilain XIV, 1050 Brussels; tel. (2) 734-56-87; fax (2) 732-07-17; e-mail ambassade.mk@skynet.be; Ambassador MUHAMMAD HALILI.

Madagascar: 276 ave de Tervueren, 1150 Brussels; tel. (2) 770-17-26; fax (2) 772-37-31; e-mail info@madagascar-embassy.eu; internet www.madagascar-embassy.eu; Chargé d'affaires a.i. IBRAHIM NORBERT RICHARD.

Malawi: 46 ave Hermann Debroux, 1160 Brussels; tel. (2) 231-09-80; fax (2) 231-10-66; e-mail embassy.malawi@skynet.be; internet www.embassymalawi.be; Ambassador BRAVE NDISALE.

Malaysia: 414A ave de Tervueren, 1150 Brussels; tel. (2) 776-03-40; fax (2) 762-50-49; e-mail malbrussels@kln.gov.my; Ambassador Dato' ZAINUDDIN YAHYA.

Maldives: Brussels; Ambassador ALI HUSSAIN DIDI.

Mali: 487 ave Molière, 1050 Brussels; tel. (2) 345-74-32; fax (2) 344-57-00; e-mail info@amba-mali.be; internet www.amba-mali.be; Ambassador IBRAHIM BOCAR BA.

Malta: 25 rue Archimède, 5e étage, 1000 Brussels; tel. (2) 343-01-95; fax (2) 230-45-83; e-mail maltaembassy.brussels@gov.mt; internet www.mfa.gov.mt/belgium; Ambassador PIERRE CLIVE AGIUS.

Mauritania: 6 ave de la Colombie, 1000 Brussels; tel. (2) 672-47-47; fax (2) 672-20-51; e-mail info@amb-mauritania.be; Ambassador MOHAMED MAHMOUD OULD BRAHIM KHLIL.

Mauritius: 68 rue des Bollandistes, 1040 Brussels; tel. (2) 733-99-88; fax (2) 734-40-21; e-mail ambmaur@skynet.be; Ambassador JAGDISH DHARAMCHAND KOONJUL.

Mexico: 94 ave F. D. Roosevelt, 1050 Brussels; tel. (2) 629-07-77; fax (2) 644-08-19; e-mail embamex@embamex.eu; internet www.embamex.eu; Ambassador SANDRA FUENTES-BERAIN.

Moldova: 57 ave F. D. Roosevelt, 1050 Brussels; tel. (2) 626-00-80; fax (2) 732-96-60; e-mail bruxelles@mfa.md; internet www.ambasadamoldova.be; Ambassador MIHAI GRIBINCEA.

Monaco: 17 place Guy d'Arezzo, 1180 Brussels; tel. (2) 347-49-87; fax (2) 343-49-20; e-mail ambassade.monaco@skynet.be; Ambassador GILLES TONELLI.

Mongolia: 18 ave Besme, 1190 Brussels; tel. (2) 344-69-74; fax (2) 344-32-15; e-mail brussels.mn.embassy@telenet.be; internet www.embassyofmongolia.be; Ambassador AVIRMEDIIN BATTÖR.

Morocco: 29 blvd St-Michel, 1040 Brussels; tel. (2) 736-11-00; fax (2) 734-64-68; e-mail sifamabruxe@skynet.be; Ambassador SAMIR ADDAHRE.

Mozambique: 97 blvd St-Michel, 1040 Brussels; tel. (2) 736-25-64; fax (2) 732-06-64; e-mail maria_manuelalucas@yahoo.com; internet www.mozambiquembassy.be; Ambassador ANA NEMBA UAIENE.

Myanmar: 9 blvd Général Wahis, 1030 Brussels; tel. (2) 701-93-80; fax (2) 705-50-48; Ambassador U THANT KYAW.

Namibia: 454 ave de Tervueren, 1150 Brussels; tel. (2) 771-14-10; fax (2) 771-96-89; e-mail info@namibiaembassy.be; internet www.namibiaembassy.be; Ambassador HANNO BURKHARD RUMPF.

Nepal: 210 ave Brugmann, 1050 Brussels; tel. (2) 346-26-58; fax (2) 344-13-61; e-mail embn@skynet.be; internet www.nepalembassy.be; Ambassador (vacant).

Netherlands: 48 ave Hermann Debroux, 1160 Brussels; tel. (2) 679-17-11; fax (2) 679-17-75; e-mail bru@minbuza.nl; internet www.nederlandseambassade.be; Ambassador HENDRIK JAN JURRIAAN (HENNE) SCHUWER.

New Zealand: 9–31 ave des Nerviens, 7e étage, 1000 Brussels; tel. (2) 512-10-40; fax (2) 513-48-56; e-mail nzemb.brussels@skynet.be; internet www.nzembassy.com/belgium; Ambassador PETER VANGELIS VITALIS.

Nicaragua: 55 ave de Wolvendael, 1180 Brussels; tel. (2) 375-65-00; fax (2) 375-71-88; e-mail sky77706@skynet.be; Ambassador MAURICIO LAUTARO SANDINO MONTES.

Niger: 78 ave F. D. Roosevelt, 1050 Brussels; tel. (2) 648-61-40; fax (2) 648-27-84; e-mail ambanigerbrux@skynet.be; Ambassador DJIBO ISSAKA.

Nigeria: 288 ave de Tervueren, 1150 Brussels; tel. (2) 762-52-00; fax (2) 762-37-63; e-mail ambassador@nigeriabrussels.be; internet www.nigeriabrussels.be; Ambassador USMAN BARAYA.

Norway: 17 rue Archimède, 1000 Brussels; tel. (2) 238-73-00; fax (2) 238-73-90; e-mail emb.brussels@mfa.no; internet www.norvege.be; Ambassador NIELS ENGELSCHIØN.

Oman: 236 ave F. D. Roosevelt, 1050 Brussels; tel. (2) 679-70-10; fax (2) 660-79-64; e-mail omanembassy@europe.com; Ambassador Sheikh GHAZI BIN SAID AL-BAHR AL-RAWAS.

Pakistan: 57 ave Delleur, 1170 Brussels; tel. (2) 673-80-07; fax (2) 675-83-94; e-mail parepbrussels@skynet.be; internet www.embassyofpakistan.be; Ambassador JALIL ABBAS JILANI.

Panama: 18 blvd Général Jacques, 1050 Brussels; tel. (2) 649-07-29; fax (2) 648-92-16; e-mail embajada.panama@skynet.be; Ambassador CARLOS CONSTANTINO AROSEMENA RAMOS.

Papua New Guinea: 430 ave de Tervueren, 1150 Brussels; tel. (2) 779-06-09; fax (2) 772-70-88; e-mail kundu.brussels@skynet.be; Ambassador PETER PULKIYE MAGINDE.

Paraguay: 475 ave Louise, BP 12, 1050 Brussels; tel. (2) 649-90-55; fax (2) 647-42-48; e-mail embapar@skynet.be; Chargé d'affaires a.i. MARIO FRANCISCO SANDOVAL FERNÁNDEZ.

Peru: 179 ave de Tervueren, 1150 Brussels; tel. (2) 733-33-19; fax (2) 733-48-19; e-mail info@embaperu.be; Ambassador CRISTINA RONQUILLO.

Philippines: 65 ave Louise, 1050 Brussels; tel. (2) 340-33-77; fax (2) 345-64-25; e-mail brussels@philembassy.be; internet www.philembassy.be; Ambassador VICTORIA SISANTE BATACLAN.

Poland: 29 ave des Gaulois, 1040 Brussels; tel. (2) 739-01-00; fax (2) 736-18-81; internet www.bruksela.polemb.net; Ambassador ARTUR HARAZIM.

Portugal: 55 ave de la Toison d'Or, 1060 Brussels; tel. (2) 533-07-00; fax (2) 539-07-73; e-mail ambassade.portugal@skynet.be; Ambassador VASCO BRAMÃO RAMOS.

Qatar: 51 rue de la Vallée, 1000 Brussels; tel. (2) 223-11-55; fax (2) 223-11-66; e-mail info@qatarembassy.be; Ambassador Sheikh MESHAL BIN HAMAD AL THANI.

Romania: 105 rue Gabrielle, 1180 Brussels; tel. (2) 345-26-80; fax (2) 346-23-45; e-mail secretariat@roumanieamb.be; internet bruxelles.mae.ro; Ambassador OVIDIU DRANGA.

Russia: 66 ave de Fré, 1180 Brussels; tel. (2) 374-34-00; fax (2) 374-26-13; e-mail amrusbel@skynet.be; internet www.belgium.mid.ru; Ambassador ALEKSANDR A. ROMANOV.

Rwanda: 1 ave des Fleurs, 1150 Brussels; tel. (2) 763-07-21; fax (2) 763-07-53; e-mail ambarwanda@gmail.com; internet www.ambarwanda.be; Ambassador ROBERT MASOZERA MUTANGUHA.

Samoa: 20 ave de l'Orée, BP 4, 1000 Brussels; tel. (2) 660-84-54; fax (2) 675-03-36; e-mail samoaembassy@skynet.be; Ambassador TUALA FALANI CHAN TUNG.

San Marino: 62 ave F. D. Roosevelt, 1050 Brussels; tel. (2) 644-22-24; fax (2) 644-20-57; e-mail ambrsm.bxl@scarlet.be; Ambassador GIAN NICOLA FILIPPI BALESTRA.

São Tomé and Príncipe: Square Montgomery, 175 ave de Tervueren, 1150 Brussels; tel. (2) 734-89-66; fax (2) 734-88-15; e-mail ambassade@saotomeeprincipe.be; Ambassador CARLOS GUSTAVO DOS ANJOS.

Saudi Arabia: 45 ave F. D. Roosevelt, 1050 Brussels; tel. (2) 649-20-44; fax (2) 647-24-92; e-mail beemb@mofa.gov.sa; Ambassador FAISAL BIN HASAN TIRAD.

Senegal: 196 ave F. D. Roosevelt, 1050 Brussels; tel. (2) 673-00-97; fax (2) 675-04-60; Ambassador PAUL BADJI.

Serbia: 11 ave Emile de Mot, 1000 Brussels; tel. (2) 647-26-52; fax (2) 647-29-41; e-mail embassy.brussels@mfa.rs; Ambassador RADOMIR DIKLIC.

Seychelles: 28 blvd Saint Michel, BP 23, 1040 Brussels; tel. (2) 733-60-55; fax (2) 732-60-22; e-mail brussels@seychellesgov.com; Ambassador VIVIANNE FOCK TAVE.

Sierra Leone: 410 ave de Tervueren, 1150 Brussels; tel. (2) 771-00-53; fax (2) 771-82-30; e-mail sierraleoneembassy@brutele.be; internet www.sierraleoneembassy.be; Ambassador CHRISTIAN S. KARGBO.

Singapore: 85 ave F. D. Roosevelt, 1050 Brussels; tel. (2) 660-29-79; fax (2) 660-86-85; e-mail singemb_bru@sgmfa.gov.sg; internet www.mfa.gov.sg/brussels; Ambassador ANIL KUMAR NAYAR.

Slovakia: 195 ave Molière, 1050 Brussels; tel. (2) 340-14-60; fax (2) 340-14-64; e-mail emb.brussel@mzv.sk; Ambassador JAN KUDERJAVY.

Slovenia: 44 rue du Commerce, 1000 Brussels; tel. (2) 213-63-37; fax (2) 213-64-29; e-mail vbr@gov.si; internet www.bruselj.veleposlanistvo.si; Ambassador ANITA PIPAN.

Solomon Islands: 17 ave Edouard Lacomble, 1040 Brussels; tel. (2) 732-70-85; fax (2) 732-68-85; e-mail siembassy@skynet.be; Ambassador JOSEPH MA'AHANUA.

South Africa: 17–19 rue Montoyer, 1040 Brussels; tel. (2) 285-44-00; fax (2) 285-44-55; e-mail embassy@southafrica.be; internet www.southafrica.be; Ambassador Dr MXOLISI NKOSI.

Spain: 19 rue de la Science, 1040 Brussels; tel. (2) 230-03-40; fax (2) 230-93-80; e-mail emb.bruselas@maec.es; internet www.maec.es/embajadas/bruselas; Ambassador SILVIA IRANZO GUTIÉRREZ.

Sri Lanka: 27 rue Jules Lejeune, 1050 Brussels; tel. (2) 344-53-94; fax (2) 344-67-37; e-mail secretariat@srilankaembassy.be; internet www.srilankaembassy.be; Ambassador RAVINATHA PANDUKABHAYA ARYASINHA.

Sudan: 124 ave F. D. Roosevelt, 1050 Brussels; tel. (2) 647-94-94; fax (2) 648-34-99; e-mail sudanbx@yahoo.com; Ambassador ELTIGANI SALIH FIDAIL.

Suriname: 379 ave Louise, BP 20, 1050 Brussels; tel. (2) 640-11-72; fax (2) 646-39-62; e-mail sur.amb.bru@online.be; Ambassador WILFRED EDUARD CHRISTOPHER.

Swaziland: 188 ave Winston Churchill, 1180 Brussels; tel. (2) 347-47-71; fax (2) 347-46-23; e-mail brussels@swaziembassy.be; internet www.swaziembassy.be; Ambassador JOEL MUSA NHLEKO.

Switzerland: 26 rue de la Loi, BP 9, 1040 Brussels; tel. (2) 285-43-50; fax (2) 230-37-81; e-mail bru.vertretung@eda.admin.ch; internet www.eda.admin.ch/bruxelles; Ambassador BÉNÉDICT DE CERJAT.

Syria: 3 ave F. D. Roosevelt, 1050 Brussels; tel. (2) 648-01-35; fax (2) 646-40-18; e-mail ambsyrie@skynet.be; internet www.syrianembassy.be; Ambassador Dr MUHAMMAD AYMAN SOUSAN.

Tajikistan: 16 blvd Général Jacques, 1050 Brussels; tel. (2) 640-69-33; fax (2) 649-01-95; e-mail tajemb-belgium@skynet.be; internet www.taj-emb.be; Ambassador RUSTAMJON A. SOLIEV.

Tanzania: 72 ave F. D. Roosevelt, 1050 Brussels; tel. (2) 640-65-00; fax (2) 640-80-26; e-mail tanzania@skynet.be; Ambassador SIMON U. R. MLAY.

Thailand: 876 Chaussée de Waterloo, 1000 Brussels; tel. (2) 640-68-10; fax (2) 648-30-66; e-mail thaibxl@thaiembassy.be; internet www.thaiembassy.be; Ambassador APICHART CHINWANNO.

Timor-Leste: 92–94 sq. Eugène Plasky, 1030 Brussels; tel. (2) 735-96-71; fax (2) 733-90-03; e-mail tlembassy.brussels@skynet.be; Ambassador NELSON SANTOS.

Togo: 264 ave de Tervueren, 1150 Brussels; tel. (2) 770-55-63; fax (2) 771-50-75; e-mail ambassade.togo@skynet.be; Ambassador FÉLIX KODJO SAGBO.

Trinidad and Tobago: 14 ave de la Faisanderie, 1150 Brussels; tel. (2) 762-94-00; fax (2) 772-27-83; e-mail info@embtrinbago.be; Ambassador MARGARET KING-ROUSSEAU.

Tunisia: 278 ave de Tervueren, 1150 Brussels; tel. (2) 771-73-95; fax (2) 771-94-33; e-mail amb.detunisie@brutele.be; Ambassador MOHAMED RIDHA FARHAT.

Turkey: 4 rue Montoyer, 1000 Brussels; tel. (2) 513-40-95; fax (2) 514-07-48; e-mail info@turkey.be; internet www.turkey.be; Ambassador ISMAIL HAKKI MUSA.

Turkmenistan: 106 blvd Reyers, 1030 Brussels; tel. (2) 648-18-74; fax (2) 648-19-06; e-mail turkmenistan@skynet.be; Ambassador KAKADJAN MOMMADOV.

Tuvalu: 17 Ave Edouard Lacomble, 2e étage, 1040 Brussels; tel. (2) 742-10-67; fax (2) 742-28-69; Ambassador TINE LEUELU.

Uganda: 317 ave de Tervueren, 1150 Brussels; tel. (2) 762-58-25; fax (2) 763-04-38; e-mail contactugandaembassy@gmail.com; Ambassador STEPHEN T. KAPIMPINA KATENTA-APULI.

Ukraine: 30–32 ave Albert Lancaster, 1180 Brussels; tel. (2) 379-21-00; fax (2) 379-21-79; e-mail emb_be@mfa.gov.ua; internet www.ukraine.be; Ambassador Dr IHOR DOLHOV.

United Arab Emirates: 73 ave F. D. Roosevelt, 1050 Brussels; tel. (2) 640-60-00; fax (2) 646-24-73; e-mail info@uaeembassy.be; internet www.uaeembassybrussels.be; Ambassador SULAIMAN HAMID SALEM AL-MAZROUI.

United Kingdom: 10 ave d'Auderghem, Oudergemselaan, 1040 Brussels; tel. (2) 287-62-11; fax (2) 287-63-55; e-mail info@britain.be; internet www.ukinbelgium.fco.gov.uk; Ambassador JONATHAN BRENTON.

USA: 27 blvd du Régent, 1000 Brussels; tel. (2) 508-21-11; fax (2) 511-27-25; internet belgium.usembassy.gov; Ambassador HOWARD W. GUTMAN.

Uruguay: 22 ave F. D. Roosevelt, 1050 Brussels; tel. (2) 640-11-69; fax (2) 648-29-09; e-mail uruemb@skynet.be; Ambassador Dr RUBEN WALTER CANCELA VILANOVA.

Uzbekistan: 99 ave F. D. Roosevelt, 1050 Brussels; tel. (2) 672-88-44; fax (2) 672-39-46; e-mail embassy@uzbekistan.be; internet www.uzbekistan.be; Ambassador BAKHTIYAR GULYAMOV.

Vanuatu: 380 ave de Tervueren, 1150 Brussels; tel. and fax (2) 771-74-94; e-mail info@embassyvanuatu.net; Ambassador ROY MICKEY JOY.

Venezuela: 10 ave F. D. Roosevelt, 1050 Brussels; tel. (2) 639-03-40; fax (2) 647-88-20; e-mail embajada@venezuela-eu.org; internet www.venezuela-eu.gob.ve; Ambassador ANTONIO GUILLERMO GARCÍA DANGLADES.

Viet Nam: 1 blvd Général Jacques, 1050 Brussels; tel. (2) 374-79-61; fax (2) 374-93-76; e-mail vnemb.brussels@skynet.be; Ambassador PHAM SANH CHAU.

Yemen: 114 ave F. D. Roosevelt, 1050 Brussels; tel. (2) 646-52-90; fax (2) 646-29-11; e-mail yemen@skynet.be; Ambassador ABD AL-WAHAB MUHAMMAD AL-SHAWKANI.

Zambia: 469 ave Molière, 1050 Brussels; tel. (2) 343-56-49; fax (2) 347-43-33; e-mail zambians_brussels@brutele.be; Ambassador INONGE M. LEWANIKA.

Zimbabwe: 11 square Joséphine Charlotte, 1200 Brussels; tel. (2) 762-58-08; fax (2) 762-96-05; e-mail zimbrussels@skynet.be; Ambassador MARGARET MUCHADA.

Judicial System

The independence of the judiciary is based on the constitutional division of power between the legislative, executive and judicial bodies, each of which acts independently. Judges are appointed by the Crown for life, and cannot be removed except by judicial sentence. The judiciary is organized on four levels, from the judicial canton to the district, regional and national courts. The lowest courts are those of the Justices of the Peace and the Police Tribunals. Each district has one of each type of district court, including the Tribunals of the First Instance, Tribunals of Commerce and Labour Tribunals, and there is a Court of Assizes in each province. There are civil and criminal Courts of Appeal and Labour Courts in five regional centres (Antwerp, Brussels, Ghent, Liège and Mons). The Constitutional Court (formerly the Court of Arbitration), which must comprise an equal number of Dutch- and French-speaking judges, ensures that legislation conforms to the Constitution and has jurisdiction in cases concerning the division of competencies between the different levels of the federal state. With the Court of Cassation, these are the highest courts in the country. The Military Court of Appeal is in Brussels.

CONSTITUTIONAL COURT

7 pl. Royale, 1000 Brussels; tel. (2) 500-12-11; internet www.const-court.be.

Presidents: MARC BOSSUYT (Dutch-speaking group), MICHEL MELCHIOR (French-speaking group).

Judges: ETIENNE DE GROOT, PIERRE NIHOUL, LUC LAVRYSEN, ROGER HENNEUSE, Baron ANDRÉ ALEN, JEAN-PAUL SNAPPE, ERIK DERYCKE, JEAN-PAUL MOERMAN, TREES MERCKX-VAN GOEY, JEAN SPREUTELS.

COURT OF CASSATION

Palais de Justice, 1 pl. Poelaert, 1000 Brussels; tel. (2) 508-62-74; fax (2) 508-69-53; internet www.cassonline.be.

First President: (vacant).

Presidents: I. VEROUGSTRAETE, C. STORCK.

Counsellors: D. BATSELÉ, R. BOES, F. CLOSE, P. CORNELIS, J. DE CODT, B. DECONINCK, B. DEJEMEPPE, M. DELANGE, E. DIRIX, A. FETTWEIS, E. FORRIER, J.-P. FRÈRE, E. GOETHALS, G. JOCQUÉ, P. MAFFEI, P. MATHIEU, C. MATRAY, K. MESTDAGH, M. REGOUT, A. SIMON, A. SMETRYNS, E. STASSIJNS, G. STEFFENS, L. VAN HOOGENBEMT, F. VAN VOLSEM, S. VELU.

Attorney-General: JEAN-FRANÇOIS LECLERCQ.

First Advocate-General: M. DE SWAEF.

Advocates-General: X. DE RIEMAECKER, G. DUBRULLE, P. DUINSLAEGER, J-M. GENICOT, A. HENKES, R. LOOP, R. MORTIER, D. THIJS, M. TIMPERMAN, D. VANDERMEERSCH, C. VANDEWAL, T. WERQUIN.

CIVIL AND CRIMINAL COURTS OF APPEAL

Antwerp: Waalse Kaai 35A, 2000 Antwerp; tel. (3) 247-97-11; fax (3) 247-97-81; internet www.juridat.be/beroep/antwerpen; Pres. MICHEL ROZIE; Attorney-Gen. Y. LIEGEOIS.

Brussels: Palais de Justice, 1 pl. Poelaert, 1000 Brussels; tel. (2) 508-65-91; fax (2) 508-64-50; internet www.juridat.be/beroep/brussel; First Pres. GUY DELVOIE; Attorney-Gen. MARC DE LE COURT.

Ghent: Gerechtsgebouw, Koophandelspl. 23, 9000 Ghent; tel. (9) 267-41-11; fax (9) 267-41-12; internet www.juridat.be/beroep/gent; First Pres. HENRI DEBUCQUOY; Attorney-Gen. FRANK SCHINS.

Liège: Palais de Justice, 16 pl. Saint Lambert, 4000 Liège; tel. (4) 232-56-36; fax (4) 232-56-37; internet www.juridat.be/appel/liege; First Pres. MARC DEWART; Attorney-Gen. CÉDRIC VISART DE BOCARME.

Mons: 1 rue des Droits de l'Homme, 7000 Mons; tel. (65) 37-90-11; fax (65) 37-93-06; internet www.juridat.be/appel/mons; First Pres. JEAN-LOUIS FRANEAU; Attorney-Gen. CLAUDE MICHAUX.

LABOUR COURTS

Antwerp: Cockerillkaai 39, 2000 Antwerp; tel. (3) 247-97-11; fax (3) 247-99-41; internet www.juridat.be/arbeidshof/antwerpen; First Pres. LOLA BOEYKENS.

Brussels: 3 pl. Poelaert, 1000 Brussels; tel. (2) 508-61-27; fax (2) 519-81-48; internet www.juridat.be/arbeidshof/brussel; First Pres. BEATRIX CEULEMANS.

Ghent: Brabantdam 33B, 9000 Ghent; tel. (9) 266-02-11; fax (9) 266-02-32; internet www.juridat.be/arbeidshof/gent; First Pres. ROGER VAN GREMBERGEN.

Liège: 89 rue St Gilles, 4000 Liège; tel. (4) 232-85-50; fax (4) 223-04-13; First Pres. JOËL HUBIN.

Mons: 1 rue des Droits de l'Homme, 7000 Mons; tel. (65) 37-92-51; fax (65) 37-92-53; First Pres. DANIEL PLAS.

Religion

CHRISTIANITY

The Roman Catholic Church

Belgium comprises one archdiocese and seven dioceses. At 31 December 2006 adherents numbered some 7,389,919 (71.2% of the total population).

Bishops' Conference

Bisschoppenconferentie van België/Conférence Episcopale de Belgique, 1 rue Guimard, 1040 Brussels; tel. (2) 509-96-94; fax (2) 509-96-95; e-mail ipid@kerknet.be; internet www.kerknet.be.

f. 1981; Pres. Most Rev. ANDRÉ-JOSEPH LÉONARD (Archbishop of Mechelen-Brussels).

Archbishop of Mechelen-Brussels: Most Rev. ANDRÉ-JOSEPH LÉONARD, Aartsbisdom, Wollemarkt 15, 2800 Mechelen; tel. (15) 29-26-11; fax (15) 20-94-85; e-mail aartsbisdom@kerknet.be; internet www.kerknet.be.

Protestant Churches

Church of England: Holy Trinity Pro-Cathedral, 29 rue Capitaine Crespel, 1050 Brussels; tel. (2) 511-71-83; fax (2) 511-10-28; e-mail admin@holytrinity.be; internet www.holytrinity.be; Senior Chaplain and Chancellor Canon Dr ROBERT INNES.

Eglise Protestante Unie de Belgique (EPUB): Brogniezstraat 44, 1070 Brussels; tel. (2) 510-61-98; fax (2) 510-61-99; e-mail info@cacpe.be; internet www.protestanet.be; f. 1979; Pres. Rev. Dr GUY LIAGRE; 50,000 mems; publ. *Mosaïque* (monthly).

Evangelical Lutheran Church in Belgium: Tabakvest 59, 2000 Antwerp; tel. (2) 233-62-50; e-mail lutherse.kerk@skynet.be; internet users.skynet.be/lutherse.kerk; f. 1939; 160 mems (2010); Pres. Rev. GIJSBERTUS VAN HATTEM.

Mission Evangélique Belge: 158 blvd Lambermont, 1030 Brussels; tel. (2) 241-30-15; fax (2) 245-79-65; e-mail information@b-e-m.org; internet www.bez-meb.be; f. 1919; Dir WILFRIED GOOSSENS; c. 12,000 mems.

Union of Baptists in Belgium (UBB): A. Liebaertstraat 85, 8400 Ostend; tel. and fax (5) 932-46-10; e-mail samuel.verhaeghel@telenet.be; f. 1922 as Union of Protestant Baptists in Belgium; mem. of the European Baptist Federation; Gen. Sec. SAMUEL VERHAEGHE; c. 1,100 mems, 31 churches.

The Orthodox Church

There are about 70,000 Greek and Russian Orthodox believers in Belgium.

Archbishop of Belgium (Ecumenical Patriarchate of Constantinople): Metropolitan PANTELEIMON OF BELGIUM, 71 ave Charbolaan, 1030 Brussels; tel. (2) 736-52-78; fax (2) 735-32-64; e-mail eglise.orthodoxe@belgacom.net; internet www.eglise-orthodoxe.be.

Archbishop of Brussels and Belgium (Moscow Patriarchate): Archbishop SIMON , 29 rue des Chevaliers, 1050 Brussels; tel. and fax (2) 513-33-74; e-mail info@archiepiskopia.be; internet www.archiepiskopia.be.

ISLAM

In 2007 there were more than 500,000 Muslims in Belgium, constituting about 5% of the total population.

Exécutif des Musulmans de Belgique/Executieve van de Moslims van België (EMB): 166–168 rue de Laaken, 1000 Brussels; tel. (2) 210-02-30; fax (2) 218-07-92; e-mail contact@embnet.be; internet www.embnet.be; f. 1999; promotes dialogue between Muslim community and the Government; Pres. SEMSETTIN UGURLU; 17 mems.

JUDAISM

The Jewish population in Belgium was estimated at between 40,000 and 50,000 in 2007.

Consistoire Central Israélite de Belgique (Central Council of the Jewish Communities of Belgium): 2 rue Joseph Dupont, 1000 Brussels; tel. (2) 512-21-90; fax (2) 512-35-78; e-mail consis@online.be; internet www.jewishcom.be; f. 1808; central body representing the 18 Jewish communities in Belgium; Chair. Prof. JULIEN KLENER; Sec.-Gen. MICHEL LAUB.

The Press

Article 25 of the Belgian Constitution states: 'The press is free; no form of censorship may ever be instituted; no cautionary deposit may be demanded from writers, publishers or printers. When the author is known and is resident in Belgium, the publisher, printer or distributor may not be prosecuted.'

There is a trend towards concentration of ownership by a number of organizations, which control chains of publications, mostly divided along linguistic lines. The largest of those organizations are as follows:

Corelio NV: Gossetlaan 30, 1702 Groot-Bijgaarden; tel. (2) 467-22-11; internet www.corelio.be; f. 1914 as NV De Standaard; fmrly De Vlaamse Uitgeversmaatschappij (VUM), present name adopted 2006; owns 5 newspapers, incl. *De Standaard*, *Het Nieuwsblad* and *De Gentenaar*; 10 magazines and 3 radio stations; Chair. THOMAS LEYSEN; CEO LUC MISSORTEN.

Groupe Rossel: 100 rue Royale, 1000 Brussels; tel. (2) 225-55-99; fax (2) 225-59-02; e-mail micheline.demeurisse@viarossel.be; internet www.rossel.be; f. 1887; newspapers and magazines; French titles: *L'Echo*, *Le Soir* and Sud Presse newspapers; also publishes *Grenz Echo* and *De Tijd*; Pres. PATRICK HURBAIN; CEO BERNARD MARCHANT.

Roularta Media Group NV: Meiboomlaan 33, 8800 Roeselare; tel. (5) 126-61-11; fax (5) 126-68-66; e-mail info@roularta.be; internet www.roularta.be; f. 1954; magazines and regional newspapers; Chair. Baron HUGO VANDAMME; CEO RIK DE NOLF.

Sanoma Magazines Belgium NV: Telecomlaan 5–7, 1831 Diegem; tel. (2) 776-22-11; fax (2) 776-23-99; e-mail info@sanoma-magazines.be; internet www.sanoma-magazines.be; periodicals; f. 2002; owned by SanomaWSOY Group (Finland); CEO AIMÉ VAN HECKE.

PRINCIPAL DAILIES

Antwerpen
(Antwerp)

Gazet van Antwerpen: Katwilgweg 2, 2050 Antwerp; tel. (3) 210-02-10; fax (3) 219-40-41; e-mail gvainfocenter@concentra.be; internet www.gva.be; f. 1891; Christian Democrat; Editor PASCAL KERKHOVE; circ. 119,005 (2011).

De Lloyd N.V.: Jan van Gentstraat 1, Postbus 102, 2000 Antwerp; tel. (3) 234-05-50; fax (3) 226-08-50; e-mail info@lloyd.be; internet www.lloyd.be; f. 1858; Dutch and French edns, with supplements in English; commerce, industry, logistics, transport (shipping, air, rail, road); Dir MICHEL SCHUURING; Editor-in-Chief PHILIPPE VAN DOOREN; circ. 10,600 (2007).

De Nieuwe Gazet: Brusselsesteenweg 347, 1730 Asse; tel. (3) 212-13-48; fax (3) 212-13-46; f. 1897; liberal; Chief Editor LUC VAN DER KELEN.

Arlon

L'Avenir du Luxembourg: 235 ave Général Patton, 6700 Arlon; tel. (63) 23-10-20; fax (63) 23-10-51; e-mail infoal@actu24.be; internet www.actu24.be; f. 1894; 100% owned by Corelio NV; Catholic; Editor-in-Chief DANIEL LAPRAILLE; circ. 103,924 (2011, with *Vers l'Avenir, Le Courrier de l'Escaut, Le Jour, Le Courrier*).

Bruxelles/Brussel
(Brussels)

La Capitale: 120 rue Royale, 1000 Brussels; tel. (2) 225-56-41; fax (2) 225-59-13; e-mail redaction.generale@sudpresse.be; internet www.lacapitale.be; f. 1944 as *La Lanterne*; present name adopted 2002; independent; owned by Sud Presse; Dir THIERRY DELHAYE; Editor-in-Chief KARIM FADOUL.

La Dernière Heure/Les Sports: 179 rue des Francs, 1000 Brussels; tel. (2) 211-28-49; fax (2) 211-28-70; e-mail dh.redaction@dh.be; internet www.dhnet.be; f. 1906; independent liberal; Dir FRANÇOIS LE HODEY; Chief Editor RALPH VANKRINKELVELDT; circ. 80,000 (2011).

L'Echo: 86C ave du Port, BP 309, 1000 Brussels; tel. (2) 423-16-11; e-mail info@lecho.be; internet www.lecho.be; f. 1881; economic and financial; Dir FREDERIK DELAPLACE; circ. 19,457 (2011).

Het Laatste Nieuws: Brusselsesteenweg 347, 1730 Asse-Kobbegem; tel. (2) 454-22-11; fax (2) 454-28-22; e-mail redactie.hln@persgroep.be; internet www.hln.be; f. 1888; Dutch; independent; Editor-in-Chief PAUL DAENEN; circ. 340,235 (2011, incl. *De Nieuwe Gazet*).

La Libre Belgique: 79 rue des Francs, 1040 Brussels; tel. (2) 744-44-44; fax (2) 211-28-32; e-mail llb.redaction@saipm.com; internet www.lalibre.be; f. 1884; independent; Editor-in-Chief VINCENT SLITS; circ. 52,473 (2011, with *La Libre Belgique—Gazette de Liège*).

De Morgen: Arduinkaai 29, 1000 Brussels; tel. (2) 556-68-11; fax (2) 520-35-15; e-mail info@demorgen.be; internet www.demorgen.be; Editor-in-Chief PETER MIJLEMANS; circ. 68,815 (2011).

Het Nieuwsblad: Gossetlaan 28, 1702 Groot-Bijgaarden; tel. (2) 467-22-50; fax (2) 466-30-93; e-mail nieuws@nieuwsblad.be; internet www.nieuwsblad.be; f. 1923; Dir PETER VANDEMEERSCH; Editor-in-Chief GUY FRANSEN; circ. 299,400 (2011, with *De Gentenaar*).

Le Soir: 100 rue Royale, 1000 Brussels; tel. (2) 225-54-32; fax (2) 225-59-10; e-mail journal@lesoir.be; internet www.lesoir.be; f. 1887; independent; Dir-Gen. BERNARD VAN MARCHANT; Editor-in-Chief DIDIER HAMANN; circ. 91,767 (2011).

De Standaard: Gossetlaan 28, 1702 Groot Bijgaarden; tel. (2) 467-22-11; fax (2) 467-32-99; e-mail hoofdredactie@standaard.be; internet www.standaard.be; f. 1914; Editor-in-Chief BART STURTEWAGEN; circ. 108,828 (2011).

De Tijd: Havenlaan 86C, Postbus 309, 1000 Brussels; tel. (2) 423-16-11; e-mail persberichten@tijd.be; internet www.tijd.be; f. 1968; economic and financial; Editor-in-Chief ISABEL ALBERS; circ. 39,660 (2011).

Charleroi

La Nouvelle Gazette (Charleroi, La Louvière, Philippeville, Namur, Nivelles); La Province (Mons): 2 quai de Flandre, 6000 Charleroi; tel. (71) 27-89-79; fax (71) 66-74-27; e-mail redaction.generale@sudpresse.be; internet www.lanouvellegazette.be; f. 1878; owned by Sud Presse; Dir THIERRY DELHAYE; Editor-in-Chief DEMETRIO SCAGLIOLA.

Vers L'Avenir Entre-Sambre et Meuse: 1 blvd du Centenaire, 5600 Philippeville; tel. (71) 66-23-40; fax (71) 66-23-49; e-mail philippeville@lavenir.net; internet www.actu24.be; f. 1900; Editor-in-Chief BRUNO MALTER.

Eupen

Grenz-Echo: Marktpl. 8, 4700 Eupen; tel. (87) 59-13-22; fax (87) 55-34-57; e-mail redaktion@grenzecho.be; internet www.grenzecho.be; f. 1927; German; independent Catholic; Dir ALFRED KÜCHENBERG; Editor-in-Chief GERARD CREMER; circ. 13,581 (2011).

Gent
(Ghent)

De Gentenaar: Kouter 150, 9000 Ghent; tel. (9) 268-72-75; fax (9) 269-09-87; e-mail de.gentenaar@nieuwsblad.be; internet www.gentenaar.be; f. 1879; Editor-in-Chief GERT DE VOS.

Hasselt

Het Belang van Limburg: Herckenrodesingel 10, 3500 Hasselt; tel. (11) 87-81-11; fax (11) 87-82-04; e-mail hbvlsecretariaat@concentra.be; internet www.hbvl.be; f. 1879; Dir LUC RADEMAKERS; Editor-in-Chief IVO VANDEKERCKHOVE; circ. 112,861 (2011).

Liège

La Libre Belgique—Gazette de Liège: 26 blvd d'Avroy, 4000 Liège; tel. (4) 290-04-80; fax (4) 290-04-81; e-mail llb.gazettedeliege@saipm.com; internet www.lalibre.be; f. 1840; Editor-in-Chief VINCENT SLITS.

La Meuse: 38 blvd de la Sauvenière, 4000 Liège; tel. (4) 220-08-40; fax (4) 220-08-59; e-mail redliege.lameuse@sudpresse.be; internet www.lameuse.be; f. 1856; owned by Sud Presse; Dir THIERRY DELHAYE; Editor-in-Chief RODOLPHE MAGIS.

Mons

La Province: 29 rue des Capucins, 7000 Mons; tel. (65) 39-49-70; fax (65) 33-84-77; e-mail redaction.generale@sudpresse.be; internet www.laprovince.be; f. 1907; owned by Sud Presse; Dir THIERRY DELHAYE; Editor-in-Chief SÉBASTIEN PONCIAU.

Namur

Le Quotidien de Namur: 134 rue de Coquelet, 5010 Namur; tel. (81) 20-82-11; fax (81) 20-83-72; internet www.lequotidiendenamur.be; f. as *La Meuse Namur*; present name adopted 2002; owned by Sud Presse; Dir THIERRY DELHAYE; Editor-in-Chief CHRISTINE BOLINNE.

Vers l'Avenir Namur et Basse Sambre: 38 route de Hannut, 5000 Namur; tel. (81) 24-88-11; fax (81) 22-00-87; e-mail infonam@actu24.be; internet www.actu24.be; f. 1918; 100% owned by Médiabel; Editor-in-Chief JEAN-FRANÇOIS PACCO.

Tournai

Le Courrier de l'Escaut: 101 ave de Maire, 7500 Tournai; tel. (69) 88-96-20; fax (69) 88-96-60; e-mail infoce@actu24.be; internet www.actu24.be; f. 1829; 100% owned by Médiabel; Editor-in-Chief JEAN-PIERRE DE ROUCK.

Verviers

Le Jour: 87 ave de Spa, 4802 Heusy; tel. (87) 32-20-90; fax (87) 32-20-89; e-mail infolj@lavenir.net; internet www.actu24.be; f. 1894; 100% owned by Médiabel; Editor-in-Chief CLAUDE GILLET.

WEEKLIES

Atlas Weekblad: Condédreef 89, 8500 Kortrijk; tel. (56) 26-10-10; fax (56) 21-35-93; e-mail atlas@atlasweekblad.be; internet www.atlasweekblad.be; f. 1946; classified advertising, regional news and sports.

Boer en Tuinder: Diestsevest 40, 3000 Leuven; tel. (16) 28-60-01; fax (16) 28-60-09; internet www.boerenbond.be; f. 1891; agriculture and horticulture; Chair. PIET VANTHEMSCHE; circ. 20,619 (2010).

De Bond: Sylvain Van Der Guchtlaan 24, 9300 Aalst; tel. (53) 82-60-80; fax (53) 82-60-90; e-mail com@publicarto.be; internet www.publicarto.be; f. 1921; general interest; Dir SONIA VERMEIRE; circ. 279,919 (2011).

Brugsch Handelsblad: 20 Sint-Jorisstraat, 8000 Brugge; tel. (50) 44-21-59; fax (50) 44-21-66; e-mail redactie.bhblad@roularta.be; internet www.kw.be; f. 1906; local news; includes *De Krant van West-Vlaanderen* as a supplement; Dir EDDY BROUCKAERT; Editor-in-Chief JAN GHEYSEN; circ. 40,000.

Ciné Télé Revue: 101 ave Reine Marie-Henriette, 1190 Brussels; tel. (2) 345-99-68; fax (2) 343-12-72; e-mail redaction@cineterevue.be; internet www.cinetelerevue.be; f. 1944 as *Theatra Ciné Revue*; present name adopted 1984; TV listings, celebrity news, family issues; circ. 359,727 (2011).

Dag Allemaal: Brandekensweg 2, 2627 Schelle; tel. (3) 880-84-50; internet www.dagallemaal.be; Tues.; general, celebrity gossip; owned by Persgroep Publishing; Editor-in-Chief ILSE BEYERS; 486,462 (2011).

Dimanche: 20 pl. de Vannes, 7000 Mons; tel. (65) 35-28-85; fax (65) 34-63-70; e-mail info@dimanche.be; internet www.dimanche.be; f. 1946; Catholic; current affairs; 22 local editions; Editor-in-Chief CHARLES DELHEZ; circ. 86,117 (2011).

European Voice: International Press Centre, Résidence Palace, rue de la Loi 155, BP 6, 1040 Brussels; tel. (2) 540-90-90; fax (2) 540-90-71; e-mail info@europeanvoice.com; internet www.europeanvoice.com; f. 1995; Thurs.; publ. by The Economist Newspaper Ltd (United Kingdom); EU policy-making, politics and business; Editor TIM KING; circ. 18,388 (2008).

Femmes d'Aujourd'hui: Telecomlaan 5–7, 1831 Diegem; tel. (2) 776-28-50; fax (2) 776-23-99; e-mail info@femmesdaujourdhui.be; internet www.femmesdaujourdhui.be; f. 1933; French; women's interest; publ. by Sanoma Magazines Belgium SA; Editor-in-Chief ANOUK VAN GESTEL; circ. 126,998 (2011).

Flair: Uitbreidingstraat 82, 2600 Berchem; tel. (3) 290-13-92; e-mail flairsec@flair.be; internet www.flair.be; women's interest; publ. by Sanoma Magazines Belgium SA; Editor-in-Chief AN BROUCKMANS; circ. (2006) 166,622 (Dutch); 62,056 (French).

Humo: Harensesteenweg 226, 1800 Vilvoorde; tel. (2) 776-24-20; fax (2) 776-23-24; e-mail redactie@humo.be; internet www.humo.be; general weekly and TV and radio guide in Dutch; circ. 259,664 (2011).

Joepie: Brandekensweg 2, 2627 Schelle; tel. (3) 880-84-65; fax (3) 844-61-52; f. 1973; owned by Persgroep Publishing; teenagers' interest; Dir-Gen. KOEN CLEMENT; Chief Editor TINNE MARANT; circ. 82,976 (2011).

Kerk en Leven: Halewijnlaan 92, 2050 Antwerp; tel. (3) 210-08-31; fax (3) 210-08-36; e-mail redactie.kerkenleven@kerknet.be; internet www.kerknet.be; f. 1942; Catholic; 5 regional edns; Editor BERT CLAERHOUT; circ. 346,874 (2011).

Knack: Raketstraat 50, 1130 Brussels; tel. (2) 702-46-51; fax (2) 702-46-52; e-mail knack@knack.be; internet www.knack.be; f. 1971; news magazine; owned by Roularta Media Group; Dir JOHAN VAN OVERTVELDT; Editor-in-Chief KARL VAN DEN BROECK; circ. 130,128 (2011).

Kortrijks Handelsblad: Doorniksewijk 83B, 8500 Kortrijk; tel. 495-50-71-35; fax (56) 27-00-12; e-mail luc.demiddele@gmail.com; regional news; owned by Roularta Media Group; includes *De Krant van West-Vlaanderen* as a supplement; Chief Editor LUC DEMIDDELE.

De Krant van West-Vlaanderen: Meiboomlaan 33, 8800 Roeselare; tel. (51) 26-66-44; fax (51) 26-65-87; e-mail jan.gheysen@kw.be; internet www.kw.be; regional news and sport; owned by Roularta Media Group; 11 different edns; included as a supplement with titles *De Weekbode*, *Het Wekelijks Nieuws*, *De Zeewacht*, *Brugsch Handelsblad*, *Kortrijks Handelsblad*; Dir EDDY BROUCKAERT; Editor-in-Chief JAN GHEYSEN; circ. 88,776 (2011).

Landbouwleven/Le Sillon Belge: 92 ave Léon Grosjean, 1140 Brussels; tel. (2) 730-34-00; fax (2) 730-33-24; e-mail info@landbouwleven.be; internet www.sillonbelge.be; f. 1952; agriculture; Editorial Man. ANDRÉ DE MOL; circ. 28,343 (2011).

Le Soir Magazine: 100 rue Royale, 1000 Brussels; tel. (2) 225-55-55; fax (2) 225-59-11; e-mail redaction@lesoirmagazine.com; internet soirmag.lesoir.be; f. 1928; independent;illustrated; Dir-Gen. DANIEL VAN WYLICK; Editor-in-Chief MICHEL MARTEAU; circ. 70,890 (2010).

Libelle: Uitbreidingstraat 82, 2600 Berchem; tel. (3) 290-14-42; fax (3) 290-14-44; e-mail libelle@libelle.be; internet www.libelle.be; f. 1945; Dutch; women's interest; publ. by Sanoma Magazines Belgium SA; Dir CHRISTINE FESTJENS; Editor-in-Chief DITTE VAN DE VELDE; circ. 278,906 (2011).

Moustique: Telecomlaan 5–7, 1831 Diegem; tel. (2) 776-25-20; fax (2) 776-23-14; e-mail telemoustique@sanoma-magazines.be; internet www.moustique.be; f. 1924; radio and TV; Dir AIMÉ VAN HECK; Editor JEAN-LUC CAMBIER; circ. 119,130 (2011).

Spirou: 52 rue Jules Destrée, 6001 Marcinelle; tel. (71) 60-05-00; fax (71) 60-05-99; e-mail spirou@dupuis.com; internet www.spirou.com; children's interest; publ. by Editions Dupuis SA; Editor-in-Chief FRÉDÉRIC NIFFLE; circ. 25,289 (2011).

Sport/Foot Magazine and Sport/Voetbal Magazine: 50 rue de la Fusée, BP 5, 1130 Brussels; tel. (2) 702-45-71; fax (2) 702-45-72; e-mail sportmagazine@roularta.be; internet www.sport.be/sportmagazine; f. 1980; Dutch and French; football; owned by Roularta Media Group; Editors-in-Chief JACQUES SYS, JOHN BAETE; circ. 66,843 (2011).

Story: Uitbreidingstraat 82, 2600 Berchem; tel. (3) 290-15-13; fax (3) 290-15-14; e-mail story@sanoma-magazines.be; internet www.storymagazine.be; f. 1975; Wed.; Dutch; women's interest; Dir AIMÉ VAN HECK; Editor-in-Chief THOMAS SIFFER; circ. 212,238 (2011).

De Streekkrant/De Weekkrant: Meiboomlaan 33, 8800 Roeselare; tel. (51) 26-61-11; fax (51) 26-68-66; e-mail streekkrant@roularta.be; internet www.streekkrant.be; f. 1949; local news; distributed free of charge; Propr Roularta Media Group; Editor JEAN-PIERRE VAN GIMST; circ. 2,551,981 (2011).

Télépro/Telepro: 50 rue de la Fusée, 1130 Brussels; tel. (87) 30-87-31; fax (87) 31-35-37; e-mail courrier@telepromagazine.be; internet www.telepro.be; f. 1954; TV listings; co-owned by Bayard Group and Roularta Media Group; Editor-in-Chief NADINE LEJAER; circ. 135,675 (2011).

TeVe-Blad: Uitbreidingstraat 82, 2600 Berchem; tel. (3) 290-14-81; fax (3) 290-14-82; e-mail teveblad@sanoma-magazines.be; internet www.teveblad.be; f. 1981; Tues.; TV listings; Editor-in-Chief JAN VAN DE VLOEDT; circ. 155,693 (2011).

Trends/Trends Tendances: Brussels Media Centre, rue de la Fusée, 50, BP 4, 1130 Brussels; tel. (2) 702-48-00; fax (2) 702-48-02; e-mail trends@trends.be; internet www.trends.be; Dutch and French; economic analysis and business news; owned by Roularta Media Group; Editor-in-Chief JOHAN VAN OVERTVELDT; circ. 54,878 (2011).

Le Vif/L'Express: rue de la Fusée 50, BP 6, 1130 Brussels; tel. (2) 702-47-01; fax (2) 702-47-02; e-mail levif@levif.be; internet www.levif.be; f. 1971; current affairs; owned by Roularta Media Group; Dir-Gen. AMID FALJAOUI; Editor-in-Chief CHRISTINE LAURENT; circ. 82,330 (2011).

De Weekbode: Meiboomlaan 33, 8800 Roeselare; tel. (51) 26-61-11; fax (51) 26-65-87; regional news; owned by Roularta Media Group; includes *De Krant van West-Vlaanderen* as a supplement; Editor-in-Chief JAN GHEYSEN.

Het Wekelijks Nieuws Kust: Meiboomlaan 33, 8800 Roeselare; tel. (51) 26-62-60; fax (51) 26-65-87; e-mail sandra.rosseel@roularta.be; internet www.kw.be; Furnes, Dixmude and Belgian West Coast local news; owned by Roularta Media Group; includes *De Krant van West-Vlaanderen* as a supplement; Editor-in-Chief SANDRA ROSSEEL.

Het Wekelijks Nieuws West: Meiboomlaan 33, 8800 Roeselare; tel. (51) 26-65-55; fax (51) 26-55-87; e-mail matthias.vanderaspoilden@roularta.be; internet www.kw.be; local newspaper; Editor MATTHIAS VANDERASPOILDEN; circ. 56,000.

De Zeewacht: Meiboomlaan 33, 8800 Roeselare; tel. (51) 26-62-74; fax (51) 26-65-87; e-mail sandra.rosseel@kw.be; internet www.kw.be; Ostend local news; owned by Roularta Media Group; includes *De Krant van West-Vlaanderen* as a supplement.

Zondag Nieuws: Brandekensweg 2, 2627 Schelle; tel. (2) 220-22-11; fax (2) 217-98-46; f. 1958; general interest; circ. 48,101.

SELECTED OTHER PERIODICALS

axelle: 111 rue de la Poste, 1030 Brussels; tel. (2) 227-13-19; fax (2) 223-04-42; e-mail axelle@viefeminine.be; internet www.axellemag.be; f. 1917; 11 a year; feminist; circ. 11,975 (2010).

Bizzy: Onder den Toren 7, 2800 Mechelen; tel. (15) 21-08-01; fax (15) 21-81-31; e-mail info@bizzy.be; internet www.bizzy.be; monthly; lifestyle magazine; circ. 257,662 (2010).

Elle België: Leuvensesteenweg 431D, 1380 Lasne; tel. (2) 379-29-90; fax (2) 379-29-99; e-mail elle@ventures.be; internet www.elle.be; monthly; fashion; Editor-in-Chief NICA BROUCKE; circ. 38,296 (2010).

Feeling: Uitbreidingstraat 82, 2600 Berchem; tel. (3) 290-13-51; fax (3) 290-13-52; e-mail feeling@feeling.be; internet www.feeling.be; monthly; publ. by Sanoma Magazines Belgium SA; women's interest; Editor-in-Chief LENE KEMPS; circ.118,922.

Goed Gevoel: Brandekensweg 2, 2627 Schelle; tel. (3) 880-84-50; e-mail redactie@goedgevoel.be; internet www.goedgevoel.be; monthly; health, psychology; owned by Persgroep Publishing; Editor-in-Chief FEMKE ROBBERECHTS; circ. 112,167 (2010).

Goedele: Uitbreidingstraat 82, 2600 Berchem; tel. (3) 290-13-23; fax (3) 290-12-01; e-mail redactie@goedelemagazine.be; internet www.goedelemagazine.be; f. 2008; monthly; lifestyle, society; Editor-in-Chief DANNY ILEGEMS; circ. 84,684 (2010).

International Engineering News (IEN Europe): Hendrik Consciencestraat 1B, 2800 Mechelen; tel. (15) 45-86-00; fax (15) 45-86-10; e-mail p.bondi@tim-europe.com; internet www.ien.eu; f. 1975; 10 a year; English; Man. Dir ORHAN ERENBERK; Editor JÜRGEN WIRTZ; circ. 50,990.

Jet Magazine: Herckenrodesingel 10, 3500 Hasselt; tel. (11) 87-85-12; fax (11) 87-84-84; e-mail jetinfo@concentra.be; internet www.jetmagazine.be; fortnightly; distributed free of charge; general; circ. (2010) 401,595 (Antwerp), 364,025 (Limburg).

Marie Claire Belgique: Telecomlaan 5-7, 1831 Diegem; tel. (2) 776-22-11; fax (2) 776-23-99; e-mail marieclaire@sanoma-magazines.be; f. 1960; monthly; women's interest; Editor-in-Chief FABIENNE WILLAERT; circ. 39,515 (2010).

Le Moniteur de l'Automobile: 56 ave Général Dumonceau, 1190 Brussels; tel. (2) 333-32-11; fax (2) 333-32-61; e-mail contact.mab@moniteurautomobile.be; internet www.moniteurautomobile.be; fortnightly; motoring; Editor-in-Chief XAVIER DAFFE; circ. 24,806 (2006).

Nest: 50 rue de la Fusée, BP 3, 1130 Brussels; tel. (2) 702-45-21; fax (2) 702-45-42; e-mail info@nest.be; internet www.nest.be; 8 a year; Dutch and French; lifestyle; owned by Roularta Media Group; Dir TESSA VERMEIREN; Editor-in-Chief PETER VANDEWEERDT; circ. 166,693 (2010).

Plus Magazine: 50 rue de la Fusée, BP 10, 1130 Brussels; tel. (2) 702-49-01; fax (2) 702-46-02; e-mail redactiie@plusmagazine.be; internet www.plusmagazine.be; monthly; Dutch and French; fmrly *Notre Temps / Onze Tijd*; senior citizens' interest; owned by Senior Publications N.V; Editor-in-Chief ANNE VANDERDONCKT; circ. 145,308 (2010).

Sélection du Reader's Digest: 20 blvd Paepsem, 1070 Brussels; tel. (2) 526-81-11; fax (2) 526-81-12; e-mail service@readersdigest.be; internet www.rdb.be; f. 1947; monthly; general; Editor-in-Chief OELE STEENKS; circ. 46,537 (2010).

Vrouw & Wereld: Langestraat 170, 1150 Brussels; tel. (2) 799-00-00; fax (2) 799-16-16; f. 1920; 11 a year; women's interest; circ. 88,900 (2010).

Vrouwen met Vaart: Remylaan 4B, 3018 Wijgmaal-Leuven; tel. (2) 624-39-99; fax (2) 624-39-09; e-mail kvlv@kvlv.be; internet www.kvlv.be; f. 1911; 10 a year; women's interest; circ. 107,925 (2010).

NEWS AGENCIES

Agence Belga (Agence Télégraphique Belge de Presse SA)/ Agentschap Belga (Belgisch Pers-telegraafagentschap NV): 8B rue F. Pelletier, 1030 Brussels; tel. (2) 743-23-11; fax (2) 735-17-44; e-mail redaction@belga.be; internet www.belga.be; f. 1920; largely owned by daily newspapers; Man. Dir EGBERT HANS; Editors-in-Chief JEAN-PIERRE BREULET, MARC HOLLANDERS.

Agence Europe SA: 36 rue de la Gare, 1040 Brussels; tel. (2) 737-94-94; fax (2) 736-37-00; e-mail info@agenceurope.com; internet www.agenceurope.info; f. 1953; daily bulletin on EU activities; Editor-in-Chief LIONEL CHANGEUR.

PRESS ASSOCIATIONS

Association belge des Editeurs de Journaux/Belgische Vereniging van de Dagbladuitgevers: 22 blvd Paepsem, bte 7, 1070 Brussels; tel. (2) 558-97-60; fax (2) 558-97-68; e-mail vdp@dagbladpers.org; e-mail www.dagbladpers.org; f. 1964; 17 mems; Pres BRUNO DE CARTIER; Gen. Secs ALEX FORDYN (Dutch), MARGARET BORIBON (French).

Association générale des Journalistes professionnels de Belgique/Algemene Vereniging van de Beroepsjournalisten in België (AGJPB/AVBB): Résidence Palace, Bloc C, 155 rue de la Loi, 1040 Brussels; tel. (2) 235-22-60; fax (2) 235-22-72; e-mail info@ajp.be; internet www.agjpb.be; f. 1978 by merger of the Association Générale de la Presse Belge and the Union Professionnelle de la Presse Belge; 4,899 mems; affiliated to International Federation of Journalists (IFJ); Nat. Secs MARTINE SIMONIS (AGJPB), POL DELTOUR (AVBB).

Association des Journalistes de la Presse Périodique/Vereniging van Journalisten van de Periodieke Pers: 54 rue Charles Martel, 1000 Brussels; tel. (2) 230-09-99; fax (2) 231-14-59; e-mail info@ajpp-vjpp.be; internet www.ajpp-vjpp.be; f. 1891; Pres. CLAUDE MUYLS.

Fédération Belge des Magazines/Federatie van de Belgische Magazines (FEBELMA): 22/8 blvd Paepsem, 1070 Brussels; tel. (2) 558-97-50; fax (2) 558-97-58; e-mail magazines@febelma.be; internet www.febelma.be; f. 1956 as Fédération Nationale des Hebdomadaires d'Information; present name adopted 1999; Pres. PATRICK DE BORCHGRAVE; Sec.-Gen. ALAIN LAMBRECHTS.

Principal Publishers

Acco CV: Blijde Inkomststraat 22, 3000 Leuven; tel. (1) 662-80-00; fax (1) 662-80-01; e-mail uitgeverij@acco.be; internet www.acco.be; f. 1960; general reference, scientific books, periodicals; Dir and Publr BART DE PRINS.

Uitgeverij Altiora Averbode NV: Abdijstraat 1, Postbus 54, 3271 Averbode; tel. (1) 378-01-82; e-mail proj@verbode.be; internet www.averbode.com; f. 1993; educational and children books; publishing dept of Uitgeverij Averbode; Int. Rights Man. JEAN-MARIE DELMOTTE.

Anthemis SA: Pl. Albert I, 9, 1300 Limal; tel. (10) 42-02-90; fax (10) 40-21-84; e-mail info@anthemis.be; internet www.anthemis.be; f. 2005; economics, law; Publrs ANNE ELOY, PATRICIA KEUNINGS.

Brepols Publishers NV: Begijnhof 67, 2300 Turnhout; tel. (1) 444-80-20; fax (1) 442-89-19; e-mail info@brepols.net; internet www.brepols.net; f. 1796; academic; Dir PAUL DE JONGH.

Editions Casterman SA: Cantersteen 47, Postbus 4, 1000 Brussels; tel. (2) 209-83-00; fax (2) 209-83-01; internet www.casterman.com; f. 1780; children's books (fiction, non-fiction, activity books), graphic books; Man. Dir LOUIS DELAS.

Davidsfonds vzw: Blijde-Inkomststraat 79–81, 3000 Leuven; tel. (1) 631-06-00; fax (1) 631-06-08; e-mail uitgeverij@davidsfonds.be; internet www.davidsfonds.be; f. 1875; general, reference, textbooks; Dir KATRIEN DE VREESE.

Groupe De Boeck SA: Belpairestraat 20, 2600 Berchem; tel. (3) 200-45-00; fax (3) 200-45-99; e-mail informatie@deboeck.com; internet www.deboeck.com; f. 1795; 100% stake acquired by Ergon Capital in 2011; French imprints: De Boeck Education, De Boeck Université, Duculot, Estem, Larcier; Dutch imprints: Uitgeverij De Boeck, Uitgeverij Larcier; educational, scientific, academic, medical, legal; Chair. ALAIN KOUCK; Man. Dir GEORGES HOYOS.

Editions Dupuis SA: 52 rue Jules Destrée, 6001 Marcinelle; tel. (7) 160-50-00; fax (7) 160-05-99; e-mail dupuis@dupuis.be; internet www.dupuis.com; f. 1898; children's fiction, periodicals and comic books for children and adults, multimedia and audiovisual; Dir-Gen. DIMITRI-NOËL KENNES.

Etablissements Emile Bruylant SA: 67 rue de la Régence, 1000 Brussels; tel. (2) 512-98-42; fax (2) 511-94-77; e-mail info@bruylant.be; internet www.bruylant.be; f. 1838; law; Pres. and Dir-Gen. JEAN VANDEVELD.

Uitgeverij EPO: Lange Pastoorstraat 25-27, 2600 Berchem; tel. (3) 239-68-74; fax (3) 218-46-04; e-mail uitgeverij@epo.be; internet www.epo.be; history, literature, travel, politics and social sciences; Dir MARTINE UYTTERHOEVEN; Publr JOS HENNES.

Groupe Erasme: 2 place Baudouin 1er, 5004 Bouge; tel. (8) 121-37-00; fax (8) 121-23-72; e-mail info@grouperasme.be; internet www.groupeerasme.be; f. 1945; imprints: Artel, D2H Didier Hatier-Hachette Education, Didier-Hatier, Erasme; school books; Dir BENOÎT DUBOIS.

Glénat Bénélux: 131 rue Saint-Lambert, 1200 Woluwe St Lambert; tel. (2) 761-26-40; fax (2) 761-26-45; internet www.glenat.com; f. 1985; owned by Glénat France; comics, magazines, books; CEO JACQUES GLÉNAT; Man. Dir HADELIN DEL MARMOL.

Editions Hemma SA: 106 rue Chevron, 4987 Chevron; tel. (86) 43-01-01; fax (86) 43-36-40; e-mail hemma@hemma.be; internet www.hemma.be; f. 1956; juveniles, educational books and materials; Dir ALBERT HEMMERLIN.

Houtekiet NV: Vrijheidstraat 33, 2000 Antwerp; tel. (3) 238-12-96; fax (3) 238-80-41; e-mail info@houtekiet.com; internet www.houtekiet.com; f. 1983; publ. by Linkeroever Uitgevers nv; Publr LEO DE HAES.

Intersentia NV: Groenstraat 31, 2640 Mortsel; tel. (3) 680-15-50; fax (3) 658-71-21; e-mail mail@intersentia.be; internet www.intersentia.com; Publrs KRIS MOEREMANS, HANS KLUWER, EWOUT LACROIX.

Die Keure NV: Kleine Pathoekeweg 3, 8000 Brugge; tel. (50) 47-12-72; fax (50) 34-37-68; e-mail info@diekeure.be; internet www.diekeure.be; f. 1948; textbooks, law, political and social sciences; Dirs B. VANDENBUSSCHE (secondary schools), NIC PAPPIJN (primary schools).

Uitgeverij De Klaproos: Ezelstraat 79, 8000 Brugge; tel. (5) 034-97-59; e-mail info@klaproos.be; internet www.klaproos.be; f. 1992; historical works; Dir SIEGFRIED DEBAEKE.

Kluwer: Ragheno Business Park, Motstraat 30, 2800 Mechelen; tel. (15) 36-10-00; fax (15) 36-11-91; e-mail info@kluwer.be; internet www.kluwer.be; law, business, scientific; subsidiary of Wolters Kluwer NV (Netherlands); CEO HENRI VAN ENGHELEN.

Uitgeverij Lannoo NV: Kasteelstraat 97, 8700 Tielt; tel. (51) 42-42-11; fax (51) 40-11-52; e-mail lannoo@lannoo.be; internet www.lannoo.com; f. 1909; general, reference; Man. Dir MATTHIAS LANNOO.

Editions du Lombard SA: 7 ave Paul-Henri Spaak, 1060 Brussels; tel. (2) 526-68-11; fax (2) 520-44-05; e-mail info@lombard.be; internet www.lelombard.be; f. 1946; graphic novels, comics; Gen. Man. FRANÇOIS PERNOT.

Manteau: Mechelsesteenweg 203, 2018 Antwerp; tel. (3) 285-72-00; fax (3) 285-72-99; e-mail info@standaarduitgeverij.be; internet www.standaarduitgeverij.be; f. 1932; literature; imprint of Standaard Uitgeverij NV; Dir ERIC WILLEMS.

Mercatorfonds: Zuidstraat 2, 1000 Brussel; tel. (2) 548-25-35; fax (2) 502-16-28; e-mail kunstboeken@mercatorfonds.be; internet www.mercatorfonds.be; f. 1965; art, ethnography, literature, music, geography and history; Dir JAN MARTENS.

Peeters: Bondgenotenlaan 153, 3000 Leuven; tel. (1) 623-51-70; fax (1) 622-85-00; e-mail peeters@peeters-leuven.be; internet www.peeters-leuven.be; f. 1857; academic; Dir P. PEETERS.

Uitgeverij Pelckmans NV: Kapelsestraat 222, 2950 Kapellen; tel. (3) 660-27-20; fax (3) 660-27-01; e-mail uitgeverij@pelckmans.be; internet www.pelckmans.be; f. 1893 as De Nederlandsche Boekhandel; present name adopted 1988; school books, scientific, general; Dirs J. PELCKMANS, R. PELCKMANS.

Plantyn NV: Motstraat 32, 2800 Mechelen; tel. (15) 36-36-36; fax (15) 36-36-37; e-mail klantendienst@plantyn.com; internet www.woltersplantyn.be; f. 1959; education; Dir DRIES VANHOVE.

Editions Racine: Tour & Taxis, Entrepôt Royal, ave du Port 86C, 1000 Brussels; tel. (2) 646-44-44; fax (2) 646-55-70; e-mail info@racine.be; internet www.racine.be; f. 1993; literature, art, history; Dir MICHÈLE POSKIN.

Roularta Books: Meiboomlaan 33, 8800 Roeselare; tel. (5) 126-61-11; fax (5) 126-68-66; e-mail jan.ingelbeen@roularta.be; internet www.roulartabooks.be; f. 1988; owned by Roularta Media Group; Publr JAN INGELBEEN.

Sanoma Magazines Belgium NV: Telecomlaan 5–7, 1831 Diegem; tel. (2) 776-22-11; fax (2) 776-23-99; e-mail info@sanoma-magazines.be; internet www.sanoma-magazines.be; periodicals; f. 2002; owned by SanomaWSOY Group (Finland); CEO AIMÉ VAN HECKE.

Snoecks NV: Begijnhoflaan 452, 9000 Ghent; tel. (9) 267-04-11; fax (9) 267-04-60; e-mail snoecks@snoecks.be; internet www.snoecks.be; f. 1782; art books, travel guides; acquired by Deckers Druk in 2006; Editor HALBE DE JONG.

Standaard Uitgeverij NV: Mechelsesteenweg 203, 2018 Antwerp; tel. (3) 285-72-00; fax (3) 285-72-99; e-mail info@standaarduitgeverij.be; internet www.standaarduitgeverij.be; f. 1924; general, fiction, non-fiction, comics, dictionaries and professional literature; Dirs LUDO STROOBANTS, JOHAN DE KONING, JOHAN VAN HULLE.

Editions Versant Sud: Pl. de l'Université 16, 1348 Louvain-la-Neuve; tel. (10) 23-54-37; fax (10) 48-35-36; e-mail info@versant-sud.com; internet www.versant-sud.com; f. 2001; independent; history, music, tourism, comics; Editor ELISABETH JONGEN.

Yoyo Books: Hagelberg 33, 2250 Olen; tel. (1) 428-23-40; fax (1) 428-23-49; e-mail jo.dupre@yoyo-books.com; internet www.yoyo-books.com; imprints: Yoyo, Allegrio; educational, cookery; Man. Dir JO DUPRÉ.

PUBLISHERS' ASSOCIATIONS

Association des Editeurs Belges (ADEB): 34 ave Huart Hamoir, 1030 Brussels; tel. (2) 241-65-80; fax (2) 216-71-31; e-mail adeb@adeb.be; internet www.adeb.be; f. 1922; asscn of French-language book publrs; Dir BERNARD GÉRARD.

Vlaamse Uitgevers Vereniging (VUV): Te Boelaerlei 37, 2140 Borgerhout; tel. (3) 287-66-92; fax (3) 281-22-40; e-mail geert

.vandenbossche@boek.be; internet www.vuv.be; asscn of Flemish-language book publrs; Dir GEERT VAN DEN BOSSCHE.

Broadcasting and Communications

TELECOMMUNICATIONS

Regulatory Authority

Institut Belge des Services Postaux et des Télécommunications/Belgisch Instituut voor Postdiensten en Telecommunicatie (Belgian Institute for Postal Services and Telecommunications—IBPT/BIPT): 35 Blvd du Rol Albert II, 1030 Brussels; tel. (2) 226-88-88; fax (2) 226-88-77; e-mail info@ibpt.be; internet www.ibpt.be; ensures regulatory frameworks are observed, consumer rights are protected and certain tasks of public interest are carried out; Chair. LUC HINDRYCKX.

Major Service Providers

Belgacom: 27B blvd du Roi Albert II, 1030 Brussels; tel. (2) 202-41-11; fax (2) 203-65-93; e-mail about@belgacom.be; internet www.belgacom.be; f. 1992; total service operator; Chair. ETIENNE SCHOUPPE; Pres. and CEO DIDIER BELLENS.

Belgacom Mobile SA (Proximus): 27B blvd du Roi Albert II, 1030 Brussels; tel. (2) 205-40-00; fax (2) 205-40-40; internet www.proximus.be; wholly owned subsidiary of Belgacom; mobile cellular telephone operator; Chair. ETIENNE SCHOUPPE.

BT Ltd (Belgium): Telecomlaan 9, 1831 Diegem; tel. (2) 700-22-11; fax (2) 700-32-11; e-mail info.belgium@bt.com; internet www.bt.be; subsidiary of BT Group plc (UK); Group Chair. Sir MICHAEL RAKE.

Cable & Wireless Belgium NV: Zaventemsesteenweg 162, 1831 Diegem; tel. (2) 627-34-00; fax (2) 627-34-01; internet www.cw.com; Man. Dir DAVID RICKETT.

KPN Group Belgium SA/NV: 105 rue Neerveld, 1200 Brussels; tel. (486) 19-99-99; fax (484) 00-62-01; e-mail help@base.be; internet www.base.be; fmrly BASE SA/NV; present name adopted in 2009; mobile cellular telephone operator; subsidiary of Koninklijke KPN NV (Netherlands); CEO ERIC HAGEMAN.

Mobistar: 3 ave du Bourgetlaan, 1140 Brussels; tel. (2) 745-71-11; fax (2) 745-70-00; internet www.mobistar.be; f. 1995; mobile cellular telephone and fixed-line operator; owned by Orange SA (France); CEO JEAN MARC HARION; 3.5m. customers (Sept. 2011).

Numericable: 26 rue des Deux Eglises, 1000 Brussels; tel. (2) 226-52-00; fax (2) 226-54-10; e-mail business-solutions@coditel.be; internet www.coditel.be; fmrly Coditel SA; acquired by Apax (France), Deficom Telecom and Altice (France) in 2011; main cable operator in the Brussels Region; Dir-Gen. PASCAL DORMAL.

Scarlet SA: Belgicastraat 5, 1930 Zaventem; tel. (2) 275-27-27; internet www.scarlet.be; f. 1997; offers fixed-line telephone and broadband internet services; acquired by Belgacom in 2008.

Telenet NV: Liersesteenweg 4, 2800 Mechelen; tel. (15) 33-30-00; fax (15) 33-39-99; internet www.telenet.be; f. 1996; total service operator; acquired UPC Belgium 2007; CEO DUCO SICKINGHE.

Verizon Belgium Luxembourg NV: Culliganlaan 2E, 1831 Diegem; tel. (2) 400-80-00; fax (2) 400-84-00; e-mail info@be.verizonbusiness.com; internet www.verizonbusiness.com/be; subsidiary of Verizon Communications (USA); Group CEO LOWELL MCADAM.

Voo: 25 rue Louvrex, 4000 Liège; internet www.voo.be; f. 2006 by merger of ALE-Télédis and Brutélé; owned by TECTEO; digital television, fixed-line telephone and broadband internet service provider; provides services to Brussels-Capital and Walloon Regions.

PUBLIC BROADCASTING ORGANIZATIONS

Flemish Community

TV Brussel: Flageygebouw, Belvédèrestraat 27A, Postbus 1, 1050 Elsene; tel. (2) 702-87-30; fax (2) 702-87-41; e-mail nieuws@tvbrussel.be; internet www.tvbrussel.be; f. 1993; broadcasts news and Dutch-language programmes in Brussels-Capital and Flanders Regions; funded by the Flemish Community; Editor-in-Chief ROBERT ESSELINCKX (acting).

Vlaamse Radio- en Televisieomroep NV (VRT): Auguste Reyerslaan 52, 1043 Brussels; tel. (2) 741-31-11; fax (2) 734-93-51; e-mail info@vrt.be; internet www.vrt.be; f. 1998; shares held by Flemish Community; operates 7 radio stations (Radio 1, Radio 2, Klara, Donna, MNM, Radio Brussel and RVi) and 3 television stations (Eén, Canvas and Ketnet); Chair. LUC VAN DEN BRANDE; Man. Dir SANDRA DE PRETER.

French Community

Radio-Télévision Belge de la Communauté Française (RTBF): 52 blvd Auguste Reyers, 1044 Brussels; tel. (2) 737-21-11; fax (2) 737-25-56; internet www.rtbf.be; operates 6 radio stations (La Première, VivaCité, Musiq'3, Classic 21, Pure FM and RTBF International) and 3 television stations (La Une, La Deux and RTBF Sat); Dir-Gen. JEAN-PAUL PHILIPPOT; Dir of Radio FRANCIS GOFFIN; Dir of Television FRANÇOIS TRON.

Télé Bruxelles: 32 rue Gabrielle Petit, 1080 Brussels; tel. (2) 421-21-21; fax (2) 421-21-22; e-mail contact@telebruxelles.be; internet www.telebruxelles.net; f. 1985; broadcasts programmes in French to Brussels-Capital and Walloon Regions; funded mainly by the French Community; Dir-Gen. MARC DE HAAN.

German-speaking Community

Belgisches Rundfunk- und Fernsehzentrum der Deutschsprachigen Gemeinschaft (BRF): Kehrweg 11, 4700 Eupen; tel. (87) 59-11-11; fax (87) 59-11-99; e-mail info@brf.be; internet www.brf.be; operates 3 radio stations (BRF1, BRF2 and BRF-DLF) and 1 television station (BRF TV); Dir ARTHUR SPODEN.

COMMERCIAL, CABLE AND PRIVATE BROADCASTING

PRIME: Liersesteenweg 4, 2800 Mechelen; tel. (2) 716-53-53; fax (2) 716-54-54; e-mail service@prime.be; internet www.prime.be; f. 1989; operated by Telenet NV; broadcasts in Dutch.

Regionale TV Media: Z.1 Research Park 120, 1731 Zellik; tel. (2) 467-58-77; fax (2) 467-56-54; e-mail contact@rtvm.be; internet www.rtvm.be; group of 11 regional news broadcasters within Flanders; commercial; Dir FRÉDÉRIC DEVOS.

RTL TVI: 2 ave Jacques Georgin, 1030 Brussels; tel. (2) 337-68-11; fax (2) 337-68-12; internet www.rtltvi.be; owned by RTL Group, Luxembourg; commercial station; broadcasts in French; Chief Exec. PHILIPPE DELUSINNE.

Vlaamse Media Maatschappij: Medialaan 1, 1800 Vilvoorde; tel. (2) 255-32-11; fax (2) 252-37-87; e-mail info@vtm.be; internet www.vtm.be; f. 1987; commercial; broadcasts in Dutch; Dir-Gen. (vacant).

Finance

(cap. = capital; res = reserves; dep. = deposits; m. = million; brs = branches; amounts in euros, unless otherwise indicated)

BANKING

L'Autorité des services et marchés financiers (The Financial Services and Markets Authority): 12–14 rue du Congrès, 1000 Brussels; tel. (2) 220-52-11; fax (2) 220-52-75; internet www.fsma.be; f. 2004 by merger; fmrly known as Commission bancaire, financière et des assurances; name changed to present in 2011; supervisory body for the financial sector; Chair., Management Bd JEAN-PAUL SERVAIS; Sec.-Gen. ALBERT NIESTEN.

Central Bank

Banque Nationale de Belgique (National Bank of Belgium): 14 blvd de Berlaimont, 1000 Brussels; tel. (2) 221-21-11; fax (2) 221-31-00; e-mail info@nbb.be; internet www.nbb.be; f. 1850; bank of issue; cap. 10m., res 2,661.8m., dep. 15,376.6m. (Dec. 2009); Gov. LUC COENE; 2 brs.

Major Commercial Banks

ABN AMRO Bank NV: Kanselarijstraat 17A, 1000 Brussels; tel. (2) 229-58-00; fax (2) 229-59-10; e-mail info@abnamro.be; internet www.abnamro.be; f. 1824; acquired by Fortis Bank (Netherlands), Banco Santander Centro Hispano (Spain), Royal Bank of Scotland PLC (UK) in 2007; Netherlands Govt acquired Dutch operations of Fortis Bank, incl. stake in ABN AMRO in 2008; Chair., Management Bd GERRIT ZALM; Chair., Supervisory Bd ARTHUR MARTÍNEZ; 7 brs.

Antwerpse Diamantbank NV/Banque Diamantaire Anversoise SA/Antwerp Diamond Bank NV: Pelikaanstraat 54, 2018 Antwerp; tel. (3) 204-72-04; fax (3) 233-90-95; e-mail jmampaey@adia.be; internet www.antwerpdiamondbank.com; f. 1934; owned by KBC Bank NV; cap. 34.4m., res 132.7m., dep. 1,322.7m. (Dec. 2010); Chair. DIRK MAMPAEY; CEO PIERRE DE BOSSCHER.

AXA Bank Europe NV: 25 blvd du Souverain, 1170 Brussels; tel. (2) 678-61-11; fax (2) 678-93-40; e-mail contact@axa-bank.be; internet www.axa.be; f. 1881 as ANHYP Bank NV; fmrly AXA Bank Belgium NV; present name adopted 2008; cap. 546.3m., res –172.6m., dep 17,941.5m. (Dec. 2010); Chair., Bd of Dirs ALFRED BOUCKAERT; CEO EUGÈNE THYSEN; 5 brs.

Banca Monte Paschi Belgio SA/NV: 24 rue Joseph II, 1000 Brussels; tel. (2) 220-72-11; fax (2) 218-83-91; e-mail info@montepaschi.be; internet www.montepaschi.be; f. 1947 as Banco di

Roma (Belgique); name changed 1992; 99% owned by Banca Monte dei Paschi di Siena SpA; cap. 50.9m., res 30.7m., dep. 1,254.2m. (Dec. 2010); Gen. Dir and Pres. of Exec. Cttee LUIGI MACCHIOLA; 1 br.

Bank J. Van Breda & Co NV: Ledeganckkaai 7, 2000 Antwerp; tel. (3) 217-53-33; fax (3) 271-10-94; e-mail info@bankvanbreda.be; internet www.bankvanbreda.be; f. 1930; present name adopted 1998; cap. 17.5m., res –4.4m., dep. 2,746.6m. (Dec. 2010); Pres., Exec. Cttee and Gen. Man. CARLO HENRIKSEN; 41 brs.

Bank Degroof SA/Banque Degroof SA: 44 rue de l'Industrie, 1040 Brussels; tel. (2) 287-91-11; fax (2) 230-67-00; e-mail info@degroof.be; internet www.degroof.be; f. 1871; present name adopted 1998; cap. 47.5m., res 465.8m., dep. 3,889.1m. (Dec. 2010; Chair. ALAIN SIAENS; CEO REGNIER HAEGELSTEEN.

Bank Delen NV/Banque Delen SA: Jan Van Rijswijcklaan 184, 2020 Antwerp; tel. (3) 244-55-66; fax (3) 216-04-91; e-mail info@delen.be; internet www.delen.be; f. 1928; name changed as above in 1996; cap. 41.8m., res 4.7m., dep. 1,030.1m. (Dec. 2010); Pres. JACQUES DELEN; Chair. JAN SUYKENS; 5 brs.

Belfius Banque & Assurances: 44 blvd Pachéco, 1000 Brussels; tel. (2) 222-11-11; fax (2) 222-11-22; internet www.dexia.be; f. 1860 as Crédit Communal de Belgique SA; present name changed from Dexia Bank Belgium 2012; Belgian Govt acquired 100% of the shares of Dexia SA in Dexia Bank Belgium in Oct. 2011; cap. 3,458.1m., res –2,308.7m., dep. 93,611.8m. (Dec. 2010); Chair., Supervisory Bd JEAN-LUC DEHAENE; Chair., Exec. Cttee JOS CLIJSTERS; 1,283 brs.

BNP Paribas Fortis: 3 Montagne du Parc, 1000 Brussels; tel. (2) 511-26-311; fax (2) 565-49-29; e-mail info@fortisbank.com; internet www.fortisbanking.be; f. 1990 as Fortis Group; present name adopted May 2009 following acquisition by BNP Paribas (France) of a 75% stake in Fortis Bank SA/NV; 25% owned by Belgian Govt; banking, insurance and investments; cap. 9,605m., res -2,012m., dep. 177,382m. (Dec. 2010); Chair. HERMAN DAEMS; CEO MAXIME JADOT; 1,081 brs.

Byblos Bank Europe SA: 10 rue Montoyer, 1000 Brussels; tel. (2) 551-00-20; fax (2) 513-05-26; e-mail byblos.europe@byblosbankeur.com; internet www.byblosbank.com.lb; f. 1976 as Byblos Arab Finance Bank (Belgium) SA; present name adopted 1998; cap. 20m., res 31.1m., dep. 551.1m. (Dec. 2010); Chair. Dr FRANÇOIS S. BASSIL; Exec. Dir SAMI HADDAD; 2 brs.

CBC Banque SA: 5 Grand-Place, 1000 Brussels; tel. (2) 547-12-11; fax (2) 547-11-10; e-mail info@cbc.be; internet www.cbc.be; f. 1958; name changed as above in 1998 following merger; cap. 89.6m., res 354.6m., dep. 9,686.9m. (Dec. 2010); Chair., Bd of Dirs JOHAN THIJS; Chair., Exec. Cttee DANIEL FALQUE; 115 brs.

Citibank Belgium NV/SA: 263 blvd Général Jacques, 1050 Brussels; tel. (2) 626-64-63; fax (2) 626-64-28; internet www.citibank.be; f. 1919; present name adopted 1992; Chair. JOSÉ DE PEÑARANDA.

Crédit Agricole SA/Landbouwkrediet NV: 251 blvd Sylvain Dupuis, 1070 Brussels; tel. (2) 558-71-11; fax (2) 558-76-23; e-mail info@credit-agricole.be; internet www.creditagricole.be; f. 1937; name changed as above in 1995; cap. 705.6m., res 242.6m., dep. 8,431m. (Dec. 2010); Pres ALAIN DIÉVAL; CEO LUC VERSELE.

Crédit Professionnel SA/Beroepskrediet NV: 6–9 ave des Arts, 1210 Brussels; tel. (2) 289-82-00; fax (2) 289-89-90; e-mail info@bkcp.be; internet www.bkcp.be; f. 1946 as Caisse Nationale de Crédit Professionnel SA; name changed as above 1997; cap. 153.9m., res 126.5m., dep. 2,900.1m. (Dec. 2010); Chair., Bd of Dirs ERIC CHARPENTIER; Chair., Exec. Bd JACQUES FAVILLIER.

Delta Lloyd Bank NV: 23 ave de l'Astronomie, 1210 Brussels; tel. (2) 229-76-00; fax (2) 229-76-99; e-mail info@dlbank.be; internet www.deltalloydbank.be; f. 1966 as Bankunie NV; above name adopted 2001; subsidiary of Delta Lloyd Group (Netherlands); cap. 248.4m., res 42.4m., dep. 4,960.7m. (Dec. 2010); Pres. JOOST MELIS.

Euroclear Bank SA: 1 blvd du Roi Albert II, 1210 Brussels; tel. (2) 326-12-11; fax (2) 326-12-87; e-mail info@euroclear.com; internet www.euroclear.com; f. 2000; 100% owned by Euroclear SA/NV; cap. 285.5m., res 584.3m., dep. 7,801.2m. (Dec. 2010); CEO PIERRE FRANCOTTE.

Europabank NV: Burgstraat 170, 9000 Ghent; tel. (9) 224-73-11; fax (9) 223-34-72; e-mail info@europabank.be; internet www.europabank.be; f. 1964; 99.9% owned by Crédit Agricole SA/Landbouwkrediet NV; cap. 1.5m., res 88.2m., dep. 661.9m. (Dec. 2010); Chair. LUC VERSELE; Pres. LUK OSTE; 44 brs.

Goffin Bank NV/Goffin Banque SA: Verlorenbroodstraat 120, 9820 Merelbeke; tel. (9) 261-02-00; fax (9) 261-02-01; e-mail info@goffinbank.be; internet www.goffinbank.be; f. 1955 as Kempische Hypotheek en Finaciering Maatschappij; present named adopted 2001; cap. 11.0m., res 0.6m., dep. 174.6m. (Dec. 2005); Pres. A. G. SAVELKOUL-LOMMAERT; Chair., Management Bd M. PIENS.

ING Belgium SA/NV: 24 ave Marnix, 1000 Brussels; tel. (2) 547-21-11; fax (2) 547-38-44; e-mail info@ing.be; internet www.ing.be; f. 1975 as Bank Brussels Lambert; acquired in 1998 by ING Group (Netherlands); name changed as above in April 2003; cap. 2,350m., res 6,202m., dep. 162,964m. (Dec. 2008); Chair., Bd of Dirs ERIC BOYER DE LA GIRODAY; CEO RALPH HAMERS; 781 brs.

KBC Bank NV: Havenlaan 2, 1080 Brussels 8; tel. (2) 429-11-11; fax (2) 429-81-31; e-mail kbc.telecenter@kbc.be; internet www.kbc.be; f. 1935 as Kredietbank NV; merged with Bank von Roeselare NV and CERA Investment Bank NV in 1998; cap. and res 10,728m., dep. 252,079m. (Dec. 2008); Chair. JAN HUYGHEBAERT; CEO JAN VANHEVEL.

Keytrade Bank SA: 100 blvd de Souverain, 1170 Brussels; tel. (2) 679-90-00; fax (2) 679-90-01; e-mail info@keytradebank.com; internet www.keytradebank.com; f. 2002 by merger of RealBank SA and VMS Keytrade.com; owned by Credit Agricole SA/Landbouwkrediet NV; cap. 28.3m., res 23.4m., dep. 1,939.6m. (Dec. 2010); Pres., CEO and Gen. Man. THIERRY TERNIER.

Santander Benelux SA/NV: 85 ave des Nerviens, 1040 Brussels; tel. (2) 286-54-11; fax (2) 230-52-32; f. 1914 as Société Hollandaise de Banque; present name adopted 2004; owned by Banco Santander Centro Hispano SA (Spain); cap. 1,139.6m., res 12.8m., dep. 6,226.1m. (Dec. 2010); Man. Dir GUILLERMO SANZ MURAT.

Development Bank

Gewestelijke Investeringsmaatschappij voor Vlaanderen (GIMV): Karel Oomsstraat 37, 2018 Antwerp; tel. (3) 290-21-00; fax (3) 290-21-05; e-mail info@gimv.be; internet www.gimv.com; f. 1980; promotes creation, restructuring and expansion of private cos; net assets 446m. (2007); Chair. URBAIN VANDEURZEN; CEO KOEN DEJONCKHEERE.

Banking Association

Association Belge des Banques et des Sociétés de Bourse/Belgische Vereniging van Banken en Beursvennootschappen (ABB/BVB): 82 rue d'Arlon, BP 5, 1040 Brussels; tel. (2) 507-68-11; fax (2) 888-68-11; e-mail info@febelfin.be; internet www.febelfin.be; f. 1936; part of Fédération Belge du Secteur Financier (FEBELFIN); Pres. FILIP DIERCKX; CEO MICHEL VERMAERKE.

STOCK EXCHANGE

Euronext Brussels SA/NV: Palais de la Bourse, 1000 Brussels; tel. (2) 509-12-11; fax (2) 509-12-12; e-mail info.be@euronext.com; internet www.euronext.com; formed in 2000 by merger of Amsterdam, Paris and Brussels exchanges, and joined in 2002 by the Lisbon stock exchange and the London futures exchange LIFFE; merged with New York Stock Exchange in 2007 to form NYSE Euronext; Chair. and CEO BRUNO COLMANT.

INSURANCE

Principal Insurance Companies

AG Insurance: 53 blvd Emile Jacqmain, 1000 Brussels; tel. (2) 664-81-11; fax (2) 664-81-50; e-mail info@aginsurance.be; internet www.aginsurance.be; f. 2006 as Fortis Insurance Belgium by merger of Fortis AG and FBAssurances; current name adopted in 2009; owned by Fortis Group; CEO ANTONIO CANO.

Allianz: Lakensestraat 35, 1000 Brussels; tel. (2) 214-61-11; internet www.allianz.be; f. 1890; insurance and financial services; CEO ROBERT FRANSSEN.

AXA: 25 blvd du Souverain, 1170 Brussels; tel. (2) 678-61-11; fax (2) 678-93-40; e-mail elly.bens@axa.be; internet www.axa.be; f. 1853; member of the AXA group; all branches; Pres. ALFRED BOUCKAERT; Chair., Exec. Cttee and Man. Dir EUGÈNE TEYSEN.

Delta Lloyd Life SA: 38 ave Fonsny, 1060 Brussels; tel. (2) 238-88-11; fax (2) 238-88-99; e-mail quality@deltalloydlife.be; internet www.deltalloydlife.be; f. 2001; by the merger of three Belgian companies; subsidiary of Delta Lloyd Group; life insurance; Chair. ONNO VERSTEGHEN; CEO JAN VAN AUTREVE.

ERGO: 1–8 blvd Bischoffsheim, 1000 Brussels; tel. (2) 535-57-11; fax (2) 535-57-00; e-mail info@ergo.be; internet www.ergo.be; f. 1960; both life and non-life insurance; Chair. Dr JOHANNES LÖRPER.

Ethias: 24 rue des Croisiers, 4000 Liège; tel. (4) 220-31-11; fax (4) 220-30-05; e-mail info@ethias.be; internet www.ethias.be; f. 1919; fmrly Société Mutuelle des Administrations Publiques (SMAP), name changed as above in 2003; institutions, civil service employees, public administration and enterprises; CEO BERNARD THIRY.

Generali Belgium SA: 149 ave Louise, 1050 Brussels; tel. (2) 403-87-00; fax (2) 403-88-99; e-mail generali_belgium@generali.be; internet www.generali.be; f. 1901; all branches; Chair. GABRIELE GALATERI DI GENOLA.

ING Life & Non-Life Belgium SA/NV: 70 cours Saint-Michel, 1040 Brussels; tel. (2) 547-77-00; fax (2) 547-70-22; e-mail telecel@ing.be; internet www.ing.be; f. 2007; as two new insurance companies ING Life Belgium SA/NV and ING Non-Life Belgium SA/NV; Chair. ERIC BOYER DE LA GIRODAY.

KBC SA/NV: Overstraetenplein 2, 3000 Leuven; tel. (07) 815-21-54; fax (03) 283-29-50; e-mail kbc24plus@verz.kbc.be; internet www.kbc.be; f. 1998; Chair. JOHAN THIJS.

Mercator Verzekeringen: Posthofbrug 16, 2600 Antwerp; tel. (3) 247-21-11; fax (3) 247-27-77; e-mail info@mercator.be; internet www.mercator.be; CEO GERT DE WINTER.

P & V: Koningsstraat 151, 1210 Brussels; tel. (2) 250-91-11; fax (2) 250-90-46; e-mail infonl@pv.be; internet www.pv.be; f. 1907; both life and non-life; Chair. GUY PEETERS.

Insurance Associations

Assuralia: 29 square de Meeûs, 1000 Brussels; tel. (2) 547-56-11; fax (2) 547-56-01; e-mail info@assuralia.be; internet www.assuralia.be; f. 1921; affiliated to Fédération des Entreprises de Belgique; Pres. BART DE SMET; 95 mems.

Fédération des Courtiers d'Assurances et Intermédiaires Financiers de Belgique (FEPRABEL): 40 ave Albert-Elisabeth, 1200 Brussels; tel. (2) 743-25-60; fax (2) 735-44-58; e-mail info@feprabel.be; internet www.feprabel.be; f. 1934; Pres. VINCENT MAGNUS; 500 mems.

Trade and Industry

GOVERNMENT AGENCIES

Flanders Investment and Trade: Gaucheretstraat 90, 1030 Brussels; tel. (2) 504-87-11; fax (2) 504-88-99; e-mail info@fitagency.be; internet www.investinflanders.com; f. 1991; promotes foreign investment in Flanders and Flemish business abroad; Man. Dir KOEN ALLAERT.

Société de Développement pour la Région de Bruxelles-Capitale (SDRB): 6 rue Gabrielle Petit, 1080 Brussels; tel. (2) 422-51-11; fax (2) 422-51-12; e-mail info@brda.be; internet www.brda.be; f. 1974; promotes economic development in the capital; Pres. L. WILLAME; Man. Dir J. MEGANCK.

Société Régionale d'Investissement de Wallonie: 13 ave Destenay, 4000 Liège; tel. (4) 221-98-11; fax (4) 221-99-99; e-mail sriw@sriw.be; internet www.sriw.be; f. 1979; promotes private enterprise in Wallonia; Chair. JEAN-PASCAL LABILLE.

PRINCIPAL CHAMBERS OF COMMERCE

There are chambers of commerce and industry in all major towns and industrial areas.

Chambre de Commerce de Bruxelles (BECI): 500 ave Louise, 1050 Brussels; tel. (2) 648-50-02; fax (2) 640-93-28; e-mail info@beci.be; internet www.beci.be; f. 1875; Pres. EMMANUEL VAN INNIS; 3,000 mems.

Chambre de Commerce et d'Industrie de Liège et de Verviers: 35 rue Renkin, 4800 Verviers; tel. (87) 29-36-36; fax (87) 26-87-80; e-mail info@ccilv.be; internet www.ccilv.be; f. 1866; Dir XAVIER CIECHANOWSKI; 2,000 mems.

Voka—Kamer van Koophandel Antwerpen-Waasland: Markgravestraat 12, 2000 Antwerp; tel. (3) 232-22-19; fax (3) 233-64-42; e-mail info@kvkaw.voka.be; internet www.voka.be; f. 1969; Pres. BERNARD VAN MILDERS; 3,000 mems.

INDUSTRIAL AND TRADE ASSOCIATIONS

Fédération des Entreprises de Belgique (VBO-FEB) (Federation of Belgian Companies): Ravensteinstraat 4, 1000 Brussels; tel. (2) 515-08-11; fax (2) 515-09-15; e-mail info@vbo-feb.be; internet www.vbo-feb.be; f. 1895; federates all the main industrial and non-industrial asscns; Chair. PIERRE ALAIN DE SMEDT; CEO RUDI THOMAES; 33 full mems.

Agoria—Fédération Multisectorielle de l'Industrie Technologique (Multisector Federation for the Technology Industry): 80 blvd Auguste Reyers, 1030 Brussels; tel. (2) 706-78-00; fax (2) 706-78-01; e-mail info@agoria.be; internet www.agoria.be; f. 1946; present name adopted 2000; more than 1,200 mem. cos; Chair. FRANCIS VERHEUGHE; CEO PAUL SOETE.

Association des Fabricants de Pâtes, Papiers et Cartons de Belgique (COBELPA) (Paper): 306 ave Louise, BP 11, 1050 Brussels; tel. (2) 646-64-50; fax (2) 646-82-97; e-mail general@cobelpa.be; internet www.cobelpa.be; f. 1940; Gen. Man. FIRMIN FRANÇOIS.

Belgian Petroleum Federation (Petroleum): 39 ave des Arts, BP 2, 1040 Brussels; tel. (2) 508-30-00; fax (2) 511-05-91; e-mail info@petrolfed.be; internet www.petrolfed.be; f. 1926; Pres. PATRICE BRÈS; Sec.-Gen. JEAN-LOUIS NIZET.

Brasseurs Belges (Belgian Brewers): Maison des Brasseurs, 10 Grand-Place, 1000 Brussels; tel. (2) 511-49-87; fax (2) 511-32-59; e-mail belgian.brewers@beerparadise.be; internet www.beerparadise.be; f. 1971; Chair. THEO VERVLOET.

Confédération Nationale de la Construction (CNC) (Civil Engineering, Road and Building Contractors and Auxiliary Trades): 34–42 rue du Lombard, 1000 Brussels; tel. (2) 545-56-00; fax (2) 545-59-00; e-mail info@confederatiebouw.be; internet www.cnc.be; f. 1946; Pres. JACQUES DE MEESTER; Man. Dir ROBERT DE MÛELENAERE; 14,000 mems.

Confédération Professionnelle du Sucre et de ses Dérivés (SUBEL) (Sugar): 182 ave de Tervueren, 1150 Brussels; tel. (2) 775-80-23; fax (2) 775-80-75; e-mail info@subel.be; internet www.subel.be; f. 1938; mems: 10 groups, 66 cos; Pres. E. KESSELS; Dir-Gen. M. ROSIERS.

Creamoda (Clothing): Leliegaarde 22, 1731 Zellik; tel. (2) 238-10-11; fax (2) 238-10-10; e-mail info@creamoda.be; internet www.belgianfashion.be; f. 1946; Dir-Gen. ERIK MAGNUS.

Fédération Belge de la Brique (Bricks): 19 rue des Chartreux, BP 19, 1000 Brussels; tel. (2) 511-25-81; fax (2) 513-26-40; e-mail info@brique.be; internet www.brique.be; f. 1947; Pres. CAMILLE VANPEE; Dir JO VAN DEN BOSSCHE; 35 mems.

Fédération Belge des Dragueurs de Gravier et de Sable (BELBAG) (Quarries): Maasstraat 82, Postbus 2, 3640 Kinrooi; tel. (8) 956-08-08; fax (8) 956-08-09; e-mail info@belbag.be; internet www.belbag.be; f. 1967; Pres. LUC SEVERIJNS.

Fédération Belge de l'Industrie de l'Automobile et du Cycle (FEBIAC) (Motor Vehicles and Bicycles): 46/6 blvd de la Woluwe, 1200 Brussels; tel. (2) 778-64-00; fax (2) 762-81-71; e-mail info@febiac.be; internet www.febiac.be; f. 1936; Sec.-Gen. ANDRÉ DECRAENE.

Fédération Belge de l'Industrie Textile, du Bois et de l'Ameublement (FEDUSTRIA) (Textiles, Wood and Furniture): 5 allée Hof-ter-Vleest, 1070 Brussels; tel. (2) 528-58-11; fax (2) 528-58-29; e-mail info@fedustria.be; internet www.fedustria.be; f. 2006 by merger of Febelbois and Fébeltex; Pres. PHILIPPE CORTHOUTS; Man. Dir FA QUIX.

Fédération Belge des Industries Chimiques et des Sciences de la Vie (Essenscia) (Chemical Industries and Life Sciences): 80 blvd Auguste Reyers, 1030 Brussels; tel. (2) 238-97-11; fax (2) 231-13-01; e-mail info@essenscia.be; internet www.essenscia.be; Pres. WOUTER DE GEEST; Man. Dir YVES VERSCHUEREN; 650 mem. cos.

Fédération Belge des Industries Graphiques (FEBELGRA) (Graphic Industries): Barastraat 175, 1070 Brussels; tel. (2) 411-22-96; fax (2) 513-56-76; e-mail febelgra.bru@skynet.be; internet www.febelgra.be; f. 1978; Pres. ARMIN VAN DER LINDEN; 750 mems.

Fédération Belgo-Luxembourgeoise de l'Industrie du Tabac (FEDETAB) (Tobacco): 7 ave Lloyd George, 1000 Brussels; tel. (2) 646-04-20; fax (2) 646-22-13; e-mail tobacco@fedetab.be; f. 1947; Pres. G. VANDERMARLIÈRE.

Fédération des Carrières de Petit Granit—Pierre Bleue de Belgique ASBL (Limestone): 1 chemin de Carrières, 7063 Neufvilles; tel. (67) 34-68-05; fax (67) 33-08-49; e-mail info@federationpierrebleue.be; internet www.federationpierrebleue.be; f. 1948; Pres. JEAN-FRANZ ABRAHAM.

Fédération d'Employeurs pour le Commerce International, le Transport et les Branches d'Activité Connexes (Employers' Federation of International Trade, Transport and Related Activities); incl. Fédération Patronale des Ports Belges: Brouwersvliet 33, Postbus 7, 2000 Antwerp; tel. (3) 221-97-11; fax (3) 232-38-26; e-mail cepa@cepa.be; internet www.cepa.be; f. 1937; Pres. MARINO VERMEERSCH; Dir RENÉ DE BROUWER.

Fédération de l'Industrie Alimentaire/Federatie Voedingsindustrie (FEVIA) (Food): 43 ave des Arts, BP 7, 1040 Brussels; tel. (2) 550-17-40; fax (2) 550-17-54; e-mail info@fevia.be; internet www.fevia.be; f. 1937; Dir-Gen. CHRIS MORIS.

Fédération de l'Industrie du Béton (FEBE) (Precast Concrete): 68 blvd du Souverain, 1170 Brussels; tel. (2) 735-80-15; fax (2) 734-77-95; e-mail mail@febe.be; internet www.febe.be; f. 1936; Pres. LUDO PANIS; Dir EDDY DANO; 80 mem. cos.

Fédération de l'Industrie Cimentière Belge (FEBELCEM) (Cement): 68, blvd du Souverain, 1170 Brussels; tel. (2) 645-52-11; fax (2) 640-06-70; e-mail info@febelcem.be; internet www.febelcem.be; f. 1949; Pres. A. JACQUEMART; Dir-Gen. ANDRÉ JASIENSKI.

Fédération des Industries Extractives et Transformatrices de Roches non-Combustibles (FEDIEX) (Extraction and processing of non-fuel rocks): 68 blvd du Souverain, 1170 Brussels; tel. (2) 511-61-73; fax (2) 511-12-84; e-mail info@fediex.org; internet www.fediex.be; f. 1942 as Union des Producteurs Belges de Chaux, Calcaires, Dolomies et Produits Connexes; name changed (as above) 1990; co-operative society; Pres. MICHEL EVRARD.

Fédération des Industries Transformatrices de Papier et Carton (FETRA) (Paper and Cardboard): 5 blvd de la Plaine, 1050 Brussels; tel. (2) 344-19-62; fax (2) 344-86-61; e-mail info@

fetra.be; internet www.fetra.be; f. 1946; Pres. Paul Pissens; Sec.-Gen. Lieve Vanlierde.

Fédération de l'Industrie du Verre (Glass): 5 blvd de la Plaine, 1050 Brussels; tel. (2) 542-61-20; fax (2) 542-61-21; e-mail info@vgi-fiv.be; internet www.vgi-fiv.be; f. 1947; Pres. Vincent Guillé; Gen. Man. Roland Deridder.

Fédération Patronale des Ports Belges: Brouwersvliet 33, Postbus 7, 2000 Antwerp 1; tel. (3) 221-99-87; fax (3) 221-99-09; e-mail rene.debrouwer@cepa.be; Pres. Paul Valkeniers; Dir René de Brouwer.

Groupement des Sablières (Sand and Gravel): Quellinstraat 49, 2018 Antwerp; tel. (3) 223-66-11; fax (3) 223-66-47; e-mail cathy.blervacq@sibelco.be; f. 1937; Pres. Alain Speeckaert.

Groupement de la Sidérurgie (Iron and Steel): 5 ave Ariane, 1200 Brussels; tel. (2) 509-14-11; fax (2) 509-14-00; e-mail gsv@steelbel.be; internet www.steelbel.be; f. 1953; Pres. Robrecht Himpe; Sec.-Gen. Robert Joos.

Lubricants Association Belgium (LAB) (Mineral Oils): 80 blvd Auguste Reyers, 1000 Brussels; tel. (2) 238-97-85; fax (2) 230-03-89; e-mail npoissonnier@essenscia.be; internet www.lubsbelgium.be; f. 1921; fmrly Industrie des Huiles Minérales de Belgique; Pres. Charles Devroey; Sec. Nathalie Poissonnier; 44 mems.

Synergrid (Gas and Electricity Grid Operators): 4 ave Palmerston, 1000 Brussels; tel. (2) 237-11-11; fax (2) 230-44-80; e-mail info@synergrid.be; internet www.synergrid.be; f. 1946; Pres. Daniel Dobbeni; Sec.-Gen. Bérénice Crabs.

Union Professionnelle des Producteurs Belges de Fibres-Ciment (Fibre-Cement): Aerschotstraat 114, 9100 Sint-Niklaas; tel. (3) 760-49-31; fax (3) 777-47-84; e-mail infod@svk.be; f. 1941; Pres. Jan Teugels; Sec. Carry Peeters.

Union Royale des Armateurs Belges (Shipowners): 8 Ernest van Dijckkaai, 2000 Antwerp; tel. (3) 232-72-32; fax (3) 231-39-97; e-mail info@brv.be; internet www.brv.be; f. 1909; Chair. Nicolas Saverys; Man. Dir Peter Verstuyft.

UTILITIES

Regulatory Authorities

Commission de Régulation de l'Electricité et du Gaz/Commissie voor de Regulering van de Elektriciteit en het Gas (CREG): 26–38 rue de l'Industrie, 1040 Brussels; tel. (2) 289-76-11; fax (2) 289-76-09; e-mail info@creg.be; internet www.creg.be; regulatory body for both gas and electricity markets; Pres. François Possemiers.

Commission de Régulation pour l'Energie en Région de Bruxelles-Capitale (BRUGEL): 92 Gulledelle, 1200 Brussels; tel. (800) 971-98; internet www.brugel.be; regulatory body for electricity and gas markets in Brussels-Capital region; Pres. Marie-Pierre Fauconnier.

Commission Wallonne pour l'Energie (CWaPE): 103–106 ave Gouverneur Bovesse, 5100 Jambes; tel. (81) 33-08-10; fax (81) 33-08-11; e-mail energie@mrw.wallonie.be; internet www.cwape.be; f. 2002; Pres. Francis Ghigny.

Vlaams reguleringsinstantie voor de elektriciteits- en gasmarkt (VREG) (Flemish Electricity and Gas Market Regulatory Authority): Graaf de Ferrarisgebouw, Koning Albert II-laan 20–19, 1000 Brussels; tel. (2) 553-13-79; fax (2) 553-13-50; e-mail info@vreg.be; internet www.vreg.be; f. 2001; responsible for regulation of distribution of gas and electricity at low voltage and production of electricity from renewable sources; Chair. André Pictoel.

Electricity

Electrabel: Regentlaan 8, 1000 Brussels; tel. (2) 518-61-11; fax (2) 518-64-00; internet www.electrabel.com; f. 1905 as Electriciteitsmaatschappij der Schelde; name changed to Ebes following merger in 1956; present name adopted 1990; generates and distributes electricity and natural gas; part of GDF Suez Group; CEO Jean-Pierre Hansen.

SPE NV (Luminus): Regentlaan 47, 1000 Brussels; tel. (2) 229-19-50; fax (2) 218-61-34; e-mail info@spe.be; internet www.spe.be; became a public company in 2000; builds, operates and maintains power plants; supplies electricity and gas under brand name Luminus; Interim CEO Christian Gosse.

Gas

Distrigas NV/SA: 10 rue de l'Industrie, 1000 Brussels; tel. (2) 557-30-01; fax (2) 557-31-12; e-mail info@distri.be; internet www.distrigas.eu; supply and sale of natural gas; f. 2001; 100% subsidiary of Eni, Italy; CEO Erwin Van Bruysel.

Fluxys NV/SA: Kunstlaan 31, 1040 Brussels; tel. (2) 282-72-11; fax (2) 230-02-39; e-mail berenice.crabs@fluxys.com; internet www.fluxys.com; owns and operates Belgian gas transmission network; CEO Walter Peeraer.

SPE NV (Luminus): see Electricity.

Total Belgium: 52 rue de l'Industrie, 1040 Brussels; tel. (2) 288-99-33; fax (2) 288-32-60; e-mail gaznat.ventes@total.com; internet www.be.total.com; CEO Michel del Marmol.

Water

Société Wallonne des Eaux: 41 rue de la Concorde, 4800 Verviers; tel. (8) 787-87; fax (8) 734-28-00; e-mail info@swde.be; internet www.swde.be; f. 1986; water production and distribution; Pres. René Thissen; Dir-Gen. Eric Van Sevenant.

Vlaamse Maatschappij voor Watervoorziening: Vooruitgangstraat 189, 1030 Brussels; tel. (2) 238-94-11; fax (2) 230-97-98; e-mail info@vmw.be; internet www.vmw.be; Chair. Luc Asselman; Dir-Gen. Bernard Breda.

TRADE UNIONS

National Federations

Algemeen Belgisch Vakverbond/Fédération Générale du Travail de Belgique (ABVV/FGTB): 42 rue Haute, 1000 Brussels; tel. (2) 506-82-11; fax (2) 506-82-29; e-mail anne.demelenne@abvv.be; internet www.abvv.be; f. 1898; 7 branch unions; affiliated to ITUC; Pres. Rudy De Leeuw; Gen. Sec. Anne Demelenne; 1,434,527m. mems (2007).

Algemeen Christelijk Vakverbond/Confédération des Syndicats Chrétiens (ACV-CSC): Haachtsesteenweg 579, 1031 Brussels; tel. (2) 246-31-11; fax (2) 246-30-10; e-mail international@acv-csc.be; internet www.acv-online.be; 13 affiliated unions; Pres. Luc Cortebeeck; Sec.-Gen. Claude Rolin; 1.7m. mems.

Algemene Centrale der Liberale Vakbonden van België/Centrale Générale des Syndicats Libéraux de Belgique (ACLVB/CGSLB) (General Federation of Liberal Trade Unions of Belgium): 72–74 blvd Poincaré, 1070 Brussels; tel. (2) 558-51-50; fax (2) 558-51-50; e-mail cgslb@cgslb.be; internet www.cgslb.be; f. 1891; present name adopted 1939; affiliated to ETUC and ITUC; Nat. Pres. Jan Vercamst; 259,367 mems (2007).

Principal Unions

ABVV Algemene Centrale/FGTB Centrale Générale (Central Union, building, timber, glass, paper, chemicals and petroleum industries): 26–28 rue Haute, 1000 Brussels; tel. (2) 549-05-49; fax (2) 514-16-91; e-mail info@accg.be; internet www.accg.be; Pres. Alain Clauwert; Gen. Sec. Jacques Michiels; 370,304 mems (2007).

ABVV Metaal (Metal Workers): Jacob Jordaenstraat 17, 1000 Brussels; tel. (2) 627-74-11; fax (2) 627-74-90; e-mail info@abvvmetaal.org; internet www.abvvmetaal.org; f. 2006; represents metal workers in Flanders; together with FGTB Métallurgistes de Wallonie–Bruxelles, forms Centrale du Métal/Centrale van Metaal; Pres. Herwig Jorissen; Gen. Sec. Ortwin Magnus; 180,914 mems (2007).

ABVV—Textiel, Kleding en Diamant/FGTB—Textile, Vêtement et Diamant (Textile, Clothing and Diamond Workers): Barrierestraat 13, 8200 Brugge; tel. (50) 72-95-70; fax (50) 72-95-80; e-mail abvvtkd.fgtbtvd@glo.be; f. 1994; Pres. Donald Wittevrongel; 38,719 mems (2007).

ACV Bouw en Industrie/CSC Bâtiment et Industrie (Building and Industrial Workers): 31 rue de Trèves, 1040 Brussels; tel. (2) 285-02-11; fax (2) 230-74-43; e-mail bouw_industrie@acv-csc.be; internet www.acvbi.be; f. 1998 by merger of the Centrale Chrétienne des Diverses Industries and the Centrale Chrétienne des Travailleurs du Bois et du Bâtiment; Pres. Luc Van Dessel; Sec.-Gen. Isabelle Parent; 230,000 mems.

ACV Energie Chemie/CSC Energie-Chimie (Chemical and Energy Workers): 31–33 rue des Trèves, 1040 Brussels; tel. (2) 285-03-03; fax (2) 285-03-20; e-mail acv-energie-chemie@acv-csc.be; internet www.acv-energie-chemie.be; f. 1912; Pres. Alfons De Potter; Gen. Sec. Italo Rodomonti.

ACV-CSC METEA (Metal and Textile Workers): 1–3 ave des Pagodes, 1020 Brussels; tel. (2) 244-99-11; fax (2) 244-99-90; e-mail metea@acv-csc.be; internet www.acv-csc-metea.be; f. 2009 after merger with ACV-CSC Textura; Pres. Marc De Wilde; 5,000 mems.

ACV Openbare Diensten/CSC Services Publics (Public Service Workers): 21 ave de l'Héliport, 1000 Brussels; tel. (2) 208-24-71; fax (2) 208-24-60; e-mail jean-paul.devos@acv-csc.be; internet www.acv-openbarediensten.be; f. 1921; Pres. Luc Hamelinck.

ACV Sporta (Sport): Kartuizersstraat 70, 1000 Brussels; tel. (2) 500-28-30; fax (2) 500-28-39; e-mail d.devos@acv-csc.be; internet www.acv-sporta.be; Nat. Sec. Dirk De Vos.

ACV Transcom/CSC Transcom (Railway, post, telecommunications, water, transport, shipping, civil aviation, radio, television and cultural workers): Galerie Agora, 105 rue Marché aux Herbes, BP 40, 1000 Brussels; tel. (2) 549-07-60; fax (2) 549-07-77; e-mail acv-transcom@acv-csc.be; internet www.acv-transcom.be; f. 2001 by merger; Pres. MARC VAN LAETHEM; 90,000 mems.

ACV Voeding en Diensten/CSC Alimentation et Services (Food and Service Industries): Kartuizersstraat 70, 1000 Brussels; tel. (2) 500-28-11; fax (2) 500-28-99; e-mail voedingendiensten@acv-csc.be; internet www.acv-voeding-diensten.be; f. 1919; Pres. PIA STALPAERT; Gen. Sec. PHILIPPE YERNA; 260,000 mems.

Belgische Transportarbeidersbond/Union Belge des Ouvriers du Transport (BTB/UBOT) (Belgian Transport Workers' Union): Paardenmarkt 66, 2000 Antwerp; tel. (3) 224-34-11; fax (3) 224-34-49; e-mail ubot@ubot-fgtb.be; internet www.ubot-fgtb.be; f. 1913; affiliated to ABVV/FGTB; Pres. IVAN VICTOR; 40,144 mems (2007).

Bond der Bedienden, Technici en Kaders van België/Syndicat des Employés, Techniciens et Cadres de Belgique (Employees, Technicians, Administrative Workers, Graphical and Paper Workers—BBTK/SETCa): 42 rue Haute, 1000 Brussels; tel. (2) 512-52-50; fax (2) 511-05-08; e-mail nationaal@setca-fgtb.be; internet www.bbtk.org; f. 1891; affiliated to ABVV/FGTB; Pres. ERWIN DE DEYN; Gen. Sec. JEAN MICHEL CAPPOEN; 373,867 mems (2007).

Centrale Générale des Services Publics/Algemene Centrale der Openbare Diensten (CGSP/ACOD) (Public Sector Workers): 9–11 place Fontainas, 1000 Brussels; tel. (2) 508-58-11; fax (2) 508-58-00; e-mail alain.lambert@cgsp.be; internet www.cgspacod.be; f. 1945; affiliated to ABVV/FGTB; Pres. KAREL STESSENS; Vice-Pres. ALAIN LAMBERT; 297,379 mems (2007).

Centrale Nationale des Employés (CNE) (Private Sector Workers): 46 rue Pépin, 5000 Namur; tel. (8) 125-90-90; fax (8) 122-50-47; e-mail raymond.coumont@acv-csc.be; internet www.cne-gnc.be; affiliated to ACV/CSC; represents private sector workers in French-speaking regions; Pres. ARLETTE PURAYE; Sec.-Gen. RAYMOND COUMONT; 120,000 mems.

Centrale Voeding-Horeca-Diensten/Centrale Alimentation-Horeca-Services (ABVV/FGTB HORVAL) (Catering and Hotel Workers): 18 rue des Alexiens, 1000 Brussels; tel. (2) 512-97-00; fax (2) 512-53-68; e-mail horval@horval.be; internet www.horval.be; f. 1912; Gen. Secs ALAIN DETEMMERMAN, TANGUI CORNU; 108,211 mems (2007).

Christelijke Onderwijscentrale (COC) (Teachers): Trierstraat 33, 1040 Brussels; tel. (2) 285-04-40; fax (2) 230-28-83; e-mail coc .brussel@acv-csc.be; internet www.coc.be; f. 1993 as a result of a merger of the Flemish wings of 3 teachers' unions; affiliated to ACV/CSC; Pres. ERIC DOLFEN; Gen. Sec. JOS VAN DER HOEVEN; 40,000 mems.

Christelijk Onderwijzersverbond (COV) (Schoolteachers): Koningsstraat 203, 1210 Brussels; tel. (2) 227-41-11; fax (2) 219-47-61; e-mail cov@acv-csc.be; internet www.cov.be; f. 1893; affiliated to ACV/CSC; Sec.-Gen. MARIANNE COOPMAN.

CSC Enseignement (Teachers): 16 rue de la Victoire, 1060 Brussels; tel. (2) 542-09-05; fax (2) 542-09-08; e-mail prosper.boulange@acv-csc.be; internet www.csc-e-fond.be; f. 1893; affiliated to ACV/CSC; Sec.-Gen. PROSPER BOULANGE; 36,000 mems.

Fédération Wallonne de l'Agriculture (FWA) (Farmers): 47 chaussée de Namur, 5030 Gembloux; tel. (81) 60-00-60; fax (81) 60-04-46; e-mail fwa@fwa.be; internet www.fwa.be; f. 2001; independent; Pres. RENÉ LADOUCE; Sec.-Gen. JEAN-PIERRE CHAMPAGNE.

FGTB Métallurgistes de Wallonie—Bruxelles (Metal Workers): rue de Namur 47, 5000 Beez; tel. (8) 126-51-11; fax (8) 126-51-22; e-mail info@mwb-fgtb.be; internet www.mwb-fgtb.be; f. 2006; represents metal workers in Walloon and Brussels-Capital regions; together with ABVV Metaal, forms Centrale du Métal/Centrale van Metaal; Pres. ANTONIO DI SANTO; Gen. Sec. NICO CUE.

Landelijke Bediendencentrale-Nationaal Verbond voor Kaderpersoneel (LBC-NVK) (Private Sector Workers): Sudermanstraat 5, 2000 Antwerp; tel. (3) 220-87-11; fax (3) 220-89-83; e-mail lbc-nvk@acv-csc.be; internet lbc-nvk.be; f. 1912; affiliated to ACV/CSC; represents private sector workers in Dutch-speaking regions; Sec.-Gen. FERRE WYCKMANS; 310,000 mems.

Nationale Unie van Openbare Diensten (NUOD)/Union Nationale des Services Publics (UNSP) (Public Sector Workers): 36 blvd Bischoffsheim, 1000 Brussels; tel. (2) 219-88-02; fax (2) 223-38-36; e-mail unsp-nuod@skynet.be; f. 1983; Pres. LUC MICHEL; Sec.-Gen. PHILIPPE LAMBERT.

Transport

RAILWAYS

The Belgian railway network is one of the densest in the world. Train services are operated by the Société Nationale des Chemins de Fer Belges (SNCB), while the infrastructure is owned and managed by Infrabel. In 2008 there were 3,536 km of standard-gauge railways, of which some 2,950 km were electrified. A high-speed railway network for northern Europe, linking Belgium, France, Germany, the Netherlands and the United Kingdom, was fully operational by November 2007.

Société Nationale des Chemins de Fer Belges/Nationale Maatschappij der Belgische Spoorwegen (SNCB/NMBS): 40 ave de la Porte de Hal, 1060 Brussels; tel. (2) 525-21-11; e-mail infocorporate@sncb.be; internet www.b-rail.be; f. 2005; 100% owned by SNCB Holding; 217m. passengers were carried in 2009; CEO MARC DESCHEEMAECKER.

Infrabel: 110 rue Bara, 1070 Brussels; tel. (2) 525-22-02; fax (2) 525-22-03; e-mail anik.cornil@infrabel.be; internet www.infrabel.be; f. 2005; responsible for rail infrastructure management; 93.6% owned by SNCB Holding, 6.4% owned by Federal Govt; CEO LUC LALLEMAND.

Thalys International: 20 place Stéphanie, 1050 Brussels; tel. (2) 548-06-00; e-mail corporate@thalys.com; internet www.thalys.com; f. 1995 as Westrail International; present name adopted 1999; operates rail passenger services between Brussels and Amsterdam (Netherlands), Cologne (Germany) and Paris (France); 62% owned by Société Nationale des Chemins de fer Français (SNCF—France), 28% by SNCB and 10% by Deutsche Bahn (Germany); CEO OLIVIER POITRENAUD.

ROADS

In 2008 there were 1,763 km of motorways and some 12,613 km of other main or national roads. There were also 1,349 km of secondary or regional roads and an additional 137,870 km of minor roads.

Société Régionale Wallonne du Transport: 96 ave Gouverneur Bovesse, 5100 Namur; tel. (81) 32-27-11; fax (81) 32-27-10; e-mail info@tec-wl.be; internet www.infotec.be; f. 1991; operates light railways, buses and trams; Dir-Gen. JEAN-MARC VANDENBROUCKE.

Société des Transports Intercommunaux de Bruxelles: 76 rue Royale, 1000 Brussels; tel. (2) 515-20-00; fax (2) 515-32-84; e-mail flauscha@stib.irisnet.be; internet www.stib.be; operates a metro service, buses and trams; operates in 19 communes in Brussels and in 11 outlying communes; Dir-Gen. ALAIN FLAUSCH.

Vlaamse Vervoermaatschappij (De Lijn): Motstraat 20, 2800 Mechelen; tel. (15) 44-07-11; fax (15) 44-89-98; e-mail marketing .cd@delijn.be; internet www.delijn.be; f. 1991; operates bus and tram services under commercial name De Lijn; Dir-Gen. ROGER KESTELOOT.

INLAND WATERWAYS

There are over 1,520 km of inland waterways in Belgium, of which 660 km are navigable rivers and 860 km are canals. Waterways administration is divided between the Flemish Region (1,055 km), the Walloon Region (450 km) and the Brussels-Capital Region (15 km).

Flemish Region:

De Scheepvaart NV: Havenstraat 44, 3500 Hasselt; tel. (11) 29-84-00; fax (11) 22-12-77; e-mail info@descheepvaart.be; internet www .descheepvaart.be; f. 2004; manages inland waterway system between Antwerp and Netherlands border; Chair. WILLY CLAES.

Waterwegen en Zeekanaal NV (W&Z): Oostdijk 110, 2830 Willebroek; tel. (3) 860-62-11; fax (3) 860-62-00; e-mail info@wenz.be; internet www.wenz.be; f. 2006 to replace Departement Leefmilieu en Infrastructuur Administratie Waterwegen en Zeewezen; Chair. ALBERT ABSILLIS; Gen. Man. ERIC VAN DEN EEDE.

Walloon Region:

Direction Générale des Voies Hydrauliques: Centre administratif du MET, 8 blvd du Nord, 5000 Namur; tel. (81) 77-29-94; fax (81) 77-37-80; e-mail jlaurent@met.wallonie.be; internet voies-hydrauliques.wallonie.be; Dir-Gen. JACQUES LAURENT.

Brussels-Capital Region:

Port de Bruxelles/Haven van Brussel: 6 place des Armateurs, 1000 Brussels; tel. (2) 420-67-00; fax (2) 420-69-74; e-mail portdebruxelles@port.irisnet.be; internet www.havenvanbrussel .irisnet.be; f. 1993; Pres. CHARLES JONET; Dir-Gen. ALFONS MOENS.

SHIPPING

The modernized port of Antwerp is the second largest in Europe and handles about 80% of Belgian foreign trade by sea and inland waterways. It is also the largest railway port and has one of the biggest petroleum refining complexes in Europe. Antwerp has

160 km of quayside and 17 dry docks. Other ports include Zeebrugge, Ostend, Ghent, Liège and Brussels.

Antwerp Port Authority: Havenhuis, Entrepotkaai 1, 2000 Antwerp; tel. (3) 205-20-11; fax (3) 205-20-28; e-mail info@portofantwerp.com; internet www.portofantwerp.com; an independent, municipally owned company, responsible for planning, development, modernization and maintenance of the port infrastructure; offers a number of ancillary services such as tugging, dredging and renting out dock cranes and floating cranes; also responsible for safe and smooth shipping movements within the dock complex, and operates the bridges and locks; CEO EDDY BRUYNINCKX.

Principal Shipping Companies

Ahlers Logistic and Maritime Services: Noorderlaan 139, 2030 Antwerp; tel. (3) 543-72-11; fax (3) 542-00-23; e-mail info@ahlers.com; internet www.ahlers.com; shipping agency, ship and crew management, forwarding; Exec. Chair. CHRISTIAN LEYSEN.

De Keyser Thornton: Brouwersvliet 25, 2000 Antwerp; tel. (3) 205-31-00; fax (3) 205-31-32; e-mail info@dkt.be; internet www.dkt.be; f. 1853; shipping agency, forwarding and warehousing services; Chair. GUY FOUCHEROT; Man. Dir PHILIP VAN TILBURG.

Manuport Group: Atlantic House, 3rd Floor, Noorderlaan 147, 2030 Antwerp; tel. (3) 204-93-00; fax (3) 204-93-01; e-mail contact@euroports.com; internet www.manuportgroup.com; forwarding, customs clearance, liner and tramp agencies, chartering, Rhine and inland barging, multi-purpose bulk/bags fertilizer, minerals and agri-bulk terminal; Pres. and CEO WALTER SIJMONS.

Transeuropa Ferries NV: Slijkensesteenweg 2, 8400 Ostend; tel. (5) 934-02-60; fax (5) 934-02-61; e-mail info@transeuropaferries.com; internet www.transeuropaferries.com; f. 2001; 5 ships; shipping, stevedoring and line representation; operates between Ostend and Ramsgate (United Kingdom).

CIVIL AVIATION

The main international airport is at Brussels, with a direct train service between the air terminal and central Brussels. There are also international airports at Antwerp, Charleroi, Kortrijk-Wevelgem, Liège and Ostend.

Brussels Airlines: b.house, Airport Building 26, Ringbaan, 1831 Diegem; tel. (2) 754-19-06; fax (2) 723-84-09; internet www.brusselsairlines.be; f. 2007 by merger of SN Brussels Airlines and Virgin Express; owned by SN Airholding; scheduled services within Europe and to Africa, Asia, the Middle East and North America; Man. Dirs MICHEL MEYFROIDT, BERNARD GUSTIN.

Tourism

Belgium has several towns of rich historic and cultural interest, such as Antwerp, Bruges, Brussels, Durbuy, Ghent, Liège, Namur and Tournai. The country's seaside towns attract many visitors. The forest-covered Ardennes region is renowned for hill-walking and gastronomy. In 2010 tourist arrivals totalled some 7.2m., while receipts from tourism totalled US $10,287m. (provisional figures).

Office de Promotion du Tourisme Wallonie et Bruxelles: 30 rue Saint-Bernard, 1060 Brussels; tel. (70) 22-10-21; fax (2) 513-69-50; e-mail info@opt.be; internet www.opt.be; f. 1981; promotion of tourism in French-speaking Belgium; Dir-Gen. VIVIANE JACOBS.

Toerisme Vlaanderen: Grasmarkt 61, 1000 Brussels; tel. (2) 504-03-90; fax (2) 513-04-75; e-mail info@toerismevlaanderen.be; internet www.visitflanders.com; f. 1985; official promotion and policy body for tourism in the Flemish Region; Administrator-Gen. PETER DE WILDE.

Defence

Belgium is a member of the North Atlantic Treaty Organization (NATO), which is headquartered in the country. As assessed at November 2011, the total strength of the Belgian armed forces was 34,336 (including 1,844 in the Medical Service and 12,619 in the Joint Service), comprising an army of 12,544, a navy of 1,590 and an air force of 5,739. Total reserves numbered 1,400. Compulsory military service was abolished in 1995. In 1996 the Belgian and Netherlands navies came under a joint operational command, based at Den Helder, Netherlands. In November 2004 the European Union (EU) defence ministers agreed to create a number of 'battlegroups' (each comprising about 1,500 men), which could be deployed at short notice to carry out peace-keeping activities at crisis points around the world. The EU battlegroups, two of which were to be ready for deployment at any one time, following a rotational schedule, reached full operational capacity from 1 January 2007. Belgium was committed to contributing troops to one battlegroup with France and another with participation from France, Germany, Luxembourg and Spain.

Defence Expenditure: Budget estimated at €2,820m. for 2012.

Chief of Defence: Gen. CHARLES-HENRI DELCOUR.

Education

Responsibility for education policy lies with the administrations of the Flemish, French and German-speaking Communities. Education may be provided by the Communities, by other public authorities (provinces and municipalities) or by private interests. All educational establishments, whether official or 'free' (privately organized), receive most of their funding from the Communities. Roman Catholic schools constitute the greatest number of 'free' establishments.

Full-time education in Belgium is compulsory between the ages of six and 16 years. Thereafter, pupils must remain in education for a further two-year period, but may do so on a part-time basis. Children may be enrolled in nursery schools, attached to elementary schools, from between the ages of two-and-a-half and three years. Elementary education begins at six years of age and consists of three courses of two years each. Secondary education, beginning at the age of 12, lasts for six years and is divided into three two-year cycles or, in a few cases, two three-year cycles. According to UNESCO, enrolment at primary schools in 2005/06 included 97.4% of children (males 97.2%; females 97.5%) in the relevant age-group, while the comparable ratio at secondary schools was estimated at 87.1% (males 88.8%; females 85.3%) in the same year.

The requirement for university entrance is a pass in the certificate of secondary education, taken after the completion of secondary studies. Reforms to the higher education system entered into effect in 2004 in both the Flemish and the French communities, introducing a three-year bachelor's degree, followed by a master's degree lasting one or two years. (Courses were previously divided into two to three years of general preparation, followed by two to three years of specialization.) There are nine university-level institutions in the French Community and seven such institutions in the Flemish Community. In 2007/08 a total of 132,611 students were enrolled in university-level establishments. Non-university institutions of higher education provide arts education, technical training and teacher training; in that year a total of 187,047 students were enrolled in such institutions. In 2006 enrolment at tertiary level was equivalent to 63% of those in the relevant age-group (males 56%; females 70%). A national study fund provides grants where necessary and about one-fifth of students receive scholarships.

Regional expenditure on education was €9,206.9m. in the Flemish Community in 2009 and €5,778.3m. in the French Community (including Brussels and Wallonia)in 2011, and was budgeted at €106.74m. in the German-speaking Community for 2008.

BELIZE

Introductory Survey

LOCATION, CLIMATE, LANGUAGE, RELIGION, FLAG, CAPITAL

Belize lies on the Caribbean coast of Central America, with Mexico to the north-west and Guatemala to the south-west. The climate is sub-tropical, tempered by trade winds. The temperature averages 24°C (75°F) from November to January, and 27°C (81°F) from May to September. Annual rainfall ranges from 1,290 mm (51 ins) in the north to 4,450 mm (175 ins) in the south. The average annual rainfall in Belize City is 1,650 mm (65 ins). Belize is ethnically diverse, the population (according to the 2000 census) consisting of 49% Mestizos (Maya-Spanish), 25% Creoles (those of predominantly African descent), 11% Amerindian (mainly Maya), 6% Garifuna ('Black Caribs', descendants of those deported from the island of Saint Vincent in 1797) and communities of Asians, Portuguese, German Mennonites and others of European descent. English is the official language and an English Creole is widely understood. Spanish is the mother-tongue of some 15% of the population but is spoken by many others. There are also speakers of Garifuna (Carib), Maya and Ketchi, while the Mennonites speak a German dialect. Most of the population profess Christianity, with about one-half being Roman Catholics. The national flag (proportions usually 3 by 5) is dark blue, with narrow horizontal red stripes at the upper and lower edges; at the centre is a white disc containing the state coat of arms, bordered by an olive wreath. The capital is Belmopan.

CONTEMPORARY POLITICAL HISTORY

Historical Context

Belize, known as British Honduras until June 1973, was first colonized by British settlers (the 'Baymen') in the 17th century, but was not recognized as a British colony until 1862. In 1954 a new Constitution granted universal adult suffrage and provided for the creation of a legislative assembly. The territory's first general election, in April 1954, was won by the only party then organized, the People's United Party (PUP), led by George Price. The PUP won all subsequent elections until 1984. In 1961 Price was appointed First Minister under a new ministerial system of government. The colony was granted internal self-government in 1964, with the United Kingdom retaining responsibility for defence, external affairs and internal security. Following an election in 1965, Price became Premier and a bicameral legislature was introduced. In 1970 the capital of the territory was moved from Belize City to the newly built town of Belmopan.

Much of the recent history of Belize has been dominated by the territorial dispute with Guatemala, particularly in the years prior to Belize's independence (see below). This was achieved on 21 September 1981, within the Commonwealth, and with Price becoming Prime Minister. However, the failure of the 1981 draft treaty with Guatemala, and the clash of opposing wings within the ruling party, undermined the dominance of the PUP, and the party's 30 years of rule ended at the general election held in December 1984. The new United Democratic Party (UDP) Government, led by Manuel Esquivel, pledged to revive Belize's economy through increased foreign investment. However, the PUP regained power following the general election of September 1989 and Price was again appointed Prime Minister.

Domestic Political Affairs

The PUP called a general election in June 1993, following recent successes at local and by-elections. However, at the election the party performed poorly, and an alliance of the UDP and the National Alliance for Belizean Rights (NABR) was able to form a Government. Esquivel was appointed Prime Minister.

The sale of citizenship, of which many Hong Kong Chinese had taken advantage, was officially ended in 1994 following criticism that the system was open to abuse. In June 1995 the Minister of Human Resources, Community and Youth Development, Culture and Women's Affairs, Phillip S. W. Goldson, was relieved of responsibility for immigration and nationality affairs, following allegations implicating him in the sale of false residence and visitor permits to nationals of the People's Republic of China and Taiwan. Reportedly, some 5,000 such permits had been issued over the previous 12-month period, and the recipients then smuggled into the USA.

The PUP Government of Said Musa

At the general election of August 1998 the PUP, led by Said Musa, won an overwhelming victory. The result reflected popular discontent with the outgoing Government's structural adjustment policies, including the introduction of value-added tax (VAT), which the PUP had pledged to repeal. Following the defeat of his party, Esquivel, who had lost his seat in the House of Representatives, resigned as leader of the UDP. He was succeeded by Dean Barrow.

In July 1999 Prime Minister Musa issued a statement rejecting allegations that Michael Ashcroft, a businessman with dual British/Belizean nationality and Belize's ambassador to the UN, had used improper influence in Belizean affairs and was involved in money-laundering. In March 2000 Ashcroft resigned his UN post after receiving a life peerage in the British House of Lords. In late 2000 the remit of an inquiry commissioned by the British Government into Belize's financial system was expanded to investigate public investment companies operating from Belize, including Ashcroft's Carlisle Holdings. In December 2001 it was announced that the Government had refused the United Kingdom's offer of £10m. of debt relief in exchange for a reform of its financial regime and an end to tax relief given to Carlisle Holdings and another company.

On 14 February 2001 the leaders of 11 Caribbean countries, including Belize, signed an agreement to establish a Caribbean Court of Justice (CCJ), based in Trinidad and Tobago. The Court was to replace the Privy Council in the United Kingdom as the final court of appeal, and would allow the execution of convicted criminals. In late October the Attorney-General defended before a panel of the Inter-American Commission on Human Rights a proposed amendment to the Constitution that would prevent prisoners sentenced to death from appealing to the Privy Council in the United Kingdom. This followed a petition to the Commission by a group of prisoners who claimed that the amendment was incompatible with the Government's obligations to an Organization of American States (OAS) treaty on human rights. The Attorney-General maintained that Belize had the right to legislate in its own domestic affairs. In July 2004 parliament approved legislation sanctioning Belize's membership of the CCJ in its original jurisdiction. However, the Government failed to garner the three-quarters' majority required to amend the Constitution that would have allowed Belize to participate fully as part of the appellate jurisdiction. In February 2010 the House of Representatives unanimously passed legislation replacing the Privy Council with the CCJ as Belize's final court of appeal. The law came into effect on 1 June.

In February 2002 the policy of economic citizenship was formally abolished. However, a report produced in July by the Ministry of Foreign Affairs substantiated claims that the immigration authorities had apparently continued the practice illegally until that month. In November a Commission of Inquiry into the economic citizenship programme reported that while no person was granted Belizean citizenship under the programme following its annulment in February, over 1,000 applications were approved during the first seven months of 2002 and a number of irregularities had been detected.

Musa became the country's first Prime Minister to be sworn in for a second term in office in 2003 following the PUP's victory in the March general election. The PUP won 22 seats in the House of Representatives, while the UDP increased its legislative representation to seven seats (from three). The PUP, which had repealed the unpopular VAT during its 1998–2003 administration, promised that, if re-elected, it would abolish sales tax on basic items and move towards the eradication of personal income tax.

Despite some implementation of pre-election pledges the PUP struggled to maintain popular support during 2004 as protracted financial crises in the Development Finance Corporation (DFC) and the Social Security Board (SSB) forced the Government to reduce spending on social projects. An audit into the SSB's financial operations found that it had made a series of unsecured loans, incurring substantial financial losses. A Senate Select Committee, established to investigate allegations of maladministration by the SSB, found evidence of negligence and recklessness in the purchase and sale of mortgage loans. The Government subsequently dismissed the SSB's General Manager and board of directors and in December it was announced that the DFC was to be dissolved.

In 2005 controversy arose over the ownership of Belize Telecommunications Ltd (BTL, later renamed Belize Telemedia Ltd). In April 2001 the Government had sold the company to Carlisle Holdings. Three years later, in April 2004, it bought back those shares and immediately sold them to US company Innovative Communication Corporation (ICC). However, in February 2005 the Government resumed control of BTL after it claimed that ICC had not met a payment deadline. ICC maintained that the default was owing to government failure to meet certain conditions regarding licensing agreements and guaranteed rates of return. In March the Chief Justice launched an inquiry into the various ownerships of BTL between April 2001 and February 2005. In March 2005 ICC was granted a temporary injunction by a court in Miami, Florida, USA, that returned control of BTL to the US company and reinstated four ICC-appointed board members. However, the Supreme Court of Belize ruled that the injunction was not enforceable in Belize. Meanwhile, members of the Belize Communication Workers' Union demanded that majority ownership of BTL be transferred to the company's employees. In mid-April the anti-Government feeling led to a strike by BTL employees and several days of violent protests by union members and students, during which shops were looted and more than 100 people were arrested. The armed forces were deployed to restore order in the capital. Protesters disrupted telephone services to large areas of the country. In June the House of Representatives approved the sale of BTL shares: 20% would be sold to employees, 12.5% to a subsidiary of Carlisle Holdings and 5% to other Belizeans. However, the Court of Appeals two months later overturned earlier supreme court rulings upholding government action in BTL, and ruled that control of the telecommunications company be returned to ICC and that all sales of BTL shares since 9 February be annulled.

Furthermore, in October 2005 Belize Water Services Company Ltd was renationalized after the Government reached agreement with the Anglo-Dutch company CASCAL to repurchase some 83% of the company for the same amount for which it sold the shares in 2001. The newly acquired shares were put on sale to the general public, with preference given to Belizean citizens.

The UDP in power

The opposition UDP won a convincing victory in the general election held on 7 February 2008, securing 25 of the 31 legislative seats and 57.0% of the valid votes cast. The PUP's representation was significantly reduced, to the six remaining seats, after obtaining 41.0% of the vote. Some 74.5% of eligible voters participated in the poll. The UDP had campaigned against what it perceived as corruption and mismanagement in the Musa administration. UDP leader Dean Barrow was sworn in as Prime Minister on 8 February. In a concurrent referendum, 61.5% of voters supported proposals for an elected Senate.

In late 2008 former Prime Minister Musa was arrested and charged with diverting US $20m. in Venezuelan grant funds, intended for social and construction projects, to the Belize Bank in order to pay the debt of the privately owned Universal Hospital. In addition, Musa's Government had initially stated that it had received the sum of $10m., a gross discrepancy from the amount Venezuela claimed to have given. Musa's case was referred to the Supreme Court; however, in June 2009 this court overturned a lower court ruling that Musa stand trial.

Rising levels of violent crime prompted Barrow to create a Ministry of Police and Public Security in June 2010. Douglas Singh was given responsibility for the new portfolio, while Carlos Perdomo, erstwhile Minister of National Security, was appointed Minister of Defence. The murder rate rose steeply in the country in 2010, from 97 to 132, while the rate of detection remained low. In an attempt to address this, in September the new security minister announced a witness protection programme. Moreover, in April 2011 the Government announced new bail restrictions, and from August the right to trial by jury was removed from defendants accused of murder, with such cases to be determined solely by a Supreme Court judge. A Caribbean Community and Common Market (CARICOM, see p. 227) initiative to address gang-related criminal activity commenced in Belize during October. Nevertheless, by December the annual murder rate had reached approximately 120.

The CCJ adjudged in July 2011 that two members of the previous PUP administration, Florencio Marin and José Coye, could be brought to trial by the Belizean Government on charges of misfeasance relating to allegedly corrupt land deals. The use of the tort system against former cabinet ministers was without precedent. Following his resignation on grounds of ill health, John Briceño was replaced as PUP leader by Francis Fonseca in October. However, some commentators claimed that Briceño had stepped down because his position had become untenable as a result of the chronic infighting and factionalism that had characterized his tenure. Fonseca was inaugurated as Leader of the Opposition in early November.

Renationalization of BTL

Controversy over the ownership of BTL continued into 2011. Following the approval of an amendment to the Telecommunications Law in the House of Representatives in August 2009, the Barrow administration announced the renationalization of the telecommunications concern. The former owners again protested against the decision, claiming it was unconstitutional, and referred the matter to the Supreme Court. In August 2010 that body ruled that the Government's decision had been lawful. In October some 45% shares in BTL went on sale to the public. A further 10% of shares were to be reserved for BTL employees. It was intended that majority ownership of the company would remain in Belizean hands. However, in June 2011 the Court of Appeal overturned the Supreme Court's 2010 judgment, declaring that the 2009 renationalization had indeed been in breach of the Constitution. In response, the Government asserted that it would only relinquish control of BTL if an enforcement order were issued—arguing that the Court of Appeal's ruling was merely 'declaratory'—and proposed a constitutional amendment to 'enshrine Belizean public ownership of the utilities'. This change to the Constitution was duly approved by the House of Representatives in October 2011, effectively ending any further legal challenges to the control of BTL by the state. (An appeal against this amendment, lodged by the Ashcroft-owned British Caribbean Bank, had been rejected by the CCJ in August.) Meanwhile, in June the financially troubled Belize Electricity Ltd was also renationalized, although its former owner, Canadian company Fortis, commenced legal action against the Government in October, claiming that this purchase had violated the Constitution.

Recent developments: 2012 elections

General and municipal elections were held on 7 March 2012. The UDP secured re-election, albeit with a much reduced majority, winning 17 of the 31 legislative seats and 49.3% of the valid votes cast. The PUP garnered almost as many votes (49.1%), but this translated into 14 seats in the House of Representatives. The People's National Party and the Vision Inspired by the People party also contested the ballot, but failed to win national representation. The UDP also performed well in the local elections, retaining control of six of the country's nine muncipalities, including Belmopan and Belize City. Prime Minister Barrow indicated that his priority at the beginning of a second term would be renegotiation of the Belize's debt-servicing agreement that comprised almost one-half gross domestic product. He also pledged to hold a plebiscite on the offshore drilling programme amid environmental concerns and low yields of petroleum.

Foreign Affairs

The frontier with Guatemala was agreed by a convention in 1859, but this was declared invalid by Guatemala in 1940. Guatemalan claims to sovereignty of Belize date back to the middle of the 19th century and were written into Guatemala's Constitution in 1945. In November 1975 and July 1977 British troops and aircraft were sent to protect Belize from the threat of Guatemalan invasion, and a battalion of troops and a detachment of fighter aircraft remained in the territory. In November 1980 the UN General Assembly overwhelmingly approved a resolution urging that Belize be granted independence (similar resolutions having been adopted in 1978 and 1979), and the United Kingdom decided to proceed with a schedule for independence, after having excluded the possibility of any cession of land to Guatemala. A tripartite conference in March 1981 appeared to produce a sound basis for a final settlement, with Guatemala accepting Belizean independence in exchange for access to the Caribbean Sea through Belize and the use of certain offshore cayes and their surrounding waters. Further tripartite talks in the same year collapsed, however, as a result of renewed claims by Guatemala to Belizean land. With Belizean independence imminent, Guatemala made an unsuccessful appeal to the UN Security Council to intervene, severing diplomatic relations with the United Kingdom and sealing its border with Belize on 7 September. Tripartite talks in January 1983 collapsed when Belize rejected Guatemala's proposal that Belize should cede the southern part of the country. This claim was subsequently suspended. Belize is a member of CARICOM, the summit conferences of which have consistently expressed support for Belize's territorial integrity against claims by Guatemala.

At independence the United Kingdom had agreed to leave troops as protection and for training of the Belize Defence Force. In 1987 renewed discussions were held between Guatemala, the United Kingdom and Belize (although Belize was still regarded by Guatemala as being only an observer at the meetings), and in 1988 the formation of a permanent joint commission (which, in effect, entailed a recognition of the Belizean state by Guatemala) was announced.

In September 1991 Belize and Guatemala signed an accord under the terms of which Belize pledged to legislate to reduce its maritime boundaries and to allow Guatemala access to the Caribbean Sea and use of its port facilities. In return, Guatemala officially recognized Belize as an independent state and established diplomatic relations, although it maintained its territorial claim over the country. In January 1992 the Maritime Areas Bill was approved in the Belizean House of Representatives. The legislation, however, had caused serious divisions within the UDP, leading to the formation of the NABR. In April 1993 Belize and Guatemala signed a non-aggression pact, affirming their intent to refrain from the threat or use of force against each other, and preventing either country from being used as a base for aggression against the other.

In January 1994 responsibility for the defence of Belize was transferred to the Belize Defence Force; all British troops were withdrawn by October, with the exception of some 180 troops who remained to organize training for jungle warfare. In March Guatemala formally reaffirmed its territorial claim to Belize, prompting the Belizean Minister of Foreign Affairs to seek talks with the British Government regarding assistance with national defence. In September 1996 the Ministers of Foreign Affairs of Belize and Guatemala conducted preliminary talks in New York, USA, concerning a resumption of negotiations on the territorial dispute. Further such discussions were conducted in 1997. In November 1998, at a meeting of ambassadors and officials of both countries, agreement was reached on the establishment of a joint commission to deal with immigration, cross-border traffic and respect for the rights of both countries' citizens.

In June 2002 the Ministers of Foreign Affairs from both countries met under OAS auspices to discuss the border dispute issue. Following further, OAS-mediated, negotiations, in early September proposals were outlined for a solution to the dispute. These included the provision that Guatemala would recognize Belize's land boundary as laid out in the treaty of 1859 and the creation of a model settlement, complete with modern amenities, for peasants and landless farmers in the border area. Guatemalan farmers occupying land within the Belizean border were to have priority rights of residency on this settlement. There was also provision for the establishment of a free trade agreement between the two countries and a Development Trust Fund, to be managed by the Inter-American Development Bank, with the money being used to alleviate poverty in the border region. In addition, Guatemala would be granted a 200 sq mile Exclusive Economic Zone in the Gulf of Honduras, although Belize and Honduras would retain fishing rights and 50% of any mineral resources discovered in the seabed. A Commission comprising Belize, Guatemala and Honduras would manage fishing in the Gulf of Honduras. However, in September 2003 the Guatemalan Government announced it would reject the OAS-proposed agreement. Delegations from the two countries met for further OAS-mediated negotiations in May 2004. In May 2005 Musa raised the possibility of bringing the dispute before the International Court of Justice (ICJ). However, in September, at the OAS headquarters in Washington, DC, USA, representatives of the two countries signed a new Agreement on a Framework of Negotiation and Confidence-Building Measures. The first meetings under the new accord were held in November in Belize, with future meetings scheduled to take place every 45 days thereafter. Following almost two years of negotiations, in March 2007 representatives of Belize and Guatemala signed a preliminary trade accord, allowing 150 products to be traded duty-free. However, a lack of progress in the talks prompted the Secretary-General of the OAS to reiterate in November the Prime Minister's suggestion that the two countries take the dispute to the ICJ. In August 2008 the Belizean foreign minister, Wilfred Elrington, announced that a referendum would be held to ascertain public support for the ICJ's intervention in the dispute; the House of Representatives finally voted to hold such a plebiscite in September 2010. Under OAS mediation, in November 2011 the foreign ministers of Belize and Guatemala agreed that concurrent referendums on the issue would be conducted by the end of 2013.

In August 2005 the Government signed a reciprocal shipboarding agreement with the USA in an attempt to prevent the transportation of weapons of mass destruction, and in February 2009 the USA agreed to provide US $1.1m. in funding for an initiative to combat organized crime and drugs-trafficking. However, in an unprecedented move, reflecting the growing significance of Belize to criminals involved in the transshipment of illegal drugs, the country was added to the USA's black list of significant drugs-producing and -trafficking nations in September 2011.

GOVERNMENT AND CONSTITUTION

The Constitution of Belize came into effect at independence on 21 September 1981. Belize is a constitutional monarchy, with the British sovereign as Head of State. Executive authority is vested in the sovereign and is exercised by the Governor-General, who is appointed on the advice of the Prime Minister, must be of Belizean nationality, and acts, in almost all matters, on the advice of the Cabinet. The Governor-General is also advised by an appointed Belize Advisory Council. Legislative power is vested in the bicameral National Assembly, comprising a Senate (12 members appointed by the Governor-General) and a House of Representatives (31 members elected by universal adult suffrage for five years, subject to dissolution). The Governor-General appoints the Prime Minister and, on the latter's recommendation, other ministers. The Cabinet is responsible to the House of Representatives.

REGIONAL AND INTERNATIONAL CO-OPERATION

Belize is a member of the Caribbean Community and Common Market (CARICOM, see p. 227), the Association of Caribbean States (see p. 448), the Organization of American States (OAS, see p. 394), the Inter-American Development Bank (IDB, see p. 334), and of the Community of Latin American and Caribbean States (see p. 462), which was formally inaugurated in December 2011. Belize is also a member of the Central American Integration System (SICA, see p. 232). Belize joined CARICOM's Caribbean Single Market and Economy (CSME), which was established on 1 January 2006. The CSME was intended to enshrine the free movement of goods, services and labour throughout the CARICOM region, although only six of the organization's 15 members were signatories to the new project from its inauguration.

Belize became a member of the UN when it became independent in 1981. The country became a contracting party to GATT (which was superseded by the World Trade Organization, WTO, see p. 433 in 1995) in 1983. As a member of the Commonwealth (see p. 239), Belize enjoys guaranteed access to the EU under the Cotonou Agreement (see p. 328), and tariff-free access to the USA under the Caribbean Basin Initiative. Belize is a member of the Group of 77 (see p. 450).

ECONOMIC AFFAIRS

In 2010, according to estimates by the World Bank, Belize's gross national income (GNI), measured at average 2008–10 prices, was US $1,288m., equivalent to US $3,740 per head (or $5,970 per head on an international purchasing-power parity basis). During 2001–10 Belize's population grew at an average annual rate of 3.3%, while in 2001–10 gross domestic product (GDP) per head increased, in real terms, at an average annual rate of 0.4%. According to the World Bank, overall GDP increased, in real terms, at an average rate of 3.7% per year in 2001–10; growth was 2.3% in 2010.

Although 38% of the country is considered suitable for agriculture, only an estimated 6.7% of the total area was used for agricultural purposes in 2009. Nevertheless, agriculture, hunting, forestry and fishing employed 20.7% of the working population in 2006 and contributed 13.2% of GDP, at constant prices, in 2010. About 31,000, or 23.8% of the working population, were engaged in the agricultural sector in 2011, according to FAO. The principal cash crops are citrus fruits, sugar cane and bananas. Agricultural policy promotes the cultivation of crops for domestic consumption and the diversification of crops for export. Maize, rice and red kidney beans are the principal domestic food crops, and the development of crops such as soybeans (soya beans), papayas, organic rice and cocoa is being encouraged. The country is largely self-sufficient in fresh meat and eggs. Belize has considerable timber reserves, particularly of tropical hardwoods, and the forestry sector is being developed. The fishing sector increased in the 2000s, largely owing to an expansion in farmed shrimp production. In 2010 marine products provided 10.8% of total export revenue. The fishing catch totalled 14,600 metric tons in 2009, according to FAO estimates. According to the World Bank, agricultural GDP increased, in real terms, by an average annual rate of 1.7% in 2001–09; sectoral GDP decreased by 2.9% in 2009, before increasing marginally, by 0.2%, in 2010.

Industry (including mining, manufacturing, construction, water and electricity) employed 15.7% of the working population in 2006 and contributed 24.1% of GDP, at constant prices, in 2010. Industrial GDP increased at an average annual rate of 6.4% in 2001–09; real industrial GDP increased by 11.0% in 2009, but growth slowed to just 0.4% in 2010.

Mining accounted for 0.5% of GDP in 2008 and employed 0.4% of the working population in 2006. Mining GDP increased at an average rate of 4.1% per year during 2000–08. The sector expanded significantly from the mid-2000s following discovery of high-quality crude petroleum in 2005; the sector recorded an increase of 19.2% in 2008.

Manufacturing (including mining and quarrying) accounted for 12.8% of GDP, at constant prices, in 2010 and employed 7.2% of the working population in 2006. Dominant activities are petroleum refining, the manufacture of clothing and the processing of agricultural products, particularly sugar cane (for sugar and rum). Manufacturing GDP increased at an average rate of 7.7% per year during 2001–09, fuelled mainly by a growth in petroleum refining; the sector recorded a increase of 6.2% in 2009, but decreased by 4.8% in 2010.

Construction accounted for 4.9% of GDP, at constant prices, in 2010 and employed 7.2% of the working population in 2006. Construction GDP increased at an average rate of 5.3% per year during 2001–09; the sector showed a sharp increase of 35.8% in 2008, largely owing to continued capital works and residential development projects financed by Chinese sources; a further increase, of 18.7%, was recorded in 2009, but the sector contracted by 5.7% in 2010.

Imports of fuels and lubricants accounted for 16.1% of the total cost of imports in 2010. Belize Natural Energy discovered Belize's first commercially viable oilfield in 2005, with proven recoverable reserves of 10m. barrels. In addition to the Mollejón hydroelectric station on the Macal River, a hydroelectric dam at Chalillo on the Macal River became operational in late 2005. The dam, operated by its Canadian contractor, Fortis Inc, before transfer to state ownership in 2031, provided an estimated 7.3 MW of electricity annually and, according to the Government, would meet Belize's energy needs for 50 years. In 2004 Hydro Maya Ltd signed a 15-year agreement to provide 2.8 MW of electricity annually to Belize Electricity Ltd (BEL). Construction of a hydroelectric dam on the Rio Grande River, to generate the required power, was completed in 2008. In 2005 Belize signed the PetroCaribe agreement with Venezuela, under which it would be allowed to purchase petroleum from that country at reduced prices. A bagasse-fuelled co-generation facility, adjacent to the Tower Hill sugar factory, began operations in late 2010. The biomass plant was expected to supply 13.5 MW to BEL and 9 MW to Belize Sugar Industries once fully operational. Many hydroelectric projects remained controversial because of their damaging impact on local ecology and on the social wellbeing of neighbouring communities.

The services sector employed 63.5% of the working population in 2006 and contributed 62.6% of GDP, at constant prices, in 2010. Tourism development is concentrated on promoting 'ecotourism', based on the attraction of Belize's natural environment, particularly its rainforests and the barrier reef, the second largest in the world. Revenue from tourism totalled US $264.4m. in 2010, compared with US $256.2m. in the previous year. The number of tourist arrivals rose by 6.8% in 2010; increases were recorded in the number of cruise ship passengers (688,165, compared with 634,697 in the previous year) and of stop-over visitors, a traditionally higher-spending sector (226,632, compared with 221,654 in 2009). The GDP of the services sector increased, in real terms, at an average annual rate of 3.7% in 2001–09; real sectoral GDP increased by 3.7% in 2010. In 2005 there were more than 27,000 registered active 'offshore' financial companies operating in Belize.

According to IMF estimates, in 2010 Belize recorded a trade deficit of US $171.5m. and a deficit of US $45.7m. on the current account of the balance of payments. In 2009 the principal source of imports was the USA (accounting for 34.7% of the total), followed by Mexico. The USA was also the principal export market, accounting for 32.4% of total exports in 2009, followed by the United Kingdom (31.7%). The principal exports in 2010 were petroleum (36.2%), orange concentrate (16.5%), bananas (12.6%), marine products (10.8%) and sugar (10.3%). The principal imports in that year were machinery and transport equipment (16.2%) and mineral fuels and lubricants (16.1%). The commercial free zone provided 18.3% of imports in 2010.

For the financial year 2010–11 there was an estimated budgetary deficit of BZ $46.2m. Belize's general government gross debt was BZ $2,309m. in 2010, equivalent to 81.4% of GDP. Belize's total external debt was estimated at $1,092m. in 2009, of which $1,063m. was public and publicly guaranteed debt. In that year the cost of servicing long-term public and publicly guaranteed debt and repayments to the IMF was equivalent to 13.3% of the value of exports of goods, services and income (excluding workers' remittances). The annual rate of inflation averaged 2.7% in 2001–10. Consumer prices fell by 1.1% in 2009, but increased by 0.9% in 2010. According to the 2010 census, some 23.1% of the total labour force were unemployed. Many Belizeans, however, work abroad, and remittances to the country from such workers are an important source of income. Emigration, mainly to the USA, is offset by the number of immigrants and refugees from other Central American countries, particularly El Salvador.

The credibility of Belize's leading financial institutions and its ability to access sources of external finance were severely damaged following a sovereign default in 2006. At the same time, the economy had to contend with restructuring in the agricultural sector (following the cessation of European Union preferential prices for sugar and bananas). However, amendments to the Income and Business Tax Act in 2007 significantly increased revenue, enabling the Government to direct 40% of total revenues from the emerging petroleum sector into budgetary operations. This sector had enjoyed impressive growth following the discovery of a large deposit of high-quality crude petroleum in 2005. The 19-MW Vaca Dam became fully operational in 2010, stimulating growth of 2.3% in that year. A recovery in oil and agricultural exports also contributed to this economic expansion. However, a constitutional amendment in October 2011, granting the Government the right to nationalize utilities was expected to deter much-needed investment, while unsustainable levels of government debt, rising inflation, high rates of poverty and uncertain prospects for the global economy were also matters of concern. The United Democratic Party Government that was re-elected in March 2012 pledged to prioritize renegotiation of Belize's burdensome debt-servicing agreement, which made up almost one-half of total debt. The IMF projected further growth of 2.5% in 2011, driven by increased activity in the agricultural, manufacturing and tourism industries, with further economic expansion of 2.8% in 2012.

PUBLIC HOLIDAYS

2013: 1 January (New Year's Day), 9 March (National Heroes' and Benefactors' Day), 29 March–1 April (Easter), 1 May (Labour Day), 24 May (Sovereign's Day), 10 September (National Day), 21 September (Independence Day), 12 October (Day of the Americas), 19 November (Garifuna Settlement Day), 25–26 December (Christmas).

Statistical Survey

Sources (unless otherwise stated): Statistical Institute of Belize, 1902 Constitution Drive, Belmopan; tel. 822-2207; internet www.statisticsbelize.org.bz; Central Bank of Belize, Gabourel Lane, POB 852, Belize City; tel. 223-6194; fax 223-6226; e-mail cenbank@btl.net; internet www.centralbank.org.bz.

AREA AND POPULATION

Area: 22,965 sq km (8,867 sq miles).

Population: 240,204 at census of 12 May 2000; 312,698 (males 157,935, females 154,763) at census of 12 May 2010.

Density (at 2010 census): 13.6 per sq km.

Population by Age and Sex (official estimates at mid-2009): *0–14:* 122,700 (males 62,600, females 60,100); *15–64:* 193,500 (males 95,100, females 98,400); *65 and over:* 17,000 (males 8,800, females 8,200); *Total* 333,200 (males 166,500, females 166,700). Note: Estimates not adjusted to take account of 2010 census results.

Districts (population at 2010 census): Belize 89,247; Cayo 72,899; Orange Walk 45,419; Corozal 40,354; Stann Creek 32,166; Toledo 30,538. Note: Figures exclude homeless (118) and institutionalized population (1,957).

Principal Towns (population at 2010 census): Belize City (former capital) 65,042; San Ignacio/Santa Elena 16,977; Orange Walk 13,400; Belmopan (capital) 13,351; San Pedro 11,510; Corozal 9,901; Dangriga (fmrly Stann Creek) 9,096; Benque Viejo 5,824; Punta Gorda 5,205.

Births, Marriages and Deaths (provisional figures, 2003): Registered live births 7,440 (birth rate 27.3 per 1,000); Registered marriages 1,713 (marriage rate 6.3 per 1,000); Registered deaths 1,277 (death rate 4.7 per 1,000). *2005* (provisional): Registered live births 8,396; Registered deaths 1,369 (Source: UN, *Population and Vital Statistics Report*).

Life Expectancy (years at birth, WHO estimates): 73 (males 71; females 76) in 2009. Source: WHO, *World Health Statistics*.

Economically Active Population (April 2006): Agriculture 18,406; Forestry 733; Fishing 2,070; Mining and quarrying 434; Manufacturing 7,363; Electricity, gas and water 879; Construction 7,390; Wholesale and retail trade and repairs 16,722; Tourism (incl. restaurants and hotels) 13,981; Transport, storage and communications 4,352; Financial intermediation 1,800; Real estate, renting and business activities 2,431; General government services 9,345; Community, social and personal services 16,041; Other 285; *Total employed* 102,233. *Total labour force* (persons aged 14 years and over, September 2009): 144,363 (employed 126,188, unemployed 18,176). *2010 Census:* Total employed 100,537; Unemployed 30,180; Total labour force 130,717 (males 79,760, females 50,957).

HEALTH AND WELFARE

Key Indicators

Total Fertility Rate (children per woman, 2009): 2.8.

Under-5 Mortality Rate (per 1,000 live births, 2009): 18.

HIV/AIDS (% of persons aged 15–49, 2009): 2.3.

Physicians (per 1,000 head, 2000): 1.1.

Hospital Beds (per 1,000 head, 2006): 1.3.

Health Expenditure (2008): US $ per head (PPP): 323.

Health Expenditure (2008): % of GDP: 4.5.

Health Expenditure (2008): public (% of total): 70.2.

Access to Water (% of persons, 2008): 99.

Access to Sanitation (% of persons, 2008): 90.

Total Carbon Dioxide Emissions ('000 metric tons, 2007): 425.0.

Carbon Dioxide Emissions Per Head (metric tons, 2007): 1.4.

Human Development Index (2011): ranking: 93.

Human Development Index (2011): value: 0.699.

For sources and definitions, see explanatory note on p. vi.

AGRICULTURE, ETC.

Principal Crops ('000 metric tons, 2010, FAO estimates): Rice, paddy 18.9; Maize 54.3; Sorghum 12.0; Sugar cane 917.7; Beans, dry 4.5; Fresh vegetables 4.0; Bananas 70.1; Plantains 3.6; Oranges 237.2; Grapefruit and pomelos 36.0; Papayas 25.1. *Aggregate Production* ('000 metric tons, may include official, semi-official or estimated data): Vegetables (incl. melons) 11.2; Fruits (excl. melons) 376.8.

Livestock ('000 head, year ending September 2010, FAO estimates): Horses 6; Cattle 95; Pigs 17; Sheep 13; Chickens 1,500.

Livestock Products ('000 metric tons, 2010, FAO estimates): Cattle meat 1.6; Chicken meat 13.0; Pig meat 1.2; Cows' milk 3.9; Hen eggs 2.1.

Forestry (2010): *Roundwood Removals* ('000 cubic metres, excl. bark, FAO estimates): Sawlogs, veneer logs and logs for sleepers 41; Fuel wood 126; Total 167. *Sawnwood Production* ('000 cubic metres, incl. railway sleepers, FAO estimates): Coniferous (softwood) 5; Broadleaved (hardwood) 30; Total 35.

Fishing ('000 metric tons, live weight, 2009): Capture 4.9 (Albacore 0.4; Caribbean spiny lobster 0.5; Stromboid conchs 2.5; Yellowfin tuna 1.0); Aquaculture 9.7 (FAO estimate) (White leg shrimp 7.3—FAO estimate); Total catch 14.6 (FAO estimate).

Source: FAO.

INDUSTRY

Production (2005, unless otherwise indicated): Raw sugar 100,435 long tons; Molasses 37,074 long tons; Cigarettes 78 million; Beer 1,891,000 gallons; Batteries 6,000; Flour 26,959,000 lb; Fertilizers 26,874,000 short tons; Garments 611,900 items; Soft drinks 4,929,000 gallons; Citrus concentrates 2,973,000 gallons (2004); Single strength juices 2,102,000 gallons (2004). Source: IMF, *Belize: Selected Issues and Statistical Appendix* (October 2006).

FINANCE

Currency and Exchange Rates: 100 cents = 1 Belizean dollar (BZ $). *Sterling, US Dollar and Euro Equivalents* (30 December 2011): £1 sterling = BZ $3.092; US $1 = BZ $2.000; €1 = BZ $2.588; BZ $100 = £32.34 = US $50.00 = €38.64. *Exchange rate*: Fixed at US $1 = BZ $2.000 since May 1976.

Budget (BZ $ million, year ending 31 March 2011): *Revenue:* Taxation 687.3 (Taxes on income and profits 256.7, Taxes on property 5.5, Taxes on goods and services 226.7, International trade and transactions 198.3); Other current revenue 96.8; Capital revenue 5.3; Total 789.3, excl. grants (54.3). *Expenditure:* Current expenditure 729.6 (Personal emoluments 300.4; Pensions 48.9; Goods and services 168.4; Debt service 111.6; Subsidies and current transfers 100.3); Capital expenditure 160.2; Total 889.8.

International Reserves (US $ million at 31 December 2010): IMF special drawing rights 30.99; Reserve position in the IMF 6.53; Foreign exchange 180.48; Total 218.00. Source: IMF, *International Financial Statistics*.

Money Supply (BZ $ million at 31 December 2010): Currency outside depository corporations 157.76; Transferable deposits 550.14; Other deposits 1,382.87; *Broad money* 2,090.78. Source: IMF, *International Financial Statistics*.

Cost of Living (Consumer Price Index; base: 2005 = 100): All items 113.5 in 2008; 112.2 in 2009; 113.2 in 2010. Source: IMF, *International Financial Statistics*.

Expenditure on the Gross Domestic Product (BZ $ million at current prices, 2008): Government final consumption expenditure 430.4; Private final consumption expenditure 1,758.8; Increase in stocks 48.2; Gross fixed capital formation 691.8; *Gross domestic expenditure* 2,929.2; Exports of goods and services 1,687.1; *Less* Imports of goods and services 1,903.4; Statistical discrepancy 4.6; *GDP at market prices* 2,717.4.

Gross Domestic Product by Economic Activity (BZ $ million at current prices, 2008): Agriculture and forestry 228.8; Fishing 59.1; Mining and quarrying 13.5; Manufacturing 339.2; Electricity and water 61.0; Construction 124.1; Wholesale and retail trade, repairs 400.7; Restaurants and hotels 117.4; Transport, storage and communications 283.4; Financial intermediation 205.3; Real estate, renting and business services 196.9; Community, social and personal services 177.0; General government services 277.6; *Sub-total* 2,484.0; Taxes, less subsidies, on products 353.6; *Less* Financial intermediation services indirectly measured 120.2; *GDP at market prices* 2,717.4.

Balance of Payments (US $ million, 2010): Exports of goods f.o.b. 475.7; Imports of goods f.o.b. –647.2; *Trade balance* –171.5; Exports of services 353.8; Imports of services –162.4; *Balance on goods and services* 20.0; Other income received 4.6; Other income paid –162.1; *Balance on goods, services and income* –137.6; Current transfers (net) 91.9; *Current balance* –45.7; Capital account (net) 5.6; Financial account (net) 27.0; Net errors and omissions 18.0; *Overall balance* 5.0 (Source: IMF, *International Financial Statistics*).

EXTERNAL TRADE

Principal Commodities (BZ $ million, 2010): *Imports c.i.f.:* Food and live animals 155.5; Mineral fuels and lubricants 230.7; Chemicals and related products 125.0; Manufactured goods 190.5; Miscellaneous manufactured articles 94.4; Machinery and transport equipment 232.6; Commercial free zone 262.5; Export processing zone 63.0; Total (incl. others) 1,435.6. *Exports f.o.b.:* Citrus concentrate 93.7; Marine products 61.7; Sugar 58.7; Bananas 71.6; Papaya 25.9; Crude petroleum 206.2; Total (incl. others) 569.3.

Principal Trading Partners (BZ $ million, 2009): *Imports c.i.f.:* USA 464.2; Mexico 136.9; United Kingdom 18.9; Canada 12.2; Total (incl. others) 1,336.4. *Exports f.o.b.* (excl. re-exports): USA 162.5; United Kingdom 158.9; Mexico 11.1; Total (incl. others) 501.2.

TRANSPORT

Road Traffic (vehicles in use, 1998): Passenger cars 9,929; Buses and coaches 416; Lorries and vans 11,339; Motorcycles and mopeds 270. *2007* (vehicles in use): Total vehicles 54,225. Source: IRF, *World Road Statistics*.

Shipping (sea-borne freight traffic, '000 metric tons, 1996): Goods loaded 255.4; Goods unloaded 277.1. *Merchant Fleet* (vessels registered at 31 December 2009): Number of vessels 430; Total displacement 1,248,204 grt (Source: IHS Fairplay, *World Fleet Statistics*).

Civil Aviation (2002): Passenger arrivals 174,038. Source: IMF, *Belize: Statistical Appendix* (April 2004).

TOURISM

Tourist Arrivals: 772,339 (cruise ship passengers 537,632, stop-over visitors 234,707) in 2008; 856,351 (cruise ship passengers 634,697, stop-over visitors 221,654) in 2009; 914,797 (cruise ship passengers 688,165, stop-over visitors 226,632) in 2010.

Tourism Receipts (US $ million): 278.5 in 2008; 256.2 in 2009; 264.4 in 2010.

COMMUNICATIONS MEDIA

Radio Receivers (1997): 133,000 in use*.

Television Receivers (2000): 44,000 in use†.

Telephones (2010): 30,300 main lines in use†.

Mobile Cellular Telephones (2010): 194,200 subscribers†.

Personal Computers (2007): 45,000 (144.5 per 1,000 persons) in use†.

Internet Subscribers (2010): 8.9†.

Broadband Subscribers (2010): 8,900†.

Book Production (1996): 107 titles*.

Non-daily Newspapers (1996): 10 (circulation 80,000)*.

* Source: UNESCO, *Statistical Yearbook*.
† Source: International Telecommunication Union.

EDUCATION

Pre-primary (2009/10 unless otherwise indicated): 182 schools (2008/09), 378 teachers, 6,596 students.

Primary (2009/10 unless otherwise indicated): 294 schools (2008/09), 2,367 teachers, 52,650 students.

Secondary (2009/10 unless otherwise indicated): 51 schools (2008/09), 1,947 teachers, 32,780 students.

Higher (1997/98, unless otherwise indicated): 12 institutions, 228 teachers, 3,581 students (2008/09).

Pupil-teacher Ratio (primary education, UNESCO estimate): 22.2 in 2009/10.

Source: fmr Ministry of Education, Youth and Sports; UNESCO Institute for Statistics.

Adult Literacy Rate (UNESCO estimates): 76.9% (males 77.1%; females 76.7%) in 2003. Source: UN Development Programme, *Human Development Report*.

Directory

The Government

HEAD OF STATE

Queen: HM Queen Elizabeth II.

Governor-General: Sir Colville Young (appointed 17 November 1993).

THE CABINET
(May 2012)

The Government is formed by the United Democratic Party.

Prime Minister and Minister of Finance and Economic Development: Dean O. Barrow.

Deputy Prime Minister and Minister of Natural Resources and of Agriculture: Gaspar Vega.

Attorney-General and Minister of Foreign Affairs: Wilfred Elrington.

Minister of Trade, Investment Promotion, Private Sector Development and Consumer Protection: Erwin Contreras.

Minister of Education, Youth and Sports: Patrick Faber.

Minister of National Security, Police and Defence: John Saldivar.

Minister of Housing and Urban Development: Michael Finnegan.

Minister of Works and Transport: Rene Montero.

Minister of Tourism and Culture: Manuel Heredia, Jr.

Minister of Health: Pablo Marin.

Minister of Labour, Local Government, Rural Development and National Emergency Management: Godwin Hulse.

Minister of the Public Service and Elections and Boundaries: Charles Gibson.

Minister of Forestry, Fisheries and Sustainable Development: Liselle Alamilla.

Minister of Human Development, Social Transformation and Poverty Alleviation: Anthony Martinez.

Minister of Energy, Science and Technology and Public Utilities: Joy Grant.

There are, in addition, six Ministers of State.

MINISTRIES

Office of the Prime Minister: Sir Edney Cain Bldg, 3rd Floor, Left Wing, Belmopan; tel. 822-2346; fax 822-0898; e-mail secretarypm@opm.gov.bz; internet www.opm.gov.bz.

Ministry of Agriculture: West Block Bldg, 2nd Floor, Belmopan; tel. 822-2241; fax 822-2409; e-mail info@agriculture.gov.bz; internet www.agriculture.gov.bz.

Ministry of Education, Youth and Sports: West Block Bldg, 3rd Floor, Belmopan; tel. 822-2380; fax 822-3389; e-mail moeducation.moes@gmail.com; internet www.moes.gov.bz.

Ministry of Energy, Science and Technology and Public Utilities: East Block Bldg, 1st Floor, Belmopan; tel. 822-3336; fax 822-0433; e-mail minister.sec@mysc.gov.bz.

Ministry of Finance and Economic Development: New Administration Bldg, Belmopan; tel. 822-2362; fax 822-2886; e-mail econdev@btl.net; internet www.mof.gov.bz.

Ministry of Foreign Affairs: NEMO Bldg, 2nd Floor, POB 174, Belmopan; tel. 822-2167; fax 822-2854; e-mail belizemfa@btl.net; internet www.mfa.gov.bz.

Ministry of Forestry, Fisheries and Sustainable Development: Sir Edney Cain Bldg, Ground Floor, Left Wing, Belmopan; tel. 822-2526; fax 822-3673; internet www.forestdepartment.gov.bz (forestry), www.agriculture.gov.bz/Fisheries_Dept.html (fisheries), www.doe.gov.bz (environment).

Ministry of Health: East Block Bldg, Independence Plaza, Belmopan; tel. 822-2068; fax 822-2942; e-mail seniorsecretary@health.gov.bz; internet health.gov.bz/moh.

Ministry of Housing and Urban Development: Sir Edney Cain Bldg, 2nd Floor, Left Wing, Belmopan; tel. 822-1039; fax 822-3337; e-mail ministry@housing.gov.bz.

Ministry of Human Development, Social Transformation and Poverty Alleviation: West Block Bldg, Independence Plaza, Belmopan; tel. 822-2161; fax 822-3175; e-mail secretary@humandev.gov.bz.

Ministry of Labour, Local Government, Rural Development and National Emergency Management: 6/8 Trinity Blvd, Belmopan; tel. 822-2297; fax 822-0156; e-mail labour.comm@labour.gov.bz.

Ministry of National Security, Police and Defence: Curl Thompson Bldg, Belmopan; tel. 822-2817; fax 822-2195; e-mail minofnatsec@mns.gov.bz.

Ministry of Natural Resources: Market Sq., Belmopan; tel. 822-3286; fax 822-2333; e-mail minister@mnrei.gov.bz; internet www.mnrei.gov.bz.

Ministry of the Public Service and Elections and Boundaries: Sir Edney Cain Bldg, Ground Floor, Left Wing, Belmopan; tel. 822-3765; fax 822-2206; e-mail ceo@mps.gov.bz; internet www.mps.gov.bz.

Ministry of Tourism and Culture: 106 South St, Belize City; tel. 227-2801; fax 227-2810; e-mail dcabelize@btl.net; internet www.belizetourism.org (tourism); www.nichbelize.org (culture).

Ministry of Trade, Investment Promotion, Private Sector Development and Consumer Protection: Sir Edney Cain Bldg, Ground Floor, Left Wing, Belmopan; tel. 822-2526; fax 822-3673; e-mail foreigntrade@btl.net.

Ministry of Works and Transport: New 2 Power Lane, Belmopan; tel. 822-2136; fax 822-3282; e-mail works@btl.net, departmentoftransport@yahoo.com.

Office of the Attorney-General: General Office, Belmopan; tel. 822-2504; fax 822-3390; e-mail agministrybze@yahoo.com.

Legislature

NATIONAL ASSEMBLY

The Senate

President: Andrea Gill.

There are 12 nominated members in addition to the current ex officio President.

House of Representatives

Speaker: Emil Arguelles.

Clerk: Herbert Panton.

General Election, 7 March 2012

	Valid votes cast	% of total	Seats
United Democratic Party (UDP)	61,903	49.33	17
People's United Party (PUP)	61,556	49.05	14
Others	2,032	1.62	—
Total valid votes*	125,491	100.00	31

* In addition, there were 4,767 blank, invalid or spoiled votes cast.

Election Commissions

Elections and Boundaries Commission: Belize City; e-mail electbound@btl.net; internet www.elections.gov.bz; f. 1978; appointed by Governor-Gen; comprises Chair. and 4 mems; separate entity to the Elections and Boundaries Dept (q.v.); Chair. Alberto August.

Elections and Boundaries Department: Charles Bartlett Hyde Bldg, Mahogany St Extension, POB 913, Belize City; tel. 222-4042; fax 222-4991; e-mail electbound@btl.net; internet www.elections.gov.bz; f. 1989; dept of the Office of the Prime Minister; Chief Elections Officer Josephine Tamai.

Political Organizations

People's National Party (PNP): 57 Main St, Punta Gorda Town, Toledo Dist; tel. 610-0978; fax 225-2571; e-mail info@pnpbelize.org; internet www.pnpbelize.org; f. 2007; Leader Wil Maheia.

People's United Party (PUP): 3 Queen St, Belize City; tel. 223-2428; fax 223-3476; internet www.pup.org.bz; f. 1950; based on organized labour; publs *The Belize Times*; Leader Francis William Fonseca; Chair. Henry Usher; Sec.-Gen. Myrtle Palacio.

United Democratic Party (UDP): South End Bel-China Bridge, POB 1898, Belize City; tel. 227-2576; fax 227-6441; e-mail unitedd@btl.net; internet www.udp.org.bz; f. 1974 by merger of People's Development Movement, Liberal Party and National Independence Party; conservative; Leader Dean Barrow; Chair. Patrick Faber.

Vision Inspired by the People (VIP): Belize City; f. 2005; Chair. Robert (Bobby) Lopez.

Diplomatic Representation

EMBASSIES AND HIGH COMMISSION IN BELIZE

Brazil: 12 Floral Park Ave, POB 548, Belmopan; tel. 822-0460; fax 822-0461; e-mail embbrazil@btl.net; internet www.embaixadadobrasilembelize.org; Ambassador Tomas Mauricio Guggenheim.

Costa Rica: 19 Orchid Garden St, POB 288, Belmopan; tel. 822-1582; fax 822-1583; e-mail embaticabz@gmail.com; Ambassador Ingrid Hermann Escribano.

Cuba: 6087 Manatee Dr., Buttonwood Bay, POB 1775, Belize City; tel. 223-5345; fax 223-1105; e-mail embacuba@btl.net; internet embacu.cubaminrex.cu/beliceing; Ambassador Manuel Javier Rubido Díaz.

El Salvador: 13 Zennia St, Cohune Walk, POB 215, Belmopan; tel. 823-3404; fax 823-3569; e-mail embasalva@btl.net; Ambassador Julio Milton Parada Dominguez.

Guatemala: 8 A St, King's Park, POB 1771, Belize City; tel. 223-3150; fax 223-5140; e-mail embbelice@minex.gob.gt; Ambassador Manuel Arturo Téllez Miralda.

Honduras: 2½ Miles, Northern Hwy, POB 285, Belize City; tel. 224-5889; fax 223-0562; e-mail embahonbe@yahoo.com; Ambassador Sandra Rosales Abella.

Mexico: 3 North Ring Rd, Embassy Sq., Belmopan; tel. 822-2480; fax 822-2487; e-mail embamexbze@btl.net; internet www.sre.gob.mx/belice; Ambassador Mario Velázquez Suarez.

Nicaragua: 1 South St, Belize City; tel. and fax 227-0335; e-mail embanicbelize@btl.net; Ambassador Gilda Maria Bolt Gonzalez (resident in El Salvador).

Taiwan (Republic of China): 20 North Park St, POB 1020, Belize City; tel. 227-8744; fax 223-3082; e-mail embroc@btl.net; internet www.taiwanembassy.org/bz; Ambassador David Wu.

United Kingdom: Embassy Sq., POB 91, Belmopan; tel. 822-2146; fax 822-2761; e-mail brithicom@btl.net; internet ukinbelize.fco.gov.uk; High Commissioner Patrick Ashworth.

USA: Floral Park Rd, POB 286, Belmopan; tel. 822-4011; fax 822-4012; e-mail embbelize@state.gov; internet belize.usembassy.gov; Ambassador Vinai K. Thummalapally.

Venezuela: 17 Orchid Garden St, POB 49, Belmopan; tel. 822-2384; fax 822-2022; e-mail embaven@btl.net; Chargé d'affaires Gabriel Sánchez.

Judicial System

Summary Jurisdiction Courts (criminal jurisdiction) and District Courts (civil jurisdiction), presided over by magistrates, are established in each of the six judicial districts. Summary Jurisdiction Courts have a wide jurisdiction in summary offences and a limited jurisdiction in indictable matters. Appeals lie to the Supreme Court, which has jurisdiction corresponding to the English High Court of Justice and where a jury system is in operation. From the Supreme Court further appeals lie to a Court of Appeal, established in 1967, which holds an average of four sessions per year. Since 1 June 2010 final appeals are made to the Caribbean Court of Justice, based in Trinidad and Tobago, rather than to the Privy Council in the United Kingdom.

Court of Appeal: Belize City; tel. 227-2907; internet www.belizelaw.org; Pres. Manuel Sosa; Justices of Appeal Douglas Mendes, Boyd Carey, Dennis Morrison, Brian Alleyne.

Magistrates' Court: Paslow Bldg, Belize City; tel. 227-7164; Chief Magistrate Margaret Gabb-MacKenzie.

Supreme Court: Supreme Court Bldg, Belize City; tel. 227-7256; fax 227-0181; e-mail chiefjustice@btl.net; internet www.belizelaw.org/supreme_court/chief_justice.html; Registrar Velda Flowers; Chief Justice Kenneth Benjamin.

Religion

CHRISTIANITY

Most of the population are Christian, the largest denomination being the Roman Catholic Church.

Belize Council of Churches: 149 Allenby St, POB 508, Belize City; tel. 227-7077; f. 1957 as Church World Service Cttee; present name adopted 1984; 9 mem. churches, 4 assoc. bodies; Pres. Rev. LeRoy Flowers.

The Roman Catholic Church

According to the latest available census figures (2000), some 50% of the population are Roman Catholics. Belize comprises the single diocese of Belize City-Belmopan, suffragan to the archdiocese of Kingston in Jamaica. The Bishop participates in the Antilles Episcopal Conference (whose secretariat is based in Port of Spain, Trinidad and Tobago).

Bishop of Belize City-Belmopan: DORICK MCGOWAN WRIGHT, Bishop's House, 144 North Front St, POB 616, Belize City; tel. 223-2122; fax 223-1922; e-mail episkopos@btl.net.

The Anglican Communion

Anglicans in Belize, accounting for some 5% of the population at the 2000 census, belong to the Church in the Province of the West Indies, comprising eight dioceses. The Archbishop of the Province is the Bishop of the North Eastern Caribbean and Aruba, resident in St John's, Antigua and Barbuda.

Bishop of Belize: Rt Rev. PHILIP S. WRIGHT, Rectory Lane, POB 535, Belize City; tel. 227-3029; fax 227-6898; e-mail bzediocese@btl.net; internet www.belize.anglican.org.

Protestant Churches

According to the 2000 census, some 7% of the population are Pentecostalists, 5% Seventh-day Adventists, 4% Mennonites, 3% Baptists and 3% Methodists.

Mennonite Congregations in Belize: POB 427, Belize City; tel. 823-0137; fax 823-0101; f. 1958; in 2003 there were an estimated 3,575 mems living in 8 Mennonite settlements, the largest of which was Altkolonier Mennonitengemeinde with 1,728 mems; Bishop AARON HARDER.

Methodist Church in the Caribbean and the Americas (Belize/Honduras District) (MCCA): 75 Albert St, POB 212, Belize City; tel. 227-7173; fax 227-5870; f. 1824; c. 1,827 mems; District Pres. Rev. DAVID GOFF.

Other denominations active in the country include the Presbyterians, Moravians, Jehovah's Witnesses, the Church of God, the Nazarene Church, the Assemblies of Brethren and the Salvation Army.

OTHER RELIGIONS

There are also small communities of Hindus (367, according to the census of 2000), Muslims (243 in 2000) and Bahá'ís (205 in 2000), together accounting for less than 1% of the population.

The Press

Amandala: Amandala Press, 3304 Partridge St, POB 15, Belize City; tel. 202-4476; fax 222-4702; e-mail info@amandala.com.bz; internet www.amandala.com.bz; f. 1969; 2 a week; independent; Publr EVAN X. HYDE; Editor RUSSELL VELLOS; circ. 45,000.

Ambergris Today: Pescador Dr., POB 23, San Pedro Town, Ambergris Caye; tel. 226-3462; fax 226-3483; e-mail ambertoday@btl.net; internet www.ambergristoday.com; weekly; independent; Editor DORIAN NUÑEZ.

The Belize Times: 3 Queen St, POB 506, Belize City; tel. 224-5757; fax 223-1940; e-mail belizetime@btl.net; internet www.belizetimes.bz; f. 1956; weekly; party political paper of PUP; Editor-in-Chief MIKE RUDON, Jr; circ. 6,000.

Belize Today: Belize Information Service, East Block, POB 60, Belmopan; tel. 822-2159; fax 822-3242; monthly; official; circ. 17,000.

Government Gazette: Print Belize Ltd, 1 Power Lane, Belmopan; tel. 822-0194; fax 822-3367; e-mail admin@printbze.com; internet www.printbelize.com/content; f. 1871; official; weekly; CEO LAWRENCE J. NICHOLAS.

The Guardian: Ebony St and Bel-China Bridge, POB 1898, Belize City; tel. 207-5346; fax 227-5343; e-mail guardian@btl.net; internet www.guardian.bz; weekly; party political paper of UDP; Editor ALFONSO NOBLE; circ. 5,000.

The Reporter: 147 Allenby St, POB 707, Belize City; tel. 227-2503; fax 227-8278; e-mail editor@belizereporter.bz; internet www.reporter.bz; f. 1967; weekly; Editor ANN MARIE WILLIAMS; circ. 6,500.

The San Pedro Sun: POB 35, San Pedro Town, Ambergris Caye; tel. 226-2070; fax 226-2905; e-mail spsun@sanpedrosun.net; internet www.sanpedrosun.net; f. 1993; weekly; Editors RON SNIFFIN, TAMARA SNIFFIN.

Publishers

Angelus Press Ltd: 10 Queen St, POB 1757, Belize City; tel. 223-5777; fax 227-8825; e-mail angel@btl.net; internet www.angeluspress.com; f. 1885; owned by the Santiago Castillo Group since 1997; Gen. Man. AMPARO MASSON NOBLE.

Cubola Productions: Montserrat Casademunt, 35 Elizabeth St, Benque Viejo del Carmen; tel. 823-2083; fax 823-2240; e-mail cubolabz@btl.net; internet www.cubola.com; Dir MONTSERRAT CASADEMUNT.

Print Belize Ltd: 1 Power Lane, Belmopan; tel. 822-2293; fax 882-3367; e-mail admin@printbelize.com; internet www.printbelize.com; f. 1871; responsible for printing, binding and engraving requirements of all govt depts and ministries; publications include annual govt estimates, govt magazines and the official *Government Gazette*; CEO LAWRENCE J. NICHOLAS.

Broadcasting and Communications

TELECOMMUNICATIONS

Public Utilities Commission (PUC): regulatory body for the telecommunications sector; see Utilities—Regulatory Body.

Belize Telemedia Ltd: Esquivel Telecom Centre, St Thomas St, POB 603, Belize City; tel. 223-2868; fax 223-1800; e-mail prdept@btl.net; internet www.belizetelemedia.net; f. May 2007; fmrly Belize Telecommunications Ltd (subsidiary of Innovative Communication Corpn (ICC) until taken over by the Govt in 2005); nationalized Aug. 2009; partially privatized in 2010; Exec. Chair. NESTOR VASQUEZ.

SpeedNet Communications Ltd: 2 Bishop St, Belize City; tel. 280-1000; fax 223-1919; e-mail Smartbelizecity@speednet-wireless.com; internet www.smart-bz.com; f. 2003, commenced services in 2005; mobile cellular telecommunications provider under the brand name Smart; Man. (IT) SEAN DUNCAN.

BROADCASTING

Regulatory Authority

Belize Broadcasting Authority (BBA): 7 Gabourel Lane, Belize City; tel. and fax 223-3953; e-mail broadcasting_bze@hotmail.com; regulatory authority; part of the Ministry of Public Utilities, Transport, Communications and National Emergency Management; Chair. LOUIS LESLIE.

Radio

Love FM: 7145 Slaughterhouse Rd, POB 1865, Belize City; tel. 203-2098; fax 203-0529; e-mail lovefm@btl.net; internet www.lovefm.com; f. 1992; purchased Friends FM in 1998; CEO RENE VILLANUEVA, Sr.

Radio Krem Ltd: 3304 Partridge St, POB 15, Belize City; tel. 222-4299; fax 202-4469; e-mail kremwub@hotmail.com; internet www.krembz.com; commercial; purchased Radio Belize in 1998.

Other private radio stations broadcasting in Belize include: Estereo Amor, More FM, My Refuge Christian Radio, Radio 2000 and Voice of America.

Television

Centaur Cable Network (CTV): 31 Clarke St, Orange Walk Town, Orange Walk; tel. 670-2216; fax 322-2216; internet www.ctv3belizenews.com; f. 1989; commercial.

Channel 5 Belize: Great Belize Productions Ltd, 2882 Coney Dr., POB 1314, Belize City; tel. 223-7781; fax 223-4936; e-mail gbtv@btl.com; internet www.channel5belize.com; f. 1991; CEO AMALIA MAI.

Tropical Vision (Channel 7): 73 Albert St, Belize City; tel. 223-5589; fax 227-5602; e-mail tvseven@btl.net; internet 7newsbelize.com; commercial; Man. Dir NESTOR VASQUEZ.

Finance

(cap. = capital; res = reserves; dep. = deposits; brs = branches; amounts in BZ $, unless otherwise indicated)

BANKING

Central Bank

Central Bank of Belize: Gabourel Lane, POB 852, Belize City; tel. 223-6194; fax 223-6226; e-mail cenbank@btl.net; internet www.centralbank.org.bz; f. 1982; cap. 10m., res 23.9m., dep. 337.9m. (2009); Gov. GLENFORD YSAGUIRRE; Chair. ALAN SLUSHER.

Development Bank

Development Finance Corporation: Bliss Parade, Belmopan; tel. 822-2360; fax 822-3096; e-mail info@dfcbelize.org; internet www.dfcbelize.org; f. 1972; ceased to finance loans following a govt review in Dec. 2004; issued cap. 10m.; 5 brs.

Other Banks

Atlantic Bank Ltd: Cnr Freetown Rd and Cleghorn St, POB 481, Belize City; tel. 223-4123; fax 223-3907; e-mail atlantic@atlabank.com; internet www.atlabank.com; f. 1971; 52% owned by Honduran co Sociedad Nacional de Inversiones, SA (SONISA); dep. 161.0m., total assets 191.9m. (2001); Gen. Man. SANDRA BEDRAN; 8 brs.

Atlantic International Bank Ltd: Cnr Freetown Rd and Cleghorn St, POB 481, Belize City; tel. 223-3152; fax 223-3528; e-mail banking@atlabank.com; internet www.atlanticibl.com; affiliated to Atlantic Bank Ltd; Gen. Man. RICARDO PELAYO.

Belize Bank Ltd: 60 Market Sq., POB 364, Belize City; tel. 227-7132; fax 227-2712; e-mail bblbz@belizebank.com; internet www.belizebank.com; subsidiary of BCB Holdings; cap. US $2.1m., res US $2.1m., dep. US $489m. (March 2010); Chair. PHIL JOHNSON; 10 brs.

British Caribbean Bank International: 60 Market Sq., Belize City; tel. 227-0697; fax 227-0983; e-mail services@bcbankinternational.com; internet bcbankinternational.com; fmrly Belize Bank, Turks & Caicos.

Caye International Bank Ltd (CIBL): Coconut Dr., San Pedro, POB 11, Ambergris Caye; tel. 226-2388; fax 226-2892; e-mail cibl@btl.net; internet www.cayebank.bz; Pres. PETER A. ZIPPER; Exec. Vice-Pres. JOY A. FLOWERS.

FirstCaribbean International Bank Ltd (Barbados): 21 Albert St, POB 363, Belize City; tel. 227-7211; fax 227-8572; e-mail care@firstcaribbeanbank.com; internet www.firstcaribbeanbank.com; f. 2002 by merger of CIBC West Indies Holdings and Barclays Bank PLC Caribbean operations; Barclays relinquished its stake to CIBC in June 2006; Exec. Chair. MICHAEL MANSOOR; Exec. Dir JOHN ORR.

Heritage Bank Ltd: 106 Princess Margaret Dr., POB 1988, Belize City; tel. 223-6783; fax 223-6785; e-mail services@banking.bz; internet www.alliancebankbelize.bz; f. 2001 as Alliance Bank of Belize Ltd; name changed as above in 2010; dep. 6,876m., total assets 113.7m.; 3 brs.

Heritage International Bank and Trust Ltd: 35 Barrack Rd, POB 1867, Belize City; tel. 223-5698; fax 223-0368; e-mail services@banking.bz; internet heritageibt.com; f. 1998 as Provident Bank and Trust of Belize; name changed as above in 2010; cap. US $6.0m., res US $1.5m., dep. US $105.9m. (2004); Chair. JOY VERNON GODFREY; Pres. JOSÉ MARIN.

There is also a government savings bank. In late 2001 the Government amended the exchange-control regulations to allow foreign-currency exchange bureaux.

INSURANCE

The insurance sector is regulated by the Office of the Supervisor of Insurance, part of the Ministry of Finance.

Atlantic Insurance Company Ltd: Atlantic Bank Bldg, 3rd Floor, Cnr Cleghorn St and Freetown Rd, POB 1447, Belize City; tel. 223-2657; fax 223-2658; e-mail info@atlanticinsurancebz.com; internet www.atlanticinsurancebz.com; f. 1991; part of the Atlantic Group of Cos; holding co, Sociedad Nacional de Inversiones, SA, (SONISA); Gen. Man. MARTHA GUERRA.

Belize Insurance Centre: 212 North Front St, Belize City; tel. 227-7310; fax 227-4803; e-mail info@belizeinsurance.com; internet www.belizeinsurance.com; f. 1972; insurance broker; subsidiary of Fraser Fontaine & Kong Ltd (Jamaica); Chair. G. RICHARD FONTAINE; Gen. Man. CYNTHIA AWE.

Insurance Corporation of Belize Ltd: 7 Daly St, Belize City; tel. 224-5328; fax 223-1317; e-mail icb@icbinsurance.com; internet www.icbinsurance.com; f. 1982; general insurance; Exec. Dir ERDULFO NUÑEZ.

RF & G Insurance Co Ltd: Gordon House, 1 Coney Dr., POB 661, Belize City; tel. 223-5734; fax 223-6734; e-mail info@rfginsurancebelize.com; internet www.rfginsurancebelize.com; f. 2005 by merger of F&G Insurance and Regent Insurance; underwriters of all major classes of insurance; mem. of the Roe Group of Cos; Chair. CHRISTOPHER ROE; Man. Dir GUY HOWISON.

RF & G Life Insurance Company Ltd: Gordon House, 4th Floor, 1 Coney Dr., POB 661, Belize City; tel. 223-5734; fax 223-6734; e-mail info@rfglife.com; internet www.rfglife.com; f. 2005 through merger of the Life and Medical portfolios of F&G Insurance Co into Regent Life; mem. of the Roe Group of Cos; Chair. BRIAN D. ROE; Gen. Man. RHONDA LECKY.

Trade and Industry

STATUTORY BODIES

Banana Control Board: c/o Ministry of Agriculture, West Block Bldg, 2nd Floor, Belmopan; management of banana industry; in 1989 it was decided to make it responsible to growers, not an independent executive.

Belize Agricultural Health Authority: Cnr Forest Dr. and Hummingbird Hwy, POB 169, Belmopan; tel. 822-0818; fax 822-0271; e-mail baha@btl.net; internet www.baha.bz; CEO GABINO CANTO; Man. Dir MICHAEL THOMAS.

Belize Marketing and Development Corporation (BMDC): 117 North Front St, POB 633, Belize City; tel. 227-7402; fax 227-7656; f. 1948 as Belize Marketing Board to encourage the growing of staple food crops; renamed as above in 2003; promotes domestic produce; Man. Dir ROQUE MAI.

Coastal Zone Management Authority and Institute (CZMAI): POB 1884, Belize City; tel. 223-0719; fax 223-5738; e-mail czmbze@btl.net; internet www.coastalzonebelize.org; Man. Dir VIRGINIA VASQUEZ (acting).

Pesticides Control Board (PCB): Central Farm, Cayo District; tel. 824-2640; fax 824-3486; e-mail pcbinfo@btl.net; internet www.pcbbelize.com; Chair. EUGENE WAIGHT.

DEVELOPMENT ORGANIZATION

Belize Trade and Investment Development Service (BELTRAIDE): 14 Orchid Garden St, Belmopan; tel. 822-3737; fax 822-0595; e-mail beltraide@belizeinvest.org.bz; internet www.belizeinvest.org.bz; f. 1986 as a joint govt and private sector institution to encourage export and investment; Exec. Chair. MICHAEL SINGH.

CHAMBERS OF COMMERCE

American Chamber of Commerce of Belize: 5½ Miles Western Hwy, Cucumber Beach, Marina, POB 75, Belize City; tel. 222-4344; fax 222-4265; e-mail office@amchambelize.org; internet www.amchambelize.org; Pres. PHIL HAHN; Sec. CON MURPHY.

Belize Chamber of Commerce and Industry (BCCI): 4792 Coney Dr., Withfield Tower, 1st Floor, POB 291, Belize City; tel. 223-5330; fax 223-5333; e-mail bcci@belize.org; internet www.belize.org; f. 1920; Pres. KAY MENZIES; Sec. ASHANTI MARTIN; 300 mems.

EMPLOYERS' ASSOCIATIONS

Banana Growers' Association: Big Creek, Independence Village, Stann Creek District; tel. 523-2000; fax 523-2112; e-mail banana@btl.net; Chair. EUGENE ZABANEH.

Belize Citrus Growers Association (BCGA): Mile 9, Stann Creek Valley Rd, POB 7, Dangriga, Stann Creek District; tel. 522-3585; fax 522-2686; e-mail cga@belizecitrus.org; internet www.belizecitrus.org; f. 1967; Chair. ECCLESTON IRVING; CEO HENRY N. ANDERSON.

Belize Livestock Producers' Association (BLPA): 47½ miles Western Hwy, POB 183, Belmopan; tel. 822-3883; e-mail blpa@btl.net; internet www.blpabz.org; f. 1972; Chair. Dr ERROL VANZIE.

Belize Sugar Cane Farmers' Association (BSCFA): 34 San Antonio Rd, Orange Walk; tel. 322-2005; fax 322-3171; f. 1959 to assist cane farmers and negotiate with the Sugar Cane Board and manufacturers on their behalf; Dir ALFREDO ORTEGA; CEO CARLOS MAGANA; 16 district brs.

United Cane Farmers' Association: Orange Walk; f. 2009; breakaway faction of the BSCFA; Rep. WILFREDO MAGAÑA.

UTILITIES

Regulatory Body

Public Utilities Commission (PUC): 41 Gabourel Lane, POB 300, Belize City; tel. 223-4938; fax 223-6818; e-mail info@puc.bz; internet www.puc.bz; f. 1999; regulatory body, headed by commissioners; replaced the Offices of Electricity Supply and of Telecommunications following enaction of the Public Utilities Commission Act in 1999; Chair. JOHN AVERY.

Electricity

Belize Electricity Co Ltd (BECOL): 115 Barrack Rd, POB 327, Belize City; tel. 227-0954; fax 223-0891; e-mail bel@btl.net; internet www.fortisinc.com; wholly owned subsidiary of Fortis Inc (Canada); operates Mollejón 25.2-MW hydroelectric plant and Chalillo 7.3-MW hydroelectric facility, which supply electricity to Belize Electricity Ltd (BEL—see below); Pres. and CEO H. STANLEY MARSHALL.

Belize Electricity Ltd (BEL): 2½ miles Northern Hwy, POB 327, Belize City; tel. 227-0954; fax 223-0891; e-mail pr@bel.com.bz; internet www.bel.com.bz; fmrly Belize Electricity Board, changed name upon privatization in 1992; nationalized in 2011; 70.2% owned by the Govt of Belize and 26.9% owned by Social Security Board; Pres. and CEO JEFFREY LOCKE; Chair. RODWELL WILLIAMS; 251 employees.

Water

Belize Water Services Ltd: Central American Blvd, POB 150, Belize City; tel. 222-4757; fax 222-4759; e-mail bws_ceosec@btl.net; internet www.bws.bz; f. 1971 as Water and Sewerage Authority (WASA); changed name upon privatization in 2001; renationalized in Oct. 2005 prior to partial reprivatization in early 2006; Chair. HERMAN LONGSWORTH; Sec. ALVAN HAYNES.

TRADE UNIONS

National Trade Union Congress of Belize (NTUCB): POB 2359, Belize City; tel. 822-0677; fax 822-0283; e-mail ntucb@btl.net; Pres. DYLAN RENEAU; Gen. Sec. JAVIER ROBERTS.

Principal Unions

Belize Communications Workers' Union (BCWU): POB 1291, Belize City; tel. 223-4809; fax 224-4300; e-mail bcwu@btl.net; f. 1989; Pres. PAUL PERRIOTT; Gen. Sec. EMILY TURNER.

Belize Energy Workers' Union: c/o Belize Electricity Ltd, 2½ miles Northern Hwy, POB 1066, Belize City; tel. 227-0954; e-mail bewunion@gmail.com; Pres. MARVIN MORA; Gen. Sec. DORLA STAINE.

Belize National Teachers' Union: NGO Crescent, POB 382, Belize City; tel. 223-4811; fax 223-5233; e-mail admin@bntubelize.org; internet www.bntubelize.org; f. 1970 following merger between the British Honduras Union of Teachers' (BHUT) and the Catholic Education Association (CEA); adopted present name in 1976; Pres. JAIME PANTI; Exec. Sec. GEORGE FRAZER; 1,000 mems.

Belize Water Services Workers' Union: Belize City; tel. 223-4809; e-mail bwswu@yahoo.com; Pres. LORELEI WESTBY.

Belize Workers' Union: Tate St, Orange Walk Town; tel. 822-2327; e-mail bwu@btl.net; Pres. JULIO GONGORA; Sec. IAN LEIVA.

Christian Workers' Union: 107B Cemetery Rd, POB 533, Belize City; tel. 227-2150; fax 227-8470; e-mail cwu@btl.net; f. 1962; general; Pres. ANTONIO GONZÁLEZ; Gen. Sec. JAMES MCFOY; 1,000 mems.

Public Service Union of Belize: Hilltop Complex, POB 458, Belmopan; tel. 802-3885; fax 822-0283; e-mail belizepsu@btl.net; f. 1922; public workers; Pres. JACQUELINE WILLOUGHBY-SANCHEZ; Gen. Sec. MARIO CALIZ; 1,600 mems.

Transport

Department of Transport: NEMO Bldg, Belmopan; tel. 822-2135; fax 822-3317; e-mail departmentoftransport@yahoo.com; Commr GARRET MURILLO.

RAILWAYS

There are no railways in Belize.

ROADS

There are 2,872 km of roads, of which some 2,210 km (1,600 km of gravel roads, 300 km of improved earth roads and 310 km of unimproved earth roads) are unpaved. A double-lane bridge was built over the Sibun River in 2004, and over Silver Creek in 2006. The Middlesex Bridge over Stann Creek was reconstructed at a cost of BZ $2.2m. in 2010. There are four major highways that connect all the major cities and towns and lead to the Mexican and Guatemalan borders. In 2011 work began on the BZ $48m. Southern Highway connecting the south of the country to the Guatemala border. The project was financed by the Kuwaiti Fund for Economic Development and the Development Fund of the Organization of Petroleum Exporting Countries.

SHIPPING

There is a deep-water port at Belize City and a second port at Commerce Bight, near Dangriga (formerly Stann Creek), to the south of Belize City. There is a port for the export of bananas at Big Creek and additional ports at Corozal and Punta Gorda. Nine major shipping lines operate vessels calling at Belize City, including the Carol Line (consisting of Harrison, Hapag-Lloyd, Nedlloyd and CGM). A project to develop a cruise ship port at Port Loyola at a cost of BZ $963.5m. commenced in 2007; however, a dispute between the operating companies and the Government of that time severely compromised future development.

Belize Ports Authority: 120 North Front St, POB 633, Belize City; tel. 223-0752; fax 223-0710; e-mail bzportauth@btl.net; internet www.portauthority.bz; f. 1980; Commr of Ports Maj. (retd) J. M. A. FLOWERS.

Marine & Services Ltd: Blake Bldg, Suite 203, Cnr Hudson and Eyre St, POB 611, Belize City; tel. 227-2113; fax 227-5404; e-mail info@marineservices.bz; internet www.marineservices.bz; f. 1975; shipping and cargo services, cruise line agent; Man. JOSE GALLEGO.

Port of Belize Ltd: Caesar Ridge Rd, POB 2674, Belize City; tel. and fax 223-2439; fax 223-3571; e-mail info@portofbelize.com; internet www.portofbelize.com; operates the main port facility; CEO ARTURO VASQUEZ; Deputy CEO FRANZINE WAIGHT.

CIVIL AVIATION

Philip S. W. Goldson International Airport, 16 km (10 miles) from Belize City, can accommodate medium-sized jet-engined aircraft. There are 37 airstrips for light aircraft on internal flights near the major towns and offshore islands.

Belize Airports Authority (BAA): POB 1564, Belize City; tel. 225-2045; fax 225-2439; e-mail bzeaa@btl.net; CEO PABLO ESPAT; Gen. Man. KENWORTH TILLET.

Department of Civil Aviation: POB 367, Belize City; tel. 225-2052; fax 225-2533; e-mail dcabelize@btl.net; internet www.civilaviation.gov.bz; f. 1931; Dir JOSE A. CONTRERAS.

Maya Island Air: Municipal Airstrip, Bldg 1, 2nd Floor, POB 458, Belize City; tel. 223-1140; fax 223-0576; e-mail regional@mayaislandair.com; internet www.mayaregional.com; f. 1961 as merger between Maya Airways Ltd and Island Air; operated by Belize Air Group; internal services, centred on Belize City, and charter flights to neighbouring countries; CEO LOUIS ZABANEH; Gen. Man. CARLOS VARGAS.

Tropic Air: San Pedro, POB 20, Ambergris Caye; tel. 226-2012; fax 226-2338; e-mail reservations@tropicair.com; internet www.tropicair.com; f. 1979; operates internal services and services to Guatemala; Chair. CELI MCCORKLE.

Tourism

The main tourist attractions are the beaches and the barrier reef, diving, fishing and the Mayan archaeological sites. There are nine major wildlife reserves (including the world's only reserves for the jaguar and for the red-footed booby), and government policy is to develop 'eco-tourism', based on the attractions of an unspoiled environment and Belize's natural history. The country's wildlife also includes howler monkeys and 500 species of birds, and its barrier reef is the second largest in the world. There were 5,789 hotel rooms in Belize in 2006. In 2010 there were 914,797 tourist arrivals, of which some 688,165 were cruise ship passengers and 226,632 were stop-over visitors. Tourism receipts totalled US $264.4m. in 2010.

Belize Tourism Board: 64 Regent St, POB 325, Belize City; tel. 227-2420; fax 227-2423; e-mail info@travelbelize.org; internet www.belizetourism.org; f. 1964; fmrly Belize Tourist Bureau; 8 mems; CEO LINDSAY GARBUTT; Dir (Tourism) SELENI MATUS.

Belize Tourism Industry Association (BTIA): 10 North Park St, POB 62, Belize City; tel. 227-1144; fax 227-8710; e-mail info@btia.org; internet www.btia.org; f. 1985; promotes sustainable tourism; Pres. JIM SCOTT; Exec. Dir WENDY LEMUS; 500 mems.

Defence

The Belize Defence Force was formed in 1978 and was based on a combination of the existing Police Special Force and the Belize Volunteer Guard. Military service is voluntary, but provision has been made for the establishment of National Service, if necessary, to supplement normal recruitment. As assessed at November 2011, the regular armed forces totalled approximately 1,050 and there were some 700 militia reserves. In 1994 all British forces were withdrawn from Belize, and in 2008 some 30 troops remained to organize training for jungle warfare. On 28 November 2005 the Belize National Coast Guard Service was inaugurated to combat drugs-trafficking, illegal immigration and illegal fishing in Belize's territorial waters. The Coast Guard comprised 58 volunteer officers from the Belize Defence Force, the Belize Police Department, the Customs and Excise Department, the National Fire Service, the Department of Immigration and Nationality Services, the Port Authority and the Fisheries Department.

Defence Budget: an estimated BZ $32m. in 2012.

Belize Defence Force Commandant: Brig.-Gen. DARIO TAPIA.

Education

Education is compulsory for all children for a period of 10 years between the ages of five and 14 years. Primary education, beginning at five years of age and lasting for eight years, is provided free of charge, principally through subsidized denominational schools under government control. In 2008/09 enrolment at primary institutions included 97% of children in the relevant age-group. Secondary education, beginning at the age of 13, lasts for four years. Enrolment at secondary schools in 2008/09 included 65% of students in the relevant age-group (males 62%; females 68%).

In 2008/09 there were 3,581 students enrolled in 12 other educational institutions, which included technical, vocational and teacher-training colleges. There is an extra-mural branch of the University of the West Indies in Belize. In 2000 the University of Belize was formed through the amalgamation of five higher education institutions, including the University College of Belize and Belize Technical College. Government expenditure on education in the financial year 2011/12 was projected at BZ $191.9m.

BENIN

Introductory Survey

LOCATION, CLIMATE, LANGUAGE, RELIGION, FLAG, CAPITAL

The Republic of Benin is a narrow stretch of territory in West Africa. The country has an Atlantic coastline of about 100 km (60 miles), flanked by Nigeria to the east and Togo to the west; its northern borders are with Burkina Faso and Niger. Benin's climate is tropical, and is divided into three zones: the north has a rainy season between July and September, with a hot, dry season in October–April; the central region has periods of abundant rain in May–June and in October; and there is year-round precipitation in the south, the heaviest rains being in May–October. Average annual rainfall in Cotonou is 1,300 mm. French is the official language, but each of the indigenous ethnic groups has its own language. Bariba and Fulani are the major languages in the north, while Fon and Yoruba are widely spoken in the south. It is estimated that 38% of the people are Christians, mainly Roman Catholics, 24% are Muslims, while 23% follow traditional beliefs and customs. The national flag (proportions 2 by 3) has a vertical green stripe at the hoist, with equal horizontal stripes of yellow over red in the fly. The administrative capital is Porto-Novo, but most government offices and other state bodies are presently in the economic capital, Cotonou.

CONTEMPORARY POLITICAL HISTORY

Historical Context

Benin, called Dahomey until 1975, was formerly part of French West Africa. It became a self-governing republic within the French Community in December 1958, and an independent state on 1 August 1960. The early years of independence were characterized by chronic political instability and by periodic regional unrest, fuelled by long-standing rivalries between north and south.

Elections in December 1960 were won by the Parti dahoméen de l'unité, whose leader, Hubert Maga (a northerner), became the country's first President. In October 1963 Maga was deposed in a coup led by Col (later Gen.) Christophe Soglo, Chief of Staff of the Army. Soglo served as interim Head of State until January 1964, when Sourou-Migan Apithy, a southerner and former Vice-President, was elected President. Another southerner, Justin Ahomadegbé, became Prime Minister. In November 1965 Gen. Soglo forced Apithy and Ahomadegbé to resign. A provisional Government was formed, but a further military intervention, in December, resulted in Soglo again assuming power. In December 1967 industrial unrest precipitated another coup, led by Maj. (later Lt-Col) Maurice Kouandété. Lt-Col Alphonse Alley, hitherto Chief of Staff, became interim Head of State, and Kouandété Prime Minister.

A new Constitution, providing for a return to civilian rule, was approved by referendum in March 1968; however, the presidential election held in May was declared void, and in June the military regime nominated Dr Emile-Derlin Zinsou as President. In December 1969 Zinsou was deposed by Kouandété, then Commander-in-Chief of the Army, and a three-member military Directoire assumed power. In March 1970 a presidential election was abandoned when counting revealed roughly equal support for the three main candidates—Ahomadegbé, Apithy and Maga—to whom the Directoire ceded power in May: it was intended that each member of this Presidential Council would act as Head of State, in rotation, for a two-year period. Maga was the first to hold this office and was succeeded in May 1972 by Ahomadegbé.

In October 1972 the civilian leadership was deposed by Maj. (later Brig.-Gen.) Mathieu Kérékou, Deputy Chief of Staff of the armed forces and a northerner. In September 1973 a Conseil national révolutionnaire (CNR) was established. Strategic sectors and financial institutions were acquired by the State, under Kérékou's regime, which pursued Marxist-based policies. In late 1975 the Parti de la révolution populaire du Bénin (PRPB) was established as the sole party, and Dahomey was renamed the People's Republic of Benin.

In August 1977 the CNR adopted a *Loi fondamentale* decreeing new structures in government. Elections to a new 'supreme authority', the Assemblée nationale révolutionnaire (ANR), took place in November 1979, when a single list of 336 'People's Commissioners' was approved by 97.5% of voters. At the same time a Comité exécutif national (CEN) was established to replace the CNR. The PRPB designated Kérékou as the sole candidate for President of the Republic, and in February 1980 the ANR unanimously elected him to this office. A gradual moderation in Benin's domestic policies followed. At legislative elections in June 1984 the single list of People's Commissioners was approved by 98% of voters, and in July the ANR re-elected Kérékou, again the sole candidate, as President.

In January 1987 Kérékou resigned from the army to become a civilian Head of State. At elections to the ANR in June 1989 89.6% of voters endorsed the single list of PRPB-approved candidates. In August the ANR re-elected Kérékou (once again the sole candidate) as President. At the end of the year Kérékou instituted major political changes, abandoning Marxism-Leninism as the official state ideology.

Domestic Political Affairs

In February 1990 delegates at a conference of the 'active forces of the nation' voted to adopt a 'national charter' that was to form the basis of a new constitution. An interim Haut conseil de la République (HCR) was appointed to assume the functions of the ANR. Among the members of the HCR were former Presidents Ahomadegbé, Maga and Zinsou. Presidential and legislative elections, to be held in the context of a multi-party political system, were scheduled for early 1991. A former official of the World Bank (who had briefly been Minister of Finance and Economic Affairs in the mid-1960s), Nicéphore Soglo, was designated interim Prime Minister. The conference also voted to change the country's name to the Republic of Benin. The HCR was inaugurated in March 1990 and Soglo appointed a transitional Government; of the previous administration, only Kérékou remained in office. Legislation permitting the registration of political parties was promulgated in August.

A national referendum on the draft Constitution was conducted on 2 December 1990. Voters were asked to choose between two proposed documents, one of which incorporated a clause stipulating upper and lower age-limits for presidential candidates, and would therefore prevent the candidatures of Ahomadegbé, Maga and Zinsou. It was reported that 95.8% of those who voted approved one or other of the versions, with 79.7% of voters favouring the age-restriction clause.

Following legislative elections on 17 February 1991, the largest grouping in the new 64-member Assemblée nationale was an alliance of three pro-Soglo parties, which secured 12 seats. Kérékou and Soglo were among 13 candidates at the first round of the presidential election on 10 March. Soglo, who won 36.2% of the total votes cast, received his greatest support in the south of the country, while Kérékou, who received 27.3% of the overall vote, was reported to have secured the support of more than 80% of voters in the north. Soglo and Kérékou proceeded to a second round of voting on 24 March, when Soglo was elected President, with 67.7% of the total votes cast. Soglo was inaugurated as President on 4 April.

In July 1992 Soglo, who had previously asserted his political neutrality, had made public his membership of a political party, La renaissance du Bénin (RB), formed by his wife, Rosine Soglo, earlier that year; he was appointed leader of the RB in July 1994.

In November 1994 the Assemblée nationale voted to establish an independent electoral supervisory body, the Commission électorale nationale autonome (CENA), despite resistance from Soglo, who also opposed a planned increase in the number of deputies from 64 to 83. Some 31 political organizations participated in the legislative elections held on 28 March 1995. In mid-April the Constitutional Court annulled the results of voting for 13 seats on the grounds of irregularities. Following by-elections in May, the RB held 20 seats in the Assemblée nationale, and other supporters of Soglo 13. Opposition parties held 49 seats, the most prominent being the Parti du renouveau démocratique (PRD), with 19 seats, and the Front d'action pour le renouveau et le développement—Alafia (FARD—Alafia), with

10; the latter had attracted considerable support from Kérékou supporters in the north, although the former President had not actively campaigned in the election.

The first round of the presidential election, on 3 March 1996, was contested by seven candidates at which Soglo secured 35.7% of the valid votes and Kérékou 33.9%, followed by the leader of the PRD, Adrien Houngbédji (19.7%). The rate of participation by voters was 86.9%. Most of the defeated candidates quickly expressed their support for Kérékou. The second round of voting took place on 18 March. Several days later the Constitutional Court announced Kérékou's election, with 52.5% of the valid votes. Some 78.1% of those eligible had voted.

Elections to the 83 seats in the Assemblée nationale, were held on 30 March 1999, and international monitors reported that the elections had been conducted peacefully and democratically. The combined opposition parties won a slender majority in the legislature, with 42 seats. The RB won the largest number of seats, with 27, principally in the south and centre, while FARD—Alafia, the Parti social-démocrate (PSD) and other parties loyal to the President performed strongly in the north and west. The rate of participation by voters was in excess of 70%. Houngbédji was elected Speaker of the new assembly.

The 2001 presidential election

In the period preceding the March 2001 presidential election, Soglo was widely regarded as the sole credible challenger to Kérékou. In the first round of the election, held on 4 March, Kérékou gained the largest share of the vote, but failed to secure an absolute majority; a second round, to be contested by Kérékou and Soglo, the second-placed candidate, was scheduled for 18 March. As campaigning proceeded, the Constitutional Court conducted a review of the election results declared by the CENA. Revised provisional results of the first round gave Kérékou 45.4% of the votes cast, Soglo 27.1%, Houngbédji 12.6% and Bruno Amoussou 8.6%. Following the declaration of the revised results, which indicated a participation rate of around 80%, there were calls for a boycott of the second round of voting, owing to alleged irregularities in the conduct of the first round. Soglo appealed to the Constitutional Court to annul the disputed results, and to rerun the election. On 16 March Soglo, having had his appeal rejected, withdrew his candidature. The Government postponed the second round of the election, which was thus to be contested by Kérékou and Houngbédji, until 22 March. However, on 19 March Houngbédji also declared his dissatisfaction with the conduct of the election and withdrew from the second round. Consequently, Amoussou, who had previously declared his support for Kérékou, was now to challenge him for the presidency. Nine opposition members of the CENA resigned in protest at the conduct of the election. Voter participation in the second round of voting, duly held on 22 March, was significantly lower than in the first round, at about 55%. Two days after polling the CENA announced that Kérékou had won 84.1% of the valid votes cast. Kérékou was declared President for a further term, despite allegations that the depleted CENA was not qualified to organize the election.

Following the legislative elections held on 30 March 2003, a secure pro-presidential majority in the Assemblée nationale was formed for the first time since the introduction of multi-party elections in Benin. Pro-Kérékou parties and alliances won 52 of the 83 elective seats, and in mid-April the PRD, which had secured 11 seats, announced that it would, henceforth, also support the Government. The Union pour le Bénin du futur (UBF) emerged as the largest single party, with 31 seats. The representation of the RB, the largest party in the outgoing assembly, was reduced from 27 to 15 seats. Nine other parties or alliances won representation in the elections. It was reported that as many as one-half of the deputies elected to the new legislature had not served in the outgoing assembly. Among the new deputies elected was the President's son, Modeste Kérékou. The formation of a new Government was announced in mid-June 2003: Amoussou was appointed to the most senior ministerial post in the new Government, as Minister of State, responsible for Planning and Development.

In February 2005 President Kérékou effected a major cabinet reorganization. Amoussou was removed from the Government and was replaced as Minister of State, responsible for Planning and Development by Zul Kifl Salami. During the course of 2005 the forthcoming presidential election (due to be held in March 2006) was the principal focus of political debate in Benin. In late 2005 senior members of the Government stated that a lack of budgetary funds could prevent the election from being held as scheduled, and suggested that presidential polling be held concurrently with the legislative elections scheduled for 2007. In January 2006 civil servants staged two days of strike action in protest against any such postponement. Moreover, the appointment, in late January, of Col (retd) Martin Dohou Azonhiho as Minister of State, responsible for National Defence, resulted in further controversy; Azonhiho, who had held several senior positions in Kérékou's military and Marxist governments from the mid-1970s had, prior to his appointment, been a vocal proponent of the postponement of the elections, and had served a prison sentence for embezzlement, prior to his release on parole in 2001. However, in January 2006 Kérékou, who was constitutionally prohibited from standing, announced that funding for the elections would be forthcoming, and at the end of the month the Constitutional Court approved 26 of the 29 presidential candidacies presented to it.

The first Boni Yayi administration

The first round of presidential polling was held, as scheduled, on 5 March 2006. The CENA announced the results of voting on 12 March, several days later than expected. Boni Yayi, who had recently resigned as President of the Banque Ouest-Africaine de Développement (BOAD) to contest the election, received the largest share of the votes cast (35.6%), followed by Houngbédji, with 24.1%. Amoussou was placed third, with 16.2%, while Léhadi Vinagnon Vitoun Soglo, one of two sons of Nicéphore and Rosine Soglo to contest the election, was fourth, with 8.4%. Around 75% of the electorate voted. Yayi and Houngbédji progressed to a run-off poll, scheduled for 19 March. International monitors described the election as broadly free and fair. Following the confirmation of the results by the Constitutional Court, the CENA requested that the second round of voting be postponed until 22 March; however Kérékou overruled the decision of the Constitutional Court to delay and voting duly proceeded on 19 March. According to the results of the second round, announced several days later by the Constitutional Court, Yayi was overwhelmingly elected as President, obtaining 74.5% of the votes cast; he was inaugurated as Head of State on 6 April. On 9 April Yayi appointed a new, 22-member Council of Ministers, of which 13 members were not affiliated to any political party. The most senior position, to which Pascal Irénée Koupaki was appointed, was that of Minister of Development, Economy and Finance.

Legislative elections were held on 31 March 2007, following a delay of one week, owing to organizational difficulties. According to provisional results released by the Constitutional Court in mid-April, the Force cauris pour un Bénin émergent (FCBE), a pro-Yayi coalition of some 20 parties, took 35 of the 83 seats, while the Alliance pour une dynamique démocratique, of which Soglo's RB was a member, secured 20 seats. The PRD won 10 seats and a further nine parties or alliances secured parliamentary representation. The rate of voter participation was recorded at 58.7%. In June President Yayi named his new Government; of the 17 new appointments the most notable included Soulé Mana Lawani, who was awarded the finance portfolio, and Moussa Okanla, who became Minister of Foreign Affairs, African Integration, Francophone Affairs and Beninois Abroad. Koupaki was again appointed to the most senior position, namely that of Minister of State, in charge of Planning, Development and the Evaluation of Public Action.

A new, enlarged, 30-member Council of Ministers named in October 2008 included several opposition party members. The most notable changes were the appointments of Armand Zinzindohoué and Soulé Mana Lawani to the interior and public security and the economy and finance portfolios, respectively.

In mid-2009, following the emergence of a financial scandal concerning the construction of infrastructure for the 10th summit of the Community of Sahel-Saharan States (CEN-SAD, see p. 449) held in Cotonou in 2008, Yayi, who had pledged to combat corruption during his election campaign, dismissed Lawani and the Minister of Town Planning, Housing, Land Reform and the Fight against Coastal Erosion, François Noudégbéssi, owing to mismanagement of government funds and alleged irregularities in the tendering process. Idrissou Daouda, hitherto the Managing Director of the Banque centrale des états de l'Afrique de l'ouest was named as Lawani's replacement.

In mid-June 2010 Yayi effected a cabinet reorganization appointing eight new ministers, including Modeste Kérékou, the son of former head of state Mathieu Kérékou, as Minister of Youth, Sports and Leisure. Yayi also re-appointed Noudégbéssi, who had been cleared by a commission of enquiry of any wrongdoing, to his former position, while Daouda retained his post as Minister of the Economy and Finance. The following month a further financial scandal was revealed and some 100,000 people protested in Cotonou appealing for the Government to recover the failed investments of Investment Consultancy and Computing Services, a company that was perceived as having ties with the Government, and which had promised interest returns of up to 50%, but had caused losses of more than 100,000m. francs CFA in deposits, defrauding between 50,000 and 70,000 small investors. Zinzindohoué was subsequently dismissed from the Government and responsibility for his vacated portfolio was assumed on an acting basis by Minister of Industry Candide Azanaï. In August it was reported that over one-half of the members of the Assemblée nationale had requested that impeachment proceedings be brought against President Yayi; however, this demand was refused by the President of the Assemblée, Mathurin Nago.

In preparation for presidential elections scheduled for March 2011, France and the European Union contributed financial support of €400,000 and 2,000m. francs CFA, respectively, for the implementation of a digital electoral list. By the end of 2010 a number of presidential candidates had been announced: the Conference of Presidents of the parties of the opposition Union fait la nation (UN) declared Houngbédji as its candidate, and in January 2011 Christian Adovelande, President of the Economic Community of West African States (ECOWAS, see p. 264) Banque d'Investissement et de Développement, was nominated to take over leadership at the BOAD allowing its former head, Abdoulaye Bio Tchané, to declare his candidacy for the presidency. Furthermore, a coalition of opposition parties, trade unions and non-governmental organizations, including the UN and Bio Tchané's movement, united to form the Front de défense de la démocratie with the stated aim of ensuring Yayi's defeat.

Recent developments: Yayi re-elected

The presidential election was held on 13 March 2011 (having been postponed by seven days as a result of organizational problems) and was contested by 14 candidates. Yayi secured 53.1% of the votes cast and was re-elected to the presidency. Houngbedji was placed second with 35.6% of the votes, while Bio Tchané took 6.1%. No other candidate won more than 1.5% of the votes cast. The rate of voter participation was officially recorded at 84.8% of the registered electorate. Following the release of the results, Houngbédji publicly denounced the outcome and there were protests outside the office of the CENA, causing ECOWAS to voice deep concern over rising tensions and call upon all candidates to refrain from undermining the electoral process. Legislative elections took place on 30 April; results validated by the Constitutional Court on 12 May gave the FCBE 41 of the 83 parliamentary seats. The UN became the second largest party in the legislature having taken 31 seats. On 28 May President Yayi announced the composition of the new Government, which had been reduced in membership from 35 to 26 ministers. It included eight women, among them Marie-Elise Gbédo, as Keeper of the Seals, Minister of Justice, Legislation and Human Rights, and Government Spokesperson, and Madina Séphou as Minister of Industry, Commerce and Small and Medium-sized Enterprises; a member of the opposition, Blaise Ahanhanzo-Glèlè, was awarded the environment, housing and town planning portfolio. Honouring his election campaign promise to establish the role of Prime Minister, Yayi appointed Koupaki to lead the Council of Ministers.

In October 2011 the Assemblée nationale approved legislation removing the right to strike from customs officers, military and paramilitary personnel (including public officials working in the forestry and water industries). The Confédération Générale des Travailleurs du Bénin and the opposition denounced the measure as the beginning of a raft of intimidatory tactics against trade unions, and was regarded as a response to a 48-hour strike by customs officers at the Port of Cotonou in mid-September. The new law was also seen as paving the way for a series of structural adjustments to come in 2012 in a drive to develop business and private initiative by modernizing administrative structures and applying results-based management in compliance with IMF demands.

In mid-April 2012 President Yayi carried out a minor reorganization of the Government, assuming personal responsibility for the defence portfolio. The most notable other change was the dismissal of Adidjatou Mathys as Minister of the Economy and Finance. She was replaced by Jonas Gbian, hitherto the Minister of Energy, Mining and Petroleum Research, Water and the Development of Renewable Energy Sources.

Foreign Affairs

Benin maintains generally good relations with neighbouring countries and joined the CEN-SAD in March 2002. None the less, in mid-2000 a long-term dispute between Benin and Niger, over the ownership of various small islands in the Niger river, erupted after Nigerien soldiers reportedly sabotaged the construction of a Beninois administrative building on Lété Island. Meetings between representatives of the two Governments and arbitration by the Organization of African Unity (now the African Union, see p. 189) failed to resolve the dispute, and in April 2002 the two countries officially ratified an agreement (signed in 2001) to refer the dispute to the International Court of Justice (ICJ) in The Hague, Netherlands, for arbitration. Benin and Niger filed confidential written arguments with the Court, and in November 2003 a five-member Chamber formed to consider the case held its first public sitting. Both countries subsequently submitted counter-arguments, and a third written pleading was submitted by both parties in December of that year. (In June the UN had awarded Benin and Niger US $350,000 each towards the cost of resolving their dispute.) In July 2005 the ICJ issued a final ruling to the effect that 16 of the 25 disputed islands, including Lété, belonged to Niger; the Governments of both countries announced their acceptance of the ruling.

Benin and Nigeria launched joint police patrols along their common border in August 2001. However, renewed concerns about cross-border crime resulted in the unilateral closure, by the Nigerian authorities, of the frontier in August 2003. The border was reopened later that month, and the Beninois and Nigerian authorities announced a series of measures intended to enhance co-operation to combat cross-border crime, including restrictions of certain types of export trade from Benin to Nigeria. Following his inauguration in April 2006 President Yayi's first official foreign visit was to Nigeria, and in August he signed a treaty with President Gen. Olusegun Obasanjo regarding the maritime boundary between the two countries. In February 2007 the two Presidents, along with the President of Togo, Faure Gnassingbé, announced the formation of a Co-Prosperity Alliance Zone aimed at the further integration of their economies and the promotion of peace, stability and development in West Africa. In April 2009 the Nigerian Senate requested that troops be deployed to stop cross-border incursions from Benin; in one such incident, involving 2,000 Beninois villagers, the entire village of Tungar-Kungi in northern Kebbi State was destroyed leaving 1,500 people (mostly women and children) displaced. In 2011 Nigeria and Benin also launched joint sea patrols following a sharp increase in piracy attacks in their maritime area, which, in August, resulted in international insurers classifying the zone as one of a 'war risk'.

An ongoing border dispute between Benin and Burkina Faso came close to armed conflict in 2005, and there was further tension in 2007 following the death of an inhabitant of the contested area while in custody in Benin. In March 2008 the two countries appeared to have settled the long-running dispute at a meeting of high-level officials, where it was pledged that neither side would make any 'visible sovereignty act' in the contested territory (such as building paramilitary or police stations) and that joint security patrols would be carried out at the common border. However, in September 2009 two villages remained in dispute and both countries agreed to refer the issue to the ICJ. Pending a decision by that body, the 68-sq km area was to remain neutral and to be administered and financed jointly.

From late April 2005 thousands of Togolese sought refuge in Benin, having fled the violence that followed a presidential election in that country (see Contemporary Political History of Togo). In December the office of the UN High Commissioner for Refugees (UNHCR) estimated that some 26,632 Togolese refugees had fled to Benin. In April 2007 Benin, Togo and UNHCR signed an agreement on the voluntary repatriation of the remaining refugees, and by the end of 2010 it was reported that only 5,912 remained in Benin.

In July 2011 President Yayi, along with the Heads of State of Côte d'Ivoire, Guinea and Niger met with US President Barack Obama in Washington, DC, who promised them 'stalwart' support on economic and security matters in the future. France also pledged financial support to Benin in October to be used in training local forces and supplying two surveillance aircraft to combat piracy that threatened the functioning of the Port of Cotonou. At Yayi's request a team of UN officials were sent to the area to assess the piracy threat in November.

CONSTITUTION AND GOVERNMENT

The Constitution of the Republic of Benin, which was approved in a national referendum on 2 December 1990, provides for a civilian, multi-party political system. Executive power is vested in the President of the Republic, who is elected by direct universal adult suffrage with a five-year mandate, renewable only once. The legislature is the 83-member Assemblée nationale, which is similarly elected, for a period of four years, by universal suffrage. The President of the Republic appoints the Council of Ministers, subject to formal parliamentary approval.

For the purposes of local administration, Benin is divided into 12 departments, each administered by a civilian prefect. These departments are further divided into a total of 77 communes.

REGIONAL AND INTERNATIONAL CO-OPERATION

Benin is a member of the African Union (see p. 189), of the Economic Community of West African States (ECOWAS, see p. 264), of the West African organs of the Franc Zone (see p. 333), of the Community of Sahel-Saharan States (CEN-SAD, see p. 449), of the African Petroleum Producers' Association (APPA, see p. 444), of the Conseil de l'Entente (see p. 449) and of the Niger Basin Authority (see p. 451).

Benin became a member of the UN in 1960, and was admitted to the World Trade Organization (WTO, see p. 433) in 1996. Benin participates in the Group of 77 (G77, see p. 450) developing countries.

ECONOMIC AFFAIRS

In 2010, according to estimates by the World Bank, Benin's gross national income (GNI), measured at average 2008–10 prices, was US $6,945m., equivalent to $780 per head (or $1,580 on an international purchasing-power parity basis). During 2001–10, it was estimated, the population increased at an average annual rate of 3.1%, while gross domestic product (GDP) per head increased, in real terms, by an average of 0.8% per year. Overall GDP increased, in real terms, at an average annual rate of 3.9% in 2001–10; growth in 2010 was 3.0%.

According to the African Development Bank (AfDB), agriculture (including forestry and fishing) contributed 35.1% of GDP in 2010. In mid-2012 an estimated 42.4% of the labour force were employed in the sector, according to FAO. The principal cash crops are cotton (exports of which accounted for an estimated 13.2% of total exports in 2008, according to the AfDB), oil palm and cashew nuts. Benin is normally self-sufficient in basic foods; the main subsistence crops are cassava, yams and maize. In September 2011 plans were adopted that aimed to increase rice production from 152,000 metric tons in 2010 to 550,000 from 2015 onwards; this included the purchase of two processing plants at Malanville and Glazoué. According to the AfDB, agricultural GDP increased at an average annual rate of 4.2% in 2000–07; growth in 2010 was 8.9%.

According to the AfDB, industry (including mining, manufacturing, construction and power) contributed 14.4% of GDP in 2010 and engaged 13.0% of the employed labour force at the time of the 2002 census. According to the AfDB, industrial GDP increased at an average annual rate of 5.1% in 2000–07; it grew by 7.8% in 2007.

Mining contributed only 0.3% of GDP in 2010, according to the AfDB, and engaged 1.4% of the employed labour force in 2002. Petroleum reserves, were estimated at some 22m. barrels in 2000. Marble and limestone are also exploited commercially. There are also deposits of gold, phosphates, natural gas, iron ore, silica sand, peat and chromium. The GDP of the mining sector declined at an average annual rate of 28.6% in 1994–2001; growth in mining GDP was 7.0% in 2010, according to the AfDB.

The manufacturing sector, which contributed 8.4% of GDP in 2010, engaged 9.0% of the employed labour force in 2002. The sector is based largely on the processing of primary products (principally cotton-ginning and oil-palm processing). Construction materials and some simple consumer goods are also produced for the domestic market. According to the AfDB, manufacturing GDP increased at an average annual rate of 4.3% in 2000–07; it increased by 14.9% in 2010.

Construction contributed 4.5% of GDP in 2010 and engaged 2.5% of the employed labour force at the time of the 2002 census. According to the AfDB, the sector's GDP grew by 7.0% in 2010.

Benin is at present highly dependent on imports of electricity from Ghana. In March 2009 the Chinese corporation Sinohydro signed a deal with the Communauté Electrique du Bénin (CEB) to develop the 147-MW Adjarala hydroelectric installation, a second dam, on the Mono River. The plant, operated jointly with Togo, was due to be functional by 2013, making it less likely that the delayed and over budget West African Gas Pipeline project that was to transport natural gas from Nigeria to the two countries would be completed. According to World Bank estimates, in 2008 99.3% of Benin's electricity production was derived from petroleum. In 2009 the World Bank approved a grant of US $1.82m. to upgrade the electrical network and a Nigerian firm signed an agreement in September, granting it exclusive right of way concession with the CEB, which operates the high voltage power lines in both Benin and Togo. The total cost of the rehabilitation project was estimated at €73.2m. Imports of mineral fuels and lubricants accounted for 21.6% of the value of total imports in 2006.

According to the AfDB the services sector contributed 50.5% of GDP in 2010, and engaged 39.8% of the employed labour force in 2002. The port of Cotonou, taken over in 2009 by a French group on a 25-year concession, is of considerable importance as an entrepôt for regional trade. According to the AfDB, the GDP of the services sector increased at an average annual rate of 4.0% in 2000–07; the output of the sector increased by 4.6% in 2007.

In 2010, according to IMF estimates, Benin recorded a visible trade deficit of 295,700m. francs CFA, while there was a deficit of 224,700m. francs CFA on the current account of the balance of payments. In 2006 the principal source of imports (17.2%) was France; other major sources were the People's Republic of China, Côte d'Ivoire, Ghana, the United Kingdom and Togo. The principal market for exports in that year was China (24.0%); other important purchasers were Nigeria, India, Niger and Côte d'Ivoire. The principal exports in 2006 were cotton (amounting to 42.3% of total exports), tobacco, edible fruit and animal and vegetable oils. The main imports in that year were mineral fuels and lubricants (21.6% of the total) cereals, and cement.

In 2010, according to preliminary figures from the IMF, Benin recorded an estimated overall budgetary deficit of 99,200m. francs CFA. Benin's general government gross debt was 1,010,290m. francs CFA in 2010, equivalent to 31.1% of GDP. The country's total external debt at the end of 2009 was US $1,073m., of which $990.0m. was public and publicly guaranteed debt. In 2009 the cost of servicing long-term public and publicly guaranteed debt and repayments to the IMF was equivalent to 7.3% of the value of exports of goods, services and income (excluding workers' remittances). The annual rate of inflation increased by an average of 2.8% per year in 2001–10, according to ILO estimates. Consumer prices increased by 0.4% in 2010. According to the 2002 census, 0.7% of the total labour force was unemployed.

The global financial crisis of the late 2000s adversely affected the Beninois economy, reducing GDP growth from 5.0% in 2008 to 2.7% in 2009. Furthermore, devastating floods in 2010, which displaced 200,000 people and destroyed 128,000 ha of crops, resulted in a further reduction in growth, to 2.6%. Nevertheless, the IMF expected economic recovery to accelerate in 2011, with GDP growth estimated at 4.0%. A number of internationally funded infrastructure projects were undertaken, including the construction of a dry port in the commune of Tori-Bossito, which would reduce storage time spent by freight in Cotonou docks. Also, the long awaited international airport at Glo Djigbé finally began construction with South African funding. The airport, due to be completed by 2013, was intended to provide facilities to process 900 passengers per hour (in both arrivals and departures) and 12,000 tons of freight per year. A total of 140m. francs CFA worth of development aid from China was granted to facilitate trade and relaunch agriculture, and the World Bank approved a loan of US $7.5m. to encourage private sector-led trade through the provision of insurance, re-insurance and related services. The Port of Cotonou remained the main contributor to the country's economy, although it was affected by industrial action (see Recent Developments) and piracy attacks in 2011. Nevertheless, Malian businesses were encouraged to use Cotonou in place of the Port of Abidjan during the political crisis in Côte d'Ivoire in 2011, and a structural reform was adopted to make the port at Cotonou a 'one-stop shop', thus increasing customs revenue collection. In an address to the nation in November President Yayi announced the creation of a Council of Food and Nutrition; the measure was viewed as an essential factor in aiding the economic development of Benin as statistics demonstrated that 85% of illnesses were linked directly to food, and that strengthening human capital would lead to increased economic productivity. In a further positive development, in December the Government agreed to put in place a three-year plan to relaunch growth in the sectors of agriculture, education, local development and infrastructure.

PUBLIC HOLIDAYS

2013: 1 January (New Year's Day), 10 January (Vodoun national holiday), 16 January (Martyrs' Day, anniversary of mercenary attack on Cotonou), 29 March (Good Friday), 1 April (Easter Monday and Youth Day), 1 May (Workers' Day), 9 May (Ascension Day), 20 May (Whit Monday), 1 August (Independence Day), 7 August* (Id al-Fitr, end of Ramadan), 15 August (Assumption), 14 October* (Id al-Adha, Feast of the Sacrifice), 26 October (Armed Forces Day), 1 November (All Saints' Day), 30 November (National Day), 25 December (Christmas Day), 31 December (Harvest Day).

* These holidays are dependent on the Islamic lunar calendar and may vary by one or two days from the dates given.

Statistical Survey

Source (unless otherwise stated): Institut National de la Statistique et de l'Analyse Economique, BP 323, Cotonou; tel. 21-30-82-43; fax 21-30-82-46; e-mail insae@insae-bj.org; internet www.insae-bj.org.

Area and Population

AREA, POPULATION AND DENSITY

Area (sq km)	112,622*
Population (census results)	
15–29 February 1992	4,915,555
11 February 2002	
Males	3,284,119
Females	3,485,795
Total	6,769,914
Population (UN estimates at mid-year)†	
2010	8,849,892
2011	9,099,924
2012	9,351,837
Density (per sq km) at mid-2012	83.0

* 43,484 sq miles.

† Source: UN, *World Population Prospects: The 2010 Revision*.

POPULATION BY AGE AND SEX
(UN estimates at mid-2012)

	Males	Females	Total
0–14	2,039,460	2,013,366	4,052,826
15–64	2,464,787	2,550,250	5,015,037
65 and over	113,299	170,675	283,974
Total	4,617,546	4,734,291	9,351,837

Source: UN, *World Population Prospects: The 2010 Revision*.

ETHNIC GROUPS

2002 (percentages): Fon 39.2 (incl. Fon 17.6; Goun 6.3; Aïzo 4.3; Mahi 3.5; Ouémè 2.5; Torri 2.4; Kotafon 1.4; Tofin 1.3); Adja 15.2 (incl. Adja 8.7; Sahouè 2.6; Xwla 1.4; Mina 1.2); Yoruba 12.3 (incl. Nagot 6.8; Yoruba 1.8; Idaasha 1.5; Holli-Djè 1.4); Bariba 9.2 (incl. Bariba 8.3); Peulh 6.9 (incl. Peulh Fulfuldé 5.5); Otamari 6.1 (incl. Berba 1.4; Ditamari 1.3; Waama 1.0); Yoa Lokpa 4.5 (incl. Yoa 1.8; Lokpa 1.2); Dendi 2.5 (incl. Dendi 2.4); Others 2.7.

ADMINISTRATIVE DIVISIONS
(2012, official projections)

Département	Area (sq km)	Population	Population density (per sq km)
Alibori	25,683	720,812	28.1
Atacora	20,459	759,992	37.1
Atlantique	3,233	1,108,944	343.0
Borgou	25,310	1,001,724	39.6
Collines	13,561	741,326	54.7
Couffo	2,404	725,644	301.8
Donga	10,691	484,230	45.3
Littoral	79	920,013	11,645.7
Mono	1,396	498,028	356.8
Ouémé	2,835	1,010,855	356.6
Plateau	1,865	563,151	302.0
Zou	5,106	829,898	162.5
Total	112,622	9,364,617	83.2

PRINCIPAL TOWNS
(Communes, 2007)

Cotonou	781,902	Bohicon	132,953
Porto-Novo (capital)	262,808	Tchaourou	125,614
Djougou	213,833	Savalou	123,151
Banikoara	178,726	Malanville	119,475
Parakou	176,106	Ketou	118,153
Aplahoue	137,533	Kalale	117,591
Seme-Kpodji	135,473		

Mid-2009 (incl. suburbs, UN estimates): Cotonou 815,041; Porto Novo 276,993 (Source: UN, *World Urbanization Prospects: The 2009 Revision*).

BIRTHS AND DEATHS
(annual averages, UN estimates)

	1995–2000	2000–05	2005–10
Birth rate (per 1,000)	44.0	42.2	40.7
Death rate (per 1,000)	14.6	13.4	12.4

Source: UN, *World Population Prospects: The 2010 Revision*.

2002: Birth rate 41.2 per 1,000; Death rate 12.3 per 1,000.

Life expectancy (years at birth, WHO estimates): 57 (males 54; females 60) in 2009 (Source: WHO, *World Health Statistics*).

ECONOMICALLY ACTIVE POPULATION
(persons aged 10 years and over, 1992 census)

	Males	Females	Total
Agriculture, hunting, forestry and fishing	780,469	367,277	1,147,746
Mining and quarrying	609	52	661
Manufacturing	93,157	67,249	160,406
Electricity, gas and water	1,152	24	1,176
Construction	50,959	696	51,655
Trade, restaurants and hotels	36,672	395,829	432,501
Transport, storage and communications	52,228	609	52,837
Finance, insurance, real estate and business services	2,705	401	3,106
Community, social and personal services	126,122	38,422	164,544
Sub-total	1,144,073	870,559	2,014,632
Activities not adequately defined	25,579	12,917	38,496
Total employed	1,169,652	883,476	2,053,128
Unemployed	26,475	5,843	32,318
Total labour force	1,196,127	889,319	2,085,446

Source: ILO, *Yearbook of Labour Statistics*.

2002 (census results): Total employed 2,811,753 (males 1,421,474, females 1,390,279); Unemployed 19,123 (males 12,934, females 6,189); Total labour force 2,830,876 (males 1,434,408, females 1,396,468).

Mid-2012 (estimates in '000): Agriculture, etc. 1,630; Total labour force 3,846 (Source: FAO).

Health and Welfare

KEY INDICATORS

Total fertility rate (children per woman, 2009)	5.4
Under-5 mortality rate (per 1,000 live births, 2009)	118
HIV/AIDS (% of persons aged 15–49, 2009)	1.2
Physicians (per 1,000 head, 2004)	0.04
Hospital beds (per 1,000 head, 2005)	0.5
Health expenditure (2008): US $ per head (PPP)	61
Health expenditure (2008): % of GDP	4.1
Health expenditure (2008): public (% of total)	51.7
Access to water (% of persons, 2008)	75
Access to sanitation (% of persons, 2008)	12
Total carbon dioxide emissions ('000 metric tons, 2007)	3,872.8
Carbon dioxide emissions per head (metric tons, 2007)	0.5
Human Development Index (2011): ranking	167
Human Development Index (2011): value	0.427

For sources and definitions, see explanatory note on p. vi.

Agriculture

PRINCIPAL CROPS
('000 metric tons)

	2008	2009	2010
Rice, paddy	109.4	150.6	162.2*
Maize	978.1	1,205.2	1,235.9*
Millet	36.3	27.4	28.6*
Sorghum	142.0	124.0	127.5*
Sweet potatoes	72.9	63.7	62.0*
Cassava (Manioc)	3,611.2	3,996.4	4,147.4*
Yams	2,527.3	2,370.9	2,389.9*
Sugar cane	40.9	40.9*	40.9*
Beans, dry	143.6	115.9*	162.5*
Cashew nuts, with shell*	62	49.5	69.7
Groundnuts, with shell	115.6	121.0†	117.0†
Coconuts	20.3†	17.5†	17.2*
Oil palm fruit*	255	260	260
Seed cotton	244.6	229.0*	224.9*
Cottonseed†	135	120	110
Tomatoes	184.5	159.0	154.6*
Chillies and peppers, green	46.1	25.8	25.0*
Okra	48.1	49.1*	39.9*
Pineapples	135.0	222.2	220.8*
Cotton (lint)*	100.0	91.5	76.3

* FAO estimate(s).
† Unofficial figure(s).

Aggregate production ('000 metric tons, may include official, semi-official or estimated data): Total cereals 1,268 in 2008, 1,508 in 2009, 1,555 in 2010; Total roots and tubers 6,214 in 2008, 6,434 in 2009, 6,602 in 2010; Total pulses 191 in 2008, 154 in 2009, 205 in 2010; Total vegetables (incl. melons) 389 in 2008, 376 in 2009, 338 in 2010; Total fruits (excl. melons) 283 in 2008, 386 in 2009, 399 in 2010.

Source: FAO.

LIVESTOCK
('000 head, year ending September)

	2008	2009	2010
Cattle	1,908	1,954	2,005*
Sheep	781	791	800*
Goats	1,549	1,580*	1,620*
Pigs	330	340	354
Chickens	15,286	16,000*	16,500*

* FAO estimate.

Source: FAO.

LIVESTOCK PRODUCTS
('000 metric tons, FAO estimates)

	2008	2009	2010
Cattle meat	24.0	28.1	28.7
Goat meat	4.9	5.0	5.1
Pig meat	4.3	4.4	4.6
Chicken meat	17.1	17.9	17.9
Game meat	6.8	7.3	7.8
Cows' milk	29.7	30.5	32.0
Goats' milk	7.7	7.9	8.2
Hen eggs	13.8	13.1	14.0

Source: FAO.

Forestry

ROUNDWOOD REMOVALS
('000 cubic metres, excl. bark)

	2007	2008	2009
Sawlogs, veneer logs and logs for sleepers	130	130*	130*
Other industrial wood*	297	297	297
Fuel wood*	6,141	6,184	6,228
Total*	6,568	6,611	6,655

* FAO estimate(s).

2010: Production assumed to be unchanged from 2009 (FAO estimates).

Source: FAO.

SAWNWOOD PRODUCTION
('000 cubic metres, incl. railway sleepers)

	2005	2006	2007
Total (all broadleaved)	31*	146	84

* FAO estimate.

2008–10: Production assumed to be unchanged from 2007 (FAO estimates).

Source: FAO.

Fishing

('000 metric tons, live weight)

	2007	2008	2009
Capture*	36.4	37.5	38.9
Tilapias*	10.9	10.9	10.9
Black catfishes*	1.5	1.5	1.5
Torpedo-shaped catfishes*	1.5	1.5	1.5
Mullets*	2.2	2.2	2.2
Sardinellas	0.5*	0.4	0.8
Bonga shad*	1.7	1.7	1.7
European anchovy	0.5*	n.a.	n.a.
Freshwater crustaceans*	4.6	4.6	4.6
Penaeus shrimps*	2.4	2.4	2.4
Aquaculture	0.2	0.2*	0.4
Total catch (incl. others)*	36.6	37.7	39.3

* FAO estimate(s).

Note: Figures exclude catches by Beninois canoes operating from outside the country.

Source: FAO.

Mining

	2006	2007	2008
Clay ('000 metric tons)	72.2	77.3	77.0
Gold (kg)	24	19	20
Gravel ('000 cu m)	10.6	25.3	25.0

2009: Production assumed to be unchanged from 2008 (estimates).

Source: US Geological Survey.

Industry

SELECTED PRODUCTS
('000 metric tons, unless otherwise indicated)

	2007	2008	2009
Cement (hydraulic)	1,550	1,500	1,500
Beer of barley*	117.0	120.0	124.4
Palm oil†	40	42	44
Palm kernel oil†	11.7	12.4	13.2

* Estimates.
† Unofficial figures.

Beer of sorghum ('000 metric tons): 32.8 in 2000; 35.0 in 2001; 41.8 in 2002 (Source: FAO).

Salted, dried or smoked fish ('000 metric tons): 2.0 in 2001; 2.0 in 2002; 2.4 in 2003 (Source: FAO).

Electric energy (million kWh): 128 in 2006; 132 in 2007; 136 in 2008.

Sources: US Geological Survey; FAO; UN Industrial Commodity Statistics Database.

Finance

CURRENCY AND EXCHANGE RATES

Monetary Units
100 centimes = 1 franc de la Communauté financière africaine (CFA).

Sterling, Dollar and Euro Equivalents (30 December 2011)
£1 sterling = 783.813 francs CFA;
US $1 = 506.961 francs CFA;
€1 = 655.957 francs CFA;
10,000 francs CFA = £12.76 = $19.73 = €15.24.

Average Exchange Rate (francs CFA per US $)
2009 472.186
2010 495.277
2011 471.866

Note: An exchange rate of 1 French franc = 50 francs CFA, established in 1948, remained in force until January 1994, when the CFA franc was devalued by 50%, with the exchange rate adjusted to 1 French franc = 100 francs CFA. This relationship to the French currency remained in effect with the introduction of the euro on 1 January 1999. From that date, accordingly, a fixed exchange rate of €1 = 655.957 francs CFA has been in operation.

BUDGET
('000 million francs CFA)

Revenue	2009	2010*	2011†
Tax revenue	500.4	525.9	578.0
Taxes on international trade and transactions‡	259.3	278.4	304.0
Direct and indirect taxes	241.2	247.5	273.9
Non-tax revenue	75.4	77.1	72.0
Total	575.8	603.0	650.0

Expenditure	2009	2010*	2011†
Salaries	225.9	238.7	270.0
Pensions and scholarships	39.8	43.6	53.0
Other expenditure and current transfers	212.7	204.4	211.6
Investment	302.3	177.2	233.0
Budgetary contribution	221.6	101.2	133.0
Financed from abroad	80.7	76.0	100.0
Interest due	15.6	17.7	29.9
External debt	8.2	8.1	7.6
Net lending	12.7	20.6	—
Total	809.0	702.2	797.5

* Preliminary figures.
† Projections.
‡ Including value-added taxes on imports.

2012 (projections): Total revenues 710.0; Total expenditure (incl. net lending) 843.9 (Current expenditure 614.2, Capital expenditure and net lending 229.7).

Source: IMF, *Benin: Second Review Under the Three-Year Arrangement Under the Extended Credit Facility and Request for a Waiver of the Nonobservances of a Continuous Performance Criterion — Staff Report; Staff Supplement; Press Release; and Statement by the Executive Director for Benin* (September 2011).

INTERNATIONAL RESERVES
(excluding gold, US $ million at 31 December)

	2008	2009	2010
IMF special drawing rights	0.1	77.9	76.6
Reserve position in IMF	3.4	3.4	3.4
Foreign exchange	1,259.9	1,148.5	1,120.1
Total	1,263.4	1,229.8	1,200.1

Source: IMF, *International Financial Statistics*.

MONEY SUPPLY
('000 million francs CFA at 31 December)

	2008	2009	2010
Currency outside banks	361.6	339.7	347.6
Demand deposits at deposit money banks	378.1	415.2	449.0
Checking deposits at post office	8.9	8.9	9.1
Total money (incl. others)	750.2	764.3	806.2

Source: IMF, *International Financial Statistics*.

COST OF LIVING
(Consumer Price Index in Cotonou; base: 2000 = 100)

	2007	2008	2009
Food, beverages and tobacco	112.6	132.9	140.3
Clothing	102.0	102.2	102.1
Rent*	131.4	137.7	141.5
All items (incl. others)	120.8	130.3	133.2

* Including water, electricity, gas and other fuels.

2010: Food, beverages and tobacco 141.6; All items (incl. others) 133.7.

Source: ILO.

NATIONAL ACCOUNTS
('000 million francs CFA at current prices)

Expenditure on the Gross Domestic Product

	2008	2009	2010
Government final consumption expenditure	351.9	376.8	403.6
Private final consumption expenditure	2,262.4	2,431.2	2,648.0
Gross fixed capital formation	596.5	663.8	724.5
Change in inventories	13.4	44.3	28.5
Total domestic expenditure	3,224.2	3,516.1	3,804.6
Exports of goods and services	583.3	644.8	797.4
Less Imports of goods and services	833.0	899.6	971.6
GDP in purchasers' values	2,974.7	3,261.4	3,630.3

Gross Domestic Product by Economic Activity

	2008	2009	2010
Agriculture	956.2	1,056.3	1,171.6
Mining and quarrying	7.1	7.8	8.5
Manufacturing	218.4	244.4	281.3
Electricity, gas and water	29.1	34.1	40.3
Construction	124.8	139.0	151.8
Wholesale and retail trade, restaurants and hotels	398.3	433.3	490.5
Finance, insurance and real estate	360.9	388.1	420.9
Transport and communication	254.3	278.1	309.5
Public administration and defence	380.2	413.6	468.2
Sub-total	2,729.3	2,994.7	3,342.6
Indirect taxes	295.6	322.0	351.9
Less Imputed bank service charge.	50.3	55.4	64.2
GDP in purchasers' values	2,974.7	3,261.4	3,630.3

Source: African Development Bank.

BALANCE OF PAYMENTS
('000 million francs CFA)

	2008	2009	2010*
Exports of goods f.o.b.	290.1	348.9	405.7
Imports of goods f.o.b.	-696.5	-699.9	-701.4
Trade balance	-406.4	-351.0	-295.7
Exports of services	237.8	171.0	180.6
Imports of services	-228.5	-234.2	-245.2
Balance on goods and services	-397.1	-414.2	-360.4
Income (net)	-5.1	-15.5	-8.9
Balance on goods, services and income	-402.2	-429.7	-369.3
Private unrequited transfers	73.4	32.4	45.8
Public unrequited transfers	88.6	119.7	98.8
Current balance	-240.2	-277.6	-224.7
Capital account (net)	21.6	28.8	19.2
Medium- and long-term public capital	66.4	46.6	68.3
Medium- and long-term private capital	45.0	5.0	30.0
Foreign direct investment	77.8	48.7	58.2
Portfolio investment	9.4	37.6	30.1
Deposit money banks	16.9	-40.2	-57.5
Short-term capital	34.1	27.8	90.0
Net errors and omissions	16.9	38.7	11.4
Statistical discrepancy	—	33.3	—
Overall balance	47.9	-51.3	25.0

* Estimates.

Source: IMF, *Benin: Second Review Under the Three-Year Arrangement Under the Extended Credit Facility and Request for a Waiver of the Nonobservances of a Continuous Performance Criterion — Staff Report; Staff Supplement; Press Release; and Statement by the Executive Director for Benin* (September 2011).

External Trade

PRINCIPAL COMMODITIES
(distribution by HS, US $ million)

Imports c.i.f.	2004	2005	2006
Meat and meat products	56.3	48.0	44.1
Cereals	54.6	101.2	112.9
Animal and vegetable oils	18.7	25.4	44.3
Palm oil	14.4	11.9	29.3
Salt, sulphur, earth, stone, plaster, lime and cement	36.8	47.7	52.0
Cement, etc.	28.9	41.9	45.0
Mineral fuels, oils, distillation products, etc.	205.6	183.7	217.2
Petroleum oils	142.0	122.8	154.0
Pharmaceutical products	39.3	34.6	40.1
Cotton	41.8	36.4	36.8
Woven cotton fabrics	36.8	35.1	34.9
Clothing, textile articles, etc.	34.4	39.7	47.8
Nuclear reactors, boilers, machinery, etc.	45.3	32.8	31.7
Electrical, electronic equipment	53.7	32.8	35.8
Vehicles other than railway, tramway	44.1	42.6	43.2
Cars (incl. station wagons)	23.3	25.8	27.7
Total (incl. others)	893.8	898.7	1,003.3

Exports f.o.b.	2004	2005	2006
Edible fruit, nuts, peel of citrus fruit, melons	17.2	20.3	16.8
Oil seed, oleagic fruits, grain, seed, fruit, etc.	6.1	6.3	6.9
Animal and vegetable oils	3.3	9.3	15.5
Sunflower, cotton-seed oil	1.7	7.6	8.8
Tobacco and manufactured tobacco substitutes	19.3	19.4	35.4
Salt, sulphur, earth, stone, plaster, lime and cement	11.9	11.7	9.9
Cotton	207.1	169.8	95.0
Pearls, precious stones, metals, coins, etc.	0.7	7.0	6.9
Iron and steel	7.9	7.6	9.7
Total (incl. others)	298.3	288.2	224.6

Source: Trade Map-Trade Competitiveness Map, International Trade Centre, www.intracen.org/marketanalysis.

PRINCIPAL TRADING PARTNERS
(US $ million)

Imports c.i.f.	2004	2005	2006
Belgium	43.5	40.2	35.7
Brazil	9.0	9.8	11.8
Bahrain	4.7	9.0	7.5
Cameroon	9.6	10.0	9.0
China, People's Repub.	59.6	79.1	85.4
Côte d'Ivoire	62.5	62.4	69.0
France	194.6	165.4	172.9
Germany	15.5	18.2	15.0
Ghana	63.9	64.4	68.4
Hong Kong	0.9	4.6	11.1
India	9.2	14.1	22.9
Indonesia	8.4	6.9	11.2
Italy	14.4	10.7	10.6
Japan	13.8	20.3	28.2
Malaysia	8.8	5.4	16.8
Netherlands	26.2	27.5	26.0
Nigeria	35.9	26.8	41.3
Norway	8.0	13.9	12.4
Senegal	18.1	7.6	12.0
South Africa	19.7	6.3	10.5
Spain	23.5	15.6	17.6
Sweden	4.1	3.3	13.8
Switzerland	20.6	23.4	35.7
Thailand	37.5	59.8	39.1
Togo	39.9	50.8	53.2
United Kingdom	46.7	51.4	63.3
USA	18.2	9.8	14.4
Total (incl. others)	893.8	898.7	1,003.3

Exports f.o.b.	2004	2005	2006
Bangladesh	7.5	1.2	0.1
Burkina Faso	4.3	2.2	8.1
Chad	2.0	4.1	3.6
China, People's Repub.	93.1	104.2	53.9
Côte d'Ivoire	1.1	4.5	12.9
Denmark	3.2	2.4	4.4
France	3.6	8.4	7.6
Ghana	3.4	5.4	8.7
India	21.9	19.9	19.4
Indonesia	24.3	10.5	3.9
Italy	3.6	4.2	2.1

Exports f.o.b.—*continued*	2004	2005	2006
Mali	7.3	7.6	7.6
Morocco	3.1	2.1	3.7
Niger	17.8	15.1	16.1
Nigeria	13.6	16.6	19.6
Pakistan	6.0	1.6	2.0
Portugal	3.8	3.2	5.2
Senegal	2.6	0.4	2.8
Singapore	3.7	4.2	1.8
South Africa	3.7	2.6	2.5
Spain	2.0	4.3	2.1
Sweden	1.9	3.1	0.8
Switzerland	2.0	4.9	1.2
Thailand	14.2	10.5	9.6
Togo	14.4	9.9	5.7
Viet Nam	10.0	4.4	2.6
Total (incl. others)	298.3	288.2	224.6

Source: Trade Map-Trade Competitiveness Map, International Trade Centre, www.intracen.org/marketanalysis.

Transport

RAILWAYS
(traffic)

	1998	1999	2000
Passengers carried ('000)	699.8	n.a.	n.a.
Passenger-km (million)	112.0	82.2	156.6
Freight ton-km (million)	218.7	269.0	153.2

Source: mainly IMF, *Benin: Statistical Appendix* (August 2002).

2001 (traffic, million): Passenger-km 101; Net ton-km 316 (Source: UN, *Statistical Yearbook*).

2002 (traffic, million): Net ton-km 482 (Source: UN, *Statistical Yearbook*).

ROAD TRAFFIC
(motor vehicles in use)

	1994	1995	1996
Passenger cars	26,507	30,346	37,772
Buses and coaches	353	405	504
Lorries and vans	5,301	6,069	7,554
Road tractors	2,192	2,404	2,620
Motorcycles and mopeds	220,800	235,400	250,000

2007: Passenger cars 149,310; Buses and coaches 1,114; Lorries and vans 35,656; Motorcycles and mopeds 15,600.

Source: IRF, *World Road Statistics*.

SHIPPING

Merchant Fleet
(registered at 31 December)

	2007	2008	2009
Number of vessels	6	6	7
Total displacement (grt)	1,003	1,003	1,271

Source: IHS Fairplay, *World Fleet Statistics*.

International Sea-borne Freight Traffic
(at Cotonou, including goods in transit, '000 metric tons)

	2004	2005	2006
Goods loaded	488.2	596.1	514.3
Goods in transit	n.a.	n.a.	2.1
Goods unloaded	3,520.6	4,556.8	4,854.8
Goods in transit	n.a.	n.a.	2,462.1

Source: IMF, *Benin: Selected Issues and Statistical Appendix* (August 2008).

CIVIL AVIATION
(traffic on scheduled services, domestic and international)*

	1999	2000	2001
Kilometres flown (million)	3	3	1
Passengers carried ('000)	84	77	46
Passenger-km (million)	235	216	130
Total ton-km (million)	36	32	19

* Including an apportionment of the traffic of Air Afrique.

Source: UN, *Statistical Yearbook*.

Tourism

FOREIGN VISITORS BY COUNTRY OF ORIGIN*

	2006	2007	2008
Angola	10,880	10,921	3,504
Austria	1,308	1,745	295
Belgium	3,360	3,900	1,910
Burkina Faso	4,020	4,470	10,600
Burundi	2,036	1,240	74
Cameroon	12,500	11,600	7,244
Central African Republic	600	1,047	1,445
Chad	2,400	1,932	1,481
Congo, Republic	32,114	33,896	12,468
Côte d'Ivoire	15,800	14,745	12,940
France	12,115	14,641	15,846
Gabon	2,050	4,244	10,287
Germany	1,700	2,000	2,718
Ghana	9,500	8,300	4,196
Guinea	620	1,967	1,740
Madagascar	1,988	1,148	332
Malawi	1,700	890	12
Mali	1,470	1,400	1,729
Niger	6,900	7,700	5,240
Nigeria	22,200	22,900	21,150
Senegal	1,586	2,880	4,111
Togo	11,146	9,988	6,667
Tunisia	1,727	1,500	1,342
USA	277	1,200	1,448
Total (incl. others)	180,006	186,394	188,000

* Arrivals of non-resident tourists at national borders, by country of residence.

Receipts from tourism (US $ million, incl. passenger transport): 121.6 in 2006; 206.3 in 2007; 216.0 in 2008.

Source: World Tourism Organization.

Communications Media

	2008	2009	2010
Telephones ('000 main lines in use)	115.3	127.1	133.4
Mobile cellular telephones ('000 subscribers)	3,625.4	5,033.3	7,074.9
Internet subscribers ('000)	9.4	19.4	n.a.
Broadband subscribers	2,000	3,000	26,100

Personal computers 60,000 (7.1 per 1,000 persons) in 2007.

Source: International Telecommunication Union.

Television receivers ('000 in use): 272 in 2000 (Source: UNESCO, *Statistical Yearbook*).

2004: Daily newspapers 34 (average circulation 3,000 copies); Non-daily newspapers 24 (average circulation 2,000 copies) (Source: UNESCO Institute for Statistics).

1999: Radio receivers ('000 in use): 2,661; Periodicals 106 (average circulation 110,000 copies) (Sources: UNESCO, *Statistical Yearbook* and Institute for Statistics).

Book production: 84 titles (42,000 copies) in 1994 (first editions only); 9 titles in 1998. (Sources: UNESCO, *Statistical Yearbook*, UNESCO Institute for Statistics.).

Education

(2009/10 unless otherwise indicated)

	Institutions	Teachers	Students ('000)		
			Males	Females	Total
Pre-primary	283[1]	2,928	48.1	49.2	97.3
Primary	4,178[2]	38,540	957.1	830.8	1,787.9
Secondary	145[3]	14,410[4]	281.2[5]	154.3[5]	435.4[5]
Tertiary	n.a.	955[6]	n.a.	n.a.	42.6[7]

[1] 1995/96.
[2] 1999/2000.
[3] 1993/94.
[4] 2003/04.
[5] 2004/05.
[6] 2000/01.
[7] 2005/06.

Source: UNESCO, *Statistical Yearbook* and Institute for Statistics.

Pupil-teacher ratio (primary education, UNESCO estimate): 46.4 in 2009/10 (Source: UNESCO Institute for Statistics).

Adult literacy rate (UNESCO estimates): 41.7% (males 54.2%; females 29.1%) in 2009 (Source: UNESCO Institute for Statistics).

Directory

The Government

HEAD OF STATE

President: Dr Boni Yayi (inaugurated 6 April 2006; re-elected 13 March 2011).

COUNCIL OF MINISTERS

(May 2012)

President, Head of Government, in charge of National Defence: Dr Boni Yayi.

Prime Minister, responsible for the Co-ordination of Government Action, the Evaluation of Public Policy, Denationalization and Social Dialogue: Pascal Irénée Koupaki.

Minister of State, in charge of Presidential Affairs: Issifou Kogui N'Douro.

Minister of the Interior and Public Security: Benoît Assouan Dègla.

Keeper of the Seals, Minister of Justice, Legislation and Human Rights, and Government Spokesperson: Marie-Elise Gbédo.

Minister of Decentralization, Local Government, Administration and Land Settlement: Raphaël Edou.

Minister of Foreign Affairs, African Integration, Francophone Affairs and Beninois Abroad: Nassirou Arifari Bako.

Minister of Economic Analysis, Development and Planning: Marcel de Souza.

Minister of the Economy and Finance: Jonas Gbain.

Minister of Agriculture, Stockbreeding and Fisheries: Katé Sadaï.

Minister of Industry, Commerce and Small and Medium-sized Enterprises: Madina Séphou.

Minister of Energy, Mining and Petroleum Research, Water and the Development of Renewable Energy Sources: Sofiatou Onifade Babamoussa.

Minister of Health: Akoko Kindé Gazard.

Minister of Nursery and Primary Education: Eric N'Dah.

Minister of Secondary Education, Technical and Professional Training and the Integration of Youths: Alassane Soumanou.

Minister of Higher Education and Scientific Research: François Adébayo Abiola.

Minister of Labour and the Civil Service: Maïmouna Kora Zaki.

Minister of Youth, Sports and Leisure: Didier Aplogan.

Minister of Microfinance and Youth and Women's Employment: Reckya Madougou.

Minister of the Environment, Housing and Town Planning: Blaise Ahanhanzo-Glèlè.

Minister in charge of Relations with the Institutions: Safiatou Bassabi.

Minister of Public Works and Transport: Lambert Koty.

Minister-delegate at the Presidency, in charge of the Maritime Economy and Ports: Valentin Djènontin.

Minister of Information and Communication Technology: Max Ahouèkè.

Minister of Culture, Literacy, Crafts and Tourism: Jean-Michel Abimbola.

Minister of Administrative and Institutional Reform: Martial Sounton.

Minister of the Family, Social Affairs, National Solidarity, the Disabled and Senior Citizens: Fatouma Amadou Djibril.

MINISTRIES

Office of the President: BP 1288, Cotonou; tel. 21-30-00-90; fax 21-30-06-36; internet www.gouv.bj.

Ministry of Administrative and Institutional Reform: rue du Collège Père Aupiais, BP 3010, Cotonou; tel. 21-30-80-14; fax 21-30-18-51; e-mail mrai@reforme.gouv.bj; internet www.reforme.gouv.bj.

Ministry of Agriculture, Stockbreeding and Fisheries: 03 BP 2900, Cotonou; tel. 21-30-04-10; fax 21-30-03-26; e-mail sgm@agriculture.gouv.bj; internet www.agriculture.gouv.bj.

Ministry of Culture, Literacy, Crafts and Tourism: Cotonou.

Ministry of Decentralization, Local Government, Administration and Land Settlement: Cotonou; tel. 21-30-40-30.

Ministry of the Economy and Finance: BP 302, Cotonou; tel. 21-30-02-81; fax 21-31-18-51; e-mail sgm@finance.gouv.bj; internet www.finances.bj.

Ministry of Energy, Mining and Petroleum Research, Water and the Development of Renewable Energy Sources: Cotonou.

Ministry of the the Environment, Housing and Town Planning: 01 BP 3621, Cotonou; tel. 21-31-55-96; fax 21-31-50-81; e-mail sg@environnement.gouv.bj.

Ministry of the Family, Social Affairs, National Solidarity, the Disabled and Senior Citizens: 01 BP 2802, Cotonou; tel. 21-31-67-08; fax 21-31-64-62.

Ministry of Foreign Affairs, African Integration, Francophone Affairs and Beninois Abroad: Zone Résidentielle, route de l'Aéroport, 06 BP 318, Cotonou; tel. 21-30-09-06; fax 21-38-19-70; e-mail infos@maebenin.bj; internet www.maebenin.bj.

Ministry of Health: Immeuble ex-MCAT, 01 BP 882, Cotonou; tel. 21-33-21-41; fax 21-33-04-64; e-mail sgm@sante.gouv.bj; internet www.ministeresantebenin.com.

Ministry of Higher Education and Scientific Research: 01 BP 348, Cotonou; tel. 21-30-06-81; fax 21-30-57-95; e-mail sgm@recherche.gouv.bj; internet www.mesrs.bj.

Ministry of Industry, Commerce and Small and Medium-sized Enterprises: BP 363, Cotonou; tel. and fax 21-30-30-24; e-mail mic@mic.bj; internet www.mic.bj.

Ministry of Information and Communication Technology: Cotonou.

Ministry of the Interior and Public Security: BP 925, Cotonou; tel. 21-30-11-06; fax 21-30-01-59.

Ministry of Justice, Legislation and Human Rights: BP 2493, Cotonou; tel. 21-30-08-90; fax 21-30-18-21; e-mail sgm@justice.gouv.bj; internet www.justice.gouv.bj.

Ministry of Labour and the Civil Service: BP 907, Cotonou; tel. 21-31-26-18; fax 21-31-06-29; e-mail sgm@travail.gouv.bj; internet www.travail.gouv.bj.

Ministry of Microfinance and Youth and Women's Employment: BP 302, Cotonou; tel. 21-30-02-81; fax 21-30-18-51.

Ministry of National Defence: BP 2493, Cotonou; tel. 21-30-08-90; fax 21-30-18-21.

Ministry of Nursery and Primary Education: 01 BP 10, Porto-Novo; tel. 20-21-33-27; fax 20-21-50-11; e-mail sgm@enseignement.gouv.bj; internet www.enseignement.gouv.bj.

Ministry of Planning, Development and the Evaluation of Public Action: Cotonou; internet www.developpement.bj.

Ministry of Public Works and Transport: Cotonou.

Ministry of Secondary Education, Technical and Professional Training and the Integration of Youths: 10 BP 250, Cotonou; tel. and fax 21-30-56-15.

Ministry of Small and Medium-sized Enterprises and the Promotion of the Private Sector: Cotonou.

Ministry of Town Planning, Housing, Land Reform and the Fight against Coastal Erosion: Cotonou.

Ministry of Trade: BP 363, Cotonou; tel. 21-30-76-46; fax 21-30-30-24; e-mail sgm@commerce.gouv.bj; internet www.commerce.gouv.bj.

Ministry of Youth, Sports and Leisure: 03 BP 2103, Cotonou; tel. 21-30-36-14; fax 21-38-21-26; internet www.mjsl.bj.

President and Legislature

PRESIDENT

Presidential Election, 13 March 2011

Candidate	Votes	% of votes
Boni Yayi	1,579,550	53.14
Adrien Houngbédji	1,059,396	35.64
Abdoulaye Bio Tchané	182,484	6.14
Issa Salifou	37,219	1.25
Christian Eunock Lagnidé	19,221	0.65
François Janvier Yahouédéhou	16,591	0.56
Others*	77,984	2.62
Total	2,972,445	100.00

* There were eight other candidates.

LEGISLATURE

Assemblée nationale

BP 371, Porto-Novo; tel. 20-21-22-19; fax 20-21-36-44; e-mail assemblee.benin@yahoo.fr; internet www.assembleebenin.org.

President: MATHURIN NAGO.

General Election, 30 April 2011

Party	Seats
Force cauris pour un Bénin émergent (FCBE)	41
Union fait la Nation (UN)	31
Alliance Amana	2
Alliance Cauris	2
Alliance forces dans l'unité (AFU)	2
Union pour la Bénin (UB)	2
Union pour la relève-Force espoir (UPR-FE)	2
Alliance G13 Baobab	1
Total	83

Election Commission

Commission électorale nationale autonome (CENA): 01 BP 443, Cotonou; tel. 21-31-69-90; e-mail info@cena-benin.org; internet www.cena-benin.org; f. 1994; 25 mems, of whom 18 are appointed by the Assemblée nationale, 2 by the President of the Republic, 2 by civil society; there are additionally 4 members of the Commission's permanent administrative secretariat; Chair. PASCAL TODJINOU.

Advisory Council

Conseil économique et social (CES): ave Jean-Paul II, 08 BP 679, Cotonou; tel. 21-30-03-91; fax 21-30-03-13; e-mail noc@ces-benin.org; internet www.ces-benin.org; f. 1994; 30 mems, representing the executive, legislature and 'all sections of the nation'; reviews all legislation relating to economic and social affairs; competent to advise on proposed economic and social legislation, as well as to recommend economic and social reforms; Pres. RAPHIOU TOUKOUROU.

Political Organizations

The registration of political parties commenced in August 1990. In mid-2002 there were more than 160 registered parties. Some 19 political parties or alliances contested the 2011 legislative elections.

Alliance pour une dynamique démocratique (ADD): Leader NICÉPHORE SOGLO.

Mouvement africain pour la démocratie et le progrès (MADEP): BP 1509, Cotonou; tel. 21-31-31-22; f. 1997; Leader El Hadj SÉFOU L. FAGBOHOUN.

Parti social-démocrate (PSD): Leader BRUNO AMOUSSOU.

Rassemblement démocratique pour le développement—Nassara (RDD—Nassara): Leader RAMATOU BABA MOUSSA.

La renaissance du Bénin (RB): BP 2205, Cotonou; tel. 21-31-40-89; f. 1992; Chair. ROSINE VIEYRA SOGLO.

Union des forces démocratiques (UFD): Parakou; f. 1994; Leader SACCA GEORGES ZIMÉ.

Alliance étoile: f. 2002; Leader SACCA LAFIA.

Union pour la démocratie et la solidarité nationale (UDS): BP 1761, Cotonou; tel. 21-31-38-69; Pres. SACCA LAFIA.

Les verts du Bénin—Parti écologiste du Bénin: 06 BP 1336, Cotonou; tel. and fax 21-35-19-47; e-mail greensbenin@yahoo.fr; internet www.greensbenin.org; f. 1995; Pres. TOUSSAINT HINVI; Sec. PIERRE AHOUANOZIN.

Alliance des forces du progrès (AFP): Assemblée nationale, BP 371, Porto-Novo; Leader VALENTIN ADITI HOUDE.

Alliance impulsion pour le progrès et la démocratie (Alliance IPD): 04 BP 0812, Cotonou; tel. 21-35-20-03; f. 1999; Leader THÉOPHILE NATA.

Alliance MDC-PS-CPP: Assemblée nationale, BP 371, Porto-Novo; Leader DAMIEN ZINSOU MODÉRAN ALAHASSA.

Congrès du peuple pour le progrès (CPP): Quartier Houéyiho, villa 061, cité BCEAO, BP 1565, Cotonou; tel. 21-38-52-55; Leader JEAN GOUNONGBÉ.

Mouvement pour le développement par la culture (MDC): Quartier Zogbohoué, BP 10, Cotonou; Pres. CODJO ACHODÉ.

Parti du salut (PS): 06 BP 11, Cotonou; tel. 21-36-02-56; f. 1994; Leader DAMIEN MODÉRAN ZINSOU ALAHASSA.

Alliance du renouveau (AR): Leader MARTIN DOHOU AZONHIHO.

Coalition pour un Bénin émergent (CBE): Leader VENANCE GNIGLA.

Force cauris pour un Bénin émergent (FCBE): tel. 95-86-11-00; e-mail fcbe@gmail.com; internet www.fcbe2007.org; Pres. EXPÉDIT HOUESSOU; Sec.-Gen. DAVID NAHOUAN.

Force clé: Carré 315, ScoaGbéto, 01 BP 1435, Cotonou; tel. 21-35-09-36; f. 2003 on basis of Mouvement pour une alternative du peuple; Leader LAZARE SÈHOUÉTO.

Force espoir (FE): Leader ANTOINE DAYORI.

G13: f. 2008 by fmr supporters of President Yayi; Leader ISSA SALIFOU.

Mouvement pour le développement et la solidarité (MDS): BP 73, Porto-Novo; Leader SACCA MOUSSÉDIKOU FIKARA.

Nouvelle Alliance: Cotonou; f. 2006; Leader CORENTIN KOHOUE.

Parti pour la démocratie et le progrès social (PDPS): Leader EDMOND AGOUA.

Parti du renouveau démocratique (PRD): Immeuble Babo Oganla, 01 BP 1157, Porto-Novo; tel. 21-30-07-57; f. 1990; Leader ADRIEN HOUNGBÉDJI.

Rassemblement pour la démocratie et le panafricanisme (RDP): 03 BP 1050, Cotonou; tel. 21-32-02-83; fax 21-32-35-71; e-mail cotrans@leland.bj; f. 1995; Pres. DOMINIQUE O. HOUNGNINOU; Treas. JANVIER SETANGNI.

Restaurer l'espoir (RE): Leader CANDIDE AZANNAÏ.

Union pour le Bénin du futur (UBF): 03 BP 1972, Cotonou; tel. 21-33-12-23; e-mail amoussou@avu.org; f. 2002 by supporters of then Pres. Kérékou; separate faction, UBF 'Aller plus loin', formed Oct. 2004 under leadership of JOSEPH GANDAHO, comprising more than 30 pro-presidential parties and asscns; further, smaller, faction, the 'Alliance UBF' formed April 2005, led by ALAIN ADIHOU; Co-ordinator BRUNO AMOUSSOU.

Front d'action pour le renouveau, la démocratie et le développement—Alafia (FARD—Alafia): 01 BP 3238, Cotonou; tel. 21-33-34-10; f. 1994; Sec.-Gen. DANIEL TAWÉMA.

Union nationale pour la démocratie et le progrès (UNDP): Chair. EMILE DERLIN ZINSOU.

Union pour la relève (UPR): Gbégamey; internet www.uprbenin.org; Leader ISSA SALIFOU.

Diplomatic Representation

EMBASSIES IN BENIN

China, People's Republic: 2 route de l'Aéroport, 01 BP 196, Cotonou; tel. 21-30-07-65; fax 21-30-08-41; e-mail prcbenin@serv.eit.bj; internet bj.chineseembassy.org; Ambassador TAO WEIGUANG.

Congo, Democratic Republic: Carré 221, Ayélawadjè, Cotonou; tel. 21-30-00-01.

Cuba: ave de la Marina, face Hôtel du Port, 01 BP 948, Cotonou; tel. 21-31-52-97; fax 21-31-65-91; e-mail embacuba@benin.cubaminrex.cu; internet emba.cubaminrex.cu/benin; Ambassador OSCAR GENARO COET BLACKSTOCK.

Denmark: Lot P7, Les Cocotiers, 04 BP 1223, Cotonou; tel. 21-30-38-62; fax 21-30-38-60; e-mail cooamb@um.dk; internet www.ambcotonou.um.dk; Ambassador GERT MEINECKE.

Egypt: Lot G26, route de l'Aéroport, BP 1215, Cotonou; tel. 21-30-08-42; fax 21-30-14-25; Ambassador RAMADAN MOHAMED E. BAKR.

France: ave Jean-Paul II, BP 966, Cotonou; tel. 21-30-02-25; fax 21-30-15-47; e-mail ambafrance.cotonou@diplomatie.gouv.fr; internet www.ambafrance-bj.org; Ambassador HERVÉ BESANCENOT.

Germany: 7 ave Jean-Paul II, 01 BP 504, Cotonou; tel. 21-31-29-67; fax 21-31-29-62; e-mail info@cotonou.diplo.de; internet www.cotonou.diplo.de; Ambassador LUDWIG LINDEN.

Ghana: route de l'Aéroport, Lot F, Les Cocotiers, BP 488, Cotonou; tel. 21-30-07-46; fax 21-30-03-45; e-mail ghaemb02@leland.bj; Ambassador MODESTUS AHIABLE.

Holy See: 08 BP 400, Cotonou; tel. 21-30-03-08; fax 21-30-03-10; e-mail nonciaturebenin@gmail.com; Apostolic Nuncio Archbishop MICHAEL AUGUST BLUME (Titular Archbishop of Alexanum).

Japan: Villa A2, Complexe CEN-SAD, Laico-Benin, blvd de la Marina, Cotonou; tel. 21-30-59-86; fax 21-30-59-94.

Korea, Democratic People's Republic: Cotonou; Ambassador KIM PYONG GI.

Kuwait: Cotonou; Ambassador FAEYEZ MISHARI AL-JASSIM.

Libya: Carré 36, Cotonou; tel. 21-30-04-52; fax 21-30-03-01; Ambassador TOUFIK ASHOUR ADAM.

Netherlands: ave Pape Jean Paul II, route de l'Aéroport, derrière le Tri Postal, 08 BP 0783, Cotonou; tel. 21-30-04-39; fax 21-30-41-50; e-mail cot@minbuza.nl; internet www.ambassadehollande-cotonou.org; Ambassador W. WOUTER PLOMP.

Niger: derrière l'Hôtel de la Plage, BP 352, Cotonou; tel. 21-31-56-65; Ambassador LOMPO SOULEYMANE.

Nigeria: ave de France, Marina, BP 2019, Cotonou; tel. 21-30-11-42; fax 21-30-11-13; Ambassador EZEKEIL O. OLADEJI.

South Africa: Marina Hotel, blvd de la Marina, 01 BP 1901, Cotonou; tel. 21-30-72-17; fax 21-30-70-58; e-mail foreign@intnet.bj; Chargé d'affaires a.i. KGOSIETSILE CHARLES KEEPILE.

Russia: Zone résidentielle, ave de la Marina, face Hôtel du Port, BP 2013, Cotonou; tel. 21-31-28-34; fax 21-31-28-35; e-mail ambrusben@mail.ru; internet www.benin.mid.ru; Ambassador YURII GRASHCHENKOV.

USA: rue Caporal Anani Bernard, 01 BP 2012, Cotonou; tel. 21-30-06-50; fax 21-30-03-84; e-mail irccotonou@state.gov; internet cotonou.usembassy.gov; Ambassador JAMES KNIGHT.

Judicial System

Constitutional Court: BP 2050, Cotonou; tel. 21-31-16-10; fax 21-31-37-12; e-mail cconstitutsg@yahoo.fr; internet www.gouv.bj/institutions/cour_constitutionnelle/presentation.php; f. 1990; inaug. 1993; 7 mems; 4 appointed by the Assemblée nationale, 3 by the President of the Republic; exercises highest jurisdiction in constitutional affairs; determines the constitutionality of legislation, oversees and proclaims results of national elections and referendums, responsible for protection of individual and public rights and obligations, charged with regulating functions of organs of state and authorities; Pres. ROBERT DOSSOU; Sec.-Gen. MARCELLINE-CLAIRE GBÈHA AFOUDA.

High Court of Justice: 01 BP 2958, Porto-Novo; tel. 20-21-26-81; fax 20-21-27-71; tel. hcjbenin@intnet.bj; internet www.gouv.bj; f. 1990; officially inaugurated in 2001; comprises the 6 members of the Constitutional Court (other than its President), 6 deputies of the Assemblée nationale and the First President of the Supreme Court; competent to try the President of the Republic and members of the Government in cases of high treason, crimes committed in, or at the time of, the exercise of their functions, and of plotting against state security; Pres. Prof. THÉODORE HOLO.

Supreme Court: 01 BP 330, Cotonou; tel. and fax 20-21-26-77; fax 20-21-32-08; e-mail info@coursupreme.gouv.bj; internet www.coursupreme.gouv.bj; f. 1960; highest juridical authority in administrative and judicial affairs and in matters of public accounts; competent in disputes relating to local elections; advises the executive on jurisdiction and administrative affairs; comprises a President (appointed by the President of the Republic, after consultation with the President of the Assemblée nationale, senior magistrates and jurists), presidents of the component chambers, a public prosecutor, 4 assistant procurators-fiscal, counsellors and clerks; Pres. OUSMANE BATOKO; Attorney-Gen. JEAN-BAPTISTE MONSI; Pres. of the Judicial Chamber JACQUES MAYABA; Pres. of the Administrative Chamber GRÉGOIRE Y. ALAYÈ; Pres. of the Chamber of Accounts JUSTIN BIOKOU; Chief Clerk FRANÇOISE TCHIBOZO-QUENUM.

Religion

Religious and spiritual cults, which were discouraged under Kérékou's military regime, re-emerged as a prominent force in Beninois society during the 1990s. At the time of the 2002 census it was estimated that some 38% of the population were Christians (mainly Roman Catholics), 24% were Muslims, and 17% followed the traditional *vodoun* religion, with a further 6% being adherents of other traditional religions.

CHRISTIANITY

The Roman Catholic Church

Benin comprises two archdioceses and eight dioceses. An estimated 27.6% of the population were Roman Catholics.

Bishops' Conference

Conférence Episcopale du Bénin, Archevêché, 01 BP 491, Cotonou; tel. 21-30-66-48; fax 21-30-07-07; e-mail cepiscob@usa.net; Pres. Most Rev. ANTOINE GANYÉ (Bishop of Dassa-Zoumé).

Archbishop of Cotonou: Most Rev. ANTOINE GANYÉ, Archevêché, 01 BP 491, Cotonou; tel. 21-30-01-45; fax 21-30-07-07; e-mail mhlagbot@yahoo.fr.

Archbishop of Parakou: PASCAL N'KOUÉ, Archevêché, BP 75, Parakou; tel. 23-61-02-54; fax 23-61-01-09; e-mail archeveche@borgou.net.

Protestant Church

There are an estimated 257 Protestant mission centres in Benin.

Eglise Protestante Méthodiste en République du Bénin (EPMB): 54 ave Mgr Steinmetz, 01 BP 34, Cotonou; tel. and fax 21-31-11-42; e-mail epmbenin@intnet.bj; f. 1843; Pres. Rev. Dr SIMON K. DOSSOU; Sec. Rev. Dr CÉLESTIN GB. KIKI; 101,000 mems (1997).

VODOUN

The origins of the traditional *vodoun* religion can be traced to the 14th century. Its influence is particularly strong in Latin America and the Caribbean, owing to the shipment of slaves from the West African region to the Americas in the 18th and 19th centuries.

Communauté Nationale du Culte Vodoun (CNCV): Ouidah; Pres. HOUNGUÈ TOWAKON GUÈDÉHOUNGUÈ II.

ISLAM

Union Islamique du Bénin (UIB): Cotonou; Pres. Imam El Hadj MOHAMED AMED SANNI; Sec.-Gen. FAÏSSOU ADÉGBOLA.

BAHÁ'Í FAITH

National Spiritual Assembly: BP 1252, Cotonou.

The Press

In 2010 there were some 75 dailies and periodicals recognized by the Haute Autorité de l'Audiovisuel et de la Communication in Benin.

DAILIES

Actu-Express: 01 BP 2220, Cotonou; tel. 97981047 (mobile); internet www.actuexpress.com; Dir of Publication Médéric François Gohoungo.

L'Adjinakou: Lot AC, Parcelle 1 Avakpa-Tokpa, Immeuble Radio école APM, 03 BP 105, Porto-Novo; tel. 20-22-06-76; e-mail adjinakou2004@yahoo.com; internet www.journal-adjinakou-benin.info; f. 2003; Dir of Publication Maurille Agbokou.

L'Araignée: siège du cyber DOPHIA, face Cité Houeyiho, 01 BP 1357, Cotonou; tel. 21-30-64-12; fax (44) 21-32-18-84; e-mail info@laraignee.org; internet www.laraignee.org; f. 2001; online only; politics, public affairs, culture, society, sport; Dir of Publishing Félix Aniwanou Hounsa; Editor-in-Chief Willéandre Houngbédji.

L'Aurore: face Clinique Boni, 05 BP 464, Cotonou; tel. 21-33-70-43; e-mail laurore1998@yahoo.fr; Dir Patrick Adjamonsi; circ. 1,500.

L'Autre Quotidien: Lot 115 Z, rue Capitaine Anani, Face PNUD, Zone Résidentielle, 01 BP 6659, Cotonou; tel. 21-31-01-99; fax 21-31-02-05; e-mail lautreredaction@yahoo.fr; internet www.lautrequotidien.com; Dir Romain Toï; Editor-in-Chief Léon Brathier.

Bénin-Presse Info: 01 BP 72, Cotonou; tel. 21-31-26-55; fax 21-31-13-26; e-mail abpben@bow.intnet.bj; internet www.gouv.bj/presse/abp/index.php; bulletin of Agence Bénin-Presse; Dir Yaovi R. Hounkponou; Editor-in-Chief Joseph Vodounon.

Le Confrère de la Matinée: Esplanade du Stade de l'Amitié, Cotonou; tel. 21-04-20-14; e-mail info@leconfrere.com; internet www.leconfrere.com; Dir of Publication Faustin Babatoundé Adjagba.

Djakpata: Quartier Todote C/410, Maison Bokononhui, 02 BP 2744, Cotonou; tel. 21-32-43-73; e-mail quotidiendjakpata@yahoo.fr; internet djakpata.info; Editor Cyrille Saïzonou.

Les Echos du Jour: Carré 136, Sodjatimè, 08 BP 718, Cotonou; tel. 21-33-18-33; fax 21-33-17-06; e-mail echos@intnet.bj; independent; Dir Maurice Chabi; Editor-in-Chief Sébastien Dossa; circ. 3,000.

Fraternité: face Station Menontin, 05 BP 915, Cotonou; tel. 21-38-47-70; fax 21-38-47-71; e-mail fraternite@fraternite-info.com; internet www.fraternite-info.com; Dir-Gen. Malick Seibou Gomina; Editor-in-Chief Brice U. Houssou.

L'Informateur: Etoile Rouge, Bâtiment Radio Star, Carré 1072c, 01 BP 5421, Cotonou; tel. and fax 21-32-66-39; f. 2001; Dir Clément Adéchian; Editor-in-Chief Brice Guèdè.

Le Matin: Carré 54, Tokpa Hoho, 06 BP 2217, Cotonou; tel. 21-31-10-80; fax 21-33-42-62; e-mail lematinonline@moncourrier.com; f. 1994; independent; Dir Moïse Dato; Editorial Dir Ignace Fanou.

Le Matinal: Carré 153–154, Atinkanmey, 06 BP 1989, Cotonou; tel. 90-94-83-32; e-mail infodumatinal@yahoo.fr; internet www.actubenin.com; f. 1997; daily; Dir-Gen. Maximin Tchibozo; Editor-in-Chief Napoléon Maforikan; circ. 5,000.

La Nation: Cadjèhoun, 01 BP 1210, Cotonou; tel. 21-30-02-99; fax 21-30-34-63; e-mail onipben@intnet.bj; internet www.gouv.bj/presse/lanation/index.php; f. 1990; official newspaper; Dir Akuété Assevi; Editor-in-Chief Hubert O. Akponikpe; circ. 4,000.

La Nouvelle Tribune: Immeuble Zonon, Lot 1498, P Quartier Missogbè à Vêdoko, 09 BP 336, Cotonou; tel. 21-38-34-88; e-mail redaction@lanouvelletribune.info; internet www.lanouvelletribune.info; f. 2001; Dir-Gen. and Dir of Publication Vincent Foly; Editorial Dir Emmanuel S. Tachin.

L'Oeil du Peuple: Carré 743, rue PTT, Gbégamey, 01 BP 5538, Cotonou; tel. 21-30-22-07; e-mail loeildupeuple@yahoo.fr; Dir Celestin Abissi; Editor-in-Chief Paul Agboyidou.

Le Point au Quotidien: 332 rue du Renouveau, 05 BP 934, Cotonou; tel. 90-91-69-45; fax 21-32-25-31; e-mail info@lepointauquotidien.com; independent; Dir and Editor-in-Chief Fernando Hessou; circ. 2,000.

La Presse du Jour: 01 BP 1719, Cotonou; tel. 21-30-51-75; internet www.lapressedujour.net; Dir of Publication Pascal Hounkpatin.

Le Progrès: 05 BP 708, Cotonou; tel. 21-32-52-73; e-mail journalprogres@hotmail.com; internet www.leprogres.info; f. ; Dir of Publication Ludovic Agbadja.

Le Républicain: Les Presses d'Afrique, Carré 630, Tanto, 05 BP 1230, Cotonou; tel. and fax 21-33-83-04; e-mail lerepublicain@lerepublicain.org; independent; Editor-in-Chief Isidore Zinsou.

La Tribune de la Capitale: Lot 03-46, Parcelle E, Houinmè, Maison Onifadé, Catchi, 01 BP 1463, Porto-Novo; tel. 20-22-55-69; e-mail latribunedelacapitale@yahoo.fr; internet www.latribunedelacapitale.com; Dir of Publication Seth Evariste Hodonou; Editor-in-Chief Kpakoun Charles.

PERIODICALS

Afrique Identité: ave du Canada, Lot 1069 T, 02 BP 1215, Cotonou; Dir Angelo Ahouanmagma; Editorial Dir Serge Auguste Loko.

Agri-Culture: 03 BP 0380, Cotonou; tel. and fax 21-36-05-46; e-mail agriculture@uva.org; f. 1999; monthly; Editor-in-Chief Joachim Saïzonou; circ. 1,000.

L'Autre Gazette: 02 BP 1537, Cotonou; tel. 21-32-59-97; e-mail collegi@beninweb.org; Editor-in-Chief Wilfried Ayibatin.

L'Avenir: Carré 911, 02 BP 8134, Cotonou; tel. 21-32-21-23; fortnightly; political analysis; Dir Claude Firmin Gangbe.

Bénin Info: 06 BP 590, Cotonou; tel. 21-32-52-64; fortnightly; Dir Romain Toi.

Le Canard du Golfe: Carré 240, Midombo, Akpakpa, 06 BP 59, Cotonou; tel. 21-32-72-33; e-mail lecanardugolfe@yahoo.fr; satirical; weekly; Dir F. L. Tingbo; Editor-in-Chief Emmanuel Sotikon.

Le Continental: BP 4419, Cotonou; tel. 21-30-04-37; fax 21-30-03-21; Editor-in-Chief Arnauld Houndete.

La Croix du Bénin: Centre Paul VI, 01 BP 105, Cotonou; tel. and fax 21-32-11-19; e-mail andrequenum@yahoo.com; internet www.lacroixdubenin.com; f. 1946; twice a week; Roman Catholic; Editor Rev. Dr André S. Quenum.

Emotion Magazine: 06 BP 1404, Cotonou; tel. 95-40-17-07; fax 21-32-21-33; e-mail emomagazine@yahoo.fr; f. 1998; every 2 months; cultural and social affairs; Dir of Publication Eric Sessinou Huannou; Editor-in-Chief Bernard Hermann Zannou; circ. 3,000 (2006).

La Gazette du Golfe: Immeuble La Gazette du Golfe, Carré 902e, Sikècodji, 03 BP 1624, Cotonou; tel. 21-32-68-44; fax 21-32-52-26; e-mail gazettedugolfe@serv.eit.bj; f. 1987; weekly; Dir Ismaël Y. Soumanou; Editor Marcus Boni Teiga; circ. 18,000 (nat. edn), 5,000 (int. edn).

Le Gongonneur: 04 BP 1432, Cotonou; tel. 90-90-60-95; fax 21-35-04-22; e-mail dahoun@yahoo.com; f. 1998; owned by Prix Etoile Internationale à la Qualité; Dir Mathias C. Sossou; Editor-in-Chief Gaffarou Radji.

Le Héraut: 03 BP 3417, Cotonou; tel. 21-36-00-64; e-mail franck.kouyami@auf.org; internet leheraut.org; monthly; current affairs; analysis; produced by students at Université nationale du Bénin; Dir Geoffrey Gounou N'Goye; Editor-in-Chief Gabriel Dideh.

Initiatives: 01 BP 2093, Cotonou; tel. 21-31-22-61; fax 21-31-59-50; e-mail cepepe@firstnet1.com; 6 a year; journal of the Centre de Promotion et d'Encadrement des Petites et Moyennes Entreprises.

Journal Officiel de la République du Bénin: BP 59, Porto-Novo; tel. 20-21-39-77; f. 1890; present name adopted 1990; official govt bulletin; fortnightly; Dir Afize Désiré Adamo.

Madame Afrique: Siège Mefort Inter Diffusion, Carré 1066, quartier Cadjehoun, 05 BP 1914, Cotonou; tel. 97-68-22-90; e-mail madafric@yahoo.fr; f. 2000; monthly; women's interest; Dir of Publication Bernard G. Zanklan.

Le Magazine de l'Entreprise: BP 850, Cotonou; tel. 21-30-80-79; fax 21-30-47-77; e-mail oliviergat@hotmail.com; f. 1999; monthly; business; Dir A. Victor Fakèyè.

Opérateur Économique: ave du Général de Gaulle, 01 BP 31, Cotonou; tel. 21-31-20-81; fax 21-31-22-99; monthly; published by Chambre de Commerce et d'Industrie du Bénin; Dir Wassi Mouftaou.

Le Perroquet: Carré 478, Quartier Bar-Tito, 03 BP 880, Cotonou; tel. 21-32-18-54; e-mail leperroquet2003@yahoo.fr; internet www.leperroquet.fr.gd; f. 1995; 2 a month; independent; news and analysis; Dir Damien Houessou; Editor-in-Chief Charles Richard Nzi; circ. 4,000 (2004).

La Réplique: BP 1087, Porto-Novo; tel. and fax 20-21-45-77; Dir Emile Adechina; Editor-in-Chief Jerôme Aklamavo.

Le Temps: Kouhounou, 04 BP 43, Cotonou; tel. 21-30-55-06; 2 a month; Dir Yaya Yolou; Editor-in-Chief Guy Condé.

Press Association

Union des Journalistes de la Presse Privée du Bénin (UJPB): blvd de la République, près Cadmes Plus, 03 BP 383, Cotonou; tel. 21-32-52-73; e-mail ujpb@h2com.com; internet www.h2com.com/ujpb; f. 1992; asscn of independent journalists; Pres. Agapit N. Maforikan.

NEWS AGENCY

Agence Bénin-Presse (ABP): BP 72, Cotonou; tel. and fax 21-31-26-55; e-mail abpben@intnet.bj; internet www.abp.gouv.bj; f. 1961; nat. news agency; Dir YAOVI R. HOUNKPONOU.

Publishers

AFRIDIC: 01 BP 269, 01 Porto-Novo; tel. 20-22-32-28; f. 1996; poetry, essays, fiction; Dir ADJIBI JEAN-BAPTISTE.

Editions de l'ACACIA: 06 BP 1978, Cotonou; tel. 21-33-04-72; e-mail zoundin@yahoo.fr; f. 1989; fmrly Editions du Flamboyant; literary fiction, history, popular science; Dir OSCAR DE SOUZA.

Editions des Diasporas: 04 BP 792, Cotonou; e-mail camouro@yahoo.fr; poetry, essays; Editor CAMILLE AMOURO.

Editions Ruisseaux d'Afrique: 04 BP 1154, Cotonou; tel. and fax 90-94-79-25; fax 21-30-31-86; e-mail ruisseau@leland.bj; f. 1992; children's literature; Dir BÉATRICE GBADO.

Editions Souvenir: 01 BP 2589, Porto-Novo; tel. 97-88-49-04; e-mail editsouvenir@voila.fr; youth and adult literature; Dir JEAN-BAPTISTE KUNDA LI FUMU'NSAMU.

Graphitec: 04 BP 825, Cotonou; tel. and fax 21-30-46-04; e-mail lewado@yahoo.com.

Imprimerie Notre Dame: BP 109, Cotonou; tel. 21-32-12-07; fax 21-32-11-19; f. 1974; Roman Catholic publs; Dir BARTHÉLÉMY ASSOGBA CAKPO.

Société Tunde: 06 BP 1925, Cotonou; tel. 21-30-15-68; fax 21-30-42-86; e-mail tunde.sa@tunde-sa.com; internet www.tunde-sa.com; f. 1986; economics, management; Pres. BABATOUNDÉ RASAKI OLLOFINDJI; Dir-Gen. ALFRED LAMBERT SOMA.

Star Editions: 01 BP 367, Recette principale, Cotonou; tel. 90-94-66-28; fax 21-33-05-29; e-mail star_editions@yahoo.fr; business, economics, science, poetry; Editor JOACHIM ADJOVI.

GOVERNMENT PUBLISHING HOUSE

Office National d'Edition, de Presse et d'Imprimerie (ONEPI): 01 BP 1210, Cotonou; tel. 21-30-02-99; fax 21-30-34-63; f. 1975; Dir-Gen. INNOCENT ADJAHO.

Broadcasting and Communications

TELECOMMUNICATIONS

Benin's fixed-line telephone sector is dominated by the state operator, Bénin Télécoms. In 2011 there were five providers of mobile cellular telephone services, of which four were privately owned and one, Libercom, was state-owned. At December 2007 there were 110,254 subscribers to fixed-line telephone services, while at June 2010 there were 6.3m subscribers to mobile telephone services.

Autorité Transitoire de Régulation des Postes et Télécommunications (ATRPT): ave Steinmetz, Von opposé ancien Air Gabon, Immeuble Suzanne Loko, 01 BP 2034, Cotonou; tel. 21-31-72-76; fax 21-31-72-76; e-mail infos@atrpt.bj; internet www.atrpt.bj; f. 2007; Pres. FIRMIN DJIMENOU.

Bénin Télécoms: Ganhi, 01 BP 5959, Cotonou; tel. 21-31-20-45; fax 21-31-38-43; e-mail sp.dgbttelecoms@intnet.bj; internet www.benintelecoms.bj; f. 2004 to assume responsibility for telecommunications activities of fmr Office des Postes et des Télécommunications, in advance of proposed transfer of 55% stake to private ownership scheduled for Jan. 2009; Dir-Gen. URBAIN FADÉGNON (acting); 110,254 subscribers (Dec. 2007).

Bell Bénin Communications (BBCOM): 02 BP 1886, Gbégamey; tel. 21-30-52-84; fax 21-30-84-84; internet www.bellbenin.net; f. 2002; mobile cellular telephone operator; Chief Exec. ISSA SALIFOU; 443,550 subscribers (2008).

Glo Mobile Bénin: Aïdjèdo, Lot 817 Parcelle C, ave de la Libération, 01 BP 8050, Cotonou; tel. 21-32-44-56; Dir-Gen. FEMMY OGUNLUSI; 560,090 subscribers (2008).

Libercom: blvd Saint-Michel, face Hall des Arts et de la Culture, 01 BP 5959, Cotonou; tel. 21-31-46-48; fax 21-31-49-42; e-mail renseignements@libercom.bj; internet www.libercom.bj; f. 2000; mobile cellular telephone operator in Cotonou and Porto-Novo; Dir-Gen. ISIDORE DÉGBÈLO; 194,888 subscribers (2008).

MTN Bénin: 01 BP 5293, Cotonou; tel. 21-31-66-41; internet www.mtn.bj; f. 2000 as BéninCell; renamed as Areeba in 2005; mobile cellular telephone operator in Cotonou, Porto-Novo and Parakou under network name Areeba; owned by Mobile Telephone Network International (South Africa); CEO MOHAMAD BADER; 267,583 subscribers (2005).

Moov Bénin: Immeuble Kougblenou, 5è étage, ave Mgr Steinmetz, Cotonou; e-mail moov@moov.bj; internet www.moov.bj; f. 2000 as Telcel Bénin; mobile cellular telephone operator in Cotonou, Porto-Novo, Abomey, Lokossa, other regions of southern Benin and in Parakou; Dir-Gen. TALIBI HAÏDRA; 950,584 subscribers (2008).

BROADCASTING

Since 1997 the Haute Autorité de l'Audiovisuel et de la Communication has issued licences to private radio and television stations.

Haute Autorité de l'Audiovisuel et de la Communication (HAAC): 01 BP 3567, Cotonou; tel. 21-31-17-45; fax 21-31-17-42; e-mail infohaac@haacbenin.org; internet www.haacbenin.org; f. 1994; Pres. THÉOPHILE NATA.

Radio

In early 2002 there were nine commercial radio stations, 17 non-commercial stations and five rural or local stations broadcasting in Benin.

Office de Radiodiffusion et de Télévision du Bénin (ORTB): 01 BP 366, Cotonou; tel. 21-30-46-19; fax 21-30-04-48; e-mail drp@ortb.bj; internet www.ortb.bj; state-owned; radio programmes broadcast from Cotonou and Parakou in French, English and 18 local languages; Dir-Gen. JULIEN PIERRE AKPAKI; Dir of Radio CHRISTIAN DE SOUZA.

Atlantic FM: 01 BP 366, Cotonou; tel. 21-30-20-41; Dir JOSEPH OGOUNCHI.

Radiodiffusion nationale du Bénin: BP 366, Cotonou; tel. 21-30-10-96; f. 1953; Dir MOUFALIOU LIADY.

Radio Régionale de Parakou: BP 128, Parakou; tel. 23-61-07-73; Dir SÉNI SOUROU.

Bénin-Culture: BP 21, Association pour l'Institutionnalisation de la Mémoire et de la Pensée Intellectuelle Africaine, 01 BP 21, Porto-Novo; tel. 20-22-69-34; Head of Station ARMAND COVI.

Golfe FM-Magic Radio: 03 BP 1624, Cotonou; tel. 21-32-42-08; fax 21-32-42-09; e-mail golfefm@serv.eit.bj; internet www.eit.bj/golfefm.htm; Dir ISMAËL SOUMANOU.

Radio Afrique Espoir: Carré 123, 03 BP 203, Porto-Novo; tel. 20-21-34-55; fax 20-21-32-63; e-mail afespoir@intnet.bj; Dir RAMANOU KOUFERIDJI.

Radio Carrefour: 03 BP 432, Cotonou; tel. 21-32-70-50; fax 22-51-16-55; e-mail chrisdavak@yahoo.fr; f. 1999; production and broadcast of radio and television programmes; Dir-Gen. CHRISTOPHE DAVAKAN.

Radio FM-Ahémé: BP 66, Bopa, Mono; tel. 95-05-58-18; f. 1997; informative, cultural and civic education broadcasts; Dir AMBROISE COKOU MOUSSOU.

Radio Immaculée Conception: BP 88, Allada; tel. 21-36-80-97; e-mail satric@immacolata.com; internet www.immacolata.com; operated by the Roman Catholic Church of Benin; broadcasts to Abomey, Allada, Bembéréke, Cotonou, Dassa-Zoume, Djougou and Parakou; Dir Fr ALFONSO BRUNO.

Radio Maranatha: 03 BP 4113, Cotonou; tel. and fax 21-32-58-82; e-mail maranatha.fm@serv.eit.bj; internet www.eit.to/RadioMaranatha.htm; operated by the Conseil des Eglises Protestantes Evangéliques du Bénin; Dir Rev. CLOVIS ALFRED KPADE.

Radio Planète: 02 BP 1528, Immeuble Master Soft, Cotonou; tel. 21-30-30-30; fax 21-30-24-51; internet www.planetefm.com; Dir JANVIER YAHOUEDEHOU.

Radio Solidarité FM: BP 135, Djougou; tel. 23-80-11-29; fax 23-80-15-63; Dir DAOUDA TAKPARA.

Radio Tokpa: Dantokpa, Cotonou; tel. 21314532; internet www.radiotokpa.net; Dir-Gen. GUY KPAKPO.

La Voix de la Lama: 03 BP 3772, Cotonou; tel. 21-37-12-26; fax 21-37-13-67; e-mail voix_delalama@yahoo.fr; f. 1998; non-commercial FM station, broadcasting on 103.8 Mhz from Allada; Dir SÉRAPHINE DADY.

La Voix de l'Islam: 08 BP 134, Cotonou; tel. 21-31-11-34; fax 21-31-51-79; e-mail islamben@leland.bj; operated by the Communauté musulmane de Zongo; Dir El Hadj MAMAN YARO.

Radio Wêkê: 05 BP 436, Cotonou; tel. 20-21-38-40; fax 20-21-37-14; e-mail issabadarou@hotmail.com; Promoter ISSA BADAROU-SOULÉ.

Benin also receives broadcasts from Africa No. 1, the British Broadcasting Corporation World Service and Radio France International.

Television

ORTB: (see Radio); Dir of Television STÉPHANE TODOME.

ATVS: BP 7101, Cotonou; tel. 21-31-43-19; owned by African Television System-Sobiex; Dir JACOB AKINOCHO.

LC2 Media (LC2): 05 BP 427, Cotonou; tel. 21-33-47-49; fax 21-33-46-75; e-mail lc2@lc2tv.com; internet www.lc2tv.com; commenced broadcasts 1997; CEO CHRISTIAN LAGNIDE; Man. NADINE LAGNIDE WOROU.

Telco: 44 ave Delorme, 01 BP 1241, Cotonou; tel. 21-31-34-98; e-mail telco@serv.eit.bj; relays 5 int. channels; Dir JOSEPH JÉBARA.

TV+ International/TV5: 01 BP 366, Cotonou; tel. 21-30-10-96; Dir CLAUDE KARAM.

Finance

(cap. = capital; res = reserves; dep. = deposits; m. = million; br(s). = branch(es); amounts in francs CFA)

BANKING

In 2009 there were 12 banks and one financial institution in Benin.

Central Bank

Banque centrale des états de l'Afrique de l'ouest (BCEAO): ave Jean-Paul II, BP 325, Cotonou; tel. 21-31-24-66; fax 21-31-24-65; e-mail akangni@bceao.int; internet www.bceao.int; HQ in Dakar, Senegal; f. 1962; bank of issue for the mem. states of the Union économique et monétaire ouest-africaine (UEMOA, comprising Benin, Burkina Faso, Côte d'Ivoire, Guinea-Bissau, Mali, Niger, Senegal and Togo); cap. 134,120m., res 1,474,195m., dep. 2,124,051m. (Dec. 2009); Gov. KONÉ TIÉMOKO MEYLIET; Dir in Benin ALAIN FAGNON KOUTANGNI; br. at Parakou.

Commercial Banks

Bank of Africa—Bénin (BOAB): ave Jean-Paul II, 08 BP 0879, Cotonou; tel. 21-31-32-28; fax 21-31-31-17; e-mail information@boabenin.com; internet www.boabenin.com; f. 1990; owned by BOA Group; cap. 9,000m., res 19,285m., dep. 429,487m. (Dec. 2009); Chair. PAULIN L. COSSI; Dir-Gen. CHEIKH TIDIANE N'DIAYE; 28 brs.

Banque Atlantique du Bénin: rue du Gouverneur Bayol, 08 BP 0682 Cotonou; tel. 21-31-10-18; fax 21-31-31-21; e-mail babn_support@banqueatlantique.net; internet www.banqueatlantique.net; cap. 6,500m., res –1,324m., dep. 74,079m. (2009); Chair. DOSSONGUI KONÉ; 6 brs.

Banque Internationale du Bénin (BIBE): carrefour des Trois Banques, ave Giran, 03 BP 2098, Jéricho, Cotonou; tel. 95-07-01-02; fax 21-31-23-65; e-mail bibedi@leland.bj; internet www.bibebank.net; f. 1989; owned by Nigerian commercial interests; cap. 9,000m., dep. 48,577m. (Dec. 2002); Chair. Dr G. A. T. OBOH; Man. Dir JEAN-PAUL K. AIDDO; 4 brs.

Continental Bank—Bénin (La Continentale): ave Jean-Paul II, carrefour des Trois Banques, 01 BP 2020, Cotonou; tel. 21-31-24-24; fax 21-31-51-77; e-mail contact@cbankbenin.com; f. 1993 to assume activities of Crédit Lyonnais Bénin; 43.61% state-owned; full transfer to private sector ownership proposed; cap. 3,600m., res 2,720m., dep. 43,407m. (Dec. 2007); Pres. FOGAN SOSSAH; Dir-Gen. GWEN OLOKÉ-ABIOLA; 13 brs.

Diamond Bank Bénin: 308 rue du Révérend Père Colineau, 01 BP 955, Cotonou; tel. 21-31-79-27; fax 21-31-79-33; e-mail info@benin.diamondbank.com; internet www.benin.diamondbank.com; f. 2001; 80% owned by Diamond Bank (Nigeria); cap. and res 1,939m., total assets 20,645m. (Dec. 2003); Chair. PASCAL GABRIEL DOZIE; Dir-Gen. BENEDICT IHEKIRE; 9 brs.

Ecobank Bénin: rue du Gouverneur Bayol, 01 BP 1280, Cotonou; tel. 21-31-40-23; fax 21-31-33-85; e-mail ecobankbj@ecobank.com; internet www.ecobank.com; f. 1989; 79% owned by Ecobank Transnational Inc (operating under the auspices of the Economic Community of West African States); total assets 600,067m., dep. 259,943.6m. (Dec. 2008); Pres., Chair. and Dir RAPHIOU TOUKOUROU; Man. Dir CHEIKH TRAVALY; 6 brs.

Orabank Bénin SA (FBB): ave du Gouverneur Général Ponty, 01 BP 2700, Cotonou; tel. 21-31-31-00; fax 21-31-31-02; e-mail secretariat.fbbj@financial-bank.com; internet benin.financial-bank.com; f. 1996; 93.18% owned by Oragroup (Togo), 5.11% owned by Caisse Nationale de Sécurité Sociale; cap. 2,500.0m., dep. 58,661.8m., total assets 61,862.0m. (Dec. 2006); Pres. GABRIEL OUSMANE MOUSSA; Dir-Gen. RIZWAN HAÏDER; 8 brs.

Finadev: ave du Commandant Decoeur, 01 BP 6335, Cotonou; tel. 21-31-40-81; fax 21-31-79-22; e-mail info.bj@finadev-groupe.com; f. 1998; 25% owned by Financial Bank Bénin, 25% owned by FMO (Netherlands); cap. and res 1,016.0m., total assets 6,254.6m. (Dec. 2005); Pres. RÉMY BAYSSET; Dir-Gen. CHRISTINE WESTERCAMP; 4 brs.

Société Générale de Banques au Bénin (SGBBE): ave Clozel, Quartier Ganhi, 01 BP 585, Cotonou; tel. 21-31-83-00; fax 21-31-82-95; e-mail hotline.sogebenin@socgen.com; internet www.sogebenin.com; f. 2002; 67% owned by Genefitec, a wholly owned subsidiary of Groupe Société Générale (France); cap. and res 2,044.0m., total assets 25,503.0m. (Dec. 2003); Pres. GILBERT MEDJE; Dir-Gen. CHRISTIAN METAUX; 4 brs.

Savings Bank

Caisse Nationale d'Epargne: Cadjèhoun, route Inter-Etat Cotonou-Lomé, Cotonou; tel. 21-30-18-35; fax 21-31-38-43; e-mail fdossou@opt.bj; internet www.cne.opt.bj; state-owned; cap. and res 948.0m., total assets 27,512.5m. (Dec. 2002); Pres. CHARLES PRODJINOTHO; Dir ZAKARI BOURAHIMA.

Credit Institutions

Crédit du Bénin: 08 BP 0936, Cotonou; tel. 21-31-30-02; fax 21-31-37-01; Man. Dir GILBERT HOUNKPAIN.

Crédit Promotion Bénin: 03 BP 1672, Cotonou; tel. 21-31-31-44; fax 21-31-31-66; wholly owned by private investors; cap. 150m., total assets 409m. (Dec. 1998); Pres. BERNARD ADIKPETO; Man. Dir DÉNIS OBA CHABI.

Equipbail Bénin: blvd Jean-Paul II, 08 BP 0690, Cotonou; tel. 21-31-11-45; fax 21-31-46-58; e-mail equip.be@bkofafrica.com; internet www.bkofafrica.net/equipbail.htm; f. 1995; 58.7% owned by Bank of Africa—Bénin; cap. and res 1,229.2m., total assets 5,966.3m. (Dec. 2006); Pres. PAUL DERREUMAUX.

Financial Institution

Caisse Autonome d'Amortissement du Bénin: BP 59, Cotonou; tel. 21-31-47-81; fax 21-31-53-56; e-mail caa@firstnet.bj; f. 1966; govt owned; manages state funds; Man. Dir ADAM DENDE AFFO.

STOCK EXCHANGE

Bourse Régionale des Valeurs Mobilières (BRVM): Antenne Nationale des Bourses du Bénin, Immeuble Chambre de Commerce et d'Industrie du Bénin, ave Charles de Gaulle, 01 BP 2985, Cotonou; tel. 21-31-21-26; fax 21-31-20-77; e-mail patioukpe@brvm.org; internet www.brvm.org; f. 1998; nat. branch of BRVM (regional stock exchange based in Abidjan, Côte d'Ivoire, serving the member states of UEMOA); Man. in Benin PAULINE ATIOUKPE.

INSURANCE

In 2008 there were 13 insurance companies in Benin.

Allianz Bénin Assurances: Carré 5, ave Delorme, 01 BP 5455, Cotonou; tel. 21-31-67-35; fax 21-31-67-34; e-mail allianz.benin@allianz-bj.com; internet www.allianz-africa.com/benin; f. 1998; Dir-Gen. CYRIL CHOPPIN DE JANVRY.

A&C Bénin: Carré 21, 01 BP 3758, ave Delorme, Cotonou; tel. 21-31-09-32; fax 21-31-08-70; e-mail info@acbenin.com; internet www.acbenin.com; f. 1996; broker specializing in all branches of insurance; Man. Dir JUSTIN HUBERT AGBOTON.

Africaine des Assurances: Place du Souvenir, 01 BP 3128, Cotonou; tel. 21-30-04-83; fax 21-30-14-06; e-mail assuraf@intnet.bj; internet www.africaine-assur.com; Pres. ANTOINE ZOUNON; Dir-Gen. VINCENT MAFORIKAN.

Africaine Vie Bénin: 01 BP 2040, Cotonou; tel. 21-30-39-93; fax 21-30-02-91; e-mail trmetinhoue@yahoo.fr; f. 2006; Dir-Gen. ROLAND MÊTINHOUÉ.

ASA Bénin: 01 BP 5508, Cotonou; tel. and fax 21-30-00-40; internet asabenin.org; fmrly Société Nationale d'Assurance; Sec.-Gen. ARMAND YEHOUENOU.

Assurances et Réassurance du Golfe de Guinée (ARGG): 04 BP 0851, Cadjehoun, Cotonou; tel. 21-30-56-43; fax 21-30-55-55; e-mail argg@intnet.bj; internet arggbenin.org; non-life insurance and re-insurance; Man. Dir PAULIN HOUECHENOU.

Avie Assurances: Immeuble Notre-Dame, ave Clozel, 01 BP 7061, Cotonou; tel. 21-31-83-55; fax 21-31-83-57; e-mail contact@avieassur.com; f. 2004; Dir-Gen. EVELYNE MARIE S. FASSINOU.

Colina Vie Bénin: Lot 636, Quartier Les Cocotiers, 04 BP 1419, Cotonou; tel. 21-30-85-23; fax 21-30-55-46; e-mail benin@groupecolina.com; Dir-Gen. MARIAM NASSIROU.

Fédérale d'Assurances (FEDAS): 01 BP 4201, Cotonou; tel. 21-31-56-77; fax 21-31-49-79; e-mail fedasbenin@yahoo.fr; f. 1998; Dir-Gen. FAISSOU ADEYEMAN.

Gras Savoye Bénin: Immeuble Aboki Hounkpehedji, 1er étage, ave Mgr Steinmetz, face de l'Immeuble Kougblenou, 01 BP 294 RP Cotonou; tel. 21-31-69-22; fax 21-31-69-79; e-mail gsbenin@leland.bj; affiliated to Gras Savoye (France); Man. GUY BIHANNIC.

Nouvelle Société Interafricaine d'Assurances du Bénin: Immeuble Kougblénou, ave Mgr Steinmetz, 08 BP 0258, Cotonou; tel. 21-31-33-69; fax 21-31-35-17; e-mail nsab@nsiabenin.com; f. 1997; Dir-Gen. ALAIN LATH HOUNGUE.

SOBAC: Carré 5, ave Delorme, 01 BP 544, Cotonou; tel. 21-31-67-35; fax 21-31-67-34; e-mail sobac@intnet.bj; affiliate of AGF (France).

Union Béninoise d'Assurance-Vie: Place du Souvenir, 08 BP 0322, Cotonou; tel. 21-30-02-12; fax 21-30-07-69; e-mail uba@ubavie.com; f. 1994; cap. 500m.; 53.5% owned by Groupe SUNU (France); Man. Dir VENANCE AMOUSSOUGA.

Trade and Industry

GOVERNMENT AGENCIES

Cellule des Opérations de Dénationalisation (COD): 02 BP 8140, Cotonou; tel. 21-31-59-18; fax 21-31-23-15; Co-ordinator VICTORIN DOSSOU-SOGNON.

Centre Béninois du Commerce Extérieur (CBCE): pl. du Souvenir, BP 1254, Cotonou; tel. 21-30-13-20; fax 21-30-04-36; e-mail cbce@bow.intnet.bj; internet www.cbce.africa-web.org; f. 1988; provides information to export cos.

Centre Béninois de la Recherche Scientifique et Technique (CBRST): 03 BP 1665, Cotonou; tel. 21-32-12-63; fax 21-32-36-71; e-mail cbrst@yahoo.fr; internet www.cbrst-benin.org; f. 1986; promotes scientific and technical research and training; 10 specialized research units; Dir-Gen. BIAOU FIDÈLE DIMON.

Centre de Promotion de l'Artisanat: à côté du Hall des Arts et de la Culture, 01 BP 2651, Cotonou; tel. 21-30-34-32; fax 21-30-34-91; e-mail cpainfos@ifrance.com; internet www.cpabenin.bj; f. 1987; Dir LATIFOU ALASSANE.

Centre de Promotion et d'Encadrement des Petites et Moyennes Entreprises (CEPEPE): face à la Mairie de Xlacondji, 01 BP 2093, Cotonou; tel. 21-31-22-61; fax 21-31-59-50; e-mail cepepe@firstnet.bj; internet www.cepepe.org; f. 1989; promotes business and employment; offers credits and grants to small businesses; undertakes management training and recruitment; publishes bi-monthly journal, *Initiatives*; Dir-Gen. THÉOPHILE CAPO-CHICHI.

Conseil d'Analyse Economique: Palais de la Marina, 01 BP 2028, Cotonou; tel. 21-30-08-07; fax 21-30-18.03; e-mail contact@caebenin.org; internet www.caebenin.org/web; f. 2006; Pres. FULBERT AMOUSSOUGA GERO.

Institut National de Recherches Agricoles du Bénin (INRAB): 01 BP 884, Cotonou; tel. 21-30-02-64; fax 21-30-37-70; e-mail inrabdg4@intnet.bj; internet www.inrab.bj.refer.org; f. 1992; undertakes research into agricultural improvements; publicizes advances in agriculture; Dir DAVID YAO ARODOKOUN.

Office Béninois de Recherches Géologiques et Minières (OBRGM): 04 BP 1412, Cotonou; tel. 21-31-03-09; fax 21-31-41-20; e-mail nestorved@yahoo.fr; internet www.energie.gouv.bj/obrgm/index.htm; f. 1996 as govt agency responsible for mining policy, exploitation and research; Dir-Gen. CYRIAQUE TOSSA.

Office National d'Appui à la Sécurité Alimentaire (ONASA): PK3, route de Porto-Novo, 06 BP 2544, Cotonou; tel. 21-33-15-02; fax 21-33-02-93; e-mail onasa@onasa.org; internet www.onasa.org; f. 1992; distribution of cereals; Pres. IMAROU SALÉ; Dir-Gen. IRENÉE BIO ABOUDOU.

Office National du Bois (ONAB): PK 3,5 route de Porto-Novo, 01 BP 1238, Cotonou; tel. 21-33-16-32; fax 21-33-39-83; e-mail contact@onab-benin.net; internet www.onab-benin.net; f. 1983; reorganized and partially privatized in 2002; forest devt and management, manufacture and marketing of wood products; industrial activities privatized in 2009; Dir-Gen. Dr CLEMENT KOUCHADE.

DEVELOPMENT ORGANIZATIONS

Agence Béninoise pour la Réconciliation et le Développement: 04 BP 0409, Cotonou; tel. 21-30-68-82; AMONKÈ AYICHATOU BEEN FAFOUMI.

Agence Française de Développement (AFD): blvd de France, 01 BP 38, Cotonou; tel. 21-31-35-80; fax 21-31-20-18; e-mail afdcotonou@groupe-afd.org; internet www.afd.fr; fmrly Caisse Française de Développement; Country Dir FULVIO MAZZEO.

France Volontaires: BP 344, Recette Principale, Cotonou; tel. 21-30-06-21; fax 21-30-07-78; e-mail afvpbn@intnet.bj; internet www.france-volontaires.org; f. 1964; name changed as above in 2009; Nat. Delegate RÉMI HALLEGOUËT.

Mission de Coopération et d'Action Culturelle (Mission Française d'Aide et de Coopération): BP 476, Cotonou; tel. 21-30-08-24; administers bilateral aid from France; Dir BERNARD HADJADJ.

Projet d'Appui au Développement des Micro-entreprises (PADME): C/647 Cadjehoun, rue de la Polyclinique les Cocotiers, 08 BP 712, Cotonou; tel. 21-30-30-47; fax 21-30-23-78; internet www.padmebenin.org; f. 1994; Dir-Gen. RENÉ AZOKLI.

SNV Bénin (Société Néerlandais de Développement): 01 BP 1048, Carré 107, Zone Résidentielle, Rue du PNUD, Cotonou; tel. 21-31-21-22; fax 21-31-35-59; e-mail benin@snvworld.org; internet www.snvbenin.bj; Country Dir DELLAPHINE B. RAUCH-HOUEKPON.

CHAMBER OF COMMERCE

Chambre de Commerce et d'Industrie du Bénin (CCIB): ave du Général de Gaulle, 01 BP 31, Cotonou; tel. 21-31-20-81; fax 21-31-32-99; e-mail ccib@bow.intnet.bj; internet www.ccibenin.org; f. 1908; present name adopted 1962; Pres. ATAOU SOUFIANO; brs at Parakou, Mono-Zou, Natitingou and Porto-Novo.

EMPLOYERS' ORGANIZATIONS

Conseil National des Chargeurs du Bénin (CNCB): 06 BP 2528, Cotonou; tel. 21-31-59-47; fax 21-31-59-60; e-mail cncb@intnet.bj; internet www.cncbenin.com; f. 1983; represents interests of shippers; Dir-Gen. PIERRE GANSARÉ.

Conseil National du Patronat du Bénin (CNP–Bénin): 01 BP 1260, Cotonou; tel. 21-30-74-06; fax 21-30-83-22; e-mail cnpbenin@yahoo.fr; internet www.cnpbenin.org; f. 1984 as Organisation Nationale des Employeurs du Bénin; Pres. SÉBASTIEN AJAVON; Sec.-Gen. VICTOR FAKEYE.

Fédération des Unions de Producteurs du Bénin (FUPRO): Route Nationale 2, SACLO, BP 372, Bohicon; tel. 51-07-00; fax 51-09-46; e-mail fuproben@leland.bj; internet www.fuproben.org; Pres. LÉPOLD LOKOSSOU; Sec.-Gen. JACQUES DJIMA BONOU.

Fondation de l'Entrepreneurship du Bénin (FEB): pl. du Québec, 08 BP 1155, Cotonou; tel. 21-31-35-37; fax 21-31-37-26; e-mail fonda@intnet.bj; internet www.placequebec.org; non profit-making org.; encourages the devt of the private sector and of small and medium-sized businesses; Dir PIERRE DOVONOU LOKOSSOU.

Syndicat National des Commerçants et Industriels Africains du Bénin (SYNACIB): BP 367, Cotonou; Pres. URBAIN DA SILVA.

UTILITIES

Communauté Electrique du Bénin (CEB): Vedoko, BP 537, Cotonou; tel. 21-30-06-75; f. 1968; jt venture between Benin and Togo to exploit energy resources in the 2 countries; Dir-Gen. DJIBRIL SALIFOU.

Société Béninoise d'Énergie Électrique (SBEE): 01 BP 2047, Cotonou; tel. 21-31-21-45; fax 21-31-50-28; f. 1973; state-owned; production and distribution of electricity and water; separation of electricity and water sectors pending, prior to proposed privatization of electricity operations; Dir-Gen. MARIUS Z. HOUNKPATIN.

Société Nationale des Eaux du Bénin (SONEB): 92 ave Pope Jean-Paul II, 216 RP Cotonou; tel. 21-31-20-60; fax 21-31-11-08; e-mail info@soneb.com; internet www.soneb.com; f. 2003 to assume water activities of Société Béninoise d'Electricité et d'Eau; operates under supervision of Ministry responsible for water resources; utilises about 60 systems of drinkable water adductions, feeding 69 municipalities; Pres. EMILE LOUIS PARAÏSO; Dir-Gen. ADRIEN TODOMÈ DOSSOU.

TRADE UNIONS

Centrale Syndicale des Travailleurs du Bénin (CSTB): 03 BP 0989, Cotonou; tel. 21-30-13-15; fax 21-33-26-01; actively opposes privatization and the influence of the international financial community; linked to the Parti Communiste du Bénin; Sec.-Gen. GASTON AZOUA.

Centrale des Syndicats Autonomes du Bénin (CSA—Bénin): 1 Blvd St Michel, Bourse du Travail, 04 BP 1115, Cotonou; tel. 21-30-31-82; fax 21-30-23-59; e-mail csabenin@intnet.bj; internet csa-benin.org; principally active in private sector enterprises; Sec.-Gen. DIEUDONNÉ LOKOSSOU.

Centrale des Syndicats du Secteur Privé et Informel du Bénin (CSPIB): 03 BP 2961, Cotonou; tel. 21-33-53-53; Sec.-Gen. CHRISTOPHE C. DOVONON.

Centrale des Syndicats Unis du Bénin (CSUB): Cotonou; tel. 21-33-10-27; Sec.-Gen. JEAN SOUROU AGOSSOU.

Confédération Générale des Travailleurs du Bénin (CGTB): 06 BP 2449, Cotonou; tel. 21-31-73-11; fax 21-31-73-10; e-mail cgtbpdd@bow.intnet.bj; principally active in public administration; Sec.-Gen. PASCAL TODJINOU; 33,275 mems (2002).

Confédération des Organisations Syndicales Indépendantes du Bénin (COSI—Benin): Bourse du Travail, 03 BP 1218, Cotonou; tel. 21-30-39-65; fax 21-33-27-82; e-mail cosibenin@intnet.bj; Sec.-Gen. GOERGES KAKAÏ GLELE.

Union Nationale des Syndicats de Travailleurs du Bénin (UNSTB): 1 blvd Saint-Michel, BP 69, Recette Principale, Cotonou; tel. and fax 21-30-36-13; e-mail unstb@unstb.org; internet www.unstb.org; principally active in public administration; sole officially recognized trade union 1974–90; 40,000 members in 2005, of which 25,000 in the informal sector; Sec.-Gen. EMMANUEL ZOUNON.

Transport

RAILWAYS

In 2006 there were 758 km of railway track in operation. There are plans to extend the 438-km Cotonou–Parakou line to Dosso, Niger.

Organisation Commune Bénin-Niger des Chemins de Fer et des Transports (OCBN): BP 16, Cotonou; tel. 21-31-28-57; fax 21-31-41-50; e-mail ocbn@intnet.bj; f. 1959; 50% owned by Govt of Benin, 50% by Govt of Niger; total of 579 track-km; main line runs for 438 km from Cotonou to Parakou in the interior; br. line runs westward via Ouidah to Segboroué (34 km); also line of 107 km from Cotonou via Porto-Novo to Pobé (near the Nigerian border); extension to the Republic of Niger proposed; Dir-Gen. RIGOBERT AZON.

ROADS

In 2011 there were some 30,000 km of roads, including 1,823 km of paved roads.

Agence Générale de Transit et de Consignation (AGETRAC): blvd Maritime, BP 1933, Cotonou; tel. 21-31-32-22; fax 21-31-29-69; e-mail agetrac@leland.bj; f. 1967; goods transportation and warehousing.

Compagnie de Transit et de Consignation du Bénin (CTCB Express): Cotonou; f. 1986; Pres. SOULÉMAN KOURA ZOUMAROU.

Fonds Routier du Bénin: Cotonou; internet www.fondsroutier.bj; Dir-Gen. SYLVESTRE KOCHOFA.

SHIPPING

The main port is at Cotonou. In 2006 the port handled some 5.4m. metric tons of goods. In 2009 the merchant fleet of Benin comprised seven vessels, with a total displacement of 1,271 grt.

Port Autonome de Cotonou (PAC): BP 927, Cotonou; tel. 21-31-28-90; fax 21-31-28-91; e-mail pac@leland.bj; internet www.portdecotonou.com; f. 1965; state-owned port authority; Dir-Gen. JOSEPH AHANHANZO.

Association pour la Défense des Intérêts du Port de Cotonou (AIPC) (Communauté Portuaire du Bénin): Port Autonome de Cotonou; tel. 21-31-17-26; fax 21-31-28-91; f. 1993; promotes, develops and co-ordinates port activities at Cotonou; Pres. ISSA BADAROU-SOULÉ; Sec.-Gen. CAMILLE MÉDÉGAN.

Compagnie Béninoise de Navigation Maritime (COBENAM): pl. Ganhi, 01 BP 2032, Cotonou; tel. 21-31-27-96; fax 21-31-09-78; e-mail cobenam@elodia.intnet.bj; f. 1974 by Govts of Algeria and Dahomey (now Benin); 100% state-owned; Pres. ABDEL KADER ALLAL; Man. Dir ARMAND PRIVAT KANDISSOUNON.

Maersk Bénin: Maersk House, Zone OCBN Lot 531, Parcelle B, 01 BP 2826, Cotonou; tel. 21-31-39-93; fax 21-31-56-60; e-mail coocuscal@maersk.com; internet www.maerskline.com/bj; subsidiary of Maersk Line (Denmark); Dir DAVID SKOV.

SDV Bénin: route du Collège de l'Union, Akpakpa, 01 BP 433, Cotonou; tel. 21-31-21-19; fax 21-31-59-26; e-mail sdvbenin@bow.intnet.bj; f. 1986; affiliated to SDV Group (France); Pres. J. F. MIGNONNEAU; Dir-Gen. R. PH. RANJARD.

Société Béninoise d'Entreprises Maritimes (SBEM): BP 1733, Cotonou; tel. 21-31-23-57; fax 21-31-59-26; warehousing, storage and transportation; Dir RÉGIS TISSER.

Société Béninoise des Manutentions Portuaires (SOBEMAP): blvd de la Marina, BP 35, Cotonou; tel. 21-31-41-45; fax 21-31-53-71; e-mail infos@sobemap.com; internet www.sobemap.com; f. 1969; state-owned; Dir-Gen. SOUMANOU SÉIBOU TOLÉBA.

Société Béninoise Maritime (SOBEMAR): Carré 8, Cruintomé, 08 BP 0956, Cotonou; tel. 21-31-49-65; fax 21-31-52-51; e-mail adm@sobemar-benin.com; internet www.navitrans.fr; f. 1992; Pres. RODOLPHE TORTORA.

CIVIL AVIATION

There is an international airport at Cotonou-Cadjehoun and there are secondary airports at Parakou, Natitingou, Kandi, Savè, Porga and Djougou.

Aviation Civile du Bénin: 01 BP 305, Cotonou; tel. 21-30-92-17; fax 21-30-45-71; e-mail anacaero@anac.bj; internet www.anac.bj; Dir-Gen. ARISTIDE DE SOUZA.

Trans Air Bénin (TAB): ave Jean Paul II, Lot No 14, Les Cocotiers, Cotonou; tel. 21-00-61-65; fax 21-30-92-75; e-mail transairbenin@aol.com; f. 2000; regional flights; Dir BRICE KIKI.

Tourism

Benin's rich cultural diversity and its national parks and game reserves are the principal tourist attractions. About 188,000 tourists visited Benin in 2008. Receipts from tourism were estimated at US $216.0m. in that year.

Direction de la Promotion et des Professions Touristiques: BP 2037, Cotonou; tel. 21-32-68-24; fax 21-32-68-23; internet www.benintourism.com.

Defence

As assessed at November 2011, the Beninois Armed Forces numbered an estimated 4,750 active personnel (land army 4,300, navy about 200, air force 250). Paramilitary forces comprised a 2,500-strong gendarmerie. Military service is by selective conscription, and lasts for 18 months.

Defence Expenditure: Estimated at 34,900m. francs CFA in 2011.

Chief of Defence Staff: Brig.-Gen. CHABI A. BONI.

Chief of Staff of the Army: Col DOMINIQUE M. AHOUANDJINOU.

Chief of Staff of the Navy: Capt. FERNAND MAXIME AHOYO.

Chief of Staff of the Air Force: Col CAMILLE MICHODJEHOUN.

Education

The Constitution of Benin obliges the state to make a quality compulsory primary education available to all children. Primary education was declared free of charge in 2006. Primary education begins at six years of age and lasts for six years. Secondary education, beginning at 12 years of age, lasts for up to seven years, comprising a first cycle of four years and a second of three years. According to UNESCO estimates, primary enrolment in 2009/10 included 94% of children in the appropriate age-group, while enrolment at secondary schools in 2000/01 included 20% of children in the appropriate age-group (males 26%; females 13%). In the 1990s the Government sought to extend the provision of education. In 1993 girls in rural areas were exempted from school fees, and in 1999 the Government created a 500m. francs CFA fund to increase female enrolment. The Université Nationale du Bénin, at Cotonou, was founded in 1970 and a second university, in Parakou, opened in 2001. In 2005/06 a total of 42,600 students were enrolled at tertiary education institutes. According to UNESCO estimates, in 2007 spending on education represented 15.9% of total budgeted government expenditure.

BHUTAN

Introductory Survey

LOCATION, CLIMATE, LANGUAGE, RELIGION, FLAG, CAPITAL

The Kingdom of Bhutan lies in the Himalaya range of mountains, with Tibet (the Xizang Autonomous Region), part of the People's Republic of China, to the north and India to the south. The average monthly temperature ranges from 4.4°C (40°F) in January to 17°C (62°F) in July. Rainfall is heavy, ranging from 150 cm (60 ins) to 300 cm (120 ins) per year. The official language is Dzongkha, spoken mainly in western Bhutan. Written Dzongkha is based on the Tibetan script. The state religion is Mahayana Buddhism, primarily the Drukpa school of the Kagyupa sect, although Nepalese settlers, who comprise about one-quarter of the country's total population, practise Hinduism. The Nepali-speaking Hindus dominate southern Bhutan and are referred to as southern Bhutanese. The national flag (proportions 2 by 3) is divided diagonally from the lower hoist to the upper fly, so forming two triangles, one yellow and the other orange, with a white dragon superimposed in the centre. The capital is Thimphu.

CONTEMPORARY POLITICAL HISTORY

Historical Context

Following decades of domestic strife and warfare, the first hereditary King of Bhutan was installed in December 1907. An Anglo-Bhutanese Treaty, signed in 1910, placed Bhutan's foreign relations under the supervision of the Government of British India. After India became independent, this treaty was replaced in August 1949 by the Indo-Bhutan Treaty of Friendship, whereby Bhutan agreed to seek the advice of the Government of India with regard to its foreign relations but remained free to decide whether or not to accept such advice. King Jigme Dorji Wangchuck, who was installed in 1952, established the National Assembly (tshogdu chenmo) in 1953 and a Royal Advisory Council (lodoi tsokde) in 1965. He formed the country's first Council of Ministers (lhengye zhungtshog) in 1968. Bhutan became a member of the UN in 1971 and of the Non-aligned Movement in 1973.

King Jigme Dorji Wangchuck died in 1972 and was succeeded by the Western-educated, 16-year-old Crown Prince, Jigme Singye Wangchuck. The new King introduced the concept of 'Gross National Happiness' (GNH) to his country, a measure of Bhutan's prosperity that sought to balance material progress with spiritual well-being; the four pillars of GNH were defined as the promotion of sustainable development, the preservation and promotion of cultural values, the conservation of the natural environment and the establishment of good governance. He also stated his wish to preserve the Indo-Bhutan Treaty and further to strengthen friendship with India. In 1979, however, during the Non-aligned Conference and later at the UN General Assembly, Bhutan voted in opposition to India, in favour of Chinese policy. In 1983 India and Bhutan signed a new trade agreement concerning overland trade with Bangladesh and Nepal. India raised no objection to Bhutan's decision to negotiate directly with the People's Republic of China over the Bhutan–China border, and discussions between Bhutan and China were begun in 1984 (see below).

When Chinese authority was established in Tibet (Xizang) in 1959, Bhutan granted asylum to more than 6,000 Tibetan refugees. As a result of allegations that many refugees were engaged in spying and subversive activities, the Bhutanese Government decided in 1976 to disperse them in small groups, introducing a number of Bhutanese families into each settlement. In June 1979 the National Assembly approved a directive establishing the end of the year as a time limit for the refugees to decide whether to acquire Bhutanese citizenship or accept repatriation to Tibet. By September 1985 most of the Tibetans had chosen Bhutanese citizenship, and the remainder were to be accepted by India. A revised Citizenship Act, adopted by the National Assembly in 1985, confirmed residence in Bhutan in 1958 as a fundamental basis for automatic citizenship (as provided for by the 1958 Nationality Act), but this was to be interpreted flexibly. Provision was also made for citizenship by registration for Nepalese immigrants who had resided in the country for at least 20 years (15 years if employed by the Government) and who could meet linguistic and other tests of commitment to the Bhutanese community.

Domestic Political Affairs

Important institutional changes were introduced in mid-1998, whereby King Jigme relinquished his role as head of government (while remaining Head of State) in favour of a smaller elected Council of Ministers, which was to enjoy full executive power under the leadership of a Chairman (elected by ministers, on a rotational basis, for a one-year term in office) who would be head of government. An act to regulate the Council of Ministers was presented to the National Assembly in mid-1999 and was subjected to extensive discussion and amendment. The rules as finally endorsed explicitly specified that the King had full power to dissolve the Council of Ministers.

At the 11th summit of the South Asian Association for Regional Cooperation (SAARC, see p. 420), held in Kathmandu, Nepal, in January 2002, the incumbent Chairman of the Council of Ministers, Lyonpo Khandu Wangchuk, was referred to as 'Prime Minister' of Bhutan, a title that subsequently became accepted usage. In accordance with a decree issued by King Jigme in September 2001, a committee to draft a written constitution for Bhutan was inaugurated in November. The 39-member committee was chaired by the Chief Justice and included the Chairman and members of the Royal Advisory Council, five government representatives, the Speaker of the National Assembly, representatives from each of the 20 local districts and two lawyers from the High Court. In December 2002 the preliminary draft of the constitution was presented by the committee to King Jigme; the King subsequently referred the draft to the Prime Minister for further scrutiny, envisaging widespread public debate. In November 2004 King Jigme presented a fourth draft of the proposed constitution to the Council of Ministers for discussion; the 34-article draft was made available for public review in March 2005.

Meanwhile, the creation of four new ministerial positions (as part of a general reorganization of ministries) was announced in June 2003, bringing the total number of ministers to 10. In October 2004 the Crown Prince, Dasho Jigme Khesar Namgyel Wangchuck, was formally installed as the chhoetse penlop (heir to the throne) at a ceremony held at the Trongsa Dzong Buddhist monastery. In December a ban on sales of tobacco throughout the kingdom came into effect, making Bhutan the first country in the world to declare such a policy. Imports of tobacco were permitted for private consumption, although these attracted a duty of between 100%–200%, depending on the country of origin. In February 2005 a complete ban on smoking in public places was announced. In December King Jigme announced that he intended to abdicate in favour of his son in 2008, the year in which Bhutan intended to hold its first national elections under the provisions of its new constitution. Meanwhile, appointments to the country's first constitutional posts were announced at the end of 2005, in advance of the document's formal adoption. Dasho Kuenzang Wangdi became the country's first Chief Election Commissioner, while an Anti-Corruption Commission was also created.

The fifth draft of the Constitution, which was published in August 2005, provided for, among other things: the establishment of a democratic constitutional monarchy in accordance with the principle of hereditary succession; the establishment of a parliament consisting of the monarch, a 25-member National Council (upper house) and a 47-member National Assembly (lower house), with members of the latter body to be elected by universal secret ballot from constituencies with approximately equivalent populations; and for two political parties to be represented in the National Assembly, the election campaigns of which would be funded by the State. Within the National Council, 20 members—one representing each of the 20 electoral districts—were to be directly elected by a national vote, with the remaining five 'eminent members' to be selected by royal appointment.

In September 2006 the incumbent Minister of Foreign Affairs, Lyonpo Khandu Wangchuk, succeeded Lyonpo Sangay Ngedup as Prime Minister of Bhutan. Later in the month Chief Election Commissioner Wangdi announced that all registered parties would be able to contest the first round of the 2008 general election, following which the two parties with the largest number of votes would compete for parliamentary seats in the second and third rounds. A draft list of about 400,000 potential voters had already been prepared and electoral registration forms were subsequently sent out. In January 2007 it was announced that 'mock' elections would be held: the first round took place on 21 April, and was followed by a second stage on 28 May. In March details were announced of the 47 constituencies for the National Assembly. Meanwhile, on 9 December 2006 King Jigme issued a kasho (a royal decree) in which he formally transferred his responsibilities as Head of State to Crown Prince Jigme Khesar Namgyel, who succeeded to the throne on 21 December. In his first public speech King Jigme Khesar promised to continue on the path towards the establishment of parliamentary democracy.

In June 2007 the King instructed the Chief Election Commissioner to conduct elections for the National Council in December of that year, a primary round for the National Assembly in February 2008, and a general election for the Assembly in March 2008. The Election Commission declared itself open to receive party nominations from 1 July 2007. In that month the Prime Minister and Minister of Foreign Affairs, Lyonchhen Khandu Wangchuk, tendered the resignation of himself and six other ministers prior to joining the political process. Lyonpo Kinzang Dorji, hitherto Minister of Works and Human Settlement, assumed the role of Prime Minister at the head of a greatly diminished Council of Ministers. The National Assembly was dissolved on 31 July, and, prompted by the depleted status of the Council of Ministers, from August the Royal Advisory Council similarly stood dissolved, in advance of the proposed October termination, in preparation for the inauguration of the new governmental structure.

Candidates in the National Council elections campaigned without party affiliation, and the Election Commission ruled that only university graduates from approved institutions were eligible to stand. The latter restriction meant that the requisite minimum of two candidates was not available in five electoral districts before the date of the election, 31 December 2007. Consequently, a second stage of voting was held in these districts on 29 January 2008. Overall, some 53% of registered voters participated in the ballot. The 20 successful candidates, four of whom were women, were to serve five-year terms. An additional five members of the National Council were to be appointed by the King.

By January 2008 only two parties had successfully registered with the Election Commission ahead of elections to the National Assembly—the Druk Phuensum Tshogpa (DPT), led by former Prime Minister and Minister of Home and Cultural Affairs Lyonpo Jigmi Yozer Thinley, and the People's Democratic Party (PDP), headed by former Prime Minister and Minister of Agriculture Lyonpo Sangay Ngedup. A third party, the recently formed Bhutan National Party, had its application for registration cancelled, while the application of the Bhutan People's United Party (established by a breakaway faction of the DPT) was rejected by the Election Commission in November 2007. Consequently, the Commission announced that elections to the new National Assembly would be completed in one day (rather than in two rounds as originally envisaged) and the election date was set as 24 March 2008.

A series of bomb blasts occurred in Bhutan in January and February 2008. On 20 January four bombs were detonated in different locations, including one in the capital Thimphu, and a further explosion occurred behind a government office in Samtse district on 4 February. No one was seriously hurt in the incidents. Leaflets of the Bhutan Communist Party (Marxist-Leninist-Maoist) (BCP—MLM) were recovered from the site of the February explosion, and police subsequently raided two training camps in southern Bhutan and arrested eight members of the party, which officials believed was attempting to disrupt preparations for the general election. A group entitled the United Revolutionary Front of Bhutan (URFB), which had reportedly been established in April 2007 and was believed to be the military wing of the BCP—MLM, claimed responsibility for the series of bomb blasts in January 2008. The URFB also stated that it was responsible for a bomb explosion in the Sarpang district in late December which killed four Bhutanese forest guards.

Democratic elections and a new Constitution

The DPT won an overwhelming majority in the elections to the National Assembly, which were held as scheduled on 24 March 2008, securing 45 of the 47 legislative seats and 67% of valid votes cast, while the PDP, the only other party contesting the ballot, won a mere two seats (despite almost universal expectation that representation would be roughly evenly split). Voter turn-out was high, with 79.4% of the electorate participating in the polling. Lyonpo Jigmi Yozer Thinley was subsequently nominated as Prime Minister by the DPT, and his premiership was endorsed by the King on 9 April. The new Council of Ministers was installed two days later and included key appointments for a number of former ministers: Khandu Wangchuk, who had previously served two terms as Prime Minister, was appointed Minister of Economic Affairs, while the finance portfolio was assigned to Wangdi Norbu, who had formerly held the same post. Ugyen Tshering and Yeshey Zimba were appointed as Minister of Foreign Affairs and Minister of Works and Human Settlement, respectively. The opening session of the first Parliament of Bhutan was inaugurated as a joint session of the National Assembly and the National Council on 8 May, and it concluded on 29 July. The draft Constitution was debated throughout May, and was formally signed on 18 July. After agreement on the Constitution, the bicameral Parliament discussed six bills, which were eventually adopted as the National Council Act, the National Assembly Act, the Election Act, the Election Fund Act, the Parliamentary Entitlements Act and the National Referendum Act. The Parliament also approved the 2008/09 national budget, as well as agreements for the establishment of a SAARC food bank and a South Asia University.

The formal coronation of Jigme Khesar Namgyel Wangchuck as the fifth hereditary king of Bhutan took place in Thimphu on 6 November 2008, and was attended by hundreds of foreign dignitaries, including the President of India.

The second session of the Bhutanese National Assembly was held in December 2008–January 2009 (the National Council met concurrently but separately). The Assembly confirmed that a government sub-committee (which had already been established and which was composed of the ministers of education, foreign affairs, and home and cultural affairs) should be responsible for reviewing the security clearance certificate (SCC) issue. It was widely agreed that security should be given priority in light of the 2008 bomb blasts in the south of the country. (It was subsequently reported that the Royal Bhutan Police were planning to establish an élite special forces counter-terrorism unit.) In September 2009, as part of the country's ongoing programme of decentralization and devolution of power, the Local Government Act of Bhutan was approved by Parliament. The Act established 20 dzongkhag tshogdus (district councils) to function as the highest decision-making body in each of Bhutan's dzongkhags. The dzongkhag tshogdus, which were ultimately to be under the authority of the Ministry of Home and Cultural Affairs, were to be assigned a variety of tasks, including the promotion of local business, the preservation of culture and tradition, the protection of public health, the coordination of government agency activities, and the review of local government regulations and ordinances. The dzongkhag tshogdus were also to be responsible for the supervision of the dzongdas (district officers), who are appointed by the Royal Civil Service Commission and act as the chief executive of each dzongkhag.

In September 2009 six districts in eastern Bhutan were struck by a powerful earthquake which killed 12 people and seriously damaged more than 6,000 homes and public buildings.

Recent developments

In June 2010 the Minister of Finance announced the introduction of additional taxes in his budget address to the National Assembly. The Opposition Leader, Tshering Tobgay, objecting to the Minister's attempt to implement the tax measures without allowing the Assembly to discuss and vote on the proposals, instigated a legal challenge against the Government. The case, which was heard in the Thimphu High Court, represented Bhutan's first constitutional court case. The High Court ruled that the Government was in violation of constitutional procedures by not introducing the revised tax schedule as a money bill subject to discussion and vote. The Government appealed to the Supreme Court, which, in February 2011, upheld and revised the lower court's decision. In March those who had paid additional taxes were invited to apply for refunds.

In December 2010 the Council of Ministers approved plans for Bhutan's full accession to the International Labour Organization; it was hoped that membership would enable the country to gain access to technical assistance covering a variety of labour and market issues.

The Tobacco Control Act, which was passed by an overwhelming majority of Assembly members in June 2010, came into effect in January 2011; the Act resolved several implementation problems arising from the 2005 ban on smoking in public places. Personal possession and use of tobacco products was allowed, under conditions, but only on production of a customs receipt (valid for one month) to show legal and duty-paid acquisition. The Act laid down mandatory prison terms for possession of unauthorized products (which were regarded as having been smuggled). In early 2011 the case of a 23-year-old monk, who was apprehended with 48 packets of chewing tobacco and subsequently sentenced to three years' imprisonment (the lightest penalty permissible), provoked a major outcry; the accused claimed ignorance of the Act and stated that the tobacco was for personal consumption.

In February 2010 the King issued a kasho establishing the Bhutan Media Foundation (BMF), which was supported by an initial royal grant of Nu 15m. The BMF was created to strengthen Bhutanese media through training aided by scholarships. It was also expected to promote the readership of printed media through subscription grants, the publication of dzongkhag-level (i.e. local) editions of newspapers, and the functioning of journalists' associations and press clubs. The BMF was inaugurated in March 2011. In February the Kidu Foundation was established under the patronage of the King, with the stated goal of 'complementing' the Government's efforts in the development of education, the rule of law, democracy, the media, environmental protection and cultural heritage. The Foundation was to be funded by voluntary donations; the Government of India announced a contribution of Rs 150m. to support its launch. These initiatives were regarded by some observers as the gradual development of a separate administration, centred on the King, in parallel to the elected DPT Government, which undermined the principles of Bhutan's fledgling democracy. However, others saw these developments as a reflection of the expected leadership role of the monarch in helping to strengthen institutions in contemporary Bhutan.

In 2011 Bhutan's first democratic local government elections (which were originally scheduled to be held in 2008) took place, on a non-party-membership basis, throughout the country. The polling was to appoint officials to the lower levels of local government—the gewog tshogdes (village councils) and the thromdes (mayoralties). In January elections were completed for the mayoralties of four large towns (Thimphu, Phuentsholing, Samdrup Jongkhar and Gelephu), after issues with residence qualifications and a shortage of qualified candidates were resolved. (All candidates were required to pass functional literacy and administrative skills tests.) Further local elections took place nation-wide in late June 2011, following the long-delayed confirmation of local government electoral boundaries. The Election Commission reported that around 56% of the electorate had participated in the polling, which, according to official observers, was conducted in a peaceful and proper manner. Although some 1,104 representatives were elected to various lower levels of local government, owing to a general lack of eligible candidates, a total of 373 positions remained vacant after the elections. Comprehensive local government polls—including elections to the 20 recently created dzongkhag tshogdus—were declared by the Election Commission to be possible only after 2013 (i.e. after the next parliamentary election). In January 2012 it was reported that a new political party, the Social Democratic Party (SDP), had been established; the SDP was mainly composed of former PDP members and civil servants and was led by Dr Tandin Dorji (himself an erstwhile member of the PDP). According to the Election Commission, another two new political parties (one of which was named as the Druk Mitsher Tshogpa) were in the process of registering.

Meanwhile, on 13 October 2011 the highly popular King Jigme Khesar married a Bhutanese commoner, Jetsun Pema, in an elaborate Buddhist ceremony at a monastic fortress in Punakha. Following their marriage, the young couple embarked on a nine-day state visit to India.

In a move that was widely viewed as a vital step towards the establishment of good governance and accountability, a Right to Information bill was submitted to the National Council in March 2012 and was scheduled to be presented for discussion in May.

Assamese Militancy

By mid-1998 the most pressing security issue confronting the country was the perceived threat from the presence of Assamese (Asomese) tribal (Bodo) and Maoist (United Liberation Front of Assam—ULFA) militants from India, who had established military training bases in the jungle border regions of south-eastern Bhutan. Concern was expressed regarding a brief Indian military incursion into Bhutanese territory in a raid on suspected militants (for which the Government of India subsequently apologized). In mid-1999 the Bhutanese Minister of Home Affairs reported that recent talks with ULFA leaders had elicited the response that members of the ULFA had been forced to enter Bhutanese territory in 1992, but that they were not ready to leave Bhutan for at least another 18 months. They asserted that they were determined to fight until independence for Assam (Asom), India, was achieved, but offered to reduce their military presence in Bhutan. After detailed discussion, assembly members decided that all supplies of food and other essentials to the ULFA and National Democratic Front of Bodoland (NDFB) must be stopped, that any Bhutanese who assisted the militants should be punished according to the National Security Act, and that discussions should continue with the ULFA to seek a peaceful withdrawal of these forces from Bhutan. In July 2000 the National Assembly adopted a resolution stating that the problem should be solved through peaceful means, but that if negotiations failed military force should be used to evict the insurgents from Bhutanese territory. Some groups of militants began to return to India. However, most ULFA and Bodo militants, who had hitherto refrained from carrying out violent activities in Bhutan, were angered by the Assembly's decision. In December some 13 people were killed when members of the Bodo Liberation Tigers (a group allegedly supported by the Indian security forces) attacked a convoy of Bhutanese vehicles on the Bhutan–India border. The act was perceived as a warning to the Bhutanese Government not to shelter ULFA and NDFB militants.

Following discussions in June 2001, representatives of the ULFA agreed to seven points, including the removal of four of their nine military camps in Bhutan by December 2001 and the reduction in strength of the cadres in the remaining camps. In late December the Royal Bhutan Army (RBA) confirmed that the four designated ULFA camps had been abandoned. Initially, however, the whereabouts of the militants was unknown and there were concerns that they had repositioned their camps elsewhere in Bhutan. In mid-2002 it was reported that the ULFA had opened a new camp on a mountain ridge above the main Samdrup Jongkhar–Trashigang highway. In the mean time, the NDFB had three main camps and four mobile camps between Lhamoizingkha and Daifam. The Minister of Home Affairs also reported that the Indian militant Kamtapur Liberation Organization (KLO) had established camps in Bhangtar sub-district (dungkhag) and near Piping in Lhamoizingkha sub-district. The KLO armed militants were Rajbansi tribals of north Bengal, India, bordering Chhukha and Samtse districts, who were campaigning for separate statehood for the Kamtapuris. The Minister of Home Affairs stressed that the presence of armed militants in Bhutan remained a grave threat.

In mid-2003 the ULFA was reported to have increased its total number of camps inside Bhutan to eight, with an estimated 1,560 militants; the NDFB had eight camps, with about 740 militants; and the KLO had three camps in Bhutan, with an estimated 430 militants. The Council of Ministers approved a contingency budget of up to Nu 2,000m. in the event of military action. King Jigme informed the Assembly that India had given its assurance that the Indian army would not enter Bhutan without the permission of the Council of Ministers and the National Assembly. The Bhutanese Government subsequently made further efforts to seek a peaceful resolution to the issue by directly addressing the three armed groups. However, negotiations with representatives of the ULFA and of the NDFB in the latter half of 2003 proved fruitless, while the KLO continued to fail to respond to any initiatives taken by the Bhutanese Government.

A 48-hour notice to leave Bhutan, issued to the militants by the Government on 13 December 2003, went unheeded. Accordingly, on 15 December the RBA launched simultaneous attacks on most of the training camps (which now totalled 30), concentrating on the elimination of the general headquarters of the ULFA. By the end of the month the Government reported that all of the camps had been captured and destroyed (14 of the camps belonged to the ULFA, the NDFB operated 11 camps and the KLO had five camps). Large quantities of armaments and ammunition were seized during the operation. In February 2004 the Chief of Staff of the Indian Army stated that the offensive, which had resulted in the deaths of at least 420 insurgents, had been highly successful. In March it was reported that the RBA had launched another offensive against the remaining militants. In September a bomb explosion in Gelephu killed two people (both of Indian nationality) and injured a further 27; the NDFB was believed to have been responsible for the attack. Meanwhile, more than 100 people in a number of locations in Bhutan were convicted of aiding and abetting the insurgents and were sentenced to prison terms of various lengths. However, in late 2008 the Assam police force expressed its concern that the militants had re-established camps in southern Bhutan, after a bomb that had killed 30 people in Assam in October was linked to dissident groups based in Bhutan. The Bhutanese Government, for its part, claimed to have no evidence of any renewal in Assamese insurgent activity within its borders.

Ethnic Unrest, the Southern Bhutanese and the Refugee Camps in Nepal

The violent ethnic Nepalese agitation in India for a 'Gurkha homeland' in the Darjiling-Kalimpong region during the late 1980s and the populist movement in Nepal in 1988–90 (see the chapters on India and Nepal, respectively) spread into Bhutan in 1990. Ethnic unrest became apparent in that year when a campaign of intimidation and violence, directed by militant Nepalese against the authority of the Government in Thimphu, was initiated. In September thousands of southern Bhutanese villagers, and Nepalese who entered Bhutan from across the Indian border, organized demonstrations in border towns in southern Bhutan to protest against domination by the indigenous Buddhist Drukpa. The 'anti-nationals' (ngolops), as they were called by the Bhutanese authorities, demanded a greater role in the country's political and economic life and were bitterly opposed to official attempts to strengthen the Bhutanese sense of national identity through an increased emphasis on Tibetan-derived, rather than Nepalese, culture and religion (including a formal dress code, Dzongkha as the sole official language, etc.). Bhutanese officials, by contrast, viewed the southerners as recent arrivals who abused the hospitality of their hosts through acts of violence and the destruction of development infrastructure.

Most southern villagers were relatively recent arrivals from Nepal, and many of them had made substantial contributions to the development of the southern hills. The provision of free education and health care by the Bhutanese Government for many years attracted Nepalese who had been struggling to survive in their own country and who came to settle illegally in Bhutan. This population movement was largely ignored by local administrative officials, many of whom accepted incentives to disregard the illegal nature of the influx. The Government's policy of encouraging a sense of national identity, together with rigorous new procedures (introduced in 1988) to check citizenship registration, revealed the presence of thousands of illegal residents in southern Bhutan—many of whom had lived there for a decade or more, married local inhabitants and raised families. During the ethnic unrest in September 1990 the majority of southern villagers were coerced into participating in the demonstrations by groups of armed and uniformed young men (including many of Nepalese origin who were born in Bhutan). Many of these dissidents, including a large number of students and former members of the RBA and of the police force, had fled Bhutan in 1989 and early 1990 and had taken up residence in tea gardens and villages in eastern Nepal. Following the demonstrations that took place in Bhutan in September–October 1990, other ethnic Nepalese left Bhutan. In January 1991 more than 200 persons, claiming to be Bhutanese refugees, reportedly arrived in the Jhapa district of eastern Nepal. In September, at the request of the Nepalese Government, the office of the UN High Commissioner for Refugees (UNHCR, see p. 74) inaugurated a relief programme providing food and shelter for more than 300 people in the ad hoc camps. By December the number of people staying in the camps had risen to about 6,000. This number was substantially augmented by landless and unemployed Nepalese, who had been expelled from Assam (Asom) and other eastern states of India. The small and faction-ridden ethnic Nepalese Bhutan People's Party (BPP) purported to lead the agitation for 'democracy' but presented no clear set of objectives and attracted little support from within Bhutan itself.

Between 1988 and the end of 1999 King Jigme personally authorized the release of more than 1,700 militants captured by the authorities. The King asserted that, while he had an open mind regarding the question of the pace and extent of political reform (including a willingness to hold discussions with any discontented minority group), his Government could not tolerate pressures for change if based on intimidation and violence. Although several important leaders of the dissident movement remained in custody, the King stated that they would be released upon a return to normal conditions of law and order. Violence continued in the disturbed areas of Samtse, Chhukha, Tsirang, Sarpang and Gelephu throughout the early 1990s, and companies of trained militia volunteers were posted to these areas to relieve the forces of the regular army.

A number of southern Bhutanese officials (including the Director-General of Power, Bhim Subba, and the Managing Director of the State Trading Corporation, R. B. Basnet) absconded in June 1991 (on the eve of the publication of departmental audits) and went directly to Nepal, where they reportedly sought political asylum on the grounds of repression and atrocities against southern Bhutanese. These accusations were refuted by the Government in Thimphu. The former Secretary-General of the BPP, D. K. Rai, was tried by the High Court in Thimphu in May 1992 and was sentenced to life imprisonment for terrorist acts; a further 35 defendants received lesser sentences. Tek Nath Rizal, who had founded the People's Forum for Human Rights–Bhutan (the precursor to the BPP) in exile in Nepal in 1989 and who was alleged to be primarily responsible for the ethnic unrest, came to trial (having been held in prison since November 1989), and was sentenced to life imprisonment in November 1993, having been found guilty of offences against the Tsawa Sum ('the country, the King, and the people'). (Rizal, together with 40 other 'political prisoners', was pardoned by the King and released from prison in December 1999; he decided to remain in Thimphu.)

In 1991 'Rongthong' Kinley Dorji (also styled Kuenley or Kunley), a former Bhutanese businessman accused of unpaid loans and of acts against the State, had absconded to Nepal and joined the anti-Government movement. In 1992 he established and became President of the Druk National Congress, claiming human rights violations in Bhutan. Following the signing of an extradition treaty between India and Bhutan in December, Kinley was arrested by the Indian authorities during a visit to Delhi in April 1997; he remained in detention until June 1998, when he was released on bail while his case was being examined by the Indian courts. Meanwhile, the extradition treaty was read to the 75th Assembly in July 1997, when demands for Kinley Dorji's return to Bhutan for trial were unanimously supported (as they were also at the 76th Assembly in 1998 and the 77th Assembly in 1999). Finally, in April 2010 the Delhi High Court ruled against the extradition proceedings and Kinley was absolved of all pending charges.

In late 1991 and throughout 1992 several thousand legally settled villagers left southern Bhutan for the newly established refugee camps in eastern Nepal. The Bhutanese Government alleged that the villagers were being enticed or threatened to leave their homes by militants based outside Bhutan, in order to augment the population of the camps and gain international attention; the dissidents, by contrast, claimed that the Bhutanese Government was forcing the villagers to leave. The formation of the Bhutan National Democratic Party (BNDP), including members drawn from supporters of the BPP and with R. B. Basnet as its President, was announced in Kathmandu in February 1992. Incidents of ethnic violence, almost all of which involved infiltration from across the border by ethnic Nepalese who had been trained and dispatched from the camps in Nepal, reportedly diminished substantially in the first half of 1993, as talks continued between Bhutanese and Nepalese officials regarding proposals to resolve the issues at stake. The Nepalese Government steadfastly refused to consider any solution that did not include the resettlement in Bhutan of all ethnic Nepalese 'refugees' living in the camps (by November 1993 the number of alleged ethnic Nepalese refugees from Bhutan totalled about 85,000). This proposal was rejected by the Bhutanese Government, which maintained that the majority of the camp population merely claimed to be from Bhutan, had absconded from Bhutan (and thus forfeited their citizenship, according to Bhutan's citizenship laws), or had departed voluntarily after selling their properties and surrendering their citizenship papers and rights. The deadlock was broken, however, when a joint statement was signed by the two countries' Ministers of Home Affairs in July, which committed each side to establishing a 'high-level committee' to work towards a settlement and, in particular, to fulfilling the following mandate prior to undertaking any other related activity: to determine the different categories of people claiming to have come from Bhutan in the refugee camps in eastern Nepal (which now numbered eight); and to specify the positions of the two Governments on each of these categories, which would provide the basis for the resolution of the problem. The two countries held their first meeting of the ministerial joint committee (MJC) (at foreign minister level) regarding the issue in Kathmandu in October, at which it was agreed that four categories would be established among the people in the refugee camps: '(i) bona fide Bhutanese who have been evicted forcefully; (ii) Bhutanese who emigrated; (iii) non-Bhutanese; and (iv) Bhutanese who have committed criminal acts' (henceforth referred to as Categories I, II, III and IV, respectively). Further meetings were held in 1994. Following the election of a new Government in Nepal in November of that year, however, little progress was made at MJC meetings held in the first half of 1995. Nepal's communist Government demanded that all persons in the camps (regardless of status) be accepted by Bhutan; the Bhutanese authorities, on the other hand, were prepared to accept only the unconditional return of any bona fide Bhutanese citizens who had left the country involuntarily. Nevertheless, diplomatic exchanges continued in the latter half of the year, despite serious political instability in Nepal.

During 1996–98 two rounds of MJC talks were held, but both proved relatively fruitless. At the eighth round of negotiations, which was held in Kathmandu in September 1999, the Bhutanese Minister of Foreign Affairs agreed that some of those previously classified as voluntary emigrants (under Category II) might be reclassified as Category I (according to the Bhutanese Government, the number of people in this category totalled only about 3,000, while the Nepalese Government claimed that all of the camp dwellers—who now numbered about 100,000—had been compelled to leave Bhutan).

At the 10th round of MJC negotiations, held in December 2000, it was agreed that nationality would be verified on the basis of the head of the refugee family for those under 25 years of age, and that refugees over 25 years of age would be verified on an individual basis. This important advance in bilateral negotiations signified a major concession by Bhutan, which had hitherto insisted that verification be conducted on an individual basis. By the end of January 2001 a Joint Verification Team (JVT), consisting of five officials each from the Nepalese and Bhutanese Governments, had concluded the inspection of the refugee camps. Verification of the nationalities of 98,897 people claiming refugee status (including some 13,000 minors born in the camps) began at the end of March, commencing with the Khudanabari camp. However, as a result of subsequent disagreements between the two sides over the categorization of the refugees, the process had come to a standstill by the end of the year.

In January 2003 Bhutan hosted the 12th meeting of the MJC, at which the two Governments finally harmonized their positions on each of the four categories. Details of the results of the verification process at Khudanabari were published in June: only 2.4% of the camp's inhabitants were classified as belonging to Category I (forcefully evicted Bhutanese people); 70.5% to Category II (Bhutanese who had emigrated); 24.2% to Category III (non-Bhutanese people); and 2.8% to Category IV (Bhutanese who had committed criminal acts). Arrangements were made to conduct the repatriation to Bhutan of most of the families in Category I by the end of the year. The MJC also decided that Bhutan would be fully responsible for any Category I persons, while Category II people could apply for either Bhutanese or Nepalese citizenship, in accordance with the respective laws. However, in December the Bhutanese members of the JVT, while explaining procedures to Category I residents of the Khudanabari camp, were attacked by several thousand other camp members protesting against the terms and conditions of the agreement. The JVT members were subsequently withdrawn to Thimphu, the repatriation process was halted, and talks between Bhutan and Nepal were suspended. In March 2004 Tek Nath Rizal, who now held the position of Chairman of the Human Rights Council of Bhutan (established in 2003), began a hunger strike in Nepal, with the intention of drawing international attention to the plight of the refugees. Rizal ended his strike in the following month after receiving assurances from the Nepalese Government that it would attempt to enlist the involvement of UNHCR and India in restarting the stalled repatriation process. In September Rizal led a Nepalese delegation to the headquarters of UNHCR in Geneva, Switzerland, in a further attempt to raise the international profile of the refugees. In the following month the US Assistant Secretary of State for Population, Refugees and Migration visited the area and held discussions on how to end the stalemate. In October 2006 the US Government offered to resettle (after interviews and screening) as many as 60,000 of the refugees over a period of three to four years. This met with a mixed response: some argued that third-country resettlement would amount to an exoneration of Bhutan's actions, while others welcomed the proposal. In the following month Australia, Canada and New Zealand also offered asylum to the refugees, although proposed intake numbers were not supplied. UNHCR, which had urged Bhutan to allow repatriation, and the Nepalese Government began a census of the estimated 106,000 refugees in the Jhapa and Morang districts of Nepal in November. In the same month the much-anticipated resumption of MJC negotiations was postponed indefinitely—once at the request of Bhutan and a second time owing to the unsettled political situation in Nepal. The refugee issue was at the top of the agenda at the 86th session of Bhutan's National Assembly, which began in December. The Bhutanese Prime Minister, Lyonchhen Khandu Wangchuk, expressed concern about the alleged infiltration of the refugee camps by terrorists and radicals, suggesting that repatriation of the refugees would challenge security and stability in Bhutan; the Nepalese Government and Bhutanese refugee groups, however, denied the veracity of the claim.

In January 2007 the Bhutanese Movement Steering Committee, a prominent refugee organization, urged the Nepalese Government to terminate discussions with Bhutan and to resolve the matter with the help of India. In May an attempt by a group of 15,000 refugees to cross the Mechi bridge on the Indo–Nepalese border was foiled by Indian troops, who reportedly killed two people and injured a further 60. The march was organized by the National Front for Democracy, a coalition of exiled Bhutanese political groups, to coincide with the second round of 'mock' elections in Bhutan (see above). Following a visit to the refugee camps in November, the US Assistant Secretary of State for Population, Refugees and Migration stated that the refugees were confronted by 'severe intimidation' from political leaders who were opposed to the offers of resettlement abroad on the grounds that this would undermine their political struggle to settle all the 'camp people' in Bhutan. Nevertheless, in February 2008 Nepal began issuing exit permits to those who had opted for resettlement, and in March the first group of refugees left the camps for the USA and New Zealand. According to the International Organization for Migration, between January 2008 and February 2009 more than 10,000 people claiming to be from Bhutan were resettled overseas (more than 9,000 in the USA), with many more expected to follow. At the 15th SAARC summit held in Colombo, Sri Lanka, in August 2008, Bhutan's Prime Minister, Jigmi Yozer Thinley, met with his Nepalese counterpart, G. P. Koirala; the two leaders agreed that their respective Governments would resume the stalled MJC talks regarding the refugee problem. During the following two years or so, however, there was no official resumption of negotiations and no further progress was made with respect to the refugee problem. In April 2011 during a visit to Kathmandu in his capacity as Chairman of SAARC, Jigmi Yozer Thinley held talks with the Nepalese Prime Minister, Jhala Nath Khanal, in the course of which both leaders pledged their commitment to the resumption of MJC talks (at a date to be decided through diplomatic means).

Unconfirmed reports from Kathmandu, Nepal, in late 2010 suggested that 'Rongthong' Kinley Dorji (see above) had been appointed leader of a joint front of exiled dissident groups, comprising the Bhutanese Movement Steering Committee, the BPP and the BNDP, which advocated repatriation of all refugees claiming to be from Bhutan. In October 2011, however, it was reported that the veteran dissident had died while undergoing medical treatment in India.

In early 2011 the Nepalese Government announced plans to convert the seven camps in eastern Nepal into two by the end of 2012. According to UNHCR, by mid-January 2012 approximately 59,000 persons claiming Bhutanese refugee status had been resettled in third countries since November 2007: the USA had accepted the largest number (around 50,000), followed by Canada, Australia, New Zealand, Norway, Denmark, the Netherlands and the United Kingdom. At that time some 54,652 persons remained in seven camps in Nepal, around 78% of whom had expressed an interest in third-country resettlement. In 2012

UNHCR was expected to facilitate the resettlement of up to 16,000 refugees.

Foreign Affairs

In December 2006 Bhutan and India concluded most of a border demarcation process that had been instigated more than four decades earlier, with the signing of some 62 strip maps and plans for boundary markers and pillars. In 2007 Indo-Bhutanese relations entered a new phase: a revised India-Bhutan Friendship Treaty, which was signed in February and ratified in March, ensured greater autonomy for Bhutan in external and military affairs and increased economic co-operation between the two countries, including free trade. The Treaty also allowed Bhutan to import arms from and through India, and guaranteed equality of justice for citizens of each country when residing in the other. Relations between the two countries were further strengthened in May 2008 when the Indian Prime Minister, Dr Manmohan Singh, paid an official visit to Bhutan, during which he dedicated the Tala Hydroelectric Project, the largest joint venture between India and Bhutan to date, to the two countries. King Jigme Khesar made a state visit to India in December 2009, in the course of which several important agreements were signed between the two countries relating to co-operation in further education, the provision of hydroelectric power, air transport, the prevention of illicit drugs-trafficking and the development of the IT sector. During the visit an agreement was also signed to construct a strategically important 20-km railway line linking the two countries across the foothills of the Himalayas. Bhutan's first railway line, which was to be funded and built by India, was to run between Hasimara in West Bengal to Toribari in south Bhutan.

Following the relaxation of many policies in the People's Republic of China from 1978, and anticipating improved relations between India and China, Bhutan moved cautiously to assert positions on regional and world affairs that took into account the views of India but were not necessarily identical to them. Discussions with China regarding the formal delineation and demarcation of Bhutan's northern border began in 1984, and substantive negotiations commenced in 1986. At the 12th round of talks, held in Beijing, China, in December 1998, the Ministers of Foreign Affairs of Bhutan and China signed an official interim agreement (the first agreement ever to be signed between the two countries) to maintain peace and tranquillity in the Bhutan–China border area and to observe the status quo of the border as it was prior to May 1959, pending a formal agreement on the border alignment. Meanwhile, demarcation of Bhutan's southern border was agreed with India, except for small sectors on the Bhutan–Sikkim border, in the middle zone (between Sarpang and Gelephu) and in the eastern zone of Arunachal Pradesh and the de facto China–India border. Following a series of bilateral negotiations between Bhutan and China in the first half of the 2000s, the disputed border area, which was 1,128 sq km during the early rounds of talks, was subsequently reduced to 764 sq km in four pasture areas in the north-west of Bhutan—namely the Doklam, Sinchulumpa, Charithang and Dramana areas. However, road construction and maintenance work carried out by China in the disputed border area caused some tension from 2004, with the Bhutanese Government expressing concern that the work encroached upon its territory. In addition, the Bhutanese authorities alleged that the Chinese army had, on around 40 occasions during 2008–09, intruded into Bhutan's border patrol camps. Following a hiatus of three years, boundary negotiations were resumed in January 2010, during which the experts from each side agreed to arrange a joint field-survey exercise to help harmonize reference points and place-names in the disputed sectors. An expert group meeting in Beijing in July concluded that ongoing disagreements regarding a mutually acceptable common claim line would have to be resolved before the Bhutan–China border issue could be finalized. Reports of continuing differences at the local level along the border, largely relating to differences over grazing lands and harvesting cordyceps (a type of mushroom), were aired in the National Assembly in December.

In response to the increasing volume of bilateral trade between Bhutan and Nepal, a draft preferential trade agreement was drawn up by the two countries in March 2010. A second round of talks on the issue was held in Thimphu in May 2011. In a further reflection of the growing ties of the two states, in 2010 Nepal proposed opening a diplomatic mission in the Bhutanese capital.

Bangladesh's Prime Minister, Sheikh Hasina Wajed, made a three-day state visit to Bhutan in November 2009, during which the existing Bhutan-Bangladesh Trade Agreement was renewed for a further five years. The two sides also discussed the possibility of Bhutan exporting electricity to Bangladesh. Amicable relations between the two countries were further strengthened following a five-day state visit made to Bangladesh by King Jigme Khesar in March 2011.

The 16th SAARC summit was held in Thimphu on 28–29 April 2010. Bhutan had previously declined to host the meeting, on the grounds that its facilities were inadequate, but in the event the Thimphu meeting was rated as highly successful by the leaders in attendance. In his keynote speech, Bhutan's Prime Minister, Jigmi Yozer Thinley, warned that SAARC was in danger of 'losing focus' through an excessively bureaucratic approach, and proposed a study to rationalize the Association's procedures. The Prime Minister, who, as head of the hosting government, was to chair the SAARC Council until the next summit, in the Maldives in November 2011, described the 2010 summit as 'important in the enhancement of the country's sovereignty'. The establishment of a new SAARC Development Fund (SDF), the permanent secretariat of which was to be located in Thimphu, was announced at the 16th summit. The SDF was created to fund regional projects involving poverty alleviation and economic development; Bhutan's projected contribution was US $15m. payable over five years.

CONSTITUTION AND GOVERNMENT

In 2007–08 Bhutan underwent a transition from a modified form of constitutional monarchy to a democratic constitutional monarchy in accordance with the principle of hereditary succession and a bicameral legislature. The former system of government, in place until 2007, was unusual in that power was shared by the monarchy (assisted by the Royal Advisory Council—lodoi tsokde), the Council of Ministers (lhengye zhungtshog) and the National Assembly (tshogdu chenmo). The Head Abbot (je khenpo) and Bhutan's 3,000–4,000 Buddhist monks were represented in the National Assembly by six delegates elected from the central and regional monastic bodies. A special committee was convened in late 2001 to prepare a draft written constitution. A completed first draft was formally presented to King Jigme Singye Wangchuck in December 2002. The formal registration of political parties began in mid-2007, and the National Assembly and Royal Advisory Council were both subsequently dissolved. In accordance with the provisions of the draft Constitution, Bhutan's first general election took place in March 2008, and was followed by the installation of a new Council of Ministers and a bicameral legislature, composed of a National Council (upper house) and National Assembly (lower house). The National Council comprises 20 members elected by universal suffrage for a five-year term in office, together with five royal nominees; none of the members of the National Council are affiliated to any political party. The National Assembly consists of 47 representatives with party affiliations, who are elected for a term of five years by adult franchise from each district in proportion to its population. The final version of the draft Constitution was adopted by the new Parliament (comprising the King and both legislative houses) in July 2008.

There are 20 local districts (dzongkhags), each headed by a dzongda (district officer, in charge of administration and law and order) and a drangpon (magistrate, in charge of judicial matters, formerly known as a thrimpon). Dzongdas are appointed by the Royal Civil Service Commission and are responsible to the Commission and the Ministry of Home and Cultural Affairs. Drangpons answer to the authority of the High Court. In September 2009 the Local Government Act of Bhutan established 20 dzongkhag tshogdus (district councils) to function as the highest decision-making body in each of Bhutan's dzongkhags. Seven of the districts are further sub-divided into sub-districts (dungkhags), and the next level down of administrative unit in all districts is the block (gewog) of several villages; in early 2012 there were a total of 205 gewogs in Bhutan, although in 2011 plans were announced to divide or merge a number of blocks. According to the 2009 Local Government Act, each gewog is administered by a gewog tshogde (gewog council), which is subordinate to the dzongkhag tshogdu. The gewog tshogde is composed of a gup (headman), a mangmi (deputy), and between five and eight democratically elected tshogpas (village elders). The gewogs, in turn, are divided into chiwogs for elections and thromdes (municipalities) for administration.

REGIONAL AND INTERNATIONAL CO-OPERATION

Bhutan is a member of the Asian Development Bank (ADB, see p. 210), the Colombo Plan (see p. 449), BIMSTEC (Bay of Bengal Initiative for Multi-Sectoral Technical and Economic

Cooperation) and the South Asian Association for Regional Cooperation (SAARC, see p. 420), all of which seek to improve regional cooperation, particularly in economic development. Having joined the UN in 1971, Bhutan is also a member of the Economic and Social Commission for Asia and the Pacific (ESCAP, see p. 40). In early 2011 the Bhutan Government began the accession process to join the International Labour Organization (ILO, see p. 141) and expected to become a member within two years.

ECONOMIC AFFAIRS

In 2010, according to estimates by the World Bank, Bhutan's gross national income (GNI), measured at average 2007–10 prices, was US $1,361m., equivalent to $1,880 per head (or $4,950 per head on an international purchasing-power parity basis). During 2001–10, it was estimated, the population increased at an average annual rate of 2.4%, while gross domestic product (GDP) per head rose, in real terms, by an average of 6.1% per year. Overall GDP increased, in real terms, at an average annual rate of 8.6% in 2001–10. According to the Asian Development Bank (ADB), GDP grew by 9.3% in in the financial year ending 30 June 2010 and by 8.3% in 2010/11.

Agriculture (including livestock and forestry) contributed an estimated 18.7% of GDP in 2009. About 59.5% of the employed labour force were engaged in the sector in 2010. The principal sources of revenue in the agricultural sector are apples, oranges, potatoes, ginger and cardamom. Timber production is also important; about 60% of the total land area is covered by forest. Agricultural GDP increased, in real terms, at an average annual rate of 1.9% in 2001–09; it declined by 0.7% in 2008, but grew by 2.7% in 2009.

Industry (including mining, manufacturing, utilities and construction) engaged about 6.7% of the employed labour force in 2010, and contributed an estimated 43.2% of GDP in 2009. Industrial GDP increased at an average annual rate of 10.9% in 2001–09; growth in the sector was 6.1% in 2008, largely owing to increased capacity in the electricity and water sector, and 3.6% in 2009.

Mining and quarrying contributed an estimated 2.3% of GDP in 2009, and employed just 0.3% of the labour force in 2010. Calcium carbide is the most significant mineral export (contributing 3.8% of total export revenue in 2008). Mineral products (including fuels) accounted for 12.0% of total exports in 2009. Gypsum, coal, limestone, slate and dolomite are also mined. Mining GDP increased at an average rate of 8.8% per year in 2001–09; it rose by 20.0% in 2008, but declined by 6.9% in 2009.

Manufacturing contributed 8.4% of GDP in 2009, and the sector employed 3.9% of the employed labour force in 2010. The most important sectors are base metals and related products and cement production. Small-scale manufacturers produce, inter alia, textiles, soap, matches, candles and carpets. Manufacturing GDP increased at an average annual rate of 8.8% in 2001–09; the sector grew by 8.5% in 2008 and by 6.9% in 2009.

Construction contributed 12.6% of GDP in 2009, although a mere 0.9% of the employed population were engaged in the sector in 2010. Construction GDP increased at an average annual rate of 3.8% in 2001–09; the sector contracted by 10.2% in 2008, but grew by 16.5% in 2009.

Energy is derived principally from hydroelectric power. Bhutan's potential hydroelectric production capacity has been estimated at up to 30,000 MW. A number of hydroelectric power installations, developed in partnership with India, provide electricity for domestic consumption and also for export to India (see below). In 2009 exports of electricity provided 42.0% of total export revenue, while in the same year the value of imports of mineral products (including fuels) was equivalent to 19.8% of total import costs.

The services sector contributed 38.1% of GDP in 2009, and the sector employed about 33.9% of the employed labour force in 2010. The tourism sector has become increasingly significant with tourist arrivals rising from 17,342 in 2006 to 26,938 in 2010 (revenue from tourism grew from US $13m. in 2004 to $35m. in 2010). The GDP of the services sector increased at an average annual rate of 9.2% in 2001–09; sectoral GDP rose by 4.7% in 2008 and by 13.3% in 2009.

In the financial year ending 30 June 2010, according to provisional official estimates, Bhutan recorded a visible trade deficit of Nu 13,938.2m. (There has been a series of widening annual deficits in recent years as a result of increased import costs). In 2009/10, according to provisional estimates, there was a deficit of Nu 8,754.9m. on the current account of the balance of payments. In 2009 the principal source of imports (providing an estimated 77.7% of the total) was India, which was also the main market for exports (accounting for an estimated 93.5% of the total). The principal exports in 2009 were hydroelectric power (42.0% of total exports), base metals and related products, and mineral products (including fuels). The principal imports in 2009, accounting for 20.5% of total merchandise imports, were machinery, mechanical appliances and electrical appliances and equipment; mineral products (including fuels), base metals and related products, and transport vehicles and equipment were also significant imports.

According to revised estimates, the 2009/10 budget recorded a deficit of Nu 4,090.5m., equivalent to 6.7% of GDP for 2009. According to the World Bank, Bhutan's total external debt amounted to US $762m. at the end of 2010. The average annual rate of inflation was 4.7% in 2008–10, according to official figures. Consumer prices increased by 5.5% in 2010, according to official estimates. The unemployment rate was 3.3% in 2010.

Bhutan's economic development has been guided by a series of five-year plans. Under the 10th Plan (2008–13) the Government pledged to provide electricity to all rural households lacking power; to extend the road network; to reduce poverty (according to a UN Development Programme report published in 2007, some 23.2% of the country's population were classified as poor); and to improve local governance and service delivery. Bhutan is primarily dependent upon the sale of electricity (principally to India) to earn rupees for regional expenditure, and on the continued influx of foreign tourists to earn hard currency for expenses outside the region. The Government hoped to attract as many as 100,000 tourists per year to the country by 2013. The completion of the Chhukha (1988), Kurichhu (2002) and Tala (2008) hydroelectric power (HEP) projects helped to stimulate growth in the industrial sector and contributed to strong economic growth in the mid-2000s. In late 2011 Bhutan and India reiterated their commitment to achieving the target of 10,000 MW of power-generation in Bhutan by 2020. In early 2012 four Indian-funded HEP projects were in progress—the 670 MW Chamkharchhu-I HEP, the 180 MW Bunakha HEP, the 486 MW Kholongchhu HEP and the 600 MW Wangchhu HEP. Indian government funding of the four projects was forecast to total some US $438m. in 2012/13. In 1999 Bhutan was opened up to foreign investment, although the stock exchange remained closed to external investors. According to the ADB, foreign direct investment (FDI) in Bhutan totalled US $73m. in 2006/07, but had declined to $11m by 2009/10. In mid-2009 the Government announced that it was planning to permit FDI of 100% in certain sectors in an attempt to attract more foreign investors (particularly from India). Greater liberalization was also to be introduced in Bhutan's financial sector. In early 2010 two new commercial banks, the Tashi Bank (T Bank) and the Druk Punjab National Bank Ltd (which was jointly owned by the Indian Punjab National Bank and Bhutanese investors), commenced operations in Thimphu. Bhutan's first information technology park, Thimphu TechPark—the Bhutan Innovation and Technology Centre—was inaugurated in November 2011. It was anticipated that the project, which was forecast to cost around Nu 250m., would generate significant foreign investment and promote employment opportunities for young Bhutanese citizens. From late 2011, mainly as a result of excessive imports from India fuelled by the increasing amount of loans provided by Bhutanese financial institutions, Bhutan was faced with a severe shortage in the supply of Indian rupees.

PUBLIC HOLIDAYS

2013: The usual Buddhist holidays are observed, as well as the Winter Solstice (2 January), Losar (Tibetan New Year, 12 February), the Birthday of the fifth King Jigme Khesar Namgyel Wangchuck (21–23 February), the Birthday of the late third King Jigme Dorji Wangchuck (2 May), the Anniversary of the death of the late third King (7 August), Blessed Rainy Day (September), two days for Thimphu Tsechu (September/October, in Thimphu district only), the movable Hindu feast of Dussehra (14 October), the Coronation Day of the fifth King (1 November), the Birthday of the fourth King Jigme Singye Wangchuck and Constitution Day (11 November) and the National Day of Bhutan (17 December).

Statistical Survey

Source (unless otherwise stated): National Statistics Bureau, POB 338, Thimphu; tel. (2) 322753; fax (2) 323069; internet www.nsb.gov.bt.

Area and Population

AREA, POPULATION AND DENSITY

Area (sq km)	38,394*
Population (census results)	
30–31 May 2005†	
Males	364,482
Females	307,943
Total	672,425
Population (official projected estimates)	
2010	695,822
2011	708,265
2012	720,679
Density (per sq km) at 2012	18.8

* 14,824 sq miles.

† Including adjustment for estimated 37,443 persons with no permanent residence; the enumerated total was 634,982. The number of Bhutanese nationals was 552,996.

POPULATION BY AGE AND SEX

(official estimates at mid-2012)

	Males	Females	Total
0–14	109,456	107,516	216,972
15–64	248,628	220,822	469,450
65 and over	17,470	16,787	34,257
Total	375,554	345,125	720,679

DISTRICTS

(official population projections at mid-2012)

	Area ('000 sq km)*	Population	Density (per sq km)
Bumthang	2.6	18,126	7.0
Chhukha	1.7	84,203	49.5
Dagana	1.3	26,060	20.0
Gasa	4.2	3,522	0.8
Haa	1.7	12,962	7.6
Lhuentse	2.8	16,980	6.1
Mongar	1.9	42,117	22.2
Paro	1.2	41,174	34.3
Pemagatshel	0.5	24,362	48.7
Punakha	0.9	26,541	29.5
Samdrup Jongkhar	2.2	38,708	17.6
Samtse	1.5	67,525	45.0
Sarpang	2.2	43,042	19.6
Thimphu	1.8	108,933	60.5
Trashigang	2.2	54,036	24.6
Trashi Yangtse	1.4	19,951	14.3
Trongsa	1.7	15,240	9.0
Tsirang	0.6	20,894	34.8
Wangdue Phodrang	3.8	35,628	9.4
Zhemgang	2.0	20,672	10.3
Total	38.4	720,679	18.8

* Data approximated from percentage distribution.

PRINCIPAL TOWNS

(official figures at 2005 census)

Thimphu (capital)	79,185	Gelephu	9,199
Phuentsholing	20,537	Wangdue	6,714

2007 (official estimate at 1 January): Thimphu 95,000.

BIRTHS AND DEATHS

(annual averages, UN estimates)

	1995–2000	2000–05	2005–10
Birth rate (per 1,000)	29.2	25.2	21.5
Death rate (per 1,000)	9.9	7.9	7.2

Source: UN, *World Population Prospects: The 2010 Revision*.

2005 census (year ending 31 May 2005): Live births 12,538 (birth rate 20 per 1,000); Deaths 4,498 (death rate 7 per 1,000).

Life expectancy (years at birth, WHO estimates): 63 (males 62; females 65) in 2009 (Source: WHO, *World Health Statistics*).

EMPLOYMENT

('000 persons)

	2003	2004	2005
Agriculture and forestry	167.2	132.8	108.6
Mining and quarrying	0.4	0.1	2.8
Manufacturing	4.5	12.6	4.9
Electricity, gas and water supply	1.0	1.0	4.1
Construction	2.9	6.9	30.9
Wholesale and retail trade; repairs of motor vehicles and personal and household goods	6.9	4.8	6.7
Hotels and restaurants	1.3	1.4	4.0
Transport, storage and communications	0.2	2.6	8.1
Financial intermediation	0.3	2.5	2.3
Public administration and defence; compulsory social security	19.5	10.0	17.5
Education	3.5	3.9	7.8
Health and social work	2.7	2.4	2.5
Other community, social and personal service activities	11.4	29.1	48.7
Total	221.8	210.1	249.0

Source: Royal Monetary Authority of Bhutan, *Annual Report*.

2005 census: Total employed 308,998; Unemployed 7,236; Total labour force 316,234.

2010 (economically active population, labour force survey, '000 persons): Agriculture and forestry 190.8; Mining and quarrying 0.9; Manufacturing 12.5; Electricity, gas and water 5.3; Construction 2.8; Wholesale and retail trade; repairs of motor vehicles and personal and household goods 30.9; Hotels and restaurants 4.1; Transport, storage and communications 9.5; Financial intermediation 2.5; Real estate, renting and business activities 13.4; Public administration and defence 26.3; Education 9.8; Health and social work 5.3; Other community, social and personal service activities 6.7; Private households with employed persons 0.3; *Total employed* 320.9; Unemployed 11.0; *Total labour force* 331.9. Note: Employed persons include those engaged in at least one hour's work during week prior to survey.

Health and Welfare

KEY INDICATORS

Total fertility rate (children per woman, 2009)	2.6
Under-5 mortality rate (per 1,000 live births, 2009)	79
HIV/AIDS (% of persons aged 15–49, 2009)	0.2
Physicians (per 1,000 head, 2007)	0.3
Hospital beds (per 1,000 head, 2007)	1.8
Health expenditure (2008): US $ per head (PPP)	263
Health expenditure (2008): % of GDP	5.5
Health expenditure (2008): public (% of total)	82.5
Access to water (% of persons, 2008)	92
Access to sanitation (% of persons, 2008)	65
Total carbon dioxide emissions ('000 metric tons, 2007)	578.9
Carbon dioxide emissions per head (metric tons, 2007)	0.9
Human Development Index (2011): ranking	141
Human Development Index (2011): value	0.522

For sources and definitions, see explanatory note on p. vi.

Agriculture

PRINCIPAL CROPS
('000 metric tons)

	2008	2009	2010*
Rice, paddy	77	66	62
Maize	69	61	55
Potatoes	55	49	54
Sugar cane	13*	13*	13
Oranges	25†	30†	31
Apples	5	7	7
Nutmeg, mace and cardamom	8*	9*	10

* FAO estimate(s).
† Unofficial figure.

Aggregate production ('000 metric tons, may include official, semi-official or estimated data): Total cereals 166 in 2008, 143 in 2009, 134 in 2010; Total roots and tubers 77 in 2008, 75 in 2009, 80 in 2010; Total vegetables (incl. melons) 21 in 2008, 25 in 2009, 26 in 2010; Total fruits (excl. melons) 53 in 2008, 59 in 2009, 61 in 2010.

Source: FAO.

LIVESTOCK
('000 head, year ending September)

	2008	2009	2010
Horses*	20	19	19
Asses and mules*	27	27	27
Cattle	326	307	303*
Buffaloes*	2	2	1
Pigs	25	22	20*
Sheep	13	12	12
Goats	39	39	40*
Chickens	198	240*	245*

* FAO estimate(s).

Source: FAO.

LIVESTOCK PRODUCTS
('000 metric tons, FAO estimates)

	2008	2009	2010
Cattle meat	5.1	5.1	5.1
Pig meat	1.0	1.0	1.0
Cows' milk	44.9	45.2	51.0
Buffaloes' milk	0.4	0.4	0.4
Hen eggs	0.3	0.3	0.3

Source: FAO.

Forestry

ROUNDWOOD REMOVALS
('000 cubic metres, excl. bark)

	2007	2008	2009
Sawlogs, veneer logs and logs for sleepers	188	168	168
Other industrial wood	112	88	88
Fuel wood*	4,663	4,723	4,783
Total*	4,964	4,980	5,040

* FAO estimates.

2010: Production assumed to be unchanged from 2009 (FAO estimates).

Source: FAO.

SAWNWOOD PRODUCTION
('000 cubic metres, incl. railway sleepers)

	2006*	2007	2008
Coniferous (softwood)	12	9	9
Broadleaved (hardwood)	6	12	18
Total	18	21	27

* FAO estimates.

2009–10: Production assumed to be unchanged from 2008 (FAO estimates).

Source: FAO.

Fishing

(metric tons, live weight, capture of freshwater fishes, FAO estimates)

	2007	2008	2009
Total catch	200	180	180

Source: FAO.

Mining

('000 metric tons unless otherwise indicated)

	2008	2009	2010
Dolomite	1,248	1,029	1,192
Limestone	584	591	716
Gypsum	248	300	344
Coal	124	49	88
Marble (sq m)	1,143	31	—
Slate (sq m)	764	1,765	—
Quartzite	95	83	105
Talc	56	64	26

Source: US Geological Survey.

Industry

GROSS SALES AND OUTPUT OF SELECTED INDUSTRIES
(million ngultrum)

	2008	2009	2010
Penden Cement Authority	1,327.5	1,784.6	1,936.6
Bhutan Ferro Alloys	1,898.8	1,711.8	1,920.0
Bhutan Fruit Products	560.8	201.2	169.8
Army Welfare Project*	302.1	327.8	573.8
Bhutan Carbide and Chemicals	1,877.3	1,158.5	1,404.1
Bhutan Board Products	397.8	413.7	298.9
Eastern Bhutan Coal Company	337.7	197.3	243.6
Druk Satair Corporation Ltd	338.5	468.8	473.6

* Manufacturer of alcoholic beverages.

Source: Royal Monetary Authority of Bhutan.

Electric energy (million kWh, year ending 30 June): 1,972.2 in 1995/96; 1,838.4 in 1996/97; 1,800.0 in 1997/98 (Source: Department of Power, Royal Government of Bhutan).

Revenue from the Chhukha, Basochhu, Kurichhu and Tala Hydroelectric Projects (million ngultrum): 11,885.5 (Internal consumption 852.9, Exports 11,032.6) in 2008; 10,991.6 (Internal consumption 919.1, Exports 10,072.5) in 2009; 11,219.1 (Internal consumption 909.5, Exports 10,309.5) in 2010.

Source: Department of Power, Royal Government of Bhutan.

Finance

CURRENCY AND EXCHANGE RATES

Monetary Units
100 chetrum (Ch) = 1 ngultrum (Nu).

Sterling, Dollar and Euro Equivalents (30 December 2011)
£1 sterling = 82.345 ngultrum;
US $1 = 53.260 ngultrum;
€1 = 68.913 ngultrum;
1,000 ngultrum = £12.14 = $18.78 = €14.51.

Average Exchange Rate (ngultrum per US $)
2009 48.405
2010 45.726
2011 46.671

Note: The ngultrum is at par with the Indian rupee, which also circulates freely within Bhutan. The foregoing figures relate to the official rate of exchange, which is applicable to government-related transactions alone. Since April 1992 there has also been a market rate of exchange, which values foreign currencies approximately 20% higher than the official rate of exchange.

GOVERNMENT FINANCE

(general government transactions, million ngultrum, year ending 30 June)

Revenue	2005/06	2006/07	2007/08
Tax revenue	4,124.7	4,266.9	5,238.4
Direct taxes	2,420.1	2,829.0	3,386.8
Business income tax	356.5	367.7	464.9
Corporate income tax	1,363.3	1,566.9	1,817.3
Royalties	407.4	498.6	573.0
Indirect taxes	1,704.6	1,437.9	1,851.6
Bhutan sales tax	662.8	765.5	831.0
Excise duties	879.5	519.4	877.7
Non-tax revenue	2,778.2	5,815.3	7,107.6
Fees, dividends and profits	2,610.4	5,640.0	7,023.3
Dividends	1,542.4	2,123.2	2,479.8
Capital revenue	167.8	175.3	84.4
Other	124.5	—	35.5
Total revenue	7,027.4	10,082.2	12,381.5
Grants	6,424.7	6,000.9	5,935.4
From India	3,417.2	4,024.3	4,671.1
Total revenue and grants	13,452.2	16,083.1	18,316.9

Expenditure*	2005/06	2006/07	2007/08
Ministries	9,247.3	9,580.8	13,537.3
Agriculture	1,286.2	1,134.6	1,236.9
Education	631.9	684.5	694.3
Finance	1,570.8	1,724.7	4,493.2
Foreign Affairs	226.5	236.9	281.5
Health	1,248.2	1,166.6	1,332.3
Home Affairs	692.5	803.8	948.7
Information and Communications	374.1	262.5	245.1
Labour and Human Resources	215.7	265.8	237.4
Trade and Industry	701.6	681.8	782.6
Works and Human Settlement	2,299.8	2,619.6	3,285.2
Non-ministerial organizations	993.6	1,372.3	2,004.7
Council for Religious Affairs	226.2	241.0	285.8
Royal University of Bhutan	289.7	326.4	424.1
Office of the Election Commission	7.4	156.6	303.4
Local government	3,073.8	4,213.0	4,151.1
Total	13,314.6	15,166.1	19,693.0

* Excluding lending minus repayments (million ngultrum): 456.3 in 2005/06; 629.3 in 2006/07; –1,779.6 in 2007/08.

2008/09: *Revenue:* Tax revenue 6,482.4; Non-tax revenue 7,566.6; Other 2,818.9; Grants 6,575.1 (From India 4,394.9); Total revenue and grants 23,443.0. *Expenditure (incl. lending minus repayments):* Total 22,350.5.

2009/10 (revised figures): *Revenue:* Tax revenue 9,411.4; Non-tax revenue 5,958.8; Other 567.6; Grants 10,423.4 (From India 6,146.2); Total revenue and grants 26,361.1. *Expenditure (incl. lending minus repayments):* Total 30,451.6.

Source: partly Royal Monetary Authority of Bhutan, *Annual Report*.

FOREIGN EXCHANGE RESERVES

(at 31 December)

	2008	2009	2010
Indian rupee reserves (million Indian rupees)	3,407.9	5,519.3	6,035.2
Royal Monetary Authority	2,291.9	3,830.4	4,919.3
Bank of Bhutan	847.9	1,222.3	424.0
Bhutan National Bank	268.1	466.6	172.3
T Bank Limited	—	—	89.5
Druk PNB Limited	—	—	430.0
Rupee reserves expressed as dollars (US $ million)	70.1	118.4	133.6
Convertible currency reserves (US $ million)	669.7	782.7	868.6
Royal Monetary Authority	644.2	760.1	843.8
Bank of Bhutan	16.3	8.5	7.8
Bhutan National Bank	9.2	14.0	11.8
T Bank Limited	—	—	0.1
Druk PNB Limited	—	—	5.0
Total reserves (US $ million)	739.8	901.1	1,002.2

Source: Royal Monetary Authority of Bhutan.

MONEY SUPPLY

(million ngultrum at 31 December)

	2008	2009	2010
Currency outside depository corporations	4,097	4,981	5,609
Transferable deposits	10,067	17,653	23,465
Other deposits	16,937	21,914	22,912
Broad money	31,102	44,548	51,987

Source: IMF, *International Financial Statistics*.

COST OF LIVING

(Consumer Price Index at 31 December, excluding rent; base: 30 September 2003 = 100)

	2008	2009	2010
Food	140.1	155.1	163.2
Non-food items	131.2	131.9	139.5
All items	134.0	139.3	146.9

Source: Royal Monetary Authority of Bhutan.

NATIONAL ACCOUNTS

(million ngultrum at current prices)

Expenditure on the Gross Domestic Product

	2007	2008	2009
Government final consumption expenditure	9,454.8	10,372.6	13,082.1
Private final consumption expenditure	18,864.1	21,761.6	23,202.2
Statistical discrepancy for consumption expenditure account	3,906.8	6,466.5	3,674.6
Changes in stocks	–1,289.0	623.3	–73.2
Gross fixed capital formation	19,537.8	21,164.5	25,301.2
Total domestic expenditure	50,474.5	60,388.5	65,186.9
Exports of goods and services	27,186.5	25,488.5	39,639.1
Less Imports of goods and services	31,905.6	40,944.9	40,945.9
Statistical discrepancy*	3,701.2	9,780.9	–2,656.6
GDP in purchasers' values	49,456.6	54,713.0	61,223.5
GDP at constant 2000 prices	30,596.7	38,088.0	40,650.6

* Referring to the difference between the expenditure and production methodologies.

Gross Domestic Product by Economic Activity

	2007	2008	2009
Agriculture, forestry and livestock	9,234.1	10,078.3	11,158.7
Mining and quarrying	890.5	1,252.0	1,392.0
Manufacturing	4,033.2	4,593.4	5,017.2
Electricity and water	10,082.0	11,520.9	11,816.4
Construction	6,781.0	6,251.0	7,469.7
Wholesale and retail trade	2,497.1	2,694.7	2,935.3
Restaurants and hotels	368.1	569.2	537.6
Transport, storage and communications	4,468.8	5,365.8	5,989.9
Finance, insurance and real estate and business services	4,105.4	4,576.6	4,962.1
Public administration	3,370.2	3,762.7	4,728.4
Education and health	1,941.6	2,167.7	3,235.0
Personal services and recreational activities	241.9	267.7	276.4
Sub-total	48,013.9	53,100.0	59,518.7
Taxes, less subsidies, on products	1,442.5	1,613.1	1,704.8
GDP at current prices	49,456.6	54,713.0	61,223.5

BALANCE OF PAYMENTS

(million ngultrum, year ending 30 June, estimates)

	2007/08	2008/09	2009/10*
Merchandise exports f.o.b.	24,170.8	24,657.5	25,401.8
Merchandise imports c.i.f.	–27,092.4	–28,980.0	–39,340.0
Trade balance	–2,921.6	–4,322.4	–13,938.2
Exports of services	2,206.9	2,700.0	3,205.3
Imports of services	–3,769.5	–3,603.4	–4,220.5
Balance on goods and services	–4,484.2	–5,225.9	–14,953.4
Other income received	1,419.9	1,012.6	761.0
Other income paid	–2,730.0	–2,762.0	–3,414.3
Balance on goods, services and income	–5,794.3	–6,975.3	–17,606.7
Current transfers received	6,780.2	7,730.8	10,414.7
Current transfers paid	–2,066.2	–1,704.3	–1,562.9
Current balance	–1,080.2	–948.7	–8,754.9
Capital transfers	635.5	1,413.2	3,719.5
Direct investment from abroad	1,198.3	710.8	534.6
Foreign aid (net of loans)	1,015.0	4,193.3	2,215.2
Other loans	2,801.9	–1,252.2	547.1
Net errors and omissions	–2,613.4	1,578.3	6,139.8
Overall balance	1,957.0	5,694.8	4,401.4

* Provisional.

Source: Royal Monetary Authority of Bhutan, *Annual Report*.

OFFICIAL DEVELOPMENT ASSISTANCE

(US $ million)

	2000	2001	2002
Bilateral donors	33.7	42.5	42.9
Multilateral donors	19.6	18.0	30.6
Total received	53.3	60.5	73.5
Grants	42.5	47.1	52.0
Loans	10.8	13.4	21.5
Per caput assistance (US $)	25.9	28.3	33.4

Total received: 89.6 in 2005; 94.2 in 2006; 89.2 in 2007.

Source: UN, *Statistical Yearbook for Asia and the Pacific*.

External Trade

PRINCIPAL COMMODITIES

(million ngultrum)

Imports	2007	2008	2009
Animal products	685.7	789.2	992.7
Fruit, vegetables and cereal crops (incl. tea, coffee and spices)	990.9	1,131.9	1,295.0
Vegetable fats and oils	2,055.0	966.2	414.1
Processed foods and beverages (incl. alcohol)	928.0	1,002.2	1,161.1
Mineral products (incl. fuels)	3,838.8	5,028.2	5,059.9
Chemical products (incl. medicines and pharmaceuticals)	732.3	909.1	970.9
Plastics and rubber products	731.6	812.4	840.1
Wood, woodpulp and products thereof	677.0	1,021.1	1,179.8
Textiles, clothing and footwear	510.6	640.2	384.1
Articles of stone, plaster, cement, etc.	327.0	342.5	371.1
Pearls and products of precious and semi-precious metal and stones	760.9	110.2	138.1
Base metals and articles of base metals	4,057.9	3,776.2	4,405.6
Machinery, mechanical appliances and electrical appliances and equipment	3,663.7	4,151.4	5,230.8
Transport vehicles and equipment	1,437.9	2,187.7	2,448.4
Total (incl. others)	21,745.6	23,495.1	25,523.0

Exports	2007*	2008	2009
Fruit, vegetables and cereal crops (incl. tea, coffee and spices)	591.1	703.7	1,130.2
Processed foods and beverages (incl. alcohol)	376.1	283.0	326.0
Mineral products (incl. fuels)	2,079.9	2,476.0	2,872.8
Chemical products (including medicines and pharmaceuticals)	783.9	895.2	1,051.8
Plastics and rubber products	285.9	214.2	308.4
Wood, woodpulp and products thereof	319.8	311.7	323.8
Textiles, clothing and footwear	461.1	294.3	67.1
Base metals and articles of base metals	6,343.2	5,535.3	7,061.9
Magnetic discs, cards, tapes and media (recorded and unrecorded)	4,451.3	0.0	—
Electricity†	10,034.3	11,032.6	10,072.5
Total (incl. others)	27,859.0	22,590.6	23,973.9

* Excluding trade with Nepal.

† Trade with India only.

Source: Royal Monetary Authority of Bhutan, *Annual Report*.

PRINCIPAL TRADING PARTNERS

(million ngultrum)

Imports c.i.f.	2007	2008	2009
China, People's Republic	402.7	844.7	487.3
Germany	125.4	285.0	222.7
India	15,099.5	17,339.5	19,840.8
Indonesia	1,306.8	244.3	68.6
Japan	460.1	1,098.9	558.5
Korea, Republic	644.5	286.7	383.8
Malaysia	193.4	207.1	374.5
Russia	731.4	n.a.	n.a.
Singapore	1,109.7	964.8	744.0
Sweden	306.2	240.7	462.4
Thailand	224.9	410.8	348.9
Total (incl. others)	21,745.4	23,495.1	25,522.9

Exports f.o.b.	2007	2008	2009
Bangladesh	469.6	632.4	758.0
Hong Kong	2,764.3	105.3	677.6
India	22,732.7	21,480.0	22,415.5
Nepal	54.3	195.8	84.8
Singapore	683.8	n.a.	n.a.
Total (incl. others)	27,913.4	22,590.6	23,973.9

Source: Royal Monetary Authority of Bhutan, *Annual Report*.

Transport

ROAD TRAFFIC
(registered vehicles, excl. military)

	2007	2008	2009
Heavy vehicles	4,494	4,627	5,745
Medium vehicles	520	649	863
Light vehicles	19,792	23,687	29,189
Two-wheelers	7,464	7,731	8,438
Taxis	2,218	2,481	3,032
Industrial and plant	633	725	1,118
Others (incl. tractors)	582	759	915
Total	35,703	40,659	49,300

CIVIL AVIATION
(traffic on scheduled services)

	2003	2004	2005
Kilometres flown (million)	2	2	2
Passengers carried ('000)	36	45	49
Passenger-km (million)	56	69	74
Total ton-km (million)	5	6	7

Source: UN, *Statistical Yearbook*.

Passengers carried (Druk Air only): 110,137 in 2006; 121,711 in 2007; 119,105 in 2008; 118,084 in 2009.

Tourism

FOREIGN VISITORS BY COUNTRY OF ORIGIN*

	2006	2007	2008
Australia	774	1,181	1,524
Austria	484	443	472
Canada	375	588	852
China, People's Republic	362	504	1,069
France	708	738	1,402
Germany	1,074	1,456	1,717
Italy	648	614	751
Japan	1,815	2,008	2,743
Netherlands	389	497	915
Singapore	180	350	667
Spain	281	444	803
Switzerland	427	396	597
Thailand	776	707	627
United Kingdom	1,950	2,193	2,758
USA	5,018	5,773	6,941
Total (incl. others)	17,342	21,094	27,636

Total foreign visitors: 23,480 in 2009; 26,938 in 2010.
* Figures relate to tourists paying in convertible currency.

Tourism receipts (US $ million): 29.9 in 2007; 38.8 in 2008; 31.9 in 2009; 35.0 in 2010.

Source: Royal Monetary Authority of Bhutan, *Annual Report*.

Communications Media

	2008	2009	2010
Telephones ('000 main lines in use)	27.5	26.3	26.3
Mobile cellular telephones ('000 subscribers)	253.4	338.9	394.3
Internet subscribers ('000)	6.0	6.7	9.8
Broadband subscribers ('000)	2.1	3.1	8.7

Personal computers: 17,000 (25.1 per 1,000 persons) in 2007.

Radio receivers ('000 in use): 37 in 1997.

Television receivers ('000 in use): 13.5 in 2000.

Sources: International Telecommunication Union; UNESCO, *Statistical Yearbook*.

Education

(2011)

	Institutions	Teachers	Students
Community primary schools	266	1,380	29,569
Primary schools	91	999	22,510
Lower secondary schools	93	2,002	50,102
Middle secondary schools	57	1,654	40,097
Higher secondary schools	44	1,402	28,799
Institutes*	20	1,055	11,039
Non-formal education (NFE) centres	740	834	12,968
Daycare centres	94	122	1,520

* Including tertiary education (excluding students studying abroad), vocational institutes and Sanskrit Pathshala.

Source: Ministry of Education, Thimphu.

Pupil-teacher ratio (primary education, UNESCO estimate): 27.7 in 2008/09 (Source: UNESCO Institute for Statistics).

Adult literacy rate (UNESCO estimates): 55.6% (males 67.1%; females 42.2%) in 2007 (Source: UNESCO Institute for Statistics).

Directory

The Government

HEAD OF STATE

Druk Gyalpo ('Dragon King'): HM JIGME KHESAR NAMGYEL WANGCHUCK (succeeded to the throne on 21 December 2006).

LHENGYE ZHUNGTSHOG
(Council of Ministers)
(May 2012)

The Government is formed by the Druk Phuensum Tshogpa (DPT) (Bhutan Peace and Prosperity Party).

Prime Minister: Lyonchhen JIGMI YOZER THINLEY.

Minister of Works and Human Settlement: Lyonpo YESHEY ZIMBA.

Minister of Economic Affairs: Lyonpo KHANDU WANGCHUK.

Minister of Finance: Lyonpo WANGDI NORBU.

Minister of Foreign Affairs: Lyonpo UGYEN TSHERING.

Minister of Health: Lyonpo ZANGLEY DUKPA.

Minister of Home and Cultural Affairs: Lyonpo MINJUR DORJI.

Minister of Education: Lyonpo THAKUR SINGH POWDYEL.

Minister of Agriculture and Forests: Lyonpo PEMA GYAMTSHO.

Minister of Information and Communications: Lyonpo NANDALAL RAI.

Minister of Labour and Human Resources: Lyonpo DORJI WANGDI.

MINISTRIES AND OTHER MAJOR GOVERNMENT BODIES

Ministry of Agriculture and Forests: POB 252, Thimphu; tel. (2) 323765; fax (2) 324520; e-mail pgyamtsho@moa.gov.bt; internet www.moaf.gov.bt.

Ministry of Economic Affairs: Tashichhodzong, POB 141, Thimphu; tel. (2) 322211; fax (2) 323617; e-mail khandu_wangchuk@hotmail.com; internet www.moea.gov.bt.

Ministry of Education: POB 112, Thimphu; tel. (2) 323825; fax (2) 326424; e-mail minister@education.gov.bt; internet www.education.gov.bt.

Ministry of Finance: Tashichhodzong, POB 117, Thimphu; tel. (2) 324867; fax (2) 333976; e-mail wnorbu@mof.gov.bt; internet www.mof.gov.bt.

Ministry of Foreign Affairs: Gyalyong Tshokhang, POB 103, Thimphu; tel. (2) 322771; e-mail ugyen@mofa.gov.bt; internet www.mfa.gov.bt.

Ministry of Health: Kawangsa, POB 108, Thimphu; tel. (2) 323973; fax (2) 323113; e-mail zangleydukpa@health.gov.bt; internet www.health.gov.bt.

Ministry of Home and Cultural Affairs: Tashichhodzong, POB 133, Thimphu; tel. (2) 322301; fax (2) 335905; e-mail lmd@mohca.gov.bt; internet www.mohca.gov.bt.

Ministry of Information and Communications: POB 278, Thimphu; tel. (2) 322144; fax (2) 324860; e-mail secretary@moic.gov.bt; internet www.moic.gov.bt.

Ministry of Labour and Human Resources: Thongsel Lam, Lower Motithang, POB 1036, Thimphu; tel. (2) 333867; fax (2) 326731; e-mail doe@molhr.gov.bt; internet www.molhr.gov.bt.

Ministry of Works and Human Settlement: POB 791, Thimphu; tel. (2) 327998; fax (2) 323122; e-mail mowhs@mowhs.gov.bt; internet www.mowhs.gov.bt.

Anti-Corruption Commission: POB 1113, Thimphu; tel. (2) 334863; fax (2) 334865; e-mail quedenly333@yahoo.com; internet www.anti-corruption.org.bt; f. 2006; Chair. Dasho Aum NETEN ZANGMO; Commrs THINLAY WANGDI, KEZANG JAMTSHO.

Cabinet Secretariat: Tashichhodzong, Thimphu; tel. (2) 321437; fax (2) 321438; e-mail cabinet@druknet.bt; internet www.cabinet.gov.bt.

Gross National Happiness Commission: Convention Centre, POB 127, Thimphu; tel. (2) 326786; fax (2) 322928; e-mail ktshiteem@pc.gov.bt; internet www.gnhc.gov.bt; f. 2008 to replace Planning Commission (f. 1971); Chair. Lyonchhen JIGMI YOZER THINLEY; Vice-Chair. Lyonpo WANGDI NORBU; Sec. KARMA TSHITEEM.

His Majesty's Secretariat: Tashichhodzong, Thimphu; tel. (2) 335530; fax (2) 335519; Sec. Dasho AGAY UGEN DORJI TRONGSA DRONGYER.

National Environment Commission: POB 466, Thimphu; tel. (2) 323384; fax (2) 323385; e-mail secretary@nec.gov.bt; internet www.nec.gov.bt; Hon. Dep. Minister Dr UGYEN TSHEWANG.

National Land Commission: Thimphu; tel. (2) 321217; fax (2) 336063; e-mail sangaykhandu@hotmail.com; internet www.land.gov.bt; f. 2007; Sec. SANGAY KHANDU.

Royal Audit Authority: POB 191, Kawajangsa, Thimphu; tel. (2) 322111; fax (2) 323491; e-mail bhutanaudit@bhutanaudit.gov.bt; internet www.bhutanaudit.gov.bt; f. 1985; Auditor-Gen. UGEN CHEWANG.

Royal Civil Service Commission: POB 163, Thimphu; tel. (2) 322491; fax (2) 323086; internet www.rcsc.gov.bt; f. 1982 under Royal Charter; successor to Dept of Manpower; Chair. Lyonpo THINLEY GYAMTSHO; Commrs PRITHIMAN PRADHAN, KINLEY YANGZOM, BACHU PHUB DORJI, SANGAY DORJI.

Royal Privy Council (Gyal Doen Tshokdey): Thimphu; tel. (2) 337336; fax (2) 337258; f. 2009; Chair. Lyonpo CHENKYAB DORJI; Mems Dasho NADO RINCHEN, Dasho SANGAY WANGCHUG, Dr JAGAR DORJI.

Legislature

NATIONAL COUNCIL (UPPER HOUSE)

Within the National Council, 20 members—one representing each of the 20 electoral districts—were directly elected by a national vote, with the remaining five 'eminent persons' selected by royal appointment. The first round of elections to the National Council was held on 31 December 2007 in 15 districts, and a second round, held on 29 January 2008 in the five remaining districts, completed the voting process.

Chairperson: Thrizin NAMGAY PENJOR.

Vice-Chairperson: SONAM KUENGA.

NATIONAL ASSEMBLY (LOWER HOUSE)

Speaker: Dasho TSHOGPON JIGME TSHULTIM.

Deputy Speaker: YANGKHU TSHERING.

Opposition Leader: Lyonpo TSHERING TOBGAY.

General Election, 24 March 2008

Party	% of votes	Seats
Druk Phuensum Tshogpa (DPT)	67	45
People's Democratic Party (PDP)	33	2
Total	100	47

Election Commission

Election Commission of Bhutan: Thimphu; tel. (2) 334761; fax (2) 334763; e-mail cec@election-bhutan.org.bt; internet www.election-bhutan.org.bt; f. 2006; appointed by the King; Chief Election Commr Dasho KUNZANG WANGDI; Election Commrs Dasho CHOGYAL DAGO RIGDZIN, Aum DEKI PEMA.

Political Organizations

Having previously been banned in accordance with long-standing legislation, the formal registration of political parties commenced in July 2007. However, by March 2008, only two parties—the Druk Phuensum Tshogpa (DPT) and the People's Democratic Party (PDP)—had successfully registered with the Election Commission.

Druk Phuensum Tshogpa (DPT) (Bhutan Peace and Prosperity Party): Chang Lam, Thimphu; tel. (2) 336336; fax (2) 335845; e-mail dpt@druknet.bt; internet www.dpt.bt; f. 2007 following merger of short-lived All People's Party and Bhutan People's United Party; Pres. Lyonchhen JIGMI YOZER THINLEY; Gen. Sec. Lyonpo THINLEY GYAMTSHO.

People's Democratic Party (PDP): Drizang Lam, Lower Motithang, Thimphu; tel. (2) 335557; fax (2) 335757; e-mail info@pdp.bt; internet www.pdp.bt; f. 2007 in asscn with a minister of the outgoing Govt; Pres. Lyonpo TSHERING TOBGAY; Sec.-Gen. SONAM JATSO.

Outside of Bhutan, there are a number of anti-Government organizations, composed principally of Nepali-speaking former residents of Bhutan, based in Kathmandu, Nepal, and New Delhi, India.

Bhutan Communist Party (Marxist-Leninist-Maoist) (BCP—MLM): Nepal; f. 2003; advocates complete revolution in Bhutan; Gen. Sec. VIKALPA.

Bhutan Gurkha National Liberation Front (BGNLF): Nepal; f. 1994; mem. National Front for Democracy in Bhutan, a coalition also involving the BPP and the DNC; Vice-Pres. D. R. KATEL; Gen. Sec. LALIT PRADHAN.

Bhutan National Democratic Party (BNDP): POB 3334, Kathmandu, Nepal; tel. (1) 525682; f. 1992; also has offices in Delhi and Varanasi, India, and in Thapa, Nepal; Pres. D. N. S. DHAKAL; Gen. Sec. Dr HARI P. ADHIKARI.

Bhutan People's Party (BPP): POB 13, Anarmani-4, Bhadrapur Rd, Birtamode, Jhapa, Nepal; tel. and fax (23) 542561; e-mail bpparty@ntc.net.np; internet www.bhutanpeoplesparty.org; f. 1990 as a successor to the People's Forum for Human Rights–Bhutan (f. 1989); advocates unconditional release of all political prisoners, judicial reform, freedom of religious practices, linguistic freedom, freedom of press, speech and expression, and equal rights for all ethnic groups; Pres. BALA RAM POUDYAL; Gen. Sec. DURGA GIRI.

Druk National Congress (DNC): Boudha 6, POB 5754, Kathmandu, Nepal; tel. (1) 2298060; e-mail dnc2006@gmail.com; internet www.bhutandnc.com; f. 1994; advocates democracy and human rights in Bhutan; Pres. KESANG LHENDUP; Gen. Sec. KARMA DUPTHO.

Human Rights Organization of Bhutan (HUROB): Patan Dhoka, POB 172, Lalitpur, Kathmandu, Nepal; tel. (1) 525046; fax (1) 526038; f. 1991; documents alleged human rights violations in Bhutan and co-ordinates welfare activities in eight refugee camps in Nepal for ethnic Nepalese claiming to be from Bhutan; Chair. S. B. SUBBA; Gen. Sec. OM DHUNGEL.

Diplomatic Representation

EMBASSIES IN BHUTAN

Bangladesh: POB 178, Upper Choubachu, Thimphu; tel. (2) 222362; fax (2) 322629; e-mail bdoot@druknet.bt; Ambassador IMTIAZ AHMED.

India: India House Estate, POB 193, Thimphu; tel. (2) 322162; fax (2) 323195; e-mail eoihoc@druknet.bt; internet www.indianembassythimphu.bt; Ambassador PAVAN KUMAR VARMA.

Kuwait: Thimphu; Ambassador NUMAIR AL-GURAINI.

Judicial System

Bhutan has Civil and Criminal Codes, which are based on those laid down by the Shabdrung Ngawang Namgyal in the 17th century. An independent judicial authority was established in 1961, but law was mostly administered at the district level until 1968, when the High Court was set up. A substantially revised Civil and Criminal Procedure Code was endorsed by the National Assembly in 2001. In accordance with the law, a National Judicial Commission was established in 2003. The principal role of this new body was to professionalize further the appointment and tenure of judges in the court system. Following the promulgation of the new Constitution in July 2008, the Supreme Court of Bhutan (which was to consist of a Chief Justice and four magistrates, or drangpons) was established as the highest appellate authority in the country. In February 2010 the first Chief Justice of the Supreme Court, Lyonpo Sonam Tobgye (the incumbent Chief Justice of the High Court), and three drangpons were sworn in, following their appointment by a Royal Commission. In March the National Judicial Commission was belatedly appointed and was expected to appoint the final member of the Supreme Court and to fill vacancies in the High Court in due course.

All citizens have the right to make informal appeal for redress of grievances directly to the King, through the office of the gyalpoi zimpon (court chamberlain).

SUPREME COURT

The Supreme Court is a Court of Record and acts as the guardian of the Constitution. The Court exercises jurisdiction outside Bhutan on the basis of international law principles.

Chief Justice of the Supreme Court: Lyonpo SONAM TOBGYE, Kuengachholing State Guest House, Thimphu.

HIGH COURT

Established in 1968 to review appeals from Lower Courts, although some cases are heard at the first instance. The Full Bench is presided over by the Chief Justice. There are normally eight other judges (drangpons), who are appointed by the King on the recommendation of the National Judicial Commission. Three judges form a quorum.

Chief Justice of the High Court: SANGAY KHANDU (acting), Thimphu; tel. (2) 322344; fax (2) 322921; internet www.judiciary.gov.bt.

OFFICE OF THE ATTORNEY-GENERAL

Office of the Attorney-General: POB 1045, Thori Lam, Lower Motithang, Thimphu; tel. (2) 326889; fax (2) 324606; e-mail oag@oag.gov.bt; internet www.oag.gov.bt; f. 2006; fmrly Office of Legal Affairs; Chief Prosecutor (vacant); Attorney-Gen. PHUNTSHO WANGDI.

Religion

The state religion is Mahayana Buddhism, but the southern Bhutanese are predominantly followers of Hinduism. The main monastic group, the Central Monastic Body (comprising about 1,600 monks in Thimphu and Punakha), led by an elected Head Abbot (je khenpo), is directly supported by the State and spends six months of the year at Tashichhodzong and at Punakha, respectively. A further 2,120 monks, who are members of the District Monastic Bodies, are sustained by the lay population. Religious proselytizing, in any form, is illegal.

Commission for Religious Organizations (Chhoedey Lhentshog): c/o Department of Culture, Ministry of Home and Cultural Affairs, POB 233, Thimphu; f. 2009.

Council for Ecclesiastical Affairs (Dratshang Lhentshog): POB 254, Thimphu; tel. (2) 322754; fax (2) 323867; e-mail dratshang@druknet.bt; f. 1984, replacing the Central Board for Monastic Studies, to oversee the national memorial chorten (a mound-like structure containing Buddhist relics) and all Buddhist meditational centres and schools of Buddhist studies, as well as the Central and District Monastic Bodies; daily affairs of the Council are run by the Central Monastic Secretariat; Chair. His Holiness the 70th Je Khenpo Trulku JIGME CHOEDRA; Sec. KARMA PENJOR.

Hindu Dharma Samudaya of Bhutan (HDSB): Motithang, Thimphu; f. 2007; promotes Hindu religion and values; Chair. Dasho MEGHRAJ GURUNG; Exec. Dir DIPENDRA GIRI.

The Press

In February 2012 there were eleven newspapers licensed in Bhutan. Some of the main newspapers and periodicals are listed below.

Bhutan Observer: POB 1112, Norzin Lam, Thimphu; tel. (2) 334891; fax (2) 327981; e-mail info@bhutanobserver.bt; internet www.bhutanobserver.bt; f. 2006; weekly newspaper; publ. in English and Dzongkha; Man. Dir TENZIN WANGDI; Man. Editor NEEDRUP ZANGPO.

Bhutan Times: POB 1365, Top Floor, Etho Metho Plaza, Norzim Lam, Thimphu; tel. (2) 335006; fax (2) 328451; e-mail bttimes@druknet.bt; internet www.bhutantimes.bt; f. 2006; weekly newspaper; publ. by Bhutan Times Ltd; English and Dzongkha edns; publ. *Bhutan NOW* magazine; Chair. UGEN TSHECHUP; Man. Ed. NAMKHAI NORBU.

Bhutan Today: POB 1532, Thimphu; tel. (2) 336806; fax (2) 336805; internet www.bhutantoday.bt; f. 2008; daily newspaper; Publr and Chair. NGAWANG DORJI; Man. Dir TENZIN DORJI.

Bhutan Youth: POB 1694, Thimphu; tel. (2) 332032; fax (2) 332033; e-mail bhutanyouth@gmail.com; internet www.bhutanyouth.bt; f. 2010; weekly; youth-related issues and news; CEO YANGCHEN DEMA DUKPA; Editor SUNNY TOBGAY.

The Bhutanese: Changangkha, Thegchen Lam, POB 1694, Thimphu; tel. (2) 332032; fax (2) 332033; e-mail editor.thebhutanese@gmail.com; internet www.thebhutanese.bt; f. 2012; bi-weekly; English; CEO TENZING LAMSANG.

Business Bhutan: Norzim Lam, POB 1190, Thimphu; tel. (2) 339904; fax (2) 339882; e-mail editor@businessbhutan.bt; internet www.businessbhutan.bt; f. 2009; weekly newspaper; English and Dzongkha edns; CEO TSHERING WANGCHUK; Editor TASHI DORJI.

Druk Neytshuel: Thimphu; f. 2010; weekly; the country's first exclusively Dzongkha newspaper; CEO SINGYE DORJI; Chief Editor CHUNGDU TSHERING.

Drukpa: POB 885, Thimphu; tel. (2) 324177; fax (2) 324178; e-mail drukpaletters@gmail.com; internet www.drukpa.bt; f. 2009; monthly news magazine; Publr JIGME TSHULTIM, Jr; Editor MITRA RAJ DHITAL.

The Journalist: POB 1336, Norzim Lam, Thimphu; tel. (2) 327540; fax (2) 321680; e-mail iamthejournalist@gmail.com; internet www.thejournalist.bt; f. 2009; weekly Sunday newspaper; CEO SONAM GYELTSHEN; Editor PEKEY SAMAL.

Kuensel Corporation: POB 204, Thimphu; tel. (2) 322483; fax (2) 322975; e-mail editor@kuensel.com.bt; internet www.kuenselonline.com; f. 1965 as a weekly govt bulletin; reorg. as a national weekly newspaper in 1986; became autonomous corporation in 1992 (previously under Dept of Information), incorporating former Royal Government Press; six issues weekly from 2009; in English and Dzongkha; offered 49% of shares to public in 2006, while Government retained controlling 51%; Man. Dir CHENCHO TSHERING; Editor PHUNTSHO WANGDI.

PRESS ASSOCIATIONS

Bhutan Media Foundation (BMF): POB 1655, Thori Lam, Thimphu; tel. (2) 331705; fax (2) 331702; e-mail bhutanmediafoundation@gmail.com; internet www.bmf.bt; f. 2010; estd through a Royal Charter; works to foster media growth; Chair. CHENCHO TSHERING; Exec. Dir LILY WANGCHHUK.

Bhutan Media Foundation (BMF): POB 1655, Thori Lam, Thimphu; tel. (2) 331705; fax (2) 331702; e-mail bhutanmediafoundation@gmail.com; internet www.bmf.bt; f. 2010; estd through a Royal Charter; works to foster media growth; Chair. CHENCHO TSHERING; Exec. Dir LILY WANGCHHUK.

Publishers

Absolute Bhutan Books: POB 698, Thimphu; tel. (2) 335336; fax (2) 332007; e-mail abs@druknet.bt; internet www.absolutebhutanbooks.com.bt; publ. of books and journals; CEO LILY WANGCHUK.

KMT Printers and Publishers: Thimphu; tel. (2) 325026; fax (2) 324081; publs incl. books, journals and textbooks; organizer of National Book Fair, Thimphu; Gen. Man. PEMA TASHI; Man. Dir LOPEN KINZANG THINLEY.

Rabsell Media Services: POB 1321, Thimphu; tel. (2) 334641; publr of books on history of Bhutanese royal family; co-publr of Discover Bhutan magazine; Gen. Man. TSHERING WANGCHUCK.

Broadcasting and Communications

TELECOMMUNICATIONS

In April 2011, according to the Ministry of Information and Communications, there were 419,926 mobile cellular telephone subscribers (59.3% of the total population) and 27,152 fixed-line subscribers.

Bhutan Infocomm and Media Authority (BICMA): POB 1072, Olakha, Thimphu; tel. (2) 321506; fax (2) 326909; e-mail bca@druknet.bt; internet www.bicma.gov.bt; f. 2000 as Bhutan Telecommunications Authority under Bhutan Telecommunications Act; telecommunications and media regulatory body; regulatory remit extended to include Information and Communication Technology and media services in 2005; began operations as autonomous authority, independent of Ministry of Information and Communications, from 1 January 2007; Dir SONAM PHUNTSHO.

Bhutan Telecom Ltd: 2/28 Drophen Lam, Thimphu; tel. (2) 322678; fax (2) 328160; e-mail bt@bt.bt; internet www.telecom.net.bt; f. 2000; state-owned public corpn; fmr regulatory authority and monopoly provider of telecommunications services; latterly a provider of fixed-line, mobile and internet services; responsible for the development of national telecommunications infrastructure; Chair. LAM DORJI; Man. Dir THINLEY DORJI.

B-Mobile: Drophen Lam, POB 134, Thimphu; tel. (2) 320194; fax (2) 320193; e-mail mkto@telecom.net.bt; internet www.telecom.net.bt; f. 2002; offered mobile cellular tel. services from Nov. 2003; covered Thimphu and most of Paro by mid-2004; coverage extended to all 20 districts by early 2008; more than 167,000 subscribers (2008); subsidiary of Bhutan Telecom Ltd; Gen. Man. TANDI WANGCHUK.

DrukNet: 2/28 Drophen Lam, POB 134, Thimphu; tel. (2) 326998; fax (2) 328160; e-mail info@druknet.bt; internet www.druknet.bt; f. 1999; internet service provider; subsidiary of Bhutan Telecom Ltd; Head GANGA SHARMA; Gen. Man. TSHERING NORBU.

Tashi InfoComm Ltd (TashiCell): POB 1502, Norzim Lam, Thimphu; tel. 77889977 (mobile); fax (2) 336318; e-mail mail@tashicell.com; internet www.tashicell.com; f. 2008; first privately owned mobile cellular tel. co in Bhutan; initially covered seven districts; 60,000 subscribers (2010); Chair. WANGCHUK DORJI; Exec. Dir TASHI TSHERING.

BROADCASTING

Radio

Following the passage of an Information, Communications and Media Act in June 2006, the country's first private radio stations were granted FM operating licences. By June 2011 there were six private stations in operation.

Bhutan Broadcasting Service (BBS): POB 101, Thimphu; tel. (2) 323071; fax (2) 323073; e-mail bbs@bbs.com.bt; internet www.bbs.com.bt; f. 1973 as Radio Nat. Youth Asscn of Bhutan (NYAB); became autonomous corpn in 1992 (previously under Dept of Information), but remains 100% state-owned; short-wave radio station broadcasting daily in Dzongkha, Sharchopkha, Nepali (Lhotsamkha) and English; FM broadcasts are 24 hours a day in Dzongkha, seven hours a day in Nepali and Sharchopkha and 12 hours a day in English; a television service was launched in 1999; in early 2012 a second TV channel (BBS 2) was launched; Chair. Aum SANGAY ZAM; Man. Dir THINLEY DORJI.

Centennial Radio 101 FM: Ground Floor, Karma Tshongkhang Bldg, Thimphu; f. 2008; news, current affairs, music and entertainment programmes; CEO DORJI WANGCHUK.

Kuzoo FM: POB 419, Thimphu; tel. (2) 335984; fax (2) 335263; e-mail fm@kuzoo.net; internet www.kuzoo.net; f. 2006; broadcasts 24 hours a day on FM in Dzongkha and English; news, information and entertainment programmes.

Radio Valley: Rabten Lam, above Pension Board Colony, POB 224/225, Thimphu; tel. (2) 335733; fax (2) 335744; e-mail the_soundweaver@hotmail.com; internet www.radiovalley.bt; f. 2007; broadcasts 12 hours a day on FM; music, entertainment and information programmes to be broadcast upon commencement of full operations; Founder KINLEY CHOZOM.

Television

Television was officially introduced as recently as 1999, when the state broadcaster BBS launched a limited service (in Dzongkha and English) in Thimphu. A nation-wide television service via satellite commenced in 2006, allowing BBS to broadcast to almost 40 countries. BBS broadcasts are limited to 10 hours a day and consist principally of national news and documentaries. In 1999 the Government issued the first licences to cable television operators. By mid-2007, according to official figures, there were 52 cable television operators providing more than 30 channels. Limited 'direct-to-home' private satellite services were approved in 2009.

Bhutan Broadcasting Service (BBS): see Radio

Finance

(cap. = capital; auth. = authorized; p.u. = paid up; res = reserves; dep. = deposits; m. = million; brs = branches; amounts in ngultrum)

BANKING

Central Bank

Royal Monetary Authority (RMA): POB 154, Thimphu; tel. (2) 323111; fax (2) 322847; e-mail rmarsd@rma.org.bt; internet www.rma.org.bt; f. 1982; bank of issue; frames and implements official monetary policy, co-ordinates the activities of financial institutions and holds foreign-exchange deposits on behalf of the Govt; cap. 21m., res 709m., dep. 14,656m. (June 2007); Gov. and Chair DAW TENZIN.

Commercial Banks

Bank of Bhutan Ltd: Samdrup Lam, POB 75, Phuentsholing; tel. (5) 252225; fax (5) 252955; e-mail bobho1@druknet.bt; internet www.bob.bt; f. 1968; 20% owned by the State Bank of India and 80% by the Govt of Bhutan; wholly managed by Govt of Bhutan from 1997; cap. 400m., res 1,643m., dep. 22,178m. (Dec. 2009); Chair. KARMA W. PENJOR; 26 brs and 3 extension counters.

Bhutan National Bank Ltd (BNB): POB 439, Thimphu; tel. (2) 328577; fax (2) 328839; internet www.bnb.com.bt; f. 1996; Bhutan's second commercial bank; partially privatized in 1998; 13.6% owned by Govt and 20.1% by Asian Development Bank; cap. 355.5m., res 933.2m., dep. 14,601.4m. (2008); Chair. UGYEN NAMGYAL; CEO KIPCHU TSHERING; 10 brs.

Druk PNB Bank Ltd: Norzim Lam, Thimphu; tel. (2) 324497; fax (2) 333156; e-mail corporate@drukpnbbank.bt; internet www.drukpnbbank.bt; f. 2010; 51% owned by Punjab National Bank (India), 19% by local promoters and 30% by Bhutanese public; share cap. 300m. (2011); CEO N. K. ARORA; three brs.

Tashi Bank Ltd (T Bank Ltd): TCC Complex Bldg, Norzin Lam, POB 631, Thimphu; tel. 17117664 (mobile); fax (2) 336236; internet www.tbank.com.bt; f. 2010; 60% owned by three mems of Tashi Group, 40% owned by public; share cap. 220m. (2010); CEO TSHERING DORJI.

Development Bank

Bhutan Development Finance Corporation (BDFC): POB 256, Thimphu; tel. (2) 322579; fax (2) 323428; e-mail info@bdfcl.com.bt; internet www.bdfcl.com.bt; f. 1988; provides industrial loans and short- and medium-term agricultural loans; 93.50% state-owned; cap. p.u. 100m., receivable loans 2,220.9m. (2008); Chair. Dasho NIMA WANGDI; Man. Dir NGAWANG GYETSE; three regional offices, 29 brs and two sub-brs.

STOCK EXCHANGE

Royal Securities Exchange of Bhutan Ltd (RSEB): POB 742, Thimphu; tel. (2) 323994; fax (2) 323849; e-mail rseb@druknet.bt; internet www.rsebl.org.bt; f. 1993; supervised by the Royal Monetary Authority; open to Bhutanese nationals only; 21 listed cos (2010); Chair. DAW TENZIN; CEO DORJI PHUNTSHO.

INSURANCE

Bhutan Insurance Ltd: Chorten Lam, POB 779, Thimphu; tel. (2) 339893; fax (2) 339895; e-mail info@bhutaninsurance.com.bt; internet www.bhutaninsurance.com.bt; f. 2009; 40% owned by private investors, 60% to be offered to public shareholders; provides personal, commercial and industrial insurance, and motor vehicle third-party liability insurance; Man. Dir and CEO TSHERING GYALTSHEN; Gen. Man. DAMDI DORJI.

Royal Insurance Corporation of Bhutan Ltd: POB 315, Thimphu; tel. (2) 322426; fax (2) 323677; e-mail insure@druknet.bt; internet www.ricb.com.bt; f. 1975; provides general and life insurance and credit investment services; Chair. DASHO PENJORE; CEO DASHO NAMGYAL LHENDUP; 10 brs and development centres.

Trade and Industry

GOVERNMENT AGENCIES

Druk Holding and Investments Ltd (DHI): POB 1127, Motithang, Thimphu; tel. (2) 336257; fax (2) 336259; e-mail info@dhi.bt; internet www.dhi.bt; f. 2007 to manage the existing and future investments of the Govt; managed an initial grouping of 14 cos in sectors incl. hydropower, banking, minerals and natural resources; cap. p.u. Nu 44,268.3m (2009); Chair. Lyonpo OM PRADHAN; CEO KARMA YONTEN.

Food Corporation of Bhutan (FCB): POB 80, Phuentsholing; tel. (5) 252241; fax (5) 252289; e-mail drukfood@druknet.bt; f. 1974; activities include procurement and distribution of food grains and other essential commodities through appointed FCB agents; marketing of surplus agricultural and horticultural produce through FCB-regulated market outlets; logistics concerning World Food Programme food aid; maintenance of buffer stocks to offset any emergency food shortages; maintenance of SAARC Food Security Reserve Stock; exporting oranges and potatoes; Chair. TENZIN CHOPHEL; Man. Dir KUNZANG NAMGYEL; 20 outlets and 68 agents.

Natural Resources Development Corporation Ltd (NRDCL): POB 192, Thimphu; tel. (2) 323834; fax (2) 325585; e-mail info@nrdcl.bt; internet www.nrdcl.bt; fmrly Forestry Devt Corpn; renamed as above in 2007; fixes price of sand and timber; oversees quarrying and mining of sand, stone and other natural resources; Chair. PHUNTSHO NORBU; CEO SANGAY GYALTSHEN.

State Trading Corpn of Bhutan Ltd (STCB): POB 76, Phuentsholing; tel. (5) 252745; fax (5) 252619; e-mail stcbl@druknet.bt; internet www.stcb.bt; f. 1969; manages imports and exports of vehicles, IT and construction materials on behalf of the Govt; 51% govt-owned; initial public offering of 49% of shares in 1997; Man. Dir DORJI NAMGAY; brs in Thimphu (POB 272; tel. (2) 324785; fax (2) 322953; e-mail stcbthim@druknet.bt) and Kolkata (Calcutta), India (e-mail stcbkol@vsnl.net).

CHAMBER OF COMMERCE

Bhutan Chamber of Commerce and Industry (BCCI): Doebum Lam, POB 147, Thimphu; tel. (2) 322742; fax (2) 323936; e-mail bccihrd@gmail.com; internet www.bcci.org.bt; f. 1980; reorg. 1988; promotion of trade and industry and privatization, information dissemination, private-sector human resource devt; 14 exec. mems; 20-mem. district exec. cttee; Pres. TOPGYAL DORJI; Sec.-Gen. PHUB TSHERING.

INDUSTRIAL AND TRADE ASSOCIATIONS

Association of Bhutanese Industries: POB 54, Phuentsholing; tel. (5) 251340; fax (5) 251341; e-mail abi@abibhutan.com; internet www.abibhutan.com; Pres. Dasho RINCHEN DORJI.

Bhutan Exporter Association: POB 256, Phuentsholing; tel. (5) 251917; fax (5) 251918; e-mail bea@druknet.bt; Pres. GALEY NIMA.

Construction Association of Bhutan: Thimphu; tel. (2) 327830; fax (2) 327831; e-mail cab@druknet.bt; internet www.cab.org.bt; f. 2000; Chair. UGEN TSECHUP DORJI.

Handicraft Association of Bhutan: POB 870, Thimphu; tel. (5) 17110557; e-mail hab@druknet.bt; f. 2005; Chair. TSHERING DEM ONGDI.

Wood Based Industries Association: POB 1601, Phuentsholing; tel. (2) 337364; Pres THUBDRUP GYELTSHEN.

UTILITIES

Electricity

Bhutan Electricity Authority (BEA): c/o Ministry of Economic Affairs, Tashichhodzong, POB 1557, Thimphu; tel. (2) 327317; fax (2) 328757; e-mail bea@druknet.bt; internet www.bea.gov.bt; f. 1991; regulates the electricity supply industry; CEO KARMA TSHERING.

Department of Energy: c/o Ministry of Economic Affairs, Tashichhodzong, POB 141, Thimphu; tel. (2) 322279; fax (2) 328278; internet www.moea.gov.bt/doe.php; Dir-Gen. YESHEY WANGDI.

Bhutan Power Corporation Ltd: POB 580, Thimphu; tel. (2) 325095; fax (2) 322279; e-mail hr@bpc.bt; internet www.bpc.bt; f. 2002; responsible for ensuring electricity supply for the whole country at an affordable cost by 2020 and for providing uninterrupted transmission access for export of surplus power; operations in 19 districts; Chair. ZIMPON PENJORE; Man. Dir BHARAT TAMANG YONZEN.

Druk Green Power Corpn Ltd: POB 1351, Thimphu; tel. (2) 336413; fax (2) 336342; internet www.drukgreen.bt; f. 2008 on amalgamation of management of Basochhu Hydropower Corpn, Chhukha Hydropower Corpn and Kurichhu Project Authority; assumed control of Tala Hydroelectric Project Authority in April 2009; combined installed capacity 1,480 MW; Dagachhu Project (114 MW) to be commissioned in near future; intended to manage all future power projects in Bhutan; cap. p.u. Nu 6,855m. (2009); Chair. KARMA TSHITEEM; Man. Dir Dasho CHHEWANG RINZIN.

Water

Thimphu City Corporation (Water Supply Unit): POB 215, Thimphu; tel. (2) 324710; fax (2) 324315; e-mail tda@druknet.bt; internet www.tcc.gov.bt; f. 1982; responsible for water supply of Thimphu municipality; Head BHIMLAL DHUNGEL.

TRADE UNIONS

Under long-standing legislation, trade union activity is illegal in Bhutan. In early 2007 a Labour Act was passed, permitting (among other things) the formation of 'workers' associations'.

Transport

ROADS AND TRACKS

In June 2005 there were 4,392.5 km of roads in Bhutan, of which 2,461.3 km were black-topped and included 1,579 km designated national highways. Surfaced roads link the important border towns of Phuentsholing, Gelephu, Sarpang and Samdrup Jongkhar in southern Bhutan to towns in West Bengal and Assam (Asom) in India. There is a shortage of road transport. Yaks, ponies and mules are still the chief means of transport on the rough mountain tracks. A Roads Sector Master Plan (2007–27) envisaged the construction of 2,587.4 km of feeder roads throughout Bhutan, a second East–West Highway (794 km) stretching from Sipsu to Jomotshankha, and 410 km of highways to improve inter-connectivity between districts. It was hoped that 75% of the country's rural population would live within half a day's walk of the nearest road by the end of the 10th Five-Year Plan in 2013.

Road Safety and Transport Authority: Thimphu; tel. (2) 321282; fax (2) 321281; e-mail director@rsta.gov.bt; internet www.rsta.gov.bt; f. 1995; under Ministry of Information and Communications; regulates all motor vehicle activities and surface transport services; Dir TASHI NORBU.

Transport Corpn of Bhutan: Phuentsholing; tel. (5) 252476; f. 1982; subsidiary of Royal Insurance Corpn of Bhutan; operates direct coach service between Phuentsholing and Kolkata (Calcutta), India, via Siliguri, India.

RAILWAY

In late 2009 an agreement was signed by Bhutan and India to construct a strategically important 20-km railway line linking the two countries across the foothills of the Himalayas. Bhutan's first railway line, which was to be funded and built by India, was to run between Hasimara in West Bengal to Toribari in south Bhutan.

CIVIL AVIATION

There is an international airport at Paro, and a runway strip at Trashigang. There are also some 30 helicopter landing pads, which are used, by arrangement with the Indian military and aviation authorities, solely by government officials. The Council of Ministers approved the operation of a domestic helicopter service to improve mobility and to promote tourism; by mid-2003 five domestic heliports had been surveyed and found acceptable. Two domestic airports, at Yonphula (34 km south of Trashigang) and Bumthang became operational in late 2011; a third domestic airport, at Gelephu, was under construction, with completion expected by mid-2012. In December 2011 Bhutan's first private airline, Tashi Air (also known as Bhutan Airlines), launched domestic services from Paro to Bumthang and Yonphula.

Department of Civil Aviation: c/o Ministry of Information and Communications, Woochu, Paro; tel. and fax (8) 271407; fax (8) 271909; e-mail aviation@druknet.bt; internet www.dca.gov.bt; state-owned; f. 1986; Dir-Gen. PHALA DORJI.

Druk Air Corpn Ltd (Royal Bhutan Airlines): Head Office, Nemeyzampa, PO Paro; tel. (8) 271856; fax (8) 271861; e-mail drukair@druknet.bt; internet www.drukair.com.bt; national airline; f. 1981; became fully operational in 1983; services from Paro to Delhi, Kolkata, Bagdora and Gaya (winter only) in India, Bangladesh, Nepal and Thailand; charter services available; Chair. KESANG WANGDI; Man. Dir TANDIN JAMTSHO.

Tashi Air (Bhutan Airlines): Phuentsholing; tel. (5) 252109; fax (5) 252110; e-mail tashi@tashigroup.bt; internet www.tashigroup.bt; f. 2011; owned by the Tashi Group; CEO Capt. DAVID YOUNG.

Tourism

Bhutan was opened to tourism in 1974. Tourists travel in organized 'package', cultural or trekking tours, or individually, accompanied by trained guides; independent, unaccompanied travel is not permitted within the kingdom. In 1991 the Government began transferring the tourism industry to the private sector and licences were issued to new private tourism operators. The Association of Bhutan Tour Operators (ABTO) was established in 2000 to act as a forum for co-ordinating tourism issues among the travel agencies. In 2008 the Tourism Council of Bhutan was established as an autonomous inter-governmental agency, replacing the Department of Tourism, to optimize the role of the industry. The previously closed north-east region of Merak-Sakteng was opened to tour groups from September 2010. In 2010 the total number of foreign visitors was 26,938 and receipts from tourism increased by almost 10% to reach about US $35m. According to the Tourism Council of Bhutan, in 2011 tourist arrivals rose significantly: 36,765 international tourists visited the kingdom (excluding business travellers and regional tourists) and receipts from tourism increased to $47.7m.

Tourism Council of Bhutan (TCB): POB 126, Thimphu; tel. (2) 323251; fax (2) 323695; e-mail dot@tourism.gov.bt; internet www.tourism.gov.bt; f. 2008 to replace the Department of Tourism; autonomous inter-governmental agency; manages and develops the tourism industry; Chair. JIGME YOZER THINLEY; Dir-Gen. KESANG WANGDI.

Association of Bhutanese Tour Operators (ABTO): POB 938, Thimphu; tel. (2) 322862; fax (2) 325286; e-mail abto@druknet.bt; internet www.abto.org.bt; f. 2000 to provide forum for mems' views and to unite, supervise and co-ordinate activities of mems; Exec. Dir SONAM DORJI; 245 mem. tour operators (March 2011).

Defence

The strength of the Royal Bhutan Army (RBA), which was established in the 1950s and which is under the direct command of the King, was officially said to number 9,021 at June 2007. Membership of the RBA is based on voluntary recruitment augmented by a form of conscription. The RBA includes the Royal Bodyguards, an élite branch of the armed forces responsible for the security of the King, the royal family, and other high-ranking officials. Regular army training facilities are provided, on a functional basis, by an Indian military training team (IMTRAT), whose main personnel are stationed at Haa. The RBA and the Royal Bhutan Police were significantly strengthened from 2000 owing to the growing numbers of armed Indian militants who had established military camps on southern Bhutanese territory. In 2007, however, army officials proposed a reduction in military personnel to 8,000. In addition, the National Assembly resolved that recruitment and training of militia should be renewed.

No reference is made in the Indo-Bhutan Treaty to any aid by India for the defence of Bhutan. In November 1958, however, the Prime Minister of India declared that any act of aggression against Bhutan would be regarded as an act of aggression against India.

Expenditure on Public Order and Safety: 552.7m. ngultrum in 2003/04.

Supreme Commander in Chief of the Royal Bhutan Army: HM JIGME KHESAR NAMGYEL WANGCHUCK.

Chief of Operations, Royal Bhutan Army: Goongloen Wogma BATOO TSHERING.

Commandant of the Royal Bodyguards: Goongloen Wogma DHENDUP TSHERING.

Education

Traditionally, education in Bhutan was purely monastic, and the establishment of the contemporary state education system was the result of the reforming zeal of the third King, Jigme Dorji Wangchuck. The proposed outlay on education under the Tenth Plan (2008–13) was Nu 10,333.5m. (equivalent to about 7.0% of total expenditure). In 2008/09 Government expenditure on education totalled Nu 3,605.5m. (15.6% of total expenditure). In 2010 there were 52 privately operated schools (the majority in Thimphu), including 25 kindergartens; these schools were under the supervision of the Ministry of Education. English is the medium of instruction, and Dzongkha is a compulsory subject.

The total number of enrolled students in Bhutan was 14,000 in 1974. By 2010, however, the total had risen to more than 170,000. All schools are co-educational and follow a syllabus that initially reflected British and Indian practices, but in recent times education at both primary and secondary levels has become increasingly localized, in order to take into account national needs. Primary education begins with a pre-primary year (the minimum entry age being six years) and lasts for seven years. Secondary education lasts a further six years, with two years spent at each of three levels, following a 2002 reclassification of secondary schools into lower, middle and higher secondary schools. Tertiary education includes various first degree courses offered by 10 colleges under the supervision of the Royal University of Bhutan (RUB), which was established in 2003.

In 2008/09 the total enrolment at primary and secondary schools was equivalent to an estimated 86% of the school-age population. In the same year, enrolment at primary schools included 88% of children in the relevant age-group (boys 87%; girls 89%), while the ratio for secondary enrolment was 47% of pupils in the relevant age-group (boys 45%; girls 48%). Enrolment at primary schools (excluding community primary schools) increased from 9,039 (including only 456 girls) in 1970 to 24,586 (including 12,201 girls) in 2010. Between 1970 and 2010, enrolment at secondary schools increased from 714 (boys 690; girls 24) to 115,587 (boys 57,833; girls 57,754). In 2010 there were 30,232 pupils in community primary schools. In 2010 girls' enrolment was nearing that of boys at all levels, averaging just over 50% of total enrolment at all levels of secondary education.

BOLIVIA

Introductory Survey

LOCATION, CLIMATE, LANGUAGE, RELIGION, FLAG, CAPITAL

The Plurinational State of Bolivia is a land-locked state in South America, bordered by Chile and Peru to the west, by Brazil to the north and east, and by Paraguay and Argentina to the south. The climate varies, according to altitude, from humid tropical conditions in the northern and eastern lowlands, which are less than 500 m (1,640 ft) above sea level, to the cool and cold zones at altitudes of more than 3,500 m (about 11,500 ft) in the Andes mountains. The official languages are Spanish, Quechua and Aymará. Almost all of the inhabitants profess Christianity, and the great majority are adherents of the Roman Catholic Church. The national civil flag (proportions 2 by 3) has three equal horizontal stripes, of red, yellow and green. The state flag has, in addition, the national coat of arms in the centre of the yellow stripe. The legal capital is Sucre. The administrative capital and seat of government is La Paz.

CONTEMPORARY POLITICAL HISTORY

Historical Context

The Incas of Bolivia were conquered by Spain in 1538 and, although there were many revolts against Spanish rule, independence was not achieved until 1825. Bolivian history has been characterized by recurrent internal strife, resulting in a lengthy succession of presidents, and frequent territorial disputes with its neighbours, including the 1879–83 War of the Pacific between Bolivia, Peru and Chile, which resulted in the loss of Bolivia's coastline, and the Chaco Wars of 1928–30 and 1932–35 against Paraguay.

Domestic Political Affairs

At a presidential election in 1951 the largest share of the vote was won by Dr Víctor Paz Estenssoro, the candidate of the Movimiento Nacionalista Revolucionario (MNR), who had been living in Argentina since 1946. He was denied permission to return to Bolivia and contested the election *in absentia*. However, he failed to gain an absolute majority, and the incumbent President transferred power to a junta of army officers. This regime was overthrown in 1952, when a popular uprising enabled Paz Estenssoro to return from exile and assume the presidency. His Government, a coalition of the MNR and the Labour Party, committed itself to profound social revolution. The coalition nationalized the tin mines and introduced universal suffrage and land reform. Dr Hernán Siles Zuazo, a leading figure in the 1952 revolution, was elected President for the 1956–60 term, and Dr Paz Estenssoro was again elected President in 1960. However, the powerful trade unions came into conflict with the Government, and in 1964, following widespread strikes and disorder, Paz Estenssoro was overthrown by the Vice-President, Gen. René Barrientos Ortuño, who was supported by the army. After serving with Gen. Alfredo Ovando Candía as Co-President under a military junta, Gen. Barrientos resigned in January 1966 to campaign for the presidency; he was elected in July.

President Barrientos encountered strong opposition from left-wing groups, including mineworkers' unions. There was also a guerrilla uprising in south-eastern Bolivia, led by Dr Ernesto ('Che') Guevara, the Argentine-born revolutionary who had played a leading role in the Castro regime in Cuba. However, the insurgency was suppressed by government troops, with the help of US advisers, and guerrilla warfare ended in October 1967, when Guevara was captured and killed. In April 1969 President Barrientos was killed in an air crash and Dr Luis Adolfo Siles Salinas, the Vice-President, succeeded to the presidency. In September, however, Siles Salinas was deposed by the armed forces, who reinstated Gen. Ovando. He was forced to resign in October 1970, when, after a power struggle between right-wing and left-wing army officers, Gen. Juan José Torres González, who had support from leftists, emerged as President, pledging support for agrarian reform and worker participation in management. A 'People's Assembly', formed by Marxist politicians, radical students and leaders of trade unions, was allowed to meet and demanded the introduction of extreme socialist measures, causing disquiet in right-wing circles. President Torres was deposed in August 1971 by Col (later Gen.) Hugo Banzer Suárez, who drew support from the right-wing Falange Socialista Boliviana and a section of the MNR, as well as from the army. In June 1973 President Banzer announced an imminent return to constitutional government, but elections were later postponed to June 1974. The MNR withdrew its support and entered into active opposition.

Following an attempted military coup in June 1974, all portfolios within the Cabinet were assigned to military personnel. After another failed coup attempt in November, President Banzer declared that elections had been postponed indefinitely and that his military regime would retain power until at least 1980. All political and union activity was banned. Political and industrial unrest in 1976, however, led Banzer to announce that elections would be held in July 1978. Allegations of fraud rendered the elections void, but Gen. Juan Pereda Asbún, the armed forces candidate in the elections, staged a successful military coup. In November his right-wing Government was overthrown in another coup, led by Gen. David Padilla Aranciba, Commander-in-Chief of the Army, with the support of national left-wing elements.

Presidential and congressional elections were held in July 1979. The presidential poll resulted in almost equal support for two ex-Presidents, Siles Zuazo and Paz Estenssoro, who were now leading rival factions of the MNR. An interim Government was formed under Walter Guevara Arce, but this administration was overthrown on 1 November by a right-wing army officer, Col Alberto Natusch Busch. He withdrew 15 days later after failing to gain the support of the Congreso (Congress), which elected Dra Lidia Gueiler Tejada, President of the Cámara de Diputados (Chamber of Deputies), as interim Head of State pending further elections.

The result of the 1980 presidential election was inconclusive, and in July, before the Congreso could meet to decide between the two main contenders (again Siles Zuazo and Paz Estenssoro), a military junta led by an army commander, Gen. Luis García Meza, staged a coup—the 189th in Bolivia's 154 years of independence. In August 1981 a military uprising forced Gen. García to resign. In September the junta transferred power to another army commander, Gen. Celso Torrelio Villa, who declared his intention to return the country to democracy within three years. Labour unrest, provoked by Bolivia's severe economic crisis, was appeased by restitution of trade union and political rights, and a mainly civilian Cabinet was appointed in April 1982. Elections were scheduled for April 1983. The political liberalization disturbed the armed forces, who attempted to create a climate of violence, and President Torrelio resigned in July 1982, amid rumours of an impending coup. The junta installed the less moderate Gen. Guido Vildoso Calderón, the Army Chief of Staff, as President. Unable to resolve the worsening economic crisis or to control a general strike, in September the military regime announced that power would be handed over in October to the Congreso that had originally been elected in 1980. Siles Zuazo was duly elected President by the Congreso, and was sworn in for a four-year term in October 1982.

A return to democratic rule

President Siles Zuazo appointed a coalition Cabinet consisting of members of his own party, the Movimiento Nacionalista Revolucionario de Izquierda (MNRI), the Movimiento de la Izquierda Revolucionaria (MIR) and the Partido Comunista de Bolivia (PCB). Economic aid from the USA and Europe was resumed, but the Government found itself unable to fulfil the expectations that had been created by the return to democratic rule. The entire Cabinet resigned in August 1983, and the President appointed a Cabinet in which the number of portfolios that were held by the right-wing of the MNRI, the Partido Demócrata Cristiano (PDC) and independents was increased. The MIR joined forces with the MNR and with business interests in rejecting the Government's policy of complying with IMF conditions for assistance, which involved harsh economic measures. The Government lost its majority in the Congreso and was confronted by strikes and mass labour demonstrations. In November the opposition-dominated Senado Nacional (Senate) approved an increase of 100% in the minimum wage, in defiance of the Government's austerity measures. Following a 48-hour general strike, the whole Cabinet resigned once again in December, in anticipation of an opposition motion of censure. In January 1984 President Siles Zuazo appointed a new coalition Cabinet, including 13 members of the previous Government.

At elections in July 1985, amid reports of electoral malpractice and poor organization, the right-wing Acción Democrática Nacionalista (ADN), whose presidential candidate was the former dictator Gen. Hugo Banzer Suárez, received 29% of the votes cast, and the MNR obtained 26%, while the MIR was the leading left-wing party. At a further round of voting in the Congreso in August, an alliance between the MNR and the leading left-wing groups, including the MIR, enabled Víctor Paz Estenssoro of the MNR to return to the presidency. The armed forces pledged their support for the new Government.

On taking office in August 1985, the new Government immediately introduced a very strict economic programme, designed to reduce inflation, which was estimated to have reached 14,173% in the year to August. The trade union confederation, the Central Obrera Boliviana (COB), rejected the programme and called an indefinite general strike in September. The Government responded by declaring the strike illegal and by ordering a 90-day state of siege throughout Bolivia. Leading trade unionists were detained or banished, and thousands of strikers were arrested. The strike was called off in October, when union leaders agreed to hold talks with the Government. Demonstrations and strikes in protest against the Government's austerity measures were held throughout 1986 and 1987, culminating in April 1988 with a national hunger strike, called by the COB.

Presidential and congressional elections took place in May 1989. No candidate had gained the requisite absolute majority, but Gen. Banzer Suárez of the ADN withdrew his candidacy in order to support his former adversary, Jaime Paz Zamora of the MIR, in a congressional vote. Paz Zamora was duly elected to the presidency in August and a coalition Government of 'national unity', the Acuerdo Patriótico, was then formed.

From 1988 the Government increased its attempts to reduce the illegal production of coca. As a result, during 1989 clashes between the drugs-control troops, Unidad Móvil de Patrullaje Rural (UMOPAR), and drugs-traffickers intensified, particularly in the coca processing region of northern Beni. By the middle of the year, however, it became clear that the Government had failed to attain the targets of its coca eradication programme, having encountered staunch opposition from the powerful coca growers' organizations. Paz Zamora was critical of the militaristic approach of the USA to coca eradication and emphasized the need for economic and social support. In May 1990, however, he accepted US $35m. in military aid from the USA.

In March 1991 the reputation of the Government was seriously undermined when three of its senior officials were forced to resign amid allegations of corruption. Moreover, the appointment in February of Col Faustino Rico Toro as the new head of Bolivia's anti-drugs-trafficking force had provoked widespread outrage. In addition to his alleged connections with illegal drugs-traffickers, Rico was accused of having committed human rights abuses during his tenure as Chief of Army Intelligence in 1980–81. Rico resigned from his new position in March. Later that month, following accusations by the USA linking them with illegal drugs-traffickers, the Minister of the Interior, Migration and Justice and the Chief of Police also resigned. In July the Government announced a decree granting a 120-day amnesty to drugs-traffickers to surrender voluntarily. In return, they were offered minimum prison sentences and the guarantee that they would not risk extradition to the USA. As many as seven of the country's most powerful drugs-traffickers were reported to have taken advantage of the amnesty.

In April 1993 the Supreme Court found the former military dictator Gen. Luis García Meza guilty on 49 charges of murder, human rights abuses, corruption and fraud, and sentenced him, *in absentia*, to 30 years' imprisonment. Similar sentences were imposed on 14 of his collaborators. García Meza was extradited from Brazil in 1994 and began his prison sentence in March 1995.

A presidential election was held in June 1993. Again, no candidate secured the requisite absolute majority, so a congressional vote was scheduled to take place in August to decide between the two main contenders, Sánchez de Lozada of the MNR and Banzer Suárez, who was supported by both the ADN and the MIR. However, Banzer withdrew from the contest, thereby leaving Sánchez de Lozada's candidacy unopposed. At legislative elections, conducted simultaneously, the MNR secured the most seats in the bicameral Congreso, although it had to form a coalition with the Unión Cívica Solidaridad (UCS) and the Movimiento Bolivia Libre (MBL) in order to secure a congressional majority.

In early 1995 government plans to privatize much of the education system and to restrict teachers' rights to union membership provoked industrial action by teachers nation-wide. In response to a call by the COB for an indefinite strike the Government declared a state of siege for 90 days. Military units were deployed throughout the country, and 370 union leaders were arrested and banished to remote areas. The state of siege was extended by a further 90 days in July, owing to continued civil unrest, which had become particularly intense in the Chapare valley of Cochabamba, where UMOPAR forces had begun to occupy villages and to destroy coca plantations. Violent clashes between peasant farmers and UMOPAR personnel between July and September resulted in the arrest of almost 1,000 coca growers. Human rights organizations expressed alarm at the number of peasants killed and injured in the UMOPAR campaign.

Continued opposition to the Government's capitalization programme led to further industrial unrest and a general strike in 1996. In April more than 100,000 transport workers undertook a series of strikes and demonstrations in protest at the sale of the Eastern Railway to a Chilean company. Riots in La Paz resulted in damage to Chilean-owned railway property, which prompted threats from the Chilean Government to withdraw its investment from Bolivia. In December a group of miners occupied a pit at Amayapampa in northern Potosí to protest at the actions of the mine's Canadian operators, who, they alleged, had failed to pay local taxes and had caused damage to the environment. When troops arrived at the site to remove the miners 10 protesters were killed and 50 others injured in ensuing violent clashes.

A presidential election was held in June 1997. The MNR's candidate was Juan Carlos Durán, the MIR presented Paz Zamora, while Banzer Suárez was the nominee of the ADN. In the event, Banzer secured 22% of the total votes, Durán won 18% and Paz Zamora received 17%. At legislative elections held concurrently the ADN failed to secure a majority of seats; however, it subsequently formed a pact with the MIR, the UCS and Condepa to form a congressional majority and, as a result, Banzer was elected President for a newly extended term of five years.

In early 1998 coca producers in the Cochabamba region announced their rejection of the Government's new anti-coca policy, claiming that an agreement, signed in the previous year, to provide alternative development programmes had not been honoured. Moreover, many observers believed that similar policies had been ineffective, as, despite the provision of US finance worth US $500m. since 1990 to eradicate the crop, there had been no net reduction in coca production in Bolivia. Violent clashes ensued when army and police personnel converged on the region in April 1998 to implement the eradication programme. More than 1,000 coca growers undertook an 800-km protest march from Chapare to La Paz in August. Demonstrations and road-blocks by coca growers in La Paz and Cochabamba during September were disrupted by security forces, leading to violent confrontations. The relocation of the headquarters of the armed forces from La Paz to Cochabamba in 1999 was widely interpreted as a further measure against coca growing.

The Government was put under further pressure in September 2000 when striking teachers demanding higher salaries were joined by peasants protesting against the Government's plan to tax water used for crop irrigation. Violence ensued between the protesters and riot police, resulting in at least 10 fatalities. In late 2000 the Government acceded to coca growers' demands for a halt to the construction of new military bases in the Chapare region; however, the process of coca eradication intensified.

President Banzer resigned owing to ill health in August 2001. The Vice-President, Jorge Quiroga Ramírez, assumed the presidency and immediately replaced 12 of the 16 members of the Government; almost one-half of the new Cabinet was not affiliated to any political party.

A presidential election was held in June 2002. The main contenders were Sánchez de Lozada, again representing the MNR, Manfred Reyes Villa of the centre-right Nueva Fuerza Republicana and Juan Evo Morales Aima, a coca grower leader, representing the left-wing Movimiento al Socialismo—Instrumento Político por la Soberanía de los Pueblos (MAS). In the event, Sánchez de Lozada won the largest share of the ballot (23%). Morales, who opposed the Government's free market economic policy and its coca eradication programme, performed unexpectedly well, coming second with 21% of the votes cast. As no candidate had achieved an absolute majority, however, the Congreso voted to appoint Sánchez de Lozada to the presidency once more. Following his inauguration in August, Sánchez de Lozada formed a fragile coalition Government dominated by MNR and MIR members.

In light of renewed US pressure to intensify eradication efforts, in September 2002 the Government held inconclusive talks with coca growers' representatives, led by Morales. The USA had threatened to suspend preferential access to certain US markets, agreed under the Andean Trade Promotion and Drug Eradication Act (ATPDEA), if Bolivia failed to meet the agreed eradication targets. In January 2003 coca growers staged roadblocks and demonstrations in protest against the Government's coca eradication policies and in ensuing clashes with the police at least 10 people were killed.

In February 2003 the Government's proposal to raise income tax rates increased popular dissatisfaction still further. The new measure—known as an *impuestazo*, or 'tax shock'—drew widespread condemnation from representatives of middle- and lower-income groups, and prompted civil unrest. Following the Government's dismissal of their 40% wage-increase demand, approximately 7,000 armed police officers joined civilian protests in central La Paz. During the ensuing confrontation with military personnel some 32 people were killed and the President was forced to withdraw to safety. The riots prompted the resignation, on 19 February, of the entire Cabinet. In the following month the Government withdrew the proposed *impuestazo*.

Civil unrest and the presidency of Carlos Mesa

Increasing civil unrest in El Alto, an industrial suburb of La Paz, prompted by dissatisfaction with the Government's management of Bolivia's natural energy resources, culminated in military intervention, resulting in the deaths of some 36 people on 12 October 2003. The following day protests in La Paz fuelled by the events in El Alto resulted in more violent clashes with the army, and a further 13 deaths. The violent suppression of the protests prompted the resignation of the Vice-President, Carlos Mesa Gisbert, and the Minister of Economic Development, and the COB declared an indefinite general strike. On 15 October, in an attempt to restore order, the Government announced that it would hold a referendum on gas exports and would revise existing energy legislation. Nevertheless, the civil unrest continued unabated and the death toll rose to an estimated 74. On 17 October Sánchez de Lozada resigned as President and fled to the USA. The Congreso approved erstwhile Vice-President Mesa to succeed him. Mesa was sworn in as President on 18 October.

President Mesa appointed a Cabinet largely composed of independent technocrats, and notably restored the indigenous affairs portfolio abolished in February 2003. He pledged to re-examine the contentious gas export plan and reiterated the previous administration's pledges to hold a referendum on a proposed pipeline through Chile. Mesa announced plans to reduce the coca eradication programme, attracting the cautious approval of peasant and coca growers' leaders, although the US Government announced its opposition to the policy. In September 2004 President Mesa announced a new anti-drugs strategy that would receive some US $969m. in funding over the following four years. Instead of forcible eradication, the cultivation of alternative crops would be encouraged. Accordingly, in November the Government signed an agreement with Evo Morales (in his capacity as leader of the coca growers) to suspend the programme of forcible eradication in the Chapare region. In October the Congreso voted to prosecute former President Sánchez de Lozada and his Government over the decision to deploy troops to quell the civil unrest in October 2003 in El Alto. In May 2009 the Congreso voted to suspend the President of the Supreme Court, Eddy Fernández, for failing to open a trial on charges of genocide against the former President and his associates. Nevertheless, in August 2011 the Ministers of Labour and Sustainable Development in the Sánchez de Lozada administration each received three-year gaol terms (subsequently suspended) for their involvement in the violent suppression of the 2003 protests, while five senior military officers were given prison sentences of up to 15 years after being convicted on genocide charges. However, Sánchez de Lozada and most of the members of his former Cabinet continued to reside abroad, outside of the reach of the Bolivian judicial system.

In July 2004 a referendum was held on energy policy. The electorate was asked if it agreed with the abrogation of the hydrocarbons law that had been reintroduced by President Sánchez de Lozada; if state intervention in the oil and gas industry should be increased; if the state oil company, Yacimientos Petrolíferos Fiscales Bolivianos (YPFB), should reclaim shares in privatized energy companies; if Bolivia's gas reserves should be used as a negotiating tool to regain access to the Pacific Ocean; and if reform of the energy sector under broadly left-wing principles should be allowed to proceed. All five of the Government's proposals were accepted, but, despite this clear mandate for change, the resulting draft legislation caused great controversy. Specifically, there was disagreement as to whether extant contracts with energy sector companies should be voided and rewritten to provide for greater state control and revenue. Although various congressional, popular and indigenous groups strongly supported such moves, several foreign companies (notably, BP and Repsol) and foreign government delegations acting in their interests (notably, those of the USA, Brazil, Spain and the United Kingdom) voiced their opposition to any proposals they considered illegal under international law.

Also in late 2004 a broad-based coalition that included politicians, employers and trade unions from Santa Cruz and the oil- and gas-producing department of Tarija made increasingly vociferous demands for a referendum on greater regional autonomy or even full secession. This grouping was also opposed to an increased role for central government in the energy sector, fearing that this would deter foreign investment. In furtherance of the aim for autonomy, a widely supported general strike was held in Santa Cruz and Tarija in November. Civil unrest intensified in the following month, after the Government's announcement of significant increases in fuel prices was met with public protests across the country. The COB demanded President Mesa's resignation and announced that it was to organize an indefinite nation-wide general strike from mid-January 2005. Throughout early 2005 the country suffered severe disruption from roadblocks and other acts of civil disobedience by protesters demanding, *inter alia*, a decrease in the price of fuel and a dramatic increase in government revenues from the hydrocarbons sector. In the face of such public opposition, President Mesa announced that the fuel increases would be reduced from 23% to 15%. However, this was not enough to appease the protesters in Santa Cruz, where at a mass rally the Comité Cívico pro Santa Cruz declared Santa Cruz to be autonomous and announced that it was to establish a provincial interim government. On the same day President Mesa announced that provincial gubernatorial elections would be held on 12 June (departmental prefects were hitherto appointed by the President). However, this measure first required approval by referendum in order to be constitutional, and a constituent assembly was duly appointed. Confronted with continued protests, on 8 March Mesa submitted his resignation to the Congreso, although this was rejected after an agreement was signed by the major congressional groups. On 16 March Evo Morales appealed for a temporary cessation of the roadblocks following the approval by the upper house of legislation that provided for a state royalty of 18% on hydrocarbons at the point of extraction and a further tax of 32%. Final approval of the legislation was given by the lower house on 5 May. Nevertheless, throughout April and May blockades, demonstrations and marches caused great disruption and shortages of goods and services nation-wide. Considering his position untenable, on 6 June President Mesa submitted his resignation to the Congreso, which was accepted. Owing to fears of exacerbating the civil conflict, the speakers of the Senado Nacional and the Cámara de Diputados both waived their constitutional right to assume the presidency, which was instead assumed in a temporary capacity by a less partisan figure, Eduardo Rodríguez Veltzé, hitherto President of the Supreme Court.

The Government of Evo Morales

Legislative and presidential elections were held on 18 December 2005. Evo Morales, candidate of the MAS, was elected to the presidency with 54% of valid votes cast, while former Vice-President Jorge Quiroga Ramírez of the conservative Poder Democrático y Social (PODEMOS) received 29% of the ballot. The MAS also secured the most votes in the concurrent legislative elections, winning 72 of 130 seats in the Cámara de Diputados and 12 of the 27 seats in the Senado Nacional. Despite Morales' close alignment with the left-wing regimes of Venezuela and Cuba and his opposition to US counter-narcotics policy, the US Administration expressed its desire to work closely with the new Government.

Upon taking office on 22 January 2006, President Morales reiterated his electoral pledge to 'refound' the Bolivian state, by drafting a new constitution. To this end, in March a Government-sponsored enabling law was approved by the Congreso. The legislation would allow for the election of a constituent assembly and a concurrently held referendum on regional autonomy. The referendums were held on 2 July. The MAS garnered 54.4% of the valid votes cast, which translated into 137 seats in the 255-seat Constituent Assembly, considerably short of the two-thirds' majority President Morales needed to be sure of gaining approval for his proposed reforms. PODEMOS secured only 15.0% of the ballot, or 60 seats, leaving it reliant on the support of other opposition parties to block government proposals. In the vote on regional autonomy, four of the country's nine departments were in favour of further devolution—Beni, Pando, Santa Cruz and Tarija. The Constituent Assembly convened on 6 August and was to draft a proposed constitution by August 2007, which would then be put to another referendum for approval. However, in early September 2006 opposition members withdrew from the Assembly after MAS representatives endorsed a resolution that decisions would need approval only by a simple majority, rather than the two-thirds' majority originally agreed. The impasse was ended in mid-November, after 10 independent members of the Assembly aligned themselves with the pro-Government bloc: it was agreed that the final proposed text of the constitution would require the approval of two-thirds of the members, but that individual clauses only needed a majority decision. Following further opposition, however, in January 2007 it was agreed that any individual clauses not accepted by a two-thirds' majority would also be put to a referendum, as well as the constitution as a whole.

In November 2006 the President attempted to weaken the power of the regional prefects (six of whom were from opposition parties) by proposing legislation that would allow the Congreso to censure and dismiss departmental heads. The Government claimed the move would allow it better to distribute revenues from oil-producing regions to poorer areas. In response, the Governor of Cochabamba, Manfredo Reyes Villa, announced that a further referendum on autonomy should be held in the region. A majority of the electorate in Cochabamba had voted against autonomy in July; however, if another vote returned a different result, it would put the pro-autonomy departments into a majority. Government supporters in Cochabamba held a massive rally against the proposal in January 2007, demanding Reyes Villa's resignation. The protests and subsequent counter-protests descended into violence, with over 100 people injured and two killed. Reyes Villa was forced to flee the department, taking refuge in Santa Cruz, although he refused to resign.

Meanwhile, on 1 May 2006 President Morales issued a decree establishing the state's ownership of the hydrocarbons sector and increasing taxes for foreign companies operating in the sector from 50% to 82%. Foreign companies had 180 days to sign new contracts with the state hydrocarbons company YPFB or else cease operations in Bolivia. Although the announcement was widely viewed as 'nationalization' of the hydrocarbons sector, foreign concerns would be allowed to remain in the country as minority share-holders. In the following month Morales issued another decree giving the state the power to seize land it deemed unproductive, in order to redistribute it to landless farmers. It was estimated that some 20m.–30m. ha of land could be affected. In the face of much protest from land-owners, particularly in eastern Bolivia, the President pledged that productive farms would be left alone, as would any land gained legally. In early November the Congreso approved a draft version of the reform, prompting protests from land-owning organizations. Then, at the end of the month, the Government succeeded in gaining senate approval for the law (and for numerous new contracts with foreign oil companies). The new contracts with the foreign oil concerns were approved in April 2007.

The Constituent Assembly finally came into operation in February 2007. Morales' proposals for the new constitution included new rights of determination for the indigenous majority, with their own political systems and legally recognized leaders, greater state control of the economy, the election of supreme court judges by popular vote (rather than their appointment by the Congreso) and the allowance of two consecutive five-year terms for Presidents. By July, however, disagreements over a proposal to transfer the seat of government back from La Paz to Sucre (where it had been located until 1899) led to disruption. A demonstration in La Paz, one of the largest in the country's history, was held in protest against the proposal. In August MAS delegates on the Assembly voted to exclude the issue from the agenda, prompting several weeks of unrest in Sucre. Some observers believed that the issue of relocating the capital from the poor western highlands to the relatively prosperous eastern region was being used by critics of Morales to sabotage his attempts to establish a more inclusive constitution, in which the country's wealth was more evenly distributed. Failure to agree on the issue, however, led to continued unrest during November. Opposition governors from six of the country's nine departments approved a resolution urging civil disobedience in response to Morales' plans to use profits from the hydrocarbons tax to fund a new pension scheme, diverting income that was previously sent to regional prefects. Meanwhile, some 10,000 supporters of Morales marched from El Alto to the opposition-controlled Senado in La Paz, condemning the delegates in Sucre for stalling progress on the new constitution. The constitution was approved on 9 December by the required two-thirds of members present, although not by two-thirds of the membership, owing to a boycott by opposition delegates. Claims of procedural irregularities led the opposition to denounce the vote as illegal.

In February 2008 President Morales approved legislation setting 4 May as the date for an initial national referendum on the draft constitution. However, resistance from the PODEMOS-led opposition—particularly regional prefects of the affluent 'media luna' region (Bolivia's gas-rich eastern lowlands, comprising four of the nine regional departments) who claimed the charter favoured the country's indigenous population, and announced concurrent referendums on proposals for greater regional autonomy—provoked considerable political turmoil. The Corte Nacional Electoral (CNE—National Electoral Court), Bolivia's supreme electoral authority, subsequently ruled that all referendums were to be postponed indefinitely owing, *inter alia*, to the logistical obstacles to public consultations at such short notice. Nevertheless, the authorities in Santa Cruz held a referendum on the autonomy proposal on 4 May. The Government, which claimed that the referendum was illegal and unconstitutional, urged voters to abstain. Referendums on the respective autonomy proposals were subsequently held in Beni and Pando on 1 June, and in Tarija on 22 June. In all three plebiscites, which, like the one in Santa Cruz, were deemed illegal by the Government, roughly four-fifths of votes cast were in favour of autonomy. Only days after the Santa Cruz vote, the opposition-controlled Senado approved legislation that instituted recall referendums for the President, Vice-President and departmental Prefects, in an attempt to force Morales to resign and thus postpone indefinitely a referendum to approve the constitution. In fact, the recall referendums, which were held on 10 August, resulted in a decisive victory for Morales and Vice-President Alvaro García Linera, whose continuance in office was supported by some 67% of valid votes according to provisional results.

The ongoing constitutional crisis descended into violence in September 2008. Opponents of Morales raided government buildings, set up roadblocks, sabotaged gas pipelines and fought with government supporters in the opposition-controlled departments of Beni, Pando, Santa Cruz, Chuquisaca and Tarija. In one incident on 11 September in Pando at least 18 government supporters were ambushed and shot dead and many others were injured or found to be missing. In response the Government imposed martial law and the Prefect of the department, Leopoldo Fernández, was arrested and charged with ordering the massacre. The heads of state of the 12 member countries of UNASUR (the Union of South American Nations) held an emergency summit in Chile on 15 September in response to the crisis, at which they declared their overwhelming support for Morales and stated that their nations would not tolerate any attempts to destabilize the Government.

Following further negotiations in late 2008 between the Government and a moderate faction of PODEMOS, agreement was secured on the final draft constitution and a referendum finally took place on 25 January 2009. Some 61% of the electorate voted in favour of the new Constitution, with support being highest in the western highlands, where the indigenous majority is concentrated, while the eastern lowlands rejected the charter. Thousands of Bolivians took to the streets to celebrate the approval of the historic new Constitution, which Morales described as 'refounding a new united Bolivia'. Legislation on electoral reform and the new Constitution was signed into law on 9 February. Under the new charter three new ministries were created, one of which, the Ministry of Autonomy, was charged with the task of restructuring local government and overseeing land reform. An electoral law was finally approved by the opposition-dominated Senado in mid-April, which allowed for a presidential ballot to be held on 6 December. The legislation also set out the framework for votes on autonomy to be held in five regions.

Morales' second term

Morales was decisively re-elected as President on 6 December 2009, receiving 64.2% of the total votes cast, compared with Manfred Reyes Villa, candidate of the newly formed right-wing Plan Progreso para Bolivia–Convergencia Nacional, who garnered 26.5% of the ballot. The legislative election held concurrently resulted in a majority for the MAS in both chambers, with 88 of the 130 seats in the Cámara de Diputados and 26 of the 36 seats in the newly enlarged Senado Nacional. An estimated 95% of the eligible voters participated in the poll. Morales' victory, and particularly his party's new majority in the Senado, was seen as a powerful mandate for his ongoing programme of socialist reforms. Morales announced a reorganization of cabinet portfolios in January 2010, which allocated 10 positions to women (compared with four in his previous administration). Three senior members of the previous Cabinet were omitted. These included Walker San Miguel, the former Minister of National Defence, who had attracted criticism from some of Morales' supporters because of his association with the Sánchez de Lozada administration and the privatization process, and the former Minister of the Interior, Alfredo Rada, who had failed to prevent Manfred Reyes and José Luis Paredes, two leading opponents of the Government who faced corruption charges, from fleeing the country following the elections.

Gubernatorial and municipal elections were held on 4 April 2010 and resulted in further success for the MAS. The MAS won six of the nine gubernatorial posts and secured a comfortable majority in the municipal ballot, with the party continuing to garner most of its support from rural areas. Shortly after the elections, the CNE altered the electoral legislation, which resulted in the MAS being awarded an additional 33 local assembly seats. Protests were held in the affected regions, but the CNE argued that the changes were in accordance with the Constitution.

The elections carried added significance since they facilitated a key principle enshrined in the new Constitution, namely the decentralization of government. This process was formalized in July 2010, when the legislature approved an autonomy framework law delineating the responsibilities of the new four-tier local governance system (comprising departmental, regional, municipal and indigenous levels). Morales' opponents censured the legislation for disregarding the 2008 autonomy referendums held in the 'media luna' region and criticized its vagueness, particularly in relation to the allocation of fiscal resources. Controversially, the autonomy law also barred those accused of corruption, or other 'formal' charges, from public office. This rule was enforced to suspend the opposition Governors of Tarija and Beni in December 2010 and December 2011, respectively, and also to remove two opposition mayors. Moreover, in late 2011 the sole remaining opposition Governor, Rubén Costas of Santa Cruz, was charged with contempt of court, and an investigation begun into the Governor's financial affairs following allegations of corruption.

The approval of the autonomy law marked the end of a flurry of legislation that established the legal foundations for the new Constitution to come into effect. Laws adopted to this end, the *leyes orgánicas* (organic laws), included a judicial reform bill, to improve efficiency in the courts and permit the establishment of separate indigenous judicial systems, and new electoral rules, which politically empowered social movements (generally perceived as MAS affiliates) and restricted referendums.

Meanwhile, the Government's announcement in May 2010 of a 5% increase in public sector salaries precipitated nation-wide protests orchestrated by the COB, which demanded pay rises of up to 25% and had up until this point been a strong supporter of the Morales administration. The Government entered into negotiations with the COB following the latter's threat of an indefinite strike, and, in what was viewed as a triumph for Morales, a deal was agreed whereby the 5% rise was maintained in exchange for a proposed reduction in the retirement age and additional wage increases for the lowest paid workers.

Mass demonstrations and blockades took place in the poverty-stricken and traditionally pro-MAS department of Potosí in August 2010. The protests, initially organized to demand government intervention to resolve a border dispute with the neighbouring department of Oruro concerning control of a mineral-rich region in Potosí and reportedly involving up to 100,000 people, escalated into protests against a perceived lack of government investment. Several foreign-owned mining companies were forced to suspend operations as a result of the unrest. An agreement to end the demonstrations was eventually reached with the local civic committee after the Government committed to investing in infrastructure and industry and to the creation of a commission to investigate the border issue.

Former President Jorge Quiroga Ramírez was sentenced, *in absentia*, to 32 months' imprisonment in September 2010 for 'defamation and slander' after he accused the government-owned Banco Unión of corruption in 2009. Furthermore, in September 2011 Quiroga and another former President, Sánchez de Lozada, were charged with concluding unfavourable deals with foreign hydrocarbons companies during their tenures in office.

In October 2010 Morales promulgated a contentious anti-racism law, which gave the Government the authority to fine or shut down media outlets that disseminated 'racist and discriminatory ideas'. The legislation was widely viewed as an attempt by Morales to weaken the country's media corporations, predominantly owned by right-wing elements fiercely critical of the Morales administration. In addition to vehement opposition from the local media, the bill also prompted expressions of concern from the UN and national and international press freedom organizations, which feared that the legislation could be misused by the authorities to silence legitimate political debate. The approval of new telecommunications legislation in July 2011, which granted the state greater control over radio and television frequencies, attracted further criticism from media groups; concern was also expressed regarding a stipulation that allowed the authorities, under certain circumstances, to monitor telecommunications networks.

In December 2010 the pension system was nationalized and the age of retirement was reduced substantially, to 58 years (hitherto 65 years for men and 60 years for women). Opponents argued that lowering the retirement age was not financially viable. Later that month the Government announced that fuel subsidies would be withdrawn, resulting in petrol prices increasing by up to 83%. Nation-wide protests were rapidly organized by trade unions in response to this highly unpopular decision, and the Government was forced to reinstate the subsidies shortly afterwards. Seemingly in response to this incident, Luis Fernando Vincenti Vargas, the Minister of Hydrocarbons and Energy, was replaced by José Luis Gutiérrez in a minor cabinet reorganization in January 2011. Further government changes were implemented by Morales in the following month, and a new Ministry of Communications was established. In April María Cecilia Chacón Rendón was appointed as Minister of National Defence, the first woman to assume that position. Morales effected another cabinet reorganization in June, as part of which Claudia Peña Claros became the new Minister of Autonomy, thereby fulfilling the President's pledge to achieve ministerial gender equality. Meanwhile, there were further demonstrations and strikes throughout the country in April, organized by the COB to demand greater increases in the minimum wage and public sector salaries than those proposed by the Government. Following almost two weeks of nation-wide disruption, a compromise deal was agreed in mid-April and the protests were discontinued.

Recent developments: judicial reform

Unprecedented elections were conducted on 16 October 2011 to appoint senior judicial personnel to serve in, *inter alia*, the Supreme Court and the Constitutional Court. (In the interim, prior to the elections, Morales had controversially been given the power to appoint high-ranking judges.) Morales asserted that the vote would ensure judicial independence, but all of the candidates had been pre-selected by the MAS-controlled legislature. Although the rate of participation by the electorate was high, the majority of ballots were spoiled or left blank in accordance with an opposition-led protest campaign against the Government. This outcome was regarded as a significant defeat for Morales, whose popularity had declined dramatically since late 2010.

The Role of Coca in Recent Bolivian Politics

One of Morales' campaign pledges was to legalize the cultivation of coca. On taking office, the new President appointed a former coca grower, Felipe Cáceres García, to lead the country's anti-narcotics effort. In May 2006, following negotiations with representatives from the main coca growing regions, the Government announced that voluntary eradication was to resume. However, growers in the Caranavi region were allowed to cultivate about 1,600 sq m of coca per household, a compromise already extended to the Chapare and Yungas regions. In December Morales announced that the amount of land legally permitted for coca cultivation would be increased from 12,000 ha to 20,000 ha by 2010. The decision was criticized in a 2007 US report, which also berated Morales for advocating the industrialization of coca production. In December the Constituent Assembly approved a measure urging the UN to decriminalize coca and to refrain from 'using the name of the sacred leaf in their products'. The motion resulted from complaints that the US-based multinational drinks company Coca-Cola used the name 'coca' to promote its products while exports of Bolivian products containing coca were banned. After making an unsuccessful attempt in January 2011 to remove a clause in the 1961 UN Single Convention on Narcotic Drugs banning the chewing of coca leaves, Bolivia withdrew from the agreement in June. The Government claimed that the Convention was in breach of the 2007 UN Declaration on the Rights of Indigenous People and Bolivia's new Constitution, both of which enshrined the cultural significance of coca consumption in Bolivian society.

Indigenous Peoples' Rights

The issue of the participation of the Aymara, Quechua and Guaraní indigenous peoples in Bolivia's public life reached a critical phase in the early 21st century, following limited progress in the 1990s. Government decrees issued in 1990 acknowledging as Indian territory more than 1.6m. ha of tropical rainforest in northern Bolivia constituted an unprecedented act of recognition of Indian land rights. In 2002 the Sánchez de Lozada administration announced a Land Reform Programme, under which some 1.2m. ha were to be bought by the Government and redistributed to some 11,000 landless families, at a cost of approximately US $2,500m. Despite government claims that some 500,000 ha of land was available for redistribution, landless peasants continued to occupy farms illegally throughout 2004. In August land owned by the multinational hydrocarbons company BP was occupied until the Government agreed to accelerate the process of land redistribution. There was an unprecedented level of indigenous political participation in the 2004 municipal elections in 2004; in sharp contrast to the elections of 1999, in which candidates from just 18 parties stood, over 400 'citizen organizations' fielded candidates. A large majority of constituencies were won by these candidates.

The election in December 2005 of Bolivia's first President of indigenous descent, Evo Morales, was seen as a key development in indigenous peoples' political participation. In 2006, following the issuing of a decree on land reform (see above), Morales handed over title deeds to 3.1m. ha of land in the east of the country to indigenous leaders. The gesture was largely symbolic, but it was expected that the land reform would grant indigenous and landless farmers almost 200,000 sq km of land by 2011. The 2009 Constitution granted far-reaching powers to the country's indigenous majority in relation to government, the judiciary and land ownership. In August of that year, in line with the provisions of the new Constitution, Morales enacted the Law of Indigenous Autonomies, which detailed the conditions under which indigenous people could vote for autonomy. Local referendums on this issue took place alongside the general election of December. In June 2010 the legislature adopted a judicial reform bill, which most notably granted indigenous peoples the right to establish judicial structures in accordance with traditional principles, separate from and equal to the national justice system. This controversial law was denounced by right-wing opponents, who highlighted a series of lynchings to draw parallels between indigenous justice and vigilantism. Further legislation was approved in December, limiting the range of crimes under the jurisdiction of indigenous communities and banning lynchings. The hitherto strong relations between the Morales administration and indigenous groups deteriorated in mid-2011 as a result of a government scheme to build a major road through indigenous territory in Cochabamba. Approximately 1,000 indigenous rights activists, who claimed that the construction of the highway breached multiple constitutional protections guaranteed to their communities and to the environment, began a 500-km protest march from Beni to La Paz in August. The police attempted to stop the march by force in the following month, prompting widespread condemnation of the authorities and the resignations of Minister of National Defence Cecilia Chacón Rendón and Minister of the Interior Sacha Sergio Llorenti Soliz (who were replaced by Rubén Saavedra Soto and Wilfredo Franz Chávez Serrano, respectively). The march continued, none the less, reaching La Paz in October. Under increasing pressure, Morales terminated the highway project later that month, although the episode had severely damaged his popularity. Nevertheless, in February 2012 the legislature approved a non-binding referendum in Cochabamba on the road project. The volte-face followed a march on La Paz by supporters of the highway. The plebiscite was due to take place by 10 May, although in late April this deadline was extended by 90 days.

Foreign Affairs

Regional relations

Bolivia's relations with Peru and Chile have been dominated by the long-standing issue of possible Bolivian access to the Pacific Ocean. An agreement with Peru, completed in 1993, granted Bolivia free access from its border town of Desaguadero to the Pacific port of Ilo, Peru, until 2091. In 2004 the Presidents of Bolivia and Peru signed a declaration of intent to create a special zone in Ilo for the exportation of Bolivian gas (see Economic Affairs). In 2010 Peru broadened the scope of the original 1993 agreement, granting Bolivia permission to construct docks, storage facilities, a free trade area and a naval academy.

Bolivia's desire to regain sovereign access to the Pacific has continued to impair relations with Chile. The Chilean Government's decision in 2004 to privatize the port of Arica elicited vehement objections from the Mesa administration, which feared this would adversely affect Bolivia's external trade, owing to significant increases in port tariffs (supposedly in contravention of the 1904 treaty that guaranteed duty-free passage of Bolivian goods through Arica). Although bilateral relations had improved during Morales' presidency, leading some observers to speculate on the possibility of a permanent access agreement, the new Chilean administration of Sebastián Piñera announced in December 2010 that it would not grant Bolivia sovereign rights to any part of its territory. Morales, frustrated by this impasse, threatened to refer the matter to the International Court of Justice in 2011, precipitating a sharp deterioration in relations.

In May 2009 Bolivia signed a border agreement with Paraguay, resolving a dispute over the Chaco region that had led to war between the two countries during the 1920s and 1930s, in which more than 100,000 people had died. Bolivia and Brazil concluded an agreement to combat drugs-trafficking along their shared border in March 2011, and a further memorandum of understanding was signed in October. Brazil pledged to provide Bolivia with training and equipment, and Brazilian unmanned aircraft commenced surveillance operations in Bolivian territory. Bolivia also signed border security agreements with Paraguay and Peru in late 2011.

Other external relations

Allegations by the Government that the US ambassador had given support to opposition activists in the 'media luna' region led to a deterioration in the already strained relationship between Bolivia and the USA in 2008. President Morales announced the expulsion of the ambassador in September. Relations between the two countries continued to deteriorate with Morales' decision to suspend indefinitely all operations by the US Drug Enforcement Administration, which it accused of spying and of fomenting political unrest in the country. The US Government rejected Morales' claims and in retaliation announced the suspension of Bolivia from the ATPDEA trade programme. TIn July 2009 the US Administration of Barack Obama announced the permanent withdrawal of trade privileges for Bolivian goods in the USA under the ATPDEA. This decision was widely criticized in Bolivia, and Morales accused Obama of dishonesty in his stated pledge to work towards an equal partnership between the USA and Latin America. Nevertheless, in November 2011 Bolivia and the USA pledged to re-establish diplomatic relations.

Bolivia and Iran established closer bilateral relations in 2007 following the signing of an industrial co-operation agreement and the investment by Iran of US $1,000m. in technology and trade and industry projects in Bolivia. The presidents of the two countries also signed a framework agreement expressing support for nuclear research for peaceful energy purposes. The US Government expressed concern at Iran's apparently increasing influence in the region. Following discussions between President Morales and the Iranian Minister of Industries and Mines, Ali Akbar Mehrabian, in La Paz in 2010, Iran agreed to lend the Bolivian Government $254m. to finance a variety of mining projects. Further agreements, including an additional $276m.

loan for industrial development schemes in Bolivia, were signed by Morales and his Iranian counterpart, Mahmoud Ahmadinejad, during a visit to Iran in October. The Argentine Government expressed its disapproval of the presence of the Iranian Minister of Defence and Armed Forces Logistics, Brig.-Gen. Ahmad Vahidi, at an official Bolivian military engagement in May 2011. Argentine officials alleged that Vahidi, who was subsequently ejected from Bolivia, had been involved in a deadly bomb attack against an Argentine Jewish centre in 1994. Bolivia formally apologized for the incident.

In February 2009 President Morales made an official visit to Russia, where he held discussions with that country's President and Prime Minister. The visit, which was the first of its kind from a Bolivian head of state, aimed to secure investment from Russia, including some US $4,500m. for Bolivia's energy sector.

President Morales made an official visit to Spain in September 2009, during which the Spanish Government agreed to cancel some US $85m. of Bolivian debt and to provide further investment in the country's energy sector. The Spanish Minister of Foreign Affairs and Co-operation, Trinidad Jiménez García-Herrera, met her Bolivian counterpart in La Paz in November 2010 and signed a co-operation accord, pledging to provide Bolivia with $445m. in funding over the following five years.

CONSTITUTION AND GOVERNMENT

A revised Constitution was signed into law in February 2009, which provided for greater autonomy for indigenous communities, enshrined state control over key economic sectors (most notably natural resources), imposed restrictions on the size of land holdings, removed Roman Catholicism as the state religion and aimed to make the judiciary more transparent and accountable. It also enlarged the Senado Nacional and allowed the President, who is elected by direct suffrage for a five-year term, to seek re-election for a second consecutive term. Legislative power is held by the bicameral Congreso Nacional (Congress), comprising a Senado Nacional (Senate), with 36 members and a Cámara de Diputados (Chamber of Deputies), comprising 130 members. Both houses are elected for a five-year term by universal adult suffrage. Executive power is vested in the President and the Cabinet, which is appointed by the President. If no candidate gains an absolute majority of votes, the President is chosen by the Congreso. The country is divided, for administrative purposes, into nine departments, each of which is governed by a prefect.

REGIONAL AND INTERNATIONAL CO-OPERATION

In May 1991 Bolivia was one of five Andean Pact countries to sign the Caracas Declaration providing the foundation for a common market. Bolivia is a member of the Andean Community (see p. 197). In 1997 a free trade agreement with Mercosur (see p. 428), equivalent to associate membership of the organization, came into effect. The country is also a member of the Organization of American States (OAS, see p. 394), of the Latin American Integration Association (ALADI, see p. 362), and of the Community of Latin American and Caribbean States (see p. 462), which was formally inaugurated in December 2011. In December 2004 Bolivia was one of the founder signatories to the agreement signed in Cusco, Peru, creating the South American Community of Nations (Comunidad Sudamericana de Naciones), intended to promote greater regional economic integration and further the unification of Mercosur and the Andean Community. A treaty for the community—referred to as the Union of South American Nations (UNASUR) since its reinvention at the first South American Energy Summit of 16 April 2007—was signed by heads of state meeting in Brasília, Brazil, in May 2008, with full functionality of economic union tentatively scheduled for 2019.

Bolivia became a member of the UN in 1945. The country has been a member of the World Trade Organization (see p. 433) since September 1995. Bolivia is a member of the Group of 77 (see p. 450) organization of developing states.

ECONOMIC AFFAIRS

In 2010, according to World Bank estimates, Bolivia's gross national income (GNI), measured at average 2008–10 prices, totalled US $17,982m., equivalent to about $1,810 per head (or $4,610 per head on an international purchasing-power parity basis). During 2001–10, it was estimated, the population grew at an average annual rate of 1.8% per year, while gross domestic product (GDP) per head increased at an average annual rate of 2.3% per year. Bolivia's overall GDP increased, in real terms, at an average annual rate of 4.1% in 2001–10; GDP increased by a preliminary 4.1% in 2010.

Agriculture (including forestry and fishing) contributed 12.4% of GDP in 2010, according to preliminary figures. According to FAO estimates, 40.6% of the economically active population were engaged in agriculture in mid-2012. The principal cash crop is soya, particularly soya oil. During 2001–10 agricultural GDP increased at an average annual rate of 2.5%; sectoral GDP increased by an estimated 3.7% in 2009, but decreased by a preliminary 1.2% in 2010.

Industry (including mining, manufacturing, construction and power) provided 35.8% of GDP in 2010, according to preliminary figures. According to International Labour Organization (ILO) estimates, some 19.7% of the working population was employed in industry in 2007. In 2001–10 industrial GDP increased at an average annual rate of 5.3%; the sector grew by an estimated 3.8% in 2010.

Mining (including petroleum exploration) contributed 16.7% of GDP in 2010, according to preliminary figures. The sector employed about 1.5% of the working population in 2007. President Evo Morales' policy of bringing the country's hydrocarbons sector under state control led to a significant decrease in foreign investment, although revenue from mineral resources remained relatively high. Natural gas accounted for a preliminary 40.2% of export earnings in 2010. Zinc, silver, tin, gold, wolfram and antimony are the major mineral exports. Exports of zinc and silver earned a preliminary US $888.1m. and $684.2m., respectively, in 2010. In 2001–10 the GDP of the mining sector increased at an estimated average annual rate of 7.3%, according to preliminary official figures; mining GDP contracted by 2.0% in 2009, mainly owing to a fall in earnings from petroleum and natural gas, but increased by an estimated 4.0% in 2010.

In 2010 manufacturing accounted for 13.4% of GDP, according to preliminary figures. In 2007 the sector engaged some 11.0% of the working population. The GDP of this sector increased during 2001–10 at an average annual rate of 4.2%; it increased by 2.6% in 2010.

The construction sector accounted for 3.2% of GDP in 2010, according to preliminary figures, and engaged 6.8% of the economically active population in 2007, according to the ILO. During 2001–10 construction GDP increased at an average annual rate of 5.0%, according to preliminary official figures; construction GDP increased by 7.5% in 2010.

Energy is derived principally from natural gas and hydroelectricity. In 2009 electricity generation totalled 6,000m. kWh, according to provisional figures issued by the US Energy Information Administration (EIA). Hydroelectricity accounted for 36.6% of Bolivia's total installed generating capacity in 2008 (2.3 GW), with thermal power stations accounting for most of the remainder (60.5%). According to EIA, in 2010 production of crude petroleum averaged a reported 47,170 barrels per day. Output declined by 9.9% in 2009, but increased by 4.4% in 2010. In that year imports of mineral products comprised a preliminary 12.1% of total merchandise imports. Earnings from exports of mineral products (including gas and petroleum) accounted for a preliminary 43.4% of total export earnings in the same year. At the end of 2010 the country's proven reserves of gas stood at 281,000m. cu m. In December 2009 the Government announced plans to exploit the country's considerable reserves of lithium (estimated at some 20m. metric tons in 2010), an essential component of electric vehicle batteries, which is found in the Salar de Uyuni salt flats. Morales expressed his intention to manufacture the batteries in Bolivia, rather than merely to export the raw material, in order to maximize revenue from the commodity.

The services sector accounted for 51.8% of GDP in 2010, according to preliminary figures. According to ILO, it engaged some 44.2% of the employed population in 2007. During 2001–10 the GDP of the services sector increased at an average annual rate of 3.3%; the sector expanded by 5.2% in 2010.

In 2010 Bolivia recorded a visible trade surplus of US $1,283.7m., and there was a surplus of $873.7m. on the current account of the balance of payments. In 2010 the main sources of imports were Brazil (18.6%), the USA, Argentina, the People's Republic of China, Peru, Japan, Chile and Venezuela. Brazil was also the main recipient of exports (34.6%) in that year, followed by the USA, Argentina, Japan, Peru, Belgium (including Luxembourg), South Korea and Venezuela. The principal imports in that year included machinery and transport equipment (34.1%), base metals and their manufactures, and chemicals and chemical products. The principal legal exports were mineral fuels and lubricants (43.4%) and crude materials (inedible, 29.1%). It was estimated that a large proportion of Bolivia's export earnings came from the illegal trade in coca and its derivatives (mainly cocaine).

In 2009 Bolivia's overall budget deficit amounted to a preliminary 4,924.7m. bolivianos, equivalent to some 4.0% of GDP in the same year. Bolivia's general government gross debt was 50,473m. bolivianos in 2010, equivalent to 36.6% of GDP. Bolivia's total external debt at the end of 2009 was US $5,745m., of which $2,545m. was long-term public debt. The cost of servicing long-term public and publicly guaranteed debt and repayments to the IMF in that year was equivalent to 5.4% of the total value of exports of goods, services and income (excluding workers' remittances). According to ILO, in 2001–10 the average annual rate of inflation was 5.2%. Consumer prices increased by 2.5% in 2010. According to official estimates, some 7.5% of the labour force was unemployed in 2008.

Despite ongoing political problems, Bolivia's economy performed well during 2007–11. The hydrocarbons sector supplied a large portion of this growth, both directly—via export receipts—and indirectly, as the state increased its stake in production, a move that enabled large fiscal surpluses. The global recession from late 2008 had a negligible impact on the Bolivian economy, largely owing to the underdeveloped financial system and comparatively low levels of short-term capital investment. Hydrocarbons exports and foreign direct investment both increased in 2010, and GDP growth was estimated at 4.1%. With hydrocarbons revenues critical to Morales' economic agenda, a series of new exploration projects was announced, and several significant gas deposits were discovered during 2011. Investment in the gas and mining sectors remained buoyant in 2011, hydrocarbon production levels continued to increase, and gas exports were forecast to rise following the inauguration in June of a new pipeline connecting Bolivia and Argentina. However, inflation rose sharply in that year as a result of higher food prices, increases in the minimum wage and public sector salaries, and loose monetary policy. In an effort to boost agricultural production and reduce food price inflation, in mid-2011 the Government pledged to invest US $5,000m. in the agricultural sector over the next 10 years and announced plans to provide financial support to farmers. The IMF projected strong GDP growth of 4.5% for both 2011 and 2012, although poverty and income inequality, while decreasing, still posed enormous challenges.

PUBLIC HOLIDAYS

2013: 1 January (New Year), 22 January (Plurinational State Foundation Day), 12–13 February (Carnival), 29 March (Good Friday), 1 May (Labour Day), 30 May (Corpus Christi), 21 June (Aymara New Year/Summer Solstice), 16 July (La Paz only), 6 August (Independence), 14 September (Cochabamba only), 24 September (Santa Cruz and Pando only), 2 November (All Souls' Day), 25 December (Christmas).

Statistical Survey

Sources (unless otherwise indicated): Instituto Nacional de Estadística, José Carrasco 1391, Casilla 6129, La Paz; tel. (2) 222-2333; internet www.ine.gob.bo; Banco Central de Bolivia, Avda Ayacucho, esq. Mercado, Casilla 3118, La Paz; tel. (2) 240-9090; fax (2) 240-6614; e-mail bancocentraldebolivia@bcb.gob.bo; internet www.bcb.gob.bo.

Area and Population

AREA, POPULATION AND DENSITY

Area (sq km)	
Land	1,084,391
Inland water	14,190
Total	1,098,581*
Population (census results)†	
3 June 1992	6,420,792
5 September 2001	
Males	4,123,850
Females	4,150,475
Total	8,274,325
Population (official projections)	
2008	10,027,644
2009	10,227,299
2010	10,426,154
Density (per sq km) at 2010	9.5

* 424,164 sq miles.

† Figures exclude adjustment for underenumeration. This was estimated at 6.92% in 1992.

POPULATION BY AGE AND SEX

(official projections, 2010)

	Males	Females	Total
0–14	1,903,360	1,830,821	3,734,181
15–64	3,086,854	3,128,450	6,215,304
65 and over	211,760	264,909	476,669
Total	5,201,974	5,224,180	10,426,154

DEPARTMENTS

(official projections, 2010)

	Area (sq km)*	Population	Density (per sq km)	Capital ('000)
Beni	213,564	445,234	2.1	Trinidad (92,587)
Chuquisaca	51,524	650,570	12.6	Sucre (284,032)
Cochabamba	55,631	1,861,924	33.5	Cochabamba (618,376)
La Paz	133,985	2,839,946	21.2	La Paz (835,361)
Oruro	53,588	450,814	8.4	Oruro (216,724)
Pando	63,827	81,160	1.3	Cobija (41,948)
Potosí	118,218	788,406	6.7	Potosí (154,693)
Santa Cruz	370,621	2,785,762	7.5	Santa Cruz de la Sierra (1,616,063)
Tarija	37,623	522,339	13.9	Tarija (194,313)
Total	1,098,581	10,426,154	9.5	

* As at 2001 census.

PRINCIPAL TOWNS

(official projections, 2010)

Santa Cruz de la Sierra	1,616,063	Sacaba	155,668
El Alto	953,253	Potosí	154,693
La Paz (administrative capital)	835,361	Yacuiba	112,096
Cochabamba	618,376	Quillacollo	99,050
Sucre (legal capital)	284,032	Montero	96,106
Oruro	216,724	Trinidad	92,587
Tarija	194,313	Riberalta	87,501

BIRTHS AND DEATHS
(annual averages, UN estimates)

	1995–2000	2000–05	2005–10
Birth rate (per 1,000)	32.6	30.3	27.4
Death rate (per 1,000)	8.9	8.1	7.5

Source: UN, *World Population Prospects: The 2010 Revision*.

Life expectancy (years at birth, WHO estimates): 68 (males 66; females 70) in 2009 (Source: WHO, *World Health Statistics*).

ECONOMICALLY ACTIVE POPULATION
(labour force survey, '000 persons aged 10 years and over)

	2005	2006	2007
Agriculture, hunting, forestry and fishing	1,643.6	1,797.4	1,686.7
Mining and quarrying	71.0	55.5	72.4
Manufacturing	465.5	477.8	514.9
Electricity, gas and water supply	13.9	13.0	15.4
Construction	275.3	248.1	316.3
Wholesale and retail trade; repair of motor vehicles, motorcycles and personal and household goods	629.3	647.3	673.8
Hotels and restaurants	171.4	186.7	159.3
Transport, storage and communications	256.3	251.5	272.4
Financial intermediation	13.1	23.3	28.0
Real estate, renting and business activities	104.6	152.0	136.9
Public administration and defence; compulsory social security	91.1	115.2	152.3
Education	192.7	217.9	222.9
Health and social work	64.0	96.9	109.3
Other community, social and personal service activities	153.0	147.5	149.0
Private households with employed persons	108.3	119.6	160.7
Extra-territorial organizations and bodies	4.0	0.6	1.9
Total employed	4,257.2	4,550.3	4,672.4
Unemployed	245.2	243.5	255.0
Total labour force	4,502.4	4,793.8	4,927.4
Males	2,468.2	2,624.6	2,699.4
Females	2,034.2	2,169.2	2,228.0

Source: ILO.

Health and Welfare

KEY INDICATORS

Total fertility rate (children per woman, 2009)	3.4
Under-5 mortality rate (per 1,000 live births, 2009)	51
HIV/AIDS (% of persons aged 15–49, 2009)	0.2
Physicians (per 1,000 head, 2001)	1.2
Hospital beds (per 1,000 head, 2006)	1.1
Health expenditure (2008): US $ per head (PPP)	194
Health expenditure (2008): % of GDP	4.5
Health expenditure (2008): public (% of total)	65.7
Access to water (% of persons, 2008)	86
Access to sanitation (% of persons, 2008)	25
Total carbon dioxide emissions ('000 metric tons, 2007)	13,179.4
Carbon dioxide emissions per head (metric tons, 2007)	1.4
Human Development Index (2011): ranking	108
Human Development Index (2011): value	0.663

For sources and definitions, see explanatory note on p. vi.

Agriculture

PRINCIPAL CROPS
('000 metric tons)

	2008	2009	2010*
Wheat	200.0	239.4	310.7
Rice, paddy	337.8	395.7	362.7
Barley	73.2	74.1	75.0
Maize	1,001.8	813.6	981.7
Sorghum	404.4	314.2	403.2
Potatoes	748.0	762.7	782.8
Cassava (Manioc)	361.3	363.1	364.5
Sugar cane	7,009.2	7,437.7	7,437.7
Brazil nuts	42.6*	39.1*	39.1
Chestnuts	58.4*	53.6*	53.6
Soybeans (Soya beans)	1,259.7	1,499.4	1,637.0
Sunflower seeds	273.2	206.5	153.0
Tomatoes	122.7	123.6	121.3
Pumpkins, squash and gourds	20.5	19.9	18.2
Onions, dry	33.2	33.7	36.1
Peas, green	24.9	25.5	25.0
Carrots and turnips	29.6	29.0	27.6
Maize, green	34.9	35.6	36.8
Watermelons	5.1	5.3	5.6
Bananas	183.3	188.9	194.6
Plantains	451.2	466.4	464.2
Oranges	93.4	95.6	100.7
Tangerines, mandarins, clementines and satsumas	38.6	40.0	42.8
Lemons and limes	28.4	28.6	26.9
Grapes	32.7	33.6	37.0
Papayas	7.6	7.7	7.9
Coffee, green	27.3	28.3	29.1

* FAO estimate(s).

Aggregate production ('000 metric tons, may include official, semi-official or estimated data): Total cereals 2,053 in 2008, 1,874 in 2009, 2,173 in 2010; Total roots and tubers 1,169 in 2008, 1,185 in 2009, 1,190 in 2010; Total vegetables (incl. melons) 377 in 2008, 380 in 2009, 385 in 2010; Total fruits (excl. melons) 902 in 2008, 929 in 2009, 944 in 2010.

Source: FAO.

LIVESTOCK
('000 head, year ending September)

	2007	2008	2009
Horses	465	470*	475*
Asses*	635	635	635
Mules*	82	82	82
Cattle	7,894	7,904	8,080
Pigs	2,592	2,655†	2,760†
Sheep	9,177	9,333	9,530
Goats	1,960	1,979†	2,002†
Chickens	73,388	76,263	83,852
Ducks*	295	295	295
Turkeys*	155	155	155

* FAO estimate(s).
† Unofficial figure.

2010: Figures assumed to be unchanged from 2009 (FAO estimates).

Source: FAO.

LIVESTOCK PRODUCTS
('000 metric tons)

	2008	2009	2010*
Cattle meat	248.7	254.6	247.3
Sheep meat*	20.0	21.0	21.3
Goat meat*	5.8	5.8	5.8
Pig meat	114.5	117.2	117.5
Chicken meat*	166.3	166.1	168.3
Cows' milk	260.0*	290.0	302.4
Sheep's milk*	31.1	31.7	33.5
Goats' milk*	11.9	11.9	11.3
Hen eggs	65.4†	68.6†	68.5
Wool, greasy*	7.9	7.1	6.6

* FAO estimate(s).
† Unofficial figure.

Source: FAO.

Forestry

ROUNDWOOD REMOVALS
('000 cubic metres, excl. bark)

	2007	2008	2009
Sawlogs, veneer logs and logs for sleepers	910*	910*	910†
Fuel wood†	2,289	2,309	2,329
Total†	3,199	3,219	3,239

* Unofficial figure.
† FAO estimate(s).

2010: Production assumed to be unchanged from 2009.

Source: FAO.

SAWNWOOD PRODUCTION
('000 cubic metres, incl. railway sleepers)

	2004	2005	2006
Coniferous (softwood)*	1	1	2
Broadleaved (hardwood)	402	408	459
Total*	403	409	461

* Unofficial figures.

2007–10: Production assumed to be unchanged from 2006 (FAO estimates).

Source: FAO.

Fishing

(metric tons, live weight)

	2006*	2007	2008
Capture	6,350	6,000*	6,797*
Freshwater fishes	5,200	4,851	5,787
Rainbow trout	300	299*	160
Silversides (sand smelts)*	850	850	850
Aquaculture	455	585	631*
Rainbow trout	230	130	194
Total catch	6,805	6,585*	7,428*

* FAO estimate(s).

Note: Figures exclude crocodiles and alligators, recorded by number rather than by weight. The number of spectacled caimans caught was: 44,443 in 2006; 49,115 in 2007; 51,618 in 2008.

Note: No data were available for 2009.

Source: FAO.

Mining

(metric tons unless otherwise indicated; figures for metallic minerals refer to the metal content of ores)

	2007	2008	2009
Crude petroleum ('000 barrels)	15,027	14,233*	12,330*
Natural gas (million cu m)	15,230	15,374*	13,500†
Copper	606	731	882*
Tin	15,972	17,320	19,581*
Lead	22,798	81,602	84,537*
Zinc	214,053	383,618	430,879*
Tungsten (Wolfram)	1,107	1,148	1,023*
Antimony	3,881	3,905	2,990*
Silver (kg)	524,989	1,113,764	1,325,700*
Gold (kg)	8,818	8,405	7,217*

* Preliminary figure.
† Estimate.

Source: US Geological Survey.

Industry

SELECTED PRODUCTS
('000 42-gallon barrels unless otherwise indicated)

	2007	2008	2009
Cement ('000 metric tons)	1,739	1,985	2,292*
Liquefied petroleum gas	895	685†	645†
Distillate fuel oil	4,880	5,050†	4,100†
Kerosene	131	130†	100†
Motor spirit (petrol)	4,558	5,390†	5,530†

* Preliminary figure.
† Estimate.

Electric energy (million kWh): 4,778 in 2005.

2001 (provisional): Flour ('000 metric tons) 788; Carbonated drinks ('000 hl) 1,996; Beer ('000 hl) 1,586; Cigarettes (packets) 75,373; Alcohol ('000 litres) 29,099.

Source: partly US Geological Survey.

Finance

CURRENCY AND EXCHANGE RATES

Monetary Units
100 centavos = 1 boliviano (B).

Sterling, Dollar and Euro Equivalents (30 December 2011)
£1 sterling = 10.684 bolivianos;
US $1 = 6.910 bolivianos;
€1 = 8.941 bolivianos;
100 bolivianos = £9.36 = $14.47 = €11.18.

Average Exchange Rate (bolivianos per US $)
2009 7.02
2010 7.02
2011 6.94

GENERAL BUDGET
(national treasury budget, million bolivianos, preliminary)

Revenue (all current)	2007	2008	2009
Tax revenue	12,679.5	14,379.2	15,271.7
Internal	11,691.1	13,357.4	14,108.5
Customs	746.8	780.6	922.4
Duties on hydrocarbons	1,152.6	1,085.8	2,636.5
Other current revenue	384.2	354.6	1,166.2
Repayment of loans	23.3	n.a.	n.a.
Current transfers	252.8	672.6	n.a.
Grants	402.0	236.1	328.4
Total	14,894.4	16,728.3	19,402.8

Expenditure	2007	2008	2009
Current expenditure	15,617.6	18,851.9	23,443.7
Personal services	8,310.7	9,187.7	10,731.1
Goods and services	727.4	890.2	1,088.0
Interest on debt	2,243.3	2,781.9	2,396.0
External	1,059.8	1,063.1	834.2
Internal	1,183.5	1,718.8	1,561.8
Current transfers	4,336.2	5,992.2	8,619.9
Payments	3,472.6	3,877.2	4,440.8
Capital expenditure	287.0	417.7	883.8
Total	15,904.6	19,269.6	24,327.5

INTERNATIONAL RESERVES
(US $ million at 31 December)

	2008	2009	2010
Gold (national valuation)	794.5	997.6	1,596.2
IMF special drawing rights	42.3	258.5	254.0
Reserve position in IMF	13.7	13.9	13.7
Foreign exchange	6,871.4	7,311.3	7,866.2
Total	7,721.9	8,581.3	9,730.1

Source: IMF, *International Financial Statistics*.

MONEY SUPPLY
(million bolivianos at 31 December)

	2008	2009	2010
Currency outside depository corporations	15,807	17,080	22,485
Transferable deposits	19,279	18,723	22,763
Other deposits	37,483	45,334	47,774
Securities other than shares	—	—	140
Broad money	72,569	81,137	93,162

Source: IMF, *International Financial Statistics*.

COST OF LIVING
(Consumer Price Index for urban areas; base: 2000 = 100)

	2006	2007	2008
Food and beverages	122.2	138.9	174.5
Fuel and light	124.1	125.5	n.a.
Clothing and footwear	119.1	125.1	134.1
Rent	112.7	113.1	n.a.
All items (incl. others)	121.6	132.2	150.7

2009: Food 124.1; All items (incl. others) 155.8.

2010: Food 127.8; All items (incl. others) 159.7.

Source: ILO.

NATIONAL ACCOUNTS
(million bolivianos at current prices, preliminary)

Expenditure on the Gross Domestic Product

	2008	2009	2010
Government final consumption expenditure	16,025.0	17,904.5	19,069.9
Private final consumption expenditure	75,100.3	79,733.2	85,894.4
Increase in stocks	366.9	598.9	599.4
Gross fixed capital formation	20,818.1	20,059.7	22,849.1
Total domestic expenditure	112,310.3	118,296.3	128,412.8
Exports of goods and services	54,199.4	43,484.0	56,787.4
Less Imports of goods and services	45,815.9	40,053.5	47,324.6
GDP at market prices	120,693.8	121,726.7	137,875.6
GDP at constant 1990 prices	30,277.8	31,294.3	32,585.7

Gross Domestic Product by Economic Activity

	2008	2009	2010
Agriculture, hunting, forestry and fishing	12,603.3	13,575.5	14,325.1
Mining and quarrying	17,181.5	15,779.3	19,332.4
Manufacturing	13,479.7	14,140.7	15,538.6
Electricity, gas and water	2,436.6	2,631.4	3,010.7
Construction	2,792.6	3,027.8	3,679.4
Trade	8,468.5	8,779.1	10,195.3
Transport, storage and communications	10,147.0	10,723.5	12,375.6
Finance, insurance, real estate and business services	10,062.3	10,642.8	11,997.9
Government services	12,600.9	14,507.8	16,423.2
Other services	7,597.5	8,308.4	9,056.3
Sub-total	97,369.7	102,116.1	115,934.5
Value-added tax / Import duties	27,123.7	23,562.6	26,423.1
Less Imputed bank charge	3,799.7	3,951.9	4,481.9
GDP in purchasers' values	120,693.8	121,726.7	137,875.6

BALANCE OF PAYMENTS
(US $ million)

	2008	2009	2010
Exports of goods f.o.b.	6,526.5	4,917.6	6,290.5
Imports of goods f.o.b.	–4,764.1	–4,143.6	–5,006.8
Trade balance	1,762.4	774.0	1,283.7
Exports of services	499.7	515.5	549.6
Imports of services	–1,017.2	–1,015.3	–1,151.9
Balance on goods and services	1,245.0	274.2	681.4
Other income received (net)	–536.4	–673.7	–888.9
Balance on goods, services and income	708.6	–399.6	–207.5
Current transfers received (net)	1,284.1	1,213.1	1,081.3
Current balance	1,992.7	813.5	873.7
Capital account (net)	9.7	110.5	–7.2
Direct investment (net)	509.3	420.0	650.8
Portfolio investment assets	–208.1	–153.6	90.1
Other investment assets (net)	69.1	–196.7	119.1
Net errors and omissions	1.5	–453.6	–802.3
Overall balance	2,374.2	540.2	924.3

Source: IMF, *International Financial Statistics*.

External Trade

PRINCIPAL COMMODITIES
(distribution by SITC, US $ million)

Imports c.i.f.	2008	2009	2010*
Food and live animals	402.2	356.3	369.4
Crude materials (inedible) except fuels	84.2	51.7	62.2
Mineral fuels, lubricants, etc.	579.1	501.1	653.2
Chemicals and related products	868.4	781.8	946.2
Basic manufactures	988.5	885.8	1,049.7
Machinery and transport equipment	1,771.7	1,586.3	1,841.8
Miscellaneous manufactured articles	323.6	310.0	398.3
Total (incl. others)	5,100.2	4,577.4	5,393.3

Exports f.o.b.	2008	2009	2010*
Food and live animals	577.8	678.3	684.8
Crude materials (inedible) except fuels	1,712.6	1,691.8	2,021.3
Mineral fuels, lubricants, etc.	3,548.7	2,135.2	3,014.9
Animal and vegetable oils, fats and waxes	290.3	248.3	281.0
Basic manufactures	421.9	290.5	523.7
Machinery and transport equipment	1.6	1.4	6.2
Miscellaneous manufactured articles	145.1	145.1	160.7
Total (incl. others)	6,932.9	5,399.6	6,952.1

* Preliminary.

PRINCIPAL TRADING PARTNERS
(US $ million)

Imports c.i.f.	2008	2009	2010*
Argentina	729.8	628.5	699.5
Brazil	925.3	788.6	1,001.0
Chile	350.6	246.7	303.6
China, People's Republic	445.1	415.6	536.5
Colombia	111.7	98.9	118.0
France (incl. Monaco)	57.1	43.0	86.2
Germany	92.0	98.1	111.2
Italy	45.1	44.5	67.6
Japan	501.7	319.7	316.7
Korea, Republic	31.3	25.4	42.3
Mexico	109.9	96.7	127.6
Paraguay	46.8	28.0	30.5
Peru	354.4	322.0	388.5
Spain	55.4	48.8	61.9
Sweden	98.4	97.8	57.2
USA	552.4	627.7	713.3
Venezuela	253.2	308.8	298.7
Total (incl. others)	5,100.2	4,577.4	5,393.3

Exports	2008	2009	2010*
Argentina	493.3	433.9	553.4
Belgium-Luxembourg	157.4	189.6	379.7
Brazil	3,023.1	1,667.5	2,406.9
Canada	87.3	69.9	88.4
Chile	78.1	75.0	83.1
China, People's Republic	129.4	130.6	208.4
Colombia	216.2	291.5	240.8
Japan	214.3	303.5	460.3
Korea, Republic	812.5	494.9	367.1
Panama	24.7	57.6	39.0
Peru	275.9	288.4	391.7
Switzerland (incl. Liechtenstein)	162.1	167.3	166.4
United Kingdom	90.0	74.3	101.3
USA	486.9	471.0	690.4
Venezuela	250.0	291.5	360.6
Total (incl. others)	6,932.9	5,399.6	6,952.1

* Preliminary.

Transport

RAILWAYS
(traffic)

	2002	2003	2004
Passenger-km (million)	280	283	286
Net ton-km (million)	873	901	1,058

Source: UN, *Statistical Yearbook*.

ROAD TRAFFIC
(motor vehicles in use at 31 December)

	2002	2003	2004
Passenger cars	26,229	127,222	138,729
Buses	27,226	43,588	49,133
Lorries and vans	30,539	225,028	251,801
Motorcycles	1,125	15,467	19,426

2007: Passenger cars 174,912; Buses 6,996; Lorries and vans 468,763; Motorcycles 34,982.

Source: IRF, *World Road Statistics*.

SHIPPING

Merchant Fleet
(registered at 31 December)

	2007	2008	2009
Number of vessels	75	56	59
Total displacement ('000 grt)	102.9	74.7	122.0

Source: IHS Fairplay, *World Fleet Statistics*.

CIVIL AVIATION
(traffic on scheduled services)

	2005	2006	2007
Kilometres flown (million)	22	13	4
Passenger-km (million)	1,903	1,413	287
Freight ton-km (million)	25	11	1

Source: UN Commission for Latin America and the Caribbean, *Statistical Yearbook*.

Passengers carried (million): 1.9 in 2005; 1.4 in 2006; 1.7 in 2007; 1.7 in 2008; 1.5 in 2009 (Source: World Bank, World Development Indicators database).

Tourism

ARRIVALS AT HOTELS
(regional capitals only)

Country of origin	2004	2005	2006
Argentina	36,320	41,610	54,622
Brazil	29,745	32,400	35,077
Canada	8,120	8,297	10,745
Chile	14,948	19,234	26,515
France	24,416	25,167	27,304
Germany	19,804	20,308	23,707
Israel	12,149	9,405	12,171
Italy	8,480	8,101	9,744
Japan	7,469	7,226	7,505
Netherlands	9,764	8,625	9,651
Peru	68,739	77,380	84,867
Spain	12,140	11,974	17,531
Switzerland	8,531	8,519	9,964
United Kingdom	20,616	20,801	22,650
USA	38,066	37,758	41,378
Total (incl. others)	390,888	413,267	496,489

Tourism receipts (US $ million, excl. passenger transport): 292 in 2007; 275 in 2008; 279 in 2009 (provisional).

Source: World Tourism Organization.

Communications Media

	2008	2009	2010
Telephones ('000 main lines in use)	789.0	804.2	848.2
Mobile cellular telephones ('000 subscribers)	5,038.6	6,464.4	7,179.3
Internet subscribers ('000)	n.a.	351.1	n.a.
Broadband subscribers ('000)	79.3	96.1	95.9

Source: International Telecommunication Union.

Personal computers: 220,000 (24.0 per 1,000 persons) in 2005 (Source: International Telecommunication Union).

Television receivers ('000): 990 in use in 2000 (Source: International Telecommunication Union).

Radio receivers ('000): 5,250 in use in 1997 (Source: UNESCO, *Statistical Yearbook*).

Daily newspapers: 18 in 1996 (average circulation 420,000 copies) (Source: UNESCO, *Statistical Yearbook*).

Education

(2007/08 unless otherwise indicated, estimates)

	Institutions	Teachers	Students ('000) Males	Females	Total
Pre-primary	2,294*	6,126†	117.2	112.7	229.9
Primary	12,639‡	62,430†	771.3	737.1	1,508.4
Secondary: general	n.a.	57,912†	544.7	514.9	1,059.6
Secondary: technical/vocational	n.a.	2,148§	17.3‖	32.3‖	49.6‖
Tertiary†	n.a.	15,685	193.8	158.8	352.6

* 1988.

† 2006/07.

‡ 1987.

§ 2003/04.

‖ 2002/03.

Pupil-teacher ratio (primary education, UNESCO estimate): 24.2 in 2006/07.

Adult literacy rate (UNESCO estimates): 90.7% (males 95.0%; females 86.8%) in 2008.

Source: UNESCO Institute for Statistics.

Directory

The Government

HEAD OF STATE

President: JUAN EVO MORALES AIMA (took office 22 January 2006, re-elected 6 December 2009).

Vice-President: ALVARO MARCELO GARCÍA LINERA.

THE CABINET

(May 2012)

The Cabinet is composed of members of the Movimiento al Socialismo.

Minister of Foreign Affairs and Worship: DAVID CHOQUEHUANCA CÉSPEDES.

Minister of the Interior: CARLOS GUSTAVO ROMERO BONIFAZ.

Minister of National Defence: RUBÉN SAAVEDRA SOTO.

Minister of Justice: CECILIA LUISA AYLLÓN QUINTEROS.

Minister of Economy and Public Finance: LUIS ALBERTO ARCE CATACORA.

Minister of Development Planning: ELBA VIVIANA CARO HINOJOSA.

Minister of the Presidency: JUAN RAMÓN QUINTANA.

Minister of Autonomy: CLAUDIA PEÑA CLAROS.

Minister of Institutional Transparency and the Fight against Corruption: NARDI SUXO ITURRY.

Minister of Health and Sport: JUAN CARLOS CALVIMONTES.

Minister of Labour, Employment and Social Security: DANIEL SANTALLA TÓRREZ.

Minister of Education: ROBERTO AGUILAR GÓMEZ.

Minister of Rural Development and Lands: NEMESIA ACHACOLLO TOLA.

Minister of Hydrocarbons and Energy: JUAN JOSÉ SOSA SORUCO.

Minister of Mines and Metallurgy: MARIO VIRREIRA.

Minister of Public Works, Services and Housing: VLADIMIR SÁNCHEZ ESCOBAR.

Minister of Water and the Environment: FELIPE QUISPE QUENTA.

Minister of the Legal Defence of State: ELIZABETH ARISMENDI CHUMACERO.

Minister of Culture: PABLO CÉSAR GROUX CANEDO.

Minister of Productive Development and Plural Economy: ANA TERESA MORALES OLIVERA.

Minister of Communications: AMANDA DÁVILA.

MINISTRIES

Office of the President: Palacio de Gobierno, Calle Ayacucho, esq. Comercio s/n, La Paz; tel. and fax (2) 220-2321; e-mail correo@presidencia.gob.bo; internet www.presidencia.gob.bo.

Office of the Vice-President: Edif. de la Vicepresidencia del Estado, Calle Ayacucho, esq. Mercado 308, Casilla 7056, La Paz; tel. (2) 214-2000; fax (2) 220-1211; internet www.vicepresidencia.gob.bo.

Ministry of Autonomy: Edif. Cámara Nacional de Comercio, 11°, Avda Mariscal Santa Cruz 1392, Casilla 1397, La Paz; tel. (2) 211-0930; fax (2) 211-3613; e-mail administrador@autonomia.gob.bo; internet www.autonomia.gob.bo.

Ministry of Communications: Edif. La Urbana, 4°, Avda Camacho 1485, La Paz; tel. (2) 220-0402; fax (2) 220-0509; e-mail comunicacion@comunicacion.gob.bo; internet www.comunicacion.gob.bo.

Ministry of Culture: Palacio Chico, Calle Ayacucho, esq. Potosí, Casilla 7846, La Paz; tel. (2) 220-0910; fax (2) 220-2628; e-mail despacho@minculturas.gob.bo; internet www.minculturas.gob.bo.

Ministry of Development Planning: Avda Mariscal Santa Cruz, esq. Oruro 1092, Casilla 12814, La Paz; tel. (2) 211-6000; fax (2) 231-7320; e-mail comunicacion@planificacion.gov.bo; internet www.planificacion.gov.bo.

Ministry of Economy and Public Finance: Edif. Palacio de Comunicaciones, 19°, CP 3744, La Paz; tel. (2) 220-3434; fax (2) 235-9955; e-mail ministro_web@economiayfinanzas.gob.bo; internet www.economiayfinanzas.gob.bo.

Ministry of Education: Avda Arce 2147, Casilla 3116, La Paz; tel. and fax (2) 244-2414; e-mail webmaster@minedu.gob.bo; internet www.minedu.gob.bo.

Ministry of Foreign Affairs and Worship: Plaza Murillo, Calle Ingavi, esq. Calle Junín, La Paz; tel. (2) 240-8900; fax (2) 240-8905; e-mail mreuno@rree.gob.bo; internet www.rree.gob.bo.

Ministry of Health and Sport: Plaza del Estudiante, esq. Cañada Strongest s/n, La Paz; tel. (2) 249-0554; fax (2) 248-6654; e-mail info@sns.gov.bo; internet www.sns.gov.bo.

Ministry of Hydrocarbons and Energy: Edif. Palacio de Comunicaciones, 12°, Avda Mariscal Santa Cruz, esq. Calle Oruro, La Paz; tel. (2) 237-4050; fax (2) 214-1307; e-mail minehidro@hidrocarburos.gob.bo; internet www.hidrocarburos.gob.bo.

Ministry of Institutional Transparency and the Fight against Corruption: Edif. Capitán Ravelo, 3°–9°, Calle Capitán Ravelo 2101, esq. Montevideo, La Paz; tel. 211-5773; fax 215-3084; internet www.transparencia.gob.bo.

Ministry of the Interior: Avda Arce 2409, esq. Belisario Salinas 2409, Casilla 7110, La Paz; tel. (2) 244-0466; fax (2) 237-1334; e-mail mail@mingobierno.gob.bo; internet www.mingobierno.gob.bo.

Ministry of Justice: Avda 16 de Julio (El Prado) 1769, La Paz; tel. (2) 212-4725; fax (2) 231-5468; e-mail ministerio@justicia.go.bo; internet www.justicia.gob.bo.

Ministry of Labour, Employment and Social Security: Calle Yanacocha, esq. Mercado, Zona Central, La Paz; tel. (2) 240-8606; fax (2) 237-1387; e-mail info@mintrabajo.gob.bo; internet www.mintrabajo.gob.bo.

Ministry of the Legal Defence of State: Edif. Hansa, 4°, Avda Mariscal Santa Cruz, La Paz; tel. and fax (2) 211-8454; e-mail mdle@defensalegal.gob.bo; internet www.defensalegal.gob.bo.

Ministry of Mines and Metallurgy: Edif. Palacio de Comunicaciones, 14°, Avda Mariscal Santa Cruz, Casilla 8686, La Paz; tel. (2) 231-0846; fax (2) 239-1241; e-mail mineria@mineria.gob.bo; internet www.mineria.gob.bo.

Ministry of National Defence: Calle 20 de Octubre 2502, esq. Pedro Salazar, La Paz; tel. (2) 243-2525; fax (2) 243-3153; e-mail utransparencia@mindef.gob.bo; internet www.mindef.gob.bo.

Ministry of the Presidency: Palacio de Gobierno, Calle Ayacucho, esq. Comercio s/n, La Paz; tel. (2) 215-3913; fax (2) 237-1388; e-mail correo@presidencia.gob.bo; internet www.presidencia.gob.bo.

Ministry of Productive Development and Plural Economy: Edif. Centro de Comunicaciones, 20°, Avda Mariscal Santa Cruz, esq. Calle Oruro, La Paz; tel. (2) 212-4235; fax (2) 212-4240; e-mail contacto@produccion.gob.bo; internet www.produccion.gob.bo.

Ministry of Public Works, Services and Housing: Edif. Centro de Comunicaciones, 5°, Avda Mariscal Santa Cruz, esq. Calle Oruro, La Paz; tel. (2) 211-9999; internet www.oopp.gob.bo.

Ministry of Rural Development and Lands: Avda Camacho 1471, entre Calle Bueno y Loaysa, La Paz; tel. (2) 211-1103; fax (2) 211-1067; e-mail despacho@agrobolivia.gov.bo; internet www.agrobolivia.gov.bo.

Ministry of Water and the Environment: Capitán Castrillo 434, entre Calles 20 de Octubre y Héroes del Acre, Zona San Pedro, La Paz; tel. (2) 211-5571; fax (2) 211-8582; e-mail gary.suarez@minagua.gov.bo; internet www.mmaya.gob.bo.

President and Legislature

PRESIDENT

Election, 6 December 2009

Candidate	Valid votes	% of valid votes cast
Juan Evo Morales Aima (MAS)	2,943,209	64.22
Manfred Reyes Villa Leopoldo Fernández (PPB—CN)	1,212,795	26.46
Samuel Doria Medina (UN)	258,971	5.65
René Joaquino Suárez González (AS)	106,027	2.31
Others	61,784	1.35
Total (incl. others)*	4,582,786	100.00

* In addition, there were 156,290 blank votes and 120,364 spoiled votes.

ASAMBLEA LEGISLATIVA PLURINACIONAL

President of the Senado Nacional: ANA MARÍA ROMERO DE CAMPO (MAS).

President of the Cámara de Diputados: HÉCTOR ARCE (MAS).

General Election, 6 December 2009

Party	Seats: Cámara de Diputados	Senado Nacional
Movimiento al Socialismo (MAS)	88	26
Plan Progreso para Bolivia—Convergencia National (PPB—CN)	37	10
Frente de Unidad Nacional (UN)	3	—
Alianza Social (AS)	2	—
Total	130	36

Governors

DEPARTMENTS
(May 2012)

Beni: HAISEN RIBERA LEIGUE (acting).

Chuquisaca: ESTEBAN URQUIZU CUÉLLAR.

Cochabamba: EDMUNDO NOVILLO AGUILAR.

La Paz: CÉSAR HUGO COCARICO YANA.

Oruro: SANTOS JAVIER TITO VÉLIZ.

Pando: LUIS ADOLFO FLORES ROBERTS.

Potosí: FÉLIX GONZÁLEZ BERNAL.

Santa Cruz de la Sierra: RUBÉN DARÍO COSTAS AGUILERA.

Tarija: LINO CONDORI ARAMAYO.

Election Commission

Corte Nacional Electoral (CNE): Avda Sánchez Lima, esq. Pedro Salazar, Sopocachi, CP 8748, La Paz; tel. (2) 242-4221; fax (2) 241-6710; e-mail cne@cne.org.bo; internet www.cne.org.bo; Pres. ANTONIO JOSÉ I. COSTAS SITIC.

Political Organizations

Acción Democrática Nacionalista (ADN): Edif. Illimani II, No 2512, Of. 12, Avda 6 de agosto y Pedro Salazar, La Paz; f. 1979; right-wing; Leader GUILLERMO FORTÚN SUÁREZ.

Alianza Social (AS): Calle Fortunato Gumiel s/n, Potosí; tel. (2) 622-6150; internet alianzasociallapaz.blogspot.com; f. 2006; Leader RENÉ JOAQUINO CABRERA.

Bolivia Social Demócrata (BSD): Edif. Arco Iris, planta baja, Of. 01, Calle Yanacocha 441, La Paz; tel. (2) 247-0768; e-mail rimech@hotmail.com; internet www.boliviasocialdemocrata.org; f. 2003; Pres. Dr RIME FRANCISCO CHOQUEHUANCA AGUILAR.

Comité Cívico de Tarija (CCT): Tarija; right-wing autonomist grouping; Pres. PATRICIA GALARZA.

Comité pro Santa Cruz (CSC): Avda Cañada Strongest 70, CP 1801, Santa Cruz; tel. (3) 334-2777; fax (3) 334-1812; internet www.comiteprosantacruz.org.bo; f. 1950; right-wing autonomist grouping; Pres. Dr HERLAND VACA DÍEZ BUSCH.

Consenso Popular (CP): alle Solíz de Olguín 447, esq. Avda Velarde, Santa Cruz; e-mail oscarortizantelo@gmail.com; internet www.consenso-popular.bo; f. 2009; fmr dissident grouping of PODEMOS; Leader OSCAR ORTIZ ANTELO.

Frente Revolucionario de Izquierda (FRI): Avda Busch 1191 y Pasaje Jamaica, Miraflores, La Paz; tel. (2) 222-5488; e-mail waltervr2002@yahoo.es; left-wing; f. 1978; Leader OSCAR ZAMORA MEDINACELI.

Frente de Unidad Nacional (UN): Calle Fernando Guachalla, esq. Jacinto Benavente 2190, La Paz; tel. and fax (2) 211-5110; e-mail info@unidad-nacional.com; internet www.unidad-nacional.com; f. 2003; left-wing; Leader SAMUEL DORIA MEDINA.

Frente para la Victoria (FPV): Edif. Ugarte de Ingeniería, Penthouse 1, Calle Loayza, La Paz; e-mail fpvbolivia@hotmail.com; f. 2006; Leader ELISEO RODRÍGUEZ PARI.

Movimiento sin Miedo (MSM): Calle 20 de Octubre y Conchitas, frente al colegio Bolívar, La Paz; tel. 70514444 (mobile); e-mail landaeta93@hotmail.com; internet www.bolivian.com/msm/index.html; f. 1999; left-wing; Leader JUAN DEL GRANADO COSÍO.

Movimiento Nacionalista Revolucionario (MNR): Avda Hernando Siles 21, Curva Sur del Estado Hernando Siles, La Paz; tel. (2) 212-8475; fax (2) 212-8479; e-mail mnr@bolivian.com; internet www.bolivian.com/mnr; f. 1942; centre-right; Leader MIRTHA QUEVEDO ACALINOVIC; Sec.-Gen. FRANKLIN ANAYA VÁZQUEZ; 165,000 mems.

Movimiento al Socialismo (MAS): Calle Benedicto Vincenti 960, Sopocachi, La Paz; tel. 72970205 (mobile); e-mail info@masbolivia.com; internet www.masbolivia.com; f. 1987; also known as the Movimiento al Socialismo—Instrumento Político por la Soberanía de los Pueblos (MAS—IPSP); left-wing; promotes equality for indigenous people, peasants and workers; Leader JUAN EVO MORALES AIMA.

Partido Demócrata Cristiano (PDC): Calle Colón 812, 2°, esq. Sucre, Casilla 4345, La Paz; tel. 70655693 (mobile); e-mail josuva2002@hotmail.com; f. 1954; contested the 2009 election in alliance with PODEMOS; Pres. JORGE SUÁREZ VARGAS.

Partido Obrero Revolucionario (POR): Correo Central, La Paz; internet www.por-bolivia.org; f. 1935; Trotskyist; Leader GUILLERMO LORA.

Plan Progreso para Bolivia—Convergencia Nacional (PPB—CN): Plaza del Estudiante 1907, Of. Radio Ciudad, Zona Central, La Paz; tel. 71520200 (mobile); e-mail jlparedesm@hotmail.com; internet www.planprogreso.org; f. 2007; Leader JOSÉ LUIS PAREDES MUÑOZ.

Poder Democrático y Social (PODEMOS): La Paz; right-wing; split into two factions in 2009; contested the 2009 elections in alliance with the PDC; Leader JORGE SUAREZ VARGAS.

Unión Cívica Solidaridad (UCS): Edif. La Primera Bloque B, 17°, Of. 7 y 8, Avda Mariscal Santa Cruz 1364, La Paz; tel. (2) 236-0297; fax (2) 237-2200; e-mail unidadcivicasolidaridad@hotmail.com; f. 1989; populist; Leader JOHNNY FERNÁNDEZ SAUCEDO; 102,000 mems.

Diplomatic Representation

EMBASSIES IN BOLIVIA

Argentina: Calle Aspiazú 497, esq. Sánchez Lima, Casilla 64, La Paz; tel. (2) 241-7737; fax (2) 242-2727; e-mail ebolv@mrecic.gov.ar; Chargé d'affaires a.i. JORGE LUIS GÓMEZ.

Brazil: Edif. Multicentro, Torre B, Avda Arce s/n, esq. Rosendo Gutiérrez, Sopocachi, Casilla 429, La Paz; tel. (2) 216-6400; fax (2) 244-0043; e-mail embajadabrasil@brasil.org.bo; internet www.brasil.org.bo; Ambassador MARCEL FORTUNA BIATO.

China, People's Republic: Calle 1 8532, Los Pinos, Calacoto, Casilla 10005, La Paz; tel. (2) 279-3851; fax (2) 279-7121; e-mail emb-china@kolla.net; Ambassador SHEN ZHILIANG.

Colombia: Calle 9, No 7835, Casilla 1418, Calacoto, La Paz; tel. (2) 278-4491; fax (2) 279-6011; e-mail elapaz@cancilleria.gov.co; internet www.embajadaenbolivia.gov.co; Ambassador MARTHA CECILIA PINILLA PERDOMO.

Cuba: Calle Gobles 6246, entre calles 11 y 12, Bajo Irpavi, Zona Sur, La Paz; tel. (2) 272-1646; fax (2) 272-3419; e-mail embacuba@acelerate.com; internet www.cubadiplomatica.cu/bolivia; Ambassador ROLANDO ANTONIO GÓMEZ GONZÁLEZ.

Denmark: Edif. Fortaleza, 9°, Avda Arce 2799, esq. Cordero, Casilla 9860, La Paz; tel. (2) 243-2070; fax (2) 243-3150; e-mail lpbamb@um.dk; internet www.amblapaz.um.dk; Ambassador MORTEN ELKJÆR.

Ecuador: Calle 10, No 8054, Calacoto, Casilla 406, La Paz; tel. (2) 278-4422; fax (2) 277-1043; e-mail eecuabolivia@mmrree.gov.ec; Ambassador RICARDO ULCUANGO.

Egypt: Avda Ballivián 599, esq. Calle 12, Casilla 2956, La Paz; tel. (2) 278-6511; fax (2) 278-4325; e-mail embajadaegipto@acelerate.com; Ambassador HANI MUHAMMAD BASYONI MAHMOUD.

France: Avda Hernando Silés 5390, esq. Calle 8 de Obrajes, Casilla 717, La Paz; tel. (2) 214-9900; fax (2) 214-9901; e-mail information@ambafrance-bo.org; internet www.ambafrance-bo.org; Ambassador MICHEL PINARD.

Germany: Avda Arce 2395, esq. Belisario Salinas, Casilla 5265, La Paz; tel. (2) 200-1500; fax (2) 244-1441; e-mail info@la-paz.diplo.de; internet www.la-paz.diplo.de; Ambassador Dr PHILIPP SCHAUER.

Holy See: Avda Arce 2990, San Jorge, Casilla 136, La Paz; tel. (2) 243-1007; fax (2) 243-2120; e-mail nunciaturabolivia@gmail.com; Apostolic Nuncio Most Rev. GIAMBATTISTA DIQUATTRO (Titular Archbishop of Giru Mons).

Iran: Calle 9, No 21, entre Avda Costanera y Avda Los Sauces, Calacoto, La Paz; tel. (2) 277-5749; fax (2) 277-5747; e-mail iranbolivi@yahoo.com; Ambassador ALIREZA GHEZILI.

Italy: Calle 5 (Jordán Cuellar) 458, Obrajes, Casilla 626, La Paz; tel. (2) 278-8506; fax (2) 278-8178; e-mail segreteria.lapaz@esteri.it; internet www.amblapaz.esteri.it; Ambassador LUIGI DE CHIARA.

Japan: Calle Rosendo Gutiérrez 497, esq. Sánchez Lima, Casiila 2725, La Paz; tel. (2) 241-9110; fax (2) 241-1919; e-mail coopjapon@acelerate.com; internet www.bo.emb-japan.go.jp; Ambassador TOSHIO WATANABE.

Korea, Republic: Edif. Torre Lucía, 6°, Calle 13, Calacoto, La Paz; tel. (2) 211-0361; fax (2) 211-0365; e-mail coreabolivia@gmail.com; internet bol.mofat.go.kr; Ambassador CHUN YOUNG-WOOK.

Mexico: Avda Ballivián 1174, entre Calles 17 y 18, Calacoto, Casilla 430, La Paz; tel. (2) 277-1871; fax (2) 277-1855; e-mail embamex@embamexbolivia.org; internet www.sre.gob.mx/bolivia; Chargé d'affaires a.i. CLAUDIA VELASCO.

Netherlands: Edif. Hilda, 7°, Avda 6 de Agosto 2455, Casilla 10509, La Paz; tel. (2) 244-4040; fax (2) 244-3804; e-mail lap@minbuza.nl; internet bolivia.nlambassade.org; Chargé d'affaires a.i. HANS GLAUBITZ.

Panama: Calle 10, No 7853, Calacoto, Casilla 678, La Paz; tel. (2) 278-7334; fax (2) 279-7290; e-mail empanbol@ceibo.entelnet.bo; internet www.empanbol.org; Ambassador AFRANIO HERRERA GARCÍA.

Paraguay: Edif. Illimani II, 1°, Of. 101, Avda 6 de Agosto, esq. Pedro Salazar, Sopocachi, Casilla 882, La Paz; tel. (2) 243-3176; fax (2) 243-2201; e-mail embaparbolivia@mre.gov.py; Chargé d'affaires a.i. OSVALDO BITTAR VICIOSO.

Peru: Calle Fernando Guachalla 300, Sopocachi, Casilla 668, La Paz; tel. (2) 244-1250; fax (2) 244-1240; e-mail embbol@caoba.entelnet.bo; internet www.embaperubolivia.com; Ambassador SILVIA ELENA ALFARO ESPINOSA.

Russia: Avda Walter Guevara Arce 8129, Calacoto, Casilla 5494, La Paz; tel. (2) 278-6419; fax (2) 278-6531; e-mail embrusia@acelerate.com; Ambassador LEONID E. GOLUBEV.

Spain: Avda 6 de Agosto 2827, Casilla 282, La Paz; tel. (2) 243-3518; fax (2) 243-2752; e-mail emb.lapaz@maec.es; internet www.maec.es/embajadas/lapaz; Ambassador RAMÓN SANTOS MARTÍNEZ.

Sweden: Edif. Multicine, 11°, Avda Arce 2631, La Paz; tel. (2) 297-9630; fax (2) 297-9631; e-mail ambassaden.la-paz@foreign.ministry.se; internet www.swedenabroad.com; Ambassador MARIE ANDERSSON DE FRUTOS.

Switzerland: Calle 13, esq. Avda 14 de Setiembre, Obrajes, Casilla 9356, La Paz; tel. (2) 275-1225; fax (2) 214-0885; e-mail paz.vertretung@eda.admin.ch; internet www.eda.admin.ch/lapaz; Ambassador PASCAL AEBISCHER.

United Kingdom: Avda Arce 2732, Casilla 694, La Paz; tel. (2) 243-3424; fax (2) 243-1073; e-mail ukinbolivia@gmail.com; internet www.ukinbolivia.fco.gov.uk; Ambassador NIGEL BAKER, ROSS PATRICK DENNY.

USA: Avda Arce 2780, Casilla 425, La Paz; tel. (2) 216-8000; fax (2) 216-8111; e-mail consularlapaz@state.com; internet bolivia.usembassy.gov; Chargé d'affaires a.i. JOHN S. CREAMER.

Uruguay: Edif. Monroy Velez, 7°, Calle 21, San Miguel 8350, Calacoto, La Paz; tel. (2) 279-1482; fax (2) 279-3976; e-mail urulivia@acelerate.com; Ambassador CARLOS MARIO FLANAGAN BENTOS.

Venezuela: Calle 12, esq. Costanerita 1000, Obrajes, Casilla 441, La Paz; tel. (2) 278-8501; fax (2) 278-8254; e-mail embvzla@acelerate.com; Ambassador CRISBEYLEE GONZÁLES HERNÁNDEZ.

Judicial System

In October 2011, following a constitutional amendment, direct elections were held to elect judges to the constitutional court, supreme court, council of magistrates and a newly established agro-environmental court. The judges took up their posts in January 2012.

CONSTITUTIONAL COURT

Tribunal Constitucional de Bolivia: Avda del Maestro 300, Sucre; tel. (4) 644-0455; fax (4) 642-1871; e-mail tribunal@tc.gob.bo; internet www.tribunalconstitucional.gob.bo; f. 1994; seven mems; Pres. Dr ERNESTO FÉLIX MUR.

SUPREME COURT

Corte Suprema de Justicia

Parque Bolívar, Casilla 211 y 321, Sucre; tel. (4) 645-3200; fax (4) 646-2696; e-mail cortesuprema@poderjudicial.gob.bo; internet suprema.poderjudicial.gob.bo.

Judicial power is vested in the Supreme Court. There are nine judges and a further nine alternates, directly elected for a term of six years. The court is divided into five chambers. One chamber deals with civil cases, two chambers deal with criminal cases, a further two deal with administrative and social cases. The President of the Supreme Court presides over joint sessions of the courts and attends the joint sessions for cassation cases.

President of the Supreme Court of Justice: Dra BEATRIZ ALCIRA SANDOVAL DE CAPOBIANCO.

AGRO-ENVIRONMENTAL COURT

The Agro-Environmental Court was founded in 2011. It comprises seven judges, elected by popular vote for a six-year term.

DISTRICT COURTS

There is a District Court sitting in each Department, and additional provincial and local courts to try minor cases.

ATTORNEY-GENERAL

In addition to the Attorney-General at Sucre (appointed by the President on the proposal of the Senate), there is a District Attorney in each Department as well as circuit judges.

Attorney-General: MARIO URIBE MELENDRES.

Religion

CHRISTIANITY

The Roman Catholic Church

Some 83% of the population are Roman Catholics. Bolivia comprises four archdioceses, six dioceses, two Territorial Prelatures and five Apostolic Vicariates.

Bishops' Conference

Conferencia Episcopal Boliviana, Calle Potosí 814, Casilla 2309, La Paz; tel. (2) 240-6855; fax (2) 240-6941; e-mail asc@scbbs-bo.com.

f. 1972; Pres. Cardinal JULIO TERRAZAS SANDOVAL (Archbishop of Santa Cruz de la Sierra).

Archbishop of Cochabamba: Most Rev. TITO SOLARI CAPELLARI, Avda Heroínas 152, esq. Zenteno Anaya, Casilla 129, Cochabamba; tel. (4) 425-6562; fax (4) 425-0522; e-mail arzobispado@iglesia.org; internet www.iglesiacbba.org.

Archbishop of La Paz: Most Rev. EDMUNDO LUIS FLAVIO ABASTOFLOR MONTERO, Calle Ballivián 1277, Casilla 259, La Paz; tel. (2) 220-3690; fax (2) 220-3840; e-mail arzonslp@ceibo.entelnet.bo; internet www.arzobispadolapaz.org.

Archbishop of Santa Cruz de la Sierra: Cardinal JULIO TERRAZAS SANDOVAL, Calle Ingavi 49, Casilla 25, Santa Cruz; tel. (3) 332-4416; fax (3) 333-0181; e-mail asc@scbbs-bo.com.

Archbishop of Sucre: Most Rev. JESÚS GERVASIO PÉREZ RODRÍGUEZ, Calle Bolívar 702, Casilla 205, Sucre; tel. (4) 645-1587; fax (4) 646-0336; e-mail arzsucre@mara.scr.entelnet.bo.

The Anglican Communion

Within the Iglesia Anglicana del Cono Sur de América (Anglican Church of the Southern Cone of America), Bolivia forms part of the diocese of Peru. The Bishop is resident in Lima, Peru.

Protestant Churches

Baptist Union of Bolivia: Casilla 2199, La Paz; tel. (2) 222-9538; Pres. Rev. AUGUSTO CHUIJO.

Convención Bautista Boliviana (Baptist Convention of Bolivia): Casilla 3147, Santa Cruz; tel. and fax (3) 334-0717; f. 1947; Pres. EIRA SORUCO DE FLORES.

Iglesia Evangélica Luterana Boliviana: Calle Rio Pirai 958, La Paz; tel. (2) 238-1858; fax (2) 238-0073; e-mail ielb@ielbbolivia.org; internet www.ielbbolivia.org; Pres. Rev. LUIS CRISTÓBAL ALEJO FERNÁNDEZ.

Iglesia Evangélica Metodista en Bolivia (Evangelical Methodist Church in Bolivia): Casillas 356 y 8347, La Paz; tel. (2) 249-1628; fax (2) 249-1624; autonomous since 1969; 10,000 mems; Bishop Rev. CARLOS INTIPAMPA.

BAHÁ'Í FAITH

National Spiritual Assembly of the Bahá'ís of Bolivia: Casilla 1613, La Paz; tel. (2) 278-5058; fax (2) 278-2387; e-mail noticias@bahai.org.bo; internet bahai.org.bo; mems resident in 5,161 localities; Gen. Sec. BADÍ HERNÁNDEZ.

The Press

DAILY NEWSPAPERS

Cochabamba

Opinión: Calle General Acha 252, Casilla 287, Cochabamba; tel. (4) 425-4400; fax (4) 441-5121; e-mail opinion@opinion.com.bo; internet www.opinion.com.bo; f. 1985; Dir EDWIN TAPIA FRONTANILLA; Chief Editor ANTONIO RIVERA M.

Los Tiempos: Edif. Los Tiempos, Plaza Quintanilla, Casilla 525, Cochabamba; tel. (4) 425-4562; fax (4) 425-4577; e-mail contactos@lostiempos.com; internet www.lostiempos.com; f. 1943; morning; independent; Dir FERNANDO CANELAS TÁRDIO; Man. Editor ALCIDES FLORES MONCADA; circ. 19,000.

La Paz

El Diario: Calle Loayza 118, Casilla 5, La Paz; tel. (2) 215-0900; fax (2) 215-0902; e-mail redinfo@diario.net; internet www.eldiario.net; f. 1904; morning; conservative; Dir ANTONIO CARRASCO GUZMÁN; Man. Editor RODRIGO TICONA ESPINOZA; circ. 55,000.

Jornada: Edif. Almirante Grau 672, Zona San Pedro, Casilla 1628, La Paz; tel. (2) 248-8163; fax (2) 248-7487; e-mail cartas@jornadanet.com; internet www.jornadanet.com; f. 1964; evening; independent; Dir DAVID RÍOS ARANDA; circ. 11,500.

La Prensa: Mayor Lopera 230, Villa Fátima, Casilla 5614, La Paz; tel. (2) 221-8821; fax (2) 221-8851; e-mail laprensa@laprensa.com.bo; internet www.laprensa.com.bo; Pres. JUAN CARLOS RIVERO J.; Chief Editor CARLOS MORALES PEÑA.

La Razón: Colinas de Santa Rita, Alto Auquisamaña (Zona Sur), Casilla 13100, La Paz; tel. (2) 277-1415; fax (2) 277-0908; e-mail jcrocha@la-razon.com; internet www.la-razon.com; f. 1990; Dir EDWIN HERRERA S.; Man. Editor PATRICIA CUSICANQUI H.; circ. 35,000.

Oruro

La Patria: Avda Camacho 1892, Casilla 48, Oruro; tel. (2) 525-0781; fax (2) 525-0782; e-mail info@lapatria.com.bo; internet www.lapatriaenlinea.com; f. 1919; morning; independent; Dir ENRIQUE MIRALLES BONNECARRERE; circ. 6,000.

Potosí

El Potosí: Calle Cochabamba 35 (Junto a Unidad Sanitaria), Potosí; tel. (2) 622-2601; fax (2) 622-7835; e-mail elpotosi@entelnet.bo; internet www.elpotosi.net; f. 2001; Pres. GONZALO CANELAS TARDÍO; Man. Editor GUILLERMO BULLAÍN IÑIGUEZ.

Santa Cruz

El Deber: Avda El Trompillo 1144, 2º, Casilla 2144, Santa Cruz; tel. (3) 353-8000; fax (3) 353-9053; e-mail web@eldeber.com.bo; internet www.eldeberdigital.com; f. 1953; morning; independent; Dir Dr PEDRO RIVERO MERCADO; Man. Editor TUFFÍ ARÉ VÁZQUEZ; circ. 35,000.

El Día: Avda Cristo Redentor 3355, Casilla 5344, Santa Cruz; tel. (3) 343-4040; fax (3) 342-4041; e-mail eldia@eldia.com.bo; internet www.eldia.com.bo; f. 1987; Dir EDUARDO BOWLES; Man. Editor RÓGER CUÉLLAR.

La Estrella del Oriente: Calle Republiquetas 353, Santa Cruz; tel. (3) 332-9011; fax (3) 332-9012; e-mail central@laestrelladeloriente.com; internet www.laestrelladeloriente.com; f. 1864; Pres. CARLOS SUBIRANA SUÁREZ; Dir (vacant).

El Mundo: Parque Industrial MZ-7, Casilla 1984, Santa Cruz; tel. (3) 346-4646; fax (3) 346-3322; e-mail redaccion@mail.elmundo.com.bo; internet www.elmundo.com.bo; f. 1979; morning; owned by Santa Cruz Industrialists' Asscn; Dir GERMÁN CASASSA ZAPATA; Chief Editor BENITO JESÚS ESPÍNDOLA; circ. 15,000.

Sucre

Correo del Sur: Calle Kilómetro 7, No 202, Casilla 242, Sucre; tel. (4) 646-3202; fax (4) 646-0152; e-mail publicidad_impresa@correodelsur.com; internet www.correodelsur.com; f. 1987; Dir MARCO ANTONIO DIPP MUKLED; Man. Editor RAYKHA FLORES COSSIO.

PERIODICALS

Actualidad Boliviana Confidencial (ABC): Fernando Guachalla 969, Casilla 648, La Paz; f. 1966; weekly; Dir HUGO GONZÁLEZ RIOJA; circ. 6,000.

ANF-Notas: Edif. Mariscal de Ayacucho, 5°, Of. 501, Calle Loayza 233, Casilla 5782, La Paz; tel. (2) 233-5577; fax (2) 233-7607; internet www.noticiasfides.com; f. 1963; publ. by ANF; weekly; political analysis; Editor JOSÉ GRAMUNT DE MORAGAS.

Aquí: Casilla 10937, La Paz; tel. (2) 234-3524; fax (2) 235-2455; f. 1979; weekly; circ. 10,000.

Bolivia Libre: Edif. Esperanza, 5°, Avda Mariscal Santa Cruz 2150, Casilla 6500, La Paz; fortnightly; govt organ.

Carta Cruceña de Integración: Casilla 3531, Santa Cruz de la Sierra; weekly; Dirs HERNÁN LLANOVARCED A., JOHNNY LAZARTE J.

Comentarios Económicos de Actualidad (CEA): Casilla 312097, La Paz; tel. (2) 242-4766; fax (2) 242-4772; e-mail veceba@caoba.entelnet.bo; f. 1983; fortnightly; articles and economic analyses; Editor GUIDO CÉSPEDES.

Información Política y Económica (IPE): Calle Comercio, Casilla 2484, La Paz; weekly; Dir GONZALO LÓPEZ MUÑOZ.

Informe R: La Paz; weekly; Editor SARA MONROY.

El Noticiero: Sucre; weekly; Dir DAVID CABEZAS; circ. 1,500.

Prensa Libre: Sucre; tel. (4) 646-2447; fax (4) 646-2768; e-mail prelibre@mara.scr.entelnet.bo; f. 1989; weekly; Dir JULIO PEMINTEL A.

Servicio de Información Confidencial (SIC): Elías Sagárnaga 274, Casilla 5035, La Paz; weekly; publ. by Asociación Nacional de Prensa; Dir JOSÉ CARRANZA.

Siglo XXI: La Paz; weekly.

Unión: Sucre; weekly; Dir JAIME MERILES.

Visión Boliviana: Calle Loayza 420, Casilla 2870, La Paz; 6 a year.

PRESS ASSOCIATIONS

Asociación Nacional de la Prensa: Claudio Aliaga 1290, 2°, San Miguel, La Paz; tel. (2) 279-4208; internet www.anpbolivia.com; f. 1976; private; Pres. MARCO ANTONIO DIPP MUKLED; Exec. Dir JUAN JAVIER ZEBALLOS GUTIÉRREZ.

Asociación de Periodistas de La Paz: Avda 6 de Agosto 2170, Edif. Las Dos Torres, Casilla 477, La Paz; tel. (2) 243-0345; fax (2) 243-6006; internet www.aplp.org.bo; f. 1929; Pres. RONALDO GREBE LÓPEZ; Vice-Pres. MARIÁN DELINA OTAZÚ.

NEWS AGENCIES

Agencia Boliviana de Información: Avda Camacho 1485, Casilla 6500, La Paz; tel. (2) 211-3782; fax (2) 220-4370; e-mail abi@abi.bo; internet www.abi.bo; govt-owned; Dir JORGE REY CUBA AKIYAMA; Man. Editor RUBÉN DAVID SANDI LORA.

Agencia de Noticias Fides (ANF): Edif. Mariscal de Ayacucho, 5°, Of. 501, Calle Loayza, Casilla 5782, La Paz; tel. (2) 236-5152; fax (2) 236-5153; internet www.noticiasfides.bo; f. 1963; owned by the Roman Catholic Church; Dir JOSÉ GRAMUNT DE MORAGAS; Editors JAIME LOAYZA ZEGARRA (morning), (vacant) (evening).

Publishers

Editorial los Amigos del Libro: Edif. Alba I, 3°, Of. 312, Calle España O-153, Cochabamba; tel. (4) 425-6005; fax (4) 450-4151; e-mail gutten@librosbolivia.com; internet www.librosbolivia.com; f. 1945; general; Gen. Man. INGRID GUTTENTAG.

Editorial Bruño: Loayza 167, Casilla 4809, La Paz; tel. (2) 233-1254; fax (2) 233-5043; f. 1964; Dir IGNACIO LOMA GUTIÉRREZ.

Editorial Comunicarte: Avda Cañoto 360, Santa Cruz; tel. (3) 332-3111; fax (3) 336-9332; e-mail comunicarte@comunicarte.com.bo; internet www.comunicarte.com.bo; Gen. Man. ANA MARÍA ARTIGAS.

Editorial Don Bosco: Villa Tejada Rectangular, Avda La Paz, esq. Avda Cívica, Casilla 4458, La Paz; tel. (2) 281-7325; fax (2) 281-7294; e-mail editorialdonbosco@gmail.com; internet www.editorial-donbosco.com; f. 1896; social sciences and literature.

Editorial Gente Comun: Villa Fátima, Avda de las Américas 764, La Paz; tel. (2) 221-4493; e-mail marcel@editorialgentecomun.com; internet editorialgentecomun.com; Man. Dir ARIEL MUSTAFÁ.

Editorial Icthus: Calle Miguel Angel Valda 121, Sucre; tel. (4) 642-7345; e-mail icthus@entelnet.bo; internet www.innset.com.bo; f. 1967; general and textbooks; Man. Dir FABIOLA GORENA.

Editorial Verbo Divino: Avda Juan de la Rosa O-2216, Casilla 191, Cochabamba; tel. (4) 428-6297; fax (4) 442-0733; e-mail info@verbodivino-bo.com; internet www.verbodivino-bo.com; f. 1997; Christian literature; part of Grupo Editorial Verbo Divino; Gen. Man. PEDRO PITURA.

El Pauro Ediciones: Calle Vallegrande 424, Santa Cruz; tel. (3) 339-4916; e-mail elpauroed@cotas.com.bo; internet elpauroediciones.com; Gen. Man. MAGDALENA MÁRQUEZ.

Gisbert y Cía, SA: Calle Comercio 1270, Casilla 195, La Paz; tel. (2) 220-2626; fax (2) 220-2911; e-mail info@libreriagisbert.com; internet www.libreriagisbert.com; f. 1907; textbooks, history, law and general; Pres. ANTONIO SCHULCZEWSKI GISBERT; Promotions Man. MARÍA DEL CARMEN SCHULCZEWSKI; Admin. Man. SERGIO GARCÍA.

Grupo Editorial La Hoguera: Edif. Gabriela, 2°, Calle Beni 678, Santa Cruz; tel. (3) 335-4426; fax (3) 311-7821; e-mail lahoguera@lahoguera.com; internet www.lahoguera.com; f. 1990; Pres. ALFONSO CORTEZ; Dir-Gen. MAURICIO MÉNDEZ.

Idearia: Calle 8, Este 19, Barrio Hamacas, Santa Cruz; tel. (3) 339-8381; e-mail idearia@idearia.net; internet www.idearia.net; children's literature and magazines; Gen. Man. GABRIELA ICHASO.

Librería Editorial Juventud: Plaza Murillo 519, Casilla 1489, La Paz; tel. (2) 240-6248; f. 1946; textbooks and general; Dir GUSTAVO URQUIZO MENDOZA.

Martínez Acchini, SRL Libros: Edif. Illampu, Avda Arce 2132, La Paz; tel. (2) 244-1112; internet martinezacchini.com; f. 1975; Man. Dir ERNESTO MARTÍNEZ.

Master Bolivia: Calle Velasco 268, Santa Cruz; tel. (3) 333-2413; fax (3) 311-2260; e-mail info@masterbolivia.com; internet masterbolivia .com.

Plural Editores: Calle Rosendo Gutiérrez 595, esq. Avda Ecuador, La Paz; tel. (2) 241-1018; e-mail plural@plural.bo; internet www .plural.bo; Dir MAURICIO SOUZA.

Rodel Ediciones: Calle Mandioré 46, Santa Cruz; tel. (3) 337-8689; fax (3) 337-0246; e-mail info@rodelediciones.com; internet rodelediciones.com; Pres. JORGE LUIS RODRÍGUEZ.

Santillana de Ediciones, SA: Calle 13, No 8078, Calacoto, La Paz; tel. (2) 277-4242; fax (2) 277-1056; e-mail info@santillanabo.com; internet www.santillanabo.com; f. 1994; Gen. Man. CAROLA OSSIO.

PUBLISHERS' ASSOCIATION

Cámara Boliviana del Libro: Calle Capitán Ravelo 2116, Casilla 682, La Paz; tel. and fax (2) 211-3264; e-mail cabolib@entelnet.bo; internet www.camaralibrolapaz.org.bo; f. 1947; Pres. ERNESTO MARTÍNEZ ACCHINI; Vice-Pres. CARLA MARÍA BERDEGUÉ; Gen. Man. ANA PATRICIA NAVARRO.

Broadcasting and Communications

TELECOMMUNICATIONS

Regulatory Authorities

Autoridad de Fiscalización y Control Social de Transportes y Telecomunicaciones (ATT): Calle 13, Nos 8260 y 8280, entre Sauces y Costanera, Calacoto, Casilla 6692, La Paz; tel. (2) 277-2266; fax (2) 277-2299; e-mail informaciones@att.gob.bo; internet www.att .gob.bo; supervises and regulates the activities and services provided by telecommunications operators; Exec. Dir PEDRO CLIFFORD PARAVICINI HURTADO.

Superintendencia de Telecomunicaciones: Calle 13, No 8260, Calacoto, La Paz; tel. (2) 277-2266; fax (2) 277-2299; e-mail supertel@ ceibo.entelnet.bo; internet www.sittel.gov.bo; f. 1995; govt-controlled broadcasting authority; Supt JORGE NAVA AMADOR.

Major Operators

Bolitel, SRL (Bolivia Telecomunicación, SRL): Calle Nueva América 3000, Santa Cruz; tel. (3) 364-2424; fax (3) 364-3973; e-mail gerencia@bolitelsrl.com; internet www.libre.com.bo; f. 2008; part of the UNAGRO corpn; Man. MAURICIO PINTO.

Empresa Nacional de Telecomunicaciones, SA (ENTEL): Calle Federico Suazo 1771, Casilla 4450, La Paz; tel. (2) 214-1010; fax (2) 239-1789; e-mail contacto@entelsa.entelnet.bo; internet www.entel .bo; f. 1965; privatized under the Govt's capitalization programme in 1995; reverted to state ownership in 2008; Pres. CARLOS REYES MONTAÑO; Gen. Man. ROY ROQUE MÉNDEZ.

Tigo (Telefónica Celular de Bolivia): Avda Viedma 648, Santa Cruz; tel. (3) 333-5227; fax (3) 335-8790; e-mail atencionalcliente@tigo.com .bo; internet www.tigo.com.bo; f. 2005; part of Millicom International Cellular, SA (MIC); Chief Officer, Latin America MARIO ZANOTTI.

Viva GSM (NuevaTel PCS de Bolivia, SA): Edif. Multicentro, Calle Capitán Ravelo, esq. R. Gutiérrez 2289, Casilla 11875, Sopocachi, La Paz; tel. (2) 244-2420; fax (2) 244-2353; e-mail infoa@nuevatel.com; internet www.nuevatel.com; f. 1999; Regional Man. VIRGINIA RETAMOSO.

BROADCASTING

Regulatory Authority

Asociación Boliviana de Radiodifusoras (ASBORA): Edif. Jazmín, 10°, Avda 20 de Octubre 2019, Casilla 5324, La Paz; tel. (2) 236-5154; fax (2) 236-3069; broadcasting authority; Pres. RAÚL NOVILLO ALARCÓN.

Radio

Educación Radiofónica de Bolivia (ERBOL): Edif. Smith, Calle Ballivián 1323, 4°, Casilla 5946, La Paz; tel. (2) 204-0111; fax (2) 220-3888; e-mail erbol@erbol.com.bo; internet www.erbol.com.bo; f. 1967; asscn of 28 educational radio stations in Bolivia; Dir ANDRÉS GÓMEZ VELA.

Radio Fides: La Paz; e-mail sistemas@radiofides.com; internet www.radiofides.com; f. 1939; network of 28 radio stations; Roman Catholic; Pres. EDUARDO PÉREZ IRIBARNE.

Red Patria Nueva: Avda Camacho 1485, 6°, La Paz; tel. (2) 220-0473; fax (2) 200-390; e-mail illimani@comunica.gov.bo; internet www.patrianueva.bo; f. 1932 as Compañía Radio Boliviana; govt-owned network; broadcasts across the country, often as Radio Illimani; Dir IVÁN MALDONADO CORTÉZ.

Television

ATB Red Nacional (Canal 9): Avda Argentina 2057, Casilla 9285, La Paz; tel. and fax (2) 222-9922; e-mail noticias@atb.com.bo; internet www.atb.com.bo; f. 1984; privately owned television network; part of Grupo Prisa, SA; Man. ROXANA ALCOBA.

Bolivisión (Canal 4): Parque Demetrio Canelas 1543, Casilla 6067, Cochabamba; tel. (4) 428-4318; fax (4) 428-4319; e-mail jimmystrauch@redbolivision.tv; internet www.redbolivision.tv.bo; f. 1997; privately owned television network; Exec. Pres. ERNESTO ASBÚN GAZAUI; Gen. Man. JEANNETTE ARRÁZOLA RIVERO.

Red Uno: Calle Romecín Campos 592, Sopocachi, La Paz; tel. (2) 242-1111; fax (2) 241-0939; e-mail notivision@reduno.com.bo; internet www.reduno.com.bo; f. 1985; commercial television station; offices in La Paz, Santa Cruz and Cochabamba; Dir MARIO ROJAS; Gen. Man. JULIO ROMERO.

Televisión Boliviana (TVB—Canal 7): Edif. La Urbana, 6°, Avda Camacho 1485, Casilla 900, La Paz; tel. (2) 220-3404; fax (2) 220-3973; e-mail info@boliviatv.bo; internet www.boliviatv.bo; f. 1969; govt network operating stations in La Paz, Oruro, Cochabamba, Potosí, Chuquisaca, Pando, Beni, Tarija and Santa Cruz; Gen. Man. IRGUEN PASTÉN.

Televisión Universitaria (Canal 13): Edif. Hoy, 12°–13°, Avda 6 de Agosto 2170, Casilla 13383, La Paz; tel. and fax (2) 244-1313; e-mail canal13@umsa.bo; internet tvu.umsa.bo; f. 1980; educational programmes; stations in Oruro, Cochabamba, Potosí, Sucre, Tarija, Beni and Santa Cruz; Dir OMAR GÓMEZ LIZARRO.

Unitel (Canal 9): Km 5, Carretera antigua a Cochabamba, Santa Cruz; tel. (3) 352-7686; fax (3) 352-7688; e-mail canal9@unitel.com .bo; internet www.unitel.tv; f. 1997; privately owned television network; Gen. Man. YAMILE IBAÑEZ CORREA.

Finance

(cap. = capital; res = reserves; dep. = deposits; m. = million; br(s) = branch(es); amounts are in bolivianos, unless otherwise stated)

BANKING

Supervisory Authority

Autoridad de Supervisión del Sistema Financiero: Plaza Isabel la Católica 2507, Casilla 447, La Paz; tel. (2) 243-1919; fax (2) 243-0028; e-mail asfi@asfi.gov.bo; internet www.asfi.gov.bo; f. 1928; fmrly Superintendencia de Bancos y Entidados Financieras; name changed as above in 2009; Exec. Dir Lic. REYNALDO YUJRA SEGALES.

Central Bank

Banco Central de Bolivia: Avda Ayacucho, esq. Mercado, Casilla 3118, La Paz; tel. (2) 240-9090; fax (2) 240-6614; e-mail bancocentraldebolivia@bcb.gob.bo; internet www.bcb.gob.bo; f. 1911 as Banco de la Nación Boliviana; name changed as above in 1928; bank of issue; cap. 515.7m., res 7,807.9m., dep. 47,441.2m. (Dec. 2009); Pres. MARCELO ZABALAGA ESTRADA; Gen. Man. EDUARDO PARDO.

Commercial Banks

Banco Bisa, SA: Avda 16 de Julio 1628, Casilla 1290, La Paz; tel. (2) 231-7272; fax (2) 239-0033; e-mail bancobisa@grupobisa.com; internet www.bisa.com; f. 1963; cap. 731.1m., res 141.5m., dep. 7,850.3m. (Dec. 2010); Pres., CEO and Chair. Ing. JULIO LEÓN PRADO.

Banco de Crédito de Bolivia, SA: Calle Colón, esq. Mercado 1308, Casilla 907, La Paz; tel. (2) 233-0444; fax (2) 231-9163; e-mail cnavarro@bancred.com.bo; internet www.bancodecredito.com.bo; f. 1993 as Banco Popular del Perú, SA; name changed as above 1994; owned by Banco de Crédito del Perú; cap. 315.5m., res 234.1m., dep. 6,813.4m. (Dec. 2010); Chair. DIONISIO ROMERO; Gen. Man. DIEGO A. CAVERO BELAUNDE; 8 brs.

Banco Económico, SA-SCZ: Calle Ayacucho 166, Casilla 5603, Santa Cruz; tel. (3) 315-5500; fax (3) 336-1184; e-mail baneco@baneco .com.bo; internet www.baneco.com.bo; f. 1990; dep. US $244.9m., cap. US $24.4m., total assets US $269.3m. (Dec. 2006); Pres. IVO MATEO KULJIS FÜCHTNER; 25 brs.

Banco Ganadero, SA-Santa Cruz: Calle Bolivar 99, esq. Beni, Santa Cruz; tel. (3) 336-1616; fax (3) 336-1617; internet www.bg.com .bo; f. 1994; cap. 148.5m., res 17.7m., dep. 3,702.9m. (Dec. 2009); Pres. JORGE MARCOS SALVADOR; Gen. Man. RONALD GUTIÉRREZ LÓPEZ.

Banco Mercantil Santa Cruz, SA: Calle Ayacucho, esq. Mercado 295, Casilla 423, La Paz; tel. (2) 240-9040; fax (2) 240-9158; e-mail asalinas@bancomercantil.com.bo; internet www.bmsc.com.bo;

f. 1905 as Banco Mercantil, SA; acquired Banco Santa Cruz in 2006 and changed name as above; cap. 413.3m., res 296.9m., dep. 10,827.2m. (Dec. 2010); Exec. Vice-Pres. ALBERTO VALDES ANDREATTA; Pres. EMILIO UNZUETA ZEGARRA; 37 brs.

Banco Nacional de Bolivia: Avda Camacho, esq. Colón 1296, Casilla 360, La Paz; tel. (2) 233-2323; fax (2) 231-0695; e-mail info@bnb.com.bo; internet www.bnb.com.bo; f. 1871; 67.27% owned by Grupo Bedoya; cap. 549.5m., res 57.2m., dep. 8,800.7m. (Dec. 2010); Pres. IGNACIO BEDOYA SÁENZ; Gen. Man. PABLO BEDOYA SÁENZ; 9 brs.

Banco Solidario, SA (BancoSol): Calle Nicolás Acosta 289, Casilla 13176, La Paz; tel. (2) 248-4242; fax (2) 248-6533; e-mail info@bancosol.com.bo; internet www.bancosol.com.bo; f. 1992; cap. 147.7m., res 36.8m., dep. 2,935.1m. (Dec. 2009); Gen. Man. KURT KÖNIGSFEST SANABRIA.

Banco Unión, SA: Calle Loayza 255, Edif. de Ugarte Ingeniería, 10°, Of. 1001, La Paz; e-mail info@bancounion.com.bo; internet www.bancounion.com.bo; f. 1982; cap. 132.9m., res 124.2m., dep. 3,876.4m. (Dec. 2009); Pres. FERNANDO ARTEAGA MONTERO; Gen. Man. MARCIA VILLARROEL GONZÁLES; 9 brs.

Credit Institution

PRODEM: Avda Camacho 1277, esq. Colón, La Paz; tel. (2) 211-3227; fax (2) 214-7632; e-mail info@prodemffp.com.bo; internet www.prodemffp.com; f. 2000; microcredit institution; Gen. Man. JOSÉ NOEL ZAMORA; 250 brs.

Banking Association

Asociación de Bancos Privados de Bolivia (ASOBAN): Edif. Cámara Nacional de Comercio, 15°, Avda Mariscal Santa Cruz, esq. Colombia 1392, Casilla 5822, La Paz; tel. (2) 237-6164; fax (2) 239-1093; e-mail info@asoban.bo; internet www.asoban.bo; f. 1957; Pres. KURT KÖENIGSFEST SANABRIA; Vice-Pres ANTONIO VALDA, MIGUEL NAVARRO; 18 mems.

STOCK EXCHANGE

Bolsa Boliviana de Valores, SA: Calle Montevideo 142, Casilla 12521, La Paz; tel. (2) 244-3232; fax (2) 244-2308; e-mail info@bolsa-valores-bolivia.com; internet www.bbv.com.bo; f. 1989; Pres. JOSÉ TRIGO VALDIVIA; Gen. Man. JAVIER ANEIVA.

INSURANCE

Supervisory Authority

Autoridad de Fiscalización y Control de Pensiones y Seguros (APS): Edif. Torres Gundlach Este, 6°, Calle Reyes Ortiz, esq. Federico Zuazo, Casilla 10794, La Paz; tel. (2) 233-1212; fax (2) 231-2223; e-mail contactenos@aps.gob.bo; internet www.aps.gob.bo; Exec. Dir JAVIER LIJERÓN LOAYZA.

Major Companies

Alianza, Cía de Seguros y Reaseguros, SA: Avda 20 de Octubre 2680, esq. Campos, Zona San Jorge, Casilla 1043, La Paz; tel. (2) 243-2121; fax (2) 243-2713; e-mail info@alianzaseguros.com; internet www.alianza.com.bo; f. 1991; Exec. Dir ALEJANDRO YBARRA CARRASCO.

Alianza Vida Seguros y Reaseguros, SA: Avda Viedma 21, esq. Melchor Pinto, Casilla 7181, Santa Cruz; tel. (3) 337-5656; fax (3) 337-5666; e-mail vida@alianzaseguros.com; internet www.alianza.com.bo; f. 1999; Gen. Man. ALEJANDRO YBARRA CARRASCO.

Bisa Seguros y Reaseguros, SA: Edif. San Pablo, 13°, Avda 16 de Julio 1479, Casilla 3669, La Paz; tel. (2) 235-2123; fax (2) 214-8724; e-mail JZeballos@grupobisa.com; internet www.bisaseguros.com; f. 1991; part of Grupo Bisa; Pres. JULIO LEÓN PRADO; Exec. Vice-Pres. ALEJANDRO MACLEAN CÉSPEDES.

La Boliviana Ciacruz de Seguros y Reaseguros, SA: Edif. La Boliviana Ciacruz, Calle Colón 288, Casilla 628, La Paz; tel. (2) 220-3131; fax (2) 220-4087; e-mail info@lbc.bo; internet www.lbc.bo; f. 1964; owned by Zurich Bolivia group; all classes; Pres. GONZALO BEDOYA HERRERA; Vice-Pres. RODRIGO BEDOYA DIEZ DE MEDINA.

Bupa Insurance (Bolivia), SA: Calle 9 este, No 9, esq. Pasillo A, Zona Equipetrol, Santa Cruz; tel. (3) 341-2842; fax (3) 341-2832; e-mail bolivia@bupa.com.bo; internet bolivia.ihi.com; health insurance; Pres. ANTHONY CABRELLI; Gen. Man. DIEGO NORIEGA.

Cía de Seguros y Reaseguros Fortaleza, SA: Avda Arce 2799, esq. Cordero, La Paz; tel. and fax (2) 243-4142; e-mail grupo@grupofortaleza.com.bo; internet www.grupofortaleza.com.bo; Pres. GUIDO EDWIN HINOJOSA CARDOSO; Gen. Man. MARTHA O. LUCCA SUÁREZ.

Credinform International, SA de Seguros: Edif. Credinform, Calle Potosí, esq. Ayacucho 1220, Casilla 1724, La Paz; tel. (2) 231-5566; fax (2) 220-3917; e-mail credinform@credinformsa.com; internet www.credinformsa.com; f. 1954; all classes; Pres. Dr ROBÍN BARRAGÁN PELÁEZ; Gen. Man. MIGUEL ANGEL BARRAGÁN IBARGÜEN.

Latina Seguros Patrimoniales, SA: Avda Monseñor Rivero 223, esq. Asunción, Casilla 3087, Santa Cruz; tel. (3) 371-6565; fax (3) 371-6905; e-mail latinaseguros@latinaseguros.com.bo; internet www.latina-seguros.com.bo; f. 2007; part of Grupo Nacional Vida; Exec. Vice-Pres. JOSÉ LUÍS CAMACHO MISERENDINO; Gen. Man. RAMIRO JESÚS QUIROGA SAN MARTÍN.

Nacional Vida Seguros de Personas, SA: Avda Monseñor Rivero 223, esq. Asunción, Santa Cruz; tel. (3) 371-6262; fax (3) 333-7969; e-mail nacionalvida@nacionalvida.com.bo; internet www.nacionalvida.com.bo; f. 1999; Pres. MARIO AVELINO MORENO VIRUEZ; Gen. Man. LUIS ALVARO TOLEDO PEÑARANDA.

Seguros Illimani, SA: Edif. Mariscal de Ayacucho, 10°, Calle Loayza 233, Casilla 133, La Paz; tel. (2) 220-3040; fax (2) 239-1149; e-mail info@segurosillimani.com.bo; internet www.segurosillimani.com.bo; f. 1979; all classes; Exec. Pres. FERNANDO ARCE G.

La Vitalicia: Edif. Hoy, Avda 6 de Agosto 2860, Casilla 8424, La Paz; tel. (2) 212-5355; fax (2) 211-3480; e-mail aibanez@grupobisa.com; internet www.lavitaliciaseguros.com; f. 1988; part of Grupo Bisa; Pres. JULIO LEÓN PRADO; Exec. Vice-Pres. LUIS ALFONSO IBAÑEZ MONTES.

Zurich Boliviana Seguros Personales, SA: Edif. La Boliviana Ciacruz, Calle Colón 288, Casilla 4297, La Paz; tel. (2) 220-0028; fax (2) 220-0515; e-mail info@zurich-boliviana.com; internet www.bolivianaciacruz.com.bo/ZURICH; owned by Zurich Bolivia group; Pres. GONZALO BEDOYA HERRERA; Vice-Pres. JORGE ALVAREZ POL.

Insurance Association

Asociación Boliviana de Aseguradores: Edif. Castilla, 5°, Of. 510, Calle Loayza, esq. Mercado 250, Casilla 4804, La Paz; tel. (2) 220-1014; fax (2) 220-1088; e-mail aba@ababolivia.org; internet www.ababolivia.org; f. 1950; Pres. ALEJANDRO YBARRA CARRASCO; Gen. Man. Dr JUSTINO AVENDAÑO RENEDO.

Trade and Industry

DEVELOPMENT ORGANIZATIONS

Centro de Estudios para el Desarrollo Laboral y Agrario (CEDLA): Avda Jaimes Freyre 2940, esq. Muñoz Cornejo, Casilla 8630, La Paz; tel. (2) 241-2429; fax (2) 241-4625; e-mail jgomez@cedla.org; internet www.cedla.org; f. 1985; agrarian and labour development; Exec. Dir JAVIER GÓMEZ AGUILAR.

Fondo Nacional de Desarrollo Regional (FNDR): Calle Pedro Salazar, esq. Andrés Muñoz 631, Casilla 12613, La Paz; tel. (2) 241-7575; fax (2) 242-2267; e-mail transparencia@fndr.gob.bo; internet www.fndr.gob.bo; f. 1987; promotes local and regional devt, offering financing and support; assumed temporary responsibility for water supply in La Paz in Jan. 2007 following annulment of contracts with private water cos; Exec. Dir EDSON VALDA GÓMEZ.

CHAMBERS OF COMMERCE

Cámara de Comercio e Industria de Pando: Avda Teniente Coronel Cornejo 80, Casilla 277, Cobija; tel. (3) 842-3139; fax (3) 842-2291; e-mail cicpando@entelnet.bo; Pres. NEMESIO RAMÍREZ.

Cámara de Comercio de Oruro: Edif. Cámara de Comercio, Pasaje Guachalla, La Plata, Casilla 148, Oruro; tel. (2) 525-2615; fax (2) 525-0606; e-mail camacor@coteor.net.bo; f. 1895; Pres. FERNANDO DEHNE FRANCO; Gen. Man. VÍCTOR HUGO RODRÍGUEZ GARCÍA; 165 mems.

Cámara de Comercio y Servicios de Cochabamba: Calle Sucre E-0336, Casilla 493, Cochabamba; tel. (4) 425-7715; fax (4) 425-7717; e-mail gerencia@cadeco.org; internet www.cadeco.org; f. 1922; Pres. NELSON ZEGARRA VILLEGAS.

Cámara Departamental de Comercio de Beni: Casilla 96, Trinidad; tel. (3) 462-2399; fax (3) 462-0910; Pres. MARCO ANTONIO SALINAS IÑIGUEZ; Sec.-Gen. JUAN MAGARELLI ANNESE.

Cámara Departamental de Industria, Comercio y Servicios de Tarija: Calle Bolívar, entre Mendez y Suipacha, Zona Central, Casilla 74, Tarija; tel. (4) 664-2737; fax (4) 611-3636; e-mail caincotar@entelnet.bo; internet www.cictja.org; f. 2005; Pres. VÍCTOR FERNÁNDEZ.

Cámara de Exportadores de La Paz (CAMEX): Avda Arce 2021 esq. Goitia, Sopocachi, Casilla 789, La Paz; tel. (2) 244-4310; fax (2) 244-2842; e-mail info@camexbolivia.com; internet www.camexbolivia.com; f. 1993; Pres. GUILLERMO POU MUNT.

Cámara de Exportadores de Santa Cruz (CADEX): Avda Velarde 131, Santa Cruz; tel. (3) 332-1509; e-mail cadex@cadex

.org; internet www.cadex.org; f. 1986; Gen. Man. OSWALDO BARRIGA KARLBAUM.

Cámara de Industria y Comercio de Chuquisaca: Calle España 64, 2°, Casilla 33, Sucre; tel. (4) 645-1194; fax (4) 645-1850; f. 1923; Pres. MARCELO CUELLAR; Gen. Man. LORENZO CATALÁ SUBIETA.

Cámara de Industria, Comercio, Servicios y Turismo de Santa Cruz (CAINCO): Torre Cainco, Avda Las Américas, 7°, Casilla 180, Santa Cruz; tel. (3) 333-4555; fax (3) 334-2353; e-mail cainco@cainco.org.bo; internet www.cainco.org.bo; f. 1915; Pres. ELAR EDUARDO PAZ VARGAS.

Cámara Nacional de Comercio: Edif. Cámara Nacional de Comercio, Avda Mariscal Santa Cruz 1392, 1° y 2°, Casilla 7, La Paz; tel. (2) 237-8606; fax (2) 239-1004; e-mail cnc@boliviacomercio.org.bo; internet www.boliviacomercio.org.bo; f. 1929; 30 brs and special brs; Pres. OSCAR ALBERTO CALLE ROJAS.

Cámara Nacional de Exportadores (CANEB): Avda Arce 2017, esq. c. Goitia, Casilla 12145, La Paz; tel. (2) 244-3529; fax (2) 244-1491; e-mail secretaria@caneb.org.bo; internet www.caneb.org.bo; f. 1969; fmrly Asociación Nacional de Exportadores de Bolivia; adopted current name in 1993; Pres. GORAN VRANICIC.

Cámara Nacional de Industrias de Bolivia: Edif. Cámara Nacional de Comercio, 14°, Avda Mariscal Santa Cruz 1392, Casilla 611, La Paz; tel. (2) 237-4477; fax (2) 236-2766; e-mail ragreda@bolivia-industry.com; internet www.bolivia-industry.com; f. 1937; eight depts throughout Bolivia; Pres. ARMANDO GUMUCIO KARSTULOVIC.

INDUSTRIAL AND TRADE ASSOCIATIONS

Asociación Nacional de Exportadores de Café (ANDEC): Calle Nicaragua 1638, Casilla 9770, La Paz; tel. (2) 224-4290; fax (2) 224-4561; e-mail andec@caoba.entelnet.bo; controls the export, quality and marketing of coffee producers; Exec. Pres. CARMEN DONOSO DE ARAMAYO.

Cámara Agropecuaria del Oriente: Avda Roca y Coronado s/n, (Predios de Fexpocruz), Casilla 116, Santa Cruz; tel. (3) 352-2200; fax (3) 352-2621; e-mail cao@cotas.com.bo; internet www.cao.org.bo; f. 1964; agriculture and livestock asscn for eastern Bolivia; Gen. Man. EDILBERTO OSINAGA ROSADO.

Cámara Boliviana de Hidrocarburos: Radial 17 1/2 y Sexto Anillo, Casilla 3920, Santa Cruz; tel. (3) 353-8799; fax (3) 357-7868; e-mail cbh@cbh.org.bo; internet www.cbh.org.bo; f. 1986; Pres. JOSÉ MAGELA BERNARDES.

Cámara Forestal de Bolivia: Prolongación Manuel Ignacio Salvatierra 1055, Casilla 346, Santa Cruz; tel. (3) 333-2699; fax (3) 333-1456; e-mail camaraforestal@cfb.org.bo; internet www.cfb.org.bo; f. 1969; represents the interests of the Bolivian timber industry; Pres. PEDRO COLANZI SERRATE.

EMPLOYERS' ASSOCIATIONS

Asociación Nacional de Mineros Medianos: Calle Pedro Salazar 600, esq. Presbítero Medina, Casilla 6190, La Paz; tel. (2) 241-7522; fax (2) 241-4123; e-mail anmm@caoba.entelnet.bo; f. 1939; asscn of 14 private medium-sized mining cos; Pres. HUMBERTO RADA; Sec.-Gen. Dr EDUARDO CAPRILLES.

Confederación de Empresarios Privados de Bolivia (CEPB): Calle Méndez Arcos 117, Plaza España, Zona Sopacachi, Casilla 4239, La Paz; tel. (2) 242-0999; fax (2) 242-1272; e-mail cepb@cepb.org.bo; internet www.cepb.org.bo; largest national employers' org.; Pres. RODRIGO AGREDA; Exec. Sec. ANDRÉS TÓRREZ VILLA-GÓMEZ.

STATE HYDROCARBON COMPANY

Corporación Minera de Bolivia (COMIBOL): Avda Camacho 1396, esq. Loayza, La Paz; tel. (2) 268-2100; fax (2) 235-7979; e-mail comibol@comibol.gov.bo; internet www.comibol.gov.bo; f. 1952; state mining corpn; owns both mines and processing plants; Pres. HUGO MIRANDA RENDÓN; 26,000 employees.

Empresa Metalúrgica Vinto (EMV): Carretera Potosí Km 7, Casilla 612, Oruro; tel. (2) 527-8094; fax (2) 527-8024; e-mail info@vinto.gob.bo; internet www.vinto.gob.bo; f. 1966; smelting of non-ferrous minerals and special alloys; majority of shares previously owned by Glencore (Switzerland); renationalized in 2007; took control of Glencore-owned Vinto-Antimony plant in 2010 following renationalization; Gen. Man. RAMIRO VILLAVICENCIO NIÑO DE GUZMÁN; 950 employees.

UTILITIES

Electricity

Autoridad de Fiscalización y Control Social de Electricidad (AE): Avda 16 de Julio 1571, Zona Central, La Paz; tel. (2) 231-2401; fax (2) 231-2393; e-mail autoridaddeelectricidad@ae.gob.bo; internet www.ae.gob.bo; f. 1994; fmrly Superintendencia de Electricidad; regulates the electricity sector; Exec. Dir MARIO GUERRA MAGNUS.

Alternative Energy Systems Ltd (Talleres AES): Calle Manuel Cespedes 0451, Condominio Mistic, Casilla 1C, Cochabamba; tel. and fax (4) 441-3124; e-mail aesbol@freeyellow.com; internet aesbol.freeyellow.com; f. 1986; specialist manufacturers of alternative energy products including small water turbines, equipment for small hydro plants and pumping stations; Gen. Man. MIGUEL ALANDIA.

Compañía Boliviana de Energía Eléctrica, SA (COBEE): Avda Hernando Siles 5635, Casilla 353, La Paz; tel. (2) 278-2474; fax (2) 278-5920; e-mail cobee@cobee.com; internet www.cobee.com; f. 1925; largest private power producer and distributor, serving the areas of La Paz and Oruro; generated 27.2% of Bolivia's total electricity output in 2002; mainly hydroelectric; Pres. and Gen. Man. RENÉ SERGIO PEREIRA.

Compañía Eléctrica Central Bulo Bulo, SA (CECBB): Avda San Martín 1700, Centro Empresarial Equipetrol Norte, 6°, Casilla 6428, Santa Cruz; tel. (3) 366-3606; fax (3) 366-3601; e-mail ramon.bascope@chaco.com.bo; f. 1999; generator co; owned by Empresa Petrolera Chaco, SA; 101.2 MW capacity in 2002; Gen. Man. RAMÓN BASCOPE PARADA.

Compañía Eléctrica Sucre, SA (CESSA): Calle Ayacucho 254, Sucre; tel. (4) 645-3126; fax (4) 646-0292; e-mail cessa@mara.scr.entelnet.bo; internet www.cessasucre.com; f. 1924; electricity distributor; Pres. MILTON BARÓN; Gen. Man. ALFREDO DEHESA.

Cooperativa Rural de Electrificación Ltda (CRE): Avda Busch, esq. Honduras, Santa Cruz; tel. (3) 336 6666; fax (3) 332 4936; e-mail webmaster@cre.com.bo; internet www.cre.com.bo; f. 1965; electricity distributor; Gen. Man. CARMELO PAZ DURÁN; Sec.-Gen. JOSÉ ERNESTO ZAMBRANA.

Electropaz: Avda Illimani 1973, Miraflores, Casilla 10511, La Paz; tel. (2) 222-2200; fax (2) 222-3756; e-mail cpacheco@electropaz.com.bo; internet www.electropaz.com.bo; f. 1995; distributor serving La Paz area; Gen. Man. Ing. MAURICIO VALDEZ CÁRDENAS.

Empresa Nacional de Electricidad, SA (ENDE): Avda Ballivián 503, Edif. Colón, 8°, Casilla 565, Cochabamba; tel. (4) 452-0317; fax (4) 452-0318; e-mail ende@ende.bo; internet www.ende.bo; f. 1962; former state electricity co; privatized under the Govt's capitalization programme in 1995 and divided into three arms concerned with generation, transmission and distribution, respectively; Gen. Man. NELSON CABALLERO; The following companies were renationalized in May 2010 and placed under the control of ENDE:

Empresa Corani, SA: Avda Oquendo 654, Edif. Las Torres Sofer I, 9°, Casilla 5165, Cochabamba; tel. (4) 423-5700; fax (4) 425-9148; e-mail corani@corani.com; internet www.corani.com; f. 1995; generator co; 802.60 GWh generation in 2006 in conjunction with Santa Isabel; Pres. FREDERICK P. RENNER.

Empresa Eléctrica Valle Hermoso, SA (EVH): Calle Tarija 1425, esq. Adela Zamudio, Cala Cala, Cochabamba; tel. (4) 424-0544; fax (4) 428-6838; e-mail central@evh.com.bo; internet www.evh.com.bo; f. 1995; generator co; 347.41 MW capacity in 2002; Pres. ENRIQUE HERRERA SORIA.

Empresa de Generación Guaracachi, SA (EGSA): Avda Brasil y Tercer Anillo Interno, Casilla 336, Santa Cruz; tel. (3) 346-4632; fax (3) 346-5888; e-mail central@egsa.com.bo; internet www.guaracachi.com.bo; f. 1995; generator co; 445 MW capacity in 2008; Pres. PETER EARL.

Empresa de Luz y Fuerza Eléctrica Cochabamba, SA (ELFEC): Avda Heroínas 0-686, Casilla 89, Cochabamba; tel. (4) 420-0125; fax (4) 425-9427; e-mail sugerencias@elfec.com; internet www.elfec.com; f. 1908; electricty distributor; Gen. Man. JAVIER DE UDAETA.

Hidroeléctrica Boliviana, SA: Avda Fuerza Naval 22, Zona Calcoto, La Paz; tel. (2) 277-0765; fax (2) 277-0933; e-mail hb@hidrobol.com; internet www.hidrobol.com; 317 GWh generation in 2008; Gen. Man. Ing. ANGEL ZANNIER CLAROS.

Gas

Numerous distributors of natural gas exist throughout the country, many of which are owned by the petroleum distributor, Yacimientos Petrolíferos Fiscales Bolivianos (YPFB).

Yacimientos Petrolíferos Fiscales Bolivianos (YPFB): Calle Bueno 185, 6°, Casilla 401, La Paz; tel. and fax (2) 237-0210; e-mail webmaster@ypfb.gov.bo; internet www.ypfb.gov.bo; f. 1936; exploration, drilling, production, refining, transportation and distribution of petroleum; partially privatized in 1996; Pres. CARLOS VILLEGAS QUIROGA; 4,900 employees.

Water

Autoridad de Fiscalización y Control Social de Agua Potable y Saneamiento Básico (AAPS): Edif. Cámara de Comercio, Avda Mariscal Santa Cruz 1392, 4° y 16°, Casilla 4245, La Paz; tel. (2) 231-0801; fax (2) 231-0554; e-mail contactos@aaps.gob.bo; internet www.aaps.gob.bo; f. 1999; fmrly Superintendencia de Saneamiento Básico (SISAB); decentralized regulatory authority for urban water supplies and grants service concessions and licences; Exec. Dir JAMES AVILA.

Empresa Pública Social de Agua y Saneamiento (EPSAS): Avda de las Américas 705, Villa Fátima, Casilla 9359, La Paz; tel. (2) 221-0295; fax (2) 221-2454; e-mail info@epsas.com.bo; internet www.epsas.com.bo; f. 2007; state-owned water and sewerage provider in La Paz and El Alto; Gen. Man. VÍCTOR RICO.

TRADE UNIONS

Central Obrera Boliviana (COB): Edif. COB, Calle Pisagua 618, Casilla 6552, La Paz; tel. (2) 352-426; fax (2) 281-201; e-mail postmast@cob-bolivia.org; f. 1952; main union confederation; 800,000 mems; Exec. Sec. PEDRO MONTES.

Affiliated unions:

Central Obrera Departamental de La Paz: Plaza Zalles 284, Estación Central, La Paz; tel. (2) 245-8741; e-mail codlp@hotmail.com; Exec. Sec. SALUSTIANO LAURA.

Confederación Sindical Unica de los Trabajadores Campesinos de Bolivia (CSUTCB): Avda Saavedra 2045, Miraflores, Casilla 11589, La Paz; tel. (2) 224-6232; fax (2) 224-6300; e-mail csutcbbolivia@gmail.com; internet www.csutcb.org; f. 1979; peasant farmers' union; Exec. Sec. LUIS GABRIEL MORALES.

Federación Sindical de Trabajadores Mineros de Bolivia (FSTMB): Plaza Venezuela 147, Casilla 14565, La Paz; tel. (2) 235-9656; fax (2) 231-7764; e-mail fstmb1944@hotmail.com; internet sites.google.com/site/fstmb2003/; f. 1944; mineworkers' union; Leader MIGUEL ZUBIETA; Exec. Sec. GUIDO MISMA CRISPIN; 27,000 mems.

Confederación General de Trabajadores Fabriles de Bolivia (CGTFB): Avda Armentia 452, Casilla 21590, La Paz; tel. (2) 228-1524; fax (2) 228-5783; e-mail cgtfb@hotmail.com; f. 1951; manufacturing workers' union; Exec. Sec. ANGEL ASTURIZAGA.

Transport

RAILWAYS

Empresa Nacional de Ferrocarriles (ENFE): Estación Central de Ferrocarriles, Plaza Zalles, Casilla 428, La Paz; tel. (2) 232-7401; fax (2) 239-2677; f. 1964; privatized in 1995; renationalized in 2010; total networks: 3,698 km (2008); Andina network: 2,274 km; Oriental (Eastern) network: 1,424 km; Pres. JOSÉ MANUEL PINTO CLAURE.

Empresa Ferroviaria Andino, SA: Calle Quintin Barrios 791, entre Avda Ecuador y Calle Cervantes, Plaza España, Casilla 4350, La Paz; tel. and fax (2) 241-4400; fax (2) 241-8516; e-mail efasa@fca.com.bo; internet www.fca.com.bo; f. 1996; Pres. MIGUEL SEPÚLVEDA CAMPOS; Gen. Man. EDUARDO MACLEAN ABAROA.

Empresa Ferroviaria Oriental, SA (FCOSA): Avda Montes Final s/n, Casilla 3569, Santa Cruz; tel. (3) 338-7000; fax (3) 338-7105; e-mail ferroviaria@fo.com.bo; internet www.fo.com.bo; f. 1996; Chair. RAFAEL ENRIQUE ABREU ANSELMI; Gen. Man. RICARDO FERNANDEZ DURÁN.

ROADS

In 2004 Bolivia had some 62,479 km of roads, of which an estimated 3,979 km (6.6%) were paved. Almost the entire road network is concentrated in the *altiplano* region and the Andes valleys. The Pan-American Highway, linking Argentina and Peru, crosses Bolivia from south to north-west. In 2010 the Administradora Boliviana de Carreteras commenced work on consolidating the Corredor al Norte, which would integrate the departments of La Paz, Beni and Pando. Also known as the Corredor Amazónico, the 1,357-km stretch would also improve Bolivia's connections with neighbouring countries.

Administradora Boliviana de Carreteras (ABC): Edif. Centro de Comunicaciones, 8°, Avda Mariscal Santa Cruz, La Paz; tel. (2) 235-7220; fax (2) 239-1764; e-mail abc@abc.gob.bo; internet www.abc.gob.bo; f. 2006; planning and devt of national highways; Pres. LUIS SÁNCHEZ.

INLAND WATERWAYS AND SHIPPING

By agreement with Paraguay in 1938, Bolivia has an outlet on the River Paraguay. This arrangement, together with navigation rights on the Paraná, gives Bolivia access to the River Plate and the sea. The River Paraguay is navigable for vessels of 12-ft draught for 288 km beyond Asunción, in Paraguay, and for smaller boats another 960 km to Corumbá in Brazil.

Bolivia has duty-free access to the Brazilian coastal ports of Belém and Santos and the inland ports of Corumbá and Port Velho, as well as to free port facilities at Rosario, Argentina, on the River Paraná, and to the Peruvian port of Ilo. Most of Bolivia's foreign trade is handled through the ports of Matarani (Peru), Antofagasta and Arica (Chile), Rosario and Buenos Aires (Argentina) and Santos (Brazil). An agreement between Bolivia and Chile to reform Bolivia's access arrangements to the port of Arica came into effect in 1996. In 2010 Bolivia's fleet totalled 59 vessels.

CIVIL AVIATION

Bolivia has 30 airports, including the two international airports at La Paz (El Alto) and Santa Cruz (Viru-Viru).

Dirección General de Aeronaútica Civil: Edif. Multicine, 9°, Avda Arce 2631, Casilla 9360, La Paz; tel. (2) 244-4450; fax (2) 211-9323; internet www.dgac.gob.bo; f. 1947; Exec. Dir Gen. LUIS COIMBRA BUSCH.

AeroSur: Avda Irala 616, Casilla 3104, Santa Cruz; tel. (3) 336-4446; fax (3) 363-1384; e-mail ventas@aerosur.com; internet www.aerosur.com; f. 1992 by merger of existing charter cos following deregulation; privately owned; Pres. SERGIO SANZETENEA; Gen. Man. CARLOS MEYER.

Boliviana de Aviación: Calle Jordán 202, esq. Nataniel Aguirre, Cochabamba; tel. (4) 411-4643; fax (4) 411-6477; e-mail ventasweb@boa.bo; internet boa.bo; f. 2007; state-owned; Gen. Man. RONALD SALVADOR CASSO CASSO.

Transportes Aéreos Bolivianos (TAB): El Alto, Internacional Aeropuerto, Casilla 12237, La Paz; tel. (2) 284-0556; e-mail tabair@tabairlines.com; internet www.tabairlines.com; f. 1977; regional scheduled and charter cargo services; Gen. Man. LUIS GUERECA PADILLA.

Transportes Aéreos Militares: Avda Montes 738, esq. Jose Maria Serrano, La Paz; tel. (2) 268-1101; fax (2) 268-1102; internet www.tam.bo; internal passenger and cargo services; Dir-Gen. REMBERTO DURÁN.

Tourism

Bolivia's tourist attractions include Lake Titicaca, at 3,810 m (12,500 ft) above sea level, pre-Incan ruins at Tiwanaku, Chacaltaya, in the Andes mountains, which has the highest ski-run in the world, and the UNESCO World Cultural Heritage Sites of Potosí and Sucre. In 2006 some 496,489 foreign visitors arrived at hotels in Bolivian regional capitals. In 2009 receipts from tourism totalled US $279m., according to provisional figures. Tourists come mainly from South American countries, the USA and Europe.

Asociación Boliviana de Agencias de Viajes y Turismo (ABAVYT): Calle Boliviar 27, 2°, Zonca Central, Santa Cruz; tel. (3) 332-7110; fax (3) 332-1634; e-mail abavyt@acelerate.com; f. 1984; Pres. LOURDES OMOYA BENITEZ.

Dirección General de Turismo: Edif. Cámara Nacional de Comercial, Avda Mariscal Santa Cruz, 11°, Casilla 1868, La Paz; tel. (2) 236-3326; fax (2) 220-2628; Vice-Minister of Tourism MARKO MARCELO MACHICAO BANKOVIC.

Defence

As assessed at November 2011, Bolivia's armed forces numbered 46,100: army 34,800 (including 25,000 conscripts), navy 4,800, air force 6,500. There was also a paramilitary force numbering 37,100. Military service, lasting one year, is selective.

Defence Expenditure: budgeted at 2,500m. bolivianos in 2010.

Commander-in-Chief of the Armed Forces: Adm. TITO ROGER GANDARILLAS SALAZAR.

General Commander of the Army: Maj.-Gen. ANTONIO CUETO CALDERÓN.

General Commander of the Air Force: Maj.-Gen. LIBORIO FLORES ENRÍQUEZ ESPINOZA.

General Commander of the Naval Forces: Vice-Adm. RAÚL VISCARRA ESCÓBAR.

Education

Primary education, beginning at six years of age and lasting for eight years, is officially compulsory and is available free of charge. Secondary education, which is not compulsory, begins at 14 years of age and lasts for up to four years. In 2006/07 enrolment at primary schools included 94% of pupils in the relevant age-group. In 2007/08 enrolment at secondary schools included 69% of students in the relevant age-group. There are eight state universities and two private universities. The Government of Evo Morales, which took office in 2006, launched an education programme, 'Yo sí puedo', to alleviate levels of illiteracy, which was followed by 'Yo sí puedo seguir' in 2011 to provide alternative education for adults. The provision for education in the 2012 central government budget was 11,000m. bolivianos.

BOSNIA AND HERZEGOVINA

Introductory Survey

LOCATION, CLIMATE, LANGUAGE, RELIGION, FLAG, CAPITAL

Bosnia and Herzegovina is situated in south-eastern Europe. It is bounded by Croatia to the north, west and south-west, by Serbia to the east and by Montenegro to the south-east. There is a short south-western coastline on the Adriatic Sea, and an exclave of Croatia, around Dubrovnik, lies to the south-east. Bosnia and Herzegovina is a largely mountainous territory with a continental climate and steady rainfall throughout the year; in areas nearer the coast the climate is more Mediterranean. The designated official languages (all of which were, in the 20th century, considered to be variants of Serbo-Croat) are Bosnian, Croatian and Serbian. Bosnian and Croatian are written in the Latin script, while Serbian has traditionally been written in the Cyrillic script, but is sometimes also written in the Latin script. The Muslims (Bosniaks), the majority of whom belong to the Sunni sect, are the largest religious grouping in Bosnia and Herzegovina, comprising 43.7% of the population in 1991. Religious affiliation is roughly equated with ethnicity, the Serbs (31.4% of the population) belonging to the Serbian Orthodox Church and the Croats (17.3%) mostly being members of the Roman Catholic Church. The national flag (proportions 1 by 2) consists of two unequal vertical sections of blue, separated by a yellow triangle, which is bordered on the left by a diagonal line of nine white, five-pointed stars. The capital is Sarajevo.

CONTEMPORARY POLITICAL HISTORY

Historical Context

The provinces of Bosnia and Herzegovina formed part of the Turkish Osmanlı (Ottoman) Empire for almost 400 years, but, following the Congress of Berlin of 1878, were administered by the Habsburg Empire of Austria-Hungary, which formally annexed the territories in 1908. The population of the provinces was composed of a mixture of Orthodox Christian Serbs, Roman Catholic Croats and Muslims (also known, subsequently, as Bosniaks). Serbian expansionist aims caused tension from the late 19th century, and in 1914, following the assassination of the heir to the Habsburg throne by a Bosnian Serb extremist in Sarajevo, Austria-Hungary declared war on Serbia, precipitating the First World War. On 4 December 1918 the Kingdom of Serbs, Croats and Slovenes was proclaimed, under the Serbian monarchy. Bitter disputes ensued between Serbs and Croats, and in 1929 King Aleksandar imposed a dictatorship, formally renaming the country Yugoslavia in October.

Although proscribed in 1921, the Communist Party of Yugoslavia (CPY) operated clandestinely, and in 1937 Josip Broz (Tito) became its General Secretary. During the Second World War (1939–45) intense fighting took place in Bosnia and Herzegovina, which was incorporated into a fascist Independent State of Croatia in 1941. From 1943 Tito's Partisan movement dominated most of Bosnia and Herzegovina, which, after the war, became one of the six constituent republics of the Yugoslav federation. In the 1960s Tito sought to maintain a balance of power between the ethnic groups in both Bosnia and Herzegovina and the Socialist Federal Republic of Yugoslavia (SFRY—as the country was renamed in 1963) as a whole. Slav Muslims were granted a recognized official ethnic status, as a nation of Yugoslavia, prior to the 1971 census. In that year a collective state presidency was established for Bosnia and Herzegovina, with a regular rotation of posts.

Domestic Political Affairs

Communal affiliation proved to be a decisive factor in the elections held to the republican legislature, the Skupština Republike Bosne i Hercegovine (Assembly of the Republic of Bosnia and Herzegovina), in November and December 1990. The three main ethnically based parties emerged as the largest parties in the Skupština: the (principally Muslim) Party of Democratic Action (PDA), with 86 seats; the Serbian Democratic Party (SDP), with 72 seats; and the Croatian Democratic Union of Bosnia and Herzegovina (CDU—BH), with 44 seats. These parties also took all the seats on the directly elected seven-member collective Presidency, forming a coalition administration. On 20 December the leader of the PDA, Alija Izetbegović, was named President of the Presidency, while members of the CDU—BH and the SDP were to be President of the Executive Council (Prime Minister) and President of the Skupština, respectively.

Following the declarations of independence by Slovenia and Croatia in June 1991, and the ensuing conflict, particularly in Croatia, Serb-dominated territories in Bosnia and Herzegovina declared their intent to remain within the Yugoslav federation. On 16 September a 'Serb Autonomous Region' (SAR) of Bosnian Krajina, based in the north-western city of Banja Luka, was proclaimed; this SAR was formed on the basis of a Serb 'Community of Municipalities of Bosnian Krajina', which had been formed in April, and which had announced its unification with the neighbouring 'SAR of Krajina' in Croatia in June. As tension intensified, the formation of further SARs was proclaimed, amid accusations that Serb nationalist elements sought to establish a 'Greater Serbia', with the support of the Yugoslav People's Army (JNA). In October the JNA assumed effective control of the southern city of Mostar, north-west of the predominantly Serb 'Old' Herzegovina.

In early October 1991 both the republican Presidency (with the dissenting votes of the Bosnian Serb members) and the PDA proposed that the republic declare its independence. Later that month the Serb deputies rejected a resolution in the Skupština to that end, and withdrew from the chamber. On 15 October the remaining parliamentarians approved a resolution declaring the sovereignty of Bosnia and Herzegovina. In response, the SARs, which rejected the declaration of sovereignty, declared that, henceforth, only the federal laws and Constitution would apply on their territory. On 24 October the Serb deputies of the republican legislature announced that they were to form their own Narodna skupština (National Assembly). On 9–10 November a referendum, organized by this body, indicated overwhelming support among Bosnian Serbs for remaining in a common state with Serbs elsewhere in Yugoslavia. On 9 January 1992 the formation of a 'Serb Republic (Republika Srpska) of Bosnia and Herzegovina', comprising Serb-held areas of the republic (about 65% of the total area), was proclaimed, headed by Radovan Karadžić, the leader of the SDP. The republican Government immediately declared this secessionist Republic, based in Banja Luka, to be illegal; in August it was renamed 'Republika Srpska', removing any reference to Bosnia and Herzegovina from its title. Meanwhile, in a republic-wide referendum on 29 February–1 March, boycotted by the majority of Bosnian Serbs, 99.4% of the participating 63% of the electorate expressed support for the independence of Bosnia and Herzegovina, which was then duly declared by Izetbegović.

Subsequently, renewed Serb–Muslim tension led to clashes in Sarajevo and elsewhere. On 18 March 1992, following mediation by the European Community (EC, now European Union—EU, see p. 276), the leaders of the Serb, Croat and Muslim communities signed an agreement providing for the division of Bosnia and Herzegovina into three autonomous units. In April fighting between the JNA on one side, and Muslim and Croat forces on the other, intensified, particularly after the EC and the USA recognized Bosnia and Herzegovina's independence on 7 April; Serb troops besieged Sarajevo and launched mortar attacks on the city, while Serb fighters and irregular troops conducted a campaign of 'ethnic cleansing' in the east and north-west of Bosnia. Izetbegović requested foreign military intervention to support the Government, but the UN, while deploying a UN Protection Force (UNPROFOR) in Croatia, decided against the deployment of a peace-keeping force in Bosnia and Herzegovina. On 20 May the Government of Bosnia and Herzegovina declared the JNA to be an 'occupying force' and announced the formation of a republican army. Two days later Bosnia and Herzegovina was admitted to the UN. On 30 May the UN imposed economic sanctions against the recently established Federal Republic of Yugoslavia (comprising Serbia and Montenegro), in response to its involvement in the conflict in Bosnia and Herzegovina. In early June, in an apparent effort to placate the UN, Serbian leaders in Belgrade (the Yugoslav and Serbian capital) ordered the Bosnian Serbs to end their siege of Sarajevo.

The proclamation, on 3 July 1992, by Croats in western and central Bosnia and Herzegovina, of an autonomous 'Croat Community of Herzeg-Bosna', covering about 30% of the territory of the country and headed by Mate Boban, was immediately declared to be illegal by Izetbegović. Izetbegović and President Franjo Tuđman of Croatia signed a co-operation agreement in late July. Under this accord, the Governments of Bosnia and Herzegovina and of Croatia formed a Joint Defence Committee in September, and repeated demands that the UN end an armaments embargo (which had been imposed on the SFRY in September 1991, and which was subsequently determined to apply to all regions formerly contained therein). After several months of increasing tensions, hostilities erupted between Croats and Muslims in October, and Croat forces captured the towns of Mostar, Novi Travnik and Vitez. Mostar was subsequently proclaimed capital of Herzeg-Bosna, with the city effectively being split into Croat- and Muslim-controlled zones, the Serb population of the city (around 20% of the pre-conflict population) having largely fled. In November the Croatian Government admitted that Croatian army units had been deployed in Bosnia and Herzegovina, and accordingly became a signatory to the latest cease-fire agreement in the Republic. In December the UN Human Rights Commission declared that Bosnian Serbs were largely responsible for violations of human rights in Bosnia and Herzegovina. (Television broadcasts of concentration camps in Serb-held areas of the Bosnian Krajina had provoked international outrage in August.) Later in December the UN Security Council unanimously adopted a resolution condemning the atrocities, particularly the widespread rape of Bosniak women, and demanding access to all Serb detention camps.

Geneva peace proposals

In January 1993 the Co-Chairmen of the Geneva Peace Conference (a permanent forum for talks on the conflict), Lord (David) Owen (a former British Secretary of State for Foreign and Commonwealth Affairs) and Cyrus Vance (the UN mediator and a former US Secretary of State), visited Belgrade for talks with the President of Serbia, Slobodan Milošević. Their aim was to persuade him to convince the Bosnian Serbs to agree to a division of Bosnia and Herzegovina into 10 provinces (with three provinces allocated to each ethnic group and Sarajevo as a province with special status). The peace plan was approved by Boban, and, in part, by Izetbegović, but was rejected by Karadžić. In mid-January Milošević attended the peace talks in Geneva, Switzerland, for the first time. Karadžić, under pressure from Milošević and the President of Yugoslavia, agreed to the constitutional proposals included in the plan and, subsequently, to the military arrangements. On 19–20 January the Bosnian Serb Narodna skupština, based at Pale, near Sarajevo, voted to accept the general principles of the Vance-Owen plan. On 22 February the UN Security Council adopted a resolution providing for the establishment of an international court to try alleged war criminals for acts committed since 1991 in the territories formerly included in the SFRY. On 31 March the UN Security Council adopted a resolution permitting the taking of 'all necessary measures' by UN member states or regional organizations to enforce a 'no-fly zone' imposed on the airspace of Bosnia and Herzegovina in October 1992. In March 1993 Izetbegović agreed to both the military arrangements and the proposed territorial divisions included in the Vance-Owen plan. In April, however, the Bosnian Serb assembly rejected the territorial arrangements, incurring international disapproval. In early May Karadžić signed the Vance-Owen plan in Geneva, but two days later it was rejected by the Bosnian Serb assembly.

In May 1993 the USA, France, Russia, Spain and the United Kingdom signed a communiqué declaring that the arms embargo on the post-SFRY states would continue and that international armed forces would not intervene in the conflict; they proposed instead, with effect from 22 July, the creation of six designated 'safe areas' (Sarajevo, Bihać, Tuzla, Goražde, Srebrenica and Žepa), in which disarmed Bosniaks—who, unlike the Bosnian Serbs and Croats, lacked substantial external military support—would be settled. In June a UN Security Council resolution permitted UNPROFOR to use force, including air power, in response to attacks against these 'safe areas'. In that month a joint Serb-Croat offensive began against the predominantly Bosniak town of Maglaj. In July intense fighting between Croats and Bosniaks for the control of Mostar commenced. Meanwhile, in June new peace proposals were announced in Geneva by Owen and Thorvald Stoltenberg (who had replaced Vance as the UN mediator), under which Bosnia and Herzegovina would become a confederation of three ethnically determined states. Izetbegović refused to discuss the tripartite division of Bosnia and boycotted the remainder of the Geneva talks.

On 30 July 1993 the three factions reached a constitutional agreement in Geneva on the reconstruction of Bosnia and Herzegovina as a confederation of three states, under a central government with limited powers. Sarajevo would be placed under UN administration for a two-year transitional period. However, fighting continued, and in early August the three Croat members of the state presidency (including the Prime Minister, who was consequently dismissed from that post) left the delegation to Geneva, instead joining the Croatian negotiators. On 28 August a 'Croat Republic of Herzeg-Bosna' was proclaimed in Grude, which proceeded to accept the Owen-Stoltenberg plan on condition that the Serbs and Bosniaks also accepted it. On the same day the Bosnian Serb assembly also voted in favour of the plan. On 31 August, however, the Skupština Republike Bosne i Hercegovine rejected the plan. On 10 September Fikret Abdić, a Bosniak member of the state presidency, announced the creation of an 'Autonomous Province of Western Bosnia' in the north-western region around Bihać. On 27 September Abdić was elected 'President' of the 'province' by a 'Constituent Assembly'. Abdić (who signed a peace agreement with representatives of the Bosnian Serbs) was subsequently dismissed from the state presidency of Bosnia and Herzegovina. Izetbegović imposed martial law on the area, and government forces attacked troops under Abdić's command.

In February 1994 the shelling of a Sarajevo market place, killing at least 68 people, prompted the UN to threaten military intervention against Serb forces. Following the issuing of an ultimatum by the North Atlantic Treaty Organization (NATO, see p. 370), the Bosnian Serbs withdrew most of their heavy weaponry from a 20-km 'exclusion zone' around the city, which, however, remained blockaded. Moreover, the exclusion zone was frequently violated. In late February NATO forces near Banja Luka shot down four Serb aircraft, which had violated the UN prohibition of non-humanitarian flights over the country—the first aggressive military action ever taken by NATO. Bosnian Serb forces continued to shell Maglaj throughout March, and several of the 'safe areas' were also bombarded. Following a cease-fire agreed by the republican Government and Herzeg-Bosna in late February, Haris Silajdžić (Prime Minister of Bosnia and Herzegovina since October 1993) and Kresimir Zubak (who had replaced Boban as the leader of Herzeg-Bosna) signed an agreement on 18 March, in Washington, DC, USA, providing for the creation of a Federation on those territories in Bosnia and Herzegovina controlled by Croats and Bosniaks. A further agreement was signed by Izetbegović and Tuđman, providing for the eventual creation of a loose confederation of the Federation and Croatia. In late March the accords were approved by the Herzeg-Bosna assembly, and the new Constitution was ratified by the Skupština Republike Bosne i Hercegovine. In April, in response to the continued shelling of the 'safe area' of Goražde by Bosnian Serb forces, UN-sanctioned air-strikes were launched by NATO aircraft on Serb ground positions. However, Serb forces captured Goražde later that month, prompting strong criticism from the Russian Government, which for the first time indicated that it would not oppose the use of force against the Bosnian Serbs. Bosnian Serb forces withdrew from Goražde in late April. On 26 April a new negotiating forum, the Contact Group, comprising representatives from France, Germany, Russia, the United Kingdom and the USA, was established.

In May 1994 the Ustavotvorna skupština Federacije Bosne i Hercegovine (Constituent Assembly of the Federation of Bosnia and Herzegovina) elected Zubak to the largely ceremonial post of President of the Federation at its inaugural meeting. Ejup Ganić, a Bosniak, was elected Vice-President of the Federation (he was concurrently a Vice-President of the collective Presidency of the Republic of Bosnia and Herzegovina), and Silajdžić was appointed Prime Minister of the Federation. A joint Government of the Federation and the Republic, led by Silajdžić, was appointed in June.

Following negotiations in Geneva in June 1994, a one-month republic-wide cease-fire was declared. By the end of the month, however, following repeated violations, government forces had captured Serb-held areas of central Bosnia. The Contact Group presented new peace proposals in July, according to which the Federation would be granted 51% of the country's territory. Sensitive areas, including Sarajevo, Srebrenica, Goražde and

Brčko, would be placed under UN and EU administration. On 17 July Izetbegović and Tuđman endorsed the Contact Group plan, which was also approved by the Skupština Republike Bosne i Hercegovine, but the Bosnian Serb Narodna skupština rejected proposals requiring the Bosnian Serbs to cede around one-third of the territory they controlled. Milošević criticized Bosnian Serb opposition to the plan, and in early August Yugoslavia announced the closure of its borders with Bosnia and Herzegovina. On 5 August NATO air-strikes (the first since April) were launched against Bosnian Serb targets, in response to attacks against UN forces and the renewed shelling of Sarajevo. In late August 96% of participants of a referendum held in the Bosnian Serb-held areas reportedly voted to reject the Contact Group plan; this rejection was unanimously approved by the Bosnian Serb assembly on 1 September. Meanwhile, on 21 August Bihać was captured by the government army of Bosnia and Herzegovina. In December the Contact Group issued proposals based on the July peace plan, which indicated the possibility of confederal links between a Bosnian Serb polity and Yugoslavia or Serbia. On 31 December the Bosnian Serb authorities and the republican Government signed a four-month cease-fire agreement, to take effect from the following day. While the cease-fire was generally observed during January 1995, intense fighting continued in the Bihać enclave between government forces and troops loyal to Abdić, who was supported by troops from the adjoining 'Republic of Serb Krajina' in Croatia. In February the USA refused to continue negotiations with Karadžić until the Bosnian Serb authorities had accepted the Contact Group plan.

On 20 February 1995 representatives of the Bosnian Serbs and the Croatian Serbs signed a military pact, guaranteeing mutual assistance in the event of attack and providing for the establishment of a joint Supreme Defence Council. In early March, in response, a formal military alliance was announced between the armies of Croatia, the authorities of Herzeg-Bosna and the Government of the Republic of Bosnia and Herzegovina. On 8 April President Zubak of the Federation and Ganić, the Vice-President of both the Federation and of Bosnia and Herzegovina, signed an agreement in Bonn, Germany, on the implementation of principles for the entity. On 25 May, following a UN request in response to the continued bombardment of Sarajevo, NATO aircraft carried out strikes on Bosnian Serb ammunition depots. Serb forces responded by shelling five of the six 'safe areas' and, following further NATO air-strikes on 26 May, undertook a massive bombardment of Tuzla, killing at least 70 people. Bosnian Serb troops subsequently disarmed and took hostage 222 UNPROFOR personnel in Goražde. In June NATO and European defence ministers agreed to form a 10,000-strong 'rapid reaction force' for Bosnia and Herzegovina, which would operate under UN command from mid-July, so as to provide 'enhanced protection' to UNPROFOR. Meanwhile, the release of the remaining hostages coincided with the withdrawal of UNPROFOR from Bosnian Serb-controlled territory around Sarajevo.

On 11 July 1995 the eastern 'safe area' of Srebrenica was captured by Bosnian Serb fighters, after Dutch UNPROFOR troops based in the town were taken hostage, despite NATO air-strikes on Bosnian Serb tanks approaching the town. Following the capture of Srebrenica, an estimated 7,000–8,000 Muslim male civilians were massacred by Bosnian Serb forces, the largest atrocity to take place in Europe since the end of the Second World War.

Bihać was attacked on 20 July 1995, in a concerted effort by Bosnian Serbs, Croatian Serbs, and rebel Bosniaks led by Abdić, precipitating the signature of a military co-operation agreement between Izetbegović and Tuđman two days later. Croatian and Herzeg-Bosna troops subsequently launched attacks on Serb positions around Bihać, thereby blocking supply routes into the Serb-controlled Krajina enclave.

Croatian government forces invaded the Croatian Serb-held Krajina on 4 August 1995, and rapidly recaptured the entire enclave. On 6–7 August the siege of Bihać was ended by Bosnian government and Croatian troops. On 9 August a further peace initiative, devised by Richard Holbrooke, a US Assistant Secretary of State, was announced by the USA; the proposals, based on the Contact Group plan of 1994, allowed the Bosnian Serbs to retain control of Srebrenica and Žepa, the latter of which they had captured in late July. On 28 August a mortar attack on a market in central Sarajevo, attributed to Bosnian Serb forces, resulted in at least 38 deaths. Two days later NATO responded by commencing a series of air-strikes ('Operation Deliberate Force') on Serb positions throughout Bosnia and Herzegovina, which continued for several weeks.

On 8 September 1995 the Ministers of Foreign Affairs of Bosnia and Herzegovina, Croatia and Yugoslavia (the latter acting on behalf of the Bosnian Serbs), meeting in Geneva under the auspices of the Contact Group, signed an agreement determining the basic principles for a peace accord. These principles included the continuing existence of Bosnia and Herzegovina within its present borders, but comprising two administrative units, known as entities: the Federation of Bosnia and Herzegovina; and Republika Srpska, each of which was largely to retain its existing Constitution. In mid-September 'Operation Deliberate Force' was suspended, following the withdrawal of Bosnian Serb weaponry from the 'exclusion zone' around Sarajevo (the air-strikes also led to a marked reduction in the extent of the territory controlled by Bosnian Serb forces). Agreement on further basic principles for a peace accord was reached by the Ministers of Foreign Affairs of Bosnia and Herzegovina, Croatia and Yugoslavia, meeting in New York, USA, on 26 September. Within the central state parliament, Republika Srpska was to be apportioned one-third of the seats; the Federation was to control two-thirds of the seats (legislative decisions were only to be implemented, however, with the approval of at least one-third of the deputies of each entity). A collective presidency was also to be organized according to the one-third Serb to two-thirds Bosniak-Croat proportional division. A 60-day cease-fire took effect on 12 October.

The Dayton accords

On 1 November 1995 peace negotiations between the three warring parties in the conflict began in Dayton, Ohio, USA. A comprehensive peace agreement was reached on 21 November, when Izetbegović, Tuđman and Milošević (the latter representing both Yugoslavia and the Bosnian Serbs) initialled a General Framework Agreement for Peace in Bosnia and Herzegovina, dividing the country, to be known officially as Bosnia and Herzegovina, between the Federation of Bosnia and Herzegovina, with 51% of the territory, and Republika Srpska, with 49%. Whereas the Government of Republika Srpska was to be highly centralized, with a directly elected presidency and no level of local government other than that of municipality, power in the Federation was devolved to 10 cantonal administrations, as well as to municipalities. The Federation was to have a bicameral legislature, whereas that of Republika Srpska was to be unicameral. A state government (encompassing the whole country) was to have a democratically elected collective presidency and a parliament. The agreement stipulated the right of all refugees and displaced persons to return to their homes and either to have seized property returned to them or to receive fair compensation. Several suburbs of Sarajevo were to form part of Republika Srpska, although most of the city was to be in the Federation. No agreement was reached on control of the Posavina corridor, surrounded by Federation territory, connecting the northern sector of Republika Srpska with the southern sector, including the town of Brčko and its river-port; the three sides agreed to place the issue under international arbitration. An international, NATO-commanded, 60,000-strong Implementation Force (IFOR) was to be mandated to oversee the withdrawal of the warring parties from zones of separation and to monitor the agreed exchanges of territory. It was estimated that around 200,000 people had been killed in the conflict in Bosnia and Herzegovina, and some 2.7m. (out of a total population of 4.4m. at the 1991 census) were believed to have been displaced.

Following the initialling of the Dayton peace accords, the UN suspended the remaining economic sanctions against Yugoslavia and voted to remove gradually the arms embargo against the post-SFRY states. At a conference on the implementation of the accords, held in London, United Kingdom, in early December 1995, it was agreed that an Organization for Security and Co-operation in Europe (OSCE, see p. 388) mission would organize and monitor parliamentary elections in Bosnia and Herzegovina and that the Contact Group would be replaced by a Peace Implementation Council (PIC) based in Brussels, Belgium. The Swedish former Prime Minister and EU envoy to the peace talks, Carl Bildt, was appointed High Representative of the International Community in Bosnia and Herzegovina, with responsibility for the implementation of the civilian aspects of the accords. On 14 December the Dayton peace agreement was formally signed by Izetbegović, Tuđman and Milošević, and by President Bill Clinton of the USA and a number of European political leaders in Paris, France. The formal transfer of power from UNPROFOR to IFOR took place on 20 December.

On 30 January 1996 Hasan Muratović was elected by the state assembly as Prime Minister of Bosnia and Herzegovina, following the resignation from the premiership of Silajdžić; a new state Government was appointed on the same day, and a new federation Government was appointed one day later. In mid-February, in response to unrest in Mostar (where tensions between Croats and Bosniaks remained intense), an emergency summit meeting took place in Rome, Italy, at which Izetbegović, Tuđman and Milošević reaffirmed their adherence to the Dayton agreement. A joint Croat-Bosniak security patrol, accompanied by officers from the UN International Police Task Force (IPTF) and Western European Union (WEU), subsequently began operating in Mostar.

By the end of April 1996 substantial progress had been made in the implementation of the military aspects of the Dayton agreement. However, the exchange of territory between the two entities did not proceed as envisaged. From January there had been a mass exodus of Serbs from the suburbs of Sarajevo that were to be transferred to the control of the Federation. The Republika Srpska authorities in Pale were criticized for using intimidation to coerce the Serb inhabitants of these districts to resettle in towns in regions of Republika Srpska from which Muslims had been driven during the war. By late March only about 10% of the pre-war Serb population in Sarajevo remained.

In May 1996 Bosniak and Croat leaders, meeting in Washington, DC, agreed on the merger of their armed forces and the return of refugees. The agreement on a unified federation army was the principal precondition for the implementation of a US-sponsored training programme intended to give it equivalent military capabilities to that of Republika Srpska's armed forces. Given that Karadžić had been indicted by the International Criminal Tribunal for the former Yugoslavia (ICTY, see p. 22), based in The Hague, Netherlands, for war crimes, notably responsibility for the massacre at Srebrenica in July 1995, his continued position as President of Republika Srpska (and that of Gen. Ratko Mladić as head of the armed forces) was in breach of the Dayton agreement, which prohibited indicted war criminals from holding public office. Karadžić subsequently delegated some of his powers to his deputy, Dr Biljana Plavšić.

In June 1996 Croats in Mostar announced a new Government of Herzeg-Bosna, in contravention of agreements that the autonomous state would be dissolved. At a summit meeting of the Presidents of Bosnia and Herzegovina, Croatia and Serbia, convened by the USA in Geneva in August, Tuđman and Izetbegović agreed on the full establishment of federation institutions by the end of the month. In late June 1996 Western European countries issued an ultimatum to Karadžić to resign, on penalty of the reimposition of sanctions against Republika Srpska that had been suspended in April. In defiance of this, the SDP re-elected Karadžić as party leader. At the end of June Karadžić announced his temporary resignation and the appointment of Plavšić as the acting President of Republika Srpska. It was then confirmed that Karadžić would not contest the election to the presidency of Republika Srpska, and Plavšić was nominated as the SDP candidate. In mid-July the ICTY issued arrest warrants for Karadžić and Mladić. Following intensive negotiations convened by Holbrooke with Milošević and Bosnian Serb leaders, on 19 July Karadžić resigned from the presidency and as head of the SDP.

Post-conflict elections

In August 1996 the OSCE announced that municipal elections were to be postponed, in response to evidence that the Republika Srpska authorities were forcibly registering displaced Serbs in formerly Muslim-dominated localities. Elections were held on 14 September to the state presidency and Predstavnički dom/ Zastupnički dom (Predstavnički dom—House of Representatives, the lower chamber of the bicameral Parlamentarna skupština Bosne i Hercegovine—Parliamentary Assembly of Bosnia and Herzegovina). Elections also took place at entity level, to the Republika Srpska presidency and legislature, to cantonal authorities within the Federation and to the Predstavnički dom Federacije/Zastupnički dom Federacije (Predstavnički dom Federacije—Federation House of Representatives, the lower chamber of a bicameral Parlament Federacije—Federation Parliament). At the election to the state collective Presidency, Izetbegović won 80% of the Bosniak votes cast; Zubak (contesting the election as the candidate of the CDU—BH) 88% of the Croat votes; and Momčilo Krajišnik (of the SDP) 67% of the Serb votes. Having received the largest number of votes of the three winning presidential candidates, Izetbegović became Chairman of the Presidency. The PDA and the CDU—BH dominated both the Federation section of the Predstavnički dom and the Predstavnički dom Federacije; none the less, an alliance of social democratic Bosniak and Croat parties, the Joint List of Bosnia and Herzegovina, and the Party for Bosnia and Herzegovina (led by Silajdžić) won a significant number of votes in the elections to both the state and Federation legislatures. The SDP secured a majority of votes in both the Serb section of the Predstavnički dom and in the Narodna skupština Republike Srpske. Plavšić was elected President of Republika Srpska, receiving 59% of the votes cast. Following the OSCE's endorsement of the election results, on 1 October the UN Security Council decided to remove sanctions against Yugoslavia and Republika Srpska. The inauguration of the state presidency took place on 5 October. In November Plavšić announced that she had dismissed Gen. Mladić as Commander of the Bosnian Serb armed forces.

Following a Peace Implementation Conference, held in London, it was announced that IFOR would be replaced by a Stabilization Force (SFOR) from 20 December 1996. In mid-December the Presidency appointed the two Co-Prime Ministers of the state Council of Ministers: Silajdžić, and Boro Bosić of the SDP. Later in the month the dissolution of Herzeg-Bosna was announced and a Federation Prime Minister elected. The state Council of Ministers was appointed by the Co-Prime Ministers and approved at the inaugural session of the bicameral Parlamentarna skupština (comprising the indirectly elected Dom Naroda—House of Peoples—and the Predstavnički dom) on 3 January 1997.

On 28 February 1997 Krajišnik signed, on behalf of Republika Srpska, an agreement with Yugoslavia to foster mutual economic co-operation and to collaborate on regional security. The accord was ratified by the Narodna skupština Republike Srpske in March, despite Plavšić's opposition. In June Bildt was replaced as High Representative by Carlos Westendorp. In July Plavšić announced the dissolution of the Narodna skupština, scheduling parliamentary elections for September; this measure followed the assembly's opposition to the suspension of the entity's Minister of Internal Affairs by Plavšić (who was expelled from the SDP in response). In August the Constitutional Court ruled that Plavšić's dissolution of the legislature had been illegal; the Narodna skupština proceeded to vote to disregard future decrees by her. At municipal elections, held on 13–14 September in both entities, three main nationalist parties, the PDA, the CDU—BH and the SDP, received the majority of the votes cast.

Elections to the Narodna skupština Republike Srpske were held on 22–23 November 1997, under the supervision of the OSCE. Although the representation of the SDP was much reduced, to 24 seats, it remained the largest party in the legislature. A newly formed electoral alliance, the Coalition for a Single and Democratic Bosnia and Herzegovina, which included the PDA and the Party for Bosnia and Herzegovina, secured 16 seats, while the Serb National Alliance (SNA), recently established by Plavšić, and the Serb Radical Party (SRP) each received 15 seats. At the inaugural session of the new assembly on 27 December, Plavšić nominated Mladen Ivanić, an economist with no political affiliation, as premier. However, in January 1998, following the failure of inter-party talks, Milorad Dodik, the leader of the Party of Independent Social Democrats of Republika Srpska (PISD), secured sufficient parliamentary support to form a new government. At the end of January Dodik announced that government bodies were to be transferred from Pale to Banja Luka. In June the UN Security Council officially voted in favour of extending the mandate of SFOR indefinitely, with six-monthly reviews.

In April 1998 the OSCE dissolved the municipal assembly of Srebrenica in Republika Srpska, owing to its failure to assist in the resettlement of displaced Muslims there; a provisional executive council, headed by a senior OSCE official, was established to replace the assembly. In June Krajišnik criticized a motion by the Narodna skupština expressing no confidence in its Speaker, Dragan Kalinić, and Deputy Speaker. Kalinić was subsequently elected as Chairman of the SDP, following the resignation of the incumbent.

Tensions between the state and Republika Srpska authorities

In September 1998 elections took place to the state presidency and legislature, to the presidency and legislature of Republika Srpska, and to the Predstavnički dom Federacije. Izetbegović was re-elected as the Bosniak member of the collective Presidency. The Chairman of the Socialist Party of Republika Srpska (SPRS, a member of the SNA-led Accord Coalition), Živko Radišić, replaced Krajišnik, and the Chairman of the CDU—BH, Ante Jelavić, was elected as the Croat member of the Presidency. In the election to the presidency of Republika Srpska, the Chairman of the SRP, Dr Nikola Poplasen, defeated Plavšić. The SDP retained 19 of the 83 seats in the Narodna skupština, while the Coalition for a Single and Democratic Bosnia and Herzegovina won 15 seats; the latter also secured 14 of the 42 seats in the Predstavnički dom and 68 of the 140 seats in the Predstavnički dom Federacije.

On 13 October 1998 the state presidency was inaugurated. Poplasen took office as President of Republika Srpska. The Accord Coalition, which held 32 seats in the Narodna skupština Republike Srpske, rejected Poplasen's nomination of Kalinić as Prime Minister of the entity, and supported the reappointment of Dodik to the post. In December the Parlament Federacije re-elected Ganić as President (to which post he had been elected in December 1997) and a new Federation Council of Ministers was established. In January 1999 the Narodna skupština rejected Poplasen's nomination of Brane Miljus, a member of the PISD, as Prime Minister of Republika Srpska.

In February 1999 Westendorp declared that supreme command of the armed forces of the two entities was to be transferred to the members of the collective state presidency. However, the Republika Srpska Government announced that Poplasen would remain Commander of the entity's armed forces, pending a ruling by the state Constitutional Court. In March Poplasen proposed a motion in the Narodna skupština Republike Srpske, in an attempt to instigate Dodik's dismissal. Westendorp announced Poplasen's removal from office, on the grounds that he had exceeded his authority. In the same month international arbitrators ruled that Serb control of Brčko would end, and that the town would henceforth be governed jointly by Republika Srpska and the Federation, under international supervision. The Narodna skupština rejected both the ruling on Brčko and Westendorp's decision to remove Poplasen from office. (It subsequently withdrew its opposition to Poplasen's dismissal, and Mirko Šarović, the incumbent Vice-President, provisionally assumed the presidential office.) In April a new multi-ethnic municipal Government was elected in Brčko. In March 2000 Brčko was established as a neutral district, and an Interim District Government was established.

In June 1999 NATO announced that the strength of the SFOR contingent was to be reduced to about 16,500. In August Wolfgang Petritsch, hitherto the Austrian ambassador to Yugoslavia, succeeded Westendorp as High Representative. In February 2000 the SPRS withdrew from the Accord Coalition of Republika Srpska, after Dodik dismissed the SPRS Deputy Prime Minister, Tihomir Gligorić. In March a senior Bosnian Croat commander, Gen. Tihomir Blaškić, was sentenced by the ICTY to 45 years' imprisonment (the most severe sentence issued by the Tribunal) for war crimes perpetrated against Muslims in 1992–93. (In July 2004 the ICTY reduced Blaskić's sentence to nine years on appeal, reversing most of the convictions against him on the grounds that he had not been responsible for atrocities perpetrated by forces under his command.) In April 2000 Krajišnik was arrested by SFOR troops and extradited to the ICTY. (His trial commenced at the ICTY in February 2004; he pleaded not guilty to eight charges, including two relating to genocide.)

At local elections, held on 8 April 2000, the SDP won control of 49 of the 145 municipal councils, the CDU—BH secured 25 and the PDA 23; the multi-ethnic Social Democratic Party of Bosnia and Herzegovina (SDP BiH) made significant electoral gains in the Federation. In the same month the Predstavnički dom approved the restructuring of the state Council of Ministers, which was to comprise a Chairman (appointed by the collective Presidency for an eight-month term) and five ministers. In June a new state Council of Ministers was appointed, after the Predstavnički dom confirmed the nomination of a non-party candidate, Spasoje Tusevljak, as Chairman.

In September 2000 the Narodna skupština Republike Srpske adopted a motion, proposed by the SDP, expressing no confidence in Dodik's administration. However, the Government submitted a legal challenge to the entity's Constitutional Court and announced that it would remain in office pending forthcoming legislative elections. In October Izetbegović retired from the collective state presidency. A member of the CDU—BH, Martin Raguž, subsequently became Chairman of the Council of Ministers, replacing Tusevljak.

A downturn in support for the nationalist parties

On 11 November 2000 elections to the Predstavnički dom, to the legislatures of both entities and to the presidency of Republika Srpska took place. The results of elections to the Predstavnički dom and the Predstavnički dom Federacije demonstrated a relative decline in support for the nationalist parties. In elections to the 42-member Predstavnički dom, the SDP BiH secured nine seats, the PDA eight seats, the SDP six seats and the CDU—BH five seats, while in the 140-member Predstavnički dom Federacije the PDA won 38 seats, the SDP BiH 37 seats, the CDU—BH 25 seats and the Party for Bosnia and Herzegovina 21 seats. The SDP secured 31 of the 83 seats in the Narodna skupština Republike Srpske, while the SPRS and the Party of Democratic Progress of Republika Srpska (PDP) each received 11 seats. Mirko Šarović, the SDP candidate, was elected to the presidency of Republika Srpska, with some 49.8% of the votes cast, defeating Dodik. The SDP subsequently announced that it was to establish a parliamentary coalition with the PDP, the SPRS and the PDA, thereby securing a majority in the Narodna skupština.

In December 2000 Šarović designated Ivanić, who was now the leader of the PDP, as Prime Minister of Republika Srpska. In the following month Ivanić formed the entity's first multi-ethnic Council of Ministers. Meanwhile, the SDP BiH established parliamentary coalitions with a further nine non-nationalist parties (the Alliance for Change), which in total held 17 seats in the Predstavnički dom and 69 seats in the Predstavnički dom Federacije.

In January 2001 Plavšić surrendered to the ICTY, following her indictment in April 2000 on charges of involvement in the organization of genocide and deportation against Bosniaks and Croats in 1991–92. In February 2001 three Bosnian Serbs were sentenced to terms of imprisonment by the ICTY for crimes against humanity perpetrated against Bosniak women in Foča in 1992 (the first case at the Tribunal concerning systematic rape and sexual enslavement). In the same month a former Herzeg-Bosna official received a custodial term of 25 years for authorizing crimes against humanity to be committed against Bosniaks in 1993–94.

On 22 February 2001 the Predstavnički dom approved a new state Council of Ministers, after endorsing the nomination by the Presidency of SDP BiH candidate Božidar Matić as Chairman. On 28 February the Predstavnički dom Federacije elected Karlo Filipović, of the SDP BiH, as federation President. The new federation Government notably included several members of the Alliance for Change. Meanwhile, in response to the rejection of Raguž's candidacy to the state premiership, a newly formed grouping of parties led by the CDU—BH, the self-styled 'Croat People's Assembly', declared self-government in three Croat-majority cantons. Petritsch subsequently dismissed Jelavić from the collective Presidency. Many Croat members of the armed forces and local officials also declared support for the Croat People's Assembly. On 28 March the Predstavnički dom voted to appoint Jozo Križanović of the SDP BiH as the Croat member of the collective Presidency. Following negotiations with federal and international community officials, however, the Croat alliance agreed to end its boycott of state institutions in May.

In June 2001 Matić resigned as Chairman of the Council of Ministers. On 7 July the state legislature accepted the nomination of Zlatko Lagumdžija, the leader of the SDP BiH and the hitherto Minister of Foreign Affairs, as Chairman of the Council of Ministers, and the legislation was approved in the following month. In August the ICTY obtained its first conviction on charges of genocide, sentencing a former senior Serb army officer, Radislav Krstić, to 46 years' imprisonment for his responsibility for the massacre at Srebrenica in 1995. (In 2004 his sentence was reduced to 35 years on appeal.) In October 2001 the Narodna skupština Republike Srpske adopted legislation requiring its security forces actively to pursue and to extradite war crime suspects to the ICTY. In November Milošević—who had been extradited to the ICTY in June and had been charged with crimes against humanity relating to Croatia in 1991–92 and to Kosovo in 1999—was additionally indicted on the basis of responsibility for genocide in Bosnia and Herzegovina in 1992–95. (Milošević died in March 2006, while still on trial.)

In March 2002 Dragan Mikerević of the PDP was appointed to the rotating chairmanship of the state Council of Ministers. Later in March the leading political parties, under pressure from Petritsch, agreed on constitutional reforms (implemented the following month), to ensure the representation at all levels of government of Bosniaks, Croats and Serbs throughout the country. A Vijeće naroda (Council of Peoples—comprising eight

Bosniaks, eight Croats, eight Serbs and four others) was established within the Narodna skupština Republike Srpske (which was to elect the members of the Council); among the principal duties of the Council was to be the selection of the entity's delegates to the state Dom Naroda.

Lord Ashdown as High Representative

In late May 2002 Petritsch appointed eight judges to a new Court of Bosnia and Herzegovina, which was to become the country's highest judicial organ. On the same day Lord Ashdown, a British politician and former diplomat, succeeded Petritsch as High Representative, being additionally appointed to a new position, that of EU Special Representative for Bosnia and Herzegovina. In June Ashdown dismissed the federation Deputy Prime Minister and Minister of Finance, Nikola Grabovac, while the Republika Srpska Minister of Finance, Milenko Vracar, tendered his resignation, following pressure from Ashdown, who had criticized official malpractice in both entities. In September 2002 an organ of the Republika Srpska Government issued a report disputing the veracity of the Srebrenica massacre and claiming that only some 2,000 members of the republican armed forces had been killed (mainly in military operations) in the region. The report was strongly condemned as a fabrication by the Bosniak community and by Ashdown. In October a Bosnian Serb former official, Milan Simić, was sentenced to five years' imprisonment on charges of having committed torture in 1992.

On 5 October 2002 elections were conducted to the state presidency, the presidency of Republika Srpska, the state and entity legislatures, and to the federation cantonal assemblies. In the three ballots to the state presidency, the Chairman of the PDA, Sulejman Tihić, was elected the Bosniak member, while Dragan Čović of the CDU—BH became the Croat member and Šarović of the SDP the Serb member. Dragan Čavić of the SDP was elected President of Republika Srpska. The SDP BiH-led alliance lost its majority in the Predstavnički dom following the polls, and the PDA became the largest single party, with 10 seats. The PDA also secured the highest number of seats (32) in the Predstavnički dom Federacije (which was reduced in size to 98 deputies), while the CDU—BH, contesting the elections in alliance with the Croatian Christian Democratic Union—Bosnia and Herzegovina, obtained 16 seats. The SDP BiH and the Party for Bosnia and Herzegovina each won 15 seats. In the elections to the Narodna skupština Republike Srpske, the SDP remained the largest party, with 26 seats, while the Alliance of Independent Social Democrats (AISD—as the PISD had become) obtained 19. At the end of October both the Minister of Defence and the army Chief of the General Staff of Republika Srpska resigned, after it emerged that an aviation company owned by the Republika Srpska authorities had exported military equipment to Iraq, in contravention of a UN armaments embargo.

In November 2002 Mitar Vasiljević, the Bosnian Serb former leader of a paramilitary group, was sentenced to 20 years' imprisonment at the ICTY on two charges relating to atrocities perpetrated against Bosniaks in 1992–94. (In February 2004 his sentence was reduced to 15 years.) In December 2002 Čavić nominated Mikerević as Prime Minister of Republika Srpska. Also in December Ashdown introduced new legislation to strengthen the powers of the state Government: two new ministries, of security and justice, were to be established and the Prime Minister was henceforth to be appointed for a four-year term (replacing the system of rotation between the three ethnic representatives). At the end of 2002 the mandate of the principally civilian security force, the UN Mission in Bosnia and Herzegovina (UNMIBH), officially expired, and the UN transferred responsibility for peace-keeping to an EU Police Mission, which was to supervise the reorganization and training of the country's security forces.

In January 2003 the Predstavnički dom approved the appointment of Adnan Terzić of the PDA as Chairman of the state Government and a new Council of Ministers was formed. Although this Government was dominated by the three main nationalist parties, representatives of the PDP and the Party for Bosnia and Herzegovina were also included to ensure a legislative majority. Subsequently, the Narodna skupština Republike Srpske approved Mikerević's nomination as entity Prime Minister and the formation of a new Government, which, in accordance with recently approved constitutional amendments, comprised eight Serb, five Bosniak and three Croat representatives. Later that month the Predstavnički dom Federacije elected Niko Lozančić, a Croat, to the presidency and a Bosniak and a Serb to the office of joint Vice-President. The appointment of a new federation Government, led by Ahmet Hadžipašić, was approved in February.

On 27 February 2003 the ICTY sentenced Plavšić to 11 years' imprisonment on the charge of crimes against humanity. On 2 April Šarović resigned as the Serb member of the state presidency, after being implicated in illicit exports to Iraq and alleged espionage activities by the Republika Srpska military. Ashdown announced the abolition of the Republika Srpska Supreme Military Council; command of the armed forces was transferred provisionally to the entity's President. Ashdown also removed all references of statehood from the Constitution of Republika Srpska. On 10 April the Predstavnički dom confirmed the nomination of Borislav Paravać, also of the SDP, to replace Šarović.

In July 2003 Željko Mejakić, the Bosnian Serb commander of the Omarska detention camp (who had originally been indicted in 1995), was transferred to the ICTY, having surrendered to the authorities in Serbia. At the end of July a former mayor of Prijedor, Dr Milomir Stakić, was sentenced to life imprisonment by the ICTY for his involvement in the campaign of 'ethnic cleansing' of non-Serbs from the region (involving the killing of 1,500 people and deportation of a further 20,000) in 1992–95. In October the international community pledged to finance the establishment of a new war crimes court in Sarajevo, which would assume competence for a number of less important trials pending at the ICTY. During a state visit to Sarajevo in November 2003 Svetozar Marović, the President of Serbia and Montenegro (as Yugoslavia had been renamed in February), issued a formal apology for the atrocities committed against Bosnian civilians during the conflict. In December a Bosnian Serb former army commander, Momir Nikolić, was sentenced at the ICTY to 27 years' imprisonment for his involvement in the Srebrenica massacre. Also in December Gen. Stanislav Galić, the Bosnian Serb commanding officer in 1992–94, was sentenced to 20 years' imprisonment on charges related to the siege of Sarajevo.

Bosnian Serb authorities issue apology for Srebrenica massacre

In January 2004 Ashdown issued a decree providing for the reunification of Mostar (divided between six Croat- and Bosniak-controlled municipalities since 1993) into a single administration, thereby fulfilling one of the preconditions for signature of a Stabilization and Association Agreement (SAA) with the EU. In February 2004 Ashdown announced the dismissals of three security officials of Republika Srpska and the removal of Mirko Šarović from the presidium of the SDP, owing to suspicions of their complicity in attempts to prevent Karadžić's capture. The SDP refused to approve Šarović's dismissal, and the party's leader, Dragan Kalinić, subsequently resigned in protest at Ashdown's decision. In mid-March the Predstavnički dom approved the nomination of Nikola Radovanović of the SDP as the first state Minister of Defence (following the rejection, at the insistence of Ashdown, of two extreme nationalist candidates). At the end of the month the state Constitutional Court ruled that the renaming since 1992 of some 13 municipalities in Republika Srpska with variants of the prefix 'Srpski' (Serb) was unconstitutional; the entity authorities subsequently agreed to rename these districts. In April 2004 Ashdown dismissed the Republika Srpska army Chief of Staff, who had failed to provide information required by a commission investigating the Srebrenica massacre. In June Ashdown dismissed 60 Republika Srpska officials, including the Minister of the Interior, who were reportedly implicated in the continued failure of the authorities to locate and apprehend Karadžić. In September the ICTY sentenced Radislav Brđanin, the self-styled Deputy Prime Minister of Republika Srpska in 1992, to 32 years' imprisonment for involvement in crimes committed against Croats and Muslims in the Krajina region, although he was acquitted of the charge of genocide. In municipal elections, held in October 2004, the PDA received the highest level of support in the Federation, while in Republika Srpska the SDP lost support to the AISD. In mid-October the commission established by the Republika Srpska authorities to investigate the Srebrenica massacre submitted a final report acknowledging that Bosnian Serb forces had, on that occasion, killed an estimated 7,800 Muslim males. In November the Republika Srpska Government issued an official apology for the Srebrenica massacre.

On 22 November 2004 the UN Security Council approved a resolution authorizing the establishment of a new peace-keeping contingent under the command of the EU, and in December SFOR officially transferred authority to the new, 7,000-member EU Force (EUFOR). In December NATO rejected for the second time Bosnia and Herzegovina's application to join the 'Partnership for Peace' (PfP) programme. Ashdown responded by announcing the acceleration of military reforms: the entity Ministries of Defence were to be abolished by 2005, while a single police force under the state Minister of Security was to replace the three existing police and security agencies. In addition, Ashdown removed nine Republika Srpska security officials accused of complicity in the evasion from arrest of war crime suspects, and the USA imposed travel restrictions on the leadership of the PDP and the SDP. On 17 December Mikerević resigned as Prime Minister of Republika Srpska in protest at the dismissals. Ivanić tendered his resignation from his post in the state Government as Minister of Foreign Affairs, although neither his resignation, nor those that had been threatened by other members of the state Government, were accepted. On 8 January 2005 Cavić nominated Pero Bukejlović of the SDP as Prime Minister of Republika Srpska.

In February 2005 the Narodna skupština Republike Srpske approved the SDP-dominated entity Government nominated by Bukejlović. Ivanić announced that the PDP was to remain in the state-level administration, and in March his threat of resignation and those of the other ministers were formally withdrawn. Later that month the Croat member of the state Presidency, Dragan Čović, was charged with corruption during his former tenure as federation Minister of Finance; he was removed from office by Ashdown in March. In May Ivo Miro Jović became the new Croat member of the state presidency.

The new War Crimes Chamber of the Court of Bosnia and Herzegovina commenced operations in March 2005. In June the Republika Srpska army Chief of General Staff was dismissed at the request of NATO and EUFOR commanders, following incidents during military induction ceremonies, in which new Republika Srpska army recruits had refused to pledge allegiance to Bosnia and Herzegovina. In July a special defence reform commission endorsed legislation providing for the establishment of a joint multi-ethnic army with a unified command structure by 2007; the entity Ministries of Defence and system of military conscription were to be abolished. In August 2005 the Narodna skupština Republike Srpske approved the transfer of entity defence powers to the state Government, with effect from January 2006. In October the Narodna skupština finally approved the proposals for police reform, which were subsequently adopted by the Parlamentarna skupština Bosne i Hercegovine.

On 19 October 2005 the European Commissioner responsible for Enlargement, Olli Rehn, recommended that the Government of Bosnia and Herzegovina be invited to begin discussions on the signature of an SAA with the EU; these officially opened in November (with progress remaining conditional on implementation of the police and other reforms). Meanwhile, in October the former Chairman of the CDU—BH and a former member of the Presidency, Ante Jelavić, was sentenced to 10 years' imprisonment for the embezzlement of public funds in 1997, while serving as Minister of Defence in the federation Government. (In August 2006 his conviction was overturned on a legal technicality, and he evaded a further trial by fleeing to Croatia.) The federation and Republika Srpska Ministries of Defence and armed forces were officially dissolved on 1 January 2006, when authority over the military was transferred to the central state authorities.

On 26 January 2006, after Ivanić announced the withdrawal of the PDP's support for the Republika Srpska Government in the Narodna skupština Republike Srpske, a motion of no confidence, initiated by the AISD, was approved by 44 deputies in the 83-member chamber. On 31 January a German politician and former government minister, Dr Christian Schwarz-Schilling, succeeded Ashdown as High Representative; Schwarz-Schilling announced his intention of pursuing a less interventionist approach than his predecessor. On 4 February Čavić nominated Dodik as the new Prime Minister of Republika Srpska; Dodik subsequently formed a new administration, which was approved by the Narodna skupština on 28 February. In March, following the convening of US-supported discussions in Sarajevo in January, the principal parties reached agreement on a number of draft constitutional reforms, which included replacement of the tripartite Presidency with a single rotating president and two vice-presidents, to be elected by the legislature. However, on 26 April the Parlamentarna skupština narrowly failed to approve the reforms by the requisite majority of two-thirds of deputies, after four dissenting CDU—BH representatives formed a breakaway party, the Croatian Democratic Union 1990 of Bosnia and Herzegovina (CDU 1990).

Proposals for the closure of the Office of the High Representative

In June 2006 Schwarz-Schilling announced plans for the closure of the Office of the High Representative at the end of June 2007, although the position of EU Special Representative (to which Schwarz-Schilling also had been appointed simultaneously) was to continue. The elections at national, entity and cantonal level, held on 1 October 2006, were pronounced by the OSCE to have been conducted satisfactorily. In the ballot for the Bosniak member of the tripartite presidency, Silajdžić was elected by 62.8% of the votes cast, defeating the incumbent Bosniak representative, Tihić. Nebojša Radmanović, a member of the AISD, secured the post of Serb member of the Presidency, with 53.3%, while the SDP candidate took only 24.2% of votes. The successful Croat candidate, Željko Komšić, won 39.6% of the votes cast, defeating the incumbent Croat member of the presidency, Jović, who received 26.1%. In the election to the 42-member Predstavnički dom, the PDA secured nine seats, while the Party for Bosnia and Herzegovina increased its representation to eight seats, the AISD obtained seven seats, and the SDP BiH five seats. The PDA also remained the leading party in the Predstavnički dom Federacije, with 28 seats; the Party for Bosnia and Herzegovina won 24 seats, and the SDP BiH 17 seats. The AISD achieved the largest representation in the Narodna skupština Republike Srpske, with 41 seats, two fewer than required for an absolute majority, while the SDP won only 17 seats. Milan Jelić of the AISD was elected to the Republika Srpska presidency with 48.8% of the votes cast, defeating Čavić.

In October 2006 Krajišnik was convicted at the ICTY on five charges of crimes against humanity and sentenced to 27 years' imprisonment; however, he was acquitted of genocide and complicity in genocide. (In March 2009 his sentence was reduced on appeal to a term of 20 years; in September he was transferred to a prison in the United Kingdom, and in February 2010 it was announced that he was entitled to apply for early release under British law.) The three members of the collective presidency were inaugurated on 6 November 2006. The new Narodna skupština Republike Srpske was installed on 9 November, and Jelić was inaugurated on the same day. In mid-November Jelić nominated Dodik as Prime Minister of Republika Srpska. Dodik renewed the ruling coalition of the AISD with the PDP and PDA, and a new Government was approved by the Narodna skupština on 30 November.

Following a summit meeting on 14 December Bosnia and Herzegovina, together with Montenegro and Serbia, was admitted to the NATO PfP programme. The ICTY Prosecutor, Carla Del Ponte, criticized NATO's decision and declared that the co-operation of Bosnia and Herzegovina, in particular of the Republika Srpska authorities, with the Tribunal continued to be unsatisfactory. In December the EU announced a staged reduction in EUFOR troops, from 6,000 to 2,500.

On 3 January 2007 agreement was reached on the appointment of Nikola Špirić of the AISD as Chairman of the state Council of Ministers, and his Government was approved by the Predstavnički dom on 9 February. At the end of January the Constitutional Court of Bosnia and Herzegovina abolished the coats of arms and flags of both Republika Srpska and the Federation, and the anthem of Republika Srpska, after both entity Governments failed to comply with a previous court ruling that the symbols should represent equally the three constituent ethnic groups. On 28 February 2007 the PIC announced that the operations of the Office of the High Representative, which had been expected to end in June, were to be extended for a further year, although Schwarz-Schilling was to leave the post as scheduled. A new five-party coalition federation Government, headed by Nedžad Branković of the PDA (hitherto the Minister of Transport and Communications), was approved in the Predstavnički dom Federacije on 30 March.

In May 2007 a Serb war criminal, Radovan Stanković, who had been sentenced to 20 years' imprisonment by the Court of Bosnia and Herzegovina after being transferred from the ICTY, escaped from custody near Foča. In the same month a former Bosnian Serb army officer, Zdravko Tolimir, believed to be a close associate of Mladić and to be assisting his evasion of capture, was arrested in Republika Srpska, and extradited to the ICTY. (Tolimir's trial began in February 2010.) On 1 July 2007 a Slovakian diplomat, Miroslav Lajčák, officially succeeded Schwarz-Schilling as High Representative. In the same month the state and entity Governments signed an accord on public administration reform, which was required for the disbursement of EU funds and was also a precondition for the signature of an

SAA. In August Lajčák insisted that agreement be reached on the police reforms by the end of September in order to allow the completion of negotiations on the SAA in 2007. A new police reform plan, agreed between Silajdžić and Dodik shortly before the stipulated date, was rejected by Lajčák as being insufficient to meet the main conditions stipulated by the EU.

In October 2007 Lajčák announced a number of measures for reforming parliamentary and government decision-making procedures, including new regulations to prevent representatives of one ethnic group from obstructing the adoption of legislation. On 1 November Špirić resigned from the state premiership in protest at Lajčák's decision, after the PIC expressed support for the reforms. At the end of November Bosnian Serb leaders (who had initially threatened to boycott institutions) ended resistance to the proposed legislation. Following an agreement by the political leaders to proceed with police reforms in accordance with the EU criteria, the SAA was initialled on 4 December, with its signature remaining dependent on the implementation of the reforms.

On 9 December 2007 an election to the Republika Srpska presidency was conducted, following the death of Jelić at the end of September; Rajko Kuzmanović of the AISD secured 41.3% of the votes cast, defeating nine candidates, including Ognjen Tadić of the SDP (with 34.8%). At his presidential inauguration on 28 December, Kuzmanović stated his opposition to any further transfer of powers to central government from the entities. On the same day Špirić was reappointed to the state premiership. On 20 February 2008 the Predstavnički dom approved the unchanged Council of Ministers reappointed by Špirić. A further police reform plan, proposed by Lajčák, was approved by the Predstavnički dom on 10 April and by the Dom Naroda on 16 April; the compromise agreement abandoned the stipulation for the creation of a single police force, and provided for the establishment of seven state-level co-ordination bodies, with authority over the entity police forces. EU officials welcomed the measure as fulfilment of the final requirement for signature of the SAA.

On 8 May 2008 the Central Election Commission announced that elections to municipal councils and mayoralties nationwide, and to the Assemblies of Brčko and Banja Luka, and the City Council of Mostar were to take place on 5 October. On 16 June Bosnia and Herzegovina officially signed the SAA with the EU. Following a meeting in Sarajevo in late June, PIC officials announced that the mandate of the Office of the High Representative would continue until the Government completely fulfilled a number of stipulated objectives and conditions.

The arrest of Radovan Karadžić

In June 2008 a former Bosnian Serb police commander and close aide to Karadžić and Mladić, Stojan Zupljanin, was arrested in Serbia; he was subsequently transferred to the ICTY on 12 charges relating to crimes committed against Croats and Muslims in the Bosnian Krajina region. (The trial of Zupljanin and his associate, Mićo Stanišić, who had surrendered to the authorities in March 2005, began in September 2009.) On 21 July 2008 the office of Serbian President Boris Tadić unexpectedly announced that Karadžić had been arrested in an operation by Serbian security officers; it was subsequently revealed that he had been a long-term resident of Belgrade. Karadžić was transferred to the War Crimes Panel of the Belgrade District Court and was extradited to the ICTY on 30 July. Appearing before the Tribunal on the following day, he refused to recognize its jurisdiction, and alleged that, under a private agreement reached with Richard Holbrooke in 1996, he had been guaranteed immunity from prosecution if he left politics. (Holbrooke had strenuously denied such claims.) (In February 2009 the ICTY approved an amended indictment of 11 charges against Karadžić, including two counts of genocide, of which one related to war crimes in 1992 and one to the massacre of Srebrenica. In March a plea of not guilty was entered on his behalf.)

The overall voter turn-out in local elections, which were conducted on 5 October 2008, was recorded at 55%, with lower levels in principal towns. Council of Europe observers concluded that the elections had been organized in accordance with international standards, but criticized the level of nationalist campaigning and lack of public debate on local issues preceding the poll. The AISD again performed strongly in Republika Srpska, securing 39 mayoralties overall, including that of Banja Luka, while the PDA received 36 mayoralties, gaining support from the CDU—BH, which obtained 16 mayoralties. (In February 2009 the Brčko Assembly finally elected Dragan Pajić of the AISD as the new mayor.)

On 23 January 2009 Lajčák announced his resignation from the Office of the High Representative to assume the post of Slovakian Minister of Foreign Affairs, at the invitation of the Slovakian Prime Minister. The Austrian ambassador to Slovenia, Valentin Inzko, was proposed as his successor. Later in January Dodik, Tihić and Čović, who had resumed constitutional discussions at the end of 2008, issued a statement on an agreement envisaging the redivision of the country into four regions and three administrative levels. In February 2009, however, Dodik withdrew from the discussions, after Tihić and Čović rejected his demand that the right of Bosnian Serbs to secession following a referendum be recognized in a new constitution. (Discussions between Bosnian political leaders and international community officials continued from October without agreement.)

On 11 March 2009 EU member states approved the appointment of Inzko as EU Special Representative for the period of one year; he officially assumed the post of High Representative on 26 March. On the same day, following an agreement between the main ethnic party leaders in January, the state legislature adopted a constitutional amendment officially incorporating Brčko's status as a neutral self-governing district into the Constitution. On 27 May Branković resigned from the post of federation Prime Minister, following charges against him and former premier Edhem Bičakčić of misappropriating entity funds to obtain real estate. Mustafa Mujezinović of the PDA was approved as the new federation Prime Minister on 25 June.

In July 2009 a Serb paramilitary leader, Milan Lukić (who had been extradited from Argentina in February 2006), received a term of life imprisonment at the ICTY for war crimes committed in Višegrad in 1992–94, while his cousin Sredoje was sentenced to 30 years' imprisonment. In September it was announced that Plavšić (who had been transferred to a Swedish prison after her sentence) was to be granted early release under Swedish law; associations representing Bosnian war victims expressed outrage at the decision, which had been approved by the ICTY. She was released on 27 October. Karadžić's trial officially began in late October; however, he refused to appear at the opening session, claiming that he had been allowed insufficient time to prepare his defence.

In June 2009, meanwhile, a resolution adopted by the Narodna skupština Republike Srpske, obligating the entity's institutions and officials to oppose any future transfer of powers to the central state, was repealed by Inzko on the grounds that it was in violation of the Constitution. In November the PIC concluded that the conditions required for the closure of the Office of the High Representative of the International Community had not yet been met, and stated that the eventual closure of that office might necessitate a concomitant strengthening in the powers of the EU Special Representative. On 18 December Mostar City Council, which had proved unable to form a coalition administration following the municipal elections of October 2008, finally elected Ljubo Bešlić of the CDU—BH as mayor, after Inzko ordered that the voting be conducted by a simple majority rather than a two-thirds majority. Also in December 2009 Inzko extended the mandate of international judges and prosecutors working in the Court of Bosnia and Herzegovina, thereby overruling a vote in the state legislature in October. Dodik condemned his decision, and later that month it was rejected as unconstitutional by the Narodna skupština Republike Srpske, which demanded that a referendum be conducted on the issue in Republika Srpska. Later that month the European Court of Human Rights (ECHR) ruled that the state Constitution discriminated against members of minority ethnic groups, upholding a complaint by two Bosnians of Roma and Jewish origin, respectively, on the grounds that only Serbs, Croats and Bosniaks were entitled to contest elections to the state presidency and upper legislative chamber. On 10 February 2010 the Predstavnički dom voted in favour of amending the Constitution and electoral code in accordance with the Court's ruling. On the same day legislation allowing Republika Srpska wide-ranging powers on the organization of referendums was adopted by the Narodna skupština, despite protests by the international community. When the legislation was referred to the Vijeće naroda for approval on 23 February, however, the Bosniak members of the council voted to oppose the legislation. Meanwhile, on 22 February, EU foreign ministers voted to extend Inzko's mandate as EU Special Representative for a further six months. On 21 April the Constitutional Court of Republika Srpska ruled that the legislation on referendums approved by the Narodna skupština was valid and legitimate, rejecting the motion of the Bosniak members of the Vijeće naroda.

In May 2010 the appellate chamber of the Court of Bosnia and Herzegovina acquitted a Bosnian Serb former commander of the special police, Miloš Stupar, of charges relating to the 1995 Srebrenica massacre, thereby reversing his conviction in July 2008 (when he had been sentenced to 40 years' imprisonment). In June 2010 two Bosnian Serb former senior security officers were convicted by the ICTY on charges of genocide and other war crimes at Srebrenica and both sentenced to life imprisonment, while a further five military and police officers received lesser terms. In August Inzko's mandate as EU Special Representative was extended for a further year. In November the Roma complainant to the ECHR announced that he would submit a further case for compensation at the Court following the failure of Bosnia and Herzegovina to implement the December 2009 ruling.

The 2010 elections

Elections to the state presidency, the presidency of Republika Srpska, the state and entity legislatures, and to the federation cantonal assemblies were conducted on 3 October 2010. Clashes between Croat and Bosniak youths in Mostar were reported. In the election to the state presidency, Bakir Izetbegović of the PDA was elected as the Bosniak member, with 34.9% of votes cast, defeating Fahrudin Radončić of the newly established Union for a Better Future of Bosnia and Herzegovina (30.5% of votes) and the incumbent Silajdžić of the Party for Bosnia and Herzegovina (25.1%); Komšić of the SDP BiH was re-elected as the Croat member, with 60.6% of votes cast; and Radmanović of the AISD was re-elected as the Serb member, with 48.9% of votes, narrowly defeating Ivanić of the PDP. Silajdžić's replacement by Bakir Izetbegović (the son of Alija Izetbegović), who was regarded as a moderate, was welcomed by international observers. Dodik was elected as President of Republika Srpska, with 50.5% of votes cast; Emil Vlajki of the (predominately Serb) PDP and Enes Suljkanović of the SDP BiH were elected as the entity's Croat and Bosniak Vice-Presidents, respectively. In the elections to the Predstavnički dom, the SDP BiH and the AISD won eight seats each, while the PDA received seven seats. The SDP BiH significantly increased its representation in the Predstavnički dom Federacije, to 28 seats, replacing the PDA (which took 23 seats) as the leading party in the chamber. The AISD remained the dominant party in the Narodna skupština Republike Srpske, with a slightly reduced representation of 37 seats, while the SDP received 18 seats. In the elections of the Federations's 10 cantons, the SDP BiH won 61 and the PDA 55 seats of the contested 289 seats in the cantonal assemblies.

The three members of the collective state presidency were sworn in on 10 November 2010. On 15 November, after the new Narodna skupština Republike Srpske was convened, Dodik was inaugurated as President of Republika Srpska; he declared that the entity would accept no further legislation or resolutions imposed by the High Representative and stated that he sought the eventual independence from Bosnia and Herzegovina of Republika Srpska. On 24 November Dodik nominated Aleksandar Džombić, hitherto the Republika Srpska Minister of Finance, to succeed him as the entity's Prime Minister. On 29 December the Narodna skupština approved a new Government, headed by Džombić and principally comprising representatives of the AISD. However, in January 2011 the Bosniak members of the Vijeće naroda opposed the appointment of the new Government, claiming that for none of the entity's six main institutions to be headed by a Bosniak breached the constitutional right of constituent peoples to equal representation. In the same month, pending a decision by the Bosnian Constitutional Court, Inzko suspended legislation, adopted by the Narodna skupština in the previous September, which stipulated that Republika Srpska would manage all forms of property within its territory. Local elections took place in eight municipalities on 16 January. At the end of that month the Republika Srpska Constitutional Court ruled against the challenge of the Bosniak members of the Vijeće naroda, allowing the installation of Džombić's administration to proceed. Meanwhile, the 12 parties represented in the Predstavnički dom had failed to reach agreement on the formation of a state-level coalition government, with the SDP BiH and the AISD (which had formed a parliamentary alliance with the SDP) remaining in conflict over the appointment of a new prime minister. In the Federation, on 17 March the Dom Naroda Federacije (Federation House of Peoples—upper chamber of the federation legislature) elected Živko Budimir of the extreme nationalist Croatian Party of Rights of Bosnia and Herzegovina as federation President and endorsed a new entity Government, largely comprising members of the SDP BiH and the PDA, and under the premiership of SDP BiH Secretary-General, Nermin Nikšić. Following their boycott of the entity's new legislature, the two main Croat parties, the CDU—BH and CDU 1990, denounced the election as illegitimate, on the grounds that three Croat-dominated cantons had failed to nominate their delegates to the Dom Naroda Federacije. On 24 March the Central Election Commission, upholding a complaint by outgoing federation President Borjana Krišto of the CDU—BH, annulled the election of Budimir; however, Inzko subsequently reversed the decision of the Commission.

On 13 April 2011, following an initiative by Dodik, the Narodna skupština Republike Srpske voted in support of a referendum being conducted in the entity on legislation imposed by the High Representative that the AISD considered to be biased against Serbs, notably concerning the Court of Bosnia and Herzegovina and Prosecutor's Office. Inzko warned that he would prohibit the planned referendum, which was also strongly opposed by the US Administration and the EU. On 13 May Dodik announced that the planned referendum in Republika Srpska had been postponed, following a meeting in Banja Luka that day with the EU High Representative for Foreign Affairs and Security Policy, Catherine Ashton, who had issued pledges that the EU would establish a commission to consider judicial reform in Bosnia and Herzegovina. On 2 June the Narodna skupština approved Dodik's proposal to cancel the referendum. Meanwhile, on 26 May Serbian security forces arrested Mladić in a village in northern Serbia; he was extradited to the ICTY five days later (after his claim that he was medically unfit was rejected by the authorities), and his trial commenced on 3 June.

Recent developments: delayed appointment of the state government

At the beginning of July 2011 the Chief Prosecutor, Milorad Barašin, was suspended from office by the High Judicial and Prosecutorial Council, pending an investigation into his alleged connections with arms traffickers. In early July an appeals court in The Hague ruled that the Dutch state was responsible for the deaths of three Bosnian Muslims, who had been ceded to Bosnian Serb forces by Dutch members of the peace-keeping force prior to the massacre at Srebrenica in 1995; the Dutch Government was ordered to pay compensation to the relatives of the three men. After the failure in June 2011 of a candidate for the state premiership, Slavo Kukić of the SDP, to secure approval in the Predstavnički dom, unsuccessful discussions between the leaders of the six principal parties on the formation of a state-level Council of Ministers took place in Sarajevo and Brčko in September, with continuing disagreement between the main Croat parties and the SDP BiH over the allocation of portfolios. It was reported that federation President Budimir had additionally proposed the creation of a separate Croat entity—thereby threatening to undermine the existing Federation. In late October a Serbian national, subsequently named as Mevlid Jašarević and believed to be a member of the Wahhabi Islamic movement, staged an armed assault against the US embassy in Sarajevo, shooting and injuring a police officer, before being overpowered and arrested. In November a number of suspected associates of Jašarević were arrested, and large amounts of armaments were seized in a police operation against suspected Wahhabi members in the north-eastern village of Gornja Maoča. On 28 December, following several further meetings, it was announced that the six main political party leaders had finally agreed on the formation of a new state Council of Ministers, having reached a compromise arrangement whereby the new administration would be chaired by a Croat representative, and comprise a further two Croats, four Bosniaks and three Serbs. On 12 January 2012 the nomination by the collective Presidency of an economist and former federation Vice-President, Vjekoslav Bevanda of the CDU—BH, as the new Chairman was approved in the Predstavnički dom. On 1 February the AISD and SDP proposed a motion at the Republika Srpska legislature for the abolition of the Court of Bosnia and Herzegovina and Prosecutor's Office, following the Chief Prosecutor's decision to abandon a criminal investigation against 14 former senior officials regarding a May 1992 incident, in which JNA and Serbian soldiers were killed. On 10 February a new Council of Ministers, headed by Bevanda, was finally approved in the Predstavnički dom; its members included former premiers Lagumdžija of the SDP BiH as Minister of Foreign Affairs and Spirić of the AISD as Minister of Finance and the Treasury.

Foreign Affairs

Regional relations

Bosnia and Herzegovina established diplomatic relations with the Federal Republic of Yugoslavia in December 2000, following the overthrow of the Government of Slobodan Milošević. On 27 February 2006 a case submitted to the International Court of Justice (ICJ, see p. 25) at The Hague, Netherlands, in 1993 by Bosnia and Herzegovina against Yugoslavia (represented by Serbia, as its successor state), claiming reparations for acts of genocide perpetrated against the Bosniak population in 1992–95, finally commenced. On 26 February 2007 the ICJ ruled that the Serbian state was not directly responsible for genocide or complicity in genocide in Bosnia and Herzegovina in 1992–95. However, the Court declared that Serbia was in violation of its obligation under international law by having failed to prevent the 1995 massacre in Srebrenica and to co-operate fully with the ICTY. In May 2007 the newly appointed Serbian Minister of Foreign Affairs, Vuk Jeremić, met his Bosnian counterpart for discussions in Sarajevo, in an initiative to improve bilateral relations. In February 2010 it was announced that Serbia had accepted the appointment of a new Bosnian ambassador (the post having remained vacant since 2007). In March 2010 Ejup Ganić, the former President of the Federation of Bosnia and Herzegovina, was arrested at an airport in London in response to a request for extradition issued by Serbia on war crimes charges relating to an attack on a Yugoslav army convoy near Sarajevo in May 1992. (In July 2010 a court in London rejected the Serbian authorities' attempt to extradite Ganić from the United Kingdom, describing it as being politically motivated.) On 31 March the Serbian legislature narrowly adopted a resolution condemning the Srebrenica massacre of July 1995 and formally apologizing for Serbia's failure to prevent it. Following several meetings between the Bosnian and Serbian Ministers of Foreign Affairs with Turkish mediation, in April 2010 the Chairman of the Bosnian collective Presidency Silajdžić, the Serbian President, Boris Tadić, and Turkish President, Abdullah Gül, met in İstanbul, Turkey; Silajdžić and Tadić pledged to continue to improve relations between their countries and signed a declaration agreeing to resolve outstanding disputes. Meanwhile, following a 'special relations' agreement signed by Republika Srpska and Serbia in September 2006, a series of economic co-operation accords were reached by the two Governments.

In December 2000 a Free Trade Agreement was signed between Bosnia and Herzegovina and Croatia. The delineation of a small border area on the Adriatic Sea, including the status of Neum and the Croatian port of Ploče, remained under dispute with Croatia.

Following Kosovo's unilateral declaration of independence from Serbia on 17 February 2008, the Bosnian Presidency announced that it would not extend recognition to Kosovo in the near future, owing to the opposition of the Serb population. Large-scale protests against Kosovo's independence were staged in Banja Luka, and secessionist sentiments increased within Republika Srpska; on 21 February the Narodna skupština Republike Srpske adopted a resolution denouncing the declaration. After the subsequent recognition of Kosovo's independence by the USA and leading EU member states, Republika Srpska Prime Minister Dodik attended a nationalist protest rally in Belgrade and intensified demands for a referendum on the proposed secession of Republika Srpska. In early 2009 the Bosnian Government, together with Serbia, announced that it refused to recognize new passports issued by Kosovo's authorities. In July 2010 the ICJ issued a non-binding, advisory opinion that Kosovo's declaration of independence had not breached international law; the decision was denounced by the Serbian and Republika Srpska authorities.

Other external relations

Following the beginning of discussions with the European Commission on visa liberalization in May 2008, the Commission announced in November 2009 that Bosnia and Herzegovina had failed to meet the criteria for the abolishment of visa requirements for Bosnian citizens, urging further efforts to combat corruption and improve border controls. Meanwhile, during a visit to the country in May, US Vice President Joe Biden emphasized the USA's commitment towards its future, but also strongly criticized the renewal of nationalist rhetoric by some Bosnian politicians. On 22 April NATO announced the extension of a Membership Action Plan (MAP) to Bosnia and Herzegovina, although a number of questions concerning the registration of the ownership of military property remained unresolved. In November the EU officially agreed to end visa requirements for citizens of Bosnia and Herzegovina (and Albania), with effect from mid-December; it was also decided that monitoring mechanisms would be applied for the two countries to verify compliance with regulations. Nevertheless, an EU progress report on Bosnia and Herzegovina, released later that month, concluded that the authorities had demonstrated little willingness to meet obligations for EU integration. In October 2011 the European Commission issued a progress report citing the continued failure to form a state-level Council of Ministers (see above) as the principal obstacle to progress in stipulated reforms.

CONSTITUTION AND GOVERNMENT

In accordance with the General Framework Agreement for Peace in Bosnia and Herzegovina ('the Dayton accords'), signed in December 1995, Bosnia and Herzegovina is a single state, which consists of two autonomous entities: the Federation of Bosnia and Herzegovina and Republika Srpska. In March 2000, following completion of a demilitarization process, the north-eastern town of Brčko was established as a neutral district and placed under joint Serb, Croat and Bosniak authority. Its status was confirmed under a constitutional amendment adopted in March 2009. A civilian High Representative of the International Community in Bosnia and Herzegovina oversees government institutions and the implementation of the peace accords. Since 2002 the High Representative of the International Community has concurrently served as a Special Representative of the European Union. The state Government of Bosnia and Herzegovina has a three-member collective Presidency of one Bosniak, one Croat and one Serb. Members of the Presidency are directly elected for a term of four years, and are eligible to serve for only two consecutive terms. Chairmanship of the Presidency is rotated between the members every eight months. The bicameral Parlamentarna skupština Bosne i Hercegovine (Parliamentary Assembly of Bosnia and Herzegovina) comprises the Dom Naroda (House of Peoples) and the Predstavnički dom (House of Representatives). The Predstavnički dom/Zastupnički dom has 42 deputies, who serve for a four-year term, of whom 28 are directly elected from the Federation and 14 are directly elected from Republika Srpska. The Dom Naroda has 15 deputies, who serve for a four-year term, of whom 10 are selected by the federation legislature and five by the Republika Srpska legislature. The Presidency appoints a Chairman of the state Council of Ministers (subject to the approval of the Predstavnički dom/Zastupnički dom), who subsequently appoints the other ministers.

The Federation of Bosnia and Herzegovina and Republika Srpska each retain an executive presidency, government and legislature. The bicameral Parlament Federacije (Federation Parliament) has a 98-member Predstavnički dom Federacije/Zastupnički dom Federacije (Federation House of Representatives), which is directly elected for a four-year term, and a 58-member Dom Naroda Federacije (Federation House of Peoples), comprising 17 Serb, 17 Bosniak, 17 Croat and seven other deputies, who are elected by the assemblies of each of the 10 cantons within the Federation. The Parlament Federacije elects a President and two joint Vice-Presidents, comprising one Bosniak, one Croat and one Serb, for a term of four years. Each canton of the Federation has an elected assembly, President, and Government.

The legislature of Republika Srpska comprises an 83-member Narodna skupština Republike Srpske (National Assembly of Republika Srpska), which is directly elected for a four-year term. This Assembly elects 28 delegates, of whom eight are Bosniaks, eight Croats, eight Serbs, and four representatives of other ethnic groups, to a Vijeće naroda (Council of Peoples), which is responsible, *inter alia*, for electing the entity's representatives to the Dom Naroda. The President and two Vice-Presidents of Republika Srpska are directly elected, for a four-year term.

The judicial system of each entity comprises a Constitutional Court, a Supreme Court and local district courts. The Court of Bosnia and Herzegovina is the country's highest judicial organ, and includes both national and international judges.

Bosnia and Herzegovina comprises a total of 143 municipalities, of which 79 are in the Federation, 63 in Republika Srpska, and 1 in Brčko district.

REGIONAL AND INTERNATIONAL CO-OPERATION

Bosnia and Herzegovina is a member of the Organization for Security and Co-operation in Europe (OSCE, see p. 388), the Council of Europe (see p. 256) and the Central European Free Trade Agreement (CEFTA, see p. 448). In 2006 the North Atlantic Treaty Organization (NATO, see p. 370) invited Bosnia and Herzegovina to join its 'Partnership for Peace' programme. In 2008 Bosnia and Herzegovina, together with Montenegro, joined the Adriatic Charter, a US-supported initiative that had been established by Albania, Croatia and the former Yugoslav republic of Macedonia in 2003 for accelerated military reform and regional security co-operation in the process of integration into NATO. Bosnia and Herzegovina signed a Stabilization and Association Agreement with the European Union (EU, see p. 276) in June 2008.

Bosnia and Herzegovina was admitted to the UN in 1992. The country became a non-permanent member of the UN Security Council in January 2010.

ECONOMIC AFFAIRS

In 2010, according to World Bank estimates, Bosnia and Herzegovina's gross national income (GNI), measured at average 2008–10 prices, was US $18,015m., equivalent to $4,790 per head (or $8,970 per head on an international purchasing-power parity basis). During 2001–10, it was estimated, the population of Bosnia and Herzegovina remained constant, while gross domestic product (GDP) per head increased, in real terms, by an average annual rate of 4.0%. According to World Bank estimates, overall GDP increased, in real terms, at an average annual rate of 4.0% in 2001–10; real GDP declined in 2010 by 3.1%, but increased by 0.8% in 2010.

Agriculture (including forestry and fishing) contributed 8.4% of GDP in 2010, according to preliminary figures, and 21.2% of the employed labour force was engaged in the sector in May 2009. The major agricultural products are tobacco and fruit, and the livestock sector is also significant. Foodstuffs and live animals comprised 18.4% of total imports in 2010. According to World Bank estimates, the GDP of the agricultural sector increased, in real terms, at an average annual rate of 3.6% in 2001–10. The sector's GDP declined by 0.8% in 2009, but grew by 0.5% in 2010.

Industry (mining, manufacturing, utilities and construction) contributed 26.1% of GDP in 2010, according to preliminary figures. Some 31.4% of the employed labour force was engaged in the industrial sector in May 2009. According to World Bank estimates, industrial GDP increased, in real terms, at an average annual rate of 5.2% in 2001–10. Industrial GDP declined in 2009 by 5.6%, but increased by 0.5% in 2010.

The mining and quarrying sector contributed 2.4% of GDP in 2010, according to preliminary figures, and the sector engaged 3.3% of the employed population in March 2003. The sector's GDP increased, in real terms, by 7.0% in 2010, according to preliminary official estimates. Bosnia and Herzegovina possesses extensive mineral resources, including iron ore, lignite, copper, lead, zinc and gold.

According to preliminary figures, manufacturing contributed 13.2% of GDP in 2010, and the sector engaged 23.9% of the employed population in March 2003. The manufacturing sector is based largely on the processing of iron ore, non-ferrous metals, coal, and wood and paper products. Manufacturing GDP increased, according to World Bank estimates, in real terms, at an average annual rate of 5.7% in 2001–10. Manufacturing GDP declined by 6.9% in 2009, but increased by 0.5% in 2010.

The construction sector contributed 5.2% of GDP in 2010, according to preliminary figures, and 5.5% of the employed population were engaged in the sector in March 2003. The sector's GDP decreased by an estimated 9.7% in 2010, according to preliminary official figures.

The civil conflict resulted in the destruction of much of the electric power system in Bosnia and Herzegovina. In 2008 some 64.4% of electricity production was derived from coal and 34.3% from hydroelectric power. Mineral fuels accounted for 0.2% of total imports in 2010.

The services sector contributed 65.5% of GDP in 2010, according to preliminary official estimates, and the sector engaged some 47.3% of the employed labour force in May 2009. According to World Bank estimates, the GDP of the services sector increased, in real terms, at an average annual rate of 3.1% in 2001–10. The GDP of the services sector declined by 4.3% in 2010.

In 2010 Bosnia and Herzegovina recorded a visible trade deficit of US $4,293.2m., and there was a deficit of $1,008.5m. on the current account of the balance of payments. In 2010 the principal source of imports was Croatia (which accounted for 15.1% of total imports); other important suppliers were Serbia and Montenegro, Germany, Italy and Slovenia. In that year the main market for exports was Germany (which accounted for 15.3% of the total); other significant purchasers were Croatia, Serbia and Montenegro, Italy, Slovenia and Austria. The principal imports in 2010 were basic manufactures (accounting for 29.3% of the total), mineral fuels and lubricants, machinery and transport equipment and food and live animals. The principal exports in 2010 were basic manufactures (accounting for 46.0% of total exports), mineral fuels and lubricants, machinery and transport equipment, miscellaneous manufactured articles and food and live animals.

Bosnia and Herzegovina's overall budget surplus for 2010 was KM 634.2m. Bosnia and Herzegovina's general government gross debt was KM 9,685m. in 2010, equivalent to 39.7% of GDP. The country's total external debt was estimated at US $9,583m. in 2009, of which $3,569m. was public and publicly guaranteed debt. In that year, the cost of debt-servicing was equivalent to about 2.8% of the value of exports of goods and services. Consumer prices decreased by 3.1% in 2010. The rate of unemployment was some 27.6% in November 2011.

During 2002 the High Representative imposed a series of economic regulations, with the ultimate aim of unifying the telecommunications, banking, and tax and customs administrations throughout the country, as a prerequisite for eventual membership of the European Union—EU (see p. 276). In 2006 a single-rate value-added tax came into effect. A Stabilization and Association Agreement (SAA), signed with the EU in June 2008, was expected to bring significant benefits to domestic business conditions. However, in January 2009 EU officials warned the Bosnian authorities of an absence in progress in implementing reforms required under the SAA. Meanwhile, the impact of the international financial crisis on the country's fiscal balance became apparent from late 2008. In July 2009 the IMF approved a stand-by credit arrangement, totalling US $1,570m., in order to strengthen the country's financial sector. However, in May 2010 the IMF delayed the extension of a disbursement under the credit arrangement, after the Federation failed to implement numerous austerity measures, as a result of trade union and popular pressure; the entity's parliament finally approved the required legislation in July and the IMF approved a further disbursement in October. Despite the official approval of visa liberalization for Bosnia and Herzegovina in November, the EU concluded in that month that little progress had been made by the authorities towards meeting the criteria for EU integration, particularly in the area of constitutional reform. Following state and entity elections in October 2010, the continued failure to establish a state-level government deterred foreign investment and was cited by the European Commission in October 2011 as the principal obstacle to progress in reforms. In November the European Commission announced that it was to grant pre-accession funds of some €200m. during 2012–13 to support government reform efforts. A new state Council of Ministers was finally formed in February 2012. The IMF considered, meanwhile, that the country's economic recovery, which had begun in mid-2010, was being weakened by the negative effects of the ongoing debt crisis in the euro area, projecting real GDP growth at 1.7% for 2011 and 0.7% for 2012.

PUBLIC HOLIDAYS

2013: 1 January (New Year), 6–7 January (Serbian Orthodox Christmas), 1 March (Independence Day), 29 March–1 April (Catholic Easter), 1–2 May (Labour Day), 3–6 May (Orthodox Easter), 9 May (Victory Day), 7 August* (Ramadan Bayram, end of Ramadan), 14 October* (Kurban Bayram, Feast of the Sacrifice), 1 November (Catholic All Saints' Day), 21 November (General Framework Agreement Day), 25 November (National Statehood Day), 25 December (Catholic Christmas).

*These holidays are dependent on the Islamic lunar calendar and may vary by one or two days from the dates given.

Statistical Survey

Source (unless otherwise stated): Agencija za statistiku Bosne i Hercegovine, 71000 Sarajevo, trg Bosne i Hercegovine 1; tel. and fax (33) 2206222; e-mail bhas@bih.net.ba; internet www.bhas.ba.

Area and Population

AREA, POPULATION AND DENSITY

Area (sq km)	
Land	51,197
Inland water	12
Total	51,209*
Population (census results)	
31 March 1981	4,124,008
31 March 1991	
Males	2,183,795
Females	2,193,238
Total	4,377,033
Population (estimates at mid-year)†	
2009	3,842,566
2010	3,843,126
2011	3,839,737
Density (per sq km) at mid-2011	75.0

* 19,772 sq miles.

† Including estimates for Republika Srpska and Brčko District.

2010 (Republika Srpska only, official estimate at 31 December): 1,433,038.

2010 (Brčko District only, estimate at 31 December): 75,674.

Mid-2011 (Federation only, official estimate): 2,338,270.

POPULATION BY AGE AND SEX

(household budget survey, 2007)

	Males	Females	Total
0–17	383,839	361,664	745,503
18–64	1,076,349	1,105,045	2,181,394
65 and over	224,061	296,199	520,260
Total	1,684,249	1,762,908	3,447,157
Federation of Bosnia and Herzegovina	1,079,998	1,133,785	2,213,783
0–17	261,306	247,762	509,068
18–64	692,567	718,480	1,411,047
65 and over	126,125	167,543	293,668
Republika Srpska	571,049	595,124	1,166,173
0–17	115,719	106,828	222,547
18–64	362,412	366,017	728,429
65 and over	92,918	122,279	215,197
Brčko District	33,202	33,999	67,201
0–17	6,814	7,074	13,888
18–64	21,370	20,548	41,918
65 and over	5,018	6,377	11,395

POPULATION BY ETHNIC GROUP

(according to official declaration of nationality, 1991 census, provisional)

	Number	% of total population
Muslim	1,905,829	43.7
Serb	1,369,258	31.4
Croat	755,892	17.3
Yugoslav	239,845	5.5
Others	93,750	2.1
Total	4,364,574	100.0

CANTONS WITHIN THE FEDERATION

(official estimates at mid-2011)

Canton	Population	Principal city (with population)
Bosna-Podrinje	32,818	Goražde (30,017)
Central Bosnia	254,003	Travnik (54,771)
Herzegovina-Neretva	224,902	Mostar (111,602)
Posavina	39,585	Orašje (19,468)
Sarajevo	438,757	Sarajevo (311,161)
Tuzla	499,221	Tuzla (131,768)
Una-Sana	287,835	Bihać (61,491)
West Herzegovina	81,414	Široki Brijeg (26,304)
Zenica-Doboj	399,856	Zenica (127,202)
'Canton 10'*	79,879	Livno (31,785)
Total	2,338,270	

* Formerly known as Herceg-Bosna Canton.

Source: Federation of Bosnia and Herzegovina Office of Statistics.

PRINCIPAL TOWNS

(population estimates)

Sarajevo (capital)	311,161*	Cazin	62,632*
Banja Luka	224,647†	Bihać	61,491*
Tuzla	131,768*	Gradišca	61,440†
Zenica	127,202*	Živinice	55,507*
Mostar	111,602*	Travnik	54,771*
Bijeljina	109,211†	Gračanica	52,319*
Prijedor	98,570†	Zvornik	51,688†
Doboj	80,464†	Lukavac	50,845*

* Estimate for mid-2011 (Source: Federation of Bosnia and Herzegovina Office of Statistics). The figure for Sarajevo excludes those areas of the city ('East Sarajevo') located in Republika Srpska.

† Estimate for 31 December 2004 (Source: Republika Srpska Institute of Statistics).

BIRTHS, MARRIAGES AND DEATHS

	Registered live births		Registered marriages		Registered deaths	
	Number	Rate (per 1,000)	Number	Rate (per 1,000)	Number	Rate (per 1,000)
2003	35,234	9.2	20,733	5.4	31,757	8.3
2004	35,151	9.1	22,252	5.8	32,616	8.5
2005	34,627	9.0	21,698	5.6	34,402	9.0
2006	34,033	8.9	21,501	5.6	33,221	8.6
2007	33,835	8.8	23,494	6.1	35,044	9.1
2008	34,176	8.9	22,151	5.8	34,026	8.9
2009	34,550	9.0	20,633	5.4	34,904	9.1
2010	33,528	8.7	19,541	5.1	35,118	9.1

Note: Rates are based on official mid-year estimates of de facto population.

Life expectancy (years at birth, WHO estimates): 76 (males 73; females 78) in 2009 (Source: WHO, *World Health Statistics*).

EMPLOYMENT

(labour force survey at 31 March 2003)

	Males	Females	Total
Agriculture, hunting and forestry	14,503	3,447	17,950
Fishing	393	98	491
Mining and quarrying	18,203	2,051	20,254
Manufacturing	92,867	55,958	148,825
Electricity, gas and water supply	19,013	4,999	24,012
Construction	29,500	4,857	34,357
Wholesale and retail trade; repair of motor vehicles, motorcycles and personal and household goods	40,062	35,432	75,494
Hotels and restaurants	9,703	9,543	19,246
Transport, storage and communications	30,123	8,973	39,096
Financial intermediation	3,949	6,317	10,266
Real estate, renting and business activities	8,725	4,657	13,382
Public administration and defence; compulsory social security	26,565	20,351	46,916
Education	19,875	28,042	47,917
Health and social work	13,211	27,565	40,776
Other community, social and personal service activities	13,904	7,997	21,901
Sub-total	340,596	220,287	560,883
Activities not adequately defined	42,773	18,164	60,937
Total	383,369	238,451	621,820

Registered unemployed at mid-year: 530,190 in 2007; 489,730 in 2008; 492,718 in 2009.

2009 (labour force survey at May, '000 persons aged 15 years and over): Agriculture 182; Industry 270; Services 406; *Total employed* 859; Unemployed 272; *Total labour force* 1,132 (males 703, females 428).

2010 (labour force survey at November, '000 persons aged 15 years and over): Total employed 843; Unemployed 315; *Total labour force* 1,158.

2011 (labour force survey at November, '000 persons aged 15 years and over): Total employed 816; Unemployed 311; *Total labour force* 1,127.

Health and Welfare

KEY INDICATORS

Total fertility rate (children per woman, 2009)	1.2
Under-5 mortality rate (per 1,000 live births, 2009)	14
HIV/AIDS (% of persons aged 15–49, 2007)	<0.1
Physicians (per 1,000 head, 2005)	1.4
Hospital beds (per 1,000 head, 2005)	3.0
Health expenditure (2008): US $ per head (PPP)	937
Health expenditure (2008): % of GDP	10.3
Health expenditure (2008): public (% of total)	58.2
Access to water (% of persons, 2008)	99
Access to sanitation (% of persons, 2008)	95
Total carbon dioxide emissions ('000 metric tons, 2007)	29,000.6
Carbon dioxide emissions per head (metric tons, 2007)	7.7
Human Development Index (2011): ranking	74
Human Development Index (2011): value	0.733

For sources and definitions, see explanatory note on p. vi.

Agriculture

PRINCIPAL CROPS

('000 metric tons)

	2008	2009	2010
Wheat	240.5	255.8	145.4
Barley	77.8	77.2	50.1
Maize	1,004.4	962.9	853.4
Rye	11.1	12.2	7.4
Oats	40.9	34.6	19.8
Potatoes	428.6	413.7	378.7
Beans, dry	13.2	14.9	12.6
Soybeans (Soya beans)	8.4	8.2	8.0
Cabbages and other brassicas	86.2	81.7	80.7
Tomatoes	40.7	46.3	36.6
Chillies and peppers, green	39.9	40.3	38.4
Onions, dry	38.5	39.4	37.2
Garlic	6.9	7.0	6.3
Carrots and turnips	27.6	21.0	22.9
Watermelons*	27.0	26.6	27.0
Grapes	23.9	25.6	23.2
Apples	51.9	71.5	71.7
Pears	21.7	24.8	22.9
Plums	132.6	155.8	157.6
Tobacco, unmanufactured	3.1	2.4	1.9

* FAO estimates.

Aggregate production ('000 metric tons, may include official, semi-official or estimated data): Total cereals 1,374.7 in 2008, 1,390.7 in 2009, 1,104.1 in 2010; Total roots and tubers 428.6 in 2008, 413.7 in 2009, 378.7 in 2010; Total vegetables (incl. melons) 795.3 in 2008, 771.4 in 2009, 738.4 in 2010; Total fruits (excl. melons) 271.6 in 2008, 324.2 in 2009, 321.3 in 2010.

Source: FAO.

LIVESTOCK

('000 head, year ending September)

	2008	2009	2010
Horses	22.9	21.2	19.3
Cattle	459.2	457.7	462.4
Pigs	502.2	529.1	590.4
Sheep	1,030.5	1,054.7	1,046.0
Chickens*	14,900	17,260	19,700
Ducks*	400	460	530
Geese and guinea fowls*	485	560	630
Turkeys*	400	460	330

* Unofficial figures.

Source: FAO.

LIVESTOCK PRODUCTS

('000 metric tons)

	2008	2009	2010
Cattle meat	26.3	23.4	23.4
Sheep meat	1.6	1.6	2.0
Pig meat	8.5	9.7	13.3
Chicken meat	28.9	33.2	37.6
Cows' milk	760.1	797.8	715.6
Sheep's milk	19.4	18.4	18.9
Hen eggs*	26.2	23.6	20.8

* Unofficial figures.

Source: FAO.

Forestry

ROUNDWOOD REMOVALS

('000 cubic metres, excluding bark)

	2008	2009	2010
Sawlogs, veneer logs and logs for sleepers	2,041	1,597	1,658
Pulpwood	285	322	488
Other industrial wood	245	181	208
Fuel wood	1,440	1,329	1,260
Total	4,011	3,429	3,614

Source: FAO.

SAWNWOOD PRODUCTION

('000 cubic metres, including railway sleepers)

	2008	2009	2010
Coniferous (softwood)	650	509	505
Broadleaved (hardwood)	355	272	260
Total	1,005	781	765

Source: FAO.

Fishing

(metric tons, live weight)

	2005	2006	2007*
Capture	2,005*	2,005*	2,005
Aquaculture	7,070	7,621	7,620
Common carp	2,450	2,740	2,740
Rainbow trout	3,720	3,880	3,880
Total catch	9,075*	9,626*	9,625

* FAO estimate(s).

2008–09: Figures assumed to be unchanged from 2007 (FAO estimates).

Source: FAO.

Mining

('000 metric tons unless otherwise indicated)

	2008	2009	2010
Brown coal and lignite	11,244	11,515	10,976
Iron ore: metal content*	622	678	588
Bauxite	1,018	556	828
Barite (Barytes) concentrate (metric tons)	54	30	57
Salt	555	556	663
Gypsum (crude)	150	74	65

* Estimates.

Source: US Geological Survey.

Industry

SELECTED PRODUCTS

('000 metric tons unless otherwise indicated)

	2001	2002	2003
Beer	480*	652*	1,316†
Cigarettes	690*	662*	5,062†
Crude steel‡	139	115	166
Aluminium (metal ingot)‡	95	102	113
Cement‡	704	913	890
Electric energy (million kWh)	10,327	10,785	11,250

* Excluding figures for the Federation.
† New series, not comparable with previous years' data.
‡ Source: US Geological Survey.

Source: UN Industrial Commodity Statistics Database.

2004 ('000 metric tons, unless otherwise indicated): Electric energy (million kWh) 12,734; Crude steel 75; Aluminium (metal ingot) 121; Cement 1,045 (Sources: US Geological Survey; UN Industrial Commodity Statistics Database).

2005 ('000 metric tons, unless otherwise indicated): Electric energy (million kWh) 12,637; Crude steel 289; Aluminium (metal ingot) 131; Cement 1,026 (Sources: US Geological Survey; UN Industrial Commodity Statistics Database).

2006 ('000 metric tons, unless otherwise indicated): Electric energy (million kWh) 13,346; Crude steel 490; Aluminium (metal ingot) 136; Cement 1,226 (Sources: UN Industrial Commodity Statistics Database; US Geological Survey).

2007 ('000 metric tons): Electric energy (million kWh) 11,824; Crude steel 533; Aluminium (metal ingot) 147; Cement 1,283 (Sources: US Geological Survey; UN Industrial Commodity Statistics Database).

2008 ('000 metric tons): Electric energy (million kWh) 13,261; Crude steel 608; Aluminium (metal ingot) 156; Cement 1,406 (Sources: US Geological Survey; UN Industrial Commodity Statistics Database).

2009 ('000 metric tons): Crude steel 519; Aluminium (metal ingot) 130; Cement 1,074 (Source: US Geological Survey).

2010 ('000 metric tons): Crude steel 593; Aluminium (metal ingot) 150; Cement 949 (Source: US Geological Survey).

Finance

CURRENCY AND EXCHANGE RATES

Monetary Units

100 pfeninga = 1 konvertibilna marka (KM or convertible marka).

Sterling, Dollar and Euro Equivalents (30 December 2011)

£1 sterling = KM 2.337;
US $1 = KM 1.512;
€1 = KM 1.956;
KM 100 = £42.79 = $66.16 = €51.13.

Average Exchange Rate (KM per US $)

2009 1.4079
2010 1.4767
2011 1.4069

Note: The new Bosnia and Herzegovina dinar (BHD) was introduced in August 1994, with an official value fixed at 100 BHD = 1 Deutsche Mark (DM). The DM, the Croatian kuna and the Yugoslav dinar also circulated within Bosnia and Herzegovina. On 22 June 1998 the BHD was replaced by the KM, equivalent to 100 of the former units. The KM was thus at par with the DM. From the introduction of the euro, on 1 January 1999, the German currency had a fixed exchange rate of €1 = DM 1.95583.

CONSOLIDATED BUDGET

(KM million)*

Revenue	2008	2009	2010
Tax revenue	5,946.3	5,351.9	5,640.2
Taxes on income, profits and capital gains	280.1	548.2	721.7
Taxes on payroll and work-force	487.0	173.4	—
Taxes on property	124.9	95.8	87.2
Taxes on goods, services, international trade and transactions	5,018.8	4,522.1	4,824.2
Other taxes	35.4	12.4	7.2
Social security contributions	3,568.7	3,638.6	3,813.0
Grants	39.3	48.3	48.5
Other revenue	1,348.7	1,303.7	1,360.9
Total	10,903.1	10,342.5	10,862.5

Expenditure†	2008	2009	2010
Compensation of employees	3,022.3	3,155.2	3,169.8
Use of goods and services	2,462.0	2,489.4	2,593.1
Interest payments	123.6	123.9	122.7
Subsidies and grants	439.6	418.5	476.7
Social security benefits	3,898.9	3,951.0	3,770.3
Other expenditure	606.8	526.5	707.7
Total	10,553.3	10,664.5	10,840.2

* Figures represent a consolidation of the budgetary accounts of: the central state Government; the federation and cantonal authorities and social security and road maintenance funds in the Federation; the central republican authorities, local and district administrations, social security and road maintenance funds in Republika Srpska; the central government and health insurance and employment funds in Brčko District.
† Excluding net lending (KM million): –493.1 in 2008; –1,070.0 in 2009; –611.9 in 2010.

Source: Central Bank of Bosnia and Herzegovina, *Annual Statement of Government Operations*.

INTERNATIONAL RESERVES

(US $ million at 31 December)

	2008	2009	2010
Foreign exchange	4,464	4,544	4,383
Total	4,464	4,544	4,383

Source: IMF, *International Financial Statistics*.

MONEY SUPPLY
(KM million at 31 December)

	2008	2009	2010
Currency outside banks	2,302	2,009	2,210
Demand deposits at banks	3,581	3,728	3,979
Total money (incl. others)	6,330	6,352	6,795

Source: IMF, *International Financial Statistics*.

COST OF LIVING
(Consumer Price Index; annual averages; base: previous year = 100)

	2008	2009	2010
Food and non-alcoholic beverages	112.1	99.1	99.3
Clothing and footwear	97.9	96.1	95.4
Housing, utilities and fuels	108.5	103.9	103.1
All items (incl. others)	107.4	99.6	102.1

Source: Central Bank of Bosnia and Herzegovina, *Statistical Bulletin*.

All items (Consumer Price Index; base: December of previous year = 100): 103.8 in 2008; 100.0 in 2009; 103.1 in 2010.

NATIONAL ACCOUNTS
(KM million at current prices, estimates)

Expenditure on the Gross Domestic Product

	2008	2009	2010
Government final consumption expenditure	5,570.5	5,734.1	5,779.8
Private final consumption expenditure	22,724.5	21,873.5	22,084.3
Gross capital formation	7,953.5	5,837.6	5,419.8
Total domestic expenditure	36,248.6	33,445.2	33,283.9
Exports of goods and services	9,102.4	7,733.6	9,192.3
Less Imports of goods and services	17,235.4	13,283.7	14,521.7
GDP in purchasers' values	28,115.6	27,895.2	27,954.5

Note: GDP estimates may differ from respective figures for GDP by economic activity owing to differing methods of data compilation.

Gross Domestic Product by Economic Activity

	2008	2009	2010*
Agriculture, hunting and forestry	1,842.6	1,759.4	1,733.4
Fishing	8.0	10.4	6.4
Mining and quarrying	512.3	500.4	491.7
Manufacturing	2,827.4	2,588.5	2,757.3
Electricity, gas and water	1,022.0	1,061.5	1,098.9
Construction	1,340.2	1,269.1	1,082.7
Wholesale and retail trade; repair of motor vehicles, motorcycles, etc.	3,300.0	3,143.1	3,242.7
Hotels and restaurants	496.7	484.5	491.1
Transport, storage and communications	1,661.5	1,648.9	1,698.3
Financial intermediation	852.2	869.0	883.6
Real estate, renting and business activities	2,059.5	2,158.7	2,207.1
Public administration and defence	2,191.3	2,349.2	2,274.2
Education	1,114.6	1,160.5	1,181.2
Health and social welfare	1,091.8	1,095.4	1,135.1
Other community, social and personal service activities	473.8	493.8	527.6
Sub-total	20,794.0	20,592.5	20,811.4
Less Financial intermediation services indirectly measured	682.9	675.8	674.9
Gross value added in basic prices	20,111.1	19,916.7	20,136.5
Taxes, *less* subsidies, on products	4,606.5	4,087.0	4,349.1
GDP in market prices†	24,717.6	24,003.7	24,485.5

* Preliminary figures.

† Comprising (KM million): Federation 15,647.0 in 2008, 15,230.6 in 2009, 15,615.1 in 2010 (preliminary); Republika Srpska 8,489.3 in 2008, 8,223.0 in 2009, 8,307.0 in 2010 (preliminary); Brčko District 548.2 in 2007, 581.3 in 2008, 550.2 in 2009, 563.5 in 2010 (preliminary).

BALANCE OF PAYMENTS
(US $ million)

	2008	2009	2010
Exports of goods f.o.b.	5,194.0	4,079.9	4,937.0
Imports of goods f.o.b.	−12,291.3	−8,833.7	−9,230.2
Trade balance	−7,097.3	−4,753.8	−4,293.2
Exports of services	1,672.3	1,443.9	1,283.6
Imports of services	−692.3	−646.6	−588.5
Balance on goods and services	−6,117.4	−3,956.4	−3,598.0
Other income received	1,174.8	836.0	598.5
Other income paid	−502.6	−257.5	−267.3
Balance on goods, services and income	−5,445.2	−3,378.0	−3,266.8
Current transfers received	3,080.4	2,531.7	2,497.2
Current transfers paid	−239.9	−228.6	−238.9
Current balance	−2,604.6	−1,074.9	−1,008.5
Capital account (net)	296.7	255.4	212.5
Direct investment abroad	−16.4	−5.5	−43.7
Direct investment from abroad	981.8	240.1	231.5
Portfolio investment assets	−8.8	−188.8	−91.3
Other investment assets	−510.8	−206.0	344.5
Other investment liabilities	1,548.0	452.5	33.9
Net errors and omissions	34.7	59.5	76.2
Overall balance	−279.5	−467.7	−244.9

Source: IMF, *International Financial Statistics*.

External Trade

SELECTED COMMODITIES
(KM million*)

Imports	2008	2009	2010
Food and live animals	2,620.2	2,389.0	2,502.4
Vegetable products	704.1	526.0	602.2
Prepared foodstuffs	1,411.2	1,376.4	1,425.2
Mineral fuels, lubricants, etc.	2,836.9	1,999.3	2,743.9
Chemicals and related products	1,395.2	1,260.6	1,345.7
Basic manufactures	4,956.4	3,604.2	3,989.0
Plastics and rubber	777.7	648.1	725.1
Wood and wood products	597.4	507.1	526.4
Textiles and textile articles	737.3	664.9	708.1
Articles of stone, plaster, cement and asbestos	379.4	285.1	283.6
Base metals and articles thereof	1,974.3	1,075.0	1,209.2
Machinery and transport equipment	3,886.4	2,644.9	2,519.9
Machinery and mechanical appliances	2,610.8	1,840.2	1,764.3
Transport equipment	1,275.6	804.7	755.6
Total (incl. others)	16,292.5	12,355.2	13,616.2

Exports	2008	2009	2010
Food and live animals	410.0	452.8	553.1
Prepared foodstuffs	220.1	233.9	260.9
Mineral fuels, lubricants, etc.	808.5	861.7	1,215.7
Basic manufactures	3,467.0	2,524.4	3,263.4
Wood and wood products	639.0	550.4	630.1
Textiles and textile articles	332.0	323.5	316.0
Footwear and headgear	369.0	345.9	412.4
Base metals and articles thereof	1,798.6	1,047.2	1,609.0
Machinery and transport equipment	1,002.2	758.7	850.4
Machinery and mechanical appliances	793.5	618.8	696.3
Transport equipment	208.7	139.9	154.0
Miscellaneous manufactured articles	530.1	537.5	678.2
Total (incl. others)	6,711.7	5,531.2	7,095.5

* Figures from the Customs Administration of the Federation, the Customs Administration of Republika Srpska and the Customs Service of Brčko District, not including adjustments.

Source: Central Bank of Bosnia and Herzegovina.

Ministry of Civil Affairs: 71000 Sarajevo, trg Bosne i Hercegovine 1; tel. (33) 492532; fax (33) 221074; e-mail zorica.rulj@mcp.gov.ba; internet www.mcp.gov.ba.

Ministry of Communications and Transport: 71000 Sarajevo, trg Bosne i Hercegovine 1; tel. (33) 284750; fax (33) 284751; e-mail info@mkt.gov.ba; internet www.mkt.gov.ba.

Ministry of Defence: 71000 Sarajevo, Hamdije Kreševljakovića 98; tel. (33) 285500; fax (33) 206094; e-mail info@mod.gov.ba; internet www.mod.gov.ba.

Ministry of Finance and the Treasury: 71000 Sarajevo, trg Bosne i Hercegovine 1; tel. (33) 205345; fax (33) 202930; e-mail trezorbih@mft.gov.ba; internet www.trezorbih.gov.ba.

Ministry of Foreign Affairs: 71000 Sarajevo, Musala 2; tel. (33) 281100; fax (33) 227156; e-mail info@mvp.gov.ba; internet www.mfa.gov.ba.

Ministry of Foreign Trade and Economic Relations: 71000 Sarajevo, Musala 9; tel. (33) 220093; fax (33) 220091; e-mail info@mvteo.gov.ba; internet www.mvteo.gov.ba.

Ministry of Human Rights and Refugees: 71000 Sarajevo, trg Bosne i Hercegovine 1; tel. (33) 202600; fax (33) 206140; e-mail kabmin@mhrr.gov.ba; internet www.mhrr.gov.ba.

Ministry of Justice: 71000 Sarajevo, trg Bosne i Hercegovine 1; tel. (33) 223501; fax (33) 223504; e-mail info@mpr.gov.ba; internet www.mpr.gov.ba.

Ministry of Security: 71000 Sarajevo, trg Bosne i Hercegovine 1; tel. (33) 213623; fax (33) 213628; e-mail glasnogovornik@msb.gov.ba; internet www.msb.gov.ba.

Federation Government

Office of the Federation Presidency (Mostar): 88000 Mostar, Ante Starčevića bb; tel. and fax (36) 318905; e-mail info@predsjednikfbih.gov.ba; internet www.predsjednikfbih.org.

Office of the Federation Presidency (Sarajevo): 71000 Sarajevo, Musala 9; tel. and fax (33) 206656; e-mail info@predsjednikfbih.gov.ba; internet www.predsjednikfbih.org.

Office of the Prime Minister: 71000 Sarajevo, Alipašina 41; tel. (33) 650457; fax (33) 664816; e-mail kabprem@fbihvlada.gov.ba; internet www.fbihvlada.gov.ba.

Ministry of Agriculture, Water Management and Forestry: 71000 Sarajevo, Maršala Tita 15; tel. (33) 443338; fax (33) 226434; e-mail kabinet@fmpvs.gov.ba; internet www.fmpvs.gov.ba.

Ministry of Culture and Sport: 71000 Sarajevo, ul. Obala Maka Dizdara 2; tel. (33) 254153; fax (33) 254151; e-mail munevera.becirovic@fmksa.com; internet www.fmks.gov.ba.

Ministry of Development, Entrepreneurship and Crafts: 88000 Mostar, ul. Ante Starčevića bb; tel. (36) 449120; fax (36) 449122; e-mail fmrpo@fmrpo.gov.ba; internet www.fmrpo.gov.ba.

Ministry of Displaced Persons and Refugees: 71000 Sarajevo, Alipašina 41; tel. (33) 212986; fax (33) 220437; e-mail kabinet@fmroi.gov.ba.

Ministry of Education and Science: 88000 Mostar, Ante Starčevića bb; tel. (36) 355700; fax (33) 355742; e-mail info@fmon.gov.ba; internet www.fmon.gov.ba.

Ministry of Energy, Mining and Industry: 88000 Mostar, Alekse Šantića bb; tel. (36) 513800; fax (36) 580015; e-mail fmeri-so@bih.net.ba.

Ministry of the Environment and Tourism: 71000 Sarajevo, Alipašina 41; tel. (33) 562870; fax (33) 201602; e-mail fmoit@gov.ba; internet www.fmoit.gov.ba.

Ministry of Finance: 71000 Sarajevo, Mehmeda Spahe 5; tel. (33) 253400; fax (33) 203152; e-mail info@fmf.gov.ba; internet www.fmf.gov.ba.

Ministry of Health: 71000 Sarajevo, Maršala Tita 9; tel. and fax (33) 226635; e-mail kab.moh@bih.net.ba; internet www.fmoh.gov.ba.

Ministry of Internal Affairs: 71000 Sarajevo, Mehmeda Spahe 7; tel. and fax (33) 280020; e-mail info@fmup.gov.ba; internet www.fmup.gov.ba.

Ministry of Justice: 71000 Sarajevo, Valtera Perića 15; tel. (33) 213151; fax (33) 213155; e-mail info@fmp.gov.ba; internet www.fmp.gov.ba.

Ministry of Labour and Social Policy: 71000 Sarajevo, Vilsonovo šetalište 10; tel. (33) 661782; fax (33) 661783; e-mail info@fmrsp.gov.ba; internet www.fmrsp.gov.ba.

Ministry of Physical Planning: 71000 Sarajevo, Maršala Tita 9A; tel. (33) 227188; fax (33) 226420; e-mail info@fmpu.gov.ba; internet www.fmpu.gov.ba.

Ministry of Trade: 88000 Mostar, Ante Starčevića bb; tel. (36) 310148; fax (36) 318684; e-mail desnica.radivojevic@fmt.gov.ba; internet www.fmt.gov.ba.

Ministry of Transport and Communications: 88000 Mostar, Braće Fejića bb; tel. (36) 550025; fax (36) 550024; e-mail fmpik@fmpik.gov.ba; internet www.fmpik.gov.ba.**Ministry of Veterans and the Disabled of the War of Defensive Liberation:** 71000 Sarajevo, Alipašina 41; tel. (33) 212932; fax (33) 222679; e-mail kabinet@bih.net.ba; internet www.fmbi.gov.ba.

Republika Srpska Government

Office of the President: 78000 Banja Luka, Bana Milosavljevića 4; tel. (51) 248101; fax (51) 248161; e-mail info@predsjednikrs.net; internet www.predsjednikrs.net.

Office of the Prime Minister: 78000 Banja Luka, trg Republike Srpske 1; tel. (51) 339102; fax (51) 339119; e-mail kabinet@vladars.net; internet www.vladars.net.

Ministry of Administration and Local Government: 78000 Banja Luka, trg Republike Srpske 1; tel. (51) 339545; fax (51) 339648; e-mail muls@muls.vladars.net; internet www.vladars.net/sr-SP-Cyrl/Vlada/Ministarstva/muls.

Ministry of Agriculture, Forestry and Water Management: 78000 Banja Luka, trg Republike Srpske 1; tel. (51) 338415; fax (51) 338865; e-mail mps@mps.vladars.net; internet www.vladars.net/sr-SP-Cyrl/Vlada/Ministarstva/mps.

Ministry of Economic Affairs and Regional Co-operation: 78000 Banja Luka, trg Republike Srpske 1; tel. (51) 339324; fax (51) 339647; e-mail meoi@meoi.vladars.net; internet www.vladars.net/sr-SP-Cyrl/Vlada/Ministarstva/meoi.

Ministry of Education and Culture: 78000 Banja Luka, trg Republike Srpske 1; tel. (51) 338461; fax (51) 338853; e-mail mp@mp.vladars.net; internet www.vladars.net/sr-SP-Cyrl/Vlada/Ministarstva/mpk.

Ministry of the Family, Youth and Sport: 78000 Banja Luka, trg Republike Srpske 1; tel. (51) 338332; fax (51) 338846; e-mail mpos@mpos.vladars.net; internet www.vladars.net/sr-SP-Cyrl/Vlada/Ministarstva/mpos.

Ministry of Finance: 78000 Banja Luka, trg Republike Srpske 1; tel. (51) 339155; fax (51) 339645; e-mail mf@mf.vladars.net; internet www.vladars.net/sr-SP-Cyrl/Vlada/Ministarstva/mf.

Ministry of Health and Social Welfare: 78000 Banja Luka, trg Republike Srpske 1; tel. (51) 339486; fax (51) 339652; e-mail ministarstvo-zdravlja@mzsz.vladars.net; internet www.vladars.net/sr-SP-Cyrl/Vlada/Ministarstva/MZSZ.

Ministry of Industry, Energy and Mining: 78000 Banja Luka, trg Republike Srpske 1; tel. (51) 339581; fax (51) 339651; e-mail mier@mier.vladars.net; internet www.vladars.net/sr-SP-Cyrl/Vlada/Ministarstva/mper.

Ministry of Internal Affairs: 78000 Banja Luka, Desanke Maksimović 4; tel. (51) 334391; fax (51) 334392; e-mail goga.davidovic@mup.vladars.net; internet www.mup.vladars.net.

Ministry of Justice: 78000 Banja Luka, trg Republike Srpske 1; tel. (51) 339325; fax (51) 339650; e-mail mpr@mpr.vladars.net; internet www.vladars.net/sr-SP-Cyrl/Vlada/Ministarstva/mpr.

Ministry of Labour and the Protection of War Veterans: 78000 Banja Luka, Kralja Petra I Karađorđevića 100; tel. (51) 338602; fax (51) 338845; e-mail mpb@mpb.vladars.net; internet www.vladars.net/sr-SP-Cyrl/Vlada/Ministarstva/mpb.

Ministry of Physical Planning, Civil Engineering and the Environment: 78000 Banja Luka, trg Republike Srpske 1; tel. (51) 339592; fax (51) 339653; e-mail kabinetministra@mgr.vladars.net; internet www.vladars.net/sr-SP-Cyrl/Vlada/Ministarstva/mgr.

Ministry of Refugees and Displaced Persons: 78000 Banja Luka, trg Republike Srpske 1; tel. (51) 338642; fax (51) 338847; e-mail mirl@mirl.vladars.net; internet www.vladars.net/sr-SP-Cyrl/Vlada/Ministarstva/mirl.

Ministry of Science and Technology: 78000 Banja Luka, Administrativni Centar Vlade RS; tel. (51) 338709; fax (51) 338856; e-mail mnk@mnk.vladars.net; internet www.vladars.net/sr-SP-Cyrl/Vlada/Ministarstva/mnk.

Ministry of Trade and Tourism: 78000 Banja Luka, trg Republike Srpske 1; tel. (51) 338769; fax (51) 338864; e-mail mtt@mtt.vladars.net; internet www.vladars.net/sr-SP-Cyrl/Vlada/Ministarstva/MTT.

Ministry of Transport and Communications: 78000 Banja Luka, trg Republike Srpske 1; tel. (51) 339603; fax (51) 339649; e-mail msv@msv.vladars.net; internet www.vladars.net/sr-SP-Cyrl/Vlada/Ministarstva/msv.

Brčko District

Office of the Principal Deputy High Representative of the International Community and International Supervisor of Brčko District: 76100 Brčko, Musala bb; tel. (49) 240300; fax (49) 217560; internet www.ohr.int/ohr-offices/brcko.

Office of the Government of Brčko District: 76100 Brčko, bul. Mira 1; tel. (49) 240600; fax (49) 205142; e-mail gradonacelnik@bdcentral.net; internet www.bdcentral.net.

The Presidency

STATE PRESIDENCY*

Election, 3 October 2010

	Votes	% of votes
Bosniak Candidates		
Bakir Izetbegović (PDA)	162,831	34.86
Fahrudin Radončić (UBF)	142,387	30.49
Haris Silajdžić (PBH)	117,240	25.10
Others	44,581	9.55
Total	467,039	100.00
Croat Candidates		
Željko Komšić (SDP BiH)	337,065	60.61
Borjana Krišto (CDU—BH)	109,758	19.74
Martin Raguž (CDU 1990)	60,266	10.84
Jerko Ivanković-Lijanović (PPWB)	45,397	8.16
Others	3,625	0.65
Total	556,111	100.00
Serb Candidates		
Nebojša Radmanović (AISD)	295,629	48.92
Mladen Ivanić (PDP)	285,951	47.31
Rajko Papović (Alliance for a Democratic Srpska)	22,790	3.77
Total	604,370	100.00

* The Presidency of Bosnia and Herzegovina comprises three members: one Bosniak, one Croat and one Serb. The Serb is elected from within Republika Srpska, and the Bosniak and Croat members from within the Federation of Bosnia and Herzegovina. The position of Chairman of the Presidency is filled on a rotating basis for a term of eight months by each member of the Presidency.

REPUBLIKA SRPSKA PRESIDENCY

Election, 3 October 2010

Candidate	Votes	% of votes
Milorad Dodik (AISD)	319,618	50.52
Ognjen Tadić (SDP)	227,239	35.92
Others	85,817	13.56
Total	632,674	100.00

Legislature

STATE LEGISLATURE

The **Parlamentarna Skupština Bosne i Hercegovine** (Parliamentary Assembly of Bosnia and Herzegovina) comprises two chambers: a directly elected lower chamber, the **Predstavnički dom/ Zastupnički dom** (House of Representatives) and an indirectly elected **Dom naroda** (House of Peoples).

Predstavnički dom/Zastupnički dom (House of Representatives)

71000 Sarajevo, trg Bosne i Hercegovine 1; tel. (33) 284402; fax (33) 286054; e-mail branka.todorovic@parlament.ba; internet www.parlament.ba.

The Predstavnički dom/Zastupnički dom has 42 deputies directly elected for a four-year term, of whom 28 are elected from the Federation and 14 from Republika Srpska.

Speaker: MILORAD ŽIVKOVIĆ.

General Election, 3 October 2010

Party	% of votes FBiH*	% of votes RS†	% of votes Overall	Seats
SDP BiH	26.07	2.96	17.33	8
AISD	0.86	43.30	16.92	8
PDA	19.40	2.64	13.05	7
SDP	—	22.19	8.40	4
UBF	12.16	1.02	7.95	4
CDU—BH	10.99	0.38	6.97	3
PBH	7.25	2.04	5.28	2
Croatian Coalition‡	4.86	0.08	3.05	2
PDP	—	6.45	2.44	1
PPBW	4.81	—	2.99	1
DPA	0.11	4.59	1.80	1
DPC	1.45	0.05	0.92	1
Others	12.04	14.30	12.90	—
Total	100.00	100.00	100.00‖	42

* Federation of Bosnia and Herzegovina.
† Republika Srpska.
‡ A coalition of the CDU 1990 and the CPR BH.
‖ A total of 1,641,569 valid votes were cast, of which 1,020,293 were cast in the Federation of Bosnia and Herzegovina and 621,276 were cast in Republika Srpska.

Dom naroda (House of Peoples)

71000 Sarajevo, trg Bosne i Hercegovine 1; tel. (33) 284454; fax (33) 286056; e-mail marin.vukoja@parlament.ba; internet www.parlament.ba.

There are 15 deputies in the Dom naroda (House of Peoples), of whom 10 are elected by the Dom naroda Federacije (Federation House of Peoples) and five by the Vijeće naroda (Council of Peoples) of the Narodna skupština Republike Srpske (National Assembly of Republika Srpska).

Speaker: DRAGAN ČOVIĆ.

FEDERATION LEGISLATURE

The **Parlamentarna Federacije** (Federation Parliament) comprises two chambers: a directly elected lower chamber, the **Predstavnički dom Federacije/Zastupnički dom Federacije** (Federation House of Representatives) and an indirectly elected **Dom Naroda Federacije** (Federation House of Peoples). Each of the 10 cantons also has an elected assembly.

Predstavnički dom Federacije/Zastupnički dom Federacije (Federation House of Representatives)

71000 Sarajevo, Hamdije Kreševljakovića 3; tel. (33) 263585; fax (33) 223623; e-mail kabinet.predsjedavajuceg@parlamentfbih.gov.ba; internet www.parlamentfbih.gov.ba.

The 98 deputies of the Predstavnički dom Federacije/Zastupnički dom Federacije are directly elected for a four-year term.

Speaker: DENIS ZVIZDIĆ.

General Election, 3 October 2010

Party	Votes	% of votes	Seats
SDP BiH	251,053	24.53	28
PDA	206,926	20.22	23
UBF	121,697	11.89	13
CDU—BH	108,943	10.64	12
PBH	78,086	7.63	9
PPWB	48,286	4.72	5
Croatian Coalition*	47,941	4.68	5
Party of Democratic Activities	19,254	1.88	1
DPC	15,082	1.47	1
AISD	9,505	0.93	1
Others	116,819	11.41	—
Total	1,023,529	100.00	98

* A coalition of the CDU 1990 and the CPR BH.

Dom Naroda Federacije (Federation House of Peoples)

71000 Sarajevo, Hamdije Kreševljakovića 3; tel. (33) 203246; fax (33) 205547; e-mail izmirhadziavdic@parlamentfbih.gov.ba; internet www.parlamentfbih.gov.ba.

The 51-member Dom Naroda Federacije comprises 17 Bosniak, 17 Croat, 10 Serb and seven other deputies, who are elected by the cantonal assemblies.

Speaker: KAROLINA PAVLOVIĆ.

REPUBLIKA SRPSKA LEGISLATURE

The legislature of Republika Srpska comprises the monocameral, directly elected **Narodna Skupština Republike Srpske** (National Assembly of Republika Srpska).

Narodna skupština Republike Srpske (National Assembly of Republika Srpska)

51000 Banja Luka, Vuka Karadžića 2; tel. (51) 338104; fax (51) 301087; internet www.narodnaskupstinars.net.

Speaker: IGOR RADOJIČIĆ.

Election, 3 October 2010

Party	Votes	% of votes	Seats
AISD	240,727	38.00	37
SDP	120,136	18.97	18
PDP	47,806	7.55	7
DPA	38,547	6.09	6
SP–Party of United Pensioners alliance	26,824	4.23	4
DP	21,604	3.41	3
SDP BiH	19,297	3.05	3
PDA	16,861	2.66	2
PDPRS	13,440	2.12	2
SRPRS	15,166	2.39	1
Others	73,021	11.53	—
Total	633,429	100.00	83

The Narodna skupština Republike Srpske elects 28 delegates to a Vijeće naroda (Council of Peoples), who are responsible for, *inter alia*, nominating the entity's representatives to the state Dom Naroda. These 28 members comprise eight Bosniaks, eight Croats, eight Serbs and four others.

Vijeće naroda Republike Srpske (Council of Peoples of Republika Srpska): 51000 Banja Luka, Vuka Karadžića 4; tel. (51) 247446; fax (51) 247653; e-mail predsjedavajuci@vijecenarodars.net; internet www.vijecenarodars.net; Chair. MOMIR MALIĆ.

BRČKO DISTRICT

Note: residents of Brčko District are entitled to vote in elections to state institutions, to those of the Entity that they are a citizen of, and in elections to the local district institutions.

Election Commission

Centralna Izborna Komisija Bosne i Hercegovine (Central Election Commission of Bosnia and Herzegovina): 71000 Sarajevo, Danijela Ozme 7; tel. (33) 251300; fax (33) 251329; e-mail kontakt@izbori.ba; internet www.izbori.ba; independent; Pres. IRENA HADŽIABDIĆ.

Political Organizations

Alliance of Independent Social Democrats (AISD) (Savez nezavisnih socijaldemokrata—SNSD): 78000 Banja Luka, Petra Kočića 5; tel. (51) 318492; fax (51) 318495; e-mail snsd@snsd.org; internet www.snsd.org; f. 1997 as Party of Independent Social Democrats; present name adopted 2001, following merger with Democratic Socialist Party; Chair. MILORAD DODIK; Sec.-Gen. RAJKO VASIĆ.

Croatian Democratic Union 1990 of Bosnia and Herzegovina (CDU 1990) (Hrvatska Demokratska Zajednica 1990—HDZ 1990): 88000 Mostar, Nikole Šubića Zrinjskog 11/I; tel. (36) 449730; fax (36) 449737; e-mail hdz1990@tel.net.ba; internet www.hdz1990.org; f. 2006 by fmr mems of the Croatian Democratic Union of Bosnia and Herzegovina; contested 2010 legislative elections as mem. of Croatian Coalition; Pres. BOŽO LJUBIĆ.

Croatian Democratic Union of Bosnia and Herzegovina (CDU—BH) (Hrvatska Demokratska Zajednica Bosne i Hercegovine—HDZ BiH): 88000 Mostar, Kneza Domagoja bb; tel. (36) 310701; fax (36) 333574; e-mail hdzbih@hdzbih.org; internet www.hdzbih.org; f. 1990; affiliate of the CDU in Croatia; adopted new party statute May 2007; Croat nationalist party; Pres. DRAGAN ČOVIĆ.

Croatian Party of Rights of Bosnia and Herzegovina (CPR BH) (Hrvatska stranka Prava BiH): 88320 Ljubuški, Fra Petra Bakule 2; tel. and fax (39) 831020; e-mail info@hsp-posusje.com; internet www.hsp-posusje.com; Croat nationalist; contested 2010 legislative elections as mem. of Croatian Coalition; Pres. Dr ZVONKO JURIŠIĆ.

Democratic Party (DP) (Demokratska Partija): 78000 Banja Luka, ul. Mrkalja Save 4; tel. (51) 217000; e-mail demokratska.partija@gmail.com; internet www.dp-rs.org; f. 2009; Pres. DRAGAN ČAVIĆ.

Democratic People's Alliance (DPA) (Demokratski Narodni Savez—DNS): 78000 Banja Luka, Aleja Svetog Save 20; tel. (51) 219033; fax (51) 219020; internet www.dnsrs.org; f. 2000 by fmr mems of the Serb National Alliance; Chair. Dr MARKO PAVIĆ.

Democratic People's Community of Bosnia and Herzegovina (DPC) (Demokratska narodna zajednica BiH—DNZ BiH): 77230 Velika Kladuša, Sulejmana Topića 7; tel. (37) 775340; fax (37) 770307; e-mail dnzbih@gmail.com; internet www.dnzbih.ba; f. 1993; Chair. RIFAT DOLIĆ.

Party for Bosnia and Herzegovina (PBH) (Stranka za Bosnu i Hercegovinu): 71000 Sarajevo, Fra Grge Martića 2/II; tel. and fax (33) 573470; fax (33) 475597; e-mail zabih@zabih.ba; internet www.zabih.ba; f. 1996; integrationist; Pres. HARIS SILAJDŽIĆ.

Party of Democratic Action (PDA) (Stranka Demokratske Akcije—SDA): 71000 Sarajevo, Mehmeda Spahe 14; tel. (33) 216906; fax (33) 225363; e-mail sda@bih.net.ba; internet www.sda.ba; f. 1990; moderate Bosniak nationalist party that supports admission of Bosnia and Herzegovina to the European Union and formation of a Republic of Bosnia and Herzegovina as a decentralized state composed of multi-ethnic regions, with Bosniaks, Croats and Serbs as members of a common Bosnian nation; Chair. SULEJMAN TIHIĆ; Sec.-Gen. AMIR ZUKIĆ.

Party of Democratic Activities (Stranka Demokratske Aktivnosti—A-SDA): 77220 Cazin, Cazinskih Brigada; tel. and fax (37) 512005; e-mail info@asda.ba; internet www.asda.ba; f. 2008 by fmr mems of Party of Democratic Action (q.v.); supports greater integration with Europe, state involvement in the economy; Pres. ISMET KURTAGIĆ.

Party of Democratic Progress of Republika Srpska (PDP) (Partija Demokratskog Progresa Republike Srpske): 78000 Banja Luka, ul. Prvog Krajiškog Korpusa 130; tel. (51) 346210; fax (51) 300956; e-mail pdp@blic.net; internet www.pdpinfo.net; f. 1999; moderate, supports equal rights for all ethnic groups, supports closer co-operation of Republika Srpska with the European Union; Chair. MLADEN IVANIĆ.

People's Democratic Party of Republika Srpska (PDPRS) (Narodna Demokratska Stranka Republike Srpske): 78000 Banja Luka, Miloša Obilića 9; tel. and fax (51) 465675; e-mail info@ndsrs.org; internet ndsrs.org; Chair. KRSTO JANDRIĆ.

People's Party Working for Betterment (PPWB) (Narodna stranka Radom za boljitak): 71000 Sarajevo, Zmaja od Bosne 4; tel. (33) 212540; fax (33) 212610; e-mail zaboljitak@zaboljitak.ba; internet www.zaboljitak.ba; f. 2001; Leader MLADEN IVANKOVIĆ-LIJANOVIĆ.

Serbian Democratic Party (SDP) (Srpska demokratska stranka—SDS BiH): 78000 Banja Luka, Nikole Tesle 1B; tel. (51) 225130; fax (51) 212984; e-mail sds@teol.net; internet www.sdsrs.com; f. 1990; allied to SDP of Serbia; Serb nationalist party; Chair. MLADEN BOSIĆ.

Serbian Radical Party of Republika Srpska (SRPRS) (Srpska Radikalna Stranka Republike Srpske—SRS): 78000 Banja Luka, Vidovdanska 53; tel. (51) 219428; e-mail kontakt@srs-rs.org; internet www.srs-rs.org; radical Serb nationalist, supports the notion of a 'Greater Serbia'; Chair. MILANKO MIHAJLICA.

Social Democratic Party of Bosnia and Herzegovina (SDP BiH) (Socijaldemokratska Partija BiH): 71000 Sarajevo, Alipašina 41; tel. (33) 563900; fax (33) 563901; e-mail generalni.sekretar@sdp-bih.org.ba; internet www.sdp.ba; Chair. Dr ZLATKO LAGUMDŽIJA; Sec.-Gen. NERMIN NIKŠIĆ.

Socialist Party (SP) (Socijalistička Partija): 78000 Banja Luka, Jovana Dulića 25; tel. (51) 328750; fax (51) 328753; e-mail info@socijalisti.ba; internet www.socijalisti.ba; f. 1993 as br. of Socialist Party of Serbia; fmrly Socialist Party of Republika Srpska; Chair. PETAR ĐOKIĆ.

Union for a Better Future of Bosnia and Herzegovina (UBF) (Savez za bolju budućnost BiH—SBB): 71000 Sarajevo, Tešanjska 24A; tel. (33) 942550; fax (33) 942560; e-mail info@sbbbh.ba; internet www.sbbbh.ba; f. 2009; Pres. FAHRUDIN RADONČIĆ.

Diplomatic Representation

EMBASSIES IN BOSNIA AND HERZEGOVINA

Austria: 71000 Sarajevo, Džidžikovac 7; tel. (33) 279400; fax (33) 668339; e-mail sarajewo-ob@bmeia.gv.at; internet www.austrijska-ambasada.ba; Ambassador DONATUS KÖCK.

Bulgaria: 71000 Sarajevo, Radnička 30; tel. (33) 668191; fax (33) 668189; e-mail possar@bih.net.ba; internet www.mfa.bg/bg/116/; Ambassador ANDREY S. TRANSKI.

China, People's Republic: 71000 Sarajevo, Braće Begića 17; tel. (33) 215102; fax (33) 215108; e-mail emprcbh@bih.net.ba; Ambassador WANG FUGUO.

Croatia: 71000 Sarajevo, Mehmeda Spahe 16; tel. (33) 251640; fax (33) 472434; e-mail croemb.sarajevo@mvpei.hr; internet ba.mvp.hr; Ambassador TONČI STANIČIĆ.

Czech Republic: 71000 Sarajevo, Franjevačka 19; tel. (33) 447525; fax (33) 447526; e-mail sarajevo@embassy.mzv.cz; internet www.mzv.cz/sarajevo; Ambassador TOMÁŠ SZUNYOG.

Denmark: 71000 Sarajevo, Splitska 9; tel. (33) 665901; fax (33) 665902; e-mail sijamb@um.dk; internet www.ambsarajevo.um.dk; Ambassador KIRSTEN GEELAN.

Egypt: 71000 Sarajevo, Nurudina Gackića 58; tel. (33) 666498; fax (33) 666499; e-mail eg.em.sa@bih.net.ba; Ambassador AHMED EL-SAYED KHATTAB.

France: 71000 Sarajevo, Kapetanović Ljubušak 18; tel. (33) 282050; fax (33) 282052; e-mail ambsarajevo.presse@diplomatie.gouv.fr; internet www.ambafrance-ba.org; Ambassador ROLAND GILLES.

Germany: 71000 Sarajevo, Skenderija 3; tel. (33) 565300; fax (33) 206400; e-mail info@sarajevo.diplo.de; internet www.sarajewo.diplo.de; Ambassador JOACHIM SCHMIDT.

Greece: 71000 Sarajevo, Obala Maka Dizdara I; tel. (33) 203516; fax (33) 203512; e-mail greekemb@bih.net.ba; internet www.mfa.gr/Sarajevo; Ambassador PROCOPIOS D. MANTZOURANIS.

Holy See: 71000 Sarajevo, Pehlivanuša 9; tel. (33) 551055; fax (33) 551057; e-mail nunbosnia@bih.net.ba; Apostolic Nuncio ALESSANDRO D'ERRICO (Titular Archbishop of Hyccarum).

Hungary: 71000 Sarajevo, Splitska 2; tel. (33) 205302; fax (33) 268930; e-mail hung.emb@bih.net.ba; internet www.mfa.gov.hu/emb/sarajevo; Ambassador LÁSZLÓ TÓTH.

Iran: 71000 Sarajevo, Obala Maka Dizdara 6; tel. (33) 650210; fax (33) 663910; e-mail iries2@bih.net.ba; Ambassador ALI LAKI.

Italy: 71000 Sarajevo, Čekaluša 39; tel. (33) 218022; fax (33) 659368; e-mail ambsara@bih.net.ba; Ambassador RAIMONDO DE CARDONA.

Japan: 71000 Sarajevo, Bistrik 9; tel. (33) 209580; fax (33) 209583; e-mail japanbih@bih.net.ba; Ambassador FUTAO MOTAI.

Libya: 71000 Sarajevo, Drinska 8; tel. (33) 660387; fax (33) 663620; e-mail libija1@bih.net.ba; Ambassador SALEM A. A. FINNIR.

Macedonia, former Yugoslav republic: 71000 Sarajevo, Splitska 57; tel. and fax (33) 206004; e-mail sarajevo@mfa.gov.mk; Ambassador RAMI REXHEPI.

Malaysia: 71000 Sarajevo, Radnička 4A; tel. (33) 201578; fax (33) 667713; e-mail malsrjevo@kln.gov.my; Ambassador ZULKIFLI ADNAN.

Montenegro: 71000 Sarajevo, Talirovića 4; tel. (33) 239925; fax (33) 239928; e-mail ambcg1@bih.net.ba; Ambassador DRAGAN ĐUROVIĆ.

Netherlands: 71000 Sarajevo, Grbavička 4; tel. (33) 562600; fax (33) 223413; e-mail sar@minbuza.nl; internet www.mfa.nl/sar; Ambassador SWEDER VAN VOORST TOT VOORST.

Norway: 71000 Sarajevo, Ferhadija 20; tel. (33) 254000; fax (33) 666505; e-mail emb.sarajevo@mfa.no; internet www.norveska.ba; Ambassador JAN BRAATHU.

Pakistan: 71000 Sarajevo, Emerika Bluma 17; tel. (33) 211836; fax (33) 211837; e-mail parepsarajevo@yahoo.com; internet www.mofa.gov.pk/bosnia; Ambassador SALEEM JAUHAR.

Poland: 71000 Sarajevo, Dola 13; tel. (33) 201142; fax (33) 233796; e-mail beata.zatovic@msz.gov.pl; internet www.sarajewo.polemb.net; Chargé d'affaires a.i. EMANUELA SUPROWICZ.

Portugal: 71000 Sarajevo, Čobanija 12/1; tel. (33) 200835; fax (33) 233796; e-mail embaport@bih.net.ba; Ambassador ANTÓNIO BOTELHO DE SOUSA.

Qatar: 71000 Sarajevo, Dajanli Ibrahim-bega 23; tel. (33) 565810; fax (33) 205351; e-mail qr.embassy@bih.net.ba; Ambassador MUBARAK KLEEFIEK KHALED AL-HAJRI.

Romania: 71000 Sarajevo, Tahtali sokak 13–15; tel. (33) 207447; fax (33) 668940; e-mail rumunska@bih.net.ba; Ambassador (vacant).

Russia: 71000 Sarajevo, Urjan Dedina 93; tel. (33) 668147; fax (33) 668148; e-mail rusembbih@bih.net.ba; internet www.sarajevo.mid.ru; Ambassador ALEKSANDR A. BOTSAN-KHARCHENKO.

Saudi Arabia: 71000 Sarajevo, Koševo 44; tel. (33) 211861; fax (33) 212204; e-mail saudiembassy@epn.ba; Ambassador EID MUHAMMAD A. AL-THAKAFI.

Serbia: 71000 Sarajevo, Obala Maka Dizdara 3A; tel. (33) 260080; fax (33) 221469; e-mail srbamba@bih.net.ba; Ambassador NINOSLAV STOJADINOVIĆ.

Slovakia: 71000 Sarajevo, Skopljanska 7; tel. (33) 716440; fax (33) 716410; e-mail emb.sarajevo@mzv.sk; internet www.sarajevo.mfa.sk; Ambassador MIROSLAV MOJŽITA.

Slovenia: 71000 Sarajevo, Bentbaša 7; tel. (33) 271260; fax (33) 271270; e-mail vsa@gov.si; internet sarajevo.veleposlanistvo.si; Ambassador ANDREJ GRASSELLI.

Spain: 71000 Sarajevo, Maguda 18; tel. (33) 584000; fax (33) 239155; e-mail embaspa@bih.net.ba; Ambassador ALEJANDRO ENRIQUE ALVARGONZÁLEZ SAN MARTÍN.

Sweden: 71000 Sarajevo, Ferhadija 20; tel. (33) 276030; fax (33) 276060; e-mail ambassaden.sarajevo@foreign.ministry.se; internet www.swedenabroad.se/sarajevo; Ambassador BOSSE HEDBERG.

Switzerland: 71000 Sarajevo, Josipa Štadlera 15; tel. (33) 275850; fax (33) 570120; e-mail vertretung@sar.rep.admin.ch; internet www.eda.admin.ch/sarajevo; Ambassador ANDRÉ SCHALLER.

Turkey: 71000 Sarajevo, Hamdije Kreševljakovića 5; tel. and fax (33) 445260; e-mail turksa@bih.net.ba; Ambassador VEFAHAN OCAK.

United Kingdom: 71000 Sarajevo, Tina Ujevića 8; tel. (33) 282200; fax (33) 282203; e-mail britemb@bih.net.ba; internet ukinbih.fco.gov.uk; Ambassador MICHAEL TATHAM.

USA: 71000 Sarajevo, ul. Roberta C. Frasurea 1; tel. (33) 704000; fax (33) 659722; e-mail bhopa@state.gov; internet sarajevo.usembassy.gov; Ambassador PATRICK S. MOON.

Judicial System

The Court of Bosnia and Herzegovina, which was officially inaugurated on 27 January 2003, represents the country's highest judicial organ. The judicial system of each entity comprises a Constitutional Court, a Supreme Court and local district courts.

Court of Bosnia and Herzegovina: 71000 Sarajevo, Kraljice Jelene 88; tel. (33) 707100; fax (33) 707301; e-mail pios@sudbih.gov.ba; internet www.sudbih.gov.ba; inaugurated 2003; state-level court; comprises 53 judges (51 national and 2 international); 3 divisions (Criminal, Administrative and Appellate); War Crimes Chamber est. 2005; Pres. KRESO MEDDŽIDA.

Constitutional Court of Bosnia and Herzegovina: 71000 Sarajevo, Reisa Dzemaludina Causevića 6; tel. (33) 251226; fax (33) 561134; e-mail info@ccbh.ba; internet www.ccbh.ba; f. 1997; nine mems appointed until the age of 70, three of whom are non-nationals selected by the President of the European Court of Human Rights, and six of whom are nationals; four of the latter are elected by the Predstavnički dom Federacije/Zastupnički dom Federacije and two by the Narodna skupština Republike Srpske; Pres. MIODRAG SIMOVIĆ.

Office of the Prosecutor of Bosnia and Herzegovina: 71000 Sarajevo, Kraljice Jelene 88; tel. (33) 707100; fax (33) 707463; e-mail info@tuzilastvobih.gov.ba; internet www.tuzilastvobih.gov.ba; Chief Prosecutor JADRANKA LOKMIĆ-MISIRAČA (acting).

FEDERATION OF BOSNIA AND HERZEGOVINA

Constitutional Court of the Federation of Bosnia and Herzegovina: 71000 Sarajevo, Valtera Perića 15; tel. (33) 251650; fax (33) 251651.

Supreme Court of the Federation of Bosnia and Herzegovina: 71000 Sarajevo, Valtera Perića 15; tel. (33) 226751; fax (33) 226755; e-mail info@vsfbih.ba; internet www.vsfbih.ba; four chambers; Pres. AMIR JAGANJAĆ.

Office of the Federation Prosecutor: 71000 Sarajevo, Valtera Perića 11; tel. (33) 214990; Prosecutor ZDRAVKO KNEŽEVIĆ.

REPUBLIKA SRPSKA

Constitutional Court of Republika Srpska: 78000 Banja Luka, Kralja Alfonsa 11; tel. (51) 301218; e-mail ustsudrs@inecco.net; internet www.ustavnisud.org; nine mems; Pres. MIRKO ZOVKO.

Supreme Court of Republika Srpska: 78000 Banja Luka, Aleja Svetog Save bb; tel. (51) 211690; fax (51) 226071; e-mail vrhovnisudrs@vrhovnisudrs.com; internet www.vrhovnisudrs.com; Pres. ŽELIMIR BARIĆ.

Office of the Chief Prosecutor of Republika Srpska: 78000 Banja Luka, Kralja Petra I Karađorđevića 12; tel. (51) 218827; fax (51) 218834; e-mail rjt@inecco.net; Prosecutor AMOR BUKIĆ.

Religion

The dominant religion in Bosnia and Herzegovina is Islam, but around one-half of the population are Christian, either adhering to the Serbian Orthodox Church or the Roman Catholic Church. There is a small Jewish community.

ISLAM

Islamic Community of Bosnia and Herzegovina (Islamska Zajednica u Bosni i Hercegovini): 71000 Sarajevo, Reisa Demaludina

Čaueviċa 2; tel. (33) 200355; fax (33) 441573; internet www.rijaset .ba; Reis-ul-ulema Dr MUSTAFA EFENDI CERIĆ.

CHRISTIANITY

The Serbian Orthodox Church

Metropolitan of Dabrobosna: NICOLAJ (MRDA), 71000 Sarajevo, Zelenih Beretki 3; tel. and fax (71) 210518; e-mail info@ mitropolijadabrobosanska.org; internet www .mitropolijadabrobosanska.org.

The Roman Catholic Church

Bosnia and Herzegovina comprises one archdiocese and two dioceses. At 31 December 2008 adherents of the Roman Catholic Church numbered 458,861, representing about 15.4% of the total population.

Bishops' Conference: 71000 Sarajevo, Kaptol 32; tel. and fax (33) 666867; e-mail kaptolka@bih.net.ba; f. 1995; Pres. Cardinal VINKO PULJIĆ (Archbishop of Vrhbosna, Sarajevo).

Archbishop of Vrhbosna, Sarajevo: Cardinal VINKO PULJIĆ, 71000 Sarajevo, Kaptol 7; tel. (33) 218823; fax (33) 212937; e-mail kaptolka@bih.net.ba.

The Press

PRINCIPAL DAILIES

Capital: 78000 Banja Luka, Vlašićka 25C; tel. and fax (51) 281407; e-mail info@capital.ba; internet www.capital.ba; Editor-in-Chief SINIŠA VUKELIĆ.

Dnevni Avaz (Daily Herald): 71000 Sarajevo, Tešanjska 24B; tel. (33) 281393; fax (33) 281414; e-mail redakcija@avaz.ba; internet www.dnevniavaz.ba; f. 1995; Editor-in-Chief SEAD NUMANOVIĆ; circ. 15,700 (2001).

Dnevni List (Daily News): 88000 Mostar, Kralja Petra Krešimira 66/2; tel. (36) 313370; fax (36) 333437; e-mail national-holding@tel .net.ba; internet www.dnevni-list.ba; Editor-in-Chief DARIO LUKIĆ.

Fokus: 78000 Banja Luka, Jovana Raškovića 16; tel. (51) 243900; fax (51) 243945; e-mail redakcija@fokus.ba; internet www.fokus.ba; Editor-in-Chief DALIBOR ĐEKIĆ.

Glas Srpske (Voice of Republika Srpska): 78000 Banja Luka, Skendera Kulenovića 1; tel. (51) 342900; fax (51) 342910; e-mail dopisnik@glassrpske.com; internet www.glassrpske.com; fmrly *Glas Srpski* (Serbian Voice); Editor-in-Chief MIRJANA KUSMUK; Deputy Editor-in-Chief PERICA PEĆANAC.

Jutarnje Novine (Morning News): Sarajevo; e-mail irfan_ljevakovic@jutarnje.ba; fmrly *Vecernje Novine* (Evening News); Dir IRFAN LJEVAKOVIĆ; circ. 10,000 (2001).

Nezavisne novine (The Independent): 78000 Banja Luka, Braće Pišteljića 1; tel. (51) 331800; fax (51) 331810; e-mail desk@nezavisne .com; internet www.nezavisne.com; f. 1995; Editor-in-Chief BORJANA RADMANOVIĆ-PETROVIĆ; circ. 7,500 (2001).

Oslobođenje (Liberation): 71000 Sarajevo, Džemala Bijedića 185; tel. (33) 468054; fax (33) 468090; e-mail info@oslobodjenje.de; internet www.oslobodjenje.ba; f. 1943; morning; Editor-in-Chief VILDANA SELIMBEGOVIĆ.

San (Dream): 71000 Sarajevo, Bistrik 9; tel. (33) 254300; fax (33) 254301; e-mail redakcija@san.ba; internet www.san.ba; Editor-in-Chief MENSUR OSMOVIĆ.

Tuzlanski List: 75000 Tuzla, Maršala Tita 34; tel. (35) 360020; fax (35) 319912; e-mail redakcija@tuzlanskilist.ba; internet www .tuzlanskilist.ba; f. 2007; Editor-in-Chief SNEŽANA AGIĆ.

WEEKLY NEWSPAPERS

Dani (Days): 71000 Sarajevo, Džemala Bijedića 185; tel. (33) 276900; fax (33) 651789; e-mail info@bhdani.com; internet www.bhdani.com; independent; political and cultural; Man. Editor DRAGAN STANOJLOVIĆ; circ. 25,000.

Hercegovačke Novine (Herzegovina News): 88000 Mostar, Krpića 3; tel. and fax (36) 581124; e-mail novine@hercegovacke.ba; internet www.hercegovacke.ba; Editor-in-Chief ALIJA LIZDE; circ. 15,000 (2010).

Slobodna Bosna (Free Bosnia): 71000 Sarajevo, Čekaluša Čikma 6; tel. (33) 444041; fax (33) 444895; e-mail sl.bos@bih.net.ba; internet www.slobodna-bosna.ba; independent; national and international politics; Editor SENAD AVDIĆ; circ. 28,000 (2001).

Start: 71000 Sarajevo, La Benevolencije 6; tel. and fax (33) 260210; e-mail redakcija@startbih.info; internet www.startbih.info; f. 1998; independent; Editor-in-Chief DARIO NOVALIĆ.

PERIODICALS

Auto Magazin: 71000 Sarajevo, Skenderpašina 25; tel. (33) 261430; fax (33) 261431; e-mail info@automagazin.ba; internet www .automagazin.ba; monthly; Editor DREN MILINOVIĆ.

Buka: 78000 Banja Luka, Aleja Svetog Save 24; tel. and fax (51) 222210; e-mail buka@blic.net; internet www.6yka.com; internet magazine published by the Banja Luka Centre for Informational Decontamination of the Young (Centar za informativnu dekontaminaciju mladih iz Banjaluke); Editor-in-Chief ALEKSANDAR TRIFUNOVIĆ.

Business Magazine: 71000 Sarajevo, Muhameda ef. Pandže 67; tel. (33) 557115; fax (33) 223165; e-mail marketing@business-magazin .ba; internet www.business-magazin.ba; f. 2006; two a month; Editor-in-Chief AIDA DELIĆ.

Gracija: 71000 Sarajevo, Skenderija 31A; tel. (33) 261710; fax (33) 261711; e-mail redakcija@gracija.ba; internet www.gracija.ba; women's affairs; bi-weekly; Editor-in-Chief OZREN KEBO.

Gusto: 71000 Sarajevo, Zmaja od Bosne 7–7A; tel. (33) 279312; fax (33) 279310; e-mail marketing@gusto.ba; internet www.gusto.ba; f. 2008; gastronomy; monthly; Editor SARA KRAJINA-JAZVIĆ.

Info: 71000 Sarajevo, Trebevićka 18; tel. and fax (33) 211673; internet www.info.ba; f. 1997; information technology; monthly; Editor-in-Chief GORAN MILIĆ.

In Store: 71000 Sarajevo, Hasana Brkića 2; tel. (33) 710616; fax (33) 710615; e-mail instore.magazine@altermedia.ba; internet www .instore.ba; trade; monthly; Editor-in-Chief SAMIRA MURATOVIĆ.

Magazine: 71000 Sarajevo, Zmaja od Bosne 7–7A; tel. (33) 279313; fax (33) 279310; e-mail info@magazine.ba; internet www.magazine .ba; lifestyle; monthly; Dir MUAMER KUČUK; circ. 20,000 (2010).

Naša Ognjišta—Hrvatski katolički mjesečnik (Our Hearth—Croat Catholic Monthly): 80240 Tomislavgrad, trg fra Mije Čuića 1; tel. (34) 352295; fax (34) 352808; e-mail nasa.ognjista@tel.net.ba; internet www.nasa-ognjista.com; f. 1971; monthly; Editor-in-Chief GABRIJEL MIOČ.

Naša Riječ (Our Word): 72000 Zenica, Kralja Tvrtka I/1; tel. (32) 408003; fax (32) 403055; e-mail redakcija@nasarijec.ba; internet www.nasarijec.ba; f. 1956; weekly; Editor-in-Chief SAJTO ĆEHOVIĆ.

Novi Izraz (New Expression): 7100 Sarajevo, Vrazova 1; tel. (33) 200155; fax (33) 217854; e-mail krugpen@bih.net.ba; internet www .penbih.ba; f. 1992 as successor to *Izraz*; literary and art criticism; monthly; published by P. E. N. Centar Bosne i Hercegovine; Editor-in-Chief HANIFA KAPIDŽIĆ-OSMANAGIĆ.

Novi Reporter (New Reporter): 78000 Banja Luka, Duška Koščice 49; tel. (51) 229922; fax (51) 229921; e-mail rep@inecco.net; internet www.novireporter.com; f. 2003 as successor to *Reporter*; independent; Editor-in-Chief SLAVA GOVEDARICA.

Odjek (Echo): 71000 Sarajevo, Obala Maka Dizdara 2; tel. and fax (33) 204463; e-mail redakcija@odjek.ba; internet www.odjek.ba; arts, science and society; quarterly; Editor-in-Chief NERMINA KURSPAHIĆ.

Sarajevske Sveske (Sarajevo Notebook): Mediacentar Sarajevo, 71000 Sarajevo, Kolodvorska 3; tel. and fax (33) 715860; e-mail sarajevske.sveske@media.ba; internet www.sveske.ba; bi-monthly; literature and social issues; Editor-in-Chief VELIMIR VISKOVIĆ.

Svjetlo Riječi (Light of the Word): 71000 Sarajevo, Zagrebačka 18; tel. (33) 726200; fax (33) 812247; e-mail redakcija@svjetlorijeci.ba; internet www.svjetlorijeci.ba; f. 1983; Franciscan; monthly; Dir MILJENKO PETRIČEVIĆ; Editor-in-Chief IVAN ŠARČEVIĆ.

Zehra: 71000 Sarajevo, Zenička 3; tel. (33) 651401; fax (33) 712545; e-mail magazinzehra@gmail.com; internet www.zehra.ba; f. 2001; monthly; family and society; published by women's org., Kewser; Editor MEDIHA DŽAKMIĆ.

Zrno (The Grain): 71000 Sarajevo, Trg sarajevske olimpijade; tel. (61) 485106; e-mail zrno@zrno.ba; internet www.zrno.ba; weapons, technology and security; in Croatian; monthly.

NEWS AGENCIES

FENA—Federalna Novinska Agencija (Federation News Agency): 71000 Sarajevo, Cemalusa 1; tel. (33) 445247; fax (33) 265460; e-mail direktor@fena.ba; internet www.fena.ba; f. 2000; Dir FARUK BORIĆ; Editor-in-Chief ZORAN ILIĆ.

NINA—Nezavisna Informativna Novinska Agencija (Independent Information and News Agency): 88000 Mostar, Kralja Petra Krešimira IV 66/2; tel. (36) 324280; fax (36) 313377; e-mail nina@ nina.ba; internet www.nina.ba; f. 2003; independent; Dir MIROSLAV RAŠIĆ; Editor-in-Chief ŽELJKO MARJANOVIĆ.

ONASA Independent News Agency: 71000 Sarajevo, Zmaja od Bosna 4; tel. (33) 276580; fax (33) 276599; e-mail onasa@onasa.com .ba; internet www.onasa.com.ba; f. 1994; Gen. Man. ELVIRA BEGOIĆ.

SNRA—Novinska Agentsija Republike Srpske (News Agency of Republika Srpska): 76300 Bijeljina, Sofke Nikolić 51; tel. (55)

211177; fax (55) 201810; internet www.snra.rs; f. 1992; bureaux in Banja Luka and East Sarajevo; Man. Dir DRAGAN DAVIDOVIĆ.

Publishers

Sarajevo Publishing: 71000 Sarajevo, Obala Kulina Bana 4; tel. (33) 220809; fax (33) 217164; e-mail redakcija@sarajevopublishing.ba; internet www.sarajevopublishing.ba; f. 1950; history, literature, philosophy and culture; Dir MUSTAFA ALAGIĆ.

Službeni List BiH Sarajevo: 71000 Sarajevo, Džemala Bijedića 39/III; tel. and fax (33) 722061; e-mail info@sllist.ba; internet www.sllist.ba; publishes legislation and other official publications; Dir MEHMEDALIJA HUREMOVIĆ.

Svjetlost (Light): 71000 Sarajevo, Petra Preradovića 3; tel. (33) 212144; fax (33) 272352; internet www.svjetlost.ba; f. 1945; textbooks and literature, religion; Dir SAVO ZIROJEVIĆ.

TKD Šahinpašić: 71020 Sarajevo, Vreoca b.b.; tel. (33) 771180; fax (33) 771188; e-mail info@btcsahinpasic.com; internet www.btcsahinpasic.com; f. 1989; contemporary literature, philosophy and children's books; publishers, importers, exporters and retailers; Dir-Gen. TAJIB ŠAHINPAŠIĆ.

Zoro (Sarajevo): 71000 Sarajevo, Šenoina 14; tel. (33) 214454; fax (33) 213879; e-mail zorosa@bih.net.ba; internet www.zoro.hr; f. 1994 in Zagreb (Croatia); Dir SAMIR FAZLIĆ.

PUBLISHERS' ASSOCIATION

Asscn of Publishers and Booksellers of Bosnia and Herzegovina: 71000 Sarajevo, Maršala Tita 9A; tel. (33) 207945; fax (33) 266630; e-mail ibrosa@bih.net.ba; internet www.uik.ba; f. 2005; Pres. IBRAHIM SPAHIĆ.

Broadcasting and Communications

TELECOMMUNICATIONS

Three principal service providers of telecommunications operate in Bosnia and Herzegovina: BH Telecom, which operates chiefly in Sarajevo and in Bosniak-majority cantons of the Federation; HT Mostar in Croat-majority cantons of the Federation; and Telekom Srpske in Republika Srpska.

BH Telecom d.d. Sarajevo: 71000 Sarajevo, Obala Kulina Bana 8; tel. (33) 232651; fax (33) 221111; e-mail nedzad.residbegovic@bhtelecom.ba; internet www.bhtelecom.ba; 90% owned by Govt of Federation of Bosnia and Herzegovina; operates mobile cellular network under the brand name 'BH Mobile'; Dir-Gen. NEDŽAD REŠIDBEGOVIĆ.

Eronet: 88000 Mostar, Tvrtka Miloša bb; tel. (39) 633800; fax (39) 663391; e-mail korisnicka.sluzba@hteronet.ba; internet www.eronet.ba; f. 1996; 51% owned by HT Mostar, 49% owned by T-Hrvatski Telecom (Croatia); mobile cellular telecommunications; provides coverage in western, southern, central and northern regions of Bosnia and Herzegovina.

HT Mostar—Hrvatske telekomunikacije Mostar: 88000 Mostar, Zagrebačka 6; tel. and fax (36) 318155; e-mail prodaja-mostar@hteronet.ba; internet www.ht.ba; f. 1995; 50.1% owned by Govt of Federation of Bosnia and Herzegovina, 39.1% by T-Hrvatski Telekom (Croatia); Pres. VILIM PRIMORAC.

M:Tel: 78000 Banja Luka, Mladena Stojanovića 4; e-mail korisnicka.podrska@mtel.ba; internet www.mtel.ba; f. 1999; fmrly Mobi's; subsidiary of Telekom Srpske; present name adopted 2007; mobile cellular communications; provides coverage in a majority of regions of Bosnia and Herzegovina; Gen. Dir PREDRAG ĆULIBRK; 506,500 subscribers (2003).

Telekom Srpske: 78000 Banja Luka, Kralja Petra I Karađorđevića 61A; tel. (51) 240100; fax (51) 211150; e-mail korisnicki.servis@mtel.ba; internet www.mtel.ba; 65% share owned by Telekom Srbija (Serbia); Dir-Gen. PREDRAG ĆULIBRK.

BROADCASTING

Regulatory Authority

Communications Regulatory Agency (Regulatorna agencija za komunikacije—RAK): 71000 Sarajevo, Mehmeda Spahe 1; tel. (33) 250600; fax (33) 713080; e-mail info@rak.ba; internet www.rak.ba; f. 2001; Dir-Gen. KEMAL HUSEINOVIĆ.

Radio and Television

In 2010 there were 144 registered radio stations, of which 63 were publicly owned. At that time there were 44 registered terrestrial television stations, of which 14 were publicly owned.

Alternativna Televizija Informisanje: 78000 Banja Luka, Gunduliceva 33; tel. and fax (51) 348248; e-mail info@atvbl.com; internet www.atvbl.com; f. 1996; Dir NATAŠA TEŠANOVIĆ.

NTV Hayat: 71320 Sarajevo,Vogošća, Jošanička 55; tel. (33) 492900; fax (33) 492911; e-mail elvir@hayat.ba; internet www.hayat.ba; f. 1991; broadcasts 4 channels; Dir-Gen. ELVIR ŠVRAKIĆ.

Public Broadcasting Service of Bosnia and Herzegovina: 71000 Sarajevo, Bulevar Meše Selimovića 12; tel. (33) 461522; e-mail belmin.karamehmedovic@bhrt.ba; internet www.bhrt.ba; f. 1945; Dir-Gen. MEHMED AGOVIĆ; Dir of Radio SENADA ĆUMUROVIĆ; Dir of TV BELMIN KARAMEHMEDOVIĆ.

Radio-Televizija Federacije Bosne i Hercegovine (Radio and Television of the Federation of Bosnia and Herzegovina): 71000 Sarajevo, Bulevar Meše Selimovića 12; tel. (33) 464070; fax (33) 455103; e-mail press@rtvfbih.ba; internet www.rtvfbih.ba/loc; Dir-Gen. DŽEMAL ŠABIĆ; Dir of Radio LEJLA TAFRO-SEFIĆ; Dir of Television ZVONIMIR JUKIĆ.

Radio-Televizija Republike Srpske (RTRS) (Radio and Television of Republika Srpska): 78000 Banja Luka, Kralja Petra I Karađorđevića 129; tel. (51) 339800; fax (51) 339924; e-mail rtrs@rtrs.tv; internet www.rtrs.tv; f. 1992; Gen. Man. DRAGAN DAVIDOVIĆ.

Studio 99: 71000 Sarajevo, Skenderija; tel. (33) 221101; fax (33) 262690; e-mail oko22@ntv99.ba; internet www.ntv99.ba; f. 1995; independent radio and TV station; political and current affairs; Editor-in-Chief ADIL KULENOVIĆ.

Finance

(cap. = capital; res = reserves; dep. = deposits; m. = million; amounts in konvertibilna marka—KM, convertible marka; brs = branches)

BANKING

In 2008 31 banks were operating in Bosnia and Herzegovina (of which 21 were licensed by the Banking Agency of the Federation and 10 by the Banking Agency of Republika Srpska).

Central Bank

Central Bank of Bosnia and Herzegovina: 71000 Sarajevo, Maršala Tita 25; tel. (33) 278222; fax (33) 215094; e-mail contact@cbbh.ba; internet www.cbbh.ba; f. 1997; cap. 25.0m., res 477.4m., dep. 3,437.7m. (Dec. 2009); Gov. KEMAL KOZARIĆ.

Selected Banks

Hypo Alpe-Adria-Bank a.d. Banja Luka: 78000 Banja Luka, Aleja Svetog Save 13; tel. (51) 336500; fax (51) 336518; e-mail bank.bl.bih@hypo-alpe-adria.rs.ba; internet www.hypo-alpe-adria.ba; f. 2002; 99.6% owned by Hypo Alpe-Adria-Bank International AG (Austria); cap. 125.8m., res 19.2m., dep. 1,391.6m. (Dec. 2009); Dir SAMUEL VLČAN.

Hypo Alpe-Adria-Bank d.d.: 88000 Mostar, Kneza Branimira 2B; tel. (36) 444200; fax (36) 444235; e-mail bank.bih@hypo-alpe-adria.com; internet www.hypo-alpe-adria.ba; f. 1999; present name adopted 2001; subsidiary of Hypo Alpe-Adria-Bank International AG (Austria); cap. 193.0m., res 8.2m., dep. 1,955.7m. (Dec. 2009); Dir MICHAEL VOGT.

NLB Razvojna Banka a.d.: 78000 Banja Luka, Milana Tepića 4; tel. (51) 221610; fax (51) 221623; e-mail info@nlbrazvojnabanka.com; internet www.nlbrazvojnabanka.com; f. 1998; present name adopted 2006; 50.6% stake owned by NLB d.d. (Slovenia); cap. 52.0m., res 21.9m., dep. 931.6m. (Dec. 2009); Gen. Dir RADOVAN BAJIĆ; 13 brs.

NLB Tuzlanska Banka d.d. Tuzla: 75000 Tuzla, Maršala Tita 34; tel. (35) 259259; fax (35) 302802; e-mail info@nlbtuzlanskabanka.ba; internet www.nlbtuzlanskabanka.ba; f. 1990; present name adopted 2006; 96.3% owned by NLB d.d. (Slovenia); cap. 38.6m., res 22.9m., dep. 665.0m. (Dec. 2009); Man. ALMIR ŠAHINPAŠIĆ; 20 brs.

Nova Banka a.d. Banja Luka: 78000 Banja Luka, Kralja Alfonsa XIII 37A; tel. (55) 230300; fax (55) 201410; e-mail office@novabanka.com; internet www.novabanka.com; f. 1992; fmrly Nova Banka a.d. Bijeljina; present name adopted 2007; cap. 53.2m., res 10.0m., dep. 584.3m. (Dec. 2009); Pres. GORAN RADANOVIĆ; Gen. Man. MILAN RADOVIĆ.

Raiffeisen Bank d.d. Bosna i Hercegovina: 71000 Sarajevo, Danijela Ozme 3; tel. (33) 287100; fax (33) 213851; e-mail info.rbbh@rbb-sarajevo.raiffeisen.at; internet www.raiffeisenbank.ba; f. 1992; present name adopted 2000; cap. 241.8m., res 125.1m., dep. 3,682.3m. (Dec. 2009); Pres. Dr MICHAEL G. MÜLLER.

UniCredit Bank d.d.: 88000 Mostar, Kardinala Štepinca bb; tel. (36) 312112; fax (36) 356227; e-mail info@unicreditgroup.ba; internet www.unicreditbank.ba; f. 1992; 66% owned by Zagrebačka Banka d.d. Zagreb (Croatia); present name adopted 2008; cap. 119.1m., res 249.5m., dep. 2,726.2m. (Dec. 2009); Chief Exec. BERISLAV KUTLE.

Volksbank BH d.d.: 71000 Sarajevo, Fra Anđela Zvizdovića 1; tel. (33) 295601; fax (33) 295603; e-mail info@volksbank.ba; internet www.volksbank.ba; cap. 47.0m., res 38.9m., dep. 651.6m. (Dec. 2009); Dir REINHOLD KOLLAND.

Banking Agencies

Banking Agency of the Federation of Bosnia and Herzegovina (Agencija za Bankarstvo Federacije Bosne i Hercegovine): 71000 Sarajevo, Koševo 3; tel. (33) 721400; fax (33) 668811; e-mail agencija@fba.ba; internet www.fba.ba; f. 1996; Chair. HARIS IHTIJAREVIĆ; Dir ZLATKO BARŠ.

Banking Agency of Republika Srpska (Agencija za Bankarstvo Republike Srpske): 78000 Banja Luka, Vase Pelagića 11A; tel. (51) 218111; fax (51) 216665; e-mail office@abrs.ba; internet www.abrs.ba; f. 1998; Chair. of Bd MIRJANA JAĆIMOVIĆ; Dir SLAVICA INJAC.

INSURANCE

In 2008 there were 25 insurance companies operating in Bosnia and Herzegovina, including the following:

Aura Osiguranje d.d. Banja Luka: 78000 Banja Luka, Knjaza Miloša 10A; tel. (51) 344777; fax (51) 344770; e-mail auraos@teol.net; internet www.auraosiguranje.com; f. 2007; non-life; Chair. of Bd ZORAN TUNJIĆ.

Bosna Sunce Osiguranje d.d. Sarajevo: 71000 Sarajevo, trg Međunarodnog Prijateljstva 20; tel. (33) 755450; fax (33) 755490; e-mail info@bosna-sunce.ba; internet www.bosna-sunce.ba; life and non-life; Chair. ŽELJKO PERVAN; 6 brs.

Drina Osiguranje d.d.: 75446 Milići, trg rudara 1; tel. and fax (56) 741610; e-mail office@drina-osiguranje.com; internet www.drina-osiguranje.com; f. 1996; non-life; Dir MILE MATIĆ; 9 brs.

Jahorina Osiguranje d.d.: 71420 Pale, ul. Svetosavska; tel. (57) 201320; fax (57) 201321; e-mail direkcija@jahorinaosiguranje.com; internet www.jahorinaosiguranje.com; f. 1992; non-life; Dir-Gen. MIROSLAV MIŠKIĆ.

Kosig Dunav Osiguranje d.d. Banja Luka: 78000 Banja Luka, Veselina Masleše 26; tel. (51) 246100; fax (51) 211686; e-mail info@dunav.ba; internet www.dunav.ba; Man. Dir SAŠA ČUDIĆ.

Lido Osiguranje d.d. Sarajevo: 71210 Ilidža, Hifzi Bjelevca 82/1; tel. (33) 776388; fax (33) 776399; e-mail info@lido-osiguranje.com; internet www.lido-osiguranje.com; f. 1994; non-life; Dir-Gen. HALID ĐULIĆ; 11 brs in the Federation of Bosnia and Herzegovina.

Sarajevo Osiguranje d.d. Sarajevo: 71000 Sarajevo, Čobanija 14; tel. (33) 203270; fax (33) 664142; e-mail info@sarajevoosiguranje.ba; internet www.sarajevoosiguranje.ba; life and non-life, insurance and reinsurance; Dir-Gen. MIDHAT TERZIĆ; 13 brs.

Triglav BH Osiguranje d.d.: 71000 Sarajevo, ul. Dolina 8; tel. (33) 252111; fax (33) 252179; e-mail info@triglavbh.ba; internet www.triglavbh.ba; f. 2002; subsidiary of Triglav (Slovenia); Chair. of Management FEJSAL HRUSTANOVIĆ; 8 brs.

STOCK EXCHANGES

Sarajevo Stock Exchange (Sarajevska berza-burza): 71000 Sarajevo, Đoke Mazalića 4; tel. (33) 251462; fax (33) 559460; e-mail contact@sase.ba; internet www.sase.ba; f. 2002; Dir-Gen. ZLATAN DEDIĆ.

Banja Luka Stock Exchange (Banjalučka berza): 78000 Banja Luka, Petra Kočića bb; tel. (51) 326040; fax (51) 326056; e-mail office@blberza.com; internet www.blberza.com; f. 2001; Chief Exec. MILAN BOŽIĆ.

Trade and Industry

GOVERNMENT AGENCIES

Foreign Investment Promotion Agency of Bosnia and Herzegovina (FIPA): 71000 Sarajevo, Tešanjska 24A, Avaz Twist Tower; tel. (33) 278080; fax (33) 278081; e-mail fipa@fipa.gov.ba; internet www.fipa.gov.ba; f. 1999; Dir JELICA GRUJIĆ.

Federation of Bosnia and Herzegovina

Privatization Agency of the Federation of Bosnia and Herzegovina (Agencija za privatizaciju u Federaciji BiH—APF): 71000 Sarajevo, Alipašina 41; tel. (33) 212884; fax (33) 212883; e-mail apfbih@bih.net.ba; internet www.apf.com.ba; Dir ENES GANIĆ.

Securities Commission of the Federation of Bosnia and Herzegovina (Komisija za vrijednosne papire Federacije Bosne i Hercegovine): 71000 Sarajevo, Cemalusa 9/2; tel. (33) 203862; fax (33) 211655; e-mail info@komvp.gov.ba; internet www.komvp.gov.ba; f. 1999; Pres. HASAN ĆELAM.

Republika Srpska

Republika Srpska Directorate for Privatization: 78000 Banja Luka, Mladena Stoganovića 4; tel. (51) 308311; fax (51) 311245; e-mail dip@inecco.net; Dir BORISLAV OBRADOVIĆ.

Republika Srpska Securities Commission (Komisija za khartije od vrijednosti Republike Srpske): 78000 Banja Luka, Vuka Karadžića 6; tel. (51) 218362; fax (51) 218361; e-mail kontakt@secrs.gov.ba; internet www.secrs.gov.ba; Pres. MIODRAG JANDRIĆ.

DEVELOPMENT ORGANIZATION

Federation Development Planning Institution (Federacija BiH Federalni zavod za programiranje razvoja): 71000 Sarajevo, Cemalusa 9/3; tel. (33) 667272; fax (33) 212625; e-mail info@fzzpr.gov.ba; internet www.fzzpr.gov.ba; Dir LJUBIŠA ĐAPAN.

CHAMBERS OF COMMERCE

Chamber of Commerce of Bosnia and Herzegovina (Privredna Komora BiH): 71000 Sarajevo, Branislava Đurđeva 10; tel. (33) 566222; fax (33) 214292; e-mail mahirh@komorabih.ba; internet www.komorabih.ba; Pres. VESELIN POLJAŠEVIĆ.

Chamber of Commerce of the Federation of Bosnia and Herzegovina—Mostar (Privredna Komora FBiH—Mostar): 88000 Mostar, Zagrebačka 10; tel. (36) 332963; fax (36) 332966; e-mail gkfbih@tel.net.ba; internet www.kfbih.com; Sec. ŽELJANA BEVANDA.

Chamber of Commerce of the Federation of Bosnia and Herzegovina—Sarajevo (Privredna Komora FBiH—Sarajevo): 71000 Sarajevo, Branislava Đurđeva 10; tel. (33) 217782; fax (33) 217783; e-mail info@kfbih.com; internet www.kfbih.com; f. 1999; Pres. JAGO LASIĆ.

Chamber of Commerce of Republika Srpska (Privredna komora RS): 78000 Banja Luka, Đure Daničića 1/2; tel. (51) 215744; fax (51) 215565; e-mail info@komorars.ba; internet www.komorars.ba; Pres. BORKO ĐURIĆ.

UTILITIES

Electricity

Elektroprivreda BiH: 71000 Sarajevo, Vilsonovo Šetalište 15; tel. (33) 751000; fax (33) 751008; internet www.elektroprivreda.ba; generation, transmission and distribution of electric energy; Gen. Man. AMER JERLAGIĆ.

Gas

BH-Gas: 71000 Sarajevo, Hamdije Cemerlića 2/1; tel. (33) 279000; fax (33) 661621; e-mail management@bh-gas.ba; internet www.bh-gas.ba; f. 1997; Man. Dir ALMIR BEČAREVIĆ.

Water

Vodno Područje Slivova Rijeke Save: 71000 Sarajevo, ul. Grbavička 4/3; tel. (33) 565400; fax (33) 565423; e-mail info@voda.ba; internet www.voda.ba; Dir SEJAD DELIĆ.

TRADE UNIONS

Confederation of Independent Trade Unions of Bosnia and Herzegovina (Savez samostalnih sindikata Bosne i Hercegovine—SSSBiH): 71000 Sarajevo, Obala Kulina Bana 1; tel. (33) 202029; fax (33) 442321; e-mail sssbih@sindikatbih.ba; internet www.sindikatbih.ba; Chair. ISMET BAJRAMOVIĆ.

Confederation of Trade Unions of Republika Srpska (Savez sindikata Republike Srpske—SSRS): 78000 Banja Luka, Srpska 32; tel. (51) 214543; fax (51) 304241; e-mail ssrs-bl@blic.net; internet www.savezsindikatars.org; f. 1992; Pres. RANKA MISIĆ.

Transport

RAILWAYS

In 2009 there were 1,016 km of railway lines in Bosnia and Herzegovina.

Željeznice Federacije Bosne i Hercegovine (ŽFBH) (Railways of the Federation of Bosnia and Herzegovina): 71000 Sarajevo, Musala 2; tel. (33) 251120; fax (33) 652396; e-mail kabinez@bih.net.ba; internet www.zfbh.ba; CEO Dr NEDŽAD OSMANAGIĆ.

Željeznice Republike Srpske (ŽRS) (Railways of Republika Srpska): 74000 Doboj, Svetog Save 71; tel. (53) 241369; fax (53) 222247; e-mail zrs.kp@doboj.net; internet www.zrs-rs.com; Dir-Gen. PETKO STANOJEVIĆ.

ROADS

Bosnia and Herzegovina's road network covers some 22,600 km, including 3,788 km of main roads and 4,842 km of regional roads.

CIVIL AVIATION

The country has an international airport at Sarajevo, and three smaller civil airports, at Tuzla, Banja Luka and Mostar.

Department of Civil Aviation of Bosnia and Herzegovina: 78000 Banja Luka, Vojvode Pere Krece bb; tel. (51) 921222; fax (51) 921520; e-mail bhdca@bhdca.gov.ba; internet www.bhdca.gov.ba; f. 1997; Dir-Gen. ĐORĐE RATKOVIĆ.

Federation Civil Aviation Department (FEDCAD) (Federalna Direkcija za Civilnu Avijaciju): 88000 Mostar, Ante Starčevića bb; tel. (36) 449230; fax (36) 327811; e-mail info@fedcad.gov.ba; internet www.fmpik.gov.ba/sektori/civ_avio.html; Dir AMADEO MANDIĆ.

Republika Srpska Civil Aviation Department (RSCAD): 78250 Laktaši, Mahovljani bb, Banja Luka International Airport; tel. (51) 337500; fax (51) 337503; e-mail rscad@rscad.org; internet www.rscad.org; Dir DAMIR ĆOPIĆ.

B&H Airlines: 71000 Sarajevo, Kurta Schorka 36; tel. (33) 460783; fax (33) 466338; e-mail nrecica@bhairlines.ba; internet www.bhairlines.ba; f. 1994 as Air Bosna; ceased operations in 2003, relaunched as B&H Airlines in 2005; 51% state-owned; regular services to Croatia, Germany, Switzerland and Turkey; Dir-Gen. NUĐŽEIM REČICA.

Tourism

Bosnia and Herzegovina has many sites of potential interest to tourists, including mountain scenery, rivers and waterfalls, the historic cities of Sarajevo, Mostar, Travnik, Trebinje and Jajce. There were 310,942 foreign tourist arrivals in 2009, when receipts from tourism (including passenger transport) totalled US $761m.

Tourism Asscn of the Federation of Bosnia and Herzegovina: 71000 Sarajevo, Branilaca Sarajeva 21/2; tel. (33) 252900; fax (33) 252901; e-mail media@tourism.ba; internet www.bhtourism.ba.

Tourism Organization of Republika Srpska (Turistička organizacija Republike Srpske): 78000 Banja Luka, Bana Milosavljevića 8; tel. (51) 229720; fax (51) 229721; e-mail tors@teol.net; internet www.turizamrs.org.

Defence

As assessed at November 2011, the active armed forces of Bosnia and Herzegovina numbered 10,577, including an army of 9,205, air-force and air-defence brigades of 872, and 500 joint forces. Bosnia and Herzegovina was admitted to the 'Partnership for Peace' (PfP) programme of the North Atlantic Treaty Organization (NATO) on 14 December 2006.

An EU Force (EUFOR), authorized to maintain peace and to support the country's progress towards European integration, established in 2004 comprised around 1,468 personnel from 26 countries (including five non-EU member states) as assessed at November 2011.

Defence Expenditure: Budgeted at KM 353m. in 2010.

Chief of Joint Defence Staff of the Bosnia and Herzegovina Armed Forces: Lt-Gen. MILADIN MILOJČIĆ.

Commander of the European Union Force (EUFOR—ALTHEA) in Bosnia and Herzegovina: Maj.-Gen. BERNHARD BAIR.

Education

A nine-year system of elementary education is free and compulsory for children between the ages of six and 15 years. Secondary education is provided in general secondary schools, vocational schools, and technical schools. The entities and the District of Brčko have separate ministries of education, and authority over schooling in the Federation is further divided between the 10 cantons. In 2008/09 enrolment at primary schools included 87% of children in the relevant age-group, while secondary education enrolment was equivalent to 91% of children in the relevant age-group. In 2010/11 336,429 pupils were enrolled in a total of 1,942 primary schools, while 151,680 students were enrolled in 310 institutions of secondary education. Some 107,537 students were enrolled in 41 higher education institutions, including eight universities.

BOTSWANA

Introductory Survey

LOCATION, CLIMATE, LANGUAGE, RELIGION, FLAG, CAPITAL

The Republic of Botswana is a land-locked country in southern Africa, with South Africa to the south and east, Zimbabwe to the north-east and Namibia to the west and north. A short section of the northern frontier adjoins Zambia. The climate is generally sub-tropical, with hot summers. Annual rainfall averages about 457 mm (18 ins), varying from 635 mm (25 ins) in the north to 228 mm (9 ins) or less in the western Kalahari desert. The country is largely near-desert, and most of its inhabitants live along the eastern border, close to the main railway line. English is the official language, and Setswana the national language. Most of the population follow traditional animist beliefs, but several Christian churches are also represented. The national flag (proportions 2 by 3) consists of a central horizontal stripe of black, edged with white, between two blue stripes. The capital is Gaborone.

CONTEMPORARY POLITICAL HISTORY

Historical Context

Botswana was formerly Bechuanaland, which became a British protectorate, at the request of the local rulers, in 1885. It was administered as one of the High Commission Territories in southern Africa, the others being the colony of Basutoland (now Lesotho) and the protectorate of Swaziland. The British Act of Parliament that established the Union of South Africa in 1910 also allowed for the inclusion in South Africa of the three High Commission Territories, on condition that the local inhabitants were consulted. Until 1960 successive South African Governments asked for the transfer of the three territories, but the native chiefs always objected to such a scheme. Bechuanaland became the independent Republic of Botswana, within the Commonwealth, on 30 September 1966, with Sir Seretse Khama, the leader of the Botswana Democratic Party (BDP) taking office as the country's first President. The BDP won elections to the National Assembly, with little opposition, in 1969, 1974 and 1979.

Domestic Political Affairs

Upon Khama's death in July 1980, Dr Quett Masire (later Sir Ketumile Masire), hitherto Vice-President and Minister of Finance, was appointed to the presidency. Following elections to the National Assembly in September 1984, at which the BDP again achieved a decisive victory, Masire was re-elected President by the legislature. In October 1989 the BDP received 65% of the votes cast at a general election to the National Assembly, winning 27 of the 30 elective seats (the remaining three seats were won by the principal opposition party, the Botswana National Front—BNF), and the new legislature re-elected Masire for a third term as President.

At the general election held in October 1994 the BDP, which received 53.1% of the votes cast, won 26 of the 40 available seats, while the BNF, which obtained 37.7% of the votes, increased its representation to 13 seats. More than 70% of registered voters participated in the election. The National Assembly subsequently re-elected Masire to the presidency.

In August 1997 the National Assembly formally adopted a constitutional amendment restricting the presidential mandate to two terms of office and providing for the automatic succession to the presidency of the Vice-President, in the event of the death or resignation of the President. In September a national referendum endorsed further revisions, lowering the age of eligibility to vote from 21 to 18 years and providing for the establishment of an independent electoral commission. In November Masire announced his intention to retire from politics in March 1998. In accordance with the amended Constitution, Vice-President Festus Mogae was inaugurated as President on 1 April 1998, pending elections to be held in 1999, and subsequently appointed a new Cabinet, in which the only new minister was Lt-Gen. Seretse Khama Ian Khama, son of Sir Seretse Khama and hitherto Commander of the Botswana Defence Force (BDF). Khama received the portfolio of presidential affairs and public administration, and was later designated as Mogae's Vice-President, subject to his election to the National Assembly. Ponatshego Kedikilwe, the Chairman of the BDP, was appointed Minister of Finance and Development Planning. Khama was elected to the National Assembly in July, and was sworn in as Vice-President in the same month.

Meanwhile, hostility between Kenneth Koma, the leader of the BNF, and his deputy, Michael Dingake, had led to a split in the party. In June 1998 the Botswana Congress Party (BCP) was formed, under the leadership of Dingake and the following month the BCP was declared the official opposition, after 11 of the BNF's 13 deputies joined the new party.

At the general election, held in mid-October 1999, the BDP received 57.2% of the votes and increased its representation in the National Assembly from 26 to 33 seats, while the number of seats held by the BNF (with 26.0% of the votes) fell significantly, to only six seats. The BCP (having received 11.9%) obtained just one seat; 77.3% of the electorate participated in the polls. Mogae was re-elected to the presidency by the National Assembly on 20 October.

In November 2001 a number of changes to the structure and conditions of service of the judiciary were approved in a national referendum, although less than 5% of the electorate were reported to have participated in the vote. Ethnic tensions arose over a clause providing for an increase in the retirement age for judges. Pitso Ya Batswana, a Tswana nationalist group, claimed that this proposal was evidence of the over-representation in the judiciary and other professions of the Kalanga people, who constituted approximately 10% of the population, and that the referendum represented an attempt by the Kalanga community to advance its own interests. However, the Kalanga, together with numerous other ethnic groups, were not recognized in the Constitution as one of the eight tribes with the right to be represented in the House of Chiefs, Botswana's second legislative house. The Government had established a constitutional commission in July 2000 to investigate allegations of discrimination against minority groups, including the Kalanga, Wayeyi and San (see below). On the basis of the recommendations of this commission, in December 2001 the Government presented a number of draft constitutional amendments. Under the proposals, the House of Chiefs would be renamed the Ntlo ya Dikgosi and its membership increased from 15 to 35, comprising 30 members elected by senior tribal authorities and five members appointed by the President. Elections to the Ntlo ya Dikgosi would be held every five years. In April 2002 the draft amendments were revised to allow the eight paramount chiefs to retain their ex officio status in the chamber. The proposed amendments were submitted to the legislature in late 2003. Approval of the increase in membership was announced in late December 2005.

In June 2002 the National Assembly approved legislation providing for an expansion in its directly elected membership from 40 to 57, with effect from the next general election, and a gradual increase in both the number of ministries, from 12 to 16, and in the number of assistant ministers, from four to eight.

At the election to the newly enlarged legislature, held on 30 October 2004, the BDP secured 44 seats, although it obtained a smaller share of the vote (51.7%) than at the previous general election. The BNF received 26.1% of the votes cast and increased its representation to 12 seats, while the BCP (with 16.6%) retained its solitary parliamentary seat. The rate of voter participation was recorded at 74.6%. President Mogae was sworn in for a second and final term of office on 2 November. Eleven new appointees were included in the reorganized Cabinet.

In January 2007 President Mogae effected a reorganization of the Cabinet. Most notably, Daniel Kwelagobe was appointed to the newly created post of Minister for Public Service in the Office of the President, responsible for the Public Service, the Ombudsman, the Independent Electoral Commission and the National AIDS Co-ordinating Agency, while Kedikilwe assumed the minerals, energy and water affairs portfolio, replacing Charles Tibone, who became Minister of Labour and Home Affairs.

Recent developments: the Khama presidency

In July 2007 President Mogae announced that, as expected, he would relinquish the presidency in March 2008. In accordance with the Constitution, Vice-President Khama was sworn in as his successor on 1 April. Lt-Gen Mompati Merafhe, hitherto Minister of Foreign Affairs and International Co-operation, was appointed to the vice-presidency and a new Cabinet was named, which resulted in the removal of five ministers. Later in April Kwelagobe was appointed Chairman of the BDP.

Despite the dominant status of the BDP in national politics, the party was increasingly affected by internal divisions. In September 2009 factional rivalry within the BDP resulted in the dismissal of Gomolemo Motswaledi, who was eventually replaced as Secretary-General of the party in November by Thato Kwerepe. Motswaledi had challenged Khama's decision to appoint five additional members to the party's central committee in an attempt to reduce the influence of Kwelagobe, whose supporters had secured the majority of executive positions on the committee. Motswaledi was subsequently suspended from the BDP for a period of five years.

Meanwhile, at the elections to the National Assembly, which took place on 16 October 2009, the BDP secured 53.3% of the valid votes cast, thus increasing the number of seats it held in the legislature by one, to 45. The BNF's representation was reduced from 12 seats to just six (the party took 21.9% of votes), while the BCP (with 19.2%) won four seats, compared with the one seat it secured in 2004. Observers from the Southern African Development Community declared the elections 'credible, peaceful, free and fair'. On 20 October President Khama was inaugurated for his first full five-year term of office and the following day he appointed a new Cabinet, which featured five new ministers. Merafhe retained the vice-presidency, while Lesego Motsumi replaced Kwelagobe as Minister of Presidential Affairs and Public Administration.

Continuing factionalization within the BDP precipitated the creation of the Botswana Movement for Democracy (BMD), which separated from the ruling party in May 2010. The BMD was formed by four BDP parliamentarians, dissatisfied with Khama's autocratic leadership style and his treatment of Motswaledi, and portrayed itself as a younger, more progressive political alternative, utilizing the internet to spread its message. A further four elected BDP members, along with several councillors, defected to the BMD in mid-2010, making the splinter party the largest opposition grouping in the National Assembly. (Interim deputy leader of the BMD Botsalo Ntuane was officially named Leader of the Opposition in November.) Two of the defectors subsequently rejoined the BDP, however, with the BMD claiming that they had been seduced by financial incentives and offers of ministerial jobs, allegations that the ruling party denied. Following the large number of party defections during the year, Motsumi proposed legislation in November to discourage members of the National Assembly from changing political affiliation. If adopted, the law would require defectors to relinquish their seats and stand for re-election. Meanwhile, the main opposition parties—the BMD, the BCP, the BNF and the Botswana People's Party—held discussions in 2010 with the aim of forming an informal coalition to challenge the dominance of the BDP. However, opposition co-operation efforts suffered a reverse in September, when the BDP candidate in the Tonota North by-election comprehensively defeated the BCP's representative, who had been supported by the other coalition parties. Mutual mistrust and ideological differences among the opposition groups continued to undermine the cohesion of the coalition. None the less, in mid-2011 the three main opposition parties decided to ally themselves against the BDP for the forthcoming general elections in 2014, and at the inaugural congress of the BMD in May 2011 Motswaledi was elected as the party's first President.

Meanwhile, the Minister of Defence, Justice and Security, and cousin of the President, Brig. Dikgakgamatso Seretse, tendered his resignation at the end of August 2010 after allegedly failing to reveal his role as a director of a company that had been awarded government supply contracts, in contravention of anti-corruption legislation. Seretse was charged by public prosecutors with corruption in October. Motsumi was assigned responsibility for Seretse's portfolios on an acting basis.

Khama announced a rearranged Cabinet in October 2011. Edwin Batsu was replaced as Minister of Justice, Defence and Security by Ramadeluka Seretse. Batsu replaced Peter Siele as Minister of Labour and Home Affairs, while Siele was appointed Minister of Local Government. Lebonaamang Mokalake became the Minister of Lands and Housing, replacing Nonofo Molefhi, who was appointed Minister of Transport and Communications.

Some 100,000 civil servants began industrial action in April 2011 in response to the Government's refusal to increase wages by 16%. The unprecedented civil action—the country's first national strike—was believed to have adversely affected the health and education sectors, although Government was quick to downplay the crisis. The strike was organized by the Botswana Federation of Public Sector Unions (BFPSU), which maintained that the Government had not increased wages for public sector workers for three consecutive years. The public sector is Botswana's largest employer, and in order to maintain services, the Government redeployed members of the police and military, prompting the trade unions to accuse them of intimidation and the use of illegal substitute workers. Meanwhile, the Industrial Court ordered all workers in essential service sectors back to work. In May many doctors, nurses, pharmacists and cleaners lost their jobs as a result of the strike action, which finally ended in June with the unions accepting a wage increase of 3%. In September the BFPSU requested that the courts reinstate about 2,600 workers from the public sector who had lost their jobs as a result of the industrial action. Following the end of the strike the Labour Ministry classified teachers and diamond workers (among others) as providing essential services in order that they would not be able to take part in future strikes.

Indigenous Peoples' Rights

The Government's attempts to relocate San (Bushmen) people from their homeland within the Central Kalahari Game Reserve to a new settlement outside the Reserve provoked international concern from 1996. It was claimed that officials had forced many San to move by disconnecting water supplies and threatening military intervention; 2,160 San had been resettled by mid-2001, according to reports. At the end of January 2002 the Government withdrew services to the remaining San living in the Reserve (estimated to number 500–700), in accordance with a decision announced in August 2001. A legal appeal brought to a halt the process of relocation but the return of hunting rights to the San was rejected on a technicality in April 2002. In August a delegation from the European Union (EU, see p. 276) accused the Government of providing false information about the number of San remaining in the Reserve, and of failing to fulfil their human rights requirements, including the supply of fresh water. In October the Government awarded some P2m. in compensation to more than 3,000 San who had been removed from the Reserve. In late 2002 Survival International, a lobby group for the rights of indigenous peoples, alleged that the Government had relocated the San in order to allow mining companies to explore for diamonds in the Reserve; the Government vehemently rejected these claims, maintaining that it was acting in the socio-economic interests of the San. Some 243 San commenced legal action against the Government in late 2003 in order to be permitted to live in the Reserve. In mid-2005 the Government removed a clause in the Constitution granting protection to San and other minorities, and some analysts argued that this was designed to undermine the court challenge. In December 2006 the High Court ruled that the removal of the San from the Reserve had been 'unlawful and unconstitutional' and confirmed their right to live on the Reserve, but also decreed that the Government was not obliged to provide services to them. Following the announcement of the decision some 100 San returned to the Reserve, although it was reported that the Government was attempting to limit the number of returnees. In June 2008 Khama reasserted the Government's firm stance on the issue and maintained that the authorities would not provide the San with any amenities in the Reserve. The Government attracted criticism in July 2010 when it defeated a legal challenge by San demanding the right to reopen a well on the Reserve, which had been sealed by the authorities. The ruling also denied the San the right to drill other water-holes, forcing them to rely upon water transported from distant settlements. The San announced their intention to contest the verdict. In protest against the Government's conduct, in November Survival International appealed for a boycott of Botswana diamonds. In January 2011 the Botswana Court of Appeal ruled that the San were entitled to use the existing well on the Reserve and also granted them permission to drill for new sources of water.

Foreign Affairs

From independence, it was the Botswana Government's stated policy not to permit any guerrilla groups to operate from its territory. Relations with South Africa deteriorated in May 1984,

2009 the Government announced plans to open up the Central Kgalagadi Game Reserve to mineral exploration, granting some 100 mining licences to 14 foreign companies. Other immediate government priorities included the creation of new employment opportunities and the maintenance of macroeconomic stability and financial discipline. Nevertheless, the HIV/AIDS pandemic represents a significant threat to continued economic growth, diminishing the work-force and depleting government resources through expenditure on projects to counter the disease. Approximately one-quarter of the population between the ages of 15 and 49 was believed to be infected with HIV in 2009, although World Health Organization figures showed an increase in life expectancy, to an estimated 61 years, in 2009. The use of antiretroviral drugs has increased among the infected population, and at December 2010 it was estimated that antiretroviral drugs coverage had reached at least 80% of the infected population. Following three years of budget deficits as a result of the global economic crisis, which reduced diamond sales and foreign direct investment in the country, a budget surplus of 0.9% of GDP was forecast for 2012. The economy also returned to growth in 2010, following a contraction in 2009. Furthermore, in 2011 GDP was estimated to have increased by almost 6%, according to the IMF, although the Ministry of Finance revised its growth projection for 2012 down to 4.4%. Uncertainty in the diamond sector was blamed, as revenue from sales of this mineral declined by some 70% between June and December 2011. Government proposals to reduce spending—from 36% of GDP in 2011 to 33% in 2012—were to include a 5% cut in all ministries' wage bills over the following three years, if diamond sales failed to recover. This appeared likely further to strain relations between the Government and the public sector unions, which organized the country's first national strike in April 2011 (see Recent Developments).

PUBLIC HOLIDAYS

2013: 1–2 January (New Year), 29 March–1 April (Easter), 1 May (Labour Day), 9 May (Ascension Day), 1 July (Sir Seretse Khama Day), 15–16 July (President's Day), 30 September (Botswana Day), 25–26 December (Christmas).

Statistical Survey

Source (unless otherwise stated): Central Statistics Office, Private Bag 0024, Gaborone; tel. 352200; fax 352201; e-mail csobots@gov.bw; internet www.cso.gov.bw.

Area and Population

AREA, POPULATION AND DENSITY

Area (sq km)	581,730*
Population (census results)	
17 August 2001	
Males	813,583
Females	867,280
Total	1,680,863†
9-18 August 2011 (preliminary)	2,038,228
Density (per sq km) at 2011 census	3.5

* 224,607 sq miles.

† Excluding 60,716 non-Batswana enumerated at the time of the census.

POPULATION BY AGE AND SEX

(UN estimates at mid-2012)

	Males	Females	Total
0–14	330,388	325,115	655,503
15–64	671,019	641,202	1,312,221
65 and over	36,387	49,126	85,513
Total	1,037,794	1,015,443	2,053,237

Source: UN, *World Population Prospects: The 2010 Revision*.

DISTRICTS AND SUB-DISTRICTS

(population at 2011 census, preliminary)

Central		Kweneng West	47,841
Bobonong	70,806	*North-East*	
Boteti	56,209	Francistown	100,079
Mahalapye	117,492	North-East	59,829
Orapa	9,544	*North-West*	
Selebi-Phikwe	49,724	Chobe	23,449
Serowe/Palapye	188,174	Ngamiland West	61,748
Sowa Town	3,599	Ngamiland East†	96,356
Tutume	144,895	*South-East*	
Ghanzi		Gaborone	227,333
Ghanzi*	43,370	Lobatse	29,032
Kgalagadi		South-East	92,843
Kgalagadi North	20,484	*Southern*	
Kgalagadi South	30,016	Barolong	55,103
Kgatleng		Jwaneng	18,063
Kgatleng	92,247	Ngwaketse	129,462
Kweneng		Ngwaketse West	13,697
Kweneng East	256,833	**Total**	2,038,228

* Including Central Kalahari Game Reserve (CKGR) sub-district.

† Including Delta sub-district.

PRINCIPAL TOWNS

(population at 2011 census, preliminary)

Gaborone (capital)	227,333	Selebi-Phikwe	49,724
Francistown	100,079	Serowe	47,447
Molepolole	67,598	Kanye	45,196
Mogoditshane	57,637	Mochudi	44,339
Maun	55,784	Mahalapye	41,316

BIRTHS AND DEATHS

(annual averages, UN estimates)

	1995–2000	2000–05	2005–10
Birth rate (per 1,000)	28.6	25.5	24.2
Death rate (per 1,000)	11.0	14.9	12.6

Source: UN, *World Population Prospects: The 2010 Revision*.

2001 (12 months prior to August 2001 census): Births 53,735 (birth rate 41.1 per 1,000); deaths 20,823 (death rate 12.4 per 1,000) (Source: UN, *Demographic Yearbook*).

2006: Crude birth rate 29.7; crude death rate 11.2.

Life expectancy (years at birth, WHO estimates): 61 (males 59; females 62) in 2009 (Source: WHO, *World Health Statistics*).

EMPLOYMENT

(number of persons aged 7 years and over, 2006 labour force survey)

	Males	Females	Total
Agriculture, hunting, forestry and fishing	98,805	62,561	161,367
Mining and quarrying	12,457	1,716	14,173
Manufacturing	16,010	19,962	35,973
Electricity, gas and water supply	2,626	1,537	4,163
Construction	23,111	4,476	27,587
Wholesale and retail trade; repair of motor vehicles, motorcycles and personal and household goods	27,924	49,478	77,401
Hotels and restaurants	3,770	10,898	14,667
Transport, storage and communications	10,496	5,555	16,050
Financial intermediation	3,018	5,406	8,424
Real estate, renting and business services	15,554	9,701	25,255
Public administration and defence; compulsory social security	34,539	25,618	60,157
Education	15,182	28,063	43,245
Health and social work	5,393	8,609	14,002

—continued	Males	Females	Total
Other community, social and personal service activities	5,213	5,342	10,554
Private households with employed persons	7,208	18,027	25,235
Extra-territorial organizations and bodies	456	439	895
Total employed	281,762	257,388	539,150

Mid-2012 ('000 persons, FAO estimates): Agriculture, etc. 326; Total labour force 783 (Source: FAO).

Health and Welfare

KEY INDICATORS

Total fertility rate (children per woman, 2009)	2.8
Under-5 mortality rate (per 1,000 live births, 2009)	57
HIV/AIDS (% of persons aged 15–49, 2009)	24.8
Physicians (per 1,000 head, 2004)	0.4
Hospital beds (per 1,000 head, 2007)	2.4
Health expenditure (2008): US $ per head (PPP)	1,053
Health expenditure (2008): % of GDP	7.6
Health expenditure (2008): public (% of total)	78.2
Access to water (% of persons, 2008)	95
Access to sanitation (% of persons, 2008)	60
Total carbon dioxide emissions ('000 metric tons, 2007)	4,994.0
Carbon dioxide emissions per head (metric tons, 2007)	2.6
Human Development Index (2011): ranking	118
Human Development Index (2011): value	0.633

For sources and definitions, see explanatory note on p. vi.

Agriculture

PRINCIPAL CROPS
('000 metric tons)

	2008	2009	2010*
Maize	9.0	13.2	14.1
Sorghum	23.6	37.6	41.0
Sunflower seed	8.1	6.0†	3.7
Roots and tubers	99.7*	87.6*	99.4
Pulses	2.3	2.5*	2.3

* FAO estimate(s).
† Unofficial figure.

Aggregate production ('000 metric tons, may include official, semi-official or estimated data): Total cereals 35.9 in 2008, 55.9 in 2009, 60.5 in 2010; Total vegetables (incl. melons) 31.7 in 2008, 25.8 in 2009, 28.0 in 2010; Total fruits (excl. melons) 7.9 in 2008, 6.0 in 2009, 5.9 in 2010.

Source: FAO.

LIVESTOCK
('000 head, year ending September)

	2008	2009	2010*
Cattle	2,222	2,467	2,550
Horses	38	38	38
Asses	330*	330*	330
Sheep	188	170	153
Goats	1,880	2,000*	2,100
Pigs	14	13	13
Poultry	4,800*	5,000*	5100

* FAO estimate(s).

LIVESTOCK PRODUCTS
('000 metric tons)

	2008	2009	2010
Cattle meat*	36.0	36.0	37.0
Goat meat	5.5	5.5	5.5*
Chicken meat*	6.6	5.8	6.8
Other meat*	8.0	8.5	9.1
Cows' milk*	108.2	112.4	114.2
Goats' milk*	4.8	3.9	4.1
Hen eggs*	4.5	4.3	4.5

* FAO estimate(s).

Source: FAO.

Forestry

ROUNDWOOD REMOVALS
('000 cubic metres, excl. bark, FAO estimates)

	2007	2008	2009
Industrial wood	105.0	105.0	105.0
Fuel wood	669.0	673.9	678.6
Total	774.0	778.9	783.6

2010: Production assumed to be unchanged from 2009 (FAO estimates).

Source: FAO.

Fishing

(metric tons, live weight)

	2006	2007	2008
Tilapias	52	82	61
Torpedo-shaped catfishes	25	37	23
Other freshwater fishes	4	3	2
Total catch	81	122	86

2009: Figures assumed to be unchanged from 2008 (FAO estimates).

Source: FAO.

Mining

(metric tons, unless otherwise indicated)

	2008	2009	2010
Hard coal	909,511	737,798	988,240
Copper ore*†	23,146	24,382	n.a.
Nickel ore†	28,940	29,616	n.a.
Gold (kg)	3,176	1,626	1,774
Cobalt*†	337	342	252
Salt	170,994	241,114	346,761
Diamonds ('000 carats)	32,595	17,733	22,019
Soda ash (natural)	263,566	215,188	240,898
Sand and gravel ('000 cu m)‡	3,000§	3,000§	n.a.

* Figures refer to the metal content of matte; product smelted was granulated nickel-copper-cobalt matte.
† Figures refer to the nickel content of matte and include some product not reported as milled.
‡ Source: US Geological Survey.
§ Estimate.

Source (unless otherwise stated): Bank of Botswana, *Annual Report 2010*.

Industry

SELECTED PRODUCTS

	2001	2002	2003
Beer ('000 hl)	1,692	1,396	1,198
Soft drinks ('000 hl)	431	389	405
Electric energy (million kWh)	1,010	1,060	1,133

Electric energy (million kWh): 991 in 2004; 971 in 2005; 1,042 in 2006; 721 in 2007; 631 in 2008.

Source: UN Industrial Commodity Statistics Database.

Finance

CURRENCY AND EXCHANGE RATES

Monetary Units
100 thebe = 1 pula (P).

Sterling, Dollar and Euro Equivalents (30 December2011)
£1 sterling = 11.636 pula;
US $1 = 7.526 pula;
€1 = 9.738 pula;
100 pula = £8.59 = $13.29 = €10.27.

Average Exchange Rate (pula per US $)
2009 7.1551
2010 6.7936
2011 6.8382

BUDGET
(million pula, year ending 31 March)

Revenue*	2009/10	2010/11†	2011/12‡
Taxation	26,773.9	26,060.3	31,205.2
Mineral revenue	9,088.4	9,317.0	11,197.0
Customs and excise	7,931.0	6,003.7	8,458.0
Non-mineral income taxes	5,560.6	5,805.9	5 998.2
Other taxes	4,193.8	4,933.7	5,552.0
General sales tax/VAT	3,943.5	4,668.4	5,252.0
Other current revenue	2,480.4	3,707.7	2,582.5
Interest	32.1	48.4	34.9
Other property income	1,107.7	866.5	605.4
Fees, charges, etc.	1,237.1	1,653.9	1,864.8
Sales of fixed assets and land	103.6	1,138.9	77.4
Total	29,254.3	29,768.0	33,787.7

Expenditure§	2009/10	2010/11†	2011/12‡
General services (incl. defence)	9,737.0	10,251.7	10,618.4
Social services	17,969.2	17,711.5	18,882.7
Education	9,299.9	10,224.5	9,634.1
Health	3,372.1	3,397.9	4,594.8
Housing, urban and regional development	3,480.4	2,446.8	3,112.0
Food and social welfare programme	727.1	704.5	744.9
Other community and social services	1,089.8	937.9	796.8
Economic services	8,388.5	8,991.9	8,495.8
Agriculture, forestry and fishing	1,185.0	1,064.8	1,108.5
Mining	768.6	166.7	686.6
Electricity and water supply	1,857.2	3,732.5	2,731.8
Roads	1,900.5	1,849.5	1,927.2
Others	2,677.3	2,178.5	2,041.8
Transfers	3,394.6	3,553.5	3,031.4
Deficit grants to local authorities	3,024.8	3,053.9	2,473.9
Interest on public debt	369.8	499.6	557.5
Total	39,489.2	40,508.5	41,028.2

* Excluding grants received (million pula): 768.8 in 2009/10; 520.3 in 2010/11 (estimate); 310.3 in 2011/12 (budget forecast).

† Estimates.

‡ Budget forecasts.

§ Including net lending (million pula): 751.7 in 2009/10; –26.6 in 2010/11 (estimate); –94.2 in 2011/12 (budget forecast).

Source: Bank of Botswana, *Annual Report 2010*.

INTERNATIONAL RESERVES
(US $ million at 31 December)

	2008	2009	2010
IMF special drawing rights	60.93	145.57	143.19
Reserve position in IMF	13.06	17.79	20.86
Foreign exchange	9,044.66	8,540.60	7,721.16
Total	9,118.64	8,703.96	7,885.21

Source: IMF, *International Financial Statistics*.

MONEY SUPPLY
(million pula at 31 December)

	2008	2009	2010
Currency outside depository corporations	1,103	1,145	1,241
Transferable deposits	6,666	5,963	8,023
Other deposits	31,459	31,609	33,596
Broad money	39,228	38,717	42,860

Source: IMF, *International Financial Statistics*.

COST OF LIVING
(Consumer Price Index; base: 2000 = 100)

	2008	2009	2010
Food (incl. beverages)	207.7	237.4	246.1
Clothing (incl. footwear)	122.2	132.6	143.2
Fuel	288.9	284.6	320.6
All items (incl. others)	196.6	212.5	227.3

Source: ILO.

NATIONAL ACCOUNTS
(million pula at current prices, provisional figures)

Expenditure on the Gross Domestic Product

	2008	2009	2010
Government final consumption expenditure	17,339	20,077	21,141
Private final consumption expenditure	31,897	36,689	42,737
Increase in stocks	7,050	1,726	2,068
Gross fixed capital formation	21,252	23,372	26,051
Total domestic expenditure	77,538	81,865	91,997
Exports of goods and services	38,657	26,273	32,949
Less Imports of goods and services	35,131	35,629	40,111
Statistical discrepancy	10,916	9,587	16,100
GDP in purchasers' values	91,981	82,096	100,935
GDP at constant 1993/94 prices	25,484	24,227	25,970

Gross Domestic Product by Economic Activity

	2008	2009	2010
Agriculture, hunting, forestry and fishing	2,025	1,947	2,348
Mining and quarrying	37,515	21,464	31,561
Manufacturing	3,111	3,343	3,857
Water and electricity	2,341	2,409	2,824
Construction	3,571	4,313	5,169
Trade, restaurants and hotels	10,102	11,328	13,110
Transport, post and telecommunications	3,401	4,050	4,443
Finance, insurance and business services	9,462	10,302	11,586
Government services	13,676	15,364	16,782
Social and personal services	3,156	3,765	4,194
Sub-total	88,359	78,285	95,874
Less Imputed bank service charge.	4,160	4,563	4,835
GDP at basic prices	84,199	73,722	91,039
Import duties	4,582	4,610	5,183
Taxes on products	3,586	4,204	5,212
Less Subsidies on products	387	439	499
GDP in purchasers' values	91,981	82,096	100,935

Source: Bank of Botswana, *Annual Report 2010*.

BALANCE OF PAYMENTS
(US $ million)

	2008	2009	2010
Exports of goods f.o.b.	4,800.1	3,435.0	4,633.3
Imports of goods f.o.b.	-4,364.9	-4,003.2	-4,841.7
Trade balance	435.1	-568.3	-208.5
Exports of services	871.8	496.0	394.5
Imports of services	-783.0	-952.2	-876.6
Balance on goods and services	524.0	-1,024.5	-690.6
Other income received	474.7	352.4	413.0
Other income paid	-1,171.3	-455.0	-655.6
Balance on goods, services and income	-172.7	-1,127.1	-933.2
Current transfers received	1,399.3	1,153.5	1,396.2
Current transfers paid	-358.9	-547.6	-417.2
Current balance	867.8	-521.3	45.9
Capital account (net)	76.3	89.2	19.0
Direct investment abroad	91.1	-65.2	-0.3
Direct investment from abroad	902.4	824.1	265.0
Portfolio investment assets	322.9	347.8	396.8
Portfolio investment liabilities	-29.5	17.7	17.8
Other investment assets	-1,194.6	-1,142.6	-1,217.8
Other investment liabilities	-9.3	38.6	-96.2
Net errors and omissions	144.0	699.9	609.5
Overall balance	1,171.0	288.5	39.8

Source: IMF, *International Financial Statistics*.

External Trade

PRINCIPAL COMMODITIES
(million pula, provisional figures)

Imports c.i.f.	2008	2009	2010
Food, beverages and tobacco	4,277.3	4,435.7	4,812.0
Fuels	6,006.5	4,515.8	5,520.0
Chemicals and rubber products	3,739.0	3,753.3	4,206.4
Wood and paper products	1,205.8	1,332.3	1,314.9
Textiles and footwear	1,413.3	1,504.0	1,562.5
Metals and metal products	2,799.0	2,391.2	2,854.9
Machinery and electrical equipment	6,269.2	5,795.0	6,760.2
Vehicles and transport equipment	3,822.9	4,219.0	3,704.9
Total (incl. others)	35,443.4	33,560.7	38,450.4

Exports f.o.b.	2008	2009	2010
Meat and meat products	608.8	808.4	1,082.9
Diamonds	20,793.3	15,234.1	21,779.9
Copper-nickel matte	5,925.4	3,621.2	4,231.3
Textiles	1,817.8	1,417.6	1,118.5
Vehicles and parts	453.9	491.1	500.6
Total (incl. others)	32,892.0	24,317.7	32,040.5

PRINCIPAL TRADING PARTNERS
(million pula, provisional figures)

Imports c.i.f.	2008	2009	2010
SACU*	27,611.9	25,757.9	28,304.5
Zimbabwe	322.2	272.0	258.3
United Kingdom	2,143.2	2,042.7	3,563.2
Other Europe	26.2	1.7	195.2
Korea, Repub.	43.8	46.9	55.2
USA	458.1	726.5	506.9
Total (incl. others)	35,443.4	33,560.7	38,450.4

Exports f.o.b.	2008	2009	2010
SACU*	6,414.3	3,573.6	4,381.5
Zimbabwe	1,457.7	1,085.4	1,194.9
Other Africa	32.0	18.3	2.9
United Kingdom	18,267.0	13,061.8	17,710.1
Other Europe	4.2	1.0	2.1
USA	328.1	321.5	385.1
Total (incl. others)	32,892.0	24,317.7	32,040.5

* Southern African Customs Union, of which Botswana is a member; also including Lesotho, Namibia, South Africa and Swaziland.

Transport

RAILWAYS
(traffic)

	2007	2008	2009*
Number of passengers ('000)	382.8	391.1	97.6
Freight ('000 metric tons)	1,750.7	1,759.5	971.0

* Preliminary figures.

Passenger-km (million): 528.1 in 2002; 572.0 in 2003.

Freight net ton-km (million): 920.2 in 2003; 636.7 in 2004 (Source: International Road Federation, *World Road Statistics*).

ROAD TRAFFIC
(registered vehicles)

	2007	2008	2009*
Cars	104,926	120,783	135,334
Light duty vehicles	82,916	88,547	91,826
Trucks	12,819	15,324	17,209
Buses	10,019	10,889	11,590
Tractors	2,835	3,371	4,057
Others (incl. trailers, motorcycles and tankers)	16,548	17,584	20,623
Total	230,063	256,498	280,639

* Estimates.

CIVIL AVIATION
(traffic on scheduled services, million)

	2007	2008	2009
Kilometres flown	4	4	4
Passenger-km	116	118	113
Total ton-km	10	11	10

Source: UN, *Statistical Yearbook*.

Passengers carried: 609,715 in 2007; 645,823 in 2008; 772,186 in 2009.

Freight carried (metric tons): 1,098.2 in 2007; 1,067.8 in 2008; 936.9 in 2009.

Tourism

FOREIGN TOURIST ARRIVALS

Country of origin	2004*	2006	2007
Namibia	57,542	78,530	64,298
South Africa	626,207	516,329	479,473
United Kingdom	24,069	23,860	19,690
Zambia	72,492	126,201	80,592
Zimbabwe	576,328	499,869	652,292
Total (incl. others)	1,522,807	1,425,994	1,455,151

* Data for 2005 were not available.

Total arrivals ('000): 1,500 in 2008; 1,553 in 2009.

Receipts from tourism (US $ million, excl. passenger transport): 546 in 2007; 553 in 2008; 452 in 2009.

Source: World Tourism Organization.

Office of the Attorney-General

Private Bag 009, Gaborone; tel. 3954700; fax 3957089.

Attorney-General: Dr ATHALIAH MOLOKOMME.

Religion

In 2006, according to official figures, the majority of the population aged 10 years and above were Christians (approximately 62%); an estimated 2% held animist beliefs. There are Islamic mosques in Gaborone and Lobatse. Hinduism and the Bahá'í Faith are also represented.

CHRISTIANITY

Botswana Council of Churches (Lekgotla la Dikereke mo Botswana): POB 355, Gaborone; tel. and fax 3951981; e-mail bots.christ.c@info.bw; f. 1966; Pres. Rev. MPHO MORUAKGOMO; Gen. Sec. DAVID J. MODIEGA; 24 mem. churches and orgs.

The Anglican Communion

Anglicans are adherents of the Church of the Province of Central Africa, covering Botswana, Malawi, Zambia and Zimbabwe. The Church comprises 15 dioceses, including one in Botswana. The current Archbishop of the Province is the Bishop of Northern Zambia. The Province was established in 1955, and the diocese of Botswana was formed in 1972. There were some 10,500 adherents at mid-2000.

Bishop of Botswana: Rt Rev. MUSONDA TREVOR S. MWAMBA, POB 769, Gaborone; tel. 3953779; fax 3952075; e-mail info@anglicanbotswana.org.bw.

Protestant Churches

There were an estimated 178,000 adherents in the country at mid-2000.

African Methodist Episcopal Church: POB 141, Lobatse; tel. 5407520; e-mail mobeat@bpc.bw; Presiding Elder Rev. MOSES P. LEKHORI.

Evangelical Lutheran Church in Botswana (Kereke ya Luthere ya Efangele mo Botswana): POB 1976, Serotologane St, Plot 28570, Gaborone; tel. 3164612; fax 3164615; e-mail elcb@info.bw; f. 1979; Bishop Dr COSMOS MOENGA; 43 congregations; 18,650 mems (2010).

Evangelical Lutheran Church in Southern Africa (Botswana Diocese): Bontleng, POB 201012, Gaborone; tel. and fax 302144; f. 1982; Bishop Rev. G. EKSTEEN.

Methodist Church of Southern Africa (Gaborone Circuit): POB 260, Gaborone; tel. 3167627; Circuit Supt Rev. ODIRILE E. MERE.

United Congregational Church of Southern Africa (Synod of Botswana): POB 1263, Gaborone; tel. 3952491; synod status since 1980; Chair. Rev. D. T. MAPITSE; Sec. Rev. M. P. P. DIBEELA; c. 24,000 mems.

Other denominations active in Botswana include the Church of God in Christ, the Dutch Reformed Church, the Mennonite Church, the United Methodist Church and the Seventh-day Adventists.

The Roman Catholic Church

Botswana comprises one diocese and one apostolic vicariate. The metropolitan see is Bloemfontein, South Africa. The church was established in Botswana in 1928, and adherents comprised some 5% of the total population. The Bishop participates in the Southern African Catholic Bishops' Conference, currently based in Pretoria, South Africa.

Bishop of Gaborone: Rt Rev. VALENTINE TSAMMA SEANE, POB 218, Bishop's House, Plot 162, Queens Rd, Gaborone; tel. 3912958; fax 3956970; e-mail gabs.diocese@botsnet.bw.

Vicar Apostolic of Francistown: Rt Rev. FRANKLYN NUBUASAH, POB 702, Tsane Rd, 14061 Area W, Francistown; tel. 2413601; fax 2417183; e-mail catholicoffice@botsnet.bw.

The Press

DAILY NEWSPAPERS

Dikgang tsa Gompieno (Daily News): 37795 Wellie Seboni Dr., Private Bag BR 139, Gaborone; tel. 3653500; fax 3901675; e-mail dailynews@gov.bw; internet www.dailynews.gov.bw; f. 1964; Mon.–Fri.; publ. by Dept of Information and Broadcasting; Setswana and English; Acting Editor THEBEYAME RAMOROKA; circ. 60,000.

Mmegi/The Reporter: Segogwane Way, Plot 8901, Broadhurst, Private Bag BR 50, Gaborone; tel. 3974784; fax 3905508; e-mail dikgang@mmegi.bw; internet www.mmegi.bw; f. 1984 as *Mmegi wa Dikgang*; daily; publ. by Dikgang Publishing Co; Setswana and English; Man. Editor TITUS MBUYA; circ. 20,000; also publishes the weekly *Mmegi Monitor* (f. 2000, Monday, circ. 16,000).

PERIODICALS

Botswana Advertiser/Northern Advertiser: 5647 Nakedi Rd, Broadhurst Industrial, POB 130, Gaborone; tel. 3914788; fax 3182957; e-mail sales@northernadvertiser.co.bw; internet www.theadvertiser.co.bw; f. 1971; owned by Screen Print (Pty) Ltd; weekly; English; circ. 90,000 (*Botswana Advertiser*), 35,000 (*Northern Advertiser*); Gen. Man. MARTIN CHIBANDA.

The Botswana Gazette: 125 Sedimosa House, Millennium Park, Kgale View, POB 1605, Gaborone; tel. 3912833; fax 3972283; e-mail info@gazettebw.com; internet www.gazette.bw; f. 1985; publ. by News Co Botswana; weekly; Man. Dir CLARA OLSEN; Editor AUBREY LUTE; circ. 17,000.

Botswana Guardian: Plot 14442, Kamushungo Rd, G-West Industrial Site, POB 1641, Gaborone; tel. 3908432; fax 3908457; internet www.botswanaguardian.co.bw; f. 1983; weekly; publ. by Pula Printing & Publishing (Pty) Ltd; English; Editor OUTSA MOKONE; circ. 21,505.

Business and Financial Times: Unit 9, Plot 64, Gaborone International Commerce Park, POB 402396, Gaborone; tel. 3939911; fax 3939910; e-mail businesstimes@botsnet.bw; internet www.businesstimes.co.bw; Publr JAFFAR KATERYA MBUI; Editor JIMMY SWIRA.

The Clarion: POB 397, Gaborone; tel. 3930709; fax 3930708; Editor SELLO MOTSETA.

Fame Magazine: F5, Fairground Mall, POB 2214, Gaborone; tel. and fax 3907711; e-mail kudadi@yahoo.com.

Flair Magazine: Plot 22055, Mocha House, Unit Z, POB 21606, Gaborone; tel. 3911349; fax 3911359; monthly; Editor BOITSHEPO BALOZWI.

Francistown News and Reviews: POB 632, Francistown; tel. and fax 2412040; weekly; English.

Kutlwano: Willie Sebonie Rd, Private Bag BR 139, Gaborone; tel. 3653500; fax 3653630; e-mail kutlwano@gov.bw; monthly; publ. by Dept of Information Services; Setswana and English; Editor BOME MATSHABA; circ. 15,000.

The Midweek Sun: Plot 14442, Kamushungo Rd, G-West Industrial Site, POB 00153, Gaborone; tel. 3908408; fax 3908457; internet www.midweeksun.co.bw; f. 1989; weekly; English; Editor MIKE MOTHIBI; circ. 17,971.

Mokgosi Newspaper: Plot 134, Madirelo, Tlokweng, POB 46530, Gaborone; tel. 3936868; fax 3936869; e-mail mokgosi@mmegi.bw.

The Ngami Times: Mabudutsa Ward, Private Bag BO 30, Maun; tel. 6864807; fax 6860257; e-mail tnt@info.bw; internet www.ngamitimes.com; f. 1999; owned by The Ngami Times Printing and Publishing Co Botswana (Pty) Ltd; weekly; English; Editor NORMAN CHANDLER.

The Oriental Post: Gaborone; f. 2009; weekly; Chinese; Dir MILES NAN.

Sunday Standard: Postnet Kgale View, Private Bag 351, Suite 287, Gaborone; tel. 3188784; fax 3188795; internet www.sundaystandard.info; Editor OUTSA MOKONE.

Sunday Tribune: POB 41458, Gaborone; tel. and fax 3926431; weekly.

Tautona Times: Office of the President, PMB 001, Gaborone; tel. 71318598; e-mail jramsay@gov.bw; f. 2003; weekly; electronic press circular publ. by the Office of the Pres.; Communications Co-ordinator Dr JEFF RAMSAY.

The Voice: Plot 170, Unit 7, Commerce Park, POB 40415, Gaborone; tel. 3161585; fax 3932822; e-mail voicebw@yahoo.com; internet www.thevoicebw.com; f. 1992 as *The Francistowner*; weekly; Publr BEATA KASALE; Man. Editor DONALD MOORE; Editor EMANG BOKHUTLO; circ. 30,000.

Wena Magazine: POB 201533, Gaborone; tel. and fax 3907678; e-mail environews@it.bw; f. 1998; 6 a year; English and Setswana; environmental issues; Editor and Publr FLORA SEBONI-MMEREKI; circ. c. 8,000.

The Zebra's Voice: National Museum, 331 Independence Ave, Private Bag 00114, Gaborone; tel. 3974616; fax 3902797; e-mail bemotswakhumo@gov.bw; internet www.botswana-museum.gov.bw; f. 1980; twice a year; cultural affairs; Editor BERLINAH MOTSWAKHUMO; circ. 5,000.

NEWS AGENCY

Department of Information Services, Botswana Press Agency (BOPA): Private Bag BR 139, Gaborone; tel. 3653525; fax 3653626; e-mail bopa@gov.bw; f. 1981; News Editor MABEL KEBOTSAMANG.

PRESS ORGANIZATIONS

Botswana Journalists' Association (BOJA): POB 60518, Gaborone; tel. 3974435; e-mail penlite@info.bw; internet www.botswanamedia.bw/boja.htm; f. 1977; represents professional journalists; Chair. SECHELE SECHELE; Sec.-Gen. RAMPHOLO MOLEFHE; 55 mems (1999).

Botswana Media Consultative Council (BMCC): POB 2679, Gaborone; tel. 71624382; e-mail botswanamedia@info.bw; internet www.botswanamedia.bw; f. 1998; promotes the devt of a democratic media; Chair. Dr JEFF RAMSAY; Exec. Sec. ANTOINETTE O. CHIGODORA; 40 mem. orgs (1999).

Publishers

A. C. Braby (Botswana) (Pty) Ltd: Unit 3/A/2, Western Industrial Estate, 22100 Phase 4 Industrial, POB 1549, Gaborone; tel. 3971444; fax 3973462; e-mail customercare@brabys.co.za; internet www.brabys.com/bw/; business directories.

Bay Publishing: POB 832, Gaborone; tel. and fax 3937882; e-mail baybooks@it.bw; f. 1994; Dir LENE BAY.

Botsalo Books: Gaborone International Commerce Park, Kgale, Plot 59/60, Unit 5, POB 1532, Gaborone; tel. 3912576; fax 3972608; e-mail botsalo@botsnet.bw; internet www.abcdafrica.com/botsalobooks.

The Botswana Society (BotSoc): Kgale Siding Office 1A, Kgale, POB 71, Gaborone; tel. and fax 3919745; fax 3919673; e-mail botsoc@info.bw; internet www.botsoc.org.bw; f. 1968; archaeology, arts, history, law, sciences; Chair. JOSEPH TSONOPE.

Heinemann Educational Botswana (Pty) Ltd: Plot 20695, Unit 4, Magochanyana Rd, POB 10103, Village Post Office, Gaborone; tel. 3972305; fax 3971832; e-mail hein@info.bw; internet www.heinemann.co.za; Man. Dir LESEDI SEITEI.

Lentswe la Lesedi (Pty): POB 2365, Gaborone; tel. 314017; fax 314634; e-mail publisher@lightbooks.net; f. 1992.

Lightbooks Publishers: Digitec House, 685 Botswana Rd, The Mall, POB 2365, Gaborone; tel. 3903994; fax 3914017; e-mail publisher@lightbooks.net; internet www.lightbooks.net; f. 1992; commercial publishing division of Lentswe la Lesedi (Pty); scholarly, research, women's issues, journals, reports; Publr CHARLES BEWLAY.

Longman Botswana (Pty) Ltd: Plot 14386, West Industrial Site, New Lobatse Rd, POB 1083, Gaborone; tel. 3922969; fax 3922682; e-mail connie.burford@pearsoned.com; f. 1981; subsidiary of Pearson Education, UK; educational; Man. Dir J. K. CHALASHIKA.

Macmillan Botswana Publishing Co (Pty) Ltd: Plot 50635, Block 10, Airport Rd, POB 1155, Gaborone; tel. 3911770; fax 3911987; e-mail uiterwijkw@macmillan.bw; Man. Dir WIM UITERWIJK.

Medi Publishing: Phakalane Phase 1, Medie Close, Plot No. 21633, POB 47680, Gaborone; tel. 3121110; e-mail medi@it.bw; f. 1995; scholarly; Publishing Dir PORTIA TSHOAGONG.

Mmegi Publishing House (MPH): Plot 8901, Segogwane Way, Broadhurst, Private Bag BR 50, Gaborone; tel. 3952464; fax 3184977; e-mail editor@mmegi.bw; internet www.mmegi.bw; owned by Dikgang Publishing Co; academic and general.

Printing and Publishing Co (Botswana) (Pty) Ltd (PPCB): Plot 5634 Nakedi Rd, Broadhurst Industrial, POB 130, Gaborone; tel. 3912844; fax 3913054; e-mail ppcb@info.bw; internet www.ppcb.co.bw; educational; Man. Dir Y. MUSSA; Gen. Man. GAVIN BLAMIRE.

GOVERNMENT PUBLISHING HOUSE

Department of Government Printing and Publishing Service: Private Bag 0081, Gaborone; tel. 353202; fax 312001; Dir O. ANDREW SESINYI.

Broadcasting and Communications

TELECOMMUNICATIONS

Botswana Telecommunications Authority (BTA): 206–207 Independence Ave, Private Bag 00495, Gaborone; tel. 3957755; fax 3957976; e-mail pro@bta.org.bw; internet www.bta.org.bw; f. 1996; independent regulator for the telecommunications industry; Chair. Dr BOTSWIRI OUPA TSHEKO; CEO THARI G. PHEKO.

Botswana Telecommunications Corpn (BTC): POB 700, Gaborone; tel. 3958000; fax 3913355; internet www.btc.bw; f. 1980; state-owned; privatization pending; fixed-line telecommunications provider; Chair. LEONARD MUSA MAKWINJA; CEO PAUL TAYLOR.

Mascom: Tsholetsa House, Plot 4705/6, Botswana Rd, Main Mall, Private Bag BO298, Bontleng, Gaborone; tel. 3903396; fax 3903445; e-mail backoffice@mascom.bw; internet www.mascom.bw; f. 1998; 60% owned by DECI; 40% owned by Econet Wireless; mobile cellular telecommunications provider; CEO JOSE VIEIRA COUCEIRO.

Orange Botswana: Camphill Bldg, Plot 43002/1, Private Bag BO64, Bontleng, Gaborone; tel. 3163370; fax 3163372; internet www.orange.co.bw; f. 1998 as Vista Cellular; present name adopted in 2003; 49% owned by Orange SA, France; 46% owned by Mosokelatsebeng Cellular; mobile cellular telecommunications provider; CEO ELISABETH MEDOU BADANG.

BROADCASTING

The Department of Information and Broadcasting operates 21 radio stations across the country from bureaux in Gaborone, Kanye, Serowe and Francistown. The National Broadcasting Board was preparing to issue three further licences for private commercial radio stations in addition to those already held by Yarona FM and GABZ FM.

Department of Information and Broadcasting: Private Bag 0060, Gaborone; tel. 3658000; fax 564416; e-mail otsiang@btv.gov.bw; internet www.dib.gov.bw; f. 1978 following merger between Information Services and Radio Botswana; Dir O. ANDREW SESINYI.

Radio

Radio Botswana (RB1): Private Bag 0060, Gaborone; tel. 3952541; fax 3957138; e-mail rbeng@info.bw; state-owned; f. 1965; fmrly Radio Bechuanaland; culture, entertainment, news and current affairs programmes; broadcasts 18 hours daily in Setswana and English; Dir ANDREW SESINYI; Head of Programmes M. GABAKGORE.

Radio Botswana (RB2) (FM 103): Private Bag 0060, Gaborone; tel. 3653000; fax 3653346; e-mail mmphusu@gov.bw; f. 1992; contemporary entertainment; Head of Programmes MONICA MPHUSU.

GABZ FM 96.2: Private Bag 319, Gaborone; tel. 3956962; fax 3181443; e-mail feedback@gabzfm.co.bw; internet www.gabzfm.com; f. 1999; owned by Thari Investment; entertainment, news and politics; broadcasts in Setswana and English; Man. Dir KENNEDY OTSHELENG.

Yarona FM 106.6: POB 1607, Gaborone; tel. 3912305; fax 3901063; e-mail info@yaronafm.co.bw; internet www.yaronafm.co.bw; f. 1999; owned by Copacabana Investment; Station Man. DUMI LOPANG.

Television

Botswana Television (BTV): Private Bag 0060, Gaborone; tel. 3658000; fax 3900051; e-mail marketing@btv.gov.bw; internet www.btv.gov.bw; f. 2000; broadcasts local and international programmes 8 hours daily (Mon.–Fri.) and 10 hours (Sat.–Sun.); 60% local content; Gen. Man. MOLEFHE SEJOE.

E-Botswana: Plot 53996, Mogochama St, opposite Coca Cola, POB 921, Gaborone; tel. 3957654; fax 3901875; e-mail info@ebotswana.co.bw; internet www.ebotswana.co.bw; f. 1988; present name adopted 2010; operated by Gaborone Broadcasting Co (Pty) Ltd; 49% owned by Sabido (South Africa); Setswana and English; rebroadcasts foreign TV programmes; Man. Dir MIKE KLINCK.

Finance

(cap. = capital; res = reserves; dep. = deposits; m. = million; brs = branches; amounts in pula, unless otherwise stated)

In 2010 there were 10 commercial banks, 1 investment bank and 4 financial institutions in Botswana.

BANKING

Central Bank

Bank of Botswana: POB 712, Private Bag 154,17938 Khama Cres., Gaborone; tel. 3606301; fax 3974859; e-mail selwej@bob.bw; internet www.bankofbotswana.bw; f. 1975; bank of issue; cap. 25m., res 34,609.1m., dep. 20,898.3m. (Dec. 2009); Gov. LINAH MOHOHLO.

Commercial Banks

ABN AMRO Bank (Botswana) Ltd: Private Bag 254, Gaborone; tel. 3692911; fax 3692933; f. 2009; Man. Dir MAXIMILIAAN TERWINDT.

BancABC: ABC House, Tholo Office Park, Plot 50669, Fairground Office Park, POB 00303, Gaborone; tel. 3905455; fax 3902131; e-mail abcbw@africanbankingcorp.com; internet www.africanbankingcorp.com; f. 1989 as ulc (Pty) Ltd; name changed to African Banking Corpn (Pty) Ltd in 2001; present name adopted in 2009; subsidiary of ABC Holdings Ltd; financial services and investment banking; operates in Botswana, Mozambique, Tanzania, Zambia and Zimbabwe; cap. 34.1m., res 6.1m., dep. 1,405.0m. (Dec. 2009); Chair. HOWARD BUTTERY; CEO DOUGLAS MUNATSI.

Bank Gaborone Ltd: Plot 5129, Pilane/Queens Rd, The Mall, Private Bag 00325, Gaborone; tel. 3671500; fax 3904007; e-mail info@bankgaborone.co.bw; internet www.bankgaborone.co.bw; f. 2006; Chair. J. C. BRANDT; Man. Dir ANDRÉ BARNARD.

Bank of Baroda (Botswana) Ltd: AKD House, Plot 1108, Queens Rd, The Main Mall, Bontleng, POB 21559, Gaborone; tel. 3188878; fax 3188879; e-mail botswana@barodabank.co.bw; internet www.bankofbaroda.co.bw; f. 2001; subsidiary of the Bank of Baroda, India; Man. Dir DEBABROTO MITRA; Chief Man. R. N. BOKADE.

Barclays Bank of Botswana Ltd: Barclays House, 6th Floor, Plot 8842, Khama Cres., POB 478, Gaborone; tel. 3952041; fax 3913672; e-mail botswana.customerservice@barclays.com; internet www.barclays.com/africa/botswana; f. 1975 as local successor to Barclays Bank Int. Ltd; 74.9% owned by Barclays Bank PLC, UK; cap. 17.1m., res 71.4m., dep. 10,541.0m. (Dec. 2009); Chair. BLACKIE MAROLE; Man. Dir THULISIZWE JOHNSON; 52 brs.

Capital Bank Ltd: Plot 17954, Old Lobatse Rd, POB 5548, Gaborone; tel. 3907801; fax 3922818; internet www.capitalbank.co.bw; f. 2007; cap. 58.5m., dep. 518.9m. (Dec. 2009); CEO SRIRAM GADE.

First National Bank of Botswana Ltd: Finance House, 5th Floor, Plot 8843, Khama Cres., POB 1552, Gaborone; tel. 3642600; fax 3906130; e-mail ddesilva@fnbbotswana.co.bw; internet www.fnbbotswana.co.bw; f. 1991; 69.5% owned by First Nat. Bank Holdings Botswana Ltd; cap. 51.0m., res 1,107.4m., dep. 10,566.6m. (June 2010); Chair. PREMCHAND DEPAL SHAH; CEO LORATO BOAKGOMO-NTAKHWANA; 18 brs.

Kingdom Bank Africa Limited: Plot 115, Unit 23, Kgale Mews International Financial Park, POB 45078, Riverwalk, Gaborone; tel. 3906926; fax 3906874; e-mail kbal@kingdombotswana.co.bw; internet www.kingdombotswana.com; f. 2003; 52.57% owned by Brotherhood Holdings Ltd; cap. US $5.1m., res. –1.9m., dep. $6.6m. (Dec. 2009); Chair. MICHAEL MCNAUGHT; Man. Dir SIBONGINKOSI MOYO.

Stanbic Bank Botswana Ltd: Stanbic House, 1st Floor, Plot 50672, Fairground (off Machel Dr.), Private Bag 00168, Gaborone; tel. 3901600; fax 3900171; e-mail stanbic@mega.bw; internet www.stanbic.co.bw; f. 1992; subsidiary of Standard Bank Investment Corpn Africa Holdings Ltd; cap. 23.1m., res 9.6m., dep. 3,617.4m. (Dec. 2006); Man. Dir D. W. KENNEDY; Exec. Dir T. FERREIRA; 6 brs.

Standard Chartered Bank Botswana Ltd: Standard House, 5th Floor, Plots 1124–1127, The Mall, POB 496, Gaborone; tel. 3601500; fax 3918299; internet www.standardchartered.com/bw; f. 1975; 75% owned by Standard Chartered Holdings (Africa) BV, Amsterdam; cap. 44.5m., res 60.0m., dep. 7,512.6m. (Dec. 2009); Man. Dir DAVID CUTTING; 11 brs; 5 agencies.

Other Banks

Botswana Savings Bank: Tshomarelo House, POB 1150, Gaborone; tel. 3912555; fax 3952608; e-mail marketing@bsb.bw; internet www.bsb.bw; f. 1992; cap. and res 48.4m., dep. 101.5m. (March 2000); Chair. F. MODISE; Man. Dir LANDRICK OTENG SIANGA.

Letshego: POB 318, Gaborone; tel. 3180635; fax 3957949; e-mail letshego@info.bw; internet www.letshego.co.bw; f. 1998; microfinance; 43.8% owned by Micro Provident Ltd; 34.9% owned by the Int. Finance Corpn, Netherlands Devt Finance Co, Pan-African Investment Partners and Pan-Commonwealth African Partners; total assets 328.0m. (Oct. 2005); Chair. LEGODILE E. SEREMA; Man. Dir FREDRICK MMELESI.

National Development Bank: Development House, Plot 1123, The Mall, POB 225, Gaborone; tel. 3952801; fax 3974446; e-mail bmojalemotho@ndb.bw; internet www.ndb.bw; f. 1963; cap. 77.7m., res 49.8m. (March 2009); Chair. LESEDI SEITEI (acting); CEO LORATO C. MORAPEDI; 3 brs.

STOCK EXCHANGE

Botswana Stock Exchange: Exchange House, Office Block 6 Plot 64511, Fairgrounds, PMB 00417, Gaborone; tel. 3180201; fax 3180175; e-mail enquiries@bse.co.bw; internet www.bse.co.bw; f. 1989; commenced formal functions of a stock exchange in 1995; Chair. LIPALESA SIWAWA; CEO Dr HIRAN MENDIS; 27 cos and 32 securities firms listed in 2004.

INSURANCE

In 2010 there were 15 insurance companies in Botswana.

Botswana Eagle Insurance Co Ltd: Eagle House, Plot 54479, Fairgrounds, POB 1221, Gaborone; tel. 3188888; fax 3188911; e-mail john.main@botswanaeagle.co.za; f. 1976; subsidiary of Zurich Insurance Co South Africa Ltd, fmrly South African Eagle Insurance Co Ltd; Man. JOHN MAIN.

Botswana Insurance Co. Ltd: BIC House, Gaborone Business Park, Plot 50372, Gaborone Show Grounds, POB 715, Gaborone; tel. 3600500; fax 3972867; internet www.bic.co.bw; f. 1975; Man. Dir DZIKAMANI NGANUNU.

Botswana Insurance Holdings Ltd (BIHL): Block A, Fairground Office Park, POB 336, Gaborone; tel. 3645100; fax 3905884; f. 1975; 54% owned by African Life Assurance Co Ltd (Aflife), South Africa; total assets 80.8m. (Dec. 2006); Chair. BATSHO DAMBE-GROTH; CEO REGINA SIKALESELE-VAKA.

Botswana Life Insurance Ltd: Block A, Fairground Office Park, Plot 50676, Gaborone; tel. 3645100; fax 3905884; e-mail Webmaster@blil.co.bw; internet www.botswanalifeinsurance.com; subsidiary of BIHL; life insurance; CEO CATHERINE LESETEDI-LETEGELE.

General Insurance Botswana (GIB): 767 Tati Rd, Private Bag 00315, Gaborone; tel. 3184310; fax 3950008; internet www.gib.co.bw; Man. Dir SOPHIE K. TSHEOLE.

Hollard Insurance Botswana: Plot 50676, 2nd Floor, Block A, BIFM Bldg, Fairgrounds Business Park, POB 45029, Gaborone; tel. 3958023; fax 3958024; internet www.hollard.co.bw; Man. THEMBA MPOFU.

Metropolitan Life of Botswana Ltd: Standard House, 1st Floor, Queens Rd, Main Mall, Private Bag 231, Gaborone; tel. 3624300; fax 3624423; e-mail omothibatsela@metropolitan.co.bw; internet www.metropolitan.co.bw; f. 1996; 75% owned by Metropolitan South Africa, 25% owned by the Botswana Devt Corpn; Man. Dir OUPA MOTHIBATSELA.

Mutual and Federal Insurance Co of Botswana Ltd: Bldg B, Fairground Office Park, Private Bag 00347, Gaborone; tel. 3903333; fax 3903400; e-mail jbekker@mf.co.za; f. 1994; subsidiary of Mutual and Federal, South Africa; Man. Dir JACK BEKKER.

Regent Insurance Botswana: Plot 50370, Twin Towers, East Wing Fairgrounds Office Park, Private Bag BR 203, Gaborone; tel. 3188153; fax 3188063; Man. Dir A. A. BOTES; also **Regent Life Botswana**, life insurance.

Trade and Industry

GOVERNMENT AGENCIES

Botswana Housing Corpn (BHC): Plot 4773, cnr Mmaraka and Station Rds, POB 412, Gaborone; tel. 3605100; fax 3952070; e-mail info@bhc.bw; internet www.bhc.bw; f. 1971; provides housing for central govt and local authority needs and assists with private sector housing schemes; Chair. MACLEAN C. LETSHWITI; CEO MOOTIEMANG R. MOTSWAISO.

Citizen Entrepreneurial Development Agency (CEDA): Leseding House, 1st Floor, Plot 204, Independence Ave, Private Bag 00504, Gaborone; tel. 3170895; fax 3170896; e-mail info@ceda.co.bw; internet www.ceda.co.bw; f. 2001; develops and promotes citizen-owned enterprises; provides business training and financial assistance; Chair. LUCAS PHIRIE GAKALE; CEO THABO PRINCE THAMANE.

Competition Authority: Private Bag 00101, Gaborone; tel. 3934278; e-mail competitionauthority@gmail.com; f. 2011; monitors, controls and prohibits anti-competitive trade or business practices; CEO THULA GILBERT KAIRA.

Department of Town and Regional Planning: Private Bag 0042, Gaborone; tel. 3658596; fax 3913280; e-mail rchephethe@gov.bw; f. 1972; responsible for physical planning policy and implementation; Dir R. CHEPHETHE.

Public Enterprises Evaluation and Privatisation Agency (PEEPA): Twin Towers, East Wing, 2nd Floor, Fairground Office Park, Private Bag 00510, Gaborone; tel. 3188807; fax 3188662; e-mail peepa@peepa.co.bw; internet www.peepa.co.bw; f. 2001; responsible for commercializing and privatizing public parastatals; Acting CEO KGOTLA RAMAPHANE.

DEVELOPMENT ORGANIZATIONS

Botswana Council of Non-Governmental Organisations (BOCONGO): Bonokopila House, Plot 53957, Machel Dr., Private Bag 00418, Gaborone; tel. 3911319; fax 3912935; e-mail bocongo@bocongo.org.bw; internet www.bocongo.org.bw; Chair. Rev. BIGGIE BUTALE; 84 mem. orgs.

Botswana Development Corpn Ltd: Moedi, Plot 50380, Gaborone International Showgrounds (off Machel Dr.), Private Bag 160, Gaborone; tel. 3651300; fax 3904193; e-mail enquiries@bdc.bw; internet www.bdc.bw; f. 1970; Chair. SOLOMON. M. SEKWAKWA; Man. Dir MARIA M. NTHEBOLAN.

Botswana Export Development and Investment Authority (BEDIA): Plot 28, Matsitama Rd, The Main Mall, POB 3122, Gaborone; tel. 3181931; fax 3181941; e-mail bedia@bedia.bw; internet www.bedia.co.bw; f. 1997; promotes and facilitates local and foreign investment; Chair. MORAGO NGIDI; CEO JACOB NKATE.

Botswana International Financial Services Centre (Botswana IFSC): Plot 50676, Block B, Fairground Office Park, Private

Bag 160, Gaborone; tel. 3605000; fax 3913075; e-mail ifsc@ifsc.co.bw; internet www.botswanaifsc.com; f. 2003; govt-owned; facilitates and promotes the devt of cross-border financial services based in Botswana; CEO ALAN P. BOSHWAEN.

Integrated Field Services: Ministry of Trade and Industry, Private Bag 004, Gaborone; tel. 3953024; fax 3971539; promotes industrialization and rural devt; Dir B. T. TIBONE.

RETENG: the Multicultural Coalition of Botswana: POB 402786, Gaborone; tel. 71654345; fax 3937779; f. 2003; umbrella org. composed of human rights advocacy and conservation groups, and public service and private sector unions; Sec.-Gen. Prof. LYDIA NYATHI-RAMAHOBO.

CHAMBER OF COMMERCE

Botswana National Chamber of Commerce and Industry: POB 20344, Gaborone; tel. 3952677; Dir MODIRI J. MBAAKANYI.

INDUSTRIAL AND TRADE ASSOCIATIONS

Botswana Agricultural Marketing Board (BAMB): Plot 130, Unit 3–4, Gaborone International Finance Park, Private Bag 0053, Gaborone; tel. 3951341; fax 3952926; internet www.bamb.co.bw; Chair. D. TIBE; CEO MASEGO MPHATHI.

Botswana Meat Commission (BMC): Plot 621, 1 Khama Ave, Private Bag 4, Lobatse; tel. 5330321; fax 5332228; internet www.bmc.bw; f. 1966; slaughter of livestock, export of hides and skins, carcasses, frozen and chilled boneless beef; operates tannery and beef products cannery; CEO DAVID FELAPAU; Gen. Man. JOHNSON BOJOSI.

EMPLOYERS' ORGANIZATIONS

Botswana Confederation of Commerce, Industry and Manpower (BOCCIM): BOCCIM House, Old Lobatse Rd, Plot 5196, POB 432, Gaborone; tel. 3953459; fax 3973142; e-mail publicrelations@boccim.co.bw; internet www.boccim.co.bw; f. 1971; Pres. ALEX LETLHOGONOLO MONCHUSI; CEO MARIA MACHAILO-ELLIS; 2,000 mems.

Botswana Teachers' Union (BTU): Plot 0019, BTU Rd, Mogoditshane; BTU Centre, Private Bag 0019, Mogoditshane; tel. 3906774; fax 3909838; e-mail btu@it.bw; internet www.btu.co.bw; f. 1937 as the Bechuanaland Protectorate African Teachers' Asscn; present name adopted 1966; Pres. SIMON MAPULELO; Sec.-Gen. IBO NANA KENOSI; 13,000 mems.

UTILITIES

Electricity

Botswana Power Corpn (BPC): Motlakase House, Macheng Way, POB 48, Gaborone; tel. 3603000; fax 3973563; e-mail contact@bpc.bw; internet www.bpc.bw; f. 1971; parastatal; operates power station at Morupule (132 MW); Chair. EWETSE RAKHUDU; Acting CEO JACOB N. RALERU.

Water

Department of Water Affairs: Khama Cres., Private Bag 0018, Gaborone; tel. 3656600; fax 3972738; e-mail dwa@global.bw; provides public water supplies for rural areas.

Water Utilities Corpn: Private Bag 00276, Gaborone; tel. 3604400; fax 3973852; e-mail metsi@wuc.bw; internet www.wuc.bw; f. 1970; 100% state-owned; supplies water to main urban centres; Chair. NOZIPHO MABE; Chief Exec. FRED MAUNGE.

CO-OPERATIVES

Department for Co-operative Development: POB 86, Gaborone; tel. 3950500; fax 3951657; e-mail vmosele@gov.bw; f. 1964; promotes marketing and supply, consumer, dairy, horticultural and fisheries co-operatives, thrift and loan societies, credit societies, a co-operative union and a co-operative bank; Commissioner VIOLET MOSELE.

TRADE UNIONS

Botswana Federation of Trade Unions (BFTU): POB 440, Gaborone; tel. and fax 3952534; f. 1977; Pres. ALLEN KEITSENG; Sec.-Gen. GAZHANI MHOTSHA; 25,000 mems (2001).

Affiliated Unions

Botswana Bank Employees' Union (BOBEU): Ext. 4, South Ring Rd, Dilalelo, POB 111, Gaborone; tel. 3905893; fax 3973146; e-mail bobeu@botsnet.bw; Gen. Sec. KEITSHOKILE BASOTI.

Botswana Construction Workers' Union: POB 1508, Gaborone; tel. 352534; fax 357790; Gen. Sec. JOSHUA KESIILWE.

Botswana Diamond Sorters and Valuators' Staff Union (BDSVU): POB 1186, Gaborone; Gen. Sec. JACOB MPASOPI.

Botswana Hotel, Wholesalers, Furniture, Agricultural and Commercial General Workers' Union (BHWFACGWU): POB 62, Gaborone; tel. 3911874; fax 3959360; f. 2006 by merger of Botswana Agricultural Marketing Board Workers' Union, Botswana Commercial and Gen. Workers' Union (f. 1988), Botswana Hotel Travel and Tourism Union, and Botswana Wholesale Furniture and Retail Workers' Union.

Botswana Mining Workers' Union (BMWU): POB 86, Orapa; tel. 2970331; fax 2970067; Chair. CHIMBIDZANI CHIMIDZA; Sec.-Gen. JACK TLHAGALE.

Botswana Postal Services Workers' Union (BOPSWU): POB 87, Gaborone; Chair. MOLEFE LESOLE.

Botswana Power Corpn Workers' Union (BPCWU): Private Bag 0053, Gaborone; Gen. Sec. KABELO MOEPENG.

Botswana Railways Amalgamated Workers' Union (BRAWU): POB 181, Gaborone; Chair. LETLAMPONA MOKGALAJWE.

Botswana Telecommunications Employees' Union (BOTEU): Gaborone; Pres. NATHANIEL KEBALEFETSE.

National Amalgamated Local and Central Government, Parastatal, Statutory Body and Manual Workers' Union (NALCPMWU): Ext. 15, Plot No. 4946/7, Jawara Rd, POB 374, Gaborone; tel. 352790; fax 357790; e-mail nalcg.pwu@info.bw; Chair. DAVID OTHUSITSE BINA TSALAILE; Gen. Sec. SIMON KGAOGANANG.

Other affiliated unions include: the Air Botswana Employees' Union; the Botswana Beverages and Allied Workers' Union; the Botswana Central Bank Staff Union; the Botswana Housing Corpn Staff Union; the Botswana Institute of Development Management Workers' Union; the Botswana Manufacturing and Packaging Workers' Union; the Botswana Meat Industry Union; the Botswana National Development Bank Staff Union; the Botswana Private Medical and Health Services Workers' Union; the Botswana Savings Bank Employees' Union; the Botswana Vaccine Institute Staff Union; and the Rural Industry Promotions Co Workers' Union.

Principal Non-affiliated Unions

Botswana Landboard and Local Authority Health Union (BLLAHU): Private Bag 40, Francistown; tel. and fax 2413312; internet www.bulgsa.org.bw; fmrly the Botswana Unified Local Govt Service Asscn; renamed in 2007 on achieving union status; Pres. PELOTSHWEU A. D. S. BAENG; Sec.-Gen. MOSHE NOGA.

Botswana Sectors of Educators Trade Union (BOSETU): Unit 5, Commerce Park, Broadhurst, POB 404341, Gaborone; tel. 3937472; fax 3170845; f. 1986 as Botswana Fed. for Secondary School Teachers; Pres. SHANDUKANI HLABANO; Sec.-Gen. TOBOKANI RARI.

The BLLAHU, the BOSETU and three other unions (the Botswana Public Employees Union, the Botswana Teachers Union and the National Amalgamated Local Government, and Central Government and Parastatals Union) form the Botswana Federation of Public Service Unions (BOFEPUSU).

Transport

RAILWAYS

The 960-km railway line from Mafikeng, South Africa, to Bulawayo, Zimbabwe, passes through Botswana and has been operated by Botswana Railways (BR) since 1987. In 2010 there were 888 km of 1,067-mm-gauge track within Botswana, including three branches serving the Selebi-Phikwe mining complex (56 km), the Morupule colliery (16 km) and the Sua Pan soda-ash deposits (175 km). Through its links with Transnet, which operates the South African railways system, and the National Railways of Zimbabwe, BR provides connections with Namibia and Swaziland to the south, and an uninterrupted rail link to Zambia, the Democratic Republic of the Congo, Angola, Mozambique, Tanzania and Malawi to the north. However, freight traffic on BR was severely reduced following Zimbabwe's construction, in 1999, of a rail link from Bulawayo to Beitbridge, on its border with South Africa. In April 2009 BR suspended all passenger services owing to continuing losses. In 2010 plans were under way for the construction of a trans-Kalahari railway linking the Mmamabula coal deposits in Botswana with the port of Walvis Bay, Namibia. A 1,100-km railway project linking Botswana with a new port in southern Mozambique was also under consideration.

Botswana Railways (BR): Private Bag 52, Mahalapye; tel. 4711375; fax 4711385; e-mail info@botrail.bw; internet www.botswanarailways.co.bw; f. 1986; Chair. RAYMOND WATSON; CEO TAOLO SEBONEGO.

ROADS

In 2011 there were 25,798 km of roads, including 8,916 km of secondary roads. Some 33% of the road network was paved, including a main road from Gaborone, via Francistown, to Kazungula, where the borders of Botswana, Namibia, Zambia and Zimbabwe meet. The construction of a 340-km road between Nata and Maun was completed in the late 1990s. Construction of the 600-km Trans-Kalahari Highway, from Jwaneng to the port of Walvis Bay on the Namibian coast, commenced in 1990 and was completed in 1998. A car-ferry service operates from Kazungula across the Zambezi river into Zambia.

Department of Road Transport and Safety: Private Bag 0054, Gaborone; tel. 3905442; e-mail amotshegwe@gov.bw; internet www.roadtransport.gov.bw; responsible for national road network; responsible to the Ministry of Works and Transport; Dir O. M. B. MOSIGI (acting).

CIVIL AVIATION

The main international airport is at Gaborone. Four other major airports are located at Kasane, Maun, Francistown and Ghanzi. In 2000 there were also 108 airfields throughout the country. Scheduled services of Air Botswana are supplemented by an active charter and business sector. In 2011 there were some 14 non-scheduled air operators in Botswana.

Civil Aviation Authority of Botswana (CAAB): Plot 61920, Letsema Office Park, POB 250, Gaborone; tel. 3688200; fax 3913121; e-mail caab@caab.co.bw; internet www.caab.co.bw; f. 2009; Chair. MARK SAMPSON; CEO (vacant).

Air Botswana: POB 92, Sir Seretse Khama Airport, Gaborone; tel. 3952812; fax 3974802; internet www.airbotswana.co.bw; f. 1972; 45% state-owned; transfer to private sector suspended in October 2007; domestic services and regional services to countries in eastern and southern Africa; Chair. G. N. THIPE; Gen. Man. SAKHILE NYONI-REILING; 150,000 passengers per year.

Moremi Air: 1st Floor, Maun Airport Bldg, Private Bag 187, Maun; tel. 6863632; fax 6862078; e-mail info@moremiair.com; internet www.moremiair.com; air charter operator; Gen. Man. KELLY SEROLE.

Tourism

There are five game reserves and three national parks, including Chobe, near Victoria Falls, on the Zambia–Zimbabwe border. Efforts to expand the tourism industry include plans for the construction of new hotels and the rehabilitation of existing hotel facilities. In 2008 foreign tourist arrivals were estimated at 1.6m. Receipts from tourism totalled $452m. in that year.

Botswana Tourism Board: Plot 50676, Fairground Office Park, Block B, Ground Floor, Gaborone; tel. 3913111; fax 3959220; e-mail board@botswanatourism.co.bw; internet www.botswanatourism.co.bw; f. 2003; CEO MYRA SEKGOROROANE.

Department of Wildlife and National Parks: POB 131, Gaborone; tel. 3971405; fax 3912354; e-mail dwnp@gov.bw; Dir J. MATLHARE.

Hospitality and Tourism Association of Botswana (HATAB): Private Bag 00423, Gaborone; tel. 3957144; fax 3903201; internet www.hatab.bw; f. 1982; fmrly Hotel and Tourism Asscn of Botswana; CEO MORONGOE NTLOEDIBE-DISELE.

Defence

Military service is voluntary. Botswana established a permanent defence force in 1977. As assessed at November 2011, the total strength of the Botswana Defence Force (BDF) was some 9,000, comprising an army of 8,500 and an air force of 500. In addition, there was a paramilitary police force of 1,500. There are plans to enlarge the strength of the army to 10,000 men. In March 2007 Botswana began recruiting women into the BDF for the first time.

Defence Expenditure: Budgeted at P3,680m. in 2012.

Defence Force Commander: Maj.-Gen. TEBOGO H. C. MASIRE.

Education

Although education is not compulsory, enrolment ratios are high. Primary education begins at six years of age and lasts for up to seven years. Secondary education, beginning at the age of 13, lasts for a further five years, comprising a first cycle of three years and a second of two years. In 2010 a total of 331,196 pupils were enrolled in primary education, while in 2009 a total of 171,986 pupils were enrolled in secondary education. A total of 16,239 pupils were enrolled in tertiary education in 2005/06. According to UNESCO estimates, enrolment at primary schools in 2006/07 included 86% of children in the relevant age-group (boys 85%; girls 86%), while the ratio for secondary enrolment in the same year was 59% (boys 55%; girls 63%). The Government aims to provide universal access to 10 years of basic education. Botswana has the highest teacher-pupil ratio in Africa, but continues to rely heavily on expatriate secondary school teachers. School fees were abolished in 1987. However, in October 2005 legislation was approved to reintroduce fees for secondary education from January 2006. Tertiary education is provided by the University of Botswana (which was attended by 14,676 students in 2009/10) and the affiliated College of Technical and Vocational Education. There are also more than 40 other technical and vocational training centres, including the Institutes of Health Sciences, the Botswana College of Agriculture, the Roads Training College, the Colleges of Education (Primary and Secondary), and the Botswana Institute of Administration and Commerce. Expenditure on education by the central Government in 2010/11 was budgeted at P10,036.5m. (representing 25.6% of total expenditure by the central Government).

BRAZIL

Introductory Survey

LOCATION, CLIMATE, LANGUAGE, RELIGION, FLAG, CAPITAL

The Federative Republic of Brazil, the fifth largest country in the world, lies in central and north-eastern South America. To the north are Venezuela, Colombia, Guyana, Suriname and French Guiana, to the west Peru and Bolivia, and to the south Paraguay, Argentina and Uruguay. Brazil has a very long coastline on the Atlantic Ocean. Climatic conditions vary from hot and wet in the tropical rainforest of the Amazon basin to temperate in the savannah grasslands of the central and southern uplands, which have warm summers and mild winters. In Rio de Janeiro temperatures are generally between 17°C (63°F) and 29°C (85°F). The official language is Portuguese. Almost all of the inhabitants profess Christianity, and about 74% are adherents of the Roman Catholic Church. The national flag (proportions 7 by 10) is green, bearing, at the centre, a yellow diamond containing a blue celestial globe with 26 white five-pointed stars (one for each of Brazil's states), arranged in the pattern of the southern firmament, below an equatorial scroll with the motto 'Ordem e Progresso' ('Order and Progress'), and a single star above the scroll. The capital is Brasília.

CONTEMPORARY POLITICAL HISTORY

Historical Context

Formerly a Portuguese possession, Brazil became an independent monarchy in 1822, and a republic in 1889. A federal constitution for the United States of Brazil was adopted in 1891. Following social unrest in the 1920s, the economic crisis of 1930 resulted in a major revolt, led by Dr Getúlio Vargas, who was installed as President. He governed the country as a benevolent dictator until forced to resign by the armed forces in December 1945. During Vargas's populist rule, Brazil enjoyed internal stability and steady economic progress. He established a strongly authoritarian corporate state, similar to fascist regimes in Europe, but in 1942 Brazil entered the Second World War on the side of the Allies.

A succession of ineffectual presidential terms (including another by Vargas, who was re-elected in 1950) failed to establish stable government in the late 1940s and early 1950s. President Jânio Quadros, elected in 1960, resigned after only seven months in office, and in September 1961 the Vice-President, João Goulart, was sworn in as President. Military leaders suspected Goulart, the leader of the Partido Trabalhista Brasileiro (PTB), of communist sympathies, and they were reluctant to let him succeed to the presidency. As a compromise, the Constitution was amended to restrict the powers of the President and to provide for a Prime Minister. However, following the appointment of three successive premiers during a 16-month period of mounting political crisis, the system was rejected when a referendum, conducted in January 1963, approved a return to the presidential system of government.

Following a period of economic crisis, exacerbated by allegations of official corruption, the left-wing regime of President Goulart was overthrown in April 1964 by a bloodless right-wing military coup led by Gen. (later Marshal) Humberto Castelo Branco, the Army Chief of Staff, who was promptly elected President by the National Congress (Congresso Nacional). In October 1965 President Castelo Branco assumed dictatorial powers, and all political parties were banned. In December, however, two artificially created parties, the pro-Government Aliança Renovadora Nacional (ARENA) and the opposition Movimento Democrático Brasileiro (MDB), were granted official recognition. President Castelo Branco nominated as his successor the Minister of War, Marshal Artur da Costa e Silva, who was elected in October 1966 and took office in March 1967 as President of the redesignated Federative Republic of Brazil (a new Constitution was introduced simultaneously). The ailing President da Costa e Silva was forced to resign in September 1969 and was replaced by a triumvirate of military leaders.

Domestic Political Affairs

The military regime granted the President wide-ranging powers to rule by decree. In October 1969 the ruling junta introduced a revised Constitution, vesting executive authority in an indirectly elected President. The Congresso Nacional, suspended since December 1968, was recalled and elected Gen. Emílio Garrastazu Médici as President. Médici was succeeded as President by Gen. Ernesto Geisel and Gen. João Baptista de Figueiredo, respectively. Despite the attempts of both Presidents to pursue a policy of *abertura*, or opening to democratization, opposition to military rule intensified throughout the 1970s and early 1980s. In November 1982 the government-sponsored Partido Democrático Social (PDS) suffered significant losses at elections to the Câmara dos Deputados (Chamber of Deputies), state governorships and municipal councils. However, the PDS secured a majority of seats in the Senado Federal (Federal Senate) and, owing to pre-election legislation, seemed set to enjoy a guaranteed majority in the electoral college, scheduled to choose a successor to Gen. Figueiredo in 1985.

However, in July 1984 Vice-President Antônio Chaves de Mendonça and the influential Marco de Oliveira Maciel, a former Governor of Pernambuco, formed an alliance of liberal PDS members with members of the Partido do Movimento Democrático Brasileiro (PMDB), which, in December, became an official political party, the Partido Frente Liberal (PFL). At the presidential election, conducted in January 1985, the PFL candidate, Tancredo Neves, was elected as Brazil's first civilian President for 21 years. However, after Neves died before being inaugurated, the PFL vice-presidential candidate, José Sarney, took office as President in April. In May the Congresso Nacional approved a constitutional amendment restoring direct elections by universal suffrage.

Support for Sarney's Government was demonstrated in November 1986 at elections to the Congresso Nacional, which was to operate as a Constitutional Assembly (Assembleia Constitucional). In June 1988 the Assembly approved a presidential mandate of five years. The first round of voting for the presidential election was provisionally set for 15 November 1989, thereby enabling Sarney to remain in office until March 1990. This de facto victory for the President led to the resignations of some leading members of the PMDB, who formed a new centre-left party, the Partido da Social Democracia Brasileira (PSDB). The Constitution was approved by the Congresso Nacional on 22 September 1988 and promulgated in October. Among its 245 articles were provisions transferring many hitherto presidential powers to the legislature. In addition, censorship was abolished, as was the National Security Law, whereby many political dissidents had been detained, and the principle of habeas corpus was recognized. However, the Constitution offered no guarantees of land reform, and was thought by many to be nationalistic and protectionist.

Brazil's first presidential election by direct voting since 1960 took place on 15 November 1989. The main contenders were the conservative Fernando Collor de Mello, of the newly formed Partido de Reconstrução Nacional (PRN), Luiz Inácio Lula da Silva of the left-wing Partido dos Trabalhadores (PT) and Leonel Brizola of the centre-left Partido Democrático Trabalhista (PDT). At a second round in December, contested by the two leading candidates, Collor de Mello defeated Lula, with 53% of the votes cast. Following his inauguration on 15 March 1990, the new President announced an ambitious programme of economic reform, entitled 'New Brazil' (known as the 'Collor Plan'), with the principal aim of reducing inflation, which had reached a monthly rate of more than 80%. A second economic plan was implemented in February 1991. In March Collor de Mello announced a new Plan for National Reconstruction, which envisaged further deregulation and rationalization of many state-controlled areas.

Collor de Mello's position became increasingly precarious towards the end of 1991, after accusations of mismanagement of federal funds were made against his wife and several associates. Allegations of high-level corruption persisted into 1992, and in May the President became the focus of further revelations, which appeared to implicate him in a number of corrupt practices orchestrated by his election campaign treasurer. The Congresso Nacional established a special commission of inquiry to investigate the affair and in September, after the commission had delivered its report, and bolstered by massive popular support, a congressional committee authorized the initiation of impeachment proceedings against the President. On 29 September the Câmara dos Deputados voted to proceed with the impeachment of the President for abuses of authority and position, prompting the immediate resignation of the Cabinet. On 2 October Collor de Mello surrendered authority to Vice-President Itamar Franco for a six-month period, pending a final pronouncement regarding his future in office by the Senado.

In December 1992 the Senado voted overwhelmingly to proceed with Collor de Mello's impeachment and to indict the President for 'crimes of responsibility'. At the opening of the impeachment trial on 29 December, however, Collor de Mello resigned from the presidency; Franco was sworn in to serve the remainder of his term. On the following day the Senado announced the removal of the former President's political rights (including immunity from prosecution). In January 1993 the Supreme Federal Court announced that Collor de Mello was to stand trial as an ordinary citizen on charges of 'passive corruption and criminal association', and in December the Court endorsed the Senado's eight-year ban on his holding public office. In December 1994, however, the tribunal voted to acquit Collor de Mello of the charges, owing to insufficient evidence. In January 1998 the former President was cleared of charges of illegal enrichment.

The withdrawal of the PDT from the ruling coalition in April 1993 was followed by that of the Partido Socialista Brasileiro (PSB) in August, and in the following month the PMDB national council narrowly defeated a motion to end its association with the Government. The fragility of the Government was exacerbated by a corruption scandal in October, in which numerous senior politicians were implicated in a fraudulent scheme in which political influence was allegedly exercised in order to secure state projects for construction companies in exchange for bribes. In April 1994 the Congresso Nacional concluded a review of the Constitution, having adopted six amendments, including a reduction in the length of the presidential term from five to four years.

Allegations of corruption and misconduct preceding the elections in October 1994 forced the replacement of the vice-presidential running mates of both Minister of the Economy Fernando Henrique Cardoso and of Lula and the withdrawal from the contest of the presidential candidate of the Partido Liberal (PL). Cardoso, whose candidacy was supported by the PFL, the PTB, the PL and the business community, won the presidential contest in the first round, following a campaign that had focused largely on the success of his economic initiatives, which included the introduction of a new currency, the real.

Cardoso's presidency

Cardoso was inaugurated as President on 1 January 1995. Opposition to the ongoing programme of economic stabilization and to renewed efforts by the Government to introduce constitutional amendments, including those that would end state monopolies in the telecommunications and petroleum sectors, resulted in a general strike in May. A number of amendments, including to the petroleum and telecommunication sectors, were none the less subsequently approved by the Senado.

By December 1995, however, Cardoso's integrity had been seriously compromised by the alleged involvement of a number of his political associates in irregular financial transactions organized by the Banco Econômico, and by an influence-peddling scandal arising from the award to a US company of the contract for development of an Amazon Regional Surveillance System (Sivam). Investigation of the so-called 'pink folder' of politicians, recovered from the ailing Banco Econômico, continued during 1996, as the banking sector was plunged into further crisis. In March it was revealed that the Government had withheld details of a US $5,000m. fraud perpetrated at the Banco Nacional a decade earlier. Moreover, it emerged that the Government had extended a recent credit facility of $5,800m. to the bank in order to facilitate its merger with UNIBANCO in 1995.

Cardoso's own popularity benefited from the success of the Government's attempts to control inflation. In June 1996 the Government announced details of the next phase of its massive divestment programme. Several companies in the power sector and 31 ports were among those state concerns to be offered for sale. In July the Government announced that the state telecommunications company, Telebrás, together with large sections of the rail and power networks, would be privatized by the end of 1998. In March 1997 legislation was approved ending the long-standing monopoly of Petróleo Brasileiro, SA (Petrobras) over the petroleum industry. In mid-1997 a constitutional amendment to permit the President to stand for re-election in 1998 was approved by the Senado, and was swiftly ratified by Cardoso.

In October 1998 Cardoso, again the PSDB's candidate, became the first President to be re-elected for a second consecutive term. At the concurrent legislative elections, the PSDB also performed well, securing 99 of the 513 seats in the lower chamber, while its electoral allies—the PFL, PMDB, Partido Progressista (PP) and PTB—won a total of 278 seats, bringing the coalition's total representation to 377.

In January 1999 Itamar Franco, the newly elected Governor of Minas Gerais, declared that the state was defaulting on its debt to the federal Government, indirectly precipitating the devaluation of the Brazilian currency. In the same month the Congresso Nacional endorsed long-proposed reforms to the country's munificent pension system, considerably enhancing the prospects of President Cardoso's programme of fiscal austerity. However, the Government suffered a set-back in March following the withdrawal of the PTB from the ruling coalition. In August demonstrations against the Government's economic and social policies culminated in the arrival in Brasília of as many as 100,000 marchers, comprising political opponents led by the PT, trade unionists and landless individuals.

In October 1999 a congressional commission of inquiry into allegations of organized crime exposed a nation-wide criminal network that allegedly encompassed politicians, government officials, judges, police officers, business executives and banking officials. Embarrassed by the scale of the revelations (which extended to reports of drugs-trafficking within the parliament building), President Cardoso announced the establishment of a new anti-corruption force to combat organized crime. In an effort to improve accountability and to strengthen congressional powers of investigation, the Senado approved a constitutional amendment to restrict presidential use of provisional measures, to which successive Governments had frequently resorted as a means to circumvent the cumbersome legislative process. In October 2001 Jader Barbalho, the President of the Senado, resigned his post after it emerged that he had been involved in corrupt activities while Governor of the state of Pará in the 1980s.

At the presidential election of 6 October 2002, Lula, once again the PT's candidate, secured 46% of the votes cast in the first round. José Serra, the government-backed PMDB candidate, was second placed, with 23% of the ballot, followed by PSB nominee Anthony Garotinho, with 18%, and Ciro Gomes, the candidate of the centre-left PPS, with 12%. Aided by the support of Garotinho, Gomes and Sarney, Lula defeated Serra in a second round of voting on 27 October, securing 61% of the votes cast (the largest ever proportion of the vote since the system's introduction in 1945). At the congressional elections, also held on 6 October, Lula's party took 91 of the 513 seats in the Câmara dos Deputados and increased its representation in the Senado to 14 seats. The PFL secured 84 lower house seats, followed by the PMDB (74 seats) and the PSDB (71 seats). The PFL's representation in the Senado remained unchanged, at 19 seats; however, the number of PMDB senators decreased, from 27 seats to 19, as did the PSDB's upper house representation, from 16 to 11 seats.

Lula's first term in office

President Lula took office on 2 January 2003. The new President needed support from the centrist parties in order to form a Government, and duly entered a coalition agreement with the PFL and the PMDB. Lula's new Cabinet was dominated by members of the PT, although it also included representatives from the PPS, PDT, PSB and the PL. Lula affirmed his intention to proceed with a promised 'zero hunger' poverty alleviation programme, to effect public sector pension reform, and to modernize Brazil's tax system. Immediate spending cuts in all areas of government were announced in order to fund the anti-hunger campaign. The Government proposed taxing public sector pensions and raising the retirement age, provoking discontent among government workers and the PT's traditional allies in the trade union movement. Nevertheless, although the Government was forced to make several alterations to the legislation, it was approved by the Câmara dos Deputados in August and by the Senado in December.

Changes to the tax system, which included standardizing the rate of value-added tax (which varied between states) and replacing the federal property tax with a state levy, were approved by the Câmara dos Deputados in September 2003 and, following a number of concessions by the Government, by the Senado in December. In January 2004 the first of three stages of tax reform came into effect.

In February 2004 evidence emerged that the former deputy of Cabinet Chief José Dirceu, Waldomiro Diniz, had offered government contracts in exchange for contributions towards the 2002 presidential campaign from the head of an illegal gambling operation in the state of Rio de Janeiro. Diniz was dismissed from his post and a criminal investigation was begun, as was a federal parliamentary investigation into the affair. The final report of the parliamentary investigation, published in June 2006, recommended that Diniz, as well as former Minister of Finance Antônio Palocci (see below) and a close associate of the President, Paulo Okamoto, be indicted on corruption charges.

Divisions within the governing coalition emerged in December 2004, when the Minister of National Integration, Ciro Gomes, resigned after his party, the PPS, announced its departure from the coalition, accusing the Government of being 'too conservative'. One day later members of the PMDB also voted to leave the coalition Government, citing Lula's failure to pursue an active social policy. However, the party's two cabinet members and several of its senators and deputies refused to abide by the decision (the vote was ruled invalid by the high court).

In June 2005 a videotape was shown on national television that appeared to show proof that bribes had been offered to employees of the state-run postal service, the Empresa Brasileira de Correios e Telégrafos, and the reinsurance company, IRB-Brasil Resseguros, in return for contracts. A recipient of the bribes accused Roberto Jefferson, the President of the PTB, of organizing the cash incentive scheme; Jefferson denied the allegation and, in turn, accused the PT leadership of running a system of institutional bribery in 2003 and 2004. Under this scheme, deputies from other parties allegedly received a monthly allowance ('*mensalão*') for supporting government-sponsored legislation. Jefferson cited President Lula's Cabinet Chief, José Dirceu, as the organizer of the *mensalão* scheme. In mid-June 2005 Dirceu resigned, followed in July by Sílvio Pereira, Delúbio Soares and José Genoíno, respectively Secretary-General, Treasurer and President of the PT. Dirceu was replaced as Cabinet Chief by Dilma Vana Rousseff, a former PT activist who had previously held the mines and energy portfolio. In order to maintain the support of the PMDB, Lula was forced to effect further cabinet reshuffles in July, which increased the number of ministries held by that party, at the expense of the PT.

In August 2005 Valdemar Costa Neto, the President of the PL, a party allied to the Government, resigned owing to his alleged involvement in the *mensalão* scheme. Costa Neto claimed that the President had been aware of the irregular practices in his party. Lula's problems worsened when his Minister of Finance, Antônio Palocci, was also accused of having accepted illegal payments from a waste management company while he was mayor of Ribeirão Preto. At the end of August Jefferson further alleged that the PT also received payments from a state-owned electricity company. The President was dealt a further blow in September when his Vice-President and Minister of Defence, José Alencar Gomes da Silva, announced that he was leaving the PL, citing the party's involvement in the *mensalão* scandal. A report published in the same month by the two congressional investigation committees into the *mensalão* and post office corruption scandals recommended that 18 deputies, including Dirceu, be impeached for their role in the affairs. All but one of the deputies belonged to the PT or allied parties. In mid-September the legislature voted to dismiss Jefferson from the Câmara dos Deputados. One week later Severino Cavalcanti, the President of the Câmara dos Deputados (and a member of the PP), resigned following allegations that he too had accepted bribes, although this was unconnected to the *mensalão* scandal.

In November 2005 the congressional committee investigating the corruption scandals concluded its inquiry. It found that the PT had given money to deputies from pro-Government parties in return for legislative support. It also reported that public funds had been illegally transferred through the Banco do Brasil to the PT. It recommended that former PT Treasurer Soares be charged in relation to the bribes and related money-laundering. In December José Dirceu was finally dismissed from the Câmara dos Deputados after deputies voted to impeach him.

After being implicated in a series of corruption scandals, Palocci finally resigned as Minister of Finance in March 2006, when it was revealed that he had leaked the financial details of a man who had accused him of frequenting parties also attended by prostitutes. He was replaced by Guido Mantega, President of the Banco Nacional do Desenvolvimento Econômico e Social and a former minister, who announced that he would continue existing economic policy. In August 2009 the Supreme Federal Court narrowly ruled that there was insufficient evidence to charge Palocci with violating banking secrecy legislation.

In May 2006 a sustained outbreak of violence in São Paulo paralysed the city and led to an estimated 138 deaths. The rioting had been prompted by an organized uprising in gaols in the region by gang members displeased at being transferred to higher-security institutions. In response, the Senado approved stricter legislation on gang membership and organized crime. Nevertheless, some 25 people were murdered in a similiar wave of co-ordinated violent crime in Rio de Janeiro in December. A further 21 people, all thought to be gang members, were killed in a further outbreak of violence in the city in April 2007. In June the Government initiated a security plan, intended to combat youth crime in particular, and announced an expansion of the National Security Force, an élite federal body that provided additional troops to over-deployed state police forces.

Lula continued to enjoy high levels of popularity among voters in the months preceding the 2006 presidential election. However, in the first round of voting, held on 1 October, he failed to secure the necessary amount of votes to avoid a run-off ballot, garnering 48.6% of the valid votes cast, while Geraldo Alckmin, the former Governor of the state of São Paulo and the PSDB's candidate, won 41.6% of the ballot. The next highest placed nominee was Heloísa Helena, a former PT member who stood as an anti-corruption candidate for the Partido Socialismo e Liberdade, with just 6.9% of the votes. It was widely accepted that the numerous corruption scandals involving his Government had cost Lula a first round victory. Nevertheless, in a second round ballot on 29 October Lula comfortably secured a second term in office, attracting some 60.8% of the valid votes. In the congressional elections, also held on 1 October, the PMDB (which did not put forward a presidential candidate) won the most seats, 89, in the 513-seat lower chamber, while the PT returned 83 deputies. The PSDB and the PFL both secured 65 seats, followed by the PP with 42 and the PFL (an ally of the PSDB) with 27. Some 27 seats were contested in the 81-seat Senado: following voting the PMDB held 20 upper house seats, the PFL and the PSDB 16 each, the PT 12, and the PTB and the PDT four each. Lacking an absolute majority in the Congresso, the President immediately announced that he intended to govern 'by consensus' in his second term. To this end, in November 2006 he secured the congressional support of the PT and of most of the factions of the internally divided PMDB.

Lula's second term

President Lula was inaugurated on 1 January 2007. The President declared that his main priority in his second term in office would be economic growth and the poverty alleviation programmes initiated in his first term, in particular the successful Bolsa Família (Family Allowance) cash transfer programme.

Cases of corruption continued to affect the Government in Lula's second term. In May 2007 a police investigation into embezzlement of federal funds implicated the Minister of Mines and Energy, Silas Rondeau, as well as two state governors. Rondeau resigned in response to the accusation, although he maintained his innocence, and was replaced in January 2008 by Edison Lobão. Later in May 2007 an article in the magazine *Veja* alleged that the President of the Senado, Renan Calheiros, a close ally of Lula, had accepted bribes from the construction company Mendes Júnior. The Senado's ethics committee recommended the impeachment of Calheiros, but a substantial majority of senators voted not to indict the chamber's President in a secret ballot held in September. Calheiros did agree to a temporary leave of absence in October, and in November the ethical committee again recommended that he be deprived of his seat after evidence emerged implicating him in further illegal practices; however, Calheiros resigned as President in December, shortly before the Senado voted against his impeachment. (He was replaced by Garibaldi Alves Filho.) The controversy surrounding Calheiros contributed to the Senado's rejection, later in December, of legislation to extend a temporary tax on financial transactions for a further four-year period, representing the Government's first major defeat in the Congresso Nacional since Lula gained power. Meanwhile, Walfrido dos Mares Guia, the Minister of Institutional Relations, also resigned in November after being accused by the public prosecution service of fraud in a

1998 gubernatorial election, and was succeeded by José Múcio Monteiro Filho.

In August 2007 the Supreme Federal Court indicted 40 people on charges related to the *mensalão* affair, including Jefferson, Dirceu, Soares and Genoíno. (The trial of 38 of those first indicted commenced in 2011; a ruling was expected in early 2012.)

Marina Silva resigned as Minister of the Environment in May 2008, citing difficulties she had faced in implementing government policy, having unsuccessfully opposed a series of federal infrastructure projects on ecological grounds. She was replaced by Carlos Minc Baumfeld, who had hitherto held the same portfolio in the state of Rio de Janeiro. Further government changes took place in June and July. Municipal elections held on 5 and 26 October resulted in gains for both the PMDB (which won the greatest number of votes and of mayoralties) and the PT, and a decline in the share of the vote for the PSDB and the Democratas (DEM—as the PFL had been renamed in 2007).

In February 2009 the PMDB's candidates, Michel Temer, the party's President, and José Sarney, a former President of the republic (1985–90), secured the presidencies of both the Câmara dos Deputados and the Senado, respectively, despite an earlier agreement by the PMDB to support the PT's candidate in the upper house election. The PMDB strengthened its position further by gaining control of an additional two states in February and April, bringing its total to nine, following the impeachment of the Governors of Paraíba (of the PSDB) and Maranhão (of the PDT), after they were found guilty by the Higher Electoral Court of bribing voters in the gubernatorial elections in 2006.

Tension between senators of the PMDB and the PT delayed the passage of legislation in the first half of 2009, amid mutual allegations of corruption, including the misuse of arrangements to compensate legislators for expenses. It also emerged that appointed employees of the Senado had been paid R $6.2m. in overtime in January 2009, when the upper house was in recess. In March Sarney initiated a review of the Senado's administrative structure, which revealed that 'secret directives' had been issued to appoint political associates of senators to administrative positions in the upper house and to reinstate officials who had been dismissed following accusations of corruption. In June the newspaper *O Estado de São Paulo* reported that more than 600 'secret directives' had been issued since 1995. Although senators from all the major parties were alleged to have benefited from these directives, attention was focused particularly on Sarney, who had also presided over the Senado in 1995–97, when the practice was believed to have been introduced, and several of whose relatives were alleged to have been on the upper chamber's payroll despite not having worked there. As the allegations against Sarney mounted, the PSDB and the DEM withdrew their support for him in late June. However, Lula, who hoped to secure the support of Sarney's PMDB for his preferred successor, Cabinet Chief Rousseff, in the 2010 presidential election, staunchly defended the senate President, and in August the chamber's ethics committee decided not to investigate the accusations any further.

Meanwhile, in May 2009, at the behest of the PSDB, the Senado initiated a congressional inquiry into allegations of corruption at Petrobras. However, the work of the committee appointed to conduct the investigation subsequently stalled, as members allied to the Government failed to attend meetings. It was speculated that the President feared that the inquiry might prove damaging to Rousseff, who had been responsible for appointing the company's Administrative Council, in her previous position as Minister of Mines and Energy, and remained Chairperson of the Board of Directors. In August Lula submitted to the Congresso Nacional a proposed new regulatory framework for the exploitation of major offshore petroleum and natural gas reserves discovered in late 2007, envisaging overall state control and the extensive involvement of Petrobras. The framework was approved and signed into law in December 2010, shortly before Lula left office. Petrobras was to be the sole operator for all new projects in the offshore fields and was to hold a minimum 30% stake in all new joint venture agreements. However, Lula vetoed a plan to divide the income from royalties and tax revenue related to the oil sector equally between all states and municipalities, whether oil-producing (Rio de Janeiro, Espírito Santo and São Paulo) or not. (Attempts to resolve the royalties issue provoked renewed controversy in November 2011 when more than 100,000 people, led by Governor Sérgio Cabral, participated in a protest in Rio de Janeiro against a new proposal to increase the share of royalties received by non-producing states.)

A corruption scandal emerged in late November 2009, involving the Governor of the Federal District of Brasília, José Roberto Arruda of the DEM, and a number of other politicians from various parties. Arruda, who resigned from the DEM in the following month, was accused of receiving illegal payments from lobbyists and companies seeking to win contracts for public works projects. He was arrested in February 2010, together with several close associates, and his gubernatorial mandate was revoked by the regional electoral court in March.

Meanwhile, a new national human rights programme proposed in December 2009 caused divisions within the Cabinet and considerable controversy among several sectors of society, particularly the armed forces, which opposed the planned creation of a truth commission to investigate human rights abuses committed by the military regime of 1964–85 and the possible annulment of an amnesty law approved in 1979. After the military Chiefs of Staff and Minister of Defence, Nelson Jobim, threatened to resign in protest, President Lula promised a 'political solution', subsequently deciding to remove the most contested elements of the legislation prior to submitting it to the Congresso Nacional. (In a ruling in April 2010, the Supreme Court voted to uphold the 1979 amnesty law.)

2010 general election

Lula strongly supported Rousseff's candidacy for the PT presidential nomination throughout 2009 and early 2010: his regular attendance, with Rousseff, at the inauguration of infrastructure projects funded under the Government's Growth Acceleration Programme (Programa de Aceleração do Crescimento—PAC), which was principally co-ordinated by the Cabinet Chief, prompted opposition parties to accuse the President of using the events to campaign prematurely on Rousseff's behalf. (The Higher Electoral Court upheld a complaint by the PSDB to that effect in March 2010, fining Lula R $5,000.) Rousseff announced in April 2009 that she had been diagnosed with lymphatic cancer, but she remained in her post while undergoing treatment, which was successfully completed in September. The Government and Rousseff suffered a reverse in September when the Court of Audit recommended the suspension of 41 government projects, including 13 being undertaken under the PAC, on suspicion of 'grave accounting irregularities'. In October, however, the PMDB agreed to support Rousseff's presidential bid in return for the vice-presidential candidacy.

Rousseff was confirmed as the PT's presidential candidate at a party congress in February 2010. In the following month she accompanied Lula at the presentation of the second phase of the PAC, which envisaged public and private investments amounting to some R $958,900m. in 2011–14 and R $632,000m. after 2014, with priority given to energy, housing and transport projects. Serra stood down as Governor of São Paulo at the end of March, officially declaring his presidential candidacy for the PSDB in April. Rousseff and eight other ministers also resigned from the Government in order to run for office in the general election in October. Erenice Guerra, hitherto Executive Secretary of the Office of the Civilian Cabinet, succeeded Rousseff as Cabinet Chief. Former Minister of the Environment Marina Silva, who had resigned from the PT in 2009, after more than 30 years of membership, confirmed her presidential candidacy for the Partido Verde in May. By this time opinion poll ratings for Rousseff (whose vice-presidential candidate was to be the PMDB leader, Temer) were beginning to equal, or even surpass, those for Serra, who had been the most popular of the potential candidates throughout 2009 and early 2010. Meanwhile, Rousseff and Lula (whose own approval ratings consistently exceeded 80%) were repeatedly fined by the Higher Electoral Court for their promotion of Rousseff's candidacy prior to the start of the official campaign period in July. A number of controversies subsequently threatened to damage Rousseff's electoral prospects, including claims that government officials had illegally accessed the tax and bank account details of several senior PSDB politicians and of members of Serra's family and passed them to Rousseff's campaign team, which had earlier been accused of preparing to disseminate false allegations about Serra. Moreover, Rousseff's successor, Guerra, was forced to resign as Cabinet Chief in September, following corruption allegations implicating members of her family and officials in the Office of the Civilian Cabinet. None the less, Rousseff remained ahead in the polls.

In the first round of voting in the presidential election, held on 3 October 2010, Rousseff failed to secure sufficient votes to avoid a run-off ballot, winning 46.9% of the valid votes cast, while Serra obtained 32.6%. In third place, securing a far greater share of the ballot than forecast, was Marina Silva, with 19.3% of the valid votes cast. The six other candidates all took less than 1% of the ballot. Some 81.9% of the electorate participated in the poll. Rousseff defeated Serra in a second round of voting on 31 October, receiving 56.0% of the valid votes cast. A turn-out of 78.5% was recorded. The PT and its allies also performed well at the congressional elections, held concurrently with the first round of the presidential vote, securing a majority of seats in both chambers. The PT became the largest party in the 513-member Câmara dos Deputados, with 88 seats, while the PMDB won 79, the Partido da República (PR) and the PP 41 each, the PSB 34 and the PDT 28. The opposition PSDB and DEM secured 53 and 43 seats, respectively, in the lower house. The PT also increased its representation in the Senado (where 54 of the 81 seats were contested), to 15 seats, while the PMDB retained the most upper house seats, with 20; following the election, other allied parties held an additional 19 seats, including the PR, the PP and the PDT, with four each, and the PSB, with three. The PSDB was represented by 11 senators, and the DEM and the PTB by six each. In gubernatorial elections, 16 of the 27 governors elected were deemed to be supportive of Rousseff. In late October the Supreme Federal Court ruled that legislation enacted in June rendering politicians convicted of committing electoral violations and crimes involving the use of public funds ineligible for public office for eight years was valid and should be applied retroactively. Both the legislation and the verdict were controversial: the former because it appeared to contravene the constitutional right to the presumption of innocence until all appeals are heard; and the latter because it was only reached through the President of the Court's use of exceptional measures after the judges failed to reach a majority decision.

Recent developments: Rousseff's first year in office

Rousseff took office as Brazil's first female President on 1 January 2011. Her 37-member coalition Government included 17 ministers from the PT and six from the PMDB, as well as representatives of the PP, the PSB, the PDT, the PR and the PC do B and a number of independents. The new administration was expected broadly to continue the social and economic policies of its predecessor, with the reform of the education sector and the eradication of extreme poverty identified as particular priorities. This continuity was signalled by the retention of several ministers from the outgoing Cabinet, including those responsible for finance, defence, mines and energy, education, and labour and employment, while Antônio Palocci, Rousseff's election campaign manager and Lula's Minister of Finance until his resignation in 2006 (see above), notably returned to the Government as Cabinet Chief.

Rousseff's first year in office was marked by the resignations of seven ministers from her Cabinet, in six cases following their alleged implication in corruption scandals (although they all refuted the accusations against them). First to stand down, in June 2011, was Palocci, after a newspaper reported that his personal wealth had increased 20-fold during 2006–10, when he had worked as a political consultant while also serving as a deputy in the Câmara dos Deputados. Palocci denied any wrongdoing, citing a desire not to damage the President as his reason for resigning. He was replaced as Cabinet Chief by Gleisi Hoffmann, a PT senator. Palocci's departure from office was followed in July 2011 by that of the Minister of Transport, Alfredo Nascimento, the President of the PR, amid allegations of irregularities in the granting of public works contracts by his ministry. Paulo Sérgio Passos, hitherto Executive Secretary in the Ministry of Transport, succeeded Nascimento. Two PMDB ministers resigned in August: the Minister of Defence, Nelson Jobim, after reportedly criticizing government colleagues; and the Minister of Agriculture, Livestock and Food Supply, Wagner Rossi, following accusations that he had accepted bribes and free air travel from agricultural companies. Celso Amorim, who had been Minister of Foreign Affairs throughout Lula's presidency, was appointed to head the Ministry of Defence, while Mendes Ribeiro replaced Rossi. In a further set-back for Rousseff, which reflected the difficulty of maintaining unity in the multi-party Government, the PR announced its withdrawal from the ruling coalition that month, on the grounds that it was not sufficiently valued as a partner. The Government retained its congressional majorities, however, and the PR allowed Passos, its only representative in the Cabinet, to remain in his post, noting that he had not been nominated by the party but was an appointee of the President. A series of nation-wide protests against corruption took place on 7 September, Independence Day, attended by several thousand people. One week later the Minister of Tourism, Pedro Novais of the PMDB, resigned from the Cabinet over accusations that he had used public funds to employ domestic staff; in the previous month, moreover, Novais's deputy minister and more than 30 other officials at the Ministry of Tourism had been arrested in connection with a separate investigation into alleged embezzlement of public funds. Gastão Vieira, a PMDB deputy, was appointed to replace Novais. The Minister of Sport, Orlando Silva of the Partido Comunista do Brasil (PC do B), stood down from office in late October, after the Supreme Federal Court initiated an investigation into allegations of his involvement in a ministry scheme in which illicit payments were received from non-governmental organizations (NGOs) seeking to participate in a programme promoting sports among disadvantaged children. José Aldo Rebelo, also of the PC do B, was appointed Minister of Sport. Finally, in early December Carlos Lupi, the PDT Minister of Labour and Employment, became the seventh minister to resign from Rousseff's Cabinet, when he and other officials at his ministry were also accused, *inter alia*, of demanding payments from NGOs in return for funding or government contracts. Paulo Roberto Dos Santos Pinto succeeded Lupi in an acting capacity. The Government suffered yet another casualty in early February 2012 when the Minister of Cities, Mário Negromonte, resigned after allegations of corruption appeared in the media.

Most of the ministers who left the Cabinet during Rousseff's 13 months in office were notably first appointed by Lula, and President Rousseff's popularity remained high in December, according to opinion polls, despite the numerous scandals affecting her Government, indicating public admiration for her professed 'zero tolerance' approach to corruption. However, some commentators criticized the President for reacting to corruption revealed by the media, and only once it had developed into a scandal, rather than actively attempting to uncover ministerial wrongdoing, while at the same time acknowledging that her ability to act was constrained by the need to maintain good relations with the various coalition parties.

Meanwhile, notwithstanding the instability caused by the tensions and frequent changes within her Cabinet, Rousseff attempted to proceed with implementing the pledges made during her election campaign. In June 2011 she launched the Brasil Sem Miséria (Brazil Without Poverty) social welfare plan, which aimed to lift 16.2m. Brazilians out of extreme poverty by 2014, partly through the expansion of existing initiatives, such as the Bolsa Família programme, and by increasing access to essential services, including utilities, education, health care and housing. A new centrist party, the Partido Social Democrático (PSD), led by the mayor of São Paulo, Gilberto Kassab (formerly of the DEM), pledged its legislative support for Rousseff's governing coalition following its registration in September 2011. Comprising dissidents from the opposition DEM and PSDB, among other parties, the PSD became the third largest party in the Câmara dos Deputados, displacing the PSDB. Legislation providing for the creation of a National Truth Commission, which had provoked controversy when first proposed during Lula's presidency (see Lula's Second Term), was finally approved by the Congresso Nacional in October and enacted by Rousseff in November. With a two-year mandate, the Commission was to investigate human rights violations committed in Brazil between 1946 and 1988.

Land Occupations

From the mid-1990s the Landless Peasant Movement, the Movimento dos Trabalhadores Rurais Sem-Terra (MST), came to increasing prominence. During 1995 the MST organized a number of illegal occupations of disputed land in support of demands for an acceleration of the Government's programme of expropriation of uncultivated land for distribution to landless rural families. Rapidly deteriorating relations between the authorities and the MST were exacerbated in April 1996 by the violent intervention of the local military police in a demonstration in the state of Pará, which resulted in the deaths of 19 demonstrators. Widespread public outrage prompted the Government to announce new measures to accelerate the process of land reform in April 1997. In March 1998 thousands of activists occupied government premises in a campaign that led to the suspension of São Paulo's land expropriation proceedings. In May 2000 more than 30,000 members of the MST occupied a number of public buildings prompting the Government to introduce legislation preventing further land invasions.

Following the election of Lula to the presidency in October 2002, the MST, a traditional supporter of the PT, agreed to a temporary suspension of illegal land occupations. However, in March 2003 the MST declared its autonomy from the Government and resumed its policy of land invasions. In January 2007 the Government announced that it had reached 95% of its landless resettlement targets in 2003–06; however, this figure was disputed by landless organizations. Following a truce with the PT during Lula's re-election campaign in 2006, in April 2007 the MST again resumed its policy of land invasions. In February 2009 four security guards were killed during land occupations by MST members in Pernambuco state and some 2,000 activists from a dissident group within the MST invaded 20 plantations across eastern areas of São Paulo state. Following the killings in Pernambuco, the President of the Supreme Federal Court, Gilmar Ferreira Mendes, controversially alleged that militant groups linked to the MST were illicitly receiving public funding. Further land invasions in the state of Pará in April ended in violent clashes with the security forces. In October, following the destruction of a productive farm in São Paulo state by MST members, the opposition succeeded in initiating a congressional investigation into the disbursement of government funds to the movement and the alleged use of such funds to finance criminal activities.

Environmental Issues

The murder, in December 1988, of Francisco (Chico) Mendes, the leader of the rubber tappers' union and a pioneering ecologist, brought Brazil's environmental problems to international attention. Widespread concern was expressed that large-scale development projects, together with the 'slash-and-burn' farming techniques of cattle ranchers, peasant smallholders and loggers, and the release of large amounts of mercury into the environment by an estimated 60,000 gold prospectors (*garimpeiros*) in the Amazon region, presented a serious threat to the survival of both the indigenous Indians and the rainforest. International criticism of the Government's poor response to the threat to the environment persisted into the 2000s. Of particular concern to many international observers was the plight of the Yanomami Indian tribe in Roraima. It was estimated that, since the arrival of the *garimpeiros* in the region, some 10%–15% of the Yanomami's total population had been exterminated as a result of pollution and disease, introduced to the area by the gold prospectors. Legislation to provide greater protection for Brazil's natural resources, through the establishment of criminal penalties for illegal activities, was introduced in February 1998. In August 2002 Cardoso's Government created the world's biggest national park in the Tumucumaque Mountains. In September 2003 President Lula was criticized by environmentalists following the announcement of a four-year government infrastructure plan, which aimed to increase electricity output and improve transport links in the Amazon region. It was claimed that the plan would accelerate rainforest destruction. In April 2005, despite protests by farmers, the Government approved the creation of an Indian reservation of 1.75m. ha, Raposa Serra do Sol, in northern Roraima. The constitutionality of the reservation was contested in the Supreme Federal Court by a group of farmers and others affected by its creation; however, in March 2009 the Court ruled in favour of maintaining the reservation as a single unbroken territory. The judgment meant that the farmers and all other non-indigenous inhabitants of the designated area would be required to leave. A report published by the international environmentalist group Greenpeace in June accused the Brazilian Government of being complicit in the destruction of the rainforest through its financial support for the expansion of cattle ranching in the Amazon region. In late 2009 the Government pledged to reduce Brazil's annual rate of deforestation by some 80% by 2020, to less than 4,000 sq km per year.

A contract for the construction of the Belo Monte hydroelectric dam on the Xingu river, in the state of Pará, was signed in August 2010, despite concerns regarding the project's potential social and environmental impact, as well as its economic viability. A court in Pará suspended the contract in February 2011, on the grounds that the developers, Norte Energia, had failed to meet environmental standards. This ruling was overturned in March, however, allowing preparatory work on the 11,000-MW dam to commence, and in June permission for construction work was granted by the state environmental agency. In September a judge barred Norte Energia from undertaking any infrastructure work that would interfere with the natural flow of the Xingu river, ruling in favour of an appeal by a fisheries group that the dam would affect fish stocks, but he reversed his decision in December, stating that Norte Energia had demonstrated that the project would not harm fishing.

In May 2011, following the murders of several environmental campaigners in the Amazon region, the Government promised increased protection for such activists, establishing a ministerial working group to monitor investigations into the killings. In the same month the Câmara dos Deputados approved controversial amendments to the forestry code, essentially easing restrictions designed to protect the rainforest. The proposals notably provided for a reduction in the amount of forest that farmers were required to conserve on their land and for partial amnesty from fines imposed on those who deforested illegally prior to 2008. In December 2011 the Senado approved a revised version of the bill, which was then approved by the Câmara dos Deputados in late April 2012 prior to enactment by the President. Environmentalists urged Rousseff to veto the changes. Meanwhile, official figures indicated an 11% year-on-year decrease in deforestation in the Amazon region between August 2010 and July 2011, with the area cleared amounting to 6,238 sq km, the lowest level recorded since monitoring began in 1988.

Foreign Affairs

Regional relations

In 1990 a series of bilateral trade agreements was signed with Argentina, representing the first stage in a process which led to the establishment of a Southern Common Market (Mercado Comum do Sul—Mercosul, see p. 428), also to include Paraguay and Uruguay. Mercosul came into effect on 1 January 1995, following the signing, by the Presidents of the four member nations, of the Ouro Prêto Protocol. Customs barriers on 80%–85% of mutually exchanged goods were removed immediately.

Relations between Brazil and Bolivia threatened to become strained in May 2006, after President Evo Morales of Bolivia announced the effective nationalization of his country's hydrocarbons industry. The state-owned Petrobras was a significant investor in Bolivia's petroleum and gas sectors: although the Brazilian Government accepted the 82% tax increase on profits, it refused to accept any increases in the cost of gas imports, or any expropriation of Petrobras assets in Bolivia. Relations had improved by August 2009, when Morales and Lula signed bilateral agreements on energy (allowing Brazil to reduce the amount of gas purchased from Bolivia), trade in textiles and transport infrastructure, and pledged to increase co-operation in combating drugs-trafficking. An agreement on joint efforts to combat drugs-trafficking was signed in March 2011, followed by a further memorandum of understanding on co-operation in this area in October. Brazil was notably to provide unmanned aircraft to monitor its border with Bolivia.

In July 2009 President Lula and his Paraguayan counterpart, Fernando Lugo, signed an agreement aimed at ending a dispute over the Itaipú hydroelectric plant on their joint border. Under the accord, Brazil was to triple the amount it paid Paraguay for surplus electricity from Itaipú and to allow Paraguay to sell energy direct to Brazilian utility companies, rather than solely through the state-controlled enterprise Centrais Elétricas Brasileiras, SA (Eletrobrás). However, the Brazilian Government refused Paraguayan demands for a renegotiation of the terms of the 1973 bilateral Treaty of Itaipú (not due to expire until 2023), which provided for an equal division of the electricity generated at Itaipú, but obliged each country to sell any of its allocation that remained unused to the other at below the market rate. The agreement was finally ratified by the Brazilian Congresso Nacional in May 2011, just days before President Rousseff made her first official visit to Paraguay.

Other external relations

At the fifth Ministerial Conference of the World Trade Organization (WTO), held in Cancún, Mexico, in September 2003, Brazil led a group of countries opposed to the policy of subsidizing agricultural products as practised by the USA and the European Union. This group of developing nations, which came to be known as the Group of 20 (G20), demanded an end to subsidies in industrialized countries, in return for opening up their markets. The failure of the Doha round of WTO negotiations in 2007 was partly attributed to Brazilian–US failure to reach consensus on agricultural subsidies. On several occasions in 2009, in response to the global financial crisis and resulting economic downturn, Lula advocated reform of international financial institutions, including greater representation for major emerging economies, and a resumption of stalled WTO negotiations on trade liberalization. Similar demands were made at the first summit meeting of the leaders of the BRIC group of nations (comprising Brazil, Russia, India and the People's Republic of China), which was held in Yekaterinburg, Russia, in June. The Lula administration had greatly expanded trade links with

China, particularly in the energy sector, and in March 2009 that country became Brazil's principal trading partner. Further bilateral agreements on trade and energy co-operation were signed by Brazilian and Chinese officials at the second BRIC summit, which was held in Brasília in April 2010. In December of that year the IMF Board of Governors approved reforms that, subject to the approval of member states, would increase the voting powers of the BRIC countries within the Fund. At the third summit of the BRICS group (which had been renamed following the inclusion of South Africa), held in Sanya, China, in April 2011, participants urged the implementation of the proposed IMF reforms. While in China, the Brazilian delegation concluded agreements on Chinese investment in a number of Brazilian manufacturing projects, Brazil already constituting the largest recipient of Chinese foreign direct investment in 2010. In addition, in a joint communiqué marking President Rousseff's visit to China, her first overseas trip since taking office, China expressed its support for Brazil's bid for a permanent seat on the UN Security Council.

Brazil is a significant contributor to UN peace-keeping activities: in June 2004 the country dispatched 1,200 troops to Haiti to cope with the deteriorating security situation there, and took command of the UN peace-keeping troops stationed in the country. Brazil served as a non-permanent member of the UN's Security Council in 2010–11; the country has campaigned for a permanent seat on the Security Council. Brazil's opposition to imposing further UN sanctions on Iran over the latter's nuclear programme frustrated the US Administration during the first half of 2010 (although, as a non-permanent member of the Security Council, Brazil did not have the power of veto), as did its involvement in brokering an agreement, signed in May, to allow Iran to send low-enriched uranium to Turkey in return for reactor fuel. None the less, Brazilian-US relations remained cordial, and a bilateral defence co-operation agreement was signed in April of that year. President Rousseff sought to strengthen relations with the USA after taking office in January 2011. This was achieved to some extent during a visit to Brazil by US President Barack Obama in March, when talks focused largely on increasing bilateral trade and investment. Obama acknowledged Brazil's rising global significance, but failed fully to endorse the country's aspiration to secure a permanent seat on the UN Security Council, instead expressing 'appreciation' of this desire. Addressing the UN General Assembly in New York, USA, in September, Rousseff reiterated Brazil's aim of becoming a permanent member of the Security Council, as well as demands for an increased role for emerging economies in multilateral financial institutions and in addressing the international economic crisis.

Lula pursued closer relations with France, signing a new strategic partnership plan with that country during a visit to Brazil by the French Prime Minister, Nicolas Sarkozy, in December 2008. A strategic military co-operation agreement was signed by the two leaders in September 2009.

CONSTITUTION AND GOVERNMENT

Under the Constitution, which was promulgated on 5 October 1988, the country is a federal republic comprising 26 states and a Federal District (Brasília). Legislative power is exercised by the bicameral Congresso Nacional (National Congress), comprising the Senado Federal (Federal Senate—members elected by the majority principle in rotation for eight years) and the Câmara dos Deputados (Chamber of Deputies—members elected by a system of proportional representation for four years). The number of deputies is based on the size of the population. Election is by universal adult suffrage. Executive power is exercised by the President, elected by direct ballot for four years. The President appoints and leads the Cabinet. Each state has a directly elected Governor and an elected legislature. Judicial power is exercised by the Supreme Federal Court; the Higher Court of Justice; the regional federal courts; labour courts; electoral courts; military courts; and the courts of the states. For the purposes of local government, the states are divided into municipalities.

REGIONAL AND INTERNATIONAL CO-OPERATION

Brazil is a member of the Latin American Integration Association (see p. 362), of the Southern Common Market (Mercado Comum do Sul—Mercosul, see p. 428), of the Union of South American Nations (see p. 466) (União das Nações Sul-Americanas, UNASUR) and the associated South American Defence Council, and of the Community of Latin American and Caribbean States (see p. 462), which was formally inaugurated in December 2011.

Brazil was a founder member of the UN in 1945. As a contracting party to the General Agreement on Tariffs and Trade, Brazil joined the World Trade Organization (see p. 433) on its establishment in 1995. Brazil participates in the Group of 20 (G20, see p. 454) leading industrialized and developing nations, and is also a member of the Association of Tin Producing Countries, of the Cairns Group (see p. 504), and of the Comunidade dos Países de Língua Portuguesa (see p. 463). Brazil is a member of the Inter-American Development Bank (see p. 334) and the Organization of American States (see p. 394).

ECONOMIC AFFAIRS

In 2010, according to estimates by the World Bank, Brazil's gross national income (GNI), measured at average 2008–10 prices, was US $1,830,392m., equivalent to US $9,390 per head (or $10,920 per head on an international purchasing-power parity basis). During 2001–10, it was estimated, the population increased at an average annual rate of 1.1%, while gross domestic product (GDP) per head increased, in real terms, by an average of 2.7% per year. Overall GDP increased, in real terms, at an average annual rate of 3.8% in 2001–10; real GDP declined by 0.6% in 2009, but grew by 7.5% in 2010.

Agriculture (including hunting, forestry and fishing) contributed 5.3% of GDP in 2010 and engaged 17.0% of the economically active population, according to official figures, in 2009. The principal cash crops are sugar cane, soya beans, coffee, tobacco and cocoa beans. Subsistence crops include wheat, maize, rice, potatoes, beans, cassava and sorghum. Beef and poultry production are also important, as is fishing (particularly tuna, crab and shrimp). In 2005 the Congresso Nacional approved a law permitting the use of genetically modified crops. During 2001–10, according to the World Bank, agricultural GDP increased at an average annual rate of 3.7%; the sector's GDP decreased by 4.6% in 2009, but increased by 8.0% in 2010.

Industry (including mining, manufacturing, construction and power) provided 28.1% of GDP in 2010 and employed 36.0% of the working population in 2009. During 2001–10, according to the World Bank, industrial GDP increased at an average annual rate of 3.2%; the sector's GDP decreased by 6.7% in 2009, mainly owing to decreased contribution of mining activities caused by the global economic slowdown, but increased by 11.8% in 2010.

Mining contributed 3.0% of GDP in 2010. The GDP of the mining sector grew by 10.4% in 2002. The major mineral exports are iron ore (haematite—in terms of iron content, Brazil is the largest producer in the world), manganese, tin and aluminium. Gold, phosphates, platinum, uranium, copper and coal are also mined. In 2010 Brazil supplied an estimated 87.0% of the world's total output of columbium and was among the largest producers of bauxite, graphite, iron ore, manganese, niobium, tantalum and tin. In 2009 gold production totalled 65,000 kg, compared with 55,000 kg in the previous year. Copper output stood at 217,600 metric tons in 2009, a 1.1% fall on 2008. The state-run oil company Petróleo Brasileiro, SA (Petrobras) estimated Brazil's reserves of petroleum to be 15,283m. 42-gallon barrels in 2010 following discoveries of oil in the pre-salt layer off the coast of Rio de Janeiro.

Manufacturing contributed 16.2% of GDP in 2010 and engaged 13.9% of the economically active population in 2009. There is considerable state involvement in a broad range of manufacturing activity. While traditionally dominant areas, including textiles and clothing, footwear and food- and beverage-processing, continue to contribute a large share to the sector, more recent developments in the sector have resulted in the emergence of machinery and transport equipment (including road vehicles and components, passenger jet aircraft and specialist machinery for the petroleum industry), construction materials (especially iron and steel), wood and sugar cane derivatives, and chemicals and petrochemicals as significant new manufacturing activities. According to the World Bank, manufacturing GDP increased at an average rate of 2.9% per year in 2001–10; the sector's GDP declined by 8.2% in 2009 and by 11.9% in 2010.

Construction provided 5.7% of GDP in 2010 and employed 7.5% of the working population in 2009.

In 2008, according to the World Bank, 79.8% of total electricity production was provided by hydroelectric power. Other energy sources, including petroleum, coal and nuclear power, accounted for the remaining 20.2%. Attempts to exploit further the country's vast hydroelectric potential were encouraged by the completion of ambitious dam projects at Itaipú, on the border with Paraguay (expected to produce as much as 35% of Brazil's total electricity requirements when fully operational), and at Tucuruí, on the Tocantins river. According to official figures, imports of mineral fuels and lubricants comprised 14.8% of the value of total merchandise imports in 2009.

The services sector contributed 66.6% of GDP in 2010 and engaged 60.9% of the employed labour force in 2009. Tourism was an important contributor to the economy. Tourism receipts (excluding passenger transport) totalled a provisional US $5,919m. in 2010. In that year foreign tourists reached 5,161,379, a 7.5% increase on the total in 2009. According to the World Bank, the GDP of the services sector increased at an average rate of 3.9% per year in 2001–10; the sector's GDP increased by 2.1% in 2009 and by 5.5% in 2010.

According to official estimates, in 2010 Brazil recorded a trade surplus of US $20,221m., and there was a deficit of $47,365m. on the current account of the balance of payments. In 2008 the principal source of imports (14.9%) was the USA, which was also the principal market for exports (14.0%). Other major trading partners were the People's Republic of China, Argentina, the Netherlands, Mexico and Japan. The principal exports in 2008 were iron ore and concentrates, crude petroleum and fuels, and soya beans and related products. The principal imports in that year were mineral fuels and lubricants, chemicals and pharmaceutical goods, and minerals.

The 2010 federal budget recorded expenditure of R $643,908m. and revenue of R $919,773m., creating a surplus which was 7.3% of the total GDP. Brazil's general government gross debt was R $2,456,350m. in 2010, equivalent to 65.2% of GDP. Brazil's external debt was US $276,932m. at the end of 2009, of which US $87,317m. was long-term public debt. The cost of servicing long-term public and publicly guaranteed debt and repayments to the IMF in that year was equivalent to 7.0% of the value of exports of goods, services and income. According to the International Labour Organization (ILO), the annual rate of inflation averaged 6.0% in 2001–10. Consumer prices increased by 5.1% in 2010. The ILO indicated an average unemployment rate of 8.3% of the labour force in 2009.

On taking office in January 2011, President Dilma Vana Rousseff pledged to continue the economic policies of her predecessor, Luiz Inácio Lula da Silva. She announced a new plan aimed at eradicating extreme poverty, while existing programmes, such as the Growth Acceleration Programme (Programa de Aceleração do Crescimento), were extended. Rousseff inherited a rapidly expanding economy, which was recovering strongly from the recession of late 2008 and early 2009 after several years of relative economic stability. This recovery was driven by increasing domestic demand and investment, as well as rising prices for Brazil's commodity exports. However, there were concerns regarding the strength of the the national currency, the real, and mounting inflationary pressures. The central bank gradually raised its benchmark interest rate to 12.5% between April 2010 and July 2011 (having lowered it to a record low of 8.75% in July 2009) in an effort to contain inflation, which reached a rate of 7.3% on a year-on-year basis in September 2011. In March and May 2010, and again in February 2011, the Government announced reductions in expenditure totalling R $31,800m. for 2010 and R $50,000m. for 2011 in a further bid to cool the economy. However, citing a deteriorating global economic outlook and the expectation of a downward trend in inflation, the central bank lowered the interest rate three times between August and November 2011, to 11.0%. As anticipated, year-on-year inflation began to decelerate in late 2011, reaching 6.5% by the end of the year. In August the Government announced a plan to enhance the competitiveness of manufacturing companies, which had suffered as a result of the continued strength of the real; the measures included tax reductions for Brazilian-made products and stricter import controls. In December the central bank forecast that GDP growth in 2011 would slow to 3.0%, from 7.5% in 2010, amid a weakening industrial performance, before accelerating slightly to 3.5% in 2012. Meanwhile, the unemployment rate remained low, at 5.2% in November 2011 (compared with 8.3% for 2009 as a whole).

PUBLIC HOLIDAYS

2013: 1 January (New Year's Day—Universal Confraternization Day), 11–13 February (Carnival), 29 March (Good Friday), 21 April (Tiradentes Day—Discovery of Brazil), 1 May (Labour Day), 30 May (Corpus Christi), 7 September (Independence Day), 12 October (Our Lady Aparecida, Patron Saint of Brazil), 2 November (All Souls' Day), 15 November (Proclamation of the Republic), 20 November (Death of Zumbi dos Palmares—Black Awareness Day), 25 December (Christmas Day).

Other local holidays include 20 January (Foundation of Rio de Janeiro) and 25 January (Foundation of São Paulo).

Statistical Survey

Sources (unless otherwise stated): Economic Research Department, Banco Central do Brasil, SBS, Quadra 03, Bloco B, 70074-900 Brasília, DF; tel. (61) 3414-1074; fax (61) 3414-2036; e-mail coace.depec.@bcb.gov.br; internet www.bcb.gov.br; Instituto Brasileiro de Geografia e Estatística (IBGE), Centro de Documentação e Disseminação de Informações (CDDI), Rua Gen. Canabarro 706, 2° andar, Maracanã, 20271-201 Rio de Janeiro, RJ; tel. (21) 2142-4781; fax (21) 2142-4933; e-mail ibge@ibge.bov.br; internet www.ibge.gov.br.

Area and Population

AREA, POPULATION AND DENSITY

Area (sq km)	8,514,877*
Population (census results)†	
1 August 2000	169,590,693
1 August 2010 (preliminary)	
Males	93,406,990
Females	97,348,809
Total	190,755,799
Density (per sq km) at census of 1 August 2010	22.4

* 3,287,611 sq miles.

† Excluding Indian jungle population (numbering 45,429 in 1950).

POPULATION BY AGE AND SEX

(official projected estimates at mid-2012)

	Males	Females	Total
0–14	24,517,381	23,804,152	48,321,533
15–64	65,683,496	68,404,697	134,088,193
65 and over	6,117,415	7,999,152	14,116,567
Total	96,318,292	100,208,001	196,526,293

Note: Estimates not revised to take account of the 2010 census results.

ADMINISTRATIVE DIVISIONS

(population at census of 1 August 2010, preliminary results)

State	Area (sq km)	Population	Density (per sq km)	Capital
Acre (AC)	152,581	733,559	4.8	Rio Branco
Alagoas (AL)	27,768	3,120,494	112.4	Maceió
Amapá (AP)	142,815	669,526	4.7	Macapá
Amazonas (AM)	1,570,746	3,483,985	2.2	Manaus
Bahia (BA)	564,693	14,016,906	24.8	Salvador
Ceará (CE)	148,826	8,452,381	56.8	Fortaleza
Distrito Federal (DF)	5,802	2,570,160	443.0	Brasília
Espírito Santo (ES)	46,078	3,514,952	76.3	Vitória
Goiás (GO)	340,087	6,003,788	17.7	Goiânia
Maranhão (MA)	331,983	6,574,789	19.8	São Luís
Mato Grosso (MT)	903,358	3,035,122	3.4	Cuiabá
Mato Grosso do Sul (MS)	357,125	2,449,024	6.9	Campo Grande
Minas Gerais (MG)	586,528	19,597,330	33.4	Belo Horizonte
Pará (PA)	1,247,690	7,581,051	6.1	Belém
Paraíba (PB)	56,440	3,766,528	66.7	João Pessoa
Paraná (PR)	199,315	10,444,526	52.4	Curitiba
Pernambuco (PE)	98,312	8,796,448	89.5	Recife
Piauí (PI)	251,529	3,118,360	12.4	Teresina

State—*continued*	Area (sq km)	Population	Density (per sq km)	Capital
Rio de Janeiro (RJ)	43,696	15,989,929	366.0	Rio de Janeiro
Rio Grande do Norte (RN)	52,797	3,483,985	66.0	Natal
Rio Grande do Sul (RS)	281,749	10,693,929	38.0	Porto Alegre
Rondônia (RO)	237,576	1,562,409	6.6	Porto Velho
Roraima (RR)	224,299	450,479	2.0	Boa Vista
Santa Catarina (SC)	95,346	6,248,436	65.5	Florianópolis
São Paulo (SP)	248,209	41,262,199	166.2	São Paulo
Sergipe (SE)	21,910	2,068,017	94.4	Aracaju
Tocantins (TO)	277,621	1,383,445	5.0	Palmas
Total	8,514,877	190,755,799	22.4	—

PRINCIPAL TOWNS
(population at census of 1 August 2010, preliminary results)*

São Paulo	11,253,503	Jaboatão dos Guararapes	644,620
Rio de Janeiro	6,320,446	São José dos Campos	629,921
Salvador	2,675,656	Ribeirão Preto	604,682
Brasília (capital)	2,570,160	Uberlândia	604,013
Fortaleza	2,452,185	Contagem	603,442
Belo Horizonte	2,375,151	Sorocaba	586,625
Manaus	1,802,014	Aracaju	571,149
Curitiba	1,751,907	Feira de Santana	556,642
Recife	1,537,704	Cuiabá	551,098
Porto Alegre	1,409,351	Juíz de Fora	516,247
Belém	1,393,399	Joinville	515,288
Goiânia	1,302,001	Londrina	506,701
Guarulhos	1,221,979	Niterói	487,562
Campinas	1,080,113	Ananindeua	471,980
São Luís	1,014,837	Belford Roxo	469,332
São Gonçalo	999,728	Campos dos Goytacazes	463,731
Maceió	932,748	São João de Meriti	458,673
Duque de Caxias	855,048	Aparecida de Goiânia	455,657
Teresina	814,230	Caxias do Sul	435,564
Natal	803,739	Porto Velho	428,527
Nova Iguaçu	796,257	Florianópolis	421,240
Campo Grande	786,797	Santos	419,400
São Bernardo do Campo	765,463	Mauá	417,064
João Pessoa	723,515	Vila Velha	414,586
Santo André	676,407	Serra	409,267
Osasco	666,740	São José do Rio Preto	408,258

* Figures refer to *municípios*, which may contain rural districts.

BIRTHS, MARRIAGES AND DEATHS
(official estimates based on annual registrations)

	Live births		Marriages	Deaths	
	Number*	Rate (per 1,000)	Number	Number	Rate (per 1,000)
2003	3,426,727	19.2	748,981	993,685	5.6
2004	3,329,120	18.4	806,968	1,013,657	5.6
2005	3,329,431	18.2	835,846	996,931	5.4
2006	3,172,000	17.1	889,828	1,023,814	5.5
2007	3,080,266	16.4	916,006	1,036,405	5.5
2008	3,107,927	16.4	959,901	1,060,365	5.6
2009	3,045,696	15.9	935,116	1,083,399	5.7
2010	2,985,406	15.7	977,620	1,132,701	5.1

* Including births registered but not occurring during that year: 604,265 in 2003; 510,202 in 2004; 448,243 in 2005; 368,062 in 2006; 324,895 in 2007; 309,885 in 2008; 281,054 in 2009; 224,445 in 2010.

Life expectancy (years at birth, WHO estimates): 73 (males 70; females 77) in 2009 (Source: WHO, *World Health Statistics*).

ECONOMICALLY ACTIVE POPULATION
('000 persons aged 10 years and over, labour force sample survey at September)*

	2007	2008	2009
Agriculture, hunting, forestry and fishing	16,579	16,100	15,715
Industry (excl. construction)	13,846	13,995	13,598
Manufacturing industries	13,105	13,266	12,815
Construction	6,107	6,905	6,895
Commerce and repair of motor vehicles and household goods	16,309	16,093	16,484
Hotels and restaurants	3,351	3,592	3,623
Transport, storage and communication	4,374	4,596	4,436
Public administration	4,504	4,531	4,754
Education, health and social services	8,379	8,539	8,681
Domestic services	6,732	6,626	7,223
Other community, social and personal services	3,711	4,083	3,928
Other activities	6,684	7,134	7,150
Sub-total	90,577	92,194	92,487
Activities not adequately defined	209	201	202
Total employed	90,786	92,395	92,689
Unemployed	8,060	7,106	8,421
Total labour force	98,846	99,500	101,110

* Data coverage excludes rural areas of Acre, Amapá, Amazonas, Pará, Rondônia and Roraima.

Health and Welfare

KEY INDICATORS

Total fertility rate (children per woman, 2009)	1.8
Under-5 mortality rate (per 1,000 live births, 2009)	21
HIV/AIDS (% of persons aged 15–49, 2007)	0.6
Physicians (per 1,000 head, 2000)	1.2
Hospital beds (per 1,000 head, 2002)	2.6
Health expenditure (2008): US $ per head (PPP)	875
Health expenditure (2008): % of GDP	8.4
Health expenditure (2008): public (% of total)	44.0
Access to water (% of persons, 2008)	97
Access to sanitation (% of persons, 2008)	80
Total carbon dioxide emissions ('000 metric tons, 2007)	368,015.8
Carbon dioxide emissions per head (metric tons, 2007)	1.9
Human Development Index (2011): ranking	84
Human Development Index (2011): value	0.718

For sources and definitions, see explanatory note on p. vi.

Agriculture

PRINCIPAL CROPS
('000 metric tons)

	2008	2009	2010
Wheat	6,027	5,055	6,037
Rice, paddy	12,061	12,652	11,309
Barley	237	201	274
Maize	58,933	50,720	56,060
Oats	239	253	368
Sorghum	2,004	1,854	1,505
Buckwheat*	60	53	57
Potatoes	3,677	3,444	3,595
Sweet potatoes	548	477	479
Cassava (Manioc)	26,703	24,404	24,354
Yams*	253	231	232
Sugar cane	645,300	672,157	719,157
Beans, dry	3,461	3,487	3,202
Brazil nuts, with shell	31	37	37
Cashew nuts, with shell	243	221	102
Soybeans (Soya beans)	59,833	57,345	68,518
Groundnuts, with shell	313	256	230
Coconuts	2,960	2,960	2,706
Oil palm fruit	1,091	1,122	1,122*
Castor oil seed	122	91	93

—continued	2008	2009	2010
Sunflower seed	148	101	80
Tomatoes	3,868	4,310	3,691
Onions, dry	1,367	1,512	1,556
Garlic	92	87	105
Watermelons	1,995	2,065	1,870
Cantaloupes and other melons	340	403	365
Bananas	6,998	6,783	6,978
Oranges	18,538	17,619	19,112
Tangerines, mandarins, clementines and satsumas	1,080	1,094	1,123
Lemons and limes	965	900	1,020
Grapefruit and pomelos*	71	67	72
Apples	1,124	1,223	1,276
Peaches and nectarines	239	216	221
Grapes	1,421	1,365	1,306
Guavas, mangoes, mangosteens	1,155	1,198	1,189
Avocados	147	139	152
Pineapples	2,569	2,206	2,120
Persimmons	173	172	164
Cashew-apple*	1,691	1,593	1,716
Papayas	1,890	1,793	1,871
Coffee, green	2,797	2,440	2,874
Cocoa beans	202	218	233
Mate	435	443	426
Sisal	246	280	236
Tobacco, unmanufactured	851	863	781
Natural rubber	202	212	222

* FAO estimate(s).

Aggregate production ('000 metric tons, may include official, semi-official or estimated data): Total cereals 79,752 in 2008, 70,914 in 2009, 75,731 in 2010; Total roots and tubers 31,181 in 2008, 28,556 in 2009, 28,661 in 2010; Total vegetables (incl. melons) 10,131 in 2008, 11,074 in 2009, 10,032 in 2010; Total fruits (excl. melons) 38,790 in 2008, 37,124 in 2009, 39,287 in 2010.

Source: FAO.

LIVESTOCK

('000 head, year ending September)

	2008	2009	2010
Cattle	202,307	205,260	209,541
Buffaloes	1,147	1,135	1,185
Horses	5,542	5,497	5,514
Asses	1,131	1,031	1,002
Mules	1,314	1,276	1,277
Pigs	36,819	38,046	38,957
Sheep	16,630	16,812	17,381
Goats	9,355	9,164	9,313
Chickens	1,202,020	1,233,860	1,238,910
Ducks*	3,600	3,600	3,600
Turkeys*	23,000	23,000	23,000

* FAO estimates.

Source: FAO.

LIVESTOCK PRODUCTS

('000 metric tons)

	2008	2009	2010
Cattle meat	6,621	6,662	6,977
Sheep meat*	79	80	81
Goat meat*	29	30	30
Pig meat	2,636	2,930	3,078
Horse meat*	21	22	22
Chicken meat	10,216	9,940	10,693
Cows' milk	28,441	30,008	31,667
Goats' milk*	140	144	148
Hen eggs†	1,845	1,922	1,948
Other poultry eggs	95	115	139
Natural honey	38	39	45*
Wool, greasy	12	11	10*

* FAO estimate(s).

† Unofficial figures.

Source: FAO.

Forestry

ROUNDWOOD REMOVALS

('000 cubic metres, excl. bark, FAO estimates)

	2007	2008	2009
Sawlogs, veneer logs and logs for sleepers	52,243	49,355	49,015
Pulpwood	60,964	58,182	65,346
Other industrial wood	8,313	7,853	7,799
Fuel wood	139,831	140,916	141,989
Total	261,351	256,306	264,149

2010: Production assumed to be unchanged from 2009 (FAO estimates).

Source: FAO.

SAWNWOOD PRODUCTION

('000 cubic metres, incl. railway sleepers)

	2006	2007	2008*
Coniferous (softwood)	9,078	9,577	9,532
Broadleaved (hardwood)	14,719	14,837	15,455
Total	23,797	24,414	24,987

* Unofficial figures.

2009–10: Production assumed to be unchanged from 2008 (FAO estimates).

Source: FAO.

Fishing

('000 metric tons, live weight)

	2007	2008	2009
Capture	783.2	791.9	825.4
Characins	92.3	85.9	84.3
Freshwater siluroids	40.1	38.8	35.6
Weakfishes	50.2	46.7	51.5
Whitemouth croaker	44.4	41.5	45.8
Brazilian sardinella	55.9	74.6	83.3
Aquaculture	289.1	365.4*	415.6*
Common carp	36.6	67.6	80.9
Tilapias	95.1	111.1	133.0
Whiteleg shrimp	65.0	70.3	65.2
Total catch	1,072.2	1,157.2*	1,241.0*

* FAO estimate.

Note: Figures exclude aquatic mammals, recorded by number rather than by weight. The number of whales and dolphins caught was: 1,799 in 2007; 27 in 2008; 25 in 2009. Also excluded are crocodiles: the number of broad-nosed, black and spectacled caimans caught was: 10,254 in 2007; 7,024 in 2008; 6,569 in 2009.

Source: FAO.

Mining

('000 metric tons unless otherwise indicated)

	2007	2008	2009[1]
Hard coal[2]	6,133	6,474	6,500
Crude petroleum ('000 barrels)	638,018	876,000	938,780
Natural gas (million cu m)	15,831	18,642	18,375
Iron ore:[3]			
gross weight	354,674	351,677	310,000
metal content	235,504	233,514	206,100
Copper (metric tons)	218,367	220,000	217,600
Nickel ore (metric tons)[4]	58,317	67,116	67,000
Bauxite	25,461	28,098	25,628
Lead concentrates (metric tons)[4]	24,574	25,286	24,600
Zinc (metric tons)	265,126	248,874	270,700
Tin concentrates (metric tons)[4]	9,634	10,558	10,600
Chromium ore (metric tons)[5]	253,254	256,300	246,900
Tungsten concentrates (metric tons)[4]	537	550	550
Ilmenite (metric tons)	130,000	130,000	130,000
Rutile (metric tons)	3,000	3,000	3,000
Zirconium concentrates (metric tons)[6]	26,739	26,739	26,700

—continued	2007	2008	2009[1]
Silver (kg)[7]	36,000	36,500	36,500
Gold (kg)	47,743	55,000	65,000
Bentonite (beneficiated)	239	239	239
Kaolin (beneficiated)	2,530	2,800	2,674
Magnesite (beneficiated)	399	399	399
Phosphate rock[8]	6,185	6,343	6,800
Potash salts[9]	424	383	383
Fluorspar (Fluorite) (metric tons)[10]	65,924	63,573	63,600
Barite (Barytes) (beneficiated) (metric tons)	13,311	7,321	7,300
Quartz (natural crystals) (metric tons)	22,561	22,600	22,600
Salt (unrefined):			
marine	5,365	5,370	5,400
rock	1,621	1,650	1,650
Gypsum and anhydrite (crude)	1,923	1,923	1,950
Graphite (natural) (metric tons)[2]	77,163	77,200[11]	77,200
Asbestos (fibre) (metric tons)	254,204	287,673	282,032
Mica (metric tons)[11]	4,000	4,000	4,000
Vermiculite concentrates (metric tons)	18,952	20,089	20,100
Talc (crude)	401	401	401
Pyrophyllite (crude)[11]	200	200	200
Diamonds, gem and industrial ('000 carats)[11,12]	182	182	200

[1] Preliminary figures.
[2] Figures refer to marketable products.
[3] Includes sponge iron (metric tons) 270,000 in 2005–09 (estimates).
[4] Figures refer to the metal content of ores and concentrates.
[5] Figures refer to the chromic oxide (Cr_2O_3) content.
[6] Including production of baddeleyite-caldasite.
[7] Figures refer to primary production only. The production of secondary silver (in kg, estimates): was: 32,000 in 2007; 32,500 in 2008; 32,500 in 2009 (preliminary figure).
[8] Figures refer to the gross weight of concentrates. The phosphoric acid (P_2O_5) content (in '000 metric tons) was: 2,185 in 2007; 2,242 in 2008; 2,400 in 2009 (preliminary figure).
[9] Figures refer to the potassium oxide (K_2O) content.
[10] Acid-grade and metallurgical-grade concentrates.
[11] Estimated production.
[12] Figures refer to officially reported diamond output plus official Brazilian estimates of diamond output by independent miners (*garimpeiros*).

Source: US Geological Survey.

Industry

SELECTED PRODUCTS

('000 metric tons unless otherwise indicated)

	2007	2008	2009
Beef—fresh or chilled	3,425	3,229	3,476
Frozen poultry meats and giblets	5,464	5,662	5,687
Sugar (granulated)	18,230	17,812	17,583
Beer ('000 hl)	100,203	110,521	12,587
Soft drinks ('000 hl)	126,422	140,966	142,041
Gas-diesel oil (distillate fuel oil, '000 cu m)	40,658	42,572	45,949
Residual fuel oils ('000 cu m)	26,817	28,879	30,720
Naphthas for petrochemicals ('000 cu m)	11,915	11,165	9,187
Liquefied petroleum gas	12,171	11,820	12,159
Ethylene—unsaturated	2,830	2,498	2,772
Fertilizers with nitrogen, phosphorus and potassium	18,377	17,989	15,057
Chemical wood pulp, cellulose	7,894	9,118	9,856
Iron	10,504	10,041	5,028
Iron ore*	456,453	427,499	315,744
Hot rolled coils of carbon steel—uncoated	6,345	6,831	4,961
Motor vehicles (units)	2,473,586	n.a.	n.a.
Trucks (units)†	106,235	126,437	100,832
Motorcycles (units)	1,759,425	1,938,073	1,391,865
Mobile cellular telephones ('000 units)	68,433	68,327	55,854

* Prepared forms, including concentrates, ball bearings, etc.
† Vehicles with diesel engines and maximum load capacity in excess of five metric tons.

Electric energy (million kWh): 419,336 in 2006; 445,094 in 2007; 463,120 in 2008 (Source: UN Industrial Commodity Statistics Database).

Finance

CURRENCY AND EXCHANGE RATES

Monetary Units
100 centavos = 1 real (plural: reais).

Sterling, Dollar and Euro Equivalents (30 December 2011)
£1 sterling = 2.899 reais;
US $1 = 1.875 reais;
€1 = 2.426 reais;
100 reais = £34.49 = $53.33 = €41.22.

Average Exchange Rates (reais per US $)
2009 1.9994
2010 1.7592
2011 1.6742

Note: In March 1986 the cruzeiro (CR $) was replaced by a new currency unit, the cruzado (CZ $), equivalent to 1,000 cruzeiros. In January 1989 the cruzado was, in turn, replaced by the new cruzado (NCZ $), equivalent to CZ $1,000 and initially at par with the US dollar (US $). In March 1990 the new cruzado was replaced by the cruzeiro (CR $), at an exchange rate of one new cruzado for one cruzeiro. In August 1993 the cruzeiro was replaced by the cruzeiro real, equivalent to CR $1,000. On 1 March 1994, in preparation for the introduction of a new currency, a transitional accounting unit, the Unidade Real de Valor (at par with the US $), came into operation, alongside the cruzeiro real. On 1 July 1994 the cruzeiro real was replaced by the real (R $), also at par with the US $ and thus equivalent to 2,750 cruzeiros reais.

BUDGET

(R $ million)

Revenue	2008	2009	2010
National treasury revenues	551,344	555,054	705,297
Gross revenues*	564,723	569,846	719,531
Taxes and welfare contributions	484,702	n.a.	n.a.
Restitutions	–13,388	–14,737	14,135
Fiscal incentives	–1	–55	99
Social security revenues	163,355	182,008	211,968
Urban	158,383	177,444	207,154
Rural	4,973	4,564	4,814
Central bank revenues	1,959	2,242	2,508
Total	716,658	739,305	919,773

Expenditure	2008	2009	2010
Transfers to state and local governments	133,076	127,684	140,678
Treasury expenditures	295,907	344,437	245,344
Payroll*	130,829	151,653	166,486
Worker support fund (FAT)	21,026	27,433	30,311
Economic subsidies and grants†	5,980	5,190	7,875
Assistance benefits (LOAS/RMV)	16,036	18,946	22,234
Other current and capital expenditures	120,993	140,035	171,196
Transfer to central bank	1,043	1,180	1,242
Social security benefits	199,562	224,876	254,859
Central bank expenditures	2,431	2,872	3,027
Sovereign Fund of Brazil‡	14,244	—	—
Total	645,220	699,869	643,908

* Excludes the employer share of federal civil service payments from revenues originating in contributions to the Social Security Plan (CPSS) and personnel outlays.
† Includes judicially determined repayments related to the Rural Unified and Industrial Unified initiatives.
‡ Expenses related to paid-in capital for the Fiscal Investment and Stabilization Fund (FFIE) from the Sovereign Fund of Brazil.

Source: Ministério da Fazenda, Brasília, DF.

CENTRAL BANK RESERVES

(US $ million at 31 December)

	2008	2009	2010
Gold (national valuation)	940	1,175	1,519
IMF special drawing rights	1	4,527	4,450
Foreign exchange	192,842	231,888	280,570
Total	193,783	237,590	286,539

Source: IMF, *International Financial Statistics*.

MONEY SUPPLY

(R $ million at 31 December)

	2008	2009	2010
Currency outside depository corporations	92,360	105,793	121,969
Transferable deposits	130,017	143,099	159,005
Other deposits	1,695,406	1,971,278	2,239,882
Securities other than shares	24,621	29,481	74,434
Broad money	1,942,404	2,249,651	2,595,291

Source: IMF, *International Financial Statistics*.

COST OF LIVING

(Consumer Price Index; base: 2000 = 100)

	2004	2005	2006
Food	146.5	151.0	151.0
Clothing and footwear	135.2	147.3	156.1
Rent	148.6	158.3	165.7
All items (incl. others)	141.7	151.4	157.8

2007: Food 161.2; All items (incl. others) 163.5.

2008: Food 182.3; All items (incl. others) 172.8.

2009: Food 192.9; All items (incl. others) 181.2.

2010: All items 190.4.

Source: ILO.

NATIONAL ACCOUNTS

(R$ million at current prices)

National Income and Product

	2008	2009	2010
Gross domestic product (GDP) in market prices	3,032,204	3,239,404	3,770,085
Wages and salaries	1,041	1,218	879
Primary incomes received from abroad (net)	−72,815	−65,296	−69,042
Gross national income (GNI)	2,960,429	3,175,327	3,701,921
Current transfers received from abroad (net)	7,916	6,684	4,912
Net national disposable income	2,968,345	3,182,010	3,706,834

Expenditure on the Gross Domestic Product

	2008	2009	2010
Final consumption expenditure	2,398,945	2,666,753	3,045,956
Households	1,786,840	1,979,751	2,248,625
General government	612,105	687,001	797,333
Gross capital formation	627,497	577,846	763,012
Gross fixed capital formation	579,531	585,317	733,713
Changes in inventories	47,967	−7,471	29,300
Total domestic expenditure	3,026,443	3,244,599	3,808,968
Exports of goods and services	414,296	355,654	409,868
Less Imports of goods and services	408,533	360,847	448,750
GDP in market prices	3,032,204	3,239,404	3,770,085

Gross Domestic Product by Economic Activity

	2008	2009	2010
Agriculture, hunting, forestry and fishing	152,612	157,232	171,177
Mining and quarrying	83,499	51,065	95,886
Manufacturing	429,063	465,264	523,617
Electricity, gas and water	80,875	86,586	103,873
Construction	126,552	146,784	182,478
Trade, restaurants and hotels	323,375	349,061	404,007
Transport, storage and communications	129,013	134,233	161,936
Information services	98,037	99,742	103,978
Financial intermediation, insurance, and related services	175,379	202,216	242,410
Real estate and renting	210,291	233,757	252,823
Government, health and education services	406,958	456,425	522,776
Other services	364,798	412,015	462,220
Gross value added in basic prices	2,580,449	2,794,378	3,227,180
Taxes, less subsidies, on products	451,754	445,026	542,904
GDP in market prices	3,032,204	3,239,404	3,770,085

BALANCE OF PAYMENTS

(US $ million)

	2008	2009	2010
Exports of goods f.o.b.	197,942	152,995	201,915
Imports of goods f.o.b.	−173,107	−127,705	−181,694
Trade balance	24,836	25,290	20,221
Exports of services	30,451	27,728	31,821
Imports of services	−47,140	−46,974	−62,628
Balance on goods and services	8,146	6,044	−10,586
Other income received	12,511	8,826	7,353
Other income paid	−53,073	−42,510	−46,919
Balance on goods, services and income	−32,416	−27,640	−50,152
Current transfers received	5,317	4,736	4,661
Current transfers paid	−1,093	−1,398	−1,873
Current balance	−28,192	−24,302	−47,365
Capital account (net)	1,055	1,129	1,119
Direct investment abroad	−20,457	10,084	−11,519
Direct investment from abroad	45,058	25,949	48,438
Portfolio investment assets	1,900	4,125	−4,784
Portfolio investment liabilities	−767	46,159	67,795
Financial derivatives assets	298	322	133
Financial derivatives liabilities	−610	−166	−245
Other investment assets	−5,269	−30,376	−42,575
Other investment liabilities	8,143	14,064	41,301
Net errors and omissions	1,810	591	−3,217
Overall balance	2,969	47,578	49,080

Source: IMF, *International Financial Statistics*.

External Trade

PRINCIPAL COMMODITIES

(US $ million)

Imports f.o.b.	2006	2007	2008
Capital goods	18,924	25,125	35,932
Industrial machinery	5,310	7,356	10,992
Parts of capital goods for industry	2,109	4,186	5,420
Moveable transport equipment	1,405	1,882	3,487
Parts and accessories of industrial machinery	1,352	1,825	2,418
Consumer goods	11,955	16,027	22,526
Non-durable goods	5,879	7,776	9,816
Foodstuffs	1,728	2,082	2,812
Pharmaceuticals	2,171	2,908	3,493
Durable goods	6,076	8,251	12,710
Passenger vehicles	1,914	3,121	5,343
Mineral fuels and lubricants	15,197	20,085	31,464
Raw materials and intermediate goods	45,274	59,381	83,056
Chemicals and pharmaceutical goods	12,240	15,672	21,185
Intermediate goods and parts thereof	7,818	8,839	11,132
Minerals	9,205	11,631	15,447
Transport equipment, parts and spares	553	768	990
Agricultural products (excl. foodstuffs)	3,036	5,529	10,955
Total (incl. others)	91,351	120,617	172,978

Exports f.o.b.	2006	2007	2008
Basic goods	40,285	51,596	73,028
Iron ore and concentrates	8,949	10,558	16,539
Crude petroleum and fuels	6,894	8,905	13,556
Soybeans and products thereof	5,663	6,709	10,952
Coffee (not roasted)	2,928	3,378	4,131
Beef and poultry	7,082	8,935	n.a.
Semi-manufactured goods	19,523	21,800	27,073
Sugar (raw)	3,936	3,130	3,650
Iron and steel in primary forms	2,277	2,340	4,002
Wood pulp	2,479	3,012	3,901
Manufactured goods	75,018	83,943	92,683
Passenger cars	4,597	4,653	4,916
Aeroplanes	3,241	4,719	5,495
Parts and accessories for motor vehicles and tractors	2,972	3,186	3,510
Flat-rolled products of iron or non-alloy steel	2,718	2,532	1,921
Devices, transmitters, receivers and components	3,068	2,353	2,550
Total (incl. others)	137,807	160,649	197,942

PRINCIPAL TRADING PARTNERS
(US $ million)*

Imports f.o.b.	2006	2007	2008
Argentina	8,053	10,404	13,258
Belgium-Luxembourg	997	1,191	1,689
Canada	1,194	1,708	3,210
Chile	2,866	3,462	3,952
China, People's Republic	7,990	12,621	20,044
France	2,838	3,525	4,678
Germany	6,503	8,669	12,027
Italy	2,570	3,348	4,613
Japan	3,840	4,609	6,807
Korea, Republic	3,106	3,391	5,413
Mexico	1,310	1,979	3,125
Netherlands	786	1,116	1,477
Paraguay	296	434	657
Spain	1,431	1,843	2,472
United Kingdom	1,417	1,956	2,551
USA	14,817	18,888	25,810
Uruguay	618	786	1,018
Total (incl. others)	91,351	120,617	172,978

Exports f.o.b.	2006	2007	2008
Argentina	11,740	14,417	17,606
Belgium-Luxembourg	3,015	3,912	4,494
Canada	2,281	2,362	1,866
Chile	3,914	4,264	4,792
China, People's Republic	8,402	10,749	16,403
France	2,669	3,472	4,126
Germany	5,691	7,211	8,851
Italy	3,836	4,464	4,765
Japan	3,895	4,321	6,115
Korea, Republic	1,963	2,047	3,119
Mexico	4,458	4,260	4,281
Netherlands	5,749	8,841	10,483
Paraguay	1,234	1,648	2,488
Spain	2,330	3,476	4,074
United Kingdom	2,829	3,301	3,792
USA	24,773	25,314	27,648
Uruguay	1,013	1,288	1,644
Total (incl. others)	137,807	160,649	197,942

* Imports by country of purchase; exports by country of last consignment.

Transport

RAILWAYS
(figures are rounded)

	2003	2004	2005
Passengers ('000)			
Long distance	1,553	1,557	1,451
Metropolitan	133,900	141,900	144,300
Passenger-km ('000, long distance only)	469,330	475,186	451,943
Freight ('000 metric tons)	345,111	377,776	388,592
Freight ton-km (million)	182,644	205,711	221,633

Source: Agência Nacional de Transportes Terrestres (ANTT), Ministério dos Transportes, Brasília.

ROAD TRAFFIC
(motor vehicles in use at 31 December)

	2004	2005	2006
Passenger cars	24,936,541	26,309,256	27,868,564
Lorries	1,636,535	1,703,715	1,768,221
Vans	1,218,922	1,674,532	2,036,030
Coaches	2,661,614	2,441,858	2,328,596
Motorcycles and mopeds	7,039,675	8,070,148	9,360,696
Total (incl. others)	39,240,875	42,071,961	45,372,640

2007 (motor vehicles in use at 31 December): Passenger cars 30,282,855; Vans and lorries 5,709,063; Buses and coaches 1,985,761; Motorcycles and mopeds 10,921,686; Total 48,899,365 (Source: IRF, *World Road Statistics*).

SHIPPING

Merchant Fleet
(registered at 31 December)

	2007	2008	2009
Number of vessels	538	569	592
Total displacement ('000 grt)	2,290	2,359	2,378

Source: IHS Fairplay, *World Fleet Statistics*.

International Sea-borne Freight Traffic
('000 metric tons)

	2003	2004	2005
Goods loaded	376,188	417,723	452,742
Goods unloaded	194,602	202,997	196,677

CIVIL AVIATION
(embarked passengers, mail and cargo)

	2006	2007	2008
Number of passengers ('000)	47,702	51,029	56,205
Passenger-km (million)*	49,218	52,045	n.a.
Freight ton-km ('000)†	7,728,482	7,832,290	8,403,749

* Source: UN Economic Commission for Latin America and the Caribbean, *Statistical Yearbook*.

† Including mail.

Source: mostly Departamento de Aviação Civil (DAC), Comando da Aeronáutica, Ministério da Defesa, Brasília.

Tourism

FOREIGN TOURIST ARRIVALS

Country of origin	2008	2009	2010
Argentina	1,017,675	1,211,159	1,399,592
Bolivia	84,072	83,454	99,359
Canada	62,681	63,296	64,188
Chile	240,087	170,491	200,724
France	214,440	205,860	199,719
Germany	254,264	215,595	226,630
Italy	265,724	253,545	245,491
Japan	81,270	66,655	59,742

Country of origin—*continued*	2008	2009	2010
Mexico	77,193	68,028	67,616
Netherlands	81,936	75,518	76,411
Paraguay	217,709	180,373	194,340
Portugal	222,558	183,697	189,065
Spain	202,624	174,526	179,340
Switzerland	61,169	72,736	69,995
United Kingdom	181,179	172,643	167,355
USA	625,506	603,674	641,377
Uruguay	199,403	189,412	228,545
Total (incl. others)	5,050,099	4,802,217	5,161,379

Source: Instituto Brasileiro de Turismo—EMBRATUR, Brasília.

Receipts from tourism (US $ million, excl. passenger transport): 5,785 in 2008; 5,305 in 2009; 5,919 in 2010 (provisional) (Source: World Tourism Organization).

Communications Media

	2008	2009	2010
Telephones in use ('000 main lines)	41,235.2	41,497.0	42,141.4
Mobile cellular telephones ('000 subscribers)	150,641.4	173,959.4	202,944.0
Internet subscribers ('000)	27,522.6	22,909.2	20,992.4
Broadband subscribers ('000)	9,680.8	11,295.5	13,266.3

Personal computers: 30,000,000 (161.2 per 1,000 persons) in 2005.

Source: International Telecommunication Union.

Radio receivers ('000 in use): 71,000 in 1997 (Source: UNESCO, *Statistical Yearbook*).

Television receivers ('000 in use): 58,283 in 2000 (Source: International Telecommunication Union—ITU).

Book production ('000 titles): 21,689 in 1998 (Source: UNESCO Institute for Statistics).

Daily newspapers: 532 (average circulation, '000 copies): 6,552 in 2004 (Source: UNESCO Institute for Statistics).

Non-daily newspapers: 2,472 in 2004 (Source: UNESCO Institute for Statistics).

Education

(2009 unless otherwise indicated)

	Institutions	Teachers	Students
Pre-primary	106,563	309,881*	6,699,109
Literacy classes (Classe de Alfabetização)†	27,670	37,508	598,589
Primary	152,251	1,665,341*	31,512,884
Secondary	25,923	519,935*	8,288,520
Higher‡	2,252	338,890	5,080,056

* 2006 figure.
† 2003 figures.
‡ Preliminary figures for 2008.

Source: Ministério da Educação, Brasília.

Pupil-teacher ratio (primary education, UN estimate): 23 in 2007/08 (Source: UNESCO Institute for Statistics).

Adult literacy rate (UNESCO estimates): 90.0% (males 89.8%; females 90.2%) in 2008 (Source: UNESCO Institute for Statistics).

Directory

The Government

HEAD OF STATE

President: DILMA VANA ROUSSEFF (PT) (took office 1 January 2011).

Vice-President: MICHEL MIGUEL ELIAS TEMER LULIA (PMDB).

THE CABINET
(May 2012)

The Cabinet is composed of members of the Partido dos Trabalhadores (PT), the Partido do Movimento Democrático Brasileiro (PMDB), the Partido Progressista (PP), the Partido Socialista Brasileiro (PSB), the Partido da República (PR), the Partido Comunista do Brasil (PCdoB) and Independents.

Cabinet Chief: GLEISI HELENA HOFFMAN (PT).

Minister of Foreign Affairs: ANTÔNIO DE AGUIAR PATRIOTA (PT).

Minister of Justice: JOSÉ EDUARDO CARDOZO (PT).

Minister of Finance: GUIDO MANTEGA (PT).

Minister of Defence: CELSO AMORIM (PT).

Minister of Agriculture, Livestock and Food Supply: ALBERTO MENDES RIBEIRO FILHO (PMDB).

Minister of Agrarian Development: GILBERTO JOSÉ SPIER VARGAS (PT).

Minister of Labour and Employment: CARLOS BRIZOLA NETO (PDT).

Minister of Transport: PAULO SERGIO DE OLIVEIRA PASSOS (PR).

Minister of Cities: AGUINALDO VELLOSO BORGES RIBEIRO (PP).

Minister of Planning, Budget and Administration: MIRIAM BELCHIOR (PT).

Minister of Mines and Energy: EDISON LOBÃO (PMDB).

Minister of Culture: ANNA MARIA BUARQUE DE HOLLANDA (Ind.).

Minister of the Environment: IZABELLA MÔNICA VIEIRA TEIXEIRA (Ind.).

Minister of Development, Industry and Foreign Trade: FERNANDO PIMENTEL (PT).

Minister of Education: ALOÍZIO MERCADANTE (PT).

Minister of Health: ALEXANDRE ROCHA SANTOS PADILHA (PT).

Minister of National Integration: FERNANDO BEZERRA DE SOUSA COELHO (PSB).

Minister of Social Security: GARIBALDI ALVES FILHO (PMDB).

Minister of Social Development and the Fight against Hunger: TEREZA CAMPELO (PT).

Minister of Communications: PAULO BERNARDO SILVA (PT).

Minister of Science, Technology and Innovation: MARCO ANTÔNIO RAUPP (Ind.).

Minister of Sport: JOSÉ ALDO REBELO FIGUEIREDO (PCdoB).

Minister of Tourism: GASTÃO VIEIRA (PMDB).

Minister of Fisheries and Aquaculture: MARCELO BEZERRA CRIVELLA (PR).

Attorney-General: ROBERTO MONTEIRO GURGEL SANTOS.

Comptroller-General: JORGE HAGE SOBRINHO.

Chief Minister of the Office of Institutional Security: Gen. JOSÉ ELITO CARVALHO SIQUEIRA.

SECRETARIES

Secretary of Strategic Affairs: MOREIRA FRANCO.

Secretary of Civil Aviation: WAGNER BITTENCOURT.

Secretary of Social Communication: HELENA CHAGAS.

Secretary of Human Rights: MARIA DO ROSÁRIO.

Secretary of Policies for the Promotion of Racial Equality: LUIZA HELENA DE BAIRROS.

Secretary of Women's Policies: ELEONORA MENICUCCI DE OLIVEIRA.

Secretary of Ports: JOSÉ LEÔNIDAS CRISTINO.

Secretary of Institutional Relations: IDELI SALVATTI.

Secretary-General: GILBERTO CARVALHO.

MINISTRIES AND SECRETARIATS

Office of the President: Palácio do Planalto, 3° andar, Praça dos Três Poderes, 70150-900 Brasília, DF; tel. (61) 3411-1200; fax 3411-2222; e-mail protocolo@planalto.gov.br; internet www.presidencia.gov.br.

Office of the Civilian Cabinet: Palácio do Planalto, 4° andar, Praça dos Três Poderes, 70150-900 Brasília, DF; tel. (61) 3411-1221; fax (61) 3411-2222; e-mail casacivil@planalto.gov.br; internet www.casacivil.planalto.gov.br.

Ministry of Agrarian Development: Esplanada dos Ministérios, Bloco A, 8º andar, Ala Norte, 70050-902 Brasília, DF; tel. (61) 2020-0002; fax (61) 2020-0061; e-mail miguel.rossetto@mda.gov.br; internet www.mda.gov.br.

Ministry of Agriculture, Livestock and Food Supply: Esplanada dos Ministérios, Bloco D, Anexo B, 70043-900 Brasília, DF; tel. (61) 3218-2828; fax (61) 3218-2401; e-mail gm@agricultura.gov.br; internet www.agricultura.gov.br.

Ministry of Cities: Edif. Telemundi II, 14º andar, Setor de Autarquias Sul, Quadra 01, Lote 01/06, Bloco H, 700700-10 Brasília, DF; tel. (61) 2108-1000; fax (61) 2108-1415; e-mail cidades@cidades.gov.br; internet www.cidades.gov.br.

Ministry of Communications: Esplanada dos Ministérios, Bloco R, 8° andar, 70044-900 Brasília, DF; tel. (61) 3311-6000; fax (61) 3311-6731; e-mail imprensa@mc.gov.br; internet www.mc.gov.br.

Ministry of Culture: Esplanada dos Ministérios, Bloco B, 4° andar, 70068-900 Brasília, DF; tel. (61) 2024-2000; fax (61) 3225-9162; e-mail gm@cultura.gov.br; internet www.cultura.gov.br.

Ministry of Defence: Esplanada dos Ministérios, Bloco Q, 70049-900 Brasília, DF; tel. (61) 3312-4000; fax (61) 3225-4151; e-mail faleconosco@defesa.gov.br; internet www.defesa.gov.br.

Ministry of Development, Industry and Foreign Trade: Esplanada dos Ministérios, Bloco J, 70053-900 Brasília, DF; tel. (61) 2027-7000; fax (61) 2027-7230; e-mail asint@desenvolvimento.gov.br; internet www.desenvolvimento.gov.br.

Ministry of Education: Esplanada dos Ministérios, Bloco L, 8º andar, Sala 805, 70047-900 Brasília, DF; tel. (61) 2022-7842; fax (61) 2022-7858; e-mail acsgabinete@mec.gov.br; internet www.mec.gov.br.

Ministry of the Environment: Esplanada dos Ministérios, Bloco B, 5°–9° andares, 70068-900 Brasília, DF; tel. (61) 2028-1057; fax (61) 2028-1756; e-mail webmaster@mma.gov.br; internet www.mma.gov.br.

Ministry of Finance: Esplanada dos Ministérios, Bloco P, 5° andar, 70048-900 Brasília, DF; tel. (61) 3412-2000; fax (61) 3412-1721; e-mail gabinete.df.gmf@fazenda.gov.br; internet www.fazenda.gov.br.

Ministry of Fisheries and Aquaculture: SBS Quadra 2, Lote 10, Bloco J, 70043-900 Brasília DF; tel. (61) 2023-3000; fax (61) 2023-3914; e-mail comunicacao@mpa.gov.br; internet www.mpa.gov.br.

Ministry of Foreign Affairs: Palácio do Itamaraty, Térreo, Esplanada dos Ministérios, Bloco H, 70170-900 Brasília, DF; tel. (61) 3411-8006; fax (61) 3225-8002; e-mail imprensa@itamaraty.gov.br; internet www.itamaraty.gov.br.

Ministry of Health: Esplanada dos Ministérios, Bloco G, 70058-900 Brasília, DF; tel. (61) 3315-3200; fax (61) 3224-2563; e-mail leandro.viegas@saude.gov.br; internet www.saude.gov.br.

Ministry of Justice: Esplanada dos Ministérios, Bloco T, 70064-900 Brasília, DF; tel. (61) 3429-3000; fax (61) 3224-0954; e-mail acs@mj.gov.br; internet www.mj.gov.br.

Ministry of Labour and Employment: Esplanada dos Ministérios, Bloco F, 5° andar, 70059-900 Brasília, DF; tel. (61) 3317-6000; fax (61) 3317-8245; e-mail ouvidoria@mte.gov.br; internet www.mte.gov.br.

Ministry of Mines and Energy: Esplanada dos Ministérios, Bloco U, 70065-900 Brasília, DF; tel. (61) 3319-5555; fax (61) 3319-5074; e-mail gabinete@mme.gov.br; internet www.mme.gov.br.

Ministry of National Integration: Esplanada dos Ministérios, Bloco E, 8º andar, 70067-901 Brasília, DF; tel. (61) 3414-5814; fax (61) 3321-5914; e-mail impresa@integracao.gov.br; internet www.integracao.gov.br.

Ministry of Planning, Budget and Administration: Esplanada dos Ministérios, Bloco K, 7º andar, 70040-906 Brasília, DF; tel. (61) 2020-4102; fax (61) 2020-5009; e-mail ministro@planejamento.gov.br; internet www.planejamento.gov.br.

Ministry of Science, Technology and Innovation: Esplanada dos Ministérios, Bloco E, 4° andar, 70067-900 Brasília, DF; tel. (61) 3317-7500; fax (61) 3317-7764; e-mail webgab@mct.gov.br; internet www.mct.gov.br.

Ministry of Social Development and the Fight against Hunger: Esplanada dos Ministérios, Bloco C, 5° andar, 70046-900 Brasília, DF; tel. (61) 3433-1029; e-mail ministro.mds@mds.gov.br; internet www.mds.gov.br.

Ministry of Social Security: Esplanada dos Ministérios, Bloco F, 8º andar, 70059-900 Brasília, DF; tel. (61) 2021-5000; fax (61) 2021-5407; e-mail gm.mps@previdencia.gov.br; internet www.mps.gov.br.

Ministry of Sport: Esplanada dos Ministérios, Bloco A, 70054-906 Brasília, DF; tel. (61) 3217-1800; fax (61) 3217-1707; e-mail gabmin@esporte.gov.br; internet www.esporte.gov.br.

Ministry of Tourism: Esplanada dos Ministérios, Bloco U, 2º e 3º andar, 70065-900 Brasília, DF; tel. (61) 2023-7024; fax (61) 2023-7096; e-mail ouvidoria@turismo.gov.br; internet www.turismo.gov.br.

Ministry of Transport: Esplanada dos Ministérios, Bloco R, 6º andar, 70044-900 Brasília, DF; tel. (61) 2029-7000; fax (61) 2029-7876; e-mail paulo.passos@transportes.gov.br; internet www.transportes.gov.br.

Office of Institutional Security: Brasília, DF.

Secretariat-General of the Presidency: Praça dos Três Poderes, Palácio do Planalto, 4º andar, 70150-900 Brasília, DF; tel. (61) 3411-1225; e-mail sg@planalto.gov.br; internet www.secretariageral.gov.br.

Secretariat of Civil Aviation: Brasília, DF.

Secretariat of Human Rights: Edif. Parque Cidade Corporate, Torre A, 10º andar, Setor Comercial Sul B, Quadra 9, Lote C, 70308-200 Brasília, DF; tel. (61) 2025-3536; fax (61) 2025-3106; e-mail direitoshumanos@sedh.gov.br; internet www.direitoshumanos.gov.br.

Secretariat of Institutional Relations: Palácio do Planalto, 4º andar, Sala 404, Praça dos Três Poderes, 70150-900 Brasília, DF; tel. (61) 3411-1585; fax (61) 3411-1503; e-mail sri.gabinete@planalto.gov.br; internet www.relacoesinstitucionais.gov.br.

Secretariat of Policies for the Promotion of Racial Equality: Esplanada dos Ministérios, Bloco A, 9º andar, 70054-906 Brasília, DF; tel. (61) 2025-7043; fax (61) 3226-5625; e-mail seppir.imprensa@planalto.gov.br; internet www.seppir.gov.br.

Secretariat of Ports: Centro Empresarial Varig, Pétala C Mezanino, Sala 1403, SCN Quadra 04, Bloco B, 70714-900 Brasília, DF; tel. (61) 3411-3704; fax (61) 3326-3025; e-mail faleconosco@portosdobrasil.gov.br; internet www.portosdobrasil.gov.br.

Secretariat of Social Communication: Esplanada dos Ministérios, Bloco A, 70054-900 Brasília, DF; tel. (61) 3411-1279; fax (61) 3226-8316; internet www.secom.gov.br.

Secretariat of Strategic Affairs: Esplanada dos Ministérios, Bloco O, 7° andar, 8° e 9° andares, 70052-900 Brasília, DF; tel. (61) 3411-4674; e-mail falecomministro.sae@presidencia.gov.br; internet www.sae.gov.br.

Secretariat of Women's Policies: Via N1 Leste, Pavilhão das Metas, Praça dos Tres Poderes, Zona Cívico-Administrativa, 70150-908 Brasília, DF; tel. (61) 3411-4246; fax (61) 3327-7464; e-mail spmulheres@spmulheres.gov.br; internet www.sepm.gov.br.

President and Legislature

PRESIDENT

Election, First Round, 3 October 2010

Candidate	Votes	% of valid votes
Dilma Vana Rousseff (PT)	47,651,434	46.91
José Serra (PSDB)	33,132,283	32.61
Marina Silva (PV)	19,636,359	19.33
Plínio de Arruda Sampaio (PSOL)	886,816	0.87
José Maria Eymael (PSDC)	89,350	0.09
José Maria de Almeida (PSTU)	84,609	0.08
Levy Fidelix (PRTB)	57,960	0.06
Ivan Pinheiro (PCB)	39,136	0.04
Rui Costa Pimenta (PCO)	12,206	0.01
Total*	101,590,153	100.00

* In addition, there were 3,479,340 blank and 6,124,254 spoiled votes.

Election, Second Round, 31 October 2010

Candidate	Votes	% of valid votes
Dilma Vana Rousseff (PT)	55,725,529	56.04
José Serra (PSDB)	43,711,388	43.96
Total*	99,436,917	100.00

* In addition, there were 2,452,597 blank ballots and 4,689,428 spoiled ballots.

CONGRESSO NACIONAL

Câmara dos Deputados

Chamber of Deputies: Palácio do Congresso Nacional, Edif. Principal, Praça dos Três Poderes, 70160-900 Brasília, DF; tel. (61) 3216-0000; internet www.camara.gov.br.

President: Marco Aurélio Spall Maia (PT).

The Chamber has 513 members who hold office for a four-year term.

General Election, 3 October 2010

Party	Votes	% of valid votes	Seats
Partido dos Trabalhadores (PT)	16,289,199	16.9	88
Partido do Movimento Democrático Brasileiro (PMDB)	12,537,252	13.0	79
Partido da Social Democracia Brasileira (PSDB)	11,477,380	11.9	53
Democratas (DEM)	7,301,171	7.6	43
Partido da República (PR)	7,311,655	7.6	41
Partido Progressista (PP)	6,330,062	6.6	41
Partido Socialista Brasileiro (PSB)	6,851,053	7.1	34
Partido Democrático Trabalhista (PDT)	4,854,602	5.0	28
Partido Trabalhista Brasileiro (PTB)	4,038,239	4.2	21
Partido Social Cristão (PSC)	3,072,546	3.2	17
Partido Verde (PV)	3,710,366	3.8	15
Partido Comunista do Brasil (PC do B)	2,748,290	2.8	15
Partido Popular Socialista (PPS)	2,536,809	2.6	12
Partido Republicano Brasileiro (PRB)	1,633,500	1.7	8
Partido da Mobilização Nacional (PMN)	1,086,705	1.1	4
Partido Socialismo e Liberdade (PSOL)	1,142,737	1.2	3
Partido Trabalhista do Brasil (PT do B)	642,422	0.7	3
Partido Humanista da Solidariedade (PHS)	764,412	0.8	2
Partido Renovador Trabalhista Brasileira (PRTB)	307,925	0.3	2
Partido Republicano Progressista (PRP)	307,188	0.3	2
Partido Trabalhista Cristão (PTC)	595,431	0.6	1
Partido Social Liberal (PSL)	499,963	0.5	1
Total (incl. others)	96,580,011	100.0	513

Senado Federal

Federal Senate: Palácio do Congresso Nacional, Praça dos Três Poderes, 70165-900 Brasília, DF; tel. (61) 3311-4141; fax (61) 3311-3190; e-mail webmaster.secs@senado.gov.br; internet www.senado.gov.br.

President: José Sarney (PMDB).

The 81 members of the Senate are elected by the 26 states and the Federal District (three senators for each) according to the principle of majority. The Senate's term of office is eight years, with elections after four years for one-third of the members and after another four years for the remaining two-thirds.

In the elections of 3 October 2010 54 seats were contested. In that month the PMDB was represented by 20 senators, the PT by 15, the PSDB by 11, the PTB and the DEM by six each, the PR, the PP and the PDT by four each, the PSB by three, the PSOL and the PC do B by two each and the PRB, the PPS, the PSC and the PMN by one each.

Governors

STATES

(April 2012)

Acre: Sebastião Afonso Viana Macedo Neves (PT).

Alagoas: Teotônio Brandão Vilela Filho (PSDB).

Amapá: Carlos Camilo Góes Capiberibe (PSB).

Amazonas: Omar José Abdel Aziz (PMN).

Bahia: Jacques Wagner (PT).

Ceará: Cid Gomes (PSB).

Espírito Santo: Renato Casagrande (PSB).

Goiás: Marconi Ferreira Perillo Júnior (PSDB).

Maranhão: Roseana Sarney (PMDB).

Mato Grosso: Silval Cunha Barbosa (PMDB).

Mato Grosso do Sul: André Puccinelli (PMDB).

Minas Gerais: Antônio Augusto Junho Anastasia (PSDB).

Pará: Simão Robson Oliveira Jatene (PSDB).

Paraíba: Ricardo Vieira Coutinho (PSB).

Paraná: Carlos Alberto Richa (PSDB).

Pernambuco: Eduardo Henrique Accioly Campos (PSB).

Piauí: Wilson Nunes Martins (PSB).

Rio de Janeiro: Sérgio de Oliveira Cabral Filho (PMDB).

Rio Grande do Norte: Rosalba Ciarlini Rosado (DEM).

Rio Grande do Sul: Tarso Fernando Herz Genro (PT).

Rondônia: Confúcio Aires de Moura (PMDB).

Roraima: José de Anchieta Júnior (PSDB).

Santa Catarina: João Raimundo Colombo (DEM).

São Paulo: Geraldo Alckmin Filho (PSDB).

Sergipe: Marcelo Déda Chagas (PT).

Tocantins: José Wilson Siquiera Campos (PSDB).

FEDERAL DISTRICT

Brasília: Agnelo Santos Queiroz Filho (PT).

Election Commission

Tribunal Superior Eleitoral (TSE): Praça dos Tribunais Superiores, Bloco C, 70096-900 Brasília, DF; tel. (61) 3316-3000; fax (61) 3316-3002; e-mail webmaster@tse.gov.br; internet www.tse.gov.br; f. 1945; Pres. Enrique Ricardo Lewandowski; Inspector Gen. Elections Aldir Guimarães Passarinho Junior.

Political Organizations

Democratas (DEM): Senado Federal, Anexo 1, 26° andar, 70165-900 Brasília, DF; tel. (61) 3311-4305; fax (61) 3224-1912; e-mail democratas25@democratas.org.br; internet www.dem.org.br; f. 1985 as the Partido da Frente Liberal; refounded in 2007 under present name; Pres. José Agripino Maia; Sec.-Gen. Onyx Lorenzoni.

Partido Comunista do Brasil (PC do B): Rua Rego Freitas 192, 01220-907 São Paulo, SP; tel. and fax (11) 3054-1800; e-mail comitecentral@pcdob.org.br; internet www.pcdob.org.br; f. 1922; Pres. José Renato Rabelo; Sec.-Gen. Walter Sorrentino; 185,000 mems.

Partido Democrático Trabalhista (PDT): Rua do Teatro 39, Praça Tiradentes, 20010-190 Rio de Janeiro, RJ; tel. (21) 2232-1016; fax (21) 2232-0121; e-mail fio@pdt.org.br; internet www.pdt.org.br; f. 1980; fmrly the Partido Trabalhista Brasileiro, renamed 1980 when that name was awarded to a dissident group following controversial judicial proceedings; mem. of Socialist International; Pres. Carlos Lupi; Sec.-Gen. Manoel Dias.

Partido da Mobilização Nacional (PMN): Rua Martins Fontes, 197, 3° andar, Conj. 32, 01050-906 São Paulo, SP; tel. (11) 3214-4261; fax (11) 3120-2669; e-mail pmn33@pmn.org.br; internet www.pmn.org.br; f. 1984; Pres. Oscar Noronha Filho; Sec.-Gen. Telma Ribeiro dos Santos.

Partido do Movimento Democrático Brasileiro (PMDB): Câmara dos Deputados, Edif. Principal, Ala B, Sala 6, Praça dos Três Poderes, 70160-900 Brasília, DF; tel. (61) 3215-9206; fax (61) 3215-9220; e-mail pmdb@pmdb.org.br; internet www.pmdb.org.br; f. 1980 by moderate elements of fmr Movimento Democrático Brasileiro; merged with Partido Popular in 1982; Pres. Michel Temer; Sec.-Gen. Mauro Lopes; factions include the Históricos and the Movimento da Unidade Progressiva (MUP).

Partido Popular Socialista (PPS): SCS, Quadra 7, Bloco A, Edif. Executive Tower, Sala 826/828, Pátio Brasil Shopping, Setor Comercial Sul, 70307-901 Brasília, DF; tel. (61) 3218-4123; fax (61) 3218-4112; e-mail pps23@pps.org.br; internet www.pps.org.br; f. 1922; Pres. Roberto João Pereira Freire; Sec.-Gen. Rubens Bueno.

Partido Progressista (PP): Senado Federal, Anexo 1, 17° andar, Sala 1704, 70165-900 Brasília, DF; tel. (61) 3311-3041; fax (61) 3322-6938; e-mail pp@pp.org.br; internet www.pp.org.br; f. 1995 as Partido Progressista Brasileiro by merger of Partido Progressista Reformador, Partido Progressista and Partido Republicano Progressista; adopted present name 2003; right-wing; Pres. FRANCISCO DORNELLES; Sec.-Gen. BENEDITO DOMINGOS.

Partido da República (PR): SCN, Edif. Liberty Mall, Quadra 02, Bloco D, Torre A, Salas 601/606, Asa Norte, 70712-903 Brasília, DF; tel. and fax (61) 3202-9922; e-mail pr22@partidodarepublica.org.br; internet www.partidodarepublica.org.br; f. 2006 by merger of Partido Liberal and Partido de Reedificação da Ordem Nacional; Pres. ALFREDO PEREIRA DO NASCIMENTO; Sec.-Gen. VALDEMAR COSTA NIETO.

Partido Republicano Brasileiro (PRB): SDS, Bloco L 30, Edif. Miguel Badya, 3° andar, Sala 320, 70394-901 Brasília, DF; tel. and fax (61) 3223-9069; e-mail faleconosco@prb10.org.br; internet www.prb10.org.br; f. 2005 as Partido Municipalista Renovador; name changed as above in 2006; political wing of Igreja Universal do Reino de Deus; Pres. MARCOS ANTÔNIO PEREIRA; Sec.-Gen. EVANDRO GARLA.

Partido Social Cristão (PSC): Rua Pouso Alegre 1388, Santa Teresa, 31015-030 Belo Horizonte, MG; tel. (31) 3467-1390; fax (31) 3467-6522; e-mail psc@psc.org.br; internet www.psc.org.br; f. 1970 as Partido Democrático Republicano; Pres. VITOR JORGE ADBALA NÓSSEIS; Sec.-Gen. ANTONIO OLIBONI.

Partido da Social Democracia Brasileira (PSDB): SGAS, Quadra 607, Edif. Metrópolis, Asa Sul, Cobertura 2, 70200-670 Brasília, DF; tel. (61) 3424-0500; fax (61) 3424-0515; e-mail tucano@psdb.org.br; internet www.psdb.org.br; f. 1988; centre-left; formed by dissident mems of parties incl. the PMDB, PFL, PDT, PSB and PTB; Pres. SÉRGIO GUERRA; Sec.-Gen. RODRIGO DE CASTRO.

Partido Social Liberal (PSL): SCS, Quadra 01, Bloco E, Edif. Ceará, Sala 1004, 70303-900 Brasília, DF; tel. (61) 3322-1721; fax (61) 3032-6832; e-mail contato@pslnacional.org.br; internet www.pslnacional.org.br; f. 1994; Pres. LUCIANO CALDAS BIVAR; Sec.-Gen. ROBERTO SIQUEIRA GOMES.

Partido Socialismo e Liberdade (P-SOL): SCS, Quadra 1, Bloco E, Edif. Ceará, Salas 1203–04, 70303-900 Brasília, DF; tel. (61) 3963-1750; fax (61) 3039-6356; e-mail secretariageral@psol50.org.br; internet psol50.org.br; f. 2004 by fmr PT mems; Pres. IVAN VALENTE; Secs-Gen. EDILSON FRANCISCO DA SILVA, MARIO AGRA JUNIOR.

Partido Socialista Brasileiro (PSB): SCLN 304, Bloco A, Sobreloja 1, Entrada 63, 70736-510 Brasília, DF; tel. and fax (61) 3327-6405; e-mail psb@psbnacional.org.br; internet www.psbnacional.org.br; f. 1945 as the Esquerda Democrática, renamed 1947; Pres. EDUARDO HENRRIQUE ACCIOLY CAMPOS; Sec.-Gen. JOSÉ RENATO CASAGRANDE.

Partido dos Trabalhadores (PT): SCS, Quadra 2, Bloco C, Edif. Toufic, Sala 256, 70302-000 São Paulo, SP; tel. (11) 3213-1313; fax (11) 3213-1360; e-mail presidencia@pt.org.br; internet www.pt.org.br; f. 1980; first independent labour party; associated with the *autêntico* br. of the trade union movt; 500,000 mems; Pres. RUI FALCÃO; Sec.-Gen. ELÓI PIETÁ.

Partido Trabalhista Brasileiro (PTB): SEPN, Quadra 504, Bloco A, Edif. Ana Carolina, Sala 100, Cobertura, 70730-521 Brasília DF; tel. (61) 2101-1414; fax (61) 2101-1400; e-mail ptb@ptb.org.br; internet www.ptb.org.br; f. 1980; Pres. ROBERTO JEFFERSON MONTEIRO FRANCISCO; Sec.-Gen. ANTÔNIO CARLOS DE CAMPOS MACHADO.

Partido Trabalhista Cristão (PTC): SCS, Quadra 8, Edif. Venâncio 2000, Bloco B-50, Salas 133–35, 70333-900 Brasília, DF; tel. (61) 3039-6791; fax (61) 3039-6382; e-mail ptcnacional@gmail.com; internet www.ptcnacional.com.br; f. 1989 as the Partido da Reconstrução Nacional, renamed 1997; Christian party; Pres. DANIEL S. TOURINHO; Sec.-Gen. RIVAILTON PINTO VELOSO DA SILVA.

Partido Verde (PV): Edif. Miguel Badya, Bloco L, Sala 218, Asa Sul, 70394-901 Brasília, DF; tel. (61) 3366-1569; e-mail nacional@pv.org.br; internet www.pv.org.br; Pres. JOSÉ LUIS DE FRANÇA PENNA; Organizing Sec. CARLA PIRANDA.

Other political parties include the Partido da Causa Operária (PCO; internet www.pco.org.br), the Partido Republicano Progressista (PRP; internet www.prp.org.br), Democrata Cristão (PSDC; internet www.psdc.org.br), the Partido Trabalhista do Brasil (PT do B; internet www.ptdob.org.br) and the Partido Humanista da Solidariedade (PHS; internet www.phs.org.br).

OTHER ORGANIZATIONS

Movimento dos Trabalhadores Rurais Sem Terra (MST): Alameda Barão de Limeira, 1232 Campos Elíseos, 01202-002 São Paulo, SP; tel. (11) 3361-3866; e-mail semterra@mst.org.br; internet www.mst.org.br; landless peasant movt; Pres. JOÃO PEDRO STÉDILE; Nat. Co-ordinator GILMAR MAURO.

Other rural movements include the Organização da Luto no Campo (OLC) and the Movimento de Liberação dos Sem Terra (MLST), a dissident faction of the MST.

Diplomatic Representation

EMBASSIES IN BRAZIL

Albania: SMDB, Conj. 4, Lote 3, Casa D, Lago Sul, 71680-040 Brasília, DF; tel. (61) 3364-0519; e-mail embassy.brasilia@mfa.gov.al; Ambassador TATIANA GJONAJ.

Algeria: SHIS, QI 09, Conj. 13, Casa 01, Lago Sul, 70472-900 Brasília, DF; tel. (61) 3248-4039; fax (61) 3248-4691; e-mail sanag277@terra.com.br; Ambassador DJAMEL-EDDINE OMAR BENNAOUM.

Angola: SHIS, QL 06, Conj. 5, Casa 01, 71620-055 Brasília, DF; tel. (61) 3248-4489; fax (61) 3248-1567; e-mail embangola@embaixadadeangola.com.br; internet www.embaixadadeangola.com.br; Ambassador NELSON MANUEL COSME.

Argentina: SES Quadra 803, Lote 12, 70200-030 Brasília, DF; tel. (61) 3212-7600; fax (61) 3364-7666; e-mail ebras@mrecic.gov.br; internet www.brasil.embajada-argentina.gov.ar; Ambassador LUIS MARÍA KRECKLER.

Armenia: SHIS, QL 28, Conj. 3, Casa 04, South Lake, 71665-235 Brasilia, DF; e-mail armgenconsulatesan-paulo@mfa.am; Ambassador ASHOT YEGHIAZARIAN.

Australia: SES, Av. Das Nações, Quadra 801, Conj. K, Lote 7, 70200-010 Brasília, DF; tel. (61) 3226-3111; fax (61) 3226-1112; e-mail embaustr@dfat.gov.au; internet www.brazil.embassy.gov.au; Ambassador BRETT HACKETT.

Austria: SES, Av. das Nações, Quadra 811, Lote 40, 70426-900 Brasília, DF; tel. (61) 3443-3111; fax (61) 3443-5233; e-mail brasilia-ob@bmeia.gv.at; internet www.embaixadadaaustria.com.br; Ambassador HANS-PETER GLANZER.

Barbados: SHIS, QI 13, Conj. 10, Casa 03, Lago Sul, 71635-100 Brasília, DF; tel. (61) 3526-8310; e-mail brasilia@foreign.gov.bb; Ambassador YVETTE GODDARD.

Belarus: SHS Quadra 2, Bloco J, Apto 1106, Bonaparte Blupoint Hotel, 70322-901 Brasília, DF; tel. (61) 3321-3141; fax (61) 3226-7401; e-mail belarus.emb@terra.com.br; Ambassador LEONID KRUPETS.

Belgium: SES, Av. das Nações, Quadra 809, Lote 32, 70422-900 Brasília, DF; tel. (61) 3443-1133; fax (61) 3443-1219; e-mail brasilia@diplobel.org; internet www.diplomatie.be/brasilia; Ambassador CLAUDE MISSON.

Benin: SHIS, QI 9, Conj. 11, Casa 24, Lago Sul, 71625-110 Brasília, DF; tel. (61) 3248-2192; fax (61) 3263-0739; e-mail ambabeninbrasilia@yahoo.fr; Ambassador ISIDORE BENJAMIN AMÉDÉE MONSI.

Bolivia: SHIS, QI 19, Conj. 13, Casa 19, Lago Sul, 71655-130 Brasília, DF; tel. (61) 3366-3432; fax (61) 3366-3136; e-mail embolivia@embolivia.org.br; internet www.embolivia.org.br; Ambassador JOSÉ ALBERTO GONZÁLES SAMANIEGO.

Botswana: SHIS, QI 09, Conj. 17, Casa 16, Lago Sul, 70316-000 Brasília, DF; tel. (61) 3366-5563; fax (61) 3248-6713; Ambassador DIABI JACOB MMUALEFE.

Bulgaria: SEN, Av. das Nações, Quadra 801, Lote 08, 70432-900 Brasília, DF; tel. (61) 3223-6193; fax (61) 3323-3285; e-mail bulgaria@linkexpress.com.br; internet www.mfa.bg/brazil; Ambassador NIKOLAY TZATCHEV.

Burkina Faso: SHIS QI 09, Conj. 13, Casa 12, Lago Sul, 71605-001 Brasília, DF; tel. (61) 3366-4636; fax (61) 3366-3210; e-mail amburkinabras@gmail.com; internet www.burkina.org.br; Ambassador ALAIN FRANCIS GUSTAVE ILBOUDO.

Cameroon: SHIS, QI 09, Conj. 07, Casa 01, 71625-070 Brasília, DF; tel. (61) 3248-5403; fax (61) 3248-0443; e-mail embcameroun@embcameroun.org.br; internet www.embcameroun.org.br; Ambassador MARTIN AGBOR MBENG.

Canada: SES, Av. das Nações, Quadra 803, Lote 16, 70410-900 Brasília, DF; tel. (61) 3424-5400; fax (61) 3424-5490; e-mail brsla@international.gc.ca; internet www.canadainternational.gc.ca/brazil; Ambassador JAMAL KHOKHAR.

Cape Verde: SHIS, QL 14, Conj. 03, Casa 08, Lago Sul, 71640-035 Brasília, DF; tel. (61) 3248-0543; fax (61) 3364-4059; e-mail embcvbrasil@embcv.org.br; internet www.embcv.org.br; Ambassador DANIEL ANTÓNIO PEREIRA.

Chile: SES, Av. das Nações, Quadra 803, Lote 11, Asa Sul, 70407-900 Brasília, DF; tel. (61) 2103-5151; fax (61) 3322-0714; e-mail embchile@embchile.org.br; internet chileabroad.gov.cl/brasil; Ambassador JORGE MONTERO FIGUEROA.

China, People's Republic: SES, Av. das Nações, Quadra 813, Lote 51, Asa Sul, 70443-900 Brasília, DF; tel. (61) 2198-8200; fax (61) 3346-3299; e-mail chinaemb_br@mfa.gov.cn; internet br.china-embassy.org/por; Ambassador LI JINZHANG.

Colombia: SES, Av. das Nações, Quadra 803, Lote 10, 70444-900 Brasília, DF; tel. (61) 3226-8997; fax (61) 3224-4732; e-mail ebrasili@cancilleria.gov.co; internet www.embajadaenbrasil.gov.co; Ambassador MARÍA ELVIRA POMBO HOLGUÍN.

Congo, Democratic Republic: SHIS, QL 13, Conj. 08, Casa 21, Lago Sul, CP 71635-080 Brasília, DF; tel. (61) 3365-4822; fax (61) 3365-4823; e-mail ambaredeco@ig.com.br; Chargé d'affaires a.i. BAUDOUIN MAYOLA MA LULENDO.

Congo, Republic: SHIS, QL 8, Conj. 05, Casa 06, Lago Sul, 71620-255 Brasília, DF; tel. and fax (61) 3532-0440; e-mail ambacobrazza@gmail.com; Ambassador LOUIS SYLVAIN GOMA.

Costa Rica: SRTV/N 701, Conj. C, Ala A, Salas 308/310, Edif. Centro Empresarial Norte, 70719-903 Brasília, DF; tel. (61) 3032-8450; fax (61) 3032-8452; e-mail embcr.brasil@gmail.com; Ambassador VICTOR MONGE CHACÓN.

Côte d'Ivoire: SEN, Av. das Nações, Lote 09, 70473-900 Brasília, DF; tel. (61) 3321-7320; fax (61) 3321-1306; e-mail cotedivoire@cotedivoire.org.br; internet www.cotedivoire.org.br; Ambassador SYLVESTRE AKA AMON KASSI.

Croatia: SHIS, QI 09, Conj. 11, Casa 03, 71625-110 Brasília, DF; tel. (61) 3248-0610; fax (61) 3248-1708; e-mail croemb.brasilia@mvpei.hr; Ambassador DRAGO STAMBUK.

Cuba: SHIS, QI 05, Conj. 18, Casa 01, Lago Sul, 71615-180 Brasília, DF; tel. (61) 3248-4710; fax (61) 3248-6778; e-mail embacuba@uol.com.br; internet embacu.cubaminrex.cu/brasil; Ambassador CARLOS RAFAEL ZAMORA RODRIGUEZ.

Cyprus: Naoum Plaza Hotel, Quarto 1611, Brasília, DF; tel. (61) 3322-4545; fax (61) 3322-4949; Ambassador MARTHA A. MAVROMMATIS.

Czech Republic: SHIS, QI 9, Conj. 16, Casa 3, Lago Sul, 71625-160 Brasília, DF; tel. (61) 3242-7785; fax (61) 3242-7833; e-mail brasilia@embassy.mzv.cz; internet www.mzv.cz/brasilia; Ambassador IVAN JANČÁREK.

Denmark: SES, Av. das Nações, Quadra 807, Lote 26, 70200-900 Brasília, DF; tel. (61) 3878-4500; fax (61) 3878-4509; e-mail bsbamb@um.dk; internet www.ambbrasilia.um.dk; Ambassador SVEND ROED NIELSEN.

Dominican Republic: SHIS, QL 06, Conj. 07, Casa 02, 71626-075 Brasília, DF; tel. (61) 3248-1405; fax (61) 3364-3214; e-mail embaixada@republicadominicana.org.br; internet www.republicadominicana.org.br; Ambassador HÉCTOR DIONISIO PÉREZ FERNÁNDEZ.

Ecuador: SHIS, QL 10, Conj. 08, Casa 01, 71630-085 Brasília, DF; tel. (61) 3248-5560; fax (61) 3248-1290; e-mail embeq@solar.com.br; internet www.embequador.org.br; Ambassador HORACIO SEVILLA BORJA.

Egypt: SEN, Av. das Nações, Lote 12, 70435-900 Brasília, DF; tel. (61) 3323-8800; fax (61) 3323-1039; e-mail embegito@opengate.com.br; internet www.opengate.com.br/embegito; Ambassador AHMED HASSAN IBRAHIM DARWISH.

El Salvador: SHIS, QL 10, Conj. 01, Casa 15, Lago Sul, 71630-015 Brasília, DF; tel. (61) 3364-4141; fax (61) 3364-2459; e-mail elsalvador@embelsalvador.brte.com.br; Ambassador RINA DEL SOCORRO ANGULO.

Equatorial Guinea: SHIS, QL 10, Conj. 09, Casa 01, Lago Sul, 70630-095 Brasília, DF; tel. (61) 3364-4185; fax (61) 3364-1641; e-mail embaixada@embrge.brtdata.com.br; Ambassador TEODORO BIYOGO NSUÉ OKOMO.

Fiji: QL 20, Conj. 2, Casa 16, Lago Sul, 71650-125 Brasília, DF; tel. (61) 3548-8100; Ambassador CAMA TUIQILAQILA TUILOMA.

Finland: SES, Av. das Nações, Quadra 807, Lote 27, 70417-900 Brasília, DF; tel. (61) 3443-7151; fax (61) 3443-3315; e-mail sanomat.bra@formin.fi; internet www.finlandia.org.br; Ambassador JARÍ LUOTO.

France: SES, Av. das Nações, Quadra 801, Lote 04, 70404-900 Brasília, DF; tel. (61) 3222-3999; fax (61) 3222-3917; e-mail france@ambafrance.org.br; internet ambafrance-br.org/france_bresil; Ambassador YVES EDOUARD SAINT-GEOURS.

Gabon: SHIS, QL 09, Conj. 09, Casa 19, Lago Sul, 71625-160 Brasília, DF; tel. (61) 3248-3536; fax (61) 3248-2241; e-mail embgabao@yahoo.com.br; Ambassador JÉRÔME ANGOUO.

Georgia: SHIS, QI 5, Conj. 11, Casa 01, Lago Sul, 71615-030 Brasília, DF; tel. (61) 3366-1101; fax (61) 3366-1161; e-mail brazil.emb@mfa.gov.ge; Ambassador OTAR BERDZENISHVILI.

Germany: SES, Av. das Nações, Quadra 807, Lote 25, 70415-900 Brasília, DF; tel. (61) 3442-7089; fax (61) 3443-7508; e-mail info@alemanja.org; internet www.brasilia.diplo.de; Ambassador WILFRIED GROLIG.

Ghana: SHIS, QL 10, Conj. 08, Casa 02, 71630-085 Brasília, DF; tel. (61) 3248-6047; fax (61) 3248-7913; e-mail ghaembra@zaz.com.br; Ambassador Brig.-Gen. WALLACE GBEDEMAH.

Greece: SES, Av. das Nações, Quadra 805, Lote 22, 70480-900 Brasília, DF; tel. (61) 3443-6573; fax (61) 3443-6902; e-mail gremb.bra@mfa.gr; internet www.emb-grecia.org.br; Ambassador DIMITRI ALEXANDRAKIS.

Guatemala: SHIS, QI 07, Conj. 13, Casa 09, Lago Sul, 71615-330 Brasília, DF; tel. (61) 3248-4175; fax (61) 3248-6678; e-mail embaguate.brasil@gmail.com; Ambassador MANUEL ESTUARDO ROLDÁN BARILLAS.

Guinea: SHIS, QL 02, Conj. 07, Casa 09, Lago Sul, 71610-075 Brasília, DF; tel. (61) 3365-1301; fax (61) 3365-4921; e-mail ambaguibrasil@terra.com.br; Ambassador MOHAMED YOULA.

Guinea-Bissau: SHIS QL 02, Conj. 3, Casa 18, Lago Sul, 71610-035 Brasília, DF; tel. (61) 3366-1098; fax (61) 3366-1554; Ambassador EUGÉNIA PEREIRA SALDANHA ARAÚJO.

Guyana: SHIS, QI 05, Conj. 19, Casa 24, 71615-190 Brasília, DF; tel. (61) 3248-0874; fax (61) 3248-0886; e-mail embguyana@embguyana.org.br; internet www.embguyana.org.br; Ambassador KELLAWAN LALL.

Haiti: SHIS, QI 11, Conj. 06, Casa 13, Lago Sul, 71625-260 Brasília, DF; tel. (61) 3248-6860; fax (61) 3248-7472; e-mail embhaiti@terra.com.br; Ambassador IDALBERT PIERRE-JEAN.

Holy See: SES, Av. das Nações, Quadra 801, Lote 01, 70401-900 Brasília, DF; tel. (61) 3223-0794; fax (61) 3224-9365; e-mail nunapost@solar.com.br; Apostolic Nuncio Most Rev. GIOVANNI D'ANIELLO (Titular Archbishop of Pesto).

Honduras: SHIS, QI 19, Conj. 07, Casa 34, Lago Sul, 71655-070 Brasília, DF; tel. (61) 3366-4082; fax (61) 3366-4618; e-mail embaixadahonduras@gmail.com; Ambassador AVA ROSSANA GUEVARA PINTO.

Hungary: SES, Av. das Nações, Quadra 805, Lote 19, 70413-900 Brasília, DF; tel. (61) 3443-0836; fax (61) 3443-3434; e-mail mission.brz@kum.hu; internet www.mfa.gov.hu/emb/brasilia; Ambassador Dr CSABA SZIJJARTO.

India: SHIS, QL 08, Conj. 08, Casa 01, 71620-285 Brasília, DF; tel. (61) 3248-4006; fax (61) 3248-7849; e-mail indemb@indianembassy.org.br; internet www.indianembassy.org.br; Ambassador BELLUR SHAMARAO PRAKASH.

Indonesia: SES, Av. das Nações, Quadra 805, Lote 20, 70479-900 Brasília, DF; tel. (61) 3443-8800; fax (61) 3443-6732; e-mail contato@embaixadadaindonesia.org; internet www.embaixadadaindonesia.org; Ambassador SUDARYOMO HARTOSUDARMO.

Iran: SES, Av. das Nações, Quadra 809, Lote 31, 70421-900 Brasília, DF; tel. (61) 3242-5733; fax (61) 3224-9640; e-mail secretaria@irembassy.com; internet brasilia.mfa.gov.ir; Ambassador MOHAMMAD ALI GHANEZADEH EZABADI.

Iraq: SES, Av. das Nações, Quadra 815, Lote 64, 70430-900 Brasília, DF; tel. (61) 3346-2822; fax (61) 3346-7034; e-mail brzemb@iraqmfamail.com; Ambassador BAKER FATTAH HUSSEIN.

Ireland: SHIS, QL 12, Conj. 05, Casa 09, Lago Sul, 71630-255 Brasília, DF; tel. (61) 3248-8800; fax (61) 3248-8816; e-mail brasiliaembassy@dfa.ie; internet www.embaixada-irlanda.org.br; Ambassador FRANK SHERIDAN.

Israel: SES, Av. das Nações, Quadra 809, Lote 38, 70424-900 Brasília, DF; tel. (61) 2105-0500; fax (61) 2105-0555; e-mail info@brasilia.mfa.gov.il; internet brasilia.mfa.gov.il; Ambassador RAFAEL ELDAD.

Italy: SES, Av. das Nações, Quadra 807, Lote 30, 70420-900 Brasília, DF; tel. (61) 3442-9900; fax (61) 3443-1231; e-mail ambasciata.brasilia@esteri.it; internet www.ambbrasilia.esteri.it; Ambassador GHERARDO LA FRANCESCA.

Jamaica: Brasília, DF; Ambassador ALISON STONE ROOFE.

Japan: SES, Av. das Nações, Quadra 811, Lote 39, 70425-900 Brasília, DF; tel. (61) 3442-4200; fax (61) 3442-2499; e-mail consularjapao@yawl.com.br; internet www.br.emb-japan.go.jp; Ambassador AKIRA MIWA.

Jordan: SHIS, QI 09, Conj. 18, Casa 14, Lago Sul, 71625-180 Brasília, DF; tel. (61) 3248-5414; fax (61) 3248-1698; e-mail emb.jordania@apis.com.br; Ambassador RAMEZ ZAKI ODEH GOUSSOUS.

Kenya: SHIS, QL 10, Conj. 08, Casa 08, Lago Sul, 71630-085 Brasília, DF; tel. (61) 3364-0691; fax (61) 3364-0978; e-mail brazil@mfa.go.ke; internet www.kenyaembassy.com.br; Ambassador PETER KIRIMI KABERIA.

Korea, Democratic People's Republic: SHIS, QI 25, Conj. 10, Casa 11, Lago Sul, 71660-300 Brasília, DF; tel. (61) 3367-1940; fax (61) 3367-3177; e-mail embrpdcoreia@hotmail.com; Ambassador RI HWA GUN.

Korea, Republic: SEN, Av. das Nações, Lote 14, 70436-900 Brasília, DF; tel. (61) 3321-2500; fax (61) 3321-2508; e-mail emb-br@mofat.go.kr; internet bra-brasilia.mofat.go.kr; Ambassador KYONG-LIM CHOI.

Kuwait: SHIS, QI 05, Chácara 30, Lago Sul, 71600-550 Brasília, DF; tel. (61) 3213-2333; fax (61) 3248-0969; e-mail kuwait@opendf.com.br; Ambassador YOUSEF AHMAD ABDULSAMAD.

Lebanon: SES, Av. das Nações, Quadra 805, Lote 17, 70411-900 Brasília, DF; tel. (61) 3443-5552; fax (61) 3443-8574; e-mail embaixada@libano.org.br; internet www.libano.org.br; Ambassador FOUAD EL-KHOURY GHANEM.

Libya: SHIS, QI 15, Chácara 26, Lago Sul, 71600-750 Brasília, DF; tel. (61) 3248-6710; fax (61) 3248-0598; e-mail emblibia@terra.com.br; Ambassador SALEM OMAR ABDULLAH AZ-ZUBAIDI.

Malawi: SHIS, QI 15, Conj. 1, Casa 03, Lago Sul, 71635-230 Brasília, DF; tel. (61) 3366-1337; fax (61) 3365-2149; e-mail malawiembassybrasil@bol.com.br; Ambassador FRANCIS MOTO.

Malaysia: SHIS, QI 05, Chácara 62, Lago Sul, 70477-900 Brasília, DF; tel. (61) 3248-5008; fax (61) 3248-6307; e-mail mwbrasilia@terra.com.br; internet www.kln.gov.my/perwakilan/brasilia; Ambassador SUDHA DEVI.

Mauritania: SHIS, QI 9, conj. 14, casa 3, Lago Sul, 71925-140 Brasília, DF; tel. (61) 3797-3995; fax (61) 3263-6944; e-mail ambarimbrasilia@mauritania.org.br; internet www.mauritania.org.br; Ambassador KABA MOUHAMED ALIOU.

Mexico: SES, Av. das Nações, Quadra 805, Lote 18, 70412-900 Brasília, DF; tel. (61) 3204-5200; fax (61) 3204-5201; e-mail embamexbra@cabonet.com.br; internet portal.sre.gob.mx/brasil; Ambassador ALEJANDRO DE LA PEÑA NAVARRETE.

Morocco: SEN, Av. das Nacões, Quadra 801, Lote 02, Asa Norte, 70432-900 Brasília, DF; tel. (61) 3321-3994; fax (61) 3321-0745; e-mail sifamabr@onix.com.br; internet www.embmarrocos.org.br; Ambassador MUHAMMAD LOUAFA.

Mozambique: SHIS, QL 12, Conj. 07, Casa 09, Lago Sul, 71630-275 Brasília, DF; tel. (61) 3248-4222; fax (61) 3248-3917; e-mail embamoc-bsb@uol.com; internet www.mozambique.org.br; Ambassador MURADE ISAAC MIGUIGY MURARGY.

Myanmar: SHIS, QI 13, Conj. 08, Casa 09, Lago Sul, 71635-080 Brasília, DF; tel. (61) 3248-3747; fax (61) 3364-2747; e-mail mebrsl@brnet.com.br; Ambassador HTEIN WIN.

Namibia: SHIS QI 09, Conj. 08, Casa 11, Lago Sul, 71625-080 Brasília, DF; tel. (61) 3248-6274; fax (61) 3248-7135; e-mail info@embassyofnamibia.org.br; internet www.embassyofnamibia.org.br; Ambassador LINEEKELA JOSEPHAT MBOTI.

Nepal: SHIS QI 11, Conj.03, Casa 20, Lago Sul, 71625-230 Brasília, DF; tel. (61) 3541-1232; fax (61) 3541-1229; e-mail embaixadanepal@gmail.com; Ambassador PRADHUMNA BIKRAM SHAH.

Netherlands: SES, Av. das Nações, Quadra 801, Lote 05, 70405-900 Brasília, DF; tel. (61) 3961-3200; fax (61) 3961-3234; e-mail bra@minbuza.nl; internet www.mfa.nl/brasil; Ambassador KEES PIETER RADE.

New Zealand: SHIS, QI 09, Conj. 16, Casa 01, 71625-160 Brasília, DF; tel. (61) 3248-9900; fax (61) 3248-9916; e-mail zelandia@nwi.com.br; internet www.nzembassy.com/brazil; Ambassador JEFFREY MCALISTER.

Nicaragua: SHIS, QL 22, Conj. 10, Casa 13, Lago Sul, 71650-305 Brasília, DF; tel. (61) 3366-3297; fax (61) 3366-5213; e-mail mromerom@cancilleria.gob.ni; Ambassador SARA MARÍA TÓRREZ RUIZ.

Nigeria: SEN, Av. das Nações, Lote 05, 70800-400 Brasília, DF; tel. (61) 3208-1700; fax (61) 3226-5192; e-mail admin@nigerianembassy-brazil.org; internet www.nigerianembassy-brazil.org; Ambassador VINCENT AMERIB-OKUN OKOEDION.

Norway: SES, Av. das Nações, Quadra 807, Lote 28, 70418-900 Brasília, DF; tel. (61) 3443-8720; fax (61) 3443-2942; e-mail emb.brasilia@mfa.no; internet www.noruega.org.br; Ambassador TURID B. RODRIGUES EUSÉBIO.

Pakistan: SHIS, QL 12, Conj. 02, Casa 19, Lago Sul, 71630-225 Brasília, DF; tel. (61) 3364-1632; fax (61) 3248-0246; e-mail parepbrasilia@yahoo.com; internet www.pakistan.org.br; Ambassador NASRULLAH KHAN (designate).

Panama: SES, Av. das Nações, Quadra 803, Lote 9, 70200-030 Brasília, DF; tel. (61) 3323-2885; fax (61) 3248-2834; e-mail empanamabr@embaixada.brte.com.br; Ambassador GABRIELA GARCÍA CARRANZA.

Paraguay: SES, Av. das Nações, Quadra 811, Lote 42, 70427-900 Brasília, DF; tel. (61) 3242-3732; fax (61) 3242-4605; e-mail secretaria@embaparaguai.org.br; internet www.embaparaguai.org.br; Ambassador EVELIO FERNÁNDEZ ARÉVALOS.

Peru: SES, Av. das Nações, Quadra 811, Lote 43, 70428-900 Brasília, DF; tel. (61) 3242-9933; fax (61) 3225-9136; e-mail embperu@embperu.org.br; internet www.embperu.org.br; Ambassador JORGE PORFIRIO BAYONA MEDINA.

Philippines: SEN, Av. das Nações, Lote 01, 70431-900 Brasília, DF; tel. (61) 3223-5143; fax (61) 3226-7411; e-mail brasiliape@turbo.com.br; Ambassador EVA G. BETITA.

Poland: SES, Av. das Nações, Quadra 809, Lote 33, 70423-900 Brasília, DF; tel. (61) 3212-8000; fax (61) 3242-8543; e-mail embaixada@polonia.org.br; internet www.polonia.org.br; Ambassador JACEK JUNOSZA KISIELEWSKI.

Portugal: SES Sul, Av. das Nações, Quadra 801, Lote 02, 70402-900 Brasília, DF; tel. (61) 3032-9600; fax (61) 3032-9642; e-mail embaixadadeportugal@embaixadadeportugal.org.br; internet www.embaixadadeportugal.org.br; Ambassador FRANCISCO MARIA DE SOUSA RIBEIRO TELLES.

Qatar: SHIS, QL 20, Conj. 01, Casa 19, Lago Sul, 71650-115 Brasília, DF; tel. (61) 3366-1005; fax (61) 3366-1115; e-mail qatarbsb@embcatar.org.br; Ambassador JAMAL NASSER SULTAN AL-BADR.

Romania: SEN, Av. das Nações, Lote 06, 70456-900 Brasília, DF; tel. (61) 3226-0746; fax (61) 3226-6629; e-mail romenia@solar.com.br; Ambassador DIANA ANCA RADU.

Russia: SES, Av. das Nações, Quadra 801, Lote A, 70476-900 Brasília, DF; tel. (61) 3223-3094; fax (61) 3226-7319; e-mail emb@embrus.brte.com.br; internet www.brazil.mid.ru; Ambassador SERGUEY POGÓSSOVITCH AKOPOV.

Saudi Arabia: SHIS, QL 10, Conj. 09, Casa 20, 70471-900 Brasília, DF; tel. (61) 3248-3523; fax (61) 3284-1142; e-mail bremb@mofa.gov.sa; internet www.saudiembassy.org.br; Ambassador MUHAMMAD AMIN BIN ALI BIN MUHAMMAD KURDI.

Senegal: SEN, Av. das Nações, Lote 18, 70800-400 Brasília, DF; tel. (61) 3223-6110; fax (61) 3322-7822; e-mail senebrasilia@senebrasilia.com.br; internet www.senebrasilia.org.br; Ambassador EL HADJ ABDOUL AZIZ NDIAYE.

Serbia: SES, Av. das Nações, Quadra 803, Lote 15, 70409-900 Brasília, DF; tel. (61) 3223-7272; fax (61) 3223-8462; e-mail embaixadaservia@terra.com.br; Ambassador LJUBOMIR MILIC.

Slovakia: SES Av. das Nações, Quadra 805, Lote 21B, 70200-902 Brasília, DF; tel. (61) 3443-1263; fax (61) 3443-1267; e-mail eslovaca@brasil.mfa.sk; Ambassador BRANISLAV HITKA.

Slovenia: SHIS, QL 8, Conj. 8, Casa 07, Lago Sul, 71620-285 Brasília, DF; tel. (61) 3365-1445; fax (61) 3365-1440; e-mail vbi@gov.si; Ambassador MILENA ŠMIT.

South Africa: SES, Av. das Nações, Quadra 801, Lote 06, 70406-900 Brasília, DF; tel. (61) 3312-9500; fax (61) 3322-8491; e-mail brasilia.general@foreign.gov.za; internet www.africadosul.org.br; Ambassador MOHAKAMA NYANGWENI MBETE.

Spain: SES, Av. das Nações, Quadra 811, Lote 44, 70429-900 Brasília, DF; tel. (61) 3701-1600; fax (61) 3242-1781; e-mail emb.brasilia@maec.es; Ambassador MANUEL DE LA CÁMARA HERMOSO.

Sri Lanka: SHIS, QI 09, Conj. 09, Casa 07, Lago Sul, 71625-090 Brasília, DF; tel. (61) 3248-2701; fax (61) 3364-5430; e-mail lankaemb@yawl.com.br; Ambassador MAHINDA BALASURIYA (designate).

Sudan: SHIS, QI 11, Conj. 5, Casa 13, Lago Sul, 71625-250 Brasília, DF; tel. (61) 3248-4835; fax (61) 3248-4833; e-mail sudanbrasilia@yahoo.com; Ambassador ABD ELGHANI ELNAIM AWAD ELKARIM.

Suriname: SHIS, QI 09, Conj. 08, Casa 24, 71625-080 Brasília, DF; tel. (61) 3248-6706; fax (61) 3248-3791; e-mail surinameemb@terra.com.br; Ambassador MARLON FAISAL MOHAMED HOESEIN.

Sweden: SES, Av. das Nações, Quadra 807, Lote 29, 70419-900 Brasília, DF; tel. (61) 3442-5200; fax (61) 3443-1187; e-mail ambassaden.brasilia@foreign.ministry.se; internet www.suecia.org.br; Ambassador MAGNUS ROBACH.

Switzerland: SES, Av. das Nações, Quadra 811, Lote 41, 70448-900 Brasília, DF; tel. (61) 3443-5500; fax (61) 3443-5711; e-mail bra.vertretung@eda.admin.ch; internet www.dfae.admin.ch/brasilia; Ambassador WILHELM MEIER.

Syria: SEN, Av. das Nações, Lote 11, 70434-900 Brasília, DF; tel. (61) 3226-0970; fax (61) 3223-2595; e-mail embsiria@uol.com.br; Ambassador MOHAMMAD KHADOUR.

Tanzania: SHIS, QI 09, Conj. 16, Casa 20, Lago Sul, 71615-190 Brasília, DF; tel. (61) 3364-2629; fax (61) 3248-3361; e-mail tanrepbrasilia@yahoo.com.br; Ambassador FRANCIS AMBAKISYE MALAMBUGI.

Thailand: SEN, Av. das Nações, Lote 10, 70433-900 Brasília, DF; tel. (61) 3224-6943; fax (61) 3223-7502; e-mail thaiemb@mfa.go.th; internet www.thaiembassy.org/brasilia; Ambassador THARIT CHARUNGVAT.

Timor-Leste: SHIS, QI 11, Conj. 10, Casa 19, Lago Sul, 71625-300 Brasília, DF; tel. and fax (61) 3366-2755; e-mail embaixada@embaixadatimorleste.com.br; Ambassador DOMINGOS FRANCISCO DE JESUS DE SOUSA.

Trinidad and Tobago: SHIS, QL 02, Conj. 02, Casa 01, 71665-028 Brasília, DF; tel. (61) 3365-1132; fax (61) 3365-1733; e-mail trinbagoemb@gmail.com; Ambassador Dr HAMZA RAFEEQ.

Tunisia: SHIS, QI 11, Conj. 06, Casa 06, Lago Sul, 71625-260 Brasília, DF; tel. (61) 3248-7366; fax (61) 3248-7355; e-mail at .brasilia@terra.com.br; Ambassador MOHAMED EL MESTIRI.

Turkey: SES, Av. das Nações, Quadra 805, Lote 23, 70452-900 Brasília, DF; tel. (61) 3242-1850; fax (61) 3242-1448; e-mail turquia@ conectanet.com.br; internet www.turquia.org.br; Ambassador DURMUŞ ERSIN ERÇIN.

Ukraine: SHIS, QI 05, Conj. 04, Casa 02, Lago Sul, 71615-040 Brasília, DF; tel. (61) 3365-1457; fax (61) 3365-2127; e-mail emb_br@ mfa.gov.ua; internet www.mfa.gov.ua/brazil; Ambassador ROSTYSLAV TRONENKO.

United Arab Emirates: SHIS, QI 05, Chácara 54, 70800-400 Brasília, DF; tel. (61) 3248-0717; fax (61) 3248-7543; e-mail uae@ uae.org.br; internet www.uae.org.br; Ambassador YOUSEF ALI AL-USAIMI.

United Kingdom: SES, Av. das Nações, Quadra 801, Conj. K, Lote 08, 70408-900 Brasília, DF; tel. (61) 3329-2300; fax (61) 3329-2369; e-mail press.brasilia@fco.gov.uk; internet ukinbrazil.fco.gov.uk; Ambassador ALAN CHARLTON.

USA: SES, Av. das Nações, Quadra 801, Lote 03, 70403-900 Brasília, DF; tel. (61) 3312-7000; fax (61) 3312-7676; e-mail ircbsb@state.gov; internet brasilia.usembassy.gov; Ambassador THOMAS A. SHANNON, Jr.

Uruguay: SES, Av. das Nações, Quadra 803, Lote 14, 70450-900 Brasília, DF; tel. (61) 3322-1200; fax (61) 3322-6534; e-mail urubras@ emburuguai.org.br; internet www.emburuguai.org.br; Ambassador CARLOS DANIEL AMORÍN TENCONI.

Venezuela: SES, Av. das Nações, Quadra 803, Lote 13, 70451-900 Brasília, DF; tel. (61) 2101-1011; fax (61) 3321-0871; e-mail emb@ embvenezuela.org.br; internet www.embvenezuela.org.br; Ambassador MAXIMILIAN SANCHEZ ARVELAIZ.

Viet Nam: SHIS, QI 09, Conj. 10, Casa 01, Lago Sul, 71625-100 Brasília, DF; tel. (61) 3364-5876; fax (61) 3364-5836; e-mail embavina@yahoo.com; internet www.vietnamembassy-brazil.org/ vi; Ambassador DUONG NGUYÊN TUONG.

Zambia: SHIS, QL 10, Conj. 6, Casa 10, Lago Sul, 71630-065 Brasília, DF; tel. and fax (61) 3248-3277; e-mail zambiansbrasil@ embaixadazambia.org.br; Ambassador CYNTHIA JANGULO.

Zimbabwe: SHIS, QI 03, Conj. 10, Casa 13, Lago Sul, 71605-300 Brasília, DF; tel. (61) 3365-4801; fax (61) 3365-4803; e-mail zimbrasilia@uol.com.br; Ambassador THOMAS SUKUTAI BVUMA.

Judicial System

The judicial powers of the State are held by the following: the Supreme Federal Court, the Higher Court of Justice, the five Regional Federal Courts and Federal Judges, the Higher Labour Court, the 24 Regional Labour Courts, the Conciliation and Judgment Councils and Labour Judges, the Higher Electoral Court, the 27 Regional Electoral Courts, the Electoral Judges and Electoral Councils, the Higher Military Court, the Military Courts and Military Judges, the Courts of the States and Judges of the States, the Court of the Federal District and of the Territories and Judges of the Federal District and of the Territories.

The Supreme Federal Court comprises 11 ministers, nominated by the President and approved by the Senado. Its most important role is to rule on the final interpretation of the Constitution. The Supreme Federal Court has the power to declare an act of Congress void if it is unconstitutional. It judges offences committed by persons such as the President, the Vice-President, members of the Congresso Nacional, Ministers of State, its own members, the Attorney-General, judges of other higher courts, and heads of permanent diplomatic missions. It also judges cases of litigation between the Union and the States, between the States, or between foreign nations and the Union or the States, disputes as to jurisdiction between higher Courts, or between the latter and any other court, in cases involving the extradition of criminals, and others related to the writs of habeas corpus and habeas data, and in other cases.

The Higher Court of Justice comprises 33 members, appointed by the President and approved by the Senado. Its jurisdiction includes the judgment of offences committed by State Governors. The Regional Federal Courts comprise at least seven judges, recruited when possible in the respective region and appointed by the President of the Republic. The Higher Labour Court comprises 17 members, appointed by the President and approved by the Senado. The judges of the Regional Labour Courts are also appointed by the President. The Regional Electoral Courts are composed of seven members. The Higher Military Court comprises 15 life members, appointed by the President and approved by the Senado: three from the navy, four from the army, three from the air force and five civilian members. The States are responsible for the administration of their own justice, according to the principles established by the Constitution.

SUPREME FEDERAL COURT

Supremo Tribunal Federal: Praça dos Três Poderes, 70175-900 Brasília, DF; tel. (61) 3217-3000; fax (61) 3217-4412; internet www .stf.jus.br.

President: ANTONIO CEZAR PELUSO.

Vice-President: CARLOS AYRES DE FREITAS BRITTO.

Justices: JOSÉ CELSO DE MELLO FILHO, MARCO AURELIO MENDES DE FARIAS MELLO, ELLEN GRACIE NORTHFLEET, CARLOS AYRES DE FREITAS BRITTO, JOAQUIM BENEDITO BARBOSA GOMES, ENRIQUE RICARDO LEWANDOWSKI, CÁRMEN LÚCIA ANTUNES ROCHA, JOSÉ ANTÔNIO DIAS TOFFOLI, LUIZ FUX.

Procurator-General: ROBERTO MONTEIRO GURGEL SANTOS.

Religion

CHRISTIANITY

Conselho Nacional de Igrejas Cristãs do Brasil (CONIC) (National Council of Christian Churches in Brazil): Edif. Ceará, Sala 713, SCS, Quadra 01, Bloco E, 70303-900 Brasília, DF; tel. and fax (61) 3321-8341; e-mail conic.brasil@terra.com.br; internet www .conic.org.br; f. 1982; eight mem. churches; Pres. Pastor CARLOS AUGUSTO MÖLLER; Exec. Sec. Rev. LUIZ ALBERTO BARBOSA.

The Roman Catholic Church

Brazil comprises 44 archdioceses, 212 dioceses (including one each for Catholics of the Maronite, Melkite and Ukrainian Rites), 12 territorial prelatures and one personal apostolic administration. The Archbishop of São Sebastião do Rio de Janeiro is also the Ordinary for Catholics of other Oriental Rites in Brazil (estimated at 10,000 in 1994). According to the latest available census figures (2000), some 74% of the population are Roman Catholics.

Bishops' Conference: Conferência Nacional dos Bispos do Brasil, SES, Quadra 801, Conj. B, 70401-900 Brasília, DF; tel. (61) 2103-8300; fax (61) 2103-8303; e-mail cnbb@cnbb.org.br; internet www .cnbb.org.br; f. 1952; statutes approved 2002; Pres. GERALDO LYRIO ROCHA (Archbishop of Mariana, MG); Sec.-Gen. DIMAS LARA BARBOSA.

Latin Rite

Archbishop of São Salvador da Bahia, BA, and Primate of Brazil: MURILO SEBASTIÃO RAMOS KRIEGER, Cúria Metropolitana, Rua Martin Afonso de Souza 270, 40100-050 Salvador, BA; tel. (71) 328-6699; fax (71) 328-0068; e-mail gma@atarde.com.br.

Archbishop of Aparecida, SP: Cardinal RAYMUNDO DAMASCENO ASSIS.

Archbishop of Aracaju, SE: JOSÉ PALMEIRA LESSA.

Archbishop of Belém do Pará, PA: ALBERTO TAVEIRO CORRÊA.

Archbishop of Belo Horizonte, MG: WALMOR OLIVEIRA DE AZEVEDO.

Archbishop of Botucatu, SP: MAURÍCIO GROTTO DE CAMARGO.

Archbishop of Brasília, DF: SÉRGIO DA ROCHA.

Archbishop of Campinas, SP: AIRTON JOSÉ DOS SANTOS.

Archbishop of Campo Grande, MS: DIMAS LARA BARBOSA.

Archbishop of Cascavel, PR: MAURO APARECIDO DOS SANTOS.

Archbishop of Cuiabá, MT: MILTON ANTÔNIO DOS SANTOS.

Archbishop of Curitiba, PR: MOACYR JOSÉ VITTI.

Archbishop of Diamantina, MG: JOÃO BOSCO OLIVER DE FARIA.

Archbishop of Feira de Santana, BA: ITAMAR NAVILDO VIAN.

Archbishop of Florianópolis, SC: WILSON TADEU JÖNCK.

Archbishop of Fortaleza, CE: JOSÉ ANTÔNIO APARECIDO TOSI MARQUES.

Archbishop of Goiânia, GO: WASHINGTON CRUZ.

Archbishop of Juiz de Fora, MG: GIL ANTÔNIO MOREIRA.

Archbishop of Londrina, PR: ORLANDO BRANDES.

Archbishop of Maceió, AL: ANTÔNIO MUNIZ FERNANDES.

Archbishop of Manaus, AM: LUIZ SOARES VIEIRA.

Archbishop of Mariana, MG: GERALDO LYRIO ROCHA.

Archbishop of Maringá, PR: ANUAR BATTISTI.

Archbishop of Montes Claros, MG: JOSÉ ALBERTO MOURA.

Archbishop of Natal, RN: JAIME VIEIRA ROCHA.

Archbishop of Niterói, RJ: JOSÉ FRANCISCO REZENDE DIAS.

Archbishop of Olinda e Recife, PE: ANTONIO FERNANDO SABURIDO.

Archbishop of Palmas, PR: (vacant).

Archbishop of Paraíba, PB: ALDO DE CILLO PAGOTTO.

Archbishop of Passo Fundo, RS: PEDRO ERCÍLIO SIMON.

Archbishop of Pelotas, RS: JACINTO BERGMANN.

Archbishop of Porto Alegre, RS: DADEUS GRINGS.

Archbishop of Porto Velho, RO: ESMERALDO BARRETO DE FARIAS.

Archbishop of Pouso Alegre, MG: RICARDO PEDRO CHAVES PINTO FILHO.

Archbishop of Ribeirão Preto, SP: JOVIANO DE LIMA JÚNIOR.

Archbishop of Santa Maria, RS: HÉLIO ADELAR RUBERT.

Archbishop of São Luís do Maranhão, MA: JOSÉ BELISÁRIO DA SILVA.

Archbishop of São Paulo, SP: Cardinal ODILO PEDRO SCHERER.

Archbishop of São Sebastião do Rio de Janeiro, RJ: ORANI JOÃO TEMPESTA.

Archbishop of Sorocaba, SP: EDUARDO BENES DE SALES RODRIGUES.

Archbishop of Teresina, PI: JACINTO FURTADO DE BRITO SOBRINHO.

Archbishop of Uberaba, MG: ALOÍSIO ROQUE OPPERMANN.

Archbishop of Vitória, ES: LUIZ MANCILHA VILELA.

Archbishop of Vitória da Conquista, BA: LUIS GONZAGA SILVA PEPEU.

Maronite Rite

Bishop of Nossa Senhora do Líbano em São Paulo, SP: EDGAR MADI.

Melkite Rite

Bishop of Nossa Senhora do Paraíso em São Paulo, SP: FARES MAAKAROUN.

Ukrainian Rite

Bishop of São João Batista em Curitiba, PR: VALDOMIRO KOUBETCH.

The Anglican Communion

Anglicans form the Episcopal Anglican Church of Brazil (Igreja Episcopal Anglicana do Brasil), comprising eight dioceses.

Igreja Episcopal Anglicana do Brasil: Av. Ludolfo Boehl 256, Teresópolis, 91720-150 Porto Alegre, RS; tel. and fax (51) 3318-6200; internet www.ieab.org.br; f. 1890; 103,021 mems (1997); Primate Rt Rev. MAURÍCIO JOSÉ ARAÚJO DE ANDRADE; Sec.-Gen. Rev. FRANCISCO DE ASSIS DA SILVA.

Protestant Churches

According to the 2000 census, 15% of the population are Evangelical Christians.

Igreja Cristã Reformada do Brasil (Christian Reformed Church of Brazil): Rua Domingos Rodrigues, 306/Lapa, 05075-000 São Paulo, SP; tel. (11) 3260-7514; f. 1932; Pres. Rev. ANTÔNIO BONZOI; 500 mems.

Igreja Evangélica de Confissão Luterana no Brasil (IECLB): Rua Senhor dos Passos 202, 4° andar, 90020-180 Porto Alegre, RS; tel. (51) 3284-5400; fax (51) 3284-5419; e-mail presidencia@ieclb.org.br; internet www.luteranos.org.br; f. 1949; 717,000 mems; Pres. Pastor Dr WALTER ALTMANN; Vice-Pres. Pastor HOMERO SEVERO PINTO.

Igreja Evangélica Congregacional do Brasil: Rua Dom Pedro 1616, 85960-000 Marechal Cândido Rondon, PR; tel. (45) 254-2448; e-mail web@iecb.org.br; internet www.iecb.org.br; f. 1942; 148,836 mems (2000); Pres. Rev. H. DORIVAL L. SEIDEL.

Igreja Evangélica Luterana do Brasil: Av. Cel. Lucas de Oliveira 894, Bairro Mont'Serrat, 90440-010 Porto Alegre, RS; tel. (51) 3332-2111; fax (51) 3332-8145; e-mail ielb@ielb.org.br; internet www.ielb.org.br; f. 1904; 233,416 mems; Pres. Rev. PAULO MOISÉS NERBAS; Sec. Rev. Dr RONY RICARDO MARQUARDT.

Igreja Maná do Brasil: Travesa da Imprensa 26, Centro 12900-460 Bragança Paulista, SP; tel. (11) 4032-8104; e-mail adm_brasil@igrejamana.com; internet www.igrejamana.com.

Igreja Metodista do Brasil: Av. Piassanguaba 3031, Planalto Paulista, 04060-004 São Paulo, SP; tel. (11) 2813-8600; fax (11) 2813-8632; e-mail sede.nacional@metodista.org.br; internet www.metodista.org.br; 136,470 mems (2002); Exec. Sec. Bishop JOÃO CARLOS LOPES.

Igreja Presbiteriana Unida do Brasil (IPU): Av. Jeronimo Monteiro 400, Edif. Vitória Center, 1210/1, 29010-360 Vitória, ES; tel. and fax (27) 3256-6598; e-mail ipu@ipu.org.br; internet www.ipu.org.br; f. 1978; Moderator Rev. ENOC TEIXEIRA WENCESLAU.

BAHÁ'Í FAITH

Comunidade Bahá'í do Brasil (Bahá'í Community of Brazil): SHIS, QL 08, Conj. 02, CP 7035, 71620-970 Brasília, DF; tel. (61) 3364-3594; fax (61) 3364-3470; e-mail info@bahai.org.br; internet www.bahai.org.br; f. 1965; Sec. CARLOS ALBERTO SILVA.

BUDDHISM

Sociedade Budista do Brasil (Buddhist Society—Rio Buddhist Vihara): Dom Joaquim Mamede 45, Lagoinha, Santa Tereza, 20241-390 Rio de Janeiro, RJ; tel. (21) 2526-1411; e-mail sbbrj@yahoo.com; internet www.geocities.com/sbbrj; f. 1972; Pres. JORGE ALOICE GOMES.

OTHER RELIGIONS

Sociedade Taoísta do Brasil (Daoist Society): Rua Cosme Velho 355, Cosme Velho, 22241-090 Rio de Janeiro, RJ; tel. (21) 2225-2887; e-mail info@taoismo.org.br; internet www.taoismo.org.br; f. 1991.

The Press

The most striking feature of the Brazilian press is the relatively small circulation of newspapers in comparison with the size of the population. The newspapers with the largest circulations are *O Dia* (250,000), *O Globo* (350,000), *Folha de São Paulo* (287,627), and *O Estado de São Paulo* (242,000). The low circulation is mainly owing to high costs resulting from distribution difficulties. In consequence, there are no national newspapers. In 2004 a total of 532 daily newspaper titles, with an average circulation of 6,552,000, and 2,472 non-daily newspapers were published in Brazil.

DAILY NEWSPAPERS

Belém, PA

O Liberal: Av. 25 de Setembro 2473, Marco, 66093-000 Belém, PA; tel. (91) 3216-1138; e-mail redacao@orm.com.br; internet www.orm.com.br/oliberal; f. 1946; Pres. LUCIDEA MAIORANA; circ. 20,000.

Belo Horizonte, MG

Diário do Comércio: Av. Américo Vespúcio 1660, Nova Esperança, 31230-250 Belo Horizonte, MG; tel. (31) 3469-2049; fax (31) 3469-2043; e-mail redacaodc@diariodocomercio.com.br; internet www.diariodocomercio.com.br; f. 1932; Editor OSIRES FECCI.

Estado de Minas: Av. Getúlio Vargas 291, 8º andar, 30112-020 Belo Horizonte, MG; tel. (31) 3263-5800; fax (31) 3263-5424; e-mail gerais.em@uai.com.br; internet www.uai.com.br/em; f. 1928; morning; independent; Chief Editor JOSEMAR GIMENEZ RESENDE; circ. 65,000.

Hoje em Dia: Rua Padre Rolim 652, Santa Efigênia, 30130-916 Belo Horizonte, MG; tel. (31) 3236-8000; fax (31) 3236-8010; e-mail comercial@hojeemdia.com.br; internet www.hojeemdia.com.br; Editorial Dir CARLOS LINDENBURG.

Blumenau, SC

Jornal de Santa Catarina: Rua Bahia 2291, 89031-002 Blumenau, SC; tel. (48) 3221-1400; fax (48) 3221-1405; e-mail redacao@santa.com.br; internet www.santa.com.br; f. 1971; Dir (vacant); circ. 25,000.

Brasília, DF

Correio Brasiliense: SIG, Quadra 02, Lote 340, 70610-901 Brasília, DF; tel. (61) 3214-1100; fax (61) 3214-1157; e-mail geral@correioweb.com.br; internet www.correiobraziliense.com.br; f. 1960; Pres. and Dir ÁLVARO TEIXEIRA DA COSTA; circ. 30,000.

Jornal de Brasília: SIG, Trecho 1, Lotes 585/645, 70610-400 Brasília, DF; tel. (61) 3343-8000; fax (61) 3226-6735; e-mail redacao@jornaldebrasilia.com.br; internet www.jornaldebrasilia.com.br; f. 1972; Editor-in-Chief JORGE EDUARDO ANTUNES; circ. 25,000.

Campinas, SP

Correio Popular: Rua 7 de Setembro 189, Vila Industrial, 13035-350 Campinas, SP; tel. (19) 3736-3050; fax (19) 3234-8984; e-mail webmaster@rac.com.br; internet www.cpopular.com.br; f. 1927; Editorial Dir NELSON HOMEM DE MELLO; circ. 40,000.

Curitiba, PR

O Estado do Paraná: Rua João Tschannerl 800, Jardim Mercês, Vista Alegre, 80820-010 Curitiba, PR; tel. (41) 3331-5000; fax (41)

3335-2838; e-mail oestado@parana-online.com.br; internet www.parana-online.com.br; f. 1951; Pres. PAULO CRUZ PIMENTEL; Dir Supt YVONNE LUNARDELLI PIMENTEL; circ. 15,000.

Gazeta do Povo: Rua Pedro Ivo 459, Centro, 80010-020 Curitiba, PR; tel. (41) 3321-5000; fax (41) 3321-5300; e-mail atendimento@tudoparana.com; internet www.gazetadopovo.com.br; f. 1919; Vice-Pres. GUILHERME CUNHA PEREIRA; circ. 45,000.

Tribuna do Paraná: Rua João Tschannerl 800, Jardim Mercês, Vista Alegre, 80820-010 Curitiba, PR; tel. (41) 3331-5000; fax (41) 3335-2838; e-mail tribuna@parana-online.com.br; internet www.parana-online.com.br; f. 1956; Man. Editor RAFAEL TAVARES; circ. 15,000.

Fortaleza, CE

Diário do Nordeste: Editora Verdes Mares Ltda, Praça da Impresa, C.G.C. 07209-299 Fortaleza, CE; tel. (85) 3266-9773; fax (85) 3266-9797; e-mail aloredacao@diariodonordeste.com.br; internet diariodonordeste.globo.com; Editorial Dir ILDEFONSO RODRIGUES.

Jornal O Povo: Av. Aguanambi 282, 60055 Fortaleza, CE; tel. (85) 3255-6250; fax (85) 3231-5792; e-mail centraldeatendimento@opovo.com.br; internet opovo.uol.com.br; f. 1928; evening; Exec. Editor FÁTIMA SUDÁRIO; Editor-in-Chief ERICK GUIMARÃES; circ. 20,000.

Goiânia, GO

Diário da Manhã: Av. Anhanguera 2833, Setor Leste Universitário, 74610-010 Goiânia, GO; tel. (62) 3267-1000; internet www.dm.com.br; f. 1980; Editor BATISTA CUSTÓDIO; circ. 16,000.

O Popular: Rua Thómas Edson, Quadra 07, Setor Serrinha, 74835-130 Goiânia, GO; tel. (62) 3250-1220; fax (62) 3250-1270; e-mail dca@opopular.com.br; internet www.opopular.com.br; f. 1938; Editor ELISÂNGELA NASCIMENTO; circ. 65,000.

João Pessoa, PB

Correio da Paraíba: Av. Pedro II, Centro, João Pessoa, PB; tel. (83) 3216-5000; fax (83) 3216-5009; e-mail assinante@portalcorreio.com.br; internet www.correiodaparaiba.com.br; Exec. Dir BEATRIZ RIBEIRO.

Londrina, PR

Folha de Londrina: Rua Piauí 241, 86010-420 Londrina, PR; tel. (43) 3374-2020; fax (43) 3339-1412; e-mail editorial@folhadelondrina.com.br; internet www.bonde.com.br/folha; f. 1948; Editor-in-Chief OSWALD PETRIN; circ. 40,000.

Manaus, AM

A Crítica: Av. André Araújo 1924A, Aleixo-Cidade das Comunicações, 69060-001 Manaus, AM; tel. (92) 3643-1200; fax (92) 3643-1234; internet www.acritica.com.br; f. 1949; Dir RITA ARAÚJO CALDERARO; circ. 19,000.

Natal, RN

Diario de Natal: Av. Deodoro da Fonseca 245, Petrópolis, 59012-600 Natal, RN; tel. (84) 4009-0166; e-mail redacao.rn@diariosassociados.com.br; internet www.diariodenatal.com.br; Exec. Editor JULISKA AZEVEDO.

Niterói, RJ

O Fluminense: Rua da Conceição 188, Loja 118, Niterói Shopping, Niterói, RJ; tel. (21) 2620-6168; fax (21) 2620-8636; e-mail redacao@ofluminense.com.br; internet www.ofluminense.com.br; f. 1878; Man. Editor SANDRA DUARTE; circ. 80,000.

A Tribuna: Rua Barão do Amazonas 31, Ponta D'areia, 2403-0111 Niterói, RJ; tel. (21) 2719-1886; e-mail icarai@urbi.com.br; internet www.atribunarj.com.br; f. 1936; daily; Dir-Supt GUSTAVO SANTANO AMÓRO; circ. 10,000.

Palmas, TO

O Girassol: Av. Teotônio Segurado 101 Sul, Conj. 01, Edif. Office Center, Lote 06, Sala 408, 77015-002 Palmas, TO; tel. and fax (63) 3225-5456; e-mail ogirassol@uol.com.br; internet www.ogirassol.com.br; Editor-in-Chief WILBERGSON ESTRELA GOMES; Exec. Editor SONIELSON LUCIANO DE SOUSA.

Porto Alegre, RS

Zero Hora: Av. Ipiranga 1075, Azenha, 90169-900 Porto Alegre, RS; tel. (51) 3218-4300; fax (51) 3218-4700; e-mail geral@zerohora.com.br; internet www.zerohora.com.br; f. 1964; Editorial Dir RICARDO STEFANELLI; circ. 165,000 (Mon.), 170,000 (weekdays), 240,000 (Sun.).

Recife, PE

Diário de Pernambuco: Rua do Veiga 600, Santo Amaro, 50040-110 Recife, PE; tel. (81) 2122-7555; fax (81) 2122-7544; e-mail faleconosco@diariodepernambuco.com.br; internet www.diariodepernambuco.com.br; f. 1825; morning; independent; Editorial Dir VERA OGANDO; circ. 47,000.

Ribeirão Preto, SP

Jornal Tribuna da Ribeirão Preto: Rua São Sebastião 1380, Centro, 14015-040 Ribeirão Preto, SP; tel. and fax (16) 3632-2200; e-mail tribuna@tribunariberao.com.br; internet www.tribunaribeirao.com.br; Editor HILTON HARTMANN; circ. 16,000.

Rio de Janeiro, RJ

O Dia: Rua Riachuelo 359, Centro, 20235-900 Rio de Janeiro, RJ; fax (21) 2507-1228; internet odia.terra.com.br; f. 1951; morning; centrist labour; Editor-in-Chief ALEXANDRE FREELAND; circ. 250,000 (weekdays), 500,000 (Sun.).

O Globo: Rua Irineu Marinho 35, CP 1090, 20233-900 Rio de Janeiro, RJ; tel. (21) 2534-5000; fax (21) 2534-5510; internet oglobo.globo.com; f. 1925; morning; Editor-in-Chief RODOLFO FERNANDES; circ. 350,000 (weekdays), 600,000 (Sun.).

Jornal do Brasil: Av. Paulo de Frontin 568, Fundos, Rio Comprido, 20261-243 Rio de Janeiro, RJ; tel. (21) 2323-1000; e-mail jb@jbonline.com.br; internet www.jbonline.terra.com.br; f. 1891; print edn suspended July 2010, online only; Catholic, liberal; NELSON TANURE; Vice-Pres. RICARDO CARVALHO.

Jornal dos Sports: Rua Pereira de Almeida 88, Praça de Bandeira, 20260-100 Rio de Janeiro, RJ; tel. (21) 2563-0363; e-mail redacao@jsports.com.br; internet jsports.uol.com.br; f. 1931; morning; sporting daily; Editor THIAGO VIANA; circ. 39,000.

Salvador, BA

Correio da Bahia: Rua Professor Aristides Novis 123, Federação, 40210-630 Salvador, BA; tel. (71) 3533-3030; fax (71) 3203-1045; e-mail comercial@correiodabahia.com.br; internet www.correiodabahia.com.br; f. 1978; Editor-in-Chief SERGIO COSTA.

A Tarde: Rua Prof. Milton Cayres de Brito 204, Caminho das Árvores, 41820-570 Salvador, BA; tel. (71) 3340-8500; fax (71) 3231-8800; e-mail suporte@atarde.com.br; internet www.atarde.com.br; f. 1912; evening; Editor-in-Chief FLORISVALDO MATTOS; circ. 54,000.

Santarém, PA

O Impacto—O Jornal da Amazônia: Av. Presidente Vargas 3728, Caranazal, 68040-060 Santarém, PA; tel. (93) 3523-3330; fax (93) 3523-9131; e-mail oimpacto@oimpacto.com.br; internet www.oimpacto.com.br; Editor-in-Chief JERFFESON ROCHA.

Santo André, SP

Diário do Grande ABC: Rua Catequese 562, Bairro Jardim, 09090-900 Santo André, SP; tel. (11) 4435-8100; fax (11) 4434-8250; e-mail online@dgabc.com.br; internet www.dgabc.com.br; f. 1958; Exec. Editor MARCELO RUIZ; circ. 78,500.

Santos, SP

A Tribuna: Rua João Pessoa 129, 2º e 3º andares, Centro, 11013-900 Santos, SP; tel. (13) 2102-7000; fax (13) 3219-7329; e-mail atribuna@atribuna.com.br; internet www.atribuna.com.br; f. 1984; Exec. Editor ARMINDA AUGUSTO; Editor-in-Chief CARLOS CONDE; circ. 40,000.

São Luís, MA

O Imparcial: Empresa Pacotilha Ltda, Rua Assis Chateaubriand s/n, Renascença 2, 65075-670 São Luís, MA; tel. (98) 3212-2000; e-mail redacao@oimparcial.com.br; internet www.oimparcial.com.br; f. 1926; Editor-in-Chief PEDRO HENRIQUE FREIRE; circ. 8,000.

São Paulo, SP

DCI (Diário Comércio, Indústria e Serviços): Rua Bacaetava 191, 1° andar, 04705-010 São Paulo, SP; tel. (11) 5094-5200; fax (11) 5095-5308; e-mail redacao@dci.com.br; internet www.dci.com.br; f. 1933; morning; Editorial Dir MÁRCIA RAPOSO; circ. 50,000.

Diário do Comércio: Associação Comercial de São Paulo, Rua Boa Vista 51, 6° andar, Centro, 01014-911 São Paulo, SP; tel. (11) 3244-3322; fax (11) 3244-3046; e-mail faleconosco@dcomercio.com.br; internet www.dcomercio.com.br; Pres. GUILHERME AFIF DOMINGOS.

Diário de São Paulo: Rua Major Quedinho 90, Centro, São Paulo, SP; tel. (11) 3235-7800; internet www.diariosp.com.br; f. 1884; fmrly *Diário Popular*; evening; owned by O Globo; Editor-in-Chief NELSON NUNES; circ. 90,000.

O Estado de São Paulo: Av. Celestino Bourroul 68, 1° andar, 02710-000 São Paulo, SP; tel. (11) 3856-5400; fax (11) 3856-2940; e-mail falecom.estado@grupoestado.com.br; internet www.estado.com.br; f. 1875; morning; independent; Editor JULIO DE MESQUITA NETO; circ. 242,000 (weekdays), 460,000 (Sun.).

Folha de São Paulo: Alameda Barão de Limeira 425, 6° andar, Campos Elíseos, 01202-900 São Paulo, SP; tel. (11) 3224-4759; fax (11) 3224-7550; e-mail falecomagente@folha.com.br; internet www.folha.uol.com.br; f. 1921; morning; Editor CAMILA MARQUES; circ. 287,627 (weekdays), 342,614 (Sun.).

Jornal da Tarde: Av. Eng. Caetano Álvares 55, Bairro do Limão, 02598-000 São Paulo, SP; tel. (11) 3856-2234; fax (11) 3856-2940; e-mail pergunta.jt@grupoestado.com.br; internet www.jt.com.br; f. 1966; evening; independent; Dir FERNÃO LARA MESQUITA; circ. 120,000, 180,000 (Mon.).

Vitória, ES

A Gazeta: Rua Charic Murad 902, 29050 Vitória, ES; tel. (27) 3321-8333; fax (27) 3321-8720; e-mail ahees@redegazeta.com.br; internet gazetaonline.globo.com; f. 1928; Exec. Editor ANDRÉ HEES; circ. 19,000.

PERIODICALS

Rio de Janeiro, RJ

Antenna-Eletrônica Popular: Av. Marechal Floriano 151, Centro, 20080-005 Rio de Janeiro, RJ; tel. (21) 2223-2442; fax (21) 2263-8840; e-mail antenna@anep.com.br; internet www.anep.com.br; f. 1926; monthly; telecommunications and electronics, radio, TV, hi-fi, amateur and CB radio; Dir MARIA BEATRIZ AFFONSO PENNA; circ. 15,000.

Conjuntura Econômica: Rua Barão de Itambi 60, 7º andar, Botafogo, 22231-000 Rio de Janeiro, RJ; tel. (21) 2559-6040; fax (21) 2559-6039; e-mail conjunturaeconomica@fgv.br; internet www.fgv.br/ibre/cecon; f. 1947; monthly; economics and finance; published by Fundação Getúlio Vargas; Editor-in-Chief CLAUDIO CONCEIÇÃO; circ. 15,000.

ECO21: Av. Copacabana 2, Gr. 301, 22010-122 Rio de Janeiro, RJ; tel. (21) 2275-1490; e-mail eco21@eco21.com.br; internet www.eco21.com.br; f. 1990; monthly; ecological issues; Editor RENÉ CAPRILES.

São Paulo, SP

Ana Maria: Editora Abril, Av. das Nações Unidas 7221, 05425-902 São Paulo, SP; tel. (11) 3037-2000; fax (11) 3037-4734; e-mail anamaria.abril@atleitor.com.br; internet mdemulher.abril.com.br/revistas/anamaria; weekly; women's interest; Editor-in-Chief LIDICE-BAH; circ. 222,171.

Caros Amigos: Rua Paris 856, Sumaré, 01257-040 São Paulo, SP; tel. (11) 2594-0355; fax (11) 2594-0351; e-mail atendimento@carosamigos.com.br; internet www.carosamigos.com.br; f. 1997; monthly; political; Editor HAMILTON OCTAVIO DE SOUZA; circ. 37,000.

Caras: Editora Abril, Av. das Nações Unidas 7221, 05425-902 São Paulo, SP; tel. (11) 3037-2000; fax (11) 3037-4734; e-mail redacaoonline@caras.com.br; internet www.caras.com.br; f. 1993; weekly; celebrities; Dir EDGARDO MARTOLIO; circ.308,465.

CartaCapital: Alameda Santos 1800, 7º B, 01418-200 São Paulo, SP; tel. (11) 3474-0161; e-mail redacao@cartacapital.com.br; internet www.cartacapital.com.br; f. 1994; weekly; politics and economics; Editor-in-Chief MINO CARTA; circ. 32,570.

Casa e Jardim: Av. Jaguaré 1485, 05346-902 São Paulo, SP; tel. (11) 3767-7000; fax (11) 3767-7936; e-mail casaejardim@edglobo.com.br; internet revistacasaejardim.globo.com; f. 1953; monthly; homes and gardens, illustrated; Editor-in-Chief ARTUR DE ANDRADE; circ. 100,811.

Claudia: Editora Abril, Av. das Nações Unidas 7221, Pinheiros, 05425-902 São Paulo, SP; tel. (11) 3037-2000; fax (11) 5087-2100; e-mail claudia.abril@atleitor.com.br; internet claudia.abril.com.br; f. 1962; monthly; women's interest; Editor-in-Chief LÚCIA BARROS; circ. 402,940.

Contigo!: Editora Abril, Av. das Nações Unidas 7221, 5° andar, 05425-902 São Paulo, SP; tel. (11) 3037-2000; fax (11) 3037-4734; e-mail contigo.abril@atleitor.com.br; internet contigo.abril.com.br; f. 1963; weekly; entertainment and celebrity news; Dir FELIX FASSONE; circ. 148,569.

Criativa: Av. Jaguaré 1485, 05346-902 São Paulo, SP; tel. (11) 3767-7812; fax (11) 3767-7771; e-mail criativa@edglobo.com.br; internet revistacriativa.globo.com; monthly; women's interest; Editor-in-Chief MARIANA WEBER; circ. 100,314.

Digesto Econômico: Associação Comercial de São Paulo, Rua Boa Vista 51, Centro, 01014-911 São Paulo, SP; tel. (11) 3244-3092; fax (11) 3244-3355; e-mail admdiario@acsp.com.br; internet www.acsp.com.br; fortnightly; Pres. ELVIO ALIPRANDI; Chief Editor JOÃO DE SCANTIMBURGO.

Elle: Editora Abril, Av. das Nações Unidas 7221, 16° andar, Pinheiros, 05425-902 São Paulo, SP; tel. (11) 3037-3545; fax (11) 3037-5451; e-mail elle.abril@atleitor.com.br; internet www.elle.com.br; f. 1988; monthly; women's interest; Editor-in-Chief ELIANA SANCHEZ; circ. 100,000.

Época: Av. Jaguaré 1485, 05346-902 São Paulo, SP; tel. (11) 3767-7000; e-mail epocadir@edglobo.com.br; internet revistaepoca.globo.com; f. 1998; news weekly; Editor HELIO GUROVITZ; circ. 416,744.

Exame: Editora Abril, Av. das Nações Unidas 7221, Pinheiros, 05425-902 São Paulo, SP; tel. (11) 3037-2000; fax (11) 3037-2027; e-mail redacao.exame@abril.com.br; internet www.exame.com.br; f. 1967; 2 a week; business; Editorial Dir CLÁUDIA VASSALLO; circ. 168,300.

ISTOÉ: Rua William Speers 1088, 05067-900 São Paulo, SP; tel. (11) 3618-4200; fax (11) 3618-4324; e-mail leitor@istoe.com.br; internet www.istoe.com.br; politics and current affairs; Editorial Dir CARLOS JOSÉ MARQUES; circ. 340,764.

Máquinas e Metais: Alameda Olga 315, 01155-900 São Paulo, SP; tel. (11) 3824-5300; fax (11) 3666-9585; e-mail infomm@arandanet.com.br; internet www.arandanet.com.br; f. 1964; monthly; machine and metal industries; Editor JOSÉ ROBERTO GONÇALVES; circ. 15,000.

Marie Claire: Av. Jaguaré 1485, 05346-902 São Paulo, SP; tel. (11) 3767-7000; fax (11) 3767-7833; e-mail mclaire@edglobo.com.br; internet revistamarieclaire.globo.com; monthly; women's interest; Editorial Dir MÔNICA DE ALBUQUERQUE LINS SERINO; circ. 199,831.

Micromundo-Computerworld do Brasil: Rua Caçapava 79, 01408 São Paulo, SP; tel. (11) 3289-1767; e-mail editor@computerworld.com.br; internet www.computerworld.com.br; f. 1976; bimonthly; computers; Editor FABIANA MONTE; circ. 38,000.

Nova Escola: Editora Abril, Av. das Nações Unidas 7221, 6° andar, 05425-902 São Paulo, SP; tel. (11) 3037-2000; fax (11) 3037-4322; e-mail novaescola@atleitor.com.br; internet revistaescola.abril.com.br; f. 1986; monthly; education; Dir GABRIEL GROSSI; circ. 451,125.

Placar: Editora Abril, Av. das Nações Unidas 7221, 14° andar, Pinheiros, 05425-902 São Paulo, SP; tel. (11) 3037-2000; fax (11) 5087-2100; e-mail placar.abril@atleitor.com.br; internet placar.abril.com.br; f. 1970; monthly; soccer; Editor SÉRGIO XAVIER; circ. 127,000.

Quatro Rodas: Av. das Nações Unidas 7221, 14° andar, 05425-902 São Paulo, SP; fax (11) 3037-5039; internet quatrorodas.abril.com.br; f. 1960; monthly; motoring; Editor SÉRGIO BEREZOVSKY; circ. 190,139.

Revista O Carreteiro: Rua Palacete das Aguias 395, Vila Alexandria, 04635-021 São Paulo, SP; tel. (11) 5035-0000; fax (11) 5031-8647; e-mail revista@ocarreteiro.com.br; internet www.revistaocarreteiro.com.br; f. 1970; monthly; transport; Editor JOÃO GERALDO; circ. 100,000.

Saúde: Editora Abril, Av. das Nações Unidas 7221, 16° andar, Pinheiros, 05425-902 São Paulo, SP; tel. (11) 3037-4885; fax (11) 3037-4867; e-mail saude.abril@atleitor.com.br; internet saude.abril.com.br; monthly; health; Editor LÚCIA HELENA DE OLIVEIRA; circ. 183,250.

Superinteressante: Editora Abril, Avenida das Nações Unidas 7221, 8º andar, 05425-902 São Paulo, SP; tel. (11) 3037-2000; fax (11) 3037-5891; e-mail superleitor.abril@atleitor.com.br; internet super.abril.com.br; f. 1987; monthly; popular science; Dir SÉRGIO GWERCMAN; circ. 354,947.

Veja: Editora Abril, Av. das Nações Unidas 7221, Pinheiros, 05425-902 São Paulo, SP; tel. (11) 3347-2121; fax (11) 3037-5638; e-mail veja@abril.com.br; internet vejaonline.abril.com.br; f. 1968; news weekly; Editor EURÍPEDES ALCÂNTARA; circ. 1,099,078.

Viva Mais: Editora Abril, Av. das Nações Unidas 7221, 05425-902 São Paulo, SP; tel. (11) 3037-2000; fax (11) 3037-4734; e-mail vivamais.abril@atleitor.com.br; internet mdemulher.abril.com.br; weekly; women's interest; Editor MÔNICA KATO; circ. 219,940.

NEWS AGENCIES

Agência o Estado de São Paulo: Av. Eng. Caetano Alvares 55, Bairro do Limão, 02588-900 São Paulo, SP; tel. (11) 3856-3500; fax (11) 3856-2940; internet www.estadao.com.br; Rep. SAMUEL DIRCEU F. BUENO.

Agência O Globo: Rua Irineu Marinho 70, 4° andar, Cidade Nova, 20230-901 Rio de Janeiro, RJ; tel. (21) 2534-5656; e-mail agenciaoglobo@oglobo.com.br; internet www.agenciaoglobo.com.br; f. 1974; Man. RICARDO MELLO.

Agência JB (Agência Jornal do Brasil): Av. Paulo de Frontin 568, Fundos, Rio Comprido, 20261-243 Rio de Janeiro, RJ; tel. (21) 2101-4148; fax (21) 2101-4428; e-mail ajb@jb.com.br; internet www.agenciajb.com.br; f. 1966; Exec. Dir EDGAR LISBOA.

Folhapress: Alameda Barão de Limeira 401, 4° andar, Campos Elíseos, 01202-900 São Paulo, SP; tel. (11) 3224-3123; fax (11) 3224-4778; e-mail folhapress@folhapress.com.br; internet www.folhapress.com.br; Gen. Man. RAIMUNDO CUNHA.

PRESS ASSOCIATIONS

Associação Brasileira de Imprensa (ABI): Rua Araújo Porto Alegre 71, Centro, 20030-012 Rio de Janeiro, RJ; tel. (21) 2282-1292; e-mail abi@abi.org.br; internet www.abi.org.br; f. 1908; asscn for journalistic rights and assistance; 4,000 mems; Pres. MAURÍCIO AZÊDO.

Associação Nacional de Editores de Revistas (ANER): Rua Deputado Lacerda Franco 300, 15°, Conj. 155, 05418-000 São Paulo, SP; tel. (11) 3030-9390; fax (11) 3030-9393; e-mail info@aner.org.br; internet www.aner.org.br; f. 1986; Pres. ROBERTO MUYLAERT; Exec. Dir MARIA CÉLIA FURTADO.

Federação Nacional dos Jornalistas (FENAJ): SCLRN 704, Bloco F, Loja 20, 70730-536 Brasília, DF; tel. (61) 3244-0650; fax (61) 3242-6616; e-mail fenaj@fenaj.org.br; internet www.fenaj.org.br; f. 1946; represents 31 regional unions; Pres. SÉRGIO MURILLO DE ANDRADE.

Publishers

Aymará Edições e Tecnologia, Ltda: Rua Lamenha Lins 1709, Rebouças, 80220-080 Curitiba, PR; tel. (41) 3213-3500; fax (41) 3213-3501; e-mail debora.nunes@aymara.com.br; internet www.aymara.com.br; academic; Pres. ANDRÉ CALDEIRA.

Barsa Planeta Internacional: Av. Francisco Matarazzo 1500, 4° andar, Edif. New York, Centro Empresarial Agua Branca, 05001-100 São Paulo, SP; tel. (11) 3225-1990; fax (11) 3225-1960; e-mail atendimento@barsaplaneta.com.br; internet brasil.planetasaber.com; f. 1949; reference books.

Cengage Learning: Condomínio E-Business Park, Rua Werner Siemens 111, Prédio 20, Espaço 04, Lapa de Baixo, 05069-900 São Paulo, SP; tel. (11) 3665-9900; fax (11) 3665-9901; e-mail milagros.valderrama@cengage.com; internet www.cengage.com.br; f. 1960 as Editora Pioneira; architecture, computers, political and social sciences, business studies, languages, children's books; Dir MILAGROS VALDERRAMA.

Cortez Editora: Rua Monte Alegre 1074, 05014-001 São Paulo, SP; tel. (11) 3611-9696; fax (11) 3864-0111; e-mail erivan@cortezeditora.com.br; internet www.cortezeditora.com.br; f. 1980; children's literature, linguistics and social sciences; Dir ERIVAN GOMES.

Ediouro Publicações, SA: Rua Nova Jerusalém 345, CP 1880, Bonsucesso, 21042-235 Rio de Janeiro, RJ; tel. (21) 3882-8416; fax (21) 3882-8200; e-mail livros@ediouro.com.br; internet www.ediouro.com.br; f. 1939; part of Empresas Ediouro; general interest, leisure magazines, textbooks; Pres. JORGE CARNEIRO.

Editora Abril, SA: Av. das Nações Unidas 7221, Pinheiros, 05425-902 São Paulo, SP; tel. (11) 3037-2000; fax (11) 5087-2100; e-mail abril@abril.com.br; internet www.abril.com.br; f. 1950; magazines; Pres. and Editorial Dir ROBERTO CIVITA.

Editora Atica, SA: Rua Barão de Iguape 110, 01507-900 São Paulo, SP; tel. (11) 3346-3000; fax (11) 3277-4146; e-mail editora@atica.com.br; internet www.atica.com.br; f. 1965; acquired by Grupo Abril in 2004; textbooks, Brazilian and African literature; Pres. VICENTE PAZ FERNANDEZ.

Editora Atlas, SA: Rua Conselheiro Nébias 1384, 01203-904 São Paulo, SP; tel. (11) 3357-9144; fax (11) 3331-7830; e-mail atendimento@editora-atlas.com.br; internet www.editoraatlas.com.br; f. 1944; business administration, economics, accounting, law, education, social sciences; Pres. LUIZ HERRMANN, Jr.

Editora Blucher: Rua Pedroso Alvarenga 1245, 4° andar, 04531-012 São Paulo, SP; tel. (11) 3078-5366; fax (11) 3079-2707; e-mail eduardo@blucher.com.br; internet www.blucher.com.br; f. 1957; science and engineering; Dir EDUARDO BLÜCHER.

Editora do Brasil, SA: Rua Conselheiro Nébias 887, Campos Elíseos, CP 4986, 01203-001 São Paulo, SP; tel. (11) 3226-0211; fax (11) 3222-5583; e-mail editora@editoradobrasil.com.br; internet www.editoradobrasil.com.br; f. 1943; education; Pres. MARIA APPARECIDA CAVALCANTE COSTA.

Editora Brasiliense, SA: Rua Mourato Coelho 111, Pinheiros, 05417-010 São Paulo, SP; tel. and fax (11) 3087-0000; e-mail brasilienseedit@uol.com.br; internet www.editorabrasiliense.com.br; f. 1943; education, racism, gender studies, human rights, ecology, history, literature, social sciences; Pres. YOLANDA C. DA SILVA PRADO.

Editora Campus-Elsevier: Rua Sete de Setembro 111, 16° andar, 20050-002 Rio de Janeiro, RJ; tel. (21) 3970-9300; fax (21) 2507-1991; e-mail info@elsevier.com.br; internet www.campus.com.br; f. 1976; business, computing, non-fiction; imprint of Elsevier since 2002; Pres. CLAUDIO ROTHMULLER; Dir IGDAL PARNES.

Editora Canção Nova: Rua São Bento 43, Centro, 01011-000 São Paulo, SP; tel. (11) 3106-9080; e-mail editora@cancaonova.com; internet editora.cancaonova.com; f. 1996; spiritual literature and children's books; Dir CRISTIANA MARIA NEGRÃO.

Editora Delta, SA (Mundo da Criança): Av. Nilo Peçanha 50, Centro 2817, 20020-100 Rio de Janeiro, RJ; tel. (21) (21) 2533-6673; e-mail faleconosco@mundodacrianca.com; internet www.mundodacrianca.com; f. 1930; reference books; Pres. ANDRÉ KOOGAN BREITMAN.

Editora Educacional Brasileira, SA: Rua Brasílio Itibere 3920, Água Verde, 80240-060 Curitiba, PR; tel. (41) 3342-1414; e-mail editoraeducacional@yahoo.com.br; f. 1963; biology, textbooks and reference books.

Editora FTD, SA: Rua Rui Barbosa 156, Bairro Bela Vista, 01326-010 São Paulo, SP; tel. (11) 3253-5011; fax (11) 3288-0132; e-mail ftd@ftd.com.br; internet www.ftd.com.br; f. 1902; textbooks; Pres. DÉLCIO AFONSO BALESTRIN; Dir CECILIANY ALVES.

Editora Globo, SA: Av. Jaguaré 1485, 3° andar, 05346-902 São Paulo, SP; tel. (11) 3767-7400; fax (11) 3767-7870; e-mail globolivros@edglobo.com.br; internet globolivros.globo.com; f. 1957; fiction, engineering, agriculture, cookery, environmental studies; Dir-Gen. FREDERIC ZOGHAIB KACHAR.

Editora Lê, SA: Rua Januária 437, Floresta, 31110-060 Belo Horizonte, MG; tel. (31) 3423-3200; fax (31) 2517-3003; e-mail editora@le.com.br; internet www.le.com.br; f. 1967; textbooks; Dir JOSÉ ALENCAR MAYRINK.

Editora Manole: Av. Ceci 672, Tamboré, 06460-120 Barueri, SP; tel. (11) 4196-6000; e-mail info@manole.com.br; internet www.manole.com.br; includes the imprints Minha Editora and Amarilys Editora; Dir AMARYLIS MANOLE.

Editora Melhoramentos, Ltda: Rua Tito 479, Vila Romana, 05051-000 São Paulo, SP; tel. (11) 3874-0800; fax (11) 3874-0855; e-mail sac@melhoramentos.com.br; internet www.livrariamelhoramentos.com.br; f. 1890; general non-fiction, children's books, dictionaries; Dir BRENO LERNER.

Editora Michalany, Ltda: Rua Laura dos Anjos Ramos 420, Jardim Santa Cruz—Interlagos, 04455-350 São Paulo, SP; tel. (11) 5611-3414; fax (11) 5614-1592; e-mail smmeditora@uol.com.br; f. 1965; biographies, economics, textbooks, geography, history, religion, maps; Dir DOUGLAS MICHALANY.

Editora Moderna, Ltda: Rua Padre Adelino 758, Belenzinho, 03303-904 São Paulo, SP; tel. (11) 2790-1300; fax (11) 2602-5510; e-mail faleconosco@moderna.com.br; internet www.moderna.com.br; f. 1968; Pres. RICARDO ARISSA FELTRE.

Editora Nova Fronteira, SA: Rua Nova Jerusalém 345, Bonsucesso, 21042-230 Rio de Janeiro, RJ; tel. (21) 2131-1111; fax (21) 2537-2009; e-mail sac@novafronteira.com.br; internet www.novafronteira.com.br; f. 1965; acquired by Empresas Ediouro in 2006; fiction, psychology, history, politics, science fiction, poetry, leisure, reference; Exec. Dir MAURO PALERMO.

Editora Positivo: Rua Major Heitor Guimarães 174, Seminário, 80400-120 Curitiba, PR; tel. (41) 3212-3500; fax (41) 3336-5135; e-mail vendas@editorapositivo.com.br; internet www.editorapositivo.com.br; f. 1980; Dir-Gen. EMERSON SANTOS.

Editora Record, SA: Rua Argentina 171, São Cristóvão, CP 884, 20921-380 Rio de Janeiro, RJ; tel. (21) 2585-2000; fax (21) 2585-2085; e-mail record@record.com.br; internet www.record.com.br; f. 1942; part of Grupo Editorial Record; general fiction and non-fiction, education, textbooks, fine arts; Pres. SÉRGIO MACHADO.

Editora Revista dos Tribunais, Ltda: Rua do Bosque 820, 01136-000 São Paulo, SP; tel. (11) 3613-8400; fax (11) 3613-8450; e-mail sac@rt.com.br; internet www.rt.com.br; f. 1912; acquired by Thomson Reuters in 2010; law and jurisprudence books and periodicals; Pres. GONZALO LISSARRAGUE; CEO BELINELO ANTONIO.

Editora Rideel, Ltda: Av. Casa Verde 455, Casa Verde, 02519-000 São Paulo, SP; tel. and fax (11) 2238-5100; e-mail sac@rideel.com.br; internet www.rideel.com.br; f. 1971; general; Dir ITALO AMADIO.

Editora Saraiva: Rua Henrique Schaumann 270, Cerqueira César, 05413-909 São Paulo, SP; tel. (11) 3613-3000; fax (11) 3611-3308; e-mail saceditorasaraiva@editorasaraiva.com.br; internet www.editorasaraiva.com.br; f. 1914; education, textbooks, law, economics, general fiction and non-fiction; Pres. JORGE EDUARDO SARAIVA.

Editora Scipione, Ltda: Av. Otaviano Alves de Lima 4400, Freguesia do Ó, 02909-900 São Paulo, SP; tel. (11) 3990-1788; e-mail scipione@scipione.com.br; internet www.scipione.com.br; f. 1983; owned by Editora Abril, SA; school books, literature, reference; Chair. DOUGLAS DURAN; Dir LUIZ ESTEVES SALLUM.

Editora Vozes, Ltda: Rua Frei Luís 100, CP 90023, Centro, 25689-900 Petrópolis, RJ; tel. (24) 2233-9000; fax (24) 2231-4676; e-mail editorial@vozes.com.br; internet www.universovozes.com.br; f. 1901; Catholic publrs; theology, philosophy, history, linguistics, science, psychology, fiction, education, etc.; Dir ANTÔNIO MOSER.

Global Editora: Rua Pirapitingüi 111, Liberdade, 01508-020 São Paolo, SP; tel. (11) 3277-7999; fax (11) 3277-8141; e-mail global@

globaleditora.com.br; internet www.globaleditora.com.br; f. 1973; Dir LUIZ ALVES JÚNIOR.

Instituto Brasileiro de Edições Pedagógicas, Ltda (Editora IBEP): Av. Alexandre Mackenzie 619, Jaguaré, 05322-000 São Paulo, SP; tel. (11) 2799-7799; fax (11) 6694-5338; e-mail editoras@ibep-nacional.com.br; internet www.editoraibep.com.br; f. 1965; part of Grupo IBEP; textbooks; Dirs JORGE YUNES, PAULO CORNADO MARTI.

Lex Editora, SA: Rua da Consolação 77, Centro, 01301-000 São Paulo, SP; tel. (11) 2126-6000; fax (11) 2126-6020; e-mail editorial@lex.com.br; internet www.lex.com.br; f. 1937; legislation and jurisprudence; Pres. CARLOS SERGIO SERRA; Exec. Dir FÁBIO PAIXÃO.

Pallas Editora: Rua Frederico de Albuquerque 56, Higienópolis, 21050-840 Rio de Janeiro, RJ; tel. and fax (21) 2270-0186; e-mail pallas@pallaseditora.com.br; internet www.pallaseditora.com.br; f. 1980; Afro-Brazilian culture; Pres. CRISTINA FERNANDES WARTH.

Yendis Editora: Rua Major Carlos del Prete 510, 09530-000 Sao Caetano do Sul, SP; tel. (11) 4224-9400; fax (11) 4224-9403; e-mail max@yendis.com.br; internet www.yendis.com.br; Dir MAXWELL MEDEIROS FERNANDES.

PUBLISHERS' ASSOCIATIONS

Associação Brasileira de Difusão do Livro (ABDL) (Brazilian Association of Door-to-Door Booksellers): Rua Marquês de Itu 408-71, CP 01223-000, São Paulo, SP; internet www.abdl.com.br; f. 1987; non-profit org.; Pres. LUÍS ANTONIO TORELLI.

Associação Brasileira de Editores de Livros Escolares (Abrelivros): Rua Funchal 263, Conj. 61/62, Vila Olímpia, 04551-060 São Paulo, SP; tel. and fax (11) 3826-9071; e-mail contato@abrelivros.org.br; internet www.abrelivros.org.br; f. 1991; 28 mems; Pres. JORGE YUNES; Gen. Man. BEATRIZ GRELLET.

Associação Brasileira do Livro (ABL): Av. 13 de Maio 23, 16° andar, Sala 1619/1620, 20031-000 Rio de Janeiro, RJ; tel. and fax (21) 2240-9115; e-mail abralivro@uol.com.br; internet www.abralivro.com.br; f. 1955; Pres. ADENILSON JARBAS CABRAL.

Câmara Brasileira do Livro: Rua Cristiano Viana 91, Pinheiros, 05411-000 São Paulo, SP; tel. and fax (11) 3069-1300; e-mail cbl@cbl.org.br; internet www.cbl.org.br; f. 1946; Pres. ROSELY BOSCHINI.

Sindicato Nacional dos Editores de Livros (SNEL): Rua da Ajuda 35, 18° andar, Centro, 20040-000 Rio de Janeiro, RJ; tel. (21) 2533-0399; fax (21) 2533-0422; e-mail snel@snel.org.br; internet www.snel.org.br; 200 mems; Pres. SONIA MACHADO JARDIM.

There are also regional publishers' associations.

Broadcasting and Communications

TELECOMMUNICATIONS

Regulatory Authority

Agência Nacional de Telecomunicações (ANATEL): SAUS Quadra 06, Blocos C, E, F e H, 70070-940 Brasília, DF; tel. (61) 2312-2000; fax (61) 2312-2264; e-mail biblioteca@anatel.gov.br; internet www.anatel.gov.br; f. 1998; regional office in each state; Pres. RONALDO MOTA SARDENBERG.

Major Operators

AT&T Brazil: Torre Sul, 7°, Rua James Joule 65, São Paulo, SP; tel. (11) 3885-0080; internet www.att.com.br; Vice-Pres. (Caribbean and Latin America) MARY LIVINGSTON.

Claro: Rua Florida 1970, Bairro Cidade Monções, 40432-544 São Paulo, SP; internet www.claro.com.br; f. 2003 by mergers; owned by América Móvil, SA de CV (Mexico); mobile cellular provider; 30.2m. subscribers (2007); CEO CARLOS ZENTENO DE LOS SANTOS.

CTBC (Companhia de Telecomunicações do Brasil Central): Rua Machado de Assis 333, Centro, 38400-112 Uberlândia, MG; tel. (34) 3256-2033; fax (34) 3236-7723; e-mail tatianes@ctbc.com.br; internet www.ctbc.com.br; f. 1954; owned by Grupo Algar; mobile and fixed line provider in central Brazil; Pres. DIVINO SEBASTIÃO DE SOUZA.

Empresa Brasileira de Telecomunicações, SA (Embratel): Av. Presidente Vargas 1012, CP 2586, 20179-900 Rio de Janeiro, RJ; tel. (21) 2519-8182; e-mail cmsocial@embratel.net.br; internet www.embratel.com.br; f. 1965; operates national and international telecommunications system; owned by Telmex (Teléfonos de Mexico, SA); Exec. Dir ANTONIO JOÃO FILHO.

Oi (Tele Norte Leste Participações, SA): Rua Lauro Müller 116, 22° andar, Botafogo, Rio de Janeiro, RJ; tel. (21) 2815-2921; fax (21) 2571-3050; internet www.novaoi.com.br; f. 1998 as Tele Norte Leste; fixed line and mobile operator; Pres. JOSÉ MAURO METTRAU CARNEIRO DA CUNHA; CEO LUIZ EDUARDO FALCO.

Sercomtel Celular, SA: Rua João Cândido 555, 86010-000 Londrina, PR; e-mail casc@sercomtel.com.br; internet www.sercomtelcelular.com.br; f. 1998; mobile cellular network provider; Pres. FERNANDO LOPES KIREEFF.

Telefônica SP: Rua Martiniano de Carvalho 851, Bela Vista, 01321-000 São Paulo, SP; tel. (11) 3549-7200; fax (11) 3549-7202; e-mail telefonicabr@telefonica.com.br; internet www.telefonica.com.br; fmrly Telecomunicações de São Paulo (Telesp), privatized in 1998; subsidiary of Telefónica, SA (Spain); 41m. customers; Pres. ANTONIO CARLOS VALENTE.

Telemig Celular: internet www.telemigcelular.com.br; mobile cellular provider in Minas Gerais; 2.6m. customers.

Vivo: Av. Chucri Zaidan 2460, 5°, 04583-110 São Paulo, SP; tel. (11) 5105-1001; internet www.vivo.com.br; owned by Telefónica Móviles, SA of Spain; Telefónica bought Portugal Telecom's share in 2010; mobile telephones; Pres. ROBERTO OLIVEIRA DE LIMA; 24.6m. customers.

TIM (Telecom Italia Mobile): Av. das Américas 3434, 5° andar, Barra da Tijuca, 22640-102 Rio de Janeiro, RJ; internet www.tim.com.br; f. 1998 in Brazil; subsidiary of Telecom Italia (Italy); mobile cellular provider; 24.1m. customers (2006); Pres. GABRIELE GALATERI DI GENOLA; Dir LEANDRO GUERRA.

BROADCASTING

Empresa Brasil de Comunicação (EBC): SCRN 702/3, Bloco B, 70323-900 Brasília, DF; tel. (61) 3799-5200; e-mail comunicacao@ebc.com.br; internet www.ebç.com.br; f. 1975, as Empresa Brasileira de Radiodifusão (RADIOBRÁS); re-established as above in 2007; state-run radio and television network; manages public broadcasters; Pres. TEREZA CRUVINEL; Exec. Sec. RICARDO COLLAR.

Radio

The main broadcasting stations in Rio de Janeiro are: Rádio Nacional, Rádio Globo, Rádio Eldorado, Rádio Jornal do Brasil, Rádio Tupi and Rádio Mundial. In São Paulo the main stations are Rádio Bandeirantes, Rádio Mulher, Rádio Eldorado, Rádio Gazeta and Rádio Excelsior; and in Brasília: Rádio Nacional, Rádio Alvorada, Rádio Planalto and Rádio Capital.

The state-run corporation Empresa Brasil de Comunicação (q.v.) owns the following radio stations:

Rádio Nacional AM de Brasília: CP 259, 70710-750 Brasília, DF; tel. (61) 3799-5167; fax (61) 3799-5169; e-mail centraldoouvinte@ebc.com.br; f. 1958; Man. CRISTINA GUIMARÃES.

Rádio Nacional da Amazônia: CP 258, 70359-970 Brasília, DF; f. 1977; Regional Man. SOFÍA HAMMOE; Co-ordinator LUCIANA COUTO.

Rádio Nacional FM de Brasília: CP 070747, 70720-502 Brasília, DF; e-mail ouvinte@radiomec.com.br; f. 1976; broadcasts to the Federal District and surrounding areas; Man. CARLOS SENNA.

Rádio Nacional do Rio de Janeiro: Rua de Relação 18, Lapa, 20231-110 Rio de Janeiro, RJ; tel. (21) 2117-6208; e-mail cao@radiomec.com.br; f. 2004; Regional Man. ANTONIO GRASSI.

Television

The main television networks are:

RBS TV: Rua do Acampamento 2550, Passo do Príncipe, 96425-250 Bagé, RS; tel. (53) 3240-5300; fax (53) 3240-5305; internet www.rbs.com.br; f. 1957; major regional network; operates Canal Rural and TVCOM; Group Pres. NELSON PACHECO SIROTSKY.

TV Bandeirantes: Rádio e Televisão Bandeirantes Ltda, Rua Radiantes 13, Morumbi, 05699-900 São Paulo, SP; tel. (11) 3742-3011; fax (11) 3745-7622; e-mail cat@band.com.br; internet www.band.com.br; 65 TV stations and repeaters throughout Brazil; Pres. JOÃO CARLOS SAAD.

TV Brasil Internacional (TVBI): CP 08840, 70312-970 Brasília, DF; tel. (61) 3799-5889; fax (61) 3799-5888; e-mail tvbrasilinternacional@ebc.com.br; internet www.tvbrasil.ebc.com.br/internacional; f. 2010; owned by Empresa Brasil de Comunicação (EBC); broadcasts internationally via satellite in Portuguese; Dir-Gen. NELSON BREVE; Exec. Advisor MAX GONÇALVES.

TV Nacional/TV Brasil (Canal 2): Rua da Relação 18, Lapa, 20231-110 Rio de Janeiro, RJ; tel. (21) 2117-6208; e-mail sap@tvbrasil.org.br; internet www.tvbrasil.org.br; public tv station; broadcasts to the Federal District and surrounding areas; operated by Empresa Brasil de Comunicação (EBC); Dir-Gen. PAULO RUFINO.

TV Record—Rádio e Televisão Record, SA: Rua de Bosque 1393, Barra Funda, 01136-001 São Paulo, SP; tel. (11) 3660-4761; fax (11) 3660-4756; e-mail tvrecord@rederecord.com.br; internet rederecord.r7.com; f. 1953; Dir JOÃO BATISTA RODRIGUES SILVA.

TV Rede Globo: Rua Lopes Quintas 303, Jardim Botânico, 22460-010 Rio de Janeiro, RJ; tel. (21) 2444-4725; fax (21) 2294-2092; e-mail cgcom-br@tvglobo.com.br; internet redeglobo.globo.com; f. 1965; 8 stations; national network; Dir ROBERTO IRINEU MARINHO.

TV SBT—Sistema Brasileira de Televisão—Canal 4 de São Paulo, SA: Av. Das Comunicações 4, Vila Jaraguá, Osasco, 06278-

905 São Paulo, SP; tel. (11) 7087-3000; fax (11) 7087-3509; internet www.sbt.com.br; 107 local TV channels; Pres. LUIZ SEBASTIÃO SANDOVAL.

Broadcasting Associations

Associação Brasileira de Emissoras de Rádio e Televisão (ABERT): Edif.Via Esplanada, SAF/SUL Quadra 02, Lote 04, Bloco D, Sala 101, 70770-600 Brasília, DF; tel. (61) 2104-4600; fax (61) 2104-4611; e-mail abert@abert.org.br; internet www.abert.org.br; f. 1962; Pres. EMANUEL SOARES CARNEIRO; Exec. Dir LUIS ROBERTO ANTONIK.

There are regional associations for Bahia, Ceará, Goiás, Minas Gerais, Rio Grande do Sul, Santa Catarina, São Paulo, Amazonas, Distrito Federal, Mato Grosso and Mato Grosso do Sul (combined), and Sergipe.

Finance

(cap. = capital; res = reserves; dep. = deposits; m. = million; brs = branches; amounts in reais, unless otherwise stated)

BANKING

Conselho Monetário Nacional (CMN): Setor Bancário Sul, Quadra 03, Bloco B, Edif. Sede do Banco do Brasil, 21° andar, 70074-900 Brasília, DF; tel. (61) 3414-1945; fax (61) 3414-2528; e-mail cmn@bcb.gov.br; f. 1964 to formulate monetary policy and to supervise the banking system; Pres. GUIDO MANTEGA (Minister of Finance).

Central Bank

Banco Central do Brasil: SBS, Quadra 03, Mezanino 01, Bloco B, 70074-900 Brasília, DF; tel. (61) 3414-1414; fax (61) 3223-1033; e-mail secre.surel@bcb.gov.br; internet www.bcb.gov.br; f. 1965; est. to execute the decisions of the Conselho Monetário Nacional; bank of issue; total assets 1,157,596.2m. (Dec. 2009); Gov. ALEXANDRE TOMBINI; 10 brs.

State Commercial Banks

Banco do Brasil, SA: SBS, Quadra 01, Bloco C, Lote 32, Edif. Sede III, 70073-901 Brasília, DF; tel. (61) 3102-1124; fax (61) 3102-1435; e-mail ri@bb.com.br; internet www.bb.com.br; f. 1808; cap. 33,077.9m., res 17,362.6m., dep. 384,625.1m. (Dec. 2010); Pres. and Vice-Chair. ALDEMIR BENDINE.

Banco do Estado do Pará: Edif. Banpará, 4° andar, Av. Presidente Vargas 251, Campina, 66010-000 Belém, PA; tel. (91) 3210-3233; fax (91) 3241-7163; internet www.banparanet.com.br; f. 1961; cap. 105.8m., res 158.2m., dep. 1,639.5m. (Dec. 2010); Pres. AUGUSTO SÉRGIO AMORIM COSTA; 24 brs.

Banco do Estado do Rio Grande do Sul, SA (Banrisul): Rua Caldas Junior 108, 7° andar, 90018-900 Porto Alegre, RS; tel. (51) 3215-2501; fax (51) 3215-1715; e-mail cambio_dg@banrisul.com.br; internet www.banrisul.com.br; f. 1928; cap. 2,900m., res 955.2m., dep. 20,543.8m. (Dec. 2010); Pres. TÚLIO LUIZ ZAMIN; 352 brs.

Banco do Nordeste do Brasil, SA: Av. Pedro Ramalho 5700, Passaré, 60740-000 Fortaleza, CE; tel. (85) 3299-3000; fax (85) 3299-3674; e-mail info@banconordeste.gov.br; internet www.banconordeste.gov.br; f. 1952; cap. 1,851m., res 326.3m., dep. 9,064.2m. (Dec. 2010); Pres. JURANDIR SANTIAGO; 186 brs.

BANESTES, SA—Banco do Estado do Espirito Santo: Edif. Palas Center, Bloco B, 9° andar, Av. Princesa Isabel 574, Centro, 29010-931 Espirito Santo, ES; tel. (27) 3383-1545; fax (27) 3383-1398; e-mail ri@banestes.com.br; internet www.banestes.com.br; f. 1937; cap. 436.3m., res 353.6m., dep. 7,751.2m. (Dec. 2010); CEO BRUNO PESSANHA NEGRIS.

Private Banks

Banco ABC Brasil, SA: Av. Juscelino Kubitschek 1400, 3°–5° andares, 04543-000 São Paulo, SP; tel. (11) 3170-2000; fax (11) 3170-2001; e-mail sac.abcbrasil@abcbrasil.com.br; internet www.abcbrasil.com.br; f. 1989 as Banco ABC—Roma SA; 84% owned by Arab Banking Corpn BSC (Bahrain); cap. 1,004.4m., res 343.5m., dep. 3,721.8m. (Dec. 2010); Pres. and Gen. Man. TITO ENRIQUE DA SILVA NETO; 4 brs.

Banco Alfa de Investimento, SA: Alameda Santos 466, Cerqueira César, 01418-000 Paraíso, SP; tel. (11) 3175-5074; fax (11) 3171-2438; e-mail alfanet@alfanet.com.br; internet www.alfanet.com.br; f. 1998; cap. 446m., res 591.9m., dep. 3,386.7m. (Dec. 2010); Pres. PAULO GUIHERME MONTEIRO LOBATO RIBEIRO; 12 brs.

Banco da Amazônia, SA: Av. Presidente Vargas 800, 3° andar, 66017-000 Belém, PA; tel. (91) 4008-3421; fax (91) 4008-3243; e-mail cambio@bancoamazionia.com.br; internet www.bancoamazonia.com.br; f. 1942; state-owned; cap. 1,219.6m., res 713.9m., dep. 2,344.7m. (Dec. 2010); Pres. ABIDIAS JOSÉ DE SOUZA JÚNIOR; 104 brs.

Banco BBM, SA: Av. Tancredo Neves 1632, Caminho das Arvores, 41820-020 Salvador, BA; tel. (71) 4009-6000; fax (71) 4009-6001; internet www.bancobbm.com.br; f. 1858; est. as Banco de Bahia; present name adopted 1998; cap. 487.8m., dep. 465.4m. (Dec. 2010), res 244.7m. (Dec. 2009); Pres. PEDRO HENRIQUE MARIANI BITTENCOURT; 6 brs.

Banco BMG, SA: Av. Alvares Cabral 1707, Santo Agostinho, 30170-001 Belo Horizonte, MG; tel. (31) 3290-3000; fax (31) 3290-3100; e-mail bancobmg@bancobmg.com.br; internet www.bancobmg.com.br; f. 1930; cap. 1,399.7m., res 937.1m., dep.5,625.4m. (Dec. 2010); Pres. FLÁVIO PENTAGNA GUIMARÃES; 14 brs.

Banco Bradesco, SA: Cidade de Deus, Vila Yara, 06029-900 Osasco, SP; tel. (11) 3684-4011; fax (11) 3684-4630; internet www.bradesco.com.br; f. 1943; est. as Banco Brasileiro de Descontos; present name adopted 1989; cap. 30,000m., res 18,042.8m., dep. 334,619.5m. (Dec. 2010); Chair. LÁZARO DE MELLO BRANDÃO; CEO LUIZ CARLOS TRABUCO CAPPI; 3,628 brs.

Banco Brascan, SA: Av. Almirante Barroso 52, 30° andar, Centro, 20031-000 Rio de Janeiro, RJ; tel. (21) 3231-3000; fax (21) 3231-3231; internet www.bancobrascan.com.br; f. 1968; cap. 169.0m., res 20.8m., dep. 228m. (Dec. 2010); Pres. VALDECYR GOMES.

Banco BTG Pactual, SA: Torre Corcovado, 6°, Praia de Botafago 501, 22250-040 Rio de Janeiro, RJ; tel. (21) 3262-9600; fax (21) 2514-8600; internet www.btgpactual.com; f. 1983; fmrly Banco UBS Pactual; present name adopted 2008 following acquisition by BTG Pactual; cap. 2,971.3m., res 2,631.2m., dep. 52,537.9m. (Dec. 2010); Pres. ANDRÉ ESTEVES; 5 brs.

Banco Dibens, SA: Rua Boa Vista 162, 6° andar, Centro, 01014-000 São Paulo, SP; tel. (11) 5019-8101; fax (11) 5019-8103; internet www.dibens.com.br; f. 1989; jtly owned by UNIBANCO and Grupo Verdi; cap. 179.2m., res 23.6m., dep. 1,420.3m. (Dec. 2005); Pres. CARLOS HENRIQUE ZANVETTOR; 23 brs.

Banco Fibra: Av. Presidente Juscelino Kubitschek 360, 4°–9° andares, 04543-000 São Paulo, SP; tel. (11) 3847-6700; fax (11) 3847-6962; e-mail bancofibra@bancofibra.com.br; internet www.bancofibra.com.br; f. 1989; cap. 806.4m., res –12.0m., dep. 6,169.3m. (Dec. 2010); CEO ANTONIO DE LIMA NETO.

Banco Finasa BMC, SA: Av. das Nações Unidas 12995, 25° andar, 04578-000 São Paulo, SP; tel. (11) 5503-7711; fax (11) 3523-0037; internet www.bradescopromotora.com.br; f. 1939; est. as Banco Mercantil de Crédito, SA; renamed Banco BMC SA in 1990; adopted current name in 2008 after merger with Bank Finasa; owned by Banco Bradesco; cap. 22,010.0m., res 536.1m., dep. 37,976.0m. (Dec. 2008); Pres. LÁZARO DE MELLO BRANDÃO.

Banco Industrial do Brasil: Av. Juscelino Kubitschek 1703, 2°–4° andares, Itaim Bibi, 04543-000 São Paulo, SP; tel. (11) 3049-9671; fax (11) 3049-9810; internet www.bancoindustrial.com.br; f. 1994; cap. 360.5m., res 47m., dep. 1,157m. (Dec. 2010); Pres. CARLOS ALBERTO MANSUR.

Banco Industrial e Comercial, SA (Bicbanco): Av. Paulista 1048, Bela Vista, 01310-100 São Paulo, SP; tel. (11) 2173-9000; fax (11) 2173-9101; internet www.bicbanco.com.br; f. 1938; cap. 1,434.2m., res 255.0m., dep. 5,600.3m. (Dec. 2008); Pres. JOSÉ BEZERRA DE MENEZES; 30 brs.

Banco Indusval, SA (Banco Indusval Multistock): Rua Boa Vista, 7°–12° andares, Centro, 01014-000 São Paulo, SP; tel. (11) 3315-6777; fax (11) 3315-0130; e-mail banco@indusval.com.br; internet www.indusval.com.br; f. 1980; cap. 370.9m., res 55.4m., dep. 1,501.5m. (Dec. 2010); Pres. MANOEL FELIX CINTRA NETO.

Banco Itaú BBA, SA: Av. Brig. Faria Lima 3400, 3° ao 8° andar, 04538-132 São Paulo, SP; tel. (11) 3708-8000; fax (11) 3708-8172; e-mail bancoitaubba@itaubba.com.br; internet www.itaubba.com.br; f. 1967; est. as Banco do Estado de Minas Gerais, SA; acquired by Banco Itaú in 2002; present name adopted 2004; cap. 4,224m., res 2,162.5m., dep. 92,474m. (Dec. 2010); Pres. and CEO CANDIDO BOTELHO BRACHER; 6 brs.

Banco Mercantil do Brasil, SA: Rua Rio de Janerio 680, Centro, 30160-912 Belo Horizonte, MG; tel. (31) 3057-4450; fax (31) 3079-8422; e-mail sac@mercantil.com.br; internet www.mercantil.com.br; f. 1943; est. as Banco Mercantil de Minas Gerais, SA; cap. 332.7m., res 340.4m., dep. 6,825.7m. (Dec. 2010); Pres. MILTON DE ARAÚJO; 171 brs.

Banco Paulista, SA: Av. Brigadeiro Faria Lima, 1355 Jardim Paulistano, 2° andar, 01452-002 São Paulo, SP; tel. (11) 3299-2000; fax (11) 3299-2362; e-mail cambiobp@bancopaulista.com.br; internet www.bancopaulista.com.br; f. 1989; cap. 107.0m., res 2.4m., dep. 727.9m. (Dec. 2010); Pres. ALVARO AUGUSTO VIDIGAL.

Banco de Pernambuco, SA (Bandepe): Edif. Bandepe, 5° andar, Cais do Apolo 222, Bairro do Recife, 50030-230 Recife, PE; tel. (11) 3174-9957; fax (11) 3174-7101; internet www.bandepe.com.br; f. 1938; est. as Banco do Estado de Pernambuco; present name adopted 2000; owned by Grupo Santander Brasil; cap. 2,768.4m., res 150.3m., dep. 1,095.8m. (Dec. 2005); Pres. JOSE DE MENEZES BERENGUER NETO; 66 brs.

Banco Pine, SA: Eldorado Business Tower, Av. das Nações Unidas 8501, 30° andar, 05425-070 São Paulo, SP; tel. (11) 3372-5200; fax (11) 3372-5404; e-mail bancopine@uol.com.br; internet www.bancopine.com.br; f. 1997; cap. 422.6m., res 432.6m., dep. 6,094.5m. (Dec. 2010); Chair. NORBERTO NOGUEIRA PINHEIRO.

Banco Real, SA: Av. Brigadeiro Luís Antônio 1824, 9° andar, 01317-002 Bela Vista, SP; tel. (11) 3174-9615; fax (11) 3174-7052; internet www.bancoreal.com.br; f. 1925; acquired by Grupo Santander (Spain) in 2008; cap. 7,593.7m., res 2,092.0m., dep. 73,754.7m. (Dec. 2006); 847 brs.

Banco Rural, SA: Rua Rio de Janeiro 927, 14º andar, 30160-041 Belo Horizonte, MG; tel. (31) 2126-5000; fax (31) 2126-5096; e-mail rural002@rural.com.br; internet www.bancorural.com.br; f. 1964; est. as Banco Rural de Minas Gerais; present name adopted 1980; cap. 368m., res 77.3m., dep. 3,115.4m. (Dec. 2010); Pres. PLAUTO GOUVÊA; 22 brs.

Banco Safra, SA: Av. Paulista 2100, 9° andar, 01310-930 São Paulo, SP; tel. (11) 3175-7309; fax (11) 3175-8466; internet www.safra.com.br; f. 1940; cap. 2,245.4m., res 3,368.2m., dep. 39,502.1m. (Dec. 2010); Pres. CARLOS ALBERTO VIEIRA; 98 brs.

Banco Santander, SA: Av. Presidente Juscelino Kubitschek, 2041 Vila Olimpia, 04543-011 São Paulo, SP; tel. (11) 3553-5447; fax (11) 3553-7778; internet www.santander.com.br; f. 2006; est. as Banco Santander Banespa, SA by merger; present name adopted 2007; owned by Banco Santander, SA (Spain); cap. 62,828.2m., res 2,022.7m., dep. 128,475.7m. (Dec. 2010); Pres. FABIO COLLETTI BARBOSA.

Banco Société Générale Brasil, SA: Av. Paulista 2300, 9° andar, Cerqueira Cesar, 01310-300 São Paulo, SP; tel. (11) 3217-8000; fax (11) 3217-8090; e-mail faleconosco@sgcib.com; internet www.sgbrasil.com.br; f. 1981; est. as Banco Sogeral; present name adopted 2001; cap. 1,404.9m., res 24.4m., dep. 2,181.9m. (Dec. 2009); Pres. FRANÇOIS DOSSA.

Banco Votorantim, SA: Av. das Nações Unidas 14171, Torre A, 18° andar, Vila Gertrudes, 04794-000 São Paulo, SP; tel. (11) 5171-1000; fax (11) 5171-1900; e-mail sac@bancovotorantim.com.br; internet www.bancovotorantim.com.br; f. 1991; cap. 4,026.8m., res 4,362m., dep. 23,630.4m. (Dec. 2010); Pres. WILSON MASAO KUZUHARA.

Banif—Banco Internacional do Funchal (Brasil), SA: Rua Minas de Prata 30, 16°–17° andares, 04552-080 São Paulo, SP; tel. (11) 3165-2000; fax (11) 3167-3960; e-mail bc_matriz@bancobanif.com.br; internet www.bancobanif.com.br; f. 1999 as Banco Banif Primus, SA; present name adopted 2005; owned by Banif Comercial SGPS, SA (Portugal); cap. 173.4m., res 3.2m., dep. 1,192.1m. (Dec. 2010); Pres. ANTONIO JÚLIO MACHADO RODRIGUES.

Itaú Unibanco Holding, SA: Praça Alfredo Egydio de Souza Aranha 100, Torre Itaúsa, 04344-902 São Paulo, SP; tel. (11) 5019-8101; fax (11) 5019-8103; e-mail investor.relations@itau-unibanco.com.br; internet www.itau.com.br; f. 1944; est. as Banco Central de Crédito; renamed Banco Itaú, SA in 1973; named changed as above in 2008 following merger with Unibanco; cap. 40,175.0m., res 406.0m., dep. 366,234.3m. (Dec. 2008); Pres. and CEO ROBERTO SETUBAL; 3,044 brs.

Development Banks

Banco de Desenvolvimento de Minas Gerais, SA (BDMG): Rua da Bahia 1600, 30160-907 Belo Horizonte, MG; tel. (31) 3219-8000; fax (31) 3226-3292; internet www.bdmg.mg.gov.br; f. 1962; owned by the state of Minas Gerais; long-term credit operations; cap. 1,003.2m., res 20m., total assets 2,345.6m. (Dec. 2010); Pres. PAULO DE TARSO ALMEIDA PAIVA.

Banco Nacional do Desenvolvimento Econômico e Social (BNDES): Av. República do Chile 100, Centro, 20031-917 Rio de Janeiro, RJ; tel. (21) 2172-7447; fax (21) 2172-6266; e-mail gerai@bndes.gov.br; internet www.bndes.gov.br; f. 1952 to act as main instrument for financing of govt devt schemes and to support programmes for the devt of the national economy; socio-environmental devt and the modernization of public administration; cap. 20,260.8m., res 7,367.1m., dep. 50,530.3m. (Dec. 2009); Chair. LUCIANO COUTINHO.

Investment Bank

Banco Fininvest, SA: Rua da Passagem 170, 7° andar, 20030-021 Rio de Janeiro, RJ; tel. (21) 3097-4725; fax (21) 3820-5323; internet www.fininvest.com.br; f. 1961 as Fininvest SA Crédito Financiamento e Investimento; present name adopted 1989; owned by Unibanco; cap. 3,165.8m., res 674.7m., dep. 937.7m. (Dec. 2008); Pres. ALVARO OSÓRIO LONGO MUSA DOS SANTOS.

State-owned Savings Bank

Caixa Econômica Federal: SBS, Quadra 04, Lotes 3–4, 16° andar, 70092-900 Brasília, DF; tel. (61) 3206-3171; fax (61) 3206-9732; e-mail genit@caixa.gov.br; internet www.caixa.gov.br; f. 1861; cap. 12,473.7m., res 2,963.2m., dep. 261,561.2m. (Dec. 2010); Pres. JORGE FONTES HEREDA; 2,500 brs.

Foreign Banks

Banco Sumitomo Mitsui Brasileiro, SA: Av. Paulista 37, 11° andar, Paraiso, 01311-902 São Paulo, SP; tel. (11) 3178-8000; fax (11) 3178-8194; internet www.smbcgroup.com.br; f. 1958; present name adopted 2001; cap. 667.8m., res 11.8m., dep. 786.2m. (Dec. 2010); Pres. TERUHISA KONISHI; 1 br.

Banco de Tokyo-Mitsubishi UFJ Brasil, SA: Av. Paulista 1274, Bela Vista, 01310-925 São Paulo, SP; tel. (11) 3268-0211; fax (11) 3268-0453; internet www.br.bk.mufg.jp; f. 1972 as Banco de Tokyo; cap. 186.9m., res 118.7m., dep. 493.3m. (Dec. 2010); Pres. TOSHIFUMI MURATA; 2 brs.

Deutsche Bank SA—Banco Alemão: Av. Brigadeiro Faria Lima 3900, 13–15° andares, Itaim Bibi, 04598-132 São Paulo, SP; tel. (11) 2113-5000; fax (11) 2113-5100; internet www.deutsche-bank.com.br; f. 1911; cap. 415.2m., res 575.3m., dep. 4,613.8m. (Dec. 2010); Pres. BERNANDO PARNES.

HSBC Bank Brasil SA-Banco Multiplo: Edif. Palácio Avenida, 4° andar, Travessa Oliveira Belo 34, Centro, 80020-030 Curitiba, PR; tel. (41) 3321-6161; fax (41) 3321-6075; internet www.hsbc.com.br; f. 1997; cap. 5,211.3m., res 2,579.2m., dep. 77,765.9m. (Dec. 2010); Pres. BERNANDO PARNES; 939 brs.

Banking Associations

Associação Nacional dos Bancos de Investimentos (ANBID): Edif. Eldorado Business Tower, Av. das Nações Unidas 8501, 21° andar, 05425-070 São Paulo, SP; tel. (11) 3471-4200; fax (11) 3471-4230; e-mail anbid@anbid.com.br; internet www.anbid.com.br; investment banks; Pres. MARCELO FIDÊNCIO GIUFRIDA; Supt LUIZ KAUFMAN.

Federação Brasileira dos Bancos: Avda Brigadeiro Faria Lima 1485, 14° andar, Torre Norte, Pinheiros, 01452-921 São Paulo, SP; tel. (11) 3244-9800; fax (11) 3031-4106; e-mail imprensa@febraban.org.br; internet www.febraban.org.br; f. 1966; Pres. MURILO PORTUGAL; Dir-Gen. WILSON ROBERTO LEVORATO; 120 mems.

Sindicato dos Bancos dos Estados do Rio de Janeiro e Espírito Santo: Rua do Ouvidor 50, 20° andar, 20040-004 Rio de Janeiro, RJ; tel. (21) 2253-1538; fax (21) 2253-6032; e-mail aberj@aberj.com.br; internet www.aberj.com.br; f. 1935; Pres. CARLOS ALBERTO VIEIRA.

Sindicato dos Bancos dos Estados de São Paulo, Paraná, Mato Grosso e Mato Grosso do Sul: Rua Líbero Badaró 293, 13° andar, 01905 São Paulo, SP; f. 1924; Pres. PAULO DE QUEIROZ.

There are other banking associations in Maceió, Salvador, Fortaleza, Belo Horizonte, João Pessoa, Recife and Porto Alegre.

STOCK EXCHANGES

Comissão de Valores Mobiliários (CVM): Rua 7 de Setembro 111, Centro, 20050-901 Rio de Janeiro, RJ; tel. (21) 3554-8686; fax (21) 3554-8211; e-mail ouvidor@cvm.gov.br; internet www.cvm.gov.br; f. 1977 to supervise the operations of the stock exchanges and develop the Brazilian securities market; regional offices in Brasília and São Paulo; Chair. MARIA HELENA DOS SANTOS FERNANDES DE SANTANA.

BM&F BOVESPA, SA: Praça Antônio Prado 48, Rua XV e Novembro, 275 Centro, 01010-901 São Paulo, SP; tel. (11) 2565-4000; e-mail ri@bmfbovespa.com.br; internet www.bmfbovespa.com.br; f. 2008 by merger of Bolsa de Mercadorias e Futuros (BM&F—Mercantile and Futures Exchange) and Bolsa de Valores de São Paulo (BOVESPA—São Paulo Stock Exchange); offices in Brasília, Rio de Janeiro, Porto Alegre, Campo Grande, Santos, New York (USA) and Shanghai (People's Republic of China); Pres. ARMENIO FRAGA NETO; CEO EDEMIR PINTO.

There are commodity exchanges at Paraná, Porto Alegre, Vitória, Recife, Santos and São Paulo.

INSURANCE

Supervisory Authorities

Conselho de Recursos do Sistema Nacional de Seguros Privados, de Previdência Abierta e de Capitalização (CRSNSP): Av. Presidente Vargas 730, 20071-900 Rio de Janeiro, RJ; tel. (21) 3233-4115; internet www.fazenda.gov.br/portugues/orgaos/crsnsp/crsnsp.html; f. 1966 as Conselho Nacional de Seguros Privados (CNSP); changed name in 1998; part of the Ministry of Finance; Pres. FRANCISCO TEIXEIRA DE ALMEIDA; Sec. THERESA CHRISTINA CUNHA MARTINS.

Superintendência de Seguros Privados (SUSEP): Av. Presidente Vargas, 730 Centro, 20071-900 Rio de Janeiro, RJ; tel. (21) 3233-4000; e-mail gabinete.rj@susep.gov.br; internet www.susep.gov.br; f. 1966; part of the Ministry of Finance; offices in Brasília, São Paulo and Porto Alegre; Pres. GUIDO MANTEGA (Minister of Finance); Supt PAULO DOS SANTOS.

Principal Companies

The following is a list of the principal national insurance companies, selected on the basis of assets. The total assets of insurance companies operating in Brazil were R $283,040m. in May 2011.

Bradesco Seguros e Previdência, SA: Rua Barão de Itapagipe 225, 20261-901 Rio de Janeiro, RJ; tel. (21) 2503-1101; fax (21) 2293-9489; internet www.bradescoseguros.com.br; f. 1934; general; Pres. MARCO ANTONIO ROSSI.

Bradesco Vida e Previdência, SA: Cidade de Deus s/n, Vila Yara, São Paulo, SP; tel. (11) 3684-2122; fax (11) 3684-5068; internet www.bradescoprevidencia.com.br; f. 2001; life insurance; Pres. LÚCIO FLÁVIO DE OLIVEIRA.

Brasilprev Seguros e Prevedência, SA: Rua Alexandre Dumas 1671, 04717-004 São Paulo, SP; tel. (11) 5185-4240; e-mail atendimento@brasilprev.com.br; internet www.brasilprev.com.br; f. 1993; all classes; 50% owned by Banco do Brasil; Pres. SÉRGIO ROSA.

Caixa Seguros: Edif. No 1, 15° andar, SCN Quadra 01, Bloco A, Asa Norte, 70711-900 Brasília, DF; tel. (61) 2192-2400; fax (61) 3328-0600; internet www.caixaseguros.com.br; f. 1967; fmrly Sasse, Cia Nacional de Seguros; adopted current name 2000; general; Pres. THIERRY MARC CLAUDE CLAUDON.

Caixa Vida e Previdência, SA: Edif. Numero 1, 13° andar, SCN Quadra 1, Bloco A, 70711-900 Brasília, DF; tel. (61) 2192-2400; fax (61) 3328-0600; internet www.caixavidaeprevidencia.com.br; part of Caixa Seguros group; Dir JUVÊNCIO CAVALCANTE BRAGA.

Cia de Seguros Aliança do Brasil, SA (BB Seguros): Rua Manuel da Nóbrega 1280, 9° andar, 04001-004 São Paulo, SP; tel. (11) 4689-5638; e-mail imprensa@aliancadobrasil.com.br; internet www.aliancadobrasil.com.br; f. 1996; Pres. ROBERTO BARROSO.

HSBC Vida e Previdência (Brasil), SA: Rua Teniente Francisco Ferreira de Souza 805, Bloco 1, Ala 4, Vila Hauer, 81630-010 Curitaba, PR; tel. (41) 3777-4400; fax (41) 3523-2320; e-mail spariz@hsbc.com.vr; internet www.hsbc.com.br; f. 1938; all classes; Supt Dir FERNANDO ALVES MOREIRA.

Icatu Hartford Seguros, SA: Praça 22 de Abril 36, 20021-370 Rio de Janeiro, RJ; tel. (21) 3824-3900; fax 3824-6678; e-mail atendimento_internet@icatuseguros.com.br; internet www.icatuseguros.com.br; Pres. MARIA SILVIA BASTOS MARQUES.

IRB-Brasil Resseguros: Av. Marechal Câmara 171, Castelo, 20020-901 Rio de Janeiro, RJ; tel. (21) 2272-0200; fax (21) 2272-2800; e-mail info@irb-brasilre.com.br; internet www.irb-brasilre.com.br; f. 1939; state-owned reinsurance co; fmrly Instituto de Resseguros do Brasil; Pres. LEONARDO ANDRÉ PAIXÃO.

Itaú Seguros, SA: Praça Alfredo Egydio de Souza Aranha 100, Bloco A, 04344-920 São Paulo, SP; tel. (11) 5019-3322; fax (11) 5019-3530; e-mail itauseguros@itauseguros.com.br; internet www.itauseguros.com.br; f. 1921; all classes; Pres. ROBERTO EGYDIO SETUBAL; Supt MARCOS DE BARROS LISBOA.

Liberty Seguros, SA: Rua Dr Geraldo Campos Moreira 110, 04571-020 São Paulo, SP; tel. (11) 5503-4000; fax (11) 5505-2122; internet www.libertyseguros.com.br; f. 1906; general; Pres. LUIS EMILIO MAURETTE.

Marítima Seguros, SA: Rua Col Xavier de Toledo 114 e 140, 10° andar, São Paulo, SP; tel. (11) 3156-1000; fax (11) 3156-1712; internet www.maritima.com.br; f. 1943; Pres. FRANCISCO CAIUBY VIDIGAL; Exec. Dir MARIO JORGE PEREIRA.

Porto Seguro Cia de Seguros Gerais: Rua Guaianazes 1238, 12° andar, Campos Elíseos, 01204-001 São Paulo, SP; tel. (11) 3366-5963; fax (11) 3366-5175; internet www.portoseguro.com.br; f. 1945; life, automotive and risk; Pres. JAYME BRASIL GARFINKEL.

Santander Seguros, SA: internet www.santander.com.br; part of Banco Santander.

Sul América Cía Nacional de Seguros, SA: Rua da Beatriz Larragoiti Lucas 121, Cidade Nova, 20211-903 Rio de Janeiro, RJ; tel. (21) 2506-8585; fax (21) 2506-8807; internet www.sulamerica.com.br; f. 1895; life and risk; Chair. PATRICK ANTONIO DE LARRAGOITI LUCAS; CEO THOMAZ LUIZ CABRAL DE MENEZES.

Tokio Marine Seguradora, SA: Rua Samapiao Viana 44, 04004-902 Paraíso, SP; tel. (11) 3054-7000; internet www.tokiomarine.com.br; f. 1969 as Real Seguros, SA; adopted current name 2008; owned by Tokio Marine Holdings (Japan); general; Pres. AKIRA HARASHIMA.

Insurance Associations

Confederação Nacional das Empresas de Seguros Gerais, Previdência Privada e Vida, Saúde Suplementar e Capitalização (CNseg): Rua Senador Dantas 74, 12° andar, Centro, 20031-205 Rio de Janeiro, RJ; tel. (21) 2510-7777; e-mail suporte@cnseg.org.br; internet www.viverseguro.org.br; f. 1951 as Federação Nacional das Empresas de Seguros Privados e de Capitalização; reformulated as above 2008; four subordinate feds; Pres. JORGE HILÁRIO GOUVÊA VIEIRA.

Federação Nacional de Capitalização (FenaCap): Pres. PAULO ROGÉRIO CAFFARELLI.

Federação Nacional de Previdência Privada e Vida (FenaPrevi): Pres. MARCO ANTONIO ROSSI.

Federação Nacional de Saúde Suplementar (FenaSaúde): Pres. MARCIO SERÔA DE ARAUJO CORIOLANO.

Federação Nacional de Seguros Gerais (FenSeg): Pres. JAYME BRASIL GARFINKEL.

Federação Nacional dos Corretores de Seguros Privados e de Resseguros, de Capitalização, de Previdência Privada e das Empresas Corretoras de Seguros e de Resseguros (FENACOR): Rua Senador Dantas 74, 10° andar, 20031-205 Rio de Janeiro, RJ; tel. (21) 3077-4777; fax (21) 3077-4799; e-mail presidencia@fenacor.com.br; internet www.fenacor.com.br; f. 1975; Pres. ARMANDO VERGÍLIO DOS SANTOS, Jr.

Trade and Industry

GOVERNMENT AGENCIES

Agência Nacional de Petróleo, Gás Natural e Biocombustíveis (ANP): Av. Rio Branco 65, 12° andar, 20090-004 Rio de Janeiro, RJ; tel. (21) 2112-8100; fax (21) 2112-8129; internet www.anp.gov.br; f. 1998; regulatory body of the petroleum, natural gas and biofuels industries; Dir-Gen. HAROLDO BORGES RODRIGUES LIMA.

Agência de Promoção de Exportações do Brasil (APEX Brasil): Edif. Apex-Brasil, SBN, Quadra 02, Lote 11, 70040-020 Brasília, DF; tel. (61) 3426-0202; fax (61) 3426-0263; e-mail apex@apexbrasil.com.br; internet www.apexbrasil.com.br; f. 2003; promotes Brazilian exports; CEO MAURICIO BORGES.

Câmara de Comércio Exterior (CAMEX): Ministério do Desenvolvimento, Indústria e Comércio Exterior, Bloco J, 70053-900 Brasília, DF; tel. (61) 2109-7483; e-mail camex@desenvolvimento.gov.br; internet www.desenvolvimento.gov.br; f. 2003; part of Ministry of Development, Industry and Foreign Trade; formulates and co-ordinates export policies; Exec. Sec. EMILIO GAROFALO.

Companhia de Pesquisa de Recursos Minerais (CPRM): Av. SGAN, Quadra 603, Conj. J, Parte A, 1° andar, 70830-030 Brasília, DF; tel. (61) 2192-8252; fax (61) 3224-1616; e-mail cprmsede@df.cprm.gov.br; internet www.cprm.gov.br; mining research, attached to the Ministry of Mines and Energy; regional offices in Belém, Belo Horizonte, Goiânia, Manaus, Porto Alegre, Recife, Salvador and São Paulo; Pres. CLAUDIO SCLIAR; Exec. Dir MANOEL BARRETTO DA ROCHA NETO.

Conselho Nacional de Desenvolvimento Científico e Tecnológico (CNPq): Edif. Sede CNPq, 3° andar, Sala 300, SEPN 507, Bloco B, 70740-901 Brasília, DF; tel. (61) 2108-9000; fax (61) 2108-9394; e-mail presidencia@cnpq.br; internet www.cnpq.br; f. 1951; scientific and technological development council; Pres. GLAUCIUS OLIVA.

Conselho Nacional de Desenvolvimento Rural Sustentável (CONDRAF): Edif. Palácio do Desenvolvimento, 8° andar, SBN, Quadra 01, Bloco D, 70057-900 Brasília, DF; tel. (61) 2191-9880; e-mail condraf@mda.gov.br; internet sistemas.mda.gov.br/condraf; f. 2000 to promote sustainable rural development; Pres. AFONSO BANDEIRA FLORENCE (Minister of Agrarian Development).

Departamento Nacional da Produção Mineral (DNPM): SAN, Quadra 1, Bloco B, 3° andar, 70041-903 Brasília, DF; tel. (61) 3312-6666; fax (61) 3225-8274; e-mail dire@dnpm.gov.br; internet www.dnpm.gov.br; f. 1934; responsible for geological studies and control of exploration of mineral resources; part of Ministry of Mines and Energy; Dir-Gen. SÉRGIO AUGUSTO DÂMASO DE SOUSA.

Empresa Brasileira de Pesquisa Agropecuária (EMBRAPA): Edif. Sede, Parque Estação Biológica (PqEB) s/n, Av. W3 Norte (final), CP 40315, 70770-901 Brasília, DF; tel. (61) 3448-4433; fax (61) 3448-4890; e-mail presid@sede.embrapa.br; internet www.embrapa.br; f. 1973; attached to the Ministry of Agriculture and Food Supply; agricultural research; Pres. PEDRO ANTONIO ARRAES PEREIRA.

Instituto Brasileiro de Geografia e Estatística (IBGE): Av. Franklin Roosevelt 166, 10° andar, Castelo, 20271-201 Rio de Janeiro, RJ; tel. (21) 2142-4503; fax (21) 2142-4933; e-mail ibge@ibge.gov.br; internet www.ibge.gov.br; f. 1936; produces and analyses statistical, geographical, cartographic, geodetic, demographic and socio-economic information; Pres. (IBGE) EDUARDO PEREIRA NUNES; Exec. Dir SÉRGIO DA COSTA CÔRTES.

Instituto Brasileiro do Meio Ambiente e Recursos Naturais Renováveis (IBAMA): Edif. Sede IBAMA, SCEN Trecho 2, 70818-900 Brasília, DF; tel. (61) 3316-1001; fax (61) 3226-1025; e-mail presid.sede@ibama.gov.br; internet www.ibama.gov.br; f. 1989; responsible for the annual formulation of national environmental plans; authorizes environmentally sensitive devt projects; Pres. CURT TRENNEPOHL.

Instituto Nacional de Colonização e Reforma Agraria (INCRA): Edif. Palácio do Desenvolvimento, SBN, Quadra 01, Bloco D, 70057-900 Brasília, DF; tel. (61) 3411-7474; fax (61) 3411-7404; e-mail publico@incra.gov.br; internet www.incra.gov.br; f. 1970; land reform agency; Pres. CELSO LISBOA DE LACERDA.

Instituto Nacional de Metrologia, Normalização e Qualidade Industrial (INMETRO): Rua Santa Alexandrina 416, 10° andar, Rio Comprido, 20261-232 Rio de Janeiro, RJ; tel. (21) 2563-2800; fax (21) 2563-2970; e-mail caint@inmetro.gov.br; internet www.inmetro.gov.br; f. 1973; part of Ministry of Development, Industry and Foreign Trade; Pres. JOÃO ALZIRO HERZ DA JORNADA.

Instituto Nacional da Propriedade Industrial (INPI): Praça Mauá 7, 18° andar, Centro, 20081-240 Rio de Janeiro, RJ; tel. (21) 2139-3000; fax (21) 2263-2539; e-mail inpipres@inpi.gov.br; internet www.inpi.gov.br; f. 1970; part of Ministry of Development, Industry and Foreign Trade; intellectual property, etc.; Pres. JORGE DE PAULA COSTA ÁVILA.

Instituto de Pesquisa Econômica Aplicada (IPEA): Av. Presidente Antônio Carlos 51, 15° andar, 20020-010 Rio de Janeiro, RJ; tel. (21) 3804-8000; fax (21) 2240-1920; e-mail faleconosco@ipea.gov.br; internet www.ipea.gov.br; also has an office in Brasília; f. 1970; economics and planning institute; Pres. MARCIO POCHMANN.

REGIONAL DEVELOPMENT ORGANIZATIONS

Companhia de Desenvolvimento dos Vales do São Francisco e do Parnaíba (CODEVASF): Edif. Manoel Novaes, SGAN, Quadra 601, Conj. 1, 70830-901 Brasília, DF; tel. (61) 3312-4611; fax (61) 3312-4680; e-mail orlandoc@codevasf.gov.br; internet www.codevasf.gov.br; f. 1974; promotes integrated development of resources of São Francisco and Parnaíba Valley; part of Ministry of National Integration; Pres. CLEMENTINO DE SOUZA COELHO.

Superintendência do Desenvolvimento da Amazônia (SUDAM): Av. Almirante Barroso 426, Marco, 66090-900 Belém, PA; tel. (91) 4008-5442; fax (91) 4008-5456; e-mail gabinete@ada.gov.br; internet www.ada.gov.br; f. 2001 to co-ordinate the devt of resources in Amazon region; Dir-Gen. DJALMA BEZERRA MELLO.

Superintendência de Desenvolvimento do Nordeste (SUDENE): Praça Ministro João Gonçalves de Souza s/n, Engenho do Meio, 50670-900 Recife, PE; tel. (81) 2102-2114; fax (81) 2102-2575; e-mail gabinete@sudene.gov.br; internet www.sudene.gov.br; f. 2007 to replace Agência de Desenvolvimento do Nordeste (f. 2001); Supt PAULO SÉRGIO DE NORONHA FONTANA.

Superintendência da Zona Franca de Manaus (SUFRAMA): Av. Ministro João Gonçalves de Souza s/n, Distrito Industrial, 69075-830 Manaus, AM; tel. (92) 3321-7000; fax (92) 3237-6549; e-mail cas@suframa.gov.br; internet www.suframa.gov.br; assists in the development of the Manaus Free Zone; Supt FLÁVIA SKROBOT BARBOSA GROSSO.

AGRICULTURAL, INDUSTRIAL AND TRADE ORGANIZATIONS

Associação Brasileira do Alumínio (ABAL): Rua Humberto I 220, 4° andar, Vila Mariana, 04018-030 São Paulo, SP; tel. (11) 5904-6450; fax (11) 5904-6459; e-mail aluminio@abal.org.br; internet www.abal.org.br; f. 1970; represents aluminium producing and processing cos; 66 mem. cos; Pres. ADJARMA AZEVEDO.

Associação Brasileira de Celulose e Papel—Bracelpa: Rua Olimpíadas, 66, 9° and Bairro Vl. Olímpia São Paulo, São Paulo, SP; tel. (11) 3018-7800; fax (11) 3018-7813; e-mail faleconosco@bracelpa.org.br; internet www.bracelpa.org.br; f. 1932; pulp and paper asscn; Exec. Dir ELIZABETH CARVALHAES.

Associação Brasileira das Indústrias de Óleos Vegetais (Abiove) (Brazilian Association of Vegetable Oil Industries): Av. Vereador José Diniz 3707, 7° andar, Conj. 73, 04603-004 São Paulo, SP; tel. (11) 5536-0733; fax (11) 5536-9816; e-mail abiove@abiove.com.br; internet www.abiove.com.br; f. 1981; 10 mem. cos; Pres. CARLO LOVATELLI.

Associação Brasileira dos Produtores de Algodão (ABRAPA): Edif. Antônio Ernesto de Salvo, Térreo, SGAN, Quadra 601, Lote K, 70830-903 Brasília, DF; tel. (61) 2109-1606; fax (61) 2109-1607; e-mail faleconosco@abrapa.com.br; internet www.abrapa.com.br; f. 1999; cotton producers' asscn; Pres. SÉRGIO DE MARCO.

Associação Comercial do Rio de Janeiro (ACRJ): Rua da Calendária 9, 11°–12° andares, Centro, 20091-020 Rio de Janeiro, RJ; tel. and fax (21) 2514-1229; e-mail acrj@acrj.org.br; internet www.acrj.org.br; f. 1820; Pres. ANTENOR BARROS LEAL.

Associação Comercial de São Paulo (ACSP): Rua Boa Vista 51, Centro, 01014-911 São Paulo, SP; tel. (11) 3244-3322; fax (11) 3244-3355; e-mail infocem@acsp.com.br; internet www.acsp.com.br; f. 1894; Pres. ROGÉRIO PINTO COELHO AMATO.

Associação de Comércio Exterior do Brasil (AEB) (Brazilian Foreign Trade Association): Av. General Justo 335, 4° andar, 20021-130 Rio de Janeiro, RJ; tel. (21) 2544-0048; fax (21) 2544-0577; e-mail aebbras@aeb.org.br; internet www.aeb.org.br; exporters' asscn; Pres. JOSÉ AUGUSTO DE CASTRO.

Associação Nacional dos Fabricantes de Veículos Automotores (ANFAVEA): Av. Indianópolis 496, 04062-900 São Paulo, SP; tel. (11) 2193-7800; fax (11) 2193-7825; internet www.anfavea.com.br; f. 1956; motor vehicle manufacturers' asscn; Pres. CLEDORVINO BELINI.

Centro das Indústrias do Estado de São Paulo (CIESP): Av. Paulista 1313, 01311-923 São Paulo, SP; tel. (11) 3549-3232; e-mail atendimento@ciesp.com.br; internet www.ciesp.org.br; f. 1928; asscn of small and medium-sized businesses; Pres. PAULO ANTONIO SKEF.

Confederação da Agricultura e Pecuária do Brasil (CNA): SGAN, Quadra 601, Modulo K, 70830-903 Brasília, DF; tel. (61) 2109-1400; fax (61) 2109-1490; e-mail cna@cna.org.br; internet www.canaldoprodutor.com.br; f. 1964; national agricultural confederation; Pres. KÁTIA REGINA DE ABREU.

Confederação Nacional do Comércio (CNC): Av. General Justo 307, 20021-130 Rio de Janeiro, RJ; tel. (21) 3804-9200; e-mail cncrj@cnc.com.br; internet www.portaldocomercio.org.br; national confederation comprising 35 affiliated federations of commerce; Pres. ANTÔNIO JOSÉ DOMINGUES DE OLIVEIRA SANTOS.

Confederação Nacional da Indústria (CNI) (National Confederation of Industry): Edif. Roberto Simonsen, SBN, Quadra 01, Bloco C, 70040-903 Brasília, DF; tel. (61) 3317-9993; fax (61) 3317-9994; e-mail sac@cni.org.br; internet www.cni.org.br; f. 1938; national confederation of industry comprising 27 state industrial federations; membership of some 1,016 employers' unions; Pres. ROBSON BRAGA DE ANDRADE; Exec. Dir JOSÉ AUGUSTO COELHO FERNANDES.

Conselho dos Exportadores de Café Verde do Brasil (CECAFE): Av. Nove de Julho 4865, Torre A, Conj. 61, Chácara Itaim, 01407-200 São Paulo, SP; tel. (11) 3079-3755; fax (11) 3167-4060; e-mail cecafe@cecafe.com.br; internet www.cecafe.com.br; f. 1999 through merger of Federação Brasileira dos Exportadores de Café and Associação Brasileira dos Exportadores de Café; council of green coffee exporters; Pres. JOÃO ANTÔNIO LIAN; Dir-Gen. GUILHERME BRAGA ABREU PIRES FILHO.

Federação das Indústrias do Estado do Rio de Janeiro (FIRJAN): Centro Empresarial FIRJAN, Av. Graça Aranha 1, Rio de Janeiro, RJ; tel. (21) 2563-4389; e-mail centrodeatendimento@firjan.org.br; internet www.firjan.org.br; Pres. EDUARDO EUGENIO GOUVÊA VIEIRA; regional manufacturers' asscn; 103 affiliated syndicates representing almost 16,000 cos.

Federação das Indústrias do Estado de São Paulo (FIESP): Av. Paulista 1313, 01311-923 São Paulo, SP; tel. (11) 3549-4499; e-mail relacionamento@fiesp.org.br; internet www.fiesp.org.br; regional manufacturers' asscn; Pres. PAULO ANTONIO SKAF.

Instituto Aço Brasil: Av. Rio Branco 181, 28° andar, 20040-007 Rio de Janeiro, RJ; tel. (21) 3445-6300; fax (21) 2262-2234; e-mail acobrasil@acobrasil.org.br; internet www.acobrasil.org.br; f. 1963; fmrly Instituto Brasileiro de Siderurgia (IBS); steel cos' org.; Pres. ANDRÉ BIER GERDAU JOHANNPETER; Exec. Chair MARCO POLO DE MELLO LOPES.

Instituto Brasileiro do Mineração (IBRAM) (The Brazilian National Mining Association): SHIS, Quadra 12, Conj. 0, Casa 4, 71630-205 Brasília, DF; tel. (61) 3364-7200; fax (61) 3364-7272; e-mail ibram@ibram.org.br; internet www.ibram.org.br; f. 1976 to foster the development of the mining industry; Pres. and Dir PAULO CAMILLO VARGAS PENNA.

Instituto Nacional de Tecnologia (INT): Av. Venezuela 82, 8° andar, 20081-312 Rio de Janeiro, RJ; tel. (21) 2123-1100; fax (21) 2123-1284; e-mail dcom@int.gov.br; internet www.int.gov.br; f. 1921; co-operates in national industrial development; Dir DOMINGOS MANFREDI NAVEIRO.

Serviço de Apoio às Micro e Pequenas Empresas (Sebrae): SEPN, Quadra 515, Lote 03, Bloco C, Asa Norte, 70770-530 Brasília, DF; tel. (61) 3348-7100; fax (61) 3347-3581; internet www.sebrae.com.br; f. 1972; supports small and medium-sized enterprises; Exec. Dir LUIZ EDUARDO PEREIRA BARRETTO FILHO.

União Democrática Ruralista (UDR): Av. Col Marcondes 983, 6° andar, Sala 62, Centro, 19010-080 Presidente Prudente, SP; tel. (11) 3221-1082; fax (11) 3232-4622; e-mail udr.org@uol.com.br; internet www.udr.org.br; landowners' org.; Pres. LUIZ ANTÔNIO NABHAN GARCIA.

União da Industria de Cana-de-Açúcar (UNICA): Av. Brigadeiro Faria Lima 2179, 9° andar, Jardim Paulistano, 01452-000 São Paulo, SP; tel. (11) 3093-4949; fax (11) 3812-1416; e-mail unica@

unica.com.br; internet www.unica.com.br; f. 1997; sugar and bioethanol asscn; offices in Washington, DC, USA, and Brussels, Belgium; Pres. MARCOS SAWAYA JANK; Exec. Dir EDUARDO LEÃO DE SOUSA.

STATE HYDROCARBONS COMPANIES

Petróleo Brasileiro, SA (Petrobras): Av. República do Chile 65, Centro, 20031-912 Rio de Janeiro, RJ; tel. (21) 3224-1510; fax (21) 3224-6055; e-mail sac@petrobras.com.br; internet www.petrobras.com.br; f. 1953; production of petroleum and petroleum products; owns 16 oil refineries; net profit US $16,645m. (2009); CEO MARIA DAS GRAÇAS SILVA FOSTER; Sec.-Gen. HÉLIO SHIGUENOBU FUJIKAWA; 53,933 employees; subsidiary cos are Petrobras Transporte, SA (Transpetro), Petrobras Comercializadora de Energia, Ltda, Petrobras Negócios Eletrônicos, SA, Petrobras International Finance Company (PIFCO) and Downstream Participações, SA, and cos listed below:

Petrobras Biocombustível, SA (Petrobras Biofuel): Av. República do Chile 65, Centro, 20031-912 Rio de Janeiro, RJ; tel. (21) 3224-1510; fax (21) 3224-6055; e-mail biocombustivel@petrobras.com.br; internet www.petrobrasbiocombustivel.com.br; f. 2008; three biodiesel plants in Candeias, Quixadá and Montes Claros; Pres. JOSÉ SÉRGIO GABRIELLI DE AZEVEDO.

Petrobras Distribuidora, SA: Rua General Canabarro 500, Maracanã, 20271-900 Rio de Janeiro, RJ; tel. (21) 3876-4477; fax (21) 3876-4977; internet www.br.com.br; f. 1971; distribution of all petroleum by-products; Pres. JOSÉ LIMA DE ANDRADE NETO; 3,758 employees.

Petrobras Gás, SA (Gaspetro): Av. República do Chile 65, Centro, 20031-912 Rio de Janeiro, RJ; tel. (21) 3534-0439; fax (21) 3534-1080; e-mail sac@petrobras.com.br; internet www.gaspetro.com.br; f. 1998; Pres. JOSÉ SÉRGIO GABRIELLI DE AZEVEDO; Dir (Gas and Energy) MARIA DAS GRAÇAS SILVA FOSTER.

Petrobras Química, SA (Petroquisa): Av. República do Chile 65, 9° andar, Centro, 20031-912 Rio de Janeiro, RJ; tel. (21) 3224-1455; fax (21) 2262-1521; e-mail contato.petroquisa@petrobras.com.br; internet www.petroquisa.com.br; f. 1968; petrochemicals industry; controls 27 affiliated companies and four subsidiaries; Pres. JOSÉ SÉRGIO GABRIELLI DE AZEVEDO.

Pré-Sal Petróleo, SA: f. 2010; state-owned; manages exploration of petroleum and natural gas beneath the salt layer along the Brazilian coast; Pres. EDISON LOBÃO (Minister of Mines and Energy).

UTILITIES

Regulatory Agencies

Agência Nacional de Energia Elétrica (ANEEL): SGAN 603, Módulo J, 70830-030 Brasília, DF; tel. (61) 2192-8600; e-mail aneel@aneel.gov.br; internet www.aneel.gov.br; f. 1939 as Conselho Nacional de Águas e Energia Elétrica, present name adopted 1996; Dir-Gen. NELSON JOSÉ HÜBNER MOREIRA.

Comissão Nacional de Energia Nuclear (CNEN): Rua General Severiano 90, Botafogo, 22290-901 Rio de Janeiro, RJ; tel. (21) 2173-2000; fax (21) 2173-2003; e-mail corin@cnen.gov.br; internet www.cnen.gov.br; f. 1956; state org. responsible for management of nuclear power programme; Pres. ODAIR DIAS GONÇALVES.

Electricity

Ampla Energia e Serviços, SA (Ampla): Praça Leoni Ramos 1, Bloco 1, 7º andar, São Domingos, 24210-205 Niterói, RJ; tel. (21) 2613-7000; fax (21) 2613-7153; e-mail ampla@ampla.com; internet www.ampla.com; f. 1907; fmrly Companhia de Eletricidade do Estado do Rio de Janeiro-CERJ; privatized in 1996; present name adopted in 2004; Pres. MARCELO LLÉVENES.

CPFL Energia, SA (Companhia Paulista de Força e Luz): Rua Gomes de Carvalho 1510, 14º andar, Conj. 1402, 04547-005 Vila Olímpia, SP; tel. (19) 3756-8018; fax (19) 3252-7644; internet www.cpfl.com.br; provides electricity through govt concessions; operates 21 subsidiaries for generation, distribution and commercialization of energy in the electricity sector; Pres. MURILO CESAR LEMOS DOS SANTOS PASSOS; Exec. Dir WILSON PINTO FERREIRA JÚNIOR.

Centrais Elétricas Brasileiras, SA (Eletrobras): Av. Presidente Vargas 409, 13º andar, Centro, 20071-003 Rio de Janeiro, RJ; tel. (21) 2514-5151; fax (21) 2514-6479; e-mail pr@eletrobras.gov.br; internet www.eletrobras.com; f. 1962; holding company responsible for planning, financing and managing Brazil's electrical energy programme; 54% govt-owned; Pres. JOSÉ ANTONIO MUNIZ LOPES; controls six electricity generation and transmission subsidiaries and six distribution subsidiaries:

Eletrobras Amazonas Energia: Av. Sete de Setembro 2414, Cachoeirinha, 69005-141 Manaus, AM; tel. (92) 3621-1201; fax (92) 3633-2406; internet www.amazonasenergia.gov.br; f. 1895; became subsidiary of Eletronorte in 1997 as Manaus Energia; name changed as above in 2010; electricity distribution; Exec. Dir PEDRO CARLOS HOSKEN VIEIRA.

Eletrobras CGTEE (Companhia de Geração Térmica de Energia Elétrica): Rua Sete de Setembro 539, 90010-190 Porto Alegre, RS; tel. (51) 3287-1500; fax (51) 3287-1566; internet www.cgtee.gov.br; f. 1997; became part of Eletrobras in 2000; generation and transmission; Pres. VALTER LUIZ CARDEAL DE SOUZA; Exec. Dir SERENO CHAISE.

Eletrobras Chesf (Companhia Hidro Eléctrica do São Francisco): 333 Bongi, Rua Delmiro Golveia, 50761-901 Recife, PE; tel. (81) 3229-2000; fax (81) 3229-2390; e-mail chesf@chesf.com.br; internet www.chesf.gov.br; f. 1948; generation and transmission; Pres. UBIRAJARA ROCHA MEIRA; Exec. Dir DILTON DA CONTI OLIVEIRA.

Eletrobras Distribuição Acre (ELETROACRE): Rua Valério Magalhães 226, Bairro do Bosque, 69909-710 Rio Branco, AC; tel. (68) 3212-5700; fax (68) 3223-1142; e-mail ouvidoria@eletroacre.com.br; internet www.eletroacre.com.br; f. 1965; electricity distribution; Exec. Dir PEDRO CARLOS HOSKEN VIEIRA.

Eletrobras Distribuição Alagoas (CEAL): Av. Fernandes Lima 3349, Gruta de Lourdes, 57057-900 Maceió, AL; tel. (82) 2126-9247; fax (82) 2126-9326; e-mail ape@ceal.com.br; internet www.ceal.com.br; f. 1961; electricity distribution; Exec. Dir PEDRO CARLOS HOSKEN VIEIRA.

Eletrobras Distribuição Rondônia, SA (CERON): Av. Imigrantes 4137, Industrial, 76821-063 Porto Velho, RO; tel. (69) 3216-4000; internet www.ceron.com.br; f. 1968; electricity distribution; Exec. Dir PEDRO CARLOS HOSKEN VIEIRA.

Eletrobras Distribuição Roraima (Boa Vista Energia): Av. Capitão Ene Garcêz 691, Centro, 69310-160 Boa Vista, RR; tel. (95) 2621-1400; e-mail frvcarvalho@boavistaenergia.gov.br; internet www.boavistaenergia.gov.br; f. 1997; subsidiary of Eletronorte; electricity distribution; Exec. Dir PEDRO CARLOS HOSKEN VIEIRA.

Eletrobras Distribuição Piauí (CEPISA): Av. Maranhão 759, Sul, 64001-010 Teresina, PI; tel. (86) 3228-8000; internet www.cepisa.com.br; f. 1962; 99% of shares bought by Eletrobras in 1997; distributor of electricity in state of Piauí; Exec. Dir PEDRO CARLOS HOSKEN VIEIRA.

Eletrobras Eletronorte: SCN, Quadra 6, Conj. A, Blocos B e C, Entrada Norte 2, Asa Norte, 70716-901 Brasília, DF; tel. (61) 3429-5151; fax (61) 3328-1463; e-mail ouvidoria@eln.gov.br; internet www.eln.gov.br; f. 1973; generation and transmission; serves Amapá, Acre, Amazonas, Maranhão, Mato Grosso, Pará, Rondônia, Roraima and Tocantins; Pres. ASTROGILDO FRAGUGLIA QUENTAL; Exec. Dir JOSIAS MATOS DE ARAUJO.

Eletrobras Eletronuclear: Rua da Candelária 65, Centro, 20091-906 Rio de Janeiro, RJ; tel. (21) 2588-7000; fax (21) 2588-7200; internet www.eletronuclear.gov.br; f. 1997 by fusion of the nuclear branch of Furnas with Nuclebrás Engenharia (NUCLEN); operates two nuclear facilities, Angra I and II; Angra III scheduled to be commissioned in 2015; Pres. MIGUEL COLASUONNO; Exec. Dir OTHON LUIZ PINHEIRO DA SILVA.

Eletrobras Eletrosul: Rua Deputado Antônio Edu Vieira 999, Pantanal, 88040-901 Florianópolis, SC; tel. (48) 3231-7000; fax (48) 3234-4040; internet www.eletrosul.gov.br; f. 1968; generation and transmission; Pres. VALTER LUIZ CARDEAL DE SOUZA; Exec. Dir EURIDES LUIZ MESCOLOTTO.

Eletrobras Furnas: Rua Real Grandeza 219, Bloco A, 16° andar, Botafogo, 22281-900 Rio de Janeiro, RJ; tel. (21) 2528-3112; fax (21) 2528-5858; e-mail webfurnas@furnas.com.br; internet www.furnas.com.br; f. 1957; generation and transmission; Pres. FLÁVIO DECAT; Exec. Dir CARLOS NADALUTTI FILHO.

Companhia de Eletricidade do Estado da Bahia (COELBA): Av. Edgard Santos 300, 300 Narandiba, 41186-900 Salvador, BA; tel. (71) 3370-5130; fax (71) 3370-5135; internet www.coelba.com.br; f. 1960; Pres. JOILSON RODRIGUES FERREIRA CHAVES; Exec. Dir MOISÉS AFONSO SALES FILHO.

Companhia Energética de Brasília (CEB): SIA/SAPS, Trecho 01, Lotes C, Asa Sul, 71215-000 Brasília, DF; tel. (61) 3363-4011; fax (61) 3363-2657; e-mail info@ceb.com.br; internet www.ceb.com.br; generation and distribution of electric energy in Distrito Federal; also operates gas distribution co CEBGAS; Pres. and CEO PAULO VICTOR RADA DE REZENDE.

Companhia Energética do Ceará (COELCE): Rua Padre Valdevino 150, 1º andar, Joaquim Távora, 60135-040 Fortaleza, CE; tel. (85) 3247-1444; fax (85) 3216-4088; e-mail gercom@coelce.com.br; internet www.coelce.com.br; f. 1971; part of Endesa (Spain); Pres. ABEL ROCHINHA.

Companhia Energética do Maranhão (CEMAR): Av. Coronel Colares Moreira 477, Renascença II, 65075-441 São Luis, MA; tel. (98) 3217-2211; fax (98) 3321-7161; e-mail corporativo@cemar-ma.com.br; internet www.cemar-ma.com.br; f. 1958 as Centrais

Elétricas do Maranhão; changed name as above in 1984; owned by PPL Global, Inc (USA); Exec. Dir AUGUSTO MIRANDA DA PAZ JÚNIOR.

Companhia Energética de Minas Gerais (CEMIG): Av. Barbacena 1200, 5° andar, Ala B1, Bairro Santo Agostinho, 30161-970 Belo Horizonte, MG; tel. (31) 3299-4900; fax (31) 3299-3700; e-mail atendimento@cemig.com.br; internet www.cemig.com.br; f. 1952; 51% state-owned, 33% owned by Southern Electric Brasil Partipações, Ltda; Exec. Dir DJALMA BASTOS DE MORAIS.

Companhia Energética de Pernambuco (CELPE): Av. João de Barros 111, Sala 301, Boa Vista, 50050-902 Recife, PE; tel. (81) 3217-5168; e-mail celpe@celpe.com.br; internet www.celpe.com.br; state distributor of electricity; Pres. JOILSON RODRIGUES FERREIRA; Exec. Dir LUIZ ANTÔNIO CIARLINI.

Companhia Energética de São Paulo (CESP): Av. Nossa Senhora do Sabará 5312, Bairro Pedreira, 04447-011 São Paulo, SP; tel. (11) 5613-2100; fax (11) 3262-5545; e-mail inform@cesp.com.br; internet www.cesp.com.br; f. 1966; Pres. DILMA SELI PENA; Exec. Dir VILSON DANIEL CHRISTOFARI.

Companhia Paranaense de Energia (COPEL): Rua Coronel Dulcídio 800, 80420-170 Curitiba, PR; tel. (41) 3331-5050; fax (41) 3331-4376; e-mail copel@copel.com; internet www.copel.com; f. 1954; state distributor of electricity and gas; Pres. LÉO DE ALMEIDA NEVES; Exec. Dir RAUL MUNHOZ NETO.

Eletropaulo Metropolitana Eletricidade de São Paulo, SA (AES Eletropaulo): Av. Lourenço Marques 158, 3º andar, Vila Olímpia, 04547-100 São Paulo, SP; tel. (11) 2195-2000; fax (11) 2195-2511; e-mail administracao@eletropaulo.com.br; internet www.aeseletropaulo.com.br; f. 1899; acquired by AES in 2001; Pres. and Exec. Dir BRITALDO PEDROSA SOARES.

Energisa Minas Gerais: Praça Rui Barbosa 80, Centro, 36770-901 Cataguases, MG; tel. (32) 3429-6000; fax (32) 3429-6317; e-mail secretaria@energisa.com.br; internet www.minasgerais.energisa.com.br; f. 1905 as Companhia Força e Luz Cataguazes-Leopoldina, adopted current name in 2008; subsidiary of Grupo Energisa, SA; concerned with generation and distribution of electrical energy; Pres. IVAN MÜLLER BOTELHO; Exec. Dir GABRIEL ALVES PEREIRA JÚNIOR.

Espírito Santo Centrais Elétricas, SA (EDP Escelsa): Rua José Alexandre Buaiz 160, 8º andar, Enseada do Suá, 29050-955 Vitória, ES; tel. (27) 3321-9000; fax (27) 3322-9109; e-mail escelsa@enbr.com.br; internet www.escelsa.com.br; f. 1968; subsidiary of EDB; Pres. ANTÓNIO MANUEL BARRETO PITA DE ABREU; Exec. Dir MIGUEL NUNO FERREIRA SETAS.

Indústrias Nucleares do Brasil, SA (INB): Rua Mena Barreto 161, Botafogo, 22271-100 Rio de Janeiro, RJ; tel. (21) 2536-1600; fax (21) 2537-9391; e-mail inbrio@inb.gov.br; internet www.inb.gov.br; f. 1988; Pres. ODAIR DIAS GONÇALVES; Exec. Dir ALFREDO TRANJAN FILHO.

Itaipu Binacional: Av. Tancredo Neves 6731, 85866-900 Foz de Iguaçu, PR; tel. (45) 3520-5252; fax (45) 3520-3015; e-mail itaipu@itaipu.gov.br; internet www.itaipu.gov.br; f. 1974; jtly owned by Brazil and Paraguay; hydroelectric power station on Brazilian–Paraguayan border; 92,245 GWh produced in 2011; Dir-Gen. (Brazil) JORGE MIGUEL SAMEK; Dir-Gen. (Paraguay) EFRAÍN ENRÍQUEZ GAMÓN.

LIGHT—Serviços de Eletricidade, SA: Av. Marechal Floriano 168, CP 0571, 20080-002 Rio de Janeiro, RJ; tel. (21) 2211-7171; fax (21) 2233-1249; e-mail light@lightrio.com.br; internet www.lightrio.com.br; f. 1905; electricity generation and distribution in Rio de Janeiro; fmrly state-owned, sold to a Brazilian-French-US consortium in 1996; controlled by EdF (France) from 2002; in 2006 79.4% holding sold to Brazilian group Rio Minas Energia Participaçoes, SA (RME) with EdF retaining 10% share; generating capacity of 850 MW; Pres. SÉRGIO ALAIR BARROSO; Exec. Dir JERSON KELMAN.

Gas

Companhia Distribuidora de Gás do Rio de Janeiro (CEG): Av. Pedro II 68, São Cristóvão, 20941-070 Rio de Janeiro, RJ; tel. (21) 2585-7575; fax (21) 2585-7070; internet www.ceg.com.br; f. 1969; gas distribution in the Rio de Janeiro region; privatized in 1997; Pres. SERGIO ARANDA MORENO; Exec. Dir BRUNO ARMBRUST.

Companhia de Gás de Alagoas, SA (ALGÁS): Rua Artur Vital da Silva, 04, Gruta de Lourdes, 57052-790 Maceió, AL; tel. (82) 3218-7767; fax (82) 3218-7742; e-mail algas@algas.com.br; internet www.algas.com.br; 51% state-owned; Exec. Dir GERSON FONSECA.

Companhia de Gás de Bahia (BAHIAGÁS): Av. Tancredo Neves 450, Edif. Suarez Trade, 20° andar, Caminho das Arvores, 41820-901 Salvador, BA; tel. (71) 3206-6000; fax (71) 3206-6001; e-mail atendimento@bahiagas.com.br; internet www.bahiagas.com.br; f. 1991; 51% state-owned; Pres. WILSON ALVES DE BRITO FILHO; Exec. Dir DAVIDSON DE MAGALHÃES SANTOS.

Companhia de Gás do Ceará (CEGÁS): Av. Santos Dumont 7700, 5°–8° e 11° andares, Manoel Dias Branco, 60190–800 Fortaleza, CE; tel. (85) 3266–6900; fax (85) 3265-2026; e-mail ouvidoria@cegas.com.br; internet www.cegas.com.br; 51% owned by the state of Amazonas; Pres. Dr JOSÉ REGO FILHO.

Companhia de Gás de Minas Gerais (GASMIG): Av. do Contorno 6594, 10º andar, Funcionários, 30110-044 Belo Horizonte, MG; tel. (31) 3265-1000; fax (31) 3265-1103; e-mail gasmig@gasmig.com.br; internet www.gasmig.com.br; Exec. Dir MÁRCIO AUGUSTO VASCONCELOS NUNES.

Companhia de Gás de Pernambuco (COPERGÁS): Av. Mal. Mascarenhas de Morais 533, Imbiribeira, 51150-904 Recife, PE; tel. (81) 3184-2000; e-mail copergas@copergas.com.br; internet www.copergas.com.br; 51% state-owned; Exec. Dir ALDO GUEDES.

Companhia de Gás do Rio Grande do Sul (SULGÁS): Rua 7 de Setembro 1069, Edif. Santa Cruz, 5° andar, Centro, 90010-190 Porto Alegre, RS; tel. (51) 3287-2200; fax (51) 3287-2205; internet www.sulgas.rs.gov.br; f. 1993; 51% state-owned; 49% owned by Petrobras; Pres. DANIEL ANDRADE; Exec. Dir ANTÔNIO GREGÓRIO GOIDANICH.

Companhia de Gás de Santa Catarina (SCGÁS): Rua Antônia Luz 255, Centro Empresarial Hoepcke, 88010-410 Florianópolis, SC; tel. (48) 3229-1200; fax (48) 3229-1230; internet www.scgas.com.br; f. 1994; 51% state-owned; Exec. Dir IVAN CÉSAR RANZOLIN.

Companhia de Gás de São Paulo (COMGÁS): Rua Olimpíadas 205, 10° andar, Vila Olímpia, 04551-000 São Paulo, SP; tel. (11) 4504-5000; fax (11) 4504-5027; e-mail investidores@comgas.com.br; internet www.comgas.com.br; f. 1978; distribution in São Paulo of gas; sold in 1999 to consortium including British Gas PLC and Royal Dutch Shell Group; Chair. NELSON LUIZ COSTA SILVA; Exec. Dir LUIS AUGUSTO DOMENECH.

Companhia Paraibana de Gás (PBGÁS): Av. Presidente Epitácio Pessoa 4756, Cabo Branco, 58045-001 João Pessoa, PB; tel. (83) 3247-7609; fax (83) 3247-2244; e-mail cicero@pbgas.com.br; internet www.pbgas.pb.gov.br; f. 1995; 51% state-owned; Exec. Dir ANTÔNIO CARLOS FERNANDES REGIS.

Companhia Paranaense de Gás (COMPAGÁS): Rua Pasteur 463, Edif. Jatobá, 7° andar, Batel, 80250-080 Curitaba, PR; tel. (41) 3312-1900; fax (41) 3312-1922; e-mail compagas@compagas.com.br; internet www.compagas.com.br; f. 1998; 51.0% owned by Copel Participaçoes, SA, 24.5% by Gaspetro and 24.5% by Mitsui Gás e Energia do Brasil; Pres. Dr ANTÔNIO FERNANDO KREMPEL; Exec. Dir STÊNIO JACOB.

Companhia Potiguar de Gás (POTIGÁS): Av. Brancas Dunas 485, Lojas 1 e 2, Salas de 101 a 106, Candelária, 59064-720 Natal, RN; tel. (84) 3204-8500; fax (84) 3206-8504; e-mail mauricio@potigas.com.br; internet www.potigas.com.br; 17% state-owned; Pres. FRANCISCO CIPRIANO DE PAULA SEGUNDO; Exec. Dir NELSON HERMÓGENES DE MEDEIROS FREIRE.

Companhia Rondoniense de Gás, SA (RONGÁS): Av. Carlos Gomes 1223, Sala 403, 4° andar, Centro, 78900-030 Porto Velho, RO; tel. and fax (69) 3229-0333; e-mail rongas@rongas.com.br; internet www.rongas.com.br; f. 1997; 17% state-owned; Exec. Dir JOSÉ SANGUANINI.

Empresa Sergipana de Gás, SA (EMSERGÁS): Av. Heráclito Rollemberg 1712, Conj. Augusto Franco, 49030-640 Farolândia, SE; tel. (79) 3243-8500; fax (79) 3243-8508; e-mail emsergas@infonet.com.br; internet www.sergipegas.com.br; f. 1993; 51% state-owned; Exec. Dir FERNANDO AKIRA OTA.

Water

Águas e Esgotos do Piauí (AGESPISA): Av. Marechal Castelo Branco 101, Norte, Cabral, 64000-810 Teresina, PI; tel. (86) 3216-6300; fax (86) 3216-8182; e-mail marcosvenicius@agespisa.com.br; internet www.agespisa.com.br; f. 1962; state-owned; water and waste management; Exec. Dir MARCOS VENÍCIUS MEDEIROS COSTA.

Companhia de Agua e Esgosto de Ceará (CAGECE): Av. Dr Lauro Vieira Chaves 1030, Vila União, 60420-280 Fortaleza, CE; tel. (85) 3101-1805; fax (85) 3101-1834; e-mail asimp-cagece@cagece.com.br; internet www.cagece.com.br; f. 1971; state-owned; water and sewerage services; Pres. JOAQUIM CARTAXO FILHO; Exec. Dir HENRIQUE VIEIRA COSTA LIMA.

Companhia Algoas Industrial (CINAL): Rodovia Divaldo Suruagy, BR 424, Km 12, 57160-000 Marechal Deodoro, AL; tel. (82) 3218-2500; fax (82) 3269-1199; e-mail airton@cinal.com.br; internet www.cinal.com.br; f. 1982; management of steam and treated water; Pres. ROBERTO PRISCO PARAÍSO RAMOS; Exec. Dir FRANCISCO CARLOS RUGA.

Companhia Espírito Santense de Saneamento (CESAN): Av. Governador Bley 186, Edif. BEMGE, 3º andar, Centro, 29010-150 Vitória, ES; tel. (27) 2127-5353; fax (27) 2127-5000; e-mail comunica@cesan.com.br; internet www.cesan.com.br; f. 1968; state-owned; construction, maintenance and operation of water supply and sewerage systems; Exec. Dir PAULO RUY VALIM CARNELLI.

Companhia Estadual de Aguas e Esgotos (CEDAE): Rua Sacadura Cabral 103, 9° andar, 20081-260 Rio de Janeiro, RJ; tel. (21) 2332-3600; fax (21) 2296-0416; internet www.cedae.rj.gov.br; f. 1975;

state-owned; water supply and sewerage treatment; Pres. ALBERTO JOSÉ MENDES GOMES; Exec. Dir WAGNER GRANJA VICTER.

Companhia Pernambucana de Saneamento (COMPESA): Rua da Aurora 777, Boa Vista, 50040-905 Recife, PE; tel. (81) 3412-9693; fax (81) 3412-9181; internet www.compesa.com.br; state-owned; management and operation of regional water supply in the state of Pernambuco; Pres. JOÃO BOSCO DE ALMEIDA.

Companhia Riograndense de Saneamento (CORSAN): Rua Caldas Júnior 120, 18° andar, 90010-260 Porto Alegre, RS; tel. (51) 3215-5600; e-mail ascom@corsan.com.br; internet www.corsan.com.br; f. 1965; state-owned; management and operation of regional water supply and sanitation programmes; Exec. Dir LUIS ZAFFALON.

Companhia de Saneamento Básico do Estado de São Paulo (SABESP): Rua Costa Carvalho 300, Pinheiros, 05429-000 São Paulo, SP; tel. (11) 3388-8200; fax (11) 3813-0254; internet www.sabesp.com.br; f. 1973; state-owned; supplies basic sanitation services for the state of São Paulo, including water treatment and supply; Pres. DILMA SELI PENA; Exec. Dir GESNER JOSÉ DE OLIVEIRA FILHO.

TRADE UNIONS

Central Unica dos Trabalhadores (CUT): Rua Caetano Pinto 575, Brás, 03041-000 São Paulo, SP; tel. (11) 2108-9200; fax (11) 2108-9310; e-mail duvaier@cut.org.br; internet www.cut.org.br; f. 1983; central union confederation; left-wing; 3.5m. mems; Pres. ARTUR ENRIQUE DA SILVA SANTOS; Gen. Sec. QUINTINO SEVERO MARQUES.

Confederação Nacional dos Metalúrgicos (Metal Workers): Av. Antártico, 480-Jardim do Mar, São Bernardo do Campo, 09726-150 São Paulo, SP; tel. (11) 4122-7700; e-mail cnmcut@cnmcut.org.br; internet www.cnmcut.org.br; f. 1992; Pres. PAULO CAYRES; Gen. Sec. JOÃO CAYRES.

Confederação Nacional das Profissões Liberais (CNPL) (Liberal Professions): SCS, Quadra 02, Bloco D, Edif. Oscar Niemeyer, 9º andar, 70316-900 Brasília, DF; tel. (61) 2103-1683; fax (61) 2103-1684; e-mail secretaria@cnpl.org.br; internet www.cnpl.org.br; f. 1953; 260,000 mems (2007); Pres. FRANSCISCO ANTONIO FEIJÓ; Sec.-Gen. JOSÉ ALBERTO ROSSI.

Confederação Nacional dos Trabalhadores na Indústria (CNTI) (Industrial Workers): SEP/NORTE, Quadra 505, Conj. A, 70730-540 Brasília, DF; tel. (61) 3448-9900; fax (61) 3448-9956; e-mail cnti@cnti.org.br; internet www.cnti.org.br; f. 1946; Pres. JOSÉ CALIXTO RAMOS; Sec.-Gen. APRÍGIO GUIMARÃES.

Confederação Nacional dos Trabalhadores no Comércio (CNTC) (Commercial Workers): Av. W/5 Sul, SGAS Quadra 902, Bloco C, 70390-020 Brasília, DF; tel. (61) 3217-7100; fax (61) 3217-7122; e-mail cntc@cntc.com.br; internet www.cntc.com.br; f. 1946; Pres. ANTÔNIO ALVES DE ALMEIDA.

Confederação Nacional dos Trabalhadores em Transportes Aquaviários e Aéreos, na Pesca e nos Portos (CONTTMAF) (Maritime, River and Air Transport Workers): SDS, Edif. Venâncio V, Grupos 501/503, 70393-900 Brasília, DF; tel. (61) 3226-5263; fax (61) 3322-6383; e-mail conttmaf@conttmaf.org.br; internet www.conttmaf.org.br; f. 1957; Pres. SEVERINO ALMEIDA FILHO; Sec.-Gen. ODILON DOS SANTOS BRAGA.

Confederação Nacional dos Trabalhadores em Comunicações e Publicidade (CONTCOP) (Communications and Advertising Workers): SCS, Quadra 02, Edif. Serra Dourada, Sala 705–709, 70300-902 Brasília, DF; tel. (61) 3224-7926; fax (61) 3224-5686; e-mail faleconosco@contcop.org.br; internet www.contcop.org.br; f. 1964; 350,000 mems; Pres. ANTÔNIO MARIA THAUMATURGO CORTIZO; Sec.-Gen. BENEDITO ANTONIO MARCELLO.

Confederação Nacional dos Trabalhadores nas Empresas de Crédito (CONTEC) (Workers in Credit Institutions): SEP-SUL, Av. W/4, EQ 707/907, Conj. A/B, 70390-078 Brasília, DF; tel. (61) 3244-5833; fax (61) 3224-2743; e-mail contec@contec.org.br; internet www.contec.org.br; f. 1958; Pres. LOURENÇO FERREIRA DO PRADO; Sec.-Gen. GILBERTO ANTONIO VIEIRA.

Confederação Nacional dos Trabalhadores em Estabelecimentos de Educação e Cultura (CNTEEC) (Workers in Education and Culture): SAS, Quadra 4, Bloco B, 70070-908 Brasília, DF; tel. (61) 3321-4140; fax (61) 3321-2704; internet www.cnteec.org.br; f. 1966; Pres. MIGUEL ABRÃO NETO.

Confederação Nacional dos Trabalhadores na Agricultura (CONTAG) (Agricultural Workers): SMPW, Quadra 01, Conj. 02, Lote 02, Núcleo Bandeirante, 71735-102 Brasília, DF; tel. (61) 2102-2288; fax (61) 2102-2299; e-mail contag@contag.org.br; internet www.contag.org.br; f. 1964; represents 25 state feds and 3,630 syndicates, 15m. mems; Pres. ALBERTO ERCÍLIO BROCH; Sec.-Gen. DAVID WYLKERSON RODRIGUES DE SOUZA.

Federação Nacional dos Trabalhadores em Empresas dos Correios e Similares (FENTECT) (Postal Workers): SDS, Edif. Venâncio V, Bloco R, Loja 60, 70393-900 Brasília, DF; tel. and fax (61) 3323-8810; e-mail fentect@fentect.org.br; internet www.fentect.org.br; f. 1989; Sec.-Gen. JOSÉ RIVALDO DA SILVA.

Força Sindical (FS): Rua Rocha Pombo, 94 Liberdade, 01525-010 São Paulo, SP; tel. and fax (11) 3348-9000; e-mail secgeral@fsindical.org.br; internet www.fsindical.org.br; f. 1991; 2.1m. mems (2007); Pres. PAULO PEREIRA DA SILVA; Sec.-Gen. JOÃO CARLOS GONÇALVES.

União Geral dos Trabalhadores (UGT): Rua Aguiar de Barrios, 144 Bela Vista, 01316-020 São Paulo, SP; tel. (11) 2111-7300; fax (11) 2111-7501; e-mail ugt@ugt.org.br; internet www.ugt.org.br; f. 2007 by merger of Confederação Geral dos Trabalhadores with two other unions; Pres. RICARDO PATAH; Sec.-Gen. FRANCISCO CANINDÉ PEGADO DO NASCIMENTO.

Transport

Ministério dos Transportes: see section on the Government (Ministries).

Agência Nacional de Transportes Terrestres (ANTT): Edif. Phenícia, SBN, Quadra 2, Bloco C, Lote 17, 70040-020 Brasília, DF; tel. (61) 3410-8100; fax (61) 3410-1189; e-mail ouvidoria@antt.gov.br; internet www.antt.gov.br; f. 2002; govt agency; oversees road and rail infrastructure; Dir-Gen. BERNARDO FIGUEIREDO.

RAILWAYS

In 2008 there were 29,817 km of railway lines. There are also railways owned by state governments and several privately owned railways. In 2005 railways accounted for 25% of all traffic. Construction of a new high-speed rail link connecting Rio de Janeiro, São Paulo and Campinas was originally scheduled to begin in late 2010, although rising costs and delays meant this was postponed until 2013. The estimated cost of the project was R $38,000m.

América Latina Logistica do Brasil, SA (ALL): Rua Emilio Bertolini 100, Vila Oficinas, Cajuru, Curitiba, PR; tel. (41) 2141-7555; e-mail caall@all-logistica.com; internet www.all-logistica.com; f. 1997; 6,586 km in 2003; acquired Ferrovia Novoeste, SA in 2006; Pres. WILSON FERRO DE LARA; Dir-Gen. PAULO LUIZ ARAÚJO BASÍLIO.

Ferrovia Bandeirante, SA (Ferroban): Av. Paulista 1.499, 17º andar, Sala 5, São Paulo, SP; tel. (11) 3138-2048; fax (11) 3138-2054; f. 1971 by merger of five railways operated by São Paulo State; transferred to private ownership in 1998; fmrly Ferrovia Paulista; 4,236 km open in 2003; Dir JOÃO GOUVEIA FERRÃO NETO.

Associação Nacional dos Transportadores Ferroviários (ANTF): Edif. CNT, Torre A, 6° andar, Sala 605, Quadra 01, Bloco J, 70070-010 Brasília, DF; tel. (61) 3226-5434; fax (61) 3221-0135; e-mail imprensa@antf.org.br; internet www.antf.org.br; promotes railway devt; 11 mem. cos; Pres. EDUARDO PARENTE; Exec. Dir RODRIGO VILAÇA.

Cia Brasileira de Trens Urbanos (CBTU): Estrada Velha da Tijuca 77, Usina, 20531-080 Rio de Janeiro, RJ; tel. (21) 2575-3399; fax (21) 2571-6149; e-mail imprensa@cbtu.gov.br; internet www.cbtu.gov.br; f. 1984; fmrly responsible for suburban networks and metro systems throughout Brazil; operates 5 metro systems; Pres. FRANCISCO COLOMBO.

Metrô BH (Superintendência de Trens Urbanos de Belo Horizonte): Rua Janúaria 181m, 31110-060 Belo Horizonte, MG; tel. (31) 3250-3900; fax (31) 3250-4053; e-mail stu-bh@cbtu.gov.br; f. 1981 as DEMETRÔ; present name adopted 2003; operates 3 lines; Supt. JOSÉ DÓRIA.

METROREC (Superintendência de Trens Urbanos de Recife): Rua José Natário 478, Areias, 50900-000 Recife, PE; tel. (81) 2102-8500; fax (81) 3455-4422; e-mail ouvidoria@metrorec.com.br; internet www2.cbtumetrorec.gov.br; f. 1985; 71 km open in 2010; Supt RICARDO BELTRÃO.

Superintendência de Trens Urbanos de João Pessoa (GTU/JOP): Praça Napoleão Laureano 1, Varadouro, 58010-040 João Pessoa, PB; tel. (83) 3241-4240; fax (83) 3241-6388; e-mail gecomjp@cbtu.gov.br; internet joaopessoa.cbtu.gov.br; 30 km; Supt. LUCÉLIO CARTAXO.

Superintendência de Trens Urbanos de Maceió (STU/MAC): Rua Barão de Anadia 121, Centro, 57020-630 Maceió, AL; tel. (82) 2123-1700; e-mail gecommac@cbtu.gov.br; internet maceio.cbtu.gov.br; 32 km; Supt. MARCELO DE AGUIAR GOMES.

Superintendência de Trens Urbanos de Natal (STU/NAT): Praça Augusto Severo, 302 Ribeira, 59012-380 Natal, RN; tel. (84) 3221-3355; fax (84) 3211-4122; e-mail stunat@cbtu.gov.br; internet natal.cbtu.gov.br; f. 1984; 56 km; Supt ERLY BASTOS.

Cia Cearense de Transportes Metropolitanos, SA (Metrofor): Rua 24 de Maio 60, 60020-001 Fortaleza, CE; tel. (85) 3101-7100; fax (85) 3101-4744; e-mail metrofor@metrofor.ce.gov.br; internet www.metrofor.ce.gov.br; f. 1997; 46 km; Pres. RÔMULO DOS SANTOS FORTES.

Cia do Metropolitano de São Paulo: Rua Boa Vista 175, 01014-001, São Paulo, SP; tel. (11) 3291–7800; fax (11) 3371-7329; e-mail ouvidoria@metrosp.com.br; internet www.metro.sp.gov.br; f. 1968; 4-line metro system, 61.3 km open in 2007; Dir-Gen. SÉRGIO HENRIQUE PASSOS AVELLEDA.

Cia Paulista de Trens Metropolitanos (CPTM): Av. Paulista 402, 5° andar, 01310-000 São Paulo, SP; tel. (11) 3371-1530; fax (11) 3285-0323; e-mail usuario@cptm.sp.gov.br; internet www.cptm.sp.gov.br; f. 1992 to incorporate suburban lines fmrly operated by the CBTU and FEPASA; 286 km; Pres. Dr JURANDIR FERNANDES; Dir-Gen. MARIO MANUEL SEABRA RODRIGUES BANDEIRA.

Empresa de Trens Urbanos de Porto Alegre, SA: Av. Ernesto Neugebauer 1985, 6º andar, Humaitá, 90250-140 Porto Alegre, RS; tel. (51) 3363-8000; fax (51) 3363-8166; e-mail atendimento@trensurb.com.br; internet www.trensurb.gov.br; f. 1985; 33.8 km open in 2004; Pres. ROBERTO DE OLIVEIRA MUNIZ; Dir-Gen. HUMBERTO KASPER.

Estrada de Ferro do Amapá (EFA): Av. Santana 429, Porto de Santana, 68925-000 Macapá, AP; tel. (96) 281-1845; fax (96) 281-1175; f. 1957; operated by Indústria e Comércio de Minérios, SA; 194 km open in 2007; Dir Supt JOSÉ LUIZ ORTIZ VERGULINO.

Estrada de Ferro Campos do Jordão: Rua Martin Cabral 87, CP 11, 12400-020 Pindamonhangaba, SP; tel. (12) 3642-3233; fax (12) 242-2499; internet www.efcj.sp.gov.br; f. 1914; operated by the Tourism Secretariat of the State of São Paulo; Dir SILVIO CAMARGO.

Estrada de Ferro Carajás: Av. Graça Aranha 26, 20030-000 RJ; tel. (21) 3814-4477; fax (21) 3814-4040; f. 1985 for movement of minerals from the Serra do Carajás to the port at Ponta da Madeira; operated by Vale, SA (CVRD); 892 km open in 2002; Supt JUARES SALIBRA.

Estrada de Ferro do Jari: Vila Munguba s/n, Monte Dourado, 68230-000 Pará, PA; tel. (91) 3736-6526; fax (91) 3736-6490; e-mail ascarvalho@jari.com.br; f. 1979; transportation of timber; 70 km open; Operations Man. PABLO ASSIS GUZZO.

Estrada de Ferro Paraná-Oeste, SA (FERROESTE): Av. Iguaçú 420, 7° andar, Rebouças, 80230-902 Curitiba, PR; tel. (41) 3281-9800; fax (41) 3233-2147; e-mail ferroest@pr.gov.br; internet www.ferroeste.pr.gov.br; f. 1988; serves the grain-producing regions in Paraná and Mato Grosso do Sul; privatized in 1996; 248 km in 2005; Pres. MAURICIO QUERINO THEODORO.

Estrada de Ferro Vitória-Minas: Av. Aarão Reis 423, Centro, Belo Horizonte, MG; tel. (31) 273-5976; fax (31) 3279-4676; f. 1942; operated by Vale, SA (CVRD); transport of iron ore, general cargo and passengers; 905 km open in 2003; Dir ALVARO ALBERGARIA.

Ferrovia Centro Atlântica, SA: Rua Sapucaí 383, Floresta 30150-904, Belo Horizonte, MG; tel. (31) 3279-5323; fax (31) 3279-5709; e-mail thiers@centro-atlantica.com.br; internet www.fcasa.com.br; f. 1996 following the privatization of Rede Ferroviária Federal, SA; owned by Vale, SA (CVRD) since 2003; industrial freight; 8,000 km; Dir-Gen. MARCELLO SPINELLI.

Ferrovia Norte-Sul: Av. Marechal Floriano 45, Centro, 20080-003 Rio de Janeiro, RJ; tel. (21) 2291-2185; fax (21) 2263-9119; e-mail valecascom@ferrovianortesul.com.br; 2,066 km from Belém to Goiânia; Dir JOSÉ FRANCISCO DAS NEVES.

Ferrovia Tereza Cristina, SA (FTC): Rua dos Ferroviários 100, Bairro Oficinas, 88702-230 Tubarão, SC; tel. (48) 3621-7724; fax (48) 3621-7747; e-mail comunicacao@ftc.com.br; internet www.ftc.com.br; 164 km in 2007; Man. Dir BENONY SCHMITZ FILHO.

Metrô Rio: Av. Presidente Vargas 2000, Col. Centro, 20210-031 Rio de Janeiro, RJ; tel. (21) 3211-6300; e-mail sac@metrorio.com.br; internet www.metrorio.com.br; 2-line metro system; operated by Opportans Concessão Metroviária, SA.

MRS Logística, SA: Praia de Botafogo 228, Sala 1201E, Ala B, Botafogo, 22359-900 Rio de Janeiro, RJ; tel. (21) 2559-4610; e-mail daf@mrs.com.br; internet www.mrs.com.br; f. 1996; 1,974 km in 2003; CEO EDUARDO PARENTE.

Transnordestina Logística, SA: Av. Francisco de Sá 4829, Bairro Carlito Pamplona, 60310-002 Fortaleza, CE; tel. (85) 4008-2500; fax (85) 4008-2525; e-mail kerley@cfn.com.br; internet www.cfn.com.br; fmrly Cia Ferroviária do Nordeste; changed name as above in 2008; subsidiary of Grupo CSN (Cia Siderúrgica Nacional); 4,534 km in 2003; Dir-Gen. TUFI DAHER FILHO.

Transporte Urbano do Distrito Federal (DFTRANS): SAIN, Estação Rodoferroviária, Ala Sul, Sobreloja, 70631-900 Brasília, DF; tel. (61) 3043-0401; e-mail ouvidoriadftrans@yahoo.com.br; internet www.dftrans.df.gov.br; the first section of the Brasília metro, linking the capital with the western suburb of Samambaia, was inaugurated in 1994; Dir MARCO ANTONIO CAMPANELLA.

ROADS

In 2009 there were 1,596,683 km of roads in Brazil, of which 207,462 km were paved. Brasília has been a focal point for inter-regional development, and paved roads link the capital with every region of Brazil. The building of completely new roads has taken place predominantly in the north. Roads are the principal mode of transport, accounting for 58% of traffic in 2005. Major projects include the Interportos Highway, linking the ports of Paraná, Paranagua, Antonina and the future port terminals of Pontal and Emboguaçu. A 3.5-km bridge linking Manaus with Iranduba over the Rio Negro, a tributary of the Amazon, was inaugurated in October 2011. In January 2011 a 2,600-km road, linking Rio Branco, the capital of Acre, with Nazca on the coast of Peru, was opened.

Departamento Nacional de Infra-Estrutura de Transportes (DNIT) (National Roads Development): Edif. Núcleo dos Transportes, SAN, Quadra 3, Bloco A, Lote A, 70040-902 Brasília, DF; tel. (61) 3315-4000; fax (61) 3315-4050; e-mail diretoria.geral@dnit.gov.br; internet www.dnit.gov.br; f. 1945 to plan and execute federal road policy and to supervise state and municipal roads in order to integrate them into the national network; Dir-Gen. JORGE ERNESTO PINTO FRAXE; Exec. Dir TARCÍSIO GOMES DE FREITAS.

INLAND WATERWAYS

River transport plays only a minor part in the movement of goods. There are three major river systems, the Amazon, the Paraná and the São Francisco, with a total of 28,000 km of waterways. The Amazon is navigable for 3,680 km, as far as Iquitos in Peru, and ocean-going ships can reach Manaus, 1,600 km upstream. Plans have been drawn up to improve the inland waterway system, and one plan is to link the Amazon and Upper Paraná to provide a navigable waterway across the centre of the country.

Agência Nacional de Transportes Aquaviários (ANTAQ): Edif. ANTAQ, SEPN, Quadra 514, Conj. E, 70760-545 Brasília, DF; tel. (61) 2029-6500; fax (61) 3447-1040; e-mail asc@antaq.gov.br; internet www.antaq.gov.br; Dir-Gen. FERNANDO ANTÔNIO BRITO FIALHO.

Administração das Hidrovias do Nordeste (AHINOR): Rua da Paz 561, Centro, 65020-450 São Luiz, MA; tel. and fax (98) 3231-5122; fax (98) 3232-6707; e-mail ahinor@elo.com.br; internet www.ahinor.gov.br; Pres. JOSÉ OSCAR FRAZÃO FROTA.

Administração da Hidrovia do Paraguai (AHIPAR): Rua Treze de Junho 960, 79300-040 Corumbá, MS; tel. (67) 3234-3200; fax (67) 3231-2661; internet www.ahipar.gov.br; Supt ANTÔNIO PAULO DE BARROS LEITE.

Administração da Hidrovia do Paraná (AHRANA): Av. Brig. Faria Lima 1912, 16° andar, Jardim Paulistano, 01451-000 São Paulo, SP; tel. (11) 2106-1600; fax (11) 3815-5435; e-mail ahrana@ahrana.gov.br; internet www.ahrana.gov.br; Supt ANTONIO BADIH CHENIN.

Administração da Hidrovia do São Francisco (AHSFRA): Praça do Porto 70, Distrito Industrial, 39270-000 Pirapora, MG; tel. (38) 3741-2555; fax (38) 3741-3046; e-mail superint@ahsfra.gov.br; internet www.ahsfra.gov.br; Supt SEBASTIÃO JOSÉ MARQUES DE OLIVEIRA.

Administração das Hidrovias da Amazônia Ocidental (AHIMOC): Rua Marquês de Santa Cruz 264, Centro, 69005-050 Manaus, AM; tel. (92) 3633-3061; fax (92) 3232-5156; e-mail ahimoc@ahimoc.com.br; internet www.ahimoc.com.br; Supt. SEBASTIÃO DA SILVA REIS.

Administração das Hidrovias da Amazônia Oriental (AHIMOR): Rua Joaquim Nabuco 8, Nazaré, 66055-300 Belém, PA; tel. (91) 3039-7700; fax (91) 3039-7721; e-mail ahimor@ahimor.gov.br; internet www.ahimor.gov.br; Supt ALBERTINO DE OLIVEIRA E SILVA.

Administração das Hidrovias do Sul (AHSUL): Praça Oswaldo Cruz 15, 3° andar, Sala 311–314, 90030-160 Porto Alegre, RS; tel. (51) 3225-0700; fax (51) 3226-9068; e-mail ahsul@uol.com.br; internet www.ahsul.com.br; Supt JOSÉ LUIZ FAY DE AZAMBUJA.

Administração das Hidrovias do Tocantins e Araguaia (AHITAR): ACSE Conj. 02, Lote 33, 1º andar, Sala 02, 77020-024 Palmas, TO; tel. (62) 3215-3171; fax (62) 3213-1904; e-mail ahitar@terra.com.br; internet www.ahitar.gov.br; Supt TARLES JUNQUEIRA CALEMAN.

SHIPPING

There are more than 40 deep-water ports in Brazil, all but one of which (Imbituba) are directly or indirectly administered by the Government. The majority of ports are operated by state-owned concerns (Cia Docas do Pará, Estado de Ceará, Estado do Rio Grande do Norte, Bahia, Paraíba, Espírito Santo, Rio de Janeiro and Estado de São Paulo), while a smaller number (including Suape, Cabedelo, São Sebastião, Paranaguá, Antonina, São Francisco do Sul, Porto Alegre, Itajaí, Pelotas and Rio Grande) are administered by state governments.

The ports of Santos, Rio de Janeiro and Rio Grande have specialized container terminals handling more than 1,200,000 TEUs (20-ft equivalent units of containerized cargo) per year. Santos is the major container port in Brazil, accounting for 800,000 TEUs annually. The ports of Paranaguá, Itajaí, São Francisco do Sul, Salvador, Vitória and Imbituba cater for containerized cargo to a lesser extent.

Total cargo handled by Brazilian ports in 2005 amounted to 6m. metric tons.

Brazil's merchant fleet comprised 592 vessels, with a combined aggregate displacement of some 2,377,821 grt, in December 2009.

Departamento de Marinha Mercante: Coordenação Geral de Transporte Maritimo, Av. Rio Branco 103, 6° e 8° andar, 20040-004 Rio de Janeiro, RJ; tel. (21) 2221-4014; fax (21) 2221-5929; Dir DÉBORA TEIXEIRA.

Port Authorities

Administração do Porto de Manaus (SNPH): Rua Marquês de Santa Cruz 25, Centro, 69005-050 Manaus, AM; tel. (92) 2123-4350; fax (92) 2123-4358; e-mail falecom@portodemanaus.com.br; internet www.portodemanaus.com.br; private; operates the port of Manaus; Dir ALESSANDRO BRONZE.

Administração do Porto de São Francisco do Sul (APSFS): Av. Eng. Leite Ribeiro 782, CP 71, 89240-000 São Francisco do Sul, SC; tel. (47) 3471-1200; fax (47) 3471-1211; e-mail porto@apsfs.sc.gov.br; internet www.apsfs.sc.gov.br; Pres. PAULO CÉSAR CORTES CORSI.

Administração dos Portos de Paranaguá e Antonina (APPA): Av. Conde Matarazzo 2500, 83370-000 Antonina, PR; Av. Ayrton Senna da Silva 161D, Pedro II, 83203-800 Paranaguá, PR; tel. (41) 3420-1100; fax (41) 3423-4252; e-mail superintendencia@appa.pr.gov.br; internet www.portosdoparana.pr.gov.br; Supt. AIRTON VIDAL MARON.

Cia Docas do Espírito Santo (CODESA): Av. Getúlio Vargas 556, Centro, 29010-945 Vitória, ES; tel. (27) 3132-7360; fax (27) 3132-7311; e-mail dirpre@codesa.gov.br; internet www.portodevitoria.com.br; f. 1983; Dir-Gen. CLOVIS LASCOSQUE.

Cia das Docas do Estado de Bahia (CODEBA): Av. da França 1551, Comércio, 40010-000 Salvador, BA; tel. (71) 3320-1100; fax (71) 3320-1375; e-mail business@codeba.com.br; internet www.codeba.com.br; f. 1977; port authority of state of Bahia and administers the ports of Salvador, Aratu and Ilhéus; CEO JOSÉ MUNIZ REBOUÇAS.

Cia Docas do Estado de Ceará (CDC): Praça Amigos da Marinha s/n, Mucuripe, 60182-640 Fortaleza, CE; tel. (85) 3266-8800; internet www.docasdoceara.com.br; administers the port of Fortaleza; Dir-Gen. PAULO ANDRÉ DE CASTRO HOLANDA.

Cia Docas do Estado de São Paulo (CODESP): Av. Conselheiro Rodrigues Alves s/n, Macuco, 11015-900 Santos, SP; tel. (13) 3202-6565; fax (13) 3202-6411; internet www.portodesantos.com; administers the ports of Santos, Charqueadas, Estrela, Cáceres and Corumbá/Ladário, and the waterways of Paraná (AHRANA), Paraguai (AHIPAR) and the South (AHSUL); Dir-Gen. JOSÉ ROBERTO CORREIA SERRA.

Cia Docas de Imbituba (CDI): Av. Presidente Vargas 100, CP 01, 88780-000 Imbituba, SC; tel. (48) 3355-8900; fax (48) 3255-0701; e-mail docas@cdiport.com.br; internet www.cdiport.com.br; private sector concession to administer the port of Imbituba until 2012; Pres. NILTON GARCIA DE ARAUJO; Port Administrator JEZIEL PAMATO DE SOUZA.

Cia Docas do Pará (CDP): Av. Presidente Vargas 41, 2° andar, Centro, 66010-000 Belém, PA; tel. (91) 3182-9029; fax (91) 3182-9139; e-mail asscom@cdp.com.br; internet www.cdp.com.br; f. 1967; administers the ports of Belém, Miramar, Santarém Obidos, Altamira, São Francisco, Marabá and Vila do Conde; Dir-Gen. CARLOS J. PONCIANO DA SILVA.

Cia Docas da Paraíba (DOCAS-PB): Porto de Cabedelo, Rua Presidente João Pessoa s/n, Centro, 58310-000 Cabedelo, PB; tel. (83) 3250-3000; fax (83) 3250-3001; e-mail gvp@docaspb.com.br; internet www.docaspb.com.br; administers the port of Cabedelo; Dir-Gen. WILBUR JÁCOME.

Cia Docas do Rio de Janeiro (CDRJ): Rua do Acre 21, Centro, 20081-000 Rio de Janeiro, RJ; tel. (21) 2219-8617; fax (21) 2253-0528; e-mail aleconosco@portosrio.gov.br; internet www.portosrio.gov.br; administers the ports of Rio de Janeiro, Niterói, Itaguaí and Angra dos Reis; Dir-Gen. JORGE LUZ DE MELLO.

Cia Docas do Rio Grande do Norte (CODERN): Av. Hildebrando de Góis 220, Ribeira, 59010-700 Natal, RN; tel. (84) 4005-5311; e-mail administrativo@codern.com.br; internet www.codern.com.br; administers the ports of Areia Branca, Natal and Maceió; Dir-Gen. PEDRO TERCEIRO DE MELO.

Empresa Maranhense de Administração Portuária (EMAP): Av. dos Portugueses s/n, Itaquí, 65085-370 São Luís, MA; tel. (98) 3216-6000; fax (98) 3216-6060; e-mail csl@emap.ma.gov.br; internet www.emap.ma.gov.br; f. 2001 to administer port of Itaquí as concession from the state of Maranhão; Pres. LUIZ CARLOS FOSSATI.

Sociedade de Portos e Hidrovias do Estado de Rondônia (SOPH): Rua Terminal dos Milagres 400, Bairro da Balsa, 78900-750 Porto Velho, RO; tel. (69) 3229-2134; fax (69) 3229-3904; e-mail soph@soph.ro.gov.br; internet www.soph.ro.gov.br; operates the port of Porto Velho; Dir-Gen. MATEUS SANTOS COSTA.

SUAPE—Complexo Industrial Portuário Governador Eraldo Gueiros: Rodovia PE-060, Km 10, Engenho Massangana, 55590-972 Ipojuca, PE; tel. (81) 3527-5000; fax (81) 3527-5066; e-mail imprensa@suape.pe.gov.br; internet www.suape.pe.gov.br; administers the port of Suape; Pres. GERALDO JULIO.

Superintendência do Porto de Itajaí: Rua Blumenau 5, Centro, 88305-101 Itajaí, SC; tel. (47) 3341-8000; fax (47) 3341-8075; e-mail atendimento@portoitajai.com.br; internet www.portoitajai.com.br; Supt ANTÐNIO AYRES DOS SANTOS, Jr; Exec. Dir HEDER CASSIANO MORITZ.

Superintendência do Porto de Rio Grande (SUPRG): Av. Honório Bicalho s/n, CP 198, 96201-020 Rio Grande do Sul, RS; tel. (53) 3231-1366; fax (53) 3231-1857; e-mail dirceu.lopes@portoriogrande.com.br; internet www.portoriogrande.com.br; f. 1996; Supt DIRCEU DA SILVA LOPES.

Superintendência do Porto de Tubarão: Ponta de Tubarão, CP 1078, 29072-970 Vitória, ES; tel. (27) 3335-4666; fax (27) 3335-3535; operated by Vale, SA (CVRD); handles iron ore cargoes; Exec. Dir TITO MARTINS.

Superintendência de Portos e Hidrovias do Estado do Rio Grande do Sul (SPH): Av. Mauá 1050, 4° andar, 90010-110 Porto Alegre, RS; tel. and fax (51) 3288-9200; e-mail executiva@sph.rs.gov.br; internet www.sph.rs.gov.br; f. 1921; administers the ports of Porto Alegre, Porto Pelotas, Porto Cachoeira, the São Gonçalo canal and other waterways; Dir-Supt PEDRO HOMERO FLORES OBELAR.

Private Companies

Aliança Navegação e Logística, Ltda: Rua Verbo Divino 1547, Bairro Chácara Santo Antônio, 04719-002 São Paulo, SP; tel. (11) 5185-3100; fax (11) 5185-5624; e-mail alianca@sao.alianca.com.br; internet www.alianca.com.br; f. 1951; cargo services to Argentina, Uruguay, Europe, Baltic, Atlantic and North Sea ports; Pres. ARSÊNIO CARLOS NÓBREGA.

Cia Libra de Navegação: Av. Rio Branco, 4, 6° e 7° andares, 20090-000 Rio de Janeiro; tel. and fax (21) 2213-9700; e-mail atendimento.brasil@csavgroup.com; internet www.libra.com.br.

Cia de Navegação da Amazônia (CNA): Edif. Vieiralves Business Center, Rua Salvador 120, 11° andar, Adrianópolis, Manaus, AM; tel. (92) 2125-1200; fax (92) 2125-1212; internet www.cnamazon.com.br; f. 1942; Exec. Pres. RENÉ LEVY AGUIAR.

Cia de Navegação Norsul: Av. Augusto Severo 8, 8° andar, 20021-040 Rio de Janeiro, RJ; tel. (21) 2139-0505; fax (21) 2507-1547; e-mail norsul@norsul.com; internet www.norsul.com; f. 1963; largest private fleet; owns and operates more than 28 vessels; Pres. CARLOS TEMKE.

Petrobras Transporte, SA (TRANSPETRO): Edif. Visconde de Itaboraí, Av. Presidente Vargas 328, 20091-060 Rio de Janeiro, RJ; tel. (21) 3211-7848; e-mail ouvidoria@transpetro.com.br; internet www.transpetro.com.br; f. 1998; absorbed the Frota Nacional de Petroleiros (FRONAPE) in 1999; transport of petroleum and related products; 53 vessels; Pres. JOSÉ SERGIO DE OLIVEIRA MACHADO.

Wilson Sons Agência Marítima: Rua Jardim Botânico 518, 3° andar, 22461-000 Rio de Janeiro, RJ; tel. (21) 2126-4222; fax (21) 2126-4190; e-mail box@wilsonsons.com.br; internet www.wilsonsons.com.br; f. 1837; shipping agency, port operations, towage, small shipyard; CEO AUGUSTO CEZAR TAVARES BAIÃO.

CIVIL AVIATION

There were 2,498 airports and airstrips and 857 helipads in 2006. Of the 67 principal airports, 22 are international, although most international traffic is handled by the two airports at Rio de Janeiro and two at São Paulo. In 2012 the Government reached agreement with foreign consortia to expand or upgrade the two São Paulo airports and the airport at Brasília. There were 18,024 aircraft registered in Brazil in 2008.

Agência Nacional de Aviação Civil: Edif. Parque Cidade Corporate Torre A, SCS, Quadra 09, Lote C, 70308-200 Brasília, DF; tel. (61) 3314-4105; internet www.anac.gov.br; f. 2006; Dir-Pres. MARCELO PACHECO DOS GUARANYS.

Empresa Brasileira de Infra-Estrutura Aeroportuária (Infraero): Estrada do Aeroporto, Setor de Concessionárias, Lote 5, Edif. Sede, 71608-900 Brasília, DF; tel. (61) 3312-3222; fax (61) 3321-0512; e-mail webmaster@infraero.gov.br; internet www.infraero.gov.br; Pres. GUSTAVO DO VALE.

Principal Airlines

Avianca: Av. Marechal Câmara 160, Sala 1532, Centro, 20020-080 Rio de Janeiro, RJ; tel. (21) 2544-2181; fax (21) 2215-7181; e-mail reservas@avianca.com.br; internet www.avianca.com.br; f. 1998 as Oceanair Linhas Aéreas, Ltda; changed name as above 2010; domestic services; Pres. JOSÉ EFROMOVICH.

Azul Linhas Aéreas Brasileiras: São Paulo, SP; tel. (11) 4831-1245; e-mail imprensa@voeazul.com.br; internet www.voeazul.com .br; f. 2009; Pres. DAVID NEELEMAN.

GOL Transportes Aéreos, SA: Rua Tamios 246, Jardim Aeropuerto, 04630-000 São Paulo, SP; tel. (11) 5033-4200; e-mail faleconosco@golnaweb.com.br; internet www.voegol.com.br; f. 2001; low-cost airline, acquired VARIG, SA in 2007; Man. Dir CONSTANTINO OLIVEIRA JÚNIOR.

Líder Aviação, SA: Av. Santa Rosa 123, São Luiz, 31270-750 Belo Horizonte, MG; tel. (31) 3490-4500; fax (31) 3490-4600; internet www .lideraviacao.com.br; f. 1958 as Líder Táxi Aéreo; changed name as above 2005; helicopters and small jets; Pres. JOSÉ AFONSO ASSUMPÇÃO.

TAM Linhas Aéreas, SA (TAM Airlines—TAM): Av. Jurandir 856, Lote 4, 1° andar, Jardim Ceci, 04072-000 São Paulo, SP; tel. (11) 570-5700; e-mail tamimprensa@tam.com.br; internet www.tam.com.br; f. 1976; scheduled passenger and cargo services from São Paulo to destinations throughout Brazil and in Argentina, Paraguay, Europe and the USA; CEO MARCO ANTONIO BOLOGNA.

TRIP Linhas Aéreas: Av. Brigadeiro Faria Lima 2601, 9º andar, Paulistano, 01451-001 São Paulo, SP; tel. (11) 3643.2700; internet www.voetrip.com.br; f. 1998; part of Grupos Caprioli; Pres. JOSÉ MARIO CAPRIOLI.

Tourism

In 2010 some 5.2m. tourists visited Brazil. In 2010 receipts from tourism totalled US $5,919m, according to provisional figures. Rio de Janeiro, with its famous beaches, is the centre of the tourist trade. Like Salvador, Recife and other towns, it has excellent examples of Portuguese colonial and modern architecture. The modern capital, Brasília, incorporates a new concept of city planning and is the nation's showpiece. Other attractions are the Iguaçu Falls, the seventh largest (by volume) in the world, the tropical forests of the Amazon basin and the wildlife of the Pantanal.

Associação Brasileira da Indústria de Hotéis (ABIH): Edif. América Office Tower, 17º andar, Salas 1712 e 1713, SCN, Quadra 01, Bloco F, 70711-905 Brasília, DF; tel. and fax (61) 3326-1177; e-mail secretariaabih@abih.com.br; internet www.abih.com.br; f. 1936; hoteliers' asscn; Pres. ENRICO FERMI TORQUATO.

Federação Nacional de Turismo (FENACTUR): Largo do Arouche 290, 6° andar, São Paulo, SP; tel. (11) 3331-4590; fax (11) 3221-6947; e-mail fenactur@uol.com.br; internet www.fenactur.com .br; f. 1990; Pres. MICHEL TUMA NESS.

Instituto Brasileiro de Turismo (EMBRATUR): Edif. Embratur, 3° andar, SCN, Quadra 02, Bloco G, 70712-907 Brasília, DF; tel. (61) 3429-7777; fax (61) 3429-7710; e-mail presidencia@embratur .gov.br; internet www.braziltour.com; f. 1966; Pres. FLÁVIO DINO DE CASTRO E COSTA.

Defence

As assessed at November 2011, Brazil's armed forces numbered 318,480: army 190,000 (including 70,000 conscripts); navy 59,000 (including at least 3,200 conscripts; also including 2,500 in the naval air force and 15,000 marines); and air force 69,480. Reserves numbered 1,340,000 and there were some 395,000 in the paramilitary Public Security Forces, state militias under army control. Military service lasts for 12 months and is compulsory for men between 18 and 45 years of age.

Defence Budget: R $63,700m. in 2012.

Chief of Staff of the Air Forces: Gen. JUNITI SAITO.

Chief of Staff of the Army: Lt-Gen. ENZO MARTINS PERI.

Chief of Staff of the Navy: Adm. JÚLIO SOARES DE MOURA NETO.

Education

Education is free in official schools at primary and secondary level. Primary education is compulsory between the ages of six and 14 years and lasts for nine years. Secondary education begins at 15 years of age and lasts for three years. In 2008 enrolment in primary schools included 94% of children in the relevant age-group, while enrolment in secondary schools included 82% of those in the relevant age-group. The federal Government is responsible for higher education, and in 2009 there were 186 universities, of which 100 were state-administered. Numerous private institutions exist at all levels of education. Federal government expenditure on education was R $7,746.2m. in 2010.

BRUNEI

Introductory Survey

LOCATION, CLIMATE, LANGUAGE, RELIGION, FLAG, CAPITAL

The Sultanate of Brunei (Negara Brunei Darussalam) lies in South-East Asia, on the north-west coast of the island of Borneo (most of which comprises the Indonesian territory of Kalimantan). It is surrounded and bisected on the landward side by Sarawak, one of the two eastern states of Malaysia. The country has a tropical climate, characterized by consistent temperature and humidity. Annual rainfall averages about 2,540 mm (100 ins) in coastal areas and about 3,300 mm (130 ins) in the interior. Temperatures are high: average daily temperatures range from 24°C (75°F) to 32°C (90°F). The principal language is Malay, although Chinese is also spoken and English is widely used. The Malay population (an estimated 66.0% of the total in 2010) are mainly Sunni Muslims. Most of the Chinese in Brunei (11.0% of the population in 2010) are Buddhists, and some are adherents of Confucianism and Daoism. Europeans and Eurasians are predominantly Christians, and the majority of indigenous tribespeople (Iban, Dayak and Kelabit—3.6% of the population in 2006) adhere to various animist beliefs. The flag (proportions 1 by 2) is yellow, with two diagonal stripes, of white and black, running from the upper hoist to the lower fly; superimposed in the centre is the state emblem (in red, with yellow Arabic inscriptions). The capital is Bandar Seri Begawan (formerly Brunei Town).

CONTEMPORARY POLITICAL HISTORY

Historical Context

Brunei, a traditional Islamic monarchy, formerly included most of the coastal regions of North Borneo (now Sabah) and Sarawak, which later became states of Malaysia. During the 19th century the rulers of Brunei ceded large parts of their territory to the United Kingdom, reducing the sultanate to its present size. In 1888, when North Borneo became a British Protectorate, Brunei became a British Protected State. In accordance with an agreement made in 1906, a British Resident was appointed to the court of the ruling Sultan as an adviser on administration. Under this arrangement, a form of government that included an advisory body, the State Council, emerged.

Brunei was invaded by Japanese forces in December 1941, but reverted to its former status in 1945, when the Second World War ended. The British-appointed Governor of Sarawak was High Commissioner for Brunei from 1948 until the territory's first written Constitution was promulgated in September 1959, when a further agreement was made between the Sultan and the British Government. The United Kingdom continued to be responsible for Brunei's defence and external affairs until the Sultanate's declaration of independence in 1984.

In December 1962 a large-scale revolt broke out in Brunei and in parts of Sarawak and North Borneo. The rebellion was undertaken by the 'North Borneo Liberation Army', an organization linked with the Parti Rakyat Brunei (PRB—Brunei People's Party), led by Sheikh Ahmad Azahari, which was strongly opposed to the planned entry of Brunei into the Federation of Malaysia. The rebels proclaimed the 'revolutionary State of North Kalimantan', but the revolt was suppressed, after 10 days' fighting, with the aid of British forces from Singapore. A state of emergency was declared, the PRB was banned, and Azahari was given asylum in Malaya. In the event, the Sultan of Brunei, Sir Omar Ali Saifuddin III, decided in 1963 against joining the Federation. From 1962 he ruled by decree, and the state of emergency remained in force. In October 1967 Saifuddin, who had been Sultan since 1950, abdicated in favour of his son, Hassanal Bolkiah. Under an agreement signed in November 1971, Brunei was granted full internal self-government.

In December 1975 the UN General Assembly adopted a resolution advocating British withdrawal from Brunei, the return of political exiles and the holding of a general election. Negotiations in 1978, following assurances by Malaysia and Indonesia that they would respect Brunei's sovereignty, resulted in an agreement (signed in January 1979) that Brunei would become fully independent within five years. Independence was duly proclaimed on 1 January 1984, and the Sultan took office as Prime Minister and Minister of Finance and of Home Affairs, presiding over a cabinet of six other ministers (including two of the Sultan's brothers and his father, the former Sultan).

The Chinese population, which controlled much of Brunei's private commercial sector but had become stateless since independence, appeared threatened in 1985, when the Sultan indicated that Brunei would become an Islamic state in which the indigenous, mainly Malay, inhabitants, known as *bumiputras* ('sons of the soil'), would receive preferential treatment.

Domestic Political Affairs

In May 1985 a new political party, the Parti Kebangsaan Demokratik Brunei (PKDB—Brunei National Democratic Party), was formed, comprising business executives loyal to the Sultan. However, the Sultan forbade employees of the Government (about 40% of the country's working population) to join the party, which based its policies on Islam and a form of liberal nationalism; persons belonging to the Chinese community were also excluded from membership. Divisions within the new party led to the formation of a second group, the Parti Perpaduan Kebangsaan Brunei (PPKB—Brunei National Solidarity Party), in February 1986. This party, which also received the Sultan's official approval, placed greater emphasis on co-operation with the Government, and was open to both Muslim and non-Muslim ethnic groups.

During 1985–86 the adoption of a more progressive style of government became apparent. The death of Sir Omar Ali Saifuddin, the Sultan's father, in September 1986 was expected to accelerate modernization. In October the cabinet was enlarged to 11 members, and commoners and aristocrats were assigned portfolios that had previously been held by members of the royal family. In February 1988, however, the PKDB was dissolved by the authorities after it had demanded the resignation of the Sultan as head of government (although not as head of state), an end to the 26-year state of emergency and the holding of democratic elections. The official reason for the dissolution of the party was its connections with a foreign organization, the Pacific Democratic Union. The leaders of the PKDB, Abdul Latif Hamid and Abdul Latif Chuchu, were arrested, under the provisions of the Internal Security Act, and detained until March 1990. Abdul Latif Hamid died in May of that year.

In 1990 the Government encouraged the population to embrace *Melayu Islam Beraja* (MIB—Malay Islamic Monarchy) as the state ideology. This affirmation of traditional Bruneian values for Malay Muslims was widely believed to be a response to an increase in social problems, including alcohol and narcotics abuse. Muslims were urged to adhere more closely to the tenets of Islam, greater emphasis was laid on Islamic holiday celebrations, and the distribution of alcohol was discouraged.

In 1994 a constitutional committee, appointed by the Government and chaired by the Minister of Foreign Affairs, Prince Mohamed Bolkiah, submitted a recommendation that the Constitution be amended to provide for an elected legislature. In February 1997 the Sultan replaced his brother, Prince Jefri Bolkiah, as Minister of Finance. It was rumoured that the Sultan's assumption of the finance portfolio was due to alleged financial disagreements rather than Prince Jefri's frequently criticized lifestyle. In March the Sultan and Prince Jefri denied accusations of misconduct made by a former winner of a US beauty contest, Shannon Marketic. A US court granted the Sultan immunity from legal action in August, owing to his status as a foreign head of state; this immunity was extended to Prince Jefri in March 1998. Similar allegations against Prince Jefri, submitted to a court in Hawaii, resulted in an undisclosed financial settlement, following the judge's rejection of Prince Jefri's claims to immunity. Further allegations concerning the extravagant lifestyle of Prince Jefri emerged in a court case in the United Kingdom in February, in which Jefri was being sued for £80m. by two former business associates, Watche (Bob) and Rafi Manoukian. The Manoukian brothers claimed that Prince Jefri had reneged on two property agreements; Prince Jefri was counter-suing them for £100m., alleging that they had exploited their relationship with him to amass considerable wealth. The case, which was unreported in Brunei, was also settled out of court for an undisclosed sum.

On 10 August 1998 the Sultan's son, Prince Haji Al-Muhtadee Billah Bolkiah, was installed as the heir to the throne. Meanwhile, Prince Jefri, who had left Brunei in April, was removed as Chairman of the Brunei Investment Agency (BIA) in July, following the collapse of his business conglomerate, the Amedeo Development Corporation. (Amedeo was formally liquidated in July 1999, with reported debts of at least US $3,500m.) Prince Jefri, who was also removed from the boards of seven communications companies, claimed that he was the victim of a conspiracy of conservative Islamists, led by his estranged brother, Prince Mohamed Bolkiah (the Minister of Foreign Affairs), and the Minister of Education, Pehin Dato' Haji Abdul Aziz bin Pehin Haji Umar. Prince Jefri's removal from positions of authority took place amid a more rigorous enforcement of the ban on alcohol and the confiscation from retailers of non-Islamic religious artefacts. In September Abdul Aziz, who had replaced Prince Jefri as Chairman of the BIA, announced that large amounts of government funds had been misappropriated during Prince Jefri's tenure. After many months of self-imposed exile, Prince Jefri returned to Brunei in January 2000. In the following month the Government and the BIA began civil proceedings against him, alleging his improper withdrawal and use of substantial BIA funds while Minister of Finance and Chairman of the BIA; 71 other people were named in the action, including Prince Jefri's eldest son, Prince Muda Abdul Hakeem. In May an out-of-court settlement was reached whereby the assets that had been acquired by Prince Jefri with funds derived from the BIA were to be returned to the State. These assets were sold for £5.5m. at a public auction in August 2001.

In 2000 a new political party, Parti Kesedaran Rakyat (PAKAR—People's Consciousness Party), was established. PAKAR outwardly pledged its support to the Sultan and the system of governance, but was critical of administrative deficiencies. In October of that year Haji Awang Kassim, Prince Jefri's former confidential secretary, who was also former deputy managing director of the BIA and a prominent figure in Amedeo management, was arrested, following his extradition from the Philippines. Civil proceedings were also instigated against another six of Prince Jefri's former colleagues. In the mean time, the legal dispute over responsibility for Amedeo's huge losses continued. In October 2001 the Sultan requested his newly created local company, Global Evergreen, to resolve the long-standing dispute with more than 300 creditors who were owed an estimated B $1,000m. Negotiations proceeded swiftly, and creditors were strongly recommended to accept a new, highly favourable offer whereby they would be repaid on a 'sliding scale' according to the magnitude of their claim. The settlement brought to an end much of the legal contention arising from the closure of the company.

In March 2004 it was reported that a businessman and two retired senior army and police intelligence officers had been imprisoned without trial under the Internal Security Act for allegedly 'leaking' government secrets. The police officer was also accused of treason, having allegedly provided classified documents to a foreign country.

Reconvening of the Legislative Council

In September 2004 the 21-member Legislative Council, suspended in 1983 prior to Brunei's declaration of independence, was reconvened and approved a series of constitutional amendments. These envisaged, among other changes, the direct election of 15 members of an expanded 45-member Legislative Council, although the remaining 30 members would be appointed by the Sultan. However, no schedule was established for the holding of the elections, nor was there any reference to an end to the national state of emergency that had been in place since 1962.

In May 2005 the Sultan effected a major cabinet reorganization, in which four prominent ministers were dismissed, including the Minister of Home Affairs and Special Adviser to the Prime Minister, Pehin Dato' Haji Isa Ibrahim (who was replaced by Pehin Dato' Haji Adanan bin Mohammad Yusof), and the Minister of Education, Pehin Dato' Haji Abdul Aziz (replaced by Pehin Dato' Haji Abdul Rahman Taib). Crown Prince Haji Al-Muhtadee Billah Bolkiah was appointed to the newly formed position of Senior Minister at the Prime Minister's Office. The changes also included the creation of a new Ministry of Energy and the appointment of the first ethnic Chinese official within the Bruneian cabinet, Pehin Dato' Lim Jock Seng, who was installed as the Minister of Foreign Affairs II. The Sultan also appointed 10 new Deputy Ministers, including two from the corporate sector.

In September 2005 the Sultan dissolved the existing Legislative Council and appointed 29 new members. The enlargement of the Council received widespread approval, but by 2012 there was still no indication of a date for the holding of elections. In March 2006 the Legislative Council held a six-day session principally for the purpose of approving the National Budget. The Council convened in March each year, thereafter. In May the Government announced that state laws governing the granting of citizenship to foreign nationals resident in Brunei were to be relaxed. Henceforth, any foreign male national married to a Bruneian woman for 15 years, if he had been born in Brunei (or for 20 years if born outside Brunei), could apply for permanent citizenship. Furthermore, foreign nationals possessing professional skills of direct benefit to the country and those contributing to Brunei's economic growth and commanding assets and/or investments worth in excess of B $500,000 (approximately US $319,040) would also be eligible. However, all applicants would still be required to demonstrate both written and oral proficiency in Malay and be expected to possess a comprehensive understanding of Bruneian culture.

Recent developments

In August 2006 the number of legal political organizations in Brunei was increased to three upon the establishment of the Parti Pembangunan Bangsa (PPB, or National Development Party—NDP). Founded by the former Secretary-General of the PRB, Muhammad Yasin Affendy bin Abdul Rahman, the PPB—the stated goal of which was to support the Government by promoting adherence to the values of MIB—held its first congress in April 2006. However, in 2007 both the PPKB and PAKAR were deregistered—PAKAR in March, as a result of the internal leadership disputes that had resulted in the party splitting into two opposing factions, and the PPKB in November, following its failure to supply annual reports to the relevant authority. The PPKB appealed against its deregistration but this was rejected in February 2008 by the Minister of Home Affairs, thereby confirming the dissolution and consolidating the PPB's status as the only active party within the country. The PPB's fifth party congress was held in June 2010, but the party remained largely ineffectual. Owing to ill health, Yasin Affendy resigned as the PPB's President in February 2011, and was subsequently replaced, on an interim basis, by Malai Hassan Othman.

Meanwhile, in 2004 the BIA had initiated further legal proceedings against Prince Jefri, alleging that he had failed to relinquish ownership of properties in Europe and the USA as prescribed by the out-of-court settlement of 2001. Prince Jefri disputed the legitimacy of the BIA's actions, and the case was referred to the Privy Council in London, where the Prince was now resident. In November 2007 the Privy Council, which remained Brunei's highest court of appeal, dismissed Prince Jefri's defence as 'hopeless' and ruled that he return assets valued at more than US $1,000m. Citing Prince Jefri's continued failure to honour the court ruling, the Sultanate referred the case to the High Court of England and obtained an order compelling Prince Jefri to attend a five-day hearing for contempt of court in June 2008. When Prince Jefri failed to appear at the proceedings, the presiding judge issued a warrant for his arrest. Prince Jefri returned to Brunei in October 2009, whereupon he visited the Sultan, prompting speculation that relations between the two brothers might have improved and that the ongoing legal dispute might soon be resolved. Photographs published in local media during 2010–11 of the Prince in the company of the Sultan and other members of the royal family appeared to confirm suggestions that a reconciliation between the brothers had been achieved.

In November 2010, however, controversy re-emerged when court proceedings involving Prince Jefri opened at a New York state court. The Prince had filed a lawsuit against Thomas Derbyshire and Faith Zaman Derbyshire, a British husband-and-wife legal team whom he had employed during 2004–06 to supervise the sale of a number of luxury properties, claiming that his former advisers had illegally diverted some US $7m. of his personal wealth for their own uses. The couple denied any wrongdoing and filed a countersuit in which they claimed that they were owed $21m. in unpaid legal fees. Following a five-week trial, the jury ruled in December 2010 that Prince Jefri was owed $54,000 in improperly charged expenses by Derbyshire and Zaman, but dismissed the Prince's claim that the pair had defrauded him, and ordered him to pay them the $21m. that it found he owed in unpaid fees. Prince Jefri expressed his intention to appeal against the verdict, but in November 2011 it was reported that he had abandoned his appeal, appearing to conclude the scandal, which had proved to be of considerable embarrassment to the Bruneian royal family.

In various *titah* (royal addresses) in the second half of the 2000s, the Sultan repeatedly stressed the need to revive the religious education system, insisting that emphasis be given to the teaching of Islamic religious knowledge in schools. In August 2007 the Sultanate's first Islamic University, Universiti Islam Sultan Sharif Ali (UNISSA), welcomed its first intake of students, but was criticized by the Sultan in a *titah* in November 2009 for placing too little emphasis on the teachings of the Koran. Meanwhile, in August 2008 the reallocation of three cabinet portfolios was announced. In August of the following year Datin Hayati Salleh was appointed to the position of Attorney-General, a role that had been conferred with ministerial status in 2005, thus becoming the first woman to attain full cabinet rank in Brunei (although Princess Hajah Masna, Brunei's ambassador-at-large, had sometimes served as Minister of Foreign Affairs in an acting capacity).

A major cabinet reorganization was implemented in May 2010. Significant appointments included that of Pehin Dato' Paduka Haji Badaruddin bin Haji Othman, hitherto Deputy Minister of Religious Affairs, as the new Minister of Home Affairs and of Pehin Dato' Haji Col (retd) Mohammad Yasmin bin Haji Umar, formerly Deputy Minister of Defence, as Minister of Energy at the Prime Minister's Office. Pengiran Dato' Dr Haji Mohammad bin Haji Abdul Rahman, previously Deputy Minister of Education, was appointed Minister of Religious Affairs, in place of Pehin Zain Serudin, who left the Council of Cabinet Ministers after 24 years' service. Another notable departure was that of Pehin Abdul Rahman Taib, a cabinet minister since independence in 1984 (initially as Minister of Development, and as Minister of Education since 1986). Datin Adina Othman, hitherto Director of the Community Development Department within the civil service, was appointed Deputy Minister of Culture, Youth and Sports, thereby becoming the second woman to attain full ministerial status in Brunei (after Attorney-General Salleh).

Meanwhile, in a televised address to commemorate Brunei's National Day in February 2010, the Sultan emphasized the importance of well-managed economic policies and favourable investment conditions in order to promote overall economic growth. In a *titah* in July, the Sultan announced the establishment of the Autoriti Monetari Brunei Darussalam (AMBD), which was to be responsible for overseeing monetary policy, supervising financial institutions and currency management. Crown Prince Al-Muhtadee Bolkiah was appointed Chairman of the AMBD, which was formally inaugurated on 1 January 2011; the Prince retained the post of Senior Minister at the Prime Minister's Office.

Haji Mohammed Yassin resigned as Speaker of the Legislative Council in February 2011 and was replaced by Pehin Dato' Haji Isa Ibrahim, the former Minister of Home Affairs and Special Adviser to the Prime Minister. In the following month the Sultan decreed that, following the undermining of Islamic jurisprudence by British intervention during the colonial era, Bruneian law must henceforth be more closely aligned with Syariah (*Shari'a*—Islamic) law, which had constituted the main body of law in Brunei prior to the implementation of British civil law. A working committee was thus to be established to ensure that criminal justice was restructured according to the requirements of Islamic teachings, and any discrepancies between existing civil legislation and Syariah law were to be eliminated. In April the Sultan appointed Princes Abdul Azim, Abdul Malik and Abdul Mateen to the Privy Council, appearing to indicate the potential emergence of a new generation of Bruneian leaders. Two former cabinet ministers, Pehin Abdul Aziz Umar and Pehin Mohd Zain Serudin, were also appointed to the Council.

Foreign Affairs

Regional relations

Brunei has developed close relations with the members of the Association of Southeast Asian Nations (ASEAN, see p. 214), in particular Singapore, with which it has concluded numerous bilateral agreements, including a memorandum of understanding (MOU) signed in March 2009 to bolster co-operation in the fields of agriculture, biodiversity research and nature conservation, and a separate agreement, signed in June of that year, that was intended to promote policy and regulatory exchanges related to digital media, as well as business collaborations among government and private entities.

Conflicting claims (from Brunei, the People's Republic of China, Malaysia, the Philippines, Taiwan and Viet Nam) to all, or some, of the uninhabited Spratly Islands, situated in the South China Sea, were a source of tension in the region. Brunei was the only claimant not to have stationed troops on the islands, which are not only strategically important but also possess potentially large reserves of petroleum. During the 1990s attempts to resolve the dispute through a negotiated settlement resulted in little progress, and military activity in the area increased. However, during the annual ASEAN summit meeting held in Cambodia, in November 2002, the members of the grouping signed an agreement with China approving a 'code of conduct' for the islands. Following the ASEAN summit meeting held in Viet Nam in October 2010, it was announced that China and the ASEAN member states had agreed to adopt a more legally binding code of conduct for the islands, which it was hoped would reduce political and security instability in the region and strengthen regional co-operation. An agreement on guidelines for the establishment of such a code of conduct was signed in July 2011 following talks, held in Bali, Indonesia, between ASEAN ministers responsible for foreign affairs and Chinese foreign officials.

Protracted land and maritime border disputes between Brunei and Malaysia were deemed by the Governments of both countries to have been concluded by the signing of an Exchange of Letters in March 2009 by the Sultan and the then Malaysian Prime Minister, Abdullah Badawi. As well as the final settlement of the maritime border between Brunei and Malaysia, the agreement also provided for, *inter alia*, the establishment of a joint petroleum revenue area and the eventual demarcation of the common land border. Relations with Malaysia were further boosted by the signing, in October 2010, of an MOU intended to bolster co-operation in higher education and, in December of that year, of a bilateral agreement providing for the joint development of two petroleum blocks off the coast of Borneo.

At the end of the seventh summit meeting of ASEAN leaders, hosted by Brunei in November 2001, the Sultanate pledged its support for a programme proposed by Philippine President Gloria Arroyo, which sought to encourage close regional co-operation in countering international terrorism in the aftermath of the September suicide attacks on the USA; ASEAN leaders subsequently signed a Declaration on Counter-Terrorism with the USA. Brunei was due to resume the annually rotating chair of ASEAN in 2013. Meanwhile, in January 2010 the Sultanate hosted an ASEAN Tourism Forum summit meeting.

Relations with China, with which full diplomatic relations were established in late 1991, have strengthened in recent years. In September 2004, during an official visit to the People's Republic, the Sultan and Chinese President Hu Jintao signed several MOUs, which were intended to increase co-operation in areas such as trade and investment, education and judicial affairs. During a reciprocal visit to Brunei by President Hu in April 2005, several more bilateral agreements were signed, under the terms of which the need for diplomatic and official visas for travel between the two countries was waived; other areas of focus included energy, public health, tourism, education and military training. One indirect consequence of this burgeoning relationship was the temporary closure in 2006 of the Taiwanese Economic and Cultural Representative Office in Bandar Seri Begawan. In January 2011 Brunei's ambassador-at-large, Princess Hajah Masna, urged a deepening of relations with China, and announced that the Bruneian and Chinese Governments were planning several events and initiatives to commemorate the 20th anniversary of the establishment of diplomatic relations, including the designation of the year 2011 as a 'Year of Friendship' between the two countries. During a visit to Bandar Seri Begawan by Chinese Premier Wen Jiabao in November of that year, Wen emphasized the growing importance of Chinese-Bruneian co-operation, which, he asserted, had engendered tangible benefits to both countries and had helped to promote regional stability and prosperity, a view that was echoed by the Sultan, who appealed for a further deepening of bilateral relations. Premier Wen also held discussions with other prominent members of the Bruneian royal family during his stay.

Japan remained a major market for Bruneian exports, and in July 2007 the Sultan and Japanese Prime Minister Shinzo Abe signed a free trade agreement—the Brunei-Japan Economic Partnership Agreement (BJEPA)—in the Japanese capital,

Tokyo. Bilateral relations were further consolidated during a meeting between the Sultan and Japanese Emperor Akihito in Tokyo in November 2010. Meanwhile, in April 2009 Brunei and the Philippines signed an MOU that was intended to increase bilateral co-operation in a number of areas, including agriculture and farming-related trade and investment; a further MOU, pertaining to the field of information and communications technology, was signed between the two countries in July 2010.

Other external relations

Relations with the United Kingdom became strained during 1983, following the Brunei Government's decision, in August, to transfer the management of its investment portfolio from the British Crown Agents to the newly created BIA. However, normal relations were restored in September, when the British Government agreed that a battalion of Gurkha troops, stationed in Brunei since 1971, should remain in the country after independence, at the Sultanate's expense, specifically to guard the oil- and gasfields.

In July 1990, in response to the uncertainty over the future of US bases in the Philippines, Brunei offered the USA the option of operating its forces from Brunei. A bilateral MOU was subsequently signed, providing for up to three visits a year to Brunei by US warships. Under the terms of the memorandum, Bruneian and US armed forces engage in regular joint military exercises and training programmes. Senior-level state visits to the USA in recent years have included those of the Sultan to Washington, DC, in December 2002 and to New York in November 2008 and that of the Crown Prince to Washington, DC, and New York in September 2011, during which he addressed the UN General Assembly, expressing his Government's desire for a 'fair and equitable two-state solution to the situation in Palestine'. Meanwhile, bilateral tension was provoked in June 2010 by the inclusion of Brunei on the USA's Trafficking in Persons Report, an annual document containing a list of countries perceived by the US Administration to be a significant destination for forced labour and prostitution.

Diplomatic relations were established with numerous countries in 2005–11, including Venezuela in July 2005; Iceland and Estonia in April and May 2006, respectively; Afghanistan in February 2007; Kenya in August 2008; Trinidad and Tobago in November 2009; Georgia and the Dominican Republic in March and August 2010, respectively; and Fiji and Palau in April and December 2011, respectively. Meanwhile, Brunei's relations with other Islamic nations continued to develop; in April 2006 the Sultan made his first state visits to Qatar and the United Arab Emirates, and in April 2009 he made official visits to Kuwait and Oman. In October 2011 the Sultan revisited Kuwait in order to attend the 10th Ministerial Meeting of the Asia Cooperation Dialogue—established in 2002 to promote Asian co-operation at a continental level and to help to integrate separate regional organizations such as ASEAN, the Gulf Cooperation Council and the South Asian Association for Regional Cooperation.

The Sultan paid an official visit to France in June 2008, where he had discussions with President Nicolas Sarkozy, as a result of which links were established between the respective special forces units of the Bruneian and French militaries. In December the then Russian President, Vladimir Putin, signed an order to open an embassy in Brunei. During a visit to Russia in October 2009, the Sultan met with Prime Minister Putin and President Dmitrii Medvedev, signing several bilateral agreements intended to improve co-operation in the areas of defence, the economy, education and tourism. The embassy was formally opened in April 2010. During a visit to Bandar Seri Begawan by a high-ranking Russian delegation in October 2011, discussions were held with a number of Bruneian officials, including Minister of Religious Affairs Pengiran Dato' Dr Haji Mohammad bin Haji Abdul Rahman, on further strengthening bilateral relations, with a particular emphasis on religious affairs co-operation.

CONSTITUTION AND GOVERNMENT

The 1959 Constitution confers supreme executive authority on the Sultan. He is assisted and advised by four Constitutional Councils: the Religious Council, the Privy Council, the Council of Cabinet Ministers and the Council of Succession. Following the rebellion of 1962, certain provisions of the Constitution (including those pertaining to elections and to a fifth Council, the Legislative Council) were suspended, and the Sultan has since ruled by decree. However, in September 2004 the 21-member Legislative Council was convened for the first time since the country became independent in 1984 and approved several constitutional amendments, including one providing for the direct election of 15 members of an expanded 45-member Legislative Council. The remaining members were to be appointed by the Sultan. In September 2005 the Sultan appointed a new, enlarged Legislative Council comprising 29 members. At early 2012 no schedule had been established for the holding of the elections.

REGIONAL AND INTERNATIONAL CO-OPERATION

Brunei is a member of the Association of Southeast Asian Nations (ASEAN, see p. 214), of the Asia-Pacific Economic Co-operation (APEC, see p. 204) forum, of the Asian Development Bank (ADB, see p. 210), and of the UN's Economic and Social Commission for Asia and the Pacific (ESCAP, see p. 40).

Brunei became a member of the UN in 1984, and was admitted to the World Trade Organization (WTO) in 1995. Brunei participates in the Group of 77 (G77, see p. 450) developing countries. In 2007 Brunei was admitted to the International Labour Organization (ILO, see p. 141). Brunei is also a member of the Organization of the Islamic Conference (OIC, see p. 404) and of the Non-aligned Movement (see p. 464).

ECONOMIC AFFAIRS

In 2009, according to estimates by the World Bank, Brunei's gross national income (GNI), measured at average 2007–09 prices, was US $12,461m., equivalent to US $31,800 per head (or US $49,730 on an international purchasing-power parity basis). In 2001–10, it was estimated, the population increased by an annual average of 2.0%. Gross domestic product (GDP) per head, in real terms, decreased by an annual average of 0.9% during 2001–09. According to the Asian Development Bank (ADB), Brunei's overall GDP increased at an estimated average annual rate of 1.2% during 2001–10. Real GDP expanded by 2.6% in 2010 and by 2.9% in 2011.

Agriculture (including forestry and fishing) employed just over 0.5% of the working population in 2011, according to FAO estimates, and provided 0.8% of GDP in 2010. The principal crops include rice, cassava, bananas and pineapples. According to figures from the ADB, in 2001–10 the GDP of the agricultural sector increased, in real terms, at an estimated average annual rate of 1.9%; agricultural GDP increased by 5.6% in 2009, but declined by 5.8% in 2010.

Industry (comprising mining, manufacturing, construction and utilities) employed 21.4% of the working population, according to the results of the 2001 census, and contributed 66.8% of GDP in 2010. According to figures from the ADB, total industrial GDP decreased at an average annual rate of 0.7% in 2001–10. Industrial GDP decreased by 5.0% in 2009, but increased by 1.7% in 2010.

Brunei's economy has continued to rely almost entirely on its petroleum and natural gas resources. According to the 2001 census, mining and quarrying employed only 2.7% of the working population. The contribution to GDP of the sector increased from 47.3% in 2009 to 50.8% in 2010. Proven reserves of petroleum at the end of 2010 amounted to 1,100m. barrels, sufficient to sustain production at that year's levels (averaging 172,000 barrels per day) for more than 17 years. Output of natural gas in 2010 totalled an estimated 12,200m. cu m. According to industry sources, proven reserves at the end of that year totalled 301,000m. cu m (a level sustainable for nearly 25 years). In 2009, according to estimates from the IMF, exports of oil and gas accounted for 96.1% of total exports. According to figures from the ADB, the GDP of the mining sector decreased by an annual average of 1.4% in 2001–10, declining by 3.4% in 2009, before increasing by 1.6% in 2010. Commercial operations at Brunei's inaugural petrochemical plant, a methanol production facility at the Sungai Liang Industrial Park in Belait district, commenced in May 2010.

The manufacturing sector employed 8.5% of the working population, according to the 2001 census, and contributed 12.1% of GDP in 2010. The textile and garment industry provides modest revenue; other industries include cement, mineral water, canned food, dairy products, silica sands products, footwear and leather products, the design and manufacture of printed circuits, publishing and printing. According to ADB figures, during 2001–10 manufacturing GDP increased by an annual average of 0.2%. The GDP of this sector declined by 9.8% in 2009, but increased by 1.5% in 2010.

Construction employed 8.4% of the working population, according to the 2001 census, and contributed 3.1% of GDP in

2010. According to figures from the ADB, the GDP of the sector increased at an average annual rate of 3.4% during 2001–10; sectoral GDP decreased by 4.1% in 2009, but increased by 2.4% in 2010.

Services employed 77.2% of the working population, according to the 2001 census, and provided an estimated 32.5% of GDP in 2010. In that year the sector comprising wholesale and retail trade contributed 3.7% of GDP, and the finance sector contributed 3.5%. In addition to efforts to develop Brunei as a financial centre, the tourism sector was also being actively promoted, and in 2008 receipts from tourism totalled US $241m. In 2008 a total of 225,757 tourists visited Brunei. During 2001–10, according to the ADB, the combined GDP of the service sectors increased, in real terms, at an average annual rate of 3.9%. The GDP of the services sector increased by 2.1% in 2009 and by 3.8% in 2010.

In 2009 Brunei recorded a visible trade surplus of US $4,889.5m., predominantly attributable to receipts from petroleum exports. In the same year there was a surplus of US $3,977.4m. on the current account of the balance of payments. In 2009 the principal source of imports (providing 25.6%) was Singapore; other major suppliers were Malaysia (19.4%), the USA, Japan and the People's Republic of China. The principal market for exports in that year was Japan, which accounted for 46.1% of total exports (mainly natural gas on a long-term contract); other significant purchasers were the Republic of Korea (also a purchaser of natural gas), Indonesia and Australia. In 2009 principal imports comprised machinery and transport equipment, basic manufactures, food and live animals and miscellaneous manufactured articles; principal exports were mineral fuels and lubricants.

For the fiscal year ending March 2011 there was a projected budgetary deficit of B $1,024m. The ADB estimated the fiscal surplus at the equivalent of 17.5% of GDP in 2010/11. Brunei has no external public debt. Annual inflation averaged 0.4% in 2001–08. According to the ADB, consumer prices increased by 1.1% in 2009, by 0.4% in 2010 and by 2.0% in 2011. Foreign workers, principally from Malaysia and the Philippines, have helped to ease the labour shortage that results from the small size of the population, and comprised about 41% of the labour force in 2000. However, the rate of unemployment was 2.7% in 2010, reflecting a shortage of non-manual jobs for the well-educated Bruneians.

The Government's ninth National Development Plan, encompassing the period 2007–12, identified eight strategic areas of focus: education, economics, security, institutional development, local business development, infrastructural development, social security and the environment. Expenditure of B $9,500m. was allocated to the plan, which formed part of the Wawasan (National Vision) Brunei 2035, a long-term development strategy intended to improve per caput incomes and to diversify economic activities. The country's diversification strategy included the promotion of the Brunei Halal brand on world markets. In addition to the area of Islamic financial services, the Government hoped to extend the programme beyond food products to items such as pharmaceuticals. However, a lack of local raw materials constituted a severe impediment to such ambitions. The 1.9% contraction in GDP registered in 2008 was attributed not only to the global economic slowdown and to a weakening of international petroleum prices, but also to production constraints arising from extensive upgrading work being carried out on Brunei's oil facilities. The value of oil and gas exports declined by 33% in 2009, leading to a further contraction, of 1.8%, in GDP. Following a recovery in 2010, when GDP increased by 2.6%, growth accelerated to 2.9% in 2011; the ADB forecast an increase of 2.6% in GDP for 2012. In December 2011 the Chinese company Zhejiang Hengyi Group was awarded the development rights for a US $2,500m. oil refinery and aromatics cracker project to be located at Pulau Muara Besar. Following completion of the first phase of the project, which was to include petroleum products, paraxylene and benzene, and which was expected to create more than 800 jobs (the majority of which were to be offered to local workers), the Chinese firm planned a further investment of US $3,500m. to expand the refinery to allow for the production of olefins. This second phase was expected to lead to the creation of a further 1,200 employment opportunities. The tourism industry was expected to be negatively affected by the unexpected announcement by Royal Brunei Airlines in mid-2011 that it was to suspend its services to several destinations, including several prominent Australian and New Zealand cities. Meanwhile, following the establishment in January 2011 of the Autoriti Monetari Brunei Darussalam, which was to perform the functions of a central bank, it was confirmed that the currency interchangeability agreement with Singapore was to remain in place. The arrangement was expected to help mitigate inflationary pressures, as was the Government's continuation of subsidies on various consumer items.

PUBLIC HOLIDAYS

2013 (provisional): 1 January (New Year's Day), 23 January* (Hari Mouloud, Birth of the Prophet), 11 February† (Chinese New Year), 25 February (for National Day), 31 May (Royal Brunei Armed Forces Day), 5 June* (Israk Mikraj, Ascension of the Prophet Muhammad), 8 July* (Beginning of Ramadan), 15 July (Sultan's Birthday), August* (Memperingati Nuzul Al-Quran, Anniversary of the Revelation of the Koran), 7 August* (Hari Raya Aidilfitri, end of Ramadan), 14 October* (Hari Raya Aidiladha, Feast of the Sacrifice), 4 November* (Hijrah, Islamic New Year).

* These holidays are dependent on the Islamic lunar calendar and may vary by one or two days from the dates given.

† The first day of the first moon of the lunar calendar.

Statistical Survey

Sources (unless otherwise stated): Department of Economic Planning and Development, Prime Minister's Office, Block 2A, Jalan Ong Sum Ping, Bandar Seri Begawan BA 1311; tel. 2244433; fax 2230236; e-mail info@jpke.gov.bn; Brunei Economic Development Board, Block 2K, Bangunan Keraajan, Jalan Ong Sum Ping, Bandar Seri Begawan BA 1311; tel. 2230111; fax 2230063; e-mail info@bedb.com.bn; internet www.bedb.com.bn.

AREA AND POPULATION

Area: 5,765 sq km (2,226 sq miles); *By District:* Brunei/Muara 570 sq km (220 sq miles), Seria/Belait 2,725 sq km (1,052 sq miles), Tutong 1,165 sq km (450 sq miles), Temburong 1,305 sq km (504 sq miles).

Population (excluding transients afloat): 260,482 at census of 7 August 1991; 332,844 (males 168,925, females 163,919) at census of 21 August 2001; 414,400 (males 219,100, females 195,300) in 2010 (official estimate at mid-year). *By District* (official estimates at mid-2010): Brunei/Muara 290,100; Seria/Belait 68,300; Tutong 45,800; Temburong 10,200; Total 414,400.

Density (at mid-2010): 71.9 per sq km.

Population by Age and Sex (UN estimates at mid-2012): *0–14:* 105,618 (males 54,732, females 50,886); *15–64:* 291,520 (males 145,668, females 145,852); *65 and over:* 15,755 (males 7,998, females 7,757); *Total* 412,893 (males 208,398, females 204,495) (Source: UN, *World Population Prospects: The 2010 Revision*). *Population by Age* ('000 persons at mid-2010, official estimates): *0–19:* 141.9; *20–64:* 257.3; *65 and over:* 14.4; *Total* 414.4. Note: Totals may not be equal to the sum of components, owing to rounding.

Ethnic Groups (official estimates at mid-2010): Malay 273,600, Chinese 45,400, Others 95,400, Total 414,400.

Principal Towns: Bandar Seri Begawan (capital): population 27,285 at 2001 census; Kuala Belait: population 21,200 at 1991 census; Seria: population 21,100 at 1991 census; Tutong: population 13,000 at 1991 census. *Mid-2009* (incl. suburbs, UN estimate): Bandar Seri Begawan 22,228 (Source: UN, *World Urbanization Prospects: The 2009 Revision*).

Births, Marriages and Deaths (2010): Live births 6,412 (birth rate 15.5 per 1,000); Marriages 2,634; Deaths 1,208 (death rate 2.9 per 1,000).

Life Expectancy (years at birth, WHO estimates): 77 (males 76; females 77) in 2009. Source: WHO, *World Health Statistics*.

Economically Active Population (persons aged 15 years and over, 2001 census, provisional): Agriculture, hunting, forestry and fishing 1,994; Mining and quarrying 3,954; Manufacturing 12,455; Electricity, gas and water 2,639; Construction 12,301; Trade, restaurants and hotels 20,038; Transport, storage and communications 4,803; Financing, insurance, real estate and business services 8,190; Community, social and personal services 79,880; *Total employed* 146,254 (males 85,820, females 60,434); Unemployed 11,340 (males 6,734, females 4,606); *Total labour force* 157,594 (males 92,554, females 65,040). *2010:* Total employed 193,500; Unemployed 5,300; Total labour force 198,800.

HEALTH AND WELFARE

Key Indicators

Total Fertility Rate (children per woman, 2009): 2.1.

Under-5 Mortality Rate (per 1,000 live births, 2009): 7.

HIV/AIDS (% of persons aged 15–49, 2005): <0.1.

Physicians (per 1,000 head, 2002): 1.1.

Hospital Beds (per 1,000 head, 2005): 3.0.

Health Expenditure (2008): US $ per head (PPP): 1,131.

Health Expenditure (2008): % of GDP: 2.3.

Health Expenditure (2008): public (% of total): 85.5.

Total Carbon Dioxide Emissions ('000 metric tons, 2007): 7,599.1.

Carbon Dioxide Emissions Per Head (metric tons, 2007): 19.7.

Human Development Index (2011): ranking: 33.

Human Development Index (2011): value: 0.838.

For sources and definitions, see explanatory note on p. vi.

AGRICULTURE, ETC.

Principal Crops ('000 metric tons, 2010): Rice, paddy 1.4 (FAO estimate). *Aggregate Production* ('000 metric tons, may include official, semi-official or estimated data): Total vegetables (incl. melons) 9.9; Total fruits (excl. melons) 7.5.

Livestock ('000 head, 2010, FAO estimates): Cattle 1.0; Buffaloes 4.6; Sheep 3.8; Goats 3.0; Pigs 1.3; Chickens 16,000.

Livestock Products ('000 metric tons, 2010, FAO estimates): Cattle meat 0.6; Chicken meat 18.9; Hen eggs 7.2.

Forestry ('000 cubic metres, 2010, FAO estimates): *Roundwood Removals:* Sawlogs, veneer logs and logs for sleepers 96.3; Other industrial roundwood 11.0; Fuel wood 11.7; Total 119.0. *Sawnwood Production:* Total (all broad-leaved) 50.9.

Fishing (metric tons, live weight, 2009, FAO estimates): Capture 2,358; Aquaculture 433 (Blue Shrimp 320); *Total catch* 2,791.

Source: FAO.

MINING

Production (2009, estimates): Crude petroleum ('000 barrels, incl. condensate) 61,000; Natural gas (million cu m, gross) 12,100. Source: US Geological Survey.

INDUSTRY

Production ('000 metric tons, 2008, unless otherwise indicated): Motor spirit (petrol) 217; Distillate fuel oils 187; Residual fuel oil 91; Cement 220 (2009, estimate); Electric energy (million kWh) 3,423. Sources: mainly UN Industrial Commodity Statistics Database; and US Geological Survey.

FINANCE

Currency and Exchange Rates: 100 sen (cents) = 1 Brunei dollar (B $). *Sterling, US Dollar and Euro Equivalents* (30 December 2011): £1 sterling = B $2.011; US $1 = B $1.301; €1 = B $1.683; B $100 = £49.73 = US $76.88 = €59.42. *Average Exchange Rate* (Brunei dollars per US $): 1.4546 in 2009; 1.3635 in 2010; 1.2579 in 2011. Note: The Brunei dollar is at par with the Singapore dollar.

Budget (B $ million, year ending 31 March 2011, projected figures): *Revenue:* Tax revenue 2,841 (Oil and gas sector 2,530); Non-tax revenue 1,790 (Oil and gas sector 1,324); Total 4,631. *Expenditure:* Current expenditure 4,074 (Wages and salaries 1,819, Other annual recurrent charges 1,586, Charged expenditure 669); Capital expenditure 1,581 (Special expenditure charges 531; Development expenditure 1,050); Total 5,655. Source: IMF, *Brunei Darussalam: Statistical Appendix* (June 2011).

International Reserves (excl. gold, US $ million at 31 December 2010): IMF special drawing rights 333.23; Reserve position in IMF 21.06; Foreign exchange 1,208.87; *Total* 1,563.16. Source: IMF, *International Financial Statistics*.

Money Supply (B $ million at 31 December 2010): Currency outside depository corporations 824.5; Transferable deposits 2,992.6; Other deposits 8,755.9; Securities other than shares 0.0; *Broad money* 12,573.0. Source: IMF, *International Financial Statistics*.

Cost of Living (Consumer Price Index; base: 2005 = 100): All items 103.3 in 2008; 104.4 in 2009; 104.8 in 2010. Source: Asian Development Bank.

Gross Domestic Product (B $ million at constant 2000 prices): 11,753.8 in 2008; 11,546.4 in 2009; 11,846.5 in 2010.

Expenditure on the Gross Domestic Product (B $ million in current prices, 2010): Government final consumption expenditure 3,780.7; Private consumption expenditure 3,908.6; Changes in inventories 0.7; Gross fixed investment 2,677.6; *Total domestic expenditure* 10,367.6; Exports of goods and services 13,736.6; *Less* Imports of goods and services 5,544.7; Statistical discrepancy –1,692.1; *GDP in purchasers' values* 16,867.3.

Gross Domestic Product by Economic Activity (B $ million in current prices, 2010): Agriculture, hunting, forestry and fishing 128.2; Mining and quarrying 8,571.7; Manufacturing 2,035.5; Electricity, gas and water 131.5; Construction 524.1; Wholesale and retail trade 623.2; Transport and communications 576.3; Finance 583.4; Public administration 2,312.5; Others 1,381.0; *GDP in purchasers' values* 16,867.3.

Balance of Payments (US $ million, 2009): Exports of goods 7,171.9; Imports of goods –2,282.4; *Trade balance* 4,889.5; Exports of services 914.9; Imports of services –1,434.2; *Balance on goods and services* 4,370.2; Other income received 316.3; Other income paid –264.2; *Balance on goods, services and income* 4,422.2; Current transfers (net) –444.8; *Current balance* 3,977.4; Capital account (net) –10.9; Direct investment (net) 325.6; Portfolio investment (net) 139.3; Other investment assets 644.4; Other investment liabilities 498.1; Net errors and omissions –5,420.0; *Overall balance* 153.7. Source: IMF, *International Financial Statistics*.

EXTERNAL TRADE

Principal Commodities (US $ million, 2009): *Imports c.i.f.:* Food and live animals 290; Chemicals 192; Basic manufactures 537; Machinery and transport equipment 950; Miscellaneous manufactured articles 246; Total (incl. others) 2,400. *Exports f.o.b.:* Mineral fuels 6,888; Machinery and transport equipment 152; Miscellaneous manufactured articles 78; Total (incl. others) 7,169 (Source: IMF, *Brunei Darussalam: Statistical Appendix*—June 2011).

Principal Trading Partners (US $ million, 2009): *Imports:* China, People's Republic 140; Japan 214; Malaysia 465; Singapore 614; Thailand 95; USA 312; Total (incl. others) 2,400. *Exports:* Australia 524; Indonesia 772; Japan 3,305; Republic of Korea 829; Singapore 184; Thailand 138; Total (incl. others) 7,169 (Source: IMF, *Brunei Darussalam: Statistical Appendix*—June 2011).

TRANSPORT

Road Traffic (registered vehicles, 2007): Passenger cars 252,679; Lorries and vans 16,744; Buses 1,522; Motorcycles and mopeds 12,177. Source: IRF, *World Road Statistics*.

Merchant Fleet (displacement, '000 grt at 31 December): 483.2 in 2007; 494.0 in 2008; 500.0 in 2009. Source: IHS Fairplay, *World Fleet Statistics*.

International Sea-borne Shipping (freight traffic, '000 freight tons, 2010): Goods loaded 23.7; Goods unloaded 1,024.5. Note: One freight ton equals 40 cu ft (1.133 cu m) of cargo.

Civil Aviation (2009): Kilometres flown (million) 28; Passengers carried ('000) 999; Passenger-km (million) 3,431; Total ton-km (million) 399. *2010:* Passengers carried ('000) 1,929.3. Source: mainly UN, *Statistical Yearbook*.

TOURISM

Foreign Visitor Arrivals by Nationality (tourist arrivals at national borders, 2008): Australia 25,732; Canada 2,244; China, People's Republic 27,652; Germany 2,056; India 3,402; Japan 4,489; Korea, Republic 17,548; New Zealand 9,427; United Kingdom 16,192; USA 3,408; Total (incl. others) 225,757.

Tourism Receipts (US $ million, excl. passenger transport): 224 in 2006; 233 in 2007; 241 in 2008.

Source: World Tourism Organization.

COMMUNICATIONS MEDIA

Radio Receivers (2000, estimate): 362,712 in use.

Television Receivers (2000, estimate): 216,223 in use.

Telephones (2010): 79,901 main lines in use. Source: International Telecommunication Union.

Mobile Cellular Telephones ('000 subscribers, 2010): 435.1. Source: International Telecommunication Union.

Personal Computers: 33,000 (89.2 per 1,000 persons) in 2005. Source: International Telecommunication Union.

Internet Subscribers ('000, 2009): 100.1. Source: International Telecommunication Union.

Broadband Subscribers ('000, 2010): 21.7. Source: International Telecommunication Union.

Book Production (1992): 25 titles; 56,000 copies. *1998:* 38 titles. Source: UNESCO, *Statistical Yearbook*.

Newspapers (2002 unless otherwise indicated): Daily 2 (with total circulation of 25,000 copies) in 2004; Non-daily: English 2 (with circulation of 22,000 copies); Malay 3 (with circulation of 39,500 copies); Malay and English 1 (with circulation of 10,000 copies) (Source: partly UNESCO Institute for Statistics).

Other Periodicals (1998): 15 (estimated combined circulation 132,000 copies per issue).

EDUCATION

Pre-primary and Primary (2010): 199 schools (incl. some schools also offering secondary education), 4,562 teachers and 57,293 pupils.

General Secondary (2010): 38 schools (excl. schools offering primary education also), 4,375 teachers and 39,844 pupils.

Nursing/Technical/Vocational (2010): 13 colleges, 533 teachers and 3,398 students.

Teacher Training (2008): 1 college, 37 teachers and 437 students.

Higher Education (2010): 5 institutes; 637 teachers and 5,903 students.

Pupil-teacher Ratio (primary education, UNESCO estimate): 11.3 in 2009/10. Source: UNESCO Institute for Statistics.

Adult Literacy Rate (UNESCO estimates): 95.3% (males 96.8%; females 93.7%) in 2009. Source: UNESCO Institute for Statistics.

Directory

The Government

HEAD OF STATE

Sultan and Yang Di-Pertuan: HM Sultan Haji HASSANAL BOLKIAH (succeeded 5 October 1967; crowned 1 August 1968).

COUNCIL OF CABINET MINISTERS
(May 2012)

Prime Minister, Minister of Defence and of Finance: HM Sultan Haji HASSANAL BOLKIAH.

Senior Minister at the Prime Minister's Office: HRH Prince Haji AL-MUHTADEE BILLAH BOLKIAH.

Minister of Energy at the Prime Minister's Office: Pehin Dato' Haji Col (retd) MOHAMMAD YASMIN BIN Haji UMAR.

Minister of Foreign Affairs and Trade: HRH Prince Haji MOHAMED BOLKIAH.

Minister of Home Affairs: Pehin Dato' Paduka Haji BADARUDDIN BIN Haji OTHMAN.

Minister of Education: Pehin Dato' Seri Haji ABU BAKAR BIN Haji APONG.

Minister of Industry and Primary Resources: Pehin Dato' Paduka Haji YAHYA BIN Haji BAKAR.

Minister of Religious Affairs: Pengiran Dato' Dr Haji MOHAMMAD BIN Haji ABDUL RAHMAN.

Minister of Development: Pehin Dato' Seri Haji SUYOI BIN Haji OSMAN.

Minister of Health: Pehin Dato' Seri Haji ADANAN BIN Pehin Dato' Haji MOHAMMAD YUSOF.

Minister of Culture, Youth and Sports: Pehin Dato' Haji HAZAIR BIN Haji ABDULLAH.

Minister of Communications: Pehin Dato' Paduka Haji ABDULLAH BIN Haji BAKAR.

Minister of Finance II: Pehin Dato' Seri Haji ABDUL RAHMAN BIN Haji IBRAHIM.

Minister of Foreign Affairs and Trade II: Pehin Dato' Seri Paduka LIM JOCK SENG.

MINISTRIES

Prime Minister's Office (Jabatan Perdana Menteri): Blk 2D, Ong Sum Ping Complex, Bandar Seri Begawan BA 1000; tel. 2223626; fax 2233743; e-mail info.jpm@jpm.gov.bn; internet www.jpm.gov.bn.

Ministry of Communications (Kementerian Perhubungan): Jalan Menteri Besar, Bandar Seri Begawan BB 3910; tel. 2383838; fax 2380127; e-mail info@mincom.gov.bn; internet www.mincom.gov.bn.

Ministry of Culture, Youth and Sports (Kementerian Kebudayaan, Belia dan Sukan): Simpang 336-17, Jalan Kebangsaan, Bandar Seri Begawan BA 1210; tel. 2382911; fax 2380652; e-mail info@kkbs.gov.bn; internet www.kkbs.gov.bn.

Ministry of Defence (Kementerian Pertahanan): Bolkiah Garrison, Bandar Seri Begawan BB 3510; tel. 2386352; fax 2382110; e-mail info@mindef.gov.bn; internet www.mindef.gov.bn.

Ministry of Development (Kementerian Pembangunan): Old Airport, Jalan Berakas, Bandar Seri Begawan BB 3510; tel. 2383222; fax 2380298; e-mail info@mod.gov.bn; internet www.mod.gov.bn.

Ministry of Education (Kementerian Pendidikan): Old Airport, Berakas, Bandar Seri Begawan BB 3510; tel. 2381133; fax 2380050; e-mail feedback@moe.edu.bn; internet www.moe.edu.bn.

Ministry of Energy: Office of the Prime Minister, Tingkat 5, Bahirah Bldg, Jalan Menteri Besar, Bandar Seri Begawan BB 3910; tel. 2384488; fax 2384444; e-mail energy@jpm.gov.bn; internet www.energy.gov.bn.

Ministry of Finance (Kementerian Kewangan): Tingkat 15, Bangunan Kementerian Kewangan, Commonwealth Dr., Jalan Kebangsaan, Bandar Seri Begawan BB 3910; tel. 2383950; fax 2226132; e-mail administration@mof.gov.bn; internet www.mof.gov.bn.

Ministry of Foreign Affairs and Trade (Kementerian Hal Ehwal Luar Negeri dan Perdagangan): Jalan Subok, Bandar Seri Begawan BD 2710; tel. 2261293; fax 2262904; e-mail info@mfa.gov.bn; internet www.mfa.gov.bn.

Ministry of Health (Kementerian Kesihatan): Jalan Menteri Besar, Commonwealth Dr., Bandar Seri Begawan BB 3910; tel. 2381640; fax 2381440; e-mail prohealth@moh.gov.bn; internet www.moh.gov.bn.

Ministry of Home Affairs (Kementerian Hal Ehwal Dalam Negeri): Jalan James Pearce, Bandar Seri Begawan BS 8610; tel. 2223225; fax 2241367; e-mail info@home-affairs.gov.bn; internet www.home-affairs.gov.bn.

Ministry of Industry and Primary Resources (Kementerian Perindustrian dan Sumber-sumber Utama): Jalan Menteri Besar, Bandar Seri Begawan BB 3910; tel. 2380599; fax 2382474; e-mail helpdesk@bruneimipr.gov.bn; internet www.bruneimipr.gov.bn.

Ministry of Religious Affairs (Kementerian Hal Ehwal Ugama): Jalan Menteri Besar, Jalan Berakas, Bandar Seri Begawan BB 3910; tel. 2382525; fax 2382330; e-mail info@religious-affairs.gov.bn; internet www.religious-affairs.gov.bn.

Legislature

THE LEGISLATIVE COUNCIL

In September 2005 the Sultan dissolved the existing Legislative Council and appointed a new Council comprising 29 members. The Council usually convenes annually, in March.

Speaker: Pehin Dato' Haji ISA IBRAHIM.

Political Organizations

At early 2012 there was only one legally registered political organization in Brunei.

Parti Pembangunan Bangsa (PPB) (National Development Party): Limbaruh Hijau, Simpang 323, Jalan Jerudong, Kampong Jerudong, Brunei Muara, BG 3122; tel. 2610703; fax 2610701; e-mail aspirasi@aspirasi-ndp.com; internet www.aspirasi-ndp.com; f. 2005; 2,000 mems; Pres. MALAI HASSAN OTHMAN (acting); Gen. Sec. Haji RAMLI.

Political organizations that have officially ceased activities include: Parti Rakyat Brunei (PRB—Brunei People's Party), banned in 1962 and leaders all exiled; Barisan Kemerdeka'an Rakyat (BAKER—People's Independence Front), f. 1966 but no longer active; Parti Perpaduan Kebangsaan Rakyat Brunei (PERKARA—Brunei People's National United Party), f. 1968 but no longer active; Parti

Kebangsaan Demokratik Brunei (PKDB—Brunei National Democratic Party—BNDP), f. 1985 and dissolved by government order in 1988; Parti Kesedaran Rakyat (PAKAR—People's Consciousness Party), f. 2000 and subsequently split into two opposing factions, prior to being deregistered in 2007; and Parti Perpaduan Kebangsaan Brunei (PPKB—Brunei National Solidarity Party—BNSP), f. 1986 but deregistered in 2008.

Diplomatic Representation

EMBASSIES AND HIGH COMMISSIONS IN BRUNEI

Australia: Level 6, DAR Takaful IBB Utama, Jalan Pemancha, Bandar Seri Begawan BS 8711; tel. 2229435; fax 2221652; e-mail austhicom.brunei@dfat.gov.au; internet www.bruneidarussalam.embassy.gov.au; High Commissioner MARK SAWERS.

Bangladesh: 10 Simpang 83-20, Jalan Sungai Akar, Kampong Sungai Akar, Bandar Seri Begawan BC 3915; tel. 2342420; fax 2342421; e-mail bdoot@brunet.bn; internet www.hcbangladesh.org.bn; High Commissioner M. SHAMEEM AHSAN.

Cambodia: 7 Simpang 1444-14, Jalan Beribi, Gadong, Bandar Seri Begawan BE 1118; tel. 2426450; fax 2426452; e-mail camemb.brn@mfa.gov.kh; Ambassador CHHAY SOKHAN.

Canada: 5th Floor, Jalan McArthur Bldg, 1 Jalan McArthur, Bandar Seri Begawan BS 8711; tel. 2220043; fax 2220040; e-mail bsbgn@international.gc.ca; internet www.canadainternational.gc.ca/brunei_darussalam; High Commissioner WENDELL SANFORD.

China, People's Republic: 1, 3 & 5 Simpang 462, Kampong Sungai Hanching, Jalan Muara, Bandar Seri Begawan BC 2115; tel. 2339609; fax 2335710; e-mail chinaemb_bn@mfa.gov.cn; internet bn.chineseembassy.org/eng; Ambassador ZHENG XIANGLIN.

France: Kompleks Jalan Sultan, Units 301–306, 3rd Floor, 51–55 Jalan Sultan, Bandar Seri Begawan BS 8811; tel. 2220960; fax 2243373; e-mail france@brunet.bn; internet www.ambafrance-bn.org; Ambassador LOUIS LE VERT.

Germany: Kompleks Yayasan Sultan Haji Hassanal Bolkiah, Blk A, 2nd Floor, Unit 2.01, Jalan Pretty, Bandar Seri Begawan BS 8711; tel. 2225547; fax 2225583; e-mail prgerman@brunet.bn; internet www.bandar-seri-begawan.diplo.de; Ambassador Dr BERND MORAST.

India: Baitussyifaa, Simpang 40-22, Jalan Sungai Akar, Bandar Seri Begawan BC 3915; tel. 2339947; fax 2339783; e-mail hicomind@brunet.bn; internet www.hcindiabrunei.org.bn; High Commissioner LALDUHTHLANA RALTE.

Indonesia: Simpang 528, Lot 4498, Kampong Sungai Hanching Baru, Jalan Muara, Bandar Seri Begawan BC 2115; tel. 2330180; fax 2330646; e-mail kbribsb@brunet.bn; internet www.kemlu.go.id/bandarseribegawan; Ambassador HANDRIYO KUSUMO PRIYO.

Iran: 2 Jalan Dato Ratna, Kampong Kiarong BE 1318; tel. 2424873; fax 2424875; e-mail iranemb1@brunet.bn; Ambassador MOHAMMAD REZA HAVASELI ASTIANI.

Japan: 1 & 3 Jalan Jawatan Dalam, Lot 37355, 33 Simpang 122, Kampong Kiulap, Bandar Seri Begawan BE 1518; tel. 2229265; fax 2229481; e-mail embassy@japan.com.bn; internet www.bn.emb-japan.go.jp; Ambassador NORIKI HIROSE.

Korea, Republic: 17 Simpang 462, Kampong Hancing Baru, Jalan Muara, Bandar Seri Begawan BC 2115; tel. 2330248; fax 2330254; e-mail brunei@mofat.go.kr; internet brn.mofat.go.kr; Ambassador CHOI BYUNG-KOO.

Kuwait: Lot 4144, 21 & 25 Simpang 40, Jalan Elia Fatimah, Kampong Kiarong, Gadong BE 1318; tel. 2457176; fax 2457179; e-mail kuwait@brunet.bn; Ambassador GHASSAN MOHAMMED ABDURRAHMAN AL-DUWAISAN.

Laos: 159 Simpang 336, Kampong Sungai Akar, Jalan Kebangsaan, Bandar Seri Begawan BB 4313; tel. 2384382; fax 2384381; e-mail laosemba@brunet.bn; Ambassador SOUVANNA PHOUYAVONG.

Malaysia: 61 Simpang 336, Jalan Kebangsaan, Kampong Sungai Akar, Bandar Seri Begawan BA 1211; tel. 2381095; fax 2381278; e-mail malbrnei@kln.gov.my; internet www.kln.gov.my/perwakilan/seribegawan; High Commissioner Dato' ABDULLAH SANI BIN OMAR.

Myanmar: 14 Lot 2185/46292, Simpang 212, Jalan Kampong Rimba, Gadong, Bandar Seri Begawan BE 3119; tel. 2451960; fax 2451963; e-mail myanmar@brunet.bn; Ambassador THURA THET OO MUANG.

Oman: 35 Simpang 100, Kampong Pengkalan, Jalan Tungku Link, Gadong, Bandar Seri Begawan BE 3719; tel. 2446953; fax 2446956; e-mail omnembsb@brunet.bn; Ambassador SAYYID FAKHRI MOHAMMED AL-SAID.

Pakistan: 8 Simpang 31, Jalan Bunga Jasmine, Kampong Beribi, Gadong, Bandar Seri Begawan BE 1118; tel. 2424600; fax 2424606; e-mail hcpak@brunet.bn; internet www.mofa.gov.pk/brunei; High Commissioner MUHAMMAD IJAZ HUSSEIN AWAN (designate).

Philippines: 17 Simpang 336, Jalan Kebangsaan, Bandar Seri Begawan BA 1210; tel. 2241465; fax 2237707; e-mail bruneipe@brunet.bn; internet www.philippineembassybrunei.net; Ambassador NESTOR Z. OCHOA.

Qatar: Lot 188897, Simpang 898, Kampong Jangsak, Gadong, Bandar Seri Begawan; tel. 2447777; fax 2443333; Chargé d'affaires AHMAD IBRAHIM AL-ABDULLAH.

Russia: The Holiday Lodge Hotel, 97192, Kampong Jerudong, Jalan Palau Kubu, Bandar Seri Begawan; tel. 2611413; fax 2411424; e-mail ruembr@yandex.ru; Ambassador VIKTOR A. SELEZNEZ.

Saudi Arabia: 1 Simpang 570, Jalan Muara, Kampong Salar, Bandar Seri Begawan BU 1429; tel. 2792821; fax 2792826; e-mail saudibru@brunet.bn; Ambassador MOHAMMED JAMIL ABDUL JALEEL HASHIM.

Singapore: 8 Simpang 74, Jalan Subok, Bandar Seri Begawan; tel. 2262741; fax 2262752; e-mail singhc_bwn@sgmfa.gov.sg; internet www.mfa.gov.sg/brunei; High Commissioner JOSEPH K. H. KOH.

Thailand: 2 Simpang 682, Jalan Tutong, Kampong Bunut, Bandar Seri Begawan BF 1320; tel. 2653108; fax 2653032; e-mail thaiemb@brunet.bn; Ambassador APICHART PHETCHARATANA.

United Kingdom: Kompleks Yayasan Sultan Haji Hassanal Bolkiah, Blk D, 2nd Floor, Unit 2.01, Bandar Seri Begawan BS 8711; tel. 2222231; fax 2234315; e-mail brithc@brunet.bn; internet ukinbrunei.fco.gov.uk; High Commissioner ROBERT FENN.

USA: Simpang 336-52-16-9, Jalan Kebangsaan, Bandar Seri Begawan BC 4115; tel. 2384616; fax 2384604; e-mail amembassy_bsb@state.gov; internet brunei.usembassy.gov; Ambassador DANIEL L. SHIELDS, III.

Viet Nam: 9 Simpang 148-3, Jalan Telanai, Bandar Seri Begawan BA 2312; tel. 2651580; fax 2651574; e-mail vnembassy@yahoo.com; internet www.vietnamembassy-brunei.org; Ambassador PHAM BINH MAN.

Judicial System

SUPREME COURT

The Supreme Court consists of the Court of Appeal and the High Court. Syariah (*Shari'a*) courts coexist with the Supreme Court and deal with Islamic laws.

Office of the Supreme Court

Km 11/2, Jalan Tutong, Bandar Seri Begawan BA 1910; tel. 2243939; fax 2241984; e-mail judiciarybn@hotmail.com; internet www.judicial.gov.bn.

Chief Registrar: Haji ROSTAINA Pengiran Haji DURAMAN.

The Court of Appeal

Composed of the President and two Commissioners appointed by the Sultan. The Court of Appeal considers criminal and civil appeals against the decisions of the High Court and the Intermediate Court. The Court of Appeal is the highest appellate court for criminal cases. In civil cases an appeal may be referred to the Judicial Committee of Her Majesty's Privy Council in London if all parties agree to do so before the hearing of the appeal in the Brunei Court of Appeal.

President: JOHN BARRY MORTIMER.

The High Court

Composed of the Chief Justice and judges sworn in by the Sultan as Commissioners of the Supreme Court. In its appellate jurisdiction, the High Court considers appeals in criminal and civil matters against the decisions of the Subordinate Courts. The High Court has unlimited original jurisdiction in criminal and civil matters.

Chief Justice: Dato' Seri Paduka Haji KIFRAWI KIFLI.

OTHER COURTS

Intermediate Courts

Intermediate Courts have jurisdiction to try all offences other than those punishable by the death sentence and civil jurisdiction to try all actions and suits of a civil nature where the amount in dispute or value of the subject/matter does not exceed B $100,000

The Subordinate Courts

Presided over by the Chief Magistrate and magistrates, with limited original jurisdiction in civil and criminal matters and civil jurisdiction to try all actions and suits of a civil nature where the amount in dispute does not exceed B $50,000 (for Chief Magistrate) and B $30,000 (for magistrates).

Chief Magistrate: ABDULLAH SOEFRI BIN Pengiran Haji ABIDIN.

The Courts of Kathis

Deal solely with questions concerning Islamic religion, marriage and divorce. Appeals lie from these courts to the Sultan in the Religious Council.

Chief Kathi: Dato' Seri Setia Haji SALIM BIN Haji BESAR.

Attorney-General: Datin Paduka Hajah HAYATI Dato' Seri Paduka Haji MOHD SALLEH, Attorney-General's Chambers, The Law Bldg, Km 1, Jalan Tutong, Bandar Seri Begawan BA 1910; tel. 2244872; fax 2223100; e-mail info@agc.gov.bn; internet www.agc.gov.bn.

Solicitor-General: Datin Paduka MAGDALENE CHONG.

Religion

The official religion of Brunei is Islam, and the Sultan is head of the Islamic community. The majority of the Malay population are Muslims of the Shafi'is school of the Sunni sect; at the 1991 census Muslims accounted for 67.2% of the total population. The Chinese population is either Buddhist (accounting for 12.8% of the total population at the 1991 census), Confucianist, Daoist or Christian. Large numbers of the indigenous ethnic groups practise traditional animist forms of religion. The remainder of the population are mostly Christians, generally Roman Catholics, Anglicans or members of the American Methodist Church of Southern Asia. At the 1991 census Christians accounted for 10.0% of the total population.

ISLAM

Supreme Head of Islam: HM Sultan Haji HASSANAL BOLKIAH (Sultan and Yang Di-Pertuan).

CHRISTIANITY

The Anglican Communion

Within the Church of the Province of South East Asia, Brunei forms part of the diocese of Kuching (Malaysia).

The Roman Catholic Church

Brunei comprises a single apostolic vicariate. At 31 December 2007 there were an estimated 18,427 adherents in the country, equivalent to 5.0% of the population.

Prefect Apostolic: Rev. CORNELIUS SIM, Church of Our Lady of the Assumption, Jalan Kumbang Pasang, Bandar Seri Begawan BS 8670; tel. 2222261; fax 2238938; e-mail frcsim@brunet.bn.

The Press

NEWSPAPERS

Borneo Bulletin: Locked Bag No. 2, MPC (Old Airport, Berakas), Bandar Seri Begawan BB 3510; tel. 2451468; fax 2451461; e-mail borneobulletin@brunet.bn; internet www.brunet.bn/news/bb; f. 1953; daily; English; independent; owned by QAF Group; Editor PRABHAKAR NATARAJAN; circ. 20,000 (weekdays), 25,000 (Sat.), 20,000 (Sun.).

Brunei Darussalam Newsletter: Dept of Information, Prime Minister's Office, Istana Nurul Iman, Berakas, Bandar Seri Begawan BB 3510; tel. 2383400; fax 2382012; e-mail bd.newsletter@information.gov.bn; internet www.information.gov.bn/bdnewsletter; monthly; English; govt newspaper; distributed free; Editor SASTRA SARINI BINTI Haji JULAINI; circ. 3,000.

The Brunei Times: Wisma Haji Mohd Taha, 3rd Floor, Jalan Gadong, Bandar Seri Begawan BE 4119; tel. 2428333; fax 2428555; e-mail bruneitimes@bt.com.bn; internet www.bt.com.bn; f. 2006; daily; English; Editor-in-Chief Haji BUJANG BIN MASU'UT.

Daily News Digest: Dept of Information, Prime Minister's Office, Istana Nurul Iman, Bandar Seri Begawan BA 1000; English; govt newspaper.

Media Permata: Locked Bag No. 2, MPC (Old Airport, Berakas), Bandar Seri Begawan BB 3510; tel. 2451468; fax 2451461; e-mail mediapermata@brunet.bn; internet www.brunei-online.com/mp; f. 1995; daily (not Sun.); Malay; owned by QAF Group; Editor MUHAMMAD NOOR; circ. 10,000.

Pelita Brunei: Dept of Information, Prime Minister's Office, Old Airport, Berakas, Bandar Seri Begawan BB 3510; tel. 2383941; fax 2381004; e-mail e.pelita@yahoo.com; internet www.pelitabrunei.gov.bn; f. 1956; 3 a week (Mon., Wed. and Sat.); Malay; govt newspaper; distributed free; Editor Haji JAAFAR BIN Haji IBRAHIM; circ. 27,500.

Salam: c/o Brunei Shell Petroleum Co Sdn Bhd, Jalan Utara, Panaga, Seria KB 3534; tel. 3373018; fax 3374189; e-mail editorial@shell.com; internet www.bsp.com.bn/main/mediacentre/publications.asp; f. 1953; monthly; Malay and English; distributed free to employees and shareholders of the Brunei Shell Petroleum Co Sdn Bhd; Exec. Editor KHAIRUL ANWAR ISMAIL; circ. 46,000.

Publishers

Borneo Printers & Trading Sdn Bhd: POB 2211, Bandar Seri Begawan BS 8674; tel. 2651387; fax 2654342; e-mail bptl@brunet.bn.

Brunei Press Sdn Bhd: Lots 8 & 11, Perindustrian Beribi II, Jalan Gadong, Bandar Seri Begawan BE 1118; tel. 2451468; fax 2451462; e-mail brupress@brunet.bn; internet www.bruneipress.com.bn; f. 1953; Gen. Man. REGGIE SEE.

Capital Trading & Printing Pte Ltd: POB 1089, Bandar Seri Begawan; tel. 2244541.

Leong Bros: 52 Jalan Bunga Kuning, POB 164, Seria; tel. 322381.

Offset Printing House: Lot Q37, 4 Simpang 5, Lambak Kanan Industrial Area, Berakas, Bandar Seri Begawan BB 1714; tel. 2390797; fax 2390798; e-mail offset@brunei.bn; f. 1980; Gen. Man. KENNY TEO.

GOVERNMENT PUBLISHING HOUSES

Dewan Bahasa dan Pustaka (Language and Literature Bureau): c/o Ministry of Culture, Youth and Sports, Berakas BB 3510; tel. 2382511; fax 2381817; e-mail pengarahdbp@brunet.bn; internet www.dbp.gov.bn; f. 1961; publs incl. children's books, textbooks, novels, poetry and translations of foreign works; promotion and preservation of Malayan literature and folklore; library services; Dir-Gen. Datuk TERMUZI ABDUL AZIZ.

Jabatan Percetakan Kerajaan (Government Printing Dept): Prime Minister's Office, Bandar Seri Begawan BB 3510; tel. 2382541; fax 2381141; e-mail info@printing.gov.bn; internet www.printing.gov.bn; f. 1975; Dir Haji DAUD BIN Haji AHMAD.

Broadcasting and Communications

TELECOMMUNICATIONS

Authority for Info-Communications Technology Industry (AITI): Blk B14, Simpang 32–35, Kampong Anggrek Desa, Jalan Berakas, Bandar Seri Begawan BB 3713; tel. 2323232; fax 2382447; e-mail info@aiti.gov.bn; internet www.aiti.gov.bn; f. 2003; assumed responsibility for regulating and representing telecommunications industry following corporatization of Dept of Telecommunications of Brunei in April 2006; also entrusted with devt of ICT industry; Chair. ALAIHUDDIN BIN Haji MOHAMMED TAHA.

B-Mobile Communications Sdn Bhd (b-mobile): Old Airport, Berakas, Bandar Seri Begawan BB 3510; tel. 2221010; fax 2384040; e-mail contact@bmobile.com.bn; internet www.bmobile.com.bn; f. 2005; 3G mobile service provider; jt venture between Telekom Brunei Bhd (TelBru) and QAF Comserve.

DST Communications Sdn Bhd: Jalan Tungku Link, Bandar Seri Begawan BE 3619; tel. 2410888; fax 2410142; e-mail dstmarketing@simpur.net.bn; internet www.dst-group.com/dstcom; mobile and internet broadband services provider; mem. of DST Group; signed agreement with Alcatel in 2003 to improve provision of mobile services in Brunei; Chief Operating Officer (DST Group) Haji MARSAD BIN Haji ISMAIL.

Telekom Brunei Bhd (TelBru): Jalan Lapangan Terbang Lama, Berakas, Bandar Seri Begawan BB 3510; tel. 2321321; fax 2382444; e-mail info@telbru.com.bn; internet www.telbru.com.bn; fmrly Jabatan Telekom Brunei (Dept of Telecommunications of Brunei); name changed as above upon corporatization in April 2006; telecommunications services provider; Chair. Dato' Paduka Haji HISHAM BIN Haji MOHAMMAD HANIFAH; CEO UMAR ALI Haji ABDULLAH (acting).

BROADCASTING

Radio

KRISTALfm: Jalan Tungku Link, Bandar Seri Begawan BE 3619; tel. 2410888; fax 2411788; e-mail kristalfm@dst-group.com; internet www.kristal.fm; f. 1999; subsidiary of Kristal Media Sdn Bhd; mem. of DST Group; two networks; Malay and English.

Radio Televisyen Brunei (RTB): Prime Minister's Office, Jalan Elizabeth II, Bandar Seri Begawan BS 8610; tel. 2243111; fax 2241882; e-mail gts@rtb.gov.bn; internet www.rtb.gov.bn; f. 1975; five radio networks; Malay, Chinese (Mandarin), English and Arabic; also broadcasts on the internet; Dir Haji MOHAMAD YUNOS BIN Haji BOLHASSAN.

Television

Kristal Astro Sdn Bhd: Unit 1-345, 1st Floor, Gadong Properties Centre, Gadong, Bandar Seri Begawan BE 4119; tel. 2456828; fax 2420682; f. 2000; jt venture between Kristal Sdn Bhd and Malaysian Measat Broadcast Network Systems Sdn Bhd; provides more than 30 digital satellite subscription channels.

Kristal TV: DST Network Sdn Bhd, Unit 1-345, 1st Floor, Gadong Properties Centre, Gadong, Bandar Seri Begawan BE 4119; tel. 2456828; fax 2420682; f. 1999; 14 TV channels.

Radio Televisyen Brunei (RTB): Prime Minister's Office, Jalan Elizabeth II, Bandar Seri Begawan BS 8610; tel. 2243111; fax 2241882; e-mail director@rtb.gov.bn; internet www.rtb.gov.bn; f. 1975; five TV channels; five radio channels; Dir Haji MOHAMAD YUNOS BIN Haji BOLHASSAN.

Finance

(cap. = capital; res = reserves; dep. = deposits; brs = branches; amounts in Brunei dollars unless otherwise stated)

BANKING

In 2008 there were 11 banks in operation, including six foreign and two 'offshore' banks. In January 2011 the Monetary Authority of Brunei Darussalam formally assumed responsibility for the functions of the Brunei Currency and Monetary Board.

Autoriti Monetari Brunei Darussalam (AMBD) (Monetary Authority of Brunei Darussalam): Bandar Seri Begawan; f. 2011; performs functions of central bank; responsible for monetary policy, supervision of financial institutions and currency management; Chair. HRH Prince Haji AL-MUHTADEE BILLAH BOLKIAH; Man. Dir Haji MOHD ROSLI bin Haji SABTU.

Commercial Banks

Baiduri Bank Bhd: Blk A, Units 1–4, Kiarong Complex, Lebuhraya Sultan Hassanal Bolkiah, Bandar Seri Begawan BE 1318; tel. 2268300; fax 2455599; e-mail bank@baiduri.com; internet www.baiduri.com; f. 1994; cap. 100m., res 14.8m., dep. 1,795.5m. (Dec. 2008); Chair. Pengiran Anak ISTERI Pengiran Anak Hajjah ZARIAH; Gen. Man. PIERRE IMHOF; 11 brs.

Bank Islam Brunei Darussalam: Lot 159, Bangunan IBB, Jalan Pemancha, POB 2725, Bandar Seri Begawan BS 8711; tel. 2235687; fax 2235722; internet www.bibd.com.bn; f. 1981; est. as Island Devt Bank; fmrly Islamic Bank of Brunei; merged with Islamic Devt Bank of Brunei Bhd in 2006; practises Islamic banking principles; Chair. Dato' Seri Setia Haji ABDULLAH BIN BEGAWAN MUDIM Dato' Paduka Haji BAKAR; Man. Dir JAVED AHMED; 14 brs.

Foreign Banks

Citibank NA (USA): Darussalam Complex, 12–15 Jalan Sultan, Bandar Seri Begawan BS 8811; tel. 2243983; fax 2237344; e-mail glen.rase@citi.com; Country Head GLEN RASE; 2 brs.

The Hongkong and Shanghai Banking Corpn Ltd (HSBC) (Hong Kong): Jalan Sultan, cnr Jalan Pemancha, Bandar Seri Begawan BS 8670; tel. 2252252; fax 2241316; e-mail hsbc@hsbc.com.bn; internet www.hsbc.com.bn; f. 1947; acquired assets of Nat. Bank of Brunei in 1986; CEO TAREQ MUHMOOD; 10 brs.

Maybank (Malaysia): 1 Jalan McArthur, Bandar Seri Begawan BS 8711; tel. 2242494; fax 2225404; e-mail maybank@brunet.bn; f. 1960; Country Man. GEOFFREY LIM CHEE TIONG; 3 brs.

RHB Bank Bhd (Malaysia): Kompleks Yayasan Sultan Haji Hassanal Bolkiah, Blk D, Unit G.02, Jalan Pretty, Bandar Seri Begawan BS 8711; tel. 2222515; fax 2237487; e-mail apandi_klompot@rhbbank.com.my; fmrly Sime Bank Bhd; Country Man. APANDI BIN KLOMPOT; 1 br.

Standard Chartered Bank (United Kingdom): Kompleks Jalan Sultan, 1st Floor, 51–55 Jalan Sultan, POB 186, Bandar Seri Begawan BS 8811; tel. 2228400; fax 2220103; e-mail scb.brunei@bn.standardchartered.com; internet www.standardchartered.com/bn; f. 1958; CEO TIEW SIEW CHUEN; 7 brs.

United Overseas Bank Ltd (Singapore): Units 10–11, Bangunan D'Amin Jaya, Lot 54989, Kampong Kiarong, Bandar Seri Begawan BE 1318; tel. 2225477; fax 2240792; f. 1973; Gen. Man. GEORGE LAI TED MIN; 2 brs.

'Offshore' Banks

The Brunei International Financial Centre (BIFC—see Government Agencies), under the Ministry of Finance, supervises the activities of the 'offshore' banking sector in Brunei.

Royal Bank of Canada: 1 Jalan McArthur, 4th Floor, Unit 4A, Bandar Seri Begawan BS 8711; tel. 2224366; fax 2224368; Gen. Man. SUHAILA KANI.

Sun Hung Kai International Bank (Brunei) Ltd (Hong Kong): Bandar Seri Begawan; e-mail cs@shkf.com; f. 2004; Dir PAK HUNG MAK.

STOCK EXCHANGE

International Brunei Exchange Ltd (IBX): The Empire, Muara-Tutong Highway, Jerudong BG 3122; tel. 2611222; fax 2611020; e-mail info@ibx.com.bn; f. 2001; CEO B. C. YONG.

INSURANCE

General Companies

Audley Insurance Co Sdn Bhd: Ministry of Finance Bldg, 9th Floor, Commonwealth Dr., Jalan Kebangsaan, Bandar Seri Begawan BB 3910; tel. 2383535; fax 2383548; e-mail audley@bia.com.bn; Man. Dir Datuk HAJAH UMI SALAMAH Haji ISMAIL.

Etiqa Insurance Bhd: B7, Ground Floor, Shakirin Kompleks, Kampong Kiulap, Bandar Seri Begawan BE 1518; tel. 2443393; fax 2427451; e-mail tsangpy@brunet.bn; fmrly known as Malaysia National Insurance Bhd; Man. TSANG POH YEE.

MBA Insurance Sdn Bhd: First Floor, Units 15–17, Lot 9784, Bangunan Haji Hassan Abdullah, Kampong Menglait, Jalan Gadong, Bandar Seri Begawan BE 3978; tel. 2441535; fax 2441534; e-mail mbabrunei@brunet.bn; Gen. Man. SHIM WEI HSUING.

Mitsui Sumitomo Insurance (Malaysia) Bhd: Unit 311, 3rd Floor, Kompleks Mohamad Yussof, Km 4, Jalan Tutong, Bandar Seri Begawan; tel. 2223632; fax 2220965; Sr Exec. DAVID ENG.

National Insurance Co Bhd: Units 12 and 13, Blk A, Regent Sq., Simpang 150, Kampong Kiarong BE1318; tel. 2226222; fax 2429888; e-mail insurance@national.com.bn; internet www.national.com.bn; f. 1969; Gen. Man. KOLJA KLAWUNN.

South East Asia Insurance (B) Sdn Bhd: Unit 2, Blk A, Abdul Razak Complex, 1st Floor, Jalan Gadong, Bandar Seri Begawan BE 3919; tel. 2443842; fax 2420860; Gen. Man. SHIM WEI HSIUNG.

Standard Insurance (B) Sdn Bhd: 2 Bangunan Hasbullah I, Ground Floor, Bandar Seri Begawan BE 3719; tel. 2450077; fax 2450076; e-mail feedback@standard-ins.com; internet www.standard-ins.com; Man. PAUL KONG.

Tokio Marine Insurance Singapore Ltd: Unit A1 & A2, 1st Floor, Blk A, Bangunan Hau Man Yong, Simpang 88, Kampong Kiulap, Bandar Seri Begawan BE 1518; tel. 2236100; fax 2236102; e-mail davidwong@tmasiainsurance.com; f. 1929; Br. Man. DAVID WONG KOK MIN.

Life Companies

American International Assurance Co Ltd: Unit 509, Wisma Jaya Bldg, 5th Floor, 85–94 Jalan Pemancha, Bandar Seri Begawan BS 8811; tel. 2239112; fax 2221667; e-mail Kenneth-WC.Ling@aia.com; Gen. Man. PETER LIM.

The Great Eastern Life Assurance Co Ltd: Unit 18, Blk B, Bangunan Habza Simpang 150, Kampong Kiarong, Bandar Seri Begawan BA 1318; tel. 2233118; fax 2238118; e-mail helenyeo@lifeisgreat.com.bn; Man. HELEN YEO.

TM Asia Life Singapore Ltd: Unit 2, 1st Floor, Blk D, Abdul Razak Complex, Jalan Gadong, Bandar Seri Begawan BE 4119; tel. 2423755; fax 2423754; e-mail tmasialife@brunet.bn; fmrly Asia Life Assurance Society Ltd; Br. Man. JOSEPH WONG SIONG LION.

Takaful (Composite Insurance) Companies

Insurans Islam TAIB Sdn Bhd: Perbadanan TAIB, Jalan Sultan, Bandar Seri Begawan BS 8811; tel. 2232222; fax 2237729; e-mail ict@insuranstaib.com.bn; internet www.insuranstaib.com.bn; f. 1993; provides Islamic insurance products and services; Gen. Man. OSMAN MOHAMAD JAIR.

Takaful Bank Pembangunan Islam Sdn Bhd (TBPISB): Unit 10, Komplex Seri Kiulap, Kampong Kiulap, Gadong, Bandar Seri Begawan BE 1518; tel. 2237220; fax 2237045; internet www.takafulbpisb.com; f. 2001; fmrly Takaful IDBB Sdn Bhd; name changed as above in 2003; Islamic life and non-life insurance products; Chair. Pehin Dato' Haji AHMAD WALLY SKINNER; Man. Dir Haji AISHATUL AKMAR SIDEK.

Takaful IBB Bhd: Levels 2 & 7–8, Dar Takaful IBB Utama, Jalan Pemancha, Bandar Seri Begawan BS 8711; tel. 2239338; fax 2451808; e-mail takaful@brunet.bn; f. 1993; Chair. Pehin Dato' Haji ABU BAKAR BIN Haji APONG DAUD.

Insurance Association

General Insurance Association of Negara Brunei Darussalam (GIAB): Unit C2-2, Blk C, Shakirin Complex, Kampong Kiulap, Bandar Seri Begawan BE 1518; tel. 2237898; fax 2237858; e-mail giab@brunet.bn; internet www.giab.com.bn; f. 1986; 15 mems; Chair. HELEN YEO.

Trade and Industry

GOVERNMENT AGENCIES

Brunei International Financial Centre (BIFC): Tingkat 14, Ministry of Finance, Commonwealth Dr., Jalan Kebangsaan, Bandar Seri Begawan BB 3910; tel. 2383747; fax 2383787; e-mail bifc@mof.gov.bn; internet www.mof.gov.bn/english/bifc; f. 2000; regulates international financial sector and encourages devt of Brunei as investment destination; Dir MOHAMED ROSLI SABTU.

Brunei Investment Agency (BIA): Tingkat 11, Bangunan Kementerian Kewangan, Commonwealth Dr., Jalan Kebangsaan, Bandar Seri Begawan BB 3910; tel. 2383535; fax 2383539; e-mail dramin.abdullah@bia.com.bn; f. 1983; Chair. Pehin Dato' Haji ABU BAKAR BIN Haji APONG; Man. Dir Haji MOHAMMAD AMIN LIEW ABDULLAH.

DEVELOPMENT ORGANIZATIONS

Brunei Economic Development Board (BEDB): Blk 2K, Bangunan Kerajaan, Jalan Ong Sum Ping, Bandar Seri Begawan, BA 1311; tel. 2230111; fax 2230063; e-mail info@bedb.com.bn; internet www.bedb.com.bn; f. 2001; promotes Brunei as an investment destination; facilitates and assists industrial devt; under control of Prime Minister's Office since late 2010; Chair. Dato' Paduka Haji ALI Haji BIN APONG; CEO Dato' Paduka VINCENT CHEONG.

Brunei Industrial Development Authority (BINA): Ministry of Industry and Primary Resources, Km 8, Jalan Gadong, Bandar Seri Begawan BE 1118; tel. 2444100; fax 2423300; e-mail bruneibina@brunet.bn; internet www.bina.gov.bn; f. 1996; Dir Pengiran SHARIFUDDIN BIN Pengiran Haji METALI.

Brunei Islamic Trust Fund (Tabung Amanah Islam Brunei): Bangunan Kewangaan Utama, Jalan Sultan, Bandar Seri Begawan BS 8811; tel. 2232222; fax 2240316; e-mail administration@taib.com.bn; internet www.taib.com.bn; f. 1991; promotes trade and industry; Chair. Dato' Paduka Dr Haji MAT SUNY Haji MUHAMMAD HUSSEIN.

Semaun Holdings Sdn Bhd: Unit 10, Blk B, Warisan Mata-Mata Complex, Kampong Mata-Mata, Gadong, Bandar Seri Begawan BE 1718; tel. 2456064; fax 2456070; e-mail semaun@brunet.bn; internet www.semaunholdings.com; f. 1994; promotes industrial and commercial devt through direct investment in key industrial sectors; 100% govt-owned; bd of dirs is composed of ministers and senior govt officials; chaired by Minister of Industry and Primary Resources; Man. Dir Hajah ASMAH Binti Haji SAMAN.

CHAMBERS OF COMMERCE

Brunei Darussalam International Chamber of Commerce and Industry: Unit 401–403A, 4th Floor, Wisma Jaya, Jalan Pemancha, Bandar Seri Begawan BS 8811; tel. 2236601; fax 2228389; Chair. Haji AHMAD BIN Haji ISA; Sec. Haji SHAZALI BIN Dato' Haji SULAIMAN; 30 mems.

Brunei Malay Chamber of Commerce and Industry: Suite 301, 2nd Floor, Bangunan Guru-Guru Melayu Brunei, Jalan Kianggehi, Bandar Seri Begawan 1910; tel. 2227297; fax 2227278; f. 1964; Pres. Haji RAZALI BIN Haji JOHARI; 160 mems.

Chinese Chamber of Commerce: Chinese Chamber of Commerce Bldg, 4th Floor, 72 Jalan Roberts, Bandar Seri Begawan BS 8711; tel. 2235494; fax 2235493; e-mail ccc@brunet.bn; Pres. Dr CHAN SUI KIAT.

Indian Chamber of Commerce: Unit 13–15, Blk B, Delima Jaya Complex, Kampong Serusop, Jalan Muara, Bandar Seri Begawan BB 2313; tel. and fax 2340972; fax 2340976; Pres. NAZEER AHMAD.

National Chamber of Commerce and Industry of Brunei Darussalam (NCCIBD): Unit 1, Blk D, Beribi Industrial Complex 1, Jalan Gadong, Bandar Seri Begawan BE 1118; tel. 2421840; fax 2421839; e-mail nccibd@brunet.bn; internet www.nccibd.com; Pres. Haji RAZALI BIN Haji JOHARI; Sec.-Gen. Haji ABDUL SAMAN AHMAD.

STATE HYDROCARBON COMPANIES

Brunei LNG Sdn Bhd (BLNG): Lumut, Seria KC 2935; tel. 3236901; fax 3236892; e-mail enquiry@bruneilng.com; internet www.blng.com.bn; f. 1969; natural gas liquefaction; owned jtly by the Brunei Govt (50%), Shell and Mitsubishi Corpn; operates LNG plant at Lumut, which has a capacity of 7.2m. metric tons per year; Man. Dir and CEO Haji SALLEH BOSTAMAN Haji ZAINAL ABIDIN.

Brunei National Petroleum Co Sdn Bhd (PetroleumBrunei): Unit 1.01, 1st Floor, Blk D, Kompleks Yayasan Sultan Haji Hassanal Bolkiah, Jalan Pretty, Bandar Seri Begawan BS 8711; tel. 2230720; fax 2230654; e-mail pb@pb.com.bn; internet www.pb.com.bn; f. 2001; wholly govt-owned; CEO MOHAMMED JA'AFAR BIN Haji BAKAR.

Brunei Shell Marketing Co Bhd: Ground & 12th Floor, PGGMB Bldg, Jalan Kianggeh, Bandar Seri Begawan BS 8811; tel. 2229304; fax 2240470; e-mail edyzurina.awang@shell.com; internet www.bsm.com.bn; f. 1978; est. from Shell Marketing Co of Brunei Ltd as jt venture between Shell and the Bruneian Govt; markets petroleum and chemical products throughout Brunei; Man. Dir MAT SUNY Haji MOHD HUSSEIN.

Brunei Shell Petroleum Co Sdn Bhd (BSP): Jalan Utara, Panagia, Seria KB 3534; tel. 3373999; fax 3372040; internet www.bsp.com.bn; f. 1957; the largest industrial concern in the country; 50% state holding; Man. Dir GRAHAEME HENDERSON.

Jasra International Petroleum Sdn Bhd: RBA Plaza, 2nd Floor, Jalan Sultan, Bandar Seri Begawan; tel. 2228968; fax 2228929; petroleum exploration and production; Man. Dir ROBERT A. HARRISON.

TRADE UNIONS

All trade unions must be registered with the Government. Authorization for affiliation with international trade union organizations is required. In 2008 the three officially registered trade unions were all in the petroleum sector, which collectively represented about 1,500 workers (less than 1% of the total work-force). Two of the unions, representing the sector's office workers, were reported to be inactive.

Brunei Oilfield Workers' Union: XDR/11, BSP Co Sdn Bhd, Seria KB 3534; f. 1964; 470 mems; Pres. SUHAINI Haji OTHMAN; Sec.-Gen. ABU TALIB BIN Haji MOHAMAD.

Transport

RAILWAYS

There are no public railways. The Brunei Shell Petroleum Co Sdn Bhd maintains a 19.3-km section of light railway between Seria and Badas.

ROADS

In 2010 there were 3,029 km of roads in Brunei (excluding roads maintained by the Brunei Shell Petroleum Co Sdn Bhd), of which 80.1% were permanent. The main highway connects Bandar Seri Begawan, Tutong and Kuala Belait.

Land Transport Department: Jalan Beribi Gadong, Bandar Seri Begawan BE 1110; tel. 2451979; fax 2424775; e-mail latis@brunet.bn; internet www.land-transport.gov.bn; f. 1962; Dir MOHAMMAD RIZA BIN Haji MOHAMMAD YUNOS.

SHIPPING

Most sea traffic is handled by a deep-water port at Muara, 28 km from the capital. It has a container terminal, warehousing, freezer facilities and cement silos. In September 2007 a cruise ship centre was opened at Muara. The port at Kuala Belait takes shallow-draught vessels and serves mainly the Shell petroleum field and Seria. The jetty at Lumut handles liquefied natural gas (LNG) carriers.

Four main rivers, with numerous tributaries, are an important means of communication in the interior. Water taxis operate daily to the Temburong district.

Shipping Association of Brunei Darussalam (SABD): POB 476, Bandar Seri Begawan BS 8670; tel. 2421572; fax 2421453; e-mail seatradefang@brunet.bn; Pres. Haji RAZALI BIN Haji JOHARI; Sec.-Gen. FANG TECK SIONG.

Bee Seng Shipping Co: 7 Blk D, Sufri Complex, Km 2, Jalan Tutong, POB 1777, Bandar Seri Begawan; tel. 2220055; fax 2221815; e-mail beeseng@beeseng.com.

Brunei Gas Carriers Sdn Bhd (BGC): Setia Kenangan Office Blk, 7th Floor, Setia Kenangan Complex, Kampong Kuilap, Bandar Seri Begawan BE 1518; e-mail bgc@brunet.bn; internet www.syarikatbgc.com; f. 1998; LNG shipping co; owned jtly by the Prime Minister's Corpn (80%), Shell Gas BV (10%) and Mitsubishi subsidiary Diamond Gas Carriers BV (10%); one vessel operated by Shell Int. Trading and Shipping Co Ltd; Man. Dir KOH HUI LING (acting).

Brunei Shell Tankers Sdn Bhd: Seria KB 3534; tel. 3372722; f. 1986; owned jtly by the Prime Minister's Corpn (50%), Shell Petroleum Ltd (25%) and Diamond Gas BV (25%); seven vessels operated by Shell Int. Trading and Shipping Co Ltd; delivers LNG to domestic customers; Man. Dir Dr GRAHAEME HENDERSON.

Harper Wira Sdn Bhd: B2, 1st Floor, Bangunan Pehin, Simpang 27, Lot 12284, Km 3, Jalan Gadong, Bandar Seri Begawan 3180; tel. and fax 2448529.

IDS Borneo Sdn Bhd: Bangunan Inchcape Borneo, Km 4, Jalan Gadong, Bandar Seri Begawan; tel. 2422396; fax 2232537; f. 1856; Gen. Man. LO FAN KEE.

Pansar Co Sdn Bhd: Unit A6, 2nd Floor, Bangunan Urairah, Kampong Kiulap Mukim, Jalan Gadong, Bandar Seri Begawan BE 1518; tel. 2233641; fax 2233643; e-mail pscbwn-admin@pansar.com.my.

Seatrade Shipping Co: POB 476, Bandar Seri Begawan BS 8670; tel. 2421457; fax 2425824; e-mail seatradefang@brunet.bn.

Silver Line (B) Sdn Bhd: 2nd Floor, 6 Abdul Razak Complex, Simpang 137, Jalan Gadong, Bandar Seri Begawan BE 4119; tel. 2445069; fax 2430276; e-mail silvline@brunet.bn.

Tri-Star Shipping and Trading Co Sdn Bhd: Unit 16, Simpang 584, Jalan Tutong, Bandar Seri Begawan; tel. 2653013; fax 2652685; e-mail enquiry@tristarbrunei.com; internet www.tristarbrunei.com.

CIVIL AVIATION

There is an international airport at Berakas, near Bandar Seri Begawan. The Brunei Shell Petroleum Co Sdn Bhd operates a private airfield at Anduki for helicopter services.

Department of Civil Aviation: Brunei International Airport, Bandar Seri Begawan BB 2513; tel. 2330142; fax 2340971; e-mail info@civil-aviation.gov.bn; internet www.civil-aviation.gov.bn; Dir Haji OMARALI BIN Haji MOHAMMED JA'AFAR.

Royal Brunei Airlines (RBA) Ltd: RBA Plaza, Jalan Sultan, POB 737, Bandar Seri Begawan BS 8671; tel. 2212222; fax 2244737; e-mail feedback@rba.com.bn; internet www.bruneiair.com; f. 1974; operates services within the Far East and to the Middle East, Australia and Europe; Chair. Dato' LIM JOCK SENG; CEO ROBERT YANG.

Syabas Aviation Services Sdn Bhd: Unit 47, 1st Floor, Haji Uthman Kompleks, Simpang 13, Jalan Lapangan Terbang Antarabangsa, Bandar Seri Begawan BB 2513; tel. 2342657; fax 2342658; e-mail info@syabasaviation.com; internet syabasaviation.com; f. 2009; Chair. ABAS MOHAMMED.

Tourism

Tourist attractions in Brunei include the flora and fauna of the rain forest and the national parks, as well as mosques and water villages. In 2008 the number of tourist arrivals was estimated at 225,757, and international tourist receipts totalled US $241m.

Brunei Tourism: c/o Ministry of Industry and Primary Resources, Jalan Menteri Besar, Bandar Seri Begawan BB 3910; tel. 2382822; fax 2382824; e-mail info@bruneitourism.travel; internet www.bruneitourism.travel; CEO Sheikh JAMALUDDIN BIN Sheikh MOHAMMED.

Defence

As assessed at November 2011, the total strength of the Royal Brunei Malay Regiment was 7,000 (including 700 women): army 4,900; navy 1,000; air force 1,100. Military service (for which only ethnic Malays are eligible) is voluntary. Paramilitary forces comprise an estimated 2,250, of whom an estimated 400–500 belong to the Gurkha Reserve Unit and 1,750 are members of the Royal Brunei Police. A Gurkha battalion of the British army guards the petroleum and gas fields. Singaporean troops operate a training school in Brunei.

Defence Expenditure: B $514m. in 2011.

Commander of the Royal Brunei Armed Forces: Maj.-Gen. Haji AMINUDDIN IHSAN ABIDIN.

Commander of the Royal Brunei Land Force: Col YUSSOF BIN Haji ABD RAHMAN.

Commander of the Royal Brunei Navy: Col Haji ABDUL HALIM BIN Haji MOHAMED HANIFAH.

Commander of the Royal Brunei Air Force: Col JOFRI BIN Haji ABDULLAH.

Education

Education is free and is compulsory for 12 years from the age of five years. Islamic studies form an integral part of the school curriculum. There are three official languages of instruction, Malay, English and Chinese (Mandarin), with schools being divided accordingly. In 2009/10 enrolment at pre-primary level included 65% of children in the relevant age-group (males 64%; females 65%), while enrolment at primary level in 2007/08 included 93% of children in the relevant age-group (males 93%; females 93%). Enrolment at secondary level in 2008/09 included 97% of pupils in the relevant age-group (males 95%; females 99%). In 2010 there were 199 pre-primary and primary schools, 38 secondary schools, 13 vocational colleges and five higher education institutions. In the budget for 2010/11 the Government allocated B $638m. to the Ministry of Education.

BULGARIA

Introductory Survey

LOCATION, CLIMATE, LANGUAGE, RELIGION, FLAG, CAPITAL

The Republic of Bulgaria lies in the eastern Balkans, in south-eastern Europe. It is bounded by Romania to the north, by Turkey and Greece to the south, by Serbia to the west and by the former Yugoslav republic of Macedonia to the south-west. The country has an eastern coastline on the Black Sea. The climate is one of fairly sharp contrasts between winter and summer. Temperatures in Sofia are generally between −5°C (23°F) and 28°C (82°F). The official language is Bulgarian, a Southern Slavonic language, written in the Cyrillic alphabet. Minority languages include Turkish and Macedonian. The majority of the population is Christian; most are members of the Bulgarian Orthodox Church, although there is a substantial minority of Muslims. The national flag (proportions 2 by 3) has three equal horizontal stripes, of white, green and red. The capital is Sofia.

CONTEMPORARY POLITICAL HISTORY

Historical Context

After almost 500 years of Ottoman rule, Bulgaria declared itself an independent kingdom in 1908. In both the First and Second World Wars, Bulgaria allied itself with Germany, and in 1941 joined in the occupation of Yugoslavia. Soviet troops occupied Bulgaria in 1944. In September the Fatherland Front, a left-wing alliance formed in 1942, seized power, with help from the USSR, and installed a Government, led by Kimon Georgiev. In September 1946 the monarchy was abolished following a popular referendum, and a republic was proclaimed. The first post-war elections were held in October, when the Fatherland Front won 364 seats—277 of which were held by the Bulgarian Communist Party (BCP)—in the 465-member Narodno Sobranie (National Assembly). In November Georgi Dimitrov, the First Secretary of the BCP, became Chairman of the Council of Ministers (Prime Minister) in a Government formed by the Fatherland Front. All opposition parties were abolished and a new Constitution was adopted in December 1947, when Bulgaria was designated a People's Republic. Dimitrov was replaced as Prime Minister by Vasil Kolarov in March 1949, but remained leader of the BCP until his death in July. His successor as party leader, Vulko Chervenkov, became Prime Minister in February 1950.

Todor Zhivkov succeeded Chervenkov as leader of the BCP in 1954, although Chervenkov remained Prime Minister until 1956, when he was replaced by Anton Yugov. Following an ideological struggle within the BCP, Zhivkov was Prime Minister from 1962 until 1971, when, after the adoption of a new Constitution, he became the first President of the newly formed State Council. At a BCP Congress in 1981 the party's leader was restyled General Secretary. In June, following elections to the Narodno Sobranie, a new Government was formed: Grisha Filipov, a member of the BCP's Political Bureau, succeeded Stanko Todorov, who had been Prime Minister since 1971. In March 1986 Filipov was replaced by Georgi Atanasov, a former Vice-President of the State Council.

In local elections in March 1988, the nomination of candidates other than those endorsed by the BCP was permitted. Candidates presented by independent public organizations and workers' collectives obtained about one-quarter of the total votes cast. On 10 November 1989 Zhivkov was removed from his post of General Secretary of the BCP and from the Political Bureau. He was replaced as General Secretary by Petar Mladenov, Minister of Foreign Affairs since 1971, who also became President of the State Council. In mid-November 1989 the Narodno Sobranie voted to abolish part of the penal code prohibiting 'anti-State propaganda' and to grant an amnesty to those convicted under its provisions. Zhivkov was subsequently denounced by the BCP, and an investigation into corruption during his tenure was initiated. In 1990 Zhivkov was arrested on charges of embezzlement of state funds. (In January 1994 Zhivkov was sentenced to seven years' imprisonment on these charges, but in February 1996 his appeal against the sentence was upheld.)

Domestic Political Affairs

In early December 1989 Angel Dimitrov became leader of the Bulgarian Agrarian People's Union (BAPU, the sole legal political party apart from the BCP, with which it was originally allied); the BAPU was subsequently reconstituted as an independent opposition party. In mid-December the BCP proposed amendments to the Constitution and the adoption of a new electoral law to permit free elections to be held. In January 1990 the Narodno Sobranie voted to remove from the Constitution the article guaranteeing the BCP's dominant role in society and approved legislation permitting citizens to form independent groups and to stage demonstrations. Discussions regarding political and economic reforms commenced in that month between the BCP, the BAPU and the Union of Democratic Forces (UDF), which comprised several dissident and independent groups. In February the BCP adopted a new manifesto, pledging its commitment to the separation of party and state, and the introduction of a multi-party system, while retaining its Marxist orientation. Nevertheless, the new Council of Ministers, appointed on 8 February, was composed solely of BCP members, chaired by Andrei Lukanov, who was regarded as an advocate of reform.

In February 1990 some 200,000 supporters of the UDF protested in Sofia to demand the end of BCP rule. Following discussions in March, with the participation of the BAPU and other political and public organizations, it was finally agreed that Mladenov was to be re-elected as President, pending elections to a Velikoto Narodno Sobranie (Grand National Assembly), which would be empowered to approve a new constitution. It was also decided to dissolve the State Council. In April the Narodno Sobranie adopted an electoral law, together with legislation that guaranteed the right to form political parties. Meanwhile, the BCP was reconstituted as the Bulgarian Socialist Party (BSP).

Elections to a 400-member Velikoto Narodno Sobranie were held in two rounds in June 1990. The BSP won 211 seats, while the UDF obtained 144. The Movement for Rights and Freedoms (MRF), which had been established earlier in 1990 to represent the country's Muslim minority (principally ethnic Turks), secured 23 seats. The BAPU won 16 seats. In July Mladenov resigned as President, following a campaign of protests led by students. Zhelyu Zhelev, the Chairman of the UDF, was elected to replace him in August. Zhelev was succeeded as Chairman of the UDF first by Petar Beron, and, from December, by Filip Dimitrov.

In November 1990 16 BSP delegates to the Velikoto Narodno Sobranie formed a separate group, as a result of which the party no longer held an absolute majority. Following a general strike prompted by increased economic hardship, Lukanov's Government resigned at the end of the month. A new 'Government of national consensus' was formed in December, comprising members of the BSP, the UDF, the BAPU and four independents, and chaired by Dimitar Popov, a lawyer with no party affiliation.

Meanwhile, in November 1990 the Velikoto Narodno Sobranie voted to rename the country the Republic of Bulgaria and to remove from the national flag the state emblem, which included communist symbols. The Velikoto Narodno Sobranie adopted a new Constitution in July 1991; it subsequently voted to dissolve itself. The new Constitution provided for elections to be held, on an ad hoc basis, to a Velikoto Narodno Sobranie, the sole body empowered to adopt a new constitution and sanction territorial changes or certain constitutional amendments, although the permanent legislative body was to be the Narodno Sobranie. The Constitution stipulated a five-year residency qualification for presidential candidates, effectively disqualifying the candidacy of Simeon Sakskoburggotski (Saxe-Coburg Gotha—'Simeon II'), the pretender to the Bulgarian throne, who had lived in exile since 1946. At the elections to the new, 240-seat Narodno Sobranie, held on 13 October 1991, the UDF obtained 110 seats, narrowly defeating an alliance led by the BSP, which won 106 seats. The MRF secured 24 seats. The new Council of Ministers, composed principally of UDF members, was announced in November. Dimitrov, the leader of the UDF, was elected Chairman of the new Government. A direct presidential election was held in January 1992, in two rounds; Zhelev was re-elected for a five-year term, receiving 53% of the votes cast in the 'run-off' poll.

In April 1992 the Government adopted legislation restoring ownership of land and property that had been transferred to the state during 1947–62 (the deadline for property restitution was extended by three years in 1995); legislation approving the privatization of state-owned companies followed. In May Dimitrov implemented an extensive reorganization of the Council of Ministers. Meanwhile, relations between President Zhelev and the UDF became increasingly strained. In October MRF and BSP deputies in the Narodno Sobranie defeated the Government in a motion of confidence proposed by Dimitrov. In December the MRF nominated an academic, Prof. Lyuben Berov, hitherto an economic adviser to Zhelev, as Prime Minister. The UDF accused Berov of collaborating with the former communist regime and organized a large rally to protest against his candidacy. Although the majority of UDF deputies abstained, Berov was approved as Prime Minister on 30 December, heading a Council of Ministers principally composed of 'technocrats'.

In March 1993 a breakaway faction of the UDF formed a new, pro-Berov organization, the New Union for Democracy (NUD). Demonstrations were subsequently staged by the UDF in Sofia and several other cities in June, accusing Zhelev of attempting to restore communism, and demanding immediate elections. In June the Vice-President, Blaga Dimitrova, resigned. The crisis subsided when three votes expressing no confidence in Berov's Government, proposed by the UDF in the Narodno Sobranie, proved unsuccessful.

In September 1994 Berov's Government submitted its resignation, owing to criticism of the organization of the privatization programme, and in October Zhelev dissolved the Narodno Sobranie. At the general election, which was held on 18 December, the BSP (in alliance with two small parties) obtained an outright majority in the Narodno Sobranie, with 125 seats; the UDF won 69 seats. A new Government, headed by the Chairman of the BSP, Zhan Videnov, was appointed in January 1995.

In March 1995 the Government drafted a programme for mass privatization. At municipal elections in October–November, the ruling coalition won 195 of a total of 255 mayoralties, although the UDF secured the mayoralties in the country's three main cities. In January 1996 an unsuccessful motion of no confidence in the Videnov administration, led to the resignations of the Deputy Prime Minister and two ministers. In October former Prime Minister Andrei Lukanov was assassinated.

In the first round of the presidential election, held on 27 October 1996, Petar Stoyanov, a lawyer and senior member of the UDF, secured 44.1% of the votes cast; Ivan Marazov of the BSP, the candidate of a newly formed electoral alliance, Together for Bulgaria, received only 27.0% of the votes. In the second round of voting, which took place on 3 November, Stoyanov was elected to the presidency, with 59.7% of the votes cast.

Decline in BSP support

In December 1996 the UDF staged a series of demonstrations to demand early legislative elections and the resignation of the Government. On 21 December Videnov tendered his resignation as Prime Minister and BSP leader. Georgi Parvanov, who was a supporter of Videnov, subsequently replaced him as Chairman of the BSP. At the end of December the Narodno Sobranie voted to accept the resignation of Videnov's Government. The UDF, however, intensified its campaign of demonstrations.

On 19 January 1997 Stoyanov was inaugurated as President. Nikolai Dobrev relinquished the BSP mandate to form a government, owing to concern that protests and strikes by UDF supporters might escalate into civil conflict. The legislature approved recommendations by the consultative National Security Council that the President should appoint an interim council of ministers, dissolve the Narodno Sobranie and schedule legislative elections. In March the interim Government, led by the Mayor of Sofia, Stefan Sofiyanski, announced that Videnov was to be charged with criminal negligence as a result of government policies that had caused severe grain shortages in 1995–96; the Minister of Agriculture under Videnov was also prosecuted.

At the elections to the Narodno Sobranie, conducted on 19 April 1997, the UDF secured 137 seats, while the BSP (which again contested the elections in alliance with other parties, as the Democratic Left) obtained only 58 seats. Later in April the UDF nominated the party Chairman, Ivan Kostov, as Prime Minister, and in May he was confirmed in that position by the Narodno Sobranie.

Local government elections took place in October 1999: the UDF won 31.3% of the votes cast and the BSP secured 29.4%. In January 2001, in advance of presidential and legislative elections, the BSP attempted to consolidate support by forming an alliance, the Coalition for Bulgaria, with smaller leftist and nationalist groups. In April the former monarch, Simeon Sakskoburggotski, who had returned to Bulgaria at the beginning of the month, was not permitted to register his new National Movement as a party. In May, however, the Movement was permitted to form an alliance with two smaller, registered parties, the Party of Bulgarian Women and the Oborishte Party for National Revival, as the National Movement Simeon II (NMSII), in order to participate in the legislative elections. Sakskoburggotski (who was not permitted officially to lead the Movement) asserted that he had no desire to restore the monarchy, and pledged to combat official corruption and reform the economy, in order to fulfil the criteria for membership of the European Union (EU, see p. 276).

In the general election, held on 17 June 2001, the NMSII obtained 120 seats, while the UDF secured only 51 seats. The NMSII held just one seat fewer than the 121 required to secure an absolute majority in the Narodno Sobranie, and it approached the MRF (which held 21 legislative seats) and the UDF as potential partners. The MRF agreed to be represented in the government, but the UDF refused to participate in an administration that included members of the MRF; the BSP subsequently became an informal coalition partner. Sakskoburggotski was sworn in as Prime Minister on 24 July. The Council of Ministers, in which two ministerial portfolios were allocated to both the MRF and the BSP, was approved by the Narodno Sobranie on the same day. Kostov subsequently resigned his leadership of the UDF. In March 2002 five members of the Narodno Sobranie left the NMSII, in protest at Sakskoburggotski's perceived failure to fulfil electoral pledges. In April the NMSII was finally legally registered as a political party, and Sakskoburggotski was elected as its Chairman.

Meanwhile, in the first round of voting in the presidential election held on 11 November 2001 Parvanov, contesting the election for the Coalition for Bulgaria, won 36.4% of the votes cast, and the incumbent, Stoyanov, who stood as an independent candidate, secured 34.9% of the votes. However, the rate of participation by the electorate was just 39.2% (less than the 50% demanded by the Constitution). Parvanov confirmed his victory in a second round of voting on 18 November, in which he obtained 54.1% of the votes cast; the rate of voter participation was some 54.6%. Parvanov took office on 22 January 2002.

Following efforts by the Supreme Administrative Court to suspend the sales of both the state tobacco company, Bulgartabac, and the Bulgarian Telecommunications Company in late 2002, in January 2003 the Narodno Sobranie approved controversial legislation removing the Court's power to prevent the privatization of principal state enterprises, which was, instead, to be decided by the Government, with the approval of the legislature. In February the Narodno Sobranie voted to override a presidential veto, and an appeal was subsequently lodged at the Constitutional Court by Parvanov, the UDF and the BSP; in April the Court ruled that the amendments to the privatization bill had been unconstitutional. Meanwhile, in February five legislative deputies had left the NMSII, alleging widespread corruption within the Government, thereby reducing the governing coalition's legislative majority to just 10 seats.

The return of the BSP

In municipal elections, conducted in October–November 2003, the BSP and the UDF secured the majority of seats. In January 2004 Ekaterina Mihailova resigned her position as deputy leader of the UDF, in protest at the leadership of Nadezhda Mihailova. Mihailova was re-elected to the party leadership in February, prompting 26 UDF members, including the party's former Chairman, Kostov, to leave the party. Kostov subsequently founded a new party, Democrats for a Strong Bulgaria (DSB).

In February 2005 the Narodno Sobranie voted by a narrow majority to dismiss its Chairman, Ognyan Gerdzhikov. Gerdzhikov had been accused of systematically violating the Narodno Sobranie's rules of procedure, after he refused to allow parliament to discuss the failed sale of Bulgartabac to British American Tobacco. He was replaced by Borislav Velikov. In the same month, in an attempt to strengthen the ruling coalition before the legislative elections due to take place later that year, the Prime Minister reorganized the Council of Ministers; Milko Kovachev, hitherto Minister of Energy and Energy Resources, was appointed as Deputy Prime Minister and Minister of the Economy.

At the elections to the Narodno Sobranie, held on 25 June 2005, the BSP-led Coalition for Bulgaria secured 82 of the 240 seats in the legislature and 34.2% of the votes cast; the NMSII received 53 seats and 22.1% of the votes, and the MRF secured 34 seats and 14.2% of the votes. A newly formed coalition of extreme right-wing and nationalist parties, the Attack National Union (Attack—subsequently the Attack Party), secured 21 seats (8.8% of the votes). The rate of participation by the electorate was relatively low, at 55.7%. On 16 August the Narodno Sobranie approved a three-party coalition Government led by BSP leader Sergei Stanishev. The new Council of Ministers comprised nine members of the BSP, five members of the NMSII, three members of the MRF and one independent minister. Each of the three coalition partners nominated a Deputy Prime Minister. Meanwhile, in July Georgi Pirinski, a former Minister of Foreign Affairs and Deputy Chairman of the BSP, was elected as the new Chairman of the Narodno Sobranie.

In October 2005 former President Stoyanov was appointed as leader of the UDF, replacing Mihailova. The first round of presidential voting, held on 22 October 2006 and contested by seven candidates, proved inconclusive because the rate of electoral participation was below the requisite 50%. The first-placed candidate, the incumbent, Parvanov, who secured some 64.1% of the votes cast, progressed to a 'run-off' vote against Volen Siderov of Attack (who secured 21.5% of the votes cast) on 29 October. Parvanov won 76.0% of the votes in the second round of voting (which had no minimum required rate of participation), thereby becoming the first post-communist President of Bulgaria to be elected to a second term of office. Parvanov was inaugurated on 22 January 2007.

At elections to the European Parliament in May 2007, both the UDF and the DSB failed to secure representation, prompting the resignations of Stoyanov and Kostov from the leadership of their respective parties; the BSP and the Citizens for European Development of Bulgaria (GERB), a newly established centre-right opposition party unofficially headed by the Mayor of Sofia, Boyko Borisov, each secured five of the 18 available seats. The NMSII obtained one seat, and in the following month reconstituted itself as the National Movement for Stability and Progress (NMSP). In June Stanishev announced that he had accepted the resignation of the Minister of the Economy and Energy, Rumen Ocharov, following allegations against him of corruption, and the Minister of Justice, Georgi Petkanov. At municipal elections, which were conducted on 28 October and 4 November, GERB won the mayoral polls in the country's principal towns, with Borisov re-elected as Mayor of Sofia.

A new State Agency for National Security was established in December 2007 to investigate cases of corruption and organized crime. In April 2008 the Minister of the Interior, Rumen Petkov, resigned from the Government, after allegations emerged of endemic corruption. The BSP, the MRF and the NMSP reached agreement on a government reorganization, in which four ministers (including Petkov) were replaced. Hitherto ambassador to Germany, Meglena Plugchieva was appointed to the new post of Deputy Prime Minister, with responsibility for EU funds, while Mihail Mikov became Minister of the Interior. In May a new political organization, Bulgarian New Democracy, was created by former members of the NMSP, including 16 deputies who had left the party a few months earlier owing to their opposition to the NMSP leadership. None the less, the ruling three-party coalition retained a large majority in the Narodno Sobranie. In January 2009 more than 2,000 people attended an anti-Government demonstration outside the parliament building in Sofia to protest against the perceived failure to reduce corruption and poverty; police detained around 160 people. On the following day 15 opposition deputies participated in a second demonstration, which took place peacefully.

In April 2009 the Narodno Sobranie approved the introduction of a mixed system of voting in legislative elections: 31 of the 240 deputies were to be directly elected by majority vote, while the remaining seats continued to be distributed by proportional representation. At elections to the European Parliament held on 7 June, GERB secured five of the 17 seats allocated to Bulgaria, with 24.4% of the votes cast, while the BSP-led Coalition for Bulgaria took four (18.5% of the votes) and the MRF three (14.1%). Attack and the NMSP each obtained two seats, with the remaining seat won by the recently formed Blue Coalition, led by the UDF and the DSB. A rate of participation of 37.5% was recorded.

The 2009 legislative elections

In the general election held on 5 July 2009, GERB won 39.7% of the votes cast and 116 of the 240 seats; the Coalition for Bulgaria received 17.7% of the votes and 40 seats, the MRF secured 14.4% of the votes and 38 seats, while the NMSP failed to obtain representation. GERB's electoral campaign had focused on pledges to combat corruption and to revive the economy. Attack, the Blue Coalition and the centre-right Order, Law and Justice party (founded in late 2005) secured 21, 15 and 10 seats, respectively. At 60.9%, the rate of voter participation was notably higher than at the 2005 elections. Tsetska Tsacheva, of GERB, was elected to chair the new Narodno Sobranie at its first session on 14 July. A minority GERB Government, led by Borisov and supported by Attack, the Blue Coalition and Order, Law and Justice, was approved by the legislature on 27 July. The new Council of Ministers included two Deputy Prime Ministers: Tsvetan Tsvetanov, the Chairman of GERB, who was also appointed as Minister of the Interior, and Simeon Dyankov, hitherto a senior economist at the World Bank, who was also allocated the finance portfolio. In February 2010 a recount of votes at 23 Turkish polling stations led to a ruling by the Constitutional Court that increased the number of parliamentary seats held by GERB to 117, and reduced the representation of the MRF by one seat, to 37.

Borisov swiftly introduced measures intended to fulfil his electoral promise to address corruption. In August 2009 a six-member ministerial council, chaired by Simeon Dyankov, was established to manage all resources received from the EU, while the Ministry of the Interior and the police force initiated a joint project aimed at detecting and preventing the misuse of EU funds. The Government also instigated investigations into alleged corruption by the previous Government. In November the Prosecutor-General sought the removal by the Narodno Sobranie of the immunity from prosecution of former Prime Minister Stanishev and of the former Minister of Labour and Social Policy, Emilia Maslarova; both denied any wrongdoing and voluntarily surrendered their immunity.

Also in November 2009 Yordanka Fandakova, a candidate of GERB and Minister of Education, Youth and Science, was elected Mayor of Sofia; Sergey Ignatov was appointed to replace her in the Council of Ministers. Prime Minister Borisov made further changes to the Government in January 2010, following the resignation of the Minister of Foreign Affairs, Rumyana Zheleva. Nikolay Mladenov, hitherto Minister of Defence, was appointed as Minister of Foreign Affairs, and the defence portfolio was taken by his former deputy, Anyu Angelov. Meanwhile, also in January Borisov was elected as Chairman of GERB, with Tsvetanov as his deputy; Borisov had been barred from assuming the official leadership of the party while holding the position of Mayor of Sofia. In mid-March Tomislav Donchev, hitherto Mayor of the central city of Gabrovo, was appointed to the new position of Minister for the Management of EU Funds.

The GERB Government

In late February 2010 Maslarova was charged with embezzlement and abuse of power. In early 2010 indictments were also issued against former Minister of Agriculture and Food Valeri Tsvetanov, who was accused of abuse of power between April 2008 and July 2009, and against former Minister of Defence Nikolai Tsonev, who was accused of defrauding the state of some 8m. leva by signing agreements for the delivery of military equipment in early 2009. In July 2010 former premier Stanishev was formally charged in connection with the loss of classified information in 2005–09. In November 2010 the city court in Sofia acquitted Tsonev of the charges against him. Later in November a new, independent commission was established to investigate high-level corruption.

Meanwhile, the Government survived a motion of no confidence in October 2010. In November it was reported that Parvanov had launched a new movement, the Alternative for Bulgarian Revival, which included former members of the BSP; he accused GERB of incompetence and poor leadership at a time of economic crisis. In December it emerged that almost one-half of the members of Bulgaria's diplomatic service had co-operated with the communist-era security services. The Narodno Sobranie subsequently voted in favour of the recall of 33 ambassadors. Bozhidar Dimitrov, who was also known to have collaborated with the security services, resigned from his post as Minister without Portfolio in late December. In January 2011 illicitly obtained recordings released in the media appeared to implicate members of the Government, including Borisov, in corrupt practices, and to reveal severe internal divisions. The Government, which denied the authenticity of the recordings, subsequently won two votes of confidence in the Narodno Sobranie. In February a bomb exploded outside the offices of opposition newspaper *Galeria*, which had notably published transcripts of the illicit recordings. The Director of the State Agency for National Security subsequently tendered his resignation. In March a large-scale anti-Government demonstration was organized by the BSP in Sofia, in protest at economic hardship. In June the Government survived a further parliamentary motion of no confidence.

In late September 2011 the death of a young man, who was believed to have been murdered by the driver of a minibus in the southern village of Katunitsa, precipitated attacks against the property of a local Roma organized crime leader, who was revealed to have links with the driver. The violence escalated, and anti-Roma protests took place in several cities, including Sofia; many demonstrators were arrested. In early October the office of the UN High Commissioner for Human Rights expressed serious concern that violent protests were being directed against the entire Roma community, in response to a crime perpetrated by an individual.

Recent developments: the 2011 presidential election

The first round of the presidential election held on 23 October 2011 was contested by 18 candidates; Rosen Plevneliev of GERB (who had previously held the position of Minister of Regional Development and Public Works) secured 40.1% of the votes cast, while the BSP candidate, Ivaylo Kalfin, received 29.0%. (Parvanov, having served two terms in office, was prohibited from seeking re-election.) At the consequent second round of voting, contested by the two leading candidates on 30 October, Plevneliev was elected to the presidency with 52.6% of the votes cast. The rate of participation by the electorate was estimated at 48.3%. Municipal elections were conducted in two rounds concurrently with the presidential voting: GERB retained control of the principal towns, including the mayoralties of Sofia and Burgas. On 14 December the Constitutional Court officially ruled the results of the presidential election to be legitimate, despite opposition claims of irregularities, particularly relating to the disenfranchisement of eligible voters. Plevneliev was inaugurated on 22 January 2012.

In early December 2011 the Narodno Sobranie voted to adopt controversial pension reforms, which included proposals for a gradual increase in the retirement age from 2012. Opposition parties strongly opposed the measures, while the two main trade union federations, which had previously negotiated an agreement with the Government allowing the retirement age to remain unchanged until 2021, began a campaign of national protests. In January 2012 a 'special court' that was designed to expedite trials relating to organized crime opened in Sofia; more than 400 cases were expected to be referred to the court by the end of that year.

Foreign Affairs

Regional relations

Bulgaria's establishment of formal relations with the former Yugoslav republic of Macedonia (FYRM) in January 1992 prompted harsh criticism from the Greek Government, although relations with Greece appeared to improve thereafter. In November 1993 the FYRM expressed its desire to establish full diplomatic relations with Bulgaria, and in the following month Bulgaria announced that it was to open an embassy in the FYRM and relax border procedures between the two states. In February 1999 Prime Minister Kostov and the Prime Minister of the FYRM, Ljubčo Georgievski, signed a declaration pledging that neither country had a territorial claim on the other. In March the Ministers of Defence of Bulgaria and the FYRM signed a joint declaration providing for increased military co-operation, in connection with the aim of both countries to join the North Atlantic Treaty Organization (NATO, see p. 370).

Bulgaria's relations with Serbia were strained in March 2008, following the Bulgarian Government's decision to recognize Kosovo's independence, which had been unilaterally declared by the former Serbian province in the previous month. None the less, in September the Governments of Bulgaria, Serbia and Romania signed an agreement on co-operation in combating cross-border crime.

Relations between Bulgaria and Russia improved in 1992, following the signature of co-operation agreements, and the visit of the Russian President, Boris Yeltsin, to Sofia in August. In April 1998 the Bulgarian Government signed an agreement with the Russian national gas company, Gazprom, providing for the supply and transit of Russian gas. In December 2000 Russia expressed its disappointment at Bulgaria's decision to terminate, in accordance with conditions for accession to the EU, a 1978 bilateral agreement on visa-free travel, with effect from June 2001. However, in March 2003 Russian President Vladimir Putin visited Bulgaria, resulting in strongly enhanced economic relations, despite failing to persuade Bulgaria to withdraw its support for US-led military action in Iraq (see below). In March 2007 the Russian, Bulgarian and Greek Governments signed an agreement in the Greek capital, Athens, on the construction of a pipeline to transport Russian petroleum from the Bulgarian Black Sea port of Burgas to Alexandroupolis, on the Greek Aegean coast. This agreement was finalized during an official visit to Bulgaria by President Putin in early 2008, when the two countries also signed an accord on Bulgaria's participation in Russia's so-called South Stream project, which was being pursued jointly with Italian energy company Eni and involved the establishment of a pipeline to deliver Russian natural gas to Italy and Austria, via Bulgaria. Nevertheless, in July 2009 the Governments of Bulgaria, Austria, Hungary, Romania and Turkey signed an agreement on the construction of the 3,300-km Nabucco pipeline, which was designed to transport natural gas from Central Asia through Turkey to Europe, thus reducing dependence on Russian supplies. In November 2010 Putin, now premier of Russia, visited Sofia, and he and Prime Minister Boyko Borisov signed an agreement on the establishment of a joint company for the construction of the South Stream pipeline route. In December 2011, however, the Bulgarian Government announced its withdrawal from the Burgas–Alexandroupolis pipeline, citing concerns over the project's financial and economic viability.

Relations with Turkey were intermittently strained from the mid-1980s, when the Zhivkov regime began a campaign of forced assimilation of Bulgaria's ethnic Turkish minority (an estimated 9% of the total population). In May 1989 Bulgarian militia units violently suppressed demonstrations by an estimated 30,000 ethnic Turks in eastern Bulgaria, and in June more than 80,000 ethnic Turks were expelled from Bulgaria, although the Bulgarian authorities claimed that the Turks had chosen to settle in Turkey. By mid-August an estimated 310,000 Bulgarian Turks had crossed into Turkey, and in late August the Turkish Government closed the border. In the following month a substantial number of the Bulgarian Turks, disillusioned with conditions in Turkey, began to return to Bulgaria. The Turkish Government repeatedly proposed that discussions with the Bulgarian Government be held, under the auspices of the UN High Commissioner for Refugees, to establish the rights of the Bulgarian Turks and to formulate a clear immigration policy. Finally, Bulgaria agreed to negotiations, and friendly relations between Bulgaria and Turkey were restored by late 1991.

Meanwhile, in December 1989 some 6,000 Pomaks (ethnic Bulgarian Muslims) held demonstrations to demand religious and cultural freedoms, as well as an official inquiry into alleged atrocities against Pomaks during Zhivkov's tenure of office. In January 1990 anti-Turkish demonstrations were held in the Kurdzhali district of southern Bulgaria, in protest at the Government's declared intention to restore civil and religious rights to the ethnic Turkish minority. Despite continuing demonstrations by Bulgarian nationalist protesters, in March the Narodno Sobranie approved legislation that permitted ethnic Turks and Pomaks to use their original, non-Slavic names. This development was welcomed by the Turkish Government. Nevertheless, inter-ethnic disturbances continued, particularly in the Kurdzhali region, during 1990. In May 1992 Prime Minister Dimitrov visited Turkey, and the two countries signed a treaty of friendship and co-operation. In July 1995 a visit by President Süleyman Demirel of Turkey to Bulgaria indicated a significant improvement in Bulgarian-Turkish relations. In June 1998 the Narodno Sobranie ratified an agreement demarcating the border between Bulgaria and Turkey (which had been signed during an official visit to Sofia by the Turkish Prime Minister, Mesut Yılmaz, in December 1997). In February 2001 Bulgaria and Turkey signed a joint protocol on combating terrorism and organized crime.

Negotiations on Bulgaria's accession to the EU began in March 2000. In March 2004 the European Parliament praised Bulgaria's reform efforts and endorsed the planned date of 2007 for Bulgaria's accession, and in June Bulgaria (along with Romania) officially concluded the negotiation process with the EU. Bulgaria and Romania signed formal accession agreements with the EU on 25 April 2005. In October the European Commission emphasized that Bulgaria's accession to the EU remained dependent on its ability, *inter alia*, to combat organized crime and reform the judicial system. Bulgaria (and Romania) formally acceded to the EU on 1 January 2007. However, many existing EU members imposed extensive labour market restrictions; only nine countries guaranteed unlimited access to migrant workers from Bulgaria and Romania following their accession (the Czech Republic and Italy removed their labour market restrictions in January 2012). Additional constraints on membership rights, together with domestic power deficits following the closure of two nuclear reactors at the end of 2006, in compliance with EU accession preconditions, provoked some animosity between Bulgaria and the original bloc members and led to reciprocal restrictions against economic migrants from those countries refusing or limiting access to Bulgarians. In early 2008, with continuing domestic electricity shortages, the Government initiated an official campaign to gain support for the reopening of the nuclear reactors, despite the opposition of the EU. The severe gas shortages experienced in January 2009 (see Contemporary Political History) prompted President Parvanov to renew demands for the reactivation of the closed reactors. The European Commission suspended nearly €500m. in development aid to Bulgaria in July 2008, after releasing a report that strongly criticized the country's continued failure to reduce levels of organized crime and corruption, including the alleged misuse of EU funds by public officials. In November €220m. of this funding was forfeited. After taking office in July 2009, the administration of Boyko Borisov introduced measures aimed at improving the management of EU funds (see Contemporary Political History). In September, during a visit to Brussels, Belgium, by a government delegation led by Borisov, it was announced that the European Commission was to resume farm subsidy payments and other agricultural aid to Bulgaria. Further suspended funds, amounting to some €340m., were released in November. In June 2011 the European Parliament voted in support of the admission of Bulgaria and Romania to the EU's Schengen area (which would allow the abolition of visa requirements within the EU for citizens of those states). However, at a meeting of EU ministers of internal affairs in Brussels in September, Finland and the Netherlands vetoed membership of the zone for the two states, owing to continuing concerns over issues including corruption and organized crime.

Other external relations

Bulgaria's relations with the USA strengthened during 2002, and in February 2003 the Narodno Sobranie voted to allow US forces to make use of Bulgarian airspace, as well as the airbase at Sarafovo, on the Black Sea, for military operations during the impending US-led campaign to remove the regime of Saddam Hussain in Iraq; Bulgaria had previously offered its support to the USA during its military campaign in Afghanistan from late 2001. Bulgaria dispatched some 470 troops to support the US-led military campaign in Iraq, which commenced in March 2003. The troops were withdrawn after the Iraqi parliamentary elections in December 2005. In February 2006 the Narodno Sobranie approved the deployment of a 155-member mission to maintain security at a refugee camp in Ashraf, Iraq; the mission was withdrawn in December 2008. Bulgarian troops continued to participate in the NATO-led International Security Assistance Force in Afghanistan, their contingent numbering 602 in early 2012. Meanwhile, a defence co-operation agreement on the sharing of Bulgarian military bases with US troops was signed by Kalfin and the US Secretary of State, Condoleezza Rice, in Sofia in April 2006, and entered into force in June; further agreements on the joint use of military facilities were signed in early 2008. Several bilateral accords were signed during an official visit to the USA by Bulgarian Prime Minister Stanishev in June 2008.

In the first half of 2011 the Bulgarian Government sent a frigate to the Mediterranean Sea to participate in the NATO operation to enforce the arms embargo imposed against Libya. The embargo had been put in place in an effort to protect civilians from attack by forces loyal to Libyan leader Col Muammar al-Qaddafi, who was killed in October (see Libya).

CONSTITUTION AND GOVERNMENT

The Constitution of the Republic of Bulgaria took effect upon its promulgation, on 13 July 1991. Legislative power is held by the unicameral Narodno Sobranie (National Assembly), comprising 240 members, who are elected for four years by universal adult suffrage. The President of the Republic (Head of State) is directly elected for a period of five years, and is also Supreme Commander-in-Chief of the Armed Forces. The Council of Ministers, the highest organ of state administration, is elected by the Narodno Sobranie. The judicial branch of government is independent. The Supreme Court of Cassation exercises supreme judicial responsibility for the application of the law by all courts, while the Supreme Administrative Court rules on all challenges to the legality of acts of any organ of government. For local administration purposes, Bulgaria comprises 28 regions (divided into a total of 259 municipalities).

REGIONAL AND INTERNATIONAL CO-OPERATION

Bulgaria is a member of the European Bank for Reconstruction and Development (EBRD, see p. 271), of the Council of Europe (see p. 256) and of the Organization of the Black Sea Economic Co-operation (BSEC, see p. 402). In January 2007 Bulgaria acceded to the European Union (EU, see p. 276).

Bulgaria became a member of the UN in 1955, and was admitted to the World Trade Organization (WTO, see p. 433) in 1996. In 2004 Bulgaria joined the North Atlantic Treaty Organization (NATO, see p. 370).

ECONOMIC AFFAIRS

In 2010, according to estimates by the World Bank, Bulgaria's gross national income (GNI), measured at average 2008–10 prices, was US $47,159m., equivalent to $6,250 per head (or $13,250 per head on an international purchasing-power parity basis). During 2001–10, it was estimated, the population decreased at an average rate of 0.5% per year, while gross domestic product (GDP) per head increased, in real terms, at an average annual rate of 4.6%. According to the World Bank, Bulgaria's overall GDP increased, in real terms, by an average of 4.0% annually during 2001–10. Real GDP declined by 5.5% in 2009, but increased by 0.2% in 2010.

According to preliminary figures, agriculture (including hunting, forestry and fishing) contributed 5.4% of GDP in 2010. The sector engaged 7.5% of the employed labour force in 2008. In 1990 private farming was legalized, and by the end of 1999 some 96% of farmland had been restituted, in its former physical boundaries, to former owners and their heirs. The principal crops are wheat, sunflower seeds, maize, barley, grapes, potatoes, watermelons and tomatoes. Bulgaria is a major exporter of wine, and there is a large exportable surplus of processed agricultural products. According to the World Bank, during 2001–10 the average annual GDP of the agricultural sector declined, in real terms, by 1.1%; the GDP of the sector declined by 3.5% in 2009, but increased by 3.0% in 2010.

According to preliminary figures, industry (including mining, manufacturing, construction and utilities) provided some 31.4% of GDP in 2010. The sector engaged 36.4% of the employed labour force in 2008. According to the World Bank, industrial GDP increased, in real terms, at an average annual rate of 4.7% in 2001–10. Real industrial GDP declined by 7.2% in 2009, but increased by 3.5% in 2010.

In 2005 mining accounted for some 1.6% of GDP, while in 2008 mining and quarrying engaged 1.0% of the employed labour force. Coal, iron ore, copper, manganese, lead and zinc are mined, and petroleum is extracted on the Black Sea coast.

According to World Bank estimates, the manufacturing sector contributed 16.1% of GDP in 2010. The sector engaged 22.9% of the employed labour force in 2008. The GDP of the manufacturing sector increased at an average annual rate of 5.3%, in real terms, in 2001–10. The GDP of the sector declined by 4.0% in 2009, but increased by 5.0% in 2010.

According to preliminary figures, the construction sector contributed 7.5% of GDP in 2010, and it engaged 10.1% of the employed labour force in 2008. The GDP of the sector increased at an average annual rate of 6.7% in 2000–09, in real terms. Sectoral GDP declined by 16.7% in 2010.

Bulgaria's production of primary energy in 2006 was equivalent to 53.1% of gross consumption. Coal and nuclear power, the latter produced by the country's sole nuclear power station, at Kozloduy, are the main domestic sources of energy. Four of the plant's six reactors were closed by 2006, in compliance with conditions for membership of the European Union (EU, see p. 276). Bulgaria's proven coal reserves stood at 2,366m. metric tons at the end of 2010. In 2008 nuclear power provided 35.4% of electric energy, while coal accounted for 52.1% of electricity production. Crude petroleum and natural gas comprised 20.2% of the value of merchandise imports in 2010.

According to preliminary figures, in 2010 the services sector contributed some 63.3% of GDP. In 2008 the sector engaged 56.1% of the employed labour force. Tourism revenue increased significantly from 2002. Revenue totalled US $4,831m. in 2008, compared with $3,317m. in 2006. The real GDP of the services sector increased at an annual average rate of 5.1% during 2001–10, according to the World Bank. The real GDP of the sector declined by 0.6% in 2009, but increased by 0.9% in 2010.

In 2010 Bulgaria recorded a visible trade deficit of US $3,217.4m., and there was a deficit of $578.0m. on the current account of the balance of payments. In that year the principal sources of imports were Russia (which provided 17.0% of the total), Germany, Italy, Romania, Turkey, the People's Republic of China and Greece. The main market for exports in 2010 was Germany (taking 10.6% of the total); Italy, Romania, Turkey and Greece were also significant purchasers. The principal exports in 2010 were metals (including iron and steel), petroleum products, clothing and footwear, raw materials for the food industry, and food. The principal imports in that year were crude petroleum and natural gas, machines and equipment, plastics and rubber, and ores.

According to IMF estimates, in 2009 Bulgaria recorded a budgetary deficit of 330m. new leva (equivalent to 3.9% of GDP). Bulgaria's general government gross debt was 12,240m. new leva in 2010, equivalent to 17.4% of GDP. Bulgaria's total external debt in 2009 was US $40,582m., of which $4,772m. was public and publicly guaranteed debt. In that year the cost of debt-servicing was equivalent to 2.0% of the value of exports of goods, services and income. The annual rate of inflation averaged 5.8% in 2001–10. Consumer prices increased by 5.3% in 2010. According to Bulgaria's National Statistical Institute, 10.2% of the labour force were registered as unemployed in 2010.

Large inflows of foreign investment followed the conclusion, in 2004, of negotiations on Bulgaria's membership of the EU and continued after accession at the beginning of 2007, allowing infrastructure projects to proceed rapidly. The new, centre-right Government that took office in July 2009 swiftly announced measures aimed at improving the fiscal position. The 2009 budget deficit exceeded the threshold of 3% of GDP imposed by the EU on countries hoping to join the exchange rate mechanism (ERM II), with the eventual aim of adopting the euro. In July 2010 Bulgaria's budget deficit triggered the EU's Excessive Deficit Procedure (EDP), which compels countries to correct errors relating to fiscal policy. Bulgaria swiftly introduced measures to reduce the deficit, to 2.5% of GDP in 2011 and to 1.3% in 2012. In December 2011 the Government announced its withdrawal from a longstanding agreement on the construction of a pipeline to transport Russian petroleum from the Bulgarian Black Sea port of Burgas to Alexandroupolis, on the Greek Aegean coast, citing concerns over the project's financial and economic viability, and environmental considerations. In March 2012, moreover, Bulgaria announced that long-standing plans for the construction of a new nuclear power plant at Belene were to be formally abandoned. Meanwhile, although GDP growth had resumed in 2010, continuing uncertainties in the external environment (with an ongoing debt crisis in the euro area in early 2012) were considered to be hampering the country's recovery; the IMF projected growth of 1.9% for 2011. However, the IMF welcomed the Government's progress in imposing greater fiscal control in order to meet its budget deficit target for 2011, and its decision to bring forward plans for the initiation of extensive pension reforms, including a gradual increase in the retirement age, to January 2012.

PUBLIC HOLIDAYS

2013: 1 January (New Year), 3 March (National Day), 1 May (Labour Day), 5–6 May (Eastern Orthodox Easter), 6 May (St George's Day), 24 May (Education Day), 6 September (Unification Day), 22 September (Independence Day), 24–26 December (Christmas).

Statistical Survey

Sources (unless otherwise indicated): National Statistical Institute, 1038 Sofia, ul. P. Volov 2; tel. (2) 985-77-00; fax (2) 985-76-40; e-mail info@nsi.bg; internet www.nsi.bg; Bulgarian National Bank, 1000 Sofia, pl. Knyaz Aleksandar I 1; tel. (2) 914-59; fax (2) 980-24-25; e-mail press_office@bnbank.org; internet www.bnb.bg; Center for Economic Development, 1408 Sofia, ul. J. K. Ivan Vazov 1/9; tel. (2) 953-42-04; e-mail stat@ced.bg; internet www.stat.bg.

Area and Population

AREA, POPULATION AND DENSITY

Area (sq km)*	110,994†
Population (census results)	
1 March 2001	7,928,901
1 February 2011	
Males	3,586,571
Females	3,777,999
Total	7,364,570
Density (per sq km) at 2011 census	66.4

* Including territorial waters of frontier rivers (261.4 sq km).

† 42,855 sq miles.

POPULATION BY AGE AND SEX

(population at 2011 census)

	Males	Females	Total
0–14	501,718	473,554	975,272
15–64	2,530,872	2,497,029	5,027,901
65 and over	553,981	807,416	1,361,397
Total	3,586,571	3,777,999	7,364,570

ETHNIC GROUPS

(2011 census)

	Number	%
Bulgarian	5,664,624	76.9
Turkish	588,318	8.0
Roma	325,343	4.4
Others*	786,285	10.7
Total	7,364,570	100.0

* Including 53,391 (0.7% of the total) who chose not to be defined by ethnic group.

ADMINISTRATIVE REGIONS

(population at 2011 census)

	Area (sq km)	Population	Density (per sq km)
City Oblast			
Sofia City	1,038.8	1,291,591	1,243.3
Oblasts			
Blagoevgrad	6,468.8	323,552	50.0
Burgas	7,610.6	415,817	54.6
Dobrich	4,692.5	189,677	40.4
Gabrovo	2,069.5	122,702	59.3
Haskovo	4,032.0	246,238	61.1
Kardzhali	4,023.0	152,808	38.0
Kyustendil	3,004.2	136,686	45.5
Lovech	4,131.0	141,422	34.2
Montana	3,587.6	148,098	41.3
Pazardzhik	4,382.2	275,548	62.9
Pernik	2,356.7	133,530	56.7
Pleven	4,187.1	269,752	64.4
Plovdiv	5,595.1	683,027	122.1

—continued	Area (sq km)	Population	Density (per sq km)
Razgrad	2,647.9	125,190	47.3
Ruse	2,625.9	235,252	89.6
Shumen	3,376.5	180,528	53.5
Silistra	2,878.1	119,474	41.5
Sliven	3,731.7	197,473	52.9
Smolyan	3,520.6	121,752	34.6
Sofia	7,389.4	247,489	33.5
Stara Zagora	4,905.6	333,265	67.9
Targovishche	2,756.0	120,818	43.8
Varna	3,822.8	475,074	124.3
Veliko Tarnovo	4,693.5	258,494	55.1
Vidin	3,112.3	101,018	32.5
Vratsa	4,189.1	186,848	44.6
Yambol	4,165.1	131,447	31.6
Total	110,993.6	7,364,570	66.4

Note: Each oblast is named after its capital city.

PRINCIPAL TOWNS
(population at 2011 census, preliminary)

Sofia (capital)	1,270,284	Sliven	89,848
Plovdiv	331,796	Dobrich*	89,472
Varna	330,486	Shumen	82,557
Burgas (Bourgas)	197,301	Pernik	81,052
Ruse (Roussé)	146,609	Khaskovo	74,843
Stara Zagora	136,363	Pazardzhik	70,882
Pleven	106,011	Veliko Tarnovo	68,197

* Known as Tolbukhin in 1949–90.

BIRTHS, MARRIAGES AND DEATHS

	Registered live births		Registered marriages		Registered deaths	
	Number	Rate (per 1,000)	Number	Rate (per 1,000)	Number	Rate (per 1,000)
2006	73,978	9.6	26,159	4.3	113,438	14.8
2007	75,349	9.8	29,640	3.9	113,004	14.8
2008	77,712	10.2	27,722	3.6	110,523	14.5
2009	80,956	10.7	25,923	3.4	108,068	14.3
2010	75,513	10.0	24,286	3.2	110,165	14.6

Life expectancy (years at birth, WHO estimates): 74 (males 70; females 77) in 2009 (Source: WHO, *World Health Statistics*).

ECONOMICALLY ACTIVE POPULATION
(labour force survey, '000 persons aged 15 years and over)

	2005	2006	2007
Agriculture, hunting, forestry and fishing	265.4	252.2	245.4
Mining and quarrying	36.9	38.2	35.5
Manufacturing	728.7	745.1	766.5
Electricity, gas and water supply	64.0	58.9	60.4
Construction	190.6	230.0	292.3
Wholesale and retail trade; repair of motor vehicles, motorcycles and personal and household goods	447.1	494.0	519.2
Hotels and restaurants	150.2	156.4	163.0
Transport and communications	213.9	220.3	220.0
Financial intermediation	37.8	39.1	43.7
Real estate, renting and business activities	141.6	147.1	163.2
Public administration and defence; compulsory social security	214.1	225.0	238.9
Education	207.2	214.9	217.5
Health and social work	159.6	163.8	161.7
Other community, social and personal service activities	120.8	125.1	125.3
Sub-total	2,977.9	3,110.0	3,252.6

—continued	2005	2006	2007
Activities not adequately defined	2.1	—	—
Total employed	2,980.0	3,110.0	3,252.6
Unemployed	334.2	305.7	240.2
Total labour force	3,314.2	3,415.8	3,492.8
Males	1,773.9	1,809.2	1,852.2
Females	1,540.3	1,606.5	1,640.6

2008 ('000 persons aged 15 years and over): Agriculture, hunting, forestry and fishing 251.2; Mining and quarrying 35.0; Manufacturing 769.7; Electricity, gas, and water 79.1; Construction 340.3; Services 1,885.4; Total employed 3,360.7 (males 1,792.9, females 1,567.8); Unemployed 199.7 (males 103.9, females 95.8); Total labour force 3,560.4 (males 1,896.8, females 1,663.6).

Source: ILO.

2009 ('000 persons aged 15 years and over): Total employed 3,253.6; Unemployed 238.0; Total labour force 3,491.6 (males 1,862.4, females 1,629.2).

2010 ('000 persons aged 15 years and over): Total employed 3,052.8; Unemployed 348.0; Total labour force 3,400.9 (males 1,804.7, females 1,596.2).

Health and Welfare

KEY INDICATORS

Total fertility rate (children per woman, 2009)	1.4
Under-5 mortality rate (per 1,000 live births, 2009)	11
HIV/AIDS (% of persons aged 15–49, 2009)	0.1
Physicians (per 1,000 head, 2006)	3.7
Hospital beds (per 1,000 head, 2006)	6.2
Health expenditure (2008): US $ per head (PPP)	974
Health expenditure (2008): % of GDP	7.1
Health expenditure (2008): public (% of total)	57.8
Total carbon dioxide emissions ('000 metric tons, 2007)	51,739.3
Carbon dioxide emissions per head (metric tons, 2007)	6.8
Human Development Index (2011): ranking	55
Human Development Index (2011): value	0.771

For sources and definitions, see explanatory note on p. vi.

Agriculture

PRINCIPAL CROPS
('000 metric tons)

	2008	2009	2010
Wheat	4,632.2	3,976.9	3,994.9
Rice, paddy	38.6	43.4	56.0
Barley	878.0	858.7	833.3
Maize	1,368.4	1,290.8	2,044.1
Rye	14.8	18.9	17.5
Oats	54.5	30.7	40.0
Triticale (wheat-rye hybrid)	20.5	17.2	26.3
Potatoes	353.1	231.7	251.1
Beans, dry	2.4	1.7	1.4
Sunflower seed	1,300.7	1,318.0	1,596.1
Cabbages and other brassicas	64.9	39.4	78.9
Asparagus*	6.3	6.5	6.5
Tomatoes	134.1	104.2	114.6
Pumpkins, squash and gourds	4.3	4.3	14.8
Cucumbers and gherkins	62.6	78.0	65.7
Aubergines (eggplants)	7.1	16.6	10.7
Chillies and peppers, green	59.5	71.5	69.1
Onions, dry	16.0	8.2	19.1
Beans, green	6.9	5.7	4.3
Carrots and turnips	13.4	14.6	10.6
Mushrooms and truffles	1.4	1.7	1.6
Watermelons	93.3	110.7	70.8
Apples	23.5	35.5	43.2

—continued	2008	2009	2010
Apricots	13.0	7.6	11.6
Sweet cherries	16.1	17.5	25.0
Peaches and nectarines	14.9	17.2	24.5
Plums and sloes	14.3	17.2	33.7
Strawberries	8.6	8.6	5.7
Grapes	363.5	281.3	230.2
Tobacco, unmanufactured	42.2	51.3	41.1

* FAO estimates.

Aggregate production ('000 metric tons, may include official, semi-official or estimated data): Total cereals 7,015.6 in 2008, 6,243.1 in 2009, 7,026.8 in 2010; Total roots and tubers 353.1 in 2008, 231.7 in 2009, 251.1 in 2010; Total vegetables (incl. melons) 527.6 in 2008, 502.7 in 2009, 509.8 in 2010; Total fruits (excl. melons) 475.1 in 2008, 405.9 in 2009, 396.3 in 2010.

Source: FAO.

LIVESTOCK
('000 head at 1 January each year)

	2008	2009	2010
Horses	168.3	175.1	112.8
Asses*	130.0	130.0	130.0
Cattle	602.1	564.9	563.0
Pigs	888.6	783.6	729.8
Sheep	1,526.4	1,474.8	1,400.3
Goats	495.5	429.8	360.8
Chickens	16,426	15,765	16,002

* FAO estimates.

Source: FAO.

LIVESTOCK PRODUCTS
('000 metric tons)

	2008	2009	2010
Cattle meat	19.9	21.9	19.6
Sheep meat	15.8	13.3	13.3
Goat meat	5.1	4.1	3.7
Pig meat	73.7	73.7	70.5
Poultry meat*	108.5	129.2	106.9
Cows' milk	1,143.2	1,073.4	1,124.4
Buffaloes' milk	7.2	7.0	7.9
Sheep's milk	88.2	87.2	85.0
Goats' milk	77.5	64.1	60.4
Hen eggs	93.7	88.7	89.3
Other poultry eggs	0.5	0.2	0.4
Honey	11.4	9.5	10.6
Wool: greasy*	7.2	7.4	7.0

* FAO estimates.

Source: FAO.

Forestry

ROUNDWOOD REMOVALS
('000 cubic metres, excl. bark)

	2008	2009	2010
Sawlogs, veneer logs and logs for sleepers	1,579	952	1,320
Pulpwood	1,706	1,225	1,613
Other industrial wood	94	47	78
Fuel wood	2,692	2,375	2,657
Total	6,071	4,599	5,668

Source: FAO.

SAWNWOOD PRODUCTION
('000 cubic metres, incl. sleepers)

	2008*	2009	2010
Coniferous (softwood)	465	334	448*
Broadleaved (hardwood)	178	113	185
Total	643	447	633

* Unofficial figure(s).

Source: FAO.

Fishing

('000 metric tons, live weight)

	2007	2008	2009
Capture	8.9	8.9	7.6
Common carp	0.5	0.5	0.8
European sprat	3.0	4.3	4.6
Sea snails	4.3	2.9	2.2
Aquaculture	4.0	5.2	4.3
Common carp	1.2	1.5	1.9
Rainbow trout	1.7	1.8	2.4
Total catch	12.9	14.1	11.9

Source: FAO.

Mining

('000 metric tons, unless otherwise indicated)

	2007	2008	2009
Other hard coal	18	19	18*
Lignite	25,325	26,008	24,700*
Other brown coal	2,834	2,643	2,500*
Crude petroleum	24	23	24
Natural gas (million cu metres)	295	218	12
Copper ore†	116	109	110*
Copper concentrate†	110	105	105
Lead—mine output†	15	15	18
Lead concentrate†	16.4	13.0	13.0*
Zinc—mine output†	10.0	10.0	12.0
Zinc concentrate*†	12.2	10.6	10.7
Silver—mine output (kilograms)*†	55	55	55
Gold (kilograms)‡	3,964	4,160	4,300*
Bentonite	99	178	160*
Kaolin (raw)	1,631	1,530	1,400*
Salt (unrefined)	2,000	2,100	1,900*
Gypsum and anhydrite (crude)	234	210	190*

* Estimated production.

† Figures relate to the metal content of ores and concentrates.

‡ Figures relate to metal production.

Iron ore: gross weight ('000 metric tons): 83 in 2004.

Iron ore: metal content ('000 metric tons): 27 in 2004.

Barite (Barytes) ('000 metric tons): 237 in 2004.

Source: US Geological Survey.

Industry

SELECTED PRODUCTS
('000 metric tons unless otherwise indicated)

	2006	2007	2008
Wheat flour	414	424	423
Refined sugar	207	155	225
Wine ('000 hectolitres)	1,930	2,063	1,852
Beer ('000 hectolitres)	4,778	5,284	5,409
Cigarettes (million)	17,353	20,763	17,766
Cotton yarn (metric tons)*	3.7	3.0	1.0
Woven cotton fabrics†‡	24,058	25,551	16,859
Wool yarn (metric tons)*	1,881	1,307	1,391
Woven woollen fabrics‡	14,922	6,407	n.a.
Footwear (excl. rubber, '000 pairs)	4,998	5,222	5,357
Chemical wood pulp	130	130	130
Nitrogenous fertilizers§	191	185	n.a.
Clay building bricks (million)	354	425	n.a.
Cement	4,064	4,383	4,904
Crude steel (ingots)‖	2,124	1,909	1,330
Pig iron, steel-making (incl. foundry)‖	1,147	1,069	441

—continued	2006	2007	2008
Lathes (number)	2,008	2,075	1,816
Fork-lift trucks (number)¶	1,948	2,206	1,360
Electric energy (million kWh)	45,843	43,297	45,037

* Other than sewing thread. Figures for wool include yarn of man-made staple.
† Pure and mixed fabrics, after undergoing finishing processes.
‡ Million square metres.
§ Nitrogen (N) content.
‖ Source: US Geological Survey.
¶ Both electric and motor fork-lift trucks.

2009: Crude steel (ingots) 726.

Source: mostly UN Industrial Commodity Statistics Database.

Finance

CURRENCY AND EXCHANGE RATES

Monetary Units

100 stotinki (singular: stotinka) = 1 new lev (plural: leva).

Sterling, Dollar and Euro Equivalents (30 December 2011)

£1 sterling = 2.337 new leva;
US $1 = 1.512 new leva;
€1 = 1.956 new leva;
100 new leva = £42.79 = $66.16 = €51.13.

Average Exchange Rate (new leva per US $)

2009 1.4067
2010 1.4774
2011 1.4065

Note: On 5 July 1999 a new lev, equivalent to 1,000 old leva, was introduced. In January 1999 the value of the old lev had been linked to the German currency, the Deutsche Mark (DM), when an official exchange rate of 1 DM = 1,000 old leva was established. The new lev was thus at par with the DM. From the establishment of the euro, on 1 January 1999, the German currency had a fixed exchange rate of €1 = 1.95583 DM.

GOVERNMENT FINANCE

(general government operations, cash basis, million new leva)

Summary of Balances

	2007	2008	2009
Revenue	23,348	26,495	24,676
Less Expense	18,633	21,157	21,997
Net cash inflow from operating activities	4,715	5,338	2,679
Less Purchases of non-financial assets	3,467	4,072	3,318
Sales of non-financial assets	712	648	309
Cash surplus/deficit	1,960	1,915	–330

Revenue

	2007	2008	2009
Taxes	14,772	17,169	15,335
Taxes on income, profits and capital gains	3,641	4,200	3,813
Taxes on goods and services	10,097	11,724	10,438
General taxes on goods and services	6,599	7,485	6,433
Excises	3,315	4,052	3,844
Social contributions	4,890	5,393	5,273
Grants	1,172	761	1,171
Other revenue	2,514	3,173	2,896
Total	23,348	26,495	24,676

Expense/Outlays

Expense by economic type	2007	2008	2009
Compensation of employees	4,611	5,392	5,752
Use of goods and services	3,976	4,341	3,572
Interest	631	585	521
Subsidies	781	879	894
Social benefits	7,507	8,650	9,920
Other expense	1,127	1,309	1,338
Total	18,633	21,157	21,997

Outlays by functions of government*	2007	2008	2009
General public services	2,684	2,858	2,999
Defence	1,286	1,325	1,130
Public order and safety	1,736	1,904	1,871
Economic affairs	2,674	2,911	2,204
Transport	1,764	1,982	1,502
Environmental protection	143	755	833
Housing and community amenities	677	754	854
Health	2,720	2,831	2,634
Recreation, culture and religion	483	602	538
Education	2,179	2,765	2,838
Social protection	6,807	7,876	9,105
Total	21,388	24,580	25,005

* Including purchases of non-financial assets.

Source: IMF, *Government Finance Statistics Yearbook*.

INTERNATIONAL RESERVES

(US $ million at 31 December)

	2008	2009	2010
Gold*	1,107.2	1,399.5	1,812.5
IMF special drawing rights	6.5	957.7	940.8
Reserve position in IMF	51.6	52.9	52.2
Foreign exchange	16,757.4	16,116.8	14,427.5
Total	17,922.7	18,526.9	17,233.0

* Valued at market-related prices.

Source: IMF, *International Financial Statistics*.

MONEY SUPPLY

(million new leva at 31 December)

	2008	2009	2010
Currency outside depositary corporations	8,030	7,115	7,356
Transferable deposits	11,837	11,011	11,032
Other deposits	25,876	29,511	32,283
Securities other than shares	82	100	75
Broad money	45,825	47,737	50,746

Source: IMF, *International Financial Statistics*.

COST OF LIVING

(Consumer Price Index; base: 2000 = 100)

	2006	2007	2008
Food	123.4	140.0	163.4
Fuel and light	162.0	170.2	191.9
Clothing	102.6	109.8	121.1
Rent	139.5	144.8	160.9
All items (incl. others)	139.0	150.7	169.3

2009: Food 162.3; All items (incl. others) 174.0.

2010: Food 161.7; All items (incl. others) 178.2.

Source: ILO.

NATIONAL ACCOUNTS

(million new leva at current prices)

Expenditure on the Gross Domestic Product

	2008	2009	2010*
Government final consumption expenditure	11,730	11,351	11,406
Private final consumption expenditure	45,766	42,942	42,844
Gross fixed capital formation	23,283	19,724	16,546
Changes in inventories	2,732	339	1,018
Total domestic expenditure	83,511	74,356	71,814
Exports of goods and services	40,342	32,458	40,733
Less Imports of goods and services	54,557	38,493	42,074
GDP in market prices	69,295	68,322	70,474

* Preliminary figures.

Gross Domestic Product by Economic Activity

	2008	2009	2010*
Agriculture, hunting, forestry and fishing	4,132	2,841	3,249
Construction	5,386	5,411	4,523
Other industry	12,601	12,983	14,511
Wholesale and retail trade; repair of motor vehicles and household goods; hotels and restaurants; transport and communications	15,446	15,115	15,200
Finance, real estate, renting and business activities	11,555	12,945	13,714
Other services	8,613	9,400	9,449
Gross value added in basic prices	57,733	58,695	60,646
Taxes, less subsidies, on products	11,562	9,626	9,829
GDP in market prices	69,295	68,322	70,474

* Preliminary figures.

Note: Financial intermediation services indirectly measured assumed to be distributed by activity.

BALANCE OF PAYMENTS
(US $ million)

	2008	2009	2010
Exports of goods f.o.b.	22,484.2	16,377.6	20,608.2
Imports of goods f.o.b.	–35,107.7	–22,152.9	–23,825.6
Trade balance	–12,623.5	–5,775.3	–3,217.4
Exports of services	7,991.1	6,896.1	6,909.9
Imports of services	–5,957.7	–5,043.1	–4,472.1
Balance on goods and services	–10,590.1	–3,922.3	–779.6
Other income received	1,450.1	1,118.0	840.0
Other income paid	–4,028.9	–2,779.2	–2,674.8
Balance on goods, services and income	–13,168.9	–5,583.5	–2,614.4
Current transfers received	2,421.1	2,164.9	2,766.7
Current transfers paid	–1,097.7	–839.8	–730.4
Current balance	–11,845.5	–4,258.5	–578.0
Capital account (net)	419.6	654.9	391.3
Direct investment abroad	–792.4	136.2	–236.0
Direct investment from abroad	9,979.1	3,389.2	2,167.5
Portfolio investment assets	–399.9	–774.7	–738.8
Portfolio investment liabilities	–241.4	–93.0	–19.9
Financial derivatives assets	–132.5	–55.2	–29.6
Financial derivatives liabilities	56.9	27.5	–3.3
Other investment assets	198.5	–903.3	482.7
Other investment liabilities	8,933.2	–127.1	–1,663.7
Net errors and omissions	–4,272.1	2,011.2	–377.5
Overall balance	1,903.6	7.2	–605.3

Source: IMF, *International Financial Statistics*.

External Trade

PRINCIPAL COMMODITIES
(€ million)

Imports c.i.f.	2008	2009	2010
Furniture and household appliances	968.2	710.9	672.8
Medicines and cosmetics	732.8	735.6	801.5
Automobiles	549.9	170.0	182.4
Ores	904.1	722.9	965.3
Iron and steel	1,333.5	503.7	636.0
Textiles	1,198.7	933.7	927.3
Plastics and rubber	1,112.1	794.1	970.4
Machines and equipment	2,377.7	1,506.2	1,347.8
Electrical machines	875.4	718.5	771.1
Vehicles	1,662.3	558.5	574.2
Spare parts and equipment	807.0	550.9	746.7
Crude petroleum and natural gas	4,298.6	2,588.5	3,083.4
Total (incl. others)	25,093.5	16,875.7	19,161.4

Exports f.o.b.	2008	2009	2010
Food	617.7	670.5	840.5
Clothing and footwear	1,384.0	1183.5	1,359.7
Furniture and household appliances	568.1	560.9	573.8
Iron and steel	940.2	437.7	662.1
Other metals	1,788.0	1,218.7	1,787.0
Chemicals	413.9	217.9	258.9
Textiles	472.3	379.0	322.3
Raw materials for the food industry	967.2	920.2	1,307.6
Machines and equipment	798.5	541.4	704.2
Petroleum products	2,041.9	1,191.3	1,695.1
Other mineral fuels and electricity	458.9	321.9	434.2
Total (incl. others)	15,203.8	11,699.3	15,588.3

PRINCIPAL TRADING PARTNERS
(€ million)

Imports c.i.f.	2008	2009	2010
Austria	595.1	423.6	393.3
Belgium	334.8	274.9	269.4
Brazil	209.6	164.2	109.3
China	1,331.4	908.2	1,044.8
Czech Republic	475.9	431.7	342.3
France	913.0	662.5	650.2
Germany	2,750.1	1,865.6	2,003.3
Greece	1,167.9	931.1	1,032.4
Hungary	493.3	359.4	387.1
Italy	1,977.9	1,334.4	1,457.3
Japan	344.6	174.0	176.3
Netherlands	424.7	311.8	340.6
Poland	568.4	392.5	437.8
Romania	1,185.6	790.2	1,133.1
Russia	4,430.7	2,614.5	3,257.4
Spain	446.5	311.2	361.0
Sweden	204.1	112.6	138.6
Switzerland	231.5	182.3	202.8
Turkey	1,407.2	935.2	1,058.0
Ukraine	839.1	357.5	456.6
United Kingdom	431.6	241.7	289.5
USA	496.4	314.9	292.5
Total (incl. others)	25,093.5	16,875.7	19,161.4

Exports f.o.b.	2008	2009	2010
Austria	312.9	229.5	293.8
Belgium	897.3	663.8	587.3
France	623.1	524.1	628.4
Germany	1,383.3	1,320.4	1,658.9
Greece	1,508.2	1,117.8	1,236.7
Italy	1,272.0	1,092.6	1,509.9
Macedonia, former Yugoslav republic	342.7	239.2	331.2
Netherlands	216.1	185.1	235.6
Poland	290.3	183.8	267.5
Romania	1,102.9	1,010.1	1,441.2
Russia	412.6	293.5	443.5
Serbia	707.0	414.9	585.8
Spain	340.8	375.4	415.9
Turkey	1,338.7	846.5	1,325.4
United Kingdom	319.1	229.8	303.3
USA	237.1	182.9	213.4
Total (incl. others)	15,203.8	11,699.3	15,588.3

Transport

RAILWAYS
(traffic)

	2008	2009	2010
Passengers carried ('000)	33,757.8	31,360.2	30,101.9
Passenger-kilometres (million)	2,334.9	2,144.3	2,099.7
Freight carried ('000 metric tons)	19,715.5	13,284.4	12,939.5
Freight net ton-kilometres (million)	4,693.3	3,144.5	3,063.5

ROAD TRAFFIC
(motor vehicles in use at 31 December)

	2002	2003	2004
Passenger cars	2,254,222	2,309,343	2,438,383
Buses and coaches	44,255	43,687	36,000
Lorries and vans	262,641	293,487	317,681
Motorcycles and mopeds	220,296	n.a.	137,955

2008: Passenger cars 2,366,196; Buses and coaches 24,622; Lorries and vans 291,161; Motorcycles 106,911.

Source: International Road Federation, *World Road Statistics*.

INLAND WATERWAYS
(traffic)

	2000	2001	2002
Passengers carried ('000)	76	67	60
Passenger-kilometres (million)	1	—	—
Freight carried ('000 metric tons)	1,846	1,300	1,621
Freight ton-kilometres (million)	397	365	571

SHIPPING

Merchant Fleet
(registered at 31 December)

	2007	2008	2009
Number of vessels	139	136	107
Total displacement ('000 grt)	911.1	876.1	522.8

Source: IHS Fairplay, *World Fleet Statistics*.

Sea-borne Traffic
(international and coastal)

	2000	2001	2002
Freight ('000 metric tons)	18,619	16,737	15,557
Freight ton-kilometres (million)	74,391	67,551	60,814

CIVIL AVIATION
(traffic)

	2003	2004	2005
Passengers carried ('000)	311	476	654
Kilometres flown (million)	7	11	14
Passenger-kilometres (million)	457	747	1,123
Total ton-kilometres (million)	42	71	105

Source: UN, *Statistical Yearbook*.

2006: Passengers carried ('000) 808.5; Total ton-kilometres (million) 3.4 (Source: World Bank, World Development Indicators database).

2007: Passengers carried ('000) 855.2; Total ton-kilometres (million) 3.0 (Source: World Bank, World Development Indicators database).

2008: Passengers carried ('000) 1,073.5; Total ton-kilometres (million) 2.3 (Source: World Bank, World Development Indicators database).

Tourism

ARRIVALS OF FOREIGN VISITORS
(including same day visitors)

Country of origin	2008	2009	2010
Czech Republic	167,738	197,863	184,440
Germany	759,660	898,352	853,430
Greece	881,458	924,220	1,017,914
Israel	105,882	106,825	131,144
Macedonia, former Yugoslav republic*	323,400	310,113	409,970
Poland	257,713	304,659	294,131
Romania*	1,769,194	1,398,694	1,445,342
Russia	296,918	295,713	389,864
Serbia and Montenegro*	311,666	217,940	307,838
Sweden	118,913	65,148	48,992
United Kingdom	370,908	316,928	309,482
Total (incl. others)	8,532,972	7,872,805	8,374,034

* Includes 'shuttle traders'.

Tourism receipts (US $ million, incl. passenger transport): 3,317 in 2006; 3,975 in 2007; 4,831 in 2008 (Source: World Tourism Organization).

Communications Media

	2007	2008	2009
Telephones ('000 main lines in use)	2,300.4	2,189.8	2,205.4
Mobile cellular telephones ('000 subscribers)	9,897.5	10,500.2	10,575.7
Internet subscribers ('000)	647.6	853.0	973.7
Broadband subscribers ('000)	629.1	843.5	969.7
Book production*:			
titles	6,648	6,767	6,491
copies ('000)	4,797	4,646	5,971
Newspapers:			
titles	448	438	436
total circulation ('000 copies)	338,590	370,789	355,600
Magazines:†			
titles	817	775	745
total circulation ('000 copies)	17,944	14,708	11,401

* Including pamphlets.
† Including bulletins.

Television receivers (number in use): 3,692,000 in 2000.

Personal computers: 835,660 (109.6 per 1,000 persons) in 2008.

Sources: partly UN, *Statistical Yearbook*, UNESCO, *Statistical Yearbook*, and International Telecommunication Union.

Education

(2010/11)

	Institutions	Teachers	Students
Kindergartens	5,200*	19,579	223,186
General and special schools:			
primary	156	14,780	255,086
basic	1,429	n.a.	n.a.
lower secondary	13	19,867	219,980
upper secondary	166	26,903†	303,375
combined schools	411	n.a.	n.a.
Vocational	484	13,841	161,536
Colleges	9	1,375	25,511‡
Universities and equivalent	44	21,057	255,659§

* Excluding dependent half-day kindergartens.
† Including teaching staff in interschools centres.
‡ Qualification degree 'specialist'.
§ Including 3,850 post-graduates studying for 'specialist' degrees.

Pupil-teacher ratio (primary education, UNESCO estimate): 16.1 in 2007/08 (Source: UNESCO Institute for Statistics).

Adult literacy rate (UNESCO estimates): 98.3% (males 98.7%; females 98.0%) in 2008 (Source: UNESCO Institute for Statistics).

Directory

The Government

HEAD OF STATE AND VICE-PRESIDENT

President: Rosen Plevneliev (took office 22 January 2012).
Vice-President: Margarita Popova.

COUNCIL OF MINISTERS
(May 2012)

Prime Minister: Boyko Borisov.

Deputy Prime Minister and Minister of the Interior: Tsvetan Tsvetanov.

Deputy Prime Minister and Minister of Finance: Simeon Dyankov.

Minister of Foreign Affairs: Nikolay Mladenov.

Minister of Education, Youth and Science: Sergey Ignatov.

Minister of the Economy, Energy and Tourism: Delyan Dobrev.

Minister of Defence: Anyu Angelov.

Minister of Justice: Diana Kovacheva.

Minister of Labour and Social Policy: Totyu Mladenov.

Minister of Transport, Information Technology and Communications: Ivaylo Moskovski.

Minister of Regional Development and Public Works: Liliyana Pavlova.

Minister of the Environment and Water: Nona Karadzhova.

Minister of Agriculture and the Food Industry: Miroslav Naydenov.

Minister of Health: Desislava Atanasova.

Minister of Culture: Vezhdi Rashidov.

Minister of Physical Education and Sport: Svilen Neykov.

Minister for the Management of EU Funds: Tomislav Donchev.

Note: The Chairmen of the State Agencies for Youth and Sport, Tourism and Information and Communications Technologies are also members of the Council of Ministers.

MINISTRIES

Office of the President: 1123 Sofia, bul. Dondukov 2; tel. (2) 923-93-33; e-mail press@president.bg; internet www.president.bg.

Council of Ministers: 1194 Sofia, bul. Dondukov 1; tel. (2) 940-29-99; fax (2) 980-20-56; e-mail gis@government.bg; internet www.government.bg.

Ministry of Agriculture and the Food Industry: 1040 Sofia, bul. Hristo Botev 55; tel. (2) 985-11-238; fax (2) 980-91-19; e-mail press@mzh.government.bg; internet www.mzh.government.bg.

Ministry of Culture: 1040 Sofia, bul. A. Stamboliyski 17; tel. (2) 940-09-00; fax (2) 981-81-45; e-mail press@mc.government.bg; internet www.mc.government.bg.

Ministry of Defence: 1092 Sofia, ul. Dyakon Ignatiy 3; tel. (2) 922-09-22; fax (2) 987-96-93; e-mail presscntr@mod.bg; internet www.mod.bg.

Ministry of the Economy, Energy and Tourism: 1000 Sofia, ul. Slavyanska 8; tel. (2) 940-70-01; fax (2) 987-21-90; e-mail e-docs@mee.government.bg; internet www.mee.government.bg.

Ministry of Education, Youth and Science: 1540 Sofia, bul. Knyaz Dondukov 2a; tel. (2) 921-77-99; fax (2) 988-24-85; e-mail press_mon@mon.bg; internet www.minedu.government.bg.

Ministry of the Environment and Water: 1000 Sofia, bul. Maria Luiza 22; tel. (2) 940-62-31; fax (2) 986-25-33; e-mail contact@moew.government.bg; internet www.moew.government.bg.

Ministry of Finance: 1040 Sofia, ul. G. S. Rakovski 102; tel. (2) 985-920-22; fax (2) 987-05-81; e-mail feedback@minfin.bg; internet www.minfin.bg.

Ministry of Foreign Affairs: 1040 Sofia, ul. Al. Zhendov 2; tel. (2) 948-20-18; fax (2) 297-136-20; e-mail vtcherneva@mfa.bg; internet www.mfa.government.bg.

Ministry of Health: 1000 Sofia, pl. Sv. Nedelya 5; tel. (2) 930-011-01; fax (2) 981-26-39; e-mail minister@mh.government.bg; internet www.mh.government.bg.

Ministry of the Interior: 1000 Sofia, ul. 6-ti Septemvri 29; tel. (2) 982-50-00; fax (2) 982-20-47; e-mail info@mvr.bg; internet www.mvr.bg.

Ministry of Justice: 1040 Sofia, ul. Slavyanska 1; tel. (2) 923-75-55; fax (2) 981-91-57; e-mail pr@justice.government.bg; internet www.mjeli.government.bg.

Ministry of Labour and Social Policy: 1051 Sofia, ul. Triaditsa 2; tel. (2) 811-94-43; fax (2) 988-44-05; e-mail mlsp@mlsp.government.bg; internet www.mlsp.government.bg.

Ministry of Physical Education and Sport: 1040 Sofia, bul. Vasil Levski 75; tel. (2) 930-05-75; fax (2) 988-40-32.

Ministry of Regional Development and Public Works: 1000 Sofia, ul. Kiril i Metodiy 17–19; tel. (2) 940-54-30; fax (2) 987-25-17; e-mail press@mrrb.government.bg; internet www.mrrb.government.bg.

Ministry of Transport, Information Technology and Communications: 1000 Sofia, ul. Dyakon Ignatiy 9; tel. and fax (2) 988-50-94; e-mail mmarkova@mtitc.government.bg; internet www.mtitc.government.bg.

President

Presidential Election, First Round, 23 October 2011

Candidate	Votes	% of votes
Rosen Plevneliev (Citizens for European Development of Bulgaria)	1,349,380	40.11
Ivaylo Kalfin (Bulgarian Socialist Party)	974,300	28.96
Meglena Kuneva (Independent)	470,808	14.00
Others	569,590	16.93
Total	3,364,078	100.00

Second Round, 30 October 2011

Candidate	Votes	% of votes
Rosen Plevneliev (Citizens for European Development of Bulgaria)	1,698,136	52.58
Ivaylo Kalfin (Bulgarian Socialist Party)	1,531,193	47.42
Total	3,229,329	100.00

Legislature

Narodno Sobranie
(National Assembly)

1169 Sofia, pl. Narodno Sobranie 2; tel. (2) 939-39; fax (2) 981-31-31; e-mail infocenter@parliament.bg; internet www.parliament.bg.

Chairman: Tsetska Tsacheva Dangovska.

General Election, 5 July 2009*

Party	Votes	% of votes	Seats
Citizens for European Development of Bulgaria	1,678,583	39.89	117
Coalition for Bulgaria†	748,114	17.78	40
Movement for Rights and Freedoms	592,381	14.08	37
Attack Party	395,707	9.40	21
Blue Coalition‡	285,647	6.79	15
Order, Law and Justice	174,570	4.15	10
LIDER Political Party—Liberal Initiative for Democratic European Development	137,790	3.27	—
National Movement for Stability and Progress	127,470	3.03	—
Others	67,575	1.61	—
Total	4,207,837	100.00	240

* On 16 February 2010 the Constitutional Court ruled that some 18,358 votes that had been cast by overseas voters in Turkey were null and void. Consequently, the parliamentary representation of the Movement for Rights and Freedoms was reduced by one seat, and that of the Citizens for European Development of Bulgaria increased by one seat. The information provided in this table represents the revised results, in accordance with the ruling of the Constitutional Court.

† A coalition of eight parties, led by the Bulgarian Socialist Party.

‡ A coalition of five parties, led by the Union of Democratic Forces and Democrats for a Strong Bulgaria.

Election Commission

Central Election Committee: 1169 Sofia, pl. A. Battenberg 1; tel. (2) 987-92-42; fax (2) 986-64-56; internet www.cikipvr.org; Chair. SNEZHANA NACHEVA.

Political Organizations

Agrarian National Union—People's Union (Zemedelski Naroden Sayuz—ZNS): 1000 Sofia, bul. N. I. Vapstarov 23; tel. and fax (2) 987-05-77; e-mail office@zns.bg; internet www.zns.bg; fmrly Bulgarian Agrarian Nat. Union—People's Union; present name adopted 2006; Pres. STEFAN LICHEV.

Attack Party (Partiya Ataka): 1000 Sofia, ul. Vrabcha 1; tel. and fax (2) 980-55-70; e-mail atakacentrala@abv.bg; internet www.ataka.bg; f. 2005 as Attack Nat. Union by coalition of the Nat. Movement for the Salvation of the Fatherland, the Bulgarian Nat. Patriotic Party and the Union of Patriotic Forces and Militaries of the Defence Reserve; subsequently constituted as a political party; nationalist, populist, anti-Western; Leader VOLEN SIDEROV.

Bulgarian New Democracy (BND) (Balgarska Nova Demokratsia): 1169 Sofia, Krasno Selo, ul. Knyaginya Klementina 21; tel. and fax (2) 856-61-65; e-mail bnd2008@abv.bg; internet www.bnd.bg; f. 2008 by fmr mems of the Nat. Movement for Stability and Progress; centre-right; Chair. NIKOLAY SVINAROV.

Bulgarian Social Democrats (Balgarski Sotsialdemokrati): 1000 Sofia, ul. Aksakov 31; tel. and fax (2) 988-15-69; e-mail sdms@pbs-d.bg; internet www.pbs-d.bg; fmrly Bulgarian Social Democratic Party (United); contested 2009 legislative elections as part of the Coalition for Bulgaria; Pres. GEORGI ANASTASOV.

Bulgarian Socialist Party (BSP) (Balgarska Sotsialisticheska Partiya): 1000 Sofia, ul. Positano 20; tel. (2) 810-72-00; fax (2) 981-21-85; e-mail bsppress@bsp.bg; internet www.bsp.bg; f. 1891 as the Bulgarian Social Democratic Party (BSDP); renamed as above in 1990; contested 2009 legislative elections as part of the Coalition for Bulgaria; Chair. SERGEY STANISHEV.

Citizens for European Development of Bulgaria (Grazhdani za evropeysko razvitie na Balgariya—GERB): 1463 Sofia, pl. Balgariya 1, NDK Administration Bldg 17; tel. (2) 490-13-13; fax (2) 490-09-51; e-mail pr@gerb.bg; internet www.gerb.bg; f. 2006; centre-right; Chair. KOYKO MORISOV.

Communist Party of Bulgaria (Komunisticheska Partiya na Balgariya): 1000 Sofia, ul. Tsar Kaloyan 10; tel. and fax (2) 981-60-93; e-mail comparty@abv.bg; internet www.comparty-bg.com; f. 1996; breakaway party of fmr Bulgarian Social Democratic Party; contested 2009 legislative elections as part of the Coalition for Bulgaria; Chair. ALEKSANDAR PAUNOV.

Democratic Party (Demokraticheskata Partiya): 1303 Sofia, bul. Botev 61; tel. (2) 930-80-30; fax (2) 930-80-31; internet www.demparty.eu; re-formed 1990; Chair. ALEKSANDAR PRAMATARSKI.

Democrats for a Strong Bulgaria (DSB) (Demokrati za silna Balgariya): 1000 Sofia, bul. Vitosha 18; tel. (2) 400-99-21; fax (2) 980-53-34; e-mail dsb@dsb.bg; internet www.dsb.bg; f. 2004; right-wing; contested 2009 legislative elections as part of the Blue Coalition; Chair. IVAN KOSTOV.

The Greens (Zelenite): 1412 Sofia, ul. Biser 7; e-mail info@zelenite.bg; internet www.zelenite.bg; f. 2008; Co-Chair. ANDREY KOVACHEV, PETKO KOVACHEV, DENICA PETROVA.

IMRO—Bulgarian National Movement (VMRO—Balgarsko natsionalno dvizhenie—VMRO—BND): 1301 Sofia, ul. Pirotska 5; tel. (2) 980-25-82; fax (2) 980-25-83; e-mail vmro@vmro.org; internet www.vmro.org; f. 2000; fmrly Inner Macedonian Revolutionary Org.—Bulgarian Nat. Movement; in March 2010 it was reported that a splinter group had been formed, under the leadership of Petko Atansov; Chair. KRASSIMIR KARAKACHANOV.

LIDER Political Party—Liberal Initiative for Democratic European Development (Politicheska Partia LIDER): Sofia, bul. Cherni Vrykh 39; tel. and fax (2) 421-11-55; e-mail lider@lider-bg.org; internet www.lider-bg.org; f. 2007; Chair. KANCHO FILIPOV.

Movement for Rights and Freedoms (MRF) (Dvizhenie za Prava i Svobodi—DPS): 1301 Sofia, bul. Al. Stamboliyski 45A; tel. (2) 811-44-32; fax (2) 811-44-60; e-mail press@dpa.bg; internet www.dps.bg; f. 1990 to represent interests of Muslim minority in Bulgaria; supported integration of Bulgaria into the European Union (EU) and North Atlantic Treaty Organization (NATO); Pres. AKHMED DOGAN.

National Movement for Stability and Progress (NMSP) (Natsionalno dvizhenie za stabilnost i vazhod—NDSV): 1000 Sofia, ul. Vrabcha 23; tel. (2) 921-81-83; fax (2) 921-81-81; e-mail presscenter@ndsv.bg; internet www.ndsv.bg; f. 2001 by supporters of the former monarch; registered as a political party, Nat. Movement Simeon II, in 2002; name changed June 2007; Pres. KHRISTINA KHRISTOV.

The New Time (Novoto vreme): Sofia, bul. 6 Septembri 7A; tel. (89) 999-76-26; e-mail party@novotovreme.bg; internet www.novotovreme.bg; f. 2003 by fmr mems of Nat. Movement Simeon II; Leader EMIL KOSHLUKOV.

Order, Law and Justice (Red, zakonnost i spravedlivost—RZS): 1000 Sofia, bul. Knyaz Dondukov 15; tel. (2) 981-03-07; fax (2) 981-10-89; e-mail centrala@rzs.bg; internet www.rzs.bg; f. 2005; Leader YANE YANEV.

Union of Democratic Forces (UDF) (Sayuz na Demokratichnite Sili—SDS): 1000 Sofia, bul. Rakovski 134; tel. (2) 930-61-32; fax (2) 981-01-19; e-mail presscenter@sds.bg; internet www.sds.bg; f. 1989; supported the integration of Bulgaria into the EU; pro-market; contested 2009 legislative elections as part of the Blue Coalition; Chair. MARTIN DIMITROV.

Union of Free Democrats (Sayuz na svobodnite demokrati—SSD): 1000 Sofia, bul. Levski 91; tel. (2) 989-59-99; fax (2) 989-69-99; e-mail ssd_centrala@abv.bg; internet www.ssd.bg; f. 2001 as a breakaway faction of the Union of Democratic Forces; supports greater integration of Bulgaria into the EU and NATO; Leader STEFAN SOFIANSKI.

Diplomatic Representation

EMBASSIES IN BULGARIA

Afghanistan: 1700 Sofia, Simeonovsko shose 57/3; tel. (2) 962-51-93; fax (2) 962-74-86; e-mail embassy_in_sofia@yahoo.com; Ambassador MOHAMMAD DAOUD PANJSHIRI.

Albania: 1504 Sofia, ul. Krakra 10; tel. (2) 943-38-57; fax (2) 943-30-69; e-mail aembassy.sofia@mfa.gov.al; Ambassador PETRIT KARABINA.

Algeria: 1000 Sofia, ul. Slavyanska 16; tel. (2) 980-22-50; fax (2) 981-03-28; e-mail ambalgsf@abv.bg; Ambassador AHMED BOUTACHE.

Argentina: 1040 Sofia, ul. D. Tsankov 36, Interpred B, 8th Floor, POB 635; tel. (2) 971-25-39; fax (2) 969-30-28; e-mail arebulg@mbox.contact.bg; Ambassador GUILLERMO AZRAK.

Armenia: 1111 Sofia, ul. Zagorichane 3; tel. and fax (2) 946-12-72; fax (2) 946-12-74; e-mail armembsof@omega.bg; Ambassador ARSEN SKHOIAN.

Austria: 1000 Sofia, ul. Shipka 4; tel. (2) 932-90-32; fax (2) 981-05-67; e-mail sofia-ob@bmeia.gv.at; Ambassador GERHARD REIWEGER.

Azerbaijan: 1113 Sofia, zh. k. Iztok, ul. Charlz Darvin 6; tel. (2) 817-00-70; fax (2) 817-00-77; e-mail sefirlik@azerembsof.com; Ambassador EMIL KARIMOV.

Belarus: 1505 Sofia, kv. Reduta, ul. N. Karadzhov 3; tel. and fax (2) 973-31-00; e-mail bulgaria@mfa.gov.by; internet www.bulgaria.belembassy.org; Ambassador VYACHESLAV H. KACHANOV.

Belgium: 1407 Sofia, ul. Dzheyms Baucher 103; tel. (2) 988-72-90; fax (2) 963-36-38; e-mail sofia@diplobel.fed.be; internet www.diplomatie.be/sofia; Ambassador MARC MICHIELSEN.

Bosnia and Herzegovina: 1000 Sofia, ul. Al. Zhendov 1; tel. (2) 973-37-75; fax (2) 973-37-29; e-mail ambihsofia@dir.bg; Ambassador Lt-Gen. SIFET PODZIĆ.

Brazil: 1000 Sofia, bul. Knyaz Dondukov 54B; tel. (2) 971-98-19; fax (2) 971-28-18; e-mail brasemb.sofia@itamaraty.gov.br; internet sofia.itamaraty.gov.br; Ambassador WASHINGTON LUÍS PEREIRA-DE-SOUSA.

China, People's Republic: 1113 Sofia, ul. A. fon Khumbolt 7; tel. (2) 973-38-73; fax (2) 971-10-81; e-mail chnemb_bg@live.cn; internet www.chinaembassy.bg; Ambassador GUO YEZHOU.

Croatia: 1504 Sofia, ul. Veliko Tarnovo 32; tel. (2) 861-12-12; fax (2) 946-13-55; e-mail croemb.sofia@mvp.hr; internet bg.mvp.hr; Ambassador DANIJELA BARIŠIĆ.

Cuba: 1113 Sofia, ul. K. Sharkelov 1; tel. (2) 872-09-96; fax (2) 872-04-60; e-mail secretaria@embacuba-bg.com; internet www.cubadiplomatica.cu/bulgaria/en/home.aspx; Ambassador TERESITA CAPOTE CAMACHO.

Cyprus: 1164 Sofia, ul. Dzheimz Baucher i Plachkovitsa 1A/1; tel. (2) 961-77-30; fax (2) 862-94-70; e-mail cyprus@mbox.contact.bg; Ambassador STAVROS AMVROSIOU.

Czech Republic: 1504 Sofia, bul. Ya. Sakazov 9; tel. (2) 948-68-00; fax (2) 948-68-18; e-mail sofia@embassy.mzv.cz; internet www.mzv.cz/sofia; Ambassador PAVEL VACEK.

Denmark: 1504 Sofia, bul. Dondukov 54, POB 37; tel. (2) 917-01-00; fax (2) 980-99-01; e-mail sofamb@um.dk; internet www.ambsofia.um.dk; Ambassador KAARE ERHARD JANSON.

Egypt: 1000 Sofia, ul. 6-ti Septemvri 5; tel. (2) 988-15-09; fax (2) 980-12-63; e-mail egembsof@spnet.net; Ambassador OLFAT FARAH.

Estonia: 1000 Sofia, ul. Bacho Kiro 26–30, et. 6; tel. (2) 937-99-00; fax (2) 937-99-09; e-mail embassy.sofia@mfa.ee; internet www.sofia.vm.ee; Ambassador TOOMAS KUKK.

Finland: 1000 Sofia, ul. Bacho Kiro 26–28, 5th Floor; tel. (2) 810-21-10; fax (2) 810-21-20; e-mail sanomat.sof@formin.fi; internet www.finland.bg; Ambassador TARJA LAITIAINEN.

France: 1504 Sofia, ul. Oborishte 27–29; tel. (2) 965-11-00; fax (2) 965-11-20; e-mail presse@ambafrance-bg.org; internet www.ambafrance-bg.org; Ambassador PHILIPPE AUTIÉ.

Georgia: 1113 Sofia, kv. Lozenets, ul. Krichim 65; tel. (2) 868-54-04; fax (2) 868-34-27; e-mail bulgaria.emb@mfa.gov.ge; internet www.bulgaria.mfa.gov.ge; Ambassador MIKHEIL UKLEBA.

Germany: 1113 Sofia, ul. F. Zholio-Kyuri 25; tel. (2) 918-38-00; fax (2) 963-16-58; e-mail info@sofia.diplo.de; internet www.sofia.diplo.de; Ambassador MATTHIAS HÖPFNER.

Greece: 1504 Sofia, ul. San Stefano 33; tel. (2) 843-30-85; fax (2) 946-12-49; e-mail info@greekembassy-sofia.org; internet info.greekembassy-sofia.org; Ambassador THRASSYVOULOS STAMATOPOULOS.

Holy See: 1000 Sofia, ul. 11-ti Avgust 6, POB 9; tel. (2) 981-21-97; fax (2) 981-61-95; e-mail nunziatura.bulgaria@gmail.com; Apostolic Nuncio JANUARIUSZ BOLONEK (Titular Archbishop of Madaurus).

Hungary: 1000 Sofia, ul. 6-ti Septemvri 57; tel. (2) 963-11-35; fax (2) 963-21-10; e-mail embassy.sof@kum.hu; internet www.mfa.gov.hu/emb/sofia; Ambassador JUDIT LÁNG.

India: 1421 Sofia, kv. Lozenets, ul. Sv. Sedmochislenitsi 23; tel. (2) 963-56-75; fax (2) 963-56-86; e-mail ambassador@indembsofia.org; internet www.indembsofia.org; Ambassador DIVYABH MANCHANDA.

Indonesia: 1700 Sofia, Iosef Valdkhart 5; tel. (2) 962-52-40; fax (2) 962-44-18; e-mail kbrisofia@indonesia.bg; internet www.indonesia.bg; Ambassador BUNYAN SAPTOMO.

Iran: 1087 Sofia, ul. V. Levski 77; tel. (2) 987-85-46; fax (2) 981-41-72; e-mail iranembassy@abv.bg; Ambassador GHOLAMREZA MOGHADDAM.

Iraq: 1113 Sofia, ul. A. Chekhov 21; tel. (2) 973-33-48; fax (2) 971-11-97; e-mail sofemb@mofaml.gov.iq; Ambassador SAAD ALI.

Ireland: 1000 Sofia, ul. Bacho Kiro 26–30; tel. (2) 985-34-25; fax (2) 983-33-02; e-mail sofiaembassy@dfa.ie; internet www.embassyofireland.bg; Ambassador JOHN ROWAN.

Israel: 1463 Sofia, pl. Balgariya 1, NDK Administration Bldg, 7th floor; tel. (2) 951-50-44; fax (2) 952-11-01; e-mail info@sofia.mfa.gov.il; internet sofia.mfa.gov.il; Ambassador NOAH GAL-GENDLER.

Italy: 1000 Sofia, ul. Shipka 2; tel. (2) 921-73-00; fax (2) 980-37-17; e-mail ambasciata.sofia@esteri.it; internet www.ambsofia.esteri.it; Ambassador STEFANO BENAZZO.

Japan: 1113 Sofia, ul. Lyulyakova gradina 14; tel. (2) 971-27-08; fax (2) 971-10-95; e-mail emb-jp-bl@geobiz.net; internet www.bg.emb-japan.go.jp; Ambassador M. MAKOTO ITO.

Kazakhstan: 1000 Sofia, ul.Galichitsa 38; tel. (2) 862-41-52; fax (2) 862-41-70; e-mail kazembassy@bulpost.net; internet www.kazembassy.bulpost.net; Chargé d'affaires a.i. TEMIRTAY IZBASTIN.

Korea, Democratic People's Republic: 1756 Sofia, kv. Darvenitsa, ul. Sofiysko pole 3; tel. (2) 975-33-40; fax (2) 974-61-11; e-mail koembg@yahoo.com; Ambassador ZU UANG HUAN.

Korea, Republic: 1040 Sofia, bul. D. Tsankov 36, et. 7A; tel. (2) 971-21-81; fax (2) 971-33-88; e-mail korean-embassy@mofat.go.kr; internet bgr.mofat.go.kr; Ambassador CHUN BEE-HO.

Kuwait: 1700 Sofia, Simeonovsko shose 15; tel. (2) 962-56-89; fax (2) 962-45-84; e-mail kuwaitembassy-bulgaria@hotmail.com; Ambassador FAISAL AL-ADWANI.

Lebanon: 1113 Sofia, ul. F. Zholio-Kyuri 155/13; tel. (2) 971-27-23; fax (2) 973-34-97; e-mail amblibansofia@gmail.com; Ambassador MICHELINE ABI SAMRA.

Libya: 1784 Sofia, Mladost 1, bul. A. Sakharov 1; tel. (2) 974-35-56; fax (2) 974-32-73; e-mail libya_embbg@yahoo.com; Chargé d'affaires a.i. ISSA OMAR ASHUR.

Lithuania: 1000 Sofia, ul. Alabin 38; tel. (2) 980-61-04; fax (2) 980-61-05; e-mail amb.bg@urm.lt; internet bg.mfa.lt; Chargé d'affaires DARIUS GAIDYS.

Macedonia, former Yugoslav republic: 1113 Sofia, ul. F. Zholio-Kyuri 17/2/1; tel. (2) 870-15-60; fax (2) 971-28-32; e-mail sofia@mfa.gov.mk; Ambassador BLAGOJ HANDZISKI.

Moldova: 1142 Sofia, bul. G. S. Rakovski 152; tel. (2) 935-60-11; fax (2) 980-64-75; e-mail secretary@ambasadamd.org; Ambassador ALEXANDRU PRIGORSCHI.

Mongolia: 1113 Sofia, ul. F. Zholio-Kyuri 52; tel. (2) 865-90-12; fax (2) 963-07-45; e-mail mongemb@gmail.com; Ambassador TSERENDORJIIN GANKHUYAG.

Morocco: 1421 Sofia, ul. Chervena stena 1/1; tel. (2) 865-11-26; fax (2) 865-48-11; e-mail ambmarsofia@mbox.contact.bg; Ambassador AZIZA LIMAME.

Netherlands: 1504 Sofia, ul. Oborishte 15; tel. (2) 816-03-00; fax (2) 816-03-01; e-mail sof@minbuza.nl; internet www.netherlandsembassy.bg; Ambassador KAREL VAN KESTEREN.

Norway: 1000 Sofia, vul. Bacho Kiro 26–30; tel. (2) 803-61-00; fax (2) 803-61-99; e-mail emb.sofia@mfa.no; internet www.norvegia.bg; Ambassador TOVE SKARSTEIN.

Poland: 1000 Sofia, ul. Khan Krum 46; tel. (2) 987-26-10; fax (2) 987-29-39; e-mail sofia.amb.sekretariat@msz.gov.pl; internet www.sofia.polemb.net; Ambassador LESZEK HENSEL.

Portugal: 1000 Sofia, ul. Pozitano 7/3, et. 5; tel. (2) 448-41-10; fax (2) 448-41-02; e-mail embpor@sofia.dgaccp.pt; Ambassador VERA MARIA FERNANDES.

Qatar: Sofia; Ambassador MUHAMMAD ALI SAID AL-NUAYMI.

Romania: Sofia, bul. Mihai Eminesku 4; tel. (2) 971-28-58; fax (2) 973-34-12; e-mail ambsofro@vip.bg; internet sofia.mae.ro; Ambassador PĂCUREȚU ANTON.

Russia: 1113 Sofia, bul. D. Tsankov 28; tel. (2) 963-09-14; fax (2) 963-41-03; e-mail info@russia.bg; internet www.russia.bg; Ambassador YURII N. ISAKOV.

Serbia: 1504 Sofia, ul. Veliko Tarnovo 3; tel. (2) 946-16-33; fax (2) 946-10-59; e-mail sofia@emb-serbia.com; internet www.emb-serbia.com; Ambassador ALEKSANDAR CRKVENJAKOV.

Slovakia: 1504 Sofia, bul. Ya. Sakazov 9; tel. (2) 942-92-10; fax (2) 942-92-35; e-mail emb.sofia@mzv.sk; internet www.mzv.sk/sofia; Ambassador KAROL MISTRÍK.

South Africa: 1000 Sofia, ul. Bacho Kiro 26; tel. (2) 939-50-15; fax (2) 939-50-17; e-mail sofia.admin@foreign.gov.za; Ambassador SHEILA M. CAMERER.

Spain: 1504 Sofia, ul. Sheynovo 27, POB 381; tel. (2) 943-36-20; fax (2) 946-12-01; e-mail emb.sofia@maec.es; internet www.embespbg.com; Ambassador (vacant).

Sudan: 1113 Sofia, ul. F. Zholio-Kyuri 19/156/1, ap. 2; tel. (2) 971-29-91; fax (2) 971-70-38; e-mail scgs@online.bg; internet sudansof.org; Ambassador ELTAIB ABULGAZIM FADOUL ABULGAZIM.

Switzerland: 1504 Sofia, ul. Shipka 33, POB 132; tel. (2) 942-01-00; fax (2) 946-16-22; e-mail sof.vertretung@eda.admin.ch; internet www.eda.admin.ch/sofia; Ambassador REGINA ESCHER.

Syria: 1700 Sofia, Simeonovsko shose 13A; tel. (2) 962-57-42; fax (2) 962-43-14; e-mail syrianembassy@mbox.contact.bg; Chargé d'affaires SALAH SOUKKAR.

Turkey: 1000 Sofia, bul. V. Levski 80; tel. (2) 935-55-00; fax (2) 981-93-58; e-mail turksofya@spnet.net; Ambassador İSMAIL ARAMAZ.

Ukraine: 1618 Sofia, Ovcha Kupel, ul. Boryana 29; tel. (2) 818-68-28; fax 955-52-47; e-mail emb_bg@mfa.gov.ua; internet www.mfa.gov.ua/bulgaria; Ambassador MYKOLA BALTAZHI.

United Kingdom: 1000 Sofia, ul. Moskovska 9; tel. (2) 933-92-22; fax (2) 933-92-19; e-mail information@british-embassy.bg; internet ukinbulgaria.fco.gov.uk; Ambassador JONATHAN ALLEN.

USA: 1407 Sofia, ul. Kozyak 16; tel. (2) 937-51-00; fax (2) 937-53-20; e-mail sofia@usembassy.bg; internet bulgaria.usembassy.gov; Ambassador JAMES WARLICK.

Venezuela: 1421 Sofia, ul. Arsenalski 11, 4th Floor; tel. (2) 963-16-37; fax (2) 963-16-42; e-mail embavenezuela@abv.bg; Ambassador RAFAEL ANGEL BARRETO CASTILLO.

Viet Nam: 1113 Sofia, ul. Zhetvarka 1; tel. and fax (2) 963-36-58; e-mail vnemb.bg@mofa.gov.vn; internet www.mofa.gov.vn/vnemb.bg; Ambassador TRAN VAN THINH.

Yemen: 1784 Sofia, Mladost 1, bul. A. Sakharov 3; tel. (2) 870-41-19; fax (2) 974-34-63; e-mail yemb-sofia@mofa.gov.ye; Chargé d'affaires AHMED AL-KADASI.

Judicial System

The 1991 Constitution provides for justice to be administered by the Supreme Court of Cassation, the Supreme Administrative Court, courts of appeal, courts of assizes, military courts and district courts. The main legal officials are the justices, or judges, of the higher courts, the prosecutors and investigating magistrates. The judicial system is independent, most appointments being made or recommended by the Supreme Judicial Council, a permanent, supervisory body. The military courts handle cases involving military personnel. Administrative courts review appeals of government acts. The Supreme Judicial Council comprises 25 members, who serve a 5-year term; 11 members are elected by the Narodno Sobranie (National Assembly) and 11 are elected by the judiciary. The Chairmen of the two Supreme Courts and the Prosecutor-General are senior *ex officio* members. The Supreme Judicial Council is responsible for all judicial appointments and administers the judiciary. The Constitutional Court is the final arbiter of constitutional issues. It comprises 12 judges, who serve 9-year terms, four of whom are appointed by the President, four by the Narodno Sobranie and four by the Supreme Courts. A new 'special court' opened in Sofia in January 2012, designed to expedite organized crime trials.

Supreme Court of Cassation (Varkhoven kasatsionen sad): 1000 Sofia, bul. Vitosha 2; tel. (2) 987-17-34; fax (2) 987-60-24; internet www.vks.bg; Chair. LAZAR GRUEV.

Supreme Administrative Court (Varkhoven Administrariven Sad): 1301 Sofia, bul. A. Stamboliyski 18; tel. (2) 988-49-02; fax (2) 981-87-51; e-mail programata.gk@gmail.com; internet www.sac.government.bg; Chair. GEORGI KOLEV.

Constitutional Court (Konstitutsionen Sad): 1594 Sofia, bul. Dondukov 1; tel. (2) 987-50-08; fax (2) 987-19-86; e-mail s.petrova@constcourt.bg; internet www.constcourt.bg; Chair. EVGENIY TANCHEV.

Supreme Judicial Council (Vissh Sadeben Savet): 1000 Sofia, ul. Saborna 9; tel. (2) 930-49-57; fax (2) 981-91-76; e-mail vss_adm@inet.bg; internet www.vss.justice.bg.

Office of the Prosecutor-General: 1061 Sofia, bul. Vitosha 2; tel. (2) 986-76-71; fax (2) 981-58-32; e-mail infocenter@prb.bg; internet www.prb.bg; Prosecutor-Gen. Dr BORIS VELCHEV.

Religion

Most of the population professes Christianity, the main denomination being the Bulgarian Orthodox Church. The 1991 Constitution guarantees freedom of religion, although Eastern Orthodox Christianity is declared to be the 'traditional religion in Bulgaria'. There is a significant Islamic minority, most of whom are ethnic Turks, although there are also some ethnic Bulgarian Muslims, known as Pomaks. There is a small Jewish community.

CHRISTIANITY

Bulgarian Orthodox Church: 1090 Sofia, ul. Oborishte 4, Synod Palace; tel. (2) 987-56-11; fax (2) 989-76-00; f. 865; autocephalous Exarchate 1870 (recognized 1945); administered by the Bulgarian Patriarchy; 11 dioceses in Bulgaria and two dioceses abroad (Diocese of North and South America and Australia, and Diocese of West Europe), each under a Metropolitan; Chair. of the Bulgarian Patriarchy Patriarch MAKSIM.

Armenian Apostolic Orthodox Church: Sofia 1080, ul. Nishka 31; tel. (2) 988-02-08; 20,000 adherents (1996); administered by Bishop DIRAYR MARDIKIYAN, resident in Bucharest, Romania; Chair. of the Diocesan Council in Bulgaria OWANES KIRAZIAN.

The Roman Catholic Church

The Latin (Roman) Rite, which is organized in two dioceses, both directly responsible to the Holy See, had an estimated 63,000 adherents at 31 December 2008. The Byzantine-Slav (Eastern) Rite is organized in one apostolic exarchate, which had 10,000 adherents at that time.

Bishops' Conference: 1606 Sofia, ul. Lulin Planina 5; tel. (2) 953-04-06; fax (2) 952-61-86; e-mail proykov@gmail.com; internet www.catholic-bg.org; f. 1991; Pres. Most Rev. CHRISTO NIKOLOV PROYKOV (Titular Bishop of Briula).

Latin Rite

Bishop of Nicopolis: Most Rev. PETKO CHRISTOV, 7000 Ruse, ul. Bratya Simeonovi 26A; tel. (82) 83-52-45; fax (82) 82-28-81; e-mail dio_nicop@elits.rousse.bg.

Bishop of Sofia and Plovdiv: Most Rev. GEORGI ZHOVCHEV, 4000 Plovdiv, bul. Maria Luisa 3; tel. (32) 62-20-42; fax (32) 62-15-22; e-mail manolov@seznam.cz.

Byzantine Rite

Apostolic Exarch of Sofia: CHRISTO PROYKOV (Titular Bishop of Briula), 1606 Sofia, ul. Lulin Planina 5; tel. (2) 953-04-06; fax (2) 952-61-86; e-mail cproykov@technolink.bg.

ISLAM

National Muslim Conference: 1000 Sofia, ul. Bratya Miladinovi 27; tel. (2) 981-60-01; fax (2) 980-30-58; e-mail gl.mufti@genmuftibg.net; internet www.genmuftibg.net; f. 1909; an estimated 1,200 imams; Chair. SHABANALI AHMED; Grand Mufti MUSTAFA HADZHI.

JUDAISM

Central Jewish Theological Council: 1000 Sofia, ul. Ekzarkh Yosif 16; tel. (2) 983-12-73; fax (2) 983-50-85; e-mail sofia_synagogue@mail.orbitel.bg; internet www.sofiasynagogue.com; Head ROBERT DJERASSI.

The Press

There were 436 newspapers and 745 periodicals, including bulletins, published in 2009.

PRINCIPAL DAILIES

24 Chasa (24 Hours): 1504 Sofia, bul. Tsarigradsko 47; tel. (2) 942-25-14; fax (2) 942-28-19; internet www.24chasa.bg; f. 1991; wholly owned by Westdeutsche Allgemeine Zeitung (Germany); Editor-in-Chief BORISLAV ZYUMBULEV (acting); circ. 330,000.

Capital Daily: 1000 Sofia, ul. I Vazov 16; tel. (2) 461-54-14; fax (2) 461-52–32; e-mail pisma@capital.bg; internet www.capital.bg; f. 2011 through merger of the print editions of *Dnevnik* and *Pari*; Editor-in-Chief STANKA TOSHEVA; Managing Editor IVAN BEDROV.

Chernomorsky Far (The Black Sea Lighthouse): 8000 Burgas Oblast, Pomorie, ul. Milin Kamak 7; tel. (56) 96-03-32; fax (56) 96-03-31; e-mail far@chfar.com; internet far.bourgas.org; f. 1958; regional independent; Chief Editor RUMYANA EMANUILIDU.

Dneven Trud (Daily Labour): 1000 Sofia, bul. Dondukov 52; tel. (2) 980-12-69; fax (2) 980-26-26; internet www.trud.bg; f. 1936; owned by Westdeutsche Allgemeine Zeitung (Germany); Editor TOSHO TOSHEV.

Dnevnik (The Daily): 1000 Sofia, ul. I. Vazov 16; tel. (2) 461-53-00; fax (2) 461-52-35; e-mail dnevnik@dnevnik.bg; internet www.dnevnik.bg; f. 2001; online only from 2011; Chief Editor VELISLAVA POPOVA.

Duma (Word): 1000 Sofia, bul. Tsarigradsko shose 113A; tel. (2) 970-52-00; fax (2) 975-26-04; e-mail duma@duma.bg; internet www.duma.bg; f. 1990; Chief Editor IVELIN NIKOLOV.

Monitor: 1784 Sofia, bul. Tsarigradsko shose 113A; tel. (2) 960-22-09; fax (2) 975-24-44; e-mail monitor@monitor.bg; internet www.monitor.bg; f. 1998; Editorial Dir IRENA KRASTEVA.

Narodno Delo (People's Cause): 9000 Varna, bul. Miladinovi 68; tel. (52) 66-36-03; fax (52) 61-50-80; e-mail office@narodnodelo.bg; internet www.narodnodelo.bg; f. 1944; 6 a week; regional independent; business, politics and sport; Chief Editor ANGEL PETRICHEV; circ. 20,000 (Oct. 2009).

Novinar: 1505 Sofia, ul. Oborishte 44; tel. and fax (2) 943-45-32; e-mail novinar@novinar.bg; internet www.novinar.net; f. 1992; Editorial Dir LYUBEN DILOV-SIN.

Sega: 1463 Sofia, pl. Balgaria 1; tel. (2) 428-23-00; e-mail prepress@segabg.com; internet www.segabg.com; f. 1998; Chief Editor TEODORA PEEVA.

Standart News: 1404 Sofia, bul. Balgaria 49, Biznis tsentar 'Vitosha'; tel. (2) 960-43-43; fax (2) 960-43-12; e-mail agency@standartnews.com; internet www.standartnews.com; f. 1992; Chief Editor NEVEN KOLANDANOVA.

Trud (Labour): 1000 Sofia, bul. Dondukov 52; tel. (2) 921-42-12; fax (2) 980-11-40; internet www.trud.bg; f. 1936; organ of the Confederation of Independent Trade Unions in Bulgaria; Editor-in-Chief NIKOLA KITSEVSKI (acting); circ. 200,000.

PRINCIPAL PERIODICALS

168 Chasa (168 Hours): 1504 Sofia, bul. Tsarigradsko 47; tel. (2) 433-92-88; fax (2) 433-93-15; f. 1990; weekly; business, politics, entertainment; owned by Westdeutsche Allgemeine Zeitung (Germany); Editor-in-Chief NIKOLAY PENCHEV; circ. 93,000.

AMICA: 1504 Sofia, bul. Shipka 21; tel. (2) 946-02-14; fax (2) 946-12-87; e-mail amica@amica.bg; internet www.amica.bg; fashion; monthly; in Bulgarian; owned by Bulgarian Textile; Editor-in-Chief BOGDANA ZLATEVA; circ. 20,000 (2007).

Az Buki (Alphabet): 1113 Sofia, bul. Tsarigradsko 125; tel. and fax (2) 870-52-98; e-mail azbuki@minedu.government.bg; f. 1991; weekly; for schools; sponsored by the Ministry of Education, Youth and Science; Editor-in-Chief ZLATOMIR ZLATANOV; circ. 4,000 (2009).

Bankera: 1421 Sofia, ul. Tsvetna gradina 5; tel. (2) 440-94-40; fax (2) 963-20-28; e-mail info@banker.bg; internet www.banker.bg; banking and finance; weekly; Editor BISTRA GEORGIEVA.

Bulka (Bride): 1784 Sofia, POB 138; tel. (89) 787-77-63; e-mail bulka@gbg.bg; internet www.spisaniebulka.com; quarterly; fashion and weddings; owned by 75 GROUP Ltd; Chief Editor VIOLETA TSACHEVA.

Durzhaven Vestnik (State Gazette): 1169 Sofia, bul. A. Battenberg 1; tel. (2) 939-35-03; fax (2) 981-17-11; e-mail dv@parliament.bg; internet dv.parliament.bg; f. 1879; 2 a week; official publication of the Republic of Bulgaria; 2 bulletins of parliamentary proceedings and the publ. in which all legislation is promulgated; Editor-in-Chief ISKRA KOEVA; circ. 8,000.

EVA: 1000 Sofia, Hristo Belchev 1/5; tel. (2) 987-34-39; fax (2) 980-94-54; e-mail eva@eva.bg; internet www.eva.bg; fashion and lifestyle; monthly; in Bulgarian; Editor-in-Chief MILENA POPOVA.

Galeria (Gallery): Sofia, Tsarigradsko Shosse 17; f. 2009; weekly; politics; Editor-in-Chief KRISTINA PATRASHKOVA.

Ikonomichesky Zhivot (Economic Life): 1000 Sofia, bul. Dondukov 11; tel. (2) 987-95-06; fax (2) 987-65-60; e-mail ikonzhiv@dir.bg; f. 1966; weekly; independent; marketing and finance; Editor-in-Chief VASIL ALEKSIEV; circ. 10,000.

Kultura (Culture): 1164 Sofia, kv. Lozenets, ul. Milin Kamak 14; tel. (2) 963-21-06; fax (2) 963-21-05; e-mail kultura@online.bg; internet www.kultura.bg; f. 1957; weekly; arts, publicity and cultural affairs; Chief Editor KOPRINKA CHERVENKOVA; circ. 5,000.

Napravi Sam (Do It Yourself): 1527 Sofia, ul. Panayot Volov 11; tel. and fax (2) 943-41-28; e-mail office@newteck.bg; internet www.newteck.bg/doitself; f. 1981; monthly; Editor-in-Chief GEORGI BALANSKI; circ. 8,000.

Novo Vreme (New Time): 1000 Sofia, ul. Pozitano 20; tel. (2) 810-72-70; fax (2) 810-72-69; e-mail novovreme@novovreme.com; internet www.novovreme.com; f. 1897; 6 a year; organ of the Bulgarian Socialist Party; Editor-in-Chief I. BORISOV.

Pro i Anti: 1000 Sofia, pl. Slaveykov 11; tel. (2) 980-44-45; fax (2) 963-42-36; e-mail v.proanti@gmail.com; f. 1991; weekly; politics, culture; Editor VASIL STANILOV; circ. 7,000.

Sofia Ekho (Sofia Echo): 1000 Sofia, ul. Kiril i Metodii 64; tel. (2) 801-26-72; e-mail editor@sofiaecho.com; internet www.sofiaecho.com; f. 1997; weekly; business, law, property, travel and tourism, lifestyle and sports; in Bulgarian and English; owned by the media company Economedia; Editor-in-Chief CLIVE LEVIEV-SAWYER; circ. 3,000 (2008).

Starshel (The Hornet): 1000 Sofia, pl. Slaveykov 4; tel. and fax (2) 988-08-16; e-mail info@starshel.bg; internet www.starshel.bg; f. 1946; weekly; satirical; Chief Editor MIKHAIL VESHIM; circ. 45,200.

Tema: 1000 Sofia, bul. Vitosha 19; tel. (2) 933-09-10; fax (2) 933-09-39; e-mail tema@temanews.com; internet www.temanews.com; society, economics, politics; weekly; Chief Editor VALERI ZAPRYANOV; circ. 10,000.

Tsarkoven Vestnik (Church Newspaper): 1000 Sofia, ul. Oborishte 4; tel. (2) 87-56-11; f. 1900; weekly; organ of the Bulgarian Orthodox Church; Editor-in-Chief DIMITAR KIROV; circ. 4,000.

Zhenata Dnes (Women Today): 1164 Sofia, bul. Dzheims Bauchar 23; tel. and fax (2) 969-41-97; e-mail jenatadnes@rispress.com; internet www.jenatadnes.com; f. 1946; monthly; Chief Editor MIRA BADZHEVA; circ. 50,000.

NEWS AGENCIES

Balgarska Telegrafna Agentsia (BTA) (Bulgarian Telegraph Agency): Sofia, bul. Tsarigradsko 49; tel. (2) 988-17-19; fax (2) 988-54-63; e-mail bta@bta.bg; internet www.bta.bg; f. 1898; official news agency; domestic, Balkan and international news in Bulgarian and English; also economic and sports news; publishes weekly surveys of science and technology, international affairs, literature and art; Gen. Dir MAKSIM MINCHEV.

Sofia News Agency: 1000 Sofia, ul. Khan Asparuh 54; tel. (2) 421-11-51; internet www.novinite.com; f. 2001; English language news provider; part of One Click Media Group; Man. Dir MAXIM BEHAR.

Sofia-Press Agency: 1000 Sofia, ul. Slavyanska 29/7; tel. (2) 988-28-78; e-mail office@sofia-press.com; internet www.sofia-press.com; f. 1967; publishes socio-political and scientific literature, fiction, children's and tourist literature, publs on the arts, a newspaper, magazines and bulletins in foreign languages.

PRESS ASSOCIATIONS

Bulgarian Journalists' Union: 1000 Sofia, Graf Ignatiev 4; tel. (2) 987-35-31; fax (2) 988-30-47; e-mail sbj_bg@mail.bg; internet www.sbj-bg.eu; f. 1944; Pres. MILEN VALKOV.

Union des Journalistes Bulgares Podkrepa: 1000 Sofia, Angel Kantchev 2; tel. (2) 987-21-98; fax (2) 987-05-57; e-mail journalist@podkrepa.org; Pres. RENETA NIKOLOVA.

Publishers

Balgarski Hudozhnik (Bulgarian Artist) Publishing House: 1504 Sofia, ul. Shipka 6; tel. (2) 944-61-15; fax (2) 946-02-12; e-mail info@sbhart.com; internet www.sbhart.com; f. 1952; owned by Union of Bulgarian Artists (q.v.); art books, children's books; Chair. LYUBEN GENOV.

Balgarski Pisatel (Bulgarian Writer) Publishing House: 1000 Sofia, ul. 6-ti Septemvri 35; tel. (2) 87-58-73; fax (2) 87-24-95; publishing house of the Union of Bulgarian Writers; Bulgarian fiction and poetry, literary criticism; Dir GERTCHO ATANASOV.

Khristo G. Danov State Publishing House (Darzhavno Izdatelstvo 'Khristo G. Danov'): 4005 Plovdiv, ul. S. Chalakov 1; tel. (32) 63-25-52; fax (32) 26-05-60; f. 1855; fiction, poetry, literary criticism; Dir NACHO KHRISTOSKOV.

Prof. Marin Drinov Academic Publishing House (Bulgarian Academy of Sciences) (Izdatelstvo na Bulgarskata Akademiya na Naukite 'Prof. Marin Drinov'): 1113 Sofia, ul. G. Bonchev 6; tel. (2) 872-09-22; fax (2) 870-40-54; e-mail aph@aph.bas.bg; internet www.baspress.com; f. 1869; scientific works and periodicals of the Bulgarian Academy of Sciences; Dir MARTIN KRASTEV.

Medizina i Fizkultura (Medicine and Physical Culture) Publishing House (Izdatelstvo 'Medizina i Fizkultura'): 1000 Sofia, pl. Slaveykov 11; tel. and fax (2) 987-13-08; e-mail medpubl@abv.bg; internet www.medpubl.com; f. 1956; privately owned; medicine; Dir EMILIA NIKOLOVA.

Military Publishing House (Voenno Izdatelstvo): 1080 Sofia, ul. I. Vazov 12; tel. (2) 987-39-34; fax (2) 980-27-79; e-mail plamstoyanov@abv.bg; internet www.vi-books.com; f. 1888; Dir PLAMEN STOYANOV.

Narodna Kultura (National Culture) Publishing House: 1000 Sofia, ul. A. Kanchev 1, POB 421; tel. (2) 987-80-63; e-mail nauk-izk@sigma-bg.com; f. 1944; general; Dir PETAR MANOLOV.

Nauka i Izkustvo (Sciences and Arts) Publishing House: 1000 Sofia, pl. Slaveykov 11; tel. (2) 987-47-90; fax (2) 987-24-96; e-mail nauk_izk@sigma-bg.com; f. 1948; language and psychology; Man. LORETA PUSHKAROVA.

Prosveta (Enlightenment) Publishing House: 1618 Sofia, ul. Zemedelska 2; tel. (2) 818-20-20; fax (2) 818-20-19; e-mail prosveta@prosveta.bg; internet www.prosveta.bg; f. 1945; educational publishing house; Chair. JOANA TOMOVA.

Reporter Publishing House: 1784 Sofia, bul. Tsarigradsko 113; tel. (2) 975-23-82; fax (2) 975-23-84; e-mail reporter7@abv.bg; f. 1990; private publishers of fiction and documentary literature; Man. KRUM BLAGOV.

RIVA Publishers: 1000 Sofia, ul. Graf Ignatiyev 53B; tel. (2) 986-56-86; e-mail riva@rivapublishers.com; internet www.rivapublishers.com; f. 1990; history, philosophy, social sciences, literature and musicology.

Sinodalno (Synodal) Publishing House: 1000 Sofia, ul. Oborishte 4; tel. (2) 87-56-11; religious publishing house; Dir ANGEL VELITEHKOV.

Tangra TanNakRa: 1124 Sofia, POB 1832; tel. (2) 986-44-19; fax (2) 986-69-45; e-mail mail@tangra-bg.org; internet www.tangra-bg.org; history.

Technica Publishing House: 1000 Sofia, pl. Slaveykov 1; tel. (2) 987-12-83; fax (2) 987-49-06; e-mail office@technica-bg.com; internet www.technica-bg.com; f. 1958; textbooks for professional, higher and university education, technical literature, dictionaries and handbooks; Exec. Man. MARIA TSANKOVA.

Zemizdat Publishing House: 1504 Sofia, bul. Tsarigradsko 47; tel. (2) 44-18-29; f. 1949; specializes in works on agriculture, shooting, fishing, forestry, livestock-breeding, environmental studies, and popular scientific literature and textbooks; Dir PETAR ANGELOV.

PUBLISHERS' ASSOCIATION

Bulgarian Book Association: 1463 Sofia, Vitosha Blv.; tel. (2) 958-15-25; fax (2) (2) 958-92-11; e-mail office@abk.bg; internet www.abk.bg; f. 1994; Chair. VESSELIN TODOROV; Sec. SILVA PAPAZIAN.

Broadcasting and Communications

TELECOMMUNICATIONS

The fixed telephony market contracted in the late 2000s. In 2009 three companies providing mobile telecommunications networks and services: Cosmo Bulgaria Mobile EAD, Mobitel and Vivacom.

Communications Regulation Commission (CRC): 1000 Sofia, ul. Gurko 6; tel. (2) 949-24-18; fax (2) 971-27-29; e-mail info@crc.bg; internet www.crc.bg; f. 2002; Chair. VESELIN BOZHKOV.

Cosmo Bulgaria Mobile EAD (Globul): 1766 Sofia, bul. Mladost 4; tel. (2) 942-80-00; fax (2) 415-41-23; e-mail customercare@globul.bg; internet www.globul.bg; f. 2001; subsidiary of Cosmote Group (Greece); Chief Exec. ATHANASIOS KATSIROUBAS; 2.4m. subscribers (Sept. 2006).

Mobikom (Radiotelecommunication Company Mobikom): 1000 Sofia, POB 101; tel. (2) 974-40-27; fax (2) 960-56-13; f. 1992; owned by Vivacom; Man. Dir JOHN MUNNERY.

Mobiltel EAD: 1309 Sofia, Ilinden, ul. Kukush 1/8; tel. (88) 808-80-88; fax (88) 850-08-85; e-mail pr@mobiltel.bg; internet www.mtel.bg; f. 1994; owned by Telekom Austria AG from 2006; provides mobile and fixed telecommunications services, digital TV and high-speed internet; 5.3m. subscribers (Nov. 2011); CEO ANDREAS MAIERHOFER.

Vivacom: 1784 Sofia, Tsarigradsko shosse 115; tel. (2) 949-46-24; fax (2) 952-10-98; e-mail pc@btc.bg; internet www.vivacom.bg; 90%

owned by AIG Investments (USA); formerly known as Bulgarian Telecommunications Co (BTC); merged with BTC Mobile (Vivatel) in Jan. 2009; name changed as above in Sept. 2009; Chair. PIERRE MELLINGER; CEO BERNARD MOSCHENI; 23,000 employees.

BROADCASTING

National Radio and Television Council: 1504 Sofia, ul. San Stefano 29; Dir IVAN BORISLAVOV.

Association of Bulgarian Broadcasters (ABBRO): 1463 Sofia, pl. Balgaria 1; tel. (2) 946-16-20; fax (2) 916-63-51; e-mail office@abbro-bg.org; internet www.abbro-bg.org; f. 1997; independent non-profit org.; represents 60 private media companies, incl. 160 radio and TV stations; Exec. Dir GRISHA KAMBUROV.

Radio

In 2009 there were 86 licensed, local radio stations, and two principal nationwide stations, Bulgaria National Radio (BNR) and Darik Radio. At the end of 2008 BNR and Darik Radio reached 96% and 95% of the population, respectively.

Bulgarian National Radio (Balgarsko Natsionalno Radio): 1040 Sofia, bul. D. Tsankov 4; tel. (2) 933-66-38; fax (2) 933-67-15; internet www.bnr.bg; f. 1929; two Home Service programmes; local stations at Blagoevgrad, Plovdiv, Shumen, Stara Zagora and Varna; Foreign Service broadcasts in Bulgarian, Albanian, Arabic, English, French, German, Greek, Russian, Serbian, Spanish and Turkish; Dir VALERI TODOROV.

BG Radio: 1000 Sofia, POB 48; tel. (2) 952-38-07; fax (2) 952-38-45; e-mail office@bgradio.net; internet www.bgradio.net; f. 2001; commercial music station; wholly owned by Metromedia Int. Telecommunications Inc (USA); Chief Exec. NIKOLAY YANCHOVICHIN.

Television

At the end of 2009 there were 20 terrestrial television broadcasters. Of these, the three most significant were the state-owned Bulgarian National Television, and two private stations, bTV and Nova Television. There were also 532 cable television operators, offering a total of 2,811 channels.

bTV: 1463 Sofia, pl. Balgaria 1, NDK Administration Bldg; tel. (2) 917-68-00; fax (2) 917-68-86; internet www.btv.bg; f. 2000; daily transmission of commercial news, family entertainment and locally produced programmes, on bTV channel; owned by Central European Media Enterprises; Gen. Dir VICKY POLITOVA.

Bulgarian National Television (Bulgarska Natsionalna Televiziya): 1504 Sofia, ul. San Stefano 29; tel. (2) 944-49-99; fax (2) 946-12-10; internet www.bnt.bg; f. 1959; daily transmission of programmes on Channel 1 and Efir 2 and on the satellite channel TV Bulgaria; Dir VYARA ANKOVA; 3,000 employees.

Nova Television: 1592 Sofia, bul. Christopher Columbus 41, Porsche Business Centre; tel. (2) 805-00-00; e-mail office@ntv.bg; internet www.ntv.bg; f. 1994; privately owned; news and entertainment; CEO SVETLANA VASSILEVA.

Finance

(cap. = capital; res = reserves; dep. = deposits; m. = million; brs = branches; amounts in new leva)

BANKING

At mid-2009 30 commercial banks were licensed to operate in Bulgaria (of which six were branches of foreign banks).

Central Bank

Bulgarian National Bank (Bulgarska Narodna Banka): 1000 Sofia, pl. Knyaz Aleksandar I 1; tel. (2) 914-59; fax (2) 980-24-25; e-mail press_office@bnbank.org; internet www.bnb.bg; f. 1879; bank of issue; cap. 20.0m., res 4,326.7m., dep. 12,315.1m. (Dec. 2010); Gov. IVAN ISKROV; 3 brs.

Commercial Banks

Central Co-operative Bank (Tsentralna Kooperativna Banka): 1086 Sofia, bul. G. S. Rakovski 103; tel. (2) 926-61-07; fax (2) 988-81-07; e-mail office@ccbank.bg; internet www.ccbank.bg; f. 1991; cap. 83.2m., res 60.6m., dep. 2,015.0m. (Dec. 2010); Chair. of Managing Bd IVO KAMENOV; 49 brs.

Corporate Commercial Bank (Korporativna Targovska Banka): 1000 Sofia, ul. Graf Ignatiev 10, POB 632; tel. (2) 937-56-06; fax (2) 980-89-48; e-mail corpbank@corpbank.bg; internet www.corpbank.bg; f. 1989; cap. 60.0m., res 215.8m., dep. 1,747.8m. (Dec. 2009); Chair. of Supervisory Bd TZVETAN VASILEV; 10 brs.

DSK Bank (Banka DSK): 1036 Sofia, ul. Moskovska 19; tel. (2) 700-10-375; fax (2) 980-64-77; e-mail call_center@dskbank.bg; internet www.dskbank.bg; f. 1951 as State Savings Bank; present name adopted 1998; provides general retail banking services throughout the country; wholly owned by Nat. Savings and Commercial Bank—OTP Bank (Hungary); cap. 154.0m., res 1,082.7m., dep. 6,516.7m. (Dec. 2009); Chair. and Chief Exec. VIOLINA MARINOVA; 352 brs and offices.

EIBank—Economic and Investment Bank (SIBank—Stopanka i investitsionna banka): 1000 Sofia, ul. Slavyanska 2; tel. (2) 939-92-40; fax (2) 981-25-26; e-mail info@hq.eibank.bg; internet www.eibank.bg; f. 1994; present name adopted 2000; 75% owned by KBC Bank NV (Belgium); cap. 69.7m., res 126.5m., dep. 1,586.0m. (Dec. 2008); Chair. and Exec. Dir VASSIL SIMOV; 16 brs.

Eurobank EFG Bulgaria (Postbank): 1048 Sofia, bul. Tsar Osvoboditel 14; tel. (2) 816-60-00; fax (2) 988-81-10; e-mail contact@postbank.bg; internet www.postbank.bg; f. 2007 by merger of Postbank and DZI Bank; 63.6% owned by EFG Eurobank Ergasias SA (Greece); cap. 246.2m., res 230.3m., dep. 4,888.5m. (Dec. 2008); Chief Exec. ANTONIOS C. HASSIOTIS.

First Investment Bank (Parva Investitsionna Banka): 1797 Sofia, bul. Dragan Tzankov 37; tel. (2) 817-11-00; fax (2) 970-95-97; e-mail call@fibank.bg; internet www.fibank.bg; f. 1993; 20% owned by the European Bank for Reconstruction and Development; cap. 110.0m., res 159.5m., dep. 3,540.5m. (Dec. 2009); Chair. of Supervisory Bd GEORGI DIMITROV MUTAFCHIEV; 102 brs.

Investbank: 1404 Sofia, bul. Bulgaria 83A; tel. (2) 818-61-44; fax (2) 854-81-99; e-mail office@ibank.bg; internet www.ibank.bg; f. 1994; present name adopted 2002; cap. 80.0m., res 22.5m., dep. 898.0m. (Dec. 2009); Chair. of Supervisory Bd PETIA SLAVOVA; 60 brs.

Municipal Bank (Obshchinska Banka): 1000 Sofia, ul. Vrabcha 6; tel. (2) 930-01-11; fax (2) 930-02-70; e-mail contacts@municipalbank.bg; internet www.municipalbank.bg; f. 1996; 67% owned by the Municipality of Sofia; cap. 25.0m., res 21.4m., dep. 684.7m. (Dec. 2009); Chair. of Supervisory Bd DIMITAR KOLEV; 63 brs.

Piraeus Bank Bulgaria AD: 1000 Sofia, bul. Vitosha 3; tel. (2) 700-12-002; fax (2) 981-85-79; e-mail customerservice@piraeusbank.bg; internet www.piraeusbank.bg; f. 1994; 99.8% owned by Piraeus Bank (Greece); cap. 316.7m., res 18.2m., dep. 3,086.3m. (Dec. 2009); CEO ATHANASIOS KOUTSOPOULOS; 65 brs.

Raiffeisenbank (Bulgaria) EAD: 1504 Sofia, ul. Gogol 18–20; tel. (2) 700-10-100; fax (2) 943-45-28; internet www.rbb.bg; f. 1994; 100% owned by Raiffeisen Int. Bank Holding AG (Austria); cap. 603.4m., res 71.4m., dep. 4,373.0m. (Dec. 2009); Chair. and Exec. Dir MOMCHIL ANDREEV.

Société Générale Expressbank AD Varna: 9000 Varna, bul. Vl. Varnenchik 92; tel. (52) 68-61-00; fax (52) 60-16-81; e-mail sgeb.contact@socgen.com; internet www.sgeb.bg; f. 1993; present name adopted 2005; 97.95% owned by Société Générale (France); cap. 33.7m., res 98.6m., dep. 2,418.8m. (Dec. 2009); CEO PHILIPPE LHOTTE; 20 brs.

UniCredit Bulbank AD: 1000 Sofia, pl. Sveta Nedelia 7; tel. (2) 923-21-11; fax (2) 988-46-36; e-mail pr@unicreditgroup.bg; internet www.unicreditbulbank.bg; f. 1964; present name adopted 2007; 86.1% owned by Bank Austria Creditanstalt AG (Austria); cap. 239.2m., res 1,201.9m., dep. 9,566.9m. (Dec. 2009); Chair. and Chief Exec. LEVON HAMPARTZOUMIAN; 91 brs.

United Bulgarian Bank (Obedinena Balgarska Banka): 1040 Sofia, ul. Sv. Sofia 5; tel. (2) 811-28-00; fax (2) 988-08-22; e-mail info@ubb.bg; internet www.ubb.bg; f. 1992; universal commercial bank; 99.9% owned by National Bank of Greece SA; cap. 76.0m., 0.1m., dep. 6,743.1m. (Dec. 2009); Chair. IOANNIS GEORGIOS PEHLIVANIDIS; 134 brs.

STOCK EXCHANGE

Bulgarian Stock Exchange: 1303 Sofia, ul. Triushi 10; tel. (2) 937-09-34; fax (2) 937-09-46; e-mail bse@bse-sofia.bg; internet www.bse-sofia.bg; f. 1997; Chair. ASEN YAGODIN; CEO IVAN TAKEV.

INSURANCE

Bulstrad: 1000 Sofia, pl. Pozitano 5; tel. (2) 985-66-10; fax (2) 985-61-03; e-mail public@bulstrad.bg; internet www.bulstrad.bg; f. 1961; 31% owned by TBIH Group (Netherlands); all classes of insurance and reinsurance; Chair. of Bd and Chief Exec. RUMEN YANCHEV; 14 brs.

DZI Insurance: 1000 Sofia, Georgi Benkovski St 3; tel. (2) 981-57-99; fax (2) 987-45-33; e-mail general.ins@dzi.bg; internet www.dzi.bg; f. 1946; privatization approved in 2002; all areas of insurance; Chair. of Bd NEDYALKO CHANDUROV; 27 agencies, 101 brs.

Evroins: 1592 Sofia, bul. Christopher Columbus 43; tel. (2) 965-15-25; fax (2) 965-15-26; e-mail office@euroins.bg; internet www.euroins.bg; f. 1996; business and general insurance; Chair. of Supervisory Bd VIOLETA DARAKOVA; 87 agencies and offices.

Municipal Insurance Co (Obshchinska Zastrakhovatelna Kompaniya): 1301 Sofia, bul. Sveta Sofia 7, 5th Floor; tel. (2) 981-31-22;

fax (2) 981-43-51; e-mail headoffice@ozk.bg; internet www.ozk.bg; f. 1996; Exec. Dir ALEKSANDER LICHEV.

Uniqa Insurance Plc Bulgaria: 1612 Sofia, ul. Yunak 11–13; tel. (2) 915-63-33; fax (2) 915-63-00; e-mail info@uniqa.bg; internet www.uniqa.bg; f. 1992; subsidiary of Uniqa (Austria); fmrly Vitosha-Zhivot (Vitosha Life) Insurance Co; CEO and Chair. NIKOLAI GENCHEV; 10 agencies, 28 brs.

Trade and Industry

GOVERNMENT AGENCY

Privatization and Post-privatization Control Agency: 1113 Sofia, bul. Dr G. M. Dimitrov 52A; tel. (2) 970-16-15; fax (2) 970-16-80; f. 2010 by merger of the Privatization Agency and the Agency for Post-privatization Control; Exec. Dir EMIL KARANIKOLOV.

INTERNATIONAL FREE TRADE ZONES

Burgas Free Trade Zone: 8000 Burgas, ul. Trapezitsa 5, POB 154; tel. (56) 84-20-47; fax (56) 84-15-62; e-mail info@freezonebourgas.com; internet www.freezonebourgas.com; f. 1989; Exec. Dir VASSILIY SKRIPKA.

Dragoman Free Trade Zone: 2210 Dragoman, ul. Z. Stoianov 16; tel. and fax (2) 954-93-39.

Plovdiv Free Trade Zone: 4003 Plovdiv, ul. Vasil Levski 242A, POB 75; tel. (32) 90-62-33; fax (32) 96-08-33; e-mail frzone@mbox.contact.bg; internet www.freezone-plovdiv.com; f. 1990; Exec. Dir VASIL CHUCHULEV.

Ruse (Rousse) Free Trade Zone: 7000 Ruse, Tutrakan bul. 71, POB 107; tel. (82) 88-08-00; fax (82) 83-11-12; e-mail manager@freezone-rousse.bg; internet www.freezone-rousse.bg; f. 1988; Exec. Dir DIMITAR NEDYALKOV.

Svilengrad Free Trade Zone: 6500 Svilengrad, bul. Bulgaria 60; tel. (359) 379-74-45; fax (359) 379-75-41; e-mail sbz@svilengrad.com; f. 1990; Exec. Dir DIMO HARAKCHIEV.

Vidin Free Trade Zone: 3700 Vidin; tel. (94) 60-20-60; fax (94) 60-20-46; e-mail ftzvd@vidin.net; f. 1988; Gen. Man. K. MARINOV.

CHAMBER OF COMMERCE

Bulgarian Chamber of Commerce and Industry (BCCI): 1058 Sofia, ul. Iskar 9; tel. (2) 987-26-31; fax (2) 987-32-09; e-mail bcci@bcci.bg; internet www.bcci.bg; f. 1895; promotes economic relations and business contacts between Bulgarian and foreign cos and orgs; organizes participation in international fairs and exhibitions; publishes economic publs in Bulgarian and foreign languages; organizes foreign trade advertising and publicity; provides legal and economic consultations, etc.; registers all Bulgarian cos trading internationally (more than 46,945 at the end of 2006); Pres. TSVETAN SIMEONOV; 28 regional chambers.

EMPLOYERS' ASSOCIATIONS

Bulgarian Industrial Association—Union of Bulgarian Business (Balgarska Stopanska Kamara—Sayuz na balgarskiya biznes): 1000 Sofia, ul. Alabin 16–20; tel. (2) 932-09-11; fax (2) 987-26-04; e-mail office@bia-bg.com; internet www.bia-bg.com; f. 1980; assists Bulgarian economic enterprises with promotion and foreign contacts; economic analysis; legal and arbitration services; intellectual property protection; training and qualifications; Chair. and Exec. Pres. BOZHIDAR DANEV.

Employers' Association of Bulgaria (EABG) (Sayuz na Rabotodatelite v Balgariya): 1202 Sofia, ul. Industrialna 11; tel. (2) 917-88-68; fax (2) 917-88-61; f. 2000; Chair. VASIL VASILEV.

Union for Private Economic Enterprise in Bulgaria (UPEE) (Sayuz za Stopansko Initsiativa—SSI): 1407 Sofia, ul. T. Notchev 30; tel. (2) 962-47-84; fax (2) 962-13-76; e-mail bborisov@unwe.acad.bg; internet www.ssi-bg.org; f. 1989; voluntary asscn of private enterprises; Pres. Dr BORISLAV BORISOV; 140 brs.

Vazrazhdane (Renaissance) Union of Bulgarian Private Entrepreneurs (UPBE) (Vazrazhdane sayuz na chastnite predpremachi): 1504 Sofia, bul. Dondukov 68; tel. (2) 926-24-17; fax (2) 926-74-12; e-mail vuzrazdane@union-vuzrazdane.com; internet www.union-vuzrazdane.eu; f. 1989; Chair. VANIYA TODOROVA.

UTILITIES

Electricity

National Electricity Company (Natsionalna Elektricheska Kompania—NEK): 1040 Sofia, ul. Veslets 5; tel. (2) 926-36-36; fax (2) 980-12-43; e-mail nek@nek.bg; internet www.nek.bg; f. 1991; wholly state-owned subsidiary of Bulgarian Energy Holding EAD; responsible for hydroelectric power generation; national transmission of electricity; centralized purchase and sale of electrical energy; supervision of national power system; Chair. of Bd EVGENY NAGELOV; Exec. Dir KRASSIMIR PARVANOV.

Gas

Bulgargaz: 1336 Sofia, bul. P. Vladigerov 66, POB 3; tel. (2) 939-64-00; fax (2) 925-03-94; e-mail hq@bulgargaz.bg; internet www.bulgargaz.bg; f. 1973; renamed 1990; state-owned subsidiary of Bulgarian Energy Holding EAD; import, transmission, distribution, storage and transit of natural gas; Chair. VORIS TODOROV; Exec. Dir DIMITAR GOGOV.

Overgaz: 1407 Sofia, ul. F. Kutev 5; tel. (2) 428-33-54; fax (2) 962-17-24; e-mail press@overgas.bg; internet www.overgas.bg; f. 1992; 50% owned by Gazprom (Russia) (q.v.), 50% by Overgas Holding AD (Bulgaria); controlling interest in five local gas distribution cos; Exec. Dir SASHO DONTCHEV.

TRADE UNION CONFEDERATIONS

Confederation of Independent Trade Unions in Bulgaria (CITUB) (Konfederatsia na Nezavisitimite Sindikati v Bulgaria—KNSB): 1040 Sofia, bul. Makedonia 1; tel. (2) 401-05-01; fax (2) 988-59-69; e-mail pldimitrov@citub.net; internet knsb-bg.org; f. 1904; name changed from Bulgarian Professional Union and independence declared from all parties and state structures in 1990; Chair. PLAMEN DIMITROV (acting); Sec. MILADIN STOYNOV; 250,010 mems (2007).

Podkrepa (Support) Trade Union Confederation of Labour: 1000 Sofia, ul. A. Kanchev 2; tel. (2) 987-68-82; fax (2) 987-05-57; e-mail intdept@podkrepa.org; internet www.podkrepa.org; f. 1989; 36 regional and 24 branch union orgs; Chair. Dr KONSTANTIN TRENCHEV; 155,350 mems (2011).

Transport

RAILWAYS

In 2009 there were 4,150 km of railway lines.

Bulgarian State Railways EAD (Balgarski Darzhavni Zheleznitsi—BDZh/BDZ): 1080 Sofia, ul. I. Vazov 3; tel. (2) 981-11-10; fax (2) 981-71-51; e-mail bdz@bdz.bg; internet www.bdz.bg; f. 1888; operates passenger and freight railway services; wholly state-owned; Chair. of Bd of Dirs GEORGI PETARNEICHEV; Exec. Dir PENCHO POPOV; 17,832 employees (2006).

National Railway Infrastructure Company (Natsionalna Kompania 'Zhelezoputna Infrastruktura'): 1233 Sofia, bul. Maria Luiza 110; tel. (2) 932-34-13; e-mail office@rail-infra.bg; internet www.rail-infra.bg; f. 2002 to assume infrastructure responsibilities of Bulgarian State Railways; Chair. ATANAS TONEV; Dir-Gen. ANTON GINEV.

Railway Administration Executive Agency (Zhelezoputna Administratsiya): 1080 Sofia, ul. Gurko 5; tel. (2) 940-94-28; fax (2) 987-67-69; e-mail iaja@mtitc.government.bg; internet www.iaja.government.bg; f. 2001; regulatory and control functions; Exec. Dir VESELIN VASILEV.

ROADS

There were 19,435 km of roads in Bulgaria in 2009, of which 418 km were motorways; 98.6% of the road network was paved. Two international motorways traverse the country, and a motorway links Sofia to the coast.

SHIPPING AND INLAND WATERWAYS

At December 2009 Bulgaria's merchant fleet had 107 vessels, with a total displacement of 522,785 grt. The largest Black Sea ports in Bulgaria are at Varna and Burgas. The Danube (Dunav) River is the main waterway, with Ruse (Rousse) and Lom the two main ports.

Bulgarian Ports National Co (BPA) (Natsionalna Kompania 'Pristanishta'): 1000 Sofia, ul. Gen. Gurko 5; tel. (2) 940-97-73; fax (2) 987-94-80; e-mail bpa@port.bg; internet www.port.bg; f. 2000; Gen. Dir Capt. PEYCHO MANOLOV.

Bulgarian River Shipping Co (Parakhodstvo Balgarsko Rechno Plavane): 7000 Ruse, pl. Otets Paisiy 2; tel. (82) 833-37-77; fax (82) 822-21-30; e-mail main@brp.bg; internet www.brp.bg; f. 1935; shipment of cargo and passengers on the Danube; storage, handling and forwarding of cargo; 100% privately owned; Exec. Dir DRAGOMIR KOCHANOV.

Bulgarski Morski Flot Co: 9000 Varna, ul. Panaguirishte 17; tel. (52) 22-63-16; fax (52) 22-53-94; carriage of goods and passengers on waterways; Dir-Gen. ATANAS YONKOV.

Burgas (Bourgas) Port Authority: 8000 Burgas, ul. A. Battenberg 1; tel. (56) 82-22-22; fax (56) 82-21-56; e-mail headoffice@port-burgas.com; internet www.port-burgas.com; Chair. NELY BENEVA; Exec. Dir ARGIR BOIADJIEV.

Navigation Maritime Bulgare: 9000 Varna, Primorski bul. 1; tel. (52) 68-33-72; fax (52) 68-39-32; e-mail office@navbul.com; internet www.navbul.com; f. 1892; scheduled for privatization; sea transport and ship repair; owns 78 tankers, bulk carriers, and container, ferry, cargo and passenger vessels with a capacity of 1.35m. dwt; owns Varna shipyard; Dir-Gen. Capt. HRISTO DONEV; 5,000 employees.

Varna Port Authority: 9000 Varna, pl. Slaveykov 1; tel. (52) 69-22-32; fax (52) 63-29-53; e-mail headoffice@port-varna.bg; internet port-varna.bg; Exec. Dir DANAIL PAPAZOV.

CIVIL AVIATION

There are three international airports in Bulgaria, at Sofia, Varna and Burgas, and seven other airports for domestic services.

Civil Aviation Administration (Grazhdanska Vazdukhoplavatelna Administratsiya): 1000 Sofia, ul. Dyakon Ignatiy 9; tel. (2) 937-10-47; fax (2) 980-53-37; e-mail caa@caa.bg; internet www.caa.bg; Dir-Gen. TILKO PETROV.

Bulgaria Air: 1540 Sofia, bul. Brussels 1, Sofia Airport; tel. (2) 402-03-06; fax (2) 937-32-54; e-mail office@air.bg; internet www.air.bg; f. 2002 as successor to Balkan Bulgarian Airlines (Balkanair); 99.99% owned by Balkan Hemus Group; international passenger and cargo services; Chief Exec. YANKO GEORGIEV.

Tourism

Bulgaria's tourist attractions include the resorts on the Black Sea coast, mountain scenery, ski resorts and historic centres. In 2010 there were 8,374,034 foreign visitor arrivals. Receipts from tourism (including passenger transport) totalled an estimated US $4,831m. in 2008.

Bulgarian Tourist Chamber: 1000 Sofia, ul. Sv. Sofia 8; tel. (2) 987-40-59; fax (2) 986-51-33; e-mail btch@btch.org; internet www.btch.org; f. 1990; assists tourism enterprises, provides training, and co-ordinates non-governmental orgs; Chair. TSVETAN TONCHEV.

State Agency for Tourism: 1052 Sofia, ul. Slavianska 8; tel. (2) 933-58-14; e-mail secretary@bulgariatravel.org; internet www.tourism.government.bg; Chair. ANELIYA KRUSHKOVA.

Defence

The total strength of the armed forces, as assessed at November 2011, was 31,315, comprising an army of 16,304, an air force of 6,706, a navy of 3,471, and 4,834 centrally controlled staff. There were also 34,000 paramilitary forces, and a total of 303,000 reserves. Bulgaria joined the North Atlantic Treaty Organization's (NATO) 'Partnership for Peace' programme of military co-operation in 1994 and became a full member of the Alliance on 29 March 2004. The modernization of the national defence force, and its operation on a professional basis, which were stipulated as preconditions of Bulgaria's accession to the EU, were agreed in November 2006. Compulsory military service was officially ended on 1 December 2007.

Defence Expenditure: Budgeted at 1,010m. new leva in 2012.

Chief of the General Staff: Gen. SIMEON HRISTOV SIMEONOV.

Education

Education is free and compulsory between the ages of seven and 16 years. Children between the ages of three and six years may attend kindergartens (in 2009/10 some 74.3% of pre-school age children attended). A 12-year system of schooling was introduced in 1998. Primary education (grades one to four), beginning at seven years of age, lasts for four years. Secondary education (grades five to 12), from 11 years of age, lasts for up to eight years, comprising two cycles of four years each. Secondary education is undertaken at general schools, which provide a general academic course, or vocational and technical schools, and art schools, which offer specialized training. In addition, basic schools cover both primary and lower secondary grades, while combined schools can cater for pupils from grades one to 12. In 2009/10, according to official figures, primary enrolment included 93.4% of children in the relevant age-group, while enrolment at lower secondary and upper secondary schools included 82.4% and 78.6%, respectively, of those in the relevant age-group. In 2009/10 enrolment in universities and equivalent higher institutions was 33.1% of those in the relevant age-group. In 2010/11 there were a total of 44 universities and equivalent higher educational institutions, with a total enrolment of 255,659 students (including 3,850 post-graduates studying for 'specialist' degrees), and an additional nine colleges. Tuition fees for university students were introduced in mid-1999. General government expenditure on education in 2009 amounted to 2,838m. new leva (representing 11.3% of total spending).

BURKINA FASO

Introductory Survey

LOCATION, CLIMATE, LANGUAGE, RELIGION, FLAG, CAPITAL

Burkina Faso is a land-locked state in West Africa, bordered by Mali to the west and north, by Niger to the east, and by Benin, Togo, Ghana and Côte d'Ivoire to the south. The climate is hot and mainly dry, with an average temperature of 27°C (81°F) in the dry season (December–May). A rainy season occurs between June and October. Levels of rainfall are generally higher in the south than in the north; average annual rainfall in Ouagadougou is 718 mm (28 ins). The official language is French, and there are numerous indigenous languages (principally Mossi), with many dialects. The majority of the population are Muslims (61%), while some 23% are Christians, mainly Roman Catholics, and 15% follow animist beliefs. The national flag (proportions 2 by 3) has two equal horizontal stripes, of red and green, with a five-pointed gold star in the centre. The capital is Ouagadougou.

CONTEMPORARY POLITICAL HISTORY

Historical Context

Burkina Faso became a self-governing republic (as Upper Volta) within the French Community in December 1958 and achieved independence on 5 August 1960, with Maurice Yaméogo as President. In January 1966 Yaméogo was deposed in a *coup d'état*, led by Lt-Col (later Gen.) Sangoulé Lamizana, the army Chief of Staff, who took office as President and Prime Minister. The new regime dissolved the legislature, suspended the Constitution and established a Conseil suprême des forces armées. A new Constitution, approved by referendum in June 1970, provided for a return to civilian rule after a four-year transitional period. The Union démocratique voltaïque (UDV) won 37 of the 57 seats in elections for an Assemblée nationale, held in December. In early 1971 Lamizana appointed the UDV leader, Gérard Ouédraogo, as Prime Minister at the head of a mixed civilian and military Council of Ministers.

In February 1974 Lamizana announced that the army had again assumed power and a 65-member Conseil national consultatif pour le renouveau was formed. Political activity resumed in October 1977, and in the following month a referendum approved a draft Constitution providing for a return to civilian rule. The UDV won 28 of the 57 seats at elections to a new Assemblée nationale, held in April 1978, while the Union nationale pour la défense de la démocratie (UNDD), led by Hermann Yaméogo (the son of the former President), secured 13 seats. In May Lamizana was elected President, and in July the Assemblée elected Lamizana's nominee, Dr Joseph Conombo, as Prime Minister.

In November 1980 Lamizana was overthrown in a bloodless coup, led by Col Saye Zerbo, and a new Government, comprising both army officers and civilians, was formed. Opposition to the Zerbo regime soon emerged, and in November 1982 Zerbo was deposed by a group of non-commissioned army officers. Maj. Jean-Baptiste Ouédraogo emerged as leader of the new regime, and a predominantly civilian Government was formed. A power struggle within the Government became apparent with the arrest, in May 1983, of radical left-wing elements, including Capt. Thomas Sankara, the recently appointed Prime Minister. Sankara and his supporters were released following a rebellion by commandos under the leadership of Capt. Blaise Compaoré.

In August 1983 Sankara seized power in a violent coup. A Conseil national révolutionnaire (CNR) was established, and Jean-Baptiste Ouédraogo and other opponents of the new administration were placed under house arrest. Compaoré, as Minister of State at the Presidency, became the regime's second-in-command. Administrative, judicial and military reforms were announced, and citizens were urged to join Comités pour la défense de la révolution, which played an important role in consolidating Sankara's position. In August 1984 the country was renamed Burkina Faso ('Land of the Incorruptible Men').

In December 1985 a long-standing border dispute with Mali erupted into a six-day war that left some 50 people dead. The conflict centred on a reputedly mineral-rich area known as the Agacher strip. Following a cease-fire, arranged by the regional defence grouping, Accord de non-agression et d'assistance en matière de défense, and as a result of an interim decision on the dispute delivered by the International Court of Justice (ICJ) in January 1986, troops were withdrawn from the Agacher area; both countries accepted the ICJ's ruling, made in December, that the territory be divided equally between the two.

Domestic Political Affairs

In October 1987 a self-styled Front populaire (FP), led by Compaoré, overthrew the CNR in a coup, in which Sankara was killed. A predominantly civilian Council of Ministers included seven members of the previous administration. Compaoré became Head of State. In April 1989 a new political grouping, the Organisation pour la démocratie populaire/Mouvement du travail (ODP/MT), was established, under the leadership of Clément Oumarou Ouédraogo. The dismissal of government members who had declined to join the new party was an indication that the ODP/MT was to assume a prominent role in Compaoré's regime.

In August 1989 an amnesty was proclaimed for all political prisoners. In the following month it was announced that the Commander-in-Chief of the Armed Forces and Minister of People's Defence and Security, Maj. Jean-Baptiste Boukary Lingani, and the Minister of Economic Promotion, Capt. Henri Zongo, had been executed, together with two others, following the discovery of a plot to overthrow Compaoré. It was widely believed that Lingani and Zongo had been opposed to aspects of economic reform, notably the principle of co-operation with the IMF and the World Bank (funding negotiations with which had begun in 1988). Compaoré subsequently assumed personal responsibility for defence.

The first congress of the FP, in March 1990, sanctioned the establishment of a commission to draft a new constitution that would define a process of 'democratization'. In April Oumarou Ouédraogo was dismissed from the Council of Ministers and replaced as Secretary for Political Affairs of the FP and as Secretary-General of the ODP/MT by Roch Marc-Christian Kaboré, hitherto Minister of Transport and Communications. The final draft of the Constitution, which was completed in late 1990, referred to Burkina Faso as a 'revolutionary, democratic, unitary and secular state'. Multi-party legislative and presidential elections, by universal suffrage, were to take place, while provision was made for the establishment of a second, appointed and consultative chamber of the legislature, the Chambre des représentants. In March 1991 the ODP/MT adopted Compaoré as the party's presidential candidate and renounced its Marxist-Leninist ideology. In May a congress was convened to restructure the FP and to provide for the separation, upon the adoption of the draft constitution, of the functions of the FP and the organs of state. Delegates also approved the rehabilitation of Maurice Yaméogo, and an appeal was made to all political exiles to return to Burkina.

About 49% of the registered electorate voted in the constitutional referendum, which took place on 2 June 1991: of these, 93% were reported to have endorsed the new Constitution, which thereby took effect on 11 June. A transitional Government, in which the ODP/MT retained a dominant role, was subsequently appointed, its most senior member being Kaboré (as Minister of State, responsible for the Co-ordination of Government Action). In July Hermann Yaméogo (who had been a senior member of the FP in early 1990, but was subsequently expelled from the organization), now leader of the Alliance pour la démocratie et la fédération (ADF), and several other representatives of parties outside the FP were appointed to the Government. In August, however, Yaméogo (who had announced his intention to contest the presidency) was one of three government members who resigned in protest against proposed electoral procedures. Seven further opposition members resigned from the transitional administration in September and joined the Coordination des forces démocratiques (CFD).

A presidential election proceeded on 1 December 1991, when Compaoré (who had resigned from the army to contest the presidency as a civilian) was elected, unopposed, with the support of 90.4% of those who voted. The CFD claimed that an abstention rate of 74.7% reflected the success of its appeal for a boycott of the poll. Compaoré was inaugurated as President on 24 December and four opposition members were appointed to the Government in February 1992, including Hermann Yaméogo as Minister of State.

Some 27 political parties contested the legislative elections, which were held on 24 May 1992. The ODP/MT won 78 of the 107 seats in the Assemblée des députés du peuple (ADP), and nine other parties secured representation. The rate of participation by voters was reported to have been around 35%. In June Compaoré appointed Youssouf Ouédraogo, hitherto President of the Economic and Social Council, as Prime Minister. Although his Council of Ministers included representatives of seven political parties, the ODP/MT was allocated most strategic posts.

In March 1994 Ouédraogo resigned, apparently prompted by the failure of the Government to negotiate a settlement for salary increases acceptable to workers' representatives, following the 50% devaluation of the CFA franc in January. Kaboré was appointed as the new premier. In February 1996 Kadré Désiré Ouédraogo, hitherto Deputy Governor of the Banque centrale des états de l'Afrique de l'ouest, replaced Kaboré as Prime Minister. At this time the ODP/MT and 10 other parties merged to form the Congrès pour la démocratie et le progrès (CDP), which was dominated by close allies of Compaoré, and the new premier subsequently joined the party.

Constitutional amendments and a new electoral code were approved by the ADP in January 1997. Notably, restrictions were removed on the renewal of the Head of State's mandate (hitherto renewable only once), the number of parliamentary seats was to be increased to 111 with effect from the forthcoming elections, and the ADP was renamed the Assemblée nationale. At elections to that body in May the CDP won a resounding victory, securing 101 seats.

Several prominent opposition figures, among them Hermann Yaméogo, whose party had become the Alliance pour la démocratie et la fédération—Rassemblement démocratique africain (ADF—RDA), and Joseph Ki-Zerbo, the leader of the principal opposition party in the legislature, the Parti pour la démocratie et le progrès (PDP), declined to participate in the presidential election held on 15 November 1998. Compaoré was challenged by two minor candidates and provisional results confirmed his decisive victory, with 87.5% of the valid votes cast. Despite the appeal by a prominent opposition coalition, the Groupe du 14 février (G-14f), for a boycott, the rate of voter participation, at 56.1%, was considerably higher than in 1991. A new Government, again headed by Ouédraogo, was appointed in January 1999.

The political climate deteriorated rapidly after Norbert Zongo, the managing editor of the newspaper *L'Indépendant*, was found dead, together with three colleagues, in December 1998. Zongo, a frequent critic of the Compaoré regime, had been investigating allegations that David Ouédraogo, a driver employed by François Compaoré, younger brother and special adviser of the President, had been tortured and killed by members of the presidential guard. However, the commission of inquiry set up to investigate the deaths stated that it was unable to prove the identity of the perpetrators.

Political reform

In June 1999 Compaoré established a Collège des sages, composed of Burkinabè state elders, and religious and ethnic leaders. The 16-member Collège was to promote national reconciliation and to investigate unpunished political crimes since independence. In mid-June the Collège ordered the arrest of the three members of the presidential guard accused of the murder of David Ouédraogo. The Collège's report, published in August, recommended the formation of both a government of national unity and a 'commission of truth and justice' to oversee the transition to a truly plural political system and to investigate unresolved political murders, including that of Sankara. The Collège further recommended the creation of a commission to investigate possible political reforms. Opposition organizations rejected the proposed amnesty for those implicated during the investigations of the commission of truth and justice and criticized the need for the President to assent to any proposed reforms. Meanwhile, proposals to form a government of national unity were impeded by the demands of most opposition parties that legal action be expedited in the cases of David Ouédraogo and Norbert Zongo. Thus, the reshuffled Council of Ministers, announced in October, included just two representatives of the opposition. In November, the two advisory commissions, the formation of which had been recommended by the Collège des sages, were inaugurated. Despite official assurances that the commissions' findings would be binding, the G-14f refused to participate.

In January 2000 the ruling CDP organized a public demonstration in favour of the proposals made by the commission on political reform, including a restriction of the presidential mandate to no more than two successive terms. The Assemblée nationale subsequently voted to revise the electoral code and to accord greater powers to a restructured independent electoral commission: the Commission électorale nationale indépendante (CENI). The opposition, however, criticized what they perceived to be the limited nature of the reforms and expressed their determination to boycott any elections until the Ouédraogo and Zongo cases had been fully resolved. The commission on national reconciliation published its report in February, urging the prosecution of those suspected of involvement in the embezzlement of public funds and in political killings. The commission also called for greater freedom of speech, of the press, and of assembly, the resolution of legal proceedings in the Ouédraogo and Zongo cases, the enactment of an amnesty law, and the construction of a monument to former President Sankara.

The Assemblée nationale approved revisions to the electoral code in April 2000; under the new regulations, which introduced a system of proportional representation, 90 deputies would be elected from regional lists, while 21 would be elected from a national list. The new legislation also reduced the presidential mandate from seven to five years, renewable only once. However, as the new limits were not to take effect until the next election, Compaoré would be permitted to contest the presidential elections due in 2005 and 2010. In addition, the Assemblée approved significant judicial reforms, which provided for the abolition of the Supreme Court and the replacement of its four permanent chambers with four new state institutions: a Constitutional Council, a Council of State, a Court of Appeal and a National Audit Court.

In November 2000 Prime Minister Kadré Désiré Ouédraogo resigned; he was succeeded by Paramanga Ernest Yonli, hitherto the Minister of the Civil Service and Institutional Development. Compaoré subsequently formed a 36-member Council of Ministers, including 12 members of the opposition.

Meanwhile, the trial of the soldiers accused of murdering David Ouédraogo began in August 2000. The military tribunal sentenced two members of Compaoré's presidential guard, including Marcel Kafando, head of the guard at the time of Ouédraogo's death, to 20 years' imprisonment, with a third member sentenced to 10 years'. In February 2001 Kafando was charged with arson and the murder of Norbert Zongo and three others. In March, at a rally attended by some 30,000 people, President Compaoré apologized for 176 unpunished crimes allegedly committed by state representatives since independence in 1960. This act constituted the most significant element of a 'day of forgiveness' that had been proposed by the Collège des sages, but which was boycotted by, among others, relations of Sankara and Zongo. Dissatisfaction at the Government's failure to resolve the Zongo case continued, and in June 2001 several thousand people participated in a demonstration in Ouagadougou calling for those whom they believed to have ordered the killing of Zongo, including François Compaoré, to be brought to justice. However, in August, following the appointment of two of their members to the CENI, the constituent parties of the G-14f announced their intention to contest the forthcoming legislative elections. Michel Tapsoba, a human rights activist, was elected as Chairman of the CENI in the following month. In November it was announced that the judicial investigation into Kafando's alleged involvement in Zongo's death had been hampered by the poor health of the defendant. (In August 2006 an appeals court confirmed the dismissal of all charges against Kafando.)

In February 2002 the Assemblée nationale adopted a constitutional amendment, providing for the abolition of the Chambre des représentants, following the failure to appoint replacement representatives for those whose terms had expired in December 2001. On 5 May some 30 parties contested elections to the Assemblée nationale. The CDP remained the largest party, securing 57 of the 111 seats, with 49.5% of the votes cast, although its representation was much reduced. The ADF—RDA won 17 seats, with 12.6% of the votes cast, becoming the largest opposition party, followed by the PDP—PS (as the PDP had become, following its merger with the Parti socialiste burkinabè in mid-2001), with 10 seats. Kaboré was elected as President of the Assemblée nationale in June, prior to the reappointment of Yonli as Prime Minister. Despite the slim majority held by the CDP in the Assemblée nationale and the precedent set by the inclusion of ministers from opposition parties in the outgoing administration, the new 31-member Government did not contain any representatives of the opposition.

In October 2003 the Government announced that the authorities had prevented a planned *coup d'état*. By January 2004 some 15 members of the armed forces, including several members of the presidential guard, and two civilians, notably Norbert Tiendrébéogo, the Chairman of the Front des forces sociales (FFS), had been arrested on suspicion of involvement in the alleged plot. The reputed leader of the group, Capt. Luther Ouali, was subsequently convicted of treason and complicity with a foreign power and sentenced to 10 years' imprisonment.

The 2005 presidential election

In March 2005 it was announced that the first round of the presidential election would take place on 13 November. Local elections, which had previously also been expected to be held in early November, were postponed until 12 February 2006. In the following months a number of candidates for the presidency emerged, including three candidates representing a 12-party opposition alliance, known as Alternance 2005, namely: Hermann Yaméogo now of the Union nationale pour la démocratie et le développement (UNDD); Philippe Ouédraogo of the Parti africain de l'indépendance; and Bénéwendé Stanislas Sankara of the Union pour la renaissance—Mouvement sankariste. Other candidates included Tiendrébéogo, for the FFS, and Prof. Ali Lankoandé (who had recently succeeded Ki-Zerbo as the party's President) for the PDP—PS. In June Compaoré announced his intention to seek a further term as the candidate of the CDP (28 smaller parties also declared their support for Compaoré); this announcement, although widely anticipated, was a cause of some controversy, and prompted several opposition parties, including those of Alternance 2005, to demand a ruling by the Constitutional Court as to whether the constitutional amendments approved in 2000 (which, notably, restricted Presidents to two terms of office) applied retroactively.

Following a ruling by the Constitutional Court in October 2005 confirming that Compaoré was entitled to contest both the forthcoming election, and that scheduled to be held in 2010, Hermann Yaméogo announced that he was to withdraw from the contest (although his name remained on the ballot paper), and the UNDD called for a campaign of civil disobedience against what it termed a 'forceful step towards the installation of an absolute republican monarch'.

The presidential election was held, as scheduled, on 13 November 2005. According to official results, Compaoré obtained an overwhelming victory, securing 80.4% of the votes cast; the second-placed candidate was Sankara, with just 4.9%. Around 57% of the registered electorate participated in the election, and international election observers declared themselves largely satisfied with the conduct of the election, although some concern was expressed at relatively low levels of voter registration. Compaoré was inaugurated to a further term of office on 20 December. In January 2006 he reappointed Yonli as Prime Minister, heading a new Government that included several members of opposition parties, although many of the principal positions remained unchanged from the outgoing administration.

The premiership of Tertius Zongo

A total of 47 parties contested the legislative elections held on 6 May 2007. The CDP increased its majority in the Assemblée nationale, securing 73 of the 111 available seats (16 more than in the 2002 elections); the ADF—RDA took 14 and the remaining seats were shared by 11 parties. Voter turn-out was reported to be 56.4%. The following month Prime Minister Yonli tendered his resignation and that of his Government. President Compaoré subsequently named Tertius Zongo, hitherto the Burkinabè ambassador to the USA, as Yonli's successor and in mid-June a new Council of Ministers was sworn in.

The civil unrest of 2006 involving demonstrations against escalating fuel prices was followed in February 2008 by protests over the rising cost of living, particularly the sharp increase in food prices (in the year to March the price of corn had reportedly doubled). In Banfora, Ouahigouya and Bobo-Dioulasso rioters attacked government offices, shops and petrol stations; the violence lasted for two days, leading to hundreds of arrests. The Government responded by suspending import taxes on certain staple goods rather than lowering prices. Violent protests took place in Ouagadougou later in February after opposition groups called for a day of strikes and civil action in the capital. Further arrests were made, including that of the leader of the opposition Rassemblement démocratique et populaire, Thibault Nana, who was alleged to have organized the demonstration. In early March it was reported that 29 people had been sentenced to between three and 36 months in prison for their parts in the protests, amid accusations that protesters had been abused while in custody and denied proper legal representation. A new coalition of civil society organizations, including human rights groups and trade unions, was formed, and on 15 March led a demonstration in the capital to demand an increase in salaries and a reduction in the price of basic goods, threatening a two-day general strike if the Government did not comply. Similar demonstrations took place in other towns but there were no repeats of the violence that had occurred in February, and no arrests were made. The Government continued to refuse to meet the demands of the protesters and the two-day strike commenced peacefully on 8 April, although it did not precipitate a change in the Government's stance. In December it was reported that the cost of rice was 30% higher than it had been in the previous year, despite a local harvest of 235,800 metric tons in 2008, more than three times that of 2007, when just 69,000 tons were harvested.

In April and May 2009 the Assemblée nationale adopted several amendments to the electoral system, including a stipulation that women comprise at least 30% of political organizations' candidate lists for legislative and municipal elections, and a reduction in the percentage of votes that parties are required to secure in elections to be eligible for state funding from 5% to 3%. Also approved was a specification that the official leader of the parliamentary opposition should not come from a party supportive of the Government (the ADF—RDA had hitherto provided the holder of this position, being the second largest party in the legislature, despite its support for Compaoré's administration).

Recent developments: the 2010 presidential election

In February 2010 the Government announced that the first round of voting for the presidential elections would take place on 21 November. Electoral lists were to be established between 1 and 21 March; however, a low registration rate (20%) in this period led to a prorogation to 15 April. By the end of the electoral registration process the CENI announced that only 3.3m. out of some 14m. citizens eligible to vote had registered. Also in March a minor government reorganization took place predominantly affecting those ministries responsible for financial matters: Adrien Koné became Minister of Labour and Social Security, while François Marie Didié Zoundi was appointed Minister-delegate to the Minister of the Economy and Finance, responsible for the Budget. Furthermore, Léonce Koné resigned from his position as head of the Banque Agricole et Commerciale du Burkina to become Minister of Industry, Trade, Business Promotion and Crafts. Meanwhile, Coalition 37 was formed by 15 political parties opposed to plans by the Government to revise Article 37 of the Constitution, adopted in 2000 (see above), which restricted the presidential election term to two mandates.

In August 2010 the ruling CDP approved Compaoré's candidature for the presidency and requested that the constitutional limitation on the number of presidential terms that could be served be abolished. In October legislation was adopted postponing municipal elections scheduled to take place in April 2011 in order that they be held concurrently with legislative elections in May 2012. According to provisional results released by the CENI four days after the presidential election (which was held as scheduled on 21 November 2010) took place, Compaoré recorded an overwhelming victory, securing 80.2% of the votes cast. His closest rivals, the deputy mayor of Dori, Hama Arba Diallo, and Sankara took just 8.2% and 6.3% of the votes, respectively. The rate of voter participation was recorded at some 55%. Diallo and Sankara were among four defeated candidates who contested the results of the ballot; however, on 4 December the Constitutional Council announced its rejection of their appeals and on 8 December confirmed Compaoré as the winner of the election, having made only minor adjustments to the number of votes attributed to the seven candidates.

On 21 December 2010 Compaoré was sworn in for what was scheduled to be his final, five-year presidential term. Prime Minister Zongo announced his resignation, and that of his Government, on 12 January 2011, but was reappointed to the premiership the following day, and on 16 January a new, 38-member Council of Ministers was named. It included eight new appointees but was again formed by members of the CDP. The former President of the Assemblée nationale, Bognessan Arsène

Ye joined the Government as Minister of State, Minister at the Presidency, in charge of Political Reform, and was to oversee constitutional changes and the creation of an upper chamber of the legislature. Léonce Koné was replaced by Patiendé Arthur Kafando, formerly head of the Société nationale des postes (Sonapost), while the hitherto Director-General of the Société Nationale Burkinabè d'Electricité, Salif Lamoussa Kaboré, was appointed Minister of Mines, Quarries and Energy. The former President of the Appeals Court and Secretary-General of the Justice Ministry, Jérôme Traoré became Minister of Justice, Keeper of the Seals.

During the first half of 2011 there were numerous outbreaks of severe unrest that threatened Compaoré's administration. The death of a student, Justin Zongo, in police custody in the town of Koudougou, some 75 km west of Ouagadougou, provoked violent protests in late February, in which six people were reportedly killed. The Governor of the Centre-ouest region, of which Koudougou is the capital, was subsequently dismissed. Military strife followed in late March, when troops from two army camps protested in Ouagadougou, and tensions escalated on 14 April, when a mutiny by members of the presidential guard, over unpaid housing and food allowances, prompted Compaoré to flee Ouagadougou for several hours. Compaoré responded the following day, upon his return to the capital, by dismissing his Government and imposing an overnight curfew. The Chief of the General Staff of the Armed Forces and the head of the presidential guard were also replaced. On 18 April Luc Adolphe Tiao, hitherto ambassador to France, was appointed as the new Prime Minister, and although a new Government (reduced in size from 38 to 29 ministers) was announced on 21 April, it was not functional until mid-May. Yipènè Djibril Bassolet, who had served as Minister of Foreign Affairs and Regional Co-operation in Zongo's first administration, returned to that post, while Compaoré himself assumed responsibility for the defence portfolio. Later in April protests were carried out by students and members of the police force and a reported 10,000 civilians participated in nation-wide protests against high food and fuel prices. In early May the Government introduced a series of emergency measures aimed at allaying public discontent over the high cost of living, including a reduction in the prices of certain staple foodstuffs and a 10% cut in taxes on salaries. Nevertheless, on 14 May thousands of women staged a further anti-government protest; two days later the curfew was lifted.

Throughout the unrest analysts had highlighted a culture of impunity that needed to be addressed, and from mid-2011 numerous individuals were punished for their roles in the disturbances. In early June Compaoré replaced 13 regional governors, while in July 566 soldiers were discharged from the armed forces and 217 were detained on charges of rebellion. Three police officers were jailed in August for their involvement in the death of Zongo, and in September the military chiefs in the regions of Kaya and Bobo-Dioulasso were also replaced. A number of economic measures were also taken by the Government in late 2011 to mollify dissent: a 5% increase in salary and pension benefits was announced for public sector workers (although trade unions had demanded a 30% rise) and the Government pledged to create 50,000 new jobs, alongside 45,000 apprenticeships for young people, by the end of 2014.

Meanwhile, the CENI was also overhauled. In June 2011 opposition members resigned from the CENI citing a lack of confidence in the ability of its President to organize transparent legislative elections in May 2012. Initially measures were announced for CENI members to be replaced before the end of their current mandate, which was due to expire at the end of September 2011; however, a law was passed in July dissolving the current composition of the Commission. In early August Barthélemy Kéré was elected as the new President of the CENI, and in October it was announced that the legislative and municipal elections had been deferred until November 2012 to allow for a system of biometric voter cards to be introduced.

Foreign Affairs

Compaoré has, in recent years, gained wide recognition for his efforts as a regional mediator and as a proponent of inter-African conflict-resolution initiatives. Most recently, after opposition protesters were killed at a rally in September 2009 in Conakry, Guinea, the Economic Community of West African States (ECOWAS, see p. 264) appointed Compaoré to mediate in the crisis. In the early 1990s, however, relations with some members of ECOWAS were difficult, owing to the Compaoré Government's support for Charles Taylor's rebel National Patriotic Front of Liberia (NPFL) and Burkina's refusal to participate in the military intervention by the ECOWAS cease-fire monitoring group (ECOMOG) in Liberia. Nevertheless, in February 1997 the Burkinabè legislature approved legislation authorizing the participation of military personnel in ECOMOG, and members of the country's military subsequently remained in Liberia to assist in the training of new armed forces. In early 1999 President Ahmed Tejan Kabbah of Sierra Leone and the Nigerian Government alleged that Burkina Faso and Liberia were co-operating to provide support and supply arms to the rebel fighters of the Revolutionary United Front (RUF) in Sierra Leone. In early 2000 a report to the UN Security Council accused Burkina of having supplied weapons to the RUF in exchange for diamonds on several occasions. It was also alleged that Burkina had supplied weapons to Liberia and to Angolan rebel groups, despite international embargoes on the supply of weapons to those countries. The report was strenuously denied by the Burkinabè Government. Two missions from the UN Security Council visited Burkina Faso in mid-2000, at the invitation of the Burkinabè authorities, to investigate the claims regarding the breaching of arms embargoes against Angola and Sierra Leone. Although Compaoré, in May 2001, criticized a decision by the UN to impose travel restrictions on Liberian officials, relations with the Taylor Government subsequently deteriorated. In July 2002 the Burkinabè Government hosted a conference intended to promote a peaceful resolution of the political crisis in Liberia, at which Taylor's Government was not represented. Moreover, Compaoré stated that he regarded Taylor's resignation as President of Liberia in August 2003 as a positive development, which would encourage the stabilization of the region.

In early November 1999 a dispute over land rights between Burkinabè settlers in the south-west of Côte d'Ivoire and the indigenous minority Krou population led to the violent and systematic expulsion from the region of several hundred Burkinabè plantation workers. Several deaths were reported, and some 20,000 expatriates subsequently returned to Burkina. Following the *coup d'état* in Côte d'Ivoire in December, the military authorities assured the Government of Burkina that the expulsions would cease and that measures would be taken in order to allow workers to return. None the less, tensions between the two countries intensified as the former Prime Minister of Côte d'Ivoire, Alassane Ouattara, was excluded from participation in the Ivorian presidential election of October 2000 because of his Burkinabè origins. Following a coup attempt in Abidjan in early January 2001, which the Ivorian Government attributed to the influence of unnamed, neighbouring states, attacks on Burkinabè expatriates in Côte d'Ivoire reportedly increased; by late January it was reported that up to 10,000 Burkinabè were returning to Burkina each week. In early July a meeting between Compaoré and the Ivorian President, Laurent Gbagbo, in Sirte, Libya, was reported to have defused tensions somewhat between the two countries.

Following the outbreak of unrest in northern Côte d'Ivoire in mid-September 2002, Gbagbo again alleged that an unnamed, neighbouring country was implicated in the rebellion; these allegations were widely believed to refer to Burkina, although the Burkinabè Government denied any involvement in the uprising. However, in late November, following an attack on the residence of the Burkinabè President in Abidjan, the Ivorian Minister of Agriculture and Rural Development met Compaoré to express the Ivorian Government's regret for the attack. A statement by Compaoré in an interview with the French newspaper *Le Parisien*, in late January 2003, to the effect that the restoration of peace in Côte d'Ivoire would necessitate the resignation of Gbagbo as President of that country, led to a further deterioration in relations between the two countries. As a result of the upsurge in violence in Côte d'Ivoire, at least 350,000 Burkinabè citizens were reported to have fled Côte d'Ivoire for Burkina by mid-2003. The Burkinabè authorities closed the common border of the two countries in September 2002, reopening it in September 2003. Relations between the two countries subsequently became more cordial, and in late 2003 Compaoré hosted meetings with several prominent Ivorian leaders, including Gbagbo, Prime Minister Seydou Diarra and former rebel leader Guillaume Soro, emphasizing the need to develop bilateral co-operation. In March 2007 Compaoré brokered a peace agreement between Gbagbo and Soro which provided for the reunification of the country, the disarmament of rebels and the dismantling of militia groups, and the establishment of an electoral timetable. In December 2008 Compaoré was again instrumental in the signing of a further accord between Gbagbo and Soro (who had been appointed Prime Minister in April 2007) to integrate rebel troops into the Ivorian police force. Following the Ivorian presidential election run-off of November 2010 and Gbagbo's refusal to relinquish the presidency to the internationally recognized victor, Alassane Ouattara, Compaoré was among a number of African heads of state who endorsed attempts by ECOWAS and the African Union to seek Gbagbo's removal from power. The political crisis in Côte d'Ivoire had significant negative economic consequences for Burkina according to an IMF report in October 2011, largely in terms of transportation costs as alternative methods of transport were sought after the closure of the railroad system and for small companies relying on imported spare parts from the neighbouring country.

During 2003–04 the Mauritanian President Col Maaouiya Ould Sid'Ahmed Taya and his administration repeatedly accused the Government of Burkina Faso of supporting a series of attempted *coups d'état* in Mauritania. The Burkinabè authorities denied claims that, in collaboration with Libya, they had provided refuge, funding, arms and training facilities to the rebels, particularly Saleh Ould Hnana and Capt. Abderahmane Ould Mini, who admitted attempting to overthrow President Taya's regime during the trial of 181 suspects which commenced in Mauritania in late 2004. Also among the accused, tried *in absentia*, was Sidi Mohamed Mustapha Ould Limam Chavi, a Mauritanian-born adviser to President Compaoré. In protest at the alleged conduct of the Burkinabè Government, President Taya did not attend the 10th Summit of La Francophonie, held in Ouagadougou in November 2004. Relations between Burkina Faso and Mauritania improved following the overthrow of Taya's regime in August 2005, with the new President, Col Ely Ould Mohamed Vall, attending President Compaoré's inauguration to a new term of office in December. In March 2006 Compaoré consolidated relations by paying a state visit to Nouakchott, the Mauritanian capital.

After a meeting held in the Beninois town of Porga in March 2008, ministers from Burkina Faso and Benin announced that a long-running border dispute between the two countries had been resolved, with a commitment from both sides that neither would make any further 'visible sovereignty acts' (including building police stations or displaying national flags) in the 68-sq km contested zone. In 2009 a 10-km area of border that remained in dispute was referred to the ICJ (see Benin Contemporary Political History).

CONSTITUTION AND GOVERNMENT

Under the terms of the Constitution of June 1991, as subsequently revised, executive power is vested in the President and in the Government, and is counterbalanced by a legislative Assemblée nationale, and by an independent judiciary. Presidential and legislative elections are conducted by universal adult suffrage, in the context of a multi-party political system. The President is elected for a seven-year term, and delegates to the Assemblée nationale are elected for a five-year term. In April 2000 the Assemblée nationale adopted legislation, effective from the next elections, which reduced the presidential mandate from seven to five years, renewable only once, and introduced a system of proportional representation for elections to the Assemblée nationale, according to which 90 deputies would be elected from a regional list, while 21 would be elected from a national list. The President is empowered to appoint a Prime Minister; however, the Assemblée nationale has the right to veto any such appointment.

An amendment to the electoral code in April 2004 changed the electoral unit from the region to the province. Each province is administered by a civilian governor.

REGIONAL AND INTERNATIONAL CO-OPERATION

Burkina Faso is a member of numerous regional organizations, including the Economic Community of West African States (ECOWAS, see p. 264), the West African organs of the Franc Zone (see p. 333), the Community of Sahel-Saharan States (see p. 449), the Conseil de l'Entente (see p. 449), the Liptako–Gourma Integrated Development Authority (see p. 451), and the Permanent Inter-State Committee on Drought Control in the Sahel (CILSS, see p. 452).Burkina Faso is also a member of the African Union (see p. 189)

Burkina Faso became a member of the UN in 1960 and was admitted to the World Trade Organization (WTO, see p. 433) in 1995. Burkina participates in the Group of 77 (G77, see p. 450) developing countries. In May 2008 the country was elected to sit on the 47-member UN Human Rights Council for a term of three years, and in 2012 Burkina began a three-year term on the UN Economic and Social Council (UNESCO).

ECONOMIC AFFAIRS

In 2010, according to estimates by the World Bank, Burkina Faso's gross national income (GNI), measured at average 2008–10 prices, was US $9,031m., equivalent to $550 per head (or $1,250 on an international purchasing-power parity basis). During 2001–10, it was estimated, the population increased at an average annual rate of 3.0%, while gross domestic product (GDP) per head increased, in real terms, by an average of 2.6% per year. Overall GDP increased, in real terms, at an average annual rate of 5.6% in 2001–10; growth in 2010 was 9.2%.

Agriculture (including forestry and fishing) contributed an estimated 34.8% of GDP in 2009, according to the African Development Bank (AfDB). According to FAO estimates, 92.0% of the employed labour force were engaged in agriculture in mid-2012. The principal cash crop is cotton (exports of which accounted for an estimated 28.2% of the value of total exports in 2009). Smaller amounts of other crops, including karité nuts (sheanuts) and sesame seed, are also exported. The main subsistence crops are sorghum, millet and maize. Burkina is almost self-sufficient in basic foodstuffs in non-drought years. Livestock-rearing is of considerable significance, contributing 9.7% of GDP in 2002 and an estimated 9.0% of export revenue in 2005. According to the AfDB, during 2000–07 agricultural GDP increased at an average annual rate of 5.3%. Agricultural GDP increased by 1.9% in 2009.

Industry (including mining, manufacturing, construction and power) contributed an estimated 23.6% of GDP in 2009, according to the AfDB, but engaged only 3.1% of the employed labour force in 2005. According to the AfDB, during 2000–07 industrial GDP increased at an average annual rate of 8.7%; industrial GDP increased by 6.4% in 2007.

Although Burkina has considerable mineral resources, extractive activities accounted for just 2.8% of GDP in 2009, according to the AfDB, and engaged only 0.3% of the employed labour force in 2005. However, the development of reserves of gold (exports of which contributed an estimated 35.7% of the value of total exports in 2009) has brought about an increase in the sector's economic importance, while there is considerable potential, subject to the development of an adequate infrastructure, for the exploitation of manganese, zinc and limestone. In mid-2007 it was reported that the recently reopened gold mine at Taparko-Bouroum had yielded its first metal for 20 years. Gold production amounted to some 13,181 kg in 2009, according to the US Geological Survey. The country's other known mineral reserves include phosphates, silver, lead and nickel. Between 2007 and 2010 six gold mines and one manganese mine began production. An increase in the number of exploration permits granted (537 in 2008 and 599 in 2009, compared with only 350 between 2003 and 2007) and a rise in market prices resulted in a significant increase in gold production, and the commodity replaced cotton as Burkina's primary export product.

The manufacturing sector engaged only 2.0% of the employed labour force in 2005, and contributed 12.0% of GDP in 2009, according to the AfDB. The sector is dominated by the processing of primary products: major activities are cotton-ginning, the production of textiles, food-processing (including milling and sugar-refining), brewing and the processing of tobacco and of hides and skins. Motorcycles and bicycles are also assembled. According to the AfDB, manufacturing GDP increased at an average annual rate of 8.8% in 2000–07; the GDP of the sector increased by 10.6% in 2008 and by 0.4% in 2009.

The construction and public works sector engaged only 0.4% of the employed labour force in 1996, and contributed 7.4% of GDP in 2009, according to the AfDB. The sector grew by 4.8% in 2009.

In 2007 some 81.9% of Burkina's total electricity production came from hydroelectric sources; the remainder (19.1%) was derived from thermal power stations (using imported fuel). The country's hydropower capacity is being expanded, and in 2000 the interconnection of the south of Burkina Faso with the electricity network of Côte d'Ivoire was finalized (although supply was disrupted by the Ivorian political crisis in 2011); a link with Ghana's electricity grid is also planned. Imports of petroleum accounted for an estimated 23.6% of the value of total merchandise imports in 2009.

The services sector contributed an estimated 41.6% of GDP in 2009, according to the AfDB, and engaged 12.3% of the employed labour force in 2005. According to the AfDB, the GDP of the services sector increased at an average annual rate of 5.0% in 2000–07; growth was 2.7% in 2006.

According to the IMF, in 2010 Burkina recorded a visible trade deficit of 144,100m. francs CFA, while there was a deficit of an estimated 152,200m. francs CFA on the current account of the balance of payments. In 2008 the principal source of imports was Côte d'Ivoire (which provided 14.5% of the total) and other major trading partners were France, the People's Republic of China, the USA and India. The principal market for exports in that year was Switzerland (taking 39.3% of exports). Other major trading partners were France and Côte d'Ivoire. The principal exports in 2008 were textiles and clothing (41.1% of the total), pearls, gems and precious metals, and vegetable products. In the same year the principal imports were mineral products, machinery and transport materials, chemical products, base metals, vegetable products, and prepared foodstuffs and beverages.

In 2011 Burkina was projected to have an estimated overall budget deficit of 183,800m. francs CFA. Burkina's general government gross debt was 1,185,170m. francs CFA in 2010, equivalent to 27.1% of GDP. Burkina's total external debt was US $1,835m. at the end of 2009, of which $1,725m. was public and publicly guaranteed debt. In that year the cost of servicing long-term public and publicly guaranteed debt and repayments to the IMF was equivalent to 1.7% of the value of exports of goods, services and income (excluding workers' remittances). In 2000–10 the average annual rate of inflation was 2.8%. Consumer prices increased by 2.7% in 2009 but decreased by 2.4% in 2010. Some 71,280 people were unemployed in 1996, according to the national census, equivalent to only 1.4% of the total labour force. According to official figures the unemployed population represented 2.7% in 2005 and the inactive population represented 13.4%, giving a combined rate of 16.2%.

Burkina Faso remains one of the poorest nations in the world and, largely owing to its very poor health and education indicators, was ranked 181st out of 187 countries on the UN Development Programme's 2011 human development index. Economic activity in the late 2000s was negatively affected by the global economic crisis, and GDP growth declined from 5.0% in 2008 to 3.5% in 2009. In mid-2010 a new Extended Credit Facility (ECF) worth US $67.7m. was agreed with the IMF for fiscal consolidation to sustain macroeconomic stability: $10.9m. was disbursed immediately for structural reforms supporting the private sector. Nevertheless, the IMF produced an optimistic end of year report in 2011, predicting that GDP would be maintained above 5.5% in 2012, due to expansion in the mining sector, high global gold prices and high capital inflows. The annual inflation rate, however, was projected to rise from 1.4% in 2011 to 2.0% in 2012 and this was forecast to be accompanied by a current account deficit of 6.9%, a significant increase on the 3.6% of the previous year. Poor rains in 2009 had led to a 17% decline in cereal production and in 2010 many dams burst, resulting in the flooding of 2,000 ha of agricultural land in eastern Burkina and 400 ha in the centre of the country. Continuing difficult agricultural conditions were exacerbated in 2011 by social unrest and rises in global oil and food prices (maize rose by 8%, sorghum by 5% and millet by 3%) while the country also suffered from droughts. In an attempt to forestall further agricultural decline, in the early 2010s a seed procurement and distribution programme to 100,000 farmers was carried out by the UN, organized by FAO and in part funded by the European Union. Furthermore, government subsidies were put in place to supply 100,000 ploughs to smallholders, one-half of whom were women. This supplemented funds of $54.5m. made available by the World Bank for the period 2010–15 to combat food insecurity, and the Government also requested that companies in the mining industry—the overwhelming majority of which were foreign owned—include measures to help fight poverty in their investment plans.

PUBLIC HOLIDAYS

2013: 1 January (New Year's Day), 4 February (Mouloud, Birth of the Prophet), 8 March (International Women's Day), 1 April (Easter Monday), 1 May (Labour Day), 9 May (Ascension Day), 5 August (Independence Day), 7 August* (Aid es Segheir, end of Ramadan), 15 August (Assumption), 1 November (All Saints' Day), 14 October* (Aid el Kebir—Tabaski, Feast of the Sacrifice), 11 December (Proclamation of the Republic), 25 December (Christmas).

* These holidays are dependent on the Islamic lunar calendar and may vary by one or two days from the dates given.

Statistical Survey

Source (except where otherwise stated): Institut National de la Statistique et de la Démographie, 555 blvd de la Révolution, 01 BP 374, Ouagadougou 01; tel. 50-32-49-76; fax 50-32-61-59; e-mail insd@cenatrin.bf; internet www.insd.bf.

Area and Population

AREA, POPULATION AND DENSITY

Area (sq km)	274,200*
Population (census results)	
10 December 1996	10,312,609
9–23 December 2006	
Males	6,768,739
Females	7,248,523
Total	14,017,262
Population (UN estimates at mid-year)†	
2010	16,468,714
2011	16,967,845
2012	17,481,982
Density (per sq km) at mid-2012	63.8

* 105,870 sq miles.

† Source: UN, *World Population Prospects: The 2010 Revision.*

POPULATION BY AGE AND SEX
(UN estimates at mid-2012)

	Males	Females	Total
0–14	4,014,128	3,873,958	7,888,086
15–64	4,515,626	4,682,298	9,197,924
65 and over	156,291	239,681	395,972
Total	8,686,045	8,795,937	17,481,982

Source: UN, *World Population Prospects: The 2010 Revision.*

ETHNIC GROUPS

1995 (percentages): Mossi 47.9; Peul 10.3; Bobo 6.9; Lobi 6.9; Mandé 6.7; Sénoufo 5.3; Gourounsi 5.0; Gourmantché 4.8; Tuareg 3.1; others 3.1 (Source: La Francophonie).

PROVINCES
(population at 2006 census)

	Population	Capital	Population of capital
Balé	213,423	Boromo	29,849
Bam	275,191	Kongoussi	70,840
Banwa	269,375	Solenzo	121,819
Bazèga	238,425	Kombissiri	67,964
Bougouriba	101,479	Diébougou	42,067
Boulgou	543,570	Tenkodogo	124,985
Boulkiemdé	505,206	Koudougou	138,209
Comoé	407,528	Banfora	109,824
Ganzourgou	319,380	Zorgho	48,096
Gnagna	408,669	Bogandé	84,838
Gourma	305,936	Fada N'Gourma	124,577
Houet	955,451	Bobo-Dioulasso (rural)	64,075
Ioba	192,321	Dano	46,469
Kadiogo	1,727,390	Ouagadougou	1,475,223
Kénédougou	285,695	Orodara	31,632
Komandjari	79,507	Gayéri	48,757
Kompienga	75,867	Pama	37,296
Kossi	278,546	Nouna	73,006
Koulpélogo	258,667	Ouargaye	32,658
Kouritenga	329,779	Koupéla	58,411

—continued	Population	Capital	Population of capital
Kourwéogo	138,217	Boussé	43,352
Léraba	124,280	Sindou	18,280
Loroum	142,853	Titao	66,717
Mouhoun	297,350	Dédougou	86,965
Nahouri	157,071	Pô	51,552
Namentenga	328,820	Boulsa	81,967
Nayala	163,433	Toma	29,451
Noumbiel	70,036	Batié	31,963
Oubritenga	238,775	Ziniaré	62,972
Oudalan	195,964	Gorom-Gorom	106,346
Passoré	323,222	Yako	80,926
Poni	256,931	Gaoua	52,733
Sanguié	297,036	Réo	61,960
Sanmatenga	598,014	Kaya	117,122
Séno	264,991	Dori	106,808
Sissili	208,409	Léo	51,037
Soum	347,335	Djibo	60,042
Sourou	220,622	Tougan	67,589
Tapoa	342,305	Diapaga	32,620
Tuy	228,458	Houndé	76,998
Yagha	160,152	Sebba	32,374
Yatenga	553,164	Ouahigouya	125,030
Ziro	175,915	Sapouy	55,968
Zondoma	166,557	Gourcy	81,226
Zoundwéogo	245,947	Manga	33,042
Total	14,017,262		

PRINCIPAL TOWNS
(population at 2006 census)

Ouagadougou (capital)	1,475,223	Kaya	54,365
Bobo-Dioulasso	489,967	Tenkodogo	44,491
Koudougou	88,184	Fada N'gourma	41,785
Banfora	75,917	Dédougou	38,862
Ouahigouya	73,153	Houndé	34,669

Mid-2010 (incl. suburbs, UN estimate): Ouagadougou 1,907,951 (Source: UN, *World Urbanization Prospects: The 2009 Revision*).

BIRTHS AND DEATHS
(annual averages, UN estimates)

	1995–2000	2000–05	2005–10
Birth rate (per 1,000)	45.8	44.9	43.9
Death rate (per 1,000)	15.6	14.2	12.6

Source: UN, *World Population Prospects: The 2010 Revision*.

Life expectancy (years at birth, WHO estimates): 52 (males 49; females 56) in 2009 (Source: WHO, *World Health Statistics*).

ECONOMICALLY ACTIVE POPULATION
(1996 census, persons aged 10 years and over)

	Males	Females	Total
Agriculture, hunting, forestry and fishing	2,284,744	2,229,124	4,513,868
Mining and quarrying	2,946	1,033	3,979
Manufacturing	46,404	25,161	71,565
Electricity, gas and water	2,279	534	2,813
Construction	20,678	398	21,076
Trade, restaurants and hotels	98,295	126,286	224,581
Transport, storage and communications	20,024	556	20,580
Finance, insurance, real estate and business services	10,466	2,665	13,131
Community, social and personal services	76,690	27,236	103,926
Sub-total	2,562,526	2,412,993	4,975,519
Activities not adequately defined	15,104	13,712	28,816
Total employed	2,577,630	2,426,705	5,004,335
Unemployed	51,523	19,757	71,280
Total labour force	2,629,153	2,446,462	5,075,615

Mid-2012 ('000, estimates): Agriculture, etc. 7,394; Total labour force 8,035 (Source: FAO).

Health and Welfare

KEY INDICATORS

Total fertility rate (children per woman, 2009)	5.8
Under-5 mortality rate (per 1,000 live births, 2009)	166
HIV/AIDS (% of persons aged 15–49, 2009)	1.2
Physicians (per 1,000 head, 2004)	0.05
Hospital beds (per 1,000 head, 2006)	0.9
Health expenditure (2008): US $ per head (PPP)	82
Health expenditure (2008): % of GDP	5.9
Health expenditure (2008): public (% of total)	59.1
Access to water (% of persons, 2008)	76
Access to sanitation (% of persons, 2008)	11
Total carbon dioxide emissions ('000 metric tons, 2007)	1,692.8
Carbon dioxide emissions per head (metric tons, 2007)	0.1
Human Development Index (2011): ranking	181
Human Development Index (2011): value	0.331

For sources and definitions, see explanatory note on p. vi.

Agriculture

PRINCIPAL CROPS
('000 metric tons)

	2008	2009	2010
Rice, paddy	195.1	213.6	232.9
Maize	1,013.6	894.6	1,133.5
Millet	1,255.2	970.9	1,147.9
Sorghum	1,875.1	1,521.5	1,990.2
Sweet potatoes	73.2	81.5	92.5
Yams	42.3	80.9	97.6
Sugar cane*	455	455	455
Cow peas, dry*	300.0	325.0	432.4
Bambara beans	55.6	44.7	59.5
Groundnuts, with shell	346.3	330.6	340.2
Okra*	22	18	21
Cotton lint*	266.0	183.0	190
Cottonseed†	315	265	250
Seed cotton	720.7	483.9	529.6

* FAO estimates.
† Unofficial figures.

Aggregate production ('000 metric tons, may include official, semi-official or estimated data): Total cereals 4,358.5 in 2008, 3,626.6 in 2009, 4,522.7 in 2010; Total pulses 375.6 in 2008, 385.8 in 2009, 513.3 in 2010; Total roots and tubers 121.9 in 2008, 168.0 in 2009, 196.4 in 2010; Total vegetables (incl. melons) 275.3 in 2008, 217.4 in 2009, 281.3 in 2010; Total fruits (excl. melons) 90.2 in 2008, 100.0 in 2009, 96.5 in 2010.

LIVESTOCK
('000 head, year ending September)

	2008	2009	2010*
Cattle	8,072	8,234	9,845
Sheep	7,770	8,003	8,050
Goats	11,634	11,983	12,378
Pigs	2,083	2,125	1,920
Chickens	35,359	37,000*	39,000
Horses	38	38	38
Asses	1,009	1,030	1,030
Camels	16*	17	17

* FAO estimate(s).

Source: FAO.

LIVESTOCK PRODUCTS
('000 metric tons, FAO estimates)

	2008	2009	2010
Cattle meat	106.6	110.5	133.5
Sheep meat	18.0	18.3	19.0
Goat meat	30.8	31.8	32.6
Pig meat	30.0	30.6	27.7
Chicken meat	33.8	35.4	35.4
Cows' milk	201.7	209.0	219.4
Goats' milk	42.5	43.8	45.6
Hen eggs	48.7	51.1	52.0

Source: FAO.

Forestry

ROUNDWOOD REMOVALS

('000 cubic metres, excluding bark, FAO estimates)

	2007	2008	2009
Sawlogs, veneer logs and logs for sleepers	73	73	73
Other industrial wood	1,098	1,098	1,098
Fuel wood	11,573	12,418	12,600
Total	12,744	13,589	13,771

2010: Production assumed to be unchanged from 2009 (FAO estimates).

Source: FAO.

SAWNWOOD PRODUCTION

('000 cubic metres)

	2005	2006	2007
Total (all broadleaved)	1.1	0.7	5.2

2008–10: Production assumed to be unchanged from 2007 (FAO estimates).

Source: FAO.

Fishing

(metric tons, live weight)

	2007	2008	2009
Capture	10,200	11,093	11,800
Freshwater fishes	10,200	11,093	11,800
Aquaculture	298	405*	205
Total catch	10,498	11,498*	12,005

* FAO estimate.

Source: FAO.

Mining

(estimates)

	2007	2008	2009
Cement (metric tons)	30,000	30,000	30,000
Gold (kg)	2,250	7,633*	13,181*

* Includes artisanal mining, which was estimated to be 1,600 kilograms.

Source: US Geological Survey.

Industry

SELECTED PRODUCTS

(metric tons, unless otherwise indicated)

	2000	2001	2002
Edible oils	17,888	19,452	19,626
Shea (karité) butter	186	101	21
Flour	12,289	13,686	10,005
Pasta	211	n.a.	n.a.
Sugar	43,412	46,662	47,743
Beer ('000 hl)	494	500	546
Soft drinks ('000 hl)	221	222	250
Cigarettes (million packets)	85	78	78
Printed fabric ('000 sq m)	275	n.a.	n.a.
Soap	12,079	9,240	9,923
Matches (cartons)	9,358	4,956	3,009
Bicycles (units)	22,215	17,718	20,849
Mopeds (units)	16,531	19,333	19,702
Tyres ('000)	397	599	670
Inner tubes ('000)	2,655	3,217	2,751
Electric energy ('000 kWh)	390,352	365,503	364,675

Electric energy ('000 kWh): 612,712 in 2007; 619,400 in 2008; 699,790 in 2009.

Source: mainly IMF, *Burkina Faso: Selected Issues and Statistical Appendix* (September 2005).

Raw sugar ('000 metric tons): 40 in 2006–08 (Source: UN Industrial Commodity Statistics Database).

Finance

CURRENCY AND EXCHANGE RATES

Monetary Units

100 centimes = 1 franc de la Communauté financière africaine (CFA).

Sterling, Dollar and Euro Equivalents (30 December 2011)

£1 sterling = 783.813 francs CFA;
US $1 = 506.961 francs CFA;
€1 = 655.957 francs CFA;
10,000 francs CFA = £12.76 = $19.73 = €15.24.

Average Exchange Rate (francs CFA per US $)

2009 472.186
2010 495.277
2011 471.866

Note: An exchange rate of 1 French franc = 50 francs CFA, established in 1948, remained in force until January 1994, when the CFA franc was devalued by 50%, with the exchange rate adjusted to 1 French franc = 100 francs CFA. This relationship to French currency remained in effect with the introduction of the euro on 1 January 1999. From that date, accordingly, a fixed exchange rate of €1 = 655.957 francs CFA has been in operation.

BUDGET

('000 million francs CFA)

Revenue*	2009	2010†	2011‡
Tax revenue	494.6	565.7	614.4
Income and profits	106.7	133.6	158.2
Domestic goods and services	282.9	318.4	337.9
International trade	89.7	96.8	101.1
Non-tax revenue	44.5	115.5	97.4
Total	539.1	681.3	711.7

Expenditure§	2009	2010†	2011‡
Current expenditure	499.1	530.9	635.2
Wages and salaries	228.4	245.8	269.3
Goods and services	95.1	90.8	104.4
Interest payments	16.9	21.4	23.4
Current transfers	158.8	172.9	238.1
Capital expenditure	457.4	531.2	596.6
Expenditure carried forward from previous year	0.0	67.7	0.0
Total	956.4	1,129.8	1,231.8

* Excluding grants received ('000 million francs CFA): 232.4 in 2009; 198.9 in 2010 (estimated); 330.0 in 2011 (projected).

† Estimated figures.

‡ Programmed figures.

§ Excluding net lending ('000 million francs CFA): 3.2 in 2009; –6.2 in 2010 (estimated); –6.3 in 2011 (projected).

Source: IMF, *Burkina Faso: Second Review Under the Three-Year Arrangement Under the Extended Credit Facility and Request for Modification of Performance Criteria—Staff Report; Press Release on the Executive Board Discussion; and Statement by the Executive Director for Burkina Faso* (July 2011).

INTERNATIONAL RESERVES

(excluding gold, US $ million at 31 December)

	2008	2009	2010
IMF special drawing rights	0.1	75.4	74.2
Reserve position in IMF	11.4	11.7	11.5
Foreign exchange	916.1	1,208.8	982.5
Total	927.6	1,295.8	1,068.2

Source: IMF, *International Financial Statistics*.

MONEY SUPPLY

('000 million francs CFA at 31 December)

	2008	2009	2010
Currency outside banks	213.6	251.8	215.1
Demand deposits at deposit money banks*	282.9	356.0	437.9
Checking deposits at post office	4.8	5.5	3.9
Total money (incl. others)	503.2	615.1	659.2

* Excluding the deposits of public establishments of an administrative or social nature.

Source: IMF, *International Financial Statistics*.

COST OF LIVING

(Consumer Price Index; base: 2000 = 100)

	2007	2008	2009
Food, beverages and tobacco	117.9	145.4	149.2
Clothing	115.1	118.4	122.5
Housing, water, electricity and gas	114.8	128.7	142.6
All items (incl. others)	118.5	131.1	134.6

2010: Food (incl. beverages) 152.7; All items (incl. others) 131.4.

Source: ILO.

NATIONAL ACCOUNTS

('000 million francs CFA in current prices)

Expenditure on the Gross Domestic Product

	2007	2008	2009
Government final consumption expenditure	774	748	778
Private final consumption expenditure	2,214	2,687	2,764
Gross fixed capital formation	688	728	824
Change in stocks	27	114	50
Total domestic expenditure	3,703	4,277	4,416
Exports of goods and services	342	336	434
Less Imports of goods and services	807	953	1,010
GDP in purchasers' values	3,238	3,660	3,840

Gross Domestic Product by Economic Activity

	2007	2008	2009
Agriculture, livestock, forestry and fishing	971	1,170	1,230
Mining	15	66	100
Manufacturing	328	417	425
Electricity, gas and water	35	46	48
Construction and public works	179	238	260
Wholesale and retail trade, restaurants and hotels	359	405	405
Finance, insurance and real estate	46	50	53
Transport and communications	172	158	188
Public administration and defence	723	582	601
Other services	172	230	225
Sub-total	3,000	3,362	3,535
Indirect taxes	285	335	346
Less Imputed bank service charge	48	38	40
GDP in purchasers' values	3,238	3,660	3,840

Source: African Development Bank.

BALANCE OF PAYMENTS

('000 million francs CFA)

	2008	2009*	2010*
Exports of goods f.o.b.	310.3	425.2	701.8
Imports of goods f.o.b.	–711.7	–652.8	–845.9
Trade balance	–401.4	–227.6	–144.1
Services (net)	–211.6	–192.1	–249.0
Balance on goods and services	–613.0	–419.7	–393.1
Income (net)	15.1	17.1	8.7
Balance on goods, services and income	–597.9	–402.6	–384.4
Private unrequited transfers (net)	57.0	62.5	61.9
Official unrequited transfers (net)	126.3	173.5	170.2
Current balance	–414.6	–166.6	–152.2
Capital account (net)	85.5	113.7	77.9
Financial account†	311.7	272.8	182.6
Net errors and omissions	–17.7	–30.6	–29.0
Overall balance	–35.1	189.3	79.3

* Projections.

† Including portfolio investment and direct foreign investment.

Source: IMF, *Burkina Faso: Second Review Under the Three-Year Arrangement Under the Extended Credit Facility and Request for Modification of Performance Criteria—Staff Report; Press Release on the Executive Board Discussion; and Statement by the Executive Director for Burkina Faso* (July 2011).

External Trade

PRINCIPAL COMMODITIES

('000 million francs CFA)

Imports f.o.b.	2006	2007	2008
Vegetable products	59.0	61.0	74.5
Prepared foodstuffs and beverages	38.8	42.7	50.5
Mineral products	184.5	196.0	236.6
Chemical products	95.7	93.1	110.1
Plastics and articles thereof	24.3	27.9	28.4
Textiles and clothing	13.8	15.0	24.1
Base metals and articles of base metal	49.3	58.0	80.4
Machinery and transport materials	153.2	203.9	219.9
Total (incl. others)	674.5	761.4	902.8

Exports f.o.b.	2006	2007	2008
Animals and animal products	3.5	2.5	9.7
Vegetable products	23.3	36.5	29.0
Prepared foodstuffs and beverages	6.5	7.0	9.8
Textiles and clothing	166.9	148.1	90.8
Pearls, gems and precious metals	4.7	4.6	55.6
Machinery and electrical equipment	2.6	7.2	5.4
Total (incl. others)	221.0	227.5	221.1

PRINCIPAL TRADING PARTNERS

('000 million francs CFA)*

Imports c.i.f.	2006	2007	2008
Belgium-Luxembourg	19.9	19.0	22.5
Benin	5.4	5.5	5.5
Brazil	13.5	9.7	10.0
China, People's Repub.	31.6	62.7	89.5
Côte d'Ivoire	136.2	126.9	131.2
France	117.6	116.1	122.4
Germany	19.0	20.4	19.3
Ghana	21.6	26.7	39.0
India	31.1	49.5	50.0
Italy	10.2	14.2	15.6
Japan	19.6	21.4	30.8
Netherlands	10.2	19.2	28.4
Pakistan	13.4	8.5	2.4
Russia	14.3	5.6	3.5
Senegal	6.9	7.9	6.5
Spain	8.5	13.1	14.0
Thailand	9.7	6.7	24.0
Togo	26.3	29.4	33.2
USA	25.3	49.6	59.8
Total (incl. others)	674.5	761.4	902.8

Exports f.o.b.	2006	2007	2008
Belgium-Luxembourg	19.9	25.7	8.6
Benin	2.3	8.0	8.5
Côte d'Ivoire	8.2	9.2	13.5
France	39.4	32.2	19.3
Ghana	8.2	20.0	9.9
Mali	5.8	5.8	5.1
Niger	6.9	5.8	7.8
Switzerland	57.7	60.9	86.8
Togo	13.5	10.1	5.0
United Kingdom	20.4	13.0	8.5
Total (incl. others)	221.0	227.5	221.1

* Figures refer to recorded trade only.

Transport

RAILWAYS

	2007	2008	2009
Freight carried ('000 metric tons)	907.4	832.7	871.6
Freight ton-km ('000)	840,374	779,620	820,784
Passengers ('000 journeys)	500*	n.a.	n.a.

* Estimate.

ROAD TRAFFIC
('000 motor vehicles in use)

	2007	2008	2009
Passenger cars	97.1	103.6	110.9
Vans	23.0	24.6	26.1
Trucks	14.2	15.0	15.8
Tractors, trailers and semi-trailers	17.2	17.7	18.6
Motorbikes and mopeds	356.5	447.4	551.3

CIVIL AVIATION
(traffic on scheduled services)*

	2003	2004	2005
Kilometres flown (million)	1	1	1
Passengers carried ('000)	54	61	66
Passenger-km (million)	29	33	37
Total ton-km (million)	3	3	3

* Including an apportionment of the traffic of Air Afrique.

Source: UN, *Statistical Yearbook*.

Passengers carried ('000): 77.8 in 2007; 80.5 in 2008; 79.3 in 2009 (Source: World Bank, World Development Indicators database).

Tourism

FOREIGN VISITORS BY COUNTRY OF ORIGIN*

	2006	2007	2008
Belgium	7,454	8,345	6,435
Benin	9,233	10,442	9,043
Canada	6,088	7,025	5,500
Côte d'Ivoire	15,659	18,009	14,904
France	81,532	80,054	63,395
Germany	5,914	6,562	6,181
Ghana	5,819	6,359	6,622
Guinea	4,003	3,707	3,333
Italy	6,806	7,405	5,990
Mali	14,103	12,512	10,125
Mauritania	2,188	2,022	1,819
Netherlands	3,575	3,657	3,743
Niger	13,044	11,406	9,858
Nigeria	4,653	4,010	4,172
Senegal	10,724	9,584	8,688
Switzerland	4,534	3,869	4,030
Togo	8,854	7,664	7,871
United Kingdom	3,424	3,942	4,377
USA	7,855	10,250	7,792
Total (incl. others)	263,978	288,965	225,651

* Arrivals at hotels and similar establishments.

Receipts from tourism (US $ million, incl. passenger transport): 45.4 in 2005; 55.1 in 2006; 57.4 in 2007.

Source: World Tourism Organization.

Communications Media

	2008	2009	2010
Telephones ('000 main lines in use)	148.2	152.5	144.0
Mobile cellular telephones ('000 subscribers)	3,024.2	3,823.6	5,707.8
Internet subscribers ('000)	15.5	23.4	28.7
Broadband subscribers ('000)	10.3	11.9	14.2

Personal computers: 90,000 (6.3 per 1,000) in 2006.

Source: International Telecommunication Union.

Television receivers ('000 in use): 140 in 2000 (Source: UNESCO, *Statistical Yearbook*).

Radio receivers ('000 in use): 370 in 1997 (Source: UNESCO, *Statistical Yearbook*).

Daily newspapers (national estimates): 4 (average circulation 14,200 copies) in 1997; 4 (average circulation 14,500 copies) in 1998; 5 in 2004 (Source: UNESCO Institute for Statistics).

Non-daily newspapers: 9 (average circulation 42,000 copies) in 1995 (Source: UNESCO, *Statistical Yearbook*).

Book production: 12 titles (14,000 copies) in 1996 (first editions only); 5 in 1997 (Sources: UNESCO, *Statistical Yearbook*, UNESCO Institute for Statistics).

Education

(2009/10 unless otherwise indicated)

	Institutions	Teachers	Students ('000)		
			Males	Females	Total
Pre-primary	147*	1,776†	22.1	20.9	43.0
Primary	9,726‡	42,870	1,089.9	957.7	2,047.6
Secondary (general)	922‡	14,953	295.5	216.1	511.6
Secondary (technical and vocational)	119‡	2,827	13.9	12.5	26.4
Tertiary	52‡	2,889	34.9	16.3	51.2

* 1997/98.
† 2007/08.
‡ 2008/09.

Source: mostly UNESCO Institute for Statistics.

Pupil-teacher ratio (primary education, UNESCO estimate): 47.8 in 2009/10 (Source: UNESCO Institute for Statistics).

Adult literacy rate (UNESCO estimates): 28.7% (males 36.7%; females 21.6%) in 2007 (Source: UNESCO Institute for Statistics).

Directory

The Government

HEAD OF STATE

President: BLAISE COMPAORÉ (assumed power as Chairman of the Front populaire 15 October 1987; elected President 1 December 1991; re-elected 15 November 1998, 13 November 2005 and 21 November 2010).

COUNCIL OF MINISTERS
(May 2012)

President and Minister of National Defence and War Veterans: BLAISE COMPAORÉ.

Prime Minister: LUC ADOLPHE TIAO.

Minister of State, Minister in charge of Parliamentary Affairs and Political Reform: BONGNESSAN ARSÈNE YE.

Minister of Foreign Affairs and Regional Co-operation: YIPÈNÈ DJIBRIL BASSOLET.

Minister of the Economy and Finance: LUCIEN MARIE NOËL BEMBAMBA.

Minister of Agriculture, Water Resources and Fisheries: LAURENT GOUINDÉ SÉDEGO.

Minister of Transport, Posts and the Digital Economy: GILBERT G. NOËL OUÉDRAOGO.

Minister of Justice, Keeper of the Seals: SALAMATA SAWAGOGO TAPSOBA.

Minister of Territorial Administration, Decentralization and National Security: JÉRÔME BOUGOUMA.

Minister of Mines, Quarries and Energy: ABDOULAYE LAMOUSSA SALIF KABORÉ.

Minister of Culture and Tourism: BABA HAMA.

Minister of Communication and Government Spokesperson: ALAIN EDOUARD TRAORÉ.

Minister of Housing and Town Planning: YACOUBA BARRY.

Minister of Industry, Trade and Crafts: PATIENDÉ ARTHUR KAFANDO.

Minister of Infrastructure and Improving Access to Isolated Regions: JEAN BERTIN OUÉDRAOGO.

Minister of Health: ADAMA TRAORÉ.

Minister of Secondary and Higher Education: Prof. ALBERT OUÉDRAOGO.

Minister of Scientific Research and Innovation: GNISSA ISAÏE KONATÉ.

Minister of National Education and Literacy: KOUMBA BOLY BARRY.

Minister of the Civil Service, Labour and Social Security: SOUNGALO APPOLINAIRE OUATTARA.

Minister of the Environment and Sustainable Development: JEAN COULDIATY.

Minister of Youth, Professional Training and Employment: ACHILLE MARIE JOSEPH TAPSOBA.

Minister of Social Action and National Solidarity: CLÉMENCE TRAORÉ SOME.

Minister of Human Rights and Civic Promotion: ALBERT OUÉDRAOGO.

Minister of Animal Resources: JÉRÉMIE OUÉDRAOGO.

Minister for the Promotion of Women: NESTORINE SANGARÉ COMPAORÉ.

Minister of Sport and Leisure: YACOUBA OUÉDRAOGO.

Minister-delegate to the Minister of Agriculture, Water Resources and Fisheries, responsible for Agriculture: ABDOULAYE COMBARY.

Minister-delegate to the Minister of the Economy and Finance, responsible for the Budget: FRANÇOIS MARIE DIDIER ZOUNDI.

Minister-delegate to the Minister of Territorial Administration, Decentralization and National Security, responsible for Local Communities: TOUSSAINT ABEL COULIBALY.

Minister-delegate to the Minister of Foreign Affairs and Regional Co-operation, responsible for Regional Co-operation: VINCENT ZAKANÉ.

Minister-delegate to the Minister of National Education and Literacy, responsible for Literacy: ZAKARIA TIEMTORÉ.

MINISTRIES

Office of the President: 03 BP 7030, Ouagadougou 03; tel. 50-30-66-30; fax 50-31-49-26; e-mail info@presidence.bf; internet www.presidence.bf.

Office of the Prime Minister: 03 BP 7027, Ouagadougou 03; tel. 50-32-48-89; fax 50-33-05-51; e-mail webmaster@primature.gov.bf; internet www.gouvernement.gov.bf.

Ministry of Agriculture, Water Resources and Fisheries: 03 BP 7005, Ouagadougou 03; tel. 50-32-41-14; fax 50-31-08-70; internet www.agriculture.gov.bf.

Ministry of Animal Resources: 03 BP 7026, Ouagadougou 03; tel. 50-39-96-15; fax 50-31-84-75; e-mail pinidie.banaon@mra.gov.bf; internet www.mra.gov.bf.

Ministry of the Civil Service and State Reform: Immeuble de la Modernisation, 922 ave Kwamé N'Krumah, 03 BP 7006, Ouagadougou 03; tel. 50-30-19-52; fax 50-30-19-55; internet www.fonction-publique.gov.bf.

Ministry of Communication and Government Spokesperson: 387 ave Georges Conseiga, 01 BP 5175, Ouagadougou 01; tel. 50-49-00-00; fax 50-33-73-87; internet www.mptic.gov.bf.

Ministry of Culture and Tourism: 11 BP 852, CMS, Ouagadougou 11; tel. 50-33-09-63; fax 50-33-09-64; e-mail mctc@cenatrin.bf; internet www.culture.gov.bf.

Ministry of Defence and War Veterans: 01 BP 496, Ouagadougou 01; tel. 50-30-72-14; fax 50-31-36-10; internet www.defense.gov.bf.

Ministry of the Economy and Finance: 395 avenue Ho Chi Minh, 01 BP 7008, Ouagadougou 01; tel. 50-32-42-11; fax 50-31-27-15; e-mail webmaster@finances.gov.bf; internet www.finances.gov.bf.

Ministry of the Environment and Sustainable Development: 565 rue Agostino Neto, Koulouba, 03 BP 7044, Ouagadougou 03; tel. 50-32-40-74; fax 50-30-70-39; internet www.environnement.gov.bf.

Ministry of Foreign Affairs and Regional Co-operation: rue 988, blvd du Faso, 03 BP 7038, Ouagadougou 03; tel. 50-32-47-34; fax 50-30-87-92; e-mail webmaster.mae@mae.gov.bf; internet www.mae.gov.bf.

Ministry of Health: 03 BP 7035, Ouagadougou 03; tel. 50-32-61-88; internet www.sante.gov.bf.

Ministry of Housing and Town Planning: Ouagadougou; tel. and fax 50-30-57-86.

Ministry of Industry, Trade and Crafts: 01 BP 514, Ouagadougou 01; tel. 50-32-48-28; fax 50-31-70-53; internet www.commerce.gov.bf.

Ministry of Infrastructure and Improving Access to Isolated Regions: 03 BP 7011, Ouagadougou 03; tel. 50-30-73-33; fax 50-31-84-08; internet www.mith.gov.bf.

Ministry of Justice and the Promotion of Human Rights: 01 BP 526, Ouagadougou 01; tel. 50-32-48-33; fax 50-31-71-37; e-mail webmestre@justice.bf; internet www.justice.gov.bf.

Ministry of Labour and Social Security: 01 BP 7016, Ouagadougou 01; tel. 50-30-09-60; fax 50-31-88-01; e-mail emploi@metss.gov.bf; internet www.emploi.gov.bf.

Ministry of Mines, Quarries and Energy: 01 BP 644, Ouagadougou 01; tel. 50-31-84-29; fax 50-31-84-30; internet www.mines.gov.bf.

Ministry of National Education and Literacy: 03 BP 7032, Ouagadougou 03; tel. 50-30-66-00; fax 50-31-42-76; internet www.meba.gov.bf.

Ministry of Parliamentary Affairs and Political Reform: 01 BP 2079, Ouagadougou 01; tel. 50-32-40-70; fax 50-30-78-94; e-mail cab_mrp@yahoo.fr; internet www.mrp.gov.bf.

Ministry for the Promotion of Women: 01 BP 303, Ouagadougou 01; tel. 50-30-01-04; fax 50-30-01-02; e-mail secretariat@mpf.gov.bf; internet www.mpf.gov.bf.

Ministry of Scientific Research and Innovation: Ouagadougou.

Ministry of Secondary and Higher Education: 03 BP 7047, Ouagadougou 03; tel. 50-32-45-67; fax 50-32-61-16; e-mail laya.saw@messrs.gov.bf; internet www.messrs.gov.bf.

Ministry of Security: 01 BP 6466, Ouagadougou 01; tel. 50-31-68-91; fax 50-33-02-97; e-mail infos@secu.gov.bf; internet www.securite.gov.bf.

Ministry of Social Action and National Solidarity: 01 BP 515, Ouagadougou 01; tel. 50-30-68-75; fax 50-31-67-37; internet www.action-sociale.gov.bf.

Ministry of Sport and Leisure: 03 BP 7035, Ouagadougou 03; tel. 50-32-47-86; fax 50-33-08-18; internet www.sports.gov.bf.

Ministry of Territorial Administration, Decentralization and National Security: 01 BP 526, Ouagadougou 01; tel. 50-32-48-33; fax 50-31-72-00; internet www.matd.gov.bf.

Ministry of Transport, Posts and the Digital Economy: 03 BP 7011, Ouagadougou 03; tel. 50-30-73-33; fax 50-31-84-08.

Ministry of Youth, Professional Training and Employment: 01 BP 7016, Ouagadougou 01; tel. 50-30-09-60; fax 30-31-84-80; internet www.emploi.gov.bf.

President and Legislature

PRESIDENT

Presidential Election, 21 November 2010

Candidate	Votes	% of votes
Blaise Compaoré	1,357,315	80.15
Hama Arba Diallo	138,975	8.21
Bénéwendé Stanislas Sankara	107,310	6.34
Boukary Kaboré	39,186	2.31
Maxime Kaboré	25,077	1.48
Pargui Emile Paré	14,560	0.86
Ouampoussoga François Kaboré	10,962	0.65
Total	1,693,385	100.00

LEGISLATURE

Assemblée nationale

01 BP 6482, Ouagadougou 01; tel. 50-31-46-84; fax 50-31-45-90.

President: ROCH MARC CHRISTIAN KABORÉ.

General Election, 6 May 2007

Parties	% of total votes*	National list seats	Total seats†
CDP	58.85	9	73
ADF—RDA	10.70	2	14
UPR	4.30	1	5
UNIR—MS	3.89	1	4
CFD/B‡	2.34	1	3
PDS	3.28	1	2
PDP—PS	2.51	—	2
RDB	2.09	—	2
UPS	1.74	—	2
PAREN	1.29	—	1
RPC	1.15	—	1
UDPS	1.03	—	1
PAI	0.83	—	1
Total (incl. others)	100.00	15	111

* Including votes from regional and national party lists.

† Including seats filled by voting from regional lists, totalling 96.

‡ The Coalition des forces démocratiques du Burkina, an electoral alliance of six parties.

Election Commission

Commission électorale nationale indépendante (CENI): 01 BP 5152, Ouagadougou 01; tel. 50-30-00-52; fax 50-30-80-44; e-mail ceni@fasonet.bf; internet www.ceni.bf; f. 2001; 15 mems; Pres. BARTHÉLEMY KÉRÉ.

Advisory Council

Conseil économique et social: 01 BP 6162, Ouagadougou 01; tel. 50-32-40-91; fax 50-31-06-54; e-mail ces@ces.gov.bf; internet www.ces.gov.bf; f. 1985; present name adopted in 1992; 90 mems; Pres. THOMAS SANON.

Political Organizations

A total of 47 political parties contested the legislative elections held in May 2007.

Alliance pour la démocratie et la fédération—Rassemblement démocratique africain (ADF—RDA): 01 BP 1991, Ouagadougou 01; tel. 50-30-52-00; f. 1990 as Alliance pour la démocratie et la fédération; absorbed faction of Rassemblement démocratique africain in 1998; several factions broke away in 2000 and in mid-2003; Pres. GILBERT NOËL OUÉDRAOGO.

Congrès pour la démocratie et le progrès (CDP): 1146 ave Dr Kwamé N'Krumah, 01 BP 1605, Ouagadougou 01; tel. 50-31-50-18; fax 50-31-43-93; e-mail contact@cdp-burkina.org; internet www.cdp-burkina.org; f. 1996 by merger, to succeed the Organisation pour la démocratie populaire/Mouvement du travail as the principal political org. supporting Pres. Compaoré; social democratic; Pres. ROCH MARC CHRISTIAN KABORÉ.

Convention nationale du progrès du Burkina: f. 2009; Pres. MOUSSA BOLY.

Convention panafricaine sankariste (CPS): BP 44, Bokin; tel. 40-45-72-93; f. 1999 by merger of 4 parties, expanded in 2000 to include 2 other parties; promotes the policies of fmr Pres. Sankara; Pres. NONGMA ERNEST OUÉDRAOGO.

Front des forces sociales (FFS): BP 255, Ouagadougou; tel. 50-32-32-32; f. 1996; Sankarist; member of the Groupe du 14 février and opposition Collectif d'organisations démocratiques de masse et de partis politiques; Chair. NORBERT MICHEL TIENDRÉBÉOGO.

Front patriotique pour le changement (FPC): BP 8539, Ouagadougou; tel. 70-25-32-45; Pres. TAHIROU IBRAHIM ZON.

Mouvement du peuple pour le socialisme—Parti fédéral (MPS—PF): BP 3448, Ouagadougou; tel. 50-36-50-72; f. 2002 by split from PDP—PS; Leader Dr PARGUI EMILE PARÉ.

Parti africain de l'indépendance (PAI): Ouagadougou; tel. 50-33-46-66; f. 1999; Sec.-Gen. SOUMANE TOURÉ.

Parti pour la démocratie et le progrès—Parti socialiste (PDP—PS): 11 BP 26, Ouagadougou 11; tel. and fax 50-31-14-10; e-mail pdp-ps@fasonet.bf; f. 2001 by merger of the Parti pour la démocratie et le progrès and the Parti socialiste burkinabè; Nat. Pres. Dr FRANÇOIS KABORÉ.

Parti pour la démocratie et le socialisme (PDS): Ouagadougou; tel. 50-34-34-04; Pres. BA SAMBO.

Parti de la renaissance nationale (PAREN): Ouagadougou; tel. 50-43-12-26; f. 2000; social-democratic; Pres. KILACHIA LAURENT BADO.

Rassemblement démocratique et populaire (RDP): Ouagadougou; tel. 50-36-02-98; Pres. THIBAUT NANA.

Rassemblement pour le développement du Burkina (RDB): Pres. CÉLESTIN SEYDOU COMPAORÉ.

Rassemblement populaire des citoyens (RPC): Ouagadougou; f. 2006; promotes an alternative style of politics; Pres. ANTOINE OUARÉ.

Union pour la démocratie et le progrès: f. 2010; Pres. ZÉPHIRIN DIABRÉ; Sec.-Gen. DENIS NIKIÈMA.

Union pour la démocratie et le progrès social (UDPS): Ouagadougou; Leader FIDÈLE HIEN.

Union nationale pour la démocratie et le développement (UNDD): 03 BP 7114, Ouagadougou 03; tel. 50-31-15-15; internet www.undd.org; f. 2003 by fmr mems of the ADF—RDA (q.v.); liberal; Pres. Me HERMANN YAMÉOGO.

Union des partis sankarist (UPS).

Union pour le Progrès et le Changement (UPC): Ouagadougou; f. 2010; Pres. ZÉPHIRIN DIABRÉ.

Union pour la renaissance—Parti sankariste (UNIR—PS): Ouagadougou; tel. 50-36-30-45; f. 2000 as Union pour la renaissance—Mouvement sankariste; renamed as above in 2009; Pres. BÉNÉWENDÉ STANISLAS SANKARA.

Union pour la république (UPR): Ouagadougou; Leader TOUSSAINT ABEL COULIBALY.

Diplomatic Representation

EMBASSIES IN BURKINA FASO

Algeria: Secteur 13, Zone du Bois, 295 ave Babanguida, 01 BP 3893, Ouagadougou 01; tel. 50-36-81-81; fax 50-36-81-79; Ambassador ABDELKRIM BENCHIAH.

Belgium: Immeuble Me Benoit Sawadogo, 994 rue Agostino Neto, Koulouba, 01 BP 1624, Ouagadougou 01; tel. 50-31-21-64; fax 50-31-06-60; e-mail ouagadougou@diplobel.fed.be; internet www.diplomatie.be/ouagadougou; Ambassador ADRIEN THÉATRE.

Canada: rue Agostino Neto, 01 BP 548, Ouagadougou 01; tel. 50-31-18-94; fax 50-31-19-00; e-mail ouaga@dfait-maeci.gc.ca; internet www.dfait-maeci.gc.ca/burkina_faso; Ambassador IVAN ROBERTS.

Chad: Ouagadougou; Ambassador BRAHIM MAHAMAT IMAM.

Côte d'Ivoire: pl. des Nations Unies, 01 BP 20, Ouagadougou 01; tel. 50-31-82-28; fax 50-31-82-30; Ambassador ABDOU TOURÉ.

Cuba: rue 4/64, La Rotonde, Secteur 4, Ouagadougou; tel. 50-30-64-91; fax 50-31-73-24; e-mail embacuba.bf@fasonet.bf; Ambassador ANA MARIA ROVIRA INGIDUA.

Denmark: 316 ave Pr. Joseph Ki-Zerbo, 01 BP 1760, Ouagadougou 01; tel. 50-32-85-40; fax 50-32-85-77; e-mail ouaamb@um.dk; internet www.ambouagadougou.um.dk; Ambassador BIRGITTE NYGAARD MARKUSSEN.

Egypt: Zone du Conseil de L'Entente, blvd du Faso, 04 BP 7042, Ouagadougou 04; tel. 50-30-66-39; fax 50-31-38-36; Ambassador AHMAD ABDEL WAHED ZAIN.

France: ave du Trésor, 01 BP 504, Ouagadougou 01; tel. 50-49-66-66; fax 50-49-66-09; e-mail ambassade@ambafrance-bf.org; internet www.ambafrance-bf.org; Ambassador Gen. EMMANUEL BETH.

Germany: 399 ave Joseph Badoua, 01 BP 600, Ouagadougou 01; tel. 50-30-67-31; fax 50-31-39-91; e-mail amb.allemagne@fasonet.bf; Ambassador ULRICH HOCHSCHILD.

Ghana: 22 ave d'Oubritenga, 01 BP 212, Ouagadougou 01; tel. 50-30-76-35; e-mail embagna@fasonet.bf; Ambassador Chief MANDEAYA BAWUMIA.

Holy See: Tange Saabé, BP 1902, Ouagadougou 01; tel. 50-31-63-56; fax 50-31-63-55; e-mail nuntiusapbn@yahoo.it; Ambassador VITO RALLO (Titular Archbishop of Alba).

Korea, Democratic People's Republic: Ouagadougou; Ambassador KIL MUN YONG.

Libya: 01 BP 1601, Ouagadougou 01; tel. 50-30-67-53; fax 50-31-34-70; Ambassador ABD AL-NASSER SALEH MUHAMMAD YOUNES.

Mali: 2569 ave Bassawarga, 01 BP 1911, Ouagadougou 01; tel. 50-38-19-22; Ambassador (vacant).

Mauritania: Ouagadougou; Ambassador MOHAMED OULD SID AHMED LEKHAL.

Morocco: Ouaga 2000 Villa B04, pl. de la Cotière, 01 BP 3438, Ouagadougou 01; tel. 50-37-40-16; fax 50-37-41-72; e-mail maroc1@fasonet.bf; Ambassador FARHAT BOUAAZA.

Netherlands: 415 ave Dr Kwamé N'Krumah, 01 BP 1302, Ouagadougou 01; tel. 50-30-61-34; fax 50-30-76-95; e-mail oua@minbuza.nl; internet burkinafaso.nlambassade.org; Ambassador ERNST ALBERT NOORMAN.

Nigeria: rue de l'Hôpital Yalgado, 01 BP 132, Ouagadougou 01; tel. 50-36-30-15; Ambassador (vacant).

Saudi Arabia: Ouaga 2000, rue de la Francophonie, Villa M05, 01 BP 2069, Ouagadougou 01; tel. 50-37-42-06; fax 50-37-42-10; e-mail saudiembassy@liptinfor.bf; Ambassador DAHIR MOOTISH ALANZI.

Senegal: Immeuble Espace Fadima, ave de la Résistance du 17 Mai, 01 BP 3226, Ouagadougou 01; tel. 50-31-14-18; fax 50-31-14-01; Ambassador MAMADOU MAKHTAR GUEYE.

South Africa: Villa 1110, Hotel Sofitel, Ouagadougou; tel. 50-37-60-98; fax 50-37-60-97; e-mail ouagadougou@foreign.gov.za; Ambassador L. S. GANTSHO.

Sweden: 11 BP 755, CMS, Ouagadougou; tel. 50-49-61-70; e-mail ambassaden.ouagadougou@sida.se; internet www.swedenabroad.com/ouagadougou; Ambassador CARIN WALL.

Taiwan (Republic of China): 994 rue Agostino Neto, 01 BP 5563, Ouagadougou 01; tel. 50-31-61-95; fax 50-31-61-97; e-mail ambachine@fasonet.bf; Ambassador ZHANG MING-ZHONG.

Turkey: Ouagadougou; Ambassador AYDIN SEFA AKAY.

USA: ave Sembene Ousmane, Ouaga 2000, Secteur 15, Ouagadougou; tel. 50-49-53-00; fax 50-49-56-28; e-mail amembouaga@state.gov; internet ouagadougou.usembassy.gov; Ambassador THOMAS DOUGHERTY.

Judicial System

In accordance with constitutional amendments approved by the Assemblée nationale in April 2000, the Supreme Court was abolished; its four permanent chambers were replaced by a Constitutional Council, a Council of State, a Court of Cassation and a National Audit Court, all of which commenced operations in December 2002. Judges are accountable to a Higher Council, under the chairmanship of the President of the Republic, in which capacity he is officially responsible for ensuring the independence of the judiciary. A High Court of Justice is competent to try the President and members of the Government in cases of treason, embezzlement of public funds, and other crimes and offences.

Constitutional Council: 40 ave de la Nation, 11 BP 1114, Ouagadougou 11; tel. 50-30-05-53; fax 50-30-08-66; e-mail conseil@conseil-constitutionnel.gov.bf; internet www.conseil-constitutionnel.gov.bf; f. 2002 to replace Constitutional Chamber of fmr Supreme Court; Pres. DÉ ALBERT MILLOGO; Sec.-Gen. HONIBIPÈ MARIAM MARGUERITE OUÉDRAOGO.

Council of State: 01 BP 586, Ouagadougou 01; tel. 50-30-64-18; e-mail webmaster@conseil-etat.gov.bf; internet www.conseil-etat.gov.bf; f. 2002 to replace Administrative Chamber of fmr Supreme Court; comprises 2 chambers: a Consultative Chamber and a Chamber of Litigation; First Pres. HARIDIATA SERE DAKOURÉ; Pres. of Consultative Chamber THÉRÈSE SANOU TRAORÉ; Pres. of Chamber of Litigation VENANT OUEDRAOGO.

Court of Cassation: 05 BP 6204, Ouagadougou 05; tel. 50-31-20-47; fax 50-31-02-71; e-mail webmaster@courcassation.bf; internet www.cour-cassation.gov.bf; f. 2002 to replace Judicial Chamber of fmr Supreme Court; First Pres. CHEICK DIMKINSEDO OUÉDRAOGO.

High Court of Justice: Ouagadougou; f. 1998; comprises 6 deputies of the Assemblée nationale and 3 magistrates appointed by the President of the Court of Cassation; Pres. DIM-SONGDO BONAVENTURE OUÉDRAOGO; Vice-Pres. SIBILA FRANCK COMPAORÉ.

National Audit Court: 01 BP 2534, Ouagadougou 01; tel. 50-30-36-00; fax 50-30-35-01; e-mail infos@cour-comptes.gov.bf; internet www.cour-comptes.gov.bf; f. 2002 to replace Audit Chamber of fmr Supreme Court; comprises 3 chambers, concerned with: local government organs; public enterprises; and the operations of the State; First Pres. NOUMOUTIÉ HERBERT TRAORÉ; Procurator-Gen. THÉRÈSE TRAORÉ SANOU; Pres of Chambers PASCAL SANOU, SÉNÉBOU RAYMONDD MANUELLA OUILMA TRAORÉ, SABINE OUEDRAOGO YETA.

Religion

The Constitution provides for freedom of religion, and the Government respects this right in practice. The country is a secular state. Islam, Christianity and traditional religions operate freely without government interference. According to the 2006 census, some 60.5% of the population are Muslims, 23.2% are Christians and 15.3% follow animist beliefs, with the remaining population being adherents of other religions or practising no religion.

ISLAM

Association Islamique Nouroul Islam: BP 262, Ouagadougou; tel. 50-31-28-88.

CHRISTIANITY

The Roman Catholic Church

Burkina Faso comprises three archdioceses and 12 dioceses. Some 19% of the total population are Roman Catholics.

Bishops' Conference

Conférence des Evêques de Burkina Faso et du Niger, 01 BP 1195, Ouagadougou 01; tel. 50-30-60-26; fax 50-31-64-81; e-mail ccbn@fasonet.bf; internet www.egliseduburkina.org.

f. 1966; legally recognized 1978; Pres. Most Rev. SÉRAPHIN FRANÇOIS ROUAMBA (Archbishop of Koupéla).

Archbishop of Bobo-Dioulasso: Most Rev. PAUL YEMBOARO OUÉDRAOGO, Archevêché, Lafiaso, 01 BP 312, Bobo-Dioulasso; tel. 20-97-00-35; fax 20-97-19-50; e-mail lafiaso@fasonet.bf.

Archbishop of Koupéla: Most Rev. SÉRAPHIN FRANÇOIS ROUAMBA, Archevêché, BP 51, Koupéla; tel. 40-70-00-30; fax 40-70-02-65; e-mail ardiokou@fasonet.bf.

Archbishop of Ouagadougou: Most Rev. PHILIPPE OUÉDRAOGO, Archevêché, 01 BP 1472, Ouagadougou 01; tel. 50-30-67-04; fax 50-30-72-75; e-mail untaani@fasonet.bf.

Protestant Churches

Some 4.2% of the population are Protestants.

Assemblées de Dieu du Burkina Faso: 01 BP 458, Ouagadougou 01; tel. 50-34-35-45; fax 50-34-28-71; e-mail adlagengo@fasonet.bf; f. 1921; Pres. Pastor MICHEL OUÉDRAOGO.

Fédération des Eglises et Missions Evangéliques (FEME): BP 108, Ouagadougou; tel. 50-36-14-26; e-mail feme@fasonet.bf; f. 1961; 10 churches and missions, 82,309 adherents; Pres. Pastor SAMUEL YAMÉOGO.

BAHÁ'Í FAITH

Assemblée spirituelle nationale: 01 BP 977, Ouagadougou 01; tel. 50-34-29-95; e-mail gnampa@fasonet.bf; Nat. Sec. JEAN-PIERRE SWEDY.

The Press

Direction de la presse écrite: Ouagadougou; govt body responsible for press direction.

DAILIES

24 Heures: 01 BP 3654, Ouagadougou 01; tel. 50-31-41-08; fax 50-30-57-39; f. 2000; privately owned; Dir BOUBAKAR DIALLO.

Bulletin de l'Agence d'Information du Burkina: 01 BP 2507, Ouagadougou 01; tel. 50-32-46-40; fax 50-33-73-16; e-mail infos@aib.bf; internet www.aib.bf; f. 1964 as L'Agence Voltaïque de Presse; current name adopted in 1984; Dir JAMES DABIRÉ.

L'Express du Faso: 01 BP 1, Bobo-Dioulasso 01; tel. 20-97-93-26; e-mail kami.express@caramail.com; internet www.lexpressdufaso.com; f. 1998; privately owned; Dir of Publication KAMI MOUNTAMOU; circ. 2,000 (2010).

L'Observateur Paalga (New Observer): 01 BP 584, Ouagadougou 01; tel. 50-33-27-05; fax 50-31-45-79; e-mail lobs@fasonet.bf; internet www.lobservateur.bf; f. 1973; privately owned; also a Sunday edn, *L'Observateur Dimanche*; Dir EDOUARD OUÉDRAOGO; circ. 8,000 (2010).

Le Pays: Cité 1200 logements, 01 BP 4577, Ouagadougou 01; tel. 50-36-20-46; fax 50-36-03-78; e-mail lepays91@yahoo.fr; internet www.lepays.bf; f. 1991; independent; Dir-Gen. BOUREIMA JÉRÉMIE SIGUE; Editor-in-Chief MAHOROU KANAZOE; circ. 12,000 (2010).

Sidwaya Quotidien (Daily Truth): 5 rue du Marché, 01 BP 507, Ouagadougou 01; tel. 50-31-22-89; fax 50-31-03-62; e-mail daouda.ouedraogo@sidwaya.bf; internet www.sidwaya.bf; f. 1984; state-owned; Dir-Gen. IBRAHIMAN SAKANDÉ; Editor-in-Chief VICTORIEN AIMAR SAWADOGO; circ. 5,000 (2010).

PERIODICALS

L'Aurore: 01 BP 5104, Ouagadougou 01; tel. 70-25-22-81; e-mail enitiema@yahoo.fr; Dir of Publication ELIE NITIÈMA.

Bendré (Drum): 16.38 ave du Yatenga, 01 BP 6020, Ouagadougou 01; tel. 50-33-27-11; fax 50-31-28-53; e-mail bendrekan@hotmail.com; internet www.journalbendre.net; f. 1990; weekly; current affairs; Dir SY MOUMINA CHERIFF; circ. 2,000 (2010).

Evasion: Cité 1200 logements, 01 BP 4577, Ouagadougou 01; tel. 50-36-17-30; fax 50-36-03-78; e-mail lepays91@yahoo.fr; internet www.lepays.fr; f. 1996; publ. by Editions le Pays; weekly; current affairs; Dir-Gen. BOUREIMA JÉRÉMIE SIGUE; Editor-in-Chief CHRISTINE SAWADOGO.

L'Evènement: 01 BP 1860, Ouagadougou 01; tel. and fax 50-31-69-34; e-mail bangreib@yahoo.fr; internet www.evenement-bf.net; f. 2001; bimonthly; Dir of Publication GERMAIN BITTIOU NAMA; Editor-in-Chief NEWTON AHMED BARRY; circ. 6,000 (2010).

Fasozine: Ouagadougou; tel. 50-30-76-01; fax 50-31-69-73; e-mail ecrire@fasozine.com; internet www.fasozine.com; f. 2005; Dir of Publication MORIN YAMONGBE.

L'Hebdomadaire: Ouagadougou; tel. 50-31-47-62; e-mail hebdcom@fasonet.bf; internet www.hebdo.bf; f. 1999; Fridays; Dir ZÉPHIRIN KPODA; Editor-in-Chief DJIBRIL TOURÉ.

L'Indépendant: 01 BP 5663, Ouagadougou 01; tel. 50-33-37-75; e-mail sebgo@fasonet.bf; internet www.independant.bf; f. 1993 by Norbert Zongo; weekly, Tuesdays; Dir LIERMÉ DIEUDONNÉ SOMÉ; Editor-in-Chief TALATO SIID SAYA; circ. 5,000 (2010).

Le Journal du Jeudi (JJ): 01 BP 3654, Ouagadougou 01; tel. 50-31-41-08; fax 50-30-01-62; e-mail info@journaldujeudi.com; internet www.journaldujeudi.com; f. 1991; weekly; satirical; Dir BOUBAKAR DIALLO; Editor-in-Chief DAMIEN GLEZ; circ. 10,000.

Laabaali: Association Tin Tua, BP 167, Fada N'Gourma; tel. 40-77-01-26; fax 40-77-02-08; e-mail info@tintua.org; internet www.tintua.org/Liens/Laabali.htm; f. 1988; monthly; promotes literacy, agricultural information, cultural affairs; Gourmanche; Dir of Publishing BENOÎT B. OUOBA; Editor-in-Chief SUZANNE OUOBA; circ. 4,000.

Le Marabout: 01 BP 3564, Ouagadougou 01; tel. 50-31-41-08; e-mail info@marabout.net; f. 2001; monthly; publ. by the Réseau africain pour la liberté d'informer; pan-African politics; satirical; Dir BOUBAKAR DIALLO; Editor-in-Chief DAMIEN GLEZ.

L'Opinion: 01 BP 6459, Ouagadougou 01; tel. and fax 50-30-89-49; e-mail zedcom@fasonet.bf; internet www.zedcom.bf; weekly; Dir of Publishing ISSAKA LINGANI.

San Finna: Immeuble Photo Luxe, 12 BP 105, Ouagadougou 12; tel. and fax 50-35-82-64; e-mail sanfinna@yahoo.fr; internet www.sanfinna.com; f. 1999; Mondays; independent; current affairs, international politics; Editor-in-Chief MATHIEU N'DO.

Sidwaya Hebdo (Weekly Truth): 5 rue du Marché, 01 BP 507, Ouagadougou 01; tel. 50-31-22-89; fax 50-31-03-62; e-mail daouda.ouedraogo@sidwaya.bf; internet www.sidwaya.bf; f. 1997; state-owned; weekly; Editor-in-Chief DAOUDA E. OUÉDRAOGO.

Sidwaya Magazine (Truth): 5 rue du Marché, 01 BP 507, Ouagadougou 01; tel. 50-31-22-89; fax 50-31-03-62; e-mail daouda.ouedraogo@sidwaya.bf; internet www.sidwaya.bf; f. 1989; state-owned; monthly; Editor-in-Chief DAOUDA E. OUÉDRAOGO; circ. 2,500.

La Voix du Sahel: 01 BP 5505, Ouagadougou 01; tel. 50-33-20-75; e-mail voixdusahel@yahoo.fr; privately owned; Dir of Publication PROMOTHÉE KASSOUM BAKO.

Votre Santé: Cité 1200 logements, 01 BP 4577, Ouagadougou 01; tel. 50-36-20-46; fax 50-36-03-78; e-mail lepays91@yahoo.fr; internet www.lepays.fr; f. 1996; publ. by Editions le Pays; monthly; Dir-Gen. BOUREIMA JÉRÉMIE SIGUE; Editor-in-Chief ALEXANDRE LE GRAND ROUAMBA.

NEWS AGENCY

Agence d'Information du Burkina (AIB): 01 BP 2507, Ouagadougou 01; tel. 50-32-46-39; fax 50-33-73-16; e-mail aib.redaction@mcc.gov.bf; internet www.aib.bf; f. 1964; fmrly Agence Voltaïque de Presse; state-controlled; Dir JOLIVET EMMAÜS.

PRESS ASSOCIATIONS

Association Rayimkudemdé—Association Nationale des Animateurs et Journalistes en Langues Nationales du Burkina Faso (ARK): Sigh-Noghin, Ouagadougou; f. 2001; Pres. RIGOBERT ILBOUDO; Sec.-Gen. PIERRE OUÉDRAOGO.

Centre National de Presse—Norbert Zongo (CNP—NZ): 04 BP 8524, Ouagadougou 04; tel. and fax 50-34-37-45; internet www.cnpress-zongo.net; f. 1998 as Centre National de Presse; centre of information and documentation; provides journalistic training; incorporates Association des Journalistes du Burkina (f. 1988); Dir ABDOULAYE DIALLO.

Publishers

Editions Contact: 04 BP 8462, Ouagadougou 04; tel. 76-61-28-72; e-mail contact.evang@cenatrin.bf; f. 1992; evangelical Christian and other books in French.

Editions Découvertes du Burkina (ADDB): 06 BP 9237, Ouagadougou 06; tel. 50-36-22-38; e-mail jacques@liptinfor.bf; human and social sciences, poetry; Dir JACQUES GUÉGANÉ.

Editions Firmament: 01 BP 3392, Ouagadougou 01; tel. 50-38-44-25; e-mail brkabore@uemoa.int; f. 1994; literary fiction; Dir ROGER KABORÉ.

Editions Flamme: 04 BP 8921, Ouagadougou 04; tel. 50-34-15-31; fax 70-21-10-28; e-mail flamme@fasonet.bf; f. 1999; owned by the Assembleés de Dieu du Burkina Faso; literature of Christian interest in French, in Mooré and in Dioula; Dir Pastor ZACHARIE DELMA.

Editions Gambidi: 01 BP 5743, Ouagadougou 01; tel. 50-36-59-42; politics, philosophy; Dir JEAN-PIERRE GUINGANÉ.

Graphic Technic International & Biomedical (GTI): 01 BP 3230, Ouagadougou 01; tel. and fax 50-31-67-69; medicine, literary, popular and children's fiction, poetry; Dir-Gen. SAWADOGO N. TASSERE.

Editions Hamaria: 01 BP 6788, Ouagadougou 01; tel. 50-34-38-04; sciences, fiction.

Presses Africaines SA: 01 BP 1471, Ouagadougou 01; tel. 50-30-71-75; general fiction, religion, primary and secondary textbooks; Man. Dir A. WININGA.

Editions Sankofa et Gurli: 01 BP 3811, Ouagadougou 01; tel. 70-24-30-81; e-mail sankogur@hotmail.com; f. 1995; literary fiction, social sciences, African languages, youth and childhood literature; in French and in national languages; Dir JEAN-CLAUDE NABA.

Editions Sidwaya: BP 507, Ouagadougou 01; tel. 50-31-22-89; fax 50-31-03-62; internet www.sidwaya.bf; f. 1998 to replace Société Nationale d'Editions et de Presse; state-owned; transfer to private ownership proposed; general, periodicals; Dir IBRAHIMAN SAKANDÉ.

Broadcasting and Communications

TELECOMMUNICATIONS

Regulatory Authority

Autorité de régulation des communications électroniques et des postes (ARCEP): ave Dimdolobsom, porte 43, rue 3 angle rue 48, 01 BP 6437, Ouagadougou 01; tel. 50-37-53-60; fax 50-37-53-64; e-mail secretariat@arcep.bf; internet www.arce.bf; f. 2009 to replace Autorité nationale de régulation des télécommunications (ARTEL); Pres. of the Council of Administration BÉLI MATHURIN BAKO; Dir-Gen. SIBIRI OUATTARA.

Service Providers

Airtel Burkina Faso: ave du Président Aboubacar Sangoulé Lamizana, 01 BP 6622, Ouagadougou 01; tel. 50-33-14-00; fax 50-33-14-06; e-mail info@bf.airtel.com; internet africa.airtel.com/burkina; f. 2001; fmrly Zain Burkina Faso, present name adopted 2010; mobile cellular telephone operator in Ouagadougou, Bobo-Dioulasso and

235 other towns; acquired by Bharti Airtel (India) in 2010; Dir-Gen. JOHN NDEGO; 1m. subscribers (Feb. 2008).

Office National des Télécommunications (ONATEL): ave de la Nation, 01 BP 10000, Ouagadougou 01; tel. 50-49-44-02; fax 50-31-03-31; e-mail dcrp@onatel.bf; internet www.onatel.bf; 51% owned by Maroc Telecom (Morocco, Vivendi); 23% state owned; Pres. PAUL BALMA; Dir-Gen. MOHAMMED MORCHID.

TELMOB: tel. 49-42-41; fax 50-49-42-78; e-mail wema.d@onatel.bf; internet www.telmob.bf; f. 2002; mobile cellular telephone operator in 19 cities; Dir DIEUDONNÉ WEMA; 400,000 subscribers (Dec. 2006).

Telecel-Faso: 396 ave de la Nation, 08 BP 11059, Ouagadougou 086; tel. 50-33-35-56; fax 50-33-35-58; e-mail infos@telecelfaso.bf; internet www.telecelfaso.bf; f. 2000; mobile cellular telephone operator in Ouagadougou, Bobo-Dioulasso and 19 other towns; 80% owned by Orascom Telecom (Egypt); Dir-Gen. DIMITRI W. OUÉDRAOGO; 80,000 subscribers (Dec. 2003).

BROADCASTING

In 2010 there were some 112 radio stations and 14 television stations operating in Burkina Faso.

Regulatory Authority

Conseil supérieur de la Communication (Higher Council of Communication): 290 ave Ho Chi Minh, 01 BP 6618, Ouagadougou 01; tel. 50-30-11-24; fax 50-30-11-33; e-mail info@csi.bf; internet www.csi.bf; f. 1995 as Higher Council of Information, present name adopted 2005; Pres. MARIE NOËLLIE BÉATRICE DAMIBA; Sec.-Gen. JEAN-PAUL KONSEIBO.

Radio

Radiodiffusion-Télévision du Burkina (RTB): 01 BP 2530, Ouagadougou 01; tel. 50-31-83-53; fax 50-32-48-09; internet www.rtb.bf; f. 2001; Dir-Gen. YACOUBA TRAORÉ.

Horizon FM: 01 BP 2714, Ouagadougou 01; tel. 50-33-23-23; fax 50-30-21-41; e-mail hfm@grouphorizonfm.com; internet www.grouphorizonfm.com; f. 1990; private commercial station; broadcasts in French, English and 8 vernacular languages; operates 10 stations nationally; Dir JUDITH IDA SAWADOGO.

Ouaga FM: blvd France-Afrique, Ouagadougou; tel. 50-37-51-21; fax 50-37-61-77; internet www.ouagafm.bf; Pres. JOACHIM BAKY; Dir-Gen. ZAKARIDJA GNIENHOUN.

Radio Nationale du Burkina (La RNB): 03 BP 7029, Ouagadougou 03; tel. 50-32-43-02; fax 50-31-04-41; e-mail radio@rtb.bf; internet www.radio.bf; f. 1959; state radio service; comprises national broadcaster of informative and discussion programmes, music stations *Canal Arc-En-Ciel* and *Canal Arc-en-Ciel Plus*, and 2 regional stations, broadcasting in local languages, in Bobo-Dioulasso and Gaoua; Dir OUÉZIN LOUIS OULON.

Radio Evangile Développement (RED): 04 BP 8050, Ouagadougou 04; tel. 50-43-51-56; e-mail redbf@laposte.net; internet www.red-burkina.org; f. 1993; broadcasts from Ouagadougou, Bobo-Dioulasso, Ouahigouya, Léo, Houndé, Koudougou, Yako and Fada N'Gourma; evangelical Christian; Dir-Gen. ETIENNE KIEMDE.

Radio Locale-Radio Rurale: 03 BP 7029, Ouagadougou 03; tel. 50-31-27-81; fax 40-79-10-22; f. 1969; community broadcaster; local stations at Diapaga, Djibasso Gasson, Kongoussi, Orodara and Poura; Dir-Gen. BÉLIBIÉ SOUMAÏLA BASSOLE.

Radio Maria: BP 51, Koupela; tel. and fax 40-70-00-10; e-mail administration.bur@radiomaria.org; internet www.radiomaria.org; f. 1993; Roman Catholic; Dir BELEMSIGRI PIERRE CLAVER.

Radio Pulsar: Ave Léo Frobenius, 01 BP 5976, Ouagadougou 01; tel. 50314199; e-mail info@monpulsar.com; internet www.monpulsar.com; f. 1996; Dir FRANÇOIS YESSO.

Radio Salankoloto-Association Galian: 01 BP 1095, Ouagadougou 01; tel. 50-31-64-93; fax 50-31-64-71; e-mail radiosalankoloto@cenatrin.bf; f. 1996; community broadcaster; Dir ROGER NIKIÉMA.

Radio Vive le Paysan: BP 75, Saponé; tel. 50-40-56-21; fax 50-30-52-80; e-mail a2oyigde@yahoo.fr; f. 1995; Dir ADRIEN VITAUX.

Radio la Voix du Paysan: BP 100, Ouahigouya; tel. 40-55-04-11; fax 40-55-01-62; community broadcaster; f. 1996; Pres. BERNARD LÉDÉA OUÉDRAOGO.

Savane FM: 10 BP 500, Ouagadougou 10; tel. 50-43-37-43; internet www.savanefm.bf; Dir-Gen. CHARLEMAGNE ABISSI.

Television

BF1: Ouagadougou; f. 2010; Dir-Gen. LÉOPOLD KOHOUN.

La Télévision Nationale du Burkina: 955 blvd de la Révolution, 01 BP 2530, Ouagadougou 01; tel. 50-31-83-53; fax 50-32-48-09; e-mail television@rtb.bf; internet www.tnb.bf; branch of Radiodiffusion-Télévision du Burkina (q.v.); broadcasts 75 hours per week; Dir PASCAL YEMBOINI THIOMBIANO.

Télévision Canal Viim Koéga—Fréquence Lumière: BP 108, Ouagadougou; tel. 50-30-76-40; e-mail cvktv@cvktv.org; internet www.cvktv.org; f. 1996; operated by the Fédération des Eglises et Missions Evangéliques; broadcasts 6 hours daily (Mon.–Fri.).

TV Canal 3: ave Kwamé N'Krumah, 11 BP 340, Ouagadougou 11; tel. 50-30-06-55; e-mail info@tvcanal3.com; internet www.tvcanal3.com; f. 2002.

TV Maria: Ouagadougou; f. 2009; Roman Catholic; Dir RACHEL ZONGO.

TVZ Africa: 145 ave de Kossodo, 01 BP 70170, Ouagadougou 01; tel. 70-26-28-20; internet www.tvzafrica.com; commercial broadcaster; Pres. and Dir-Gen. MOUSTAPHA LAABLI THIOMBIANO.

Finance

(cap. = capital; res = reserves; dep. = deposits; m. = million; br(s). = branch(es); amounts in francs CFA)

BANKING

In 2009 there were 11 banks and 5 financial institutions in Burkina Faso.

Central Bank

Banque centrale des états de l'Afrique de l'ouest (BCEAO): ave Bassawarga, BP 356, Ouagadougou; tel. 50-30-60-15; fax 50-31-01-22; e-mail webmaster@bceao.int; internet www.bceao.int; HQ in Dakar, Senegal; f. 1962; bank of issue for the mem. states of the Union économique et monétaire ouest-africaine (UEMOA, comprising Benin, Burkina Faso, Côte d'Ivoire, Guinea-Bissau, Mali, Niger, Senegal and Togo); cap. 134,120m., res 1,474,195m., dep. 2,124,051m. (Dec. 2009); Gov. KONÉ TIÉMOKO MEYLIET; Dir in Burkina Faso BOLO SANOU; br. in Bobo-Dioulasso.

Other Banks

Bank of Africa—Burkina Faso (BOA—B): 770 ave du President Sangoule Lamizana, 01 BP 1319, Ouagadougou 01; tel. 50-30-88-70; fax 50-30-88-74; e-mail boadg@fasonet.bf; internet www.boaburkinafaso.com; f. 1998; cap. 5,000.0m., res 2,428.8m., dep. 158,062.3m. (Dec. 2009); Chair. MICHEL F. KAHN; 20 brs.

Banque Agricole et Commerciale du Burkina (BAC-B): 2 ave Gamal Abdel Nasser, Secteur 3, 01 BP 1644, Ouagadougou 01; tel. 50-33-33-33; fax 50-31-43-52; e-mail bacb@bacb.bf; internet www.bacb.bf; f. 1980; fmrly Caisse Nationale de Crédit Agricole du Burkina (CNCA-B); present name adopted 2002; 25% state-owned; cap. 3,500m., res 898m., dep. 70,108m. (Dec. 2006); Pres. TIBILA KABORE; Chair. and Gen. Man. LÉONCE KONÉ; 4 brs.

Banque Commerciale du Burkina (BCB): 653 ave Dr Kwamé N'Krumah, 01 BP 1336, Ouagadougou 01; tel. 50-30-78-78; fax 50-31-06-28; e-mail bcb@bcb.bf; internet www.bcb.bf; f. 1988; 50% owned by Libyan Arab Foreign Bank, 25% state-owned, 25% owned by Caisse Nationale de Sécurité Sociale; cap. 26,125m., res –6,555m., dep. 73,391m. (Dec. 2009); Pres. JACQUES ZIDA; Gen. Man. ABDULLA EL MOGADAMI; 4 brs.

Banque Internationale du Burkina (BIB): 1340 ave Dimdolobsom, 01 BP 362, Ouagadougou 01; tel. 75-35-20-95; fax 75-35-20-94; e-mail info@bibburkinafaso.net; internet www.bibburkinafaso.net; f. 1974; 25% owned by Fonds Burkina de Développement Economique et Social, 24.2% owned by Holding COFIPA (Mali), 22.8% state owned; cap. 12,000.0m., res –4,761.3m., dep. 156,775.9m. (Dec. 2009); Pres. and Dir-Gen. GASPARD-JEAN OUÉDRAOGO; 21 brs.

Banque Internationale pour le Commerce, l'Industrie et l'Agriculture du Burkina (BICIA—B): 479 ave Dr Kwamé N'Krumah, 01 BP 08, Ouagadougou 01; tel. 50-31-31-31; fax 50-31-19-55; e-mail biciabq@fasonet.bf; internet www.biciab.bf; f. 1973; affiliated to BNP Paribas (France); 25% state-owned; cap. 5,000m., res 7,338m., dep. 127,687m. (Dec. 2008); Pres. MICHEL KOMPAORÉ; Dir-Gen. LUC VIDAL; 11 brs.

Ecobank Burkina: Immeuble espace Fadima, 633 rue Ilboudo Waogyande, 01 BP 145, Ouagadougou 01; tel. 50-32-83-28; fax 50-31-89-81; e-mail ecobankbf@ecobank.com; internet www.ecobank.com; f. 1996; 82% owned by Ecobank Transnational Inc.; dep. 108,167.5m. (Dec. 2008); Chair. ANDRÉ BAYALA; Dir-Gen. ROGER DAH-ACHINANON.

Société Générale de Banques au Burkina (SGBB): 248 rue de l'Hôtel de Ville, 01 BP 585, Ouagadougou 01; tel. 50-32-32-32; fax 50-31-05-61; e-mail sgbb.burkina@socgen.com; internet www.sgbb.bf; f. 1998; 50% owned by Partie Burkinabè, 44% owned by Société Générale (France), 6% owned by FINADEI; cap. and res 5,510m., total assets 95,927m. (Dec. 2004); Dir-Gen. PATRICK DELAILLE.

Credit Institutions

Burkina Bail, SA: 1035 ave du Dr Kwamé N'Krumah, Immeuble SODIFA, 01 BP 1913, Ouagadougou 01; tel. 50-33-26-33; fax 50-30-70-02; e-mail info@burkinabail.bf; internet www.burkinabail.bf; f. 1998; 47% owned by BIB, 34% owned by FMO and 18% owned by Cauris Investissement; cap. 1,000m., total assets 9,276m. (Dec. 2007); CEO KOUAFILANN ABDOULAYE SORY.

Réseau des Caisses Populaires du Burkina (RCPB): Ouagadougou; tel. 50-30-48-41; internet www.rcpb.bf; f. 1972; Dir-Gen. DAOUDA SAWADOGA; 450,000 mems (2006), 104 co-operatives.

Société Burkinabè de Financement (SOBFI): Immeuble Nassa, 1242 ave Dr Kwamé N'Krumah, 10 BP 13876, Ouagadougou 10; tel. 50-31-80-04; fax 50-33-71-62; e-mail sobfi@fasonet.bf; f. 1997; cap. 500.0m., total assets 2,850.9m. (Dec. 2002); Pres. DIAWAR DIACK.

Bankers' Association

Association Professionnelle des Banques et Etablissements Financiers du Burkina (APBEF-B): 1021 ave de la Cathédrale, 01 BP 6215, Ouagadougou 01; tel. 50-31-20-65; fax 50-31-20-66; e-mail apbef@fasonet.bf; f. 1967; Vice-Pres. MAMADI NAPON.

STOCK EXCHANGE

Bourse Régionale des Valeurs Mobilières (BRVM): s/c Chambre de Commerce, d'Industrie et d'Artisanat du Burkina, 01 BP 502, Ouagadougou 01; tel. 50-30-87-73; fax 50-30-87-19; e-mail louedraogo@brvm.org; internet www.brvm.org; f. 1998; national branch of BRVM (regional stock exchange based in Abidjan, Côte d'Ivoire, serving the member states of UEMOA); Man. LÉOPOLD OUÉDRAOGO.

INSURANCE

In 2008 there were 10 insurance companies in Burkina Faso.

Allianz Burkina Assurances: 99 ave Léo Frobénius, 01 BP 398, Ouagadougou 01; tel. 50-30-62-04; fax 50-31-01-53; e-mail allianz.burkina@allianz-bf.com; internet www.allianz-burkina.com; f. 1978; name changed as above in 2009; subsidiary of Allianz (France); non-life insurance and reinsurance; cap. 400m.; Dir-Gen. PHILIPPE AUDOUIN; also **Allianz Burkina Assurances Vie**, life insurance; Dir-Gen. PHILIPPE AUDOUIN.

Générale des Assurances: 01 BP 6275, Ouagadougou 01; tel. 50-30-06-40; fax 50-30-87-17; e-mail g.assur@fasonet.bf; Dir-Gen. (life insurance) SIMON PIERRE GOUEM; Dir-Gen. (non-life insurance) JEAN-PAUL OUÉDRAOGO.

Gras Savoye Burkina Faso: ave de la Résistance du 17 mai, 01 BP 1304, Ouagadougou 01; tel. 50-30-51-69; fax 50-30-51-73; affiliated to Gras Savoye (France); Dir-Gen. LAURENT SAWADOGO.

Raynal SA: ave du Dr Kwamé N'Krumah, 01 BP 6131, Ouagadougou 01; tel. 50-30-25-12; fax 50-30-25-14; e-mail raynal-sa@raynal-sa.com; Dir-Gen. REYNATOU ELÉONOR BADO YAMEOGO.

Société Nationale d'Assurances et de Réassurances (SONAR): 284 ave de Loudun, 01 BP 406, Ouagadougou 01; tel. 50-33-46-66; fax 50-30-89-75; e-mail sonarinfo@sonar.bf; internet www.sonar.bf; f. 1974; 42% owned by Burkinabè interests, 33% by French, Ivorian and US cos, 22% state-owned; life and non-life; cap. 720m. (SONAR-IARD, non-life), 500m. (SONAR-Vie, life); Dir-Gen. ANDRÉ B. BAYALA; 9 brs and sub-brs.

Union des Assurances du Burkina (UAB): 08 BP 11041, Ouagadougou 08; tel. 50-31-26-15; fax 50-31-26-20; e-mail uab@fasonet.bf; f. 1991; 11% owned by AXA Assurances Côte d'Ivoire; cap. 1,000m.; Pres. APPOLINAIRE COMPAORÉ; Dir-Gen. (non-life insurance) JEAN DASMASCÈNE NIGNAN; Dir-Gen. (life insurance) SOUMAÏLA SORGHO.

Trade and Industry

GOVERNMENT AGENCIES

Bureau des Mines et de la Géologie du Burkina (BUMIGEB): 4186 route de Fada N'Gourma, 01 BP 601, Ouagadougou 01; tel. 50-36-48-02; fax 50-36-48-88; e-mail bumigeb@cenatrin.bf; internet www.bumigeb.bf; f. 1978; restructured 1997; research into geological and mineral resources; Pres. BOURI ROGER ZOMBRE; Dir-Gen. PASCALE DIENDÉRÉ.

Commission de Privatisation: 01 BP 6451, Ouagadougou 01; tel. 50-33-58-93; fax 50-30-77-41; Pres. PLACIDE SOME.

Comptoir Burkinabè des Métaux Précieux (CBMP): Ouagadougou; tel. 50-30-75-48; fax 50-31-56-34; promotes gold sector, liaises with artisanal producers; transfer to private management pending; Dir-Gen. YACOUBA BARRY.

Office National d'Aménagement des Terroirs (ONAT): 01 BP 3007, Ouagadougou 01; tel. 50-30-61-10; fax 50-30-61-12; f. 1974; fmrly Autorité des Aménagements des Vallées des Voltas; integrated rural devt, incl. economic and social planning; Man. Dir ZACHARIE OUÉDRAOGO.

Office National des Barrages et des Aménagements Hydro-agricoles (ONBAH): 03 BP 7056, Ouagadougou 03; tel. 50-30-89-82; fax 50-31-04-26; f. 1976; control and devt of water for agricultural use, construction of dams, water and soil conservation; state-owned; Dir-Gen. AÏZO TINDANO.

Office National du Commerce Extérieur (ONAC): 30 ave de l'UEMOA, 01 BP 389, Ouagadougou 01; tel. 50-31-13-00; fax 50-31-14-69; e-mail info@onac.bf; internet www.tradepoint.bf; f. 1974; promotes and supervises external trade; Man. Dir BAYA JUSTIN BAYILI; br. at Bobo-Dioulasso.

DEVELOPMENT ORGANIZATIONS

Agence Française de Développement (AFD): 52 ave de la Nation, 01 BP 529, Ouagadougou 01; tel. 50-30-60-92; fax 50-31-19-66; e-mail afdouagadougou@bf.groupe-afd.org; internet www.afd.fr; Country Dir PATRICE TRANCHANT.

Autorité de régulation des marchés publics: 01 BP 2080, Ouagadougou 01; tel. 50-30-69-01; e-mail armp@armp.bf; internet www.armp.bf; f. 2007; Perm. Sec. MAMADOU GUIRA.

Bureau d'Appui aux Micro-entreprises (BAME): BP 610, Bobo-Dioulasso; tel. 20-97-16-28; fax 20-97-21-76; f. 1991; supports small business; Dir FÉLIX SANON.

Cellule d'Appui à la Petite et Moyenne Entreprise d'Ouagadougou (CAPEO): 01 BP 6443, Ouagadougou 01; tel. 50-31-37-62; fax 50-31-37-64; internet www.spid.com/capeo; f. 1991; supports small and medium-sized enterprises.

France Volontaires: 01 BP 947, Ouagadougou 01; tel. 50-30-70-43; fax 50-30-10-72; internet www.france-volontaires.org; f. 1973 as Association Française des Volontaires du Progrès; name changed as above in 2009; supports small business; Nat. Delegate EUGÈNE SOME.

Promotion du Développement Industriel, Artisanal et Agricole (PRODIA): Secteur 8, Gounghin, 01 BP 2344, Ouagadougou 01; tel. 50-34-31-11; fax 50-34-71-47; f. 1981; supports small business; Dir MAMADOU OUÉDRAOGO.

CHAMBERS OF COMMERCE

Chambre de Commerce, d'Industrie et d'Artisanat du Burkina Faso: 118/220 ave de Lyon, 01 BP 502, Ouagadougou 01; tel. 50-30-61-14; fax 50-30-61-16; e-mail ccia-bf@ccia.bf; internet www.ccia.bf; f. 1948; Pres. ALIZÈTA OUÉDRAOGO; Dir-Gen. FRANCK TAPSOBA; brs in Bobo-Dioulasso, Koupéla and Ouahigouya.

Chambre des Mines du Burkina (CMB): Ouagadougou; f. 2011; Pres. ELIE OUÉDRAOGO.

EMPLOYERS' ORGANIZATIONS

Club des Hommes d'Affaires Franco-Burkinabé: Ambassade de France au Burkina Faso, 01 BP 4382, Ouagadougou 01; tel. 50-31-32-73; fax 50-31-32-81; internet www.chafb.bf; f. 1990; represents 65 major enterprises and seeks to develop trading relations between Burkina Faso and France; Pres. EDDIE KOMBOIGO.

Conseil National du Patronat Burkinabè (CNPB): 1221 ave du Dr Kwame N'Krumah, 01 BP 1482, Ouagadougou 01; tel. 50-33-03-09; fax 50-30-03-08; e-mail cnpb@liptinfor.bf; f. 1974; comprises 70 professional groupings; Pres. El Hadj OUMAROU KANAZOE; Sec.-Gen. PHILOMÈNE YAMEOGO.

Groupement Professionnel des Industriels (GPI): Immeuble CBC, 641 ave Koubemba, 01 BP 5381, Ouagadougou 01; tel. and fax 50-30-11-59; e-mail gpi@fasonet.bf; internet www.gpi.bf; f. 1974; Pres. (vacant).

Fédération Nationale des Exportateurs du Burkina (FENEB): 01 BP 389, Ouagadougou 01; tel. 50-31-13-00; fax 50-31-14-69; e-mail fofseydou@hotmail.com; Permanent Sec. SEYDOU FOFANA.

Jeune Chambre Internationale du Burkina Faso: Immeuble Kanazoe, ave du Travail, 11 BP 136, Ouagadougou; tel. 78-85-40-41; e-mail kroser73@yahoo.fr; internet www.jci.cc/local/burkina; f. 1976; org. of entrepreneurs aged 18–40; affiliated to Junior Chambers International, Inc; Exec. Pres. K. RODOLPHE S. DJIGUIMDE.

Maison de l'Entreprise du Burkina Faso (MEBF): rue 3-1119, porte 132, 11 BP 379, Ouagadougou 11; tel. 50-39-80-60; fax 50-39-80-62; e-mail info@me.bf; internet www.me.bf; f. 2002; promotes devt of the private sector; Pres. ALAIN ROGER COEFE; Dir-Gen. ISSAKA KARGOUGOU.

Syndicat des Commerçants Importateurs et Exportateurs du Burkina (SCIMPEX): ave Kadiogo, Secteur 2, Immeuble CBC, 1er étage, 01 BP 552, Ouagadougou 01; tel. 50-31-18-70; fax 50-31-30-36; e-mail scimpex@fasonet.bf; internet www.scimpex-bf.com; f. 1959; Pres. LASSINÉ DIAWARA.

Union Nationale des Producteurs de Coton du Burkina Faso (UNPCB): 02 BP 1677, Bobo-Dioulasso 02; tel. 20-97-33-10; fax 20-97-20-59; e-mail unpcb@fasonet.bf; internet www.abcburkina.net/unpcb/unpcb_index.htm; f. 1998; Pres. KARIM TRAORÉ.

UTILITIES

Electricity

Société Générale de Travaux et de Constructions Electriques (SOGETEL): Zone Industrielle, Gounghin, 01 BP 429, Ouagadougou 01; tel. 50-30-23-45; fax 50-34-25-70; e-mail sogetel@cenatrin.bf; internet www.cenatrin.bf/sogetel; transport and distribution of electricity.

Société Nationale Burkinabè d'Électricité (SONABEL): 55 ave de la Nation, 01 BP 54, Ouagadougou 01; tel. 50-30-61-00; fax 50-31-03-40; e-mail courrier@sonabel.bf; internet www.sonabel.bf; f. 1984; state-owned; partial privatization proposed; production and distribution of electricity; Dir-Gen. SIENGUI APOLLINAIRE KI.

Water

Office National de l'Eau et de l'Assainissement (ONEA): 01 BP 170, Ouagadougou 01; tel. 50-43-19-00; fax 50-43-19-11; e-mail onea@fasonet.bf; internet www.oneabf.com; f. 1977; storage, purification and distribution of water; transferred to private management (by Veolia Water Burkina Faso) in 2001; Dir-Gen. HAROUNA YAMBA OUIBIGA.

Veolia Water Burkina Faso: 06 BP 9525, Ouagadougou 06; tel. and fax 50-34-03-00; manages operation of water distribution and sewerage services; subsidiary of Veolia Environnement (France).

CO-OPERATIVE

Union des Coopératives Agricoles et Maraîchères du Burkina (UCOBAM): 01 BP 277, Ouagadougou 01; tel. 50-30-65-27; fax 50-30-65-28; e-mail ucobam@zcp.bf; internet www.ucobam.bf; f. 1968; comprises 8 regional co-operative unions (6,500 mems, representing 35,000 producers); production and marketing of fruit, vegetables, jams and conserves; Dir-Gen. YASSIA OUEDRAOGO.

TRADE UNIONS

Confédération Générale du Travail Burkina (CGTB): 01 BP 547, Ouagadougou 01; tel. and fax 50-31-36-71; e-mail info@cgtb.bf; internet www.cgtb.bf; f. 1988; confed. of several autonomous trade unions; Sec.-Gen. TOLÉ SAGNON.

Confédération Nationale des Travailleurs Burkinabè (CNTB): BP 445, Ouagadougou; tel. 50-31-23-95; e-mail cntb@fasonet.bf; f. 1972; Sec.-Gen. AUGUSTIN BLAISE HIEN; 10,000 mems.

Confédération Syndicale Burkinabè (CSB): 01 BP 1921, Ouagadougou 01; tel. and fax 50-31-83-98; e-mail cosybu2000@yahoo.fr; f. 1974; mainly public service unions; Sec.-Gen. JEAN MATHIAS LILIOU.

Organisation Nationale des Syndicats Libres (ONSL): 01 BP 99, Ouagadougou 01; tel. and fax 50-34-34-69; e-mail onslbf@yahoo.fr; f. 1960; Sec.-Gen. PAUL NOBILA KABORÉ; 6,000 mems.

Union Syndicale des Travailleurs Burkinabè (USTB): BP 381, Ouagadougou; tel. and fax 50-33-73-09; f. 1958; Sec.-Gen. MAMADOU NAMA; 35,000 mems in 45 affiliated orgs.

Transport

RAILWAY

In 2010 the total length of track in operation was 622 km.

SITARAIL—Transport Ferroviaire de Personnes et de Marchandises: rue Dioncolo, 01 BP 5699, Ouagadougou 01; tel. 50-31-07-35; fax 50-30-85-21; 67% owned by Groupe Bolloré, 15% state-owned, 15% owned by Govt of Côte d'Ivoire; national branch of SITARAIL (based in Abidjan, Côte d'Ivoire); responsible for operations on the railway line between Kaya, Ouagadougou and Abidjan (Côte d'Ivoire); Regional Dir MOURAMANE FOFANA.

Société de Gestion du Patrimoine Ferroviaire du Burkina (SOPAFER—B): 93 rue de la Culture, 01 BP 192, Ouagadougou 01; tel. 50-31-35-99; fax 50-31-35-94; e-mail dgsopafer@liptinfor.bf; f. 1995; railway network services; Dir-Gen. AHAMADO OUÉDRAGO.

ROADS

In 2004 there were an estimated 92,495 km of roads, including 15,271 km of highways.

Fonds d'Entretien Routier du Burkina (FER): 01 BP 2517, Ouagadougou 01; Dir-Gen. MAMADOU OUATTARA.

Société Africaine de Transports Routiers (SATR): 01 BP 5298, Ouagadougou 01; tel. 50-34-08-62.

Société Nationale du Transit du Burkina (SNTB): 474 rue Ilboudo Waogyandé, 01 BP 1192, Ouagadougou 01; tel. 50-49-30-00; fax 50-30-85-21; f. 1977; 82% owned by Groupe SAGA (France), 12% state-owned; road haulage and warehousing; Dir-Gen. RÉGIS TISSIER.

Société de Transport en Commun de Ouagadougou (SOTRACO): 2257 ave du Sanematenga, 01 BP 5665 Ouagadougou 01; tel. 50-35-67-87; fax 50-35-66-80; e-mail sotraco@fasonet.bf; internet sotraco-bf.net; f. 2003; Dir-Gen. BOUREIMA TARNAGDA.

CIVIL AVIATION

There are international airports at Ouagadougou and Bobo-Dioulasso, 49 small airfields and 13 private airstrips. Plans were announced in 2006 for the construction of a new international airport at Donsin, 35 km north-east of the capital; the first phase of the project from 2007–11 was to cost some 115,000m. francs CFA. Two subsequent phases were projected to extend until 2023. Ouagadougou airport handled an estimated 2,756,367 passengers and 4,105 metric tons of freight in 2005.

Air Burkina: 29 ave de la Nation, 01 BP 1459, Ouagadougou 01; tel. 50-49-23-70; fax 50-31-31-65; e-mail resa@airburkina.bf; internet www.air-burkina.com; f. 1967 as Air Volta; 56% owned by Aga Khan Group, 14% state-owned; operates domestic and regional services; Dir MOHAMED GHELALA.

Tourism

Burkina Faso, which possesses some 2.8m. ha of nature reserves, is considered to provide some of the best opportunities to observe wild animals in West Africa. Some big game hunting is permitted. Several important cultural events are also held in Burkina Faso: the biennial pan-African film festival, FESPACO, is held in Ouagadougou, as is the biennial international exhibition of handicrafts, while Bobo-Dioulasso hosts the biennial week of national culture. In 2008 there were 225,651 foreign visitors. Receipts from tourism were estimated at US $57.4m. in 2007.

Office National du Tourisme Burkinabè (ONTB): ave Frobénius, BP 1318, Ouagadougou; tel. 50-31-19-59; fax 50-31-44-34; e-mail ontb@ontb.bf; internet www.ontb.bf; Dir-Gen. SOULÉMANE OUEDRAOGO.

Defence

National service is voluntary, and lasts for two years on a part-time basis. As assessed at November 2011, the armed forces numbered 11,200 (army 6,400, air force 600, paramilitary gendarmerie 4,200). There was also a 'security company' of 250 and a part-time people's militia of 45,000.

Defence Expenditure: Estimated at 62,400m. francs CFA in 2010.

Chief of the General Staff of the Armed Forces and Chief of Staff of the Army: Col-Maj. HONORÉ NABÉRÉ TRAORÉ.

Education

Education is provided free of charge, and is officially compulsory for 10 years between the ages of six and 16. Primary education begins at six years of age and lasts for six years, comprising three cycles of two years each. Secondary education, beginning at the age of 13, lasts for a further seven years, comprising a first cycle of four years and a second of three years. Enrolment levels are among the lowest in the region. According to UNESCO estimates, in 2008/09 primary enrolment included 60% (boys 64%; girls 57%) of children in the relevant age-group, while in 2009/10 secondary enrolment included only 16% of children in the appropriate age-group (boys 18%; girls 14%). There are three state-owned higher education institutions: a university in Ouagadougou, a polytechnic university at Bobo-Dioulasso and an institute of teacher training at Koudougou. There are also 11 private higher education institutions. The number of students enrolled at tertiary-level institutions in 2009/10 was 51,200. In 2011 spending on education was budgeted at 23.3% of total budgeted government expenditure.

BURUNDI

Introductory Survey

LOCATION, CLIMATE, LANGUAGE, RELIGION, FLAG, CAPITAL

The Republic of Burundi is a land-locked country lying on the eastern shore of Lake Tanganyika, in central Africa, a little south of the Equator. It is bordered by Rwanda to the north, by Tanzania to the south and east, and by the Democratic Republic of the Congo (formerly Zaire) to the west. The climate is tropical (hot and humid) in the lowlands, and cool in the highlands, with an irregular rainfall. The population is composed of three ethnic groups: the Hutu (85%), the Tutsi (14%) and the Twa (1%). The official languages are French and Kirundi, while Swahili is used, in addition to French, in commercial circles. Some 70% of the inhabitants profess Christianity, with the great majority of the Christians being Roman Catholics. A large minority still adhere to traditional animist beliefs. The national flag (proportions 3 by 5) consists of a white diagonal cross on a background of red (above and below) and green (hoist and fly), with a white circle, containing three green-edged red stars, in the centre. The capital is Bujumbura.

CONTEMPORARY POLITICAL HISTORY

Historical Context

Burundi (formerly Urundi) became part of German East Africa in 1899. In 1916 the territory was occupied by Belgian forces from the Congo (now the Democratic Republic of the Congo, DRC). Subsequently, as part of Ruanda-Urundi, it was administered by Belgium under a League of Nations mandate and later as a UN Trust Territory. Elections in September 1961, conducted under UN supervision, were won by the Union pour le progrès national (UPRONA). Internal self-government was granted in January 1962 and full independence on 1 July, when the two parts of the Trust Territory became separate states, as Burundi and Rwanda. Tensions between Burundi's two main ethnic groups, the Tutsi (traditionally the dominant tribe, despite representing a minority of the overall population) and the Hutu, escalated during 1965. Following an unsuccessful attempt by the Hutu to overthrow the Tutsi-dominated Government in October, nearly all the Hutu political élite were executed, eliminating any significant participation by the Hutu in Burundi's political life until the late 1980s (see below).

Burundi was declared a republic in June 1966, and UPRONA became the sole legal party in July 1974. However, in 1976 members of the armed forces, led by Lt-Col (later Col) Jean-Baptiste Bagaza, effected a *coup d'état*. Bagaza was appointed President by the Supreme Revolutionary Council (composed of army officers), and a new Council of Ministers was formed. The first national congress of UPRONA was held in December 1979, and a party Central Committee, headed by Bagaza, was elected to take over the functions of the Supreme Revolutionary Council in January 1980. A new Constitution, adopted by national referendum in November 1981, provided for the establishment of a unicameral legislature, the Assemblée nationale. The first legislative elections were held in October 1982. Having been re-elected President of UPRONA in July 1984, Bagaza, the sole candidate, was elected President of Burundi in August, winning 99.6% of the votes cast.

In September 1987 Bagaza was deposed in a military coup, led by Maj. Pierre Buyoya, who accused Bagaza of corruption. Buyoya immediately formed a Comité militaire pour le salut national (CMSN) to administer the country. The Constitution was suspended, and the Assemblée nationale was dissolved. On 2 October Buyoya was inaugurated as President of the Third Republic.

In August 1988 tribal tensions erupted into violence in the north of the country when groups of Hutus, claiming Tutsi provocation, slaughtered hundreds of Tutsis in the towns of Ntega and Marangara. The Tutsi-dominated army was immediately dispatched to the region to restore order, and large-scale tribal massacres occurred. In October Buyoya announced government changes, including the appointment of a Hutu, Adrien Sibomana, as Prime Minister, and established a committee to investigate the massacres; nevertheless, political tension persisted.

Domestic Political Affairs

In May 1990, in response to a new draft charter on national unity, Buyoya announced plans to replace military rule with a 'democratic constitution under a one-party government'. In December, at an extraordinary national congress of UPRONA, the CMSN was abolished and its functions transferred to an 80-member Central Committee, with Buyoya as Chairman and with a Hutu, Nicolas Mayugi, as Secretary-General. At a referendum in February 1991 the draft charter on national unity was overwhelmingly approved. Later in the month a ministerial reorganization, in which Hutus received 12 of the 23 government portfolios, was viewed with scepticism by political opponents. Proposals to establish a multi-party parliamentary system, which was to operate in conjunction with a renewable five-year presidential mandate, received the support of more than 90% of the voters in a referendum held on 9 March 1992, and the new Constitution was promulgated on 13 March.

In an extensive government reorganization in April 1992, Hutus were appointed to 15 of the 25 ministries, while Buyoya relinquished the defence portfolio. In the same month Buyoya approved legislation relating to the creation of new political parties in accordance with the new Constitution. New political parties were to be obliged to demonstrate impartiality with regard to ethnic or regional origin, gender and religion, and were to refrain from militarization. In October Buyoya announced the creation of a 33-member electoral commission, which included representatives of the eight recognized political parties.

A presidential election on 1 June 1993 was won, with 64.8% of the votes cast, by Melchior Ndadaye, the candidate of the Front pour la démocratie au Burundi (FRODEBU), who was supported by the Rassemblement du peuple burundien (RPB), the Parti du peuple and the Parti libéral; Buyoya received 32.4% of the vote as the UPRONA candidate, with support from the Rassemblement pour la démocratie et le développement économique et social (RADDES) and the Parti social démocrate. Elections for 81 seats in the Assemblée nationale were conducted on 29 June. FRODEBU again emerged as the most successful party, with 71% of the votes and 65 of the seats in the new legislature. UPRONA, with 21.4% of the votes, secured the remaining 16 seats. Ndadaye, Burundi's first Hutu Head of State, assumed the presidency on 10 July. A Tutsi, Sylvie Kinigi, became Prime Minister, while the new Council of Ministers included a further six Tutsi representatives.

On 21 October 1993 more than 100 army paratroopers swiftly overwhelmed supporters of the Government and occupied the presidential palace and the headquarters of the national broadcasting company. Ndadaye and several other prominent Hutu politicians and officials were detained and subsequently killed by the insurgents, who later proclaimed François Ngeze, one of the few Hutu members of UPRONA and a minister in the Government of former President Buyoya, as head of a Comité national du salut public (CNSP). While members of the Government sought refuge abroad and in the offices of foreign diplomatic missions in Bujumbura, the armed forces declared a state of emergency, closing national borders and the capital's airport. However, international condemnation of the coup, together with the scale of renewed tribal violence, undermined support for the insurgents from within the armed forces, and precipitated the collapse of the CNSP, which was dissolved on 25 October. Kinigi ended the curfew, but remained in hiding and urged the deployment of an international force in Burundi to protect the civilian Government. On 28 October the UN confirmed that the Government had resumed control of the country. Ngeze and 10 coup leaders were arrested, while some 40 other insurgents were believed to have fled to Zaire (now the DRC). Meanwhile, following division within FRODEBU, a 'hardline' leader, Léonard Nyangoma, established a new party, Conseil national pour la défense de la démocratie (CNDD), with an armed wing, the Forces pour la défense de la démocratie (FDD).

In early November 1993 several members of the Government, including the Prime Minister, left the French embassy with a small escort of French troops, and on 8 November Kinigi met with 15 of the 17 surviving ministers, in an attempt to address the humanitarian crisis arising from the massacre and displacement of hundreds of thousands of Burundians following the failed coup. On the same day the Constitutional Court officially recognized the presidential vacancy resulting from the murder of both Ndadaye and his constitutional successor, Giles Bimazubute, the Speaker of the Assemblée nationale, and stated that presidential power should be exercised by the Council of Ministers, pending a presidential election, which was to be conducted within three months. In December the Minister of External Relations and Co-operation, Sylvestre Ntibantunganya (who had succeeded Ndadaye as leader of FRODEBU), was elected Speaker of the Assemblée nationale.

Meanwhile, in November 1993, following repeated requests by the Government for an international contribution to the protection of government ministers in Burundi, the Organization of African Unity (OAU—now the African Union—AU, see p. 189) agreed to the deployment of a protection force, to comprise some 180 civilian and military personnel. In December opposition parties, including UPRONA and the RADDES, organized demonstrations in protest at the deployment of the contingent, scheduled for January 1994, claiming that it infringed Burundi's sovereignty. As a compromise, in March the Government secured a significant reduction in the size of the mission, to comprise a military contingent of 47 and 20 civilian observers; it was finally deployed in February 1995.

In early January 1994 FRODEBU deputies in the Assemblée nationale approved a draft amendment to the Constitution, allowing a President of the Republic to be elected by the Assemblée nationale, in the event of the Constitutional Court's recognition of a presidential vacancy. UPRONA deputies, who had boycotted the vote, expressed concern that such a procedure represented election by indirect suffrage, in direct contravention of the terms of the Constitution. The continued boycott of the Assemblée nationale by UPRONA deputies forced the postponement, on 10 January, of an attempt by FRODEBU deputies to elect their presidential candidate, the Minister of Agriculture and Livestock, Cyprien Ntaryamira. Three days later, none the less, following the successful negotiation of a political truce with opposition parties, Ntaryamira was elected President by the Assemblée nationale. A Tutsi Prime Minister, Anatole Kanyenkiko, was appointed in early February, and the composition of a new multi-party Council of Ministers was subsequently agreed.

Ethnic violence

On 6 April 1994, returning from a regional summit meeting in Dar es Salaam, Tanzania, Ntaryamira and three government ministers were killed when the aircraft of the Rwandan President, Juvénal Habyarimana, in which they were travelling, was the target of a rocket attack above Kigali airport, Rwanda, and exploded on landing. Habyarimana, who was also killed, was widely acknowledged to have been the intended victim of the attack. In contrast to the violent chaos that erupted in Rwanda (q.v.) in the aftermath of the death of Habyarimana, Burundians responded positively to appeals for calm issued by Ntibantunganya, the Speaker of the Assemblée nationale, who, on 8 April, was confirmed (in accordance with the Constitution) as interim President for a three-month period.

Having discounted the possibility of organizing a general election, owing to security considerations, in June 1994 all major political parties joined lengthy negotiations to establish a procedure for the restoration of the presidency. The mandate of the interim President was extended for three months by the Constitutional Court in July, and by the end of August it had been decided that a new President would be elected by a broadly representative commission. A new power-sharing agreement, the Convention of Government, was announced on 10 September. Detailing the terms of government for a four-year transitional period (including the allocation of 45% of cabinet posts to opposition parties), it was incorporated into the Constitution on 22 September. The Convention also provided for the creation of a Conseil de sécurité nationale (CSN—National Security Council), which was formally inaugurated on 10 October. On 30 September the Convention elected Ntibantunganya to the presidency from a list of six candidates. Ntibantunganya's appointment was endorsed by the Assemblée nationale, and he was formally inaugurated on 1 October. In February 1995 Antoine Nduwayo, a UPRONA candidate selected in consultation with other opposition parties, was appointed Prime Minister by presidential decree. A new coalition Council of Ministers was announced on 1 March, but political stability was undermined immediately by the murder of the Hutu Minister of Energy and Mines, Ernest Kabushemeye.

An escalation in the scale and frequency of incidents of politically and ethnically motivated violence during 1995 prompted renewed concern that the security crisis would precipitate a large-scale campaign of ethnic massacres similar to that in Rwanda during 1994. Government-sponsored military initiatives were concentrated in Hutu-dominated suburbs of Bujumbura and in the north-east, where a campaign was waged against the alleged insurgent activities of the Parti de libération du peuple hutu (PALIPEHUTU—a small, proscribed, Hutu opposition group based in Tanzania), resulting in the deaths of hundreds of Hutu civilians. In June 1995 a report published by the human rights organization Amnesty International claimed that national security forces in Burundi had collaborated with extremist Tutsi factions in the murder of thousands of Hutus since 1993. Increased security measures announced by Ntibantunganya in the same month included restrictions on a number of civil liberties.

By early 1996 reports of atrocities perpetrated against both Hutu and Tutsi civilians by dissident elements of the Tutsi-led armed forces (including militia known as the *Sans Echecs*) and by extremist Hutu rebel groups had become almost commonplace in rural areas. In December 1995 the UN Secretary-General urged the Security Council to sanction some form of international military intervention in Burundi to address the crisis.

Representatives of some 13 political parties (including FRODEBU and UPRONA) participated in discussions conducted in Mwanza, Tanzania, in April 1996, with mediation from the former President of Tanzania, Julius Nyerere. Talks resumed in Mwanza in early June; UPRONA, with support from an informal coalition of seven smaller, predominantly Tutsi parties (the Rassemblement unitaire), accused FRODEBU deputies of seeking to abrogate the Convention of Government, a charge that was strenuously denied by FRODEBU following the talks. At a conference of regional powers in Arusha, Tanzania, in late June, it was reported that Ntibantunganya and Nduwayo had requested foreign intervention to protect government installations. By early July a regional technical commission to examine the request for 'security assistance' (comprising regional defence ministers, but not representatives of the Burundian armed forces) had convened in Arusha and had reached preliminary agreement, with UN support, for an intervention force. Meanwhile, significant differences with regard to the mandate of such a force had emerged between Ntibantunganya and Nduwayo (who suggested that the President was attempting to neutralize the country's military capability). At a mass rally in Bujumbura of Tutsi-dominated opposition parties, the Prime Minister joined other leaders in rejecting foreign military intervention. Some days later, however, full endorsement of the Arusha proposal for intervention was recorded by member nations of the OAU at a summit meeting convened in Yaoundé, Cameroon.

Political and ethnic enmities intensified still further when reports of a massacre of more than 300 Tutsi civilians at Bugendana, allegedly committed by Hutu extremists, including heavily armed Rwandan Hutu refugees, emerged shortly after the UN accused the Burundian authorities of collaborating with the Rwandan administration in a new initiative of (largely enforced) repatriation of Rwandan refugees in Burundi. While FRODEBU members made an urgent appeal for foreign intervention to contain the increasingly violent civil and military reaction to these events, students (with the support of the political opposition) staged further protests against regional military intervention, and in support of demands for the removal of the country's leadership.

Military coup: Buyoya declared transitional President

In late July 1996 the armed forces were extensively deployed in the capital in a military coup. A statement made by the Minister of National Defence, Lt-Col Firmin Sinzoyiheba, criticized the failure of the administration to safeguard national security, and announced the suspension of the Assemblée nationale and all political activity, the imposition of a nation-wide curfew and the closure of national borders and the airport at Bujumbura. Former President Buyoya was declared interim President of a transitional republic, and immediately sought to reassure former ministers and government officials that their safety would be guaranteed by the new regime. Ntibantunganya conveyed his refusal to relinquish office, but Nduwayo resigned, attributing his failure to effect national reconciliation principally to

Ntibantunganya's ineffective leadership. In response to widespread external condemnation of the coup, Buyoya announced that a largely civilian government of national unity would be promptly installed, and that future negotiations with all Hutu groups would be considered. The forced repatriation of Rwandan Hutu refugees was halted with immediate effect.

Despite the appointment at the end of July 1996 of Pascal-Firmin Ndimira, a Hutu member of UPRONA, as Prime Minister, and an urgent attempt by Buyoya to obtain regional support, the leaders of Ethiopia, Kenya, Rwanda, Tanzania, Uganda and Zaire, meeting in Arusha, under OAU auspices, declared their intention to impose stringent economic sanctions against the new regime unless constitutional government was restored immediately. In early August sanctions were imposed, and in the same month the composition of a new 23-member, multi-ethnic Cabinet was announced. In mid-August Buyoya declared that an expanded transitional Assemblée nationale, incorporating existing elected deputies, would be inaugurated during September for a three-year period, but sanctions were maintained due to the continued suspension of the Constitution. Buyoya was formally sworn in as President on 27 September.

By late 1996 the military action in eastern Zaire had led to the repatriation of 30,000 Burundians and had severely weakened FDD fighting capacity, although some rebel activity continued from Tanzania. In January 1997 the office of the UN High Commissioner for Refugees (UNHCR) reported that the army had massed more than 100,000 (mainly Hutu) civilians in camps, as part of a 'regroupment' scheme, which the authorities claimed to be an initiative to protect villagers in areas of rebel activity.

Six ministers were replaced in a reorganization of Ndimira's Government in May 1997, and in August a new post of Minister of the Peace Process was created. Nevertheless, civil unrest continued and on 1 January 1998 an attack on Bujumbura airport by more than 1,000 Hutu rebels resulted in at least 250 deaths. Similar attacks, although on a smaller scale, continued during early 1998. Following the announcement in late February that a regional summit, held in Kampala, Uganda, had voted to maintain the sanctions on Burundi, President Buyoya announced the impending repeal of travel restrictions that had been applied to former Presidents Bagaza and Ntibantunganya, and to the Speaker of the Assemblée nationale, Léonce Ngendakumana.

Following negotiations between the Government and the Assemblée nationale concerning the expiry of FRODEBU's electoral mandate in June 1998, Buyoya and Ngendakumana publicly signed a political accord, and a new transitional Constitution was promulgated on 6 June. The new charter provided for institutional reforms, including the creation of two vice-presidencies to replace the office of Prime Minister, the enlargement of the Assemblée nationale from 81 to 121 seats, and the creation of a seven-member Constitutional Court. In accordance with the transitional Constitution, Buyoya was inaugurated as President on 11 June. On the following day the two Vice-Presidents were appointed: Frédérique Bavuginyumvira, a senior member of FRODEBU, who was allocated responsibility for political and administrative affairs, and Mathias Sinamenye (a Tutsi and hitherto the Governor of the central bank), with responsibility for economic and social issues. A new 22-member Council of Ministers included 13 Hutus and eight Tutsis. The newly enlarged Assemblée nationale, which was inaugurated in mid-July, incorporated nine representatives from smaller political parties, together with 27 civilian representatives and 21 new representatives of FRODEBU to replace those who had been killed or had fled into exile.

Buyoya attended the fourth Arusha summit meeting on the Burundi conflict in April 1997, where the leaders of the Great Lakes countries agreed to ease economic sanctions in the interest of alleviating conditions for the civilian population. The full revocation of sanctions was made dependent on the opening of direct, unconditional peace talks between the Burundian Government and opposition. Initial optimism that inter-party discussions, commencing in Arusha in August 1997, would achieve progress in ending the political crisis diminished as the Buyoya Government became increasingly hostile to the mediation of Nyerere, claiming him to be biased in favour of the opposition. After it became evident that the sanctions would not be revoked immediately upon the opening of negotiations, the Buyoya Government announced that it would not be attending the Arusha talks, stating that it required more time to prepare, and the session was subsequently abandoned. Nyerere openly condemned the stance of the Buyoya regime, appealing for wider international assistance in resolving the crisis.

In May 1998 dissension between the political and military wings of the CNDD resulted in a division of the organization, into a faction headed by Nyangoma (which retained the name CNDD) and a larger faction comprising most of its armed forces, led by the FDD Chief of Staff, Jean-Bosco Ndayikengurukiye (which became known as the CNDD—FDD).

At a regional summit meeting, which took place in Arusha in January 1999, following an appeal from the UN Security Council earlier in the month, regional Heads of State voted to suspend the economic sanctions, although they emphasized that the eventual lifting of the sanctions would be dependent on progress made at inter-party peace talks. In May Buyoya announced his proposals for reconciliation; these included a 10-year transitional period during which he would occupy the presidency for the first five years and a Hutu representative would assume the post for the second five years. The plan also envisaged the extension of the Assemblée nationale to include Hutu rebel factions, the creation of an upper legislative chamber, the establishment of communal police forces, to resolve the issue of Tutsi-dominated defence and security forces, and the establishment of a national truth commission. Buyoya's opponents dismissed the proposals, citing his failure to honour his commitment to return the country swiftly to civilian rule in 1996 and the absence of any reference to elections in his plan. A round of discussions took place in Arusha in July; Nyerere criticized the lack of progress achieved at the negotiations, and the failure of the commissions to reach agreement. The absence from the negotiations of the two most significant rebel movements, the CNDD—FDD and an armed wing of PALIPEHUTU, known as Forces nationales de libération (FNL), was also viewed as a major impediment to agreement on a peace plan. Further talks at Arusha in September were impeded by the escalation of violence throughout the country, particularly around Bujumbura. Subsequent discussions were postponed, owing to the death of Nyerere in mid-October. All the participating parties expressed their commitment to the process, and nine organizations, including FRODEBU and UPRONA, created a movement for peace and solidarity, the Convergence nationale pour la paix et réconciliation (CNPR). In December regional Heads of State, meeting in Arusha, nominated the former President of South Africa, Nelson Mandela, as the new mediator of the peace negotiations.

In January 2000 a major cabinet reorganization was effected. Peace negotiations (the first to be attended by Mandela) resumed in Arusha in late February. Mandela criticized Tutsi domination of public office and urged equal representation of Hutu and Tutsi in the armed forces, while also denouncing Hutu rebel attacks on civilians. At a further round of discussions, which commenced in Arusha in late March, agreement was reached on draft proposals for a new ethnically balanced armed force. (Nevertheless, government forces continued attacks against Hutu rebel positions, prompting fierce fighting south of Bujumbura.) Following a meeting with Buyoya in Johannesburg, South Africa, in June, Mandela announced that the Burundian President had agreed to ensure equal representation of Hutu and Tutsi in the armed forces.

In July 2000 Ndayikengurukiye, as leader of the CNDD—FDD, for the first time accepted an invitation by Mandela to participate in the peace negotiations. In the same month the drafting of a peace accord was finalized; the agreement stipulated the terms for the establishment of a transitional government for a period of three years, the integration of former Hutu rebels into the armed forces, and the creation of an electoral system that would ensure power-sharing between the Tutsi and the Hutu. At a summit meeting, which was attended by several regional Heads of State in Arusha, negotiating groups were presented with the draft peace agreement, which included compromise proposals on unresolved issues. However, the CNDD—FDD demanded the release by the authorities of political prisoners and bilateral negotiations with the armed forces, as a precondition to the cessation of hostilities. (The FNL had again failed to attend the discussions.) On 28 August the peace agreement was formally endorsed by representatives of the Government, the Assemblée nationale, seven Hutu political associations and seven Tutsi parties. The remaining three Tutsi groups that had attended the previous negotiations subsequently signed the accord at cease-fire discussions, which took place in Nairobi, Kenya, in late September, following assurances by Mandela that measures would be taken to ensure that the Hutu rebels cease hostilities. At the same time an Implementation and Monitoring Committee, comprising representatives of the negotiating parties, and international and civil society representatives, was established. Following the conclusion of these discussions, a statement was issued, demanding that the CNDD—FDD and FNL suspend rebel activity and sign the peace agreement.

In January 2001 14 of the 19 signatories of the peace accord agreed on the composition of a new Assemblée nationale, which would allocate Hutu parties 60% and Tutsi 40% representation in the legislature. Nevertheless, hostilities between government troops and Hutu rebels continued, and at the end of February the FNL launched an offensive on the northern outskirts of Bujumbura, which resulted in some 50,000 civilians fleeing to the centre of the capital. Government forces had regained control of Bujumbura by early March, but heavy fighting continued in regions outlying the capital. Later that month CNDD—FDD forces launched a major attack against the principal town of Gitega, 100 km east of Bujumbura, which was repelled by government troops. On 18 April, while Buyoya was attending peace negotiations with the CNDD—FDD leadership in Gabon, Tutsi army officers seized control of the state radio station in Bujumbura and announced that the Government had been overthrown. Troops loyal to Buyoya rapidly suppressed the coup attempt, and about 40 members of the armed forces were subsequently arrested in connection with the uprising.

Peace agreement and power-sharing Government

In late July 2001 Mandela chaired a peace summit of regional Heads of State in Arusha at which the signatory groups to the Arusha accord finally reached agreement on the nature of the transitional leadership. A new multi-party transitional government, according the Hutu and Tutsi ethnic groups balanced representation, was to be installed on 1 November. The Secretary-General of FRODEBU, Domitien Ndayizeye, was nominated to the vice-presidency of the transitional administration. Buyoya was to continue in the office of President for 18 months (from 1 November), after which time he was to transfer the office to Ndayizeye. However, the CNDD—FDD and the FNL persisted in rejecting the peace accord and announced that they would continue hostilities against the transitional authorities, while one of the principal Tutsi opposition parties, the Parti pour le redressement national (PARENA), refused to join the proposed new government.

Following further negotiations in Arusha and in Pretoria, South Africa, in early October 2001, agreement was reached on the composition of the new 26-member transitional Government. FRODEBU and UPRONA were the most dominant parties in the new power-sharing administration, while portfolios were allocated to a further 13 parties that had signed the Arusha agreement. (In total, Hutus received 14 of the 26 ministerial posts.) On 29 October a transitional Constitution, which was drafted by a technical law commission and included principles incorporated in the previous Constitution of 1992 and the Arusha peace accord, was formally adopted by the Assemblée nationale. The new transitional Constitution provided for the establishment of an upper legislative chamber, the Sénat, and four new commissions to assist in the peace and reconciliation process. Former combatants belonging to political movements were to be integrated into the armed and security forces during the transitional period. Also at the end of October the South African Government dispatched troops to Burundi as part of a proposed 700-member contingent, in an effort, initiated by Mandela, to enforce national security and support the transitional authorities. In a reversal to the peace efforts, however, the CNDD—FDD had divided, with the emergence of a new faction, led by Maj. Jean-Pierre Nkurunziza, which commanded the support of most of the movement's combatants.

On 1 November 2001 the newly established transitional Government was officially installed, as scheduled. However, the FNL continued to launch attacks on the outskirts of Bujumbura, despite the deployment of the South African troops. In January 2002 the Constitutional Court endorsed the nomination to the transitional Assemblée nationale of a number of deputies, representing civil society and 14 of the political parties that had signed the peace agreement. (FRODEBU and UPRONA retained their seats in the chamber.) Jean Minani, the Chairman of FRODEBU, was subsequently elected Speaker of the Assemblée nationale. At the end of that month the Constitutional Court approved the establishment of a 51-member Sénat.

Efforts to bring about a cease-fire in the civil conflict continued, with a series of meetings in Pretoria in February 2002, which were attended by representatives of the Government and armed forces, and both factions of the CNDD—FDD (but not by the FNL). In March a further regional summit meeting was convened in Dar es Salaam, which the FNL and Nkurunziza's CNDD—FDD faction again boycotted. In response to the continued lack of progress in peace efforts, FRODEBU issued a statement in April condemning the Government's failure to suppress the rebel militia. The South African Deputy President, Jacob Zuma (who had replaced Mandela as the principal mediator), hosted a new series of consultations between the militia groups and the Burundi Government in Pretoria later that month. However, both the FNL and Nkurunziza's faction refused to participate. Further discussions between government and rebel delegations regarding the implementation of a cease-fire were scheduled to take place in Dar es Salaam in August. Early that month, following an attempt to remove the FNL 'hardline' leader, Agathon Rwasa, from his post, the movement divided: a new faction, led by Alain Mugabarabona, emerged, while Rwasa remained in control of most of the combatants. The peace negotiations, which commenced on 12 August, were attended for the first time by Mugabarabona's FNL faction and both CNDD—FDD factions. At the end of that month, however, renewed fighting between FNL supporters and government troops was reported on the outskirts of Bujumbura.

A summit meeting on Burundi (attended by regional Presidents), which was convened in Dar es Salaam on 7 October 2002, resulted in a cease-fire agreement between the Government, and Ndayikengurukiye's CNDD—FDD and Mugabarabona's FNL faction. Negotiations with the main CNDD—FDD continued, amid hostilities between government and rebel forces in central and northern Burundi. The authorities placed Bagaza (now the leader of PARENA) under house arrest, on suspicion of involvement with several attacks in Bujumbura. Also in November Maj.-Gen. Vincent Niyungeko, hitherto Chief of Staff of the armed forces, became the new Minister of Defence.

On 3 December 2002, following mediation from Uganda and South Africa, the Government finally reached a cease-fire agreement with the CNDD—FDD, which was scheduled to enter into effect at the end of that month. Under the Arusha agreement, the rebel factions were to be reconstituted as political parties, while Buyoya was to relinquish the presidency to Ndayizeye at the end of April 2003. However, the cease-fire agreement was not imposed at the end of December 2002, owing to delays in the arrival of observers from the AU. Hostilities between government and CNDD—FDD forces continued, particularly in Gitega, and Nkurunziza, attributing responsibility for the failure to implement the accord to the Government, suspended further discussions. In February 2003 the AU Cease-fire Observer Mission, comprising 35 monitors (from Burkina Faso, Mali, Togo and Tunisia), arrived in Bujumbura, with a mandate to monitor the peace agreement. In late April the first 100 members of an AU Mission in Burundi (AMIB) arrived in the country; the contingent (which was to comprise troops from South Africa, Ethiopia and Mozambique) was to assist in the enforcement of the cease-fire between the Government and the rebel factions. Despite the reported reluctance of Buyoya to relinquish the presidency, Ndayizeye was officially inaugurated as President for the scheduled period of 18 months on 30 April. On the same day Alphonse-Marie Kadege was appointed Vice-President. On 5 May Ndayizeye appointed a representative of Mugabarabona's FNL faction and Ndayikengurukiye's CNDD—FDD faction to the transitional Council of Ministers, as part of a government reorganization. In May the Government announced that it had ended the ban on PARENA activities, imposed in November 2002.

In October 2003, under the mediation of Zuma and the South African President, Thabo Mbeki, Ndayizeye signed an agreement with Nkurunziza on political, military and security power-sharing. The CNDD—FDD faction was to be allocated four ministerial portfolios, 40% of army officers' posts, the vice-presidency of the Assemblée nationale, three provincial governorships, and two ambassadorial posts, while former CNDD—FDD combatants were to be demobilized. Mugabarabona and Ndayikengurukiye issued a statement condemning the accord, which was finally approved by the legislature on 22 October. On 16 November the Government and Nkurunziza's CNDD—FDD signed a final comprehensive peace agreement, endorsing the accords of December 2002, and of October and November 2003. On the same day regional Heads of State issued an ultimatum to Rwasa (as leader of the only rebel faction to remain in conflict with the Government) to join the peace process. Later that month Ndayizeye reorganized the Government of national unity to include four representatives of Nkurunziza's CNDD—FDD faction, including Nkurunziza himself, who was appointed to the third most senior post, Minister of State with responsibility for Good Governance and State Inspection.

In January 2004 Ndayizeye established a 33-member Joint Military High Command, comprising 20 members of the existing armed forces and 13 of the former CNDD—FDD. In mid-January fighting between government troops and FNL combatants in Bujumbura Rural province resulted in the displacement of some 10,000 civilians. Later that month negotiations between Ndayizeye and an FNL delegation, convened in Oisterwijk, Netherlands, ended without agreement on a cease-fire being reached. The FNL continued to refuse to recognize the transitional authorities, and clashes between government and rebel forces continued in early February. In March the AU renewed the mandate of AMIB (which was due to expire at the beginning of April) for a further month, and urged the UN Security Council to authorize the deployment of UN peace-keeping troops in Burundi. In April Nkurunziza announced the suspension of CNDD—FDD participation in the transitional institutions, on the grounds that the Government had failed to implement the November 2003 power-sharing accord. In May the UN Security Council approved the replacement of the AMIB mission with a UN contingent, the Opération des Nations Unies au Burundi (ONUB). With a maximum strength of 5,650 military personnel, ONUB officially commenced deployment on 1 June.

In July 2004 the International Monitoring Committee charged with overseeing the implementation of the power-sharing arrangements urged political parties to reach consensus in efforts to adopt a new constitution (necessary to allow elections to proceed). A draft power-sharing accord (which provided for a Government and Assemblée nationale of 60% Hutu and 40% Tutsi composition) was reached in Pretoria later that month, but was rejected by predominantly Tutsi parties. (Also in July the CNDD—FDD announced the resumption of its participation in the Government of national unity.) On 6 August the accord, which would allow elections to proceed on 31 October, was signed in Pretoria by 20 of the 30 delegations, with Tutsi parties, notably UPRONA, refusing to accept the proposed power-sharing arrangements. A five-member Commission électorale nationale indépendante (CENI) was established at the end of August. In September initial regional peace discussions were conducted in Bujumbura. Following the massacre of refugees at the Gatumba camp in August (see below), however, government forces launched attacks against FNL troop positions during that month.

Nkurunziza becomes President

In September 2004 the International Criminal Court (ICC, see p. 342) announced that Burundi had ratified the signatory treaty, allowing prosecutions for civilian massacres to proceed. Meanwhile, the main political groupings continued to fail to reach agreement on a proposed new constitution, with 11 Tutsi parties, including UPRONA, objecting to the parliamentary ethnic representation vested in the draft. In mid-October the CENI announced that legislative elections, scheduled to take place at the end of that month, were to be postponed until 22 April 2005. On 20 October 2004 a new interim 'post-transitional' Constitution was officially adopted by Ndayizeye, after its approval by both chambers of the legislature. The new Constitution, which was to extend the mandate of the transitional organs of government from 1 November until the elections in April 2005, and which enshrined the power-sharing principles of a Government and Assemblée nationale of 60% Hutu and 40% Tutsi composition, was endorsed at a referendum on 28 February 2005 by some 92% of votes cast (with an estimated 88% of the electorate participating in the ballot). Legislative elections were to proceed on 22 April, to be followed by the election of a President by the new Assemblée nationale and Sénat. (Under the terms of the Constitution, subsequent Presidents were to be directly elected.) However, the legislature failed to approve the new electoral code until late April, and the Government subsequently announced that Ndayizeye's mandate was to be extended to allow a further postponement of the elections. According to the new schedule, after local government elections in June, elections were to be conducted to the Assemblée nationale on 4 July, and to the Sénat on 19 July, followed by the election of a President by the new legislature on 19 August. Meanwhile, at the end of December 2004 the Government had announced the creation of a new Forces de défense nationales and of a new police force, comprising equal numbers of the existing Tutsi-dominated armed forces and Hutu former rebel combatants (mainly CNDD—FDD); a Tutsi was appointed head of the new army, while the post of deputy commander was allocated to a Hutu.

On 3 June 2005 communal government elections were conducted under the transitional schedule; of the 3,225 contested seats, the CNDD—FDD secured 1,781, FRODEBU 822, and UPRONA 260 seats. Elections to a reduced number of 100 seats in the Assemblée nationale took place, as scheduled, on 4 July 2005, and received the approval of international observers. According to official results, the CNDD—FDD won 59 seats, FRODEBU 25 and UPRONA 10 seats. A further 18 deputies were subsequently nominated in accordance with the constitutional requirements of balance of ethnic representation (60% Hutu and 40% Tutsi) and a minimum 30% representation of women; in effect, the Twa ethnic group was allocated three seats, while the CNDD—FDD, FRODEBU and UPRONA each received five additional seats. The CNDD—FDD won 30 of the 34 contested seats in elections to the Sénat, which followed on 29 July, while FRODEBU won only four seats; four former Presidents were subsequently allocated seats, and the Twa ethnic group was designated three seats. In early August the authorities and political parties agreed to expand the chamber to 49 deputies, in order to guarantee the stipulated minimum representation of women; the four political parties with the highest votes each nominated two women to the additional seats. On 19 August a joint session of the Assemblée nationale and the Sénat elected Nkurunziza as President; the sole candidate, he secured about 81.5% of votes cast. Nkurunziza was officially inaugurated on 26 August and subsequently formed a 20-member Government in accordance with the terms of the Constitution, comprising a 60% Hutu and 40% Tutsi balance of representation, with a minimum 30% of women.

In September 2005 the FNL leadership refused an offer by the new Government to enter into reconciliation negotiations. In following months the Government consequently increased military efforts to suppress rebel activity, particularly in the provinces of Bujumbura Rural and Bubanza where the movement was based, causing large displacement of civilians from these regions. As a result of increasing support within the FNL for reconciliation with the Government, Rwasa was ousted from the leadership in December, and was replaced by Jean-Bosco Sindayigaya, who announced that he was prepared to enter into unconditional negotiations with the authorities. However, Rwasa continued to head a smaller faction of the FNL opposed to negotiations and sporadic hostilities continued in early 2006. In December 2005 the UN Security Council extended the mandate of ONUB for a further six months.

In January 2006 Nkurunziza ordered the provisional release of 'political prisoners' imprisoned in connection with the coup attempt of 1993, with the stated aim of promoting national reconciliation. In March the President of FRODEBU, Léonce Ngendakumana, ordered its representatives to withdraw from the Government and legislature, in protest at the failure of the CNDD—FDD to consult with other coalition parties, and at decisions which he considered to be contrary to democratic principles; however, the three FRODEBU ministers refused to resign from their posts, and were subsequently expelled from the party. Raising concerns about the stability of the administration, in early March Nkurunziza announced that senior members of the armed and security forces had planned a coup attempt against him. No arrests were made, however, and the claims were dismissed by opposition parties. Later that month Nkurunziza replaced two CNDD—FDD ministers for alleged corruption and mismanagement. Also in March Rwasa agreed to enter into peace negotiations, providing that they constituted direct dialogue with Nkurunziza. In May, following a request from Nkurunziza that South Africa assist in the negotiations, Mbeki appointed the South African Minister of Safety and Security, Charles Nqakula, as mediator. Negotiations commenced in Dar es Salaam later that month. In June government and FNL delegations signed a framework accord for a cessation of hostilities; however, discussions continued throughout July without agreement being reached on a cease-fire. On 30 June the UN Security Council adopted a resolution authorizing the extension of ONUB's mandate to the end of 2006, when the mission was to withdraw and be replaced by a UN office, the Bureau Intégré des Nations Unies au Burundi (BINUB).

In August 2006 several prominent politicians, including former President Ndayizeye, former Vice-President Kadege and FNL faction leader Mugabarabona were arrested on suspicion of involvement in a coup attempt, and subsequently charged. In September, after Rwasa agreed to abandon demands for the restructured armed forces to comprise a higher proportion of Hutus, he and Nkurunziza signed a comprehensive cease-fire agreement, under the aegis of Mbeki, in Dar es Salaam. A Joint Verification and Monitoring Committee, composed of UN officials, together with representatives of the FNL and the Governments of Burundi, South Africa, Tanzania and Uganda, was established at the beginning of October to supervise the implementation of the cease-fire. (Owing to a boycott by the FNL members, however, the Committee subsequently failed to commence operations.)

Also in September 2006 the Second Vice-President, Alice Nzomukunda, a member of the CNDD—FDD, tendered her resignation, citing her opposition to the arrests in connection with the alleged conspiracy to overthrow the Government; she was replaced by Marina Barampama. At the end of 2006 ONUB duly withdrew and BINUB was installed for an initial period of one year (which was subsequently extended), with authorization to continue the process of peace consolidation, including support for the demobilization and reintegration of former combatants and reform of the security sector. Some 850 South African peace-keeping troops previously belonging to ONUB were transferred to the authority of the AU, which announced plans to increase the size of the contingent deployed in the country to 1,700.

In January 2007 Ndayizeye, Kadege and three other suspects were acquitted of the charges of conspiring to overthrow Nkurunziza's Government; however, Mugabarabona was convicted and sentenced to 20 years' imprisonment, while a further defendant received a term of 15 years. The outcome of Ndayizeye's trial precipitated political unrest, with ruling party leaders, particularly the Chairman of the CNDD—FDD, Hussein Radjabu, suspected of fabricating the conspiracy involving opposition figures in order to suppress dissent. The Minister of Development Planning and National Reconstruction (a member of the CNDD—FDD) was removed following an investigation into the sale of a presidential airplane, and subsequently fled abroad, causing further controversy. At the end of January, after discussions in Dar es Salaam, the FNL leadership agreed, in principle, to accept the terms for the implementation of the cease-fire agreement.

In mid-February 2007 Barampama was dismissed from the post of Second Vice-President, after pledging her support to Radjabu, who had been removed from the chairmanship of the CNDD—FDD at a special congress of the party earlier that month. Gabriel Ntiszerana, hitherto the Governor of the central bank, was appointed to replace her as Second Vice-President. In April Radjabu was arrested and detained on charges of recruiting and arming demobilized troops and planning to launch an attack on state forces. (In April 2008 he was convicted by the Supreme Court and sentenced to 13 years in prison.)

The peace process

In consultation with international partners the Government developed a Priority Action Programme (PAP) aimed at enforcing the terms of a cease-fire agreement and supporting social and economic reconstruction projects. In June 2007 Rwasa became the last of the rebel leaders to sign the cease-fire agreement drawn up in 2006. However, the following month FNL leaders deserted their roles in a joint monitoring group that had been established to oversee the implementation of the cease-fire, further delaying the peace process, and in September fighting resumed between rebel insurgents. In light of the continued impasse between the Government and opposition parties over the terms of a power-sharing agreement, and the increasing unrest among rebel groups, international observers appealed for renewed peace talks. In October Nkurunziza issued a statement announcing that a power-sharing compromise had been reached; the agreement pledged to guarantee the rights of political parties to meet freely and reinstate members of the opposition who had previously been dismissed from the Government.

President Nkurunziza installed a new, 21-member Council of Ministers (which included eight new ministers) in July 2007, in an effort to address concerns over allegations of corruption and human rights abuses. The reorganization was, however, denounced by members of the opposition, who claimed that the move failed to resolve the issues of corruption. In August First Vice-President Martin Nduwimana was expelled from UPRONA amid allegations that he had been attempting to sabotage the party, and in the same month the Governor of the central bank, Isaac Bizimana, was arrested for allegedly embezzling state funds. In November Nduwimana resigned from the Government, and was replaced by Yves Sahinguvu. Later that month Nkurunziza announced further changes to the composition of the Government, which included the appointment of Vénant Kamana, hitherto Minister at the Presidency, as Minister of the Interior.

Heavy fighting between rival factions of the FNL in September 2007 threatened to destabilize the peace process, with at least 20 people reported to have been killed when FNL dissidents attacked rebels loyal to Rwasa. There was a resumption of hostilities between the rebels and government forces in April and early May 2008 when FNL units launched attacks on a number of military positions and towns, and shelled Bujumbura. Casualties were reported on both sides and a number of civilians were also killed, with thousands more displaced; the Burundian armed forces responded by bombing rebel positions in the north of the country. None the less, in late May a cease-fire was signed between the Government and the FNL, and four days later Rwasa returned to Burundi from Tanzania, where he had been living in exile. The following month, at a ceremony in Rugazi Commune to mark the start of the cantonment of FNL fighters, he declared that the armed struggle against the Government had officially ended. Furthermore, at a summit in Bujumbura in December, the FNL agreed to remove the word 'Hutu' from the name of its political wing, the PALIPEHUTU, in accordance with the constitutional ban on such ethnic terminology. This signified a breakthrough in the peace process, and at the same summit Nkurunziza confirmed that he would award government positions to members of the FNL and would release political prisoners and prisoners of war.

Meanwhile, the political situation had deteriorated following FRODEBU's withdrawal, in February 2008, from the Assemblée nationale in protest at the dismissal of that body's first Vice-President, Alice Nzomukunda, which resulted in the opposition occupying the majority of seats in the legislature. Later that month 46 members of the Assemblée nationale sent a letter to the UN Secretary-General, Ban Ki-Moon, expressing their concerns about the security situation in Burundi and requesting international protection from persecution by the Government. In March there were a series of grenade attacks on the homes of four opposition party members (all of whom were signatories to the letter), which some observers claimed was a co-ordinated attempt on behalf of the governing party to intimidate the political opposition.

In June 2008 the Constitutional Court expelled 22 deputies from the Assemblée nationale, who had defected from the ruling CNDD—FDD party in early 2007 in response to Radjabu's dismissal as Chairman, and the Government's purge of his supporters. The Court's ruling was widely viewed as part of a government plan to undermine the opposition and remain in power until elections scheduled for 2010. There was further concern regarding an apparent crackdown on the opposition in November 2008, when Alexis Sinduhije, a journalist and leader of the opposition Mouvement pour la sécurité et la démocratie, was arrested, along with 30 other members of the party. In December the Assemblée nationale approved a new penal code, which was praised by human rights groups for abolishing capital punishment, as well as defining and prohibiting torture, but also criticized for criminalizing homosexual activity and permitting arbitrary detention.

In January 2009 Nkurunziza reorganized the Council of Ministers; notably, Minister of the Interior Kamana was replaced by Edouard Nduwimana, formerly the governor of Kayanza province, while Augustin Nsanze was appointed Minister of External Relations and International Co-operation, replacing Antoinette Batumubwira. A new CENI, comprising two civil society activists and one representative each from the CNDD—FDD, FRODEBU and UPRONA, was officially appointed in early April. Rwasa symbolically surrendered his weapons at a special ceremony in Bubanza on 18 April, marking the start of the demobilization of FNL combatants, under a agreement between the FNL and the Government whereby 3,500 FNL combatants would be integrated into the national army and police force and a further 5,000 would be demobilized. (However, an estimated 10,000 FNL supporters who were not recognized by the authorities as former combatants remained at large.) The FNL was formally registered as a political party on 21 April. In June Nkurunziza appointed several senior FNL officials to government posts, including Rwasa, who became head of the National Social Security Institute.

The 2010 elections

In December 2009 the Chairman of CENI announced that the first round of a direct presidential election was to take place on 28 June 2010, on the expiry of Nkurunziza's term of office, and was to be followed by elections to the Assemblée nationale on 23 July and to the Sénat on 28 July. A voter registration process was undertaken in January. Meanwhile, reports emerged of division within the FNL, following Rwasa's government appointment, between his supporters and a faction led by the party's spokesman, Pasteur Habimana, which declared that it no longer recognized Rwasa as Chairman. The FNL selected Rwasa as its presidential candidate in that month, while FRODEBU chose Ndayizeye. Nkurunziza was elected as the presidential candidate by the CNDD—FDD at a special congress in late April. Also in April, despite strong opposition from the main FNL, Habimana's faction of the FNL, led by his associate, Jacques Kenese, officially registered as a party, known as FNL Iragi rya Gahutu.

A number of grenade attacks, which prompted the arrest of some 130 suspects, were reported during the campaign period prior to communal government elections. Following the elections on 24 May 2010, it was announced that the CNDD—FDD had secured 64% of votes cast, with the FNL receiving only 14%, UPRONA 6%, and FRODEBU 5% of the votes. While a European Union (EU, see p. 276) observer mission reported that the communal elections had generally proceeded in accordance with international standards, the opposition denounced the results as fraudulent and demanded that the elections be repeated. All principal opposition parties subsequently withdrew from the electoral process in protest at the alleged malpractice, and the five opposition candidates who had registered to contest the presidential election, including Rwasa and Ndayizeye, announced that they would boycott the poll.

Prior to the presidential election in June 2010, at least two prominent members of the CNDD—FDD and an opposition activist were killed in further numerous grenade attacks, mainly directed against CNDD—FDD local offices. The Government ordered the arrest of large numbers of opposition members, particularly of the FNL (which denied any involvement in the attacks), and banned all opposition party gatherings. The presidential election took place, as scheduled, on 28 June. The Constitutional Court confirmed the official results of the election on 8 July, according to which Nkurunziza (who had contested the election as the sole candidate) was re-elected with 91.6% of votes cast. The rate of voter participation was estimated at 77.0% of the registered electorate. At the elections to the Assemblée nationale, which took place on 23 July, the CNDD—FDD increased its number of seats to 81, while UPRONA took 17 and FRODEBU-Nyakuri (a small, pro-Government, breakaway faction of FRODEBU) five. A further three deputies from the Twa ethnic group were subsequently nominated in accordance with the constitutional requirements of balance of ethnic representation. At the elections to the Sénat on 28 July, the CNDD—FDD secured 32 of the 34 available seats; the remaining two seats were won by UPRONA. A further four seats were allocated to former Presidents and three to the Twa ethnic group, increasing the total number of senators to 41. At the beginning of August government supporters within the FNL announced that Rwasa had been deposed as party leader and replaced by a presidential adviser, Emmanuel Miburo. On 30 August Nkurunziza appointed a new Government, which included 10 new ministers, notably Thérence Sinunguruza of UPRONA as First Vice-President.

In late 2010 sporadic unrest continued in rural areas and in early November the Prosecutor-General announced the establishment of a commission to investigate reports of a number of extrajudicial killings by members of the armed forces, including that of a local FNL leader in Bujumbura province. Upon the expiry of BINUB's mandate in mid-December, the UN Security Council adopted a resolution authorizing the establishment of a reduced, 15-member body, the new UN Office in Burundi (BNUB), for an initial 12-month period, beginning on 1 January 2011.

Recent developments: further unrest

In June 2011 EU ambassadors addressed an official protest to the Burundian Government at 20 incidences of politically motivated extrajudicial killings and a number of torture cases allegedly committed by security officials between June 2010 and March 2011. In October the authorities stated, following a preliminary inquiry, that Rwasa (who was believed to be in hiding in the DRC) had organized an attack at a bar in the town of Gatumba, near the border with the DRC, in September; a total of 39 people had been killed in the incident, which followed a series of attacks previously attributed by the Government to armed bandits. The trial of 21 defendants suspected of perpetrating the killings began in Bujumbura High Court in mid-October but was adjourned until December. Also in October principal international human rights organizations demanded that the Government provide financial support to a newly established National Independent Human Rights Commission and end restrictions on media reporting, also citing arrests and legal measures undertaken by the authorities against a number of independent journalists and civil activists in previous months.

In early November 2011 Nkurunziza effected an extensive government reorganization, in which six new ministers were appointed. Notably, head of police Gabriel Nizigama was awarded the post of Minister of Public Security, while Laurent Kavakure, hitherto a senior presidential adviser, became Minister of External Relations and International Co-operation. Following the abolition of the Ministry of Planning for Economic Development, Minister of Finance Clotilde Nizigama assumed the additional portfolio. In December one of the defendants accused of participating in the bar attack in September claimed that he had been recruited by senior police officials, who had planned to eliminate an FNL rebel commander. On 20 December the UN Security Council adopted a resolution extending the mandate of BNUB until mid-February 2013, emphasizing that further action was required to address the continuing human rights violations.

Foreign Affairs

The cross-border movement of vast numbers of refugees, provoked by regional ethnic and political violence, has dominated recent relations with Rwanda, Tanzania and the DRC (formerly Zaire), and has long been a matter of considerable concern to the international aid community. The uprising by Laurent-Désiré Kabila's Alliance des forces démocratiques pour la libération du Congo-Zaïre (AFDL) in eastern Zaire in January 1997 resulted in the return of large numbers of refugees to Burundi, reportedly undermining the operations from Zaire of FDD combatants. Moreover, the seizure of power by the AFDL in May was welcomed by the Buyoya regime, which moved to forge close relations with Kabila's DRC. Burundi initially denied any involvement in the civil war that commenced in the DRC in August, but by 1999 some 3,000 Burundian troops were reported to be stationed in the east of the country, with the aim of destroying CNDD—FDD camps. (The CNDD—FDD supported the DRC Government in the civil war and used the conflict as an opportunity to regroup and rearm.) In June the DRC instituted proceedings against Burundi, together with Rwanda and Uganda, at the International Court of Justice in The Hague, Netherlands, accusing them of acts of armed aggression in contravention of the terms of both the UN Charter and the Charter of the OAU. In February 2001, however, the DRC abandoned proceedings against Burundi and Rwanda. In January 2002 the Burundian Government made a formal commitment to withdraw all troops (reported to number about 1,000) from the DRC, while the DRC authorities pledged to end their alliance with the CNDD—FDD. In mid-2004 intensified hostilities in eastern DRC resulted in the flight of a further 30,000 refugees to Burundi. In August some 160 Banyamulenge (Congolese Tutsi) were massacred at a refugee camp at Gatumba, near the border between the two countries. Although the FNL admitted responsibility for the atrocity (which prompted the further exodus of both Burundian Tutsis and Banyamulenge refugees to Rwanda), the Governments of Burundi and Rwanda maintained that Hutu militia operating within the DRC were involved. In 2009 Burundi, the DRC and UNHCR signed a tripartite agreement providing for the voluntary repatriation of Burundian and Congolese refugees; UNHCR estimated that some 24,000 refugees originating from the DRC remained in Burundi at the end of 2011.

With improvement in the security situation in Burundi, the Tanzanian authorities began a UNHCR-supervised programme in 2003 to repatriate Burundian refugees. In early 2008 the Tanzanian Government announced an initiative (commended by UNHCR), under which the remaining Burundian refugees would be permitted to remain in the country and apply for Tanzanian citizenship, or be repatriated; it was reported that some 55,000 had decided to return to Burundi. By October 2009 some 53,500 long-term Burundian refugees had been repatriated under the UNHCR programme since March 2008, while some 162,000 Burundian refugees had applied for Tanzanian citizenship. In April 2010 the Tanzanian Government pledged to grant Tanzanian citizenship to the 162,000 Burundians who had registered. In December 2011 the Tanzanian Government announced that it had suspended the resettlement of naturalized Burundi refugees in a number of regions, owing to concerns over their suspected connections with rebel and criminal activities.

In December 2006 the Presidents of Burundi, Kenya, Uganda, the DRC and Rwanda signed a Pact of Security, Stability and Development in the Great Lakes Region, which was welcomed by

Finance

URRENCY AND EXCHANGE RATES

onetary Units
100 centimes = 1 Burundian franc.

Sterling, Dollar and Euro Equivalents (30 November 2011)
£1 sterling = 2,078.5 francs;
US $1 = 1,331.7 francs;
€1 = 1,786.9 francs;
10,000 Burundian francs = £4.81 = $7.50 = €5.60.

Average Exchange Rate (Burundian francs per US dollar)
2008 1,185.691
2009 1,230.179
2010 1,230.748

GOVERNMENT FINANCE

(central government operations, '000 million Burundian francs)

Summary of balances	2006	2007*	2008†
Revenue	178.8	197.6	249.8
Less Expenditure and net lending	361.0	407.9	558.0
Overall balance (commitment basis)	−182.2	−210.4	−308.2
Change in arrears	−13.7	−21.9	−17.5
External (interest)	−1.8	−0.4	—
Domestic	−11.9	−21.5	−17.5
Overall balance (cash basis)	−195.9	−232.3	−325.7
Grants	169.0	221.5	302.2
Overall balance after grants‡	−30.8	−16.3	−23.4

Revenue	2006	2007*	2008†
Tax revenue	163.4	182.6	232.0
Income tax	45.9	53.5	60.3
Taxes on goods and services	83.9	92.3	124.3
Taxes on international trade	29.7	33.7	43.2
Non-tax revenue	15.4	15.0	17.8
Total	178.8	197.6	249.8

Expenditure and net lending	2006	2007*	2008†
Current expenditure	221.5	261.2	330.2
Compensation of employees	93.9	114.0	141.2
Goods and services	63.8	70.7	93.1
Transfers and subsidies	39.5	46.7	65.6
Interest payments	24.3	29.9	30.3
DDR project§	23.5	12.2	23.5
Capital expenditure	116.8	134.8	208.8
Net lending	−0.8	−0.3	−4.5
Total	361.0	407.9	558.0

* Estimates.
† Budget forecast.
‡ Including errors and omissions.
§ Demobilization, disarmament and reintegration.

Source: IMF, *Burundi: 2008 Article IV Consultation and Request for Three-Year Arrangement Under the Poverty Reduction and Growth Facility - Staff Report; Public Information Notice and Press Release on the Executive Board Discussion; and Statement by the Executive Director for Burundi* (August 2008).

INTERNATIONAL RESERVES

(US $ million at 31 December)

	2008	2009	2010
Gold*	0.84	1.06	1.36
IMF special drawing rights	0.15	104.48	112.77
Reserve position in IMF	0.55	0.56	0.55
Foreign exchange	265.00	217.00	217.41
Total	266.54	323.10	332.09

* Valued at market-related prices.
† Excluding gold reserves.

Source: IMF, *International Financial Statistics*.

MONEY SUPPLY

(million Burundian francs at 31 December)

	2008	2009	201[illegible]
Currency outside depository corporations	112,624	120,916	139,10[illegible]
Transferable deposits	333,546	389,094	470,67[illegible]
Other deposits	111,501	128,426	155,47[illegible]
Broad money	557,670	638,435	765,25[illegible]

Source: IMF, *International Financial Statistics*.

COST OF LIVING

(Consumer Price Index for Bujumbura; base: January 2000 = 100)

	2005	2006	2007
Food	139.4	139.5	151.6
Clothing	126.7	125.9	119.1
Rent	163.2	176.6	195.5
All items (incl. others)	144.8	148.6	161.0

Source: ILO.

NATIONAL ACCOUNTS

('000 million Burundian francs at current prices)

Expenditure on the Gross Domestic Product

	2007	2008	2009
Government final consumption expenditure	156	156	163
Private final consumption expenditure	1,286	1,292	1,361
Gross fixed capital formation	198	201	210
Change in inventories	18	18	18
Total domestic expenditure	1,658	1,667	1,752
Exports of goods and services	91	86	71
Less Imports of goods and services	360	281	285
GDP in purchasers' values	1,389	1,473	1,539

Gross Domestic Product by Economic Activity

	2007	2008	2009
Agriculture, hunting, forestry and fishing	566	583	646
Mining and quarrying	6	6	7
Manufacturing	126	127	139
Electricity, gas and water	9	9	9
Construction	19	47	51
Trade, restaurants and hotels	141	144	160
Finance, insurance and real estate	33	34	37
Transport and communications	221	218	225
Public administration and defence	116	114	123
Other services	22	23	25
GDP at factor cost	1,259	1,305	1,422
Indirect taxes	170	207	163
Less Imputed bank service charge	40	38	46
GDP in purchasers' values	1,389	1,473	1,539

Source: African Development Bank.

BALANCE OF PAYMENTS

(US $ million)

	2008	2009	2010
Exports of goods f.o.b.	69.6	66.0	101.2
Imports of goods f.o.b.	−335.5	−343.0	−438.4
Trade balance	−265.8	−277.0	−337.2
Export of services	83.3	49.9	79.5
Import of services	−258.8	−176.6	−168.2
Balance on goods and services	−441.3	−403.7	−425.9

the UN Security Council as a significant measure towards regional stabilization. In the same month the East African Community (EAC, see p. 449) officially accepted the membership applications of Burundi and Rwanda. In November 2009 the Heads of State of Tanzania, Kenya, Uganda, Rwanda and Burundi signed a common market protocol in Arusha, allowing the free movement of goods, services, people and capital within the EAC. The common market protocol officially entered into force in July 2010. Burundi for the first time hosted an EAC summit meeting in November 2011, when plans to adopt a single currency in 2012 were under discussion.

CONSTITUTION AND GOVERNMENT

Following the coup of 25 July 1996, the Constitution of March 1992 was suspended. A peace agreement, which was signed by representatives of the incumbent Government, the Assemblée nationale and 17 political groupings on 28 August 2000, provided for the installation of a transitional administration, in which power-sharing between the Hutu and Tutsi ethnic groups was guaranteed (see Contemporary Political History). Under an interim 'post-transitional' Constitution, which was officially adopted by the President on 20 October 2004, legislative elections were conducted in July 2005, and a President, elected by the new Assemblée nationale and the Sénat, was inaugurated on 26 August. The Assemblée nationale comprised 118 deputies, of whom 100 were elected for a term of five years, and the remainder nominated according to constitutional requirements for a proportion of 60% Hutu and 40% Tutsi representatives, and a minimum 30% of women, while three seats were allocated to the Twa ethnic group. The Sénat comprised 49 deputies, of whom 34 were elected (two deputies by ethnically balanced colleges from each of the country's provinces) for a term of five years, and the remainder nominated according to constitutional requirements for balance of ethnic representation and minimum representation of women. The President, who is Head of State and is henceforth directly elected, appoints two Vice-Presidents, and, in consultation with them, the Government.

For the purposes of local government, Burundi comprises 17 provinces (administered by civilian Governors), each of which is divided into districts and further subdivided into communes. Each district has a council, which is directly elected for a term of five years.

REGIONAL AND INTERNATIONAL CO-OPERATION

Burundi is a member of the African Union (see p. 189) and, with neighbouring states Rwanda and the DRC, is a member of the Economic Community of the Great Lakes Countries (see p. 449). Burundi is also a member of the Common Market for Eastern and Southern Africa (see p. 237), and of the International Coffee Organization (see p. 445). In December 2006 Burundi, together with Rwanda, was admitted to the East African Community (see p. 449).

Burundi was admitted to the UN in 1962, and joined the World Trade Organization (WTO, see p. 433) in 1995. Burundi participates in the Group of 77 (G77, see p. 450) developing countries

ECONOMIC AFFAIRS

In 2010, according to estimates by the World Bank, Burundi's gross national income (GNI), measured at average 2008–10 prices, was US $1,402m., equivalent to $170 per head (or $400 per head on an international purchasing-power parity basis). During 2001–10, it was estimated, the population increased at an average annual rate of 2.9%, while gross domestic product (GDP) per head increased, in real terms, by an average of 0.4% per year. Overall GDP increased, in real terms, at an average annual rate of 3.3% in 2001–10; growth was 3.9% in 2010.

Agriculture (including forestry and fishing) contributed an estimated 45.4% of GDP in 2009, according to the African Development Bank (AfDB). According to FAO, some 89.1% of the labour force were estimated to be employed in the sector in mid-2012. The principal cash crops are coffee and its substitutes (which accounted for 35.2% of export earnings in 2009) and cane sugar. The main subsistence crops are sweet potatoes and cassava. Although Burundi is traditionally self-sufficient in food crops, population displacement (a consequence of the political crisis) resulted in considerable disruption in the sector. The livestock-rearing sector was also severely affected by the civil war. During 2000–07, according to the AfDB, agricultural GDP increased at an average annual rate of 1.4%; it grew by 3.5% in 2009.

Industry (comprising mining, manufacturing, construction and utilities) engaged 21.8% of the employed labour force in 1991. According to the AfDB, the sector contributed an estimated 14.5% of GDP in 2009. Industrial GDP declined at an average annual rate of 6.2% in 2000–07; it declined by 7.5% in 2007.

Mining and power engaged 0.1% of the employed labour force in 1990 and, according to the AfDB, mining and quarrying contributed just 0.5% of GDP in 2009. Gold (alluvial), tin, tungsten and columbo-tantalite are mined in small quantities, although much activity has hitherto been outside the formal sector. Burundi has important deposits of nickel (estimated at 5% of world reserves), vanadium and uranium. In addition, petroleum deposits have been discovered. The GDP of the mining sector increased at an average annual rate of 3.4% in 1997–2001, according to IMF estimates; growth in 2001 was an estimated 14.3%. According to the AfDB, growth in the mining sector of 7.8% was recorded in 2009.

Manufacturing engaged 1.2% of the employed labour force in 1990 and, according to the AfDB, contributed an estimated 9.7% of GDP in 2009. The sector consists largely of the processing of foodstuffs and agricultural products (coffee, cotton, tea and the extraction of vegetable oils), and of textiles and leather products. Manufacturing GDP increased at an average annual rate of 3.9% in 2000–07. Manufacturing GDP increased by 6.3% in 2009.

According to the AfDB, the construction sector contributed 3.6% of GDP in 2009. The sector engaged only 0.7% of the employed labour force in 1990. The sector grew by 3.5% in 2009.

Energy is derived principally from hydroelectric power (an estimated 38.6% of electricity consumed in 2001 was imported). Peat is also exploited as an additional source of energy. Imports of mineral fuels and lubricants comprised 2.3% of the value of imports in 2009.

The services sector contributed an estimated 40.1% of GDP in 2009, according to the AfDB. The sector engaged only 4.4% of the employed labour force in 1990. The GDP of the services sector increased at an average annual rate of 2.6% in 2000–07; growth was negligible in 2007.

In 2010 Burundi recorded a trade deficit of US $337.2m., and there was a deficit of $323.1m. on the current account of the balance of payments. In 2009 the principal source of imports (13.5%) was Belgium; other important suppliers in that year were the People's Republic of China, Kenya, Uganda, India, France and Japan. The principal market for exports in 2009 was Switzerland and Liechtenstein (18.3%); other important markets were Tanzania, Germany, Kenya, the DRC and Belgium. The main imports in 2009 were machinery and transport equipment, basic manufactures, chemicals and related products, and food and live animals. The principal exports in that year were food and live animals (especially coffee) and machinery and transport equipment.

In 2008 the budget deficit was estimated at 23,400m. Burundian francs, equivalent to 0.5% of GDP. Burundi's general government gross debt was 788,709m. Burundian francs in 2009, equivalent to 48.2% of GDP. Burundi's external debt at the end of 2009 was US $518m., of which $420m. was public and publicly guaranteed debt. The cost of debt-servicing long-term public and publicly guaranteed debt and repayments to the IMF in that year was equivalent to 1.7% of the value of exports of goods, services and income (excluding workers' remittances). According to ILO, the annual rate of inflation averaged 7.0% in 2000–07. Consumer prices increased by 6.5% in 2010, according to the AfDB.

Following a period of extended conflict in Burundi from the mid-1990s, the transitional power-sharing Government installed in 2001 oversaw the beginning of an economic recovery (despite continuing hostilities in parts of the country). In August 2005 the IMF and the World Bank's International Development Association (IDA) officially agreed that, in view of progress demonstrated in economic stabilization and commitment to structural reforms, Burundi had qualified for interim debt relief under the enhanced initiative for heavily indebted poor countries (HIPC), thereby enabling it to reduce the unsustainably high external debt-servicing burden. Rebel activity in the country finally ended in May 2008, with the signing of a cease-fire agreement between the Government and the remaining principal rebel movement. In July the IMF approved a further Poverty Reduction and Growth Facility arrangement providing for total disbursements of about US $71.6m. In January 2009 the IMF and World Bank announced that Burundi had made sufficient progress to reach completion point under the HIPC initiative and had become eligible for further debt relief from the IMF, IDA and the African Development Fund under a multilateral debt relief initiative. International endorsement of the conduct of elections in mid-2010 improved prospects for Burundi, which had also begun to benefit from greater integration within the East African Community (EAC, see p. 449). By the end of 2011 trade between EAC member states (which had officially established a common market in July 2010) was estimated to have doubled since 2005, although infrastructure development and improvement of transport systems remained a priority for the organization; the adoption of a common currency by June 2012 was envisaged. In July 2011 the IMF issued a favourable sixth review of the Government's economic programme financed by the Fund under its extended credit facility, enabling the disbursement of a further tranche of about $10.5m.; the authorities were urged to continue prioritization of social spending in order to mitigate the domestic effects of rising fuel and food prices. In October the British Department for International Development announced its controversial decision to end its bilateral aid programme in Burundi in 2012. Modest GDP growth of about 4.2% was projected by the IMF for 2011; uncertainties in the global economy, with weaker growth in trading partners and lower aid flows, were considered to endanger Burundi's economic progress.

PUBLIC HOLIDAYS

2013: 1 January (New Year's Day), 5 February (Unity Day), 1 April (Easter Monday), 1 May (Labour Day), 9 May (Ascension Day), 1 July (Independence Day), 15 August (Assumption), 7 August* (Id al-Fitr, end of Ramadan), 18 September (Victory of UPRONA Party), 13 October (Rwagasore Day), 21 October (Ndadaye Day), 1 November (All Saints' Day), 25 December (Christmas).

* These holidays are dependent on the Islamic lunar calendar and may vary by one or two days from the dates given.

Statistical Survey

Area and Population

AREA, POPULATION AND DENSITY

Area (sq km)	27,834*
Population (census results)†	
16–30 August 1990	5,139,073
16–31 August 2008	
Males	3,838,045
Females	4,039,683
Total	7,877,728
Population (UN estimates at mid-year)‡	
2010	8,382,849
2011	8,575,172
2012	8,749.386
Density (per sq km) at mid-2012	314.3

* 10,747 sq miles.
† Excluding adjustment for underenumeration.
‡ Source: UN, *World Population Prospects: The 2010 Revision*.

POPULATION BY AGE AND SEX
(UN estimates at mid-2012)

	Males	Females	Total
0–14	1,633,838	1,627,731	3,261,569
15–64	2,565,574	2,670,233	5,235,807
65 and over	99,329	152,681	252,010
Total	4,298,741	4,450,645	8,749,386

Source: UN, *World Population Prospects: The 2010 Revision*.

Principal Towns: Bujumbura (capital), population 235,440 (census result, August 1990). *1978:* Gitega 15,943 (Source: Banque de la République du Burundi). *Mid-2009* (urban population, incl. suburbs, UN estimate): Bujumbura 454,866 (Source: UN, *World Urbanization Prospects: The 2009 Revision*).

BIRTHS AND DEATHS
(UN estimates, annual averages)

	1995–2000	2000–05	2005–10
Birth rate (per 1,000)	40.0	36.0	34.3
Death rate (per 1,000)	17.9	16.1	14.8

Source: UN, *World Population Prospects: The 2010 Revision*.

Life expectancy (years at birth, WHO estimates): 50 (males 49; females 51) in 2009 (Source: WHO, *World Health Statistics*).

ECONOMICALLY ACTIVE POPULATION*
(persons aged 10 years and over, 1990 census)

	Males	Females	Total
Agriculture, hunting, forestry and fishing	1,153,890	1,420,553	2,574,443
Mining and quarrying	1,146	39	1,185
Manufacturing	24,120	9,747	33,867
Electricity, gas and water	1,847	74	1,921
Construction	19,447	290	19,737
Trade, restaurants and hotels	19,667	6,155	25,822
Transport, storage and communications	8,193	311	8,504
Financing, insurance, real estate and business services	1,387	618	2,005
Community, social and personal services	68,905	16,286	85,191
Sub-total	1,298,602	1,454,073	2,752,675
Activities not adequately defined	8,653	4,617	13,270
Total labour force	1,307,255	1,458,690	2,765,945

* Figures exclude persons seeking work for the first time, totalling 13,832 (males 9,608, females 4,224), but include other unemployed persons.

Source: UN, *Demographic Yearbook*.

Mid-2012 (estimates in '000): Agriculture, etc. 3,852; Total labour force 4,333 (Source: FAO).

Health and Welfare

KEY INDICATORS

Total fertility rate (children per woman, 2009)	4.5
Under-5 mortality rate (per 1,000 live births, 2009)	166
HIV/AIDS (% of persons aged 15–49, 2009)	3.3
Physicians (per 1,000 head, 2004)	0.03
Hospital beds (per 1,000 head, 2006)	0.70
Health expenditure 2008): US $ per head (PPP)	50
Health expenditure (2008): % of GDP	13.0
Health expenditure (2008): public (% of total)	40.0
Access to water (% of persons, 2008)	72
Access to sanitation (% of persons, 2008)	46
Total carbon dioxide emissions ('000 metric tons, 2006)	197.9
Carbon dioxide emissions per head (metric tons, 2006)	0.0
Human Development Index (2011): ranking	185
Human Development Index (2011): value	0.316

For sources and definitions, see explanatory note on p. vi.

Agriculture

PRINCIPAL CROPS
('000 metric tons)

	2008	2009	2010
Wheat	8.1	8.6	9.0
Rice, paddy	74.5	78.4	83.0
Maize	117.7	120.4	126.4
Millet*	11.0	11.2	11.7
Sorghum	79.8	81.2	83.0
Potatoes	28.9	10.6	9.3
Sweet potatoes	900.4	484.2	303.4
Cassava (Manioc)	577.1	235.4	187.9
Taro (Coco yam)	58.3	44.5	18.5
Yams	9.9	5.6	3.1
Sugar cane	189.2	132.8	131.7
Beans, dry	189.7	202.9	201.6
Peas, dry	30.9	37.3	31.5
Groundnuts, with shell*	8.8	8.0	10.2
Oil palm fruit*	16.5	15.5	15.5
Bananas	1,760.0	620.0	136.6
Coffee, green	7.3	25.1	6.8
Tea	6.7	6.7	8.0

* FAO estimates.

Aggregate production ('000 metric tons, may include official, semi-official or estimated data): Total cereals 291.1 in 2008, 299.8 in 2009, 313.2 in 2010. Total roots and tubers 1,574.6 in 2008, 780.3 in 2009, 522.2 in 2010. Total vegetables (incl. melons) 372.8 in 2008, 442.0 in 2009, 403.0 in 2010. Total fruits (excl. melons) 1,873.8 in 2008, 733.8 in 2009, 238.5 in 2010.

Source: FAO.

LIVESTOCK
('000 head, year ending September)

	2008	2009	2010
Cattle	472	554	596
Pigs	167	203	245
Sheep	281	292	296
Goats	1,617	1,687	2,163
Chickens*	4,950	5,000	5,050

* FAO estimates.

Source: FAO.

LIVESTOCK PRODUCTS
('000 metric tons, FAO estimates)

	2008	2009	2010
Cattle meat	13.0	15.2	15.6
Sheep meat	0.6	0.7	0.7
Goat meat	6.1	6.4	6.4
Pig meat	9.8	12.0	12.0
Chicken meat	6.9	6.9	6.9
Cows' milk	22.0	26.0	25.6
Sheep's milk	0.7	0.8	0.8
Goats' milk	16.1	16.9	17.6
Hen eggs	3.1	2.8	3.0

Source: FAO.

Forestry

ROUNDWOOD REMOVALS
('000 cubic metres, excl. bark, FAO estimates)

	2007	2008	2009
Sawlogs, veneer logs and logs for sleepers	307	307	307
Other industrial wood	576	576	576
Fuel wood	8,822	8,965	9,111
Total	9,705	9,848	9,994

2010: Production assumed to be unchanged from 2009 (FAO estimates).

Source: FAO.

SAWNWOOD PRODUCTION
('000 cubic metres, incl. railway sleepers)

	2005	
Coniferous (softwood)	18.0*	
Broadleaved (hardwood)*	65.0	
Total*	83.0	8.

* FAO estimate(s).

2008–10: Production assumed to be unchanged from 2007 (FA

Source: FAO.

Fishing

(metric tons, live weight)

	2007	2008	
Capture	16,700	17,766	1
Freshwater perches	3,600	3,169	
Dagaas	12,000	13,181	13
Aquaculture	200	200	
Total catch (incl. others)	16,900	17,966	17,9

Source: FAO.

Mining

(metric tons, unless otherwise indicated)

	2007	2008	2009*
Tin ore†	2	21	21
Tantalum and niobium (columbium) concentrates‡	51.6	83.9	84.0
Gold (kg)*†	750	750	750
Peat	7,489	9,764	9,800

* Estimates.
† Figures refer to the metal content of ores.
‡ The estimated tantalum content (in metric tons) was 10.0 in 2007, 16.4 in 2008 and 16.4 in 2009 (estimate).

Source: US Geological Survey.

Industry

SELECTED PRODUCTS
('000 metric tons, unless otherwise indicated)

	2008	2009	2010
Beer ('000 hl)	1,368.7	1,366.5	1,665.2
Soft drinks ('000 hl)	285.0	287.1	319.9
Cottonseed oil ('000 litres)	33.6	31.5	26.5
Sugar	18.2	14.3	18.9
Cigarettes (million)	436.1	514.2	457.8
Paint	0.5	0.5	0.5
Polyethylene film (metric tons)	23.8	17.5	1.6
Soap (metric tons)	5,671.4	6,000.8	5,202.5
Plastic racks ('000)	367.6	361.1	393.2
Moulds (metric tons)	26.0	26.7	39.1
PVC tubing (metric tons)	104.4	139.9	143.1
Steel tubing (metric tons)	68.5	n.a.	n.a.
Electric energy (million kWh)	111.8	121.1	142.0

Source: Banque de la République du Burundi.

—continued	2008	2009	2010
Other income received	10.9	1.4	1.1
Other income paid	–15.2	–18.4	–12.0
Balance on goods, services and income	–445.6	–420.7	–436.8
Current transfers received	94.3	162.1	127.2
Current transfers paid	–2.0	–3.2	–13.6
Current balance	–353.3	–261.9	–323.1
Capital account (net)	67.0	82.2	75.7
Direct investment abroad	–0.6	—	—
Direct investment from abroad	3.8	0.3	0.8
Other investment assets	–30.8	–28.9	–43.6
Other investment liabilities	20.0	–718.8	106.2
Net errors and omissions	57.8	–103.6	8.1
Overall balance	–236.1	–1,030.6	–175.9

Source: IMF, *International Financial Statistics.*

External Trade

PRINCIPAL COMMODITIES

(US $ million)

Imports c.i.f.	2007	2008	2009
Food and live animals	46.5	27.1	38.8
Maize, unmilled	14.3	1.8	0.1
Beverages and tobacco	2.6	2.8	2.0
Beverages	1.8	2.0	2.0
Mineral fuels, lubricants and related materials	118.4	10.4	8.0
Chemicals and related products	43.0	52.6	55.3
Medicinal and pharmaceutical products	25.4	32.0	29.7
Basic manufactures	79.7	76.4	87.0
Machinery and transport equipment	103.6	107.4	112.1
Road vehicles	66.5	34.0	36.7
Miscellaneous manufactured articles	19.9	25.8	26.7
Total (incl. others)	423.0	315.2	344.8

Exports f.o.b.	2007	2008	2009
Food and live animals	52.9	48.9	53.8
Coffee and coffee substitutes	38.5	39.5	39.7
Cane sugar, raw	6.2	1.4	1.8
Beverages and tobacco	1.8	3.4	2.9
Beer made from malt	0.8	1.5	1.4
Crude materials (inedible), except fuels	9.8	12.1	8.1
Hides and skins	3.7	2.8	1.6
Mineral fuels, lubricants and related materials	5.9	1.1	1.6
Petroleum	5.9	1.1	1.6
Basic manufactures	2.6	1.2	1.0
Machinery and transport equipment	20.7	11.4	13.0
Road vehicles	14.3	7.9	9.5
Other transport equipment	0.6	—	0.3
Miscellaneous manufactured articles	8.0	0.8	2.0
Arms and ammunition	0.5	—	—
Total (incl. others)	156.2	141.8	112.9

Source: UN, *International Trade Statistics Yearbook.*

PRINCIPAL TRADING PARTNERS

(US $ million)

Imports c.i.f.	2007	2008	2009
Belgium	47.6	54.6	46.5
China, People's Repub.	16.6	23.2	32.3
Denmark	3.7	3.8	8.3
Egypt	5.1	8.5	14.0
France (incl. Monaco)	15.6	28.8	18.4
Germany	9.2	21.1	6.2
India	14.2	15.9	19.4
Italy	6.4	6.7	12.9
Japan	29.4	15.2	17.3
Kenya	33.5	27.6	32.1
Netherlands	4.8	5.1	3.9
Pakistan	4.9	0.2	1.8
Russia	0.7	0.3	0.6
Saudi Arabia	116.1	1.5	4.4
South Africa	10.4	10.2	4.6
Tanzania	10.1	15.7	15.2
Thailand	4.5	1.2	—
Turkey	1.0	0.9	2.0
Uganda	45.4	30.3	29.7
United Kingdom	3.3	4.1	4.1
USA	4.1	2.8	9.3
Zambia	6.4	3.0	11.7
Total (incl. others)	423.0	315.2	344.8

Exports f.o.b.	2007	2008	2009
Albania	3.1	0.4	—
Belgium	3.8	8.6	6.3
Congo, Democratic Repub.	14.7	5.9	7.0
Ethiopia	0.5	—	—
France (incl. Monaco)	3.6	0.6	1.0
Germany	3.5	5.7	8.4
Japan	3.8	0.2	0.2
Kenya	11.2	7.6	7.3
Mozambique	—	0.2	—
Nepal	0.1	—	—
Netherlands	0.5	1.3	1.0
Pakistan	—	0.1	—
Rwanda	10.4	4.5	4.7
South Africa	2.9	0.1	0.1
Sudan	3.2	1.1	—
Switzerland and Liechtenstein	17.0	21.7	20.7
Tanzania	2.0	2.2	9.5
United Kingdom	7.6	0.2	0.6
Total (incl. others)	156.2	141.8	112.9

Source: UN, *International Trade Statistics Yearbook.*

Transport

ROAD TRAFFIC

('000 motor vehicles in use, estimates)

	1998	1999	2000
Passenger cars	6.6	6.9	7.0
Commercial vehicles	9.3	9.3	9.3

2001–03 ('000 motor vehicles in use): Figures assumed to be unchanged from 2000.

Source: UN, *Statistical Yearbook.*

2007 ('000 motor vehicles in use): Passenger cars 15,466; Vans and lorries 32,717; Motorcycles and mopeds 11,302 (Source: IRF, *World Road Statistics*).

LAKE TRAFFIC
(Bujumbura, '000 metric tons)

	2008	2009	2010
Goods:			
arrivals	107.3	167.6	222.9
departures	8.5	5.8	22.7

Source: Banque de la République du Burundi.

CIVIL AVIATION
(traffic on scheduled services)

	1996	1997	1998
Passengers carried ('000)	9	12	12
Passenger-km (million)	2	8	8

Source: UN, *Statistical Yearbook*.

Tourism

TOURIST ARRIVALS BY REGION*

	2004	2005	2006
Africa	1,333	49,473	140,868
Americas	5,908	9,956	4,025
Asia	4,528	4,023	10,062
Europe	29,409	29,486	32,199
Unspecified	92,050	55,480	14,087
Total	133,228	148,418	201,241

* Including Burundian nationals residing abroad.

Tourism receipts (US $ million, incl. passenger transport): 1.6 in 2006; 2.3 in 2007; 1.6 in 2008; 1.7 in 2009.

Source: World Tourism Organization.

Communications Media

	2008	2009	2010
Telephones ('000 main lines in use)	30.4	31.5	32.6
Mobile cellular telephones ('000 subscribers)	480.6	838.4	1,150.5
Internet subscribers ('000)	0.06	0.06*	n.a.
Broadband subscribers	200	200	200

* Estimate.

Personal computers: 65,000 (8.5 per 1,000 persons) in 2006.

Television receivers ('000 in use): 200 in 2001.

Radio receivers ('000 in use): 140 in 1997.

Daily newspapers: 1 in 2004.

Non-daily newspapers: 5 in 1998 (circulation 8,000 copies).

Sources: mainly International Telecommunication Union; UNESCO, *Statistical Yearbook*.

Education

(2009/10)

	Teachers	Students		
		Males	Females	Total
Pre-primary	1,617	27,581	27,522	55,103
Primary	36,557	931,034	918,827	1,849,861
Secondary:				
General	10,143	186,342	135,770	322,112
Technical and vocational	1,132	9,893	5,572	15,465
Higher	1,784	18,917	10,352	29,269

Institutions (1988/89): Primary 1,512; Secondary 400.

Source: UNESCO Institute for Statistics.

Pupil-teacher ratio (primary education, UNESCO estimate): 50.6 in 2009/10 (Source: UNESCO Institute for Statistics).

Adult literacy rate (UNESCO estimates): 66.6% (males 72.6%; females 60.9%) in 2009 (Source: UNESCO Institute for Statistics).

Directory

The Government

HEAD OF STATE

President: Maj. JEAN-PIERRE NKURUNZIZA (inaugurated 26 August 2005; re-elected 28 June 2010).

First Vice-President: THÉRENCE SINUNGURUZA.

Second Vice-President: GERVAIS RUFYIKIRI.

COUNCIL OF MINISTERS
(May 2012)

The Government comprises members of the Conseil national pour la défense de la démocratie—Forces pour la défense de la démocratie (CNDD—FDD), the Front pour la démocratie au Burundi (FRODEBU-Nyakuri), the Union pour le progrès national (UPRONA) and independents.

Minister of the Interior: EDOUARD NDUWIMANA (CNDD—FDD).

Minister of Public Security: GABRIEL NIZIGAMA (CNDD—FDD).

Minister of External Relations and International Co-operation: LAURENT KAVAKURE (CNDD—FDD).

Minister at the Presidency, in charge of Good Governance and Privatization: ISSA NGENDAKUMANA.

Minister at the Presidency, in charge of East African Community Affairs: HAFSA MOSSI (CNDD—FDD).

Minister of Justice, Keeper of the Seals: PASCAL BARANDAGIYE (CNDD—FDD).

Minister of Finance and Planning for Economic Development: TABU ABDALLAH MANIRAKIZA (CNDD—FDD).

Minister of Communal Development: MARTIN MANIRAKIZA.

Minister of National Defence and War Veterans: Maj.-Gen. PONTIEN GACIYUBWENGE (Ind.).

Minister of Public Health and the Fight against AIDS: Dr SABINE NTAKARUTIMANA (CNDD—FDD).

Minister of Higher Education and Scientific Research: Dr JULIEN NIMUBONA (UPRONA).

Minister of Primary and Secondary Education, Professional and Vocational Training and Literacy: SÉVERIN BUZINGO (CNDD—FDD).

Minister of Agriculture and Livestock: ODETTE KAYITESI (CNDD—FDD).

Minister of Telecommunications, Information, Communications and Relations with Parliament: CONCILIE NIBIGIRA (UPRONA).

Minister of Water, the Environment, Territorial Development and Town Planning: JEAN-MARIE NIBIRANTIJE (CNDD—FDD).

Minister of Commerce, Industry, Posts and Tourism: VICTOIRE NDIKUMANA (UPRONA).

Minister of Energy and Mines: CÔME MANIRAKIZA (CNDD—FDD).

Minister of Civil Service, Labour and Social Security: ANNONCIATE SENDAZIRASA (CNDD—FDD).

Minister of Transport, Public Works and Equipment: MOÏSE BUKUMI.

Minister of Youth, Sports and Culture: JEAN-JACQUES NYENIMIGABO.

Minister of National Solidarity, Human Rights and Gender: CLOTILDE NIRAGIRA.

MINISTRIES

Office of the President: Bujumbura; tel. 22226063; internet www.presidence.bi.

Ministry of Agriculture and Livestock: Bujumbura; tel. 22222087.

Ministry of Civil Service, Labour and Social Security: BP 1480, Bujumbura; tel. 22225645; fax 22228715.

Ministry of Commerce, Industry, Posts and Tourism: BP 492, Bujumbura; tel. 22225330; fax 22225595.

Ministry of Energy and Mines: BP 745, Bujumbura; tel. 22225909; fax 22223337.

Ministry of External Relations and International Co-operation: Bujumbura; tel. 22222150.

Ministry of Finance: ave des Non-Aligens, BP 1830, Bujumbura; tel. 22225142; fax 22223128; internet www.finances.gov.bi.

Ministry of Higher Education and Scientific Research: Bujumbura.

Ministry of the Interior: Bujumbura.

Ministry of Justice: ave des Palmiers, Bujumbura; tel. 22222148.

Ministry of National Defence and War Veterans: Bujumbura.

Ministry of National Solidarity, Human Rights and Gender: BP 224, Bujumbura; tel. 22225394; fax 22224193; e-mail ministre@miniplan.bi; internet www.cslpminiplan.bi.

Ministry of Planning and Communal Development: Bujumbura; internet www.miniplan.bi.

Ministry of Primary and Secondary Education, Professional and Vocational Training and Literacy: Bujumbura.

Ministry of Public Health and the Fight against AIDS: rue Pierre Ngendandumwe, Bujumbura.

Ministry of Public Security: Bujumbura.

Ministry of Telecommunications, Information, Communications and Relations with Parliament: BP 2870, Bujumbura.

Ministry of Transport, Public Works and Equipment: BP 2000, Bujumbura; tel. 22222923; fax 22226900.

Minister of Water, the Environment, Territorial Development and Town Planning: BP 631, Bujumbura; tel. 22224976; fax 22228902; e-mail nduwi_deo@yahoo.fr.

Ministry of Youth, Sports and Culture: Bujumbura; tel. 22226822.

President and Legislature

PRESIDENT

A presidential election was held on 28 June 2010 at which Jean-Pierre Nkurunziza, representing the Conseil national pour la défense de la démocratie—Forces pour la défense de la démocratie, was the sole candidate. According to results confirmed by the Constitutional Court on 8 July, Nkurunziza secured 2,482,219 of the 2,709,941 votes cast, equating to 91.60%. (There were 29,195 invalid votes cast.)

SÉNAT

President: GABRIEL NTISEZERANA (CNDD—FDD).

First Vice-President: PERSILLE MWIDOGO (CNDD—FDD).

Second Vice-President: PONTIEN NIYONGABO (UPRONA).

Elections, 28 July 2010

Party	Seats*
CNDD—FDD	32
UPRONA	2
Total	34

* In accordance with constitutional requirements for balance of ethnic representation and a minimum 30% representation of women, a further four seats were allocated to former Presidents and three to the Twa ethnic group, increasing the total number of senators to 41.

ASSEMBLÉE NATIONALE

President: PIE NTAVYOHANYUMA (CNDD—FDD).

First Vice-President: MO-MAMO KARERWA (CNDD—FDD).

Second Vice-President: FRANÇOIS KABURA (UPRONA).

Elections, 23 July 2010

Party	Seats*
CNDD—FDD	81
UPRONA	17
FRODEBU-Nyakuri	5
Total	103

* In accordance with constitutional requirements for balance of ethnic representation and a minimum 30% representation of women, a further three seats were allocated to the Twa ethnic group, increasing the total number of deputies to 106. The CNDD—FDD, FRODEBU-Nyakuri and UPRONA each received an additional seat.

Election Commission

Commission électorale nationale indépendante (CENI): BP 1128, Bujumbura; tel. 22274464; tel. info@ceniburundi.bi; internet www.ceniburundi.bi; f. 2004; independent; 5 mems; Chair. PIERRE CLAVER NDAYICARIYE; Vice-Chair. MARGUERITTE BUKURU.

Political Organizations

Political parties are required to demonstrate firm commitment to national unity, and impartiality with regard to ethnic or regional origin, gender and religion, in order to receive legal recognition. By 2009 the number of registered political parties had increased to 42; these included former rebel organizations.

Alliance burundaise-africaine pour le salut (ABASA): Bujumbura; f. 1993; Tutsi; Leader TÉRENCE NSANZE.

Alliance démocratique pour le changement au Burundi (ADC—Ikibiri): Bujumbura; f. 2010; coalition of 12 opposition parties, including Front pour la démocratie au Burundi (FRODEBU); Pres. LÉONCE NGENDAKUMANA.

Alliance libérale pour le développement (ALIDE): f. 2001; Leader JOSEPH NTIDENDEREZA.

Alliance des Vaillants (AV—Intware) (Alliance of the Brave): Bujumbura; f. 1993; Tutsi; Leader ANDRÉ NKUNDIKIJE.

Conseil national pour la défense de la démocratie (CNDD): Bujumbura; e-mail cndd_bur@usa.net; internet www.club.euronet.be/pascal.karolero.cndd.burundi; f. 1994; Hutu; Pres. LÉONARD NYANGOMA.

Conseil national pour la défense de la démocratie—Forces pour la défense de la démocratie (CNDD—FDD): fmr armed wing of the Hutu CNDD; split into 2 factions in Oct. 2001, one led by JEAN-BOSCO NDAYIKENGURUKIYE and the other by JEAN-PIERRE NKURUNZIZA; Nkurunziza's faction incl. in Govt Nov. 2003, following peace agreement; registered as political org. Jan. 2005; Chair. JÉRÉMIE NGENDAKUMANA; Sec.-Gen. GÉLASE NDABIRABE.

Forces nationales de libération (FNL): fmr armed wing of Hutu Parti de libération du peuple hutu (PALIPEHUTU, f. 1980); split in Aug. 2002 and in Dec. 2005; cease-fire with Govt announced Sept. 2006; formally registered as a political organization in 2009; Chair. EMMANUEL MIBURO.

Forces nationales de libération—Iragi rya Gahutu: f. 2009; Leader JACQUES KENESE.

Front national de libération Icanzo (FNL Icanzo): reconstituted Dec. 2002 from fmr faction of Forces nationales de libération; Leader Dr ALAIN MUGABARABONA.

Front pour la démocratie au Burundi (FRODEBU): Bujumbura; internet www.frodebu.bi; f. 1992; split in June 1999; Hutu; Chair. LÉONCE NGENDAKUMANA.

FRODEBU-Nyakuri: Bujumbura; f. 2008; Leader JEAN MINANI.

KAZE—Force pour la défense de la démocratie (KAZE—FDD): f. May 2004; reconstituted as a political party from a faction of the armed CNDD—FDD (see above); Leader JEAN-BOSCO NDAYIKENGURUKIYE.

Mouvement pour la réhabilitation du citoyen—Rurenzangemero (MRC—Rurenzangemero): Bujumbura; f. June 2001; regd Nov. 2002; Leader Lt-Col EPITACE BAYAGANAKANDI.

Mouvement pour la sécurité et la démocratie: tel. 29550803; e-mail msdburundi@yahoo.fr; internet msdburundi.org; ALEXIS SINDUHIJE; Sec.-Gen. ODETTE NTAHIRAJA.

Mouvement socialiste panafricaniste—Inkinzo y'Ijambo Ry'abarundi (MSP—Inkinzo) (Guarantor of Freedom of Speech in Burundi): Bujumbura; f. 1993; Tutsi; Chair. TITE BUCUMI.

Parti libéral (PL): BP 2167, Bujumbura; tel. 22214848; fax 22225981; e-mail liberalburundi@yahoo.fr; f. 1992; Hutu; Leader GAËTAN NIKOBAMYE.

Parti pour le développement et la solidarité des travailleurs (PML-Abanyamwete): Bujumbura; f. Oct. 2004; Leader PATRICIA NDAYIZEYE.

Parti pour la réconciliation du peuple (PRP): Bujumbura; f. 1992; Tutsi; Leader MATHIAS HITIMANA.

Parti pour le redressement intégral du Burundi (PARIBU): Bujumbura; f. Sept. 2004; Leader BENOÎT NDORIMANA.

Parti pour le redressement national (PARENA): Bujumbura; f. 1994; Leader JEAN-BAPTISTE BAGAZA.

Parti social démocrate (PSD): Bujumbura; f. 1993; Tutsi; Leader GODEFROID HAKIZIMANA.

Rassemblement pour la démocratie et le développement économique et social (RADDES): Bujumbura; f. 1992; Tutsi; Chair. JOSEPH NZEYZIMANA.

Union pour la paix et le développement (Zigamibanga): f. Aug. 2002; Leader ZEDI FERUZI.

Union pour le progrès national (UPRONA): BP 1810, Bujumbura; tel. 22225028; f. 1958 following the 1961 elections; the numerous small parties which had been defeated merged with UPRONA, which became the sole legal political party in 1966; party activities were suspended following the coup of Sept. 1987, but resumed in 1989; Chair. ALOYS RUBUKA.

Diplomatic Representation

EMBASSIES IN BURUNDI

Belgium: 9 blvd de la Liberté, BP 1920, Bujumbura; tel. 22226176; fax 22223171; e-mail bujumbura@diplobel.fed.be; internet www.diplomatie.be/bujumbura; Ambassador JOZEF SMETS.

China, People's Republic: 675 sur la Parcelle, BP 2550, Bujumbura; tel. 22224307; fax 22213735; e-mail chinaemb_bi@mfa.gov.cn; Ambassador YU XUZHONG.

Egypt: 31 ave de la Liberté, BP 1520, Bujumbura; tel. 22223161; fax 22222918; Ambassador ABDEL MONE'M OMAR ABDEL MONE'M.

France: 60 ave de l'UPRONA, BP 1740, Bujumbura; tel. 22203000; fax 22203010; e-mail cad.bujumbura-amba@diplomatie.gouv.fr; internet www.ambafrance-bi.org; Ambassador JOËL LOUVET.

Germany: 22 rue 18 septembre, BP 480, Bujumbura; tel. 22257777; fax 22221004; e-mail info@buju.diplo.de; Ambassador JOSEPH WEISS.

Holy See: 46 ave des Travailleurs, BP 1068, Bujumbura; tel. 22225415; fax 22223176; e-mail na.burundi@diplomat.va; Apostolic Nuncio FRANCO COPPOLA (Titular Archbishop of Vinda).

Kenya: PTA Bank Bldg, 2nd Floor, West Wing Chaussée du Prince Louis Rwagasore, BP 5138, Mutanga, Bujumbura; tel. 22258160; fax 22258161; e-mail information@kenyaembassy.bu; Ambassador BENJAMIN A. W. MWERI.

Korea, Democratic People's Republic: BP 1620, Bujumbura; tel. 22222881; Ambassador SOON CHUN LEE.

Russia: 78 blvd de l'UPRONA, BP 1034, Bujumbura; tel. 22226098; fax 22222984; e-mail ustas@cbinf.com; Ambassador VLADIMIR TIMOFEEV.

Rwanda: 40 ave de la RDC, BP 400, Bujumbura; tel. 22228755; fax 22215426; e-mail ambabuja@minaffet.gov.rw; internet www.burundi.embassy.gov.rw; Ambassador AUGUSTIN HABIMANA.

South Africa: ave de la Plage, Quartier Asiatique, BP 185, Bujumbura; tel. 22248220; fax 22248219; e-mail bujumbura@foreign.gov.za; Ambassador MDU LEMBEDE.

Tanzania: 855 rue United Nations, BP 1653, Bujumbura; tel. 22248632; fax 22248637; e-mail tanzanrep@usan-bu.net; Ambassador Dr JAMES NZAGI.

USA: ave des Etats-Unis, BP 1720, Bujumbura; tel. 22223454; fax 22222926; e-mail jyellin@bujumbura.us-state.gov; internet burundi.usembassy.gov; Ambassador PAMELA JO HOWELL SLUTZ.

Judicial System

Constitutional Court: BP 151, Bujumbura; comprises a minimum of 7 judges, who are nominated by the President for a 6-year term; Pres. CHRISTINE NZEYIMANA.

Supreme Court: BP 1460, Bujumbura; tel. and fax 22213544; court of final instance; 3 divisions: ordinary, cassation and administrative; Pres. (vacant).

Courts of Appeal: Bujumbura, Gitega and Ngozi.

Tribunals of First Instance: There are 17 provincial tribunals and 123 smaller resident tribunals in other areas.

Religion

Some 70% of the population are Christians, the majority of whom are Roman Catholics. Anglicans number about 60,000. There are about 200,000 other Protestant adherents, of whom about 160,000 are Pentecostalists. About 23% of the population adhere to traditional beliefs, which include the worship of the god Imana. About 10% of the population are Muslims. The Bahá'í Faith is also active in Burundi.

CHRISTIANITY

Conseil National des Eglises Protestantes du Burundi (CNEB): BP 17, Bujumbura; tel. 22224216; fax 22227941; e-mail cneb@cbninf.com; f. 1935; 10 mem. churches; Pres. Rt Rev. ISAAC BIMPENDA (Anglican Bishop of Gitega); Gen. Sec. Rev. NOAH NZEYIMANA.

The Anglican Communion

The Church of the Province of Burundi, established in 1992, comprises five dioceses.

Archbishop of Burundi and Bishop of Matana: Most Rev. BERNARD NTAHOTURI, BP 447, Bujumbura; tel. 22924595; fax 22229129; e-mail ntahober@cbinf.com.

Provincial Secretary: Rev. PEDACULI BIRAKENGANA, BP 447, Bujumbura; tel. 22270361; fax 22229129; e-mail peab@cbinf.com.

The Roman Catholic Church

Burundi comprises two archdioceses and six dioceses. Some 69% of the total population are Roman Catholics.

Bishops' Conference

Conférence des Evêques Catholiques du Burundi, 5 blvd de l'UPRONA, BP 1390, Bujumbura; tel. 22223263; fax 22223270; e-mail cecab@cbinf.com.

f. 1980; Pres. Rt Rev. EVARISTE NGOYAGOYE (Archbishop of Bujumbura).

Archbishop of Bujumbura: Rt Rev. EVARISTE NGOYAGOYE, BP 690, Bujumbura; tel. 22231476; fax 22231165; e-mail dicabu@cni.cbinf.com.

Archbishop of Gitega: Most Rev. SIMON NTAMWANA, Archevêché, BP 118, Gitega; tel. 22402160; fax 22402620; e-mail archigi@bujumbura.ocicnet.net.

Other Christian Churches

Union of Baptist Churches of Burundi: Rubura, DS 117, Bujumbura 1; 87 mem. churches; Pres. PAUL BARUHENAMWO; mems 25,505 (2005).

Other denominations active in the country include the Evangelical Christian Brotherhood of Burundi, the Free Methodist Church of Burundi and the United Methodist Church of Burundi.

BAHÁ'Í FAITH

National Spiritual Assembly: BP 1578, Bujumbura; tel. 79955840; e-mail bahaiburundi@yahoo.fr; Sec. DENIS NDAYIZEYE.

The Press

Conseil national de la communication (CNC): Immeuble Marcoil, blvd de l'UPRONA, Bujumbura; tel. 22259064; fax 22259066; e-mail info@cnc-burundi.org; internet cnc-burundi.org; f. 2001 under the terms of the transitional Constitution; responsible for ensuring press freedom; Pres. VESTINE NAHIMANA.

NEWSPAPER

Le Renouveau du Burundi: BP 2573, Bujumbura; tel. 22226232; f. 1978; daily; French; govt-owned; Dir THADDÉE SIRYUYUMUNSI; circ. 2,500 (2004).

PERIODICALS

Arc-en-Ciel: Bujumbura; weekly; French; Editor-in-Chief THIERRY NDAYISHIMIYE.

Au Coeur de l'Afrique: Association des conférences des ordinaires du Rwanda et Burundi, BP 1390, Bujumbura; fax 22223027; e-mail cnid@cbinf.com; bimonthly; education; circ. 1,000.

Bulletin Économique et Financier: BP 482, Bujumbura; bimonthly.

Bulletin Mensuel: Banque de la République du Burundi, Service des études, BP 705, Bujumbura; tel. 22225142; monthly.

Iwacu: ave de France 6, BP 1842, Bujumbura; tel. 22258957; fax 79991474; internet www.iwacu-burundi.org; f. 2008; weekly; publ. by the Union Burundaise des Journalistes; Editor-in-Chief Antoine Kaburahe.

In-Burundi: c/o Cyber Média, BP 5270, ave du 18 septembre, Bujumbura; tel. 2244464; current affairs internet publication; Editor-in-Chief Edgar C. Mbanza.

Ndongozi Y'uburundi: Catholic Mission, BP 690, Bujumbura; tel. 22222762; fax 22228907; fortnightly; Kirundi.

Revue Administration et Juridique: Association d'études administratives et juridiques du Burundi, BP 1613, Bujumbura; quarterly; French.

PRESS ASSOCIATIONS

Association Burundaise des Femmes Journalistes (AFJO): ave Kunkiko, BP 2414, Bujumbura; tel. 79949460; fax 22254920; e-mail nijembazi@yahoo.fr; Pres. Espérance Nijembazi.

Union Burundaise des Journalistes (UBJ): Bujumbura; fmrly Association Burundaise des Journalistes (ABJ), present name adopted 2009; Pres. Alexandre Niyungeko; Sec.-Gen. Bertrand Bihizi.

NEWS AGENCY

Agence Burundaise de Presse (ABP): ave Nicolas Mayugi, BP 2870, Bujumbura; tel. 22213083; fax 22222282; e-mail abp@cbinf.com; internet www.abp.info.bi; f. 1975; publ. daily bulletin.

Publishers

Editions Intore: 19 ave Matana, BP 2524, Bujumbura; tel. 22223499; e-mail anbirabuza@yahoo.fr; f. 1992; philosophy, history, journalism, literature, social sciences; Dir Dr André Birabuza.

IMPARUDI: ave du 18 septembre 3, BP 3010, Bujumbura; tel. 22223125; fax 22222572; e-mail imparudi.1982@yahoo.fr; f. 1950; Dir-Gen. Théoneste Mutambuka.

Imprimerie la Licorne: 29 ave de la Mission, BP 2942, Bujumbura; tel. 22223503; fax 22227225; f. 1991.

Les Presses Lavigerie: 5 ave de l'UPRONA, BP 1640, Bujumbura; tel. 22222368; fax 22220318.

Régie de Productions Pédagogiques: BP 3118, Bujumbura II; tel. 22226111; fax 22222631; e-mail rpp@cbinf.com; f. 1984; school textbooks; Dir Abraham Mbonerane.

GOVERNMENT PUBLISHING HOUSE

Imprimerie Nationale du Burundi (INABU): BP 991, Bujumbura; tel. 22224046; fax 22225399; f. 1978; Dir Nicolas Nijimbere.

Broadcasting and Communications

In 2011 there were five providers of cellular mobile telephone communications services. The state-owned ONATEL provided fixed-line services. In 2010 there were 1.7m. mobile telephone subscribers.

TELECOMMUNICATIONS

Agence de Régulation et de Contrôle des Télécommunications (ARCT): 360 ave Patrice Lumumba, BP 6702, Bujumbura; tel. 22210276; fax 22242832; Dir-Gen. Joseph Nsegana.

Direction Générale des Transports, Postes et Télécommunications: BP 2390, Bujumbura; tel. 22225422; fax 22226900; govt telecommunications authority; Dir-Gen. Vital Narakwiye.

Econet Wireless Burundi: 21 blvd du 28 Novembre, BP 431, Bujumbura; tel. 22243131; fax 22243535; internet www.econet.bi; formerly Spacetel; mobile and fixed telecommunications services and products, satellite services and internet solutions; Dir-Gen. Darlington Mandivenga.

Leo Burundi: 1 pl. de l'Indépendance, BP 5186, Bujumbura; e-mail feliciten@leo.bi; internet www.leo.bi; f. 1993; fmrly Telecel Burundi, Leo Burundi is the trade name of U-Com Burundi; mobile telephone service provider; a subsidiary of Orascom Telecom Holding; Dir-Gen. Raymond Laforce.

Office National des Télécommunications (ONATEL): ave du Commerce, BP 60, Bujumbura; tel. 22223196; fax 22226917; e-mail onatel@cbinf.com; f. 1979; Dir-Gen. Salvator Nizigiyimana.

ONAMOB: Bujumbura; mobile cellular telephone operator owned by ONATEL.

Smart Mobile: Immeuble White Stone, blvd de l'Uprona Centre, BP 3150, Bujumbura; internet lacellsu.com; f. 2010; trade name of Lacell SU; Dir-Gen. Bhupendra Bhandari.

Tempo Africell: ave de la RDC, Bujumbura; tel. 78872872; e-mail africell@cbinf.com; internet www.tempo.bi; f. 1999 as Africell; name changed as above in 2008 following acquisition by VTEL Holdings (United Arab Emirates); mobile cellular telephone service provider; CEO Yanal Abzack.

BROADCASTING

In 2010 there were some 15 private radio stations and one private television channel operating in Burundi, in addition to the state-run Radiodiffusion et Télévision Nationale du Burundi.

Radio

Radio Bonesha FM: BP 5314, Bujumbura; tel. 22217068; e-mail umwizero@cbinf.com; f. 1996 as Radio Umwizero; EU-funded, private station promoting national reconciliation, peace and devt projects; broadcasts 9 hours daily in Kirundi, Swahili and French; Dir Hubert Vieille.

Radio Isanganiro: 27 ave de l'Amitié, BP 810, Bujumbura; tel. 22246595; fax 22246600; e-mail isanganiro@isanganiro.org; internet www.isanganiro.org; f. Nov. 2002; controlled by Association Ijambo, f. by Studio Ijambo (see below); broadcasts on 89.7 FM frequency, in Kirundi, French and Swahili; services cover Bujumbura area, and were to be extended to all Great Lakes region; Dir Vincent Nkeshimana.

Radio Publique Africaine (RPA): Bujumbura; tel. 79920704; e-mail nfo@rpa-radioyacu.org; internet www.rpa-radiyoyacu.org; f. 2001 with the aim of promoting peace; independent; Dir Alexis Sinduhije.

Radio Renaissance FM: Bujumbura; f. 2003; Dir-Gen. Innocent Muhozi.

Radio Sans Frontières Bonesha FM: Association Radio Sans Frontières 47, Chemin P. L. Rwagasore, BP 5314, Bujumbura; internet www.bonesha.bi; Dir Corneille Nibaruta.

Rema FM: Bujumbura; f. 2008.

Studio Ijambo (Wise Words): 27 ave de l'Amitié, BP 6180, Bujumbura; tel. 22219699; e-mail burundi@sfcg.org.bi; internet www.studioijambo.org; f. 1995 by Search for Common Ground; promotes peace and reconciliation.

Voix de la Révolution/La Radiodiffusion et Télévision Nationale du Burundi (RTNB): BP 1900, Bujumbura; tel. 22223742; fax 22226547; internet www.rtnb.bi; f. 1960; govt-controlled; daily radio broadcasts in Kirundi, Swahili, French and English; Pres. Salvator Nizigiyimana; Dir-Gen. Channel Sabimbona.

Television

Télé Renaissance: Bujumbura; f. 2008; Dir-Gen. Innocent Muhozi.

Voix de la Révolution/La Radiodiffusion et Télévision Nationale du Burundi (RTNB): BP 1900, Bujumbura; tel. 22223742; fax 22226547; internet www.rtnb.bi; f. 1960; govt-controlled; television service in Kirundi, Swahili, French and English; Pres. Salvator Nizigiyimana; Dir-Gen. Channel Sabimbona.

Finance

(cap. = capital; res = reserves; dep. = deposits; m. = million; brs = branches; amounts in Burundian francs)

BANKING

In 2010 there were 10 commercial banks and 22 microfinancial institutions in Burundi.

Central Bank

Banque de la République du Burundi (BRB): ave du Gouvernement, BP 705, Bujumbura; tel. 22225142; fax 22223128; e-mail brb@brb.bi; internet www.brb-bi.net; f. 1964 as Banque du Royaume du Burundi; state-owned; bank of issue; cap. 11,000m., res 21,780m., dep. 169,043m. (Dec. 2009); Gov. Gaspard Sindayigaya; First Vice-Gov. Melchior Wagara; 2 brs.

Commercial Banks

Banque Burundaise pour le Commerce et l'Investissement SARL (BBCI): blvd du Peuple Murundi, BP 2320, Bujumbura; tel. 22223328; fax 22223339; e-mail bbci@cbinf.com; f. 1988; cap. and res 2,645.8m., total assets 14,016.2m. (Dec. 2003); Pres. Celeslin Mizero; Dir-Gen. Charles Nihangaza.

Banque Commerciale du Burundi SM (BANCOBU): 84 chaussée Prince Louis Rwagasore, BP 990, Bujumbura; tel. 22222317; fax 22221018; e-mail info@bancobu.com; internet www.bancobu.com; f. 1960; cap. 6,820.0m., res 7,065.4m., dep. 82,091.1m. (Dec. 2009); Pres. ALEXIS NTACONZOBA; Dir-Gen. JEAN CIZA; 8 brs.

Banque de Crédit de Bujumbura SM: ave Patrice Emery Lumumba, BP 300, Bujumbura; tel. 22201111; fax 22201115; e-mail info@bcb.bi; internet www.bcb.bi; f. 1964; cap. 7,000.0m., res 3,949.6m., dep. 144,333.8m. (Dec. 2009); Pres. CLOTILDE NIRAGIRA; Gen. Man. THARCISSE RUTUMO; 8 brs.

Banque de Financement et de Leasing S.A.: blvd de la Liberté, BP 2998, Bujumbura; tel. 22243206; fax 22225437; e-mail finalease@cbinf.com; cap. and res 1,400.5m., total assets 8,578.4m. (Dec. 2003); Pres. AUDACE BIREHA; Dir-Gen. ERIC BONANE RUBEGA.

Banque de Gestion et de Financement SA: 1 blvd de la Liberté, BP 1035, Bujumbura; tel. 22221349; fax 22221351; e-mail bgf@onatel.bi; f. 1996; cap. 1,029.0m., res 986.1m., dep. 19,791.7m. (Dec. 2006); Pres. BÉDE BEDETSE; Gen. Man. MATHIAS NDIKUMANA.

Ecobank Burundi: 6 rue de la Science, BP 270, Bujumbura; tel. 22226351; fax 22225437; e-mail ecobankbi@ecobank.com; internet www.ecobank.com; cap. 7,000.1m., res 564.4m., dep. 38,044.6m. (Dec. 2009); Chair. ISAAC BUDABUDA; Man. Dir STEPHANE DOUKOURE.

Interbank Burundi SARL: 15 rue de l'Industrie, BP 2970, Bujumbura; tel. 22220629; fax 22220461; e-mail info@interbankbdi.com; internet www.interbankbdi.com; f. 1993; cap. and res 9,385.1m., total assets 117,387.0m. (Dec. 2006); Pres. GEORGES COUCOULIS; Dir-Gen. CALLIXTE MUTABAZI.

Development Bank

Banque Nationale pour le Développement Economique SARL (BNDE): 3 ave du Marché, BP 1620, Bujumbura; tel. 22222888; fax 22223775; e-mail bnde@cbinf.com; internet www.bndesm.com; f. 1966; 40% state-owned; cap. 6,190.1m., res 811.3m., dep. 6,526.1m. (Dec. 2009); Chair. and Man. Dir DONATIEN NIJIMBERE.

Co-operative Bank

Banque Coopérative d'Epargne et de Crédit Mutuel (BCM): BP 1340, Bujumbura; operating licence granted in April 1995; Vice-Pres. JULIEN MUSARAGANY.

Financial Institutions

Fonds de Promotion de L'Habitat Urbain (FPHU): ave de la Liberté, BP 1996, Bujumbura; tel. 22224986; fax 22223225; e-mail info@fphu.bi; internet www.fphu.bi; cap. 818m. (2005); Dir-Gen. AUDACE BUKURU.

Société Burundaise de Financement: 6 rue de la Science, BP 270, Bujumbura; tel. 22222126; fax 22225437; e-mail sbf@cbinf.com; cap. and res 2,558.9m., total assets 11,680.4m. (Dec. 2003); Pres. ASTÈRE GIRUKWIGOMBA; Dir-Gen. DARIUS NAHAYO.

INSURANCE

In 2010 there were six insurance companies in Burundi.

Société d'Assurances du Burundi (SOCABU): 14–18 rue de l'Amitié, BP 2440, Bujumbura; tel. 22226520; fax 22226803; e-mail socabu@socabu.bi; internet www.socabu-assurances.com; f. 1977; cap. 180m.; Man. Dir ONÉSIME NDUWIMANA.

Société Générale d'Assurances et de Réassurance (SOGEAR): BP 2432, Bujumbura; tel. 22222345; fax 22229338; f. 1991; Pres. BENOÎT NDORIMANA; Dir-Gen. L. SAUSSEZ.

Union Commerciale d'Assurances et de Réassurance (UCAR): BP 3012, Bujumbura; tel. 22223638; fax 22223695; e-mail ucar@cbinf.com; f. 1986; cap. 150m.; Chair. Lt-Col EDOUARD NZAMBIMANA; Dir-Gen. PASCAL NTAMASHIMIKIRO.

Trade and Industry

GOVERNMENT AGENCIES

Agence Burundaise de Promotion des Investissements: Quartier Kigobe, BP 7057, Bujumbura; tel. 22275996; e-mail info@burundi-investment.com; internet www.burundi-investment.com; f. 2009; Dir-Gen. LIBÉRAT MFUMUKEKO.

Agence de Promotion des Echanges Extérieurs (APEE): 27 rue de la Victoire, BP 3535, Bujumbura; tel. 22225497; fax 22222767; e-mail apee@cbinf.com; promotes and supervises foreign exchanges.

Agence Régulateur de la Filière Café (ARFIC): 279 blvd de Tanzanie, BP 450, Bujumbura; tel. 22223193; fax 22225532; f. 2009 to replace the Office du Café du Burundi, f. 1964; contributes to policy formulation for the coffee sector and supervises coffee plantations and coffee exports; Dir EVARISTE NGAYEMPORE.

Office National du Commerce (ONC): Bujumbura; f. 1973; supervises international commercial operations between the Govt of Burundi and other states or private orgs; also organizes the import of essential materials; subsidiary offices in each province.

Office National du Logement (ONL): BP 2480, Bujumbura; tel. 22226074; f. 1974 to supervise housing construction.

Office du Thé du Burundi (OTB): 52 blvd de l'UPRONA, Bujumbura; tel. 22224228; fax 22224657; e-mail otb@cbinf.com; f. 1979; supervises production and marketing of tea; Man. Dir ALEXIS NZOHABONIMANA.

DEVELOPMENT ORGANIZATIONS

Agence Française de Développement (AFD): Immeuble Old East, BP 2740, Bujumbura; tel. 222255931; internet www.afd.fr; Gen. Man. CLEMENCE VIDAL DE LA BLACHE.

Compagnie Financière pour le Développement SA: Bldg INSS, 1 route Nationale, BP 139, Ngozi; tel. 22302279; fax 22302296; Pres. ABBÉ EPHREM GIRUKWISHAKA.

Fonds de National d'Investissement Communal (FONIC): blvd du 28 Novembre, BP 2799, Bujumbura; tel. 22221963; fax 22243268; e-mail fdc@cbinf.com; internet www.fonic.bi; f. 2007 to replace Fonds de Développement Communal; Pres. DOMITIEN NDIHOKUBWAYO.

Fonds de Promotion de l'Habitat Urbain: 6 ave de la Liberté, BP 1996, Bujumbura; tel. 22227676; fax 22223225; e-mail info@fphu.bi; internet www.fphu.bi; cap. 818m. Burundian francs; Pres. IDI KARIM BUHANGA; Dir-Gen. BUKURU AUDACE.

Institut des Sciences Agronomiques du Burundi (ISABU): BP 795, Bujumbura; tel. 22227349; fax 22225798; e-mail dgisabu@cbinf.com; f. 1962 for the scientific development of agriculture and livestock; Dir-Gen. MARIE GORETTI MIREREKANO.

Observatoire des Filières Agricoles du Burundi (OFB): 7 ave Imbo, Quartier Asiatique, BP 5, Bujumbura; tel. 22251865; fax 22250567; e-mail info@ofburundi.org; internet www.ofburundi.org; f. 2004; provides information on Burundi's agricultural sector and facilitates dialogue between key figures and orgs; Co-ordinator PATRICE NTAHOMPAGAZE.

Office National de la Tourbe (ONATOUR): route de l'aéroport, BP 2360, Bujumbura; tel. 22226480; fax 22226709; e-mail kariyo@yahoo.fr; f. 1977 to promote the exploitation of peat deposits; Dir-Gen. YVETTE KARIYO.

Société d'Economie pour l'Exploitation du Quinquina au Burundi (SOKINABU): 16 blvd Mwezi Gisabo, BP 1783, Bujumbura; tel. 22223469; fax 22218160; e-mail chiastos@yahoo.fr; f. 1975 to develop and exploit cinchona trees, the source of quinine; Dir CHRISTIAN REMEZO.

INDUSTRIAL AND TRADE ASSOCIATIONS

Association des Commerçants du Burundi (ACOBU): 254 ave du Commerce, Rohero, BP 6373, Bujumbura; tel. 22248663; Pres. CONSTANTIN NDIKUMANA.

Association des Employeurs du Burundi (AEB): 187 rue de la Mission, BP 141, Bujumbura; tel. 221119; fax 248190; e-mail assoaeb64@yahoo.fr; Pres. ALOYSE KIRAHUZI; Exec. Sec. GASPARD NZISABIRA.

Association des Femmes Entrepreneurs du Burundi (AFAB): 127 ave Kunkiko, Rohero II, BP 1628, Bujumbura; tel. 22242784; Pres. CONSOLATA NDAYISHIMIYE.

Association des Industriels du Burundi (AIB): 187 rue de la mission, Rohero, BP 141, Bujumbura; tel. 22221119; fax 22220643; e-mail aib.burundi@yahoo.fr; Pres. ECONIE NIJEMBERE; Exec. Sec. JEAN PAUL NTUHURUMURYANGO.

CHAMBER OF COMMERCE

Chambre Fédérale de Commerce et d'Industrie du Burundi (CFCIB): ave du 18 Septembre, BP 313, Bujumbura; tel. 22222280; fax 22227895; e-mail ccib@ccib.bi; internet www.cfcib.org; f. 2010 to replace Chambre de Commerce, d'Industrie, d'Agriculture et d'Artisanat du Burundi (CCIB; f. 1923); Pres. CONSOLATA NDAYISHIMIYE; 130 mems.

UTILITY

Régie de Distribution d'Eau et d'Electricité (REGIDESO): Ngozi, Bujumbura; tel. 22302222; state-owned distributor of water and electricity services; Dir PASCAL NDAYISHIMIYE.

TRADE UNIONS

Confédération des Syndicats du Burundi (COSYBU): ave du 18 Septembre, Ex Hôtel Central 8, BP 220, Bujumbura; tel. and fax 22248190; e-mail cosybu@yahoo.fr; Pres. THARCISSE GAHUNGU; 32 mem. asscns.

Confédération des Syndicats libres du Burundi (CSB): BP 1570, Bujumbura; tel. 222229; e-mail csb sq2001@vahoo.fr; Pres. THARCISSE NIBOGORA; Sec.-Gen. MATHIAS RUVARI.

Transport

RAILWAYS

There are no railways in Burundi. Plans have been under consideration since 1987 for the construction of a line passing through Uganda, Rwanda and Burundi, to connect with the Kigoma–Dar es Salaam line in Tanzania. This rail link would relieve Burundi's isolated trade position.

ROADS

In 2004 Burundi had a total of 12,322 km of roads, of which 5,012 km were national highways and 282 km secondary roads. In 2008 some 31.7% of all roads were paved.

Office des Transports en Commun (OTRACO): BP 1486, Bujumbura; tel. 22231313; fax 22232051; 100% govt-owned; operates public transport; Dir-Gen. NICODÈME NIZIGIYIMANA.

INLAND WATERWAYS

Bujumbura is the principal port for both passenger and freight traffic on Lake Tanganyika, and the greater part of Burundi's external trade is dependent on the shipping services between Bujumbura and lake ports in Tanzania, Zambia and the Democratic Republic of the Congo.

Société Concessionnaire de l'Exploitation du Port de Bujumbura (EPB): BP 59, Bujumbura; tel. 22226036; e-mail bujaport@cbinf.com; f. 1967; 43% state-owned; controls Bujumbura port; Dir-Gen. MÉTHODE SHIRAMBERE.

CIVIL AVIATION

The international airport at Bujumbura is equipped to take large jet-engined aircraft.

Air Burundi: 40 ave du Commerce, BP 2460, Bujumbura; tel. 22223460; fax 22223452; e-mail reservation@airburundi.com; internet www.airburundi.org; f. 1971 as Société de Transports Aériens du Burundi; state-owned; operates charter and scheduled passenger services to destinations throughout central Africa; CEO MELCHIOR NAHIMANA; Man. Dir ELIE NTACORIGIRA.

Tourism

Tourism is relatively undeveloped. The annual total of tourist arrivals declined from 125,000 in 1991 to only 10,553 in 1997. Total arrivals increased gradually thereafter, reaching 74,116 in 2003 and increasing to an estimated 201,241 in 2006. Tourism receipts amounted to an estimated US $1.7m. in 2009.

Office National du Tourisme (ONT): 2 ave des Euphorbes, BP 902, Bujumbura; tel. and fax 22224208; e-mail info@burunditourisme.net; internet www.burunditourisme.net; f. 1972; responsible for the promotion and supervision of tourism; Dir DÉO NGENDAHAYO.

Defence

Burundi's armed forces, as assessed at November 2011, comprised an army of 20,000 and a paramilitary force of 31,050 gendarmes (including a 50-strong marine police force). At the end of 2004 the Government had officially established a reconstituted armed forces (Forces de défense nationales—FDN—comprising equal proportions of Hutus and Tutsis), which incorporated some 23,000 former rebel combatants, and a new police force. In April 2003 the deployment of the first members of an AU Mission in Burundi (AMIB) commenced; the contingent (which comprised mainly South African troops, with reinforcements from Ethiopia and Mozambique) was mandated to assist in the enforcement of the cease-fire between the Government and rebel factions. In May 2004 the UN Security Council approved the deployment of a Opération des Nations Unies au Burundi (ONUB—with a maximum authorized strength of 5,650 military personnel), to replace AMIB. Under a resolution of 30 June 2006, the UN Security Council ended the mandate of ONUB at the end of December, when it was replaced by a UN office, the Bureau Intégré des Nations Unies au Burundi (BINUB). BINUB was established for an initial period of one year, with authorization to continue peace consolidation, including support for the demobilization and reintegration of former combatants and reform of the security sector. BINUB's mandate was subsequently extended until 31 December 2010. In mid-December the Security Council replaced BINUB with the United Nations Office in Burundi, with effect from 1 January 2011 and with an initial mandate of 12 months. Meanwhile, some 100 Burundian troops were sent to Somalia in December 2007 as part of the African Union Mission to Somalia (AMISOM), a peace-keeping force established at the beginning of that year in an attempt to stabilize the war-torn country. By late 2010 the AU force, comprised 7,250 soldiers, including 3,000 from Burundi. In 2012 a total of 4,411 troops were stationed abroad, of which five were observers.

Defence Expenditure: Budgeted at 79,700m. Burundian francs in 2011.

Chief of Staff of the Forces de défense nationales: Maj.-Gen. GODEFROID NIYOMBARE.

Chief of Staff of the Gendarmerie: Col SALVATOR NDAYIYUNVIYE.

Education

Education is provided free of charge. Kirundi is the language of instruction in primary schools, while French is used in secondary schools. Primary education, which is officially compulsory, begins at seven years of age and lasts for six years. Secondary education begins at the age of 13 and lasts for up to seven years, comprising a first cycle of four years and a second of three years. In 2008/09, according to UNESCO estimates, 99% of children in the relevant age-group (males 98%; females 100%) were enrolled at primary schools. In 2005 it was announced that primary education would be provided for free by the state, vastly increasing enrolment in the following years. Enrolment at secondary schools in 2009/10 was equivalent to only an estimated 16% of the population (males 18%; females 15%). In 2002/03 11,915 students were enrolled at the University of Bujumbura. There are also private universities at Ngozi and Bujumbura, the Université de Ngozi, the Université Lumière de Bujumbura, the Université du Lac Tanganyika and Hope Africa University. The total number of students enrolled in higher education in 2009/10 was 29,269. Public expenditure on education in 2008 was equivalent to 22.3% of total government expenditure.

CAMBODIA

Introductory Survey

LOCATION, CLIMATE, LANGUAGE, RELIGION, FLAG, CAPITAL

The Kingdom of Cambodia occupies part of the Indo-Chinese peninsula in South-East Asia. It is bordered by Thailand and Laos to the north, by Viet Nam to the east and by the Gulf of Thailand to the south. The climate is tropical and humid. There is a rainy season from June to November, with the heaviest rainfall in September. The temperature is generally between 20°C and 36°C (68°F to 97°F), with March and April usually the hottest months; the annual average temperature in Phnom-Penh is 27°C (81°F). The official language is Khmer, which is spoken by almost everybody except the Vietnamese and Chinese minorities. The state religion is Theravada Buddhism. The national flag (proportions 2 by 3) consists of three horizontal stripes, of dark blue, red (half the depth) and dark blue, with a stylized representation (in white) of the temple of Angkor Wat, showing three of its five towers, in the centre. The capital is Phnom-Penh.

CONTEMPORARY POLITICAL HISTORY

Historical Context

The Kingdom of Cambodia became a French protectorate in the 19th century and was incorporated into French Indo-China. In April 1941 Norodom Sihanouk, then aged 18, succeeded his grandfather as King. In May 1947 he promulgated a Constitution which provided for a bicameral Parliament, including an elected National Assembly. Cambodia became an Associate State of the French Union in November 1949 and attained independence on 9 November 1953. In order to become a political leader, King Sihanouk abdicated in March 1955 in favour of his father, Norodom Suramarit, and became known as Prince Sihanouk. He founded a mass movement, the Sangkum Reastr Niyum (Popular Socialist Community), which won all the seats in elections to the National Assembly in 1955, 1958, 1962 and 1966. King Suramarit died in April 1960, and in June Parliament elected Prince Sihanouk as head of state. Prince Sihanouk's Government developed good relations with the People's Republic of China and with North Viet Nam, but it was highly critical of the USA's role in Asia. From 1964, however, the Government was confronted by an underground Marxist insurgency movement, the Khmers Rouges, while it also became increasingly difficult to isolate Cambodia from the war in Viet Nam.

Domestic Political Affairs

In March 1970 Prince Sihanouk was deposed by a right-wing coup, led by the Prime Minister, Lt-Gen. (later Marshal) Lon Nol. The new Government pledged itself to the removal of foreign communist forces and appealed to the USA for military aid. Sihanouk went into exile and formed the Royal Government of National Union of Cambodia (GRUNC), supported by the Khmers Rouges. Sihanoukists and the Khmers Rouges formed the National United Front of Cambodia (FUNC). Their combined forces, aided by South Viet Nam's National Liberation Front and North Vietnamese troops, posed a serious threat to the new regime, but in October 1970 Marshal Lon Nol proclaimed the Khmer Republic. In June 1972 he was elected the first President. During 1973 several foreign states recognized GRUNC as the rightful government of Cambodia. In 1974 the republican regime's control was limited to a few urban enclaves, besieged by GRUNC forces, mainly Khmers Rouges, who gained control of Phnom-Penh on 17 April 1975. Prince Sihanouk became head of state again but did not return from exile until September. The country was subjected to a prearranged programme of radical social deconstruction immediately after the Khmers Rouges' assumption of power; towns were largely evacuated, and their inhabitants forced to work in rural areas. During the following three years an estimated 1.7m. people died as a result of ill-treatment, hunger, disease and executions.

A new Constitution, promulgated in January 1976, renamed the country Democratic Kampuchea, and established a republican form of government; elections for a 250-member People's Representative Assembly were held in March 1976. In April Prince Sihanouk resigned as head of state, and GRUNC was dissolved. The Assembly elected Khieu Samphan, formerly Deputy Prime Minister, to be President of the State Presidium (head of state). The little-known Pol Pot (formerly Saloth Sar) became Prime Minister. The Communist Party of Kampuchea (CPK), with Pol Pot as the Secretary of its Central Committee, became the ruling organization.

After 1975 close links with China developed, while relations with Viet Nam deteriorated. In 1978, following a two-year campaign of raids across the Vietnamese border by the Khmers Rouges, the Vietnamese army launched a series of offensives into Kampuchean territory. In December 1978 Viet Nam invaded Kampuchea, supported by the Kampuchean National United Front for National Salvation (KNUFNS—a communist-led movement opposed to Pol Pot, the establishment of which had been announced earlier that month).

On 7 January 1979 Phnom-Penh was captured by Vietnamese forces, and three days later the People's Republic of Kampuchea was proclaimed. A People's Revolutionary Council was established, with Heng Samrin, leader of the KNUFNS, as President. The CPK was replaced as the governing party by the Kampuchean People's Revolutionary Party (KPRP). However, the Khmer Rouge forces remained active in the western provinces, near the border with Thailand, and conducted sporadic guerrilla activities elsewhere in the country. Several groups opposing both the Khmers Rouges and the Heng Samrin regime were established, including the Khmer People's National Liberation Front (KPNLF), headed by a former Prime Minister, Son Sann. In July, claiming that Pol Pot's regime had been responsible for 3m. deaths, the KPRP administration sentenced Pol Pot and his former Minister of Foreign Affairs, Ieng Sary, to death *in absentia*. In January 1980 Khieu Samphan assumed the premiership of the deposed Khmer Rouge regime, while Pol Pot became Commander-in-Chief of the armed forces. In 1981 the CPK was reportedly dissolved and was replaced by the Party of Democratic Kampuchea (PDK).

During the early years of the KPRP regime Viet Nam launched regular offensives on the Thai–Kampuchean border against the united armed forces of Democratic Kampuchea, the coalition Government-in-exile of anti-Vietnamese resistance groups formed in June 1982. Thousands of Kampuchean refugees crossed the border into Thailand; in turn, a large number of Vietnamese citizens subsequently settled on Kampuchean territory. The coalition Government-in-exile, of which Prince Sihanouk became President, Khieu Samphan (PDK) Vice-President and Son Sann (KPNLF) Prime Minister, received the support of China and of member states of the Association of Southeast Asian Nations (ASEAN, see p. 214), while retaining the Kampuchean seat in the UN General Assembly.

In the mid-1980s an increasingly conciliatory relationship between the USSR and China led to a number of diplomatic exchanges, aimed at reconciling the coalition Government-in-exile with the Government in Phnom-Penh, led by the General Secretary of the KPRP, Heng Samrin, but the Heng Samrin Government rejected peace proposals from ASEAN and the coalition Government-in-exile. In September 1987 the Chinese Government stated that it would accept a Kampuchean 'government of national reconciliation' under Prince Sihanouk, but that the presence of Vietnamese troops in Kampuchea remained a major obstacle. The USSR also declared that it was 'prepared to facilitate a political settlement' in Kampuchea. In October, having announced its readiness to conduct negotiations with some PDK leaders (but not Pol Pot), the Heng Samrin Government offered Prince Sihanouk a government post and issued a set of peace proposals, which included the complete withdrawal of Vietnamese troops, internationally observed elections and the formation of a coalition government. In December 1987 Prince Sihanouk and Hun Sen, the Chairman of the Council of Ministers in the Heng Samrin Government, met in France for private discussions. The meeting ended in a joint communiqué, stating that the conflict was to be settled politically by negotiations involving all the Kampuchean parties.

Under increasing pressure from the USSR and China, the four Kampuchean factions participated in a series of 'informal meetings', held in Indonesia, which were also attended by representatives of Viet Nam, Laos and the six ASEAN members. At the first of these meetings, in July 1988, Viet Nam advanced its deadline for a complete withdrawal of its troops from Kampuchea to late 1989. In April 1989 the National Assembly in Phnom-Penh ratified several constitutional amendments, whereby the name of the country was changed to the State of Cambodia, a new national flag, emblem and anthem were introduced, Buddhism was reinstated as the state religion, and the death penalty was abolished. In July 1989 the Paris International Conference on Cambodia (PICC) met for the first time. The PICC agreed to send a UN reconnaissance party to Cambodia to study the prospects for a cease-fire and the installation of a peace-keeping force.

The Paris Peace Agreement and election of 1993

The withdrawal of Vietnamese forces, completed on schedule in September 1989, was followed by renewed offensives into Cambodia by the resistance forces, particularly the PDK. In November, following substantial military gains by the PDK, the UN General Assembly adopted a resolution supporting the formation of an interim government in Cambodia, which would include members of the PDK; however, the resolution retained a clause, introduced in 1988, relating to past atrocities committed by the organization. The resolution also cast doubt on the Vietnamese withdrawal (since it had not been monitored by the UN) and, in reference to the alleged presence of 1m. Vietnamese settlers in Cambodia, condemned 'demographic changes' imposed in the country. An Australian peace initiative was unanimously approved by the five permanent members of the UN Security Council in January 1990. In February Prince Sihanouk declared that the coalition Government-in-exile would henceforth be known as the National Government of Cambodia.

In July 1990 the USA withdrew its support for the National Government of Cambodia's occupation of Cambodia's seat at the UN. In August the UN Security Council endorsed the framework for a comprehensive settlement in Cambodia. The agreement provided for UN supervision of an interim government, military arrangements for the transitional period, free elections and guarantees for the future neutrality of Cambodia. A special representative of the Secretary-General of the UN was to control the proposed UN Transitional Authority in Cambodia (UNTAC). The UN would also assume control of the Ministries of Foreign Affairs, National Defence, Finance, the Interior and Information, Press and Culture.

At a fourth 'informal meeting', held in Indonesia in September 1990, the four Cambodian factions accepted the UN proposals. They also agreed to the formation of the Supreme National Council (SNC), with six representatives from the Phnom-Penh Government and six from the National Government of Cambodia. SNC decisions were to be taken by consensus, effectively allowing each faction the power of veto, and the SNC was to occupy the Cambodian seat at the UN General Assembly. Prince Sihanouk was subsequently elected to the chairmanship of the SNC, and resigned as leader of the resistance coalition and as President of the National Government of Cambodia (positions to which Son Sann was appointed). Agreement was also reached on the four factions reducing their armed forces by 70% and the remaining 30% being placed in cantonments under UN supervision; the introduction of a system of multi-party democracy; the Phnom-Penh Government abandoning its demand for references to genocide to be included in a draft plan; and the holding of elections to a constituent assembly, which would subsequently become a legislative assembly comprising 120 seats.

Following the release of political prisoners by the Phnom-Penh Government in October 1991, including former 'reformist' associates of Hun Sen (who had been arrested in 1990 and replaced by supporters of the more conservative chairman of the National Assembly, Chea Sim), a congress of the KPRP was convened at which the party changed its name to the Cambodian People's Party (CPP). The communist insignia was removed from its emblem, Heng Samrin was replaced as Chairman of the Central Committee (formerly the Politburo) by Chea Sim and Hun Sen was elected as Vice-Chairman.

On 23 October 1991 the four factions signed the UN peace agreement in Paris—commonly known as the Paris Peace Agreement—under the auspices of the PICC. The UN Advance Mission in Cambodia (UNAMIC), comprising 300 men, was in position by the end of 1991. The agreement also provided for the repatriation, under the supervision of the UN High Commissioner for Refugees, of the estimated 340,000 Cambodian refugees living in camps in Thailand. In November Prince Sihanouk returned to Phnom-Penh, accompanied by Hun Sen. The CPP and the United National Front for an Independent, Neutral, Peaceful and Co-operative Cambodia (FUNCINPEC), led by Prince Sihanouk, subsequently formed an alliance and announced their intention to establish a coalition government. (The alliance was abandoned in December, in response to objections from the KPNLF and the PDK.) The four factions endorsed the reinstatement of Prince Sihanouk as head of state of Cambodia. In late November, however, an attack by demonstrators on Khieu Samphan on his return to Phnom-Penh led senior PDK officials to flee to the Thai capital of Bangkok where the SNC met and agreed that, henceforth, officials of the party would occupy the SNC headquarters in Phnom-Penh with members of UNAMIC. Further demonstrations followed. Having reached an agreement with representatives of the UN Security Council, by March 1992 the Phnom-Penh Government had released all remaining political prisoners. The UN Security Council expanded UNAMIC's mandate to include mine-clearing operations, and in February authorized the dispatch of a 22,000-member peace-keeping force to Cambodia to establish UNTAC. In March UNAMIC transferred responsibility for the implementation of the peace agreement to UNTAC.

The refugee repatriation programme, which began in March 1992, was threatened by repeated cease-fire violations, which were concentrated in the central province of Kampong Thom. In response to the PDK's continued obduracy to the peace-keeping operation, in August Yasushi Akashi (who had been appointed UN Special Representative to Cambodia in charge of UNTAC in January 1992) affirmed that the legislative elections would proceed without the participation of the PDK if it continued to refuse to co-operate. The UN set a deadline for compliance of 15 November. By the end of November, however, no consensus had been reached, and the Security Council adopted a resolution condemning PDK obduracy. The Security Council approved an embargo on the supplies of petroleum products to the PDK and endorsed a ban on the export of timber (a principal source of income for the party). However, the PDK announced the formation of a subsidiary party to contest the forthcoming elections, the Cambodian National Unity Party, led by Khieu Samphan and Son Sen. The Phnom-Penh Government subsequently launched an offensive against the PDK in northern and western Cambodia, recovering much of the territory gained by the PDK since the signing of the peace agreement in October 1991. There were also continuing attacks by the PDK on ethnic Vietnamese, and, following several rural massacres, thousands of Vietnamese took refuge in Viet Nam. Under the repatriation programme for refugees on the Thai border, 360,000 refugees had been returned to Cambodia by the end of April 2003.

Meanwhile, by the final deadline at the end of January 1993 20 parties, excluding the PDK, had registered to contest the elections. On 23–28 May about 90% of the electorate participated in the elections to the Constituent Assembly. The PDK offered support to the FUNCINPEC Party but, owing to the massive voter participation in the election, Prince Sihanouk abandoned his proposals for the inclusion of the PDK in a future Government. Despite CPP allegations of irregularities, UNTAC rejected requests for fresh elections in at least four provinces. In early June, without prior consultation with the UN and disregarding the incomplete election results, Prince Sihanouk announced the formation of a new Government, with himself as Prime Minister and Prince Norodom Ranariddh and Hun Sen as joint Deputy Prime Ministers. The coalition was created and renounced within hours, owing to objections from Prince Ranariddh, who had not been consulted, and to suggestions by UN officials that it was tantamount to a coup. Two days later the official results of the election were released: the FUNCINPEC Party had secured 58 seats with 46% of the votes cast, the CPP 51 seats (38%), the Buddhist Liberal Democratic Party (BLDP, founded by the KPNLF) 10 seats (3%) and a breakaway faction from the FUNCINPEC Party, MOLINAKA (National Liberation Movement of Cambodia), one seat. Despite the UN's endorsement of the election as fair, the CPP refused to dissolve the State of Cambodia Government in Phnom-Penh. Prince Norodom Chakrapong (a son of Prince Sihanouk who had been appointed to the Council of Ministers of the Phnom-Penh Government in December 1991) subsequently led a secessionist movement in seven provinces in the east and north-east of the country, which was reportedly sanctioned by the CPP leadership in an attempt to secure a power-sharing agreement with the FUNCINPEC Party.

On 14 June 1993, at the inaugural session of the Constituent Assembly, Prince Sihanouk was proclaimed head of state, and 'full and special' powers were conferred on him. The Assembly adopted a resolution declaring null and void the overthrow of Prince Sihanouk 23 years previously and recognizing him retroactively as head of state of Cambodia during that period. The secessionist movement collapsed, and an agreement was reached on the formation of an interim government, with Hun Sen and Prince Ranariddh as Co-Chairmen of the Provisional National Government of Cambodia. Prince Chakrapong returned to Phnom-Penh, where he was reconciled with Prince Sihanouk, and the CPP officially recognized the election results.

The PDK had immediately accepted the results of the election and supported the formation of a coalition government, but continued to engage in military action to support its demands for inclusion in a future government. In August the newly formed Cambodian National Armed Forces (later restyled the Royal Cambodian Armed Forces), which had been created through the merger of the forces of the other three factions in June, initiated a successful offensive against PDK positions in north-western Cambodia. The Government rejected an appeal for urgent discussions by the PDK after government forces had captured PDK bases, insisting that the party surrender unconditionally the estimated 20% of Cambodian territory under its control.

The new Constitution and National Assembly

In September 1993 the Constituent Assembly adopted a new Constitution, which provided for an hereditary monarchy. Prince Sihanouk duly promulgated the Constitution, thus terminating the mandate of UNTAC (whose personnel left the country by mid-November). The Constituent Assembly became the National Assembly, and Prince Sihanouk acceded to the throne of the new Kingdom of Cambodia. Chea Sim was elected Chairman of the National Assembly. Government ministers were to be chosen from parties represented in the National Assembly, thus precluding the involvement of the PDK. At the end of October the National Assembly approved the new Royal Government of Cambodia (previously endorsed by King Sihanouk), in which Prince Ranariddh was named First Prime Minister and Hun Sen Second Prime Minister. Subsequent initiatives to incorporate the PDK into the new Government failed, owing to objections from various parties. In May 1994 King Sihanouk threatened to stop negotiating with the PDK and the Government to end the fighting in the north-west of the country, which had reached a severity not witnessed since 1989, and forced the postponement of proposed peace talks in Pyongyang, the Democratic People's Republic of Korea (North Korea). Following the failure of peace talks held in May and June 1994, the Government ordered the PDK to leave Phnom-Penh and closed the party's mission in the capital.

In July 1994 the Government claimed to have suppressed a coup attempt led by Prince Chakrapong and Gen. Sin Song, a former Minister of National Security under the State of Cambodia. Following a personal appeal from King Sihanouk, Prince Chakrapong, who protested his innocence, was exiled from Cambodia, while Gen. Sin Song was placed under arrest. (Gen. Sin Song escaped from prison in September and was captured by Thai authorities in November.) Hun Sen also suspected Deputy Prime Minister and Minister of the Interior Sar Kheng of involvement in the alleged revolt; however, Sar Kheng was protected by his powerful brother-in-law, Chea Sim. The coup attempt was also used by the increasingly divided Government as a pretext to suppress criticism of the regime.

Despite King Sihanouk's continued advocacy of national reconciliation, in July 1994 the National Assembly adopted legislation outlawing the PDK (while allowing for an immediate six-month amnesty for the lower ranks of the party). In response, the PDK formed a Provisional Government of National Unity and National Salvation of Cambodia (PGNUNSC), under the premiership of Khieu Samphan, which was to co-ordinate opposition to the Government in Phnom-Penh from its headquarters in the northern province of Preah Vihear. In October Sam Rainsy was dismissed as Minister of Finance, apparently owing to his efforts to combat corruption at senior levels. Prince Sirivudh subsequently resigned as Minister of Foreign Affairs in protest at Rainsy's removal, and criticized the FUNCINPEC Party, of which he was Secretary-General, for submitting too readily to CPP demands, as it became increasingly apparent that real power lay with the former communists.

Following his expulsion from the FUNCINPEC Party in May 1995 and from the National Assembly in June, Rainsy formed a new party, the Khmer Nation Party (KNP). Meanwhile, the National Assembly adopted the revised draft of a stringent press law, which imposed substantial fines and prison sentences for reporting issues affecting 'national security' or 'political stability'. In October Prince Sirivudh was also expelled from the National Assembly and charged with conspiring to assassinate Hun Sen. He was allowed to go into exile in France in December on condition that he refrain from political activity, and in January 1996 he was convicted and sentenced to 10 years' imprisonment *in absentia* on charges of criminal conspiracy and possession of unlicensed firearms. Also in January the Government began to adopt repressive measures against the KNP. In March Rainsy nominally merged the KNP with a defunct but still legally registered party, in an attempt to gain legal status. However, in April the Government ordered all parties without parliamentary representation to close their offices. Several KNP officials were assassinated during the year.

In August 1996 the prominent PDK leader Ieng Sary, together with two military divisions that controlled the PDK strongholds of Pailin and Malai, defected from the movement and negotiated a peace agreement with the Government. Ieng Sary denied responsibility for the atrocities committed during Pol Pot's regime, and was granted a royal amnesty in September. He then formed a new political organization, the Democratic National United Movement (DNUM), while his supporters retained control of Pailin and Malai, despite efforts by troops loyal to the PDK leadership to recapture the region (where lucrative mineral and timber resources were situated). An estimated 2,500 PDK troops transferred allegiance to the Government in October. Former PDK troops (numbering about 4,000) were integrated into the national army in November.

In September 1996 the partial dissolution of the PDK increased tensions within the ruling coalition: as the FUNCINPEC Party appeared more successful than the CPP at recruiting former PDK commanders and cadres, Hun Sen became concerned that the alliance between the royalists and the PDK as former resistance forces would be re-established. In February 1997 Prince Ranariddh sent a helicopter mission to Anlong Veng to negotiate with the central PDK faction; however, PDK members opposed to peace talks ambushed the helicopter, killing the majority of the Prince's emissaries. Meanwhile, the two Prime Ministers were stockpiling weapons, violations of human and civil rights were becoming increasingly prevalent, corruption was rampant and labour unrest was widespread. In March Rainsy led a demonstration outside the National Assembly. The rally was attacked by assailants who threw four grenades, killing 19 and injuring more than 100 protesters. Rainsy, who was himself among the injured, accused Hun Sen of organizing the attack.

In April 1997 Ung Phan, a former CPP member who had joined the FUNCINPEC Party in the early 1990s, led a rebellion against the party leadership of Prince Ranariddh, with the support of Hun Sen. The National Assembly, which was due to adopt legislation pertaining to elections scheduled for 1998, was unable to convene, as the FUNCINPEC Party refused to attend until its dissident members were expelled from the Assembly, whereas the CPP insisted on their retention. In June the dissident FUNCINPEC members formed a rival FUNCINPEC Party.

In May 1997 Khieu Samphan announced the creation of a new political party, the National Solidarity Party, which would support the National United Front (an alliance founded in February by Prince Ranariddh) at the next election. Prince Ranariddh declared that, if the notorious former leadership of the PDK were excluded, he would welcome such an alliance. However, Hun Sen deemed the potential alliance to be a threat to the CPP and, following the seizure of a shipment of weapons destined for Prince Ranariddh, accused the Prince of illegally importing weapons to arm PDK soldiers. The PDK was divided over the issue of peace negotiations. Pol Pot ordered the death of the Minister of National Defence, Son Sen, and also that of Ta Mok, the south-western regional army commander. Following the execution of Son Sen and his family, many PDK commanders rallied behind Ta Mok, and fighting erupted between the two factions. Pol Pot and his supporters fled into the jungle, with Khieu Samphan as a hostage, but were captured by Ta Mok's forces and returned to the PDK base at Anlong Veng, near the Thai border. In June Prince Ranariddh claimed that Pol Pot was under arrest and that Khieu Samphan would surrender. In July Pol Pot was condemned by a 'people's court' for 'destroying national unity' and for the killing of Son Sen and his family.

In early July 1997, following several attempts by CPP troops to detect the presence of PDK soldiers in FUNCINPEC units, CPP forces disarmed a unit of Prince Ranariddh's bodyguards, and Prince Ranariddh left the country. On 5 July serious fighting erupted in Phnom-Penh, and on 6 July, the day on which Khieu Samphan had been scheduled to broadcast the PDK's agreement with the FUNCINPEC Party to end its resistance and rejoin the political system, Hun Sen appeared on television to demand Prince Ranariddh's arrest (on charges of negotiating with the PDK, introducing proscribed PDK troops into Phnom-Penh and secretly importing weapons to arm those forces) and to urge FUNCINPEC officials to select another leader. More than 24 hours of violence then ensued. The UN subsequently claimed that it had documentary evidence showing that at least 43 people, principally from the royalist army structure, had been murdered by forces loyal to Hun Sen after the events of 5–6 July. Many more FUNCINPEC and KNP officials, as well as many FUNCINPEC members of the legislature, fled the country.

King Sihanouk's appeals for a settlement were rejected by Hun Sen. Prince Ranariddh announced from Paris that a resistance movement was being organized in western Cambodia. Meanwhile, Hun Sen began negotiations with certain prominent members of the FUNCINPEC Party who remained in Phnom-Penh in an effort to attain the two-thirds' majority of the National Assembly necessary for the investiture of a new government. By the end of July 1997 the National Assembly had reconvened, with 98 of the 120 deputies present, including 40 of the 58 FUNCINPEC deputies. Hun Sen protested to the international community that his actions did not constitute a *coup d'état*, as he had not abolished the Constitution or the monarchy and had not dissolved the Government or the National Assembly. King Sihanouk, who had been in China since February, insisted on remaining neutral and accepted that Chea Sim should continue to sign royal decrees in his absence. In August the National Assembly voted to remove Ranariddh's legal immunity (a warrant subsequently being issued for his arrest) and elected Ung Huot, the FUNCINPEC Minister of Foreign Affairs, to the post of First Prime Minister.

Troops loyal to Prince Ranariddh, led by Gen. Nhiek Bun Chhay (the former military Deputy Chief of Staff and a principal negotiator with the PDK), were swiftly forced into the north-west of the country by CPP troops. They regrouped near the Thai border in an effective alliance with PDK troops under Ta Mok. Prolonged fighting took place for control of the town of O'Smach, about 70 km west of Anlong Veng, which was the last base for the resistance coalition led by Prince Ranariddh, the Union of Cambodian Democrats. At the end of August 1997 King Sihanouk arrived in Siem Reap. Hun Sen rejected another proposal from the King to act as a mediator in peace talks, insisting that Ranariddh be tried for his alleged crimes.

In September 1997 Hun Sen announced a cabinet reorganization that effectively removed remaining supporters of Prince Ranariddh from the Government. However, in a secret ballot the National Assembly failed by 13 votes to approve the changes by the required two-thirds' majority. Hun Sen continued to encourage the return of all opposition representatives who had fled the country in July, except Ranariddh and Gen. Nhiek Bun Chhay. In late 1997 Rainsy returned to Cambodia and agreed to co-operate with Hun Sen. In December the National Assembly voted to postpone local and legislative elections from May until July 1998 and to increase the number of seats from 120 to 122. In February 1998 Rainsy withdrew the KNP from the electoral process in protest at the unlawful methods allegedly employed by Hun Sen, including the registration of a breakaway faction of the KNP bearing an identical title and logo and the fatal shooting in January of a KNP official and his daughter. The KNP was subsequently restyled the Sam Rainsy Party (SRP).

Hun Sen and Ranariddh agreed to the terms of a Japanese peace proposal in February 1998, which provided for the severance of Ranariddh's links with the PDK, the implementation of a cease-fire in the north-west (which came into effect on 27 February), a royal pardon for Ranariddh if he were convicted *in absentia* of the charges against him, and his guaranteed safe return to participate in the general election. Ranariddh was convicted in March of illegally importing weapons and of conspiring with the proscribed PDK, and sentenced to 30 years' imprisonment and a fine of US $54m. for damage caused on 5–6 July 1997. At the formal request of Hun Sen, King Sihanouk granted Ranariddh a royal pardon, but no amnesty was accorded to Gen. Nhiek Bun Chhay or Serei Kosal, the commanders of Ranariddh's troops in the north-west, who were also found guilty. Ranariddh returned to Phnom-Penh at the end of March 1998, but the FUNCINPEC Party had been severely weakened by the killing of many of its senior personnel, the closure of its offices and the defection of some principal officials.

In March 1998 several divisions of PDK troops mutinied against their leader, Ta Mok, surrendering control of the PDK headquarters, Anlong Veng, to government troops; during the ensuing clashes thousands of civilians were evacuated to Thailand. Pol Pot died on 15 April, shortly after his comrades had offered to surrender him for trial by an international tribunal. It was later reported that he had committed suicide. Ta Mok announced that he was prepared to reach agreement with the Government but demanded autonomy for Anlong Veng. Despite sporadic clashes between the remnants of the PDK and government forces, the grouping was practically defunct by the end of the year, following further significant defections in October and December. In late December Nuon Chea (Pol Pot's former deputy) and Khieu Samphan defected to the Government, seeking sanctuary in Pailin, an area still effectively controlled by Ieng Sary. In February 1999 a final 4,332 PDK troops surrendered to the Co-Ministers of National Defence in Anlong Veng, although Ta Mok remained in the border area.

The coalition Government of 1998–2003

The campaign period for the July 1998 election was characterized by intimidation and violence. All demonstrations were banned, as was the dissemination of political information by private news media. However, the election, which took place relatively peacefully on 26 July, was deemed free and fair by the UN-co-ordinated Joint International Observer Group; 90% of the 5,395,024 registered voters (representing 98% of the population of voting age) participated in the poll, which was contested by 39 parties. Under a newly introduced modified system of proportional representation that favoured larger parties, the CPP secured 64 seats (with 41.4% of the popular vote), the FUNCINPEC Party 43 seats (31.7%) and the SRP 15 seats (14.3%). Hun Sen proposed a three-party coalition, but this was rejected by Ranariddh and Rainsy.

In August 1998 Rainsy was detained for questioning, following a grenade explosion at the Ministry of the Interior. Several thousand Cambodians took part in a peaceful demonstration in Phnom-Penh, organized by Rainsy, to denounce alleged electoral fraud and to demand the removal of Hun Sen. Following a grenade attack on a disused residence of Hun Sen, the protesters were violently dispersed by security forces in September. Hun Sen ordered the arrest of Rainsy on charges of murder, prompting the latter to take refuge under the protection of the UN. Both Rainsy and Ranariddh abandoned demands for a recount. Sporadic violence continued, and Hun Sen announced that the FUNCINPEC Party and the SRP would be expelled from the National Assembly if they failed to attend its inauguration on 24 September. Following a rocket-propelled grenade attack on a convoy of vehicles en route to the convening ceremony of the National Assembly, Ranariddh and Rainsy fled to Thailand. The situation continued to deteriorate in October with the arrest, torture and execution of many opposition supporters. Ranariddh subsequently agreed to return to Cambodia to attend a meeting with Hun Sen, under the auspices of King Sihanouk, from which Rainsy was excluded.

In November 1998 agreement was reached on the formation of a CPP-FUNCINPEC coalition Government, which would be supported by 107 of the 122 deputies, with Hun Sen as Prime Minister and Ranariddh as the Chairman of the National Assembly. The accord also provided for the creation of a Senate (to be presided over by Chea Sim), the reintegration of resistance soldiers into the armed forces, royal pardons for Gen. Nhiek Bun Chhay and Serei Kosal, as well as Prince Sirivudh and Prince Chakrapong, and restitution for property damaged during the fighting of July 1997. Ranariddh was duly elected Chairman of the National Assembly, with two CPP deputies. The new Royal Government included Co-Ministers for the influential Ministries of Defence and of the Interior, while the CPP controlled the foreign affairs and finance portfolios and the FUNCINPEC Party assumed responsibility for information and health. Rainsy became the official leader of the opposition. The Senate held its inaugural session in March 1999. Representation in the 61-member upper chamber was proportionate to elected strength in the National Assembly; the CPP was allocated 31 seats, the FUNCINPEC Party 21 and the SRP seven, with a further two members being appointed by the King. Chea Sim was duly elected as Chairman, and Gen. Nhiek Bun Chhay became one of the three Deputy Chairmen.

Reform of the Royal Cambodian Armed Forces began in January 1999 with Hun Sen's resignation as Commander-in-

Chief. He was replaced by the former Chief of the General Staff, Gen. Ke Kimyan. By the end of September 15,551 'ghost' troops (soldiers who had been killed or had deserted, but whose pay continued to be collected by senior officers) had been removed from the army payroll. Plans announced in November 1999 provided for the demobilization of 11,500 troops in 2000, followed by a further 10,000 in both 2001 and 2002.

In March 1999 Ta Mok was captured near the Thai border and placed in detention. In May Kang Khek Ieu (also known as Duch or Kaing Guek Eav), the director of the Tuol Sleng detention centre where more than 15,000 detainees had been tortured and executed during the Democratic Kampuchean regime, was arrested and charged with belonging to a proscribed organization. Following delays in the establishment of a tribunal to try former Khmer Rouge leaders for atrocities committed during 1975–79 (see The Khmer Rouge Tribunal), in August 1999 the National Assembly approved legislation extending pre-trial detention for those accused of genocide and crimes against humanity from six months to three years. In September both Ta Mok and Duch were formally charged with genocide under a 1979 decree of the People's Republic of Kampuchea, and in the first half of 2002 both were also charged with having committed crimes against humanity. In July 2006, however, Ta Mok died. Between 1999 and 2002, meanwhile, a number of senior Khmer Rouge leaders were convicted in connection with the abduction and murder of three foreign tourists, and were sentenced to life imprisonment.

The office of the UN Secretary-General's special envoy to Cambodia was closed in December 1999 at the request of the Cambodian Government, despite UN pleas that it remain open for a further year. However, the Cambodian Government had agreed in August to extend the mandate of the representative of the UN High Commissioner for Human Rights in Cambodia.

In November 2000 dozens of armed men launched an attack on official buildings in Phnom-Penh. At least seven of the gunmen were killed in the raid, responsibility for which was subsequently claimed by the US-based Cambodian Freedom Fighters organization, led by Chhun Yasith (a naturalized citizen of the USA who had fled Cambodia in 1982, having reportedly witnessed the execution of his father by the Khmers Rouges in the late 1970s); the organization was vehemently opposed to Prime Minister Hun Sen, who it argued was obstructing democratic reform in Cambodia. Chhun Yasith alleged that the principal intention of the attack had been to disrupt the forthcoming visit of the President of Viet Nam, Tran Duc Luong (which had originally been scheduled for late November, but which was later postponed until November 2001). In June–July 2001 the trial of 32 of those accused of participating in the apparent coup attempt of November 2000 took place, amid accusations, notably by Sam Rainsy, that the Government had played a part in fomenting the violence so as to facilitate the intimidation of political opponents by local leaders. Three US citizens, among those on trial, were sentenced to life imprisonment *in absentia*; 27 Cambodians were given sentences ranging from three years to life, while two people were released owing to lack of evidence. Following a second mass trial, a further 26 Cambodian nationals were imprisoned in November 2001 for terms of up to 15 years. In February 2002 a further 20 people (including one US citizen) were convicted and imprisoned in connection with the attempted coup. In June 2005 Chhun Yasith was arrested in California, USA; he was subsequently indicted on charges of conspiracy to kill, and to destroy property, in a foreign country, of conspiracy to use a weapon of mass destruction outside the USA and of engaging in a military expedition against a nation with which the USA was at peace. He was convicted on all four charges by a Californian court in April 2008, and was sentenced to life imprisonment in June 2010.

Cambodia's first multi-party local elections took place in February 2002. Polling for the 1,621 *khum* (communes) resulted in an overwhelming victory for the CPP, which secured control of 1,598 *khum*. The SRP won control of 13 and the FUNCINPEC Party 10. Despite numerous allegations of intimidation and electoral irregularities, the opposition parties accepted the results; however, according to election monitors, the elections could be deemed neither free nor fair. At least 20 of the candidates who planned to mount a challenge to Hun Sen and the ruling CPP had been fatally shot in the course of the election campaign, during which the opposition had been denied access to the state-controlled media.

The 2003 election, King's abdication and new Senate

Following its disappointing performance in the local elections of 2002, a rift developed within the FUNCINPEC Party. As an indirect result, in May Prince Chakrapong, one of the sons of King Sihanouk, founded a new political party, the Prince Norodom Chakrapong Khmer Soul party. Meanwhile, in June the FUNCINPEC Party was weakened further by the defection of one of its founding members, Hang Dara, who announced the formation of the Hang Dara Movement Democratic Party to contest the next general election.

On 27 July 2003 23 political parties contested elections to the 123-member National Assembly. The CPP secured 73 seats (failing to secure the two-thirds' majority necessary to form a single-party government), while the FUNCINPEC Party won 26 seats and the SRP 24. The FUNCINPEC Party and the SRP both refused to enter into a multi-party government and, instead, agreed to form the Alliance of Democrats to oppose the CPP. Initially, the Alliance insisted that it would agree to form a tripartite government only if Hun Sen tendered his resignation as Prime Minister. The stalemate continued, angering King Sihanouk, who indicated his displeasure by failing to attend the inauguration of the National Assembly, an event also boycotted by both opposition parties. A series of talks convened by the King between leading figures in the CPP and the opposition resulted in the conclusion of a provisional agreement by the three parties in November regarding the formation of a joint administration, although disagreement continued as to the details of the proposed arrangement. In December the three parties finally began negotiations on the formation of a new government, and the first session of the incoming National Assembly took place later in that month. However, the CPP continued to reject opposition demands concerning the composition of a new administration, insisting that Hun Sen would continue as Prime Minister. With elections scheduled for March, in early 2004 King Sihanouk announced that he had approved a request by the Chairman of the Senate, Chea Sim, to extend the Senate's mandate by one year in order to avert a constitutional crisis. The impasse was finally ended when the CPP and the FUNCINPEC Party signed a power-sharing agreement in June. The formation of a new, 207-member coalition Government (in which the CPP held 136 posts and the FUNCINPEC Party 71) was ratified by the National Assembly in July, and Hun Sen was confirmed as Prime Minister by royal decree. Prince Ranariddh of the FUNCINPEC Party was appointed President of the National Assembly, which was boycotted by the SRP in protest at its exclusion from the new Government.

Meanwhile, a series of shootings of prominent opposition supporters in the aftermath of the legislative elections was believed to have been co-ordinated by the CPP. In January 2004 the leader of the Free Trade Union of Workers of the Kingdom of Cambodia (FTUWKC), Chea Vichea, a prominent opponent of Hun Sen, was murdered in Phnom-Penh; two men were subsequently arrested. In August 2005 the two defendants were convicted of Chea Vichea's murder, following a trial during which no defence witnesses had been called and no forensic evidence had been admitted. Both men were sentenced to 20 years' imprisonment.

In October 2004 King Sihanouk unexpectedly announced his intention to abdicate, owing to ill health. The Royal Council of the Throne was convened and subsequently appointed one of Sihanouk's sons, Prince Norodom Sihamoni, to the throne. Sihamoni's coronation took place later in that month.

In February 2005 the National Assembly voted to strip Sam Rainsy and two other SRP members—Cheam Channy and Chea Poch—of their parliamentary immunity, leaving them open to several defamation lawsuits. The SRP conducted another parliamentary boycott in protest, which lasted until August, when 16 of the party's 24 National Assembly members resumed their seats, stating that they felt compelled to use the appropriate channels to challenge corruption within the Government and to speak out about other issues of concern to the Cambodian people. In the same month Cheam Channy was sentenced to seven years' imprisonment for attempting to form a military group with the aim of overthrowing the Government. In December Sam Rainsy was sentenced *in absentia* to 18 months' imprisonment for defaming leaders of the ruling coalition. In February 2006 King Sihamoni granted royal pardons to both Sam Rainsy and Cheam Channy. Rainsy returned to Cambodia later that month, whereupon he met separately with Hun Sen and Prince Ranariddh to discuss their differences.

Meanwhile, in January 2006 the country's first Senate elections were held. The ballot was open only to parliamentarians and members of local administrative bodies, with the general public being ineligible to vote. The CPP received 7,854 of the

11,352 votes cast, securing 45 of the 57 seats determined by election. The FUNCINPEC Party took 10 seats and the SRP just two. A further four senators were appointed by the National Assembly and King Sihamoni. In September the National Assembly approved a law whereby legislators would no longer be granted immunity from prosecution if they expressed opinions that threatened 'the good customs of society, law and order, and national security'.

In October 2006 Prince Ranariddh was ousted as President of the FUNCINPEC Party, amid allegations of corruption and bribery expressed by the Secretary-General of the party, Gen. Nhiek Bun Chhay. It was this involvement in crime, Nhiek Bun Chhay claimed, that had led to a recent disintegration of the working relationship between Prince Ranariddh and Prime Minister Hun Sen; however, Prince Ranariddh adamantly denied any wrongdoing. Keo Puth Rasmey, the son-in-law of Norodom Sihanouk and at that time Cambodian ambassador to Germany, was elected as the new party President, and was subsequently also appointed as Deputy Prime Minister of the Kingdom. In November the FUNCINPEC Party filed a lawsuit against Prince Ranariddh, accusing him of embezzling approximately US $3.6m. from party coffers. In the following month Prince Ranariddh lost his seat in the National Assembly, following his decision to assume control of the Khmer Front Party, now renamed the Norodom Ranariddh Party (NRP); according to laws governing the National Assembly, any member who left his or her political party was obliged to relinquish his or her Assembly seat. Two of Prince Ranariddh's supporters—Prince Chakrapong and Chhim Seak Leng—were also removed from their seats in the Senate and the National Assembly, respectively. In March 2007 Prince Ranariddh, who was by then living in self-imposed exile in Malaysia, was found guilty *in absentia* of defrauding FUNCINPEC in a property transaction. In the same month, furthermore, he was formally charged with contravening a new monogamy law, which many observers regarded as having been deliberately directed against the Prince's long-standing extramarital relationship. However, Ranariddh was subsequently acquitted after it emerged that his marriage had never been formally registered and did not, therefore, have legal status.

At the second *khum* elections, held on 1 April 2007, the CPP retained control of the majority of the local posts; the party secured a total of 7,993 local positions, including 1,591 of the available commune chief posts. The SRP won 2,660 posts, of which 28 were at the level of chief. The NRP failed to win any of the senior positions of commune chief, and its candidates were elected to occupy only 425 other positions. Although conditions were more stable than in 2002, the level of voter participation declined from 87% to less than 68%.

In December 2007 the Special Representative of the UN Secretary-General for Human Rights in Cambodia, Yash Ghai—a Kenyan professor of constitutional law—concluded, following his fourth visit to the country, that the human rights situation was deteriorating; he expressed particular concern with regard to the numerous land expropriations and illegal forced evictions that had left thousands of families homeless. The weakness of the country's judicial system, the prevalence of corruption and the dearth of official land records (most of which had been destroyed by the Khmers Rouges) remained major issues. International human rights organizations, including Human Rights Watch (a US-based non-governmental organization—NGO), expressed their deep concern at recent developments, urging the Cambodian Government to fulfil its international obligations.

Recent developments: the 2008 election and beyond

As widely anticipated, the CPP secured a resounding victory at the legislative elections held on 27 July 2008, winning 90 seats in the 123-member National Assembly, with 58.1% of the votes cast. The SRP secured only 26 seats (21.9% of the votes), while the new Human Rights Party (HRP), formed by Kem Sokha in 2007, was placed third, taking three seats; the NRP and the FUNCINPEC Party won two seats each. Some 75% of the electorate was reported to have participated in the election, which was described as relatively peaceful. Election monitors from the European Union criticized aspects of the electoral process, including the CPP's involvement in the media and the National Electoral Commission's removal of thousands of voters from the electoral roll, but suggested that irregularities had no significant effect on the result. According to Human Rights Watch, the CPP had used both intimidation and employment incentives to promote the defection of SRP members to its own ranks, and had also targeted journalists who had been critical of the CPP. One journalist was fatally shot by unidentified gunmen in July.

Hun Sen was re-elected Prime Minister by the National Assembly in September 2008; his cabinet was largely unchanged, and the CPP's coalition with the FUNCINPEC Party remained intact. A few days later, at the request of Hun Sen, King Sihamoni granted a royal pardon to Prince Ranariddh, overruling his 2007 fraud conviction (see above), which had been upheld by the Supreme Court in July 2008. Prince Ranariddh issued a statement thanking both the King and the Prime Minister for their clemency; he returned to Cambodia at the end of September, whereupon he announced his withdrawal from active politics. The NRP was subsequently renamed the Nationalist Party (NP). In December King Sihamoni appointed Prince Ranariddh as President of the Supreme Privy Advisory Council, a position that effectively precluded him from resuming his political career.

A minor cabinet reorganization in March 2009 included the appointment as a Deputy Prime Minister without Portfolio of Gen. Ke Kimyan, who had been dismissed as Commander-in-Chief of the Royal Cambodian Armed Forces and replaced by his deputy, Gen. Pol Saroeun, in January. Also in March Surya Subedi, a Nepalese professor of international and human rights law at a British university, was appointed as the UN Special Rapporteur for Human Rights in Cambodia, following Yash Ghai's resignation in 2008 after months of insults from the Cambodian Government. Subedi made his first visit to Cambodia in July, whereupon he concluded that improvements to the human rights situation were urgently needed, particularly with regard to the judiciary and 'core political rights', including freedom of speech and peaceful assembly. However, he welcomed the Government's willingness to engage constructively with him.

Three SRP members were stripped of their parliamentary immunity from prosecution in 2009, prompting widespread accusations that the Government was using the courts as a political instrument for dealing with dissenters. In June the National Assembly voted to suspend the immunity from prosecution of Mu Sochua and Ho Vann. Mu Sochua was convicted of defaming Hun Sen in August, and was fined 6.5m. riels, while Ho Vann was charged with defamation by a group of 22 senior military officers whose training he had described in a local newspaper as 'useless'; he was acquitted in September owing to a lack of evidence. (An appeal by Mu Sochua against the verdict against her was rejected by the Supreme Court in June 2010.) In October 2009 Sam Rainsy was charged with racial incitement and destruction of public property after leading a group of protesters at the Cambodian–Vietnamese border decrying alleged Vietnamese encroachment on Cambodian territory; Rainsy was reported to have encouraged his supporters to uproot border markings that he claimed had been illegally positioned by Viet Nam during the ongoing bilateral border demarcation process (see Foreign Affairs). In November the National Assembly voted to strip the opposition leader of his immunity from prosecution. Rainsy declared that he would not attend any court proceedings, denouncing the court as a political tool of the ruling party, and was convicted *in absentia* in January 2010 and sentenced to two years' imprisonment; two local villagers were also convicted, each receiving a one-year prison sentence (later reduced by two months).

The Government filed a new lawsuit against Rainsy in February 2010, alleging that he had forged official documents and disseminated false information about the ongoing border dispute with Viet Nam. The allegations related to government claims that the opposition leader had posted a 'manipulated' map of the Cambodian–Vietnamese border on the SRP's website in order 'fraudulently' to claim that Viet Nam was encroaching upon Cambodia's sovereign territory. Rainsy, who was reported to be living in self-imposed exile in Europe, denied the charges, insisting that he had obtained the map from a popular internet site. None the less, in September Rainsy was convicted of the fresh charges *in absentia* and sentenced to 10 years' imprisonment; he was also ordered to pay a fine of 5m. riels, as well as 60m. riels in compensation to the Government for discrediting its reputation. SRP spokesperson Yim Sovann denounced the verdict as an attempt to negate the popularity of the opposition in advance of legislative elections due to be held in 2013 and 'a huge set-back for democracy in Cambodia'. In a statement issued from the United Kingdom, Rainsy rejected the claims against him, decrying his conviction as a 'verdict from a kangaroo court (that) reflects Phnom-Penh's subservience to (the Vietnamese Government)'. The two-year sentence imposed on Rainsy in January

2010 was upheld by the Supreme Court in March 2011, prompting the National Assembly to announce the loss of Rainsy's parliamentary status and privileges.

A new penal code, which had been signed into law in November 2009, was implemented in December 2010. Controversial new articles that appeared to outlaw criticism of court decisions and public officials elicited severe criticism from human rights organizations. The Cambodian League for the Promotion and Defense of Human Rights (LICADHO) dismissed the new code as 'vague and highly subjective' and a 'set-back for freedom of expression issues' in the country. Further consternation was provoked by draft legislation pertaining to NGO activity, the details of which were publicized later that month. A spokesperson for the Ministry of the Interior stated that the legislation was intended to increase transparency among the country's hundreds of NGOs; however, some rights groups claimed that the more stringent registration and reporting regulations proposed by the draft legislation would restrict the activities of NGOs, particularly smaller, more community-based groups. Nevertheless, the bill was widely considered to be less restrictive than similar legislation proposed in 2005.

Following months of public speculation, in December 2010 Prince Ranariddh announced the resumption of his political career at the head of the NP, which later that month readopted its former name, the Norodom Ranariddh Party. Given Prince Ranariddh's very public ousting from FUNCINPEC in 2006 (see The 2003 election, King's abdication and new Senate), the development appeared to jeopardize existing plans for a merger between the NRP and FUNCINPEC. The Prince claimed that the FUNCINPEC leadership, including party President Keo Puth Rasmey and Secretary-General Gen. Nhiek Bun Chhay, had lost popular support, implying that it would be in FUNCINPEC's best interests if they were to step down. Meanwhile, Hun Sen issued a warning that any FUNCINPEC government officials who attempted to defect to the NRP would be relieved of their government positions. In a rare public speech, addressing party members in November 2011, Prince Ranariddh stated that his aim in returning to the political fray was to reunite monarchists across the country and to force the creation of a coalition government with the ruling CPP following the legislative elections due in 2013. The Prince also criticized Gen. Nhiek Bun Chhay, reiterating claims that the latter had been responsible for his ousting from FUNCINPEC in 2006.

Meanwhile, during a meeting of the FUNCINPEC Party Permanent Committee in February 2011, three party officials—Phorn Chantha, Suong Phally and Yim Savy—distributed documents purporting to show Gen. Nhiek Bun Chhay's involvement in the mismanagement and embezzlement of party property and funds since 2008. Nhiek Bun Chhay adamantly refuted the allegations and filed a defamation suit against the three officials, who, he asserted, were planning to defect to the NRP and had consequently forged the documents and fabricated the case against him to win favour with Prince Ranariddh. Amid the ensuing claims of an internal fissure within FUNCINPEC, it was reported in the *Phnom Penh Post* in March 2011 that 127 FUNCINPEC party activists in Kampong Cham province had defected to the NRP in that month. However, a FUNCINPEC spokesperson denied the claim, contending that such reports were a gross exaggeration fabricated by the NRP as a means of fomenting division within Prince Ranariddh's former party.

At the second indirect elections to the Senate, which were held on 29 January 2012 and contested only by the CPP and the SRP, the CPP gained one additional seat compared with the 2006 polls, securing 46 of the 57 elective seats (with 8,880 of the 11,383 valid votes cast), while the SRP increased its representation from two seats to 11. A further four senators were appointed by the National Assembly and the King. In early 2012 preparations were also under way for Cambodia's third *khum* elections, which were scheduled to be held on 3 June. In late October 2011 the Committee for Free and Fair Elections in Cambodia (Comfrel—established in 1995 as a permanent election-monitoring organization) had noted with concern a significant number of 'irregularities' in the voter registration process, which took place during September and October, and an 'imbalance' in political broadcasting, with the ruling CPP dominating television and radio broadcasts.

The Khmer Rouge Tribunal

The detention of Ta Mok in March and of Duch in May 1999 (see Domestic Political Affairs) resulted in increased domestic and international pressure for the establishment of a tribunal to try former Khmer Rouge leaders for atrocities committed during 1975–79. However, the Cambodian Government was reluctant to indict former Khmer Rouge leaders who had surrendered, for fear that former PDK members might revert to armed insurrection. Furthermore, Hun Sen insisted that any trials take place within the existing Cambodian court structure, while the UN favoured an international tribunal. In April 1999, however, Hun Sen conceded that UN-appointed foreign judges could take part in a trial in Cambodia, although he still favoured the nomination of a Cambodian prosecutor.

Agreement was reached in early 2000 on a formula for the establishment of the tribunal. The final version of the legislation was endorsed by the National Assembly in July 2001 and signed into law by King Sihanouk in August, after receiving the approval of the Constitutional Council. Meanwhile, in June Prime Minister Hun Sen accused the UN of interfering with Cambodian sovereignty, a view that was reiterated by Prince Ranariddh. In February 2002 the UN unexpectedly announced that it had decided to abandon negotiations with the Cambodian Government over a UN role in the establishment of a joint tribunal, claiming that the legal framework created by the Government did not conform to international standards of justice and would not ensure either the independence or impartiality of proceedings. In response, the Government stated that it intended to proceed with the trials and would make no further concessions to the UN in order to facilitate the establishment of a tribunal. However, in July Hun Sen announced that Cambodia was prepared to compromise with the UN by amending the laws that would govern the establishment of any tribunal. Following exploratory talks in January 2003, and the subsequent recommencement of negotiations in March, in June the two sides concluded a formal agreement providing for the establishment of a bicameral tribunal, composed of a Trial Chamber and a Supreme Court Chamber. Under the legislation approved in 2001, only those individuals deemed 'most responsible' for the atrocities of 1975–78 were to be put on trial, thereby implicitly exempting significant numbers of middle- and lower-ranking former Khmer Rouge officials from prosecution. After a significant delay, owing to the prolonged political dispute that had arisen following the 2003 elections (see Domestic Political Affairs), the legislation establishing the tribunal was finally ratified by the Cambodian legislature and promulgated by the King in October 2004. In December UN officials arrived in Cambodia to begin preparatory work.

Efforts to establish the tribunal (officially known as the Extraordinary Chambers in the Courts of Cambodia—ECCC) were accelerated from March 2006, in which month Kofi Annan submitted to the Cambodian Government a list of international candidates for judicial positions within the tribunal. In July the 17 local and 13 international judges and prosecutors selected by the Cambodian Supreme Council of Magistracy—the country's highest judicial body, responsible for all judicial and prosecutorial appointments—were formally sworn in by King Sihamoni; later that month the two newly appointed co-prosecutors began their formal investigations, with former King Sihanouk stating that he would be willing to testify against the Khmers Rouges. At a meeting held in November, however, Cambodian and international judges failed to agree on internal rules governing the operations of the ECCC, further delaying the proceedings. In December Human Rights Watch alleged that Cambodian government interference was responsible for halting the process; the NGO urged the ECCC's judicial personnel to revise the draft rules so as to ensure that all trials would be conducted publicly, that defendants could not be sentenced *in absentia* and that the defence counsel would remain independent. In June 2007 agreement was finally reached on the tribunal's rules of procedure, and in July Duch became the first former leader of the Khmers Rouges to be formally charged with crimes against humanity, in what became known as Case 001.

In August 2007 the removal by royal decree of the President of the Court of Appeal, Ly Louch Leng, following allegations of bribery, and her replacement by You Bunleng, a judge previously appointed to serve with the ECCC, was widely regarded as seriously jeopardizing the independence and efficiency of the judiciary. Yash Ghai, the Special Representative of the UN Secretary-General for Human Rights in Cambodia, and Leandro Despouy, the UN's Special Rapporteur on the Independence of Judges and Lawyers, issued a statement questioning the Cambodian authorities' decision to make the appointment without due regard for the country's Constitution. Concerns were reiterated regarding the composition of the Supreme Council of Magistracy, which included a government minister and an official of the ruling party, and the appointment in August of four new members, through executive rather than constitutional channels, further diminished confidence in the system.

In the latter part of 2007 former Khmer Rouge leaders Nuon Chea, Ieng Sary and Khieu Samphan were charged with war crimes and crimes against humanity. Ieng Thirith, former Minister of Social Affairs and wife of Ieng Sary, was also charged with crimes against humanity. In a report released in October, the UN criticized Cambodia's management of the proceedings, in particular the engagement of excessive numbers of apparently unqualified staff, warning that it would withdraw from the trials process if changes were not implemented. In November, in its first public session, the tribunal began its consideration of Duch's request for bail, his lawyers arguing that his detention without trial for eight years had been a breach of international standards of justice; the request was rejected in December. In the same month Buddhist monks and nuns, joined by members of the Muslim and Christian communities which had been similarly repressed during the 1970s, took part in a march to the tribunal building to demonstrate their support for an acceleration of the protracted process of bringing to justice those responsible for the atrocities of the late 1970s.

Duch was formally indicted in August 2008 and, following a preliminary hearing in February 2009, his trial began in March. Duch admitted responsibility, and apologized, for the part that he had played in the torture and execution of inmates as governor of the Tuol Sleng detention centre (see The coalition Government of 1998–2003). However, Duch claimed that he had been merely 'a cog in a running machine', and, in his closing statement on the final day of the trial, asked to be released on the grounds that he had co-operated fully with the ECCC and had been incarcerated since 1999, seemingly casting doubt on the sincerity of his claims during the trial that he felt 'excruciating remorse' for his actions and wished to seek the forgiveness of the victims' relatives. In June 2009 the court had heard the testimony of Vann Nath, one of only a few prisoners who survived incarceration at the Tuol Sleng camp, who described the 'inhumane' conditions under which the inmates had been detained before most were executed. (Following a period of ill health, Vann Nath died in September 2011.) The trial was concluded in November 2009, and, following protracted delays, Duch was convicted of war crimes and crimes against humanity in July 2010 and sentenced to 30 years' imprisonment (reduced from 35 years on account of Duch's illegal detention prior to the establishment of the ECCC in 2007). However, this was to be reduced by 11 years owing to time already spent incarcerated, effectively shortening the term of imprisonment to 19 years. The tribunal's President, Nil Nonn, explained that the decision not to award a life sentence (the maximum punishment to which the tribunal had recourse) was due to several mitigating factors, among them Duch's 'co-operation with the chamber, admission of responsibility, limited expressions of remorse, the coercive environment in Democratic Kampuchea and the potential for rehabilitation'.

Opinion on the sentence handed down to Duch was divided. While some argued that the conviction indicated that those guilty of atrocities during the Khmer Rouge regime would not avoid justice, and that the legal process in itself represented a vital, cathartic element in Cambodia's efforts to move on from its troubled past, many insisted that anything short of life imprisonment for Duch represented a gross insult to his many thousands of victims. Others criticized the decision to spend nearly US $150m. on funding the judicial process in a country in which gross domestic product per caput stood at just $650 in 2009.

In August 2010 it was announced that prosecutors were appealing against the 30-year prison sentence. Later that month Duch's lawyers also appealed against the conviction, arguing that the tribunal lacked jurisdiction since it was mandated to prosecute only the most senior leaders and those 'most responsible' for the atrocities committed during 1975–78, while Duch, they insisted, was just one of more than 100 prison guards serving during the Khmer Rouge regime and had merely been following orders. However, the prosecution team maintained that, as governor of the infamous Tuol Sleng detention camp, to which those deemed most dangerous to the Khmer Rouge regime had been sent and where no more than 15 detainees were thought to have survived, Duch had been one of the main protagonists of the regime's atrocities. Following an appeal hearing in March–April 2011, in early February 2012 the ECCC's Supreme Court Chamber ruled that the original sentence had been too lenient given the gravity of Duch's crimes and increased his sentence to one of life imprisonment.

In September 2010 the four other defendants awaiting trial by the ECCC—Nuon Chea, Khieu Samphan, Ieng Sary and Ieng Thirith (collectively known as Case 002)—were formally indicted for genocide, crimes against humanity and war crimes. The four defendants, who were to be tried together, denied the charges against them; however, their final appeal was rejected in January 2011. Following a preliminary hearing in June, it was announced in September that the four defendants' trial was to be held in a number of stages, the first of which was to consider charges involving the forced movement of people and crimes against humanity, while subsequent trials would focus on the remaining charges, including genocide. In November, two days prior to the opening of the trial, medical experts deemed Ieng Thirith unfit to stand trial owing to poor mental health—she was reported to be suffering from dementia and Alzheimer's disease—and ordered that she be released. (However, in December the ECCC ruled that she remain in detention and be transferred to a medical facility for treatment in the hope that she might subsequently become fit to stand trial.) The trial of Nuon Chea, Khieu Samphan and Ieng Sary opened two days later as planned. Almost 4,000 civil parties, primarily the relatives of victims of the Khmer Rouge regime, were to give evidence during the court proceedings, which were not expected to be concluded before 2013.

Meanwhile, during a meeting with UN Secretary-General Ban Ki-Moon in October 2010, Prime Minister Hun Sen, himself a former junior Khmer Rouge cadre, was reported to have stated that he would not allow further prosecutions to be pursued by the ECCC beyond the long-anticipated second trial, arguing that such action would pose a threat to stability in Cambodia; several prominent Cambodian government officials, including Deputy Prime Minister and Minister of Foreign Affairs and International Co-operation Hor Nam Hong and Minister of Information Kieu Kanharith, publicly stated that pursuing all but the most senior former Khmer Rouge leaders would constitute a breaching of the tribunal's stipulated remit. However, a spokesperson for the UN-sponsored tribunal appeared to rebuff such comments, stating: 'The court does not seek permission and endorsement for its work. It simply follows the legal process described in the law and the agreement relating to this court.' The comments came amid ongoing investigations into two other complaints (known as Cases 003 and 004) filed against five other former Khmer Rouge officials still at large—former Khmer Rouge navy commander Meas Mut, former air force commander Sou Met, former district chief Im Chaem, and former zone deputy secretaries Ta Tith and Ta An. However, as of early 2012 the complaints had received no support from either the Cambodian ECCC co-prosecutor, Chea Leang, or the Cambodian ECCC co-investigating judge, You Bunleng. In June 2011 You Bunleng and the international co-investigating judge, Siegfried Blunk of Germany, had rejected a request for further investigation by the international co-prosecutor, Andrew Cayley of the United Kingdom, on the grounds that Cayley had failed formally to register a disagreement on the issue that he had with Chea Leang. Chea Leang's continued refusal to investigate new cases had provoked accusations by some observers that he was wilfully obstructing the ECCC's activity in order to serve the Hun Sen Government's agenda. Similar accusations levelled against Blunk precipitated the German's resignation from the ECCC in October; Blunk defended his conduct as international co-investigating judge, blaming Cambodian government interference for his reticence in pursuing new cases. Human Rights Watch welcomed Blunk's resignation, but appealed for You Bunleng to step down as well, arguing that justice could not be obtained while he remained on the tribunal. Blunk was subsequently replaced by Laurent Kasper-Ansermet of Switzerland, who had served as a reserve judge since February. However, hopes that the new appointment might facilitate the bringing of new cases before the ECCC appeared likely to be frustrated. In January 2012 Kasper-Ansermet issued a statement to the media in which he accused You Bunleng of preventing him from disclosing key information about Cases 003 and 004; shortly thereafter, You Bunleng issued his own public statement, in which he expressed 'deep disappointment' with the conduct of Kasper-Ansermet, who, as the reserve international co-investigating judge, lacked 'legal accreditation to undertake any procedural action or measure with respect to the Case Files' and failed to comprehend the legal principles and common practices of the ECCC. The dispute prompted Kasper-Ansermet's resignation from the ECCC in March. Meanwhile, Hun Sen continued to resist the idea of bringing any further charges against former Khmer Rouge leaders and insisted that no member of his Government was under any obligation to provide testimony to the ECCC.

Foreign Affairs

Regional relations

Regional relations were severely affected by the events of July 1997. ASEAN decided to postpone indefinitely Cambodia's admission to the grouping, which had been scheduled for that month, while Japan, like others in the international donor community, suspended all but humanitarian assistance. At the end of July Hun Sen invited ASEAN to mediate in the Cambodian crisis and held discussions with the grouping in early August. Prior to the ASEAN summit meeting in Viet Nam in December 1998, Singapore, Thailand and the Philippines remained opposed to Cambodia's immediate accession to the organization. However, the host country then announced that Cambodia had been accepted as the 10th member of ASEAN. Cambodia duly acceded to ASEAN in April 1999.

In August 2002, following a meeting of ASEAN in Brunei, Cambodia became a signatory to an anti-terrorism pact originally drawn up by Malaysia, Indonesia and the Philippines in May of that year; the pact was intended to increase regional co-operation on security issues. In November the country hosted the annual ASEAN summit meeting, which was also attended by the Republic of Korea (South Korea), Japan and the People's Republic of China, as well as India, which was present for the first time. During the meeting a framework agreement was signed to establish an ASEAN-China free trade area by 2010; the accord, which was intended to 'bring the countries together in a mutually dependent and beneficial relationship in an increasingly borderless global environment', was duly implemented in January 2010.

Relations between Cambodia and the People's Republic of China (which had formerly supported the PDK) improved from the mid-1990s. China continued to provide support, and in November 2000 President Jiang Zemin paid a two-day official visit to Cambodia, the first by a Chinese head of state in more than 35 years. In August 2005 King Sihamoni undertook an official visit to China, and Chinese Premier Wen Jiabao made a reciprocal visit to Phnom-Penh in April 2006. Cambodia prompted international censure in December 2009 when, before their claims for asylum had been heard, it decided to deport 20 Uygur refugees to China, following coercion from the Chinese Government and despite objections from human rights groups and the UN. The members of the Turkic-speaking Muslim minority group had fled to Cambodia in the previous month, claiming that they were being persecuted by the Chinese Government following violent clashes in July between Uygur and Han Chinese in Urumqi, in the Xinjiang region of China. Several of the refugees had declared in written statements gathered by the Office of the UN High Commissioner for Refugees that they feared the imposition of the death penalty if forced to return to China. Two days later China and Cambodia signed 14 agreements for grants and loans, totalling an estimated US $1,000m., prompting suggestions that the former had abused its position as Cambodia's largest foreign investor to persuade the Cambodian Government to deport the refugees. Following the US Government's decision to suspend the delivery of military vehicles and uniforms in protest at the repatriation of the Uygur from Cambodia to China, in May China and Cambodia signed an agreement whereby China would supply the 257 vehicles and 50,000 uniforms; the delivery was received by Cambodia in the following month. Also in June a memorandum of understanding (MOU) intended to increase road and bridge infrastructure co-operation was signed between Cambodia and China; the Cambodian Minister of Public Works and Transport, Tram Eav Toek, hailed the agreement as a reflection of the strengthening co-operation between the two countries. According to the Chairman of Cambodia's National Assembly, Heng Samrin, the bilateral trade volume for the first eight months of 2011 totalled $1,430m. (almost equal to that recorded for the whole of 2010) and was expected to reach $2,000m. by year-end. Between 1994 and mid-2011 China was reported to have provided Cambodia with more than $8,000m. in foreign direct investment.

Thailand remained neutral following the events in Cambodia of mid-1997, but extended humanitarian assistance to the estimated 35,000 Cambodian refugees who crossed into Thailand to avoid the fighting. In January 2003 demonstrators attacked the Thai embassy and several Thai-owned businesses in Phnom-Penh, having been provoked by comments, wrongly attributed to a Thai actress, that implied that the temples at Angkor Wat had been stolen from Thailand. The violence escalated, prompting the Thai Government to withdraw its ambassador, together with more than 500 Thai nationals resident in Cambodia, and to downgrade diplomatic relations. Prime Minister Hun Sen subsequently issued a formal apology to the Thai Government. In April the Thai ambassador returned to Phnom-Penh, and in mid-2003 the Cambodian and Thai Cabinets held an unprecedented joint meeting. In September almost all of those Cambodians who had been imprisoned for their involvement in the riots were released, and in October 2004 the Thai embassy in Phnom-Penh reopened. Hun Sen visited Bangkok in May 2005 to commemorate the 55th anniversary of bilateral relations. An MOU pertaining to information and broadcasting was signed by the two countries in October of that year and a second MOU, which provided for a single tourist visa valid for both countries, was signed in the following month. Following the removal of the Government of Thaksin Shinawatra in a military coup in September 2006, Hun Sen stated that relations between the two countries remained unchanged and that Cambodia respected the right of Thailand to resolve its domestic affairs without international interference.

Cambodian-Thai relations were severely tested when the Preah Vihear temple, located on the bilateral border, was declared a World Heritage Site by UNESCO in July 2008. An International Court of Justice (ICJ) ruling in 1962 had awarded Cambodia ownership of the temple, but sovereignty of the surrounding area remained a point of contention, and the Thai Government's initial approval of Cambodia's application to UNESCO, without parliamentary consent, had caused dissatisfaction in Thailand. In July the Thai ambassador to the UN accused the Cambodian Government of employing 'guerrilla tactics' in an attempt to redraw the bilateral border. As the situation escalated, soldiers from both countries were deployed to the area; following discussions between the two sides, most of the troops were withdrawn in August, but in October the confrontation resulted in the deaths of two Cambodian soldiers. Later that month senior members of the Cambodian and Thai Governments agreed to seek a peaceful resolution to the matter, and in November plans for a border demarcation process and the full withdrawal of all remaining troops were drawn up. In February 2009 Hun Sen met with Thai Prime Minister Abhisit Vejjajiva in Hua Hin, Thailand, to discuss energy co-operation in the Gulf of Thailand, prompting hopes of an improvement in relations. However, four Thai soldiers were reported to have been killed during an exchange of fire across the border in April. In the same month the Joint Border Committee (JBC) of Cambodia and Thailand convened to discuss plans to accelerate the process of border demarcation; following the two-day meeting, a JBC spokesman announced that both sides had agreed to plant border posts in July; by early 2012, however, little discernible progress had been made to this end, and minor skirmishes in the disputed area continued to be reported during the latter half of 2009 and into 2010. During an official visit to the disputed area around the Preah Vihear temple in February 2010, Hun Sen accused Thailand of planning to invade Cambodia and urged Cambodian troops to continue to protect the country's borders from 'the enemy'.

Meanwhile, in October 2009 Hun Sen had incensed Thai officials at the ASEAN summit meeting, held in Hua Hin, by declaring that Thaksin (who had been convicted *in absentia* of corruption and sentenced to two years' imprisonment by the Thai Supreme Court in October 2008) was welcome to seek refuge in Cambodia. Following the Cambodian Government's decision to appoint Thaksin as an economic adviser in late October 2009, Thailand recalled its ambassador from Phnom-Penh in early November, accusing the Cambodian Government of interfering in Thailand's internal affairs; Cambodia recalled its own ambassador in Bangkok on the following day. In mid-November Thai diplomats presented Cambodian officials with an extradition request for Thaksin, a request that was summarily rejected by the Cambodian Government on the grounds that Thaksin's conviction had been 'politically motivated'. Later that same day a Thai national was arrested by the Cambodian authorities and charged with espionage; Siwarak Chotipong, an employee at a Cambodian air traffic services company, was alleged to have stolen the private flight schedule of Thaksin and to have given it to the first secretary at the Thai embassy in Phnom-Penh. The first secretary was promptly expelled from Cambodia, with Thailand responding in kind. Siwarak was convicted in early December and sentenced to seven years' imprisonment; however, he was released just a few days later, having been granted a royal pardon by King Sihamoni, reportedly at the request of Thaksin. In mid-December a Thai Government spokesman announced that the Thai ambassador would return to Phnom-Penh if Cambodia 'corrected its stated opinions' of Thai politics and of the Thai justice system, and rescinded the appointment of Thaksin as economic adviser. Hun Sen responded by stating that normal bilateral relations would not be restored until Thailand's current Government had been voted out of office, accusing the Abhisit Government of using the dispute over Thaksin as a distraction from the more serious issue of border demarcation.

Nevertheless, diplomatic relations between Cambodia and Thailand were fully restored following the announcement in August 2010 that Thaksin had resigned from his economic advisory position in Cambodia, and the respective ambassadors returned to their posts. A subsequent series of meetings between Hun Sen and Abhisit on the sidelines of regional and international conferences from September, at which the two leaders were reported to have discussed the Preah Vihear issue and measures to prevent future border disputes, led to a further amelioration in relations. However, tensions once again escalated in mid-October, when a senior Thai investigator alleged that 11 members of the anti-Government Red Shirt movement who had been arrested earlier that month on suspicion of involvement in alleged assassination plots—the intended targets of which had included Abhisit—had received training at a Cambodian military base. The Cambodian Government adamantly denied the claims, which were based on witness statements arising from the arrest in early October of 11 men in Thailand's northern Chiang Mai province. In December Thailand's Commander-in-Chief of the Army, Gen. Prayuth Chanocha, dismissed Cambodian claims that Thai troops had been withdrawn from the disputed area; however, Gen. Prayuth did confirm an 'adjustment' of Thai troops in the area, which he stated had been made in response to similar action by Cambodia. Fighting broke out again in contested border areas in mid-April 2011, and by the beginning of May at least 18 Cambodian and Thai soldiers were reported to have been killed in the latest bout of violence. The Cambodian Government refuted claims by Thai Minister of Foreign Affairs Kasit Piromya that Cambodia was 'the aggressor', insisting that its soldiers were merely acting in self-defence. ASEAN Secretary-General Surin Pitsuwan appealed for the immediate holding of formal dialogue, cautioning that the reputation of the regional bloc would be jeopardized should a complete cessation of hostilities not be swiftly secured. A tentative truce was declared in early May, and the Cambodian–Thai border crossing near the Preah Vihear site was reopened. In the same month Cambodian and Thai representatives appeared before the ICJ in connection with the border dispute, with both sides stating that they would respect the ultimate decision of the Court; however, in June the Thai Government formally denounced the 1972 UNESCO World Heritage Convention. In July 2011 the ICJ ordered the withdrawal of all Cambodian and Thai military personnel from the disputed area around the Preah Vihear site and the establishment of a demilitarized zone therein, which would be monitored by ASEAN-appointed observers.

Tensions were further exacerbated when a Cambodian court convicted two members of a Thai nationalist movement on espionage charges and, in February 2011, sentenced them both to eight years in prison. However, the entry into office of Yingluck Shinawatra, sister of Thaksin, as Thailand's Prime Minister in August, following elections in July, engendered hopes of a new era in Cambodian-Thai relations. While at early 2012 it remained too early to ascertain to what extent such hopes might prove founded, an official visit to Cambodia by Yingluck in September 2011 did appear to indicate a significant amelioration in relations. At a meeting held during her stay, the new premier and the Cambodian Minister of Information, Kieu Kanharith, agreed that both countries must adhere to the ICJ's rulings on the bilateral border dispute, including the redeployment of all military personnel away from the Preah Vihear site; the two also agreed to bolster co-operation in the fields of trade and investment and cross-border crime. Following a meeting in December between the Cambodian and Thai ministers responsible for foreign affairs, Hor Nam Hong and Surapong Towijakchaikul, respectively, Hor Nam Hong indicated that the two Thai nationals imprisoned on espionage charges in February might be released early through a prisoner exchange programme, pending an agreement between the two countries' Governments.

In April 1995 Cambodia, Thailand, Viet Nam and Laos signed an agreement providing for the establishment of the Mekong River Commission (see p. 451), which was to co-ordinate the sustainable development of the resources of the Lower Mekong River Basin. In October 1999 the leaders of Cambodia, Laos and Viet Nam convened in the Laotian capital for their first 'unofficial' Indo-Chinese summit meeting. In November 2005 Prime Minister Hun Sen visited Viet Nam to discuss various bilateral issues, and the two countries signed a supplementary border treaty to complement an existing treaty signed by Cambodia and Viet Nam in 1985; the new agreement envisaged that the demarcation of the border between the two countries would be finalized by December 2008. However, in March 2008 it was announced that the project was behind schedule, with only about 30 of the 340 border markers having been installed, and it was not expected to be completed until the end of 2012. King Sihamoni made his first official visit to Viet Nam in March 2006. In December 2009 bilateral co-operation agreements were signed on power generation, industry, mining and maritime transport; later that month, at a conference co-hosted by the Vietnamese Ministry of Planning and Investment and the Cambodian Development Council, more than 60 agreements and contracts were signed, intended to promote Vietnamese investment in Cambodia and estimated to be worth US $6,000m. At a five-nation regional summit meeting held in Cambodia in November 2010, Cambodia, Laos, Myanmar, Thailand and Viet Nam signed the Phnom Penh Declaration, which was intended to improve economic co-operation among the regional neighbours; the agreement pertained to numerous fields of activity, including agriculture, industry and the energy sector, the environment, investment and trade facilitation, transport, tourism and public health. The five states also expressed their support for the elimination of visa requirements for 30-day visits by citizens within the five countries, while Cambodia and Thailand signed an agreement exempting Cambodian and Thai citizens holding ordinary passports from visa requirements, in order to facilitate the flow of businesspeople and tourists. At a tripartite ministerial meeting on anti-narcotics co-operation held in December, Cambodia, Laos and Viet Nam agreed to intensify co-operation in order to combat the circulation, production, farming and smuggling of drugs within the three countries. In June 2011 the Cambodian Government signed an agreement with the Laotian and Vietnamese Governments providing for the establishment of a trilateral economic development zone; however, critics argued that the agreement, which called for an acceleration of the border demarcation process, could result in the ceding of sovereign Cambodian territory to its regional neighbours.

Cambodia's relations with Japan continued to improve, following policy talks between the two in 1998–99, which culminated in the Japanese Government's resumption of direct funding to Cambodia in 1999; during the 2000s Japan was a leading donor of development aid to the country. In 2005/06, in addition to its contribution of US $22m. towards the financing of the Khmer Rouge trials, Japan provided aid totalling almost $115m., pledging a similar amount for 2006/07. In June 2008 Japan provided an additional $3m. to the ECCC, following a plea by the latter for more funding from the international donor community, and in March 2009 Japan provided further 'urgent' funding to the ECCC to enable local Cambodian staff to be paid. Burgeoning bilateral relations were reflected by the first-ever official visit to Japan of King Sihamoni, in May 2010; during his stay, the King met with Japanese Emperor Akihito and prominent political leaders, among them Prime Minister Yukio Hatoyama, and discussed, *inter alia*, regional and international security issues. Shortly after the commencement of the trial against four former Khmer Rouge leaders in November 2011 (see The Khmer Rouge Tribunal), the Japanese Government announced the disbursement of a further $2.9m. to support the activities of the ECCC.

Other external relations

As with its regional relations, Cambodia's relations with countries further afield were greatly impeded by the events of July 1997. Like Japan, the USA and many European donors (including Germany) suspended all but humanitarian assistance, and in October 1998 the US House of Representatives adopted a resolution accusing Hun Sen of genocide. A further significant consequence was the decision of the UN Accreditation Committee to leave Cambodia's seat at the UN vacant; however, following the formation of a coalition Government in November 1998, Cambodia regained its seat in December.

Following bilateral policy consultations in early 1999, Germany resumed financial aid to Cambodia, as did many within the international donor community. During the 2000s Germany was one of Cambodia's principal bilateral donors, providing significant financial assistance for a wide range of developmental and humanitarian projects, as well as support for the Khmer Rouge trials.

US direct funding to Cambodia remained suspended until February 2007. In the same month, for the first time in more than 30 years, a US navy frigate docked in Cambodia, visiting the port of Sihanoukville. Although bilateral relations were hampered by Cambodia's decision to deport 20 Uygur refugees to China in December 2009 (see Regional relations), the damage appeared to be limited and brief. In May 2010 a US $1.8m. peace-keeping training centre, funded by the US Department of Defense, was opened in the Cambodian capital. Furthermore, in July the USA and Cambodia co-organized the 'Angkor Sentinel 10' military exercises, involving 1,200 soldiers from 23 countries. Speaking at the event's inauguration, which coincided with the 60th anniversary of US-Cambodian relations, the US ambassador to Cambodia emphasized the commitment of the US Government to deepening its defence relations and other links with Cambodia. Human Rights Watch and other rights organizations urged the Administration of US President Barack Obama to suspend military aid to Cambodia until the latter country had achieved significant progress on its human rights record. During a visit to Phnom-Penh in November, US Secretary of State Hillary Clinton stated that Cambodia should take care to maintain a foreign policy that was not 'too dependent' on China. She also urged the Cambodian Government not to resist efforts to widen the mandate of the ECCC to include the prosecution of lower- and middle-ranking members of the Khmers Rouges, and to do more to improve Cambodia's human rights record. However, given the deepening nature of Sino-Cambodian relations, it was feared by some observers that the US Administration's commitment to the promotion of human rights in Cambodia might be overshadowed by its desire to foster closer strategic relations with Phnom-Penh and thereby to contain China's influence in Cambodia and the wider Asian-Pacific region.

Cambodia has sought to enhance relations with South Asian states in recent years. In April 2004 Prime Minister Hun Sen held formal talks with his Pakistani counterpart, Zafarullah Khan Jamali, at which the pair agreed to deepen multilateral relations in order more effectively to address regional stability and security concerns. In December 2010 the Cambodian legislature adopted draft legislation pertaining to the ASEAN-India Framework Agreement on Comprehensive Economic Cooperation, which had been signed by India and the member states of ASEAN during the second ASEAN-India summit, hosted in Bali, Indonesia, in October 2003. The key objectives of the agreement included the removal of bilateral trade tariffs on a wide range of goods and services (including the elimination of tariffs on 90% of agricultural products by 2016), the creation of a transparent and liberal investment regime, and a deepening of trade and investment co-operation.

Meanwhile, in June 2007 the inaugural session of the Cambodia Development Cooperation Forum (CDCF) was held in Phnom-Penh. Chaired solely by the Cambodian Government, the new forum replaced the Consultative Group of international donors and was to complement the implementation of the National Strategic Development Plan. Attended by about 25 delegations from the international community, the first meeting resulted in a total of US $689m. being pledged by foreign donors, for the first time including China. A total of $951.5m. was pledged at the second CDCF meeting, held in December 2008. A further $1,100m. was pledged at the third meeting, held in June 2010. In August 2011 the fourth meeting, which had been scheduled to be convened in December of that year, was indefinitely postponed at the request of the Cambodian Government. This development was widely believed to have been linked to the announcement by the World Bank earlier in August that it was suspending the provision of new loans to Cambodia, in response to the forced eviction of thousands of residents living around Boeung Kak lake in Phnom-Penh to make way for a luxury residential and commercial property development. One of the companies involved in the development was a Chinese firm alleged to have close links with Hun Sen. The World Bank further stated that it would resume funding only when the Cambodian Government halted such evictions and agreed to compensate all those who had already been evicted. Appearing eager to downplay the significance of the development, a Cambodian government spokesperson stated that the Government had already, in late 2010, expressed its view that the Bank was 'not a proper help to Cambodia in the cause of development'.

CONSTITUTION AND GOVERNMENT

The Kingdom of Cambodia is a constitutional monarchy. The monarch is the head of state and is selected by the Throne Council from among descendants of three royal lines. Legislative power is vested in the 123-member National Assembly, the lower chamber, which is elected for a term of five years by universal adult suffrage, and the 61-member Senate, the upper chamber, 57 members of which are elected by parliamentarians and members of local administrative bodies, while the remaining four members are appointed by the National Assembly and the King. Executive power is held by the Cabinet (the Royal Government of Cambodia), headed by the Prime Minister, who is appointed by the King at the recommendation of the Chairman of the National Assembly from among the representatives of the majority party.

For local administration the Kingdom of Cambodia is divided into provinces, municipalities and districts, known as *khan*, *khum* and *sangkat*.

REGIONAL AND INTERNATIONAL CO-OPERATION

Cambodia is a member of the Association of Southeast Asian Nations (ASEAN, see p. 214), of the Asian Development Bank (ADB, see p. 210), of the Mekong River Commission (see p. 451), and of the Colombo Plan (see p. 449). Cambodia is also a member of the UN's Economic and Social Commission for Asia and the Pacific (ESCAP, see p. 40).

Cambodia became a member of the UN in 1955, and was admitted to the World Trade Organization (WTO, see p. 433) in 2004. Cambodia participates in the Group of 77 (G77, see p. 450) developing nations, and is also a member of the International Labour Organization (ILO, see p. 141) and of the Non-aligned Movement (see p. 464).

ECONOMIC AFFAIRS

In 2010, according to the World Bank, Cambodia's gross national income (GNI), measured at average 2008–10 prices, was US $10,686m., equivalent to $760 per head (or $2,040 per head on an international purchasing-power parity basis). During 2001–10, it was estimated, the population increased at an average annual rate of 1.2%, while gross domestic product (GDP) per head increased, in real terms, by an average of 6.5% per year during the same period. Cambodia's overall GDP increased, in real terms, at an average annual rate of 8.0% during 2001–10. According to the Asian Development Bank (ADB), GDP increased by 6.0% in 2010 and by 6.8% in 2011.

According to the ADB, agriculture (including forestry and fishing) contributed 36.0% of GDP in 2010. In 2007, according to the IMF, the sector engaged 55.9% of the economically active population. In 2010 production of paddy rice, a significant source of export revenue, was 8.2m. metric tons. Other important crops include cassava, maize, sugar cane and bananas. Rubber and timber are also major export commodities. However, forestry reserves continued to be depleted and reafforestation remained inadequate. The fishing sector was also adversely affected by deforestation, which caused the silting up of lakes and rivers, resulting in reductions in freshwater fishing catches. According to ADB data, agricultural GDP increased, in real terms, at an average annual rate of 5.1% during 2001–10. The GDP of the agricultural sector increased by 4.0% in 2010 and by 3.3% in 2011.

According to the ADB, industry (including mining, manufacturing, construction and utilities) contributed 23.0% of GDP in 2010. In 2007 15.4% of the employed labour force were engaged in this sector, according to the IMF. In real terms, according to figures from the ADB, industrial GDP increased at an average annual rate of 10.0% during 2001–10. Sectoral GDP rose by 13.6% in 2010 and by 13.9% in 2011.

In 2010, according to the ADB, mining and quarrying contributed less than 0.7% of GDP. This sector employed 0.3% of the working population in 2007, according to the IMF. Cambodia's mineral resources include phosphates, gemstones, iron ore, bauxite, silicon, manganese ore and gold. Cambodia hoped to commence the exploitation of its offshore petroleum reserves in late 2012. The country also has substantial reserves of natural gas. According to figures from the ADB, the GDP of the mining sector increased, in real terms, at an average annual rate of 20.0% during 2001–10; growth in the mining sector's GDP increased by 20.0% in 2009 and by 28.0% in 2010.

Manufacturing contributed 15.9% of GDP in 2010, according to the ADB, and employed 11.3% of the labour force in 2007, according to the IMF. The sector is dominated by rice milling and the production of garments, household goods, textiles, tyres and pharmaceutical products. The manufacture of clothing, mostly for export, grew rapidly from the mid-1990s, and in late 2008 approximately 350,000 workers were engaged in garment manufacture. The total value of garment exports increased from US $1,144m. in 2001 to $2,943m. in 2007. According to ADB figures, the GDP of the manufacturing sector increased, in real terms, at an average annual rate of 10.1% during 2001–10. Manufacturing GDP declined by 15.5% in 2009, but grew by 29.5% in 2010.

According to the ADB, construction contributed 6.1% of GDP in 2010. The sector engaged 3.6% of the employed labour force in 2007, according to the IMF. During 2001–10, according to figures from the ADB, the GDP of the sector increased at an average annual rate of 8.4%; sectoral GDP increased by 5.0% in 2009, but decreased by 25.5% in 2010.

Household energy is derived principally from timber. Most commercial energy used in Cambodia is imported. In 2008 only 20% of Cambodian households had access to electricity. Cambodia has significant hydropower potential. In 2008 petroleum accounted for 96.5% of electricity output. Imports of petroleum products accounted for 7.6% of the cost of total merchandise imports in 2008.

The services sector contributed 41.0% of GDP in 2010, according to the ADB, and engaged 28.7% of the economically active population in 2007, according to the IMF. The tourism sector has become increasingly significant since 2000. Foreign tourist arrivals rose by 14.9% to reach 2.9m. in 2011, when receipts amounted to US $1,912m. In real terms, the GDP of the services sector increased at an average annual rate of 8.5% during 2001–10, according to data from the ADB. The sector's rate of growth reached 3.3% in 2010 and 5.0% in 2011.

In 2009 Cambodia recorded a visible trade deficit of US $1,573.9m., while there was a deficit of $865.6m. on the current account of the balance of payments. In 2010, according to the ADB, the principal source of imports was Thailand (27.1%). Other major sources were Singapore, the People's Republic of China, Hong Kong and Viet Nam. In the same year the principal market for exports was the USA (47.8%); other important purchasers were Canada, the United Kingdom and Germany. The principal exports in 2007 were garments (accounting for about three-quarters of the total), rice, rubber and fish, along with logs and sawn timber. The country's imports included petroleum products, vehicles, cigarettes, motorcycles, cement and clothing.

According to IMF estimates, Cambodia's overall budget deficit in 2010 was projected at 2,584m. riels. Cambodia's general government gross debt was 14,283,760m. riels in 2010, equivalent to 29.9% of GDP. The Cambodia Development Cooperation Forum (CDCF), which superseded the Consultative Group of international donors in 2007, has continued to provide support (see Contemporary Political History). According to the ADB, Cambodia's external public debt was estimated at US $3,611m. at the end of 2011. In that year the cost of servicing external public debt was equivalent to 1.2% of the value of exports of goods and services. The annual rate of inflation in Phnom-Penh averaged 6.2% during 2001–08. Consumer prices declined by 0.7% in 2009 but increased by 4.0% in 2010 and by 5.5% in 2011, according to the ADB. The unemployment rate was estimated at 7.1% in 2004.

The Cambodian economy has remained narrowly based on the tourism and garment industries, both of which were adversely affected by the global recession of 2008/09. The Government introduced various measures to counter the economic downturn, including tax concessions for the tourism sector and for garment manufacturers. However, its attempts to reduce levels of poverty, particularly in rural areas, were impeded by an unexpectedly sharp rise (of 25%) in consumer prices in 2008 and by the ensuing adverse economic conditions. Inflationary pressures subsided in 2009 but re-emerged in 2010–11, as the costs of food and fuel again increased; inflation was forecast to reach 5% in 2012. As plans for the exploitation of Cambodia's petroleum reserves proceeded, analysts continued to express doubts with regard to the future administration of income from these resources. Having decreased by more than 20% in 2009, the value of exports of Cambodian garments to the USA rose by 19% in 2010. The garment sector remained a leading recipient of investment finance. According to the World Bank, total foreign direct investment increased from US $530.2m. in 2009 to $782.6m. in 2010. Light industry was further encouraged by the establishment of special economic zones. Cambodia's long-awaited inaugural stock exchange—the Cambodia Securities Exchange—was launched in July 2011, representing an important step forward in the development of the country's financial sector; trading on the exchange, which was 55% owned by the Cambodian Government and 45% owned by the South Korean stock exchange, commenced in April 2012. In December 2011 the ADB announced the provision of a $15m. loan intended to promote further reform of the Cambodian financial sector. Following the resumption of robust growth in 2010, GDP increased by 6.8% in 2011, underpinned by strong increases in exports of garments, footwear and milled rice and a rise in tourist arrivals; the ADB forecast growth of 6.5% for 2012. However, observers noted that, in order to achieve sustained growth in the coming years, Cambodia would have to diversify its economy; overcome serious infrastructural shortcomings; promote private sector investment and encourage public-private partnerships; and improve economic and financial competitiveness, in part by addressing widespread governance issues.

PUBLIC HOLIDAYS

2013 (provisional): 1 January (International New Year's Day), 7 January (Victory Day over the Genocide Regime), 25 February (Meak Bochea Day), 8 March (International Women's Day), 13 April (Cambodian New Year), 1 May (Labour Day), 9 May (Royal Ploughing Ceremony), 13 May (King Sihamoni's Birthday), 25 May (Visaka Buchea Day), 3 June (for International Children's Day), 18 June (Former Queen's Birthday), 24 September (Constitution Day), 14 October (Bonn Pchum Ben), 29 October (Anniversary of Coronation of King Sihamoni), 31 October (Former King Sihanouk's Birthday), 11 November (for Independence Day), 27 November (Water Festival), 10 December (Human Rights Day).

Statistical Survey

Source (unless otherwise stated): National Institute of Statistics, Ministry of Planning, Sangkat Boeung Keng Kang 1, blvd Monivong, Phnom-Penh; tel. (23) 216538; fax (23) 213650; e-mail census@camnet.com.kh; internet www.nis.gov.kh.

Area and Population

AREA, POPULATION AND DENSITY

Area (sq km)	181,035*
Population (census results)†	
3 March 1998	11,437,656
3 March 2008	
Males	6,516,054
Females	6,879,628
Total	13,395,682
Population (UN estimates at mid-year)‡	
2010	14,138,255
2011	14,305,182
2012	14,478,320
Density (per sq km) at mid-2012	80.0

* 69,898 sq miles; figure includes Tonlé Sap lake (approx. 3,000 sq km).
† Excluding adjustments for underenumeration.
‡ Source: UN, *World Population Prospects: The 2010 Revision*.

POPULATION BY AGE AND SEX

(UN estimates at mid-2012)

	Males	Females	Total
0–14	2,263,491	2,173,010	4,436,501
15–64	4,612,131	4,842,840	9,454,971
65 and over	216,793	370,055	586,848
Total	7,092,415	7,385,905	14,478,320

Source: UN, *World Population Prospects: The 2010 Revision*.

PROVINCES

(population at 2008 census)

	Area (sq km)*	Population	Density (per sq km)
Banteay Meanchey	6,679	677,872	101.5
Battambang	11,702	1,025,174	87.6
Kampong Cham	9,799	1,679,992	171.4
Kampong Chhnang	5,521	472,341	85.6
Kampong Spueu	7,017	716,944	102.2
Kampong Thom	13,814	631,409	45.7
Kampot	4,873	585,850	120.2
Kandal	3,568	1,265,280	354.6
Kep	336	35,753	106.4
Koh Kong	11,160	117,481	10.5
Kratie	11,094	319,217	28.8
Mondul Kiri	14,288	61,107	4.3
Oddar Meanchey	6,158	185,819	30.2
Pailin	803	70,486	87.8
Phnom-Penh	290	1,327,615	4,578.0
Preah Vihear	13,788	171,139	12.4
Prey Veng	4,883	947,372	194.0
Pursat	12,692	397,161	31.3
Ratanak Kiri	10,782	150,466	14.0
Siem Reap	10,299	896,443	87.0
Sihanoukville (Preah Sihanouk)	868	221,396	255.1
Stung Treng	11,092	111,671	10.1
Svay Rieng	2,966	482,788	162.8
Takeo	3,563	844,906	237.1
Total	178,035	13,395,682	75.2

* Excluding Tonlé Sap lake (approx. 3,000 sq km).

PRINCIPAL TOWNS

(population at 1998 census)

Phnom-Penh (capital)	999,804	Bat Dambang (Battambang)	139,964
Preah Sihanouk (Sihanoukville)*	155,690	Siem Reab (Siem Reap)	119,528

* Also known as Kampong Saom (Kompong Som).

Mid-2010 ('000, incl. suburbs, UN estimate): Phnom-Penh 1,562,498 (Source: UN, *World Urbanization Prospects: The 2009 Revision*).

BIRTHS AND DEATHS

(annual averages, UN estimates)

	1995–2000	2000–05	2005–10
Birth rate (per 1,000)	30.3	25.1	23.3
Death rate (per 1,000)	10.2	9.1	8.3

Source: UN, *World Population Prospects: The 2010 Revision*.

2004: Live births 384,267; Deaths 124,391 (Source: UN, *Population and Vital Statistics Report*).

Life expectancy (years at birth, WHO estimates): 61 (males 57; females 65) in 2009 (Source: WHO, *World Health Statistics*).

EMPLOYMENT

('000 persons)

	2005	2006	2007
Agriculture, forestry and fishing	4,655	4,619	4,670
Mining and quarrying	19	20	22
Manufacturing	789	870	944
Electricity, gas and water	17	19	21
Construction	234	260	299
Wholesale and retail trade	1,104	1,140	1,196
Restaurants and hotels	43	61	86
Transport and communications	206	217	228
Financial intermediation	23	32	32
Real estate and renting	16	18	20
Public administration	185	184	185
Education	113	120	128
Health and social work	43	49	57
Other social services	89	108	123
Other services	341	336	343
Total employed	7,878	8,053	8,354

Source: IMF, *Cambodia: Statistical Appendix* (February 2009).

2010 ('000 persons): Agriculture 5,122.7; Manufacturing 599.5; Mining 49.6; Others 1,314.5; *Total employed* 7,086.3 (Source: Asian Development Bank).

Health and Welfare

KEY INDICATORS

Total fertility rate (children per woman, 2009)	2.9
Under-5 mortality rate (per 1,000 live births, 2009)	88
HIV/AIDS (% of persons aged 15–49, 2009)	0.5
Physicians (per 1,000 head, 2000)	0.2
Hospital beds (per 1,000 head, 2004)	0.1
Health expenditure (2008): US $ per head (PPP)	118
Health expenditure (2008): % of GDP	5.7
Health expenditure (2008): public (% of total)	23.8
Access to water (% of persons, 2008)	61
Access to sanitation (% of persons, 2008)	29
Total carbon dioxide emissions ('000 metric tons, 2007)	4,437.1
Carbon dioxide emissions per head (metric tons, 2007)	0.3
Human Development Index (2011): ranking	139
Human Development Index (2011): value	0.523

For sources and definitions, see explanatory note on p. vi.

Agriculture

PRINCIPAL CROPS
('000 metric tons)

	2008	2009	2010
Rice, paddy	7,175.5	7,586.0*	8,245.3
Maize	611.9	924.0*	1,411.5
Sweet potatoes	39.6	78.9	79.4
Cassava (Manioc)	3,676.2	3,497.3*	4,247.4
Beans, dry	38.6	44.6	71.2
Soybeans (Soya beans)	108.4	137.3	156.6
Groundnuts, with shell	25.5	21.8	22.0
Sesame seed	27.3	34.5	29.9
Coconuts	70.9*	71.0†	76.4†
Sugar cane*	385.2	350.0	365.6
Tobacco, unmanufactured	17.4	13.5	14.6
Natural rubber	31.7	37.4	37.5†
Oranges†	55.7	50.4	53.0
Guavas, mangoes and mangosteens†	59.0	58.6	56.0
Pineapples†	22.9	22.6	22.0
Bananas†	130.0	130.0	159.0

* Unofficial figure(s).
† FAO estimate(s).

Aggregate production ('000 metric tons, may include official, semi-official or estimated data): Total cereals 7,787.3 in 2008, 8,510.0 in 2009, 9,656.9 in 2010; Total roots and tubers 3,753.1 in 2008, 3,615.9 in 2009, 4,370.0 in 2010; Total vegetables (incl. melons) 460.4 in 2008; 468.7 in 2009, 480.3 in 2010; Total fruits (excl. melons) 347.9 in 2008; 343.9 in 2009; 355.9 in 2010.

Source: FAO.

LIVESTOCK
('000 head, year ending September)

	2008	2009	2010
Horses*	28	28	28
Cattle	3,458	3,589	3,484
Buffaloes	746	740	702
Pigs	2,216	2,126	2,057
Chickens	16,928	17,000*	17448
Ducks*	7,000	7,000	7000

* FAO estimate(s).

Source: FAO.

LIVESTOCK PRODUCTS
('000 metric tons, FAO estimates)

	2008	2009	2010
Cattle meat	62.4	64.7	62.9
Buffalo meat	10.4	10.3	9.8
Pig meat	110.0	105.0	100.0
Chicken meat	19.0	19.0	19.5
Cows' milk	23.8	24.5	27.0
Hen eggs	16.8	15.8	17.6
Other poultry eggs	3.8	3.8	4.8

Source: FAO.

Forestry

ROUNDWOOD REMOVALS
('000 cubic metres, excl. bark, FAO estimates)

	2008	2009	2010
Sawlogs, veneer logs and logs for sleepers	105	105	70
Other industrial wood	13	13	13
Fuel wood	8,735	8,586	8,586
Total	8,853	8,704	8,668

Source: FAO.

SAWNWOOD PRODUCTION
('000 cubic metres, incl. railway sleepers)

	2006	2007	2008
Total (all broadleaved)	2	4	10

2009–10: Production assumed to be unchanged from 2008 (FAO estimate).

Source: FAO.

Fishing

('000 metric tons, live weight)

	2007*	2008	2009
Capture	458.5	431.0	465.0
Freshwater fishes	394.5	364.6	389.7
Marine fishes	41.5	45.3	55.4
Natantian decapods	12.4	11.0	7.0
Aquaculture*	35.3	40.0	50.0
Total catch*	493.7	471.0	515.0

* FAO estimates.

Note: Figures exclude crocodiles, recorded by number rather than by weight. The total number of estuarine crocodiles caught was: 128,945 in 2007; 156,500 in 2008; 185,000 in 2009. Also excluded are aquatic plants.

Source: FAO.

Mining

('000 metric tons)

	2007	2008	2009
Gravel	36.3	37.5*	41.8
Limestone*	1,000.0	1,000.0	1,000.0
Sand (construction material)	329.0	6,581.5	14,035.8
Salt (unrefined)	76.7	78.0*	n.a.

* Estimate(s).

Source: US Geological Survey.

Industry

SELECTED PRODUCTS

	2007	2008	2009
Plywood ('000 cu m)*†	12	12	12
Electric energy (million kWh)‡	1,349.3	1,484.1	1,234.6

* Source: FAO.
† FAO estimates.
‡ Source: Electricity Authority of Cambodia.

2010: Plywood ('000 cu m) 5 (FAO estimate).

Finance

CURRENCY AND EXCHANGE RATES

Monetary Units
100 sen = 1 riel.

Sterling, Dollar and Euro Equivalents (30 November 2011)
£1 sterling = 6,297.8 riels;
US $1 = 4,035.0 riels;
€1 = 5,414.2 riels;
10,000 riels = £1.59 = $2.48 = €1.85.

Average Exchange Rate (riels per US $)
2008 4,054.17
2009 4,139.33
2010 4,184.92

BUDGET
('000 million riels)

Revenue	2006	2007	2008*
Tax revenue	2,372	3,343	3,241
Direct taxes	331	480	486
Trade tax	644	903	858
Value-added tax	836	1,093	1,120
Excise duties	418	617	587
Non-tax revenue	681	705	710
Forestry	2	0	10
Quota auction/garment licences, etc.	88	118	90
Tourism income	59	78	118
Casino royalties	77	75	69
Posts and telecommunications	83	78	61
Passports and visas	95	122	132
Capital revenue	377	117	157
Total	3,431	4,165	4,109

Expenditure	2006	2007	2008*
Current expenditure	2,527	3,043	3,569
Salaries	975	1,058	1,242
Operating costs	974	1,129	945
Economic transfers	137	65	73
Social transfers	34	501	441
Interest	50	70	75
Provincial expenditure	220	220	207
Other current expenditure	176	1	586
Statistical discrepancy	–39	—	—
Capital expenditure	1,716	2,121	2,111
Locally financed	381	436	711
Externally financed	1,336	1,682	1,400
Total	4,244	5,164	5,680

* Budget projections.

Source: IMF, *Cambodia: Statistical Appendix* (February 2009).

2008 ('000 million riels): *Revenue:* Tax revenue 4,494 (Direct taxes 654, Indirect taxes 3,433, Provincial taxes 259, Other 148); Non-tax revenue 769; Capital revenue 200; Total 5,463. *Expenditure:* Current expenditure 4,097 (Wages 1,438, Non-wage 2,311, Provincial expenditure 347); Capital expenditure 2,654; Total 6,751 (Source: IMF, *Cambodia: 2010 Article IV Consultation—Staff Report; Staff Supplement; Public Information Notice on the Executive Board Discussion; and Statement by the Executive Director*—February 2011).

2009 ('000 million riels, budget figures): *Revenue:* Tax revenue 4,177 (Direct taxes 746, Indirect taxes 3,300, Provincial taxes 131); Non-tax revenue 870; Capital revenue 135; Total 5,182. *Expenditure:* Current expenditure 4,663 (Wages 1,730, Non-wage 2,577, Provincial expenditure 357); Capital expenditure 2,759; Total 7,422 (Source: IMF, *Cambodia: 2010 Article IV Consultation—Staff Report; Staff Supplement; Public Information Notice on the Executive Board Discussion; and Statement by the Executive Director*—February 2011).

2010 ('000 million riels, budget figures): *Revenue:* Tax revenue 4,763 (Direct taxes 968, Indirect taxes 3,663, Provincial taxes 131); Non-tax revenue 774; Capital revenue 300; Total 5,837. *Expenditure:* Current expenditure 5,300 (Wages 2,092, Non-wage 2,882, Provincial expenditure 326); Capital expenditure 3,121; Total 8,421 (Source: IMF, *Cambodia: 2010 Article IV Consultation—Staff Report; Staff Supplement; Public Information Notice on the Executive Board Discussion; and Statement by the Executive Director*—February 2011).

INTERNATIONAL RESERVES
(US $ million at 31 December)

	2008	2009	2010
Gold (national valuation)	349.01	437.32	547.01
IMF special drawing rights	0.11	107.39	105.43
Foreign exchange	2,291.44	2,743.74	3,149.68
Total	2,640.56	3,288.45	3,802.12

Source: IMF, *International Financial Statistics*.

MONEY SUPPLY
('000 million riels at 31 December)

	2008	2009	2010
Currency outside depository corporations	2,305.00	3,008.57	3,103.56
Transferable deposits	2,241.74	2,572.67	3,030.17
Other deposits	7,355.51	10,556.17	13,440.93
Broad money	11,902.26	16,137.41	19,574.66

Source: IMF, *International Financial Statistics*.

COST OF LIVING
(Consumer Price Index for Phnom-Penh at January; base: October-December 2006 = 100)

	2009	2010	2011
Food and non-alcoholic beverages	137.6	148.4	153.8
Clothing and footwear	109.5	112.8	115.0
Housing and utilities	113.4	118.8	122.1
Household furnishings, etc.	115.2	120.8	122.6
Medical care and health expenses	109.7	115.1	116.7
Transport	101.8	116.1	121.4
Communication	76.3	72.9	73.8
Recreation and culture	104.0	103.9	103.4
Education	131.6	139.4	140.2
All items	125.4	134.1	138.5

NATIONAL ACCOUNTS
('000 million riels at current prices)

Expenditure on the Gross Domestic Product

	2008	2009	2010
Government final consumption expenditure	2,364.7	3,446.9	3,929.4
Private final consumption expenditure	33,341.4	32,792.1	35,384.5
Change in stocks	566.4	566.4	566.4
Gross fixed capital formation	7,246.7	8,669.9	7,530.6
Total domestic expenditure	43,519.2	45,475.3	47,410.9
Exports of goods and services	27,507.4	25,804.6	31,083.7
Less Imports of goods and services	28,444.9	27,121.8	31,683.8
Statistical discrepancy	–613.4	–1,092.2	–868.3
GDP in purchasers' values	41,968.4	43,065.8	45,942.7
GDP at constant 2000 prices	28,667.5	28,692.4	30,380.8

Gross Domestic Product by Economic Activity

	2008	2009	2010
Agriculture, hunting, forestry and fishing	13,745.1	14,420.0	15,547.0
Mining and quarrying	164.6	195.9	284.0
Manufacturing	6,441.1	6,207.6	6,848.1
Electricity, gas and water	211.9	229.7	251.6
Construction	2,571.5	2,693.7	2,518.6
Trade, hotels and restaurants	5,618.8	5,811.6	6,358.0
Transport, storage and communications	3,102.0	3,223.6	3,433.1
Finance, real estate and other business activities	549.5	594.1	670.1
Public administration	767.8	768.5	806.9
Other services	6,263.0	6,303.9	6,426.3
Sub-total	39,435.3	40,448.6	43,143.7
Less Imputed bank service charge	420.9	471.9	529.1
GDP at factor cost	39,014.4	39,976.7	42,614.6
Indirect taxes, *less* subsidies	2,953.9	3,089.3	3,328.2
GDP in purchasers' values	41,968.4	43,065.8	45,942.7

Source: Asian Development Bank.

BALANCE OF PAYMENTS
(US $ million)

	2007	2008	2009
Exports of goods f.o.b.	4,088.5	4,708.0	4,301.8
Imports of goods f.o.b.	−5,438.9	−6,508.4	−5,875.8
Trade balance	−1,350.4	−1,800.4	−1,573.9
Exports of services	1,547.5	1,645.1	1,624.9
Imports of services	−915.4	−1,035.8	−1,022.4
Balance on goods and services	−718.3	−1,191.1	−971.5
Other income received	112.2	108.4	55.6
Other income paid	−476.2	−583.0	−523.8
Balance on goods, income and services	−1,082.2	−1,665.7	−1,439.7
Current transfers received	620.3	642.8	595.5
Current transfers paid	−25.8	−27.9	−21.3
Current balance	−487.7	−1,050.8	−865.6
Capital account (net)	258.3	232.7	311.6
Direct investment abroad	−1.1	−20.5	−18.8
Direct investment from abroad	867.3	815.2	530.2
Portfolio investment assets	−6.5	−11.6	−7.6
Other investment assets	−780.6	312.4	−346.7
Other investment liabilities	602.4	290.8	533.9
Net errors and omissions	−28.9	−45.9	−34.7
Overall balance	423.2	522.4	102.2

Source: IMF, *International Financial Statistics*.

External Trade

PRINCIPAL COMMODITIES
(US $ million)

Imports c.i.f.	2005	2006	2007
Cigarettes	80	103	108
Petroleum products	164	212	273
Motorcycles	55	93	108
Vehicles	90	105	172
Clothing	45	47	55
Cement	44	53	54
Total (incl. others)	4,230	5,123	5,874

Exports f.o.b.	2005	2006	2007
Crude rubber	119	175	157
Logs and sawn timber	16	18	21
Clothing	2,261	2,727	2,943
Fish	76	90	105
Rice	177	332	411
Total (incl. others)	2,910	3,694	4,089

Note: Totals include imports for re-export and estimates for unrecorded items.

Source: IMF, *Cambodia: Statistical Appendix* (February 2009).

PRINCIPAL TRADING PARTNERS
(US $ million)

Imports c.i.f.	2008	2009	2010
China, People's Republic	934.9	881.3	1,482.0
Hong Kong	589.6	484.2	645.4
Indonesia	96.2	145.5	239.5
Japan	114.7	118.9	174.1
Korea, Republic	229.4	209.1	214.9
Malaysia	122.5	132.0	135.7
Singapore	303.8	209.0	2,436.1
Thailand	696.9	464.8	2,574.4
USA	219.4	90.6	168.9
Viet Nam	471.0	493.5	507.2
Total (incl. others)	4,419.8	3,896.3	9,487.2

Exports f.o.b.	2008	2009	2010
Canada	292.0	195.8	346.6
Germany	138.1	108.8	294.6
Hong Kong	839.9	1,646.3	20.4
Japan	32.1	79.5	190.1
Netherlands	151.5	144.9	55.9
Singapore	113.3	482.3	143.3
Spain	123.7	105.5	109.2
United Kingdom	155.7	179.7	315.0
USA	1,970.9	1,552.8	2,183.6
Viet Nam	169.3	115.5	118.7
Total (incl. others)	5,127.6	4,984.3	4,567.1

Note: Data reflect the IMF's direction of trade methodology and, as a result, the totals may not be equal to those presented for trade in commodities.

Source: Asian Development Bank.

Transport

RAILWAYS
(traffic)

	1997	1998	1999
Freight carried ('000 metric tons)	16	294	259
Freight ton-km ('000)	36,514	75,721	76,171
Passengers ('000)	553	438	431
Passenger-km ('000)	50,992	43,847	49,894

Source: Ministry of Economy and Finance, Phnom-Penh.

2000: Passenger-km (million) 15; Freight ton-km (million) 91 (Source: UN, *Statistical Yearbook*).

2005: Passenger-km (million) 45 (Source: World Bank, World Development Indicators database).

ROAD TRAFFIC
(estimated number of motor vehicles in use)

	2002	2003	2004
Passenger cars	209,128	219,602	235,298
Buses and coaches	3,196	3,269	3,502
Trucks	29,968	30,448	31,946
Other vehicles	421	428	440
Motorcycles and mopeds	586,278	619,748	646,944

Sources: Ministry of Public Works and Transport, Phnom-Penh, and Phnom-Penh Municipal Traffic Police.

SHIPPING

Merchant Fleet
(registered at 31 December)

	2007	2008	2009
Number of vessels	881	939	963
Displacement ('000 grt)	2,059.8	2,096.2	1,963.9

Source: IHS Fairplay, *World Fleet Statistics*.

International Sea-borne Freight Traffic
(estimates, '000 metric tons)

	1988	1989	1990
Goods loaded	10	10	11
Goods unloaded	100	100	95

Source: UN, *Monthly Bulletin of Statistics*.

Tourism

FOREIGN TOURIST ARRIVALS BY COUNTRY OF RESIDENCE

Country of residence	2008	2009	2010
Australia	99,087	96,678	93,588
Canada	36,891	36,340	38,718
China, People's Repub.	129,626	128,210	177,636
France	97,517	105,437	113,285
Germany	59,903	59,916	62,864
Japan	163,806	146,286	151,795
Korea, Republic	266,525	197,725	289,702
Malaysia	80,738	77,759	89,952
Philippines	39,294	49,079	56,156
Singapore	40,945	41,273	45,709
Taiwan	83,000	72,119	91,229
Thailand	109,020	102,018	96,277
United Kingdom	98,093	106,837	103,087
USA	145,079	148,482	146,005
Viet Nam	209,516	316,202	466,695
Total (incl. others)	2,125,465	2,161,577	2,508,289

Tourism receipts (US $ million, incl. passenger transport): 1,595 in 2008, 1,561 in 2009, 1,786 in 2010.

Source: Ministry of Tourism, Phnom-Penh.

Communications Media

	2008	2009	2010
Telephones ('000 main lines in use)	43.1	54.2	358.8
Mobile cellular telephones ('000 subscribers)	4,237.0	6,268.0	8,150.8
Internet subscribers ('000)	19.1	n.a.	n.a.
Broadband subscribers ('000)	16.6	30.0	35.7

Personal computers: 52,000 (3.6 per 1,000 persons) in 2007.

Television receivers ('000 in use): 98 in 1999; 99 in 2000.

Radio receivers ('000 in use): 1,120 in 1995; 1,300 in 1996; 1,340 in 1997.

Sources: UNESCO, *Statistical Yearbook* and International Telecommunication Union.

Education

(2009/10 unless otherwise indicated)

	Institutions*	Teachers	Students		
			Males	Females	Total
Pre-primary	n.a.	5,211†	57,499	57,459	114,958
Primary	5,915	48,223†	1,186,561	1,085,966	2,272,527
Secondary	594	30,258‡	488,683‡	386,437‡	875,120‡
General	411	27,856‡	497,402	428,386	925,788
Vocational	183	2,402‡	10,080‡	8,840‡	18,920‡
Tertiary†	n.a.	6,086	80,505	42,128	122,633

* 2002/03 data.
† 2007/08 data.
‡ 2006/07 data.

Sources: IMF, *Cambodia: Statistical Appendix* (October 2004); UNESCO Institute for Statistics.

Pupil-teacher ratio (primary education, UNESCO estimate): 48.4 in 2009/10 (Source: UNESCO Institute for Statistics).

Adult literacy rate (UNESCO estimates): 77.6% (males 85.1%; females 70.9%) in 2008 (Source: UNESCO Institute for Statistics).

Directory

The Government

HEAD OF STATE

King: HM King Norodom Sihamoni (appointed by the Royal Council of the Throne on 14 October 2004).

ROYAL GOVERNMENT OF CAMBODIA

(May 2012)

A coalition of the Cambodian People's Party (CPP) and the FUNCINPEC Party.

Prime Minister: Hun Sen (CPP).

Permanent Deputy Prime Minister and Minister of National Assembly-Senate Relations and Inspection: Men Sam On (CPP).

Deputy Prime Minister and Minister of Economy and Finance: Keat Chhon (CPP).

Deputy Prime Minister and Minister of the Interior: Sar Kheng (CPP).

Deputy Prime Minister and Minister of National Defence: Gen. Tea Banh (CPP).

Deputy Prime Minister and Minister of Foreign Affairs and International Co-operation: Hor Nam Hong (CPP).

Deputy Prime Minister and Minister in Charge of the Council of Ministers: Dr Sok An (CPP).

Deputy Prime Minister and Minister of Royal Palace Affairs: Kong Sam Ol (CPP).

Deputy Prime Ministers without Portfolio: Gen. Nhiek Bun Chhay (FUNCINPEC), Yim Chhay Ly (CPP), Bin Chhin (CPP), Ke Kimyan.

Senior Ministers: Cham Prasidh (CPP), Chhay Thon (CPP), Keat Chhon (CPP), Im Chhun Lim (CPP), Dr Mok Mareth (CPP), Nhim Vannda (CPP), Tav Senghuo (CPP), Om Yintieng (FUNCINPEC), Khun Haing (FUNCINPEC), Nuth Sokhom (CPP), Kol Pheng (FUNCINPEC), Sun Chanthol (FUNCINPEC), Veng Sereivuth (FUNCINPEC), Ly Thuch (FUNCINPEC), Serei Kosal (FUNCINPEC).

Minister of Agriculture, Forestry and Fisheries: Dr Chan Sarun (CPP).

Minister of Commerce: Cham Prasidh (CPP).

Minister of Culture and Fine Arts: Him Chaem (CPP).

Minister of Education, Youth and Sport: Im Sithy (CPP).

Minister of Environment: Dr Mok Mareth (CPP).

Minister of Health: Mam Bun Heng (CPP).

Minister of Industry, Mines and Energy: Suy Sem (CPP).

Minister of Information: Kieu Kanharith (CPP).

Minister of Justice: Ang Vong Vathna (CPP).

Minister of Labour and Vocational Training: Vorng Soth (CPP).

Minister of Land Management, Urban Planning and Construction: Im Chhun Lim (CPP).

Minister of Planning: Chhay Than (CPP).

Minister of Posts and Telecommunications: So Khun (CPP).

Minister of Public Works and Transport: Tram Eav Toek (CPP).

Minister of Religions and Cults: MIN KHIN (CPP).

Minister of Rural Development: CHEA SOPHARA (CPP).

Minister of Social Affairs, Veterans and Youth Rehabilitation: ITH SAM HENG (CPP).

Minister of Tourism: THONG KHON (CPP).

Minister of Water Resources and Meteorology: LIM KEAN HOR (CPP).

Minister of Women's Affairs: Dr OENG KANTHA PHAVY (FUNCINPEC).

Secretary of State for Public Functions: PECH BUN THIN (CPP).

Secretary of State for Civil Aviation: MAO HAS VANNAL (FUNCINPEC).

MINISTRIES

Office of the Council of Ministers: 41 blvd Confédération de la Russie, Sangkat Toeuk Thla, Khan Sen Sok, Phnom-Penh; tel. (12) 804442; fax (23) 880624; e-mail ocm@cambodia.gov.kh; internet www.cambodia.gov.kh.

Ministry of Agriculture, Forestry and Fisheries: 200 blvd Norodom, Sangkat Tonle Bassac, Khan Chamkarmon, Phnom-Penh 12301; tel. (23) 211351; fax (23) 217320; e-mail info@maff.gov.kh; internet www.maff.gov.kh.

Ministry of Commerce: blvd Confédération de la Russie, Sangkat Toeuk Thla, Khan Sen Sok, Phnom-Penh; tel. (23) 866088; fax (23) 866188; e-mail moccab@moc.gov.kh; internet www.moc.gov.kh.

Ministry of Culture and Fine Arts: 227 blvd Norodom, Phnom-Penh; tel. and fax (23) 218148; e-mail info@mcfa.gov.kh; internet www.mcfa.gov.kh.

Ministry of Economy and Finance: 60 rue 92, Sangkat Wat Phnom, Khan Duan Penh, Phnom-Penh; tel. (23) 724664; fax (23) 427798; e-mail admin@mef.gov.kh; internet www.mef.gov.kh.

Ministry of Education, Youth and Sport: 80 blvd Preah Norodom, Phnom-Penh; tel. and fax (23) 210134; e-mail info@moeys.gov.kh; internet www.moeys.gov.kh.

Ministry of Environment: 48 blvd Sihanouk, Sangkat Tonle Bassac, Khan Chamkarmon, Phnom-Penh; tel. (23) 427894; fax (23) 427844; e-mail moe-cabinet@camnet.com.kh; internet www.camnet.com.kh/moe.

Ministry of Foreign Affairs and International Co-operation: 3 rue Samdech Hun Sen, Sangkat Tonle Bassac, Khan Chamkarmon, Phnom-Penh; tel. (23) 214441; fax (23) 216144; e-mail mfaic@mfa.gov.kh; internet www.mfaic.gov.kh.

Ministry of Health: 151–153 blvd Kampuchea Krom, Phnom-Penh; tel. (23) 722873; fax (23) 426841; e-mail webmaster@moh.gov.kh; internet www.moh.gov.kh.

Ministry of Industry, Mines and Energy: 45 blvd Preah Norodom, Khan Duan Penh, Phnom-Penh; tel. (23) 211141; fax (23) 428263; e-mail info@mime.gov.kh; internet www.mime.gov.kh.

Ministry of Information: 62 blvd Monivong, Phnom-Penh; tel. and fax (23) 430514; e-mail info@information.gov.kh; internet www.information.gov.kh.

Ministry of the Interior: 275 blvd Norodom, Khan Chamkarmon, Phnom-Penh; tel. (23) 721190; fax (23) 726052; e-mail info@interior.gov.kh; internet www.interior.gov.kh.

Ministry of Justice: 240 blvd Sothearos, Phnom-Penh; tel. (23) 360327; fax (23) 364119; e-mail moj@cambodia.gov.kh; internet www.moj.gov.kh.

Ministry of Labour and Vocational Training: 3 blvd Confédération de la Russie, Sangkat Toeuk Thla, Khan Sen Sok, Phnom-Penh; tel. (23) 884375; e-mail mlv@cambodia.gov.kh; internet www.mlv.gov.kh.

Ministry of Land Management, Urban Planning and Construction: 771–773 blvd Monivong, Boeung Trabek, Khan Chamkarmon, Phnom-Penh; tel. (23) 880780; e-mail mlmupc@camnet.com.kh; internet www.mlmupc.gov.kh.

Ministry of National Assembly-Senate Relations and Inspection: rue Jawaharlal Nehru 215, Phnom-Penh; tel. (23) 884261; fax (23) 884264; e-mail mnasrl@cambodia.gov.kh.

Ministry of National Defence: blvd Confédération de la Russie, cnr rue 175, Sangkat Toeuk Thla, Khan Sen Sok, Phnom-Penh; tel. and fax (23) 883184; e-mail info@mond.gov.kh; internet www.mond.gov.kh.

Ministry of Planning: 386 blvd Monivong, Sangkat Boeung Keng Kang 1, Phnom-Penh; tel. (23) 212049; fax (23) 210698; e-mail mop@cambodia.gov.kh; internet www.mop.gov.kh.

Ministry of Posts and Telecommunications: Sangkat Wat Phnom, cnr rues 13 & 102, Phnom-Penh; tel. (23) 426510; fax (23) 426011; e-mail mptc@cambodia.gov.kh; internet www.mptc.gov.kh.

Ministry of Public Works and Transport: cnr blvd Norodom, rue 106, Phnom-Penh; tel. (23) 427845; e-mail mpwt@online.com.kh; internet www.mpwt.gov.kh.

Ministry of Religions and Cults: Preah Sisowath Quay, cnr rue 240, Phnom-Penh; tel. (23) 725099; fax (23) 725699; e-mail morac@cambodia.gov.kh; internet www.morac.gov.kh.

Ministry of Rural Development: blvd Confédération de la Russie, cnr rue 169, Sangkat Toeuk Thla, Khan Sen Sok, Phnom-Penh; tel. and fax (23) 880007; e-mail mrd@cambodia.gov.kh; internet www.mrd.gov.kh.

Ministry of Social Affairs, Veterans and Youth Rehabilitation: 788B blvd Monivong, Phnom-Penh; tel. (23) 726103; fax (23) 726086; internet www.mosvy.gov.kh.

Ministry of Tourism: 3 blvd Monivong, Phnom-Penh 12258; tel. (23) 213741; fax (23) 220704; e-mail admin@mot.gov.kh; internet www.mot.gov.kh.

Ministry of Water Resources and Meteorology: 47 blvd Norodom, Phnom-Penh; tel. (23) 724289; fax (23) 426345; e-mail mowram@cambodia.gov.kh; internet www.mowram.org/temp.

Ministry of Women's Affairs: rue 47, Sangkat Sras Chork, Khan Daun Penh, Phnom-Penh; tel. (23) 430992; e-mail mwva@online.com.kh.

Legislature

PARLIAMENT

National Assembly

blvd Samdech Sothearos, cnr rue 240, Phnom-Penh; tel. (23) 214136; fax (23) 217769; e-mail kimhenglong@cambodian-parliament.org; internet www.national-assembly.org.kh.

Chairman: HENG SAMRIN.

Election, 27 July 2008

	% of votes	Seats
Cambodian People's Party	58.11	90
Sam Rainsy Party	21.91	26
Human Rights Party	6.62	3
FUNCINPEC Party	5.05	2
Norodom Ranariddh Party	5.62	2
Total	100.00*	123

* Including others.

Senate

Chamkarmon State Bldg, blvd Norodom, Phnom-Penh; tel. (23) 211441; fax (23) 211446; e-mail info@senate.gov.kh; internet www.senate.gov.kh.

President: CHEA SIM (CPP).

First Vice-President: SAY CHHUM (CPP).

Second Vice-President: TEP NGORN (CPP).

Election, 29 January 2012

	Seats
Cambodian People's Party	46
Sam Rainsy Party	11
King's appointees	2
National Assembly's appointees	2
Total	61

Note: 57 of the 61 Senators were chosen by means of an electoral college system.

Election Commission

National Election Committee (NEC): blvd Preah Norodom, Khan Chamkarmon, Phnom-Penh; tel. (12) 855018; fax (23) 214374; e-mail necinfo@forum.org.kh; internet www.necelect.org.kh; independent body, appointed by royal decree; Chair. IM SUOSDEY.

Political Organizations

Cambodian People's Party (CPP) (Kanakpak Pracheachon Kampuchea): 203 blvd Norodom, Sangkat Tonle Bassac, Khan Chamkarmon, Phnom-Penh; tel. and fax (23) 215801; e-mail cpp@camnet.com.kh; internet www.thecpp.org; f. 1951; known as the Kampuchean People's Revolutionary Party (KPRP) 1979–91; name changed as above in 1991; 30-mem. Standing Cttee of the Cen. Cttee; Cen. Cttee of 268 full mems; Hon. Chair. of Cen. Cttee HENG SAMRIN; Chair. of Cen. Cttee CHEA SIM; Vice-Chair. HUN SEN; Chair. of Permanent Cttee SAY CHHUM.

Solidarity Front for Development of the Cambodian Motherland (SFDCM): Phnom-Penh; f. 1978; est. as Kampuchean National United Front for National Salvation (KNUFNS); name changed to Kampuchean United Front for National Construction and Defence (KUFNCD) in 1981, and to United Front for the Construction and Defence of the Kampuchean Fatherland (UFCDKF) in 1989; present name adopted in 2006; mass org. supporting policies of the CPP; an 89-mem. Nat. Council and a seven-mem. hon. Presidium; Chair. of Nat. Council HENG SAMRIN; Gen. Sec. of Nat. Council MIN KHIN.

Farmers' Party: 21 rue 528, Sangkat Boeung Kak I, Khan Chamkarmon, Phnom-Penh; tel. (16) 333200; Pres. PON PISITH.

FUNCINPEC Party (United National Front for an Independent, Neutral, Peaceful and Co-operative Cambodia Party): 11 blvd Monivong (93), Sangkat Sras Chak, Khan Daun Penh, BP 1444, Phnom-Penh; tel. (23) 428864; fax (23) 218547; e-mail funcinpec@funcinpec.org; FUNCINPEC altered its title to the FUNCINPEC Party when it adopted political status in 1992; the party's military wing was the National Army of Independent Cambodia (fmrly the Armée Nationale Sihanoukiste—ANS); merged with the Son Sann Party in Jan. 1999; Pres. KEO PUTH RASMEY; Sec.-Gen. Gen. NHIEK BUN CHHAY.

Hang Dara Movement Democratic Party: 16 rue 430, Sangkat Phsar Doeum Thkov, Khan Chamkarmon, Phnom-Penh; tel. (12) 672007; f. 2002; breakaway faction of the FUNCINPEC Party; Pres. HANG DARA.

Human Rights Party (HRP): 72–74 rue 598, Sangkat Boeung Kak II, Khan Tol Kok, Phnom-Penh; tel. (23) 884649; e-mail hrpcambodia@yahoo.com; internet www.hrpcambodia.info; f. 2007; Pres. KEM SOKHA.

Indra Buddra City Party: Commune, Chbarmon District, Kampong Spueu; tel. (12) 710331; Pres. NOREAK RATANAVATHANO.

Khmer Democratic Party (Kanakpak Pracheathippatei Khmer): 79A rue 186, Sangkat Touek Laak III, Khan Tuol Kok, Phnom-Penh; tel. (12) 842947; Pres. OUK PHURIK.

Khmer M'chas Srok (Khmer Sovereign): 14A rue Keo Chea, Phnom-Penh; tel. (23) 62365; fax (23) 27340; e-mail khmer.mchas.srok@gmail.com; internet www.khmer-mchas-srok.org; fmrly Khmer Neutral Party; Pres. SAKHONN CHAK.

Khmer Republican Party (KRP): 282 rue 371, Phoum Obekaam, Sangkat Taek Thla, Khan Russey Keo, Phnom-Penh; tel. (23) 350842; e-mail krp2005@gmail.com; f. 2006; Pres. LON RITH.

League for Democracy Party: 61A rue 608, Sangkat Boeung Kak II, Khan Tuol Kok, Phnom-Penh; tel. (12) 897600; e-mail info@leadparty.org; internet www.camldp.org; f. 2006; Pres. KHEM VEASNA; Sec.-Gen. OK VETH.

Norodom Ranariddh Party (NRP): 27 blvd Mao Tse Toung, Khan Chamkarmon, Phnom-Penh; tel. and fax (11) 559088; fax (23) 218795; e-mail skpstaff@yahoo.com; f. 2002; est. as Khmer Front Party; present name adopted 2006; renamed Nationalist Party late 2008; reverted to present name Dec. 2010; Pres. Prince NORODOM RANARIDDH; Vice-Pres. Prince NORODOM CHAKRAPONG.

Rice Party (Svor): 69 blvd Sothearos, Sangkat Tonle Bassac, Khan Chamkarmon, Phnom-Penh 12301; tel. (11) 860060; e-mail riceparty@asia.com; f. 1992; Pres. NHOUNG SEAP.

Sam Rainsy Party (SRP): 71 blvd Sothearos, Sangkat Tonle Bassac, Khan Chamkarmon, Phnom-Penh; tel. (23) 217452; fax (23) 211336; e-mail srphq@online.com.kh; internet www.samrainsyparty.org; f. 1995; est. as Khmer Nation Party; present name adopted 1998; Pres. SAM RAINSY; Sec.-Gen. KE SOVANNROTH.

Sangkum Jatiniyum Front Party: 40 rue 566, Boeung Kak II, Khan Tuol Kok, Phnom-Penh; tel. (12) 762207; internet sjfparty.free.fr; f. 1997; fmrly the Khmer Unity Party; Delegate-Gen. HRH Samdech SISOWATH THOMICO; Sec.-Gen. SUTHER DINA.

Diplomatic Representation

EMBASSIES IN CAMBODIA

Australia: 16B rue Nat. Assembly, Sangkat Tonle Bassac, Khan Chamkarmon, Phnom-Penh; tel. (23) 213470; fax (23) 213413; e-mail australian.embassy.cambodia@dfat.gov.au; internet www.cambodia.embassy.gov.au; Ambassador PENNY RICHARDS.

Brunei: 237 rue Pasteur 51, Sangkat Boeung Keng Kang 1, Khan Chamkarmon, Phnom-Penh; tel. (23) 211457; fax (23) 211456; e-mail brunei@online.com.kh; Ambassador Pengiran Dato' Paduka Haji ABU BAKAR BIN Pengiran Seri Indera Pengiran Haji ISMAIL.

Bulgaria: 227–229 blvd Norodom, Phnom-Penh; tel. (23) 217504; fax (23) 212792; e-mail bulgembpnp@online.com.kh; internet www.mfa.bg/en/39; Chargé d'affaires IVAN PETKOV.

China, People's Republic: 156 blvd Mao Tse Toung, Phnom-Penh; tel. (23) 720920; fax (23) 720922; e-mail chinaemb_kh@mfa.gov.cn; internet kh.china-embassy.org/chn; Ambassador PAN GUANGXUE.

Cuba: 96–98 rue 214, Sangkat Veal Vong, Khan 7 Makara, Phnom-Penh; tel. (23) 213965; fax (23) 217428; e-mail embacambodia1@online.com.kh; internet embacuba.cubaminrex.cu/cambodia; Ambassador JOSÉ RAMÓN RODRIGUEZ VARONA.

France: 1 blvd Monivong, BP 18, Phnom-Penh; tel. (23) 430020; fax (23) 430037; e-mail ambafrance.phnom-penh-amba@diplomatie.gouv.fr; internet www.ambafrance-kh.org; Ambassador CHRISTIAN CONNAN.

Germany: 76–78 rue Yougoslavie (rue 214), BP 60, Phnom-Penh; tel. (23) 216381; fax (23) 427746; e-mail info@phnom-penh.diplo.de; internet www.phnom-penh.diplo.de; Ambassador Dr WOLFGANG MOSER.

India: 5 rue 466, Phnom-Penh; tel. (23) 210912; fax (23) 210914; e-mail embindia@online.com.kh; internet www.indembassyphnompenh.org; Ambassador RAJESH K. SACHDEVA.

Indonesia: 1 rue 466, cnr blvd Norodom, BP 894, Phnom-Penh; tel. (23) 216148; fax (23) 217566; e-mail indoembassy-phnompenh@clickmail.com.kh; internet www.kemlu.go.id/phnompenh; Ambassador SOEHARDJONO SASTROMIHADJO.

Japan: 194 blvd Preah Norodom, Sangkat Tonle Bassac, Khan Chamkarmon, BP 21, Phnom-Penh; tel. (23) 217161; fax (23) 216162; e-mail eojc@online.com.kh; internet www.kh.emb-japan.go.jp; Ambassador MASAFUMI KUROKI.

Korea, Democratic People's Republic: 39 blvd Samdech Suramarith, Phnom-Penh; tel. and fax (15) 217013; Ambassador HONG KI CHOL.

Korea, Republic: 50–52 rue 214, Sangkat Boeung Raing, Khan Daun Penh, BP 2433, Phnom-Penh; tel. (23) 211900; fax (23) 219200; e-mail cambodia@mofat.go.kr; internet khm.mofat.go.kr; Ambassador KIM HAN-SOO.

Laos: 15–17 blvd Mao Tse Toung, Khan Chamkarmon, BP 19, Phnom-Penh; tel. (23) 982632; fax (23) 720907; e-mail laoembpp@camintel.com; Ambassador YASENG LAO.

Malaysia: 5 rue 242, Sangkat Chaktomouk, Khan Daun Penh, Phnom-Penh; tel. (23) 216176; fax (23) 426101; e-mail malppenh@kln.gov.my; internet www.kln.gov.my/web/khm_phnom-penh; Ambassador Datuk Pengiran Haji MOHD TAHIR NASRUDDIN.

Myanmar: 181 blvd Preah Norodom, Sangkat Boeung Keng Kang 1, Khan Chamkarmon, Phnom-Penh; tel. (23) 223761; fax (23) 223763; e-mail mephnompenh@yahoo.com; Ambassador CHO HTUN AUNG.

Pakistan: 45 rue 310, Sangkat Boeung Keng Kang 1, Phnom-Penh; tel. (23) 996890; fax (23) 992113; e-mail parep.cambodia@yahoo.com; internet www.mofa.gov.pk/cambodia; Ambassador FAZAL-UR-RAHMAN KAZI.

Philippines: 15 rue 422, Khan Chamkarmon, Sangkat Tonle Bassac, Phnom-Penh; tel. (23) 222203; fax (23) 215143; e-mail phnompenhpe@ezecom.com.kh; Ambassador NOE A. WONG.

Russia: 213 blvd Samdech Sothearos, Phnom-Penh; tel. (23) 210931; fax (23) 216776; e-mail russemba@gmail.com; internet www.embrusscambodia.mid.ru; Ambassador ALEKSANDR IGNATOV.

Singapore: 129 blvd Preah Norodom, Phnom-Penh; tel. (23) 221875; fax (23) 210862; e-mail singemb_pnh@sgmfa.gov.sg; internet www.mfa.gov.sg/phnompenh; Ambassador S. PREMJITH.

Sweden: POB 68, Phnom-Penh; tel. (23) 212259; fax (23) 212867; e-mail ambassaden.phnompenh@foreign.ministry.se; Ambassador ANNE HÖGLUND.

Thailand: 196 blvd Preah Norodom, Sangkat Tonle Bassac, Khan Chamkarmon, Phnom-Penh; tel. (23) 726306; fax (23) 726303; e-mail thaipnp@mfa.go.th; internet www.thaiembassy.org/phnompenh; Ambassador SOMPONG SANGUANBUN.

United Kingdom: 27–29 rue 75, Sangkat Srah Chak, Khan Daun Penh, Phnom-Penh; tel. (23) 427124; fax (23) 427125; e-mail britemb@online.com.kh; internet ukincambodia.fco.gov.uk/en; Ambassador MARK GOODING.

USA: 1 rue 96, Sangkat Wat Phnom, Khan Daun Penh, Phnom-Penh; tel. (23) 728000; fax (23) 728600; e-mail ACSPhnomPenh@state.gov; internet cambodia.usembassy.gov; Ambassador WILLIAM E. TODD.

Viet Nam: 436 blvd Monivong, Khan Chamkarmon, Phnom-Penh; tel. (23) 726274; fax (23) 726495; e-mail banbientap@mofa.gov.vn; internet www.vietnamembassy-cambodia.org; Ambassador NGO ANH DUNG.

Judicial System

An independent judiciary was established under the 1993 Constitution. A council for legal and judicial reform was created in 2003 to co-ordinate the implementation of reforms. A new criminal law code took effect in December 2010, replacing the penal code implemented by the UN Transitional Authority in Cambodia in 1992. The highest judicial body is the Supreme Council of Magistracy.

Supreme Court: 222 blvd Trasak Phaem, Sangkat Boeung Keng Kang I, Khan Chamkarmon, Phnom-Penh; tel. and fax (23) 212828; Pres. DITH MUNTY.

Religion

The Government of Democratic Kampuchea banned all religious activity in 1975. Under a constitutional amendment of 1989, Buddhism was reinstated as the national religion and was retained as such under the 1993 Constitution.

BUDDHISM

The principal religion of Cambodia is Theravada Buddhism (Buddhism of the 'Tradition of the Elders'), the sacred language of which is Pali. In 2010 about 93% of the population were Buddhists.

Great Supreme Patriarch: Ven. Patriarch TEP VONG.

Supreme Patriarchs: Ven. Patriarch BOU KRY (Thammayut Nikaya sect), Ven. Patriarch NON NGET (Maha Nikaya sect).

CHRISTIANITY

The Roman Catholic Church

Cambodia comprises the Apostolic Vicariate of Phnom-Penh and the Apostolic Prefectures of Battambang and Kampong Cham. At December 2010 the Christian community constituted 2% of the population.

Vicar Apostolic of Phnom-Penh: Rev. OLIVIER SCHMITTHAEUSLER (Titular Bishop of Catabum Castra), 787 blvd Monivong (rue 93), BP 123, Phnom-Penh; tel. and fax (23) 212462; e-mail evecam@forum .org.kh.

ISLAM

Islam is practised by a minority in Cambodia; in 2010 there were an estimated 464,000 Muslims.

The Press

According to Cambodia's Press Law, newspapers, magazines and foreign press agencies are required to register with the Department of Media at the Ministry of Information.

NEWSPAPERS

Areyathor (Civilization): 52 rue Lyuk Lay, Sangkat Chey, Chummneah, Phnom-Penh; tel. (23) 913662; f. 1994; 2 a week; Editor LEANG HI.

Business News: 28B rue 75, Sangkat Sraas Chak, Khan Daun Penh, Phnom-Penh 12201; tel. and fax (23) 990110; e-mail editor@businessnews-bd.com; weekly; English; Editor-in-Chief BALA CHANDRAN.

Cambodge Nouveau: 58 rue 302, Sangkat Boeung Keng Kang 1, Khan Chamkarmon, Phnom-Penh 12302; tel. (23) 214610; e-mail cn@forum.org.kh; internet www.cambodgenouveau.com; f. 1994; monthly; French; politics, economics and business; Editor-in-Chief ALAIN GASCUEL.

Cambodge Soir: 26CD rue 302, Sangkat Boeung Keng Kang 1, Khan Chamkarmon, Phnom-Penh 12302; tel. and fax (23) 362654; e-mail cambodgesoirpnh@online.com.kh; f. 1994; daily; French and Khmer; publ. suspended Sept. 2010; Editor-in-Chief PIERRE GILLETTE.

Cambodia Daily: 129 rue 228, Phnom-Penh; tel. (23) 426602; fax (23) 426573; e-mail aafc@camnet.com.kh; internet www .cambodiadaily.com; f. 1993; Mon.–Sat.; English and Khmer; distributed free of charge within Cambodia; Editor-in-Chief KEVIN DOYLE; Publr BERNARD KRISHER; circ. 3,500.

Cambodia New Vision: BP 158, Phnom-Penh; tel. (23) 219898; fax (23) 360666; e-mail cabinet1b@camnet.com.kh; internet www.cnv .org.kh; f. 1998; official newsletter of the Cambodian Govt.

Cambodia Sin Chew Daily: 107 blvd Josep Broz Tito, rue 214, Sangkat Boeung Prolit, Khan 7 Makara, Phnom-Penh 12258; tel. (23) 212628; fax (23) 211728; e-mail sinchew_daily@online.com.kh; internet www.sinchew-i.com/cambodia; f. 2000; daily; Chinese; Editor CHARLES SHAW.

Chakraval: 3 rue 181, Sangkat Tumnop Teuk, Khan Chamkarmon, Phnom-Penh; tel. (12) 669629; fax (23) 720141; e-mail chakraval@hotmail.com; f. 1992; daily; Khmer; Publr KEO SOPHORN; Editor NGOUN CHANMUNY.

The Commercial News: 394 blvd Preah Sihanouk, Phnom-Penh; tel. (23) 721665; fax (23) 721709; e-mail tcnews@online.com.kh; internet www.tcnewscambodia.com; f. 1993; Chinese; Chief Editor LIU XIAO GUANG; circ. 8,000.

Jian Hua Daily: 116–118 blvd Kampuchea Krom, Sangkat Monorom, Khan 7 Makara, Phnom-Penh 12251; tel. (23) 883801; fax (23) 883797; e-mail jianhuadaily@hotmail.com; internet www .jianhuadaily.com; daily; Chinese; Editor-in-Chief XENG ZUANG RONG.

Kampuchea Thmey (New Cambodia): 805 blvd Kampuchea Krom, rue 128, Sangkat Tuk Laak 1, Khan Tuol Kok, Phnom-Penh 12156; tel. (23) 6624141; fax (23) 726617; e-mail kampucheathmey@mail2world.com; internet www.kampucheathmey.com; daily; Editor-in-Chief KEV NAVY.

Kampuchea Thnai Nes (Cambodia Today Newspaper): 21 rue 163, Sangkat Veal Vong, Khan 7 Makara, Phnom-Penh 12253; tel. and fax (23) 364882; e-mail cambodiatoday@online.com.kh; daily; Editor-in-Chief HONG NARA.

Koh Santepheap (Island of Peace): 41E rue 338, Sangkat Boeung Tumpun, Khan Meanchey, Phnom-Penh 12351; tel. (23) 211818; fax (23) 220155; e-mail kohdaily@gmail.com; internet www .kohsantepheapdaily.com.kh; daily; Khmer; Dir THONG UY PANG.

Mekong News: POB 623, 576 National Rd 2, Sangkat Chak Angre Krom, Khan Menachey, Phnom-Penh; tel. (23) 425353; fax (23) 425363; e-mail mrcs@mrcmekong.org; f. 2005; quarterly; English and Khmer; publ. by Mekong River Commission Secretariat, distributed free of charge; Editor and Publr M. NOOR ULLAH.

Neak Chea: 1 rue 158, Oukghna Toeung Kang, Beng Raing Daun Penh, Phnom-Penh; tel. (23) 218653; fax (23) 217229; e-mail adhoc@forum.org.kh; 2 a month; Khmer; bulletin of Cambodia Human Rights and Devt Asscn.

Phnom Penh Post: 888 Bldg F, 8th Floor, Phnom Penh Center, cnr Sothearos & Sihanouk Blvd, Sangkat Tonle Bassac, Khan Chamkarmon, Phnom-Penh; tel. (23) 214311; fax (23) 214318; e-mail bernie.leo@phnompenhpost.com; internet www.phnompenhpost .com; f. 1992; fortnightly; English; Editor-in-Chief BERNIE LEO.

Pracheachon (The People): 101 blvd Norodom, Phnom-Penh; tel. (23) 723665; f. 1985; 2 a week; organ of the CPP; Editor-in-Chief SOM KIMSUOR; circ. 50,000.

Raja Bori News: 76 rue 57, Sangkat Boeung Kak II, Khan Tuol Kok, Phnom-Penh 12152; tel. (12) 840993; weekly; Editor-in-Chief KIM SOMLOT.

Rasmei Angkor (Light of Angkor): 25/25Z rue 372, Sangkat Boeung Salang, Khan Tuol Kok, Phnom-Penh 12160; tel. (11) 637609; e-mail raksmeiangkor@yahoo.com; f. 1992; 3 a week; Editor-in-Chief EN CHAN SIVUTHA.

Rasmei Kampuchea (Light of Cambodia): T. B. R. Printing Co Ltd, 474 blvd Preah Monivong, Sangkat Tonle Bassac, Khan Chamkarmon, Phnom-Penh 12301; tel. and fax (23) 7266555; e-mail rasmei_kampuchea@yahoo.com; daily; f. 1993; local newspaper in northern Cambodia; Editor PEN SAMITHY.

Sahasa Wat Thmey (New Millennium): 48AE blvd Oknha Chun, Sangkat Chaktomuk, Khan Daun Penh, Phnom-Penh 12207; tel. (16) 719551; e-mail sahasawatthmey@mail2world.com; f. 2004; 3 a week; Editor-in-Chief MANN BUNTHOEUN.

Samleng Thmei (New Voice): 91 rue 139, Sangkat Veal Vong, Khan 7, Phnom-Penh; tel. (15) 920589; Khmer; Editor KHUN NGOR.

Samleng Yuvachun (Voice of Khmer Youth): 251 rue 261, Sangkat Tuk Laak 2, Khan Tuol Kok 12200, Phnom-Penh 12309; tel. (12) 859142; fax (23) 997470; e-mail khmeryouthnews@yahoo.com; f. 1993; Editor-in-Chief UK SUN HENG.

Udomkate Khmer (Khmer Ideal): 17 blvd Samdech Sothearos, Sangkat Tuk Laak 3, Khan Tuol Kok, Phnom-Penh 12158; tel. (12) 851478; daily; Editor-in-Chief HOR SOK LEN.

PERIODICALS

Angkor Thom: 105 rue 324, Sangkat Boeung Salang, Khan Tuol Kok, Phnom-Penh 12253; tel. (23) 996421; fax (23) 996441; e-mail vuthyrith@angkorthommagazine.com; internet ekhmermagazines .com; f. 1998; 3 a month; Khmer; news, current affairs, arts and sport; Editor-in-Chief SING VUTHYRITH; circ. 30,000.

Bayon Pearnik: 3 rue 174, Sangkat Phsar Thmei 3, Khan Daun Penh, Phnom-Penh 312210; tel. (12) 803968; e-mail bp@forum.org .kh; internet www.bayonpearnik.com; f. 1996; monthly; English; news for expatriates and tourists; Publr and Editor-in-Chief ADAM PARKER.

Cambodian Scene: 41 blvd Sang Kreach Tieng, rue 222, Sangkat Boeung Raing, Khan Daun Penh, Phnom-Penh 12211; tel. (23)

224488; fax (23) 222266; e-mail publisher@cambodianscene.com; internet www.cambodianscene.com; every 2 months; English; tourism, culture and entertainment guide; Publr and Editor-in-Chief MOEUN NHEAN.

L'Echo du Cambodge: 42 blvd Preah Norodom, Sangkat Phsar Thmei 2, Khan Daun Penh, Phnom-Penh 12206; e-mail echoducambodge@yahoo.fr; monthly; English and French; Editor-in-Chief MARCEL ZARCA.

Indradevi: 167 blvd Mao Tse Toung, Sangkat Tuol Svay Prey 2, Khan Chamkarmon, Phnom-Penh 12309; tel. and fax (23) 215808; e-mail indradevi@camnet.com.kh; f. 2000; Editor-in-Chief CHHEM SARITH.

Kambuja: Kambuja Dept, Agence Kampuchea Presse, Ministry of Information, 62 blvd Preah Monivong, Sangkat Wat Phnom, Khan Daun Penh, Phnom-Penh 12202; tel. and fax (23) 427945; e-mail akp@camnet.com.kh; monthly; Khmer; publ. by the AKP; devt, education and int. affairs; Editor-in-Chief NERK SARAT.

Khmer Apsara: 143A Khum Pring Kang Cheung, Sangkat Chom Chao, Khan Dangkor, Phnom-Penh 12405; tel. (17) 391087; e-mail khmer_apsara01@yahoo.com; internet www.khmerapsaramagazine.com; f. 2005; monthly; Khmer; entertainment, fashion, technology, health and culture; Editor-in-Chief EN SOPHANNA.

Pracheaprey (Popular): 71–73 rue 70, Sangkat Sras Chak, Phnom-Penh; tel. (12) 890613; fax (12) 890614; e-mail popularmagazine@online.com.kh; f. 2000; 3 a month; Khmer; news, current affairs, politics, arts, science and sport; Editor-in-Chief PRACH SIM.

Samay Thmei (Modern): 127 rue 357, Sangkat Chbar Ampheou 2, Khan Meanchey, Phnom-Penh 12355; tel. (23) 359969; fortnightly; Khmer; fashion, contemporary living, sports and entertainment; Editor-in-Chief EK SAMAT.

Suorsadey Magazine: 13A rue 222, Sang Kreach Tieng, Phnom-Penh; tel. (23) 224488; fax (23) 222266; f. 2009; quarterly; tourism, culture and entertainment guide; Editor MOEN NHEAN.

NEWS AGENCY

Agence Kampuchea Presse (AKP): 62 blvd Monivong, Phnom-Penh; tel. (23) 430564; fax (23) 427945; e-mail akp@camnet.com.kh; internet www.camnet.com.kh/akp; f. 1978; Dir-Gen. KIT-KIM HUON.

ASSOCIATIONS

Cambodian Association for the Protection of Journalists (CAPJ): BP 816, 58 rue 336, Sangkat Phsar Doeum Kor, Khan Tuol Kok, Phnom-Penh; tel. (15) 997004; fax (23) 215834; e-mail umsarin@hotmail.com; Pres. UM SARIN.

Club of Cambodian Journalists: 226 rue 155, Sangkat Tuol Tumpong 1, Khan Chamkarmon, Phnom-Penh; tel. and fax (23) 224094; e-mail ccj@online.com.kh; internet www.ccj.com.kh; f. 2000; Pres. PEN SAMITTHY; Sec.-Gen. PRACH SIM.

Khmer Journalists' Association: 170C rue 167, Sangkat Tuol Tom Poung 2, Khan Chamkarmon, Phnom-Penh 12311; tel. (23) 987622; e-mail mondulkeo@yahoo.com; f. 1979; Pres. TATH LY HOK.

Press Council of Cambodia: 127 blvd Norodom, Sangkat Tonle Bassac, Khan Chamkarmon, Phnom-Penh; tel. (12) 910425; f. 2008; est. as an umbrella body for more than 15 journalists' asscns; Pres. SOK SOVANN.

Broadcasting and Communications

TELECOMMUNICATIONS

Cambodia Advance Communications Co Ltd (CADCOMMS): 825ABC blvd Preah Monivong, Sangkat Phsar Damthkov, Khan Chamkarmon, Phnom-Penh; tel. (13) 300313; fax (13) 300317; e-mail info@qbmore.com; internet www.qbmore.com; f. 2006; operates mobile services; Chief Information Officer SANDOS NONG.

Camintel: 1 cnr Terak Vithei Sisowath & Vithei Phsar Dek, Phnom-Penh; tel. (23) 986986; fax (23) 986277; e-mail support@camintel.com; internet www.camintel.com; f. 1995; jt venture between the Ministry of Posts and Telecommunications and Indonesian co Indosat; operates domestic telephone network and internet; CEO KANG NAM KOOK; Man. Dir CHOI DEUG MAN.

Mfone Co Ltd: 721 blvd Preah Monivong, Sangkat Boeung Keng Kang 3, Khan Chamkarmon, Phnom-Penh; tel. (23) 303333; fax (23) 361111; e-mail sales@mfone.biz; internet www.mfone.com.kh; f. 1993; fmrly Cambodia Shinawatra Co Ltd; subsidiary of Shenington Investments Pte Ltd and Asia Mobile Holdings Pte Ltd; provides fixed line, mobile (incl. third generation—3G) and internet services; CEO SUTTISAK KHNDHIKAJANA.

MobiTel: 33 blvd Preah Sihanouk, BP 2468, Phnom-Penh; tel. (12) 800800; fax (12) 801801; e-mail helpline@mobitel.com.kh; internet www.mobitel.com.kh; f. 1998; wholly owned by The Royal Group since Nov. 2009; operates national GSM 900 mobile network under trade name Cellcard; CEO DAVID SPRIGGS.

Smart Mobile: 464A blvd Monivong, Sangkat Tonle Bassac, Khan Chamkarmorn, Phnom-Penh; tel. (10) 201000; fax (23) 868882; e-mail info@smart.com.kh; internet www.smart.com.kh; operates GSM mobile services; CEO THOMAS HUNDT.

Telekom Malaysia International (Cambodia) Co Ltd: cnr Sihanouk & Sothearos, Sangkat Tonle Bassac, Khan Chamkarmon, Phnom-Penh; tel. (16) 880002; internet www.hello.com.kh; f. 1992; est. as Cambodia Samart Communication; name changed as above following acquisition by Telekom Malaysia Bhd in 2006; operates a national mobile network under trade name Hello; CEO MUHAMMED YUSOFF ZAMRI.

BROADCASTING

Radio

There is a single government radio station, the National Radio of Cambodia, and many local private radio stations, which emerged following the deregulation of broadcasting services in 1979.

Apsara Radio (FM 97 MHz): 69 rue 57, Sangkat Boeung Keng Kang 1, Khan Chamkarmon, Phnom-Penh; tel. (12) 303002; fax (23) 214302; internet www.apsaratv.com.kh; f. 1996; linked to Cambodian People's Party; Khmer; Dir-Gen. SOK EYSAN.

Bayon Radio (FM 95 MHz): 3 rue 466, Sangkat Tonle Bassac, Khan Chamkarmon, Phnom-Penh; tel. (12) 682222; fax (23) 363795; internet www.bayontv.com.kh; f. 1998; linked to Prime Minister Hun Sen; Dir-Gen. HUN MANA; Deputy Dir-Gen. HUOT KHEANGVENG.

Beehive Radio (Sambok Khmoum): 44G rue 360, Sangkat Boeung Keng Kang 1, Khan Chamkarmon, Phnom-Penh; tel. (16) 458599; fax (23) 210439; e-mail sbk105kh@gmail.com; internet www.sbk.com.kh; f. 1996; broadcasts incl. news programmes from Voice of America and Radio Free Asia; Dir-Gen. MAM SONANDO.

Family FM 99.5 MHz (Krusa FM): Phnom-Penh; e-mail febcam@bigpond.com.kh; internet www.febc.org; f. 2002; controlled by Far East Broadcasting Co; religious and educational programmes from a Christian perspective; Dir SAMOEUN INTAL.

FM 90 MHz: 65 rue 178, Phnom-Penh; tel. (16) 709090; fax (23) 368623; news, music and educational programmes; affiliated to the FUNCINPEC Party; Dir-Gen. NHIM BUN THON; Dep. Dir-Gen. TUM VANN DET.

FM 107 MHz: 18 rue 562, Boeung Kak 1, Khan Toul Kork, Phnom-Penh; tel. (23) 880874; fax (23) 881935; e-mail info@tv9.com.kh; internet www.tv9.com.kh; news and music; Dir-Gen. KHUN HAING.

National Radio of Cambodia (RNK) (Radio National Kampuchea): Bldg 6, Sangkat Wat Phnom, cnr rues 19 & 102, Phnom-Penh; tel. (23) 722869; fax (23) 427319; internet www.rnk.gov.kh; f. 1978; fmrly Vithyu Samleng Pracheachon Kampuchea (Voice of the Cambodian People); controlled by the Ministry of Information; domestic service in Khmer; broadcasts on both AM and FM frequencies; daily external services in English, French, Lao, Vietnamese and Thai; Dir-Gen. TAN YAN.

New Life Radio FM 89.5 MHz: 4 rue 95, Sangkat Boueng Keng Kong II, Khan Chamkarmon, Phnom-Penh; tel. (23) 212593; e-mail newliferadio@camnet.com.kh.

Phnom-Penh Municipality Radio (103 MHz): 2 blvd Confédération de la Russie, Phnom-Penh; tel. (23) 725205; fax (23) 360800; Gen. Man. KHAMPUN KEOMONY.

Royal Cambodian Armed Forces Radio (RCAF Radio) (FM 98.0 MHz): c/o Borei Keila, rue 169, Sangkat Vealvong, Phnom-Penh; tel. (23) 306064; fax (23) 884245; f. 1994; Dir THA TANA; News Editor SENG KATEKA.

Ta Prohm Radio (FM 90.5 MHz): 27B rue 472, Phnom-Penh; tel. (23) 993206; e-mail taprohm@yahoo.com; f. 2003; launched by FUNCINPEC Party as opposition radio station; broadcasts news programmes in Khmer to Phnom-Penh and surrounding area; Propr EAR LIMSUOR.

Women's Radio FM 102 MHz: 30 rue 488, Sangkat Phsar Demthkov, Khan Chamkarmon, Phnom-Penh; POB 497, Phnom-Penh; tel. (23) 212264; fax (23) 223597; e-mail fm102@wmc.org.kh; internet www.wmc.org.kh; f. 1999; independent; radio station of Women's Media Centre of Cambodia; Exec. Dir CHEA SUNDANETH.

There are also several private local radio stations.

Television

Apsara Television (TV11): 69 rue 57, Sangkat Boeung Keng Kang 1, Khan Chamkarmon, Phnom-Penh; tel. (23) 303002; fax (23) 214302; e-mail tv11@camnet.com.kh; internet www.apsaratv.com.kh; broadcasts for 14 hours per day on weekdays, and for 16 hours per day at weekends, in Khmer; linked to Cambodian People's Party; Dir-Gen. SOK EYSAN.

Bayon Television (TV27): 3 rue 466, Sangkat Tonle Bassac, Khan Chamkarmon, Phnom-Penh; tel. (12) 682222; fax (23) 363795; e-mail bayontv@camnet.com.kh; internet www.bayontv.com.kh; linked to Prime Minister Hun Sen; Dir-Gen. HUN MANA.

Cambodian Television Network (CTN): POB 2468, Phnom-Penh 12104; tel. (12) 999434; e-mail tv@ctn.com.kh; internet www.ctn.com .kh; f. 2003; wholly owned by The Royal Group; operates two free-to-air stations, CTN and MYTV; CTN International available internationally via satellite; Propr KITH MENG; Gen. Man. GLEN FELGATE.

Cambodian Television Station Channel 9 (TV9): 18 rue 562, Phnom-Penh; tel. (23) 880874; fax (23) 368212; e-mail info@tv9.com .kh; internet www.tv9.com.kh; f. 1992; Dir-Gen. KHOUN ELYNA; News Editor PHAN TITH.

National Television of Cambodia (TVK): 62 blvd Preah Monivong, Phnom-Penh; tel. and fax (12) 554535; e-mail tvk@camnet.gov .kh; internet www.tvk.gov.kh; f. 1983; broadcasts in Khmer, 24 hours per day (TVK) and 12 hours per day (TVK2); Dir-Gen. (Head of Television) KEM GUNAWADH.

Phnom-Penh Municipality Television (TV3): 2 blvd Confédération de la Russie, Phnom-Penh; tel. (12) 814323; fax (23) 360800; e-mail tv3@kcsradio.com; internet www.tv3.com.kh; jt venture between Phnom Penh Municipality and KCS Cambodia Co Ltd (Thailand); Dir-Gen. KHAMPHUN KEOMONY.

Royal Cambodian Armed Forces Television (TV5 Cambodia): Prek Tloeng Village, Prek Kampoes, Kandal Stoeng, Kandal; tel. (23) 303925; fax (23) 994385; e-mail info@ch5cambodia.com; internet www.ch5cambodia.com; f. 1995; jt venture between Royal Cambodian Armed Forces and MICA Media Co; also operates an FM radio service.

Finance

(cap. = capital; res = reserves; dep. = deposits; brs = branches; amounts in US dollars unless otherwise stated)

BANKING

In 2012 there were 43 banks (excluding the central bank) operating in Cambodia, comprising: seven specialized banks; 32 locally incorporated private banks; and four branches of foreign banks.

Central Bank

National Bank of Cambodia (NBC): 22–24 blvd Preah Norodom, BP 25, Phnom-Penh; tel. (23) 722563; fax (23) 426117; e-mail info@ nbc.org.kh; internet www.nbc.org.kh; f. 1954; est. as National Bank of Cambodia; name changed to People's National Bank of Cambodia in 1979; name reverted to above in 1992; cap. 100,000m. riels, res 6,537,600m. riels, dep. 3,875,862m. riels (June 2007); Gov. CHEA CHANTO; Dep. Gov. NEAV CHANTHANA.

Specialized Banks

First Investment Specialized Bank (FISB): 72 blvd Preah Sihanouk, Sangkat Tonle Bassac, Khan Daun Penh, Phnom-Penh; tel. (23) 222281; fax (23) 221112; e-mail service@fibank.com.kh; internet www.fibank.com.kh; f. 2005; cap. 12m. (Dec. 2009); Chair. and CEO NEAK OKNHA; Gen. Man. YIP SOREIYOS.

Peng Heng SME Bank: 74 blvd Norodom, Sangkat Chey Chumneas, Khan Daun Penh, Phnom-Penh; tel. (23) 219243; fax (23) 219185; e-mail pengheng@camnet.com.kh; f. 2001.

Rural Development Bank: 9–13 rue 7, Sangkat Chaktomouk, Khan Daun Penh, BP 1410, Phnom-Penh; tel. (23) 220810; fax (23) 224628; e-mail admin@rdb.com.kh; internet www.rdb.com.kh; f. 1998; state-owned; provides credit to rural enterprises; Chair. and CEO SON KOUN THOR.

Private Banks

ACLEDA Bank PLC: 61 blvd Monivong, Sangkat Srah Chork, Khan Duan Penh, BP 1149, Phnom-Penh; tel. (23) 430999; fax (23) 430555; e-mail acledabank@acledabank.com.kh; internet www .acledabank.com.kh; f. 1993; became specialized bank Oct. 2000; awarded commercial banking licence Dec. 2003; provides financial services to all sectors; cap. 68.1m., res 28.0m., dep. 702.0m. (Dec. 2009); Chair. CHEA SOK; Pres. and CEO IN CHANNY; 234 brs.

Advanced Bank of Asia Ltd: 148 blvd Preah Sihanouk, Sangkat Boeung Keng Kang 1, Khan Chamkarmon, Phnom-Penh; tel. (23) 225333; fax (23) 216333; e-mail info@ababank.com; internet www .ababank.net; f. 1996; CEO MADI AKMAMBET.

Cambodia Asia Bank Ltd: 439 blvd Monivong, Ground Floor, Phnom-Penh; tel. (23) 220000; fax (23) 426628; e-mail cab@cab.com .kh; internet www.cab.com.kh; incorporated in 1992; cap. 13.0m., dep. 13.9m. (Dec. 2009); Man. WONG TOW FOCK.

Cambodia Mekong Bank: 6 blvd Monivong, Khan Daun Penh, Phnom-Penh; tel. and fax (23) 217122; e-mail ho.mailbox@ mekongbank.com; f. 1994; cap. 37.0m., dep. 18.2m. (Dec. 2009); Chair. MICHAEL C. STEPHEN; Pres. and CEO KHOV BOUN CHHAY.

Cambodian Commercial Bank Ltd: 26 blvd Preah Monivong, Sangkat Phsar Thmei 2, Khan Daun Penh, Phnom-Penh; tel. (23) 426145; fax (23) 426116; e-mail ccbpp@online.com.kh; f. 1991; cap. 13m., dep. 115.2m. (Dec. 2009); Chair. NABHENGBHASANG KRISHNAMRA; Dir and Gen. Man. NATTHAWUT CHAKANAN; 4 brs.

Cambodian Public Bank (Campu Bank): Campu Bank Bldg 23, rue Kramoun Sar 114, Sangkat Phsar Thmei 2, Khan Daun Penh, Phnom-Penh; tel. (23) 222880; fax (23) 222887; e-mail campuhoe@ campubank.com.kh; internet www.campubank.com.kh; f. 1992; cap. 90m., dep. 751m. (Dec. 2009); wholly owned subsidiary of Public Bank Bhd, Malaysia; Chair. (non-exec.) Tan Sri Dato' Sri Dr HONG PIOW TEH; Country Head PHAN YING TONG.

Canadia Bank PLC: 315 rue Preah Ang Duong, cnr blvd Monivong, Khan Daun Penh, Phnom-Penh; tel. (23) 868222; fax (23) 222830; e-mail canadia@canadiabank.com.kh; internet www.canadiabank .com; f. 1991; est. as Canadia Gold and Trust Corpn Ltd; present name adopted 2004; cap. 50.6m. riels, res 32.3m. riels, dep. 411.6m. riels (2001); Pres. and CEO PUNG KHEAV SE; 26 brs.

Foreign Trade Bank: 3 rue Kramoun Sar, Sangkat Phsar Thmei 1, Khan Daun Penh, Phnom-Penh; tel. (23) 724466; fax (23) 426108; e-mail info@ftbbank.com; internet www.ftbbank.com; f. 1979; removed from direct management of Nat. Bank of Cambodia in 2000; scheduled for privatization; Chair. OKNHA PUNG KHEAV SE; Gen. Man. LOK ONUMTEAV OUK MALY.

Singapore Banking Corporation Ltd: 68 rue Samdech Pan 214, Sangkat Boeung Raing, Khan Daun Penh, BP 688, Phnom-Penh; tel. (23) 211211; fax (23) 212121; e-mail info@sbc-bank.com; internet www.sbc-bank.com; f. 1992; cap. 17m., dep. 32.8m. (Dec. 2009); Pres. ANDY KUN SWEE TIONG; Chair. KUN KAY HONG.

Union Commercial Bank PLC: UCB Bldg, 61 rue 130, Sangkat Phsar Chas, Khan Daun Penh, Phnom-Penh; tel. (23) 427995; fax (23) 427997; e-mail ucbhq@ucb.com.kh; internet www.ucb.com.kh; f. 1994; cap. 14.1m., res 2.0m., dep. 114.1m. (Dec. 2009); Chair. and Pres. YUM SUI SANG; 4 brs.

Vattanac Bank: 89 blvd Preah Norodom, Sangkat Boeung Raing, Khan Daun Penh, Phnom-Penh; tel. (23) 212727; fax (23) 216687; e-mail service@vattanacbank.com; internet www.vattanacbank .com; f. 2002; cap. 13m., dep. 102.7m. (Dec. 2007); Chair. SAM ANG; Pres. CHHUN LEANG.

Bankers' Association

The Association of Banks in Cambodia: 1 rue Kramuon Sar (rue 114), Sangkat Phsar Thmei 1, Khan Daun Penh, Phnom-Penh; tel. (23) 218610; fax (23) 224310; e-mail secretariat@abc.org.kh; internet www.abc.org.kh; f. 1994; Chair. PUNG KHEAV SE.

STOCK EXCHANGE

The Cambodia Securities Exchange, a joint venture between the Government and the Korea Exchange (KRX—Republic of Korea), was launched in July 2011.

Stock Exchange

Cambodia Securities Exchange (CSX): 25th Floor, Canadia Tower, 315 rue Preah Ang Duong, Khan Daun Penh, Phnom-Penh; tel. (23) 958888; fax (23) 955558; e-mail info@csx.com.kh; internet www.csx.com.kh; f. 2011; 55% govt-owned and 45% owned by Korea Exchange; trading began in April 2012; CEO HONG SOK HOUR.

Supervisory Body

Securities and Exchange Commission of Cambodia (SECC): 99 rue 598, Sangkat Phnom-Penh Thmei, Khan Sen Sok, Phnom-Penh; tel. (23) 885611; fax (23) 885622; e-mail sovy_va@secc.gov.kh; internet www.secc.gov.kh; f. 2007; govt-owned; Gen. Dir MING BANKOSAL; Dir SOVY VA.

INSURANCE

Asia Insurance (Cambodia) Ltd: 5 rue 13, Sangkat Wat Phnom, Khan Daun Penh, Phnom-Penh 12201; tel. (23) 427981; fax (23) 216969; e-mail email@asiainsurance.com.kh; internet www .asiainsurance.com.kh; f. 1996; Gen. Man. PASCAL BRANDT-GAGNON.

Cambodia National Insurance Company (CAMINCO): cnr rues 106 & 13, Sangkat Wat Phnom, Khan Daun Penh, Phnom-Penh; tel. (23) 722043; fax (23) 427810; e-mail info@caminco.com.kh; internet www.caminco.com.kh; f. 1990; fmrly 100% state-owned; since 2008 75% owned by Viriyah BVB Insurance PLC (Cambodian co est. by local businessman Duong Vibol), 25% state-owned; Chair. LOK CHHUM TEV OKNHA SAT NAVY; Man. Dir DUONG VIBOL.

Forte Insurance (Cambodia) PLC: 325 blvd Mao Tse Toung, BP 565, Phnom-Penh; tel. (23) 885077; fax (23) 986922; e-mail info@

forteinsurance.com; internet www.forteinsurance.com; f. 1996; Man. Dir CARLO CHEO; Gen. Man. YOUK CHAMROEUNRITH.

Infinity General Insurance PLC: 126 blvd Preah Norodom, Phnom-Penh; tel. (23) 999888; fax (23) 999123; e-mail cs@infinity.com.kh; internet www.infinityinsurance.com.kh.

Trade and Industry

DEVELOPMENT ORGANIZATIONS

Council for the Development of Cambodia (CDC): Government Palace, quai Sisowath, Sangkat Wat Phnom, BP 1225, Phnom-Penh; tel. (23) 981241; fax (23) 981161; e-mail cdc-cmb@camnet.com.kh; internet www.cdc-crdb.gov.kh; f. 1994; Chair. HUN SEN; Sec.-Gen. SOK CHENDA.

Cambodian Investment Board (CIB): Government Palace, quai Sisowath, Sangkat Wat Phnom, Phnom-Penh; tel. (23) 981156; fax (23) 428426; e-mail cdc.cib@bigpond.com.kh; internet www.cambodiainvestment.gov.kh; f. 1993; part of CDC; sole body responsible for approving foreign investment in Cambodia; Chair. HUN SEN; Sec.-Gen. SUON SITTHY.

Cambodian National Petroleum Authority (CNPA): 13–14 blvd Confédération de la Russie, Sangkat Toeuk Thla, Khan Sen Sok, Phnom-Penh; tel. (23) 890569; fax (23) 890569; internet cnpa-cambodia.com; f. 1999; Chair. SOK AN; Dir-Gen. TE DUONG TARA.

National Information Communications Technology Development Authority (NiDA): 113 rue 214, Sangkat Bong Prolet, Khan 7 Makara, Phnom-Penh; tel. (12) 812282; fax (23) 216793; e-mail info@nida.gov.kh; internet www.nida.gov.kh; f. 2000; promotes IT and formulates policy devt; Chair. HUN SEN; Sec.-Gen. Dr PHU LEEWOOD.

CHAMBER OF COMMERCE

Cambodia Chamber of Commerce: 7D blvd Confédération de la Russie, Khan Tuol Kok, Phnom-Penh; tel. (23) 880795; fax (23) 881757; e-mail info@ppcc.org.kh; internet www.ppcc.org.kh; f. 1995; Pres. KITH MENG; Dir-Gen. NGUON MENG TECH.

INDUSTRIAL AND TRADE ASSOCIATIONS

Garment Manufacturers' Association in Cambodia (GMAC): 175 blvd Jawaharlal Nehru (rue 215), Sangkat Phsar Doeum Kor, Khan Tuol Kok 12159, Phnom-Penh; tel. (23) 882860; fax (23) 331183; e-mail info@gmac-cambodia.org; internet www.gmac-cambodia.org; Chair. VAN SOU IENG; Sec.-Gen. KEN LOO.

Trade Promotion Department: Ministry of Commerce, 65–69 rue 136, Sangkat Phsar Kandal 2, Khan Daun Penh, Phnom-Penh; tel. (23) 216948; fax (23) 211745; e-mail info@tpd.gov.kh; internet www.tpd.gov.kh; Dir SEUN SOTHA.

UTILITIES

Electricity

Electricité du Cambodge (EDC): EDC Bldg, rue 19, Sangkat Wat Phnom, Khan Daun Penh, Phnom-Penh; tel. (23) 723971; fax (23) 426018; e-mail edchq@edc.com.kh; internet www.edc.com.kh; f. 1996; state-owned; Chair. TUN LEAN; Man. Dir KEO ROTTANAK.

Electricity Authority of Cambodia (EAC): 2 rue 282, Sangkat Boeung Keng Kang 1, Khan Chamkarmon, Phnom-Penh; tel. (23) 217654; fax (23) 214144; e-mail admin@eac.gov.kh; internet www.eac.gov.kh; f. 2001; regulatory authority; Chair. Dr TY NORIN.

Water

Phnom-Penh Water Supply Authority (PPWSA): rue 108, Phnom-Penh 12201; tel. (23) 724046; fax (23) 428969; e-mail eksonnchan@ppwsa.com.kh; f. 1996; autonomous public enterprise; Dir-Gen. EK SONN CHAN.

TRADE UNIONS

Cambodia Federation of Independent Trade Unions (CFITU): 45 rue 63, Sangkat Boeung Keng Kang 1, Khan Chamkarmon, Phnom-Penh; tel. (23) 213356; e-mail cfitu@online.com.kh; f. 1979 as Cambodia Fed. of Trade Unions; changed name as above in 1999; Chair. ROS SOK.

Cambodia Labour Union Federation (CLUF): 78 rue 474, Sangkat Boeung Trabek, Khan Chamkarmon, Phnom-Penh; tel. (23) 866682; f. 1999; Pres. SOM AUN.

Cambodian Independent Teachers' Association (CITA): 54E rue 95, Sangkat Boeung Keng Kang 3, Khan Chamkarmon, Phnom-Penh; tel. and fax (23) 217544; e-mail cita@online.com.kh; internet www.the-ccu.org; f. 2000; Pres. RONG CHHUN; Gen. Sec. CHEA MUNI.

Cambodian Labor Organization (CLO): 425 rue 310, Sangkat Boeung Keng Kang 2, Khan Chamkarmon, Phnom-Penh; tel. and fax (23) 218132; e-mail clo@forum.org.kh; f. 1995.

Cambodian Labour Confederation: No. 2, 3G rue 26BT, Tnotchrum Village, Sangkat Boeung, Tompun, Khan Meanchey, Phnom-Penh; tel. (12) 998906; e-mail c.l.ccambodia@online.com.kh; internet clccambodia.org; f. 2006; Pres. ATH THORN.

Cambodian Union Federation (CUF): 16 rue 11 (New World City), Phoum Tropaintling, Sangkat Chomchao, Khan Dongkor, Phnom-Penh; tel. (12) 837789; fax (23) 884329; e-mail CUF@online.com.kh; internet cuf-cctu.org; f. 1997; est. with CPP support in response to formation of FTUWKC; Pres. CHUON MOMTHOL.

Cambodian Union Federation of Building and Wood Workers: 18A rue 112, Sangkat Phsar Depo 3, Khan Tuol Kok, Phnom-Penh; tel. (23) 842382; fax (23) 882453; f. 2001; Pres. SOK SOVANDEITH; Sec.-Gen. KEN CHENGLANG.

Coalition of Cambodia Apparel Workers' Democratic Union: 6C rue 476, Sangkat Tuol Tompoung 1, Khan Chamkarmon, Phnom-Penh; tel. and fax (23) 210481; e-mail c.cawdu@online.com.kh; f. 2001; Pres. ATH THUN.

Free Trade Union of Workers of the Kingdom of Cambodia (FTUWKC): 16A rue 360, Sangkat Boeung Keng Kang 3, Khan Chamkarmon, Phnom-Penh; tel. and fax (23) 216870; e-mail contact@ftuwkc.org; internet www.ftuwkc.org; f. 1996; fmrly Free Trade Union of Khmer Workers; Pres. CHEA MONY; Gen. Sec. SREY KIM HENG.

National Independent Federation Textile Union of Cambodia (NIFTUC): 120AE rue 432, Sangkat Toul Tompoung 2, Khan Chamkarmon, Phnom-Penh; tel. (12) 994908; e-mail niftuc_2006@yahoo.com; f. 1999; Pres. MORM NHIM.

Transport

RAILWAYS

Toll Royal Railways: Central Railway Station, Railway Sq., Sangkat Srach Chak, Khan Daun Penh, Phnom-Penh; tel. (23) 992379; fax (23) 992353; e-mail sonyka.bunny@tollgroup.com; internet www.tollroyalrailway.com; two single-track lines: the original 385-km Phnom-Penh to Poipet line (incl. 48-km Sisophon–Poipet link); and a redeveloped 254-km line between Phnom-Penh and Sihanoukville, a 117-km section of which, linking Phnom-Penh and Kampot, reopened in late 2010; jt venture between Toll (55%) and Royal Group (45%) under 30-year concession agreement with Cambodian govt; Pres. and Dir-Gen. SOKHOM PHEAKAVANMONY; CEO DAVID KERR.

ROADS

In 2004 the total road network was 38,257 km in length, of which 4,757 km were highways and 5,700 km were secondary roads; about 6.3% of the road network was paved. A road bridge across the Mekong River opened in 2001.

INLAND WATERWAYS

The major routes are along the Mekong River, and up the Tonlé Sap River into the Tonlé Sap (Great Lake), covering, in all, about 2,400 km. The inland ports of Neak Luong, Kampong Cham and Prek Kdam have been supplied with motor ferries.

SHIPPING

The main port is Sihanoukville, on the Gulf of Thailand, which has 11 berths and can accommodate vessels of 10,000–15,000 tons. Phnom-Penh port lies some distance inland. Koh Kong port, near the border with Thailand, serves as a docking bay for vessels entering Cambodia from Singapore, Malaysia and Thailand.

Phnom Penh Autonomous Port: Preah Sisowath, Sangkat Sras Chak, Khan Daun Penh; tel. and fax (23) 427802; e-mail ppapmpwt@online.com.kh; internet www.ppap.com.kh; state-owned; Chair. and CEO HEI BAVY.

Sihanoukville Autonomous Port (PAS): Terak Vithei Samdech Akka Moha Sena Padei Techo HUN SEN Sangkat No 3, Sihanoukville, Preah Sihanouk; tel. (34) 933416; fax (34) 933693; e-mail pasplan@pas.gov.kh; internet www.pas.gov.kh; Chair. and CEO LOU KIM CHHUN.

CIVIL AVIATION

There are international airports at Pochentong, serving nearby Phnom-Penh, and at Siem Reap.

State Secretariat of Civil Aviation (SSCA): 62 blvd Norodom, Phnom-Penh; tel. and fax (23) 211019; e-mail sengvany@camnet.com.kh; internet www.civilaviation.gov.kh; Dir-Gen. MAO HAS VANNAL.

Cambodia Angkor Air: 1–2, 294 blvd Mao Tse Tong, Phnom-Penh; tel. (23) 6666786; fax (23) 424496; internet www.cambodiaangkorair.com; f. 2009; national carrier; jt venture with Viet Nam Airlines; Chair. and CEO TRINH NGOC THANH.

PMT Air: 118 rue 2013, Sangkat Kakab, Khan Dong Kar, Phnom-Penh; tel. and fax (23) 23890322; e-mail tiket@pmtair.com; internet www.pmtair.com; f. 2003; domestic and international services.

Royal Khmer Airlines: 36B, 245 blvd Mao Tse Toung, Sangkat Boeung Trabek, Khan Chamkarmon, Phnom-Penh; tel. (23) 994888; fax (23) 994508; e-mail rudy@royalkhmerairlines.com; internet www.royalkhmerairlines.com; f. 2000; jt venture with Indonesia; domestic and international services; CEO RUDYANTO WIDJAJA.

Royal Phnom-Penh Airways: 209 rue 19, Sangkat Chey Chumneah, Khan Daun Penh, Phnom-Penh; tel. (23) 215565; fax (23) 217420; e-mail ppenhairw@bigpond.com.kh; f. 1999; scheduled and charter passenger flights to domestic and regional destinations; Chair. Prince NORODOM CHAKRAPONG.

Siem Reap Airways International: 65 rue 214, Sangkat Boeung Raing, Khan Daun Penh, Phnom-Penh; tel. (23) 723962; fax (23) 720522; internet www.siemreapair.com; f. 2000; scheduled domestic and international passenger services; CEO PRASERT PRASARTTONG-OSOTH.

Tourism

Cambodia's attractions include the ancient temples of Angkor and the beaches of Sihanoukville. Receipts from tourism totalled US $1,912m. in 2011. In that year visitor arrivals reached 2.9m. Major sources of visitors included Viet Nam, South Korea, the People's Republic of China and Japan. The number of rooms available in hotels and guest houses was estimated to have exceeded 40,000 in 2010.

Directorate-General of Tourism: 3 blvd Monivong, Phnom-Penh; tel. (23) 427130; fax (23) 426107; f. 1988; Dir-Gen. THITH CHANTHA.

Defence

As assessed at November 2011, the total strength of the Royal Cambodian Armed Forces was estimated to be 124,300 (including provincial forces): army 75,000, navy 2,800, air force 1,500 and provincial forces about 45,000. Paramilitary forces are organized at village level and numbered some 67,000 men and women in 2011. The defence budget for 2011 was 1,230,000m. riels.

Supreme Commander of the Royal Cambodian Armed Forces: King NORODOM SIHAMONI.

Commander-in-Chief: Gen. POL SAROEUN.

Education

In 2003/04 there were 1,345 pre-primary institutions. In 2002/03 there were 5,915 primary schools, 411 general secondary schools and 183 vocational secondary schools. In 2009/10 a total of 114,958 children were attending pre-primary schools, and primary pupils totalled 2,272,527. Secondary students totalled 875,120 in 2006/07. In 2009/10 enrolment at pre-primary level included 13% of children in the relevant age-group (males 13%; females 13%). Primary education is compulsory for nine years between the ages of six and 15. Enrolment at primary level included 96% of children in the relevant age-group (males 96%; females 95%) in 2009/10. Secondary education comprises two cycles, each lasting three years. Enrolment at secondary level included 35% of children in the relevant age-group (males 37%; females 33%) in 2006/07.

Institutions of higher education include Phnom-Penh University, an arts college, a technical college, a teacher-training college, a number of secondary vocational schools and an agricultural college.

The budget for 2012 allocated 1,007,626m. riels to the Ministry of Education, Youth and Sport.

CAMEROON

Introductory Survey

LOCATION, CLIMATE, LANGUAGE, RELIGION, FLAG, CAPITAL

The Republic of Cameroon lies on the west coast of Africa, with Nigeria to the west, Chad and the Central African Republic to the east, and the Republic of the Congo, Equatorial Guinea and Gabon to the south. The climate is hot and humid in the south and west, with average temperatures of 26°C (80°F). Annual rainfall in Yaoundé averages 4,030 mm (159 ins). The north is drier, with more extreme temperatures. The official languages are French and English; many local languages are also spoken, including Fang, Bamileke and Duala. Approximately 53% of Cameroonians profess Christianity, 25% adhere to traditional religious beliefs, and about 22%, mostly in the north, are Muslims. The national flag (proportions 2 by 3) has three equal vertical stripes, of green, red and yellow, with a five-pointed gold star in the centre of the red stripe. The capital is Yaoundé.

CONTEMPORARY POLITICAL HISTORY

Historical Context

In 1919 the former German protectorate of Cameroon (Kamerun) was divided into two zones: a French-ruled area in the east and south, and a smaller British-administered area in the west. In 1946 the zones were transformed into UN Trust Territories, with British and French rule continuing in their respective areas. French Cameroons became an autonomous state within the French Community in 1957. Under the leadership of Ahmadou Ahidjo, a northerner who became Prime Minister in 1958, the territory became independent, as the Republic of Cameroon, on 1 January 1960. The first election for the country's National Assembly, held in April 1960, was won by Ahidjo's party, the Union camerounaise. In May the new National Assembly elected Ahidjo to be the country's first President.

British Cameroons, comprising a northern and a southern region, was attached to neighbouring Nigeria, for administrative purposes, prior to Nigeria's independence in October 1960. Plebiscites were held, under UN auspices, in the two regions of British Cameroons in February 1961. The northern area voted to merge with Nigeria (becoming the province of Sardauna), while the south voted for union with the Republic of Cameroon, which took place on 1 October 1961.

The enlarged country was named the Federal Republic of Cameroon, with French and English as joint official languages. It comprised two states: the former French zone became East Cameroon, while the former British portion became West Cameroon. John Ngu Foncha, the Prime Minister of West Cameroon and leader of the Kamerun National Democratic Party, became Vice-President of the Federal Republic. Under the continuing leadership of Ahidjo, who (as the sole candidate) was re-elected President in May 1965, the two states became increasingly integrated. In September 1966 the two governing parties and several opposition groups combined to form a single party, the Union nationale camerounaise (UNC). Ahidjo was re-elected as President in March 1970, and Solomon Muna (who had replaced Foncha as Prime Minister of West Cameroon in 1968) became Vice-President.

In June 1972, following the approval by referendum of a new Constitution, the federal system was ended, and the country was officially renamed the United Republic of Cameroon. A centralized political and administrative system was rapidly introduced, and in May 1973 a new National Assembly was elected for a five-year term. After the re-election of Ahidjo as President in April 1975, the Constitution was revised, and a Prime Minister, Paul Biya (a bilingual Christian southerner), was appointed in June. In April 1980 Ahidjo was unanimously re-elected to the presidency for a fifth five-year term of office.

Ahidjo resigned as President in November 1982, and nominated Biya as his successor. In January 1984 Biya was re-elected as President of the Republic. The post of Prime Minister was subsequently abolished, and it was announced that the country's name was to revert to the Republic of Cameroon.

Domestic Political Affairs

In April 1984 rebel elements in the presidential guard attempted to overthrow the Biya Government. After three days of intense fighting, in which hundreds of people were reported to have been killed, the rebellion was suppressed by forces loyal to the President; a total of 51 defendants subsequently received death sentences. Following extensive changes within the military hierarchy, the UNC Central Committee and the leadership of state-controlled companies, Biya reorganized his Government in July and introduced more stringent press censorship. In March 1985 the UNC was renamed the Rassemblement démocratique du peuple camerounais (RDPC).

Presidential and legislative elections were held in April 1988. Biya was re-elected unopposed to the presidency, securing 98.8% of the votes cast. In the elections to the National Assembly voters were presented with a choice of RDPC-approved candidates; 153 of the 180 deputies elected were new members.

In February 1990 11 people were arrested in connection with their alleged involvement in an unofficial opposition organization, the Social Democratic Front (SDF). In June, in response to mounting civil unrest, Biya stated that he envisaged the future adoption of a multi-party system and announced a series of reforms, including the abolition of laws governing subversion, the revision of the law on political associations, and the reinforcement of press freedom. In December the National Assembly adopted legislation whereby Cameroon officially became a multi-party state.

In April 1991, in response to increasing pressure for political reform, the National Assembly approved legislation granting a general amnesty for political prisoners and reintroducing the post of Prime Minister. Biya subsequently appointed Sadou Hayatou, hitherto Secretary-General at the Presidency, to the position. Hayatou named a transitional Government, principally composed of members of the former Cabinet. However, the Government's refusal to comply with demands for an unconditional amnesty for all political prisoners and for the convening of a national conference prompted the organization of a general strike in June. The Government placed seven of Cameroon's 10 provinces under military rule, prohibited opposition gatherings, and later in June, following continued civil disturbances, banned several opposition parties, alleging that they were responsible for terrorist activities. The observance of the general strike declined in subsequent months.

Towards constitutional reform

Following negotiations, in mid-November 1991 the Government and about 40 of the 47 registered opposition parties signed an agreement providing for the establishment of a committee to draft constitutional reforms. The opposition undertook to suspend the campaign of civil disobedience, while the Government agreed to end the ban on opposition meetings and to release all prisoners who had been arrested during anti-Government demonstrations. The Government revoked the ban on opposition gatherings later in November, and in December ended military rule. In February 1992 those opposition parties that had not accepted the agreement in November 1991 formed the Alliance pour le redressement du Cameroun (ARC), and announced that they were to boycott the forthcoming elections.

Legislative elections took place on 1 March 1992, at which the RDPC won 88 of the National Assembly's 180 seats, while the Union nationale pour la démocratie et le progrès (UNDP) obtained 68, the extreme left-wing Union des populations camerounaises (UPC) 18 and the Mouvement pour la défense de la République (MDR) six seats. The RDPC subsequently formed an alliance with the MDR, thereby securing an absolute majority in the National Assembly. In April Biya formed a 25-member Cabinet, principally comprising members of the previous Government and including five MDR members; Simon Achidi Achu, an anglophone member of the RDPC, was appointed Prime Minister.

In August 1992 Biya announced that the presidential election, scheduled for May 1993, was to be brought forward to 11 October 1992. In September Biya promulgated legislation regulating the election of the President that prohibited the formation of electoral alliances. Shortly before the election two of the seven opposition candidates withdrew in favour of the Chairman of the SDF, John Fru Ndi, who received the support of the ARC. Despite opposition allegations of malpractice on the part of the Government it was announced that Biya had been re-elected by 39.9% of the votes cast, while Fru Ndi had secured 35.9%, prompting violent demonstrations by opposition supporters in many areas. Biya was inaugurated as President on 3 November and pledged to implement further constitutional reforms. At the end of November Biya appointed a new 30-member Cabinet, which, in addition to three members of the MDR, included representatives of the UPC, the UNDP and the Parti national du progrès.

In April 1993 the Government promulgated draft constitutional amendments that provided for the installation of a democratic political system, with the establishment of new organs of government, including an upper legislative chamber, to be known as the Senate, and restricted the power vested in the President (who was to serve a maximum of two five-year terms of office). The draft legislation retained a unitary state, but, in recognition of demands by supporters of federalism, envisaged a more decentralized system of local government. Constitutional discussions resumed in December 1994, but were boycotted by the opposition, which cited limitations in the agenda of the debate. Nevertheless, in early 1995 the recently formed Consultative Constitutional Review Committee submitted revised constitutional amendments to Biya for consideration.

In July 1995 members of a new anglophone organization, the Southern Cameroons National Council (SCNC, which demanded that the former portion of the British Cameroons that had amalgamated with the Republic of Cameroon in 1961 be granted autonomy), staged a demonstration in Bamenda. In August representatives of anglophone movements officially presented their demands for the establishment of an independent, English-speaking republic of Southern Cameroons to the UN; the organizations claimed that the plebiscite of 1961, whereby the former southern portion of British Cameroons had voted to merge with the Republic of Cameroon on terms of equal status, had been rendered invalid by subsequent francophone domination.

In October 1995 a special congress of the RDPC re-elected Biya as leader of the party for a further term of five years. In December the National Assembly adopted the revised constitutional amendments, submitted by Biya earlier that month, which increased the presidential mandate from five to seven years (while restricting the maximum tenure of office to two terms) and provided for the establishment of a Senate. In September Achu was replaced as Prime Minister by Peter Mafany Musonge, the General Manager of the Cameroon Development Corporation, and a new Cabinet was appointed.

In January 1997 the Government postponed the legislative elections (which had been scheduled to take place in March) owing to organizational difficulties. The elections, which were contested by 46 political parties, took place on 17 May. The announcement of provisional results (which attributed a large majority of seats to the RDPC) prompted opposition claims of widespread electoral malpractice; however, the Supreme Court rejected opposition appeals against RDPC victories and in early June the official election results were announced: the RDPC had secured 109 of the 180 seats in the legislature, while the SDF had obtained 43, the UNDP 13 and the Union démocratique du Cameroun (UDC) five seats. The Cabinet remained virtually unchanged from the previous administration. In August further polls were conducted in seven constituencies where the results had been annulled, owing to alleged irregularities; the RDPC won all of the seats, thus increasing its representation in the National Assembly to 116 seats.

It was announced in September 1997 that the presidential election would be held on 12 October. Shortly afterwards the SDF, the UNDP and the UDC declared a boycott of all elections, in protest against the absence of an independent electoral commission. At the election, which was contested by seven candidates, Biya was re-elected, winning 92.6% of the votes cast. The level of voter participation in the election was much disputed, with official sources asserting that 81.4% of the electorate took part, while opposition leaders claimed that the abstention rate was higher than 80%. Biya was formally inaugurated on 3 November. In December, having reappointed Musonge as Prime Minister, Biya made major changes to the composition of the Cabinet. The new Government included representatives from four of the country's many political groups, although the RDPC retained 45 of the 50 ministerial posts.

Parliamentarians staged a sit-in outside the National Assembly in November 2000 after the security forces prevented a protest march from proceeding. The march had been organized by the SDF in support of demands for the creation of an independent electoral commission. In the following month the National Assembly adopted legislation on the establishment of a National Elections Observatory (NEO) and on the regulation of state funding for political parties and electoral campaigns. However, five opposition parties boycotted the vote on the elections observatory, claiming that it would be unconstitutional, as it would perform the same functions as the Constitutional Council, and criticizing the President's role in appointing its 11 members. Nevertheless, in October the NEO was inaugurated.

Legislative elections, contested by some 47 parties, were held on 30 June 2002. The RDPC's majority increased to 133 seats, while its closest rival, the SDF, secured 21 seats, the UDC five, the UPC three and the UNDP only one seat. Electoral turn-out was reported to be less than 50%, and the elections were boycotted by the SCNC. Voting for the remaining 17 seats was cancelled by the Supreme Court, in response to complaints of various irregularities in the nine constituencies concerned. Opposition parties alleged widespread electoral fraud, however, and demanded that the elections be declared void. The SDF initially refused to participate in the newly elected legislature, although in mid-July Fru Ndi announced the end of the boycott, provoking internal conflict within his party. Several SDF senior officials subsequently resigned from the party and formed the Alliance des forces progressistes, claiming that Fru Ndi's unilateral decision to end the boycott had been inspired by covert plans to join the Government. In August there was an extensive cabinet reorganization, in which 18 new members of government were appointed. On 15 September voting took place for the 17 legislative seats that had remained vacant since June; the RDPC secured a further 16 seats, increasing its majority to 149 of the 180 seats in the National Assembly, while the SDF won the remaining seat.

Biya's third term

Despite a constitutional limit of two terms in office, on 11 October 2004 Biya was again re-elected to the presidency, securing 70.9% of the vote. Fru Ndi (SDF) and Adamou Ndam Njoya (UDC) were attributed just 17.4% and 4.5% of the vote, respectively. Although opposition groups strongly contested the validity of the result, accusing Biya and his allies of large-scale electoral fraud, a delegation of electoral observers composed of former members of the US Congress declared the elections to have been fairly conducted.

In December 2004 President Biya appointed a new Cabinet and, notably, an English-speaking Prime Minister, Ephraïm Inoni, hitherto Assistant Secretary-General of the Presidency. Despite the appointment of Inoni, representatives of Cameroon's anglophone community demanded increased representation in government to counterbalance what they perceived as a disproportionate number of francophone ministers. The new administration was again comprised largely of members of the RDPC.

In July 2005 the National Assembly approved legislation harmonizing the penal code in Cameroon. Hitherto, the anglophone and francophone regions of Cameroon had been subject to distinct penal codes. The new, unique penal code was to combine elements of the Napoleonic, British and pre-colonial legal traditions. Although the measure was broadly welcomed as beneficial to national unity, unrest and secessionist sympathies grew throughout 2005 among anglophones of southern Cameroon. In October public celebrations in Bui County commemorating the anniversary of southern British Cameroons' union with the Republic of Cameroon in 1961 led to violent confrontations. Subsequently, more than 100 SCNC leaders and members, including the movement's National Chairman, Ette Otun Ayamba, were arrested.

At legislative elections held in July 2007 the RDPC consolidated its majority in the National Assembly, winning 152 of the 180 seats available. However, opposition parties denounced the results; it was reported that in some areas no opposition party ballot papers were made available and that members of the RDPC had been observed bribing and intimidating voters. The results in five constituencies were subsequently annulled and new polls were held on 30 September. Provisional results indicated that the RDPC had secured 13 of the 17 seats contested, giving it a total of 153 seats in the National Assembly; the SDF retained its position as the second largest party with 16 seats, while the UNDP took six seats.

In January 2008 it was reported that public meetings and demonstrations had been prohibited in the province of Littoral, including its capital, Douala, where several opposition parties and civil society organizations had been intending to organize protests against government plans to seek the abolition of the constitutional limitation on presidential terms that would allow Biya to stand for re-election in 2011. In late February 2008 rioting erupted in Douala as a nation-wide strike by transport workers staged in protest against recent significant rises in the prices of fuel and basic products coincided with political opposition to constitutional reform. Despite a decision to end the strike after two days, following a slight reduction in fuel prices, the unrest spread to other cities, including Yaoundé. By the end of the month order had been restored in Douala and Yaoundé, where large numbers of heavily armed troops had been deployed, although three people were reportedly killed in clashes with the security forces in the western towns of Bamenda and Bafang. According to official figures, a total of 40 people died and more than 1,500 were arrested during the violence, although one human rights group claimed that more than 100 people had been killed. In March the Government announced a series of measures intended to allay popular discontent, including a 15% increase in the salaries of civil servants and military employees, the suspension of duties on imports of certain basic foodstuffs and a reduction in electricity tariffs. In July 2009 further reductions to the cost of staple goods, such as rice, fish and salt, were announced in an attempt to avoid further unrest.

Meanwhile, in April 2008 the National Assembly approved a number of constitutional amendments, including the controversial removal of the restriction on presidential terms, in a vote boycotted by SDF deputies, who denounced the revisions as a 'constitutional coup'. Protests followed in a number of cities. In August 2008 Fru Ndi was brought to trial for his alleged involvement in the murder of a member of a rival SDF faction in May 2006. Fru Ndi denied the accusations, claiming that they were politically motivated and aimed at preventing him from contesting the 2011 presidential election.

In June 2009 a Cabinet reorganization was effected in which several ministers were redeployed, and nine ministers were replaced. Most notably Philémon Yang, a long-standing anglophone member of the presidential circle, succeeded Inoni as Prime Minister.

A World Bank report published in September 2009 stated that, despite the Epervier anti-corruption campaign that had been put in place in 2004 by Inoni, fraud and institutional corruption were still the largest obstacles to development and investment in Cameroon. Following the convictions and arrests of over 130 officials in 2008, a number of high-profile scandals involving ministers and officials were made public in late 2009 and early 2010, including the arrest of the recently replaced Minister of Education, Haman Adama, and seven regional officials from Douala who were accused of misappropriation of public funds. The Yaoundé branch of the Banque des états de l'Afrique centrale was under investigation for the alleged embezzlement of funds by officials based there and in Paris, France, while President Biya was severely criticized in the French press for the extravagant cost of his visit to the country in September 2009, having two months earlier accepted €537m. in French aid.

Recent developments: the 2011 presidential election

Elections Cameroon (ELECAM), which had been signed into law in 2006 to replace the NEO, became fully functional in January 2010. Shortly thereafter Mboua Massock of the Nouvelle dynamique nationaliste Africaine (a political-cultural opposition movement), who had in 2009 announced his intention to stand in the upcoming presidential election, commenced a protest march from Douala across seven of the 10 regions of the country to popularize 12 electoral demands. These included the holding of two rounds of voting, the computerization of electoral files, and respect for the presidential term of office. However, within the first weeks of the march he was arrested on three separate occasions. The electoral body's impartiality was also called into question—11 of its 12 board members had been selected from the governing party—and in April 2010 a coalition of 10 opposition parties and 10 civil associations appealed for its dissolution.

The registration process for the 2011 presidential poll began in August 2010 and opposition leader Fru Ndi announced his intention to seek a postponement of the elections if some 11 demands were not met: among these were the introduction of biometric data on voters' cards and registers; the participation of all political parties at all levels of decision making regarding the poll; financial autonomy for ELECAM; non-participation of government officials in the election campaign; and the introduction of the right to vote for Cameroon nationals living abroad. This latter stipulation was met in July 2011, when legislation permitting electoral participation by the diaspora was adopted by the National Assembly. Meanwhile, in February the Government established the Agency for the Regulation of Supplies of Basic Consumption Goods, which would impose price controls on staple foodstuffs during inflationary periods, ostensibly to offset a potential source of social disorder prior to the election. Costly fuel subsidies were also maintained during the pre-election period.

In early October 2011, just one week before voting in the presidential poll was due to commence, over 200 SCNC supporters were arrested for attending an 'unauthorized protest' in Buéa. In a similar incident in April, at least 14 members of the SCNC had been detained after participating in a meeting that was viewed by the authorities as illegal.

The presidential election was duly held on 9 October 2011, amid opposition concerns regarding the constitutionality of Biya standing for a further term in office, the impartiality of ELECAM and the credibility of the rules governing the election. As expected, Biya secured another resounding victory, winning 78.0% of the votes cast, while Fru Ndi of the SDF secured 10.7% of the ballot and Garga Haman Adji of the Alliance pour la démocratie et le développement 3.2%; 20 other candidates, underlining the fragmented nature of the opposition, each received under 2% of the vote, including Ayah Paul Abine (1.3%), who had resigned from the RDPC in January following death threats after he had announced his intention to compete against Biya for the right to become the party's presidential nominee. According to official figures, the rate of participation by the electorate was 65.8%. The SDF and other opposition parties complained of widespread procedural irregularities, but, in spite of demands for their annulment, the Supreme Court upheld the election results. While noting numerous deficiencies, international observers were generally satisfied with the conduct of the poll.

In November 2011 the Commission Nationale Anticorruption published a report accusing numerous high-ranking public officials, including government ministers, of corrupt practices. Most notably, Minister of Public Works Bernard Messengue Avom was accused of embezzling US $30m. after issuing fraudulent construction contracts. President Biya established a judicial inquiry to examine the allegations and pledged that legal action would be brought against those responsible.

Biya implemented a cabinet reorganization in December 2011. Among several significant changes, Alamine Ousmane Mey, hitherto the General Manager of Afriland First Bank, was appointed as Minister of Finance, replacing Lazare Essimi Menye, who was given responsibility for the agricultural and rural development portfolio, while Emmanuel Nganou Djoumessi became Minister of the Economy, Planning and Land Settlement, and Emmanuel Bonde was assigned to head the Ministry of Mines, Industry and Technological Development. This focus on the economic portfolios indicated the priorities of the new Government, which was again headed by Yang.

Human rights

A report published by a human rights organization in 2009 cited alleged instances of extra-judicial killings by government forces, prisoners dying while being held in custody, protesters being beaten and journalists being imprisoned without trial. In January Lewis Medjo, editor of the weekly publication *La Détente Libre*, had been sentenced to a three-year gaol term for 'spreading false news', and in April 50 people were arrested in Bamenda for holding an illegal rally. In May 2010 security forces prevented the staging of a rally by hundreds of members of the Union des Journalists du Cameroun demanding the immediate release of all reporters being held and that media cases be tried in civil rather than criminal courts. They also protested against a number of arrests; in December 2009 Jean Bosco Talla, director of the weekly newspaper *Germinal*, had been arrested for 'attacking the honour' of the President; two independent journalists jailed in February 2010 claimed that they had been tortured by intelligence agents; and in April there were three further arrests of journalists investigating corruption at the presidential level, one of whom, Germain Cyrille Ngota (managing editor of the *Cameroon Express*), had died while in custody. Following the exertion of significant political pressure by France, the USA and a number of international journalist organizations, the Government announced that a judicial inquiry into Ngota's death would be held. In September the inquiry reported that Ngota, having been allegedly diagnosed with HIV, had died in gaol from medical complications associated with the disease, although his family and press freedom organizations rejected this assertion. Reports continued to emerge during 2011 of further arrests of journalists, particularly those investigating high-level corruption.

Foreign Affairs

Regional relations

In 1991 the Nigerian Government claimed that Cameroon had annexed nine Nigerian fishing settlements, following a long-standing border dispute, based on a 1913 agreement between Germany and the United Kingdom that ceded the Bakassi peninsula in the Gulf of Guinea (a region of strategic and economic significance) to Cameroon. In December 1993 some 500 Nigerian troops were dispatched to the region, in response to a number of incidents in which Nigerian nationals had been killed by Cameroonian security forces. Later that month the two nations agreed to establish a joint patrol in the disputed area, and to investigate the incidents. In February 1994, however, Cameroon announced that it was to submit the dispute for adjudication by the UN, the Organization of African Unity (OAU, now the African Union, see p. 189) and the International Court of Justice (ICJ, see p. 25), based in The Hague, Netherlands. Subsequent reports of clashes between Cameroonian and Nigerian forces in the region prompted fears of a full-scale conflict, and in September the Cameroonian Government submitted additional claims to territory in north-eastern Nigeria to the ICJ.

In February 1996 Cameroon and Nigeria agreed to refrain from further military action, and delegations from the two countries began discussions with Togolese mediation. In March the ICJ ordered both nations to cease military operations in the region, to withdraw troops to former positions, and to co-operate with a UN investigative mission, which was to be dispatched to the area. Nevertheless, both nations continued to reinforce their contingents in the region, and in December and again in May 1997 the Nigerian authorities claimed that Cameroonian troops had resumed attacks in the region. Further clashes were reported in late 1997 and early 1998.

Relations between Cameroon and Nigeria began to improve in late 1998, and in November the International Committee of the Red Cross organized an exchange of prisoners between the two sides. Although the two countries reportedly agreed to resolve the dispute 'in a fraternal way', both countries presented evidence of their claims at public hearings in The Hague in February and March 2002.

In October 2002 the ICJ issued its final verdict on the demarcation of the land and maritime boundary between Cameroon and Nigeria, notably ruling in favour of Cameroon's sovereignty over the Bakassi peninsula, citing the 1913 Anglo-German partition agreement, while upholding Nigeria's offshore boundary claims. Despite having no option to appeal, Nigeria refused to accept the Court's decision, and troop deployments began to increase on both sides of the border. In mid-November, however, at a meeting in Geneva, Switzerland, mediated by the Secretary-General of the UN, Kofi Annan, the Presidents of Cameroon and Nigeria signed a joint communiqué announcing the creation of a bilateral commission, to be headed by a UN Special Representative, with a mandate to achieve a peaceful solution to the Bakassi peninsula dispute. At its inaugural meeting in Yaoundé in December, the commission agreed on a 15-point peace agenda and decided to establish a sub-committee to undertake the demarcation of the boundary. In August 2003 Nigeria and Cameroon adopted a framework for the demilitarization of the Bakassi region and in December the Nigerian Government ceded control of 32 villages on its north-eastern border to Cameroon, but sovereignty over the disputed territory with petroleum resources remained under discussion.

In January 2004 the two countries agreed to establish joint security patrols in the disputed region, and, following a meeting in Yaoundé in July, it was confirmed that Nigerian troops would withdraw from Bakassi by 15 September. However, the Nigerian Government subsequently reneged on this agreement following legal appeals by Bakassi residents regarding the constitutional legality of ceding land held by Nigerians. The Nigerian Federal High Court rejected this appeal in October but by the end of December the Nigerian Government had still not withdrawn troops from the disputed peninsula, citing difficulties over demarcating maritime boundaries. A new agreement for the withdrawal of Nigerian troops from the peninsula was reached in October 2005 by the bilateral commission. In December the UN Office in West Africa announced that 260 km of the disputed border had been demarcated. In June 2006, at a UN-mediated summit in New York, USA, it was agreed that Nigeria would withdraw its troops from the Bakassi peninsula within 60 days. In August a ceremony marked the transfer of the area to Cameroon after Nigeria completed its troop withdrawal from the disputed region. Nigerian police were to remain in control of the southern and eastern parts of the region until August 2008. In August 2008 Nigeria formally ceded control of the Bakassi peninsula and the first border marker was laid in December 2009. Nevertheless, reports of deaths and harassment of Nigerian nationals in the area continued and there were an estimated 1,500 displaced people at the Ekpri Ikang camp by the end of 2009. In spite of this, in 2011 preliminary work was underway on bilateral transportation and petroleum exploration schemes in the Bakassi region, although the border had still not been fully demarcated by the end of the year.

Relations between Cameroon and Equatorial Guinea have become strained in recent years. The construction of the Cameroon–Chad petroleum pipeline has led to diminished fishing areas inshore, resulting in Cameroonian fishermen travelling further out to sea and thus closer to Equatorial Guinean waters in search of their catch. An armed assault against the presidential palace in Equatorial Guinea in February 2009 led to a further deterioration in relations and the common maritime border was temporarily sealed.

Other external relations

In May 2009, during a visit of the French Prime Minister, François Fillon, to Cameroon, the two countries signed a new defence agreement, replacing the accord in place since 1974 that provided for French military intervention in Cameroon. The new agreement, which formed part of French President Nicolas Sarkozy's Africa policy of moving away from protecting France's spheres of historical and colonial influence, referred to the establishment of a 'strategic partnership' between the two countries. France would thenceforth provide logistical support to the Cameroon armed forces in terms of equipment and technical assistance through training.

CONSTITUTION AND GOVERNMENT

Under the amended 1972 Constitution, the Republic of Cameroon is a multi-party state. Executive power is vested in the President, as Head of State, who is elected by universal adult suffrage for a term of seven years; there is no limit on the number of terms that may be served. Legislative power is held by the National Assembly, which comprises 180 members and is elected for a term of five years. In December 1995 constitutional amendments provided for the establishment of an upper legislative chamber (to be known as the Senate). The Cabinet is appointed by the President. Local administration is based on 10 provinces, each with a governor who is appointed by the President.

REGIONAL AND INTERNATIONAL CO-OPERATION

Cameroon is a member of the African Union (see p. 189), of the Central African organs of the Franc Zone (see p. 333) and of the Communauté économique des états de l'Afrique centrale (CEEAC, see p. 449).

Cameroon became a member of the UN in 1960, and was admitted to the World Trade Organization (WTO, see p. 433) in 1995. Cameroon participates in the Group of 77 (G77, see p. 450) developing countries and in 2009 was elected to the UN Human Rights Council for a three-year term. Cameroon is also a member of the International Cocoa Organization (see p. 445) and of the International Coffee Organization (see p. 445).

ECONOMIC AFFAIRS

In 2010, according to estimates by the World Bank, Cameroon's gross national income (GNI), measured at average 2008–10 prices, was US $23,169m., equivalent to $1,180 per head (or $2,230 per head on an international purchasing-power parity basis). During 2001–10, it was estimated, the population increased at an average annual rate of 2.3%, while gross domestic product (GDP) per head increased, in real terms, by an average of 0.9% per year. Overall GDP increased, in real terms, at an average annual rate of 3.1% in 2001–10; growth in 2010 was 2.6%.

Agriculture (including hunting, forestry and fishing) contributed 23.3% of GDP in 2009, according to the African Development Bank (AfDB). An estimated 45.2% of the labour force were employed in agriculture in mid-2012, according to FAO. The principal cash crops are cocoa beans (which accounted for 6.2% of export earnings in 2006) and cotton (2.3%). The principal subsistence crops are cassava, plaintains, maize and sorghum; Cameroon is not, however, self-sufficient in cereals. In 1995 an estimated 42% of the country's land area was covered by forest, but an inadequate transport infrastructure has impeded the development of the forestry sector. In 2010 an accord was signed with the European Union (EU, see p. 276), to which Cameroon exports 80% of its wood, with the aim of combating illegal logging and introducing a system of traceability by 2012. During 2001–07, according to the World Bank, the real GDP of the agricultural sector increased at an average annual rate of 3.4%; growth in 2007 was 3.9%.

Industry (including mining, manufacturing, construction and power) employed 8.9% of the labour force in 1990, and contributed 29.7% of GDP in 2009, according to the AfDB. During 2001–07, according to the World Bank, industrial GDP declined at an average annual rate of 0.6%; growth in 2007 was 0.1%.

According to the AfDB, mining contributed 7.9% of GDP in 2009. The sector employed only 0.1% of Cameroon's working population in 1985, although this number was believed to have grown considerably in recent years. Receipts from the exploitation of the country's petroleum reserves constitute a principal source of government revenue. Deposits of limestone are also quarried. Significant reserves of natural gas, bauxite, iron ore, uranium and tin remain largely undeveloped. However, the extraction of bauxite at Ngaoundere and iron ore at Mbalamtwo was scheduled to begin in 2012, and in 2009 a joint Cameroon-North Korean company had also discovered deposits of gem quality and industrial diamonds; mining began in 2010. Furthermore, a French company was also granted rights for petroleum exploration in Rio del Rey in the recently ceded Bakassi region (see Foreign Affairs). According to the IMF, the GDP of the mining sector increased by an average of 2.5% per year in 1995/96–2000/01; growth in 2000/01 was 0.6%.

Manufacturing contributed an estimated 16.1% of GDP in 2009, according to the AfDB. The sector employed an estimated 7% of the working population in 1995. The sector is based on the processing of both indigenous primary products (petroleum-refining, agro-industrial activities) and of imported raw materials (an aluminium smelter uses alumina imported from Guinea). According to the World Bank, manufacturing GDP increased at an average annual rate of 4.4% in 2001–04; growth in 2004 was 4.0%.

Construction contributed 4.7% of GDP in 2009, according to the AfDB. The sector employed 1.8% of the employed labour force in 1985.

In 2008 hydroelectric power installations supplied 76.2% of Cameroon's energy. A further 15.9% was produced by petroleum sources and 7.7% by gas. In 2006 imports of mineral fuels accounted for 32.1% of the value of total imports.

Services contributed 46.9% of GDP in 2009, according to the AfDB. The sector engaged 14.7% of the employed labour force in 1985. During 2001–07 the GDP of the services sector increased at an average annual rate of 6.3%; growth in 2007 was 5.0%.

In 2010 Cameroon recorded a visible trade deficit of US $177.4m., and there was a deficit of $856.3m. on the current account of the balance of payments. In 2006 the principal source of imports (23.3%) was Nigeria; other major suppliers were France and the People's Republic of China. Spain was the principal market for exports in that year, taking 25.9% of the total; other significant purchasers were Italy, France, the USA and the Netherlands. The principal exports in 2006 were crude petroleum and oils and cocoa beans. The principal imports in that year were mineral fuels and lubricants, food and live animals, machinery and transport equipment, manufactured goods, and chemicals and related products. In January 2009 Cameroon signed an interim economic partnership agreement with the EU to liberalize 80% of imports from the EU market for a period of 15 years.

In 2011 there was a budget deficit of 150,000m. francs CFA. Cameroon's general government gross debt was 1,349,510m. francs CFA in 2010, equivalent to 12.1% of GDP. Cameroon's total external debt in 2009 was US $2,941m., of which $2,128m. was public and publicly guaranteed debt. In 2009 the cost of servicing long-term public and publicly guaranteed debt and repayments to the IMF was equivalent to 1.4% of the value of exports of goods, services and income (excluding workers' remittances). According to ILO, the annual rate of inflation averaged 2.9% in 2000–10; consumer prices increased by 8.5% in 2009 and by 1.3% in 2010. An estimated 7.5% of the labour force were unemployed in 2001.

Cameroon's potential for continued economic development has been hindered by its poor physical infrastructure, endemic fraud and corruption, and a consistent decline in petroleum output. Production volumes decreased from a peak of 185,000 barrels per day (b/d) in the mid-1980s to 64,000 b/d in 2010. Although output was forecast to rise during 2012–14 as new oilfields entered into production, a subsequent return to the long-term downward trend was projected. Meanwhile, to address the infrastructural problems that were inhibiting economic growth, the Government embarked upon an ambitious public works programme, which was ongoing in 2011. Roads were to be modernized, a deep-water harbour at Kribi was to be built (in a venture that was expected to generate 30,000 jobs in its construction phase), water and telecommunications networks were to be extended, and new power plants were to be established. The IMF estimated that real GDP expanded by 3.2% during 2010 (up from 2.0% in 2009), reflecting rising demand for Cameroon's commodity exports, the high price of oil on international markets and increases in agricultural productivity. These trends continued in 2011, when real GDP growth was forecast to reach 3.8%, according to the IMF. Cocoa farmers enjoyed a record harvest during the 2010/11 season and exports increased as a result, although severe weather conditions and disease were reportedly having a negative impact on the 2011/12 crop. Prospects in the near term appeared broadly favourable, with an expected (temporary) rise in oil output, numerous infrastructural projects underway, and increased efforts by the Government to attract foreign investment and stabilize the country's finances. However, due to its export-driven economy, Cameroon remained susceptible to a deterioration in global economic conditions. The IMF projected real GDP growth of 4.5% in 2012, while the Government's Strategy Document for Growth and Employment foresaw an annual GDP growth rate of 5.5% between 2010 and 2020, and significant resources were being targeted at securing a three-fold increase in the production of electrical power by 2020, which would facilitate a number of energy-intensive mining operations.

PUBLIC HOLIDAYS

2013: 1 January (New Year), 11 February (Youth Day), 29 March (Good Friday), 1 April (Easter Monday), 1 May (Labour Day), 9 May (Ascension Day), 20 May (National Day), 7 August* (Djoulde Soumae, end of Ramadan), 15 August (Assumption), 14 October* (Festival of Sheep), 25 December (Christmas).

* These holidays are dependent on the Islamic lunar calendar and may vary by one or two days from the dates given.

Statistical Survey

Source (unless otherwise stated): Direction de la Prévision, Ministère de l'Economie et des Finances, BP 18, Yaoundé; tel. 2223-4040; fax 2223-2150.

Area and Population

AREA, POPULATION AND DENSITY

Area (sq km)	475,442*
Population (census results)	
9 April 1987	10,493,655
11 November 2005	
Males	8,408,495
Females	8,643,639
Total	17,052,134
Population (UN estimates at mid-year)†	
2010	19,598,889
2011	20,030,359
2012	20,468,945
Density (per sq km) at mid-2012	43.1

* 183,569 sq miles.

† Source: UN, *World Population Prospects: The 2010 Revision*.

POPULATION BY AGE AND SEX

(UN estimates at mid-2012)

	Males	Females	Total
0–14	4,154,615	4,099,424	8,254,039
15–64	5,738,378	5,755,453	11,493,831
65 and over	327,700	393,375	721,075
Total	10,220,693	10,248,252	20,468,945

Source: UN, *World Population Prospects: The 2010 Revision*.

PROVINCES

(population at 1987 census)

	Urban	Rural	Total
Centre	877,481	774,119	1,651,600
Littoral	1,093,323	259,510	1,352,833
West	431,337	908,454	1,339,791
South-West	258,940	579,102	838,042
North-West	271,114	966,234	1,237,348
North	234,572	597,593	832,165
East	152,787	364,411	517,198
South	104,023	269,775	373,798
Adamaoua	178,644	316,541	495,185
Far North	366,698	1,488,997	1,855,695
Total	3,968,919	6,524,736	10,493,655

PRINCIPAL TOWNS

(population at 1987 census)

Douala	810,000	Bamenda	110,000
Yaoundé (capital)	649,000	Nkongsamba	85,420
Garoua	142,000	Kumba	70,112
Maroua	123,000	Limbé	44,561
Bafoussam	113,000		

Mid-2010 ('000, incl. suburbs, UN estimates): Douala 2,125; Yaoundé 1,801 (Source: UN, *World Urbanization Prospects: The 2009 Revision*).

BIRTHS AND DEATHS

(annual averages, UN estimates)

	1995–2000	2000–05	2005–10
Birth rate (per 1,000)	38.0	38.0	37.2
Death rate (per 1,000)	14.6	15.3	15.0

Source: UN, *World Population Prospects: The 2010 Revision*.

Life expectancy (years at birth, WHO estimates): 51 (males 51; females 51) in 2009 (Source: WHO, *World Health Statistics*).

ECONOMICALLY ACTIVE POPULATION

(persons aged six years and over, mid-1985, official estimates)

	Males	Females	Total
Agriculture, hunting, forestry and fishing	1,574,946	1,325,925	2,900,871
Mining and quarrying	1,693	100	1,793
Manufacturing	137,671	36,827	174,498
Electricity, gas and water	3,373	149	3,522
Construction	65,666	1,018	66,684
Trade, restaurants and hotels	115,269	38,745	154,014
Transport, storage and communications	50,664	1,024	51,688
Financing, insurance, real estate and business services	7,447	562	8,009
Community, social and personal services	255,076	37,846	292,922
Sub-total	2,211,805	1,442,196	3,654,001
Activities not adequately defined	18,515	17,444	35,959
Total in employment	2,230,320	1,459,640	3,689,960
Unemployed	180,016	47,659	227,675
Total labour force	2,410,336	1,507,299	3,917,635

Source: ILO, *Yearbook of Labour Statistics*.

Mid-2012 ('000, estimates): Agriculture, etc. 3,574; Total labour force 7,914 (Source: FAO).

Health and Welfare

KEY INDICATORS

Total fertility rate (children per woman, 2009)	4.5
Under-5 mortality rate (per 1,000 live births, 2009)	154
HIV/AIDS (% of persons aged 15–49, 2009)	5.3
Physicians (per 1,000 head, 2004)	0.2
Hospital beds (per 1,000 head, 2006)	1.5
Health expenditure (2008): US $ per head (PPP)	117
Health expenditure (2008): % of GDP	5.3
Health expenditure (2008): public (% of total)	22.7
Access to water (% of persons, 2008)	74
Access to sanitation (% of persons, 2008)	47
Total carbon dioxide emissions ('000 metric tons, 2008)	4,070.7
Carbon dioxide emissions per head (metric tons, 2008)	0.2
Human Development Index (2011): ranking	150
Human Development Index (2011): value	0.482

For sources and definitions, see explanatory note on p. vi.

Agriculture

PRINCIPAL CROPS

('000 metric tons)

	2008	2009	2010
Rice, paddy	72	115*	175*
Maize	1,395	1,450*	1,674
Millet	75†	65*	55†
Sorghum	931†	980*	900†
Potatoes	145	147*	151
Sweet potatoes	236	230*	242*
Cassava (Manioc)	2,883	2,950*	3,024
Yams	400	400*	410
Taro (Coco yams)	1,482	1,450*	1,470
Sugar cane*	1,450	1,450	1,450
Beans, dry	271	275*	285
Groundnuts, with shell	484	457†	460†
Oil palm fruit*	1,555	1,600	1,575
Melonseed*	62	60	62

—continued	2008	2009	2010
Tomatoes	572	570*	576
Pumpkins, squash and gourds*	142	145	146
Onions, dry	112	113*	115
Bananas	1,078	1,000*	950
Plantains	2,501	2,450*	2,604
Avocados*	55	54	56
Pineapples	126	127	137
Coffee, green	51	48†	67
Cocoa beans	229	236	264
Natural rubber	53	52	55

* FAO estimate(s).
† Unofficial figure.

Aggregate production ('000 metric tons, may include official, semi-official or estimated data): Total cereals 2,474 in 2008, 2,531 in 2009, 2,805 in 2010; Total roots and tubers 5,183 in 2008, 5,215 in 2009, 5,336 in 2010; Total vegetables (incl. melons) 1,829 in 2008, 1,846 in 2009, 1,865 in 2010; Total fruits (excl. melons) 3,886 in 2008, 3,760 in 2009, 3,879 in 2010.

Source: FAO.

LIVESTOCK
('000 head, year ending September)

	2008	2009	2010*
Horses	15	17	17
Asses	40	40	40
Cattle	5,046	5,000	5,700
Pigs	1,500	1,630	1,680
Sheep*	3,800	3,800	3,800
Goats*	4,400	4,400	4,400
Chickens	44,929	44,754	45,000

* FAO estimate(s).

Source: FAO.

LIVESTOCK PRODUCTS
('000 metric tons)

	2008	2009	2010
Cattle meat	109.6	109.6	124.0*
Sheep meat	13.3	12.7	16.5
Goat meat	17.7	16.9	20.1
Pig meat	32.6	31.1	37.8*
Chicken meat	67.7	63.9	68.0*
Game meat*	62.1	66.2	66.5
Cows' milk	170.0	170.1	175.0
Sheep's milk*	17.7	18.3	18.6
Goats' milk*	45.3	47.2	48.0
Hen eggs*	14.9	14.9	15.0
Honey*	3.8	4.2	4.2

* FAO estimate(s).

Source: FAO.

Forestry

ROUNDWOOD REMOVALS
('000 cubic metres, excl. bark, FAO estimates, unless otherwise indicated)

	2007	2008	2009
Sawlogs, veneer logs and logs for sleepers	2,274*	2,266	2,266
Other industrial wood	350	350	350
Fuel wood	9,648	9,733	9,818
Total	12,272	12,349	12,434

* Unofficial figure.

2010: Production assumed to be unchanged from 2009 (FAO estimates).

Source: FAO.

SAWNWOOD PRODUCTION
('000 cubic metres, incl. railway sleepers)

	2006	2007	2008
Total (all broadleaved)	702*	773†	773†

* FAO estimate.
† Unofficial figure.

2009–10: Production assumed to be unchanged from 2008 (FAO estimates).

Source: FAO.

Fishing

('000 metric tons, live weight)

	2007	2008*	2009*
Capture*	138.6	138.0	138.0
Freshwater fishes	74.4	74.0	74.0
Cassava croaker	0.1	0.1	0.1
Bobo croaker	0.3	0.3	0.3
Sardinellas	2.1	2.1	2.1
Bonga shad	41.5	41.4	41.4
Aquaculture*	0.3	0.3	0.4
Total catch*	139.0	138.3	138.4

* FAO estimates.

Source: FAO.

Mining

	2007	2008	2009
Crude petroleum (million barrels)	30.4	29.7	30.0
Gold (kg)*	2,000	1,800	1,800
Pozzolan ('000 metric tons)	600	600	600
Limestone ('000 metric tons)	100	100	100

* From artisanal mining.

Source: US Geological Survey.

Industry

SELECTED PRODUCTS
('000 metric tons unless otherwise indicated)

	2006	2007	2008
Palm oil	193	172*	185†
Raw sugar	126	100	100
Veneer sheets ('000 cu m)	47†	85*	85†
Plywood ('000 cu m)	40†	32*	32†
Jet fuels	71	73	85
Motor spirit (petrol)	320	390	399
Kerosene	300	331	261
Gas-diesel (distillate fuel) oil	569	694	658
Residual fuel oils	354	387	380
Lubricating oils	0	0	0
Petroleum bitumen (asphalt)	0	0	0
Liquefied petroleum gas	22	19	17
Cement	1,127	1,209	982
Aluminium (unwrought)	91	90	n.a.
Electric energy (million kWh)	5,106	5,753	5,551

* Unofficial figure.
† FAO estimate.

2009 ('000 cu metres unless otherwise indicated, unofficial figures): Veneer sheets 79; Plywood 24; Palm oil ('000 metric tons) 182.

2010 ('000 cu metres, FAO estimates): Veneer sheets 85; Plywood 32.

Sources: UN Industrial Commodity Statistics Database; FAO.

Finance

CURRENCY AND EXCHANGE RATES

Monetary Units
100 centimes = 1 franc de la Coopération financière en Afrique centrale (CFA).

Sterling, Dollar and Euro Equivalents (30 December 2011)
£1 sterling = 783.813 francs CFA;
US $1 = 506.961 francs CFA;
€1 = 655.957 francs CFA;
10,000 francs CFA = £12.76 = $19.73 = €15.24.

Average Exchange Rate (francs CFA per US $)

2009	472.186
2010	495.277
2011	471.866

Note: An exchange rate of 1 French franc = 50 francs CFA, established in 1948, remained in force until January 1994, when the CFA franc was devalued by 50%, with the exchange rate adjusted to 1 French franc = 100 francs CFA. This relationship to French currency remained in effect with the introduction of the euro on 1 January 1999. From that date, accordingly, a fixed exchange rate of €1 = 655.957 francs CFA has been in operation.

BUDGET
('000 million francs CFA)

Revenue*	2010	2011†	2012‡
Petroleum revenue	497	415	663
Non-petroleum revenue	1,372	1,576	1,665
Direct taxes	343	—	404
Special tax on petroleum products	83	89	95
Taxes on international trade	253	—	300
Other taxes on goods and services	612	—	768
Non-tax revenue (excluding privatization proceeds)	81	97	97
Total	1,869	1,991	2,328

Expenditure	2010	2011†	2012‡
Current expenditure	1,611	1,565	1,750
Wages and salaries	634	665	734
Other goods and services	613	479	534
Interest on public debt	33	45	48
Subsidies and transfers	331	376	434
Capital expenditure	456	680	702
Externally financed investment	100	206	196
Domestically financed investment	315	429	441
Restructuring	42	45	65
Total	2,067	2,245	2,452

* Excluding grants received ('000 million francs CFA): 71 in 2010; 104 in 2011 (budget figure); 88 in 2012 (projected figure).
† Budget figures.
‡ Projected figures.

Source: IMF, *Cameroon: 2011 Article IV Consultation—Staff Report; Debt Sustainability Analysis; Informational Annex; Public Information Notice on the Executive Board Discussion; and Statement by the Executive Director for Cameroon* (September 2011).

INTERNATIONAL RESERVES*
(US $ million at 31 December)

	2008	2009	2010
IMF special drawing rights	4.56	243.71	27.13
Reserve position in IMF	1.26	1.32	1.34
Foreign exchange	3,080.57	3,430.49	3,614.17
Total	3,086.38	3,675.52	3,642.64

* Excluding reserves of gold (30,000 troy ounces in 2008).

Source: IMF, *International Financial Statistics*.

MONEY SUPPLY
('000 million francs CFA at 31 December)

	2008	2009	2010
Currency outside banks	430.64	447.50	501.65
Demand deposits at deposit money banks	902.17	992.84	1,089.71
Total money (incl. others)	1,358.00	1,451.41	1,602.08

Source: IMF, *International Financial Statistics*.

COST OF LIVING
(Consumer Price Index; base: 2000 = 100)

	2006	2007	2008
Food	117.9	119.1	130.0
Clothing	100.4	100.3	100.8
Electricity, gas and other fuels	119.3	120.4	124.6
All items	116.2	117.2	123.5

2009: All items 127.2.

2010: All items 128.9.

Source: ILO.

NATIONAL ACCOUNTS

Expenditure on the Gross Domestic Product
('000 million francs CFA at current prices)

	2007	2008	2009
Government final consumption expenditure	993	1,127	1,243
Private final consumption expenditure	7,170	7,840	8,304
Gross capital formation	1,702	1,842	1,965
Change in inventories	–7	60	80
Total domestic expenditure	9,858	10,869	11,592
Exports of goods and services	2,343	2,520	1,770
Less Imports of goods and services	2,409	2,946	2,322
GDP in purchasers' values	9,792	10,444	11,040

Gross Domestic Product by Economic Activity
('000 million francs CFA at current prices)

	2007	2008	2009
Agriculture	2,066	2,257	2,391
Mining and quarrying	958	926	807
Manufacturing	1,340	1,447	1,653
Electricity, gas and water	99	102	100
Construction	293	315	485
Wholesale and retail trade, restaurants and hotels	1,976	2,053	2,059
Finance, insurance and real estate	513	609	648
Transport and communication	470	518	534
Public administration and defence	342	458	507
Other services	1,011	1,007	1,060
Sub-total	9,068	9,692	10,244
Indirect taxes	772	811	856
Less Imputed bank service charge	47	61	60
GDP in purchasers' values	9,792	10,444	11,040

Source: African Development Bank.

BALANCE OF PAYMENTS
(US $ million)

	2008	2009	2010
Exports of goods f.o.b.	5,890.0	4,169.9	4,485.2
Imports of goods f.o.b.	–5,424.0	–4,559.0	–4,662.6
Trade balance	466.0	–389.2	–177.4
Exports of services	1,483.7	1,248.9	1,159.3
Imports of services	–2,668.3	–1,779.9	–1,745.6
Balance on goods and services	–718.6	–920.2	–763.7
Other income received	65.8	131.4	93.1
Other income paid	–394.5	–608.5	–331.7
Balance on goods, services and income	–1,047.3	–1,397.2	–1,002.3

—*continued*	2008	2009	2010
Current transfers received	774.6	532.0	334.3
Current transfers paid	–177.0	–253.5	–188.3
Current balance	–449.7	–1,118.7	–856.3
Capital account (net)	146.5	184.1	147.0
Direct investment abroad	47.3	140.8	35.8
Direct investment from abroad	–24.2	668.3	–0.6
Portfolio investment assets	–39.3	–97.2	–10.8
Portfolio investment liabilities	–1.4	–0.7	85.2
Other investment assets	–66.4	–100.9	550.6
Other investment liabilities	449.2	394.4	–132.8
Net errors and omissions	205.1	159.7	188.8
Overall balance	267.0	229.8	6.8

Source: IMF, *International Financial Statistics*.

External Trade

PRINCIPAL COMMODITIES
(US $ million)

Imports c.i.f.	2004	2005	2006
Food and live animals	407.3	464.1	508.9
Cereals and cereal preparations	211.9	267.2	285.1
Mineral fuels, lubricants, etc.	427.7	720.2	1,010.1
Petroleum, petroleum products and related materials	423.3	714.3	995.5
Crude petroleum and oils	366.5	657.9	925.4
Chemicals and related products	312.4	301.3	348.7
Manufactured goods	327.3	381.4	400.9
Iron and steel	60.7	89.5	93.4
Tubes, pipes and fittings	12.8	29.9	28.1
Machinery and transport equipment	642.3	548.7	537.9
Road vehicles	198.8	191.3	184.2
Total (incl. others)	2,406.3	2,735.2	3,150.5

Exports f.o.b.	2004	2005	2006
Food and live animals	443.6	393.3	414.5
Coffee, tea, cocoa, spices, etc.	344.7	310.4	329.4
Cocoa and cocoa products	266.7	245.2	260.6
Cocoa beans (raw, roasted)	230.1	209.6	221.9
Crude materials, inedible, except fuels	309.8	329.6	594.3
Textile fibres and wastes	144.5	132.6	103.9
Raw cotton (not carded or combed)	144.5	132.6	103.7
Mineral fuels, lubricants, etc.	1,156.3	1,211.6	2,203.5
Petroleum, petroleum products and related materials	1,156.2	1,211.5	2,203.5
Crude petroleum and oils	1,018.7	839.6	1,781.7
Petroleum products (refined)	137.5	371.9	421.4
Manufactured goods	162.5	161.8	238.5
Aluminium	114.1	123.9	161.2
Total (incl. others)	2,476.8	2,440.6	3,576.4

Source: UN, *International Trade Statistics Yearbook*.

PRINCIPAL TRADING PARTNERS
(US $ million, estimates)

Imports c.i.f.	2004	2005	2006
Belgium	118.1	106.0	127.6
Brazil	35.9	70.4	86.1
China, People's Repub.	110.6	143.2	199.8
Côte d'Ivoire	32.1	25.5	67.2
Finland	62.7	6.6	6.8
France (incl. Monaco)	539.7	509.3	540.4
Germany	111.2	104.1	108.1
India	26.6	34.2	60.7
Italy	69.2	77.9	83.6
Japan	111.4	90.3	86.3
Mauritania	27.9	42.1	43.9
Netherlands	54.9	46.5	42.3
Nigeria	292.8	605.5	735.4
South Africa	36.3	40.3	43.4
Spain	35.3	36.6	33.8
Thailand	54.9	68.6	39.7
Turkey	22.4	18.3	18.2
United Kingdom	50.0	52.8	41.9
USA	127.1	133.3	90.3
Total (incl. others)	2,406.3	2,735.2	3,150.5

Exports f.o.b.	2004	2005	2006
Belgium	96.3	114.5	122.1
Chad	27.7	26.2	28.7
China, People's Repub.	62.8	68.4	121.5
Congo, Democratic Repub.	20.9	27.3	98.6
Congo, Repub.	22.5	20.9	23.5
France (incl. Monaco)	334.6	300.3	380.9
Gabon	37.7	28.3	16.8
Germany	21.9	26.1	28.6
India	17.2	10.0	6.1
Ireland	27.0	20.6	7.7
Italy	284.3	327.1	825.9
Netherlands	211.6	212.4	226.8
Nigeria	24.8	15.8	21.3
South Africa	20.4	54.4	22.8
Spain	263.7	453.9	927.6
Turkey	27.7	14.3	19.1
United Kingdom	97.7	132.7	70.2
USA	141.6	111.1	227.8
Total (incl. others)	2,476.8	2,440.6	3,576.4

Source: UN, *International Trade Statistics Yearbook*.

Transport

RAILWAYS
(traffic, year ending 30 June)

	2001	2002	2003
Freight ton-km (million)	1,159	1,179	1,090
Passenger-km (million)	303	308	322

Source: UN, *Statistical Yearbook*.

2006 (million): Passengers carried 1.1; Passenger-km 357; Freight ton-km 1,076 (Source: World Bank, World Development Indicators database).

ROAD TRAFFIC
('000 motor vehicles in use, estimates)

	2001	2002	2003
Passenger cars	134.5	151.9	173.1
Commercial vehicles	51.1	37.4	57.4

Source: UN, *Statistical Yearbook*.

2005 ('000 motor vehicles in use): Passenger cars 174,865; Buses and coaches 15,613; Vans and lorries 56,207; Motorcycles and mopeds 65,574 (Source: IRF, *World Road Statistics*).

SHIPPING

Merchant Fleet
(registered at 31 December)

	2007	2008	2009
Number of vessels	66	64	64
Total displacement ('000 grt)	55.3	16.5	16.2

Source: IHS Fairplay, *World Fleet Statistics*.

International Sea-borne Freight Traffic
(freight traffic at Douala, '000 metric tons)

	2006	2008	2009
Goods loaded	6,468	2,160	1,824
Goods unloaded	13,416	4,848	5,352

Note: Data for 2007 were not available.

Source: UN, *Monthly Bulletin of Statistics*.

CIVIL AVIATION
(traffic on scheduled services)

	2004	2005	2006
Kilometres flown (million)	11	12	12
Passengers carried ('000)	356	384	425
Passenger-km (million)	720	797	861
Total ton-km (million)	88	97	108

Source: UN, *Statistical Yearbook*.

Passengers carried ('000): 453.1 in 2007; 470.6 in 2008; 466.1 in 2009 (Source: World Bank, World Development Indicators database).

Tourism

FOREIGN VISITORS BY COUNTRY OF ORIGIN*

	2004	2005	2006
Belgium	3,885	3,046	3,129
Canada	2,399	2,760	1,969
France	40,611	33,650	32,362
Italy	4,426	4,211	3,329
Netherlands	4,217	2,951	2,724
Switzerland	5,668	3,715	2,089
United Kingdom	5,818	5,076	4,146
USA	9,194	7,242	7,030
Total (incl. others)	189,856	176,372	184,549

* Arrivals at hotels and similar establishments.

Receipts from tourism (US $ million, incl. passenger transport): 231 in 2006; 254 in 2007; 165 in 2008.

Source: World Tourism Organization.

Communications Media

	2008	2009	2010
Telephones ('000 main lines in use)	255.3	435.4	539.5
Mobile cellular telephones ('000 subscribers)	6,160.9	8,004.1	8,636.7
Internet users ('000)	725.0	749.6	n.a.
Broadband subscribers	900	900	1,000

Personal computers: 200,000 (11.2 per 1,000 persons) in 2005.

Radio receivers ('000 in use): 2,270 in 1997.

2004: Daily newspapers 10; Non-daily newspapers 250.

Sources: mainly UNESCO, *Statistical Yearbook*; International Telecommunication Union.

Education

(2009/10 unless otherwise indicated)

			Students ('000)		
	Institutions	Teachers	Males	Females	Total
Pre-primary	1,371*	14,522	157.8	158.9	316.7
Primary	9,459*	76,655	1,895.5	1,614.9	3,510.4
Secondary:					
general	700*	21,650†	533.5‡	476.3‡	1,009.8‡
technical/ vocational	324*	21,543†	161.8‡	97.1‡	258.9‡
Universities	6§	3,020	121.8	98.5	220.3

* 1997/98.

† 2005/06.

‡ 2008/09.

§ 1996/97.

Source: UNESCO Institute for Statistics.

Pupil-teacher ratio (primary education, UNESCO estimate): 45.8 in 2009/10 (Source: UNESCO Institute for Statistics).

Adult literacy rate (UNESCO estimates): 75.9% (males 84.0%; females 67.8%) in 2008 (Source: UNESCO Institute for Statistics).

Directory

The Government

HEAD OF STATE

President: PAUL BIYA (took office 6 November 1982; elected 14 January 1984; re-elected 24 April 1988, 11 October 1992, 12 October 1997; 11 October 2004; and 9 October 2011).

CABINET

(May 2012)

The Government is a coalition of the Rassemblement démocratique du peuple camerounais (RDPC), the Front pour le salut national du Cameroun (FSNC), the Union nationale pour la démocratie et le progrès (UNDP) and the Alliance nationale pour la démocratie et le progrès (ANDP).

Prime Minister: PHILÉMON YANG (RDPC).

Deputy Prime Minister, Minister-delegate at the Presidency in charge of Relations with the Assemblies: AMADOU ALI (RDPC).

Ministers of State

Minister of State, Minister of Tourism and Leisure: MAIGARI BELLO BOUBA (UNDP).

Minister of State, Minister of Justice and Keeper of the Seals: LAURENT ESSO.

Ministers

Minister of Territorial Administration and Decentralization: RÉNÉ EMMANUEL SADI.

Minister of Social Affairs: CATHERINE LOUISE MARINETTE BAKANG MBOCK (RDPC).

Minister of Agriculture and Rural Development: LAZARE ESSIMI MENYE.

Minister of Art and Culture: AMA TUTU MUNA (RDPC).

Minister of Trade: LUC MAGLOIRE MBANGA ATANGANA.

Minister of Communication: BAKARY ISSA TCHIROMA.

Minister of Estates and Land Affairs: JACQUELINE KOUNG A. BISSIKE.

Minister of Water and Energy: BASILE ATANGANA KOUNA.

Minister of the Economy, Planning and Land Settlement: EMMANUEL NGANOU DJOUMESSI (RDPC).

Minister of Basic Education: YOUSSOUF ADIDJA ALIM.

Minister of Livestock, Fisheries and Animal Industries: Dr TAIGA.

Minister of Employment and Professional Training: ZACHARIE PÉRÉVET (RDPC).

Minister of Secondary Education: LOUIS BAPES BAPES (RDPC).

Minister of Higher Education: JACQUES FAME NDONGO (RDPC).

Minister of the Environment, the Protection of Nature and Sustainable Development: PIERRE HÉLÉ (RDPC).

Minister of Finance: ALAMINE OUSMANE MEY.

Minister of Public Service and Administrative Reform: Michel Ange Angouin (RDPC).

Minister of Forests and Wildlife: Philip Ngwese Ngole (RDPC).

Minister of Housing and Urban Development: Jean Claude Mbwetchou (RDPC).

Minister of Youth and Civic Education: Ismaël Bidoung Kpwatt.

Minister of Mines, Industry and Technological Development: Emmanuel Bonde.

Minister of Small and Medium-Sized Enterprises, Social Economy and Crafts: Laurent Serge Etoundi Ngoa (RDPC).

Minister of Posts and Telecommunications: Jean-Pierre Byiti Bi Essam.

Minister of Women's Affairs and the Family: Marie Thérèse Abena Ondua.

Minister of Scientific Research and Innovation: Madeleine Tchuenté (RDPC).

Minister of External Relations: Pierre Moukoko Mbonjo.

Minister of Public Health: André Mama Fouda (RDPC).

Minister of Sports and Physical Education: Adoum Garoua.

Minister of Transport: Robert Nkili.

Minister of Labour and Social Security: Grégoire Owona.

Minister of Public Works: Patrice Amba Salla.

Ministers-delegate

Minister-delegate at the Presidency, in charge of Defence: Edgard Alain Mebe Ngo'o.

Minister-delegate at the Presidency, in charge of the Contrôle Superieur de l'État: Henri Eyebe Ayissi.

Minister-delegate at the Presidency, in charge of Public Markets: Abba Sadou.

Minister-delegate at the Ministry of Territorial Administration and Decentralization, in charge of Decentralized Territorial Collectivities: Jules Doret Ndongo (RDPC).

Minister-delegate at the Ministry of Agriculture and Rural Development, in charge of Rural Development: Clémentine Antoinette Ananga Messina.

Minister-delegate at the Ministry of the Environment, the Protection of Nature and Sustainable Development: Nana Aboubakar Djalloh (UNDP).

Minister-delegate at the Ministry of the Economy, Planning and Land Settlement, in charge of Planning: Abdoulaye Yaouba.

Minister-delegate at the Ministry of Finance: Pierre Titti.

Minister-delegate at the Ministry of Justice, Keeper of the Seals: Jean Pierre Fogui.

Minister-delegate at the Ministry of External Relations, in charge of Relations with the Commonwealth: Joseph Dion Ngute (RDPC).

Minister-delegate at the Ministry of External Relations, in charge of Relations with the Islamic World: Adoum Gargoum (RDPC).

Minister-delegate at the Ministry of Transport: Mefiro Oumarou.

Secretaries of State

Secretary of State for Defence, in charge of the National Gendarmerie: Jean Baptiste Bokam.

Secretary of State for Defence, in charge of Former Combatants and War Victims: Issa Koumpa.

Secretary of State for Basic Education: Benoît Ndong Soumhet.

Secretary of State for Secondary Education, in charge of Normal Education: Moulouna Foutsou.

Secretary of State for Forests and Wildlife: Alhadji Koulsoumi Boukar.

Secretary of State for Housing and Urban Development, in charge of Urban Development: Marie Rose Dibong.

Secretary of State for Justice, in charge of Prisons: Jérôme Penbaga Dooh.

Secretary of State for Industry, Mines and Technological Development: Calistus Gentry Fuh.

Secretary of State for Public Health, in charge of the Fight Against Epidemics and Pandemics: Alim Hayatou (RDPC).

Secretary of State for Public Works, in charge of Roads: Hans Nyetam Nyetam.

Other Officials with the Rank of Minister

Ministers, chargés de mission at the Presidency: Hamadou Moustapha, Paul Atanga Nji, Victor Mengot Arrey Nkongho, Philippe Mbarga Mboa.

MINISTRIES

Correspondence to ministries not holding post boxes should generally be addressed c/o the Central Post Office, Yaoundé.

Office of the President: Palais de l'Unité, Yaoundé; tel. 2223-4025; internet www.camnet.cm/celcom/homepr.htm.

Office of the Prime Minister: Yaoundé; tel. 2223-8005; fax 2223-5735; e-mail spm@spm.gov.cm; internet www.spm.gov.cm.

Ministry of Agriculture and Rural Development: Quartier Administratif, Yaoundé; tel. 2223-1190; fax 2222-5091.

Ministry of Art and Culture: Quartier Hippodrome, Yaoundé; tel. 2222-6579; fax 2223-6579.

Ministry of Basic Education: Quartier Administratif, Yaoundé; tel. 2223-4050; fax 2223-1262.

Ministry of Communication: Quartier Hippodrome, Yaoundé; tel. 2223-3974; fax 2223-3022; e-mail mincom@mincom.gov.cm; internet www.mincom.gov.cm.

Ministry of Defence: Quartier Général, Yaoundé; tel. 2223-4055.

Ministry of the Economy, Planning and Land Settlement: Yaoundé; e-mail lecinfosminepat@gmail.com; internet www.minepat.info.

Ministry of Employment and Professional Training: Yaoundé; tel. 2222-0186; fax 2223-1820.

Ministry of the Environment, the Protection of Nature and Sustainable Development: Yaoundé.

Ministry of Estates and Land Affairs: Yaoundé.

Ministry of External Relations: Yaoundé; tel. 2220-3850; fax 2220-1133; internet www.diplocam.gov.cm.

Ministry of Finance: BP 13750, Quartier Administratif, Yaoundé; tel. and fax 7723-2099; internet www.camnet.cm/investir/minfi/.

Ministry of Forests and Wildlife: BP 1341, Yaoundé; tel. 2220-4258; fax 2222-9487; e-mail onadef@camnet.cm; internet www.camnet.cm/investir/envforet/index.htm.

Ministry of Higher Education: 2 ave du 20 mai, BP 1457, Yaoundé; tel. 2222-1770; fax 2222-9724; e-mail aowono@uycdc.uninet.cm; internet www.mineup.gov.cm.

Ministry of Justice: Quartier Administratif, Yaoundé; tel. 2223-4292; fax 2223-0005; e-mail jpouloumou@yahoo.fr.

Ministry of Labour and Social Security: Yaoundé.

Ministry of Livestock, Fisheries and Animal Industries: Yaoundé; tel. 2222-3311.

Ministry of Mines, Industry and Technological Development: Quartier Administratif, BP 955, Yaoundé; tel. 2223-3404; fax 2223-3400; e-mail minmee@camnet.cm; internet www.camnet.cm/investir/minmee.

Ministry of Posts and Telecommunications: Quartier Administratif, Yaoundé; tel. 2223-0615; fax 2223-3159; internet www.minpostel.gov.cm.

Ministry of Public Health: Quartier Administratif, Yaoundé; tel. and fax 2222-0233; internet www.minsante.gov.cm.

Ministry of Public Service and Administrative Reform: Yaoundé; tel. 2222-0356; fax 2223-0800.

Ministry of Public Works: Quartier Administratif, Yaoundé; tel. 2222-1916; fax 2222-0156.

Ministry of Secondary Education: Yaoundé.

Ministry of Scientific Research and Innovation: Yaoundé; tel. 2222-1334; fax 2222-1336; internet www.minresi.net.

Ministry of Small and Medium-Sized Enterprises, Social Economy and Crafts: BP 6096, Yaoundé; tel. 2223-2388; fax 2223-2180; e-mail enngoal1@yahoo.fr; internet www.minpmeesa.cm.

Ministry of Social Affairs: Quartier Administratif, Yaoundé; tel. 2222-5867; fax 2222-1121.

Ministry of Sports and Physical Education: POB 1016, Yaoundé; tel. 2223-1201; fax 2223-2610; e-mail minsepinfos@yahoo.fr.

Ministry of Technical and Professional Training: Yaoundé.

Ministry of Territorial Administration and Decentralization: Quartier Administratif, Yaoundé; tel. 2223-4090; fax 2222-3735.

Ministry of Tourism and Leisure: BP 266, Yaoundé; tel. 2222-4411; fax 2222-1295; e-mail mintour@camnet.cm; internet www.mintour.gov.cm.

Ministry of Trade: Yaoundé; tel. 2223-0216.

Ministry of Transport: Quartier Administratif, Yaoundé; tel. 2222-8709; fax 2223-2238; e-mail minetatcam@gmail.com; internet www.mint.gov.cm.

Ministry of Urban Development and Housing: Yaoundé; tel. 2223-2282.

Ministry of Water and Energy: Quartier Administratif, BP 955, Yaoundé; tel. 2223-3404; fax 2223-3400; e-mail minmee@camnet.cm; internet www.camnet.cm/investir/minmee.

Ministry of Women's Affairs and the Family: Quartier Administratif, Yaoundé; tel. 2223-2550; fax 2223-3965; e-mail cab_minproff@yahoo.fr; internet www.minproff.gov.cm.

Ministry of Youth and Civic Education: Quartier Administratif, Yaoundé; tel. 2223-3257; e-mail minjes@minjes.gov.cm; internet www.minjes.gov.cm.

President and Legislature

PRESIDENT

Election, 9 October 2011

Candidate	Votes	% of votes
Paul Biya (RDPC)	3,772,527	77.99
Ni John Fru Ndi (SDF)	518,175	10.71
Garga Haman Adji (ADD)	155,348	3.21
Adamou Ndam Njoya (UDC)	83,860	1.73
Ayah Paul Abine (PAPE)	61,158	1.26
Others*	246,181	5.09
Total	4,837,249	100.00

* There were 18 other candidates.

NATIONAL ASSEMBLY

President: CAVAYE YÉGUIÉ DJIBRIL.

General Election, 22 July 2007

Party	Seats
Rassemblement démocratique du peuple camerounais (RDPC)	140
Social Democratic Front (SDF)	14
Union démocratique du Cameroun (UDC)	4
Union nationale pour la démocratie et le progrès (UNDP)	4
Mouvement progressiste (MP)	1
Total	163*

* The results of voting in five constituencies (for 17 seats) were annulled, owing to irregularities. By-elections were held on 30 September 2007 at which the RDPC won 13 seats; the SDF and the UNDP each secured two seats.

Election Commission

Elections Cameroon (ELECAM): BP 13506, Yaoundé; tel. 2221-2540; fax 2221-2539; e-mail elecam@elecam.cm; internet www.elecam.cm; f. 2006 to replace Observatoire national des élections/National Elections Observatory; 12 mems appointed by the Head of State in consultation with political parties represented in the National Assembly and civil society; Pres. SAMUEL FONKAM AZU'U; Sec.-Gen. MOHAMAN SANI TANIMOU.

Political Organizations

At December 2011 a total of 271 political parties were registered with the Minister of Territorial Administration and Decentralization, of which the most important are listed below:

Action for Meritocracy and Equal Opportunity Party (AMEC): BP 20354, Yaoundé; tel. 9991-9154; fax 2223-4642; e-mail Tabijoachim@yahoo.fr; Leader JOACHIM TABI OWONO.

Alliance pour la démocratie et le développement (ADD): BP 231, Garoua; Sec.-Gen. GARGA HAMAN ADJI.

Alliance des forces progressistes (AFP): BP 4724, Douala; f. 2002; Leader BERNARD MUNA.

Alliance nationale pour la démocratie et le progrès: BP 5019, Yaoundé; tel. and fax 220-9898; Pres. HAMADOU MOUSTAPHA.

Cameroon Anglophone Movement (CAM): advocates a federal system of govt.

Démocratie intégrale au Cameroun (DIC): BP 8282, Douala; tel. 7785-1712; f. 1991; Sec.-Gen. ANNETTE ESSAKA.

Front pour le salut national du Cameroun (FSNC): Yaoundé; f. 2007; Pres. BAKARY ISSA TCHIROMA.

Mouvement africain pour la nouvelle indépendance et la démocratie (MANIDEM): BP 10298, Douala; tel. 3342-0076; fax 9996-0229; f. 1995; fmrly a faction of the UPC; Leader ANDRÉ BANDA KANI.

Mouvement pour la défense de la République (MDR): BP 6438, Yaoundé; tel. 2220-8982; f. 1991; Leader DAKOLE DAÏSSALA.

Mouvement des démocrates camerounais pour la paix (MDCP): BP 3274, Yaoundé; tel. 2220-8173; f. 2000; Leader GAMEL ADAMOU ISSA.

Mouvement pour la démocratie et le progrès (MDP): BP 8379, Douala; tel. 2239-1174; f. 1992; Pres. ARON MUKURI MAKA; Sec.-Gen. RENÉ MBANDA MANDENGUE.

Mouvement pour la jeunesse du Cameroun (MLJC): BP 26, Eséka; tel. 7714-8750; fax 2228-6019; Pres. DIEUDONNÉ TINA; Sec.-Gen. JEAN LÉONARD POM.

Mouvement pour la libération et le développement du Cameroun (MLDC): BP 886, Edéa; tel. 3346-4431; fax 3346-4847; f. 1998 by a breakaway faction of the MLJC; Leader MARCEL YONDO.

Mouvement progressiste (MP): BP 2500, Douala; tel. 9987-2513; e-mail djombyves@yahoo.fr; f. 1991; Pres. JEAN JACQUES EKINDI.

Nouvelle force populaire (NFP): BP 1139, Douala; f. 2002; Leader LÉANDRE DJINO.

Parti des démocrates camerounais (PDC): BP 6909, Yaoundé; tel. 2222-2842; f. 1991; Leader LOUIS-TOBIE MBIDA; Sec.-Gen. GASTON BIKELE EKANI.

Parti libéral-démocrate (PLD): BP 4764, Douala; tel. 3337-3792; f. 1991; Pres. JEAN ROBERT LIAPOE; Sec.-Gen. JEAN TCHUENTE.

Parti républicain du peuple camerounais (PRPC): BP 6654, Yaoundé; tel. 2222-2120; f. 1991; Leader ANDRÉ ATEBA NGOUA.

Parti socialiste camerounais (PSC): BP 12501, Douala; Sec.-Gen. EMMANUEL ELAME.

Rassemblement camerounais pour la république: BP 452, Bandjoun; tel. 3344-1349; f. 1992; Leader SAMUEL WAMBO.

Rassemblement démocratique du peuple camerounais (RDPC): Palais des Congrès, 2e étage, BP 867, Yaoundé; tel. and fax 2221-2417; fax 2221-2508; e-mail rdpcpdm@rdpcpdm.cm; internet www.rdpcpdm.cm; f. 1966 as Union nationale camerounaise by merger of the Union camerounaise, the Kamerun National Democratic Party and four opposition parties; adopted present name in 1985; sole legal party 1972–90; Pres. PAUL BIYA; Sec.-Gen. RÉNÉ EMMANUEL SADI.

Social Democratic Front (SDF): BP 490, Mankon, Bamenda; tel. 3336-3949; fax 3336-2991; e-mail webmaster@sdfparty.org; internet www.sdfparty.org; f. 1990; Chair. NI JOHN FRU NDI; Sec.-Gen. Dr ELIZABETH TAMAJONG.

Social Democratic Movement (SDM): BP 7655, Yaoundé; tel. 9985-9372; f. 1995; breakaway faction of the Social Democratic Front; Leader SIGA ASANGA.

Southern Cameroons National Council (SCNC): BP 131, Eyumojock; tel. 796-4888; e-mail scnc@scncforsoutherncameroons.net; internet www.scncforsoutherncameroons.net; f. 1995; supports the establishment of an independent republic in anglophone Cameroon; Chair. Chief ETTE OTUN AYAMBA.

Union démocratique du Cameroun (UDC): BP 1638, Yaoundé; tel. 2222-9545; fax 2222-4620; f. 1991; Leader ADAMOU NDAM NJOYA.

Union des forces démocratiques du Cameroun (UFDC): BP 7190, Yaoundé; tel. 2223-1644; f. 1991; Leader VICTORIN HAMENI BIELEU.

Union des mouvements socialistes: f. 2011; Leader PIERRE KWEMO.

Union nationale pour la démocratie et le progrès (UNDP): BP 656, Douala; tel. 2220-9898; f. 1991; split in 1995; Chair. MAIGARI BELLO BOUBA; Sec.-Gen. PIERRE FLAMBEAU NGAYAP.

Union nationale pour l'indépendance totale du Cameroun (UNITOC): BP 1301, Yaoundé; tel. 2222-8002; f. 2002; Pres. DANIEL TATSINFANG; Sec.-Gen. JEAN CLAUDE TIENTCHEU FANSI.

Union des populations camerounaises (UPC): BP 1348, Yaoundé; tel. 2745-5043; f. 1948; Pres. Dr SAMUEL MACH-KIT; Sec.-Gen. MOUKOKO PRISO.

Diplomatic Representation

EMBASSIES AND HIGH COMMISSIONS IN CAMEROON

Algeria: 433 rue 1828, Quartier Bastos, BP 1619, Yaoundé; tel. 2221-5351; fax 2231-5354; Ambassador TOUFIK MILAT.

Brazil: rue 1828, Quartier Bastos, BP 16227, Yaoundé; tel. 2220-1085; fax 2220-2048; e-mail embiaunde@cameroun-online.com; Ambassador ROBERTO PESSOA DACOSTA.

Canada: Immeuble Stamatiades, pl. de l'Hôtel de Ville, BP 572, Yaoundé; tel. 2223-2311; fax 2222-1090; e-mail yunde@international.gc.ca; internet www.cameroon.gc.ca; High Commissioner BENOÎT-PIERRE LARAMÉE.

Central African Republic: 41 rue 1863, Quartier Bastos, Montée du Carrefour de la Vallée Nlongkak, BP 396, Yaoundé; tel. and fax 2220-5155; Chargé d'affaires a.i. JEAN WENZOUÏ.

Chad: Quartier Bastos, BP 506, Yaoundé; tel. 2221-0624; fax 2220-3940; e-mail ambatchad_yaounde@yahoo.fr; Ambassador ANDRÉ SEKIMBAYE BESSANE.

China, People's Republic: Nouveau Bastos, BP 1307, Yaoundé; tel. 2221-0083; fax 2221-4395; e-mail chinaemb_cm@mfa.gov.cn; Ambassador XUE JINWEI.

Congo, Democratic Republic: BP 632, Yaoundé; tel. 2220-5103; Chargé d'affaires a.i. FRANÇOIS LUAMBO.

Congo, Republic: Rheinallée 45, BP 1422, Yaoundé; tel. 2221-2458; fax 2221-1733; Ambassador ERIC EPENI OBONDZO.

Côte d'Ivoire: rue 1983, Résidence 140, Quartier Bastos, BP 1715, Yaoundé; tel. 2221-3291; fax 2221-3592; e-mail contact@ambaci-cam.org; internet www.ambacicam.org; Ambassador DOSSO ADAMA.

Egypt: 718 rue 1828, Quartier Bastos, BP 809, Yaoundé; tel. 2220-3922; fax 2220-2647; Ambassador IBRAHIM MOUSTAPHA HAFEZ.

Equatorial Guinea: 82 rue 1851, Quartier Bastos, BP 277, Yaoundé; tel. and fax 2221-0804; Ambassador PEDRO ELA NGUEMA BUNA.

France: Plateau Atémengué, BP 1631, Yaoundé; tel. 2222-7900; fax 2222-7909; e-mail chancellerie.yaounde-amba@diplomatie.gouv.fr; internet www.ambafrance-cm.org; Ambassador BRUNO GAIN.

Gabon: Quartier Bastos, Ekoudou, BP 4130, Yaoundé; tel. 2220-2966; fax 2221-0224; Ambassador MICHEL MANDOUGOUA.

Germany: Nouvelle Route Bastos, Bastos-Usine, BP 1160, Yaoundé; tel. 2221-0056; fax 2221-6211; e-mail info@jaun.diplo.de; internet www.jaunde.diplo.de; Ambassador REINHARD BUCHHOLZ.

Holy See: rue du Vatican, BP 210, Yaoundé (Apostolic Nunciature); tel. 2220-0475; fax 2220-7513; e-mail nonce.cam@sat.signis.net; Apostolic Pro-Nuncio Most Rev. PIERO PIOPPO (Titular Archbishop of Torcello).

Israel: rue du Club Olympique à Bastos 154, Longkak, BP 5934, Yaoundé; tel. 2221-1291; fax 2221-0823; e-mail info@yaounde.mfa.gov.il; internet yaounde.mfa.gov.il; Ambassador MICHAEL ARBEL.

Italy: Plateau Bastos, BP 827, Yaoundé; tel. 2220-3376; fax 2221-5250; e-mail ambasciata.yaounde@esteri.it; internet www.ambyaounde.esteri.it; Ambassador STEFANO PONTESILLI.

Japan: 1513 rue 1828, Quartier Bastos, Ekoudou, BP 6868, Yaoundé; tel. 2220-6202; fax 2220-6203; Ambassador TSUTOMU ARAI.

Korea, Democratic People's Republic: Yaoundé; Ambassador KIM RYONG YONG.

Korea, Republic: BP 13286, Yaoundé; tel. 2220-3756; fax 2220-3757; e-mail korean.embassy.yaounde@gmail.com; Ambassador (vacant).

Liberia: Quartier Bastos, Ekoudou, BP 1185, Yaoundé; tel. 2221-1296; fax 2220-9781; Ambassador MASSA JAMES.

Libya: Quartier Nylon Nlongkak, Quartier Bastos, BP 1980, Yaoundé; tel. 2220-4138; fax 2221-4298; Chargé d'affaires a.i. IBRAHIM O. AMAMI.

Morocco: 32 rue 1793, Quartier Bastos, BP 1629, Yaoundé; tel. 2220-5092; fax 2220-3793; e-mail ambmaroccam@yahoo.fr; Ambassador LAHCEN SAIL.

Nigeria: Quartier Bastos, BP 448, Yaoundé; tel. 2222-3455; fax 2223-5551; e-mail nhc_yde@yahoo.com; High Commissioner PHILIP ALI DAUDA.

Russia: Quartier Bastos, BP 488, Yaoundé; tel. 2220-1714; fax 2220-7891; e-mail consrusse@camnet.cm; Ambassador AKHMEDOV STANISLAS.

Saudi Arabia: rue 1951, Quartier Bastos, BP 1602, Yaoundé; tel. 2221-2675; fax 2220-6689; Ambassador MAHMOOD BIN HOSAIN QATTAN.

South Africa: rue 1801, Quartier Bastos, BP 1636, Yaoundé; tel. 2220-0438; fax 2220-0995; e-mail yaounde@foreign.gov.za; High Commissioner N. M. TSHEOLE.

Spain: blvd de l'URSS, Quartier Bastos, BP 877, Yaoundé; tel. 2220-3543; fax 2220-6491; e-mail embespcm@mail.mae.es; Ambassador ARTURO SPIEGELBERG DE ORTUETA.

Switzerland: BP 1169, Yaoundé; tel. 2220-5067; fax 2220-9386; Ambassador URS BERNER.

Tunisia: rue de Rotary, Quartier Bastos, BP 6074, Yaoundé; tel. 2220-3368; fax 2221-0507; e-mail at.yaounde@camnet.cm; Ambassador ABDERRAZAK LANDOULSI.

Turkey: blvd de l'URSS 1782, Quartier Bastos, BP 35155, Yaoundé; tel. 2220-6775; fax 2220-6778; Ambassador ATILAY ERSAN.

United Kingdom: ave Winston Churchill, BP 547, Yaoundé; tel. 2222-0545; fax 2222-0148; e-mail BHC.yaounde@fco.gov.uk; internet ukincameroon.fco.gov.uk; High Commissioner BHARAT JOSHI.

USA: ave Rosa Parks, BP 817, Yaoundé; tel. and fax 2220-1500; internet yaounde.usembassy.gov; Ambassador ROBERT PORTER JACKSON.

Judicial System

The independence of the judiciary is enshrined in the Constitution and judicial power is exercised by the Supreme Court, courts of appeal and tribunals. The President of the Republic guarantees the independence of the judicial power and appoints members of the bench and of the legal department. He is assisted in this task by the Higher Judicial Council (HJC), which gives him its opinion on all nominations for the bench and on disciplinary action against judicial and legal officers. The HJC is composed of six members who serve five-year terms. Justice is rendered in Cameroon by: courts of first instance; high courts; military courts; courts of appeal and the Supreme Court.

Supreme Court

Yaoundé; tel. 2222-0164; fax 2222-0576; internet www.coursupreme.cm.

Consists of a president, 9 titular and substitute judges, a procureur général, an avocat général, deputies to the procureur général, a registrar and clerks.

President: ALEXIS DIPANDA MOUELLE.

Attorney-General: MARTIN RISSOUCK MOULONG.

Religion

It is estimated that 53% of the population are Christians (an estimated 26% of those are Roman Catholics), 25% adhere to traditional religious beliefs, and 22% are Muslims.

CHRISTIANITY

Protestant Churches

Conseil des Eglises Protestantes du Cameroun (CEPCA): BP 491, Yaoundé; tel. and fax 2223-8117; e-mail femec_org@yahoo.fr; f. 1968; name changed as above in 2005; 11 mem. churches; Pres. Rev. Dr ROBERT NGOYECK; Admin. Sec. Rev. Dr PHILIPPE NGUETE.

Church of the Lutheran Brethren of Cameroon: POB 16, Garoua; tel. and fax 2227-2573; e-mail eflcsynode@yahoo.fr; Pres. Rev. ROBERT GOYEK DAGA; 105,994 mems (2010).

Eglise évangélique du Cameroun (Evangelical Church of Cameroon—EEC): 13 rue Alfred Saker, Akwa, Centenaire, BP 89, Douala; tel. 3342-3611; fax 3342-4011; e-mail eec@eeccameroun.org; internet www.eeccameroun.org; f. 1957; 2m. mems; Pres. Rev. ISAAC BATOMEN HENGA; Sec. Rev. JEAN SAMUEL HENDJE TOYA.

Eglise presbytérienne camerounaise (Presbyterian Church of Cameroon): BP 519, Yaoundé; tel. 3332-4236; independent since 1957; comprises 4 synods and 16 presbyteries; Gen. Sec. Rev. Dr MASSI GAM'S.

Eglise protestante africaine (African Protestant Church): BP 26, Lolodorf; e-mail epacameroun@yahoo.fr; f. 1934; Pres. Rev. FRANÇOIS PUASSE.

Evangelical Lutheran Church of Cameroon: POB 6, Ngaoundere-Adamaoua; tel. 2225-2066; fax 2225-2299; e-mail evequenational_eelc@yahoo.fr; Pres. Rev. Dr THOMAS NYIWE; 253,000 mems (2010).

Presbyterian Church in Cameroon: BP 19, Buéa; tel. 3332-2487; fax 332-2754; e-mail pcc_modoffice19@yahoo.com; 1,800,000 mems; 302 ministers; Moderator Rt Rev. Dr NYANSAKO-NI-NKU.

Union des Eglises baptistes du Cameroun (Union of Baptist Churches of Cameroon): New Bell, BP 6007, Douala; tel. 3342-4106; e-mail mbangueeboa@yahoo.fr; autonomous since 1957; Gen. Sec. Rev. EMMANUEL MBANGUE EBOA.

Other Protestant churches active in Cameroon include the Cameroon Baptist Church, the Cameroon Baptist Convention, the Presbyterian Church in West Cameroon and the Union of Evangelical Churches of North Cameroon. The Eglise Evangélique du Cameroun (EEC) et Union des Eglises Baptistes du Cameroun (UEBC) have also formed a Conseil des Eglises Baptistes et Evangéliques du Cameroun (CEBEC).

The Roman Catholic Church

Cameroon comprises five archdioceses and 19 dioceses. Some 26% of the total population are Roman Catholics.

Bishops' Conference

Conférence Episcopale Nationale du Cameroun, BP 1963, Yaoundé; tel. 2231-1592; fax 2231-2977; e-mail cenc20042003@yahoo.ca.

f. 1989; Pres. Most Rev. JOSEPH ATANGA (Archbishop of Bertoua); Sec.-Gen. SÉBASTIEN MONGO BEHONG.

Archbishop of Bamenda: Most Rev. CORNELIUS FONTEM ESUA, Archbishop's House, BP 82, Bamenda; tel. 3336-1241; fax 3336-3487; e-mail archbishopshouse@yahoo.com.

Archbishop of Bertoua: Most Rev. JOSEPH ATANGA, Archevêché, BP 40, Bertoua; tel. 2224-1748; fax 2224-2585.

Archbishop of Douala: SAMUEL KLEDA, Archevêché, BP 179, Douala; tel. 3342-3714; fax 3343-1837; e-mail mikjp2004@yahoo.fr.

Archbishop of Garoua: Most Rev. ANTOINE NTALOU, Archevêché, BP 272, Garoua; tel. 2227-1353; fax 2227-2942; e-mail archigaroua@yahoo.fr.

Archbishop of Yaoundé: Most Rev. SIMON-VICTOR TONYÉ BAKOT, Archevêché, BP 207, Yaoundé; tel. 2201-1048; fax 2221-9735; e-mail simonvita2000@yahoo.fr.

BAHÁ'Í FAITH

National Spiritual Assembly: 4230 Yaoundé; tel. 2223-0575; e-mail nsacameroon@yahoo.com; mems in 1,744 localities.

The Press

DAILIES

Cameroon Tribune: route de l'Aéroport, BP 1218, Yaoundé; tel. 2230-4147; fax 2230-4362; e-mail cameroon-tribune@cameroon-tribune.cm; internet www.cameroon-tribune.cm; f. 1974; govt-controlled; French and English; Publr MARIE CLAIRE NNANA; Man. Editor RAOUL DIEUDONNÉ LEBOGO NDONGO; circ. 25,000.

Mutations: South Media Corporation, 183 rue 1,055, Pl. Repiquet, BP 12348, Yaoundé; tel. 2222-5104; fax 2222-9635; e-mail journalmutations@yahoo.fr; internet quotidienmutations.info; daily; French; independent; Publr ALAIN BLAISE BATONGUÉ.

The Post: POB 91, Buéa; tel. 3332-3287; fax 7773-8904; e-mail thepostnp@yahoo.com; internet www.thepostwebedition.com; bi-weekly; independent; English; Publr FRANCIS WACHE; Editor CHARLY NDI CHIA.

Le Quotidien: BP 13088, Douala; tel. 3339-1189; fax 3339-1819; French; circ. 29,000.

PERIODICALS

Accord Magazine: BP 3696, Messa, Yaoundé; tel. 9969-0600; e-mail accordmag@hotmail.com; popular culture.

Affaires Légales: BP 3681, Douala; tel. 3342-5838; fax 3343-2259; monthly; legal periodical.

L'Anecdote: face collège Vogt, BP 25070, Yaoundé; tel. 2231-3395; e-mail journalanecdote@yahoo.com; weekly; conservative; Editor-in-Chief FRANÇOIS BIKORO.

Aurore Plus: BP 7042, Douala; tel. 3342-9261; fax 3342-4917; e-mail jouraurplus@yahoo.fr; 2 a week; Dir MICHEL MICHAUT MOUSSALA.

Les Cahiers de Mutations: South Media Corporation, 183 rue 1,055, Pl. Repiquet, BP 12348, Yaoundé; tel. 2222-5104; fax 2222-9635; monthly; Dir ROGER ALAIN TAAKAM.

Cameroon Outlook: BP 124, Limbé; f. 1969; 3 a week; independent; English; Editor JÉRÔME F. GWELLEM; circ. 20,000.

Cameroon Panorama: BP 46, Buéa; tel. 3332-2240; e-mail cainsbuea@yahoo.com; f. 1962; monthly; English; Roman Catholic; Editor Rev. Fr MOSES TAZOH; circ. 4,500.

Cameroon Review: BP 408, Limbé; monthly; Editor-in-Chief JÉRÔME F. GWELLEM; circ. 70,000.

Cameroon Times: BP 408, Limbé; f. 1960; weekly; English; Editor-in-Chief JÉRÔME F. GWELLEM; circ. 12,000.

Le Combattant: Yaoundé; weekly; independent; Editor BENYIMBE JOSEPH; circ. 21,000.

Dikalo: BP 4320, Douala; tel. 3337-2122; fax 3337-1906; f. 1991; independent; 2 a week; French; Publications Dir TETTEH M. ARMAH; Editor HENRI EPEE NDOUMBE.

Ecovox: BP 1256, Bafoussam; tel. 3344-6668; fax 3344-6669; e-mail ecovox@cipcre.org; internet www.cipcre.org/ecovox; 2 a year; French; ecological news.

L'Effort Camerounais: BP 15231, Douala; tel. 3343-2726; fax 3343-1837; e-mail leffortcamerounais@yahoo.com; internet www.leffortcamerounais.com; bi-monthly; Catholic; f. 1955; Editor-in-Chief IRENEAUS CHIA CHONGWAIN.

La Gazette: BP 5485, Douala; 2 a week; Editor ABODEL KARIMOU; circ. 35,000.

The Herald: BP 1218, Yaoundé; tel. 2231-5522; fax 2231-8497; 3 a week; English; Dir Dr BONIFACE FORBIN; circ. 1,568.

Al Houda: BP 1638, Yaoundé; quarterly; Islamic cultural review.

Le Jeune Observateur: Yaoundé; f. 1991; Editor JULES KOUM KOUM.

J'informe: Yaoundé; tel. 9993-6605; fax 2220-5336; f. 2002; weekly; French; Editor DELOR MAGELLAN KAMGAING.

Journal Officiel de la République du Cameroun: BP 1603, Yaoundé; tel. 2220-1719; fax 2220-2959; weekly; official govt notices; Man. Editor JOSEPH MARCEL; circ. 4,000.

Le Messager: rue des Écoles, BP 5925, Douala; tel. 3342-0214; fax 3342-0439; internet www.lemessager.net; f. 1979; 3 a week; independent; Man. Editor (vacant); circ. 20,000.

The Messenger: BP 15043, Douala; English-language edn of *Le Messager*; Editor HILARY FOKUM.

Nleb Ensemble: Imprimerie Saint-Paul, BP 763, Yaoundé; tel. 2223-9773; fax 2223-5058; f. 1935; fortnightly; Ewondo; Dir Most Rev. JEAN ZOA; Editor JOSEPH BEFE ATEBA; circ. 6,000.

La Nouvelle Expression: 12 rue Prince de Galles, BP 15333, Douala; tel. 3343-2227; fax 3343-2669; internet www.lanouvelleexpression.net; 3 a week; independent; French; Man. Editor SÉVERIN TCHOUNKEU.

La Nouvelle Presse: face mairie de Yaoundé VIème/Biyem-Assi, BP 2625, Messa, Yaoundé; tel. 9996-6768; e-mail lanvellepresse@iccnet.cm; f. 2001; weekly; Publications Dir JACQUES BLAISE MVIE.

Nyanga: route de l'Aéroport, BP 1218, Yaoundé; tel. 2230-4147; fax 2230-4362; publ. by the Société de Presse et d'Editions du Cameroun (SOPECAM); Dir EMMANUEL TATAW.

Ouest Echos: BP 767, Bafoussam; tel. and fax 3344-1091; e-mail ouechos@wagne.net; internet www.wagne.net/ouestechos; weekly; regional; Dir MICHEL ECLADOR PÉKOUA.

Recherches et Études Camerounaises: BP 193, Yaoundé; monthly; publ. by Office National de Recherches Scientifiques du Cameroun.

La Sentinelle: BP 24079, Douala; tel. and fax 3339-1627; weekly; lifestyle; circ. 3,200.

Le Travailleur/The Worker: BP 1610, Yaoundé; tel. 2222-3315; f. 1972; monthly; French and English; journal of Organisation Syndicale des Travailleurs du Cameroun/Cameroon Trade Union Congress; Sec.-Gen. LOUIS SOMBES; circ. 10,000.

Le Triomphe: BP 1862, Douala; tel. 3342-8774; f. 2002; weekly; Publications Dir SIPOWA CONSCIENCE PARFAIT.

Weekly Post: BP 30420, Yaoundé; tel. 2206-7649; e-mail weeklyp@yahoo.com; internet weeklypost1.tripod.com; English; f. 1992; independent; Editor-in-Chief BISONG ETAHOBEN.

NEWS AGENCY

CamNews: c/o SOPECAM, BP 1218, Yaoundé; tel. 2230-3830; fax 2230-4362; Dir JEAN NGANDJEU.

PRESS ASSOCIATIONS

Association des Journalistes Indépendants du Cameroun (AJIC): BP 2996, Yaoundé; tel. 2222-3572; independent journalists' asscn; Pres. CÉLESTIN LINGO.

Conseil Camerounais des Médias (CCM): Yaoundé; internet www.ccm-info.org; f. 2005; created by the UJC to strengthen the quality and independence of journalism in Cameroon; 9 mems; Pres. PIERRE ESSAMA ESSOMBA; Sec.-Gen. PIERRE-PAUL TCHINDJI.

Union des Journalistes du Cameroun (UJC): Yaoundé; Pres. CÉLESTIN LINGO.

Publishers

AES Presses Universitaires d'Afrique: BP 8106, Yaoundé; tel. 2222-0030; fax 2222-2325; e-mail aes@iccnet.cm; internet www

.aes-pua.com; f. 1986; literature, social sciences and law; Dir-Gen. SERGE DONTCHUENG KOUAM.

Editions Akoma Mba: ave Germaine Ahidjo 20189, Yaoundé; tel. 9992-2955; fax 2222-4343; e-mail akomamba@hotmail.com; educational; Dir EDMOND VII MBALLA ELANGA.

Editions Clé (Centre de Littérature Evangélique): BP 1501, ave Maréchal Foch, Yaoundé; tel. 2222-3554; fax 2223-2709; e-mail editionscle@yahoo.fr; internet www.wagne.net/cle; f. 1963; African and Christian literature and studies; school textbooks; medicine and science; general non-fiction; Dir Dr MARCELIN VOUNDA ETOA.

Editions Ndzé: BP 647, Bertoua; tel. 9950-9295; fax 2224-2585; e-mail editions@ndze.com; internet www.ndze.com; fiction; Commercial Dir ALEXIS LIMBONA.

Editions Semences Africaines: BP 5329, Yaoundé-Nlongkak; tel. 9917-1439; e-mail renephilombe@yahoo.fr; f. 1974; fiction, history, religion, textbooks; Man. Dir RÉNÉ LÉA PHILOMBE.

New Times Publishing House: Presbook Compound, BP 408, Limbé; tel. 3333-3217; f. 1983; publishing and book-trade reference; Dir and Editor-in-Chief JÉRÔME F. GWELLEM.

Presses de l'Université catholique d'Afrique Centrale (PUCAC): BP 11628, Yaoundé; tel. 2230-5508; fax 2230-5501; e-mail p_ucac@yahoo.fr; internet www.pucac.com; Man. GABRIEL TSALA ONANA.

GOVERNMENT PUBLISHING HOUSES

Centre d'Edition et de Production pour l'Enseignement et la Recherche (CEPER): BP 808, Yaoundé; tel. 7723-1293; f. 1967; transfer pending to private ownership; general non-fiction, science and technology, tertiary, secondary and primary educational textbooks; Man. Dir JEAN CLAUDE FOUTH.

Imprimerie Nationale: BP 1603, Yaoundé; tel. 2223-1277; Dir AMADOU VAMOULKE.

Société de Presse et d'Editions du Cameroun (SOPECAM): route de l'Aéroport, BP 1218, Yaoundé; tel. 2230-4147; fax 2230-4362; e-mail mclairennana@yahoo.fr; f. 1977; under the supervision of the Ministry of Communication; Pres. PAUL TESSA; Dir-Gen. MARIE CLAIRE NNANA.

Broadcasting and Communications

TELECOMMUNICATIONS

In early 2011 there were three operators of telecommunication services in Cameroon: one fixed-line and two mobile cellular. In mid-2011 the Government was planning to issue licences to three new mobile operators. In December 2011 a new company, Eto'o Télécom, announced that it was to commence operations under the brand name Set Télécom.

Agence de Régulation des Télécommunications (ART): Immeuble Balanos, rue Valéry Giscard d'Estaing, BP 6132, Yaoundé; tel. 2223-0380; fax 2223-3748; e-mail art@art.cm; internet www.art.cm; f. 1998; regulatory authority; Dir-Gen. JEAN LOUIS BEH MENGUE.

Cameroon Telecommunications (CAMTEL): BP 1571, Yaoundé; tel. 2223-4065; fax 2223-0303; e-mail camtel@camnet.cm; internet www.camtel.cm; f. 1999 by merger of INTELCAM and the Dept of Telecommunications; 51% privatization pending; Pres. NFON VICTOR MUKETE; Dir-Gen. DAVID NKOTO EMANE.

Mobile Telephone Networks (MTN) Cameroon Ltd: 360 rue Drouot, Bonamouti, Akwa, BP 15574, Douala; tel. 7900-9000; fax 7900-9040; internet www.mtncameroon.net; f. 1999 as CAMTEL Mobile; acquired by MTN in 2000; mobile cellular telephone operator; 70% owned by MTN Ltd, 30% owned by Broadband Telecom Ltd; CEO KARL OLUTOKUN TORIOLA.

Orange: Immeuble CBC, ave Kennedy, Yaoundé; tel. 2222-4956; e-mail contact@orange.cm; internet www.orange.cm; mobile cellular telephone and internet operator; Dir-Gen. JEAN BARDET.

BROADCASTING

Radio

Office de Radiodiffusion-Télévision Camerounaise (CRTV): BP 1634, Yaoundé; tel. 2221-4077; fax 2220-4340; e-mail infos@crtv.cm; internet www.crtv.cm; f. 1987; broadcasts in French and English; satellite broadcasts commenced in Jan. 2001, reaching some 80% of the national territory; Pres. of Council of Administration BAKARY ISSA TCHIROMA (Minister of Communication); Dir-Gen. AMADOU VAMOULKE.

Radio Bertoua: BP 260, Bertoua; tel. 2224-1445; fax 2224-2275; Head of Station BAIVE NYONG PHILIP.

Radio Buéa: BP 86, Buéa; tel. 3332-2615; programmes in English, French and 15 vernacular languages; Man. PETERSON CHIA YUH; Head of Station GIDEON MULU TAKA.

Radio Douala: BP 986, Douala; tel. 3342-6060; programmes in French, English, Duala, Bassa, Ewondo, Bakoko and Bamileke; Dir BRUNO DJEM; Head of Station LINUS ONANA MVONDO.

Radio Garoua: BP 103, Garoua; tel. 2227-1167; programmes in French, Hausa, English, Foulfouldé, Arabic and Choa; Dir BELLO MALGANA; Head of Station MOUSSA EPOPA.

Radio Ngaoundere: BP 135, Ngaoundéré; tel. 2225-2148.

Radio Yaoundé FM 94: BP 1634, Yaoundé; tel. 2220-2089; fax 2220-4340; e-mail fm94@crtv.cm; Head of Station LOUISE POM.

There are also provincial radio stations at Abong Mbang, Bafoussam, Bamenda, Ebolowa and Maroua.

Television

Television programmes from France were broadcast by the Office de Radiodiffusion-Télévision Camerounaise from early 1990.

Office de Radiodiffusion-Télévision Camerounaise (CRTV): see Radio.

Finance

(cap. = capital; res = reserves; dep. = deposits; m. = million; brs = branches; amounts in francs CFA)

BANKING

In 2010 there were 12 licensed banks in Cameroon.

Central Bank

Banque des Etats de l'Afrique Centrale (BEAC): 736 ave Monseigneur Vogt, BP 1917, Yaoundé; tel. 2223-4060; fax 2223-3329; e-mail beac@beac.int; internet www.beac.int; f. 1973; bank of issue for mem. states of the Communauté économique et monétaire de l'Afrique centrale (CEMAC, fmrly Union douanière et économique de l'Afrique centrale): Cameroon, the Central African Repub., Chad, the Repub. of the Congo, Equatorial Guinea and Gabon; cap. 88,000m., res 227,843m., dep. 4,110,966m. (Dec. 2007); Gov. LUCAS ABAGA NCHAMA; Dir in Cameroon JEAN-MARIE BENOÎT MANI (acting); 5 brs in Cameroon.

Commercial Banks

Afriland First Bank: 1063 pl. de l'Indépendance, BP 11834, Yaoundé; tel. 2223-3068; fax 2222-1785; e-mail firstbank@afrilandfirstbank.com; internet www.afrilandfirstbank.com; formerly Caisse Commune d'Epargne et d'Investissement (CCEI); SBF & Co (36.62%), FMO (19.80%), private shareholders (43.58%); cap. and res 10,017m., total assets 161,293m. (Dec. 2003); Pres. Dr PAUL KAMMOGNE FOKAM; Gen. Man. ALAMINE OUSMANE MEY.

Banque Internationale du Cameroun pour l'Epargne et le Crédit (BICEC): ave du Général de Gaulle, BP 1925, Douala; tel. 3343-6000; fax 3343-1226; e-mail bicec@bicec.banquepopulaire.com; internet www.bicec.com; f. 1962 as Banque Internationale pour le Commerce et l'Industrie du Cameroun; name changed as above in 1997, following restructuring; 52.5% owned by Groupe Banques Populaires (France); cap. 6,000m., res 37,729m., dep. 438,081m. (Dec. 2009); Pres. JEAN-BAPTISTE BOKAM; Gen. Man. PASCAL REBILLARD; 32 brs.

Citibank N.A. Cameroon: 96 rue Flatters, Bonanjo, BP 4571, Douala; tel. 3342-2777; fax 3342-4074; internet www.citigroup.com; f. 1997; Dir-Gen. ASIF ZAIDI; COO WILSON CHOLA.

Commercial Bank Cameroon SA (CBC): ave du Général de Gaulle, BP 59, Douala; tel. 3342-0202; fax 3343-3800; e-mail cbcbank@cbc-bank.com; internet www.cbc-bank.com; f. 1997; cap. 7,000.0m., res 4,596.2m., dep. 156,758.3m. (Dec. 2005); Pres. YVES MICHEL FOTSO.

Ecobank Cameroun SA (Togo): blvd de la Liberté, BP 582, Douala; tel. 3343-8251; fax 3343-8609; e-mail ecobankcm@ecobank.com; internet www.ecobank.com; f. 2001; cap. 6,250.0m., res 2,171.2m., dep. 206,611.9m. (Dec. 2009); Chair. ANDRÉ FOTSO; Man. Dir ASSIONGBON EKUE; 24 brs.

Highland Corporation Bank SA: Immeuble Hôtel Hilton, blvd du 20 mai, BP 10039, Yaoundé; tel. 2223-9287; fax 2232-9291; e-mail atnjp@camnet.cm; internet pcnet.ifrance.com/pcnet/hcb; f. 1995; 100% privately owned; cap. 1,500m. (Dec. 1999); Exec. Pres. PAUL ATANGA NJI; Asst Dir-Gen. JOHANES MBATI.

Société Commerciale de Banque Cameroun SA: 530 rue du Roi George, BP 300, Douala; tel. 3343-5400; fax 3342-5413; e-mail ca_scb@scbcameroun.com; f. 1989 as Société Commerciale de Banque—Crédit Lyonnais Cameroun; renamed Crédit Lyonnais Cameroun SA in 2002, and as above in 2007; 35% state-owned; cap. 6,000.0m., res 13,131.1m., dep. 294,167.7m. (Dec. 2009); Pres. MARTIN ARISTIDE OKOUDA; Gen. Man. FRANCIS DUBUS.

Société Générale de Banques au Cameroun (SGBC): 78 rue Joss, BP 4042, Douala; tel. 3342-7010; fax 3343-0353; e-mail sgbcdla@camnet.cm; internet www.sgbc.cm; f. 1963; 25.6% state-owned; cap. 6,250m., res 26,524m., dep. 389,967m. (Dec. 2009); Chair. MATHURIN NDOUMBÉ EPÉE; Dir-Gen. ALEXANDRE MAYMAT; 15 brs.

Standard Chartered Bank Cameroon SA: blvd de la Liberté, BP 1784, Douala; tel. 3343-5200; fax 3342-2789; e-mail Paul.Sagnia@cm.standardchartered.com; internet www.standardchartered.com/cm; f. 1980 as Boston Bank Cameroon; name changed 1986; 100% owned by Standard Chartered Bank (United Kingdom); cap. 7,000m., res 5,797m., dep. 127,823m. (June 2005); CEO MATHIEU MANDENG; 2 brs.

Union Bank of Cameroon, Ltd (UBC): NWCA Ltd Bldg, 2nd Floor, Commercial Ave, BP 110, Bamenda, Douala; tel. 3336-2316; fax 3336-2314; e-mail ubc@unionbankcameroon.com; internet www.unionbankcameroon.com; f. 2000; share cap. 5,000m. (2005); Pres. GABRIEL IKOMÉ NJOH; Gen. Man. ABRAHAM NDOFOR.

United Bank for Africa Cameroon: blvd de la Liberté-Akwa, BP 2088, Douala; tel. 3343-3683; fax 3343-3707; e-mail ubacameroon@ubagroup.com; internet www.ubagroup.com/ubacameroon; Dir-Gen. EMEKE E. IWERIEBOR.

Development Banks

Banque de Développement des Etats de l'Afrique Centrale: see Franc Zone.

Crédit Foncier du Cameroun (CFC): 484 blvd du 20 mai 1972, BP 1531, Yaoundé; tel. 2223-5216; fax 2223-5221; f. 1977; 75% state-owned; cap. 6,000m. (Dec. 2007); provides assistance for low-cost housing; Chair. JULES DORET NDONGO; Gen. Man. CAMILLE EKINDI; 10 brs.

Société Nationale d'Investissement du Cameroun (SNI): pl. Ahmadou Ahidjo, BP 423, Yaoundé; tel. 2222-4422; fax 2223-1332; e-mail sni@sni.cm; internet www.sni.cm; f. 1964; state-owned investment and credit agency; cap. 22,000m., total assets 33,341m. (June 2003); Chair. SIMON ACHIDI ACHU; Dir-Gen. YAOU AISSATOU.

Financial Institutions

Caisse Autonome d'Amortissement du Cameroun: BP 7167, Yaoundé; tel. 2222-2226; fax 2222-0129; e-mail caa@caa.cm; internet www.caa.cm; f. 1985; cap. 5,000m. (1998); Dir-Gen. EVOU MEKOU DIEUDONNÉ.

National Financial Credit Company Cameroon (NFCC): BP 6578, Yaoundé; tel. 2222-4806; fax 2222-8781; e-mail national_financial_credit@yahoo.com; cap. and res 2,350m., total assets 9,338m.; Pres. ABEY JEROME ONGHER; Gen. Man. AWANGA ZACHARIA.

Société Camerounaise de Crédit Automobile (SOCCA): rue du Roi Albert, BP 554, Douala; tel. 3342-7478; fax 3342-1219; e-mail socca@socca-cm.cm; internet www.giefca.com/english/cameroun.htm; f. 1959; cap. and res 4,770m., total assets 23,748m. (Dec. 2003); Dir-Gen. JOHANN BAUDOT.

Société Camerounaise de Crédit-Bail (SOCABAIL): rue du Roi Albert, BP 554, Douala; tel. 3342-7478; fax 3342-1219; e-mail soccabail@camnet.cm; cap. 500m., res 1,343m., total assets 5,880m. (June 1999); Pres. ALAIN GUYON.

STOCK EXCHANGE

Bourse des Valeurs de Douala (Douala Stock Exchange): 1450 blvd de la Liberté, BP 442, Douala; tel. 3343-8583; fax 3353-8584; e-mail dsx@douala-stock-exchange.com; internet www.douala-stock-exchange.com; f. 2003; 23% state-owned; Chair. BÉNÉDICT BELIBI; Dir-Gen. PIERRE EKOULÉ MOUANGUÉ.

INSURANCE

In 2010 there were 24 insurance companies in Cameroon.

Activa Assurances: rue du Prince du Galles 1385, BP 12970, Douala; tel. 3343-4503; fax 3343-4572; e-mail activa.assur@camnet.cm; f. 1999; all branches except life insurance; cap. 400m.; 66% owned by Cameroonian investors, 33% by Ivorian investors; Chair. JEAN KACOU DIAGOU; Gen. Man. RICHARD NZONLIÉ LOWE; also **Activa Vie**, life insurance.

Allianz Cameroun: rue Manga Bell, BP 105, Douala; tel. 3350-2000; fax 3350-2001; e-mail allianz.cameroun@allianz-cm.com; internet www.allianz-africa.com/cameroun; formerly AGF Cameroun Assurances; all classes of insurance; Dir-Gen. BERNARD GIRARDIN (life insurance).

Association des Sociétés d'Assurances du Cameroun (ASAC): BP 1136, Douala; tel. and fax 3342-0668; e-mail contact@asac-cameroun.org; internet asac-cameroun.org; Pres. MARTIN N. FONCHA; Sec.-Gen. GEORGES MANDENG LIKENG.

AXA Assurances Cameroun: 309 rue Bebey-Eyidi, BP 4068, Douala; e-mail axa.cameroun@axacameroun.com; internet www.axacameroun.com; tel. 3342-6772; fax 3342-6453; f. 1974 as Compagnie Camerounaise d'Assurances et de Réassurances; renamed as above in June 2000; Pres. SANDA OUMAROU; Dir-Gen. THIERRY KEPEDEN.

Beneficial Life Insurance SA: BP 2328, Douala; tel. 3342-8408; fax 3342-7754; e-mail beneficial@iccnet.cm; f. 1974; Dir-Gen. ALLEN ROOSEVELT BROWN.

Chanas Assurances: BP 109, Douala; tel. 3342-1474; fax 3342-9960; e-mail chanas@iccnet2000.com; internet www.chanas-assurances.com; f. 1999; Pres. and Dir-Gen. JACQUELINE CASALEGNO.

Colina All Life: blvd de la Liberté, BP 267, Douala; tel. 3343-0904; fax 3343-1237; e-mail colinaalllife@groupecolina.com; internet www.groupecolina.com; f. 1996; life insurance; Dir-Gen. MARTIN FONCHA.

Colina La Citoyenne Cameroun: 34 rue Dinde, BP 12125, Douala; tel. 3342-4446; fax 3342-4727; e-mail citoyenne@groupecolina.com; internet colina.cawad.com; f. 1986; non-life insurance; Dir-Gen. PROTAIS AYANGMA AMANG.

Compagnie Nationale d'Assurances (CNA): BP 12125, Douala; tel. 3342-4446; fax 3342-4727; f. 1986; all classes of insurance; cap. 600m.; Chair. THÉODORE EBOBO; Man. Dir PROTAIS AYANGMA AMANG.

General and Equitable Assurance Cameroon Ltd (GEACAM): 56 blvd de la Liberté, BP 426, Douala; tel. 3342-5985; fax 3342-7103; cap. 300m.; Pres. V. A. NGU; Man. Dir J. CHEBAUT.

Société Africaine d'Assurances et Réassurances (SAAR): BP 1011, Douala; tel. 3343-1765; fax 3343-1759; internet www.saar-assurances.com; f. 1990; Pres. Dr PAUL K. FOKAM; Dir-Gen. GEORGES LÉOPOLD KAGOU; also **SAAR-Vie**, life insurance; Dir-Gen. FERDINAND MENG.

Société Camerounaise d'Assurances et de Réassurances (SOCAR): 1450 blvd de la Liberté, BP 280, Douala; tel. 3342-5584; fax 3342-1335; f. 1973; cap. 800m.; Chair. J. YONTA; Man. Dir R. BIOUELE.

Trade and Industry

GOVERNMENT AGENCY

Conseil économique et social: BP 1058, Yaoundé; tel. 2223-2474; advises the Govt on economic and social problems; comprises 150 mems, who serve a 5-year term, and a perm. sec.; Pres. LUC AYANG; Sec.-Gen. ESSOME BIKOU RENÉ.

DEVELOPMENT ORGANIZATIONS

Agence Française de Développement (AFD): Immeuble Flatters, rue de la Radio, BP 2283, Douala; tel. 3342-9959; fax 3342-9959; e-mail afddouala@groupe-afd.org; internet www.afd.fr; fmrly Caisse Française de Développement; Man. GILLES CHAUSSE.

Cameroon Development Corporation (CAMDEV): Bota Area, Limbé; tel. 3333-2251; fax 3333-2680; e-mail info@cdc-cameroon.com; internet www.cdc-cameroon.com; f. 1947; reorg. 1982; cap. 15,626m. francs CFA; statutory corpn established to acquire and develop plantations of tropical crops for local and export markets; operates 3 palm oil mills and 5 rubber factories; Chair. Chief OKIAH NAMATA ELANGWE; Gen. Man. HENRY NJALLA QUAN.

Direction Générale des Grands Travaux du Cameroun (DGTC): BP 6604, Yaoundé; tel. 2222-1803; fax 2222-1300; f. 1988; commissioning, implementation and supervision of public works contracts; Chair. JEAN FOUMAN AKAME; Man. Dir MICHEL KOWALZICK.

Hévéa-Cameroun (HEVECAM): BP 1298, Douala and BP 174, Kribi; tel. 3346-1919; f. 1975; state-owned; devt of 15,000 ha rubber plantation; 4,500 employees; transferred to private ownership in 1997; Pres. ELIE C. NYOKWEDI MALONGA; Man. Dir JEAN-MARC SEYMAN.

Institut de Recherche Agricole pour le Développement (IRAD): BP 2067, Yaoundé; tel. and fax 2222-3538; e-mail contact@irad-cameroun.org; internet www.irad-cameroon.org; Dir-Gen. NOÉ WOIN.

Institut de Recherche pour le Développement (IRD): 1095 rue Joseph Essono Mballa, Quartier Elig Essono, BP 1857, Yaoundé; tel. 2220-1508; fax 2220-1854; e-mail cameroun@ird.fr; internet www.cameroun.ird.fr; f. 1984; Rep. in Cameroon Dr XAVIER GARDE.

Mission d'Aménagement et d'Equipement des Terrains Urbains et Ruraux (MAETUR): 716 ave Winston Churchill, Quartier Hippodrome, BP 1248, Yaoundé; tel. 2222-3113; fax 2223-3190; e-mail maetur@maetur.cm; internet www.maetur.cm; f. 1977; Pres. ABDOULAYE ABOUBAKARY; Dir-Gen. EMMANUEL ETOUNDI OYONO.

Mission d'Aménagement et de Gestion des Zones Industrielles: Yaoundé; internet www.magzicameroun.com; state-owned industrial land authority; Dir CHRISTOL GEORGES MANON.

Mission de Développement de la Province du Nord-Ouest (MIDENO): BP 442, Bamenda; Gen. Man. JOHN B. NDEH.

Office Céréalier dans la Province du Nord: BP 298, Garoua; tel. 2227-1438; f. 1975 to combat effects of drought in northern Cameroon and stabilize cereal prices; Pres. Alhadji MAHAMAT; Dir-Gen. GILBERT GOURLEMOND.

Office National du Cacao et du Café (ONCC): BP 3018, Douala; tel. 3342-9482; fax 3342-0002; Dir-Gen. MICHAËL NDOPING.

Service de Coopération et d'Action Culturelle: BP 1616, Yaoundé; tel. 2223-0412; fax 2222-5065; e-mail mission.coop@camnet.cm; administers bilateral aid from France; Dir YVON ALAIN.

Société de Développement du Cacao (SODECAO): BP 1651, Yaoundé; tel. 2230-4544; fax 2230-3395; e-mail sodecaodg@gmail.com; internet www.sodecao.cm; f. 1974; reorg. 1980; cap. 425m. francs CFA; devt of cocoa, coffee and food crop production in the Littoral, Centre, East and South provinces; Pres. JOSEPH-CHARLES DOUMBA; Dir-Gen. JÉRÔME MVONDO.

Société de Développement du Coton (SODECOTON): BP 302, Garoua; tel. 2227-1556; fax 2227-2026; f. 1974; Chair. HAOUNAYE GOUNOKO; Man. MOHAMMED IYA.

Société de Développement de l'Elevage (SODEVA): BP 50, Kousseri; cap. 50m. francs CFA; Dir Alhadji OUMAROU BAKARY.

Société de Développement et d'Exploitation des Productions Animales (SODEPA): BP 1410, Yaoundé; tel. 2220-0810; fax 2220-0809; e-mail courrier@sodepa.org; internet www.sodepa.org; f. 1974; cap. 375m. francs CFA; devt of livestock and livestock products; Man. Dir DIEUDONNÉ BOUBA NDENGUE.

Société de Développement de la Haute-Vallée du Noun (UNVDA): BP 25, N'Dop, North-West Province; f. 1970; cap. 1,380m. francs CFA; rice, maize and soya bean cultivation; Dir-Gen. SAMUEL BAWE CHI WANKI.

Société d'Expansion et de Modernisation de la Riziculture de Yagoua (SEMRY): BP 46, Yagoua; tel. 2229-6213; internet semry.com; f. 1971; cap. 4,580m. francs CFA; commercialization of rice products and expansion of rice-growing in areas where irrigation is possible; Pres. AHMADOU TIDJANI; Dir-Gen. MARC ATANA.

Société Immobilière du Cameroun (SIC): ave de l'Indépendance, BP 387, Yaoundé; BP 924, Douala; BP 94, Garoua; tel. 2223-3411; fax 2222-5119; e-mail sic@sicameroun.com; internet www.sicameroun.com; f. 1952; cap. 1,000m. francs CFA; housing construction and devt; Pres. ABDOULAYE HAMAN ADJI; Dir-Gen. BONIFACE NGOA NKOU.

CHAMBERS OF COMMERCE

Chambre d'Agriculture, des Pêches, de l'Élevage et des Forêts du Cameroun (CAPEF): BP 6620, Yaoundé; tel. 2222-0441; fax 2222-2025; e-mail cfe_cameroun@yahoo.fr; f. 1955; 120 mems; Pres. JANVIER MONGUI SOSSOMBA; Sec.-Gen. BERNARD NWANA SAMA; other chambers at Ebolowa, Bertoua, Douala, Ngaoundere, Garoua, Maroua, Buéa, Bamenda and Bafoussam.

Chambre de Commerce, d'Industrie, des Mines et de l'Artisanat du Cameroun (CCIMA): rue de Chambre de Commerce, BP 4011, Douala; also at BP 36, Yaoundé; BP 211, Limbé; BP 59, Garoua; BP 944, Bafoussam; BP 551, Bamenda; BP 824, Ngaoundere; BP 86, Bertoua; tel. 3342-6855; fax 3342-5596; e-mail siege@ccima.net; internet www.ccima.net; f. 1921; 160 mems; Pres. CHRISTOPHE EKEN; Sec.-Gen. SAÏDOU ABDOULAYE BOBBOY.

EMPLOYERS' ORGANIZATIONS

Association Professionnelle des Établissements de Crédit du Cameroun (APECCAM): BP 133, Yaoundé; tel. 2223-5401; fax 2223-5402; Pres. FRANCIS DUBUS; Sec.-Gen. BÉNÉDICT BELIBI.

Groupement des Femmes d'Affaires du Cameroun (GFAC): BP 1940, Douala; tel. 2223-4059; fax 2221-1041; e-mail gfacnational@yahoo.fr; f. 1985; Pres. FRANÇOISE FONING.

Groupement Inter-Patronal du Cameroun (GICAM): rue des Ministres, Bonanjo, BP 829, Douala; tel. 3342-3141; fax 3342-4591; e-mail gicam@legicam.org; internet www.legicam.org; Pres. OLIVIER BEHLE.

Mouvement des Entrepreneurs du Cameroun (MECAM): BP 12443, Douala; tel. 3339-5000; fax 3339-5001; Pres. DANIEL CLAUDE ABATÉ.

Syndicat des Commerçants Importateurs-Exportateurs du Cameroun (SCIEC): 16 rue Quillien, BP 562, Douala; tel. 3342-0304; Pres. EMMANUEL UGOLINI; Treas. MICHEL CHUPIN.

Syndicat des Industriels du Cameroun (SYNDUSTRICAM): BP 673, Douala; tel. 3342-3058; fax 3342-5616; e-mail syndustricam@camnet.cm; f. 1953; Pres. CHARLES METOUCK; Sec.-Gen. BEKE BIHEGE.

Syndicat des Producteurs et Exportateurs de Bois du Cameroun: BP 570, Yaoundé; tel. 2220-2722; fax 2220-9694; f. 1939; Pres. CARLO ORIANI.

Syndicat Professionnel des Entreprises du Bâtiment, des Travaux Publics et des Activités Annexes: BP 1134, Yaoundé; BP 660, Douala; tel. and fax 2220-2722; Sec.-Gen. FRANCIS SANZOUANGOU.

UTILITIES

Electricity

Electricity Development Corpn: Immeuble Stamatiadès, BP 15111, Yaoundé; tel. 2223-1930; fax 2223-1113; e-mail info@edc-cameroon.org; internet edc-cameroon.org; f. 2006; state-owned; Pres. VICTOR MENGOT; Dir-Gen. Dr THÉODORE NSANGOU.

Société Nationale d'Electricité du Cameroun (SONEL): BP 4077, 63 ave de Gaulle, Douala; tel. 3342-5444; fax 3342-2209; e-mail sonel@camnet.cm; f. 1974; 56% owned by AES Sirocco, 44% state-owned; Gen. Man. JEAN-DAVID BILE.

Water

Cameroon Water Utilities Corpn (Camwater): BP 4077, Douala; tel. 3342-5444; fax 3342-2247; f. 1967; 73% state-owned; Pres. AMADOU ALI; Dir-Gen. BASILE ATANGANA KOUNA.

PRINCIPAL CO-OPERATIVE ORGANIZATIONS

Centre National de Développement des Entreprises Coopératives (CENADEC): Yaoundé; f. 1970; promotes and organizes the co-operative movement; bureaux at BP 43, Kumba and BP 26, Bamenda; Dir JACQUES SANGUE.

Union Centrale des Coopératives Agricoles de l'Ouest (UCCAO): ave Samuel Wanko, BP 1002, Bafoussam; tel. 3344-4296; fax 3344-1845; e-mail uccao@uccao-cameroun.com; internet www.uccao-cameroon.com; f. 1958; marketing of cocoa and coffee; 120,000 mems; Pres. JACQUES FOTSO KANKEU; Gen. Man. FRANÇOIS MEFINJA FOKA.

West Cameroon Co-operative Association Ltd: BP 135, Kumba; founded as central financing body of the co-operative movement; provides short-term credits and agricultural services to mem. socs; policy-making body for the co-operative movement in West Cameroon; 142 mem. unions and socs representing c. 45,000 mems; Pres. Chief T. E. NJEA.

TRADE UNION FEDERATIONS

Confederation of Cameroon Trade Unions (CCTU): BP 1610, Yaoundé; tel. 2222-3315; f. 1985; fmrly the Union Nationale des Travailleurs du Cameroun (UNTC); Pres. JEAN-MARIE ZAMBO AMOUGOU.

Confédération des Syndicats Autonomes du Cameroun (CSAC): Yaoundé; Pres. COLLINS VEWESSEE; Sec.-Gen. PIERRE LOUIS MOUANGUE.

Union des Syndicats Libres du Cameroun (USLC): BP 13306, Yaoundé; tel. 2234196; Pres. FLAUBERT MOUSSOLÉ.

Other trade union federations include the Union Générale des Travailleurs du Cameroun (UGTC), the Confédération Camerounaise du Travail (CCT), the Confédération générale du travail-Liberté du Cameroun (CGT-L), the Confédération des Syndicats Indépendants du Cameroun (CSIC) and the Confédération des Travailleurs Unis du Cameroun (CTUC).

Transport

RAILWAYS

In 2010 there were some 1,103 km of track—the West Line running from Douala to Nkongsamba (166 km), with a branch line leading south-west from Mbanga to Kumba (29 km), and the Transcameroon railway, which runs from Douala to Ngaoundere (885 km), with a branch line from Ngoumou to Mbalmayo (30 km). There were also plans for the construction of a 450-km railway linking Mbalam with Kribi.

CAMRAIL: Gare Centrale de Bessengué, blvd de la Réunification, BP 766, Douala; tel. 3340-6045; fax 3340-8252; e-mail didier.vandenbon@camrail.net; internet www.camrail.net; f. 1999; passenger and freight transport; Pres. HAMADOU SALI; Dir-Gen. QUENTIN GÉRARD.

Office du Chemin de Fer Transcamerounais: BP 625, Yaoundé; tel. 2222-4433; supervises the laying of new railway lines and improvements to existing lines, and undertakes relevant research; Dir-Gen. LUC TOWA FOTSO.

ROADS

In 2011 there were an estimated 52,743 km of roads, of which 8.4% were paved. In August of that year the Government stated its intention to pave 3,500 km of new roads by 2020.

Fonds Routier du Cameroun: BP 6221, Yaoundé; tel. 2222-4752; fax 2222-4789; e-mail contact@fonds-routier.cm; f. 1996; Dir-Gen. PIERRE TITTI.

Société Camerounaise de Transport Urbain (SOCATUR): BP 1347, Douala; tel. 3340-1297; fax 3340-1297; f. 2000; bus operator in Douala; Dir-Gen. JEAN ERNEST NGALLÉ BIBEHE.

SHIPPING

There are seaports at Kribi and Limbé-Tiko, a river port at Garoua, and an estuary port at Douala-Bonabéri, the principal port and main outlet, which has 2,510 m of quays and a minimum depth of 5.8 m in the channels and 8.5 m at the quays. Total handling capacity is 7m. metric tons annually. The first phase of the Kribi Deep Sea Port commenced in December 2010 after a concessionary loan of CFA 207,000m. was granted by the Export and Import Bank of China. Plans for a similar deep sea port project at Limbé-Tiko were under way in 2011.

Autorité Portuaire Nationale (APN): BP 11538 Yaoundé; tel. 2223-7316; fax 2223-7314; Dir-Gen. JOSUÉ YOUMBA.

Port Autonome de Douala (PAD): 81 rue de la Chambre de Commerce, BP 4020, Douala; tel. 3342-0133; fax 3342-6797; e-mail portdouala@iccnet2000.com; Chair. SHEY JONES YEMBE; Dir-Gen. EMMANUEL ETOUNDI OYONO.

Camtainer: Para-maritime Area, Douala Port, BP 4993, Douala; tel. 3342-7704; fax 3342-7173; e-mail camtainer@douala1.com; internet www.camnet.cm/investir/transpor/camtenair/sommaire.htm; f. 1984; Chair. JOSEPH TSANGA ABANDA; Man. ZACHARIE KUATE.

Compagnie Maritime Camerounaise SA (CMC): BP 3235, Douala; tel. 3342-8540; fax 3342-5842.

Conseil National des Chargeurs du Cameroun (CNCC): BP 1588, Douala; tel. 3343-6767; fax 3343-7017; e-mail info@cncc-cam.org; internet www.cncc-cam.org; f. 1975; promotion of the maritime sector; Gen. Man. AUGUSTE MBAPPE PENDA.

Consignation et Logistique du Golfe de Guinée (CLGG): BP 4054, Douala; tel. 3342-0064; fax 3342-2181; e-mail agencies@camshipinc.com; f. 1975; privatized Feb. 1997; 6 vessels trading with Western Europe, USA, Far East and Africa; Chair. RENÉ MBAYEN; Man. Dir PAUL VAN DYCK.

Delmas Cameroun: rue Kitchener, BP 263, Douala; tel. 3342-4750; fax 3342-8851; f. 1977; Pres. JEAN-GUY LE FLOCH; Dir-Gen. DANY CHUTAUX.

MAERSK CAMEROUN SA—Douala: BP 12414, Douala; tel. 3342-1185; fax 3342-1186; Dir-Gen. DAVID WARE.

Société Africaine de Transit et d'Affrètement (SATA): Douala; tel. 3342-8209; f. 1950; Man. Dir RAYMOND PARIZOT.

Société Agence Maritime de l'Ouest Africain Cameroun (SAMOA): 5 blvd de la Liberté, BP 1127, Douala; tel. 3342-1680; f. 1953; shipping agents; Dir JEAN PERRIER.

Société Camerounaise de Manutention et d'Acconage (SOCAMAC): BP 284, Douala; tel. 3342-4051; e-mail socamac@camnet.cm; internet www.camnet.cm/investir/transpor/socamac/socamac.htm; f. 1976; freight handling; Pres. MOHAMADOU TALBA; Dir-Gen. HARRY J. GHOOS.

Société Camerounaise de Transport et d'Affrètement (SCTA): BP 974, Douala; tel. 3342-1724; f. 1951; Pres. JACQUES VIAULT; Dir-Gen. GONTRAN FRAUCIEL.

Société Camerounaise de Transport Maritime: BP 12351, Douala; tel. 3342-4550; fax 3342-4946.

Société Ouest-Africaine d'Entreprises Maritimes—Cameroun (SOAEM—Cameroon): 5 blvd de la Liberté, BP 4057, Douala; tel. 3342-5269; fax 3342-0518; f. 1959; Pres. JACQUES COLOMBANI; Man. Dir JEAN-LOUIS GRECIET.

SOCOPAO Cameroun: BP 215, Douala; tel. 3342-6464; f. 1951; shipping agents; Pres. VINCENT BOLLORE; Man. Dir E. DUPUY.

Transcap Cameroun: BP 4059, Douala; tel. 3342-7214; f. 1960; Pres. RENÉ DUPRAZ; Man. Dir MICHEL BARDOU.

CIVIL AVIATION

There are international airports at Douala, Garoua and Yaoundé; there are, in addition, 11 domestic airports, as well as a number of secondary airfields.

Cameroon Civil Aviation Authority (CCAA): BP 6998 Yaoundé; tel. 2230-3090; fax 2230-3362; e-mail contact@ccaa.aero; internet www.ccaa.aero; Pres. MAXIMIN PAUL NKOUE NKONGO; Dir-Gen. PIERRE TANKAM.

Aéroports du Cameroun (ADC): Nsimalen, BP 13615, Yaoundé; tel. 2223-4521; fax 2223-4520; e-mail adc@iccnet.cm; internet aeroportsducameroun.com; f. 1999; manages major airports; 63% state-owned; Dir-Gen. ROGER NTONGO ONGUENE.

Cameroon Airlines Corpn (CAMAIRCO): f. 2008 to replace Cameroon Airlines; commenced operations in March 2011; Chair. PHILEMON YANG; Dir-Gen. ALEX VAN ELK.

Tourism

Tourists are attracted by Cameroon's cultural diversity and by its national parks, game reserves and sandy beaches. In 2006 184,549 tourists visited Cameroon. In 2008 receipts from tourism totalled US $165m.

Ministry of Tourism and Leisure: see Ministries.

Defence

As assessed at November 2011, Cameroon's armed forces were estimated to total 14,200 men (army 12,500, navy 1,300, air force 400). There was also a 9,000-strong paramilitary force.

Defence Expenditure: Estimated at 164,000m. francs CFA in 2011.

Commander-in-Chief of the Armed Forces: PAUL BIYA.

Education

Since independence, Cameroon has achieved one of the highest rates of school attendance in Africa, but provision of educational facilities varies according to region. Education, which is bilingual, is provided by the Government, missionary societies and private concerns. Primary education in state schools is available free of charge, and the Government provides financial assistance for other schools. It begins at six years of age, and lasts for six years. Secondary education, beginning at the age of 12, lasts for a further seven years, comprising two cycles of four years and three years in the Francophone sub-system and of five years and two years in the Anglophone sub-system. In 2009/10, according to UNESCO estimates, 94% were enrolled at primary schools. In 2008/09 the number of pupils enrolled at secondary schools totalled some 1.3m. There are seven universities, six of which are state-owned. There were 220,300 students enrolled at the state-owned universities in 2009/10 and they employed a total of 3,020 teachers in that year. In 2008/09 expenditure on education was budgeted at 15.5% of total government spending.

CANADA

Introductory Survey

LOCATION, CLIMATE, LANGUAGE, RELIGION, FLAG, CAPITAL

Canada occupies the northern part of North America (excluding Alaska and Greenland) and is the second largest country in the world, after Russia. It extends from the Atlantic Ocean to the Pacific. Except for the boundary with Alaska in the north-west, Canada's frontier with the USA follows the upper St Lawrence Seaway and the Great Lakes, continuing west along latitude 49°N. The climate is an extreme one, particularly inland. Winter temperatures drop well below freezing but summers are generally hot. Rainfall varies from moderate to light and there are heavy falls of snow. The two official languages are English and French, the mother tongues of 57.2% and 21.8%, respectively, at the general census in 2006. About 45% of the population are Roman Catholics. The main Protestant churches are the United Church of Canada and the Anglican Church of Canada. Numerous other religious denominations are represented. The national flag (proportions 1 by 2) consists of a red maple leaf on a white field, flanked by red panels. The capital is Ottawa.

CONTEMPORARY POLITICAL HISTORY

Historical Context

The Liberals, led by Pierre Trudeau, were returned to office at general elections in 1968, 1972, 1974, and again in 1980 after a short-lived minority Progressive Conservative Party (PC) administration. Popular support for the Liberals, however, was undermined by an economic recession, and the PC, led by Brian Mulroney, obtained a substantial legislative majority at a general election held in September 1984.

During 1986 the persistence of high rates of unemployment, together with the resignations in discordant circumstances of five cabinet ministers, led to a fall in the PC Government's popularity. Popular support for the Government further declined, in response to criticism by the Liberals and the New Democratic Party (NDP) of the Government's negotiation of a new US-Canadian trade treaty, which the Liberals and the NDP viewed as overly advantageous to US business interests and potentially damaging to Canada's national identity, and which was approved by the House of Commons in August 1988. Nevertheless, in a general election in November the PC was re-elected, although with a reduced majority, and full legislative ratification of the free trade agreement followed in December. In February 1990 the federal Government opened negotiations with Mexico, to achieve a lowering of trade barriers. The US Government joined these discussions, and in December 1992 Canada, the USA and Mexico finalized terms for a tripartite North American Free Trade Agreement (NAFTA, see p. 369), with the aim of creating a free trade zone encompassing the whole of North America.

In the province of Québec, where four-fifths of the population speak French as a first language and which maintains its own cultural identity, the question of political self-determination has long been a sensitive issue. At provincial elections in 1976 the separatist Parti Québécois (PQ) came to power, and in 1977 made French the official language of education, business and government in Québec. In December 1985 the PQ was replaced by the Liberals as the province's governing party. The Liberals retained power at provincial elections in 1989. However, political support for separatist aspirations was extended to the federal Parliament in May 1990, when seven PC members representing Québec constituencies, led by Lucien Bouchard (a former member of Mulroney's Cabinet), broke away from the party and formed the independent Bloc Québécois (BQ), with the object of acting in the interests of a 'sovereign Québec'. The BQ later expanded, with disaffected Liberal support, to nine members.

In 1982 the British Parliament transferred to Canada authority over all matters contained in British statutes relating to Canada, opening the way for institutional reform and the redistribution of legislative powers between Parliament and the provincial legislatures. All the provinces except Québec eventually accepted constitutional provisions that included a charter of rights and a formula for constitutional amendments, whereby such amendments would require the support of at least seven provinces representing more than 50% of the population. Québec, however, maintained that its legislature could exercise the right to veto constitutional provisions.

Domestic Political Affairs

Following the return to office in 1985 of the Liberals in Québec, the federal Government adopted new initiatives to include Québec in the constitutional arrangements. In April 1987 Mulroney and the provincial premiers met at Meech Lake, Québec, to negotiate a constitutional accommodation for Québec. The resultant agreement, the Meech Lake Accord, recognized Québec as a 'distinct society' within the Canadian federation, and granted each of the provinces substantial new powers in the areas of federal parliamentary reform, judicial appointments and the creation of new provinces. The Accord was subject to ratification, not later than June 1990, by the federal Parliament and all provincial legislatures.

Opposition to the Meech Lake arrangements, on the grounds that they afforded too much influence to Québec and failed to provide Inuit and Indian minorities with the same measure of protection as francophone groups, began to emerge in March 1990. Despite the adoption of a number of compromise amendments, the provinces of Manitoba and Newfoundland upheld their opposition and the Meech Lake Accord duly lapsed in late June. The Québec Government responded by refusing to participate in future provincial conferences, and by appointing a commission to examine the province's political choices. In September 1991 the federal Government announced a new series of constitutional reform proposals, which, unlike the Meech Lake Accord, would require the assent of only seven provinces representing 50% of the total population. Under the new plan, Québec was to be recognized as a distinct society in terms of its language, culture and legal system, while each province would have full control of its cultural affairs. Native peoples were to receive full self-government within 10 years, inter-provincial trade barriers were to be abolished, and the federal Senate was to become an elected body with limited powers of legislative veto, except in matters involving natural resources, in which it would have full powers of veto. The reform proposals also included the creation of a Council of Federation to resolve disputes between the provinces and federal Government. The Québec provincial Government expressed initial reservations about the plan on economic grounds.

In March 1992 an all-party committee of the federal Parliament recommended new constitutional proposals providing for a system of 'co-operative federalism', which would grant Québec powers of veto over future constitutional changes, together with exclusive jurisdiction over the main areas of its provincial affairs. This plan was rejected by the Québec Government, while the western provinces, which sought increased representation in a reformed Senate, were unwilling to concede a constitutional veto to Québec until after these changes were carried out. In August a new programme of constitutional reforms, the Charlottetown Agreement, was finalized for submission to a national referendum. The proposals, which were endorsed by all of the provincial premiers as well as the leaders of the three main political parties, provided for an equal and elected Senate, a guarantee in perpetuity to Québec of one-quarter of the seats in the federal House of Commons (regardless of future movements in population), as well as three of the nine seats on the Supreme Court of Canada. There was also to be recognition of provincial jurisdiction in cultural affairs, and increased provincial powers over certain economic affairs and immigration. The inherent right to self-government of the Indian and Inuit population was also to be recognized.

Despite the apparent political consensus, considerable opposition to the Charlottetown Agreement became evident. Disagreements emerged on a regional basis, as well as among NDP and Liberal supporters, and aspects of the proposed constitution were opposed by the PQ and the BQ, and by the Reform Party (RP), a conservative-populist movement that led opposition in the western provinces. At the referendum, which took place in

October 1992, the proposals were defeated by a margin of 54% to 45%.

The defeat of the Charlottetown Agreement, together with the persistence of adverse economic conditions, led to a rapid erosion in the prestige of the Government, and in the Prime Minister's personal popularity. In February 1993 Mulroney announced that he was to relinquish office in June. He was succeeded by the former Minister of Defence and Veterans' Affairs, Kim Campbell, who became Canada's first female Prime Minister.

The Campbell Government proved unable to restore the PC's political standing, and a general election was scheduled for October 1993. The election resulted in a decisive victory for the Liberals, led by Jean Chrétien. PC representation in the new Parliament was reduced to only two seats. The BQ, with 54 seats, became the official opposition party, and declared that it would pursue the achievement of full sovereignty for Québec. Campbell, who lost her seat in the federal Parliament, resigned as PC leader and was succeeded by Jean Charest.

In December 1993, following the renegotiation of certain treaty protocols with the US Government, NAFTA, which had received Canadian legislative ratification in June, was formally promulgated, to take effect from January 1994.

Separatism in Québec

The issue of separatism in Québec was reopened by provincial elections held in September 1994, in which the PQ, led by Jacques Parizeau, defeated the incumbent Liberal administration. Parizeau, whose campaign had included an undertaking that a new referendum on independence would be held during 1995, was supported at federal level by the BQ, although the federal Government asserted that considerable uncertainty was felt within Québec over the possible economic consequences of secession. In June 1995 the PQ and the BQ, together with a smaller provincial nationalist group, the Action Démocratique du Québec (ADQ), agreed a framework for the province's proposed independence, and in September the referendum received provincial legislative approval.

In the referendum, held on 30 October 1995, the sovereignty proposals were defeated by a margin of only 50,000 votes; in a turn-out of 93% of eligible voters, 49% were in favour of the sovereignty plan, and 51% opposed. Parizeau announced his intention to resign. In February 1996 Lucien Bouchard, having resigned from the federal House of Commons and relinquished the leadership of the BQ, succeeded Parizeau as Premier of Québec and leader of the PQ. In September 1997 Bouchard refused to attend a conference of provincial premiers and territorial commissioners, at which a seven-point framework on Canadian unity was agreed. The conference, held in Calgary, recognized the 'unique character' of Québec, but asserted that any future change in the constitutional powers of one province should be applicable to all provinces. By June 1998 the resultant 'Calgary Declaration' had been endorsed by the legislatures of all provinces except Québec.

The Supreme Court, which had been requested in February 1998 to rule on the legality of a unilateral secession by Québec, declared in August that no province had the right, in constitutional or international law, to leave the federation without prior negotiations with the federal and provincial governments, and that secession would require the approval of the federal legislature, together with that of seven of the 10 provinces. It was further stated that an obligation would exist for negotiation with Québec if a clear majority of its voters expressed a wish to leave the federation.

In March 1998 Jean Charest resigned as leader of the PC, to accept the leadership of the Liberal Party of Québec. The Liberals narrowly won the provincial legislative election in November.

In January 2001 Bouchard announced his resignation as Premier of Québec, once a successor had been elected. He also resigned as a member of the provincial legislature and as leader of the PQ, stating that he had failed in his intention to achieve independence for the province. The BQ had lost several seats in Québec to the Liberals at the 2000 federal general election, and opinion polls continued to show a decline in support for independence. In March 2001 Bernard Landry of the PQ, hitherto Minister of Finance in the province, was elected Premier of Québec.

Continuing Liberal rule 1997–2006

The Liberals were re-elected at a general election held in June 1997, although with a reduced majority in the House of Commons. The RP replaced the BQ as the main opposition party.

In March 2000 members of the RP voted to form the Canadian Alliance (CA), an organization conceived at a convention held in September 1998 with the aim of uniting the major right-wing parties. The PC declined to join the CA, although a number of that party's prominent members chose to do so. In July Stockwell Day, a former PC member, was elected leader of the CA.

In October 2000 Prime Minister Chrétien announced that a general election would be held on 27 November, despite his Government's mandate being valid until June 2002. At the election, Chrétien's Liberals won 172 of the 301 seats in the House of Commons. The CA secured 66 seats, while the BQ obtained 38, the NDP 13 and the PC 12. The results demonstrated an increasing political polarization between the country's east and centre and its west—the CA won 50 of the 60 seats available in the two westernmost provinces, British Columbia and Alberta, but only two in Ontario (the Liberals being elected in 100 of the 103 constituencies in that province).

In May 2001, in British Columbia, the NDP, which had been in government since 1991, was roundly defeated in provincial elections, retaining just two seats in the 79-seat Legislative Assembly. The Liberal Party secured the remaining 77 seats. The provincial party leader, Gordon Campbell, became Premier.

In July 2001, following several months of internal dissent in the party owing to its poor performance in the 2000 legislative elections, 13 CA members resigned from the party in protest at Day's refusal to resign the leadership. Day eventually resigned in December, and was succeeded by Stephen Harper.

Legislative elections were held in 10 of the 13 provinces and territories in late 2002 and throughout 2003. In April 2003 Charest became Premier of Québec when the Liberal Party secured a majority in the provincial legislature. In October the Liberals assumed control of Ontario from the PC; Dalton McGuinty was appointed provincial Premier. Later in the same month the PC assumed power from the Liberals in elections in Newfoundland and Labrador (as the province had officially been renamed in December 2001); Danny Williams became Premier.

In December 2003 former Minister of Finance Paul Martin succeeded Chrétien as Prime Minister and as leader of the Liberal Party following the latter's retirement. In the same month the PC and CA announced that they had merged at federal level to form a new party, the Conservative Party of Canada; Stephen Harper was elected leader of the new party in March 2005.

Legislation defining marriage as 'a heterosexual or homosexual union' was approved by the House of Commons in June 2005 by 158 to 133 votes; the bill received senate approval in the following month. Thus, Canada became only the third country in the world to legalize same-sex marriages (after the Netherlands and Belgium).

From 2002 the Liberal Government was subject to persistent accusations of corruption. In February 2004 a report by the office of the Auditor-General concluded that the Government had misappropriated funds during a state campaign intended to promote national unity in Québec in 1997–2001. It was alleged that contracts worth some C $100m. had been awarded to advertising companies in Québec with links to the Liberal Party, and that some of these contracts were false. Prime Minister Martin denied any involvement in the affair, which coincided with his time as Minister of Finance in the Chrétien Government, and ordered a public inquiry. Nevertheless, the so-called 'sponsorship scandal' was widely believed to have affected support for the Liberal Party in the general election that was held on 28 June 2004. The incumbent party failed to obtain a parliamentary majority. The level of voter participation was the lowest ever recorded, at 60.9% of the electorate. Prime Minister Martin formed the first minority Government in Canada since 1979.

The Commission of Inquiry into the alleged misappropriation of campaign funds in Québec held public hearings from September 2004, receiving testimony from politicians, civil servants, and advertising and communications executives. As details emerged of alleged fraud and systemic mismanagement of sponsorship deals, the Government came under increasing pressure from opposition parties to hold a fresh election. In April 2005 Prime Minister Martin announced that a general election would be held within 30 days of the publication of the Commission's report. In May, with the support of the NDP, the Government narrowly avoided a parliamentary defeat in a vote on the 2006 budget that was treated as a motion of confidence. The budget was approved by 153 votes to 152.

The first part of the Commission of Inquiry's report into the sponsorship scandal was published on 1 November 2005. The report concluded, *inter alia*, that the Liberal Party had obtained election funds illegally. Although there was no evidence to link former Prime Minister Chrétien to any wrongdoing, he was held politically accountable for the failures in management; Prime Minister Martin and the current Liberal Government were exonerated. However, in late November the Conservatives tabled a motion of no confidence in the Government. Having lost the support of the NDP earlier in the month—according to the NDP, because of differences over health policy—the Government was defeated by 171 votes to 133, thus precipitating a general election. Parliament was dissolved by the new Governor-General, Michaëlle Jean, who had succeeded Adrianne Clarkson in September.

The 2006 general election

At the general election, held on 23 January 2006, the Conservative Party won 124 of the 308 seats, an increase of 25. As expected, the Liberals' parliamentary representation fell, by 32 seats to 103 seats. In contrast, the NDP increased its share of seats by 10, to 29 seats. The BQ, which was only represented in Québec, won 51 seats, a slight decrease from the 54 seats it held previously. There was one independent seat. Conservative leader Stephen Harper was declared Prime Minister-elect, but was forced to form a minority Government. Voter turn-out was some 64.9% of the electorate.

Harper was sworn into office on 6 February 2006. His new Federal Ministry included Peter MacKay as Minister of Foreign Affairs and David Emerson as Minister of International Trade; the latter, a former minister in the Liberal Government, had defected to the Conservatives following the election. The new Prime Minister pledged that his first piece of legislation on taking office would be the introduction of a Federal Accountability Act. The proposal reflected the conclusions of the Commission of Inquiry, the final part of which was released on 1 February. The report made 19 recommendations towards improving executive answerability, including: reform of the Government's decision-making process; a curtailment of the powers of the Prime Minister; and an increase in the authority of the federal Parliament. In the same month Martin stood down as Liberal Party leader; he was succeeded by Stéphane Dion.

In November 2006 the House of Commons voted by an overwhelming margin to approve legislation introduced by Prime Minister Harper recognizing Québec as a 'nation within a united Canada'. Although the resolution was largely seen as symbolic, the Minister for Intergovernmental Affairs, Michael D. Chong, resigned from the Cabinet in protest at the legislation's recognition of what he described as 'ethnic nationalism'.

In August 2007 Minister of National Defence Gordon O'Connor, who had encountered criticism over Canada's continuing military involvement in the US-led 'war on terror' in Afghanistan (see Foreign Affairs), was replaced by Peter MacKay. O'Connor assumed responsibility for the national revenue portfolio, and Maxime Bernier was appointed as MacKay's successor as Minister of Foreign Affairs. In October the Government survived three votes of confidence in the House of Commons.

A number of provinces and territories held legislative elections in 2007–08. In Québec on 26 March 2007, Jean Charest, leader of the Québec Liberal Party, was re-elected Premier; however, the Liberals failed to secure a parliamentary majority, precipitating the formation of a minority Government, the first in 129 years in that province. The ADQ defeated the PQ to become the official opposition, although the formation of government was almost equally divided between the three parties. The ruling NDP, led by Gary Doer, was returned to power in Manitoba in elections held on 22 May, while in Prince Edward Island the opposition Liberal Party defeated the ruling PC. The Liberal Party leader, Robert Ghiz, was duly sworn in as Premier in June. In Newfoundland and Labrador, however, Premier Danny Williams's PC won an overwhelming majority in an election held on 9 October, securing a second successive term. The following day a provincial ballot in Ontario returned the Liberals to government. In the same month Floyd Roland was elected the new Premier of the Northwest Territories following elections to the Legislative Assembly. In Saskatchewan, Brad Wall became Premier after his Saskatchewan Party won a majority in the provincial election of 7 November. Finally, in March 2008 the Conservatives were re-elected to serve an 11th consecutive term in Alberta; Edward Stelmach was sworn in as Premier.

Former Prime Minister Brian Mulroney was the subject of corruption allegations in November 2007, regarding C $300,000 he reportedly received in payments from businessman Karlheinz Schreiber in 1993–94. Mulroney denied receiving any money while still in office. In April 2008 the House of Commons' ethics committee recommended a broad public inquiry into the allegations. Public hearings by a federal Commission of Inquiry commenced in March 2009. Testifying in May, Mulroney admitted receiving $225,000 from Schreiber, but claimed that this was payment for the international promotion of military vehicles to be manufactured in Canada by a German company represented by Schreiber, rather than for illegal domestic lobbying. In a report issued at the end of May 2010 the head of the Commission, Associate Chief Justice Jeffrey Oliphant, concluded that Mulroney, in his secretive dealings with Schreiber, was guilty of infringing federal ethics guidelines; Oliphant highlighted Mulroney's acceptance of three large cash payments. However, the report found that the transactions had occurred after the former premier's resignation in June 1993.

Harper's Government was undermined in May 2008 by the resignation of the Minister of Foreign Affairs, Maxime Bernier, after it was revealed that he had left sensitive North Atlantic Treaty Organization (NATO) documents at the house of his girlfriend, Julie Couillard, who had been accused of having links with known gangs. He was replaced by David Emerson.

The 2008 general election and subsequent events

Parliament was dissolved on 7 September 2008 on the request of Prime Minister Harper, who was seeking a functional mandate for his party after two-and-a-half years of minority government. At a general election on 14 October, the Conservative Party secured 37.6% of the vote and 143 of the 308 seats, an increase of 16 but still short of the 155 required for a majority. The Liberal Party won 26.2% of the ballot, securing 77 seats, the BQ garnered 49 and the NDP won 37, while two were secured by independent candidates. Turn-out was 59.1%, the lowest participation rate ever recorded.

Harper suspended Parliament for a second time in three months in December 2008, thus avoiding a scheduled no confidence vote in which his minority Government had been expected to be defeated. The Liberal Party and the NDP had intended to form a coalition administration with support from the BQ, having proposed the vote on the grounds that the Conservative Government had failed adequately to address adverse economic conditions. A few days later the leader of the Liberal Party, Stéphane Dion, announced that he was to resign. He was replaced, initially in an acting capacity, by Michael Ignatieff, whose leadership of the party was ratified in May 2009. Meanwhile, following the criticism of its response to the economic downturn, the Government announced a programme of stimulus measures costing some C $40,000m. over two years, which received the approval of Parliament in February.

Meanwhile, in November 2008 Eva Aariak was selected as the new Premier of Nunavut. In Québec, following early legislative elections called by the minority Liberal administration in December, Jean Charest was elected to a third term as Premier and the Liberals secured a majority in the provincial legislature. In legislative elections conducted in British Columbia in mid-May 2009, the Liberal Party, led by Premier Gordon Campbell, secured a third successive term in office. Earlier that month the House of Assembly of Nova Scotia approved a vote of no confidence in Rodney MacDonald's minority PC Government over its proposed budget. The NDP, led by Darrell Dexter, was victorious in elections held in the province in June, and Dexter duly replaced MacDonald as Premier of the province. Greg Selinger was elected as leader of the NDP in Manitoba and inaugurated as provincial Premier in October.

At the beginning of October 2009 the House of Commons rejected, by 144 votes to 117, a motion of no confidence in the Government tabled by the Liberal Party, which again accused Harper's administration of economic mismanagement. Although the BQ had supported the Liberal motion, the NDP abstained from voting, allowing the Conservative Government to survive. The Conservatives performed well in by-elections to fill four vacant seats in the House of Commons in November, increasing their representation to 145 seats.

Parliament was suspended again at Harper's request in December 2009, until early March 2010. The Prime Minister claimed that more time was required to review economic policy prior to the presentation of the 2010 budget, but opposition parties accused the Government of attempting to evade questions regarding the alleged torture of prisoners in Afghanistan transferred into local custody by Canadian soldiers (see Foreign Affairs). Public discontent was also evident: demonstrations were held throughout Canada in late January 2010 in protest against the legislative suspension. Meanwhile, Harper effected a government reorganization in mid-January. Among the changes, Peter Van Loan, hitherto Minister of Public Safety, was appointed as Minister of International Trade.

In June 2010 Canada hosted two major international forums on economic co-operation: the annual summit of the Group of Eight (G8) was held in Huntsville, Ontario on 25–26 June, and was immediately followed by a summit meeting of the Group of 20 (G20) in Toronto. In order to protect visiting officials and control the activities of anti-summit protesters, the authorities mounted what was described as the nation's largest and most expensive security operation. The provincial government in Ontario granted extended powers of search and arrest to the security services for the duration of the summit. None the less, a series of protests commenced in Toronto from mid-June, and large demonstrations on 26–27 June escalated into extensive civil disorder, as some protesters were embroiled in violent clashes with the security forces; there were also widespread reports of acts of vandalism aimed at business interests in the city centre. The unrest prompted the largest mass arrests in Canada's history, as more than 1,000 people were detained. More than 800 detainees were released within 48 hours; however, the severity of the security response was strongly criticized by civil rights organizations.

In provincial elections in New Brunswick in September 2010 the PC overturned the Liberal Party's majority, winning 42 of the Legislative Assembly's 55 seats. David Alward was sworn in as Premier on 12 October. In November the Premier of British Columbia, Gordon Campbell of the Liberal Party, announced his intention to resign after almost 10 years in office. The announcement followed growing political opposition to the Liberals' introduction of a harmonized sales tax. In February 2011 Christy Clark won the Liberal Party's provincial leadership contest; she was sworn in as Premier of British Columbia in March. In November 2010 Newfoundland and Labrador Premier Danny Williams announced his resignation; Kathy Dunderdale, the province's deputy premier and Minister of Natural Resources, was sworn in as Premier in December.

At the beginning of October 2010 David Johnston, an author and former academic, was sworn in as Governor-General of Canada, succeeding Michaëlle Jean, who had held the post since 2005.

In May 2010 an opposition-sponsored Climate Change Accountability Act was passed in the House of Commons; the act required a reduction in emissions of greenhouse gases to 25% below 1990 levels by 2020. However, the bill was defeated by Conservatives in the Senate in November. The intervention of the upper house in the passage of the legislation, which was described as 'undemocratic' by opposition politicians, was defended by Prime Minister Harper, who insisted that the legislation was 'irresponsible'. Peter Kent was appointed Minister of the Environment in January 2011, replacing Jim Prentice, who had resigned in November 2010. In his inaugural speech, Kent insisted that Canadian environmental regulations would, by necessity, be aligned with those of the USA. (For further background information on climate change policy, see Regional Relations.)

Recent developments: the 2011 general election

In early 2011 the tenure of the minority Government appeared increasingly insecure as a series of misconduct allegations were levelled against the Conservatives. In February four officials were charged with financial irregularities relating to the Conservative's 2006 general election campaign. In early March the Speaker of the House, Peter Milliken, approved two opposition motions that accused the Government of being in contempt of Parliament: the administration had allegedly failed to disclose full details of federal spending on crime prevention, and Minister of International Co-operation Beverley Oda was accused of misleading the House over investigations into her role in the falsification of a document on foreign-aid funding. In mid-March the parliamentary Standing Committee on Procedure and House Affairs confirmed that the Government's conduct constituted contempt of Parliament. The collapse of the minority Government appeared all but inevitable when the three main opposition parties indicated their intention to vote against the 2011 federal budget, which was presented to the House on 22 March. On 25 March the Liberals presented a parliamentary motion charging Harper's administration with contempt of Parliament and expressing no confidence in the Government; the motion was carried by 156 votes to 145. A general election was scheduled for 2 May.

Despite the fact that Harper's Government was the first in Canada's history to be declared in contempt of Parliament, opinion polls showed no reduction in support for the Conservatives. In the event, the general election on 2 May 2011 produced a dramatic transformation in the political status quo. According to the final results, the Conservative Party won an overall majority for the first time, with 166 out of 308 available seats (an increase of 23 seats on the previous election in October 2008). Both the Liberals and the BQ suffered heavy electoral losses: the Liberals retained just 34 seats, compared with 77 at the 2008 election; the BQ held only four seats, compared with 49 in 2008. Michael Ignatieff, leader of the Liberal Party, and his BQ counterpart, Gilles Duceppe, both failed to secure re-election, and each subsequently resigned his respective party leadership. The NDP recorded an impressive increase in support and became for the first time the largest opposition party: the party increased its representation in the House from 37 seats to 103, enjoying particularly large gains in Québec, where it secured 59 out of 75 seats. In British Columbia a candidate of the Green Party of Canada secured the party's first seat in the federal Parliament. Voter turn-out was recorded at 61.1%. Harper announced a new Federal Ministry in mid-May 2011. Most notably, John Baird replaced the unseated Lawrence Cannon as Minister of Foreign Affairs, although the other key portfolios remained unaltered. Robert Rae was elected as the Liberal Party's interim leader in late May (a permanent replacement for Ignatieff was not expected to be chosen until 2013). NDP leader Jack Layton died of cancer in August 2011; Nycole Turmel assumed Layton's duties on an interim basis. In March 2012 Thomas Mulcair was elected as the new leader of the NDP and, therefore, became the official opposition leader in the House of Commons. Meanwhile, in December 2011 Daniel Paillé won the BQ's leadership election, and in the following month the ADQ was absorbed by the recently founded Coalition Avenir Québec.

In June 2011 the Government proposed new measures to reform the Senate. Voluntary elections would be held in the provinces and territories to nominate potential senators, who, if selected by the Prime Minister, would serve non-renewable, nine-year terms. Opposition parties criticized the proposals for introducing additional costly elections, for lacking a framework to resolve conflicts between the upper and lower houses, and for failing to address provincial inequalities in relation to the distribution of Senate seats. In a controversial move to re-emphasize Canada's traditional connections with the British monarchy, in August Minister of National Defence Peter MacKay proclaimed that the Maritime Command and the Air Command would be redesignated, respectively, as the Royal Canadian Navy and the Royal Canadian Air Force, titles not used since 1968.

Seven provincial and territorial legislative elections were conducted during October–November 2011. Dalton McGuinty won a third term as Premier of Ontario, although the Liberals failed to retain their majority in the provincial legislature, while the NDP, under Greg Selinger, secured a fourth consecutive tenure in office in Manitoba. In Saskatchewan, Premier Brad Wall and his Saskatchewan Party were re-elected for a second term, as were Premier Robert Ghiz and the Liberals in Prince Edward Island. The Conservative administration in Newfoundland and Labrador, led by Kathy Dunderdale, was elected to serve a third successive term. The Yukon territorial election was won by the Yukon Party, and incumbent Premier Darrell Pasloski—who had assumed the premiership in June after triumphing in the Yukon Party's leadership contest in the previous month—was sworn in for a full term in October. Robert McLeod was elected as the new Premier of the Northwest Territories. Meanwhile, in early October Alison Redford was selected as the new Progressive Conservative leader in Alberta and hence became Premier of the province shortly thereafter. In April 2012 Redford's Conservatives were re-elected to serve a 12th consecutive term in Alberta. The Conservatives won a convincing, albeit somewhat reduced, majority, with 61 out of 87 seats in the provincial legislature; the right-wing Wildrose Alliance Party, who had failed to win a single seat in the 2008 ballot, secured 17 seats and replaced the Liberals as the largest opposition party in the province.

Legislation increasing the number of seats in the House of Commons, from 308 to 338, was promulgated in December 2011, although this change would not come into effect until the next general election (expected to take place in 2015). The Fair

Representation Act partially redressed the imbalances in the allocation of seats among the provinces, with Alberta, British Columbia, Ontario and Québec all receiving additional seats to reflect their growing populations; however, in spite of this move, Alberta, British Columbia and Ontario would remain under-represented in the lower house.

Land Treaty Claims

The question of land treaty claims by Canada's indigenous peoples came to prominence in the latter part of the 20th century, when disputes over land rights arose in Ontario, Manitoba and Québec. In September 1988, following 13 years of negotiations, the federal Government formally transferred to indigenous ownership an area covering 673,000 sq km in the Northwest Territories. In the Yukon Territory, an area of 41,000 sq km (representing 8.6% of the Territory's land) was transferred to indigenous control. At the same time, debate had begun to intensify on the formulation of a new constitutional status for the Northwest Territories, in which a population of only 58,000 (of which Inuit and other indigenous peoples comprised about one-half) occupied an area comprising one-third of Canada's land mass. In December 1991 specific terms for the creation of a semi-autonomous Nunavut Territory, covering an area of 2.2m. sq km, to the east of a boundary running northwards from the Saskatchewan–Manitoba border, were agreed by Inuit representatives and the federal Government, and in May 1992 a plebiscite on a proposal to divide the Northwest Territories into two self-governing units was approved by the territories' residents.

A formal agreement to settle all outstanding land treaty claims was finalized by the federal Government in May 1993, providing for Nunavut to come into official existence on 1 April 1999. Elections to a new, 17-seat legislature for Nunavut, to be located at Iqaluit, were held in February 1999, and the new territorial Government took office in April. In December 1997 the Supreme Court awarded legal title to 57,000 sq km of ancestral land to two native groups in British Columbia, and in the following month the federal Government offered a formal apology to all native groups for past mistreatment and injustices. The principle of 'aboriginal title', established by the Supreme Court ruling, was again exercised in April 1999 in British Columbia under the Nisga'a Agreement. The Agreement transferred some 2,000 sq km of land, together with substantial powers of self-government and C $196m., to 5,500 Nisga'a people; in return, they ceded their wider aboriginal title. In August 2003 Prime Minister Chrétien signed an agreement that would transfer powers of self-government and 39,000 sq km of land to some 3,000 Tlicho people in the Northwest Territories; the agreement was ratified by the federal Parliament in February 2005. At a summit in British Columbia in November, Prime Minister Martin pledged to spend C $4,300m. over the next 10 years on measures to reduce poverty and improve health, education and housing among the Indian and Inuit communities. An agreement worth C $350m., transferring powers of self-government to 5,300 Inuit people in northwest Labrador, came into effect on 1 December.

In February 2006 an agreement was reached to protect some 1.8m. ha of land in British Columbia, incorporating the Great Bear rainforest. Ecosystem-based management would allow controlled resource development in 4.6m. ha of surrounding territory. An accord between the federal Government and the native Cree Indian communities of Québec was announced in July 2007; the agreement, which required ratification by both parties, would grant the communities increased powers of self-government, and guaranteed federal government investment in the region over the next 20 years.

Foreign Affairs

Regional relations

Recent administrations have sought to emphasize Canada's independence from the USA in matters of foreign policy, while continuing the increased co-operation in areas such as trade and environmental protection. In the last two decades of the 20th century a number of bilateral environmental agreements were signed, including accords on gaseous emissions, both domestically and in the USA (which move northwards into Canada to produce environmentally destructive 'acid rain'), and the elimination of industrial pollution from the Great Lakes, in conjunction with the implementation of a number of domestic environmental-improvement programmes. Canada assumed a leading role in the establishment, with seven other circumpolar countries, of the Arctic Council (see p. 448), which commenced operation in September 1996. The aims of the Council include the protection of the environment of the polar region, the formation of co-ordinated policies governing its future, and the safeguarding of the interests of its indigenous population groups. In 1997, at the third Conference of the Parties to the Framework Convention on Climate Change (World Meteorological Organization, see p. 179), held in Kyoto, Japan, Canada undertook to implement reductions of its emissions of greenhouse gases to 6% below 1990 levels by the year 2012. In December 2002 the Government ratified the Protocol, despite opposition from the gas and petroleum industries and the province of Alberta. However, by April 2007 the country's greenhouse gas emissions were reportedly 30% greater than those recorded in 1990, and the Martin administration conceded that Canada would be unable to satisfy its obligations prescribed under the Kyoto Protocol by 2012. At the end of April 2007, a government initiative targeting a 20% reduction in current emissions from 2006 levels by 2020 was undertaken. In January 2010 the Minister of the Environment, Jim Prentice, announced that Canada's target for lowering emissions would be amended to match that of the USA, which was considering a 17% reduction from 2005 levels by 2020. To avoid financial penalties (totalling C $13,600m. according to the Government) for failing to attain emissions reduction targets, in December 2011 Canada became the first signatory to the Kyoto Protocol to withdraw from the agreement. This decision attracted international criticism and was also censured by environmental groups and Canada's opposition parties. The Harper administration claimed that the Kyoto targets were unrealistic and damaging to Canada's economy and argued that the Protocol was ineffective since significant polluters such as the USA and China were not obliged to reduce their greenhouse gas emissions.

Canada, which maintains significant economic and commercial links with Cuba and operates a policy of 'constructive engagement' in its relations with that country, adopted a prominent role in international opposition to efforts, initiated by the US Government in March 1996, to penalize investors whose business in any way involves property in Cuba that was confiscated from US citizens following the 1959 revolution. The imposition of these measures, known as the Helms-Burton Act, led in July 1996 to the exclusion from the USA of nine Canadian businessmen involved in nickel-mining operations in Cuba. The Canadian Government responded by introducing legislation prohibiting Canadian companies from compliance with the Helms-Burton Act, and refused to recognize foreign court rulings arising from the Act. With Mexico, which also conducts significant trade with Cuba, Canada co-ordinated a joint challenge to the US Government through NAFTA dispute procedures. In November 1996 Canada actively promoted a resolution by the UN General Assembly condemning the US trade sanctions against Cuba and, in the same month, joined the European Union (EU) in a complaint against the embargo to the World Trade Organization (WTO, see p. 433). In April 1998, following an official visit to Cuba by Prime Minister Chrétien, the Canadian Government signed a series of co-operation agreements with Cuba. However, relations between the two countries subsequently experienced a marked decline, owing to increasing concern in Canada at the Cuban Government's human rights record, particularly in relation to the treatment of political prisoners. In July 1999 the Canadian Government stated that it would implement no further assistance programmes to Cuba that did not clearly further the protection of human rights, and it was indicated that Canada would not support the participation of Cuba in the Organization of American States (OAS, see p. 394). However, bilateral relations subsequently improved, and the Canadian Government welcomed a resolution adopted by the OAS General Assembly in June 2009 that revoked the decision made in 1962 to suspend Cuba from the organization's activities.

Meanwhile, relations with the USA improved in June 1999 following the resolution of a long-standing disagreement over the demarcation of salmon-fishing rights off the Pacific coast. However, in September 2000 a dispute arose over the USA's threat to impose export tariffs on Canadian timber, which, the USA claimed, was subsidized by the Canadian Government, and which undercut the price of US timber. Canada requested a WTO investigation into US anti-subsidy policies, after the USA imposed duties of 32% on softwood lumber imports from Canada in response. In August 2001 Canada won a preliminary victory at the WTO, which adopted a report agreeing that the Government was not subsidizing exports. Canada hoped to remove US duties and replace an earlier quota agreement, which expired in March 2001, with a system based on free trade; however, the USA imposed tariffs of 27% on softwood lumber imports from Canada in May 2002. Negotiations to resolve the issue failed, and in January 2004 the Canadian Government rejected a US proposal to remove the duties in exchange for quotas limiting Canadian exports to the US market. In August the WTO ruled that Canada could retaliate with trade sanctions. In August 2005 a NAFTA panel ordered the USA to remove the duties on Canadian softwood and to refund some US $4,000m. already collected. However, the USA refused to comply and in this case received support from the WTO. The trade dispute was resolved in April 2006 when the USA agreed to remove its tariffs and refund the US $4,000m. in duties collected; in return, Canada agreed to restrict its share of the US timber market to 34%. The USA's prohibition of the use of foreign-produced iron, steel and other manufactured goods in projects funded by a US $787,000m. fiscal stimulus programme approved by the US Congress in February 2009 prompted considerable concern in Canada, owing to the importance to the Canadian economy of trade with the USA. Prime Minister Harper sought to secure the exemption of Canadian producers and suppliers from the so-called 'buy American' provision, and in February 2010 a bilateral agreement was signed that allowed Canadian companies to participate in some US state and local infrastructure projects for the remainder of the stimulus programme in exchange for access for US companies to construction contracts in Canada.

Following the terrorist attacks on the USA on 11 September 2001 Canada and the USA increased co-operation on intelligence and security matters: under the 'Smart Border Declaration' signed by the two countries in December, 400 US National Guards were to be deployed at 43 crossings along both sides of the 6,400-km (4,000-mile) Canada–USA border. In the same month extensive anti-terrorist legislation was also introduced.

In February 2005 Prime Minister Martin announced that Canada would not participate in a controversial US missile defence programme. However, in 2004 Martin's Government had acceded to a US request to allow installations of the North American Aerospace Defense Command (NORAD—a binational military organization established by the two countries in 1958) to be integrated into the anti-missile warning system, which was regarded as tantamount to Canadian participation. In May 2006 the House of Commons voted to renew the NORAD agreement and to make it a permanent arrangement, subject to review every four years.

In February 2011 Prime Minister Harper and US President Barack Obama announced details of a framework agreement on border co-operation, which envisioned a fully integrated and jointly operated North American security perimeter. Political opponents claimed that the agreement represented a serious threat to Canada's national sovereignty, on the grounds that it would force Canada to adopt US policy on immigration and security, and would enable US border guards to operate within Canadian territory. These claims were rejected by Harper, who insisted that the initiative would be mutually beneficial, on economic and security grounds. An action plan to implement the border agreement was announced by Harper and Obama in December.

In mid-2007 Russian explorers participating in a research expedition descended to the floor of the Arctic Ocean and planted their nation's flag directly under the North Pole. The incident was widely interpreted, not least in Canada, as an attempt to stake a territorial claim to the Arctic seabed and the vast mineral and energy resources believed to exist therein. Such interpretations were refuted by the Russian authorities. Nevertheless, the Conservative Government of Stephen Harper has pursued an increasingly assertive approach in its defence of Canadian maritime sovereignty in the Arctic. In July 2007 the Government announced its intention to commission up to eight Arctic patrol ships, with ice-breaking capabilities, which would enable the Navy to maintain year-round patrols of Canada's northern waters. In mid-2011 construction contracts for the vessels were awarded, and the first ships were expected to be launched in 2013. Further plans aimed at consolidating Canada's presence in the far north included the construction of a naval training facility and the development of a deep-water port in locations adjacent to the Northwest Passage. In early 2012 several territorial disputes involving Canada remained open: a long-running dispute with Denmark concerning ownership of Hans Island, a small uninhabited island located in the strategic strait between Greenland and Ellesmere Island, Nunavut; a disagreement with the USA concerning delineation of their joint maritime border in the Beaufort Sea; and an ongoing debate with several nations regarding Canada's claimed sovereignty over the Northwest Passage. In early 2011 Canadian-Danish negotiations on the Hans Island issue were reported to be making good progress, with plans for a joint-mapping project on the adjacent seabed under discussion. Under the terms of the UN Convention on the Law of the Sea (UNCLOS), Canada was required to submit its sovereignty claims to the Arctic seabed by 2013 (ten years after ratification of the convention).

Other external relations

There have been recurrent disagreements between Canada and France concerning the boundary of disputed waters near the French-controlled islands of Saint Pierre and Miquelon, off the southern coast of Newfoundland and Labrador. In June 1992 an international arbitration tribunal presented its report, generally regarded as favourable to Canada, and in December 1994 the two countries agreed a 10-year accord on the allocation of fishing rights around the islands. In September 2001 France and Canada held talks on energy exploration in the waters off Saint Pierre and Miquelon; geologists believed there were large petroleum and natural gas deposits between the islands and Newfoundland and Labrador and Nova Scotia. In May 2009 the French Government lodged a claim at the UN Commission on the Limits of the Continental Shelf to areas of seabed beyond its existing Exclusive Economic Zone (EEZ) around Saint Pierre and Miquelon. The Canadian Government insisted that the matter had been definitively resolved by the arbitration tribunal in 1992.

In 1994 the Canadian Government vigorously contested a decision by the EU unilaterally to award itself almost 70% of the internationally agreed quota of Greenland halibut caught in the north-west Atlantic fishing grounds. It declared that it would act to prevent EU fishing trawlers (principally from Spain and Portugal) from overfishing the already seriously depleted stocks of Greenland halibut and announced that Canada was extending its maritime jurisdiction beyond its EEZ, already extending 200 nautical miles (370 km) from the coastline. This action was rejected by the EU as contrary to international law. (In November 2003 Canada ratified the UN Convention on the Law of the Sea—UNCLOS—which establishes the limit of the EEZ as being 200 nautical miles from the coastline. In July 2006 the Government announced that it would undertake an underwater survey to identify the outer edge of the continental shelf; under the terms of UNCLOS countries have the right to exploit natural resources on and under the seabed up to an identifiable shelf edge where it extends beyond the EEZ.)

In February 1995 the Canadian Government warned the EU that force would be used if necessary to ensure that total catches by EU vessels did not exceed the Northwest Atlantic Fishing Organization (NAFO)-agreed quota and, in the following month, its enforcement vessels impounded a Spanish trawler fishing in international waters. The EU responded by suspending all official political contacts with Canada, pending the trawler's release. The impasse was eased by the release of the trawler in the following month, when it was agreed to initiate quota allocation negotiations. A resolution was reached in April, under which Canada and EU countries each consented to accept 41% of the 1996 Greenland halibut quota. It was agreed that independent observers would monitor the activities of trawlers in the north-west Atlantic fishing zone. In early 2002 the Canadian Government imposed a ban on all vessels from Estonia and the Faroe Islands from entering Canadian ports, accusing those fleets of violating NAFO-agreed shrimp quotas off the eastern coast of the country. In September the Government extended the ban to any foreign vessel that violated NAFO-agreed quotas. The ban on the Estonian fleet was lifted in December. In July 2006 the EU and Canada announced that they would begin joint inspection patrols to combat illegal fishing and to enforce the NAFO Regulatory Area.

The EU is Canada's second largest trading partner, after the USA. Negotiations with the EU concerning a Comprehensive Economic and Trade Agreement (CETA) commenced in mid-2009 and were expected to be concluded during 2012. An EU ban on trade in seal products, which had entered into force in August 2010, prompted Canada (a major supplier of such items) to refer the matter to the WTO in February 2011. A similar ban came into effect in Russia, Belarus and Kazakhstan in August, placing the future of the Canadian sealing industry in serious jeopardy. A further obstacle to the CETA was an EU directive, under discussion in early 2011, which would classify oil sands as a 'carbon intensive' fuel, thus impeding future European imports of Canadian oil.

Some 750 Canadian troops were deployed in Afghanistan in February 2002 as part of the US-led international forces present in that country, although all Canadian forces had returned home by November. However, in August 2003 around 1,900 Canadian troops were sent to Afghanistan as part of a NATO-led mission to protect the interim Government there and suppress militant resistance. By late 2006 Canada had committed C $1,000m. to fund reconstruction and poverty reduction and to strengthen governance in Afghanistan, over a 10-year period. In July 2011 Canadian combat operations in Afghanistan were officially terminated and the approximately 3,000 Canadian armed forces personnel in the country were withdrawn. According to reports, 157 Canadian soldiers had died in Afghanistan since 2001, while the cost of the mission was estimated at US $11,000m. The Government pledged that Canadian forces would continue to participate in humanitarian and development projects. Furthermore, up to 950 military personnel were to be deployed in training programmes for the Afghan security forces.

In February 2007 Canada became embroiled in allegations relating to the abuse of Afghan detainees by military personnel. Under the Access to Information Act, the Department of National Defence released documents on 6 February apparently providing evidence of the violent mistreatment by military police officers of three prisoners held in Canadian custody near Qandahar, Afghanistan, during an interrogation exercise. A government inquiry into the scandal was immediately commenced and endorsed by NATO in April. In the same month the human rights organization Amnesty International alleged that Canadian military forces had been aware that prisoners transferred from Canadian custody into Afghan custody had been subject to abuse. An agreement allowing Canadian military access to any prisoner originally detained by Canadian forces was reached in the following month. Meanwhile, appeals launched in the Supreme Court by three suspected al-Qa'ida operatives, who had been detained in Canada between 2001 and 2003, returned a unanimous ruling in February 2007 that the Government had contravened Canada's Charter of Rights and Freedoms by ratifying legislation in 2002 that permitted the use of undisclosed evidence by the authorities to justify the indefinite detention, or deportation, of non-Canadian terrorist suspects without recourse to trial. The judgment had been suspended by one year to enable Parliament to amend the Immigration and Refugee Protection Act, while on 27 February the renewal of two further pieces of anti-terrorism legislation, due to expire on 1 March, was opposed by the federal legislature. Controversy regarding the treatment of detainees transferred from Canadian to Afghan custody re-emerged in November 2009, when Richard Colvin, a senior Canadian diplomat who had been based in Afghanistan in 2006–07, alleged that the Canadian authorities had been complicit in the torture of prisoners and that his complaints regarding abuse had been 'mostly ignored'. Colvin's testimony, before a parliamentary committee, prompted opposition demands for a public inquiry, but was dismissed by the Government. In December the House of Commons adopted a motion requiring the release of uncensored documents concerning the Afghan detainees to the committee considering the issue. After initially refusing to comply with the motion, in June 2011 the Government finally released some 4,000 pages of partially redacted documents, proclaiming that they exonerated the military of any malpractice and that the matter was now closed. However, opposition parties expressed concern that a reported 36,000 pages of documents relating to the abuse allegations still remained classified and appealed for a further investigation.

In February 2011 Canada placed economic sanctions on the Libyan regime of Col Muammar al-Qaddafi and recalled the Canadian ambassador in Tripoli following attempts by the Libyan authorities to suppress violently a popular uprising. To protect the civilian population from attacks by Qaddafi's forces, in the following month the Canadian military intervened in Libya as part of an international coalition established to enforce a 'no-fly zone' over the country (authorized under UN Security Council Resolution 1973). In June the Canadian Government recognized the rebel 'National Transitional Council of Libya' and pledged aid of C $2m., while in August Qaddafi-appointed diplomats were expelled from Canada. John Baird, the Canadian Minister of Foreign Affairs, announced further funding of $10m. during a visit to Libya in October. The coalition military action, which included Canadian air-strikes, heavily contributed to the final defeat of the Qaddafi regime later that month, prompting critics to claim that the alliance had breached the terms of the UN mandate. At the end of October the UN Security Council terminated the mission, and Canadian forces returned home. The Government estimated the cost of Canada's military intervention at $50m.

At a conference held in Ottawa in December 1997, Canada became the first signatory of the Ottawa Convention, a treaty agreed by 121 countries, undertaking to discontinue the use of land-mines and providing for the destruction of existing stockpiles. Humanitarian concerns remained at the forefront of Canadian foreign policy—in late 2011 Canadian humanitarian or peace-keeping forces were deployed in the following locations: Afghanistan, Côte d'Ivoire, Cyprus, the Democratic Republic of the Congo, Haiti, the Golan Heights, Kosovo, Sinai and East Jerusalem, Sierra Leone, South Sudan and Sudan.

CONSTITUTION AND GOVERNMENT

Canada is a federal parliamentary state. Under the Constitution Act 1982, which was enacted as Schedule B to the Canada Act (UK) 1982, and which entered into force on 17 April 1982, executive power is vested in the British monarch, as Head of State, and may be exercised by her representative, the Governor-General, whom she appoints on the advice of the Canadian Prime Minister. The federal Parliament comprises the Head of State, a nominated Senate (a maximum of 112 members, appointed on a regional basis) and a House of Commons (308 members, elected by universal adult suffrage for single-member constituencies). According to the terms of the Fair Representation Act, which was promulgated in December 2011, the number of members in the House of Commons was to be increased to 338 from the next general election, expected to be held in 2015. A Parliament may last no longer than five years. The Governor-General appoints the Prime Minister and, on the latter's recommendation, other ministers to form the Federal Ministry. The Prime Minister should have the confidence of the House of Commons, to which the Cabinet is responsible. Canada comprises 10 provinces (each with a Lieutenant-Governor and a legislature, which may last no longer than five years, from which a Premier is chosen), and three territories constituted by Act of Parliament.

REGIONAL AND INTERNATIONAL CO-OPERATION

Canada is a member of the Organization of American States (see p. 394) and of the Inter-American Development Bank (see p. 334). Together with Mexico and the USA, Canada is a signatory to the North American Free Trade Agreement (NAFTA, see p. 369), which entered into force in 1994 and had been fully implemented by 2008. Canada has also sought to expand trade in Latin America, concluding free trade agreements with Chile, Colombia, Costa Rica, Panama and Peru. Free trade negotiations have also been conducted with the Dominican Republic, El Salvador, Guatemala, Honduras and Nicaragua and with members of the Caribbean Community and Common Market (see p. 227).

Canada was a founder member of the UN in 1945. As a contracting party to the General Agreement on Tariffs and Trade, Canada joined the World Trade Organization (see p. 433) on its establishment in 1995. Canada is a member of The Commonwealth (see p. 239), of the North Atlantic Treaty Organization (see p. 370) and of the Organisation for Economic Co-operation and Development (see p. 379). The country also participates in the Group of Eight (G8, see p. 463) leading industrialized nations and in the Group of 20 (G20, see p. 454). Canada has concluded a free trade accord with the members of the European Free Trade Association (see p. 450) and, in 2009, commenced negotiations aimed at reaching a similar agreement with the European Union (see p. 276).

ECONOMIC AFFAIRS

In 2009, according to estimates by the World Bank, Canada's gross national income (GNI), measured at average 2007–09 prices, was US $1,415,436m., equivalent to US $41,950 per head (or US $37,280 on an international purchasing-power parity basis). The country's population increased at an average annual rate of 1.0% in 2001–10, while gross domestic product (GDP) per head increased, in real terms, by an average of 0.8% per year. Overall GDP increased, in real terms, at an average rate of 1.9% per year in 2001–10. The economy declined by 2.5% in 2009 but grew by 3.1% in 2010.

Agriculture (including forestry and fishing) contributed 1.6% of GDP in 2010, according to the UN, and the sector (excluding forestry and fishing) engaged 1.8% of the economically active population in 2010. In terms of farm receipts, the principal crops are wheat and canola (rapeseed), which, together with livestock production (chiefly cattle and pigs) and timber, provide an important source of export earnings. Canada is a leading world exporter of forest products and of fish and seafood. The production of furs is also important. In real terms, the GDP of the agricultural sector increased at an average annual rate of 1.0% in 2001–10; the sector's GDP increased by 1.3% in 2010.

Industry (including mining, manufacturing, construction and power) provided 29.0% of GDP in 2010, according to the UN, and the sector (including forestry and fishing) employed 20.2% of the economically active population in 2010. Industrial GDP decreased, in real terms, at an average annual rate of 0.1% in 2001–10. Industrial GDP increased by 5.3% in 2010.

According to the UN, mining (including power) provided 10.5% of GDP in 2010. The mining sector (together with forestry, fishing, petroleum and gas) employed only 1.9% of the economically active population in 2010. Canada is a major world producer of zinc, asbestos, nickel, potash and uranium. Gold, silver, iron, copper, cobalt and lead are also exploited. There are considerable reserves of petroleum and natural gas in Alberta's oil sands, off the Atlantic coast and in the Canadian Arctic islands. At the end of 2010 the country's proven natural gas reserves were estimated at 1,727,450m. cu m. Proven oil reserves were put at 32,073m. barrels in 2010 and crude oil production totalled 3.34m. barrels per day in the same year. These figures included estimated reserves of some 26,500m. barrels 'under active development' in Alberta's oil sands in 2010. However, additional 'established reserves' from Canada's oil sands measured an estimated 143,100m. barrels in 2010. When total oil sands reserves are included, Canada holds the world's third largest reported oil reserves (after Venezuela and Saudi Arabia). The GDP of the mining sector (including power) increased, in real terms, at an average annual rate of 0.2% in 2001–10. Mining GDP increased by 3.5% in 2010.

Manufacturing contributed 11.4% of GDP in 2010, according to the UN, and employed 10.2% of the economically active population in that year. The principal branches of manufacturing in 2010, measured by the value of shipments, were transport equipment (accounting for 16.1% of the total), food products, refined petroleum and coal industries, chemical products, primary metal industries, and fabricated metal products. The GDP of the sector declined, in real terms, at an average rate of 1.7% per year in 2001–10. Manufacturing GDP increased by 5.3% in 2010.

Construction contributed 7.2% of GDP in 2010, according to UN figures, and employed 7.1% of the economically active population in 2010. During 2001–10 the GDP of the sector increased at an average annual rate of 3.4%. Construction GDP increased by 8.1% in 2010.

Energy is derived principally from hydroelectric power (which provided 58.7% of the electricity supply in 2008) and from geothermal and nuclear power stations. In 2006 Canada's total energy production (including nuclear energy) totalled an estimated 639,841m. kWh. In 2009 energy products accounted for 9.7% of imports. In August 2009 Suncor Energy and Petro-Canada merged under the name Suncor, creating Canada's first major oil conglomerate.

Services provided 69.4% of GDP in 2010, according to the UN, and engaged 78.1% of the economically active population in 2010. The combined GDP of the service sectors increased, in real terms, at an average rate of 2.7% per year in 2001–10. Services GDP increased by 2.6% in 2010.

In 2010 Canada recorded a visible trade deficit of US $8,682m. The current account of the balance of payments also showed a deficit of US $49,307m. in that year. In 2010 the USA accounted for 73.3% of Canada's total exports and 62.8% of total imports; the countries of the European Union (EU, see p. 276) and Japan were also important trading partners. The principal exports in that year were industrial goods and materials (23.8%), energy products, and machinery and equipment. The principal imports were machinery and equipment (27.5%), industrial goods and materials, and automotive products.

For the financial year 2008/09 there was a consolidated budget surplus of C $2,421m. Canada's general government gross debt was C $1,363,910m. in 2010, equivalent to 84.0% of GDP. The annual rate of inflation averaged 2.0% in 2001–10. Consumer prices increased by an average of 1.8% in 2010. The rate of unemployment averaged 8.0% in 2010.

A sustained period of buoyancy enjoyed by the Canadian economy from the mid-1990s continued into the mid-2000s. The economic success was underpinned by stringent financial policy, low rates of domestic inflation, high international commodity prices and by the beneficial effects of the North American Free Trade Agreement on Canadian exports to the USA. Real GDP declined by 2.8% in 2009, amid a global economic downturn; however, a robust recovery in 2010, with real GDP increasing by an estimated 3.2%, was attributed by the IMF to effective macroeconomic intervention and the resilience of the financial sector. In the fiscal year 2009/10 a consolidated budget deficit of C $55,600m. was recorded—an almost ten-fold increase when compared with 2008/09, when a budget deficit had been incurred for the first time in more than ten years. A significant portion of the deficit was ascribed to the commencement of a two-year economic stimulus programme in February 2009. According to the Government, the federal budget was not forecast to return to surplus before 2015/16. The predominance of trade with the USA traditionally compensated for deficits with other major trading partners, allowing Canada to record substantial trade surpluses in the early 2000s. However, Canada was therefore vulnerable to failures in the US economy, and in 2009 recorded its first annual trade deficit since 1975. Although the deficit widened in 2010, the balance of trade returned to surplus in December, following strong exports of energy products to the USA. The IMF estimated that real GDP expansion slowed in 2011, to 2.2%. Although levels of investment and domestic consumption remained robust in that year, and the unemployment rate continued its downward trend, growth was hindered by the volatile global economic climate and the rising value of the local currency, both of which had a negative impact on exports. The reduction of stimulus spending, as part of a broader effort by the Government to lower the budget deficit, also acted as a constraint on economic expansion. Growth in real GDP was forecast by the IMF to slow further in 2012, to 1.9%. Meanwhile, in an attempt to encourage business investment, the federal rate of corporate income tax was reduced to 15% in January 2012 (from 22% in 2007). Also in that month, the US Department of State rejected a Canadian plan to build a 2,700-km oil pipeline, 'Keystone XL', connecting the Alberta oil sands with markets in the USA. The US authorities declared that further time was needed to assess thoroughly the environmental impact of the project; a revised proposal was expected to be submitted in due course. Another proposed pipeline project, between Alberta and British Colombia, which would facilitate the export of Canadian oil to Asia, was under consideration in 2012. However, both projects have been criticized by environmentalists since oil sands production is considered more polluting than conventional petroleum operations.

PUBLIC HOLIDAYS*

2013: 1 January (New Year's Day), 29 March (Good Friday), 1 April (Easter Monday), 20 May (Victoria Day), 1 July (Canada Day), 2 September (Labour Day), 14 October (Thanksgiving Day), 11 November (Remembrance Day), 25 December (Christmas Day), 26 December (Boxing Day).

*Standard public holidays comprise the listed days, together with any other day so proclaimed by individual provinces or territories.

Statistical Survey

Source (unless otherwise stated): Statistics Canada, Ottawa, ON K1A 0T6; tel. (613) 951-8116; fax (613) 951-0581; internet www.statcan.gc.ca.

The following Statistics Canada resources have been adapted for use in this survey (with permission). [SC1]: *Land and freshwater area, by province and territory*; internet www.statcan.ca/english/Pgdb/phys01.htm. [SC2]: *Population and Dwelling Counts, for Canada, Provinces and Territories, 2006 and 2001 Censuses - 100% Data*; internet www12.statcan.ca/english/census06/data/popdwell/Table.cfm?T=101. [SC3a]: *Population by sex and age group*; internet www40.statcan.gc.ca/l01/cst01/demo10a-eng.htm. [SC3b]: *Population by year, by province and territory*; internet www40.statcan.ca/l01/cst01/demo02a.htm. [SC4]: *Population of census metropolitan areas (2001 Census boundaries)*; internet www40.statcan.ca/l01/cst01/demo05a.htm. [SC5]: *Births and birth rate, by province and territory*; internet www40.statcan.ca/l01/cst01/demo04a.htm. [SC6]: *Marriages by province and territory*; internet www40.statcan.ca/l01/cst01/famil04.htm. [SC7]: *Deaths and death rate, by province and territory*; internet www40.statcan.ca/l01/cst01/demo07a.htm. [SC8]: *Employment by industry*; internet www40.statcan.ca/l01/cst01/econ40.htm. [SC9]: *Labour force characteristics*; internet www40.statcan.ca/l01/cst01/econ10.htm. [SC10]: *Field and speciality crops*; internet www40.statcan.ca/l01/cst01/prim11b.htm. [SC11]: *Fur production, by province and territory*; internet www40.statcan.ca/l01/cst01/prim46a.htm. [SC12]: *Manufacturing shipments, by subsector*; internet www40.statcan.ca/l01/cst01/manuf11.htm. [SC13]: *Consolidated government revenue and expenditures*; internet www40.statcan.ca/l01/cst01/govt48a.htm. [SC14]: *Gross domestic product, income-based*; internet www40.statcan.ca/l01/cst01/econ03.htm. [SC15]: *Gross domestic product, expenditure-based*; internet www40.statcan.ca/l01/cst01/econ04.htm. [SC16]: *Real gross domestic product, expenditure-based*; internet www40.statcan.ca/l01/cst01/econ05.htm. [SC17]: *Gross domestic product at basic prices by industry*; internet www40.statcan.ca/l01/cst01/econ41.htm. [SC18]: *Imports of goods on a balance-of-payments basis, by product*; internet www40.statcan.ca/l01/cst01/gblec05.htm. [SC19]: *Exports of goods on a balance-of-payments basis, by product*; internet www40.statcan.ca/l01/cst01/gblec04.htm. [SC20]: *Imports, exports and trade balance of goods on a balance-of-payments basis, by country or country grouping*; internet www40.statcan.ca/l01/cst01/gblec02a.htm. [SC21]: *Motor vehicle registrations, by province and territory*; internet www40.statcan.ca/l01/cst01/trade14a.htm. All data were retrieved January 2012.

Area and Population

AREA, POPULATION AND DENSITY

Area (sq km)	
Land	8,965,121*
Inland water	n.a.
Total	n.a.
Population (census results)†	
16 May 2006	
Males‡	15,475,970
Females‡	16,136,925
Total	31,612,897
10 May 2011	33,476,688
Density (per sq km) at 2011 census	3.7§

* 3,461,451 sq miles; area of inland water was recorded at 891,163 sq km in 2005, but a full breakdown was not available at 2011 census.

† Excluding census data for one or more incompletely enumerated Indian reserves or Indian settlements and excluding adjustment for underenumeration.

‡ Figures are rounded to nearest 5.

§ Land area only.

Sources: Statistics Canada, [SC1], [SC2], [SC3b].

POPULATION BY AGE AND SEX
('000, official postcensal estimates at 1 July 2011)

	Males	Females	Total
0–14	2,897.4	2,747.4	5,644.9
15–64	11,992.0	11,872.4	23,864.5
65 and over	2,214.6	2,758.8	4,973.4
Total	17,104.0	17,378.6	34,482.8

Note: Totals may not be equal to the sum of components, owing to rounding.

Source: Statistics Canada [SC3a].

PROVINCES AND TERRITORIES
(population at 2011 census)

	Land area (sq km)	Population	Density (per sq km)	Capital
Provinces:				
Alberta	640,082	3,645,257	5.7	Edmonton
British Columbia	922,509	4,400,057	4.8	Victoria
Manitoba	552,330	1,208,268	2.2	Winnipeg
New Brunswick	71,377	751,171	10.5	Fredericton
Newfoundland and Labrador	370,511	514,536	1.4	St John's
Nova Scotia	52,939	921,727	17.4	Halifax
Ontario	908,608	12,851,821	14.1	Toronto
Prince Edward Island	5,686	140,204	24.7	Charlottetown
Québec	1,356,547	7,903,001	5.8	Québec
Saskatchewan	588,239	1,033,381	1.8	Regina
Territories:				
Northwest Territories	1,143,793	41,462	0.0	Yellowknife
Nunavut Territory	1,877,788	31,906	0.0	Iqaluit
Yukon Territory	474,713	33,897	0.1	Whitehorse
Total	8,965,121	33,476,688	3.7	—

Sources: Statistics Canada, [SC1], [SC3b].

PRINCIPAL METROPOLITAN AREAS
(population at 2011 census)

Toronto	5,583,064	London	474,786
Montréal	3,824,221	St Catharines–Niagara	392,184
Vancouver	2,313,328	Halifax	390,328
Ottawa–Gatineau (capital)	1,236,324	Oshawa	356,177
Calgary	1,214,839	Victoria	344,615
Edmonton	1,159,869	Windsor	319,246
Québec	765,706	Saskatoon	260,600
Winnipeg	730,018	Regina	210,556
Hamilton	721,053	Sherbrooke	201,890
Kitchener	477,160		

Source: Statistics Canada, [SC4].

BIRTHS, MARRIAGES AND DEATHS
(year ending 30 June, unless otherwise indicated)

	Registered live births*		Registered marriages†		Registered deaths*	
	Number	Rate (per 1,000)	Number	Rate (per 1,000)	Number	Rate (per 1,000)
2003/04	337,762	10.6	147,391	4.7	228,829	7.2
2004/05	339,270	10.6	146,242	4.5	229,906	7.2
2005/06	346,082	10.7	145,842	4.5	225,489	7.0
2006/07	360,916	11.0	147,084	4.5	233,825	7.1
2007/08	373,695	11.2	148,296‡	4.4	236,525	7.1
2008/09	380,767	11.3	148,831‡	4.4	239,930	7.1
2009/10	383,585	11.2	n.a.	n.a.	244,677	7.2
2010/11‡	386,013	11.2	n.a.	n.a.	252,561	7.3

* Including Canadian residents temporarily in the USA but excluding US residents temporarily in Canada.

† Figures refer to the first of the two years, from January to December.

‡ Preliminary figure(s).

Sources: Statistics Canada, [SC3b], [SC5], [SC6], [SC7].

Life expectancy (years at birth, WHO estimates): 81 (males 79; females 83) in 2009 (Source: WHO, *World Health Statistics*).

ECONOMICALLY ACTIVE POPULATION*
(annual averages, '000 persons aged 15 years and over)

	2008	2009	2010
Agriculture	323.6	316.1	300.7
Forestry, fishing, mining, petroleum and gas	344.6	317.9	329.4
Utilities	151.5	147.6	148.3
Construction	1,231.0	1,160.8	1,217.2
Manufacturing	1,962.7	1,781.8	1,744.3
Trade	2,684.9	2,652.2	2,677.8
Transportation and warehousing	848.9	816.2	805.7
Finance, insurance, real estate and leasing	1,073.6	1,092.1	1,095.7
Professional, scientific and technical services	1,189.3	1,191.9	1,266.7
Business, building and other support services	685.0	654.9	672.2
Educational services	1,186.3	1,188.8	1,217.8
Health care and social assistance	1,893.0	1,949.2	2,030.7
Information, culture and recreation	758.4	769.6	766.0
Accommodation and food services	1,080.6	1,056.6	1,058.4
Other services	748.3	787.0	753.5
Public administration	925.7	930.3	956.4
Total employed	17,087.4	16,813.1	17,041.0
Unemployed	1,116.5	1,516.0	1,484.1
Total labour force	18,203.9	18,329.0	18,525.1

* Figures exclude military personnel, inmates of institutions, residents of the Yukon, Northwest and Nunavut Territories, and Indian Reserves.

Sources: Statistics Canada, [SC8], [SC9].

Health and Welfare

KEY INDICATORS

Total fertility rate (children per woman, 2008)	1.6
Under-5 mortality rate (per 1,000 live births, 2008)	6
HIV/AIDS (% of persons aged 15–49, 2009)	0.2
Physicians (per 1,000 head, 2000)	2.1
Hospital beds (per 1,000 head, 1999)	3.9
Health expenditure (2007): US $ per head (PPP)	3,900
Health expenditure (2007): % of GDP	10.1
Health expenditure (2007): public (% of total)	70.0
Total carbon dioxide emissions ('000 metric tons, 2007)	556,884.0
Carbon dioxide emissions per head (metric tons, 2007)	16.9
Human Development Index (2011): ranking	6
Human Development Index (2011): value	0.908

For sources and definitions, see explanatory note on p. vi.

Agriculture

PRINCIPAL CROPS
('000 metric tons)

	2009	2010	2011
Wheat	26,847.6	23,166.8	25,261.4
Barley	9,517.2	7,605.3	7,755.7
Corn for grain	9,561.2	11,714.5	10,688.7
Rye	280.5	232.4	194.7
Oats	2,906.1	2,479.5	2,997.1
Peas, dry	3,379.4	3,018.2	2,115.6
Soybeans	3,506.8	4,345.3	4,246.3
Sunflower seed	101.9	67.6	19.8
Rapeseed (Canola)	12,889.2	12,773.3	14,164.5
Canary seed	196.1	153.5	102.3
Lentils	1,510.2	1,947.1	1,532.0
Linseed	930.1	423.0	368.3
Mustard seed	208.3	186.8	124.8
Tame hay	25,022.0	32,681.4	31,410.4

Source: Statistics Canada, [SC10].

LIVESTOCK
('000 head at 1 July)

	2008	2009	2010
Horses*	385	385	385
Cattle	13,895	13,180	13,013
Pigs	13,810	12,180	11,835
Sheep	825	808	803
Chickens*	165,000	165,000	165,000
Ducks*	1,200	1,200	1,200
Turkeys*	5,880	5,600	5,600

* FAO estimates.

Source: FAO.

LIVESTOCK PRODUCTS
('000 metric tons)

	2008	2009	2010
Cattle meat	1,288.1	1,251.9	1,272.3
Sheep meat	16.2	16.4	15.8
Pig meat	1,947.8	1,943.4	1,925.9
Horse meat*	18	18	18
Chicken meat	1,041.2	1,036.1	1,048.5
Turkey meat	180.0	166.5	159.0
Cows' milk†	8,140	8,213	8,243
Hen eggs	419.0	422.0	428.5

* FAO estimates.
† Unofficial figures.

Source: FAO.

Forestry

ROUNDWOOD REMOVALS
('000 cubic metres)

	2008	2009	2010*
Sawlogs, veneer logs and logs for sleepers	109,333	91,324	106,149
Pulpwood	21,237	21,653	21,365
Other industrial wood	1,662	2,376	2,045
Fuel wood	2,715	2,903	2,903
Total	134,947	118,255	132,461

* Unofficial figures.

Source: FAO.

SAWNWOOD PRODUCTION
('000 cubic metres, incl. railway sleepers)

	2008	2009	2010
Coniferous (softwood)*	40,437	32,007	37,712
Broadleaved (hardwood)	1,111	813	955
Total	41,548	32,820	38,667

* Unofficial figures.

Source: FAO.

Fur Industry

NUMBER OF PELTS PRODUCED
('000)

	2007	2008	2009
Alberta	100.7	n.a.	n.a.
British Columbia	n.a.	170.1	162.7
Manitoba	139.9	150.3	124.5
New Brunswick	74.4	84.1	85.6
Newfoundland and Labrador	156.6	100.4	191.7
Northwest Territories	20.4	31.4	27.5
Nova Scotia	1,226.0	1,262.8	1,404.3
Nunavut Territory	8.4	7.3	4.5
Ontario	497.3	517.1	537.1
Prince Edward Island	46.9	51.9	63.9
Québec	248.0	261.8	278.2
Yukon Territory	4.2	4.5	2.3
Total (incl. others)	2,839.1	2,776.5	3,010.7

Source: Statistics Canada, [SC11].

Fishing

('000 metric tons, live weight)

	2008	2009	2010
Cod	28	21	19
Herring	152	168	159
Mackerel	30	42	38
Clams	25	32	28
Scallop*	68	63	60
Lobster	59	58	63
Shrimp	167	139	165
Queen Crab	94	97	84
Hake	89	69	59
Salmon	5	19	24
Canada total (incl. others)	920	915	898

* Includes meat with roe.

Note: Figures exclude landings of aquatic plants and animals ('000 metric tons): 20 in 2008; 46 in 2009; 40 in 2010.

Source: Department of Fisheries and Oceans, Ottawa.

Mining

('000 metric tons unless otherwise indicated)

	2008	2009	2010*
Metallic:			
Bismuth (metric tons)	71	87	92
Cadmium (metric tons)	313	322	278
Cobalt (metric tons)	4,809	2,275	2,119
Copper	584	470	498
Gold (kilograms)	94,909	96,573	97,104
Iron ore	32,102	31,728	37,001
Lead	87	71	58
Molybdenum (metric tons)	8,229	9,116	8,261
Nickel	246	132	149
Platinum group (kilograms)	22,764	10,925	9,612
Selenium (metric tons)	191	131	79
Silver (metric tons)	709	609	543
Uranium (metric tons)	8,703	10,133	10,152
Zinc	705	670	599
Non-metallic:			
Gypsum	5,819	3,568	2,717
Lime	2,046	1,613	1,913
Nepheline syenite	646	527	581
Potash (K_2O)	10,379	4,297	9,788
Salt	14,224	14,676	10,820
Sulphur, in smelter gas	746	543	593
Sulphur, elemental	6,880	6,435	6,355
Fuels:			
Coal	67,750	62,935	67,876
Structural materials:			
Cement	13,604	10,831	11,692
Stone	153,556	153,038	147,643

* Provisional figures.

Source: Natural Resources Canada.

2010: Natural gas (million cubic metres) 159,829; Crude petroleum ('000 metric tons) 162,776 (Source: BP, *Statistical Review of World Energy 2011*).

Industry

VALUE OF SHIPMENTS
(C $ million)

	2008	2009	2010
Food industries	76,608.0	78,649.0	80,493.1
Beverage and tobacco products industries	10,307.0	10,549.7	10,686.0
Textile mills	1,827.0	1,502.7	1,538.9
Textile product mills	2,159.0	1,583.2	1,687.0
Leather and allied products industries	426.7	366.4	395.6
Paper industries	28,636.8	24,938.3	26,470.1
Printing, publishing and allied industries	10,283.4	9,252.4	8,749.0
Refined petroleum and coal products industries	82,490.9	59,093.7	68,083.1
Chemical and chemical products industries	48,638.8	41,067.8	43,883.3
Plastics and rubber products industries	23,334.7	19,061.8	20,906.4
Clothing industries	2,646.2	2,213.2	2,294.6
Wood product industries	21,522.0	16,703.8	18,850.9
Non-metallic mineral products industries	14,129.2	11,638.2	12,990.3
Primary metal industries	53,840.6	33,901.8	41,963.2
Fabricated metal products industries	36,439.0	29,292.4	30,645.0
Machinery industries (excl. electrical machinery)	32,260.3	27,256.7	28,888.7
Computer and electronic products industries	17,278.4	15,510.1	15,491.6
Electrical equipment, appliance and component industries	10,486.6	9,404.2	9,640.9
Transportation equipment industries	96,403.1	74,646.8	85,293.4
Furniture and fixture industries	12,342.7	10,427.7	10,713.8
Other manufacturing industries	9,909.2	9,606.3	10,182.1
Total	591,969.7	486,666.3	529,847.0

Source: Statistics Canada, [SC12].

Electric energy (net production, million kWh): 612,594 in 2006; 639,841 in 2007; 651,324 in 2008 (Source: UN Industrial Commodity Statistics Database).

Finance

CURRENCY AND EXCHANGE RATES

Monetary Units:
100 cents = 1 Canadian dollar (C $).

Sterling, US Dollar and Euro Equivalents (30 December 2011):
£1 sterling = C $1.5786;
US $1 = C $1.0210;
€1 = C $1.3211;
C $100 = £63.35 = US $97.9 = €75.7.

Average Exchange Rate (C $ per US $):
2009 1.1431
2010 1.0302
2011 0.9895

BUDGET

(C $ million, year ending 31 March)*

Revenue	2006/07	2007/08	2008/09
Income taxes	245,867	269,467	248,655
Property and related taxes	51,277	53,882	54,862
Consumption taxes	105,809	111,684	107,150
Health insurance premiums	3,268	3,457	3,390
Contributions to social security plans	74,697	77,740	80,010
Other taxes	20,489	21,129	21,807
Sales of goods and services	44,913	49,685	53,168
Investment income	50,122	52,436	57,793
Other revenue from own sources	8,151	8,070	6,836
Total own source revenue	604,592	647,552	633,672

Expenditure	2006/07	2007/08	2008/09
General government services	20,857	21,505	22,822
Protection of persons and property	46,396	50,689	50,790
Transport and communications	26,280	29,966	32,197
Health	107,497	114,245	121,577
Social services	174,290	187,734	190,276
Education	87,455	92,722	95,732
Resource conservation and industrial development	21,078	21,360	19,975
Environment	14,420	15,516	16,933
Recreation and culture	15,008	15,809	16,306
Labour, employment and immigration	2,619	2,917	2,395
Housing	4,942	5,544	6,120
Foreign affairs and international assistance	6,500	6,211	6,508
Regional planning and development	2,338	2,524	2,775
Research establishments	2,023	2,332	2,268
Debt charges	45,578	45,715	43,634
Other expenditures	894	1,303	945
Total expenditure	578,174	616,090	631,251

* Figures refer to the consolidated accounts of federal, provincial and territorial governments.

Source: Statistics Canada, [SC13].

INTERNATIONAL RESERVES

(US $ million at 31 December)

	2008	2009	2010
Gold*	95	119	153
IMF special drawing rights	991	9,212	9,054
Reserve position in IMF	1,249	2,424	3,056
Foreign exchange	41,537	42,602	44,888
Total	43,872	54,357	57,151

* National valuation.

Source: IMF, *International Financial Statistics*.

MONEY SUPPLY

(C $ million at 31 December*)

	2006	2007	2008
Currency outside depository corporations	43,870	44,740	48,610
Transferable deposits	515,470	452,820	566,410
Other deposits	1,791,510	1,257,500	1,404,760
Broad money	2,350,840	1,755,050	2,019,770

* Figures rounded to the nearest $10m.

Source: IMF, *International Financial Statistics*.

COST OF LIVING

(Consumer Price Index; base: 2000 = 100)

	2007	2008	2009
Food	119.9	124.1	130.2
Water, electricity, gas and other fuels	134.2	143.6	133.4
Clothing	95.4	93.5	93.1
Rent	109.8	111.7	113.4
All items	116.9	119.6	119.9

2010: Food 132.0; All items (incl. others) 122.1.

Source: ILO.

NATIONAL ACCOUNTS

National Income and Product

(C $ million at current prices)

	2008	2009	2010
Compensation of employees	818,563	814,707	849,618
Net operating surplus and mixed income	481,228	401,760	447,198
Domestic factor incomes	1,299,791	1,216,467	1,296,816
Consumption of fixed capital	209,257	219,445	229,331
Gross domestic product (GDP) at factor cost	1,509,048	1,435,912	1,526,147
Indirect taxes, less subsidies	94,190	92,862	98,667
Statistical discrepancy	180	211	–206
GDP at market prices	1,603,418	1,528,985	1,624,608

Gross national income (C $ '000 million): 1,587.73 in 2008; 1,507.99 in 2009; 1,593.97 in 2010 (Source: IMF, *International Financial Statistics*).

Gross national disposable income (C $ '000 million): 1,587.36 in 2008; 1,505.81 in 2009; 1,591.53 in 2010 (Source: IMF, *International Financial Statistics*).

Expenditure on the Gross Domestic Product

(C $ million at current prices)

	2008	2009	2010
Government final consumption expenditure	315,977	337,735	353,569
Private final consumption expenditure	890,601	898,215	940,620
Changes in inventories	5,896	–6,954	2,255
Gross fixed capital formation	366,702	326,001	358,480
Total domestic expenditure	1,579,176	1,554,997	1,654,924
Exports of goods and services	563,075	439,527	478,132
Less Imports of goods and services	538,654	465,328	508,653
Statistical discrepancy	–179	–211	205
GDP at market prices	1,603,418	1,528,985	1,624,608

Gross Domestic Product by Economic Activity

(C $ million at chained 2002 prices)

	2008	2009	2010
Agriculture, hunting, forestry and fishing	30,008	28,082	28,486
Mining, petroleum and gas extraction	56,538	52,125	54,967
Manufacturing	171,785	150,431	158,326
Electricity, gas and water	33,044	32,191	32,624
Construction	74,875	68,011	73,467
Wholesale trade	69,628	65,268	68,822
Retail trade	73,293	72,774	75,634
Transportation and warehousing	57,884	55,338	57,569
Finance, insurance, real estate and leasing	245,547	251,128	257,488
Professional, scientific and technical services	60,209	59,623	59,948
Administration and support, waste management and remediation services	31,025	29,860	30,329
Education	60,140	61,219	62,539
Health care and social assistance	78,715	80,888	82,761
Information and cultural industries	44,940	44,848	45,240
Arts, entertainment and recreation	11,215	11,272	11,359
Accommodation and food services	26,846	26,094	26,611
Public administration	71,447	73,742	75,390
Other services	32,039	31,920	32,329
Statistical discrepancy	608	–1,603	41
GDP at basic prices	1,229,786	1,193,211	1,233,930

Sources: Statistics Canada, [SC14], [SC15], [SC16], [SC17].

BALANCE OF PAYMENTS
(US $ million)

	2008	2009	2010
Exports of goods f.o.b.	461,651	324,521	393,183
Imports of goods f.o.b.	–417,849	–328,915	–401,865
Trade balance	43,803	–4,394	–8,682
Exports of services	68,359	60,089	69,166
Imports of services	–88,791	–79,268	–91,255
Balance on goods and services	23,371	–23,572	–30,770
Other income received	66,799	48,754	60,021
Other income paid	–82,802	–62,813	–75,988
Balance on goods, services and income	7,368	–37,631	–46,738
Current transfers received	9,882	7,591	8,999
Current transfers paid	–10,873	–9,984	–11,569
Current balance	6,376	–40,024	–49,307
Capital account (net)	4,324	3,344	4,620
Direct investment abroad	–81,163	–42,899	–39,130
Direct investment from abroad	57,877	22,465	23,587
Portfolio investment assets	8,390	–6,282	–14,017
Portfolio investment liabilities	31,582	97,720	114,112
Other investment assets	–35,619	–35,740	–46,845
Other investment liabilities	12,931	12,106	9,650
Net errors and omissions	–2,930	–218	1,145
Overall balance	1,769	10,470	3,815

Source: IMF, *International Financial Statistics*.

External Trade

PRINCIPAL COMMODITIES
(C $ million)

Imports f.o.b.	2008	2009	2010
Agricultural and fishing products	28,511.3	29,347.9	29,578.9
Energy products	53,173.4	33,950.6	40,548.6
Crude petroleum	34,176.5	20,932.7	23,837.3
Industrial goods and materials	92,087.9	75,068.3	86,926.3
Metals and metal ores	32,588.8	24,749.4	33,094.6
Chemicals and plastics	32,061.2	27,116.8	28,971.6
Machinery and equipment (excl. automotive products)	122,641.8	107,897.2	113,877.5
Industrial and agricultural machinery	34,276.5	27,810.4	30,187.4
Aircraft and other transportation equipment	17,530.4	15,692.4	14,608.0
Office machines and equipment	14,415.1	12,385.9	13,254.3
Automotive products	71,958.5	55,320.9	68,712.9
Passenger automobiles and chassis	25,979.4	18,749.1	22,267.4
Trucks and other motor vehicles	15,137.3	12,828.9	16,861.5
Motor vehicle parts	30,841.9	23,742.8	29,584.1
Other consumer goods	57,608.1	57,517.7	57,770.5
Total (incl. others)	443,777.2	374,080.9	413,832.8

Exports f.o.b.	2008	2009	2010
Agricultural and fishing products	40,859.0	37,237.9	36,937.6
Energy products	125,727.8	79,834.6	90,886.1
Crude petroleum	60,969.7	42,503.1	50,111.2
Natural gas	33,046.0	15,748.6	15,619.4
Forestry products	25,354.5	19,528.8	21,851.4
Lumber and sawmill products	8,868.8	6,768.4	8,110.6
Newsprint and other paper and paperboard products	10,087.3	8,152.9	7,424.5
Industrial goods and materials	111,321.1	79,145.3	96,488.8
Chemicals, plastics and fertilizers	35,709.8	25,607.1	30,113.5
Metals and alloys	39,978.7	28,029.5	36,085.6
Machinery and equipment (excl. automotive products)	92,214.3	80,157.9	76,095.3
Industrial and agricultural machinery	23,171.6	19,153.4	18,032.7
Aircraft and other transportation equipment	20,079.6	19,333.7	17,758.0
Automotive products	61,155.8	43,811.0	56,783.2
Passenger automobiles and chassis	34,076.3	26,286.6	37,603.2
Trucks and other motor vehicles	7,334.2	3,757.7	2,309.7
Motor vehicle parts	19,745.3	13,766.7	16,870.3
Other consumer goods	18,171.5	17,935.0	16,427.7
Total (incl. others)	488,754.1	369,343.2	404,834.2

Sources: Statistics Canada, [SC18], [SC19].

PRINCIPAL TRADING PARTNERS
(C $ million, balance of payments basis)

Imports	2008	2009	2010
Japan	11,671.8	9,329.2	10,067.2
United Kingdom	11,232.9	8,529.6	9,560.6
USA	281,535.0	236,289.6	259,952.7
Other European Union countries	35,461.4	30,240.5	30,788.3
Other OECD countries	27,380.4	25,961.7	29,012.9
Other countries	76,495.7	63,730.4	74,451.1
Total	443,777.2	374,080.9	413,832.8

Exports	2008	2009	2010
Japan	11,784.3	8,861.8	9,716.6
United Kingdom	14,029.3	13,046.0	16,985.8
USA	370,015.3	271,108.7	296,672.0
Other European Union countries	25,173.5	19,010.3	19,475.8
Other OECD countries	20,748.6	16,690.6	17,908.3
Other countries	47,013.1	40,625.8	44,075.7
Total	488,754.1	369,343.2	404,834.2

Source: Statistics Canada, [SC20].

Transport

RAILWAYS
(revenue traffic)

	2007	2008	2009
Passengers carried ('000)*	4,478	4,899	4,538
Passenger-km (million)*	1,468	1,588	1,439
Freight carried ('000 metric tons)	306,623	289,114	244,062
Net freight ton-km ('000)	361,619	346,457	307,880

* Intercity trains only.

Source: Railway Association of Canada, *Railway Trends*.

ROAD TRAFFIC
('000 vehicles registered at 31 December)

	2009
On-road motor vehicle registrations	21,387.1
Passenger cars and light trucks	19,877.0
Heavy trucks	829.7
Buses	85.6
Motorcycles and mopeds	594.9
Trailers	5,747.3
Other (off-road, construction, farm vehicles, etc.)	1,920.9
Total vehicle registrations	29,055.3

Note: Light trucks are defined as vehicles weighing less than 4,500 kilograms; heavy trucks are those weighing 4,500 kilograms and over.

Source: Statistics Canada, [SC21].

INLAND WATER TRAFFIC
(St Lawrence Seaway, '000 gross registered metric tons)

	2008	2009	2010
Montréal-Lake Ontario	29,353	24,231	29,999
Welland Canal	33,580	32,514	36,808

Source: St Lawrence Seaway Management Corpn.

SHIPPING

Merchant Fleet
(registered at 31 December)

	2007	2008	2009
Number of vessels	927	938	934
Total displacement ('000 grt)	2,768.0	2,961.9	2,992.8

Source: IHS Fairplay, *World Fleet Statistics*.

CIVIL AVIATION
(scheduled services)

	2007	2008	2009
Kilometres flown (million)	1,111	1,137	1,105
Passengers carried ('000)	52,104	53,719	52,584
Passenger-km (million)	107,280	110,602	107,371
Total ton-km (million)	11,970	12,243	11,904

Source: UN, *Statistical Yearbook*.

Tourism

FOREIGN TOURIST ARRIVALS BY COUNTRY OF RESIDENCE

	2007	2008	2009
Australia	219,592	238,802	204,383
China, People's Republic	152,200	159,927	160,833
France	374,785	420,895	407,653
Germany	306,638	319,895	309,684
Hong Kong	113,404	128,139	107,410
India	101,724	110,890	107,959
Japan	330,931	276,091	197,752
Korea	200,388	183,895	138,150
Mexico	247,106	266,295	168,724
Netherlands	121,651	121,050	109,133
United Kingdom	908,806	854,404	710,513
USA	13,375,201	12,503,880	11,667,233
Total (incl. others)	17,934,881	17,142,102	15,737,150

Tourism receipts (US $ million, excl. passenger transport): 15,668 in 2008; 13,707 in 2009; 15,787 in 2010 (provisional).

Source: World Tourism Organization.

Communications Media

	2008	2009	2010
Telephones ('000 main lines in use)	18,250.0	17,625.0	17,021.3
Mobile cellular telephones ('000 subscribers)	22,092.5	23,811.9	24,037.4
Internet subscribers ('000)	10,163.3	10,713.6	10,953.3
Broadband subscribers ('000)	9,842	10,274	10,139

Personal computers ('000 in use): 22,390 in 2005.

Television receivers ('000 in use): 21,486 in 2002.

Daily newspapers: 103 in 2004 (circulation 5,578,000).

Book production (titles): 22,941 in 1999.

Sources: International Telecommunication Union; UN, *Statistical Yearbook*; UNESCO Institute for Statistics.

Education

(2007/08 unless otherwise indicated, UNESCO estimates)

		Students		
	Teachers	Males	Females	Total
Pre-primary	28,624*	251,160	238,263	489,423
Primary	141,045*	1,128,890	1,071,313	2,200,203
Secondary	376,830	1,382,183	1,285,951	2,668,134
Tertiary	132,230†	577,784‡	748,927‡	1,326,711‡

* 1999/2000 figure.

† 2001/02 figure.

‡ 2003/04 figure.

Source: UNESCO Institute for Statistics.

Directory

The Government

HEAD OF STATE

Queen: HM Queen ELIZABETH II.

Governor-General: DAVID LLOYD JOHNSTON (took office on 1 October 2010).

FEDERAL MINISTRY
(May 2012)

The Government is formed by the Conservative Party of Canada.

Prime Minister: STEPHEN J. HARPER.

Leader of the Government in the Senate: MARJORY LEBRETON.

Leader of the Government in the House of Commons: PETER VAN LOAN.

Minister of Justice and Attorney-General of Canada: ROBERT D. NICHOLSON.

Minister of Foreign Affairs: JOHN BAIRD.

Minister of National Defence: PETER G. MACKAY.

Minister of Labour: LISA RAITT.

Minister of Veterans' Affairs: STEVEN BLANEY.

Minister of Citizenship, Immigration and Multiculturalism: JASON KENNEY.

Minister of Agriculture and Agri-Food and Minister for the Canadian Wheat Board: GERRY RITZ.

Minister of Natural Resources: JOE OLIVER.

Minister of Fisheries and Oceans and Minister for the Atlantic Gateway: KEITH ASHFIELD.

Minister of Public Safety: VIC TOEWS.

Minister of National Revenue: GAIL SHEA.

Minister of the Environment: PETER KENT.

Minister of Intergovernmental Affairs and President of the Queen's Privy Council for Canada: PETER PENASHUE.

Minister of Human Resources and Skills Development: DIANE FINLEY.

Minister of Canadian Heritage and Official Languages: JAMES MOORE.

Minister of Aboriginal Affairs and Northern Development: JOHN DUNCAN.

President of the Treasury Board and Minister for the Federal Economic Development Initiative for Northern Ontario: TONY CLEMENT.

Minister of Industry and Minister of State (Agriculture): CHRISTIAN PARADIS.

Minister of Transport, Infrastructure and Communities and Minister of the Economic Development Agency of Canada for the Regions of Quebec: DENIS LEBEL.

Minister of Health and Minister of the Canadian Northern Economic Development Agency: LEONA AGLUKKAQ.

Minister of Finance: JAMES M. FLAHERTY.

Minister of International Co-operation: BEVERLEY J. ODA.

Minister of International Trade and Minister for the Asia-Pacific Gateway: EDWARD FAST.

Minister of Public Works and Government Services and Minister for Status of Women: RONA AMBROSE.

Associate Minister of National Defence: JULIAN FANTINO.

Minister of State and Chief Government Whip: GORDON O'CONNOR.

Minister of State of Foreign Affairs (Americas and Consular Affairs): DIANE ABLONCZY.

Minister of State (Finance): TED MENZIES.

Minister of State (Small Business and Tourism): MAXIME BERNIER.

Minister of State (Sport): BAL GOSAL.

Minister of State (Seniors): ALICE WONG.

Minister of State (Transport): STEVEN JOHN FLETCHER.

Minister of State (Western Economic Diversification): LYNNE YELICH.

Minister of State (Democratic Reform): TIM UPPAL.

Minister of State (Science and Technology) (Federal Economic Development Agency for Southern Ontario): GARY GOODYEAR.

Minister of State (Atlantic Canada Opportunities Agency) (La Francophonie): BERNARD VALCOURT.

MINISTRIES

Office of the Prime Minister: Langevin Block, 80 Wellington St, Ottawa, ON K1A 0A2; tel. (613) 941-6888; fax (613) 941-6900; e-mail pm@pm.gc.ca; internet www.pm.gc.ca.

Agriculture and Agri-Food Canada: 1341 Baseline Rd, Ottawa, ON K1A 0C5; tel. (613) 773-1000; fax (613) 773-1081; e-mail info@agr.gc.ca; internet www.agr.gc.ca.

Atlantic Canada Opportunities Agency (ACOA): Blue Cross Centre, 3rd Floor, 644 Main St, POB 6051, Moncton, NB E1C 9J8; tel. (506) 851-2271; fax (506) 851-7403; e-mail information@acoa-apeca.gc.ca; internet www.acoa-apeca.gc.ca.

Canada Economic Development for the Regions of Québec: Edifice Dominion Sq., 1255 rue Peel, bureau 900, Montréal, QC H3B 2T9; tel. (514) 283-6412; fax (514) 283-3302; internet www.dec-ced.gc.ca.

Canada Revenue Agency: Office of the Minister of National Revenue, 7th Floor, 555 McKenzie Ave, Ottawa, ON K1A 0L5; tel. (613) 952-9184; internet www.cra-arc.gc.ca.

Canadian Heritage: 15 rue Eddy, Gatineau, QC K1A 0M5; tel. (819) 997-0055; fax (819) 953-5382; internet www.pch.gc.ca.

Canadian Northern Economic Development Agency (CanNor): Iqaluit, NU; tel. (866) 553-0554; fax (866) 817-3977; e-mail infopubs@ainc-inac.gc.ca; internet www.north.gc.ca; devt of the northern territories; brs in Yellowknife and Whitehorse; Pres. NICOLE JAUVIN.

Citizenship and Immigration Canada: Jean Edmonds Towers, 21st Floor, 365 Laurier Ave West, Ottawa, ON K1A 1L1; tel. (613) 954-1064; fax (613) 957-2688; e-mail minister@cic.gc.ca; internet www.cic.gc.ca.

Department of Finance Canada: East Tower, 19th Floor, 140 O'Connor St, Ottawa, ON K1A 0G5; tel. (613) 992-1573; fax (613) 943-0938; e-mail finpub@fin.gc.ca; internet www.fin.gc.ca.

Department of Justice Canada: East Memorial Bldg, 284 Wellington St, Ottawa, ON K1A 0H8; tel. (613) 957-4222; fax (613) 954-0811; e-mail webadmin@justice.gc.ca; internet www.canada.justice.gc.ca.

Department of National Defence: National Defence HQ, Maj.-Gen. George R. Pearkes Bldg, 101 Colonel By Dr., Ottawa, ON K1A 0K2; tel. (613) 995-2534; fax (613) 992-4739; e-mail dnd_mdn@forces.gc.ca; internet www.forces.gc.ca.

Environment Canada: Informathèque, 351 blvd St Joseph, place Vincent-Massey, 8e étage, Gatineau, QC K1A 0H3; tel. (819) 997-2800; fax (819) 994-1412; e-mail enviroinfo@ec.gc.ca; internet www.ec.gc.ca.

Fisheries and Oceans Canada: Centennial Towers, 13th Floor, 200 Kent St, Station 13E228, Ottawa, ON K1A 0E6; tel. (613) 993-0999; fax (613) 990-1866; e-mail info@dfo-mpo.gc.ca; internet www.dfo-mpo.gc.ca.

Foreign Affairs and International Trade Canada: Lester B. Pearson Bldg, 125 Sussex Dr., Ottawa, ON K1A 0G2; tel. (613) 944-4000; fax (613) 996-9709; e-mail enqserv@international.gc.ca; internet www.international.gc.ca.

Health Canada: 0900C2, Ottawa, ON K1A 0K9; tel. (866) 225-0709; fax (613) 941-5366; e-mail info@hc-sc.gc.ca; internet www.hc-sc.gc.ca.

Human Resources and Skills Development Canada: Phase IV, 140 promenade du Portage, Gatineau, QC K1A 0J9; tel. (819) 994-6313; fax (819) 953-7260; internet www.hrsdc.gc.ca; manages the Labour Program.

Indian and Northern Affairs Canada: Terrasses de la Chaudière, 10 rue Wellington, Tour Nord, Gatineau, QC; Ottawa, ON K1A 0H4; tel. (819) 997-0811; fax (866) 817-3977; e-mail infopubs@ainc-inac.gc.ca; internet www.ainc-inac.gc.ca.

Industry Canada: C. D. Howe Bldg, 11th Floor, East Tower, 235 Queen St, Ottawa, ON K1P 5G8; tel. (613) 954-5031; fax (613) 954-2340; e-mail info@ic.gc.ca; internet www.ic.gc.ca.

Natural Resources Canada: 580 Booth St, Ottawa, ON K1A 0E4; tel. (613) 995-0947; fax (613) 996-9094; e-mail questions@nrcan.gc.ca; internet www.nrcan-rncan.gc.ca.

Public Safety Canada: 269 Laurier Ave West, Ottawa, ON K1A 0P8; tel. (613) 944-4875; fax (613) 954-5186; e-mail communications@ps-sp.gc.ca; internet www.ps-sp.gc.ca.

Public Works and Government Services Canada: 11 rue Laurier, PDP III, Gatineau, QC K1A 0S5; tel. (819) 956-3115; fax (819) 956-9062; e-mail questions@tpsgc-pwgsc.gc.ca; internet www.tpsgc-pwgsc.gc.ca.

Status of Women Canada: McDonald Bldg, 10th Floor, 123 Slater St, Ottawa, ON K1P 1H9; tel. (613) 995-3783; fax (613) 947-0761; e-mail infonational@swc-cfc.gc.ca; internet www.swc-cfc.gc.ca.

Transport Canada: 330 Sparks St, Ottawa, ON K1A 0N5; tel. (613) 990-2309; fax (613) 954-4731; e-mail questions@tc.gc.ca; internet www.tc.gc.ca.

Treasury Board: Strategic Communications and Ministerial Affairs, L'Esplanade Laurier, 9th Floor, East Tower, 140 O'Connor St, Ottawa, ON K1A 0R5; tel. (613) 957-2400; fax (613) 941-4000; e-mail info@tbs-sct.gc.ca; internet www.tbs-sct.gc.ca.

Veterans Affairs Canada: 161 Grafton St, POB 7700, Charlottetown, PE C1A 8M9; tel. (866) 522-2122; fax (902) 566-8508; e-mail information@vac-acc.gc.ca; internet www.vac-acc.gc.ca.

Western Economic Diversification Canada: Canada Pl., 9700 Jasper Ave, Suite 1500, Edmonton, AB T5J 4H7; tel. (780) 495-4164; fax (403) 495-4557; e-mail info@wd-deo.gc.ca; internet www.wd-deo.gc.ca.

Federal Legislature

THE SENATE

Speaker: Noël A. Kinsella.

Seats at Mar. 2012

Conservative Party	59
Liberal Party	41
Progressive Conservative	1
Independent	2
Vacant	2
Total	105

HOUSE OF COMMONS

Speaker: Andrew Scheer.

General Election, 2 May 2011, official results

	% of votes	Seats at election	Seats at Mar. 2012
Conservative Party	39.6	166	165
New Democratic Party	30.6	103	101
Liberal Party	18.9	34	35
Bloc Québécois	6.1	4	4
Green Party	3.9	1	1
Independent	—	—	1
Vacant	—	—	1
Total (incl. Independent and others)	100.0	308	308

Provincial Legislatures

ALBERTA

Lieutenant-Governor: Donald S. Ethell.

Premier: Alison Redford.

Election, 23 April 2012

	Seats at election
Progressive Conservative	61
Wildrose Alliance Party	17
Liberal	5
New Democratic Party	4
Total	87

BRITISH COLUMBIA

Lieutenant-Governor: Steven L. Point.

Premier: Christy Clark.

Election, 12 May 2009

	Seats at election	Seats at Mar. 2012
Liberal	49	47
New Democratic Party	35	34
Independent	1	2
Vacant	—	2
Total	85	85

MANITOBA

Lieutenant-Governor: Phillip S. Lee.

Premier: Greg Selinger.

Election, 4 October 2011

	Seats
New Democratic Party	37
Progressive Conservative	19
Liberal	1
Total	57

NEW BRUNSWICK

Lieutenant-Governor: Graydon Nicholas.

Premier: David Alward.

Election, 27 September 2010

	Seats
Progressive Conservative	42
Liberal	13
Total	55

NEWFOUNDLAND AND LABRADOR

Lieutenant-Governor: John Crosbie.

Premier: Kathy Dunderdale.

Election, 11 October 2011

	Seats
Progressive Conservative	37
Liberal	6
New Democratic Party	5
Vacant	—
Total	48

NOVA SCOTIA

Lieutenant-Governor: John James Grant.

Premier: Darrell Dexter.

Election, 9 June 2009

	Seats at election	Seats at Mar. 2012
New Democratic Party	31	31
Liberal	11	13
Progressive Conservative	10	7
Independent	—	1
Vacant	—	—
Total	52	52

ONTARIO

Lieutenant-Governor: David C. Onley.

Premier: Dalton McGuinty.

Election, 6 October 2011

	Seats
Liberal	53
Progressive Conservative	37
New Democratic Party	17
Vacant	—
Total	107

PRINCE EDWARD ISLAND

Lieutenant-Governor: H. Frank Lewis.

Premier: Robert Ghiz.

Election, 3 October 2011

	Seats
Liberal	22
Progressive Conservative	5
Total	27

QUÉBEC

Lieutenant-Governor: PIERRE DUCHESNE.

Premier: JEAN CHAREST.

Election, 8 December 2008

	Seats at election	Seats at Mar. 2012
Liberal	66	64
Parti Québécois	51	44
Action Démocratique du Québec	7	—
Coalition Avenir Québec	—	9
Independents	—	6
Québec Solidaire	1	1
Vacant	—	1
Total	125	125

SASKATCHEWAN

Lieutenant-Governor: Dr GORDON L. BARNHART.

Premier: BRAD WALL.

Election, 7 November 2011

	Seats
Saskatchewan Party	49
New Democratic Party	9
Vacant	—
Total	58

Territorial Legislatures

NORTHWEST TERRITORIES

Commissioner: GEORGE L. TUCCARO.

Premier: BOB MCLEOD.

The Legislative Assembly consists of 19 independent members without formal party affiliation.

NUNAVUT TERRITORY

Commissioner: ANN M. HANSON.

Premier: EVA AARIAK.

The Legislative Assembly consists of 19 independent members without formal party affiliation.

YUKON TERRITORY

Commissioner: DOUGLAS GEORGE PHILLIPS.

Premier: DARRELL PASLOSKI.

Election, 11 October 2011

	Seats
Yukon Party	11
New Democratic Party	6
Liberal	2
Vacant	—
Total	19

Election Commission

Elections Canada: Jackson Bldg, 257 Slater St, Ottawa, ON K1A 0M6; tel. (613) 993-2975; fax (613) 954-8584; e-mail info@elections.ca; internet www.elections.ca; f. 1920; independent; Chief Electoral Officer MARC MAYRAND.

Political Organizations

Action Démocratique du Québec: 740 rue Sainte-Maurice, bureau 108, Montréal, QC H3C 1L5; tel. (514) 270-4413; fax (514) 270-4469; e-mail adq@adq.qc.ca; internet www.adq.qc.ca; f. 1994; provincial nationalist; Leader GÉRARD DELTELL; Pres. CHRISTIAN LÉVESQUE.

Bloc Québécois: 3730 blvd Crémazie Est, 4e étage, Montréal, QC H2A 1B4; tel. (514) 526-3000; fax (514) 526-2868; e-mail capitale@bloc.org; internet www.blocquebecois.org; f. 1990 by group of seven Progressive Conservative MPs representing Québec constituencies in federal Parliament; seeks negotiated sovereignty for Québec; Leader VIVIAN BARBOT (acting).

Canadian Action Party: 333 Sockeye Creek, St Terrace, BC V8G 0G5; tel. (705) 727-9827; e-mail info@canadianactionparty.ca; internet www.canadianactionparty.ca; f. 1997; Leader CHRISTOPHER PORTER (acting); Pres. FRED WILSON.

Christian Heritage Party of Canada: POB 4958, Station E, Ottawa, ON K1S 5J1; tel. (819) 281-6686; fax (819) 281-7174; e-mail nationaloffice@chp.ca; internet www.chp.ca; f. 1986; Leader JIM HNATIUK; Pres. TOM KROESBERGEN (acting).

Communist Party of Canada: 290A Danforth Ave, Toronto, ON M4K 1N6; tel. (416) 469-2446; fax (416) 469-4063; e-mail info@cpc-pcc.ca; internet www.communist-party.ca; f. 1921; Leader MIGUEL FIGUEROA.

Conservative Party of Canada: 130 Albert St, Suite 1204, Ottawa, ON K1P 5G4; tel. (613) 755-2000; fax (613) 755-2001; internet www.conservative.ca; f. 2003 by merger of federal brs of Canadian Alliance and Progressive Conservative Party of Canada; Leader STEPHEN J. HARPER; Pres. JOHN WALSH.

Green Party of Canada: 75 Albert St, Suite 305, Ottawa, ON K1P 5E7; POB 997, Station B, Ottawa, ON K1P 5R1; tel. (613) 562-4916; fax (613) 482-4632; e-mail info@greenparty.ca; internet www.greenparty.ca; f. 1983; environmentalist; Leader ELIZABETH MAY.

Liberal Party of Canada: 81 Metcalfe St, Suite 600, Ottawa, ON K1P 6M8; tel. (613) 237-0740; fax (613) 235-7208; e-mail info@liberal.ca; internet www.liberal.ca; Interim Leader BOB RAE; Pres. ALFRED APPS.

Libertarian Party of Canada: 1111 Davis Dr., Suite 425, Newmarket, ON L3Y 9E5; tel. (416) 283-7589; e-mail info@libertarian.ca; internet www.libertarian.ca; f. 1974; supports the extension of individual freedoms; Leader KATRINA CHOWNE; Pres. JOHN SHAW.

Marijuana Party: 5535 ave Bourbonnière, Montréal, QC H1X 2N3; tel. (514) 507-5188; e-mail info@marijuanaparty.ca; internet www.marijuanaparty.ca; f. 2000; radical; campaigns for the legalization of marijuana; Leader BLAIR T. LONGLEY.

Marxist-Leninist Party of Canada: 1867 Amherst St, Montréal, QC H2L 3L7; tel. and fax (514) 522-1373; e-mail office@mlpc.ca; internet www.mlpc.ca; f. 1970; publishes *The Marxist-Leninist Daily* (English and French); Nat. Leader ANNA DI CARLO.

New Democratic Party of Canada (NDP): 279 Laurier Ave West, Suite 300, Ottawa, ON K1P 5J9; tel. (613) 236-3613; fax (613) 230-9950; internet www.ndp.ca; f. 1961; social democratic; Leader THOMAS MULCAIR; Pres. REBECCA BLAIKIE.

Parti Québécois: 1200 ave Papineau, bureau 150, Montréal, QC H2K 4R5; tel. (514) 526-0020; fax (514) 526-0272; e-mail info@pq.org; internet www.pq.org; f. 1968; social democratic; seeks political sovereignty for Québec; Leader PAULINE MAROIS; Pres. RAYMOND ARCHAMBAULT.

Saskatchewan Party: 324 McDonald St, Regina, SK S4N 6P6; tel. (306) 359-1638; fax (306) 359-9832; e-mail info@saskparty.com; internet www.saskparty.com; f. 1997; provincial; Leader BRAD WALL; Pres. GARY MESCHISHNICK.

Socialist Party of Canada: POB 4280, Victoria, BC V8X 3X8; e-mail spc@iname.com; internet www.worldsocialism.org/canada; f. 1905; publ. *Imagine* (occasional journal); Gen. Sec. JOHN AYERS; Treas. STEVE SZALAI.

Wildrose Alliance Party of Alberta: 919 Centre St NW, Suite 408, Calgary, AB T2E 2P6; tel. (888) 262-1888; fax (866) 620-4791; e-mail info@wildrosealliance.ca; internet www.wildrosealliance.ca; f. 2008 by merger of Alberta Alliance and Wildrose Alliance Party of Alberta; provincial; Leader DANIELLE SMITH; Pres. HAL WALKER.

Yukon Party: 211 Elliott St, POB 31113, Whitehorse, YT Y1A 5P7; tel. (867) 668-6505; e-mail info@yukonparty.ca; internet www.yukonparty.ca; provincial; Leader DARELL PASLOSKI; Pres. JONAS SMITH.

Diplomatic Representation

EMBASSIES AND HIGH COMMISSIONS IN CANADA

Afghanistan: 240 Argyle Ave, Ottawa, ON K2P 1B9; tel. (613) 563-4223; fax (613) 563-4962; e-mail contact@afghanemb-canada.net; internet www.afghanemb-canada.net; Ambassador BARNA KARIMI.

Albania: 130 Albert St, Suite 302, Ottawa, ON K1P 5G4; tel. (613) 236-3053; fax (613) 236-0804; e-mail embassy.ottawa@mfa.gov.al; Ambassador ELIDA PETOSHATI.

Algeria: 500 Wilbrod St, Ottawa, ON K1N 6N2; tel. (613) 789-8505; fax (613) 789-1406; e-mail ambalgcan@rogers.com; internet www.embassyalgeria.ca; Ambassador SMAIL BENAMARA.

Angola: 189 Laurier Ave East, Ottawa, ON K1N 6P1; tel. (613) 234-1152; fax (613) 234-1179; e-mail info@embangola-can.org; internet www.embangola-can.org; Ambassador AGOSTINHO TAVARES DA SILVA NETO.

Antigua and Barbuda, Dominica, Grenada, Montserrat, Saint Christopher and Nevis, Saint Lucia and Saint Vincent and the Grenadines (Eastern Caribbean High Commission): 130 Albert St, Suite 700, Ottawa, ON K1P 5G4; tel. (613) 236-8952; fax (613) 236-3042; e-mail echcc@travel-net.com; High Commissioner BRENDON CALVERT BROWNE.

Argentina: 81 Metcalfe St, 7th Floor, Ottawa ON K1P 6K7; tel. (613) 236-2351; fax (613) 235-2659; e-mail embargentina@argentina-canada.net; internet www.canada.embajada-argentina.gov.ar; Chargé d'affaires a.i. JOSÉ NESTOR URETA.

Armenia: 7 Delaware Ave, Ottawa, ON K2P 0Z2; tel. (613) 234-3710; fax (613) 234-3444; e-mail embottawa@rogers.com; internet www.armembassycanada.ca; Ambassador ARMEN YEGANIAN.

Australia: 50 O'Connor St, Suite 710, Ottawa, ON K1P 6L2; tel. (613) 236-0841; fax (613) 236-4376; internet www.ahc-ottawa.org; High Commissioner LOUISE HAND.

Austria: 445 Wilbrod St, Ottawa, ON K1N 6M7; tel. (613) 789-1444; fax (613) 789-3431; e-mail ottawa-ob@bmeia.gv.at; internet www.austro.org; Ambassador WERNER BRANDSTETTER.

Azerbaijan: 275 Slater St, Suite 904, Ottawa, ON K1P 5H9; tel. (613) 288-0497; fax (613) 230-8089; e-mail azerbaijan@azembassy.ca; internet www.azembassy.ca; Chargé d'affaires a.i. FARID SHAFIYEV.

Bahamas: 50 O'Connor St, Suite 1313, Ottawa, ON K1P 6L2; tel. (613) 232-1724; fax (613) 232-0097; e-mail ottawa-mission@bahighco.com; internet www.bahighco.ca; High Commissioner MICHAEL DOUGLAS SMITH.

Bangladesh: 340 Albert St, Suite 1250, Ottawa, ON K1R 7Y6; tel. (613) 236-0138; fax (613) 567-3213; e-mail bangla@rogers.com; internet www.bdhc.org; High Commissioner A. M. YAKUB ALI.

Barbados: 55 Metcalfe St, Suite 470, Ottawa, ON K1P 6L5; tel. (613) 236-9517; fax (613) 230-4362; e-mail ottawa@foreign.gov.bb; High Commissioner EDWARD EVELYN GREAVES.

Belarus: 130 Albert St, Suite 600, Ottawa, K1P 5G4; tel. (613) 233-9994; fax (613) 233-8500; e-mail canada@belembassy.org; internet www.canada.belembassy.org; Chargé d'affaires a.i. ROMAN SOBOLEV.

Belgium: 360 Albert St, 8th Floor, Suite 820, Ottawa, ON K1R 7X7; tel. (613) 236-7267; fax (613) 236-7882; e-mail ottawa@diplobel.fed.be; internet www.diplomatie.be/ottawa; Ambassador BRUNO VAN DER PLUIJM.

Benin: 58 Glebe Ave, Ottawa, ON K1S 2C3; tel. (613) 233-4429; fax (613) 233-8952; e-mail ambaben@benin.ca; internet www.benin.ca; Ambassador HONORÉ THÉODORE AHIMAKIN.

Bolivia: 130 Albert St, Suite 416, Ottawa, ON K1P 5G4; tel. (613) 236-5730; fax (613) 236-8237; e-mail mbolivia-ottawa@rree.gov.be; Ambassador EDGAR JOSÉ TORREZ-MOSQUEIRA.

Bosnia and Herzegovina: 130 Albert St, Suite 805, Ottawa, ON K1P 5G4; tel. (613) 236-0028; fax (613) 236-1139; e-mail embassyofbih@bellnet.ca; internet www.bhembassy.ca; Ambassador BILJANA GUTIĆ-BJELICA.

Brazil: 450 Wilbrod St, Ottawa, ON K1N 6M8; tel. (613) 237-1090; fax (613) 237-6144; e-mail mailbox@brasembottawa.org; internet www.brasembottawa.org; Ambassador PIRAGIBE DOS SANTOS TARRAGO.

Brunei: 395 Laurier Ave East, Suite 400, Ottawa, ON K1N 6R4; tel. (603) 234-5656; fax (603) 234-4397; e-mail bhco@bellnet.ca; High Commissioner RAKIAH Haji ABDUL LAMIT.

Bulgaria: 325 Stewart St, Ottawa, ON K1N 6K5; tel. (613) 789-3215; fax (613) 789-3524; e-mail mailmn@storm.ca; Ambassador EVGUENI S. STOYTCHEV.

Burkina Faso: 48 Chemin Range Rd, Ottawa, ON K1N 8J4; tel. (613) 238-4796; fax (613) 238-3812; e-mail burkina.faso@sympatico.ca; internet www.burkinafaso.ca; Ambassador AMADOU ADRIEN KONÉ.

Burundi: 325 Dalhousie St, Suite 815, Ottawa, ON K1N 7G2; tel. (613) 789-0414; fax (613) 789-9537; e-mail ambabucanada@infonet.ca; Chargé d'affaires a.i. JUSTINE SEMONDE.

Cameroon: 170 Clemow Ave, Ottawa, ON K1S 2B4; tel. (613) 236-1522; fax (613) 238-3885; e-mail cameroun@rogers.com; High Commissioner ANU'A-GHEYLE SOLOMON AZOH-MBI.

Chile: 50 O'Connor St, Suite 1413, Ottawa, ON K1N 6L2; tel. (613) 235-4402; fax (613) 235-1176; e-mail echileca@chile.ca; internet www.chile.ca; Ambassador ROBERTO IBARRA.

China, People's Republic: 515 St Patrick St, Ottawa, ON K1N 5H3; tel. (613) 789-3434; fax (613) 789-1911; e-mail chinaemb_ca@mfa.gov.cn; internet www.chinaembassycanada.org; Ambassador ZHANG JUNSAI.

Colombia: 360 Albert St, Suite 1002, Ottawa, ON K1R 7X7; tel. (613) 230-3760; fax (613) 230-4416; e-mail embajada@embajadacolombia.ca; internet www.embajadacolombia.ca; Ambassador CLEMENCIA FURERO UCROS.

Congo, Democratic Republic: 18 Range Rd, Ottawa, ON K1N 8J3; tel. (613) 230-6391; fax (613) 230-1945; e-mail ambardcongocan@rogers.com; internet www.ambardcongocanada.ca; Ambassador DOMINIQUE KILUFYA KAMFWA.

Costa Rica: 325 Dalhousie St, Suite 407, Ottawa, ON K1N 7G2; tel. (613) 562-2855; fax (613) 562-2582; e-mail embcr@costaricaembassy.com; internet www.costaricaembassy.com; Ambassador LUIS CARLOS DELGADO.

Côte d'Ivoire: 9 Marlborough Ave, Ottawa, ON K1N 8E6; tel. (613) 236-9919; fax (613) 563-8287; e-mail info@canada.diplomatie.gouv.ci; internet www.canada.diplomatie.gouv.ci; Ambassador N'GORAN KOUAME.

Croatia: 229 Chapel St, Ottawa, ON K1N 7Y6; tel. (613) 562-7820; fax (613) 562-7821; e-mail croemb.ottawa@mvpei.hr; internet ca.mfa.hr; Ambassador VESELKO GRUBIŠIĆ.

Cuba: 388 Main St, Ottawa, ON K1S 1E3; tel. (613) 563-0141; fax (613) 563-0068; e-mail cuba@embacubacanada.net; internet embacu.cubaminrex.cu/Default.aspx?tabid=73; Ambassador TERESITA DE JÉSUS VICENTE SOTOLONGO.

Czech Republic: 251 Cooper St, Ottawa, ON K2P 0G2; tel. (613) 562-3875; fax (613) 562-3878; e-mail ottawa@embassy.mzv.cz; internet www.czechembassy.org; Ambassador KAREL ZEBRAKOVSKY.

Denmark: 47 Clarence St, Suite 450, Ottawa, ON K1N 9K1; tel. (613) 562-1811; fax (613) 562-1812; e-mail ottamb@um.dk; internet www.ambottawa.um.dk; Ambassador ERIK VILSTRUP LORENZEN.

Dominica: (see entry for Antigua and Barbuda).

Dominican Republic: 130 Albert St, Suite 418, Ottawa, ON K1P 5G4; tel. (613) 569-9893; fax (613) 569-8673; e-mail info@drembassy.org; internet www.drembassy.org; Ambassador JOSÉ DEL CARMEN UREÑA ALMONTE.

Ecuador: 50 O'Connor St, Suite 316, Ottawa, ON K1P 6L2; tel. (613) 563-8206; fax (613) 235-5776; e-mail mecuacan@rogers.com; internet www.embassyecuador.ca; Ambassador ANDRES TERAN-PARRAL.

Egypt: 454 Laurier Ave East, Ottawa, ON K1N 6R3; tel. (613) 234-4931; fax (613) 234-9347; e-mail egyptemb@sympatico.ca; internet www.mfa.gov.eg/Missions/canada/OTTAWA/Embassy/en-GB; Ambassador WAEL AHMED KAMAL ABOUL MAGD.

El Salvador: 209 Kent St, Ottawa, ON K2P 1Z8; tel. (613) 238-2939; fax (613) 238-6940; e-mail elsalvadorottawa@rree.gob.sv; internet embajadacanada.rree.gob.sv; Ambassador OSCAR MAURICIO DUARTE GRANADOS.

Eritrea: 75 Albert St, Suite 610, Ottawa, ON K1P 5E7; tel. (613) 234-3989; fax (613) 234-6213; Ambassador GHIRMAI GHEBREMARIAM ABBAI.

Estonia: 260 Dalhousie St, Suite 210, Ottawa, ON K1N 7E4; tel. (613) 789-4222; fax (613) 789-9555; e-mail embassy.ottawa@mfa.ee; internet www.estemb.ca; Ambassador MARINA KALJURAND.

Ethiopia: 151 Slater St, Suite 210, Ottawa, ON K1P 5H3; tel. (613) 235-6637; fax (613) 235-4638; e-mail info@embassyofethiopia.net; internet www.embassyofethiopia.net; Chargé d'affaires a.i. ALMAZ AMAHA TESFAY.

Finland: 55 Metcalfe St, Suite 850, Ottawa, ON K1P 6L5; tel. (613) 288-2233; fax (613) 288-2244; e-mail embassy@finland.ca; internet www.finland.ca; Ambassador RISTO ENSIO PIIPPONEN.

France: 42 Sussex Dr., Ottawa, ON K1M 2C9; tel. (613) 789-1795; fax (613) 562-3735; e-mail politique@ambafrance-ca.org; internet www.ambafrance-ca.org; Ambassador PHILIPPE ANDRÉ FRANÇOIS E. ZELLER.

Gabon: 4 Range Rd, POB 368, Ottawa, ON K1N 8J5; tel. (613) 232-5301; fax (613) 232-6916; e-mail ambgabon@sprint.ca; Chargé d'affaires a.i. FRANÇOIS EBIBI MBA.

Georgia: 150 Metcalfe St, Suite 2101, Ottawa ON K2P 1P1; tel. (613) 421-0460; fax (613) 680-0394; Ambassador LEVAN METREVELI.

Germany: 1 Waverley St, Ottawa, ON K2P 0T8; tel. (613) 232-1101; fax (613) 594-9330; e-mail info@ottawa.diplo.de; internet www.ottawa.diplo.de; Ambassador GEORG M. WITSCHEL.

Ghana: 153 Gilmour St, Ottawa, ON K2P 0N8; tel. (613) 236-0871; fax (613) 236-0874; e-mail ghanacom@ghc-ca.com; internet www.ghc-ca.com; High Commissioner (vacant).

Greece: 76–80 MacLaren St, Ottawa, ON K2P 0K6; tel. (613) 238-6271; fax (613) 238-5676; e-mail embassy@greekembassy.ca; internet www.greekembassy.ca; Ambassador ELEFTHERIOS ANGHELOPOULOS.

Grenada: (see entry for Antigua and Barbuda).

Guatemala: 130 Albert St, Suite 1010, Ottawa, ON K1P 5G4; tel. (613) 233-7188; fax (613) 233-0135; e-mail embassy1@

embaguate-canada.com; internet www.embaguate-canada.com; Ambassador GEORGES DE LA ROCHE PLIHAL.

Guinea: 483 Wilbrod St, Ottawa, ON K1N 6N1; tel. (613) 789-8444; fax (613) 789-7560; e-mail infos@ambaguinee-canada.org; Chargé d'affaires a.i. HAWA DIAKITÉ.

Guyana: Burnside Bldg, 151 Slater St, Suite 309, Ottawa, ON K1P 5H3; tel. (613) 235-7249; fax (613) 235-1447; e-mail guyanahcott@rogers.com; internet www.guyanamissionottawa.org; High Commissioner HARRY NARINE NAWBATT.

Haiti: 130 Albert St, Suite 1500, Ottawa, ON K1P 5G4; tel. (613) 238-1628; fax (613) 238-2986; e-mail bohio@bellnet.ca; Ambassador FRANTZ LIAUTAUD.

Holy See: Apostolic Nunciature, 724 Manor Ave, Rockcliffe Park, Ottawa, ON K1M 0E3; tel. (613) 746-4914; fax (613) 746-4786; e-mail apostolic.nunciature@rogers.com; Nuncio Most Rev. PEDRO LÓPEZ QUINTANA (Titular Archbishop of Agropoli).

Honduras: 151 Slater St, Suite 805, Ottawa, ON K1P 5H3; tel. (613) 233-8900; fax (613) 232-0193; e-mail embhonca@embassyhonduras.ca; internet www.embassyhonduras.ca; Ambassador SOFIA LASTENIA CERRATO RODRIGUEZ.

Hungary: 299 Waverley St, Ottawa, ON K2P 0V9; tel. (613) 230-2717; fax (613) 230-7560; e-mail mission.ott@mfa.gov.hu; internet www.mfa.gov.hu/kulkepviselet/CA/en/mainpage.htm; Ambassador LÁSZLÓ CSABA PORDÁNY.

Iceland: Constitution Sq., 360 Albert St, Suite 710, Ottawa, ON K1R 7X7; tel. (613) 482-1944; fax (613) 482-1945; e-mail icemb.ottawa@utn.stjr.is; internet www.iceland.org/ca; Ambassador THORDUR AEGIR OSKARSSON.

India: 10 Springfield Rd, Ottawa, ON K1M 1C9; tel. (613) 744-3751; fax (613) 744-0913; e-mail hicomind@hciottawa.ca; internet www.hciottawa.ca; High Commissioner SHASHISHEKHAR M. GAVAI.

Indonesia: 55 Parkdale Ave, Ottawa, ON K1Y 1E5; tel. (613) 724-1100; fax (613) 724-1105; e-mail info@indonesia-ottawa.org; internet www.indonesia-ottawa.org; Ambassador DIENNE HARDIANTI MOEHARIO.

Iran: 245 Metcalfe St, Ottawa, ON K2P 2K2; tel. (613) 235-4726; fax (613) 232-5712; e-mail executive@salamiran.org; internet www.salamiran.org; Chargé d'affaires a.i. KAMBIZ SHEIKH HASSANI.

Iraq: 215 McLeod St, Ottawa, ON K2P 0Z8; tel. (613) 236-9177; fax (613) 236-9641; e-mail media@iraqembassy.ca; internet www.iraqembassy.ca; Ambassador ABDULRAHMAN HAMID AL-HUSSAINI.

Ireland: 130 Albert St, 11th Floor, Suite 1105, Ottawa, ON K1P 5G4; tel. (613) 233-6281; fax (613) 233-5835; e-mail embassyofireland@rogers.com; Ambassador JOHN RAYMOND BASSETT.

Israel: 50 O'Connor St, Suite 1005, Ottawa, ON K1P 6L2; tel. (613) 567-6450; fax (613) 567-9878; e-mail info@ottawa.mfa.gov.il; internet www.embassyofisrael.ca; Ambassador MIRIAM ZIV.

Italy: 275 Slater St, 21st Floor, Ottawa, ON K1P 5H9; tel. (613) 232-2401; fax (613) 233-1484; e-mail ambasciata.ottawa@esteri.it; internet www.ambottawa.esteri.it; Ambassador ANDREA MELONI.

Jamaica: 151 Slater St, 10th Floor, Suite 1000, Ottawa, ON K1P 5H3; tel. (613) 233-9311; fax (613) 233-0611; e-mail hc@jhcottawa.ca; internet www.jhcottawa.ca; High Commissioner SHEILA IVOLINE SEALY MONTEITH.

Japan: 255 Sussex Dr., Ottawa, ON K1N 9E6; tel. (613) 241-8541; fax (613) 241-4261; e-mail infocul@embjapan.ca; internet www.ca.emb-japan.go.jp; Ambassador KAORU ISHIKAWA.

Jordan: 100 Bronson Ave, Suite 701, Ottawa, ON K1R 6G8; tel. (613) 238-8090; fax (613) 232-3341; e-mail jordan@on.aibn.com; internet www.embassyofjordan.ca; Ambassador BASHEER FAWWAZ ZOUBI.

Kazakhstan: 56 Hawthorne Ave, Ottawa, ON K1S 0B1; tel. (613) 788-3705; fax (613) 788-3702; e-mail kazconscan@on.aibn.com; internet kazembassy.ca; Ambassador KONSTANTIN ZHIGALOV.

Kenya: 415 Laurier Ave East, Ottawa, ON K1N 6R4; tel. (613) 563-1773; fax (613) 233-6599; e-mail kenyahighcommission@rogers.com; internet www.kenyahighcommission.ca; High Commissioner SIMON NABUKWESI.

Korea, Republic: 150 Boteler St, Ottawa, ON K1N 5A6; tel. (613) 244-5010; fax (613) 244-5043; e-mail canada@mofat.go.kr; internet can-ottawa.mofat.go.kr; Ambassador JOO-HONG NAM.

Kuwait: 333 Sussex Dr., Ottawa, ON K1N 1J9; tel. (613) 780-9999; fax (613) 780-9905; e-mail info@embassyofkuwait.ca; internet www.embassyofkuwait.ca; Ambassador ALI HUSSAIN SALEH AL-SAMMAK.

Latvia: 350 Sparks St, Suite 1200, Ottawa, ON K1R 7S8; tel. (613) 238-6014; fax (613) 238-7044; e-mail embassy.canada@mfa.gov.lv; internet www.ottawa.am.gov.lv; Ambassador JURIS AUDARIŅŠ.

Lebanon: 640 Lyon St, Ottawa, ON K1S 3Z5; tel. (613) 236-5825; fax (613) 232-1609; e-mail info@lebanonembassy.ca; internet www.lebanonembassy.ca; Chargé d'affaires a.i. GEORGES ABOU ZEID.

Lesotho: 130 Albert St, Suite 1820, Ottawa, ON K1P 5G4; tel. (613) 234-0770; fax (613) 234-5665; e-mail lesotho.ottawa@bellnet.ca; High Commissioner MATHABO THERESIA TSEPA.

Libya: 81 Metcalfe St, Suite 1000, Ottawa, ON K1P 6K7; tel. (613) 842-7519; fax (613) 842-8627; e-mail info@libyanembassy.ca; internet www.libyanembassy.ca; Chargé d'affaires a.i. ABUBAKER KARMOS.

Lithuania: 150 Metcalfe St, Suite 1600, Ottawa, ON K2P 1P1; tel. (613) 567-5458; fax (613) 567-5315; e-mail litemb@storm.ca; internet www.lithuanianembassy.ca; Ambassador GINTĖ BERNADETA DAMUŠIS.

Macedonia, former Yugoslav republic: 130 Albert St, Suite 1006, Ottawa, ON K1P 5G4; tel. (613) 234-3882; fax (613) 233-1852; e-mail emb.macedonia.ottawa@sympatico.ca; Ambassador LJUBEN TEVDOVSKI.

Madagascar: 3 Raymond St, Ottawa, ON K1R 1A3; tel. (613) 567-0505; fax (613) 567-2882; e-mail ambamadcanada@bellnet.ca; internet www.madagascar-embassy.ca; Ambassador SIMON CONSTANT HORACE.

Malaysia: 60 Boteler St, Ottawa, ON K1N 8Y7; tel. (613) 241-5182; fax (613) 241-5214; e-mail malottawa@kln.gov.my; internet www.kln.gov.my/perwakilan/ottawa; High Commissioner HAYATI BINTI ISMAIL.

Mali: 50 Goulburn Ave, Ottawa, ON K1N 8C8; tel. (613) 232-1501; fax (613) 232-7429; e-mail ambassadedumali@rogers.com; internet www.ambamalicanada.org; Ambassador AMI TRAORE.

Mexico: 45 O'Connor St, Suite 1000, Ottawa, ON K1P 1A4; tel. (613) 233-8988; fax (613) 235-9123; e-mail info@embamexcan.com; internet www.sre.gob.mx/canada; Ambassador FRANCISCO JAVIER BARRIO TERRAZAS.

Mongolia: 151 Slater St, Suite 503, Ottawa, ON K1P 5H3; tel. (613) 569-3830; fax (613) 569-3916; e-mail mail@mongolembassy.org; internet www.ottawa.mfat.gov.mn; Ambassador TUNDEVDORJIIN ZALAA-UUL.

Montserrat: (see entry for Antigua and Barbuda).

Morocco: 38 Range Rd, Ottawa, ON K1N 8J4; tel. (613) 236-7391; fax (613) 236-6164; e-mail info@ambamaroc.ca; internet www.ambamaroc.ca; Ambassador NOUZHA CHEKROUNI.

Myanmar: 85 Range Rd, Suite 902/903, Ottawa, ON K1N 8J6; tel. (613) 232-9990; fax (613) 232-6999; e-mail meottawa@rogers.com; Ambassador KYAW TIN.

Nepal: 408 Queen St, Ottawa, ON K1R 5A7; tel. (613) 680-5513; fax (613) 422-5149; e-mail nepalembassy@rogers.com; internet www.nepalembassy.ca; Ambassador BHOJ RAJ GHIMIRE.

Netherlands: 350 Albert St, Suite 2020, Ottawa, ON K1R 1A4; tel. (613) 237-5031; fax (613) 237-6471; e-mail nid@the-netherlands.org; internet ottawa.the-netherlands.org; Ambassador WILHELMUS JULIUS PETRUS GEERTS.

New Zealand: Clarica Centre, 99 Bank St, Suite 727, Ottawa, ON K1P 6G3; tel. (613) 238-5991; fax (613) 238-5707; e-mail info@nzhcottawa.org; internet www.nzembassy.com/canada; High Commissioner ANDREW PETER NEEDS.

Niger: 38 Blackburn Ave, Ottawa, ON K1N 8A3; tel. (613) 232-4291; fax (613) 230-9808; e-mail ambanigeracanada@rogers.com; internet www.ambanigeracanada.ca; Ambassador NANA AÏCHA MOUCTARI FOUMAKOYE.

Nigeria: 295 Metcalfe St, Ottawa, ON K2P 1R9; tel. (613) 236-0522; fax (613) 236-0529; e-mail chancery@nigeriahcottawa.com; internet www.nigeriahcottawa.com; High Commissioner OJO MADUEKWE.

Norway: 90 Sparks St, Suite 532, Ottawa, ON K1P 5B4; tel. (613) 238-6571; fax (613) 238-2765; e-mail emb.ottawa@mfa.no; internet www.emb-norway.ca; Ambassador ELSE BERIT EIKELAND.

Pakistan: 10 Range Rd, Ottawa, ON K1N 8J3; tel. (613) 238-7881; fax (613) 238-7296; e-mail parepottawa@rogers.com; internet www.pakmission.ca; High Commissioner MIAN GUL AKBAR ZEB.

Panama: 130 Albert St, Suite 300, Ottawa, ON K1P 5G4; tel. (613) 236-7177; fax (613) 236-5775; e-mail embassyofpanama@gmail.com; internet www.embassyofpanama.ca; Chargé d'affaires, a.i. JUVENTINO CABALLERO APARICIO.

Paraguay: 151 Slater St, Suite 501, Ottawa, ON K1P 5H3; tel. (613) 567-1283; fax (613) 567-1679; e-mail consularsection@embassyofparaguay.ca; internet www.embassyofparaguay.ca; Ambassador MANUEL SCHAERER KANONNIKOFF.

Peru: 130 Albert St, Suite 1901, Ottawa, ON K1P 5G4; tel. (613) 238-1777; fax (613) 232-3062; e-mail emperuca@bellnet.ca; internet www.embassyofperu.ca; Ambassador JOSÉ ANTONIO BELLINA ACEVEDO.

Philippines: 130 Albert St, Suite 606, Ottawa, ON K1P 5G4; tel. (613) 233-1121; fax (613) 233-4165; e-mail embassyofphilippines@rogers.com; internet www.philembassy-ottawa.com; Ambassador LESLIE B. GATAN.

Poland: 443 Daly Ave, Ottawa, ON K1N 6H3; tel. (613) 789-0468; fax (613) 789-1218; e-mail ottawa@polishembassy.ca; internet www.polishembassy.ca; Ambassador ZENON KOSINIAK-KAMYSZ.

Portugal: 645 Island Park Dr., Ottawa, ON K1Y 0B8; tel. (613) 729-0883; fax (613) 729-4236; e-mail embportugal@dgaccp.org; internet www.embportugal-ottawa.org; Ambassador PEDRO LUÍS MOITINHO DE ALMEIDA.

Qatar: 150 Metcalfe St, 8th Floor, Suite 800, Ottawa ON K2P 1P1; tel. (613) 241-4917; fax (613) 241-3304; e-mail ottawa@mofa.gov.qa; Ambassador SALEM MUBARAK ALSHAFI.

Romania: 655 Rideau St, Ottawa, ON K1N 6A3; tel. (613) 789-3709; fax (613) 789-4365; e-mail romania@romanian-embassy.com; internet ottawa.mae.ro; Ambassador ELENA STEFOI.

Russia: 285 Charlotte St, Ottawa, ON K1N 8L5; tel. (613) 235-4341; fax (613) 236-6342; e-mail rusemb@magma.ca; internet www.rusembcanada.mid.ru; Ambassador GEORGII MAMEDOV.

Rwanda: 121 Sherwood Drive, Ottawa, ON K1Y 3V1; tel. (613) 569-5420; fax (613) 569-5421; e-mail generalinfo@ambarwaottawa.ca; internet www.ambarwaottawa.ca; High Commissioner EDDA MUKABAGWIZA.

Saint Christopher and Nevis: (see entry for Antigua and Barbuda).

Saint Lucia: (see entry for Antigua and Barbuda).

Saint Vincent and the Grenadines: (see entry for Antigua and Barbuda).

Saudi Arabia: 201 Sussex Dr., Ottawa, ON K1N 1K6; tel. (613) 237-4100; fax (613) 237-0567; e-mail caemb@mofa.gov.sa; Ambassador OSAMA BIN AHMAD SANOUSI.

Senegal: 57 Marlborough Ave, Ottawa, ON K1N 8E8; tel. (613) 238-6392; fax (613) 238-2695; e-mail ambassn@sympatico.ca; Ambassador AMADOU TIDIANE WONE.

Serbia: 17 Blackburn Ave, Ottawa, ON K1N 8A2; tel. (613) 233-6289; fax (613) 233-7850; e-mail diplomat@yuemb.ca; internet www.serbianembassy.ca; Ambassador ZORAN VELJIĆ.

Slovakia: 50 Rideau Terrace, Ottawa, ON K1M 2A1; tel. (613) 749-4442; fax (613) 749-4989; e-mail ottawa@slovakembassy.ca; internet www.ottawa.mfa.sk; Ambassador MILAN KOLLÁR.

Slovenia: 150 Metcalfe St, Suite 2200, Ottawa, ON K2P 1P1; tel. (613) 565-5781; fax (613) 565-5783; e-mail vot@gov.si; internet ottawa.embassy.si; Chargé d'affaires a.i. LUKA KOVAČEC.

South Africa: 15 Sussex Dr., Ottawa, ON K1M 1M8; tel. (613) 744-0330; fax (613) 741-1639; e-mail rsafrica@southafrica-canada.ca; internet www.southafrica-canada.ca; High Commissioner MOHAU NTHISANA PHEKO.

Spain: 74 Stanley Ave, Ottawa, ON K1M 1P4; tel. (613) 747-2252; fax (613) 744-1224; e-mail emb.ottawa@mae.es; internet www.embaspain.ca; Ambassador EUDALDO MIRAPEIX Y MARTÍNEZ.

Sri Lanka: 333 Laurier Ave West, Suite 1204, Ottawa, ON K1P 1C1; tel. (613) 233-8449; fax (613) 238-8448; e-mail slhcit@rogers.com; internet www.srilankahcottawa.org; High Commissioner CHITRANGANEE WAGISWARA.

Sudan: 354 Stewart St, Ottawa, ON K1N 6K8; tel. (613) 235-4000; fax (613) 235-6880; e-mail sudanembassy-canada@rogers.com; internet www.sudanembassy.ca; Chargé d'affaires a.i. MUSA ABDELRAHIM MOHAMED ADAM.

Sweden: 377 Dalhousie St, Ottawa, ON K1N 9N8; tel. (613) 244-8200; fax (613) 241-2277; e-mail sweden.ottawa@foreign.ministry.se; internet www.swedishembassy.ca; Ambassador TEPPO MARKUS TAURIAINEN.

Switzerland: 5 Marlborough Ave, Ottawa, ON K1N 8E6; tel. (613) 235-1837; fax (613) 563-1394; e-mail ott.vertretung@eda.admin.ch; internet www.eda.admin.ch/canada; Ambassador ULRICH LEHNER.

Syria: 46 Cartier St, Ottawa, ON K2P1J3; tel. (613) 569-5556; fax (613) 569-3800; e-mail info@syrianembassy.ca; internet www.syrianembassy.ca; Chargé d'affaires a.i. BASHAR AKBIK.

Tanzania: 50 Range Rd, Ottawa, ON K1N 8J4; tel. (613) 232-1500; fax (613) 232-5184; e-mail tzottawa@synapse.net; High Commissioner ALEX CRESCENT MASSINDA.

Thailand: 180 Island Park Dr., Ottawa, ON K1Y 0A2; tel. (613) 722-4444; fax (613) 722-6624; e-mail contact@thaiembassy.ca; internet www.thaiembassy.ca; Ambassador UDOMPHOL NINNAD.

Togo: 12 Range Rd, Ottawa, ON K1N 8J3; tel. (613) 238-5916; fax (613) 235-6425; e-mail ambatogoca@hotmail.com; Chargé d'affaires, a.i. PANEYBESSE ALLI.

Trinidad and Tobago: 200 First Ave, Ottawa, ON K1S 2G6; tel. (613) 232-2418; fax (613) 232-4349; e-mail ottawa@ttmissions.com; internet www.ttmissions.com; High Commissioner PHILIP ANTHONY BUXO.

Tunisia: 515 O'Connor St, Ottawa, ON K1S 3P8; tel. (613) 237-0330; fax (613) 237-7939; e-mail atottawa@comnet.ca; Chargé d'affaires, a.i. HATEM BOUJEMAA.

Turkey: 197 Wurtemburg St, Ottawa, ON K1N 8L9; tel. (613) 244-2470; fax (613) 789-3442; e-mail turkishottawa@mfa.gov.tr; internet www.turkishembassy.com; Ambassador RAFET AKGÜNAY.

Uganda: 231 Cobourg St, Ottawa, ON K1N 8J2; tel. (613) 789-7797; fax (613) 789-8909; internet ugandahighcommission.com; High Commissioner GEORGE M. ABOLA.

Ukraine: 310 Somerset St West, Ottawa, ON K2P 0J9; tel. (613) 230-2961; fax (613) 230-2400; e-mail emb_ca@ukremb.ca; internet www.ukremb.ca; Chargé d'affaires, a.i. MYKHAILO M. KHOMENKO.

United Arab Emirates: World Exchange Plaza, 45 O'Connor St, Suite 1800, Ottawa, ON K1P 1A4; tel. (613) 565-7272; fax (613) 5658007; e-mail safara@uae-embassy.com; internet www.uae-embassy.com; Ambassador MUHAMMAD ABDULLAH MUTLEQ AL-GHAFLI.

United Kingdom: 80 Elgin St, Ottawa, ON K1P 5K7; tel. (613) 237-1530; fax (613) 237-7980; e-mail generalenquiries@britainincanada.org; internet www.britainincanada.org; High Commissioner ANDREW POCOCK.

USA: 490 Sussex Dr., POB 866, Station B, Ottawa, ON K1P 5T1; tel. (613) 238-5335; fax (613) 688-3080; internet ottawa.usembassy.gov; Ambassador DAVID C. JACOBSON.

Uruguay: 130 Albert St, Suite 1905, Ottawa, ON K1P 5G4; tel. (613) 234-2727; fax (613) 233-4670; e-mail embassy@embassyofuruguay.ca; internet embassyofuruguay.ca; Ambassador ELBIO OSCAR ROSSELLI FRIERI.

Venezuela: 32 Range Rd, Ottawa, ON K1N 8J4; tel. (613) 235-5151; fax (613) 235-3205; e-mail info.canada@misionvenezuela.org; internet www.misionvenezuela.org; Chargé d'affaires, a.i. ANA CAROLINA RODRÍGUEZ.

Viet Nam: 470 Wilbrod St, Ottawa, ON K1M 6M8; tel. (613) 236-0772; fax (613) 236-2704; e-mail vietem@istar.ca; internet www.vietnamembassy-canada.ca; Ambassador LE SY VUONG HA.

Yemen: 54 Chamberlain Ave, Ottawa, ON K1S 1V9; tel. (613) 729-6627; fax (613) 729-8915; e-mail info@yemenincanada.ca; internet www.yemenincanada.ca; Ambassador KHALED MAHFOODH ABDULLAH BAHAH.

Zambia: 151 Slater St, Suite 205, Ottawa, ON K1B 5H3; tel. (613) 232-4400; fax (613) 232-4410; e-mail embzamb@aol.com; High Commissioner BOBBY MBUNJI SAMAKAI.

Zimbabwe: 332 Somerset St West, Ottawa, ON K2P 0J9; tel. (613) 237-4388; fax (613) 563-8269; e-mail zimembassy@bellnet.ca; internet www.zimbabweembassy.ca; Ambassador FLORENCE ZANO CHIDEYA.

Judicial System

FEDERAL COURTS

The Supreme Court of Canada: Supreme Court Bldg, 301 Wellington St, Ottawa, ON K1A 0J1; tel. (613) 995-4330; fax (613) 996-3063; e-mail reception@scc-csc.gc.ca; internet www.scc-csc.gc.ca; ultimate court of appeal in both civil and criminal cases throughout Canada. The Supreme Court is also required to advise on questions referred to it by the Governor-General in Council. Important questions concerning the interpretation of the Constitution Act, the constitutionality or interpretation of any federal or provincial law, the powers of Parliament or of the provincial legislatures, among other matters, may be referred by the Government to the Supreme Court for consideration.

In most cases, appeals are heard by the Court only if leave to appeal is given from any final judgment of the highest court of last resort in a province or territory, or of the Federal Court of Appeal. Such leave, or permission, will be given by the Court when a case involves a question of public importance. There are cases, however, where leave is not required. In criminal cases, for example, there may be an automatic right of appeal where one judge in the provincial court of appeal dissents on a question of law.

Chief Justice of Canada: BEVERLEY MCLACHLIN.

Puisne Judges: LOUIS LEBEL, MARIE DESCHAMPS, MORRIS J. FISH, ROSALIE SIBERMAN ABELLA, MARSHALL ROTHSTEIN, THOMAS ALBERT CROMWELL, MICHAEL J. MOLDAVER, ANDROMACHE KARAKATSANIS.

The Federal Court: Supreme Court Bldg, Kent and Wellington Sts, Ottawa, ON K1A 0H9; tel. (613) 996-6795; fax (613) 952-7226; e-mail reception@cas-satj.gc.ca; internet www.fct-cf.gc.ca; has jurisdiction in claims against the Crown, claims by the Crown, miscellaneous cases involving the Crown, claims against or concerning crown officers and servants, relief against Federal Boards, Commissions, and other tribunals, interprovincial and federal-provincial disputes, industrial or industrial property matters, admiralty, income tax and estate tax appeals, citizenship appeals, aeronautics, interprovincial works and undertakings, residuary jurisdiction for relief if there is no other Canadian court that has such jurisdiction, and jurisdiction in specific matters conferred by federal statutes.

Chief Justice: PAUL S. CRAMPTON.

The Federal Court of Appeal: Supreme Court Bldg, Kent and Wellington Sts, Ottawa, ON K1A 0H9; tel. (613) 996-6795; fax (613) 952-7226; e-mail reception@cas-satj.gc.ca; internet www.fca-caf.gc.ca; has jurisdiction on appeals from the Trial Division, appeals from Federal Tribunals, review of decisions of Federal Boards and Commissions, appeals from Tribunals and Reviews under Section 28 of the Federal Court Act, and references by Federal Boards and Commissions. The Court has one central registry and consists of the principal office in Ottawa and local offices in major centres throughout Canada.

Chief Justice: PIERRE BLAIS.

PROVINCIAL AND TERRITORIAL COURTS

Alberta

Court of Appeal

Chief Justice of Alberta: CATHERINE A. FRASER (Edmonton).

Court of Queen's Bench

Chief Justice: NEIL C. WITTMAN (Calgary).
Associate Chief Justice: JOHN D. ROOKE (Calgary).

British Columbia

Court of Appeal

Chief Justice of British Columbia: LANCE SIDNEY GEORGE FINCH.

Supreme Court

Chief Justice: ROBERT J. BAUMAN.
Associate Chief Justice: ANNE W. MACKENZIE.

Manitoba

Court of Appeal

Chief Justice of Manitoba: RICHARD J. SCOTT.

Court of Queen's Bench

Chief Justice: GLENN D. JOYAL.
Associate Chief Justice: WILLIAM J. BURNETT.
Associate Chief Justice (Family Division): LORI A. DOUGLAS.

New Brunswick

Court of Appeal

Chief Justice of New Brunswick: J. ERNEST DRAPEAU.

Court of Queen's Bench

Chief Justice: DAVID D. SMITH (Moncton).

Newfoundland and Labrador

Supreme Court—Court of Appeal

Chief Justice of Newfoundland and Labrador: J. DEREK GREEN.

Trial Division

Chief Justice: DAVID B. ORSBORN.

Northwest Territories

Court of Appeal

Chief Justice: CATHERINE A. FRASER (Edmonton, Alberta).

Supreme Court

Judges of the Supreme Court: J. EDWARD RICHARD, VIRGINIA A. SCHULER, LOUISE A. M. CHARBONNEAU, KARAN M. SHANER.

Nova Scotia

Court of Appeal

Chief Justice of Nova Scotia: MICHAEL MACDONALD.

Supreme Court

Chief Justice: JOSEPH PHILLIP KENNEDY.
Associate Chief Justice: DEBORAH K. SMITH.

Supreme Court—Family Division

Associate Chief Justice (Family Division): LAWRENCE I. O'NEIL.

Nunavut Territory

Court of Appeal

Chief Justice: CATHERINE A. FRASER (Alberta).

Court of Justice

Judges of the Court of Justice: S. COOPER, R. G. KILPATRICK, E. D. JOHNSON, N. A. SHARKEY.

Ontario

Court of Appeal

Chief Justice of Ontario: WARREN K. WINKLER.
Associate Chief Justice of Ontario: DENNIS R. O'CONNOR.

Court of Justice

Chief Justice: HEATHER FORSTER SMITH.
Associate Chief Justice: J. DOUGLAS CUNNINGHAM.

Prince Edward Island

Supreme Court—Appeal Division

Chief Justice of Prince Edward Island: DAVID H. JENKINS.

Supreme Court—Trial Division

Chief Justice: JACQUELINE R. MATHESON.

Québec

Court of Appeal

Chief Justice of Québec: NICOLE DUVAL HESLER.

Superior Court

Chief Justice: FRANÇOIS ROLLAND.
Associate Chief Justice: ROBERT PIDGEON.

Saskatchewan

Court of Appeal

Chief Justice of Saskatchewan: JOHN KLEBUC.

Court of Queen's Bench

Chief Justice: R. D. LAING (Saskatoon).

Yukon Territory

Court of Appeal

Chief Justice: LANCE S. G. FINCH (British Columbia).

Supreme Court

Judge of the Supreme Court: L. F. GOWER HUDSON (Whitehorse).

Religion

CHRISTIANITY

According to the 2001 census, about 59% of the population belong to the three main Christian churches: Roman Catholic, United and Anglican. Numerous other religious denominations are active in Canada.

Canadian Council of Churches/Conseil canadien des églises: 47 Queen's Park Cres. East, Toronto, ON M5S 2C3; tel. (416) 972-9494; fax (416) 927-0405; e-mail delph@ccc-cce.ca; internet www.ccc-cce.ca; f. 1944; 22 mem. churches, one assoc. mem., two affiliate mems; Pres. Rev. BRUCE ADEMA (Christian Reformed Church in North America); Gen. Sec. Rev. Dr KAREN HAMILTON.

The Anglican Communion

The Anglican Church of Canada (L'Eglise anglicane du Canada) comprises 30 dioceses in four ecclesiastical provinces (each with a Metropolitan archbishop). The Church had about 800,000 members in 30 dioceses in 2007.

General Synod of the Anglican Church of Canada: 80 Hayden St, Toronto, ON M4Y 3G2; tel. (416) 924-9192; fax (416) 968-7983; e-mail information@national.anglican.ca; internet www.anglican.ca; f. 1893; Gen. Sec. The Venerable MICHAEL THOMPSON.

Primate of the Anglican Church of Canada: Most Rev. FRED HILTZ.

Province of British Columbia and Yukon: Metropolitan Most Rev. JOHN E. PRIVETT (Archbishop of Kootenay).

Province of Canada: Metropolitan Most Rev. CLAUDE E. W. MILLER (Bishop of Fredericton).

Province of Ontario: Metropolitan Most Rev. COLIN JOHNSON (Archbishop of Toronto).

Province of Rupert's Land: Metropolitan Most Rev. DAVID ASHDOWN (Archbishop of Keewatin).

The Orthodox Churches

According to census figures, there were some 479,620 members of Eastern Orthodox churches in Canada in 2001.

Greek Orthodox Metropolis of Toronto (Canada): 86 Overlea Blvd, Toronto, ON M4H 1C6; tel. (416) 429-5757; fax (416) 429-4588; e-mail metropolis@gocanada.org; internet www.gocanada.org; 215,175 mems (2001); Metropolitan Archbishop SOTIRIOS ATHANASSOULAS.

Ukrainian Orthodox Church of Canada: 9 St John's Ave, Winnipeg, MB R2W 1G8; tel. (204) 586-3093; fax (204) 582-5241; e-mail consistory@uocc.ca; internet www.uocc.ca; f. 1918; 281 parishes; 32,720 mems (2001); Primate His Eminence YURIJ; Chancellor Rev. VICTOR LAKUSTA.

The Russian, Belarusian, Polish, Romanian, Serbian, Coptic, Antiochian and Armenian Churches are also represented in Canada.

The Roman Catholic Church

For Catholics of the Latin rite, Canada comprises 18 archdioceses (including one directly responsible to the Holy See), 46 dioceses and one territorial abbacy. There are also one archdiocese and four dioceses of the Ukrainian rite. In addition, the Maronite, Melkite and Slovak rites are each represented by one diocese (all directly responsible to the Holy See). In December 2006 the Roman Catholic Church had about 13.8m. adherents in Canada.

Canadian Conference of Catholic Bishops/Conférence des évêques catholiques du Canada: 2500 Don Reid Dr., Ottawa, ON K1H 2J2; tel. (613) 241-9461; fax (613) 241-8117; e-mail cecc@cccb.ca; internet www.cccb.ca; f. 1943 as Canadian Catholic Conference; officially recognized 1948; restyled as above 1977; Pres. Rt Rev. PIERRE MORISSETTE (Bishop of Baie-Comeau); Gen. Sec. Mgr PATRICK POWERS.

Latin Rite

Archbishop of Edmonton: Most Rev. RICHARD SMITH.

Archbishop of Gatineau: Most Rev. PAUL-ANDRÉ DUROCHER.

Archbishop of Grouard-McLennan: Most Rev. GÉRARD PETTIPAS.

Archbishop of Halifax: Most Rev. ANTHONY MANCINI.

Archbishop of Keewatin-Le Pas: Most Rev. SYLVAIN LAVOIE.

Archbishop of Kingston: Most Rev. BRENDAN M. O'BRIEN.

Archbishop of Moncton: Most Rev. ANDRÉ RICHARD.

Archbishop of Montréal: Cardinal CHRISTIAN LÉPINE.

Archbishop of Ottawa: Most Rev. TERRENCE PRENDERGAST.

Archbishop of Québec: Most Rev. GÉRALD CYPRIEN LACROIX.

Archbishop of Regina: Most Rev. DANIEL J. BOHAN.

Archbishop of Rimouski: Most Rev. PIERRE-ANDRÉ FOURNIER.

Archbishop of St Boniface: Most Rev. ALBERT LEGATT.

Archbishop of St John's, NL: Most Rev. MARTIN WILLIAM CURRIE.

Archbishop of Sherbrooke: Most Rev. LUC CYR.

Archbishop of Toronto: Most Rev. THOMAS COLLINS.

Archbishop of Vancouver: Most Rev. MICHAEL MILLER.

Archbishop of Winnipeg: Most Rev. V. JAMES WEISGERBER.

Ukrainian Rite

Ukrainian Catholic Archeparchy of Winnipeg (Metropolitan See of Canada): 233 Scotia St, Winnipeg, MB R2V 1V7; tel. (204) 338-7801; fax (204) 339-4006; e-mail chancery@archeparchy.ca; internet www.archeparchy.ca; 126,200 mems (2001); Archeparch-Metropolitan of Winnipeg Most Rev. LAWRENCE HUCULAK.

The United Church of Canada

The United Church of Canada (l'Eglise Unie du Canada) was founded in 1925 with the union of Methodist, Congregational and 70% of Presbyterian churches in Canada. The Evangelical United Brethren of Canada joined in 1968. It is the largest Protestant denomination in Canada. In 2003 there were 3,584 congregations and 608,243 confirmed members (although, according to 2001 census figures, 2.8m. people identified themselves as adherents of the United Church).

Moderator: Rt Rev. MARDI TINDAL.

General Secretary: NORA SANDERS, 3250 Bloor St West, Suite 300, Toronto, ON M8X 2Y4; tel. (416) 231-5931; fax (416) 231-3103; e-mail info@united-church.ca; internet www.united-church.ca.

Other Christian Churches

Canadian Baptist Ministries: 7185 Millcreek Dr., Mississauga, ON L5N 5R4; tel. (905) 821-3533; fax (905) 826-3441; e-mail communications@cbmin.org; internet www.cbmin.org; more than 1,000 churches; 250,000 mems (2008); Pres. Rev. BRENDA HALK; Gen. Sec. Rev. Dr SAM CHAISE.

Christian Reformed Church in North America (Canadian Council): 3475 Mainway, POB 5070, Burlington, ON L7R 3Y8; tel. (905) 336-2920; fax (905) 336-8344; e-mail crcna@crcna.org; internet www.crcna.org; f. 1857; 256 congregations; 75,600 mems (2010); Dir in Canada Rev. BRUCE ADEMA.

Church of Jesus Christ of Latter-day Saints (Mormon): 28 St South, Suite 2410, Lethbridge, AB T1K 2V9; tel. (403) 328-8552; f. 1832; 481 congregations; 166,505 mems in Canada (2004); Dir GORDON GEDLAMAN.

Evangelical Lutheran Church in Canada (ELCIC): 393 Portage Ave, Suite 302, Winnipeg, MB R3B 3H6; tel. (204) 984-9157; fax (204) 984-9185; e-mail info@elcic.ca; internet www.elcic.ca; f. 1986 by merger of the fmr Evangelical Lutheran Church of Canada and Lutheran Church in America—Canada Section; 611 congregations; 148,863 mems (2010); Nat. Bishop Rev. SUSAN JOHNSON, Vice-Pres. SHEILA HAMILTON.

Lutheran Church—Canada: 3074 Portage Ave, Winnipeg, MB R3K 0Y2; tel. (204) 895-3433; fax (204) 897-4319; e-mail pres_sec@lutheranchurch.ca; internet www.lutheranchurch.ca; f. 1988 by three Canadian congregations of the Lutheran Church—Missouri Synod; more than 325 congregations; 51,650 mems (2010); Pres. Rev. ROBERT BUGBEE.

Pentecostal Assemblies of Canada: 2450 Milltower Court, Mississauga, ON L5N 5Z6; tel. (905) 542-7400; fax (905) 542-7313; e-mail info@paoc.org; internet www.paoc.org; f. 1919; 1,103 congregations; 236,000 mems; Gen. Supt Rev. DAVID WELLS.

Presbyterian Church in Canada: 50 Wynford Dr., Toronto, ON M3C 1J7; tel. (416) 441-1111; fax (416) 441-2825; e-mail pccweb@presbycan.ca; internet www.presbyterian.ca; f. 1875; 997 congregations; 125,509 mems (2003); Prin. Clerk Rev. STEPHEN KENDALL.

Religious Society of Friends: 91A Fourth Ave, Ottawa, ON K1S 2L1; tel. (613) 235-8553; fax (613) 235-1753; e-mail cym-office@quaker.ca; internet www.quaker.ca; Clerk of Canadian Yearly Meeting CAROL DIXON.

Seventh-day Adventist Church in Canada: 1148 King St East, Oshawa, ON L1H 1H8; tel. (905) 433-0011; fax (905) 433-0982; e-mail communications@sdacc.org; internet www.adventist.ca; 356 congregations, 63,132 mems (2011); f. 1901; Pres. MARK JOHNSON; Sec. CATHY ANDERSON.

BAHÁ'Í FAITH

Bahá'í Community of Canada: 7200 Leslie St, Thornhill, ON L3T 6L8; tel. (905) 889-8168; fax (905) 889-8184; e-mail secretariat@cdnbnc.org; internet www.ca.bahai.org; f. 1902; 30,000 mems (2004); Sec.-Gen. KAREN MCKYE.

BUDDHISM

Jodo Shinshu Buddhist Temples of Canada: 11786 Fentiman Pl., Richmond, BC V7E 6M6; tel. (604) 272-3330; fax (604) 272-6865; e-mail jsbtcheadquarters@shaw.ca; internet www.bcc.ca; f. 1905; fmrly Buddhist Churches of Canada; Bishop GRANT IKUTA.

ISLAM

According to the Canadian Islamic Congress, there were an estimated 750,000 Muslims in Canada in 2006.

Ahmadiyya Muslim Jama'at (Canada): 10610 Jane St, Maple, ON L6A 3A2; tel. (905) 303-4000; fax (905) 832-3220; e-mail info@ahmadiyya.ca; internet www.ahmadiyya.ca; f. 1965; Pres. LAL KHAN MALIK; Gen. Sec. Dr ASLAM DAUD.

Canadian Islamic Congress (CIC): 877 Shefford Rd, Gloucester, Ottawa, ON K1J 8H9; tel. (613) 680-2867; fax (613) 680-2902; e-mail cicnp@canadianislamiccongress.com; internet www.canadianislamiccongress.com; f. 1998; Chair. and Nat. Pres. WAHIDA VALIANTE.

Canadian Muslim Union (CMU): Toronto, ON; tel. (416) 558-4777; e-mail secretary@muslimunion.ca; internet www.muslimunion.ca; f. 2006 following split from the Muslim Canadian Congress; Sec.-Gen. EL-FAROUK KHAKI.

Council of Muslim Communities of Canada (CMCC): 1521 Trinity Dr., Unit 16, Mississauga, ON L5T 1P6; tel. and fax (416)

564-1566; fax (416) 564-1544; f. 1971; umbrella org. representing c. 30 communities nation-wide; Pres. HANNY HASSAN.

Organization of North American Shi'a Itha-Asheri Muslim Communities (NASIMCO): 9200 Dufferin St, POB 20078, Concord, ON L4K 0C0; tel. (905) 763-7512; fax (905) 763-7509; e-mail director@nasimco.org; internet www.nasimco.org; Pres. GULAMABBAS NAJAFI; Sec. HABIB M. HABIB.

JUDAISM

According to census figures, there were some 329,995 Jews in Canada in 2001.

Canadian Council for Reform Judaism (CCRJ): 3845 Bathurst St, Suite 301, Toronto, ON M3H 3N2; tel. (416) 630-0375; fax (416) 630-5089; e-mail ccrj@urj.org; internet urj.org/ccrj; f. 1988; Pres. CAROLE STERLING; Exec. Dir Rabbi SHARON L. SOBEL.

United Synagogue of Conservative Judaism: 1000 Finch Ave West, Suite 508, Toronto, ON M3J 2V5; tel. (416) 667-1717; fax (416) 667-1818; e-mail canadian@uscj.org; internet www.uscj.org; Pres. PAUL KOCHBERG.

SIKHISM

There were some 278,410 Sikhs in Canada, according to 2001 census figures.

Canadian Sikh Council (CSC): 4103 Sherbrooke St West, Montréal, QC H3Z1A7; tel. (416) 630-0375; fax (416) 630-5089; e-mail info@sikhcouncil.ca; internet www.sikhcouncil.ca; f. 2001; Dir Dr MANJIT SINGH.

World Sikh Organization of Canada (WSO Canada): 1183 Cecil Ave, Ottawa, ON K1H 7Z6; tel. (613) 521-1984; fax (613) 521-7454; e-mail info@worldsikh.org; internet worldsikh.org; f. 1984; Pres. PREM SINGH VINNING.

The Press

Traditionally the daily press in Canada was essentially local in coverage, influence and distribution. In October 1998 publication began of Canada's first national newspaper, the *National Post*. A national edition of the Toronto *Globe and Mail*, established in 1981, was also available coast to coast, as was (from 1988) a national edition of the *Financial Post*.

Chain ownership has traditionally been predominant: in 2010 some 54% of daily newspaper circulation was represented by two major groups, Postmedia Network Inc and Quebecor Media Inc. Quebecor, including its subsidiaries Sun Media Corpn and Osprey, owned 36 daily newspapers (and controlled 23% of total paid daily newspaper circulation), Postmedia Network Inc (which had bought CanWest's entire newspaper division in 2010) owned 13 (with the greatest share of total circulation, at 31%).

In 2010 there were 96 daily newspapers, with a combined daily circulation of some 4.0m.; of these only two were independent. In 2011 there were 28 free daily newspapers, with a combined daily circulation of almost 1.6m. In the same year the Canadian Community Newspaper Association comprised 763 weekly and twice-weekly community newspapers, serving mainly the more remote areas of the country. These newspapers had a combined daily circulation of almost 14m. per week in 2010.

There were numerous periodicals for business, trade, professional, recreational and special interest readership, although periodical publishing, particularly, suffered from substantial competition from publications originating in the USA. In 2009 1,276 consumer titles and 777 business titles were published in Canada. The principal industry association, Magazines Canada, comprised more than 370 member titles in 2010.

The following are among the principal newspaper publishing groups:

Gesca Limitée: 7 rue St-Jacques, Montréal, QC H2Y 1K9; e-mail recherchemarketing@lapresse.ca; internet publicite.gesca.ca; wholly owned subsidiary of the Power Corpn of Canada; owns 7 daily newspapers (average daily circ. 420,776); Chair. and Co-CEO PAUL DESMARAIS, Jr; Pres. and Co-CEO ANDRÉ DESMARAIS.

Postmedia Network Inc: 1450 Don Mills Rd, Don Mills, ON M3B 3R5; tel. (416) 383-2300; internet www.postmedia.com; f. 2010 to acquire the newspaper division of CanWest Global Communications Corpn; owns 13 English-language daily newspapers and 35 community newspapers in Canada; Dir and Chair. RON OSBORNE.

Quebecor Media Inc: 612 rue St-Jacques, Montréal, QC H3C 4M8; tel. (514) 954-0101; e-mail webmaster@quebecor.com; internet www.quebecor.com; f. 1965; acquired Osprey Media Group Inc in 2007; through its subsidiaries Sun Media Corpn and Osprey Media Group, publishes 36 English- and French-language dailies and over 284 community papers; television, cable, telecommunications and publishing interests in 17 countries; Pres. and CEO PIERRE KARL PÉLADEAU.

Osprey Media: 100, Renfrew Dr., Suite 110, Markham, ON L3R 9R6; tel. (905) 752-1132; 20 dailies and 34 non-daily newspapers, magazines and other publications.

Sun Media Corpn: 333 King St East, Toronto, ON M5A 3X5; tel. (416) 947-2222; e-mail qi_info@quebecor.com; internet www.sunmedia.ca; f. 1965; 43 community dailies and over 250 community weeklies; Pres. and CEO PIERRE KARL PÉLADEAU.

Torstar Corpn: 1 Yonge St, Toronto, ON M5E 1P9; tel. (416) 869-4010; fax (416) 869-4183; e-mail torstar@torstar.ca; internet www.torstar.com; f. 1958; incorporates the Star Media Group and Metroland Media Group; owns 4 daily newspapers (daily circ. 450,383), 10 weekly publs, and 95 community newspapers; Chair. JOHN A. HONDERICH; Pres. and CEO DAVID P. HOLLAND.

Transcontinental Media: 1100 blvd René-Lévesque ouest, 24th Floor, Montréal, QC H3B 4X9; tel. (514) 954-4000; fax (514) 954-4016; e-mail contact-media@transcontinental.ca; internet www.transcontinentalmedia.com; f. 1978; publs 10 dailies (daily circ. 97,878) and more than 125 weekly, fortnightly and monthly newspapers (circ. 2.4m.); Chair. RÉMI MARCOUX; Pres. and CEO FRANÇOIS OLIVIER.

PRINCIPAL DAILY NEWSPAPERS

Alberta

Calgary Herald: 215 16th St, SE, POB 2400, Station M, Calgary, AB T2P 0W8; tel. (403) 235-7100; fax (403) 235-7379; e-mail calgaryherald@reachcanada.com; internet www.canada.com/calgaryherald; f. 1883; owned by Postmedia Network Inc; Publr MALCOLM KIRK; Editor-in-Chief LORNE MOTLEY; circ. Mon. to Fri. 133,435, Sat. 126,380, Sun. 120,610 (2010).

Calgary Sun: 2615 12th St, NE, Calgary, AB T2E 7W9; tel. (403) 410-1010; fax (403) 250-4176; e-mail callet@calgarysun.com; internet www.calgarysun.com; f. 1980; owned by Sun Media Corpn; Publr and CEO GORDON NORRIE; Editor-in-Chief JOSÉ RODRIGUEZ; circ. Mon. to Fri. 37,249, Sat. 40,886, Sun. 52,589 (2010).

Daily Herald-Tribune: 10604 100th St, Postal Bag 3000, Grande Prairie, AB T8V 6V4; tel. (780) 532-1110; fax (780) 532-2120; e-mail frinne@bowesnet.com; internet www.dailyheraldtribune.com; f. 1913; owned by Sun Media Corpn; evening; Publr KENT KEEBAUGH; Man. Editor JEFF MCCOSHEN; circ. Mon. to Fri. 5,631 (2010).

Edmonton Journal: 10006 101st St, POB 2421, Edmonton, AB T5J 2S6; tel. (780) 429-5100; fax (780) 429-5536; internet www.edmontonjournal.com; f. 1903; owned by Postmedia Network Inc; Publr JOHN CONNOLLY; Editor-in-Chief LUCINDA CHODAN; circ. Mon. to Fri. 108,156, Sat. 109,985, Sun. 105,383 (2010).

Edmonton Sun: 4990 92nd Ave, Suite 250, Edmonton, AB T6B 3A1; tel. (780) 468-0100; fax (780) 468-0128; e-mail mailbag@edmsun.com; internet www.edmontonsun.com; f. 1978; owned by Sun Media Corpn; Editor-in-Chief JOSÉ RODRIGUEZ; Man. Editor DONNA HARKER; circ. Mon. to Fri. 44,865, Sat. 43,227, Sun. 55,858 (2010).

Fort McMurray Today: 8550 Franklin Ave, Bag 4008, Fort McMurray, AB T9H 3G1; tel. (780) 743-8186; fax (780) 715-3820; e-mail editorial@fortmcmurraytoday.com; internet www.fortmcmurraytoday.com; owned by Sun Media Corpn; evening; Publr TIM O'ROURKE; circ. Mon. to Fri. 2,061 (2010).

Lethbridge Herald: 504 Seventh St South, POB 670, Lethbridge, AB T1J 2H1; tel. (403) 328-4411; fax (403) 328-4536; e-mail calbrecht@lethbridgeherald.com; internet www.lethbridgeherald.com; f. 1907; evening and Sun.; Gen. Man. BOB CAREY; Man. Editor CRAIG ALBRECHT; circ. Mon. to Fri. 16,386, Sat. 16,117, Sun. 14,575 (2010).

Medicine Hat News: 3257 Dunmore Rd, SE, POB 10, Medicine Hat, AB T1A 7E6; tel. (403) 527-1101; fax (403) 527-1244; e-mail apoirier@medicinehatnews.com; internet www.medicinehatnews.com; f. 1887; evening; Publr MICHAEL J. HERTZ; Man. Editor ALAN POIRIER; circ. Mon. to Fri. 11,742 (2010).

Red Deer Advocate: 2950 Bremner Ave, Bag 5200, Red Deer, AB T4R 1M9; tel. (403) 343-2400; fax (403) 341-6560; e-mail editorial@reddeeradvocate.com; internet www.reddeeradvocate.com; f. 1894; Publr FRED GORMAN; Man. Editor JOHN STEWART; circ. Mon. to Fri. 14,027, Sat. 13,852 (2010).

British Columbia

Alberni Valley Times: 4918 Napier St, POB 400, Port Alberni, BC V9Y 3H5; tel. (250) 723-8171; fax (250) 723-0586; e-mail lpatterson@avtimes.net; internet www.canada.com/albernivalleytimes; Publr (vacant); Man. Editor CALE COWAN; circ. Mon. to Fri. 4,104 (2010).

Daily Bulletin: 335 Spokane St, Kimberley, BC V1A 1Y9; tel. (250) 427-5333; fax (250) 427-5336; e-mail bulletin@cyberlink.bc.ca; internet www.dailytownsman.com; f. 1932; evening; Publr BRIAN SIMS; Editor CAROLYN GRANT; circ. 2,000.

Daily Courier: 550 Doyle Ave, Kelowna, BC V1Y 7V1; tel. (250) 762-4445; fax (250) 762-3866; e-mail terry.armstrong@ok.bc.ca; internet www.kelownadailycourier.ca; f. 1904; morning; Publr TERRY ARMSTRONG; Man. Editor JON MANCHESTER; circ. Mon. to Fri. 13,605, Sat. 13,797, Sun. 13,131 (2010).

Daily Townsman: 822 Cranbrook St North, Cranbrook, BC V1C 3R9; tel. (250) 426-5201; fax (250) 426-5003; e-mail townsman@cyberlink.bc.ca; internet www.dailytownsman.com; evening; Publr BRIAN SIMS; Editor BARRY COULTER; circ. 4,000.

Kamloops Daily News: 393 Seymour St, Kamloops, BC V2C 6P6; tel. (250) 372-2331; fax (250) 374-3884; e-mail kamloopsnews@telus.net; internet www.kamloopsnews.ca; f. 1930; evening; Publr TIM SHOULTS; Editor MEL ROTHENBURGER; circ. Mon. to Sat. 12,627 (2010).

Nanaimo Daily News: 2575 McCullough Rd, Nanaimo, BC V9S 5W5; tel. (250) 729-4200; fax (250) 729-4247; e-mail dnews@island.net; internet www.nanaimodailynews.com; f. 1874; evening; Publr CURT DUDDY; Man. Editor CALE COWAN; circ. Mon. to Sat. 6,209 (2010).

Penticton Herald: 186 Nanaimo Ave West, Suite 101, Penticton, BC V2A 1N4; tel. (250) 492-4002; fax (250) 492-2403; e-mail editor@pentictonherald.ca; internet www.pentictonherald.ca; f. 1906 as Penticton Press; morning; Man. Editor JAMES MILLER; Gen. Man. ANDRÉ MARTIN; circ. Mon. to Fri. 7,014, Sat. 6,980, Sun. 6,439 (2010).

Prince George Citizen: 150 Brunswick St, POB 5700, Prince George, BC V2L 5K9; tel. (250) 562-2441; fax (250) 562-7453; e-mail info@pgcitizen.ca; internet www.princegeorgecitizen.com; f. 1916; morning; Publr HUGH NICHOLSON; Editor DAVE PAULSON; circ. Mon. to Sat. 12,161 (2010).

The Province: 200 Granville St, Suite 1, Vancouver, BC V6C 3N3; tel. (604) 605-2000; fax (604) 605-2308; e-mail wmoriarty@theprovince.com; internet www.theprovince.com; f. 1898; owned by Postmedia Network Inc; Publr KEVIN BENT; Editor-in-Chief WAYNE MORIARTY; circ. Mon. to Fri. 157,184, Sun. 172,234 (2010).

Sing Tao Daily News (Eastern Canada Edition): 8508 Ash St, Vancouver, BC V6P 3M2; tel. (604) 321-1111; fax (604) 321-1178; e-mail vanadmin@singtao.ca; internet news.singtao.ca; f. 1978; Chinese; Editor VICTOR HO; circ. Mon. to Sun. 45,000.

Times Colonist: 2621 Douglas St, Victoria, BC V8T 4M2; tel. (250) 380-5211; fax (250) 380-5353; e-mail customerservice@timescolonist.com; internet www.timescolonist.com; f. 1980 by merger of British Colonist (f. 1858) and Victoria Daily Times (f. 1884); owned by Postmedia Network Inc; Publr BOB MCKENZIE; Editor-in-Chief DENISE HELM (acting); circ. Tue. to Fri. 63,759, Sat. 60,869, Sun. 60,350 (2010).

Trail Daily Times: 1163 Cedar Ave, Trail, BC V1R 4B8; tel. (250) 368-8551; fax (250) 368-8550; e-mail editor@trailtimes.ca; internet www.trailtimes.ca; evening; Publr BARB BLATCHFORD; Editor GUY BERTRAND; circ. Mon. to Fri. 5,002 (2010).

The Vancouver Sun: 200 Granville St, Suite 1, Vancouver, BC V6C 3N3; tel. (604) 605-2000; fax (604) 605-2308; e-mail pgraham@vancouversun.com; internet www.vancouversun.com; f. 1886; owned by Postmedia Network Inc; Pres. and Publr KEVIN D. BENT; Editor-in-Chief PATRICIA GRAHAM; circ. Mon. to Fri. 173,837, Sat. 202,844 (2010).

World Journal (Vancouver): 2288 Clark Dr., Vancouver, BC V5N 3G8; tel. (604) 876-1338; fax (604) 876-9191; e-mail bcwebmaster@worldjournal.com; internet www.worldjournal.com; f. 1976; Chinese; Publr WILSON CHIEN; circ. 10,000.

Manitoba

Brandon Sun: 501 Rosser Ave, Brandon, MB R7A 0K4; tel. (204) 727-2451; fax (204) 725-0976; e-mail jperreau@brandonsun.com; internet www.brandonsun.com; f. 1882; evening and Sun.; Publr ERIC LAWSON; Man. Editor JAMES O'CONNOR; circ. Mon. to Fri. 13,520, Sat. 14,847, Sun. 22,990 (2010).

Daily Graphic: 1941 Saskatchewan Ave West, POB 130, Portage La Prairie, MB R1N 3B4; tel. (204) 857-3427; fax (204) 239-1270; e-mail editor.dailygraphic@shawcable.com; internet www.portagedailygraphic.com; owned by Sun Media Corpn; evening; Publr BARRY CLAYTON; Man. Editor CLARISE KLASSEN; circ. Mon. to Fri. 1,655 (2010).

Winnipeg Free Press: 1355 Mountain Ave, Winnipeg, MB R2X 3B6; tel. (204) 697-7000; fax (204) 697-7375; e-mail bob.cox@freepress.mb.ca; internet www.winnipegfreepress.com; f. 1872; morning; Publr BOB COX; Editor MARGO GOODHAND; circ. Mon. to Fri. 119,478, Sat. 161,538, Sun. 132,205 (2010).

Winnipeg Sun: 1700 Church Ave, Winnipeg, MB R2X 3A2; tel. (204) 694-2022; fax (204) 697-0759; e-mail kevin.klein@sunmedia.ca; internet www.winnipegsun.com; f. 1980; owned by Sun Media Corpn; Publr and CEO KEVIN KLEIN; Editor-in-Chief STEPHEN RIPLEY; circ. Mon. to Fri. 25,325, Sat. 25,986, Sun. 29,697 (2010).

New Brunswick

L'Acadie Nouvelle: 476 blvd St-Pierre ouest, CP 5536, Caraquet, NB E1W 1B7; tel. (506) 727-4444; fax (506) 727-7620; e-mail infos@acadienouvelle.com; internet an.capacadie.com; f. 1984; French; Publr GILLES GAGNÉ; Editor-in-Chief JEAN SAINT-CYR; circ. Mon. to Fri. 20,178 (2010).

The Daily Gleaner: 984 Prospect St, POB 3370, Fredericton, NB E3B 2T8; tel. (506) 452-6671; fax (506) 452-7405; e-mail news@dailygleaner.com; internet dailygleaner.canadaeast.com; f. 1881; morning; Publr NANCY COOK; Man. Editor CATHERINE METCALFE; circ. Mon. to Fri. 20,424, Sat. 20,922 (2010).

Telegraph-Journal: 210 Crown St, POB 2350, Saint John, NB E2L 3V8; tel. (506) 633-5599; fax (506) 648-2654; e-mail newsroom@nbpub.com; internet www.telegraphjournal.com; Man. Editor RON BARRY; circ. Mon. to Fri. 32,352, Sat. 34,305 (2010).

The Times and Transcript: 939 Main St, POB 1001, Moncton, NB E1C 8P3; tel. (506) 859-4905; fax (506) 859-4904; e-mail news@timestranscript.com; internet timestranscript.canadaeast.com; f. 1983; Mon. to Sat. evening, Sat. morning; Publr ERIC LAWSON; Man. Editor AL HOGAN; circ. Mon. to Fri. 35,251, Sat. 38,114 (2010).

Newfoundland and Labrador

The Telegram: 430 Topsail Rd, POB 86, St John's, NL A1E 4N1; tel. (709) 364-6300; fax (709) 364-3939; e-mail telegram@thetelegram.com; internet www.thetelegram.com; f. 1879; evening; Publr and Gen. Man. CHARLES STACEY; Man. Editor KERRY HANN; circ. Mon. to Fri. 20,432, Sat. 36,715 (2010).

The Western Star: 106 West St, POB 460, Corner Brook, NL A2H 6E7; tel. (709) 634-4348; fax (709) 634-9824; e-mail newsroom@thewesternstar.com; internet www.thewesternstar.com; f. 1900; Publr and Gen. Man. TRINA BURDEN; Man. Editor TROY TURNER; circ. Mon. to Fri. 5,883, Sat. 6,725 (2010).

Nova Scotia

Amherst Daily News: 147 South Albion St Town Sq., POB 280, Amherst, NS B4H 2X2; tel. (902) 667-5102; fax (902) 667-0419; e-mail bworks@amherstdaily.com; internet www.amherstdaily.com; f. 1893; Publr RICHARD RUSSELL; Man. Editor BRAD WORKS; circ. Mon. to Fri. 2,622 (2010).

Cape Breton Post: 255 George St, POB 1500, Sydney, NS B1P 6K6; tel. (902) 564-5451; fax (902) 562-7077; e-mail edit@cbpost.com; internet www.capebretonpost.com; f. 1901; Publr ANITA DELAZZER; Man. Editor FRED JACKSON; circ. Mon. to Fri. 20,490, Sat. 21,473 (2010).

ChronicleHerald: 2717 Joseph Howe Dr., POB 610, Halifax, NS B3J 2T2; tel. (902) 426-2811; fax (902) 426-3382; e-mail reception@herald.ca; internet thechronicleherald.ca; f. 1875; Publr GRAHAM W. DENNIS; Editor-in-Chief BOB HOWSE; circ. Mon. to Fri. 107,857, Sat. 111,427, Sun. 94,054 (2010).

The News: 352 East River Rd, POB 159, New Glasgow, NS B2H 5E2; tel. (902) 752-3000; fax (902) 752-1945; e-mail news@ngnews.ca; internet www.ngnews.ca; f. 1910; fmrly known as *The Evening News*; evening; Publr RICHARD RUSSELL; Man. Editor DAVE GLENEN; circ. Mon. to Fri. 5,880 (2010).

Truro Daily News: 6 Louise St, POB 220, Truro, NS B2N 5C3; tel. (902) 893-9405; fax (902) 895-6106; e-mail news@trurodaily.com; internet www.trurodaily.com; f. 1891; evening; Publr RICHARD RUSSELL; Man. Editor CARL FLEMING; circ. Mon. to Fri. 5,453 (2010).

Ontario

Barrie Examiner: 571 Bayfield St North, Barrie, ON L4M 4Z9; tel. (705) 726-6537; fax (705) 726-5414; internet www.thebarrieexaminer.com; f. 1864; owned by Sun Media Corpn; evening; Man. Editor MIKE BEAUDIN; circ. Mon. to Fri. 4,603, Sat. 4,700 (2010).

Beacon Herald: 16 Packham Rd, POB 430, Stratford, ON N5A 6T6; tel. (519) 271-2220; fax (519) 271-1026; e-mail jkastner@bowesnet.com; internet www.stratfordbeaconherald.com; f. 1854; owned by Sun Media Corpn; evening; Publr DAVE CARTER; Man. Editor JOHN KASTNER; circ. Mon. to Fri. 7,833, Sat. 8,158 (2010).

Brockville Recorder and Times: 2479 Parkedale Ave, POB 10, Brockville, ON K6V 5T8; tel. (613) 342-4441; fax (613) 342-4456; e-mail editor@recorder.ca; internet www.recorder.ca; f. 1821; owned by Sun Media Corpn; evening; Publr BOB PEARCE; Editor-in-Chief BARRY RAISON; circ. Tue. to Fri. 8,876, Sat. 9,252 (2010).

Chatham Daily News: 138 King St West, POB 2007, Chatham, ON N7M 1E3; tel. (519) 354-2000; fax (519) 436-0949; e-mail news@chathamdailynews.ca; internet www.chathamdailynews.ca; f. 1862; owned by Sun Media Corpn; evening; Publr and Gen. Man. DEAN MUHARREM; Man. Editor BRUCE CORCORAN; circ. Tue. to Fri. 8,005, Sat. 8,281 (2010).

Chronicle Journal: 75 Cumberland St South, Thunder Bay, ON P7B 1A3; tel. (807) 343-6200; fax (807) 345-9409; e-mail julio.gomes@chroniclejournal.com; internet www.chroniclejournal.com; Publr and Gen. Man. COLIN J. BRUCE; Man. Editor JULIO HELENO GOMES; circ. Mon. to Fri. 26,267, Sat. 27,160, Sun. 22,855 (2012).

Daily Observer: 100 Crandal St, POB 190, Pembroke, ON K8A 0B1; tel. (613) 732-3691; fax (613) 732-2226; e-mail editor@thedailyobserver.ca; internet www.thedailyobserver.ca; f. 1855; owned by Sun Media Corpn; evening; Publr STEVE GLOSTER; Man. Editor PETER LAPINSKIE; circ. Tue. to Fri. 4,179, Sat. 4,772 (2010).

The Daily Press: 187 Cedar South, Timmins, ON P4N 7G1; tel. (705) 268-5050; fax (705) 268-7373; internet www.timminspress.com; f. 1933; owned by Sun Media Corpn; Publr and Gen. Man. BRUCE COWAN; Man. Editor TOM PERRY; circ. Mon. to Fri. 6,632, Sat. 6,714 (2010).

Le Droit: 47 rue Clarence, bureau 222, CP 8860, succursale Terminus, Ottawa, ON K1G 3J9; tel. (613) 562-0111; fax (613) 562-7539; e-mail ledroit@ledroit.com; internet www.cyberpresse.ca; f. 1913; Publr JACQUES PRONOVOST; Man. Editor ANDRÉ LAROCQUE; circ. Mon. to Fri. 36,698, Sat. 38,422 (2010).

The Expositor: 195 Henry St, Brantford, ON N3S 5C9; tel. (519) 756-2020; fax (519) 756-4911; e-mail publisher@theexpositor.com; internet www.brantfordexpositor.ca; f. 1852; owned by Sun Media Corpn; Publr and Gen. Man. MIKE WALSH; Man. Editor JOHN CHAMBERS; circ. Mon. to Fri. 16,131, Sat. 16,940 (2010).

The Globe and Mail: 444 Front St West, Toronto, ON M5V 2S9; tel. (416) 585-5000; fax (416) 585-5085; e-mail newsroom@globeandmail.ca; internet www.globeandmail.com; f. 1844; Publr and CEO PHILLIP CRAWLEY; Editor-in-Chief JOHN STACKHOUSE; circ. Mon. to Fri. 306,654, Sat. 373,416 (2010).

Guelph Mercury: 8–14 Macdonnell St, Guelph, ON N1H 6P7; tel. (519) 823-9838; fax (519) 767-1681; e-mail editor@guelphmercury.com; internet news.guelphmercury.com; f. 1854; evening; Publr PAUL MCCUAIG; Man. Editor PHIL ANDREWS; circ. Mon. to Fri. 11,324, Sat. 12,274 (2010).

Hamilton Spectator: 44 Frid St, Hamilton, ON L8N 3G3; tel. (905) 526-3333; fax (905) 526-0147; internet www.thespec.com; f. 1846; Publr DANA ROBBINS; Editor-in-Chief PAUL BERTON; circ. Mon. to Fri. 90,150, Sat. 99,542 (2010).

Intelligencer: 199 Front St, Suite 535, Century Pl., Belleville, ON K8N 5H5; tel. (613) 962-9171; fax (613) 962-9652; e-mail bglisky@intelligencer.ca; internet www.intelligencer.ca; f. 1870; owned by Sun Media Corpn; evening; Publr and Gen. Man. JOHN KNOWLES; Man. Editor BILL GLISKY; circ. Mon. to Fri. 9,657, Sat. 9,948 (2010).

The Kingston Whig-Standard: 6 Cataraqui St, POB 2300, Kingston, ON K7L 4Z7; tel. (613) 544-5000; fax (613) 530-4122; e-mail whiglocal@thewhig.com; internet www.thewhig.com; f. 1834; owned by Sun Media Corpn; Publr RON LAURIN; circ. Mon. to Fri. 20,291, Sat. 23,888 (2010).

Lindsay Post: 17 William St South, Lindsay, ON K9V 3A3; tel. (705) 324-2113; fax (705) 324-0174; e-mail jbain@thepost.ca; internet www.thepost.ca; evening; Publr ANDY WHEELER; Man. Editor JASON BAIN; circ. 4,831.

London Free Press: 369 York St, POB 2280, London, ON N6A 4G1; tel. (519) 679-1111; fax (519) 667-4528; e-mail letters@lfpress.com; internet www.lfpress.com; f. 1849; owned by Sun Media Corpn; Publr and CEO SUSAN MUSZAK; Editor-in-Chief JOE RUSCITTI; circ. Mon. to Fri. 67,498, Sat. 79,407 (2010).

Ming Pao Daily News: 1355 Huntingwood Dr., Scarborough, ON M1S 3J1; tel. (416) 321-0088; fax (416) 321-9663; e-mail newsdesk@mingpaotor.com; internet www.mingpaotor.com; f. 1993; Chinese; Editor-in-Chief RICHARD KWOK-KAI NG; circ. Mon. to Fri. 68,600, Sat. 97,000, Sun. 102,000.

National Post: 1450 Don Mills Rd, Suite 300, Don Mills, ON M3B 3R5; tel. (416) 383-2300; fax (416) 383-2305; e-mail queries@nationalpost.com; internet www.nationalpost.com; f. 1998; incorporates the *Financial Post* (f. 1907); national newspaper with printing centres in nine cities; owned by Postmedia Network Inc; Publr DOUGLAS KELLY; Editor-in-Chief STEPHEN MEURICE; circ. Mon. to Fri. 161,340, Sat. 142,798 (2010).

Niagara Falls Review: 4801 Valley Way, POB 270, Niagara Falls, ON L2E 6T6; tel. (905) 358-5711; fax (905) 356-0785; e-mail pconradi@nfreview.com; internet www.niagarafallsreview.ca; f. 1879; owned by Sun Media Corpn; morning; Publr MARK CRESSMAN; Man. Editor STEVEN GALLAGHER; circ. Mon. to Fri. 10,658, Sat. 10,749 (2010).

North Bay Nugget: 259 Worthington St, POB 570, North Bay, ON P1B 3B5; tel. (705) 472-3200; fax (705) 472-1438; e-mail news@nugget.ca; internet www.nugget.ca; f. 1909; owned by Sun Media Corpn; evening; Publr DAN JOHNSON; Man. Editor STEVE HARDY; circ. Mon. to Fri. 11,534, Sat. 12,395 (2010).

Northern Daily News: 8 Duncan Ave, POB 1030, Kirkland Lake, ON P2N 3L4; tel. (705) 567-5321; fax (705) 567-6162; e-mail news@northernnews.ca; internet www.northernnews.ca; f. 1922; evening; Publr and Gen. Man. TIM CRESWELL; Man. Editor JOE O'GRADY; circ. 3,379.

Northumberland Today: 99 King St West, POB 400, Cobourg, ON K9A 2M4; tel. (905) 372-0131; fax (905) 372-4966; e-mail editor@northumberlandtoday.com; internet www.northumberlandtoday.com; f. 2009 by merger of the *Cobourg Star* (f. 1834), *Colborne Chronicle* (f. 1959) and *Port Hope Evening Guide* (f. 1878); owned by Sun Media Corpn; evening; Group Publr MARK HOLMES; Man. Editor SHARIE LYNN FLEMING; circ. 4,933 (2010).

Orillia Packet and Times: 425 West St North, Suite 15, Orillia, ON L3V 7R2; tel. (705) 325-1355; fax (705) 325-4033; internet www.orilliapacket.com; f. 1926 by merger; owned by Sun Media Corpn; evening; Publr and Gen. Man. JOHN HAMMILL; Editor RANDY LUCENTI; circ. Mon. to Fri. 5,336, Sat. 5,407 (2010).

Ottawa Citizen: 1101 Baxter Rd, POB 5020, Ottawa, ON K2C 3M4; tel. (613) 829-9100; fax (613) 726-1198; e-mail subscriberservices@ottawacitizen.com; internet www.ottawacitizen.com; f. 1845 as *The Packet*; owned by Postmedia Network Inc; Publr and Editor-in-Chief GERRY NOTT; Exec. Editor GRAHAM GREEN; circ. Mon. to Fri. 123,109, Sat. 119,072, Sun. 108,461 (2010).

Ottawa Sun: POB 9729, Station T, Ottawa, ON K1G 5H7; tel. (613) 739-7000; fax (613) 739-9383; e-mail rick.gibbons@ott.sunpub.com; internet www.ottawasun.com; owned by Sun Media Corpn; Publr RICK GIBBONS; Editor-in-Chief MITCHELL AXELRAD; circ. Mon. to Fri. 39,295, Sat. 30,593, Sun. 34,745 (2010).

Peterborough Examiner: 730 Kingsway, Peterborough, ON K9J 8L4; tel. (705) 745-4641; fax (705) 743-4581; e-mail newsroom@peterboroughexaminer.com; internet www.thepeterboroughexaminer.com; f. 1847; owned by Sun Media Corpn; evening; Publr and Gen. Man. DARREN MURPHY; Man. Editor ED N. ARNOLD; circ. Mon. to Fri. 13,417, Sat. 14,291 (2010).

The Record: 160 King St East, Kitchener, ON N2G 4E5; tel. (519) 894-2231; fax (519) 894-3912; e-mail pmccuaig@therecord.com; internet www.therecord.com; f. 1878; evening; Publr PAUL MCCUAIG; Editor-in-Chief LYNN HADDRALL; circ. Mon. to Fri. 64,485, Sat. 71,963.

St Catharines Standard: 17 Queen St, St Catharines, ON L2R 5G5; tel. (905) 684-7251; fax (905) 684-6032; e-mail akriluck@stcatharinesstandard.ca; internet www.stcatharinesstandard.ca; f. 1891; owned by Sun Media Corpn; evening; Publr JUDY BULLIS; Man. Editor WENDY METCALFE; circ. Mon. to Fri. 19,011, Sat. 21,269 (2010).

St Thomas Times-Journal: 16 Hincks St, St Thomas, ON N5R 5Z2; tel. (519) 631-2790; fax (519) 631-5653; e-mail news@stthomastimesjournal.com; internet www.stthomastimesjournal.com; f. 1882; owned by Sun Media Corpn; evening; Publr BEV PONTON; Man. Editor ROSS PORTER; circ. Tue. to Fri. 4,168, Sat. 4,069 (2010).

Sarnia Observer: 140 Front St South, POB 3009, Sarnia, ON N7T 7M8; tel. (519) 344-3641; fax (519) 332-2951; e-mail rhilts@theobserver.ca; internet www.theobserver.ca; f. 1853; owned by Sun Media Corpn; evening; Publr DARYL C. SMITH; Man. Editor ROD HILTS; circ. Mon. to Fri. 12,745, Sat. 14,447 (2010).

Sault Star: 145 Old Garden River Rd, POB 460, Sault Ste Marie, ON P6A 5M5; tel. (705) 759-3030; fax (705) 942-8690; e-mail ssmstar@saultstar.com; internet www.saultstar.com; f. 1912; owned by Sun Media Corpn; evening; Pres. and Publr LOU A. MAULUCCI; Editor FRANK RUPNIK; circ. Mon. to Fri. 13,790, Sat. 14,153 (2010).

Sentinel-Review: 16 Brock St, POB 1000, Woodstock, ON N4S 3B4; tel. (519) 537-2341; fax (519) 537-3049; e-mail sentinelreview@bowesnet.com; internet www.woodstocksentinelreview.com; f. 1886; owned by Sun Media Corpn; evening; Publr ANDREA DEMEER; Man. Editor BRUCE URQUHART; circ. Mon. to Sat. 7,700 (2010).

Simcoe Reformer: 50 Gilbertson Dr., POB 370, Simcoe, ON N3Y 4L2; tel. (519) 426-5710; fax (519) 426-9255; e-mail refedit@bowesnet.com; internet www.simcoereformer.ca; f. 1858; owned by Sun Media Corpn; evening; Group Publr MIKE WALSH; Man. Editor KIMBERLEY NOVAK; circ. 5,650 (2010).

Sing Tao Daily News: 417 Dundas St West, Toronto, ON M5T 1G6; tel. (416) 596-8140; fax (416) 599-6688; e-mail singtao@singtao.ca; internet www.singtao.ca; Chinese; Editor-in-Chief ROBERT LEUNG; circ. Mon. to Sun. 160,693.

Standard-Freeholder: 1150 Montreal Rd, Cornwall, ON K6J 1E2; tel. (613) 933-3160; fax (613) 933-3664; e-mail news@standard-freeholder.com; internet www.standard-freeholder.com; owned by Sun Media Corpn; Publr and Gen. Man. MILTON S. ELLIS; Man. Editor ANDREW CARROLL; circ. Mon. to Fri. 10,685, Sat. 10,907 (2010).

Sudbury Star: 33 MacKenzie St, Sudbury, ON P3C 4Y1; tel. (705) 674-5271; fax (705) 674-6834; e-mail bmacleod@thesudburystar.com; internet www.thesudburystar.com; f. 1909; owned by Sun

Media Corpn; evening; Publr and Gen. Man. DAVID KILGOUR; Man. Editor BRIAN MACLEOD; circ. Mon. to Fri. 13,315, Sat. 14,333 (2010).

Sun Times: 290 Ninth St East, POB 200, Owen Sound, ON N4K 5P2; tel. (519) 376-2250; fax (519) 376-7190; internet www.owensoundsuntimes.com; f. 1853 as *The Times*; owned by Sun Media Corpn; evening; Publr CHERYL A. MCMENEMY; Man. Editor MICHAEL DEN TANDT; circ. Mon. to Fri. 12,458, Sat. 12,737 (2010).

Toronto Star: 1 Yonge St, Toronto, ON M5E 1E6; tel. (416) 367-2000; fax (416) 869-4328; e-mail city@thestar.ca; internet www.thestar.com; f. 1892; Publr JOHN D. CRUICKSHANK; Editor-in-Chief MICHAEL COOKE; circ. Mon. to Fri. 266,125, Sat. 417,809, Sun. 295,589 (2010).

Toronto Sun: 333 King St East, Toronto, ON M5A 3X5; tel. (416) 947-2222; fax (416) 947-1664; e-mail torsun.editor@sunmedia.ca; internet www.torontosun.com; f. 1971; owned by Sun Media Corpn; Publr MIKE POWER; Editor-in-Chief JAMES WALLACE; circ. Mon. to Fri. 141,163, Sat. 123,510, Sun. 187,433 (2010).

Welland Tribune: 228 East Main St, POB 278, Welland, ON L3B 5P5; tel. (905) 732-2411; fax (905) 732-3660; e-mail tribme@wellandtribune.ca; internet www.wellandtribune.ca; f. 1863; owned by Sun Media Corpn; Publr KEN KOYAMA; Man. Editor ANGUS SCOTT; circ. Mon. to Fri. 10,205, Sat. 10,296 (2010).

Windsor Star: 167 Ferry St, Windsor, ON N9A 4M5; tel. (519) 255-5743; fax (519) 255-5515; internet www.windsorstar.com; f. 1918; owned by Postmedia Network Inc; Publr JIM VENNEY; Editor MARTY BENETEAU; circ. Mon. to Fri. 59,281, Sat. 62,689 (2010).

World Journal (Toronto): 7755 Warden Ave, Unit 9, Markham, ON L3R 0N3; tel. (416) 778-0888; fax (416) 778-1037; e-mail webmaster@worldjournal.com; internet www.worldjournal.com; f. 1976; Chinese; Pres. DAVID TING; Editor-in-Chief PAUL CHANG; circ. 38,000.

Prince Edward Island

Guardian: 165 Prince St, POB 760, Charlottetown, PE C1A 4R7; tel. (902) 629-6000; fax (902) 566-3808; e-mail comments@theguardian.pe.ca; internet www.theguardian.pe.ca; f. 1887; Publr DON BRANDER; Man. Editor GARY MACDOUGALL; circ. Mon. to Fri. 17,291, Sat. 19,187 (2010).

The Journal Pioneer: 316 Water St, POB 2480, Summerside, PE C1N 4K5; tel. (902) 436-2121; fax (902) 436-0784; e-mail newsroom@journalpioneer.com; internet www.journalpioneer.com; f. 1865; evening; Publr SANDY RUNDLE; Man. Editor MIKE TURNER; circ. Mon. to Fri. 7,745, Sat. 8,014 (2010).

Québec

Le Devoir: 2050 rue de Bleury, 9e étage, Montréal, QC H3A 3M9; tel. (514) 985-3333; fax (514) 985-3360; e-mail redaction@ledevoir.com; internet www.ledevoir.com; Publr BERNARD DESCÔTEAUX; Editor-in-Chief JOSÉE BOILEAU; circ. Mon. to Fri. 28,438, Sat. 47,327 (2010).

The Gazette: 1010 rue Ste-Catherine ouest, Suite 200, Montréal, QC H3B 5L1; tel. (514) 987-2222; fax (514) 987-2270; e-mail readtheg@montrealgazette.com; internet www.montrealgazette.com; f. 1778; owned by Postmedia Network Inc; English; Publr ALAN ALLNUTT; Man. Editor CATHERINE WALLACE; circ. Mon. to Fri. 155,063, Sat. 166,297, Sun. 153,041 (2010).

Le Journal de Montréal: 4545 rue Frontenac, Montréal, QC H2H 2R7; tel. (514) 521-4545; fax (514) 525-4542; e-mail transmission@journalmtl.com; internet www.canoe.com/journaldemontreal; f. 1964; owned by Sun Media Corpn; Publr and Editor LYNE ROBITAILLE; Editor-in-Chief DANY DOUCET; circ. Mon. to Fri. 206,476, Sat. 228,340, Sun. 209,175 (2010).

Le Journal de Québec: 450 ave Béchard, Vanier, QC G1M 2E9; tel. (418) 683-1573; fax (418) 683-8886; e-mail commentaires@journaldequebec.com; internet lejournaldequebec.canoe.ca; f. 1967; owned by Sun Media Corpn; Publr and CEO DANIEL HOUDE; circ. Mon. to Fri. 206,476, Sat. 228,340, Sun. 209,175 (2010).

Le Nouvelliste: 1920 rue Bellefeuille, CP 668, Trois Rivières, QC G9A 3Y2; tel. (819) 376-2501; fax (819) 376-0946; e-mail information@lenouvelliste.qc.ca; internet www.cyberpresse.ca/le-nouvelliste; f. 1920; Pres. and Publr ALAIN TURCOTTE; Editor-in-Chief STÉPHAN FRAPPIER; circ. Mon. to Fri. 43,745, Sat. 46,514 (2010).

La Presse: 7 rue St-Jacques, Montréal, QC H2Y 1K9; tel. (514) 285-7070; fax (514) 285-6930; e-mail avosaffaires@lapresseaffaires.com; internet www.cyberpresse.ca/actualites/regional/montreal; f. 1884; Pres. and Editor GUY CREVIER; circ. Mon. to Fri. 202,389, Sat. 264,678 (2010).

Le Quotidien du Saguenay-Lac-St-Jean: 1051 blvd Talbot, Chicoutimi, QC G7H 5C1; tel. (418) 545-4474; fax (418) 690-8824; e-mail redaction@lequotidien.com; internet www.cyberpresse.ca/le-quotidien; f. 1973; Editor-in-Chief MICHEL SIMARD; circ. Mon. to Fri. 26,913, Sat. 28,084, Sun. 36,007 (2010).

The Record: 1195 Galt St East, CP 1200, Sherbrooke, QC J1G 1Y7; tel. (819) 569-9525; fax (819) 821-3179; e-mail newsroom@sherbrookerecord.com; internet www.sherbrookerecord.com; f. 1897; Publr and Man. Editor SHARON MCCULLY; Editor DANIEL COULOMBE; circ. Mon. to Fri. 4,123 (2010).

Le Soleil: 410 blvd Charest est, CP 1547, succursale Terminus, Québec, QC G1K 7J6; tel. (418) 686-3233; fax (418) 686-3280; e-mail redaction@lesoleil.com; internet www.cyberpresse.ca/le-soleil; f. 1896; Publr CLAUDE GAGNON; Editor-in-Chief PIERRE-PAUL NOREAU; circ. Mon. to Fri. 76,336, Sat. 102,089, Sun. 81,270 (2010).

La Tribune: 1950 rue Roy, Sherbrooke, QC J1K 2X8; tel. (819) 564-5450; fax (819) 564-8098; e-mail redaction@latribune.qc.ca; internet www.cyberpresse.ca/la-tribune; f. 1910; Pres. and Publr LOUISE BOISVERT; Editor-in-Chief MAURICE CLOUTIER; circ. Mon. to Fri. 32,551, Sat. 35,316 (2010).

La Voix de L'Est: 76 rue Dufferin, Granby, QC J2G 9L4; tel. (450) 375-4555; fax (450) 777-4865; e-mail redaction@lavoixdelest.qc.ca; internet www.cyberpresse.ca/la-voix-de-lest; f. 1945; Pres. and Publr GUY GRANGER; circ. Mon. to Fri. 14,828, Sat. 16,451 (2010).

Saskatchewan

Daily Herald: 30 10th St East, Prince Albert, SK S6V 0Y5; tel. (306) 764-4276; fax (306) 763-3331; e-mail editorial@paherald.sk.ca; internet www.paherald.sk.ca; f. 1894; Publr, Gen. Man. and Editor IAN JENSEN; circ. Mon. to Fri. 5,470, Sat. 5,842 (2010).

Leader-Post: 1964 Park St, POB 2020, Regina, SK S4P 3C4; tel. (306) 781-5211; fax (306) 565-2588; e-mail readerservice@leaderpost.com; internet www.leaderpost.com; f. 1883; owned by Postmedia Network Inc; Publr MARTY KLYNE; Editor-in-Chief JANICE DOCKHAM; circ. Mon. to Fri. 46,535, Sat. 48,686 (2010).

StarPhoenix: 204 Fifth Ave North, Saskatoon, SK S7K 2P1; tel. (306) 657-6231; fax (306) 657-6437; e-mail citydesk@thestarphoenix.com; internet www.thestarphoenix.com; f. 1902; owned by Postmedia Network Inc; Publr DALE BRIN; Editor STEVE GIBB; circ. Mon. to Fri. 52,208, Sat. 54,845 (2010).

Times Herald: 44 Fairford St West, POB 3000, Moose Jaw, SK S6H 1V1; tel. (306) 692-6441; fax (306) 692-2101; e-mail enews@mjtimes.sk.ca; internet www.mjtimes.sk.ca; f. 1889; evening; Publr and Gen. Man. ROB CLARK; circ. Mon. to Sat. 6,475 (2010).

Yukon Territory

Whitehorse Star: 2149 Second Ave, Whitehorse, Yukon, YT Y1A 1C5; tel. (867) 667-4481; fax (867) 668-7130; e-mail star@whitehorsestar.com; internet www.whitehorsestar.com; f. 1900; evening; Publr JACKIE PIERCE; Editor JIM BUTLER; circ. Mon. to Fri. 1,990 (2010).

SELECTED PERIODICALS

Alberta

Oilweek: 2nd Floor, 55 Ave, Suite 816, NE, Calgary, AB T2E 6Y4; tel. (403) 209-3500; fax (403) 245-8666; e-mail webmaster@junewarren.com; internet www.oilweek.com; monthly magazine; f. 1948; Publr AGNES ZALEWSKI; Man. Editor DALE LUNAN; circ. 7,500.

Ukrainski Visti (Ukrainian News): 12227 107th Ave, Suite 1, Edmonton, AB T6B 1R2; tel. (780) 488-3693; fax (780) 488-3859; e-mail ukrnews@compusmart.ab.ca; f. 1929; fortnightly; Ukrainian and English; Publr and Editor MARCO LEVYTSKY; circ. 3,274.

British Columbia

BC Outdoors—Sport, Fishing and Outdoor Adventure: OP Publishing Ltd, 200 West Esplanade, Suite 500, North Vancouver, BC V7M 1A4; tel. (604) 998-3310; fax (604) 998-3320; e-mail subscriptions@oppublishing.com; internet www.bcosportfishing.com; f. 1945; 6 a year; Publr MARK YELIC; Editor MIKE MITCHELL; circ. 13,615.

Pacific Yachting: OP Publishing Ltd, 200 West Esplanade, Suite 500, North Vancouver, BC V7M 1A4; tel. (604) 998-3310; fax (604) 998-3320; e-mail editor@pacificyachting.com; internet www.pacificyachting.com; f. 1968; monthly; Editor DALE MILLER; circ. 14,291.

Vancouver Magazine: 2608 Granville St, Suite 560, Vancouver, BC V6H 3V3; tel. (604) 877-7732; fax (604) 877-4848; e-mail mail@vancouvermagazine.com; internet www.vanmag.com; f. 1967; 11 a year; Publr KIM PEACOCK; Editor-in-Chief GARY STEPHEN ROSS; circ. 60,000.

Western Living: 2608 Granville St, Suite 560, Vancouver, BC V6H 3V3; tel. (604) 877-7732; fax (604) 877-4838; e-mail wlmail@westernlivingmagazine.com; internet www.westernlivingmagazine.com; f. 1971; 10 a year; Editor-in-Chief ANICKA QUIN; circ. 192,350.

WestWorld BC: 4180 Lougheed Hwy, 4th Floor, Burnaby, BC V5C 6A7; tel. (604) 299-7311; fax (604) 299-9188; e-mail arose@

canadawide.com; f. 1974; quarterly; travel and sport; Publr and Pres. PETER LEGGE; Exec. Editor ANNE ROSE; circ. 540,000.

Manitoba

Canada's History: Bryce Hall, University of Winnipeg, 515 Portage Ave, Winnipeg, MB R3B 2E9; tel. (204) 988-9300; fax (204) 988-9309; e-mail editors@canadashistory.ca; internet www.canadashistory.ca; f. 1920 as *The Beaver—Canada's History Magazine*, present name adopted 2010; 6 a year; Canadian history; Publr, Pres. and CEO DEBORAH MORRISON; Editor MARK REID; circ. 37,956.

Cattlemen: 1666 Dublin Ave, Winnipeg, MB R3H 0H1; tel. and fax (204) 954-1400; fax (204) 954-1422; e-mail gren@fbcpublishing.com; internet www.canadiancattlemen.ca; f. 1938; 13 a year; animal husbandry; Editor GREN WINSLOW; circ. 14,636.

Country Guide: 1666 Dublin Ave, Winnipeg, MB R3H 0H1; tel. (204) 944-5754; fax (204) 954-1422; e-mail tbutton@twinbanks.com; internet www.country-guide.ca; f. 1882; 10 a year; agriculture; two editions: *Western Edition* and *Eastern Edition*; Publr BOB WILCOX; Editor TOM BUTTON; circ. 21,751.

Grainews: 1666 Dublin Ave, Winnipeg, MB R3H 0H1; tel. (204) 954-1400; fax (204) 944-1422; e-mail lyndsey@fbcpublishing.com; internet www.grainews.ca; f. 1975; 17 a year; grain and cattle farming; Editor LYNDSEY SMITH; circ. 20,974.

Kanada Kurier: 955 Alexander Ave, POB 1054, Winnipeg, MB R3C 2X8; tel. (204) 774-1883; fax (204) 783-5740; f. 1889; weekly; German language and culture; Publr E. ROTZETTER; Editor MARION SCHIRRMANN; circ. 7,442.

The Manitoba Co-operator: 1666 Dublin Ave, Winnipeg, MB R3H 0H1; tel. (204) 954-1400; fax (204) 954-1422; e-mail laura@fbcpublishing.com; internet www.manitobacooperator.ca; f. 1925; owned by Farm Business Communications, a subsidiary of Glacier Ventures International Corpn; weekly; for the farming community; Editor LAURA RANCE; circ. 11,877 (March 2010).

New Brunswick

Brunswick Business Journal: 175 General Manson Way, Miramichi, NB E1N 6K7; tel. (506) 622-2600; internet nbbusinessjournal.canadaeast.com; f. 1984; monthly; Man. Editor NANCY COOK.

Newfoundland and Labrador

Atlantic Business Magazine: 95 Le Marchand Rd, Suite 302, St John's, NL A1C 2H1; tel. (709) 726-9300; fax (709) 726-3013; e-mail dchafe@atlanticbusinessmagazine.com; internet www.atlanticbusinessmagazine.com; f. 1987; 6 a year; business; Publr HUBERT HUTTON; Exec. Editor DAWN CHAFE; circ. 37,000.

Northwest Territories

L'Aquilon: POB 456, Yellowknife, NT X1A 2N4; tel. (867) 873-6603; fax (867) 873-6663; e-mail direction_aquilon@mac.com; internet www.aquilon.nt.ca; f. 1986; weekly; Editor ALAIN BESSETTE; circ. 1,000.

Hay River Hub: 8–4 Courtoreille St, Hay River, NT X0E 1G2; tel. (867) 874-6577; fax (867) 874-2679; e-mail editor@hayriverhub.com; internet www.hayriverhub.com; f. 1973; weekly; Publr CHRIS BRODEUR; Editor PATRICK TESKEY; circ. 3,000.

Northern News Services: 5108 50th St, POB 2820, Yellowknife, NT X1A 2R1; tel. (867) 873-4031; fax (867) 873-8507; e-mail nnsl@nnsl.com; internet www.nnsl.com; f. 1945 as *News/North*; weekly; Publr JACK SIGVALDASON; Man. Editor BRUCE VALPY; circ. 11,000.

Slave River Journal: 207 McDougal Rd, POB 990, Fort Smith, NT X0E 0P0; tel. (867) 872-3000; fax (867) 872-2754; e-mail admin@srj.ca; internet www.srj.ca; f. 1978; weekly; Publr and Man. Editor DON JAQUE; circ. 2,750.

Yellowknifer: POB 2820, Yellowknife, NT X1A 2R1; tel. (867) 873-4031; fax (867) 873-8507; e-mail nnsl@nnsl.com; internet www.nnsl.com; weekly; Publr JACK SIGVALDASON; Man. Editor BRUCE VALPY; circ. 6,200.

Nova Scotia

Canadian Forum: 5502 Atlantic St, Halifax, NS B3H 1G4; tel. (902) 421-7022; fax (902) 425-0166; f. 1920; 10 a year; political, literary and economic; Editor ROBERT CLUDOS; circ. 9,000.

Progress: 1660 Hollis St, Penthouse, Suite 1202, Halifax, NS B3J 1V7; tel. (902) 494-0999; fax (902) 494-0997; e-mail progress@progressmedia.ca; internet progressmedia.ca; f. 1993; 8 a year; regional business; Editor PAMELA SCOTT-CRACE; circ. 22,477 (June 2010).

Nunavut Territory

Kivalliq News: Rankin Inlet, NU; tel. (867) 645-3223; fax (867) 645-3225; e-mail kivalliqnews@nnsl.com; internet www.nnsl.com; f. 1994; weekly; owned by Northern News Services; English and Inuktitut; Publr JACK SIGVALDASON; Man. Editor BRUCE VALPY; circ. 1,400.

Nunatsiaq News: POB 8, Iqaluit, NU X0A 0H0; tel. (867) 979-5357; fax (867) 979-4763; e-mail editor@nunatsiaqonline.ca; internet www.nunatsiaq.com; f. 1973; weekly; English and Inuktitut; Publr MICHAEL ROBERTS; Editor JIM BELL; circ. 8,000.

Ontario

Anglican Journal: 80 Hayden St, Toronto, ON M4Y 3G2; tel. (416) 924-9192; fax (416) 921-4452; e-mail letters@anglicanjournal.com; internet www.anglicanjournal.com; f. 1875; monthly; official publ. of the Anglican Church of Canada; Editor KRISTIN JENKINS; circ. 205,000.

Better Farming: 21400 Service Rd, Vankleek Hill, ON K0B 1R0; tel. (613) 678-2232; fax (613) 678-5993; e-mail admin@betterfarming.com; internet www.betterfarming.com; f. 1999; 10 a year; Publr PAUL NOLAN; Man. Editor ROBERT C. IRWIN; circ. 38,083 (June 2010).

CAmagazine: The Canadian Institute of Chartered Accountants, 277 Wellington St West, Toronto, ON M5V 3H2; tel. (416) 977-3222; fax (416) 204-3409; e-mail camagazineinfo@cica.ca; internet www.camagazine.com; f. 1911; 10 a year; English and French; Publr CAIRINE M. WILSON; Editor-in-Chief OKEY CHIGBO; circ. 90,413 (June 2010).

Campus Canada: 5397 Eglington Ave West, Suite 101, Toronto, ON M9C 5K6; tel. (416) 928-2909; fax (416) 928-1357; internet www.campus.ca; f. 1983; quarterly; 30 campus edns; Man. Editor CHRISTIAN PEARCE; circ. 145,000.

Canada Gazette: Canada Gazette Directorate, Public Works and Govt Services Canada, 5th Floor, 350 Albert St, Ottawa, ON K1A 0S5; tel. (613) 996-1268; fax (613) 991-3540; e-mail info.gazette@pwgsc-tpsgc.gc.ca; internet canadagazette.gc.ca; f. 1841; weekly; official newspaper of the Govt of Canada; English and French; Editor-in-Chief JOSÉE BOISVERT.

Canadian Architect: 12 Concorde Pl., Suite 800, Toronto, ON M3C 4J2; tel. (416) 510-6807; fax (416) 510-5140; e-mail editors@canadianarchitect.com; internet www.canadianarchitect.com; f. 1955; monthly; Publr TOM ARKELL; Editor IAN CHODIKOFF; circ. 14,000.

Canadian Art: 215 Spadina Ave, Suite 320, Toronto, ON M5T 2C7; tel. (416) 368-8854; fax (416) 368-6135; e-mail info@canadianart.ca; internet www.canadianart.ca; quarterly; Editor RICHARD RHODES; Man. Editor BRYNE MCLAUGHLIN; circ. 17,385.

Canadian Bar Review/Revue du Barreau canadien: Canadian Bar Foundation, 500–865 Carling Ave, Ottawa, ON K1S 5S8; tel. (613) 237-2925; fax (613) 237-0185; e-mail review@cba.org; internet www.cba.org; f. 1923; quarterly, comprising 3 online issues and 1 yearly consolidated vol.; Editor Prof. BETH BILSON; circ. 36,000.

Canadian Business: 1 Mount Pleasant Rd, 11th Floor, Toronto, ON M4Y 2Y5; tel. (416) 764-1200; fax (416) 764-1255; e-mail help@canadianbusiness.com; internet www.canadianbusiness.com; f. 1928; 18 a year; owned by Rogers Media; Publr KENNETH WHYTE; Editor and Assoc. Publr STEVE MAICH; circ. 80,536.

Canadian Chemical News: 130 Slater St, Suite 550, Ottawa, ON K1P 6E2; tel. (613) 232-6252; fax (613) 232-5862; e-mail magazine@accn.ca; internet www.accn.ca; f. 1949; 10 a year; Editor JODI DI MENNA; Chair. and Pres. JOE SCHWARCZ; circ. 6,500.

Canadian Electronics: Annex Publishing & Printing Inc, 240 Edward St, Aurora, ON L4G 3S9; tel. (905) 727-0077; fax (905) 727-0017; e-mail ce@clbmedia.ca; internet www.electronicsincanada.com; f. 1986; 7 a year; Publr KLAUS PIRKER; Editorial Dir MIKE EDWARDS; circ. 20,990 (June 2010).

Canadian Geographic: 1155 Lola St, Suite 200, Ottawa, ON K1K 4C1; tel. (613) 745-4629; fax (613) 744-0947; e-mail editorial@canadiangeographic.ca; internet www.canadiangeographic.ca; f. 1930; 6 a year; publ. of the Royal Canadian Geographical Soc; Publr ANDRÉ PRÉFONTAINE; Editor-in-Chief ERIC HARRIS; circ. 186,805.

Canadian Home Workshop: 54 St Patrick St, Toronto, ON M5T 1V1; tel. (416) 599-2000; fax (416) 599-0800; e-mail editorial@canadianhomeworkshop.com; internet www.canadianhomeworkshop.com; f. 1977; owned by Cottage Life Media Inc; 6 a year; home improvement; Editor-in-Chief and Brand Man. DOUGLAS THOMSON; Man. Editor MATTHEW PIORO; circ. 125,015.

Canadian House & Home: 511 King St West, Suite 120, Toronto, ON M5V 2Z4; tel. (416) 591-0204; fax (416) 591-1630; e-mail chheditorial@hhmedia.com; internet www.houseandhome.com; f. 1982; 12 a year; Pres. and Publr LYNDA REEVES; Editor-in-Chief SUZANNE DIMMA; circ. 244,436.

Canadian Jewish News (CJN): 1500 Don Mills Rd, Suite 205, North York, ON M3B 3K4; tel. (416) 391-1836; fax (416) 391-0829; e-mail cjninfo@gmail.com; internet www.cjnews.com; f. 1971;

weekly; Gen. Man. GARY LAFORET; Editor MORDECHAI BEN-DAT; circ. 41,000.

Canadian Living: 25 Sheppard Ave West, Suite 100, North York, ON M2N 6S7; tel. (416) 733-7600; fax (416) 733-3398; e-mail letters@canadianliving.com; internet www.canadianliving.com; f. 1975; monthly; Editor-in-Chief SUSAN ANTONACCI; circ. 505,665.

Canadian Medical Association Journal (CMAJ): 1867 Alta Vista Dr., Ottawa, ON K1G 5W8; tel. (613) 731-8610; fax (613) 565-5471; e-mail pubs@cma.ca; internet www.cmaj.ca; f. 1911; 25 a year; Editor-in-Chief Dr RAJENDRA KALE (interim); Man. Editor LEESA D. SULLIVAN; circ. 73,711 (March 2010).

Canadian Musician (CM): 23 Hannover Dr., Suite 7, St Catharines, ON L2W 1A3; tel. (905) 641-3471; fax (888) 665-1307; e-mail mail@nor.com; internet www.canadianmusician.com; f. 1979; 6 a year; Editor ANDREW KING; circ. 27,000.

Canadian Nurse/L'infirmière canadienne: 50 Driveway, Ottawa, ON K2P 1E2; tel. (613) 237-2133; fax (613) 237-3520; e-mail info@infirmiere-canadienne.com; internet www.canadian-nurse.com; f. 1905 as journal of the Canadian Nurses' Asscn; publ. in separate French and English edns since 2000; 9 a year; Editor-in-Chief LISA BRAZEAU; Editor JODY JOHNSTONE; circ. 134,000 (January 2011).

Canadian Pharmacists Journal (CPJ): 1785 Alta Vista Dr., Ottawa, ON K1G 3Y6; tel. (613) 523-7877; fax (613) 523-0445; e-mail cpj@pharmacists.ca; internet www.pharmacists.ca/content/hcp/resource_centre/cpj/cpj_contacts.cfm; f. 1868; fmrly *Canadian Pharmaceutical Journal*; 6 a year; Publr JAMES DE GASPÉ BONAR; Editor-in-Chief ROSEMARY M. KILLEEN; circ. 15,000.

Canadian Travel Press Weekly: 310 Dupont St, Toronto, ON M5R 1V9; tel. (416) 968-7252; fax (416) 968-2377; e-mail ctpeditorial@baxter.net; internet www.travelpress.com; 46 a year; Editor-in-Chief EDITH BAXTER; Exec. Editor ROBERT MOWAT; circ. 25,000.

Chatelaine: 1 Mount Pleasant Rd, 8th Floor, Toronto, ON M4Y 2Y5; tel. (416) 764-1888; fax (416) 764-2891; internet www.chatelaine.com; f. 1928; publ. by Rogers Publishing Inc; monthly; women's journal; Publr KEN WHYTE; Editor-in-Chief JANE FRANCISCO; circ. 544,413.

ComputerWorld Canada: 55 Town Centre Ct, Suite 302, Scarborough, ON M1P 4X4; tel. (416) 290-0240; fax (416) 290-0238; e-mail general@itworldcanada.com; internet www.itworldcanada.com; f. 1984; 25 a year; Editor-in-Chief SHANE SCHICK; circ. 42,000.

Fashion: 111 Queen St East, Suite 320, Toronto, ON M5C 1S2; tel. (416) 364-3333; fax (416) 594-3374; internet www.fashionmagazine.com; f. 1996 as Elm Street; ceased publication in 2004 but continued to publish quarterly fashion supplement *Elm Street The Look* until 2006 when magazine relaunched under above name; publ. by St Jospeh Media; monthly; women's interest; Editor-in-Chief CERI MARSH.

Flare: 1 Mount Pleasant Rd, 8th Floor, Toronto, ON M4Y 2Y5; tel. (416) 764-1829; fax (416) 764-2866; e-mail laura.lanktree@flare.rogers.com; internet www.teenflare.com; f. 1980; monthly; fashion, beauty and health; Publr KERRY MITCHELL; Editor-in-Chief and Assoc. Publr LISA TANT; circ. 135,489.

The Hockey News: Transcontinental Publishing, 25 Sheppard Ave West, Suite 100, North York, ON M2N 6S7; tel. (416) 340-8000; fax (416) 340-2786; e-mail editorial@thehockeynews.com; internet www.thehockeynews.com; f. 1947; 34 a year; Man. Editor JASON KAY; circ. 100,027.

Holstein Journal: 9040 Leslie St, Suite 310, Richmond Hill, ON L4B 3M4; tel. (905) 886-4222; fax (905) 886-0037; e-mail subs@holsteinjournal.com; internet www.holsteinjournal.com; f. 1938; publ. by The Holstein Journal Group, Inc; monthly; news and information pertaining to Holstein dairy cattle; Publr G. PETER ENGLISH; Editor BONNIE E. COOPER; circ. 4,223.

Journal of the Canadian Dental Association: 1815 Alta Vista Dr., Ottawa, ON K1G 3Y6; tel. (613) 523-1770; fax (613) 523-7736; e-mail jokeefe@cda-adc.ca; internet www.cda-adc.ca/jcda; f. 1935; 11 a year; Editor Dr JOHN P. O'KEEFE; circ. 20,000.

Kanadai Magyarsag (Hungarian-Canadians): 74 Advance Rd, Etobicoke, ON M8Z 2T7; tel. (416) 233-3131; fax (416) 233-5984; e-mail magyarsag@wellerpublishing.com; internet canadahun.com; weekly; Publr IRENE VOROSVARY; Editor and Man. CSABA GAAL; circ. 9,800.

Legion Magazine: 86 Aird Pl., Kanata, ON K2L 0A1; tel. (613) 591-0116; fax (613) 591-0146; e-mail editor@legionmagazine.com; internet www.legionmagazine.com; f. 1926; 6 a year; publ. for Canadian veterans and Legionnaires; Gen. Man. JENNIFER MORSE; circ. 2,323,308.

Maclean's: 1 Mount Pleasant Rd, 11th Floor, Toronto, ON M4Y 2Y5; tel. (416) 764-1300; fax (416) 764-1332; e-mail letters@macleans.ca; internet www2.macleans.ca; f. 1905 as *The Business Magazine*; present name adopted in 1911; weekly; Publr and Editor-in-Chief KENNETH WHYTE; Editor MARK STEVENSON; circ. 340,610.

The Northern Miner: 80 Valleybrook Dr., Toronto, ON M3B 2S9; tel. (416) 442-2122; fax (416) 442-2191; e-mail northernminer2@northernminer.com; internet www.northernminer.com; f. 1915; owned by the Business Information Group; weekly; Publr DOUGLAS DONNELLY; Editor JOHN CUMMING; circ. 11,000.

Now: 189 Church St, Toronto, ON M5B 1Y7; tel. (416) 364-1300; fax (416) 364-1166; e-mail web@nowtoronto.com; internet www.nowtoronto.com; f. 1981; weekly; young adult; Publr and Editor MICHAEL HOLLETT; CEO and Editor ALICE KLEIN; circ. 115,911.

Ontario Medical Review (OMA): 150 Bloor St West, Suite 900, Toronto, ON M5S 3C1; tel. (416) 599-2580; fax (416) 340-2944; e-mail info@oma.org; internet www.oma.org; f. 1922; monthly; publ. of the Ontario Medical Asscn; Editor JEFF HENRY; Man. Editor ELIZABETH PETRUCELLI; circ. 29,000.

Oral Health: 12 Concorde Pl., Suite 800, Toronto, ON M3C 4J2; tel. (416) 510-6785; fax (416) 510-5140; e-mail cwilson@oralhealthjournal.com; internet www.oralhealthjournal.com; f. 1911; monthly; dentistry; Sr Publr MELISSA SUMMERFIELD; Editorial Dir CATHERINE WILSON; circ. 21,000 (2010).

Quill & Quire: POB 819, Markham, ON L3P 8A2; tel. (416) 364-3333; fax (416) 595-5415; e-mail swoods@quillandquire.com; internet www.quillandquire.com; f. 1935; 10 a year; book publishing industry; Publr ALISON JONES; Editor STUART WOODS; circ. 5,000.

Style: 1106–60 Bloor St West, Toronto, ON M4W 3B8; tel. (416) 203-7900; fax (416) 703-6392; e-mail bryan@rivegauchemedia.com; internet www.style.ca; f. 1888; monthly; fashion and clothing trade; owned by Rive Gauche Media; Pres. OLIVIER FELICIO; Editor BRYAN SOROKA; circ. 12,000.

Style at Home: Transcontinental Media Inc, 25 Sheppard Ave West, Suite 100, Toronto, ON M2N 6S7; tel. (416) 733-7600; fax (416) 218-3632; e-mail letters@styleathome.com; internet www.styleathome.com; f. 1997; 12 a year; owned by Transcontinental Media Inc; Editor ERIN MCLAUGHLIN; circ. 230,002.

Toronto Life Magazine: 111 Queen St East, Suite 320, Toronto, ON M5C 1S2; tel. (416) 364-3333; fax (416) 861-1169; e-mail editorial@torontolife.com; internet www.torontolife.com; f. 1966; monthly; Publr SHARON MCAULEY; Editor SARAH FULFORD; circ. 95,000.

Tribute Magazine: 71 Barber Greene Rd, Don Mills, Toronto, ON M3C 2A2; tel. (416) 445-0544; fax (416) 445-2894; e-mail generalinfo@tribute.ca; internet www.tribute.ca; f. 1981; 9 a year; entertainment; Editor-in-Chief SANDRA I. STEWART; circ. 500,000.

TV Guide: POB 815, Markham Station, Markham ON L3P 7Z7; tel. (416) 733-7600; fax (416) 733-3632; e-mail tvguide@indas.on.ca; internet www.tvguide.ca; f. 1976; weekly; Publr CAROLINE ANDREWS; Editor AMBER DOWLING; circ. 243,695.

Québec

L'Actualité: 1200 ave McGill College, bureau 800, Montréal, QC H3B 4G7; tel. (514) 843-2564; fax (514) 843-2186; e-mail redaction@lactualite.rogers.com; internet www.lactualite.com; f. 1976; monthly; current affairs; Publr and Editor-in-Chief CAROLE BEAULIEU; circ. 163,572.

Affaires Plus: 1100 blvd René-Lévesque ouest, 24e étage, Montréal, QC H3B 4X9; tel. (514) 392-9000; fax (514) 392-4726; e-mail aplus@transcontinental.ca; internet www.affairesplus.com; f. 1978; monthly; Editor-in-Chief DANIEL GERMAIN; circ. 76,274 (June 2010).

Le Bulletin des Agriculteurs: 1 Place du Commerce, Suite 320, Nuns' Island, QC H3E 1A2; tel. (514) 766-9554; fax (514) 766-2665; e-mail info@lebulletin.rogers.com; internet www.lebulletin.com; f. 1918; monthly; Editor-in-Chief YVON THÉRIEN; circ. 12,270 (June 2010).

Châtelaine: 1200 ave McGill College, bureau 800, Montréal, QC H3B 4G7; tel. (514) 845-5141; fax (514) 843-2185; e-mail redaction@chatelaine.rogers.com; internet fr.chatelaine.com; f. 1960; monthly; Publr KENNETH WHYTE; Dir and Gen. Man. KAT PETERSON; circ. 544,413.

CIM Magazine: 3500 blvd de Maisonneuve ouest, bureau 1250, Montréal, QC H3Z 3C1; tel. (514) 939-2710; fax (514) 939-2714; e-mail cim@cim.org; internet www.cim.org; 8 a year; fmrly *CIM Bulletin*; publ. by the Canadian Inst. of Mining, Metallurgy and Petroleum; Editor-in-Chief ANGELA HAMLYN; circ. 10,460.

Il Cittadino Canadese: 5960 Jean-Talon est, bureau 209, Montréal, QC H1S 1M2; tel. (514) 253-2332; fax (514) 253-6574; e-mail journal@cittadinocanadese.com; internet www.cittadinocanadese.com; f. 1941; weekly; Italian; Publr and Editor BASILIO GIORDANO; circ. 38,500.

Commerce: 1100 blvd René-Lévesque ouest, 24e étage, Montréal, QC H3B 4X9; tel. (514) 392-9000; fax (514) 392-1489; e-mail commerce@transcontinental.ca; f. 1898; monthly; Editor-in-Chief DIANE BÉRARD; circ. 40,135.

Harrowsmith Country Life: 3100 blvd Concorde est, Suite 213, Laval, QC H7E 2B8; tel. (450) 665-0271; fax (450) 665-2974; e-mail info@harrowsmithcountrylife.ca; internet www.harrowsmithcountrylife.ca; f. 1976; 6 a year; Editor TOM CRUICKSHANK; circ. 126,862.

Le Lundi: 7 chemin Bates, Outrement, QC H2V 1A6; tel. (514) 270-1100; fax (514) 270-5395; f. 1976; weekly; Editor MICHAEL CHOINIÈRE; circ. 25,037.

Photo Life: 185 St Paul St, Québec City, QC G1K 3W2; tel. (800) 905-7468; fax (800) 664-2739; e-mail editor@photolife.com; internet www.photolife.com; f. 1976; 6 a year; Editorial Dir VALÉRIE RACINE; circ. 55,000.

Le Producteur de Lait Québecois: 555 blvd Roland-Therrien, Longueuil, QC J4H 4G3; tel. (450) 679-8483; fax (450) 670-4788; e-mail fplq@upa.qc.ca; internet www.lait.org/zone3/producteur/index.asp; f. 1980; 10 a year; dairy farming; publ. by Fédération des producteurs de lait du Québec; Publr LOIC HAMON; Editor-in-Chief JEAN VIGNEAULT; circ. 12,000.

Québec Science: 1251 rue Rachel est, Montréal, QC H2J 2J9; tel. (514) 843-8356; fax (514) 843-4897; e-mail courrier@quebecscience.qc.ca; internet www.quebecscience.qc.ca; f. 1969; 10 a year; Editor-in-Chief RAYMOND LEMIEUX; circ. 32,000.

Le Quotidien: Saguenay, QC G7H 5C1; tel. (418) 545-4474; fax (418) 690-8805; e-mail msimard@lequotidien.com; internet www.cyberpresse.ca/le-quotidien; f. 1964; weekly; also publishes *Le Progrès Dimanche*; Pres. and Editor MICHEL SIMARD; circ. 132,800 (2009).

Reader's Digest: 1100 blvd René-Lévesque ouest, Montréal, QC H3B 5H5; tel. (514) 934-0751; fax (514) 940-3637; internet www.readersdigest.ca; f. 1947; monthly; English edn; Pres. and CEO TONY CIOFFI; Editor-in-Chief ROBERT GOYETTE; circ. 597,229.

Rénovation Bricolage: 7 chemin Bates, Outremont, QC H2V 4V7; fax (514) 848-0309; e-mail renobrico@tva-publications.com; internet tva.canoe.ca/groupetva/filiales/tva_publications.html; f. 1976; 9 a year; Publr and Editor CLAUDE LECLERC; Editor-in-Chief VINCENT ROY; circ. 31,489.

Sélection du Reader's Digest: 1100 blvd René-Lévesque ouest, Montréal, QC H3B 5H5; tel. (514) 940-0751; fax (514) 940-7340; e-mail manon.sylvain@readersdigest.com; internet www.selection.ca; f. 1947; monthly; Pres. and CEO TONY CIOFFI; Editor-in-Chief ROBERT GOYETTE; circ. 249,843.

La Terre de Chez Nous: 555 blvd Roland-Therrien, Longueuil, QC J4H 3Y9; tel. (450) 679-8483; fax (450) 670-4788; e-mail laterre@laterre.ca; internet www.laterre.ca; f. 1929; weekly; agriculture and forestry; Editor-in-Chief RICHELLE FORTIN; circ. 35,576.

TV Hebdo: 7 chemin Bates, Outremont, QC H2V 4V7; tel. (514) 848-7000; fax (514) 848-7070; e-mail tvhebdo@tvapublications.com.com; internet www.tvhebdo.com; f. 1960; weekly; Editor-in-Chief JEAN-LOUIS PODLESAK; circ. 81,007.

Saskatchewan

Farm Light & Power: 2230 15th Ave, Regina, SK S4P 1A2; tel. (306) 525-3305; fax (306) 757-1810; f. 1959; monthly; Editor TOM BRADLEY; circ. 71,000.

Western Producer: 2310 Millar Ave, POB 2500, Saskatoon, SK S7K 2C4; tel. (306) 665-3544; fax (306) 934-2401; e-mail newsroom@producer.com; internet www.producer.com; f. 1923; weekly; agriculture; Editor JOANNE PAULSON; circ. 74,000.

Yukon Territory

Yukon News: 211 Wood St, Whitehorse, YT Y1A 2E4; tel. (867) 667-6285; fax (867) 668-3755; e-mail rmostyn@yukon-news.com; internet www.yukon-news.com; f. 1960; 3 a week; Editor RICHARD MOSTYN; circ. 8,000.

NEWS AGENCY

The Canadian Press: 36 King St East, Toronto, ON M5C 2L9; tel. (416) 364-0321; fax (416) 364-0207; internet www.cp.org; f. 1917; national news co-operative; 99 newspaper mems; Editor-in-Chief SCOTT WHITE.

PRESS ASSOCIATIONS

Canadian Business Press (CBP): 2100 Banbury Cres., Oakville, ON L6H 5P6; tel. (416) 239-1022; fax (416) 239-1076; e-mail admin@cbp.ca; internet www.cbp.ca; f. 1920; Chair. JOHN KERR; Exec. Dir KAREN DALTON; over 170 mems.

Canadian Community Newspapers Association (CCNA): 890 Yonge St, Suite 200, Toronto, ON M4W 3P4; tel. (416) 482-1090; fax (416) 482-1908; e-mail info@ccna.ca; internet www.newspaperscanada.ca; f. 1919; in Jan. 2011 est. Newspapers Canada, a jt initiative with the Canadian Newspaper Asscn, to represent interests of all newspaper members; Chair. MIKE WILLISCRAFT; Pres. PAUL MACNEILL; 7 regional asscns; more than 700 mems.

Canadian Newspaper Association (CNA): 890 Yonge St, Suite 200, Toronto, ON M4W 3P4; tel. (416) 923-3567; fax (416) 923-7206; e-mail info@cna-acj.ca; internet www.newspaperscanada.ca; f. 1996; in Jan. 2011 est. Newspapers Canada, a jt initiative with the Canadian Community Newspapers Asscn, to represent interests of all newspaper members; Chair. PETER KVARNSTROM; Pres. and CEO JOHN HINDS.

Magazines Canada (The Magazine Asscn of Canada): 425 Adelaide St West, Suite 700, Toronto, ON M5V 3C1; tel. (416) 504-0274; fax (416) 504-0437; internet www.magazinescanada.ca; f. 1973 as the Canadian Magazine Publrs Asscn; present name adopted 2005; represents over 370 of the country's consumer titles; CEO MARK JAMISON; Gen. Man. and Publr BARBARA ZATYKO.

Publishers

Thomas Allen and Son Ltd: 390 Steelcase Rd East, Markham, ON L3R 1G2; tel. (905) 475-9126; fax (905) 475-4255; e-mail info@t-allen.com; internet www.thomasallen.ca; f. 1916; Pres. and CEO JIM ALLEN.

Annick Press Ltd: 15 Patricia Ave, Toronto, ON M2M 1H9; tel. (416) 221-4802; fax (416) 221-8400; e-mail annickpress@annickpress.com; internet www.annickpress.com; f. 1975; children's; Dir RICK WILKS.

Arsenal Pulp Press Book Publishers Ltd: 211 East Georgia St, Suite 101, Vancouver, BC V6A 1Z6; tel. (604) 687-4233; fax (604) 687-4283; e-mail info@arsenalpulp.com; internet www.arsenalpulp.com; f. 1982; literary fiction and non-fiction, cultural studies, gay and lesbian; Publr BRIAN LAM.

Editions Bellarmin: 7333, pl. des Roseraies, Suite 100, Anjou, QC H1M 2X6; tel. (514) 745-4290; fax (514) 745-4299; e-mail editions@fides.qc.ca; internet www.fides.qc.ca; f. 1891; religious, educational, politics, sociology, ethnography, history, sport, leisure; Dir-Gen. STÉPHANE LAVOIE.

Black Rose Books: CP 1258, succursale pl. du Parc, Montréal, QC H2W 2R3; tel. (514) 844-4076; e-mail info@blackrosebooks.net; internet www.blackrosebooks.net; f. 1969; politics, social studies, humanities; Pres. JACQUES ROUX.

Borealis Press Ltd: 8 Mohawk Cres., Nepean, ON K2H 7G6; tel. (613) 829-0150; fax (613) 829-7783; e-mail drt@borealispress.com; internet www.borealispress.com; f. 1972; Canadian fiction and non-fiction, drama, juvenile, poetry; Pres. FRANK TIERNEY.

Breakwater Books: 100 Water St, POB 2188, St John's, NL A1C 6E6; tel. (709) 722-6680; fax (709) 753-0708; e-mail info@breakwaterbooks.com; internet www.breakwaterbooks.com; f. 1973; fiction, non-fiction, children's, educational, folklore; Pres. REBECCA ROSE.

Broadview Press: 280 Perry St, Unit 5, POB 1243, Peterborough, ON K9J 7H5; tel. (705) 743-8990; fax (705) 743-8353; e-mail customerservice@broadviewpress.com; internet www.broadviewpress.com; f. 1985; English studies and philosophy; Pres. and CEO DON LEPAN.

Canada Law Book: 1 Corporate Plaza, 2075 Kennedy Rd, Toronto, ON M1T 3V4; tel. (416) 609-3800; fax (416) 298-5085; e-mail najat@canadalawbook.ca; internet www.canadalawbook.ca; f. 1855; law reports, law journals, legal textbooks, online legal research services, etc.; Pres. (vacant).

Les Editions CEC, Inc: 9001 blvd Louis-H. La Fontaine, Anjou, Montreal, QC H1J 2C5; tel. (514) 351-6010; fax (514) 351-3534; e-mail infoped@ceceditions.com; internet www.editionscec.com; f. 1956; textbooks; Pres. and Dir-Gen. CHRISTIAN JETTÉ.

Chenelière Education: 5800 rue Saint-Denis, bureau 900, Montréal, QC H2S 3L5; tel. (514) 273-1066; fax (514) 276-0324; e-mail jrochefort@cheneliere.ca; internet www.cheneliere.ca; textbooks; Pres. JACQUES ROCHEFORT.

Coach House Books: 80 bpNichol Lane, behind 401 Huron St, Toronto, ON M5S 3J4; tel. (416) 979-2217; fax (416) 977-1158; e-mail mail@chbooks.com; internet www.chbooks.com; f. 1965; fiction, poetry, drama; Publr STAN BEVINGTON; Editor-in-Chief ALANA WILCOX.

Crabtree Publishing Co, Ltd: 616 Welland Ave, St Catharines, ON L2M 5V6; tel. (905) 682-5221; fax (905) 682-7166; e-mail custserv@crabtreebooks.com; internet www.crabtreebooks.com; f. 1978; children's non-fiction; Pres. PETER A. CRABTREE; Gen. Man. JOHN SIEMENS.

D&M Publishers Inc: 2323 Québec St, Suite 201, Vancouver, BC V5T 4S7; tel. (604) 254-7191; fax (604) 254-9099; e-mail dm@dmpibooks.com; internet www.dmpibooks.com; f. 1964 as Douglas & McIntyre Publrs; imprints incl. Greystone Books, New Society

Publrs; general non-fiction, literary fiction; Publr SCOTT MCINTYRE; Pres. MARK SCOTT.

The Dundurn Group: 3 Church St, Suite 500, Toronto, ON M5E 1M2; tel. (416) 214-5544; fax (416) 214-5556; e-mail info@dundurn.com; internet www.dundurn.com; f. 1972; drama and performing arts, history, reference, fiction and non-fiction; Pres. KIRK HOWARD.

Fenn Publishing Co Ltd: 34 Nixon Rd, Bolton, ON L7E 1W2; internet www.hbfenn.com; fiction and non-fiction; Pres. HAROLD FENN; Publr C. JORDAN FENN.

Editions Fides: 7333 pl. des Roseraies, Suite 100, Anjou, QC H1M 2X6; tel. (514) 745-4290; fax (514) 745-4299; e-mail editions@fides.qc.ca; internet www.fides.qc.ca; f. 1937; juvenile, history, theology, textbooks and literature; Dir-Gen. STÉPHANE LAVOIE.

Fifth House Publishers Ltd: 195 Allstate Pkwy, Markham, ON L3R 4T8; e-mail stewart@fifthhousepublishers.ca; internet www.fifthhousepublishers.ca; f. 1982; imprint of Fitzhenry & Whiteside Ltd; native, literary and non-fiction; Publr STEPHANIE STEWART.

Fitzhenry & Whiteside Ltd: 195 Allstate Pkwy, Markham, ON L3R 4T8; tel. (905) 477-9700; fax (905) 477-2834; e-mail godwit@fitzhenry.ca; internet www.fitzhenry.ca; f. 1966; children's fiction and non-fiction, textbooks, trade, educational, poetry; Pres. SHARON FITZHENRY.

Harlequin Enterprises Ltd: 225 Duncan Mill Rd, Don Mills, ON M3B 3K9; tel. (416) 445-5860; fax (416) 445-8655; e-mail CustomerService@Harlequin.com; internet www.eharlequin.com; f. 1949; fiction, paperbacks; imprints: Silhouette, MIRA Books, Red Dress Ink, LUNA Books, HQN Books, Steeple Hill Books, Steeple Hill Café, Kimani Press, Spice and Harlequin Ginger Blossom; Chair. and CEO DONNA M. HAYES.

HarperCollins Canada Ltd: 1995 Markham Rd, Scarborough, ON M1B 5M8; tel. (416) 321-2241; fax (416) 321-3033; internet www.harpercollins.ca; f. 1989; trade, bibles, dictionaries, juvenile, paperbacks; Pres. and CEO DAVID KENT.

Editions de l'Hexagone: 1010 rue de la Gauchetière est, Montréal, QC H2L 2N5; tel. (514) 523-7993; fax (514) 282-7530; e-mail adpcommandes@messageries-adp.com; internet www.edhexagone.com; f. 1953; part of Quebecor Media Inc; literature; Editor MARTIN BALTHAZAR.

Institut de Recherches Psychologiques, Inc/Institute of Psychological Research, Inc: 1304 rue Fleury Est, Montréal, QC H2C 1R3; tel. (514) 382-3000; fax (514) 382-3007; e-mail pierre@irpcanada.com; internet www.irpcanada.com; f. 1964; educational and psychological; Dir PAUL-JULIEN GROLEAU.

Key Porter Books: 6 Adelaide St East, 10th Floor, Toronto, ON M5C 1H6; tel. (416) 862-7777; fax (416) 862-2304; e-mail rob.howard@keyporter.com; internet www.keyporter.com; f. 1979; majority owned by H. B. Fenn and Co Ltd; general trade; Publr and Vice-Pres. JORDAN FENN.

Leméac Editeur: 4609 rue d'Iberville, 1e étage, Montréal, QC H2H 2L9; tel. (514) 525-5558; fax (514) 524-3145; e-mail lemeac@lemeac.com; internet www.lemeac.com; f. 1957; literary, academic, theatre, general; Gen. Dir LISE P. BERGEVIN.

Lidec Inc: 4350 ave de l'Hôtel-de-Ville, Montréal, QC H2W 2H5; tel. (514) 843-5991; fax (514) 843-5252; e-mail lidec@lidec.qc.ca; internet www.lidec.qc.ca; f. 1965; educational, textbooks; Pres. MARC-AIMÉ GUÉRIN.

Formac Publishing Ltd: 5502 Atlantic St, Halifax, NS B3H 1G4; tel. (902) 421-7022; fax (902) 425-0166; e-mail jlorimer@formac.ca; internet www.formac.ca; f. 1971; urban and labour studies, maritime studies, children's, general non-fiction; Publr JAMES LORIMER.

McClelland and Stewart Ltd: 75 Sherbourne St, 5th Floor, Toronto, ON M5A 2P9; tel. (416) 598-1114; fax (416) 598-7764; e-mail editorial@mcclelland.com; internet www.mcclelland.com; f. 1906; trade and illustrated; Pres. and Publr DOUG PEPPER; Chair. AVIE J. BENNETT.

McGill-Queen's University Press: 1010 Sherbrooke St West, Suite 1720, Montréal, QC H3A 2R7; tel. (514) 398-3750; fax (514) 398-4333; e-mail mqup@mcgill.ca; internet mqup.mcgill.ca; f. 1960; scholarly and general interest; Exec. Dir PHILIP J. CERCONE.

McGraw-Hill Ryerson Ltd: 300 Water St, Whitby, ON L1N 9B6; tel. (905) 430-5000; fax (905) 430-5191; internet www.mcgrawhill.ca; f. 1944; general; three divisions: educational publishing, higher education and professional publishing; Exec. Vice-Pres. GORDON DYER.

Nelson Education: 1120 Birchmount Rd, Scarborough, ON M1K 5G4; tel. (416) 752-9448; fax (416) 752-8101; e-mail inquire@nelson.com; internet www.nelson.com; f. 1914; owned by OMERS Capital Partners; retailing, consumer affairs, textbooks; Pres. GREG NORDAL.

Editions du Noroît: 4609 rue d'Iberville, Suite 202, Montréal, QC H2H 2L9; tel. (514) 727-0005; fax (514) 723-6660; e-mail lenoroit@lenoroit.com; internet www.lenoroit.com; f. 1971; poetry; Dir PAUL BÉLANGER.

Oberon Press: 145 Spruce St, Suite 205, Ottawa, ON K1R 6P1; tel. and fax (613) 238-3275; e-mail oberon@sympatico.ca; internet www.oberonpress.ca; f. 1966; poetry, fiction and general non-fiction; Pres. MICHAEL MACKLEM.

Oxford University Press Canada: 8 Sampson Mews, Suite 204, Don Mills, ON M3C 0H5; tel. (416) 441-2941; fax (416) 444-0427; e-mail customer.service.ca@oup.com; internet www.oupcanada.com; f. 1904; general, education, scholarly, Canadiana; Pres. DAVID STOVER.

Pearson Canada Assessment: 55 Horner Ave, Toronto, ON M8Z 4X6; tel. (866) 335-8418; fax (416) 644-2166; e-mail cs.canada@pearson.com; internet pearsonassess.ca; f. 1922; medical, educational, scholarly; Pres. and Publr AURELIO PRIFITERA; Gen. Man. SCOTT PAWSON.

Pearson Education Canada, Inc: 26 Prince Andrew Pl., Toronto, ON M3C 2T8; tel. (416) 447-5101; fax (416) 443-0948; e-mail webinfo.pubcanada@pearsoned.com; internet www.pearsoned.ca; educational; Pres. ALLAN REYNOLDS.

Penguin Group (Canada): 90 Eglinton Ave East, Suite 700, Toronto, ON M4P 2Y3; tel. (416) 925-2249; fax (416) 925-0068; e-mail info@penguin.ca; internet www.penguin.ca; f. 1974; division of Pearson; Pres. MIKE BRYAN; Chair. J. ROBERT PRICHARD.

Pippin Publishing Corpn: POB 242, Don Mills, ON M3C 2S2; tel. (416) 510-2918; fax (416) 510-3359; e-mail cynthia@pippinpub.com; internet www.pippinpub.com; f. 1995; educational and trade; Pres. JONATHAN LOVAT DICKSON.

Pontifical Institute of Mediaeval Studies: 59 Queen's Park Cres. East, Toronto, ON M5S 2C4; tel. (416) 926-7142; fax (416) 926-7292; e-mail barbara.north@utoronto.ca; internet www.pims.ca; f. 1939; scholarly publs concerning the Middle Ages; Pres. RICHARD ALWAY.

Prentice Hall Canada Inc: 1870 Birchmount Rd, Scarborough, ON M1P 2J7; tel. (416) 293-3621; fax (416) 299-2529; internet www.pearsonhighered.com; f. 1960; imprint of Pearson; trade, textbooks; Pres. BRIAN HEER.

Les Presses de l'Université Laval: Pavillon Maurice-Pollack, bureau 3103, 2305 rue de l'Université, Québec, QC G1V 0A6; tel. (418) 656-2803; fax (418) 656-3305; e-mail presses@pul.ulaval.ca; internet www.pulaval.com; f. 1950; scholarly; Gen. Man. DENIS DION.

Les Presses de l'Université de Montréal: 306 rue Saint-Zotique est, Montréal, QC H2S 1L6; tel. (514) 343-6933; fax (514) 343-2232; e-mail pum@umontreal.ca; internet www.pum.umontreal.ca; f. 1962; scholarly and general; CEO ANTOINE DEL BUSSO.

Les Presses de l'Université du Québec: Edif. le Delta I, 2875 blvd Laurier, Suite 450, Québec, QC G1V 2M2; tel. (418) 657-4399; fax (418) 657-2096; e-mail puq@puq.ca; internet www.puq.ca; f. 1969; scholarly and general; Dir-Gen. CÉLINE FOURNIER.

Random House of Canada Ltd: 1 Toronto St, Unit 300, Toronto, ON M5C 2V6; tel. (416) 364-4449; fax (416) 364-6863; internet www.randomhouse.ca; f. 1944; Chair. MARKUS DOHLE; Pres. and CEO BRAD MARTIN.

Editions du Renouveau Pédagogique, Inc: 5757 rue Cypihot, St-Laurent, QC H4S 1R3; tel. (514) 334-2690; fax (514) 334-4720; e-mail normand.cleroux@erpi.com; internet www.erpi.com; f. 1965; textbooks; Pres. NORMAND CLÉROUX.

Scholastic Canada Ltd: 175 Hillmont Rd, Markham, ON L6C 1Z7; tel. (905) 887-7323; fax (905) 472-7319; e-mail custserv@scholastic.ca; internet www.scholastic.ca; f. 1957; wholly owned subsidiary of Scholastic, Inc; imprints include North Winds Press, Éditions Scholastic; Co-Pres LINDA GOSNELL, IOLE LUCCHESE.

Sélection du Reader's Digest (Canada) Ltée/The Reader's Digest Association (Canada) Ltd: 1125 Stanley St, Montréal, QC H3B 5H5; tel. (514) 940-0751; fax (514) 940-3637; e-mail customer.service@readersdigest.com; internet www.rd.ca; Pres. and CEO TONI CIOFFI.

Editions du Septentrion: 1300 ave Maguire, Sillery, QC G1T 1Z3; tel. (418) 688-3556; fax (418) 527-4978; e-mail sept@septentrion.qc.ca; internet www.septentrion.qc.ca; f. 1988; history, essays, general; CEO GILLES HERMAN.

Simon & Schuster Canada: 166 King St East, Suite 300, Toronto, ON M5A 1J3; tel. (905) 427-8882; fax (905) 430-9446; e-mail info@simonandschuster.ca; internet www.simonandschuster.com; Pres. KEVIN HANSON.

Thistledown Press Ltd: 633 Main St, Saskatoon, SK S7H 0J8; tel. (306) 244-1722; fax (306) 244-1762; e-mail editorial@thistledownpress.com; internet www.thistledownpress.com; f. 1975; Canadian fiction, non-fiction and poetry; Publr ALLAN FORRIE.

Thompson Educational Publishing Inc: 20 Ripley Ave, Toronto, ON M6S 3N9; tel. (416) 766-2763; fax (416) 766-0398; e-mail info@thompsonbooks.com; internet thompsonbooks.com; f. 1989; textbooks; Pres. KEITH THOMPSON.

Thomson Carswell: 1 Corporate Plaza, 2075 Kennedy Rd, Toronto, ON M1T 3V4; tel. (416) 609-8000; fax (416) 298-5094; e-mail jayne

.jackson@thomsonreuters.com; internet www.carswell.com; f. 1864; fmrly Carswell-Thomson Professional Publishing Canada; legal, financial, business; Pres. and CEO DON VAN MEER.

Turnstone Press Ltd: 100 Arthur St, Suite 206, Winnipeg, MB R3B 1H3; tel. (204) 947-1555; fax (204) 942-1555; internet www.turnstonepress.com; f. 1976; literary and regional; Assoc. Publr JAMIS PAULSON.

University of Alberta Press (UAP): Ring House 2, Edmonton, AB T6G 2E1; tel. (780) 492-3662; fax (780) 492-0719; e-mail linda.cameron@ualberta.ca; internet www.uap.ualberta.ca; f. 1969; scholarly, general non-fiction; Dir LINDA D. CAMERON.

University of British Columbia Press (UBC Press): 2029 West Mall, Vancouver, BC V6T 1Z2; tel. (604) 822-5959; fax (604) 822-6083; e-mail info@ubcpress.ca; internet www.ubcpress.ca; f. 1971; law, politics, history, environmental studies, anthropology, Canadian studies, sociology, military history; Dir R. PETER MILROY.

University of Calgary Press: 2500 University Dr., NW, Calgary, AB T2N 1N4; tel. (403) 220-7578; fax (403) 282-0085; e-mail ucpress@ucalgary.ca; internet www.uofcpress.com; f. 1981; Dir DONNA LIVINGSTONE.

University of Manitoba Press: 301 St John's College, University of Manitoba, Winnipeg, MB R3T 2M5; tel. (204) 474-9495; fax (204) 474-7566; e-mail carr@cc.umanitoba.ca; internet uofmpress.ca; f. 1967; native, Arctic and Canadian history; Icelandic and Canadian literature; Dir DAVID CARR; Man. Editor GLENN BERGEN.

University of Ottawa Press/Les Presses de l'Université d'Ottawa: 542 King Edward Ave, Ottawa, ON K1N 6N5; tel. (613) 562-5246; fax (613) 562-5247; e-mail puo-uop@uottawa.ca; internet www.press.uottawa.ca; f. 1936; university texts, scholarly and literary works in English and French; Man. Editor MARIE CLAUSÉN.

University of Toronto Press Inc: 10 St Mary St, Suite 700, Toronto, ON M4Y 2W8; tel. (416) 978-2239; fax (416) 978-4738; e-mail publishing@utpress.utoronto.ca; internet www.utppublishing.com; f. 1901; scholarly books and journals; Pres., Publr and CEO JOHN YATES.

John Wiley and Sons Canada Ltd: 6045 blvd Freemont, Mississauga, ON L5R 4J3; tel. (416) 236-4433; fax (416) 236-8743; e-mail canada@wiley.com; internet ca.wiley.com; f. 1968; general and trade; CEO STEPHEN SMITH.

Wilfrid Laurier University Press: Wilfrid Laurier University, 75 University Ave West, Waterloo, ON N2L 3C5; tel. (519) 884-0710; fax (519) 725-1399; e-mail press@wlu.ca; internet www.wlupress.wlu.ca; f. 1974; academic and scholarly; Dir BRIAN HENDERSON.

GOVERNMENT PUBLISHING HOUSE

Government of Canada Publications: 350 Albert St, 5th Floor, Ottawa, ON K1A 0S5; tel. (613) 941-5995; fax (613) 954-5779; e-mail publications@pwgsc.gc.ca; internet publications.gc.ca; f. 1876; books and periodicals on numerous subjects, incl. agriculture, economics, environment, geology, history and sociology; Dir CHRISTINE LEDUC.

ORGANIZATIONS AND ASSOCIATIONS

Association of Canadian Publishers (ACP): 174 Spadina Ave, Suite 306, Toronto, ON M5T 2C2; tel. (416) 487-6116; fax (416) 487-8815; e-mail admin@canbook.org; internet www.publishers.ca; f. 1976; trade assen of Canadian-owned English-language book publrs; represents Canadian publishing internationally; 125 mems; Exec. Dir CAROLYN WOOD.

Association of Canadian University Presses/Association des Presses Universitaires Canadiennes: 10 St Mary St, Suite 700, Toronto, ON M4Y 2W8; tel. (416) 978-2239; fax (416) 978-4738; e-mail clarose@utpress.utoronto.ca; internet www.acup.ca; f. 1965; Pres. MELISSA PITTS.

Canadian Copyright Institute: 192 Spadina Ave, Suite 107, Toronto, ON M5T 2C2; tel. (416) 975-1756; fax (416) 975-1839; e-mail info@thecci.ca; internet www.canadiancopyrightinstitute.ca; 83 mems; Admin. ANNE MCCLELLAND.

Canadian Publishers' Council: 250 Merton St, Suite 203, Toronto, ON M4S 1B1; tel. (416) 322-7011; fax (416) 322-6999; e-mail jhushion@pubcouncil.ca; internet www.pubcouncil.ca; f. 1910; trade assen of Canadian-owned publrs and Canadian-incorp. subsidiaries of British and US publrs; 24 mems; Pres. DAVID SWAIL.

Broadcasting and Communications

The 1968 Broadcasting Act established the Canadian Broadcasting Corporation (CBC) as the national, publicly owned, broadcasting service and created the Canadian Radio-Television and Telecommunications Commission (CRTC) as the agency regulating radio, television and cable television. The CRTC was constituted as an independent public body under the 1985 Canadian Radio-Television and Telecommunications Act. The CRTC derives its regulatory authority over broadcasting from the 1991 Broadcasting Act, and over telecommunications from the 1987 Bell Canada Act and the 1993 Telecommunications Act, and their subsequent amendments.

Canadian Radio-Television and Telecommunications Commission (CRTC): Ottawa, ON K1A 0N2; tel. (819) 997-0313; fax (819) 994-0218; internet www.crtc.gc.ca; f. 1968; offices in Dartmouth, Edmonton, Montréal, Toronto, Regina, Vancouver and Winnipeg; regulates c. 2,000 radio, television and cable broadcasters, telecommunications carriers and telephone companies; Chair. KONRAD VON FINCKENSTEIN; Vice-Chair. (Broadcasting) TOM PENTEFOUNTAS; Vice-Chair. (Telecommunications) LEONARD KATZ; Sec.-Gen. JOHN TRAVERSY.

TELECOMMUNICATIONS

Principal Telecommunications Networks

Bell Aliant: 6 South, Maritime Centre, 1505 Barrington St, Halifax, NS B3J 2W3; tel. (902) 487-4609; fax (902) 425-0708; e-mail brenda.reid@aliant.ca; internet bell.aliant.ca; f. 2006 by merger of Aliant and Bell operations; part owned by Bell Canada and BCE; operates as Aliant in Atlantic Canada and as Bell in central Canada; world-wide communications and information technology solutions; Chair. GEORGE COPE; Pres. and CEO KAREN H. SHERIFF.

Bell Canada Enterprises Inc (BCE): 1 carrefour Alexander Graham Bell, Edif. A, 4e étage, Verdun, QC H3E 3B3; tel. (888) 932-6666; fax (514) 766-5735; e-mail bcecomms@bce.ca; internet www.bce.ca; f. 1880; provides fixed-line and mobile telecommunications, satellite and internet services; Chair. THOMAS C. O'NEILL; Pres. and CEO GEORGE COPE.

Bell Canada: POB 8716, Station A, Montréal, QC H3C 4R5; e-mail bell.direct@bell.ca; internet www.bell.ca; 80% owned by BCE; holds a monopoly in most of Québec and Ontario; CEO GEORGE COPE.

Bell Mobility: 4 Eglinton Sq., Scarborough, ON M1L 2K1; tel. (416) 755-7157; e-mail mobility@bell.ca; internet www.bellmobility.ca; mobile telecommunications; Pres. WADE OOSTERMAN.

Manitoba Telecom Services Inc (MTS): 333 Main St, POB 6666, Winnipeg, MB R3C 3V6; tel. (204) 225-5687; fax (204) 949-1244; e-mail media.relations@mtsallstream.com; internet www.mts.ca; full-service (wireline voice, data, wireless and television services) telecommunications co for Manitoba; national broadband fibre optic network of 24,300 km; Allstream (National) Division serves business customers nation-wide; Chair. DAVID LEITH; CEO PIERRE BLOUIN.

Northwestel Inc: 301 Lambert St, POB 2727, Whitehorse, YT Y1A 4Y4; tel. (867) 668-5300; fax (867) 668-7079; e-mail customerservice@nwtel.ca; internet www.nwtel.ca; f. 1979, bought by BCE Inc in 1988; provides fixed-line and mobile telecommunications services to 110,000 customers in Yukon Territory, Northwest Territories, Nunavut Territory and British Columbia; Chair. TERRY MOSEY; Pres. and CEO PAUL FLAHERTY.

Télébec: 555 ave Centrale, Val-d'Or, QC J9P 1P6; e-mail telebec@telebec.com; internet www.telebec.com; f. 1969; owned by Bell Nordiq Group Inc, subsidiary of BCE; mobile telecommunications (Télébec Mobilité) and internet services (Télébec Internet).

Glentel: 8501 Commerce Ct, Burnaby, BC V5A 4N3; tel. (604) 415-6500; fax (604) 415-6565; e-mail investors@glentel.com; internet www.glentel.com; f. 1963; wireless communications; Chair., Pres. and CEO THOMAS E. SKIDMORE.

Globalstar Canada Co: 115 Matheson Blvd West, Suite 100, Mississauga, ON L5R 3L1; tel. (905) 890-1377; fax (905) 890-2175; e-mail info@globalstar.ca; internet www.globalstar.ca; satellite voice and data communications; Chair. and CEO JAMES (JAY) MONROE, III.

Primus Telecommunications Canada Inc: 5343 Dundas St West, Suite 400, Etobicoke, ON M9B 6K5; tel. (416) 236-3636; e-mail info@primustel.ca; internet www.primustel.ca; f. 1997; long-distance, local fixed line, international and internet services; CEO ANDREW DAY.

Rogers Communications Inc: 333 Bloor St East, 10th Floor, Toronto, ON M4W 1G9; tel. (416) 935-8200; fax (877) 331-1573; e-mail customer.service@rci.rogers.com; internet www.rogers.com; f. 1986; subsidiaries: Rogers Cable and Telecom provides fixed-line telephony, cable and internet services; Rogers Wireless Inc provides wireless and mobile cellular services; Chair. and Acting CEO ALAN D. HORN; Pres. and CEO NADIR MOHAMED.

Fido: 333 Bloor St East, 10th Floor, Toronto, ON M4W 1G9; tel. (416) 935-8710; internet www.fido.ca; f. 1996; by Microcell Solutions Inc; subsidiary of Rogers Communications Inc; Gen. Man. FADEL CHBIHNA.

Saskatchewan Telecommunications International (SaskTel): POB 2121, Regina, SK S4P 4C5; tel. (411) 555-1212; fax (306) 359-

5651; internet www.sasktel.com; f. 1986; provides mobile, satellite and internet services for Saskatchewan; Chair. GRANT J. KOOK; Pres. and CEO STEVE SOUSA.

Sierra Wireless, Inc: 13811 Wireless Way, Richmond, BC V6V 3A4; tel. (604) 231-1100; fax (604) 231-1109; e-mail pr@sierrawireless.com; internet www.sierrawireless.com; f. 1993; Chair. CHARLES E. LEVINE; CEO JASON W. COHENOUR; 905 employees.

Telesat: 1601 Telesat Court, Ottawa, ON K1B 5P4; tel. (613) 748-0123; fax (613) 748-8712; e-mail info@telesat.com; internet telesat.com; f. 1969 by Act of Parliament; owns 12 satellites and operates a further 13 on behalf of customers; carrier and distributor of more than 200 TV signals in North America; provides voice and data transmission services to telecommunication carriers in North and South America and wireless data business networks in Canada and the USA; Pres. and CEO DANIEL S. GOLDBERG.

TELUS: TELUS Corpn, 555 Robson St, Vancouver, BC V6B 3K9; tel. (604) 697-8044; fax (604) 432-9681; e-mail ir@telus.com; internet www.telus.com; f. 2001 following merger of TELUS Communications and BC Telecom; Chair. BRIAN A. CANFIELD; Pres. and CEO DARREN ENTWISTLE.

TELUS Mobility: 200 Consilium Pl., Suite 1600, Scarborough, ON M1H 3J3; internet www.telusmobility.com; mobile telecommunications; incorporates Clearnet, QuébecTel and TELUS Mobility West; Pres. and CEO DARREN ENTWISTLE.

TELUS Québec: 9 rue Jules-A.-Brillant, CP 2070, Rimouski, QC G5L 7E4; tel. (514) 977-8766; e-mail sacqt@telus.com; internet www.telusquebec.com; fmrly QuébecTel; adopted current name following acquisition by TELUS corpn in 2001; telecommunications for Québec; Pres. FRANÇOIS CÔTÉ.

TerreStar Canada: 1035 Laurier Ave West, Outremont, QC H2V 2L1; tel. (514) 843-0679; fax (514) 843-0360; e-mail media@terrestar.ca; internet www.terrestar.ca; f. 2010; integrated satellite-terrestrial mobile communications services; Pres. and CEO ANDRE TREMBLAY.

Videotron Ltd: CP 11078, Succ. Centre Ville, Montréal, QC H3C 5B74M8; tel. (514) 281-1711; f. 1964; wholly owned subsidiary of Quebecor Media Inc; cable telephone, wireless telephone, internet services; Pres. and CEO ROBERT DÉPATIE.

Wind Mobile: 207 Queens Quay West, Suite 710, POB 114, Toronto, ON M5J 1A7; e-mail info@windmobile.ca; internet www.windmobile.ca; Chair. and CEO ANTHONY LACAVERA.

BROADCASTING

CBC/Radio-Canada (Canadian Broadcasting Corpn): POB 3220, Station C, Ottawa, ON K1Y 1E4; tel. (613) 288-6033; fax (613) 288-6245; e-mail liaison@cbc.ca; internet www.cbc.radio-canada.ca; f. 1936; Canada's nat. public broadcaster; financed mainly by public funds, with supplementary revenue from commercial advertising on CBC Television and other commercial sources; broadcasts via 29 services (television, radio, internet and satellite-based services); services in French, English and eight aboriginal languages; production facilities and broadcast transmitters in many locations throughout Canada; Chair. TIMOTHY W. CASGRAIN; Pres. and CEO HUBERT T. LACROIX.

French Networks: 1400 blvd René-Lévesque est, CP 6000, Montréal, QC H3C 3A8; tel. (514) 597-6000; fax (514) 597-6013; e-mail auditoire@fr.radio-canada.ca; internet www.cbc.radio-canada.ca; Exec. Vice-Pres. LOUIS LALANDE.

Radio Canada International: 1400 blvd René-Lévesque est, Montréal, QC H2L 2M2; tel. (514) 597-7500; fax 597-7760; e-mail info@rcinet.ca; internet www.rcinet.ca; f. 1945; operates short-wave, satellite and audio internet services; broadcasts in French, English, Spanish, Arabic, Russian, Mandarin and Portuguese; Dir HÉLÈNE PARENT.

Radio

CBC operates four national networks broadcasting on AM and FM, two each in English and French. CBC's Northern Service (CBC North), created in 1958, provides both national network programming in English and French, and special local and short-wave programmes, some of which are broadcast in the languages of the native Indian and Inuit peoples. CBC also operates a number of satellite and internet radio networks. CBC radio service, which is virtually free of commercial advertising, is within reach of 99.5% of the population. Radio Canada International, CBC's overseas short-wave service, broadcasts daily in nine languages and distributes recorded programmes free for use world-wide. In 2010 there were 1,208 radio and audio services authorized to broadcast in Canada.

Television

In 2010 there were 716 television services authorized to broadcast in Canada. CBC operates two national, free-to-air television networks, one in English and one in French. CBC North provides both radio and television service to inhabitants of northern Québec, the Northwest Territories, Nunavut Territory and Yukon Territory; programming is provided in Dene and Inuktitut languages as well as English and French. CBC also provides speciality services, including the CBC Newsworld network and a digital channel (bold). CBC television is available to approximately 99% of the English- and French-speaking population. Many privately owned television and radio stations have affiliation agreements with the CBC and help to distribute the national services. A number of the major private television networks also have affiliates.

Canadian Satellite Communication Inc (Cancom, now Shaw Broadcast Services) was licensed in 1981 to operate a multi-channel television and radio broadcasting service via satellite to serve remote and under-served communities. Satellite television services are also provided by Shaw Direct (a subsidiary of Shaw Communications) and Bell TV (a subsidiary of Bell Canada). Global Television Network, acquired by Shaw Communications in 2010, operates 11 stations, broadcasting to some 98.9% of the English-speaking population.

Aboriginal Peoples Television Network (APTN): 339 Portage Ave, 2nd Floor, Winnipeg, MB R3B 2C3; tel. (204) 947-9331; fax (204) 943-4829; e-mail info@aptn.ca; internet www.aptn.ca; f. 1999; fmrly Television Northern Canada—TVNC; broadcasts in English, French and a number of aboriginal languages; Chair. DANIEL VANDAL; CEO JEAN LAROSE.

Corus Entertainment Inc: Corus Quay, 25 Dockside Dr., Toronto, ON M5A 0B5; tel. (416) 479-7000; fax (416) 479-7006; e-mail investor.relations@corusent.com; internet www.corusent.com; f. 1999; operates 37 radio stations and 17 television channels, including 11 special interest television channels; Chair. HEATHER SHAW; Pres. and CEO JOHN M. CASSADAY.

W Network: Corus Quay, 25 Dockside Dr., Toronto, ON M5A 0B5; tel. (416) 479-6786; e-mail comments@wnetwork.com; internet www.wnetwork.com; f. 1995 as Women's Television Network; women's network; owned by Corus Entertainment Inc.

CTV Television Network: 9 Channel Nine Court, POB 9, Station O, Scarborough, Toronto, ON M4A 2M9; tel. (416) 384-5000; fax (416) 299-2643; e-mail programming@ctv.ca; internet www.ctv.ca; 25 privately owned affiliated stations from coast to coast (including one satellite-to-cable service), with 247 rebroadcasters; covers 99% of English-speaking Canadian TV households; owned by Bell Media; Pres. and CEO KEVIN CRULL.

CTV British Columbia (CTV): 750 Burrard St, Suite 300, Vancouver, BC V6Z 1X5; tel. (604) 608-2868; fax (604) 608-2698; e-mail bccomments@ctv.ca; internet www.ctvbc.ctv.ca; f. 1997, as VTV; rebranded in 2001; Vice-Pres. and Gen. Man. TOM HABERSTROH.

Global Television Network: 81 Barber Greene Rd, Don Mills, ON M3C 2A2; tel. (416) 446-5311; fax (416) 446-5447; e-mail globalnews.bc@globaltv.com; internet www.canada.com/globaltv; 11 stations in eight provinces; acquired by Shaw Communications in 2010.

Knowledge Network: 4355 Mathissi Pl., Burnaby, BC V5G 4S8; tel. (604) 431-3222; fax (604) 431-3387; e-mail info@knowledge.ca; internet www.knowledge.ca; f. 1981; Chair. NINI BAIRD; Pres. and CEO RUDY BUTTIGNOL.

Réseau TVA: CP 170, succursale C, Montréal, QC H2L 4P6; tel. (514) 790-0461; fax (514) 598-6085; e-mail andre.limoges@tva.ca; internet tva.canoe.com; f. 1960 as Corporation Télé-Métropole; runs the Canoë network; French-language network, with nine stations in Québec and 19 rebroadcasters serving 98% of the province and francophone communities in Ontario and New Brunswick; Pres. and CEO PIERRE DION.

RNC Media Inc: 1 pl. Ville Marie, bureau 1523, Montreal, QC H3B 2B5; tel. (514) 866-8686; fax (514) 866-8056; e-mail info@rncmedia.ca; internet www.radionord.com; f. 1948 as radio Nord Communications Inc; 16 radio stations and five television stations; Pres. and CEO PIERRE R. BROSSEAU; Man. RAYNALD BRIÈRE.

Rogers Broadcasting Ltd (Rogers Media): 333 Bloor St East, 10th Floor, Toronto, ON M4W 1G9; tel. and fax (416) 935-8200; e-mail customer.service@rci.rogers.com; internet www.rogers.com; subsidiary of Rogers Communications Inc; 51 radio stations and eight television channels; Pres. SCOTT MOORE.

Shaw Communications Inc: 630 Third Ave, SW, Suite 900, Calgary, AB T2P 4L4; tel. (403) 750-4500; fax (403) 750-4501; internet www.shaw.ca; f. 1966 as Capital Cable Television Co Ltd, present name adopted in 1993; Exec. Chair. J. R. SHAW; CEO BRADLEY SHAW.

Shaw Broadcast Services: 2055 Flavelle Blvd, Mississauga, ON L5K 1Z8; tel. (905) 403-2020; fax (905) 403-2022; e-mail don.fletcher@sjrb.ca; internet www.shawbroadcast.com; fmrly Canadian Satellite Communications Inc (Cancom); present name adopted 2006; a division of Shaw Communications Inc; responsible for providing and managing the distribution of television channels to cable companies via satellite; also operates StarChoice, a

Canadian direct broadcast satellite service; Vice-Pres. DON FLETCHER.

Taqramiut Nipingat Inc: 185 Dorval Ave, Suite 501, Dorval, QC H9S 5J9; tel. (514) 683-2330; fax (514) 683-1078; e-mail tnigeneral@taqramiut.qc.ca; internet www.taqramiut.qc.ca; f. 1975; broadcasts programming in Inuktitut, French and English to Arctic regions of Québec (Nunavik); Pres. GEORGE KAKAYUK; Dir-Gen. CLAUDE GRENIER.

TVOntario: 2180 Yonge St, POB 200, Station Q, Toronto, ON M4T 2T1; tel. (416) 484-2600; fax (416) 484-6285; e-mail asktv@tvo.org; internet www.tvo.org; f. 1970; Chair. PETER O'BRIAN; CEO LISA DE WILDE.

ASSOCIATIONS

Canadian Association of Broadcasters/L'Association canadienne des radiodiffuseurs: 45 O'Connor St, Suite 700, POB 627, Station B, Ottawa, ON K1P 5S2; tel. (613) 233-4035; fax (613) 233-6961; e-mail sbissonnette@cab-acr.ca; internet www.cab-acr.ca; f. 1926; over 600 mem. broadcasting stations; Chair. (Board of Dirs) ELMER HILDEBRAND.

Radio Advisory Board of Canada/Conseil consultatif canadien de la radio: 116 Albert St, Suite 811, Ottawa, ON K1P 5G3; tel. (613) 230-3261; fax (613) 728-3278; e-mail rabc.gm@on.aibn.com; internet www.rabc-cccr.ca; 20 mem. asscns; Gen. Man. ROGER POIRIER.

Television Bureau of Canada: 160 Bloor St East, Suite 1005, Toronto, ON M4W 1B9; tel. (416) 923-8813; fax (416) 413-3879; e-mail tvb@tvb.ca; internet www.tvb.ca; f. 1962; 150 mems; Chair. RITA FABIAN; Pres. and CEO THERESA TREUTLER.

Finance

(cap. = capital; auth. = authorized; res = reserves; dep. = deposits; m. = million; brs = branches; amounts in Canadian dollars, unless otherwise indicated)

BANKING

The Bank Act of 1980 created two categories of banking institution: Schedule I banks, in which no one interest was allowed to own more than 10% of the shares; and Schedule II banks, which are either subsidiaries of foreign financial institutions, or are banks controlled by Canadian non-bank financial institutions. In 1999 the Government adopted legislation permitting foreign banks to establish operations in Canada without their being obliged to establish Canadian-incorporated subsidiaries. Foreign bank branches (known as Schedule III banks) are prohibited from accepting deposits of less than C $150,000. The Bank Act Reform, a series of extensive changes to federal financial institutions, entered into effect in October 2001. This provided for much greater flexibility of the financial services system and also included an increase in the maximum level of single ownership in large banks from 10% to 20%, while any one interest was henceforth permitted to control as much as 65% of a medium-sized bank.

In February 2012, according to the Office of the Superintendent of Financial Institutions, the banking industry included 23 domestic banks, 26 foreign bank subsidiaries and 23 full-service foreign bank branches. At December 2009 the combined assets of all banks (excluding foreign subsidiaries) totalled C $2,662,874.4m.

Trust and loan companies, which were originally formed to provide mortgage finance and private customer loans, now occupy an important place in the financial system, offering current account facilities and providing access to money transfer services. In October 2010, according to the Office of the Superintendent of Financial Institutions, 49 trust companies and 19 loan companies, which were regulated under the federal Trust and Loan Companies Act, were operating in Canada.

Central Bank

Bank of Canada: 234 Wellington St, Ottawa, ON K1A 0G9; tel. (613) 782-7902; fax (613) 782-7713; e-mail info@bankofcanada.ca; internet www.bankofcanada.ca; f. 1934; bank of issue; cap. and res 212.9m., dep. 24,413.2m. (Dec. 2008); Gov. MARK J. CARNEY.

Commercial Banks

Schedule I Banks

Bank of Montréal: 1 First Canada Pl., 18th Floor, 100 King St West, Toronto, ON M5X 1A1; tel. (416) 867-6656; fax (416) 867-3367; e-mail feedback@bmo.com; internet www2.bmo.com; f. 1817; cap. 9,498m., res –466m., dep. 249,251m. (Oct. 2010); Chair. DAVID A. GALLOWAY; Pres. and CEO WILLIAM DOWNE; 1,280 brs; 47,000 employees.

Bank of Nova Scotia (Scotiabank): Scotia Plaza, 44 King St West, Toronto, ON M5H 1H1; tel. (416) 866-6161; fax (416) 866-3750; e-mail email@scotiabank.com; internet www.scotiabank.com; f. 1832; acquired NBG Bank Canada (Greece) in Nov. 2005; cap. 9,750m., res –4,051m., dep. 361,650m. (Oct. 2010); Chair. JOHN T. MAYBERRY; Pres. and CEO RICHARD E. WAUGH; 1,019 brs in Canada, 1,907 foreign brs.

Canadian Imperial Bank of Commerce: Commerce Court, Toronto, ON M5L 1A2; tel. (416) 980-2211; fax (416) 363-5347; internet www.cibc.com; f. 1961 by merger of Canadian Bank of Commerce (f. 1867) and Imperial Bank of Canada (f. 1875); cap. 9,959m., res –264m., dep. 246,671m. (Oct. 2010); Chair. CHARLES SIROIS; Pres. and CEO GERALD T. MCCAUGHEY; 1,100 brs in Canada.

Canadian Western Bank: 10303 Jasper Ave, Suite 3000, Edmonton, AB T5J 3X6; tel. (780) 423-8888; fax (780) 423-8897; internet www.cwbankgroup.com; f. 1988 by merger of the Bank of Alberta and the Western and Pacific Bank of Canada; cap. 489.1m., res 44.2m., dep. 10,812.7m. (Oct. 2010); Chair. ALLAN W. JACKSON; Pres. and CEO LARRY M. POLLOCK; 40 brs.

Laurentian Bank of Canada/Banque Laurentienne du Canada: Laurentian Bank Tower, 1981 ave Collège McGill, Suite 1660, Montréal, QC H3A 3K3; tel. (514) 252-1846; fax (514) 284-3988; e-mail customer_inquiries@laurentianbank.ca; internet www.laurentianbank.ca; f. 1846 as Montreal City and District Savings Bank; name changed as above 1987; cap. 469m., res 28m., dep. 19,675.5m. (Oct. 2010); Chair. DENIS DESAUTELS; Pres. and CEO REJEAN ROBITAILLE; 158 brs.

National Bank of Canada/Banque Nationale du Canada: 600 rue de la Gauchetière ouest, Montréal, QC H3B 4L2; tel. (514) 394-5000; fax (514) 394-6196; e-mail investorrelations@nbc.ca; internet www.nbc.ca; f. 1859; cap. 2,893m., res 234m., dep. 81,785m. (Oct. 2010); Chair. JEAN DOUVILLE; Pres. and CEO LOUIS VACHON; 448 brs in Canada.

Pacific and Western Bank of Canada: 140 Fullarton St, Suite 2002, London, ON N6A 5P2; tel. (519) 645-1919; fax (519) 645-2060; e-mail tellus@pwbank.com; internet www.pwbank.com; f. 1980 as Pacific and Western Trust Corpn; granted approval to become a Schedule I Bank in 2002 and name changed as above; subsidiary of Pacific and Western Credit Corpn; assets US $1,322m. (Oct. 2010); Chair. SCOTT RITCHIE; Pres. and CEO DAVID R. TAYLOR.

Royal Bank of Canada: 200 Bay St, 9th Floor, South Tower, Toronto, ON M5J 2J5; tel. (514) 974-5151; fax (514) 974-7800; internet www.rbc.com; f. 1869; bought RBTT Ltd in 2007; cap. 18,191m., res –1,946m., dep. 433,033m. (Oct. 2010); Chair. DAVID P. O'BRIEN; Pres. and CEO GORDON M. NIXON; 1,443 brs.

Toronto-Dominion Bank: Toronto-Dominion Centre, 55 King St West and Bay St, POB 1, Toronto, ON M5K 1A2; tel. (416) 982-8222; fax (416) 982-5671; e-mail customer.service@td.com; internet www.td.com; f. 1955 by merger of the Bank of Toronto (f. 1855) and the Dominion Bank (f. 1869); acquired Commerce Bancorp Inc in 2007; cap. 20,125m., res 1,218m., dep. 429,971m. (Oct. 2010); Chair. BRIAN M. LEVITT; Pres. and CEO W. EDMUND CLARKE; 953 brs.

Principal Schedule II Banks

Amex Bank of Canada (USA): 101 McNabb St, Markham, ON L3R 4H8; tel. (905) 474-0870; fax (905) 940-7702; internet www.americanexpress.com/canada; f. 1990; cap. 206m., res 8m., dep. 205m. (Dec. 2010); Chair., Pres. and CEO DENISE PICKETT.

Bank of China (Canada) (People's Republic of China): Exchange Tower, Suite 2730, 130 King St West, POB 356, Toronto, ON M5X 1E1; tel. (416) 362-2991; fax (416) 362-3047; e-mail service_ca@bank-of-china.com; internet www.boc.cn/cn/html/canada; f. 1992; cap. 65m., dep. 465m. (Dec. 2010); Pres. and CEO DASHU ZHU.

Bank of Tokyo-Mitsubishi UFJ (Canada) (Japan): Suite 1700, South Tower, Royal Bank Plaza, POB 42, Toronto, ON M5J 2J1; tel. (416) 865-0220; fax (416) 865-9511; f. Jan. 2006 through merger of Bank of Tokyo-Mitsubishi (Canada) (f. 1996) and UFJ Bank Canada (f. 2001); cap. 335m., dep. 2,437m. (Oct. 2010); Pres. and CEO TAKASHI ANDO.

BNP Paribas (Canada) (France): BNP Tower, 1981 ave McGill College, Montréal, QC H3A 2W8; tel. (514) 285-6000; fax (514) 285-6278; e-mail bnpp.canada@americas.bnpparibas.com; internet www.bnpparibas.ca; f. 2000 by merger of Banque Nationale de Paris Canada (f. 1961) into Paribas Bank of Canada (f. 1981); cap. 345m., res –3m., dep. 2,693m. (Dec. 2009); Chair. JACQUES H. WAHL; Pres. and CEO ANNE MARIE VERSTRAETEN.

Citibank Canada (USA): Suite 1100, Citibank Pl., 123 Front St West, Toronto, ON M5J 2M3; tel. (416) 947-5500; fax (416) 947-5628; internet www.citibank.com/canada; f. 1981; subsidiary of Citibank NA (USA); cap. 601m., res 15m., dep. 1,956m. (Dec. 2010); Chair. and CEO JOHN HASTINGS; 1 br.

HSBC Bank Canada: 300–885 West Georgia St, Vancouver, BC V6C 3E9; tel. (604) 685-1000; fax (604) 641-1849; e-mail info@hsbc.ca; internet www.hsbc.ca; f. 1981 as Hongkong Bank of Canada; merged with Barclays Bank of Canada in 1996; subsidiary of HSBC

Holdings plc (United Kingdom); cap. 2,171m., res 74m., dep. 52,055m. (Dec. 2010); Pres. and CEO Lindsay Gordon; c. 140 brs.

Mizuho Corporate Bank (Canada) (Japan): Suite 1102, 100 Yonge St, POB 29, Toronto, ON M5C 2W1; tel. (416) 874-0222; fax (416) 367-3452; e-mail inquiries@mizuhocbus.com; f. 1982 following merger of Dai-Ichi Kangyo Bank and Industrial Bank of Japan; name changed as above in 2002; cap. 165.2m., dep. 1,398.3m. (Oct. 2006); Pres. Takahiko Ueda; 1 br.

Société Générale (Canada): 1501 ave Collège McGill, bureau 1800, Montréal, QC H3A 3M8; tel. (514) 841-6000; fax (514) 841-6250; e-mail info.canada@sgcib.com; internet www.sgcib.com/canada; f. 1979; subsidiary of Société Générale SA (France); cap. 80m., res 34m., dep. 1,479m. (Dec. 2009); CEO Pierre Matuszewski; 3 brs.

Sumitomo Mitsui Banking Corpn of Canada (Japan): Toronto-Dominion Centre, Suite 1400, 222 Bay St, Toronto, ON M5K 1H6; tel. (416) 368-4766; fax (416) 367-3565; f. 2001 following merger of Sakura Bank and Sumitomo Bank of Canada; cap. 169m., dep. 1,249m. (Oct. 2010); Chair. Teisuke Kitayama; Pres. Minami Aida.

Development Bank

Business Development Bank of Canada: 5 pl. Ville Marie, Suite 300, Montréal, QC H3B 5E7; tel. (514) 283-5904; fax (514) 283-2872; internet www.bdc.ca; f. 1944; fed. govt corpn; total shareholders' equity 4,008m. (March 2011); Chair. John A. MacNaughton; Pres. and CEO Jean-René Halde.

Principal Trust and Loan Companies

Bank of Nova Scotia Trust Co: Scotia Plaza, 44 King St West, Toronto, ON M5H 1H1; tel. (416) 866-6161; fax (416) 866-3750; internet www.scotiabank.com; Pres. Richard E. Waugh.

Canadian Western Trust Corporation: 600–750 Cambie St, Vancouver, BC V6B 0A2; tel. (604) 685-2081; fax (604) 669-6069; e-mail informationservices@cwt.ca; internet www.cwt.ca; Vice-Pres. Adrian Baker.

CIBC Mellon: 320 Bay St, 4th Floor, POB 1, Toronto, ON M5H 4A6; tel. (416) 643-5000; e-mail generalinquiries@cibcmellon.com; internet www.cibcmellon.com; f. 1997; privately owned jt venture between CIBC and The Bank of New York Mellon; provides asset sevicing (CIBC Mellon Global Securities Services Co) and issuer services (CIBC Mellon Trust Co); Chair. Thomas C. MacMillan; Pres. and CEO Thomas S. Monahan.

Home Trust Co: 145 King St West, Suite 2300, Toronto, ON M5H 1J8; tel. (416) 360-4663; fax (416) 363-7611; e-mail inquiry.htc@hometrust.ca; internet www.hometrust.ca; f. 1977 as Home Savings and Loan Corpn; above name adopted in 2000; Pres. Martin Reid; CEO Gerald M. Soloway.

ResMor Trust Co: 3250 Bloor St West, Suite 1400, East Tower, Toronto, ON M8X 2X9; tel. (416) 640-3415; e-mail mortgagesupport@resmor.com; internet www.resmor.com; f. 1964 as Equisure Trust Co; renamed as above following acquisition in 2003 by ResMor Capital Corpn; Pres. and CEO Johanne Brossard.

TD Canada Trust: Toronto-Dominion Centre, 55 King St West, 12th Floor, POB 1, Toronto, ON M5K 1H6; tel. (416) 982-6744; fax (416) 944-5853; internet www.tdcanadatrust.com; Co-Chair. Bernie Dorval, Tim Hockey.

Savings Institutions with Provincial Charters

ATB Financial: ATB Pl., 2nd Floor, 9888 Jasper Ave, Edmonton, AB T5J 1P1; tel. (780) 408-7000; fax (780) 408-7523; e-mail apm@atb.com; internet www.atb.com; f. 1938 as Alberta Treasury Branches; name changed as above in 2002; assets 27,388m. (March 2011); Pres. and CEO David Mowat; 165 brs.

Desjardins Credit Union: 1615 Dundas St East, Whitby, ON L1N 2L1; tel. (905) 743-5790; fax (905) 743-6156; e-mail info@dcu.desjardins.com; internet www.desjardins.com/en/dcu; f. 1921, as Province of Ontario Savings Office; acquired by Desjardins Credit Union in 2003; merger with Meridian Credit Union announced in July 2011; Pres. and CEO Lionel Gauvin; Chair. Paul E. Garfinkel (acting); 21 brs.

Bankers' Organizations

Canadian Bankers Association: Commerce Court West, Suite 3000, 199 Bay St, Box 348, Toronto, ON M5L 1G2; tel. (416) 362-6092; fax (416) 362-7705; e-mail inform@cba.ca; internet www.cba.ca; f. 1891; Chair. Réjean Lévesque; Pres. and CEO Terry Campbell; 52 mems.

Institute of Canadian Bankers: Tour Scotia, 1002 rue Sherbrooke ouest, Suite 1000, Montréal, QC H3A 3M5; tel. (514) 282-9480; e-mail icb.info@csi.ca; internet www.icb.org; f. 1967; bought by CSI Global Education in 2007; provides financial training for the banking industry; Exec. Dir Marie Muldowney.

STOCK EXCHANGES

Bourse de Montréal/Montreal Exchange: Tour de la Bourse, CP 61, 800 sq. Victoria, Montréal, QC H4Z 1A9; tel. (514) 871-2424; fax (514) 871-3514; e-mail info@tmx.ca; internet www.m-x.ca; f. 1874; Chair. Jean Turmel; Pres. and CEO Alain Miquelon; 91 approved participants.

Toronto Stock Exchange (TSX): The Exchange Tower, 130 King St West, Toronto, ON M5X 1J2; tel. (416) 947-4670; fax (416) 947-4662; e-mail info@tsx.com; internet www.tsx.com; f. 1861; Chair. Wayne C. Fox; CEO Thomas Kloet; 121 mems.

TSX Venture Exchange: Fifth Ave SW, Suite 300, 10th Floor, Calgary, AB T2P 3C4; tel. (403) 218-2800; fax (403) 237-0450; e-mail info@tsx.com; internet www.tsx.ca; f. 1999 by merger of Alberta and Vancouver Stock Exchanges; incorporated Winnipeg Stock Exchange in 2000; acquired by Toronto Stock Exchange (TSX) in 2001; fmrly Canadian Venture Exchange; Pres. Linda Hohol; 68 mems.

INSURANCE

In October 2010, according to the Office of the Superintendent of Financial Institutions, 279 insurance companies were operating in Canada, including 79 life insurance companies, 17 fraternal benefit societies and 183 property and casualty companies.

Principal Companies

AIG Life Insurance Co of Canada: 60 Yonge St, Toronto, ON M5E 1H5; tel. (416) 596-3900; fax (416) 596-4143; e-mail aiglifecainfo@aig.com; internet www.aiglife.ca; owned by American International Group (AIG) Inc; Pres. and CEO Peter C. McCarthy.

Assumption Life: Assumption Pl. Bldg, 770 Main St, POB 160, Moncton, NB E1C 8L1; tel. (506) 853-6040; e-mail comments@assumption.ca; internet www.assumption.ca; f. 1903; Chair. Gilles LeBlanc; Pres. and CEO Denis Losier.

Aviva Canada Inc: 2206 Eglinton Ave East, Scarborough, ON M1L 4S8; tel. (416) 701-4409; e-mail kimberly_flood@avivacanada.com; internet www.avivacanada.com; f. 1906; fmrly known as CGU Group Canada Ltd following merger of General Accident, Commerical Union and Canadian General Insurance Group in 1999; present name adopted 2003; commercial and personal insurance; Pres. and CEO Maurice Tulloch.

Blue Cross Life Insurance Co of Canada: 644 Main St, POB 220, Moncton, NB E1C 8L3; tel. (506) 853-1811; fax (506) 853-4646; e-mail inquiry@medavie.bluecross.ca; internet www.bluecross.ca; life, accident and illness; Pres. and CEO James K. Gilligan.

The CUMIS Group Ltd: 151 North Service Rd, POB 5065, Burlington, ON L7R 4C2; tel. (905) 632-1221; e-mail customer.service@cumis.com; internet www.cumis.com; owns CUMIS General Insurance Co (f. 1980) and CUMIS Life Insurance Co (f. 1977); Chair. and CEO Kathy Bardswick.

Desjardins sécurité financière/Desjardins Financial Security: 200 rue des Commandeurs, Lévis, QC G6V 6R2; tel. (418) 828-7800; fax (418) 833-5985; e-mail info@desjardinssecuritefinanciere.com; internet www.desjardinslifeinsurance.com; fmrly Assurance-vie Desjardins-Laurentienne, merged with Imperial Life Assurance in 2001; Pres. and COO Denis Berthiaume.

Dominion of Canada General Insurance Co: 165 University Ave, Toronto, ON M5H 3B9; tel. (416) 362-7231; fax (416) 362-9918; internet www.thedominion.ca; f. 1887; Chair. Duncan N. R. Jackman; Pres. and CEO George L. Cooke.

Empire Life Insurance Co: 259 King St East, Kingston, ON K7L 3A8; tel. (613) 548-1881; fax (613) 920-5868; e-mail info@empire.ca; internet www.empire.ca; f. 1923; Chair. Duncan N. R. Jackman; Pres. and CEO Leslie (Les) C. Herr.

Equitable Life of Canada: 1 Westmount Rd North, POB 1603, Waterloo, ON N2J 4C7; tel. (519) 886-5110; fax (519) 886-5210; e-mail headoffice@equitable.ca; internet www.equitable.ca; f. 1920; Chair. Douglas W. Dodds; Pres. and CEO Ronald E. Beettam.

Federation Insurance Co of Canada: 111 Westmount Road South, POB 2000, Waterloo, ON N2J 4S4; tel. (514) 875-5790; fax (514) 875-9769; f. 1947; Pres. and CEO Noel Walpole.

GCAN Insurance Co: 181 University Ave, Suite 1000, Toronto, ON M5H 3M7; tel. (416) 682-5300; fax (416) 682-9213; e-mail central.office@gcan.ca; internet www.gcan.ca; f. 1955; Pres. and CEO Daniel P. Courtemanche.

The Great-West Life Assurance Co: 100 Osborne St North, POB 6000, Winnipeg, MB R3C 3A5; tel. (204) 946-1190; fax (204) 946-7838; e-mail contactus@gwl.ca; internet www.greatwestlife.com; f. 1891; owns London Life Insurance Co and Canada Life Assurance Co; Pres. and CEO David Allen Loney; COO (Canada) Paul A. Mahon.

Industrial Alliance Pacific Life Insurance Co: 2165 Broadway West, POB 5900, Vancouver, BC V6B 5H6; tel. (604) 734-1667; fax

(604) 739-0534; e-mail intouch@iapacific.com; internet www.iaplife.com; f. 2000; Pres. and CEO YVON CHAREST.

ING Insurance Company of Canada: 700 University Ave, Suite 1500-A, Toronto, ON M5G 0A1; tel. (416) 341-1464; fax (416) 941-5320; e-mail infoING@INGcanada.com; internet www.inginsurance.ca; CEO CHARLES BRINDAMOUR.

The Kings Mutual Insurance Co: POB 10, 220 Commercial St, Berwick, NS B0P 1E0; tel. (902) 538-3187; fax (902) 538-7271; e-mail info@kingsmutual.ns.ca; internet www.kingsmutual.ns.ca; f. 1904; Chair. DAVID DAVIES.

Kingsway General Insurance Co: 7120 Hurontario St, Suite 700, Mississauga, ON L4W 5H8; tel. (905) 677-8889; fax (905) 677-5008; e-mail caxford@kingsway-general.com; internet www.kingsway-general.com; f. 1986; incorporates York Fire and Casualty Insurance Co; Pres. and CEO JOHN L. MCGLYNN.

Manufacturers Life Insurance Co (Manulife): 500 King St North, Waterloo, ON N2J 4C6; tel. (519) 594-2660; fax (519) 747-6336; e-mail manulife_bank@manulife.com; internet www.manulife.ca; f. 1887; acquired Commercial Union Life Assurance Co of Canada in 2001; merged in 2004 with Maritime Life Assurance's holding co, John Hancock Financial Services, creating the Manulife Financial Group; Pres. and CEO PAUL ROONEY.

Metropolitan Life Insurance Co (MetLife Canada): Constitution Sq., 360 Albert St, Suite 1750, Ottawa, ON K1R 7X7; tel. (613) 237-7171; fax (613) 237-7585; internet www.metlife.com; CEO C. ROBERT HENRIKSON.

Optimum General Inc: 425 blvd de Maisonneuve ouest, bureau 1500, Montréal, QC H3A 3G5; tel. (514) 288-8725; fax (514) 288-0760; e-mail webmaster@optimum-general.com; internet www.optimum-general.com; f. 1969; fmrly the Société National d'Assurance Inc; operates Optimum West Insurance Co, Optimum Insurance Co Inc and Optimum Farm Insurance Inc; Chair. GILLES BLONDEAU; Pres. and CEO JEAN-CLAUDE PAGÉ.

Portage Mutual Insurance Co: 749 Saskatchewan Ave East, POB 340, Portage la Prairie, MB R1N 3B8; tel. (204) 857-3415; fax (204) 239-6655; e-mail info@portagemutual.com; internet www.portagemutual.com; f. 1884; Pres. and CEO JOHN G. MITCHELL.

RBC Insurance Co of Canada: West Tower, 9th Floor, 6880 Financial Dr., Mississauga, ON L5N 7Y5; internet www.rbcinsurance.com; fmrly Westbury Life; bought Unum Provident Canada and the Canadian operation of Provident Life and Accident Insurance Co in 2004; Pres. and CEO RINO D'ONOFORIO.

Royal & Sun Alliance Insurance Co of Canada: 10 Wellington St East, Toronto, ON M5E 1L5; tel. (416) 366-7511; fax (416) 367-9869; internet www.royalsunalliance.ca; f. 1851; Pres. and CEO ROWAN SAUNDERS.

The Sovereign General Insurance Co: 140 Sovereign Centre, 6700 Macleod Trail, SE, Calgary, AB T2H 0L3; tel. (403) 298-4200; fax (403) 298-4217; internet www.sovereigngeneral.com; f. 1894; COO ROB WESSELING.

Sun Life Financial Canada: 150 King St West, 6th Floor, Toronto, ON M5H 1J9; tel. (416) 979-9966; fax (416) 598-3121; e-mail service@sunlife.ca; internet www.sunlife.ca; f. 1871; merged with Clarica in 2007; Pres. KEVIN DOUGHERTY.

Transamerica Life Canada: 5000 Yonge St, Toronto, ON M2N 7J8; tel. (416) 883-5003; fax (416) 883-5520; e-mail webmaster.canada@aegoncanada.ca; internet www.transamerica.ca; f. 1927; wholly owned by Aegon NV (Netherlands); Pres. and CEO DOUGLAS W. BROOKS.

Unity Life of Canada: 1660 Tech Ave, Suite 3, Mississauga, ON L4W 5S8; tel. (905) 219-8000; fax (905) 219-8121; e-mail info@unitylife.ca; internet www.unitylife.ca; f. 1898; originally the Insurance Dept of Subsidiary High Court of the Ancient Order of Foresters, subsequently Toronto Mutual Life Insurance Co until amalgamation with its subsidiary Western Life Assurance Co in 2002; Pres. and CEO ANTHONY W. POOLE.

Wawanesa Mutual Insurance Co: 900-191 Broadway, Winnipeg, MB R3C 3P1; tel. (204) 985-3923; fax (204) 942-7724; internet www.wawanesa.com; f. 1896; Pres. and CEO KENNETH E. MCCREA.

Western Life Assurance Co: 1010-24th St East, High River, AB T1V 2A7; tel. (403) 652-4356; fax (403) 652-2673; e-mail info@westernlife.com; internet www.westernlifeassurance.net; f. 1851; fmrly Federated Life Insurance Co of Canada, present name adopted 2005; Pres. and CEO DOMINIQUE GREGOIRE.

Zurich Canada: 400 University Ave, Toronto, ON M5G 1S7; tel. (416) 586-3000; fax (416) 586-2525; internet www.zurichcanada.com; CEO ALISTER CAMPBELL.

Insurance Organizations

Advocis (Financial Advisors Association of Canada): 390 Queens Quay West, Suite 209, Toronto, ON M5V 3A2; tel. (416) 444-5251; fax (416) 444-8031; e-mail info@advocis.ca; internet www.advocis.ca; f. 2002 by merger of the Canadian Asscn of Insurance and Financial Advisors and Canadian Asscn of Financial Planners; fmrly Life Underwriters Asscn of Canada (f. 1906); Chair. ROBERT MCCULLAGH; Pres. and CEO GREG POLLOCK; c. 12,000 mems.

Assuris: 250 Yonge St, Suite 3110, POB 23, Toronto, ON M5B 2L7; tel. (416) 359-2001; fax (416) 777-9802; e-mail info@assuris.ca; internet www.assuris.ca; fmrly Canadian Life and Health Insurance Compensation Corpn (CompCorp), name changed as above in Dec. 2005; total assets 125m. (Dec. 2010); Pres. and CEO GORDON M. DUNNING; 89 mems.

Canadian Association of Mutual Insurance Companies: 311 McArthur Ave, Suite 205, Ottawa, ON K1L 6P1; tel. (613) 789-6851; fax (613) 789-7665; e-mail nlafreniere@camic.ca; internet www.camic.ca; Chair. ROB FORSYTHE; Pres. NORMAN LAFRENIÈRE; 93 mems.

Canadian Life and Health Insurance Association Inc: 1 Queen St East, Suite 1700, Toronto, ON M5C 2X9; tel. (416) 777-2221; fax (416) 777-1895; internet www.clhia.ca; f. 1894; Chair. GEORGE MOHACSI; 75 mems.

Insurance Brokers Association of Canada: 18 King St East, Suite 1210, Toronto, ON M5C 1C4; tel. (416) 367-1831; fax (416) 367-3687; e-mail ibac@ibac.ca; internet www.ibac.ca; f. 1921; Chair. FRASER LYLE; Pres. DALE REMPEL; CEO DAN DANYLUK; 11 mem. asscns.

Insurance Bureau of Canada: 777 Bay St, Suite 2400, POB 121, Toronto, ON M5G 2C8; tel. (416) 362-2031; fax (416) 361-5952; e-mail consumercentre@ibc.ca; internet www.ibc.ca; f. 1964; Pres. and CEO DON FORGERON.

Insurance Institute of Canada: 18 King St East, 16th Floor, Toronto, ON M5C 1C4; tel. (416) 362-8586; fax (416) 362-8081; e-mail iiomail@insuranceinstitute.ca; internet www.insuranceinstitute.ca; f. 1952; Chair. CHRIS FAWCUS; Pres. PETER G. HOHMAN; 36,000 mems.

Chartered Insurance Professionals' Society (CIP Society): 18 King St East, 6th Floor, Toronto, ON M5C 1C4; tel. (416) 362-8586; fax (416) 362-2692; e-mail cips@insuranceinstitute.ca; internet cip.iic-iac.org; a division of the Insurance Institute of Canada; represents c. 15,000 insurance professionals; Dir MARGARET PARENT.

LOMA Canada: 675 Cochrane Dr., East Tower, 6th Floor, Toronto, ON L3R 0B8; tel. (905) 530-2309; fax (905) 530-2001; e-mail lomacanada@loma.org; internet www.loma.org/canada; f. 1924 as Life Insurance Institute of Canada; renamed LOMA Canada in June 2006, following 2002 merger with LOMA; Pres. and CEO ROBERT A. KERZNER; Dir BRENT LEMANSKI; over 1,200 mem. cos in 84 countries.

Trade and Industry

CHAMBER OF COMMERCE

The Canadian Chamber of Commerce: 360 Albert St, Suite 420, Ottawa, ON K1R 7X7; tel. (613) 238-4000; fax (613) 238-7643; e-mail info@chamber.ca; internet www.chamber.ca; f. 1925; part of the Int. Chamber of Commerce, and of the Business and Industry Advisory Cttee to the Organisation for Economic Co-operation and Development (OECD); Chair. ROBERT YOUDEN; Pres. and CEO PERRIN BEATTY; 170,000 mems.

INDUSTRIAL AND TRADE ASSOCIATIONS

Canadian Manufacturers and Exporters: 1 Nicholas St, Suite 1500, Ottawa, ON K1N 7B7; tel. (613) 238-8888; fax (613) 563-9218; e-mail jayson.myers@cme-mec.ca; internet www.cme-mec.ca; f. 1871 as the Ontario Manufacturers' Asscn, later renamed the Canadian Manufacturers' Asscn; merged with the Canadian Exporters' Asscn in 1943 to form the Alliance of Manufacturers and Exporters Canada; present name adopted in 2000; Pres. and CEO JAYSON MYERS; Exec. Dir DIANE DEJONG; 10,000 mems.

Agriculture and Horticulture

Canada Beef Export Federation (Canada Beef): 6715 Eighth St, NE, Suite 235, Calgary, AB T2E 7H7; tel. (403) 274-0005; fax (403) 274-7275; e-mail rmeijer@canadabeef.ca; internet www.cbef.com; f. 1989; Chair. GIB DRURY; Pres. ROB MEIJER.

Canada Grains Council: 220 Portage Ave, Suite 1215, Winnipeg, MB R3C 0A5; tel. (204) 925-2130; fax (204) 925-2132; e-mail office@canadagrainscouncil.ca; internet www.canadagrainscouncil.ca; f. 1969; Chair. JEAN-MARC RUEST; 34 mems.

Canadian Federation of Agriculture/Fédération Canadienne de l'agriculture (CFA/FCA): 21 Florence St, Ottawa, ON K2P 0W6; tel. (613) 236-3633; fax (613) 236-5749; e-mail info@cfafca.ca; internet www.cfa-fca.ca; f. 1935; Pres. RON BONNETT; Exec. Dir BRIGID RIVOIRE; 22 mems.

Canadian Horticultural Council: 9 Corvus Court, Ottawa, ON K2E 7Z4; tel. (613) 226-4880; fax (613) 226-4497; e-mail webmaster@hortcouncil.ca; internet www.hortcouncil.ca; f. 1922; Pres. JACK BATES; Exec. Vice-Pres. ANNE FOWLIE.

Canadian Nursery Landscape Association/Association canadienne des pépiniéristes et des paysagistes: 7856 Fifth Line South, RR 4, Station Main, Milton, ON L9T 2X8; tel. (905) 875-1399; fax (905) 875-1840; e-mail info@canadanursery.com; internet www.canadanursery.com; f. 1922 as the Eastern Canada Nurserymen's Asscn; present name adopted in 1999; Pres. BILL VAN STENSSON; Exec. Dir VICTOR SANTACRUZ; over 3,600 mems.

Canadian Seed Growers' Association: 240 Catherine St, Suite 202, POB 8455, Ottawa, ON K1G 3T1; tel. (613) 236-0497; fax (613) 563-7855; e-mail seeds@seedgrowers.ca; internet www.seedgrowers.ca; f. 1904; Pres. GERALD GIRODAT; Exec. Dir DALE ADOLPHE; 3,700 mems (2011).

Canadian Wheat Board: 423 Main St, Station Main, POB 816, Winnipeg, MB R3C 2P5; tel. (204) 983-0239; fax (204) 983-3841; e-mail questions@cwb.ca; internet www.cwb.ca; sole marketing agency for western Canadian wheat and barley exports and for domestic sales of grains for human consumption; Chair. BRUCE JOHNSON; Pres. and CEO IAN WHITE.

National Farmers Union (NFU): 2717 Wentz Ave, Saskatoon, SK S7K 4B6; tel. (306) 652-9465; fax (306) 664-6226; e-mail nfu@nfu.ca; internet www.nfu.ca; f. 1969; Pres. TERRY BOEHM; 10,000 mems.

Union des producteurs agricoles: 555 blvd Roland-Therrien, bureau 100, Longueuil, QC J4H 3Y9; tel. (450) 679-0530; fax (450) 679-4943; e-mail upa@upa.qc.ca; internet www.upa.qc.ca; f. 1924; Pres. MARCEL GROLEAU; 44,000 mems.

Building and Construction

Canadian Construction Association: 275 Slater St, 19 Floor, Ottawa, ON K1P 5H9; tel. (613) 236-9455; fax (613) 236-9526; e-mail cca@cca-acc.com; internet www.cca-acc.com; f. 1918; Pres. MICHAEL ATKINSON; over 20,000 mems.

Canadian Institute of Steel Construction: 3760 14th Ave, Suite 200, Markham, ON L3R 3T7; tel. (905) 946-0864; fax (905) 946-8574; e-mail info@cisc-icca.ca; internet www.cisc-icca.ca; f. 1930; Chair. STEPHEN BENSON; Pres. ED WHALEN; 437 mems.

Canadian Paint and Coatings Association: 170 Laurier Ave West, Suite 608, Ottawa, ON K1P 5V5; tel. (613) 231-3604; fax (613) 231-4908; e-mail cpca@cdnpaint.org; internet www.cdnpaint.org; f. 1913; Chair. DALE CONSTANTINOFF; Pres. and CEO (vacant); 70 mems.

Canadian Precast/Prestressed Concrete Institute (CPCI): 196 Bronson Ave, Suite 100, Ottawa, ON K1R 6H4; tel. (613) 232-2619; fax (613) 232-5139; e-mail info@cpci.ca; internet www.cpci.ca; Pres. ROBERT BURAK; 26 active, 36 assoc., 12 supporting and 100 professional and student mems.

Ontario Painting Contractors Association: 211 Consumers Rd, Suite 305, Toronto, ON M2J 4G8; tel. (416) 498-1897; fax (416) 498-6757; e-mail info@ontpca.org; internet www.ontpca.org; f. 1976; Pres. THOMAS CORBETT; Exec. Dir ANDREW SEFTON; 100 mems.

Clothing and Textiles

Apparel Quebec/Vêtement Québec (Institut des manufacturiers du vêtement du Québec—IMVQ): 555 rue Chabanel ouest, Suite 1514, Montréal, QC H2N 2J2; tel. (514) 382-3846; fax (514) 940-5336; e-mail sc@vetementquebec.com; internet www.vetementquebec.com; f. 1974; Exec. Dir PATRICK THOMAS.

Canadian Apparel Federation: 151 Slater St, Suite 708, Ottawa, ON K1P 5H3; tel. (613) 231-3220; fax (613) 231-2305; e-mail info@apparel.ca; internet www.apparel.ca; f. 1977; Exec. Dir BOB KIRKE.

Canadian Textiles Institute: 222 Somerset St West, Suite 500, Ottawa, ON K2P 2G3; tel. (613) 232-7195; fax (613) 232-8722; e-mail cti@textiles.ca; internet www.textiles.ca; f. 1935; Pres. and CEO HARVEY L. PENNER; 60 mems.

Electrical and Electronics

Canadian Electrical Contractors' Association (CECA): 170 Attwell Dr., Suite 460, Toronto, ON M9W 5Z5; tel. (416) 675-3226; fax (416) 675-7736; e-mail ceca@ceca.org; internet www.ceca.org; f. 1955; Pres. COLIN CAMPBELL.

Corporation des maîtres électriciens du Québec/Corporation of Master Electricians of Québec (CMEQ): blvd Décarie, bureau 5925, Montréal, QC H3W 3C9; tel. (514) 738-2184; fax (514) 738-2192; e-mail yvon.guilbault@cmeq.org; internet www.cmeq.org; f. 1950; Pres. ANGELO TOZZI; Exec. Vice-Pres. YVON GUILBAULT.

Electrical Contractors' Association of Alberta (ECCA): 120 St, Suite 11235, Edmonton, AB T5G 2X9; tel. (780) 451-2412; fax (780) 455-9815; e-mail ecaa@ecaa.ab.ca; internet www.ecaa.ab.ca; f. 1962; Exec. Dir SHERI MCLEAN; Pres. CLEM GRATTON; over 400 mem. orgs.

Electrical Contractors' Association of British Columbia (ECABC): 3989 Henning Dr., Suite 201, Burnaby, BC V5C 6N5; tel. (604) 294-4123; fax (604) 294-4120; e-mail eca@eca.bc.ca; internet www.eca.bc.ca; f. 1952; Chair. ROBERT LASHIN; Pres. DEBORAH CAHILL.

Electrical Contractors' Association of New Brunswick, Inc: 850 Prospect St West, Suite 400, POB 322, Fredericton, NB E3B 4Y9; tel. (506) 452-7627; fax (506) 452-1786; e-mail dwe@eca.nb.ca; internet www.eca.nb.ca; Exec. Dir DAVID ELLIS.

Electrical Contractors' Association of Ontario: 170 Attwell Dr., Suite 460, Toronto, ON M9W 5Z5; tel. (416) 675-3226; fax (416) 675-7736; e-mail ecao@ecao.org; internet www.ecao.org; f. 1948; Pres. JAMES KELLETT; Exec. Vice-Pres. ERYL M. ROBERTS.

Electrical Contractors' Association of Saskatchewan: 1939 Elphinstone St, Regina, SK S4T 3N3; tel. (306) 525-0171; fax (306) 347-8595; e-mail michaelf@scaonline.ca; internet www.ecas.ca; Exec. Dir MICHAEL FOUGERE.

Canadian Electricity Association, Inc: see Utilities—Electricity

Fisheries

Fisheries Council of Canada: 170 Laurier Ave West, Suite 900, Ottawa, ON K1P 5V5; tel. (613) 727-7450; fax (613) 727-7453; e-mail info@fisheriescouncil.org; internet www.fisheriescouncil.ca; f. 1915; Pres. PATRICK MCGUINNESS; six mem. asscns, over 110 mem. cos.

Food and Beverages

Baking Association of Canada: 7895 Tranmere Dr., Suite 202, Mississauga, ON L5S 1V9; tel. (905) 405-0288; fax (905) 405-0993; e-mail info@baking.ca; internet www.baking.ca; f. 1947; Pres. and CEO PAUL HETHERINGTON; 1,400 institutional mems, 200 assoc. mems.

Brewers Association of Canada/L'Association des brasseurs du Canada: 100 Queen St, Suite 650, Ottawa, ON K1P 1J9; tel. (613) 232-9601; fax (613) 232-2283; e-mail info@brewers.ca; internet www.brewers.ca; f. 1943; Chair. BRUCE MCCUBBIN; Pres. and CEO IAN FARIS; 19 mems.

Canadian Association of Sales and Marketing Agencies/Association canadienne des agences en vente et marketing (CASMA/ACAVM): 885 Don Mills Rd, Suite 301, Toronto, ON M3C 1V9; tel. (416) 385-2322; fax (416) 510-8043; e-mail btordoff@casmaonline.ca; internet www.casmaonline.ca; f. 1942; fmrly the Canadian Food Brokers Asscn; mem. of the Asscn of Sales and Marketing Cos Int. (USA); Pres. KEITH BRAY; 70 mems, 60 assoc. mems.

Canadian Meat Council/Conseil des viandes du Canada: 1545 Carling Ave, Suite 407, Ottawa, ON K1Z 8P9; tel. (613) 729-3911; fax (613) 729-4997; e-mail info@cmc-cvc.com; internet www.cmc-cvc.com; f. 1919; Pres. SCOTT ENTZ; Exec. Dir JAMES M. LAWS; 45 regular and 60 assoc. mems.

Canadian National Millers' Association: 265 Carling Ave, Suite 200, Ottawa, ON K1S 2E1; tel. (613) 238-2293; fax (613) 235-5866; e-mail gharrison@canadianmillers.ca; internet www.canadianmillers.ca; f. 1920; Pres. GORDON HARRISON; 13 mems.

Canadian Pork Council/Conseil canadien du porc (CPC/CCP): 220 Laurier Ave West, Suite 900, Ottawa, ON K1P 5Z9; tel. (613) 236-9239; fax (613) 236-6658; e-mail info@cpc-ccp.com; internet www.cpc-ccp.com; f. 1968; Chair. JURGEN PREUGSCHAS; nine mems.

Confectionery Manufacturers Association of Canada/L'Association canadienne des fabricants confiseries (CMAC): 885 Don Mills Rd, Suite 301, Don Mills, ON M3C 1V9; tel. (416) 510-8034; fax (416) 510-8043; e-mail info@cmaconline.ca; internet www.confectioncanada.com; f. 1919; Exec. Dir LESLIE EWING; 70 mems.

Food and Consumer Products of Canada: 100 Sheppard Ave East, Suite 600, Toronto, ON M2N 6N5; tel. (416) 510-8024; fax (416) 510-8043; e-mail info@fcpc.ca; internet www.fcpc.ca; Chair. DINO BLANCO; Pres. and Gen. Man. JEAN GATTUSO; Pres. and CEO NANCY CROITORU; 150 corporate mems.

Food Processors of Canada: 350 Sparks St, Suite 900, Ottawa, ON K1R 7S8; tel. (613) 722-1000; e-mail fpc@foodprocessors.ca; internet www.foodprocessors.ca; f. 1989; fmrly Food Institute of Canada; Pres. CHRISTOPHER KYTE; 200 mems.

Forestry, Lumber and Allied Industries

Canadian Forestry Association/Association forestière canadienne (CFA/AFC): 1027 Pembroke St East, Suite 200, Pembroke, ON K8A 3M4; tel. (613) 732-2917; fax (613) 732-3386; e-mail manager@canadianforestry.com; internet www.canadianforestry.com; f. 1900; Chair. BARRY WAITO; Gen. Man. DAVE LEMKAY.

Canadian Wood Council (CWC/CCB): 99 Bank St, Suite 400, Ottawa, ON K1P 6B9; tel. (613) 747-5544; fax (613) 747-6264; e-mail info@cwc.ca; internet www.cwc.ca; f. 1959; Pres. and CEO MICHAEL GIROUX; Chair. CHRIS MCIVER; 14 mem. asscns.

Council of Forest Industries (COFI): I Business Bldg, Suite 1501, 700 West Pender St, Pender Pl., Vancouver, BC V6C 1G8; tel. (604) 684-0211; fax (604) 687-4930; e-mail info@cofi.org; internet www.cofi .org; f. 1960; Pres. and CEO JOHN ALLAN; Exec. Dir PAUL J. NEWMAN; 51 mems.

Forest Products Association of Canada/Association des produits forestiers du Canada (FPAC/APFC): 99 Bank St, Suite 410, Ottawa, ON KIP 6B9; tel. (613) 563-1441; fax (613) 563-4720; e-mail ottawa@fpac.ca; internet www.fpac.ca; f. 1913; fmrly the Canadian Pulp and Paper Asscn; Pres. and CEO AVRIM LAZAR; Exec. Dir SUSAN MURRAY; 20 mem. cos.

Ontario Forest Industries Association (OFIA): 10 King St East, Suite 300, Toronto, ON M5C 1C3; tel. (416) 368-6188; fax (416) 368-5445; e-mail info@ofia.com; internet www.ofia.com; f. 1943; merged with Canadian Lumbermen's Asscn (f. 1907) in 2009; Pres. and CEO JAMIE LIM; 12 mem. cos, 10 affiliate mems.

Hotels and Catering

Canadian Restaurant and Foodservices Association: 316 Bloor St West, Toronto, ON M5S 1W5; tel. (416) 923-8416; fax (416) 923-1450; e-mail info@crfa.ca; internet www.crfa.ca; f. 1944; Pres. and CEO GARTH WHYTE; more than 30,000 mems.

Hotel Association of Canada: 130 Albert St, Suite 1206, Ottawa, ON K1P 5G4; tel. (613) 237-7149; fax (613) 237-8928; e-mail info@hotelassociation.ca; internet www.hotelassociation.ca; f. 1913; Pres. ANTHONY P. POLLARD; 10 provincial asscns; 28 corp. mems.

Hotel and Restaurant Suppliers Association, Inc/Association des fournisseurs d'hôtels et restaurants, inc: 9300 blvd Henri Bourassa ouest, Suite 230, St-Laurent, QC H4S 1L5; tel. (514) 334-3404; fax (514) 334-1279; e-mail info@afhr.com; internet www.afhr .com; f. 1936; Pres. and CEO VICTOR FRANCOEUR.

Mining

Canadian Association of Petroleum Producers (CAPP): 350 Seventh Ave, SW, Suite 2100, Calgary, AB T2P 3N9; tel. (403) 267-1100; fax (403) 261-4622; e-mail communication@capp.ca; internet www.capp.ca; f. 1952; represents the upstream petroleum and natural gas industry; Chair. LOWELL JACKSON; Pres. DAVID COLLYER; 150 mems, 125 assoc. mems.

Canadian Gas Association: See Utilities—Gas.

Mining Association of Canada (MAC): 350 Sparks St, Suite 1105, Ottawa, ON K1R 7S8; tel. (613) 233-9392; fax (613) 233-8897; e-mail communications@mining.ca; internet www.mining.ca; f. 1935; Chair. DOUGLAS HORSWILL; Pres. and CEO PIERRE GRATTON; 31 mems, 50 assoc. mems.

Northwest Territories and Nunavut Chamber of Mines: POB 2818, Yellowknife, NT X1A 2R1; tel. (867) 669-5681; fax (867) 920-2145; e-mail officemanager@miningnorth.com; internet www .miningnorth.com; f. 1967 as Northwest Territories Chamber of Mines; present name adopted in 2000; Pres. PAMELA STRAND; Exec. Dir TOM HOEFER; 800 mems.

Ontario Mining Association: 5775 Yonge St, Suite 520, North York, ON M2M 4J1; tel. (416) 364-9301; fax (416) 364-5986; e-mail pmcbride@oma.on.ca; internet www.oma.on.ca; f. 1920; Pres. CHRIS HODGSON; 77 mems.

Petroleum Services Association of Canada: 800 Sixth Ave, SW, Suite 1150, Calgary, AB T2P 3G3; tel. (403) 264-4195; fax (403) 263-7174; e-mail info@psac.ca; internet www.psac.ca; f. 1981; Chair. BRIAN COSTON; Pres. MARK SALKELD; over 250 mems.

Yukon Chamber of Mines: 3151B Third Ave, Whitehorse, YT Y1A 1G1; tel. (867) 667-2090; fax (867) 668-7127; e-mail info@yukonminers.ca; internet www.yukonminers.ca; f. 1947; Pres. CLAIRE DEROME; Exec. Dir J. MICHAEL WARK; over 400 mems.

Pharmaceutical

Canada's Research-Based Pharmaceutical Companies/Les compagnies de recherche pharmaceutique du Canada (Rx&D): 55 Metcalfe St, Suite 1220, Ottawa, ON K1P 6L5; tel. (613) 236-0455; fax (613) 236-6756; e-mail info@canadapharma.org; internet www.canadapharma.org; f. 1914 as Canadian Asscn of Mfrs of Medicinal and Toilet Products, present name adopted 1999; Chair. DEBORAH M. BROWN; Pres. RUSSELL WILLIAMS; c. 20,000 mems.

Canadian Generic Pharmaceutical Association (CGPA): 4120 Yonge St, Suite 409, Toronto, ON M2P 2B8; tel. (416) 223-2333; fax (416) 223-2425; e-mail info@canadiangenerics.ca; internet www .canadiangenerics.ca; fmrly Canadian Drug Mfrs' Asscn; Pres. JIM KEON; Chair. BARRY FISHMAN; 18 mems.

Retailing

Retail Council of Canada: 1255 Bay St, Suite 800, Toronto, ON M5R 2A9; tel. (416) 922-6678; fax (416) 922-8011; e-mail info@retailcouncil.org; internet www.retailcouncil.org; f. 1963; Chair. DAVID RUSSELL; Pres. and CEO DIANE J. BRISEBOIS; c. 9,000 mems.

Retail Merchants' Association of Canada (Ontario) Inc: 10 Milner Business Court, Suite 401, Scarborough, ON M1B 3C6; tel. (416) 293-2100; fax (416) 293-2103; internet www.rmacanada.com; f. 1948; Exec. Dir RALPH MOYAL.

Transport

Air Transport Association of Canada: see Transport—Civil Aviation

Canadian Institute of Traffic and Transportation: 10 King St East, 4th Floor, Toronto, ON M5C 1C3; tel. (416) 363-5696; fax (416) 363-5698; internet www.citt.ca; f. 1958; Pres. CATHERINE VIGLAS; 2,000 mems.

Canadian Shippers' Council: see Transport—Shipping

Canadian Trucking Alliance: 324 Somerset St West, Ottawa, ON K2P 0J9; tel. (613) 236-9426; fax (613) 563-2701; e-mail info@cantruck.com; internet www.cantruck.com; f. 1937; CEO DAVID BRADLEY.

Canadian Vehicle Manufacturers' Association: 170 Attwell Dr., Suite 400, Toronto, ON M9W 5Z5; tel. (416) 364-9333; fax (416) 367-3221; e-mail info@cvma.ca; internet www.cvma.ca; f. 1926; Pres. MARK A. NANTAIS; 4 mems.

Railway Association of Canada: see Transport—Railways

Shipping Federation of Canada: see Transport—Shipping

Miscellaneous

Canadian Association of Importers and Exporters Inc (I. E. Canada): POB 189, Station Don Mills, ON M3C 2S2; tel. (416) 595-5333; fax (416) 595-8226; e-mail info@iecanada.com; internet www .iecanada.com; f. 1932 as the Canadian Importers and Traders Asscn; name changed as above in 2000; Chair. JOHN O'RIELLY; Pres. JOY NOTT; 750 mem. cos.

Canadian Printing Industries Association: 151 Slater St, Suite 1110, Ottawa, ON K1P 5H3; tel. (613) 236-7208; fax (613) 232-1334; e-mail info@cpia-aci.ca; internet www.cpia-aci.ca; f. 1939; Chair. DEAN MCELHINNEY; Pres. BOB ELLIOT; 789 mems.

Shipbuilding Association of Canada: 222 Queen St, Ottawa, ON K1P 5V9; tel. (613) 232-7127; fax (613) 238-5519; e-mail pcairns@cfncon.com; internet www.shipbuilding.ca; f. 1995; Chair. ANDREW MCARTHUR; Pres. PETER CAIRNS; 5 mems, 10 assoc. mems.

UTILITIES

Regulatory Authorities

Alberta Utilities Commission: Fifth Ave Pl., 4th Floor, 425 First St, SW, Calgary, AB T2P 3L8; tel. (403) 592-8845; fax (403) 592-4406; e-mail info@auc.ab.ca; internet www.auc.ab.ca; f. 2008 after realignment of Alberta Energy and Utilities Bd into two separate bodies; regulates Alberta's electric, natural gas, and water utilities; Chair. WILLIE GRIEVE; CEO BOB HEGGIE.

British Columbia Utilities Commission: 900 Howe St, 6th Floor, Box 250, Vancouver, BC V6Z 2N3; tel. (604) 660-4700; fax (604) 660-1102; e-mail commission.secretary@bcuc.com; internet www.bcuc .com; operates under and administers the Utilities Commission Act; Chair. and CEO LEONARD F. KELSEY.

Energy Resources Conservation Board: Fifth St, SW, Suite 1000, Calgary, AB T2P 0R4; tel. (403) 297-8311; fax (403) 297-7336; e-mail inquiries@ercb.ca; internet www.ercb.ca; f. 2008 after realignment of Alberta Energy and Utilities Bd into two separate bodies; regulates Alberta's oil and gas industries; Chair. DAN MCFADYEN.

Manitoba Public Utilities Board: 330 Portage Ave, Suite 400, Winnipeg, MB R3C 0C4; tel. (204) 945-2638; fax (204) 945-2643; e-mail publicutilities@gov.mb.ca; internet www.pub.gov.mb.ca; Chair. GRAHAM F. J. LANE.

National Energy Board: 444 Seventh Ave, SW, Calgary, AB T2P 0X8; tel. (403) 292-4800; fax (403) 292-5503; e-mail info@neb-one.gc .ca; internet www.neb-one.gc.ca; f. 1959; federal regulatory agency; Chair. and CEO GAÉTAN CARON; Sec. ANNE-MARIE ERICKSON.

New Brunswick Energy and Utilities Board: 15 Market Sq., Suite 1400, POB 5001, Saint John, NB E2L 4Y9; tel. (506) 658-2504; fax (506) 643-7300; e-mail rgorman@pub.nb.ca; internet www.nbeub .ca; Chair. RAYMOND GORMAN; Sec. LORRAINE R. LÉGÈRE.

Newfoundland and Labrador Board of Commissioners of Public Utilities: 120 Torbay Rd, Prince Charles Bldg, Suite E 210, POB 21040, St John's, NL A1A 5B2; tel. (709) 726-8600; fax (709)

726-9604; e-mail ito@pub.nl.ca; internet www.pub.nf.ca; Chair. and CEO ANDY WELLS.

Nova Scotia Utility and Review Board: POB 1692, Postal Unit M, Halifax, NS B3J 3S3; tel. (902) 424-4448; fax (902) 424-3919; e-mail board@gov.ns.ca; internet www.nsuarb.ca; f. 1992; Chair. PETER W. GURNHAM.

Ontario Energy Board: 2300 Yonge St, 27th Floor, POB 2319, Toronto, ON M4P 1E4; tel. (416) 481-1967; fax (416) 440-7656; e-mail boardsec@oeb.gov.on.ca; internet www.oeb.gov.on.ca; Chair. ROSEMARIE T. LECLAIR.

Prince Edward Island Regulatory and Appeals Commission: 134 Kent St, Suite 501, POB 577, Charlottetown, PE C1A 7L1; tel. (902) 892-3501; fax (902) 566-4076; e-mail info@irac.pe.ca; internet www.irac.pe.ca; f. 1991 as Public Utilities Commission; regulatory and appeal body for energy, utilities, etc.; Chair. and CEO MAURICE (MOE) RODGERSON; Vice-Chair. ALLAN RANKIN.

Québec Energy Board (Régie de l'Énergie du Québec): Tour de la Bourse, bureau 2.55, 2e étage, 800 pl. Victoria, CP 001, Montréal, QC H4Z 1A2; tel. (514) 873-2452; fax (514) 873-2070; internet www.regie-energie.qc.ca.

Saskatchewan Municipal Board: 2151 Scarth St, 4th Floor, Regina, SK S4P 3V7; tel. (306) 787-6221; fax (306) 787-1610; internet www.smb.gov.sk.ca; Chair. B. G. MCNAMEE.

Electricity

ATCO Electric: 10035 105th St, POB 2426, Edmonton, AB T5J 2V6; internet www.atcoelectric.com; fmrly Alberta Power Ltd; generates and distributes electricity in Alberta.

BC Hydro: 6911 Southpoint Dr., Burnaby, BC V3N 4X8; tel. (604) 224-9376; e-mail bob@bchydro.bc.ca; internet www.bchydro.com; f. 1961; serves 1.8m. customers in British Columbia; Chair. DAN DOYLE; Pres. and CEO CHARLES REID (acting).

Canadian Electricity Association, Inc: 350 Sparks St, Suite 1100, Ottawa, ON K1R 7S8; tel. (613) 230-9263; fax (613) 230-9326; e-mail info@electricity.ca; internet www.electricity.ca; f. 1891; Pres. and CEO PIERRE GUIMOND.

Hydro-Québec: 75 blvd René-Lévesque ouest, 19e étage, Montréal, QC H2Z 1A4; tel. (514) 289-2211; fax (514) 289-3691; e-mail cote.flavie@hydro.qc.ca; internet www.hydro.qc.ca; f. 1944; generates, transmits and distributes electricity; govt-owned supplier to 3.8m. customer accounts in Québec; sold its largest international interest, HQI Transelec Chile SA, in 2006; Chair. MICHAEL L. TURCOTTE; Pres. and CEO THIERRY VANDAL.

Manitoba Hydro: 360 Portage Ave, POB 815, Winnipeg, MB R3C 2P4; tel. (204) 474-3311; fax (204) 360-6155; e-mail publicaffairs@hydro.mb.ca; internet www.hydro.mb.ca; operates 14 hydroelectric facilities, two thermal and four diesel generating stations; Chair. VICTOR H. SCHROEDER; Pres. and CEO ROBERT B. BRENNAN.

Newfoundland and Labrador Hydro: Hydro Pl., 500 Columbus Dr., POB 12400, St John's, NL A1B 4K7; tel. (709) 737-1400; fax (709) 737-1800; e-mail hydro@nlh.nl.ca; internet www.nlh.nl.ca; publicly owned electricity wholesaler; Chair. JOHN OTTENHEIMER; Pres. and CEO ED MARTIN.

Northwest Territories Power Corporation: 4 Capital Dr., Hay River, NT X0E 1G2; tel. (867) 874-5200; fax (867) 874-5229; e-mail info@ntpc.com; internet www.ntpc.com; f. 1989; Chair. BRENDAN BELL; Pres. and CEO DAVID AXFORD.

Nova Scotia Power Inc: POB 910, Halifax, NS B3J 2W5; tel. (902) 428-6230; fax (902) 428-6110; e-mail jennifer.parker@nspower.ca; internet www.nspower.ca; fmrly Crown Corpn of Nova Scotia; privatized in 1992; distributes power to over 490,000 customers; utility subsidiary of Emera; Pres. and CEO ROB BENNETT.

Ontario Power Generation, Inc (OPG): 700 University Ave, Toronto, ON M5G 1X6; tel. (416) 592-2555; fax (416) 971-3621; e-mail webmaster@opg.com; internet www.opg.com; f. 1907 as Ontario Hydro, renamed as above in 1999; Canada's largest utility and main nuclear power producer; generating capacity of 22,000 MW; crown corpn; Chair. JAKE EPP; Pres. and CEO TOM MITCHELL.

Prince Edward Island Energy Corporation: Jones Bldg, 11 Kent St, 4th Floor, POB 2000, Charlottetown, PE C1A 7N8; tel. (902) 894-0288; fax (902) 894-0290; e-mail dwmacquarrie@gov.pe.ca; internet www.gov.pe.ca/enveng/eam-info/dg.inc.php3; Dir WAYNE MACQUARRIE.

SaskPower: 2025 Victoria Ave, Regina, SK S4P 0S1; tel. (306) 566-2121; fax (306) 566-3306; internet www.saskpower.com; f. 1929; conventional thermal, and alternative power; distributes power to over 439,000 customers; Chair. JOEL TEAL; Pres. and CEO ROBERT WATSON.

Gas

Canadian Gas Association (CGA): 350 Sparks St, Suite 809, Ottawa, ON K1R 7S8; tel. (613) 748-0057; fax (613) 748-9078; e-mail info@cga.ca; internet www.cga.ca; f. 1907; represents the natural gas delivery industry; Chair. DOUG KELLN; Pres. and CEO TIMOTHY EGAN; 200 corporate mems.

Ontario Natural Gas Association: 77 Bloor St, Suite 1104, Toronto, ON M5S 1M2; tel. (416) 961-2339; fax (416) 961-1173; e-mail onga@sympatico.ca; Chair. BERNARD JONES.

Suncor: 150 Sixth Ave, SW, POB 2844, Calgary, AB T2P 3E3; tel. (403) 296-8000; fax (403) 296-3030; e-mail info@suncormail.com; internet www.suncor.com; f. 2009 following merger of Suncor Energy (f. 1919 as Sun Co Inc, became Suncor in 1979) and Petro-Canada (f. 1975 as a Crown Corpn, privatized from 1991); natural gas and oil producer; also develops oil sands; Chair. JOHN FERGUSON; Pres. and CEO RICK L. GEORGE.

TransCanada Pipelines Ltd: 111 Fifth Ave, SW, POB 1000, Station M, Calgary, AB T2P 4K5; tel. (403) 267-6100; fax (403) 267-6444; internet www.transcanada.com; production, storage, transmission and sale of natural gas through six subsidiary cos; Pres. and CEO DOUGLAS D. BALDWIN.

Westcoast Energy Inc: 666 Burrard St, Suite 3400, Park Place, Vancouver, BC V6C 3M8; tel. (604) 488-8000; fax (604) 488-8500; internet www.westcoastenergy.com; production, storage, transmission and sale of natural gas through four operating cos in British Columbia, Alberta and Manitoba; Chair. and CEO MICHAEL E. J. PHELPS.

Water

Manitoba Water Stewardship: 200 Saulteaux Cres., POB 11, Winnipeg, MB R3J 3W3; tel. (204) 945-6398; e-mail wsd@gov.mb.ca; internet www.gov.mb.ca/waterstewardship; Minister of Water Stewardship CHRISTINE MELNICK.

Northwest Territories Water Board: POB 1500, Yellowknife, NT X1A 2R3; tel. (867) 669-2772; fax (867) 669-2719; internet infosource.gc.ca/info_1/NTW-XI-e.html.

Nunavut Water Board: Gjoa Haven, NU X0E 1J0.

Resource Management and Environmental Protection Branch, Nova Scotia Department of Environment and Labour: 5151 Terminal Rd, 5th Floor, POB 2107, Halifax, NS B3J 3B7; tel. (902) 424-2554; fax (902) 424-0503; internet www.gov.ns.ca/enla/rmep.

Saskwater: 111 Fairford St East, 2nd Floor, Suite 200, Moose Jaw, SK S6H 1C8; tel. (306) 694-3098; fax (306) 694-3207; e-mail customerservice@saskwater.com; internet www.saskwater.com; Chair. GLEN RITTINGER; Pres. DOUG MATTHIES.

Water Resources Branch, Ontario, Ministry of Environment and Energy: 135 St Clair Ave West, 1st Floor, Toronto, ON M4V 1P5; tel. (416) 325-4000; fax (416) 314-7337; e-mail picemail.moe@ontario.ca; internet www.ene.gov.on.ca/en/water/index.php; Dir Dr JAMES ASHMAN.

Water Resources Division, Prince Edward Island Department of the Environment: Jones Bldg, 11 Kent St, POB 2000, Charlottetown, PE C1A 7N8; tel. (902) 368-5000; fax (902) 368-5830; e-mail jjyoung@gov.pe.ca; Dir JIM YOUNG.

Water Resources Management Division, Newfoundland and Labrador Department of Environment and Conservation: Confederation Bldg, West Block, 4th Floor, POB 8700, St John's, NL A1B 4J6; tel. (709) 729-2563; fax (709) 729-0320; e-mail water@gov.nl.ca; internet www.env.gov.nl.ca/env/department/contact/wrmd.html; f. 1949; Dir HASEEN KHAN.

Water Stewardship Division, British Columbia Ministry of Environment: POB 9339, Station Provincial Govt, Victoria, BC V8W 9M1; tel. (250) 356-9443; fax (250) 953-3414; e-mail water.stewardship@gov.bc.ca; internet www.env.gov.bc.ca/wsd; Exec. Asst SARAH ANDREWS.

TRADE UNIONS

At the beginning of 2007 there were 4,480,020 union members in Canada, representing 30.3% of the civilian (non-agricultural) labour force. In 2000 29.5% of union members belonged to unions with headquarters in the USA.

In 2007 unions affiliated to the Canadian Labour Congress represented 70.8% of total union membership.

Canadian Labour Congress (CLC): 2841 Riverside Dr., Ottawa, ON K1V 8X7; tel. (613) 521-3400; fax (613) 521-4655; e-mail hyussuff@clc-ctc.ca; internet www.canadianlabour.ca; f. 1956; Pres. KENNETH V. GEORGETTI; Sec.-Treas. HASSAN YUSSUFF; c. 3.2m. mems (2011).

Affiliated unions with more than 15,000 members:

Amalgamated Transit Union: 61 International Blvd, Suite 210, Rexdale, ON M9W 6K4; tel. (416) 679-8846; fax (416) 679-9195; e-mail director@atucanada.ca; internet www.atucanada.ca; Dir STAN DERA; 30,000 mems (2011).

American Federation of Musicians of the United States and Canada: 150 Ferrand Dr., Suite 202, Toronto, ON M3C 3E5; tel. (416) 391-5161; fax (416) 391-5165; e-mail afmcan@afm.org; internet www.afm.org; Vice-Pres. in Canada BILL SKOLNIK; 45,000 mems (2011).

British Columbia Nurses' Union: 4060 Regent St, Burnaby, BC V5C 6P5; tel. (604) 433-2268; fax (604) 433-7945; e-mail dmcpherson@bcnu.org; internet www.bcnu.org; Pres. DEBRA MCPHERSON; 32,000 mems (2010).

British Columbia Teachers' Federation: 550 West Sixth Ave, Suite 100, Vancouver, BC V5Z 4P2; tel. (604) 871-2283; fax (604) 871-2294; e-mail susan@bctf.ca; internet bctf.ca; f. 1917; Pres. SUSAN LAMBERT; 47,021 mems (2010).

Canadian Office and Professional Employees Union/Syndicat Canadien des employees et employes professionels et de bureau (COPE/SEPB): 1200 ave Papineau, bureau 250, Montréal, QC H2K 4S6; tel. (514) 522-6511; fax (514) 522-9096; e-mail fdoyon@sepb.qc.ca; internet copesepb.ca; f. 2004 after Canadian br. of Office and Professional Employees' Union split from int. fed.; Pres. SERGE CADIEUX; 34,000 mems (2010).

Canadian Union of Postal Workers: 337 Bank St, Ottawa, ON K2P 1Y3; tel. (613) 236-7238; fax (613) 563-7861; e-mail feedback@cupw-sttp.org; internet www.cupw.ca; f. 1965; Nat. Pres. DENIS LEMELIN; 54,144 mems (2010).

Canadian Union of Public Employees (CUPE): 1375 St Laurent, Ottawa, ON K1G 0Z7; tel. (613) 237-1590; fax (613) 237-5508; e-mail cupemail@cupe.ca; internet www.cupe.ca; Nat. Pres. PAUL MOIST; 601,976 mems (2010).

Communications, Energy and Paperworkers Union of Canada/Syndicat canadien des communications, de l'energie et du papier (CEP): 301 Laurier Ave West, Ottawa, ON K1P 6M6; tel. (613) 230-5200; fax (613) 230-5801; e-mail info@cep.ca; internet www.cep.ca; Pres. DAVE COLES; Sec.-Treas. GAËTAN MÉNARD; 128,564 mems (2010).

Elementary Teachers' Federation of Ontario: 480 University Ave, Suite 1000, Toronto, ON M5G 1V2; tel. (416) 962-3836; fax (416) 642-2424; internet www.etfo.ca; f. 1998; Pres. SAM HAMMOND; 73,325 mems (2010).

FTQ Construction: 2900-565 blvd Crémazie est, Montréal, QC H2M 2V6; tel. (514) 381-7300; fax (514) 381-5173; internet www.ftqconstruction.org; f. 1980; Pres. ARNOLD GUÉRIN; Gen. Pres. YVES OUELLET; 69,914 mems (2010).

International Association of Fire Fighters: 350 Sparks St, Suite 403, Ottawa, ON K1R 7S8; tel. (613) 567-8988; fax (613) 567-8986; e-mail tburn@iaff.org; internet www.iaff.org; Gen. Pres. HAROLD A. SCHAITBERGER; 20,000 mems (2008).

International Association of Machinists and Aerospace Workers (IAM): 15 Gervais Dr., Suite 707, North York, ON M3C 1Y8; tel. (416) 386-1789; fax (416) 386-0210; e-mail info@iamaw.ca; internet www.iamaw.ca; Gen. Vice-Pres. in Canada DAVE L. RITCHIE; c. 40,000 mems (2010).

International Brotherhood of Electrical Workers: 1450 Meyerside Dr., Suite 300, Mississauga, ON L5T 2N5; tel. (905) 564-5441; fax (905) 564-8114; e-mail ivpd_01@ibew.org; internet www.ibew1st.org; Int. Vice-Pres. PHILLIP FLEMING; 57,130 mems (2010).

International Union of Operating Engineers: Suite 100, 250 Park Ave, Thunder Bay, ON P7B 5L4; tel. (807) 343-9493; internet www.iuoe.org; f. 1896; headquarters in USA; Gen. Pres. VINCENT J. GIBLIN; 41,993 mems (2010).

Labourers' International Union of North America: 44 Hughson St, South Hamilton, ON L8N 2A7; tel. (905) 522-7177; fax (905) 522-9310; e-mail joseph@liuna.ca; internet www.liuna.ca; headquarters in USA; Gen. Pres. TERENCE M. O'SULLIVAN; Vice-Pres. (Canada) JOSEPH MANCINELLI; 50,000 mems (2010).

National Automobile, Aerospace Transportation and General Workers Union of Canada (CAW–Canada): 205 Placer Court, North York, Willowdale, ON M2H 3H9; tel. (416) 497-4110; fax (416) 495-6552; e-mail caw@caw.ca; internet www.caw.ca; f. 1985; Nat. Pres. KEN LEWENZA; 195,000 mems (2010).

National Union of Public and General Employees: 15 Auriga Dr., Nepean, ON K2E 1B7; tel. (613) 228-9800; fax (613) 228-9801; e-mail national@nupge.ca; internet www.nupge.ca; Nat. Pres. JAMES CLANCY; Nat. Sec.-Treas. LARRY BROWN; 340,000 mems (2010).

Ontario English Catholic Teachers' Association: 65 St Clair Ave East, Suite 400, Toronto, ON M4T 2Y8; tel. (416) 925-2493; fax (416) 925-7764; e-mail d.thomson@oecta.on.ca; internet www.oecta.on.ca; Pres. KEVIN O'DWYER; 45,000 mems (2011).

Ontario Nurses' Association: 85 Grenville St, Suite 400, Toronto, ON M5S 3A2; tel. (416) 964-8833; fax (416) 964-8864; e-mail onamail@ona.org; internet www.ona.org; Pres. LINDA HASLAM-STROUD; 55,000 mems (2010).

Ontario Secondary School Teachers' Federation: 60 Mobile Dr., Toronto, ON M4A 2P3; tel. (416) 751-8300; fax (416) 751-3394; e-mail burgess@osstf.on.ca; internet www.osstf.on.ca; f. 1919; Pres. KENNETH CORAN; 60,000 mems (2011).

Public Service Alliance of Canada: 233 Gilmour St, Ottawa, ON K2P 0P1; tel. (613) 560-4200; fax (613) 567-0385; e-mail nat-pres@psac-afpc.com; internet www.psac-afpc.com; f. 1966; Nat. Pres. JOHN GORDON; 188,462 mems (2010).

Service Employees International Union: 2180 Steeles Ave, Suite 305, West Concord, ON L4K 2Z5; tel. (905) 695-1203; fax (905) 695-1209; e-mail stewarts@seiu.ca; internet www.seiu.ca; Int. Canadian Vice-Pres. SHARLEEN STEWART; Exec. Dir JACOB LEIBOVITCH; 92,781 mems (2010).

Teamsters Canada: 2540 Daniel-Johnson, bureau 804, Laval, QC H7T 2S3; tel. (450) 682-5521; fax (450) 681-2244; internet www.teamsters-canada.org; Canadian Pres. ROBERT BOUVIER; 140,000 mems (2011).

UNITE-HERE: 15 Gervais Dr., 3rd Floor, Suite 310, Toronto, ON M3C 1Y8; tel. (416) 384-0983; fax (416) 384-0991; e-mail mhollin@unitehere.org; internet www.uniteherecanada.org; f. 1995 by merger of Union of Needletrades, Industrial and Textile Employees and Hotel Employees and Restaurant Employees Union; Dir NICK WORHAUG; Exec. Vice-Pres. PAUL CLIFFORD; 46,000 mems (2010).

United Association of Journeymen and Apprentices of the Plumbing and Pipe Fitting Industry of the United States and Canada: 225 Metcalfe St, Suite 600, Ottawa, ON K2P 1P9; tel. (613) 565-1100; fax (613) 565-1200; e-mail uacanada@on.aibn.com; internet www.uacanada.ca; Dir of Canadian Affairs JOHN TELFORD; 49,905 mems (2010).

United Food and Commercial Workers Canada (UFCW): 61 International Blvd, Suite 300, Toronto, ON M9W 6K4; tel. (416) 675-1104; fax (416) 675-6919; e-mail ufcw@ufcw.ca; internet www.ufcw.ca; f. 1979; Nat. Pres. WAYNE HANLEY; 250,000 mems (2010).

United Steel, Paper and Forestry, Rubber, Manufacturing, Energy, Allied Industrial and Service Workers International Union (United Steelworkers): 234 Eglinton Ave East, 8th Floor, Toronto, ON M4P 1K7; tel. (416) 487-1571; fax (416) 482-5548; e-mail info@usw.ca; internet www.usw.ca; f. 1943; Nat. Dir for Canada KEN NEUMANN; c. 225,000 mems (2011).

Other Central Congresses

Centrale des syndicats démocratiques: 801 4e rue, bureau 300, Québec, QC G1J 2T7; tel. (418) 529-2956; fax (418) 529-6323; e-mail info@csd.qc.ca; internet www.csd.qc.ca; f. 1972; Pres. FRANÇOIS VAUDREUIL; Sec. JEAN-CLAUDE DUFRESNE; 74,300 mems (2012).

Centrale des syndicats du Québec: 9405 rue Sherbrooke est, Montréal, QC H1L 6P3; tel. (514) 356-8888; fax (514) 356-9999; internet www.csq.qc.net; f. 1974; name changed as above in 2000; Pres. RÉJEAN PARENT; 11 affiliated federations, 230 affiliated unions, more than 160,000 mems.

Affiliated union with more than 15,000 mems:

Fédération des syndicats de l'enseignment: 320 rue St-Joseph est, bureau 100, Québec, QC G1K 9E7; tel. (418) 649-8888; fax (418) 649-1914; e-mail fse@csq.qc.net; internet www.fse.qc.net; Pres. MANON BERNARD; 60,000 mems (2012).

Confederation of Canadian Unions: East Office Bldg, 4700 Keele St, Toronto, ON M3J 1P3; tel. (416) 736-5109; fax (416) 736-5519; e-mail contact@ccu-csc.ca; internet www.ccu-csc.ca; f. 1969; Pres. JOANIE CAMERON PRITCHETT; 7500 mems.

Confédération des syndicats nationaux: 1601 ave de Lorimier, Montréal, QC H2K 4M5; tel. (514) 598-2271; fax (514) 598-2052; e-mail csnexecutif@csn.qc.ca; internet www.csn.qc.ca; f. 1921; Pres. LOUIS ROY; 8 federated unions, 292,948 mems (2011).

Fédération du commerce: 1601 ave de Lorimier, Montréal, QC H2K 4M5; tel. (514) 598-2181; fax (514) 598-2304; e-mail diane.david@csn.qc.ca; internet www.fc.csn.qc.ca; Pres. SERGE FOURNIER; 36,274 mems (2010).

Fédération de la CSN–Construction: 2100 blvd de Maisonneuve est, 4e étage, Montréal, QC H2K 4S1; tel. (514) 598-3629; fax (514) 598-2425; e-mail sec-montreal@csnconstruction.qc.ca; internet www.csnconstruction.qc.ca; f. 1924; Pres. ALDO MIGUEL PAOLINELLI; 18,000 mems.

Fédération des employées et employés de services publics inc: 1601 ave de Lorimier, Montréal, QC H2K 4M5; tel. (514) 598-2231; fax (514) 598-2398; e-mail feesp.courrier@csn.qc.ca; internet www.feesp.csn.qc.ca; f. 1947; Pres. DENIS MARCOUX; 55,700 mems (2010).

Fédération de l'industrie manufacturière (FIM-CSN): 2100 blvd de Maisonneuve est, bureau 204, Montréal, QC H2K 4S1; tel.

(514) 529-4937; fax (514) 529-4935; e-mail fim@csn.qc.ca; internet www.fim.csn.qc.ca; f. 1944 as Fédération de la métallurgie, present name adopted 2010; Pres. ALAIN LAMPRON; Sec.-Treas. YVES GAMELIN; 11 regional offices, more than 30,000 mems.

Fédération nationale des communications: 1601 ave de Lorimier, Montréal, QC H2K 4M5; tel. (514) 598-2335; fax (514) 598-2431; e-mail chantale.larouche@fncom.org; internet www.fncom.org; f. 1972; Pres. CHANTALE LAROUCHE.

Fédération nationale des enseignantes et des enseignants du Québec (FNEEQ): 1601 ave de Lorimier, Montréal, QC H2K 4M5; tel. (514) 598-2241; fax (514) 598-2190; e-mail fneeq.reception@csn.qc.ca; internet www.fneeq.qc.ca; f. 1969; Pres. JEAN TRUDELLE; 27,000 mems (2011).

Fédération des professionnèles: 1601 ave de Lorimier, Montréal, QC H2K 4M5; tel. (514) 598-2181; internet www.fpcsn.qc.ca; f. 1964; Pres. MICHEL TREMBLAY; Sec.-Gen. LUCIE DUFOUR.

Fédération de la santé et des services sociaux: 1601 ave de Lorimier, Montréal, QC H2K 4M5; tel. (514) 598-2210; fax (514) 598-2223; e-mail fsss@fsss.qc.ca; internet www.fsss.qc.ca; Pres. FRANCINE LÉVESQUE; 122,193 mems (2010).

Affiliated union with over 15,000 members:

International Association of Bridge, Structural and Ornamental Iron Workers: 46 County Rd, Suite 4069, RR 3, Maidstone, ON N0R 1K0; tel. (519) 737-7110; fax (519) 737-7113; e-mail mdugallu700@kelcom.igs.net; internet www.ironworkerslocal700.com; Pres. ROB SCHAAFMA; 15,300 mems (2005).

Principal Unaffiliated Unions

Alberta Teachers' Association: 11010 142nd St, NW, Edmonton, AB T5N 2R1; tel. (780) 447-9400; fax (780) 455-6481; e-mail postmaster@ata.ab.ca; internet www.teachers.ab.ca; Pres. CAROL D. HENDERSON; Exec. Sec. GORDON R. THOMAS; 52,626 mems (2010).

British Columbia Teachers' Federation: 550 West Sixth Ave, Suite 100, Vancouver, BC V5Z 4P2; tel. (604) 871-2283; fax (604) 871-2294; e-mail susan@bctf.ca; internet bctf.ca; f. 1917; Pres. SUSAN LAMBERT; 47,021 mems (2010).

Canadian Telecommunications Employees' Association (CTEA): 1010 de La Gauchetière ouest (pl. du Canada), Suite 360, Montréal, QC H3B 2N2; tel. (514) 861-9963; fax (514) 861-5985; internet www.acet-ctea.com; f. 1943; Pres. BRENDA KNIGHT; 12,000 mems (2007).

Christian Labour Association of Canada (CLAC): 2335 Argentia Rd, Mississauga, ON L5N 5N3; tel. (905) 812-2855; fax (905) 812-5556; e-mail headoffice@clac.ca; internet www.clac.ca; Exec. Dir DICK HEINEN; 50,000 mems (2011).

Elementary Teachers' Federation of Ontario: 480 University Ave, Suite 1000, Toronto, ON M5G 1V2; tel. (416) 962-3836; fax (416) 642-2424; internet www.etfo.ca; f. 1998; Pres. SAM HAMMOND; 73,325 mems (2010).

Fédération interprofessionnelle de la santé du Québec: 1234 ave Papineau, Montréal, QC H2K 0A4; tel. (514) 987-1141; fax (514) 987-7273; e-mail info@fiqsante.qc.ca; internet www.fiqsante.qc.ca; f. 1987; fmrly Fédération des infirmières et d'infirmiers du Québec; Pres. RÉGINE LAURENT; c. 60,000 mems (2011).

Ontario Nurses' Association: 85 Grenville St, Suite 400, Toronto, ON M5S 3A2; tel. (416) 964-8833; fax (416) 964-8864; e-mail onamail@ona.org; internet www.ona.org; Pres. LINDA HASLAM-STROUD; 55,000 mems (2010).

Ontario Public Service Employees Union: 100 Lesmill Rd, North York, ON M3B 3P8; tel. (416) 443-8888; fax (416) 443-9670; e-mail wthomas@opseu.org; internet www.opseu.org; f. 1911; Pres. WARREN (SMOKEY) THOMAS; c. 100,000 mems (2006).

Professional Institute of the Public Service of Canada: 250 Tremblay Rd, Ottawa, ON K1G 3J8; tel. (613) 228-6310; fax (613) 228-9048; e-mail gcorbett@pipsc.ca; internet www.pipsc.ca; Pres. and CEO GARY CORBETT; 57,000 mems (2011).

Syndicat de la fonction publique Québec: 5100 blvd des Gradins, Québec, QC G2J 1N4; tel. (418) 623-2424; fax (418) 623-6109; e-mail communication@sfpq.qc.ca; internet www.sfpq.qc.ca; Gen. Pres. LUCIE MARTINEAU; c. 40,000 mems (2011).

United Nurses of Alberta: 10611 98th Ave, Suite 900, Edmonton, AB T5K 2P7; tel. (780) 425-1025; fax (780) 426-2093; e-mail provincialoffice@una.ab.ca; internet www.una.ab.ca; f. 1977; Pres. HEATHER SMITH; 24,000 mems (2009).

Transport

Owing to the size of the country, Canada's economy is particularly dependent upon its transport infrastructure. The St Lawrence Seaway allows ocean-going ships to reach the Great Lakes. In addition to an extensive railway network, the country's transport facilities are being increasingly augmented by new roads, air services and petroleum pipelines. The Trans-Canada Highway forms a main feature of a network of more than 900,000 km of roads and highways.

Canadian Transportation Agency (CTA): Ottawa, ON K1A 0N9; tel. (819) 994-0775; fax (819) 997-6727; e-mail info@otc-cta.gc.ca; internet www.cta.gc.ca; f. 1996 to replace the Nat. Transportation Agency; independent administrative tribunal responsible for dealing with and resolving transportation disputes; improving access to transportation services; and economic regulation of air, rail and marine transportation; Chair. and CEO GEOFFREY C. HARE.

RAILWAYS

Canadian Pacific Railway Ltd (CPR): Gulf Canada Sq., 401 Ninth Ave, SW, Suite 500, Calgary, AB T2P 4Z4; tel. (403) 319-7000; e-mail ed_greenberg@cpr.ca; internet www.cpr.ca; f. 1881; 26,208 km (16,300 miles) of mainline track in Canada and the north-east and mid-west of the USA; Chair. JOHN E. CLEGHORN; Pres. and CEO FRED J. GREEN.

Ontario Northland: 555 Oak St East, North Bay, ON P1B 8L3; tel. (705) 472-4500; fax (705) 476-5598; e-mail info@ontarionorthland.ca; internet www.ontarionorthland.ca; f. 1902; agency of the Govt of Ontario; operates freight and passenger rail services over 1,086 km (675 miles) of track; Commr and Chair. TED HARGREAVES; Pres. and CEO PAUL GOULET.

VIA Rail Canada Inc: Station A, POB 8116, Montréal, QC H3C 3N3; tel. (514) 871-6000; fax (514) 871-6104; e-mail customer_relations@viarail.ca; internet www.viarail.ca; f. 1978; federal govt corpn; proposed transfer to private sector postponed Oct. 2007; operates passenger services over rail routes covering 13,822 km of track throughout Canada; Chair. PAUL G. SMITH; Pres. and CEO MARC LALIBERTÉ.

Association

Railway Association of Canada: 99 Bank St, Suite 1401, Ottawa, ON K1P 6B9; tel. (613) 567-8591; fax (613) 567-6726; e-mail rac@railcan.ca; internet www.railcan.ca; f. 1917; Pres. and CEO CLIFF J. MACKAY; 60 mems.

ROADS

Provincial governments are responsible for roads within their boundaries. The federal Government is responsible for major roads in the Yukon, the Northwest Territories and Nunavut and in National Parks. In 2008 there were 1,409,000 km of roads (including, in 2004, 16,900 km of freeways and 200,400 km of highways). The Trans-Canada Highway extends from St John's, NL, to Victoria, BC.

INLAND WATERWAYS

The St Lawrence River and the Great Lakes provide Canada and the USA with a system of inland waterways extending from the Atlantic Ocean to the western end of Lake Superior, a distance of 3,769 km (2,342 miles). There is a 10.7-m (35-foot) navigation channel from Montréal to the sea and an 8.25-m (27-foot) channel from Montréal to Lake Erie. The St Lawrence Seaway (see below), which was opened in 1959, was initiated partly to provide a deep waterway and partly to satisfy the increasing demand for electric power. Power development has been undertaken by the provinces of Québec and Ontario, and by New York State. The navigation facilities and conditions are within the jurisdiction of the federal governments of the USA and Canada.

St Lawrence River and Great Lakes Shipping

St Lawrence Seaway Management Corpn: 202 Pitt St, Cornwall, ON K6J 3P7; tel. (613) 932-5170; fax (613) 932-7286; e-mail marketing@seaway.ca; internet www.greatlakes-seaway.com; f. 1998; responsible for management of the St Lawrence Seaway (f. 1959) allowing ocean-going vessels to enter the Great Lakes of North America; operated jtly with the USA; 40.8m. metric tons of freight in 2008; Chair. IAN MACGREGOR; Pres. and CEO TERENCE F. BOWLES.

Algoma Central Corpn: 62 Church St, Suite 600, St Catharines, ON L2R 3C4; tel. (905) 687-7888; fax (905) 687-7882; internet www.algonet.com; f. 1899; Pres. and CEO T. S. DOOL; 24 bulk cargo vessels.

Canada Steamship Lines (CSL): 759 square Victoria, 6th Floor, Montréal, QC H2Y 2K3; tel. (514) 982-3800; fax (514) 982-3910; e-mail info@cslmtl.com; internet www.cslcan.ca; f. 1913; Pres. LOUIS MARTEL; 19 vessels.

SHIPPING

At 31 December 2009 the Canadian merchant fleet comprised 934 vessels, with a total displacement of 2,992,800 grt.

British Columbia Ferry Services Inc (BC Ferries): 1321 Blanshard St, Victoria, BC V8W 0B7; tel. (250) 381-1401; fax (250) 381-5452; e-mail investor.relations@bcferries.com; internet www.bcferries.com; 7 passenger and car ferries; Chair. DONALD P. HAYES; Pres. and CEO DAVID L. HAHN.

Fednav Ltd: 1000 rue de la Gauchetière ouest, Montréal, QC H3B 4W5; tel. (514) 878-6500; fax (514) 878-6642; e-mail info@fednav.com; internet www.fednav.com; f. 1944; shipowners, operators, contractors, terminal operators; owned and chartered fleet of 85 vessels; Chair. LAURENCE G. PATHY; Co-Pres MARK PATHY, PAUL PATHY.

Groupe Desgagnés Inc: 21 rue du Marché-Champlain, bureau 100, Québec, QC G1K 8Z8; tel. (418) 692-1000; fax (418) 692-6044; e-mail info@desgagnes.com; internet www.groupedesgagnes.com; f. 1866; private co; 18 vessels; Chair. and CEO LOUIS-MARIE BEAULIEU.

Marine Atlantic Inc: 10 Fort William Pl., Suite 802, Baine Johnston Centre, St John's, NL A1C 1K4; tel. (709) 772-8957; fax (709) 772-8956; e-mail info@marine-atlantic.ca; internet www.marine-atlantic.ca; serves Atlantic coast of Canada; 4 vessels, incl. passenger, roll-on/roll-off and freight ferries; 405,336 passengers in 2006; Chair. ROB CROSBIE; Pres. and CEO WAYNE FOLLETT.

Associations

Canadian Shipowners Association (CSA): 350 Sparks St, Suite 705, Ottawa, ON K1R 7S8; tel. (613) 232-3539; fax (613) 232-6211; e-mail morrison@shipowners.ca; internet www.shipowners.ca; f. 1953; Pres. BRUCE BOWIE; 7 mem. cos.

Shipping Federation of Canada: 300 rue du St-Sacrement, bureau 326, Montréal, QC H27 1X4; tel. (514) 849-2325; fax (514) 849-8774; e-mail info@shipfed.ca; internet www.shipfed.ca; f. 1903; Chair. DAVID CARDIN; Pres. MICHAEL H. BROAD; 71 mems.

CIVIL AVIATION

Principal Company

Air Canada: Air Canada Centre, 7373 blvd de la Côte-Vertu ouest, Saint-Laurent, Québec, QC H4S 1Z3; tel. (514) 422-5000; e-mail media.relations@aircanada.ca; internet www.aircanada.com; f. 1937; fmrly Trans-Canada Air Lines; subsidiary of ACE Aviation Holdings Inc; acquired Canadian Airlines in Jan. 2001; operates services to 170 cities world-wide; Chair. DAVID I. RICHARDSON; Pres. and CEO CALIN ROVINESCU.

Association

Air Transport Association of Canada (ATAC): 255 Albert St, Suite 700, Ottawa, ON K1P 6A9; tel. (613) 233-7727; fax (613) 230-8648; e-mail atac@atac.ca; internet www.atac.ca; f. 1934 as the Commercial Air Transport and Mfrs' Asscn of Canada; present name adopted in 1962 following withdrawal of industrial mems; mems collectively account for more than 97% of national commercial air transport revenues; Chair. MARK WILLIAMS; Pres. and CEO JOHN MCKENNA.

Tourism

Most tourist visitors are from the USA, accounting for an estimated 11.8m. of a total 15.9m. visitors in 2010. According to the Canadian Tourism Commission, receipts from tourism in that year rose by some 3.4%, to an estimated C $11,900m.

Canadian Tourism Commission: Four Bentall Centre, 1055 Dunsmuir St, Suite 1400, Box 49230, Vancouver, BC V7X 1L2; tel. (604) 638-8300; e-mail ctx_feedback@ctc-cct.ca; internet corporate.canada.travel/ctc-cct; Chair. STEVE ALLAN; Pres. and CEO MICHELE MCKENZIE.

Tourism Industry Association of Canada: 116 Lisgar St, Suite 600, Ottawa, ON K2P 0C2; tel. (613) 238-3883; fax (613) 238-3878; e-mail info@tiac.travel; internet www.tiac.travel; f. 1930; private sector asscn, encourages travel to and within Canada; promotes devt of travel services and facilities; Chair. GOPAL RAO, Jr; Pres. and CEO DAVID F. GOLDSTEIN.

Defence

Canada co-operates with the USA in the defence of North America and is a member of the North Atlantic Treaty Organization. Military service is voluntary. As assessed at November 2011, the armed forces numbered 65,700: army 34,800, navy 11,000, air force 19,900. The Canadian Coast Guard totalled 4,500 personnel. There were 33,950 reserve troops.

Federal Defence Budget: C $21,300m. in 2012.

Chief of the Defence Staff: Gen. WALTER J. NATYNCZYK.

Commander of the Army and Chief of the Land Staff: Lt-Gen. PETER J. DEVLIN.

Commander of Maritime Command and Chief of the Maritime Staff: Vice-Adm. PAUL MADDISON.

Commander of Air Command and Chief of the Air Staff: Lt-Gen. ANDRÉ DESCHAMPS.

Education

Education policy is a provincial responsibility, and the period of compulsory school attendance varies. French-speaking students are entitled by law, in some provinces, to instruction in French. Primary, or elementary, education is for children between the ages of six and 11 or 13, while secondary, or high, schools cater for those aged 12–14 to 18. In 2008/09 some 5,088,789 pupils were enrolled in primary and secondary schools. In 2010/11 there were 95 university institutions in the country. In 2008/09 total federal, provincial and territorial government expenditure on education totalled C $95,732m., equivalent to 15.3% of total expenditure.

CAPE VERDE

Introductory Survey

LOCATION, CLIMATE, LANGUAGE, RELIGION, FLAG, CAPITAL

The Republic of Cape Verde is an archipelago of 10 islands and five islets in the North Atlantic Ocean, about 500 km (300 miles) west of Dakar, Senegal. The country lies in a semi-arid belt, with little rain and an average annual temperature of 24°C (76°F). The official language is Portuguese, of which the locally spoken form is Creole (Crioulo). Virtually all of the inhabitants profess Christianity, and some 95% are Roman Catholics. The national flag, adopted in 1992 (proportions 3 by 5), comprises five horizontal stripes: blue (half the depth) at the top, white, red, white (each one-twelfth) and blue. Superimposed, to the left of centre, is a circle of 10 five-pointed gold stars (four on the white stripes and three each on the blue stripes above and below). The capital is Cidade de Praia.

CONTEMPORARY POLITICAL HISTORY

Historical Context

The Cape Verde Islands were colonized by the Portuguese in the 15th century. From the 1950s liberation movements in Portugal's African colonies campaigned for independence, and, in this context, the archipelago was linked with the mainland territory of Portuguese Guinea (now Guinea-Bissau) under one nationalist movement, the Partido Africano da Independência do Guiné e Cabo Verde (PAIGC). The independence of Guinea-Bissau was recognized by Portugal in September 1974, but the PAIGC leadership in the Cape Verde Islands decided to pursue its independence claims separately, rather than enter into a federation with Guinea-Bissau. In December 1974 a transitional Government, comprising representatives of the Portuguese Government and the PAIGC, was formed; members of other political parties were excluded. On 30 June 1975 elections for a legislative body, the Assembleia Nacional Popular (ANP—National People's Assembly) were held, in which only PAIGC candidates were allowed to participate. Independence was granted to the Republic of Cape Verde on 5 July 1975, with Aristides Pereira, Secretary-General of the PAIGC, becoming the country's first President. Cape Verde's first Constitution was approved in September 1980.

Although Cape Verde and Guinea-Bissau remained constitutionally separate, the PAIGC supervised the activities of both states. Progress towards the ultimate goal of unification was halted by the November 1980 coup in Guinea-Bissau. The Government of Cape Verde condemned the coup, and in January 1981 the Cape Verdean wing of the PAIGC was renamed the Partido Africano da Independência de Cabo Verde (PAICV). In February Pereira was re-elected as President by the ANP, and all articles concerning an eventual union with Guinea-Bissau were removed from the Constitution. Discussions concerning reconciliation were held in June 1982, however, and diplomatic relations between the two countries were subsequently normalized.

Domestic Political Affairs

Elections to the ANP took place in December 1985. The candidates on the PAICV-approved list obtained 94.5% of the votes cast. In January 1986 Pereira was re-elected for a further five-year term as President by the ANP. In April 1990 a newly formed political organization, the Movimento para a Democracia (MpD), issued a manifesto in Paris, France, which advocated the immediate introduction of a multi-party system. Pereira subsequently announced that the next presidential election would be held, for the first time, on the basis of universal suffrage.

In July 1990 a special congress of the PAICV reviewed proposals for new party statutes and the abolition of Article 4 of the Constitution, which guaranteed the supremacy of the PAICV. Pereira also resigned as Secretary-General of the PAICV, and was later replaced by the Prime Minister, Gen. Pedro Verona Rodrigues Pires. In September the ANP approved a constitutional amendment abolishing the PAICV's monopoly of power and permitting a multi-party system. The MpD subsequently received official recognition as a political party. On 13 January 1991 the first multi-party elections to take place in lusophone Africa resulted in a decisive victory for the MpD, which secured 56 of the 79 seats in the ANP. Later that month Dr Carlos Alberto Wahnon de Carvalho Veiga, the leader of the MpD, was sworn in as Prime Minister at the head of an interim Government, mostly comprising members of the MpD. The presidential election, held in mid-February, resulted in victory for António Mascarenhas Monteiro, supported by the MpD, who secured 73.5% of the votes cast. On 25 September 1992 a new Constitution of the Republic of Cape Verde (also referred to as the 'Second Republic') came into force, enshrining the principles of multi-party democracy.

At legislative elections conducted in December 1995 the MpD secured an outright majority, taking 50 of the 72 seats in the Assembleia Nacional (AN, as the ANP had become in 1992). The PAICV won 21 seats, while the remaining seat was obtained by the Partido da Convergência Democrática (PCD), which had been formed in 1994. At a presidential election conducted in February 1996 Mascarenhas, the sole candidate, was re-elected. Veiga, meanwhile, expressed his intention to continue the policies of liberal economic and social reform that had been pursued in his previous term in office.

In municipal elections held in February 2000 the MpD sustained substantial losses, retaining only eight of 17 local councils and losing the capital to the PAICV, which re-emerged as a credible political force. Following the resignation of Pedro Pires, who announced his candidacy for the presidential election, the PAICV elected José Maria Neves as its new President in June. In the following month António Gualberto do Rosário was elected Chairman of the MpD.

In late July 2000 Veiga announced his resignation as Prime Minister and confirmed his candidacy for the presidential election scheduled to take place in early 2001; he was replaced by do Rosário. In October 2000 it was announced that the PCD, the União Caboverdiana Independente e Democrática and the Partido de Trabalho e Solidariedade were to form a coalition (the Aliança Democrática para a Mudança—ADM) to participate in the forthcoming legislative elections. At the legislative elections, held on 14 January 2001, the opposition PAICV secured 49.5% of the vote and 40 seats in the AN, compared with 40.5% (30 seats) for the MpD and 6.1% (two seats) for the ADM. A new Government, headed by Neves, was announced at the end of January. At the presidential election, conducted on 11 February, no candidate received an overall majority, necessitating a second round, held on 25 February; Pires narrowly defeated Veiga, receiving 50.01% of the valid votes cast. Appeals against the result by Veiga, who cited voting irregularities, were later rejected by the Supreme Court, which confirmed Pires as the new President. In December Agostinho Lopes was elected unopposed as the new Chairman of the MpD.

Legislative elections were held on 22 January 2006, the PAICV won 52.3% of the valid votes cast, thus securing 41 seats in the AN, while the MpD won 44.0% of the votes and took 29 seats. The União Cristã, Independente e Democrática (UCID) won two seats. The rate of voter participation was recorded at 54.5%. The MpD claimed that it had evidence of irregularities in the voting process and lodged an appeal with the Supreme Court, although international observers declared that the vote had been fair.

Pires' second term

In the presidential election held on 12 February 2006 Pires secured 51.0% of the valid votes cast, while Veiga received 49.0%. The new Council of Ministers, again headed by Neves, was appointed on 8 March. At the end of that month Agostinho Lopes resigned as leader of the MpD; Jorge Santos was subsequently elected to that position.

In September 2006 the Minister of Finance and Public Administration, João Serra, resigned, owing to ill health, and was replaced by Cristina Duarte. In the following month the PCD voted at its fourth congress to disband—a first such occurrence in the country. In November unrest was caused following a ruling by the Supreme Court that the approval of decrees on value-added tax by the Council of Ministers in the preceding year had been unconstitutional, as they should have been approved by the legislature. Consequently, the prices of fuel, electricity, water, telecommunications and transport escalated, owing to the suspension of protection from external price fluctuations. In November the Minister of the Economy, Growth and Competitiveness, João Pereira Silva, resigned following queries over the legality of certain tourism development contracts; he was succeeded by José Brito.

In mid-February 2007 the PAICV and the MpD each nominated seven deputies to a new commission charged with reaching consensus on issues that required a two-thirds majority in the AN, including constitutional reform and changes to the electoral code, in particular the membership and structure of the Comissão Nacional de Eleições (CNE—National Election Commission). After protracted negotiations a new electoral code was approved in mid-June, which included the creation of single electoral regions for each island, with the exception of Santiago (which was split into two regions). However, disagreements regarding the membership of the CNE delayed the restructuring of that body and the compilation of a new electoral census. The delay prompted the resignation in protest of the Minister of Internal Administration, Júlio Lopes Correia, who was replaced in December by Lívio Lopes, the PAICV deputy leader. In late January 2008 Correia was appointed First Vice-President of the Assembleia Nacional, replacing Mário Matos, the PAICV Secretary-General, who resigned owing to ill health. Matos was succeeded as PAICV Secretary-General by the Minister of State and of Health, Basílio Ramos.

The Government was reorganized in June 2008; only four ministers who served in the outgoing administration retained their posts. Among the key appointments were Brito, who was named Minister of Foreign Affairs, Co-operation and Communities, and Marisa Helena do Nascimento Morais, who was appointed Minister of Justice.

In early February 2010 the AN approved a number of draft changes to the Constitution. The main focus of the reform regarded the composition of the judiciary, with the proposed creation of the Conselho Superior de Magistratura Judicial (Supreme Council of Judiciary) which would approve judicial appointments. (Hitherto judges had been appointed by the Government.) Changes to the electoral code were also approved in that month. Later in February Neves restructured the Government, although the most senior positions remained unaltered.

President Pires confirmed in November 2010 that legislative elections would be held on 6 February 2011. (The presidential election was to be conducted in mid-2011.) The MpD criticized the Government in July 2010 for delays in the voter registration process for Cape Verdean citizens resident overseas; Veiga claimed that the delays would result in fewer residents abroad being able to participate in the elections. Other MpD members also accused the Government of registration irregularities and a lack of transparency. The MpD's election campaign focused on tackling unemployment and poverty by improving education levels and lowering taxes to encourage foreign investment, while the PAICV emphasized its successful infrastructure development projects and burgeoning relations with the European Union (EU).

At the elections to the AN, which were held as scheduled on 6 February 2011, the PAICV retained its legislative majority, taking 52.3% of the votes cast, although the number of seats it won was reduced to 38. The MpD won 42.2% of the votes and took 32 seats, while the UCID won two seats (4.4%). The rate of voter participation was recorded at 76.0%. In mid-March Neves announced the composition of his new Government, which was increased in size from 15 to 21 members and included six independents, appointed to head, *inter alia*, the justice and internal administration ministries. Duarte retained the finance portfolio, while Jorge Tolentino, the former ambassador to Spain, became Minister of the Presidency of the Council of Ministers and of National Defence. Ramos replaced Aristides Lima as Speaker of the AN.

Recent developments: the 2011 presidential election

The first round of the presidential election was contested between four candidates on 7 August 2011. Jorge Carlos Fonseca, a former Minister of Foreign Affairs endorsed by the MpD, secured 37.8% of the votes cast, followed by former Minister of Infrastructure, Transport and Telecommunications Manuel Inocêncio Sousa (of the PAICV) with 32.5% and two independent candidates, Aristides Lima and Joaquim Monteiro, who won 27.8% and 2.0%, respectively. Fonseca defeated Sousa in a second round of voting two weeks later, obtaining 54.2% of the ballot. International monitors, while noting some irregularities, declared that the election had been free and fair.

The participation in the election by Lima—a member of the PAICV who had chosen to stand as an independent, thereby placing himself into direct competition with Sousa, the candidate officially supported by the ruling party—created divisions within the PAICV. One consequence of this schism was the resignation in late August 2011 of the Minister of Social Development and Families, Felisberto Vieira, who, to the embarrassment of the PAICV, had publicly endorsed Lima during the election campaign. A party conference was convened in September in an attempt to promote internal unity, but, despite declarations of rapprochement, tensions remained.

Fonseca was inaugurated as President on 9 September 2011, replacing Pires (who had been constitutionally prohibited from standing in the election). This peaceful transfer of power, still a rare event in sub-Saharan Africa, was internationally recognized in October when Pires received the Mo Ibrahim Prize for Achievement in African Leadership, a high-profile annual award honouring African leaders who uphold democratic values.

Foreign Affairs

Cape Verde has traditionally professed a non-aligned stance in foreign affairs and maintains relations with virtually all the power blocs. On taking office in 1991, the MpD Government successfully sought to extend Cape Verde's range of international contacts, with special emphasis on potential new sources of development aid. In December 1996 Cape Verde became a full member of the Sommet francophone, a commonwealth comprising all the French-speaking nations of the world, and benefits in turn from membership of this body's Agence de coopération culturelle et technique. In July 2001 the new PAICV administration established diplomatic relations at ambassadorial level with the People's Republic of China; as with numerous other African countries, these relations intensified considerably from the mid-2000s. In April 2002 the Government announced its intention to seek a 'special status' for Cape Verde with the EU. With Portuguese support, Cape Verde attained special partnership status with the EU in November 2007, paving the way for greater integration and co-operation in relation to trade, development and security. In July 2010 the Government agreed to a US request to resettle a Syrian detainee, Abd-al-Nisr Mohammed Khantumani, from the USA's detention centre in Guantánamo Bay, Cuba. Critics alleged that the deal had been arranged in exchange for additional US aid, a claim denied by the Government.

The country has continued to maintain particularly close relations with Portugal and Brazil, and with other lusophone African former colonies—Angola, Guinea-Bissau, Mozambique and São Tomé and Príncipe, known collectively, with Cape Verde, as the Países Africanos da Língua Oficial Portuguesa (PALOP). In July 1996 a 'lusophone commonwealth', the Comunidade dos Países de Língua Portuguesa (CPLP), comprising the five PALOP countries together with Portugal and Brazil, was formed with the intention of benefiting each member state through joint co-operation on technical, cultural and social matters. (Timor-Leste acceded to membership of the CPLP in 2002.) In April 2010 Prime Minister Neves arrived in São Tomé and Príncipe, where he signed a number of trade agreements, and he paid an official visit to Portugal in June, signing a new friendship and co-operation accord. President Pires travelled to Mozambique in November and signed a science and technology co-operation agreement with his Mozambican counterpart. The construction of three dams on the archipelago was announced by the Government in March 2011, to be funded by a US $72m. Portuguese credit facility, while in June it was confirmed that Brazil would finance the establishment of a $220m. 'administrative city' in Praia. Brazil also pledged $3m. in August to fund a variety of environmental and infrastructural schemes on the islands. In an attempt to strengthen bilateral ties, Neves hosted discussions with José Ramos Horta, the President of Timor-Leste, and Patrice Emery Trovoada, the Prime Minister of São Tomé and Príncipe, in July and November, respectively. Neves also met with Prime Minister Carlos Gomes Júnior of Guinea-Bissau for talks during a visit to that country in November, and several economic and transportation agreements were concluded. In the previous month Guinea-Bissau had established a consulate in Praia, which it planned to upgrade to an embassy in the future. Cape Verde was a signatory to the 'Luanda Declaration' in November, which pledged greater co-operation between the CPLP member states in the fields of, *inter alia*, security, crime prevention and immigration.

CONSTITUTION AND GOVERNMENT

Under the 1992 Constitution, Cape Verde is a multi-party state, although the formation of parties on a religious or geographical basis is prohibited. Legislative power is vested in the Assembleia Nacional (National Assembly), which comprises 72 deputies, elected by universal adult suffrage for a five-year term. The Head of State is the President of the Republic, who is elected by universal suffrage for a five-year term. Executive power is vested in the Prime Minister, who is nominated by the deputies of the Assembleia Nacional, appointed by the President and governs with the assistance of a Council of Ministers. A constitutional revision, adopted in July 1999, granted the President the right to dissolve the Assembleia Nacional, created a new advisory chamber (Conselho Económico e Social), and granted the state the right to adopt Crioulo as the country's second official language.

REGIONAL AND INTERNATIONAL CO-OPERATION

Cape Verde is a member of the African Union (see p. 189), the Economic Community of West African States (see p. 264), which promotes trade and co-operation in West Africa, and is a signatory to the Lomé Convention and subsequent Cotonou Agreement (see p. 328).

Cape Verde became a member of the UN in 1975, and was admitted to the World Trade Organization (WTO, see p. 433) in 2008. Cape Verde participates in the Group of 77 (G77, see p. 450) developing countries.

ECONOMIC AFFAIRS

In 2010, according to estimates from the World Bank, Cape Verde's gross national income (GNI), measured at average 2008–10 prices, was US $1,620m., equivalent to $3,270 per head (or $3,790 per head on an international purchasing-power parity basis). During 2001–10, it was estimated, the population increased at an average annual rate of 1.2%, while gross domestic product (GDP) per head increased, in real terms, by an average of 4.9% per year. Overall GDP increased, in real terms, at an average annual rate of 6.2% in 2001–10; growth in 2010 was 5.4%.

Agriculture (including forestry and fishing) contributed an estimated 5.9% of GDP in 2010. According to FAO, the sector employed an estimated 15.7% of the total labour force in mid-2012. The staple crop is maize; sugar cane, bananas, coconuts, sweet potatoes, tomatoes, potatoes, cassava and cabbages are also cultivated. Export earnings from fish and crustaceans amounted to 2,830.9m. escudos (76.5% of the total value of exports, excluding re-exports) in 2010. Lobster and tuna are among the most important exports. In 2009 the total fish catch was 16,828 metric tons. In late 2005 an agreement was reached allowing EU vessels to fish in Cape Verdean waters; in return the EU would assist with the development of the local fishing industry. During 2001–09 the GDP of the agricultural sector increased, in real terms, at an average annual rate of 1.8%, according to the World Bank; it increased by 4.4% in 2009.

Industry (including construction and power) contributed an estimated 14.4% of GDP in 2010, and employed 24.5% of the labour force in 1990. During 2001–09, according to the World Bank, industrial GDP increased, in real terms, at an average annual rate of 10.0%; growth in 2009 was 11.2%.

Mining employed 0.3% of the labour force in 1990 and contributed 3.3% of GDP in 2007. During 2000–07 the sector's GDP increased, in real terms, at an average annual rate of 9.8%, according to official figures. Salt and pozzolana, a volcanic ash used in cement manufacture, are the main non-fuel minerals produced.

Manufacturing contributed 6.6% of GDP in 2009, according to the World Bank, and employed about 6% of the labour force in 1995. The most important branches, other than fish-processing, are clothing, footwear, rum distilling and bottling. Legislation enacted in 1999 provided for the transformation of industrial parks at Mindelo and Praia into free-trade zones, and for the establishment of a further free-trade zone on Sal island. During 2000–04 the GDP of the manufacturing sector increased, in real terms, at an average annual rate of 5.8%; a decline of 5.3% was recorded in 2007, according to official figures.

Construction contributed an estimated 7.9% of GDP in 2010 and employed 18.8% of the labour force in 1990. During 2000–07 construction GDP increased, in real terms, at an average annual rate of 8.5%, according to official figures.

Energy is derived principally from hydroelectric power and gas. Imports of fuel products comprised 11.7% of the value of total estimated imports in 2010.

Services accounted for an estimated 79.7% of GDP in 2010 and employed an estimated 50.7% of total labour in 1990. Tourism has been identified as the area with the most potential for economic development. A new international airport on Santiago, which was opened in 2005, was expected to give considerable impetus to the development of the tourism sector. The airport on São Vicente island was upgraded to international capacity in 2000. Plans were also under way for the construction of two further international airports, on São Vicente and Boa Vista. Tourist arrivals increased from 52,000 in 1998 to 336,000 in 2010. During 2001–09 the combined GDP of the services sector increased, in real terms, at an average annual rate of 5.7%, according to the World Bank; growth of 1.1% was recorded in 2009.

In 2010 Cape Verde recorded a visible trade deficit of US $678.8m., and there was a deficit of $184.3m. on the current account of the balance of payments. In 2010 the principal source of imports was Portugal (51.4%); other major suppliers were the Netherlands and Spain. In 2010 Spain was the principal recipient of exports (72.6%), while Portugal was the other major purchaser. The principal exports in 2010 were fish and crustaceans (76.5%), footwear and clothing. The principal imports in that year were manufactured food products (20.4%), construction materials, machinery, fuel and transportation products.

According to IMF estimates, budget figures for 2010 indicated a preliminary deficit of 14,643m. escudos, equivalent to 11.8% of the GDP in that year. The country's general government gross debt was 101,267m. escudos in 2010, equivalent to 73.2% of GDP. Cape Verde's total external debt at the end of 2009 was US $707m., of which $695m. was public and publicly guaranteed debt. In that year the cost of servicing long-term public and publicly guaranteed debt and repayments to the IMF was equivalent to 5.4% of the value of exports of goods, services and income (excluding workers' remittances). According to ILO, the annual rate of inflation averaged 2.8% in 2001–10. Consumer prices increased by an average of 1.0% in 2009 and by 2.1% in 2010. In 2003 unemployment affected some 21% of the labour force, according to official figures.

The IMF reported that Cape Verde appeared to be weathering the global economic slowdown, which began in the late 2000s, better than many other nations (with real GDP increasing by 3.6% in 2009) and commended the Government's 'prudent macroeconomic management'. Economic expansion in previous years had been reinforced by increases in tourism and foreign direct investment (FDI), and, in addition to significant external assistance, the country benefits from substantial remittances from emigrants. The number of tourists visiting the islands increased by some 40% between 2000 and 2005, and reached some 336,000 visitors in 2010. Using reserves built up during these years of rapid expansion, the Government implemented a counter-cyclical spending programme in 2009 to cushion the country from the effects of the global economic crisis, namely dwindling FDI and sluggish tourism and construction activity. The Government was supported in its efforts by an IMF Policy Support Instrument (PSI), approved in 2006, which was replaced by a new PSI in November 2010. The IMF reported that real GDP growth of 5.4% was achieved in 2010, based on rising exports and a recovery in the tourism sector, although FDI declined slightly. Also driving this economic expansion was the implementation of an ambitious public works programme to upgrade the archipelago's infrastructural networks. The Government anticipated that this would remove a major obstacle to future growth and would encourage further FDI. Although debt levels were rising as a result of this large-scale investment, the loans had been secured on concessionary terms. The IMF projected robust growth of 5.6% in 2011, again led by rising numbers of tourist arrivals, higher export volumes and further progress on the Government's infrastructural development scheme. Real GDP was forecast to expand by 6.4% in 2012, but Cape Verde remained vulnerable to external economic developments, particularly in the European Union, the source of most of the country's FDI and tourist arrivals.

PUBLIC HOLIDAYS

2013: 1 January (New Year), 20 January (National Heroes' Day), 1 May (Labour Day), 5 July (Independence Day), 15 August (Assumption), 1 November (All Saints' Day), 25 December (Christmas Day).

Statistical Survey

Sources (unless otherwise stated): Instituto Nacional de Estatística, Av. Amílcar Cabral, CP 116, Praia, Santiago; tel. 613960; e-mail inecv@mail.cvtelecom.cv; internet www.ine.cv; Statistical Service, Banco de Cabo Verde, Av. Amílcar Cabral 117, CP 101, Praia, Santiago; tel. 2607060; fax 2614447; e-mail apericles@bcv.cv; internet www.bcv.cv.

AREA AND POPULATION

Area: 4,033 sq km (1,557 sq miles).

Population: 436,863 (males 211,479, females 225,384) at census of 16 June 2000; 491,875 (males 243,593, females 248,282) at census of 16–30 June 2010. *By Island* (2010 census): Boavista 9,162; Brava 5,995; Fogo 37,051; Maio 6,952; Sal 25,765; Santo Antão 43,915; São Nicolau 12,817; Santiago 273,919; São Vicente 76,107; Total 491,875 (incl. 192 homeless persons).

Density (2010 census): 122.0 per sq km.

Population by Age and Sex (2010 census): *0–14:* 155,635 (males 78,159, females 77,476); *15–64:* 304,527 (males 152,833, females 151,694); *65 and over:* 31,713 (males 12,601, females 19,112); *Total* 491,875 (males 243,593, females 248,282). Note: Total includes 364 persons (216 males, 148 females) of undeclared age.

Municipalities (population at 2010 census): Boavista 9,162; Brava 5,995; Maio 6,952; Mosteiros 9,524; Paúl 6,997; Porto Novo 18,028; Praia 131,719; Ribeira Brava 7,580; Ribeira Grande 18,890; Ribeira Grande Santiago 8,325; Sal 25,779; Santa Catarina 43,297; Santa Catarina Fogo 5,299; Santa Cruz 26,617; São Domingos 13,808; São Filipe 22,248; São Lourenço Orgaos 7,388; São Miguel 15,648; São Salvador Mundo 8,677; São Vicente 76,140; Tarrafal 18,565; Tarrafal São Nicolau 5,237; *Total* 491,875.

Births and Deaths (official estimates, 2010): Live births 13,415 (birth rate 25.9 per 1,000); Deaths 2,917 (death rate 5.6 per 1,000).

Life Expectancy (years at birth, official estimates): 72.9 (males 68.9; females 76.6) in 2010.

Economically Active Population (persons aged 10 years and over, 1990 census): Agriculture, hunting, forestry and fishing 29,876; Mining and quarrying 410; Manufacturing 5,520; Electricity, gas and water 883; Construction 22,722; Trade, restaurants and hotels 12,747; Transport, storage and communications 6,138; Financial, insurance, real estate and business services 821; Community, social and personal services 17,358; *Sub-total* 96,475; Activities not adequately defined 24,090; *Total labour force* 120,565 (males 75,786, females 44,779), including 31,049 unemployed persons (males 19,712, females 11,337) (Source: ILO). *2000 Census* (persons aged 10 years and over): Total employed 144,310; Unemployed 30,334; Total labour force 174,644. *Mid-2012* (FAO estimates): Agriculture, etc. 31,000; Total (incl. others) 197,000 (Source: FAO).

HEALTH AND WELFARE

Key Indicators

Total Fertility Rate (children per woman, 2009): 2.7.

Under-5 Mortality Rate (per 1,000 live births, 2009): 27.

Physicians (per 1,000 head, 2004): 0.5.

Hospital Beds (per 1,000 head, 2005): 2.1.

Health Expenditure (2008): US $ per head (PPP): 176.

Health Expenditure (2008): % of GDP: 4.4.

Health Expenditure (2008): public (% of total): 73.1.

Access to Water (% of persons, 2008): 84.

Access to Sanitation (% of persons, 2008): 54.

Total Carbon Dioxide Emissions ('000 metric tons, 2007): 307.8.

Carbon Dioxide Emissions Per Head (metric tons, 2007): 0.6.

Human Development Index (2011): ranking: 133.

Human Development Index (2011): 0.568.

For sources and definitions, see explanatory note on p. vi.

AGRICULTURE, ETC.

Principal Crops ('000 metric tons, 2010, FAO estimates): Maize 7.6; Potatoes 4.7; Sweet potatoes 5.1; Cassava 3.7; Sugar cane 28.5; Pulses 2.8; Coconuts 5.3; Cabbages 4.9; Tomatoes 5.5; Onions, dry 2.4; Beans, green 2.8; Cucumbers and gherkins 1.3; Bananas 8.9; Guavas, mangoes and mangosteens 6.5. *Aggregate Production* ('000 metric tons, may include official, semi-official or estimated data): Vegetables (incl. melons) 20.6; Fruits (excl. melons) 20.8; Roots and tubers 13.5.

Livestock ('000 head, 2010, FAO estimates): Cattle 46.0; Pigs 238.6; Sheep 20.4; Goats 231.4; Horses 0.5; Asses 14.5; Mules 1.9; Chickens 640.

Livestock Products ('000 metric tons, 2010, FAO estimates): Pig meat 8.3; Cattle meat 0.9; Cows' milk 11.9; Goats' milk 11.4; Hen eggs 2.1.

Fishing (metric tons, live weight, 2009): Total catch 16,828 (Skipjack tuna 4,766; Yellowfin tuna 3,274).

Source: FAO.

MINING

Production (metric tons, 2009): Salt (unrefined) 1,600. Clay, gypsum, limestone and volcanic rock were also produced, at unreported levels. Source: US Geological Survey.

INDUSTRY

Production (metric tons, 2003, unless otherwise indicated): Canned fish 200; Frozen fish 900; Flour 15,901 (1999); Beer 4,104,546 litres (1999); Soft drinks 922,714 litres (1996); Cigarettes and tobacco 77 kg (1999; Paint 628,243 kg (1997); Cement 160,000 (2009); Footwear 670,676 pairs (1996); Soap 1,371,045 kg (1999); Electric energy 287m. kWh (2008). Sources: mainly UN Industrial Commodity Statistics Database, US Geological Survey and IMF, *Cape Verde: Statistical Appendix* (October 2001).

FINANCE

Currency and Exchange Rates: 100 centavos = 1 Cape Verde escudo; 1,000 escudos are known as a conto. *Sterling, Dollar and Euro Equivalents* (30 December 2011): £1 sterling = 131.763 escudos; US $1 = 85.223 escudos; €1 = 110.270 escudos; 1,000 Cape Verde escudos = £7.59 = $11.73 = €9.07. *Average Exchange Rate* (escudos per US dollar): 79.377 in 2009; 83.259 in 2010; 79.323 in 2011.

Central Government Budget (million escudos, 2010, preliminary figures): *Revenue:* Taxation 26,418 (Taxes on income and profits 7,865, Taxes on international trade 5,388, Consumption taxes 12,221, Other tax revenue 944); Non-tax revenue 3,642; Grants 8,662; Total 38,723. *Expenditure:* Recurrent 27,157 (Wages and salaries 16,180, Acquisition of goods and services 2,613, Transfers and other subsidies 5,140, Interest payments 2,174, Other recurrent expenditure 1,051); Capital 25,926; Other 282; Total 53,366. Source: IMF, *Cape Verde: First Review Under the Policy Support Instrument and Requests for Waivers of Nonobservance and Modification of Assessment Criteria—Staff Report; Supplement; and Press Release* (August 2011).

International Reserves (excluding gold, US $ million at 31 December 2010): IMF special drawing rights 10.37; Reserve position in the IMF 0.02; Foreign exchange 371.80; Total 382.19. Source: IMF, *International Financial Statistics*.

Money Supply (million escudos at 31 December 2010): Currency outside depository corporations 8,287.8; Transferable deposits 39,834.7; Other deposits 62,876.7; *Broad money* 110,999.2. Source: IMF, *International Financial Statistics*.

Cost of Living (Consumer Price Index; base: 2005 = 100): All items 117.5 in 2008; 118.6 in 2009; 121.1 in 2010. Source: IMF, *International Financial Statistics*.

Expenditure on the Gross Domestic Product (million escudos at current prices, 2010 estimates): Government final consumption expenditure 26,151.8; Private final consumption expenditure 97,973.6; Gross fixed capital formation 51,645.8; Increase in stocks 572.8; *Total domestic expenditure* 176,344.0; Exports of goods and services 26,066.5; *Less* Imports of goods and services 78,493.8; *GDP in purchasers' values* 123,916.7.

Gross Domestic Product by Economic Activity (million escudos at current prices, 2010, estimates): Agriculture and forestry 6,016.7; Fishing 831.1; Construction 9,142.0; Other industry 7,416.1; Services 91,981.4; *Sub-total* 115,387.3; Indirect taxes (net), *less* imputed bank service charge 8,529.4; *Total* 123,916.7.

Balance of Payments (US $ million, 2010): Exports of goods f.o.b. 135.34; Imports of goods f.o.b. –814.16; *Trade balance* –678.83; Exports of services 518.25; Imports of services –296.10; *Balance on goods and services* –456.68; Other income received 13.99; Other income paid –82.11; *Balance on goods, services and income* –524.80; Current transfers received 409.65; Current transfers paid –69.14;

Current balance −184.29; Capital account (net) 39.85; Direct investment abroad 0.15; Direct investment from abroad 111.70; Portfolio investment liabilities 0.01; Other investment assets −6.20; Other investment liabilities 138.20; Net errors and omissions −70.30; *Overall balance* 29.12. Source: IMF, *International Finance Statistics*.

EXTERNAL TRADE

Principal Commodities (million escudos, 2010): *Imports c.i.f.:* Consumer goods 22,606.9 (Manufactured food products 12,633.8); Intermediate goods 15,626.7 (Construction materials 7,028.3); Capital goods 10,664.7 (Machines 7,229.6; Transportation 2,967.1); Fuel imports 7,208.3 (Fuel oil 4,107.7); Other imports 5,732.4; Total 61,839.0. *Exports f.o.b.:* Fish and crustaceans 2,830.9 (Frozen 1,253.6); Clothing 367.7; Footwear 411.7; Total (incl. others) 3,699.8; Re-exports 6,385.4.

Principal Trading Partners (million escudos, 2010): *Imports c.i.f.:* Brazil 2,300.0; ECOWAS 1,148.1; Germany 276.1; Italy 1,074.9; Netherlands 10,373.9; Portugal 31,795.5; Spain 6,577.5; USA 980.7; Total (incl. others) 61,839.0. *Exports f.o.b.:* ECOWAS 21.3; Netherlands 10.4; Portugal 839.8; Spain 2,685.4; USA 59.6; Total (incl. others) 3,700.1.

TRANSPORT

Road Traffic (motor vehicles in use at 31 December 2007): Passenger cars 35,738; Buses and coaches 542; Vans and lorries 13,540; Motorcycles and mopeds 4,333 (Source: IRF, *World Road Statistics*).

Shipping: *Merchant Fleet* (registered at 31 December 2009): Number of vessels 47; Total displacement ('000 grt) 32.0 (Source: IHS Fairplay, *World Fleet Statistics*). *International Sea-borne Freight Traffic* (estimates, '000 metric tons, 1993): Goods loaded 144, goods unloaded 299 (Source: UN Economic Commission for Africa, *African Statistical Yearbook*).

Civil Aviation (traffic on scheduled services, 2009): Kilometres flown (million) 12; Passengers carried ('000) 777; Passenger-km (million) 1,216; Total ton-km (million) 115. Sources: UN, *Statistical Yearbook*.

TOURISM

Tourist Arrivals by Country of Residence (2009): Belgium and Netherlands 2,091; France 22,676; Germany 40,138; Italy 42,628; Portugal 50,617; Spain 5,646; Switzerland 2,277; United Kingdom 57,011; USA 3,935; Total (incl. others) 287,183. *2010:* Total tourist arrivals 336,000 (provisional).

Tourism Receipts (US $ million, excl. passenger transport): 350 in 2008; 292 in 2009; 289 in 2010 (provisional).

Source: World Tourism Organization.

COMMUNICATIONS MEDIA

Radio Receivers* (1997): 73,000 in use.

Television Receivers† (2000): 2,000 in use.

Telephones† (2010): 72,000 main lines in use.

Mobile Cellular Telephones† (2010): 371,900 subscribers.

Personal Computers†: 69,000 (140.3 per 1,000 persons) in 2007.

Internet Subscribers† (2010): 16,700.

Broadband Subscribers† (2010): 16,000.

Non-daily Newspapers* (2004): 5 titles.

Book Production* (1989): 10 titles.

* Source: UNESCO, *Statistical Yearbook*.
† Source: International Telecommunication Union.

EDUCATION

Pre-primary (2009/10 unless otherwise stated): 465 schools (2003/04); 1,093 teachers; 21,632 pupils.

Primary (2009/10 unless otherwise stated): 425 schools (2002/03); 3,009 teachers; 71,134 pupils.

Total Secondary (2009/10 unless otherwise stated): 33 schools (2003/04); 3,522 teachers; 61,677 pupils.

Higher (2009/10): 926 teachers; 10,144 pupils. Note: In 2002/03 a further 1,743 pupils were studying abroad.

Teacher Training (2003/04): 3 colleges; 52 teachers; 948 pupils.

Pupil-teacher Ratio (primary education, UNESCO estimate): 23.6 in 2009/10.

Adult Literacy Rate (UNESCO estimates): 84.8% (males 90.1%; females 80.2) in 2009.

Sources (unless otherwise indicated): Comunidade dos Países de Língua Portuguesa; UNESCO Institute for Statistics.

Directory

The Government

HEAD OF STATE

President: Jorge Carlos Fonseca (elected 21 August 2011; took office 9 September).

COUNCIL OF MINISTERS
(May 2012)

The Government is composed of members of the Partido Africano da Independência de Cabo Verde and independents.

Prime Minister: José Maria Pereira Neves.

Minister of State and of Health: Maria Cristina Lopes de Almeida Fontes Lima.

Minister of Finance and Planning: Cristina Duarte.

Minister of the Presidency of the Council of Ministers and of National Defence: Jorge Homero Tolentino Araújo.

Minister of Foreign Affairs: Jorge Alberto da Silva Borges.

Minister of Parliamentary Affairs: Rui Mendes Semedo.

Minister of Internal Administration: Marisa Helena do Nascimento Morais.

Minister of Justice: José Carlos Lopes Correia.

Minister of Infrastructure and the Maritime Economy: José Maria Fernandes da Veiga.

Minister of the Environment, Housing and Spatial Planning: Sara Maria Duarte Lopes.

Minister of Youth, Employment and Human Resources Development: Janira Isabel Fonseca Hopffer Almada.

Minister of Tourism, Industry and Energy: Humberto Santos de Brito.

Minister of Education and Sport: Fernanda Maria de Brito Marques.

Minister of Rural Development: Eva Verona Teixeira Ortet.

Minister of Higher Education, Science and Innovation: António Leão de Aguiar Correia e Silva.

Minister of Communities: Maria Fernanda Tavares Fernandes.

Minister of Culture: Mário Lúcio Matias de Sousa Mendes.

Secretary of State for Foreign Affairs: José Luís Rocha.

Secretary of State for Public Administration: Romeu Fonseca Modesto.

Secretary of State for Marine Resources: Adalberto Filomeno Carvalho Santos Vieira.

MINISTRIES

Office of the President: Presidência da República, Palácio do Plateau, CP 100, Plateau, Praia, Santiago; tel. 2616555; fax 2614356; internet www.presidenciarepublica.cv.

Office of the Prime Minister: Gabinete do Primeiro Ministro, Palácio do Governo, Várzea, CP 16, Praia, Santiago; tel. 2610411; fax 2613099; e-mail gab.imprensa@gpm.gov.cv; internet www.primeirominstro.cv.

Ministry of Communities: Praia, Santiago.

Ministry of Culture: Praia, Santiago; internet www.cultura.gov.cv.

Ministry of Education and Sport: Palácio do Governo, Várzea, CP 111, Praia, Santiago; tel. 2610232; fax 2610260; internet www.minedu.cv.

Ministry of the Environment, Housing and Spatial Planning: Ponta Belém, CP 115, Praia, Santiago; tel. 2615716; fax 2614054; internet www.maap.cv.

Ministry of Finance and Planning: 107 Av. Amílcar Cabral, CP 30, Praia, Santiago; tel. 2607400; e-mail aliciab@gov1.gov.cv; internet www.minfin.cv.

Ministry of Foreign Affairs: Palácio das Comunidades, Achada de Santo António, CP 60, Praia, Santiago; tel. 2607853; fax 2619270.

Ministry of Health: Largo Desastre da Assistência, Chã d'Areia, CP 719, Praia, Santiago; tel. 2612167; fax 2613112; e-mail cndsanitario@cvtelecom.cv; internet www.minsaude.gov.cv.

Ministry of Higher Education, Science and Innovation: Praia, Santiago; tel. 2610567.

Ministry of Infrastructure and the Maritime Economy: Ponta Belém, Praia, Santiago; tel. 2615709; fax 2611595; e-mail GSoares@mih.gov.cv.

Ministry of Internal Administration: Praia, Santiago.

Ministry of Justice: Rua Cidade do Funchal, CP 205, Praia, Santiago; tel. 2609900; fax 2623262; e-mail minjus@govcv.gov.cv; internet www.mj.gov.cv.

Ministry of Parliamentary Affairs: Praia, Santiago.

Ministry of the Presidency of the Council of Ministers and of National Defence: Praia, Santiago.

Ministry of Rural Development: Praia, Santiago.

Ministry of Social Development and Families: Edifício do Ministério das Finanças, 2° Esquerdo, CP 453, Plateau, Praia, Santiago; tel. 2603260; fax 2618866; e-mail madalena.neves@govcv.gov.cv; internet www.mtfs.gov.cv.

Ministry of Tourism, Industry and Energy: Praia, Santiago.

Ministry of Youth, Employment and Human Resources Development: Praia, Santiago.

President and Legislature

PRESIDENT

Presidential Election, First Round, 7 August 2011

Candidate	Votes	% of votes
Jorge Carlos Fonseca (MpD)	60,438	37.76
Manuel Inocêncio Sousa (PAICV)	51,970	32.47
Aristides Lima (Ind.)	44,500	27.80
Joaquim Monteiro (Ind.)	3,169	1.98
Total	160,077*	100.00

* The total number of votes cast declared by the CNE was 162,229, which included 964 blank votes and 885 spoiled ballots.

Presidential Election, Second Round, 21 August 2011

Candidate	Votes	% of votes
Jorge Carlos Fonseca (MpD)	97,643	54.18
Manuel Inocêncio Sousa (PAICV)	82,634	45.85
Total	180,227*	100.00

* Excluding 1,489 blank votes and 831 spoiled ballots.

LEGISLATURE

Assembleia Nacional: Achada de Santo António, CP 20A, Praia, Santiago; tel. 2608000; fax 2622660; e-mail an-cv@cvtelecom.cv; internet www.parlamento.cv.

Speaker: Basílio Ramos.

Legislative Elections, 6 February 2011

Party	Votes	% of votes	Seats
Partido Africano da Independência de Cabo Verde (PAICV)	117,967	52.68	38
Movimento para a Democracia (MpD)	94,674	42.27	32
União Cristã, Independente e Democrática (UCID)	9,842	4.39	2
Partido Socialista Democrático (PSD)	1,040	0.46	—
Partido de Trabalho e Solidariedade (PTS)	429	0.19	—
Total	223,952*	100.00	72

* Excluding 1,248 blank votes and 1,742 invalid votes.

Election Commission

Comissão Nacional de Eleições (CNE): Achada de Santo António, Praia, Santiago; tel. 2624323; e-mail cne@cne.cv; internet www.cne.cv; Pres. Rosa Carlota Martins Branco Vicente.

Political Organizations

Grupo Independente para Modernizar Sal (GIMS): Leader Jorge Figueiredo.

Movimento para a Democracia (MpD): Av. Cidade Lisboa, 4° andar, CP 90A, Praia, Santiago; tel. 2614122; e-mail mpd@mpd.cv; internet www.mpd.cv; f. 1990; advocates administrative decentralization; governing party from 1991 to 2001; formed alliance with the PCD to contest 2006 legislative and presidential elections; Chair. Carlos Veiga; Sec.-Gen. Agostinho Lopes.

Partido Africano da Independência de Cabo Verde (PAICV): Av. Amílcar Cabral, CP 22, Praia, Santiago; tel. 2612720; fax 2611410; internet www.paicv.cv; f. 1956 as the Partido Africano da Independência do Guiné e Cabo Verde (PAIGC); name changed in 1981, following the 1980 coup in Guinea-Bissau; sole authorized political party 1975–90; governing party since 2001; Pres. José Maria Pereira Neves; Sec.-Gen. Armindo Maurício.

Partido da Renovação Democrática (PRD): Praia, Santiago; f. 2000 by fmr mems of the MpD; Pres. José Luís Barbosa.

Partido Socialista Democrático (PSD): Praia, Santiago; f. 1992; Sec.-Gen. João Além.

Partido de Trabalho e Solidariedade (PTS): Praia, Santiago; f. 1998; Interim Leader Isaías Rodrigues.

União Cristã, Independente e Democrática (UCID): Achada Santo António-Frente, Restaurante 'O Poeta', Praia, Santiago; tel. 2608134; fax 2624403.

Diplomatic Representation

EMBASSIES IN CAPE VERDE

Angola: Av. OUA, Achada de Santo António, CP 78A, Praia, Santiago; tel. 2623235; fax 2623234; e-mail emb.angola@cv.telecom.cv; Ambassador Josefina Guilhermina Coelho da Cruz.

Brazil: Chã de Areia 2, CP 93, Praia, Santiago; tel. 2615607; fax 2615609; e-mail contato@embrasilpraia.org; internet www.embrasilpraia.org; Ambassador Maria Dulce Silva Barros.

China, People's Republic: Achada de Santo António, CP 8, Praia, Santiago; tel. 2623029; fax 2623047; e-mail chinaemb_cv@mfa.gov.cn; Ambassador Li Chunhua.

Cuba: Achada de Santo António, Praia, Santiago; tel. 2619408; fax 2617527; e-mail ecubacpv@cvtelecom.cv; internet emba.cubaminrex.cu/caboverdepor; Ambassador Pedro Evelio Dorta González.

France: Achada de Santo António, CP 192, Praia, Santiago; tel. 2615591; fax 2615590; internet www.ambafrance-cv.org; Ambassador Marie-Christine Glas.

Korea, Democratic People's Republic: Praia; Ambassador Ri In Sok.

Portugal: Av. OUA, Achada de Santo António, CP 160, Praia, Santiago; tel. 2623037; fax 2623222; e-mail embportpraia@gmail.com; internet www.secomunidades.pt/web/praia; Ambassador Maria da Graça Reynaud Campos Trocado Andersen Guimarães.

Russia: Achada de Santo António, CP 31, Praia, Santiago; tel. 2622739; fax 2622738; e-mail embrus@cvtelecom.cv; internet www.capeverde.mid.ru; Ambassador Alexander R. Karpushin.

Senegal: Rua Abílio Macedo, Plateau, CP 269, Praia, Santiago; tel. 2615621; fax 2612838; e-mail silcarneyni@hotmail.com; Ambassador Mamadou Fall.

USA: Rua Abílio Macedo 6, Praia, Santiago; tel. 2608900; fax 2611355; internet praia.usembassy.gov; Ambassador Marianne M. Myles.

Judicial System

Supremo Tribunal de Justiça (STJ)

Gabinete do Juiz Presidente, Edif. dos Correios, Rua Cesário de Lacerda, CP 117, Praia, Santiago; tel. 2615810; fax 2611751; e-mail stj@supremo.gov.cv; internet www.stj.cv.

f. 1975; Pres. Arlindo Almeida Medina.

Attorney-General: Franklin Afonso Furtado.

Religion

CHRISTIANITY

An estimated 95% of the population are believed to be adherents of the Roman Catholic Church. Protestant churches, among which the Church of the Nazarene is the most prominent, represent about 1% of the population.

The Roman Catholic Church

Cape Verde comprises two dioceses, directly responsible to the Holy See. The Bishops participate in the Episcopal Conference of Senegal, Mauritania, Cape Verde and Guinea-Bissau, currently based in Senegal.

Bishop of Mindelo: Rt Rev. ILDO AUGUSTO DOS SANTOS LOPES FORTES, CP 447, 2110 Mindelo, São Vicente; tel. 2318870; fax 2318872; e-mail diocesemindelo@cvtelecom.cv.

Bishop of Santiago de Cabo Verde: Rt Rev. ARLINDO GOMES FURTADO, Av. Amílcar Cabral, Largo 5 de Outubro, CP 46, Praia, Santiago; tel. 2611119; fax 2614599; e-mail diocesecv@cvtelecom.cv.

The Anglican Communion

Cape Verde forms part of the diocese of The Gambia, within the Church of the Province of West Africa. The Bishop is resident in Banjul, The Gambia.

Other Christian Churches

Church of the Nazarene: District Office, Av. Amílcar Cabral, Plateau, CP 96, Praia, Santiago; tel. 2613611.

Other churches represented in Cape Verde include the Church of the Assembly of God, the Church of Jesus Christ of Latter-day Saints, the Evangelical Baptist Church, the Maná Church, the New Apostolic Church, the Seventh-day Adventist Church and the Universal Church of the Kingdom of God.

BAHÁ'Í FAITH

National Spiritual Assembly: Rua Madragoa, Plateau, Praia, Santiago; tel. 2617739; f. 1984.

The Press

Boletim Oficial da República de Cabo Verde: Imprensa Nacional, Av. Amílcar Cabral, Calçada Diogo Gomes, CP 113, Praia, Santiago; tel. 2614150; fax 2614209; e-mail incv@gov1.gov.cv; weekly; official announcements.

O Cidadão: Praça Dr António Aurélio Gonçalves 2, Mindelo, São Vicente; tel. 2325024; fax 2325022; e-mail cidadao@caboverde.zzn.com; weekly; Editor JOSÉ MÁRIO CORREIA.

Expresso das Ilhas: Achada de Santo António, OUA Nº 21, R/C, CP 666, Praia, Santiago; tel. 2619807; fax 2619805; e-mail jornal@expressodasilhas.cv; internet www.expressodasilhas.sapo.cv; f. 2001 by the MpD; daily; Dir JOÃO DO ROSÁRIO; Editor-in-Chief JORGE MONTEZINHO.

Jornal de Cabo Verde: Prédio Gonçalves, 6º piso, Av. Cidade de Lisboa, CP 889, Praia; tel. 2601414; e-mail jornal@liberal-caboverde.com; print version of online news website O Liberal; Dir DANIEL MEDINA; circ. 7,000.

A Nação: CP 690, Palmarejo, Praia; tel. 2628677; fax 2628505; e-mail alfa_com@cvtelecom.cv; internet www.anacao.cv; f. 2007; weekly; independent; Dir ALEXANDRE SEMEDO; circ. 1,000.

Raízes: CP 98, Praia, Santiago; f. 1977; quarterly; cultural review; Editor ARNALDO FRANÇA; circ. 1,500.

A Semana: Rotunda do Palmarejo, Av. Santiago 59, CP 36C, Praia, Santiago; tel. 2629860; fax 2628661; e-mail asemana@cvtelecom.cv; internet www.asemana.publ.cv; f. 1991; weekly; independent; Editor FILOMENA SILVA; circ. 5,000.

Terra Nova: Rua Guiné-Bissau 1, CP 166, Mindelo, São Vicente; tel. 2322442; fax 2321475; e-mail terranova@cabonet.cv; f. 1975; quarterly; Roman Catholic; Editor P. ANTÓNIO FIDALGO BARROS; circ. 3,000.

There is also an online newspaper, **Visão News** (www.visaonews.com), based in the USA. Further news websites include **O Liberal** (liberal.sapo.cv), **AllCaboVerde.com** (www.noscaboverde.com), **Cabonet** (www.cabonet.org), **Sport Kriolu** (www.sportkriolu.com), dedicated to sport, and **Voz di Povo Online** (arquivo.vozdipovoonline.com).

NEWS AGENCY

Inforpress: Achada de Santo António, CP 40A, Praia, Santiago; tel. 2624313; fax 2622554; e-mail inforpress@mail.cvtelecom.cv; internet www.inforpress.publ.cv; f. 1988 as Cabopress; Pres. JOSÉ AUGUSTO SANCHES.

PRESS ASSOCIATION

Associação de Jornalistas de Cabo Verde (AJOC): Rua João Chapuzet (Travessa do mercado), CP 350A, Praia, Santiago; tel. and fax 2622121; e-mail ajoc@ajoc.org.cv; internet www.ajoc.org.cv; f. 1993; Pres. HULDA MOREIRA; 11 media cos and 159 individual mems.

Publishers

Instituto Caboverdeano do Livro e do Disco (ICL): Centro Cultural, CP 158, Praia, Santiago; tel. 2612346; books, journals, music.

GOVERNMENT PUBLISHING HOUSE

Imprensa Nacional: Av. Amílcar Cabral, Calçada Diogo Gomes, CP 113, Praia, Santiago; tel. 2612145; fax 2614209; e-mail incv@gov1.gov.cv; internet www.incv.gov.cv; Admin. JOÃO DE PINA.

Broadcasting and Communications

TELECOMMUNICATIONS

Cabo Verde Telecom (CVTelecom): Rua Cabo Verde Telecom, Várzea, CP 220, Praia, Santiago; tel. 2609200; fax 2613725; e-mail cvtelecom@cvtelecom.cv; internet www.cvtelecom.cv; f. 1995; 40% owned by Portugal Telecom; Chief Exec. ANTÓNIO PIRES CORREIA.

CVMóvel: Chã de Areia, Praia, Santiago 126-A; fax 2622509; e-mail marketing@cvt.cv; internet www.cvmovel.cv; wholly owned subsidiary of Cabo Verde Telecom providing cellular mobile services.

T+ Telecomunicações: Santiago; f. 2007; Pres. MARCO BENTO.

Regulatory Authority

Agência Nacional das Comunicações (ANAC): Edifício do MIT, Ponta Belém, CP 892, Praia, Santiago; tel. 2604400; fax 2613069; e-mail info.anac@anac.cv; internet www.anac.cv; f. 2006; Pres. DAVID GOMES.

BROADCASTING

Rádiotelevisão Caboverdiana (RTC): Rua 13 de Janeiro, Achada de Santo António, CP 1A, Praia, Santiago; tel. 2605200; fax 2605256; e-mail rtc.infos@rtc.cv; internet www.rtc.cv; govt-controlled; 40 transmitters and relay transmitters; FM transmission only; radio broadcasts in Portuguese and Creole for 24 hours daily; 1 television transmitter and 7 relay television transmitters; television broadcasts in Portuguese and Creole for 8 hours daily with co-operation of RTP Africa (Portugal) and TV5 Honde; Pres. HORÁCIO MOREIRA SEMEDO; Dir of Radio JOANA OLINDA MIRANDA; Dir of Television ÁLVARO LUDGERO ANDRADE.

Televisão de Cabo Verde: Praia, Santiago; sole television broadcaster; part of RTC; Dir ÁLVARO ANDRADE.

Praia FM: Rua Visconde de S. Januario 19, 4° andar, CP 276C, Praia, Santiago; tel. 2616356; fax 2613515; e-mail praiafm@cvtelecom.cv; internet praiafm.sapo.cv; Dir GIORDANO CUSTÓDIO.

Rádio Comercial: Av. Liberdade e Democradia 6, Prédio Gomes Irmãos, 3° esq., CP 507, Praia, Santiago; tel. 2623156; fax 2622413; e-mail multimedia.rc@cvtelecom.cv; f. 1997; Admin. HENRIQUE PIRES; Dir CARLOS FILIPE GONÇALVES.

Rádio Educativa de Cabo Verde: Achada de Santo António, Praia, Santiago; tel. 2611161; Dir LUÍS LIMA.

Rádio Morabeza: Rua São João 16, 2º andar, CP 456, Mindelo, São Vicente; tel. 2324429; fax 2324431; e-mail radiomorabeza@cvtelecom.cv; f. 1999; Dir CARLOS MONTEIRO.

Rádio Nacional de Cabo Verde (RNCV): CP 26, Praia, Santiago; tel. 2613729; Dir CARLOS SANTOS.

Rádio Nova—Emissora Cristã de Cabo Verde: CP 166, Mindelo, São Vicente; tel. 2322082; fax 2321475; internet www.radionovaonline.com; f. 2002; Roman Catholic station; Dir ANTÓNIO FIDALGO BARROS.

Voz de São Vicente: CP 29, Mindelo, São Vicente; fax 2311006; f. 1974; govt-controlled; Dir JOSÉ FONSECA SOARES.

Finance

(cap. = capital; res = reserves; dep. = deposits; m. = million; brs = branches; amounts in Cape Verde escudos, unless otherwise indicated)

BANKING

In early 2011 there were nine commercial banks and 14 international offshore financial institutions in Cape Verde.

Central Bank

Banco de Cabo Verde (BCV): Av. Amílcar Cabral 117, CP 101, Praia, Santiago; tel. 2607000; fax 2607095; e-mail avarela@bcv.cv; internet www.bcv.cv; f. 1976; bank of issue; cap. 200.0m., res –288m., dep. 28,470m. (Dec. 2009); Gov. CARLOS AUGUSTO DUARTE DE BURGO.

Other Banks

Banco Africano de Investimentos Cabo Verde SA: Edifício Santa Maria, R/C-Chã DAreia, CP 459, Praia; tel. 2601224; fax 2622810; e-mail bai@bancobai.cv; internet www.bancobai.cv; f. 2008; Pres. Dr JOSÉ DE LIMA MASSANO; Dir-Gen. Dr DAVID RICARDO TEIXEIRA PALEGE JASSE.

Banco Caboverdiano de Negócios (BCN): Av. Amílcar Cabral 97, CP 593, Praia, Santiago; tel. 2604250; fax 2614006; e-mail bcn@bcdenegocios.cv; internet www.bcncv.com; f. 1996 as Banco Totta e Açores (Cabo Verde); renamed as above in 2004; 46% owned by Banif (Portugal); cap. 900,000 escudos (Dec. 2008); 3 brs; Pres. MANUEL J. CHANTRE.

Banco Comercial do Atlântico (BCA): Praça Alexandre Albuquerque, Av. Amílcar Cabral, CP 474, Praia, Santiago; tel. 2600900; fax 2613235; e-mail bca@bca.cv; internet www.bca.cv; f. 1993; privatized in 2000; main commercial bank; cap. 1,318.6m., res 995.2m., dep. 53,688.1m. (Dec. 2009); Pres. and Gen. Man. ANTÓNIO JOAQUIM DE SOUSA; 25 brs.

Banco Espírito Santo Cabo Verde SA: Av. Cidade de Lisboa-Fazenda, CP 35, Praia, Santiago; tel. 2602626; fax 2602630; e-mail geral@bescv.cv; f. 2010; Pres. PEDRO ROBERTO MENÉRES CUDELL.

Banco Interatlântico: Av. Cidade de Lisboa, CP 131A, Praia, Santiago; tel. 2614008; fax 2614752; e-mail bi@bi.cv; internet www.bi.cv; f. 1999; cap. 600m., res 261m., dep. 14,198m. (Dec. 2009); Pres. of Exec. Comm. Dr FERNANDO MARQUES PEREIRA.

Caixa Económica de Cabo Verde, SA (CECV): Av. Cidade de Lisboa, CP 199, Praia, Santiago; tel. 2603603; fax 2612055; e-mail antonio.moreira@caixa.cv; internet www.caixa.cv; f. 1928; privatized in 1999; commercial bank; cap. 1,392.0m., res 1,522.8m., dep. 29,229.9m. (Dec. 2009); Pres. EMANUEL JESUS DA VEIGA MIRANDA; 11 brs.

Ecobank Cabo Verde: Praça Infante Dom Henrique 18, Palmarejo, CP 374C, Praia; tel. 2603660; fax 2611090; e-mail ecobankcv@ecobank.com; internet www.ecobank.com; f. 2010; Pres. EVELINE TALL; Man. Dir MAMADOU MOCTAR SALL.

STOCK EXCHANGE

Bolsa de Valores de Cabo Verde, Sarl (BVC): 16 Achada de Santo António, CP 115 A, Praia, Santiago; tel. 2603030; fax 2603038; e-mail bcv@bvc.cv; internet www.bvc.cv; f. 1998; reopened December 2005; Pres. VERÍSSIMO PINTO.

INSURANCE

Companhia Caboverdiana de Seguros (IMPAR): Sq. Amílcar Cabral, CP 344, Mindelo, S.Vicente; tel. and fax 2603134; fax 2616025; e-mail comercial@impar.cv; internet www.impar.cv; f. 1991; Pres. Dr LUÍS VASCONCELOS LOPES.

Garantia Companhia de Seguros: Chã d'Areia, CP 138, Praia, Santiago; tel. 2608600; fax 2616117; e-mail garantia@garantia.cv; internet www.garantia.cv; f. 1991; privatized in 2000; Pres. Dr ANTÓNIO JOAQUIM DE SOUSA.

Trade and Industry

GOVERNMENT AGENCIES

Agência de Regulação e Supervisão dos Produtos Farmacêuticos e Alimentares (ARFA): Achada de Santo António, CP 296A, Praia, Santiago; tel. 2626410; fax 2624970; e-mail arfa@arfa.gov.cv; internet www.arfa.cv; Pres. Eng. MIGUEL ANTÓNIO LIMA.

Agência Nacional de Segurança Alimentar (ANSA): Início Rampa Chã d'Areia à Terra Branca, 3º andar Prédio Laranja, CP 262, Praia, Santiago; tel. 2626290; fax 2626297; e-mail ansa@cvtelecom.cv; internet www.ansa.cv; food security agency; Pres. MIGUEL MONTEIRO.

Cabo Verde Investimentos (CI): Rotunda da Cruz do Papa 5, CP 89 C, Praia, Santiago; tel. 2604110; fax 2622657; e-mail Presidente@cvinvest.cv; internet www.cvinvest.cv; f. 2004; promotes public-private investment partnerships in infrastructure and tourism; Pres. and CEO JOSÉ ARMANDO DUARTE.

Comissão de Investimento Externo e Empresa Franca (CIEF): Praia, Santiago; foreign investment commission.

Gabinete de Apoio à Reestruturação do Sector Empresarial do Estado (GARSEE) (Cabo Verde Privatization): Largo do Tunis, Cruzeiro, CP 323, Praia, Santiago; tel. 2614748; fax 2612334; bureau in charge of planning and supervising restructuring and divestment of public enterprises; Project Dir Dr SÉRGIO CENTEIO.

DEVELOPMENT ORGANIZATION

Instituto Nacional de Investigação e Desenvolvimento Agrário (INIDA): CP 84, Praia, Santiago; tel. 2711147; fax 2711133; f. 1979; research and training on agricultural issues.

TRADE ASSOCIATION

Associação para a Promoção dos MicroEmpresários (APME): Fazenda, Praia, Santiago; tel. 2606056; f. 1988.

CHAMBERS OF COMMERCE

Câmara de Comércio, Indústria e Serviços de Barlavento (CCISB): Rua da Luz 31, CP 728, Mindelo, São Vicente; tel. 2328495; fax 2328496; e-mail camara.com@cvtelecom.cv; internet www.cciasb.org; f. 1996; Pres. MANUEL J. MONTEIRO.

Câmara de Comércio, Indústria e Serviços de Sotavento (CCISS): Rua Serpa Pinto 160, CP 105, Praia, Santiago; tel. 2617234; fax 2617235; e-mail cciss@cvtelecom.cv; internet www.faroldacciss.org; Pres. PAULO LIMA; Sec.-Gen. ROSÁRIO LUZ.

STATE INDUSTRIAL ENTERPRISES

Empresa Nacional de Avicultura, SARL (ENAVI): Tira Chapéu Zona Industrial, CP 135, Praia, Santiago; tel. 2627268; fax 2628441; e-mail enavi@cvtelecom.cv; poultry-farming.

Empresa Nacional de Combustíveis, SARL (ENACOL): Largo John Miller's, CP 1, Mindelo, São Vicente; tel. 2306060; fax 2323425; e-mail enacolsv@enacol.cv; internet www.enacol.cv; f. 1979; supervises import and distribution of petroleum; Pres. Dr ADALBERTO LEITE PEREIRA DE SENA; Dir CARLITOS FORTES.

Empresa Nacional de Produtos Farmacêuticos, SARL (EMPROFAC): Tira Chapéu Zona Industrial, CP 59, Praia, Santiago; tel. 2627895; fax 2627899; e-mail emprofac@cvtelecom.cv; f. 1979; state monopoly of pharmaceuticals and medical imports; Dir-Gen. ÓSCAR BAPTISTA.

UTILITIES

Electricity and Water

Empresa de Electricidade e Água, SARL (Electra): Av. Baltasar Lopes Silva 10, CP 137, Mindelo, São Vicente; tel. 2303030; fax 2324446; e-mail comercial@electra.cv; internet www.electra.cv; f. 1982; 51% govt-owned; Pres. ANTÃO FORTES.

CO-OPERATIVE

Instituto Nacional das Cooperativas: Achada de Santo António, Praia, Santiago; tel. 2616376; central co-operative org.

TRADE UNIONS

Confederação Caboverdiana dos Sindicatos Livres (CCSL): Rua Dr Júlio Abreu, CP 155, Praia, Santiago; tel. 2613928; fax 2616319; e-mail ccsl@cvtelecom.cv; f. 1992; Pres. JOSÉ MANUEL VAZ.

Federação Nacional dos Sindicatos dos Trabalhadores da Administração Pública (FNSTAP): CP 123, Praia; tel. 2614305; fax 2613629; Pres. MIGUEL HORTA DA SILVA.

Sindicato dos Transportes, Comunicações e Turismo (STCT): Praia, Santiago; tel. 2616338.

União Nacional dos Trabalhadores de Cabo Verde—Central Sindical (UNTC—CS): Av. Cidade de Lisboa, CP 123, Praia, Santiago; tel. 2614305; fax 2613629; e-mail untc@cvtelecom.cv; internet www.untc-cs.org; f. 1978; Chair. JÚLIO ASCENÇÃO SILVA.

Transport

ROADS

In 2004 there were an estimated 2,250 km of roads, of which 1,750 km were paved.

Associação Apoio aos Reclusos e Crianças de Rua (AAPR): Achada de Santo António, CP 205A, Praia, Santiago; tel. 2618441; fax 2619017; e-mail aapr@cvtelecom.cv; road devt agency.

SHIPPING

Cargo-passenger ships call regularly at Porto Grande, Mindelo, on São Vicente, and Praia, on Santiago. There were plans to upgrade the ports at Praia, Sal, São Vicente and Porto Novo (Santo Antão). There are small ports on the other inhabited islands. Cape Verde's registered merchant fleet at 31 December 2009 consisted of 47 vessels, totalling 32,000 grt.

Arca Verde (Companhia Nacional de Navegação): Rua 5 de Julho, Plateau, Santiago; tel. 2615497; fax 2615496; e-mail cnnarcaverdepra@cvtelecom.cv; shipping co; undergoing privatization.

Cabo Verde Fast Ferry (CVFF): CP 796, Chã d'Areia, Praia; tel. 2617552; fax 2617553; e-mail cvff.info@cvfastferry.com; internet www.cvfastferry.com; f. 2009; Pres. ANDY DE ANDRADE.

Cape Verde National Shipping Line, SARL (Cs Line): Rua Baltasar Lopez da Silva, CP 238, Mindelo, São Vicente.

Comissão de Gestão dos Transportes Marítimos de Cabo Verde: CP 153, São Vicente; tel. 2314979; fax 2312055.

Companhia Caboverdiana de Navegação: Rua Cristiano Sena Barcelos 3–5, Mindelo, São Vicente; tel. 2322852.

Companhia de Navegação Estrela Negra: Av. 5 de Julho 17, CP 91, Mindelo, São Vicente; tel. 2325423; fax 2315382.

Empresa Nacional de Administração dos Portos, SA (ENAPOR, SA): Av. Marginal, CP 82, Mindelo, São Vicente; tel. 2307500; fax 2324337; e-mail info@enapor.cv; internet www.enapor.cv; f. 1982; Chair. and Man. Dir FRANKLIM DO ROSÁRIO SPENCER.

Linhas Marítimas Caboverdianas (LINMAC): CP 357, Praia, Santiago; tel. 2614352; fax 2613715; Dir ESTHER SPENCER.

Seage Agência de Navegação de Cabo Verde: Av. Cidade de Lisboa, CP 232, Praia, Santiago; tel. 2615758; fax 2612524; f. 1986; Chair. CÉSAR MANUEL SEMEDO LOPES.

Transnacional, a shipping company, operates a ferry service between some islands.

CIVIL AVIATION

The Amílcar Cabral international airport, at Espargos, on Sal island, can accommodate aircraft of up to 50 tons and 1m. passengers per year. The airport's facilities were expanded during the 1990s. A second international airport, Aeroporto da Praia (renamed Aeroporto Nelson Mandela in 2012), was opened in late 2005, and São Pedro Airport, on the island of São Vicente, received its first international arrival in December 2009. There is also a small airport on each of the other inhabited islands.

Agência de Aviação Civil (AAC): 34 Av. Cidade de Lisboa, CP 371, Praia, Santiago; tel. 2603430; fax 2611075; e-mail dgeral@acivil.gov.cv; internet www.aac.cv; f. 2005; regulatory agency; Pres. VALDEMAR CORREIA.

Empresa Nacional de Aeroportos e Segurança AEREA, SA (ASA): Aeroporto Amílcar Cabral, CP 58, Ilha do Sal; tel. 2412626; fax 2411570; e-mail pca@asa.cv; internet www.asa.cv; f. 1984; state-owned; airports and air navigation; Pres. MÁRIO LOPES.

Halcyon Air: CP 142, Ilha do Sal; tel. 2412948; fax 2412362; e-mail comercial@halcyonair.com; internet flyhalcyonair.com; f. 2005; inter-island carrier; Dir-Gen. FERNANDO GIL EVORA.

Transportes Aéreos de Cabo Verde (TACV): Av. Amílcar Cabral, CP 1, Praia, Santiago; tel. 2608200; fax 2617275; e-mail pferreira@tacv.aero; internet www.tacv.cv; f. 1958; internal services connecting the 9 inhabited islands; also operates regional services to Senegal, The Gambia and Guinea-Bissau, and long-distance services to Europe and the USA; scheduled for privatization; Pres. and CEO JOÃO HIGINO SILVA; Gen. Man. PAULO FERREIRA.

A private company, Inter Island Airlines, also offers flights between the islands of Cape Verde.

Tourism

The islands of Santiago, Santo Antão, Fogo and Brava offer attractive mountain scenery. There are extensive beaches on the islands of Santiago, Sal, Boavista and Maio. Some 336,000 tourists visited Cape Verde in 2010, and in that year tourism receipts totalled some US $289m. The sector is undergoing rapid expansion, with development in a number of Zonas de Desenvolvimento Turístico Integral. In late 2003 the Government began steps to have Fogo, which contains the only live volcano on Cape Verde, designated a UNESCO World Heritage Site. Plans were unveiled in March 2004 to promote the island of Santa Luzia as an eco-tourism destination. Construction of a large tourist resort on Santiago, expected to cost €550m., commenced in early 2005. Tourist arrivals were projected to increase to about 1m. annually by 2015.

Defence

The armed forces numbered about 1,200 (army 1,000, air force less than 100, coastguard 100), as assessed at November 2011. There is also a police force, the Police for Public Order, which is organized by the local municipal councils. National service of two years is by selective conscription. In October 2002 the Government announced a programme of reform, involving the coastguard, the military police and special forces dealing with drugs-trafficking and terrorism offences.

Defence Expenditure: Budgeted at 722m. escudos in 2011.

Chief of Staff of the Armed Forces: Col ANTERO DE MATOS.

Education

Compulsory primary education begins at six or seven years of age and lasts for six years. Secondary education, beginning at 13 years of age, is divided into two cycles, the first comprising a three-year general course, the second a two-year pre-university course. There are three teacher-training units and two industrial and commercial schools of further education. According to UNESCO estimates, primary enrolment in 2009/10 included 93% of children in the relevant age-group (males 94%; females 92%), while secondary enrolment included 66% of children in the relevant age-group (males 61%; females 71%). In 2002/03 there were 1,743 Cape Verdean students studying at overseas universities. In 2002 a private university, the Universidade Jean Piaget de Cabo Verde, opened in Praia. According to UNESCO estimates, in 2005 spending on education represented 25.4% of total budgetary expenditure.

THE CENTRAL AFRICAN REPUBLIC

Introductory Survey

LOCATION, CLIMATE, LANGUAGE, RELIGION, FLAG, CAPITAL

The Central African Republic is a land-locked country in the heart of equatorial Africa. It is bordered by Chad to the north, by South Sudan and Sudan to the east, by the Democratic Republic of the Congo (formerly Zaire) and the Republic of the Congo to the south and by Cameroon to the west. The climate is tropical, with an average annual temperature of 26°C (79°F) and heavy rainfall in the south-western forest areas. The national language is Sango, but French is the official language and another 68 languages and dialects have been identified. It is estimated that about one-half of the population are Christian; another 15% are Muslims, while animist beliefs are held by an estimated 24%. The national flag (proportions 3 by 5) has four equal horizontal stripes, of blue, white, green and yellow, divided vertically by a central red stripe, with a five-pointed yellow star in the hoist corner of the blue stripe. The capital is Bangui.

CONTEMPORARY POLITICAL HISTORY

Historical Context

The former territory of Ubangi-Shari (Oubangui-Chari), within French Equatorial Africa, became the Central African Republic (CAR) on achieving self-government in December 1958. David Dacko led the country to full independence and became its first President, on 13 August 1960. In 1962 a one-party state was established, with the ruling Mouvement d'évolution sociale de l'Afrique noire (MESAN) as the sole authorized party. Dacko was overthrown on 31 December 1965 by a military coup, which brought to power his cousin, Col (later Marshal) Jean-Bédel Bokassa, Commander-in-Chief of the armed forces.

In January 1966 Bokassa formed a new Government, rescinded the Constitution and dissolved the legislature. Bokassa became Life President in March 1972 and Marshal of the Republic in May 1974. In September 1976 the Council of Ministers was replaced by the Council for the Central African Revolution, and former President Dacko was appointed personal adviser to the President. In December the Republic was renamed the Central African Empire (CAE), and a new Constitution was instituted. Bokassa was proclaimed the first Emperor, and Dacko became his Personal Counsellor. However, in September 1979, while Bokassa was in Libya, Dacko deposed him in a bloodless coup, which received considerable support from France. The country was again designated a republic, with Dacko as its President and Henri Maidou as Vice-President.

In February 1981 a new Constitution, providing for a multi-party system, was approved by referendum and promulgated by Dacko. He won a presidential election in March, amid allegations of electoral malpractice, and was sworn in for a six-year term in April. Political tension intensified in subsequent months, and on 1 September the Chief of Staff of the Armed Forces, Gen. André Kolingba, deposed Dacko in a bloodless coup. Kolingba was declared President, and an all-military Government was formed. All political activity was suspended.

Domestic Political Affairs

In March 1982 the exiled leader of the banned Mouvement pour la libération du peuple centrafricain (MLPC), Ange-Félix Patassé, returned to Bangui and was implicated in an unsuccessful coup attempt. Patassé, who had been Prime Minister under Bokassa in 1976–78 and who had contested the 1981 presidential election, sought asylum in the French embassy in Bangui, from where he was transported to exile in Togo.

In September 1985, for the first time since Kolingba's assumption of power, civilians were appointed to the Council of Ministers. In early 1986 a specially convened commission drafted a new Constitution, which provided for the creation of a sole legal political party, the Rassemblement démocratique centrafricain (RDC), and conferred extensive executive powers on the President, while defining a predominantly advisory role for the legislature. At a referendum in November some 91% of voters approved the draft Constitution and granted Kolingba a mandate to serve a further six-year term as President. The Council of Ministers was reorganized in December to include a majority of civilians. The RDC was officially established in February 1987, with Kolingba as founding President, and elections to the new Assemblée nationale took place in July, at which 142 candidates, all nominated by the RDC, contested the 52 seats.

The appointment during 1988 of former associates of Bokassa, Dacko and Patassé to prominent public offices appeared to represent an attempt by Kolingba to consolidate national unity. In August 1989, however, 12 opponents of his regime, including members of the Front patriotique oubanguien-Parti du travail and the leader of the Rassemblement populaire pour la reconstruction de la Centrafrique, Brig.-Gen. (later Gen.) François Bozizé Yangouvonda, were arrested in Benin, where they had been living in exile, and extradited to the CAR. Bozizé was subsequently found guilty of complicity in the 1982 coup attempt.

In 1990 opposition movements exerted pressure on the Government to introduce a plural political system. In December the Executive Council of the RDC recommended a review of the Constitution and the re-establishment of the premiership. Accordingly, in March 1991 Edouard Franck, a former Minister of State at the Presidency, was appointed Prime Minister, and in July the Assemblée nationale approved a constitutional amendment providing for the re-establishment of a multi-party political system. Kolingba resigned from the presidency of the RDC in the following month, in order to remain 'above parties'. In December Kolingba pardoned Bozizé.

Kolingba convened a Grand National Debate in August 1992, but it was boycotted by the influential Concertation des forces démocratiques (CFD), an alliance of opposition groupings. At the end of August the Assemblée nationale approved legislation in accordance with decisions taken by the Grand National Debate: constitutional amendments provided for the strict separation of executive, legislative and judicial powers, and Kolingba was granted temporary powers to rule by decree until the election of a new multi-party legislature. Concurrent legislative and presidential elections commenced in October, but were suspended by presidential decree and subsequently annulled by the Supreme Court, owing to alleged sabotage of the electoral process.

Patassé's presidency

Two rounds of concurrent legislative and presidential elections were held in August and September 1993 in which the MLPC won 34 of the 85 seats in the Assemblée nationale, while the RDC, in second place, secured 13 seats. Patassé, the MLPC leader and former Prime Minister, was elected President, winning 52.5% of the votes cast at a second round of voting. In October Patassé was inaugurated as President. Soon afterwards he appointed Jean-Luc Mandaba, the Vice-President of the MLPC, as Prime Minister; Mandaba formed a coalition Government, which had a working majority of 53 seats in the Assemblée nationale.

A new Constitution, which was adopted in January 1995, included provisions empowering the President to nominate senior military, civil service and judicial officials, and requiring the Prime Minister to implement policies decided by the President. In addition, provision was made for the creation of directly elected regional assemblies and for the establishment of an advisory State Council, which was to deliberate on administrative issues. Several groups in the governing coalition (notably the Mouvement pour la démocratie et le développement—MDD, led by Dacko) expressed concern at the powers afforded to the President.

In April 1995 Mandaba resigned as Prime Minister, pre-empting a threatened vote of no confidence in his administration (initiated by his own party), following accusations of corruption and incompetence. Patassé appointed Gabriel Koyambounou as the new Prime Minister, who subsequently nominated a new Council of Ministers, with an enlarged membership. In December several opposition movements (including the MDD, but not the RDC) united to form the Conseil démocratique des partis politiques de l'opposition (CODEPO), which aimed to campaign against alleged corruption and mismanagement by the Patassé regime.

In the mid-1990s the Government repeatedly failed to pay the salaries of public sector employees and members of the security forces, prompting frequent strikes and mounting political unrest. In mid-April 1996 CODEPO staged an anti-Government rally in Bangui. Shortly afterwards part of the national army mutinied in the capital and demanded the immediate settlement of all salary arrears. Patassé promised that part of the overdue salaries would be paid and that the mutineers would not be subject to prosecution. The presence of French troops (the Eléments français d'assistance opérationelle—EFAO) in Bangui contributed to the swift collapse of the rebellion. In late April Patassé appointed a new Chief of Staff of the Armed Forces, Col Maurice Regonessa, and banned all public demonstrations. In May, however, discontent resurfaced, and CODEPO organized another rally in Bangui, at which it demanded the resignation of the Government. Soon afterward the President ordered that control of the national armoury should be transferred from the regular army to the presidential guard. However, adverse reaction to this move within the ranks of the armed forces rapidly escalated into a second, more determined insurrection. Once again EFAO troops were deployed to protect the Patassé administration; some 500 reinforcements were brought in from Chad and Gabon to consolidate the resident French military presence (numbering 1,400). After five days of fierce fighting between dissident and loyalist troops, the French forces intervened to suppress the rebellion. France's military action prompted intense scrutiny of the role of the former colonial power, and precipitated large pro- and anti-French demonstrations in Bangui. Following extended negotiations, the mutineers and government representatives eventually signed an accord, providing for an amnesty for the rebels (who were to return to barracks under EFAO guard), the immediate release of hostages, and the installation of a new government of national unity. This was duly installed in June and Jean-Paul Ngoupandé, hitherto ambassador to France, was appointed as the new Prime Minister and immediately nominated a new Council of Ministers. National co-operation, however, remained elusive, as CODEPO, dissatisfied with the level of its ministerial representation, immediately withdrew from the Government.

After renewed violence in January 1997, the former transitional President of Mali, Gen. Amadou Toumani Touré was appointed as mediator and helped to create a cross-party Committee of Consultation and Dialogue. The 'Bangui Accords', drawn up by this committee, were signed towards the end of that month; these, as well as offering an amnesty to the mutineers, provided for the formation of a new government of national unity and for the replacement of the EFAO troops by peace-keeping forces from African nations. The opposition at first threatened to boycott the new Government, largely owing to the appointment of Michel Gbezera-Bria (a close associate of Patassé and hitherto the Minister of Foreign Affairs) as Prime Minister. However, with the creation of new ministerial posts for opposition politicians, a 'Government of Action' (which did not include Ngoupandé) was formed on 18 February; soon afterwards Gen. Bozizé replaced Gen. Regonessa as Chief of Staff of the Armed Forces. Also in February responsibility for peace-keeping operations was transferred from the EFAO to forces of the newly formed Mission interafricaine de surveillance des accords de Bangui (MISAB), comprising some 700 soldiers from Burkina Faso, Chad, Gabon, Mali, Senegal and Togo (with logistical support from 50 French military personnel).

In May 1997, following the deaths in police custody of three former rebels, nine ministers representing the G11 (a grouping of 11 opposition parties, including the MDD—which had left CODEPO in November 1996—and the RDC), as well as the two representatives of the former mutineers, suspended participation in the Government. In June violent clashes erupted between MISAB forces and former mutineers. Several hundred EFAO troops were redeployed on the streets of Bangui and MISAB forces launched a major offensive in the capital, capturing most of the rebel-controlled districts. This assault led to the arrest of more than 80 former mutineers, but also to some 100 deaths, both of soldiers and of civilians. Subsequently, Touré returned to Bangui in his capacity as Chairman of MISAB, and negotiated a four-day truce, which took effect at the end of June, followed by a 10-day cease-fire agreement, signed at the beginning of July; all of the former mutineers were to be reintegrated into the regular armed forces; the rebels, for their part, were to relinquish their weaponry. In September the nine representatives of opposition parties in the Council of Ministers resumed their vacant posts.

In July 1997 France announced its intention to withdraw its troops from the CAR by April 1998; the first troops left the country in October 1997. A National Reconciliation Conference, held in Bangui, in February 1998 led to the signing on 5 March of a National Reconciliation Pact by President Patassé and 40 representatives of all the country's political and social groups. The Pact restated the main provisions of the Bangui Accords and of the political protocol of June 1996. It provided for military and political restructuring, to be implemented by a civilian Prime Minister, supported by all of the country's social and political groups. The powers and position of the President were, however, guaranteed, and a presidential election was scheduled for late 1999.

The signature of the Pact facilitated the authorization, later in March 1998, by the UN Security Council of the establishment of a peace-keeping mission, the UN Mission in the Central African Republic (MINURCA), to replace MISAB. MINURCA comprised 1,345 troops from Benin, Burkina Faso, Canada, Chad, Côte d'Ivoire, Egypt, France, Gabon, Mali, Portugal, Senegal and Togo, and was granted a mandate to remain in the country for an initial period of three months. The mission was subsequently extended until the end of February 1999.

The 1998 elections

Elections to the newly reorganized Assemblée nationale took place on 22 November and 13 December 1998. The MLPC won 47 of the 109 seats in the legislature, but secured the co-operation of seven independent members. The opposition won 55 seats; however, the defection, amid allegations of bribery, of a newly elected deputy belonging to the Parti social-démocrate (PSD) gave the ruling MLPC a majority in the Assemblée. Patassé's decision to call on erstwhile Minister of Finance, Anicet Georges Dologuélé, to form a new Government provoked public demonstrations and caused the opposition formally to withdraw from the Assemblée (the boycott lasted until March 1999). Dologuélé announced the composition of a new coalition Council of Ministers in early January, but 10 opposition ministers immediately resigned in protest at the MLPC's alleged disregard for the results of the election. In mid-January Dologuélé announced the formation of another Council of Ministers, which included four members of the MDD, despite an earlier agreement made by the opposition not to accept posts in the new Government. The MDD leadership subsequently ordered its members to resign from their government positions; three of its four ministers did so.

In February 1999 the UN Security Council extended MINURCA's mandate until mid-November in order that it might assist in preparations for, and the conduct of, the presidential election, which was scheduled to be held on 29 August. France was reported to have opposed an extension of the mandate, and in February the French contingent withdrew from MINURCA (as did the troops from Côte d'Ivoire in April). The UN Secretary-General, Kofi Annan, was particularly critical of delays in the appointment of the independent electoral commission, the Commission électorale mixte indépendante (CEMI), the 27 members of which were finally approved in May. In August, at the request of bilateral creditors and the UN, a 45-member body was established to supervise the activities of the CEMI, which comprised members of both opposition and pro-Patassé parties. In the event, the election was not held until 19 September, owing to organizational problems. On 2 October the Constitutional Court announced that Patassé had been re-elected President, with 51.6% of the total votes cast. On 22 October Patassé was sworn in as President for a further six-year term. In early November recently reappointed Prime Minister Dologuélé announced the formation of a new Council of Ministers, which included members of parties loyal to Patassé, as well as independents, three opposition representatives and two members of the armed forces.

In October 1999 Kofi Annan requested that the UN Security Council authorize the gradual withdrawal of MINURCA from the CAR over a three-month period following the end of its mandate on 15 November. In December the UN announced proposals to establish a Bureau de soutien à la consolidation de la paix en Centrafrique (BONUCA), in Bangui, the role of which would be to monitor developments in the CAR in the areas of politics, socio-economics, human rights and security, as well as to facilitate dialogue between political figures. BONUCA began its operation on the same day as the final withdrawal of MINURCA, 15 February 2000, with a mandate for a one-year period. In September 2000 BONUCA's mandate was extended until the end of 2001, and in September 2001, following continued unrest, it was extended for a further one-year period.

In April 2001 Patassé dismissed the Dologuélé administration. Martin Ziguélé was appointed as Prime Minister, and a new Government was formed. In late May rebellious soldiers, thought to be supporters of Kolingba, attacked Patassé's official residence in an attempted coup. However, the insurgency was suppressed by troops loyal to Patassé, and at least 59 people were killed. Libya sent troops and helicopters, while a contingent of rebels from the Democratic Republic of the Congo (DRC, formerly Zaire) arrived to support the Patassé regime. Violence ensued throughout the country, with heavy fighting in Bangui resulting in some 300 deaths and the displacement of an estimated 60,000–70,000 civilians. In August 2002 Kolingba and 21 associates were sentenced to death *in absentia* for their alleged involvement in the coup; a further 500 defendants were reported to have received prison terms of 10–20 years.

In August 2001 the Council of Ministers was reshuffled; most notably, the Minister of National Defence, Jean-Jacques Démafouth, was replaced, following allegations regarding his involvement in the attempted coup in May (he was, however, acquitted of all charges at his trial in October 2002). In October 2001 Gen. Bozizé was dismissed from the post of Chief of Staff of the Armed Forces because of similar allegations. However, in early November violence erupted in Bangui between supporters of Bozizé and the presidential guard (supported by forces from Libya) after attempts were made to arrest Bozizé, at the request of a judicial commission of inquiry into the failed coup attempt. Efforts to mediate between Bozizé and the CAR administration were unsuccessful, and later that month Bozizé fled to the town of Sarh in southern Chad, where he was granted refuge, with about 300 of his armed supporters. Tension reportedly increased between the CAR and Chad, as security forces pursued those loyal to Bozizé along the border between the two countries. At a meeting of the Communauté économique et monétaire de l'Afrique centrale (CEMAC) in Libreville, Gabon, in December, a commission was created, chaired by President Omar Bongo of Gabon, and also comprising Presidents Idriss Deby and Denis Sassou-Nguesso of Chad and the Republic of the Congo, respectively, to find a lasting solution to the crisis in the CAR. In late December the CAR judiciary abandoned legal proceedings against Bozizé, and in January 2002, during a meeting held in Chad, a government delegation invited Bozizé and his supporters to return to the CAR. In September BONUCA's mandate was extended until December 2003.

On 25 October 2002 the northern suburbs of Bangui were invaded by forces loyal to Bozizé (who had been granted asylum in France earlier in the month, in accordance with an agreement reached at a CEMAC summit aimed at defusing tension between the CAR and Chad—see below). After five days of heavy fighting, pro-Government forces, supported by Libyan troops and some 1,000 fighters from a DRC rebel grouping, the Mouvement pour la libération du Congo (MLC), succeeded in repelling Bozizé's insurgents. Initial reports indicated that some 28 people had been killed during the fighting. None the less, by December the Patassé Government had failed fully to suppress the forces allied to Bozizé, and the CAR was effectively divided between loyalist areas in the south and east and rebel-held northern regions between the Chadian border and Bangui.

In December 2002 the first contingent of a CEMAC peacekeeping force (eventually to number 350) arrived in Bangui, and in January 2003 Libyan forces were withdrawn. Clashes were frequently claimed to have occurred between the regular CAR army and its allies, culminating in reports (denied by the CAR Government) of a massacre of MLC soldiers in December 2002. In February 2003, however, MLC fighters began to withdraw from the CAR, in response to international pressure on the Patassé Government.

Bozizé takes power

On 15 March 2003 armed supporters of Bozizé entered Bangui, encountering little resistance from government troops. President Patassé, who had been attending a regional summit in Niger, was forced to withdraw to the Cameroonian capital, Yaoundé, after shots were fired at his aeroplane as it attempted to land at Bangui. Reports suggested that casualties during the coup had numbered no more than 15 people. Following the surrender of the largely demoralized security forces in Bangui, Bozizé declared himself Head of State, dissolved the Assemblée nationale and suspended the Constitution. Although the coup was condemned by the African Union (AU, see p. 189), the UN, CEMAC, France and the USA, Bozizé insisted that his actions constituted only a 'temporary suspension of democracy' and that a new consensus government would be formed in consultation with the former opposition, human rights groups and development agencies. Following this announcement, Bozizé secured the approval of the Governments of Gabon and the Republic of the Congo at a meeting with the foreign ministers of those countries. France deployed some 300 troops in Bangui in order to assist foreign nationals intending to leave the CAR. Bozizé also gained the support of opposition parties, which pledged to oppose any attempt by Patassé to return to power. In late March Abel Goumba, the leader of the Front patriotique pour le progrès, was appointed as Prime Minister, and a new, broad-based transitional Government was subsequently formed. Despite only receiving two positions in the new Council of Ministers, in mid-April the MLPC declared that it would adhere to the transitional arrangements decreed by Bozizé.

On 30 May 2003 Bozizé inaugurated a 98-member, advisory Conseil national de transition (CNT), which included representatives of political parties, trade unions, religious organizations and human rights groups, in order to assist him in exercising legislative power during the transitional period, which was to last 18–30 months. The CNT maintained its opposition to any involvement by former President Patassé in the political process. Meanwhile, Bozizé confirmed his intention to return the country to civilian rule in January 2005, and a timetable for the resumption of democracy was announced.

In June 2003 the Government announced plans for the demobilization or integration into the CAR army of 5,700 former fighters: 1,200 loyal to Bozizé, 3,500 loyal to Patassé and 1,000 returning from exile. Meanwhile, the Government continued its investigations into widely acknowledged corruption within the country's economic institutions and civil service. In June the executive boards of the state electricity and telecommunications companies were dismissed after the reported discovery of widespread accounting irregularities, and in July 866 non-existent workers were removed from the public sector payroll. Moreover, in the same month the judicial authorities began an investigation into the whereabouts of some 4,800m. francs CFA donated by the Japanese Government for the Patassé administration's reconciliation plans, and ordered the suspension of mineral and timber interests controlled by the former President, while the Government issued guidelines obliging government officials and politicians to declare their personal assets. In August the state prosecutor issued an international arrest warrant for Patassé, now in exile in Togo, on charges including murder and embezzlement. In September BONUCA's mandate was extended until December 2004.

In December 2003 Prime Minister Goumba was appointed Vice-President, and his previous post was allocated to Célestin-Leroy Gaombalet, a former financier. Gaombalet subsequently effected a government reshuffle, in which 14 ministers retained their portfolios; the changes mainly reflected popular dissatisfaction with deteriorating public security in Bangui, and new appointees included several political figures linked to previous administrations.

An eight-member interministerial committee, headed by Prime Minister Gaombalet, was established in January 2004 to oversee the forthcoming electoral process. According to a revised schedule, a referendum on a new constitution, which was to be drafted by the CNT, would be held in November, with municipal, presidential and legislative elections to follow between December and January 2005. In early December the newly appointed Transitional Constitutional Court (TCC) oversaw the planned referendum on a new constitution, which was approved by 87.2% of those who voted. The new Constitution provided for a presidential term of five years, renewable only once, and increased powers for the Prime Minister. Following the referendum Bozizé announced that presidential and legislative elections were to be rescheduled for mid-February 2005 and that he would stand as an independent candidate for the presidency. In late December 2004 the TCC disqualified nine presidential candidates including, notably, former President Patassé and former Prime Minister Ngoupandé. However, the TCC's decision provoked popular unrest and in early January 2005 Bozizé annulled the disqualification of Ngoupandé and two other candidates.

Following administrative delays, presidential and legislative elections were held concurrently on 13 March 2005. In the presidential election Bozizé secured 43.0% of the votes cast, while the former Prime Minister Ziguélé obtained 23.5%; both proceeded to a second round of voting, held on 8 May, at which Bozizé took 64.7% of the vote. At the legislative elections the pro-Bozizé Convergence 'Kwa na kwa' (meaning 'Work and Only

Work' in Sango) secured 42 of the 105 seats in the new Assemblée nationale, while the MLPC (the principal party supporting Ziguélé) won 11 seats; 34 independent candidates were also elected. In June Bozizé announced a new Council of Ministers headed by Elie Doté. Also in that month the AU's Peace and Security Council lifted sanctions that had been imposed on the CAR in the wake of Bozizé's seizure of power in March 2003.

In April 2006 the Supreme Court confirmed that the CAR justice system was inadequate to try Patassé and his associates for the atrocities allegedly committed in the country following Bozizé's failed coup attempt of October 2002. The case was therefore referred to the International Criminal Court (ICC). In August 2006 Patassé and one of his advisers were found guilty of financial misconduct by the ICC. They were sentenced to 20 years hard labour *in absentia* and fined 7,000m. francs CFA. In late October the rebel coalition, the Union des forces démocratiques pour le rassemblement (UFDR), took control of the north-eastern town of Birao. Bozizé travelled to Chad to meet with his counterpart, Deby Itno; the two heads of state subsequently blamed the unrest on the Sudanese Government which, they claimed, supported anti-Government forces in the CAR and Chad. Chadian forces were subsequently deployed to assist the CAR military in overcoming the rebels, while the French Government agreed to provide support in the form of logistics and aerial intelligence. In late November a major government counter-offensive, in which CEMAC forces were also involved, resulted in the recapture of Birao. In mid-December Ouanda Djalle, the last town to remain under rebel control, was reclaimed, following a series of French air-strikes in the region.

In early February 2007 Abdoulaye Miskine, leader of the Front démocratique de libération du peuple centrafricain (FDPC—a faction of the UFDR), and André Ringui Le Gaillard, leader of the Armée populaire pour la restauration de la république et la démocratie (APRD), signed a peace deal with Bozizé, brokered by the Libyan leader, Col Muammar al-Qaddafi, in Sirte, Libya. Under the terms of the agreement, the rebels were to surrender their weapons and cease military activities in return for an amnesty. The agreement also committed the CAR Government to the establishment of a programme for the rehabilitation of former rebels and their integration into the CAR military. In April an accord was signed by the CAR Government and the leader of the UFDR, Zakaria Damane, on behalf of the northern rebels, granting them an amnesty and providing for the implementation of an immediate cessation of hostilities. However, the cease-fire failed to hold and the violence continued, forcing thousands more people to flee their homes and seek refuge in neighbouring Cameroon and Chad. The UN encouraged the CAR Government to continue discussions with rebel leaders to restore peace and in July Damane was appointed as an adviser to the presidency. Shortly afterwards a government reorganization was effected in which Gen. Raymond Paul Ndougou, a signatory to the April peace agreement, was named as Minister of the Interior and Public Security; Lt-Col Sylvain N'doutingaï assumed the position of Minister of Finance and the Budget, and of Mines, Energy and Hydraulics.

Prime Minister Elie Doté announced his resignation, and that of his Council of Ministers, in mid-January 2008 ahead of a planned vote of no confidence in his leadership. The country had been experiencing civil unrest for several months and a number of trade unions had earlier in January commenced a general strike in protest against unpaid salaries. Prof. Faustin-Archange Touadéra, the Rector of the University of Bangui who possessed no significant previous political experience, was named as Doté's successor and later in January a new Government was announced; many of the key portfolios remained unaltered, but three existing ministers were promoted to the status of Minister of State, including N'doutingaï, although he relinquished responsibility for finance and the budget.

A national peace process

In mid-May 2008 a peace deal was finally brokered in Libreville, Gabon, between the Government and the APRD, the last remaining rebel group outside the reconciliation process. The agreement provided for an immediate cease-fire and the eventual reintegration of rebel forces into the national army. This was followed in June by the signing of a 'global peace accord' in Libreville between the Government, the APRD and the UFDR. However, in August the APRD withdrew from the peace process, along with several other rebel factions, and violence resumed. Rebel leaders cited dissatisfaction at proposed legislation to grant amnesty to those implicated in crimes during the conflict as the reason behind the failure of the peace talks. In September the Assemblée nationale approved the new amnesty legislation, with the intent of encouraging the resumption of reconciliation talks. APRD leaders agreed to consider the terms of the new law and political dialogue resumed in early December in the presence of Patassé who had recently returned from exile.

Following 12 days of talks between some 200 representatives from the Government, the opposition, civil society groups and rebel movements, Bozizé pledged to appoint a government of national unity. In mid-January 2009 he dismissed the incumbent administration and reappointed Touadéra to the premiership. The new, 32-member Government announced on 20 January contained 13 new ministers and, most notably, included François Naoeyama of the APRD as Minister of the Environment and Ecology and Gontron Djono-Djidou-Ahabo of the UFDR as Minister of Housing and Living Conditions. The former Chief of Staff of the Armed Forces, Gen. Jules Bernard Ouandé, was appointed Minister of National Security and Public Order. However, in February the FDPC, one of the first groups to have signed the peace accord, announced its rejection of the agreement, citing government non-compliance with its terms, and Miskine declared the formation of a new rebel alliance, the Résistance nationale. Also in February the northern town of Ndélé was taken by rebel fighters from the Convention des Patriotes pour la Justice et la Paix (CPJP), formed in late 2008 under the leadership of Charles Massi, a former defence minister; control of the town was subsequently regained by the army in an operation that resulted in the flight of some 6,000 civilians. In June 2009 there were further heavy clashes in which, according to the rebels, 24 soldiers were killed, while in December government forces attacked the CPJP base pre-empting a further assault on Ndélé. Massi had been captured in Chad in June and in December was transferred to the CAR. In January 2010 the CPJP demanded that the Government prove Massi was still alive and in a later communiqué the France-based Secretary of the Forum démocratique pour la modernité, of which Massi was a member, stated that Massi had died from injuries inflicted while in custody. The CAR Government declined to issue a response.

Recent developments: the 2011 elections

Despite the ongoing violence the Government continued with its plans for peace with a three-year project to disarm, demobilize and re-integrate former rebels; the initiative was supported by the APRD and the process was to be overseen by a UN steering committee. A Commission électorale indépendante (CEI) was set up to organize legislative and presidential elections planned for 2010. Although initially a coalition of opposition parties boycotted the commission, President Bozizé acceded to their demands to annul local CEI committees that it considered had been constituted illegally. In early March a presidential decree fixed 25 April as the date for the first round of the elections; however, the opposition protested that the situation in the country was not sufficiently stable and pressed the President to retract the decree. Also in March a coup plot was uncovered implicating Patassé, who denied any involvement and denounced the accusations as an attempt to eliminate him from the presidential elections. By the end of the month the elections, which according to the UN were required to be held before April in order to comply with the Constitution and certainly before the end of the current presidential mandate which ended in June, were postponed until 16 May. At the closing date for the deposition of candidatures only Bozizé and Patassé had been put forward as, once again, the opposition had boycotted the process.

At the end of April 2010 the CEI announced that it required additional funds of €5.3m. to finance the elections and to print electoral cards, and it became apparent that the elections would be subject to a further delay. An extraordinary session of the Assemblée nationale was called to fix formalities for an extended presidential mandate up until the date when elections could reasonably be held. Legislation was swiftly adopted and the CEI unanimously decided that the polls would be held on 24 October. Bozizé, however, subsequently decreed 23 January 2011 as the election date.

The presidential and legislative elections took place as scheduled on 23 January 2011. In the presidential poll Bozizé took 64.4% of the total votes cast (thus obviating the need for a second round of voting), while his nearest challengers Patassé and Ziguélé secured 21.4% and 6.8%, respectively. A total of 35 parliamentary candidates were elected in the first round of the legislative election; however, a number of challenges by opposition parties regarding the validity of the elections were dismissed and the coalition of opposition forces boycotted the second round on 27 March. Following the conclusion of the second round, of the 105 seats available, 61 were allocated to members of Kwa na kwa, while 26 were won by independent candidates, 11 were taken by members of the 'majorité presidentielle' and two seats were secured by members of the opposition. The results in five (subsequently increased to 14) constituencies were declared void by the Constitutional Court. On 5 April the death of Patassé was announced. He had been admitted to hospital in Douala, Cameroon, en route to receive treatment in Malabo, Equatorial Guinea. Later in April Bozizé reappointed Touadéra to the premiership following the resignation of his Government the previous month. A new, 35-member Council of Ministers was announced on 22 April featuring five ministers of state. In September by-elections were held in those constituencies where the results had been annulled; Kwa na kwa secured eight seats, independents three seats, and the MLPC, the PSD and the Parti pour la Démocratie en Centrafrique each won one seat. A number of opposition parties did not participate in the by-elections in continuing protest against the allegedly fraudulent polls conducted earlier in the year.

Meanwhile, clashes between CPJP rebels and the armed forces (supported by pro-Government UFDR fighters) erupted in the north-eastern prefecture of Vakaga during April 2011. The skirmishes reportedly resulted in 27 deaths and the displacement of some 6,500 civilians, while CPJP–UFDR violence in neighbouring Bamingui-Bangoran prefecture in the previous month had left at least seven people dead and had forced a further 500 villagers to flee their homes. Nevertheless, in late April the CPJP declared a truce, which was formalized in June when a cease-fire accord was concluded with the Government, and a similar agreement was signed by a dissident CPJP faction in July. Almost 1,500 rebels, from various groupings, had been disarmed by the end of that month under the Government's demobilization programme, and there were plans for the reintegration of a further 7,500. In spite of this progress, the seizure by the CPJP of a UFDR-controlled diamond mine in Vakaga provoked renewed fighting between the two groups in September, which resulted in the deaths of at least 50 people and the displacement of an additional 4,500. The Government and the UN condemned the resumption of violence and appealed for a cease-fire, an agreement for which was duly signed by both sides in October. The Government announced that the disarmament of the CPJP and the UFDR would be completed by the end of the month.

In July 2011 two journalists were convicted of defamation and fined after accusing Jean-Francis Bozizé—the President's son and Minister-delegate at the Presidency, in charge of National Defence, War Veterans, War Victims and the Restructuring of the Armed Forces—of embezzling €5.2m. in European Union (EU) funds. Press rights organizations condemned the treatment of the journalists and declared that the legal action was in contravention of the Constitution, which ostensibly guaranteed press freedom. Human rights group Amnesty International censured the Government in October for its failure to prevent 'grave human rights violations, including possible war crimes and crimes against humanity', describing the country as 'a black hole in terms of human rights'. Minister of Justice and Moralization Firmin Findiro rejected this bleak assessment and emphasized the Government's efforts to protect civilians.

Foreign Affairs

In May 1997 the CAR recognized the administration of President Laurent Kabila in the DRC. In the same month the CAR and the DRC signed a mutual assistance pact, which provided for permanent consultation on internal security and defence. The pact also sought to guarantee border security; however, during mid-1997 armed soldiers of what had been the Zairean army were reported to be fleeing troops loyal to Kabila and crossing the Oubangui river into the CAR. In January 1999 there was a further influx to the CAR of DRC civilians fleeing the fighting between government and rebel soldiers, who were occupying the northern part of the DRC. In August the office of the UN High Commissioner for Refugees (UNHCR) estimated that the CAR was sheltering about 54,000 refugees from the DRC, Chad and Sudan. Following the attempted coup in the CAR in May 2001, UNHCR estimated that 23,000 people had escaped to the DRC; further movements were reported in the aftermath of the attempted coup of October 2002. In June 2003 Gen. Bozizé and President Joseph Kabila of the DRC agreed to re-establish existing bilateral security arrangements. In August 2004 officials from both countries met to discuss reopening the common border and, subsequently, an agreement was signed under the auspices of the UNHCR allowing some 10,000 Congolese refugees in the CAR to be repatriated. In May 2008 former Congolese Vice-President Jean-Pierre Bemba was arrested in Belgium, and in June the ICC confirmed that it had brought charges against him of war crimes and crimes against humanity for acts committed in the CAR in 2002–03. His trial opened at the ICC on 22 November 2010.

In July 2009, according to UN estimates, 1,200 Congolese fleeing attacks by the Ugandan Lord's Resistance Army (LRA), which had bases in the DRC, sought refuge in south-eastern CAR. Cross-border raids had resulted in the deaths of 10 people that month and the internal displacement of some 3,000 CAR civilians. In August 2010, after a campaign of attacks in the north-east of the country and the abduction of villagers, largely comprising children who were coerced into fighting, the CAR pledged to capture the LRA leader, Joseph Kony, with the co-operation of Uganda, France and the USA. Nevertheless, further LRA raids were reported in December and March 2011 in the south-east of the CAR. The USA deployed some 100 troops to Uganda in October to support (in a non-combat capacity) the regional military effort to subjugate the LRA and capture Kony. An unspecified number of these US Special Forces were transferred to Obo, in the south-eastern CAR prefecture of Haut-Mbomou, in December to provide assistance to the CAR military in suppressing LRA activity in the area. Counter-insurgency operations in the CAR had also been bolstered since late 2010 by the provision of French equipment and technical advice. LRA defectors asserted that the rebel group had been ensconced in Haut-Mbomou since early 2011, and Ugandan troops claimed that they had sighted Kony in the prefecture in October; US military officials also suspected that he was sheltering in the CAR.

In late 1994 the CAR and Chad agreed to ensure mutual border security. In 1994 the CAR also became the fifth member of the Lake Chad Basin Commission (see p. 451). Relations between the CAR and Chad deteriorated when armed men, led by a Chadian rebel, raided southern Chad from the CAR on 29 and 31 December 2001; four people were killed during the raids. A further outbreak of violence in the border area was reported in April 2002, which resulted in at least one fatality. Despite pledges by both countries to increase co-operation, further clashes in August resulted in the deaths of 20 CAR soldiers. An emergency CEMAC summit took place later that month, chaired by the Gabonese President, Omar Bongo, and an observer mission was dispatched to examine the security situation along the common border. At the end of August the mission reported that, although tension remained high in the region, there was no concentration of troops on the border. The CAR's decision to appoint Col Martin Khoumtan-Madji (believed by the Chadian authorities to be an alias of Abdoulaye Miskine) as the head of a special unit in the CAR military, charged with securing the common border, further strained relations, as did Chad's reputed sponsorship of forces loyal to Bozizé. In early October a CEMAC summit in Libreville, Gabon, sought to defuse tensions between the two countries; in accordance with an accord reached at the summit, Bozizé and Khoumtan-Madji were subsequently granted asylum in France and Togo, respectively. In December the first contingent of a CEMAC force was deployed in Bangui, initially to protect Patassé and later to monitor joint patrols of the border by Chadian and CAR troops. Relations between the two countries subsequently began to improve, and in January 2003 the Governments of the CAR, Chad and Sudan announced their intention to establish a tripartite committee to oversee the security and stability of their joint borders. Following Bozizé's assumption of power in the CAR in mid-March 2003, the Chadian Government dispatched some 400 troops to Bangui; 120 Chadian troops were subsequently integrated into CEMAC's operations in the CAR. In mid-2006 it was reported that rebels from Chad had attacked government forces and CEMAC units in the north-east of the CAR, close to the Sudanese border, although some sources blamed the violence in the region on CAR rebels.

In September 2007, following the adoption of UN Resolution 1778, the UN Security Council approved the deployment for a period of one year of the UN Mission in the Central African Republic and Chad (MINURCAT), with the mandate to protect refugees, displaced persons and civilians adversely affected by the uprising in the Darfur region of Sudan. MINURCAT was also to facilitate the provision of humanitarian assistance in eastern Chad and the north-east of the CAR and create favourable conditions for the reconstruction and economic and social development of those areas. The multidimensional presence was to be supported by the EU bridging military operation in Eastern Chad and North Eastern Central African Republic (EUFOR TCHAD/RCA) comprising some 4,300 troops. In March 2009 UN peace-keepers replaced the EU forces and MINURCAT's mandate was extended until March 2010. According to UN estimates there were 340,000 refugees from the CAR and Sudan living in Chad. However, at the request of the Chadian Government, MINURCAT's mandate was ended in December and all troops withdrew from the region, to be replaced by Chadian military units, causing the UN Secretary-General to express great concern for the security of citizens of both countries and also those of Sudan. There were deadly clashes later that month between CPJP rebels and government troops in Birao. A total of 71 people, including 65 rebels, were reported to have been killed, a figure refuted by the CPJP, which claimed that it had withdrawn from the town after Chadian troops, in pursuit of their own rebel forces, had fired on civilians. As many as 8,000 people fled the fighting and required humanitarian assistance. Violent attacks by Christians against Chadian Muslims took place in Bangui during late May 2011. Mosques were set ablaze, Muslim homes and shops were looted, and at least 11 people (including eight Chadians) lost their lives as a consequence of the fighting, which had been prompted by the alleged ritualistic killing of two children by a Muslim. In the following month the Minister-delegate at the Presidency, in charge of National Defence, War Veterans, War Victims and the Restructuring of the Armed Forces, Jean-Francis Bozizé, held talks with his Chadian counterpart, Bichara Issa Djadala, to discuss measures to alleviate tensions between the two communities; it was agreed that a bilateral security committee would be formed.

Relations with Sudan have been strained in recent years, ostensibly owing to the instability in the west of that country, particularly in the Darfur region. In April 2006 the CAR closed the common border, after a number of incursions into its territory from Sudanese-based rebels. Furthermore, the CAR alleged Sudanese involvement in the UFDR's capture of Birao in October (see above) and President Bozizé accused his Sudanese counterpart, Omar Hassan Ahmad al-Bashir, of attempting to destabilize the CAR. These claims were refuted by the Sudanese authorities and in August 2007, following a visit by Bozizé to Khartoum, the Sudanese capital, the two countries agreed to normalize bilateral relations and to improve border security through joint patrols. In November 2010 UNHCR and the CAR Government co-operated to airlift 3,500 Sudanese refugees, who had fled fighting in the northeast Bambari region in 2007, after conditions at their camp deteriorated. In May 2011 the Presidents of the CAR, Sudan and Chad met in Khartoum for discussions on border security. It was announced that a tripartite border force would be created to prevent smuggling and other illegal cross-border activities.

The CAR maintains amicable relations with Nigeria, and in June 1999 the two countries signed a bilateral trade agreement. The CAR is also a close ally of Libya, and in April 1999 joined the Libyan-sponsored Community of Sahel-Saharan States (see p. 449). Diplomatic relations with Libya (which had been closely allied with the Patassé Government) were resumed in July 2003, following discussions between President Bozizé and the Libyan leader, Col Muammar al-Qaddafi. In February 2010 the first meeting of a joint co-operation commission between the CAR and Cameroon took place to discuss strategies for the free movement of people and goods between the countries.

CONSTITUTION AND GOVERNMENT

Following the overthrow of President Ange-Félix Patassé in mid-March 2003, the Constitution of January 1995 was suspended, and the Assemblée nationale dissolved. The self-proclaimed Head of State, Gen. François Bozizé, appointed a Conseil national de transition, to assist him in exercising legislative power, and a transitional Government. A new Constitution was approved by referendum on 5 December 2004. Bozizé was elected to the presidency after the second round of voting in a presidential election, held on 8 May 2005. Legislative elections to a new Assemblée nationale were held concurrently with the first round of the presidential election on 13 March.

For administrative purposes, the country is divided into 14 prefectures, two economic prefectures (Gribingui and Sangha), and one commune (Bangui). It is further divided into 67 sub-prefectures and two postes de contrôle administratif. At community level there are 65 communes urbaines, 102 communes rurales and seven communes d'élevage.

REGIONAL AND INTERNATIONAL CO-OPERATION

The CAR is a member of the African Union (see p. 189), the Central African organs of the Franc Zone (see p. 333), the Community of Sahel-Saharan States (see p. 449) and of the Communauté économique des états de l'Afrique centrale (CEEAC, see p. 449).

The CAR became a member of the UN in 1960, and was admitted to the World Trade Organization (WTO, see p. 433) in 1995. The CAR participates in the Group of 77 (G77, see p. 450) developing countries. The country is also a member of the International Coffee Organization (see p. 445).

ECONOMIC AFFAIRS

In 2010, according to estimates by the World Bank, the CAR's gross national income (GNI), measured at average 2008–10 prices, was US $2,067m., equivalent to $470 per head (or $780 per head on an international purchasing-power parity basis). During 2001–10, it was estimated, the population increased at an average annual rate of 1.7%, while gross domestic product (GDP) per head, in real terms, declined at an average annual rate of 0.7%. Overall GDP increased, in real terms, at an average annual rate of 1.0% in 2001–10. It increased by 3.3% in 2010.

Agriculture (including hunting, forestry and fishing) contributed 53.5% of GDP in 2009, according to the African Development Bank (AfDB). An estimated 61.2% of the economically active population was employed in the sector in mid-2012, according to FAO estimates. The principal cash crops have traditionally been cotton (which accounted for 10.8% of export earnings in 2002, but decreased sharply to an estimated 0.8% in 2006) and coffee (only an estimated 1.0% of total exports in 2006, compared with 9.4% in 1999). Livestock and tobacco are also exported. The major subsistence crops are cassava (manioc) and yams. The Government is encouraging the cultivation of horticultural produce for export. The exploitation of the country's large forest resources represents a significant source of export revenue. Rare butterflies are also exported. According to the World Bank, agricultural GDP increased at an average annual rate of 1.4% during 2000–08. According to the AfDB, the sector's GDP increased by 1.8% in 2008, but declined by 8.9% in 2009.

Industry (including mining, manufacturing, construction and power) engaged 3.5% of the employed labour force in 1990 and, according to the AfDB, provided 13.9% of GDP in 2009. According to the World Bank, industrial GDP increased at an average annual rate of 2.0% in 2000–08; growth in 2008 was 5.7%.

Mining and quarrying engaged a labour force estimated at between 40,000 and 80,000 in the late 1990s, and contributed an estimated 2.6% of GDP in 2009, according to the AfDB. The principal activity is the extraction of predominantly gem diamonds (exports of diamonds totalled an estimated 415,000 carats in 2002 and provided some 39.7% of total export revenue in 2006). The introduction of gem-cutting facilities and the eradication of widespread 'black' market smuggling operations would substantially increase revenue from diamond mining. However, in the CAR diamonds are predominantly found in widely scattered 'alluvial' deposits (mainly in the south-west and west of the country), rather than Kimberlite deposits, which are concentrated and, thus, more easily exploited and policed. It was estimated that 50% of the potential revenue from taxes on diamond exports was lost to smuggling and corruption under the Patassé administration. In July 2003 the CAR became a participant in the Kimberley Process, an international certification scheme aimed at excluding diamonds from the world market that have been traded for arms by rebel movements in conflict zones. Deposits of gold are also exploited. The development of uranium resources may proceed, and reserves of iron ore, copper, tin and zinc have also been located, although the country's insecurity and poor infrastructure have generally deterred mining companies from attempting commercial exploitation of these reserves. The GDP of the mining sector increased by an average of 1.2% per year during 2002–06. GDP declined in 2008 by 9.2%, but increased by 68.7% in 2009, according to AfDB estimates.

The manufacturing sector engaged 1.6% of the employed labour force in 1988. Manufacturing, which, according to the AfDB, contributed 6.3% of GDP in 2009, is based on the processing of primary products. In real terms, the GDP of the manufacturing sector increased at an average annual rate of 2.2% during 2000–08, although it declined by 0.1% in 2009.

The construction sector engaged 0.5% of the employed labour force in 1988. The sector contributed 4.4% of GDP in 2009 and grew by 6.1%, according to the AfDB.

In 1999, according to preliminary figures, 97.7% of electrical energy generated within the CAR was derived from the country's two hydroelectric power installations. Imports of petroleum products comprised 16.9% of the cost of merchandise imports in 2005.

Services engaged 15.5% of the employed labour force in 1988 and, according to the AfDB, provided 32.6% of GDP in 2009. In real terms the GDP of the services sector decreased at an average rate of 1.5% per year during 2000–08; it increased by 4.9% in 2006, although growth was negligible in both 2007 and 2008.

In 2009 the CAR recorded a visible trade deficit of an estimated 63,900m. francs CFA and there was a deficit of an estimated 72,400m. francs CFA on the current account of the balance of payments. In 2005 the principal source of imports was Cameroon (providing 15.7% of the total), while the principal markets for exports were Belgium (accounting for 29.3% of the total) and France-Monaco (19.3%). Other major trading partners in that year were Cameroon, Switzerland-Liechtenstein, Israel, Italy and the Democratic Republic of the Congo. The principal exports in 2006 were diamonds and wood products. The principal imports in 2003 were petroleum and petroleum products, cereals and cereal preparations, medicinal and pharmaceutical products and road vehicles and parts.

In 2009, according to IMF projections, there was an estimated budget deficit of 27,900m. francs CFA. The CAR's general government gross debt in 2010 was 412,089m. francs CFA, equivalent to 41.9% of GDP. At the end of 2009 the CAR's total external debt was US $396.0m., of which $250.0m. was public and publicly guaranteed debt. In that year the cost of servicing long-term public and publicly guaranteed debt and repayments to the IMF was equivalent to 4.9% of the value of exports of goods, services and income (excluding workers' remittances). The annual rate of inflation averaged 3.2% in 2001–10; consumer prices increased by an average of 3.5% in 2009 and by 1.5% in 2010, according to ILO. In 1995 7.6% of the labour force were unemployed.

The CAR's land-locked position, the inadequacy of the transport infrastructure and the country's vulnerability to adverse climatic conditions and to fluctuations in international prices for its main agricultural exports have impeded sustained economic growth. Periodic reports of corruption, political instability and civil unrest have also severely disrupted economic activity and deterred foreign investment. Following his assumption of power in March 2003, President Bozizé attempted to reverse this trend and began efforts to secure financial assistance from international donors including the IMF, which approved a Poverty Reduction and Growth Facility, later known as an Extended Credit Facility. Although economic activity slowed in 2009 in response to the global financial crisis and problems with the domestic electricity network, a revival in the agricultural sector in 2010 precipitated increased real GDP growth of 3.3% (up from 1.7% in 2009), according to the IMF. However, despite this economic recovery, the country remained very poor and armed incursions restricted citizens' ability to farm and often to remain in their villages, occasioning in November 2010 the largest campaign of food distribution ever carried out in the country by the International Committee of the Red Cross reaching 55,000 residents, refugees and internally displaced persons. The IMF forecast that real GDP would expand by 3.1% in 2011, with agricultural activity again providing the impetus for this economic growth, along with rising commodity exports (principally timber and diamonds). However, with oil prices increasing and the Government holding multiple elections during 2011, the country's financial position came under pressure. Frequent outbreaks of violence throughout the year also placed a strain on public resources and discouraged inward investment. Nevertheless, in July the People's Republic of China provided a US $31m. loan to fund the construction of a new power station to alleviate the chronic power shortages in the capital, while in November the World Bank agreed to finance a $24m. agricultural development and rural poverty reduction initiative (following the approval of another $24m. loan in the previous year for urban infrastructure projects).

PUBLIC HOLIDAYS

2013: 1 January (New Year), 29 March (Anniversary of the death of Barthélemy Boganda), 1 April (Easter Monday), 1 May (May Day), 9 May (Ascension Day), 20 May (Whit Monday), 30 June (National Day of Prayer), 13 August (Independence Day), 15 August (Assumption), 1 November (All Saints' Day), 1 December (National Day), 25 December (Christmas).

Statistical Survey

Source (unless otherwise stated): Division des Statistiques et des Etudes Economiques, Ministère de l'Economie, du Plan et de la Coopération Internationale, Bangui.

Area and Population

AREA, POPULATION AND DENSITY

Area (sq km)	622,984*
Population (census results)	
8 December 1988	2,463,616
8 December 2003†	
Males	1,569,446
Females	1,581,626
Total	3,151,072
Population (UN estimates at mid-year)‡	
2010	4,401,051
2011	4,486,833
2012	4,575,585
Density (per sq km) at mid-2012	7.3

* 240,535 sq miles.

† Source: UN, Population and Vital Statistics Report.

‡ Source: UN, *World Population Prospects: The 2010 Revision*.

POPULATION BY AGE AND SEX

(UN estimates at mid-2012)

	Males	Females	Total
0–14	907,131	915,170	1,822,301
15–64	1,268,040	1,304,429	2,572,469
65 and over	79,376	101,439	180,815
Total	2,254,547	2,321,038	4,575,585

Source: UN, *World Population Prospects: The 2010 Revision*.

PRINCIPAL TOWNS

(estimated population at mid-1994)

Bangui (capital)	524,000	Carnot	41,000
Berbérati	47,000	Bambari	41,000
Bouar	43,000	Bossangoa	33,000

Mid-2009 (incl. suburbs, UN estimate): Bangui 701,597 (Source: UN, *World Urbanization Prospects: The 2009 Revision*).

BIRTHS AND DEATHS
(annual averages, UN estimates)

	1995–2000	2000–05	2005–10
Birth rate (per 1,000)	39.8	38.3	35.6
Death rate (per 1,000)	19.2	19.5	17.6

Source: UN, *World Population Prospects: The 2010 Revision*.

Life expectancy (years at birth, WHO estimates): 48 (males 49; females 48) in 2009 (Source: WHO, *World Health Statistics*).

ECONOMICALLY ACTIVE POPULATION
(persons aged 6 years and over, 1988 census)

	Males	Females	Total
Agriculture, hunting, forestry and fishing	417,630	463,007	880,637
Mining and quarrying	11,823	586	12,409
Manufacturing	16,096	1,250	17,346
Electricity, gas and water	751	58	809
Construction	5,583	49	5,632
Trade, restaurants and hotels	37,435	54,563	91,998
Transport, storage and communications	6,601	150	6,751
Financing, insurance, real estate and business services	505	147	652
Community, social and personal services	61,764	8,537	70,301
Sub-total	558,188	528,347	1,086,535
Activities not adequately defined	7,042	4,627	11,669
Total employed	565,230	532,974	1,098,204
Unemployed	66,624	22,144	88,768
Total labour force	631,854	555,118	1,186,972

Source: ILO.

Mid-2012 (estimates in '000): Agriculture, etc. 1,275; Total labour force 2,084 (Source: FAO).

Health and Welfare

KEY INDICATORS

Total fertility rate (children per woman, 2009)	4.7
Under-5 mortality rate (per 1,000 live births, 2009)	171
HIV/AIDS (% of persons aged 15–49, 2009)	4.7
Physicians (per 1,000 head, 2004)	0.1
Hospital beds (per 1,000 head, 2006)	1.2
Health expenditure (2008): US $ per head (PPP)	32
Health expenditure (2008): % of GDP	4.3
Health expenditure (2008): public (% of total)	39.3
Access to water (% of persons, 2008)	67
Access to sanitation (% of persons, 2008)	34
Total carbon dioxide emissions ('000 metric tons, 2007)	252.8
Carbon dioxide emissions per head (metric tons, 2007)	0.1
Human Development Index (2011): ranking	179
Human Development Index (2011): value	0.343

For sources and definitions, see explanatory note on p. vi.

Agriculture

PRINCIPAL CROPS
('000 metric tons)

	2008	2009	2010
Maize	146.8	151.2	150.0
Millet*	10.0	10.0	10.0
Sorghum*	40.8	50.4	40.0
Cassava (Manioc)	621.8	642.9	679.0
Taro (Coco yam)†	109.9	113.7	118.0
Rice, paddy	38.0	39.1	39.0
Yams†	402.2	415.9	435.0
Sugar cane†	95.0	95.0	95.0
Groundnuts, with shell	159.5	162.7	140.0
Oil palm fruit	14.4	9.2	4.7
Sesame seed	49.0	50.0	50.0
Melonseed†	32.4	34.1	31.1
Pumpkins, squash and gourds	32.3	32.9	30.0
Bananas†	124.9	125.0	126.0
Plantains†	82.1	85.0	88.0
Oranges†	22.0	20.9	24.0
Pineapples†	14.0	14.2	14.5
Coffee, green*	3.3	3.6	1.6
Seed cotton	2.3	7.5	10.5

* Unofficial figures.
† FAO estimates.

Aggregate production ('000 metric tons, may include official, semi-official or estimated data): Total cereals 235.5 in 2008, 250.7 in 2009, 239.0 in 2010; Total roots and tubers 1,135.0 in 2008, 1,173.6 in 2009, 1,233.2 in 2010; Total pulses 31.2 in 2008, 30.8 in 2009, 31.3 in 2010; Total vegetables (incl. melons) 97.3 in 2008, 99.2 in 2009, 95.0 in 2010; Total fruits (excl. melons) 263.9 in 2008, 268.8 in 2009, 274.6 in 2010.

Source: FAO.

LIVESTOCK
('000 head, year ending September)

	2008	2009	2010
Cattle	3,723	3,807	3,893
Goats	4,347	4,599	4,862
Sheep	351	369	388
Pigs	997	1,041	1,087
Chickens	5,869	6,117	6,376

Source: FAO.

LIVESTOCK PRODUCTS
('000 metric tons, FAO estimates)

	2008	2009	2010
Cattle meat	81.0	82.5	85.0
Sheep meat	2.0	2.1	2.2
Goat meat	16.1	17.0	18.0
Pig meat	13.5	14.3	16.0
Chicken meat	5.2	5.5	5.7
Game meat	15.8	15.9	19.7
Cows' milk	71.0	72.0	75.0
Hen eggs	1.9	1.9	1.9
Honey	15.5	16.3	14.8

Source: FAO.

Forestry

ROUNDWOOD REMOVALS
('000 cubic metres, excluding bark)

	2006	2007	2008
Sawlogs, veneer logs and logs for sleepers	524*	533†	533†
Other industrial wood*	308	308	308
Fuel wood*	2,000	2,000	2,000
Total	2,832	2,841	2,841

* FAO estimate(s).
† Unofficial figure.

2009–10: Production assumed to be unchanged from 2008 (FAO estimates).

Source: FAO.

SAWNWOOD PRODUCTION
('000 cubic metres, including railway sleepers)

	2006	2007	2008
Total (all broadleaved)	69*	95†	95†

* FAO estimate.
† Unofficial figure.

2009–10: Production assumed to be unchanged from 2008 (FAO estimate).

Source: FAO.

Fishing

('000 metric tons, live weight of capture, FAO estimates)

	2001	2002	2003
Total catch (freshwater fishes)	15.1	15.0	15.0

2004–09: Catch assumed to be unchanged from 2003 (FAO estimates).

Source: FAO.

Mining

	2007	2008	2009
Gold (kg)	10	43	61
Diamonds ('000 carats)*	467.7	377.2	311.8
Limestone ('000 metric tons)	85	85	n.a.

* Production is approximately 70% to 80% gem quality.

Source: US Geological Survey.

Industry

SELECTED PRODUCTS
('000 metric tons, unless otherwise indicated)

	2004	2005	2006
Beer ('000 hectolitres)	118.7	118.9	123.1
Sugar (raw, centrifugal)*	12	12	n.a.
Soft drinks ('000 hectolitres)	41.4	46.7	51.8
Cigarettes (million packets)	16.0	n.a.	n.a.
Palm oil*	1.7	1.7	1.7
Groundnut oil*	33.2	33.2	33.2
Plywood ('000 cubic metres)*	2.0	2.0	2.0

* FAO estimates.

Sources: IMF, *Central African Republic: Selected Issues and Statistical Appendix* (January 2008); FAO.

Groundnut oil ('000 metric tons, FAO estimates): 36.7 in 2007; 37.5 in 2008; 38.3 in 2009 (Source: FAO).

Electric energy (million kWh, estimates): 110 in 2003; 110 in 2004; 110 in 2005 (Source: UN, *Industrial Commodity Statistics Yearbook*).

Palm oil ('000 metric tons, FAO estimates): 2.5 in 2007; 1.9 in 2008; 2.0 in 2009 (Source: FAO).

Plywood ('000 metric tons, FAO estimates): 2.0 in 2007–09 (Source: FAO).

Finance

CURRENCY AND EXCHANGE RATES

Monetary Units

100 centimes = 1 franc de la Coopération financière en Afrique centrale (CFA).

Sterling, Dollar and Euro Equivalents (30 December 2011)

£1 sterling = 783.813 francs CFA;
US $1 = 506.961 francs CFA;
€1 = 655.957 francs CFA;
10,000 francs CFA = £12.76 = $19.73 = €15.24.

Average Exchange Rate (francs CFA per US $)

2009 472.186
2010 495.277
2011 471.866

Note: An exchange rate of 1 French franc = 50 francs CFA, established in 1948, remained in force until January 1994, when the CFA franc was devalued by 50%, with the exchange rate adjusted to 1 French franc = 100 francs CFA. This relationship to French currency remained in effect with the introduction of the euro on 1 January 1999. From that date, accordingly, a fixed exchange rate of €1 = 655.957 francs CFA has been in operation.

BUDGET
('000 million francs CFA)

Revenue*	2009†	2010‡	2011‡
Tax revenue	81.1	89.2	97.3
Taxes on profits and property	18.4	20.3	22.5
Taxes on goods and services	62.7	68.8	74.9
Taxes on international trade	18.2	20.8	23.6
Non-tax revenue	19.8	18.0	17.3
Total	100.9	107.2	114.6

Expenditure§	2009†	2010‡	2011‡
Current primary expenditure	79.8	103.4	98.6
Wages and salaries	39.6	46.0	49.0
Other goods and services	22.8	32.3	27.9
Transfers and subsidies	17.5	25.0	21.7
Interest payments	8.7	5.7	4.2
Capital expenditure	40.3	59.2	65.9
Domestically financed	7.4	18.4	15.4
Externally financed	32.8	40.8	50.5
Total	128.8	168.2	168.8

* Excluding grants received ('000 million francs CFA): 49.4 in 2009 (preliminary figure); 54.2 in 2010 (projected figure); 50.3 in 2011 (projected figure).
† Preliminary figures.
‡ Projections.
§ Excluding adjustment for payment arrears ('000 million francs CFA): 19.2 in 2009 (preliminary figure); 20.0 in 2010 (projected figure); 15.0 in 2011 (projected figure).

Source: IMF, *Central African Republic: Sixth Review Under the Arrangement Under the Extended Credit Facility and Financing Assurances Review—Staff Report; Debt Sustainability Analysis; Staff Supplement; Press Release on the Executive Board Discussion; and Statement by the Executive Director for Central African Republic* (October 2010).

INTERNATIONAL RESERVES
(US $ million at 31 December)

	2008	2009	2010
Gold (national valuation)	1.62	—	4.78
IMF special drawing rights	0.03	4.33	4.28
Reserve position in IMF	0.24	0.32	0.36
Foreign exchange	121.51	205.94	176.54
Total	123.40	210.59	185.96

Source: IMF, *International Financial Statistics*.

MONEY SUPPLY
('000 million francs CFA at 31 December)

	2008	2009	2010
Currency outside banks	72.91	78.71	94.41
Demand deposits at commercial and development banks	40.01	52.81	55.02
Total money (incl. others)	113.72	131.52	149.43

Source: IMF, *International Financial Statistics*.

COST OF LIVING
(Consumer Price Index for Bangui; base: 2000 = 100)

	2006	2007	2008
Food	118.9	121.1	134.9
Fuel and light	104.9	104.9	111.5
Clothing	131.0	128.1	130.6
All items (incl. others)	119.1	120.3	131.5

2009: All items 136.1.

2010: All items 138.1.

Source: ILO.

NATIONAL ACCOUNTS
(million francs CFA at current prices)

Expenditure on the Gross Domestic Product

	2007	2008	2009
Government final consumption expenditure	69,577	69,577	88,717
Private final consumption expenditure	723,842	808,394	807,055
Gross capital formation	81,450	103,163	124,129
Total domestic expenditure	874,869	981,134	1,019,901
Exports of goods and services	123,143	102,553	140,571
Less Imports of goods and services	184,544	194,480	210,468
GDP in purchasers' values	813,468	889,207	950,004

Gross Domestic Product by Economic Activity

	2007	2008	2009
Agriculture, hunting, forestry and fishing	416,396	467,646	479,574
Mining and quarrying	21,208	13,904	23,124
Manufacturing	50,991	56,271	56,206
Electricity, gas and water	6,801	5,959	6,474
Construction	31,290	36,081	39,057
Wholesale and retail trade, restaurants and hotels	98,826	108,437	115,602
Finance, insurance and real estate	49,546	54,364	57,227
Transport and communication	42,510	46,645	53,114
Public administration and defence	36,300	36,900	39,375
Other services	13,200	12,600	26,701
GDP at factor cost	767,068	838,807	896,454
Indirect taxes	46,400	50,400	53,550
GDP in purchasers' values	813,468	889,207	950,004

Note: Deduction for imputed bank service charge assumed to be distributed at origin.

Source: African Development Bank.

BALANCE OF PAYMENTS
('000 million francs CFA)

	2007	2008*	2009†
Exports of goods	85.4	65.9	57.5
Imports of goods	−120.0	−138.2	−121.4
Trade balance	−34.6	−72.3	−63.9
Services (net)	−41.5	−43.5	−43.3
Balance on goods and services	−76.1	−115.8	−107.2
Income (net)	−5.1	−9.9	−3.4
Balance on goods, services and income	−81.2	−125.7	−110.6
Current transfers (net)	30.5	34.1	38.1
Current balance	−50.7	−91.6	−72.4
Capital account (net)	25.4	29.7	406.0
Project grants	20.2	29.7	32.8
Capital grants and transfers	5.2	0.0	373.2
Financial account	−3.1	56.2	−305.4
Public sector (net)	−12.4	−17.3	−336.4
Private sector (net)	9.3	73.5	31.0
Overall balance	−28.5	−5.7	28.2

* Preliminary figures.

† Estimates.

Source: IMF, *Central African Republic: Sixth Review Under the Arrangement Under the Extended Credit Facility and Financing Assurances Review—Staff Report; Debt Sustainability Analysis; Staff Supplement; Press Release on the Executive Board Discussion; and Statement by the Executive Director for Central African Republic* (October 2010).

External Trade

PRINCIPAL COMMODITIES
(distribution by SITC, US $ million)

Imports c.i.f.	2003	2004	2005
Food and live animals	18.3	23.1	25.4
Cereals and cereal preparations	9.2	9.7	12.3
Flour of wheat or meslin	6.1	5.9	7.3
Beverages and tobacco	4.0	4.7	4.4
Tobacco and tobacco manufactures	3.1	3.2	3.1
Crude materials (inedible) except fuels	8.1	60.2	51.7
Cork and wood	1.8	50.2	46.2
Textile fibres (excl. wool tops) and waste	3.5	7.7	4.4
Mineral fuels, lubricants, etc.	11.0	24.8	31.4
Petroleum, petroleum products, etc.	10.9	24.7	31.2
Chemicals and related products	17.6	12.9	12.9
Medicinal and pharmaceutical products	13.5	6.9	8.2
Medicaments	13.1	6.1	5.8
Manufactured goods	16.0	14.9	18.7
Non-ferrous metals	1.5	1.0	1.8
Non-metallic mineral manufactures	7.2	4.7	4.6
Machinery and transport equipment	18.9	30.6	31.6
Machinery specialized for particular industries	1.1	3.8	3.8

Imports c.i.f.—*continued*	2003	2004	2005
Civil engineering and contractors' plant and equipment	0.9	2.1	1.1
General industrial machinery, equipment and parts	4.0	2.9	3.2
Telecommunications and sound equipment	1.3	2.4	3.3
Road vehicles and parts*	8.4	15.7	15.5
Passenger motor cars (excl. buses)	1.3	4.6	6.2
Motor vehicles for goods transport and special purposes	0.9	4.1	3.5
Goods vehicles (lorries and trucks)	0.9	3.3	2.6
Parts and accessories for cars, buses, lorries, etc.*	0.5	0.9	1.4
Miscellaneous manufactured articles	4.7	6.4	7.1
Total (incl. others)	99.6	179.2	186.3

* Excluding tyres, engines and electrical parts.

Exports f.o.b.	2003	2004	2005
Food and live animals	0.8	1.9	0.8
Crude materials (inedible) except fuels	40.3	86.8	67.4
Cork and wood	15.6	47.3	47.5
Textile fibres (excl. wool tops) and waste	0.9	0.2	0.3
Industrial diamonds (sorted)	23.7	39.2	19.7
Basic manufactures	23.9	15.7	40.2
Diamonds (excl. sorted industrial diamonds), unmounted	23.6	15.5	39.3
Sorted non-industrial diamonds, rough or simply worked	17.3	9.9	3.3
Machinery and transport equipment	0.2	1.1	1.5
Road vehicles	0.1	0.6	1.2
Total (incl. others)	65.7	106.6	116.2

Source: UN, *International Trade Statistics Yearbook*.

2006 ('000 million francs CFA, estimates): *Exports:* Diamonds 32.7; Coffee 0.8; Wood products 39.9; Cotton 0.7; Tobacco 0.1; Miscellaneous 8.2; Total 82.4 (Source: IMF, *Central African Republic: Selected Issues and Statistical Appendix*—January 2008).

PRINCIPAL TRADING PARTNERS
(US $ million)

Imports c.i.f.	2003	2005*
Belgium	9.1	5.8
Brazil	1.1	0.1
Cameroon	10.0	29.2
Chad	0.6	0.0
China, People's Repub.	2.5	3.4
France (incl. Monaco)	29.7	25.8
Germany	1.5	1.6
Italy	0.8	0.6
Japan	2.9	7.4
Netherlands	8.8	2.3
USA	1.3	0.8
Total (incl. others)	99.6	186.3

Exports f.o.b.	2003	2004	2005
Belgium	46.1	16.2	32.9
Cameroon	2.3	48.7	13.8
Congo, Democratic Republic	0.0	0.3	2.7
France (incl. Monaco)	4.3	35.1	21.7
Germany	4.7	0.0	0.0
Israel	0.0	0.0	5.8
Italy	0.7	0.0	8.5
Spain	0.8	0.0	0.9
Switzerland (incl. Liechtenstein)	0.9	0.0	15.9
Turkey	0.5	0.0	1.4
United Kingdom	2.0	0.0	0.0
Total (incl. others)	65.7	106.6	116.2

* Total imports 179.2 in 2004; complete data were not available for that year.

Source: UN, *International Trade Statistics Yearbook*.

Transport

ROAD TRAFFIC
(motor vehicles in use)

	1999	2000	2001
Passenger cars	4,900	5,300	5,300
Commercial vehicles	5,800	6,300	6,300

Source: UN, *Statistical Yearbook*.

2007 (motor vehicles in use at 31 December): Passenger cars 1,225; Vans and lorries 58; Motorcycles and mopeds 4,492; Total 5,775 (Source: IRF, *World Road Statistics*).

SHIPPING
(international traffic on inland waterways, metric tons)

	1996	1997	1998
Freight unloaded at Bangui	60,311	56,206	57,513
Freight loaded at Bangui	5,348	5,907	12,524
Total	65,659	62,113	70,037

Source: Banque des états de l'Afrique centrale, *Etudes et Statistiques*.

CIVIL AVIATION
(traffic on scheduled services)*

	1999	2000	2001
Kilometres flown (million)	3	3	1
Passengers carried ('000)	84	77	46
Passenger-km (million)	235	216	130
Total ton-km (million)	36	32	19

* Including an apportionment of the traffic of Air Afrique.

Source: UN, *Statistical Yearbook*.

Tourism

FOREIGN VISITORS BY COUNTRY OF ORIGIN*

	2007	2008	2009
Cameroon	1,604	2,895	4,125
Chad	740	1,275	3,221
Congo, Democratic Rep.	300	795	588
Congo, Republic	622	1,107	734
Côte d'Ivoire	418	1,024	1,116
France	4,096	6,975	4,431
Gabon	306	912	695
Italy	759	788	2,017
Senegal	564	1,127	1,662
Total (incl. others)	17,117	30,611	52,429

* Arrivals at hotels and similar establishments.

Receipts from tourism (US $ million, incl. passenger transport): 10.8 in 2007; 11.8 in 2008; 6.0 in 2009.

Source: World Tourism Organization.

Communications Media

	2008	2009	2010
Telephones ('000 main lines in use)	12.0	3.5	4.7
Mobile cellular telephones ('000 subscribers)	250.0	679.7	979.2
Internet subscribers ('000)	—	0.1	0.1

Source: International Telecommunication Union.

Personal computers: 12,000 (2.9 per 1,000 persons) in 2005 (Source: International Telecommunication Union).

Radio receivers: 283,000 in use in 1997 (Source: UNESCO, *Statistical Yearbook*).

Daily newspapers: 3 in 1996 (average circulation 6,000) (Source: UNESCO, *Statistical Yearbook*).

Non-daily newspapers: 1 in 1995 (average circulation 2,000) (Source: UNESCO, *Statistical Yearbook*).

Education

(2009/10 unless otherwise indicated)

			Students		
	Institutions*	Teachers	Males	Females	Total
Pre-primary	162	300	7,036	7,219	14,255
Primary	930	7,553	370,173	266,698	636,871
Secondary:					
general	46	1,466	51,195	30,486	81,681
vocational	n.a.	257	3,079	1,583	4,662
Tertiary	n.a.	340†	8,422	2,736	11,158

* 1990/91 figures.

† 2008/09 figure.

Source: UNESCO Institute for Statistics.

Pupil-teacher ratio (primary education, UNESCO estimate): 84.3 in 2009/10 (Source: UNESCO Institute for Statistics).

Adult literacy rate (UNESCO estimates): 55.2% (males 69.1%; females 42.1%) in 2009 (Source: UNESCO Institute for Statistics).

Directory

The Government

HEAD OF STATE

President of the Republic and Minister of National Defence, War Veterans, War Victims and the Restructuring of the Armed Forces: Gen. FRANÇOIS BOZIZÉ YANGOUVONDA (assumed power 16 March 2003; elected by direct popular vote 8 May 2005; re-elected 23 January 2011).

COUNCIL OF MINISTERS

(May 2012)

Prime Minister and Head of Government: Prof. FAUSTIN-ARCHANGE TOUADÉRA.

Minister of State for Finance and the Budget: Lt Col SYLVAIN N'DOUTINGAÏ.

Minister of State for Planning and the Economy: SYLVAIN MALICKO.

Minister of State for the Development of Transport: Col PARFAIT-ANICET M'BAYE.

Minister of State for Higher Education and Scientific Research: JEAN WILIBIRO-SACKO.

Minister of State for Posts, Telecommunications and New Technologies: ABDOU KARIM MECKASSOUA.

Minister of Agriculture and Rural Development: FIDÈLE GOUANDJIKA.

Minister of Water Resources, Forests, Hunting and Fishing: EMMANUEL BIZOT.

Minister of Foreign Affairs and Central Africans Abroad: Gen. ANTOINE GAMBI.

Minister of the Environment and Ecology: FRANÇOIS NAOUEYAMA.

Minister of Housing and Living Conditions: GONTRON DJONO-DJIDOU-AHABO.

Minister in charge of the Secretariat-General of the Government and Relations with the Institutions: MICHEL KOYT.

Minister of Professional and Technical Education and Training: DJIBRINE SALL.

Minister of Territorial Administration and Decentralization: JOSUÉ BINOUA.

Minister of Public Health, Population and the Fight against AIDS: JEAN-MICHEL MANDABA.

Minister of the Civil Service, Labour and Social Security: NOËL RAMANDAN.

Minister of National Security, Emigration-Immigration and Public Order: CLAUDE RICHARD GOUANDJA.

Minister of Trade and Industry: MARLYN MOULIOM ROOSALEM.

Minister of Equipment, Public Works and Promotion of the Regions: JEAN PROSPER WODOBODÉ.

Minister of Primary and Secondary Education and Literacy: GISÈLE ANNIE NAM.

Minister of Justice and Moralization, Keeper of the Seals: FIRMIN FINDIRO.

Minister of International Co-operation, Regional Integration and Francophone Affairs: DOROTHÉRE AIMÉE MALÉNZAPA.

Minister of Communication and Democratic and Civic Education: ALFRED TAÏNGA POLOKO.

Minister of Social Affairs, National Solidarity and the Promotion of Gender Equality: MARGUÉRITE PÉTRO KONI ZEZÉ ZARAMBAUD.

Minister of Energy and Hydraulics: LÉOPOLD MBOLI FATRAN.

Minister of Town Planning and the Reconstruction of Public Buildings: PASCAL KOYAMÉNÉ.

Minister of Tourism Development and Artisanal Industries: SYLVIE ANNICK MAZOUNGOU.

Minister of Youth, Sports, Arts and Culture: JEAN-SERGE BOKASSA.

Minister of the Promotion of Small and Medium-sized Enterprises, the Informal Sector and the Guichet Unique: ALBERTINE AGOUNDOUKOUA MBISSA.

Minister-delegate to the Minister of State for Agriculture and Rural Development, responsible for Stockbreeding and Animal Health: YOUSSOUFA YÉRIMA MANDJO.

Minister-delegate at the Presidency, in charge of National Defence, War Veterans, War Victims and the Restructuring of the Armed Forces: Col JEAN-FRANCIS BOZIZÉ.

Minister-delegate at the Presidency, in charge of Development Centres: DAVID BANZOUKOU.

Minister-delegate at the Presidency, in charge of Mines: OBED NAMSIO.

Minister-delegate at the Presidency, in charge of Civil Aviation: THÉODORE JOUSSO.

Minister-delegate at the Presidency, in charge of the Disarmament, Demobilization and Rehabilitation of Former Combatants and the National Youth Pioneers: Brig. SYLVESTRE YANGONGO.

MINISTRIES

Office of the President: Palais de la Renaissance, Bangui; tel. 21-61-46-63; internet presidencerca.com.

Ministry of Agriculture and Rural Development: Bangui; tel. 21-61-28-00.

Ministry of the Civil Service, Labour and Social Security: Bangui; tel. 21-61-21-88; fax 21-61-04-14.

Ministry of Communication and Democratic and Civic Education: Bangui.

Ministry of the Development of Transport: BP 941, Bangui; tel. 21-61-70-49; fax 21-61-46-28.

Ministry of Energy and Hydraulics: Bangui; tel. 21-61-20-54; fax 21-61-60-76.

Ministry of the Environment and Ecology: Bangui.

Ministry of Equipment, Public Works and Promotion of the Regions: Bangui.

Ministry of Finance and the Budget: BP 696, Bangui; tel. 21-61-38-05.

Ministry of Higher Education and Scientific Research: BP 791, Bangui; tel. 21-61-08-38.

Ministry of Housing and Living Conditions: Bangui.

Ministry of International Co-operation, Regional Integration and Francophone Affairs: Bangui; tel. 21-61-54-67; fax 21-61-26-06.

Ministry of Justice and Moralization: Bangui; tel. 21-61-52-11.

Ministry of National Defence, War Veterans, War Victims and the Restructuring of the Armed Forces: Bangui; tel. 21-61-00-25.

Ministry of National Security, Emigration-Immigration and Public Order: Bangui; tel. 21-61-14-77.

Ministry of Planning and the Economy: BP 912, Bangui; tel. 21-61-70-55; fax 21-61-63-98.

Ministry of Posts, Telecommunications and New Technologies: Bangui; tel. 21-61-29-66.

Ministry of Primary and Secondary Education and Literacy: Bangui.

Ministry of Professional and Technical Education and Training: Bangui.

Ministry of the Promotion of Small and Medium-sized Enterprises, the Informal Sector and the Guichet Unique: Bangui.

Ministry of Public Health, Population and the Fight against AIDS: Bangui; tel. 21-61-16-35.

Ministry of Social Affairs, National Solidarity and the Promotion of Gender Equality: Bangui; tel. 21-61-55-65.

Ministry of Territorial Administration and Decentralization: Bangui.

Ministry of Tourism Development and Artisanal Industries: Bangui; tel. 21-61-04-16.

Ministry of Town Planning and the Reconstruction of Public Buildings: Bangui; tel. 21-61-69-54.

Ministry of Trade and Industry: Bangui; tel. 21-61-10-69.

Ministry of Water Resources, Forests, Hunting and Fishing: Bangui; tel. 21-61-79-21.

Ministry of Youth, Sports, Arts and Culture: Bangui; tel. 21-61-39-69.

President and Legislature

PRESIDENT

Presidential Election, 23 January 2011

Candidate	Votes	% of votes
Gen. François Bozizé Yangouvonda	718,801	64.37
Ange-Félix Patassé	239,279	21.43
Martin Ziguélé	75,939	6.80
Emile Gros-Raymond Nakombo	51,469	4.61
Jean-Jacques Démafouth	31,184	2.79
Total	1,116,672	100.00

ASSEMBLÉE NATIONALE

Speaker: CÉLESTIN-LEROY GAOMBALET.

General Election, 23 January and 27 March 2011

Party	Seats
Kwa na kwa	61
Majorité présidentielle	11
L'opposition	2
Independents	26
Total	100*

* Following the second round of elections, five seats remained undeclared.

Election Commission

Commission électorale indépendante (CEI): Bangui; f. 2004; Pres. JOSEPH BINGUIMALÉ.

Political Organizations

Alliance pour la démocratie et le progrès (ADP): Bangui; internet alliance-democratie-progres.over-blog.com; f. 1991; progressive; Nat. Pres. EMMANUEL OLIVIER GABIRAULT.

Armée populaire pour la restauration de la république et la démocratie (APRD): Bangui; armed insurrectionary group; Leader JEAN-JACQUES DÉMAFOUTH.

Collectif des Centrafricains en France (CCF): Paris (France); f. 1984; umbrella org. for political representatives resident in France; Gen. Sec. ANDRÉ DOUNGOUMA-FOKY.

Concertation des partis politiques d'opposition (CPPO): Bangui; umbrella org. of 12 parties opposed to former President Patassé.

Conseil démocratique des partis politiques de l'opposition (CODEPO): Bangui; f. 1995; political alliance led by AUGUSTE BOUKANGA; comprises the following parties:

Mouvement démocratique pour la renaissance et l'évolution de la République Centrafricaine (MDRERC): Bangui; Chair. JOSEPH BENDOUNGA; Sec.-Gen. LÉON SEBOU.

Parti républicain centrafricain (PRC): Bangui.

Convention nationale (CN): Bangui; f. 1991; Leader DAVID GALIAMBO.

Coordination des patriotes centrafricains (CPC): Paris (France) and Bangui; f. 2003; umbrella org. for groups opposed to former President Patassé and affiliated to the uprising of March 2003; Sec.-Gen. ABDOU KARIM MÉCKASSOUA.

Forum démocratique pour la modernité (FODEM): ave Dejean, Sicai, Bangui; tel. 21-61-29-54; e-mail eric.neris@fodem.org; internet www.fodem.org; f. 1997; Pres. (vacant).

Front démocratique de libération du peuple centrafricain (FDPC): e-mail miskinedardar@yahoo.fr; internet www.centrafriquefdpc.com; Leader ABDOULAYE MISKINE.

Front patriotique pour le progrès (FPP): BP 259, Bangui; tel. 21-61-52-23; fax 21-61-10-93; f. 1972; aims to promote political education and debate; Leader ALEXANDRE GOUMBA.

Kwa na kwa (KNK): Bangui; f. 2004; formally constituted as a political party in 2009; Sec.-Gen. ELIÉ OUÉFIO.

Mouvement d'évolution sociale de l'Afrique noire (MESAN): Bangui; f. 1949; comprises two factions, MESAN and MESAN-BOGANDA, led respectively by FIDÈLE OGBAMI and JOSEPH NGBANGADIBO.

Mouvement national pour le renouveau: Bangui; Leader PAUL BELLET.

Mouvement pour la démocratie et le développement (MDD): Bangui; f. 1993; aims to safeguard national unity and the equitable distribution of national wealth; Leader LOUIS PAPENIAH.

Mouvement pour la démocratie, l'indépendance et le progrès social (MDI-PS): BP 1404, Bangui; tel. 21-61-18-21; e-mail mdicentrafrique@chez.com; internet www.chez.com/mdicentrafrique; Sec.-Gen. DANIEL NDITIFEI BOYSEMBE.

Mouvement pour la libération du peuple centrafricain (MLPC): Bangui; internet www.lemlpc.net; f. 1979; leading party in govt Oct. 1993–March 2003; Pres. MARTIN ZIGUÉLÉ; Sec.-Gen. JEAN-MICHEL MANDABA.

Nouvelle alliance pour le progrès (NAP): Bangui; internet www.centrafrique-nap.com; Leader JEAN-JACQUES DÉMAFOUTH.

Parti social-démocrate (PSD): BP 543, Bangui; tel. 21-61-59-02; fax 21-61-58-44; Leader ENOCH DERANT LAKOUÉ.

Rassemblement démocratique centrafricain (RDC): BP 503, Bangui; tel. 21-61-53-75; f. 1987; sole legal political party 1987–91; Leader (vacant).

Union des forces démocratiques pour le rassemblement (UFDR): Bangui; f. 2006; Chief of Staff ZAKARIA DAMANE.

Front démocratique centrafricain (FDC): Bangui; Leader Commdt JUSTIN HASSAN.

Groupe d'action patriotique de la libération de Centrafrique (GAPLC): Bangui; Leader MICHEL AM NONDROKO DJOTODIA.

Mouvement des libérateurs centrafricains pour la justice (MLCJ): Bangui; Leader Capt. ABAKAR SABONE.

Union des forces républicaines de Centrafrique: Bangui; f. 2006; armed insurrectionary group; Leader Lt FRANÇOIS-FLORIAN N'DJADDER-BEDAYA.

Union pour un mouvement populaire de Centrafrique (UMPCA): Pres. YVONNE M'BOÏSSONA.

Union nationale démocratique du peuple centrafricain (UNDPC): Bangui; f. 1998; Islamist fundamentalist; based in south-east CAR; Leader MAHAMAT SALEH.

Union pour le progrès en Centrafrique (UPCA): Bangui; Leader FAUSTIN YERIMA.

Diplomatic Representation

EMBASSIES IN THE CENTRAL AFRICAN REPUBLIC

Cameroon: rue du Languedoc, BP 935, Bangui; tel. 21-61-18-57; fax 21-61-16-87; Ambassador JOSEPH FOFÉ.

Chad: ave Valéry Giscard d'Estaing, BP 461, Bangui; tel. 21-61-46-77; fax 21-61-62-44; Ambassador ABDERAHIM YACOUB N'DIAYE.

China, People's Republic: ave des Martyrs, BP 1430, Bangui; tel. 21-61-27-60; fax 21-61-31-83; e-mail chinaemb_cf@mfa.gov.cn; Ambassador SUN HAICHAO.

Congo, Democratic Republic: Ambassador EMBE ISEA MBAMBE.

Congo, Republic: ave Boganda, BP 1414, Bangui; tel. 21-61-03-09; e-mail diplobrazzabangui@yahoo.fr; Ambassador GABRIEL ENTCHA-EBIA (designate).

Egypt: angle ave Léopold Sédar Senghor et rue Emile Gentil, BP 1422, Bangui; tel. 21-61-46-88; fax 21-61-35-45; e-mail ambassadedEgypt_Centreafrique@excite.com; Ambassador AZZA EL-GUIBALI.

France: blvd du Général de Gaulle, BP 884, Bangui; tel. 21-61-30-05; fax 21-61-74-04; e-mail contact@ambafrance-cf.org; internet www.ambafrance-cf.org; Ambassador JEAN-PIERRE VIDON.

Holy See: ave Boganda, BP 1447, Bangui; tel. 75041492 (mobile); e-mail nonciature.rca@hotmail.com; Apostolic Nuncio JUDE THADDEUS OKOLO (Titular Archbishop of Novica).

Japan: Temporarily closed; affairs handled through the embassy of Japan, Yaoundé, Cameroon, since October 2003.

Libya: Bangui; tel. 21-61-46-62; fax 21-61-55-25; Ambassador OMAR ISSA BARUNI.

Morocco: ave de l'indépendence, BP 1609, Bangui; tel. 21-61-39-51; fax 21-61-35-22; e-mail sifama-bg@intnet.cf; Ambassador MUSTAPHA EL-HALFAOUI.

Nigeria: ave des Martyrs, BP 1010, Bangui; tel. 21-61-07-44; fax 21-61-12-79; e-mail jimgom7@yahoo.com; Ambassador Y. T. ZARIA.

Russia: ave du Président Gamal Abdel Nasser, BP 1405, Bangui; tel. 21-61-03-11; fax 21-61-56-45; e-mail rusconsrca@yandex.ru; internet www.rca.mid.ru; Ambassador ALEKSANDR V. KASPAROV.

Sudan: ave de France, BP 1351, Bangui; tel. 21-61-38-21; Ambassador OMAR SALIH ABU BAKR.

USA: ave David Dacko, BP 924, Bangui; tel. 21-61-02-00; fax 21-61-44-94; internet bangui.usembassy.gov; Ambassador LAURENCE D. WOHLERS.

Judicial System

Supreme Court: BP 926, Bangui; tel. 21-61-41-33; highest judicial organ; acts as a Court of Cassation in civil and penal cases and as Court of Appeal in administrative cases; comprises four chambers: constitutional, judicial, administrative and financial; Pres. TAGBIA SANZIA.

Constitutional Court: BP 2104, Bangui; tel. 21-61-99-58; fax 21-61-99-52; f. 1995; Pres. MARCEL MALONGA.

There is also a Court of Appeal, a Criminal Court, 16 tribunaux de grande instance, 37 tribunaux d'instance, six labour tribunals and a permanent military tribunal.

Religion

It is estimated that 24% of the population hold animist beliefs, 50% are Christians (25% Roman Catholic, 25% Protestant) and 15% are Muslims. There is no official state religion.

CHRISTIANITY

The Roman Catholic Church

The Central African Republic comprises one archdiocese and eight dioceses. An estimated 25% of the population are Roman Catholics.

Bishops' Conference

Conférence Episcopale Centrafricaine, BP 1518, Bangui; tel. 21-61-70-72; fax 21-61-46-92; e-mail ceca_rca@yahoo.fr.

f. 1982; Pres. Most Rev. EDOUARD MATHOS.

Archbishop of Bangui: (vacant), Archevêché, BP 1518, Bangui; tel. 21-61-08-98; fax 21-61-46-92; e-mail archbangui@yahoo.fr.

Protestant Church

Eglise Évangélique Luthérienne de la République Centrafricaine: BP 100, Bouar; tel. 70-80-73-36; fax 21-31-41-70; e-mail cclrca@skyfile.com; Pres. Rev. ANDRÉ GOLIKE; 55,000 mems (2010).

Eglise Protestante du Christ Roi: rue des Missions, BP 608, Bangui; tel. 21-61-14-35; fax 21-61-35-61; e-mail sgudeac@intnet.cf; f. 1968.

The Press

The independent press is highly regulated. Independent publications must hold a trading licence and prove their status as a commercial enterprise. They must also have proof that they fulfil taxation requirements. There is little press activity outside Bangui.

DAILIES

E le Songo: Bangui; f. 1986.

Le Citoyen: BP 974, Bangui; tel. 21-61-89-16; e-mail ltdc@Yahoo.fr; independent; Dir MAKA GBOSSOKOTTO; circ. 3,000.

Le Confident: BP 427, Bangui; tel. 75-04-64-14; e-mail leconfident2000@yahoo.fr; internet www.leconfident.net; f. 2001; Mon.–Sat; Dir MATHURIN C. N. MOMET.

L'Hirondelle: Bangui; independent; Editor-in-Chief JULES YANGANDA.

Le Novateur: BP 913, Bangui; tel. 21-61-48-84; fax 21-61-87-03; e-mail ccea_ln@intnet.cf; independent; Publr MARCEL MOKWAPI; circ. 750.

PERIODICALS

Bangui Match: Bangui; monthly.

Centrafrique-Presse: BP 1058, Bangui; tel. and fax 21-61-39-57; e-mail info@centrafrique-presse.com; internet www.centrafrique-presse.com; weekly; Publr PROSPER N'DOUBA.

Le Courrier Rural: BP 850, Bangui; publ. by Chambre d'Agriculture.

Le Délit d'Opinion: Bangui; independent.

Demain le Monde: BP 650, Bangui; tel. 21-61-23-15; f. 1985; fortnightly; independent; Editor-in-Chief NGANAM NÖEL.

Journal Officiel de la République Centrafricaine: BP 739, Bangui; f. 1974; fortnightly; economic data; Dir-Gen. GABRIEL AGBA.

Nations Nouvelles: BP 965, Bangui; publ. by Organisation Commune Africaine et Mauricienne; politics and current affairs.

Le Peuple: BP 569, Bangui; tel. 21-61-76-34; f. 1995; weekly; Editor-in-Chief VERMOND TCHENDO.

Le Progrès: BP 154, Bangui; tel. 21-61-70-26; f. 1991; monthly; Editor-in-Chief BELIBANGA CLÉMENT; circ. 2,000.

Le Rassemblement: Bangui; organ of the RDC; Editor-in-Chief MATHIAS GONEVO REAPOGO.

La Tortue Déchainée: Bangui; independent; satirical; Publr MAKA GBOSSOKOTTO.

PRESS ASSOCIATION

Groupement des Editeurs de la Presse Privée Indépendante de Centrafrique (GEPPIC): Bangui; Pres. MAKA GBOSSOKOTTO.

NEWS AGENCY

Agence Centrafrique Presse (ACAP): BP 40, Bangui; tel. 21-61-22-79; internet www.acap-cf.info; f. 1960; Gen. Man. VICTOR DETO TETEYA.

Publisher

GOVERNMENT PUBLISHING HOUSE

Imprimerie Centrafricaine: ave David Dacko, BP 329, Bangui; tel. 21-61-72-24; f. 1974; Dir-Gen. SERGE BOZANGA.

Broadcasting and Communications

In 2011 there were four mobile cellular telephone operators and one fixed-line telephone operator in the country. In 2009 there were 795,097 subscribers to mobile telephone services and 9,000 subscribers to fixed-line services.

TELECOMMUNICATIONS

Agence Régulation des Télécommunications (ART): BP 1046, Bangui; tel. 21-61-56-51; fax 21-61-05-82; e-mail art-rca@art-rca.org; internet www.art-rca.org; regulatory authority; Dir Gen. Valeri Sai.

Atlantique Telecom Centrafrique SA: Immeuble Moov, ave du Président Mobutu, BP 2439 Bangui; tel. and fax 21-61-23-85; internet www.moov-rca.com; operates mobile cellular telephone services under Moov network; Dir-Gen. Souleymane Diallo (Moov Centrafrique); 248,063 subscribers.

Azur RCA: ave de l'Indépendance, Ex FNUAP, BP 1418, Bangui; tel. 21-61-33-97; fax 21-61-33-07; e-mail contact@azur-rca.com; internet www.azur-rca.com; f. 2004; fmrly Nation Link Telecom; mobile cellular telephone operator; Dir-Gen. Yannick Bourdeu; 96,499 subscribers (2009).

Orange Centrafrique: Imeuble SODIAM, ave Bathélemy Boganda, BP 863, Bangui; tel. 72-27-08-00; e-mail serviceclient@orange.cf; internet www.orange.cf; f. 2007; mobile cellular telephone operator; Pres. Michel Barré; Dir-Gen. Bruno Allassonnière; 211,657 subscribers (2009).

Société Centrafricaine de Télécommunications (SOCATEL): BP 939, Bangui; tel. 21-61-42-68; fax 21-61-44-72; e-mail dg-socatel@socatel.cf; internet www.socatel.cf; f. 1990; 60% state-owned; 40% owned by France Câbles et Radio (France Télécoms); further privatization suspended March 2003; Dir-Gen. Simon Serge Bozanga; 10,000 subscribers (2009).

Telecel: BP 939, Bangui; tel. 21-61-19-30; fax 21-61-16-99; f. 1996; mobile cellular telephone operator; Dir-Gen. Lionel Goussi; 238,868 subscribers (2009).

BROADCASTING

Radiodiffusion-Télévision Centrafricaine: BP 940, Bangui; tel. 21-61-25-88; f. 1958 as Radiodiffusion Nationale Centrafricaine; govt-controlled; broadcasts in French and Sango.

Radio Centrafrique: Bangui; tel. 75-50-36-32; e-mail yakanet.rca@gmail.com; internet www.radiocentrafrique.org; Dir-Gen David Gbanga.

Radio Ndeke Luka: community station operated by UN.

Radio Nostalgie: commercial radio station in Bangui.

Radio Notre-Dame: radio station operated by Roman Catholic Church.

Radio Rurale: community stations operating in Bouar, Nola, Berbérati and Bambari.

TELEVISION

Télévision Centrafricaine (TVCA): Bangui; tel. 21-61-61-02; Dir-Gen. Michel Ouambéti.

Finance

(cap. = capital; res = reserves; dep. = deposits; m. = million; br. = branch; amounts in francs CFA)

BANKING

In 2010 there were four commercial banks in the country.

Central Bank

Banque des Etats de l'Afrique Centrale (BEAC): BP 851, Bangui; tel. 21-61-24-00; fax 21-61-19-95; e-mail beacbgf@beac.int; internet www.beac.int; headquarters in Yaoundé, Cameroon; f. 1973; bank of issue for mem. states of the Communauté économique et monétaire de l'Afrique centrale (CEMAC, fmrly Union douanière et économique de l'Afrique centrale), comprising Cameroon, the CAR, Chad, the Repub. of the Congo, Equatorial Guinea and Gabon; cap. 88,000m., res 227,843m., dep. 4,110,966m. (Dec. 2007); Gov. Lucas Abaga Nchama; Dir in CAR Camille Kelefio.

Commercial Banks

Banque Populaire Maroco-Centrafricaine (BPMC): rue Guérillot, BP 844, Bangui; tel. 21-61-31-90; fax 21-61-62-30; e-mail bpmc@intnet.cf; f. 1991; 57.5% owned by Groupe Banque Populaire (Morocco); cap. and res 4,183m., total assets 13,331m. (Dec. 2003); Gen. Man. Mohammed Benziani.

Commercial Bank Centrafrique (CBCA): rue de Brazza, BP 59, Bangui; tel. 21-61-29-90; fax 21-61-34-54; e-mail cbcabank@cbc-bank.com; internet www.cbc-bank.com/cb_centrafrique/page.php?langue=fr; f. 1999; 54.5% owned by Groupe Fotso; 40.5% owned by CAR private shareholders; 5% owned by Commercial Bank Cameroon SA; cap. 1,500.m., res 1,856.3m., dep 22,941.2m. (Dec. 2005); Pres. Serge Psimhis; Dir-Gen. Théodore Dabanga; 1 br.

Ecobank Centrafrique: pl. de la République, BP 910, Bangui; tel. 21-61-00-42; fax 21-61-34-38; e-mail ecobankcf@ecobank.com; internet www.ecobank.com; f. 1946 as BAO; cap. 5,000m., res 845m., dep. 53,621m. (Dec. 2009); Pres. Kassimou Abou Kabassi; Man. Dir Christian Assossou.

Development Bank

Banque de Développement des Etats de l'Afrique Centrale: see Franc Zone.

Financial Institutions

Caisse Autonome d'Amortissement de la République Centrafricaine: Bangui; tel. 21-61-53-60; fax 21-61-21-82; management of state funds; Dir-Gen. Joseph Pingama.

Caisse Nationale d'Epargne (CNE): Office national des postes et de l'épargne, Bangui; tel. 21-61-22-96; fax 21-61-78-80; Pres. Simone Bodemo-Modoyangba; Dir-Gen. Ambroise Daouda; Man. Antoine Bekouanebandi.

Bankers' Association

Association Professionnelle des Banques: Bangui.

Development Agencies

Agence Française de Développement: route de la Moyenne Corniche, BP 817, Bangui; tel. 21-61-45-78; fax 21-61-03-06; e-mail afdbangui@groupe-afd.org; internet www.afd.fr; administers economic aid and finances specific development projects; Man. Jocelyn Leveneur.

Mission Française de Coopération et d'Action Culturelle: BP 934, Bangui; tel. 21-61-63-34; fax 21-61-28-24; administers bilateral aid from France; Dir Hervé Cronel.

INSURANCE

Agence Centrafricaine d'Assurances (ACA): BP 512, Bangui; tel. 21-61-06-23; f. 1956; Dir R. Cerbellaud.

Allianz Centrafrique Assurances: blvd Général de Gaulle, BP 343, Bangui; tel. 21-61-36-66; fax 21-61-33-40; e-mail allianz.centrafrique@allianz-cf.com; internet www.allianz-africa.com; f. 1988; Dir of Operations Bruno Ribeyron.

Assureurs Conseils Centrafricains (ACCAF): ave Barthélemy Boganda, BP 743, Bangui; tel. 21-61-19-33; fax 21-61-44-70; e-mail centrafrique@ascoma.com; internet www.ascoma.com; f. 1968; owned by Ascoma (Monaco); Man. Venant Ebela; Dir-Gen. Sylvain Cousin.

Entreprise d'Etat d'Assurances et de Réassurances (SIRIRI): Bangui; tel. 21-61-36-55; f. 1972; Pres. Emmanuel Dokouna; Dir-Gen. Martin Ziguélé.

Union des Assurances Centrafricaine (UAC): rue de la Victoire, BP 896, Bangui; tel. 21-61-31-02; fax 21-61-18-48; e-mail uac02@yahoo.fr; f. 1999; non-life insurance; Dir-Gen. Pathé Dione.

Trade and Industry

DEVELOPMENT ORGANIZATION

Agence Centrafricaine de Développement Agricole (ACDA): ave David Dacko, BP 997, Bangui; tel. 21-61-54-85; e-mail acda_2010@yahoo.fr; internet www.acda-rca.org; f. 1993; purchasing, transport and marketing of cotton, cotton-ginning, production of cottonseed oil and groundnut oil; Pres. Honoré Feizoure.

INDUSTRIAL AND TRADE ASSOCIATIONS

Agence de Développement de la Zone Caféière (ADECAF): BP 1935, Bangui; tel. 21-61-47-30; coffee producers' asscn; assists coffee marketing co-operatives; Dir-Gen. J. J. Nimiziambi.

Agence Nationale pour le Développement de l'Elevage (ANDE): BP 1509, Bangui; tel. 21-61-69-60; fax 21-61-50-83; assists with development of livestock; Dir-Gen. Emmanuel Namkoissé.

Bourse Internationale de Diamant de Bangui: BP 26, Bangui; tel. 21-61-58-63; fax 21-61-60-76; diamond exchange; supervised by the Ministry of Energy and Hydraulics.

Caisse de Stabilisation et de Péréquation des Produits Agricoles (CAISTAB): BP 76, Bangui; tel. 21-61-08-00; supervises marketing and pricing of agricultural produce; Dir-Gen. M. BOUNANDELE-KOUMBA.

Fédération Nationale des Eleveurs Centrafricains (FNEC): ave des Martyrs, BP 588, Bangui; tel. 21-61-23-97; fax 21-61-47-24; Pres. BI AMADOU SOUAIBOU; Sec.-Gen. YOUSSOUFA MANDJO.

Groupement des Industries Centrafricaines (GICA): BP 804, Bangui; umbrella group representing 12 principal companies of various industries; Pres. PATRICK DEJEAN.

Office National de la Forêts (ONF): BP 915, Bangui; tel. 21-61-38-27; f. 1969; reafforestation, development of forest resources; Dir-Gen. C. D. SONGUET.

CHAMBERS OF COMMERCE

Chambre d'Agriculture, d'Elevage, des Eaux, Forêts, Chasses, Pêches et du Tourisme: BP 850, Bangui; tel. 21-61-06-38; e-mail chagri_rca@hotmail.com; f. 1964; Sec.-Gen. HENRI OUIKON.

Chambre de Commerce, d'Industrie, des Mines et de l'Artisanat (CCIMA): blvd Charles de Gaulle, BP 823, Bangui; tel. 21-61-16-68; fax 21-61-35-61; e-mail ccima@intnet.cf; internet ccima-rca.com; f. 1935; Pres. ROBERT NGOKI; Treas. THÉODORE LAWSON.

EMPLOYERS' ORGANIZATION

Union Nationale du Patronat Centrafricain (UNPC): Immeuble Tropicana, 1°, BP 2180, Bangui; tel. and fax 21-61-16-79; e-mail unpc-rca@intnet.cf; Pres. GILLES GILBERT GRESENGUET.

UTILITIES

Electricity

Société Energie de Centrafrique (ENERCA): ave de l'Indépendance, BP 880, Bangui; tel. 21-61-20-22; fax 21-61-54-43; e-mail enerca@intnet.cf; f. 1967; state-owned; production and distribution of electric energy; 119.1 GWh produced for the Bangui grid in 2003; Dir-Gen. SAMUEL TOZOUI.

Water

Société de Distribution d'Eau en Centrafrique (SODECA): BP 1838, Bangui; tel. 21-61-59-66; fax 21-61-25-49; e-mail sodeca@intnet.cf; f. 1975 as the Société Nationale des Eaux; state-owned co responsible for supply, treatment and distribution of water; Dir-Gen. PAUL BELLET.

TRADE UNIONS

Confédération Chrétienne des Travailleurs de Centrafrique (CCTC): BP 939, Bangui; tel. 21-61-05-71; fax 21-61-55-81; Pres. LOUIS SALVADOR.

Confédération Nationale de Travailleurs de Centrafrique: BP 2141, Bangui; tel. 75-50-94-36; fax 21-61-35-61; e-mail cnt@intnet.cf; Sec.-Gen. JEAN-RICHARD SANDOS-OULANGA.

Confédération Syndicale des Travailleurs de Centrafrique (CSTC): BP 386, km 5, Bangui; tel. 21-61-38-69; Sec.-Gen. SABIN KPOKOLO.

Organisation des Syndicats Libres du Secteur Public, Parapublic et Privé (OSLP): BP 1450, Bangui; tel. 21-61-20-00; Sec.-Gen. GABRIEL NGOUANDJI-TANGAS.

Union Générale des Travailleurs de Centrafrique (UGTC): BP 346, Bangui; tel. 21-61-05-86; fax 21-61-17-96; Pres. CÉCILE GUÉRÉ.

Union des Journalistes: Bangui; tel. 21-61-13-38; Pres. MAKA GBOKOSSOTTO.

Union Syndicale des Travailleurs de Centrafrique (USTC): BP 1390, Bangui; tel. 21-61-60-15; e-mail vvesfon@yahoo.fr; Sec.-Gen. NOËL RAMADAN.

Transport

RAILWAYS

There are no railways at present. There are long-term plans to connect Bangui to the Transcameroon railway. A line linking Sudan's Darfur region with the CAR's Vakaga province has also been proposed.

ROADS

In 2000 there were an estimated 24,307 km of roads. Only about 3% of the total network is paved. Eight main routes serve Bangui, and those that are surfaced are toll roads. Both the total road length and the condition of the roads are inadequate for current requirements. In 1997 the European Union provided 32,500m. francs CFA to improve infrastructure in the CAR. In September a vast road improvement scheme was launched, concentrating initially on roads to the south and north-west of Bangui. The CAR is linked with Cameroon by the Transafrican Lagos–Mombasa highway. Roads are frequently impassable in the rainy season (July–October).

Bureau d'Affrètement Routier Centrafricain (BARC): Gare routière, BP 523, Bangui; tel. 21-61-20-55; fax 21-61-37-44; Dir-Gen. J. M. LAGUEREMA-YADINGUIN.

Compagnie Nationale des Transports Routiers (CNTR): Bangui; tel. 21-61-46-44; state-owned; Dir-Gen. GEORGES YABADA.

Fonds d'Entretien Routier (FER): BP 962, Bangui; tel. 21-61-62-95; fax 21-61-68-63; e-mail fondsroutier@admn.cf; f. 1981; Dir-Gen. MARIE-CLAIR BITOUANGA.

Projet Sectoriel de Transports (PST): BP 941, Bangui; tel. 21-61-62-94; fax 21-61-65-79.

TBC Cameroun SARL: BP 637, Bangui; tel. 21-61-20-16; fax 21-61-13-19; e-mail rca@tbclogistics.com; internet www.tbclogistics.com; f. 1963.

INLAND WATERWAYS

There are some 2,800 km of navigable waterways along two main water courses. The first, formed by the Congo river and its tributary the Oubangui, can accommodate convoys of barges (of up to 800 metric tons load) between Bangui and Brazzaville and Pointe-Noire in the Republic of the Congo, except during the dry season, when the route is impassable. The second is the river Sangha, also a tributary of the Congo, on which traffic is again seasonal. There are two ports, at Bangui and Salo, on the rivers Oubangui and Sangha, respectively. Bangui port has a handling capacity of 350,000 tons, with 350 m of wharfs and 24,000 sq m of warehousing. Efforts are being made to develop the Sangha upstream from Salo, to increase the transportation of timber from this area and to develop Nola as a timber port.

Agence Centrafricaine des Communications Fluviales (ACCF): BP 822, Bangui; tel. 21-61-09-67; fax 21-61-02-11; f. 1969; state-owned; supervises development of inland waterways transport system; Chair. GUY MAMADOU MARABENA.

Société Centrafricaine de Transports Fluviaux (SOCATRAF): rue Parent, BP 1445, Bangui; tel. and fax 21-61-43-15; e-mail socatraf@intnet.cf; f. 1980; 51% owned by ACCF; Man. Dir FRANÇOIS TOUSSAINT.

CIVIL AVIATION

The international airport is at Bangui-M'Poko. There are also 37 small airports for internal services.

Mondial Air Fret (MAF): BP 1883, Bangui; tel. 21-61-14-58; fax 21-61-62-62; f. 1998; Dir THÉOPHILE SONNY COLÉ.

Tourism

Although tourism remains relatively undeveloped, the CAR possesses considerable scenic attractions in its waterfalls, forests and wildlife. In 2009 52,429 tourists arrived. In that year receipts from tourism were estimated at US $6.0m.

Office National Centrafricain du Tourisme (OCATOUR): rue Roger Guérillot, BP 645, Bangui; tel. 21-61-45-66.

Defence

As assessed at November 2011, the armed forces numbered about 2,150 men (army 2,000 and air force 150). Military service is selective and lasts for two years. There was also a paramilitary gendarmerie with 1,000 members.

Defence Expenditure: Estimated at 25,500m. francs CFA in 2010.

Chief of Staff of the Armed Forces: Gen. FRANÇOIS MOBÉBOU.

Education

Education is officially compulsory for eight years between six and 14 years of age. Primary education begins at the age of six and lasts for six years. Secondary education begins at the age of 12 and lasts for up to seven years, comprising a first cycle of four years and a second of three years. In 2009/10 enrolment at primary schools included 71% of children in the relevant age-group (81% of boys; 60% of girls), according to UNESCO estimates; in 2008/09 secondary enrolment included only 11% (13% of boys; 8% of girls). In 2009/10 there were some 11,158 students enrolled in tertiary education. The provision of state-funded education was severely disrupted during the 1990s and early 2000s, owing to the inadequacy of financial resources.

CHAD

Introductory Survey

LOCATION, CLIMATE, LANGUAGE, RELIGION, FLAG, CAPITAL

The Republic of Chad is a land-locked country in north central Africa, bordered to the north by Libya, to the south by the Central African Republic, to the west by Niger, Nigeria and Cameroon, and to the east by Sudan. The climate is hot and arid in the northern desert regions of the Sahara but very wet, with annual rainfall of 5,000 mm (197 ins) in the south. The official languages are French and Arabic, and various African languages are also widely spoken. Almost one-half of the population are Muslims, living in the north. About 30% of the population are Christians. Most of the remainder follow animist beliefs. The national flag (proportions 2 by 3) has three equal vertical stripes, of dark blue, yellow and red. The capital is N'Djamena.

CONTEMPORARY POLITICAL HISTORY

Historical Context

Formerly a province of French Equatorial Africa, Chad achieved full independence on 11 August 1960. However, the sparsely populated northern territory of Borkou-Ennedi-Tibesti, accounting for some 47% of the area of Chad, remained under French military control until 1965. The first President of the independent republic was François (later Ngarta) Tombalbaye, a southerner and leader of the Parti progressiste tchadien. In 1965 a full-scale insurgency began, concentrated mainly in the north. The Muslims of northern Chad have historically been in conflict with their black southern compatriots, who are mainly Christians or animists. The banned Front de libération nationale du Tchad (FROLINAT, founded in Sudan in 1966) assumed leadership of the revolt. The rebellion was partially quelled in 1968, following French military intervention.

In 1973 several prominent figures in the regime, including Gen. Félix Malloum, the Army Chief of Staff, were imprisoned on charges of conspiracy. Also in that year Libyan troops occupied the so-called 'Aozou strip', an apparently mineral-rich region of some 114,000 sq km (44,000 sq miles) in northern Chad, over which Libya claimed sovereignty.

Domestic Political Affairs

In April 1975 Tombalbaye was killed in a military coup. Malloum was released and appointed President, leading a military regime. In early 1978 FROLINAT, which received clandestine military assistance from Libya, seized control of a large area of the north before its advance was halted by French military intervention. In August, after negotiations with Malloum, Hissène Habré, a former leader of FROLINAT, was appointed Prime Minister. However, disagreements developed between Habré (a Muslim from the north) and Malloum over the status of Muslims in Chad.

In February 1979 armed conflict broke out between Habré's Forces armées du nord (FAN) and the government armed forces, the Forces armées tchadiennes (FAT). The FAN gained control of the capital, N'Djamena, and in March Malloum resigned and fled the country. In April a provisional Government was formed, comprising representatives of several groups, including FROLINAT, the FAN and the FAT, but sporadic fighting continued. In August 11 factions formed a Gouvernement d'union nationale de transition (GUNT), with Goukouni Oueddei, the leader of FROLINAT, as President and Lt-Col (later Gen.) Wadal Abdelkader Kamougué as Vice-President.

Goukouni's authority was undermined by continual disagreements with Habré, and in March 1980 fighting resumed. In October Libyan forces intervened directly in the hostilities, in support of Goukouni. By December Habré had been defeated, and a 15,000-strong Libyan force was established in the country. In November 1981 Libyan troops were withdrawn, and a peacekeeping force was installed under the auspices of the Organization of African Unity (OAU—now the African Union—AU, see p. 189). The conflict intensified, however, and in June 1982 Habré's forces captured N'Djamena. Habré was formally inaugurated as President in October.

In August 1983 some 3,000 French troops imposed an 'interdiction line' to separate the warring factions. Although Libya and France agreed to withdraw their troops and by November all French troops had left the country, it was reported that some 3,000 Libyan troops remained. In February 1986 GUNT forces, with support from Libya, attacked government positions south of the interdiction line. Habré appealed for French military assistance, and France agreed to establish a defensive air-strike force (designated Opération Epervier) in N'Djamena and the GUNT began to disintegrate. Kamougué resigned as Vice-President in June, and in February 1987 declared his support for Habré. In October Goukouni declared himself willing to seek a reconciliation with Habré.

Following negotiations in Gabon between the Ministers of Foreign Affairs of Chad and Libya, agreement was reached, in principle, to restore diplomatic relations. However, the issues of the sovereignty of the Aozou region, the fate of Libyan prisoners of war in Chad, and the security of common borders remained unresolved. In October 1988 diplomatic relations were resumed, and the September 1987 cease-fire agreement was reaffirmed, although Chad continued to accuse Libya of violating the conditions of the agreement. In June 1989 the Government accused Libya of planning a military offensive against Chad, with the complicity of Sudan. However, the two countries held further negotiations in August in Algiers, Algeria, following which they signed an outline peace accord. Provision was made for the withdrawal of all armed forces from the Aozou region and the release of all prisoners of war. The territorial dispute was referred for adjudication by the International Court of Justice (ICJ) in The Hague, Netherlands.

In December 1989 a new Constitution was reportedly approved by 99.94% of voters in a national referendum. In endorsing the document, the electorate also approved Habré in the office of President for a further seven-year term. The new Constitution confirmed the Union nationale pour l'indépendance et la révolution as the sole legal party, and provided for the establishment of an elected legislature. Elections to this 123-seat Assemblée nationale followed in July 1990.

Deby takes power

In November 1990 the Mouvement patriotique du salut (MPS—previously styled the Forces patriotiques du salut) invaded Chad from Sudan and advanced rapidly towards N'Djamena. France reiterated its policy of non-interference in Chad's internal affairs, and on 30 November Habré and his associates fled Chad. Idriss Deby (later Idriss Deby Itno), a former Commander-in-Chief of the Armed Forces arrived in N'Djamena two days later. The Assemblée nationale was dissolved, and the Constitution suspended. Deby became interim Head of State. Several members of the former Habré regime, including Acheikh Ibn Oumar, were included in the new Government.

Following Deby's accession to power, many political organizations that had opposed Habré announced their support for the MPS. Deby announced that a smaller national army, the Armée nationale tchadienne (ANT), was to replace the FANT (as the FAN and FAT had been restyled in 1983). The French Government responded favourably to the new administration, and the Libyan and Sudanese Governments declared their support for the MPS. Deby, however, reiterated Chad's claim to the Aozou region, which remained under consideration by the ICJ. In February 1994 the ICJ ruled in favour of Chad in the issue of the sovereignty of the Aozou region. By May the withdrawal of Libyan troops from the region had been completed as scheduled; in the following month a co-operation agreement was signed by the two countries. Meanwhile, in March 1991 the Government promulgated a National Charter to operate for a 30-month transitional period, confirming Deby's appointment as President, Head of State and Chairman of the MPS, and creating a Council of Ministers and a 31-member legislative Conseil de la République.

In September 1991 forces loyal to Habré apparently entered Chad from Niger and attacked military garrisons in the north of the country. In the following month disaffected ANT troops attacked an arsenal at N'Djamena airport in an attempt to seize power. Several officials, including the Minister of the Interior, were arrested on charges connected with the incident. France reaffirmed its support for the MPS and announced that an additional 300 troops would be dispatched to Chad. Following the coup attempt, Chad abrogated a recent co-operation agreement with Libya. In December some 3,000 pro-Habré rebels of the Libya-based Mouvement pour la démocratie et le développement (MDD) attacked towns in the Lake Chad region.

A national conference was convened in January 1993. In April the conference, which had been accorded sovereign status, adopted a Transitional Charter, elected Dr Fidel Moungar, hitherto Minister of National and Higher Education, as Prime Minister, and established a 57-member interim legislature, the Conseil supérieur de la transition (CST). The leader of the Rassemblement pour la démocratie et le progrès (RDP), Lol Mahamat Choua—who had briefly served as President in 1979—was elected Chairman of the CST. Under the terms of the Transitional Charter, Deby was to remain Head of State and Commander-in-Chief of the Armed Forces for a period of one year (with provision for one extension).

In October 1993 the CST approved a motion expressing no confidence in the Moungar administration, apparently initiated by supporters of Deby. Moungar resigned, and in November the CST elected Nouradine Kassiré Delwa Coumakoye, hitherto Minister of Justice, Keeper of the Seals, as Prime Minister. In December teachers and other government employees began strike action in protest at the Government's failure to pay salary arrears. The 50% devaluation of the CFA franc, in January 1994, precipitated further unrest.

In March 1994 an Institutional Committee submitted constitutional recommendations, which included provisions for the introduction of a five-year presidential term, the installation of a bicameral legislature and a Constitutional Court, and the establishment of a decentralized administrative structure. In April the CST extended the transitional period by one year. A new electoral timetable was adopted, whereby the Government was obliged to provide funds for the organization of the elections and, by June, to adopt an electoral code, to establish a national reconciliation council, and to appoint electoral and human rights commissions. In May Deby effected a comprehensive reorganization of the Government.

In September 1994 it was reported that the Minister of Mines and Energy, Lt-Col Mahamat Garfa (who had recently been dismissed as Chief of Army Staff), had fled N'Djamena with substantial government funds and had joined rebel forces of the Conseil national de redressement du Tchad in eastern Chad; Garfa subsequently established a co-ordination of eight rebel groups operative in eastern Chad, the Alliance nationale de la résistance (ANR), while remaining in exile himself. In October Choua was replaced as Chairman of the CST by a member of the MPS, Mahamat Bachar Ghadaia.

Deby officially announced in November 1994 that the process of democratic transition would conclude on 9 April 1995, following presidential and legislative elections. In December 1994 Deby declared a general amnesty for political prisoners and opposition members in exile, notably excluding Habré. In early 1995 the CST adopted a new electoral code and approved the draft Constitution, which had been amended in accordance with recommendations made by a national conference in August 1994. In March 1995 the CST extended the transitional period for a further year and amended the National Charter to debar the incumbent Prime Minister from contesting the forthcoming presidential election or from belonging to a political party. In April the CST, which had criticized the Government's lack of progress in organizing democratic elections, voted to remove Coumakoye from the premiership, electing Djimasta Koibla, a prominent member of the Union pour la démocratie et la République (UDR), as Prime Minister. In August security forces raided the home of Saleh Kebzabo, the leader of the opposition Union nationale pour le développement et le renouveau (UNDR). In protest, an informal alliance of opposition parties, to which the UNDR belonged, announced that it was to suspend participation in the CST and demanded the resignation of the head of the security forces.

In November 1995 the Government and the MDD agreed to a cease-fire, an exchange of prisoners and the integration of a number of MDD troops into the ANT. Reconciliation discussions between the Chadian Government and its opponents were convened in Franceville, Gabon, in January 1996. In March the Government and 13 opposition groups signed a cease-fire agreement. Although it appeared that the majority of the armed movements had rejected the agreement, the conclusion of the Franceville accord allowed the electoral programme to proceed. The new Constitution was endorsed by 63.5% of votes cast at a national referendum on 31 March.

Elections under the new Constitution

In the first round of voting at the presidential election, held on 2 June 1996, Deby secured 43.9% of the votes cast, followed by Kamougué, with 12.4%, and Kebzabo, with 8.5%. Deby and Kamougué proceeded to a second round of voting on 3 July. Although most of the 13 unsuccessful first-round candidates urged a boycott of the vote, Kebzabo announced his support for Deby, who won a decisive victory, with 69.1% of votes cast. Following Deby's inauguration as President on 8 August, he reappointed Koibla as Prime Minister. Koibla named an interim Council of Ministers, which included Kebzabo as Minister of Foreign Affairs. In September representatives of the Government and the MDD signed a peace agreement in Niger.

At legislative elections held on 5 January and 23 February 1997 the MPS secured an absolute majority in the 125-member Assemblée nationale, winning 65 seats, while Kamougué's Union pour le renouveau et la démocratie (URD) secured 29 seats, and Kebzabo's UNDR 15. In May Kamougué was elected as the President of the new Assemblée nationale. Nassour Guélendouksia Ouaïdou, hitherto Secretary-General at the Presidency, was named as the new Prime Minister.

Reports emerged from late 1998 of a rebellion in the Tibesti region of northern Chad, led by the Mouvement pour la démocratie et la justice au Tchad (MDJT) of Youssouf Togoimi, who had been dismissed as Minister of the Armed Forces in 1997. In June 1999 FROLINAT announced that it was giving political and logistical support to the Tibesti rebellion. In November the MDJT announced that it had defeated ANT forces in Aozou, killing 80 and capturing 47 (a further 42 ANT troops were said to have defected to the rebellion).

Ouaïdou resigned as Prime Minister in December 1999. He was replaced by Negoum Yamassoum, whose new Government included five UNDR members, among them Kebzabo as Minister of State, Minister of Agriculture.

In July 2000 the MDJT attacked a garrison in Bardaï and proclaimed its control of four towns in Tibesti. The Prime Minister visited the region and invited MDJT negotiators to take part in peace discussions. In September Togoimi met with Deby for the first time, in Sirte, Libya. Togoimi's proposal for multilateral peace discussions, incorporating all opposition groups and Deby's administration, was followed later that month by a conference at which Deby met with representatives of some 30 organizations (including trade unions, civil society groups and political parties), styling themselves the Forces vives, who were reportedly united in their disapproval of a new electoral code (see below). However, renewed fighting broke out in October between members of the MDJT and government forces in the far north and subsequently intensified.

Meanwhile, in July 2000 the Assemblée nationale approved proposals for the creation of an independent electoral body, the Commission électorale nationale indépendante (CENI), which was to plan a reorganization of constituencies in advance of elections due to be held in 2001. An extensive reshuffle of the Government at the end of August 2000 followed the dismissal of ministers belonging to the URD, owing to their party's rejection of the new electoral code.

In February 2001 it was announced that a presidential election would take place on 20 May and that legislative elections, initially scheduled for April, would be postponed until March 2002 for financial reasons. Municipal and local elections, which would have elected the bodies that, in turn, were to elect the members of the proposed upper parliamentary chamber, the Sénat, were postponed indefinitely. In May the six opposition presidential candidates, including Kamougué and Ngarledjy Yorongar, signed an electoral pact, pledging to unite behind a single candidate in the event of a second round of voting. Meanwhile, in addition to the MPS, 27 political organizations, including the RDP, rallied behind Deby.

The 2001 presidential election

The presidential election took place, as scheduled, on 20 May 2001. Although international and national observers pronounced themselves largely satisfied with its conduct, the six opposition candidates alleged widespread fraud and malpractice. On 13 June the Constitutional Council issued the final results of the election, according to which Deby had won 63.2% of the valid votes cast, followed by Yorongar, with 16.4%. (Yorongar's supporters claimed that he had won more than one-half of the votes cast.) A turn-out of 61.4% was declared, compared with the 80.9% that had been announced initially. Following Deby's inauguration on 8 August, Yamassoum was reappointed as Prime Minister; the new Government comprised 20 representatives from the MPS, five from the RDP and 10 other allies of Deby. In January 2002 Deby announced that the legislative elections would be held on 21 April; according to the revised electoral code, the Assemblée nationale was to be enlarged to 155 members.

Reports emerged in December 2001 that the Libyan Government, which was mediating between MDJT rebels and the Chadian Government, had assured the rebels of its support. The involvement of Libya in the peace process was regarded as a major factor in the beneficial terms offered to the MDJT in a peace agreement, signed by the group's deputy leader, Adoum Togoi Abbo (a former Chadian ambassador to Libya), and the Chadian Government in early January 2002. According to the agreement, both sides would institute an immediate cease-fire and a general amnesty for prisoners. Moreover, the MDJT was to participate in the Chadian Government and other state institutions, while the rebel forces were to be regularized. However, Togoimi did not give his approval to the arrangements, and, as a split in the rebel group became evident, in early April the MDJT issued a statement accusing the Government of inhibiting the peace process by its refusal to postpone legislative elections in order to allow the appointment of MDJT representatives to the Government.

In elections to the Assemblée nationale, which took place on 21 April 2002, the MPS significantly increased its parliamentary representation, obtaining 110 seats. The RDP became the second largest party, with 12 seats, while the Fédération action pour la République (FAR) became the largest opposition party, with nine seats. Coumakoye's VIVA—Rassemblement national pour la démocratie et le progrès (VIVA—RNDP) and the UNDR each won five seats, and the URD's representation was significantly reduced, to only three seats. In mid-June Ouaïdou was elected as President of the Assemblée nationale, and Deby appointed Haroun Kabadi, a senior official in the MPS, as Prime Minister, to head a 28-member Council of Ministers.

Meanwhile, in mid-May 2002 it was reported that Togoi was being held in detention by forces loyal to Togoimi, who had confirmed his rejection of the peace agreement signed in January; MDJT commanders denied that Togoi had been killed. None the less, in early July some 200 former MDJT fighters were reported to have joined government forces. An attack, in mid-September, on the eastern village of Tissi was attributed by the Chadian Government to troops supported by the Central African Republic (CAR), although the ANR, which had been dormant for several years, claimed responsibility for the raid and, amid heightened tension with the CAR (see below), emphasized that the perpetrators of the attack were resident in Chad.

The death of Togoimi, in Libya, in September 2002, while being treated for injuries sustained in a landmine explosion in Chad in August, raised hopes that peace talks between the Government and the MDJT would be reconvened, and Deby visited the north in order to encourage a resumption of negotiations. The leadership of the MDJT was assumed, in an acting capacity, by Adoum Maurice Hel-Bongo, although a split in the organization, between those loyal to Togoi and those loyal to Hel-Bongo became evident in subsequent months. In November rebels of the Forces des organisations nationales pour l'alternance et les libertés au Tchad (FONALT), one of the constituent groups of the ANR, claimed to have killed 116 ANT soldiers in clashes near Adré, close to the borders with Sudan and the CAR, although the Chadian Government made no official confirmation or denial of these reports.

Towards a peace process

In January 2003, following negotiations in Libreville, Gabon, the Government and the ANR signed a peace memorandum. However, the FONALT rejected the terms of the accord. During the first half of 2003 reports emerged of the formation of a new 'umbrella' grouping of 'politico-military' organizations opposed to the Deby regime, the Front uni pour la démocratie et la paix (FUDP). In April Hel-Bongo resigned as acting president of the MDJT. By mid-July, when Togoi was elected as President of the FUDP, several 'politico-military' organizations had announced their affiliation to the grouping, including the MDD and the faction of the MDJT loyal to Togoi. In August the faction of the MDJT that had remained outside the FUDP elected Col Hassan Abdallah Mardigué as its leader. In September more than 200 MDJT fighters were reported to have surrendered to government forces near Fada, following the signing of a peace accord between the Minister of National Defence, Veterans and Victims of War, Gen. Mahamat Nouri, and a local MDJT commander. None the less, later in the month clashes between MDJT rebels and government troops were reported around Bardaï airport in the Tibesti region.

Meanwhile, following a minor government reorganization in May 2003, a new Council of Ministers was formed in June, headed by a close ally of Deby, Moussa Faki Mahamat, and included 11 new members; the dismissal of Kabadi as Prime Minister followed his removal from the executive committee of the MPS. In late July it was reported that the Assemblée nationale had approved legislation delegating presidential prerogatives to Faki until October, while Deby received medical treatment in France.

In December 2003 the Government signed a peace agreement with Togoi in Ouagadougou, Burkina Faso (where Togoi had been resident since 2000), providing for an immediate cease-fire, an amnesty for MDJT fighters and supporters, and for the eventual inclusion of an undisclosed number of MDJT ministers in the Chadian Government. However, 'hardline' factions of the MDJT rejected the terms of the agreement, claiming to have killed up to 30 government troops in renewed clashes in Tibesti shortly after the agreement had been signed.

In February 2004 Deby reorganized the Council of Ministers, making changes to seven government positions. Idriss Ahmed Idriss left the Ministry of the Economy and Finance to become the National Director of the regional bank, the Banque des états de l'Afrique centrale; he was replaced by Ahmat Awat Sakine, hitherto Director-General of the Treasury. Gen. Nouri retired as Minister of National Defence, Veterans and Victims of War, and was replaced by Gen. Allafouz Koni.

A number of new opposition coalitions were formed in 2004. In March six 'politico-military' organizations, including the MDD and a faction of the MDJT, formed the Union des forces pour le changement (UFC). Acheikh Ibn Oumar was named as Provisional National Co-ordinator of the new grouping, which declared itself committed to the development of national unity and the holding of fair and free elections. In April Ahmat Hassaballah Soubiane, a founder member of the MPS and the former Chadian ambassador to the USA and Canada, announced in Washington, DC, the formation of the Coalition pour la défense de la démocratie et des droits constitutionnels (CDDC). In May 25 opposition parties, including the URD, the UNDR and the RDP, announced that they had formed the Coordination des partis politiques pour la défense de la constitution (CPDC), which, like the CDDC, sought to resist Deby's proposed constitutional modifications.

Eight constitutional amendments were approved by the Assemblée nationale in May 2004, the most notable of which removed the restriction limiting the President to serving two terms of office. The changes, which required endorsement in a national referendum, were vigorously criticized by opposition parties. In June the Constitutional Council rejected an opposition appeal to annul the constitutional revisions.

Faki resigned as Prime Minister on 3 February 2005; although no official reason for his departure was issued, speculation persisted that his resignation was in response to increasing tension between the Government and the President, and followed a series of strikes held by civil servants, teachers and health workers, protesting at unpaid wages. Deby nominated Pascal Yoadimnadji, hitherto the Minister of Agriculture, as the new premier, and new ministers responsible for the economy and for education were also appointed.

On 6 June 2005, according to official results, announced later in the month, some 77.8% of the votes cast in a referendum approved the proposed constitutional amendments, which thereby took effect. Some 71.0% of the registered electorate were reported to have participated in the plebiscite. The CPDC, which had called for a boycott of the referendum, denounced the results as fraudulent and announced its intention to call a general strike. In August Deby implemented a major governmental reorganization; responsibility for defence affairs was transferred to the Office of the Presidency, with the nomination of Bichara Issa Djadallah as Minister-delegate at the Presidency, responsible for National Defence. In the same month 15 senior army officers were arrested on charges of plotting a *coup d'état*, while mutinies in the armed forces were also reported.

In mid-October 2005 the Chadian authorities announced that at least 40 soldiers had deserted their posts in N'Djamena and fled to the east of the country (opposition sources claimed the number of deserters to be as high as 500). Some 30 of the deserters were reported to have surrendered to the Chadian armed forces following clashes at Adré. The deserters formed a new 'politico-military' organization, the Socle pour le changement, l'unité nationale et la démocratie (SCUD), led by Yaya Dillo Djérou. A further rebel attack, in mid-December, on a barracks at Adré, was led by another recently formed rebel group, the Rassemblement pour la démocratie et les libertés (RDL), led by Capt. Mahamat Nour Abdelkerim, and apparently based in Sudan. In late December the RDL and SCUD were reported to have formed an alliance, the Front uni pour le changement démocratique (FUCD), under Nour's leadership.

In January 2006 the Assemblée nationale voted to approve legislation introduced by Deby that extended its mandate by 18 months, apparently because the Government lacked the funding required to hold the legislative elections that had been due in April. In February a presidential election was, none the less, scheduled for 3 May. In March the Chadian authorities announced that an attempt to assassinate Deby had been prevented; two senior army officers were arrested, while it was alleged that the plot had been devised by several other former senior officers (including several relatives of Deby) who had recently defected to join the FUCD. At the end of the month the Chief of the Land Forces, Gen. Abakar Youssouf Mahamat Itno, was killed in clashes with rebels near the Sudanese border. In mid-April the forces of the FUCD advanced on N'Djamena, and on 13 April heavy fighting broke out in the city, although government forces regained control of the city after several hours. More than 100 of the rebels (the majority of whom were reported to be Sudanese, according to official sources) were captured during the fighting, and Deby announced that Chad was to sever diplomatic relations with Sudan and work towards sealing the border between the two countries.

Deby's third term in office

The presidential election proceeded as scheduled on 3 May 2006, although a boycott was urged by opposition parties. According to results released by the Constitutional Council some three weeks later, Deby secured 64.7% of the votes cast, comfortably defeating his nearest rival, Coumakoye, who took 15.1%. The rate of voter participation was recorded at 53.1%.

In July 2006 some 54 parties and civil society groups participated in a 'national dialogue' chaired by Prime Minister Yoadimnadji; however, the meeting was boycotted by the CPDC and the FAR. Deby was sworn in for a third elected term as President on 8 August and one week later announced the composition of an enlarged Council of Ministers, appointing three candidates who stood in the presidential election in May—Coumakoye, Pahimi Padacke Albert and Ibrahim Koullamallah—to ministerial posts. Yoadimnadji retained the premiership, while Adoum Younousmi was reappointed Minister of State, Minister of Infrastructure.

Heavy fighting broke out in November 2006 between government troops and two rebel groups, the Union des forces pour la démocratie et le développement (UFDD), led by Nouri, and the Rassemblement des forces démocratique—Convention nationale Tchadienne (RAFD—CNT). The towns of Biltine and Abéché were reportedly briefly captured by the RAFD—CNT and the UFDD, respectively, before government forces re-established control. Clashes continued into December with several hundred people killed during renewed offensives. Also in December the FUCD and the Government signed a peace agreement in Tripoli, Libya, which, *inter alia*, provided for the immediate cessation of hostilities between the two sides, the release of all prisoners of war and the integration of FUCD combatants into the Chadian security forces.

On 23 February 2007 Prime Minister Yoadimnadji died from a brain haemorrhage in Paris, France, where he had been transported for medical treatment. Younousmi became Prime Minister in an acting capacity and on 26 February Coumakoye was appointed as the permanent successor to Yoadimnadji.

In August 2007 President Deby and several opposition party leaders signed an agreement on a new electoral code. The electoral system was to be reviewed under the agreement and it was anticipated that legislative elections scheduled to be held in October 2009 would be postponed until the end of that year if reforms were implemented. On 25 October 2007 the Government and four rebel movements, including the UFDD, the Rassemblement des forces pour le changement (RFC, as the RAFD—CNT had been restyled) and the Concord nationale tchadienne, concluded a peace agreement in Sirte, Libya, establishing a cease-fire. The accord granted an amnesty to all members of those organizations and permitted the rebel movements to reconstitute themselves as political parties. Under the agreement the disarmament of rebel movements was scheduled to take place in November and provision was made for their integration into the Chadian defence forces. However, in that month the cease-fire broke down following heavy fighting near Abéché between government forces and rebels from the UFDD and the RFC. Consequently, former rebel leader and Minister of National Defence Nour was dismissed from his post, amid claims that he could no longer exert control over the rebel groups.

In early February 2008 the UFDD, the RFC and the UFDD—Fondamental (UFDD—F), which had formed an anti-Government coalition of forces, advanced on N'Djamena from bases in western Sudan with the aim of overthrowing President Deby. Government troops were deployed to the boundaries of the capital to intercept the militia, and it was feared that if rebel leaders Timane Erdimi of the RFC, Gen. Nouri of the UFDD and Abdelwahid Aboud Makaye of the UFDD—F did not enter into negotiations with the Government, the deployment of the EUFOR peace-keeping mission in the region (see below) would be delayed. Heavy fighting broke out during which both sides claimed control of the capital; however, by 6 February troops loyal to Deby, with the assistance of intelligence and logistical support provided by the French military, had succeeded in repelling the rebels from N'Djamena.

In mid-April 2008 Deby dismissed Coumakoye and appointed Youssouf Saleh Abbas, a former Chadian special representative to the UN and latterly responsible for liaisons between the Government and the EUFOR mission, as Prime Minister. Later that month Abbas appointed a new Government, in which four ministerial posts were awarded to members of the CPDC, including Jean Bawoyeu Alingué and Wadal Abdelkader Kamougué, who assumed responsibility for the justice and national defence portfolios, respectively. As part of a government reorganization effected by Abbas in September, Gata Ngoulou, formerly the Secretary-General of the Banque des Etats de l'Afrique Centrale, was named as Minister of Finance and the Budget.

Resistance and peace

In December 2008 the eight main rebel movements meeting in Khartoum, Sudan, agreed a joint political manifesto to overthrow Deby's regime and establish a transitional government over a period of 18 months; in January 2009 Erdimi, the leader of the RFC, was chosen by consensus as head of the new rebel coalition, the Union des forces de la résistance (UFR). On 6 May the UFR launched an attack on Chad's eighth largest city, Am-Timan, in the south-east of the country. Violent fighting between government troops and insurgents lasted two days and resulted in 247 deaths—of which 22 were members of the military—according to government figures. A further 212 rebels were reported to have been captured, among them the UFR Deputy Chief of Staff, before government forces succeeded in repulsing the attack. In July three rebel groups that had formed the Mouvement national coalition in the previous month signed a peace treaty with Deby's Government in Tripoli, Libya.

In July 2009 a total of 30 members, selected equally from government and opposition parties, were sworn into the CENI and were tasked with preparing new elections. Meeting again in December the overwhelming majority of political parties represented in the body agreed to proceed with a 'computerized census' of the population which was to take place between 21 March and 9 May 2010. The CENI announced in January 2010 that legislative elections would take place on 28 November, followed by local elections on 12 December. A presidential election was scheduled to be held on 23 April 2011. Meanwhile, Prime Minister Abbas tendered his resignation in early March 2010, following accusations of embezzlement on the part of several government ministers, four of whom had been suspended earlier in the year. President Deby appointed Emmanuel Nadingar, hitherto Minister-delegate to the Prime Minister, responsible for Decentralization, as Abbas' replacement and Nadingar subsequently announced the formation of a new 40-member Government, which included 18 new ministers. There were two further minor reorganizations of the cabinet in October and December 2010, when the Ministry of the Interior and Public Security was split into two ministries; the Minister of National Defence was also replaced.

Recent developments: the 2011 elections

The CENI provisionally declared in June 2010 that 4.5m. people had registered to participate in the forthcoming elections, although this figure was subsequently revised to 4.8m. Nevertheless, delays to the electoral process continued throughout 2010 and in September a revised schedule was presented with a view to holding legislative, local and presidential elections in 2011. Although initially approved by the coalition of opposition parties, the President denounced the postponement as prejudicial for stability, peace and reconciliation. Finally, in October 2010 both the presidential majority (subsequently styled as the Alliance pour la renaissance du Tchad—ART—and comprising the MPS, the RDP and VIVA—RNDP) and the opposition parties agreed to the staging of legislative elections on 6 February 2011, presidential elections on 3 April and local elections on 26 June. Meanwhile, during 2010 initiatives had been undertaken to reintegrate rebels into Chadian society. A cease-fire was signed with the MDJT in April in Tripoli, Libya, with an amnesty declared for rebels and the release of prisoners of war. Furthermore, ahead of the 50th anniversary of independence celebrations in January 2011 President Deby announced an amnesty for all prisoners of war.

Legislative elections were held on 13 February 2011. A further delay of one week had been announced in mid-January following the removal of the President of the CENI, who was alleged to have fraudulently tampered with the list of parliamentary candidates. According to official results, the ART secured 132 of the 188 seats in the Assemblée nationale (legislation had been approved in August 2010 increasing the number of deputies from 155 to 188), while the UNDR took 11; the Rassemblement national pour la démocratie au Tchad—le Réveil (RNDT—le Réveil) and the URD-Parti pour la liberté et le développement alliance also both won eight seats and a further 19 political parties all secured representation in the legislature. (The Constitutional Court subsequently upheld a number of opposition complaints of electoral irregularities.)

A total of six candidates, including Deby, declared their intention to contest the presidential election; however, in mid-March 2011 the opposition candidates threatened to boycott the ballot as certain requirements regarding the compilation of voter lists had not been met. Although Deby initially refused to consider a delay, following a series of consultations it was announced that the presidential election had been rescheduled to take place on 24–25 April. The election was duly held on these dates; however, opposition demands, including for the issue of new voter registration cards, were not met and there was a consequent boycott of the poll by some candidates, including two of the most prominent opposition leaders, Kebzabo of the UNDR and the head of FAR-Parti fédération, Ngarledjy Yorongar. (Opposition leader and former Minister of Defence Kamougué died in hospital in May.) On 10 May 2011 the CENI announced that Deby had won the presidential election with about 88.7% of votes cast, while the remaining two candidates, RNDT—le Réveil leader Pahimi Padacke Albert and Nadji Madou of Alliance socialiste pour un renouveau intégral, received 6.0% and 5.3% of the votes, respectively. Both opposition candidates rejected the electoral results. According to official figures, voter turn-out was 64.2%.

Deby was sworn in for a fourth presidential term on 8 August 2011. On 13 August he reappointed Nadingar as Prime Minister, and a new Government, which included five members of the RDP and four of VIVA—RNDP, was formed on 17 August. Among the new ministers, former presidential chief of staff Bénando Tatola was appointed as Minister-delegate at the Presidency of the Republic, responsible for National Defence and War Veterans, and Christian Georges Diguimbaye, hitherto the head of the Banque Agricole et Commerciale, became Minister of Finance and the Budget. In January 2012 President Deby replaced the Minister of Energy and Petroleum and the Minister of Planning, the Economy and International Co-operation following the temporary closure of an oil refinery, which had been constructed in a joint venture with China National Petroleum Corporation (see Economic Affairs).

Foreign Affairs

Regional relations

Following the outbreak of a violent rebellion in the Darfur region of western Sudan in February 2003 (see Sudan), Deby played a major role in promoting diplomatic measures intended to restore peace to the region, meeting the Sudanese President, Lt-Gen. Omar Hassan Ahmad al-Bashir, in April, August and December. In early November Sudanese and Chadian officials agreed to establish a joint force to patrol the countries' common border, amid rising concerns about cross-border banditry associated with the rebellion. At the end of March 2004 indirect peace talks between the Sudan Liberation Movement (SLM), the Sudan Justice and Equality Movement (SJEM) and the Government, attended by international observers, commenced in Chad, and on 8 April a 45-day cease-fire was signed by representatives of the three parties. However, in late April and early May a series of clashes occurred between Chadian troops and Sudanese (principally Arab) militiamen, known as the *Janjaweed*, pursuing Sudanese rebels across the border; the Chadian Government denounced the incursions and protested to the Sudanese Government. In mid-June the Chadian Government announced that its troops had killed 69 *Janjaweed* fighters who had attacked the Chadian village of Birak, some 6 km from the Sudanese border. By December an estimated 200,000 Sudanese had fled to Chad, according to the office of the UN High Commissioner for Refugees, placing considerable strain on food and water resources in the border region. In that month the Sudanese Government concluded a cease-fire in N'Djamena with a previously unidentified rebel group, the National Movement for Reform and Development (NMRD), which described itself as a breakaway faction of the SJEM. Although it had been hoped that these negotiations would lead to the return of significant numbers of refugees to Sudan, little progress had been observed by late 2005 and violent clashes in the border area continued.

Relations between Chad and Sudan became increasingly strained in 2005, and in April President Deby accused the Sudanese Government of providing support to a 3,000-strong rebel force operating near the two countries' mutual border. In early November, following defections from the Chadian army in the previous month by soldiers in eastern regions, the Minister-delegate at the Presidency, responsible for National Defence, Bichara Issa Djadallah, announced that the Chadian authorities did not rule out the pursuit of defectors who had entered Sudan. Moreover, in late November Deby accused the Sudanese Government of complicity in providing arms and logistical support to Chadian rebels, and the Government blamed Sudan for an attack on a barracks near Adré in mid-December; although the Sudanese authorities denied any involvement in the attack, in late December Deby stated that he regarded a 'state of belligerence' as existing between the two countries. None the less, in January 2006 representatives of the Governments of both Chad and Sudan expressed a willingness to enter into negotiations to defuse tensions between the countries. Prior to agreeing to participate in any such discussions, however, the Chadian authorities demanded that Sudan conform to a number of conditions, including the disarmament of Chadian deserters in that country, the ending of Sudanese military incursions into Chadian territory, and the compensation of victims of cross-border raids. In early February Libya hosted a mini-summit on the conflict between Chad and Sudan, following which Deby, al-Bashir and the Libyan leader, Col Muammar al-Qaddafi, signed an agreement, known as the Tripoli Accord, in which, *inter alia*, the leaders of Chad and Sudan agreed to cease supporting groups hostile to the other's Government. However, following a rebel attack on the Chadian capital, N'Djamena, in mid-April, Chad announced that it was to sever diplomatic relations with Sudan with immediate effect.

Relations improved in late July 2006 when the two countries signed an agreement in N'Djamena, according to which they were not to host each other's rebel groups on their territory. In August al-Bashir attended the swearing-in ceremony of Deby and it was announced that Chad and Sudan had re-established diplomatic relations with immediate effect, and that the border between the two countries would be reopened. There were, however, numerous reports of violent incidents in the border region during late 2006 and early 2007, and in November 2006 the Governments of both Chad and the CAR appealed for the dispatch of UN peace-keeping troops to the area. The Sudanese Government expressed its vehement opposition to any such moves. In late February 2007 the UN Secretary-General, Ban Ki-Moon, proposed the deployment of an 11,000-strong UN peace-keeping mission to protect civilians and deter cross-border attacks. He also advocated the dispatch of a smaller contingent of UN military and police personnel to north-eastern CAR. However, the Chadian authorities stipulated that they would not accept a military force and requested that a civil force comprised solely of police officers be deployed to the area.

In early May 2007, following mediation by Saudi Arabia's King Abdallah, Presidents al-Bashir and Deby agreed to co-operate with the AU and the UN in their attempts to stabilize the Chad–Sudan border. Both countries approved the formation of a joint border force, and pledged to cease training and funding rebel groups and to stop all cross-border attacks. Furthermore, in June Deby announced that the Chadian Government had agreed in principle to the deployment of a European Union (EU, see p. 276) peace-keeping force along the border with Sudan. However, some rebel groups were concerned that French support for President Deby could unduly influence the force and warned that the EU troops could become a target for further violence if they did not remain impartial. In September, following the adoption of UN Resolution 1778, the UN Security Council approved the deployment of the United Nations Mission in the Central African Republic and Chad (MINURCAT), with a one-year mandate to protect refugees, displaced persons and civilians adversely affected by the uprising in Darfur. MINURCAT was also to facilitate the provision of humanitarian assistance in eastern Chad and the north-east of the CAR and create favourable conditions for the reconstruction of those areas. The mission was to be supported by the EU bridging military operation in Eastern Chad and North Eastern Central African Republic (EUFOR TCHAD/RCA) comprising some 4,300 troops, although the deployment of the EU force was delayed by the rebel assault on N'Djamena in early February 2008.

In March 2008, after the ICJ issued an arrest warrant for President al-Bashir, Sudan expelled 13 aid agencies from its territory. It was feared that the move would provoke a mass movement of refugees into eastern Chad, where aid agencies were already assisting 250,000 Sudanese refugees and 160,000 displaced Chadians. In May Chad was the subject of Sudanese accusations of supporting rebel activity in Khartoum, Sudan, and Sudan recalled its ambassador from N'Djamena. After an AU-brokered meeting convened in Dakar, Senegal, in July, the two countries agreed to resume diplomatic relations and in November ambassadors returned to their posts. Meanwhile, in October Belgium assumed command of EUFOR TCHAD/RCA, with a mandate set to last until March 2009 when EU forces were scheduled to be replaced by MINURCAT personnel. In January the Security Council extended MINURCAT's mandate until March 2010 and approved the deployment of up to 5,200 military personnel in the region as part of that force.

In May 2009 Sudan and Chad signed a bilateral agreement in Doha, Qatar, to normalize relations and end support within their borders of rebel groups hostile to the other country. However, two days after the accord was finalized the Chadian Government accused Sudan of launching a military offensive. Fighting in eastern Chad between government forces and UFR rebels resulted in 247 deaths (see above). In retaliation Chad carried out air raids along the common border and some 40 km into Sudanese territory. In February 2010, following a visit by Deby to Khartoum, Sudan and Chad agreed to end proxy wars and work together to rebuild border regions. In July al-Bashir defied an International Criminal Court (ICC) injunction by visiting Chad, a member country of the ICC. Meanwhile, MINURCAT had still not reached its recommended strength, with only approximately 3,000 soldiers deployed. Despite protestations from human rights organizations, which relied on MINURCAT for escorts, Deby finally requested that the force leave the country. In accordance with a UN Security Council resolution in May, the mandate of MINURCAT officially ended on 31 December. In December 2011 the ICC announced that Chad had not met its obligation to co-operate with the Court by again failing to arrest al-Bashir (who had visited the country to attend Deby's inauguration in August), and that it was to refer the issue to the UN Security Council.

In response to an attempted coup in the CAR in May 2001, Chad reportedly dispatched troops to defend the Government of President Ange-Félix Patassé. In early November heightened unrest broke out in the CAR, following an attempt to arrest the recently dismissed Chief of Staff of the Armed Forces, Gen. François Bozizé, in connection with the May coup attempt. Bozizé crossed into Chad, with an estimated 300 armed supporters, and was granted refuge in Sarh. Chad was subsequently involved in efforts by both the Libyan-sponsored Community of Sahel-Saharan States (see p. 449) and the Communauté économique et monétaire de l'Afrique centrale (CEMAC) to find a lasting solution to the crisis in the CAR. In late December the CAR judiciary abandoned legal proceedings against Bozizé. Meanwhile, repeated clashes were reported at the Chad–CAR border and an additional source of tension was the appointment of Col Martin Khoumtan-Madji (believed by the Chadian authorities to be an alias of Abdoulaye Miskine, a former senior member of a rebel group based in the CAR since 1998) as the head of a special unit in the CAR military, comprising some 300 soldiers, including many former Chadian rebels, and answerable directly to the presidency, charged with securing the common border of the two countries.

In early August 2002 the CAR Prime Minister, Martin Ziguélé, accused Chadian troops of launching cross-border attacks in the CAR, precipitating an emergency CEMAC summit later that month. (Chadian sources stated that the troops that had launched the attacks in the CAR were loyal to Bozizé, and not affiliated to the ANT.) A report issued by a CEMAC observer mission, at the end of August, stated that, although tension remained high in the border region, there was no concentration of troops on the border, or of foreign troops in either country. An attack by the ANR in eastern Chad (see above), in early September, was attributed by the Chadian Government to troops supported by the CAR. In early October a CEMAC summit in Libreville, Gabon, sought to defuse tensions between the two countries; in accordance with an agreement reached at the summit, Bozizé and Khoumtan-Madji were granted asylum in France and Togo, respectively; a CEMAC force was subsequently deployed to monitor joint patrols of the border by Chadian and CAR troops. Tensions thereafter abated somewhat, and in February 2003 the Presidents of Chad and the CAR met in the CAR capital Bangui in an attempt to normalize relations between the two countries. Later that month some 20,000 refugees (many of whom were Chadian nationals who had been resident in the CAR for many years) entered southern Chad, fleeing renewed fighting in the CAR. Following Bozizé's assumption of power in March, some 400 Chadian troops were reportedly dispatched to the CAR; around 120 Chadian troops were subsequently integrated into the CEMAC force that was deployed in the CAR from late 2002. However, sporadic unrest in north-eastern CAR continued; in June 2006 clashes were reported between Chadian rebel forces and CAR and CEMAC troops near Tiroungoulou, CAR, in which some 80 people were believed to have been killed. In December 2010, following the withdrawal of MINURCAT troops (see above), it was announced that Chadian troops had repelled rebel attacks in the town of Birao, on the border between the two countries. At a summit meeting in Khartoum between President Deby, Bozizé and Sudanese President al-Bashir in May 2011, it was agreed to establish a tripartite border force to address border security issues, and to encourage the voluntary return of refugees.

Further concerns regarding regional security emerged in March 2004, when clashes at the Niger–Chad border between Islamist militants belonging to the Algerian-based Groupe salafiste pour la prédication et le combat (GSPC) and Chadian and Nigerien troops resulted in the deaths of some 43 GSPC fighters and three Chadian soldiers, according to the Chadian Government. It was announced that month that the Governments of Algeria, Chad, Mali and Niger were to reinforce security co-operation in the regions of their common borders. Meanwhile, the MDJT had reportedly captured a prominent GSPC leader, Amara Saïfi (also known as Abderrazak le Para). In July it was reported that the MDJT had released Saïfi, whose faction of the GSPC had apparently united with the Chadian rebel group to fight the Chadian army. In late October 2006 the Nigerien Government announced its intention forcibly to return to Chad some 150,000 Mahamid Arabs, who had migrated to Niger from Chad over a number of years. However, following protests from the Mahamids to the AU and the UN, the Nigerien authorities stated that only those without identification papers—estimated to number about 4,000—would be required to leave Niger.

In early 1998 it was reported that Chad was to seek the extradition from Senegal of former President Habré, with a view to his prosecution in relation to human rights abuses and in connection with the embezzlement of state funds. A committee of inquiry, established by the Deby administration, held Habré's 'political police' responsible for the deaths of some 40,000 people and the torture of 200,000 others. In February 2000, following a ruling by a Senegalese court that he could be tried in that country, Habré was charged with complicity in acts of torture committed in Chad under his leadership, and placed under house arrest. The charges were dismissed in July, however, on the grounds that Senegal lacked the appropriate penal procedure to process such a case. In March 2001 the Senegalese Court of Cassation upheld this ruling, and Habré remained in Senegal. In

August 2005 Prime Minister Yoadimnadji announced that former members of Habré's security forces still working within state organizations would be removed from their posts to face trial on suspected human rights abuses, and also stated that the Government intended to introduce legislation that would provide compensation for the victims of torture and their families; this followed the publication of a report by the US-based organization Human Rights Watch, which stated that several officials suspected of complicity in human rights abuses under Habré continued to hold senior positions in the Deby administration. In September a Belgian court issued a warrant for Habré's arrest, under a law that (as amended in 2003) gave that country's courts universal jurisdiction in cases of human rights abuses and war crimes, if Belgian citizens or long-term residents were among the plaintiffs (several of the alleged victims of abuses committed under Habré's regime had been granted Belgian citizenship), and in November he was remanded into custody in Dakar by a court investigating the request for extradition. However, in late November the court ruled that it had no jurisdiction to rule on Habré's extradition; he was released but re-arrested later in the month, and the Senegalese Government announced that a decision on which judicial body was competent to rule on Habré's extradition would be taken at a forthcoming summit of AU leaders. At the summit, held in Khartoum, Sudan, in January 2006, it was agreed that Habré should not be extradited to Belgium, and a resolution calling for a panel of 'eminent African jurists' to rule on the appropriate venue for Habré's trial was approved. At an AU meeting held in Banjul, The Gambia, in July of that year it was announced that Habré was to be tried in Senegal. In July 2008 the Senegalese Assemblée nationale approved the necessary legislation allowing the trial to proceed in that country, and pre-trial preparations commenced. In August Habré was sentenced, *in absentia*, to death by a Chadian court, along with 11 rebel leaders, including Gen. Nour Adbelkerim. However, the Senegalese authorities subsequently requested international funding to meet the cost of the trial, and in February 2009 the Belgian Government appealed to the ICJ that Habré be tried in Senegal or extradited to Belgium; in February 2010 it was announced that Chad would make available to Senegal €3m. to organize a trial in that country. In November the Economic Community of West African States ruled that Senegal could not try Habré in its own courts, but could fulfil the AU mandate for his prosecution by hosting an ad hoc international tribunal. In April 2011 the Senegalese Government agreed to the creation of the proposed tribunal, but in the following month withdrew from further negotiations on the issue with the AU. In July the Government announced that it intended to extradite Habré to Chad, but reversed its decision in response to an appeal by the UN High Commissioner for Human Rights, who expressed concern that Habré might be subjected to torture if returned to Chad.

Other external relations

In early August 2006 the People's Republic of China announced that it had resumed diplomatic relations with Chad, after bilateral ties between that country and Taiwan were severed. In June 2009 China's largest energy producer began work on a major pipeline to transport crude petroleum from Koudwala to the Djarmaya refinery north of N'Djamena, and a number of other joint ventures were subsequently initiated (see Economic Affairs).

After French assistance contributed significantly to the repulsion of a rebel assault on Deby's Government in February 2008 (see above), the country's involvement in Chadian affairs was placed under scrutiny. In May 2009 a Chadian civil society delegation travelled to Paris to request French diplomatic intervention to bring pressure upon the Chadian Government to implement the 2007 agreement signed in Sirte, Libya. The French Government in response made a statement requesting that any escalation of violence be avoided: the Defence Ministry also announced that intelligence gathering, both ground and airborne, was the only role being carried out by French forces in Chad, and the French Prime Minister, François Fillon, on tour in West Africa at the time, confirmed that French troops had no role to play in Chad's internal politics. In October a report published by the French Government listed Chad as France's second largest purchaser of weapons; in 2008 Chad had purchased €13m. worth of armaments. In 2011 civil conflict in Libya affected the internal security situation, with an estimated 70,000 Libyan refugees repatriated to or via Chad during that year.

CONSTITUTION AND GOVERNMENT

A new Constitution was adopted by national referendum on 31 March 1996. Under the terms of the Constitution, the Republic of Chad is a unitary state with a multi-party political system. Executive power is vested in the President, elected by direct universal suffrage, who is the Head of State and Commander-in-Chief of the Armed Forces. The President appoints the Prime Minister, who nominates the Council of Ministers. Legislative power is vested in a unicameral legislature, the 188-member Assemblée nationale, which is elected by direct universal suffrage for a four-year term. Constitutional amendments, approved by referendum in 2005, removed the restriction limiting the President to serving two five-year terms of office and abolished the Sénat. Chad is divided into 18 administrative regions, including the capital city, N'Djamena, which is a region of special status.

REGIONAL AND INTERNATIONAL CO-OPERATION

Chad is a member of the African Union (see p. 189), the Central African organs of the Franc Zone (see p. 333) and of the Communauté économique des états de l'Afrique centrale (CEEAC, see p. 449); the Lake Chad Basin Commission (see p. 451) is based in N'Djamena.

Chad became a member of the UN in 1960, and was admitted to the World Trade Organization (WTO, see p. 433) in 1996. Chad participates in the Group of 77 (G77, see p. 450) developing countries.

ECONOMIC AFFAIRS

In 2010, according to estimates by the World Bank, Chad's gross national income (GNI), measured at average 2008–10 prices, was US $6,929m., equivalent to $620 per head (or $1,210 on an international purchasing-power parity basis). During 2001–10, it was estimated, the population increased at an average annual rate of 3.1%, while gross domestic product (GDP) per head increased, in real terms, by an average of 4.7% per year. Overall GDP increased, in real terms, at an average annual rate of 8.0% in 2001–10, according to the World Bank. GDP declined by 1.6% in 2009, but increased by 4.3% in 2010.

Agriculture contributed 19.1% of GDP in 2010, according to the African Development Bank (AfDB); some 63.4% of the labour force were employed in the sector in mid-2012, according to estimates by FAO. The principal cash crop is cotton (exports of which contributed an estimated 15.8% of total export revenue in 2003, a decline from 41.1% in 2001). The principal subsistence crops are rice, sorghum and millet. Livestock-rearing, which accounted for an estimated 21.0% of exports in 2003, also makes an important contribution to the domestic food supply. According to the World Bank, during 2000–08 agricultural GDP increased at an average annual rate of 3.1%. According to AfDB estimates, agricultural GDP declined by 6.4% in 2009, but increased by 14.6% in 2010.

Industry (including mining) contributed 51.5% of GDP in 2010, according to the AfDB. About 4.2% of the population were employed in the sector in 1990. According to the World Bank, during 2000–08 industrial GDP increased at an average annual rate of 23.7%; it increased by 144.5% in 2004, largely owing to the revenues from petroleum extraction (see below), but grew by just 5.0% in 2005, before declining by 3.7% in 2006 and by 13.6% in 2007. The sector registered a strong recovery in 2008, registering growth of 13.9% in that year.

The mining sector (including fishing, but excluding petroleum extraction) contributed 43.6% of GDP in 2010, according to the AfDB. The petroleum sector contributed some 30.0% of GDP in 2005, compared with 11.3% in 2003. For many years the only minerals exploited were natron (sodium carbonate), salt, alluvial gold and materials for the construction industry. However, long-delayed plans to develop sizeable petroleum reserves in the Doba Basin and at Sedigi, in the south of the country, were pursued in the early 2000s, and production of petroleum at Doba commenced in mid-2003 (see below). There is believed to be considerable potential for the further exploitation of gold, bauxite and uranium. During 1998–2005 the GDP of the mining sector (including fishing) increased at an average annual rate of 4.3%, according to the IMF; growth of 6.8% was recorded in 2005. According to AfDB estimates, mining GDP decreased by 5.4% in 2009, but increased by 4.2% in 2010.

According to the AfDB, the manufacturing sector (including handicrafts) contributed 5.3% of GDP in 2010. The sector operates mainly in the south of the country, and is dominated by agro-industrial activities, notably the processing of the cotton crop by the state-controlled Société Cotonnière du Tchad (COTONTCHAD). During 1998–2005 manufacturing GDP increased at an average annual rate of 0.9%, according to the IMF. The GDP of the sector declined by 0.2% in 2009, but increased by 0.8% in 2010, according to AfDB estimates.

Construction contributed 2.0% of GDP in 2010, according to AfDB estimates. The sector grew by 12.3% in that year.

Chad has historically been heavily dependent on imports of mineral fuels (principally from Cameroon and Nigeria) for the generation of electricity. The use of wood-based fuel products by most households has contributed to the severe depletion of Chad's forest resources. In 2002 only 2% of households in Chad had access to electricity.

Services contributed 29.3% of GDP in 2010, according to the AfDB. The GDP of the sector increased at an average annual rate of 8.3% in 2000–08; growth in 2008 was 6.5%.

According to the IMF, in 2010 Chad's projected trade surplus was 109,100m. francs CFA, but there was a deficit of 1,244,200m. francs CFA on the current account of the balance of payments. In 1995 Chad's principal source of imports (41.3%) was France; other major suppliers were Cameroon, Nigeria and the USA. The principal markets for exports include Cameroon and France. The principal exports in 2003 were petroleum, livestock and cotton. The principal imports in 1995 were petroleum products, road vehicles and parts, sugar and cereals.

In 2010, according to the IMF, Chad's projected budgetary deficit was 79,800m. francs CFA. Chad's general government gross debt was 1,018,560m. francs CFA in 2009, equivalent to 30.5% of GDP. Chad's external debt at the end of 2009 totalled US $1,743m., of which $1,711m. was public and publicly guaranteed debt. In that year, the cost of servicing long-term public and publicly guaranteed debt and repayments to the IMF was equivalent to 4.1% of the value of exports of goods, services and income (excluding workers' remittances). According to the ILO, consumer prices increased at an average annual rate of 3.9% in 2000–09; they rose by 10.2% in 2008, and by 10.1% in 2009.

Chad's petroleum deposits attracted considerable international interest from the late 1990s, and in late 2000 a consortium led by the US ExxonMobil Corporation began work to develop substantial petroleum resources in three fields in the Doba Basin, believed to contain reserves of approximately 900m. barrels. Operations commenced in July 2003, and a 1,070-km pipeline to transport petroleum from Doba to the port of Kribi in Cameroon was officially inaugurated in October. Output had reached some 225,000 barrels per day by late 2005 and production was expected to continue for 25–30 years. Economic growth, which fell slightly in 2009 as a result of the global downturn, recovered strongly in 2010, strengthened by the high international price of oil and a near doubling of agricultural production after favourable weather conditions (with a consequent decline in food prices). The People's Republic of China continued to be a source of major foreign investment: in December 2010 the construction of an industrial park, which was to house facilities for the petroleum industry, commenced, and in March 2011 the China Civil Engineering Construction Corporation agreed to build Chad's first railway at a cost of €5,000m. The project, primarily aimed at transporting freight, was to be carried out in two phases, ultimately to link the land-locked country to two waterways: Sudan and the Red Sea to the east and Cameroon and the Atlantic Ocean to the south-west. Significant investment in the telecommunications market was also made by Libya in 2010, which purchased a 60% stake in the Société des Télécommunications du Tchad. Chad's first oil refinery, which had been jointly constructed by the Chadian Government and China National Petroleum Corporation, commenced operations near N'Djamena in July 2011, while the authorities' extensive public investment programme continued during that year. In October, however, the Government's decision to increase the price of fuel products, after the refinery complained of severe losses, attracted domestic criticism. In November, following trade union strike action, the Government agreed to raise public sector wages significantly in the following three years. In January 2012 the Government announced that it had closed the oil refinery (prompting concerns of worsening fuel shortages in the country), after China National Petroleum Corporation refused to continue production of fuel at the price set by the authorities. Moderate GDP growth of 3.1% was projected by the IMF for 2011.

PUBLIC HOLIDAYS

2013: 1 January (New Year), 4 February* (Maloud, Birth of the Prophet), 1 April (Easter Monday), 1 May (Labour Day), 25 May ('Liberation of Africa', anniversary of the OAU's foundation), 20 May (Whit Monday), 11 August (Independence Day), 7 August* (Id al-Fitr, end of Ramadan), 15 August (Assumption), 14 October* (Id al-Adha, Feast of the Sacrifice), 1 November (All Saints' Day), 28 November (Proclamation of the Republic), 1 December (Liberation and Democracy Day, anniversary of the 1990 coup), 25 December (Christmas).

* These holidays are dependent on the Islamic lunar calendar and may vary by one or two days from the dates given.

Statistical Survey

Source (unless otherwise stated): Institut national de la statistique, des études economiques et démographiques, BP 453, N'Djamena; tel. 22-52-31-64; fax 22-52-66-13; e-mail inseed@intnet.td; internet www.inseed-tchad.org.

Area and Population

AREA, POPULATION AND DENSITY

Area (sq km)	
Land	1,259,200
Inland waters	24,800
Total	1,284,000*
Population (census result)	
8 April 1993	6,279,931
20 May–30 June 2009†	
Males	5,509,522
Females	5,666,393
Total	11,175,915
Population (UN estimates at mid-year)‡	
2010	11,227,208
2011	11,525,497
2012	11,830,573
Density (per sq km) at mid-2012	9.2

* 495,800 sq miles.

† Figures are provisional.

‡ Source: UN, *World Population Prospects: The 2010 Revision*.

POPULATION BY AGE AND SEX

(UN estimates at mid-2012)

	Males	Females	Total
0–14	2,679,928	2,660,555	5,340,483
15–64	3,054,151	3,100,712	6,154,863
65 and over	150,168	185,059	335,227
Total	5,884,247	5,946,326	11,830,573

Source: UN, *World Population Prospects: The 2010 Revision*.

ETHNIC GROUPS

1995 (percentages): Sara, Bongo and Baguirmi 20.1; Chadic 17.7; Arab 14.3; M'Bourn 6.3; Masalit, Maba and Mimi 6.1; Tama 6.1; Adamawa 6.0; Sudanese 6.0; Mubi 4.1; Hausa 2.1; Kanori 2.1; Massa 2.1; Kotoko 2.0; Peul 0.5; Others 4.5 (Source: La Francophonie).

REGIONS
(2009 census, preliminary figures)

Barh El Gazel	260,865	Mayo-Kebbi Est	769,178
Batha	527,031	Mayo-Kebbi Ouest	565,087
Borkou	97,251	Moyen-Chari	598,284
Chari-Baguirmi	621,785	N'Djamena	993,492
Ennedi	173,606	Ouaddaï	731,679
Guéra	553,795	Salamat	308,605
Hadjer-Lamis	562,957	Sila	289,776
Kanem	354,603	Tandjilé	682,817
Lac	451,369	Tibesti	21,970
Logone Occidental	683,293	Wadi Fira	494,933
Logone Oriental	796,453		
Mandoul	637,086	**Total**	11,175,915

PRINCIPAL TOWNS
(population at 1993 census)

N'Djamena (capital)	530,965	Koumra	26,702
Moundou	99,530	Pala	26,115
Sarh	75,496	Am-Timan	21,269
Abéché	54,628	Bongor	20,448
Kelo	31,319	Mongo	20,443

Mid-2010 (incl. suburbs, UN estimate): N'Djamena 808,000 (Source: UN, *World Urbanization Prospects: The 2009 Revision*).

BIRTHS AND DEATHS
(annual averages, UN estimates)

	1995–2000	2000–05	2005–10
Birth rate (per 1,000)	47.6	47.6	45.9
Death rate (per 1,000)	17.3	17.8	17.1

2001 (preliminary): Live births 397,896; Deaths 138,025.

Sources: UN, *World Population Prospects: The 2010 Revision* and *Population and Vital Statistics Report*.

Life expectancy (years at birth, WHO estimates): 48 (males 47; females 48) in 2009 (Source: WHO, *World Health Statistics*).

ECONOMICALLY ACTIVE POPULATION
('000 persons at mid-1990, ILO estimates)

	Males	Females	Total
Agriculture, hunting, forestry and fishing	1,179	1,102	2,281
Industry	105	9	115
Manufacturing	50	6	56
Services	245	100	344
Total labour force	1,529	1,211	2,740

Source: ILO.

1993 census (persons aged six years and over): Total employed 2,305,961; Unemployed 16,268; Total labour force 2,322,229.

Mid-2012 ('000, estimates): Agriculture, etc. 3,032; Total labour force 4,783 (Source: FAO).

Health and Welfare

KEY INDICATORS

Total fertility rate (children per woman, 2009)	6.1
Under-5 mortality rate (per 1,000 live births, 2009)	209
HIV/AIDS (% of persons aged 15–49, 2009)	3.4
Physicians (per 1,000 head, 2004)	0.04
Hospital beds (per 1,000 head, 2005)	0.40
Health expenditure (2008): US $ per head (PPP)	86
Health expenditure (2008): % of GDP	6.4
Health expenditure (2008): public (% of total)	50.6
Access to water (% of persons, 2008)	50
Access to sanitation (% of persons, 2008)	9
Total carbon dioxide emissions ('000 metric tons, 2007)	384.7
Carbon dioxide emissions per head (metric tons, 2007)	<0.1
Human Development Index (2011): ranking	183
Human Development Index (2011): value	0.328

For sources and definitions, see explanatory note on p. vi.

Agriculture

PRINCIPAL CROPS
('000 metric tons)

	2008	2009	2010
Rice, paddy	169.8	130.7	130.8*
Maize	226.0	209.0	208.9*
Millet	523.2	709.0*	620.9*
Sorghum	685.4	601.0	490.3*
Potatoes	42	50*	50*
Sweet potatoes*	75	90	88
Cassava (Manioc)	161	230*	231*
Taro (Coco yam)	26	33*	26*
Yams*	405	520	415
Sugar cane*	390	390	390
Beans, dry	63	80*	73*
Groundnuts, with shell	403	413*	394*
Sesame seed	39	35†	35†
Melonseed*	24	22	21
Onions, dry*	17	17	16
Dates*	19	19	19
Guavas, mangoes and mangosteens*	33	35	33

* FAO estimate(s).
† Unofficial figure.

Aggregate production ('000 metric tons, may include official, semi-official or estimated data): Total cereals 2,019 in 2008, 2,193 in 2009, 1,912 in 2010; Total pulses 109 in 2008, 125 in 2009, 122 in 2010; Total roots and tubers 709 in 2008, 922 in 2009, 810 in 2010; Total vegetables (incl. melons) 103 in 2008, 105 in 2009, 97 in 2010; Total fruits (excl. melons) 124 in 2008, 118 in 2009, 118 in 2010.

Source: FAO.

LIVESTOCK
('000 head, year ending September)

	2008	2009	2010*
Cattle	7,075	7,245	7,419
Goats	6,288	6,439	6,751
Sheep	2,886	2,956	3,027
Pigs	28*	29*	30
Horses	400	410	410
Asses	440	451	451
Camels	1,358	1,391	1,400
Chickens	5,450*	5,500*	5,550

* FAO estimate(s).

Source: FAO.

LIVESTOCK PRODUCTS
('000 metric tons, FAO estimates)

	2008	2009	2010
Cattle meat	88.7	91.1	94.8
Sheep meat	15.0	15.4	15.4
Goat meat	23.6	24.2	24.2
Cows' milk	188.1	192.6	195.6
Sheep's milk	12.4	12.7	13.1
Goats' milk	37.3	38.2	39.8
Hen eggs	3.9	4.0	4.0

Source: FAO.

Forestry

ROUNDWOOD REMOVALS
('000 cubic metres, excl. bark, FAO estimates)

	2007	2008	2009
Sawlogs, veneer logs and logs for sleepers*	14	14	14
Other industrial wood†	747	747	747
Fuel wood	6,714	6,830	6,949
Total	7,475	7,591	7,710

* Output assumed to be unchanged since 1993.
† Output assumed to be unchanged since 1999.

2010: Production assumed to be unchanged since 2009 (FAO estimates).

Source: FAO.

SAWNWOOD PRODUCTION
('000 cubic metres, incl. railway sleepers)

	1994	1995	1996
Total (all broadleaved)	2.4*	2.4	2.4

* FAO estimate.

1997–2010: Annual production as in 1996 (FAO estimates).

Source: FAO.

Fishing

('000 metric tons, live weight, FAO estimates)

	2007	2008	2009
Total catch (freshwater fishes)	45.0	40.0	40.0

Source: FAO.

Mining

	2008	2009	2010
Crude petroleum ('000 metric tons)	6,691	6,187	6,403

Source: BP, *Statistical Review of World Energy*.

Industry

SELECTED PRODUCTS

	2002	2003	2004
Sugar (centrifugal, raw, '000 metric tons)	23.1	38.0	40.0
Beer ('000 metric tons)	12.4	11.0	8.4
Cigarettes (million packs)	36.0	37.0	40.0
Electric energy (million kWh)	106.6	86.0	84.0

Source: IMF, *Chad: Selected Issues and Statistical Appendix* (January 2007).

Oil of groundnuts ('000 metric tons): 32.0 in 2008–09 (Source: FAO).

Raw sugar ('000 metric tons): 35.0 in 2005–07.

Electric energy (million kWh): 100.0 in 2005; 102.0 in 2006; 105.0 in 2007; 103.0 in 2008 (Source: UN Industrial Commodities Statistics Database).

Finance

CURRENCY AND EXCHANGE RATES

Monetary Units

100 centimes = 1 franc de la Coopération financière en Afrique centrale (CFA).

Sterling, Dollar and Euro Equivalents (30 December 2011)

£1 sterling = 783.813 francs CFA;
US $1 = 506.961 francs CFA;
€1 = 655.957 francs CFA;
10,000 francs CFA = £12.76 = $19.73 = €15.24.

Average Exchange Rate (francs CFA per US $)

2009 472.186
2010 495.277
2011 471.866

Note: An exchange rate of 1 French franc = 50 francs CFA, established in 1948, remained in force until January 1994, when the CFA franc was devalued by 50%, with the exchange rate adjusted to 1 French franc = 100 francs CFA. This relationship to French currency remained in effect with the introduction of the euro on 1 January 1999. From that date, accordingly, a fixed exchange rate of €1 = 655.957 francs CFA has been in operation.

BUDGET
('000 million francs CFA)

Revenue*	2003	2004	2005
Non-petroleum revenue	124.6	140.3	159.2
Tax revenue	113.4	122.0	138.9
Taxes on income and profits	52.4	52.5	58.9
Companies	20.3	23.5	24.2
Individuals	30.2	26.9	32.4
Employers' payroll tax	1.9	2.1	2.3
Property tax	2.5	4.1	4.2
Taxes on goods and services	20.6	25.9	26.0
Turnover tax	14.4	15.4	17.9
Tax on petroleum products	4.7	5.1	5.4
Taxes on international trade	31.3	33.8	41.1
Import taxes	27.6	33.8	41.1
Export taxes	1.6	2.0	1.6
Other revenue	11.2	18.3	20.4
Property income	2.1	2.9	1.0
Administrative fees	1.9	1.2	2.3
Non-industrial sales	2.2	3.3	2.0
Petroleum-exploitation permits and share premium	—	8.3	13.6
Petroleum revenue	—	57.7	130.4
Total	124.6	198.0	289.7

Expenditure†	2003	2004	2005
Current expenditure	149.4	154.7	187.3
Wages and salaries	73.6	80.1	101.2
Civil service	56.2	60.9	73.3
Military	17.4	19.2	27.9
Goods and services	42.6	32.4	34.2
Transfers	19.2	30.1	37.1
Interest	9.5	10.2	10.4
External	8.6	8.2	7.2
Investment expenditure	198.6	182.1	217.7
Domestically financed	28.9	48.7	68.5
Foreign financed	169.7	133.4	149.1
Total	348.0	336.8	404.9

* Excluding grants received ('000 million francs CFA): 122.7 in 2003; 69.4 in 2004; 104.2 in 2005.

† Excluding net lending ('000 million francs CFA): 76.6 in 2003; 68.0 in 2004; 53.3 in 2005.

Source: IMF, *Chad: Selected Issues and Statistical Appendix* (January 2007).

2006 ('000 million francs CFA): *Revenue:* Oil revenue 403.4; Non-oil tax revenue 143.7; Non tax revenue 10.9; Total 558.0. *Expenditure:* Current expenditure 343.4 (Wages and salaries 118.2, Goods and services 44.6, Transfers 73.0, Exceptional defence spending 92.9, Interest 14.6); Investment expenditure 198.9 (Domestically financed 88.5, Foreign financed 110.4); Total 542.3 (Source: IMF, *Chad: 2008 Article IV Consultation—Staff Report; Staff Supplement; Public Information Notice on the Executive Board Discussion; and Statement by the Executive Director for Chad* (February 2009)).

2007 ('000 million francs CFA): *Revenue:* Oil revenue 563.2; Non-oil tax revenue 188.9; Non tax revenue 12.7; Total 764.9. *Expenditure:* Current expenditure 464.2 (Wages and salaries 153.2, Goods and services 82.2, Transfers 104.2, Exceptional defence spending 111.5, Interest 13.0); Investment expenditure 245.1 (Domestically financed 154.9, Foreign financed 90.2); Total 709.3 (Source: IMF, *Chad: 2008 Article IV Consultation—Staff Report; Staff Supplement; Public Information Notice on the Executive Board Discussion; and Statement by the Executive Director for Chad* (February 2009)).

2008 ('000 million francs CFA): *Revenue:* Oil revenue 776.5; Non-oil tax revenue 200.5; Non-tax revenue 9.1; Total 986.1. *Expenditure:* Current expenditure 578.9 (Wages and salaries 184.7, Goods and services 94.4, Transfers 105.4, Exceptional defence spending 182.9, Interest 11.5); Investment expenditure 295.6 (Domestically financed 220.1, Foreign financed 75.4); Total 874.4 (Source: IMF, *Chad: 2010 Article IV Consultation—Staff Report; Staff Supplements; Public Information Notice on the Executive Board Discussion; and Statement by the Executive Director for Chad* (June 2010)).

2009 ('000 million francs CFA, estimates): *Revenue:* Oil revenue 283.8; Non-oil tax revenue 239.5; Non-tax revenue 16.3; Total 539.6. *Expenditure:* Current expenditure 634.0 (Wages and salaries 200.6, Goods and services 110.4, Transfers 109.2, Exceptional defence spending 193.0, Interest 20.8); Investment expenditure 352.8 (Domestically financed 242.1, Foreign financed 110.7); Total 986.8 (Source: IMF, *Chad: 2010 Article IV Consultation—Staff Report; Staff Supplements; Public Information Notice on the Executive Board Discussion; and Statement by the Executive Director for Chad* (June 2010)).

2010 ('000 million francs CFA, budget figures): *Revenue:* Oil revenue 463.9; Non-oil tax revenue 278.6; Non-tax revenue 14.7; Total 757.1. *Expenditure:* Current expenditure 536.5 (Wages and salaries 210.5, Goods and services 94.6, Transfers 130.6, Exceptional defence spending 82.2, Interest 18.6); Investment expenditure 300.4 (Domestically financed 219.3, Foreign financed 81.1); Total 836.9 (Source: IMF, *Chad: 2010 Article IV Consultation—Staff Report; Staff Supplements; Public Information Notice on the Executive Board Discussion; and Statement by the Executive Director for Chad* (June 2010)).

INTERNATIONAL RESERVES

(US $ million at 31 December)

	2008	2009	2010
Gold*	1.62	—	6.19
IMF special drawing rights	0.09	4.25	4.20
Reserve position in IMF	0.43	0.44	0.43
Foreign exchange	1,344.94	612.01	627.77
Total	1,347.08	616.70	638.59

* Valued at market-related prices.

Source: IMF, *International Financial Statistics*.

MONEY SUPPLY

('000 million francs CFA at 31 December)

	2008	2009	2010
Currency outside banks	287.51	280.10	333.94
Demand deposits at commercial and development banks	152.98	162.67	230.72
Total money (incl. others)	440.63	442.83	564.71

Source: IMF, *International Financial Statistics*.

COST OF LIVING

(Consumer Price Index for African households in N'Djamena; base: 2005 = 100)

	2007	2008	2009
All items	98.3	108.5	119.3

Source: IMF, *International Financial Statistics*.

NATIONAL ACCOUNTS

('000 million francs CFA)

Expenditure on the Gross Domestic Product

	2008	2009	2010
Government final consumption expenditure	279.1	311.1	315.3
Private final consumption expenditure	2,304.9	2,434.6	2,404.0
Gross fixed capital formation	989.6	1,222.4	1,594.1
Change in inventories	14.0	15.0	10.0
Total domestic expenditure	3,587.6	3,983.1	4,323.4
Exports of goods and services	2,019.9	1,418.6	1,945.3
Less Imports of goods and services	1,799.1	2,145.9	2,224.0
GDP in purchasers' values	3,808.3	3,255.9	4,044.7

Gross Domestic Product by Economic Activity

	2008	2009	2010
Agriculture	626.6	648.3	754.7
Mining and quarrying	1,849.5	1,163.3	1,721.2
Electricity, gas and water	15.7	18.8	21.0
Manufacturing	183.3	194.9	210.7
Construction	61.6	66.8	79.7
Wholesale and retail trade, restaurants and hotels	397.3	422.2	461.8
Transport and communications	59.4	61.6	65.8
Public administration and defence	356.7	402.2	434.4
Other services	174.3	186.5	193.8
GDP at factor cost	3,724.3	3,164.4	3,943.2
Indirect taxes	84.0	91.4	101.5
GDP in purchasers' values	3,803.3	3,255.9	4,044.7

Note: Deduction for imputed bank service charge assumed to be distributed at origin.

Source: African Development Bank.

BALANCE OF PAYMENTS
('000 million francs CFA)

	2008	2009*	2010†
Exports of goods f.o.b.	1,894.9	1,279.1	1,565.0
Imports of goods f.o.b.	–884.9	–1,198.9	–1,456.0
Trade balance	1,010.0	80.2	109.1
Services (net)	–912.5	–984.5	–1,043.6
Balance on goods and services	97.5	–904.3	–934.5
Factor income (net)	–744.2	–337.4	–422.6
Balance on goods, services and income	–646.7	–1,241.7	–1,357.1
Private unrequited transfers (net)	47.4	65.9	54.8
Official unrequited transfers (net)	86.1	87.3	58.1
Current balance	–513.2	–1,088.5	–1,244.2
Capital transfers	56.4	80.6	87.3
Foreign direct investment	536.7	559.6	875.5
Other medium- and long-term investments	60.3	96.3	277.4
Short-term capital	–39.1	3.1	0.0
Errors and omissions	–54.2	0.0	0.0
Overall balance	209.5	–348.9	–4.0

* Estimates.
† Projections.

Source: IMF, *Chad: 2010 Article IV Consultation—Staff Report; Staff Supplements; Public Information Notice on the Executive Board Discussion; and Statement by the Executive Director for Chad* (June 2010).

External Trade

PRINCIPAL COMMODITIES

Imports c.i.f. (US $ '000)	1995
Food and live animals	41,182
Cereals and cereal preparations	16,028
Wheat and meslin (unmilled)	8,945
Sugar, sugar preparations and honey	17,078
Refined sugars, etc.	16,825
Beverages and tobacco	7,175
Mineral fuels, lubricants, etc.	38,592
Refined petroleum products	38,551
Motor spirit (gasoline) and other light oils	6,490
Kerosene and other medium oils	8,456
Gas oils	23,318
Chemicals and related products	15,507
Medicinal and pharmaceutical products	7,789
Basic manufactures	26,190
Non-metallic mineral manufactures	7,654
Metal manufactures	8,804
Machinery and transport equipment	51,246
General industrial machinery, equipment and parts	8,175
Road vehicles (incl. air-cushion vehicles) and parts*	17,873
Parts and accessories for cars, lorries, buses, etc.*	8,253
Miscellaneous manufactured articles	27,335
Printed matter	13,565
Postage stamps, banknotes, etc.	11,622
Total (incl. others)	215,171

* Excluding tyres, engines and electrical parts.

Source: UN, *International Trade Statistics Yearbook*.

Exports ('000 million francs CFA)	2000	2001	2002*
Cotton	50.6	56.9	33.2
Livestock	48.8	49.5	52.0
Total (incl. others)	130.2	138.3	118.0

* Estimates.

Source: La Zone Franc, *Rapport Annuel 2002*.

Total imports c.i.f. (million francs CFA): 850,830 in 2008; 1,086,028 in 2009; 1,238,193 in 2010 (Source: IMF, *International Financial Statistics*).

Total exports c.i.f. (million francs CFA): 1,938,997 in 2008; 1,251,294 in 2009; 1,683,942 in 2010 (Source: IMF, *International Financial Statistics*).

PRINCIPAL TRADING PARTNERS

Imports c.i.f. (US $ '000)	1995
Belgium-Luxembourg	4,771
Cameroon	33,911
Central African Repub.	3,010
China, People's Repub.	6,251
France	88,887
Germany	2,988
Italy	6,452
Japan	5,121
Malaysia	2,234
Netherlands	2,843
Nigeria	25,269
Spain	3,402
USA	13,966
Total (incl. others)	215,171

Source: UN, *International Trade Statistics Yearbook*.

2008 (US $ '000): *Exports:* China 41.6; Japan 195.8; Taiwan 102.5; United Kingdom 1.3; United States 34,70.8; Total (incl. others) 4,275 (Source: African Development Bank).

Transport

ROAD TRAFFIC
(motor vehicles in use at 31 December)

	1994	1995*	1996*
Passenger cars	8,720	9,700	10,560
Buses and coaches	708	760	820
Lorries and vans	12,650	13,720	14,550
Tractors	1,413	1,500	1,580
Motorcycles and mopeds	1,855	2,730	3,640

* Estimates.

Source: International Road Federation, *World Road Statistics*.

2006: Passenger cars 18,867; Vans 24,874; Buses 3,278; Tractors 3,132; Motorcycles 63,036 (Source: Ministère de Travaux Publics et de Transport).

CIVIL AVIATION
(traffic on scheduled services*)

	1999	2000	2001
Kilometres flown (million)	3	3	1
Passengers carried ('000)	84	77	46
Passenger-km (million)	235	216	130
Total ton-km (million)	36	32	19

* Including an apportionment of the traffic of Air Afrique.

Source: UN, *Statistical Yearbook*.

Tourism

FOREIGN VISITORS BY NATIONALITY*

	2007	2008	2009
Belgium	326	491	335
Canada	420	42	512
Egypt	20	23	190
France	6,167	6,142	6,564
Germany	290	298	285
Italy	152	421	484
Libya	24	12	827
Saudi Arabia	8	1	—
Switzerland	178	216	36
United Kingdom	781	607	518
USA	2,760	1,699	2,579
Total (incl. others)	24,794	21,871	31,169

* Arrivals at hotels and similar establishments.

Receipts from tourism (US $ million, incl. passenger transport): 14 in 2000; 23 in 2001; 25 in 2002; n.a. in 2003–07.

Source: World Tourism Organization.

Communications Media

	2008	2009	2010
Telephones ('000 main lines in use)	45.0	58.3	51.2
Mobile cellular telephones ('000 subscribers)	1,809.0	2,281.3	2,675.3
Internet subscribers ('000)	n.a.	4.6	n.a.
Broadband subscribers	—	200	200

Television receivers ('000 in use): 10.9 in 2000.

Radio receivers ('000 in use): 1,670 in 1997.

Daily newspapers (national estimates): 2 in 1997 (average circulation 1,550 copies); 2 in 1998 (average circulation 1,560 copies).

Non-daily newspapers: 2 in 1995 (average circulation 10,000 copies); 14 in 1997; 10 in 1998.

Periodicals: 51 in 1997; 53 in 1998.

Personal computers: 16,000 (1.6 per 1,000 persons) in 2005.

Sources: International Telecommunication Union; UNESCO, *Statistical Yearbook*; UNESCO Institute for Statistics; UN, *Statistical Yearbook*.

Education

(2009/10 unless otherwise indicated)

	Institutions	Teachers	Students		
			Males	Females	Total
Pre-primary	24*	605	11,127	10,082	21,209
Primary	2,660†	30,227	973,325	706,336	1,679,661
Secondary	n.a.	14,057	318,002	130,752	448,754
Tertiary	n.a.	2,372‡	18,866	3,264	22,130

* 1994/95 figure; public institutions only.

† 1995/96.

‡ 2008/09.

Source: mainly UNESCO Institute for Statistics.

Pupil-teacher ratio (primary education, UNESCO estimate): 55.6 in 2009/10 (Source: UNESCO Institute for Statistics).

Adult literacy rate (UNESCO estimates): 33.6% (males 44.5%; females 23.1%) in 2009 (Source: UNESCO Institute for Statistics).

Directory

The Government

HEAD OF STATE

President: Gen. IDRISS DEBY ITNO (assumed office 4 December 1990; elected President 3 July 1996; re-elected 20 May 2001, 3 May 2006 and 25 April 2011).

COUNCIL OF MINISTERS

(May 2012)

Prime Minister: EMMANUEL NADINGAR.

Minister of External Relations and African Integration: MOUSSA FAKI MAHAMAT.

Minister of Finance and the Budget: CHRISTIAN GEORGES DIGUIMBAYE.

Minister of Infrastructure and Equipment: ABBAS TOLLI.

Minister of Territorial Administration and Decentralization: BACHAR ALI SOULEYMANE.

Minister of Posts and New Information Technology: JEAN BAWOYEU ALINGUÉ.

Minister of Urban and Rural Water Supply: MAHAMAT ALI ABDALLAH.

Minister of Planning, the Economy and International Co-operation: BEDOUMRA KORDIÉ.

Minister of Justice, Keeper of the Seals: Dr ABDOULAYE SABRE FADOUL.

Minister of Public Health: Dr MAMOUTH NAHOR N'GAWARA.

Minister of Agriculture and Irrigation: Dr DJIMET ADOUM.

Minister of Pastoral Development and Animal Production: AHMAT RAKHIS MANNANI.

Minister of Public Sanitation and the Promotion of Good Governance: (vacant).

Minister of Public Security and Immigration: ABDELKÉRIM AHMADAYE BAKHIT.

Minister of Information and Communication, Government Spokesperson: HASSAN SILLA BAKARI.

Minister of the Environment and Fisheries: MAHAMAT OKORMI.

Minister of Social Action, Families and National Solidarity: FATIMÉ ISSA RAMADAN.

Minister of Higher Education: Dr AHMET DJIDDA MAHAMAT.

Minister of Secondary Education: OUMAR BEN MOUSSA.

Minister of Primary and Civic Education: FAÏTCHOU ETIENNE.

Minister of Professional Training of Arts and Crafts: DAYANG MENWA ENOCH.

Minister of Youth and Sports: HAÏKAL ZAKARIA BEN DJIBRINE.

Minister of Energy and Petroleum: BRAHIM ALKHALI.

Minister of Mines and Geology: NOJITOLBAYE KLADOUMADJI.

Minister of Land Settlement, Town Planning and Housing: ASSANE NGUÉADOUM.

Minister, in charge of Microfinance for the Promotion of Women and Youth: YAKOURA MALLOUM.

Minister of the Civil Service and Labour: MAHAMAT ABBA ALI SALAH.

Minister of Transport and Civil Aviation: ABDELKÉRIM SOULEYMANE TÉRIAO.

Minister of Trade and Industry: MAHAMAT ALLAHOU TAHER.

Minister of Land Affairs and State Property: JEAN BERNARD PADARÉ.

Minister of Small and Medium-sized Enterprises: HASSAN TÉRAP.

Minister of Human and Fundamental Rights: AMINA KODJIYANA.

Minister of Tourism and Handicrafts: ABDELRASSOUL ABOUBAKAR.

Minister of Culture: KHAYAR OUMAR DÉFALLAH.

Minister-delegate at the Presidency of the Republic, responsible for National Defence and War Veterans: BÉNANDO TATOLA.

Minister, Secretary-General of the Government, in charge of Relations with the National Assembly: SAMIR ADAM ANNOUR.

Secretary of State for External Relations and African Integration: TÉDÉBÉ RUTH.

Secretary of State for Territorial Administration and Decentralization: MAHAMAT MBODOU ABDOULAYE.

Secretary of State for Finance and the Budget: ROZZI MAMAÏ.

Secretary of State for Public Health: YOUSSOUF AHMAT.

Deputy Secretary-General of the Government, responsible for Relations with the National Assembly: GAOURANG BARAMA.

MINISTRIES

Office of the President: Palais rose, BP 74, N'Djamena; tel. 22-51-44-37; fax 22-52-45-01; e-mail Contact@presidencedutchad.org; internet www.presidencedutchad.org.

Office of the Prime Minister: BP 463, N'Djamena; tel. 22-52-63-39; fax 22-52-69-77; e-mail cpcprimt@intnet.td; internet www.primature-tchad.org.

Ministry of Agriculture and Irrigation: BP 441, N'Djamena; tel. 22-52-65-66; fax 22-52-51-19; e-mail conacils@intnet.td.

Ministry of the Civil Service and Labour: BP 637, N'Djamena; tel. and fax 22-52-21-98.

Ministry of Culture: BP 519, N'Djamena; tel. 22-52-26-58.

Ministry of Energy and Petroleum: BP 816, N'Djamena; tel. 22-52-56-03; fax 22-52-36-66; e-mail mme@intnet.td; internet www.ministere-petrole.td.

Ministry of the Environment and Fisheries: BP 905, N'Djamena; tel. 22-52-60-12; fax 22-52-38-39; e-mail facdrem@intnet.td.

Ministry of External Relations and African Integration: BP 746, N'Djamena; tel. 22-51-80-50; fax 22-51-45-85; e-mail tchaddiplomatie@gmail.com; internet www.tchad-diplomatie.org.

Ministry of Finance and the Budget: BP 816, N'Djamena; tel. 22-52-68-61; fax 22-52-49-08; e-mail d.dette@intnet.td.

Ministry of Higher Education: BP 743, N'Djamena; tel. 22-51-61-58; fax 22-51-92-31.

Ministry of Human and Fundamental Rights: N'Djamena.

Ministry of Information and Communication: BP 892, N'Djamena; tel. 22-52-40-97; fax 22-52-65-60.

Ministry of Infrastructure and Equipment: N'Djamena; internet infrastructures-tchad.org.

Ministry of Justice: BP 426, N'Djamena; tel. 22-52-21-72; fax 22-52-21-39; e-mail justice@intnet.td.

Ministry of Land Affairs and State Property: N'Djamena.

Ministry of Land Settlement, Town Planning and Housing: BP 436, N'Djamena; tel. 22-52-31-89; fax 22-52-39-35.

Ministry of Microfinance for the Promotion of Women and Youth: N'Djamena.

Ministry of Mines and Geology: BP 816, N'Djamena; tel. 22-51-83-06; fax 22-52-75-60; e-mail cons.mines@intnet.td.

Ministry of National Defence: BP 916, N'Djamena; tel. 22-52-35-13; fax 22-52-65-44.

Ministry of Pastoral Development and Animal Production: BP 750, N'Djamena; tel. 22-52-89-43.

Ministry of Planning, the Economy and International Co-operation: N'Djamena; tel. 22-51-45-87; fax 22-51-51-85; e-mail spee@intnet.td.

Ministry of Posts and New Information Technology: BP 154, N'Djamena; tel. 22-52-15-79; fax 22-52-15-30; e-mail ahmatgamar1@yahoo.fr.

Ministry of Primary and Civic Education: BP 743, N'Djamena; tel. 22-51-92-65; fax 22-51-45-12.

Ministry of Professional Training of Arts and Crafts: N'Djamena.

Ministry of Public Health: BP 440, N'Djamena; tel. 22-51-51-14; fax 22-51-58-00; internet www.sante-tchad.org.

Ministry of Public Sanitation and the Promotion of Good Governance: N'Djamena.

Ministry of Public Security and Immigration: BP 916, N'Djamena; tel. 22-52-05-76.

Ministry of Secondary Education: N'Djamena.

Ministry of Small and Medium-sized Enterprises: N'Djamena.

Ministry of Social Action, Families and National Solidarity: BP 80, N'Djamena; tel. 22-52-25-32; fax 22-52-48-88.

Ministry of Territorial Administration and Decentralization: Niamey.

Ministry of Tourism and Handicrafts: BP 86, N'Djamena; tel. 22-52-44-21; fax 22-52-51-19.

Ministry of Trade and Industry: Palais du Gouvernement, BP 424, N'Djamena; tel. 22-52-21-99; fax 22-52-27-33; e-mail mdjca-dg@intnet.td.

Ministry of Transport and Civil Aviation: N'Djamena.

Ministry of Urban and Rural Water Supply: N'Djamena.

Ministry of Youth and Sports: BP 519, N'Djamena; tel. 22-52-52-90; fax 22-52-55-38.

President and Legislature

PRESIDENT

Election, 24–25 April 2011, provisional results

Candidate	Votes	% of vote
Idriss Deby Itno (MPS)	2,503,813	88.66
Pahimi Padacke Albert (RNDT—le Réveil)	170,182	6.03
Nadji Madou (ASRI)	150,220	5.32
Total	2,824,215	100.00

LEGISLATURE

Assemblée nationale

Palais du 15 janvier, BP 01, N'Djamena; tel. 22-53-00-15; fax 22-31-45-90; internet www.primature-tchad.org/ass.php.

President: NASSOUR GUÉLENDOUKSIA OUAÏDOU.

General Election, 13 February 2011

Party	Seats
Alliance pour la renaissance du Tchad (ART)*	132
Union nationale pour le développement et le renouveau (UNDR)	11
Rassemblement national pour la démocratie au Tchad—le Réveil	8
Union pour le renouveau et la démocratie-Parti pour la liberté et le développement (URD-PLD)	8
Fédération action pour la République-Parti fédération (FAR-PF)	4
Convention tchadienne pour la paix et le développement (CTPD)	2
Parti démocratique et socialiste pour l'alternance (PDSA)	2
Union pour la démocratie et la République (UDR)	2
Others†	15
Total	184‡

* Comprising the Mouvement patriotique du salut, the Rassemblement pour la démocratie et le progrès and VIVA—Rassemblement national pour la démocratie et le progrès.

† A total of 15 other parties all secured one seat each.

‡ Results in the Mayo-Boneye constituency, which was to return four deputies, were not declared by the Commission électorale nationale indépendante.

Election Commission

Commission électorale nationale indépendante (CENI): N'Djamena; internet www.ceni-td.org; f. 2000; 31 mems; Pres. YAYA MAHAMAT LIGUITA.

Political Organizations

Legislation permitting the operation of political associations, subject to official registration, took effect in October 1991. A total of 101 political organizations contested the 2011 legislative elections, of which the following were among the most important:

Action tchadienne pour l'unité et le socialisme (ACTUS): N'Djamena; e-mail actus@club-internet.fr; f. 1981; Marxist-Leninist; Sec.-Gen. Dr DJIMADOUM LEY-NGARDIGAL.

Alliance nationale pour la démocratie et le développement (ANDD): BP 4066, N'Djamena; tel. 22-51-46-72; f. 1992; Leader SALIBOU GARBA.

Alliance socialiste pour un renouveau intégral (ASRI): tel. 66-28-74-10; e-mail info@asritchad.org; internet www.asritchad.org; Pres. NADJI MADOU.

Alliance tchadienne pour la démocratie et le développement (ATD): N'Djamena; e-mail info@atd-tchad.com; Leader ABDERAMAN DJASNABAILLE.

Concord nationale tchadienne (CNT): Leader Col HASSANE SALEH AL GADAM AL JINEDI.

Convention pour la démocratie et le fédéralisme: N'Djamena; f. 2002; socialist; supports the establishment of a federal state; Leader ALI GOLHOR.

Convention tchadienne pour la paix et le développement (CTPD).

Coordination des partis politiques pour la défense de la constitution (CPDC): f. 2004 to oppose President Deby's proposed constitutional modifications; mems include the URD and the UNDR.

Fédération action pour la République-Parti fédération (FAR-PF): BP 4197, N'Djamena; tel. 66-26-89-67 (mobile); fax 22-51-78-60; e-mail yorongar@gmail.com; internet www.yorongar.com; supports the establishment of a federal republic; Leader NGARLEDJY YORONGAR.

Front pour le salut de la République (FSR): f. 2007 to unite opposition groups in attempt to oust President Deby Itno; member of the Mouvement national coalition; Pres. Col AHMAT HASSABALLAH SOUBIANE.

Mouvement patriotique du salut (MPS): Assemblée nationale, Palais du 15 janvier, BP 01, N'Djamena; e-mail administrateur@tchad-gpmps.org; internet www.tchad-gpmps.org; f. 1990 as a coalition of several opposition movements; other opposition groups joined during the Nov. 1990 offensive against the regime of Hissène Habré, and following the movement's accession to power in Dec. 1990; Pres. D'IDRISS NDELE MOUSSA; Sec.-Gen. NEGOUM YAMASSOUM.

Parti démocratique et socialiste pour l'alternance (PDSA).

Parti pour la liberté et le développement (PLD): N'Djamena; f. 1993; boycotted legislative elections in 2002; Sec.-Gen. IBN OUMAR MAHAMAT SALEH.

Rassemblement pour la démocratie et le progrès (RDP): N'Djamena; f. 1992; seeks to create a secure political environment by the establishment of a reformed national army; supported the re-election of Pres. Deby in 2001, but withdrew support from the Govt in Nov. 2003; Leader LOL MAHAMAT CHOUA.

Rassemblement national pour la démocratie au Tchad—le Réveil: Leader PAHIMI PADACKE ALBERT.

Union pour la démocratie et la République (UDR): N'Djamena; f. 1992; supports liberal economic policies and a secular, decentralized republic; boycotted legislative elections in 2002; Leader Dr JEAN BAWOYEU ALINGUÉ.

Union nationale pour le développement et le renouveau (UNDR): N'Djamena; supports greater decentralization and increased limitations on the power of the state; Pres. SALEH KEBZABOH; Sec.-Gen. CÉLESTIN TOPONA.

Union pour le renouveau et la démocratie (URD): BP 92, N'Djamena; tel. 22-51-44-23; fax 22-51-41-87; f. 1992; Leader Gen. WADAL ABDELKADER KAMOUGUÉ.

VIVA—Rassemblement national pour la démocratie et le progrès (VIVA—RNDP): N'Djamena; f. 1992; supports a unitary, democratic republic; Pres. KASSIRÉ DELWA COUMAKOYE.

A number of unregistered dissident groups (some based abroad) are also active. In 2010 these organizations, largely 'politico-military', included the following:

Alliance nationale de la résistance (ANR): f. 1996 as alliance of five movements; in early 2003 comprised eight rebel groups based in eastern Chad; signed peace agreement with Govt in Jan. 2003, although FONALT rejected this accord; Leader MAHAMAT ABBO SILECK.

Armée nationale tchadienne en dissidence (ANTD): f. 1994; Leader Col MAHAMAT GARFA.

Forces des organisations nationales pour l'alternance et les libertés au Tchad (FONALT): rejected cease-fire signed by ANR with Govt in Jan. 2003; Leader Col ABDOULAYE ISSAKA SARWA.

Coordination des mouvements armés et partis politiques de l'opposition (CMAP): internet www.maxpages.com/tchad/cmap2; f. 1999 by 13 'politico-military' orgs; a number of groups subsequently left, several of which later joined the FUDP (q.v.); Leader ANTOINE BANGUI.

Front extérieur pour la rénovation: Leader ANTOINE BANGUI.

Front de libération nationale du Tchad—Conseil provisoire de la révolution (FROLINAT—CPR): f. 1968 in Sudan; based in Algeria; Leader GOUKOUNI OUEDDEI.

Front uni pour le changement démocratique (FUCD): f. 2005; signed a peace agreement with the Govt in Dec. 2006; Leader Capt. MAHAMAT NOUR ABDELKERIM.

Rassemblement pour la démocratie et les libertés (RDL): f. 2005 in Eastern Chad; Leader Capt. MAHAMAT NOUR ABDELKERIM.

Socle pour le changement, l'unité nationale et la démocratie (SCUD): f. 2005 in Eastern Chad; Leaders TOM ERDIMI, YAYA DILLO DJÉROU.

Front uni pour la démocratie et la paix (FUDP): f. 2003 in Benin; seeks by all possible means to establish a new constitution and a transitional govt in advance of free and transparent elections; faction of MDJT (q.v.) led by Adoum Togoi Abbo claims membership, but this is rejected by principal faction of MDJT; Pres. Brig.-Gen. ADOUM TOGOI ABBO.

Conseil national de redressement du Tchad (CNR): e-mail admin@cnrdutchad.com; internet www.cnrdutchad.com; leadership of group forced to leave Benin for Togo in mid-2003; Pres. Col ABBAS KOTY YACOUB.

Convention populaire de résistance (CPR): e-mail cpr60@voila.fr; f. 2001 by fmr mems of CNR (q.v.); Leader ABDEL-AZIZ ABDALLAH KODOK.

Front national du Tchad renové (FNTR): Dabo, France; e-mail yasaid2001@yahoo.fr; internet www.maxpages.com/tchad/fntr; f. 1996; based in Dabo (France); publishes monthly bulletin, *Al-Widha*, in French and Arabic; Hon. Pres. MAHAMAT CHARFADINE; Sec.-Gen. SALAHADINE MAHADI.

Mouvement nationale des rénovateurs tchadiens (MNRT): e-mail fpls@romandie.com; democratic opposition in exile; Sec.-Gen. ALI MUHAMMAD DIALLO.

Rassemblement des forces pour le changement (RFC): internet www.rfctchad.com; f. 2006 as Rassemblement des forces démocratiques; Pres. TIMANE ERDIMI.

Union des forces pour le changement (UFC): f. 2004; advocates suspension of the 1996 Constitution and the composition of a new Charter of the Republic to develop national unity, free, transparent elections and the rule of law; National Co-ordinator ACHEIKH IBN OUMAR.

Conseil démocratique révolutionnaire (CDR): Leader ACHEIKH IBN OUMAR.

Front démocratique populaire (FDP): Leader Dr MAHAMOUT NAHOR.

Front populaire pour la renaissance nationale: Leader ADOUM YACOUB KOUKOU.

Mouvement pour la démocratie et le développement (MDD): e-mail mdd@mdd-tchad.com; internet membres.lycos.fr/mddtchad; comprises two factions, led by ISSA FAKI MAHAMAT and BRAHIM MALLAH.

Mouvement pour la démocratie et la justice au Tchad (MDJT): based in Tibesti, northern Chad; e-mail admin@mdjt.net; internet www.mdjt.net; fmr deputy leader, Brig.-Gen. ADOUM TOGOI ABBO, signed a peace agreement with Govt in Jan. 2002, although this was subsequently rejected by elements close to fmr leader, YOUSSOUF TOGOIMI (who died in Sept. 2002); split into two factions in 2003; the faction led by Togoi claimed membership of the FUDP (q.v.) and signed a peace agreement with the Govt in Dec. 2003, which was rejected by the faction led by Chair. Col HASSAN ABDALLAH MARDIGUÉ; announced a proposed merger with FROLINAT—CPR in December 2006.

Mouvement pour l'unité et la République (MUR): f. 2000 by faction of the MDD (q.v.); Pres. HASSAN DADJOULA.

Union des forces pour la démocratie et le développement (UFDD): f. 2006; Leader Gen. MAHAMAT NOURI.

Union des forces pour la démocratie et le développement—Fondamental (UFDD—F): Leader ABDELWAHID ABOUD MAKAYE.

Diplomatic Representation

EMBASSIES IN CHAD

Algeria: BP 178, rue de Paris, N'Djamena; tel. 22-52-38-15; fax 22-52-37-92; e-mail amb.algerie@intnet.td; Ambassador NADJIB MAHDI.

Cameroon: rue des Poids Lourds, BP 58, N'Djamena; tel. 22-52-28-94; Ambassador BAH OUMAROU SANDA.

Central African Republic: rue 1036, près du Rond-Point de la Garde, BP 115, N'Djamena; tel. 22-52-32-06; Ambassador DAVID NGUINDO.

China, People's Republic: BP 735, N'Djamena; tel. 22-52-29-49; fax 22-53-00-45; internet td.china-embassy.org; Ambassador YANG GUANGYU.

Congo, Democratic Republic: ave du 20 août, BP 910, N'Djamena; tel. 22-52-21-83.

Egypt: Quartier Clemat, ave Georges Pompidou, auprès rond-point de la SONASUT, BP 1094, N'Djamena; tel. 22-51-09-73; fax 22-51-09-72; e-mail am.egypte@intnet.td; Ambassador NABIH ABDELMADJID AL DAÏROUTI.

France: rue du Lt Franjoux, BP 431, N'Djamena; tel. 22-52-25-75; fax 22-52-28-55; e-mail amba.france@intnet.td; internet www.ambafrance-td.org; Ambassador BRUNO FOUCHER.

Holy See: rue de Béguinage, BP 490, N'Djamena; tel. 22-52-31-15; fax 22-52-38-27; e-mail nonceapo@intnet.td; Apostolic Nuncio Most Rev. JUDE THADDEUS OKOLO (Titular Archbishop of Novica).

Korea, Democratic People's Republic: N'Djamena; Ambassador KIM PYONG GI.

Libya: BP 1096, N'Djamena; tel. 22-51-92-89; e-mail alibya1@intnet.td; Ambassador GRÈNE SALEH GRÈNE.

Nigeria: 35 ave Charles de Gaulle, BP 752, N'Djamena; tel. 22-52-24-98; fax 22-52-30-92; e-mail nigndjam@intnet.td; Ambassador M. ARGUNGU.

Russia: 2 rue Adjutant Collin, BP 891, N'Djamena; tel. 22-51-57-19; fax 22-51-31-72; e-mail amrus@intnet.td; Ambassador VLADIMIR N. MARTYNOV.

Saudi Arabia: Quartier Aéroport, rue Jander Miry, BP 974, N'Djamena; tel. 22-52-31-28; fax 22-52-33-28; e-mail najdiat.tchad@intnet.td; Ambassador ADIL DJAMIL ARIF.

Sudan: rue de la Gendarmerie, BP 45, N'Djamena; tel. 22-52-43-59; e-mail amb.soudan@intnet.td; Ambassador ABDALLAH AL-SHEIKH.

USA: ave Félix Eboué, BP 413, N'Djamena; tel. 22-51-70-09; fax 22-51-56-54; e-mail YingraD@state.gov; internet chad.usembassy.gov; Ambassador MARK M. BOULWARE, Jr.

Judicial System

The highest judicial authority is the Supreme Court, which comprises a Judicial Chamber, an Administrative Chamber and an Audit Chamber. There is also a Constitutional Council, with final jurisdiction in matters of state. The legal structure also comprises the Court of Appeal, and magistrate and criminal courts. A High Court of Justice, which is competent to try the President or members of the Government in cases of treason, embezzlement of public funds, and certain other crimes and offences, was inaugurated in June 2003.

Supreme Court: rue 0221, Quartier Résidentiel, 1er arrondissement, BP 5495, N'Djamena; tel. 22-52-01-99; fax 22-52-51-81; e-mail ccsrp@intnet.td; internet www.coursupreme-tchad.org; Pres. ABDELRAHIM BREMÉ HAMID; Pres. of the Judicial Chamber BELKOULAYE BEN COUMAREAUX; Pres. of the Administrative Chamber OUSMAME SALAH IDJEMI; Pres. of the Audit Chamber DOLOTAN NOUDJALBAYE; Prosecutor-Gen. AHMAT AGREY.

Constitutional Council: BP 5500, N'Djamena; tel. 22-52-03-41; e-mail conseil.sg@intnet.td; internet www.primature-tchad.org/cc.php; Pres. HOUDEÏNGAR DAVID NGARIMADEN; Sec.-Gen. DARKEM JOSEPH.

Court of Appeal: N'Djamena; tel. 22-51-24-26; Pres. MAKI ADAM ISSAKA.

High Court of Justice: BP 1407, N'Djamena; tel. 22-52-33-54; fax 22-52-35-35; e-mail dchcj@intnet.td; internet www.primature-tchad.org/hdj.php; f. 2003; comprises 15 deputies of the Assemblée nationale, of whom 10 are titular judges and five supplementaries, who serve in the absence of a titular judge. All 15 are elected for the term of four years by their peers; competent to try the President and members of the Government in cases of treason, embezzlement of public funds, and certain other crimes and offences; Pres. ADOUM GOUDJA.

Religion

It is estimated that some 50% of the population are Muslims and about 30% Christians. Most of the remainder follow animist beliefs.

ISLAM

Conseil Suprème des Affaires Islamiques: POB 1101, N'Djamena; tel. 22-51-81-80; fax 22-52-58-84; Pres. CHEIKH HISSEIN HASSAN ABAKAR.

CHRISTIANITY

The Roman Catholic Church

Chad comprises one archdiocese, six dioceses and one apostolic vicariate. Approximately 9% of the total population are Roman Catholics, most of whom reside in the south of the country and in N'Djamena.

Bishops' Conference

Conférence Episcopale du Tchad, BP 456, N'Djamena; tel. 22-51-74-44; fax 22-52-50-51; e-mail secreta.cet@intnet.td.

f. 1991; Pres. Most Rev. JEAN-CLAUDE BOUCHARD (Bishop of Pala).

Archbishop of N'Djamena: Most Rev. MATTHIAS N'GARTÉRI MAYADI, Archevêché, BP 456, N'Djamena; tel. 22-51-74-44; fax 22-52-50-51; e-mail archnja@intnet.td.

Protestant Churches

Entente des Eglises et Missions Evangéliques au Tchad (EEMET): BP 2006, N'Djamena; tel. 22-51-53-93; fax 22-51-87-20; e-mail eemet@intnet.td; f. 1964; assen of churches and missions working in Chad; includes Assemblées Chrétiennes au Tchad (ACT), Assemblées de Dieu au Tchad (ADT), Eglise Evangélique des Frères au Tchad (EEFT), Eglise Evangélique au Tchad (EET), Eglise Fraternelle Luthérienne au Tchad (EFLT), Eglise Evangélique en Afrique Centrale au Tchad (EEACT), Eglise Evangélique Missionnaire au Tchad (EEMT); also five assoc. mems: Union des Jeunes Chrétiens (UJC), Groupe Biblique des Hôpitaux au Tchad (GBHT), Mission Evangélique contre la Lèpre (MECL), Croix Bleue du Tchad (CBT); Sec.-Gen. MATHIAS N'GARTÉRI MAYADI.

BAHÁ'Í FAITH

National Spiritual Assembly: BP 181, N'Djamena; tel. 22-51-47-05; e-mail ntirandaz@aol.com.

The Press

Al-Watan: N'Djamena; tel. 22-51-57-96; weekly; Editor-in-Chief MOUSSA NDORKOÏ.

Audy Magazine: BP 780, N'Djamena; tel. 22-51-49-59; f. 2000; 2 a month; women's interest; Dir TONGRONGOU AGOUNA GRÂCE.

Bulletin Mensuel de Statistiques du Tchad: BP 453, N'Djamena; monthly.

Carrefour: Centre al-Mouna, BP 456, N'Djamena; tel. 22-51-42-54; e-mail almouna@intnet.td; f. 2000; every 2 months; Dir Sister NADIA KARAKI; circ. 1,000 (2001).

Comnat: BP 731, N'Djamena; tel. 22-51-46-75; fax 22-51-46-71; quarterly; publ. by Commission Nationale Tchadienne for UNESCO.

Grenier: BP 1128, N'Djamena; tel. 22-53-30-14; e-mail cedesep@intnet.td; monthly; economics; finance; Dir KOHOM NGAR-ONE DAVID.

Info-Tchad: BP 670, N'Djamena; tel. 22-51-58-67; news bulletin issued by Agence-Info Tchad; daily; French.

La Lettre: BP 2037, N'Djamena; tel. and fax 22-51-91-09; e-mail ltdh@intnet.td; f. 1993; monthly; publ. by the Ligue Tchadienne des droits de l'Homme; Dir DOBIAN ASSINGAR.

N'Djamena Bi-Hebdo: BP 4498, N'Djamena; tel. 22-51-53-14; fax 22-52-14-98; e-mail ndjh@intnet.td; internet www.ndjh.org; f. 1989; 2 a week; Arabic and French; Dir YALDET BÉGOTO OULATAR; Editor-in-Chief DIEUDONNÉ DJONABAYE; circ. 3,500 (2001).

Notre Temps: BP 4352, N'Djamena; tel. and fax 22-51-46-50; e-mail ntemps.presse@yahoo.fr; f. 2000; weekly; opposed to the Govt of Pres. Deby Itno; Editorial Dir NADJIKIMO BENOUDJITA; circ. 3,000 (2001).

L'Observateur: BP 2031, N'Djamena; tel. and fax 22-51-80-05; e-mail observer.presse@intnet.td; f. 1997; weekly; Dir NGARADOUMBE SAMBORY; circ. 4,000 (2001).

Le Progrès: 1976 ave Charles de Gaulle, BP 3055, N'Djamena; tel. 22-51-55-86; fax 22-51-02-56; e-mail progres@intnet.td; f. 1993; daily; Dir MAHAMAT HISSÈNE; circ. 3,000 (2001).

Revue Juridique Tchadienne: BP 907, N'Djamena; internet www.cefod.org/Droit_au_Tchad/Revuejuridique/Sommaire_rjt.htm; f. 1999; Dir MAHAMAT SALEH BEN BIANG.

Tchad et Culture: BP 907, N'Djamena; tel. 22-51-54-32; fax 22-51-91-50; e-mail cefod@intnet.td; internet www.cefod.org; f. 1961; monthly; Dir RONELNGUÉ TORIAÏRA; Editor-in-Chief NAYGOTIMTI BAMBÉ; circ. 4,500 (2002).

Le Temps: face Ecole Belle-vue, Moursal, BP 1333, N'Djamena; tel. 22-51-70-28; fax 22-51-99-24; e-mail temps.presse@intnet.td; f. 1995; weekly; Publishing Dir MICHAËL N. DIDAMA; circ. 6,000 (2001).

La Voix du Paysan: BP 1671, N'Djamena; tel. 22-51-82-66; monthly; Dir DJALDI TABDI GASSISSOU NASSER.

NEWS AGENCY

Agence Tchadienne de Presse: BP 670, N'Djamena; tel. 22-52-58-67; fax 22-52-37-74; e-mail atp@infotchad.com; internet www.infotchad.com; f. 1966; Dir HASSAN ABDELKERIM BOUYEBRI.

Publishers

Grande Imprimerie du Tchad: route de Farcha, BP 691, N'Djamena; tel. 22-52-51-59.

Imprimerie AGB: ave Ornano, BP 2052, N'Djamena; tel. 22-51-21-67; e-mail agb@intnet.td.

Imprimerie du Tchad (IDT): BP 456, N'Djamena; tel. 22-52-44-40; fax 22-52-28-60; e-mail idt.tchad@intnet.td; Gen. Dir D. E. MAURIN.

Broadcasting and Communications

TELECOMMUNICATIONS

In 2011 there was one fixed-line telephone and three mobile cellular telephone operators in Chad.

Office Tchadien de Regulation des Telecommunications: BP 5808, N'Djamena; tel. 52-15-13; fax 52-15-15; e-mail otrt@intnet.td; internet www.otrt.td; regulatory authority; Dir-Gen. IDRISS SALEH BACHAR.

Société des Télécommunications du Tchad (SOTEL TCHAD): BP 1132, N'Djamena; tel. 22-52-14-36; fax 22-52-14-42; e-mail sotel@intnet.td; internet www.sotel.td; f. 2000 by merger of telecommunications services of fmr Office National des Postes et des Télécommunications and the Société des Télécommunications Internationales du Tchad; Dir-Gen. ADAM ABDERAMANE ANOU.

Salam: N'Djamena; wholly owned subsidiary of SOTEL TCHAD providing mobile cellular telephone services.

Airtel au Tchad: ave Charles de Gaulle, BP 5665, N'Djamena; tel. 22-52-04-18; fax 22-52-04-19; e-mail info.africa@airtel.com; internet africa.airtel.com/chad; f. 2000; acquired by Bharti Airtel (India) in 2010; fmrly Celtel-Tchad, subsequently Zain au Tchad, present name adopted in 2010; provides mobile cellular telecommunications in N'Djamena, Moundou and Abéché, with expansion to further regions proposed; Dir-Gen. MBAYE SYLLA KHOUMA.

Millicom Tchad: N'Djamena; internet www.millicom.com; f. 2005; 87% owned by Millicom International Cellular (Luxembourg/Sweden); operates mobile cellular telecommunications network in N'Djamena (with expansion to other cities proposed) under the brand name 'Tigo'.

BROADCASTING

Regulatory Authorities

High Council of Communication (HCC): BP 1316, N'Djamena; tel. 22-52-36-00; fax 22-52-31-51; e-mail hcc@intnet.td; f. 1994; responsible for registration and regulation of radio and television stations, in addition to the printed press; funds independent radio stations; Sec.-Gen. ADOUM GUEMESSOU.

Office National de la Radiodiffusion et de la Télévision du Tchad (ONRTV): ave Mobotu, N'Djamena; tel. 22-52-15-13; fax 22-52-15-17; internet www.onrtv.org; DOUBAÏ KLEPTOUIN.

Radio

Private radio stations have been permitted to operate in Chad since 1994, although private broadcasts did not begin until 1997. By mid-2002 15 private and community stations had received licences, of which nine had commenced broadcasts. There was, additionally, a state-owned broadcaster, with four regional stations.

Radio Nationale Tchadienne (RNT): BP 4589, N'Djamena; tel. and fax 22-51-60-71; f. 1955; state-controlled; programmes in French, Arabic and 11 vernacular languages; four regional stations; Dir HASSAN SYLLA BAKARI.

Radio Abéché: BP 36, Abéché, Ouaddaï; tel. 269-81-49.

Radio Faya-Largeau: Faya-Largeau, Borkou.

Radio Moundou: BP 122, Moundou, Logone Occidental; tel. 269-13-22; programmes in French, Sara and Arabic; Dir DIMANANGAR DJAÏNTA.

Radio Sarh: BP 270, Sarh, Bahr Kôh; tel. 268-13-61; programmes in French, Sara and Arabic; Dir BIANA FOUDA NACTOUANDI.

Union des radios privées du Tchad (URPT): N'Djamena; f. 2002 as a federation of nine private and community radio stations; Pres. ZARA YACOUB; Sec.-Gen. DJEKOURNINGA KAOUTAR LAZAR; includes the following:

DJA FM: BP 1312, N'Djamena; tel. 22-51-64-90; fax 22-52-14-52; e-mail myzara@intnet.td; f. 1999; music, cultural and informative programmes in French, Arabic and Sara; Dir ZARA YACOUB.

Radio Brakoss (Radio de l'Agriculture): Moïssala, Mandoul; f. 1996; community radio station; operations suspended by the Govt in Feb. 2004, broadcasts resumed June 2004.

Radio Duji Lohar: BP 155, Moundou, Logone Occidental; tel. 22-69-17-14; fax 22-69-12-11; e-mail cdave@intnet.td; f. 2001.

Radio FM Liberté: BP 892, N'Djamena; tel. 22-51-42-53; f. 2000; financed by nine civil society orgs; broadcasts in French, Arabic and Sara; Dir DJEKOURNINGA KAOUTAR LAZAR.

Radio Lotiko: Diocese de Sarh, BP 87, Sarh; tel. 22-68-12-46; fax 22-68-14-79; e-mail lotiko@intnet.td; internet www.lotiko.org; f. 2001; community radio station; Dir ABBÉ FIDÈLE ALLAHADOUMBAYE.

La Voix du Paysan: BP 22, Doba, Logone Oriental; f. 1996; Roman Catholic; Dir DJALDI TABDI GASSISSOU NASSER.

Television

Télévision nationale tchadienne (Télé Tchad): BP 274, N'Djamena; tel. 22-52-26-79; fax 22-52-29-23; state-controlled; broadcasts c. 38 hours per week in French and Arabic; Dir HALIMÉ ASSADYA ALI.

Broadcasts from Africa 24, Canal France International, France 24, TV5, CNN and seven Arabic television stations are also received in Chad.

Finance

(cap. = capital; res = reserves; dep. = deposits; m. = million; br(s). = branch(es); amounts in francs CFA)

BANKING

In 2009 there were nine commercial banks in Chad.

Central Bank

Banque des Etats de l'Afrique Centrale (BEAC): ave Charles de Gaulle, BP 50, N'Djamena; tel. 22-52-21-65; fax 22-52-44-87; e-mail beacndj@beac.int; internet www.beac.int; HQ in Yaoundé, Cameroon; f. 1973; bank of issue for mem. states of the Communauté économique et monétaire de l'Afrique centrale (CEMAC, fmrly Union douanière et économique de l'Afrique centrale), comprising Cameroon, the Central African Repub., Chad, the Repub. of the Congo, Equatorial Guinea and Gabon; cap. 88,000m., res 227,843m., dep. 4,110,966m. (Dec. 2007); Gov. LUCAS ABAGA NCHAMA; Dir in Chad CHRISTIAN NGARDOUM MORNONDE; brs at Moundou and Sarh.

Other Banks

Banque Agricole et Commerciale (BAC): ave el-Niméry, BP 1727, N'Djamena; tel. 22-51-90-41; fax 22-51-90-40; e-mail bast@intnet.td; f. 1997; cap. 1,200m. (2002), total assets 1,845m. (Dec. 1999); Pres. MOUHAMED OUSMAN AWAD; Dir-Gen. ABDELKADER OUSMAN HASSAN; 1 br.

Banque Commerciale du Chari (BCC): ave Charles de Gaulle, BP 757, N'Djamena; tel. 22-51-89-58; fax 22-51-62-49; e-mail bcc@intnet.td; f. 1981 as Banque Tchad-Arabe libyenne; present name adopted 1995; 50% state-owned, 50% owned by Libya Arab Foreign Bank (Libya); cap. and res 3,567m., total assets 20,931m. (Dec. 2001); Pres. BIDJERE BINDJAKI; Dir-Gen. HAMED EL MISTIRI.

Banque Sahélo-Saharienne pour l'Investissement et le Commerce (BSIC): ave Charles de Gaulle, BP 81, N'Djamena; tel. 22-52-26-92; fax 22-62-26-93; e-mail bsic@bsic-tchad.com; internet www.bsic-tchad.com; f. 2004; Pres. and Dir-Gen. ALHADJI MOHAMED ALWARFALLI.

Commercial Bank Tchad (CBT): rue du Capitaine Ohrel, BP 19, N'Djamena; tel. 22-52-28-29; fax 22-52-33-18; e-mail cbtbank@cbc-bank.com; internet www.cbc-bank.com; f. 1962; 50.7% owned by Groupe FOTSO (Cameroon), 17.5% state-owned; fmrly Banque de Développement du Tchad; cap. 4,020m., res 2,465m., dep. 38,624m. (Dec. 2005); Pres. YOUSSOUF ABBASALAH; Dir-Gen. GEORGES DJADJO; 1 br.

Orabank Tchad: ave Charles de Gaulle, BP 804, N'Djamena; tel. 22-52-26-60; fax 22-52-29-05; e-mail infitd@financial-bank.com; internet www.financial-bank.com; f. 1992; fmrly Financial Bank Tchad, name changed as above in 2012; 100% owned by Oragroup SA (Togo); cap. 4,350.0m., res 111.6m., dep. 40,191.0m. (Dec. 2009); Pres. PATRICK MESTRALLET; Dir-Gen. LOUKOUMANOU WAIDI.

Société Générale Tchadienne de Banque (SGTB): 2–6 rue Robert Lévy, BP 461, N'Djamena; tel. 22-52-28-01; fax 22-52-37-13; e-mail sgtb@intnet.td; internet www.sgtb.td; f. 1963; 30% owned by Société Générale (France), 15% by Société Générale de Banque au Cameroun; cap. and res 3,603m., total assets 36,579m. (Dec. 2003); Pres. and Dir-Gen. CHEMI KOGRIMI; 3 brs.

Bankers' Organizations

Association Professionnelle des Banques au Tchad: 2–6 rue Robert Lévy, BP 461, N'Djamena; tel. 22-52-41-90; fax 22-52-17-13; Pres. CHEMI KOGRIMI.

Conseil National de Crédit: N'Djamena; f. 1965 to formulate a national credit policy and to organize the banking profession.

INSURANCE

Assureurs Conseils Tchadiens Cecar et Jutheau: rue du Havre, BP 139, N'Djamena; tel. 22-52-21-15; fax 22-52-35-39; e-mail biliou.alikeke@intnet.td; f. 1966; Dir BILIOU ALIKEKE.

Gras Savoye Tchad: rue du Général Thillo, BP 5620, N'Djamena; tel. 22-52-00-72; fax 22-52-00-71; e-mail gras.savoye@intnet.td; affiliated to Gras Savoye (France); Man. DOMKRÉO DJAMON.

Société Mutuelle d'Assurances des Cadres des Professions Libérales et des Indépendants (SMAC): BP 644, N'Djamena; tel. 22-51-70-19; fax 22-51-70-61.

Société Tchadienne d'Assurances et de Réassurances (La STAR Nationale): ave Charles de Gaulle, BP 914, N'Djamena; tel. 22-52-56-77; fax 22-52-51-89; e-mail star@intnet.td; internet www.lastarnationale.com; f. 1977; privatized in 1996; brs in N'Djamena, Moundou and Abéché; cap. 500m.; Dir-Gen. RAKHIS MANNANY.

Trade and Industry

DEVELOPMENT ORGANIZATIONS

Agence Française de Développement (AFD): route de Farcha, BP 478, N'Djamena; tel. 22-52-70-71; fax 22-52-78-31; e-mail afdndjamena@groupe-afd.org; internet www.afd.fr; Country Dir JEAN-MARC PRADELLE.

Association Tchadienne pour le Développement: BP 470, Quartier Sabangali, N'Djamena; tel. 22-51-43-69; fax 22-51-89-23; e-mail darna.dnla@intnet.td; Dir DIGALI ZEUHINBA.

France Volontaires: BP 448, N'Djamena; tel. 22-52-20-53; fax 22-52-26-56; e-mail afvptchd@intnet.td; internet www

.france-volontaires.org; f. 1965; name changed as above in 2009; Nat. Delegate Ismaïla Diagne.

Office National de Développement Rural (ONDR): BP 896, N'Djamena; tel. 22-52-23-20; fax 22-52-29-60; e-mail psapdn@intnet .td; f. 1968; Dir Hassan Guihini Dadi.

Service de Coopération et d'Action Culturelle: BP 898, N'Djamena; tel. 22-52-42-87; fax 22-52-44-38; administers bilateral aid from France; Dir Pierre Cathala.

Société de Développement du Lac (SODELAC): BP 782, N'Djamena; tel. 22-52-35-03; f. 1967 to develop the area of Lake Chad; cap. 179m. francs CFA; Pres. Hassanty Oumar Chaib; Dir-Gen. Abbo Youssouf.

CHAMBER OF COMMERCE

Chambre de Commerce, d'Industrie, d'Agriculture, des Mines et d'Artisanat: 13 rue du Col Moll, BP 458, N'Djamena; tel. 22-52-52-64; fax 22-52-52-63; e-mail cciama_tchad@yahoo.fr; f. 1935; brs at Sarh, Moundou, Bol and Abéché; Pres. Dr Souradj Koulamallah; Dir-Gen. Bekoutou Taigam.

TRADE ASSOCIATIONS

Office National des Céréales (ONC): BP 21, N'Djamena; tel. 22-52-37-31; fax 22-52-20-18; e-mail onc1@intnet.td; f. 1978; production and marketing of cereals; Dir-Gen. Mahamat Ali Hassaballah; 11 regional offices.

Société Nationale de Commercialisation du Tchad (SONACOT): BP 630, N'Djamena; tel. 22-51-30-47; f. 1965; cap. 150m. francs CFA; 76% state-owned; nat. marketing, distribution and import-export co; Man. Dir Marbrouck Natroud.

EMPLOYERS' ORGANIZATIONS

Conseil National du Patronat Tchadien (CNPT): rue Bazelaire, angle ave Charles de Gaulle, BP 134, N'Djamena; tel. and fax 22-52-25-71; e-mail dgastat.tchad@intnet.td; Pres. Mahamat Adoum Ismael; Sec.-Gen. Marc Madengar Beremadji; 67 mem. enterprises with total work-force of 8,000 (2002).

Union des Transporteurs Tchadiens: N'Djamena; tel. 22-51-45-27.

UTILITIES

Société Nationale d'Électricité (SNE): 11 rue du Col Largeau, BP 44, N'Djamena; tel. 22-51-28-81; fax 22-51-21-34; f. 1968; state-owned; created following the dissolution of the Société Tchadienne d'Eau et d'Electricité (STEE); production and distribution of electricity; Dir-Gen. Mahamat Sénoussi Chérif.

Société Tchadienne des Eaux (STE): N'Djamena; f. 2010; Dir-Gen. Félicien Ngasna Maïngar.

TRADE UNIONS

Confédération Libre des Travailleurs du Tchad (CLTT): ave Charles de Gaulle, BP 553, N'Djamena; tel. 22-51-76-11; fax 22-52-44-56; e-mail confederationlibre@yahoo.fr; Pres. Brahim Ben Said; 22,500 mems (2001).

Union des Syndicats du Tchad (UST): BP 1143, N'Djamena; tel. 22-51-42-75; fax 22-52-14-52; e-mail ustchad@yahoo.fr; f. 1988; federation of trade unions; Pres. Michel Barka; Sec.-Gen. François Djondang.

Transport

RAILWAYS

There are no railways in Chad. In 1962 the Governments of Chad and Cameroon signed an agreement to extend the Transcameroon railway from Ngaoundere to Sarh, a distance of 500 km. Although the Transcameroon reached Ngaoundere in 1974, its proposed extension into Chad remains indefinitely postponed. In late 2011 construction was expected to commence of a 800-km railway from N'Djamena to Nyala in western Sudan, from where the existing line runs via Sudan's capital Khartoum to Port Sudan on the Red Sea. The project was to cost US $2,000m. and was partially funded by the Export Import Bank of China.

ROADS

The total length of the road network in 2006 was an estimated 40,000 km. There are also some 20,000 km of tracks suitable for motor traffic during the October–July dry season. The European Union is contributing to the construction of a highway connecting N'Djamena with Sarh and Léré, on the Cameroon border, and of a 400-km highway linking Moundou and Ngaoundere.

Coopérative des Transportateurs Tchadiens (CTT): BP 336, N'Djamena; tel. 22-51-43-55; road haulage; Pres. Saleh Khalifa; brs at Sarh, Moundou, Bangui (CAR), Douala and Ngaoundéré (Cameroon).

Fonds d'Entretien Routier: N'Djamena; internet fer-tchad.org; f. 2000; Dir Ahmed Djamalladine.

Société Générale d'Entreprise Routière (SGER): BP 175, N'Djamena; tel. and fax 22-51-55-12; e-mail itralu@intnet.td; devt and maintenance of roads; 95% owned by Arcory International (Sudan); Pres. Patrick Morin.

Société Tchadienne d'Affrètement et de Transit (STAT): 21 ave Félix Eboué, BP 100, N'Djamena; tel. 22-51-88-72; fax 22-51-74-24; e-mail stat.tchad@intnet.td; affiliated to Groupe Saga (France); road haulage.

INLAND WATERWAYS

The Chari and Logone rivers, which converge to the south of N'Djamena, are navigable. These waterways connect Sarh with N'Djamena on the Chari and Bongor and Moundou with N'Djamena on the Logone.

CIVIL AVIATION

The international airport is at N'Djamena. There are also more than 40 smaller airfields.

Autorité de l'Aviation Civile (ADAC): BP 96, N'Djamena; tel. 22-52-54-14; fax 22-52-29-09; Dir-Gen. Guelpina Ceubah.

Air Affaires Tchad: BP 256, N'Djamena; tel. 22-51-60-37; fax 22-51-06-20; e-mail airaffaires@yahoo.st; passenger and freight internal and charter flights.

Minair Tchad: ave Charles de Gaulle, BP 1239, N'Djamena; tel. 22-52-52-45; fax 22-51-07-80; e-mail abdel.ousman@intnet.td; passenger and freight air transport.

Toumaï Air Tchad (TAT): 66 ave Charles de Gaulle, 0036 rue 1020, Beck Ceccaldi, face à la Financial Bank, N'Djamena; tel. 22-52-41-07; fax 22-52-41-06; e-mail tatndj@toumaiair.com; internet www .toumaiair.com; f. 2004; scheduled passenger and cargo flights on domestic routes, and between N'Djamena and destinations in central and West Africa; Pres. and Dir-Gen. Zacharia Deby Itno.

Tourism

Chad's potential attractions for tourists include a variety of scenery from the dense forests of the south to the deserts of the north. Receipts from tourism in 2002 were estimated at US $25m. A total of 31,169 tourists visited Chad in 2009.

Direction de la promotion touristique: BP 86, N'Djamena; tel. 22-52-44-16; fax 22-52-44-19; e-mail mdtouris@intnet.td; Dir Kolmadji Blaise.

Defence

As assessed at November 2011, the Armée nationale tchadienne (ANT) was estimated to number 25,350 (army approximately 20,000, air force 350, Republican Guard 5,000). In addition, there was a 9,500-strong gendarmerie. The army has been undergoing restructuring since 1996. Military service is by conscription. Under defence agreements with France, the army receives technical and other aid: in November 2010 there were 634 French troops deployed in Chad.

Defence Expenditure: Budgeted at 63,700m. francs CFA for 2010.

Chief of Staff of the Armed Forces: Gen. Hassane Saleh al-Gadam al-Jinedi.

Chief of the Land Forces: Brig.-Gen. Massoud Dressa.

Chief of Naval Staff: Lt Mornadji Mbaissanebe.

Chief of Air Force: Brig.-Gen. Nadjita Béassoumal.

Education

Education is officially compulsory for ten years between six and 16 years of age and is provided free of charge in public institutions. Primary education begins at the age of six and lasts for six years. Secondary education, from the age of 12, lasts for seven years, comprising a first cycle of four years and a second of three years. In 2009/10 enrolment in primary education was equivalent to 90% of students in the relevant age-group, while secondary enrolment in 2009/10 was equivalent to only 26% of children in the appropriate age-group (males 36%; females 15%). The Université de N'Djamena was opened in 1971. In addition, there are several technical colleges. Some 22,130 students were enrolled at higher education institutions in 2009/10. In 2005 spending on education represented 10.1% of total budgetary expenditure.

CHILE

Introductory Survey

LOCATION, CLIMATE, LANGUAGE, RELIGION, FLAG, CAPITAL

The Republic of Chile is a long, narrow country lying along the Pacific coast of South America, extending from Peru and Bolivia in the north to Cape Horn in the far south. Isla de Pascua (Rapa Nui or Easter Island), about 3,780 km (2,350 miles) off shore, and several other small islands form part of Chile. To the east, Chile is separated from Argentina by the high Andes mountains. Both the mountains and the cold Humboldt Current influence the climate; between Arica in the north and Punta Arenas in the extreme south, a distance of about 4,000 km (2,500 miles), the average maximum temperature varies by no more than 13°C. Rainfall varies widely between the arid desert in the north and the rainy south. The language is Spanish. There is no state religion but the great majority of the inhabitants profess Christianity, and some 70% are adherents of the Roman Catholic Church. The national flag (proportions 2 by 3) is divided horizontally: the lower half is red, while the upper half has a five-pointed white star on a blue square, at the hoist, with the remainder white. The capital is Santiago.

CONTEMPORARY POLITICAL HISTORY

Historical Context

Chile was ruled by Spain from the 16th century until its independence in 1818. For most of the 19th century it was governed by a small oligarchy of landowners. Chile won the War of the Pacific (1879–83) against Peru and Bolivia. The greater part of the 20th century was characterized by the struggle for power between right- and left-wing forces.

Domestic Political Affairs

In September 1970 Dr Salvador Allende Gossens, the Marxist candidate of the left-wing Unidad Popular coalition, was elected to succeed Eduardo Frei Montalva. Allende promised to transform Chilean society by constitutional means, and imposed an extensive programme of nationalization. The Government failed to obtain a congressional majority in the elections of March 1973 and encountered a deteriorating economic situation as well as an intensification of violent opposition to its policies. Accelerated inflation led to food shortages and there were repeated clashes between pro- and anti-Government activists. The armed forces finally intervened in September 1973. President Allende died during the coup. The Congreso (Congress) was subsequently dissolved, all political activity banned and strict censorship introduced. The military junta dedicated itself to the eradication of Marxism and the 'reconstruction' of Chile, and its leader, Gen. Augusto Pinochet Ugarte, became Supreme Chief of State in June 1974 and President in December. The junta was widely criticized abroad for its repressive policies and violations of human rights. Critics of the regime were tortured and imprisoned, and several thousand were abducted or 'disappeared'. Some of those who had been imprisoned were released, as a result of international pressure, and sent into exile.

The Pinochet regime

In September 1976 three constitutional acts were promulgated with the aim of creating an 'authoritarian democracy'. All political parties were banned in March 1977, when the state of siege was extended. Following a UN General Assembly resolution, adopted in December, which condemned the Government for violating human rights, a referendum was held in January 1978 to seek endorsement of the regime's policies. Since more than 75% of the voters supported the President in his defence of Chile 'in the face of international aggression', the state of siege (in force since 1973) was ended and was replaced by a state of emergency.

At a plebiscite held in September 1980 some 67% of voters endorsed a new Constitution, drafted by the Government, although dubious electoral practices were allegedly employed. Although the new Constitution was described as providing a 'transition to democracy' and President Pinochet ceased to be head of the armed forces, additional clauses allowed him to maintain his firm hold on power until 1989. The new Constitution became effective from March 1981.

In February 1984 the Council of State, a government-appointed consultative body, began drafting a law to legalize political parties and to prepare for elections in 1989. Despite the Government's strenuous attempts to eradicate internal opposition through the introduction of anti-terrorist legislation and extensive security measures, a campaign of explosions and public protests continued throughout 1984 and 1985. A number of protesters were killed in violent clashes with security forces, and many opposition leaders and trade unionists were detained and sent into internal exile.

Throughout 1986 President Pinochet's regime came under increasing attack from the Roman Catholic Church, guerrilla organizations (principally the Frente Patriótico Manuel Rodríguez—FPMR) and international critics, including the US Administration, which had previously refrained from condemning the regime's human rights record. In September the FPMR made an unsuccessful attempt to assassinate Pinochet, precipitating the imposition of a state of siege throughout Chile, under which leading members of the opposition were detained and strict censorship was introduced. Right-wing 'death squads' reappeared, which were implicated in a series of murders following the assassination attempt.

President Pinochet clearly indicated his intention to remain in office beyond 1989 by securing, in mid-1987, the sole presidential candidacy, should it be approved by the same plebiscite that would decide the future electoral timetable. The referendum, to be held on 5 October 1988, asked if the sole candidate nominated by the Pinochet regime should be confirmed as President. If the Government lost the referendum, it would be obliged to hold open elections within one year. Opposition groups established the 'Comando por el No' campaign to co-ordinate the anti-Government vote. The official result recorded 55% of the votes cast for the anti-Pinochet campaign, and 43% for the President. Following the plebiscite, the opposition made repeated demands for changes to the Constitution, in order to accelerate the democratic process. However, Pinochet rejected the opposition's proposals, and affirmed his intention to remain in office until March 1990.

The restoration of democracy

In mid-1989 Patricio Aylwin Azócar emerged as the sole presidential candidate for the centre-left Concertación de Partidos por la Democracia (CPD, formerly the Comando por el No). Throughout 1989 the election campaign was dominated by demands from both the CPD and right-wing parties for constitutional reform. A document detailing 54 amendments ratified by the junta was finally accepted by the opposition, with some reservations, and the constitutional reforms were approved by voters in a national referendum in July. President Pinochet dismissed the possibility of his candidacy as unconstitutional, but reiterated his intention to continue as Commander-in-Chief of the Army for at least four years.

The presidential and congressional elections were conducted on 14 December 1989. In the presidential ballot, Aylwin won a clear victory over the government-supported candidate, Hernán Büchi Buc. The transfer of power took place on 11 March 1990. Two members of the outgoing junta remained as commanders of the air force and police. Without the support of the two-thirds' majority in the Congreso necessary to amend the 1981 Constitution significantly, Aylwin's new CPD administration was forced to reconcile attempts to fulfil campaign promises as quickly as possible with the need to adopt a conciliatory approach towards more right-wing parties in the Congreso.

In April 1990 the Government created a national truth and reconciliation commission, the Comisión Nacional de Verdad y Reconciliación (CNVR), to document and investigate alleged violations of human rights during the previous administration. Although Pinochet had provided for the impunity of the former military junta, it was suggested by human rights organizations that such safeguards might be circumvented by indicting known perpetrators of atrocities on charges of 'crimes against humanity', a provision that gained considerable public support following the discovery, during 1990, of a number of mass graves. The army High Command condemned the Commission for undermining the prestige of the armed forces and attempting to contravene the terms of a comprehensive amnesty declared in 1978. Although a new accord between military leaders and the Government-elect had been negotiated in January 1990, relations between the new Government and the army High Command remained tense. Pinochet became the focus for widespread disaffection with the military élite, but resisted demands for his resignation.

Escalating public and political antagonism towards the former military leadership was fuelled throughout 1990 and 1991 by further revelations of abuses of human rights and financial corruption, and erupted into widespread popular outrage following the publication, in March 1991, of the findings of the CNVR. The report documented the deaths of 2,279 alleged political opponents of the former regime who were executed, died as a result of torture or disappeared in 1973–90. (By 2011 the official death toll had been increased to over 3,000.) Those responsible were identified only by the institutions to which they belonged. However, Aylwin pledged full government co-operation for families wishing to pursue private prosecutions. The report concluded that the military Government had embarked upon a 'systematic policy of extermination' of its opponents through the illegal activities of the covert military intelligence agency, Dirección de Inteligencia Nacional (DINA). It was also highly critical of the judiciary for failing to protect the rights of individuals by refusing thousands of petitions for habeas corpus. Pinochet denounced the document and declared his opposition to government plans to make material reparation to the families of the disappeared.

In 1993 former DINA officials Gen. Manuel Contreras and Col Pedro Espinoza were convicted of the murder of Orlando Letelier, a former cabinet minister, who was assassinated in 1976 in Washington, DC, USA. In 2003 Contreras was sentenced to 15 years' imprisonment for the kidnapping of Miguel Sandoval, a left-wing activist who had disappeared in 1975; the sentence was reduced to six years in 2004, and Contreras was released from prison. However, in 2005 Contreras was sentenced to three years' imprisonment for involvement in the 'disappearance' in 1976 of schoolteacher Julia del Rosario Retamal Sepúlveda. In 2008 Contreras was given two consecutive life sentences for organizing the murders of army chief Carlos Prats and his wife in Argentina in 1974, although this was reduced to 17 years' imprisonment by the Supreme Court in July 2010.

The presidential election of December 1993 was won by the CPD candidate Eduardo Frei Ruiz-Tagle, ahead of Arturo Alessandri Besa, the candidate of the right-wing coalition, the Unión por el Progreso de Chile (UPC). However, the ruling coalition failed to make significant gains at concurrently conducted congressional elections. In August 1994 Frei presented several constitutional reform proposals to the Congreso, including the abolition of appointed senators and the introduction of an electoral system based on proportional representation. However, Frei encountered continuing opposition to constitutional reform (particularly from the right and the upper house).

In November 1995 the Government secured the support of the opposition Renovación Nacional (RN) for revised proposals for new legislation relating to human rights and constitutional reform. However, the compromised nature of the agreement provoked considerable disaffection within the RN, and within the opposition UPC alliance in general, which was effectively dissolved following internal disagreements. During 1997 government efforts to abolish the designated seats in the Senado (Senate) intensified in response to Pinochet's stated intention to assume one of the seats assigned to former Presidents on his retirement as Commander-in-Chief in March 1998. In July 1997 the Senado rejected the Government's latest petition for reform to the system of appointments. In October it was announced that Maj.-Gen. Ricardo Izurieta, previously chief of defence staff, was to succeed Pinochet as Commander-in-Chief. The announcement was made amid a number of changes in the military High Command, which appeared to confirm earlier predictions that military influence was henceforth to be concentrated in the Senado, where it would bolster the political right wing.

Legislative elections to renew all 120 seats in the Cámara de Diputados (Chamber of Deputies) and 20 of the elective seats in the Senado were conducted in December 1997. The governing CPD retained a comfortable majority in the lower house. The elections revealed a shifting balance of power within the two major political groupings, and prompted renewed criticism of the country's binomial system of voting.

Legal proceedings against Pinochet

In January 1998, in response to attempts to begin judicial proceedings against him on charges related to gross abuses of human rights, Pinochet responded by announcing that he would continue as Commander-in-Chief until 10 March, the day before he was scheduled to assume his ex officio seat in the Senado, thereby preserving the immunity from prosecution provided by the position for as long as possible. On 6 March the military High Command announced that Pinochet had been named an honorary commander-in-chief—a position with no historical precedent.

In October 1998 Pinochet was arrested during a visit to London, United Kingdom, in response to a preliminary request that he should be extradited to Spain to answer charges of 'genocide and terrorism'. The British House of Lords' hearing of the extradition appeal in November overturned an earlier ruling that Pinochet was entitled to 'sovereign immunity' as a former head of state, and in December formal extradition proceedings commenced. Further legal inquiry, however, found that only charges relating to events subsequent to December 1988 (at which time the 1984 UN Convention against Torture and Other Cruel, Inhuman or Degrading Treatment or Punishment had entered into British law) should be considered relevant, thus reducing the number of draft charges brought by Spain from 33 to three. Formal extradition proceedings were initiated in September 1999, and in October a court found that Pinochet, who remained under effective house arrest, could be lawfully extradited to Spain. However, in March 2000, after an independent doctors' report had concluded that he was physically unfit to undergo further legal proceedings, Pinochet was released, and returned to Chile.

Meanwhile, domestic attention in 1999 was once again focused on the actions of the security forces during Pinochet's regime. In June the arrest of five retired army officers (former commanders of a notorious élite army unit popularly referred to as the 'caravan of death') was ordered by an appeal court judge following renewed investigation into the disappearance of 72 political prisoners in the immediate aftermath of the 1973 coup. The decision to prosecute the five men on charges of aggravated kidnapping was considered a breakthrough in Chilean judicial practice, as the absence of physical or documented evidence of the deaths of the prisoners meant that the crimes were technically in continuance, and thus the accused men were not protected by the 1978 amnesty that guaranteed the impunity of military personnel. In July 1999 the legality of the arrests was confirmed by the Supreme Court and in September the Court ruled in favour of criminal proceedings being brought against two retired generals, Humberto Gordon Rubio and Roberto Schmied, for their alleged involvement in the murder of trade union leader Tucapel Jiménez in 1982. (In August 2002 12 former military officers, including four generals, were sentenced to terms of imprisonment for their involvement in the murder of Jiménez.) In the following month an arrest warrant was issued against Gen. (retd) Hugo Salas Wenzel, a former director of DINA, on charges of complicity in the killings in 1987 of 12 alleged members of a left-wing guerrilla group. (Salas was convicted of involvement in the killings and sentenced to life imprisonment in January 2005.) In June 2000 the Mesa de Diálogo, a roundtable discussion between human rights lawyers and the military, agreed to guarantee the anonymity of any military person offering information on the whereabouts of any 'disappeared' person.

In June 2000 the Santiago Appeal Court ruled to lift Pinochet's political immunity, and in August, in an historic judgment, the Supreme Court confirmed the decision. The judgment was made possible by changes to Chile's judiciary, several members of which had retired and had been replaced by more independent-minded judges. Foremost among these was Juan Guzmán Tapia, who vigorously took up the legal case against Pinochet and others accused of human rights' infringements. Over 200 lawsuits were filed against the former dictator. In October an Argentine judge requested the extradition of Pinochet to stand trial for the 1974 killing in Buenos Aires of former Chilean army chief Carlos Prats and his wife. In November the Supreme Court ruled that Pinochet must not leave the country, and in December Judge Guzmán indicted the former dictator on charges of aggravated kidnapping and murder in the 'caravan of death' case. In January 2001 Pinochet finally consented to a medical examination to determine whether he was mentally fit to stand trial (compulsory in Chile for all citizens over the age of 70), and was subsequently questioned by Judge Guzmán, who subsequently issued an order for the former General's arrest on charges of kidnap and murder. However, following an appeal by Pinochet, in March the Santiago Appeals Court ruled that the charges should be reduced to conspiracy to cover up the events, as opposed to responsibility for the 'caravan of death', and in July the Court ruled that the former dictator was mentally unfit to stand trial. In July 2002 the Supreme Court voted to close the case against Pinochet permanently, as he was suffering from dementia. Within days Pinochet relinquished his position as senator-for-life. However, in August 2004 the Supreme Court upheld a decision by the appeals court in May to strip Pinochet of his immunity from prosecution for the crimes allegedly committed as part of 'Plan Condor', an intelligence operation to eliminate opponents of the Latin American military dictatorships in the 1970s. Guzmán declared Pinochet to be of sufficiently sound mind to stand trial over his role in 'Plan Condor' in December, but in September 2005 the Penal Chamber of the Supreme Court ruled that the charges against Pinochet relating to 'Plan Condor' were inadmissible. In the same month US financial investigators accused Pinochet of accepting bribes totalling more than US $3.5m. from European defence contractors and in October the Supreme Court removed Pinochet's immunity from prosecution on charges of embezzlement and the use of false passports to open foreign bank accounts. In November court-appointed psychiatrists reported that Pinochet had deliberately exaggerated his dementia in order to avoid prosecution.

Gen. Pinochet died on 10 December 2006, bringing an end to the efforts to bring him to trial on various charges of human rights abuses during his rule. In January Pinochet had been charged in relation to 'Operation Colombo', an operation allegedly undertaken during his dictatorship to abduct and murder 119 opponents of the regime, after the Supreme Court had removed his immunity from prosecution on the charges in the previous month. In October he had been indicted on human rights abuses after a court ruled that he was mentally fit to face trial: some 4,500 political opponents were alleged to have been detained at the notorious Villa Grimaldi detention centre during his regime, and more than 200 people murdered there. Pinochet was charged on one count of murder, 35 kidnappings and 24 cases of torture. In November he was once again put under house arrest. Earlier in the same month the Appeals Court of Santiago also lifted his immunity from prosecution in the case of the 'disappearance' of a Spanish priest in 1974, and charges in the 'caravan of death' case were also once again brought. In addition, he was due to face trial on fraud charges relating to large sums of money that he and his wife had allegedly deposited in secret accounts.

The Government of President Lagos

At the presidential poll held in December 1999 the candidate of the CPD, Ricardo Lagos Escobar of the Partido Socialista de Chile, and the nominee of the Alianza por Chile (formed by the RN and the Unión Demócrata Independiente—UDI), Joaquín Lavín, both obtained 48% of the total votes cast. At a second round of voting in January 2000 Lagos emerged victorious with 51% of the total votes. Lagos was sworn in as President in March.

In August 2003 President Lagos announced a series of measures intended to resolve issues relating to human rights violations during the military dictatorship. These included increases in compensation paid to victims of political violence and their relatives, as well as measures to facilitate criminal prosecutions of former military personnel. In November 2004 the Supreme Court—in reference to the prosecution, on charges of involvement in 'Plan Condor', of Gen. Contreras and three other former secret policemen—again ruled against the invocation of the amnesty law in cases of 'disappearance', on the grounds that, until the body of the kidnapped person was found, such unresolved cases of abduction should be considered as ongoing. The Supreme Court's ruling opened the way for many other cases of human rights abuses to be brought. Also in November 2004, the testimonies of some 35,000 victims of abuses under the Pinochet regime were published in a report by the National Commission on Political Imprisonment and Torture. Although victims' and human rights groups welcomed the report, many criticized it for omitting the names of those accused of the abuses. Prior to the report's publication, the Commander-in-Chief of the Chilean Army, Gen. Juan Emilio Cheyre Espinosa, issued on behalf of the armed forces a public apology, in which for the first time institutional responsibility was accepted for the systematic abuse of opponents of the Pinochet regime.

In late October and early November 2004 the Senado finally approved a number of constitutional reforms. These included: the abolition of non-elected senators and of senators-for-life; the restoration of the President's power to dismiss the head of the armed forces and the police; and a reduction of the presidential term from six years to four. The constitutional reforms received final congressional approval in August 2005. Significantly, the reforms did not include changes to the binomial electoral system.

The Government of President Bachelet

At the presidential election in December 2005 the CPD's candidate, Michelle Bachelet Jeria, obtained 46% of the valid votes cast, while Sebastián Piñera Echeñique of the RN received 2% of the ballot. As no candidate obtained the requisite 50% of the ballot, a run-off election between Bachelet and Piñera was held in January 2006. Bachelet was elected President with 54% of the valid votes cast and took office in March.

In her first year in office Bachelet was confronted by unrest from various sectors of society. In May 2006, in spite of the Government's pledge to increase public spending on education, some 700,000 students attended nation-wide demonstrations in protest against the education system. Although the demonstrations were largely peaceful, the police attempted to break up the protests using water cannons and tear gas, and some 700 arrests were made. In response to the students' demands, in June the Government agreed to provide free transport for those attending school or college and to introduce grants to cover entrance examination fees for the poorest students. The unrest led to the dismissal in July of the Minister of the Interior, after the police handling of the demonstrations was criticized. The ministers responsible for education and the economy were also removed from their cabinet posts. In August workers at La Escondida copper mine went on strike to demand a higher pay increase in light of record copper prices. A settlement was reached at the end of the month, but in September teachers also instigated industrial action to demand a pay increase and in protest against the slow pace of education reform. They were joined in their protests by health workers also demanding salary increases.

Industrial unrest continued throughout 2007. As well as intermittent strikes by bus drivers in Santiago protesting over the implementation of a new public transport system, Transantiago, in June sub-contractors working at the state-owned copper company, Corporación Nacional del Cobre de Chile (CODELCO-Chile), withdrew their labour in protest against their poorer terms and conditions compared with miners employed directly by CODELCO-Chile. The dispute ended in July, but in the following month the copper workers' union, the Confederación de Trabajadores del Cobre organized a general strike in protest at the Bachelet Government's perceived neo-liberal economic policies. Demonstrations in Santiago descended into violence and led to almost 500 arrests.

A government request for a further US $92m. in funding for Transantiago was rejected by the Senado in November 2007. A Partido Demócrata Cristiano (PDC) senator Adolfo Zaldívar voted with the opposition, precipitating his expulsion from the party. In January 2008 five deputies also announced their departure from the PDC, leaving the ruling coalition in a minority in both legislative chambers. In an attempt to restore confidence in her Government, in the same month President Bachelet carried out another extensive cabinet reorganization. Congressional support for the Government was further eroded in March when Zaldívar was elected President of the opposition-controlled Senado. At municipal elections held in October the Alianza por Chile won the greatest share of the votes cast for mayors for the first time since the restoration of democracy. Continuing divisions within the ruling coalition meant that it did not present unified lists of candidates for municipal council seats.

Legislation to reform the education system was approved by the Cámara de Diputados in June 2008 with the support of both the CPD and the Alianza por Chile. Earlier in June teachers had gone on strike and students and teachers had participated in demonstrations against the reforms, claiming that they would not sufficiently reduce the inequalities inherent in the existing system, which favoured private education. The draft legislation was approved by the Senado in December.

Recent developments: the Piñera presidency

Presidential and legislative elections took place on 13 December 2009. The right-of-centre grouping, Coalición por el Cambio, secured 58 seats in the Cámara de Diputados (three short of a majority), while the CPD's representation was reduced to 57 seats. As neither grouping achieved a majority in the lower chamber, a period of intense political manoeuvring ensued. In the first round of the presidential poll Sebastián Piñera Echeñique, candidate for Coalición por el Cambio, secured 44.1% of total votes, compared with the CPD's candidate, former President Eduardo Frei Ruiz-Tagle, who won 29.6%. The popular independent candidate Marco Enríquez-Ominami Gumucio secured 20.1% of the total vote. At the second round on 17 January 2010 Piñera was victorious with 51.6% of the vote. The result was significant in marking the end of the CPD's 20-year rule and in giving Chile its first right-wing President since Pinochet. Piñera's stated priorities included the creation of jobs, the introduction of strict policies on law and order and increased investment in the business sector.

In late February 2010 a huge earthquake, measuring 8.8 on the Richter scale, struck Chile affecting a wide area centred near Concepción. According to official figures, the quake caused the deaths of more than 500 people and damaged or destroyed 370,000 homes. The outgoing Bachelet administration deployed some 14,000 members of the armed forces to the disaster area to re-establish order and prevent looting. The first priority for the incoming Government, which took office in mid-March, was to gain legislative approval for its reconstruction plan, estimated to cost US $20,000m. Among the proposals the Government put forward to fund this were tax increases, including a temporary rise in mining royalties (in exchange for a fixed lower rate in the future). However, the mining levy proved to be particularly contentious with the opposition, which accused the Piñera administration of lacking fiscal foresight. The reconstruction programme was dismissed by the Congreso in July; modified legislation was finally approved in October, after the Government agreed to reduce the duration of the fixed royalty rate.

In October 2010 international attention was focused on Chile during a successful operation to rescue 33 men from a collapsed mine near Copiapó, reportedly costing the Government up to US $20m. Although Piñera enjoyed a boost in opinion poll approval ratings owing to his strong leadership throughout the crisis, critics argued that the state's resources would have been more effectively utilized if they had been directed towards the earthquake reconstruction efforts.

There were numerous reports throughout 2010 of government property on Isla de Pascua (Rapa Nui or Easter Island) being occupied by indigenous protesters demanding land reform and immigration controls. The protesters claimed that the mainland authorities had illegally seized their historical lands. The idea of secession from Chile was also mooted by the island's indigenous leaders, a concept dismissed by the Government. Mainland police units were dispatched to the island to end the occupations, precipitating violent clashes in December between the police and the demonstrators.

To boost revenues, in January 2011 the heavily indebted state-owned petroleum company Empresa Nacional de Petróleo proposed a 17% increase in gas prices in southern Chile, prompting strikes and violent protests in Punta Arenas, which resulted in the deaths of two people and the disruption of transport links with Argentina. The Minister of the National Energy Commission, Ricardo Raineri Bernain, resigned from the Cabinet as a result of the unrest, and his duties were assumed by Minister of Mining and Energy, Laurence Golborne Riveros, a popular figure following his prominent role in the rescue of the Copiapó miners. Golborne secured an end to the protests shortly afterwards, agreeing to reduce the price increase to 3% and reinstate gas subsidies. In the same cabinet reorganization, Piñera also appointed Andrés Allamand as Minister of National Defence and Evelyn Matthei Fornet as Minister of Labour and Social Security.

Jacqueline van Rysselberghe, the Governor of Biobío and a prominent member of the UDI (part of the governing Coalición por el Cambio), was forced to resign in April 2011 following relentless pressure from the opposition CPD, which accused her of exaggerating the extent of earthquake damage in Biobío to obtain additional government funds for her region. Another UDI member, Minister of Housing and Urban Development Magdalena Matte Lecaros, resigned later that month after being implicated in the van Rysselberghe scandal; Matte had also been criticized for allegedly mishandling a construction contract for work on Transantiago. The resignations of these high-profile UDI officials signified the growing assertiveness of the left-wing opposition and also exposed tensions between the two main parties within the ruling coalition, the Renovación Nacional (RN) and the UDI, which had expected greater RN support for its members.

To improve the transparency of military expenditure, in May 2011 the Congreso Nacional abrogated a law that allocated 10% of CODELCO-Chile's export earnings to the military, a practice that had been enforced, in various forms, since 1942. Also in that month, amid widespread power shortages, local regulators approved the construction of five hydroelectric plants in southern Chile, which would boost generating capacity by some 2,750 MW at a cost of US $3,200m. However, throughout May activists concerned about the environmental consequences of the scheme staged large-scale demonstrations against this decision, some of which deteriorated into violence. An opposition-supported legal challenge prompted a local court to suspend the hydroelectric project in June, although this appeal was rejected in October and work was allowed to resume.

Student groups organized several demonstrations in Santiago in June 2011, attended by up to 80,000 people, to demand free higher education and greater government involvement and investment in the country's education system, and also to protest against private, profit-generating universities and the disparities in the standard of education received by rich and poor students. Although the President, in July, announced new measures to reduce the financial burden on students and pledged US $4,000m. in new educational funding, these proposals failed to mollify the demonstrators and the protests continued. A strike by CODELCO-Chile workers later that month, in response to alleged government plans to privatize the company, placed further pressure on the Government. A cabinet reorganization was implemented by Piñera in mid-July, in which the Minister of Education and the Minister of Mining were replaced; the President also rejected the CODELCO-Chile privatization rumours. Amid continuing, and often violent, large-scale student protests, a two-day strike was organized by the Central Unitaria de Trabajadores de Chile (CUT) in late August. The CUT claimed that 600,000 people took part in demonstrations throughout the country to demand health care, education, labour and pension reforms. However, these rallies precipitated violent clashes between the police and protesters, one of whom was killed by the security forces, and Chile's head of police was forced to resign as a result. Discussions between the Government and student representatives in September–October foundered. Riot police were deployed during a further student demonstration in mid-October, with reports that firearms and petrol bombs had been used by some demonstrators. Later that month protesters attacked the UDI's headquarters, stormed a senate meeting, forcing Minister of Education Felipe Bulnes Serrano to flee, and launched a failed attempt to occupy the Ministry of Education. Results from an unofficial plebiscite indicated strong public support for the students' demands, whereas Piñera's approval ratings had declined dramatically. The protests, while continuing, appeared to lose momentum following the approval in late November of the 2012 budget, which allocated additional funds to education; the Government also expanded the scholarship system and established a new body to regulate the quality and transparency of universities, but rejected most of the protesters' other demands. Student leaders, dissatisfied with these concessions, pledged to resume protests in early 2012. Bulnes resigned as Minister of Education in December 2011 and was replaced by Harald Beyer.

In December 2011 the Senado endorsed a constitutional amendment that would grant eligible citizens the automatic, and voluntary, right to vote in elections. (Under existing laws, voters were required to complete a registration process, following which electoral participation was mandatory.) This measure was expected to be approved by the Constitutional Court in the following month and would expand the size of the electorate by almost 5m., with the number of young voters forecast to rise significantly. Piñera was also considering reform of Chile's controversial binomial electoral system in early 2012.

Unrest among the Indigenous Mapuche Communities

A series of mining, dam and forestry projects in the 2000s prompted violent protests by the Mapuche indigenous peoples who were campaigning for the restitution of land they claimed under ancestral right. In May 2000 a Historical Truth and New Deal Commission was created to consider the demands and needs of indigenous communities. In November 2003 the Commission produced its final report, which recommended the extension of constitutional and property rights to indigenous peoples and confirmation of their entitlement to participate in national politics. In early 2004 it was alleged that damage to timber industry property and forest fires in the Biobío region were the acts of Mapuche activists opposed to the activities of the timber industry. In August five Mapuche activists were convicted under anti-terrorism legislation, while in November seven Mapuche activists (and one non-Mapuche sympathizer) were acquitted on charges of conspiring to commit terrorist acts. Meanwhile, in August, after some eight years of legal dispute between the Spanish energy company Endesa, SA, and a coalition of ecological and indigenous groups of Pehuenche ethnicity, an agreement was finally reached that would allow construction of a major hydroelectric plant in the Biobío river basin. President Bachelet put forward to the Congreso a constitutional amendment in October 2007 that would recognize indigenous ancestral lands as well as promote the rights of the country's indigenous peoples. In January 2008 the Government established a panel to address the issue of Mapuche rights; the move followed an increase in civil unrest among the indigenous population after a student was shot dead by a police officer during a demonstration at the beginning of the month. In a further attempt to improve relations between the Government and the Mapuche community, a member of the Cabinet was designated as Co-ordinator of Indigenous Policy in August 2009. This had been prompted in part by the fatal shooting of an unarmed Mapuche activist by police during an operation to evict indigenous people from a private estate in the Araucanía region. Ongoing unrest led the Government in October to announce its intention to invoke anti-terrorism laws enacted by Gen. Pinochet (which imposed penalties far stricter than those in the penal code) against individuals involved in violent disputes in the area. The Government also announced that Mapuche people believed to be involved in such activities would be ineligible for land distribution under the Government's indigenous rights programme. In August 2010 the Government declared that it had received evidence from the Colombian authorities confirming that radical Mapuches had trained with the Fuerzas Armadas Revolucionarias de Colombia—Ejército del Pueblo, a militant Colombian guerrilla group, although Mapuche representatives and high-ranking members of the Chilean police force rejected this claim. Meanwhile, in July a group of Mapuche prisoners had begun a hunger strike in protest against the controversial anti-terrorism laws that were being used to detain them without trial. Under increasing pressure, after four left-wing deputies joined the hunger strike and demonstrations were held in solidarity with the Mapuches, in September President Piñera consented to direct talks with Mapuche leaders and proposed modifications to the anti-terrorism legislation. Dissatisfied with the Government's response, Mapuche protesters in Santiago temporarily took control of UN and International Labour Organization buildings on 23 September. However, following further negotiations, on 1 October agreement was reached to end the hunger strike in exchange for government pledges to reform the anti-terrorism laws and to re-examine the terrorism charges against the prisoners. (A congressional committee had been established to facilitate the reform process in late September.) In spite of this breakthrough, in November public prosecutors invoked the Pinochet-era anti-terrorism legislation in a trial involving a Mapuche attack on several police officers. Mapuche protests resumed in March 2011, prompted by the sentencing of four high-profile Mapuches to prison terms of between 20 and 25 years after they were convicted of robbery and attempting to murder a district attorney. The four men commenced a hunger strike and lodged an appeal against their convictions with the Supreme Court, which was rejected in June (although their sentences were reduced). The prisoners ended their hunger strike shortly thereafter, following a pledge by the Government to establish a Mapuche rights commission.

Foreign Affairs

In 1991 Argentina and Chile reached a settlement regarding disputed territory in the Antarctic region. Responsibility for the contentious Laguna del Desierto region, however, was to be decided by international arbitration. In 1994 Argentina's claim to the territory was upheld by a five-member international arbitration panel. In 1998 agreement on border demarcation of the still disputed 'continental glaciers' territory in the Antarctic region was reached by the Presidents of the two countries and in 2000 both countries ratified the Mining and Co-operation Integration Treaty, allowing joint exploitation of mineral deposits along their shared border. In 2006 a bilateral group was established to resolve disagreements over energy matters. Relations between the two countries deteriorated in September 2010 when Argentina granted asylum to Sergio Galvarino Apablaza, who was wanted by the Chilean authorities in relation to the 1991 assassination of Jaime Guzmán, a prominent figure in the Pinochet regime.

Prospects for renewed diplomatic relations with Bolivia (which severed ties with Chile in 1978 over the issue of Bolivian access to the Pacific Ocean) improved under President Bachelet. However, subsequent ministerial discussions failed to produce an effective formula for the restoration of diplomatic relations. The decision in 2003 by the administration of Ricardo Lagos to privatize the port of Arica elicited vehement objections from the Bolivian Government, which feared this would lead to significant increases in port tariffs. However, bilateral discussions in 2006 included Bolivian claims to Pacific access for the first time in more than a century. In 2008 the Chilean and Bolivian Ministers of Defence signed a memorandum of understanding on defence co-operation, which both Governments described as an important step in the development of bilateral relations. However, President Piñera announced in December 2010 that he would not grant Bolivia sovereign rights to any part of Chile, an option that had been contemplated by Bachelet. Frustrated by this impasse, Bolivian President Juan Evo Morales threatened to refer the matter to the International Court of Justice in March 2011, precipitating a sharp deterioration in relations.

Relations with Peru suffered in August 2007 after a Peruvian government periodical published a map appearing to lay claim to Chilean water, prompting Chile to recall its ambassador from that country. In January 2008 Chile again recalled its ambassador after the Peruvian legislature approved legislation revising the maritime border. The issue of the maritime border between the two countries due to be considered by the International Court of Justice in 2013.

With the exception of trade with Bolivia, Chile has negotiated free trade agreements throughout the South American continent. In 1997 a free trade agreement with Canada came into effect; its terms were modified and expanded in 1998. In December 2002 Chile and the USA finally agreed on a free trade pact that would eliminate immediately all barriers on 85% of trade between the two countries, with the remaining trade restrictions being phased out within 12 years. The agreement came into effect in January 2004. In February 2003 an association agreement for political and economic co-operation between Chile and the European Union came into effect. In the same month a new free trade agreement was signed with the Republic of Korea. A free trade accord between Chile and the European Free Trade Association (see p. 450) came into effect in 2004, and in 2009 Chile became the first country in South America to sign a free trade agreement with Turkey.

CONSTITUTION AND GOVERNMENT

Chile is a republic, divided into 14 regions and a metropolitan area. Easter Island enjoys 'special territory' status within Chile. The 1981 Constitution, described as a 'transition to democracy', separated the presidency from the junta and provided for presidential elections and for the re-establishment of the bicameral legislature. Under the terms of the Constitution, executive power is vested in the President, who is directly elected for a four-year term. The President is assisted by a Cabinet. Legislative power is vested in the bicameral Congreso Nacional (National Congress), comprising the 38-member Senado (Senate) and the 120-member Cámara de Diputados (Chamber of Deputies).

REGIONAL AND INTERNATIONAL CO-OPERATION

The country is a member of the Latin American Integration Association (ALADI, see p. 362) and was admitted to the Rio Group (see p. 465) in 1990 and to the Asia-Pacific Economic Co-operation group (APEC, see p. 204) in 1994. In December 2004 Chile was one of 12 countries that were signatories to the agreement, signed in Cusco, Peru, creating the South American Community of Nations (Comunidad Sudamericana de Naciones, which was renamed Union of South American Nations—Unión de Naciones Suramericanas, UNASUR, in April 2007), intended to promote greater regional economic integration. The Senado ratified UNASUR membership in September 2010. In 2006 Chile rejoined the Andean Community of Nations (CAN, see p. 197) as an associate member; although the country had been a founding member of CAN, it had withdrawn from the organization in 1976 following a dispute. The country was a member of the Community of Latin American and Caribbean States (see p. 462), which was formally inaugurated in December 2011

Chile became a member of the UN in 1945. As a contracting party to the General Agreement on Tariffs and Trade Chile joined the World Trade Organization, WTO (see p. 433) on its establishment in 1995. In January 2010 Chile became a member of the Organization for Economic Co-operation and Development (see p. 379). Chile is a member of the Group of 77.

ECONOMIC AFFAIRS

In 2010, according to estimates by the World Bank, Chile's gross national income (GNI), measured at average 2008–10 prices, was US $170,284m., equivalent to $9,950 per head (or $13,900 per head on an international purchasing-power parity basis). During 2000–10, it was estimated, the population increased by an average of 1.0% per year, while gross domestic product (GDP) per head increased, in real terms, at an average annual rate of 2.7%. Overall GDP increased, in real terms, at an average annual rate of 3.8% in 2001–10; according to the Banco Central de Chile, real GDP declined by 1.7% in 2009, but increased by 5.2% in 2010.

Agriculture (including forestry and fishing) contributed 3.2% of GDP, according to preliminary estimates in 2010, and employed 10.3% of the employed labour force at the end of May 2011. Important subsistence crops include wheat, oats, barley, rice, beans, lentils, maize and chickpeas. Industrial crops include sugar beet, sunflower seed and rapeseed. Fruit and vegetables are also important export commodities (together contributing 14.1% of total export revenues in 2010), particularly beans, asparagus, onions, garlic, grapes, citrus fruits, avocados, pears, peaches, plums and nuts. The production and export of wine increased significantly in recent years; wine output increased by 19.6% in 2009. Forestry and fishing, and derivatives from both activities, also make important contributions to the sector. During 2001–09 agricultural GDP increased, in real terms, by an average of 4.6% per year, according to the World Bank. According to Banco Central de Chile, agricultural GDP decreased by an estimated 2.5% in 2010.

Industry (including mining, manufacturing, construction and power) contributed an estimated 42.9% of GDP, according to preliminary estimates in 2010, and accounted for 23.4% of the employed labour force at the end of May 2011. During 2001–09, according to the World Bank, industrial GDP increased by an average of 2.0% per year. According to Banco Central de Chile estimates, GDP growth in all industrial sectors contracted by 4.5% in 2009, but increased by 1.5% in 2010.

Mining contributed 19.9% of GDP, according to preliminary estimates in 2010, and engaged 2.9% of the employed labour force at the end of May 2011. Chile, with some 20% of the world's known reserves, is the world's largest producer and exporter of copper. Copper accounted for 87.5% of Chile's total export earnings in 1970, but by 2010 the contribution of copper and iron to total export earnings stood at an estimated 58.4% (some US $41,452.8m.). Gold, silver, iron ore, nitrates, molybdenum, manganese, lead and coal are also mined. According to the Banco Central de Chile, the sector remained constant during 2003–10. In real terms, the sector's GDP decreased by 1.3% in 2009, but increased by 1.2% in 2010. Petroleum and natural gas deposits have been located in the south and offshore. Chile was a major producer of lithium carbonate, producing over one-third of global output.

Manufacturing contributed 11.5% of GDP, according to preliminary estimates in 2010, and engaged 11.4% of the employed labour force at the end of May 2011. The most important branches of manufacturing are food and non-ferrous metals. Manufacturing GDP increased by an average of 2.4% per year in 2001–09. According to central bank figures, manufacturing GDP declined by 6.4% in 2009 and by a further 1.0% in 2010.

Construction contributed 8.1% of GDP, according to preliminary estimates in 2010, and engaged 8.2% of the employed labour force at the end of May 2011. According to the Banco Central de Chile, construction GDP increased by an average of 3.8% per year in 2003–10; sectoral GDP decreased by 7.9% in 2009, but increased by 3.6% in 2010.

Electric energy was derived mainly from hydroelectric power (40.5% in 2008), petroleum (26.9%), coal (23.6%) and natural gas (3.7%). Chile produces some 40% of its national energy requirements. In 2007 the Government, concerned that Chile had become increasingly reliant on imports to meet its energy needs, appropriated 32,000 sq km of land in the Magallanes region for oil and gas exploration. The area was divided into 10 blocks, which were put up for tender in 2011. In 2011 construction of five hydroelectric plants in southern Chile was approved. The controversial project (see Domestic Political Affairs) would increase generating capacity by some 2,750 MW at a cost of US $3,200m. In 2010 Chile imported mineral fuels and lubricants equivalent to some 19.4% of the value of total merchandise imports.

The services sector contributed 53.9% of GDP, according to preliminary estimates in 2010, and engaged 66.3% of the employed labour force at the end of May 2011. The financial sector continued to expand in the early 21st century, fuelled, in part, by the success of private pension funds. During 2001–09 overall services GDP increased by an average of 4.2% per year. According to the Banco Central de Chile, services GDP increased, in real terms, by an estimated 6.8% in 2010.

In 2010 Chile recorded a visible trade surplus of US $15,855m., and there was a surplus of $3,802m. on the current account of the balance of payments. In 2010 the USA was the principal source of imports (15.8%), while the People's Republic of China was the principal market for exports (24.4%). Other major trading partners were Argentina, Brazil, Japan, and the Republic of Korea. In 2010 the principal exports were non-ferrous metals (38.7% of total export revenue), metalliferous ores and metal scrap (24.5%), vegetables and fruit and fish. The principal imports in that year were machinery and transport equipment, and petroleum and petroleum products.

In 2010 there was a budgetary surplus of some 3,098,533m. pesos, equivalent to 3.0% of GDP. Chile's general government gross debt was 9,535.01m. pesos in 2010, equivalent to 9.2% of GDP. Chile's external debt totalled some US $71,646m. at the end of 2009, of which $9,282m. was long-term public and publicly guaranteed debt. In that year, the cost of servicing long-term public and publicly guaranteed debt and repayments to the IMF was equivalent to 3.4% of the value of exports of goods, services and income (excluding workers' remittances) The annual rate of inflation averaged 3.4% in 2000–09, and stood at 1.4% in 2010. Some 7.2% of the labour force were unemployed in May 2011.

In spite of a recent expansion in agricultural and industrial exports, in early 2012 Chile remained heavily dependent on exports of copper. High international copper prices resulted in Chile recording its 11th successive trade surplus in 2010. Growth in trade was buoyed by foreign direct investment and free trade agreements, although the strong copper prices led to an appreciation in the Chilean peso, which, in turn, adversely affected other merchandise exports. Following the onset of the global economic downturn in 2008, however, demand began to decline, though exports did benefit from a depreciating currency. Inflationary pressures and energy supply problems adversely affected economic growth in 2009, and real GDP contracted by 1.7%. An improvement in the global economic climate and extensive reconstruction activity following the massive earthquake that struck Concepción in February 2010 contributed to a resurgence in economic growth in 2010 and 2011. After expanding by 5.2% in 2010, the IMF reported that real GDP grew by a further 6.5% in 2011. Copper exports increased during this period, benefiting from a recovery in the copper price on international markets. Low levels of unemployment resulted in rising domestic demand, which reinforced the economic revival. Although electricity shortages were an ongoing problem, a US $3,200m. hydropower scheme received final approval in October 2011 and was expected to provide an additional 2,750 MW of generating capacity when complete. Chile remained vulnerable to fluctuations in the price of copper, but the country's economy appeared to have successfully withstood the dual challenges of the global financial crisis and the Concepción earthquake. The continuing reconstruction effort, robust internal demand and high copper prices were expected to support further GDP growth of 5.0% in 2012.

PUBLIC HOLIDAYS

2013: 1 January (New Year's Day), 29 March (Good Friday), 30 March (Holy Saturday), 1 May (Labour Day), 21 May (Navy Day—Battle of Iquique), 1 July (for Saints Peter and Paul), 16 July (Our Lady of Carmen), 15 August (Assumption), 11 September (Reconciliation Day), 18 September (Independence Day), 19 September (Army Day), 14 October (for Discovery of America), 31 October (Reformation Day), 1 November (All Saints' Day), 8 December (Immaculate Conception), 25 December (Christmas Day).

Statistical Survey

Sources (unless otherwise stated): Instituto Nacional de Estadísticas (INE), Avda Bulnes 418, Casilla 498-3, Correo 3, Santiago; tel. (2) 366-7777; fax (2) 671-2169; e-mail inesdadm@reuna.cl; internet www.ine.cl; Banco Central de Chile, Agustinas 1180, Santiago; tel. (2) 696-2281; fax (2) 698-4847; e-mail bcch@bcentral.cl; internet www.bcentral.cl.

Area and Population

AREA, POPULATION AND DENSITY*

Area (sq km)	756,096†
Population (census results)‡	
22 April 1992	13,348,401
24 April 2002	
Males	7,447,695
Females	7,668,740
Total	15,116,435
Population (official estimates at mid-year)	
2010	17,094,275
2011	17,248,450
2012	17,402,630
Density (per sq km) at mid-2012	23.0

* Excluding Chilean Antarctic Territory (approximately 1,250,000 sq km).

† 291,930 sq miles.

‡ Excluding adjustment for underenumeration.

POPULATION BY AGE AND SEX

(official estimates at mid-2011)

	Males	Females	Total
0–14	1,935,065	1,865,781	3,800,846
15–64	5,914,045	5,932,845	11,846,890
65 and over	687,794	912,920	1,600,714
Total	8,536,904	8,711,546	17,248,450

REGIONS

(2002 census)

	Area (sq km)	Population	Density (per sq km)	Capital
Tarapacá	42,225.8	238,950	5.7	Iquique
Antofagasta	126,049.1	493,984	3.9	Antofagasta
Atacama	75,176.2	254,336	3.4	Copiapó
Coquimbo	40,579.9	603,210	14.9	La Serena
Valparaíso	16,396.1	1,539,852	93.9	Valparaíso
El Libertador Gen. Bernardo O'Higgins	16,387.0	780,627	47.6	Rancagua
Maule	30,296.1	908,097	30.0	Talca
Biobío	37,068.7	1,861,562	50.2	Concepción
La Araucanía	31,842.3	869,535	27.3	Temuco
Los Lagos	48,583.6	716,739	14.8	Puerto Montt
Aisén del Gen. Carlos Ibáñez del Campo	108,494.4	91,492	0.8	Coyhaique
Magallanes y Antártica Chilena	1,382,291.1	150,826	0.1	Punta Arenas
Metropolitan Region (Santiago)	15,403.2	6,061,185	393.5	—
Los Ríos*	18,429.5	356,396	19.3	Valdivia
Arica y Parinacota*	16,873.3	189,644	11.2	Arica
Total†	2,006,096.3	15,116,435	7.5	—

* New regions created in 2007 from provinces previously contained within the Tarapacá and Los Lagos regions; census data for these regions has been reallocated, based on the data recorded for the relevant provinces, retrospectively.

† Including Chilean Antarctic Territory (approximately 1,250,000 sq km).

PRINCIPAL TOWNS

(2002 census)

Gran Santiago (capital)	4,668,473	Talca	201,797
Puente Alto	492,915	Arica	185,268
Antofagasta	296,905	Puerto Montt	175,938
Viña del Mar	286,931	Los Angeles	166,556
Valparaíso	275,982	Coquimbo	163,036
Talcahuano	250,348	Chillán	161,953
San Bernardo	246,762	La Serena	160,148
Temuco	245,347	Osorno	145,475
Iquique	216,419	Valdivia	140,559
Concepción	216,061	Calama	138,402
Rancagua	214,344		

Mid-2010 (incl. suburbs, UN estimates): Gran Santiago 5,951,554; Valparaíso 872,591 (Source: UN, *World Urbanization Prospects: The 2009 Revision*).

BIRTHS, MARRIAGES AND DEATHS

	Registered live births*		Registered marriages		Registered deaths	
	Number	Rate (per 1,000)	Number	Rate (per 1,000)	Number	Rate (per 1,000)
2002	238,981	15.3	60,971	3.9	81,079	5.2
2003	234,486	14.8	56,659	3.6	83,672	5.3
2004	230,352	14.5	53,403	3.3	86,138	5.4
2005	230,831	14.3	53,842	3.3	86,102	5.3
2006	231,383	14.2	58,155	3.5	85,639	5.2
2007	240,569	14.6	57,792	3.5	93,000	5.6
2008	246,581	14.8	56,112	3.3	90,168	5.4
2009	252,240	15.0	56,127	3.3	91,965	5.4

* Adjusted for underenumeration.

Life expectancy (years at birth, WHO estimates): 79 (males 76; females 82) in 2009 (Source: WHO, *World Health Statistics*).

ECONOMICALLY ACTIVE POPULATION*

('000 persons aged 15 years and over, March–May)

	2009	2010	2011
Agriculture, hunting, forestry and fishing	677.2	738.8	763.9
Mining and quarrying	151.0	196.2	219.2
Manufacturing	732.0	745.3	848.8
Electricity, gas and water	51.3	55.2	66.2
Construction	512.4	560.6	610.9
Trade, restaurants and hotels	1,548.6	1,693.9	1,798.0
Transport, storage and communications	504.5	509.2	541.9
Financing, insurance, real estate and business services	596.5	585.0	619.5
Community, social and personal services	1,747.2	1,887.6	1,975.7
Total employed	6,520.7	6,971.8	7,444.1
Unemployed	841.6	674.9	574.2
Total labour force	7,362.3	7,646.7	8,018.3

* Figures are based on sample surveys, covering 36,000 households, and exclude members of the armed forces. Estimates are made independently, therefore totals are not always the sum of the component parts.

Health and Welfare

KEY INDICATORS

Total fertility rate (children per woman, 2009)	1.9
Under-5 mortality rate (per 1,000 live births, 2009)	8
HIV/AIDS (% of persons aged 15–49, 2009)	0.4
Physicians (per 1,000 head, 2003)	1.1
Hospital beds (per 1,000 head, 2005)	2.3
Health expenditure (2008): US $ per head (PPP)	1,088
Health expenditure (2008): % of GDP	7.5
Health expenditure (2008): public (% of total)	44.0
Access to water (% of persons, 2008)	96
Access to sanitation (% of persons, 2008)	96
Total carbon dioxide emissions ('000 metric tons, 2007)	71,645.9
Carbon dioxide emissions per head (metric tons, 2007)	4.3
Human Development Index (2011): ranking	44
Human Development Index (2011): value	0.805

For sources and definitions, see explanatory note on p. vi.

Agriculture

PRINCIPAL CROPS
('000 metric tons)

	2008	2009	2010
Wheat	1,238	1,145	1,524
Rice, paddy	121	127	95
Barley	67	53	78
Maize	1,365	1,346	1,358
Oats	384	344	381
Potatoes	966	925	1,081
Sugar beet	1,208	1,042	1,420
Beans, dry	20	28	23
Rapeseed	67	79	44
Cabbages and other brassicas	42*	44	44*
Lettuce and chicory*	96	101	94
Tomatoes*	977	850	900
Pumpkins, squash and gourds	108*	128	137*
Chillies and peppers, green	52*	55	50*
Onions, dry	288*	295	297*
Carrots and turnips	160*	188	150*
Maize, green*	177	180	176
Watermelons*	48	50	52
Cantaloupes and other melons*	45	47	49
Oranges	160*	135*	134
Lemons and limes*	166	162	155
Apples	1,280	1,090	1,100
Pears*	185	191	180
Peaches and nectarines*	372	388	357
Plums and sloes*	234	296	298
Grapes*	2,400	2,500	2,756
Avocados*	331	328	330
Kiwi fruit*	186	227	229

* FAO estimate(s).

Aggregate production ('000 metric tons, may include official, semi-official or estimated data): Total cereals 3,273 in 2008, 3,106 in 2009, 3,569 in 2010; Total roots and tubers 977 in 2008, 935 in 2009, 1,094 in 2010; Total vegetables (incl. melons) 2,289 in 2008, 2,271 in 2009, 2,259 in 2010; Total fruits (excl. melons) 5,436 in 2008, 5,451 in 2009, 5,674 in 2010.

Source: FAO.

LIVESTOCK
('000 head, year ending September)

	2008	2009	2010
Horses*	320	320	320
Cattle*	3,800	3,900	3,900
Pigs	2,790	2,725	2,706
Sheep	3,950*	3,950*	3,644†
Goats*	740	750	750
Chickens	44,163	43,210	47,479
Turkeys*	28,500	28,500	28,500

* FAO estimate(s).
† Unofficial figure.

Source: FAO.

LIVESTOCK PRODUCTS
('000 metric tons)

	2008	2009	2010
Cattle meat	240.3	209.9	210.7
Sheep meat	11.0	10.7	10.5
Pig meat	522.4	513.7	498.5
Horse meat	8.9	7.3	7.4
Chicken meat	509.5	513.4	503.8
Cows' milk	2,550	2,350	2,530
Goats' milk*	10.0	9.6	10.3
Hen eggs	142.6†	137.0*	146.0*
Wool, greasy	9.8*	8.9*	7.8

* FAO estimate(s).
† Unofficial figure.

Source: FAO.

Forestry

ROUNDWOOD REMOVALS
('000 cubic metres, excluding bark)

	2007	2008	2009
Sawlogs, veneer logs and logs for sleepers	17,866	16,475	14,798
Pulpwood	20,359	23,232	21,323
Other industrial wood	192	171	280
Fuel wood	14,216	14,955	15,098
Total	52,633	54,833	51,499

2010: Production assumed to be unchanged from 2009 (FAO estimates).

Source: FAO.

SAWNWOOD PRODUCTION
('000 cubic metres, including railway sleepers)

	2007	2008	2009
Coniferous (softwood)	8,015	7,005	5,662
Broadleaved (hardwood)	325	301	174
Total	8,340	7,306	5,836

2010: Production assumed to be unchanged from 2009 (FAO estimates).

Source: FAO.

Fishing

('000 metric tons, live weight)

	2007	2008	2009
Capture	3,819.3	3,554.8	3,453.8
Patagonian grenadier	63.7	73.6	78.4
Araucanian herring	281.4	795.1	855.3
Anchoveta (Peruvian anchovy)	1,393.7	1,116.7	955.2
Chilean jack mackerel	1,302.8	896.2	834.9
Chub mackerel	297.2	133.0	158.5
Jumbo flying squid	124.4	145.7	56.3
Aquaculture*	779.8	843.1	792.9
Atlantic salmon	331.0*	388.8*	233.3
Coho (silver) salmon	105.5	92.3	157.0
Rainbow trout	164.4	149.4	214.7
Total catch	4,599.1*	4,398.0*	4,246.7

* FAO estimate(s).

Note: Figures exclude aquatic plants ('000 metric tons): 338.5 (capture 312.2, aquaculture 26.4) in 2007; 412.3 (capture 384.6, aquaculture 27.7) in 2008; 456.2 (capture 368.0, aquaculture 88.2) in 2009.

Source: FAO.

Mining

('000 metric tons unless otherwise indicated)

	2007	2008	2009
Copper (metal content)	5,557	5,328	5,390
Coal	288	534	636
Iron ore*	8,818	9,316	8,242
Calcium carbonate	7,196	7,295	6,012
Zinc—metal content (metric tons)	36,453	40,519	27,801
Molybdenum—metal content (metric tons)	44,912	33,687	34,925
Manganese (metric tons)†	26,808	18,273	5,722
Gold (kg)	41,527	39,162	40,834
Silver (kg)	1,936	1,405	1,301
Petroleum (crude)	931	966	1,355

* Gross weight. The estimated iron content is 61%.
† Gross weight. The estimated metal content is 32%.

Source: US Geological Survey.

Industry

SELECTED PRODUCTS

('000 metric tons unless otherwise indicated)

	2006	2007	2008
Beer ('000 hl)	4,518	5,501	7,091
Wine*	802	792	824.6
Soft drinks ('000 hl)	107	16,870	19,760
Cigarettes (million)	18,073	18,654	19,498
Non-rubber footwear ('000 pairs)	3,791	3,628	2,835
Particle board ('000 cu m)	522	515	n.a.
Mattresses ('000)	1,534	1,535	2,031
Jet fuel	660	537	511
Motor spirit (petrol)	2,482	2,349	2,230
Kerosene	58	93	77
Distillate fuel oils	3,717	3,623	3,811
Residual fuel oils	2,646	2,445	1,906
Cement	3,999.6	4,368.5	4,620.7
Tyres ('000)	4,830	5,254	5,036
Blister copper	2,024	1,936	n.a.
Refined copper, unwrought	158	124	98
Electric energy (million kWh)	55,320	58,509	58,708

2009 ('000 metric tons unless otherwise indicated): Wine 986.9*; Electric energy 58,392m. kWh.

2010 (provisional): Electric energy 60,159m. kWh.

* Source: FAO.
† Source: US Geological Survey.

Source (unless otherwise indicated): UN Industrial Commodity Statistics Database.

Finance

CURRENCY AND EXCHANGE RATES

Monetary Units

100 centavos = 1 Chilean peso.

Sterling, Dollar and Euro Equivalents (30 December 2011)

£1 sterling = 806.229 pesos;
US $1 = 521.460 pesos;
€1 = 674.717 pesos;
10,000 Chilean pesos = £12.40 = $19.18 = €14.82.

Average Exchange Rate (pesos per US $)

2009 560.860
2010 510.249
2011 483.654

GOVERNMENT FINANCE

(general government transactions, non-cash basis, million pesos)

Summary of Balances

	2008	2009	2010
Revenue	24,227,612	19,968,643	25,461,471
Less Expense	17,597,836	20,433,441	22,362,938
Net operating balance	6,629,776	–464,798	3,098,533
Less Net acquisition of non-financial assets	2,741,730	3,470,130	3,447,454
Net lending/borrowing	3,888,046	–3,934,928	–348,921

Revenue

	2008	2009	2010
Net tax revenue	17,710,171	14,720,948	18,888,577
Gross copper revenue	3,198,958	1,593,047	3,043,079
Social security contributions	1,289,225	1,371,750	1,493,987
Grants	157,623	148,874	145,356
Property income	775,478	667,469	481,437
Operating revenue	565,699	572,328	585,444
Other revenue	530,458	894,227	823,592
Total	24,227,612	19,968,643	25,461,471

Expense

Expense by economic type	2008	2009	2010
Compensation of employees	4,903,597	5,735,529	6,070,822
Use of goods and services	2,405,341	2,839,114	3,047,520
Consumption of fixed capital	782,103	887,228	972,823
Interest	439,778	475,535	537,465
Subsidies and grants	4,876,290	5,847,337	6,663,634
Social benefits	4,150,643	4,612,682	5,021,202
Other expense	40,084	36,016	49,471
Total	17,597,836	20,433,441	22,362,938

Source: Dirección de Presupuestos, Santiago.

INTERNATIONAL RESERVES

(US $ million at 31 December)

	2008	2009	2010
Gold (national valuation)	5.7	8.8	11.2
IMF special drawing rights	56.8	1,147.1	1,216.6
Reserve position in IMF	167.0	287.1	282.0
Foreign exchange	22,848.6	23,849.3	26,317.8
Total	23,072.4	25,283.5	27,827.5

Source: IMF, *International Financial Statistics*.

MONEY SUPPLY
('000 million pesos at 31 December)

	2008	2009	2010
Currency outside depository corporations	2,676.2	2,935.4	3,423.2
Transferable deposits	7,679.7	9,258.8	11,243.8
Other deposits	45,243.6	40,554.8	44,212.9
Securities other than shares	24,582.4	28,440.0	30,883.9
Broad money	80,181.8	81,189.0	89,763.8

Source: IMF, *International Financial Statistics*.

COST OF LIVING
(Consumer Price Index for Santiago; base: 2000 = 100)

	2007	2008	2009
Food (incl. beverages)	120.5	139.8	147.4
Rent, fuel and light	135.7	151.9	154.7
Clothing (incl. footwear)	81.2	81.4	70.8
All items (incl. others)	122.7	133.4	135.3

2010 (Consumer Price Index for whole country; base: 2009 = 100): Food (incl. beverages) 102.2; Rent, fuel and light 101.2; Clothing (incl. footwear) 82.5; All items (incl. others) 101.4.

Source: ILO.

NATIONAL ACCOUNTS
('000 million pesos at current prices)

Expenditure on the Gross Domestic Product

	2008	2009*	2010†
Government final consumption expenditure	10,603.2	12,405.6	13,566.6
Private final consumption expenditure	52,860.0	53,790.8	59,499.4
Increase in stocks	567.2	–1,937.6	1,538.7
Gross fixed capital formation	21,946.1	18,963.8	21,741.5
Total domestic expenditure	85,976.4	83,222.7	96,346.1
Exports of goods and services	39,866.3	35,155.0	42,030.7
Less Imports of goods and services	36,637.3	28,158.1	34,570.4
GDP in purchasers' values	89,205.5	90,219.5	103,806.4
GDP at constant 2003 prices	64,940.4	63,848.2	67,167.1

Gross Domestic Product by Economic Activity

	2008	2009*	2010†
Agriculture and forestry	2,400.0	2,395.6	2,560.5
Fishing	552.2	664.9	654.7
Mining and quarrying	15,660.3	14,046.5	19,955.5
Copper	13,842.3	12,160.7	18,012.1
Manufacturing	11,056.2	11,266.1	11,555.7
Electricity, gas and water	3,151.1	3,633.5	3,354.8
Construction	7,139.9	6,804.8	8,168.3
Trade, restaurants and hotels	7,993.9	8,163.1	9,408.4
Transport	4,653.6	4,950.3	5,953.2
Communications	1,746.4	1,650.0	1,645.4
Financial services‡	13,124.5	13,880.9	16,312.7
Sale of real estate	4,149.1	4,316.0	4,396.0
Personal services§	9,130.5	10,456.9	11,638.6
Public administration	3,640.8	4,273.6	4,626.6
Sub-total	84,398.5	86,502.2	100,230.6
Value-added tax	7,237.3	7,018.8	7,668.4
Import duties	600.7	450.0	651.8
Less Imputed bank service charge	3,030.9	3,751.4	4,744.4
GDP in purchasers' values	89,205.5	90,219.5	103,806.4

* Provisional figures.
† Preliminary figures.
‡ Including insurance, renting of property and business loans.
§ Including education.

BALANCE OF PAYMENTS
(US $ million)

	2008	2009	2010
Exports of goods f.o.b.	66,259	54,004	71,028
Imports of goods f.o.b.	–57,730	–39,888	–55,174
Trade balance	8,529	14,117	15,855
Exports of services	10,823	8,634	10,797
Imports of services	–11,787	–10,078	–11,816
Balance on goods and services	7,565	12,673	14,836
Other income received	5,928	5,345	5,995
Other income paid	–19,730	–17,011	–21,419
Balance on goods, services and income	–6,237	1,007	–588
Current transfers received	3,875	2,512	5,481
Current transfers paid	–945	–949	–1,091
Current balance	–3,307	2,570	3,802
Capital account (net)	3	15	5,641
Direct investment abroad	–8,041	–8,061	–8,744
Direct investment from abroad	15,150	12,874	15,095
Portfolio investment assets	–10,252	–13,691	–16,503
Portfolio investment liabilities	2,633	1,922	9,432
Financial derivatives assets	11,708	8,650	8,836
Financial derivatives liabilities	–12,660	–8,945	–9,759
Other investment assets	3,715	–1,412	–7,394
Other investment liabilities	6,346	6,955	3,152
Net errors and omissions	1,167	773	–536
Overall balance	6,461	1,648	3,023

Source: IMF, *International Financial Statistics*.

External Trade

PRINCIPAL COMMODITIES
(distribution by SITC, US $ million, preliminary)

Imports c.i.f.	2008	2009	2010
Food and live animals	3,749.6	2,822.7	3,714.8
Mineral fuels, lubricants, etc.	16,189.1	9,081.7	11,448.2
Petroleum, petroleum products, etc.	13,956.1	7,285.3	9,020.1
Gas, natural and manufactured	1,281.0	1,078.7	1,723.8
Chemicals and related products	6,423.7	4,594.0	5,857.3
Basic manufactures	6,536.5	4,261.8	6,470.4
Iron and steel	2,234.7	829.0	1,759.0
Machinery and transport equipment	17,177.5	13,205.0	18,728.3
Machinery specialized for particular industries	2,285.8	1,630.9	2,423.9
General industrial machinery equipment and parts	2,662.3	2,311.8	2,590.1
Office machines and automatic data-processing equipment	1,390.1	1,222.8	1,574.4
Telecommunications and sound equipment	1,893.8	1,455.5	2,357.8
Other electrical machinery apparatus, etc.	1,762.3	1,507.2	1,766.0
Road vehicles and parts*	5,176.7	3,072.8	6,319.1
Miscellaneous manufactured articles	4,307.8	3,590.1	4,859.2
Total (incl. others)	61,903.0	42,427.5	58,955.7

* Data on parts exclude tyres, engines and electrical parts.

Exports f.o.b.	2008	2009	2010
Food and live animals	10,428.2	9,402.8	9,981.4
Fish, crustaceans and molluscs and preparations thereof	3,369.7	2,977.0	2,816.5
Vegetables and fruit	4,753.8	4,127.3	4,890.4
Feeding-stuff for animals (excl. unmilled cereals)	547.3	654.1	577.1
Beverages and tobacco	1,451.4	1,438.5	1,632.8
Beverages	1,403.8	1,405.1	1,576.0
Crude materials (inedible) except fuels	18,786.4	14,942.7	21,674.6
Cork and wood	1,297.2	856.0	1,084.9
Pulp and waste paper	2,565.3	1,981.4	2,428.5
Metalliferous ores and metal scrap	14,316.0	11,425.0	17,420.4
Mineral fuels, lubricants, etc.	950.0	406.7	274.8
Chemicals and related products	3,274.2	2,162.1	2,794.9
Basic manufactures	26,802.2	21,225.5	30,030.3
Non-ferrous metals	23,575.1	19,070.8	27,492.6
Machinery and transport equipment	1,148.3	1,036.6	1,142.1
Total (incl. others)	66,455.5	53,735.4	71,028.4

PRINCIPAL TRADING PARTNERS
(US $ million, revised)

Imports c.i.f.	2008	2009	2010
Angola	1,785.8	289.6	766.4
Argentina	5,022.6	4,613.1	4,672.2
Brazil	5,275.0	2,855.4	4,632.2
Canada	963.4	726.9	708.3
China, People's Republic	6,798.3	5,135.4	8,295.8
Colombia	2,127.5	1,363.9	1,533.3
Finland	285.8	239.5	242.8
France	929.4	642.0	810.4
Germany	1,893.5	1,523.5	1,968.2
Italy	825.2	747.0	924.3
Japan	2,652.6	1,346.4	2,908.8
Korea, Republic	3,161.7	2,163.8	3,372.3
Mexico	1,748.9	1,183.9	2,037.2
Peru	1,845.8	692.1	1,330.8
Spain	932.8	1,023.8	936.8
Sweden	486.0	359.7	456.3
United Kingdom	478.9	1,032.5	966.1
USA	10,965.7	7,250.3	9,334.5
Total (incl. others)	61,903.0	42,427.5	58,955.7

Exports f.o.b.	2008	2009	2010
Argentina	982.9	719.8	986.5
Belgium	781.3	854.1	1,657.8
Brazil	3,848.8	2,725.2	4,291.6
Canada	1,386.8	1,192.3	1,391.0
China, People's Republic	9,275.1	12,486.2	17,355.4
Colombia	704.7	547.4	734.9
France	2,197.5	1,240.1	1,204.4
Germany	1,669.6	1,128.7	892.8
India	1,377.3	1,101.6	1,754.1
Italy	3,291.7	1,393.8	2,459.7
Japan	6,396.6	4,942.2	7,593.0
Korea, Republic	3,608.0	3,137.6	4,086.3
Mexico	2,210.5	1,457.7	1,844.2
Netherlands	4,122.0	2,048.5	2,559.9
Peru	1,296.9	1,457.7	1,186.6
Spain	1,737.3	1,074.3	1,293.4
United Kingdom	699.4	612.6	643.3
USA	7,947.0	6,062.4	7,002.3
Venezuela	1,212.6	751.6	541.9
Total (incl. others)	66,455.5	53,735.4	71,028.4

Transport

PRINCIPAL RAILWAYS

	2008	2009	2010*
Passenger journeys ('000)	22,210	23,275	22,020
Passenger-km ('000)	759,367	839,786	696,350
Freight ('000 metric tons)	27,185	25,492	25,215
Freight ton-km (million)	4,293	4,032	3,834

* Provisional.

ROAD TRAFFIC
(motor vehicles in use)

	2008	2009	2010
Passenger cars and jeeps (excl. taxis)	1,825,562	1,905,353	2,070,060
Minibuses and vans	153,906	156,566	164,195
Light trucks	551,913	567,445	608,507
Motorcycles and mopeds	87,545	96,213	102,314

SHIPPING

Merchant Fleet
(registered at 31 December)

	2007	2008	2009
Number of vessels	553	551	563
Total displacement ('000 grt)	908	863	849

Source: IHS Fairplay, *World Fleet Statistics*.

International Sea-borne Shipping
(freight traffic, '000 metric tons)

	2008	2009	2010
Goods loaded	46,386	48,002	48,770
Goods unloaded	40,904	35,101	41,610

CIVIL AVIATION
(traffic on scheduled services)

	2008	2009	2010
Kilometres flown (million)	147	136	154
Passengers ('000)	9,709.0	9,711.9	11,064.5
Passenger-km (million)	23,140	22,829	25,096
Freight (million ton-km)	4,279	4,249	5,306

Tourism

ARRIVALS BY NATIONALITY

	2008	2009	2010
Argentina	868,999	1,003,126	1,007,070
Bolivia	307,902	309,445	307,504
Brazil	261,080	216,801	233,644
France	62,984	63,623	63,538
Germany	75,579	67,592	67,894
Peru	252,573	269,669	308,877
Spain	61,551	56,212	53,372
United Kingdom	63,354	52,616	46,115
USA	216,280	208,566	180,215
Total (incl. others)	2,698,659	2,749,913	2,766,007

Source: Servicio Nacional de Turismo.

Tourism receipts (US $ million, excl. passenger transport): 1,674 in 2008; 1,568 in 2009; 1,636 in 2010 (provisional) (Source: World Tourism Organization).

Communications Media

	2008	2009	2010
Telephones ('000 main lines in use)	3,529.6	3,564.4	3,457.5
Mobile cellular telephones ('000 subscribers)	14,796.6	16,450.2	19,852.2
Internet subscribers ('000)	1,439.0	1,695.0	1,818.8
Broadband subscribers ('000)	1,427.2	1,654.7	1,788.5

Radio receivers ('000 in use): 5,180 in 1997.

Daily newspapers: 59 in 2004 (average circulation 816,000 copies).

Personal computers: 2,300,000 (141.1 per 1,000 persons) in 2005.

Sources: mainly UNESCO, *Statistical Yearbook*; UN, *Statistical Yearbook*; International Telecommunication Union.

Education

(2010 unless otherwise indicated)

	Institutions	Teachers	Students
Pre-primary	n.a.*	16,528†	349,720
Special primary		7,673†	145,873
Primary		75,854†	2,079,961
Secondary		49,144†	1,125,738
Adult		1,897‡	131,237†
Higher (incl. universities)	226‡	n.a.	987,643

* Many schools offer more than one level of education; a detailed breakdown is given below.

† 2004 figure.

‡ 2003 figure.

Schools (2004): Pre-primary: 640; Special 766; Primary 3,679; Secondary 517; Adult 292; Pre-primary and special 10; Pre-primary and primary 3,172; Pre-primary and secondary 1; Special and primary 22; Special and adult 3; Primary and secondary 380; Primary and adult 82; Secondary and adult 156; Pre-primary, special and primary 52; Pre-primary, primary and secondary 1,070; Pre-primary, primary and adult 261; Special, primary and secondary 2; Primary, secondary and adult 49; Pre-primary, special, primary and secondary 13; Pre-primary, special, primary and adult 7; Pre-primary, primary, secondary and adult 106; Pre-primary, special, primary, secondary and adult 5.

2008/09: *Teachers:* Pre-primary 33,220; Primary 70,044; Secondary 68,200; Tertiary 62,548. *Students:* Pre-primary 413,895; Primary 1,611,682; Secondary 1,528,200; Tertiary 876,243 (Source: UNESCO Institute for Statistics).

Pupil-teacher ratio (primary education, UNESCO estimate): 23.0 in 2008/09 (Source: UNESCO Institute for Statistics).

Adult literacy rate (UNESCO estimates): 98.6% (males 98.6%; females 98.5%) in 2009 (Source: UNESCO Institute for Statistics).

Directory

The Government

HEAD OF STATE

President: SEBASTIÁN PIÑERA ECHEÑIQUE (took office 11 March 2010).

THE CABINET
(May 2012)

A coalition of the Renovación Nacional (RN), the Unión Demócrata Independiente (UDI) and Independents.

Minister of the Interior and Public Security: RODRIGO HINZPETER KIRBERG (RN).

Minister of Foreign Affairs: ALFREDO MORENO CHARME (Ind.).

Minister of National Defence: ANDRÉS ALLAMAND (RN).

Minister of Finance: FELIPE LARRAÍN BASCUÑÁN (Ind.).

Minister, Secretary-General of the Presidency: CRISTIÁN LARROULET VIGNAU (Ind.).

Minister, Secretary-General of the Government: ANDRÉS CHADWICK (UDI).

Minister of the Economy, Development and Tourism: PABLO LONGUEIRA (UDI).

Minister of Social Development: JOAQUÍN LAVÍN INFANTE (UDI).

Minister of Education: HARALD BEYER BURGOS (Ind.).

Minister of Justice: TEODORO RIBERA (RN).

Minister of Labour and Social Security: EVELYN MATTHEI FORNET (UDI).

Minister of Public Works: LAURENCE GOLBORNE RIVEROS (Ind.).

Minister of Health: JAIME MAÑALICH MUXI (Ind.).

Minister of Housing and Urban Development: RODRIGO PÉREZ MACKENNA (Ind.).

Minister of Agriculture: LUIS MAYOL BOUCHON (Ind.).

Minister of Mining: HERNÁN DE SOLMINIHAC TAMPIER (Ind.).

Minister of Energy: JORGE BUNSTER BETTELEY (Ind.).

Minister of Transport and Telecommunications: PEDRO PABLO ERRÁZURIZ DOMÍNGUEZ (Ind.).

Minister of National Property: CATALINA PAROT DONOSO (RN).

Minister of the National Women's Service (Sernam): CAROLINA SCHMIDT ZALDÍVAR (Ind.).

Minister of the National Commission for Culture and the Arts: LUCIANO CRUZ-COKE CARVALLO (Ind.).

Minister of the Environment: MARÍA IGNACIA BENÍTEZ PEREIRA (UDI).

MINISTRIES

Ministry of Agriculture: Teatinos 40, 1°, Santiago; tel. (2) 393-5000; fax (2) 393-5135; internet www.minagri.gob.cl.

Ministry of the Economy, Development and Tourism: Avda Libertador Bernardo O'Higgins 1449, Santiago Downtown Torre II, POB 8340487, Santiago; tel. (2) 473-3400; fax (2) 473-3403; e-mail economia@economia.cl; internet www.economia.cl.

Ministry of Education: Alameda 1371, 7°, Santiago; tel. (2) 390-4000; fax (2) 380-0317; e-mail consultas@mineduc.cl; internet www.mineduc.cl.

Ministry of Energy: Edif. Santiago Downtown II, 13° y 14°, Alameda 1449, Santiago; tel. (2) 365-6800; internet www.minenergia.cl.

Ministry of Finance: Teatinos 120, 12°, Santiago; tel. (2) 473-2000; internet www.minhda.cl.

Ministry of Foreign Affairs: Teatinos 180, Santiago; tel. (2) 827-4200; internet www.minrel.gov.cl.

Ministry of Health: Enrique MacIver 541, 3°, Santiago; tel. (2) 574-0100; e-mail consulta@minsal.cl; internet www.minsal.cl.

Ministry of Housing and Urban Development: Alameda 924, POB 6513482, Santiago; tel. (2) 351-3000; fax (2) 633-7830; e-mail contactenos@minvu.cl; internet www.minvu.cl.

Ministry of the Interior and Public Security: Palacio de la Moneda, Santiago; tel. (2) 690-4000; fax (2) 699-2165; internet www.interior.cl.

Ministry of Justice: Morandé 107, Santiago; tel. (2) 674-3100; fax (2) 698-7098; internet www.minjusticia.cl.

Ministry of Labour and Social Security: Huérfanos 1273, 6°, Santiago; tel. (2) 753-0400; e-mail mintrab@mintrab.gob.cl; internet www.mintrab.gob.cl.

Ministry of Mining: Teatinos 120, 9°, Santiago; tel. (2) 473-3000; fax (2) 698-9262; internet www.minmineria.cl.

Ministry of National Defence: Edif. Diego Portales, 22°, Villavicencio 364, Santiago; tel. (2) 222-1202; fax (2) 633-0568; e-mail correo@defensa.cl; internet www.defensa.cl.

Ministry of National Property: Alameda 720, Santiago; tel. (2) 351-2100; fax (2) 351-2160; e-mail consultas@mbienes.cl; internet www.bienes.cl.

Ministry of Public Works: Morandé 59, Of. 545, Santiago; tel. (2) 449-4000; fax (2) 361-2700; internet www.mop.cl.

Ministry of Social Development: Ahumada 48, 7°, Santiago; tel. (2) 675-1400; fax (2) 672-1879; internet www.ministeriodesarrollosocial.gob.cl.

Ministry of Transport and Telecommunications: Amunátegui 139, 3°, Santiago; tel. (2) 421-3000; fax (2) 421-3552; internet www.mtt.cl.

National Commission for Culture and the Arts: Fray Camilo Henríquez 262, Santiago; tel. (2) 589-7824; internet www.consejodelacultura.cl.

National Women's Service (Sernam): Agustinas 1389, Santiago Centro, Santiago; tel. (2) 549-6100; fax (2) 549-6247; e-mail sernam@sernam.gov.cl; internet www.sernam.gov.cl.

Office of the Minister, Secretary-General of the Government: Palacio de la Moneda, Santiago; tel. (2) 690-4160; fax (2) 697-1756; e-mail cmladini@segegob.cl; internet www.segegob.cl.

Office of the Minister, Secretary-General of the Presidency: Moneda 1160, Santiago; tel. (2) 694-5855; fax (2) 694-5888; internet www.minsegpres.gob.cl.

President and Legislature

PRESIDENT

Election, 13 December 2009 and 17 January 2010

	First round % of votes	Second round % of votes
Sebastián Piñera Echeñique (Coalición por el Cambio)	44.05	51.61
Eduardo Frei Ruiz-Tagle (CPD)	29.60	48.39
Marco Enríquez-Ominami Gumucio (Ind.)	20.13	—
Jorge Arrete MacNiven (Juntos Podemos Más)	6.21	—
Total	100.00	100.00

CONGRESO NACIONAL

The Congreso Nacional is located in Valparaíso.

Senado
(Senate)

President: GUIDO GIRARDI LAVÍN (PPD).

The Senado has 38 members, who hold office for an eight-year term, with approximately one-half of the seats renewable every four years. The last election, to renew 18 of the 38 seats, was held on 13 December 2009. The table below shows the composition of the Senado following that election.

Distribution of Seats by Legislative Bloc, December 2009

	Seats
Concertación de Partidos por la Democracia (CPD)/ Juntos Podemos Más*	19
Coalición por el Cambio	16
Independents	3
Total	38

* The CPD and Juntos Podemos Más contested the congressional elections in alliance; however, the Partido Humanista, part of the Juntos Podemos Más grouping, did not participate in the alliance.

Cámara de Diputados
(Chamber of Deputies)

President: PATRICIO MELEROA ABAROA (UDI).

General Election, 13 December 2009

Legislative bloc	% of valid votes	Seats
Coalición por el Cambio	43.44	58
Unión Demócrata Independiente	—	36
Renovación Nacional	—	19
Independents	—	3
Concertación de Partidos por la Democracia (CPD)/Juntos Podemos Más*	44.36	57
Partido Demócrata Cristiano	—	19
Partido por la Democracia	—	18
Partido Socialista de Chile	—	11
Partido Radical Socialdemócrata	—	5
Partido Comunista de Chile	—	3
Independents	—	1
Chile Limpio Vote Feliz†	5.40	3
Independents	6.77	2
Total	100.00	120

* The CPD and Juntos Podemos Más contested the congressional elections in alliance; however, the Partido Humanista, part of the Juntos Podemos Más grouping, did not participate in the alliance.

† Deputies in this bloc are aligned to the Partido Regionalista de los Independientes.

Election Commissions

Servicio Electoral: Esmeralda 611, Santiago; tel. (02) 731-5500; fax (02) 639-7296; e-mail direnac@servel.cl; internet www.servel.cl; f. 1986; Dir JUAN IGNACIO GARCÍA RODRÍGUEZ.

Tribunal Calificador de Elecciones (TCE): Teatinos 391, Santiago; tel. (2) 463-8500; fax (2) 699-4464; e-mail secretaria@tribunalcalificador.cl; internet www.tribunalcalificador.cl; f. 1980; Pres. SERGIO MUÑOZ GAJARDO.

Political Organizations

Coalición por el Cambio: f. 2009 to support presidential candidacy of Sebastián Piñera; right-wing alliance.

Chile Primero: Moneda 812, Of. 1104, Santiago; tel. (2) 830-3906; e-mail contacto@chileprimero.cl; internet www.chileprimero.cl; f. 2007 by fmr mems of the PPD (q.v.); independent; Pres. VLADO MIROSEVIC; Sec.-Gen. JOSÉ CARREÑO.

Movimiento Humanista Cristiano: Nueva York 54, Of. 716, Santiago; internet www.mhcchile.cl; Pres. RICARDO MACCIONI; Sec.-Gen. CARLOS PÉREZ O.

Norte Grande: Of. 502, Washington 2562, Antofagasta; tel. and fax (55) 22-8732; internet www.cantero.cl; Leader CARLOS CANTERO OJEDA.

Renovación Nacional (RN): Antonio Varas 454, Providencia, Santiago; tel. (2) 799-4200; fax (2) 799-4212; e-mail clarrain@rn.cl; internet www.rn.cl; f. 1988; right-wing; part of the Alianza por Chile coalition (f. 1999), which, in turn, forms part of the Coalición por el Cambio; Pres. CARLOS LARRAÍN PEÑA; Sec.-Gen. MARIO DESBORDES.

Unión Demócrata Independiente (UDI): Avda Suecia 286, Providencia, Santiago; tel. (2) 241-4200; fax (2) 233-6189; e-mail contacto@udi.cl; internet www.udi.cl; f. 1989; right-wing; part of the Alianza por Chile coalition (f. 1999) which, in turn, forms part of the Coalición por el Cambio; Pres. PATRICIO MELERO; Sec.-Gen. JOSÉ ANTONIO KAST.

Concertación de Partidos por la Democracia (CPD): Londres 57, Santiago; tel. and fax (2) 639-7170; internet www.primariasconcertacion.cl; f. 1988 as the Comando por el No, an opposition front to campaign against the military regime in the plebiscite of 5 October 1988; adopted present name following plebiscite; Nat. Co-ordinator DOMINGO NAMUNCURA.

Partido Demócrata Cristiano (PDC): Alameda 1460, 2°, Santiago; tel. and fax (2) 376-0136; e-mail info@pdc.cl; internet www.pdc.cl; f. 1957; Pres. IGNACIO WALKER PRIETO; Sec. VÍCTOR MALDONADO ROLDÁN.

Partido por la Democracia (PPD): Santo Domingo 1828, Santiago; tel. and fax (2) 671-2320; e-mail presidencia@ppd.cl; internet www.ppd.cl; f. 1987; Pres. CAROLINA TOHÁ MORALES; Sec.-Gen. OSCAR CARRASCO.

Partido Radical Socialdemócrata (PRSD): Londres 57, Santiago; tel. and fax (2) 633-6928; fax (2) 638-3353; e-mail ernestov@

123mail.cl; internet www.partidoradical.cl; centre-left; Pres. JOSÉ ANTONIO GÓMEZ URRUTIA; Sec.-Gen. ERNESTO VELASCO RODRÍGUEZ.

Partido Socialista de Chile (PS): París 873, Santiago; tel. (2) 956-6700; fax (2) 956-6719; e-mail pschile@pschile.cl; internet www.pschile.cl; f. 1933; left-wing; mem. of Socialist International; Pres. OSVALDO ANDRADE LARA; Sec.-Gen. FULVIO ROSSI CIOCCA.

Juntos Podemos Más: e-mail info@podemos.cl; internet www.juntospodemosmas.cl; electoral alliance comprising:

Izquierda Cristiana de Chile (IC): Compañía 2404, Santiago; tel. (2) 672-9897; internet www.izquierdacristiana.cl; f. 1971; Pres. VÍCTOR OSORIO; Sec.-Gen. DARÍO SALAS.

Partido Comunista de Chile (PC): Avda Vicuña Mackenna 31, Santiago; tel. and fax (2) 222-2750; e-mail www@pcchile.cl; internet www.pcchile.cl; f. 1912; achieved legal status in Oct. 1990; Pres. GUILLERMO TEILLIER; Sec.-Gen. LAUTARO CARMONA.

Partido Humanista (PH): Livingstone 72, Santiago; tel. (2) 634-2614; e-mail eosorio@humanismo.cl; internet www.partidohumanista.cl; f. 1984; Pres. DANILO MONTEVERDE; Sec.-Gen. PAOLA PARRA.

Movimiento Amplio Social (MAS): Calle Padre Alonso de Ovalle 726, Santiago; internet www.movimientoampliosocial.cl; f. 2008; contested the 2009 elections in alliance with Fuerza País; Pres. ALEJANDRO NAVARRO BRAIN; Sec.-Gen. FERNANDO ZAMORANO FERNÁNDEZ.

Partido Ecologista: O'Higgins 1104, Concepción; e-mail admin@partidoecologista.cl; internet partidoecologista.cl; f. 2002; Pres. ALEJANDRO IVÁN SAN MARTÍN BRAVO; Sec.-Gen. PABLO PEÑALOZA.

Partido Progresista (PRO): Salvador 1029, Providencia; tel. (2) 204-5274; e-mail cwarner@losprogresistas.cl; internet losprogresistas.cl; f. 2010; Pres. MARCO ENRÍQUEZ-OMINAMI GUMUCIO; Sec.-Gen. CRISTIAN WARNER.

Partido Regionalista de los Independientes (PRI): Avda Miraflores 133, Of. 33, Santiago; tel. (2) 664-8772; fax (2) 664-8773; e-mail pri@pricentro.cl; internet www.pricentro.cl; f. 2006 following merger of Alianza National de Independientes and Partido de Acción Regionalista de Chile; Pres. PEDRO ARAYA GUERRERO; Sec.-Gen. HUMBERTO DE LA MAZA.

Wallmapuwen (Partido Nacionalista Mapuche): e-mail wallmapuwen@gmail.com; internet www.wallmapuwen.cl; f. 2005; campaigns for Mapuche rights; not officially registered; Pres. LUIS PENCHULEO MORALES; Sec.-Gen. HÉCTOR CUMILAF HUENTEMIL.

Diplomatic Representation

EMBASSIES IN CHILE

Algeria: Monseñor Nuncio Sotero Sanz 221, Providencia, Santiago; tel. (2) 820-2100; fax (2) 820-2121; e-mail argelia_embajada@yahoo.fr; Ambassador NOURREDINE YAZID.

Argentina: Miraflores 285, Santiago; tel. (2) 582-2500; fax (2) 639-3321; e-mail embajador@embargentina.cl; internet www.embargentina.cl; Ambassador GINÉS GONZÁLEZ GARCÍA.

Australia: Isidora Goyenechea 3621, El Golf Torre B, 12° y 13°, Casilla 33, Correo 10 Las Condes, Santiago; tel. (2) 550-3500; fax (2) 331-5960; e-mail dima-santiago@dfat.gov.au; internet www.chile.embassy.gov.au; Ambassador VIRGINIA GRAVILLE.

Austria: Barros Errazuriz 1968, 3°, Santiago; tel. (2) 223-4774; fax (2) 204-9382; e-mail santiago-de-chile-ob@bmaa.gv.at; internet www.chile-embajadadeaustria.at; Ambassador DOROTHEA AUER.

Belgium: Edif. Forum, Avda Providencia 2653, 11°, Of. 1103, Santiago; tel. (2) 232-1070; fax (2) 232-1073; e-mail santiago@diplobel.org; internet www.diplomatie.be/santiago; Ambassador DIRK VAN EECKHOUT.

Brazil: Padre Alonso Ovalle 1665, Casilla 1497, Santiago; tel. (2) 698-2486; fax (2) 671-5961; e-mail embrasil@brasembsantiago.cl; internet www.brasembsantiago.cl; Ambassador FREDERICO CEZAR DE ARAUJO.

Bulgaria: Lota 2284, Providencia, Santiago; tel. (2) 421-1244; fax (2) 421-1245; e-mail Embassy.Santiago@mfa.bg; internet www.mfa.bg/en/73; Chargé d'affaires a.i. KALIN IVANOV DIMITROV.

Canada: Edif. World Trade Center, Torre Norte, 12°, Nueva Tajamar 481, Santiago; tel. (2) 652-3800; fax (2) 652-3912; e-mail stago@international.gc.ca; internet www.canadainternational.gc.ca/chile-chili; Ambassador SARAH FOUNTAIN SMITH.

China, People's Republic: Pedro de Valdivia 550, Santiago; tel. (2) 233-9880; fax (2) 335-2755; e-mail embajadachina@entelchile.net; internet cl.china-embassy.org; Ambassador LU FAN.

Colombia: Isidora Goyenechea 3162, Of. 302, Las Condes, Santiago; tel. (2) 335-9948; fax (2) 335-8469; e-mail esantiag@cancilleria.gov.co; internet www.embajadaenchile.gov.co; Ambassador SANTIAGO FIGUEROA SERRANO.

Costa Rica: Zurich 255, Of. 85, Las Condes, Santiago; tel. (2) 334-9486; fax (2) 334-9490; e-mail embacostarica@adsl.tie.cl; Ambassador JAN RUGE MOYA.

Croatia: Ezequias Alliende 2370, Providencia, Santiago; tel. (2) 269-6141; fax (2) 269-6092; e-mail embajada@croacia.cl; Ambassador VESNA TERZIĆ.

Cuba: Avda Los Leones 1346, Providencia, Santiago; tel. (2) 367-9738; fax (2) 367-9745; e-mail emcuchil@embacuba.cl; internet www.embacuba.cl; Ambassador ILENEA DÍAZ-ARGÜELLES ALASA.

Czech Republic: Avda El Golf 254, Santiago; tel. (2) 232-1066; fax (2) 232-0707; e-mail santiago@embassy.mzv.cz; internet www.mfa.cz/santiago; Ambassador ZDENĚK KUBÁNEK.

Denmark: Jacques Cazotte 5531, Casilla 18, Centro Cívico, Vitacura, Santiago; tel. (2) 941-5100; fax (2) 218-1736; e-mail sclamb@um.dk; internet www.ambsantiago.um.dk/la; Ambassador LARS STEEN NIELSEN.

Dominican Republic: Candelaria Goyenechea 4153, Vitacura, Santiago; tel. (2) 953-5750; fax (2) 953-5758; e-mail embrepdom@erd.co.cl; Ambassador PABLO ARTURO MARIÑEZ ALVAREZ.

Ecuador: Avda Providencia 1979 y Pedro Valdivia, 5°, Casilla 16007, Correo 9, Santiago; tel. (2) 231-5073; fax (2) 232-5833; e-mail embajadaecuador@adsl.tie.cl; internet www.embajadaecuador.cl; Ambassador FRANCISCO BORJA CEVALLOS.

Egypt: Roberto del Río 1871, Providencia, Santiago; tel. (2) 274-8881; fax (2) 274-6334; e-mail embassy.santiago@mfa.gov.eg; Ambassador HAZEM AHDY KHAIRAT.

El Salvador: Coronel 2330, 5°, Of. 51, Casilla 16863, Correo 9, Santiago; tel. (2) 233-8324; fax (2) 231-0960; e-mail embasalva@adsl.tie.cl; internet www.rree.gob.sv/embajadas/chile.nsf; Ambassador AIDA ELENA MINERO REYES.

Finland: Alcántara 200, Of. 201, Las Condes, Casilla 16657, Correo 9, Santiago; tel. (2) 263-4917; fax (2) 263-4701; e-mail sanomat.snt@formin.fi; internet www.finland.cl; Ambassador ILKKA HEISKANEN.

France: Avda Condell 65, Casilla 38D, Providencia, Santiago; tel. (2) 470-8000; fax (2) 470-8050; e-mail ambassade@ambafrance-cl.org; internet www.france.cl; Ambassador MARC GIACOMINI.

Germany: Las Hualtatas 5677, Vitacura, Santiago; tel. (2) 463-2500; fax (2) 463-2525; e-mail info@santigo-de-chile.diplo.de; internet www.santiago.diplo.de; Ambassador MICHAEL GLOTZBACH.

Greece: Jorge Sexto 306, Las Condes, Santiago; tel. (2) 212-7900; fax (2) 212-8048; e-mail secretaria@mfa.gr; internet www.mfa.gr/santiag; Ambassador AGLAIA BALTA.

Guatemala: Zurich 255, Of. 55, Las Condes, Santiago; tel. (2) 586-4430; fax (2) 586-4437; e-mail embajada@guatemala.cl; internet www.guatemala.cl; Ambassador GUSTAVO ADOLFO LÓPEZ CALDERÓN.

Haiti: Zurich 255, Of. 21, Las Condes, Santiago; tel. (2) 231-3364; fax (2) 231-0967; Chargé d'affaires a.i. JEAN-VICTOR HARVEL JEAN-BAPTISTE.

Holy See: Nuncio Sótero Sanz 200, Casilla 16836, Correo 9, Santiago (Apostolic Nunciature); tel. (2) 231-2020; fax (2) 231-0868; e-mail nunciatura@iglesia.cl; Apostolic Nuncio Most Rev. IVO SCAPOLO (Titular Archbishop of Thagaste).

Honduras: Zurich 255, Of. 51, Las Condes, Santiago; tel. (2) 234-4069; fax (2) 334-7946; e-mail honduras@tie.cl; Ambassador MARÍA DEL CARMEN NASSER DE RAMOS.

India: Triana 871, Casilla 10433, Santiago; tel. (2) 235-2005; fax (2) 235-9607; e-mail info@embajadaindia.cl; internet www.embajadaindia.cl; Ambassador PRADEEP KUMAR KAPUR.

Indonesia: Avda Nueva Costanera 3318, Vitacura, Santiago; tel. (2) 207-6266; fax (2) 207-9901; e-mail kbristgo@entelchile.net; Ambassador ALOYSIUS LELE MADHAAS.

Iran: Estoril 755, Las Condes, Santiago; tel. (2) 723-3623; fax (2) 723-3632; e-mail embiranchile@mail.com; internet www.embiranchile.com; Ambassador HOUSHANG KARIMI ABHARI.

Iraq: Alsacia 150, Of. 122, Las Condes, Santiago; tel. 8-1918665 (mobile); e-mail sanemb@iraqmfamail.com; Ambassador TAHA SHOKER MAHMOOD AL-ABASSI.

Israel: San Sebastián 2812, 5°, Las Condes, Santiago; tel. (2) 750-0500; fax (2) 750-0555; e-mail amb.sec@santiago.mfa.gov.il; internet santiago.mfa.gov.il; Ambassador DAVID DADONN.

Italy: Clemente Fabres 1050, Providencia, Santiago; tel. (2) 470-8400; fax (2) 223-2467; e-mail info.santiago@esteri.it; internet www.ambsantiago.esteri.it; Ambassador VINCENZO PALLADINO.

Japan: Avda Ricardo Lyon 520, Santiago; tel. (2) 232-1807; fax (2) 232-1812; e-mail contactoembajadajapon@gmail.com; internet www.cl.emb-japan.go.jp; Ambassador HIDENORI MURAKAMI.

Jordan: Avda Presidente Errazuriz 2999, Of. 202, Las Condes, Santiago; tel. (2) 245-6210; fax (2) 245-6212; e-mail embajadadejordania@manquehue.net; Ambassador IBRAHIM AWAWDEH.

Korea, Republic: Alcántara 74, Casilla 1301, Santiago; tel. (2) 228-4214; fax (2) 206-2355; e-mail coremb@tie.cl; internet chl.mofat.go.kr; Ambassador HWANG EUI-SEUNG.

Lebanon: Alianza 1728, Vitacura, Casilla 19150, Correo 19, Santiago; tel. (2) 218-2835; fax (2) 219-3502; e-mail libano@vtr.net; Chargé d'affaires a.i. ALEJANDRO BITAR.

Malaysia: Tajamar 183, 10°, Of. 1002, Correo 35, Las Condes, Santiago; tel. (2) 233-6698; fax (2) 234-3853; e-mail mwstg@embdemalasia.cl; internet www.kln.gov.my/perwakilan/santiago; Ambassador GANESON SIVAGURUNATHAN.

Mexico: Félix de Amesti 128, Las Condes, Santiago; tel. (2) 583-8400; fax (2) 583-8484; e-mail info@emexico.cl; internet www.emexico.cl; Ambassador MARIO LEAL CAMPOS.

Morocco: Avda Juan XXIII 6152, Vitacura, Santiago; tel. (2) 218-0311; fax (2) 218-0176; e-mail ambmarch@terra.cl; Ambassador ABDELKADER CHAUI LUDIE.

Netherlands: Apoquinado 3500, 13°, Las Condes, Santiago; tel. (2) 756-9200; fax (2) 756-9226; e-mail stg@minbuza.nl; internet chile.nlembajada.org; Ambassador JOHAN VAN DER WERFF.

New Zealand: Avda Isidora Goyenechea 3000, 12°, Las Condes, Santiago; tel. (2) 616-3000; fax (2) 616-3040; e-mail embajada@nzembassy.cl; internet www.nzembassy.cl; Ambassador ROSEMARY ANNE PATERSON.

Nicaragua: Zurich 255, Of. 111, Las Condes, Santiago; tel. (2) 234-1808; fax (2) 234-5170; e-mail embanic@embajadadenicaragua.tie.cl; Ambassador MARÍA LUISA ROBLETO AGUILAR.

Norway: San Sebastián 2839, Of. 509, Casilla 2431, Santiago; tel. (2) 234-2888; fax (2) 234-2201; e-mail emb.santiago@mfa.no; internet www.noruega.cl; Ambassador MARTIN TORE BJØRNDAL.

Pakistan: Espoz 2336, Vitacura, Santiago; tel. (2) 953-8686; fax (2) 953-8691; e-mail parepsantiao@hotmail.com; Ambassador BURHANUL ISLAM.

Panama: La Reconquista 640, Las Condes, Santiago; tel. (2) 202-5439; fax (2) 202-6318; e-mail embajadapanamachile@vtr.net; Ambassador MERCEDES ALFARO DE LÓPEZ.

Paraguay: Huérfanos 886, 5°, Ofs 514–515, Santiago; tel. (2) 639-4640; fax (2) 633-4426; e-mail epychemb@entelchile.net; Ambassador TERUMI MATSUO DE CLAVEROL.

Peru: Avda Andrés Bello 1751, Casilla 16277, Providencia, Santiago; tel. (2) 339-2600; fax (2) 235-2053; e-mail embstgo@entelchile.net; Ambassador CARLOS PAREJA RÍOS.

Philippines: Félix de Amesti 367, Las Condes, Santiago; tel. (2) 208-1313; fax (2) 208-1400; e-mail embassyphil@vtr.net; Ambassador MARÍA CONSUELO PUYAT-REYES.

Poland: Mar del Plata 2055, Santiago; tel. (2) 204-1213; fax (2) 204-9332; e-mail embajador.polonia@entelchile.net; internet www.polonia.cl; Ambassador RYSZARD PIASECKI.

Portugal: Nueva Tajamar 555, Torre Norte 16°, Las Condes, Santiago; tel. (2) 203-0542; fax (2) 203-4004; e-mail embajada@embportugal.tie.cl; Ambassador JOSÉ MANUEL SANTA-MARINHA BELEZA PAES MOREIRA.

Romania: Benjamín 2955, Las Condes, Santiago; tel. (2) 231-1893; fax (2) 232-2325; e-mail embajada@rumania.tie.cl; internet www.rumania.cl; Ambassador FLORIN ANGELO FLORIAN.

Russia: Avda Américo Vespucio 2127, Vitacura, Santiago; tel. (2) 208-6254; fax (2) 206-8892; e-mail embajada@rusia.tie.cl; internet www.chile.mid.ru; Ambassador MIKHAIL ORLOVETS.

South Africa: Avda 11 de Septiembre 2353, 17°, Torre San Ramón, Santiago; tel. (2) 231-2862; fax (2) 231-3185; e-mail info.chile@foreign.gov.za; internet www.embajada-sudafrica.cl; Ambassador DUDUZILE MOERANE-KHOZA.

Spain: Avda Andrés Bello 1895, Casilla 16456, Providencia, Santiago; tel. (2) 235-2755; fax (2) 235-1049; e-mail emb.santiagodechile@mae.es; internet www.mae.es/embajadas/santiagodechile; Ambassador IÑIGO DE PALACIO ESPAÑA.

Sweden: Avda 11 de Septiembre 2353, 4°, Providencia, Santiago; tel. (2) 940-1700; fax (2) 940-1730; e-mail ambassaden.santiago-de-chile@foreign.ministry.se; internet www.embajadasuecia.cl; Ambassador EVA ZETTERBERG.

Switzerland: Avda Américo Vespucio Sur 100, 14°, Las Condes, Santiago; tel. (2) 928-0800; fax (2) 928-0135; e-mail san.vertretung@eda.admin.ch; internet www.eda.admin.ch/santiago; Ambassador YVONNEE BAUMANN.

Syria: Carmencita 111, Casilla 12, Correo 10, Santiago; tel. (2) 232-7471; fax (2) 231-1825; e-mail embajadasiria@tie.cl; Chargé d'affaires a.i. SAMI SALAMEH.

Thailand: Avda Américo Vespucio 100, 15°, Las Condes, Santiago; tel. (2) 717-3959; fax (2) 717-3758; e-mail rte.santiago@vtr.net; internet www.thaiembassy.org/santiago; Ambassador VIPAWAN NIPATAKUSOL.

Turkey: Edif. Montolin, Of. 71, Monseñor Sotero Sanz 55, Providencia, Santiago; tel. (2) 231-8952; fax (2) 231-7762; e-mail embturquia@123.cl; Ambassador HAYATI GUVEN.

United Arab Emirates: Avda Apoquindo 3039, 7°, Las Condes, Santiago; tel. (2) 790-0000; fax (2) 790-0033; e-mail archive.santiago@mofa.gov.ae; Ambassador ABDULLAH MOHAMMED AL MU'INA.

United Kingdom: Avda el Bosque Norte 0125, Santiago; tel. (2) 370-4100; fax (2) 370-4180; e-mail embsan@britemb.cl; internet ukinchile.fco.gov.uk; Ambassador JON BENJAMIN.

USA: Avda Andrés Bello 2800, Las Condes, Santiago; tel. (2) 232-2600; fax (2) 330-3710; internet chile.usembassy.gov; Ambassador ALEJANDRO DANIEL WOLFF.

Uruguay: Avda Pedro de Valdivia 711, Santiago; tel. (2) 204-7988; fax (2) 204-7772; e-mail urusgo@uruguay.cl; internet www.uruguay.cl; Ambassador PEDRO VAZ RAMELA.

Venezuela: Bustos 2021, Providencia, Santiago; tel. (2) 365-8700; fax (2) 223-1170; e-mail embavenez@embajadavenezuela.cl; internet embajadadevenezuela.cl; Ambassador MARÍA LOURDES URBANEJA DURANT.

Viet Nam: Avda Américo Vespucio Sur 833, Las Condes, Santiago; tel. (2) 244-3633; fax (2) 244-3799; e-mail sqvnchile@yahoo.com; Ambassador HA THI NGOC HA.

Judicial System

The Supreme Court consists of 21 members.

There are Courts of Appeal throughout the country whose members are appointed from a list submitted to the President of the Republic by the Supreme Court. The number of members of each court varies. Judges and ministers of the Supreme Court do not continue in office beyond the age of 75 years.

Corte Suprema

Compañía 1140, 2°, Santiago; tel. (2) 873-5000; fax (2) 873-5276; e-mail mgonzalezp@poderjudicial.cl; internet www.poderjudicial.cl.

President of the Supreme Court: RUBÉN ALBERTO BALLESTEROS CÁRCAMO.

Public Prosecutor: MÓNICA EUGENIA MALDONADO CROQUEVIELLE.

Secretary of the Court: ROSA MARÍA DEL C. PINTO EGUSQUIZA.

Religion

CHRISTIANITY

The Roman Catholic Church

According to the latest available census figures (2002), some 70% of the population aged 15 years and above are Roman Catholics. Chile comprises five archdioceses, 18 dioceses, two territorial prelatures and one apostolic vicariate.

Bishops' Conference

Conferencia Episcopal de Chile, Echaurren 4, 6°, Casilla 517-V, Correo 21, Santiago; tel. (2) 671-7733; fax (2) 698-1416; e-mail secretariageneral@episcopado.cl; internet www.iglesia.cl.

f. 1955 (statutes approved 2000); Pres. Rt Rev. ALEJANDRO GOIĆ KARMELIĆ (Bishop of Rancagua).

Archbishop of Antofagasta: PABLO LIZAMA RIQUELME, San Martín 2628, Casilla E, Antofagasta; tel. and fax (55) 26-8856; e-mail antofagasta@episcopado.cl; internet www.iglesiadeantofagasta.cl.

Archbishop of Concepción: RICARDO EZZATI ANDRELLO, Calle Barros Arana 544, Casilla 65-C, Concepción; tel. (41) 222-8173; fax (41) 223-2844; e-mail amoreno@episcopado.cl; internet www.arzobispadodeconcepcion.cl.

Archbishop of La Serena: MANUEL GERARDO DONOSO DONOSO, Los Carrera 450, Casilla 613, La Serena; tel. (51) 21-2325; fax (51) 22-5886; e-mail laserena@episcopado.cl; internet www.iglesia.cl/laserena.

Archbishop of Puerto Montt: CRISTIÁN CARO CORDERO, Calle Benavente 385, Casilla 17, Puerto Montt; tel. (65) 25-2215; fax (65) 27-1861; e-mail puertomontt@episcopado.cl; internet www.arzobispadodepuertomontt.cl.

Archbishop of Santiago de Chile: RICARDO EZZATI ANDRELLO, Erasmo Escala 1884, Casilla 30-D, Santiago; tel. (2) 696-3275; fax (2) 671-2042; e-mail curiasantiago@arzobispado.tie.cl; internet www.iglesiadesantiago.cl.

The Anglican Communion

Anglicans in Chile come within the Diocese of Chile, which forms part of the Anglican Church of the Southern Cone of America, covering Argentina, Bolivia, Chile, Paraguay, Peru and Uruguay.

Bishop of Chile: Rt Rev. HECTOR F. ZAVALA, Corporación Anglicana de Chile, Victoria Subercaseaux 41, Of. 301, Casilla 50675, Correo Central, Santiago; tel. (2) 638-3009; fax (2) 639-4581; e-mail diocesis@iach.cl; internet www.iglesiaanglicana.cl.

Other Christian Churches

According to the 2002 census, 15% of the population are Evangelical Christians, 1% are Jehovah's Witnesses and 1% are Mormons.

Iglesia Católica Apostólica Ortodoxa de la Santísima Virgen María (Orthodox Church of the Patriarch of Antioch): Avda Pedro de Valdivia 92, Providencia, Santiago; tel. (2) 231-7284; fax (2) 232-0860; e-mail iglesia@iglesiaortodoxa.cl; internet www.iglesiaortodoxa.cl; Archbishop Mgr SERGIO ABAD.

Iglesia Evangélica Luterana en Chile: Pedro de Valdivia 3420-H, Dpto 33, Ñuñoa, Casilla 167–11, Santiago; tel. (2) 223-3195; fax (2) 205-2193; e-mail secretaria@ielch.cl; internet www.ielch.cl; f. 1937; Pres. Dra GLORIA ROJAS VARGAS; 3,000 mems.

Iglesia Luterana en Chile: Avda Lota 2330, POB 16067, Correo 9, Santiago; tel. (2) 231-7222; fax (2) 231-3913; e-mail obispo@iglesialuterana.cl; internet www.iglesialuterana.cl; Pres. JÜRGEN LEIBBRANDT; 10,280 mems.

Iglesia Metodista de Chile: Sargento Aldea 1041, Casilla 67, Santiago; tel. (2) 556-6074; fax (2) 554-1763; e-mail imech.chile@metodista.cl; internet www.metodista.cl; autonomous since 1969; Bishop NEFTALÍ ARAVENA BRAVO; 9,882 mems.

Iglesia Pentecostal de Chile: Manuel Rodríguez 1155, Curicó; tel. (75) 318640; e-mail iglesia@pentecostaldechile.cl; internet www.pentecostaldechile.cl; f. 1947; Pres. Rev. SERGIO VELOSO TOLOSA; Bishop Rev. LUIS ULISES MUÑOZ MORAGA; 125,000 mems.

Jehovah's Witnesses: Avda Concha y Toro 3456, Casilla 267, Puente Alto; tel. (2) 428-2600; fax (2) 428-2609; Dir PEDRO J. LOVATO GROSSO.

Unión de Iglesias Evangélicas Bautistas de Chile: Miguel Claro 755, Providencia, Santiago; tel. (2) 264-1208; fax (2) 431-8012; e-mail centrobautista@ubach.cl; internet www.ubach.cl; f. 1908; Pres. RAQUEL CONTRERAS EDDINGER; Vice-Pres. JORGE QUINTEROS.

JUDAISM

There is a small Jewish community in Chile, numbering 14,976 at the 2002 census (less than 1% of the population).

Círculo Israelita de Santiago: Comandante Malbec 13210, Lo Barnechea, Santiago; tel. (2) 240-5000; fax (2) 243-6244; e-mail info@cis.cl; internet www.cis.cl; f. 1982; Dir-Gen. SERGIO JODORKOVSKY P.; Exec. Dir MARIO KIBLISKY.

Comunidad Israelita Sefardi de Chile: Avda Ricardo Lyon 812, Providencia, Santiago; tel. (2) 209-8086; fax (2) 204-7382; e-mail contacto@sefaradies.cl; internet www.sefaradies.cl; Sec.-Gen. LEÓN HASSÓN T.

ISLAM

There is a small Muslim community in Chile, numbering 2,894 at the 2002 census (less than 1% of the population).

Centro Islámico de Chile: Mezquita As-Salam, Campoamor 2975, esq. Chile-España, Ñuñoa, Santiago; tel. (2) 343-1376; fax (2) 343-1378; e-mail contacto@islamenchile.cl; internet www.islamenchile.cl; f. 1925 as the Sociedad Unión Musulmana; Sec. MOHAMED RUMIE.

BAHÁ'Í FAITH

National Spiritual Assembly: Manuel de Salas 356, Casilla 3731, Ñuñoa, Santiago; tel. (2) 752-3999; fax (2) 752-3999; e-mail secretaria@bahai.cl; internet www.bahai.cl.

The Press

Most newspapers of nation-wide circulation in Chile are published in Santiago.

DAILIES

Santiago

La Cuarta: Diagonal Vicuña Mackenna 1870, Casilla 2795, Santiago; tel. (2) 551-7067; fax (2) 555-7071; e-mail contacto@lacuarta.cl; internet www.lacuarta.cl; f. 1984; morning; popular; Dir DIOZEL PÉREZ; circ. 146,000.

Diario Financiero: San Crescente 81, 2°, Las Condes, Santiago; tel. (2) 339-1000; fax (2) 231-3340; e-mail suscripciones@df.cl; internet www.df.cl; f. 1988; morning; Dir GUILLERMO TURNER OLEA; Gen. Man. EDUARDO POOLEY PELIZZOLA; circ. 20,000.

Diario Oficial de la República de Chile: Casilla 81-D, Agustinas 1269, Santiago; tel. (2) 698-3969; fax (2) 698-1059; e-mail info@diariooficial.cl; internet www.diariooficial.cl; f. 1877; Dir FLORENCIO CEBALLOS BUSTOS; circ. 10,000.

Estrategia: Luis Carrera 1289, Vitacura, Santiago; tel. (2) 655-6100; fax (2) 655-6439; e-mail estrategia@edgestion.cl; internet www.estrategia.cl; f. 1978; morning; business news; Dir VÍCTOR MANUEL OJEDA; circ. 33,000.

La Hora: Avda Vicuña Mackenna 1870, Santiago; tel. (2) 550-7000; fax (2) 550-7770; e-mail contacto@lahora.cl; internet www.lahora.cl; f. 1997; Mon.–Fri; distributed free of charge; Dir JAVIER FUICA DEL CAMPO; circ. 106,000.

El Mercurio: Avda Santa María 5542, Casilla 13-D, Santiago; tel. (2) 330-1111; fax (2) 242-6965; e-mail elmercurio@mercurio.cl; internet www.elmercurio.cl; f. 1900; morning; conservative; Dir CRISTIÁN ZEGERS; circ. 154,000 (Mon.–Fri.), 232,000 (weekends).

La Nación: Agustinas 1269, Casilla 81-D, Santiago; tel. (2) 787-0100; fax (2) 698-1059; e-mail mpmoya@lanacion.cl; internet www.lanacion.cl; f. 1917 to replace govt-subsidized El Cronista; online only from Dec. 2010; owned by Soc. Periodística La Nación; Gen. Man. FRANCISCO FERES NAZARALA; Dir MARCELO CASTILLO; circ. 11,000.

Santiago Times: Avda Santa María 227, Of. 12, Santiago; tel. (2) 735-9044; fax 777-5376; e-mail editor@santiagotimes.cl; internet www.santiagotimes.cl; f. 1991; daily; national news in English; Gen. Editor BILL STOTT; 10,000 subscribers.

La Segunda: Avda Santa María 5542, Casilla 13-D, Santiago; tel. (2) 330-1111; fax (2) 242-6965; e-mail cartas@lasegunda.cl; internet www.lasegunda.com; f. 1931; owned by proprs of *El Mercurio*; evening; Dir PILAR VERGARA; circ. 40,000.

La Tercera: Avda Vicuña Mackenna 1870, Ñuñoa, Santiago; tel. (2) 550-7000; fax (2) 555-7071; e-mail latercera@copesa.cl; internet www.latercera.cl; f. 1950; morning; Dir CRISTIÁN BOFILL RODRÍGUEZ; circ. 91,000 (Mon.–Fri.), 201,000 (weekends).

Las Ultimas Noticias: Bellavista 0112, Providencia, Santiago; tel. (2) 730-3000; fax (2) 730-3331; e-mail ultimas.noticias@lun.cl; internet www.lun.cl; f. 1902; owned by the proprs of *El Mercurio*; morning; Dir AGUSTÍN EDWARDS DEL RÍO; circ. 133,000 (Mon.–Fri.), 176,000 (weekends).

Antofagasta

La Estrella del Norte: Manuel Antonio Matta 2112, Antofagasta; tel. (55) 45-3672; fax (55) 45-3671; internet www.estrellanorte.cl; f. 1966; evening; Dir SERGIO MONTIVERO; circ. 5,000.

El Mercurio de Antofagasta: Manuel Antonio Matta 2112, Antofagasta; tel. (55) 425-3600; fax (55) 425-3612; e-mail info@mercurioantofagasta.cl; internet www.mercurioantofagasta.cl; f. 1906; morning; conservative ind.; owned by Soc. Chilena de Publicaciones; Dir CARLOS RODRÍGUEZ PÉREZ; circ. 9,000.

Arica

La Estrella de Arica: San Marcos 580, Arica; tel. (58) 22-5024; fax (58) 25-2890; internet www.estrellaarica.cl; f. 1976; Dir REINALDO NEIRA RUIZ; circ. 10,000.

Atacama

Chañarcillo: Los Carrera 801, Casilla 198, Copiapó, Atacama; tel. and fax (52) 21-9044; internet www.chanarcillo.cl; f. 1992; morning; Dir ALBERTO BICHARA.

Calama

El Mercurio de Calama: Abaroa 2051, Calama; tel. (55) 45-8571; fax (55) 45-8172; e-mail cronicacalama@mercurio.cl; internet www.mercuriocalama.cl; f. 1968; owned by Soc. Chilena de Publicaciones; Dir JAVIER ORELLANA VERA; circ. 4,500 (weekdays), 7,000 (Sun.).

Chillán

La Discusión: 18 de Septiembre 721, Casilla 479, Chillán; tel. (42) 21-2650; fax (42) 21-3578; internet www.diarioladiscusion.cl; f. 1870; morning; ind.; Dir RUSSEL CABRERA PARADA; circ. 5,000.

Concepción

El Sur: Calle Freire 799, Casilla 8-C, Concepción; tel. (41) 279-4760; fax (41) 279-4761; e-mail buzon@diarioelsur.cl; internet www.elsur.cl; f. 1882; morning; ind.; Gen. Editor VICTOR TOLOZA JIMÉNEZ; Dir ERNESTO MONTALBA; circ. 28,000 (weekdays), 45,000 (Sun.).

Copiapó

El Diario de Atacama: Atacama 724A, Copiapó; tel. (52) 21-8509; fax (52) 23-2212; internet www.diarioatacama.cl; f. 1970; morning; ind.; Gen. Editor CRIATIAN ANGEL ARDILLES; Dir DAVID DOLL PINTO; circ. 6,500.

Coyhaique

El Diario de Aysén: 21 de Mayo 410, Coyhaique; tel. (67) 234-850; fax (67) 232-318; e-mail contacto@diarioaysen.cl; internet www.diarioaysen.cl; f. 1981; Dir GABRIELA VICENTINI.

Curicó

La Prensa: Merced 373, Curicó; tel. (75) 31-0453; fax (75) 31-1924; e-mail aprensa@diariolaprensa.cl; internet diariolaprensa.cl; f. 1898; morning; right-wing; Dir MANUEL MASSA MAUTINO; circ. 6,000.

Iquique

La Estrella de Iquique: Luis Uribe 452, Iquique; tel. (57) 39-9311; fax (57) 42-7975; internet www.estrellaiquique.cl; f. 1966; evening; Dir CAUPOLICÁN MÁRQUEZ VERGARA; circ. 10,000.

La Serena

El Día: Brasil 431, La Serena; tel. (51) 20-0400; fax (51) 21-9599; internet www.diarioeldia.cl; f. 1944; morning; Dir FRANCISCO PUGA VERGARA; circ. 10,800.

Los Angeles

La Tribuna: Colo Colo 464, Casilla 15-D, Los Angeles; tel. (43) 31-3315; fax (43) 31-4987; e-mail gerencia@diariolatribuna.cl; internet www.diariolatribuna.cl; f. 1958; ind; Dir CIRILO GUZMÁN DE LA FUENTE; circ. 4,200.

Osorno

El Diario Austral de Osorno: O'Higgins 870, Osorno; tel. (64) 22-2300; fax (64) 24-6244; e-mail gcanales@australosorno.cl; internet www.australosorno.cl; f. 1982; Dir RICARDO ALT; circ. 6,500 (weekdays), 7,300 (Sun.).

Ovalle

El Ovallino: Vicuña Mackena 473, Ovalle; tel. (53) 433-031; internet www.elovallino.cl; f. 1989; Dir FRANCISCO PUGA.

Puerto Montt

El Llanquíhue: Antonio Varas 167, Puerto Montt; tel. (65) 432-400; fax (65) 432-401; internet www.diariollanquihue.cl; f. 1885; Dir MAURICIO RIVAS ALVEAR; circ. 4,800 (weekdays), 5,700 (Sun.).

Punta Arenas

La Prensa Austral: Waldo Seguel 636, Casilla 9-D, Punta Arenas; tel. (61) 20-4000; fax (61) 24-7406; e-mail redaccion@laprensaaustral.cl; internet www.laprensaaustral.cl; f. 1941; morning; ind.; Gen. Editor POLY RAÍN HARO; Dir ALEJANDRO TORO; circ. 10,000 (Sun.); *El Magallanes*; f. 1894, circ. 12,000.

Quillota

El Observador: La Concepción 277, Casilla 1-D, Quillota; tel. (33) 312-096; fax (33) 311-417; e-mail elobser@entelchile.net; internet www.diarioelobservador.cl; f. 1970; Man. Dir ROBERTO SILVA BIJIT.

Rancagua

El Rancagüino: O'Carroll 518, Casilla 50, Rancagua; tel. (72) 327-400; e-mail info@elrancaguino.cl; internet www.elrancaguino.cl; f. 1915; ind.; Dir ALEJANDRO GONZÁLEZ; Gen. Man. FERNANDO REYES; circ. 10,000.

Talca

El Centro: Casa Matriz, Avda Lircay 3030, Talca; tel. (71) 51-5300; fax (71) 51-0310; e-mail diario@diarioelcentro.cl; internet www.diarioelcentro.cl; f. 1989; Dir ANTONIO FAUNDES MERINO.

Temuco

El Diario Austral de la Araucanía: Antonio Varas 945, Casilla 1-D, Temuco; tel. (45) 29-2929; fax (45) 23-9189; internet www.australtemuco.cl; f. 1916; owned by Soc. Periodística Araucanía; morning; commercial, industrial and agricultural interests; Dir JOSÉ MANUEL ALVAREZ; circ. 15,100 (weekdays), 23,500 (Sun.).

Tocopilla

La Prensa de Tocopilla: Bolívar 1244, Tocopilla; tel. (83) 81-3036; e-mail prensa@prensatocopilla.cl; internet www.prensatocopilla.cl; f. 1924; morning; ind.; Editor MARTÍN GONZÁLEZ; circ. 3,000.

Valdivia

El Diario Austral de Valdivia: Yungay 499, Valdivia; tel. (63) 24-2200; fax (63) 24-2209; internet www.australvaldivia.cl; f. 1982; Dir VERÓNICA MORENO AGUILERA; circ. 5,600.

Valparaíso

La Estrella: Esmeralda 1002, Casilla 57-V, Valparaíso; tel. (32) 226-4264; fax (32) 226-4108; internet www.estrellavalpo.cl; f. 1921; evening; ind.; Dir PEDRO URZÚA; owned by the proprs of *El Mercurio*; circ. 28,000 (weekdays), 35,000 (Sat.).

El Mercurio de Valparaíso: Esmeralda 1002, Casilla 57-V, Valparaíso; tel. (32) 226-4264; fax (32) 226-4138; e-mail info@mercuriovalpo.cl; internet www.mercuriovalpo.cl; f. 1827; owned by the proprs of *El Mercurio*; morning; Dir MARCO ANTONIO PINTO ZEPADA; circ. 65,000.

PERIODICALS

América Economía: tel. (2) 290-9400; fax (2) 206-6005; e-mail rferro@aeconomia.cl; internet www.americaeconomia.com; f. 1986; monthly; business; CEO ELÍAS SELMAN; Publr NILS STRANDBERG; Editorial Dir FELIPE ADULANTE.

CA (Ciudad/Arquitectura) Revista Oficial del Colegio de Arquitectos de Chile AG: Avda Libertador Bernardo O'Higgins 115, Santiago; tel. (2) 353-2300; fax (2) 353-2355; internet www.revistaca.cl; f. 1968; 4 a year; architecture; Dir PAULINA VILLALOBOS; circ. 3,500.

Caras: Rosario Norte 555, 18°, Santiago; tel. (2) 595-5000; e-mail revista@caras.cl; internet www.caras.cl; f. 1988; women's interest; Dir PATRICIA GUZMÁN.

Chile Agrícola: Teresa Vial 1170, Casilla 2, Correo 13, Santiago; tel. and fax (2) 522-2627; e-mail chileagricola@hotmail.com; f. 1975; 6 a year; organic farming; Dir RAÚL GONZÁLEZ VALENZUELA; circ. 7,000.

Chile Forestal: Paseo Bulnes 265, Of. 601, Santiago; tel. (2) 663-0208; fax (2) 696-6724; e-mail mariela.espejo@conaf.cl; internet www.conaf.cl; f. 1974; 6 a year; state-owned; technical information and features on forestry sector; Dir RICARDO SAN MARTÍN; Editor MARIELA ESPEJO SUAZO; circ. 4,000.

Cinegrama: Avda Holanda 279, Providencia, Santiago; tel. (2) 422-8500; fax (2) 422-8570; e-mail cinegrama@cinegrama.cl; internet www.cinegrama.cl; f. 1987; monthly; cinema; Dir JUAN IGNACIO OTO; Editor LEYLA LÓPEZ.

The Clinic: Merced 280, Of. 71, Santiago; tel. (2) 633-9584; fax (2) 639-6584; internet www.theclinic.cl; fortnightly; political and social satire; Editor PABLO VERGARA; Gen. Man. JUAN PABLO BAROS.

Conozca Más: Rosario Norte 555, 18°, Las Condes, Santiago; tel. (2) 366-7100; fax (2) 246-2810; e-mail viamail@conozcamas.cl; internet www.conozcamas.cl; monthly; science; Dir PAULA AVILES; circ. 90,000.

Cosas: Almirante Pastene 259, Providencia, Santiago; tel. (2) 364-5100; fax (2) 235-8331; e-mail info@cosas.com; internet www.cosas.com; f. 1976; fortnightly; entertainment and lifestyle; Editor OSCAR SEPÚLVEDA PACHECO; circ. 40,000.

Ercilla: Avda Holanda 279, Providencia, Santiago; tel. (2) 422-8500; fax (2) 422-8570; e-mail ercilla@holanda.cl; internet www.ercilla.cl; f. 1936; weekly; general interest; conservative; Dir JUAN IGNACIO OTO; circ. 28,000.

Paula: Vicuña Mackena 1962, Ñuñoa, Santiago; tel. (2) 550-7108; fax (2) 550-7195; e-mail cartas@paula.cl; internet www.paula.cl; f. 1967; monthly; women's interest; Dir MILENA VODANOVIC; Editor CAROLINA DÍAZ; circ. 85,000.

Punto Final: San Diego 31, Of. 606, Casilla 13954, Correo 21, Santiago; tel. and fax (2) 697-0615; e-mail punto@interaccess.cl; internet www.puntofinal.cl; f. 1965; fortnightly; politics; left-wing; Dir MANUEL CABIESES DONOSO; circ. 15,000.

¿Qué Pasa?: Vicuña Mackenna 1870, Ñuñoa, Santiago; tel. (2) 550-7523; fax (2) 550-7529; e-mail quepasa@copesa.cl; internet www.quepasa.cl; f. 1971; weekly; general interest; Dir CRISTIAN BOFILL; circ. 30,000.

Revista Mensaje: Cienfuegos 21, Santiago; tel. (2) 698-0617; fax (2) 671-7030; e-mail rrpp@mensaje.cl; internet www.mensaje.cl; f. 1951; monthly; national, church and international affairs; Dir ANTONIO DELFAU; circ. 6,000.

Vea: Avda Holanda 279, Providencia, Santiago; tel. (2) 422-8500; fax (2) 422-8572; e-mail revistavea@holanda.cl; internet www.vea.cl; f. 1939; weekly; general interest, illustrated; Dir JAIME GODOY CARTES; circ. 150,000.

PRESS ASSOCIATION

Asociación Nacional de la Prensa: Carlos Antúnez 2048, Providencia, Santiago; tel. (2) 232-1004; fax (2) 232-1006; e-mail info@anp.cl; internet www.anp.cl; f. 1951; Pres. GUILLERMO TURNER OLEA; Sec.-Gen. FERNANDO SILVA VARGAS.

NEWS AGENCIES

Agencia Chile Noticias (ACN): Carlos Antúnez 1884, Of. 104, Providencia, Santiago; tel. and fax (2) 717-9121; e-mail prensa@chilenoticias.cl; internet www.chilenoticias.cl; f. 1993; Editor NORBERTO PARRA H.

Agencia Orbe: Avda Phillips 56, Of. 66, Santiago; tel. (2) 251-7800; fax (2) 251-7801; e-mail prensa@orbe.cl; internet www.orbe.cl; f. 1955; Bureau Chief PATRICIA ESCALONA CÁCERES.

Business News Americas: San Patricio 2944, Las Condes, Santiago; tel. (2) 941-0300; fax (2) 232-9376; e-mail info@bnamericas.com; internet www.bnamericas.com; internet-based business information; CEO GREGORY BARTON.

UPI Chile Ltd: Avda Nataniel Cox 47, 9°, Santiago; tel. (2) 657-0874; fax (2) 698-6605; e-mail prensa@upi.com; internet www.upi.cl; Gen. Man. JORGEQ IRIBARREN ESPEJO.

Publishers

Carlos Quiroga Editorial: La Concepción 56, Of. 202, Providencia, Santiago; tel. and fax (2) 202-9825; e-mail cquiroga@carlosquiroga.cl; internet www.carlosquiroga.cl; children's and educational; Gen. Man. MARIANELLA MEDINA.

Edebé—Editorial Don Bosco: Avda Gen. Bulnes 35, Santiago; tel. (2) 437-8050; e-mail contacto@edebe.cl; internet www.edebe.cl; f. 1904 as Editorial Salesiana; adopted present name in 1996; general, political, biography, religious, children's; Chair. ALDO MOLTEDO; Gen. Man. PABLO MARINKOVIC.

Ediciones B Chile: Avda Las Torres 1375A, Huechuraba, Santiago; tel. (2) 729-5400; fax (2) 231-6300; e-mail mansieta@edicionesbchile.cl; internet www.edicionesbchile.cl; f. 1986; part of Grupo Zeta; children's and fiction; Gen. Man. MARILÉN WOOD.

Ediciones Mil Hojas: Avda Antonio Varas 1480, Providencia, Santiago; tel. (2) 274-3172; fax (2) 223-7544; e-mail milhojas@terra.cl; internet www.milhojas.cl; educational and reference; Dir JULIETA MELO CABELLO.

Ediciones Universitarias de Valparaíso: Universidad Católica de Valparaíso, Calle 12 de Febrero 187, Casilla 1415, Valparaíso; tel. (32) 227-3087; fax (32) 227-3429; e-mail euvsa@ucv.cl; internet www.euv.cl; f. 1970; literature, social and general sciences, engineering, education, music, arts, textbooks; Chair. PATRICIO ARANA ESPINA; Gen. Man. MARÍA TERESA VEGA SEGOVIA.

Ediciones Urano: Avda Francisco Bilbao 2790, CP 7510745, Providencia, Santiago; tel. (2) 341-7493; fax (2) 225-3896; e-mail info@edicionesurano.cl; internet www.edicionesurano.cl; f. 1983 in Spain, f. 1996 in Chile; self-help, mystical and scholarly; Gen. Man. RICARDO VLASTELICA VEGA.

Editec (Ediciones Técnicas Ltda): El Condor 844, Of. 205, Ciudad Empresarial, Huechuraba, Santiago; tel. (2) 757-4200; fax (2) 757-4201; e-mail editec@editec.cl; internet www.editec.cl; Pres. RICARDO CORTES DONOSO; Gen. Man. ROLY SOLIS SEPÚLVEDA.

Editorial Antártica, SA: San Francisco 116, Santiago; tel. (2) 639-3476; fax (2) 633-3402; e-mail consulta@antartica.cl; internet www.antartica.cl; f. 1978; Gen. Man. PAUL LABORDE U.

Editorial Borlando: Avda Victoria 155, Santiago; tel. (2) 555-9566; fax (2) 556-7100; e-mail ventas@editorialborlando.cl; internet www.editorialborlando.cl; f. 1984; scholarly, juvenile, educational and reference; Dir-Gen. SERGIO BORLANDO PORTALES.

Editorial Cuatro Vientos Ltda: Maturana 19, Metro República, entre Brasil y Cumming, Santiago; tel. (2) 672-9226; fax (2) 673-2153; e-mail editorial@cuatrovientos.cl; internet cuatrovientos.cl; f. 1980; Man. Editor JUAN FRANCISCO HUNEEUS COX.

Editorial y Distribuidora Lenguaje y Pensamiento Ltda: Avda 11 de Septiembre 1881, Of. 324, Metro Pedro de Valdivia, Santiago; tel. (2) 335-2347; e-mail contacto@lenguajeypensamiento.cl; internet www.editoriallenguajeypensamiento.cl; children's, educational; Gen. Man. MARÍA LORENA TERÁN.

Editorial Evolución, SA: Ministro Carvajal 6, Providencia, Santiago; tel. (2) 681-8072; fax (2) 236-2071; e-mail info@evolucion.cl; internet www.evolucion.cl; business and management; Dir JUAN BRAVO CARRASCO.

Editorial Fondo de Cultura Económica Chile, SA: Paseo Bulnes 152, Metro Moneda, Santiago; tel. (2) 594-4100; fax (2) 594-4101; e-mail info@fcechile.cl; internet fcechile.cl; f. 1954; Gen. Man. ÓSCAR BRAVO.

Editorial Jurídica de Chile: Ahumada 131, 4°, Santiago; tel. (2) 461-9500; fax (2) 461-9501; e-mail covalle@editorialjuridica.cl; internet www.editorialjuridica.cl; f. 1945; law; Gen. Man. PATRICIO ROJAS.

Editorial Patris: José Manuel Infante 132, Providencia, Santiago; tel. (2) 235-1343; fax (2) 235-8674; e-mail gerencia@entelchile.net; internet www.patris.cl; f. 1982; Catholic; Dir JOSÉ LUIS CORREA LIRA.

Editorial Renacimiento: Amunátegui 458, Santiago; tel. (2) 345-8300; fax (2) 345-8320; e-mail pedidos@editorialrenacimiento.com; internet www.editorialrenacimiento.com; f. 1977; Gen. Man. ALBERTO ALDEA.

Editorial San Pablo: Avda Libertador Bernardo O'Higgins 1626, Casilla 3746, Santiago; tel. (2) 720-0300; fax (2) 672-8469; e-mail alameda@san-pablo.cl; internet www.sanpablochile.cl; f. 1914; Catholic texts; Dir-Gen. BRUNO BRESSAN.

Editorial Tiempo Presente Ltda: Almirante Pastene 345, Providencia, Santiago; tel. (2) 364-5100; fax (2) 235-8331; e-mail info@cosas.com; internet www.cosas.com; Gen. Man. MATÍAS PFINGSTHORN OLIVARES.

Editorial Universitaria, SA: Avda Libertador Bernardo O'Higgins 1050, Santiago; tel. (2) 487-0700; fax (2) 487-0702; e-mail comunicaciones@universitaria.cl; internet www.universitaria.cl; f. 1947; general literature, social science, technical, textbooks; Man. Dir RODRIGO FUENTES.

Empresa Editora Zig-Zag SA: Los Conquistadores 1700, 10°, Providencia, Santiago; tel. (2) 810-7400; fax (2) 810-7452; e-mail zigzag@zigzag.cl; internet www.zigzag.cl; f. 1905; general publrs of literary works, reference books and magazines; Pres. ALFREDO VERCELLI; Gen. Man. RAMÓN OLACIREGUI.

Grupo Planeta: Avda 11 de Septiembre 2353, 16°, CP 7510058, Providencia, Santiago; tel. (2) 652-2927; fax (2) 652-2912; e-mail info@planeta.cl; internet www.editorialplaneta.cl; f. 1968; non-fiction, philosophy, psychology; Gen. Man. ELSY SALAZAR CAMPO.

Liberalia Ediciones: Avda Italia 2016, Ñuñoa, Santiago; tel. (2) 432-8003; fax (2) 326-8805; e-mail liberalia@liberalia.cl; internet www.liberalia.cl; f. 1997; Dir JAIME OXLEY MUÑOZ.

McGraw-Hill/Interamericana de Chile Ltda: Evaristo Lillo 112, 7°, Las Condes, Santiago; tel. (2) 661-3000; fax (2) 661-3020; e-mail info_chile@mcgraw-hill.com; internet www.mcgraw-hill.cl; educational and technical; Gen. Man. JOSÉ ABERG COBO.

Norma de Chile, SA: Monjitas 527, 17°, Centro, Santiago; tel. (2) 731-7500; fax (2) 632-2079; e-mail david.malhue@norma.com; internet www.librerianorma.com; f. 1960; part of Editorial Norma of Colombia; Gen. Man. DAVID MALHUE.

Pearson Educación de Chile: José Ananias 505, Macul, Santiago; tel. (2) 237-2387; fax (2) 237-3297; e-mail infopear@pearsoned.cl; Gen. Man. EDUARDO GUZMÁN BARROS.

Pehuen Editores, SA: Brown Norte 417, Ñuñoa, Santiago; tel. (2) 795-7130; fax (2) 795-7133; e-mail editorial@pehuen.cl; internet www.pehuen.cl; f. 1983; literature, sociology and photography; Pres. SEBASTIÁN BARROS CERDA; Gen. Man. JUAN MANUEL GALÁN.

RIL Editores (Red Internacional del Libro Ltda): Alférez Real 1464, Providencia, CP 750-0960, Santiago; tel. (2) 223-8100; fax (2) 225-4269; e-mail ril@rileditores.com; internet www.rileditores.com; literature, poetry, scholarly and political; f. 1991 as Red Internacional del Libro Ltda; Dir ELEONORA FINKELSTEIN; Dir of Publications DANIEL CALABRESE.

Tajamar Editores: Avda Mariano Sánchez Fontecilla 352, Las Condes, Santiago; tel. (2) 245-7026; e-mail info@tajamar-editores.cl; internet www.tajamar-editores.cl; f. 2002; literature; Gen. Man. MARÍA PAZ GAETE SILVA.

PUBLISHERS' ASSOCIATIONS

Asociación de Editores de Chile (Asociación de Editores Independientes, Universitarios y Autónomos): Centro Cultural Gabriela Mistral, Avda Libertador Bernardo O'Higgins 227, Local 2, Metro Universidad Católica, Santiago; tel. (2) 632-9210; e-mail contacto@editoresdechile.cl; internet www.editoresdechile.cl; Pres. JUAN FRANCISCO HUNEEUS COX; Exec. Dir CARMEN GLORIA ARCE.

Cámara Chilena del Libro AG: Avda Libertador Bernardo O'Higgins 1370, Of. 502, Casilla 13526, Santiago; tel. (2) 672-0348; fax (2) 687-4271; e-mail prolibro@tie.cl; internet www.camaradellibro.cl; f. 1950; Pres. EDUARDO CASTILLO GARCÍA.

Broadcasting and Communications

TELECOMMUNICATIONS

Regulatory Authority

Subsecretaría de Telecomunicaciones (Subtel): Amunátegui 139, 5°, Casilla 120, Correo 21, Santiago; tel. (2) 421-3000; fax (2) 421-

3553; e-mail subtel@subtel.cl; internet www.subtel.cl; f. 1977; part of the Ministry of Transport and Telecommunications; Under-Sec. JORGE ATTON PALMA.

Major Operators

Claro Chile, SA: Avda del Cóndor 820, Ciudad Empresarial, Comuna de Huechuraba, Santiago; tel. (2) 444-5000; fax (2) 444-5170; internet www.clarochile.cl; acquired in Aug. 2005 by América Móvil, SA de CV (Mexico); fmrly Smartcom; Gen. Man. GERARDO MUÑOZ.

CMET Telecomunicaciones: Avda Los Leones 1412, Providencia, Santiago; tel. (2) 251-3333; fax (2) 274-9573; internet www.cmet.cl; f. 1978.

Empresa Nacional de Telecomunicaciones, SA—ENTEL Chile, SA: Andrés Bello 2687, 14°, Casilla 4254, Las Condes, Santiago; tel. (2) 360-0123; fax (2) 360-3424; internet www.entel.cl; f. 1964; operates the Chilean land satellite stations of Longovilo, Punta Arenas and Coyhaique, linked to INTELSAT system; 52% owned by Telecom Italia; Pres. JUAN JOSÉ HURTADO VICUÑA; Gen. Man. RICHARD BÜCHI BUC.

Grupo GTD: Moneda 920, 11°, Santiago; e-mail soporte@gtdinternet.com; internet www.grupogtd.com; f. 1979; internet and telephone service provider; Pres. JUAN MANUEL CASANUEVA.

Movistar: Miraflores 130, Santiago; tel. (2) 661-6000; internet www.movistar.cl; privatized in 1988; owned by Telefónica, SA (Spain); fmrly known as Telefónica Chile; in 2009 adopted Movistar for all brands and products; operates fixed line, mobile and internet services; Pres. EMILIO GILOLMO LÓPEZ; Gen. Man. OLIVER FLÖGEL.

Telmex Chile: Rinconada El Salto 202, Huechuraba, Casilla 12, Santiago; tel. (2) 582-5787; fax (2) 585-5185; internet www.telmex.cl; subsidiary of Teléfonos de México, SA de CV; Pres. ALEJANDRO ROJAS PINAUD; Vice-Pres. and Gen. Man. EDUARDO DÍAZ CORONA JIMÉNEZ.

VTR GlobalCom: Reyes Lavalle 3340, 9°, Las Condes, Santiago; tel. (2) 310-1000; fax (2) 310-1560; internet www.vtr.cl; f. 1928 as Vía Transradio Chilena; present name adopted in 1999; 80% owned by Liberty Global Inc (USA), 20% owned by Cristalerías Chile of the Claro group; Exec. Pres. MAURICIO RAMOS.

BROADCASTING

Regulatory Authority

Subsecretaría de Telecomunicaciones: see Telecommunications.

Radio

Agricultura (AM y FM): Avda Manuel Rodríguez 15, Santiago; tel. (2) 392-3000; fax (2) 392-3072; internet www.radioagricultura.cl; owned by Sociedad Nacional de Agricultura; Pres. MANUEL VALDÉS VALDÉS; Gen. Man. GUIDO ERRÁZURIZ MORENO.

Beethoven FM: Avda. Santa María 2670, 2°, Providencia, Santiago; tel. (2) 571-7056; fax (2) 274-3323; e-mail director@redfm.cl; internet www.beethovenfm.cl; f. 1981; mainly classical music; affiliate stations in Viña del Mar and Temuco; Dir ADOLFO FLORES.

Bío Bío La Radio: Avda Libertador Bernardo O'Higgins 680, Concepción; tel. (41) 222-5660; fax (41) 222-6742; e-mail pandrade@laradio.cl; internet www.radiobiobio.cl; affiliate stations in Concepción, Los Angeles, Temuco, Ancud, Castro, Osorno, Puerto Montt, Santiago and Valdivia; Man. PATRICIO ANDRADE.

Duna FM: Avda Santa María 2670, 2°, Providencia, Santiago; tel. (2) 225-5494; fax (2) 225-6013; e-mail aholuigue@duna.cl; internet www.duna.cl; affiliate stations in Viña del Mar and Concepción; Pres. FELIPE LAMARCA CLARO; Dir A. HOLUIGUE.

Estrella del Mar AM: Eleuterio Ramírez 207, Ancud, Isla de Chiloé; tel. and fax (65) 62-2722; e-mail direccionrem@gmail.com; internet www.radioestrelladelmar.cl; f. 1982; station of the Roman Catholic diocese of San Carlos de Ancud; affiliate stations in Castro, Quellón, Melinka, Achao, Futaleufú, Palena and Chaitén; Exec. Dir PABLO DURÁN LEIVA.

Festival AM: Quinta 124A, 2º, Casilla 337, Viña del Mar; tel. (32) 268-4251; fax (32) 268-0266; e-mail servicios@festival.cl; internet www.festival.cl; f. 1976; Dir-Gen. SANTIAGO CHIESA HOWARD.

Horizonte: Avda Pocuro 2151, Providencia, Santiago; tel. (2) 410-5400; fax (2) 410-5460; internet www.horizonte.cl; f. 1985; affiliate stations in Arica, Antofagasta, Iquique, La Serena, Viña del Mar, Concepción, San Antonio, Temuco, Villarrica, Puerto Montt, Punta Arenas and Osorno; Dir JULIÁN GARCÍA-REYES.

IberoAmericana Radio Chile: Eliodoro Yáñez 1783, Providencia, Santiago; tel. (2) 390-2000; fax (2) 390-2047; e-mail aaguirre@iarc.cl; internet www.iarc.cl; belongs to Grupo Latino de Radio (GLR), a subsidiary of Union Radio; Exec. Dir MARCELO ZÚÑIGA VETTIGER; Communications Man. ALEJANDRA AGUIRRE C.; the media group operates 11 radio stations.

40 Principales 101.7 FM: e-mail radio@los40.cl; internet www.los40.cl.

ADN Radio Chile 91.7 FM: e-mail radio@adnradio.cl; internet www.adnradio.cl; general and sports news.

Concierto 88.5 FM: e-mail radio@concierto.cl; internet www.concierto.cl; f. 1999; 1980s music; Gen. Man. JAIME VEGA DE KUYPER.

Corazón 101.3 FM: e-mail radio@corazon.cl; internet www.corazon.cl; f. 1997.

FMDos 98.5 FM: e-mail radio@fmdos.cl; internet www.fm2.cl; popular music.

Futuro 88.9 FM: e-mail radio@futuro.cl; internet www.futuro.cl; rock music.

Imagina 88.1 FM: e-mail radio@radioimagina.cl; internet www.radioimagina.cl; women's radio.

Pudahuel 90.5 FM: e-mail radio@pudahuel.cl; internet www.pudahuel.cl; f. 1966; Pres. SUSANA MUTINELLI ANCHUBIDART; Gen. Man. JOAQUÍN BLAYA BARRIOS.

Radioactiva 92.5 FM: e-mail info@radioactiva.cl; internet www.radioactiva.cl; dance music from 1970s to 2000.

Rock & Pop 94.1 FM: e-mail contacto@rockandpop.cl; internet www.rockandpop.cl; retro classics and 1990s music.

Uno 97.1 FM: e-mail contacto@radiounochile.cl; internet www.radiounochile.cl; Chilean national music.

Infinita FM: Avda Los Leones 1285, Providencia, Santiago; tel. (2) 754-4400; fax (2) 341-6727; internet www.infinita.cl; f. 1977; affiliate stations in Santiago, Viña del Mar, Concepción and Valdivia; Gen. Man. CARLOS ALBERTO PEÑAFIEL GUARACHI.

Para Ti FM: Vial 775, Puerto Montt, Santiago; tel. (65) 317-003; internet www.radioparati.cl; 16 affiliate stations throughout Chile; Gen. Man. FELIPE MOLFINO BURKERT.

Play FM: Alcalde Dávalos 164, Providencia, Santiago; tel. (2) 630-2600; fax (2) 630-2264; e-mail asanchez@13.cl; internet www.playfm.cl; f. 2006; Dir GABRIEL POLGATI; Gen. Man. XIMENA CALLEJÓN.

Radio Carolina: Avda Santa Maria 2670, 2°, Providence, Santiago; tel. (2) 571-7000; fax (2) 571-7002; internet www.carolina.cl; f. 1975; owned by COPESA, SA; Contact HÉCTOR CABRERA.

Radio El Conquistador FM: El Conquistador del Monte 4644, Huechuraba, Santiago; tel. (2) 580-2000; e-mail radio@elconquistadorfm.cl; internet www.cqfm.cl; f. 1962; affiliate stations in Santiago, Iquique, Antofagasta, La Serena, Viña del Mar, Rancagua, Talca, Chillán, Concepción, Talcahuano, Pucón, Temuco, Villarrica, Lago Llanquihue, Osorno, Puerto Montt, Puerto Varas, Valdivia and Punta Arenas; Pres. JOAQUÍN MOLFINO.

Radio Cooperativa (AM y FM): Antonio Bellet 353, Casilla 16367, Correo 9, Santiago; tel. (2) 364-8000; fax (2) 236-0535; e-mail info@cooperativa.cl; internet www.cooperativa.cl; f. 1936; affiliate stations in Copiapó, Arica, Coquimbo, La Serena, Valparaíso, Concepción, Calama, Temuco and Castro; Pres. LUIS AJENJO ISASI; Gen. Man. SERGIO PARRA GODOY.

Radio Nacional de Chile: Santiago; tel. (2) 551-6954; fax (2) 551-6967; e-mail radionacionaldechile@gmail.com; internet www.radionacionalchile.tk; f. 1974; Gen. Man. SANTIAGO AGLIATI.

Radio Nueva Belén FM: Benavente 385, Puerto Montt; tel. (65) 25-8042; fax (65) 25-8084; e-mail nuevabelen@gmail.com; internet www.radionuevabelen.cl; f. 2005; owned by Archbishopric of Puerto Montt; Dir HÉCTOR ASENJO REYES; Gen. Man. CARLOS WAGNER CATALÁN.

Radio Polar: Bories 871, 2° y 3°, Punta Arenas; tel. (61) 24-1909; fax (61) 24-9001; e-mail secretaria@radiopolar.com; internet www.radiopolar.com; f. 1940; Pres. RENÉ VENEGAS OLMEDO.

Superandina FM: Avda Chacabuco 281, Los Andes; tel. (34) 42-2515; fax (34) 90-4091; e-mail radio@superandina.cl; internet www.superandina.cl; f. 1987; Dir JOSÉ ANDRÉS GÁLVEZ.

Universo FM: Antonio Bellet 223, Providencia, Santiago; tel. (2) 364-8000; e-mail alfredo@universo.cl; internet www.universo.cl; affiliate stations in 18 cities; Commercial Man. ALFREDO URETA Q.

Television

Corporación de Televisión de la Universidad Católica de Chile—Canal 13: Inés Matte Urrejola 0848, Providencia, Santiago; tel. (2) 251-4000; fax (2) 630-2683; internet www.canal13.cl; f. 1959; non-commercial; Pres. RENÉ CORTÁZAR; Exec. Dir DAVID BELMAR.

Corporación de Televisión de la Pontificia Universidad Católica de Valparaíso (UCV TV): Agua Santa Alta 2455, Viña del Mar; tel. (32) 276-8500; fax (32) 261-0505; e-mail direccion@ucvtv.cl; internet www.ucvtv.cl; f. 1957; Pres. BERNARDO DONOSO; Exec. Dir ENRIQUE AIMONE.

Megavisión, SA—Canal 9: Avda Vicuña Mackenna 1348, Ñuñoa, Santiago; tel. (2) 810-8000; fax (2) 551-8369; e-mail mega@mcl.cl;

internet www.mega.cl; f. 1990; Pres. RICARDO CLARO VALDÉS; Gen. Man. CRISTÓBAL BULNES SERRANO.

Red de Televisión SA/Chilevisión—Canal 11: Inés Matte Urrejola 0825, Casilla 16547, Correo 9, Providencia, Santiago; tel. (2) 461-5100; fax (2) 461-5371; e-mail contactoweb@chilevision.cl; internet www.chilevision.cl; Exec. Dir JAIME DE AGUIRRE HOFFA; Gen. Man. MARIO CONCA ROSENDE.

La Red Televisión TV: Manquehue Sur 1201, Las Condes, Santiago; tel. (2) 385-4000; fax (2) 385-4020; e-mail administracion@lared.cl; internet www.redtv.cl; f. 1991; Dir-Gen. JOSÉ MANUEL LARRAÍN.

Televisión Nacional de Chile—Canal 7: Bellavista 0990, Casilla 16104, Providencia, Santiago; tel. (2) 707-7777; fax (2) 707-7766; e-mail relaciones.publicas@tvn.cl; internet www.tvn.cl; f. 1969; govt network of 140 stations and an international satellite signal; Chair. MAURO VALDÉS; Exec. Dir DANIEL FERNÁNDEZ KOPRICH.

Broadcasting Associations

Asociación Nacional de Televisión (ANATEL): Guardia Vieja 255, Of. 1106, Providencia, Santiago; tel. (2) 331-9650; fax (2) 331-9803; e-mail info@anatel.cl; internet www.anatel.cl; 7 mem. networks; Pres. BERNARDO DONOSO RIVEROS; Sec.-Gen. HERNÁN TRIVIÑO OYARZUN.

Asociación de Radiodifusores de Chile (ARCHI): Pasaje Matte 956, 8°, Of. 801, Casilla 10476, Santiago; tel. (2) 639-8755; fax (2) 639-4205; e-mail archi@archiradios.cl; internet www.archi.cl; f. 1933; more than 1,000 affiliated stations; Nat. Pres. LUIS PARDO SAINZ; Sec.-Gen. FERNANDO OCARANZA YÑESTA.

Finance

(cap. = capital; res = reserves; dep. = deposits; m. = million; brs = branches; amounts in pesos, unless otherwise specified)

BANKING

Supervisory Authority

Superintendencia de Bancos e Instituciones Financieras: Moneda 1123, 6°, Casilla 15-D, Santiago; tel. (2) 442-6200; fax (2) 441-0914; e-mail superintendente@sbif.cl; internet www.sbif.cl; f. 1925; affiliated to Ministry of Finance; Supt CARLOS BUDNEVICH LE-FORT.

Central Bank

Banco Central de Chile: Agustinas 1180, Santiago; tel. (2) 670-2000; fax (2) 670-2099; e-mail bcch@bcentral.cl; internet www.bcentral.cl; f. 1926; under Ministry of Finance until Dec. 1989, when autonomy was granted; bank of issue; cap. and res 806,560.9m., dep. 15,274,011.2m. (Dec. 2009); Pres. RODRIGO VERGARA MONTES; Gen. Man ALEJANDRO ZURBUCHEN SILVA.

State Bank

Banco del Estado de Chile (BancoEstado): Avda Libertador Bernardo O'Higgins 1111, Casilla 240V, Santiago; tel. (2) 970-7000; fax (2) 970-5711; internet www.bancoestado.cl; f. 1953; state bank; cap. 4,000m., res 528,853m., dep. 12,538,167m. (Dec. 2007); Pres. JOSÉ LUIS MARDONES SANTANDER; CEO PABLO PIÑERA ECHENIQUE; 214 brs.

Commercial Banks

Banco BICE: Teatinos 220, Santiago; tel. (2) 692-2000; fax (2) 696-5324; e-mail webmaster@bice.cl; internet www.bice.cl; f. 1979 as Banco Industrial y de Comercio Exterior; adopted present name 1988; cap. 32,142m., res –14,237m., dep. 1,709,000m. (Dec. 2010); Pres. and Chair. BERNARDO MATTE LARRAÍN; Gen. Man. ANDRÉS ECHEVERRÍA SALAS; 18 brs.

Banco Bilbao Vizcaya Argentaria Chile: Pedro de Valdivia 100, 17°, Providencia, Santiago; tel. (2) 679-1000; fax (2) 698-5640; e-mail ascarito@bbva.cl; internet www.bbva.cl; f. 1883 as Banco Hipotecario de Fomento Nacional; controlling interest acquired by Banco Bilbao Vizcaya (Spain) in 1998; adopted current name 2003; cap. 224,795m., res 207,574m., dep. 5,634,015m. (Dec. 2009); Chair. JOSÉ SAID SAFFIE; Gen. Man. and CEO IGNACIO LACASTA CASADO; 108 brs.

Banco de Chile: Ahumada 251, Casilla 151-D, Santiago; tel. (2) 637-1111; fax (2) 637-3434; internet www.bancochile.cl; f. 1894; 35.6% owned by SAOS, SA; cap. 1,158,752m., res –149,247m., dep. 12,352,899m. (Dec. 2009); Pres. and Chair. PABLO GRANIFO LAVÍN; CEO ARTURO TAGLE QUIROZ; 422 brs.

Banco de Crédito e Inversiones (Bci): Huérfanos 1134, Casilla 136-D, Santiago; tel. (2) 692-7000; fax (2) 695-3775; e-mail webmaster@bci.cl; internet www.bci.cl; f. 1937; cap. 882,273m., res 6,623m., dep. 8,530,926m. (Dec. 2010); Pres. and Chair. LUIS ENRIQUE YARUR REY; 258 brs.

Banco Desarrollo de Scotiabank: Avda Libertador Bernardo O'Higgins 949, 3°, Casilla 320-V, Casilla 1, Santiago; tel. (2) 674-5000; fax (2) 671-5547; e-mail bdd@bandes.cl; internet www.bdd.cl; f. 1983; fmrly Banco del Desarrollo; above name adopted after acquisition by Scotiabank Chile in 2007; cap. 198,456m., res 751m., dep. 2,367,498m. (Dec. 2008); Pres. PETER CARDINAL; Gen. Man. JAMES EDWARD CALLAHAN; 83 brs.

Banco Internacional: Moneda 818, Casilla 135-D, Santiago; tel. (2) 369-7000; fax (2) 369-7367; e-mail banco@binter.cl; internet www.bancointernacional.cl; f. 1944; cap. 34,221m., res 4,370m., dep. 645,121m. (Dec. 2010); Pres. JULIO JARAQUEMADA L.; Gen. Man. JUAN ENRIQUE VILAJUANA R.

Banco Santander Chile: Bandera 140, 13°, Casilla 57-D, Santiago; tel. (2) 320-2000; fax (2) 320-8877; e-mail webmaster@santander.cl; internet www.santandersantiago.cl; f. 1926; cap. 891,303m., res –96,788m., dep. 11,795,316m. (Dec. 2010); subsidiary of Banco Santander (Spain); Chair. MAURICIO LARRAÍN GARCES; 72 brs.

Banco Security: Apoquindo 3150, Las Condes, Santiago; tel. (2) 584-4000; fax (2) 584-4058; internet www.bancosecurity.cl; f. 1981; fmrly Banco Urquijo de Chile; cap. 138,207m., res 11,004m., dep. 2,101,340m. (Dec. 2010); Pres. and Chair. FRANCISCO SILVA S.; Gen. Man. RAMÓN ELUCHANS O.; 20 brs.

Corpbanca: Rosario Norte 660, Las Condes, Casilla 80-D, Santiago; tel. (2) 687-8000; fax (2) 672-6729; e-mail corpbanca@corpbanca.cl; internet www.corpbanca.cl; f. 1871 as Banco de Concepción, current name adopted in 1997; cap. 342,379m., res –35,874m., dep. 4,488,408m. (Dec. 2010); Chair. and Pres. ALVARO SAIEH BENDECK; CEO MARIO CHAMORRO; 109 brs.

HSBC Bank (Chile): Edif. Titanium, Avda Vitacura 2872, Las Condes, Santiago; tel. (2) 332-1904; fax (2) 299-7391; e-mail ricardo.navarrete@cl.hsbc.com; internet www.hsbc.cl; f. 2003 as HSBC Bank Chile; present name adopted in 2004; cap. 92,032m., res –1,501m., dep. 706,261m. (Dec. 2010); Chair. S. K. GREEN; CEO and Gen. Man. GUSTAVO COSTA.

Scotiabank Sud Americano: Morandé 226, Casilla 90-D, Santiago; tel. (2) 692-6000; fax (2) 698-6008; e-mail scotiabank@scotiabank.cl; internet www.scotiabank.cl; f. 1944; cap. 670,469m., res 117,067m., dep. 3,094,449m. (Dec. 2008); Pres. and Chair. PETER C. CARDINAL; CEO and Gen. Man. JAMES CALLAHAN; 60 brs.

Banking Association

Asociación de Bancos e Instituciones Financieras de Chile AG: Ahumada 179, 12°, Santiago; tel. (2) 636-7100; fax (2) 698-8945; e-mail general@abif.cl; internet www.abif.cl; f. 1945; Pres. JORGE AWAD M.; Gen. Man. RICARDO MATTE E.

Other Financial Supervisory Bodies

Superintendencia de Administradoras de Fondos de Pensiones (SAFP) (Superintendency of Pension Funds): Teatinos 317, Santiago; tel. (2) 753-0100; fax (2) 753-0122; internet www.safp.cl; f. 1981; Supt SOLANGE BERSTEIN JÁUREGUI.

Superintendencia de Seguridad Social (Superintendency of Social Security): Huérfanos 1376, 5°, Santiago; tel. (2) 620-4500; fax (2) 696-4672; e-mail contacto@suseso.cl; internet www.suseso.gov.cl; f. 1927; Supt JAVIER FUENZALIDA SANTANDER.

STOCK EXCHANGES

Bolsa de Comercio de Santiago: La Bolsa 64, Casilla 123-D, Santiago; tel. (2) 399-3000; fax (2) 318-1961; e-mail chathaway@bolsadesantiago.com; internet www.bolsadesantiago.com; f. 1893; 32 mems; Pres. PABLO YRARRÁZAVAL VALDÉS; Gen. Man. JOSÉ ANTONIO MARTÍNEZ ZUGARRAMURDI.

Bolsa de Corredores—Valores de Valparaíso: Prat 798, Casilla 218-V, Valparaíso; tel. (32) 225-0677; fax (32) 221-2764; e-mail bolsadec.orred001@chilnet.cl; internet www.bovalpo.com; f. 1905; Pres. CARLOS F. MARÍN ORREGO; Man. ARIE JOEL GELFENSTEIN FREUNDLICH.

Bolsa Electrónica de Chile: Huérfanos 770, 14°, Santiago; tel. (2) 484-0100; fax (2) 484-0101; e-mail contactoweb@bolchile.cl; internet www.bolchile.cl; f. 1989; Gen. Man. JUAN CARLOS SPENCER OSSA.

INSURANCE

Supervisory Authority

Superintendencia de Valores y Seguros: Avda Libertador Bernardo O'Higgins 1449, Casilla 834-0518, Santiago; tel. (2) 617-4000; fax (2) 617-4101; internet www.svs.cl; f. 1931; under Ministry of Finance; Supt FERNANDO COLOMA CORREA.

Principal Companies

Ace Seguros, SA: Miraflores 222, 17°, Centro, Santiago; tel. (2) 549-8300; fax (2) 632-8289; e-mail melissa.tomalin@acegroup.com; internet www.acelatinamerica.com/ACELatinAmericaRoot/Chile; f. 1956; Pres. Juan Manuel Merchán; Gen. Man. Karen Oyarce.

Aseguradora Magallanes, SA: Avda Alonso de Córdova 5151, 17° y 18°, Of. 1801, Las Condes, Santiago; tel. (2) 715-4605; fax (2) 715-4860; e-mail fvarela@magallanes.cl; internet www.magallanes.cl; f. 1957; general; Pres. Eduardo Dominguez Covarrubias; Gen. Man. Fernando Varela Villaroel.

Axa Asistencia Chile: Josué Smith Solar 390, 6650378 Providencia, Santiago; tel. (2) 941-8900; fax (2) 941-8951; e-mail asistencia@axa-assistance.cl; internet www.axa-assistance.cl; f. 1994; general; Gen. Man. Marylú Forttes Valdivia.

Cardif Chile: Vitacura 2670, 13°, Las Condes, Santiago; tel. (2) 370-4800; fax (2) 370-4877; e-mail cardif@cardif.cl; internet www.cardif.cl; f. 1997; owned by BNP Paribas (France); Pres. Olivier Martin; Gen. Man. Francisco Valenzuela Cornejo.

Chilena Consolidada Seguros, SA: Avda Pedro de Valdivia 195, Casilla 16587, Correo 9, Providencia, Santiago; tel. (2) 200-7000; fax (2) 274-9933; internet www.chilena.cl; f. 1853; owned by Zurich group; general and life; Pres. Hernán Felipe Errázuriz Correa; Gen. Man. José Manuel Camposano Larraechea.

Chubb de Chile Compañía de Seguros Generales, SA: Gertrudis Echeñique 30, 4°, Ofs 41 y 42, Santiago; tel. (2) 398-7000; fax (2) 398-7090; e-mail chileinfo@chubb.com; internet www.chubb.com/chile; f. 1992; general; Gen. Man. Claudio Marcelo Rossi.

Cía de Seguros de Crédito Continental, SA: Avda Isidora Goyenechea 3162, 6°, Edif. Parque 1 Golf, Santiago; tel. (2) 636-4000; fax (2) 636-4001; e-mail seguros@continental.cl; internet www.continental.cl; f. 1990; general; Pres. Miguel Angel Poduje Sapiain; Gen. Man. Andrés Mendieta Valenzuela.

Cía de Seguros de Vida Cruz del Sur, SA: Avda El Golf 150, Las Condes, Santiago; tel. (2) 461-8000; fax (2) 461-8334; internet www.cruzdelsur.cl; f. 1992; life; Pres. José Tomás Guzmán Dumas; Gen. Man. José Antonio Llaneza Torrealba.

Consorcio, SA: Edif. Consorcio, Avda El Bosque Sur 180, Las Condes, Santiago; tel. (2) 230-4000; fax (2) 230-4050; internet www.consorcio.cl; f. 1916; life and general insurance; Pres. Juan Bilbao Hormaeche; Gen. Man. Nicolás Gellona Amunategui.

Euroamérica Seguros de Vida, SA: Apoquindo 3885, 20°, Las Condes, Santiago; tel. (2) 581-7000; fax (2) 581-7722; internet www.euroamerica.cl; f. 1962; life; Pres. Nicholas Davis Lecaros; Gen. Man. Claudio Asecio Fulgeri.

HDI Seguros, SA: Encomenderos 113, Casilla 185-D, Centro 192, Las Condes, Santiago; tel. (2) 422-9000; fax (2) 246-7567; e-mail contacto@hdi.cl; internet www.hdi.cl; f. 1989 in Chile; general; CEO Patricio Aldunate.

ING Seguros de Vida, SA: Avda Suecia 211, Providencia, Santiago; tel. (2) 252-1464; fax (2) 364-2060; e-mail centro.solucionwm@ing.cl; internet www.ingvida.cl; f. 1989; life; CEO Andrés Castro.

Mapfre Seguros: Isidora Goyenechea 3520, 14°, Casilla 7550071, Las Condes, Santiago; tel. (2) 700-4000; fax (2) 694-7565; internet www.mapfreseguros.cl; f. 1991; general; Gen. Man. Julio Domingo Souto.

MetLife Chile Seguros de Vida, SA: Agustinas 640, 9°, Casilla 111, Correo Central, Santiago; tel. (2) 640-1000; fax (2) 640-1100; internet www.metlife.cl; f. 1980 as Seguros Interamericana; subsidiary of Metlife Inc. since 2002; Country Man. Víctor Hassi Sabal.

Renta Nacional Compañías de Seguros, SA: Amunátegui 178, 2°, Centro, Santiago; tel. (2) 670-0200; fax (2) 670-0039; e-mail renta@rentanac.cl; internet www.rentanac.cl; f. 1982; life; Pres. Francisco Javier Errázuriz Talavera; Gen. Man. Jorge Sims San Román.

RSA Chile (United Kingdom): Providencia 1760, 4°, Santiago; tel. (2) 396-1000; fax (2) 396-1291; e-mail servicioaclientes@cl.rsagroup.com; internet www.rsagroup.cl; f. 2000; fmrly known as Royal & Sun Alliance Seguros; Pres. Víctor Manuel Jarpa Riveros; Gen. Man. Gonzalo Santos.

Vida Security, SA: Apoquindo 3150, 8°, Las Condes, Santiago; tel. (2) 584-2400; internet www.vidasecurity.cl; f. 2002 through merger of Seguros Security and Seguros Previsión Vida; Pres. Francisco Silva Silva; Gen. Man. Alejandro Alzérreca Luna.

Insurance Association

Asociación de Aseguradores de Chile, AG: La Concepción 322, Of. 501, Casilla 2630, Providencia, Santiago; tel. (2) 834-4900; fax (2) 834-4920; e-mail seguros@aach.cl; internet www.aach.cl; f. 1931; Pres. Fernando Cámbara Lodigiani.

Trade and Industry

GOVERNMENT AGENCIES

Comisión Nacional de Energía (CNE): Miraflores 222, 10°, Santiago; tel. (2) 797-2600; fax (2) 797-2627; internet www.cne.cl; Exec. Sec. Juan Manuel Contreras Sepúlveda.

Corporación de Fomento de la Producción (CORFO): Moneda 921, Casilla 3886, Santiago; tel. (2) 631-8200; e-mail info@corfo.cl; internet www.corfo.cl; f. 1939; holding group of principal state enterprises; grants loans and guarantees to private sector; responsible for sale of non-strategic state enterprises; promotes entrepreneurship; Pres. Pablo Longueira (Minister of the Economy, Development and Tourism); Exec. Vice-Pres. Carlos Alvarez Voullième; 13 brs.

PROCHILE (Dirección General de Relaciones Económicas Internacionales): Teatinos 180, Santiago; tel. (2) 827-5100; fax (2) 696-0639; e-mail info@prochile.cl; internet www.prochile.cl; f. 1974; bureau of international economic affairs; Dir Félix de Vicente Mingo.

Servicio Nacional de Capacitación y Empleo (SENCE) (National Training and Employment Service): Teatinos 333, 8°, Santiago; tel. (2) 870-6222; fax (2) 696-7103; internet www.sence.cl; attached to Ministry of Labour and Social Security; Nat. Dir José Miguel Berguño Cañas.

STATE CORPORATIONS

Corporación Nacional del Cobre de Chile (CODELCO-Chile): Huérfanos 1270, Casilla 150-D, Santiago; tel. (2) 690-3000; fax (2) 690-3059; e-mail comunica@codelco.cl; internet www.codelco.com; f. 1976 as a state-owned enterprise with copper-producing operational divisions at Chuquicamata, Radomiro Tomić, Salvador, Andina, Talleres Rancagua and El Teniente; attached to Ministry of Mining; Pres. Hernán de Solminihac Tampier (Minister of Mining); Exec. Pres. José Pablo Arellano Marín; 18,496 employees.

Empresa Nacional de Petróleo (ENAP): Vitacura 2736, 10°, Las Condes, Santiago; tel. (2) 280-3000; fax (2) 280-3199; e-mail webenap@enap.cl; internet www.enap.cl; f. 1950; state-owned petroleum and gas exploration and production corpn; Pres. Hernán de Solminihac Tampier (Minister of Mining); Gen. Man. Enrique Dávila Alveal; 3,286 employees.

DEVELOPMENT ORGANIZATIONS

Comisión Chilena de Energía Nuclear: Amunátegui 95, Santiago; tel. (2) 470-2500; fax (2) 470-2570; e-mail oirs@cchen.cl; internet www.cchen.cl; f. 1965; govt body to develop peaceful uses of atomic energy; concentrates, regulates and controls all matters related to nuclear energy; Pres. Renato Agurto; Exec. Dir Jaime Salas Kurte.

Corporación Nacional de Desarrollo Indígena (Conadi): Aldunate 285, Temuco, Chile; tel. (45) 641-500; fax (45) 641-520; e-mail ctranamil@conadi.gov.cl; internet www.conadi.cl; promotes the economic and social development of indigenous communities; Nat. Dir Jorge Rubio Retamal.

Corporación Nacional Forestal (CONAF): Paseo Bulnes 285, Santiago; tel. (2) 663-0000; fax (2) 225-0641; e-mail consulta@conaf.cl; internet www.conaf.cl; f. 1970 to promote forestry activities, enforce forestry law, promote afforestation, administer subsidies for afforestation projects and to increase and preserve forest resources; manages 13.97m. ha designated as National Parks, Natural Monuments and National Reserves; under Ministry of Agriculture; Exec. Dir Eduardo Vial Ruiz-Tagle.

Empresa Nacional de Minería (ENAMI): MacIver 459, 2°, Casilla 100-D, Santiago; tel. (2) 637-5278; fax (2) 637-5452; e-mail eiturra@enami.cl; internet www.enami.cl; promotes the devt of small and medium-sized mines; attached to Ministry of Mining; partially privatized; Exec. Vice-Pres. William Díaz Róman.

CHAMBERS OF COMMERCE

Cámara de Comercio de Santiago: Edif. Del Comercio, Monjitas 392, Santiago; tel. (2) 360-7000; fax (2) 633-3595; e-mail cpn@ccs.cl; internet www.ccs.cl; f. 1919; 1,300 mems; Pres. Peter Hill D.

Cámara de Comercio, Servicios y Turismo de Antofagasta: Latorre 2580, 3º, Of. 21, Antofagasta; tel. (55) 225-175; fax (55) 222-053; e-mail info@camaracomercioantofagasta.cl; internet www.camaracomercioantofagasta.cl; f. 1924; Pres. Giancarlo Coronato Mackenzie.

Cámara de Comercio, Servicios y Turismo de Temuco, AG: Vicuña Mackenna 396, Temuco; tel. (45) 210-556; fax (45) 237-047; e-mail info@camaratemuco.cl; internet www.camaratemuco.cl; Pres. Mauricio del Canto Gacitua; Sec. Teresa Cid Sepulveda.

Cámara Nacional de Comercio, Servicios y Turismo de Chile: Merced 230, Santiago; tel. (2) 365-4000; fax (2) 365-4001; internet www.cnc.cl; f. 1858; Pres. CARLOS E. JORQUIERA M.; Pres., Int. Cttee RICARDO MEWES S.; 120 mems.

Cámara de la Producción y del Comercio de Concepción: Cauplicán 567, 2°, Concepción; tel. (41) 224-1121; fax (41) 224-1440; e-mail lmandiola@cpcc.cl; internet www.cpcc.cl; f. 1927; Pres. ALBERTO MIRANDA GUERRA; Gen. Man. LEONCIO TORO ARAYA.

INDUSTRIAL AND TRADE ASSOCIATIONS

Servicio Agrícola y Ganadero (SAG): Avda Bulnes 140, 8º, Santiago; tel. (2) 345-1100; fax (2) 345-1102; e-mail dirnac@sag.gob.cl; internet www.sag.cl; under Ministry of Agriculture; responsible for the protection and devt of safe practice in the sector; Nat. Dir ANÍBAL ARIZTÍA REYES.

Servicio Nacional de Pesca (SERNAPESCA): Victoria 2832, Valparaíso; tel. (32) 281-9100; fax (32) 25-6311; e-mail informaciones@sernapesca.cl; internet www.sernapesca.cl; f. 1978; govt regulator of the fishing industry; Nat. Dir JUAN LUIS ANSOLEAGA.

Sociedad Agrícola y Servicios Isla de Pascua (SASIPA): Hotu Matu'a s/n, Hanga Roa, Isla de Pascua; tel. (32) 210-0212; e-mail atencion@sasipa.cl; internet www.sasipa.cl; f. 1966; administers agriculture and public services on Easter Island; Pres. FERNANDO JAVIER FUENTES HERNÁNDEZ; Gen. Man. PEDRO HEY ICKA.

EMPLOYERS' ORGANIZATIONS

Confederación del Comercio Detallista y Turismo de Chile, AG (CONFEDECH): Merced 380, 8°, Of. 74, Santiago; tel. (2) 639-1264; fax (2) 638-0338; e-mail comerciodetallista@confedech.cl; internet www.comerciodetallista.cl; f. 1938; retail trade; Nat. Pres. RAFAEL CUMSILLE ZAPAPA; Sec.-Gen. PEDRO ZAMORANO PIÑATS.

Confederación de la Producción y del Comercio: Monseñor Sótero Sanz 182, Providencia, Santiago; tel. (2) 231-9764; fax (2) 231-9808; e-mail procomer@entelchile.net; internet www.cpc.cl; f. 1936; Pres. LORENZO CONSTANS GORRI; Gen. Man. FERNANDO ALVEAR ARTAZA.

Affiliated organizations:

Asociación de Bancos e Instituciones Financieras de Chile AG: see Finance (Banking Association).

Cámara Nacional de Comercio, Servicios y Turismo de Chile: see Chambers of Commerce.

Cámara Chilena de la Construcción: Marchant Pereira 10, 3°, Providencia, CP 6640721, Santiago; tel. (2) 376-3300; fax (2) 371-3430; internet www.camaraconstruccion.cl; f. 1951; Pres. GASTÓN ESCALA AGUIRRE; Sec.-Gen. CARLOS URENDA ALDUNATE; 17,442 mems.

Sociedad de Fomento Fabril, FG (SOFOFA): Avda Andrés Bello 2777, 3°, Las Condes, Santiago; tel. (2) 391-3100; fax (2) 391-3200; internet www.sofofa.cl; f. 1883; largest employers' org.; Pres. ANDRÉS CONCHA RODRÍGUEZ; Sec.-Gen. CRISTÓBAL PHILIPPI; 2,500 mems.

Sociedad Nacional de Agricultura—Federación Gremial (SNA): Tenderini 187, 2°, CP 6500978, Santiago; tel. (2) 639-6710; fax (2) 633-7771; e-mail info@sna.cl; internet www.sna.cl; f. 1838; landowners' asscn; controls Radio Stations CB 57 and XQB8 (FM) in Santiago, CB-97 in Valparaíso, CD-120 in Los Angeles, CA-144 in La Serena, CD-127 in Temuco; Pres. LUIS MAYOL BOUCHON; Sec.-Gen. JUAN PABLO MATTE FUENTES.

Sociedad Nacional de Minería (SONAMI): Avda Apoquindo 3000, 5°, Santiago; tel. (2) 335-9300; fax (2) 334-9700; e-mail monica.cavallini@sonami.cl; internet www.sonami.cl; f. 1883; Pres. ALBERTO SALAS MUÑOZ; Gen. Man. FELIPE CELEDÓN MARDONES; 48 mem. cos.

CONUPIA (Confederación Gremial Nacional Unida de la Mediana y Pequeña Industria, Servicios y Artesanado): Phillips 40, 6°, Of. 63, Providencia, Santiago; tel. (2) 633-1492; e-mail secgeneral@conupia.cl; internet www.conupia.cl; f. 1966; small and medium-sized industries and crafts; Pres. PEDRO DAVIS URZÚA; Sec.-Gen. JOSÉ LUIS RAMÍREZ ZAMORANO.

UTILITIES

Comisión Nacional de Energía: see Government Agencies.

Superintendencia de Electricidad y Combustibles (SEC): Avda Libertador Bernardo O'Higgins 1449, 13°, Torre 1, Santiago; tel. (2) 756-5149; fax (2) 756-5155; e-mail pchotzen@sec.cl; internet www.sec.cl; Supt LUIS AVILA BRAVO.

Electricity

AES Gener, SA: Mariano Sánchez Fontecilla 310, 3°, Las Condes, Santiago; tel. (2) 686-8900; fax (2) 686-8991; e-mail gener@gener.cl; internet www.gener.cl; f. 1981 as Chilectra Generación, SA; privatized in 1988; current name adopted in 1998; owned by AES Corpn (USA); responsible for operation of power plants Renca, Ventanas, Laguna Verde, El Indio, Altalfal, Maitenes, Queltehues and Volcán; Pres. ANDRÉS GLUSKI WEILERT; Gen. Man. LUIS FELIPE CERÓN CERÓN; 1,121 employees (group).

Eléctrica Santiago: Jorge Hirmas 2964, Renca, Santiago; tel. (2) 680-4760; fax (2) 680-4743; e-mail electricasantiago@aes.com; internet www.electricasantiago.cl; f. 1994; operates the Renca and the Nueva Renca thermoelectric plants in Santiago; installed capacity of 379 MW; Pres. VICENTE JAVIER GIORGIO; Gen. Man. RODRIGO OSORIO BÓRQUEZ.

Empresa Eléctrica Guacolda, SA: Avda Apoquindo 3885, 10°, Las Condes, Santiago; tel. (2) 362-4000; fax (2) 464-3560; internet www.guacolda.cl; operates a thermoelectric power station in Huasco; installed capacity of 304 MW; Pres. JOSÉ FLORENCIO GUZMÁN CORREA; Gen. Man. MARCO ARRÓSPIDE RIVERA.

Energía Verde: Mariano Sánchez Fontecilla 310, 3°, Las Condes, Santiago; tel. (43) 402-700; fax (43) 402-709; internet www.energiaverde.cl; operates 2 co-generation power stations at Constitución and Laja and a steam plant at Nacimiento; supplies the Cabrero industrial plant; CEO JAIME ZUAZAGOITÍA VIANCOS.

Norgener, SA: Jorge Hirmas 2960, Renca, Santiago; tel. (2) 680-4710; fax (2) 680-4868; northern subsidiary supplying the mining industry; Exec. Dir JUAN CARLOS OLMEDO HIDALGO.

Arauco Generación: El Golf 150, 14°, Las Condes, Santiago; tel. (2) 461-7200; fax (2) 698-5987; e-mail gic@arauco.cl; internet www.arauco.cl; f. 1994 to commercialize surplus power from pulp processing facility; Pres. JOSÉ TOMÁS GUZMÁN; Gen. Man. CRISTIÁN INFANTE.

Chilquinta Energía, SA: General Cruz 222, Valparaíso; tel. (32) 250-2000; fax (32) 223-1171; e-mail contactoweb@chiquinta.cl; internet www.chilquinta.cl; f. 1997 as Energas, SA; present name adopted in 2001; owned by Inversiones Sempra and PSEG of the USA; Pres. ARTURO INFANZÓN FAVELA; Gen. Man. CRISTIÁN ARNOLDS REYES.

Compañía Eléctrica del Litoral, SA: Avda Peñablanca 540, Algarrobo, Casilla 14454, Santiago; tel. (2) 481-195; fax (2) 483-313; e-mail fmartine@litoral.cl; internet www.litoral.cl; f. 1949; Gen. Man. LUIS CONTRERAS IGLESIAS.

Compañía General de Electricidad, SA (CGE): Teatinos 280, Santiago; tel. (2) 680-7000; fax (2) 680-7104; e-mail contacto@cge.cl; internet www.cge.cl; installed capacity of 662 MW; Pres. JORGE EDUARDO MARÍN CORREA; Gen. Man. PABLO GUARDA BARROS.

Compañía Nacional de Fuerza Eléctrica, SA (CONAFE): Norte 13, Of. 810, Viña del Mar; tel. (32) 220-6100; fax (32) 227-1593; e-mail serviciocliente@conafe.cl; internet www.conafe.cl; f. 1945; Pres. JOSÉ LUIS HORNAUER HERRMANN; Gen. Man. RODRIGO VIDAL SÁNCHEZ.

E-CL, SA (Energía Esencial): El Bosque Norte 500, 9°, Vitacura, Santiago; tel. (2) 353-3200; fax (2) 353-3210; e-mail contacto@edelnor.cl; internet www.e-cl.cl; f. 1981; fmrly Edelnor; changed name as above in 2010 following merger with Electroandina; acquired by Codelco and Tractebel, SA (Belgium) in 2002; Pres. JAN FLACHET; Gen. Man. LODEWIJK VERDEYEN.

Empresa Eléctrica de Magallanes, SA (Edelmag, SA): Croacia 444, Punta Arenas; tel. (71) 40-00; fax (71) 40-77; e-mail edelmag@edelmag.cl; internet www.edelmag.cl; f. 1981; 55% owned by CGE; Pres. JORGE JORDAN FRANULIC; Gen. Man. CARLOS YÁÑEZ ANTONUCCI.

Empresas Emel, SA: Avda Libertador Bernardo O'Higgins 886, 10°, Santiago; tel. (2) 344-8000; fax (2) 344-8001; internet www.emel.cl; holding co for the Emel group of electricity cos, bought by CGE in 2007; Gen. Man. CRISTIÁN SAPHORES MARTÍNEZ; Emel group includes:

ELECDA (Empresa Eléctrica de Antofagasta, SA): José Miguel Carrera 1587, Antofagasta 1250; tel. (55) 649-100; internet www.elecda.cl; Regional Man. ORLANDO ASSAD MANRÍQUEZ.

ELIQSA (Empresa Eléctrica de Iquique, SA): Zegeres 469, Iquique; tel. (57) 40-5400; fax (57) 42-7181; e-mail eliqsa@eliqsa.cl; internet www.eliqsa.cl; Pres. PABLO GUARDA BARROS; Regional Man. JUAN CARLOS GÓMEZ GAMBOA.

EMELARI (Empresa Eléctrica de Arica, SA): Baquedano 731, Arica; tel. (58) 201-100; fax (58) 23-1105; internet www.emelari.cl; Regional Man. RICARDO MIRANDA PUEBLA.

EMELAT (Empresa Eléctrica Atacama, SA): Circunvalación Ignacio Carrera Pinto 51, Copiapó; tel. (52) 205-100; fax (52) 205-103; internet www.emelat.cl; f. 1981; distribution co; Pres. JOSÉ LUIS HORNAUER HERRMANN; Regional Man. CLAUDIO JACQUES VERGARA.

EMELECTRIC (Empresa Eléctrica de Melipilla, Colchagua y Maule): Ortúzar N° 376, Melipilla; internet www.emelectric.cl; Pres. FRANCISCO JAVIER MARÍN ESTÉVEZ; Regional Mans NOLBERTO PÉREZ PEÑA (Melipilla), JUAN CARLOS OLIVER PÉREZ (Colchagua), JUAN MANUEL ORTEGA MUÑOZ (Maule).

ENERSIS, SA: Santa Rosa 76, Casilla 1557, Vitacura, Santiago; tel. (2) 353-4400; fax (2) 378-4788; e-mail comunicacion@e.enersis.cl; internet www.enersis.cl; f. 1981; holding co for Spanish group generating and distributing electricity through its subsidiaries throughout South America; 60.62% owned by Endesa Chile; Pres. PABLO YRARRÁZAVAL VALDÉS; Gen. Man. IGNACIO ANTOÑANZAS ALVEAR; 10,957 employees.

Chilectra, SA: Santo Domingo 789, Casilla 1557, Santiago; tel. (2) 632-2000; fax (2) 639-3280; e-mail rrpp@chilectra.cl; internet www.chilectra.cl; f. 1921; transmission and distribution arm of ENERSIS; supplies distribution cos, including the Empresa Eléctrica Municipal de Lo Barnechea, Empresa Municipal de Til-Til, and the Empresa Eléctrica de Colina, SA; holds overseas distribution concessions in Argentina, Peru and Brazil; acquired by ENERSIS of Spain in 1999; Pres. JUAN MARÍA MORENO MELLADO; Gen. Man. CRISTIÁN FIERRO MONTES.

Endesa Chile: Santa Rosa 76, Casilla 1392, Santiago; tel. (2) 630-9000; fax (2) 635-4720; e-mail comunicacion@endesa.cl; internet www.endesa.cl; f. 1943; installed capacity 4,035 MW (2002); ENERSIS obtained majority control of Endesa Chile in 1999; operates subsidiaries in Pehuenche, Pangue, San Isidro y Celta; Pres. JORGE ROSENBLUT; Gen. Man. JOAQUÍN GALINDO VÉLEZ.

SAESA (Sociedad Austral de Electricidad, SA): Manuel Bulnes 441, Casilla 21-0, Osorno; tel. (64) 20-6200; fax (64) 20-6309; e-mail saesa@saesa.cl; internet www.saesa.cl; owned by PSEG Corpn of the USA; Pres. JORGE LESSER GARCÍA-HUIDOBRO; Gen. Man. FRANCISCO MUALIM TIETZ.

Gas

Abastible, SA (Abastecedora de Combustible): Avda Vicuña Mackenna 55, Providencia, Santiago; tel. (2) 693-9000; fax (2) 693-9304; internet www.abastible.cl; f. 1956; owned by COPEC; Pres. FELIPE LAMARCA CLARO; Gen. Man. JOSÉ ODONE.

Compañía de Consumidores de Gas de Santiago (GASCO, SA): 1061 Santo Domingo, Casilla 8-D, Santiago; tel. (2) 694-4444; fax (2) 694-4370; e-mail info@gasco.cl; internet www.gasco.cl; natural gas utility; supplies Santiago and Punta Arenas regions; owned by CGE; Pres. CLAUDIO HORNAUER HERRMANN; Gen. Man. GERARDO COOD SCHOEPKE.

Electrogas: Alonso de Cordova 5900, Of. 401, Las Condes, Santiago; tel. (2) 299-3400; fax (2) 299-3490; e-mail carlos.andreani@electrogas.cl; internet www.electrogas.cl/default.asp; f. 1998; subsidiary of Endesa Chile; CEO CARLOS ANDREANI LUCO.

Empresas Lipigas: Las Urbinas 53, 13°, Of. 131, Providencia, Santiago; tel. (2) 650-3582; e-mail info@empresaslipigas.cl; internet www.lipigas.cl; f. 1950; liquid gas supplier; also operates Agrogas, Enagas and Industrias Codigas; Pres. ERNESTO NOGUERA G.; Gen. Man. ANGEL MAFUCCI.

GasAndes: Avda Chena 11650, Parque Industrial Puerta Sur, San Bernardo, Santiago; tel. (2) 366-5960; fax (2) 366-5942; internet www.gasandes.com; distributes natural gas transported from the Argentine province of Mendoza via a 463-km pipeline.

GasAtacama Generación: Isidora Goyenechea 3365, 8°, Las Condes, Santiago; tel. (2) 366-3800; fax (2) 366-3802; natural gas producer and transporter; subsidiary of Endesa Chile; Man. RUDOLFO ARANEDA.

GasValpo, SA: Camino Internacional 1420, Viña del Mar; tel. (32) 227-7000; fax (32) 221-3092; e-mail info@gasvalpo.cl; internet www.gasvalpo.cl; f. 1853; owned by AGL of Australia; Pres. GREG MARTIN; Gen. Man. LUIS KIPREOS.

Linde Chile: Paseo Presidente, Errázuriz Echaurren 2631, Casilla 16953, Providencia, Santiago; tel. (2) 330-8000; fax (2) 231-8009; e-mail callcentre@cl.aga.com; internet www.linde.cl; f. 1920 as AGA Chile, SA; owned by Linde Gas Corpn of Germany; natural and industrial gases utility.

Water

Aguas Andinas, SA: Avda Presidente Balmaceda 1398, Santiago; tel. (2) 688-1000; fax (2) 698-5871; e-mail info@aguasandinas.cl; internet www.aguasandinas.cl; water supply and sanitation services to Santiago and the surrounding area; sold to a French-Spanish consortium in June 1999; Pres. FELIPE LARRAIN ASPILLAGA; Gen. Man. VÍCTOR DE LA BARRA FUENZALIDA.

Empresa de Obras Sanitarias de Valparaíso, SA (Esval): Cochrane 751, Valparaíso; tel. (32) 220-9000; fax (32) 220-9502; e-mail infoesval@entelchile.net; internet www.esval.cl; f. 1989; sanitation and irrigation co serving Valparaíso; Pres. JUAN HURTADO VICUÑA; Gen. Man. FRANCISCO OTTONE VIGORENA; 377 employees.

Sigsig Ltda (Tecnagent) (Servicios de Ingeniería Sigren y Sigren Ltda): Presidente Errázuriz 3262, Casilla 7550295, Las Condes, Santiago; tel. (2) 335-2001; fax (2) 334-8466; e-mail tecnagent@tecnagent.cl; internet www.tecnagent.cl; f. 1986; Pres. RAÚL B. SIGREN BINDHOFF; Gen. Man. RAÚL A. SIGREN ORFILA.

TRADE UNIONS

Central Unions

Central Autónoma de Trabajadores (CAT): Sazié 1761, Santiago; tel. and fax (2) 657-8533; e-mail catchile@catchile.cl; internet www.catchile.cl; 107,000 mems (2007); Pres. OSCAR OLIVOS MADARIAGA; Sec.-Gen. ALFONSO PASTENE URIBE.

Central Unitaria de Trabajadores de Chile (CUT): Alameda 1346, Centro, Santiago; tel. (2) 352-7600; fax (2) 672-0112; e-mail cutorganizacion@gmail.com; internet www.cutchile.cl; f. 1988; affiliated orgs: 20 asscns, 28 confederations, 64 federations, 35 unions; 670,000 mems (2009); Pres. ARTURO MARTÍNEZ MOLINA; Gen. Sec. JAIME GAJARDO ORELLANA.

Unión Nacional de Trabajadores: Moneda 1447, Santiago; tel. (2) 688-6344; e-mail info@untchile.cl; internet untchile.cl; Pres. DIEGO OLIVARES ARAVENA; Gen. Sec. LUIS PALOMINOS LIZAM.

Union Confederations

Agrupación Nacional de Empleados Fiscales (ANEF): Edif. Tucapel Jiménez, Alameda 1603, Santiago; tel. (2) 696-2957; fax 697-9764; e-mail info@anef.cl; internet www.anef.cl; f. 1943; affiliated to CUT; public service workers; Pres. RAÚL DE LA PUENTE PEÑA; Sec.-Gen. BERNARDO JORQUERA ROJAS.

Colegio de Profesores de Chile: Moneda 2394, Santiago; tel. (2) 470-4200; fax (2) 470-4290; e-mail contacto@colegiodeprofesores.cl; internet www.colegiodeprofesores.cl; f. 1974; 100,000 mems; Pres. JAIME GAJARDO ORELLANA; Sec.-Gen. DARÍO VÁSQUEZ SALAZAR.

Confederación Nacional Campesina: Eleuterio Ramírez 1471, Santiago; tel. and fax (2) 696-2673; affiliated to CUT; Pres. SEGUNDO STEILEN NAVARRO; Sec.-Gen. RENÉ ASTUDILLO R.

Confederación Nacional de Federaciones y Sindicatos de Gente de Mar, Portuarios y Pesqueros de Chile (CONGEMAR): José Tomás Ramos 170, Valparaíso; tel. (32) 225-7580; e-mail congemar@tie.cl; internet www.congemar.cl; affiliated to CUT; Pres. JORGE MOISES BUSTOS B.; Sec.-Gen. MARIANO VILLA PERÉZ.

Confederación Nacional de Sindicatos Agrícolas—Unidad Obrero Campesina (UOC): Eleuterio Ramírez 1463, Centro, Santiago; tel. and fax (2) 696-6342; e-mail confe.uocchile@uocchile.cl; internet www.uocchile.cl; affiliated to CUT; Pres. OLGA GUTIÉRREZ.

Confederación Nacional de Sindicatos, Federaciones y Asociaciones de Trabajadores del Sector Privado de Chile (CEPCH): Valentín Letelier 18, Centro, Santiago; tel. (2) 673-5221; e-mail convocatoriacepch@gmail.com; internet cepch.org; trade union for workers in private sector; affiliated to CUT; Pres. RUBEN VILLANUEVA LARA; Sec.-Gen. MAURICIO OLIVA CARCAMO.

Confederación Nacional de Sindicatos de Trabajadores de la Construcción, Maderas, Materiales de Edificación y Actividades Conexas (CNTC): Almirante Hurtado 2069, Centro, Santiago; tel. (2) 672-3913; fax (2) 632-2579; e-mail cntc@chile.com; internet www.cntc.cl; f. 1936; affiliated to CUT; Pres. JOSÉ SANTOS HERNANDEZ; Sec.-Gen. HECTOR VILLEGAS AREVALO.

Confederación Nacional de Sindicatos de Trabajadores Textiles, de la Confección y Vestuario (CONTEVECH): Agustinas 2349, Dpto 0555, Centro, Santiago; tel. (2) 688-2008; e-mail contevech@hotmail.es; internet contevech.blogspot.com; affiliated to CUT; Pres. JOSÉ GERMÁN SAN MARTÍN PÉREZ.

Confederación Nacional de Suplementeros de Chile (CONASUCH): Tucapel Jiménez 26, Centro, Santiago; tel. (2) 784-3444; fax (2) 784-3449; e-mail conasuch1942@gmail.com; internet conasuch.hostoi.com; f. 1942; trade union for newspaper vendors; Pres. IVÁN ENSINA CARO.

Confederación Nacional de Trabajadores del Comercio, Oficinas, Industrias y Servicios (CONSFETRACOSI): Almirante Simpson 70, Providencia, Santiago; tel. (2) 655-0301; fax (2) 222-7804; e-mail consfetracosi@gmail.com; internet consfetracosi.blogspot.com; f. 1995; affiliated to CAT; Sec.-Gen. MAGDALENA CASTILLO D.

Confederación Nacional de Trabajadores Electrometalúrgicos, Mineros y Automotrices de Chile (CONSFETEMA): Vicuña Mackenna 3101, San Joaquín, Santiago; tel. (2) 238-1732; fax (2) 553-6494; e-mail consfetema@123mail.cl; Pres. LUIS SEPÚLVEDA DEL RÍO.

Confederación Nacional de Trabajadores Forestales de Chile (CTF): Concepción; tel. and fax (41) 220-0407; internet ctf-chile.blogspot.com; f. 1988; 45,000 mems; Pres. JORGE GONZÁLEZ CASTILLO; Sec.-Gen. SERGIO GATICA ORTIZ.

Confederación Nacional de Trabajadores Metalúrgicos (CONSTRAMET): Santa Rosa 101, esq. Alonso Ovalle, Santiago; tel. (2) 664-8581; fax (2) 638-3694; e-mail secretaria@constramet.cl; internet www.constramet.cl; affiliated to CUT and the International Metalworkers' Federation; Pres. HORACIO FUENTES GONZALEZ; Sec.-Gen. ROBERTO BUSTAMENTE ROJAS.

Confederación de Sindicatos Bancarios y Afines: Agustinas 814, Of. 606, Santiago; tel. (2) 481-6122; fax (2) 481-6123; e-mail confederacionbancaria@gmail.com; internet www.bancariachile.cl; affiliated to CUT; Pres. ANDREA RIQUELME BELTRÁN; Sec.-Gen. LUIS MESINA MARÍN.

Confederación de Trabajadores del Cobre (CTC): Santiago; e-mail secretariageneral@confederaciondelcobre.cl; internet www.confederaciondelcobre.cl; f. 2007; copper workers' union; Pres. CRISTIÁN CUEVAS ZAMBRANO; Sec.-Gen. JEDRY VELIS PALMA.

Transport

RAILWAYS

In 2010 there were 6,188 km of railway lines in the country. There are railways owned by the state government and also several privately owned railways. The metropolitan transport system serves the main cities, towns and suburbs of the country.

State Railways

Empresa de los Ferrocarriles del Estado (EFE): Morandé 115, 6°, Santiago; tel. (2) 376-8500; fax (2) 776-2609; e-mail principios@efe.cl; internet www.efe.cl; f. 1851; 2,072 km of track in use (2006); Pres. VÍCTOR TOLEDO SANDOVAL; Gen. Man. FRANCO FACCILONGO FORNO.

Ferrocarriles Suburbanos de Concepción (FESUB): Avda Padre Hurtado 570, 4°, Concepción; tel. (41) 286-8015; e-mail contacto@biotren.cl; internet www.fesub.cl; f. 2008; serves Corto Laja and Regional Victoria Temuco; Pres. JOAQUÍN BRAHM BARRIL; Gen. Man. NELSON HERNÁNDEZ ROLDÁN.

Servicio de Trenes Regionales Terra, SA (TerraSur): Avda Libertador Bernardo O'Higgins 3170, andén 6, 2°, Santiago; tel. (2) 585-5000; fax (2) 585-5914; e-mail comunicaciones@terrasur.cl; internet www.terrasur.cl; Pres. GONZALO EDWARDS GUZMÁN; Gen. Man. ANTONIO DOURTHÉ CASTRILLÓN.

Transporte Ferroviario Andrés Pirazolli, SA (Transap): Exterminal Ferroviario Los Lirios, Rancagua; tel. (67) 222-2242; fax (67) 222-2039; e-mail contacto@transap.cl; internet www.transap.cl; f. 2000; freight services; Pres. MARCELO PIRAZZOLI; Gen. Man. NABIL KUNCAR.

Private Railways

Empresa de Transporte Ferroviario, SA (Ferronor): Huérfanos 587, Ofs 301 y 302, Santiago; tel. (2) 938-3170; fax (2) 638-0464; e-mail ferronor@ferronor.cl; internet www.ferronor.cl; 2,412 km of track (2009); operates cargo services only; interconnected with Argentina, Bolivia, Brazil and Paraguay; Pres. ROBERTO PIRAZZOLI; Gen. Man. JUAN CARLOS GARCÍA-HUIDOBRO.

Ferrocarril de Antofagasta (FCAB): Bolívar 255, Casillas ST, Antofagasta; tel. (55) 20-6100; fax (55) 20-6220; e-mail info@fcab.cl; internet www.fcab.cl; f. 1888; subsidiary of Grupo Antofagasta PLC (United Kingdom); operates an international railway to Bolivia and Argentina; cargo-forwarding services; track length in use 1,000 km (2011); Gen. Man. MIGUEL V. SEPÚLVEDA.

Ferrocarril del Pacífico, SA (FEPASA): Málaga 120, 5°, Las Condes, Santiago; tel. (2) 837-8000; fax (2) 837-8005; e-mail oguevara@fepasa.cl; internet www.fepasa.cl; f. 1993; privatized freight services on EFE track; 19.83% owned by EFE; Pres. OSCAR GUILLERMO GARRETÓN PURCELL; Gen. Man. GAMALIEL VILLALOBOS ARANDA.

Association

Asociación Chilena de Conservación de Patrimonio Ferroviario (ACCPF): Casilla 51996, Correo Central, Santiago; tel. (2) 699-4607; fax (2) 280-0252; e-mail info@accpf.cl; internet www.accpf.cl; f. 1986; railway preservation asscn; Pres. JOSÉ TOMÁS BRETÓN JARA; Sec.-Gen. EUGENIO TUEVE RIVERA.

METROPOLITAN TRANSPORT

Metro de Santiago: Avda Libertador Bernardo O'Higgins 1414, Santiago; tel. (2) 250-3000; fax (2) 937-2000; e-mail comunicaciones@metro.cl; internet www.metrosantiago.cl; started operations 1975; 5 lines, 84.4 km (2008); extension to 104.5 km scheduled for completion in 2010; Pres. RAPHAEL BERGOEING VELA; Gen. Man. ROBERTO BIANCHI POBLETA.

Metro Valparaíso, SA (MERVAL): Viana 1685, Viña del Mar, V Región, Valparaíso; tel. (32) 252-7511; fax (32) 252-7509; e-mail jmobando@metro-valparaiso.cl; internet www.metro-valparaiso.cl; f. 1995; Pres. VÍCTOR TOLEDO SANDOVAL; Gen. Man. MARISA KAUSEL CONTADOR.

Transantiago: Nueva York 9, 10°, Santiago; tel. (2) 428-7900; fax (2) 428-7926; internet www.transantiago.cl; f. 2005; govt scheme to co-ordinate public transport in Santiago; comprises 10 bus networks and the Metro de Santiago.

Trenes Metropolitanos, SA: Avda Libertador Bernardo O'Higgins 3170, Andén 6 de Estación Central, Santiago; tel. (2) 585-5000; fax (2) 776-3304; e-mail contacto@tmsa.cl; internet www.tmsa.cl; f. 1990; subsidiary of Empresa de los Ferrocarriles del Estado (EFE); connects Santiago with several communities near San Fernando; Pres. JUAN ESTEBAN DOÑA NOVOA; Gen. Man. CRISTIÁN MOYA SILVA.

ROADS

There were 17,269 km (10,730 miles) of paved roads in 2007. The road system includes the entirely paved Pan-American Highway, extending 3,455 km from north to south.

Dirección de Vialidad: Morandé 59, 2°, Santiago; tel. (2) 449-4000; fax (2) 441-0914; internet www.vialidad.cl; f. 1953; supervising authority; Dir MARIO FERNÁNDEZ RODRÍGUEZ.

SHIPPING

As a consequence of Chile's difficult topography, maritime transport is of particular importance. The principal ports are Valparaíso, Talcahuano, Antofagasta, San Antonio, Arica, Iquique, Coquimbo, San Vicente, Puerto Montt and Punta Arenas. Chile's merchant fleet amounted to 849,000 grt (comprising 563 vessels) at December 2009.

Supervisory Authorities

Asociación Nacional de Armadores: Blanco 869, 3°, Valparaíso; tel. (32) 221-2057; fax (32) 221-2017; e-mail info@armadores-chile.cl; internet www.armadores-chile.cl; f. 1931; shipowners' asscn; Pres. ROBERTO HETZ VORPAHL; Gen. Man. ARTURO SIERRA MERINO.

Cámara Marítima y Portuaria de Chile, AG: Blanco 869, 2°, Valparaíso; tel. (32) 225-0313; fax (32) 225-0231; e-mail info@camport.cl; internet www.camport.cl; Pres. VICTOR PINO TORCHE; Exec. Vice-Pres. RODOLFO GARCÍA SÁNCHEZ.

Dirección General de Territorio Marítimo y Marina Mercante (DIRECTEMAR): Errázuriz 537, 4°, Valparaíso; tel. (32) 220-8000; fax (32) 225-2539; e-mail transparencia@directemar.cl; internet www.directemar.cl; maritime admin. of the coast and national waters, control of the merchant navy; ship registry; Dir-Gen. Vice-Adm. MARTIN ENRIQUE LARRAÑAGA.

Cargo-handling Companies

Empresa Portuaria Antofagasta (EPA): Avda Grecia s/n, Puerto Antofagasta, Casilla 190, Antofagasta; tel. (55) 56-3756; fax (55) 56-3735; e-mail epa@puertoantofagasta.cl; internet www.puertoantofagasta.cl; f. 1998; Pres. WALDO MORA LONGA; Gen. Man. CARLOS ESCOBAR OLGUIN.

Empresa Portuaria Arica: Máximo Lira 389, Arica; tel. (58) 20-2080; fax (58) 20-2090; e-mail puertoarica@puertoarica.cl; internet www.puertoarica.cl; f. 1998; Pres. FRANCISCO JAVIER GONZÁLEZ SILVA; Gen. Man. ALDO SIGNORELLI BONOMO.

Empresa Portuaria Austral: Avda Bernardo O'Higgins 1385, Punta Arenas; tel. (61) 71-1200; fax (61) 71-1231; e-mail info@australport.cl; internet www.australport.cl; Pres. JULIO COVARRUBIAS FERNÁNDEZ; Gen. Man. IGNACIO FUGELLIE.

Empresa Portuaria Chacabuco (EMPORCHA): Avda Bernardo O'Higgins s/n, Puerto Chacabuco, XI Región; tel. (67) 35-1139; fax (67) 35-1174; e-mail info@chacabucoport.cl; internet www.chacabucoport.cl; f. 1998; Pres. GUILLERMO MARTÍNEZ BARROS; Gen. Man. ENRIQUE RUNÍN ZUÑIGA.

Empresa Portuaria Coquimbo: Melgarejo 676, Casilla 10D, Coquimbo; tel. (51) 31-3606; fax (51) 32-6146; e-mail ptoqq@entelchile.net; internet www.puertocoquimbo.cl; Pres. HUGO GRISANTI ABOGABIR.

Empresa Portuaria Iquique: Avda Jorge Barrera 62, Casilla 47D, Iquique; tel. (57) 40-0100; fax (57) 41-3176; e-mail epi@epi.cl; internet www.epi.cl; f. 1998; Pres. ANGEL CABRERA VENEGAS; Gen. Man. ALFREDO LEITON ARBEA.

Empresa Portuaria Puerto Montt: Avda Angelmó 1673, Puerto Montt, Región de los Lagos; tel. (65) 36-4500; fax (65) 36-4517; e-mail gerencia@empormontt.cl; internet www.empormontt.cl; Pres. CARLOS GUILLERMO GEISSE MACEVOY; Gen. Man. ALEX WINKLER RIETZSCH.

Empresa Portuaria San Antonio (EPSA): Alan Macowan 0245, San Antonio; tel. (35) 58-6000; fax (35) 58-6015; e-mail correo@saiport.cl; internet www.sanantonioport.cc.cl; f. 1998; Pres. PATRICIO ARRAU PONS; Gen. Man. ALVARO ESPINOSA ALMARZA.

Empresa Portuaria Talcahuano-San Vicente: Avda Blanco Encalada 547, Talcahuano; tel. (41) 272-0300; fax (41) 272-0326; e-mail eportuaria@puertotalcahuano.cl; internet www.puertotalcahuano.cl; Pres. EUGENIO GUSTAVO CANTUARIAS LARRONDO; Gen. Man. LUIS ALBERTO ROSENBERG NESBET.

Empresa Portuaria Valparaíso: Avda Errázuriz 25, 4°, Of. 1, Valparaíso; tel. (2) 244-8800; fax (2) 222-4190; e-mail comercial@epv

.cl; internet www.epv.cl; Pres. ALFONSO MUJÍCA VIZCAYA; Gen. Man. HARALD JAEGER KARL.

Principal Shipping Companies

Santiago

Agencias Universales, SA (AGUNSA): Edif. del Pacífico, 15°, Avda Andrés Bello 2687, Casilla 2511, Las Condes, Santiago; tel. (2) 460-2700; fax (2) 203-9009; e-mail agunsascl@agunsa.cl; internet www.agunsa.cl; f. 1960; maritime transportation and shipping, port and docking services; owned by Empresas Navieras, SA; Chair. JOSÉ MANUEL URENDA SALAMANCA; Gen. Man. LUIS MANCILLA PÉREZ.

Empresa Marítima, SA (Empremar Chile): Encomenderos 260, Piso 7°, Las Condes, Santiago; tel. (2) 469-6100; fax (2) 469-6199; internet www.empremar.cl; f. 1953; international and coastal services; Chair. LORENZO CAGLEVIC; Gen. Man. CRISTIÁN BERNALES.

Navimag Ferries, SA (NAVIMAG): Avda El Bosque, Norte 0440, 11°, Of. 1103/1104, Las Condes, Santiago; tel. (2) 442-3150; fax (2) 203-4025; e-mail sales@navimag.cl; internet www.navimag.com; f. 1979; part of Nisa Navegación, SA; Gen. Man. HÉCTOR HENRÍQUEZ NEGRÓN.

Ultragas Ltda: Avda El Bosque Norte 500, 20°, Las Condes, Santiago; tel. (2) 630-1009; fax (2) 232-8856; e-mail ultragas@ultragas.cl; internet www.ultragasgroup.com; f. 1960; part of Ultragas Group; tanker services; Chair. DAG VON APPEN BUROSE; CEO CHRISTIAN CSASZAR.

Valparaíso

Broom Valparaíso: Errázuriz 629, 3° y 4°, Valparaíso; tel. (32) 226-8200; fax (32) 221-3308; e-mail info@ajbroom.cl; internet www.broomgroup.com; f. 1920; shipowners and brokers; Pres. JAMES C. WELLS M.; CEO ANDRÉS NUÑEZ SORENSEN.

Cía Chilena de Navegación Interoceánica, SA (CCNI): Plaza de la Justicia 59, Valparaíso; tel. (32) 227-5500; fax (32) 225-5949; e-mail info@ccni.cl; internet www.ccni.cl; f. 1930; regular sailings to Japan, Republic of Korea, Taiwan, Hong Kong, USA, Mexico, South Pacific, South Africa and Europe; bulk and dry cargo services; owned by Empresas Navieras, SA; Chair. JOSÉ MANUEL URENDA SALAMANCA; CEO FELIPE IRARRÁZAVAL OVALLE.

Cía Sud Americana de Vapores (CSAV): Plaza Sotomayor 50, Casilla 49V, Valparaíso; tel. (32) 220-3000; fax (32) 320-3333; e-mail info@csav.com; internet www.csav.com; f. 1872; regular services world-wide; bulk and container carriers, tramp and reefer services; Chair. GUILLERMO LUKSIC CRAIG; Gen. Man. JUAN ANTONIO ALVAREZ AVENDAÑO.

Naviera Chilena del Pacífico, SA (Nachipa): Almirante Señoret 70, 6°, Casilla 370, Valparaíso; tel. (32) 250-0300; e-mail valparaiso@nachipa.com; internet www.nachipa.cl; cargo; Pres. PABLO SIMIAN ZAMORANO; Gen. Man. FELIPE SIMIAN FERNÁNDEZ.

Sudamericana Agencias Aéreas y Marítimas, SA (SAAM): Blanco 895, Valparaíso; tel. (32) 220-1000; fax (32) 220-1481; e-mail servicioalcliente@saamsa.com; internet www.saam.cl; f. 1961; cargo services; Gen. Man. ALEJANDRO GARCÍA-HUIDOBRO.

Punta Arenas

Transbordadora Austral Broom, SA: Avda Juan Williams 06450, Punta Arenas; tel. (61) 72-8100; fax (61) 72-8109; e-mail correo@tabsa.cl; internet www.tabsa.cl; f. 1968; ferry services in Chilean Antarctica; Pres. PEDRO LECAROS; Gen. Man. ALEJANDRO KUSANOVIC.

Puerto Montt

Transmarchilay, SA (Transporte Marítimo Chiloé-Aysén): Angelmo 2187, Puerto Montt; tel. (65) 27-0700; fax (65) 27-0730; e-mail transporte@tmc.cl; internet www.transmarchilay.cl; f. 1971; Pres. HARALD ROSENQVIST; Gen. Man. ALVARO CONTRERAS.

CIVIL AVIATION

There are 330 airfields in the country, of which eight have long runways. Arturo Merino Benítez, 20 km north-east of Santiago, and Chacalluta, 14 km north-east of Arica, are the principal international airports.

Regulatory Authority

Dirección General de Aeronática Civil (DGAC): Miguel Claro 1314, Providencia, Santiago; tel. (2) 439-2000; fax (2) 436-8143; internet www.dgac.gob.cl; f. 1930; Dir-Gen. Gen. JAIME ALARCÓN PÉREZ.

Principal Airlines

Aerocardal: Aeropuerto Internacional Arturo Merino Benítez, Avda Diego Barros Ortiz 2065, Pudahuel, Santiago; tel. (2) 377-7400; fax (2) 377-7405; e-mail ventas@aerocardal.com; internet www.aerocardal.com; f. 1990; executive, charter and tourist services; Gen. Man. RICARDO REAL.

Aerovías DAP: Avda Bernardo O'Higgins 891, Casilla 406, Punta Arenas; tel. (61) 61-6100; fax (61) 61-6159; e-mail ventas@aeroviasdap.cl; internet www.aeroviasdap.cl; f. 1980; domestic services; CEO ALEX PISCEVIC.

Línea Aérea Nacional de Chile (LAN-Chile): Avda Presidente Riesco 5711, 20°, Las Condes, Santiago; tel. (2) 565-2525; fax (2) 565-3890; internet www.lanchile.com; f. 1929; operates scheduled domestic passenger and cargo services, also Santiago–Easter Island; international services to French Polynesia, Spain, and throughout North and South America; Pres. IGNACIO CUETO PLAZA; CEO. ENRIQUE CUETO PLAZA.

Tourism

Chile has a wide variety of attractions for the tourist, including fine beaches, ski resorts in the Andes, lakes, rivers and desert scenery. Isla de Pascua (Easter Island) may also be visited by tourists. In 2010 there were 2,766,007 tourist arrivals. In that year receipts from tourism totalled a provisional US $1,636m.

Servicio Nacional de Turismo (SERNATUR): Avda Providencia 1550, 2°, CP 7500548, Santiago; tel. (2) 731-8419; fax (2) 236-1417; e-mail contacto@sernatur.cl; internet www.sernatur.cl; f. 1975; Nat. Dir ALVARO CASTILLA FERNÁNDEZ.

Asociación Chilena de Empresas de Turismo (ACHET): Avda Providencia 2019, Of. 42B, Santiago; tel. (2) 439-9100; fax (2) 439-9118; e-mail achet@achet.cl; internet www.achet.cl; f. 1945; 155 mems; Pres. GUILLERMO CORREA SANFUENTES; Sec.-Gen. LORENA ARRIAGADA GÁLVEZ.

Defence

As assessed at November 2011, Chile's armed forces numbered 59,059: army 35,000, navy 16,299 and air force 7,760. There were also paramilitary forces of 44,712 *carabineros*. Reserve troops numbered 40,000. Compulsory military service was ended in 2005.

Defence Expenditure: Expenditure was budgeted at 1,200,000m. pesos in 2011.

Chief of Staff of National Defence: Maj.-Gen. HERNÁN MARDONES RÍOS.

Commander-in-Chief of the Army: Gen. JUAN MIGUEL FUENTE-ALBA POBLETE.

Commander-in-Chief of the Navy: Adm. EDMUNDO GONZÁLEZ ROBLES.

Commander-in-Chief of the Air Force: Gen. RICARDO ORTEGA PERRIER.

Education

Primary education in Chile is free and compulsory for eight years, beginning at six or seven years of age. It is divided into two cycles: the first lasts for four years and provides a general education; the second cycle offers a more specialized schooling. Secondary education is divided into the humanities-science programme (lasting four years), with the emphasis on general education and possible entrance to university, and the technical-professional programme (lasting for up to six years). In 2008 enrolment at primary schools included 95% of children in the relevant age-group, while the comparable ratio for secondary enrolment was 85%. There are three types of higher education institution: universities, professional institutes and centres of technical information. In 2010 there were 987,643 students in higher education. The provision for education in the 2011 central government budget was 5,249,271m. pesos.

THE PEOPLE'S REPUBLIC OF CHINA

Introductory Survey

LOCATION, CLIMATE, LANGUAGE, RELIGION, FLAG, CAPITAL

The People's Republic of China covers a vast area of eastern Asia, with Mongolia and Russia to the north, Tajikistan, Kyrgyzstan and Kazakhstan to the north-west, Afghanistan and Pakistan to the west, and India, Nepal, Bhutan, Myanmar (formerly Burma), Laos and Viet Nam to the south. The country borders the Democratic People's Republic of Korea (North Korea) in the north-east, and has a long coastline on the Pacific Ocean. The climate ranges from subtropical in the far south to an annual average temperature of below 10°C (50°F) in the north, and from the monsoon climate of eastern China to the aridity of the north-west. The principal language is Northern Chinese (Mandarin, known as Putonghua or common speech); in the south and south-east local dialects are spoken. The Xizangzu (Tibetans), Wei Wuer (Uygurs), Menggus (Mongols) and other groups have their own languages. The traditional religions and philosophies of life are Confucianism, Buddhism and Daoism. There are also Muslim and Christian minorities. The national flag (proportions 2 by 3) is plain red, with one large five-pointed gold star and four similar but smaller stars, arranged in an arc, in the upper hoist. The capital is Beijing (Peking).

CONTEMPORARY POLITICAL HISTORY

Historical Context

The People's Republic of China was proclaimed on 1 October 1949, following the victory of Communist forces over the Kuomintang (KMT) Government, which fled to the island province of Taiwan. The new Communist regime received widespread international recognition, but it was not until 1971 that the People's Republic was admitted to the United Nations, in place of the KMT regime, as the representative of China. Most countries subsequently recognized the People's Republic, with the 'Republic of China' being confined to Taiwan.

With the establishment of the People's Republic, the leading political figure was Mao Zedong, who was Chairman of the Chinese Communist Party (CCP) from 1935 until his death in 1976. Chairman Mao, as he was known, also became head of state in October 1949, but he relinquished this post in December 1958. His successor was Liu Shaoqi, First Vice-Chairman of the CCP, who was elected head of state in April 1959. Liu was dismissed in October 1968, during the Cultural Revolution, and died in prison in 1969. The post of head of state was left vacant, and was formally abolished in January 1975, when a new Constitution was adopted. The first Premier (Head of Government) of the People's Republic was Zhou Enlai, who held this office from October 1949. Zhou was also Minister of Foreign Affairs from 1949 to 1958.

The economic progress of the early years of Communist rule enabled China to withstand the effects of the industrialization programmes of the late 1950s (the 'Great Leap Forward', which is variously estimated to have caused the death by starvation of between 14m. and 48m. people, mainly in rural areas), the drought of 1960–62 and the withdrawal of Soviet aid in 1960. To prevent the establishment of a ruling class, Chairman Mao launched the Great Proletarian Cultural Revolution in 1966. The ensuing excesses of the Red Guards prompted the army to intervene; Liu Shaoqi and Deng Xiaoping, General Secretary of the CCP, were disgraced. In 1971 an attempted coup by the Minister of National Defence, Marshal Lin Biao, was unsuccessful, and by 1973 it was apparent that Chairman Mao and Premier Zhou Enlai had retained power. In 1975 Deng Xiaoping re-emerged as first Vice-Premier and Chief of the General Staff. Zhou Enlai died in January 1976. Hua Guofeng, hitherto Minister of Public Security, was appointed Premier, and Deng was dismissed. Mao died in September. His widow, Jiang Qing, tried unsuccessfully to seize power, with the help of three radical members of the CCP's Political Bureau (Politburo). This 'Gang of Four' and six associates of Lin Biao were tried in November 1980. All were found guilty and were given long terms of imprisonment. The 10th anniversary of Mao's death was marked in September 1986 by an official reassessment of his life; while his accomplishments were praised, it was acknowledged that he had made mistakes, although most of the criticism was directed at the 'Gang of Four'.

Domestic Political Affairs

In October 1976 Hua Guofeng succeeded Mao as Chairman of the CCP and Commander-in-Chief of the People's Liberation Army (PLA). The 11th National Congress of the CCP, held in August 1977, restored Deng Xiaoping to his former posts. Deng initiated a series of economic reforms, which included replacing collective farms by individually managed units, allowing greater autonomy to state-owned enterprises, permitting the establishment of businesses by entrepreneurs, and opening the country to foreign investment, particularly through the formation (from 1980) of Special Economic Zones, initially on China's south-east coast. In September 1980 Hua Guofeng resigned as Premier, but retained his chairmanship of the CCP. The appointment of Zhao Ziyang, a Vice-Premier since April 1980, to succeed Hua as Premier confirmed the dominance of the moderate faction of Deng Xiaoping. In June 1981 Hua Guofeng was replaced as Chairman of the CCP by Hu Yaobang, former Secretary-General of the Politburo, and as Chairman of the party Central Military Commission by Deng Xiaoping. A sustained campaign by Deng to eradicate 'leftist' elements from the Politburo led to Hua's demotion to a Vice-Chairman of the CCP and, in September 1982, to his exclusion from the Politburo.

In September 1982 the CCP was reorganized and the post of Party Chairman was abolished. Hu Yaobang became, instead, General Secretary of the CCP. A year later a 'rectification' of the CCP was launched, aimed at expelling 'Maoists', who had risen to power during the Cultural Revolution, and those opposed to the pragmatic policies of Deng. China's new Constitution, adopted in December 1982, restored the office of head of state, and in June 1983 Li Xiannian, a former Minister of Finance, became President of China. In September 1986 a session of the 12th CCP Central Committee adopted a detailed resolution on the 'guiding principles for building a socialist society', which redefined the general ideology of the CCP, to provide a theoretical basis for the programme of modernization and the 'open door' policy of economic reform.

In January 1986 investigations began into reports that many officials had exploited the programme of economic reform for their own gain (see The Campaign against Corruption for subsequent offensives). A significant cultural liberalization took place in 1986, with a revival of the 'Hundred Flowers' movement of 1956–57, which had encouraged the development of intellectual debate. However, a series of student demonstrations in major cities in late 1986 was regarded by China's leaders as an indication of excessive 'bourgeois liberalization'. In January 1987 Hu Yaobang unexpectedly resigned as CCP General Secretary, being accused of 'mistakes on major issues of political principles'. Zhao Ziyang became acting General Secretary. At the 13th National Congress of the CCP, which opened in October, Deng Xiaoping retired from the Central Committee, but amendments to the Constitution of the CCP permitted him to retain the influential positions of Chairman of the State Military Commission and of the CCP Central Military Commission. A new Politburo was appointed by the Central Committee in November. The majority of its 18 members were relatively young supporters of Deng Xiaoping's policies. The membership of the new Politburo also indicated a decline in military influence in Chinese politics. The newly appointed Standing Committee of the Politburo (the highest decision-making body) was regarded, on balance, as being 'pro-reform'. In late November Li Peng was appointed Acting Premier of the State Council, in place of Zhao Ziyang. At the first session of the Seventh National People's Congress (NPC), convened in March 1988, Li Peng was confirmed as Premier, and Yang Shangkun (a member of the CCP Politburo) was elected President.

Following the death of Hu Yaobang in April 1989, students criticized the alleged prevalence of corruption and nepotism within the Government, seeking a limited degree of Soviet-style *glasnost* (openness) in public life. When negotiations between government officials and the students' leaders had failed to satisfy the protesters' demands, workers from various professions joined the demonstrations in Tiananmen Square, Beijing, which had now become the focal point of the protests. At one stage more than 1m. people congregated in the Square, as demonstrations spread to more than 20 other Chinese cities. In mid-May some 3,000 students began a hunger strike in Tiananmen Square, while protesters demanded the resignation of both Deng Xiaoping and Li Peng. The students ended their hunger strike at the request of Zhao Ziyang. On 20 May martial law was declared in Beijing. Within days, some 300,000 troops had assembled.

On 3 June 1989 a further unsuccessful attempt was made to dislodge the demonstrators, but on the following day troops of the PLA attacked protesters in and around Tiananmen Square, killing an unspecified number of people. Television evidence and eye-witness accounts suggested a death toll of between 1,000 and 5,000. The Government immediately rejected these figures, claiming that a counter-revolutionary rebellion had been taking place. Arrests and executions ensued, although some student leaders eluded capture and fled to Hong Kong. Zhao Ziyang was dismissed from all his party posts and replaced as General Secretary of the CCP by Jiang Zemin, hitherto the secretary of the Shanghai municipal party committee. Zhao was accused of participating in a conspiracy to overthrow the CCP and placed under house arrest. In November Deng resigned as Chairman of the CCP Central Military Commission, his sole remaining party position, and was succeeded by Jiang Zemin, who was hailed as the first of China's 'third generation' of communist leaders (Mao being representative of the first, and Deng of the second). In January 1990 martial law was removed in Beijing, and it was announced that a total of 573 prisoners, detained following the demonstrations, had been freed. Further groups of detainees were released subsequently. In March Deng Xiaoping resigned from his last official post, that of Chairman of the State Military Commission, and was succeeded by Jiang Zemin. An extensive military reorganization ensued. At the CCP's 14th National Congress, held in October 1992, a new 319-member Central Committee was elected. The Politburo was expanded and a new Secretariat was chosen by the incoming Central Committee. Many opponents of Deng Xiaoping's reforms were replaced.

At the first session of the Eighth NPC, convened in March 1993, Jiang Zemin was elected as the country's President, remaining CCP General Secretary. Li Peng was reappointed as Premier, and an extensive reorganization of the State Council was announced. The Congress also approved amendments to the 1982 Constitution, which included confirmation of the State's practice of a 'socialist market economy'. During 1993, however, the Government became concerned at the growing disparity between urban and rural incomes. In June thousands of peasants took part in demonstrations in Sichuan Province to protest against excessive official levies. In response to the ensuing riots, the central Government banned the imposition of additional local taxes.

In March 1995, at the third session of the Eighth NPC, the appointment of Wu Bangguo and of Jiang Chunyun as Vice-Premiers of the State Council was approved. However, in an unprecedented display of opposition neither nominee received the NPC's full endorsement. Nevertheless, the position of Jiang Zemin appeared to have been strengthened. Personnel changes in the military hierarchy later in the year were also viewed as favourable to the President. In April 1996 the Government initiated 'Strike Hard', a new campaign against crime, executing hundreds of people.

The death of Deng Xiaoping in February 1997 precipitated a period of uncertainty regarding China's future direction. President Jiang Zemin declared that the economic reforms would continue, and this was reiterated in Premier Li Peng's address to the NPC in March. Delegates at the Congress approved legislation reinforcing the CCP's control over the PLA, and revisions to the criminal code were also promulgated, whereby statutes concerning 'counter-revolutionary' acts (under which many of the pro-democracy demonstrators had been charged in 1989) were removed from the code, but were replaced by 11 crimes of 'endangering state security'. Financial offences were also included for the first time.

At the 15th National Congress of the CCP, convened in September 1997, emphasis was placed on radical reform of the 370,000 state-owned enterprises (SOEs). Delegates approved amendments to the party Constitution, enshrining the 'Deng Xiaoping Theory' of socialism with Chinese characteristics alongside 'Mao Zedong Thought' as the guiding ideology of the CCP. The Congress elected a new 344-member Central Committee, which in turn re-elected Jiang Zemin as General Secretary of the CCP and appointed a 22-member Politburo. Qiao Shi, a reformist and Jiang's most influential rival, who was ranked third in the party hierarchy, was excluded from the Politburo, reportedly because of his age, as was Gen. Liu Huaqing, China's most senior military official. Zhu Rongji, a former mayor of Shanghai, replaced Qiao Shi. Gen. Liu was replaced by a civilian, Wei Jinxiang, who was responsible for combating corruption within the CCP. The absence of the military from the Politburo, and the composition of the new Central Military Commission, confirmed Jiang's increased authority over the PLA.

At the first session of the Ninth NPC, which was held in March 1998, the number of ministry-level bodies was reduced from 40 to 29, mainly through mergers. Jiang Zemin was re-elected as President, and Hu Jintao, a member of the Standing Committee of the Politburo, was elected Vice-President. Li Peng resigned as Premier and was replaced by Zhu Rongji, who received overwhelming support from the NPC delegates. Li Peng replaced Qiao Shi as Chairman of the NPC. Zhu's appointments to a new 39-member State Council included a number of associates of Jiang Zemin.

In March 1999 the NPC ratified a number of constitutional amendments. These included the elevation of private sector and other non-state enterprises to 'important components of the socialist market economy'; a recommendation for adherence to the rule of law; and the incorporation of Deng Xiaoping's ideology into the Constitution alongside Marxism-Leninism and 'Mao Zedong Thought'. At celebrations of the 50th anniversary of the foundation of the People's Republic of China in October, a picture of Jiang Zemin was paraded alongside portraits of Mao Zedong and Deng Xiaoping: the first time that the current President had been publicly placed on a par with his predecessors. In the same month Hu Jintao was appointed a Vice-Chairman of the Central Military Commission.

In February 2000 Jiang Zemin had launched a new political theory entitled 'The Three Represents', which declared that the CCP would 'always represent the development needs of China's advanced social productive forces, always represent the onward direction of China's advanced culture and always represent the fundamental interests of the largest number of Chinese people'. However, it appeared that with the advent of social change the CCP was finding it increasingly difficult to maintain control over its members. In the following months there was harsh repression of provincial labour unrest.

At its session in March 2000, the NPC focused mainly on economic issues. In October the CCP announced a new five-year plan, under which China was to concentrate on rural development, the creation of employment, economic modernization and combating corruption. When the NPC convened in March 2001, Premier Zhu Rongji outlined plans for economic restructuring in preparation for China's membership of the World Trade Organization (WTO). The authorities renewed their action against dissent. In April Jin Ruchao was sentenced to death for his alleged involvement in a series of bomb attacks in Hebei in March, which had killed 108 people.

In May 2001 Pan Yue, a prominent intellectual who also served as a deputy director of economic reform, presented to President Jiang a plan to transform the CCP into a more broadly representative body. In a report released in June, the CCP acknowledged that its rule might be undermined by social discontent arising from the country's free-market reforms, warning that inequality and corruption were issues of increasing importance. In July President Jiang urged the modernization of the CCP and for the first time stated that business people would be welcome as party members. However, left-wing forces, which included orthodox Communists, supporters of moderate socialism, the agricultural lobby and liberals, opposed the transformation of the CCP into a more business-orientated party.

Recent developments: 'fourth generation' leadership

In July 2002 senior CCP officials met to determine the new positions to be allocated at the forthcoming party Congress. Having been postponed from September, the 16th CCP Congress was held in early November, when the long-awaited transfer of power to the 'fourth generation' leadership headed by the incoming General Secretary, Hu Jintao, was effected. A new 356-member Central Committee was elected, as well as a 24-member Politburo, the Standing Committee of which was expanded from seven to nine members, of whom Hu was the only incumbent to be retained. Jiang retained the chairmanship of the CCP Central

Military Commission, which again contained several important military allies of his. Another associate of Jiang, Gen. Liang Guanglie, hitherto Commander of the Nanjing Military Region, was appointed Chief of the PLA's General Staff. The Congress stressed continuity in policy, but introduced some economic reforms. Although state ownership would remain dominant, private businesses would be able to compete on a more equal basis. Discriminatory regulations on investment, financing, taxation, land use and foreign trade would be revised, and private property would be granted greater legal protection.

The final stage of the transfer of power to the 'fourth generation' of Chinese leadership took place during the 10th NPC, held in March 2003. Hu Jintao replaced Jiang Zemin as President, and Zeng Qinghong, who had become a full member of the Politburo in December 1999, was appointed Vice-President. Wen Jiabao, hitherto a Vice-Premier, succeeded Zhu Rongji as Premier. The new State Council also included Ma Kai as Minister of State Development and Reform Commission and Jin Renqing as Minister of Finance, both of whom had expertise in economics. Li Zhaoxing, a former ambassador to the USA and the UN, was appointed Minister of Foreign Affairs, and Gen. Cao Gangchuan became Minister of National Defence. The incoming leadership immediately confronted a new challenge with the outbreak of Severe Acute Respiratory Syndrome (SARS), a previously unknown illness (see Health Issues).

In August 2003 government directives banning media discussion of political and constitutional reform were issued. There were, none the less, some signs of reform. At district elections in Beijing in December two seats were secured by independent candidates. In March 2004 a constitutional amendment to provide legal protection of private property rights was approved by the NPC. Another important constitutional change approved at the NPC session was a new reference to the 'Three Represents' theory (see above) as a guiding ideology. Premier Wen Jiabao also outlined plans for eliminating agricultural taxation and reducing economic inequalities. (In March 2007, following several years of discussion of the contentious issue, the NPC finally approved new legislation to afford greater legal protection for private property and assets.) At a session of the 16th CCP Congress in September 2004 former President Jiang Zemin relinquished his last official post, that of Chairman of the CCP Central Military Commission, to Hu Jintao.

In April 2007 President Hu effected a reorganization of the State Council. The Minister of Foreign Affairs, Li Zhaoxing, was replaced by Yang Jiechi, a former ambassador to the USA, while Chen Lei succeeded Wang Shucheng as Minister of Water Resources. Also of note was the appointment of Wan Gang, a non-member of the CCP, as Minister of Science and Technology. (A second non-member, Chen Zhu, joined the State Council in June as Minister of Health, following the departure of Gao Qiang.) Further changes were announced in August, including the appointment of Xie Xuren as successor to Minister of Finance Jin Renqing, and the selection of Ma Wen as Minister of Supervision, following Li Zhilun's death in April.

At the 17th CCP Congress, held in October 2007, President Hu outlined plans to address the disparity between rich and poor and to amend property laws; Hu also acknowledged continuing problems such as corruption. Elections to the CCP Central Committee were followed by a plenary session of the new Committee, during which President Hu was re-elected General Secretary of the party and the composition of the Politburo and Standing Committee was determined. New appointees to the latter included Xi Jinping and Li Keqiang.

At the first session of the 11th NPC, held in March 2008, President Hu Jintao was re-elected for a second five-year term of office. Xi Jinping was elected as Vice-President, in succession to Zeng Qinghong. Wen Jiabao was confirmed as Premier for a further five-year term. A subsequent reorganization of the State Council included the appointment of Gen. Liang Guanglie as Minister of National Defence, and the elevation of the State Environmental Protection Agency to the status of ministry (one of five so-called 'super-ministries'), under Zhou Shengxian.

In May 2008 a devastating earthquake caused widespread damage and loss of life in Sichuan Province. By the end of June the number of fatalities was estimated to have exceeded 69,000, with hundreds of thousands injured and millions left homeless. A massive relief effort, supported by international rescue groups, was organized by the Government, which was relatively candid about the disaster. In view of the large number of child fatalities, the safety of building construction and regulatory frameworks, particularly for schools, was called into question. Furthermore, activists who subsequently campaigned on behalf of bereaved parents were brought to trial on charges of subversion (see Human Rights and Media Freedom).

Meanwhile, in April 2008 the journey of the Olympic torch, the traditional prelude to the Olympic Games, was beset with difficulties as protesters disrupted ceremonies around the world in an attempt to highlight the Chinese Government's alleged human rights violations, particularly in relation to Tibet. The Government also came under scrutiny with regard to issues such as media freedom (see Human Rights and Media Freedom). Nevertheless, the Olympic Games, which took place in Beijing in August, were widely deemed a major success. On the 60th anniversary of the foundation of the People's Republic in October 2009, mass celebrations in Beijing included a parade of 8,000 soldiers and extensive displays of missiles and other military equipment.

The second session of the 11th NPC, convened in March 2009, focused largely on the repercussions of the global economic crisis. Substantial increases in expenditure on health services and education facilities were among the various initiatives announced. Issues relating to economic recovery dominated the next session of the NPC, held in March 2010. In October, at the closing session of a meeting of the Central Committee of the CCP, it was announced that Vice-President Xi Jinping had been appointed a Vice-Chairman of the party's Central Military Commission.

In early 2011, meanwhile, the Chinese leadership began to acknowledge the need for a slower pace of economic growth. An increasing focus on household consumption and quality of life, particularly with regard to the environment, was envisaged, in place of the recent emphasis on investment in infrastructural projects and in manufacturing for the export market as the main sources of rapid, but uneven, economic growth. In his opening address to the annual session of the NPC in March 2011, Premier Wen Jiabao stressed the importance of social stability, emphasizing the need to reduce inflation and to curb corruption. The NPC endorsed the country's Twelfth Five-Year Plan, encompassing the period 2011–15. In an address to the nation on 1 July 2011, the 90th anniversary of the founding of the CCP, President Hu also identified corruption as a major threat to the party.

Significant changes in the political hierarchy were expected to occur in the second half of 2012, when both Hu Jintao and Wen Jiabao were due to retire after having completed their terms of office, along with five other members of the nine-member Standing Committee of the Politburo. The 18th CCP Congress, due to take place in late 2012, was to elect a new CCP Central Committee, which would then appoint a new Politburo and Standing Committee: from among the members of the latter a new President and Premier would then be appointed in early 2013. It was widely expected that Vice-President Xi Jinping would succeed Hu as General Secretary of the CCP and as President, with Li Keqiang, the First Vice-Premier, becoming Premier.

In early 2012, however, there were dramatic developments affecting other elements of the succession, which some analysts believed were linked to a power struggle at senior party level. The populist former minister Bo Xilai, a member of the Politburo, who had been the leader of the CCP in Chongqing since 2007, had been widely expected to be promoted to the Standing Committee in 2012. Bo Xilai was the son of one of the revolutionary associates of Mao Zedong, thus belonging to one of a group of powerful political families in China. He had achieved national prominence with a high-profile, aggressive campaign against organized crime in Chongqing, redistributive social policies and the revival of the use of Maoist songs. In March, however, Bo Xilai was relieved of the party leadership in Chongqing. His position had been uncertain since February when his appointee as chief of police, Wang Lijun, who had been responsible for implementing the campaign against organized crime, had fled to the US consulate in Chengdu days after losing his police post. It was suggested that he had implicated Bo Xilai's wife, Gu Kailai, in the alleged murder of a British businessman Neil Heywood in November 2011. Wang Lijun was reported to have attempted to claim asylum on the grounds that his life was endangered by his rift with Bo Xilai, but was later released to the Chinese authorities. At a press conference marking the close of the annual session of the NPC Premier Wen Jiabao, in a rare display of disunity within senior party ranks, referred directly to the incident and was critical of the leadership of Chongqing. Bo Xilai was removed from all party posts in April and placed under investigation, while his wife was remanded in custody on suspicion of having ordered the murder of Heywood, who had formerly been a friend of the family.

The Campaign against Corruption

From the 1990s there was increasing disquiet over persistent corruption within the CCP, the state bureaucracy and economic enterprises. In August 1993 the CCP initiated a major anti-corruption campaign. Hundreds of executions of officials were subsequently reported. Among the most senior culprits, in August 1998 Chen Xitong, a former member of the Politburo and of the Central Committee of the CCP, was sentenced to 16 years' imprisonment for corruption and dereliction of duty. A former Vice-Chairman of the Standing Committee of the NPC, Cheng Kejie, was executed in September 2000 for accepting large bribes. Also in September, Maj.-Gen. Ji Shengde, the former head of military intelligence of the PLA, was formally charged with having taken bribes, later receiving a prison sentence. In October, following a two-year investigation, government auditors reported the embezzlement or serious misuse of the equivalent of more than US $11,000m. of public funds by government officials.

In January 2002 Wang Xuebing, the president of China Construction Bank and an ally of Premier Zhu Rongji, was placed under investigation, and in November he was expelled from the CCP following bribery charges. In March a money-laundering and illegal loans scandal emerged at the Bank of China, the perpetrators having fled overseas. In May 2003 the Governor of Yunnan Province, Li Jiating, received a suspended death sentence for taking bribes totalling more than the equivalent of US $2,200m. Also in May, Zhou Zhengyi, chairman of a Shanghai property company, was placed under investigation amid allegations of fraudulent loan-taking. One of these loans had been received from the Bank of China in 2002. Speculation over the Bank of China's involvement in the scandal intensified following the removal of the chief executive of the bank's Hong Kong branch, Liu Jinbao, in late May. Zhou Zhengyi was found guilty in June 2004 of fabricating documents and manipulating his company's trading price on the stock market. Meanwhile, in July 2003 Yang Bin, who had been proposed for the governorship of the Sinuiju free trade area on China's border with the Democratic People's Republic of Korea (North Korea), was sentenced to 18 years' imprisonment for fraud and corruption. In October, furthermore, China's Minister of Land and Natural Resources, Tian Fengshan, was removed from office as a result of allegations of corruption.

In February 2004 the CCP announced the introduction of new regulations for the supervision of its officials. In March 2005 the Procurator-General, Jia Chunwang, announced that 30,788 government officials had been prosecuted in 2004 for work-related offences such as corruption, embezzlement and abuse of power. In the same month Zhang Enzhao, the Chairman of China Construction Bank, resigned, reportedly as a result of an investigation into allegations of corruption, and Ma De, a former senior official from Heilongjiang Province, pleaded guilty to accepting some 6m. yuan in bribes between 1992 and 2002 in exchange for helping officials to secure promotions. Following his arrest in early 2004, in August 2005 Liu Jinbao, former chief executive of the Bank of China in Hong Kong, was sentenced to death, with a two-year suspension, for embezzlement and accepting bribes.

In 2006 a major corruption case involved the Shanghai pension fund, from which more than 3,000m. yuan was said to have been misappropriated for the purposes of speculative investments. Those dismissed in connection with the scandal included the Secretary of the Shanghai Municipal Committee of the CCP, Chen Liangyu, as well as the director of the National Bureau of Statistics, Qiu Xiaohua. In September 2007 several senior officials received long prison sentences for their involvement in the scandal, and in April 2008 Chen was sentenced to 18 years' imprisonment.

In January 2007 auditors revealed that US $34.8m. had been misappropriated from funds allocated to assist the resettlement of millions of villagers displaced by the construction of the Three Gorges Dam on the River Yangtze (Changjiang) in Hubei Province, upon which work had commenced in 1994. The funding in question had allegedly been used by corrupt local officials to pay staff salaries and to clear the debts of local government departments. (In October 2007, after apparent acknowledgement by officials of the dam's potentially disastrous impact on the environment, it was announced that a further 4m. people were to be relocated.)

In March 2007 further reforms to address the problem of corruption were announced. In September the Minister of Supervision, Ma Wen, was appointed to chair the newly formed National Corruption Prevention Bureau. One of the most significant trials in 2007 was that of Zheng Xiaoyu, the former director of the State Food and Drug Administration, who was convicted of accepting bribes and of dereliction of duty; he was executed in July. The case highlighted other important issues, such as product safety and the inadequacies of food and pharmaceutical regulations in China. By October, in response to several international scandals involving the safety standards of Chinese exports, an extensive government campaign had resulted in hundreds of arrests. In June 2008 details of a five-year anti-corruption campaign were announced by the CCP, directed at state-owned corporations and illegal land seizures in particular.

In September 2008 six Chinese infants died after consuming milk contaminated with melamine, an industrial chemical that had been added to the formula to make the product appear higher in protein. About 300,000 babies were believed to have been affected, with many suffering kidney damage. The incident led to the resignation of Li Changjiang, the Director of the General Administration of Quality Supervision, Inspection and Quarantine. The extension of the scandal overseas prompted several countries to remove various imported Chinese dairy products from sale. In December the Chinese Government ordered 22 firms involved in the distribution of contaminated milk to pay compensation to the families affected. More than 20 company officials and other traders were brought to trial, including several senior executives of the Sanlu Group, the dairy company held largely responsible for the distribution of the tainted products. Stringent legislation governing food safety, in particular the use of additives, was approved in February, and a national food safety commission was established in early 2010. Meanwhile, the first compensation claim was heard in November 2009. In November 2010, however, Zhao Lianhai, who had campaigned on behalf of those affected by the contaminated product and established a website to support parents, was convicted on charges of inciting social disorder. Zhao, a former employee of the country's food quality and safety authority, was sentenced to a prison term of 30 months.

Following an investigation into the finances of Guangdong Province, in January 2009 53 CCP officials were charged in connection with the misappropriation of a total of 22m. yuan of public funds, which were alleged to have been used to finance the pursuit of personal gambling activities in Macao and Hong Kong. Several senior officials were convicted. In July Chen Tonghai, a former chairman of Sinopec, the state petroleum corporation, was sentenced to death upon his conviction of bribery; the sum in question totalled 186m. yuan. However, Chen was granted a reprieve of two years. Other cases involving senior executives included that of a former manager of China National Nuclear Corporation, Kang Rixin, who was sentenced to life imprisonment in November 2010, and that of a former vice-chairman of China Mobile, Zhang Chunjiang, who was expelled from the CCP in September. In May Huang Guangyu, a retailing magnate reputed to have become one of the country's wealthiest entrepreneurs, was found guilty of bribery, insider trading and market manipulation; he was sentenced to 14 years' imprisonment. In the same month Guo Jingyi, a senior official in the Ministry of Commerce, was sentenced to death with a two-year reprieve, having been found guilty of accepting bribes that totalled more than 8m. yuan.

In January 2010, at a session of the CCP's Central Commission for Discipline Inspection (CCDI), President Hu Jintao reiterated the importance of addressing issues such as the abuse of power, corruption, embezzlement and dereliction of duty, referring to the establishment of a more effective mechanism as a 'pressing task'. With public anger rising, particularly in view of the lack of any independent supervision of government and party officials, a new code of conduct for CCP members was issued by the party in February. In March, however, in a case that raised serious concerns with regard to the integrity of the judicial system itself, a former vice-president of the Supreme People's Court, Huang Songyou, was sentenced to life imprisonment, having been found guilty of accepting bribes from lawyers in exchange for favourable judgments. A major investigation into allegations of bribery in Chongqing, which began in mid-2009, resulted in nearly 800 prosecutions. In July 2010 the city's most senior judicial official, Wen Qiang, was executed following his conviction on charges that included rape and the protection of criminal gangs, as well as bribery. The activities of 783 judges (of whom 540 were disciplined and 113 received criminal penalties for bribery, embezzlement and abuse of power) and of 267 procurators were investigated during the course of 2010. In August the NPC expelled two legislators who were suspected of having been involved in bribery. In total it was reported that more than 146,500 officials had been penalized for disciplinary violations during 2010.

In February 2011 the former Minister of Railways became the most senior official to be placed under investigation in response to allegations of corruption. Having been dismissed by the CCP from his senior position at the Ministry of Railways early in the month, Liu Zhijun was also removed from his cabinet post and replaced by Sheng Guangzu. Liu's dismissal followed the instigation of an inquiry into allegations of widespread corruption at the Ministry. Having served as Minister of Railways since 2003, Liu was alleged to have misappropriated more than 800m. yuan, reportedly having taken substantial bribes in exchange for the allocation of contracts for the upgrading of the Chinese rail network. In addition to the seemingly rampant corruption, the case also raised the possibility of the acceptance of sub-standard construction work and attendant safety concerns, in particular following the collision of two trains in July. The accident, and the Government's apparent subsequent attempts to reduce adverse publicity, provoked unusually outspoken criticism in the state media, as well as thousands of outraged comments by domestic internet users. Other senior officials convicted of corruption in 2011 included Xu Zongheng, the former mayor of Shenzhen, who received a suspended death sentence in May, the deputy mayors of Hangzhou and Suzhou, who were both executed in July, and Zhang Zhizhong, the former executive director of Beijing's principal airport, who received a 12-year prison sentence in November. Less prominent cases of malpractice on the part of more junior officials were believed to have been the cause of numerous local protests and 'mass incidents' in recent years (see Human Rights and Media Freedom).

Human Rights and Media Freedom

The suppression of dissident activity continued during the 1990s and the early 21st century, and the issue of media freedom remained an area of much contention. In January 1991 the trials of many of those arrested during the pro-democracy protests of 1989 commenced. Most activists received relatively short prison sentences. In July 1992 Bao Tong, a senior aide of Zhao Ziyang, the former General Secretary of the CCP, was found guilty of involvement in the pro-democracy unrest of mid-1989. In February 1994 Asia Watch, an independent human rights organization based in New York, issued a highly critical report of the situation in China, detailing the cases of more than 1,700 detainees, imprisoned for their political, ethnic or religious views. In July the trial on charges of counter-revolutionary activity of 14 members of a dissident group, in detention since 1992, commenced. In December 1994 nine of the defendants received heavy prison sentences.

In February 1993 Wang Dan and Guo Haifeng, leading student activists in the 1989 demonstrations, were freed. In late 1994, however, complaining of police harassment, Wang Dan filed a lawsuit against the authorities. He was rearrested in May 1995. The imposition of an 11-year prison sentence on Wang Dan at the conclusion of his cursory trial on charges of conspiracy, in October 1996, drew international condemnation. In April 1998 he was released on medical parole and sent into exile in the USA. In May 1993, having served 12 years of a 15-year sentence, dissident activist Xu Wenli was released from prison. He was rearrested in April 1994, but released shortly afterwards. In August 1993 the arrest and expulsion from China of Han Dongfang, a trade union activist who had attempted to return to his homeland after a year in the USA, attracted much international attention.

In mid-1997 the Chinese Government repudiated reports by Amnesty International, the human rights organization, that several pro-democracy activists remained among the numerous political prisoners in China, classifying as criminals the estimated 2,000 detainees imprisoned on charges of 'counter-revolution'. In November Wei Jingsheng, whose sentencing to 14 years' imprisonment in late 1995 upon his conviction on charges of conspiring to overthrow the Government had provoked international outrage, was released on medical parole into exile in the USA. Bao Ge, a prominent Shanghai dissident and campaigner for compensation for Chinese victims of Japanese war aggression, was released from three years' imprisonment without trial in June 1997.

In September 1998 Amnesty International released a report stating that China had executed 1,876 people in 1997, more than the rest of the world combined. Also in September 1998, the UN High Commissioner for Human Rights, Mary Robinson, made an unprecedented official visit to China; her itinerary included Tibet and Hong Kong. Attempts by dissidents in Beijing and the provinces to create and register an opposition party, the Chinese Democratic Party (CDP), were suppressed by the Government, and in December at least 30 members of the CDP were detained. Three democracy activists, Xu Wenli, Qin Yongmin and Wang Youcai, were sentenced to imprisonment, provoking strong international condemnation. Human rights groups declared the release on medical parole and subsequent exile to the USA of the prominent dissident, Liu Nianchun, shortly before the conviction of the CDP activists, to be an attempt to deflect criticism of their trials. By November 1999 a further 18 CDP leaders had been convicted of subverting state power and sentenced to long prison terms.

Attempts were made by the Government in February and in November 2000 to regulate the publication of material on the internet, with the issuing of new rules first granting the regime the right to 'reorganize' or close down offending websites, and then requiring government approval prior to the posting of news bulletins. In February 2001 the trial began of the first webmaster to have been prosecuted for publishing subversive material on the internet, and between April and November of that year some 17,000 internet cafés were closed down. In June 2002 three leading internet providers were punished for disseminating harmful content and were forced to suspend a number of services.

In August 2002 the US-based group Human Rights Watch reported that growing numbers of political dissidents were being detained in mental institutions, estimating that at least 3,000 activists had been subjected to psychiatric detention in the preceding two decades. In December the authorities acknowledged that they had again arrested the US-based activist, Wang Bingzhang. Wang had disappeared in mid-2002 in Viet Nam, where he had travelled with two other Chinese dissidents, Yue Wu and Zhang Qi, in order to hold meetings with other activists. Wang was charged with espionage on behalf of Taiwan, and with terrorism, and in February he was sentenced to life imprisonment. Also in December 2002 the authorities released, on the basis of medical parole, Xu Wenli, who immediately left for the USA. In January 2003 the authorities expelled another prominent dissident, Fang Jue, to exile in the USA. He had been released from prison in July 2002, but had subsequently been detained during the CCP Congress in November. Zhang Qi had also been detained, and upon her release in March 2003 she immediately returned to the USA.

Press freedom was further restricted from mid-2003, with lists of banned topics being issued to journalists, and in August an order was issued restraining public debate on political reform and on constitutional amendments, as well as on reassessment of historical events. Despite increasing privatization of the media sector, with newspapers being required to become financially independent of the State, there were few signs that the Government was relinquishing its control over the reporting of sensitive issues. The Government also continued to exercise strict control over the internet, reportedly employing a large force to monitor web activities.

In February 2004 it was announced that foreign investment in Chinese media companies was to be allowed, on condition that foreign investors agreed to adhere to government regulations on media content. In March pro-democracy activist Wang Youcai (see above) was released and permitted to travel to the USA on medical grounds. Also in March, the NPC approved an amendment to the Constitution that introduced an explicit reference to human rights. In April a resolution condemning China's human rights record was rejected at a meeting of the UN Commission on Human Rights for the 11th time. In July a new campaign for censorship of text messages was announced, with telephone companies being required to use filtering technology to identify suspicious material. In December three leading intellectuals, Yu Jie, Liu Xiaobo and Zhang Zuhua, who were known to have expressed critical views, were detained for questioning.

In April 2005 Shi Tao, a journalist with a Changsha newspaper was sentenced to 10 years' imprisonment for 'leaking state secrets'. Shi had reportedly e-mailed to a New York website editor his notes on government instructions regarding coverage of the 15th anniversary of the suppression of the Tiananmen Square demonstrations. The internet company Yahoo! was condemned by human rights groups for apparently assisting the Chinese prosecutors in connecting the 'leaked' information to Shi's e-mail address. Also in April Ching Cheong, the Hong Kong-based China correspondent for *The Straits Times*, a Singapore newspaper, was arrested, reportedly while attempting to obtain a manuscript connected to former Premier Zhao Ziyang, who had died under house arrest in January. In May the Ministry of Foreign Affairs announced that Ching had confessed to charges of espionage, and in August he was charged with spying for Taiwan. (Ching subsequently filed an appeal, which was dismissed by the court in November 2006; none the less, he was released in February 2008.) In October 2005 it was reported that Peng Ming, a dissident based in the USA who had been arrested in Myanmar in May 2004, had been sentenced to life imprisonment on charges of terrorism and espionage. Peng, the founder of the China Federation Party, was one of the few Chinese pro-democracy activists to advocate the use of force.

In February 2005 it was reported that some 12,500 internet cafés had been shut down by the authorities in the last three months of 2004. Despite previous access issues, in May 2005 the internet search company Google obtained a licence to operate in the People's Republic. In June the Government ordered all websites and weblogs in the country to register with the authorities or risk fines and possible closure. In October the Government announced a general ban on internet material inciting 'illegal demonstrations', apparently in response to the increasing number of public protests around the country. In January 2006 Google provoked widespread criticism when the company announced that it would comply with the Chinese Government's demands to restrict access to certain websites from its Chinese-language search engine. Google sought to expand its presence in the lucrative Chinese market, but the company was subsequently accused by the authorities of disseminating pornography and other unsuitable material. In June 2009 the Government undertook to install filtering software on all new computers. In January 2010 Google revealed that, in a highly sophisticated operation, the e-mail accounts of numerous users, primarily advocates of human rights in China, had been subjected to external interference. Google then threatened to withdraw from the country, stating that it was no longer willing to censor its Chinese search engine. From March, therefore, mainland users of the Google search engine were automatically redirected to the company's Hong Kong website, which remained uncensored. In a 'new approach' in June, however, the automatic link to Hong Kong was removed, and in the following month it was announced that Google's operating licence had been renewed by the Chinese Government, thereby permitting the company to continue providing web services. The number of internet users in China was estimated to have exceeded 400m. by the end of 2010. In March 2011 the Chinese Government denied allegations that it was responsible for the disruption of the e-mail services of Google.

China's human rights situation came under increased international scrutiny prior to the holding of the Olympic Games in Beijing in 2008. The authorities' regulation of the internet continued to be a major issue. In April 2007 CCP officials were reportedly instructed to combat the 'spread of decadent and backward ideological and cultural material online'. The proliferation of weblogs drew attention to the power of the internet and its application in attempts to gain greater freedom of expression. However, weblogs remained subject to censorship. Meanwhile, in an unusual development in January, President Hu demanded an investigation into the murder of a journalist, Lan Chengzhang, outside an illegal coal mine in Shanxi Province; in June the mine's owner was given a life sentence for his involvement in the killing. In March activist Zhang Jianhong was sentenced to six years' imprisonment on charges of incitement to subversion of the State's authority, in relation to articles posted on the internet. In April 2008 Hu Jia, another prominent activist, was sentenced to imprisonment, having been convicted of 'inciting subversion of state power'; his cause attracted widespread media attention when he was awarded the annual Sakharov Prize for Freedom of Thought by the European Parliament in October. He was released, as scheduled, in June 2011, but was reported to remain under close surveillance at his home.

In November 2008 Huang Qi, who had given advice to Sichuan families that had lost children after the collapse of poorly constructed school buildings in the earthquake earlier in that year, with a view to instigating a legal case against the Government, was found guilty of 'illegally holding state secrets'. The activist received a three-year prison sentence. (In 2003 he had been sentenced to five years' imprisonment for his hosting of an online discussion forum.) Another campaigner on behalf of the earthquake victims, Tan Zuoren, was found guilty of subversion in February 2010 and sentenced to five years' imprisonment.

In February 2009, as the 20th anniversary of the Tiananmen Square protests approached, a group of activist mothers reiterated their request that the Chinese leadership show greater openness and conduct a full investigation into the events surrounding the deaths of 1989. At the end of May 2009 the expiring licences to practise of about 20 civil rights lawyers were not renewed by the authorities. Those thus prevented from continuing to practise included Jiang Tianyong, who had recently become the first independent lawyer to be appointed to represent a defendant in Tibet, charged with involvement in the recent protests (see Events in Tibet).

In September 2010 a blind human rights activist, Chen Guangcheng, was released after four years' imprisonment for allegedly 'damaging property and organizing a mob to disturb traffic'. In 2005 Chen had accused family-planning officials in Shandong Province of forcing at least 7,000 women to have late-term abortions or sterilizations. After his release his activities were closely monitored by the authorities. In February 2011, following their clandestine compilation and release of a video that confirmed that the couple's situation was tantamount to house arrest, Chen and his wife were reported to have been assaulted by security officials. Chen escaped from house arrest in April 2012 and took refuge in the US embassy in Beijing. After six days, following an agreement with the Chinese authorities regarding his future in China, he left the embassy to seek medical treatment. However, shortly afterwards, following revelations about the treatment of his family during his stay at the US embassy, he announced his desire to move with his family to the USA.

Liu Xiaobo was rearrested in December 2008 after he and more than 300 other dissidents, on the 60th anniversary of the Universal Declaration of Human Rights, signed Charter 08, an online petition demanding democratic reform in China. In December 2009 Liu was placed on trial on charges of 'inciting subversion of state power'. His conviction and immediate sentencing to a prison term of 11 years aroused international criticism. In October 2010 the announcement in Norway of the award of the annual Nobel Peace Prize to Liu Xiaobo, in recognition of his 'long and non-violent struggle for fundamental human rights in China', led to renewed demands for the dissident's release from prison. The Chinese Government submitted a formal protest to the Norwegian Government, and Liu's wife was placed under house arrest. More than 100 activists, who included eminent lawyers and academics, issued a public letter demanding Liu's release. Further controversy surrounded the Nobel award ceremony in December. The Chinese embassy in Norway urged other countries to boycott the proceedings, as a result of which as many as 19 of the 65 countries invited to the ceremony reportedly declined to attend. The announcement of China's establishment of an alternative award, the Confucius Peace Prize, drew international condemnation. (The first recipient of the new prize was to be Lien Chan, honorary Chairman of the KMT and former Vice-President of Taiwan, for his contribution to the development of cross-Straits relations). Also in December Zhang Zuhua, who remained under close police surveillance, issued a statement in which he warned that the CCP's uncompromising stance might lead to revolution. The dissident also claimed that the number of signatories of Charter 08 had reached 12,000.

In October 2010, meanwhile, shortly before an annual plenary meeting of the CCP Central Committee, it was reported that 23 party veterans, including a former secretary of Mao Zedong, had issued an appeal to the NPC for greater freedom of speech in China. Although the details of the party elders' letter were rapidly removed from the internet, the audacious initiative none the less represented a significant action in support of the ending of censorship.

In January 2010 the sentencing to nine years' imprisonment of Zhou Yongjun, following his conviction on charges of fraud, prompted international condemnation. Human rights activists maintained that the hearing of the dissident's case in Sichuan Province rather than in Hong Kong, from where Zhou had been transferred amid allegations that he had entered the territory on a false passport, contravened the policy of 'one country, two systems' (see Hong Kong for further information). In January 2012 it emerged that a leading human rights lawyer, Gao Zhisheng (who had campaigned for religious freedom, and received a suspended prison sentence in December 2006 for 'inciting subversion of state power') was now in prison in Xinjiang for violating probation conditions: his whereabouts had been unknown for most of 2011.

Meanwhile, social unrest continued to offer a challenge to the authorities. Official statistics released in 2005 estimated that in the previous year 3.7m. people had taken part in 74,000 'mass incidents' of one form or another, including labour strikes and riots. Many protests were related to land disputes; the number of illegal land seizure cases was officially estimated to have reached 31,700 in 2008. In March of that year an activist who had campaigned against the removal of land from farmers was sentenced to five years' imprisonment on subversion charges, and in the following month a protester was killed by the police at a demonstration against land seizures perpetrated by a mining company. As internet forums became an increasingly popular method of sharing information, the deaths in separate 'accidents' in December 2010 and in January 2011, respectively of a man who had led a campaign against the construction of a power station in the vicinity of his village and of a woman who had opposed the relocation of a canal, aroused much scepticism.

In December 2008, as the Government attempted to promote social stability, a major exercise aimed at addressing neighbourhood issues was implemented by the Ministry of Public Security. The operation involved the dispatch throughout China of 2m. police officers, who were to assist the public with the pursuit of individual grievances and other community matters.

Despite the introduction in 2008 of new legislation providing for better mediation and arbitration, reports of labour unrest continued to emerge. An incident in Jilin Province in July 2009, which according to some sources involved as many as 30,000 disgruntled steel workers, reportedly resulted in the beating to death of a manager of the company, who had been about to announce plans for redundancies. Unrest continued in 2010, as exemplified by a series of labour disputes. Chinese workers at Japanese-owned manufacturing plants were reported to have secured substantial pay increases as a result of strike action, during which production at both Honda and Toyota was suspended. In August Premier Wen Jiabao urged Japanese companies to address the issue of low wages. In the same month Foxconn, a Taiwanese manufacturer of electronics, announced plans to engage an additional 400,000 workers on the mainland. Amid continuing reports of protests related to working conditions at Foxconn, the announcement followed more than a dozen suicides by workers employed at its factory in southern China.

In early 2011, with renewed reports of surveillance, interrogation and arrests by the authorities (apparently mindful of the repercussions of the popular uprisings in North Africa), critics continued to maintain that, contrary to official assertions, the human rights situation in China had shown few signs of improvement. Jiang Tianyong was among dozens of lawyers and activists reported to have been detained in early 2011 in what appeared to be a new campaign of suppression. In March pro-democracy activist Liu Xianbin was sentenced to 10 years' imprisonment, having been found guilty of inciting subversion (his third such conviction since the protests of 1989). Furthermore, it was reported that the authorities were considering plans to monitor the movements of all users of mobile phones in Beijing. Critics claimed that the system would be used for the purposes of pre-empting protest rallies. The detention of the internationally renowned artist Ai Weiwei in April, ostensibly on suspicion of economic crimes, was widely deplored. Ai had criticized human rights abuses and supported the rights of alleged victims of official incompetence or corruption. He was released in June, but the authorities claimed that he had admitted tax evasion and demanded payment of 15m. yuan. Thousands of supporters contributed money to help pay the bill, and in November Ai paid part of the amount demanded, pending an appeal.

In May 2011 it was announced that a new State Internet Information Office was to assume control of internet content, replacing several other government agencies. It had become evident that, despite censorship, the internet (in particular social network sites such as Sina Weibo, which claimed in August to have 250m. registered users) was providing a major outlet for outspoken comments and criticism of the authorities. 'Cultural development guidelines' published in October ordered stricter regulation of the internet to prevent the spread of rumours and 'harmful information'. In December two activists, Chen Wei and Chen Xi, were given prison sentences after posting allegedly subversive material on the internet, and in January 2012 a writer, Li Tie, was also convicted of subversion and imprisoned. Also in January the prominent author Yu Jie left China for the USA, claiming that he had undergone surveillance and physical abuse.

During 2011 reports continued of numerous local protests at the confiscation of farmland or houses to make way for redevelopment, often aimed at local officials who were perceived to be corrupt. In July legislation was adopted imposing limits on forced evictions and the compulsory demolition of houses, to come into effect in 2012. In September 2011 protests erupted in the village of Wukan in Guangdong Province against the sale of communal land by an allegedly corrupt local official. Wukan was reportedly besieged by security forces in December, following months of protests and the death in custody of a leading protester. However, in an attempt to resolve the dispute the provincial government subsequently agreed to allow free elections in Wukan and pledged to initiate investigations into the death of Xue Jinbo and the contentious land sale. At the elections to the village committee, which took place in March 2012, several participants in the earlier protests were elected as local officials. In April two former officials were found guilty of corruption in relation to the expropriation of communal land, expelled from the CCP and ordered to repay money to the Government, although activists claimed that the sums were inadequate and the punishments too lenient.

Many other protests during 2011 were related to the grievances of migrant workers: these workers and their families, often from rural areas of China, were not entitled to the same housing, educational and social care provisions as permanent local residents, a situation which was described as a serious threat to stability in a report by a government research centre published in 2011.

Religious Affairs

The emergence of Falun Gong in the late 1990s posed new challenges to the supremacy of the CCP, which banned the popular religious sect in July 1999 on the grounds that it constituted a threat to society. The group, which was also known as Falun Dafa and embraced elements of Buddhism, mysticism and *qigong* (traditional exercise), had been established in 1992 by Li Hongzhi, who was based in the USA, and from 1999 it attracted increasing attention in China and abroad, claiming tens of millions of adherents, mainly in China. The ban imposed in 1999 was prompted by widespread demonstrations, attended by tens of thousands of supporters, in protest at the arrest of more than 100 adherents of the sect. Particularly concerned by the high level of Falun Gong membership among CCP and PLA officials, the authorities embarked on a campaign of harsh persecution of those who refused to renounce their faith. However, quiet protests continued, and in October 2000 Falun Gong was declared to be an enemy of the nation. In August 2001 the authorities sentenced 45 'die-hard' members to long prison sentences for organizing resistance. In early 2002 Falun Gong succeeded in infiltrating Chinese television broadcasts in several different cities, and in September 15 members were sentenced to between four and 20 years' imprisonment for violating anti-cult laws and damaging broadcasting equipment. In 2005 the US-based Falun Gong Information Center asserted that 2,300 practitioners had died in custody in China since the banning of the sect in 1999. The suppression of Falun Gong continued. In early 2009 it was reported that in the previous year as many as 8,000 practitioners had been detained, of whom at least 100 had died in custody, including Yu Zhou, a popular musician.

Christian churches remained subject to government supervision. In January 2000 five Catholic bishops were consecrated after being appointed by the state-controlled Chinese Catholic Patriotic Association (CCPA); this organization continued to operate independently of the Vatican, which opposed the consecration. The arrest of an archbishop belonging to the clandestine (Vatican-linked) Roman Catholic Church in February 2000 further undermined any prospect of an improvement in China's relations with the Vatican. In October Pope John Paul II canonized 120 missionary and Chinese Roman Catholic martyrs, and in the following October Catholic scholars from around the world gathered in Beijing to commemorate the 400th anniversary of the arrival of the Italian Jesuit Matteo Ricci in Beijing in 1601. The Pope expressed regret for past Vatican actions and appealed for the establishment of diplomatic relations.

By early 2003 China and the Vatican had held several sessions of informal discussions on improving bilateral relations. However, China was in confrontation with Bishop Joseph Zen Ze-kiun, the head of the Roman Catholic Church in Hong Kong, who had become increasingly critical of the central Government's administration in Hong Kong and its religious policies on the mainland. China was one of the few countries not represented at the funeral of Pope John Paul II in April 2005. In June, according to the US-based China Aid Association, police forcibly entered 100 'underground' churches in Jilin Province, detaining some 600 worshippers. The detention of members of the unofficial Catholic church in Hebei Province, apparently the most significant 'underground' church in China, also continued in 2005. Relations with the Vatican were further strained in 2006 when the Chinese Catholic church consecrated three bishops, two of whom were subsequently excommunicated by the Vatican. In July hundreds of police officers in Zhejiang were reported to have been engaged in violent clashes with around 3,000 protesters from the 'underground' Christian movement who were demonstrating against the demolition of a church claimed by the Government to be an illegal structure. Eight Christians were accused of inciting the protesters and were put on trial in December. Xu Shuangfu, the founder of another 'underground' Christian sect, who had been convicted of murdering members of a rival group, was executed in November, along with two other leaders. None the less, in August Bishop An Shuxin, who had spent more than 10 years in prison for being a member of the 'underground' Catholic Church loyal to the Pope was freed. The Archbishop of Canterbury, Dr Rowan Williams, head of the Anglican Communion, was permitted to pay an official visit to China in October.

In January 2007 Pope Benedict XVI announced that he would make efforts to restore full diplomatic relations with the People's Republic. Following a meeting in Rome to review the Roman Catholic Church's strategy towards China, the Pope stated that the Vatican was willing to engage in dialogue to overcome the 'incomprehension of the past'. In June the Pope released an open letter to all Chinese Catholics, appealing for the unity of the faith and the strengthening of links between followers of the state-controlled church and those loyal to the Vatican. Moreover, the Pope expressed a willingness to enter negotiations with the Chinese Government over issues such as the appointment of bishops. In September Father Joseph Li Shan was consecrated as Bishop of Beijing, although formal approval by the Vatican was not given. In November 2010 Joseph Guo Jincai, the vice-president of the CCPA, was consecrated Bishop of Chengde, an action which was described by the Vatican as harmful to relations. Two more bishops were appointed by the CCPA, in April and July 2011, respectively: the second of these, Joseph Huang Bingzhang, was excommunicated by the Vatican shortly after his consecration as Bishop of Shantou.

With religion apparently assuming increasing significance in Chinese society, reports of harassment of 'underground' Christians continued to emerge. Hundreds of arrests were reported during 2008, with 270 Christians being detained in Shandong Province in one operation alone. Numerous illegal churches were demolished by the authorities, but worshippers continued to meet in private homes and other clandestine venues. However, in an indication of a more conciliatory approach on the part of the Government, secret discussions were reportedly held with representatives of unofficial Protestant groups. In 2011, according to government figures, there were 18m. Protestant Christians and 6m. Catholics in China, but other sources estimated that the total number was at least 60m., including members of unregistered 'house' churches. In April of that year members of the large Shouwang unofficial Protestant church in Beijing were detained when they attempted to hold outdoor services. In July a senior Protestant pastor, Shi Enhao, the deputy chairman of the Chinese House Church Alliance, was sentenced to two years' re-education in a labour camp, for conducting illegal meetings; he was released, however, in January 2012.

Health Issues

In the early 21st century the Chinese Government confronted several serious issues of public health. First, there was increasing concern about the spread of HIV/AIDS in China. During 2001 the authorities acknowledged the seriousness of the problem. In June it was reported that as many as 500,000 people in Henan Province had been infected with HIV after selling their blood plasma to companies that had employed unhygienic practices. The authorities announced an increase in funds to counter the spread of the virus and to improve the safety of blood banks. The Government began to provide improved access to health information and to affordable health care; measures included the supply of free drugs to HIV/AIDS patients on low incomes. In December 2003 Premier Wen Jiabao publicly associated himself with the campaign against HIV/AIDS by visiting AIDS patients in a Beijing hospital on World Aids Day. In November 2006 the Ministry of Public Health announced that HIV cases in China had risen by 30% within a year, but it was stressed that this apparent rise in the number of cases was largely due to improved testing and better reporting. By the end of 2009, according to the Ministry of Public Health, a total of 740,000 mainland Chinese were living with HIV/AIDS, while the number of deaths recorded since 1985 was approaching 50,000. In April 2010 it was announced that the Government was to remove the long-standing ban on HIV-positive foreigners entering China.

By the end of April 2003 the outbreak of SARS, a hitherto unknown virus, had affected almost 3,500 people and resulted in more than 150 deaths in the People's Republic alone. The Minister of Public Health, Zhang Wenkang, and the mayor of Beijing, Meng Xuenong, were accused of having concealed the extent of the disease and were relieved of their party and state positions. The SARS epidemic was officially declared to have ended in mid-June, and the World Health Organization (WHO) removed its ban on travel to Beijing.

In November 2005 China became the fifth country to register human fatalities resulting from the epidemic of avian influenza ('bird flu') that had spread across East Asia since 2003, when two women from Anhui Province were reported to have died after contracting the virus. Earlier in the month, 6m. poultry had been culled in Liaoning Province, while the central Government had announced that it would endeavour to vaccinate all of China's 14,000m. poultry, following a series of outbreaks throughout the year. By February 2008 China had confirmed its 28th human case of the disease; 18 such cases had proved fatal. A more serious threat to public health emerged during 2009, with the appearance of a new variant of swine influenza, the A(H1N1) virus, following which the Government initiated a major vaccination programme. By March 2010 the number of cases of 'swine flu' in China was reported to have reached 127,427; a total of 796 people had died, and a further 8,320 cases were classified as severe. In 2011 it was reported that the incidence of diabetes had greatly increased in China, owing largely to dietary changes, with the disease affecting an estimated 90m. people. In the same year the number of deaths of new-born babies was reported to have declined considerably between 1996 and 2008, as had the maternal mortality rate: the improvement was attributed to a campaign to encourage mothers to choose hospital delivery.

In addition to widespread concerns about food safety and the quality of other products manufactured in China, health issues arising from the lack of adequate environmental controls were drawing increasing attention. In August 2009 two separate cases of serious environmental contamination were reported: one in Hunan Province, where the illegal levels of discharge from a manganese smelter had resulted in more than 1,350 local children being affected by lead poisoning; and a similar case in Shaanxi Province, where a metal smelter was closed down following the diagnosis of lead poisoning in more than 850 children. Similar cases were subsequently reported from elsewhere in China. In October 2011 the Government announced that it would use stricter criteria for measuring air pollution, a major problem in many Chinese cities.

In April 2009 the Government responded to public disquiet with regard to the difficulties of access to health care, particularly in rural areas, by announcing plans for a major reform of the health service. With projected expenditure of 850,000m. yuan during the 2009–11 period, thousands of new hospitals and health centres were to be built, while many existing facilities were to be upgraded. In the longer term, a programme of universal health insurance was envisaged.

Events in Tibet

Tibet (Xizang), hitherto a semi-independent region of western China, was occupied in October 1950 by Chinese Communist forces. In March 1959 there was an unsuccessful armed uprising by Tibetans opposed to Chinese rule. The Dalai Lama, the head of Tibet's Buddhist clergy and thus the region's spiritual leader, fled with some 100,000 supporters to Dharamshala, in northern India, where a government-in-exile was established. Thousands of Tibetans, including many lamas (Buddhist monks), were killed, and monasteries were destroyed. Tibet became an 'Autonomous Region' of China in September 1965. In October 1987 violent clashes occurred in Lhasa (the regional capital) between the Chinese authorities and Tibetans seeking independence; similar demonstrations followed.

In March 1989 martial law was imposed in Lhasa for the first time since 1959, after further violent clashes between separatists and the Chinese police, which resulted in the deaths of 16 protesters. In October 1989 the Chinese Government condemned as an interference in its internal affairs the award of the Nobel Peace Prize to the Dalai Lama. In May 1990 martial law was ended in Lhasa. Human rights groups claimed that during the last six months of the period of martial law as many as 2,000 people had been executed. In May 1992 a report issued by Amnesty International was critical of the Chinese authorities' violations of the human rights of the monks and nuns of Tibet. In May 1993 several thousand Tibetans were reported to have demonstrated in Lhasa against Chinese rule. A number of protesters were believed to have been killed.

In April 1994 China condemned the Dalai Lama's meeting with US President Bill Clinton during the former's lecture tour of the USA. In May 1995 the Dalai Lama's nomination of the 11th incarnation of the Panchen Lama (the second position in the spiritual hierarchy, the 10th incumbent having died in 1989) was condemned by the Chinese authorities, which banned the six-year old nominee, Gedhun Choekyi Nyima, from travelling to Dharamshala. In September 1995 it was reported that independence activists had carried out two bomb attacks in Lhasa.

China lodged a strong protest following an informal meeting between the Dalai Lama and US President Clinton in Washington, DC, in September 1995. In November the Chinese Government announced Gyaltsen (Gyaincain) Norbu as its own nominee as Panchen Lama. The boy was enthroned at a ceremony in Lhasa in December, the whereabouts of the Dalai Lama's choice remaining unknown until mid-1996, when China's ambassador to the UN in Geneva admitted that the boy was in detention in Beijing. There were violent confrontations in Tibet in May 1996, following the banning of any public display of images of the Dalai Lama. A series of minor explosions during 1996 culminated in late December with the detonation of a powerful bomb outside a government office in Lhasa.

In May 1997 it was reported that Chadrel Rinpoche, an official in the Tibetan administration and one of Tibet's most senior monks, had been sentenced to six years' imprisonment for allegedly revealing information to the Dalai Lama about the Chinese Government's search for the new Panchen Lama. In October the Dalai Lama appealed to the Chinese Government to reopen negotiations over the status of Tibet, confirming that he did not seek full independence for the region. In December the International Commission of Jurists (see p. 470) published a report accusing China of suppressing nationalist dissent and Tibetan culture, and appealed for a referendum, under the auspices of the UN, to decide the territory's future status. In April 1998 China agreed to allow envoys of the European Union (EU) to make a one-week investigatory visit to Tibet. In May the EU adopted two resolutions relating to China, condemning the sale of organs of executed prisoners and calling for a UN committee to investigate the transactions and, furthermore, urging the UN to appoint a rapporteur for Tibet issues.

During his visit to China and Hong Kong in June 1998, US President Clinton discussed the issue of Tibet with the Chinese leadership. The Government proclaimed its readiness to open negotiations if the Dalai Lama first declared both Tibet and Taiwan to be inalienable parts of China. In October the Dalai Lama admitted that since the 1960s he had received US $1.7m. annually from the US Central Intelligence Agency (CIA) to support the Tibetan separatist movement. While visiting the USA in November, the Dalai Lama had an unofficial meeting with President Clinton, and in January 1999 a new US special co-ordinator for Tibetan affairs was appointed.

In January 2000 the Chinese Government was embarrassed by the flight of the third-ranking Lama, the Karmapa, from Tibet to Dharamshala, where he requested political asylum. Ugyen Trinley Dorjie had been enthroned in 1992 at the age of seven; in an unusual development, the Karmapa had been recognized both by the Dalai Lama and by the Chinese Government. In April 2001 the Dalai Lama paid a 10-day visit to Taiwan, where he met President Chen Shui-bian and addressed the island's legislature, thus antagonizing China, which opposed any co-operation between the two 'renegade provinces'. In May the 50th anniversary of the 'peaceful liberation' of Tibet was officially commemorated; meanwhile, the Dalai Lama had a meeting with US President George W. Bush in Washington, DC. In July China's chosen Panchen Lama visited Shanghai and Zhejiang Province at the invitation of the central Government. In August Chinese troops seized the largest Tibetan monastery, Serthar, and forced thousands of monks and nuns to denounce the Dalai Lama.

In January 2002 Ngawang Choephel, a Tibetan music scholar serving an 18-year sentence on spying charges, was released, and in April the authorities freed, on medical grounds, Tanag Jigme Sangpo, who had first been imprisoned in 1965, and again since 1983, for campaigning against Chinese rule. He was believed to be the country's longest-serving political prisoner, having endured a total of 32 years in detention. In June CCP officials in Tibet formally welcomed Gyaltsen Norbu as the new Panchen Lama. In September 2002 exiled Tibetan officials visited China (including Tibet—the first such visit there since 1985): during the tour, the Dalai Lama's envoy to the USA, Lodi Gyaltsen Gyari, and the envoy to Europe, Kelsang Gyaltsen, held the first meetings with government officials since 1993. In December the authorities sentenced to death two Tibetans for their alleged role in a series of bombings in Sichuan Province during 1998–2002.

In June 2003 discussions between Chinese officials and envoys of the Dalai Lama were held. The delegation to Beijing was led by the Dalai Lama's representative in the USA, Lodi Gyaltsen Gyari. Also in June, the Indian Prime Minister acknowledged Tibet as part of China in writing for the first time. In the same month 18 Tibetans were deported to China from Nepal, despite condemnation of this action by the UN. In September US President George W. Bush held talks with the Dalai Lama. In February 2004 Phuntsog Nyidron, a Tibetan Buddhist nun believed to have received the longest sentence ever given to a female political prisoner in China, was released after 15 years in prison. In August Gyaltsen Norbu, the boy nominated by the Chinese Government as the new Panchen Lama in 1995, visited Tibet. In September 2004 a third round of talks between Chinese officials and envoys of the Dalai Lama was held in Beijing.

In September 2005 celebrations were held in Lhasa to commemorate the 40th anniversary of the establishment of the Tibet Autonomous Region. In October the construction of the 1,118-km railway link from Golmud in Qinghai Province to Lhasa was completed, thereby compounding fears that such development schemes and the considerable influx of Han Chinese (the majority ethnic group, which dominated the new economy) from neighbouring provinces were irreversibly transforming the character and culture of Tibet. By October 2006 services to Lhasa were also being offered from Shanghai and Guangzhou. However, negative global media attention was focused on the region in October, when members of an international team of mountaineers, climbing in the central Himalayas in the previous month, reported having witnessed Chinese border guards open fire on a group of Tibetans as they attempted to cross into Nepal. Video evidence of the incident in the Nangpa Pass, in which a teenage nun was killed, was subsequently released. In December a local human rights group reported that government officials and students in Tibet had been officially banned from observing an annual Buddhist festival.

In March 2007 the central Government's announcement of substantial funding to develop the region provoked a mixed reaction. The disclosure that 100,000m. yuan was to be spent on various projects, including the construction of an airport and the extension of the Lhasa railway line, prompted renewed concern in some quarters about the potential exploitation of resources and the eradication of indigenous culture. In October the presentation of the Congressional Gold Medal to the Dalai Lama in the USA precipitated violent confrontations in Tibet, between monks celebrating the occasion and the police. In March 2008, in the largest protests against Chinese rule since 1989, hundreds of monks attended rallies in Lhasa. The ensuing violence was reported to have resulted in dozens of deaths; the Chinese Government claimed that some 19 fatalities had been caused by protesters, while activists asserted that as many as 100 people had been killed by government forces. As the international community urged the Chinese Government to moderate its response, which had involved the deployment of thousands of troops, the Dalai Lama described the Government's actions as 'cultural genocide'. Further sporadic protests took place in the region and elsewhere as the Olympic torch made its symbolic journey around the world. In April 2008 nine monks were arrested in connection with a bomb attack on a government building in eastern Tibet in the previous month. Also during April, 30 people were given prison sentences for their involvement in the Lhasa riots in March. Amnesty International expressed concern in June at the uncertain fate and treatment of a large number of detainees. In May, meanwhile, representatives of the Government and the Dalai Lama attended discussions in Beijing. During his tour of Europe later in the month, the Dalai Lama indicated that some sections of the Tibetan community were dissatisfied with the lack of progress towards greater autonomy through non-violent means.

In March 2009 the central Government released a document entitled 'Fifty Years of Democratic Reform in Tibet', which attempted to emphasize the ending of the system of 'feudal serfdom' in 1959. The 50th anniversary of the establishment of Chinese rule, 28 March, was declared the first 'Serf Emancipation Day' in Tibet. With text messaging having become an important means of communication among opponents of the Chinese Government, the mobile phone network in Lhasa was temporarily curtailed, ostensibly for maintenance. In early April Tibet was reopened to foreign tour groups, following their suspension two months previously. Also in April several death sentences were meted out, as those charged in connection with the rioting of 2008 were brought to trial and convicted. Although some death sentences were commuted to life imprisonment, the Government confirmed the execution of two Tibetan prisoners in October 2009. In March 2010 the government-appointed Panchen Lama, who in the previous year had begun to make public appearances, became a member of the influential National Committee of the Chinese People's Political Consultative Conference (CPPCC). As the second anniversary of the protests of 2008 approached, a major security operation was mounted. Hundreds of Tibetans were reported to have been detained, and the authorities announced the seizure of numerous weapons. Also in March 2010 the new Governor of Tibet, Padma Choling, who in January had replaced Qiangba Puncog upon the latter's resignation, stated that Gedhun Choekyi Nyima continued to reside in Tibet; however, the Governor declined to divulge the whereabouts of the Panchen Lama chosen by the Dalai Lama 15 years previously.

The Dalai Lama, meanwhile, continued to travel extensively. In August 2009 he embarked upon on a visit to Taiwan, where he offered support to those affected by a devastating typhoon. He also undertook visits to Australia and New Zealand in December. He visited the USA in February 2010 when, in a controversial meeting, he had discussions with the US President and also Canada later in the year.

In June 2010 Karma Samdrup, an antiques dealer who had personally financed a conservation campaign in Tibet, was sentenced to 15 years' imprisonment following his conviction by a court in Xinjiang on charges of theft from ancient graves. The charges against Samdrup, a devout Buddhist and philanthropist, had first been brought in 1998 and recently revived. The activist claimed to have been tortured while awaiting trial. Shortly afterwards his environmentalist brother, Rinchen Samdrup, was sentenced to five years' imprisonment. A report released by Human Rights Watch in July 2010, based on the testimony of more than 200 Tibetan refugees, was highly critical of the Chinese authorities' use of excessive force to suppress the protests of 2008.

In March 2011 the Dalai Lama (now 76 years of age) formally announced his decision to relinquish his political responsibilities, which were to be transferred to an elected representative of the Tibetan people. However, the Dalai Lama confirmed his intention to retain his role of spiritual leader, and to determine the method whereby his eventual successor in that role would be chosen. In April it was announced that Lobsang Sangay, a research fellow at Harvard Law School in the USA, had won 55% of the votes cast by the Tibetan diaspora to defeat two other candidates and thus secure election as Prime Minister of the Tibetan government-in-exile. In July the Chinese Government announced further major investment in Tibet, amounting to 138,400m. yuan, for transport, public services and hydroelectricity. The death in March in Sichuan Province of a Tibetan monk who had set himself on fire was reported to have caused tension between local residents and security forces. By January 2012 there had been reports of at least 16 incidents of self-immolation by Tibetans in Sichuan and in Tibet itself (several of whom had died), demanding freedom and the return of the Dalai Lama from exile. The Chinese Government accused the Dalai Lama of encouraging such actions. In late January at least three Tibetans were reported to have been killed in violent confrontations between protesters and security forces in areas of Sichuan largely inhabited by ethnic Tibetans. The Chinese authorities responded by ordering stricter controls on Tibetan Buddhist monasteries and on road transport.

Events in Xinjiang

Anti-Chinese sentiment in the Xinjiang Uygur Autonomous Region intensified in the 1990s, resulting in the instigation of a new campaign by the authorities to repress the Islamist separatist movement, whose goal was to establish an independent 'East Turkestan'. Since 1949 Han Chinese had been encouraged or forced to move to the region by the central Government, thereby reducing the proportion of the indigenous Uygur population. Separatist movements such as the Xinjiang Liberation Front and the Uygur Liberation Organization (ULO) often had the support of the Uygur diaspora in Kyrgyzstan and Uzbekistan. Suppression of separatism increased in 1996, following a number of violent incidents. Hundreds of people were detained for their part in rioting and bomb attacks, and many were subsequently executed or imprisoned. Reports in late 1997 indicated that there had been a renewal of armed separatist activity, in which more than 300 people had been killed. In January 1998 13 people were executed in Xinjiang, allegedly for robbery and murder, although unofficial reports suggested that those executed were Muslim separatist demonstrators. Muslim separatists were believed to be responsible for an incendiary device deposited on a bus in Wuhan in February, which killed 16 people. Two leading activists, Yibulayin Simayi and Abudureyimu Aisha, were executed in January 1999, and a further 10 separatists were reportedly executed in May. Three Muslims were sentenced to death in September for participating in the separatist campaign, while six others received long prison sentences. In October 2000 Abduhelil Abdulmejit, a leading organizer of resistance to Chinese rule in Xinjiang who had been imprisoned three years previously, was reported to have died of pneumonia while in custody; international groups alleged that he had been tortured and murdered.

During 2001 the authorities continued the 'Strike Hard' campaign against separatists, with multiple executions reported. In August the PLA conducted large-scale military exercises involving 50,000 troops in the region. China's fears of Islamist separatism were heightened after the terrorist attacks in the USA on 11 September 2001. China stated that as many as 1,000 Uygur Islamist fighters had been trained in terrorist camps in Afghanistan operated by the al-Qa'ida network of the Saudi-born militant Osama bin Laden. Stability in Xinjiang remained crucial to China's 'go west' programme of developing the country's remote inner regions, and in late September Chinese troops began anti-guerrilla operations in the Afghan border region of Xinjiang, aimed at preventing Islamist infiltration.

In January 2002 the Government released a new report alleging links between the separatists and Osama bin Laden. In March Amnesty International reported that thousands of Muslim Uygurs had been detained since 11 September 2001, and that up to 8,000 had been given 'political education' courses. In June 2002 the authorities announced that from September Xinjiang University would no longer teach courses in the Uygur language; for 50 years students had had a choice of studying in Uygur or Mandarin. In August the USA designated the East Turkestan Islamic Movement (ETIM) a terrorist group and froze the organization's assets, in a conciliatory gesture towards the Chinese Government. The UN also added the organization to its list of terrorist organizations in September. In December 2003 China issued a 'terrorist' list that named the Eastern Turkestan Liberation Organization, the World Uygur Youth Congress and the East Turkestan Information Center, as well as the ETIM, as 'terrorist' organizations. Of these, only the ETIM was considered a terrorist movement by the USA.

In March 2004 it was reported that Rebiya Kadeer, a Uygur businesswoman and rights activist who had been imprisoned in 1999 for sending newspaper articles to her husband in the USA, would be released in 2006. (In the event she was freed in 2005, prior to a visit by the US Secretary of State.) During 2004 Erkin Alptekin (son of Isa Yusuf Alptekin, who had been head of a brief Uygur government in the 1940s) reportedly emerged as leader of a Uygur exile movement committed to achieving independence for Xinjiang by peaceful means. In September 2004 an East Turkestan government-in-exile was proclaimed by Anwar Yusuf Turani, head of the East Turkestan National Freedom Center. However, many Uygur groups did not recognize the government-in-exile.

Tension in the Xinjiang region recurred in January 2007 when 18 terrorist suspects were killed in a police operation against an alleged militants' training camp close to the Chinese border with Afghanistan and Pakistan, reportedly supervised by members of the ETIM. A few days previously the Vice-Secretary of the region's Communist Party Committee had denounced Rebiya Kadeer as a separatist, determined to 'destroy the peace and stability of Chinese society'. Kadeer, who was in exile in the USA, had been nominated for the 2006 Nobel Peace Prize. In February

2007 Ismail Semed, a Uygur activist who had previously been accused of ETIM membership, was executed, having been convicted in 2005 of trying to 'split the motherland' and possession of weapons. In January 2008 two militants, suspected of planning an attack on the forthcoming Olympic Games, were killed in a police operation in the regional capital, Urumqi, and 15 others were arrested. In March it was revealed that an attempted attack on an aircraft, en route from Xinjiang to Beijing in the previous week, had been similarly thwarted. Local officials announced in April that approximately 100 Uygurs had been arrested following a protest in late March. A further 45 were detained in April, on suspicion of planning attacks to disrupt the Olympic Games. In July, after five Uygurs were killed by security forces, bomb explosions on two buses in Kunming caused two fatalities; the attacks were reportedly linked with Uygur militants. Two Uygurs attacked and killed 16 police officers, injuring a further 16, in Kashgar in early August, days before the opening ceremony of the Olympic Games in Beijing. Suicide bombings and further outbreaks of violence were reported in the region later in the month. The two Uygur militants subsequently received the death sentence and were executed in April 2009.

In early July 2009 a protest by Uygur youths in Urumqi, apparently in response to an altercation between Han and Uygur workers in a factory in southern China in which two Uygurs had died, developed into a major confrontation between the two communities in Xinjiang. In the ensuing violence, nearly 200 people were killed and 1,700 injured. Hundreds of Han-owned shops and other buildings were attacked and seriously damaged, while numerous vehicles were destroyed by arson, in what was reported to be the worst civil unrest witnessed in China since 1989. Thousands of troops were deployed to the area, a curfew was imposed and order was swiftly restored. More than 1,500 people were believed to have been detained. State media immediately accused Rebiya Kadeer and other exiled Uygurs of inciting the attacks, declaring that the majority of those killed were Han Chinese; other sources claimed that police brutality had resulted in many Uygur deaths. The UN Secretary-General and other world leaders urged restraint, and Amnesty International pressed the Chinese Government to conduct a thorough investigation of the events.

From mid-August 2009 numerous attacks on Han Chinese by assailants using hypodermic needles were reported to hospitals in Urumqi. According to official figures, a total of 531 people were assaulted in this manner. However, no such attack appeared to have resulted in any case of poisoning, and it subsequently transpired that many cases could not be substantiated. Several deaths occurred in September, however, when thousands of Han demonstrators protested on the streets of Urumqi. Protesters demanded the resignation of the local CCP Secretary, Wang Lequan, whom they accused of failing to halt the syringe attacks. Meanwhile, access to the internet and other communication services such as text messaging within Xinjiang was severely restricted by the authorities.

About 80 people were prosecuted in connection with the unrest of July 2009. Following a series of convictions on various charges, including murder, robbery and arson, a total of 12 death sentences had been announced by mid-October; nine executions were carried out in November. In a major security operation in December, a further 94 suspects were apprehended. During the first half of 2010 two Uygur journalists and three Uygur website owners were sentenced to imprisonment after being found guilty of 'endangering state security'. In August eight people (including two alleged attackers) were killed and 15 injured in a bombing incident in the city of Aksu, reportedly perpetrated by a Uygur activist. In February 2011 four death sentences, in connection with three attacks in the latter part of 2010, were confirmed by the authorities; a further seven death sentences were approved in March 2011. In July new outbreaks of violence included an alleged attack on a police station in the city of Hotan by Uygur activists, in which 18 police and civilians were reported to have been killed; in the same month violence in Kashgar reportedly caused a further 18 deaths. The latter city had recently been designated a Special Economic Zone, intended to emulate the prospering equivalent zones in eastern China. In August the regional authorities announced a two-month 'Strike Hard' campaign to investigate and suppress suspicious activities. In September four Uygurs were sentenced to death for their part in the recent unrest. In December seven alleged kidnappers and a police officer were killed in another confrontation in southern Xinjiang.

Hong Kong, Macao and Taiwan

In September 1984, following protracted negotiations, China reached agreement with the British Government over the terms of the future administration of Hong Kong upon the territory's return to Chinese sovereignty, scheduled for mid-1997. The transfer of Hong Kong from British to Chinese administration was effected at midnight on 30 June 1997, whereupon some 4,000 troops of the PLA were deployed in the territory. In December 36 deputies from Hong Kong were directly elected to the Ninth NPC in Beijing. In June 2007 President Hu Jintao travelled to Hong Kong to attend the celebration of the 10th anniversary of the territory's transfer to Chinese sovereignty. However, tensions with regard to the pace of democratic reform in Hong Kong remained.

In June 1986 China and Portugal opened formal negotiations for the return of the Portuguese overseas territory of Macao to full Chinese sovereignty, and agreement was reached in January 1987. The agreement was based upon the 'one country, two systems' principle, which had formed the basis of China's negotiated settlement regarding the return of Hong Kong. China duly resumed sovereignty of Macao at midnight on 19 December 1999, and a PLA garrison was established in the territory. President Hu Jintao visited Macao in December 2009 on the 10th anniversary of the territory's return to Chinese rule.

Taiwan has continued to reject China's proposals for reunification, whereby the island would become a 'special administrative region' along the lines of Hong Kong and Macao. China has never relinquished its claim to sovereignty over the island and has repeatedly threatened to use military force against Taiwan in the event of any formal declaration of independence from the mainland. In March 2005 the NPC approved anti-secession legislation aimed at preventing Taiwan from declaring independence. In April–May, during an historic visit to the mainland by Lien Chan, leader of the opposition KMT, President Hu Jintao and the former Premier of Taiwan agreed to uphold their opposition to Taiwanese independence. Despite intermittent political tensions, cross-Straits business links flourished as Taiwanese investment continued to flow to the mainland. Relations between the People's Republic and Taiwan improved considerably following the election of Ma Ying-jeou of the KMT as President of Taiwan in March 2008. In a major development in June 2010, a bilateral preferential trade agreement, the Economic Co-operation Framework Agreement (ECFA), was signed in the mainland city of Chongqing. Ma's re-election to the presidency in January 2012 was welcomed by the official Chinese media.

Foreign Affairs

Relations with Japan

Japan recognized the People's Republic in 1972, and a bilateral treaty of peace and friendship was signed in 1978. However, historical issues and territorial disputes continued to affect China's relations with Japan. In 1982 China complained that passages in Japanese school textbooks sought to justify the Japanese invasion of China in 1937. In June 1989 Japan criticized the Chinese Government's suppression of the pro-democracy movement and suspended (until late 1990) a five-year aid programme to China. In April 1992 Jiang Zemin travelled to Japan, the first visit by the General Secretary of the CCP for nine years. In October Emperor Akihito made the first ever imperial visit to the People's Republic. Japan was one of many countries to criticize China's resumption of underground nuclear testing, at Lop Nor in Xinjiang Province, in October 1993. Relations were seriously strained in May 1994, when the Japanese Minister of Justice referred to the 1937 Nanjing massacre (in which more than 300,000 Chinese citizens were killed by Japanese soldiers) as a 'fabrication', and again in August, when a second Japanese minister was obliged to resign, following further controversial remarks about his country's war record. In May 1995, during a visit to Beijing, the Japanese Prime Minister expressed his deep remorse for the wartime atrocities, but offered no formal apology.

China's continuation of its nuclear-testing programme, in defiance of international opinion, prompted Japan to announce a reduction in financial aid to China. In August 1995 Japan suspended most of its grant aid to China. Following China's 'final' nuclear test in July 1996, and the declaration of a moratorium, Japan resumed grant aid in March 1997. (China signed the Comprehensive Nuclear Test Ban Treaty in September 1996.) In July 1996, however, Sino-Japanese relations were affected by a territorial dispute relating to the Diaoyu (or Senkaku) Islands, a group of uninhabited islets in the East China Sea, which China had claimed as its own since ancient times, and Japan since 1895, and to which Taiwan also laid claim. The construction of a lighthouse on one of the islands by a group of Japanese nationalists led to strong protests from the Governments of both the People's Republic and Taiwan. At a meeting with President Jiang Zemin during the Asia-Pacific Economic Cooperation (APEC, see p. 204) conference in November 1996, the Japanese Prime Minister apologized for Japanese aggression during the Second World War, and emphasized his desire to resolve the dispute over the Diaoyu Islands.

During a visit by President Jiang Zemin to Japan in November 1998, the first by a head of state from the People's Republic, the Japanese Government failed to issue an unequivocal apology for its invasion and occupation of China during 1937–45. The Japanese Prime Minister, Keizo Obuchi, undertook a reciprocal visit to the People's Republic in July 1999, when various co-operation agreements were reached.

In April 2001 NPC Chairman Li Peng cancelled a trip to Japan, apparently in response to the Japanese decision to permit former Taiwanese President Lee Teng-hui to visit Japan, and the publication of a new history textbook that attenuated Japan's wartime atrocities in China and South-East Asia. By mid-2001 China and Japan had become embroiled in trade disputes involving tariffs on imported goods. China was further antagonized by the visit of the Japanese Prime Minister, Junichiro Koizumi, to the Yasukuni Shrine, a controversial war memorial in Tokyo that glorified Japan's war dead, including several prominent war criminals. Li Peng finally visited Japan in April 2002, when he met Koizumi. In August a Tokyo court finally admitted that Japan had conducted biological warfare in China during the Second World War, but rejected the demands by 180 Chinese plaintiffs for individual compensation. In January 2003 the Diaoyu/Senkaku Islands dispute re-emerged when Japan announced plans to lease the islands to a private owner. Also in January, Prime Minister Koizumi made a further visit to the Yasukuni Shrine (see above). Two further incidents caused tensions in the Sino-Japanese relationship in 2003: in August 29 people were poisoned by chemical weapons that had been left buried in north-eastern China after the Japanese invasion of the area during the war; in September an incident involving the use of Chinese prostitutes by Japanese tourists also caused deep offence in China.

In January 2004 there was renewed conflict over the Diaoyu/Senkaku Islands when a Japanese ship fired a water cannon at a Chinese boat. In March there were protests in China following the arrest by Japanese police of seven Chinese activists who had landed on the islands. In April 2005 violent demonstrations took place across China in protest at Japan's bid for a permanent seat on the UN Security Council, as well as at the Japanese Government's approval for use in schools of history textbooks reportedly omitting mention of Japanese atrocities in China (and also Korea) during the Second World War.

A meeting between the Chinese Minister of Foreign Affairs and his Japanese counterpart in April 2006 resulted in a pledge to further Sino-Japanese co-operation and a promise to expedite negotiations on disputed gas exploration in the East China Sea. In June Japan agreed to resume low-interest loans to China, which had earlier been suspended as a result of the Chinese Government's criticisms of the Yasukuni Shrine visits. Sino-Japanese relations sharply deteriorated in August, however, following the publication of a Japanese defence policy document that was deemed to have exaggerated China's military strength and, more crucially, by Prime Minister Koizumi's visit to the Yasukuni Shrine on 15 August (the anniversary of Japan's surrender in the Second World War). The appointment of Shinzo Abe as Japanese Prime Minister in the following month led to a marked improvement in relations, largely owing to Abe's choice of Beijing for his first official overseas visit. During the trip, which took place in October, President Hu and Abe agreed to expand bilateral links in the areas of trade, investment and technology.

In April 2007 Wen Jiabao became the first Chinese Premier to address the Japanese legislature. Wen emphasized the suffering caused by the Japanese occupation and the need for amends; he also looked forward to increased co-operation between the two countries. Discussions between Wen and Abe resulted in an agreement to co-operate in fields such as the economy, defence, energy and the environment. President Hu Jintao visited Japan in May 2008, attending discussions with the Japanese Prime Minister, Yasuo Fukuda. The two leaders agreed to hold annual summit meetings, and to resolve the matter of resource development in the East China Sea. Fukuda's successor, Taro Aso, undertook an official visit to China in April 2009; discussions focused on the repercussions of the rapid deterioration in global economic conditions. Bilateral relations swiftly improved following the change of government in Japan, and in October it was reported that the two countries had entered exploratory discussions with a view to the eventual establishment of an East Asian community, similar to the EU: it was also agreed that joint studies would begin on the feasibility of a free trade agreement between China, Japan and South Korea. Ongoing bilateral issues included the disputed development of gas reserves in the East China Sea, the North Korean nuclear programme and the need for closer co-operation on matters of food safety.

In March 2010 China reiterated its claim to sovereignty over the Diaoyu/Senkaku Islands, in response to a remark by the Japanese Minister for Foreign Affairs. A major diplomatic dispute arose in September after a Chinese fishing vessel collided with a Japanese patrol boat. The captain of the Chinese trawler, who had reportedly disregarded warnings to leave the area and failed to stop for an inspection, was detained for questioning by the Japanese authorities. Bilateral exchanges were abruptly suspended. Although the captain was released a fortnight later, in the same month tensions were exacerbated by China's purchase of unusually large amounts of Japanese government bonds, prompting Japan to request a clarification of the Chinese Government's strategy. China rejected a US offer of mediation in the dispute over the Diaoyu/Senkaku Islands. In August 2011 the Chinese Government expressed 'strong dissatisfaction' with a report published by the Japanese Ministry of Defence: the document described China as increasing its regional naval capabilities and stated that Japan's coastal defences would be strengthened in response. In April 2012 China condemned plans announced by the Governor of Tokyo for the metropolitan government to purchase the islands from their private Japanese owner.

Other regional relations

During the 1990s and the early 21st century China's neighbours in South-East Asia, while benefiting from Chinese investment and trade, also displayed unease, in some cases, at China's perceived expansionism in the region. A particular source of friction was the question of the sovereignty of the Spratly Islands (Nansha or Truong Sa), situated in the South China Sea and claimed by six countries, namely Brunei, Malaysia, the Philippines, Taiwan and Viet Nam, as well as China. This strategic area, which was traversed by major international shipping routes, was believed to possess deposits of petroleum and gas, in addition to rich fishing resources. By 1994 both China and Viet Nam (which had re-established normal diplomatic relations in 1991, following many years of mutual hostility) had awarded petroleum exploration concessions to US companies, leading to increased tension among the claimants. In February 1995 it emerged that Chinese forces had occupied a reef to which the Philippines laid claim, resulting in a formal diplomatic protest from the Philippine Government. More than 60 Chinese fishermen and several vessels were subsequently detained by the Philippine authorities. Following consultations in August, China and the Philippines declared their intention to resolve their claims by peaceful means. In January 1996 the Chinese Government denied any involvement in a naval skirmish in Philippine waters, during which a ship flying the Chinese flag and a Philippine patrol boat exchanged gunfire. In November 1998 China antagonized the Philippines by building permanent structures on the disputed Mischief Reef. In late November 20 Chinese fishermen were arrested near Mischief Reef by the Philippine navy. Following Chinese protests, the men were released. In December China reiterated both its claim to sovereignty over the Spratly Islands and surrounding waters and its commitment to a peaceful solution. Discussions between the two countries in April 1999 were unsuccessful, and relations deteriorated further in May when a Chinese fishing vessel sank following a collision with a Philippine navy boat. Another Chinese fishing boat sank after colliding with a Philippine naval vessel in July. In September 2003 China proposed a joint development and petroleum exploration strategy for the Spratly Islands. In November the Philippine Government complained that China had violated the 2002 accord by installing markers in parts of the islands. There were a number of similar disputes in 2004, with China protesting against proposals by Viet Nam to conduct tourist excursions to the islands. In March 2005 the China National Offshore Oil Corporation (CNOOC), the Philippine National Oil Company and the Vietnam Oil and Gas Corporation (Petrovietnam) signed an accord pledging to conduct joint marine seismic experiments in the Spratly Islands region.

In May 1996 China declared an extension of its maritime boundaries in the South China Sea. In November 2002, in Cambodia, Prime Minister Zhu Rongji signed a significant 'declaration on the conduct of parties in the South China Sea' with members of the Association of Southeast Asian Nations (ASEAN), which aimed to avoid conflict in the area. Under this agreement, which was similar to one drafted in late 1999 but not implemented, claimants would practise self-restraint in the event of potentially hostile action (such as inhabiting the islands), effect confidence-building measures and give advance notice of military exercises in the region. However, the agreement did not include the Paracel Islands (Xisha), which in a similar territorial dispute had been seized by China from South Vietnamese forces in 1974.

Reports that China had established a new, city-level administrative division for the Spratly Islands and the Paracel Islands prompted protests in Viet Nam in December 2007. Tensions rose in May 2009 when the deadline for applications under the UN Convention on the Law of the Sea expired and the various countries formally submitted their respective claims (with the exception of Taiwan, which was not a signatory). In June eight Chinese fishing boats were briefly detained by the Indonesian authorities while operating off the Spratly Islands. China strengthened its patrols in the South China Sea, ostensibly in an attempt to counter illegal fishing activities. In various incidents during 2009–10 the Chinese navy intercepted several Vietnamese fishing vessels, operating in the area of the Paracels, and detained the crews. In January 2010 China announced plans to promote tourism on the Paracel Islands. In March 2011 the Philippine Government protested after a survey vessel, undertaking seismic testing in the South China Sea, was challenged by two Chinese patrol boats. In the same month three Philippine citizens were executed in China after having been convicted of smuggling heroin into the country, despite pleas for clemency by the President of the Philippines, Benigno Aquino. In July the two countries' ministers responsible for foreign affairs reaffirmed their commitment to the 2002 declaration concerning the South China Sea. In the same month, however, a visit to one of the disputed Spratly Islands by a group of members of the Philippine legislature was condemned by the Chinese Government as an infringement of its sovereignty. President Aquino paid an official visit to China in August 2011, accompanied by a large delegation of business leaders, one of the principal aims of the visit being to attract Chinese investment.

In June 2011 the Vietnamese navy conducted exercises in the South China Sea, claiming that the Chinese navy had been harassing Vietnamese survey vessels in the Spratlys area. In October the two countries concluded an agreement to hold meetings twice a year concerning the maritime dispute, and established emergency procedures for consultation in the event of a confrontation. The launching of China's first aircraft carrier in August was widely viewed as a further sign of China's regional assertiveness, although the vessel was not expected to be fully operational for several years.

In December 2001 President Jiang visited Myanmar, promising US $100m. in finance towards investment projects. In January 2003 the head of Myanmar's ruling council, Gen. Than Shwe, visited Beijing, where he was promised $200m. in development loans. In August, in defiance of US attempts to isolate Myanmar's leadership, 32 members of Myanmar's military junta visited Beijing for discussions. In November 2004 Soe Win, Myanmar's new Prime Minister, made an official visit to China. Various agreements were signed by Premier Wen Jiabao and his Myanma counterpart during Wen's official visit to Myanmar in June 2010. These included an agreement relating to the construction by a Chinese company of an oil and gas pipeline linking Yunnan Province to Myanmar's energy resources. In September, following the first visit of Chinese warships to the port of Yangon, Myanma leader Than Shwe undertook an official visit to Beijing, at the head of a large delegation. He and Prime Minister Thein Sein had discussions with their Chinese counterparts, focusing on trade and economic issues. In April 2011 an agreement was announced whereby a railway was to be constructed between western Myanmar and Yunnan, over a three-year period.

China was accorded the status of 'dialogue partner' with ASEAN in 1996. At the ASEAN summit meeting held in Cambodia in November 2002, an agreement to establish a free trade area by 2010 was signed with China. In October 2003 relations with ASEAN were further strengthened by the signing of a Declaration on Strategic Partnership for Peace and Prosperity, to be implemented by subsequent five-year action plans; in the same month China also signed the Association's Treaty of Amity and Co-operation, a pact for the promotion of regional stability. The free trade agreement entered into force in January 2010, and by 2015 the policy of a zero tariff for 90% of traded goods was expected to extend between China and four additional ASEAN members, namely Cambodia, Laos, Myanmar and Viet Nam. Regular joint ASEAN-China ministerial meetings take place, and a Chinese delegation attended the first ASEAN Defence Ministers' Meeting-Plus (ADMM-Plus), convened in Viet Nam in December 2010, when topics of discussion included China's territorial claims in the South China Sea.

In April 2011 the Chinese Premier, Wen Jiabao, paid official visits to Malaysia and Indonesia, during which agreements were concluded on bilateral economic co-operation and investment by China in the two countries' infrastructure.

In 1992 China established diplomatic relations with the Republic of Korea (South Korea). In June 1996 it was reported that secret discussions between representatives of South Korea and North Korea had been held in Beijing. In late 1997 China participated in quadripartite negotiations, together with the USA, North Korea and South Korea, to resolve the situation on the Korean peninsula. Further quadripartite negotiations took place during 1999. In May 2000 the North Korean leader, Kim Jong Il, visited China, and in June China welcomed the holding of the first ever inter-Korean presidential summit meeting in North Korea. Regular inter-Korean meetings followed. Kim Jong Il visited China again in January 2001, and President Jiang visited North Korea in September. During 2001, however, China increased measures to counter the growing number of North Korean refugees entering the country.

During 2002 there were tensions over the introduction of legislation to grant special rights to ethnic Koreans in China and also over China's forcible removal of North Korean refugees from South Korean diplomatic premises. In June the Chinese Government allowed 24 North Korean refugees who had been concealed in the South Korean embassy in Beijing to leave for South Korea. After the incident, the authorities began an operation against South Korean activists and missionaries who had been helping North Koreans to flee via China. In October North Korea appointed a Chinese businessman of Dutch citizenship, Yang Bin, as the new governor of its recently created Sinuiju Special Administrative Region; however, the Chinese authorities arrested him on charges of bribery and fraud, thereby preventing him from assuming the post. By 2003 China was becoming increasingly concerned about the growing diplomatic crisis between North Korea and the USA, and in July South Korean President Roh Moo-Hyun visited Beijing for discussions. Chinese diplomatic efforts played a major role in ensuring North Korean participation in the six-party talks on the issue of North Korea's nuclear programme, held in Beijing in August and attended by representatives of North and South Korea, China, the USA, Japan and Russia. The Chinese Minister of Foreign Affairs, Li Zhaoxing, paid his first visit to the North Korean capital of Pyongyang in March 2004. Relations with South Korea were affected in 2004 by a dispute over the ancient kingdom of Koguryo, believed by Koreans to have been ruled by their own ancestors, but which China claimed had been ruled by one of its own ethnic groups. In August references to Koguryo were deleted from the Chinese Ministry of Foreign Affairs website. Nevertheless, in November 2006, following an official visit to Beijing by South Korean President Roh Moo-Hyun in the previous month, it was announced that China and South Korea were to begin research on a possible bilateral free trade agreement.

Following the North Korean Government's declaration in February 2005 that it possessed nuclear weapons, the delayed fourth round of six-party disarmament talks was hosted by China, with discussions commencing in Beijing in July. China was credited with having played an important role in the conclusion of a framework agreement at the talks in September, under which North Korea agreed to disarm in exchange for various concessions; however, the agreement subsequently faltered. In October President Hu Jintao made his first official visit to North Korea as head of state, in advance of the fifth round of talks, which began in Beijing in November.

Throughout 2006 the Chinese Government continued to urge North Korea to revoke its nuclear weapons programme, but in July North Korea proceeded with a test of a long-range missile; in October the country carried out its first test of a nuclear device. Embarrassed by North Korea's disregard for its entreaties,

China surprised observers by agreeing, albeit with reservations, to the imposition of UN sanctions against the regime of Kim Jong Il. A Chinese envoy visited Pyongyang later in that month and returned with assurances that no further tests were planned. By the end of October North Korea had agreed during discussions in Beijing to return to the six-party talks. In February 2007 the six-party talks, with considerable Chinese input, resulted in an agreement that included the closure of North Korea's Yongbyon nuclear site in exchange for substantial aid. In July, following a delay of several months owing to a dispute over the release of North Korean funds held in the Macao-based Banco Delta Asia (which had allegedly been involved in corrupt financial activities on behalf of the Government of North Korea), Yongbyon was declared closed. In April 2009, however, North Korea announced its withdrawal from the six-party talks and the resumption of its nuclear programme. In the following month China joined Russia and the USA in condemning North Korea's second underground nuclear test.

In May 2010 Kim Jong Il embarked upon an official visit to China, where he was reported to have attempted to obtain additional economic assistance from the Chinese leadership. The ailing Kim unexpectedly returned to China in August, the latest of a series of unofficial visits during recent years. Following an artillery attack on South Korean territory by North Korea in November 2010, China came under renewed international pressure, notably from the USA, to exert greater influence over the North Korean Government. China's proposals for emergency consultations were rejected by the USA and other previous participants in the six-party-talks. In May 2011 Kim Jong Il made a six-day tour of China, and in June Chinese and North Korean officials announced the formation of two new economic development zones, to be created within North Korea with Chinese assistance. After Kim's death in December, the Chinese Government described him as a 'close friend', and endorsed his son, Kim Jong Un, as his successor. Following the failed launch of a rocket-mounted satellite in April 2012 (an operation generally suspected to be the testing of a long-range missile banned under UN resolutions), China did not veto condemnation of the launch by the UN Security Council. However, it called for restraint from all interested parties and subsequently President Hu Jintao reaffirmed his country's close ties to North Korea.

In January 2012 the South Korean President, Lee Myung-Bak, undertook his second state visit to China, during which he held discussions with President Hu on maintaining the stability of the Korean peninsula following Kim Jong Il's death, and it was announced that formal negotiations on a bilateral free trade agreement would begin in the near future. Joint research on the inclusion of Japan in such an agreement had begun in 2010.

In the early 21st century there was increasing competition between China and Taiwan for influence in the Pacific Islands, a region in which several countries accorded diplomatic recognition to Taiwan. China continued to provide substantial aid and investment to those Pacific nations with which it maintained diplomatic relations. Fijian leader Frank Bainimarama visited China in August 2010, and in January 2011 China agreed to finance various development projects in Fiji. China's relations with Australia, a major source of vital commodities, were strained in mid-2009 by the arrest in Shanghai of a naturalized Australian citizen, amid allegations of industrial espionage. The trial on charges of bribery and the theft of trade secrets of Stern Hu and three others concluded in March 2010. All four defendants were found guilty and received long prison sentences. In February, none the less, China and Australia resumed negotiations regarding the eventual establishment of a free trade agreement. Sino-Australian relations were tested again in early 2011, after Australia granted permission for Rebiya Kadeer, the exiled Uygur activist, to revisit the country.

In China's relations with South Asia, the long-standing border dispute with India, which gave rise to a short military conflict in 1962, remained unresolved. Discussions on the issue were held in 1988 and 1991, and in September 1993 China and India signed an agreement to reduce their troops along the frontier and to resolve the dispute by peaceful means. In August 1995 it was confirmed that the two countries were to disengage their troops from four border posts in Arunachal Pradesh. Further progress was made at discussions in October 1996, as confirmed by the visit of President Jiang Zemin to India (the first by a Chinese head of state) in November. Li Peng visited India in January 2001, and discussions were held with a view to the restoration of normal relations. Outstanding Indian concerns included the increasing levels of imports of cheap Chinese goods and the question of China's nuclear co-operation with Pakistan, while China resented India's continued hosting of Tibetan separatist organizations. However, in January 2002 Prime Minister Zhu Rongji led a business delegation to India.

In April 2003 the Indian Minister of Defence began a week-long visit to Beijing, to discuss outstanding bilateral issues, including China's support for Pakistan and Chinese observation posts in the Bay of Bengal. In June Atal Bihari Vajpayee visited Beijing, the first visit by an Indian Prime Minister in over a decade. The Indian Prime Minister officially recognized Tibet as part of China, and China agreed to trade with India's north-eastern state of Sikkim, thus implicitly recognizing India's control of that area. In November China and India held their first joint naval exercises. Further negotiations took place in 2004 in an attempt to move towards resolution of remaining border disputes, with the Chinese Minister of National Defence making an official visit to India in March and a further session of talks taking place in July. During an historic visit to India in March 2005, Chinese Premier Wen Jiabao signed an agreement aimed at resolving the border dispute. In July 2006 the reopening of the Nathu La border pass connecting the Indian state of Sikkim with Tibet represented a formal recognition by India of China's claim to Tibet and by China of India's claim to Sikkim. President Hu Jintao's visit to India in November 2006 resulted in pledges to double the value of trade exchanges by 2010, to encourage bilateral investment, to expedite feasibility studies on a joint trade agreement and to continue to work together to resolve joint border issues. In January 2008 Indian Prime Minister Manmohan Singh paid a visit to China, attending talks with President Hu and Premier Wen Jiabao and signing agreements on bilateral trade and military exercises. Singh's visit to Arunachal Pradesh in October 2009 was criticized by China, which was further antagonized by the Dalai Lama's visit to the disputed Indian state in the following month.

Sino-Indian relations were strained in August 2010 when China declined to grant a visa for a routine visit by an army general whose command included the troubled region of Jammu and Kashmir. None the less, in December Premier Wen Jiabao led a large delegation (including 400 representatives of the Chinese business sector) to India, where he had discussions with his Indian counterpart. Wen emphasized the complementary nature of the two countries' economies, identifying telecommunications and energy as sectors in which investment by Chinese companies had been of particular benefit to India. The Chinese Premier also undertook to provide Indian companies with wider access to the Chinese market in areas such as pharmaceuticals and information technology. In January 2012 renewed discussions on the two countries' border disputes resulted in an agreement to establish a joint border management mechanism to prevent the escalation of incidents into major confrontations.

In December 2001 China hosted a visit by Pakistani President Pervez Musharraf, to mark the 50th anniversary of the establishment of relations between the two countries. China and Pakistan had long been close allies, and co-operated in economic and military issues. Musharraf revisited Beijing in August 2002 and in November 2003, when various agreements were reached, including trade accords and an extradition treaty. Amid some controversy, Chinese assistance to Pakistan in the development of its nuclear energy programme continued, and in May 2004 an agreement for the construction of a second nuclear plant in Pakistan was signed. In November 2006 President Hu Jintao signed a free trade agreement with President Musharraf during a visit to the Pakistani capital of Islamabad. The visit was widely regarded as an attempt to reassure Pakistan of the continuing strength of bilateral links, particularly in view of China's growing relationship with India. Co-operation agreements signed by the two leaders aimed to treble the value of bilateral trade within five years. In October 2008 the Pakistani President, Asif Ali Zardari, visited China, securing China's assistance with the construction of a further two nuclear power stations. On President Zardari's next official visit to China, in August 2009, discussions focused on economic and trade issues. In April 2010 China and Pakistan were reported to have reached agreement on the construction of two further nuclear reactors. In December the Premier of China embarked upon a visit to Pakistan: Wen Jiabao and his Pakistani counterpart agreed further to expand bilateral trade. The Chinese Premier also expressed his support for Pakistan's attempts to combat terrorist activities.

During 2000–01 China began improving relations with the Taliban regime in Afghanistan, signing several economic and technical agreements in the expectation that the Taliban would cease supporting Islamist Uygur fighters in Xinjiang. Following the collapse of the Taliban regime in late 2001, the new Afghan Prime Minister, Hamid Karzai, visited Beijing in January 2002 to discuss Chinese aid towards the reconstruction of his country. China continued to support the reconstruction process. In 2009 Chinese corporations began developing the Aynak copper mine, the largest foreign investment project in Afghanistan. As President, Karzai revisited China in March 2010, when various agreements relating to trade and economic co-operation were signed. In October 2011 it was announced that the China National Petroleum Corporation had become the first foreign company to obtain a licence for exploration of Afghanistan's unexploited petroleum reserves, which were believed to be large.

Relations with the USA

For many years the USA refused to recognize the People's Republic, continuing to regard the Taiwanese administration as the legitimate Chinese Government. In February 1972, however, US President Richard Nixon visited the People's Republic and acknowledged that 'Taiwan is a part of China'. In January 1979 the USA formally recognized the People's Republic and severed diplomatic relations with Taiwan. Following the suppression of the pro-democracy movement in China in 1989, all senior-level government exchanges were suspended by the USA, and the export of weapons to China was prohibited. Although US President George Bush received the Chinese Minister of Foreign Affairs in Washington, DC, in November 1990, Sino-US relations deteriorated in September 1992, upon Bush's announcement of the sale of fighter aircraft to Taiwan. In August 1993 the USA imposed sanctions on China, in response to the latter's sales of technology for nuclear-capable missiles to Pakistan. The sanctions remained in force until October 1994. In June 1995, following President Clinton's highly controversial decision to grant him a visa, President Lee of Taiwan embarked upon an unofficial visit to the USA, where he met members of the US Congress. The visit resulted in the withdrawal of the Chinese ambassador from the USA. In October, at a meeting in New York, Presidents Jiang Zemin and Bill Clinton agreed to resume dialogue on various issues, the USA reaffirming its commitment to the 'one China' policy. In November the two countries reached agreement on the resumption of bilateral military contacts. In March 1996, as China began a new series of missile tests, the USA stationed two naval convoys east of Taiwan, its largest deployment in Asia since 1975. President Clinton's decision to sell anti-aircraft missiles and other defensive weapons to Taiwan was condemned by China. In February 2000 the US House of Representatives approved the Taiwan Security Enhancement Act (TSEA), establishing direct military links between the USA and Taiwan.

President Jiang Zemin visited the USA in October 1997, the first such visit by a Chinese head of state since 1985. Measures to reduce the US trade deficit with China and to accelerate China's entry into the World Trade Organization (WTO) were negotiated. In addition, the Chinese Government agreed to control the export of nuclear-related materials, in return for the removal of sanctions on the sale of nuclear-reactor technology to the People's Republic. In November 1999, after 13 years of negotiations, a bilateral trade agreement was concluded, thus facilitating China's eventual accession to the WTO.

There were initial fears that the election of George W. Bush to the presidency of the USA in late 2000 would lead to the termination of that country's recent policy of engagement with China. Relations between China and the USA were strained in May 2001 by a meeting between President Bush and the Dalai Lama in Washington, DC, and also by Taiwanese President Chen Shui-bian's stopover in New York, and in July by the conviction in China on espionage charges of Gao Zhan, a US-based Chinese scholar, and of another US-based Chinese academic, Qin Guangguang. Gao, Qin and a third academic, Li Shaomin, were freed prior to a visit by the US Secretary of State, Colin Powell.

In early September 2001 the USA sought to reduce China's fears over its national missile defence (NMD) programme by undertaking to keep China informed of its development and by abandoning its objections to China's build-up of its nuclear forces, in return for China's acceptance of the NMD. The attacks against the USA on 11 September 2001 were strongly condemned by China, which pledged its co-operation in the US-led 'war on terror'. In October Bush made his first official visit to China to attend the summit meeting of APEC, which was dominated by the issue of terrorism. However, the USA did not share China's view that Uygur and Tibetan separatists in Xinjiang and Tibet respectively were terrorists. China formally became a member of the WTO in December. At the end of 2001 President Bush signed proclamations granting China permanent normal trading relations status commencing on 1 January 2002, and also ended the Jackson-Vanik regulation preventing communist states from having normal commercial relations with the USA if they restricted emigration.

On visiting Beijing in February 2002, Bush's discussions with Jiang revealed disagreements on the issues of human rights, China's close relations with Iran, Iraq and North Korea (countries the US President had described as forming an 'axis of evil'), the USA's planned missile defence system, China's export of nuclear technology to Pakistan and US support for Taiwan. In July the USA sent a team to China to identify the remains of several US servicemen lost in the course of espionage missions conducted during the protracted period of mutual hostility known as the Cold War. A report issued in mid-July by the US Department of Defense warned that China was increasing its defence spending in order to intimidate Taiwan, while in the same month a report published by a US congressional commission stated that China had become a leading proliferator of missile technology to countries opposed to the USA, and that US corporations and their investments in China were assisting its emergence as a major economic power, to the detriment of the US trade balance. In late August China introduced the 'Regulations on Export Control of Missiles and Missile-related Items and Technologies' to curb the export of missiles and related technology, in an apparent goodwill gesture to the visiting US Deputy Secretary of State, Richard Armitage. In return, the USA designated the East Turkestan Islamic Movement a terrorist group (see Events in Xinjiang).

In October 2002 President Jiang Zemin visited the USA. The major issues discussed by Jiang and Bush were the emerging diplomatic crises over Iraq and North Korea. There was strong opposition in China to the US military intervention in Iraq in March 2003. Tensions over trade issues also increased, and during a visit to Beijing in September the US Secretary of the Treasury criticized China's refusal to revalue its currency, amid concerns that undervaluation of the yuan was having an adverse effect on the US economy by making China's exports artificially cheap. China in turn expressed strong criticism of the USA's imposition of quotas on Chinese textile exports in November 2003. In December the issue of Taiwan dominated a visit by Chinese Premier Wen Jiabao to the USA.

Increasing US concerns over China's economic strength and the trade deficit between the two countries (to the detriment of the USA) were illustrated in mid-2005 when a bid by the China National Offshore Oil Corporation to take control of a California-based oil and gas company encountered strong opposition in the US House of Representatives. The bid was regarded as potentially damaging to the security of the USA, and the company in question accepted a lower offer from a US firm. Diplomatic tension likewise arose over the huge increase in Chinese textile exports to the USA following the expiry of the WTO's Multi-Fibre Arrangement (MFA) at the end of 2004. Negotiations resulted in an agreement in November 2005 whereby limits were imposed on the rate at which the volume of Chinese clothing exports to the USA could expand. As US anxiety over the rising levels of China's military spending continued to increase, in October Donald Rumsfeld, visiting China for the first time since his appointment as US Secretary of Defense, expressed concerns at China's broadening ballistic capabilities in the Pacific region. In September, meanwhile, Hu Jintao paid his first visit as head of state to the USA, and in November President Bush reciprocated by visiting Beijing.

In February 2008 it emerged that a former employee of Boeing, the leading US aerospace corporation, had been arrested in the USA on suspicion of misappropriating confidential information on behalf of China. In a separate case, information on the USA's military sales agreements with Taiwan was alleged to have been stolen. China and the USA signed an agreement to open a 'hotline' between their respective armed forces. In October, furthermore, a US military agreement with Taiwan, envisaging the sale of defence equipment to the value of US $6,000m., resulted in China's suspension of diplomatic and military exchanges with the USA.

Following the election of Barack Obama as President of the USA in November 2008, the Chinese Government urged him to cease the sale of US weapons to Taiwan. In February 2009 the new US Secretary of State, Hillary Clinton, visited Beijing, and in a meeting with Yang Jiechi, the Minister of Foreign Affairs, she stressed the need for bilateral co-operation on various issues, including the deterioration in the global economic situation, climate change and security concerns. Tensions were raised in March when a US navy surveillance vessel was confronted by five Chinese ships in the South China Sea. China accused the US vessel of operating illegally in its exclusive economic zone. During Yang's visit to the USA later in the month the two sides agreed henceforth to collaborate more closely in order to avoid the recurrence of a similar incident. In April the two Governments initiated an annual Strategic and Economic Dialogue for bilateral discussions at a senior ministerial level. In a joint action with the EU in June, the USA lodged a formal complaint at the WTO in relation to China's imposition of restrictions on the country's exports of various raw materials, which the complainants argued were distorting international markets for certain commodities. Also in mid-2009, the US Administration urged the Chinese Government to withdraw its plan to install filtering software on all new computers, arguing that such action would violate China's free trade obligations.

In November 2009 President Obama undertook his first official visit to China. A joint statement, released following Obama's discussions with the Chinese leadership, envisaged greater bilateral co-operation in areas such as trade, global security and climate change. In January 2010 US Secretary of State Clinton urged the Chinese authorities to investigate the recent infiltration of the accounts of Google users (see Human Rights and Media Freedom). President Obama's decision to receive the Dalai Lama in Washington, DC, in February drew unusually strong condemnation from the Chinese Government. Other sources of ongoing tension in Sino-US relations in 2010 included the US Administration's decision to proceed with a major sale of defence equipment to Taiwan (a matter over which Sino-US military contacts were briefly suspended) and China's continuing refusal to implement any significant revaluation of its currency. In July the US embassy demanded the immediate release of Xue Feng, a Chinese-born US geologist sentenced to eight years' imprisonment following his conviction by a Beijing court on charges of stealing state secrets.

In January 2011, during a state visit to the USA, President Hu Jintao urged the adoption of a longer-term perspective in bilateral relations. During 2011 China (the US Government's largest foreign creditor) repeatedly expressed concern at the size of the US budget deficit, and criticized proposed US legislation to impose tariffs on goods from countries that indirectly subsidized their exports by undervaluing their currency, as China was accused of doing: the Chinese Government warned that the legislation (which was not ultimately expected to be adopted) would cause a 'trade war'. In August China accused the US Government of exaggeration in the latter's annual report on Chinese military capabilities, particularly with reference to China's expanding naval presence in the South China Sea: China had launched its first aircraft carrier in August and was predicted by the report to be planning to construct more. In September China issued an official protest at the US Government's decision to give assistance for modernizing Taiwan's air force, although the USA had not complied with Taiwan's request for the sale of new military aircraft. In November President Obama declared that the Asia-Pacific region was a 'top priority' in terms of US security, and announced that US military personnel were to be stationed in northern Australia: China's official response was that the deployment might not be 'appropriate'.

Relations with the USSR and successor states

Following the establishment of the People's Republic in 1949, China was dependent on the USSR for economic and military aid. However, as China began to develop its own form of socialism, the USSR withdrew all technical aid in 1960. In what became known as the 'Sino-Soviet Split', Chinese hostility to the USSR increased, and ideological differences were exacerbated by territorial disputes, by the Soviet invasion of Afghanistan and by the Soviet-supported Vietnamese intervention in Cambodia in the late 1970s. In 1987, however, China and the USSR signed a partial agreement concerning the exact demarcation of the disputed common border at the Amur River (Heilong Jiang). In May 1989 a full summit meeting was held in Beijing, at which normal state and party relations between China and the USSR were formally restored. During the next two years senior Chinese officials visited the USSR. In December 1991, upon the dissolution of the USSR, China recognized the newly independent states of the former union. The President of Russia, Boris Yeltsin, visited China in December 1992. In May 1994, in Beijing, Premier Li Peng and his Russian counterpart signed various co-operation agreements. In September President Jiang Zemin travelled to Moscow, the first visit to Russia by a Chinese head of state since 1957. The two sides reached agreement on the formal demarcation of the western section of the border (the eastern section having been delimited in May 1991), and each pledged not to aim nuclear missiles at the other. In June 1995 the Chinese Premier paid an official visit to Russia, where several bilateral agreements were signed.

In April 1996 in Beijing Presidents Jiang and Yeltsin signed a series of agreements, envisaging the development of closer co-operation in various fields. Together with their counterparts from Kazakhstan, Kyrgyzstan and Tajikistan, the two Presidents also signed a treaty aimed at reducing tension along their respective borders. Progress on the Sino-Russian border question and on trade matters was made during the Chinese Premier's visit to Moscow in December 1996. A further treaty on military co-operation and border demilitarization was signed by the Presidents of China, Russia, Kazakhstan, Kyrgyzstan and Tajikistan in April 1997, during a visit by President Jiang Zemin to Russia. An agreement signed during President Yeltsin's visit to Beijing in November formally ended the border dispute. In November 1998, in Moscow, representatives from Russia, China and North Korea signed an inter-governmental agreement on the delimitation of their borders along the Tumannaya River. In February 1999 11 agreements on bilateral economic and trade co-operation were signed during a visit to Russia by Premier Zhu Rongji. In June it was announced that a final accord on the demarcation of a common border between the two countries had been agreed.

Vladimir Putin, who succeeded Boris Yeltsin as Russian President in December 1999, visited Beijing in July 2000, and in September of that year NPC Chairman Li Peng visited Russia. In July 2001 Presidents Jiang and Putin signed a new 20-year Sino-Russian 'Good-neighbourly Treaty of Friendship and Co-operation' in Moscow and reaffirmed their opposition to the USA's plans for the NMD system. The Chinese Premier signed several trade agreements during a visit to Russia in September.

Russian Prime Minister Mikhail Kasyanov visited Beijing in August 2002 to discuss strategic issues, and President Putin travelled to China for discussions in December. The two countries issued a joint declaration on various global issues; they also sought to increase bilateral trade and economic co-operation. Hu Jintao visited Russia during his first overseas trip in his capacity as China's President in May 2003. Presidents Hu and Putin discussed the use of Siberian oil resources in China. President Putin's visit to China in October 2004 was dominated by the Chinese Government's wish to reach agreement on the route of a new oil pipeline, which, China hoped, would export Russian oil to Daqing, in north-eastern China. During a visit to Beijing in March 2006 President Putin appeared to favour the Daqing route, rather than a pipeline giving Japan priority.

In August 2005 the Chinese and Russian armed forces conducted joint military exercises for the first time, and 2006 was declared the 'Year of Russia in China'. In November 2006 Russian Prime Minister Mikhail Fradkov paid an official visit to China, where he signed eight agreements to expand bilateral investment, trade and technical co-operation. In particular, the two sides pledged fresh co-operation in the energy sector. President Hu paid an official visit to Russia in March 2007, marking the beginning of the 'Year of China in Russia'. Hu and President Putin signed a major agreement on bilateral trade, and declared their joint commitment to increased co-operation in a number of other fields, including technology and security. The new President of Russia, Dmitrii A. Medvedev, visited China in May 2008, signing an agreement on nuclear co-operation with President Hu. The two countries resolved a 40-year border dispute in mid-2008, when Russia recognized China's sovereignty over all of the island of Yinlong and half of the island of Heixiazi. In February 2009 China and Russia signed an agreement whereby, in exchange for Siberian oil supplies, the China Development Bank was to provide loans totalling US $25,000m. to two Russian companies, Rosneft, the state oil producer, and Transneft, holder of the country's pipeline monopoly. During a visit to Beijing by Putin (now the Russian Prime Minister) in October 2009, trade agreements valued at $3,500m. were signed. The Chinese and Russian Presidents met several times in the course of 2010, and during a visit by Medvedev to Beijing in September the two leaders celebrated the completion of their largest bilateral project, the 999-km oil pipeline between Daqing and the Russian city of Angarsk. They also signed various agreements providing for further co-operation in the field of energy. During a visit to China by Putin in October 2011 it was reported that the two Governments were close to a resolution of differences concerning exports of Russian natural gas to China, in accordance with a major agreement originally signed in 2009: implementation of the agreement, which was to cover a 30-year period, had been delayed by a dispute over pricing.

During the 1990s China steadily consolidated its relations with the former Soviet republics of Central Asia, and in 1996 China, Russia, Kazakhstan, Kyrgyzstan, and Tajikistan established the 'Shanghai Five', which became the Shanghai Co-operation Organization (SCO) at the group's annual meeting in June 2001 (when Uzbekistan became the sixth member). Both China and Russia hoped that the SCO would help to counter US influence in Central Asia.

Other external relations

Following the reversion of Hong Kong to Chinese sovereignty in mid-1997, relations between China and the United Kingdom improved significantly. The first China-EU summit meeting, which was scheduled to become an annual event, took place in London in April, prior to the Asia-Europe Meeting (ASEM). China and the EU committed themselves to greater mutual co-operation in the area of trade and economic relations. The Chinese Premier also had discussions with his British counterpart, Tony Blair, who visited China and Hong Kong in October, declaring his intention to broach the issue of human rights through 'persuasion and dialogue'. In October 1999 Jiang Zemin became the first Chinese head of state to visit the United Kingdom. This visit was part of a six-nation tour, which also included France, Portugal, Morocco, Algeria and Saudi Arabia. However, in the United Kingdom and France President Jiang's visit prompted protests by supporters of human rights. In December, during a China-EU summit meeting in Beijing, the Chinese Government rejected criticism of its human rights record. In October 2000 China concluded bilateral trade agreements with the EU necessary for WTO accession. In May 2001 Beijing hosted an EU delegation, seeking a new comprehensive partnership with China, particularly in the area of commerce. The fourth annual China-EU summit meeting took place in the Belgian capital of Brussels in early September; discussions encompassed the issue of access by EU companies to China's insurance market, the last obstacle to China's admission to the WTO (which took place in December 2001). In late October Vice-President Hu Jintao embarked upon his first official trip to the EU, visiting the United Kingdom, France, Germany and Spain. Jiang Zemin visited Germany in April 2002. In July 2003 Tony Blair undertook a visit to China, during which he sought to enhance trade links between China and the United Kingdom. In October there were developments towards greater economic co-operation between China and the EU at a China-EU summit meeting in Beijing. A new visa system was agreed to give Chinese tourists easier access to European countries. In January 2004 President Hu Jintao had discussions with French President Jacques Chirac, who expressed his support for China's opposition to a proposed referendum in Taiwan. President Hu's visit to Paris also provoked protests by French government members and human rights activists. Similarly, human rights activists and Tibetan independence groups staged demonstrations during President Hu's official visit to the United Kingdom in November 2005, as part of a trip during which he also visited Germany and Spain.

Premier Wen Jiabao made his first official visit to EU headquarters in Brussels shortly after the expansion of the Union in May 2004. In the same month Wen visited the United Kingdom and had discussions with Tony Blair on various issues, including human rights in the context of reported abuse of prisoners by British soldiers deployed in Iraq, as well as in relation to political developments in Hong Kong and mainland China. The EU continued to resist demands for the removal of a ban on weapons trade with China, which had been in place since 1989. The termination of the WTO's 10-year MFA in January 2005 resulted in a huge increase in the volume of Chinese exports of clothing to the EU, prompting the imposition of new quotas in June; however, these quotas were quickly exceeded, leading to the accumulation of large quantities of Chinese garments in European ports. In September an agreement was reached whereby 50% of the goods held in ports were released and the remaining 50% were to be offset against the quotas for 2006. However, in 2006 a fresh trade dispute arose, this time over the issue of shoe exports. In April the EU announced that it would begin imposing import duties of up to 20% on shoes from China and Viet Nam, which it accused of giving unfair subsidies to their domestic shoe manufacturers. An EU-China summit meeting held in Finland in September resulted in broad agreements to extend co-operation, including the opening of negotiations on a new Partnership and Co-operation Agreement, to replace the original Trade and Co-operation Agreement signed in 1985. In the following month the European Commission adopted a revised policy on China, urging closer engagement. In January 2007, however, the EU reiterated that its conditions for the removal of its weapons embargo on China remained unchanged. A number of European leaders visited China during 2006, including French President Jacques Chirac, German Chancellor Angela Merkel and Italian Prime Minister Romano Prodi. In September Premier Wen Jiabao visited both the United Kingdom and Germany. In September 2007, against China's wishes, Chancellor Merkel met with the Dalai Lama. In October Hu Jia, the Chinese human rights activist, was awarded the Sakharov Prize for Freedom of Thought by the European Parliament, prompting the Chinese Ministry of Foreign Affairs to accuse the body of 'gross interference in China's domestic affairs'.

In late November 2008 the Chinese Government postponed the 11th EU-China summit meeting, scheduled to be held in the French city of Lyon in the following month, citing opposition to a forthcoming meeting between the French President, Nicolas Sarkozy, and the Dalai Lama. In late January 2009 Premier Wen Jiabao embarked on a five-day visit to Europe, where his agenda included discussions on the worsening global financial crisis. Premier Wen visited Switzerland, Germany, Belgium, Spain and the United Kingdom, while notably avoiding France. In April 2010, however, President Sarkozy paid an official visit to China, one of his objectives being to reverse the recent decline in bilateral trade. President Hu Jintao visited France in November, when various bilateral co-operation agreements, encompassing areas such as energy, finance and environmental protection, were signed. In November, during an official visit to Portugal, the Chinese President offered support for the troubled Portuguese economy.

Despite pleas for clemency from the United Kingdom, in December 2009 a British citizen was executed in China following his conviction upon charges of drugs-smuggling. Supporters of Akmal Shaikh claimed that his mental health issues had been disregarded at his trial. During a visit to Beijing in March 2010 the British Secretary of State for Foreign and Commonwealth Affairs, David Miliband, raised with the Chinese leadership the case of Gao Zhisheng (see Human Rights and Media Freedom), as international concern for the lawyer's safety rose. Iran's nuclear programme was among the other issues discussed during Miliband's visit. In November 2010 David Cameron, the British Prime Minister, undertook an official visit to China, at the head of a large delegation that incorporated cabinet ministers and business representatives. Discussions with Chinese leaders included the topics of trade, finance and energy. Cameron was also reported to have raised the issue of imprisoned dissident Liu Xiaobo. In June 2011 a visit to Europe by Wen Jiabao incorporated a visit to the United Kingdom, where agreements were concluded on major investments in China by, among others, a British energy company; Wen rebuked the British Government, however, for its insistence on referring to human rights abuses in China. He then proceeded to Germany, China's largest European trading partner, where, as well as concluding important trade agreements, Wen expressed support for the euro area members in their current economic difficulties, and gave an undertaking that China would be willing to purchase European sovereign debt. In February 2012, during a visit to China by Angela Merkel, Wen stated that China was considering participation in the European Financial Stability Facility, created in 2010 to assist heavily indebted euro area countries.

In early 2012 there were increasing concerns about the circumstances surrounding the death in November 2011 of the British businessman Neil Heywood in Chongqing, which had been officially attributed to excessive alcohol consumption. In February 2012 the British Government formally requested that there be a fresh investigation into the case, and the Chinese authorities confirmed in April that two suspects had been detained on suspicion of murder.

China continued to maintain good relations with various Middle Eastern nations, despite its establishment of diplomatic links with Israel in 1992. China did not support the US-led military action against Iraq in March 2003. Relations with Iran improved, following President Muhammad Khatami's visit to

China in mid-2000. In November 2004 China signed an agreement for the development of an Iranian oilfield. As international concerns over Iran's nuclear programme intensified from 2005, China consistently opposed the imposition of sanctions against the country, one of its principal suppliers of crude petroleum. In March 2011, having abstained from the UN vote on the issue, China expressed its opposition to the multinational military intervention in Libya, following a popular uprising there. In February 2012 China imposed its veto (as did Russia) on a UN Security Council resolution that condemned the recent violent suppression of anti-Government protests in Syria.

Following the conflict between Lebanon and Israel in mid-2006, in September of that year China announced that it was to increase its force in Lebanon to 1,000 peace-keepers, its largest single such deployment since China first began contributing to UN-mandated peace-keeping forces in the 1980s. By 2009 China had become an important contributor of personnel to UN peace-keeping operations. In addition to its deployment in Lebanon, Chinese troops were also serving in the Democratic Republic of the Congo, Liberia and Sudan.

China continued to pursue closer economic relations with African nations, while adhering to the principle of non-interference in other countries' political affairs. The first Forum on China-Africa Co-operation (FOCAC) was held in Beijing in October 2000, when the People's Republic announced its decision to reduce or cancel outstanding debt totalling US $1,200m. During a state visit to China by Nigerian President Olusegun Obasanjo in April 2005 a series of bilateral economic agreements was concluded. In July President Hu Jintao signed a co-operation agreement with Robert Mugabe, President of Zimbabwe, during a visit by the latter to China. In April 2006 President Hu undertook state visits to Morocco, Nigeria and Kenya, his itinerary also including Saudi Arabia. Trade links between China and Africa were further strengthened in November when Beijing hosted the first summit meeting of FOCAC, which was attended by senior representatives from 48 African nations. China pledged to ensure that by 2010 its trade with Africa would more than double to reach $100,000m. China also announced the immediate implementation of various trade and investment agreements, including plans for major projects in Egypt, Nigeria and Zambia. However, many international critics accused China of depleting Africa's mineral resources. Meanwhile, the rapid expansion in Africa's imports from China was increasingly curbing local manufacturing activities. Premier Wen Jiabao visited seven African countries in June 2006 (including Angola, one of China's largest suppliers of petroleum), and in February 2007 President Hu embarked on an eight-nation tour of the continent, with South Africa and Sudan included in his itinerary. In May Liu Guijin was appointed as China's envoy to Africa, specifically to engage in attempts to resolve the issue of the Sudanese province of Darfur, China's support for the Sudanese Government having drawn widespread opprobrium. On his fourth visit to Africa in February 2009, during which China's commitment to regional infrastructural projects was emphasized, President Hu travelled to Mali, Senegal, Tanzania and Mauritius. At the fourth ministerial meeting of FOCAC, convened in Egypt in November, Premier Wen Jiabao committed China to the provision of low-interest loans totalling $10,000m. over a three-year period. Special concessions to the poorest African nations included China's cancellation of their debts and the introduction of a zero-tariff arrangement on nearly all Chinese imports from those countries. In January 2010 China agreed to participate in a multinational coalition of naval forces to combat the increasing incidence of piracy off the coast of Somalia.

South African President Jacob Zuma's official visit to China in August 2010 resulted in the establishment of a comprehensive strategic partnership and the signing in November of various bilateral agreements that included co-operation on energy matters. In addition to the issue of China's increasing acquisitions of mineral commodities (as exemplified in March 2010 by China's agreement with Anglo-Australian mining company Rio Tinto to develop a major iron ore mine in Guinea), another area of controversy was the increasing Chinese encroachment upon local agricultural interests. In Ethiopia, for example, China was purchasing large tracts of land for the purpose of growing crops with the intention of supplying food to the Chinese market, while in Zambia Chinese investors in the poultry industry were reported in early 2011 to have become increasingly active in local retail activities, to the detriment of Zambian chicken farmers.

In June 2011 China received a visit by the President of Sudan, Omar al-Bashir, despite the fact that a warrant had been issued by the International Criminal Court for his arrest on charges of war crimes. In August the Chinese Minister of Foreign Affairs, Yang Jiechi, visited Sudan and the newly independent South Sudan, which together constituted an important source of China's petroleum, offering to mediate between the two in their outstanding differences, particularly concerning petroleum shipments. In January 2012 the new headquarters of the African Union opened in Addis Ababa, Ethiopia, funded entirely by China.

In April 2001 President Jiang visited several Latin American nations, including Argentina, Brazil, Chile, Cuba, Uruguay and Venezuela, attempting to foster economic links. In February 2003 China hosted a visit by the Cuban President, Fidel Castro. There were developments towards close economic co-operation with Brazil in 2004, when in May President Lula da Silva visited Beijing to discuss possibilities for increasing bilateral trade, and President Hu Jintao visited Brazil in November for talks on trade. In July 2006 China concluded a free trade agreement with Chile, with the objective of giving China access to the latter's natural resources, particularly copper; China's first free trade agreement with a Latin American country duly took effect in October. In November 2008 President Hu visited Costa Rica, Cuba and Peru, where he signed trade and investment contracts. In Peru President Hu witnessed the conclusion of discussions on a bilateral free trade agreement. From 2006 China also strengthened its relations with Venezuela, a major supplier of petroleum. President Hugo Chávez undertook a six-day visit to the Chinese capital in August 2006. Venezuela was one of several Latin American countries visited by Vice-President Xi Jinping in February 2009, when various co-operation and investment agreements were signed, including arrangements for a substantial increase of Chinese imports of Venezuelan petroleum. Also in February, in a visit that further emphasized the growth of the region's strategic significance to China, Vice-Premier Hui Liangyu toured several countries of Latin America and the Caribbean; his itinerary encompassed Argentina and Ecuador. Much of China's investment funding continued to be channelled to Latin America; the region reportedly received 50% of all Chinese overseas investment in the two years 2008–09. In March 2010 CNOOC agreed to purchase a 50% stake in an Argentinian energy company, which also had interests in Bolivia and Chile. During a visit to Brazil in April 2010 President Hu signed various bilateral trade accords; agreement was also reached on the construction by China of a steel plant in Brazil. In May 2011 negotiations took place on the diversification of Brazil's exports to China: Brazil requested that more processed agricultural goods should be included, rather than raw materials.

CONSTITUTION AND GOVERNMENT

China is a unitary state. Directly under the Central Government there are 22 provinces, five autonomous regions, including Xizang (Tibet), and four municipalities (Beijing, Chongqing, Shanghai and Tianjin). The highest organ of state power is the National People's Congress (NPC). In March 2008 the first session of the 11th NPC was attended by 2,967 deputies, indirectly elected for five years by the people's congresses of the provinces, autonomous regions, municipalities directly under the Central Government, and the People's Liberation Army. The NPC elects a Standing Committee to be its permanent organ. The current Constitution, adopted by the NPC in December 1982 and subsequently amended, was China's fourth since 1949. It restored the office of head of state (President of the Republic). Executive power is exercised by the State Council (Cabinet), comprising the Premier, Vice-Premiers and other ministers heading ministries and commissions. The State Council is appointed by, and accountable to, the NPC.

Political power is held by the Chinese Communist Party (CCP). The CCP's highest authority is the Party Congress, which is convened every five years. In October 2007 the CCP's 17th National Congress elected a Central Committee of 204 full members and 167 alternate members. To direct policy, the Central Committee elected a 25-member Politburo. The incoming Standing Committee of the Politburo comprised nine members.

Provincial people's congresses are the local organs of state power. Provincial people's governments are responsible for local affairs.

REGIONAL AND INTERNATIONAL CO-OPERATION

China is a member of the Asian Development Bank (ADB, see p. 210) and of Asia-Pacific Economic Cooperation (APEC, see p. 204). In 1996 the secretariat of the Tumen River Economic Development Area (TREDA) was established in Beijing by the Governments of China, North and South Korea, Mongolia and Russia. China became an observer member of the South Asian Association for Regional Co-operation (SAARC, see p. 420) in 2005. In 2001 China was a founder member of the Shanghai Co-operation Organization (SCO—formerly known as the 'Shanghai Five'). China is also a member of the UN's Economic and Social Commission for Asia and the Pacific (ESCAP, see p. 40).

China was admitted to the UN in place of the 'Republic of China' in 1971. It is a permanent member of the UN Security Council. The country became a full member of the World Trade Organization (WTO, see p. 433) in 2001. China is also a member of the Association of Tin Producing Countries (ATPC) and of the Bank for International Settlements (BIS, see p. 224). China participates in the Group of 20 (G20, see p. 454) major industrialized and systemically important emerging market nations and in the Group of 77 (G77, see p. 450) developing countries.

ECONOMIC AFFAIRS

In 2010, according to estimates by the World Bank, China's gross national income (GNI), measured at average 2008–10 prices, was US $5,700,018m., equivalent to some $4,260 per head (or $7,570 on an international purchasing-power parity basis). During 2001–10, it was estimated, the population increased at an average annual rate of 0.6%, while gross domestic product (GDP) per head increased, in real terms, by an average annual rate of 10.1%, one of the highest growth rates in the world. Overall GDP increased, in real terms, at an average annual rate of 10.7% in 2001–10. GDP grew by 9.2% in 2011.

Agriculture (including forestry and fishing) contributed 10.1% of GDP in 2010, and in the same year accounted for 36.7% of total employment. China's principal crops are rice (production of which accounted for an estimated 29.3% of the total world harvest in 2010), maize, sweet potatoes, wheat, soybeans, sugar cane, tobacco, cotton and jute. According to the World Bank, agricultural GDP increased at an average annual rate of 4.4%, in real terms, in 2001–10. In comparison with the previous year, the sector grew by 4.5% in 2011.

Industry (including mining, manufacturing, construction and power) contributed 46.8.% of GDP and engaged 28.7% of the employed labour force in 2010. According to the World Bank, industrial GDP increased at an average annual rate of 11.6%, in real terms, in 2001–10. Compared with the previous year, industrial GDP expanded by 10.6% in 2011.

The mining sector accounted for less than 0.9% of total employment in 2002. Output in the sector accounted for some 5.3% of total industrial production in 2002. China has enormous mineral reserves and is the world's largest producer of natural graphite, antimony, tungsten and zinc. Other important minerals include coal, iron ore, molybdenum, tin, lead, mercury, bauxite, phosphate rock, diamonds, gold, manganese, crude petroleum and natural gas. Proven reserves of petroleum at the end of 2010 amounted to 14,800m. barrels, sufficient to sustain production at that year's levels (averaging 4.1m. barrels per day) for nearly 10 years.

According to the World Bank, the manufacturing sector contributed an estimated 32.4% of GDP in 2010. It accounted for 13.0% of total employment in 2002. China is a leading world producer of chemical fertilizers, cement and steel. Textiles, paper and paperboard, and motor vehicles are also important, while the information technology and electronics sectors have expanded extremely rapidly; high- and new-technology products accounted for 28.9% of total exports in 2011. The GDP of the manufacturing sector increased at an average annual rate of 11.1%, in real terms, during 2001–10, according to the World Bank. Growth in the GDP of the manufacturing sector was 9.0% in 2010, compared with the previous year.

The construction sector accounted for 6.7% of GDP in 2010. The sector engaged 4.7% of the working population in 2009. In comparison with the previous year, the construction sector's GDP grew by 12.6% in 2010 and by 10.0% in 2011.

Energy is derived principally from coal (76.5% in 2010); other sources are petroleum (9.8%), hydroelectric, nuclear and wind power (9.4%) and natural gas (4.3%). Although China is a significant oil producer, it is a major importer of crude petroleum. The 22,500-MW Three Gorges Dam hydroelectric power project on the River Yangtze (Changjiang), the world's largest hydro-electric complex, was expected to be fully operational by mid-2012; its 32 generators will have a potential annual output of 84,700m. kWh, or about 1.8% of national electric energy production at 2011 levels (in comparison with the original projection of 10%, owing to the unexpectedly rapid rise in total energy demand). The rapid development from the mid-2000s of China's nuclear power industry was temporarily affected by the accident in March 2011 at the Fukushima nuclear power plant, Japan, after which approvals for any further reactors in China were suspended. However, later that year the country's commitment to a greater reliance on nuclear energy was reaffirmed; at December 2011 26 new reactors were under construction, while a further 51 were planned. Imports of mineral fuels comprised 13.4% of the cost of total merchandise imports in 2009.

Services contributed 43.1% of GDP in 2010 and in that year engaged 34.6% of the employed labour force. Along with retail and wholesale trade, the tourism sector, especially domestic travel, has expanded rapidly. Receipts from international tourism were estimated to have increased by 5.8% compared with the previous year to reach US $48,500m. in 2011, while revenue from domestic tourism increased by 23.6% in 2011 to total an estimated 1,930.6m. yuan. In 2011 China hosted a total of 135.4m. tourists, of whom 27.1m. were classified as foreign visitors, the remainder being travellers from Hong Kong, Macao and Taiwan. During 2001–10, according to the World Bank, the GDP of the services sector increased at an average annual rate of 11.2% in real terms. Compared with the previous year, growth in the GDP of the services sector was 8.9% in 2011.

In 2010 China recorded a trade surplus of US $254,180m., and there was a surplus of $305,374m. on the current account of the balance of payments. In 2011 the principal source of imports was Japan (which provided 10.2% of total imports). Other important suppliers were the Republic of Korea (South Korea—8.6%), Taiwan (6.6%), and the USA (6.4%). The principal markets for exports in that year were the USA (18.6% of total exports), Hong Kong (15.4%) and Japan (8.5%). Most of the goods exported to Hong Kong are subsequently re-exported. The principal imports in 2011 were crude petroleum (accounting for 11.3% of total imports), iron ore (6.4%), plastics in primary form, copper and copper alloys, and refined petroleum products. The principal exports in that year were automatic data processing machines and components (accounting for 9.3% of total exports), clothing and accessories (8.1%), textiles (5.0%), mobile and car telephones and rolled steel.

In 2012 China's budget deficit was forecast at 800,000m. yuan (in comparison with 900,000m. yuan in 2011), equivalent to 1.5% of GDP. In 2011 expenditure totalled 10,374,000m. yuan was projected, with total revenue of 4,736,000,000 yuan (including 150,000m. yuan from the stabilization fund) being forecast. China's general government gross debt was 13,463,64m. yuan in 2010, equivalent to 33.8% of GDP. China's total external debt at the end of 2009 at US $428,442m., of which US $93,125m. was public and publicly guaranteed debt. In that year, the cost of servicing long-term public and publicly guaranteed debt and repayments to the IMF was equivalent to 0.6% of the value of exports of goods, services and income (excluding workers' remittances). China's foreign exchange reserves totalled US $3,181,100m. at the end of 2011. Consumer prices increased at an annual rate of 0.3% during 2001–10. Consumer prices rose by 5.4% in 2011. The official rate of urban unemployment stood at 4.1% at the end of 2011. However, as these statistics did not include workers who had been made redundant through reform of state-owned enterprises, or unemployed persons from rural areas who had migrated to urban areas in search of work, many observers estimated the urban unemployment rate to be at least 10%. In 2011 the total number of migrant workers was 252.8m.

Following the introduction in 1978 of the 'open door' policy of reform, which reduced state control of agriculture and industry and permitted foreign investment in Chinese enterprises (particularly through the newly established Special Economic Zones), the Chinese economy became one of the fastest-growing in the world, and by 2010 it had surpassed Japan to become the world's second largest economy (after the USA), and a major overseas investor. China's foreign exchange reserves were estimated at US $3,200,000m. at the beginning of 2012, by far the largest in the world: of this a major proportion was invested in US government bonds, making China the USA's principal official creditor. The value of the Chinese currency remained a contentious issue. In 2011 China continued to repudiate suggestions that its currency was undervalued and that the country's exporters were thus being afforded an unfair advantage, and resisted pressure, notably from the USA and the European Union, to implement currency reform. During 2010 and 2011 the Government undertook measures to counter speculative investment in the property market, fearing the consequences for the national economy of 'overheating' in the sector and a drastic fall in property prices. The Twelfth Five-Year Plan (2011–15), confirmed in March 2011, envisaged a period of more sustainable growth, with average annual GDP expansion being projected at 7.0%. The 2011–15 Plan accorded priority to the achievement of a more equitable distribution of China's wealth, the raising of standards of living, increased domestic consumption and improvements in social services. Energy efficiency and the reduction of carbon emissions were also addressed, and expenditure of 3,000,000m. yuan (double the allocation of 2006–10) for the purposes of environmental protection was envisaged. Inflationary pressures, particularly in relation to the costs of foodstuffs, increased in early 2011, and in March the Chinese Government acknowledged that the control of inflation had become its most important economic priority: to this end the People's Bank of China, the central bank, raised interest rates five times between October 2010 and the end of 2011. Consumer price increases reached 6.5% in July 2011, but the rate of increase slowed thereafter. During 2011 measures to reduce disparity in incomes included increasing the statutory minimum wage, raising the level of income above which income tax was to be paid, and, in November, increasing to $1 per day the level of income designated as 'poverty', below which rural citizens were entitled to various benefits. China's GDP expanded by 9.2% in 2011, but the Government reduced its target for growth to 7.5% in 2012, announcing that it aimed to rebalance the economy by focusing on domestic consumption rather than investment and exports. The IMF forecast growth of 9.2% in 2012, warning, however, that economic difficulties in the European Union (China's principal export market) could substantially reduce this.

PUBLIC HOLIDAYS

2013: 1 January (Solar New Year), 10–12 February* (Lunar New Year), 8 March (International Women's Day), 4 April (Qingming Festival), 1 May (Labour Day), 12 June (Dragon Boat Festival), 1 August (Army Day), 19 September (Mid-Autumn Festival), 1–3 October (National Days).

* From the first to the fourth day of the first moon of the lunar calendar.

Various individual regional holidays are also observed.

Statistical Survey

Source (unless otherwise stated): National Bureau of Statistics of China, 38 Yuetan Nan Jie, Sanlihe, Beijing 100826; tel. (10) 68515074; fax (10) 68515078; e-mail service@stats.gov.cn; internet www.stats.gov.cn/english/.

Note: Wherever possible, figures in this Survey exclude Taiwan. In the case of unofficial estimates for China, it is not always clear if Taiwan is included or excluded. Where a Taiwan component is known, either it has been deducted from the all-China figure or its inclusion is noted. Figures for the Hong Kong Special Administrative Region (SAR) and for the Macao SAR are listed separately. Transactions between the SARs and the rest of the People's Republic continue to be treated as external transactions.

Area and Population

AREA, POPULATION AND DENSITY

Area (sq km)	9,572,900*
Population (census results)	
1 November 2000	1,242,612,226
1 November 2010 (preliminary)	
Males	686,852,572
Females	652,872,280
Total	1,339,724,852
Population (official estimate at 31 December)†	
2011	1,347,350,000
Density (per sq km) at 31 December 2011	140.7

* 3,696,100 sq miles.

† Figure rounded to the nearest 10,000 persons.

Note: Data for population censuses do not include adjustment for under-enumeration (estimated at 0.12% for 2010); adjusted total for 2000 was 1,265,830,000.

POPULATION BY AGE AND SEX

('000, UN estimates at mid-2012)

	Males	Females	Total
0–14	138,673	114,683	253,355
15–64	509,130	475,045	984,175
65 and over	55,000	61,071	116,071
Total	702,802	650,798	1,353,601

Note: Totals may not be equal to the sum of components, owing to rounding.

Source: UN, *World Population Prospects: The 2010 Revision*.

Population by Age (at 2010 census, preliminary): *0–14* 222,459,737; *15–64* 939,616,410; *65 and over* 177,648,705; *Total* 1,339,724,852.

PRINCIPAL ETHNIC GROUPS

(at census of 1 November 2000)

	Number	%
Han (Chinese)	1,137,386,112	91.53
Zhuang	16,178,811	1.30
Manchu	10,682,262	0.86
Hui	9,816,805	0.79
Miao	8,940,116	0.72
Uygur (Uighur)	8,399,393	0.68
Tujia	8,028,133	0.65
Yi	7,762,272	0.63
Mongolian	5,813,947	0.47
Tibetan	5,416,021	0.44
Bouyei	2,971,460	0.24
Dong	2,960,293	0.24
Yao	2,637,421	0.21
Korean	1,923,842	0.16
Bai	1,858,063	0.15
Hani	1,439,673	0.12
Kazakh	1,250,458	0.10
Li	1,247,814	0.10
Dai	1,158,989	0.09
She	709,592	0.06
Lisu	634,912	0.05
Gelao	579,357	0.05
Dongxiang	513,805	0.04
Others	3,568,237	0.29
Unknown	734,438	0.06
Total	1,242,612,226	100.00

2010 census (preliminary): Han (Chinese) 1,225,932,641 (91.51% of total).

ADMINISTRATIVE DIVISIONS
(previous or other spellings given in brackets)

	Area ('000 sq km)	Population at 1 November 2010 (preliminary) Total	Density (per sq km)	Capital of province or region	Estimated population ('000) at mid-2000*
Provinces					
Sichuan (Szechwan)	487.0	80,418,200	165.1	Chengdu (Chengtu)	3,294
Henan (Honan)	167.0	94,023,567	563.0	Zhengzhou (Chengchow)	2,070
Shandong (Shantung)	153.3	95,793,065	624.9	Jinan (Tsinan)	2,568
Jiangsu (Kiangsu)	102.6	78,659,903	766.7	Nanjing (Nanking)	2,740
Guangdong (Kwangtung)	197.1	104,303,132	529.2	Guangzhou (Canton)	3,893
Hebei (Hopei)	202.7	71,854,202	354.5	Shijiazhuang (Shihkiachwang)	1,603
Hunan (Hunan)	210.5	65,683,722	312.0	Changsha (Changsha)	1,775
Anhui (Anhwei)	139.9	59,500,510	425.3	Hefei (Hofei)	1,242
Hubei (Hupeh)	187.5	57,237,740	305.3	Wuhan (Wuhan)	5,169
Zhejiang (Chekiang)	101.8	54,426,891	534.6	Hangzhou (Hangchow)	1,780
Liaoning (Liaoning)	151.0	43,746,323	289.7	Shenyang (Shenyang)	4,828
Jiangxi (Kiangsi)	164.8	44,567,475	270.4	Nanchang (Nanchang)	1,722
Yunnan (Yunnan)	436.2	45,966,239	105.4	Kunming (Kunming)	1,701
Heilongjiang (Heilungkiang)	463.6	38,312,224	82.6	Harbin (Harbin)	2,928
Guizhou (Kweichow)	174.0	34,746,468	199.7	Guiyang (Kweiyang)	2,533
Shaanxi (Shensi)	195.8	37,327,378	190.6	Xian (Sian)	3,123
Fujian (Fukien)	123.1	36,894,216†	299.7	Fuzhou (Foochow)	1,397
Shanxi (Shansi)	157.1	35,712,111	227.3	Taiyuan (Taiyuan)	2,415
Jilin (Kirin)	187.0	27,462,297	146.9	Changchun (Changchun)	3,093
Gansu (Kansu)	366.5	25,575,254	69.8	Lanzhou (Lanchow)	1,730
Hainan	34.3	8,671,518	252.8	Haikou	438‡
Qinghai (Tsinghai)	721.0	5,626,722	7.8	Xining (Hsining)	692
Autonomous regions					
Guangxi Zhuang (Kwangsi Chuang)	220.4	46,026,629	208.8	Nanning (Nanning)	1,311
Nei Monggol (Inner Mongolia)	1,177.5	24,706,321	21.0	Hohhot (Huhehot)	978
Xinjiang Uygur (Sinkiang Uighur)	1,646.9	21,813,334	13.2	Urumqi (Urumchi, Wulumuqi)	1,415
Ningxia Hui (Ninghsia Hui)	66.4	6,301,350	94.9	Yinchuan (Yinchuen)	592
Tibet (Xizang)	1,221.6	3,002,166	2.5	Lhasa (Lhasa)	134
Municipalities					
Shanghai	6.2	23,019,148	3,712.8	—	12,887
Beijing (Peking)	16.8	19,612,368	1,167.4	—	10,839
Tianjin (Tientsin)	11.3	12,938,224	1,145.0	—	9,156
Chongqing (Chungking)	82.0	28,846,170	351.8	—	4,900
Total	9,572.9	1,339,724,852§	139.9		

* UN estimates, excluding population in counties under cities' administration.
† Excluding islands administered by Taiwan, mainly Jinmen (Quemoy) and Mazu (Matsu), with 49,050 inhabitants according to figures released by the Taiwan authorities at the end of March 1990.
‡ December 1998 figure.
§ Including 2,300,000 military personnel and 4,649,985 persons with unregistered households.

PRINCIPAL TOWNS
(incl. suburbs, UN estimates, population at mid-2010)

Shanghai (Shang-hai)	16,575,110	Wenzhou	2,658,536
Beijing (Pei-ching or Peking, the capital)	12,385,263	Shijiazhuang (Shih-chia-chuang or Shihkiachwang)	2,486,936
Chongqing (Ch'ung-ch'ing or Chungking)	9,401,170	Zibo	2,455,566
Shenzhen	9,005,283	Changsha (Chang-sha)	2,414,920
Guangzhou (Kuang-chou or Canton)	8,883,865	Hefei	2,403,907
Tianjin (T'ien-chin or Tientsin)	7,884,473	Urumqi (Wulumuqi)	2,398,154
Wuhan (Wu-han or Hankow)	7,681,099	Suzhou	2,398,024
Dongguan	5,346,652	Lanzhou (Lan-chou or Lanchow)	2,284,587
Shenyang (Shen-yang or Mukden)	5,165,771	Ningbo	2,216,771
Chengdu (Chengtu)	4,960,893	Xiamen	2,206,840
Xian (Hsi-an or Sian)	4,746,755	Guiyang	2,153,908
Nanjing (Nan-ching or Nanking)	4,518,826	Xuzhou	2,141,789
Harbin (Ha-erh-pin)	4,251,063	Nanning	2,095,872
Hangzhou (Hang-chou or Hangchow)	3,860,094	Baotou	1,931,736
Changchun (Ch'ang-ch'un)	3,596,748	Jilin	1,888,374
Qingdao (Ch'ing-tao or Tsingtao)	3,323,062	Tangshan	1,870,384
Dalian (Ta-lien or Dairen)	3,305,864	Zaozhuang	1,175,057
Jinan (Chi-nan or Tsinan)	3,237,414	Anshan	1,662,528
Taiyuan (T'ai-yüan)	3,153,686	Hohhot	1,588,622
Kunming (K'un-ming)	3,115,793	Luoyang	1,539,243
Zhengzhou (Cheng-chou or Chengchow)	2,965,730	Yantai	1,526,309
Fuzhou	2,786,585	Linyi	1,426,549
Nanchang (Nan-ch'ang)	2,701,478	Datong	1,251,087
Wuxi	2,681,870		

Note: Wade-Giles or other spellings are given in parentheses.

Source: UN, *World Urbanization Prospects: The 2009 Revision*.

BIRTHS AND DEATHS
(sample surveys)

	2009	2010	2011
Birth rate (per 1,000)	11.95	11.90	11.93
Death rate (per 1,000)	7.08	7.11	7.14

2011 (rounded data): Births 16,040,000; Deaths 9,600,000.

Marriages (number registered, rounded data): 10,932,000 in 2008; 1,207,500 in 2009; 1,236,100 in 2010.

Life expectancy (years at birth, WHO estimates): 74 (males 72; females 76) in 2009 (Source: WHO, *World Health Statistics*).

EMPLOYMENT*
('000 persons at 31 December, official estimates)

	2000	2001	2002
Agriculture, forestry and fishing	333,550	329,740	324,870
Mining	5,970	5,610	5,580
Manufacturing	80,430	80,830	83,070
Electricity, gas and water	2,840	2,880	2,900
Construction	35,520	36,690	38,930
Geological prospecting and water conservancy	1,100	1,050	980
Transport, storage and communications	20,290	20,370	20,840
Wholesale and retail trade and catering	46,860	47,370	49,690
Banking and insurance	3,270	3,360	3,400
Real estate	1,000	1,070	1,180
Social services	9,210	9,760	10,940
Health care, sports and social welfare	4,880	4,930	4,930
Education, culture, art, radio, film and television broadcasting	15,650	15,680	15,650
Scientific research and polytechnic services	1,740	1,650	1,630
Government agencies, etc.	11,040	11,010	10,750
Others	56,430	58,520	62,450
Total	629,780	630,520	637,790

* In addition to employment statistics, sample surveys of the economically active population are conducted. On the basis of these surveys, the number of employed persons ('000 at 31 December) was: 755,640 (agriculture, etc. 299,230, industry 205,530, services 250,870) in 2008; 758,280 (agriculture, etc. 288,900, industry 210,800, services 258,570) in 2009; 761,050 (agriculture, etc. 279,310, industry 218,420, services 263,320) in 2010; 764,200 in 2011.

Health and Welfare

KEY INDICATORS

Total fertility rate (children per woman, 2009)	1.8
Under-5 mortality rate (per 1,000 live births, 2009)	19
HIV/AIDS (% of persons aged 15–49, 2009)	0.1
Physicians (per 1,000 head, 2003)	1.4
Hospital beds (per 1,000 head, 2006)	2.2
Health expenditure (2008): US $ per head (PPP)	265
Health expenditure (2008): % of GDP	4.3
Health expenditure (2008): public (% of total)	47.3
Access to water (% of persons, 2008)	89
Access to sanitation (% of persons, 2008)	55
Total carbon dioxide emissions ('000 metric tons, 2007)	6,533,018.3
Carbon dioxide emissions per head (metric tons, 2007)	5.0
Human Development Index (2011): ranking	101
Human Development Index (2011): value	0.687

For sources and definitions, see explanatory note on p. vi.

Agriculture

(FAO data are assumed to include Hong Kong, Macao and Taiwan; may include official, semi-official or estimated data)

PRINCIPAL CROPS
('000 metric tons)

	2008	2009	2010
Wheat	112,463	115,115	115,180
Rice, paddy	193,284	196,681	197,221
Barley	2,823	2,318	2,520*
Maize	166,035	164,108	177,549
Rye†	650	630	650
Oats†	600	580	600
Millet	1,287	1,226	1,260*
Sorghum	1,840	1,677	1,726*
Buckwheat†	600	570	590
Triticale (wheat-rye hybrid)†	383	350	270
Potatoes	70,840	73,282	74,785*
Sweet potatoes	78,443	76,773	81,176*
Cassava (Manioc)†	4,409	4,506	4,684

—*continued*	2008	2009	2010
Taro (Cocoyam)†	1,737	1,693	1,754
Sugar cane	124,918	116,251	111,454
Sugar beet	10,044	7,179	9,296
Beans, dry*	1,708	1,489	1,540
Broad beans, horse beans, dry*	1,800	1,650	1,700
Peas, dry*	1,100	960	991
Chestnuts†	1,450	1,550	1,620
Walnuts, with shell	829	979	1,061†
Soybeans (Soya beans)	15,545	14,981	15,083
Groundnuts, with shell	14,341	14,765	15,709
Coconuts	596	310†	309†
Oil palm fruit†	668	670	670
Sunflower seed	1,792	1,956	1,710*
Rapeseed	12,102	13,657	13,082
Sesame seed	586	623	588
Linseed	350	318	350†
Cabbages and other brassicas	30,918	30,215	25,218†
Asparagus†	6,353	6,502	6,969
Lettuce and chicory†	12,505	12,855	12,575
Spinach	16,640	17,550	16,025†
Tomatoes	39,939	45,366	41,865†
Cauliflowers and broccoli†	8,268	8,427	7,545
Pumpkins, squash and gourds†	6,360	6,507	6,141
Cucumbers and gherkins	42,241	44,250	40,710†
Aubergines (Eggplants)	23,748	25,913	24,504†
Chillies and peppers, green†	14,274	14,520	13,186
Onions and shallots, green†	837	887	838
Onions, dry†	20,823	21,047	20,497
Garlic	18,357	17,968	13,674
Beans, green	14,470	14,688	13,036
Peas, green	9,361	9,599	8,983†
Carrots and turnips	14,859	15,168	15,904†
Mushrooms and truffles	4,711	4,681	4,182†
Watermelons	63,025	65,002	56,650†
Cantaloupes and other melons	16068	12,225	11,333†
Grapes	7,236	8,039	8,654
Apples	29,851	31,684	33,267
Pears	13,676	14,416	15,221
Peaches and nectarines	9,564	10,170	10,721†
Plums and sloes†	5,223	5,373	5,664
Oranges	4,191	4,865	5,040*
Tangerines, mandarins, clementines and satsumas	8,948	9,746	10,121*
Lemons and limes*	919	1,014	1,051
Grapefruit and pomelos	2,606	2,768	2,869*
Guavas, mangoes and mangosteens†	3,977	4,140	4,366
Pineapples	1,386	1,477	1,519†
Persimmons	2,745	2,871	3,027†
Bananas	8,043	9,006	9,849
Tea	1,275	1,376	1,467
Chillies and peppers, dry†	252	260	254
Ginger†	329	331	334
Other spices†	77	86	82
Tobacco, unmanufactured	2,840	3,068	3,006
Jute*	47	44	40
Natural rubber	548	619	691

* Unofficial figure(s).
† FAO estimate(s).

Aggregate production ('000 metric tons, may include official, semi-official or estimated data): Total cereals 479,978.1 in 2008, 483,267.5 in 2009, 497,579.5 in 2010; Total vegetable fibres 8,142.1 in 2008, 6,804.7 in 2009, 6,330.3 in 2010; Total treenuts 2,472.6 in 2008, 2,738.0 in 2009, 2,906.4 in 2010; Total oilcrops (primary) 16,293.4 in 2008, 16,648.6 in 2009, 16,483.4 in 2010; Total pulses 4,895.9 in 2008, 4,331.1 in 2009, 4,471.5 in 2010; Total roots and tubers 155,445.5 in 2008, 156,271.4 in 2009, 162,417.8 in 2010; Total vegetables (incl. melons) 512,000.4 in 2008, 522,650.9 in 2009, 473,094.7 in 2010; Total fruits (excl. melons) 107,802.9 in 2008, 115,876.2 in 2009, 122,178.4 in 2010.

Source: FAO.

LIVESTOCK
('000 head at 31 December)

	2008	2009	2010
Horses	7,030	6,823	6,787
Asses	6,891	6,731	6,484
Cattle*	82,815	82,625	83,797
Buffaloes*	23,272	23,271	23,602
Camels	242	240	240†
Pigs	446,656	469,481	476,237
Sheep	136,436	128,557	134,021
Goats	143,595	152,499	150,708
Chickens	4,355,399*	4,502,198†	4,802,670†
Ducks	741,250*	769,427†	789,569†
Geese and guinea fowls	302,318*	316,990†	321,900†

* Unofficial figure(s).
† FAO estimate.

Source: FAO.

LIVESTOCK PRODUCTS
('000 metric tons)

	2008	2009	2010
Cattle meat*	5,841	6,061	6,236
Buffalo meat*	306	309	310
Sheep meat*	1,978	2,044	2,070
Goat meat*	1,828	1,853	1,873
Pig meat	47,190	49,874	51,720
Horse meat†	170	198	202
Rabbit meat	587	663*	669*
Chicken meat*	11,304	11,443	11,853
Duck meat*	2,504	2,644	2,736
Goose and guinea fowl meat*	2,185	2,326	2,407
Other meat†	688	704	722
Cows' milk	35,874	35,510	36,023
Buffaloes' milk†	2,950	3,000	3,100
Sheep's milk	1,096	1,589	1,724
Goats' milk†	266	272	278
Hen eggs	23,292	23,634	23,827*
Other poultry eggs	4,082	4,139	4,174*
Honey	407	407	398†
Wool, greasy	368	364	387

* Unofficial figure(s).
† FAO estimate(s).

Source: FAO.

Forestry

ROUNDWOOD REMOVALS
('000 cubic metres, excl. bark)

	2008	2009	2010
Sawlogs, veneer logs and logs for sleepers	57,249	57,249	58,920
Pulpwood	5,134	4,839	5,048
Other industrial wood	38,460	38,460	38,460
Fuel wood*	196,028	192,390	188,823
Total	296,871	292,939	291,251

* FAO estimates.

Source: FAO.

Timber production (official figures, '000 cubic metres): 69,380 in 2009; 72,830 in 2010; 72,720 in 2011.

SAWNWOOD PRODUCTION
('000 cubic metres, incl. railway sleepers)

	2008	2009	2010
Coniferous (softwood)	11,970	13,603	14,970
Broadleaved (hardwood)	16,915	19,180	22,715
Total	28,885	32,783	36,685

Source: FAO.

Fishing

('000 metric tons, live weight)

	2007	2008	2009
Capture	14,659.0	14,791.2	14,919.6
Freshwater fishes	1,574.0	1,615.3	1,526.3
Aquaculture*	31,415.1	32,731.4	34,779.9
Common carp	2,228.6	2,350.7	2,462.3
Crucian carp	1,937.1	1,955.5	2,055.5
Bighead carp	2,135.4	2,290.2	2,434.6
Grass carp (White amur)	3,556.0	3,707.1	4,081.5
Silver carp	3,075.6	3,193.3	3,484.4
Pacific cupped oyster	3,508.9	3,354.4	3,503.8
Japanese carpet shell	2,957.3	3,058.1	3,192.5
Total catch*	46,074.2	47,522.5	49,699.5

* FAO estimates.

Note: Figures exclude aquatic plants ('000 metric tons, wet weight): 10,081.2 (capture 328.6, aquaculture 9,752.6) in 2007; 10,299.9 (capture 366.1, aquaculture 9,933.8) in 2008; 10,775.5 (capture 276.2, aquaculture 10,499.3) in 2009.

Source: FAO.

Aquatic products (official figures, '000 metric tons): 47,475 (marine 25,509, freshwater 21,966) in 2007; 48,956 (marine 25,983, freshwater 22,973) in 2008; 51,164 (marine 26,816, freshwater 24,348) in 2009. The totals include artificially cultured products ('000 metric tons): 32,783 (marine 13,073, freshwater 19,710) in 2007; 34,128 (marine 13,403, freshwater 20,725) in 2008; 36,217 (marine 14,052, freshwater 22,165) in 2009. Figures include aquatic plants on a dry-weight basis ('000 metric tons): 1,388 in 2007; 1,423 in 2008; 1,484 in 2009. Freshwater plants are not included.

Mining

('000 metric tons unless otherwise indicated)

	2007	2008	2009
Coal*	2,526,000	2,802,000	2,973,000
Crude petroleum*	186,318	190,431	189,490
Natural gas (million cu m)*	69,240	80,299	85,269
Iron ore: gross weight	707,000	824,000	880,000
Copper ore†	928	940	970
Nickel ore (metric tons)†	67,000	72,000	81,000
Bauxite	30,000	35,000	40,000
Lead ore†	1,410	1,550	1,600
Zinc ore†	3,040	3,340	3,400
Tin concentrates (metric tons)†	149,000	140,000	135,000
Manganese ore†	2,000	2,200	2,400
Tungsten concentrates (metric tons)†	41,000	50,000	51,000
Molybdenum ore (metric tons)†	67,700	81,000	93,500
Vanadium (metric tons)†	45,200	46,000	52,000
Antimony ore (metric tons)†	147,000	158,000	168,000
Cobalt ore (metric tons)†	6,100	6,630	6,000
Mercury (metric tons)†	800	1,300	1,400
Silver (metric tons)†	2,700	2,800	2,900
Uranium (metric tons)†‡	712	769	750
Gold (metric tons)†	275	285	320
Magnesite	14,000	15,600	15,000
Phosphate rock§	15,100	15,200	18,000
Potash‖	2,600	2,750	3,000
Native sulphur	960	960	1,000
Fluorspar	3,200	3,250	3,200
Barite (Barytes)	4,400	4,600	3,000
Salt (unrefined)*	61,670	66,644	66,628
Gypsum (crude)	4,800	4,600	4,500
Graphite (natural)	800	800	780
Asbestos	390	380	380
Talc and related materials	2,000	2,200	2,300

* Official figures. Figures for coal include brown coal and waste. Figures for petroleum include oil from shale and coal. Figures for natural gas refer to gross volume of output.
† Figures refer to the metal content of ores, concentrates or (in the case of vanadium) slag.
‡ Data are estimates from the World Nuclear Association (London, United Kingdom).
§ Figures refer to phosphorous oxide (P_2O_5) content.
‖ Potassium oxide (K_2O) content of potash salts mined.

2010: Coal 3,235,000; Crude petroleum 203,014; Natural gas (million cu m) 94,848; Salt (unrefined) 70,378; Uranium (metric tons) 827. Note: All relevant table footnotes apply.

Source: mainly US Geological Survey.

Industry

SELECTED PRODUCTS

Unofficial Figures

('000 metric tons unless otherwise indicated)*

	2006	2007	2008
Plywood ('000 cu m)†‡	28,103	36,431	36,224
Mechanical wood pulp†‡§	790	907	1,005
Chemical and semi-chemical wood pulp†‡§	4,840	5,513	6,085
Other fibre pulp†‡	12,900	13,020	12,970
Sulphur§‖¶(a)	3,000	3,300	3,350
Sulphur§‖¶(b)	3,810	4,200	4,300
Kerosene	9,755	11,533	11,589
Residual fuel oil	17,847	19,672	17,374
Paraffin wax	2,928	3,037	2,990
Petroleum coke	9,899	10,267	10,108
Petroleum bitumen (asphalt)	10,090	10,465	10,303
Liquefied petroleum gas	17,453	19,447	19,148
Refined aluminium (primary and secondary)‖	11,700	15,400	15,900
Refined copper (primary and secondary)‖	3,000	3,600	3,900
Refined lead (primary and secondary)‖	2,720	2,790	3,200
Tin (unwrought, Sn content)‖	132	149	110
Refined zinc (primary and secondary)‖	3,170	3,740	4,000

* Figures include Hong Kong and Macao SARs, but exclude Taiwan, except where otherwise specified.

† Data from FAO.

‡ Including Taiwan.

§ Provisional or estimated figure(s).

‖ Data from the US Geological Survey.

¶ Figures refer to (a) sulphur recovered as a by-product in the purification of coal-gas, in petroleum refineries, gas plants and from copper, lead and zinc sulphide ores; and (b) the sulphur content of iron and copper pyrites, including pyrite concentrates obtained from copper, lead and zinc ores.

Lubricating oils: 5,326,000 metric tons in 2004.

Source: mainly UN Industrial Commodity Statistics Database.

2009 ('000 metric tons unless otherwise indicated): Plywood ('000 cu m) 45,327; Mechanical wood pulp 830 (estimate); Chemical and semi-chemical wood pulp 5,074 (estimate); Other fibre pulp 11,748; Refined aluminium (primary and secondary) 16,000; Refined copper (primary and secondary) 4,150; Refined lead (primary and secondary) 3,710; Tin (unwrought, Sn content) 115; Refined zinc (primary and secondary) 4,360 (Sources: FAO; US Geological Survey).

2010 ('000 metric tons unless otherwise indicated): Plywood ('000 cu m) 45,327 (estimate); Mechanical wood pulp 1,064 (estimate); Chemical and semi-chemical wood pulp 4,640 (estimate); Other fibre pulp 12,970 (Sources: FAO; US Geological Survey).

Official Figures

('000 metric tons unless otherwise indicated)

	2008	2009	2010
Edible vegetable oils	28,050.9	34,334.3	38,785.4
Refined sugar	14,326.1	13,383.5	11,175.9
Beer (million litres)	41,569.1	41,621.8	44,901.6
Cigarettes ('000 million)	2,219.9	2,290.2	2,375.3
Cotton yarn (pure and mixed)	21,709	23,935	27,170
Woven cotton fabrics (pure and mixed—million metres)	72,305	75,342	80,000
Chemical fibres	24,532.9	27,472.8	30,900.0
Paper and paperboard	84,043.0	89,651.3	98,326.3
Rubber tyres ('000)	519,569.4	656,015.6	776,118.3
Sulphuric acid	50,979.5	59,609.1	70,904.7
Caustic soda (Sodium hydroxide)	19,260.1	18,323.7	22,283.9
Soda ash (Sodium carbonate)	18,546.0	19,447.7	20,348.2
Insecticides	2,099.9	2,262.2	n.a.
Nitrogenous fertilizers (a)*	43,924.2	45,533.6	44,586.7
Phosphate fertilizers (b)*	13,855.0	15,131.4	15,329.1
Potash fertilizers (c)*	2,501.3	3,185.1	3,462.8
Synthetic rubber	2,960.3	2,749.1	3,195.2
Plastics	36,802.3	36,299.7	44,325.9
Motor spirit (gasoline)	64,347.5	71,954.8	76,760.4
Distillate fuel oil (diesel oil)	134,583.0	141,270.0	158,881.5
Coke	320,314.8	355,101.4	388,640.3
Cement	1,423,557	1,643,978	1,881,912
Pig-iron	478,244.2	552,834.6	597,333.4
Crude steel	503,057.5	572,182.3	637,229.9
—continued			
Internal combustion engines ('000 kw)	936,439.9	848,925.2	1,315,276.1
Tractors—over 20 horse-power (number)	2,844,000	3,713,000	3,835,000
Railway freight wagons (number)	57,400	42,800	48,100
Road motor vehicles ('000)	9,305.9	13,795.3	18,265.3
Bicycles ('000)	71,851.8	57,576.5	68,194.8
Electric fans ('000)	158,668.5	159,550.5	180,679.2
Mobile telephones ('000 units)	559,451.0	681,933.7	998,273.6
Microcomputers ('000)	158,537	182,151	245,845
Integrated circuits (million)	43,877	41,440	65,250
Colour television receivers ('000)	91,871	98,988	118,300
Cameras ('000)	81,930.3	84,578.1	93,277.0
Electric energy (million kWh)	3,495,761	3,714,651	420,716

* Production in terms of (a) nitrogen; (b) phosphorous oxide; or (c) potassium oxide.

Finance

CURRENCY AND EXCHANGE RATES

Monetary Units

100 fen (cents) = 10 jiao (chiao) = 1 renminbiao (People's Bank Dollar), usually called a yuan.

Sterling, Dollar and Euro Equivalents (30 December 2011)

£1 sterling = 9.742 yuan;
US $1 = 6.301 yuan;
€1 = 8.153 yuan;
100 yuan = £10.3 = $15.87 = €12.27.

Average Exchange Rate (yuan per US $)

2009 6.8314
2010 6.7703
2011 6.4615

Note: Since 1 January 1994 the official rate has been based on the prevailing rate in the interbank market for foreign exchange.

STATE BUDGET

(million yuan)*

Revenue	2008	2009	2010
Taxes	5,422,379	5,952,159	7,321,079
Personal income tax	372,231	394,935	483,727
Company income tax	1,117,563	1,153,684	1,284,354
Tariffs	176,995	148,381	202,783
Business tax	762,639	901,398	1,115,791
Consumption tax	256,827	476,122	607,155
Value-added tax	1,799,694	1,848,122	2,109,348
Non-tax revenue	710,656	899,671	989,072
Total	6,133,035	6,851,830	8,310,151
Central government	3,268,056	3,591,571	4,248,847
Local authorities	2,864,979	3,260,259	4,061,304

Expenditure	2008	2009	2010
General public services	849,083	916,421	933,716
Foreign affairs	24,072	25,094	26,922
External assistance	12,559	13,296	13,614
National defence	417,876	495,110	533,337
Public security	405,976	474,409	551,770
Armed police	66,413	86,629	93,384
Education	901,021	1,043,754	1,255,002
Science and technology	212,921	274,452	325,018
Culture, sport and media	109,574	139,307	154,270
Social safety net and employment effort	680,429	760,668	913,062
Medical and health care	275,704	399,419	480,418
Environment protection	145,136	193,404	244,198
Urban and rural community affairs	420,614	510,766	598,738
Agriculture, forestry and water conservancy	454,401	672,041	812,958
Transportation	235,400	464,759	548,847
Purchase of vehicles	100,274	108,508	154,182
Mining and quarrying, electricity and information technology	—	287,912	348,503
Commerce and services	—	—	141,314
Financial supervision		91,119	63,704

Expenditure—*continued*	2008	2009	2010
Industry, commerce and banking	622,637	—	—
Post-earthquake recovery and reconstruction	79,834	117,445	113,254
Land and weather department	—	—	133,039
Housing security	—	72,597	237,688
Management of grain and oil reserves	—	221,863	117,196
Interest payments on domestic and foreign debt	130,509	149,128	184,424
Other expenditure	294,079	320,325	270,038
Total	6,259,266	7,629,993	8,987,416
Central government	1,334,417	1,525,579	1,598,973
Local authorities	4,924,849	6,104,414	7,388,443

* The data exclude extrabudgetary transactions, totalling (in million yuan): *Revenue:* 661,725 in 2008; 641,465 in 2009; n.a. in 2010. *Expenditure:* 634,636 in 2008; 622,829 in 2009; n.a. in 2010.

Note: Omissions in data for expenditure reflect changes in classification of expenditure type during 2008–2010.

INTERNATIONAL RESERVES

(US $ million at 31 December)

	2008	2009	2010
Gold (national valuation)	4,074	9,815	9,815
IMF special drawing rights	1,199	12,510	12,344
Reserve position in IMF	2,031	4,382	6,397
Foreign exchange*	1,946,030	2,399,152	2,847,338
Total*	1,953,334	2,425,859	2,875,894

* Excluding the Bank of China's holdings of foreign exchange.

Source: IMF, *International Financial Statistics*.

MONEY SUPPLY

(million yuan at 31 December)*

	2008	2009	2010
Currency outside banking institutions	3,421,900	3,824,700	4,462,820
Demand deposits at banking institutions	13,199,820	18,319,880	22,199,340
Total money (incl. others)	16,621,710	22,144,580	26,662,150

* Figures are rounded to the nearest 10 million yuan.

Source: IMF, *International Financial Statistics*.

COST OF LIVING

(General Consumer Price Index; base: previous year = 100)

	2008	2009	2010
Food	114.3	100.7	107.2
Clothing	98.5	98.0	99.0
Housing*	102.8	100.2	104.5
All items (incl. others)	105.9	99.3	103.3

* Including water, electricity and fuels.

NATIONAL ACCOUNTS

('000 million yuan at current prices)

Expenditure on the Gross Domestic Product

	2008	2009	2010
Government final consumption expenditure	4,175.2	4,569.0	5,361.4
Private final consumption expenditure	11,059.5	12,113.0	13,329.1
Increase in stocks	1,024.1	778.3	935.1
Gross fixed capital formation	12,808.4	15,668.0	18,234.0
Total domestic expenditure	29,067.2	33,128.3	37,859.6
Exports of goods and services *Less* Imports of goods and services	2,422.9	1,503.3	1,571.1
Sub-total	31,490.1	34,502.3	39,430.7
Statistical discrepancy*	−85.6	−412.0	689.5
GDP in purchasers' values	31,404.5	34,090.3	40,120.2

* Referring to the difference between the sum of the expenditure components and official estimates of GDP, compiled from the production approach.

Gross Domestic Product by Economic Activity

	2008	2009	2010
Agriculture, forestry and fishing	3,370.2	3,522.6	4,053.3
Construction	1,874.3	2,239.9	2,671.4
Other industry*	13,026.0	13,524.0	16,086.7
Transport, storage and communications	1,636.3	1,672.7	1,896.9
Wholesale and retail trade	2,618.2	2,898.5	3,574.6
Hotels and restaurants	661.6	711.8	806.9
Financial intermediation	1,486.3	1,776.8	2,098.1
Real estate	1,473.9	1,865.5	2,231.6
Other services	5,257.7	5,878.6	6,700.8
Total	31,404.5	34,090.3	40,120.2

* Includes mining, manufacturing, electricity, gas and water.

BALANCE OF PAYMENTS

(US $ million)

	2008	2009	2010
Exports of goods f.o.b.	1,434,601	1,203,797	1,581,417
Imports of goods f.o.b.	−1,073,919	−954,287	−1,327,238
Trade balance	360,682	249,509	254,180
Exports of services	147,112	129,549	171,203
Imports of services	−158,924	−158,947	−193,321
Balance on goods and services	348,870	220,112	232,062
Other income received	101,615	108,582	144,622
Other income paid	−83,920	−101,321	−114,242
Balance on goods, services and income	366,565	227,372	262,442
Current transfers received	52,565	42,645	49,521
Current transfers paid	−6,766	−8,897	−6,588
Current balance	412,364	261,120	305,374
Capital account (net)	3,051	3,958	4,630
Direct investment abroad	−53,471	−43,898	−60,151
Direct investment from abroad	175,148	114,215	185,081
Portfolio investment assets	32,750	9,888	−7,643
Portfolio investment liabilities	9,910	28,804	31,681
Other investment assets	−106,074	9,365	−116,262
Other investment liabilities	−14,992	58,483	188,708
Net errors and omissions	20,868	−41,425	−59,760
Overall balance	479,553	400,508	471,659

Source: IMF, *International Financial Statistics*.

External Trade

PRINCIPAL COMMODITIES
(distribution by SITC, US $ million)

Imports c.i.f.	2007	2008	2009
Food and live animals	11,499.6	14,051.2	14,824.1
Crude materials (inedible) except fuels	117,915.3	166,695.1	140,821.8
Metalliferous ores and metal scrap	69,617.6	99,976.4	85,902.9
Mineral fuels, lubricants, etc.	104,930.1	169,242.0	123,962.8
Petroleum, petroleum products, etc.	99,150.5	162,374.4	109,350.7
Crude petroleum oils, etc.	79,857.5	129,330.9	89,255.6
Chemicals and related products	107,420.5	118,996.8	111,973.0
Organic chemicals	38,288.2	39,035.5	35,880.9
Basic manufactures	102,877.3	107,164.9	107,732.0
Textile yarn, fabrics, etc.	16,644.7	16,288.6	14,944.7
Iron and steel	24,144.4	27,149.0	26,476.3
Machinery and transport equipment	412,640.2	441,952.6	408,259.2
Machinery specialized for particular industries	30,597.5	31,781.1	24,885.7
General industrial machinery, equipment and parts	30,512.3	38,946.0	36,136.4
Office machines and automatic data-processing equipment	45,458.0	46,890.9	43,059.5
Telecommunications and sound equipment	35,737.9	36,896.6	34,065.2
Other electrical machinery, apparatus, etc.	209,224.7	216,810.9	199,042.8
Thermionic valves, tubes, etc.	145,263.5	148,120.6	136,924.3
Electronic microcircuits	127,901.2	129,457.3	120,164.6
Road vehicles and transport equipment *	34,928.5	39,606.8	42,798.7
Miscellaneous manufactured articles	87,330.8	97,458.0	84,935.0
Total (incl. others)	955,955.9	1,132,562.2	1,005,555.2

Exports f.o.b.	2007	2008	2009
Food and live animals	30,742.8	32,762.0	32,603.0
Mineral fuels, lubricants, etc.	19,950.9	31,772.9	20,382.8
Chemicals and related products	60,314.4	79,312.6	62,007.8
Basic manufactures	219,877.0	262,391.2	184,774.6
Textile yarn, fabrics, etc.	55,967.7	65,366.6	59,823.5
Machinery and transport equipment	577,751.4	674,065.0	591,127.5
Office machines and automatic data-processing equipment	165,880.3	176,839.1	157,320.7
Automatic data-processing machines and units	112,243.7	122,727.7	111,890.6
Telecommunications and sound equipment	146,267.5	161,947.7	148,799.0
Other electrical machinery, apparatus, etc.	128,803.9	153,398.8	134,672.5
Road vehicles and transport equipment*	53,868.6	69,151.6	59,006.5
Miscellaneous manufactured articles	296,139.2	335,235.9	298,986.2
Clothing and accessories (excl. footwear)	115,237.5	120,404.7	107,263.7
Footwear	25,305.6	29,720.4	28,016.3
Baby carriages, toys, games and sporting goods	29,019.8	34,948.8	28,166.7
Children's toys	8,485.8	8,644.0	7,783.6
Total (incl. others)	1,217,775.7	1,430,693.1	1,201,646.8

* Data on parts exclude tyres, engines and electrical parts.

Source: UN, *International Trade Statistics Yearbook*.

PRINCIPAL TRADING PARTNERS
(US $ million)*

Imports c.i.f.	2007	2008	2009
Angola	12,888.7	22,382.5	14,675.8
Australia	25,843.2	37,435.1	39,438.8
Brazil	18,339.5	29,863.4	28,281.0
Canada	10,979.1	12,673.4	12,026.2
Chile	10,280.4	11,172.8	12,790.5
France (incl. Monaco)	13,352.4	15,644.1	13,031.1
Germany	45,383.1	55,789.9	55,764.1
India	14,618.1	20,258.9	13,714.3
Indonesia	12,396.5	14,322.9	13,663.8
Iran	13,306.8	19,594.2	13,286.5
Italy	10,210.8	11,639.0	11,020.3
Japan	133,942.7	150,600.0	130,937.5
Korea, Republic	103,752.0	112,137.9	102,551.7
Malaysia	28,697.1	32,101.4	32,330.7
Philippines	23,117.8	19,504.7	11,946.6
Russia	19,688.6	23,832.8	21,283.0
Saudi Arabia	17,559.7	31,022.7	23,620.2
Singapore	17,523.7	20,171.3	17,796.6
Taiwan	101,027.2	103,338.1	85,723.0
Thailand	22,664.7	25,656.7	24,896.9
USA	69,528.7	81,585.6	77,755.1
Total (incl. others)	955,955.9	1,132,562.2	1,005,555.2

Exports f.o.b.	2007	2008	2009
Australia	17,989.7	22,247.3	20,645.6
Belgium	12,679.4	14,871.3	10,872.8
Brazil	11,398.5	18,807.5	14,118.5
Canada	19,355.7	21,795.9	17,675.1
France (incl. Monaco)	20,461.1	23,498.7	21,611.7
Germany	48,714.3	59,209.0	49,919.6
Hong Kong†	184,436.2	190,729.0	166,216.9
India	24,011.5	31,585.4	29,666.6
Indonesia	12,601.3	17,193.1	14,720.6
Italy	21,169.6	26,628.8	20,243.6
Japan	102,008.6	116,132.5	97,911.0
Korea, Republic	56,098.9	73,932.0	53,679.9
Malaysia	17,689.2	21,455.2	19,631.9
Mexico	11,717.7	13,866.5	12,299.0
Netherlands	41,417.8	45,918.6	36,682.2
Russia	28,466.2	33,075.8	17,513.8
Singapore	29,620.3	32,305.8	30,066.4
Spain	16,582.4	20,818.4	14,077.8
Thailand	12,032.9	15,636.4	13,307.1
United Arab Emirates	17,105.0	23,643.7	18,632.3
United Kingdom	31,656.3	36,072.7	31,277.4
USA	233,096.7	252,843.5	221,295.0
Viet Nam	11,895.0	15,122.1	16,300.9
Total (incl. others)	1,217,775.7	1,430,693.1	1,201,646.8

* Imports by country of origin; exports by country of consumption.
† The majority of China's exports to Hong Kong are re-exported.

Source: UN, *International Trade Statistics Yearbook*.

Transport

SUMMARY

	2008	2009	2010
Freight (million ton-km):			
railways	2,510,630	2,523,920	2,764,410
roads	3,286,820	3,718,880	4,338,970
waterways	5,026,270	5,755,670	6,842,750
Passenger-km (million):			
railways	777,860	787,890	876,220
roads	1,247,610	1,351,140	1,502,080
waterways	5,920	6,940	7,230

ROAD TRAFFIC
('000 motor vehicles in use)*

	2008	2009	2010
Passenger cars and buses	38,389.2	48,450.9	61,241.3
Goods vehicles	11,260.7	13,686.0	15,975.5
Total (incl. others)	50,996.1	62,806.1	78,018.3

* Excluding military vehicles.

SHIPPING

Merchant Fleet
(registered at 31 December)

	2007	2008	2009
Number of vessels	3,799	3,916	4,064
Total displacement ('000 grt)	24,918.5	26,811.1	30,077.1

Source: IHS Fairplay, *World Fleet Statistics*.

Sea-borne Shipping
(freight traffic, '000 metric tons)

	2008	2009	2010
Goods loaded and unloaded	4,295,990	4,754,810	5,483,580

CIVIL AVIATION

	2008	2009	2010
Passenger traffic (million)	192.5	230.5	267.7
Passenger-km (million)	288,279.9	337,523.5	403,899.6
Freight traffic ('000 metric tons)	4,076.4	4,455.3	5,630.4
Freight ton-km (million)	11,960.2	12,623.1	17,889.8
Total ton-km (million)	37,676.5	42,707.3	53,844.9

Tourism

FOREIGN VISITORS
(arrivals, '000)

Country of origin	2008	2009	2010
Australia	571.5	561.5	661.3
Canada	534.7	550.3	685.3
Germany	528.9	518.5	608.6
Indonesia	426.3	469.0	573.4
Japan	3,446.1	3,317.5	3,731.2
Korea, Republic	3,960.4	3,197.5	4,076.4
Malaysia	1,040.5	1,059.0	1,245.2
Mongolia	705.3	576.7	794.4
Philippines	795.3	748.9	828.3
Russia	3,123.4	1,743.0	2,370.3
Singapore	875.8	889.5	1,003.7
Thailand	554.3	541.8	635.5
United Kingdom	551.5	528.8	575.0
USA	1,786.4	1,709.8	2,009.6
Total (incl. others)*	24,325.3	21,937.5	26,126.9

* Excluding visitors from Hong Kong and Macao (1,013.2 in 2008, 1,000.5 in 2009 and 1,024.9 in 2010), and from Taiwan (43.9 in 2008, 44.8 in 2009 and 51.4 in 2010).

Tourism receipts (US $ million): 40,843 in 2008; 39,675 in 2009; 45,814 in 2010.

Communications Media

	2008	2009	2010
Telephones ('000 main lines in use)	340,359	313,732	294,383
Mobile cellular telephones ('000 subscribers)	641,245	747,214	859,003
Internet subscribers ('000)	95,214	111,522	n.a.
Broadband subscribers ('000)	82,879	103,978	126,337
Book production:			
titles	275,668	301,719	328,387
copies (million)	6,936	7,037	7,171
Newspaper production:			
titles	1,943	1,937	1,939
copies (million)	442,922	439,113	452,139
Magazine production:			
titles	9,549	9,851	9,884
copies (million)	3,105	3,153	3,215

Television receivers ('000 in use): 380,000 in 2000**Personal computers:** 74,110,000 (56.5 per 1,000 persons) in 2006.

Radio receivers ('000 in use): 417,000 in 1997.

Sources: International Telecommunication Union; UNESCO, *Statistical Yearbook*; UN, *Statistical Yearbook*.

Education

(2010)

	Institutions	Full-time teachers ('000)	Students ('000)
Kindergartens	150,420	1,144	29,767
Primary schools	290,597	5,646	99,407
Secondary schools	85,063	5,923	84,330
Junior secondary schools	56,479	3,530	52,759
Senior secondary schools	14,712	1,522	24,273
Vocational secondary schools	13,872	871	7,298
Special schools	1,706	40	426
Higher education	2,358	1,343	22,318

Pupil-teacher ratio (primary education, UNESCO estimate): 17.2 in 2008/09 (Source: UNESCO Institute for Statistics).

Adult literacy rate (UN estimate): 94.0% (males 96.9%; females 90.9%) in 2009 (Source: UNESCO Institute for Statistics).

Directory

The Government

HEAD OF STATE

President: HU JINTAO (elected by the 10th National People's Congress on 15 March 2003; re-elected by the 11th National People's Congress on 15 March 2008).

Vice-President: XI JINPING.

STATE COUNCIL
(May 2012)

The Government is formed by the Chinese Communist Party.

Premier: WEN JIABAO.

Vice-Premiers: LI KEQIANG, HUI LIANGYU, ZHANG DEJIANG, WANG QISHAN.

State Councillors: LIU YANDONG, LIANG GUANGLIE, MA KAI, MENG JIANZHU, DAI BINGGUO.

Secretary-General: MA KAI.
Minister of Foreign Affairs: YANG JIECHI.
Minister of National Defence: LIANG GUANGLIE.
Minister of National Development and Reform Commission: ZHANG PING.
Minister of Education: YUAN GUIREN.
Minister of Science and Technology: WAN GANG.
Minister of Industry and Information Technology: MIAO WEI .
Minister of State Ethnic Affairs Commission: YANG JING.
Minister of Public Security: MENG JIANZHU.
Minister of State Security: GENG HUICHANG.
Minister of Supervision: MA WEN.
Minister of Civil Affairs: LI LIGUO.
Minister of Justice: WU AIYING.
Minister of Finance: XIE XUREN.
Minister of Human Resources and Social Security: YIN WEIMIN.
Minister of Land and Resources: XU SHAOSHI.
Minister of Housing and Urban-Rural Construction: JIANG WEIXIN.
Minister of Railways: SHENG GUANGZU.
Minister of Transport: LI SHENGLIN.
Minister of Water Resources: CHEN LEI.
Minister of Agriculture: HAN CHANGFU.
Minister of Environmental Protection: ZHOU SHENGXIAN.
Minister of Commerce: CHEN DEMING.
Minister of Culture: CAI WU.
Minister of Health: CHEN ZHU.
Minister of National Population and Family Planning Commission: LI BIN.
Governor of the People's Bank of China: ZHOU XIAOCHUAN.
Auditor-General of the National Audit Office: LIU JIAYI.

MINISTRIES

Ministry of Agriculture: 11 Nongzhanguan Nanli, Chao Yang Qu, Beijing 100125; tel. (10) 59191830; fax (10) 59191831; e-mail webmaster_en@agri.gov.cn; internet www.agri.gov.cn.

Ministry of Civil Affairs: 147 Beiheyan Dajie, Dongcheng Qu, Beijing 100721; tel. (10) 58123114; fax (10) 65135332; internet www.mca.gov.cn.

Ministry of Commerce: 2 Dongchangan Dajie, Dongcheng Qu, Beijing 100731; tel. (10) 65284671; fax (10) 65599340; e-mail webmaster@mofcom.gov.cn; internet www.mofcom.gov.cn.

Ministry of Culture: 10 Chao Yang Men Bei Dajie, Chao Yang Qu, Beijing 100020; tel. (10) 59881114; fax (10) 65551433; e-mail webmaster@ccic.gov.cn; internet www.ccnt.gov.cn.

Ministry of Education: 37 Damucang Hutong, Xidan, Beijing 100816; tel. (10) 66096114; fax (10) 66011049; e-mail english@moe.edu.cn; internet www.moe.edu.cn.

Ministry of Environmental Protection: 115 Xizhimennei Nan Xiao Jie, Xicheng Qu, Beijing 100035; tel. (10) 66556006; fax (10) 66556010; e-mail mailbox@mep.gov.cn; internet www.mep.gov.cn.

Ministry of Finance: 3 Nansanxiang, Sanlihe, Xicheng Qu, Beijing 100820; tel. (10) 68551114; fax (10) 68551783; e-mail webmaster@mof.gov.cn; internet www.mof.gov.cn.

Ministry of Foreign Affairs: 2 Chao Yang Men, Nan Dajie, Chao Yang Qu, Beijing 100701; tel. (10) 65961114; fax (10) 65962146; e-mail webmaster@mfa.gov.cn; internet www.fmprc.gov.cn.

Ministry of Health: 1 Xizhinenwai Nan Lu, Xicheng Qu, Beijing 100044; tel. (10) 68792114; fax (10) 64012369; e-mail manager@moh.gov.cn; internet www.moh.gov.cn.

Ministry of Housing and Urban-Rural Construction: 9 Sanlihe Lu, Haidian Qu, Beijing 100835; tel. (10) 58934114; e-mail cin@mail.cin.gov.cn; internet www.cin.gov.cn.

Ministry of Human Resources and Social Security: 12 Hepinglizhong Jie, Dongcheng Qu, Beijing 100716; tel. (10) 84201114; fax (10) 64218350; internet www.mohrss.gov.cn.

Ministry of Industry and Information Technology: 13 Xichangan Dajie, Beijing 100804; tel. (10) 66014249; fax (10) 66034248; e-mail mail@miit.gov.cn; internet www.miit.gov.cn.

Ministry of Justice: 10 Chaoyangmen, Nan Dajie, Chao Yang Qu, Beijing 100020; tel. (10) 65205114; fax (10) 65205316; e-mail minister@legalinfo.gov.cn; internet www.moj.gov.cn.

Ministry of Land and Resources: 64 Funei Jie, Xisi, Beijing 100812; tel. (10) 66558407; fax (10) 66127247; e-mail webmaster@mail.mlr.gov.cn; internet www.mlr.gov.cn.

Ministry of National Defence: 20 Jingshanqian Jie, Beijing 100009; tel. (10) 66730000; fax (10) 65962146; e-mail mod@chinamil.com.cn; internet www.mod.gov.cn.

Ministry of Public Security: 14 Dongchangan Dajie, Dongcheng Qu, Beijing 100741; tel. (10) 66262114; fax (10) 65136577; e-mail gabzfwz@mps.gov.cn; internet www.mps.gov.cn.

Ministry of Railways: 10 Fuxing Lu, Haidian Qu, Beijing 100844; tel. (10) 51842281; fax (10) 63242150; internet www.china-mor.gov.cn.

Ministry of Science and Technology: 15B Fuxing Lu, Haidian Qu, Beijing 100862; tel. (10) 58881888; fax (10) 68515006; e-mail officemail@mail.most.gov.cn; internet www.most.gov.cn.

Ministry of State Security: 14 Dongchangan Dajie, Dongcheng Qu, Beijing 100741; tel. (10) 65244702.

Ministry of Supervision: 4 Zaojunmiao, Haidian Qu, Beijing 100081; tel. (10) 62114181; fax (10) 62217692; internet www.mos.gov.cn.

Ministry of Transport: Beijing 100736; tel. (10) 65292818; fax (10) 65292819; e-mail zhenglb@moc.gov.cn; internet www.mot.gov.cn.

Ministry of Water Resources: 2 Baiguang Lu, Xiang 2, Xuanwu Qu, Beijing 100053; tel. (10) 63202114; fax (10) 63202558; e-mail webmaster@mwr.gov.cn; internet www.mwr.gov.cn.

STATE COMMISSIONS

National Development and Reform Commission (NDRC): 38 Yuetannan Jie, Xicheng Qu, Beijing 100824; tel. (10) 68504409; fax (10) 68512929; e-mail ndrc@ndrc.gov.cn; internet www.ndrc.gov.cn.

National Population and Family Planning Commission: 14 Zhichun Lu, Haidian Qu, Beijing 100088; tel. (10) 62046622; fax (10) 62051865; e-mail sfpcdfa@public.bta.net.cn; internet www.npfpc.gov.cn.

State Ethnic Affairs Commission: 252 Taipingqiao Dajie, Xicheng Qu, Beijing 100800; tel. and fax (10) 66508000; fax (10) 66017375; e-mail webmaster@seac.gov.cn; internet www.seac.gov.cn.

People's Governments

PROVINCES

Governors: LI BIN (Anhui), SHU SHULIN (Fujian), LIU WEIPING (Gansu), ZHU XIAODAN (Guangdong), LIN SHUSEN (Guizhou), JIANG DINGZHI (Hainan), ZHANG QINGWEI (Hebei), WANG XIANKUI (Heilongjiang), GUO GENGMAO (Henan), WANG GUOSHENG (Hubei), XU SHOUSHENG (Hunan), LI XUEYONG (Jiangsu), LU XINSHE (Jiangxi), WANG RULIN (Jilin), CHEN ZHENGGAO (Liaoning), LUO HUINING (Qinghai), ZHAO ZHENGYONG (Shaanxi), JIANG DAMING (Shandong), WANG JUN (Shanxi), JIANG JUFENG (Sichuan), LI JIHENG (Yunnan), XIA BAOLONG (Zhejiang).

SPECIAL MUNICIPALITIES

Mayors: GUO JINLONG (Beijing), HUANG QIFAN (Chongqing), HAN ZHENG (Shanghai), HUANG XINGGUO (Tianjin).

AUTONOMOUS REGIONS

Chairmen: MA BIAO (Guangxi Zhuang), BAGATUR (Inner Mongolia—Nei Monggol), WANG ZHENGWEI (Ningxia Hui), PADMA CHOLING (Tibet—Xizang), NUR BEKRI (Xinjiang Uygur).

Legislature

QUANGUO RENMIN DAIBIAO DAHUI
(National People's Congress)

The National People's Congress (NPC) is the highest organ of state power, and is indirectly elected for a five-year term. The first plenary session of the 11th NPC was convened in Beijing in March 2008, and was attended by 2,967 deputies. The first session of the 11th National Committee of the Chinese People's Political Consultative Conference (CPPCC, www.cppcc.gov.cn, Chair. JIA QINGLIN), a revolutionary united front organization led by the Communist Party, took place simultaneously. The CPPCC holds discussions and consultations on the important affairs in the nation's political life. Members of the CPPCC National Committee or of its Standing Committee may be invited to attend the NPC or its Standing Committee as observers.

Standing Committee

In March 2008 161 members were elected to the Standing Committee, in addition to the following:

Chairman: WU BANGGUO.

Vice-Chairmen: WANG ZHAOGUO, LU YONGXIANG, UYUNQIMG, HAN QIDE, HUA JIANMIN, CHEN ZHILI, ZHOU TIENONG, LI JIANGUO, ISMAIL TILIWALDI, JIANG SHUSHENG, CHEN CHANGZHI, YAN JUNQI, SANG GUOWEI.

Secretary-General: LI JIANGUO.

Political Organizations

COMMUNIST PARTY

Zhongguo Gongchan Dang (Chinese Communist Party—CCP): Zhongnanhai, Beijing; f. 1921; 80.3m. mems (Dec. 2010); at the 17th Nat. Congress of the CCP in Oct. 2007, a new Cen. Cttee of 204 full mems and 167 alternate mems was elected; at its first plenary session the 17th Cen. Cttee appointed a new Political Bureau.

Seventeenth Central Committee

General Secretary: HU JINTAO.

Political Bureau (Politburo)

Members of the Standing Committee: HU JINTAO, WU BANGGUO, WEN JIABAO, JIA QINGLIN, LI CHANGCHUN, XI JINPING, LI KEQIANG, HE GUOQIANG, ZHOU YONGKANG.

Other Full Members: BO XILAI, Gen. GUO BOXIONG, HUI LIANGYU, LI YUANCHAO, LIU QI, LIU YANDONG, LIU YUNSHAN, WANG GANG, WANG LEQUAN, WANG QISHAN, WANG YANG, WANG ZHAOGUO, XU CAIHOU, YU ZHENGSHENG, ZHANG DEJIANG, ZHANG GAOLI.

Secretariat: XI JINPING, LIU YUNSHAN, LI YUANCHAO, HE YONG, LING JIHUA, WANG HUNING.

OTHER POLITICAL ORGANIZATIONS

China Association for Promoting Democracy: 98 Xinanli Guloufangzhuangchang, Beijing 100009; tel. (10) 64033452; f. 1945; 103,000 mems, drawn mainly from literary, cultural and educational circles; 45-mem. Cen. Cttee; Chair. of Cen. Cttee YAN JUNQI; Sec.-Gen. ZHAO GUANGHUA.

China Democratic League: 1 Beixing Dongchang Hutong, Dongcheng Qu, Beijing 100006; tel. (10) 65232757; fax (10) 65232852; e-mail bwh@dem-league.org.cn; internet www.dem-league.org.cn; f. 1941; formed from reorganization of League of Democratic Parties and Organizations of China; 196,000 mems, mainly intellectuals active in education, science and culture; Chair. JIANG SHUSHENG; Sec.-Gen. GAO SHUANPING.

China National Democratic Construction Association: 208 Jixiangli, Chaowai Lu, Chao Yang Qu, Beijing 100020; tel. (10) 85698008; fax (10) 85698007; e-mail bgt@cndca.org.cn; internet www.cndca.org.cn; f. 1945; 112,698 mems, mainly industrialists and business executives; Chair. CHEN CHANGZHI; Sec.-Gen. ZHANG JIAO.

China Zhi Gong Dang (Party for Public Interests): Beijing; e-mail czgpwz@zg.org.cn; internet www.zg.org.cn; f. 1925; reorg. 1947; 15,000 mems, mainly returned overseas Chinese and scholars; Chair. WAN GANG; Sec.-Gen. QIU GUOYI.

Chinese Communist Youth League: 10 Qianmen Dong Dajie, Beijing 100051; tel. (10) 67018132; fax (10) 67018131; e-mail gqt@gqt.org.cn; internet www.gqt.org.cn; f. 1922; 68.5m. mems; First Sec. of Cen. Cttee LU HAO.

Chinese Peasants' and Workers' Democratic Party: 55 An Wai Dajie, Beijing; tel. and fax (10) 84125629; e-mail info@ngdzy.org.cn; internet www.ngd.org.cn; f. 1930; est. as the Provisional Action Cttee of the Kuomintang; took present name in 1947; more than 102,000 mems, active mainly in public health and medicine; Chair. SANG GUOWEI.

Jiu San (3 September) Society: 14 Wan Quan Xinxin Jiayuan, Wanliu Donglu, Haidian Qu, Beijing 100089; tel. (10) 82552001; fax (10) 82552002; e-mail bwww@93.gov.cn; internet www.93.gov.cn; f. 1946; fmrly Democratic and Science Soc; more than 105,000 mems, mainly scientists and technologists; Chair. HAN QIDE; Sec.-Gen. XU GUOQUAN.

Revolutionary Committee of the Chinese Kuomintang: 84 Donghuang Chenggen Nan Jie, Dongcheng Qu, Beijing 100006; tel. (10) 65595873; fax (10) 65125886; e-mail webmaster@minge.gov.cn; internet www.minge.gov.cn; f. 1948; over 53,000 mems, mainly fmr Kuomintang mems, and those in cultural, educational, health and financial fields; Chair. ZHOU TIENONG; Sec.-Gen. QI XUCHUN.

Taiwan Democratic Self-Government League: 20 Jingshan Dongjie, Beijing 100009; tel. and fax (10) 64043293; e-mail webmaster@taimeng.org.cn; internet www.taimeng.org.cn; f. 1947; 1,600 mems; recruits Taiwanese living on the mainland; Chair. LIN WENYI; Sec.-Gen. ZHANG NING.

Diplomatic Representation

EMBASSIES IN THE PEOPLE'S REPUBLIC OF CHINA

Afghanistan: 8 Dong Zhi Men Wai Dajie, Chao Yang Qu, Beijing 100600; tel. (10) 65321582; fax (10) 65322269; e-mail afgemb_beijing@yahoo.com; Ambassador SULTAN AHMAD BAHEEN.

Albania: 28 Guang Hua Lu, Jian Guo Men Wai, Beijing 100600; tel. (10) 65321120; fax (10) 65325451; e-mail embassy.beijing@mfa.gov.al; Ambassador KUJTIM XHANI.

Algeria: 7 San Li Tun Lu, Beijing; tel. (10) 65321231; fax (10) 65321648; Ambassador HASSANE RABEHI.

Angola: 1-8-1 Tayuan Diplomatic Office Bldg, Chao Yang Qu, Beijing 100600; tel. (10) 65326968; fax (10) 65326992; Ambassador JOÃO GARCIA BIRES.

Argentina: Bldg 11, 5 Dong Wu Jie, San Li Tun, Beijing 100600; tel. (10) 65322090; fax (10) 65322319; e-mail echin@mrecic.gov.ar; Ambassador GUSTAVO ALBERTO MARTINO.

Armenia: 4-1-61 Tayuan Diplomatic Office Bldg, Chao Yang Qu, Beijing 100600; tel. (10) 65325677; fax (10) 65325654; e-mail armchinaembassy@mfa.am; Ambassador ARMEN SARGSYAN.

Australia: 21 Dong Zhi Men Wai Dajie, San Li Tun, Beijing 100600; tel. (10) 51404111; fax (10) 51404204; e-mail pubaff.beijing@dfat.gov.au; internet www.china.embassy.gov.au; Ambassador FRANCES ADAMSON.

Austria: 5 Xiu Shui Nan Jie, Jian Guo Men Wai, Beijing 100600; tel. (10) 65322061; fax (10) 65321505; e-mail peking-ob@bmeia.gv.at; internet www.bmeia.gv.at/botschaft/peking; Ambassador MARTIN SAJDIK.

Azerbaijan: Qijiayuan Diplomatic Compound, Villa No. B-3, Beijing 100600; tel. (10) 65324614; fax (10) 65324615; e-mail mailbox@azerbembassy.org.cn; internet www.azerbembassy.org.cn; Ambassador YASHAR TOFIGI ALIYEV.

Bahamas: 2-4 Tayuan Diplomatic Office Bldg, 14 Liang Ma He Lu, Beijing 100600; tel. (10) 65322922; fax (10) 65322304; e-mail info@bahamasembassy.cn; internet www.bahamasembassy.cn; Ambassador (vacant).

Bahrain: 10-06 Liang Ma Qiao Diplomatic Residence Compound, 22 Dong Fang Dong Lu, Chao Yang Qu, Beijing; tel. (10) 65326483; fax (10) 65326393; e-mail kingdombahrain@yahoo.cn; internet www.mofa.gov.bh/beijing; Ambassador BIBI SHARAF AL-ALAWI.

Bangladesh: 42 Guang Hua Lu, Beijing 100600; tel. (10) 65322529; fax (10) 65324346; e-mail bdemb@public3.bta.net.cn; internet www.bangladeshembassy.com.cn; Ambassador MUNSHI FAIZ AHMAD.

Barbados: Villa 09-02, Block A, Liang Ma Qiao Diplomatic Compound, 22 Dong Fang Dong Lu, Chao Yang Qu, 100600 Beijing; tel. (10) 85325404; fax (10) 85325437; e-mail beijing@foreign.gov.bb; Ambassador Sir LLOYD ERSKINE SANDIFORD.

Belarus: 1 Dong Yi Jie, Ri Tan Lu, Beijing 100600; tel. (10) 65321691; fax (10) 65326417; e-mail china@belembassy.org; internet www.china.belembassy.org; Ambassador VIKTOR BURYA.

Belgium: 6 San Li Tun Lu, Beijing 100600; tel. (10) 65321736; fax (10) 65325097; e-mail beijing@diplobel.fed.be; internet www.diplomatie.be/beijing; Ambassador PATRICK NIJS.

Benin: 38 Guang Hua Lu, Jian Guo Men Wai, Beijing 100600; tel. (10) 65322741; fax (10) 65325103; Ambassador SEDOZAN APITHY.

Bolivia: 2-3-2 Tayuan Diplomatic Office Bldg, Chao Yang Qu, Beijing 100600; tel. (10) 65323074; fax (10) 65324686; e-mail embolchin@public3.bta.net.cn; internet www.embolchina.com; Ambassador Gen. GUILLERMO CHALUP.

Bosnia and Herzegovina: 1-5-1 Tayuan Diplomatic Office Bldg, Chao Yang Qu, Beijing 100600; tel. (10) 65326587; fax (10) 65326418; e-mail ambbhdip@public.bta.net.cn; Ambassador AMEL KOVAČEVIĆ.

Botswana: Unit 811, IBM Tower, Pacific Century Place, 2A Gong Ti Bei Lu, Beijing 100027; tel. (10) 65391616; fax (10) 65391199; e-mail info@botswanaembassy.com; internet www.embbiz.net/com/botswana; Ambassador SASARA CHASALA GEORGE.

Brazil: 27 Guang Hua Lu, Jian Guo Men Wai, Chao Yang Qu, Beijing 100600; tel. (10) 65322881; fax (10) 65322751; e-mail brasemb.pequim@itamaraty.gov.br; internet pequim.itamaraty.gov.br; Ambassador CLODOALDO HUGUENEY FILHO.

Brunei: 1 Liang Ma Qiao Bei Jie, Chao Yang Qu, Beijing 100600; tel. (10) 65329773; fax (10) 65324097; e-mail beb@public.bta.net.cn; Ambassador MAGDALENE TEO CHEE SIONG.

Bulgaria: 4 Xiu Shui Bei Jie, Jian Guo Men Wai, Beijing 100600; tel. (10) 65321946; fax (10) 65324502; e-mail bgembassybeijing@gmail.com; internet www.mfa.bg/en/43/; Ambassador GEORGI PEYCHINOV.

Burundi: 25 Guang Hua Lu, Jian Guo Men Wai, Beijing 100600; tel. (10) 65321801; fax (10) 65322381; e-mail ambbubei@yahoo.fr; Ambassador PASCAL GASUNZU.

Cambodia: 9 Dong Zhi Men Wai Dajie, Beijing 100600; tel. (10) 65321889; fax (10) 65323507; e-mail cambassy@public2.bta.net.cn; Ambassador KHEK CAI MEALY SYSODA.

Cameroon: 7 Dong Wu Jie, San Li Tun, Beijing 100600; tel. (10) 65321828; fax (10) 65321761; e-mail acpk71@hotmail.com; Ambassador MARTIN MPANA.

Canada: 19 Dong Zhi Men Wai Dajie, Chao Yang Qu, Beijing 100600; tel. (10) 51394000; fax (10) 51394454; e-mail beijing-pa@international.gc.ca; internet www.canadainternational.gc.ca/china-chine; Ambassador DAVID MULRONEY.

Cape Verde: 6-2-121 Tayuan Diplomatic Office Bldg, Chao Yang Qu, Beijing 100600; tel. (10) 65327547; fax (10) 65327546; e-mail ecvb@163bj.com; internet bio-visa.com/program/com/cape; Ambassador JULIO CESAR FREIRE DE MORAIS.

Central African Republic: 1-1-132 Tayuan Diplomatic Office Bldg, 1 Xin Dong Lu, Chao Yang Qu, Beijing; tel. 65327353; fax 65327354; e-mail ambrcapk@yahoo.fr; Ambassador EMMANUEL TOUABOY.

Chad: 2-2-102 Tayuan Diplomatic Compound, Xin Dong Lu, Chao Yang Qu, Beijing 100600; tel. (10) 85323822; fax (10) 85322783; e-mail ambatchad.beijing@yahoo.fr; Ambassador AHMED SOUNGUI.

Chile: 1 Dong Si Jie, San Li Tun, Beijing 100600; tel. (10) 65321591; fax (10) 65323179; e-mail embachile@echilecn.com; internet chileabroad.gov.cl/china; Ambassador LUIS SCHMIDT MONTES.

Colombia: 34 Guang Hua Lu, Jian Guo Men Wai, Beijing 100600; tel. (10) 65323377; fax (10) 65321969; e-mail ebeijing@cancilleria.gov.co; internet www.embcolch.org.cn; Ambassador CARLOS URREA.

Congo, Democratic Republic: 6 Dong Wu Jie, San Li Tun, Beijing 100600; tel. (10) 65323224; fax (10) 65321360; Ambassador CHARLES MUMBALA NZANKU.

Congo, Republic: 7 Dong Si Jie, San Li Tun, Beijing 100600; tel. (10) 65321658; fax (10) 65322915; Ambassador RIGOBERT ITOUA.

Costa Rica: Jian Guo Men Wai, 1-5-41 Jiao Gong Lu, Beijing 100600; tel. (10) 65324157; fax (10) 65324546; e-mail info@embajadacrchina.org; internet www.embajadacrchina.org; Ambassador MARCO VINICIO RUIZ GUTIÉRREZ.

Côte d'Ivoire: 9 San Li Tun, Bei Xiao Jie, Beijing 100600; tel. (10) 65321223; fax (10) 65322407; Ambassador COFFIE ALAIN NICAISE PAPATCHI.

Croatia: 2-72 San Li Tun Diplomatic Office Bldg, Beijing 100600; tel. (10) 65326241; fax (10) 65326257; e-mail croemb.beijing@mvpei.hr; internet cn.mfa.hr; Ambassador ANTE SIMONIĆ.

Cuba: 1 Xiu Shui Nan Jie, Jian Guo Men Wai, Beijing 100600; tel. (10) 65321714; fax (10) 65322870; e-mail embajada@embacuba.cn; internet embacuba.cubaminrex.cu/china; Ambassador CARLOS MIGUEL PEREIRA.

Cyprus: 2-13-2 Tayuan Diplomatic Office Bldg, 14 Liang Ma He Nan Lu, Chao Yang Qu, Beijing 100600; tel. (10) 65325057; fax (10) 65324244; e-mail cyembpek@public3.bta.net.cn; Ambassador MARIOS IERONYMIDES.

Czech Republic: 2 Ri Tan Lu, Jian Guo Men Wai, Beijing 100600; tel. (10) 85329500; fax (10) 65325653; e-mail beijing@embassy.mzv.cz; internet www.mzv.cz/beijing; Ambassador LIBOR SEČKA.

Denmark: 1 Dong Wu Jie, San Li Tun, Beijing 100600; tel. (10) 85329900; fax (10) 85329999; e-mail bjsamb@um.dk; internet www.ambbeijing.um.dk; Ambassador FRIIS ARNE PETERSEN.

Djibouti: 1-1-122 Tayuan Diplomatic Office Bldg, Chao Yang Qu, Beijing; tel. (10) 65327857; fax (10) 65327858; Ambassador AHMED MOHAMED HASSAN.

Dominica: LA-06 Liang Ma Qiao Diplomatic Residence Compound, 22 Dong Fang Dong Lu, Chao Yang Qu, Beijing 100600; tel. (10) 65320848; fax (10) 65320838; e-mail dominica@dominicaembassy.com; Ambassador DAVID KING HSIU.

Ecuador: 2-62 San Li Tun Office Bldg, Chao Yang Qu, 100600 Beijing; tel. (10) 65320489; fax (10) 65324371; e-mail embecuch@public3bta.net.cn; Ambassador LEONARDO ARÍZAGA.

Egypt: 2 Ri Tan Dong Lu, Jian Guo Men Wai, Beijing 100600; tel. (10) 65321825; fax (10) 65325365; e-mail eg_emb_bj@yahoo.com; internet www.mfa.gov.eg/Beijing_Emb; Ambassador AHMED REZK.

Equatorial Guinea: 2 Dong Si Jie, San Li Tun, Beijing; tel. (10) 65323679; fax (10) 65323805; e-mail emguies@yahoo.com; Ambassador MARCOS MBA ONDO.

Eritrea: 2-10-1 Tayuan Diplomatic Office Bldg, Chao Yang Qu, Beijing 100600; tel. (10) 65326534; fax (10) 65326532; Ambassador TSEGGAI TESFATSION SEREKE.

Estonia: C-617–618 Office Bldg, Beijing Lufthansa Center, 50 Liang Ma Qiao Lu, Chao Yang Qu, Beijing 100125; tel. (10) 64637913; fax (10) 64637908; e-mail embassy.beijing@mfa.ee; internet www.peking.vm.ee; Ambassador ANDRES UNGA.

Ethiopia: 3 Xiu Shui Nan Jie, Jian Guo Men Wai, Beijing 100600; tel. (10) 65325258; fax (10) 65325591; e-mail ethchina@public3.bta.net.cn; internet www.ethiopiaemb.org.cn; Ambassador SEYOUM MESFIN.

Fiji: 1-15-2 Tayuan Diplomatic Office Bldg, 14 Liang Ma He Nan Lu, San Li Tun, Chao Yang Qu, Beijing 100600; tel. (10) 65327305; fax (10) 65327253; e-mail info@fijiembassy.org.cn; internet bio-visa.com/program/com/fiji; Ambassador Cdre ESALA TELENI.

Finland: Beijing Kerry Centre, 26/F South Tower, 1 Guanghua Lu, Beijing 100020; tel. (10) 85198300; fax (10) 85198301; e-mail sanomat.pek@formin.fi; internet www.finland.cn; Ambassador LARS BACKSTRÖM.

France: 3 Dong San Jie, San Li Tun, Chao Yang Qu, Beijing 100600; tel. (10) 85328080; fax (10) 85324841; e-mail presse@ambafrance-cn.org; internet www.ambafrance-cn.org; Ambassador SYLVIE BERMANN.

Gabon: 36 Guang Hua Lu, Jian Guo Men Wai, Beijing 100600; tel. (10) 65322810; fax (10) 65322621; Ambassador EMMANUEL MBA-ALLO.

Georgia: LA-03-02, Section A, Liang Ma Qiao Diplomatic Compound, Beijing; tel. (10) 65327518; fax (10) 65327519; e-mail geobeijing@gmail.com; internet www.china.mfa.gov.ge; Ambassador KARLO SIKHARULIDZE.

Germany: 17 Dong Zhi Men Wai Dajie, Chao Yang Qu, Beijing 100600; tel. (10) 85329000; fax (10) 65325336; e-mail embassy@peking.diplo.de; internet www.peking.diplo.de; Ambassador Dr MICHAEL SCHAEFER.

Ghana: 8 San Li Tun Lu, Beijing 100600; tel. (10) 65321319; fax (10) 65323602; e-mail ghmfa85@yahoo.com; Ambassador HELEN MAMLE KOFI.

Greece: 17/F The Place Tower, 9 Guang Hua Lu, Jian Guo Men Wai, Chao Yang Qu, Beijing 100020; tel. (10) 65872838; fax (10) 65872839; e-mail gremb.pek@mfa.gr; internet www.grpressbeijing.com; Ambassador THEODOROS GEORGAKELOS.

Grenada: T5-2-52 Tayuan Diplomatic Office Bldg, Chao Yang Qu, Beijing 100600; tel. (10) 65321208; fax (10) 65321015; e-mail grenembbeijing@yahoo.com; Ambassador F. MARCELLE GAIRY.

Guinea: 2 Xi Liu Jie, San Li Tun, Beijing 100600; tel. (10) 65323649; fax (10) 65324957; Ambassador DIARE MAMADY.

Guinea-Bissau: 2-2-101 Tayuan Diplomatic Compound, Chao Yang Qu, Beijing; tel. (10) 65327393; fax (10) 65327106; Ambassador ARAFAN ANSU CAMARA.

Guyana: 1 Xiu Shui Dong Jie, Jian Guo Men Wai, Beijing 100600; tel. (10) 65321601; fax (10) 65325741; e-mail guyemb@public3.bta.net.cn; Ambassador DAVID DABYDEEN.

Hungary: 10 Dong Zhi Men Wai Dajie, San Li Tun, Beijing 100600; tel. (10) 65321431; fax (10) 65325053; e-mail mission.pek@mfa.gov.hu; internet www.mfa.gov.hu/kulkepviselet/CN; Ambassador SÁNDOR KUSAI.

Iceland: Landmark Tower 1, 802, 8 Dongsanhuan Bei Lu, Beijing 100004; tel. (10) 65907795; fax (10) 65907801; e-mail emb.beijing@mfa.is; internet www.iceland.is/cn; Ambassador KRISTIN ÁRNADÓTTIR.

India: Tian Ze Lu, Liang Ma Qiao, Chaoyang Qu, Beijing 100600; tel. (10) 65321908; fax (10) 65324684; e-mail sscom@indianembassy.org.cn; internet www.indianembassy.org.cn; Ambassador S. JAISHANKAR.

Indonesia: 4 Dong Zhi Men Wai Dajie, Beijing 100600; tel. (10) 65325486; fax (10) 65325368; e-mail set.beijing.kbri@kemlu.go.id; internet www.kemlu.go.id/beijing; Ambassador IMRON COTAN.

Iran: 13 Dong Liu Jie, San Li Tun, Beijing 100600; tel. (10) 65322040; fax (10) 65321403; Ambassador MEHDI SAFARI.

Iraq: 25 Xiu Shui Bei Jie, Jian Guo Men Wai, Beijing 100600; tel. (10) 65323385; fax (10) 65321599; e-mail bknemb@iraqmofamail.net; Ambassador ABDUL KARIM HASHIM MUSTAFA.

Ireland: 3 Ri Tan Dong Lu, Jian Guo Men Wai, Beijing 100600; tel. (10) 65322691; fax (10) 65326857; e-mail beijing@dfa.ie; internet www.embassyofireland.cn; Ambassador DECLAN KELLEHER.

Israel: 17 Tian Ze Lu, Chao Yang Qu, Beijing 100600; tel. (10) 85320500; fax (10) 85320555; e-mail info@beijing.mfa.gov.il; internet beijing.mfa.gov.il; Ambassador AMOS NADAI.

Italy: 2 Dong Er Jie, San Li Tun, Beijing 100600; tel. (10) 85327600; fax (10) 65324676; e-mail ambasciata.pechino@esteri.it; internet www.ambpechino.esteri.it; Ambassador ATTILIO MASSIMO IANNUCCI.

Jamaica: 6-2-72 Jian Guo Men Wai Diplomatic Compound, 1 Xiu Shui Jie, Beijing 100600; tel. (10) 65320667; fax (10) 65320669; e-mail embassy@jamaicagov.cn; internet www.jamaicagov.cn; Ambassador EARLE COURTENAY RATTRAY.

Japan: 7 Ri Tan Lu, Jian Guo Men Wai, Beijing 100600; tel. (10) 65322361; fax (10) 65324625; e-mail info@eoj.cn; internet www.cn.emb-japan.go.jp; Ambassador UICHIRO NIWA.

Jordan: 5 Dong Liu Jie, San Li Tun, Beijing 100600; tel. (10) 65323906; fax (10) 65323283; e-mail beijing@fm.gov.jo; Ambassador ANMAR ABDULHALIM NAMIR HARMUD.

Kazakhstan: 9 Dong Liu Jie, San Li Tun, Beijing 100600; tel. (10) 65324189; fax (10) 65326183; e-mail kz@kazembchina.org; internet www.kazembchina.org; Ambassador IKRAM ADYRBEKOV.

Kenya: 4 Xi Liu Jie, San Li Tun, Beijing 100600; tel. (10) 65323381; fax (10) 65321770; e-mail info@kenyaembassy.cn; internet www.kenyaembassy.cn; Ambassador JULIUS LEKAKENY OLE SUNKULI.

Korea, Democratic People's Republic: 11 Ri Tan Bei Lu, Jian Guo Men Wai, Beijing 100600; tel. (10) 65321186; fax (10) 65326056; Ambassador JI JAE RYONG.

Korea, Republic: 20 Dong Fang Dong Lu, Chao Yang Qu, Beijing 100600; tel. (10) 85310700; fax (10) 85320726; e-mail chinawebmaster@mofat.go.kr; internet www.koreanembassy.cn; Ambassador LEE KYU-HYUNG.

Kuwait: 23 Guang Hua Lu, Jian Guo Men Wai, Beijing 100600; tel. (10) 65322216; fax (10) 65321607; e-mail beijing@mofa.gov.kw; Ambassador MUHAMMAD SALEH AL-THUWAIKH.

Kyrgyzstan: H-10–11 King's Garden Villas, 18 Xiao Yun Lu, Chao Yang Qu, Beijing 100125; tel. (10) 64681297; fax (10) 64681291; e-mail kyrgyz.embassy.china@gmail.com; internet www.kyrgyzstanembassy.net; Ambassador JEENBEK KULUBAYEV.

Laos: 11 Dong Si Jie, San Li Tun, Chao Yang Qu, Beijing 100600; tel. (10) 65321224; fax (10) 65326748; e-mail laoemcn@public.east.cn.net; Ambassador SOMDY BOUNKHOUM.

Latvia: Unit 71, Green Land Garden, 1A Green Land Rd, Chao Yang Qu, Beijing 100016; tel. (10) 64333863; fax (10) 64333810; e-mail embassy.china@mfa.gov.lv; internet www.latvianembassy.org.cn; Ambassador INGRIDA LEVRENCE.

Lebanon: 10 Dong Liu Jie, San Li Tun, Beijing 100600; tel. (10) 65323281; fax (10) 65322770; e-mail lebanon@public.bta.net.cn; Ambassador (vacant).

Lesotho: 302 Dong Wai Diplomatic Office Bldg, 23 Dong Zhi Men Wai Dajie, Chao Yang Qu, Beijing 100600; tel. (10) 65326843; fax (10) 65326845; e-mail lesotho-brussels@foreign.gov.ls; Ambassador RACHOBOKOANE ANTHONY THIBELI.

Liberia: Rm 013, Gold Island Diplomatic Compound, 1 Xi Ba He Nan Lu, Beijing 100028; tel. (10) 64403007; fax (10) 64403918; Ambassador NEH RITA SANGAI DUKULY TOLBERT.

Libya: 3 Dong Liu Jie, San Li Tun, Beijing 100600; tel. (10) 65323666; fax (10) 65323391; Ambassador TAHER E. A. JEHAIMI.

Lithuania: A-18 King's Garden Villas, 18 Xiaoyun Lu, Chao Yang Qu, Beijing 100125; tel. (10) 84518520; fax (10) 84514442; e-mail amb.cn@urm.lt; internet cn.mfa.lt; Ambassador LINA ANTANAVICIENE.

Luxembourg: 1701, Tower B, Pacific Century Place, 2A Gong Ti Bei Lu, Chao Yang Qu, Beijing 100027; tel. (10) 85880900; fax (10) 65137268; e-mail pekin.amb@mae.etat.lu; internet pekin.mae.lu; Ambassador CARLO KRIEGER.

Macedonia, former Yugoslav republic: 1-32 San Li Tun Diplomatic Office Bldg, Beijing 100600; tel. (10) 65327846; fax (10) 65327847; e-mail beijing@mfa.gov.mk; Ambassador OLIVER SAMBEVSKI.

Madagascar: 3 Dong Jie, San Li Tun, Beijing 100600; tel. (10) 65321353; fax (10) 65322102; e-mail ambpek@public2.bta.net.cn; Ambassador VICTOR SIKONINA.

Malawi: 503 Dong Wai Diplomatic Office Bldg, 23 Dong Zhi Men Wai Dajie, Beijing 100600; tel. (10) 65325889; fax (10) 65326022; Ambassador CHARLES ENOCH NAMONDWE.

Malaysia: 2 Liang Ma Qiao Bei Jie, Chao Yang Qu, San Li Tun, Beijing 100600; tel. (10) 65322531; fax (10) 65325032; e-mail mwbjing@kln.gov.my; internet www.kln.gov.my/web/chn_beijing; Ambassador Datuk ISKANDAR BIN SARUDIN.

Maldives: 1-5-31 Jian Guo Men Wai Diplomatic Compound, Jianwai Xiushui Lu, Chao Yang Qu, Beijing 100600; tel. (10) 85323847; fax (10) 85323746; e-mail admin@maldivesembassy.cn; internet www.maldivesembassy.cn; Ambassador AHMED LATHEEF.

Mali: 8 Dong Si Jie, San Li Tun, Beijing 100600; tel. (10) 65321704; fax (10) 65321618; e-mail ambamali@163bj.com; Ambassador N'TJI LAICO TRAORÉ.

Malta: 1-52 San Li Tun Diplomatic Compound, Gong Ti Bei Lu, Beijing 100600; tel. (10) 65323114; fax (10) 65326125; e-mail maltamembassy.beijing@gov.mt; internet www.mfa.gov.mt/china; Ambassador JOSEPH CASSAR.

Mauritania: 9 Dong San Jie, San Li Tun, Beijing 100600; tel. (10) 65321346; fax (10) 65321685; e-mail ambarim@ambarim-beijing.com; internet ambarim-beijing.com; Ambassador MOHAMED EL-HABIB BAL.

Mauritius: 202 Dong Wai Diplomatic Office Bldg, 23 Dong Zhi Men Wai Dajie, Chao Yang Qu, Beijing 100600; tel. (10) 65325695; fax (10) 65325706; e-mail mebj@public.bta.net.cn; Ambassador PAUL REYNOLD LIT FONG CHONG LEUNG.

Mexico: 5 Dong Wu Jie, San Li Tun, Beijing 100600; tel. (10) 65321717; fax (10) 65323744; e-mail embmxchn@public.bta.net.cn; internet www.sre.gob.mx/china; Ambassador JORGE EUGENIO GUAJARDO GONZÁLEZ.

Micronesia, Federated States: 1-1-11 Jian Guo Men Wai Diplomatic Compound, Chao Yang Qu, Beijing 100010; tel. (10) 65324738; fax (10) 65324609; e-mail embassy@fsmembassy.cn; Ambassador AKILLINO H. SUSAIA.

Moldova: 2-9-1 Tayuan Diplomatic Office Bldg, Chao Yang Qu, Beijing 100600; tel. (10) 65325494; fax (10) 65325379; e-mail beijing@mfa.md; Ambassador ANATOL URECHEANU.

Mongolia: 2 Xiu Shui Bei Jie, Jian Guo Men Wai, Beijing 100600; tel. (10) 65321203; fax (10) 65325045; e-mail mail@mongolembassychina.org; internet www.mongolembassychina.org; Ambassador TSEDENJAVYN SÜKHBAATAR.

Montenegro: 3-1-12 San Li Tun Diplomatic Compound, Beijing 100600; tel. (10) 65327610; fax (10) 65327662; e-mail china@mfa.gov.me; Ambassador LJILJANA TOSKOVIĆ.

Morocco: 16 San Li Tun Lu, Beijing 100600; tel. (10) 65321489; fax (10) 65321453; e-mail sifama.beijing@moroccoembassy.org.cn; Ambassador JAAFAR ALJ HAKIM.

Mozambique: 1-7-2 Tayuan Diplomatic Office Bldg, Chao Yang Qu, Beijing 100600; tel. (10) 65323664; fax (10) 65325189; e-mail embamoc@embmoz.org; Ambassador ANTÓNIO INÁCIO JÚNIOR.

Myanmar: 6 Dong Zhi Men Wai Dajie, Chao Yang Qu, Beijing 100600; tel. (10) 65320351; fax (10) 65320408; e-mail info@myanmarembassy.com; internet www.myanmarembassy.com; Ambassador TIN OO.

Namibia: 2-9-2 Tayuan Diplomatic Office Bldg, Chao Yang Qu, Beijing 100600; tel. (10) 65324810; fax (10) 65324549; e-mail namemb@eastnet.com.cn; Ambassador LEONARD NAMBAHU.

Nepal: 1 Xi Liu Jie, San Li Tun Lu, Beijing 100600; tel. (10) 65322739; fax (10) 65323251; e-mail beijing@nepalembassy.org.cn; internet www.nepalembassy.org.cn; Ambassador TANKA KARKI.

Netherlands: 4 Liang Ma He Nan Lu, Beijing 100600; tel. (10) 85320200; fax (10) 85320300; e-mail pek@minbuza.nl; internet www.hollandinchina.org; Ambassador RUDOLF BEKINK.

New Zealand: 1 Ri Tan, Dong Er Jie, Chao Yang Qu, Beijing 100600; tel. (10) 85327000; fax (10) 65324317; e-mail beijing.enquiries@mft.net.nz; internet www.nzembassy.com/china; Ambassador CARL ROBINSON WORKER.

Niger: 1-21 San Li Tun, Beijing 100600; tel. (10) 65324279; fax (10) 65327041; e-mail nigerbj@public.bta.net.cn; Ambassador ADAMOU BOUBAKAR.

Nigeria: 2 Dong Wu Jie, San Li Tun, Beijing; tel. (10) 65323631; fax (10) 65321650; e-mail nigerianembassybj@yahoo.com; internet www.nigeriaembassy.cn; Ambassador AMINU BASHIR WALI.

Norway: 1 Dong Yi Jie, San Li Tun, Beijing 100600; tel. (10) 85319600; fax (10) 65322392; e-mail emb.beijing@mfa.no; internet www.norway.cn; Ambassador SVEIN OLE SÆTHER.

Oman: 6 Liang Ma He Nan Lu, San Li Tun, Beijing 100600; tel. (10) 65323692; fax (10) 65327185; Ambassador ABDULLAH SALEH AL-SAADII.

Pakistan: 1 Dong Zhi Men Wai Dajie, San Li Tun, Beijing 100600; tel. (10) 65322504; fax (10) 65322715; e-mail info@pakembassy.cn; internet www.pakembassy.cn; Ambassador MASOOD KHAN.

Papua New Guinea: 2-11-2 Tayuan Diplomatic Office Bldg, Chao Yang Qu, Beijing 100600; tel. (10) 65324312; fax (10) 65325483; e-mail kundu_beijing@pngembassy.org.cn; internet en.pngembassy.org.cn; Ambassador CHRISTOPHER SIAOA MERO.

Peru: 1-91 San Li Tun, Bangonglou, Beijing 100600; tel. (10) 65323477; fax (10) 65322178; e-mail embaperu-pekin@rree.gob.pe; internet bio-visa.com/program/com/peru; Ambassador HAROLD FORSYTH MEJÍA.

Philippines: 23 Xiu Shui Bei Jie, Jian Guo Men Wai, Beijing 100600; tel. (10) 65321872; fax (10) 65323761; e-mail beijing.pe@dfa.gov.ph; internet www.philembassychina.org; Ambassador DOMINGO LEE.

Poland: 1 Ri Tan Lu, Jian Guo Men Wai, Chao Yang Qu, Beijing 100600; tel. (10) 65321235; fax (10) 65321745; e-mail polska@public2.bta.net.cn; internet www.pekin.polemb.net; Ambassador TADEUSZ CHOMICKI.

Portugal: 8 San Li Tun Dong Wu Jie, Beijing 100600; tel. (10) 65323242; fax (10) 65324637; e-mail embport@public2.bta.net.cn; Ambassador JOSÉ SOARES.

Qatar: A-7 Liang Ma Qiao Diplomatic Compound, Chao Yang Qu, Beijing 100600; tel. (10) 6532231; fax (10) 65325274; e-mail beijing@mofa.gov.qa; Ambassador ABDULLA A. AL-MUFTAH.

Romania: Ri Tan Lu, Dong Er Jie, Beijing 100600; tel. (10) 65323442; fax (10) 65325728; e-mail ambasada@roamb.link263.com; internet www.beijing.mae.ro; Chargé d'affaires a.i. ION DICU.

Russia: 4 Dong Zhi Men Nei, Bei Zhong Jie, Beijing 100600; tel. (10) 65322051; fax (10) 65324851; e-mail embassy@russia.org.cn; internet www.russia.org.cn; Ambassador SERGEI SERGEEVICH RAZOV.

Rwanda: 30 Xiu Shui Bei Jie, Jian Guo Men Wai, Beijing 100600; tel. (10) 65322193; fax (10) 65322006; e-mail ambabeijing@minaffet.gov.rw; internet www.china.embassy.gov.rw; Ambassador FRANÇOIS XAVIER NGARAMBE.

Samoa: 2-7-2 Tayuan Diplomatic Office Bldg, 14 Liang Ma He Nan Lu, Chao Yang Qu, Beijing 100600; tel. (10) 65321673; fax 65321642; Ambassador TAPUSALAIA TOOMATA.

Saudi Arabia: 1 Bei Xiao Jie, San Li Tun, Beijing 100600; tel. (10) 65324825; fax (10) 65325324; Ambassador YAHYA AL-ZAID.

Senegal: 305 Dong Wai Diplomatic Office Bldg, 23 Dong Zhi Men Wai Dajie, Beijing 100600; tel. (10) 65325035; fax (10) 65323730; Ambassador Gen. PAPE KHALILOU FALL.

Serbia: 1 Dong Liu Jie, San Li Tun, Beijing 100600; tel. (10) 65323516; fax (10) 65321207; e-mail embserbia@embserbia.cn; internet www.embserbia.cn; Ambassador MIOMIR UDOVICKI.

Seychelles: Rm 1105, The Spaces International Center, 8 Dong Da Qiao, Chao Yang Qu, Beijing 100020; tel. (10) 58701192; fax (10) 58701219; e-mail amb.legall@yahoo.com; Ambassador PHILIPPE LE GALL.

Sierra Leone: 7 Dong Zhi Men Wai Dajie, Beijing 100600; tel. (10) 65322174; fax (10) 65323752; e-mail slbeijing@foreignaffairs.gov.sl; Ambassador ABU BAKARR MULTI-KAMARA (designate).

Singapore: 1 Xiu Shui Bei Jie, Jian Guo Men Wai, Chao Yang Qu, Beijing 100600; tel. (10) 65321115; fax (10) 65329405; e-mail singemb_bej@sgmfa.gov.sg; internet www.mfa.gov.sg/beijing; Ambassador STANLEY LOH KA LEUNG.

Slovakia: Ri Tan Lu, Jian Guo Men Wai, Beijing 100600; tel. (10) 65321531; fax (10) 65324814; e-mail emb.beijing@mzv.sk; internet www.mzv.sk/peking; Ambassador FRANTIŠEK DLHOPOLČEK.

Slovenia: Block F, 57 Ya Qu Yuan, King's Garden Villas, 18 Xiao Yun Lu, Chao Yang Qu, Beijing 100016; tel. (10) 64681030; fax (10) 64681040; e-mail vpe@gov.si; internet beijing.embassy.si; Ambassador MARIJA ADANJA.

Somalia: 2 San Li Tun Lu, Beijing 100600; tel. and fax (10) 65321651; fax (10) 65321752; e-mail somaliaemb.beij@yahoo.com; Ambassador MOHAMMED AHMED AWIL.

South Africa: 5 Dong Zhi Men Wai Dajie, Chao Yang Qu, Beijing 100600; tel. (10) 85320000; fax (10) 65327319; e-mail embassy@saembassy.org.cn; internet www.saembassy.org.cn; Ambassador W. J. LANGA.

Spain: 9 San Li Tun Lu, Beijing 100600; tel. (10) 65323629; fax (10) 65323401; e-mail embespcn@mail.mae.es; internet www.mae.es/embajadas/pekin; Ambassador EUGENIO BREGOLAT OBIOLS.

Sri Lanka: 3 Jian Hua Lu, Jian Guo Men Wai, Beijing 100600; tel. (10) 65321861; fax (10) 65325426; e-mail lkembj@public3.bta.net.cn; internet www.slemb.com; Ambassador KARUNATILAKA AMUNUGAMA.

Sudan: 1 Dong Er Jie, San Li Tun, Beijing 100600; tel. (10) 65323715; fax (10) 65321280; Ambassador MIRGHANI MOHAMED SALIH.

Suriname: 2-2-22 Jian Guo Men Wai Diplomatic Compound, Beijing 100600; tel. (10) 65322938; fax (10) 65322941; e-mail surinamechina@gmail.com; Ambassador (vacant).

Sweden: 3 Dong Zhi Men Wai Dajie, San Li Tun, Beijing 100600; tel. (10) 65329790; fax (10) 65325008; e-mail ambassaden.peking@foreign.ministry.se; internet www.swedenabroad.com/peking; Ambassador LARS FREDÉN.

Switzerland: 3 Dong Wu Jie, San Li Tun, Beijing 100600; tel. (10) 85328888; fax (10) 65324353; e-mail bei.vertretung@eda.admin.ch; internet www.eda.admin.ch/beijing; Ambassador BLAISE GODET.

Syria: 6 Dong Si Jie, San Li Tun, Beijing 100600; tel. (10) 65321372; fax (10) 65321575; e-mail sy@syria.org.cn; internet www.syria.org.cn; Ambassador Dr KHALAF AL-JARAD.

Tajikistan: 5-1-41 Tayuan Diplomatic Office Bldg, Chao Yang Qu, Beijing 100600; tel. (10) 65322598; fax (10) 65323039; e-mail tjkemb@public2.bta.net.cn; Ambassador RASHID ALIMOV.

Tanzania: 8 Liang Ma He Nan Lu, San Li Tun, Beijing 100600; tel. (10) 65321719; fax (10) 65324351; e-mail beijing@tanzaniaembassy.org.cn; internet www.tanzaniaembassy.org.cn; Ambassador OMAR RAMADHAN MAPURI.

Thailand: 40 Guang Hua Lu, Jian Guo Men Wai, Beijing 100600; tel. (10) 65321749; fax (10) 65321748; e-mail thaibej@public.bta.net.cn; internet www.thaiembbeij.org; Ambassador PIAMSAK MILINTACHINDA.

Timor-Leste: Rm 156, Gold Island Diplomatic Compound, 1 Xi Ba He Nan Lu, Beijing 100028; tel. (10) 64403072; fax (10) 64403071; e-mail rdtlemb_beijing04@yahoo.com; Ambassador VICKY FUN HA TCHONG.

Togo: 11 Dong Zhi Men Wai Dajie, Beijing 100600; tel. (10) 65322202; fax (10) 65325884; Ambassador NOLANA TA-AMA.

Tonga: 1-2-11 Jian Guo Men Wai Diplomatic Compound, Beijing 100600; tel. (10) 65327203; fax (10) 65327204; Ambassador SIAMELIE LATU.

Tunisia: 1 Dong Jie, San Li Tun, Chao Yang Qu, Beijing 100600; tel. (10) 65322435; fax (10) 65325818; e-mail at_beijing@netchina.com.cn; Ambassador Dr MOHAMED ADEL SMAOUI.

Turkey: 9 Dong Wu Jie, San Li Tun, Beijing 100600; tel. (10) 65321715; fax (10) 65325480; e-mail embassy.beijing@mfa.gov.tr; internet beijing.emb.mfa.gov.tr; Ambassador MURAT SALIM ESENLI.

Turkmenistan: D-1 King's Garden Villas, 18 Xiao Yuan Lu, Beijing; tel. (10) 65326975; fax (10) 65326976; e-mail embturkmen@netchina.com.cn; Ambassador GRUBANNAZAR NAZAROV.

Uganda: 5 Dong Jie, San Li Tun, Beijing 100600; tel. (10) 65321708; fax (10) 65322242; Ambassador CHARLES MADIBO WAGIDOSO.

Ukraine: 11 Dong Liu Jie, San Li Tun, Beijing 100600; tel. (10) 65326359; fax (10) 65324014; e-mail gc_cnp@mfa.gov.ua; internet www.mfa.gov.ua/china; Ambassador YURII KOSTENKO.

United Arab Emirates: LA-10-04 Liang Ma Qiao Diplomatic Compound, 22 Dong Fang Dong Lu, Beijing; tel. (10) 65327651; fax (10) 65327652; e-mail beijing@mofa.gov.ae; Ambassador OMAR AHMED OUDAI NASEEB AL-BETAR.

United Kingdom: 11 Guang Hua Lu, Jian Guo Men Wai, Beijing 100600; tel. (10) 51924000; fax (10) 51924239; e-mail consular.beijing@fco.gov.uk; internet www.ukinchina.fco.gov.uk; Ambassador SEBASTIAN WOOD.

USA: 3 Xiu Shui Bei Jie, Jian Guo Men Wai, Beijing 100600; tel. (10) 85313000; fax (10) 85314200; e-mail ircacee@state.gov; internet beijing.usembassy-china.org.cn; Ambassador GARY LOCKE.

Uruguay: 1-11-2 Tayuan Diplomatic Office Bldg, Chao Yang Qu, Beijing 100600; tel. (10) 65324445; fax (10) 65327375; e-mail urubei@public.bta.net.cn; Ambassador ROSARIO PORTELL.

Uzbekistan: 11 Bei Xiao Jie, San Li Tun, Beijing 100600; tel. (10) 65326305; fax (10) 65326304; Ambassador ALISHER A. SALAHITDINOV.

Vanuatu: 3-1-11 San Li Tun Diplomatic Compound, Chao Yang Qu, Beijing 100600; tel. (10) 65320337; fax (10) 65320336; e-mail info@vanuatuembassy.org.cn; internet www.vanuatuembassy.org.cn; Ambassador WILLIE JIMMY TAPANGARARUA.

Venezuela: 14 San Li Tun Lu, Beijing 100600; tel. (10) 65321295; fax (10) 65323817; e-mail embvenez@public.bta.net.cn; internet www.venezuela.org.cn; Ambassador ROCÍO MANEIRO GONZÁLEZ.

Viet Nam: 32 Guang Hua Lu, Jian Guo Men Wai, Beijing 100600; tel. (10) 65321155; fax (10) 65325720; e-mail suquanbk@yahoo.com; internet www.vnemba.org.cn; Ambassador NGUYEN VAN THO.

Yemen: 5 Dong San Jie, San Li Tun, Beijing 100600; tel. (10) 65321558; fax (10) 65327997; e-mail info@embassyofyemen.net; internet www.embassyofyemen.net; Ambassador ABDULMALEK SULAIMAN M. AL-MUALEMI.

Zambia: 5 Dong Si Jie, San Li Tun, Chao Yang Qu, Beijing 100600; tel. (10) 65321554; fax (10) 65321891; e-mail admin@zambiaembassy-beijing.com; internet www.zambiaembassy-beijing.com; Ambassador JOYCE MWAKA CHEMBE MUSENGE.

Zimbabwe: 7 Dong San Jie, San Li Tun, Beijing 100600; tel. (10) 65323795; fax (10) 65325383; e-mail zimbei@163.bj.com; Ambassador FREDERICK M. SHAVA.

Judicial System

The general principles of the Chinese judicial system are laid down in Articles 123–135 of the 1982 Constitution.

PEOPLE'S COURTS

Supreme People's Court: 27 Dongjiaomin Xiang, Beijing 100745; tel. (10) 67550114; e-mail info@court.gov.cn; internet www.court.gov.cn; f. 1949; the highest judicial organ of the State; handles first instance cases of national importance; handles cases of appeals and protests lodged against judgments and orders of higher people's courts and special people's courts, and cases of protests lodged by the Supreme People's Procuratorate in accordance with the procedures of judicial supervision; reviews death sentences meted out by local courts, supervises the administration of justice by local people's courts; interprets issues concerning specific applications of laws in judicial proceedings; its judgments and rulings are final; Pres. WANG SHENGJUN (five-year term of office coincides with that of National People's Congress, by which the President is elected).

Local People's Courts: comprise higher courts, intermediate courts and basic courts.

Special People's Courts: include military courts, maritime courts and railway transport courts.

PEOPLE'S PROCURATORATES

Supreme People's Procuratorate: 147 Beiheyan Dajie, Beijing 100726; tel. (10) 65209114; e-mail web@spp.gov.cn; internet www.spp.gov.cn; acts for the National People's Congress in examining govt depts, civil servants and citizens, to ensure observance of the law; prosecutes in criminal cases; Procurator-Gen. CAO JIANMING (elected by the National People's Congress for a five-year term).

Local People's Procuratorates: undertake the same duties at the local level; ensure that the judicial activities of the people's courts, the execution of sentences in criminal cases and the activities of departments in charge of reform through labour conform to the law; institute, or intervene in, important civil cases that affect the interest of the State and the people.

Religion

The 1982 Constitution states that citizens enjoy freedom of religious belief and that legitimate religious activities are protected. Since 1994 all religious organizations have been required to register with the Bureau of Religious Affairs. In the late 1990s a new religious sect, Falun Gong (also known as Falun Dafa, and incorporating elements of Buddhism and Daoism) emerged and quickly gained new adherents. However, the authorities banned the group in 1999.

State Administration for Religious Affairs: 32 Beisantiao, Jiaodaokou, Dongcheng Qu, Beijing 100007; tel. (10) 64023355; fax (10) 66013565; Dir WANG ZUOAN.

ANCESTOR WORSHIP

Ancestor worship is believed to have originated with the deification and worship of all important natural phenomena. The divine and human were not clearly defined; all the dead became gods and were worshipped by their descendants. The practice has no code or dogma, and the ritual is limited to sacrifices made during festivals and on birth and death anniversaries.

BUDDHISM

Buddhism was introduced into China from India in AD 67, and flourished during the Sui and Tang dynasties (6th–8th century), when eight sects were established. The Chan and Pure Land sects are the most popular. The dominant religion of Tibet (Xizang) is Tibetan Buddhism or Lamaism, a branch of Vajrayana Buddhism.

Buddhist Association of China (BAC): f. 1953; Pres. YIN CHUAN; Sec.-Gen. XUE CHENG.

Tibetan Institute of Lamaism: Pres. BUMI JANGBALUOZHU; Vice-Pres. CEMOLIN DANZENGCHILIE.

14th Dalai Lama: His Holiness the Dalai Lama TENZIN GYATSO; spiritual leader of Tibet; fled to India following the failure of the Tibetan national uprising in 1959; resident at: Thekchen Choeling, McLeod Ganj, Dharamsala 176 219, Himachal Pradesh, India; tel. (91) 1892-21343; fax (91) 1892-21813; e-mail ohhdl@cta.unv.ernet.ind; internet www.tibet.com.

CHRISTIANITY

In the early 21st century there was a revival of interest in the Christian faith. The official Catholic Church in China operates independently of the Vatican. The 'underground' Catholic Church is recognized by the Vatican. Various Christian sects have continued to expand in China. By 2009 the number of Chinese Christians had reached an estimated 130m. Of these, 100m. were believed to be independent worshippers, with only 21m. adhering to the official Protestant Church and 5m. to the approved Catholic Church.

Three-Self Patriotic Movement Committee of Protestant Churches of China: 219 Jiujiang Lu, Shanghai 200002; tel. (21) 63210806; fax (21) 63232605; e-mail tspmccc@online.sh.cn; Chair. Rev. FU XIANWEI; Gen. Sec. Rev. XU XIAOHONG.

Catholic Church: Catholic Mission, Si-She-Ku, Beijing; Bishop of Beijing JOSEPH LI SHAN.

China Christian Council: 219 Jiujiang Lu, Shanghai 200002; tel. (21) 63210806; fax (21) 63232605; e-mail tspmccc@online.sh.cn; f. 1980; comprises provincial Christian councils; Pres. Rev. K. H. TING; Gen. Sec. Rev. KAN BAOPING.

Chinese Patriotic Catholic Association: Pres. JOHN FANG XINGYAO; Sec.-Gen. LIU BAINIAN.

CONFUCIANISM

Confucianism is a philosophy and a system of ethics, without ritual or priesthood. The respect that adherents accord to Confucius is not bestowed on a prophet or god, but on a great sage whose teachings promote peace and good order in society and whose philosophy encourages moral living.

DAOISM

Daoism was founded by Zhang Daoling during the Eastern Han dynasty (AD 125–144). Lao Zi, a philosopher of the Zhou dynasty (born 604 BC), is its principal inspiration, and is honoured as Lord the Most High by Daoists. According to unofficial sources, there were 1,600 Daoist temples in China in 2005.

China Daoist Association: Temple of the White Cloud, Xi Bian Men, Beijing 100045; tel. (10) 63406670; e-mail chinadaosim@yahoo.com.cn; internet www.taoist.org.cn; f. 1957; Pres. REN FARONG; Sec.-Gen. YUAN BINGDONG.

ISLAM

Islam was introduced into China in AD 651. There were some 20.3m. adherents in China in 2000 according to official sources, mainly among the Wei Wuer (Uygur) and Hui people, although unofficial sources estimate that the total is far higher.

Beijing Islamic Association: Dongsi Mosque, Beijing; f. 1979; Chair. Imam Al-Hadji CHEN GUANGYUAN.

China Islamic Association: Beijing 100053; tel. (10) 63546384; fax (10) 63529483; internet www.chinaislam.net.cn; f. 1953; Chair. Imam Al-Hadji CHEN GUANGYUAN; Sec.-Gen. YU ZHENGUI.

The Press

In 2009 China had 1,937 newspaper titles (including those below provincial level) and 9,851 magazines. Each province publishes its own daily newspaper. The major newspapers and periodicals are listed below.

PRINCIPAL NEWSPAPERS

Anhui Ribao (Anhui Daily): 1469 Zhongshan Lu, Hefei, Anhui 230071; tel. (551) 5179860; fax (551) 2832534; e-mail ahch2005@163.com; internet www.anhuinews.com; Editor-in-Chief SUN BANGKUN.

Beijing Ribao (Beijing Daily): 20 Jian Guo Men Nei Dajie, Beijing 100734; tel. (10) 85201843; fax (10) 65136522; internet www.bjd.com.cn; f. 1952; organ of the Beijing municipal cttee of the CCP; Dir WAN YUNLAI; Editor-in-Chief LIU ZONGMING; circ. 700,000.

Beijing Wanbao (Beijing Evening News): 20 Jian Guo Men Nei Dajie, Beijing 100734; tel. 8008108440 (mobile); fax (10) 65126581; internet www.ben.com.cn; f. 1958; Editor-in-Chief REN HUANYING; circ. 800,000.

Beijing Youth Daily: Beijing; tel. (10) 65901655; e-mail jubao@ynet.com; internet bjyouth.ynet.com; national and local news; promotes ethics and social service; circ. 3m.–4m.

Changsha Wanbao (Changsha Evening News): 161 Caie Zhong Lu, Changsha, Hunan 410005; tel. (731) 4424457; fax (731) 4445167.

Chengdu Wanbao (Chengdu Evening News): Qingyun Nan Jie, Chengdu 610017; tel. (28) 664501; fax (28) 666597; circ. 700,000.

China Economic Times: Palace St, Changping Qu, Beijing 102209; tel. (10) 81785100; fax (10) 81785120; e-mail cesnew@163.com; internet www.jjxww.com; economic news; publ. by the Development Research Centre of the State Council.

China Times: Wanda Plaza, 93 Jianguo Lu, Chaoyang Qu, Beijing 100022; tel. (10) 59250005; internet www.chinatimes.cc; f. 1989; finance; weekly.

Chongqing Ribao (Chongqing Daily): Chongqing; Dir and Editor-in-Chief LI HUANIAN.

Chungcheng Wanbao (Chungcheng Evening News): 51 Xinwen Lu, Kunming, Yunnan 650032; tel. (871) 4144642; fax (871) 4154192.

Dazhong Ribao (Dazhong Daily): Dazhong News Bldg, 4/F, 6 Luoyuan Dajie, Jinan, Shandong 250014; tel. (531) 85193611; fax (531) 2962450; internet www.dzwww.com; f. 1939; Dir XU XIYU; Editor-in-Chief LIU GUANGDONG; circ. 2,100,000.

Fujian Ribao (Fujian Daily): 84 Hualin Lu, Fuzhou, Fujian; tel. (591) 87079319; e-mail fjnet.cn@163.com; internet www.fjdaily.com; daily; Dir HUANG SHIYUN; Editor-in-Chief HUANG ZHONGSHENG.

Gansu Ribao (Gansu Daily): Gansu; tel. (931) 8157213; fax (931) 8158955; e-mail gansudaily@163.com; internet www.gansudaily.com.cn.

Gongren Ribao (Workers' Daily): Dongcheng Qu, Beijing 100718; tel. (10) 84151567; fax (10) 84151516; e-mail news@workercn.cn; internet www.workercn.cn; f. 1949; trade union activities and workers' lives; also major home and overseas news; Dir LIU YUMING; Editor-in-Chief SHENG MINGFU; circ. 2,500,000.

Guangming Ribao (Guangming Daily): 5 Dong Lu, Chongwen Qu, Zhushikou, 100062; tel. (10) 67078856; fax (10) 67078854; e-mail webmaster@gmw.cn; internet www.gmw.cn; f. 1949; literature, art, science, education, history, economics, philosophy; Editor-in-Chief YUAN ZHIFA; circ. 920,000.

Guangxi Ribao (Guangxi Daily): Guangxi Region; tel. (771) 5690995; fax (771) 5690933; e-mail newgx@gxrb.com.cn; internet www.gxnews.com.cn; Dir and Editor-in-Chief CHENG ZHENSHENG; circ. 650,000.

Guangzhou Ribao (Canton Daily): 10 Dongle Lu, Renmin Zhonglu, Guangzhou, Guangdong; tel. (20) 81919191; fax (20) 81862022; internet gzdaily.dayoo.com; f. 1952; daily; social, economic and current affairs; Editor-in-Chief LI YUANJIANG; circ. 600,000.

Guizhou Ribao (Guizhou Daily): Guiyang, Guizhou; tel. (851) 6793333; fax (851) 6625615; internet gzrb.gog.com.cn; f. 1949; Dir GAO ZONGWEN; Editor-in-Chief GAN ZHENGSHU; circ. 300,000.

Hainan Ribao (Hainan Daily): News Bldg, 9/F, Haikou, Hainan 570001; tel. (898) 66810815; fax (898) 66810545; e-mail hnrb@hndaily.com.cn; internet hnrb.hinews.cn; Dir ZHOU WENZHANG; Editor-in-Chief CHANG FUTANG.

Harbin Ribao (Harbin Daily): Harbin; internet www.harbindaily.com.

Hebei Ribao (Hebei Daily): 210 Yuhuazhong Lu, Shijiazhuang, Hebei 050013; tel. (311) 88631054; fax (311) 6046969; e-mail webmaster@hebeidaily.com; internet hebnews.cn; f. 1949; Dir GUO ZENGPEI; Editor-in-Chief PAN GUILIANG; circ. 500,000.

Heilongjiang Ribao (Heilongjiang Daily): Heilongjiang Province; tel. (451) 84656368; e-mail hljnews@hljnews.cn; internet www.hljnews.cn; Dir JIA HONGTU; Editor-in-Chief AI HE.

Henan Ribao (Henan Daily): Henan Newspaper Network Center, 10/F, 28 East Agriculture Rd, Zhengzhou, Henan 450008; tel. and fax (371) 65795870; e-mail dahenews@dahe.cn; internet www.dahe.cn; f. 1949; Dir YANG YONGDE; Editor-in-Chief GUO ZHENGLING; circ. 390,000.

Huadong Xinwen (Eastern China News): f. 1995; published by Renmin Ribao.

Huanan Xinwen (South China News): Guangzhou; f. 1997; published by Renmin Ribao.

Hubei Ribao (Hubei Daily): Metropolis Media Bldg, 13/F, 181 Wuchang Dong Wu Lu, Wuhan, Hubei 430077; tel. (27) 88567711; e-mail webmaster@cnhubei.com; internet www.cnhubei.com; f. 1949; Editor-in-Chief YAN SITIAN; circ. 800,000.

Hulunbeir Ribao (Hulunbeir Daily): 28 Victory Ave, Hahilar, Hulunbeir; tel. (470) 8252039; fax (470) 8258035; e-mail hlbrdaily@163.com; internet www.hlbrdaily.com.cn.

Hunan Ribao (Hunan Daily): 18 Furong Zhong Lu, Changsha, Hunan 410071; tel. (731) 4312999; fax (731) 4314029; Dir JIANG XIANLI; Editor-in-Chief WAN MAOHUA.

Jiangxi Ribao (Jiangxi Daily): 175 Yangming Jie, Nanchang, Jiangxi; tel. (791) 6849868; fax (791) 6849008; internet www.jxnews.com.cn/jxrb; f. 1949; Dir ZHOU JINGUANG; circ. 300,000.

Jiefang Ribao (Liberation Daily): 300 Han Kou Lu, Shanghai 200001; tel. (21) 63521111; fax (21) 63516517; e-mail info@jfdaily.com; internet www.jfdaily.com.cn; f. 1949; Editor-in-Chief JIA SHUMEI; circ. 1m.

Jiefangjun Bao (Liberation Army Daily): 34 Fuchengmenwai Dajie, Xicheng Qu, Beijing 100832; tel. (10) 68577779; fax (10) 68577779; e-mail feedback@jfjb.com.cn; internet www.chinamil.com.cn; f. 1956; official organ of the Central Military Commission; Dir Maj.-Gen. ZHANG SHIGANG; Editor-in-Chief WANG MENGYUN; circ. 800,000.

Jilin Ribao (Jilin Daily): Changchun, Jilin Province; tel. (431) 88600621; fax (431) 88600622; e-mail news@chinajilin.com.cn; internet www.chinajilin.com.cn; Dir and Editor-in-Chief YI HONGBIN.

Jingji Ribao (Economic Daily): 2 Bai Zhi Fang Dong Jie, Xuanwu Qu, Beijing 100054; tel. (10) 83512266; fax (10) 83543336; e-mail en_feedback@mail.ce.cn; internet www.ce.cn; f. 1983; financial affairs, domestic and foreign trade; administered by the State Council; Editor-in-Chief TUO ZHEN; circ. 1.2m.

Jinrong Shibao (Financial News): 18 Zhongguancun Nan Dajie, 18–22/F, Blk D, Haidan Qu, Beijing 100081; tel. (10) 82198111; fax (10) 82198029; e-mail fnweb@126.com; internet www.financialnews.com.cn.

Liaoning Ribao (Liaoning Daily): Shenyang, Liaoning Province; tel. (10) 22698539; e-mail lnd@lndaily.com.cn; internet www.lndaily.com.cn; Dir XIE ZHENGQIAN.

Nanfang Ribao (Nanfang Daily): 289 Guangzhou Da Lu, Guangzhou, Guangdong 510601; tel. (20) 87373998; fax (20) 87375806; internet nf.nfdaily.cn; f. 1949; Nanfang Daily Group also publishes *Nanfang Dushi Bao* (Southern Metropolis Daily), *Ershiyi Shiji Jingji Baodao* (21st Century Economic Herald), and weekly edn *Nanfang Zhoumou* (Southern Weekend); Dir YANG XINFENG; Editor WANG FU; circ. 1m.

Nanjing Ribao (Nanjing Daily): 223 Nanjing Lu, Shanghai 210002; tel. (25) 84499000; internet njrb.njnews.cn.

Nongmin Ribao (Peasants' Daily): Shilipu Beili, Chao Yang Qu, Beijing 100029; tel. (10) 85831572; fax (10) 85832154; e-mail zbs@farmer.com.cn; internet www.farmer.com.cn/wlb/nmrb; f. 1980; 6 a week; circulates in rural areas nation-wide; Dir ZHANG DEXIU; Editor LIU ZHENYUN; circ. 1m.

Renmin Ribao (People's Daily): 2 Jin Tai Xi Lu, Chao Yang Qu, Beijing 100733; tel. (10) 65363470; fax (10) 65363689; e-mail info@peopledaily.com.cn; internet www.people.com.cn; f. 1948; organ of the CCP; also publishes overseas edn; Pres. ZHANG YANNONG; Editor-in-Chief WU HENGQUAN; circ. 2.15m.

Shaanxi Ribao (Shaanxi Daily): 1 East Ring Rd, Xian, Shaanxi Province 710054; tel. (29) 82267114; fax (29) 82267082; e-mail sxdaily@tom.com; internet www.sxdaily.com.cn; Dir LI DONGSHENG; Editor-in-Chief DU YAOFENG.

Shanxi Ribao (Shanxi Daily): 124 Shuangtasi Jie, Taiyuan, Shanxi; tel. (351) 4281494; fax (351) 4283320; internet www.sxrb.com; CEO LIU XINYU; Editor-in-Chief HU KAIMIN; circ. 300,000.

Shenzhen Tequ Bao (Shenzhen Special Economic Zone Daily): 4 Shennan Zhonglu, Shenzhen 518009; tel. (755) 83518877; e-mail sznews@sznews.com; internet www.sznews.com; f. 1982; reports on special economic zones, as well as mainland, Hong Kong and Macao; Editor-in-Chief HUANG YANGLUE.

Sichuan Ribao (Sichuan Daily): Sichuan Daily Press Group, 70 Hongxing Zhong Lu, Erduan, Chengdu, Sichuan 610012; tel. and fax (28) 86968000; e-mail 028@scol.com.cn; internet www.sichuandaily.com.cn; f. 1952; Chair. of Bd YU CHANGQIU; Editor-in-Chief LUO XIAOGANG; circ. 8m.

Tianjin Ribao (Tianjin Daily): Tianjin Bldg, 10/F, 873 Dagu Nan Lu, Heri Qu, Tianjin 300211; tel. (22) 28201063; fax (22) 28201064; e-mail tjw@tjrb.com.cn; internet www.tianjinwe.com; f. 1949; Editor-in-Chief WANG HONG; circ. 600,000.

Wenhui Bao (Wenhui Daily): 50 Huqiu Lu, Shanghai 200002; tel. (21) 63211410; fax (21) 63230198; internet wenhui.news365.com.cn; f. 1938; Editor-in-Chief WU ZHENBIAO; circ. 500,000.

Xin Jing Bao (The Beijing News): 37 Xingfu Bei Lu, Dongcheng Qu, Beijing 100061; tel. (10) 67106666; fax (10) 67106777; e-mail shepingbj@vip.sina.com; internet www.bjnews.com.cn; f. 2003 as jt venture by owners of Guangming Ribao and Nanfang Ribao; Editor-in-chief (vacant).

Xin Min Wan Bao (Xin Min Evening News): 839 Yan An Zhong Lu, Shanghai 200040; tel. (21) 62791234; fax (21) 62473220; e-mail newmedia@wxjt.com.cn; internet xmwb.news365.com.cn; f. 1929; specializes in public policy, education and social affairs; Editor-in-Chief HU JINGJUN; circ. 1.8m.

Xinhua Ribao (New China Daily): Dacheng Plaza, 20/F, 127 Xuanwumen Xi Lu, Beijing 100031; tel. (10) 63070950; fax (10) 63070938; e-mail xhszbs@xinhuanet.com; internet www.xinhuanet.com; Editor-in-Chief HE PING; circ. 900,000.

Xinjiang Ribao (Xinjiang Daily): Daily News Bldg, 11/F, Yangtze River Rd, Urumqi, Xinjiang 830051; tel. (991) 5593345; fax (991) 5859962; e-mail info@xjdaily.com; internet www.xjdaily.com; Editor-in-Chief HUANG YANCAI.

Xizang Ribao (Tibet Daily): Lhasa, Tibet; Editor-in-Chief LI ERLIANG.

Yangcheng Wanbao (Yangcheng Evening News): 7/F, Yangcheng Wanbao Bldg, 733 Dongfeng Dong Lu, Guangzhou, Guangdong 510085; tel. (20) 87319116; fax (20) 87133836; e-mail kefu@ycwb.net; internet www.ycwb.com; f. 1957; Editor-in-Chief PAN WEIWEN; circ. 1.3m.

Yunnan Ribao (Yunnan Daily): 51 Xinwen Lu, Kunming 650032; tel. (871) 4160447; fax (871) 4156165; e-mail ynrb-zbs@yndaily.com; internet www.yndaily.com; Editor-in-Chief LUO JIE.

Zhejiang Ribao (Zhejiang Daily): Zhejiang Province; tel. (571) 85310961; e-mail zjrb@zjnews.com.cn; internet zjdaily.zjol.com.cn; f. 1949; Pres. GAO HAIHAO; Editor-in-Chief YANG DAJIN.

Zhongguo Qingnian Bao (China Youth Daily): 2 Haiyuncang, Dong Zhi Men Nei, Dongcheng Qu, Beijing 100702; tel. (10) 64098088; fax (10) 64098077; e-mail cyd@cyd.net.cn; internet www.cyol.com; f. 1951; daily; aimed at 14–40 age-group; Dir XU ZHUQING; Editor-in-Chief CHEN XIAOCHUAN; circ. 1.0m.

Zhongguo Ribao (China Daily): 15 Huixin Dong Jie, Chao Yang Qu, Beijing 100029; tel. (10) 64995000; fax (10) 64918377; internet www.chinadaily.com.cn; f. 1981; English; China's political, economic and cultural developments; world, financial and sports news; also publishes *Business Weekly* (f. 1985), *Beijing Weekend* (f. 1991), *Shanghai Star* (f. 1992), *Reports from China* (f. 1992), *21st Century* (f. 1993), *China Daily Hong Kong Edition* ; Editor-in-Chief ZHU LING; circ. 300,000.

Zhongguo Xinwen (China News): 12 Baiwanzhuang Nan Jie, Beijing 100037; tel. (10) 87826688; fax (10) 68327649; e-mail gaojian@chinanews.com.cn; internet www.chinanews.com; f. 1952; daily; current affairs; Editor-in-Chief WANG XIJIN.

SELECTED PERIODICALS

Ban Yue Tan (China Comment): Shijingshan Qu, Beijing 100043; tel. (10) 63074102; fax (10) 63074105; e-mail news_byt@xinhua.org; internet www.xinhuanet.com/banyt; f. 1980; in Chinese and Wei Wuer (Uygur); Editor-in-Chief DONG RUISHENG; circ. 6m.

Beijing Review: 24 Baiwanzhuang Lu, Xicheng Qu, Beijing 100037; tel. (10) 68996288; fax (10) 68328738; e-mail contact@bjreview.com.cn; internet www.bjreview.com.cn; f. 1958; weekly; English; also *Chinafrica* (monthly in English and French); Publr WANG GANGYI; Editor-in-Chief LII HAIBO.

BJ TV Weekly: 2 Fu Xing Men Wai Zhenwumiao Jie, Beijing 100045; tel. (10) 6366036; fax (10) 63262388; circ. 1m.

Caijing: 19/F, Prime Tower, 22 Chaoyangmenwai Lu, Beijing 100020; tel. (10) 65885047; fax (10) 65885046; e-mail newsroom@caijing.com.cn; internet www.caijing.com.cn; f. 1998; business and finance; 2 a month; Editor WANG BOMING.

China TV Weekly: 15 Huixin Dong Jie, Chao Yang Qu, Beijing 100013; tel. (10) 64214197; circ. 1.7m.

Chinese Literature Press: 24 Baiwanzhuang Lu, Beijing 100037; tel. (10) 68326010; fax (10) 68326678; e-mail chinalit@public.east.cn.net; f. 1951; monthly (bilingual in English); quarterly (bilingual in French); contemporary and classical writing, poetry, literary criticism and arts; Exec. Editor LING YUAN.

Chinese National Geography: Rm 200, Jia 11, Datun Rd, Chaoyang Qu, Beijing 100101; tel. (10) 64865566; fax (10) 64859755; e-mail bjb@cng.com.cn; internet cng.dili360.com; f. 1950; monthly; world geography, anthropology and nature; Editor LI SHUAN.

Dianying Xinzuo (New Films): 796 Huaihai Zhong Lu, Shanghai; tel. (21) 64379710; f. 1979; bi-monthly; introduces new films.

Dianzi yu Diannao (Compotech China): Beijing; tel. (10) 82563704; fax (10) 82563744; e-mail jane_ma@compotech.com.cn; internet www.compotech.com.cn; f. 1985; popular information on computers and microcomputers; Editorial Man. MALAN JUAN.

Elle (China): 14 Lane 955, Yan'an Zhong Lu, Shanghai; tel. (21) 62790974; fax (21) 62479056; internet www.ellechina.com; f. 1988; monthly; fashion; Publr and Editor-in-Chief XIAO XUE; circ. 300,000.

Guoji Xin Jishu (New International Technology): Zhanwang Publishing House, Beijing; f. 1984; also publ. in Hong Kong; international technology, scientific and technical information.

Guowai Keji Dongtai (Recent Developments in Science and Technology Abroad): Institute of Scientific and Technical Information of China, 54 San Li He Lu, Beijing 100045; tel. (10) 58882491; fax (10) 58882288; e-mail kjdt@istic.ac.cn; internet www.wanfang.com.cn; f. 1962; monthly; scientific journal; Editor-in-Chief GUO YUEHUA; circ. 40,000.

Huasheng Monthly (Voice for Overseas Chinese): 12 Bai Wan Zhuang Nan Jie, Beijing 100037; tel. and fax (10) 68315039; internet www.chinaqw.com; f. 1995; monthly; intended mainly for overseas Chinese and Chinese nationals resident abroad; Editor-in-Chief FAN DONGSHENG.

Jianzhu (Construction): Baiwanzhuang, Beijing; tel. (10) 68992849; f. 1956; monthly; Editor FANG YUEGUANG; circ. 500,000.

Jinri Zhongguo (China Today): 24 Baiwanzhuang Lu, Beijing 100037; tel. (10) 68996376; fax (10) 68328338; e-mail chinatodaynews@yahoo.com.cn; internet www.chinatoday.com.cn; f. 1952; fmrly China Reconstructs; monthly; edns in English, Spanish, French, Arabic and Chinese; economic, social and cultural affairs; illustrated; Pres. and Editor-in-Chief HUANG ZU'AN.

Liaowang (Outlook): 57 Xuanwumen Xijie, Beijing; tel. (10) 63073049; internet news.sohu.com/liaowang; f. 1981; weekly; current affairs; Gen. Man. ZHOU YICHANG; Editor-in-Chief JI BIN; circ. 500,000.

Luxingjia (Traveller): Beijing; tel. (10) 6552631; f. 1955; monthly; Chinese scenery, customs, culture.

Meishu Zhi You (Chinese Art Digest): 32 Beizongbu Hutong, East City Region, Beijing; tel. (10) 65591404; f. 1982; every 2 months; art review journal, also providing information on fine arts publs in China and abroad; Editors ZONGYUAN GAO, PEI CHENG.

Nongye Zhishi (Agricultural Knowledge): 21 Ming Zi Qian Lu, Jinan, Shandong 250100; tel. (531) 88935267; fax (531) 88550734; e-mail sdnyzs@jn-public.sd.cninfo.net; internet www.sdny.com.cn; f. 1950; fortnightly; popular agricultural science; Dir YANG LIJIAN; circ. 410,000.

Puzhi (Reader's Digest): Reader's Digest (Shanghai) Advertising Co Ltd, Raffles City Tower, Tibet Rd, Shanghai 200021; tel. (21) 61030347; fax (21) 61030388; e-mail friends@puzhi.com.cn; internet www.readersdigest.cn; f. 2008; monthly; general interest; Editor-in-Chief WANG YOU-BU.

Qiushi (Seeking Truth): 83 Beiheyan Dajie, Dongcheng Qu, Beijing 100727; tel. (10) 64037005; fax (10) 64022727; e-mail qiushi@qstheory.com; internet www.qsjournal.com.cn; f. 1988; succeeded Hong Qi (Red Flag); 2 a month; theoretical journal of the CCP; Editor-in-Chief LI BAOSHAN; circ. 1.83m.

Renmin Huabao (China Pictorial): 33 Chegongzhuang Xilu, Haidian Qu, Beijing 100044; tel. (10) 88417467; fax (10) 68412601; e-mail cnpictorial@gmail.com; internet www.chinapictorial.com.cn; f. 1950; monthly; edns: two in Chinese, one in Tibetan and 12 in foreign languages; Dir and Editor-in-Chief ZHANG JIAHUA.

Shufa (Calligraphy): 81 Qingzhou Nan Lu, Shanghai 200233; tel. (21) 64519008; fax (21) 64519015; f. 1977; every 2 months; journal on ancient and modern calligraphy; Chief Editor LU FUSHENG.

Stories: 74 Shaoxing Lu, Shanghai 200020; tel. and fax (21) 64677160; e-mail storychina@gmail.com; internet www.storychina.cn; f. 1963; bi-monthly; short stories, fiction, comics; Editor HE CHENGWEI.

Tiyu Kexue (Sports Science): 11 Tiyuguan Lu, Beijing 100061; tel. (10) 87182588; fax (10) 67181293; f. 1981; sponsored by the China Sports Science Soc; monthly; in Chinese; summary in English; Chief Officer TIAN YE; circ. 5,000.

Wenxue Qingnian (Youth Literature Journal): 27 Mu Tse Fang, Wenzhou, Zhejiang; tel. (577) 3578; f. 1981; monthly; Editor-in-Chief CHEN YUSHEN; circ. 80,000.

Window of the South: Guangzhou; tel. (20) 61036188; fax (20) 61036195; e-mail window@vip.163.com; internet www.nfcmag.com; bi-monthly; politics and current affairs; Editorial Dir ZHAO LINGMIN.

Women of China English Monthly: Rm 814, 15 Jianguonei Dajie, Beijing, 100730; tel. (10) 65103411; fax (10) 65225376; e-mail womenofchina@gmail.com; internet www.womenofchina.com.cn; f. 1956; monthly; in English; administered by All-China Women's Federation; women's rights and status, views and lifestyle, education and arts, etc.; Editor-in-Chief PENGJU YUN.

Xian Dai Faxue (Modern Law Science): Southwest University of Political Science and Law, Chongqing, Sichuan 400031; tel. (23) 67258823; fax (23) 67258826; e-mail xiandaifaxue@126.com; internet www.swupl.edu.cn; f. 1979; bi-monthly; with summaries in English; Editor-in-Chief SUN CHANGYONG.

Zhongguo Sheying (Chinese Photography): South Tower Bldg, Rm 502, 67 Campbell St, Dongheng Qu, Dongdan, Beijing 100005; tel. (10) 65252277; fax (10) 65257623; e-mail cphotoeditor@sina.com; internet www.cphoto.com.cn; f. 1957; monthly; photographs and comments; Editor WEN DANQING.

Zhongguo Zhenjiu (Chinese Acupuncture and Moxibustion): China Academy of Traditional Chinese Medicine, 16 Nan Xiao Jie, Dongzhimen Nei, Beijing 100700; tel. (10) 84014607; fax (10) 84046331; e-mail zhenjiubj@vip.sina.com; internet www.cjacupuncture.com; f. 1981; monthly; publ. by Chinese Soc. of Acupuncture and Moxibustion; abstract in English; Editor-in-Chief Prof. DENG LIANGYUE.

Other popular magazines include *Gongchandang Yuan* (Communists, circ. 1.63m.) and *Nongmin Wenzhai* (Peasants' Digest, circ. 3.54m.).

NEWS AGENCIES

Xinhua (New China) News Agency: 57 Xuanwumen Xi Dajie, Beijing 100803; tel. (10) 63071114; fax (10) 63071210; e-mail xhszbs@xinhuanet.com; internet www.xinhuanet.com; f. 1931; offices in all Chinese provincial capitals, and about 100 overseas bureaux; news service in Chinese, English, French, Spanish, Portuguese, Arabic and Russian, feature and photographic services; CNC World (China Xinhua News Network Corporation) commenced television broadcasts in Jan. 2010; 24-hour English-language news channel began broadcasting in July; Pres. LI CONGJUN; Editor-in-Chief HE PING.

Zhongguo Xinwen She (China News Service): 12 Baiwanzhuang Nan Jie, Beijing 100037; tel. (10) 87826688; fax (10) 68327649; e-mail hezuo@chinanews.com.cn; internet www.chinanews.com; f. 1952; office in Hong Kong; supplies news features, special articles and photographs for newspapers and magazines in Chinese printed overseas; services in Chinese; Dir WANG SHIGU.

PRESS ORGANIZATIONS

All China Journalists' Association: Xijiaominxiang, Beijing 100031; tel. (10) 66023981; fax (10) 66014658; Chair. TIAN CONG MING.

China Newspapers Association: Beijing; Chair. WANG CHEN.

The Press and Publication Administration of the People's Republic of China (State Copyright Bureau): 85 Dongsi Nan Dajie, East District, Beijing 100703; tel. (10) 65124433; fax (10) 65127875; Dir SHI ZONGYUAN.

Publishers

A total of 301,719 books were published in 2009.

Beijing Chubanshe Chuban Jituan (Beijing Publishing House Group): 6 Bei Sanhuan Zhong Lu, Beijing 100011; tel. (10) 58572219; fax (10) 58572220; e-mail public@bphg.com.cn; internet www.bph.com.cn; f. 1956; politics, history, law, economics, geography, science, literature, art, etc.; Dir ZHU SHUXIN; Editor-in-Chief TAO XINCHENG.

Beijing Daxue Chubanshe (Peking University Press): 205 Chengfu Lu, Zhongguancun, Haidian Qu, Beijing 100871; tel. (10) 62752033; fax (10) 62556201; e-mail zpup@pup.cn; internet www.pup.cn; f. 1979; academic and general; Pres. WANG MINGZHOU.

China International Book Trading Corpn: 35 Chegongzhuang Xilu, Beijing 100044; tel. (10) 68412045; fax (10) 68412023; e-mail cibtc@mail.cibtc.com.cn; internet www.cibtc.com.cn; f. 1949; foreign trade org. specializing in publs, including books, periodicals, art and crafts, microfilms, etc.; import and export distributors; Pres. QI PINGJIN.

China Publishing Group (CPG): 55A Dajie, Dongcheng Qu, Beijing; tel. and fax (10) 59757238; e-mail zq@cnpubg.com; internet www.cnpubg.com; f. 2002; aims to restructure and consolidate publishing sector; comprises 29 major publishing houses, including the People's Publishing House, the Commercial Press, Zhonghua Book Co, Encyclopedia of China Publishing House, China Fine Arts Publishing Group, People's Music Publishing House, SDX Joint Publishing Co, China Translation and Publishing Corpn, Orient Publishing Centre; Pres. NIE ZHENNING.

CITIC Publishing House: 8–10/F, Fusheng Bldg Tower 2, Huixindong Jie 4, Chao Yang Qu, Beijing 100029; tel. (10) 84849555; fax (10) 84849000; e-mail liyinghong@citicpub.com; internet www.publish.citic.com; f. 1988; finance, investment, economics and business; Pres. WANG BIN.

Dianzi Gongye Chubanshe (Publishing House of the Electronics Industry—PHEI): 288 Jin Jia Cun, Wanshou Nan Lu, Beijing 100036; tel. (10) 88258888; fax (10) 68159025; internet www.phei.com.cn; f. 1982; electronic sciences and technology; Pres. LIANG XIANGFENG; Vice-Pres. WANG MINGJUN.

Dolphin Books: 24 Baiwanzhuang Lu, Beijing 100037; tel. (10) 68997480; fax (10) 68993503; e-mail dolphin_books@sina.cn; internet www.dolphin-books.com.cn; f. 1986; children's books in Chinese and foreign languages; Dir WANG YANRONG.

Falü Chubanshe (Law Publishing House): Lianhuachi Xili, Fengtai Qu, Beijing 100073; tel. (10) 63939796; fax (10) 63939622; e-mail info@lawpress.com.cn; internet www.lawpress.com.cn; f. 1980; current laws and decrees, legal textbooks, translations of important foreign legal works; Pres. MIN HUANG.

Foreign Languages Press: 19 Chegongzhuang Xi Lu, Fu Xing Men Wai, Beijing 100044; tel. (10) 68413344; fax (10) 68424931; e-mail wwdinggou@cipg.org.cn; internet www.flp.com.cn; f. 1952; books in 20 foreign languages reflecting political and economic devts in China and features of Chinese culture; Pres. HU BAOMIN; Editor-in-Chief LI ZHENGUO.

Gaodeng Jiaoyu Chubanshe (Higher Education Press): 4 Dewai Dajie, Xicheng Qu, Beijing 100011; tel. (10) 82085550; fax (10) 82085552; e-mail international@hep.edu.cn; internet www.hep.edu.cn; f. 1954; academic, textbooks; Pres. LIU ZHIPENG; Editor-in-Chief ZHANG ZENGSHUN.

Gongren Chubanshe (Workers' Publishing House): Liupukeng, Andingmen Wai, Beijing; tel. (10) 64215278; f. 1949; labour movement, trade unions, science and technology related to industrial production.

Guangdong Keji Chubanshe (Guangdong Science and Technology Press): 11 Shuiyin Lu, Huanshidong Lu, Guangzhou, Guangdong 510075; tel. and fax (20) 37607770; e-mail gdkjzbb@21cn.com; internet www.gdstp.com.cn; f. 1978; natural sciences, technology, agriculture, medicine, computing, English language teaching; Dir HUANG DAQUAN.

Heilongjiang Kexue Jishu Chubanshe (Heilongjiang Science and Technology Press): 41 Jianshe Jie, Nangang Qu, Harbin 150001, Heilongjiang; tel. and fax (451) 3642127; f. 1979; industrial and agricultural technology, natural sciences, economics and management, popular science, children's and general.

Huashan Wenyi Chubanshe (Huashan Literature and Art Publishing House): 45 Bei Malu, Shijiazhuang, Hebei; tel. (0311) 22501; f. 1982; novels, poetry, drama, etc.

Kexue Chubanshe (Science Press): 16 Donghuangchenggen Beijie, Beijing 100717; tel. (10) 64034313; fax (10) 64020094; e-mail webmaster@mail.sciencep.com; internet www.sciencep.com; f. 1954; books and journals on science and technology.

Lingnan Meishu Chubanshe (Lingnan Art Publishing House): 11 Shuiyin Lu, Guangzhou, Guangdong 510075; tel. (20) 87771044; fax (20) 87771049; f. 1981; works on classical and modern painting, picture albums, photographic, painting techniques; Pres. CAO LIXIANG.

Minzu Chubanshe (The Ethnic Publishing House): 14 Anwai Hepingli Beijie, Beijing 100013; tel. and fax (10) 64211126; e-mail e56@e56.com.cn; internet www.e56.com.cn; f. 1953; books and periodicals in minority languages, e.g. Mongolian, Tibetan, Uygur, Korean, Kazakh, etc.; Editor-in-Chief HUANG ZHONGCAI.

Qunzhong Chubanshe (Masses Publishing House): Bldg 15, Part 3, Fangxingyuan, Fangzhuan Lu, Beijing 100078; tel. (10) 67633344; f. 1956; politics, law, judicial affairs, criminology, public security, etc.

Renmin Chubanshe (People's Publishing House): 8 Hepinglidongjie, Andingmenwai, Beijing; tel. (10) 4213713; f. 1950; publishes works on Marxism-Leninism, Mao Zedong Thought and Deng Xiaoping Theory, collected works and biographies of Chinese leaders, academic works in philosophy, social sciences, arts and culture, biography etc.; Dir and Editor-in-Chief XUE DEZHEN.

Renmin Jiaoyu Chubanshe (People's Education Press): 17-1 Zhongguancun Nan Dajie, Haidian, Beijing 100081; tel. (10) 58758866; fax (10) 58758877; e-mail pep@pep.com.cn; internet www.pep.com.cn; f. 1950; school textbooks, guidebooks, teaching materials, etc.

Renmin Meishu Chubanshe (People's Fine Arts Publishing House): Beijing; tel. (10) 65122371; fax (10) 65122370; f. 1951; works by Chinese and foreign painters, sculptors and other artists, picture albums, photographic, painting techniques; Dir GAO ZONGYUAN; Editor-in-Chief CHENG DALI.

Renmin Weisheng Chubanshe (People's Medical Publishing House): 19 Panjia Yuan Xi Lu, Nan Li, Chaoyang Qu, Beijing 100021; tel. (10) 59780011; fax (10) 59787588; e-mail pmphsales@pmph.com; internet www.pmph.com; f. 1953; medicine (Western and traditional Chinese), pharmacology, dentistry, public health; Pres. HU GUOCHEN.

Renmin Wenxue Chubanshe (People's Literature Publishing House): 166 Chaoyangmen, Nei Dajie, Beijing 100705; tel. (10) 65287513; fax (10) 65138394; e-mail rwbq@sina.com; internet www.rw-cn.com; f. 1951; largest publr of literary works and translations into Chinese; Pres. PAN KAIXIONG; Editor-in-Chief GUAN SHIGUANG.

Shanghai Guji Chubanshe (Shanghai Classics Publishing House): 272 Ruijin Erlu, Shanghai 200020; tel. (21) 64370011; fax (21) 64339287; e-mail guji1@guji.com.cn; internet www.guji.com.cn; f. 1956; classical Chinese literature, history, art, philosophy, geography, linguistics, science and technology.

Shanghai Jiaoyu Chubanshe (Shanghai Education Publishing House): 123 Yongfu Lu, Shanghai 200031; tel. (21) 64377165; fax (21) 64339995; e-mail webmaster@seph.com.cn; internet www.seph.com.cn; f. 1958; academic; Dir and Editor-in-Chief BAO NANLIN.

Shanghai Yiwen Chubanshe (Shanghai Translation Publishing House): 193 Fujian Lu, Shanghai 200001; tel. (21) 53594508; fax (21) 63914291; e-mail info@yiwen.com.cn; internet www.yiwen.com.cn; f. 1978; translations of foreign classic and modern literature; philosophy, social sciences, dictionaries, etc.

Shangwu Yinshuguan (The Commercial Press): 36 Wangfujing Dajie, Beijing 100710; tel. (10) 65258899; fax (10) 65134942; e-mail xxzx@cp.com.cn; internet www.cp.com.cn; f. 1897; dictionaries and reference books in Chinese and foreign languages, translations of foreign works on social sciences; Editor HU LONGBIAO; Pres. YU DIANLI.

Shaonian Ertong Chubanshe (Juvenile and Children's Publishing House): 1538 Yan An Xi Lu, Shanghai 200052; tel. (21) 62823025; fax (21) 62821726; e-mail forwardz@public4.sta.net.cn; f. 1952; children's educational and literary works, teaching aids and periodicals; Gen. Man. ZHOU SHUNPEI.

Shijie Wenhua Chubanshe (World Culture Publishing House): Dir ZHU LIE.

Wenwu Chubanshe (Cultural Relics Publishing House): 2 Dongzhimen Bei Dajie, Beijing 100007; tel. (10) 64027424; fax (10) 64010698; e-mail web@wenwu.com; internet www.wenwu.com; f. 1956; books and catalogues of Chinese relics in museums and those recently discovered; Dir SU SHISHU.

Wuhan Daxue Chubanshe (Wuhan University Press): Luojia Hill, Wuhan, Hubei; tel. (27) 68756075; fax (27) 68754094; e-mail epd@whu.edu.cn; internet www.wdp.com.cn; f. 1981; reference books, academic works, maps, audio-visual works, etc.; Pres. Prof. CHEN QINGHUI.

Xiandai Chubanshe (Modern Press): 504 Anhua Li, Andingmenwai, Beijing 100011; tel. (10) 64263515; fax (10) 64214540; f. 1981; directories, reference books, etc.; Dir ZHOU HONGLI.

Xinhua Chubanshe (Xinhua Publishing House): 8 Jungyuan Lu, Shijingshan, Beijing 100000; tel. (10) 63074407; fax (10) 63073880; e-mail wjybox@xinhuanet.com; f. 1979; social sciences, economy, politics, history, geography, directories, dictionaries, etc.; Dir LUO HAIYUAN.

Xuelin Chubanshe (Scholar Books Publishing House): 120 Wenmiao Lu, Shanghai 200010; tel. and fax (21) 63768540; f. 1981; academic, including personal academic works at authors' own expense; Dir LEI QUNMING.

Zhongguo Caizheng Jingji Chubanshe (China Financial and Economic Publishing House): 28 Fu Cheng Lu, Haidian Qu, Beijing 100142; tel. (10) 64011805; e-mail cfeph@cfeph.cn; internet www.cfeph.cn; f. 1961; finance, economics, commerce and accounting.

Zhongguo Dabaike Quanshu Chubanshe (Encyclopaedia of China Publishing House): 17 Fu Cheng Men Bei Dajie, Beijing 100037; tel. (10) 68338370; fax (10) 88390680; e-mail jxh@ecph.com.cn; internet www.ecph.com.cn; f. 1978; specializes in encyclopaedias; Dir SHAN JIFU.

Zhongguo Ditu Chubanshe (SinoMaps Press): 57 Nan Lu, Xuanwu Qu, Beijing 100055; tel. (10) 63529243; fax (10) 63529403; e-mail webmaster@sinomaps.com; internet www.sinomaps.com; f. 1954; cartographic publr; Dir ZHAO XIAOMING.

Zhongguo Funü Chubanshe (China Women Publishing House): 24A Shijia Hutong, Beijing 100010; tel. (10) 65228814; fax (10) 65133162; e-mail service@womenbooks.com.cn; internet www.womenbooks.com.cn; f. 1981; women's movement, marriage and family, child care, etc.; Editor-in-Chief YANG GUANGHUI.

Zhongguo Qingnian Chubanzongshe (China Youth Publishing Group): 21 Dongsi Shiertiao, Beijing 100708; tel. (10) 84039659; fax (10) 64031803; e-mail cyp_webmaster@126.com; internet www.cyp.com.cn; f. 1950; state-owned; literature, social and natural sciences, youth work, autobiography; also periodicals; Pres. ZHANG JINGYAN; Editor-in-Chief WEN YUXIN.

Zhongguo Shehui Kexue Chubanshe (China Social Sciences Publishing House): 158A Gulou Xidajie, Beijing 100720; tel. (10) 84029453; fax (10) 84002041; e-mail duzhe-cbs@cass.org.cn; internet www.csspw.com.cn; f. 1978; Dir MENG ZHAOYU.

Zhongguo Xiju Chubanshe (China Theatrical Publishing House): 52 Dongsi Batiao Hutong, Beijing; tel. (10) 64015815; f. 1957; traditional and modern Chinese drama.

Zhongguo Youyi Chuban Gongsi (China Friendship Publishing Corpn): e-mail tmdoxu@public.east.cn.net; Dir YANG WEI.

Zhonghua Shuju (Zhonghua Book Co): 38 Taipingqiao Xili, Fenglai Qu, Beijing; tel. (10) 63458226; f. 1912; general; Pres. LI YAN.

PUBLISHERS' ASSOCIATION

Publishers' Association of China: Beijing; tel. (10) 65246062; internet www.pac.org.cn; f. 1979; arranges academic exchanges with foreign publrs; Chair. YU YOUXIAN.

Broadcasting and Communications

TELECOMMUNICATIONS

China Mobile Communications Corpn (China Mobile): 53A Xibianmen Nei Dajie, Xuanwu Qu, Beijing 100053; tel. (10) 63604988; fax (10) 63600364; internet www.chinamobile.com; headquarters in Hong Kong; controlling shareholder in China Mobile (Hong Kong) Ltd; f. 2000; Pres. LI YUE.

China Satellite Communications Corpn Ltd (CHINA SATCOM): International Finance Centre, Haidian Qu, Beijing 100089; tel. (10) 59718188; fax (10) 59718199; internet www.chinasatcom.com; f. 2001; satellite telecommunications, radio and television services; Chair. RUI XIAOWU.

China Telecom Corpn Ltd: 31 Jinrong Jie, Xicheng Qu, Beijing 100032; tel. (10) 66428166; fax (10) 66010728; e-mail ir@chinatelecom.com.cn; internet www.chinatelecom-h.com; f. 1997; est. as a vehicle for foreign investment in telecommunications sector; restructured as a jt-stock limited company in 2002 with responsibility for fixed-line networks, via its subsidiaries, in 20 provinces, municipalities and autonomous regions; Chair. and CEO WANG XIAOCHU; Pres. YANG JIE.

China United Network Communications Co Ltd (China Unicom): 21 Financial St, Xicheng District, Beijing 100140; fax (10) 66110009; e-mail webmaster@chinaunicom.com.cn; internet www.chinaunicom.com.cn; f. 1994; fixed line and mobile telephone services; fmrly China United Telecommunications Corpn; above name adopted after merger with China Netcom Group in 2009; 273m. subscribers (2008); Chair. and CEO CHANG XIAOBING.

Netease.com: SP Tower D, 26th Floor, Tsinghua Science Park Bldg 8, 1 Zhongguancun Dong Lu, Haidan Qu, Beijing 100084; tel. (10) 82558163; fax (10) 82618163; e-mail bjsales@service.netease.com; internet corp.163.com; f. 1997; Nasdaq-listed internet portal; Founder and CEO WILLIAM DING LEI.

Sina.com: Jinmao Tower, 37th Floor, 88 Century Blvd, Pudong, Shanghai 200121; tel. (21) 50498666; fax (21) 50498806; e-mail ir@staff.sina.com.cn; internet www.sina.com.cn; Nasdaq-listed internet portal; Pres. and CEO CHARLES CHAO; Chair. YAN WANG.

Sohu.com: Sohu Internet Plaza, Park 1, Zhongguancun Dong Lu, Haidan Qu, Beijing 100084; tel. (10) 62726666; fax (10) 62726988; e-mail webmaster@contact.sohu.com; internet www.sohu.com; Nasdaq-listed internet portal; Chair. and CEO CHARLES ZHANG.

BROADCASTING

In 2007 there were 263 radio broadcasting stations and 11,384 radio transmitting and relay stations (covering 95.4% of the population). In the same year there were 287 television stations and 18,249 television transmitting and relay stations (covering 96.5% of the population).

Regulatory Authority

State Administration of Radio, Film and Television (SARFT): 2 Fu Xing Men Wai Dajie, POB 4501, Beijing 100866; tel. (10) 68513409; fax (10) 68512174; e-mail sarft@chinasarft.gov.cn; internet www.sarft.gov.cn; controls the Central People's Broadcasting Station, the Central TV Station, China Radio International, China Record Co, Beijing Broadcasting Institute, Broadcasting Research Institute, the China Broadcasting Art Troupe, etc.; Dir CAI FUCHAO.

Radio

Radio broadcasting is largely under state control; China National Radio operates the largest radio network in the country.

China National Radio (CNR): 2 Fu Xing Men Wai Dajie, Beijing 100866; tel. (10) 86093114; fax (10) 63909751; e-mail cn@cnr.cn; internet www.cnr.cn; f. 1941; domestic service in Chinese, Zang Wen (Tibetan), Min Nan Hua (Amoy), Ke Jia (Hakka), Hasaka (Kazakh), Wei Wuer (Uygur), Menggu Hua (Mongolian) and Chaoxian (Korean); Dir-Gen. YANG BO.

Radio Tianjin: 143 Weijin Rd, Heping, Tianjin; tel. (22) 23601782; e-mail radiotjworld@gmail.com; internet www.radiotj.com; f. 1949; Pres. FENG. XUIFEI.

Shaanxi Radio: 336 Chang An Nan Jie, Xian 710061; tel. (29) 85231660; e-mail sxradio6105@126.com; internet www.sxradio.com.cn.

Zhongguo Guoji Guangbo Diantai (China Radio International): 16A Shijingshan Lu, Beijing 100040; tel. (10) 68891123; fax (10) 68891232; e-mail crieng@cri.com.cn; internet www.cri.cn; f. 1941; fmrly Radio Beijing; foreign service in 61 languages and dialects incl. Arabic, Burmese, Czech, English, Esperanto, French, German, Hindi, Indonesian, Italian, Japanese, Lao, Malay, Polish, Portuguese, Russian, Spanish, Turkish and Vietnamese; Dir WANG GENGNIAN.

Television

In addition to the state-run television network, there are a number of regional and privately owned television stations. In 2006 China announced the switch to digital TV services, and by 2010 digitalization had reached above 45%.

China Central Television (CCTV): Media Centre, 11B Fuxing Lu, Haidian Qu, Beijing 100038; tel. (10) 68508381; fax (10) 68513025; e-mail cctv-9@cctv.com; internet www.cntv.com; operates under Bureau of Broadcasting Affairs of the State Council, Beijing; f. 1958; operates eight networks; 24-hour global satellite service commenced in 1996; Pres. HU ZHANFAN.

Anhui Television (AHTV): 38 Ma On Shan Rd, Heifei 230009; tel. (551) 2615582; fax (551) 2615582; e-mail webmaster@ahtv.cn; internet www.ahtv.cn; f. 1960; broadcasts eight television channels.

China Beijing Television Station (BTV): 98 Jianguo Lu, Chaoyang Qu, Beijing 100022; tel. (10) 68419922; fax (10) 68429120; e-mail btvsuggest@btv.com.cn; internet www.btv.com.cn; broadcasts 14 television channels; state-owned; Dir WANG XIAODONG.

Chongqing Television: tel. (23) 68812609; fax (23) 63850485; e-mail webmaster@ccqtv.com; internet www.ccqtv.com; f. 1961; broadcasts nine television channels.

Fujian Television: 2 Gu Tian Lu, Fuzhou 350001; tel. (591) 83310941; fax (591) 83311945; internet www.fjtv.net; f. 1960; broadcasts 10 television channels; part of the Fujian Media Group.

Gansu Television (GSTV): 226 Dong Gang Xi Lu, Lanzhou 370000; tel. (931) 8416419; fax (931) 8416499; internet www.gstv.com.cn; f. 1970; broadcasts three television channels.

Guangdong Television: Guangdong Television Centre, 331 Huan Shi Dong Lu, Guangzhou 510066; tel. (20) 83355188; e-mail gdtv@gdtv.com.cn; internet www.gdtv.com.cn; f. 1959; programmes in

Mandarin, Cantonese and English; state-owned; broadcasts 14 channels.

Guangxi Television (GXTV): 73 National Rd, Nanning 530022; tel. (771) 2196666; fax (771) 5854039; e-mail gxtv@gxtv.com.cn; internet www.gxtv.cn; f. 1970; broadcasts six television channels.

Guizhou Television (GZTV): e-mail webmaster@gztv.com; internet www.gztv.com.cn; f. 1968; broadcasts three television channels.

Hainan Television (HNTV): f. 1982; broadcasts three television channels.

Hebei Television (HEBTV): internet www.hebtv.com.cn; f. 1969; broadcasts two television channels.

Henan Television (HNTV): 2 Jing Wu Lu, Zhengzhou 450008; tel. (371) 5726212; fax (371) 5726285; e-mail hntv@hntv.ha.cn; internet www.hntv.ha.cn; f. 1969; broadcasts three television channels.

Hubei Television (HBTV): 1 Zi Jin Cun Liang Dao Jie, Wuchang, Wuhan 430071; tel. (27) 87139710; fax (27) 87139706; e-mail webmaster@hbtv.com.cn; internet www.hbtv.com.cn; f. 1960; broadcasts two television channels.

Hunan Television (HNTV): Hunan International Convention & Exhibition Center, 4th Floor, Changsha 410003; tel. (731) 82871680; fax (731) 82871686; e-mail media@hunantv.com; internet www.hunantv.com; f. 1960; broadcasts two television channels; CEO ZHANG RUOBO.

Jiangsu Broadcasting Corpn: 4 East Beijing Rd, Nanjing, Jiangsu; tel. (25) 83188185; fax (25) 83188187; e-mail info@vip.jsbc.com; internet www.jstv.com/jsbc_en/index.shtml; f. 1960; broadcasts 14 television channels; Pres. ZHOU LI.

Liaoning Television (LNTV): 10 Guang Rong Jie, Shenyang 110003; tel. (24) 23232945; fax (24) 22913733; e-mail lntv@lntv.com.cn; internet www.lntv.com.cn; f. 1959; broadcasts two television channels.

Nei Monggol Television (NMGTV): 71 Xinhua Dajie, Hohhot 010058; tel. (471) 6953000; fax (471) 6630600; e-mail info@nmtv.cn; internet www.nmtv.cn; f. 1969; broadcasts two television channels; Dir FANG GUAN.

Ningxia Television (NXTV): 66 Ningxia Lu, Beijing 750001; tel. (951) 6130011; e-mail nxtvweb@nxtv.cn; internet www.nxtv.com.cn; f. 1970; broadcasts two television channels.

Shaanxi Television (SXTV): 336 Chang An Nan Jie, Xian 710061; tel. (29) 85257538; fax (29) 5218553; e-mail webmaster@sxtvs.com; internet www.sxtvs.com; f. 1970; broadcasts seven television channels.

Shandong Television (SDTV): 81 Jingshi Lu, Jinan 250062; tel. (531) 2951295; fax (531) 2953809; e-mail webmaster@sdtv.com.cn; internet www.sdtv.com.cn; f. 1960; broadcasts six television channels.

Shanghai Media Group: 298 Weihai Lu, Shanghai; tel. (21) 62565899; internet www.smg.cn; f. 2001; est. by merger of Radio Shanghai, Eastern Radio Shanghai, Shanghai Television, Oriental Television Station and Shanghai Cable TV; broadcasts 15 television channels and 11 radio channels; Pres. LI RUIGANG.

Shanxi Television (SXTV): 318 Ying Chak Lu, Taiyuan, Shanxi 030001; tel. and fax (351) 4066178; e-mail mail@sxrtv.com; internet www.sxrtv.com; f. 1960; broadcasts two television channels; Dir DONG YUZHONG.

Sichuan Television (SCTV): 40 Dong Sheng Jie, Chengdu 610015; tel. (28) 86636065; fax (28) 86635195; e-mail webmaster@sctv.com; internet www.sctv.com; f. 1960; broadcasts nine television channels.

Xinjiang Television (XJTV): Xinjiang Television Centre 84B, 8th Floor, Urumqi 830044; tel. (991) 2577531; fax (991) 2871947; e-mail XJTVS@96669.net; internet www.xjtvs.com.cn; f. 1970; broadcasts 15 television channels; broadcasts in Mandarin, Uygur and Kazakh.

Xizang Television (XZTV): 11 Xi Lu, Lhasa; tel. (891) 6814522; internet www.xztv.net.cn; f. 1993; broadcasts two television channels; Mandarin and Tibetan.

Yunnan Television: 182 Renmin Xi Lu, Kunmin, Yunnan 650031; tel. (871) 5357842; fax (871) 5350586; e-mail webmaster@yntv.com.cn; internet www.yntv.cn; f. 1969; broadcasts nine television channels.

Zhejiang Satellite Television (ZJSTV): 111 Mo Gan Shan Lu, Hangzhou 310005; internet www.zjstv.com; f. 1960; broadcasts two television channels.

Finance

(cap. = capital; auth. = authorized; p.u. = paid up; res = reserves; dep. = deposits; m. = million; amounts in yuan unless otherwise stated)

BANKING

Regulatory Authority

China Banking Regulatory Commission: 15 Financial St, Xicheng Qu, Beijing 100140; tel. (10) 66279749; e-mail cbrclib@cbrc.gov.cn; internet www.cbrc.gov.cn; f. 2003; Chair. LIU MINGKANG.

Central Bank

People's Bank of China (PBC): 32 Chengfang Jie, Xicheng Qu, Beijing 100800; tel. (10) 66194114; fax (10) 66195370; e-mail webbox@pbc.gov.cn; internet www.pbc.gov.cn; f. 1948; bank of issue; decides and implements China's monetary policies; Gov. ZHOU XIAOCHUAN; 2,204 brs.

Other Banks

Agricultural Bank of China: 69 Jianguomen Nei Dajie, Dongcheng Qu, Beijing 100005; tel. (10) 68216807; fax (10) 68297160; e-mail 95599bj@abchina.com; internet www.abchina.com; f. 1951; serves mainly China's rural financial operations, providing services for agriculture, industry, commerce, transport, etc. in rural areas; sale of shares commenced in mid-2010; cap. 260,000m., res 23,002m.,dep. 8,320,280m. (Dec. 2009); Pres. JIANG CHAOLIANG; 28,111 brs (domestic).

Agricultural Development Bank of China: 2A Yuetanbei Jie, Xicheng Qu, Beijing 100045; tel. (10) 68081557; fax (10) 68081773; internet www.adbc.com.cn; f. 1994; cap. 165,800m. (2006); Pres. ZHENG HUI.

Bank of Beijing Co Ltd: 17C Financial St, Xicheng Qu, Beijing 100140, Beijing 100031; tel. (10) 66426928; fax (10) 66426691; internet www.bankofbeijing.com.cn; f. 1996; est. as Beijing City United Bank Corpn, changed name to Beijing City Commercial Bank Corpn Ltd in 1998, assumed present name in 2004; cap. 6,227.5m., res 22,716.4m., dep. 489,371.4m. (Dec. 2009); Chair. YAN BINGZHU; Pres. YAN XIAOYAN.

Bank of Changsha: 433 Furong Zhong Lu, Section 1, Changsha, Hunan 410005; tel. (731) 4305570; fax (731) 4305560; e-mail cscb@hncccb.com; internet www.cscb.cn; f. 1997; fmrly Changsha City Commercial Bank, name changed as above in 2008; cap. 1,173.2m., res 580.8m., dep. 60,457.9m. (Dec. 2009); Chair. ZHI YONG ZHANG; Pres. YU GUO ZHU.

Bank of China Ltd: 1 Fu Xing Men Nei Dajie, Beijing 100818; tel. (10) 66596688; fax (10) 66593777; internet www.boc.cn; f. 1912; handles foreign exchange and international settlements; operates Orient AMC (asset management corporation) since 1999; fmrly Bank of China; became shareholding co in Aug. 2004; 10% stake acquired in 2005 by a consortium headed by Royal Bank of Scotland PLC (UK); further 10% acquired by Temasek Holdings (Pvt) Ltd; cap. 253,839m., res 152,303m., dep. 7,953,385m. (Dec. 2009); Chair. XIAO GANG; Pres. LI LIHUI; 117 brs.

Bank of Chongqing: 153 Zou Rong Lu, Zou Rong Sq., Yu Zhong Qu, Chongqing 400010; tel. (23) 63836229; fax (23) 63792176; e-mail webmaster@cqcbank.com.cn; internet www.cqcbank.com.cn; f. 1996; fmrly Chongqing Commercial Bank; cap. 2,020.6m., res 640m., dep. 75,121.1m. (Dec. 2009); Pres. CHONG YI WANG; Chair. FU ZHANG.

Bank of Communications Ltd: 188 Yin Cheng Lu, Shanghai 200120; tel. (21) 58766688; fax (21) 58798398; e-mail investor@bankcomm.com; internet www.bankcomm.com; f. 1908; commercial bank; 19.9% stake was acquired by HSBC in Aug. 2004; cap. 48,994m., res 88,808m., dep. 3,034,602m. (Dec. 2009); Chair. HU HUAIBANG; Pres. NIU XIMING; 93 brs.

Bank of Hebei Co Ltd: 28 Ping An Bei Lu, Shijiazhuang, Hebei 050011; tel. (11) 88627003; fax (11) 88627075; internet www.hebbank.com; f. 1996; fmrly Shijiazhuang City Commercial Bank, name changed as above in 2009; cap. 2,000m., res 1,045.9m., dep. 50,713.6m. (Dec. 2009); Chair. QIAO ZHIQIANG.

Bank of Jiangsu Co Ltd: 55 Hongwu Lu, Nanjing, Jiangsu Province 210005; tel. (25) 58588050; fax (25) 58588055; internet www.jsbchina.cn; f. 2007; est. by merger of 13 banks; cap. 8,400m., res 5,599.1m., dep. 306,998m. (Dec. 2009); Chair. and Pres. HUANG ZHIWEI.

Bank of Ningbo Co Ltd: 294 Zhongshan Dong Lu, Ningbo 315040, Zhejiang; tel. (574) 87050028; fax (574) 87050027; e-mail inter@nbcb.cn; internet www.nbcb.com.cn; f. 1997; cap. 2,500m., res 4,978.3m., dep. 151,604m. (Dec. 2009); Chair. LU HUAYU; Pres. YU FENGYING.

Bank of Shanghai Co Ltd: 585 Zhongshan Lu (E2), Shanghai 200010; tel. (21) 68475888; fax (21) 68476111; e-mail webmaster@bankofshanghai.com.cn; internet www.bankofshanghai.com; f. 1995; est. as Shanghai City United Bank, assumed present name in 1998; cap. 2,600m., res 11,788.7m., dep. 420,059.5m. (Dec. 2009); Chair. JIANHUA FU; Pres. CHEN XIN; 209 brs.

Bank of Shaoxing Co Ltd: 20 Lao Dong Lu, Shaoxing, Zhejiang 312000; tel. (575) 85129734; fax (575) 85131190; e-mail sxsyyh@mail.sxptt.zj.cn; internet www.sxccb.com; f. 1997; fmrly Shaoxing City Commercial Bank Co Ltd, name changed as above in 2009; cap. 983.6m., res 628m., dep. 29,943m. (Dec. 2009); Pres. CHEN FANG XIAO; Chair. CHEN JUN QUAN.

Bank of Weifang Co Ltd: Shengli Lu, Weifang 261041; tel. (536) 8106161; internet www.wfccb.com; f. 1997; fmrly Weifang City Commercial Bank, name changed as above in 2009; cap. 1,396.8m., res 239.9m., dep. 28,746.9m. (Dec. 2009); Pres. WANG ZHONGUA.

BNP Paribas (China) Ltd: World Financial Center, 25/F, 100 Century Ave, Pudong Nan Lu, Shanghai 200120; tel. (21) 28962888; fax (21) 28962800; internet www.bnpparibas.com.cn; f. 1992; fmrly Int. Bank of Paris and Shanghai; name changed as above 2004; 100% owned by BNP Paribas SA (France); cap. US $520.4m., res US $40.6m., dep. US $3,452m. (Dec. 2009); Chief Exec. FRANÇOIS CRISTOFARI.

Changshu Rural Commercial Bank: 58 Century Blvd, Changshu, Jiangsu; tel. (512) 52909020; fax (512) 52962000; e-mail jscsxhc@sina.com; internet www.csrcbank.com; f. 1953; cap. 575.6m., res. 1,743.1m., dep. 36,834m. (Dec. 2009); Chair. WU JIANYA; Pres. SONG JIANMING.

China Bohai Bank: 201–205 Race Course Rd, Hexi 300204; tel. (22) 58316666; e-mail enquiry@cbhb.com.cn; internet www.cbhb.com.cn; f. 2004; 20% stake owned by Standard Chartered Bank; Chair. YANG ZILIN.

China Citic Bank Corpn Ltd: Block C, Fuhua Mansion, 8 Chao Yang Men Bei Dajie, Dongcheng Qu, Beijing 100027; tel. (10) 65558000; fax (10) 65550809; e-mail ir_cncb@citicbank.com; internet bank.ecitic.com; f. 1987; est. as Citic Industrial Bank; name changed as above in April 2007; cap. 39,033m., res 47,071m., dep. 1,632,012m. (Dec. 2009); Chair. KONG DAN; Pres. CHEN XIAOXIAN; 26 brs.

China Construction Bank Corpn (CCBC): 25 Jinrong Jie, Xicheng Qu, Beijing 100033; tel. (10) 67597114; fax (10) 66212862; e-mail ccb@bj.china.com; internet www.ccb.com; f. 1954; fmrly People's Construction Bank of China; makes payments for capital construction projects; issues loans to construction enterprises and others, incl. housing loans; handles foreign-exchange business; cap. 233,689m., res 187,674m., dep. 8,830,795m. (Dec. 2009); Chair. WANG HONGZHANG; Pres. ZHANG JIANGUO; 44 brs.

China Development Bank (CDB): 29 Fuchengmenwai Dajie, Xicheng Qu, Beijing 100037; tel. (10) 68306688; fax (10) 68306699; e-mail webmaster@cdb.com.cn; internet www.cdb.com.cn; f. 1994; merged with China Investment Bank 1998; handles low-interest loans for infrastructural projects and basic industries; Gov. JIANG CHAOLIANG; 32 brs.

China Everbright Bank: Everbright Bldg, 6 Fu Xing Men Wai Lu, Beijing 100045; tel. (10) 68098000; fax (10) 68561260; e-mail eb@cebbank.com; internet www.cebbank.com; f. 1992; est. as Everbright Bank of China; acquired China Investment Bank and assumed present name in 1999; cap. 33,434.7m., res 13,076.3m., dep. 1,078,898.3m. (Dec. 2009); Pres. GUO YOU; Chair. TANG SHUANGNING; 30 brs.

China International Capital Corporation (CICC): 28th Floor, China World Tower 2, 1 Jian Guo Men Wai Dajie, Beijing 100004; tel. (10) 65051166; fax (10) 65051156; e-mail info@cicc.com.cn; internet www.cicc.com.cn; f. 1995; international investment bank; 43.4% owned by China Jianyin Investment Ltd, 34.3% owned by Morgan Stanley; registered cap. US $100m.; Chair. LI JIANGE; CEO LEVIN ZHU.

China Merchants Bank: China Merchants Bank Tower, 49/F, 7088 Shennan Blvd, Shenzhen 518040; tel. (755) 83198888; fax (755) 83105109; e-mail office@cmbchina.com; internet www.cmbchina.com; f. 1987; cap. 19,119m., res 46,072m., dep. 1,879,231m. (Dec. 2009); Chair. FU YUNING; Pres. and CEO MA WEIHUA; 44 brs.

China Minsheng Banking Corporation: 8/F, 2 Fuxingmen Nei Dajie, Xicheng Qu, Beijing 100031; tel. (10) 58560666; fax (10) 58560635; internet www.cmbc.com.cn; first non-state national commercial bank, opened Jan. 1996; cap. 22,262m., res 54,129m., dep. 1,280,650m. (Dec. 2009); Chair. DONG WENBIAO; Pres. QI HONG; 29 brs.

China Zheshang Bank Co Ltd: 288 Qingchun Lu, Hangzhou, Zhejiang 310006; tel. (571) 95105665; fax (571) 87659108; e-mail zcbho@mail.nbptt.zj.cn; internet www.czbank.com; f. 1993; fmrly Zhejiang Commercial Bank; cap. 5,216.4m., res 3,031.9m., dep. 140,945m. (Dec. 2009); Chair. ZHANG DAYANG; Pres. GONG FANGLE.

Chinese Mercantile Bank: Ground and 23rd Floors, Dongfeng Bldg, 2010 Shennan Lu, Futian Qu, Shenzhen 518031; tel. (755) 83786833; fax (755) 83257955; e-mail service@cmbcn.com.cn; internet www.cmbcn.com.cn; f. 1993; wholly owned by ICBC (Asia) Ltd; cap. 1,650m., res 87.8m., dep. 5,721.7m. (Dec. 2009); CEO PANG KOON KWAI.

CITIC Group: Capital Mansion, 6 Xin Yuan Nan Lu, Chao Yang Qu, Beijing 100004; tel. (10) 64660088; fax (10) 64661186; e-mail g-office@citic.com.cn; internet www.citic.com; f. 1979; name changed from China International Trust and Investment Corporation in 2003; economic and technological co-operation; finance, banking, investment and trade; registered cap. 3,000m.; total assets 935,720m. (Dec. 2006); Chair. CHANG ZHENMING; Pres. TIAN GUOLI.

Export and Import Bank of China (China Exim Bank): 30 Fu Xin Men Nei Lu, Xicheng Qu, Beijing 100031; tel. (10) 83579988; fax (10) 66060636; internet www.eximbank.gov.cn; f. 1994; provides trade credits for export of large machinery, electronics, ships, etc.; Chair. and Pres. LI RUOGU.

Foshan Shunde Rural Commercial Bank Co Ltd: 38 Fengshan Zhong Lu, Guangdong, Shunde 528300; tel. (757) 22388888; fax (757) 22388226; e-mail lsbgs@sdebank.com; internet www.sdebank.com; fmrly The Rural Credit Cooperatives Union of Shunde, name changed as above in 2009; cap. 1,856.4m., res 5,144.9m., dep. 92,229.9m. (Dec. 2009).

Fujian Haixia Bank Co Ltd: 158 Liuyi Bei Lu, Fuzhou; tel. (591) 87593778; fax (591) 87585341; e-mail gyb@fuzhoubank.com; internet www.fjhxbank.com; fmrly Fuzhou City Commercial Bank Co Ltd, name changed as above in 2009; cap. 2,078.7m., res 1,568.2m., dep. 34,422.7m. (Dec. 2009); Chair. YUNLIAN GUO; Pres. JIEHONG JIANG; 30 brs.

Guangdong Development Bank: 83 Nonglinxia Lu, Dongshan Qu, Guangzhou, Guangdong 510080; tel. (20) 38322888; fax (20) 87310779; internet www.gdb.com.cn; f. 1988; 85% stake acquired by a consortium led by Citigroup Inc (USA) in Nov. 2006; cap. 11,978.8m., res 6,712.2m., dep. 630,134.9m. (Dec. 2009); Chair. DONG JIANYUE; Pres. MORRIS LI; 28 brs.

Guangxi Beibu Gulf Bank Co Ltd: 10 Qing Xiu Lu, Nanning, Guangxi Zhuang 530028; tel. (771) 6115338; fax (771) 6115383; internet www.bankofbbg.com; cap. 2,000m., res 1,038.8m., dep. 23,532.2m. (Dec. 2009); Chair. TENG CHONG; Pres. JIANPING LIU.

Hua Xia Bank: Hua Xia Bank Mansions, 22 Jianguomennei Dajie, Dongcheng Qu, Beijing 100005; tel. (10) 85238000; fax (10) 85239000; e-mail zhgjb@hxb.com.cn; internet www.hxb.com.cn; f. 1992; est. as part of Shougang Corpn; cap. 4,990.5m., res 21,469.5m., dep. 658,809.1m. (Dec. 2008); Chair. WU JIAN; Pres. FAN DAZHI; 47 brs.

Industrial and Commercial Bank of China: 55 Fu Xing Men Nei Dajie, Xicheng Qu, Beijing 100031; tel. (10) 66106070; fax (10) 66106053; e-mail webmaster@icbc.com.cn; internet www.icbc.com.cn; f. 1984; handles industrial and commercial credits and international business; operates Huarong AMC (asset management corporation) since 1999; cap. 334,019m., res 221,114m., dep. 10,834,047m. (Dec. 2009); Chair. JIANG JIANQING; Pres. YANG KAISHENG.

Industrial Bank Co Ltd: Zhong Shang Bldg, 154 Hudong Lu, Hualin, Fuzhou, Fujian 350003; tel. (591) 87839338; fax (591) 87841932; e-mail irm@cib.com.cn; internet www.cib.com.cn; f. 1982; fmrly Fujian Industrial Bank; cap. 5,000m., res 28,743.2m., dep. 1,256,140.6m. (Dec. 2009); Chair. GAO JIANPING; Pres. LI RENJIE; 48 brs.

Laishang Bank Co Ltd: 137 Longtan Dong Dajie, Laiwu, Shandong; tel. (634) 8861182; fax (634) 8681177; e-mail bgs@lsbankchina.com; internet www.lsbankchina.com; f. 1987; cap. 600m., res 703.7m., dep. 18,837.3m. (Dec. 2009); Chair LI MINSHI; Pres. TAN LEQING.

Linshang Bank Co Ltd: 336 Yimeng Lu, Linyi, Shandong; tel. (539) 8311353; fax (539) 8309052; e-mail lypfboy@sohu.com; internet www.lsbchina.com; f. 1998; fmrly Linyi City Commercial Bank Co Ltd, name changed as above in 2008; cap. 1,712m., res 214.8m., dep. 22,850.5m. (Dec. 2009); Chair. WANG JIAYU; Gen. Man. QIANG ZHAO.

Ping An Bank: Galaxy Development Centre, 15/F, 3 Fu Hua Lu, Guangdong, Futian Qu, Shenzhen; tel. (755) 82436179; fax (755) 82431019; e-mail IR@pingan.com.cn; internet bank.pingan.com; f. 1995; fmrly Shenzhen Commercial Bank; cap. 8,622.8m., res 4,481.9m., dep. 200,071.4m. (Dec. 2009); Chair. MA MINGHZE; Pres. SUN JIANYI; 45 brs.

QiLu Bank Co Ltd: 176 Shun He Lu, Jinan 250001; tel. (531) 86075850; fax (531) 81915514; e-mail boardoffice@qlbchina.com; internet www.qlbchina.com; f. 1996; fmrly Jinan City Commercial Bank Co Ltd, above name adopted in 2009; cap. 1,668.7m., res 813.1m., dep. 55,679.7m. (Dec. 2009); Chair. QIU YUNZHANG.

Shanghai Pudong Development Bank: 12 Zhongshan Dong Yi Lu, Shanghai 200002; tel. (21) 63296188; fax (21) 63232036; e-mail bdo@spdb.com.cn; internet www.spdb.com.cn; f. 1993; cap. 8,830m., res 41,907m., dep. 1,504,487.8m. (Dec. 2009); Chair. JI XIAOHUI; Pres. FU JIANHUA; 28 brs.

Shenzhen Development Bank Co Ltd: 5047 Shennan Dong Lu, Shenzhen 518001; tel. (755) 82088888; fax (755) 82081069; e-mail shudi@sdb.com.cn; internet www.sdb.com.cn; f. 1987; 18% acquired by Newbridge Capital (USA) in 2004; cap. 3,105.4m., res 12,977.3m., dep. 542,549.8m. (Dec. 2009); Chair. XIAO SUINING; Pres. FRANK NEWMAN.

Xiamen Bank Co Ltd: 101 Hubin Bei Lu, Siming, Xiamen 361012; tel. (592) 2275219; fax (592) 2275173; e-mail xmcbgc@public.xm.fj.cn; internet www.xmccb.com; f. 1996; cap. 607.5m., res 661.6m., dep. 21,149.3m. (Dec. 2009); Pres. GAO CHAOYANG.

Xiamen International Bank: 8–10 Jiang Lu, Xiamen, Fujian 361001; tel. (592) 2078888; fax (592) 2988788; e-mail xib@xib.com.cn; internet www.xib.com.cn; f. 1985; cap. 1,068m., res 1,017.8m., dep. 43,392.7m. (Dec. 2009); Chair. DING SHI DA; Pres. LU YAO MING; 3 brs.

Zhejiang Chouzhou Commercial Bank Co Ltd: Jiangbin Lu, Yiwu Leyuan, Zhejiang 322000; tel. (579) 85337701; fax (579) 85337706; e-mail intl@czcb.com.cn; internet www.czcb.com.cn; f. 2006; cap. 800m., res 1,072.7m., dep. 30,123.3m. (Dec. 2009); Chair. JIN ZIJUN; Pres. ZHOU RUIGU.

STOCK EXCHANGES

The number of companies listed on the Shanghai and Shenzhen Stock Exchanges rose from 323 in 1995 to 1,434 in 2006. A total of 1,625 Chinese companies were listed in 2008.

Stock Exchange Executive Council (SEEC): Beijing; tel. (10) 64935210; f. 1989; oversees the development of financial markets in China; mems comprise leading non-bank financial institutions authorized to handle securities; Vice-Pres. WANG BOMING.

Securities Association of China (SAC): Focus Plaza, 2/F, Tower B, 19 Financial St, Xicheng Qu, Beijing 100032; tel. (10) 66575800; fax (10) 66575827; e-mail bgs@sac.net.cn; internet www.sac.net.cn; f. 1991; 332 mems; Chair. HUANG XIANGPING.

Beijing Securities Exchange: 5 Anding Lu, Chao Yang Qu, Beijing 100029; tel. (10) 64939366; fax (10) 64936233.

Shanghai Stock Exchange: 528 Pudong Nan Lu, Shanghai 200120; tel. (21) 68808888; fax (21) 68804868; e-mail webmaster@secure.sse.com.cn; internet www.sse.com.cn; f. 1990; 870 listed cos (Dec. 2009); Chair. GENG LIANG; Pres. ZHANG YUJUN.

Shenzhen Stock Exchange: 5045 Shennan Dong Lu, Shenzhen, Guangdong 518010; tel. (755) 82083333; fax (755) 82083947; e-mail cis@szse.cn; internet www.szse.cn; f. 1991; 1,012 listed cos (June 2010); Chair. CHEN DONGZHENG; Pres. SONG LIPING.

Regulatory Authorities

Operations are regulated by the State Council Securities Policy Committee and by the following:

China Securities Regulatory Commission (CSRC): 19 Focus Plaza, Jinrong Lu, Xicheng Qu, Beijing 100033; tel. (10) 66210182; fax (10) 66210205; e-mail consult@csrc.gov.cn; internet www.csrc.gov.cn; f. 1993; Chair. SHANG FULIN.

INSURANCE

At the end of 2007 the number of insurance institutions operating in China totalled 120, of which eight were insurance group corporations, 43 were joint venture corporations and 59 were domestically funded insurance corporations. In 2007 total premiums reached 703,600m. yuan: property insurance accounted for 208,700m. yuan and life insurance for 494,900m. yuan.

Aegon-CNOOC Life Insurance Co Ltd: 15/F, Pufa Tower, 588 Pudong Nan Lu, Shanghai 200120; internet www.aegon-cnooc.com; f. 2002; jt venture between Aegon (The Netherlands) and China Nat. Offshore Oil Corpn.

Anbang Property and Casualty Insurance Co Ltd: Beijing; tel. (10) 65309999; e-mail webmaster@ab-insurance.com; internet www.ab-insurance.com; f. 2004.

AXA-Minmetals Assurance Co: 19/F China Merchants Tower, 166 Jia Zui Dong Lu, Pudong, Shanghai 200120; tel. (21) 58792288; fax (21) 58792299; internet www.axa-minmetals.com.cn; f. 1999; jt venture by Groupe AXA (France) and China Minmetals Group; CEO MA ZHEMING.

China Continent Property and Casualty Insurance Co Ltd: Shanghai; tel. (21) 58369588; internet www.ccic-net.com.cn; f. 2003; Chair. DAI FENGJU; CEO JIANG MING.

China Life Insurance Co: China Life Centre, 22–28/F, 17 Financial St, Xicheng Qu, Beijing 100140; tel. (10) 66009999; e-mail serve@e-chinalife.com; internet www.chinalife.com.cn; f. 1999; formed from People's Insurance (Life) Co, division of fmr People's Insurance Co of China—PICC; restructured into a parent company and a shareholding company Aug. 2003; initial public offering Dec. 2003; Chair. YANG MINGSHENG; Exec. Dir WAN FENG.

China Pacific Insurance Co Ltd (CPIC): 1226 Zhongshan Lu (Bei 1), Shanghai; tel. (21) 58767282; fax (21) 68870791; e-mail ir@cpic.com.cn; internet www.cpic.com.cn; f. 1991; jt-stock co; Chair. GAO GUOFU; Pres. YANG XIANGHAI.

China Taiping Insurance Group Co: Beijing; tel. (10) 63600601; fax (10) 63600605; internet www.cntaiping.com; f. 1931; fmrly China Insurance (Holdings) Co Ltd; cargo, hull, freight, fire, life, personal accident, industrial injury, motor insurance, reinsurance, etc.; 20 subsidiaries; Chair. LIN FAN; CEO KENNETH NG YU LAM.

China United Property Insurance Co: 600 Chengdu Bei Lu, Shanghai; tel. (21) 53554600; fax (21) 63276000; internet www.cicsh.com; f. 1986; fmrly Xinjiang Corpn Property Insurance Co; Gen. Man. LU FENG YUAN.

Huatai Insurance Co of China Ltd: International Business Bldg, 18/F, Tower A, 35 Financial St, Xicheng Qu, Beijing 100033; tel. (10) 59371818; fax (10) 63370081; e-mail beijing@ehuatai.com; internet www.ehuatai.com; f. 1996; est. by 63 industrial cos; Chair. and CEO WANG ZIMU.

Manulife Sinochem Life Insurance Co Ltd: Jin Mao Bldg, 21/F, 88 Century Rd, Pudong, Shanghai 200121; tel. (21) 50492288; fax (21) 50491110; e-mail cs@manulife-sinochem.com; internet www.manulife-sinochem.com; f. 1996; jt venture between Manulife (Canada) and Sinochem; Chair. MARC STERLING.

New China Life Insurance: 12 Jian Guo Man Wai Dajie, Chaoyang Qu, Beijing 100073; e-mail e@newchinalife.com; internet www.newchinalife.com; f. 1996; Chair. KANG DIAN.

PICC Property and Casualty Co Ltd: 69 Dongheyan Jie, Xuanwu Men, Beijing 100052; tel. (10) 63156688; fax (10) 63033589; e-mail webmaster@piccnet.com.cn; internet www.picc.com.cn; f. 2003; fmrly the People's Insurance Company of China; Chair. WU YAN; CEO YI WANG.

Ping An Insurance (Group) Co of China (Ping An): Galaxy Development Centre, 3 Fu Hua Lu, Futian District, Shenzhen; tel. (400) 8866338; fax (755) 82431019; e-mail IR@pingan.com.cn; internet www.pingan.com; f. 1988; 19.9% owned by HSBC Bank PLC (UK); total assets 292,519m. (June 2005); Chair. and CEO MA MINGZHE.

Sino Life Insurance: Yi Tian Rd, Fujian Qu, Shenzhen; internet www.sino-life.com; f. 2000; Chair. ZHANG JUN.

Sunlife Everbright Insurance Co Ltd: 37/F, Tianjin International Bldg, 75 Nanjing Lu, Heping Qu, Tianjin 300050; tel. (22) 23391188; fax (22) 23399929; internet www.sunlife-everbright.com; f. 1999; jt venture between Sunlife Financial (Canada) and China Everbright Group; Pres. and CEO JANET DE SILVA.

Sunshine Property and Casualty Insurance Co Ltd: 28/F, Kuntai International Mansion, 12B Chao Wai Dajie, Beijing 100020; tel. (10) 58289999; fax (10) 58289688; e-mail pinpaixuanchuan@ygbx.com; internet yangguang.sinosig.com; Pres. and Dir-Gen. ZHANG WEIGONG.

Taikang Life Insurance Co Ltd: Taikang Life Bldg, 156 Fu Xing Men Nei Dajie, Beijing 100031; tel. (10) 66429988; fax (10) 66426397; internet www.taikang.com; f. 1996; Chair. CHEN DONGSHENG.

Tianan Insurance Co Ltd: 1 Pudong Dajie, Shanghai 200120; tel. (21) 61017878; internet www.tianan-insurance.com; f. 1994; Chair. QIU QIANG.

Yongan Insurance: Jinqiao International Plaza, Tower C, 50 Keji Lu, Xian 710075; tel. (29) 87233888; fax (29) 88231200; internet www.yaic.com.cn; Chair. ZHANG DONG WU.

Regulatory Authority

China Insurance Regulatory Commission (CIRC): 15 Financial St, Xicheng Qu, Beijing 100140; tel. (10) 66286688; fax (10) 66018871; e-mail help@circ.gov.cn; internet www.circ.gov.cn; f. 1998; under direct authority of the State Council; Chair. WU DINGFU.

Trade and Industry

GOVERNMENT AGENCIES

China Council for International Investment Promotion (CCIIP): Rm 406–409, Jing Guang Centre, Hujia Lu, Chao Yang Qu, POB 8806, Beijing 100020; tel. (10) 65978801; fax (10) 65978210; e-mail msc@cciip.org.cn; internet www.cciip.org.cn; f. 2006; est. by State Council; aims to promote China's inward and outward investment; Pres. MIAO GENGSHU; Sec.-Gen. ZHOU MING.

China Investment Corpn (CIC): New Poly Plaza, 1 Chaoyangmen Bei Dajie, Dongcheng Qu, Beijing 100010; tel. (10) 64086277; fax (10) 64086908; e-mail pr@china-inv.cn; internet www.china-inv.cn; f. 2007; sovereign wealth fund; manages China's foreign-exchange reserves; Chair. LOU JIWEI; Pres. GAO XIQING.

China National Light Industry Council: 22B Fuwai Dajie, Beijing 100833; tel. (10) 68396613; fax (10) 68396264; e-mail webmaster@clii.com.cn; internet www.clii.com.cn; under supervision of State Council; Chair. CHEN SHINENG; Sec.-Gen. WANG SHICHENG.

China National Textile Industry Council (CNTIC): 12 Dong Chang An Jie, Beijing 100742; tel. (10) 65129545; under supervision of State Council; Chair. SHI WANPENG.

State Administration for Industry and Commerce: 8 San Li He Dong Lu, Xicheng Qu, Beijing 100820; tel. (10) 68013447; fax (10) 68010463; e-mail dfa@saic.gov.cn; internet www.saic.gov.cn; responsible for market supervision and administrative execution of industrial and commercial laws; functions under direct supervision of State Council.

State Administration of Foreign Exchange (SAFE): Huanrong Hotel, 18 Fucheng Lu, Haidan Qu, Beijing 100048; tel. (10) 68402265; internet www.safe.gov.cn; drafts foreign-exchange regulations, designs and implements balance of payments statistical system, manages foreign-exchange reserves; brs in Hong Kong, Singapore, London and New York; Administrator YI GANG.

State-owned Assets Supervision and Administration Commission: Beijing; tel. (10) 63192334; e-mail iecc@sasac.gov.cn; internet www.sasac.gov.cn; f. 2003; supervision and administration of state-owned assets, regulation of ownership transfers of state-owned enterprises; Chair. WANG YONG.

Takeover Office for Military, Armed Police, Government and Judiciary Businesses: Beijing; f. 1998; est. to assume control of enterprises fmrly operated by the People's Liberation Army.

CHAMBERS OF COMMERCE

All-China Federation of Industry and Commerce (All-China General Chamber of Industry and Commerce): 93 Beiheyan Dajie, Beijing 100006; tel. (10) 65136677; fax (10) 65131769; e-mail acfic@acfic.org.cn; internet www.acfic.com.cn (Chinese); www.chinachamber.org.cn (English); f. 1953; Chair. HUANG MENGFU.

China Chamber of Commerce for the Import and Export of Foodstuffs, Native Produce and Animal By-products (CFNA): Talent International Bldg, 80 Guanqumennei Jie, Chongwen Qu, Beijing 100062; tel. (10) 87109883; fax (10) 87109829; e-mail contact@cccfna.org.cn; internet www.cccfna.org.cn; f. 1988; over 5,400 mems; Pres. BIAN ZHENHU.

China Chamber of Commerce for Import and Export of Light Industrial Products and Arts-Crafts (CCCLA): 10/F, Pan Jia Yuan Da Sha Bldg, 12 Pan Jia Yuan Nanli, Chao Yang Qu, Beijing 100021; tel. (10) 67732707; fax (10) 67732698; e-mail xxb@cccla.org.cn; internet www.cccla.org.cn; f. 1988; over 6,000 mems; Chair. WANG ZHONGQI.

China Chamber of Commerce for Import and Export of Machinery and Electronic Products (CCCME): Rm 904, 9/F, Bldg 12, Pan Jia Yuan Nanli, Chao Yang Qu, Beijing; tel. (10) 58280863; fax (10) 58280860; e-mail international@cccme.org.cn; internet www.cccme.org.cn; f. 1988; more than 6,500 mems; Pres. and Sec.-Gen. ZHANG YUJING.

China Chamber of Commerce for Import and Export of Medicines and Health Products (CCCMHPIE): 11–12/F, Bldg 3, 6 Nanzhugan Hutong, Dongcheng Qu, Beijing 100010; tel. (10) 58036282; fax (10) 58036284; internet www.cccmhpie.org.cn; f. 1989; more than 1,500 mems; Pres. ZHOU XIAOMING.

China Chamber of Commerce for Import and Export of Textiles (CCCT): 12 Pan Jia Yuan Nanli, Chao Yang Qu, Beijing 100021; tel. (10) 67739246; fax (10) 67719235; e-mail info@ccct.org.cn; internet www.ccct.org.cn; f. 1988; Chair. WANG SHENYANG; over 6,300 mems.

China Council for the Promotion of International Trade (CCPIT)—China Chamber of International Commerce (CCOIC): 1 Fuxingmenwai Lu, Xicheng Qu, Beijing 100860; tel. (10) 88075000; fax (10) 68011370; e-mail webmaster@ccpit.org; internet www.ccpit.org; Chair. WAN JIFEI.

TRADE AND INDUSTRIAL ORGANIZATIONS

Beijing Urban Construction Group Co Ltd: 62 Xueyuannan Lu, Haidian, Beijing 100081; tel. (10) 62255511; fax (10) 62256027; e-mail cjp@mail.bucg.com; internet www.bucg.com; construction of civil and industrial buildings and infrastructure; Chair. LIU LONGHUA.

China Aerospace Science and Industry Corpn (CASIC): Aerospace Science and Industry Bldg 8, Fu Cheng Men Nei Dajie, Haidian Qu, Beijing 100048; tel. (10) 68373522; fax (10) 68383626; e-mail bgt@casic.com.cn; internet www.casic.com.cn; f. 1999; Gen. Man. XU DAZHE.

China Aerospace Science and Technology Corpn: 16 Fucheng Lu, Haidian Qu, Beijing 100048; tel. (10) 68767492; fax (10) 68372291; e-mail casc@spacechina.com; internet www.spacechina.com; f. 1999; Pres. MA XINGRUI.

China Association of Automobile Manufacturers: 46 San Li He, Xicheng Qu, Beijing 100823; tel. (10) 68594182; fax (10) 68595243; e-mail caam@caam.org.cn; internet www.caam.org.cn; f. 1987; Chair. HU MAOYUAN.

China Aviation Industry Corporation I: AVIC1 Plaza, 128, Jianguo Lu, Beijing 100022; tel. (10) 65665922; fax (10) 65666518; e-mail lixm@avic1.com.cn; internet www.avic1.com.cn; f. 1999; Pres. LIN ZUOMING.

China Aviation Industry Corporation II: 67 Jiao Nan Dajie, Beijing 100712; tel. (10) 64094013; fax (10) 64032109; e-mail international@avic2.com; internet www.avic2.com.cn; Pres. ZHANG HONGBIAO.

China Aviation Supplies Holding Co (CASC): 3 Tianwei Si Jie, Airport Industrial Zone A, Shunyi, Beijing 101312; tel. (10) 89455000; fax (10) 89455018; internet www.casc.com.cn; f. 1980; fmrly China Aviation Supplies Import & Export Group Corpn; aviation equipment supply services; Pres. LI HAI.

China Certification and Inspection Group Co Ltd (CCIC): Sanyuan Bldg, 18 Xibahe Dongli, Chao Yang Qu, Beijing 100028; tel. (10) 84603456; fax (10) 84603333; e-mail ccic@ccic.com; internet www.ccic.com; fmrly China National Import and Export Commodities Inspection Corpn; inspects, tests and surveys import and export commodities for overseas trade, transport, insurance and manufacturing firms; Pres. WANG FENGQING.

China Civil Engineering Construction Corpn (CCECC): 4 Beifeng Wo, Haidian Qu, Beijing 100038; tel. (10) 63263392; fax (10) 63263864; e-mail zongban@ccecc.com.cn; internet www.ccecc.com.cn; f. 1979; general contracting, provision of technical and labour services, consulting and design, etc.; Chair. LIU ZHIMING; Pres. LI YUAN.

China Construction International Inc: 9 Sanlihe Lu, Haidian Qu, Beijing; tel. (10) 68394086; fax (10) 68394097; Pres. FU RENZHANG.

China Electronics Corpn: 27 Wanshou Lu, Haidian Qu, Beijing 100846; tel. (10) 68218529; fax (10) 68213745; e-mail webmaster@cec.com.cn; internet www.cec.com.cn; Chair. XIONG QUNLI; Pres. LIU LIEHONG.

China Garment Industry Corpn: 9A Taiyanggong Beisanhuandong Lu, Chao Yang Qu, Beijing 100028; tel. (10) 64216660; fax (10) 64239134; Pres. DONG BINGGEN.

China General Technology (Group) Holding Ltd (Genertec): 23/F Genertec Plaza, 90 Xi San Huan Zhong Lu, Feng Tai Qu, Beijing 100055; tel. (10) 63348889; fax (10) 63348118; e-mail genertec@genertec.com.cn; internet www.genertec.com.cn; f. 1998; est. by merger of China Nat. Technical Import and Export Corpn, China Nat. Machinery Import and Export Corpn, China Nat. Instruments Import and Export Corpn and China Nat. Corpn for Overseas Economic Co-operation; total assets 16,000m. yuan; Chair. HE TONGXIN; Dir and Pres. LI DANG.

China Great Wall Computer Group: 18/F, Great Wall Technology Bldg, 66 East Rd, Haidian Qu, Beijing 100190; tel. (10) 59831188; fax (10) 59831133; e-mail cs@gwssi.com.cn; internet www.gwssi.com.cn; f. 1988; Pres. DU HEPING.

China Great Wall Industry Corpn: 67 Beisihuan Xilu, Haidian Qu, Beijing 100080; tel. (10) 88102000; fax (10) 88102107; e-mail cgwic@cgwic.com; internet www.cgwic.com.cn; f. 1980; international commercial wing of China Aerospace Science and Technology Corpn (CASC); Pres. YIN LIMING.

China Guangdong Nuclear Power Holding Co Ltd (CGNPC): Science Bldg, 1001 Shangbu Zhong Lu, Shenzhen 518028; e-mail webmaster_cgnpc@cgnpc.com.cn; internet www.cgnpc.com.cn; f. 1994; operates nuclear power plants; develops hydropower and wind power stations; more than 20 subsidiaries; Chair. HE YU.

China International Book Trading Corpn: see under Publishers

China International Contractors Association: Dong Zhi Men Wai Dajie, Dongcheng Qu, Beijing 100007; tel. (10) 59765260; fax (10) 59765200; e-mail webmaster@chinca.org; internet www.chinca.org; f. 1988; Chair. DIAO CHUNHE.

China International Futures Co Ltd (CIFCO): Rong Chao Business Centre, 15/F, Bldg A, 6003 Yi Tian Lu, Futian Qu, Shenzhen 518000; tel. (755) 23818333; fax (755) 23818283; e-mail cifco996@hotmail.com; internet www.szcifco.com; f. 1992; Pres. CHEN DONGHUA.

China International Telecommunication Construction Corpn (CITCC): 56 Nan Fang Zhuang, Fengtai Qu, Beijing 100079; tel. (10) 67668269; fax (10) 67668183; e-mail office@citcc.cn; internet www.citcc.cn; f. 1983; Chair. WANG QI; Gen. Man. XU CHUGUO.

China International Water and Electric Corpn (CWE): 3 Liupukang Yiqu Zhongjie, Xicheng Qu, Beijing 100120; tel. (10) 59302288; fax (10) 59302900; e-mail headoffice@cwe.cn; internet www.cwe.cn; f. 1956; est. as China Water and Electric International

Corpn, name changed 1983; imports and exports equipment for projects in the field of water and electrical engineering; undertakes such projects; provides technical and labour services; Pres. LU GUOJUN.

China Iron and Steel Industry and Trade Group Corpn (Sinosteel): Sinosteel Plaza, 8 Hai Dian Lu, Beijing 100080; tel. (10) 62686689; fax (10) 62686688; e-mail info@sinosteel.com; internet www.sinosteel.com; f. 1999; formed by merger of China National Metallurgical Import and Export Corpn, China Metallurgical Raw Materials Corpn and China Metallurgical Steel Products Processing Corpn; Pres. HUANG TIANWEN.

China Minmetals Corpn (Minmetals): 5 San Li He, Haidian Qu, Beijing 100044; tel. (10) 68495888; fax (10) 68335570; e-mail support@minmetals.com.cn; internet www.minmetals.com.cn; f. 1950; fmrly China National Metals and Minerals Import and Export Corpn, current name adopted 2004; imports and exports steel, antimony, tungsten concentrates and ferro-tungsten, zinc ingots, tin, mercury, pig-iron, cement, etc.; Pres. ZHOU ZHONGSHU.

China National Aerotechnology Import and Export Corpn: Catic Plaza, 18 Beichen Dong Lu, Chao Yang Qu, Beijing 100101; tel. (10) 84972255; fax (10) 84971088; e-mail master@catic.cn; internet www.catic.com.cn; f. 1979; exports signal flares, electric detonators, tachometers, parachutes, general purpose aircraft, etc.; Pres. MA ZHIPING.

China National Animal Breeding Stock Import and Export Corpn (CABS): 5/F Beijing News Plaza, 26 Jian Guo Men Nei Dajie, Beijing 100005; tel. (10) 65228866; fax (10) 85201555; e-mail cabs@cabs.com.cn; sole agency for import and export of stud animals including cattle, sheep, goats, swine, horses, donkeys, camels, rabbits, poultry, etc., as well as pasture and turf grass seeds, feed additives, medicines, etc.; Gen. Man. LIU XIAOFENG.

China National Arts and Crafts (Group) Corpn (CNACGC): Arts and Crafts Bldg, 103 Jixiangli, Chao Yang Men Wai, Chao Yang Qu, Beijing 100020; tel. (10) 85698808; fax (10) 85698866; e-mail info@cnacgc.com; internet www.cnacgc.com; deals in jewellery, ceramics, handicrafts, embroidery, pottery, wicker, bamboo, etc.; jointly est. by two central enterprises: China National Arts and Crafts Import & Export Corpn and China National Arts & Crafts (Group) Corpn; Pres. ZHOU ZHENGSHENG.

China National Automotive Industry Corpn (CNAIC): 46 Fucheng Lu, Haidian Qu, Beijing 100036; tel. (10) 88123968; fax (10) 68125556; Pres. CHEN XULIN.

China National Automotive Industry Import and Export Corpn (CAIEC): 265 Beisihuan Zhong Lu, Beijing 100083; tel. (10) 82379009; fax (10) 82379088; e-mail info@caiec.cn; internet www.caiec.cn; Pres. ZHANG FUSHENG; 1,100 employees.

China National Cereals, Oils and Foodstuffs Import and Export Corpn (COFCO): COFCO Fortune Plaza, 8 Chao Yang Men Wai Dajie, Chao Yang Qu, Beijing 100020; tel. (10) 85006688; fax (10) 65278612; e-mail cofcointo@cofco.com; internet www.cofco.com; f. 1952; imports, exports and processes grains, oils, foodstuffs, etc.; also hotel management and property development; Chair. NING GAONING; Pres. YU XUBO.

China National Chartering Ltd (SINOCHART): Sinotrans Plaza A, Rm 818, 43 Xi Zhi Men Bei Dajie, Beijing 100044; tel. (10) 62295052; fax (10) 62296859; e-mail sinochart@sinochart.com; internet www.sinochart.com; f. 1950; subsidiary of SINOTRANS (see below); arranges chartering of ships, reservation of space, managing and operating chartered vessels; Gen. Man. GENG CHEN.

China National Chemical Construction Corpn: Bldg No. 15, Songu, Anzhenxili, Chao Yang Qu, Beijing 100029; tel. (10) 64429966; fax (10) 64419698; e-mail cnccc@cnccc.com.cn; internet www.cnccc.com.cn; Pres. CHEN LIHUA.

China National Chemicals Import and Export Corporation (SINOCHEM): SINOCHEM Tower, 6–12/F, 28 Fu Xing Men Nei Dajie, Beijing 100031; tel. (10) 59568888; fax (10) 59568890; internet www.sinochem.com; f. 1950; import and export, domestic trade and entrepôt trade of oil, fertilizer, rubber, plastics and chemicals; Pres. LIU DESHU.

China National Coal Group Corpn: 1 Huangsi Lu, Chao Yang Qu, Beijing 100120; tel. (10) 82256688; fax (10) 82236023; e-mail zgzm@chinacoal.com; internet www.chinacoal.com; f. 1982; imports and exports coal and equipment for coal industry, joint coal development and compensation trade; fmrly known as China National Coal Industry Import and Export Corpn; Chair. and Pres. WU YAOWEN.

China National Coal Mine Corpn: 21 Bei Jie, Heipingli, Beijing 100013; tel. (10) 64217766; Pres. WANG SENHAO.

China National Complete Plant Import and Export Corpn (Group) (Complant): 9 Xi Bin He Lu, An Ding Men, Beijing 100011; tel. (10) 64253388; fax (10) 64211382; e-mail info@complant.com; internet www.complant.com; Chair. LI ZHIMIN; Gen. Man. TANG JIANGUO.

China National Electronics Import and Export Corpn: 8th Floor, Electronics Bldg, 23A Fuxing Lu, Beijing 100036; tel. (10) 68219550; fax (10) 68212352; e-mail webmaster@ceiec.com.cn; internet www.ceiec.com.cn; f. 1980; imports and exports electronics equipment, light industrial products, ferrous and non-ferrous metals; advertising; consultancy; Pres. and CEO CHEN XU.

China National Export Bases Development Corpn: Bldg 16–17, District 3, Fang Xing Yuan, Fang Zhuang Xiaoqu, Fengtai Qu, Beijing 100078; tel. (10) 67628899; fax (10) 67628803; Pres. XUE ZHAO.

China National Foreign Trade Transportation Corpn (Group) (SINOTRANS): 12/F, Sinotrans Plaza A, 43 Xi Zhi Men Bei Dajie, Beijing 100044; tel. (10) 62295900; fax (10) 62295901; e-mail office@sinotrans.com; internet www.sinotrans.com; f. 1950; agents for China's import and export corpns; arranges customs clearance, deliveries, forwarding and insurance for sea, land and air transport; Chair. ZHAO HUXIANG; Pres. LIU XIHAN.

China National Gold Group Corpn (China Gold): 1 South St, Liuyin Park, Dongcheng Qu, Beijing 100011; tel. (10) 84123635; fax (10) 84118355; e-mail cngc@chinagoldgroup.com; internet www.chinagoldgroup.com; gold mining, research and trade; Pres. SUN ZHAOXUE.

China National Instruments Import and Export Corpn (Instrimpex): Instrimpex Bldg, 6 Xi Zhi Men Wai Jie, Beijing 100044; tel. (10) 68330618; fax (10) 68318380; e-mail cnic@cnic.genertec.com.cn; internet www.instrimpex.com.cn; f. 1955; imports and exports; technical service, real estate, manufacturing, information service, etc.; Pres. AN FENGSHOU.

China National Light Industrial Products Import and Export Corpn: 910, 9th Section, Jin Song, Chao Yang Qu, Beijing 100021; tel. (10) 67766688; fax (10) 67747246; e-mail info@chinalight.com.cn; internet www.chinalight.com.cn; imports and exports household electrical appliances, audio equipment, photographic equipment, films, paper goods, building materials, bicycles, sewing machines, enamelware, glassware, stainless steel goods, footwear, leather goods, watches and clocks, cosmetics, stationery, sporting goods, etc.; Pres. PAN WANG.

China National Machine Tool Corpn: World Trade Centre, 23/F, Blk A, Dong San Huan Bei Lu, Dongcheng Qu, Beijing; tel. (10) 58257788; fax (10) 64015657; e-mail zcb@cnmtc.net; internet www.cnmtc.net; f. 1979; imports and exports machine tools and tool products, components and equipment; supplies apparatus for machine-building industry; Pres. QUAN YILU.

China National Machinery and Equipment Import and Export Corpn (Group) (CMEC): 178 Guang An Men Wai Dajie, Beijing 100055; tel. (10) 63451188; fax (10) 63261865; e-mail cmec@mail.cmec.com; internet www.cmec.com; f. 1978; imports and exports machine tools, all kinds of machinery, automobiles, hoisting and transport equipment, electric motors, photographic equipment, etc.; Pres. JIA ZHIQIANG.

China National Medicine and Health Products Import and Export Corpn (Meheco): Meheco Plaza, 18 Guangming Zhong Jie, Chongwen Qu, Beijing 100061; tel. (10) 67116688; fax (10) 67121579; e-mail meheco@meheco.com.cn; internet www.meheco.cn; Pres. ZHANG BEN ZHI.

China National Native Produce and Animal By-Products Import and Export Corpn (TUHSU): COFCO Fortune Plaza, 8 Chao Yang Men Wai Dajie, Chao Yang Qu, Beijing 100020; tel. (10) 85018181; fax (10) 85615151; e-mail tuhsu@cofco.com; internet www.tuhsu.com.cn; f. 1949; imports and exports include tea, coffee, cocoa, fibres, etc.; 9 tea brs; 23 overseas subsidiaries; Pres. WANG ZHEN.

China National Non-Ferrous Metals Import and Export Corpn (CNIEC): 12B Fuxing Lu, Beijing 100814; tel. (10) 63975588; fax (10) 63964424; Chair. WU JIANCHANG; Pres. XIAO JUNQING.

China National Nuclear Corpn: 1 Nansanxiang, Sanlihe, Beijing 100822; tel. (10) 68512211; fax (10) 68533989; e-mail xxzx@cnnc.com.cn; internet www.cnnc.com.cn; Dir SUN QIN.

China National Oil and Gas Exploration and Development Corpn: 1 Fu Cheng Men Bei Dajie, Xicheng Qu, Beijing 100034; tel. (10) 58551114; fax (10) 58551000; e-mail master@cnpcint.com; internet www.cnpc.com.cn/cnodc; subsidiary of China National Petroleum Corpn (see below); Gen. Man. BO QILIANG.

China National Packaging Import and Export Corpn: Xinfu Bldg B, 3 Dong San Huan Bei Lu, Chao Yang Qu, Beijing 100027; tel. (10) 64616359; fax (10) 64611080; e-mail info@chinapack.net; internet www.chinapack.net; handles import and export of packaging materials, containers, machines and tools; contracts for the processing and converting of packaging machines and materials supplied by foreign customers; Pres. ZHENG CHONGXIANG.

China National Petroleum Corpn (CNPC): 9 Dong Zhi Men Bei Lu, Dongcheng Qu, Beijing 100007; tel. (10) 62094114; fax (10) 62094205; e-mail admin_eng@cnpc.com.cn; internet www.cnpc.com.cn; responsible for petroleum extraction and refining in northern and western China, and for setting retail prices of petroleum products; restructured mid-1998, transferring to PetroChina Co Ltd (a publicly listed subsidiary) domestic operations in the areas of petroleum and gas exploration and devt, petroleum refining and petrochemical production, marketing, pipeline transport, and natural gas sales and utilization; acquired PetroKazakhstan in 2005; Pres. JIANG JIEMIN.

China National Publications Import and Export (Group) Corpn: 16 Gongrentiyuguandong Lu, Chao Yang Qu, Beijing; tel. (10) 65066688; fax (10) 65067100; e-mail cnpeak@cnpiec.com.cn; internet www.cnpeak.com; imports and exports books, newspapers and periodicals, records, CD-ROMs, etc.; Pres. WU JIANGJIANG.

China National Publishing Industry Trading Corpn: POB 782, 504 An Hua Li, An Ding Men Wai, Beijing 100011; tel. (10) 64210403; fax (10) 64214540; e-mail cnpitc@cnpitc.com.cn; internet www.cnpitc.com.cn; f. 1981; imports and exports publications, printing equipment technology; holds book fairs abroad; undertakes joint publication; Pres. ZHOU HONGLI.

China National Seed Group Corpn: Sinochem Tower A, 15/F, 2 Fu Xing Men Wai Dajie, Beijing 100045; tel. (10) 88079999; fax (10) 88079998; e-mail chinaseeds@sinochem.com; internet www.chinaseeds.com.cn; f. 1978; imports and exports crop seeds, including cereals, cotton, oil-bearing crops, teas, flowers and vegetables; seed production for foreign seed companies etc.; Gen. Man. ZHANG WEI.

China National Silk Import and Export Corpn: 105 Bei He Yan Jie, Dongcheng Qu, Beijing 100006; tel. (10) 65123338; fax (10) 65125125; e-mail chinasilk@chinasilk.com; internet www.chinasilk.com; 22 subsidiaries and more than 40 domestic co-operative enterprises; Gen. Man. ZHANG WEIMING.

China National Technical Import and Export Corpn: 16/F, Genertec Plaza, 90 Xi San Huan Zhong Lu, Fengtai Qu, Beijing 100055; tel. (10) 63349206; fax (10) 63373713; e-mail cntic@cntic.genertec.com.cn; internet www.cntic.com.cn; f. 1952; imports all kinds of complete plant and equipment, acquires modern technology and expertise from abroad, undertakes co-production and jt ventures, and technical consultation and updating of existing enterprises; Pres. TANG YI.

China National Textiles Import and Export Corpn: Chinatex Mansion, 19 Jian Guo Men Nei Lu, Beijing 100005; tel. (10) 65281122; fax (10) 65124711; e-mail webmaster@chinatex.com; internet www.chinatex.com; f. 1951; imports synthetic fibres, raw cotton, wool and garment accessories; exports cotton yarn, cotton fabric, knitwear and woven garments; over 30 subsidiaries; Pres. ZHAO BOYA.

China National Tobacco Import and Export Group Corpn: 9 Guang An Men Wai Dajie, Xuan Wu Qu, Beijing 100055; tel. (10) 63605290; fax (10) 63605915; internet www.cntiegc.com.cn; Chair. ZHANG HUI.

China North Industries Group Corpn (CNGC): 44 Sanlihe Lu, Beijing 100821; tel. (10) 68594210; fax (10) 68594232; e-mail webmaster@cngc.com.cn; internet www.cngc.com.cn; exports vehicles and mechanical products, light industrial products, chemical products, opto-electronic products, building materials, military products, etc.; Pres. ZHANG GUOQING.

China Railway Construction Corpn: 40 Fuxing Lu, Beijing 100855; tel. (10) 51888114; fax (10) 68217382; e-mail webmaster@crcc.cn; internet www.crcc.cn; f. 1948; state-owned; over 30 subsidiaries; design, construction, equipment installation and maintenance of railways and highways; Pres. ZHAO GUANGFA.

China Railway Group Ltd: China Railway Tower 9, 69 Fuxing Lu, Haidian Qu, Beijing 100039; tel. (10) 51845225; fax (10) 51841757; e-mail webmaster@crec.cn; internet www.crec.cn; f. 2007; est. as jt stock co; 46 subsidiaries; infrastructure construction, design, survey and consulting services; mfr of engineering equipment; Chair. LI CHANGJIN; Pres. BAI ZHONGREN.

China Road and Bridge Corpn: Zhonglu Bldg, 88C, An Ding Men Wai Dajie, Beijing 100011; tel. (10) 64280055; fax (10) 64285686; e-mail crbc@crbc.com; internet www.crbc.com; overseas and domestic building of highways, urban roads, bridges, tunnels, industrial and residential buildings, airport runways and parking areas; contracts to do surveying, designing, pipe-laying, water supply and sewerage, building, etc., and/or to provide technical or labour services; Chair. ZHANG JIANCHU; Pres. WEN GANG.

China Shipbuilding Trading Co Ltd: 8–12/F, Bldg 1, 9 Shouti Nan Lu, Haidian Qu, Beijing 100048; tel. (10) 88573688; fax (10) 88573600; e-mail webmaster@cstc.com.cn; internet www.cstc.com.cn; f. 1982; Pres. LI ZHUSHI.

China State Construction Engineering Corpn: CSCEC Mansion, 15 San Li He Dajie, Haidian Qu, Beijing 100037; tel. (10) 88082888; fax (10) 88082789; e-mail ir@cscec.com.cn; internet www.cscec.com.cn; f. 1982; Pres. YI JUN.

China State Shipbuilding Corpn (CSSC): 9 Shouti Nan Lu, Haidian Qu, Beijing 100044; tel. (10) 68038833; fax (10) 68034592; e-mail cssc@cssc.net.cn; internet www.cssc.net.cn; f. 1999; naval and civil shipbuilding; Pres. TAN ZUOJUN.

China Tea Import and Export Corpn: South Gate, Chao Yang Qu, Beijing 100020; tel. (10) 64204127; fax (10) 64204101; e-mail info@teachina.com; internet www.chinatea.com.cn; Chair. ZHU FUTANG; Gen. Man. SUN YUEHUA.

China Xinshidai (New Era) Co: Xinshidai Plaza, 26 Ping An Xi Li Dajie, Xicheng Qu, Beijing 100034; tel. (10) 88009999; fax (10) 88009779; e-mail xsd@xsd.com.cn; internet www.xsd.com.cn; f. 1980; imports and exports defence industry and civilian products; Pres. WANG XINGYE.

Daqing Petroleum Administration Bureau: Sartu Qu, Daqing, Heilongjiang; tel. (459) 814649; fax (459) 322845; Gen. Man. WANG YONGCHUN.

Maanshan Iron and Steel Co (Masteel): 8 Hongqibei Lu, Maanshan 243003, Anhui Province; tel. (555) 2888158; fax (555) 2324350; internet www.magang.com.cn; sales 34,319.9m. yuan (2006); Chair. GU JIANGUO.

PetroChina International Co Ltd (China National United Oil Corporation—Chinaoil): 27 Chengfang Lu, Xicheng Qu, Beijing 100032; tel. (10) 66227001; fax (10) 66227002; internet www.chinaoil.com.cn; international trading subsidiary of PetroChina Co Ltd; imports and exports petroleum, natural gas and refined petroleum products; Chair. DUAN WENDE; Pres. WANG LIHUA.

Shanghai International Trust Trading Corpn: 201 Zhaojiabang Lu, Shanghai 200032; tel. (21) 64033866; fax (21) 64034722; f. 1979; present name adopted 1988; handles import and export business, international mail orders, processing, assembling, compensation, trade, etc.

State Bureau of Non-Ferrous Metals Industry: 12B Fuxing Lu, Beijing 100814; tel. (10) 68514477; fax (10) 68515360; Dir ZHANG WULE.

Xinxing Oil Co (XOC): Beijing; f. 1997; exploration, development and production of domestic and overseas petroleum and gas resources; Gen. Man. ZHU JIAZHEN.

UTILITIES

Regulatory Authority

State Electricity Regulatory Commission: 86 Xichangan Dajie, Beijing 100031; tel. (10) 66058800; e-mail serc_manager@serc.gov.cn; internet www.serc.gov.cn; f. 2003; Pres. WU XINXIONG.

Electricity

Anhui Province Energy Group Co Ltd (Wenergy): 76 Ma'anshan Lu, Hefei, Anhui 230001; tel. (551) 2225678; fax (551) 2225959; e-mail webmaster@wenergy.com.cn; internet www.wenergy.com.cn.

Beijing Electric Power Corpn: Qianmen Xi Dajie, Beijing 100031; tel. (10) 63129201; internet www.bjpsc.com.

Central China Electric Power Group Co: 47 Xudong Lu, Wuchang, Wuhan 430077; tel. (27) 6813398.

Changsha Electric Power Bureau: 162 Jiefang Sicun, Changsha 410002; tel. (731) 5912121; fax (731) 5523240.

China Atomic Energy Authority: Jia 8, Fucheng 100048; e-mail webmaster@caea.gov.cn; internet www.caea.gov.cn; Chair. CHEN QUIFA.

China Guodian Corpn: 6–8 Fu Cheng Men Bei Dajie, Xicheng Qu, Beijing 100034; tel. (10) 58682000; fax (10) 58553900; e-mail cgdcb@cgdc.com.cn; internet www.cgdc.com.cn; f. 2002; transfer of Jianbi power plant from fmr State Power Corpn completed Sept. 2003; Chair. ZHU YONGPENG.

China Power Grid Development (CPG): 4 Xueyuang Nanli, Haidan Qu, Beijing; manages transmission and transformation lines for the Three Gorges hydroelectric scheme; Pres. ZHOU XIAOQIAN.

China Power Investment Corpn: Bldg 3, 28 Financial St, Xicheng Qu, Beijing 100140; tel. (10) 66298000; fax (10) 66298095; e-mail engweb@cpicorp.com.cn; internet www.zdt.com.cn; f. 2002; formed from part of the constituent businesses of fmr State Power Corpn; parent company of China Power International; Pres. LU QIZHOU.

China Southern Power Grid Co: 6 Huasui Lu, Zhujiang Xincheng, Tianhe Qu, Guangzhou 510623, Guangdong Province; tel. (20) 38121080; fax (20) 38120189; e-mail international@csg.cn; internet eng.csg.cn; f. 2002; est. from power grids in southern provinces of fmr State Power Corpn; Chair. ZHAO JIANGUO; Pres. JUN ZHONG.

China Three Gorges Project Corpn (CTGPC): 1 Jianshe Dajie, Yichang 443002, Hubei Province; tel. (717) 6276666; fax (717) 6270088; e-mail webmaster@ctgpc.com.cn; internet www.ctgpc.com; Chair. CAO GUANGJING; Pres. FI CHEN.

China Yangtze Power Co Ltd: Block B, Focus Place, 19 Financial St, Xicheng Qu, Beijing 100032; tel. (10) 58688999; fax (10) 58688888;

e-mail cypc@cypc.com.cn; internet www.cypc.com.cn; f. 2002; generation of power from the Yangtze river; manages power-generating assets on behalf of China Yangtze Three Gorges Project Development Corpn; initial public offering on the Shanghai Stock Exchange Nov. 2003; Gen. Man. ZHANG CHENG.

Chongqing Jiulong Electric Power Co Ltd: 15 Qianjinzhi Lu, Yangjiaping, Jiulongpo Qu, Chongqing 400050; tel. (23) 68787910; fax (23) 68787944; internet www.jiulongep.com; Chair. LIU WEIQING; Gen. Man. ZHENG WUSHENG.

Chongqing Three Gorges Water Conservancy and Electric Power Co Ltd: 85 Gao Suntang, Wanzhou Qu, Chongqing 400040; tel. (23) 87509622; fax (23) 58237588; internet www.cqsxsl.com; Chair. YE JIANQIAO.

Dalian Power Supply Co: 102 Zhongshan Lu, Dalian 116001; tel. (411) 2637560; fax (411) 2634430; Chief Gen. Man. LIU ZONGXIANG.

Datang Huayin Electric Power Co Ltd: 255, Third Section, Central Furong Lu, Changsha 410007; tel. (731) 5388028; internet www.hypower.com.cn; Gen. Man. WEI YUAN.

Datang International Power Generation Co Ltd: 9 Guang Ning Bo Lu, Xicheng Qu, Beijing 100140; tel. (10) 88008800; fax (10) 88008111; internet www.dtpower.com; independent power producer; Chair. ZHAI RUOYU; Pres. CAO JINGSHAN.

Fujian Electric Power Co Ltd: 4 Xingang Dao, Taijrang Qu, Fuzhou 350009; tel. and fax (591) 3268514; Gen. Man. LI WEIDONG.

Fujian Mindong Electric Power Co Ltd: 8–10/F, Hualong Bldg, 143 Huancheng Lu, Jiaocheng Qu, Ningde 352100; tel. (593) 2096666; fax (593) 2096993; internet www.mdep.com.cn; f. 2000; Chair. ZHOU DUNBIN.

Gansu Electric Power Co: Lanzhou 730050; tel. (931) 2334311; fax (931) 2331042; e-mail webmaster@gsepc.com; internet www.gsepc.com; Dir ZHANG MINGXI.

GD Power Development Co Ltd: 9/F, International Investment Plaza Tower B, 6–8 Fu Cheng Men Bei Dajie, Xicheng Qu, Beijing; tel. (10) 58682200; fax (10) 583553800; e-mail gdd1@600795.com.cn; internet www.600795.com.cn; manufacture and sale of electricity and heat, and the operation of power grids in northern, eastern, north-eastern and north-western China, as well as Yunnan and Sichuan Provinces; Chair. ZHU YONGFAN.

Guangdong Electric Power Bureau: 757 Dongfeng Dong Lu, Guangzhou 510600; tel. (20) 87767888; fax (20) 87770307.

Guangdong Electric Power Development Co Ltd: 23–26/F, South Tower, Yuedian Plaza, 2 Tian He Dong Lu, Guangzhou 510630; tel. (20) 87570251; fax (20) 85138004; internet www.ged.com.cn; Chair. LI PAN.

Guangdong Yudean Group: Yudean Plaza, 2 Tianhe Dong Lu, Guangzhou, Guangdong 510630; tel. (20) 85138888; fax (20) 85136666; e-mail ydbianjibu@gdyd.com; internet www.gdyd.com; Chair. LI PAN.

Guangxi Guiguan Electric Power Co Ltd: 126 Minzhu Lu, Nanning 530022; tel. (771) 6118880; fax (771) 6118899; e-mail ggep@ggep.com.cn; internet www.ggep.com.cn; Chair. YANG QING; Gen. Man. DAI BO.

Guangzhou Electric Power Co: 9th Floor, Huale Bldg, 53 Huale Lu, Guangzhou 510060; tel. (20) 83821111; fax (20) 83808559.

Guodian Changyuan Electric Power Co Ltd: Huazhong Electric Finance Bldg, 117 Xu Dong Jie, Wuchang Qu, Wuhan 430067, Hubei Province; tel. (27) 86610541; fax (27) 86610524; e-mail sec@cydl.com.cn; internet www.cydl.com.cn; Chair. LI QINGKUI.

Hainan Electric Power Industry Bureau: 34 Haifu Dadao, Haikou 570203; tel. (898) 5334777; fax (898) 5333230.

Huadian Energy Co Ltd: 209 Dacheng Jie, Harbin 150001; tel. (451) 53685938; fax (451) 53685915; internet www.hdenergy.com; Chair. SHUHUI REN.

Huadian Power International Corpn Ltd: 2 Xuanwumen Jie, Xicheng Qu, Beijing 100031; tel. (10) 83567888; fax (10) 83567963; e-mail hdpi@hdpi.com.cn; internet www.hdpi.com.cn; f. 1994; fmrly Shandong International Power Development, renamed as above 2003; Chair. DA HONGXING; Gen. Man. CHEN JIANHUA.

Huadong Electric Power Group Corpn: 201 Nanjing Dong Lu, Shanghai; tel. (21) 63290000; fax (21) 63290727; power supply.

Huaneng Power International: Huaneng Bldg 4, Fu Xing Men Nei Dajie, Xicheng Qu, Beijing 100031; tel. (10) 63226999; fax (10) 63226888; e-mail zqb@hpi.com.cn; internet www.hpi.com.cn; f. 1998; transfer of generating assets from fmr State Power Corpn completed Sept. 2003; Chair. CAO PEIXI; Pres. LIU GUOYUE.

Huazhong Electric Power Group Corpn: Liyuan, Donghu, Wuhan, Hubei Province; tel. (27) 6813398; fax (27) 6813143; electrical engineering; Gen. Man. LIN KONGXING.

Hunan Chendian International Development Share-holding Ltd Co: 15/F, Wanguo Bldg, Minsheng Lu, Intersection Qingnian Dajie, Chenzhou 423000; tel. (735) 2339233; fax (735) 2339269; internet www.chinacdi.com; f. 2000; electricity and gas supply and generation; Chair. FU GUO.

Inner Mongolia Electric Power Co: 28 Xilin Nan Lu, Huhehaose 010021; tel. (471) 6942222; fax (471) 6924863.

Jiangmen Electric Power Supply Bureau: 87 Gangkou Lu, Jiangmen 529030; tel. and fax (750) 3360133.

Jiangxi Electric Power Corpn: 13 Yongwai Zheng Jie, Nanchang 330006; tel. (791) 6224701; fax (791) 6224830; internet www.jepc.com.cn; f. 1993.

National Grid Construction Co: established to oversee completion of the National Grid.

North China Grid Company Ltd: 482 Guanganmen Nei Dajie, Xuanwu Qu, Beijing 100053; tel. and fax (10) 83583114; internet www.nc.sgcc.com.cn; Chair. MA ZONGLIN.

Northeast China Grid Co Ltd: 11 Shiyiwei Lu, Heping Qu, Shenyang 110003; tel. (24) 3114382; fax (24) 3872665; internet www.ne.sgcc.com.cn.

Northwest Power Construction Group Corpn: 3 Changle Xi Lu, Xian 710032; tel. (29) 82551370; fax (29) 83382405; e-mail nwepc_hr@163.com; internet www.nwepc.cn.

Shandong Electric Power Group Corpn: 150 Jinger Lu, Jinan 250001; tel. (531) 6911919; internet www.sd.sgcc.com.cn; Chair. LI TONG ZHI.

Shandong Rizhao Power Co Ltd: 1st Floor, Bldg 29, 30 Northern Section, Shunyu Xiaoqu, Jinan 250002; tel. (531) 2952462; fax (531) 2942561; subsidiary of Huaneng Power International.

Shanghai Electric Power Co Ltd: China Resource Plaza, Bldg 1, 36/F, 268 Zhongshou Nan Lu, Shanghai 200010; tel. (21) 51156666; e-mail sepco@shanghaipower.com; internet www.shanghaipower.com; Chair. ZHOU SHIPING.

Shanghai Municipal Electric Power Co (SMEPC): 1122 Yuanshen Lu, Shanghai 200122; tel. (21) 28925222; fax (21) 28926512; e-mail smepc@smepc.com; internet www.smepc.com.cn.

Shantou Electric Power Development Co: 23 Zhuchi Lu, Shantou 515041; tel. (754) 8857191; Chair. LIN WEIGUANG.

Shanxi Zhangze Electric Power Co Ltd: 197 Wuyi Lu, Taiyuan 030001; tel. (351) 4265111; fax (351) 4265112; e-mail xww@zdthb.com.cn; internet www.zhangzepower.com; Chair. JIA BIN.

Shenergy Co Ltd: 1 Fuxing Zhong Lu, Shanghai 200021; tel. (621) 63900303; fax (621) 63900456; e-mail zhengquan@shenergy.com.cn; internet www.shenergy.com.cn; f. 1992; supply and distribution of electricity and natural gas; Chair. CHOU WEIGUO.

Shenzhen Power Supply Co: 2 Yanhe Xi Lu, Luohu Qu, Shenzhen 518000; tel. (755) 5561920.

Sichuan Electric Power Co: Room 1, Waishi Bldg, Dongfeng Lu, Chengdu 610061; tel. (28) 444321; fax (28) 6661888.

Sichuan Mingxing Electric Power Co Ltd: 88 Ming Yue Lu, Sui Ning 629000; tel. (825) 2210076; fax (825) 2210017; internet www.mxdl.com.cn; f. 1988; distribution of electric power and gas; Chair. ZHANG YOUCAI.

State Grid Corpn of China: 86 Chang'an Xi Lu, Xicheng Qu, Beijing 100031; tel. and fax (10) 66597205; e-mail sgcc-info@sgcc.com.cn; internet www.sgcc.com.cn; f. 1997 from holdings of Ministry of Electric Power; fmrly State Power Corpn of China; became a grid co following division of State Power Corpn into 11 independent companies (five generating companies, four construction companies and two transmission companies) in Dec. 2002; generating assets transferred to Huaneng Group, Huadian Group, Guodian Group, China Power Investment Corpn and Datang Group; Pres. and CEO LIU ZHENYA.

Tianjin Electric Power Corpn: 39 Jinbu Dao, Hebei Qu, Tianjin 300010; tel. (22) 24406031; fax (22) 24408615; e-mail tj.sgcc-info@sgcc.com.cn; internet www.tj.sgcc.com.cn; Gen. Man. ZHANG NING.

Top Energy Co Ltd: 272 Changzhi Jie, Taiyuan, Shanxi; tel. (351) 7021857; fax (351) 7021077; e-mail top600780@sina.com; internet www.600780.net; f. 1992; Chair. CHANG XIAOGANG.

Wuhan Power Supply Co: 1053 Jiefang Dadao, Hankou 430013, Wuhan Province; tel. (27) 82403109.

Wuxi Power Supply Bureau: 8 Houxixi, Wuxi 214001; tel. (510) 2717678; fax (510) 2719182.

Xiamen Power Transformation and Transmission Engineering Co: 67 Wenyuan Lu, Xiamen 361004; tel. (592) 2046763.

Xian Power Supply Bureau: Huancheng Dong Lu, Xian 710032; tel. (29) 7271483.

Xinjiang Tianfu Thermoelectric Co Ltd: 54 Hongxing Lu, Shihezi 832000; tel. (993) 2901108; fax (993) 2901121; e-mail yj@tfrd.com.cn; internet www.tfrd.com.cn; f. 1999; generation and distribution of electricity in Shihezi, Xinjiang Uygur Autonomous Region; Chair. WEI LU.

Zhejiang Southeast Electric Power Co: 152 Tianmushan Lu, Hangzhou, Zhejiang 310007; tel. (51) 85774567; fax (51) 85774321; internet www.zsepc.com; Chair. MAO JIANHONG.

Gas

Beijing Gas Group Co Ltd: Xicheng; tel. (10) 66205589; fax (10) 66205587; e-mail bjgas@bjgas.com; internet www.bjgas.com; owned by the Hong Kong-based Beijing Enterprises Holdings Ltd; Chair. SI ZHOU.

Beijing Natural Gas Co: Bldg 5, Dixingju, An Ding Men Wai, Beijing 100011; tel. (10) 64262244.

Changchun Gas Co: 421 Yan'an Jie, Changchun 130021; tel. (431) 5937850; fax (431) 5954646; internet www.ccrq.com.cn.

Changsha Gas Co: 18 Shoshan Lu, Changsha 410011; tel. (731) 4427246.

ENN Energy Holdings Ltd: Huaxiang Lu, Langfang Economic and Technical Development Zone, Hebei 065001; tel. (316) 2598100; fax (316) 2598585; e-mail xagas_news@enn.cn; internet yw.xinaogas.com; fmrly known as Xinao Gas Holdings Ltd; Chair. WANG YUSUO.

Qingdao Gas Co: 399A Renmin Lu, Qingdao 266032; tel. (532) 4851945; fax (532) 4858653; e-mail gasoffice@qdgas.com.cn; internet www.qdgas.com.cn.

Shanghai Dazhong Public Utilities: 8/F, 1515 Zhongshan Xi Lu, Shanghai 200235; tel. (21) 64288888; fax (21) 64288727; internet www.dzug.cn; Chair. YANG GUOPING.

Shenzhen Energy Group Co Ltd: 2068 Shennan Lu, Futian Qu, Shenzhen 518031; tel. (755) 83680288; fax (755) 83680298; e-mail IR@sec.com.cn; internet www.sec.com.cn; f. 1992; Chair. GAO ZIMIN.

Wuhan Gas Co: Qingnian Lu, Hankou, Wuhan 430015; tel. (27) 5866223.

Xiamen Gas Corpn: Ming Gong Bldg, Douxi Lukou, Hubin Nan Lu, Xiamen 361004; tel. (592) 2025937; fax (592) 2033290.

Water

Beijing Municipal Water Works Bureau: 83 Cuiwei Lu, Haidian Qu, Beijing 100036; tel. (10) 68213366; fax (10) 68130728.

Changchun Water Group Co Ltd: 53 Dajing Lu, Changchun 130000; tel. (431) 88974423; e-mail ccws@changchunwater.com; internet www.changchunwater.com.

Chengdu Municipal Waterworks Co Ltd: 16 Shierqiao Jie, Shudu Dadao, Chengdu 610072; tel. (28) 77663122; fax (28) 7776876; internet www.cdwater.chengdu.gov.cn.

Guangzhou Water Supply Co: 12 Zhongshan Yi Lu, Yuexiu Qu, Guangzhou 510600; fax (20) 87159099; internet www.gzwatersupply.com; Pres. WANG JIANPING.

Haikou Water Group Co Ltd: Haidian; tel. (898) 66269271; fax (898) 66269696; internet www.haikouwater.com.

Harbin Water Co: 49 Xi Shidao Jie, Daoli Qu, Harbin 150010; tel. (451) 4610522; fax (451) 4611726.

Jiangmen Water Supply Co Ltd: 44 Jianshe Lu, Jiangmen 529000; tel. (750) 3286358; fax (750) 3286368; e-mail jmwtof@163.com; internet www.jmwater.com.

Qinhuangdao Pacific Water Co: 71 West First St, Changli, Hebei 066600; tel. (335) 2022579; fax (335) 2986924; e-mail qpwc@sinofrench.com; internet www.sinofrench.com/Qinhuangdao.htm; f. 1998; Sino-US water supply project.

Sembcorp Utilities Investment Management (Shanghai) Ltd: Unit 503–506, Fortune Gate, 1701 Beijing West Rd, Jing'an, Shanghai 200040; tel. (21) 62880822; internet www.sembcorp.com; f. 1996; treatment of wastewater, industrial water, potable water and overall water management; fmrly The China Water Co, name changed as above after acquisition by Sembcorp (Singapore) in 2010; Pres. and CEO TANG KIN FEI.

Shanghai Water Authority: 389 Jiangsu Lu, Shanghai 200050; tel. (21) 52397000; e-mail webmaster@shanghaiwater.gov.cn; internet www.shanghaiwater.gov.cn; service provider for municipality of Shanghai; Dir-Gen. ZHANG JIAYI.

Shenzhen Water Supply Group Co: 7/F Water Bldg, 1019 Shennan Zhong Lu, Shenzhen 518031; tel. (755) 82137618; fax (755) 82137830; e-mail master@waterchina.com; internet www.waterchina.com.

Tianjin Waterworks Group: 54 Jianshe Lu, Heping Qu, Tianjin 300040; tel. (22) 3393887; fax (22) 3306720; e-mail sonic356@sohu.com; internet www.jinnanwater.com.

Xian Water Co: Huancheng Xi Lu, Xian 710082; tel. (29) 4244881.

Zhanjiang Water Co: 20 Renmin Dadaonan, Zhanjiang 524001; tel. (759) 2286394.

Zhongshan Water Supply Co: 23 Yinzhu Jie, Zhuyuan Lu, Zhongshan 528403; tel. (760) 8312969; fax (760) 6326429.

Zhoushan Water Supply Co Ltd: 263 Jiefang Xi Lu, Zhoushan 316000; tel. (580) 2022769; e-mail webmaster@zswater.com; internet www.zswater.com.

Zhuhai Water Group Co Ltd: 338 Meihua Dong Lu, Zhuhai 519000; tel. (756) 8899110; e-mail zhgsdnzx@pub.zhuhai.gd.cn; internet www.zhuhai-water.com.cn.

TRADE UNIONS

At the end of 2009 the 1.84m. trade unions comprised 226.3m. members.

All-China Federation of Trade Unions (ACFTU): 10 Fu Xing Men Wai Jie, Beijing 100865; tel. (10) 68592114; fax (10) 68562030; e-mail webmaster@acftu.org.cn; internet www.acftu.org.cn; f. 1925; organized on an industrial basis; 15 affiliated national industrial unions, 30 affiliated local trade union councils; 169.94m. mems (2007); Chair. WANG ZHAOGUO; First Sec. SUN CHUNLAN.

Principal affiliated unions:

All-China Federation of Railway Workers' Unions: f. 1924; Chair. GUO YIMIN; 3.1m. mems (2006).

Chinese Agricultural, Forestry and Water Conservancy Workers' Union: f. 1933; Chair. SHENG MINGFU; 10m. mems (2008).

Chinese Aviation Workers' Union: f. 2003; Chair. GAO HONGFENG; 360,000 mems.

Chinese Defence Industry, Postal and Telecommunications Workers' Union: f. 2001; Chair. DONG XUIBIN; 6.41m. mems (2007).

Chinese Educational, Scientific, Cultural, Health and Sports Workers' Union: f. 2001; Chair. WANG XIAOLONG; 25m. mems (2007).

Chinese Energy and Chemical Workers' Union.

Chinese Financial, Commercial, Light Industry, Textile and Tobacco Workers' Union: f. 2001; Chair. JIA YANMIN; 48m. mems (2007).

Chinese Financial Workers' Union: f. 1951; Chair. HE JIESHENG; 2m. mems (2007).

Chinese Machinery, Metallurgy and Building Materials Workers' Union: f. 2001; Chair. LIU HAIHUA; 35m. mems (2007).

Chinese Seamen and Construction Workers' Union: f. 2003; Chair. WU ZIHENG; 40m. mems (2008).

Transport

RAILWAYS

The total length of railways in operation in 2009 was 65,491 km, of which 30,243 km were electrified. A 1,142-km railway linking Tibet (Xizang) with other areas of China, via Qinghai Province, was completed in 2005. The magnetic levitation ('maglev') railway linking Shanghai to Pudong International airport entered into service in 2004, and work on a 200-km 'maglev' line from Shanghai to Hangzhou was expected to start in 2011, with completion scheduled for 2014. In mid-2008 a 114-km high-speed link between Beijing and Tianjin began operating. A high-speed line from Shanghai and Hangzhou was opened in October 2010. The construction of a high-speed 1,318-km line between Beijing and Shanghai was scheduled for completion by 2012.

Ministry of Railways: see under Ministries; controls most railways through regional divisions; major routes include Beijing–Guangzhou, Tianjin–Shanghai, Manzhouli–Vladivostok, Jiaozuo–Zhicheng and Lanzhou–Badou; also line to Tibet.

City Underground Railways

Beijing Mass Transit Railway Operation Corpn Ltd: 2 Beiheyan Lu, Xicheng, Beijing 100044; tel. (10) 62293820; fax (10) 62292074; e-mail service@bjsubway.com; internet www.bjsubway.com; f. 1969; total length 142 km; projected to expand to 440 km by 2012; Gen. Man. XIE ZHENGGUANG.

Chengdu Metro Co Ltd: Chengdu; internet www.cdmetro.cn; f. 2004; network comprises seven lines and 274 km of track.

Chongqing Metro: Yuzhong Qu, Chongqing; tel. (23) 68002222; e-mail cqmetro@cta.cq.cn; internet www.cqmetro.cn; f. 2005; China's first monorail system; one operating line of 19.15 km, with further devt planned.

Guangzhou Metro: 204 Huanshi Lu, Guangzhou 510010; tel. (20) 83289033; e-mail ServiceCenter@21cn.com; internet www.gzmtr.com; opened June 1997; total length 36.6 km; network expected to comprise 9 lines and 225 km of track by 2010; Gen. Man. DING JIANLONG.

Nanjing Metro: Nanjing; internet www.nj-dt.com; f. 2005; one line of 17 km; Line 2 completed in 2009.

Shanghai Shentong Metro Group Co Ltd: Level 31, Jiu Shi Bldg, 28 Zhongshan Nan Lu, Shanghai 200010; tel. (21) 58308595; fax (21) 63300065; internet www.shmetro.com; f. 1995; 228.4 km; network planned to exceed 500 km by 2010; Pres. ZHU HUSHENG; Gen. Man. GU CHENG.

Shenzhen Metro: 1016 Metro Bldg, Futian Qu, Shenzhen; tel. (755) 23992600; fax (755) 23992555; e-mail szmc@shenzhenmc.com; internet www.szmc.net; f. 2004; Chair. HUANG RUI; Gen. Man. LIN MAODE.

Tianjin Metro Group Ltd: 3 Harmony Jiayuan, Hankou Xi Lu, Heping, Tianjin 300051; tel. (22) 87811512; fax (22) 27825588; e-mail master@tjdt.cn; internet www.tjdt.cn; f. 2000; est as Tianjin Metro Corpn; name changed as above in 2008; total planned network 154 km; Gen. Man. WANG YUJI.

Wuhan Metro Group Co Ltd: Wuhan; tel. (27) 83749024; internet www.whrt.gov.cn; f. 2004; currently one 10.2-km line, with six more lines being planned; Chair. HEPING TU; Gen. Man. LIU YUHUA.

The first stage of an underground system in Xian opened in September 2011. An underground system was also planned for Qingdao.

ROADS

In 2009 China had 3,860,080 km of highways, including 65,100 km of expressways. The programme of expressway construction to link all main cities continued; the expressway network was projected to total 55,000 km by 2020. Construction work on a bridge connecting Zhuhai with Macao and Hong Kong commenced in December 2009. Spanning nearly 50 km and comprising a six-lane expressway, the project was scheduled for completion in 2016.

INLAND WATERWAYS

In 2009 there were some 123,700 km of navigable inland waterways in China. The main navigable rivers are the Changjiang (Yangtze River), the Zhujiang (Pearl River), the Heilongjiang, the Grand Canal and the Xiangjiang.

SHIPPING

China has a network of more than 2,000 ports, of which more than 130 are open to foreign vessels. With full operation scheduled for 2020, the third stage of the biggest container port in the world, sited on the Yangshan Islands off shore from Shanghai, was completed in 2010. Other major ports include Dalian, Qinhuangdao, Tianjin, Yantai, Qingdao, Rizhao, Lianyungang, Shanghai, Ningbo, Guangzhou and Zhanjiang. In December 2009 China's merchant fleet comprised 4,064 ships, totalling 30.1m. grt.

Bureau of Water Transportation: Beijing; controls rivers and coastal traffic.

China International Marine Containers (Group) Co Ltd (CIMC): 2 Gangwan Dajie, Shekou Industrial Zone, Shenzhen, Guangdong 518067; tel. (755) 26691130; fax (755) 26692707; e-mail email@cimc.com; internet www.cimc.com; f. 1980; jt venture between China Merchants Holdings, the East Asiatic Co Ltd (EAC) and China Ocean Shipping (Group) Co (COSCO); manufacture and supply of containers, trailers and airport equipment; cap. 2,017.0m., res 7,596.8m., sales 30,938.5m. (2005); Chair. FU YUNING; Pres. MAI BOLIANG.

China National Chartering Corpn (SINOCHART): see Trade and Industrial Organizations.

China Ocean Shipping (Group) Co (COSCO): 11–12/F, Ocean Plaza, 158 Fu Xing Men Nei, Xi Cheng Qu, Beijing 100031; tel. (10) 66493388; fax (10) 66492288; internet www.cosco.com.cn; reorg. 1993, re-est. 1997; head office transferred to Tianjin late 1997; br. offices: Shanghai, Guangzhou, Tianjin, Qingdao, Dalian; 200 subsidiaries (incl. China Ocean Shipping Agency—PENAVIC) and joint ventures in China and abroad, engaged in ship-repair, container-manufacturing, warehousing, insurance, etc.; merchant fleet of 800 vessels; 47 routes; Pres. WEI JIAFU.

China Shipping (Group) Co: 700 Dong Da Ming Lu, Shanghai 200080; tel. (21) 65966666; fax (21) 65966556; e-mail cscas@cnshipping.com; internet www.cnshipping.com/english; f. 1997; state-owned shipping conglomerate; incorporates five specialized shipping fleets of oil tankers, tramps, passenger ships, container vessels and special cargo ships respectively; a total of 440 vessels with an aggregate deadweight of 20.18m. metric tons; Pres. LI SHAODE.

China Shipping Container Lines Co Ltd: 5/F, Shipping Tower, 700 Dong Da Ming Lu, Shanghai 200080; tel. (21) 65966833; fax (21) 65966498; e-mail ir@cnshipping.com; internet www.cscl.com.cn; container shipping company; 135 vessels (July 2010); Chair. LI SHAODE; Gen. Man. HUANG XIAOWEN.

China Shipping Development Co Ltd: Shanghai Maritime Bldg, 16th Floor, 700 Dong Da Ming Lu, Shanghai 200080; tel. (21) 65967160; fax (21) 65966160; e-mail csd@cnshipping.com; internet www.cnshipping.com/cndev; 50.51% owned by China Shipping (Group) Co; operates oil tankers and dry bulk cargo vessels; Chair. LI SHAODE.

Fujian Shipping Co: 151 Zhong Ping Lu, Fuzhou 350009; tel. (591) 83259900; fax (591) 83259716; e-mail fusco@fusco.com.cn; internet www.fusco.com.cn; f. 1950; transport of bulk cargo, crude petroleum products, container and related services; subsidiary of Fujian Provincial Communication Transportation Group Co Ltd; Gen. Man. YANG JINCHANG.

Guangzhou Maritime Transport (Group) Co: 308 Binjiang Zhong Lu, Guangzhou 510220; tel. (20) 84102787; fax (20) 84102187; e-mail gzmaritime@gzmaritime.com; internet www.gzmaritime.com; f. 1949; Gen. Man. YAN ZHICHONG.

CIVIL AVIATION

Air travel has continued to expand very rapidly. Following the completion of six new facilities during 2009, China had a total of 166 airports. In 2004 the establishment of private airlines was approved. Plans for the construction of a further 45 airports were announced in early 2011.

Civil Aviation Administration of China (CAAC): POB 644, 155 Dongsixi Jie, Beijing 100710; tel. (10) 64014104; fax (10) 64016918; e-mail webmaster@caac.gov.cn; internet www.caac.gov.cn; f. 1949; restructured in 1988; subsidiary of Ministry of Transport; Dir LI JIAXIANG.

Air China Ltd: Beijing International Airport, POB 644, Beijing 100621; tel. (10) 61462799; fax (10) 61462805; e-mail ir@airchina.com; internet www.airchina.com.cn; 51% owned by state-owned China Nat. Aviation Holding Co (CNAC); international and domestic scheduled passenger and cargo services; Chair. KONG DONG; Pres. CAI JIANJIANG.

Chengdu Airways Ltd: Chengdu Shuangliu International Airport, Chengdu 610202, Sichuan Province; tel. (28) 66668888; fax (28) 85706199; internet www.chengduair.cc; f. 2004; privately owned; fmrly United Eagle Airlines; name changed as above in 2010; Chair. LI JINING.

China Eastern Airlines: 92 Hongqiao Rd, Hongqiao Airport, Shanghai 200335; tel. (21) 62686268; fax (21) 62686116; e-mail ir@ceair.com; internet www.ceair.com; f. 1987; domestic services; operates flights within Asia and to the USA, Europe and Australia; Chair. LIU SHAOYONG; Pres. MA XULUN

China Eastern Airlines Wuhan (CEAW): 435 Jianshe Dajie, Wuhan 430030; tel. (87) 63603888; fax (87) 83625693; e-mail wuhanair@public.wh.hb.cn; f. 1986; fmrly Wuhan Air Lines; became China's first partly privately owned airline upon refounding in 2002; 96% owned by China Eastern Airlines; domestic services; Pres. CHENG YAOKUN.

China Eastern Xi Bei Airlines: Laodong Nan Lu, Xian 710082, Shaanxi Province; tel. (29) 88792299; fax (29) 84261622; e-mail webcnwa@mail.cnwa.com; internet www.cnwa.com; f. 1992; fmrly China Northwest Airlines; renamed following acquisition of assets by China Eastern Airlines in 2005; domestic services and flights to Macao, Singapore and Japan; Pres. GAO JUNQUI.

China Eastern Yunnan Airlines: Wujaba Airport, Kunming 650200; tel. (871) 7113007; fax (871) 7151509; internet www.c3q.com.cn; f. 1992; est. as Yunnan Airlines; renamed following acquisition of assets by China Eastern Airlines in 2005; 49 domestic services; also serves Thailand, Singapore, and Laos; Pres. XUE XIAOMING.

China General Aviation Corpn: Wusu Airport, Taiyuan 030031, Shanxi Province; tel. (351) 7040600; fax (351) 7040094; f. 1989; 34 domestic routes; Pres. ZHANG CHANGJING.

China Southern Airlines: 6 Airport Lu, Guangzhou Baiyun Int. Airport; tel. (20) 86134388; fax (20) 86137318; e-mail webmaster@csair.com; internet www.csair.com; f. 1991; merged with Zhong Yuan Airlines in 2000; acquired operations and assets of China Northern Airlines and China Xinjiang Airlines in 2004; domestic services; overseas destinations include Bangkok, Fukuoka, Hanoi, Ho Chi Minh City, Kuala Lumpur, Penang, Pyongyang, Singapore, Manila, Vientiane, Jakarta and Surabaya; Chair. SI XIANMIN; Gen. Man. TAN WENGENG

Xiamen Airlines: 22 Dai Liao Lu, Xiamen 361006, Fujian Province; tel. (592) 5739888; fax (592) 5739777; e-mail info@xiamenair.com.cn; internet www.xiamenair.com.cn; f. 1992; 60% owned by China Southern Airlines, 40% owned by Xiamen Construction and Devt Corpn; domestic services; also serves Bangkok (Thailand); Pres. YANG GUANGHUA.

China United Airlines: Dong Lu, Fengtai Qu, Beijing 100076; tel. (10) 67978899; internet www.cu-air.com; f. 2005; est. in 1986 as part of the People's Liberation Army civil transport division; closed down in 2002; resumed operations in 2005; 80% owned by Shanghai Airlines; Pres. LAN DINGSHOU.

Hainan Airlines (HNA): HNA Development Bldg, 29 Haixiu Lu, Haikou 570206, Hainan Province; tel. (898) 66739801; fax (898) 66786273; e-mail webmaster@hnair.com; internet www.hnair.com; f. 1993; leading air transport enterprise of HNA Group; 300 domestic services; international services to Korea; 14.8% owned by financier George Soros; Chair. CHEN FENG; Pres. WANG YINGMING

Changan Airlines: 16/F, Jierui Bldg, 5 South Er Huan Rd, Xian 710068, Shaanxi Province; tel. (29) 8378027; fax (29) 8707911; f. 1992; subsidiary of HNA Group; local passenger and cargo services; Pres. SHE YINING.

China Xinhua Airlines: 1 Jinsong Nan Lu, Chao Yang Qu, Beijing 100021; tel. (10) 66766027; fax (10) 67740126; e-mail infocxh@homeway.com.cn; internet www.chinaxinhuaair.com; f. 1992; subsidiary of HNA Group; Chair. LIU JIAXU; Pres. YANG JINGLIN.

Shanxi Airlines: Customs Bldg, Wusu Airport, Taiyuan 030031, Shanxi Province; subsidiary of HNA Group; Chair. QIN JIANMIN, LI QING.

Okay Airways: 16 Tianzhu Lu, Tianzhu Airport Industrial Zone, Shunyi Qu, Beijing 101312; tel. (10) 59237777; fax (10) 59237590; internet www.okair.net; f. 2004; inaugural flight 2005; China's first privately owned airline; Chair. WANG SHUSHENG.

Shandong Airlines: Shandong Aviation Mansion, 5746 Er Huan Dong Lu, Lixia Qu, Jinan 250014, Shandong Province; tel. (531) 85698666; fax (531) 85698668; e-mail webmaster@shandongair.com.cn; internet www.shandongair.com.cn; f. 1994; domestic services; Pres. SUN YUDE.

Shanghai Airlines: 212 Jiangning Lu, Shanghai 200041; tel. (21) 62558888; fax (21) 62558885; e-mail service@shanghai-air.com; internet www.shanghai-air.com; f. 1985; domestic services; also serves Phnom-Penh (Cambodia); Chair. ZHOU CHI; Pres. FAN HONGXI.

Shenzhen Airlines: Lingtian Tian, Lingxiao Garden, Shenzhen Airport, Shenzhen 518128, Guangdong Province; tel. (755) 7771999; fax (755) 7777242; e-mail wm@shenzhenair.com; internet www.shenzhenair.com; f. 1993; owned by Air China (51%), Total Logistics Co (25%) and Shenzhen Huirun Investment (24%); domestic services; Chair. CAI JIANJIANG.

Sichuan Airlines: Chengdu Shuangliu International Airport, Chengdu 610202, Sichuan Province; tel. (28) 85393566; fax (28) 85393045; e-mail scal@scal.com; internet www.scal.com.cn; f. 1986; domestic services; Pres. LAN XINGGUO.

Spring Airlines: 158 Ding Xi Lu, Shanghai; tel. (21) 62520000; fax (21) 62523734; e-mail webmaster@china-sss.com; internet www.china-sss.com; privately owned; low-cost airline; inaugural flight July 2005; Chair. and Pres. WANG ZHENGHUA.

Tourism

The tourism sector has continued to develop rapidly. Attractions include dramatic scenery and places of historical interest such as the Temple of Heaven and the Forbidden City in Beijing, the Great Wall, the Ming Tombs and the terracotta warriors at Xian. The 2008 Olympic Games were held in Beijing in August of that year. In 2009 there were 14,498 tourist hotels in operation. In 2011 China received a total of nearly 135.4m. visitors, of whom 27.1m. were foreign tourists; visitors from Hong Kong, Macao and Taiwan totalled 108.3m. Revenue from international tourism was estimated to have risen by 5.8% in 2011 to total US $48,500m., while receipts from domestic tourism increased by 23.6% to reach an estimated 1,930.6m. yuan.

China International Travel Service (CITS): 1 Dongdan Bei Dajie, Dongcheng Qu, Beijing; tel. (10) 65222991; fax (10) 65226855; e-mail info@cits.com.cn; internet www.cits.net; f. 1954; makes travel arrangements for foreign tourists; 14 subsidiary overseas cos; Pres. TONG WEI.

China National Tourism Administration (CNTA): 9A Jian Guo Men Nei Dajie, Beijing 100740; tel. (10) 65201114; fax (10) 65137871; e-mail webmaster@cnta.gov.cn; internet www.cnta.gov.cn; parastatal org. charged with co-ordinating devt and regulation of the tourism industry; five subsidiary cos; Chair. SHAO QIWEI.

Chinese People's Association for Friendship with Foreign Countries: 1 Tai Ji Chang Dajie, Beijing 100740; tel. (10) 65122474; fax (10) 65128354; internet www.cpaffc.org.cn; f. 1954; Chair. LI XIAOLIN.

Defence

China is divided into seven major military administrative units. All armed services are grouped in the People's Liberation Army (PLA). As assessed at November 2011, according to Western estimates, the regular forces totalled 2,285,000, of whom 660,000 were paramilitary forces: the army numbered 1,600,000, the navy 255,000 (including a naval air force of 26,000), the air force approximately 300,000, and the strategic missile forces 100,000. Reserves numbered some 510,000, and the People's Armed Police comprised an estimated 660,000. Military service is usually by selective conscription, and is for two years in all services. In support of international peacekeeping efforts, 218 Chinese troops were stationed in the Democratic Republic of Congo in November 2011, 344 in Lebanon, 564 in Liberia and 322 in Sudan.

Defence Expenditure: Budgeted at 583,000m. yuan for 2011.

Chairman of the CCP Central Military Commission (Commander-in-Chief): HU JINTAO.

Director of the General Political Department (Chief Political Commissar): LI JINAI.

Chief of General Staff: Gen. CHEN BINGDE.

Commander, PLA Navy: Adm. WU SHENGLI.

Commander, PLA Air Force: Gen. XU QILIANG.

Education

Fees are charged at all levels. Much importance is attached to kindergartens. Primary education begins for most children at seven years of age and lasts for six years. Secondary education usually begins at 12 years of age and lasts for six years. In 2010 nearly 29.8m. children attended kindergartens, of which there were 150,420, and 99.4m. pupils were enrolled at the 290,597 primary schools. In 2009/10 enrolment at pre-primary school was equivalent to 54% of pupils in the relevant age group (males 54%; females 54%). In the same year enrolment in primary and secondary education was equivalent to 94% of the relevant age groups (males 93%; females 96%). In 2010 there were 85,063 secondary schools, at which a total of 84.3m. pupils were enrolled. In the same year 426,000 children attended one of 1,706 special schools, while a total of 22.3m. students were enrolled in one of 2,358 higher education institutions. Private education developed quickly from the 1980s when it was first permitted. By 2004 the number of private schools was estimated at 70,000. As the Government placed increasing emphasis on higher education, this sector expanded extremely rapidly in the early years of the 21st century. In the state budget for 2010 an allocation of 1,255,002m. yuan was made to education, accounting for 14.0% of total expenditure.

CHINESE SPECIAL ADMINISTRATIVE REGIONS

HONG KONG

Introductory Survey

LOCATION, CLIMATE, LANGUAGE, RELIGION, FLAG, CAPITAL

The Special Administrative Region (SAR) of Hong Kong, as the territory became on 1 July 1997, lies in eastern Asia, off the south coast of the People's Republic of China. The SAR consists of the island of Hong Kong, Stonecutters Island, the Kowloon Peninsula and the New Territories, which are partly on the mainland. The climate is sunny and dry in winter, and hot and humid in summer. The average annual rainfall is 2,214 mm (87 ins), of which about 80% falls between May and September. The official languages are Chinese and English. Cantonese is spoken by the majority of the Chinese community, while Putonghua (Mandarin) is widely understood and of increasing significance. The main religion is Buddhism. Confucianism, Islam, Hinduism and Daoism are also practised, and there is a large Christian community. The flag of the Hong Kong SAR (proportions 2 by 3), flown subordinate to the flag of the People's Republic of China, displays a bauhinia flower consisting of five white petals, each bearing a red line and a red five-pointed star, at the centre of a red field. The administrative and business centre is Central District.

CONTEMPORARY POLITICAL HISTORY

Historical Context

Hong Kong Island was ceded to the United Kingdom under the terms of the Treaty of Nanking (Nanjing) in 1842. The Kowloon Peninsula was acquired by the Convention of Peking (Beijing) in 1860. The New Territories were leased from China in 1898 for a period of 99 years. From the establishment of the People's Republic in 1949, the Chinese Government asserted that the 'unequal' treaties giving the British control over Hong Kong were no longer valid.

Japanese forces invaded Hong Kong in December 1941, forcing the British administration to surrender. In August 1945, at the end of the Second World War, the territory was recaptured by British forces. Colonial rule was restored, with a British military administration until May 1946. Upon the restoration of civilian rule, the territory was again administered in accordance with the 1917 Constitution, which vested full powers in the British-appointed Governor. In 1946 the returning Governor promised a greater measure of self-government but, after the communist revolution in China in 1949, plans for constitutional reform were abandoned. Thus, unlike most other British colonies, Hong Kong did not proceed, through stages, to democratic rule.

Between 1949 and 1964 an estimated 1m. refugees crossed from the People's Republic to Hong Kong, imposing serious strains on Hong Kong's housing and other social services. More than 460,000 Chinese immigrants arrived, many of them illegally, between 1975 and 1980. Strict measures, introduced in October 1980, reduced the continuous flow of refugees from China, but the number of legal immigrants remained at a high level.

Domestic Political Affairs

Following a visit to Hong Kong by the British Prime Minister in September 1982, discussions between the United Kingdom and China were held regarding the territory's future status. In 1984 the United Kingdom conceded that in mid-1997, upon the expiry of the lease on the New Territories, China would regain sovereignty over the whole of Hong Kong. In September 1984 British and Chinese representatives met in Beijing and initialled a legally binding agreement, the Sino-British Joint Declaration, containing detailed assurances on the future of Hong Kong. China guaranteed the continuation of the territory's capitalist economy and life-style for 50 years after 1997. The territory, as a Special Administrative Region of the People's Republic, would be designated 'Hong Kong, China', and would continue to enjoy a high degree of autonomy, except in matters of defence and foreign affairs. It was agreed that Hong Kong would retain its identity as a free port and separate customs territory, and its citizens would be guaranteed freedom of speech, of assembly, of association, of travel and of religious belief. In December 1984, after being approved by the National People's Congress (NPC—the Chinese legislature) and the British Parliament, the agreement was signed in Beijing by the British and Chinese Prime Ministers, and in May 1985 the two Governments exchanged documents ratifying the agreement. A Joint Liaison Group (JLG), comprising British and Chinese representatives, was established to monitor the provisions of the agreement, and this group held its first meeting in July 1985. A 58-member Basic Law Drafting Committee (BLDC), including 23 representatives from Hong Kong, was formed in Beijing in June, with the aim of drawing up a new Basic Law (Constitution) for Hong Kong.

The majority of the population reportedly accepted the terms of the Joint Declaration, but the sensitive issue of the future nationality of Hong Kong residents proved controversial. The 1981 British Nationality Act had already caused alarm in the territory, where the reclassification of 2.3m. citizens was perceived as a downgrading of their status. As holders of Hong Kong residents' permits, they had no citizenship status under British laws. Following the approval of the Hong Kong agreement, the British Government announced a new form of nationality, to be effective from 1997, designated 'British National (Overseas)', which would not be transferable to descendants and would confer no right of abode in the United Kingdom.

In September 1985 indirect elections were held for 24 new members of an expanded Legislative Council (Legco), to replace the former appointees and government officials. The participation rate among the very small proportion of the population eligible to vote in the elections was low. In March 1986 municipal elections were held for the urban and regional councils, which were thus, for the first time, wholly directly elected. A new Governor, Sir David Wilson (who had played a prominent part in the Sino-British negotiations on the territory's future), formally assumed office in April 1987, following the death of his predecessor, Sir Edward Youde, in December 1986. In May 1987 the Hong Kong Government published proposals regarding the development of representative government during the final decade of British rule. Among the options that it proposed was the introduction, in 1988, of direct elections to the Legislative Council, based upon universal adult suffrage. In spite of the disapproval of the Chinese Government, in February 1988 the Hong Kong Government published, with the support of the majority of the population, a policy document on the development of representative government; the principal proposal was the introduction, in 1991, of 10 (subsequently increased) directly elected members of the Legislative Council.

In April 1988 the first draft of the Basic Law for Hong Kong was published, and a Basic Law Consultative Committee (BLCC) was established in Hong Kong, initially with 176 members, to collect public comments on its provisions, over a five-month period; the draft was to be debated by the Legislative Council and by the Parliament of the United Kingdom, but no referendum was to be held in Hong Kong, and final approval of the Basic Law rested with the NPC of China. The draft offered five options for the election of a chief executive and four regarding the composition of the future Legislative Council; however, none of these proposed that the Council be elected entirely by universal suffrage. Although the legislature would be empowered to impeach the chief executive for wrongdoing, the Chinese Government would have final responsibility for his removal.

In November 1988 the UN Commission on Human Rights criticized the British attitude to the transfer of Hong Kong, with particular reference to the lack of direct elections. A second draft of the Basic Law was approved by the Chinese NPC in February 1989, which ignored all five options previously proposed for the election of a chief executive. In May there were massive demonstrations in Hong Kong in support of the anti-Government protests taking place in China. In June, following the killing of thousands of protesters by the Chinese armed forces in Tiananmen Square in Beijing, further demonstrations and a general strike took place in Hong Kong, expressing revulsion at the massacres. The British Government refused to consider renegotiating the Sino-British Joint Declaration but, in response to demands that the British nationality laws should be changed to allow Hong Kong residents the right to settle in the United Kingdom after 1997, it announced in December 1989 that the British Parliament would be asked to enact legislation enabling as many as 50,000 Hong Kong residents (chosen on a 'points system', which was expected to favour leading civil servants, business executives and professional workers), and an estimated 175,000 dependants, to be given the right of abode in the United Kingdom. The Hong Kong authorities cautiously welcomed the announcement, but China warned prospective applicants that it would not recognize their British nationality after 1997. Despite widespread protests in Hong Kong against the scheme, the relevant legislation was approved in the British Parliament in April 1990.

Among other recommendations made by the parliamentary select committee were the introduction of a Bill of Rights for Hong Kong and an increase in the number of seats subject to direct election in the Hong Kong Legislative Council, to one-half of the total in 1991, leading to full direct elections in 1995. A draft Bill of Rights, based on the UN International Covenant on Civil and Political Rights, was published by the Hong Kong Government in March 1990. The draft was criticized in principle because its provisions would have been subordinate, in the case of conflict, to the provisions of the Basic Law. Nevertheless, the Bill of Rights entered into law in June 1991.

The transition to Chinese sovereignty

In April 1990 China's NPC approved a final draft of the Basic Law for Hong Kong: 24 of the 60 seats in the Legislative Council would be subject to direct election from 1999, and 30 seats from 2003; a referendum, to be held after 2007, would consult public opinion on the future composition of the Council, although the ultimate authority to make any changes would rest with the NPC. The British Government had agreed to co-operate with these measures by offering 18 seats for direct election in 1991 and 20 seats in 1995. Under the Basic Law, the Chief Executive of the Hong Kong Special Administrative Region (SAR), as the territory was to be designated in 1997, would initially be elected for a five-year term by a special 800-member election committee; a referendum was to be held during the third term of office in order to help to determine whether the post should be subject to a general election. However, no person with the right of residence in another country would be permitted to hold an important government post. Particular concern was expressed over a clause in the Law that would 'prohibit political organizations and groups in the Hong Kong SAR from establishing contacts with foreign political organizations or groups'.

Liberal groups founded Hong Kong's first formal political party, the United Democrats of Hong Kong (UDHK), with Martin Lee as its Chairman, in April 1990. The party subsequently became the main opposition to the conservatives, and achieved considerable success in local elections in March and May 1991, and in the territory's first direct legislative elections in September. Of the 18 seats in the Legislative Council subject to election by universal suffrage, 17 were won by members of the UDHK and like-minded liberal and independent candidates. However, only 39% of registered electors reportedly voted. Despite the party's electoral success, the Governor nominated only one of the UDHK's 20 suggested candidates when selecting his direct appointees to the Legislative Council. Changes in the membership of the Executive Council were announced in October, liberal citizens again being excluded by the Governor.

In July 1992 Christopher Patten, hitherto Chairman of the Conservative Party in the United Kingdom, took office as Governor of Hong Kong, replacing Sir David Wilson upon his retirement. Plans for democratic reform in the territory, announced by the Governor in October, included the separation of the Executive Council from the Legislative Council. The former was reorganized to include prominent lawyers and academics. At the 1995 elections to the latter, the number of directly elected members was to be increased to the maximum permissible of 20; the franchise for the existing 21 functional constituencies, representing various occupations and professions, was to be widened and nine additional constituencies were to be established, in order to encompass all categories of workers. Various social and economic reforms were also announced. In the same month Patten paid his first visit to China. The proposed electoral changes were denounced by China as a contravention of the Basic Law and of the 1984 Joint Declaration. Although Patten's programme received the general support of the Legislative Council, many conservative business leaders were opposed to the proposals.

In February 1993 China announced plans to establish a 'second stove', or alternative administration for Hong Kong, if the Governor's proposed reforms were implemented. In April the impasse was broken when the United Kingdom and China agreed to resume negotiations. In July the 57-member Preliminary Working Committee (PWC), established to study issues relating to the forthcoming transfer of sovereignty and chaired by the Chinese Minister of Foreign Affairs, held its inaugural meeting in Beijing. In December 1993, no progress in the intermittent bilateral negotiations having been made, proposed electoral reforms were submitted to the Legislative Council. The Governor's decision to proceed unilaterally was denounced by China.

In February 1994 the Legislative Council approved the first stage of the reform programme, which included the lowering of the voting age from 21 to 18 years. The second stage was presented to the Legislative Council in March 1994. In April a British parliamentary report endorsed Patten's democratic reforms. In the same month the UDHK and Meeting Point, a smaller party, merged and formed the Democratic Party of Hong Kong. In April the trial in camera of a Beijing journalist (who worked for a respected Hong Kong newspaper) on imprecise charges of 'stealing state secrets' and his subsequent severe prison sentence aroused widespread concern. Hundreds of journalists took part in a protest march through the streets of Hong Kong.

In June 1994, in an unprecedented development that reflected growing unease with Patten's style of government, the Legislative Council approved a motion of censure formally rebuking the Governor for refusing to permit a debate on an amendment to the budget. Nevertheless, at the end of the month the Legislative Council endorsed further constitutional reforms, entailing an increase in the number of its directly elected members and an extension of the franchise. Despite China's strong opposition to these reforms the People's Republic and the United Kingdom concluded an agreement on the transfer of defence sites, some of which were to be retained for military purposes and upgraded prior to 1997, while others were to be released for redevelopment. At the end of August 1994, following the issuing of a report by the PWC in the previous month, the Standing Committee of the NPC in Beijing approved a decision on the abolition, in 1997, of the current political structure of Hong Kong.

In September 1994, at elections to the 18 District Boards (the first to be held on a fully democratic basis), 75 of the 346 seats were won by the Democratic Party. The pro-Beijing Democratic Alliance for the Betterment of Hong Kong (DAB) won 37 seats, the progressive Association for Democracy and People's Livelihood (ADPL) 29 seats, and the pro-Beijing Liberal Party and Liberal Democratic Foundation 18 seats and 11 seats, respectively. Independent candidates secured 167 seats. The level of voter participation was a record 33.1%. In December 1994 the director of the State Council's Hong Kong and Macao Affairs Office and Secretary-General of the PWC, Lu Ping, formally confirmed that the Legislative Council would be disbanded in 1997. Elections for the 32 seats on the Urban Council and the 27 seats on the Regional Council took place in March 1995. The Democratic Party took 23 seats, the DAB eight seats and the ADPL also eight seats. Fewer than 26% of those eligible voted in the polls. In the same month Donald Tsang Yam-kuen was nominated as Financial Secretary; his predecessor, along with other expatriate senior officials, had been asked to take early retirement to allow for the appointment of a local civil servant. Tsang took office in September.

Following a redrafting of the legislation, in June 1995 the United Kingdom and China reached agreement on the establishment of the Court of Final Appeal. Contrary to the Governor's original wishes, this new body would not now be constituted until after the transfer of sovereignty in mid-1997. The agreement was approved by the Legislative Council in July 1995. In the same month an unprecedented motion of no confidence in the Governor was defeated at a session of the Legislative Council. At elections to the Legislative Council in September, for the first time all 60 seats were determined by election. The Democratic Party won 19 seats in total, including 12 of the 20 seats open to direct election on the basis of geographical constituencies and two of the 10 chosen by an electoral committee. The Liberal Party took nine of the 60 seats, the pro-Beijing DAB six, and the ADPL four. Independent candidates won 17 seats.

The Governor aroused much controversy in September 1995, when he urged the United Kingdom to grant the right of abode to more than 3m. citizens of Hong Kong. The proposals were rebuffed by the British Home Secretary. In October the Chinese Minister of Foreign Affairs visited London, where agreement was reached on the establishment of a liaison office to improve bilateral contacts between civil servants. China's disclosure of a plan to establish a parallel administration six months prior to the transfer of sovereignty provoked outrage in Hong Kong.

In January 1996 the 150-member Preparatory Committee of the Hong Kong SAR was formally established in Beijing to succeed the PWC. The 94 Hong Kong delegates included representatives of the territory's business and academic communities. The Democratic Party was excluded from the new body, which was to appoint a 400-member Selection Committee responsible for the choice of the territory's future Chief Executive. During a visit to the territory in March, the British Prime Minister announced that more than 2m. holders of the forthcoming Hong Kong SAR passports would be granted visa-free access to (but not residency in) the United Kingdom. The Preparatory Committee in Beijing approved a resolution to appoint a provisional body to replace the Legislative Council. As the final deadline approached, thousands of Hong Kong residents rushed to submit applications for British Dependent Territories Citizenship (BDTC), which, although conferring no right of abode in the United Kingdom, would provide an alternative travel document to the new SAR passports. In April the territory's Chief Secretary, Anson Chan, travelled to Beijing for discussions with Lu Ping. A visit to Hong Kong by Lu Ping earlier in the month had been disrupted by pro-democracy demonstrators. In early July eight pro-democracy politicians from Hong Kong, including five members of the Legislative Council, were refused entry to China to deliver a petition of 60,000 signatures against the proposed establishment of a provisional legislative body for Hong Kong. In mid-August nominations opened for candidacy for the 400-member Selection Committee. In the same month a new pro-democracy movement, The Frontier, comprising teachers, students and trade unionists, was established.

In December 1996 the second ballot for the selection of Hong Kong's Chief Executive (the first having been held in November) resulted in the choice of Tung Chee-hwa, a shipping magnate and former member of the territory's Executive Council, who obtained 320 of the 400 votes. Later in the month the Selection Committee chose the 60 members of the SAR's controversial Provisional Legislative Council (PLC). More than 30 of the new appointees were members of the existing Legislative Council, belonging mainly to the DAB and to the Liberal Party. Despite much criticism of the PLC's establishment, the new body held its inaugural meeting in Shenzhen in January 1997, and elected Rita Fan as its President.

In early 1997 the Chief Executive-designate announced the composition of the Executive Council, which was to comprise three ex-officio members (as previously) and 11 non-official members (the latter subsequently being increased to 15). Anson Chan was to remain as Chief Secretary, while Donald Tsang was to continue as Financial Secretary; Elsie Leung was to become Justice Secretary, replacing the incumbent Attorney General. China's approval of Tung Chee-hwa's recommendations that senior civil servants be retained did much to enhance confidence in the territory's future. In February, however, relations with the outgoing administration deteriorated when the Preparatory Committee voted overwhelmingly in favour of proposals to repeal or amend 25 laws.

Meanwhile, Lawrence Leung had abruptly resigned as Director of Immigration in July 1996 for 'personal reasons'. In January 1997 he cast doubt on the integrity of the Hong Kong Government when he appeared before a hearing of the Legislative Council and claimed that he had in fact been dismissed, thus contradicting the official version of his departure from office. The scandal deepened with the revelation that Leung had been found to possess undisclosed business interests. Newspaper reports alleged that Leung had been involved in espionage activities on behalf of China. The Government finally admitted that Leung had indeed been dismissed, but denied the reports of espionage.

In May 1997 the PLC approved its first legislation (a bill on public holidays), despite protests from the British Government and pro-democracy groups in Hong Kong that the PLC was not entitled to endorse laws during the transition period. However, the PLC declared that the legislation would take effect only on 1 July. Following the circulation in April of a public consultation document on proposed legislation governing civil liberties and social order, a series of amendments, relating to the holding of public demonstrations and the funding of political organizations, was announced in May.

The inauguration of the SAR and subsequent events

Shortly after the transfer of Hong Kong from British to Chinese sovereignty at midnight on 30 June 1997, the inauguration of the SAR Executive Council, the PLC and members of the judiciary was held. Some 4,000 dignitaries attended the ceremonies, although the British Prime Minister and Foreign Secretary, and the US Secretary of State, did not attend the inauguration of the PLC, to register their disapproval of its undemocratic nature. Pro-democracy groups and members of the former legislature staged peaceful demonstrations in protest at the abolition of the Legislative Council. More than 4,000 Chinese troops of the People's Liberation Army entered Hong Kong shortly after the transfer ceremony, joining the small number of Chinese military personnel that had been deployed in the territory in April; a further 500 had entered on the day of 30 June.

Details of the procedure for elections to a new Legislative Council, which would replace the PLC, were announced by the SAR Government in early July 1997. The elections were scheduled to take place in May 1998 and were to be conducted under a new system of voting. Of the 60 seats in the legislature, 20 were to be directly elected by means of a revised system of proportional representation, 30 were to be elected by functional constituencies (comprising professional and special interest groups) and 10 by an 800-member electoral college. Legislative amendments governing the electoral arrangements were approved by the PLC in late September 1997. The significant reduction of the franchise, by comparison with the 1995 legislative elections, was condemned by the Democratic Party. The appointment by indirect election of 36 Hong Kong delegates to the Chinese NPC, in December 1997, also attracted criticism.

Following the transfer of sovereignty to China, concerns continued about freedom of expression in the SAR. In March 1998 a prominent publisher and a member of the Chinese People's Political Consultative Conference (CPPCC), Xu Simin, challenged the right of the public broadcaster, Radio Television Hong Kong, to criticize government policy, while Tung Chee-hwa stated that government policies should be positively presented by the media. At the same time, Tung denied that Xu's position reflected government policy. In the same month the Secretary of Justice, Elsie Leung, was criticized following the Government's decision not to prosecute another prominent publisher and CPPCC member, Sally Aw Sian, for corruption, despite a ruling against her by the Independent Commission Against Corruption. Pro-democracy groups expressed fears regarding the independence of the Justice Department. This occurred two weeks after Leung had declined to prosecute the official Chinese news agency, Xinhua, for an alleged breach of privacy laws, after it took 10 months (despite a legal 40-day limit) to issue a denial that it possessed information pertaining to Emily Lau, the leader of The Frontier. (In March 1999 a motion of no confidence in Elsie Leung, prompted by these controversial legal decisions, was defeated in the Legislative Council.) In May 1998 two pro-democracy activists were found guilty of defacing flags of China and the Hong Kong SAR at a rally in January, the first such conviction since Hong Kong's transfer to Chinese sovereignty. In March 1999 the Court of Final Appeal ruled that the law prohibiting the defacing of the SAR flag was an unconstitutional restriction of freedom of expression. In December, however, under pressure from the Chinese Government, the Court rescinded its own decision, and the conviction was confirmed. In January 1998 a demonstration coincided with the visit of the former Chinese President, Yang Shangkun, who was regarded as one of those responsible for the Tiananmen Square massacre in 1989. Similar protests were conducted during a visit by Qiao Shi, the Chairman of the Standing Committee of the Eighth Chinese NPC, in February 1998, and in June a commemoration of the 1989 massacre took place without incident. In the following year, the 10th anniversary of the massacre was marked by a peaceful demonstration, attended by 70,000 protesters. On the second anniversary of the resumption of Chinese sovereignty, on 1 July 1999, more than 2,000 pro-democracy demonstrators protested against Chinese control. Tung Chee-hwa's unpopular policies were the subject of similar demonstrations on 1 July 2000.

Fears concerning the SAR's autonomy were exacerbated by the rapid adoption by the PLC in April 1998 of the Adaptation of Laws Bill. The Bill was ostensibly simply to replace references to the British crown in existing legislation but in practice it exempted Xinhua, the office of the Chinese Ministry of Foreign Affairs and the garrison of the People's Liberation Army from all laws unless otherwise stated. Concerns about the territory's legal autonomy were also raised in late 1998 by the conviction and execution in the People's Republic of five criminals from Hong Kong.

At the elections to the first Legislative Council of the SAR on 24 May 1998, participation (53.3% of registered voters) was the highest since the introduction of direct elections in Hong Kong. The Democratic Party and other pro-democracy parties suffered a reduction in their overall political strength in the legislature, despite winning 14 of the 20 directly elective seats. A total of 19 seats were secured by pro-democracy candidates, including 13 by the Democratic Party (nine directly elected), led by Martin Lee, which became the largest party in the Legislative Council. Lee advocated direct elections by universal suffrage for all 60 seats in the next poll, to be held in 2000. Pro-Beijing supporters dominated the functional constituencies and the election committee ballot. The pro-business Liberal Party, led by Allen Lee, failed to win a single seat in the direct elections but obtained nine in the other constituencies. The DAB also won nine seats, five of which were directly elective.

The powers of the new legislature were curbed by the Basic Law. Legislative Councillors were not permitted to introduce bills related to political expenditure, the political structure or the operation of the government. The passage of private members' bills or motions also required a majority of votes of both groups of councillors—those elected directly and those returned through functional constituencies and the election committee. At its first session in July 1998 the Legislative Council elected Rita Fan as its President. The division between the Chief Executive, who rarely consulted the legislature, and the Legislative Council became more apparent after Tung Chee-hwa's second annual policy address in October. He announced the abolition of urban and regional councils, a decision opposed by many members of the legislature.

In March 1999 Anson Chan agreed to continue serving as Chief Secretary for Administration for two years beyond her normal retirement age, until 2002, when Tung Chee-hwa's term of office was to end. In April 1999 the administration decided to abolish the municipal and regional councils, while existing district boards were to be replaced by district councils. Although the public had been dissatisfied with the performance of the municipal councils, there was resentment at the restructuring of local democracy, which was perceived as a retrograde development. The first district elections in the Hong Kong SAR took place in late November. The Democratic Party won the largest number of elected seats (86), but the pro-Beijing DAB substantially increased its representation, from 37 seats to 83.

Popular support for the SAR Government declined substantially throughout 2000, and public unrest increased. In February Tung Chee-hwa effected a reorganization of senior officials following the retirement of three officials from the civil service. In May the controversial Elsie Leung was reappointed Secretary of Justice for an additional two years. In June Tung Chee-hwa's administration was embarrassed by the resignation of Rosanna Wong as Secretary for Housing. Three days later the Legislative Council approved a vote of no confidence in Wong and one of her senior officials, holding them responsible for a series of scandals relating to sub-standard construction works. However, Wong remained a member of the Executive Council. This affair appeared to justify the resignation in April of the prominent opposition politician, Christine Loh, from the

Legislative Council. Loh had cited her frustration with the Government's reluctance to share power with the legislature.

The second elections to the Legislative Council took place on 10 September 2000. The Democratic party won the highest number of seats with 12, including nine of the now 24 directly elective seats, while the DAB obtained 11 seats. Thirty seats were elected by functional constituencies and six (reduced from 10) by an 800-member electoral college. The level of voter participation was 43.6%. At the first session of the new Legislative Council, Rita Fan was re-elected President. The Government suffered a reverse in January 2001, when Anson Chan unexpectedly announced that she was to resign, for 'personal reasons'. The widely respected Chan was succeeded as Chief Secretary for Administration in April by Donald Tsang; the latter was replaced as Financial Secretary by Antony Leung, a former banker and member of the Executive Council, who was known to be a close associate of Tung Chee-hwa.

In March 2001 the Hong Kong Government presented the new Chief Executive Election Bill, proposing the recognition of the powers of the central Government in Beijing to remove the Chief Executive and providing details of the procedure for the next election for that post, scheduled for 24 March 2002 (but see below). The new incumbent was to serve a five-year term commencing on 30 June 2002. The Bill was approved by the Legislative Council by 36 votes to 18 in July 2001 after minor amendments.

In early 2001 the Chinese Government warned that it would not allow Hong Kong to become a centre for the activities of Falun Gong, a religious sect banned on the mainland since mid-1999, and in May 2001 the Hong Kong Government increased its efforts to prevent the movement's followers from congregating in the territory in advance of a business forum. The conference was to be attended by President Jiang Zemin, former US President Bill Clinton, Thai Prime Minister Thaksin Shinawatra and hundreds of business leaders. Scores of Falun Gong followers were prevented from entering Hong Kong, although a small demonstration was permitted some 300 m from the forum venue. More than 100 Hong Kong academics urged the People's Republic to release Chinese scholars detained on the mainland in previous months (some of whom were citizens or residents of the USA, or residents of Hong Kong), including Li Shaomin and Gao Zhan, who had both been convicted for espionage. The two were freed in late July, and Li was allowed to resume his academic duties.

In November 2001 opposition groups and trade unions, led by Emily Lau, announced the formation of a coalition aimed at preventing the re-election of Tung Chee-hwa as Chief Executive. In December Lau criticized the procedures for the election of the Chief Executive as undemocratic. Despite his growing unpopularity, Tung announced his intention to stand for a second five-year term as Chief Executive, and was quickly endorsed by President Jiang Zemin. At the end of February 2002 Tung was nominated for re-election by 714 members of the 800-member Election Committee, thereby securing a second term in office without challenge. He was formally sworn in for a second term on 1 July.

In August 2002 16 Falun Gong members were convicted of obstruction, following demonstrations outside the Beijing Liaison Office—the first time that legal action had been taken against the group in the SAR. In April, and again in June, Harry Wu Hongda, a prominent US-based human rights activist, was prevented from entering Hong Kong. His deportation prompted concerns that Hong Kong's freedoms were increasingly under threat.

Plans for a major reorganization of government structures were announced in April 2002. The Executive Council was to be expanded into a cabinet-style body consisting of 14 ministers, all appointed by the Chief Executive, and which would administer the 184,000-member civil service. Critics of the proposals warned that the new system would strengthen Tung's (and therefore China's) control over the territory and compromise the independence of the professional civil service. The Legislative Council none the less adopted the changes, and a new administration was appointed in late June. The incoming Executive Council incorporated five appointees from the private sector, including Henry Tang Ying-yen, the new Secretary for Commerce, Industry and Technology, and Patrick Ho, the Secretary for Home Affairs. The portfolios of several leading officials, including Donald Tsang, the Chief Secretary for Administration, and Antony Leung, the Financial Secretary, remained unchanged.

Hong Kong observed the fifth anniversary of its reversion to the People's Republic on 1 July 2002 amid exhortations from President Jiang Zemin to Hong Kong's citizens to identify more closely with the mainland. During his visit to the SAR, Jiang also issued a rare note of criticism of the territory's Government, urging it to improve its performance. Tung Chee-hwa had described the priority of economic recovery as his greatest challenge during his second term.

In late September 2002 the Government revealed proposals for new anti-subversion laws, which it was required to introduce under Article 23 of the Basic Law, but which had thus far remained unimplemented. Chinese Vice-Premier Qian Qichen had, in June, urged the SAR Government to enact the legislation. Critics warned that the new laws would undermine civil liberties and freedom of speech. Suspicions were increased by the fact that no draft of the laws was made available to the public. The proposals sought to criminalize treason, secession, sedition and subversion, and would also give police the powers to conduct emergency 'search and entry' acts without a warrant. 'Secession' referred to attempts to break away from China, while 'subversion' was defined as threatening or using force to intimidate or overthrow the Government. The Government would also be able to ban any groups affiliated to a mainland organization that had been proscribed in the mainland by the central authorities on national security grounds. Furthermore, the legislation could also ban any 'seditious publications' that incited treason, secession or subversion, or disclosed state secrets. A maximum penalty of life imprisonment would be imposed on violators of these laws.

In December 2002 Martin Lee retired from the leadership of the Democratic Party, after completing four two-year terms (the maximum allowed), and was succeeded by a former party vice-chairman, Yeung Sum. Lee remained a member of the Legislative Council. The Hong Kong Bar Association condemned the anti-subversion laws, describing them as unacceptable and harmful to the territory's freedoms. In the same month between 20,000 and 60,000 people from a broad section of society demonstrated against the planned anti-subversion laws, and subsequent demonstrations by those in favour of the laws attracted 10,000 people. In early 2003 the Government indicated that, following the end of a three-month public consultation period, some aspects of the laws would be modified, namely provisions dealing with the possession of seditious publications, and a ban on access to state secrets.

The outbreak of Severe Acute Respiratory Syndrome (SARS, a hitherto unknown pneumonia-like illness) in Hong Kong in early 2003, which killed almost 300 people in the territory before the disease was brought under control in June, led to demands for the resignation of the Chief Executive, who was accused of mishandling the crisis. In June the Hong Kong and Beijing Governments concluded a Closer Economic Partnership Agreement (CEPA), to strengthen co-operation in trade and investment. On the sixth anniversary of Hong Kong's reversion to Chinese sovereignty, 500,000 people took part in a demonstration against the proposed anti-subversion legislation, which was due to be introduced in early July. The Chairman of the Liberal Party, James Tien, resigned from his position in the Government, stating that his party would not support the bill in the Legislative Council vote. Tung Chee-hwa subsequently postponed the introduction of the legislation. In late July two government ministers, the Secretary for Security, Regina Ip, and the Financial Secretary, Antony Leung, resigned from their positions. In early September the controversial anti-subversion bill was withdrawn by Tung Chee-hwa owing to popular opposition; this represented an indirect challenge to the authority of the Chinese Government in Hong Kong. In November, during a visit to Hong Kong, Chinese Vice-Premier Zeng Peiyan expressed China's continuing support for Tung Chee-hwa. At local government elections held in Hong Kong at the end of November the pro-Beijing DAB suffered heavy losses, prompting the resignation of the alliance's chairman, Tsang Yok-sing.

In January 2004 there were further popular protests demanding the direct election of Hong Kong's Chief Executive and of all members of the Legislative Council. In February a group of Hong Kong officials, led by Chief Secretary for Administration Donald Tsang, visited Beijing for discussions with the Chinese Government on the future political development of Hong Kong. In April the Standing Committee of the NPC in Beijing ruled that the SAR's next Chief Executive would not be chosen by direct election in 2007. The introduction of direct elections for all members of the Legislative Council in 2008 was similarly ruled out. The NPC ruling prompted protests by democracy campaigners in Hong Kong, who claimed that the decision contravened Hong Kong's Basic Law. At the end of April 2004 eight Chinese ships entered Hong Kong harbour, representing the strongest display of force by the Chinese navy since 1997.

In May 2004 there were renewed concerns over the freedom of the media after two well-known radio broadcasters, Albert Cheng and Raymond Wong, left Hong Kong, citing attempts to limit their freedom of speech and threats of violence by pro-Beijing groups. A third broadcaster, Allen Lee, who had replaced Cheng as host of a popular radio talk show, subsequently resigned as well, claiming to have been subjected to similar intimidation. Lee also resigned from his position as a Hong Kong delegate to China's NPC. In June Chief Executive Tung held discussions with pro-democracy leaders and reiterated the promise that universal suffrage would eventually be realized in Hong Kong. At the beginning of July, as many as 500,000 people, according to one estimate, took part in a demonstration demanding universal suffrage. In the same month the Secretary for Health, Welfare and Food, Yeoh Eng-kiong, resigned following the publication of a report on the 2003 SARS epidemic.

Elections to the Legislative Council were held on 12 September 2004, when 30 of the total of 60 members were directly elected. Support for the pro-democracy faction was less evident than had been expected. Of the directly elective seats, 18 were won by democratic parties and 12 by pro-Beijing parties. In the Legislative Council as a whole, pro-Beijing parties held 34 of 60 seats after the election, thus retaining their majority. Voter participation in the election was comparatively high, at 55.6%.

Recent developments: the Tsang administration

On 10 March 2005 Tung Chee-hwa resigned from the post of Chief Executive, two years before his term of office was due to end, citing ill health. However, there was speculation that the Chief Executive had been removed from his post by the central Government in Beijing owing to his unpopularity in the SAR and his perceived poor handling of the pro-democracy movement. Chief Secretary for Administration Donald Tsang occupied the role of acting Chief Executive until 25 May, whereupon he resigned in order to present his candidacy for the election of a new Chief Executive, due to be held in July. Financial Secretary Henry Tang replaced Tsang as acting Chief Executive. Meanwhile, in a controversial ruling in April, the NPC had decreed that Tung's successor would serve out only the remaining two years of his predecessor's second term, rather than being appointed to the position for a full five-year term. The two other contenders for the post, Lee Wing-tat, Chairman of the Democratic Party, and legislator Chim Pui-chung failed to secure the required 100 nominations from among the 800 members of the Election Committee, and their candidacies were thus rejected. Donald Tsang, who was endorsed by 674 of the 800 Committee members, was therefore elected unopposed to the post of Chief Executive on 16 June. Tsang's experience of public office under both the British and Chinese administrations, and his reputation for decisiveness and financial acumen, were thought to make him a popular choice among Hong Kong residents.

In September 2005 all the members of Hong Kong's Legislative Council, notably including several pro-democracy legislators whose political stance had prompted the central Government to impose a ban preventing them from travelling in mainland China, were invited on a tour of the Zhujiang (Pearl River) Delta region, in what was widely regarded as a conciliatory gesture towards the SAR's pro-democratic movement. In October Elsie Leung, Secretary for Justice since 1997, resigned. Chief Executive Tsang nominated Wong Yan-lung, a barrister with reported links to the pro-democratic Article 45 Concern Group, as her replacement, and the central Government approved the nomination. In the same month various proposals for electoral reform were published, which included the doubling of the membership of the Election Committee from 800 to 1,600 members and increasing the size of the Legislative Council from 60 to 70 members. Chief Executive Tsang endorsed the proposals, which were criticized by the pro-democracy movement for failing to set out a definite timetable for the adoption of universal suffrage. In December 2005 pro-democracy legislators were invited to mainland China to meet with senior representatives of the central Government. Two days later a large pro-democracy march (estimates of attendance varied from 63,000 to more than 250,000) took place in Hong Kong, demanding universal suffrage. Later in the month the Legislative Council voted to reject the electoral reform proposals.

Increasing dissatisfaction with the reform process led, in March 2006, to the establishment of a new political party. Founded by members of the Article 45 Concern Group, intellectuals and democracy activists, the new Civic Party became the fourth largest party in the Legislative Council. According to the leader of the new grouping, Audrey Eu, the Civic Party advocated the early introduction of full democracy to Hong Kong, although the party's manifesto contained no time frame for this process. In May, however, democracy activists were thwarted once again when the Legislative Council endorsed by 31 votes to 22 a bill to alter the term of office of the Chief Executive. Under the new legislation, the term of any Chief Executive who took office prior to the expiry of the mandate of his or her predecessor would end upon the expiry of the predecessor's term. The term of office of Donald Tsang, therefore, would end in 2007 (completing that begun by Tung in 2002), after which he would be eligible to stand for one further term only. Pro-reform activists continued to demand a change in the law to allow the Chief Executive to belong to a political party.

The continued wish for full democracy was clearly demonstrated on 1 July 2006, when thousands took to the streets of Hong Kong for the fourth annual pro-democracy march. Particularly notable was the participation of former Chief Secretary Anson Chan, who, while stressing that she did not intend to challenge the Government, demanded the introduction of universal suffrage. None the less, there were many in the SAR who opposed the activists' demands; a pro-China rally, conducted earlier on the same day, attracted a similar amount of demonstrators.

In August 2006 the Legislative Council approved a controversial surveillance law granting new powers to the authorities. The Interception of Communications and Surveillance Bill provided for measures such as the monitoring of e-mails and telephone lines, including private communications in both homes and offices. Under the new legislation, surveillance operations would require approval by judges appointed by the Hong Kong leadership, thus raising concerns about political bias. Pro-democracy legislators (who had tabled proposals for about 200 amendments to the bill, all of which were defeated), believed that the legislation would allow police officers to spy on anyone opposing the Government, in particular politicians, journalists and lawyers. The bill was approved by 32 votes to none, after pro-democracy legislators abandoned the proceedings.

Elections to determine the membership of the committee that would choose the SAR's next Chief Executive were held on 10 December 2006. Once again the ballot was restricted to the business and community sectors, with only about 5% of Hong Kong's registered electorate being eligible to vote and the level of participation being declared at 27.4%. Nevertheless, the results improved the prospects of the pro-reform camp, which unexpectedly secured 114 of the 427 contested seats on the 800-member Election Committee; the remaining 373 seats were uncontested. Having surpassed the threshold of 100 seats required to present an opposition candidate for the post of Chief Executive, the democrats were thus able to nominate Alan Leong of the Civic Party as their candidate for the forthcoming election.

Alan Leong duly received 132 formal nominations in February 2007, while Donald Tsang received 641. The unprecedented challenge mounted by Leong and the reformists, combined with the novelty of two televised debates between the candidates, contributed to an atmosphere of change, albeit marginal. At the same time, members of the pro-democracy movement criticized Leong for participating in an essentially undemocratic process, thereby lending it legitimacy. On 25 March Tsang was re-elected as Chief Executive, by an increased margin of 649–123. Leong protested against the outcome, alleging that the system had been manipulated. Meanwhile, Tsang had expressed hopes of establishing a timetable for full democracy in the SAR by 2012, but he acknowledged that he would need the support of China in order to secure this objective.

In April 2007 Tsang was formally appointed to the position of Chief Executive by Chinese Premier Wen Jiabao, and in June the composition of the Executive Council was announced. The new Council, which was sworn in during the following month, retained former Financial Secretary Henry Tang, who was promoted to Chief Secretary for Administration. The erstwhile Director of the Chief Executive's Office, John Tsang Chun-wah, was appointed to replace Tang, while Wong Yan-lung remained Secretary for Justice. New appointees included Tsang Tak-sing as Secretary for Home Affairs, and two women members, Secretary for Development Carrie Lam and Secretary for Transport and Housing Eva Cheng.

In July 2007 the Chief Executive again promised to work towards democratic reform. Speaking during the 10th anniversary of Hong Kong's transfer to Chinese sovereignty, Tsang also stressed the importance of Chinese rule. The occasion, which was attended by Chinese President Hu Jintao, was marked by festivities and, subsequently, by pro-reform demonstrations. In mid-July the Government presented a Green Paper on Constitutional Development, which was to be subject to a three-month public consultation period. Options proposed in the document included the implementation of universal suffrage for elections to the post of Chief Executive, by 2012 at the earliest. Following the completion of the consultation, it was revealed that the majority of those polled supported the introduction of direct elections to the Legislative Council as well as for the post of Chief Executive, upon the expiry of the current Government's term in 2012. Tsang's recommendations to the central Chinese Government in December 2007 were criticized for weakening these proposals to a certain extent, suggesting the holding of elections for the Chief Executive as a preliminary phase in 2012 or, perhaps preferably, 2017. The decision of the Chinese Government to consider Tsang's proposal, albeit with any implementation to be deferred until 2017, followed by the possibility of direct elections for the Legislative Council in 2020, was hailed as a positive development by Tsang, but the slow pace of reform disappointed many.

At district council elections held in November 2007 the Democratic Party and its pro-democracy allies lost more than one-quarter of the seats they had previously held. At a by-election to the Legislative Council in December, however, Anson Chan, the former Chief Secretary, was elected to the seat left vacant by the death in August of Ma Lik, the Chairman of the DAB: the result was seen as a victory for the pro-democracy movement. Ma's successor as Chairman of the DAB was Tam Yiu-chung. After only a year in office, in June 2008 the Secretary for Commerce and Economic Development, Frederick Ma, was compelled to resign for health reasons and was replaced by Rita Lau. In July the long-awaited approval by the Legislative Council of the Race Discrimination Bill, outlawing discrimination, harassment and vilification on the grounds of race, was widely welcomed. However, critics claimed that the protection thus afforded to Hong Kong's various minority groups, as well as to immigrants from mainland China, was inadequate. The Bill provided for numerous exemptions from prosecution on the grounds of discrimination for those serving in government agencies, notably in Hong Kong's immigration service and the police force.

Polling for the Legislative Council election was held on 7 September 2008. A total of 200 candidates contested the 60 seats of the Legislative Council, with 142 candidates from 53 lists standing for 30 seats in the five geographical constituencies; 14 candidates in the functional constituencies were returned to the Legislative Council unopposed. Approximately 45% of the electorate participated in the election. Pro-democracy candidates won a total of 23 seats, three fewer than previously held and significantly fewer than the number taken by pro-Beijing candidates. The DAB remained the largest single party in the legislature, securing 13 seats. However, the Liberal Party's representation was reduced, its seven seats all being won in functional constituencies only. (Moreover, its representation in the chamber was immediately decreased to six by one legislator's resignation from the party; and further reduced by three departures in October.) James Tien lost his seat in the chamber and announced his resignation as Chairman of the Liberal Party, later being replaced by Miriam Lau. Selina Chow, Vice-Chairwoman of the Liberal Party and a non-official member of the Executive Council, similarly failed to secure re-election to the Legislative Council. In October Jasper Tsang, a founder member of the DAB, was elected President of the Legislative Council, defeating Fred Li of the Democratic Party. The Frontier merged with the Democratic Party in November 2008, and in the following month Albert Ho Chun-yan, Chairman of the Democratic Party, was re-elected to head the grouping. Emily Lau, hitherto leader of The Frontier, was appointed as a Vice-Chair of the expanded Democratic Party. None of the five new members appointed to the Executive Council by Donald Tsang in January 2009 was representative of pro-democracy groups.

In early June 2009, on the 20th anniversary of the Tiananmen Square massacre in Beijing, a record number of demonstrators, estimated to total as many as 150,000, attended a vigil to commemorate the events of 1989. In late June the annual pro-democracy demonstration, held to coincide with the 12th anniversary of Hong Kong's reversion to Chinese sovereignty, was reported to have attracted as many as 76,000 people. In September three Hong Kong journalists were allegedly assaulted by the Chinese security forces and detained in western China. The journalists had been attempting to document a disturbance in the region of Xinjiang. A further five journalists were briefly detained in Xinjiang. A march in Hong Kong in support of press freedom was attended by 700 demonstrators, who included DAB members of the Legislative Council. A petition to protest against the treatment of the Hong Kong reporters, signed by 1,300 journalists and academics, was submitted to the NPC in Beijing. In December a demonstration was held to protest against the sentencing in Beijing of Liu Xiaobo, a leading advocate of democratic reform on the mainland, to 11 years' imprisonment after being found guilty of subversion. (Liu was awarded the Nobel Peace Prize in December 2010). On 1 January 2010 organizers claimed that 30,000 people had joined a march to central government offices to demand genuine universal suffrage. Further concerns with regard to human rights in Hong Kong were raised in January when another mainland dissident, Zhou Yongjun, was sentenced to nine years' imprisonment upon his conviction in Sichuan Province on charges of fraud. Alleged to have used a false Malaysian passport to enter Hong Kong from Macao in September 2008, Zhou was charged in connection with the attempted fraudulent use of a bank account. Human rights activists argued that Zhou's case should have been processed in Hong Kong and that his transfer to the mainland authorities had violated the policy of 'one country, two systems'. The case was denounced as politically motivated by Amnesty International, which noted that Hong Kong did not have an extradition agreement with mainland China. Zhou was expected to appeal against his sentence.

In September 2009 Donald Tsang stated that the election for the Chief Executive in 2017 would be held on the basis of universal suffrage, but pro-democracy groups remained sceptical. In November various proposals for political reform were presented. The Government's proposed changes, which were to be subject to a three-month public consultation period, included an increase in the number of members of the Election Committee from 800 to 1,200, to incorporate directly elected district councillors, prior to the next election for Hong Kong's Chief Executive in 2012; as before, the approval of one-eighth of the Committee's membership would be required for any nomination for the post. An expansion of the Legislative Council from 60 to 70 members was also envisaged, with one-half being directly elected in the geographical constituencies, while the remainder would continue to be chosen by the various interest groups voting in the functional constituencies. The proposals were criticized as inadequate by pro-democracy groups, which continued to press for full universal suffrage.

In a challenge to the mainland Government, in January 2010 five pro-democracy members of the Legislative Council submitted their resignation, stating that the by-elections brought about by their departure would serve as a de facto referendum on the issue of universal suffrage in Hong Kong. About 4,000 people attended a rally in support of the five legislators: two from the Civic Party, including Alan Leong, and three from the League of Social Democrats, including Raymond Wong, the group's Chairman. The by-elections took place in May, when all five candidates won back their seats; however, pro-Beijing candidates had refused to contest the elections, criticizing them as a waste of public funds, and the Democratic Party had also refused to take part; participation by the electorate was low (at about 17% of eligible voters). The central Government denounced the 'referendum' as unconstitutional. The Democratic Party, with 10 other pro-democracy organizations (but not the Civic Party or the League of Social Democrats), had, earlier in the year, formed the Alliance for Universal Suffrage, issuing a detailed 'road map' for progress towards universal suffrage.

In April 2010, meanwhile, the Hong Kong Government formally announced its proposals for electoral reform, following the period of public consultation that had begun in November 2009. The proposals were debated by the Legislative Council in June 2010. Tsang declared that, although universal suffrage was still the ultimate objective, the proposals represented significant progress towards democracy, and that, in his view, to reject them would halt any such progress. Following discussions with Tsang and with a representative of the mainland Chinese Government, the Democratic Party agreed to support the proposals, on condition that candidates for five of the 10 new seats in the Legislative Council, rather than being elected by the existing functional constituencies as originally proposed, should be nominated by members of district councils and elected by all voters who did not have a ballot in the functional constituencies (i.e. more than 90% of the electorate). This concession was accepted by Tsang and approved by the central Government. The proposals were duly adopted by the Legislative Council, with the support of eight members of the Democratic Party; a ninth member resigned from the party in protest. The League of Social Democrats and the Civic Party accused the Democratic Party of having betrayed the principles of the pro-democracy movement by voting for a system that still included functional constituencies and fell far short of universal suffrage. There were vociferous confrontations between members of the various pro-democracy parties during the annual demonstrations on the anniversary of the reversion to Chinese rule on 1 July. Martin Lee, the Democratic Party's former Chairman, also condemned the course that the party had taken, but Albert Ho, the party's incumbent leader, declared that dialogue with the mainland Government was an acceptable way to avoid deadlock in the pursuit of democracy. In August the Standing Committee of the Chinese NPC reviewed the reforms and declared them to be compatible with Hong Kong's Basic Law.

In December 2010 about 30 members of the Democratic Party, including several district councillors, resigned from the party in protest at its support for the electoral reforms. Many reportedly joined the Neo Democrats, a group established in October 2011, which declared itself not to be a political party, although it put forward several candidates for the district council elections in November (see below). The League of Social Democrats was also split by internal disagreements: in January the Chairman, Raymond Wong, resigned, and was replaced by Andrew To. Another new grouping, People Power, was established by former members of the League, including Wong, later in 2011.

In January 2011, meanwhile, the Legislative Council approved the establishment of a statutory minimum wage, amounting to HK $28 per hour, with effect from 1 May of that year; employers had argued against the measure, while trade unions had declared the amount insufficient. The minimum wage applied only to permanent residents and not to foreign workers. In April the Secretary for Commerce and Economic Development, Rita Lau, resigned for reasons of ill-health, and was replaced by Gregory So, hitherto Under-secretary in the same department. In June, at the annual commemoration of the Tiananmen Square protests, demonstrators in Hong Kong demanded the release of the artist Ai Wei Wei and other mainland activists who had recently been detained during a period of stricter security enforcement. On 1 July, during Hong Kong's annual pro-democracy rally, there were protests at a government proposal to abolish by-elections and fill any vacant seat in accordance with the previous election result: the proposal was intended to avoid the occurrence of 'referendum' by-elections such as had taken place in May 2010. The demonstrators also protested at the high cost of living, particularly with regard to property prices and recent increases in the cost of food. The Hong Kong Government announced later in July 2011 that the proposed electoral revision would be postponed.

In August 2011 the Chinese Vice-Premier, Li Keqiang, visited Hong Kong. At a forum on China's 12th Five-Year Plan (2011–15), Li undertook to liberalize the trade in services between Hong Kong and the mainland; to improve Hong Kong's status as an international centre for finance and trade; and to develop Hong Kong as an offshore centre for the Chinese currency, the renminbi. More than 200 people were arrested in the course of a protest rally that took place during Li's visit: participants claimed that the police had used excessive force. In September the Chief Secretary, Henry Tang, resigned in order to consider standing for election as Chief Executive, since Donald Tsang's term of office was to expire in the following year; Tang was replaced as Chief Secretary by Stephen Lam, hitherto Secretary for Constitutional and Mainland Affairs. Lam's previous post was assumed by Raymond Tam, until then the director of the Chief Executive's office. In October the convenor of the Executive Council, Leung Chun-ying, also resigned in order to take part in the election to the post of Chief Executive, due to take place in March 2012.

In October 2011, in his final annual policy address, Tsang, the outgoing Chief Executive, responded to public concern over property prices that were widely perceived as unaffordable, by announcing that the Government would resume a scheme (suspended in 2002) to provide subsidized housing for sale to low- and middle-income families; he also announced the provision of extra units of public rental housing, over several years. Measures were also to be taken to reduce the price of food, another popular grievance, by widening the sources of supply. Tsang identified the ageing of the population as an impending challenge, with one-quarter of Hong Kong's inhabitants expected to be over 65 years of age by 2030, and announced improvements in support and concessions for the elderly. At elections to district councils in November 2011, pro-Beijing candidates were the most successful: the DAB, in alliance with the Hong Kong Federation of Trade Unions, secured 148 of the 412 elective seats. The Democratic Party won 47, out of a total of some 90 seats estimated to have been won by pro-democracy candidates (many candidates had no formal affiliation). The chairman of the League of Social Democrats, Andrew To, resigned after his party failed to win any seats.

The election to the post of Chief Executive took place on 25 March 2012. Leung was elected as Chief Executive, securing 689 votes from the expanded Election Committee of 1,200 members, defeating Tang who gained 285 votes and the pro-democracy candidate Albert Ho, the leader of the Democratic Party, who won only 76 votes. The contest between the two candidates sanctioned by Beijing, Leung and Tang, was unprecedentedly keenly contested, owing to the coverage of the contest in the media. Tang was initially considered the Chinese Government's favoured candidate, but following revelations about his private life, notably a luxurious basement built without planning permission and an extramarital affair, Beijing's support shifted to Leung. The conduct of the election increased pressure by pro-democracy supporters for the direct election of the Chief Executive by universal suffrage, which the Chinese Government had indicated could take place in 2017.

In March 2012 Tsang, whose term as Chief Executive was to end in June, was criticized for accepting inappropriate favours from business executives. He denied any wrongdoing and pledged to co-operate with an investigation by the Independent Commission Against Corruption. None the less, the allegations heightened growing popular anxiety concerning a lack of transparency in business leaders' influence over government policy. In April Tsang survived a motion of no confidence brought against him in the Legislative Council, the first such motion against a leader since the reversion to Chinese rule in 1997. The geographical constituencies voted by 14 to seven in favour of the motion, with two abstentions, while the functional constituencies voted to reject it by 11 to four, with three abstentions.

Issues of Immigration and Asylum

Following the reversion to Chinese sovereignty, various issues relating to immigration from the mainland intermittently came to the fore. Legislation approved by the PLC in July 1997 had included the introduction of measures to restrict the immigration into the territory of mainland-born children of Hong Kong residents. However, in January 1998 a judge ruled that this new legislation contravened the Basic Law, and the ruling was upheld by the Court of Final Appeal in January 1999. Fearing that the ruling on the right of abode by the Court of Final Appeal would result in an influx of more than 1.6m. mainland Chinese, the SAR administration asked the Court in February to clarify its judgment, which apparently asserted the Court's right to overrule decisions relating to the Basic Law made by the NPC in Beijing. The Court of Final Appeal declared that it recognized the authority of the Standing Committee of the Chinese NPC. In May the Legislative Council voted to request the Standing Committee of the NPC to interpret the relevant articles of the Basic Law. In June the NPC published its interpretation, which was not retroactive, stating that the Court of Final Appeal had failed to adhere to the Basic Law in not requesting an interpretation before delivering its judgment. The NPC stipulated that mainlanders were to be granted the right of abode in Hong Kong only if at least one parent had been permanently resident in the territory at the time of their birth and that mainland children of Hong Kong parents who wished to settle in the territory had to apply for mainland approval before entering the SAR.

In August 2000 disaffected mainland Chinese immigrants seeking the right of abode in Hong Kong firebombed the Immigration Department building killing two people. In July 2001 Hong Kong's Court of Final Appeal ruled that a three-year-old boy born in Hong Kong while his mother was visiting the territory had the right to reside there. In June 2001 the Government planned to deport 5,000 migrants to the mainland, pending the outcome of a court case. The Court of Final Appeal in January 2002 announced that all except about 200 of these 5,000 people would be returned to the mainland by the end of March. Although some 400 people returned to the mainland before the 31 March deadline, approximately 4,300 refused to do so. In April, therefore, the authorities began forcibly deporting the remaining abode-seekers. The actions attracted particular criticism because they resulted in children being separated from their parents. Scores began legal proceedings against the deportations, and Bishop Joseph Zen Ze-kiun, the outspoken head of the Roman Catholic Church in Hong Kong, personally intervened on behalf of several mentally ill or sick abode-seekers who were facing expulsion. It was reported in January 2003 that some 2,302 child abode-seekers had been deported to the mainland during 2002.

In February 2003 plans were announced to ease immigration restrictions for skilled workers and business people from the Chinese mainland wishing to enter Hong Kong. The Admission Scheme for Mainland Professionals was introduced in July. Under new regulations introduced in the same month, persons holding a dependant visa were no longer entitled to take up employment in Hong Kong. Meanwhile, 18,621 mainland Chinese were refused entry to Hong Kong in 2003. The total number of illegal immigrants intercepted by the authorities notably declined, from 25,651 in 1995/96 to 3,926 in 2003/04, a reduction of nearly 85%. Reports suggested that as many as 12,000 mainland women gave birth in the SAR in 2006, in order to gain Hong Kong residency rights for their children and to circumvent the mainland's 'one child' policy. In February 2007, therefore, new rules took effect to limit the number of pregnant women from the mainland entering Hong Kong in order to give birth there. Henceforth the immigration authorities were to refuse entry to any mainland woman who appeared to be at least seven months pregnant and who was unable to provide evidence of prior hospital arrangements and advance payment of medical fees. In April 2011 a new regulation was introduced, imposing an annual quota on the number of mainland women allowed to give birth in Hong Kong, in order to reduce pressure on medical facilities: the number of babies born to mainland mothers in Hong Kong was reported to have exceeded 40,000 (or some 45% of total births) in 2010.

In September 2011 the Court of First Instance declared unconstitutional a law that denied foreign domestic helpers the right to apply for permanent residency after seven years working in Hong Kong (a right that was granted to other categories of non-Chinese nationals). There were estimated to be some 290,000 foreign domestic helpers in Hong Kong, mostly female, the majority from Indonesia and the Philippines. Opponents of the court's decision argued that it would allow domestic workers' families to settle in Hong Kong, placing additional strains on housing and welfare resources.

Following the end of the Viet Nam War in 1975, the arrival in Hong Kong of numerous Vietnamese refugees became a major issue. The influx of asylum-seekers increased substantially during the 1980s. At one stage as many as 60,000 'boat people' were interned in detention camps in Hong Kong where, under a controversial policy, the majority remained for many years with little prospect of resettlement elsewhere. Legislation to distinguish between political refugees and 'economic migrants' took effect in June 1988. In October 1991, following protracted negotiations, it was announced that Viet Nam had agreed to the mandatory repatriation of refugees from Hong Kong. The last remaining detention camp was closed in 2000, with most of the Vietnamese refugees having been resettled in other countries or repatriated.

Foreign Affairs

Despite the tensions surrounding the transfer of sovereignty during the 1990s, many citizens of Hong Kong supported the Government of the People's Republic of China in its territorial dispute with Japan regarding the Diaoyu (or Senkaku) Islands. In September 1996 a Hong Kong activist drowned during a protest against Japan's claim to the islands. As issues of patriotism assumed greater significance in Hong Kong, more than 10,000 people attended a demonstration to mourn the protester's death and to denounce Japan. In October protesters from Hong Kong joined a flotilla of small boats from Taiwan and Macao, which successfully evaded Japanese patrol vessels and raised the flags of China and Taiwan on the disputed islands.

In July 2001 Chief Executive Tung Chee-hwa visited Washington, DC, and held a meeting with US President George W. Bush, at which Hong Kong's handling of Falun Gong and other issues of freedom were discussed. In March 2004 a group of democracy activists, led by Martin Lee, visited the USA to discuss with representatives of the US Government their concerns over human rights in Hong Kong. Relations with the USA were strained in November 2007 when a US naval vessel was refused permission to dock in Hong Kong by the Chinese authorities, but such port calls were permitted to resume in January 2008. A nuclear-powered aircraft carrier, along with four other US vessels, was permitted to enter Hong Kong in February 2010, but in the same month the Chinese Government protested against sales of weapons by the USA to Taiwan and suspended official meetings between members of the Chinese and US armed forces. In November, however, a US naval vessel was allowed to make an official port visit in Hong Kong, and another did so in February 2011, when the Commander of the US Seventh Fleet stated that military contacts between the two nations were in the process of being re-established.

During a visit to Hong Kong in July 2003 the British Prime Minister, Tony Blair, expressed his support for movement towards greater democracy in Hong Kong, following mass protests earlier in the month, but also stated that it was important to maintain stability in the territory. Following the ruling of the Standing Committee of China's NPC in April, vetoing direct elections in Hong Kong, the British Foreign and Commonwealth Office issued a statement claiming that the ruling had broken the promise of a high degree of autonomy for Hong Kong that had been made by the Chinese Government in 1997. Following the adoption of electoral reforms in June 2010, the Foreign and Commonwealth Office expressed the hope that Hong Kong could now progress towards universal suffrage in the elections to be held in 2017 (for the post of Chief Executive) and 2020 (for the legislature).

In May 2004 the outspoken Bishop Joseph Zen Ze-kiun, who had been banned from visiting the mainland in 1998, was permitted to make a three-day visit to Shanghai. In March 2006 Zen was elevated to the rank of Cardinal by Pope Benedict XVI, in a potentially significant development for relations between China and the Vatican. In June 2009 Cardinal Zen urged the Chinese Government to instigate an official inquiry into the events in Tiananmen Square 20 years previously.

CONSTITUTION AND GOVERNMENT

Since 1 July 1997 the Hong Kong SAR has been administered by a Chief Executive, who is accountable to the State Council of the People's Republic of China and serves a five-year term, there being a limit of two consecutive terms. The first incumbent was chosen by a 400-member Selection Committee in December 1996. Upon the expiry of his first term in 2002, the Chief Executive was chosen by an 800-member Election Committee, which also oversaw the selection of his successor in 2005. In July 2002 a new government structure was introduced, which expanded the Executive Council into a cabinet-style body comprising 14 ex-officio members known as principal officials (each with an individual portfolio) and five non-official members, all accountable to the Chief Executive. In October 2005 the number of non-official Council members was increased to 15. Elections to the third four-year term of the 60-member Legislative Council took place in September 2004; 30 of the seats (compared with 24 in the previous legislature) were directly elective (under a system of proportional representation), with 30 seats being determined by functional constituencies (comprising professional and special interest groups). The same system was retained for the Legislative Council elections of September 2008. In June 2010 electoral reforms were adopted, according to which the Election Committee for choosing the Chief Executive was to be expanded from 800 to 1,200 members, and the Legislative Council was to be expanded from 60 to 70 members: of these, 35 were to be directly elected, and 30 elected by the same functional constituencies as in previous elections, while, in a new development, five were to be nominated by and from among members of district councils, and elected by all the members of the electorate who were not eligible to vote in other functional constituencies (about 90%).

REGIONAL AND INTERNATIONAL CO-OPERATION

Hong Kong is a member of the Asian Development Bank (ADB, see p. 210) and an associate member of the UN's Economic and Social Commission for Asia and the Pacific (ESCAP, see p. 40). Hong Kong is also a member of Asia-Pacific Economic Cooperation (APEC, see p. 204).

After 1997 Hong Kong remained a separate customs territory, within the World Trade Organization (WTO, see p. 433), which it joined in 1995. Hong Kong is also a member of the Bank for International Settlements (BIS, see p. 224).

ECONOMIC AFFAIRS

In 2010, according to estimates by the World Bank, Hong Kong's gross national income (GNI), measured at average 2008–10 prices, was US $231,658m., equivalent to US $32,780 per head (or US $47,130 on an international purchasing-power parity basis). During 2001–10, it was estimated, the population increased at an average annual rate of 0.6%; gross domestic product (GDP) per head increased, in real terms, at an average rate of 3.8% per year. Overall GDP increased, in real terms, at an average annual rate of 4.4% in 2001–10. According to official figures, GDP grew by 5.0% in 2011.

Agriculture and fishing together contributed less than 0.1% of GDP in 2010, according to official preliminary figures, and the sector employed only 0.2% of the working population in 2008. Crop production is largely restricted to vegetables, while cattle, pigs and poultry are the principal livestock. Hong Kong relies heavily on imports for its food supplies. According to figures from the World Bank, the GDP of the agricultural sector decreased at an average annual rate of 4.6% in 2001–09. According to the Asian Development Bank (ADB), the agricultural sector contracted by 4.6% in 2009, but grew by 3.9% in 2010.

Industry (including mining, manufacturing, construction and utilities) provided nearly 7.1% of GDP in 2010, according to official preliminary figures and employed 13.5% of the working population in 2008. According to the World Bank, industrial GDP declined at an average annual rate, in real terms, of 2.6% in 2001–09; industrial GDP was estimated to have decreased by 5.2% in 2009. According to the ADB, the industrial sector contracted by 5.2% in 2009, before expanding by 7.6% in 2010.

Manufacturing contributed an estimated 1.8% of GDP in 2010, according to official preliminary figures, and employed 5.4% of the working population in 2008 (4.0% in 2011). In real terms the GDP of the sector declined at an average annual rate of 2.2% in 2001–10, according to World Bank figures; manufacturing GDP declined by 7.6% in 2009, before increasing by 15.8% in 2010. The principal branches of manufacturing include textiles and clothing, plastic products, metal products and electrical machinery (particularly radio and television sets).

Construction contributed nearly 3.3% of GDP in 2010, according to official preliminary figures. In 2011 the sector employed 7.8% of the working population.

Electricity production is derived mainly from coal, which accounted for 68.2% of output in 2008. Total production of electricity reached 38,292m. kWh in 2010. Fuel imports accounted for 3.4% of the cost of Hong Kong's total merchandise imports in 2009.

The services sector plays the most important role in the economy, accounting for 92.9% of GDP in 2010, according to official preliminary figures. The sector employed 86.3% of the working population in 2008. The value of Hong Kong's invisible exports (notably financial services, tourism and shipping) was US $106,432m. in 2010. Hong Kong is regarded as a major international financial centre. Revenue from tourism totalled an estimated HK $22,951m. in 2010. The number of visitors in that year rose by 21.8% to more than 36.0m. (of whom nearly 22.7m. were from mainland China). According to World Bank figures, the GDP of the services sector increased at an average annual rate, in real terms, of 4.7% in 2001–10. According to the ADB, the sector's GDP decreased by 1.6% in 2009, but increased by 7.0% in 2010.

In 2010 Hong Kong recorded a visible trade deficit of US $42,965m., and there was a surplus of US $13,936m. on the current account of the balance of payments. Re-exports constituted 97.9% of total exports in that year. The principal sources of Hong Kong's imports in 2010 were the People's Republic of China (45.5%); the principal markets for re-exports were the People's Republic of China (52.9%). Other major trading partners included Japan, the USA, Taiwan and Singapore. In 2010 the principal exports (including re-exports) were electrical machinery, telecommunications equipment, office machines, basic manufactures, clothing, and chemicals and related products. The principal imports in that year were electrical machinery, telecommunications equipment, office machines and automatic data-processing equipment, basic manufactures and chemicals and related products.

The fiscal deficit was equivalent to 3.5% of GDP in 2011. Hong Kong's general government gross debt was HK $578,796m. in 2010, equivalent to 34.6% of GDP. The Hong Kong Government's external debt stood at US $916,622m. in 2011. Fiscal reserves were forecast to be HK $662,100m. at 31 March 2012, equivalent to 22 months of government expenditure. Consumer prices decreased at an average annual rate of 0.7% in 2001–10. The consumer price index increased by 5.3% in 2011. The rate of unemployment was 3.2% in the three months to January 2012, according to provisional official figures, while underemployment was 1.5%.

Hong Kong is a major port and one of the world's principal international financial centres. The Closer Economic Partnership Arrangement (CEPA) concluded with the Government of the People's Republic in 2003 and expanded by successive subsequent agreements, allowed the liberalization of trade in goods and services between the SAR and mainland China. The deterioration in global economic conditions in 2008/09 had an adverse impact on the Hong Kong economy. However, following the implementation of government measures to maintain and restore confidence, including providing liquidity to banks, protection for small and medium-sized enterprises, a fiscal stimulus and investment in new jobs, the SAR recovered relatively quickly. After four consecutive quarters of contraction, the economy resumed positive growth in the final quarter of 2009 and continued its recovery in 2010 and 2011. Unemployment declined from a peak of 5.5% in 2009 to 3.2% in early 2012. Substantial increases in property prices led to demands for more stringent regulation of the sector, and various measures to stabilize the housing market were announced during 2010; these included the implementation of restrictions on excessive mortgage lending. In 2011 further measures were announced to increase the supply of public rented and subsidized private housing. In August 2011 the Chinese Government stated that during its 2011–15 Five-Year Plan period it intended to increase the liberalization of trade in services between Hong Kong and the mainland, and to expand Hong Kong's role as an international financial centre, in particular as an offshore centre for the Chinese currency, the renminbi. Consumer prices increased by an average of 5.3% in 2011, but the rate of inflation was expected to slow to 3.5% in 2012. Following expansion of 5.0% in 2011, the Government envisaged economic growth of only 1%–3% in 2012. The conspicuous disparity between the richest and poorest sectors of society remained a source of public concern. In the budget for 2012/13, stimulus measures of HK $80,000m. were announced to support small and medium-sized enterprises and households. Lower-income earners were to benefit from a rebate of 75% on income tax paid in 2011/12, up to a ceiling of HK $12,000, and an increase in land supply was expected to contribute to the slowing of property price increases. A statutory minimum wage had been introduced in May 2011. The Government predicted a consolidated deficit of HK $3,400m. in 2012/13. Exports were expected to slow in 2012 as a result of the poor economic conditions in the euro area and the USA. The Government in Hong Kong planned to take advantage of the further liberalization of mainland China to develop its economy, while also pursuing other regional and international economic links.

PUBLIC HOLIDAYS

2013: 1 January (first weekday in January), 10–12 February (Chinese Lunar New Year), 29 March (Good Friday), 1 April (Easter Monday), 4 April (Ching Ming), 1 May (Labour Day), 17 May (Buddha's Birthday), 12 June (Tuen Ng, Dragon Boat Festival), 1 July (SAR Establishment Day), 20 September (Chinese Mid-Autumn Festival), 1 October (National Day), 14 October (Chung Yeung Festival), 25–26 December (Christmas).

Statistical Survey

Source (unless otherwise stated): Census and Statistics Department, 19/F, Wanchai Tower, 12 Harbour Rd, Hong Kong; tel. 25825073; fax 28271708; e-mail gen-enquiry@censtatd.gov.hk; internet www.censtatd.gov.hk.

Area and Population

AREA, POPULATION AND DENSITY

Land area (sq km)	1,104*
Population (census and by-census results)†	
14 July 2006	6,864,346
30 June 2011	
Males	3,303,015
Females	3,768,561
Total	7,071,576
Usual residents	6,859,341
Present at census	6,635,558
Absent at census	223,783
Mobile residents	212,235
Present at census	40,359
Absent at census	171,876
Density (per sq km) at 2011 census	6,405.4

* 426 sq miles.

† All residents (including mobile residents) on the census date, including those who were temporarily absent from Hong Kong. In 2006 the census recorded population by place of birth as follows: Hong Kong 4,138,844, China (other than Hong Kong) 2,298,956, Other 426,546.

POPULATION BY AGE AND SEX
(population at 2011 census)

	Males	Females	Total
0–14	426,248	397,312	823,560
15–64	2,438,510	2,868,194	5,306,704
65 and over	438,257	503,055	941,312
Total	3,303,015	3,768,561	7,071,576

DISTRICTS AND DISTRICT COUNCILS
(population at 2011 census)

	Area (sq km)	Population	Density (per sq km)
Hong Kong Island	81	1,270,876	15,690
Central and Western	13	251,519	19,348
Wanchai	10	152,608	15,261
Eastern	19	588,094	30,952
Southern	39	278,655	7,145
Kowloon	47	2,108,419	44,860
Yau Tsim Mong	7	307,878	43,983
Sham Shui Po	9	380,855	42,317
Kowloon City	10	377,351	37,735
Wong Tai Sin	9	420,183	46,687
Kwun Tong	11	622,152	56,559
New Territories	976	3,691,093	3,782
Kwai Tsing	23	511,167	22,225
Tsuen Wan	63	304,637	4,836
Tuen Mun	85	487,546	5,736
Yuen Long	139	578,529	4,162
North	137	304,134	2,220
Tai Po	148	296,853	2,006
Sha Tin	69	630,273	9,134
Sai Kung	136	436,627	3,210
Islands	176	141,327	803
Total	1,104	7,071,576*	6,405

* Including marine population (1,188).

PRINCIPAL TOWNS
(population at 1996 census)

Kowloon*	1,988,515	Tai Po	271,661
Victoria (capital)	1,011,433	Tseun Wan	268,659
Tuen Mun	445,771	Sheung Shui	192,321
Sha Tin	445,383	Tsing Yu	185,495
Kwai Chung	285,231	Aberdeen	164,439

* Including New Kowloon.

BIRTHS, MARRIAGES AND DEATHS
(numbers rounded to nearest 100 persons)

	Known live births*		Registered marriages*		Known deaths	
	Number	Rate (per 1,000)	Number	Rate (per 1,000)	Number	Rate (per 1,000)
2003	47,000	6.9	35,400	5.2	36,971	5.4
2004	49,800	7.2	41,400	6.0	36,918	5.3
2005	57,098	8.4	43,018	6.3	38,830	5.7
2006	65,626	9.6	50,328	7.3	37,457	5.5
2007	70,875	10.2	47,453	6.8	39,476	5.7
2008	78,822	11.3	47,331	6.8	41,796	6.0
2009	82,095	11.7	51,175	7.3	41,175	5.9
2010	88,584	12.5	52,558	7.4	42,194	6.0

* Numbers are rounded to the nearest 100 persons.

Life expectancy (years at birth, 2010): Males 80.0; Females 85.9.

ECONOMICALLY ACTIVE POPULATION
('000 persons aged 15 years and over, excl. armed forces)

	2006	2007	2008
Agriculture and fishing	8.2	6.4	8.3
Manufacturing	216.9	202.4	191.2
Electricity, gas and water	14.6	15.2	14.1
Construction	269.2	274.7	268.6
Wholesale, retail and import/export trades, restaurants and hotels	1,104.8	1,143.8	1,145.5
Transport, storage and communications	369.2	372.2	377.9
Financing, insurance, real estate and business services	525.7	548.0	580.0

—continued	2006	2007	2008
Community, social and personal services	892.1	921.1	933.1
Total employed	3,400.8	3,483.8	3,518.8
Unemployed	171.1	145.7	130.1
Total labour force	3,571.9	3,629.5	3,648.9
Males	1,950.6	1,958.2	1,949.4
Females	1,621.2	1,671.3	1,699.5

Source: ILO.

2009 (million persons aged 15 years and over, excl. armed forces): Total employed 3.48; Unemployed 0.2; Total labour force 3.68 (Source: Asian Development Bank).

2010 (million persons aged 15 years and over, excl. armed forces): Total employed 3.49; Unemployed 0.16; Total labour force 3.65 (Source: Asian Development Bank).

Health and Welfare

KEY INDICATORS

Total fertility rate (children per woman*, 2004)	0.9
Under-5 mortality rate (per 1,000 live births, provisional, 2007)	1.6
HIV/AIDS (% of persons aged 15–49, 2003)	0.1
Physicians (per 1,000 head, provisional, 2007)†	1.7
Hospital beds (per 1,000 head, provisional, 2007)	5.0
Total carbon dioxide emissions ('000 metric tons, 2007)	39,930.3
Carbon dioxide emissions per head (metric tons, 2007)	5.8
Human Development Index (2011): ranking	13
Human Development Index (2011): value	0.898

* Excluding female domestic helpers.
† Excluding practitioners of Chinese medicine.

For sources and definitions, see explanatory note on p. vi.

Agriculture

PRINCIPAL CROPS
('000 metric tons, FAO estimates)

	2000	2001	2002
Lettuce	5	5	5
Spinach	11	11	11
Onions and shallots (green)	4	4	4
Other vegetables	24	14	34
Fruit	4	4	4

2003–04: Figures assumed to be unchanged from 2001 (FAO estimates).

2005–10: Separate data not available for Hong Kong (see the chapter on the People's Republic of China).

Source: FAO.

Total vegetables ('000 metric tons): 25 in 2005; 21 in 2006; 19 in 2007 (Source: Asian Development Bank).

LIVESTOCK
('000 head unless otherwise indicated, year ending September, FAO estimates)

	2002	2003	2004
Cattle (head)	1,500	1,500	1,500
Pigs	100	100	100
Chickens	1,000	1,000	1,000
Ducks	250	230	250

2005–10: Separate data for Hong Kong not available (see the chapter on the People's Republic of China).

Source: FAO.

LIVESTOCK PRODUCTS
('000 metric tons)

	2002	2003	2004
Beef and veal*	14	13	13
Pig meat*	147	145	194
Poultry meat	61	58	29
Game meat†	6	6	6
Cattle hides (fresh)†	2	2	2

* Unofficial figures.
† FAO estimates.

2005–10: Separate data for Hong Kong not available (see the chapter on the People's Republic of China).

Source: FAO.

Chicken meat ('000 metric tons): 21 in 2005; 17 in 2006; 13 in 2007 (Source: Asian Development Bank).

Fishing

('000 metric tons, live weight)

	2007	2008	2009
Capture*	154.1	158.1	159.0
Lizardfishes*	5.7	5.9	5.9
Threadfin breams*	16.6	17.0	17.1
Shrimps and prawns*	4.6	4.7	4.7
Squids*	7.2	7.4	7.4
Aquaculture	4.5	4.8	4.8
Total catch*	158.7	162.9	163.8

* FAO estimates.

Source: FAO.

Industry

SELECTED PRODUCTS
('000 metric tons unless otherwise indicated)

	2005	2006	2007
Cotton yarn (other than sewing thread)	62.2	70.5	39.8
Cotton woven fabrics (million sq m)	199.8	n.a.	n.a.
Women's and girls' blouses ('000)	29,706.0	2,077.0	7,401.0
Women's and girls' dresses, not knitted or crocheted ('000)	2,609.0	n.a.	n.a.
Women's and girls' skirts, slacks and shorts ('000)	43,426.0	83,756.0	45,504.0
Men's or boys' shirts, not knitted or crocheted ('000)	72,360.0	5,702.0	21,052.0
Watches ('000)	6,099.0	9,455.0	5,029.0

2008: Women's and girls' blouses ('000) 2,011.0; Women's and girls' skirts, slacks and shorts ('000) 42,922.0; Men's or boys' shirts, not knitted or crocheted ('000) 7,627.0.

Uncooked macaroni and noodle products (instant macaroni and noodles only, '000 metric tons): 62 in 2001; 20 in 2002; 99 in 2003.

Knitted sweaters ('000): 151,965 in 2001; 113,685 in 2002; 143,143 in 2003.

Men's and boys' jackets ('000): 1,838 in 2001; 1,285 in 2002; 1,087 in 2003.

Men's and boys' trousers ('000): 14,139 in 2001; 22,696 in 2002; 11,293 in 2003.

Source: UN, *Industrial Commodity Statistics Yearbook* and Industrial Commodity Statistics Database.

Cement ('000 metric tons): 1,005 in 2005; 1,255 in 2006; 1,300 in 2007 (Source: Asian Development Bank).

Electric energy (million kWh): 38,948 in 2007; 37,990 in 2008; 38,728 in 2009; 38,292 in 2010 (Source: Asian Development Bank).

Finance

CURRENCY AND EXCHANGE RATES

Monetary Units
100 cents = 1 Hong Kong dollar (HK $).

Sterling, US Dollar and Euro Equivalents (30 December 2011)
£1 sterling = HK $12.006;
US $1 = HK $7.766;
€1 = HK $10.048;
HK $100 = £8.33 = US $12.88 = €9.95.

Average Exchange Rate (HK $ per US $)
2009 7.7518
2010 7.7692
2011 7.7840

BUDGET
(HK $ million, year ending 31 March)

Revenue	2007/08	2008/09	2009/10
Direct taxes:			
Earnings and profits tax	133,729	146,143	123,184
Indirect taxes:			
Bets and sweeps tax	13,048	12,620	12,767
Duties on petroleum products, beverages, tobacco and cosmetics	7,059	6,047	6,465
General rates (property tax)	9,495	7,175	9,957
Motor vehicle taxes	5,553	4,981	4,816
Royalties and concessions	863	2,389	1,596
Others (stamp duties, hotel accommodation tax and air passenger departure tax)	53,670	34,011	44,000
Fines, forfeitures and penalties	997	1,006	1,183
Receipts from properties and investments	11,552	12,483	12,601
Loans, reimbursements, contributions and other receipts	2,826	3,305	3,277
Operating revenue from utilities	3,344	3,320	3,438
Fees and charges	12,297	10,470	10,487
Investment income:			
General revenue account	12,005	23,352	17,893
Land Fund	9,876	14,183	11,196
Capital Works Reserve Fund (land sales and interest)	66,377	23,155	41,877
Capital Investment Fund	2,207	1,917	1,232
Loan Fund	2,098	2,101	2,276
Other capital revenue	11,469	7,904	10,197
Total government revenue	358,465	316,562	318,442

Expenditure	2007/08	2008/09	2009/10
Operating expenditure	204,734	258,007	234,367
Recurrent expenditure	120,331	129,745	134,669
Personal emoluments	46,658	49,726	50,794
Pensions	14,736	15,700	16,911
Departmental expenses	18,079	19,312	20,740
Other recurrent expenditure	40,858	45,007	46,224
Subventions	79,115	84,374	86,511
Education	26,518	28,465	29,195
Health	29,345	31,323	32,422
Universities and polytechnics	11,534	11,711	11,476
Other subventions	11,718	12,875	13,418
Non-recurrent operating expenditure	5,288	43,888	13,187
Capital expenditure	30,081	57,105	58,158
Plant, equipment and works	1,033	1,134	1,415
Subventions	1,252	1,303	1,454
Capital Works Reserve Fund	23,065	50,719	51,582
Loan fund	3,053	2,240	2,150
Other funds	1,678	1,709	1,557
Total government expenditure	234,815	315,112	292,525

INTERNATIONAL RESERVES
(US $ million at 31 December)

	2008	2009	2010
Gold (national valuation)	58	74	94
Foreign exchange*	182,469	255,768	268,649
Total	182,527	255,842	268,743

* Including the foreign-exchange reserves of the Hong Kong Special Administrative Region Government's Land Fund.

Source: IMF, *International Financial Statistics*.

MONEY SUPPLY
(HK $ '000 million at 31 December)

	2008	2009	2010
Currency outside banks	170.2	194.1	218.6
Demand deposits at banking institutions	265.1	391.1	420.4
Total money	435.3	585.2	639.0

Source: IMF, *International Financial Statistics*.

COST OF LIVING
(Consumer Price Index; base: 2000 = 100)

	2006	2007	2008
Food	100.1	104.4	115.0
Housing	86.4	88.1	91.7
Electricity, gas and other fuels	109.6	108.8	101.7
Clothing and footwear	102.5	106.8	107.7
All items (incl. others)	95.5	97.4	101.6

2009: Food 116.4; All items (incl. others) 101.9.

2010: Food 119.3; All items (incl. others) 104.4.

Source: ILO.

NATIONAL ACCOUNTS
(HK $ million at current prices)

Expenditure on the Gross Domestic Product

	2008	2009	2010
Government final consumption expenditure	139,262	142,853	147,209
Private final consumption expenditure	1,022,862	1,012,790	1,085,268
Change in stocks	8,480	22,899	38,945
Gross fixed capital formation	334,352	322,772	374,586
Total domestic expenditure	1,504,956	1,501,314	1,646,008
Exports of goods and services	3,562,628	3,164,575	3,888,108
Less Imports of goods and services	3,390,573	3,043,567	3,790,258
GDP in purchasers' values	1,677,011	1,622,322	1,743,858

Gross Domestic Product by Economic Activity

	2008	2009	2010*
Agriculture, fishing, mining and quarrying	925	1,090	948
Manufacturing	30,993	28,227	29,813
Electricity, gas and water	39,585	34,961	34,643
Construction	48,357	50,146	55,842
Wholesale, retail and import/export trades, restaurants and hotels	447,510	414,667	461,904
Transport, storage and communications	146,503	145,856	187,602
Financing, insurance, real estate and business services	421,180	409,164	453,355
Community, social and personal services	269,601	279,453	287,052
Ownership of premises	188,244	187,286	188,325
Gross domestic product at factor cost	1,592,897	1,550,851	1,699,485
Taxes on production and imports	59,919	55,967	69,906
Statistical discrepancy	24,195	15,504	–25,533
GDP in purchasers' values	1,677,011	1,622,322	1,743,858

* Preliminary figures.

BALANCE OF PAYMENTS
(US $ million)

	2008	2009	2010
Exports of goods f.o.b.	365,236	321,836	394,015
Imports of goods f.o.b.	–388,353	–348,698	–436,980
Trade balance	–23,117	–26,862	–42,965
Exports of services	92,292	86,411	106,432
Imports of services	–47,062	–44,939	–50,869
Balance on goods and services	22,113	15,610	12,598
Other income received	118,546	100,773	116,536
Other income paid	–107,845	–95,243	–111,829
Balance on goods, services and income	32,814	21,139	17,305
Current transfers received	611	469	614
Current transfers paid	–3,931	–3,646	–3,983
Current balance	29,494	17,963	13,936
Capital account (net)	2,105	4,671	5,233
Direct investment abroad	–50,549	–63,994	–76,093
Direct investment from abroad	59,614	52,395	68,915
Portfolio investment assets	–25,353	–52,086	–66,663
Portfolio investment liabilities	–12,799	9,197	5,791
Financial derivatives assets	68,601	48,542	35,215
Financial derivatives liabilities	–60,474	–45,373	–31,462
Other investment assets	46,105	97,012	–63,297
Other investment liabilities	–23,006	454	113,823
Net errors and omissions	209	2,080	3,759
Overall balance	33,948	70,860	9,153

Source: IMF, *International Financial Statistics*.

External Trade

PRINCIPAL COMMODITIES
(HK $ million)

Imports c.i.f.	2008	2009	2010
Food and live animals	92,151	100,440	117,661
Chemicals and related products	171,261	140,935	180,317
Basic manufactures	383,315	313,220	381,267
Textile yarn, fabrics, made-up articles, etc.	95,880	77,241	87,523
Machinery and transport equipment	1,615,191	1,489,438	1,923,525
Office machines and automatic data-processing equipment	265,633	246,861	322,728
Telecommunications and sound recording and reproducing apparatus and equipment	407,160	368,621	457,229
Electrical machinery, apparatus and appliances n.e.s., and electrical parts thereof	764,417	720,861	956,769
Miscellaneous manufactured articles	603,091	517,912	590,850
Clothing (excl. footwear)	144,412	120,211	129,315
Photographic apparatus, equipment and supplies, optical goods, watches and clocks	78,806	65,653	93,437
Total (incl. others)	3,025,288	2,692,356	3,364,840

Exports f.o.b.*	2008	2009	2010
Chemicals and related products	135,743	116,029	143,153
Basic manufactures	314,139	253,248	320,843
Textile yarn, fabrics, made-up articles, etc.	95,435	77,328	87,848
Machinery and transport equipment	1,580,134	1,425,941	1,823,214
Office machines and automatic data-processing equipment	279,780	249,697	332,819
Telecommunications and sound recording and reproducing apparatus and equipment	467,734	414,567	511,023
Electrical machinery, apparatus and appliances n.e.s., and electrical parts thereof	691,867	650,756	843,192
Miscellaneous manufactured articles	721,935	606,823	663,583
Clothing (excl. footwear)	217,311	176,939	186,840
Photographic apparatus, equipment and supplies, optical goods, watches and clocks	92,202	74,655	97,203
Baby carriages, toys, games and sporting goods	120,078	104,078	88,436
Total (incl. others)	2,824,151	2,469,089	3,031,019

* Including re-exports (HK $ million): 2,733,394 in 2008; 2,411,347 in 2009; 2,961,507 in 2010.

PRINCIPAL TRADING PARTNERS
(HK $ million, excl. gold)

Imports	2008	2009	2010
China, People's Republic	1,410,735	1,249,374	1,529,751
Germany	53,438	50,103	57,660
India	58,015	52,599	71,794
Japan	297,552	236,369	308,161
Korea, Republic	118,084	103,046	133,714
Malaysia	66,137	68,016	84,705
Philippines	48,406	32,596	39,713
Singapore	194,951	174,659	237,407
Taiwan	192,041	175,649	224,761
Thailand	63,756	57,589	76,304
USA	150,738	142,137	179,160
Total (incl. others)	3,025,288	2,692,356	3,364,840

Domestic exports	2008	2009	2010
Australia	1,752	1,334	1,148
China, People's Republic	34,758	26,672	31,223
Germany	1,931	512	861
Japan	2,290	1,651	2,032
Korea, Republic	1,285	1,196	1,495
Netherlands	2,252	1,863	2,639
Singapore	3,025	2,225	2,866
Switzerland	1,395	1,095	1,683
Taiwan	3,863	1,918	2,815
United Kingdom	2,723	1,239	1,554
USA	18,860	7,317	8,356
Total (incl. others)	90,757	57,742	69,512

Re-exports	2008	2009	2010
China, People's Republic	1,335,687	1,236,577	1,566,999
France	36,804	28,383	34,582
Germany	92,011	78,830	79,776
India	51,268	51,473	73,481
Japan	118,663	107,218	125,615
Korea, Republic	48,279	41,937	52,174
Netherlands	43,076	35,403	41,482
Singapore	52,290	40,028	48,113
Taiwan	51,080	52,795	65,789
United Kingdom	72,665	58,432	59,226
USA	340,395	277,920	323,733
Total (incl. others)	2,733,394	2,411,347	2,961,507

Transport

RAILWAYS
(traffic)

	2008	2009	2010
Freight ('000 metric tons):			
loaded	19	16	7
unloaded	90	68	29

Passenger journeys ('000): 3,188 in 2003.

ROAD TRAFFIC
('000 registered motor vehicles at 31 December)

	2008	2009	2010
Private cars	383	394	415
Buses (private and public)	13	13	13
Light buses (private and public)	6	6	6
Taxis	18	18	18
Goods vehicles	109	107	109
Motorcycles	38	38	38
Government vehicles (excl. military vehicles)	6	6	6
Total (incl. others)	575	584	608

Note: Figures do not include tramcars.

SHIPPING

Merchant Fleet
(registered at 31 December)

	2007	2008	2009
Number of vessels	1,242	1,371	1,529
Total displacement ('000 grt)	35,816.2	39,100.5	45,338.3

Source: IHS Fairplay, *World Fleet Statistics*.

Traffic
(2010)

	Ocean-going vessels	River vessels
Total capacity (million nrt)	803*	194†
Cargo landed ('000 metric tons)*	113,300	39,200
Cargo loaded ('000 metric tons)*	65,900	45,000

* Provisional.
† 2007.

Passenger traffic ('000, arrivals and departures by sea, 2010): Passengers landed 12,209; Passengers embarked 13,653.

Note: Includes passengers travelling to and from Macao by helicopter.

CIVIL AVIATION

	2008	2009	2010
Passengers ('000):			
arrivals	15,350	14,936	17,030
departures	14,810	14,302	16 241
Freight ('000 metric tons):			
landed	1,327	1,263	1,480*
loaded	2,301	2,084	2,650*

* Provisional.

Tourism

TOURIST ARRIVALS BY COUNTRY OF RESIDENCE
(non-resident tourist arrivals at national borders)

	2007	2008	2009
Australia	507,100	509,900	462,600
Canada	296,300	281,900	260,700
China, People's Republic	9,092,700	9,379,700	9,663,600
Germany	177,000	170,800	156,500
Indonesia	276,900	261,900	263,900
Japan	846,000	816,800	779,600
Korea, Republic	592,400	637,800	401,600
Macao	241,100	256,200	249,800
Malaysia	370,200	372,300	326,300
Philippines	439,800	451,500	455,800
Singapore	478,900	479,500	456,700
Taiwan	694,800	649,400	613,800
Thailand	290,600	298,600	303,200
United Kingdom	496,900	467,200	415,400
USA (incl. Guam)	924,100	837,600	755,800
Total (incl. others)	17,153,900	17,319,400	16,926,100

Note: Figures are rounded to the nearest 100 persons.

Receipts from tourism (US $ million, excl. passenger transport): 15,304 in 2008; 16,450 in 2009; 22,951 in 2010 (provisional).

Source: World Tourism Organization.

2010: Total arrivals 36,030,000 (mainland China 22,684,000; Taiwan 2,165,000; Macao 780,000).

Communications Media

	2008	2009	2010
Telephones ('000 in use)	4,183.0	4,277.3	4,361.7
Mobile cellular telephones ('000 subscribers)	11,580.1	12,597.2	13,793.7
Internet subscribers ('000)	2,571.8*	2,722.6	2,922.3
Broadband subscribers ('000)	1,935.5	2,022.8	2,111.1

* Estimate.

Personal computers: 4,835,300 (693.0 per 1,000 persons) in 2008.

1997 ('000 in use): Radio receivers 4,450.

2000 ('000 in use): Television receivers 3,105.

2004 (unless otherwise indicated): Daily newspapers 46; Non-daily newspapers 23; Periodicals 864 (2003).

Sources: partly UNESCO, *Statistical Yearbook;* UN, *Statistical Yearbook*; International Telecommunication Union.

Education

(2010/11 unless otherwise indicated)

	Institutions	Teachers	Students
Kindergartens	951	10,454	148,940
Primary schools	572	21,902	331,112
Secondary schools	533	29,969	449,737
Special schools	61	1,476	7,803
Institute of Vocational Education	1	1,948	62,094
Approved post-secondary college	3	266	3,376
Other post-secondary colleges	13	n.a.	9,542
UGC-funded institutions	8	5,813†*	164,857
Open University of Hong Kong	1	130†	20,196
Adult education institutions	2,344	n.a.	245,787

* 2006/07.
† Provisional figure.

Pupil-teacher ratio (primary education, UNESCO estimate): 15.2 in 2009/10 (Source: UNESCO Institute for Statistics).

Adult literacy rate (UNESCO estimates): 94.6% in 2003 (Source: UN Development Programme, *Human Development Report*).

Directory

The Government

Chief Executive: DONALD TSANG YAM-KUEN (elected unopposed 16 June 2005; re-elected 25 March 2007).

Leung Chun-ying was elected to the post of Chief Executive on 25 March 2012 and was expected to take office on 1 July.

EXECUTIVE COUNCIL
(May 2012)

Chairman: The Chief Executive.

Ex-Officio Members (Principal Officials)

Chief Secretary for Administration: STEPHEN LAM SUI-LUNG.

Financial Secretary: JOHN TSANG CHUN-WAH.

Secretary for Justice: WONG YAN-LUNG.

Secretary for Education: MICHAEL SUEN MING-YEUNG.

Secretary for Commerce and Economic Development: GREGORY SO KAM-LEUNG.

Secretary for Constitutional and Mainland Affairs: RAYMOND TAM CHI-YUEN.

Secretary for Security: AMBROSE LEE SIU-KWONG.

Secretary for Food and Health: Dr YORK CHOW YAT-NGOK.

Secretary for the Civil Service: DENISE YUE CHUNG-YEE.

Secretary for Home Affairs: TSANG TAK-SING.

Secretary for Labour and Welfare: MATTHEW CHEUNG KIN-CHUNG.

Secretary for Financial Services and the Treasury: Prof. K. C. CHAN KA-KEUNG.

Secretary for Development: CARRIE LAM CHENG YUET-NGOR.

Secretary for the Environment: EDWARD YAU TANG-WAH.

Secretary for Transport and Housing: EVA CHENG.

In addition to the above ex-officio members of the Executive Council, there were also 13 non-official members.

GOVERNMENT OFFICES

Executive Council: 1/F, Main Wing, Central Government Offices, Lower Albert Rd, Central; tel. 28102581; fax 28450176; e-mail ceo@ceo.gov.hk; internet www.ceo.gov.hk/exco.

Office of the Chief Executive: 5/F, Main Wing, Central Government Offices, Lower Albert Rd, Central; tel. 28783300; fax 25090577; e-mail ceo@ceo.gov.hk; internet www.ceo.gov.hk.

Government Secretariat: Central Government Offices, Lower Albert Rd, Central; tel. 28102900; fax 28457895.

Information Services Department: 8/F, Murray Bldg, Garden Rd, Central; tel. 28428777; fax 28459078; e-mail internet@isd.gov.hk; internet www.isd.gov.hk.

Legislature

LEGISLATIVE COUNCIL

The fourth Legislative Council since Hong Kong's transfer to Chinese sovereignty was elected on 7 September 2008. The Legislative Council comprises 60 members: 30 chosen by functional constituencies and 30 by direct election in five geographical constituencies. The term of office is four years.

President: JASPER TSANG YOK-SING.

Election, 7 September 2008 (unofficial results)

Party	Directly elective seats	Functional Constituency seats	Total seats
Democratic Alliance for the Betterment and Progress of Hong Kong	9	4	13
Democratic Party	7	1	8
Liberal Party	—	6	7
Civic Party	4	1	5
The Alliance	—	3	3
League of Social Democrats	3	—	3
Association for Democracy and People's Livelihood	1	1	2
The Frontier*	1	—	1
Hong Kong Confederation of Trade Unions	1	—	1
Hong Kong Federation of Trade Unions	—	1	1
Neighbourhood and Worker's Service Centre	1	—	1
Civic Act-up	1	—	1
Independents and others	2	13	14
Total	30	30	60

* Merged with the Democratic Party in November 2008.

Election Commission

Electoral Affairs Commission: 10/F, Harbour Centre, 25 Harbour Rd, Wanchai; tel. 28911001; fax 28274644; e-mail eacenq@reo.gov.hk; internet www.eac.gov.hk; f. 1997; Chair. BARNABAS FUNG.

Political Organizations

Alliance for Universal Suffrage: Hong Kong; internet www.universalsuffrage.hk; f. 2010; coalition of 11 pro-democracy parties and groups (incl. the ADPL, Democratic Party, Hong Kong Confederation of Trade Unions and professional groups).

Association for Democracy and People's Livelihood (ADPL): Sun Beam Commercial Bldg, Rm 1104, 469–471 Nathan Rd, Kowloon; tel. 27822699; fax 27823137; e-mail info@adpl.org.hk; internet www.adpl.org.hk; advocates democracy; Chair. BRUCE LIU; Sec.-Gen. QIN SHAN.

Citizens' Party: GPOB 321, Central; tel. 28930029; e-mail enquiry@citizensparty.org; f. 1997; urges mass participation in politics; Chair. Dr JOE WONG.

Civic Party: Unit 202, 2/F, Blk B, Sea View Bldg, 4–6 Watson Rd, North Point; tel. 28657111; fax 28652771; e-mail contact@civicparty.hk; internet www.civicparty.hk; f. 2006; pro-democracy; Chair. KENNETH CHAN; Leader ALAN LEONG.

Democratic Alliance for the Betterment and Progress of Hong Kong (DAB): SUP Tower, 15/F, 83 King's Rd, North Point; tel. 35821111; fax 35821188; e-mail info@dab.org.hk; internet www.dab.org.hk; f. 2005; formed by merger of Democratic Alliance for the Betterment of Hong Kong (f. 1992, supported return of Hong Kong to the motherland and implementation of the Basic Law) and Hong Kong Progressive Alliance (f. 1994, supported by business and professional community); pro-Beijing; Chair. TAM YIU-CHUNG; Sec.-Gen. THOMAS PANG.

Democratic Party: Hanley House, 4/F, 776–778 Nathan Rd, Kowloon; tel. 23977033; fax 23978998; e-mail dphk@dphk.org; internet www.dphk.org; f. 1994; formed by merger of United Democrats of Hong Kong (UDHK—declared a formal political party in 1990) and Meeting Point; merged with The Frontier (f. 1996) in Nov. 2008; liberal grouping; advocates democracy; Chair. ALBERT HO CHUN-YAN; Sec.-Gen. CHEUNG YIN-TUNG.

Hong Kong Democratic Foundation: POB 35588, King's Road Post Office, North Point; tel. 28696443; fax 28696318; e-mail secretariat@hkdf.org; internet www.hkdf.org; advocates democracy and an open society; Chair. ALAN LUNG KA-LUN.

League of Social Democrats/April Fifth Action: A-78, 2/F, Kam Fai Court, Kimberley Rd, Tsim Sha Tsui, Kowloon; tel. 23755338; fax 23755732; e-mail lsd@lsd.org.hk; internet www.lsd.org.hk; socialist group; anti-Beijing; Leader LEUNG KWOK-HUNG.

Liberal Party: 801–803 Manhattan Place, 23 Wang Tai Rd, Kowloon; tel. 28696833; fax 25334238; e-mail liberal@liberal.org.hk; internet www.liberal.org.hk; f. 1993; est. by mems of Co-operative Resources Centre (CRC); business-orientated; pro-Beijing; Chair. MIRIAM LAU KIN-YEE.

Neighbourhood and Worker's Service Centre: Unit 326, 3/F, West Wing, Central Government Offices, 11 Ice House St, Central; tel. 25372101; fax 25372102; e-mail legco@nwsc.org.hk; internet www.nwsc.org.hk; Chair. LEUNG YIU-CHUNG.

New Hong Kong Alliance: 4/F, 14–15 Wo On Lane, Central; tel. 27826111; fax 27706083; e-mail contact@alliance.org.hk; internet www.alliance.org.hk; pro-China; Chair. SZETO WAH.

New People's Party (NPP): Flats D–F, 11/F, China Overseas Bldg, 139 Hennessy Rd, Wanchai; tel. 31000079; fax 31000087; e-mail info@npp.org.hk; internet www.npp.org.hk; f. 2011; pro-Beijing; advocates universal suffrage, economic diversification and reduction in wealth gap; Chair. REGINA IP.

People Power: c/o The Legislative Council; e-mail admin@peoplepower.hk; internet www.peoplepower.hk; f. 2011; est. by fmr mems of League of Social Democrats; pro-democracy; Chair. LAU KA HUNG; Sec.-Gen. CHAN SO LING.

At the elections of September 2008, the Hong Kong Confederation of Trade Unions and The Hong Kong Federation of Trade Unions (see Trade and Industry), the Alliance and Civic Act-up also secured seats in the Legislative Council. A new grouping, the Neo Democrats, was established by former members of the Democratic Party in late 2010.

The Chinese Communist Party (based in the People's Republic) and the Kuomintang (Nationalist Party of China, based in Taiwan) also maintain organizations in Hong Kong.

Judicial System

The Court of Final Appeal was established on 1 July 1997 upon the commencement of the Hong Kong Court of Final Appeal Ordinance. It replaced the Privy Council in London as the highest appellate court in Hong Kong to safeguard the rule of law. The Court comprises five judges—the Chief Justice, three permanent judges and one non-permanent Hong Kong judge or one judge from another common-law jurisdiction.

The High Court consists of a Court of Appeal and a Court of First Instance. The Court of First Instance has unlimited jurisdiction in civil and criminal cases, while the District Court has limited jurisdiction. Appeals from these courts lie to the Court of Appeal, presided over by the Chief Judge or a Vice-President of the Court of Appeal with one or two Justices of Appeal. Appeals from Magistrates' Courts are heard by a Court of First Instance judge.

Chief Justice of the Court of Final Appeal: GEOFFREY MA TAO-LI.

Permanent Judges of the Court of Final Appeal: K. BOKHARY, PATRICK S. O. CHAN, R. A. V. RIBEIRO.

Chief Judge of the High Court: ANDREW CHEUNG KUI-NUNG.

Justices of Appeal: K. H. WOO, F. STOCK, D. LE PICHON, P. C. Y. CHEUNG, A. G. ROGERS, M. C. K. N. YUEN, W. C. K. YEUNG, R. C. TANG, R. A. HARTMAN, SUSAN KWAN.

OTHER COURTS

District Court: There are 32 District Judges headed by a Chief District Judge.

Magistrates' Courts: There are seven Principal Magistrates, 59 Magistrates and seven Special Magistrates, sitting in nine magistracies.

Religion

The population is predominantly Buddhist. The number of active Buddhists is estimated at between 650,000 and 700,000, and there were more than 600 temples in 2005. Confucianism and Daoism are widely practised. The three religions are frequently found in the same temple. In 2005 there were some 660,000 Christians, approximately 90,000 Muslims, 40,000 Hindus, and 8,000 Sikhs. Judaism, the Bahá'í faith and Zoroastrianism are also represented.

BUDDHISM

Hong Kong Buddhist Association: 1/F, 338 Lockhart Rd, Wanchai; tel. 25749371; fax 28340789; e-mail enquiry@hkbuddhist.org; internet www.hkbuddhist.org; Pres. Ven. KOK KWONG.

CHRISTIANITY

Hong Kong Christian Council: 9/F, 33 Granville Rd, Kowloon; tel. 23687123; fax 27242131; e-mail hkcc@hkcc.org.hk; internet www.hkcc.org.hk; f. 1954; 22 mem. orgs; Chair. Rev. NICHOLAS TAI HO-FAI; Sec. Rev. YUEN TIN-YAU.

The Anglican Communion

Primate of Hong Kong Sheng Kung Hui and Bishop of Hong Kong Island and Macao: Most Rev. PETER K. K. KWONG, Bishop's House, 1 Lower Albert Rd, Central; tel. 25265355; fax 25212199; e-mail office1@hkskh.org; internet www1.hkskh.org.

Bishop of Eastern Kowloon: Rt Rev. LOUIS TSUI, 4/F, Holy Trinity Bradbury Centre, 139 Ma Tau Chung Rd, Kowloon; tel. 27139983; fax 27111609; e-mail dek@hkskh.org; internet dek.hkskh.org.

Bishop of Western Kowloon: Rt Rev. THOMAS SOO, 15/F, Ultra Grace Commercial Bldg, 5 Jordan Rd, Kowloon; tel. 27830811; fax 27830799; e-mail dwk@hkskh.org; internet dwk.hkskh.org.

The Lutheran Church

Evangelical Lutheran Church of Hong Kong: 4/F, Lutheran Bldg, Waterloo Rd, Yau Ma Tei, Kowloon; tel. 23885847; fax 23887539; e-mail info@elchk.org.hk; internet www.elchk.org.hk; f. 1954; 16,000 mems (2011); Bishop Rev. JENNY CHAN.

Lutheran Church—Hong Kong Synod: 68 Begonia Rd, Yau Yat Chuen, Kowloon; tel. 23973721; fax 23974826; e-mail hksynod@lutheran.org.hk; internet www.lutheran.org.hk; Pres. Rev. ALLAN YUNG.

The Roman Catholic Church

For ecclesiastical purposes, Hong Kong forms a single diocese, nominally suffragan to the archdiocese of Canton (Guangzhou), China. According to Vatican sources, in December 2007 there were an estimated 352,939 adherents in the territory, representing more than 5% of the total population.

Bishop of Hong Kong: JOHN TONG HON, 12/F, Catholic Diocese Centre, 16 Caine Rd, Central; tel. 28434679; fax 25254707; e-mail bishophk@pacific.net.hk; internet www.catholic.org.hk.

The Press

At the end of 2005, according to Hong Kong government figures, there were 49 daily newspapers, including 23 Chinese-language and 13 English-language dailies, and 722 periodicals.

PRINCIPAL DAILY NEWSPAPERS

English Language

China Daily: internet www.chinadaily.com.cn/hkedition/hk.html; Hong Kong edn of China's official English-language newspaper; launched 1997; Editor-in-Chief RAY ZHOU; circ. 20,000.

International Herald Tribune: 1201 K Wah Centre, 191 Java Rd, North Point; tel. 29221188; fax 29221190; internet www.iht.com; Correspondent SYLVIA HUI; circ. 8,390 (2009).

South China Morning Post: 3/F, 1 Leighton Rd, Causeway Bay; tel. 25652222; fax 28111048; e-mail info@scmp.com; internet www.scmp.com; f. 1903; Editor-in-Chief WANG XIANGWEI; circ. 107,000.

The Standard: 3/F, Sing Tao News Corporation Bldg, 3 Tung Wong Rd, Shau Kei Wan; tel. 27982798; fax 23051765; e-mail editor@thestandard.com.hk; internet www.thestandard.com.hk; f. 1949; publ. as free newspaper since Jan. 2007; Editor-in-Chief IVAN TONG; circ. 231,018.

Target Intelligent Report: Suite 2901, Bank of America Tower, 12 Harcourt Rd, Central; tel. 25730379; fax 28381597; e-mail info@targetnewspapers.com; internet www.targetnewspapers.com; f. 1972; financial news, commentary, politics, property, litigations, etc.

Wall Street Journal Asia: 25/F, Central Plaza, 18 Harbour Rd, Wanchai; tel. 25737121; fax 28345291; e-mail wsj.ltrs@wsj.com; internet www.wsj-asia.com; f. 1976; business; Editor-in-Chief ALMAR LATOUR; circ. 80,393.

Chinese Language

Hong Kong Commercial Daily: 1/F, 499 King's Rd, North Point; tel. 25905322; fax 25658947; internet www.hkcd.com.hk; f. 1952; Chair. and CEO HUANG YANG LUE; Editor CHENG XI TIAN.

Hong Kong Daily News: 5/F, CWG Bldg, 3A Kung Ngam Village Rd, Shau Kei Wan; tel. 39216688; fax 39216686; e-mail edit@hkdailynews.com.hk; internet www.hkdailynews.com.hk; f. 1958; morning; CEO RODDY YU; Chief Editor K. K. YEUNG; circ. 120,000.

Hong Kong Economic Journal: 22/F, North Point Industrial Bldg, 499 King's Rd, North Point; tel. 28567567; fax 28111070; e-mail enquiry@hkej.com; internet www.hkej.com; Dir CHO CHI-MING; Chief Editor K. C. CHAN; circ. 30,000.

Hong Kong Economic Times: Kodak House, Block 2, 6/F, 321 Java Rd, North Point; tel. 28802444; fax 25169989; e-mail etp_info@hket.com; internet www.etpress.com.hk; f. 1988; Publr MAK PING LEUNG; Chief Editor CHAN CHO BIU; circ. 80,371.

Ming Pao Daily News: Block A, Ming Pao Industrial Centre, 15/F, 18 Ka Yip St, Chai Wan; tel. 25953111; fax 28982534; e-mail mingpao@mingpao.com; internet www.mediachinesegroup.com; f. 1959; morning; Chief Editor PAUL CHEUNG; circ. 78,258.

Oriental Daily News: Oriental Press Centre, 23 Dai Cheong St, Tai Po Industrial Estate, New Territories; tel. 36000000; fax 36001100; e-mail news@oriental.com.hk; internet orientaldaily.on.cc; Chair. C. F. MA; Editor-in-Chief LIU KOU CHOUAN; circ. 650,000.

Ping Kuo Jih Pao (Apple Daily): 8 Chun Ying St, Industrial Estate West, Tseung Kwan; tel. 29908388; fax 26239132; e-mail adnews@appledaily.com; internet appledaily.atnext.com; f. 1995; published by Next Media; Propr JIMMY LAI; Publr LOH CHAN; circ. 309,261.

Sing Pao Daily News: 3/F, CWG Bldg, 3A Kung Ngam, Village Rd, Shau Kei Wan; tel. 25702201; fax 28062091; e-mail dailynews@singpao.com.hk; internet www.singpao.com; f. 1939; morning; Chief Editor CHENG SI WEI; circ. 229,250.

Sing Tao Daily: 3/F, Sing Tao News Corpn Bldg, 3 Tung Wong Rd, Shau Kei Wan; tel. 27982323; fax 27518634; e-mail info@singtao.com; internet www.singtao.com; f. 1938; morning; Editor-in-Chief LUK KAM WING; circ. 60,000.

The Sun: Oriental Press Centre, 23 Dai Cheong St, Tai Po Industrial Estate, New Territories; tel. 36009911; fax 36009900; e-mail news@the-sun.com.hk; internet the-sun.on.cc; f. 1999; publ. by the Oriental Press Group.

Ta Kung Pao: 342 Hennessy Rd, Wanchai; tel. 25757181; fax 28345104; e-mail tkp@takungpao.com; internet www.takungpao.com; f. 1902; morning; supports People's Republic of China; Editor T. S. TSANG; circ. 150,000.

Wen Wei Po: 2–4 Hing Wai Centre, 3/F, 7 Tin Wan Praya Rd, Aberdeen; tel. 28738288; fax 28730657; e-mail editor@wenhuibao.com.hk; internet www.wenweipo.com; f. 1948; morning; Dir WANG SHUCHENG; Editor-in-Chief WONG BAK YAO; circ. 200,000.

SELECTED PERIODICALS

English Language

Asia Money: 27/F, 248 Queen's Rd East, Wanchai; tel. 29128074; fax 28656225; e-mail richard.morrow@asiamoney.com; internet www.asiamoney.com; 10 a year; Publr ANDREW COVER; Editor RICHARD MORROW.

Business Traveller Asia–Pacific: Suite 405, 4/F, Chinachem Exchange Square, 1 Hoi Wan St, Quarry Bay; tel. 25949300; fax 25196846; e-mail enquiry@businesstravellerasia.com; internet asia.businesstraveller.com; f. 1982; consumer business travel; 10 a year; Publr PEGGY TEO; Editor-in-Chief TOM OTLEY; circ. 32,439.

Electronics: 38/F, Office Tower, Convention Plaza, 1 Harbour Rd, Wanchai; tel. 28924672; fax 28240249; e-mail hktdc@hktdc.org; internet www.hktdc.com; f. 1985; 4 a year (April, June, Oct. and Dec.); publ. by the Hong Kong Trade Development Council; Chief Editor GEOFF PICKEN; circ. 90,000.

Enterprise: 38/F, Office Tower, Convention Plaza, 1 Harbour Rd, Wanchai; tel. 25844333; fax 28240249; e-mail hktdc@hktdc.org; internet www.hktdc.com; f. 1967; monthly; publ. by the Hong Kong Trade Devt Council; Chief Editor GEOFF PICKEN; circ. 150,000.

Houseware: 38/F, Office Tower, Convention Plaza, 1 Harbour Rd, Wanchai; tel. 25844333; fax 28240249; e-mail hktdc@hktdc.org; internet www.hktdc.com; f. 1983; publ. by the Hong Kong Trade Development Council; household and hardware products; 2 a year; Chief Editor GEOFF PICKEN; circ. 90,000.

Hong Kong Industrialist: Federation of Hong Kong Industries, 31/F, Billion Plaza, 8 Cheung Yue St, Cheung Sha Wan, Kowloon; tel. 27323188; fax 27213494; e-mail fhki@fhki.org.hk; internet www.industryhk.org; monthly; publ. by the Federation of Hong Kong Industries; Editor ANTHONY CHAN; circ. 6,000.

Hong Kong Special Administrative Region Government Gazette: Printing Division, Government Logistics Department, 10/F, Government Offices, 333 Java Rd, North Point; tel. 25649500; fax 28876591; e-mail info@gld.gov.hk; internet www.gld.gov.hk; weekly.

Official Hong Kong Guide (e-Newsletter): c/o HKTB, Citicorp Centre, 9–11/F, 18 Whitfield Rd, North Point; f. 1982; monthly; information on sightseeing, shopping, dining, etc. for overseas visitors; published by the Hong Kong Tourism Board.

Orientations: 815, 8/F, Zung Fu Industrial Bldg, 1067 King's Rd, Quarry Bay; tel. 25111368; fax 25074620; e-mail omag@netvigator.com; internet www.orientations.com.hk; f. 1970; 8 a year; arts of East Asia, the Indian subcontinent and South-East Asia; Publr and Editorial Dir ELIZABETH KNIGHT.

Reader's Digest (Asia Edn): Reader's Digest Association Far East Ltd, 19/F, Cyber Centre, 3 Tung Wong Rd, Shau Kei Wan; tel. 25681117; fax 96906389; e-mail friends@rdasia.com.hk; internet www.readersdigest.com.hk; f. 1963; general topics; monthly; Editor DORA CHEOK; circ. 332,000.

Sunday Examiner: 11/F, Catholic Diocese Centre, 16 Caine Rd, Central; tel. 25220487; fax 25369939; internet sundayex.catholic.org.hk; e-mail sunday@examiner.org.hk; f. 1946; religious; weekly; Editor-in-Chief Sister TERESA YUEN; Deputy Editor-in-Chief Fr JIM MULRONEY; circ. 6,500.

Textile Asia: c/o Business Press Ltd, California Tower, 11/F, 30–32 D'Aguilar St, GPOB 185, Central; tel. 25233744; fax 28106966; e-mail texasia@biznetvigator.com; internet www.textileasia-businesspress.com; f. 1970; monthly; textile and clothing industry; Publr and Editor-in-Chief MAX W. SUNG; circ. 17,000.

Travel Business Analyst: GPOB 12761, Hong Kong; tel. 25072310; e-mail TBAoffice@gmail.com; internet www.travelbusinessanalyst.com; f. 1982; monthly; travel trade; Editor MURRAY BAILEY.

Chinese Language

Affairs Weekly: Hong Kong; tel. 28950801; fax 25767842; f. 1980; general interest; Editor WONG WAI MAN; circ. 130,000.

Cheng Ming Monthly: Hennessy Rd, POB 20370, Wanchai; tel. 25740664; e-mail editor.chengmingmag@gmail.com; internet www.chengmingmag.com; current affairs; Chief Editor WAN FAI.

City Magazine: 9/F, Zung Fu Industrial Bldg, 1067 King's Rd, Quarry Bay; tel. 22509188; fax 28919719; e-mail hk@modernmedia.com.hk; internet www.cityhowwhy.com.hk; f. 1976; monthly; fashion, wine, cars, society, etc.; Publr JOHN K. C. CHAN; Chief Editor PETER WONG; circ. 30,000.

East Touch: 3/F, Sing Tao News Corpn Bldg, 3 Tung Wong Rd, Shau Kei Wan; tel. 27074471; fax 27074554; e-mail easttouch@singtaonewscorp.com; internet www.easttouch.com.hk; f. 1995; weekly; fashion, celebrity and entertainment news.

East Week: 3/F, Sing Tao News Corpn Bldg, 3 Tung Wong Rd, Shau Kei Wan; tel. 31813588; fax 21104209; e-mail info@eastweek.com.hk; internet www.eastweek.com.hk; f. 1992; weekly; publication halted in 2002; relaunched in 2003; general interest; Chair. HE ZHUGUO.

Kung Kao Po (Catholic Chinese Weekly): 16/F, 11 Catholic Parish Centre, Caine Rd, Central; tel. 25220487; fax 25213095; internet kkp.catholic.org.hk; e-mail kkp@kkp.org.hk; f. 1928; religious; weekly; Editor-in-Chief Sister TERESA YUEN.

Ming Pao Monthly: Ming Pao Industrial Centre, 15/F, Block A, 18 Ka Yip St, Chai Wan; tel. 25953111; fax 28982691; e-mail mpmeditor@mingpao.com; internet www.mingpaomonthly.com; Chief Editor KOO SIU-SUN.

Next Magazine: 8 Chun Ying St, T. K. O. Industrial Estate West, Tseung Kwan O, Kowloon; tel. 27442733; fax 29907210; internet www.nextmedia.com; internet next.atnext.com; f. 1989; weekly; news, business, lifestyle, entertainment; Editor-in-Chief LEE CHI-HO; circ. 172,708.

Open Magazine: POB 20064, Hennessy Rd; tel. 28939197; fax 28915591; e-mail open@open.com.hk; internet www.open.com.hk; f. 1990; monthly; Chief Editor JIN ZHONG; circ. 15,000.

Oriental Sunday: 10/F, Johnson Bldg, 14–16 Lee Chung St, Chai Wan; tel. 29603504; fax 29605701; e-mail anniekwan@newmediagroup.com.hk; internet www.orientalsunday.hk; f. 1991; weekly; leisure magazine; Publr TSO SUET CHUNG; circ. 120,000.

Reader's Digest (Chinese Edn): Reader's Digest Association Far East Ltd, 19/F, Cyber Centre, 3 Tung Wong Rd, Shau Kei Wan; tel. 25681117; fax 25690370; internet www.readersdigest.com.hk; f. 1965; monthly; Editor-in-Chief JOEL POON; circ. 200,000.

Today's Living: 2207, 22/F, Westlands Center, 20 Westlands Rd, Quarry Bay; tel. 28822230; fax 28823949; e-mail magazine@todaysliving.com; internet www.todaysliving.com; f. 1987; monthly; interior design; Publr and Editor-in-Chief KENNETH LI; circ. 55,000.

Yazhou Zhoukan: Block A, Ming Pao Industrial Centre, 15/F, 18 Ka Yip St, Chai Wan; tel. 25155358; fax 25059662; e-mail yzzk@mingpao.com; internet www.yzzk.com; f. 1987; international Chinese news weekly; Chief Editor YAU LOP-POON; circ. 110,000.

Yuk Long TV Weekly: Hong Kong; tel. 25657883; fax 25659958; f. 1977; entertainment, fashion, etc.; Publr TONY WONG; circ. 82,508.

NEWS AGENCIES

International News Service: 2E Cheong Shing Mansion, 33–39 Wing Hing St, Causeway Bay; tel. 25665668; Rep. AU KIT MING.

Xinhua (New China) News Agency, Hong Kong SAR Bureau: 387 Queen's Rd East, Wanchai; tel. 28314126; f. 2000; est. from fmr news dept of branch office of Xinhua (responsibility for other activities assumed by Liaison Office of the Central People's Govt in the Hong Kong SAR); Dir ZHANG GUOLIANG.

PRESS ASSOCIATIONS

Chinese Language Press Institute: 3/F, Sing Tao News Corpn Bldg, 3 Tung Wong Rd, Shau Kei Wan; tel. 27982501; fax 27953017; e-mail clpi68@yahoo.com.hk; f. 1968; Pres. Sir TIONG HIEW KING.

Hong Kong Chinese Press Association: Rm 2208, 22/F, 33 Queen's Rd, Central; tel. 28613622; fax 28661933; 13 mems; Chair. HUE PUE-YING.

Hong Kong Journalists Association: Henfa Commercial Bldg, Flat 15A, 348–350 Lockhart Rd, Wanchai; tel. 25910692; fax 25727329; e-mail hkja@hkja.org.hk; internet www.hkja.org.hk; f. 1968; 413 mems; Chair. MAK YING-TING.

Newspaper Society of Hong Kong: Rm 904, 9/F, 75–83 King's Rd, North Point; tel. 25713102; fax 25712676; e-mail secretariat@nshk.com.hk; internet www.nshk.org.hk; f. 1954; Chair. KEITH KAM; Pres. LEE CHO-JAT.

Publishers

Asia 2000 Ltd: Rm 4, 26/F, Global Trade Centre, 15 Wing Kin Rd, Kwai Chung, New Territories; tel. 25301409; fax 25261107; e-mail sales@asia2000.com.hk; internet www.asia2000.com.hk; Asian studies, politics, photography, fiction; Man. Dir MICHAEL MORROW.

Chinese University Press: Units 1–3 and 18, 9/F, Sha Tin Galleria, 18–24 Shan Mei St, Fo Tan, New Territories; tel. 29465300; fax 26036692; e-mail cup@cuhk.edu.hk; internet www.chineseupress.com; f. 1977; studies on China and Hong Kong and other academic works; Dir QI GAN.

Commercial Press (Hong Kong) Ltd: Eastern Central Plaza, 8/F, 3 Yiu Hing Rd, Shau Kei Wan; tel. 25651371; fax 25645277; e-mail info@commercialpress.com.hk; internet www.commercialpress.com.hk; f. 1897; trade books, dictionaries, textbooks, Chinese classics, art, etc.; Chair. and Man. Dir CHAN MAN HUNG.

Excerpta Medica Asia Ltd: 1601, 16/F, Leighton Centre, 77 Leighton Rd, Causeway Bay; tel. 29651300; fax 29760778; e-mail emal@excerptahk.com; subsidiary of Elsevier; f. 1980; sponsored medical publications, abstracts, journals, etc.

Hoi Fung Publisher Co: 125 Lockhart Rd, 2/F, Wanchai; tel. 25286246; fax 25286249; Dir K. K. TSE.

Hong Kong University Press: Hing Wai Centre, 14/F, 7 Tin Wan Praya Rd, Aberdeen; tel. 25502703; fax 28750734; e-mail hkupress@hku.hk; internet www.hkupress.org; f. 1956; Publr MICHAEL DUCKWORTH.

Ling Kee Publishing Co Ltd: 14/F, Zung Fu Industrial Bldg, 1067 King's Rd, Quarry Bay; tel. 25616151; fax 28111980; e-mail admin@lingkee.com; internet www.lingkee.com; f. 1956; educational and reference; Chair. B. L. AU; Man. Dir K. W. AU.

Oxford University Press (China) Ltd: Warwick House East, 18/F, 979 King's Rd, Taikoo Place, Quarry Bay; tel. 25163126; fax 25658491; e-mail elt.china.hk@oup.com; internet www.oupchina.com.hk; f. 1961; school textbooks, reference, academic and general works relating to Hong Kong, Macao, Taiwan and China; Regional Dir SIMON LI.

Taosheng Publishing House: Lutheran Bldg, 3/F, 50A Waterloo Rd, Yau Ma Tei, Kowloon; tel. 23887061; fax 27810413; e-mail taosheng@elchk.org.hk; Dir CHANG CHUN WA.

Textile Asia/Business Press Ltd: California Tower, 11/F, 30–32 D'Aguilar St, GPOB 185, Central; tel. 25233744; fax 28106966; e-mail texasia@biznetvigator.com; internet www.textileasia-businesspress.com; f. 1970; textile magazine; Man. Dir KAYSER W. SUNG.

The Woods Publishing Co: Li Yuen Bldg, 2/F, 7 Li Yuen St West, Central; tel. 25233002; fax 28453296; e-mail tybook@netvigator.com; Production Man. TONG SZE HONG.

Times Publishing (Hong Kong) Ltd: Seaview Estate, Block C, 10/F, 2–8 Watson Rd, North Point; tel. 25668381; fax 25080255; e-mail abeditor@asianbusiness.com.hk; trade magazines and directories; CEO COLIN YAM; Executive Editor JAMES LEUNG.

GOVERNMENT PUBLISHING HOUSE

Government Information Services: see Government Offices.

PUBLISHERS' ASSOCIATIONS

Hong Kong Publishers' and Distributors' Association: Flat C, 4/F, 240–246 Nathan Rd, Kowloon; tel. 23674412; 45 mems; Chair. HO KAM-LING; Sec. HO NAI-CHI.

Hong Kong Publishing Federation Ltd: Room 904, SUP Tower, 75–83 King's Rd, North Point; tel. 25786000; fax 25786838.

Hong Kong Publishing Professionals Society Ltd: 8/F, Eastern Central Plaza, 3 Yiu Hing Rd, Shaukeiwan; tel. 29766804; fax 25645270; Chair. Dr CHAN MAN HUNG.

The Society of Publishers in Asia: Hang Seng North Point Bldg, 7/F, 341 King's Rd, North Point; tel. 28071212; fax 28877026; e-mail mail@sopasia.com; internet www.sopasia.com; f. 1982; Chair. DAVE SMITH.

Broadcasting and Communications

REGULATORY AUTHORITY

A Communications Authority: 39/F, Revenue Tower, 5 Gloucester Rd, Wanchai; tel. 29616333; fax 25072218; email webmaster@ofca.gov.hk; unified regulatory body for broadcasting and telecommunications sectors, merging the functions and responsibilities of the Broadcasting Authority and the Telecommunications Authority with effect from 1 April 2012; Chair. AMBROSE HO.

TELECOMMUNICATIONS

All sectors of the Hong Kong telecommunications industry were liberalized by the early 2000s and there are no restrictions on foreign ownership. At February 2012 there were 17 companies licensed to provide local fixed carrier services, 185 internet service providers licensed to provide broadband services, and five mobile network operators: China Mobile (Hong Kong) Company Limited, CSL Limited, PCCW-HKT Telephone Ltd, Hong Kong Telecommunications (HKT) Ltd, Hutchison Telephone Company Ltd and SmarTone Mobile Communications Ltd. At December 2011 there were 14.930,948 mobile subscribers in Japan.

Asia Satellite Telecommunications Co Ltd (AsiaSat): 19/F, Sunning Plaza, 10 Hysan Ave, Causeway Bay; tel. 25000888; fax 25000895; e-mail as-mkt@asiasat.com; internet www.asiasat.com; f. 1988; Pres. and CEO WILLIAM WADE.

China Mobile Ltd: 60/F, The Center, 99 Queen's Rd, Central; tel. 31218888; fax 25119092; internet www.chinamobileltd.com; f. 1997; leading mobile services provider in mainland China, operating through its 31 subsidiaries in all 31 provinces, autonomous regions and municipalities in the People's Republic; 584m. subscribers (December 2010); Chair. and CEO XI GUOHUA.

China Unicom (Hong Kong) Ltd: 75/F, The Center, 99 Queen's Rd, Central; tel. 21262018; fax 21262016; e-mail info@chinaunicom.com.hk; internet www.chinaunicom.com.hk; f. 2000; internet and telephone service provider; operates throughout China; 57.8% shares held by Unicom Group; 303.5m. subscribers (July 2010); Chair. and CEO CHANG XIAOBING.

CSL Limited: Unit 501-8, 5/F Cyberport 3, 100 Cyberport Road; tel. 28834688; fax 29626111; e-mail customerservice@hkcsl.com; internet www.hkcsl.com; f. 1983; CEO JOSEPH O'KONEK.

Hutchison Telecommunications Hong Kong: 22/F, Hutchison House, 10 Harcourt Rd; tel. 21281188; fax 21281778; internet www.hthkh.com; Chair. CANNING FOK KIN-NING.

PCCW-HKT Telephone Ltd: 39/F, PCCW Tower, Taikoo Place, 979 King's Rd, Quarry Bay; tel. 25145084; e-mail ir@hkt.com; internet www.pccw.com; fmrly Cable and Wireless HKT Ltd, acquired by PCCW in Aug. 2000; telecommunications, multimedia, information and communications technology services provider; Chair. RICHARD LI; Group Man. Dir ALEXANDER ARENA.

SmarTone Mobile Communications Limited: 31/F, Millennium City II, 378 Kwun Tong Rd, Kwun Tong, Kowloon; tel. 28802688; fax 28816405; e-mail customer_care@smartone.com; internet www.smartone.com; CEO DOUGLAS LI.

BROADCASTING

Radio

Radio Television Hong Kong is the only public broadcaster. Digital audio broadcasting services were launched in November 2011.

Digital Broadcasting Corporation: Unit 302, Level 3, IT St, Cyberport 3, 100 Cyberport Rd; tel. 22971999; e-mail info@dbc.hk; internet www.dbc.hk; Chair. HOI-YING.

Hong Kong Commercial Broadcasting Co Ltd: 3 Broadcast Drive, KCPOB 73000, Kowloon; tel. 23394810; fax 23380021; e-mail comradio@crhk.com.hk; internet www.881903.com; f. 1959; broadcasts in English and Cantonese on three radio frequencies; Chair. G. J. HO; Dir and CEO RITA CHING-HAN CHAN.

Metro Broadcast Corpn Ltd (Metro Broadcast): Basement 2, Site 6, Whampoa Garden, Hunghom, Kowloon; tel. 36988000; fax 21239889; e-mail prenquiry@metroradio.com.hk; internet www.metroradio.com.hk; f. 1991; broadcasts on three channels in English, Cantonese and Mandarin; Man. Dir BIANCA MA.

Phoenix U Radio: 2–6 Dai King St, Tai Po Industrial Estate, Tai Po; tel. 22008888; e-mail uradio@phoenixtv.com; internet www.uradiohk.com; f. 2011; owned by the Phoenix Group.

Radio Television Hong Kong: Broadcasting House, 30 Broadcast Drive, Kowloon; tel. 23369314; fax 23380279; e-mail ccu@rthk.org.hk; internet rthk.hk; f. 1928; govt-funded; 24-hour service in English, Cantonese and Mandarin on seven radio channels; Dir ROY TANG YUN-KWONG.

Television

Hong Kong has begun the switch to digital television services; analogue broadcasting services were originally scheduled to end in 2012, but in June 2011 this was postponed until 2015.

Asia Television Ltd (ATV): 25–31 Dai Shing St, Tai Po Industrial Estate, Tai Po; tel. 29928888; fax 23380438; e-mail atv@atv.com.hk; internet www.hkatv.com; f. 1973; operates eight commercial television services (English and Chinese) and produces television programmes; Chair. WONG PO-YAN.

Hong Kong Cable Television Ltd: Cable TV Tower, 9 Hoi Shing Rd, Tsuen Wan; tel. 21126868; fax 21127878; e-mail info@i-cablecomm.com; internet www.i-cablecomm.com; f. 1993; subsidiary of i-CABLE Communications Ltd; 24-hour subscription service of news, sport and entertainment on 100 channels; carries BBC World Service Television; Chair. and CEO STEPHEN NG.

Phoenix Satellite Television: No. 9, Tower 1, Seashore Square, 18 Defeng St, Kowloon; tel. 26219888; fax 26219898; internet www.ifeng.com; f. 1995; partly owned by News Corpn (USA); Mandarin; three domestic and two international channels; CEO LIU CHANGLE.

Radio Television Hong Kong: see Radio; produces drama, documentary and public affairs programmes; also operates an educational service for transmission by two local commercial stations; Dir ROY TANG YUN-KWONG.

STAR Group Ltd: One Harbourfront, 8/F, 18 Tak Fung St, Hunghom, Kowloon; tel. 26218888; fax 26213050; e-mail corp_aff@startv.com; internet www.startv.com; f. 1990; subsidiary of News Corpn; broadcasts over 40 channels in English, Hindi, Tamil, Mandarin, Cantonese, Korean and Thai, including a range of sports programmes, music, movies, news, entertainment and documentaries; reaches more than 300m. people in 53 countries across Asia and the Middle East, with a daily audience of about 130m. people; has interests in cable systems in India and Taiwan; services also extend to terrestrial and cable TV, wireless and digital media platforms.

Television Broadcasts Ltd (TVB): TVB City, 77 Chun Choi St, Tseung Kwan O Industrial Estate, Kowloon; tel. 23352288; fax 23581300; e-mail external.affairs@tvb.com.hk; internet www.tvb.com; f. 1967; operates Chinese and English language television programme services; Chair. NORMAN LEUNG NAI PANG.

Finance

(cap. = capital; res = reserves; dep. = deposits; m. = million; brs = branches; amounts in Hong Kong dollars unless otherwise stated)

BANKING

In 2012 there were 153 licensed banks operating in Hong Kong. There were also 20 restricted licence banks (formerly known as licensed deposit-taking companies), 25 deposit-taking companies and 60 foreign banks' representative offices.

Hong Kong Monetary Authority (HKMA): 55/F, Two International Finance Centre, 8 Finance St, Central; tel. 28788196; fax 28788197; e-mail hkma@hkma.gov.hk; internet www.hkma.gov.hk; f. 1993; est. by merger of Office of the Commr of Banking and Office of the Exchange Fund; govt authority responsible for maintaining monetary and banking stability; manages official reserves in the Exchange Fund; Chief Exec. NORMAN CHAN.

Banks of Issue

Bank of China (Hong Kong) Ltd (People's Repub. of China): Bank of China Tower, 1 Garden Rd, Central; tel. 28266888; fax 28105963; internet www.bochk.com; f. 1917; became third bank of issue in May 1994; merged in Oct. 2001 with the local branches of 11 mainland banks (incl. Kwangtung Provincial Bank, Sin Hua Bank Ltd, China and the South Sea Bank Ltd, Kincheng Banking Corpn, China State Bank, National Commercial Bank Ltd, Yien Yieh Commercial Bank Ltd, Hua Chiao Commercial Bank Ltd and Po Sang Bank Ltd), to form the Bank of China (Hong Kong); cap. 43,043m., res 49,049m., dep. 1,012,119m. (Dec. 2009); CEO HE GUANGBEI; 270 brs.

The Hongkong and Shanghai Banking Corporation Ltd (HSBC): 1 Queen's Rd, Central; tel. 28221111; fax 28101112; internet www.hsbc.com.hk; f. 1865; personal and commercial banking; cap. 22,494m., res 84,063m., dep. 3,681,436m. (Dec. 2009); Chair. STUART GULLIVER; CEO ANITA FUNG; more than 600 offices world-wide.

Standard Chartered Bank: Standard Chartered Bank Bldg, 4–4A Des Voeux Rd, Central; tel. 28203333; fax 28569129; internet www.standardchartered.com.hk; f. 1859; cap. 97m., res 38,626m., dep. 608,128m. (2009); Chair. C. K. CHOW; CEO BENJAMIN HUNG; more than 500 offices worldwide.

Other Commercial Banks

Bank of East Asia Ltd: Bank of East Asia Bldg, 16/F, 10 Des Voeux Rd, Central; tel. 36083608; fax 36086000; e-mail chengwcm@hkbea.com; internet www.hkbea.com; inc in Hong Kong in 1918, absorbed United Chinese Bank Ltd in Aug. 2001, and First Pacific Bank (FPB) in April 2002; cap. 4,623m., res 23,549m., dep. 358,681m. (Dec. 2009); Chair. and Chief Exec. DAVID K. P. LI; 91 domestic brs, 23 overseas brs.

Chiyu Banking Corpn Ltd: 78 Des Voeux Rd, Central; tel. 28430111; fax 28104207; e-mail chiyu@chiyubank.com; internet www.chiyubank.com; f. 1947; mem. of Bank of China (Hong Kong); cap. 300m., res 583.3m., dep. 34,450.3m. (Dec. 2009); Chair. HE GUANGBEI; 24 brs.

Chong Hing Bank Ltd: 17–18/F, Chong Hing Bank Centre, 24 Des Voeux Rd, Central; tel. 37681021; fax 37681383; e-mail info@chbank.com; internet www.chbank.com; f. 1948; fmrly Liu Chong Hing Bank; cap. 217.5m., res 6,924m., dep. 62,280.5m. (Dec. 2009); Chair. LIU LIT-MO; CEO LIU LIT-CHI; 51 domestic brs, 3 overseas brs.

CITIC Bank International Ltd: 232 Des Voeux Rd, Central; tel. 36036633; fax 36034000; e-mail info@citicbankintl.com; internet www.citicbankintl.com; f. 1922; cap. 7,283.3m., res 203.2m., dep. 101,908.7m. (Dec. 2009); acquired Hong Kong Chinese Bank Ltd Jan. 2002; fmrly CITIC Ka Wah Bank Ltd, name changed as above in 2010; Chair. DOU JIANZHONG; CEO DOREEN CHAN HUI DOR LAM; 30 domestic brs.

Dah Sing Bank Ltd: Dah Sing Financial Centre, 36/F, 108 Gloucester Rd, Central; tel. 25078866; fax 25985052; e-mail ops@dahsing.com.hk; internet www.dahsing.com; f. 1947; cap. 3,600.0m., res 102.9m., dep. 92,684.8m. (Dec. 2009); Chair. DAVID S. Y. WONG; Man. Dir DEREK H. H. WONG; 39 domestic brs.

DBS Bank (Hong Kong) Ltd: 11/F, The Center, 99 Queen's Rd, Central; tel. 22188822; fax 21678222; e-mail hkcs@dbs.com; internet www.dbs.com.hk; f. 1938; inc in 1954 as Kwong On Bank, name changed 2000; subsidiary of the Development Bank of Singapore; cap. 7,000m., res 13,677m., dep. 193,753.2m. (Dec. 2009); acquired Dao Heng Bank and Overseas Trust Bank July 2003; Chair. KWA CHONG SENG; CEO AMY YIP; 32 brs.

Hang Seng Bank Ltd: 83 Des Voeux Rd, Central; tel. 21983422; fax 28684047; e-mail ccdca@hangseng.com; internet www.hangseng.com; f. 1933; a principal member of the HSBC group, which has an ownership of 62.14%; cap. 9,559m., res 10,946m., dep. 687,163m. (Dec. 2009); Chair. RAYMOND C. F. CH'IEN; Vice-Chair. and CEO MARGARET LEUNG; 149 brs in Hong Kong, 17 in mainland China and 1 in Macao; also rep. office in Taipei.

Industrial and Commercial Bank of China (Asia): 33/F, ICBC Tower, 3 Garden Rd, Central; tel. 25881188; fax 28051166; e-mail enquiry@icbcasia.com; internet www.icbcasia.com; f. 1964; fmrly Union Bank of Hong Kong; cap. 2,636.6m., res 10,286m., dep. 185,296m. (Dec. 2009); Chair. JIANG JIANQING; 42 brs.

Mevas Bank: 33/F, Dah Sing Financial Centre, 108 Gloucester Rd, Wanchai; tel. 31013286; fax 31013298; e-mail contactus@mevas.com; internet www.mevas.com; cap. 400m., res. 1,646m., dep. 3,632.7m. (Dec. 2009); Chair. DAVID S. Y. WONG; CEO HO MAN-CHAN.

Nanyang Commercial Bank Ltd: 151 Des Voeux Rd, Central; tel. 28520888; fax 28153333; e-mail nanyang@ncb.com.hk; internet www.ncb.com.hk; f. 1949; cap. 700m., res 19,609.2m., dep. 131,306.2m. (Dec. 2009); Chair. ZHOU ZAIQUN; 41 brs, 2 overseas brs.

Public Bank (Hong Kong) Ltd: Public Bank Centre, 2/F, 120 Des Voeux Rd, Central; tel. 25410009; fax 25452866; e-mail contact@publicbank.com.hk; internet www.publicbank.com.hk; f. 1934; fmrly Asia Commercial Bank; name changed as above June 2006; cap. 1,481.6m., res 3,387.9m., dep. 30,625.4m. (Dec. 2010); Chair. Tan Sri Dato' Sri Dr TEH HONG PIOW; CEO TAN YOKE KONG; 32 domestic brs, 3 overseas.

Shanghai Commercial Bank Ltd: 12 Queen's Rd, Central; tel. 28415415; fax 28104623; e-mail contact@shacombank.com.hk; internet www.shacombank.com.hk; f. 1950; cap. 2,000m., res 8,247.9m., dep. 95,086.6m. (Dec. 2009); Chair. LINCOLN CHU KUEN YUNG; CEO, Man. Dir and Gen. Man. DAVID SEK-CHI KWOK; 42 domestic brs, 5 overseas brs.

Standard Bank Asia Ltd: 36/F, Two Pacific Place, 88 Queensway, Central; tel. 28227888; fax 28227999; e-mail askbanking@standardbank.com.hk; internet www.standardbank.com; f. 1970; est. as Jardine Fleming & Co Ltd; renamed Jardine Fleming Bank Ltd in 1993; absorbed by Standard Bank Investment Corpn Ltd; current name adopted in July 2001; cap. US $72m., res US $62.5m., dep. US $788m. (Dec. 2009); Chair. ROB A. G. LEITH.

Tai Yau Bank Ltd: 29/F, Tai Tung Bldg, 8 Fleming Rd, Wanchai; tel. 25223296; f. 1947; cap. 300.0m., res 203.3m., dep. 1,597.5m. (Dec. 2009); Chair. KO FOOK KAU.

Wing Hang Bank Ltd: 161 Queen's Rd, Central; tel. 28525111; fax 28517127; e-mail whbpsd@whbhk.com; internet www.whbhk.com; f. 1937; cap. 295.0m., res 12,226.1m., dep. 127,416.2m. (Dec. 2009); acquired Chekiang First Bank Ltd in Aug. 2004; Chair. and Chief Exec. PATRICK Y. B. FUNG; 40 domestic brs, 13 overseas brs.

Wing Lung Bank Ltd: 45 Des Voeux Rd, Central; tel. 28268333; fax 28100592; e-mail wlb@winglungbank.com; internet www.winglungbank.com; f. 1933; cap. 1,160.9m., res 1,388.6m., dep. 98,686m. (Dec. 2009); Chair. MA WEIHUA; Exec. Dir and Chief Exec. ZHU QUI; 41 domestic brs, 4 overseas brs, 1 rep. office in China.

Principal Foreign Banks

ABN AMRO Bank NV (Netherlands): 37/F, Cheung Kong Center 2, Queens Rd, Central; tel. 37633700; fax 37633709; internet www.abnamroprivatebanking.com/hongkong; CEO (Asia) HANS DIEDEREN; 3 brs.

American Express International Inc (USA): 18/F, Cityplaza 4, 12 Taikoo Wan Rd, Taikoo Shing; tel. 22771010; internet www.americanexpress.com/hk; Senior Country Exec. DOUGLAS H. SHORT III; 3 brs.

Australia and New Zealand Banking Group Ltd: 17/F, One Exchange Square, 8 Connaught Place, Central; tel. 21768888; fax 39182211; internet www.anz.com.au/hongkong; CEO SUSAN YUEN.

Bangkok Bank Public Co Ltd (Thailand): Bangkok Bank Bldg, 28 Des Voeux Rd, Central; tel. 28016688; fax 28015679; e-mail bangkokbank@bbl.com.hk; Gen. Man. KHUN SITTHICHAI JIWATTANAKUL; 2 brs.

Bank of Communications, Hong Kong Branch: 20 Pedder St, Central; tel. 28419611; fax 28106993; e-mail enquiry@bankcomm.com.hk; internet www.bankcomm.com.hk; f. 1934; Gen. Man. FANG LIANKUI; 41 brs.

Bank of India: Ruttonjee Centre, 2/F, Dina House, 11 Duddell St, Central; tel. 25240186; fax 28771178; e-mail boihk@netvigator.com; internet www.bankofindia.com.hk; Chief Exec. B. G. KURUP.

Bank Negara Indonesia: G/F, Far East Finance Centre, 16 Harcourt Rd; tel. 28618600; fax 28656500; Gen. Man. BRAMONO DWIEDJANTO.

Bank of Tokyo-Mitsubishi UFJ Ltd (Japan): 8/F, AIG Tower, 1 Connaught Rd, Central; tel. 28236666; fax 25293821.

Barclays Capital Asia Ltd: Cheung Kong Center, 41/F, 2 Queen's Rd, Central; tel. 29032000; fax 29032999; internet www.barcap.com; f. 1972; Chair. and CEO ROBERT A. MORRICE.

BNP Paribas (France): 59–63/F, Two International Finance Centre, 8 Finance St, Central; tel. 29098888; fax 28652523; e-mail didier.balme@bnpgroup.com; internet www.bnpparibas.com.hk; f. 1958; Chief Exec. MIGNONNE CHENG; 2 brs.

Crédit Agricole Corporate and Investment Bank (France): 27/F, Two Pacific Place, 88 Queensway, Central; tel. 28267333; fax 28261270; fmrly Calyon Bank, above name adopted in 2010; Country Officer FRANÇOIS RAMEAU; 1 br.

China Construction Bank (Asia) Corpn Ltd: 16/F, York House, The Landmark, 15 Queen's Rd Central, Central; tel. 27795533; fax 25218555; internet www.asia.ccb.com; fmrly Bank of America (Asia); wholly owned subsidiary of China Construction Bank Corpn; commercial banking and retail banking; cap. 6,511m., res 9,485.1m., dep. 64,859.8m. (Dec. 2009); Pres. and CEO MIRANDA KWOK; 41 brs in Hong Kong; 9 brs in Macao.

Citibank, NA (USA): Citibank Tower, 39–40/F and 44–50/F, Citibank Plaza, 3 Garden Rd, Central; tel. 28688888; fax 25230949; internet www.citibank.com.hk; CEO (Asia Pacific) SHIRISH APTE; 26 brs.

Commerzbank AG (Germany): 29/F, Two International Finance Centre, 8 Finance St, Central; tel. 39880680; fax 39880698; internet www.commerzbank.com.hk; Man. STEFAN GÖHMANN; 1 br.

Crédit Suisse (Switzerland): 23/F, Three Exchange Square, 8 Connaught Place, Central; tel. 28414888; fax 28400012; internet www.credit-suisse.com/hk; CEO (Asia-Pacific) OSAMA ABBASI.

Deutsche Bank AG (Germany): 52/F, International Commerce Centre, 1 Austin Rd West, Kowloon; tel. 22038888; fax 22037300; internet www.db.com/hongkong; Gen. Mans Dr MICHAEL THOMAS, REINER RUSCH; 1 br.

Indian Overseas Bank: 3/F, Ruttonjee House, 11 Duddell St, Central; tel. 25227157; fax 28451549; e-mail iobsm@netvigator.com; internet www.iobhongkong.com; f. 1955; CEO SRINIVASAN KRISHNAMACHARY; 2 brs.

JP Morgan Chase Bank (USA): 39/F, One Exchange Square, Connaught Place, Central; tel. 28431234; fax 28414396.

Malayan Banking Berhad (Malaysia): 21/F, Man Yee Bldg, 68 Des Voeux Rd, Central; tel. 35188888; fax 35188889; f. 1962; trades in Hong Kong as Maybank; Gen. Man. AMOS ONG SEET JOON; 2 brs.

Mizuho Corporate Bank Ltd (Japan): 17/F, Two Pacific Place, 88 Queensway, Admiralty; tel. 21033040; fax 28101326; Man. Dir and CEO NOBORU AKATSUKA; 1 br.

National Bank of Pakistan: POB 99006, 1103 Fourseas Bldg, 208–212 Nathan Rd, Kowloon; tel. 23697355; fax 27245622; e-mail nbphkkm@netvigator.com; CEO GHULAM HUSSAIN AZHAR.

Oversea-Chinese Banking Corpn Ltd (Singapore): 9/F, 9 Queen's Rd, Central; tel. 28406200; fax 28453439; Gen. Man. BENJAMIN YEUNG; 3 brs.

Philippine National Bank: 26/F, Worldwide House, 19 Des Voeux Rd, Central; tel. 25431066; fax 25253107; e-mail pnbhkgrp@pnbhk.com; Gen. Man. RODEL BICOL; 1 br.

N. M. Rothschild and Sons (Hong Kong) Ltd: 16/F, Alexandra House, 16–20 Chater Rd, Central; tel. 25255333; fax 28106997; e-mail jackson.woo@rothschild.com.hk; cap. 308.8m., dep. 22.9m. (Dec. 2007); Chair. RUSSELL EDEY.

Société Générale Asia Ltd (France): Level 38, Three Pacific Place, 1 Queen's Rd East; tel. 21665388; fax 28682368; internet www.sgcib.hk; Head (Asia-Pacific) HIKARU OGATA.

Sumitomo Mitsui Banking Corpn (SMBC) (Japan): 7–8/F, One International Finance Centre, 1 Harbour View St, Central; tel. 22062000; fax 22062888; Gen. Man. TOSHIO MORIKAWA; 1 br.

UBAF (Hong Kong) Ltd (France): The Sun's Group Centre, 21/F, 200 Gloucester Rd, Wanchai; tel. 25201361; fax 25274256; e-mail larry.yap@ubaf.fr; cap. US $30.1m., dep. US $10.4m. (Dec. 2009); Man. Dir LARRY S. YAP.

United Overseas Bank Ltd (Singapore): 25/F, Gloucester Tower, The Landmark, 15 Queen's Rd, Central; tel. 29108888; fax 28105506; internet www.uobgroup.com/hk; Sr Vice-Pres. and CEO WEE EE CHEONG; 5 brs.

Banking Associations

Chinese Banks' Association Ltd: South China Bldg, 5/F, 1–3 Wyndham St, Central; tel. 25224789; fax 28775102; 1,666 mems; chaired by Bank of East Asia.

DTC Association (Hong Kong Association of Restricted Licence Banks and Deposit-Taking Companies): Unit 2404, 24/F, Bonham Trade Centre, 50 Bonham Strand East, Sheung Wan; tel. 25264079; fax 25230180; e-mail dtca@dtca.org.hk; internet www.dtca.org.hk; f. 1981; Sec. PUI CHONG LUND; 50 mem. banks.

Hong Kong Association of Banks: Rm 525, Prince's Bldg, Central; tel. 25211169; fax 28685035; e-mail info@hkab.org.hk; internet www.hkab.org.hk; f. 1981; est. to succeed The Exchange Banks' Asscn of Hong Kong; all licensed banks in Hong Kong are required by law to be mems of this statutory body, the function of which is to represent and further the interests of the banking sector; 132 mems; chaired by Bank of China (HK) Ltd; Sec. EVA WONG.

STOCK EXCHANGE

Hong Kong Exchanges and Clearing Ltd (HKEx): 12/F, One International Finance Centre, 1 Harbour View St, Central; tel. 25221122; fax 22953106; e-mail info@hkex.com.hk; internet www.hkex.com.hk; f. 2000; est. by merger of the Stock Exchange of Hong Kong, the Hong Kong Futures Exchange and the Hong Kong Securities Clearing Co; Chair. CHOW CHUNG-KONG; CEO CHARLES LI.

SUPERVISORY BODY

Securities and Futures Commission (SFC): 8/F, Chater House, 8 Connaught Rd, Central; tel. 28409222; fax 25217836; e-mail enquiry@sfc.hk; internet www.sfc.hk; f. 1989; regulates the securities and futures markets; Chair. EDDY FONG; CEO ASHLEY ALDER.

INSURANCE

In 2012 there were 163 authorized insurance companies, of which 98 were pure general insurers, 45 were pure long-term insurers and the remaining 20 were composite insurers. The following are among the principal companies:

ACE Insurance Ltd: 25/F, Shui On Centre, 6–8 Harbour Rd, Wanchai; tel. 31916800; fax 25603565; e-mail inquiries.hk@acegroup.com; internet www.aceinsurance.com.hk; Pres. and CEO (Asia-Pacific) DAMIEN SULLIVAN.

American Home Assurance Co: AIA Bldg, 1 Stubbs Rd, Wanchai; tel. 28321800; e-mail cs@aiu.com.hk; internet www.aiu.com.hk.

Asia Insurance Co Ltd: Worldwide House, 16/F, 19 Des Voeux Rd, Central; tel. 36069933; fax 28100218; e-mail mailbox@afh.hk; internet www.asiainsurance.com.hk; Chair. ROBIN CHAN.

Aviva Life Insurance Co Ltd: Suite 1701, Cityplaza One, 1111 King's Rd, Taikoo Shing; tel. 35509600; fax 29071787; e-mail enquiry@aviva-asia.com; internet www.aviva.com.hk; Gen. Man. ELBA TSE.

AXA General Insurance Hong Kong Ltd: 21/F, Manhattan Pl., 23 Wang Tai Rd, Kowloon Bay; tel. 25233061; fax 28100706; e-mail axahk@axa-insurance.com.hk; internet www.axa-insurance.com.hk; CEO BILLY CHAN.

Bank of China Group Insurance Co Ltd: 9/F, Wing On House, 71 Des Voeux Rd, Central; tel. 28670888; fax 25221705; e-mail info_ins@bocgroup.com; internet www.bocgroup.com/bocg-ins.

China Taiping Insurance (HK) Co Ltd: China Taiping Tower, 19/F, 8 Sunning Rd, Causeway Bay; tel. 28151551; fax 25416567; e-mail mai@mingan.com.hk; internet www.mingan.com; f. 1949; fmrly Ming An Insurance Co Ltd, name changed as above in 2009; Chair. LIN FAN; CEO CHENG KWOK PING.

Hong Kong Export Credit Insurance Corpn: South Seas Centre, Tower I, 2/F, 75 Mody Rd, Tsim Sha Tsui East, Kowloon; tel. 27329988; fax 27226277; internet www.hkecic.com; f. 1966; est. by govt to encourage and support trade; Commr RALPH LAI; Gen. Man. CYNTHIA CHIN.

HSBC Insurance (Asia) Ltd: 18/F, Tower 1, HSBC Centre, 1 Sham Mong Road, Kowloon; tel. 22886688; fax 28277636; e-mail insurance@hsbc.com.hk; internet www.insurance.asiapacific.hsbc.com; Man. Dir JASON SADLER.

MSIG Insurance (Hong Kong) Ltd: 9/F, Cityplaza One, 1111 King's Rd, Taikoo Shing; tel. 28940555; fax 28905741; e-mail hk_hotline@hk.msig-asia.com; internet www.msig.com.hk; CEO KENNETH REID.

Prudential Assurance Co Ltd: 23/F, One Exchange Square, Central; tel. 22811333; fax 29771233; e-mail service@prudential.com.hk; internet www.prudential.com.hk; life and general; CEO DEREK YUNG.

QBE Hongkong and Shanghai Insurance Ltd: 17/F, Warwick House, West Wing, Taikoo Place, 979 King's Rd, Quarry Bay; tel. 28778488; fax 36070300; e-mail info.hk@qbe.com.hk; internet www.qbe.com.hk; Gen. Man. JECKY LUI.

Royal and Sun Alliance (Hong Kong) Ltd: Dorset House, 32/F, Taikoo Place, 979 King's Rd, Quarry Bay; tel. 29683000; fax 29685111; e-mail hotline@hk.rsagroup.com; internet www.rsagroup.com.hk; Chief Exec. SIMON LEE.

Swiss Re Hong Kong Branch: 61/F, Central Plaza, 18 Harbour Rd, Wanchai; tel. 28274345; fax 28276033; acquired Mercantile and General Reinsurance in 1996; Head (Asia) MARTYN PARKER.

Zurich Insurance Group (Hong Kong): 24–27/F, One Island East, 18 Westlands Rd, Island East; tel. 29682222; fax 29680988; e-mail enquiry@hk.zurich.com; internet www.zurich.com.hk; CEO TED RIDGWAY.

Insurance Associations

Hong Kong Federation of Insurers (HKFI): 29/F, Sunshine Plaza, 353 Lockhart Rd, Wanchai; tel. 25201868; fax 25201967; e-mail hkfi@hkfi.org.hk; internet www.hkfi.org.hk; f. 1988; 87 general insurance and 47 life insurance mems; Chair. ALLAN YU.

Insurance Institute of Hong Kong: Rm 1705, Beverly House, 93–107 Lockhart Rd, Wanchai; tel. 25200098; fax 22953939; e-mail enquiry@iihk.org.hk; internet www.iihk.org.hk; f. 1967; Pres. MICHAEL HAYNES.

Trade and Industry

Hong Kong Trade Development Council: 38/F, Office Tower, Convention Plaza, 1 Harbour Rd, Wanchai; tel. 1830668; fax 28240249; e-mail hktdc@hktdc.org; internet www.hktdc.com; f. 1966; Chair. JACK SO CHAK-KWONG; Exec. Dir FREDERICK LAM.

Trade and Industry Department: Rm 912B, Trade and Industry Department Tower, 700 Nathan Rd, Kowloon; tel. 23985388; fax 23989173; e-mail lrc@tid.gov.hk; internet www.tid.gov.hk; Dir-Gen. MARIA KWAN.

DEVELOPMENT ORGANIZATIONS

Hong Kong Housing Authority: 33 Fat Kwong St, Homantin, Kowloon; tel. 27122712; fax 27114111; e-mail hkha@housingauthority.gov.hk; internet www.housingauthority.gov.hk; f. 1973; plans, builds and manages public housing; Chair. EVA CHENG; Dir of Housing D. W. PESCOD.

Hong Kong Productivity Council: HKPC Bldg, 78 Tat Chee Ave, Yau Yat Chuen, Kowloon Tong, Kowloon; tel. 27885678; fax 27885900; e-mail hkpcenq@hkpc.org; internet www.hkpc.org; f. 1967; promotes increased productivity and international competitiveness of industry; Council comprises a Chair. and 22 mems appointed by the Govt, representing managerial, labour, academic and professional interests, and govt depts associated with productivity matters; Chair. CLEMENT CHEN CHENG-JEN; Exec. Dir AGNES MAK TANG PIK-YEE.

CHAMBERS OF COMMERCE

Chinese Chamber of Commerce, Kowloon: 2/F, 8–10 Nga Tsin Long Rd, Kowloon; tel. 23822309; f. 1936; 234 mems; Chair. and Exec. Dir YEUNG CHOR-HANG.

Chinese General Chamber of Commerce: 4/F, 24–25 Connaught Rd, Central; tel. 25256385; fax 28452610; e-mail cgcc@cgcc.org.hk; internet www.cgcc.org.hk; f. 1900; 6,000 mems; Chair. JONATHAN CHOI KOON-SHUM.

Hong Kong General Chamber of Commerce: United Centre, 22/F, 95 Queensway, POB 852. Admiralty; tel. 25299229; fax 25279843; e-mail chamber@chamber.org.hk; internet www.chamber.org.hk; f. 1861; 4,000 mems; Chair. ANTHONY WU; CEO ALEX FONG.

Kowloon Chamber of Commerce: KCC Bldg, 3/F, 2 Liberty Ave, Homantin, Kowloon; tel. 27600393; fax 27610166; e-mail kcc02@hkkcc.biz.com.hk; internet www.hkkcc.org.hk; f. 1938; 1,600 mems; Chair. CHENG KWAN SUEN; Sec. of Gen. Affairs CHENG PO-WO.

FOREIGN TRADE ORGANIZATIONS

Hong Kong Chinese Importers' and Exporters' Association: Champion Bldg, 7–8/F, 287–291 Des Voeux Rd, Central; tel. 25448474; fax 25814979; e-mail info@hkciea.org.hk; internet www.hkciea.org.hk; f. 1954; 3,000 mems; Pres. ZHUANG CHENG XIN.

Hong Kong Exporters' Association: Rm 825, Star House, 3 Salisbury Rd, Tsim Sha Tsui, Kowloon; tel. 27309851; fax 27301869; e-mail exporter@exporters.org.hk; internet www.exporters.org.hk; f. 1955; not-for-profit asscn; comprises leading merchants and manufacturing exporters; 598 mems (June 2011); Chair. TOM TANG; Exec. Dir SHIRLEY SO.

INDUSTRIAL AND TRADE ASSOCIATIONS

Chinese Manufacturers' Association of Hong Kong: CMA Bldg, 64 Connaught Rd, Central; tel. 25456166; fax 25414541; e-mail info@cma.org.hk; internet www.cma.org.hk; f. 1934; promotes and protects industrial and trading interests; operates testing and certification laboratories; 3,700 mems; Pres. IRONS SZE WING-WAI.

Communications Association of Hong Kong: GPOB 13461; tel. 25042732; fax 25042752; e-mail info@cahk.hk; internet www.cahk.hk; 108 mems; Chair. Dr HUBERT CHAN.

Federation of Hong Kong Garment Manufacturers: Unit 401–403, Cheung Lee Commercial Bldg, 25 Kimberley Rd, Tsim Sha Tsui, Kowloon; tel. 27211383; fax 23111062; e-mail info@garment.org.hk; internet www.garment.org.hk; f. 1964; 120 mems; Pres. YEUNG FAN; Sec.-Gen. MICHAEL LEUNG.

Federation of Hong Kong Industries (FHKI): 31/F, Billion Plaza, 8 Cheung Yue St, Cheung Sha Wan, Kowloon; tel. 27323188; fax 27213494; e-mail fhki@fhki.org.hk; internet www.industryhk.org; f. 1960; 3,000 mems; Chair. CLIFF SUN; Dir-Gen. DENNIS T. W. YAU.

Federation of Hong Kong Watch Trades and Industries Ltd: Peter Bldg, Rm 604, 58–62 Queen's Rd, Central; tel. 25233232; fax 28684485; e-mail hkwatch@hkwatch.org; internet www.hkwatch.org; f. 1947; 650 mems; Chair. JOSEPH CHU KAI TO.

Hong Kong Association for the Advancement of Science and Technology Ltd: 2A, Tak Lee Commercial Bldg, 113–117 Wanchai Rd, Wanchai; tel. 28913388; fax 28381823; e-mail info@hkaast.org.hk; internet www.hkaast.org.hk; f. 1985; 170 mems; Pres. YUNG QILIANG.

Hong Kong Biotechnology Association Ltd: Rm 1007, 10/F, Hang Seng Bldg, 77 Des Voeux Rd, Central; tel. 28770222; fax 26201238; e-mail secretary@hkbta.org.hk; internet www.hkbta.org.hk; f. 1999; 100 mems; Chair. FRANK WAN.

Hong Kong Chinese Enterprises Association: Rm 2104–2106, Harbour Centre, 25 Harbour Rd, Wanchai; tel. 28272831; fax 28272606; e-mail info@hkcea.com; internet www.hkcea.com; f. 1991; 960 mems; Pres. FENG HONGZHENG.

Hong Kong Chinese Textile Mills Association: 11/F, 38–40 Tai Po Rd, Sham Shiu Po, Kowloon; tel. 27778236; fax 27881836; f. 1921; 150 mems; Pres. Dr ROGER NG KENG-PO.

Hong Kong Construction Association Ltd: 3/F, 180–182 Hennessy Rd, Wanchai; tel. 25724414; fax 25727104; e-mail admin@hkca.com.hk; internet www.hkca.com.hk; f. 1920; 372 mems; Pres. CONRAD WONG.

Hong Kong Electronic Industries Association Ltd: Rm 1201, 12/F, Harbour Crystal Centre, 100 Granville Rd, Tsim Sha Tsui, Kowloon; tel. 27788328; fax 27882200; e-mail hkeia@hkeia.org; internet www.hkeia.org; 310 mems; Chair. Dr K. B. CHAN; Exec. Dir ALFRED WONG.

Hong Kong Footwear Association: Kar Tseuk Bldg, 2/F, Blk A, 185 Prince Edward Rd, Kowloon; internet www.hkfootwear.org; f. 1948; over 300 mems; Pres. TOMMY FONG.

Hong Kong Garment Manufacturers Association: Unit 401–403, Cheung Lee Commercial Bldg, 25 Kimberley Rd, Tsim Sha Tsui, Kowloon; tel. 23052893; fax 23052493; e-mail sec@textilecouncil.com; f. 1987; 40 mems; Chair. PETER WANG.

Hong Kong Information Technology Federation Ltd: KITEC, 1 Trademart Dr., Kowloon Bay, Kowloon; tel. 31018197; fax 30074728; e-mail info@hkitf.com; internet www.hkitf.org.hk; over 300 mems; f. 1980; Pres. FRANCIS FONG.

Hong Kong Jewellery and Jade Manufacturers Association: Flat A, 12/F, Kaiser Estate Phase 1, 41 Man Yue St, Hunghom, Kowloon; tel. 25430543; fax 28150164; e-mail hkjja@hkjja.org; internet www.jewellery-hk.org; f. 1965; 227 mems; Pres. CHARLES CHAN; Chair. BILLY LAU.

Hong Kong Jewelry Manufacturers' Association: Unit G, 2/F, Kaiser Estate Phase 2, 51 Man Yue St, Hunghom, Kowloon; tel. 27663002; fax 23623647; e-mail enquiry@jewelry.org.hk; internet www.jewelry.org.hk; f. 1988; 345 mems; Chair. SUNNY CHAN.

Hong Kong Knitwear Exporters and Manufacturers Association: Unit 401–403, Cheung Lee Commercial Bldg, 25 Kimberley Rd, Tsim Sha Tsui, Kowloon; tel. 27552621; fax 27565672; f. 1966; 70 mems; Chair. LAWRENCE LEUNG; Exec. Sec. KARINA TSUI.

Hong Kong Optical Manufacturers' Association Ltd: 2/F, 11 Fa Yuen St, Mongkok, Kowloon; tel. 23326505; fax 27705786; e-mail hkoma@netvigator.com; internet www.hkoptical.org.hk; f. 1982; 111 mems; Pres. HUI LEUNG WAH.

Hong Kong Plastics Manufacturers Association Ltd: Rm 3, 10/F, Asia Standard Tower, 59–65 Queen's Rd, Central; tel. 25742230; fax 25742843; f. 1957; 200 mems; Chair. CLIFF SUN; Pres. JEFFREY LAM.

Hong Kong Printers Association: 1/F, 48–50 Johnston Rd, Wanchai; tel. 25275050; fax 28610463; e-mail printers@hkprinters.org; internet www.hkprinters.org; f. 1939; 400 mems; Chair. YEUNG KAM KAI.

Hong Kong Sze Yap Commercial and Industrial Association: Cosco Tower, Unit 1205–6, 183 Queen's Rd, Central; tel. 25438095; fax 25449495; e-mail gahk_ltd@hotmail.com; f. 1909; 1,082 mems; Chair. LOUIE CHICK-NAN; Sec. WONG KA CHUN.

Hong Kong Toys Council: 31/F, Billion Plaza, 8 Cheung Yue St, Cheung Sha Wan, Kowloon; tel. 27323188; fax 27213494; e-mail hktc@fhki.org.hk; internet www.toyshk.org; f. 1986; 200 mems; Chair. BERNIE TING WAI CHEUNG; Sec.-Gen. JOSEPH LI.

Hong Kong Watch Manufacturers' Association: Fu Hing Bldg, 2/F, 10 Jubilee St, Central; tel. 25225238; fax 28106614; e-mail hkwma@netvigator.com; internet www.hkwma.org; 650 mems; Pres. PAUL SO; Sec.-Gen. HUNG HAN SANG.

Information and Software Industry Association Ltd: China Overseas Bldg, 24B, 139 Hennessy Rd, Wanchai; tel. 26222867; fax 26222731; e-mail info@isia.org.hk; internet www.isia.org.hk; f. 1999; 76 mems; Chair. REGGIE WONG.

New Territories Commercial and Industrial General Association Ltd: Cheong Hay Bldg, 2/F, 107 Hoi Pa St, Tsuen Wan; tel. 24145316; fax 24934130; e-mail ntciga@netvigator.com; f. 1973; 2,663 mems; Pres. YU WAN; Chair. WAN HOK LIM; Sec.-Gen. HUANG JINHUI.

Real Estate Developers Association of Hong Kong: Worldwide House, Rm 1403, 19 Des Voeux Rd, Central; tel. 28260111; fax 28452521; f. 1965; 829 mems; Pres. Dr STANLEY HO; Chair. KEITH KERR; Sec.-Gen. LOUIS LOONG.

Textile Council of Hong Kong Ltd: 401–3, Cheung Lee Commercial Bldg, 25 Kimberley Rd, Tsim Sha Tsui, Kowloon; tel. 23052893; fax 23052493; e-mail sec@textilecouncil.com; internet www.textilecouncil.com; f. 1989; 11 mems; Chair. WILLY LIN; Exec. Dir MICHAEL LEUNG.

Toys Manufacturers' Association of Hong Kong Ltd: Rm 1302, Metroplaza, Tower 2, 223 Hing Fong Rd, Kwai Chung, New Territories; tel. 24221209; fax 31880982; e-mail info@tmhk.net; internet www.tmhk.net; f. 1996; 250 mems; Pres. SAMSON CHAM.

EMPLOYERS' ORGANIZATIONS

Employers' Federation of Hong Kong: Suite 2004, Sino Plaza, 255–257 Gloucester Rd, Causeway Bay; tel. 25280033; fax 28655285; e-mail info@efhk.org.hk; internet www.efhk.org.hk; f. 1947; 504 mems; Chair. JOHN CHAN; Exec. Dir LOUIS PONG.

Hong Kong Factory Owners' Association Ltd: Wing Wong Bldg, 11/F, 557–559 Nathan Rd, Kowloon; tel. 23882372; fax 23857129; f. 1982; 1,261 mems; Pres. HWANG JEN; Sec. CHA KIT YEN.

UTILITIES

Electricity

CLP Power Ltd: 147 Argyle St, Kowloon; tel. 26788111; fax 27604448; e-mail clp_info@clp.com.hk; internet www.clpgroup.com; f. 1918; fmrly China Light and Power Co Ltd; generation and supply of electricity to Kowloon and the New Territories; Chair. Sir MICHAEL D. KADOORIE; CEO ANDREW BRANDLER.

The Hongkong Electric Co Ltd (HK Electric): 44 Kennedy Rd; tel. 28433111; fax 28100506; e-mail mail@hkelectric.com; internet www.hkelectric.com; generation and supply of electricity to Hong Kong Island, and the islands of Ap Lei Chau and Lamma; Chair. CANNING FOK KIN-NING; Man. Dir TSO KAI SUM.

Gas

Gas Authority: all gas supply cos, gas installers and contractors are required to be registered with the Gas Authority. At the end of 2003 there were seven registered gas supply cos.

Chinese People Holdings Co Ltd: Unit 2111, 21/F, China Merchants Tower, Shun Tak Centre, 168–200 Connaught Rd, Central; tel. 29022008; fax 28030108; e-mail info@681hk.com; internet www.681hk.com; distributes and supplies natural gas in mainland China; Chair. Dr MO SHIKANG; Man. Dir JIN SONG.

The Hong Kong and China Gas Co Ltd (Towngas): 23/F, 363 Java Rd, North Point; tel. 29633388; fax 25616182; e-mail ccd@towngas.com; internet www.towngas.com; f. 1862; production, distribution and marketing of gas, water and energy related activities in Hong Kong and mainland China; operates two plants; Chair. LEE SHAU KEE; Man. Dir ALFRED CHAN WING KIN.

Water

Drainage Services Department: responsible for planning, designing, constructing, operating and maintaining the sewerage, sewage treatment and stormwater drainage infrastructures.

Water Supplies Department: 48/F, Immigration Tower, 7 Gloucester Rd, Wanchai; tel. 28294500; fax 28240578; e-mail wsdinfo@wsd.gov.hk; internet www.wsd.gov.hk; responsible for water supplies for some 7m. people living within 1,100 sq km of the Hong Kong SAR; Dir MA LEE TAK.

TRADE UNIONS

In December 2011 there were 836 trade unions in Hong Kong, comprising 788 employees' unions, 18 employers' associations and 30 mixed organizations.

Hong Kong and Kowloon Trades Union Council (TUC): 11/F, On Cheong Bldg, 456 Nathan Rd, Kowloon; tel. 23845150; fax 27705396; e-mail hktuc@yahoo.com.hk; f. 1949; 66 affiliated unions, mostly covering the catering and building trades; 30,000 mems; supports Taiwan; affiliated to ITUC; Pres. TONG WOON FAI; Gen. Sec. LEE TAK-MING.

Hong Kong Confederation of Trade Unions: Wing Wong Commercial Bldg, 19/F, 557–559 Nathan Rd, Kowloon; tel. 27708668; fax 27707388; e-mail hkctu@hkctu.org.hk; internet www.hkctu.org.hk; f. 1990; registered Feb. 1990; 90 affiliated independent unions and federations; 170,000 mems; affiliated to ITUC and IFWEA; Pres. PUN TIN CHI; Gen. Sec. LEE CHEUK-YAN.

The Hong Kong Federation of Trade Unions (HKFTU): 12 Ma Hang Chung Rd, Tokwawan, Kowloon; tel. 36525700; fax 27608477; e-mail info@ftu.org.hk; internet www.ftu.org.hk; f. 1948; 221 affiliated and associated unions, mostly in textiles, printing, insurance, construction, manufacturing, civil service, wholesale & retail, public transport and public utilities; approx. 341,000 mems; Pres. CHENG YIU-TONG; Chair. NG CHAU-PEI.

In addition, the Federation of Hong Kong and Kowloon Labour Unions has 70 affiliated unions with 41,587 mems.

Transport

Transport Department: 41/F Immigration Tower, 7 Gloucester Rd, Wanchai; tel. 28042600; fax 28240433; e-mail tdenq@td.gov.hk; internet www.td.gov.hk; Commr JOSEPH LAI.

RAILWAYS

Kowloon–Canton Railway Corpn: 8/F, Fo Tan Railway House, 9 Lok King St, Fo Tan, New Territories; tel. 26881333; fax 31241073; e-mail admin@kcrc.com; internet www.kcrc.com; f. 1982; operated by the Kowloon–Canton Railway Corpn, a public statutory body; assets controlled by MTR Corpn since 2007; also provides passenger and freight services to and from various cities on the mainland; plans for 17-km railway to link Sha Tin and Central via a new cross-harbour tunnel and thus provide the first direct rail route from the Chinese border to Hong Kong Island; Chair. K. C. CHAN; CEO Ir JAMES BLAKE.

MTR Corporation: MTR Tower, Telford Plaza, 33 Wai Strip St, Kowloon Bay; tel. 28818888; fax 27959991; internet www.mtr.com.hk; f. 1975; first section of underground mass transit railway (MTR) system opened in 1979; merged operations with Kowloon–Canton Railway Corpn in 2007; nine railway lines serving Hong Kong Island, Kowloon and New Territories; 26-km Guangzhou–Shenzhen–Hong Kong Express Rail Link to be completed by 2015; CEO JAY WALDER; Chair. Dr RAYMOND K. F. CH'IEN.

TRAMWAYS

Hong Kong Tramways Ltd: Whitty Street Tram Depot, Connaught Rd West, Western District; tel. 21186338; fax 21186038; e-mail enquiry@hktramways.com; internet www.hktramways.com; f. 1904; operates six routes and 161 double-deck trams between Kennedy Town and Shaukeiwan; Man. Dir BRUNO CHARRADE.

ROADS

In 2009 there were 2,050 km of public roads in Hong Kong. Almost all of them are concrete or asphalt surfaced. Owing to the hilly terrain, and the density of building development, the scope for substantial increase in the road network is limited. Work on a bridge linking Hong Kong's Lantau Island with Macao and Zhuhai City, in the Chinese province of Guangdong, commenced in late 2009. Spanning nearly 50 km and comprising a six-lane expressway, the project was scheduled for completion in 2016.

Highways Department: Ho Man Tin Government Offices, 5/F, 88 Chung Hau St, Ho Man Tin, Kowloon; tel. 29264111; fax 27145216; e-mail hydenquiry@1823.gov.hk; internet www.hyd.gov.hk; f. 1986; planning, design, construction and maintenance of the public road system; co-ordination of major highway and railway projects; Dir PETER LAU KA-KEUNG.

FERRIES

Conventional ferries, hoverferries, catamarans and jetfoils operate between Hong Kong, China and Macao. There is also an extensive network of ferry services to outlying districts.

Hongkong and Yaumati Ferry Co Ltd: 98 Tam Kon Shan Rd, Ngau Kok Wan, North Tsing Yi, New Territories; tel. 23944294; fax 27869001; e-mail hkferry@hkf.com; internet www.hkf.com; licensed routes on ferry services, incl. excursion, vehicular and dangerous goods; Chair. COLIN K. Y. LAM.

Shun Tak-China Travel Ship Management Ltd (TurboJET): 83 Hing Wah St West, Lai Chi Kok, Kowloon; tel. 23070880; fax 27865125; e-mail enquiry@turbojet.com.hk; internet www.turbojet.com.hk; f. 1999; operates hydrofoil services between Hong Kong, Macao and Shenzhen.

The Star Ferry Co Ltd: Star Ferry Pier, Kowloon Point, Tsim Sha Tsui, Kowloon; tel. 23677065; fax 21186028; e-mail sf@starferry.com.hk; internet www.starferry.com.hk; f. 1898; operates 8 passenger ferries between Tsim Sha Tsui and Central, the main business district of Hong Kong; between Central and Hung Hom; between Tsim Sha Tsui and Wanchai; and between Wanchai and Hung Hom; also a licensed harbour tour ferry service at Victoria Harbour; Man. Dir FRANKIE YICK.

SHIPPING

Hong Kong is one of the world's largest shipping centres and among the busiest container ports. At the end of 2009 the shipping register comprised a fleet of 1,529 vessels, totalling 45.3m. grt. The container terminals at Kwai Chung are privately owned and operated. The construction of a ninth terminal (CT9) at Kwai Chung was completed in 2004, bringing the total number of berths to 24. Lantau Island has been designated as the site for any future expansion.

Marine Department, Hong Kong Special Administrative Region Government: Harbour Bldg, 22/F, 38 Pier Rd, Central, GPOB 4155; tel. 25423711; fax 25417194; e-mail mdenquiry@mardep.gov.hk; internet www.mardep.gov.hk; Dir ROGER TUPPER.

Shipping Companies

Anglo-Eastern Ship Management Ltd: 23/F, 248 Queen's Rd East, Wanchai; tel. 28636111; fax 28612419; e-mail commercial@angloeasterngroup.com; internet www.aesm.com.hk; f. 1974; merged with Denholm Ship Management in 2001; CEO PETER CREMERS; Man. Dir MARCEL LIEDTS.

COSCO (Hong Kong) Shipping Co Ltd (CHS): 52/F, Cosco Tower, 183 Queen's Rd, Central; tel. 28098865; fax 25485653; internet www.coscochs.com.hk; established by merger of former Ocean Tramping Co Ltd and Yick Fung Shipping and Enterprise Co; owned by COSCO (Hong Kong) Group Ltd; Chair. Capt. WEI JIAFU; Man. Dir LI ZHENYU.

Fairmont Shipping (HK) Ltd: Fairmont House, 21/F, 8 Cotton Tree Dr., Central; tel. 25218338; fax 28104560; e-mail vcrmnt@fairmontshipping.com; Pres. ROBERT HO.

Hong Kong Ming Wah Shipping Co: Unit 3701, China Merchants Tower, 37/F, Shun Tak Centre, 168–200 Connaught Rd, Central; tel. 25172128; fax 25473482; e-mail mwbs@hkmw.com.hk; internet www.hkmw.com.hk; f. 1980; subsidiary of China Merchants Group; Chair. QIN XIAO; Pres. FU YUNING.

Island Navigation Corpn International Ltd: Harbour Centre, 28–29/F, 25 Harbour Rd, Wanchai; tel. 28333222; fax 28270001; Man. Dir M. H. LIANG.

Jardine Shipping Services: 24/F, Devon House, Taikoo Place, 979 King's Rd; tel. 25793001; fax 28569927; e-mail Eric.van.der.Hoeven@jardineshipping.com; internet www.jardine-shipping.com; CEO ERIC VAN DER HOEVEN.

Oak Maritime (HK) Inc Ltd: 2301 China Resources Bldg, 26 Harbour Rd, Wanchai; tel. 25063866; fax 25063563; e-mail mail01@oakhk.com; Chair. STEVE G. K. HSU; Man. Dir JACK HSU.

Orient Overseas Container Line Ltd: 31/F, Harbour Centre, 25 Harbour Rd, Wanchai; tel. 28333888; fax 25318122; e-mail hkgcsd@oocl.com; internet www.oocl.com; mem. of the Grand Alliance of shipping cos (five partners); Chair. C. C. TUNG; CEO PHILIP CHOW.

Teh-Hu Cargocean Management Co Ltd: Unit B, Fortis Bank Tower, 15/F, 77–79 Gloucester Rd, Wanchai; tel. 25988688; fax 28249339; e-mail tehhuhk@on-nets.com; f. 1974; Man. Dir KENNETH K. W. LO.

Wah Kwong Shipping Holdings Ltd: Shanghai Industrial Investment Bldg, 26/F, 48–62 Hennessy Rd, POB 283; tel. 25279227; fax 28656544; e-mail wk@wahkwong.com.hk; internet www.wahkwong.com.hk; Chair. GEORGE S. K. CHAO.

Wallem Shipmanagement Ltd: 12/F Warwick House East, Taikoo Place, 979 King's Rd, Quarry Bay; tel. 28768200; fax 28761234; e-mail wsmhk@wallem.com; internet www.wallem.com; Man. Dir JIM NELSON.

Associations

Hong Kong Cargo-Vessel Traders' Association: 21–23 Man Wai Bldg, 2/F, Ferry Point, Kowloon; tel. 23847102; fax 27820342; e-mail info@cvta.com.hk; internet www.cvta.com.hk; 978 mems; Chair. CHOW YAT-TAK; Sec. CHAN BAK.

Hong Kong Shipowners' Association: Queen's Centre, 12/F, 58–64 Queen's Rd East, Wanchai; tel. 25200206; fax 25298246; e-mail hksoa@hksoa.org.hk; internet www.hksoa.org.hk; f. 1957; 181 mems; Chair. KENNETH KOO; Man. Dir ARTHUR BOWRING.

Hong Kong Shippers' Council: Rm 2407, Hopewell Centre, 183 Queen's Rd East, Wanchai; tel. 28340010; fax 28919787; e-mail shippers@hkshippers.org.hk; internet www.hkshippers.org.hk; 63 mems; Chair. WILLY LIN; Exec. Dir SUNNY HO.

CIVIL AVIATION

The international airport on the island of Chek Lap Kok, near Lantau Island, opened in 1998. Construction of a third runway was under consideration in 2012. A new cargo terminal was scheduled to start operating in 2013. Hong Kong was served by over 100 airlines operating nearly 900 daily flights in 2012.

Airport Authority of Hong Kong: HKIA Tower, 1 Sky Plaza Rd, Hong Kong International Airport, Lantau; tel. 21887111; fax 28240717; internet www.hongkongairport.com; f. 1995; scheduled for privatization; Chair. MARVIN CHEUNG KIN-TUNG; CEO STANLEY H. C. HUI.

Civil Aviation Department: 46/F, Queensway Government Offices, 66 Queensway, Admiralty; tel. 28674332; fax 28690093; e-mail enquiry@cad.gov.hk; internet www.cad.gov.hk; Dir-Gen. NORMAN LO SHUNG-MAN.

AHK Air Hong Kong Ltd: 4/F, South Tower, Cathay Pacific City, 8 Scenic Rd, Hong Kong International Airport, Lantau; tel. 27618588; fax 27618486; e-mail ahk.hq@airhongkong.com.hk; internet www.airhongkong.com.hk; f. 1986; regional cargo carrier; wholly owned subsidiary of Cathay Pacific Airways Ltd; COO RICHARD CATER.

Cathay Pacific Airways Ltd: 7/F, North Tower, Cathay Pacific City, 8 Scenic Rd, Hong Kong International Airport, Lantau; tel. 27477222; fax 27535751; internet www.cathaypacific.com; f. 1946; services to more than 40 major cities in the Far East, Middle East, North America, Europe, South Africa, Australia and New Zealand; Chair. CHRISTOPHER D. PRATT; CEO JOHN SLOSAR.

Hong Kong Airlines Ltd: 7/F, One Citygate, 20 Tat Tung Rd, Tung Chung, Lantau; tel. 31511800; fax 31511838; e-mail crd@hkairlines.com; internet www.hkairlines.com; f. 2004; flights to mainland China, Japan, Philippines, Singapore, Indonesia, Viet Nam, Taiwan, Thailand and Moscow; Pres. YANG JIANG HONG; CEO KALID RAZACK.

Hong Kong Dragon Airlines Ltd (Dragonair): Dragonair House, 11 Tung Fai Rd, Hong Kong International Airport, Lantau; tel. 31933888; fax 31933889; internet www.dragonair.com; f. 1985; scheduled and charter flights to destinations throughout mainland China and to Bangladesh, Thailand, Cambodia, Brunei, Malaysia,

Taiwan and Japan; wholly owned subsidiary of Cathay Pacific Airways Ltd; CEO JAMES TONG.

Sky Shuttle Helicopters Ltd: Rm 1603, 16/F, China Merchants Tower, Shun Tak Centre, 200 Connaught Rd, Central; tel. 21089988; fax 21089938; e-mail info@skyshuttlehk.com; internet www.skyshuttlehk.com; f. 1990; fmrly East Asia Airlines; merged with Helicopters Hong Kong Ltd in 1998; renamed as Heli Express Ltd in 2005, and as above in 2008; operates helicopter services between Hong Kong, Macao and Shenzhen (China); CEO CHEYENNE CHAN.

Tourism

Tourism is a major source of foreign exchange. Receipts from tourism estimated US $22,951m. in 2010. Visitor arrivals rose by nearly 22% in 2010 to exceed 36.0m. (of whom almost 22.7m. travelled from mainland China). In 2010 the 175 licensed hotels offered 60,428 rooms, while tourist guesthouses totalled 619, with 5,926 rooms available. A Disneyland theme park opened in 2005.

Hong Kong Tourism Board (HKTB): 9–11/F, Citicorp Centre, 18 Whitfield Rd, North Point; tel. 28076543; fax 28060303; e-mail info@hktb.com; internet www.discoverhongkong.com; f. 1957; est. as Hong Kong Tourist Asscn; reconstituted as Hong Kong Tourism Bd in April 2001; co-ordinates and promotes the tourist industry; has govt support and financial assistance; up to 20 mems of the Bd represent the Govt, the private sector and the tourism industry; Chair. JAMES TIEN; Exec. Dir ANTHONY LAU.

Defence

In July 1997 a garrison of 4,800 troops belonging to the Chinese People's Liberation Army (PLA) was established in Hong Kong. The garrison can intervene in local matters only at the request of the Hong Kong Government, which remains responsible for internal security. A total of 7,000 Chinese troops were stationed in Hong Kong in 2007.

Defence Expenditure: Projected expenditure on internal security in 2006/07 totalled HK $92.7m.

Commander of the PLA Garrison in Hong Kong: Lt-Gen. ZHANG SHIBO.

Education

Full-time education is free and compulsory in Hong Kong between the ages of six and 15. In 2008/09 the duration of free education was extended from nine to 12 years. In 2010/11 an estimated 148,940 children attended kindergartens, which totalled 951. A total of 331,112 children attended primary schools, while secondary school pupils totalled 449,737. There are three main types of secondary school in Hong Kong: grammar, technical and pre-vocational schools. In 2009/10 total enrolment at primary and secondary schools was equivalent to 90% of the school-age population. Primary enrolment in 2009/10 included an estimated 94% of children in the relevant age-group, while the comparable ratio for secondary enrolment in the same year was 75% (males 75%, females 76%). An education reform programme was in progress from 2000, including reform of curriculum and education management, and the establishment of Project Yi Jin, a life-long learning initiative. Budgetary expenditure on general education was an estimated HK $29,195m. in the financial year 2009/10, accounting for 10.0% of total expenditure.

MACAO

Introductory Survey

LOCATION, CLIMATE, LANGUAGE, RELIGION, FLAG, CAPITAL

The Special Administrative Region (SAR) of Macao comprises the peninsula of Macao, an enclave on the mainland of southern China, and two nearby islands, Taipa, which is linked to the mainland by three bridges, and Coloane. The latter island is connected to Taipa by a causeway and by a large area of reclaimed land. The territory lies opposite Hong Kong on the western side of the mouth of the Xijiang (Sikiang) River. The climate is subtropical, with temperatures averaging 15°C in January and 29°C in July. There are two official languages, Chinese (Cantonese being the principal dialect) and Portuguese. English is also widely spoken. The predominant religions are Roman Catholicism, Chinese Buddhism, Daoism and Confucianism. The flag of the Macao SAR (proportions 2 by 3), introduced upon the territory's reversion to Chinese sovereignty in December 1999 and flown subordinate to the flag of the People's Republic of China, displays a stylized white flower below an arc of one large and four small yellow stars, above five white lines, on a green background. The executive and legislative bodies of Macao are based in the city of Macao, which is situated on the peninsula.

CONTEMPORARY POLITICAL HISTORY

Historical Context

Established by Portugal in 1557 as a permanent trading post with China, Macao became a Portuguese Overseas Province in 1951. After the military coup in Portugal in April 1974, Col José Garcia Leandro was appointed Governor of the province. A new statute, promulgated in February 1976, redefined Macao as a 'Special Territory' under Portuguese jurisdiction, but with a great measure of administrative and economic independence. Proposals to enlarge the Legislative Assembly from 17 to 21 members, thus giving the Chinese population an increased role in the administration of Macao, were abandoned when they did not receive the approval of the Government of the People's Republic of China in March 1980. China and Portugal established diplomatic relations in February 1979.

Domestic Political Affairs

Col Leandro was replaced as the territory's Governor by Gen. Nuno de Melo Egídio, Deputy Chief of Staff of Portugal's armed forces, in February 1979. In June 1981 Gen. Egídio was replaced by Cdre (later Rear-Adm.) Vasco Almeida e Costa, a Portuguese former minister and naval commander. Following a constitutional dispute in March 1984 over the Governor's plans for electoral reform (extending the franchise to the ethnic Chinese majority), the Legislative Assembly was dissolved. Elections for a new Assembly were held in August, at which the Chinese majority were allowed to vote for the first time, regardless of their length of residence in the territory. Following the elections, the Assembly was dominated by ethnic Chinese deputies.

In January 1986 Governor Almeida e Costa resigned. In May he was replaced by Joaquim Pinto Machado, whose appointment represented a departure from the tradition of military governors for Macao. However, his political inexperience placed him at a disadvantage. In May 1987 he resigned, citing 'reasons of institutional dignity' (apparently referring to the problem of corruption in the Macao administration). He was replaced in August by Carlos Melancia, a former Socialist deputy in the Portuguese legislature, who had held ministerial posts in several Portuguese governments.

The first round of negotiations between the Portuguese and Chinese Governments on the future of Macao took place in June 1986 in Beijing. Portugal's acceptance of China's sovereignty greatly simplified the issue. On 13 April 1987, following the conclusion of the fourth round of negotiations, a joint declaration was formally signed in Beijing by the Portuguese and Chinese Governments, during an official visit to China by the Prime Minister of Portugal. According to the agreement (which was formally ratified in January 1988), Macao was to become a 'special administrative region' (SAR) of the People's Republic (to be known as Macao, China) on 20 December 1999. Macao was thus to have the same status as that agreed (with effect from 1997) for Hong Kong, and was to enjoy autonomy in most matters except defence and foreign policy. A Sino-Portuguese Joint Liaison Group (JLG), established to oversee the transfer of power, held its inaugural meeting in the Portuguese capital of Lisbon in April 1988. In 1999 a Chief Executive for Macao was to be appointed by the Chinese Government, following 'elections or consultations to be held in Macao', and the territory's legislature was to contain 'a majority of elected members'. The inhabitants of Macao were to become citizens of the People's Republic of China. The Chinese Government refused to allow the possibility of dual Sino-Portuguese citizenship, although Macao residents in possession of Portuguese passports were apparently to be permitted to retain them for travel purposes. The agreement guaranteed a 50-year period during which Macao would be permitted to retain its free capitalist economy, and to be financially independent of China.

In August 1988 a Macao Basic Law Drafting Committee was formed. Comprising 30 Chinese members and 19 representatives from Macao, the Committee was to draft a law determining the territory's future constitutional status within the People's Republic of China. Elections to the Legislative Assembly were held in October. Low participation (fewer than 30% of the electorate) was recorded, and a 'liberal' grouping secured three of the seats reserved for directly elected candidates, while a coalition of pro-Beijing and conservative Macanese (lusophone Eurasian) groups won the other three.

In January 1989 it was announced that Portuguese passports were to be issued to about 100,000 ethnic Chinese inhabitants, born in Macao before October 1981, and it was anticipated that as many as a further 100,000 would be granted before 1999. Unlike their counterparts in the neighbouring British dependent territory of Hong Kong, therefore, these Macao residents (but not all) were to be granted the full rights of a citizen of the European Community (EC, now European Union—EU, see p. 276). In February 1989 President Mário Soares of Portugal visited Macao, in order to discuss the transfer of the territory's administration to China.

Following the violent suppression of the pro-democracy movement in China in June 1989, as many as 100,000 residents of Macao participated in demonstrations in the enclave to protest against the Chinese Government's action, which caused great concern in Macao. In August, however, China assured Portugal that it would honour the agreement to maintain the capitalist system of the territory after 1999.

In March 1990 the implementation of a programme to grant permanent registration to parents of 4,200 Chinese residents, the latter having already secured the right of abode in Macao, developed into chaos when other illegal immigrants demanded a similar concession. The authorities decided to declare a general amnesty, but were unprepared for the numbers of illegal residents, some 50,000 in total, who rushed to take advantage of the scheme, thereby revealing the true extent of previous immigration from China. Border security was subsequently increased, in an effort to prevent any further illegal immigration.

In late March 1990 the Legislative Assembly approved the final draft of the territory's revised Organic Law. The Law was approved by the Portuguese Assembly of the Republic in mid-April, and granted Macao greater administrative, economic, financial and legislative autonomy, in advance of 1999. The powers of the Governor and of the Legislative Assembly, where six additional seats were to be created, were therefore increased. The post of military commander of the security forces was abolished, responsibility for the territory's security being assumed by a civilian Under-Secretary.

Meanwhile, in February 1990 it was alleged that Carlos Melancia had accepted a substantial bribe from a foreign company in connection with a contract for the construction of the new airport in Macao. Although he denied any involvement in the affair, the Governor resigned, and was replaced on an acting basis by the Under-Secretary for Economic Affairs, Dr Francisco Murteira Nabo. In September 1991 it was announced that Melancia and five others were to stand trial on charges of corruption. In August 1993 the former Governor was acquitted on the grounds of insufficient evidence.

Meanwhile, many observers believed that the enclave was being adversely affected by the political situation in Lisbon, as differences between the socialist President and centre-right Prime Minister were being reflected in rivalries between officials in Macao. In an attempt to restore confidence, therefore, President Soares visited the territory in November 1990. In January 1991, upon his re-election as head of state, the President appointed Gen. Vasco Rocha Vieira (who had previously served as the territory's Chief of Staff and as Under-Secretary for Public Works and Transport) Governor of Macao. In March 1991 the Legislative Assembly was expanded from 17 to 23 members. All seven Under-Secretaries were replaced in May.

The transition to Chinese sovereignty

Following his arrival in Macao, Gen. Rocha Vieira announced that China would be consulted on all future developments in the territory. The 10th meeting of the Sino-Portuguese JLG took place in Beijing in April 1991. Topics under regular discussion included the participation of Macao in international organizations, progress towards an increase in the number of local officials employed in the civil service (hitherto dominated by Portuguese and Macanese personnel) and the status of the Chinese language. The progress of the working group on the translation of local laws from Portuguese into Chinese was also examined, a particular problem being the lack of suitably qualified bilingual legal personnel. It was agreed that Portuguese was to remain an official language after 1999. The two sides also reached agreement on the exchange of identity cards for those Macao residents who would require them in 1999. Regular meetings of the JLG continued.

In July 1991 the Macao Draft Basic Law was published. Confidence in the territory's future was enhanced by China's apparent flexibility on a number of issues. Unlike the Hong Kong Basic Law, that of Macao did not impose restrictions on holders of foreign passports assuming senior posts in the territory's administration after 1999, the only exception being the future Chief Executive. In November 1991 the Governor of Macao visited China, where it was confirmed that the 'one country, two systems' policy would operate in Macao from 1999. In March 1993 the final draft of the Basic Law of the Macao SAR was ratified by the National People's Congress (NPC) in Beijing, which also approved the design of the future SAR's flag. The adoption of the legislation was welcomed by the Governor of Macao, who reiterated his desire for a smooth transfer of power in 1999. The Chief Executive of the SAR was to be selected by local representatives. The SAR's first Legislative Council was to comprise 23 members, of whom eight would be directly elected. Its term of office would expire in October 2001, when it would be expanded to 27 members, of whom 10 would be directly elected.

Meanwhile, elections to the Legislative Assembly were held in September 1992. The level of participation was higher than on previous occasions, with 59% of the registered electorate (albeit only 13.5% of the population) attending the polls. Fifty candidates contested the eight directly elective seats, four of which were won by members of the main pro-Beijing parties, the União Promotora para o Progresso (UPP) and the União para o Desenvolvimento (UPD).

Relations between Portugal and China remained cordial. In June 1993 the two countries reached agreement on all outstanding issues regarding the construction of the territory's airport and the future use of Chinese airspace. Furthermore, Macao was to be permitted to negotiate air traffic agreements with other countries. Later in the year visits by President Soares of Portugal to Macao and by the Chinese President, Jiang Zemin, to Lisbon took place.

In April 1994, during a visit to China, the Portuguese Prime Minister received an assurance that Chinese nationality would not be imposed on Macanese people of Portuguese descent, who would be able to retain their Portuguese passports. Speaking in Macao itself, the Prime Minister expressed confidence in the territory's future. In July a group of local journalists dispatched a letter, alleging intimidation and persecution in Macao, to President Soares, urging him to intervene to defend the territory's press freedom. The journalists' appeal followed an incident involving the director of the daily *Gazeta Macaense*, who had been fined for reproducing an article from a Lisbon weekly newspaper, and now awaited trial. The territory's press had been critical of the Macao Supreme Court's decision to extradite ethnic Chinese to the mainland (despite the absence of any extradition treaty) to answer criminal charges and risk the possibility of a death sentence.

The draft of the new penal code for Macao did not incorporate the death penalty. In January 1995, during a visit to Portugal, Vice-Premier Zhu Rongji of China confirmed that the People's Republic would not impose the death penalty in Macao after 1999, regarding the question as a matter for the authorities of the future SAR. The new penal code, prohibiting capital punishment, took effect in January 1996.

On another visit to the territory in April 1995, President Soares emphasized the need for Macao to assert its identity. He also stressed the importance of three issues: the modification of the territory's legislation; the rights of the individual; and the preservation of the Portuguese language. Travelling on to Beijing, accompanied by Gen. Rocha Vieira, the Portuguese President had successful discussions with his Chinese counterpart on various matters relating to the transition.

In December 1995, while attending the celebrations to mark the inauguration of the territory's new airport, President Soares had discussions with the Chinese Vice-President, Rong Yiren. During a four-day visit to Beijing in February 1996, the Portuguese Minister of Foreign Affairs, Jaime Gama (who urged that the rights and aspirations of the people of Macao be protected), met President Jiang Zemin and other senior officials, describing the discussions as positive. While acknowledging the sound progress of recent years, Gama and the Chinese Minister of Foreign Affairs agreed on an acceleration in the pace of work of the Sino-Portuguese JLG. In the same month Gen. Rocha Vieira was reappointed Governor of Macao by the newly elected President of Portugal, Jorge Sampaio. António Guterres, the new Portuguese Prime Minister, confirmed his desire for constitutional consensus regarding the transition of Macao.

At elections to the Legislative Assembly in September 1996 the pro-Beijing UPP received 15.2% of the votes and won two of the eight directly elective seats, while the UPD won 14.5% and retained one of its two seats. The business-orientated groups were more successful: the Associação Promotora para a Economia de Macau took 16.6% of the votes and secured two seats; the Convergência para o Desenvolvimento de Macau (CODEM) and the União Geral para o Desenvolvimento de Macau each won one seat. The pro-democracy Associação de Novo Macau Democrático (ANMD) also won one seat. The level of voter participation was 64%. The 23-member legislature was to remain in place beyond the transfer of sovereignty in 1999.

From 1996 there were numerous bomb attacks and brutal assaults, including several serious attacks on local casino staff. Many attributed the alarming increase in organized crime to the opening of the airport in Macao, which was believed to have facilitated the entry of rival gangsters from mainland China, Taiwan and Hong Kong. In May 1997, following the murder of three men believed to have associations with one such group of gangsters, the Chinese Government expressed its concern at the deterioration of public order in Macao and urged Portugal to observe its responsibility to maintain the enclave's social stability during the transitional period, while pledging the enhanced co-operation of the Chinese security forces in the effort to curb organized crime in Macao.

The freedom of Macao's press was jeopardized in June 1997, when several Chinese-language newspapers, along with a television station, received threats instructing them to cease reporting on the activities of the notorious 14K triad, a 10,000-member secret society to which much of the violence had been attributed. In July an explosive device was detonated in the grounds of the Governor's palace, although it caused no serious damage. In the following month China deployed 500 armed police officers to reinforce the border with Macao in order to intensify its efforts to combat illegal immigration, contraband and the smuggling of arms into the enclave. Despite the approval in July of a law further to restrict activities such as extortion and 'protection rackets', organized crime continued unabated. In early October the police forces of Macao and China initiated a joint campaign against illegal immigration.

Meanwhile, the slow progress of the 'three localizations' (civil service, laws and the adoption of Chinese as an official language) continued to concern the Government of China. In mid-1996 almost 50% of senior government posts were still held by Portuguese expatriates. In January 1997 the Governor pledged to accelerate the process with regard to local legislation, the priority being the training of the requisite personnel. In February President Sampaio travelled to both Macao and China, where he urged respect for Macao's identity and for the Luso-Chinese declaration regarding the transfer of sovereignty. In December 1997 details of the establishment in Macao of the office of the Chinese Ministry of Foreign Affairs, which was to commence operations in December 1999, were announced. In January 1998 the Macao Government declared that the vast majority of senior civil service posts were now held by local officials.

In March 1998 the Chinese authorities reiterated their concern at the deteriorating situation in Macao. In April, by which month none of the 34 triad-related murders committed since January 1997 had been solved, the Portuguese and Chinese Governments agreed to co-operate in the exchange of information about organized criminal activities. Also in April 1998 the trial, on charges of breaching the gaming laws, of the head of the 14K triad, Wan Kuok-koi ('Broken Tooth'), was adjourned for two months, owing to the apparent reluctance of witnesses to appear in court. In early May Wan Kuok-koi was rearrested and charged with the attempted murder of Macao's chief of police, António Marques Baptista, in a car-bomb attack. The case was dismissed by a judge three days later on the grounds of insufficient evidence. Wan Kuok-koi remained in prison, charged with other serious offences. His renewed detention led to a spate of arson attacks. The Portuguese Government was reported to have dispatched intelligence officers to the enclave to reinforce the local security forces. In June Marques Baptista travelled to Beijing and Guangzhou for discussions on the problems of cross-border criminal activity and drugs-trafficking.

The Preparatory Committee for the Establishment of the Macao SAR, which was to oversee the territory's transfer to Chinese sovereignty and was to comprise representatives from both the People's Republic and Macao, was inaugurated in Beijing in May 1998. Four subordinate working groups (supervising administrative, legal, economic, and social and cultural affairs) were subsequently established. The second plenary session of the Preparatory Committee was convened in July 1998, discussions encompassing issues such as the 'localization' of civil servants, public security and the drafting of the territory's fiscal budget for 2000. In July 1998, during a meeting with the Chinese Premier, the Governor of Macao requested an increase in the mainland's investment in the territory prior to the 1999 transfer of sovereignty.

In July 1998, as abductions continued and as it was revealed, furthermore, that the victims had included two serving members of the Legislative Assembly, President Jiang Zemin of China urged the triads of Macao to cease their campaign of intimidation. The police forces of Macao, Hong Kong and Guangdong Province launched 'S Plan', an operation aiming to curb the activities of rival criminal gangs. In August, in an apparent attempt to intimidate the judiciary, the territory's Attorney-General and his wife were shot and slightly wounded. In the following month five police officers and 10 journalists who were investigating a bomb attack were injured when a second bomb exploded.

In August 1998 representatives of the JLG agreed to intensify Luso-Chinese consultations on matters relating to the transitional period. In September, in response to the increasing security problems, China unexpectedly announced that, upon the transfer of sovereignty, it was to station troops in the territory. This abandonment of a previous assurance to the contrary caused much disquiet in Portugal, where the proposed deployment was deemed unnecessary. Although the Basic Law made no specific provision for the stationing of a mainland garrison, China asserted that it was to be ultimately responsible for the enclave's defence. By October, furthermore, about 4,000 soldiers of the People's Liberation Army (PLA) were on duty at various Chinese border posts adjacent to Macao. During a one-week visit to Beijing, the territory's Under-Secretary for Public Security had discussions with senior officials, including the Chinese Minister of Public Security. In mid-October four alleged members of the 14K triad were detained without bail in connection with the May car-bombing and other incidents.

In November 1998 procedures for the election of the 200 members of the Selection Committee were established by the Preparatory Committee. Responsible for the appointment of the members of Macao's post-1999 Government, the delegates of the Selection Committee were required to be permanent residents of the territory: 60 members were to be drawn from the business and financial communities, 50 from cultural, educational and professional spheres, 50 from labour, social service and religious circles and the remaining 40 were to be former political personages.

In November 1998 raids on casinos believed to be engaged in illegal activities, conducted by the authorities, resulted in several arrests. Further violence took place in December. At the end of that month it was confirmed that Macao residents of wholly Chinese origin would be entitled to full mainland citizenship, while those of mixed Chinese and Portuguese descent would be obliged to decide between the two nationalities. In January 1999 several protesters were arrested during demonstrations to draw attention to the plight of numerous immigrant children, who had been brought illegally from China to Macao to join their legitimately resident parents and whose irregular status precluded entitlement to the territory's education, health and social services.

In January 1999 details of the composition of the future PLA garrison were disclosed. The troops were to comprise solely ground forces, totalling fewer than 1,000 soldiers and directly responsible to the Commander of the Guangzhou Military Unit. They would be permitted to intervene to maintain social order in the enclave only if the local police were unable to control major triad-related violence or if street demonstrations posed a threat of serious unrest. In March, during a trip to Macao (where he had discussions with the visiting Portuguese President), Qian Qichen, a Chinese Vice-Premier, indicated that an advance contingent of PLA soldiers would be deployed in Macao prior to the transfer of sovereignty. Other sources of contention between China and Portugal remained the unresolved question of the post-1999 status of those Macao residents who had been granted Portuguese nationality and also the issue of the court of final appeal.

In April 1999, at the first plenary meeting of the Selection Committee, candidates for the post of the SAR's Chief Executive were elected. Edmund Ho received 125 of the 200 votes, while Stanley Au garnered 65 votes. Three other candidates failed to secure the requisite minimum of 20 votes. Edmund Ho and Stanley Au, both bankers and regarded as moderate pro-business candidates, thus proceeded to the second round of voting by secret ballot, held in May. Edmund Ho received 163 of the 199 votes cast, and confirmed his intention to address the problems of law and order, security and the economy. The Chief Executive-designate also fully endorsed China's decision to deploy troops in Macao.

During 1999, in co-operation with the Macao authorities, the police forces of Guangdong Province, and of Zhuhai in particular, initiated a new offensive against the criminal activities of the triads, which had been in regular evidence with further murders throughout the year. China's desire to deploy an advance contingent of troops prior to December 1999, however, reportedly continued to be obstructed by Portugal. Furthermore, the announcement that, subject to certain conditions, the future garrison was to be granted law-enforcement powers raised various constitutional issues. Nevertheless, many Macao residents appeared to welcome the mainland's decision to station troops in the enclave. In a further effort to address the deteriorating security situation, from December Macao's 5,800-member police force was to be restructured.

In July 1999 the penultimate meeting of the JLG took place in Lisbon. In August, in accordance with the nominations of the Chief Executive-designate, the composition of the Government of the future SAR was announced by the State Council in Beijing. Appointments included that of Florinda da Rosa Silva Chan as Secretary for Administration and Justice. Also in August an outspoken pro-Chinese member of the Legislative Assembly was attacked and injured by a group of unidentified assailants in an apparently random assault. In September the Governor urged improved co-operation with the authorities of Guangdong Province in order to combat organized crime, revealing that the majority of the inmates of Macao's prisons were not permanent residents of the territory. In the same month it was reported that 90 former Gurkhas of the British army were being drafted in as prison warders, following the intimidation of local officers. Also in September the Chief Executive-designate announced the appointment of seven new members of the Legislative Council, which was to succeed the Legislative Assembly in December. While the seven nominees of the Governor in the existing Legislative Assembly were thus to be replaced, 15 of the 16 elected members (one having resigned) were to remain in office as members of the successor Legislative Council. (However, in practice the new Legislative Council continued to be known by its former name.) At the same time the composition of the 10-member Executive Council was also announced.

In October 1999 President Jiang Zemin undertook a two-day visit to Portugal, following which it was declared that the outstanding question of the deployment of an advance contingent of Chinese troops in Macao had been resolved. The advance party was to be restricted to a technical mission, which entered the territory in early December. In November the 37th and last session of the JLG took place in Beijing, where in the same month the Governor of Macao held final discussions with President Jiang Zemin.

Meanwhile, in April 1999 Wan Kuok-koi had been acquitted of charges of coercing croupiers. In November his trial on other serious charges concluded: he was found guilty of criminal association and other illegal gambling-related activities and sentenced to 15 years' imprisonment. Eight co-defendants received lesser sentences. In a separate trial Artur Chiang Calderon, a former police officer alleged to be Wan Kuok-koi's military adviser, received a prison sentence of 10 years and six months for involvement in organized crime. While two other defendants were also imprisoned, 19 were released on the grounds of insufficient evidence. As the transfer of the territory's sovereignty approached, by mid-December almost 40 people had been murdered in triad-related violence since January 1999.

The inauguration of the SAR and subsequent events

In November 1999 representatives of the JLG reached agreement on details regarding the deployment of Chinese troops in Macao and on the retention of Portuguese as an official language. At midnight on 19 December 1999, therefore, in a ceremony attended by the Presidents and heads of government of Portugal and China, the sovereignty of Macao was duly transferred; 12 hours later (only after the departure from the newly inaugurated SAR of the Portuguese delegation), 500 soldiers of the 1,000-strong force of the PLA, in a convoy of armoured vehicles, crossed the border into Macao, where they were installed in a makeshift barracks. However, prior to the ceremony it was reported that the authorities of Guangdong Province had detained almost 3,000 persons, including 15 residents of Macao, suspected of association with criminal gangs. The celebrations in Macao were also marred by the authorities' handling of demonstrations by members of Falun Gong, a religious movement recently outlawed in China. The expulsion from Macao of several members of the sect in the days preceding the territory's transfer and the arrest of 30 adherents on the final day of Portuguese sovereignty prompted strong criticism from President Jorge Sampaio of Portugal. Nevertheless, in an effort to consolidate relations with the EU, in May 2000 the first official overseas visit of the SAR's Chief Executive was to Europe, his itinerary including Portugal. The EU agreed in principle in December to grant residents of Hong Kong and Macao visa-free access to member states, subject to final approval by the European Parliament.

In March 2000, in an important change to the immigration rules, it was announced that children of Chinese nationality whose parents were permanent residents of Macao would shortly be allowed to apply for residency permits. A monthly quota of 420 successful applicants was established, while the youngest children were to receive priority. In May hundreds of demonstrators participated in a march to protest against Macao's high level of unemployment. This shortage of jobs was attributed to the territory's use of immigrant workers, mainly from mainland China and South-East Asia, who were estimated to total 28,000. Trade unions continued to organize protests, and in July (for the first time since the unrest arising from the Chinese Cultural Revolution of 1966) tear gas and water cannon were used to disperse about 200 demonstrators who were demanding that the immigration of foreign workers be halted by the Government. In the same month it was announced that, in early 2001, an office of the Macao SAR was to be established in Beijing, in order to promote links between the two Governments.

Celebrations to mark the first anniversary of the reversion to Chinese sovereignty were attended by President Jiang Zemin, who made a speech praising Macao's local administration, but warning strongly against those seeking to use either of the SARs as a base for subversion. A number of Falun Gong adherents from Hong Kong who had attempted to enter Macao for the celebrations were expelled. The same fate befell two Hong Kong human rights activists who had hoped to petition the Chinese President during his stay in Macao about the human rights situation in the People's Republic. A group of Falun Gong members in Macao, who held a protest the day before President Jiang's arrival, were detained in custody and subsequently alleged that they had suffered police brutality.

In January 2001 China urged the USA to cease interfering in its internal affairs, following the signature by President Bill Clinton of the US Macao Policy Act, which related to the control of Macao's exports and the monitoring of its autonomy. The Governor of Guangdong Province, Lu Ruihua, made an official visit to Macao in February to improve links between the two regions. At the same time, the Legislative Council announced plans to strengthen relations with legislative bodies on the mainland, and the President of the Legislative Council, Susana Chou, visited Beijing, where she held discussions with Vice-Premier Qian Qichen.

Edmund Ho visited Beijing in early March 2001 to attend the fourth session of the Ninth NPC, and held talks with President Jiang Zemin, who praised the former's achievements since the reversion of Macao to Chinese rule. The EU announced in mid-March that SAR passport holders would, from May 2001, no longer require visas to enter EU countries.

The Macao, Hong Kong and mainland police forces established a working group in March 2001 to combat cross-border crime, with a special emphasis on narcotics, and in late March the Macao, Hong Kong and Guangdong police forces conducted a joint anti-drugs operation, resulting in the arrest of 1,243 suspected traffickers and producers, and the seizure of large quantities of heroin, ecstasy and marijuana. Macao and Portugal signed an agreement in May to strengthen co-operation in the fields of economy, culture, public security and justice during the visit of the Portuguese Minister of Foreign Affairs, Jaime Gama, the most senior Portuguese official to visit Macao since its reversion to Chinese rule. In June Macao's Secretary for Security, Cheong Kuoc Va, visited Beijing and signed new accords aimed at reducing the trafficking of drugs, guns and people. In the same month Chief Executive Edmund Ho made his first official visit to the EU headquarters in the Belgian capital of Brussels, where he sought to promote contacts and exchanges between the SAR and the EU. Another major campaign against illegal activities related to the triads was conducted by the Macao, Hong Kong and Guangdong police forces in July, and in a further sign of co-operation between Macao and the mainland against crime, the two sides signed an agreement on mutual judicial co-operation and assistance in late August, the first of its kind.

Elections to the Legislative Council were held on 23 September 2001, the first since Macao's reversion to Chinese rule. The number of seats was increased from 23 to 27: seven members were appointed by the Chief Executive, 10 elected directly and 10 indirectly. Of the 10 directly elective seats, two seats each were won by the business-orientated CODEM, the pro-Beijing factions UPP and UPD and the pro-democracy ANMD. Two other factions won one seat each. Of the 10 indirectly elective seats, four were taken by representatives of business interests, two by representatives of welfare, cultural, educational, and sports interests, two by representatives of labour interests, and two by representatives of professionals.

In October 2001 China appointed Bai Zhijian as director of its liaison office in Macao, its most senior representative in the SAR, replacing the late Wang Qiren. Later in the month Cui Shiping was selected as Macao's representative in the NPC. At the same time, Edmund Ho attended the summit meeting of Asia-Pacific Economic Cooperation (APEC, see p. 204) in Shanghai, and the EU-Macao Joint Committee held a meeting in the SAR, aimed at improving trade, tourism and legal co-operation between the two entities. During late 2001, meanwhile, Macao increased co-operation with Hong Kong and the mainland in fighting crime and combating terrorism, amid reports that Russian mafias were becoming increasingly active in the SARs, and in mid-November the three police departments held an anti-drugs forum in Hong Kong.

In December 2001 the Government finally acted to end the 40-year monopoly on casinos and gambling held by Stanley Ho and his long-established company, the Sociedade de Turismo e Diversões de Macau (STDM). Under the new arrangements, some 21 companies, none of which was Chinese-owned, were to be permitted to bid for three new operating licences for casinos in the SAR. On 1 April 2002 Stanley Ho's STDM formally relinquished its 40-year monopoly on casinos. However, Ho retained influence in the gambling sector after his Sociedade de Jogos de Macau (SJM) won an 18-year licence to operate casinos.

Edmund Ho undertook a visit to Beijing in December 2001, where he and President Jiang Zemin discussed the situation in Macao. In January 2002 Ho visited the mainland city of Chongqing, seeking to reinforce economic links between the two places, and stating that Macao would play a more active role in developing the region. Also in January, the Government granted permission to the Taipei Trade and Cultural Office (TTCO) to issue visas for Taiwan-bound visitors from Macao and the mainland. In February Li Peng, Chairman of the Standing Committee of the NPC, paid an official visit to Macao, where he held discussions with the Chief Executive of the SAR. During Li's visit, a leading Macao political activist, along with several activists from the Hong Kong-based April Fifth Action group, were arrested for planning to stage protests against Li for his role in the Tiananmen Square suppression of 1989 and in favour of the release of mainland political dissidents. The Hong Kong activists were immediately deported. In March 2002 a new representative office of the Macao SAR was established in Beijing, with the aim of enhancing links between the SAR and the mainland. Wu Beiming was named as its director. At its inaugural ceremony, Edmund Ho and Chinese Vice-Premier Qian Qichen praised the 'one country, two systems' model, and the director of the central government liaison office in Macao, Bai Zhijian, suggested that Macao might become a model for Taiwan's eventual reunification with the mainland.

In December 2002 Macao selected its 12 candidates for the 10th NPC, convened in Beijing in March 2003. Edmund Ho held a meeting with the new Chinese Premier, Wen Jiabao, in March at which the future development of Macao under the policy of 'one country, two systems' was discussed. In October 2003 Chinese Vice-President Zeng Qinghong visited Macao to attend the signing ceremony of the Closer Economic Partnership Arrangement (CEPA) between Macao and the Chinese mainland.

In November 2003 Edmund Ho outlined plans for administrative reform of Macao's Government, alongside legal reform, to begin in 2004. In June 2004 it was announced that the re-election of the Chief Executive would take place in late August. Edmund Ho began his election campaign in mid-August, and was duly re-elected on 29 August, securing 296 of the 300 votes of the members of the Election Committee. In December 2004 Chinese President Hu Jintao visited Macao to mark the fifth anniversary of Macao's reunification with the People's Republic. In January 2005 President Sampaio of Portugal visited Macao, at the conclusion of an official visit to China.

In mid-2005 it was reported that the number of voters registered for the legislative election scheduled for September had reached 220,653, almost one-half of the population of the SAR and an increase of some 35% compared with the number registered for the elections of 2001. At the elections, held on 25 September, the number of seats allocated by direct suffrage was increased from 10 to 12, bringing the total number of seats in the Legislative Council to 29. The pro-democracy ANMD received the highest proportion of votes cast (18.8%) and secured two of the 12 directly elective seats. The Associação dos Cidadãos Unidos de Macau (ACUM), a citizens' association that reportedly drew a large degree of its support from immigrants from Fujian Province and advocated support for the gaming industry, also obtained two seats, while the pro-Beijing UPD and UPP retained their representation of two seats each in the legislature. Angela Leong On Kei, the wife of the influential businessman and casino owner Stanley Ho, was elected on the list of the Aliança para o Desenvolvimento de Macau (AMD). The remaining three seats were divided among Nova Esperança (NE), supported by civil servants and the ethnic Portuguese community, the União Geral para o Bem-querer de Macau (UBM) and CODEM. The turn-out was evaluated at 58.4% of registered voters. The 10 indirectly elective seats, meanwhile, were distributed as in 2001: four were allocated to representatives of business interests, and two each to representatives of labour interests), the interests of professionals and welfare, cultural, educational, and sports interests.

In September 2005 attention focused on Macao's financial sector when the US Administration asserted that the Government of the Democratic People's Republic of Korea (North Korea) had been laundering and counterfeiting money through a Macao bank, Banco Delta Asia (BDA). The Macao authorities took control of the bank pending an inquiry into its activities, and the assets held within these accounts, believed to total US $25m., were frozen. A three-month investigation by Chinese officials reportedly concluded in January 2006 that the allegations were accurate. In February it was announced that BDA was terminating its links with North Korea and that independent accountants had been appointed to monitor the bank's clients. In October an audit conducted by Ernst & Young, an international accounting company, reported that it had found no evidence to suggest that the bank had knowingly facilitated money-laundering activities. However, following the completion of an 18-month investigation, in March 2007 US Treasury officials concluded that the bank had deliberately disregarded illicit activities and ordered US banks and companies to terminate all links with BDA. The Monetary Authority of Macao expressed deep regret at this conclusion. The North Korean assets in question were to be released and transferred to a mainland Chinese bank. A Russian bank subsequently agreed to act as intermediary for the transfer of the funds, which was carried out in late June (see the Democratic People's Republic of Korea). In September the Monetary Authority of Macao announced that control of BDA was being restored to its Chairman, Stanley Au, partly because the bank had shown an improvement in its practices. The US Treasury's measures, despite a legal challenge filed by the bank, remained in effect.

Although the next elections for Macao's Legislative Council were not due to take place until the latter part of 2009, it was reported in 2006 that bogus associations were being established in an apparent attempt to influence the outcome of the future poll. The majority of these newly founded nominal organizations were sports groups, part of the category representing culture, education and sporting interests, which together with local charities would form the constituency responsible for choosing two of the Legislative Council's 10 indirectly elected members. (The three constituencies of labour, employer and professional interests would be entitled to determine the remaining eight indirectly elective seats.) The legitimacy of the SAR's Election Committee, responsible for choosing Macao's next Chief Executive in 2009, was also believed to be compromised, with 80 of its 300 members due to be selected by the constituency of culture, education and sport. A total of 207 bogus associations had reportedly been created between January and April 2006 alone, compared with 234 for the whole of 2005. Under electoral rules, such associations were required to have been established for at least three years in order to be eligible to vote, hence the proliferation of these organizations prior to the deadline in 2006.

In December 2006 a corruption scandal emerged in Macao when the Chief Executive ordered the arrest of Ao Man Long, Secretary for Transport and Public Works, and that of 11 others. Ao was subsequently charged on 76 corruption-related counts, including accepting bribes and money-laundering; he was alleged to have misappropriated 800m. patacas and to have amassed a considerable personal fortune. Ao was alleged to have collaborated with his relatives to register a number of bogus companies abroad in order to launder the bribes that he had reportedly received. In January 2008, having been found guilty of 57 of the charges against him, Ao was sentenced to 27 years' imprisonment. In June Ao's wife, three members of his family and three business associates were also convicted of various money-laundering and bribery charges. In April 2009 Ao was convicted of 23 additional charges of taking bribes and of five charges of money-laundering.

At a May Day labour rally in 2007, demonstrators protesting against alleged corruption and the use of illegal workers in the SAR proceeded to demand the resignation of Edmund Ho as Chief Executive. In this unusual display of civil unrest, there were violent clashes between thousands of protesters and several hundred police officers, armed with batons and pepper spray. Another demonstration took place in October. Amid increasing popular concern about the rapid pace of change and the perceived deterioration in the quality of life in Macao, in December hundreds attended a further protest against corruption, this time coinciding with the eighth anniversary of the establishment of the SAR. Meanwhile, in August 2007 it was alleged in the media that Edmund Ho owned shares in Many Town Company, a Hong Kong-based business with interests in STDM; the Government issued a denial, claiming that Ho's shares had been transferred to his brother in 1995. During 2007 Macao reportedly superseded Las Vegas, USA, as the world's most lucrative gambling centre. In April 2008 the Chief Executive introduced new measures that limited the number of gaming licences to six, ruling out the building of any new casinos, as the Chinese Government encouraged a shift in emphasis to other areas of the economy. During 2008 the administration attempted to alleviate the increasing cost of living by introducing a Wealth Sharing Scheme, which provided annual cash payments to residents.

In December 2008 more than 20 Hong Kong activists, who had planned to attend a demonstration against proposed legislation relating to the security of Macao, were barred from entering the SAR. In February 2009 the Legislative Council overwhelmingly approved the National Security Bill, prohibiting acts of treason, secession, sedition or subversion against the Chinese Government and outlawing the theft of state secrets. The legislation provided for prison sentences of up to 30 years for those convicted of such crimes. Fearing that the law was open to abuse by the authorities, various human rights groups, including Amnesty International, criticized the ambiguous wording of the law, particularly the reference to ill-defined 'preparatory acts'. Furthermore, shortly after the promulgation of the law in early March, the dean of the faculty of law at the University of Hong Kong, who had been invited to deliver a speech at the University of Macao, was refused entry to the territory. As fears for freedom of expression in both Macao and Hong Kong grew, the authorities of the latter SAR requested clarification of Macao's denial of entry to the law professor. Various other Hong Kong residents, including pro-democracy politicians and a photographer, were similarly prohibited from entering Macao.

Meanwhile, in January 2008 Macao conducted its election of deputies to the mainland Chinese legislature. The electoral conference, comprising more than 300 representatives of various sectors of Macao society, selected 12 deputies, who were to attend the 11th NPC, convened in Beijing in March.

Recent developments: the elections of 2009 and beyond

The election for Edmund Ho's replacement as Chief Executive of the SAR, took place in July 2009. Fernando Chui Sai On, the former Secretary for Social Affairs and Culture, was elected unopposed to the post by the Election Committee. The legislative election was held on 20 September 2009, with the level of participation reported to be 60% of the electorate. The pro-Beijing UPD won two of the 12 seats determined by direct election, while the pro-gaming ACUM and the pro-democracy Associação de Próspero Macau Democrático (APMD) took two seats each. The remaining six seats were won by: the pro-democracy ANMD; the pro-Beijing UPP; the Nova União para o Desenvolvimento de Macau (NUDM), representing the interests of the gaming sector; the NE, which continued to be supported by civil servants; the pro-business União Macau-Guangdong; and the Aliança para a Mudança, an alliance advocating public reform. Four of the 10 indirectly elective seats were taken by representatives of business interests; two by representatives of the professional sector; two by representatives of labour interests; and two by members of the social, cultural, educational and sports sector.

Fernando Chui's five-year term of office commenced on 20 December 2009. The incoming Chief Executive retained the four incumbent

Secretaries, and Cheong U was appointed as Secretary for Social Affairs and Culture. As Macao celebrated the 10th anniversary of its reversion to Chinese sovereignty, President Hu Jintao praised the achievements of the previous decade but suggested that the SAR work more closely with the Pearl River Delta region. The Chinese President also urged stronger management of the gambling industry, the diversification of the economy, the raising of living standards and the improvement of the education system.

In his first policy address, delivered in March 2010, the Chief Executive focused on issues of social welfare, announcing the continuation of various measures to provide financial support for the residents of Macao (see Economic Affairs), along with subsidies to assist disadvantaged families and other needy citizens, particularly the elderly. In an acknowledgement of increasing public concern with regard to the issue of corruption in Macao, Chui also pledged to improve the transparency and integrity of the civil service. The probity of public servants was to be more closely supervised by the Commission Against Corruption; in particular, details of the property transactions of government officials were to be made publicly available. The Commission Against Corruption subsequently agreed to establish a permanent working group with its counterparts in neighbouring Guangdong Province and in Hong Kong.

In its annual Trafficking in Persons Report, issued in May 2010, the US Department of State continued to identify Macao as a jurisdiction that had yet to become fully compliant with minimum standards for the elimination of human trafficking. However, the report acknowledged the SAR's 'significant efforts' to address the issue of commercial sexual exploitation, the principal victims of which were reported to have travelled to Macao from mainland China, Mongolia, Russia and South-East Asia, in search of employment opportunities. Macao was also identified as a source territory for women and girls subjected to forced prostitution elsewhere in Asia.

In June 2010 it was announced that, in order to assist the Chief Executive in the area of policy-making, a new government institute was to be established. This policy institute was to be responsible for conducting research on political, economic and legal issues, as well as various other matters.

During an official visit to Portugal in June 2010 Chui had discussions with President Aníbal Cavaco Silva and other senior government members. The Chief Executive's delegation included his Secretary for Economy and Finance, Francis Tam Pak Yuen, and the Secretary for Social Affairs and Culture, Cheong U, as well as representatives of Macao's business community. With the objective of revitalizing bilateral relations and of promoting co-operation in the areas of trade, investment in tourism, education and culture, it was agreed that meetings of a Joint Commission, originally envisaged under the agreement concluded in 2001 (see above), would take place annually.

Amid much public criticism, draft legislation to provide civil servants with financial aid, either if being sued or if pursuing a lawsuit on a matter arising from the performance of their public duty, was under consideration in mid-2010. Critics of the proposed legislation included Susana Chou, former President of the Legislative Assembly, who denounced it as a serious violation of the Basic Law. Media organizations, in particular, expressed concern for the freedom of the press, fearing that such a law might be used to support legal action against newspaper reporters. The most controversial parts of the proposal were subsequently abandoned by the Macao Government. In October Tam, the Secretary for Economy and Finance, held discussions with the Macao Federation of Trade Unions and undertook to conduct a study on the introduction of a statutory minimum wage.

In a policy address delivered in November 2010 the Chief Executive focused on the implementation of new measures in various areas, including the diversification of the SAR's economy, social welfare, transparency of government and regional co-operation. Chui announced that, following public consultation, the Government had decided to exclude the development of casino premises from the urban planning for newly reclaimed land; the areas in question were to be used only for the purposes of the development of residential housing, along with local industries that would help to diversify the economy. During Chui's visit to Beijing in December Premier Wen Jiabao expressed the hope that Macao would work towards the improvement of its governance and promote the diversification of its economy. The SAR's dependence on gambling was becoming a matter of urgent concern: despite recent efforts to promote conventional tourism, conferences and exhibitions, the gambling sector was by far Macao's principal source of income, contributing more than three-quarters of government revenue in 2010. Income from gambling increased by 58% in 2010, to US $23,500m. Since casinos were not permitted in mainland China, Macao attracted many mainland gamblers, including not only wealthy entrepreneurs but also senior officials and the managers of state-owned industries, some of whom were suspected of gambling with illicitly obtained funds, at a time when corruption had been identified as a major problem (see the People's Republic).

In December 2010 it was announced that the wife of the 89-year-old Stanley Ho, Angela Leong, had replaced him as managing director of SJM, Macao's principal casino operating company. In early 2011 various disputes were reported between Ho and his numerous relatives concerning the eventual control of the companies that he had founded, which not only dominated the gambling sector but also included major interests in the hotel industry, the SAR's airline and airport, ferry services to Hong Kong, bus services to the Chinese mainland, and the retail sector. In February it was reported that another casino operating company, Sands China, was under investigation by the US authorities after its former chief executive had accused the USA-based parent company of instructing him to find ways of influencing officials in Macao.

In March 2011 the Chief Executive of Macao and the Governor of the adjacent Guangdong Province signed a wide-ranging agreement providing for bilateral co-operation in various fields, including economic matters, public welfare and culture. Under the provisions of the Guangdong-Macao Co-operation Framework Agreement the two sides were to co-operate in the development of local industries, the construction of infrastructural facilities, the provision of public services and in development planning. In July the Beijing Government appointed Hu Zhengyue to replace Lu Shumin as commissioner of the Ministry of Foreign Affairs in the Macao SAR.

CONSTITUTION AND GOVERNMENT

The Macao Special Administrative Region (SAR) is governed by a Chief Executive, chosen by a 300-member Selection Committee. The Chief Executive is accountable to the State Council of China, the term of office being five years, with a limit of two consecutive terms. Upon the territory's transfer to Chinese sovereignty in December 1999, a 10-member Executive Council, appointed by the Chief Executive to assist in policy-making, assumed office. The Chief Executive is assisted in administration by five Secretaries, who hold individual portfolios. In 2001 the Legislative Council (commonly referred to as the Legislative Assembly) was expanded from 23 to 27 members, of whom 10 were directly elected, 10 indirectly elected and seven appointed by the Chief Executive, all with a mandate of four years. In 2005 the membership of the Legislative Council was increased to 29, to incorporate two additional deputies to be chosen by direct election; the composition remained unchanged at the 2009 legislative election. For the purposes of local government, the islands of Taipa and Coloane are administered separately. Macao selects 12 deputies to attend the National People's Congress in Beijing.

REGIONAL AND INTERNATIONAL CO-OPERATION

Macao is an associate member of the UN's Economic and Social Commission for Asia and the Pacific (ESCAP, see p. 40).

In 1991 Macao became a party to the General Agreement on Tariffs and Trade (GATT, subsequently superseded by the World Trade Organization—WTO, see p. 433). Macao retained its membership of WTO after December 1999. Macao also remained a 'privileged partner' of the European Union.

ECONOMIC AFFAIRS

In 2009, according to estimates by the World Bank, Macao's gross national income (GNI), measured at average 2008–10 prices, was US $21,261m., equivalent to $40,030 per head. In 2009 GNI was $57,850 per head on an international purchasing-power parity basis. During 2001–10, it was estimated, the population increased at an average annual rate of 2.4%. Gross domestic product (GDP) per head increased, in real terms, at an average annual rate of 11.5% during 2001–09. According to the World Bank, overall GDP rose, in real terms, at an average annual rate of 14.1% in 2001–09. According to official figures, GDP increased by 20.7% in 2010 and by 20.7% in 2011.

Agriculture is of minor importance, engaging only 0.2% of the economically active population in 2010. The main crops are rice and vegetables. Cattle, pigs and chickens are reared. Macao is heavily reliant on imports for its food supplies.

Industry (including mining, manufacturing, construction and public utilities) accounted for 11.0% of total GDP in 2009, according to provisional figures. In 2010 the industrial sector employed 13.7% of the economically active population. The mining sector is negligible.

According to provisional figures, the manufacturing sector contributed 1.5% of total GDP in 2009. The sector engaged 4.8% of the economically active population in 2010. The most important manufacturing industry is the production of textiles and garments. Although exports of textile items and garments have continued to decrease, from 2,469.9m. patacas in 2009 to only 1,627.3m. patacas in 2010, the sector nevertheless accounted for 23.4% of the value of total exports in the latter year. Jewellery accounted for 10.6% of export sales in 2010. The significance of other manufacturing industries, such as footwear and furniture, has declined.

According to provisional figures, the construction sector contributed 8.3% of total GDP in 2009. The sector engaged 8.6% of the economically active population in 2010.

Macao possesses few natural resources. Energy is derived principally from imported petroleum. Imports of petroleum and its products accounted for 5.9% of total import costs in 2010. The territory receives some of its electricity and water supplies from mainland China.

The services sector accounted for 89.0% of GDP in 2009, according to provisional figures, and employed 86.0% of the economically active population in 2010. At the end of 2010 a total of 44,800 workers were engaged in the gaming sector. Tourism and gambling activities make a substantial contribution to the territory's economy. In March 2008, however, a moratorium on the issuing of new gaming licences and on the building of new casinos was announced. None the less, by the end of 2009 six concessionaires were operating a total of 33 casinos in Macao, 20 of which were managed by the Sociedade de Jogos de Macau (SJM). Gross revenue from games of fortune increased from 46,047m. patacas in 2005 to 188,343m. patacas in 2010. The Government's revenue from gambling taxes reached 68,800m. patacas in 2010, representing almost 78% of total public revenue. Receipts from tourism totalled a provisional US $17,637m. in 2009. Tourist arrivals declined from almost 27.0m. in 2007 to fewer than 21.8m. in 2009. However, numbers recovered to reach nearly 25.0m. in 2010, in which year 53.0% of visitors came from mainland China and 29.9% from Hong Kong.

Legislation regulating offshore banking was introduced in 1987. A law enacted in 1995 aimed to attract overseas investment by offering the right of abode in Macao to entrepreneurs with substantial funds at their disposal. From December 1999, upon the territory's reversion to Chinese sovereignty, Macao continued to administer its own finances and was exempt from taxes imposed by central government. The pataca was retained, remaining freely convertible.

In 2010 Macao recorded a visible trade deficit of US $5,267m., but registered a surplus of US $12,233m. on the current account of the balance of payments. The principal sources of imports in 2010 were China (which supplied 31.1% of the total), followed by Hong Kong (10.5%), France, Japan and the USA. The principal market for exports was Hong Kong (which purchased 43.1%), followed by China (15.8%) and the USA (11.2%). The main exports were textiles and garments, along with machinery and apparatus. The principal imports were raw materials for industry, notably textiles, fuels, foodstuffs and other consumer goods. After December 1999 Macao retained its status as a free port and remained a separate customs territory.

The budget surplus was estimated at 50,094.2m. patacas in 2010. The average annual rate of inflation (including rents) between 2001 and 2010 was 2.7%. Consumer prices rose by 5.8% in 2011. The rate of unemployment declined to 2.0% in the period from January to March 2012.

In accordance with the Closer Economic Partnership Arrangement (CEPA), which came into effect at the beginning of 2004, successive agreements liberalized trade in goods and services between Macao and mainland China, and facilitated investment and travel between the two. Despite various attempts to diversify, gambling-related tourism has continued to dominate the economy of Macao. In November 2008, in response to the global financial crisis and the resultant decline in the SAR's gambling revenues, the Chief Executive of Macao announced a range of measures to support the economy. Small and medium-sized businesses, in particular, were to receive assistance, and various new infrastructural projects, including public housing, were announced. Subsidies were to be made available to home-buyers, in an effort to stimulate the property market, and a Wealth Sharing Scheme was introduced, whereby lump sum payments of 6,000 patacas and health care vouchers were to be distributed to all permanent residents of Macao, while non-permanent residents were to receive 3,600 patacas each: the scheme was continued in subsequent years, in the form of annual payments. In March 2010 the new Chief Executive announced further measures to reduce the tax obligations of small and medium businesses and, in order to address the lack of human resources in certain areas, plans to accelerate the granting of labour permits to foreign workers. The introduction of minimum wage legislation was under consideration in late 2010, but had still not been implemented by early 2012. Although the economy suffered a substantial contraction in the first half of 2009, in the year as a whole GDP grew by 1.7%. A robust recovery took place during 2010, in which year GDP expanded by 27.0%, with the earnings of the gambling sector increasing by 58%, to US $23,500m., contributing some 41% of GDP, while the manufacturing and construction sectors contracted. There was further strong real GDP growth of 20.7% in 2011. Income from the gambling sector increased again, by 42%, to some $33,500m. in 2011, despite restrictions placed by the Government on the number of gaming tables and on new casino developments. In 2011 the average rate of unemployment was low, at 2.5%, reflecting a shortage of labour. Inflationary pressures increased in 2011, with consumer prices rising by an average of 5.8% during the year. Efforts continued during 2011 to encourage non-gambling, longer-stay tourism and the development of Macao as a centre for conferences and trade exhibitions. Construction of a series of bridges linking Macao with Hong Kong and with Zhuhai, on the mainland, was due to be completed in 2016 and was expected to increase the speed of access to Macao for tourists and traders.

PUBLIC HOLIDAYS

2013: 1 January (New Year), 10–12 February (Chinese Lunar New Year), 29 March (Good Friday), 1 April (Easter Monday), 4 April (Ching Ming), 1 May (Labour Day), 17 May (Feast of Buddha), 12 June (Dragon Boat Festival), 20 September (Chinese Mid-Autumn Festival), 1–2 October (National Day of the People's Republic of China and day following), 14 October (Festival of Ancestors—Chung Yeung), 2 November (All Souls' Day), 8 December (Immaculate Conception), 20 December (SAR Establishment Day), 21 December (Winter Solstice), 24–25 December (Christmas).

Statistical Survey

Source (unless otherwise indicated): Direcção dos Serviços de Estatística e Censos, Alameda Dr Carlos d'Assumpção 411–417, Dynasty Plaza, 17° andar, Macao; tel. 83995311; fax 28307825; e-mail info@dsec.gov.mo; internet www.dsec.gov.mo.

AREA AND POPULATION

Area (2010): 29.7 sq km (11.47 sq miles), comprising Macao peninsula 9.3, Taipa island 6.8, Coloane island 7.6, Cotai Reclamation Area 6.0.

Population: 502,113 (males 245,167, females 256,946) according to results of by-census of 19 August 2006 (491,482 were classed as usual residents and 10,631 as mobile residents); 552,500 (males 265,100, females 287,400) at census of 12 August 2011, preliminary results (529,300 were classed as usual residents and 23,200 as mobile residents).

Density (at 2011 census): 18,602.7 per sq km.

Population by Age and Sex (at 2011 census): *0–14:* 65.9 (males 34.1, females 31.8); *15–64:* 446.6 (males 213.1, females 233.5); *65 and over:* 40.0 (males 18.0, females 22.0); *Total* 552.5 (males 265.1, females 287.4).

Population by Nationality (at by-census of August 2006): Chinese 471,484; Portuguese 8,536.

Population by Parish (at 2011 census): Santo António 122.8; São Lázaro 31.8; São Lourenço 48.8; Sé 46.8; Nossa Senhora de Fátima 218.7; Taipa 78.5; Coloane 4.3; Maritime 0.7; Total 552.5. Note: Totals may not be equal to the sum of components, owing to rounding.

Births, Marriages and Deaths (2010): Registered live births 5,114 (birth rate 9.4 per 1,000); Registered marriages 3,103 (marriage rate 5.7 per 1,000); Registered deaths 1,774 (death rate 3.3 per 1,000).

Life Expectancy (years at birth, 2007–10 average): 82.5 (males 79.4; females 85.2).

Economically Active Population (persons aged 16 years and over, 2010): Agriculture, forestry, fishing and mining 600; Manufacturing 15,300; Production and distribution of electricity, gas and water 900; Construction 27,500; Wholesale and retail trade, repair of motor vehicles, motorcycles and personal and household goods 42,300; Hotels, restaurants and similar activities 43,200; Transport, storage and communications 18,500; Financial services 7,400; Real estate, renting and services to companies 27,700; Public administration, defence and compulsory social security 21,600; Education 11,800; Health and social work 8,100; Other community, social and personal service activities 76,100; Private households with employed persons 17,100; *Total employed* 318,300; Unemployed 9,300; *Total labour force* 327,600. Note: Totals may not be equal to the sum of components, owing to rounding.

HEALTH AND WELFARE

Key Indicators

Under-5 Mortality Rate (per 1,000 live births, 2008): 3.6.

HIV/AIDS (% persons aged 15–49, 2008): 0.1.

Physicians (per 1,000 head, 2010): 2.4.

Hospital Beds (per 1,000 head, 2010): 2.1.

Human Development Index (2009): value 0.835.

For definitions, see explanatory note on p. vi.

AGRICULTURE, ETC.

(since 2004 no separate data available for livestock—see the chapter on the People's Republic of China)

Livestock ('000 head, 2004): Poultry 700 (FAO estimate).

Livestock Products ('000 metric tons, 2004): Beef and veal 1.1; Pig meat 9.6; Poultry meat 6.5 (FAO estimate); Hen eggs 1.0 (FAO estimate).

Fishing (metric tons, live weight, 2009, FAO estimates): Marine fishes 1,020; Shrimps and prawns 230; Other marine crustaceans 210; Total catch (incl. others) 1,500.

Source: FAO.

INDUSTRY

Production (2003, unless otherwise indicated): Wine 700,745 litres; Knitwear 36.18m. units; Footwear 12.13m. pairs; Clothing 230.73m. units; Furniture 5,253 units; Electric energy 1,077.0 million kWh (2010).

FINANCE

Currency and Exchange Rates: 100 avos = 1 pataca. *Sterling, Dollar and Euro Equivalents* (30 December 2011): £1 sterling = 12.376 patacas; US $1 = 8.005 patacas; €1 = 10.357 patacas; 100 patacas = £8.08 = $12.49 = €9.66. *Average Exchange Rate* (patacas per US dollar): 7.984 in 2009; 8.002 in 2010; 8.018 in 2011. Note: The pataca has a fixed link with the value of the Hong Kong dollar (HK $1 = 1.030 patacas).

Budget (million patacas, 2010, provisional): *Revenue:* Current revenue 79,388.7 (Direct taxes 68,849.2, Indirect taxes 2,202.3, Property income 2,092.0, Transfers 3,917.3, Other current revenue 2,327.9); Capital revenue 9,099.3; Total 88,488.1. *Expenditure:* Payroll 9,221.9; Goods and services 6,119.1; Current transfers 15,484.4; Other current expenditure 1,560.9; Capital expenditure 6,007.5; Total 38,393.9.

International Reserves (million patacas, 2010): Total (all foreign exchange) 190,186.8.

Money Supply (million patacas at 31 December 2010): Currency outside depository corporations 5,077.2; Transferable deposits 29,315.2; Other deposits 208,324.1; Securities other than shares 206.0; *Broad money* 242,922.6. Source: IMF, *International Financial Statistics*.

Cost of Living (Consumer Price Index; base: April 2008–March 2009 = 100): All items 100.23 in 2008; 101.40 in 2009; 104.25 in 2010.

Gross Domestic Product (million patacas at constant 2002 prices): 125,034.6 in 2007; 141,219.5 in 2008; 143,091.5 in 2009 (provisional).

Expenditure on the Gross Domestic Product (million patacas at current prices, 2010): Government final consumption expenditure 17,641.2; Private consumption expenditure 52,162.1; Changes in inventories 1,737.5; Gross fixed capital formation 28,349.6; *Total domestic expenditure* 99,890.4; Exports of goods and services 240,455.1; *Less* Imports of goods and services 114,082.2; *GDP in purchasers' values* 226,263.3.

Gross Domestic Product by Economic Activity (million patacas at current prices, 2009, provisional): Mining and quarrying 2.1; Manufacturing 1,680.8; Electricity, gas and water supply 1,464.9; Construction 9,401.4; Wholesale, retail, repair, restaurants and hotels 15,829.9; Transport, storage and communications 4,206.5; Financial intermediation, real estate, renting and business activities 26,350.4; Public administration, other community, social and personal services (incl. gaming services) 54,742.5; *GDP at basic prices* 113,678.5; Taxes on products (net) 47,295.9; Statistical discrepancy (representing the difference between the expenditure and production approaches) 4,483.1; *GDP at market prices* 165,457.5.

Balance of Payments (US $ million, 2010): Exports of goods f.o.b. 1,045; Imports of goods f.o.b. −6,312; *Trade balance* –5,267; Exports of services 28,682; Imports of services −7,544; *Balance on goods and services* 15,870; Other income received 1,106; Other income paid –4,019; *Balance on goods, services and income* 12,957; Current transfers received 97; Current transfers paid –821; *Current balance* 12,233; Capital account (net) 20; Direct investment abroad 499; Direct investment from abroad 3,530; Portfolio investment assets –1,007; Portfolio investment liabilities 164; Financial derivatives assets –8; Other investment assets –9,600; Other investment liabilities 5,189; Net errors and omissions −5,864; *Overall balance* 5,158. Source: IMF, *International Financial Statistics*.

EXTERNAL TRADE

Principal Commodities (million patacas, 2010): *Imports c.i.f.*(distribution by SITC): Live animals (excl. marine) 338.9; Vegetable and fruit 475.3; Beverages and tobacco 3,409.2 (Beverages 2,672.3); Petroleum, petroleum products, etc. 2,595.2; Textile yarn, fabrics, etc. 938.3; Iron and steel 439.3; Electrical machinery, apparatus, etc. 1,125.7; Road vehicles 2,206.2; Clothing and accessories 1,936.2; Total (incl. others) 44,118.4. *Exports f.o.b.:* Cotton garments (knitted and crocheted) 559.3; Cotton garments (excl. knitted and crocheted) 559.1; Radios, TV, image and sound recorders and reproducers 197.1; Machines and apparatus 449.0; Total (incl. others) 6,960.0 (incl. re-exports 4,570.2).

Principal Trading Partners (million patacas, 2010): *Imports c.i.f.:* Australia 421.4; China, People's Republic 13,718.3; France 4,039.8; Germany 1,321.55; Hong Kong 4,627.9; Italy 2,071.5; Japan 3,812.1; Korea, Republic 645.7; Singapore 838.6; Taiwan 1,078.3; United Kingdom 852.1; USA 2,619.0; Total (incl. others) 44,118.4. *Exports f.o.b.:* Canada 36.1; China, People's Republic 1,102.4; France 71.9; Germany 142.6; Hong Kong 3,002.6; Netherlands 77.3; United Kingdom 64.4; USA 782.1; Total (incl. others) 6,960.0 (incl. re-exports 4,570.2).

TRANSPORT

Road Traffic (motor vehicles in use, December 2010): Light vehicles 83,879; Heavy vehicles 6,335; Motorcycles 106,420.

Shipping (international sea-borne containerized freight traffic, '000 metric tons, 2010): Goods imported 147.0; Goods exported 19.5.

Civil Aviation (2010, unless otherwise indicated): Passenger arrivals 1,842,074 (2008 figure); Passenger departures 1,934,393 (2008 figure); Goods loaded (metric tons) 32,361; Goods unloaded (metric tons) 13,597.

TOURISM

Visitor Arrivals by Country of Residence (2010): China, People's Republic 13,229,100; Hong Kong 7,466,100; Taiwan 1,292,700; Total (incl. others) 24,965,400.

Receipts from Tourism (US $ million, incl. passenger transport, unless otherwise indicated): 9,755 in 2006; 13,404 in 2007; 17,093 in 2008; 17,637 in 2009 (excl.passenger transport, provisional) (Source: World Tourism Organization).

COMMUNICATIONS MEDIA

Radio Receivers (1997): 160,000 in use.

Television Receivers (2000): 125,115 in use.

Daily Newspapers (2008): 14.

Telephones (2010): 167,500 main lines in use.

Mobile Cellular Telephones (2010): 1,122,300 subscribers.

Personal Computers (2006): 192,000 (384.1 per 1,000 persons).

Internet Subscribers (2010): 132,800.

Broadband Subscribers (2010): 131,400.

Sources: partly UNESCO, *Statistical Yearbook*; International Telecommunication Union.

EDUCATION

(2009/10)

Kindergarten: 57 schools; 597 teachers; 10,038 pupils.

Primary: 70 schools; 1,686 teachers; 25,705 pupils.

Secondary: 56 schools; 2,635 teachers; 39,298 pupils.

Vocational/Technical: 10 schools; 169 teachers; 1,752 pupils.

Higher: 10 institutions; 1,963 teaching staff; 23,562 students.

Pupil-teacher Ratio (primary education, UNESCO estimate): 16.1 in 2009/10 (Source: UNESCO Institute for Statistics).

Adult Literacy Rate: 93.5% (males 96.5%, females 90.7%) in 2006 (Source: UNESCO Institute for Statistics).

Notes: For non-tertiary education, figures for schools and teachers refer to all those for which the category is applicable. Some schools and teachers provide education at more than one level. Institutions of higher education refer to those recognized by the Government of Macao Special Administrative Region.

Directory

The Government

Chief Executive: FERNANDO CHUI SAI ON (took office 20 December 2009).

SECRETARIES
(May 2012)

Secretary for Administration and Justice: FLORINDA DA ROSA SILVA CHAN.

Secretary for Economy and Finance: FRANCIS TAM PAK YUEN.

Secretary for Security: CHEONG KUOC VA.

Secretary for Social Affairs and Culture: CHEONG U.

Secretary for Transport and Public Works: LAU SI IO.

GOVERNMENT OFFICES

Office of the Chief Executive: Sede do Governo, Av. da Praia Grande; tel. 28726886; fax 28725468; internet www.gov.mo.

Executive Council: Sede do Governo, Av. da Praia Grande; tel. 28726886; fax 28726168; Sec.-Gen. HO VENG ON.

Office of the Secretary for Administration and Justice: Rua de S. Lourenço 28, Sede do Governo, 4º andar; tel. 28726886; fax 28726880; internet www.gov.mo.

Office of the Secretary for Economy and Finance: Rua de S. Lourenço 28, Sede do Governo, 3º andar; tel. 28726886; fax 28726665; internet www.gov.mo.

Office of the Secretary for Security: Calçada dos Quartéis, Quartel de S. Francisco; tel. 87997501; fax 28580702; internet www.gov.mo.

Office of the Secretary for Social Affairs and Culture: Rua de S. Lourenço 28, Sede do Governo, 2º andar; tel. 28726886; fax 28727594; internet www.gov.mo.

Office of the Secretary for Transport and Public Works: Rua de S. Lourenço 28, Edif. dos Secretários, 1° andar; tel. 28726886; fax 28727566; internet www.gov.mo.

Macao Government Information Bureau: Gabinete de Comunicação Social do Governo de Macau, Av. da Praia Grande 762–804, Edif. China Plaza, 15° andar; tel. 28332886; fax 28355426; e-mail info@gcs.gov.mo; internet www.gcs.gov.mo; Dir VICTOR CHAN CHI PING.

Economic Services Bureau: Direcção dos Serviços de Economia, Rua Dr Pedro José Lobo 1–3, Edif. Luso Internacional, 25° andar; tel. 28386937; fax 28590310; e-mail info@economia.gov.mo; internet www.economia.gov.mo; Dir SOU TIM PENG.

Legislature

LEGISLATIVE COUNCIL (LEGISLATIVE ASSEMBLY)

The Legislative Assembly was superseded by the Legislative Council under the terms of the Basic Law, implemented in 1999. In practice, however, the legislature continues to be referred to as the Legislative Assembly, which comprises 29 members: seven appointed by the Chief Executive, 12 elected directly and 10 indirectly. Members serve for four years. The Assembly chooses its President from among its members, by secret vote. At the election held on 20 September 2009 the pro-Beijing União para o Desenvolvimento (UPD) received the highest number of votes cast and secured two of the 12 directly elective seats. The Associação dos Cidadãos Unidos de Macau (ACUM), which supports the gaming industry, also took two seats, as did the pro-democracy Associação de Próspero Macau Democrático (APMD). The following six groupings each took one seat: the pro-democracy Associação de Novo Macau Democrático (ANMD); the pro-Beijing União Promotora para o Progresso (UPP); the Nova União para o Desenvolvimento de Macau (NUDM), which promotes the interests of the gaming sector; Nova Esperança (NE), supported by civil servants; the pro-business União Macau-Guangdong; and the Aliança para a Mudança, which advocates public reform. Four of the 10 indirectly elective seats were taken by representatives of business interests; two by representatives of the professional sector; two by representatives of labour interests; and two by members of the social, cultural, educational and sports sector.

Legislative Council (Legislative Assembly): Praça da Assembléia Legislativa, Edif. da Assembléia Legislativa, Aterros da Baía da Praia Grande; tel. 28728377; fax 28727857; e-mail info@al.gov.mo; internet www.al.gov.mo.

President: LAU CHEOK VA.

Political Organizations

There are no formal political parties, but various registered civic associations exist and may participate in elections for the Legislative Assembly by presenting a list of candidates (see Legislature). A total of 16 groupings contested the legislative election of September 2009.

Judicial System

Formal autonomy was granted to the territory's judiciary in 1993. A new penal code took effect in January 1996. Macao operates its own five major codes, namely the Penal Code, the Code of Criminal Procedure, the Civil Code, the Code of Civil Procedure and the Commercial Code. In 1999 the authority of final appeal was granted to Macao. The judicial system operates independently of the mainland Chinese system.

The judicial system has three tiers: the Court of Final Appeal, Intermediate Court and the First Trial Court.

President of the Court of Final Appeal: SAM HOU FAI, Praçeta 25 de Abril, Edif. dos Tribunais de Segunda Instância e Ultima Instância; tel. 83984117; fax 28326744; e-mail ptui@court.gov.mo; internet www.court.gov.mo.

Procurator-General: HO CHIO MENG.

Religion

The majority of residents profess Buddhism, and there are numerous places of worship, Daoism and Confucianism also being widely practised. The Christian community numbers about 30,000. There are small Muslim and Hindu communities.

CHRISTIANITY

The Roman Catholic Church

Macao forms a single diocese, directly responsible to the Holy See. At 31 December 2007 there were 28,242 adherents in the territory, comprising nearly 5.6% of the population.

Bishop of Macao: Rt Rev. JOSÉ LAI HUNG SENG, Paço Episcopal, Largo da Sé s/n, POB 324; tel. 28309954; fax 28309861; e-mail jesuitas@macau.ctm.net; internet www.catholic.org.mo.

The Anglican Communion

Macao forms part of the Anglican diocese of Hong Kong (q.v.).

The Press

A new Press Law, prescribing journalists' rights and obligations, was enacted in August 1990.

PORTUGUESE LANGUAGE

O Clarim: Rua Central 26A, 1° andar; tel. 28573860; fax 28307867; e-mail clarim@macau.ctm.net; internet www.oclarim.com.mo; f. 1948; weekly; Editor ALBINO BENTO PAIS; circ. 1,500.

Hoje Macau: Av. Dr Rodrigo Rodrigues 600E, Edif. Centro Comercial First National, 14° andar, Sala 1408; tel. 28752401; fax 28752405; e-mail hoje@macau.ctm.net; internet www.hojemacau.com; f. 2001; daily; Dir CARLOS MORAIS JOSÉ; circ. 1,200.

Jornal Tribuna de Macau: Av. Almeida Ribeiro 99, Edif. Comercial Nam Wah, 6° andar, Salas 603–05; tel. 28378057; fax 28337305; internet www.jtm.com.mo; f. 1998 through merger of Jornal de Macau (f. 1982) and Tribuna de Macau (f. 1982); daily; Dir JOSÉ FIRMINO DA ROCHA DINIS; circ. 1,000.

Ponto Final: Alameda Dr Carlos d'Assumpção; tel. 28339566; fax 28339563; e-mail editor@pontofinalmacau.com; daily; Publr RICARDO PINTO; Dir ISABEL CASTRO; circ. 1,500.

CHINESE LANGUAGE

Cheng Pou: Av. da Praia Grande 57–63, Edif. Heng Chang, 1° andar, Bloco E–F; tel. 28965972; fax 28965741; e-mail chengpou@macau.ctm.net; internet www.chengpou.com.mo; daily; Dir KUNG SU KAN; Editor-in-Chief LEONG CHI CHUN; circ. 5,000.

Correio de Macau: Estação Central, Largo do Senado; tel. 28574491; fax 28336603; e-mail macpost@macaupost.gov.mo; internet www.macaupost.gov.mo; f. 1989.

Jornal Informação (Son Pou): Rua de Francisco 22, Edif. Mei Fun, 1° andar; tel. 28561557; fax 28566575; e-mail sonpou@macau.ctm.net; internet www.sonpou.com.mo; weekly; Dir CHAO CHONG PENG; circ. 8,000.

Jornal San Wa Ou: Av. Venceslau de Morais 231, Edif. Industrial Nam Fong, 15° andar, Bloco E–F; tel. 28717569; fax 28717572; e-mail correiro@macau.ctm.net; internet www.waou.com.mo; daily; Dir LIN CHANG; circ. 1,500.

Jornal 'Si-Si': Av. Dr Rodrigues, Edif. Centro Comercial First National, 21° andar, Sala 2103; tel. and fax 28421333; e-mail sisinews@hotmail.com; internet www.jornalsisi.com; weekly; Dir and Editor-in-Chief CHEANG VENG PENG; circ. 3,000.

Jornal Va Kio: Rua da Alfândega 69; tel. 28345888; fax 28513724; e-mail vakiopou@macau.ctm.net; internet www.jornalvakio.com; f. 1937; daily; Publr ALICE CHIANG SAO MENG; Editor-in-Chief LEONG CHI SANG; circ. 28,000.

Ou Mun Iat Pou (Macao Daily News): Rua Pedro Nolasco da Silva 37; tel. 28371688; fax 28331998; internet www.macaodaily.com; f. 1958; daily; Dir LEI PANG CHU; Editor-in-Chief PO LOK; circ. 100,000.

O Pulso de Macau: Rua 1, 13°, Bloco B, Guang Dong Nan-Gui Jardim, Taipa; tel. 28400194; fax 28400284; e-mail pulsomacau@gmail.com; internet www.pulso.com.mo; weekly; Dir IEONG IAT FO.

Semanário Desportivo de Macau: Av. Venceslau de Morais 231, Edif. Industrial Nam Fong 7C; tel. 28354208; fax 28718285; e-mail macsport@macau.ctm.net; internet www.macausports.com.mo; weekly; sport; Dir FONG NIM LAM; Editor-in-Chief FONG NIM SEONG; circ. 2,000.

Semanário Recreativo de Macau: Av. Sidónio Pais 31D, 3° andar, Bloco A; tel. 28553216; fax 28516792; e-mail srm405@yahoo.com.hk; weekly; Dir IEONG CHEOK KUONG; Editor-in-Chief TONG IOK WA.

Seng Pou (Star): Travessa da Caldeira 9; tel. 28938387; fax 28388192; e-mail sengpou@macau.ctn.net; f. 1963; daily; Dir and Editor-in-Chief POLICARPO KOK; Deputy Editor-in-Chief TOU MAN KUM; circ. 6,000.

Si Man Pou (Jornal do Cidadão): Rua dos Pescadores, Edif. Indian Ocean, 2° Fase, Bloco 2B; tel. 28722111; fax 28722133; e-mail shemin@macau.ctm.net; internet www.shimindaily.com.mo; f. 1944; daily; Dir and Editor-in-Chief KUNG MAN; circ. 8,000.

Tai Chung Pou: Av. Leste do Hipódromo 25-69, Edif. Fok Tai, 6° andar; tel. 28939888; fax 28282322; e-mail taichung@macau.ctm.net; f. 1933; daily; Dir VONG U. KONG; Editor-in-Chief CHAN TAI PAC; circ. 8,000.

Today Macau Journal: Pátio da Barca 20, R/C; tel. 28215050; fax 28210478; e-mail todaymac@yahoo.com; internet www.todaymacao.com; daily; Dir LAM IONG CHONG; Editor-in-Chief IU VENG ION; circ. 6,000.

ENGLISH LANGUAGE

Macau Post Daily: Av. de Almeida Ribeiro 99, Edif. Nam Wah Centre, 10° andar; tel. 28331050; fax 28331104; e-mail macaupost@macau.ctm.net; internet www.macaupostdaily.com; f. 2004; Dir HARALD BRUNING.

SELECTED PERIODICALS

Agora Macau: Av. Dr Rodrigo Rodrigues 7B, Edif. Centro Comercial First National, 10° andar, Sala 1005; tel. 66283212; fax 28519236; e-mail agora28@macau.ctn.net; weekly; Chinese; Dir LAO TAT KAO.

Boletim Associação Budista Geral de Macau: Estrada de Lou Lim Ieok 2, Pou Tai Un, Ilha da Taipa; tel. 28811038; bi-monthly; Dir LEI SENG VO.

Business Intelligence: Av. da Amizade, Edif. Chong Yu 12 D; tel. 28331258; fax 28331487; e-mail admin@bizintelligenceonline.com; internet www.bizintelligenceonline.com; monthly; Chinese; Dir PAULO ALEXANDRE TEIXEIRA DE AZEVEDO.

Cáritas Ligação: Largo de Santo Agostinho 1A; tel. 28573297; bimonthly; Dir PUN CHI MENG.

Chinese Cross Currents: Macau Ricci Institute, Av. Cons. Ferreira d'Almeida 95E; tel. 28532536; fax 28568274; e-mail currents@riccimac.org; internet www.riccimac.org; f. 2004; quarterly; Chinese and English; cultural studies; Dir of Publs ARTUR WARDEGA; Editor YVES CAMUS.

Macau Business: Av. Dr Rodrigo Rodrigues 600E, Edif. Centro Comercial First National, 16° andar, Sala 1605; tel. 28331258; fax 28331487; e-mail editor@macaubusiness.com; internet www.macaubusiness.com; f. 2004; monthly; Publr PAULO A. AZEVEDO; Editor-in-Chief EMANUEL GRAÇA; circ. 32,500.

Macau Manager: Rua de Santa Clara 9, Edif. Ribeiro, 6° andar; tel. 28323233; quarterly; Chinese; published by the Macau Management Assen; Dir CHUI SAI CHEONG.

Macau Times: Rua Almirante Costa Cabral 11, Edif. Iau Fai, 11° andar A; tel. 28554978; e-mail mail@macautimes.net; internet www.macautimes.net; f. 1994; monthly; Chinese; Dir WONG TAI WAI; circ. 5,000.

Revista Mensal de Macau: Av. Dr Rodrigo Rodrigues 600E, Edif. Centro Comercial First National, 14° andar, Sala 1404; tel. 28323660; fax 28323601; e-mail contacto@revistamacau.com; internet www.revistamacau.com; f. 1987; quarterly; Portuguese; govt publication; Dir VICTOR CHAN CHI PING; Editor FERNANDO SALES LOPES.

Saúde de Macau: Rua Ferreira do Amaral 9, 2° andar; tel. 28307271; quarterly; health issues; Dir KUOK HONG NENG.

x1 Week: Av. do Infante D. Henrique 43–53A, Edif. The Macau Square, 7° andar; tel. 28710566; fax 28710565; e-mail info@x1week.com; internet www.x1week.com; computing; Dir CHAN SAO SEONG.

NEWS AGENCIES

China News Service: Rua de Londres, Edif. Zhu Kuan, 14° andar, Y/Z; tel. 28594585; fax 28594586; Correspondent HUANG HONGBIN.

Xinhua (New China) News Agency Macao SAR Branch: Av. Gov. Jaime Silvério Marques, Edif. Zhu Kuan, 13° andar V; tel. 28727710; fax 28700548; e-mail xinhua@macau.ctm.net; Dir WANG HONGYU.

PRESS ASSOCIATIONS

Associação de Imprensa de Língua Portuguesa e Inglesa de Macau: Av. do Dr Rodrigo Rodrigues 600E, Centro Comercial First National, 14° andar, Sala 1408; tel. 28752401; fax 28752405; e-mail imprensamacau@gmail.com; f. 2005; Dir PAULO AZEVEDO.

Macao Media Workers Association: Travessa do Matadouro, Edif. 3, 3B; tel. and fax 28939486; e-mail mcju@macau.ctm.net; Pres. LEI PANG CHU.

Macao Journalists Association: Rua de Jorge Alvares 7–7B, Viva Court 17A; tel. and fax 28569819; e-mail macauja@gmail.com; internet hk.myblog.yahoo.com/macaujournalist; f. 1999; Pres. ZHENG YUEMING.

Macao Journalists Club: Estrada do Repouso, Edif. Tak Fai 18B; tel. and fax 28921395; e-mail cjm@macau.ctm.net; Pres. LO SONG MAN.

Macao Media Club: Rua de Santa Clara 5–7E, Edif. Ribeiro, 4B; tel. 28330035; fax 28330036; e-mail mmedia@macau.ctn.net; Pres. CHEONG CHI SENG.

Macao Sports Press Association: Estrada de D. Maria II 1-E, Edif. Kin Chit 2G; tel. 28838206, ext. 151; fax 28718285; e-mail macsport@macau.ctm.net; Pres. LAO IU KONG.

Publishers

Associação Beneficência Leitores Jornal Ou Mun: Nova-Guia 339; tel. 28711631; fax 28711630.

Fundação Macau: Av. República 6; tel. 28966777; fax 28968658; e-mail info@fm.org.mo; internet www.fmac.org.mo; Chair. WU ZHILIANG.

Instituto Cultural de Macau: publishes literature, social sciences and history; see under Tourism.

Livros do Oriente: Av. Amizade 876, Edif. Marina Gardens, 15E; tel. 28700320; fax 28700423; e-mail livros.macau@loriente.com; internet www.loriente.com; f. 1990; publishes in Portuguese, English and Chinese on regional history, culture, etc.; Gen. Man. ROGÉRIO BELTRÃO COELHO; Exec. Man. CECÍLIA JORGE.

Universidade de Macau—Centro de Publicações: Av. Padre Tomás Pereira, SJ, Taipa; tel. and fax 83978189; e-mail pub_enquiry@umac.mo; internet www.umac.mo/pub; f. 1993; art, economics, education, political science, history, literature, management, social sciences, etc.; Head Dr RAYMOND WONG.

GOVERNMENT PUBLISHER

Imprensa Oficial: Rua da Imprensa Nacional s/n; tel. 28573822; fax 28596802; e-mail info@io.gov.mo; internet www.io.gov.mo; Dir TOU CHI MAN.

Broadcasting and Communications

TELECOMMUNICATIONS

The Government initiated a liberalization of the mobile telecommunications market in 2001. In October 2006 the Government awarded an eight-year licence for 3G operations to Hutchison Telephone (Macau) Co Ltd, and to China Unicom (Macao) Ltd, a subsidiary of the Hong Kong-based China Unicom Ltd. These services commenced in October 2007.

Companhia de Telecomunicações de Macau, SARL (CTM): Rua de Lagos, Edif. Telecentro, Taipa; tel. 28833833; fax 88913031; e-mail helpdesk@macau.ctm.net; internet www.ctm.net; f. 1981; holds local telecommunications monopoly; shareholders include Cable and Wireless (51%), Portugal Telecom (28%), and CITIC Pacific (20%); Chair. JAMES CHEESEWRIGHT; CEO VANDY POON; 806 employees.

Hutchison Telephone (Macau) Co Ltd (3 Macau): Av. Xian Xing Hai, Zhu Kuan Bldg, 8/F; tel. 8933388; fax 781282; e-mail feedback@three.com.mo; internet www.three.com.mo; f. 2001; mobile telecommunications operator; subsidiary of Hutchison Whampoa Group (Hong Kong); local capital participation; CEO HO WAI-MING.

SmarTone Mobile (Macau) Ltd: Macao; tel. 28802688; fax 25628229; e-mail customer_care@smartone.com; internet www.smartone.com.mo; f. 2001; mobile telecommunications provider; subsidiary of SmarTone Mobile Communications Ltd (Hong Kong); local capital participation; CEO PATRICK CHAN KAI-LUNG.

Regulatory Authority

Office for the Development of Telecommunications and Information Technology (GDTTI): Av. da Praia Grande 789, 3° andar; tel. 28356328; fax 83969166; e-mail ifx@gdtti.gov.mo; internet www.gdtti.gov.mo; f. 2000.

BROADCASTING

Radio and Television

Cosmos Televisão por Satélite, SARL: Av. Infante D. Henrique 29, Edif. Va Iong, 4° andar A; tel. 28785731; fax 28788234; satellite TV services; Chair. NG FOK.

Lotus TV Macau: Alameda Dr Carlos D'Assumpção 180, Tong Nam Ah Centro Comércial, 22° andar A-V; tel. 28787606; fax 28787607; e-mail lotustv@lotustv.cc; internet www.lotustv.cc; f. 2008; Dir LI ZI SONG.

Macau Cable TV Ltd: Av. Conselheiro Ferreira de Almeida 71B; tel. 28822866; e-mail enquiry@macaucabletv.com; internet www.macaucabletv.com; f. 2000; offers 70 channels from around the world; CEO ANTONIO AGUIAR.

Macau Satellite Television: c/o Cosmos Televisão por Satélite, Av. Infante D. Henrique 29, Edif. Va Iong, 4° andar A; commenced transmissions in 2000; operated by Cosmos Televisão por Satélite, SARL; domestic and international broadcasts in Chinese aimed at Chinese-speaking audiences world-wide.

Rádio Vilaverde: Macao Jockey Club, Taipa; tel. 28820338; fax 28820337; e-mail helpdesk@am738.com; internet www.am738.com; private radio station; programmes in Chinese; CEO. STANLEY LEI.

Teledifusão de Macau, SARL (TDM): Rua Francisco Xavier Pereira 157A, POB 446; tel. 28335888 (Radio), 28519188 (TV); fax 28519522; e-mail inf@tdm.com.mo; internet www.tdm.com.mo; f. 1982; owned by the Govt of the Macao SAR ; radio channels: Rádio Macau (Av. do Dr Rodrigo Rodrigues, Edif. Nam Kwong, 7° andar; tel. 28335888; fax 28343220; rmacau@tdm.com.mo), broadcasting 24 hours per day in Portuguese on TDM Canal 1 (incl. broadcasts from RTP International in Portugal) and 17 hours per day in Chinese on TDM Channel 2; Chair. Dr STANLEY HO.

Finance

(cap. = capital; res = reserves; dep. = deposits; m. = million; brs = branches; amounts in patacas unless otherwise indicated)

BANKING

Macao has no foreign-exchange controls, its external payments system being fully liberalized on current and capital transactions. The Financial System Act, aiming to improve the reputation of the territory's banks and to comply with international standards, took effect in September 1993. A total of 27 registered banks were in operation in 2009.

Issuing Authority

Autoridade Monetária de Macau (AMCM) (Monetary Authority of Macao): Calçada do Gaio 24–26, POB 3017; tel. 28568288; fax 28325432; e-mail general@amcm.gov.mo; internet www.amcm.gov.mo; f. 1989; est. as Autoridade Monetária e Cambial de Macau (AMCM), to replace the Instituto Emissor de Macau; cap. 8,324m., res 4,860m., dep. 132,183.1m. (Dec. 2009); govt-owned; Chair. ANSELMO L. S. TENG.

Banks of Issue

Banco Nacional Ultramarino (BNU), SA: Av. Almeida Ribeiro 22, POB 465; tel. 28335533; fax 28355653; e-mail markt@bnu.com.mo; internet www.bnu.com.mo; f. 1864; est. in Macao 1902; subsidiary of Caixa Geral de Depósitos (Portugal) since 2001; agent of Macao Govt; agreement whereby the Bank remains an agent of the treasury signed with the administration of the Macao SAR in 2000; to remain a note-issuing bank until 2020; cap. 400m., res 1,456.7m., dep. 24,550.4m. (Dec. 2009); Chair. Dr RODOLFO MASCARENHAS; CEO ARTUR SANTOS; 14 brs.

Bank of China: Av. Dr Mário Soares, Edif. Banco da China, R/C; tel. 28781828; fax 28781833; e-mail bocmo@bocmacao.com; internet www.bocmacau.com; f. 1950 as Nan Tung Bank, name changed 1987; authorized to issue banknotes from Oct. 1995; Gen. Man. YE YIXIN; 24 brs.

Other Commercial Banks

Banco Comercial de Macau, SA: Av. da Praia Grande 572, POB 545; tel. 87910000; fax 28332795; e-mail bcmbank@bcm.com.mo; internet www.bcm.com.mo; f. 1974; cap. 225m., res 188.3m., dep. 9,999.1m. (Dec. 2009); Chair. and Pres. DAVID SHOU-YEH WONG; CEO CHIU LUNG-MAN; 17 brs.

Banco Delta Asia (BDA), SARL: Largo de Santo Agostinho; tel. 87969600; fax 87969624; e-mail contact@bdam.com; internet www.delta-asia.com.mo; f. 1935; fmrly Banco Hang Sang; cap. 210.0m., res 173.2m., dep. 3,323.1m. (Dec. 2004); Chair. STANLEY AU; Exec. Dir DAVID LAU; 9 brs.

Banco Tai Fung, SARL: Av. Alameda Dr Carlos d'Assumpção 418, Edif. Sede Banco Tai Fung; tel. 28322323; fax 28570737; e-mail tfbsecr@taifungbank.com; internet www.taifungbank.com; f. 1971; cap. 1,000m., res 2,062m., dep. 43,098m. (Dec. 2011); Chair. HO HAO TONG; Pres. LIU DAGUO; 22 brs.

Banco Weng Hang, SA: Av. Almeida Ribeiro 241; tel. 28335678; fax 28576527; e-mail bwhhrd@whbmac.com; internet www.whbmac.com; f. 1973; subsidiary of Wing Hang Bank Ltd, Hong Kong; cap. 120m., res 1,482.6m., dep. 17,373.7m. (Dec. 2010); Chair. PATRICK YUK-BUN FUNG; Gen. Man. TAK LIM LEE; 11 brs.

China Construction Bank (Macau) Corpn Ltd: Av. Almeida Ribeiro 70–76, POB 165; tel. 83969611; fax 83969683; e-mail ccb.macau@asia.ccb.com; internet www.asia.ccb.com; f. 1937; fmrly Banco da América (Macau); cap. 500m., res 88.3m., dep. 3,563.1m. (Dec. 2008); Pres. and CEO (Asia) MIRANDA KWOK; 8 brs.

Industrial and Commercial Bank of China (Macau) Ltd (ICBC—Macau): Av. da Amizade 555, Macau Landmark, 18° andar, Torre Banco ICBC; tel. 28555222; fax 28338064; e-mail icbc@icbc.com.mo; f. 1972; est. as Seng Heng Bank Ltd; present name adopted 2009, following merger with Industrial and Commercial Bank of China; Exec. Dir PATRICK YUEN; 9 brs.

Luso International Banking Ltd: Av. Dr Mário Soares 47; tel. 28378977; fax 28711100; e-mail lusobank@lusobank.com.mo; internet www.lusobank.com.mo; f. 1974; cap. 315.6m., res 754.7m., dep. 15,030.0m. (Dec. 2009); Chair. LU YAO MING; Gen. Man. IP KAI MING; 11 brs.

Banking Association

Associação de Bancos de Macau (ABM) (Macau Association of Banks): Av. da Praia Grande 575, Edif. 'Finanças', 15/F; tel. 28511921; fax 28346049; e-mail abm@macau.ctm.net; f. 1985; Chair. YE YIXIN.

INSURANCE

ACE Seguradora, SA: Rua Dr Pedro José Lobo 1–3, Luso Bank Bldg, 17° andar, Apt 1701–02; tel. 28557191; fax 28570188; Pres. and CEO (Asia-Pacific) DAMIEN SULLIVAN.

American International Assurance Co (Bermuda) Ltd: Unit 601, AIA Tower, Av. Comercial de Macau 251A–301; tel. 89881817; fax 28315900; e-mail salina-if.ieong@aig.com; life insurance; Rep. ALEXANDRA FOO CHEUK LING.

Asia Insurance Co Ltd: 762 Av. da Praia Grande, Edif. China Plaza, 10° andar, Apt C-D; tel. 28570439; fax 28570438; e-mail asiamc@macau.ctm.net; non-life insurance; Rep. S. T. CHAN.

AXA China Region Insurance Company: Av. do Infante D. Henrique 43–53A, 20° andar, The Macau Square; tel. 28781188; fax 28780022; life insurance; CEO (Asia) MICHAEL BISHOP.

Chartis Insurance Hong Kong Ltd: Av. Comercial de Macau 251A-301, Unit 6, AIA Tower, 5° andar; tel. 28355602; fax 28355299; internet www.chartisinsurance.com.hk/macau; f. 2010; non-life insurance.

China Life Insurance (Overseas) Co Ltd: Alameda Dr Carlos D'Assumpção 263, China Civil Plaza, 22° andar A-B; tel. 28787288; fax 28787287; e-mail info@chinalife.com.mo; Gen. Man. WANG JIAN GUO.

China Taiping Insurance (Macau) Co Ltd: Av. Alameda Dr Carlos d'Assumpção 398, Edif. CNAC, 10° andar; tel. 28785578; fax 28787218; e-mail info@mo.cntaiping.com; internet www.cicmacau.com.mo; non-life insurance.

Companhia de Seguros Delta Asia, SA: Rua do Campo 39–41; tel. 28559898; fax 28921545; e-mail contact@bdam.com; internet www.delta-asia.com/macau; Chair. STANLEY AU.

Companhia de Seguros Fidelidade: Av. da Praia Grande 567, Edif. BNU, 14° andar; tel. 28374072; fax 28511085; e-mail info@fidelidademundial.com.mo; life and non-life insurance; Gen. Man. EDUARDO CLARISSEAU MESQUITA D'ABREU.

Crown Life Insurance Co: Av. da Praia Grande 287, Nam Yuet Commercial Centre, Bl. B, 8° andar; tel. 28570828; fax 28570844; Rep. STEVEN SIU.

HSBC Insurance (Asia) Ltd: Av. da Praia Grande 619, Edif. Comercial Si Toi, 1° andar; tel. 28212323; fax 28217162; non-life insurance; Rep. NORA CHIO.

ING Life Insurance Co (Macao) Ltd: Av. Almeida Ribeiro 61, 11° andar, Unit C and D; tel. 9886060; fax 9886100; e-mail customerservice@ing.com.mo; internet www.ing.com.mo; Heads LENNARD YONG, WIM HEKSTRA.

Luen Fung Hang Insurance Co Ltd (Luen Fung Hang Life Ltd): Alameda Dr Carlos d'Assumpção 398, Edif. CNAC, 4° andar; tel. 28700033; fax 28700088; e-mail info@luenfunghang.com; internet www.luenfunghang.com; life (Luen Fung Hang Life Ltd) and non-life insurance; Rep. SI CHI HOK.

Macao Life Insurance Co (Macao Insurance Company): Av. da Praia Grande 594, Edif. BCM, 10–11° andar; tel. 28555078; fax 28551074; e-mail mic@bcm.com.mo; internet www.macauinsurance.com.mo; life and non-life insurance (Macao Insurance Company); Rep. SI CHI HOK.

Manulife (International) Ltd: Av. da Praia Grande 517, Edif. Comercial Nam Tung, 8° andar, Unit B & C; tel. 3980388; fax 28323312; internet www.manulife.com.hk; CEO MICHAEL HUDDART.

MassMutual Asia Ltd: Av. da Praia Grande 517, Edif. Nam Tung 16° andar, E1–E2; tel. 28322622; fax 28322042; life insurance; Pres. MANLY CHENG.

Min Xin Insurance Co Ltd: Rua do Dr Pedro José Lobo 1–3, Luso International Bank Bldg, 27° andar, Rm 2704; tel. 28305684; fax 28305600; non-life insurance; Rep. PETER CHAN.

MSIG Insurance (Hong Kong) Ltd: Av. da Praia Grande 693, Edif. Tai Wah, 13° andar A–B; tel. 28923329; fax 28923349; internet www.msig.com.hk; wholly owned subsidiary of Mitsui Sumitomo Insurance Group Holdings Inc; CEO KENNETH REID.

QBE Insurance (International) Ltd: Rua do Comandante Mata e Oliveira 32, Edif. Associação Industrial de Macau, 8° andar B-C; tel. 28323909; fax 28323911; e-mail sally.siu@mo.qbe.com; non-life insurance; Rep. SALLY SIU.

Insurers' Associations

Federation of Macao Professional Insurance Intermediaries: Rua de Pequim 244–46, Macao Finance Centre, 6° andar G; tel. 28703268; fax 28703266; Rep. DAVID KONG.

Macao Insurance Agents and Brokers Association: Av. da Praia Grande 309, Nam Yuet Commercial Centre, 8° andar D; tel. 28378901; fax 28570848; Rep. JACK LI KWOK TAI.

Macao Insurers' Association: Av. da Praia Grande 575, Edif. 'Finanças', 15° andar; tel. 28511923; fax 28337531; e-mail info@mia-macau.com; internet www.mia-macau.com; 22 mems; Pres. SI CHI HOK.

Trade and Industry

CHAMBER OF COMMERCE

Associação Comercial de Macau (Macao Chamber of Commerce): Rua de Xangai 175, Edif. ACM, 5° andar; tel. 28576833; fax 28594513; internet www.acm.org.mo; Pres. MA IAO LAI.

INDUSTRIAL AND TRADE ASSOCIATIONS

Associação dos Construtores Civis e Empresas de Fomento Predial de Macau (Macao Association of Building Contractors and Developers): Rua do Campo 103, 5° andar; tel. 28573226; fax 28345710; e-mail info@macaudeveloper.com; internet www.macaudeveloper.com; 145 corp. mems; Pres. FONG CHI KEONG.

Associação dos Exportadores e Importadores de Macau (Macao Importers and Exporters Association): Av. Infante D. Henrique 60–62, Centro Comercial 'Central', 3° andar; tel. 28375859; fax 28512174; e-mail aeim@macau.ctm.net; internet www.macauexport.com; exporters' and importers' asscn; Pres. VITOR NG.

Associação dos Industriais de Tecelagem e Fiação de Lã de Macau (Macao Weaving and Spinning of Wool Manufacturers' Asscn): Av. da Amizade 271B, Edif. Kam Wa Kok, 6° andar A; tel. 28553378; fax 28511105; Pres. WONG SHOO KEE.

Associação Industrial de Macau (Industrial Association of Macao): Rua Dr Pedro José Lobo 34–36, Edif. AIM, 17° andar; tel. 28574125; fax 28578305; e-mail info@madeinmacau.net; internet www.madeinmacau.net; f. 1959; Pres. HO IAT SENG.

Centro de Produtividade e Transferência de Tecnologia de Macau (Macao Productivity and Technology Transfer Centre): Rua de Xangai 175, Edif. ACM, 6° andar; tel. 28781313; fax 28788233; e-mail cpttm@cpttm.org.mo; internet www.cpttm.org.mo; vocational or professional training; Pres. VITOR NG; Dir-Gen. VICTOR KUAN.

Instituto de Promoção do Comércio e do Investimento de Macau (IPIM) (Macao Trade and Investment Promotion Institute): Av. da Amizade 918, World Trade Center Bldg, 1°–4° andares; tel. 28710300; fax 28590309; e-mail ipim@ipim.gov.mo; internet www.ipim.gov.mo; Pres. JACKSON CHANG.

Ponto de Contacto da Rede Portuguesa da Enterprise Europe Network: Alameda Dr Carlos d'Assumpção 263, Edif. China Civil Plaza, 20° andar; tel. 28713338; fax 28713339; e-mail info@ieem.org.mo; internet euinfo.ieem.org.mo; f. 1992; promotes trade with European Union; fmrly Euro-Info Centre Relay of Macao; Man. LORETTA KU; Pres. JOSÉ LUÍS DE SALES MARQUES.

SDPIM (Macao Industrial Parks Development Co Ltd): Av. da Amizade 918, World Trade Center Bldg, 13° andar A & B; tel. 28786636; fax 28785374; e-mail sdpim@macau.ctm.net; internet www.sdpim.com.mo; f. 1993; Pres. of the Bd PAULINA Y. ALVES DOS SANTOS.

World Trade Center Macao, SARL: Av. da Amizade 918, Edif. World Trade Center, 16° andar; tel. 28727666; fax 28727633; e-mail wtcmc@wtc-macau.com; internet www.wtc-macau.com; f. 1995; trade information and business services, office rentals, exhibition and conference facilities; Chair. PETER LAM; Man. Dir ALBERTO EXPEDITO MARÇAL.

UTILITIES

Electricity

Companhia de Electricidade de Macau, SARL (CEM): Estrada D. Maria II 32–36, Edif. CEM; tel. 28339933; fax 28308361; e-mail e-doc@cem-macau.com; internet www.cem-macau.com; f. 1972; sole distributor; Chair. JOÃO MARQUES DA CRUZ; CEO FRANKLIN WILLEMYNS.

Water

Sociedade de Abastecimento de Aguas de Macau, SARL (SAAM) (Macao Water): Av. do Conselheiro Borja 718; tel. 28220088; fax 28234660; e-mail customer.info@macaowater.com; internet www.macaowater.com; f. 1985; jt venture with Suez Lyonnaise des Eaux; Chair. STEPHEN CLARK; Man. Dir CHIN CHEUNG.

TRADE UNIONS

Macao Federation of Trade Unions: Rua Ribeira do Patane 2; tel. 28576231; fax 28553110; Chair. CHIANG CHONG SEK.

Macao Labour Union: Pres. HO HEN KUOK.

Transport

RAILWAYS

There are no railways in Macao. A plan to connect Macao with Zhuhai and Guangzhou (People's Republic of China) is under consideration. Construction of the Zhuhai–Guangzhou section was under way in mainland China in the early 21st century. In October 2006 the Government announced plans to invest 4,200,000m. patacas in the construction of an elevated light rail system. According to reports, the project would span around 22 km, with 26 stations.

ROADS

In 2007 the public road network extended to 401 km. The peninsula of Macao is linked to the islands of Taipa and Coloane by three bridges and by a 2.2-km causeway, respectively. The first bridge (2.6 km) opened in 1974. In conjunction with the construction of an airport on Taipa (see Civil Aviation), a 4.4-km four-lane bridge to the Macao peninsula was opened in April 1994. A third link between Macao and Taipa, a double-deck bridge, opened in early 2005. A second connection to the mainland, the 1.5-km six-lane road bridge (the Lotus Bridge) linking Macao with Hengqin Island (in Zhuhai, Guangdong Province), opened to traffic in December 1999. Construction of a new bridge linking Macao with Hong Kong's Lantau Island and Zhuhai City, Guangdong Province, commenced in December 2009. To extend to nearly 50 km and comprising a six-lane expressway, the bridge was originally scheduled for completion in 2016.

SHIPPING

There are representatives of shipping agencies for international lines in Macao. There are passenger and cargo services to the People's Republic of China. Regular services between Macao and Hong Kong are run by the Hong Kong-based New World First Ferry and Shun Tak-China Travel Ship Management Ltd companies. A new terminal opened in late 1993. The port of Kao-ho (on the island of Coloane), which handles cargo and operates container services, entered into service in 1991.

Agência de Navegação Ka Fung: Av. da Praia Grande 429, South Bay Centro Comercial, 11° andar, Rm 1101; tel. 28553311; fax

28569233; e-mail info@kafung-shipping.com; internet www.kafung-shipping.com; f. 1984.

CTS Parkview Holdings Ltd: Av. Amizade, Porto Exterior, Terminal Marítimo de Macau, Sala 2006B; tel. 28726789; fax 28727112; purchased by Sociedade de Turismo e Diversões de Macau (STDM) in 1998.

DHC Logistics (Macau) Ltd: Av. de Praia Grande 619, Edif. Comercial Si Toi, 7° andar B; tel. 28788063; fax 28788093; e-mail pollywong@dhclogistics.com; internet www.dhclogistics.com.

Macao Dragon: Terminal Ferry, Taipa; tel. 82968296; internet www.macaodragon.com; f. 2010; operates two catamarans between Hong Kong and Macao; owned by Giant Dragon Sea Transport Co Ltd; Chair. DAVID LIANG.

New Line Shipping Ltd: Av. do Dr Rodrigo Rodrigues, Centro Comercial First Int., 24° andar, Rm 2404; tel. 28710250; fax 28710252; e-mail newline@macau.ctm.net; internet www.newline.com.mo; f. 2001.

STDM Shipping Dept: Av. da Amizade Terminal Marítimo do Porto Exterior; tel. 28726111; fax 28726234; e-mail shpgdept@macau.ctm.net; affiliated to STDM; Gen. Man. ALAN HO; Office Man. ALAN LI.

Association

Associação de Agências de Navegação e de Logistica de Macau (Macau Shipping and Logistics Association): Rua de Xanghai 175, Edif. ACM, 8F; tel. 28528207; fax 28302667; e-mail secretary@logistics.org.mo; internet www.logistics.org.mo; f. 1981; Pres. VONG KOK SENG.

Port Authority

Capitania dos Portos de Macau: Rampa da Barra, Quartel dos Mouros, POB 47; tel. 28559922; fax 28511986; e-mail info@marine.gov.mo; internet www.marine.gov.mo; Dir WONG SOI MAN.

CIVIL AVIATION

Macau International Airport, constructed on the island of Taipa, was officially opened in December 1995. The terminal has the capacity to handle 6m. passengers a year. By 2007 a total of 14 airlines operated flights to 25 destinations, mostly in mainland China, but also to the Democratic People's Republic of Korea, the Philippines, Singapore, Taiwan and Thailand. Helicopter services between Hong Kong and Macao are available.

Autoridade de Aviação Civil (AACM) (Civil Aviation Authority of Macao): Alameda Dr Carlos d'Assumpção 336–342, Centro Comercial Cheng Feng, 18° andar; tel. 28511213; fax 28338089; e-mail aacm@aacm.gov.mo; internet www.aacm.gov.mo; f. 1991; Pres. SIMON CHAN WENG HONG.

Administração de Aeroportos, Lda (ADA): Macau International Airport, Taipa; tel. 28861111; fax 28862222; e-mail directoraeroporto@ada.com.mo; internet www.ada.com.mo; f. 1995; owned by China National Aviation Corpn (CNAC) and ANA—Aeroportos de Portugal SA; CEO JOSÉ CARLOS ANGEJA.

CAM (Sociedade do Aeroporto Internacional de Macau, SARL): CAM Office Bldg, 4/F, Av. Wai Long, Macao International Airport; tel. 5988888; fax 28785465; e-mail mkd@macau-airport.com; internet www.macau-airport.com; f. 1989; airport owner, responsible for design, construction, development and international marketing of Macao International Airport; Chair. DENG JUN.

Air Macau: Macao Unidos Praça, Alameda Dr Carlos d'Assumpção 398, 13°–18° andar; tel. 83966888; fax 83966866; e-mail airmacau@airmacau.com.mo; internet www.airmacau.com.mo; f. 1994; controlled by China National Aviation Corpn (Group) Macao Co Ltd; services to several cities in the People's Republic of China, the Republic of Korea, the Philippines, Taiwan and Thailand; other destinations planned; Chair. ZHAO XIAO HANG; CEO ZHOU GUANG QUAN.

Tourism

In addition to the casinos, Macao's attractions include the cultural heritage and museums, dog-racing, horse-racing, and annual events such as Chinese New Year (January/February), the Macao Arts Festival (February/March), Dragon Boat Festival (May/June), the Macao International Fireworks Festival (September/October), the International Music Festival (October), the Macao Grand Prix for racing cars and motorcycles (November) and the Macao International Marathon (December). In 2007 the opening of the Las Vegas Sands Venetian casino and hotel complex provided 3,000 luxury hotel rooms. A total of 22,356 hotel rooms were available in December 2011. Visitor arrivals rose from 25.0m. in 2010 to nearly 28.0m. in 2011, the majority of tourists travelling from mainland China and from Hong Kong. Receipts from tourism (excluding passenger transport) reached a provisional US $17,637m. in 2009.

Macao Government Tourist Office (MGTO): Alameda Dr Carlos d'Assumpção 335–341, Edif. Hot Line, 12° andar; tel. 28315566; fax 28510104; e-mail mgto@macautourism.gov.mo; internet www.macautourism.gov.mo; Dir JOÃO MANUEL COSTA ANTUNES.

Instituto Cultural de Macau: Praça do Tap Seac, Edif. do Instituto Cultural; tel. 28366866; fax 28366899; e-mail postoffice@icm.gov.mo; internet www.icm.gov.mo; f. 1982; organizes performances, concerts, exhibitions, festivals, etc.; library facilities; Pres. HAN XIAOYAN.

Macau Hotel Association: Hotel Lisboa, East Wing 4F, Av. de Lisboa 2-4; tel. 28703416; fax 28703415; e-mail mhacmo@macau.ctm.net; internet www.macauhotel.org; f. 1985; aims to promote and support high quality standards and growth of tourism, in conjunction with MGTO; Dir ANTONIO SAMEIRO.

Sociedade de Turismo e Diversões de Macau (STDM), SA: Hotel Lisboa, 9th Floor, Avda de Lisboa; tel. 28574266; fax 28562285; e-mail stdmmdof@macau.ctm.net; f. 1962; operation of its casinos handled by subsidiary Sociedade de Jogos de Macau (SJM) after ending of STDM's monopoly franchise in 2002; other commercial interests include hospitality, real estate, transport, infrastructure and overseas investments; Man. Dir Dr STANLEY HO.

Defence

The budget for defence is allocated by the Chinese Government. Upon the territory's reversion to Chinese sovereignty in December 1999, troops of the People's Liberation Army (PLA) were stationed in Macao. The force comprises around 1,000 troops: a maximum of 500 soldiers are stationed in Macao, the remainder in Zhuhai, China, on the border with the SAR. The unit is directly responsible to the Commander of the Guangzhou Military Region and to the Central Military Commission. The Macao garrison is composed mainly of ground troops. Naval and air defence tasks are performed by the naval vessel unit of the PLA garrison in Hong Kong and by the air force unit in Huizhou. Subject to the request of the Macao SAR, the garrison may participate in law enforcement and rescue operations in the SAR.

Commander of the PLA Garrison in Macao: Col. ZHU QING-SHENG.

Education

The education system in Macao is structured as follows: pre-school education (lasting two years); primary preparatory year (one year); primary education (six years); and secondary education (five–six years, divided into junior secondary of three years and senior secondary of two–three years). Schooling is compulsory between the ages of five and 15, but normally lasts from the ages of three to 17. In 2009/10 schools enrolled a total of 10,038 children in kindergarten, 25,705 primary pupils and 39,298 secondary students. Enrolment for the same year at primary schools included 82% (males 81%, females 84%) of pupils in the relevant age-group, while enrolment at secondary level included 76% (males 78%, females 75%) of pupils in the relevant age-group. In 2009/10 23,562 students attended courses offered by tertiary institutions, ranging from the bacharelato (three-year courses) to doctorate programmes. The projected education budget for 2007 was 1,860m. patacas.

COLOMBIA

Introductory Survey

LOCATION, CLIMATE, LANGUAGE, RELIGION, FLAG, CAPITAL

The Republic of Colombia lies in the north-west of South America, with the Caribbean Sea to the north and the Pacific Ocean to the west. Its continental neighbours are Venezuela and Brazil to the east, and Peru and Ecuador to the south, while Panama connects it with Central America. The coastal areas have a tropical rainforest climate, the plateaux are temperate, and in the Andes mountains there are areas of permanent snow. The language is Spanish. Almost all of the inhabitants profess Christianity, and around 87% are Roman Catholics. There are small Protestant and Jewish minorities. The national flag (proportions 2 by 3) has three horizontal stripes, of yellow (one-half of the depth) over dark blue over red. The capital is Bogotá.

CONTEMPORARY POLITICAL HISTORY

Historical Context

Colombia was under Spanish rule from the 16th century until 1819, when it achieved independence as part of Gran Colombia, which included Ecuador, Panama and Venezuela. Ecuador and Venezuela seceded in 1830, when Colombia (then including Panama) became a separate republic. In 1903 the province of Panama successfully rebelled and became an independent country. For more than a century, ruling power in Colombia has been shared between two political parties, the Conservatives (Partido Conservador Colombiano, PCC) and the Liberals (Partido Liberal Colombiano, PL), whose rivalry has often led to violence. President Laureano Gómez of the PCC ruled as a dictator from 1949 until his overthrow by Gen. Gustavo Rojas Pinilla in a coup in June 1953. President Rojas established a right-wing dictatorship but, following widespread rioting, he was deposed in May 1957, when a five-man military junta took power. According to official estimates, lawlessness during 1949–58, known as 'La Violencia', caused the deaths of about 280,000 people.

Domestic Political Affairs

In an attempt to restore peace and stability, the PCC and the PL agreed to co-operate in a National Front. Under this arrangement, the presidency was to be held by the PCC and the PL in rotation, while cabinet portfolios would be divided equally between the two parties and both would have an equal number of seats in each house of the bicameral Congreso (Congress). In December 1957, in Colombia's first vote on the basis of universal adult suffrage, this agreement was overwhelmingly approved by a referendum and was subsequently incorporated in Colombia's Constitution, dating from 1886.

In May 1958 the first presidential election under the amended Constitution was won by the National Front candidate, Alberto Lleras Camargo, a PL member who had been President in 1945–46. As provided by the 1957 agreement, he was succeeded by a member of the PCC, Guillermo León Valencia, who was, in turn, succeeded by a PL candidate, Carlos Lleras Restrepo, in 1966.

At the presidential election in April 1970 the National Front candidate, Misael Pastrana Borrero (PCC), narrowly defeated Gen. Rojas, the former dictator, who campaigned as leader of the Alianza Nacional Popular (ANAPO). At concurrent congressional elections the National Front lost its majority, while ANAPO became the main opposition group in the Congreso. The result of the presidential election was challenged by supporters of ANAPO, and an armed wing of the party, the Movimiento 19 de Abril (M-19), began to organize guerrilla activity against the Government. It was joined by dissident members of a pro-Soviet guerrilla group, the Fuerzas Armadas Revolucionarias de Colombia (FARC), established in 1966. (In 1982 the FARC was renamed the Fuerzas Armadas Revolucionarias de Colombia—Ejército del Pueblo, FARC—EP, although it continued to be known by its shorter acronym.)

The bipartisan form of government ended formally with the 1974 elections, although the Cabinet remained subject to the parity agreement. The PCC and the PL together won an overwhelming majority of seats in the Congreso, and support for ANAPO was greatly reduced. The presidential election was won by the PL candidate, Alfonso López Michelsen.

The PL won a clear majority in both houses at congressional elections in February 1978, and in June the PL candidate, Julio César Turbay Ayala, won the presidential election. Turbay continued to observe the National Front agreement, and attempted to address the problems of urban terrorism and drugs-trafficking. In 1982 the guerrillas suffered heavy losses after successful counter-insurgency operations, combined with the activities of a new anti-guerrilla group associated with drugs-smuggling enterprises, the Muerte a Secuestradores (MAS, Death to Kidnappers), whose targets later became trade union leaders, academics and human rights activists.

At congressional elections in March 1982 the PL maintained its majority in both houses. In May the PCC candidate, Belisario Betancur Cuartas, won the presidential election, benefiting from a division within the PL. President Betancur declared a broad amnesty for guerrillas in November, reconvened the Peace Commission (first established in 1981) and ordered an investigation into the MAS. Despite the Peace Commission's successful negotiation of cease-fire agreements with the FARC, the M-19 (now operating as a left-wing guerrilla movement) and the Ejército Popular de Liberación (EPL) during 1984, factions of all three groups opposed to the truce continued to conduct guerrilla warfare against the authorities. The assassination of the Minister of Justice in May prompted the Government to declare a nation-wide state of siege and announce its intention to enforce its hitherto unobserved extradition treaty with the USA.

In June 1985 the M-19 formally withdrew from the cease-fire agreement. In November a dramatic siege by the M-19 at the Palace of Justice in the capital, during which more than 100 people were killed, resulted in severe public criticism of the Government and the armed forces for their handling of events. Negotiations with the M-19 were suspended indefinitely.

At congressional elections in March 1986 the traditional wing of the PL secured a clear victory over the PCC, and the PL's candidate, Virgilio Barco Vargas, was elected President in May. The large majority secured by the PL at both elections obliged the PCC to form the first formal opposition to a government for 30 years.

Hopes that an indefinite cease-fire agreement, concluded between the FARC and the Government in March 1986, would facilitate the full participation of the Unión Patriótica (UP), formed by the FARC, in the political process were largely frustrated by the Government's failure to respond effectively to a campaign of assassinations of UP members, conducted by paramilitary 'death squads'. The crisis was compounded in October 1987 by the decision of six guerrilla groups, including the FARC, the Ejército de Liberación Nacional (ELN) and the M-19, to form a joint front, the Coordinadora Guerrillera Simón Bolívar. Although the Government extended police powers against drugs dealers, its efforts were severely hampered by the Supreme Court's ruling that Colombia's extradition treaty with the USA was unconstitutional.

In September 1989 the M-19 announced that it had reached agreement with the Government on a peace treaty, under which its members were to demobilize and disarm in exchange for a general amnesty, reintegration into civilian life and firm commitments from the Barco administration that a referendum would be held to decide the question of constitutional reform and that proposals for comprehensive changes to the electoral law would be introduced in the Congreso. In October the M-19 was formally constituted as a political party, and by March 1990 all M-19 guerrilla forces had surrendered their weapons.

César Gaviria Trujillo

In March 1990 Bernardo Jaramillo, the UP candidate in the upcoming presidential ballot, was assassinated, and in April Carlos Pizarro of the M-19 became the third presidential candidate to be killed by hired assassins since August 1989. César Gaviria Trujillo of the PL was proclaimed the winner of the election in May. Some 90% of voters approved proposals for the creation of a National Constituent Assembly in a de facto referendum held simultaneously. The new President formed a Cabinet of 'national unity', and confirmed his commitment to combating drugs-trafficking.

In October 1990 the creation of the National Constituent Assembly was declared constitutionally acceptable by the Supreme Court. Alianza Democrática (AD)—M-19 candidates secured 19 of the 70 contested Assembly seats, forcing the ruling PL and the Conservatives to seek support from them for the successful enactment of reform proposals. In February 1991 the National Constituent Assembly was inaugurated. The Assembly was expanded from 70 to 74 members in order to incorporate representatives of several former guerrilla groupings. By June an agreement was reached between President Gaviria and representatives of the PL, the AD—M-19 and the conservative Movimiento de Salvación Nacional (MSN) that, in order to facilitate the process of political and constitutional renovation, the Congreso should be dissolved prematurely, pending new elections.

The new Constitution became effective on 6 July 1991. The state of siege, imposed in 1984 in response to the escalation in political and drugs-related violence, also was ended. The Constitution placed considerable emphasis upon provisions to encourage greater political participation and to eradicate electoral corruption and misrepresentation. While the Constitution was welcomed enthusiastically by the majority of the population, reservations were expressed that clauses relating to the armed forces remained largely unchanged and that provisions which recognized the democratic rights of indigenous groups did not extend to their territorial claims.

Relations with the Medellín drugs cartel, believed to be responsible for a series of assassinations of prominent citizens, improved considerably following the release, in May 1991, of its two remaining hostages. In June, following the decision to prohibit constitutionally the practice of extradition, the Government's efforts were rewarded with the surrender of Pablo Escobar, the supposed head of the Medellín cartel. Charges brought against Escobar included several of murder, kidnapping and terrorism. In July the cartel announced that its military operations were to be suspended. Hopes that Escobar's surrender might precipitate a decline in drugs-related violence were frustrated by reports that Escobar was continuing to direct cocaine cartel operations from his purpose-built prison at Envigado, and by the emergence of the powerful Cali drugs cartel.

The Liberals were the most successful party in the congressional elections of October 1991, with a clear majority of seats in both chambers. The traditional Conservative opposition suffered from a division in their support between the PCC, the MSN and the Nueva Fuerza Democrática, which together secured around one-quarter of the seats in each house.

Meanwhile, in February 1990 the Government had established the National Council for Normalization, in an attempt to repeat the success of recent peace initiatives with the M-19 in negotiations with other revolutionary groups. The EPL announced the end of its armed struggle in August and joined the political mainstream (retaining the initials EPL as Esperanza, Paz y Libertad), along with the Comando Quintín Lame and the Partido Revolucionario de Trabajadores, in 1991. Attempts to negotiate with the FARC and the ELN, however, proved fruitless, and violent clashes between the remaining guerrilla groups (now co-ordinating actions as the Coordinadora Nacional Guerrillera Simón Bolívar—CNGSB) and security forces persisted. In November Gaviria declared a 90-day state of internal disturbance, prompting the M-10 to withdraw from the Government.

As the security situation continued to deteriorate, in February 1993 the Government announced a significant increase in its budget allocation for security, and in April doubled the length of prison terms for terrorist acts. The state of internal disturbance was also extended twice. The intensification of drugs-related violence in the capital was attributed to an attempt by Pablo Escobar (who had escaped from prison in mid-1992) to force the Government to negotiate more favourable conditions for his surrender, and prompted the formation of a vigilante group, Pepe (Perseguidos por Pablo Escobar—those Persecuted by Pablo Escobar), which launched a campaign of retaliatory violence against Escobar's family, associates and property. A simultaneous and sustained assault by Pepe and by the security forces against the remnants of the Medellín cartel resulted in the death or surrender of many notable cartel members, culminating in the death of Escobar himself in December.

Ernesto Samper Pizano

Congressional elections conducted in March 1994 re-established the traditional two-party dominance of the PL and the PCC. The PL candidate, Ernesto Samper Pizano, was elected to the presidency in June. Shortly after taking office in August, allegations emerged that Samper's election campaign had been funded partly by contributions from the Cali cartel. Tape recordings of conversations were dismissed by the Prosecutor-General as insufficient proof of such contributions having been made. Emergence of a similar recording, implicating the Colombian Chief of National Police in the payment of a bribe by the Cali cartel, prompted the US Senate to vote to make the disbursement of future aid to Colombia dependent on its level of co-operation in anti-drugs programmes.

A CNGSB offensive in 1994 resulted in numerous deaths on both sides and considerable damage to infrastructure. Guerrilla activities further intensified after the new administration took office. In September, under intense international pressure, the new Government announced an initiative to address allegations of human rights abuses by the security forces; measures included the reform of the National Police and the dissolution of all paramilitary units. In November President Samper complied with a guerrilla request that imprisoned rebel leaders be moved from military installations to civilian prisons, and declared the Government's willingness to enter into negotiations.

In February 1995 President Samper reiterated his commitment to combating all illegal drugs-related activities in the country. A number of initiatives were launched in Cali, resulting in the capture of the head of the Cali drugs cartel, Gilberto Rodríguez Orejuela, and four other cartel leaders in mid-1995. Meanwhile, in April nine prominent PL politicians were suspended from the party pending investigation by the office of the Prosecutor-General into allegations of their maintaining links with the Cali cartel. It was subsequently confirmed that the Comptroller-General and the Attorney-General were also to be investigated as a result of similar allegations, while Samper's former election campaign treasurer, Santiago Medina, was arrested on charges related to the processing of drugs cartel contributions through Samper's election fund. In August the Minister of National Defence, Fernando Botero Zea, resigned, having been implicated in the affair by evidence submitted to the authorities by Medina. Medina maintained that Samper had been fully aware of the origin of the funds, an accusation denied by the President.

In May 1995 the Government extended an offer of participation in legislative and consultative processes to the FARC. Although the rebels responded positively to this proposal, negotiations were hampered by renewed FARC and ELN offensives in late May. An escalation in the number of acts of violence perpetrated by guerrilla forces and by paramilitary defence groups prompted Samper to declare a state of internal disturbance for a 90-day period. In October, however, the Constitutional Court rejected the terms of the state of emergency. Following the assassination in November of a prominent Conservative politician, the President declared a new 90-day state of internal disturbance.

In December 1995 the congressional accusations committee voted against a full-scale inquiry into allegations of Samper's use of funds proceeding from drugs cartels, on the grounds of insufficient evidence. The repercussions of the scandal, however, severely undermined the political integrity of the Government. Relations between the US Government and the Samper administration deteriorated dramatically, culminating in allegations that the US Government was attempting to destabilize the administration through the covert actions of the US Drugs Enforcement Agency. In January 1996 the PCC announced an immediate suspension of co-operation with the Government, and two PCC cabinet members resigned. Evidence collected by the Prosecutor-General was submitted to the accusations committee in February, together with four formal charges to be brought against the President. Later in the month congressional commissions of both parliamentary chambers decided to launch a new and public investigation into the matter. In March Samper testified before a new parliamentary investigation into the affair; he conceded that the Cali cartel had part-financed the campaign, albeit without his knowledge. In June the Congreso voted to acquit Samper of charges of having been aware of the part-financing of his election campaign by drugs-traffickers. The US Administration condemned the result and in the following month revoked Samper's visa to travel to the USA. During 1996 Botero, Medina and María Izquierdo, a former PL senator, were all sentenced to terms of imprisonment for their involvement in the Samper affair.

The state of internal disturbance was extended for a further 90 days in January 1996, and again in April following a CNGSB-organized nation-wide 'armed industrial strike', which occasioned as many as 40 deaths. A major offensive launched in August by FARC and ELN rebels coincided with large-scale protests by coca growers demanding a review of the coca eradication programme. Legislation approved in November 1997 permitting the extradition of Colombian nationals was strongly criticized by the US Administration as it would not have retroactive effect.

In the months preceding the October 1997 local elections the activities of guerrilla and paramilitary groups intensified. More than 40 candidates were killed, some 200 were kidnapped and as many as 1,900 withdrew after receiving death threats. In May the Government had agreed to the temporary demilitarization of part of the Caquetá department in order to secure the release of 70 members of the armed forces captured by the FARC. Voting was cancelled in numerous municipalities, while reports of secret preliminary peace negotiations between government representatives and the FARC were undermined by a major military offensive in September, in which 652 FARC guerrillas were killed and a further 1,600 were captured.

Andrés Pastrana Arango

The PL retained a narrow overall majority in both chambers of the legislature at congressional elections in March 1998. The ballot was preceded by a period of violent attacks on the security forces by guerrilla groups. The first round of the presidential election was held in May of that year. The PL candidate, Horacio Serpa Uribe, secured 35% of the valid votes cast, followed by the PCC nominee, Andrés Pastrana Arango (34%). Serpa's candidacy had been strongly opposed by the US Administration as he was alleged to have links with drugs-traffickers. Pastrana emerged victorious in the second ballot in June, and was inaugurated President in August.

In July 1998 President-elect Pastrana announced that he had held secret talks with Manuel Marulanda Vélez (alias 'Tirofijo'), the FARC leader, and that he had agreed to demilitarize five southern municipalities for a 90-day period in order to facilitate negotiations with the guerrillas. Pastrana subsequently recognized the political status of the FARC, thereby allowing the Government to negotiate with an outlawed group. None the less, FARC attacks on the security forces continued. Shortly before the negotiations began in January 1999, it was revealed that the FARC had held informal talks with government officials from the USA and Colombia. In mid-January the FARC suspended talks until the authorities provided evidence that they were taking action against paramilitary groups. In February Pastrana announced the extension of the period of demilitarization by three months.

In October 1998 representatives of the ELN, Colombian 'civil society' and the Government agreed on a timetable for preliminary peace talks, beginning in February 1999. The Government recognized the political status of the ELN, but the group did not cease hostilities. The planned peace negotiations failed to begin, however, not least because of the Government's refusal to agree to the ELN's request for further demilitarization. The ELN intensified its operations to increase pressure on the Government to accede to its demands. The guerrillas hijacked an Avianca domestic flight in April, kidnapping all 46 people on board, and abducted some 140 members of the congregation of a church in Cali in May. In June Pastrana withdrew political recognition of the ELN and made the release of hostages a precondition for future peace talks. A civilian commission was appointed subsequently by the Government to negotiate towards this end. The ELN freed the last hostage in November 2000.

Little progress was achieved in negotiations with the FARC until April 1999, as the guerrillas continued to insist that action be taken against paramilitary groups prior to a resumption of talks. The enforced resignation in that month of two senior army officers, alleged to have collaborated with paramilitary groups, appeared to appease the FARC, however, and in early May talks between Marulanda and President Pastrana resulted in an agreement on a comprehensive agenda for future peace negotiations; the period of demilitarization was again extended, but the FARC continued to pursue its military campaign. Pastrana's strategy was not supported entirely by his administration and in May Rodrigo Lloreda, the Minister of National Defence, resigned in protest at concessions granted to the FARC. The talks were subsequently postponed until October; demonstrations for peace were attended by some 10m. people throughout the country.

In March 1999 the USA decided to 'certify' Colombia's efforts to combat drugs-trafficking and in September Pastrana announced the establishment of a new anti-narcotics battalion, to be trained and financed by the USA. Collaboration between the Colombian and US authorities led to the arrest of more than 60 suspected drugs-traffickers in two major operations conducted in October and December. However, the most important progress in Colombian-US relations came in 2000 with the development of Pastrana's so-called 'Plan Colombia'. This was an ambitious, US $7,500m. project intended to strengthen the Colombian state by increasing the efficiency of the security forces and the judicial system, eliminating drugs production through both crop eradication and crop substitution, and by reducing unemployment. In July 2000 the US Congress approved a contribution to the Plan of $1,300m., including a military component of $1,000m. Human rights organizations warned of an escalation of human rights abuses following the Plan's implementation, as the main aid component was allocated to strengthening the security forces, whose links to paramilitary groups were, allegedly, yet to be severed. Colombia's Andean neighbours feared that an escalation in violence would force refugees onto their territory, and subsequently reinforced their borders.

During negotiations in September 2000 the FARC threatened to halt the peace process if plans for the US military component of Plan Colombia, to be directed against coca-growing areas of Putumayo, were implemented. The FARC effectively blockaded Putumayo from the end of that month, and succeeded in delaying the aerial spraying of coca plantations. In October the Government dismissed 388 members of the armed forces in a move designed to improve military efficiency as well as to allay accusations of corruption and violations of human rights. However, the FARC withdrew from peace talks in November to demand greater government action in combating the Autodefensas Unidas de Colombia (AUC), an organization representing most of Colombia's paramilitary groups. By the end of the year Pastrana was under increasing pressure to regain control of the demilitarized zone; a report released in December estimated a 30% increase in FARC military capacity since the zone was created. In February 2001 the FARC leadership met the President in the demilitarized zone and signed an agreement to revive the stalled negotiations and to begin discussions on a cease-fire. The new US Administration of George W. Bush refused an invitation to join the peace process, preferring instead to focus on drugs-eradication policies. In July the US House of Representatives approved a US $670m. aid package (the Andean Regional Initiative) to support Plan Colombia and to promote stability in the rest of the Andean region.

Progress was made in peace negotiations in June 2001 when the FARC signed a prisoner-exchange agreement with the Government; about 300 prisoners were released by the FARC at the end of the month. Nevertheless, in August President Pastrana signed legislation granting new powers to the military to combat guerrilla forces. In October the Government extended the existence of the demilitarized zone until January 2002, after the FARC agreed to reduce the number of kidnappings and to begin cease-fire negotiations. However, it refused demands by the FARC to remove military controls around the demilitarized zone. This impasse effectively prevented any progress being made on substantive issues such as cease-fire negotiations during the rest of the year. On 9 January 2002 Pastrana gave the FARC just 48 hours to leave the demilitarized zone. Hours before the expiry of the deadline the FARC rescinded demands for relaxed security around the demilitarized zone and agreed to recommence negotiations. However, on 20 February, following the hijacking of an aeroplane and the kidnapping of a prominent senator, Pastrana terminated peace talks and ordered the armed forces to regain control of the demilitarized zone.

In April 2000 an agreement was reached with the ELN on the establishment of a demilitarized zone, similar to that granted to the FARC, in southern Bolívar. Negotiations in Havana, Cuba, at the end of the year resulted in a preliminary agreement on the terms and conditions of the zone. The agreement was strongly opposed by the AUC and by residents of the proposed region. The prospects for a demilitarized zone were reduced after the ELN suspended negotiations with the Government in March 2001 in protest against the aerial spraying of coca in the Bolívar region. At the same time, the AUC began an offensive in the area in order to prevent the establishment of the demilitarized zone. The ELN resumed peace negotiations in April, but these faltered in August when President Pastrana suspended unofficial talks taking place in Venezuela, accusing the ELN of inflexibility. Contact between the two sides resumed in December in Cuba, and in January 2002, following a Christmas truce, negotiations on a permanent cease-fire were initiated; however, the ELN withdrew from talks in May. In mid-2004 the ELN expressed interest in re-entering negotiations, under Mexican mediation. However, the group again withdrew from talks in early 2005, allegedly in protest at Mexican criticism of Cuba. Nevertheless, in December talks towards a possible framework for peace resumed in Havana.

Alvaro Uribe Vélez

In legislative elections, held in March 2002, the most significant gains were made by independents and parties allied to Alvaro Uribe Vélez, the former Governor of Antioquia and a candidate in the forthcoming presidential election. The PL remained the largest single party in the Senado and the Cámara de Representantes, although its representation was substantially reduced. The presidential election was held in May, amid a climate of increased intimidation by both guerrilla and paramilitary groups. Uribe, a dissident member of the PL, was elected President. The PCC, the PL and a number of independents subsequently declared their support for the President-elect and his pledge to impose 'democratic security', thus giving him an overwhelming majority in both parliamentary chambers. Uribe took office in August.

Under the framework of his 'democratic security' plan, Uribe resolved to strengthen the capacity of the Government to achieve a lasting victory over the rebel groups. To this end, the new President issued a decree establishing a 'state of internal disturbance' and introducing a war tax in September 2002 (intended to raise US $750m.). The decree extended police powers to military units and designated two 'Rehabilitation and Consolidation Zones' in the north-eastern departments of Sucre, Bolívar and Arauca, within which media access and civil liberties were to be drastically curtailed. Uribe pledged to double the size of the army (to some 100,000 professional soldiers), recruit a further 100,000 police officers, create localized militias and establish a network of 'informants' to ensure public security along the road network. As a result of the measures, the President's popularity soared. In November the internal disturbance decree was renewed for a further 90-day period, despite a Constitutional Court ruling against it in July. In December the Congreso approved labour, pension and fiscal reforms that provided for an increase in military spending. Notwithstanding concerns over reports of human rights infringements by the security forces, throughout 2003 and 2004 the Government achieved apparent progress in its campaign against the rebel groups, with murder, kidnapping, massacre and terrorism rates all declining.

In December 2002 agreement was reached in the Congreso on some 15 proposed economic and political reforms, which were to be included in a national referendum. In July 2003 the Constitutional Court approved the terms of the so-called 'austerity referendum', to be held on 25 October. The proposals included: a two-year freeze on public sector salaries, and reductions in civil service pensions; the transfer of responsibility for regional finances to the federal authorities; a reduction in the number of seats in the Congreso; and an increase in prison terms for those convicted of corruption. However, participation in the referendum was below the required 25% of the electorate, in part owing to the complexity of the referendum document, but also to widespread fears of violence and to the scheduling of the referendum one day before local elections. The failure of the proposals meant that the Uribe administration had to gain congressional approval for its reforms.

In December 2003 the Congreso approved a series of anti-terrorism measures, granting extensive powers to the police and military. However, in late August 2004 the Constitutional Court ruled that the measures were unconstitutional, owing to irregularities in the congressional voting procedure. Earlier in the month the Court had also overturned parts of the Government's proposed reform to the pension system. Following these defeats, a controversial clause was added to a proposed amendment to the Constitution, to allow a President to serve two consecutive terms in office. The provision stated that the Constitutional Court was not empowered to overturn the legislation. The constitutional amendment was approved by the Congreso in December, and by the Constitutional Court in October 2005. Legislation on the framework for implementation of the amendment was approved by the Constitutional Court in November. Although the new law allowed for presidential re-election, it was intended to prevent the incumbent head of state enjoying an unfair advantage over his rivals.

Meanwhile, following the declaration of a cease-fire in December 2002, in July 2003 the leaders of the AUC declared that their federation would proceed with peace talks and disband by December 2005. Formal negotiations towards a settlement began in July 2004, and in November AUC leader Salvatore Mancuso began the demobilization of AUC combatants under the Government-sponsored programme of reinsertion to civilian society. In June 2005 the Cámara de Representantes approved legislation, the *Ley de Justicia y Paz* (Peace and Justice Law), according the status of political prisoners to demobilized paramilitaries and allowing for reduced prison sentences for demobilized paramilitaries subsequently convicted of human rights abuses. Although opposition and human rights groups were vociferous in their condemnation of the legislation, the Government maintained that such concessions were necessary to ensure the success of the peace process. Nevertheless, sustained criticism of the law, at home as well as abroad, resulted in its amendment by the Constitutional Court to strengthen provisions for the punishment of crimes committed by paramilitaries. In mid-2005 the AUC announced the indefinite suspension of demobilization, owing to concerns over the possible extradition of its leaders to the USA on drugs-trafficking charges. In November the Government issued an ultimatum that any AUC combatants not demobilized by the end of the year would be engaged in combat by the armed forces. Following protracted negotiations, the Government granted a deferral of the deadline for demobilization. The AUC resumed demobilization of its 30,000 members in December 2005; the process was formally completed in March 2006.

Legislative elections were held on 12 March 2006. The Partido Social de la Unidad Nacional (Partido de la U), a pro-Uribe group formed by former members of the PL, won significant representation in both houses, as did the two traditional parties. Cambio Radical (CR), another pro-Uribe party also fared well. At the presidential election held on 28 May Uribe secured an emphatic victory, winning 64% of the valid votes cast. The second-placed candidate, Carlos Gaviria Díaz of the left-wing Polo Democrático Alternativo (PDA), won a higher than expected 23% of the ballot, while Horacio Serpa, representing the PL, won just 12% of the votes. Uribe's new administration included a few changes in personnel, with Juan Manuel Santos Calderón, leader of the Partido de la U, appointed Minister of National Defence.

In November 2006 the Supreme Court ordered the arrest of three members of the Congreso, all supporters of the President, on charges of promoting the creation of paramilitary groups in the department of Sucre to fight left-wing rebels. The following week Salvador Arana, the Governor of Sucre, was also implicated, and later in the month other legislators were wanted for questioning over alleged links with the recently demobilized right-wing paramilitary groups, in what became known as the 'parapolitical' scandal. In February 2007 six pro-Uribe members of the legislature were arrested on charges of having links with paramilitary organizations; the Minister of Foreign Affairs, María Consuelo Araújo, was forced to resign from office as her brother was among those arrested. The reputation of the Uribe administration was further diminished later in February after Jorge Noguera, the President's former intelligence adviser and a close ally, was arrested on charges of supplying information on left-wing sympathizers to the AUC. By April 2008 62 members of the Congreso, primarily from pro-Uribe parties, were under judicial investigation in connection with the 'parapolitical' affair, some 30 of whom were being held in custody.

Relations between the Government and the Supreme Court worsened in June 2008 when the latter convicted a former deputy, Yidis Medina, of accepting bribes in exchange for her decisive vote in December 2004 in favour of the constitutional amendment that allowed President Uribe's re-election. Because Medina's conviction implicitly questioned the legitimacy of Uribe's second term in office, the Constitutional Court was asked to reconsider the amendment. In response, the President—who continued to enjoy very high popular approval ratings—accused the Supreme Court of an abuse of power and announced a referendum on the question of whether to hold a re-run of the 2006 presidential election. The referendum proposal was abandoned after the Constitutional Court upheld the legality of the amendment in July.

In December 2006 AUC leaders announced their withdrawal from the peace process in protest against their transfer to the high-security Itagüí prison. Later that month the trial began in Medellín of Mancuso, who had surrendered under the terms of the *Ley de Justicia y Paz*. AUC leaders temporarily suspended their testimonials in July 2007 in protest against the Supreme Court ruling that former paramilitaries should be tried with common crimes rather than the pardonable offence of sedition. In an apparent attempt to appease the AUC, in the following month the Uribe Government presented legislation under which some 19,000 paramilitaries would be charged with simple criminal conspiracy, thereby making them eligible for early release. In May 2008 Uribe announced the extradition of 14 senior AUC leaders to the USA on charges of drugs-trafficking, declaring that they had violated the terms of the *Ley de Justicia y Paz* by failing to tell the truth about their paramilitary activities or to provide compensation to their victims.

The prospect of a further constitutional amendment to allow President Uribe to run for a third consecutive term dominated domestic politics during 2009. Amid allegations of bribery, in September the Congreso approved a referendum on the issue, pending final authorization by the Constitutional Court. Critics of the referendum accused the Government of weakening democracy, but polls suggested that public opinion was firmly behind Uribe. However, various irregularities throughout the referendum campaign brought into doubt the legality of the plebiscite and the legitimacy of the existing electoral rules. While the Constitutional Court's deliberations on the matter continued, this uncertainty left Colombia in political deadlock. Nevertheless, the Congreso did approve a series of much-delayed political reforms in June 2009. Primarily intended to punish those parties with deputies embroiled in the 'parapolitical' scandal, the final bill was criticized for diluting these efforts to re-establish the integrity of the legislature. Despite creating an 'empty seat' to prohibit the replacement of those members under scrutiny for paramilitary connections, the measure was not retroactive and thus provided protection for deputies currently being investigated, most of whom were allies of Uribe. In addition, the reform bill relaxed the laws on party membership, ostensibly to the advantage of the major parties within Uribe's coalition by allowing them to increase their numbers from the ranks of smaller parties.

Damaging evidence of extra-judicial killings by the military was uncovered in October 2008. Soldiers had murdered civilians and disguised the victims as combatants to meet quotas, attracting domestic and international condemnation. The 'false positives' scandal escalated throughout 2009, and by mid-2010 the Attorney-General was investigating some 1,300 cases involving over 2,000 deaths, indicating widespread corruption within the military. The steady imposition during 2010–11 of lengthy prison sentences upon members of the armed forces convicted of 'false positive' murders demonstrated that progress was being made in bringing the perpetrators to justice.

Meanwhile, in February 2009 allegations emerged that the intelligence service, the Departamento Administrativo del Servicio (DAS—Administrative Department of Security), had carried out illegal surveillance of opposition politicians, trade union leaders, journalists and Supreme Court judges. Although the majority of the victims in the so-called 'chuzadas' (wiretapping) scandal were opponents of the Government, Uribe insisted that the operations were the work of rogue elements within the DAS and were not officially sanctioned. Relations between the Government and the Supreme Court, already tense, deteriorated further when it was revealed that the judge overseeing the 'parapolitical' affair was among the surveillance targets. The USA revealed in April 2010 that it would no longer be providing financial support to the DAS, while it was reported in the following month that several of Uribe's closest associates had been directly involved in the intelligence-gathering scandal, bringing into question the President's prior knowledge of the affair.

Recent developments: the Santos presidency

At the end of February 2010 the Constitutional Court ruled against a referendum on a third term for Uribe, and in early March Juan Manuel Santos Calderón, a former Minister of National Defence in Uribe's Government, was formally confirmed as the candidate for the ruling Partido de la U in the upcoming presidential election. In the same month Noemí Sanín was elected as the PCC's nominee and former Mayor of Bogotá Antanas Mockus Sivickas won the vote for the candidature of the Partido Verde (PV).

Legislative elections were held on 14 March 2010 and resulted in further gains for Santos' Partido de la U, which increased its representation in the Cámara de Representantes to 47 seats and in the Senado to 28 seats. The PCC also improved its position, winning 37 lower house seats and 22 senate seats, while the PL's representation remained virtually unaltered at 35 and 17 seats in each chamber, respectively. The Partido de Integración Nacional, formed in 2009 by a number of pro-Uribe parties but controversial owing to the large number of its members with links to politicians involved in the 'parapolitical' scandal, secured 11 seats in the Cámara and nine in the Senado, and the PV, another newcomer to the Congreso, won three and five seats, respectively. The ballot was peaceful, but monitors from the Organization of American States (OAS) reported numerous electoral irregularities. The success of the pro-Government parties in the elections was viewed as an endorsement of Uribe's policies.

Voting took place on 30 May 2010 to elect a new President. Santos secured 46.7% of the votes cast, followed by Mockus with 21.5%, necessitating a second round run-off. The other main candidates—Germán Vargas Lleras of CR, Gustavo Petro Urrego of the PDA, Noemí Sanín of the PCC and Rafael Pardo Rueda of the PL—failed to win more than 10% of the votes. The second round was held on 20 June and resulted in a comprehensive victory for Santos, who garnered 69.1% of the ballot, compared with 27.5% for Mockus. The rate of participation by the electorate was recorded at 44.3%. Mockus' anti-corruption campaign had gathered momentum as the election approached and was particularly attractive to younger voters seeking an alternative to the traditional parties, but the popularity of Santos' platform, based on the continuation of the 'Uribismo' project, proved to be insurmountable. The OAS declared that it was satisfied with the conduct of the elections. Santos assumed the presidency on 7 August and announced that the priorities of his new Government were economic growth, job creation, and the improvement of relations with Venezuela and Ecuador; pledges of congressional support by the PCC, the PL and CR provided Santos with the necessary backing to effect his political agenda.

In October 2010 the Attorney-General ruled that nine high-profile members of the Uribe administration would be prohibited from assuming official positions owing to misconduct. Uribe's subsequent acceptance of responsibility for their actions prompted a congressional committee to initiate an inquiry into the former President's involvement in the 'chuzadas' scandal. (Uribe attended a preliminary hearing in August 2011 and again rejected accusations that he had authorized the DAS surveillance operations, while in November the Prosecutor-General began a separate investigation into Uribe's alleged complicity.) In November 2010 María del Pilar Hurtado Afanador, Uribe's appointee to head the DAS between 2007 and 2008, was granted asylum in Panama after claiming that her life was at risk in Colombia. In late November, in a controversial statement condemning the Colombian judicial system for an alleged lack of impartiality, Uribe declared his support for Hurtado's decision to flee the country (indeed, media reports claimed that the former President had explicitly advised her to seek asylum). The former President's comments attracted criticism from the Attorney-General, the leaders of the PL and the PCC, and, most notably, President Santos. By August 2011 three senior DAS officials had been sentenced to eight-year gaol terms for their involvement in the 'chuzadas' affair, two of whom alleged that they had been following Hurtado's instructions. The former DAS Director had been charged in May with organizing illegal surveillance operations, and in December the Government requested her extradition from Panama. The Agencia Nacional de Inteligencia (ANI) was established on 1 January 2012, to replace the discredited DAS, which Santos had dissolved on the previous day. The ANI was given a much narrower mandate, with many of the DAS's powers and resources being transferred to other government departments and the police.

Heavy rains caused by the La Niña climate pattern, which resulted in mudslides and flooding nation-wide, forced Santos to declare a state of emergency in December 2010. Some 300 people had been killed by the disaster by the end of the year, and over 300,000 houses had been damaged or destroyed. Using his emergency powers, Santos increased taxes to raise funding for the extensive reconstruction operation, which was estimated to cost US $5,000m. Nearly 100 people lost their lives in further flooding in April 2011, by which point an estimated 2m. civilians had been displaced by the disaster. Santos described the floods as the 'worst natural tragedy in Colombia's history'.

In February 2011 Santos announced a new security strategy to address the growing problem of the Bandas Criminales Emergentes (Bacrim or Emerging Criminal Gangs—organized groups involved in the illegal drugs trade, formed mainly by recently demobilized AUC combatants). The Government asserted that the main focus of the security forces would be shifted from defeating the guerrilla insurgency to combating the Bacrim's activities, underlining the severity of the threat posed by these criminal groups.

Mario de Jesús Uribe Escobar, a cousin of former President Uribe and an erstwhile Senate President, received a seven-and-a-half-year prison term in February 2011 after been convicted of involvement in the 'parapolitical' scandal. In September another of Uribe's close associates—Jorge Noguera, the Director of the DAS between 2002 and 2005—was held responsible for the 2004 murder of a left-wing activist, Alfredo Correa de Andreis, and was given a 25-year prison sentence. Noguera had provided the AUC with confidential information that was then used by the paramilitary group to locate and assassinate Correa de Andreis.

Legislation was adopted in May 2011 to facilitate the transfer of reparation payments from the state to the victims of human rights abuses committed by guerrillas, paramilitaries or the security forces during the various post-1985 internal conflicts. Land that had been seized illegally after 1990 (estimated to total at least 2m. ha) was also to be restituted to the original title holders. While UN Secretary-General Ban Ki-Moon welcomed the new legislation, critics argued that the law would be too expensive to implement and claimed that it equated the actions of the armed forces with those of illegal organizations. A further concern was the large number of land restitution campaigners who had been murdered during 2011, presumably targeted by armed groups unwilling to comply with the terms of the victims law.

The Ministry of the Interior and Justice was divided into separate ministries in mid-2011. Germán Vargas Lleras, who had hitherto headed the joint ministry, was appointed as Minister of the Interior, and Juan Carlos Esguerra of the PL became the new Minister of Justice and Law. Juan Carlos Pinzón replaced Rodrigo Rivera Salazar as Minister of National Defence in September following the latter's resignation in the previous month. Meanwhile, the PDA was left as the sole opposition party in the Congreso in July, after the PV joined the governing coalition.

In regional elections held on 30 October 2011 the Partido de la U secured four governorships, five departmental capitals and 259 mayoralties, and the PL also performed strongly, winning six, seven and 181 mandates, respectively. Gustavo Francisco Petro Urrego, a former M-19 militant representing the recently formed Movimiento Progresista, won the politically significant mayoralty of Bogotá. Right-wing 'Uribista' candidates performed poorly in the elections. Voting was conducted peacefully, although over 40 candidates had been murdered during pre-election campaigning. On the day after the elections Santos appointed PL President Rafael Pardo Rueda to head the newly re-established Ministry of Labour.

'Democratic security' and the FARC

In April 2004 the Government announced the initiation of the so-called 'Plan Patriota', a largely US-funded military campaign in which some 17,000 troops were to be deployed in the traditional FARC strongholds of Caquetá, Guaviare, Meta and Putumayo. In May the UN Special Envoy to Colombia expressed concerns that Plan Patriota could lead to increased numbers of internally displaced refugees and human rights abuses. Nevertheless, in September the Government announced the capture of nearly 6,000 alleged insurgents and the death of some 1,500 others as a result of the Plan Patriota. In spite of the success of the Plan, in December 2005 President Uribe pledged to demilitarize 180 sq km of a south-eastern department in order to facilitate an exchange of FARC prisoners for hostages held by the guerrillas. (An estimated 3,000 civilians had been kidnapped, among them foreigners and politicians, including Ingrid Betancourt, a former presidential candidate, in February 2002.) However, in the wake of a car bomb attack in Bogotá in late 2006, the Goverment withdrew from talks and Uribe announced that the hostages would be freed by military means. In July some 450 FARC fighters stormed a police station, killing 17 officials, while in December the group launched its most lethal attack on the armed forces since Uribe took office, killing almost 30 soldiers who had been deployed to destroy coca crops in the south of the country.

In an effort to re-engage the FARC in the peace process, in June 2007 President Uribe ordered the release of some 150 imprisoned members of the group. Weeks later, however, the FARC announced that 11 of 12 deputies from Valle del Cauca, kidnapped in 2002, had been killed in crossfire in a battle with an 'unidentified military group'. Although the FARC appeared to implicate either the armed forces or a paramilitary group in the deputies' deaths, Sigifredo López, the only surviving Valle del Cauca deputy, freed in February 2009, corroborated the Government's claim that the rebels had been responsible for the killings. Two high-profile hostages were released by the FARC to Venezuelan officials in January 2008, and in February the FARC freed four further captives; their release followed a series of anti-FARC demonstrations in Colombia and throughout the world, in which several million people participated. In March Colombian armed forces launched a raid on a FARC training camp in Ecuador, killing 17 rebels, including the group's second-in-command, Raúl Reyes; the attack provoked a crisis in relations with Ecuador and Venezuela (see below). The FARC was further debilitated later in that month by the death of its commander-in-chief, Marulanda. In July, moreover, the Government secured a major victory against the FARC when special forces rescued the group's highest-profile hostage, Betancourt, along with 14 other captives. The manner of their rescue—the troops, posing as members of a humanitarian organization, had convinced the rebel officer in charge of the hostages that they were under instructions from the FARC's new commander, Guillermo León Sáenz Vargas ('Alfonso Cano'), to convey the captives to him by helicopter—was interpreted as further evidence that the guerrilla group's command structure had been severely weakened. A steady stream of hostage releases by the FARC during the first half of 2009, followed in August by a statement of the group's willingness to initiate talks with the Government, raised hopes for fresh dialogue. However, the Government remained sceptical of engaging with the rebels, fearing that any abatement in the operations against the FARC would provide the group with the opportunity to rebuild. Uribe made a token offer of new talks in April, but the precondition of a cease-fire was, as expected, rejected by the rebels.

In December 2009 the FARC and the ELN, in spite of a history of conflict and division, announced a cease-fire and revealed that they would henceforth unite forces against the military. Although clearly damaged by the Government's aggressive 'democratic security' initiatives, the FARC still possessed the ability to orchestrate attacks, and in a high-profile incident on 21 December Luis Francisco Cuellar, the Governor of Caquetá, was kidnapped and murdered. Uribe responded by authorizing an air-strike on 1 January 2010 on two FARC bases in Meta, resulting in the deaths of 31 rebels. Guaviare gubernatorial candidate José Alberto Pérez Restrepo was wounded and six of his associates were killed during a failed kidnapping raid carried out by FARC rebels in February. Nevertheless, two further hostages were released by the FARC at the end of March. Uribe welcomed this development, but downplayed the possibility of future negotiations.

Following his inauguration in August 2010, President Santos reiterated his intention to continue Uribe's 'democratic security' policies, and his tough stance on the FARC was symbolized by his refusal to designate a High Commissioner for Peace. In September the FARC and the ELN initiated a series of co-ordinated attacks. In response, the Government rapidly organized counter-operations against the rebels and established a Consejo de Seguridad Nacional (National Security Council). Santos secured a major victory on 22 September, when senior FARC leader and military commander Víctor Suárez ('Mono Jojoy') was killed during an attack by the security forces on a rebel base in Meta. None the less, FARC activity continued, although there was a noticeable shift in tactics by the guerrilla group, with fewer direct attacks and a greater use of bombings and ambushes, perceived by Santos as a sign of the FARC's declining military capabilities. In May 2011 the Government announced that it intended to end the guerrilla insurgency (and eliminate the major Bacrim groups) by 2014 through the implementation of an ambitious new security strategy, the Política Integral de Seguridad y Defensa para la Prosperidad (Integral Policy on Security and Defence for Prosperity), essentially an extension of the 'democratic security' campaign. The Santos administration made significant progress towards this objective on 4 November 2011, when FARC commander Sáenz Vargas was killed during a military raid on a rebel encampment in Cauca. Santos hailed this development as 'the most crushing blow against the FARC in its entire history' and urged the group to disband. Unsurprisingly, this demand was firmly rejected, and Rodrigo Londoño Echeverri ('Timochenko') became the new FARC leader later that month. In mid-November the military seized the FARC's primary transmitter, terminating the group's radio broadcasts. During a clash with the armed forces in late November, the FARC murdered four captive members of the security forces, after holding them hostage for over 12 years, prompting condemnation from the Government, the UN and human rights organizations. In the following month widely attended anti-FARC protest marches were held in Colombia, the USA and Europe, underlining the deep unpopularity of the guerrilla movement. A FARC proposal to resume negotiations was rejected by Santos in January 2012. FARC released its 10 remaining security force captives at the beginning of April; however, the group still held more than 400 civilians hostage.

Foreign Affairs

Regional relations

Colombia has a long-standing border dispute with Venezuela. Relations between the countries improved following the signing, in 1989, of a border integration agreement, which included a provision on joint co-operation in the campaign to eradicate drugs-trafficking. In 1990 the San Pedro Alejandrino agreement, signed by the two countries, sought to initiate the implementation of recommendations made by existing bilateral border commissions. Colombia's efforts to improve relations with Venezuela were hampered by the activities of FARC guerrillas in the border region, leading the two countries to sign an agreement to improve border co-operation in 1997. Agreements were subsequently signed by the two countries to strengthen military co-operation and intelligence sharing. In 2000 relations deteriorated, owing to Venezuelan President Hugo Chávez's opposition to Plan Colombia and accusations by Colombia that Venezuela was covertly aiding the guerrilla forces. Following the appointment of President Uribe, relations improved: in 2002 Chávez and Uribe agreed on measures to promote bilateral trade and, notably, to establish a system to deal with problems on their common border. However, relations were severely strained in December 2004 following the arrest of Rodrigo Granda Escobar, the supposed international spokesperson of the FARC. It was subsequently alleged by the Venezuelan Government that Granda, although ultimately arrested in Cúcuta, was first kidnapped in Venezuela by Venezuelan and Colombian agents in the pay of the Colombian Government and with the collusion of US intelligence services. Both the Uribe Government and the US Administration denied all accusations of wrongdoing. Although Chávez recalled the Venezuelan ambassador to Colombia in January 2005 and imposed restrictions on trade and passage between the two countries, bilateral relations were normalized in February. In August 2007 Chávez was invited to mediate between the Colombian Government and the FARC to effect an exchange of prisoners and hostages, although the initiative was cancelled by President Uribe in November, reportedly because Chávez had made contact with Colombian military leaders against Uribe's expressed wishes. Bilateral relations deteriorated rapidly, and Chávez again recalled his ambassador to Colombia. Tensions increased after Chávez requested that the Colombian guerrilla groups be accorded belligerent, rather than terrorist, status in January 2008. Furthermore, in March, Uribe's claim that computers taken during a raid on a FARC camp in Ecuador (see below) indicated that Chávez had pledged some US $30m.-worth of petroleum to the rebel group prompted the Venezuelan President to expel the Colombian ambassador in Caracas and to dispatch troops to the border. The two countries restored diplomatic relations after Colombia announced it would not pursue charges against Chávez in the International Criminal Court. Relations, already strained by the impending US base deal (see below), reached a new nadir in July 2009 when Chávez suspended diplomatic ties with Colombia after Venezuela was accused of supplying weapons to the FARC, a charge vehemently denied by the Venezuelan President. Chávez imposed an informal trade blockade upon Colombia, and cross-border commerce declined sharply as a result. During the first half of 2010 further allegations of Venezuelan-FARC links emerged. In July, at an OAS summit meeting, Colombian officials publicly accused the Venezuelan Government of providing shelter to large numbers of FARC and ELN guerrillas. Chávez immediately severed diplomatic relations with Colombia. However, tensions eased in August following the inauguration of Santos, who adopted a more conciliatory stance towards Venezuela. Santos and Chávez agreed to restore diplomatic relations and establish a number of joint committees to discuss economic and security concerns. A second round of constructive discussions in November resulted in the signing of several economic accords and the formation of a commission to combat drugs-trafficking: a bilateral anti-drugs-smuggling agreement was signed in January 2011. In a further act of rapprochement, from late 2010 Chávez began to comply with Colombian requests for the extradition of alleged guerrillas sheltering in Venezuela. The Colombian authorities reciprocated in May 2011 by transferring an alleged drugs-trafficker to Caracas. Later that month joint mediation by Santos and Chávez resulted in a breakthrough in the political crisis in Honduras. Further economic bilateral co-operation agreements were concluded in November.

Ecuador has repeatedly objected to incursions by Colombian combatants into its territory, and to the Colombian Government's policy of aerial spraying of drugs crops in departments on the border between the two countries. In November 2005 the Uribe administration agreed to a temporary cessation of aerial fumigation in border areas from January 2006. In December, however, Colombia resumed its crop-spraying programme along the border, which Ecuador described as a hostile act. Following intervention by the OAS (see p. 394), the diplomatic crisis was resolved after Colombia agreed to give notice of any aerial fumigation conducted in the border area. The raid by Colombian forces on a FARC camp in Ecuador in March 2008 provoked an angry response from the Ecuadorean administration, which expelled the Colombian ambassador in Quito, withdrew its own ambassador from Bogotá, and sent troops to the Colombian–Ecuadorean border. Tensions were further exacerbated by the Colombian Government's claim that documents seized in the raid proved that the Ecuadorean President, Rafael Correa, was interested in establishing official relations with FARC and that a member of his Government had met Reyes for discussions. President Correa dismissed the claims, asserting that his Government's involvement had been solely on humanitarian grounds as part of efforts to secure the release of hostages. The stand-off was ended by an OAS resolution that included a clause that Colombian troops would not launch any further incursions into Ecuadorean territory; however, Colombian–Ecuadorean relations remained suspended. In January 2009 Colombia reinforced security along its border with Ecuador by deploying some 27,000 troops. Bilateral relations deteriorated further in July when a video was made public in which a FARC leader apparently admitted to making financial contributions to Correa's election campaign; both Correa and the FARC dismissed the video as fraudulent. (However, according to documents recovered during the 2008 raid, published in May 2011, the FARC had indeed made a US $100,000 campaign contribution.) Nevertheless, partial diplomatic relations were restored in November 2009. Economic concerns played a major role in the rapprochement: Uribe was eager to offset the rapid decline in exports to Venezuela (see above) with increased trade with Ecuador. President Santos made efforts to improve ties with Ecuador, and a number of bilateral committees were relaunched following his inauguration. In November 2010 the Government handed over to the Ecuadorean authorities a dossier containing detailed information about the 2008 raid, precipitating the normalization of diplomatic ties on 26 November. Relations continued to improve in 2011, and two bilateral border security agreements were signed in June and December. Also in the latter month, Santos and Correa pledged to create a joint commission to delineate officially their maritime boundaries.

In 1980 Nicaragua laid claim to the Colombian-controlled islands of Providencia and San Andrés. Colombia has a territorial dispute with Honduras over cays in the San Andrés and Providencia archipelago. In 1986 the Colombia and Honduras agreed a delimitation treaty of marine and submarine waters in the Caribbean Sea. Ratification of the treaty, which strengthened Colombia's claim to the islands of Providencia and San Andrés, in 1999angered Nicaragua, which filed a complaint with the International Court of Justice (ICJ). In December 2007 the ICJ dismissed Nicaragua's claim to the San Andrés archipelago, although it had yet to rule on jurisdiction on the other disputed waters.

Other external relations

The USA renewed and extended the Andean Trade Promotion and Drug Eradication Act (ATPDEA) with Colombia every year since its inception in 2002 (when it succeeded the Andean Trade Preference Act). The ATPDEA offered commercial incentives to those Andean countries deemed co-operative in US counter-narcotics policy. The ATPDEA expired in February 2011, but was renewed again in October. In the same month a free trade agreement between the USA and Colombia, signed in November

2006, was finally ratified by the US Congress. The delay was in part owing to concerns over Colombia's human rights record. The agreement was expected finally to be implemented in 2012.

In October 2009 an agreement was signed with the USA granting the US military access to seven bases in Colombia to assist the Uribe administration in its efforts to address drugs-trafficking and the insurgency. Although the deal was popular with the public and strengthened relations with the USA, it proved to be highly contentious with Colombia's neighbours: Argentina, Brazil, Bolivia, Ecuador and, in particular, Venezuela expressed concern at the US military presence in the region. The Government argued that the agreement was merely an extension of existing initiatives with the USA, emphasizing that the scope of US military operations would not stray beyond combating drugs and the insurgency within Colombia's borders. However, regional suspicions intensified when the details of the deal were disclosed in November, as it became apparent that no clear restrictions had been put in place to limit US activity. In August 2010 the Constitutional Court rejected the assertion that the US base deal was an extension of earlier arrangements, judging it to be a new agreement and therefore unconstitutional since it had not received congressional ratification.

CONSTITUTION AND GOVERNMENT

A new 380-article Constitution took effect in July 1991. Executive power is exercised by the President (assisted by a Cabinet), who is elected for a four-year term by universal adult suffrage. A 1995 amendment allowed for the re-election of the President for a second term of office. Legislative power is vested in the bicameral Congress, consisting of the Senado (Senate—102 members elected for four years) and the Cámara de Representantes (House of Representatives—161 members elected for four years). Judicial power is ultimately exercised by the Supreme Court of Justice. The integrity of the State is ensured by the Constitutional Court. The Council of State serves as the supreme consultative body for the Government in matters of legislation and administration. The country is divided into 32 Departments and one Capital District.

REGIONAL AND INTERNATIONAL CO-OPERATION

Colombia has been a member of the UN since its inception in 1945. It acceded to the World Trade Organization (see p. 433) in April 1995. Colombia is a member of the Organization of American States (see p. 394), the Latin American Integration Association (see p. 362), the Andean Community (see p. 197), the Association of Caribbean States (see p. 448), and of the Community of Latin American and Caribbean States (see p. 462), which was formally inaugurated in December 2011. The country belongs to the Inter-American Development Bank (see p. 334). In December 2004 Colombia was one of 12 countries that were signatories to the agreement, signed in Cusco, Peru, creating the South American Community of Nations (Comunidad Sudamericana de Naciones, which was renamed Union of South American Nations—Unión de Naciones Suramericanas, UNASUR, in April 2007), intended to promote greater regional economic integration. The country is a member of the Group of 77 (see p. 450) organization of developing states.

ECONOMIC AFFAIRS

In 2010, according to estimates by the World Bank, Colombia's gross national income (GNI), measured at average 2008–10 prices, was US $255,290m., equivalent to $5,510 per head (or $9,000 per head on an international purchasing-power parity basis). During 2001–10, it was estimated, the population increased at an average annual rate of 1.5%; however, average annual growth of gross domestic product (GDP) per head, in real terms, was 2.8% in 2001–10. Colombia's overall GDP increased, in real terms, by an average of 4.4% per year in 2001–10; GDP grew by 4.3% in 2010.

Agriculture (including hunting, forestry and fishing) contributed 7.0% of GDP in 2010 and employed 17.6% of the labour force in 2008. The principal cash crops are coffee (which accounted for 4.7% of official export earnings in 2010), cocoa, sugar cane, bananas, tobacco, cotton and cut flowers. Rice, cassava, plantains and potatoes are the principal food crops. Timber and beef production are also important. During 2001–10, according to World Bank estimates, agricultural GDP increased at an average annual rate of 2.2%; the GDP of the sector declined by 0.4% in 2009, but increased by 1.5% in 2010.

Industry (including mining, manufacturing, construction and power) employed 19.8% of the labour force in 2008 and contributed 36.2% of GDP in 2010. According to the World Bank, during 2001–10 real industrial GDP increased at an estimated average annual rate of 4.2%; sectoral GDP increased by 4.8% in 2010.

Mining employed 0.9% of the labour force in 2008 and contributed 8.9% of GDP in 2010. Petroleum, natural gas, coal, nickel, emeralds and gold are the principal minerals exploited. At the end of 2010 Colombia's proven oil reserves stood at 1,900m. barrels. Silver, platinum, iron, lead, zinc, copper, mercury, limestone and phosphates are also mined. During 2001–10 the real GDP of the mining sector increased at an average annual rate of 4.2%; the GDP of the sector increased by a provisional 11.1% in 2010, according to official estimates.

Manufacturing contributed 14.9% of GDP in 2010 and employed 13.4% of the labour force in 2008. According to World Bank estimates, during 2001–10 manufacturing GDP increased at an average annual rate of 3.1%. Manufacturing GDP increased by 4.5% in 2010. Based on the value of output, the most important branches of manufacturing were food products, beverages, chemical products, textiles and transport equipment.

The construction sector contributed 8.1% of GDP in 2010, and engaged 5.0% of the employed labour force in 2008. During 2001–10, according to official figures, the GDP of the sector increased at an annual rate of 8.6%; according to official estimates, construction GDP increased by a provisional 1.7% in 2010.

Hydroelectricity provided 82.8% of Colombia's electricity requirements in 2008. The country is self-sufficient in petroleum and coal, and these minerals together accounted for 56.5% of export revenues in 2010.

The services sector contributed 56.8% of GDP in 2010 and engaged 62.7% of the labour force in 2008. According to the World Bank, during 2001–10 the combined GDP of the services sector increased, in real terms, at an average rate of 4.7% per year; the GDP of the sector increased by 4.5% in 2010.

In 2010 Colombia recorded a visible trade surplus of US $2,150m., but there was a deficit of $9,032m. on the current account of the balance of payments. The country's principal market for imports in 2010 was the USA, which provided 25.8% of total imports. The USA was also the biggest market for exports, providing 42.1% of total export revenue in the same year. Other important trading partners in that year were the People's Republic of China, Brazil, Mexico and Germany. The principal exports in 2010 were petroleum and its derivatives, coal, textiles, metal manufactures and chemicals. The principal imports in the same year were mechanical and electrical equipment, chemical products, vehicles and transport equipment, metals and metal manufactures and prepared foodstuffs, beverages and tobacco. A significant amount of foreign exchange is believed to be obtained from illegal trade in gold, emeralds and, particularly, cocaine.

In 2010 there was an estimated public sector deficit of 14,692.3m. pesos, equivalent to 2.7% of GDP. Colombia's general government gross debt was 196,973,230m. pesos in 2010, equivalent to 36.0% of GDP. Colombia's external debt amounted to US $52,223m. at the end of 2009, of which $35,364m. was public and publicly guaranteed debt. In that year, the cost of servicing long-term public and publicly guaranteed debt and repayments to the IMF was equivalent to 9.6% of the value of exports of goods, services and income (excluding workers' remittances). During 2001–10 the average annual rate of inflation was 5.6%; consumer prices increased by an annual average of 2.4% in 2010. Some 11.4% of the labour force were unemployed in 2008.

The high levels of investment that sustained the economic expansion in Colombia in 2004–08 evaporated with the onset of the world-wide financial crisis in 2008. Industrial production, exports and remittances from abroad all declined significantly during 2009, and this economic slowdown was exacerbated by the informal trade blockade imposed by Venezuela. In an attempt to revive domestic demand, the Government introduced a fiscal stimulus programme, and this, combined with an improvement in the international economic climate, precipitated a recovery from late 2009. Economic activity accelerated in 2010—driven by increased investment, rising oil prices and increased output in the mining and manufacturing sectors—and real GDP grew by 4.3% in that year. The administration of President Santos, which took office in August, rapidly repaired relations with Venezuela and Ecuador, a policy that was expected to yield significant commercial benefits. However, extensive flooding devastated large parts of the country in late 2010–early 2011, and Santos increased taxes in an attempt to raise the estimated US $5,000m. required to finance the reconstruction programme. Although the agricultural sector was badly affected by the flooding, with widespread damage caused to crops and farmland, a bumper 2010/11 coffee harvest was recorded. The IMF estimated that real GDP expanded by 4.9% in 2011, supported by robust internal demand, high prices for Colombia's export commodities and increased mining activity. Oil output rose during that year and several significant petroleum discoveries were announced. Although the economy had recovered well from the global financial crisis, Colombia remained vulnerable to further turbulence on international markets, particularly in key commodities such as oil, coal and coffee. Therefore, as a precautionary measure, the country was granted a $6,200m. IMF Flexible Credit Line in May 2011. Increasing petroleum production, strong inflows of foreign direct investment and the ratification by the USA of a long-awaited bilateral free trade agreement in October were all expected to stimulate the Colombian economy in the near term, and the IMF projected real GDP growth of 4.5% in 2012.

PUBLIC HOLIDAYS

2013: 1 January (New Year's Day), 7 January (for Epiphany), 25 March (for St Joseph's Day), 28 March (Maundy Thursday), 29 March (Good Friday), 1 May (Labour Day), 13 May (for Ascension Day), 3 June (for Corpus Christi), 10 June (for Sacred Heart of Jesus), 1 July (for SS Peter and Paul), 22 July (for Independence), 7 August (Battle of Boyacá), 19 August (for Assumption), 14 October (for Discovery of the Americas), 4 November (for All Saints' Day), 11 November (Independence of Cartagena), 9 December (for Immaculate Conception), 25 December (Christmas Day).

Statistical Survey

Sources (unless otherwise stated): Departamento Administrativo Nacional de Estadística (DANE), Transversal 45 No 26-70, Interior I-CAN, Bogotá, DC; tel. (1) 597-8300; fax (1) 597-8399; e-mail dane@dane.gov.co; internet www.dane.gov.co; Banco de la República, Carrera 7A, No 14-78, 5°, Apdo Aéreo 3531, Bogotá, DC; tel. (1) 343-1111; fax (1) 286-1686; e-mail wbanco@banrep.gov.co; internet www.banrep.gov.co.

Area and Population

AREA, POPULATION AND DENSITY

Area (sq km)	1,141,748*
Population (census results)	
24 October 1993†	37,635,094
30 June 2005‡	
Males	21,169,835
Females	21,718,757
Total	42,888,592
Population (official projections at mid-year)	
2010	45,509,584
2011	46,044,601
2012	46,581,823
Density (per sq km) at mid-2012	40.8

* 440,831 sq miles.

† Revised figure, including adjustment for underenumeration. The enumerated total was 33,109,840 (males 16,296,539, females 16,813,301) in 1993.

‡ A 'census year' was conducted between 22 May 2005 and 22 May 2006, and a 'conciliated' total for 30 June 2005 was finally published in May 2007 (the original enumerated total was 41,298,706) incorporating adjustments for underenumeration, geographical undercoverage and underlying natural growth trends.

POPULATION BY AGE AND SEX

(official projections at mid-2012)

	Males	Females	Total
0–14	6,603,408	6,319,582	12,922,990
15–64	14,928,873	15,470,414	30,399,287
65 and over	1,464,806	1,794,740	3,259,546
Total	22,997,087	23,584,736	46,581,823

DEPARTMENTS

(census of 30 June 2005)*

Department	Area (sq km)	Population	Capital (with population†)
Amazonas	109,665	67,726	Leticia (32,450)
Antioquia	63,612	5,682,276	Medellín (2,233,660)
Arauca	23,818	232,118	Arauca (74,385)
Atlántico	3,388	2,166,156	Barranquilla (1,113,016)
Bolívar	25,978	1,878,993	Cartagena (895,400)
Boyacá	23,189	1,255,311	Tunja (152,419)
Caldas	7,888	968,740	Manizales (368,433)
Caquetá	88,965	420,337	Florencia (142,123)
Casanare	44,640	295,353	Yopal (103,754)
Cauca	29,308	1,268,937	Popayán (258,653)
César	22,905	903,279	Valledupar (348,990)
Chocó	46,530	454,030	Quibdó (110,032)
Córdoba	25,020	1,467,929	Montería (381,525)
Cundinamarca	22,623	2,280,037	Bogotá‡
Guainía	72,238	35,230	Puerto Inírida (15,827)
La Guajira	20,848	681,575	Riohacha (169,311)
Guaviare	42,327	95,551	San José del Guaviare (45,573)
Huila	19,890	1,011,418	Neiva (315,332)
Magdalena	23,188	1,149,917	Santa Marta (414,387)
Meta	85,635	783,168	Villavicencio (384,131)
Nariño	33,268	1,541,956	Pasto (383,846)
Norte de Santander	21,658	1,243,975	Cúcuta (585,919)
Putumayo	24,885	310,132	Mocoa (36,185)
Quindío	1,845	534,552	Armenia (272,574)
Risaralda	4,140	897,509	Pereira (428,397)
San Andrés y Providencia Islands	44	70,554	San Andrés (55,426)
Santander del Sur	30,537	1,957,789	Bucaramanga (509,918)
Sucre	10,917	772,010	Sincelejo (236,780)
Tolima	23,562	1,365,342	Ibagué (495,246)
Valle del Cauca	22,140	4,161,425	Cali (2,075,380)
Vaupés	65,268	39,279	Mitú (17,641)
Vichada	100,242	55,872	Puerto Carreño (12,897)
Capital District			
Bogotá, DC	1,587	6,840,116	—
Total	1,141,748	42,888,592	—

* A 'census year' was conducted between 22 May 2005 and 22 May 2006, and a 'conciliated' total for 30 June 2005 was finally published in May 2007 (the original enumerated total was 41,298,706) incorporating adjustments for underenumeration, geographical undercoverage and underlying natural growth trends.

† These amended figures for 11 November 2005 include an adjustment for geographical undercoverage and were announced in November 2006, prior to the publication of the final conciliated figures for 30 June 2005.

‡ The capital city, Bogotá, exists as the capital of a department as well as the Capital District. The city's population is included only in Bogotá, DC.

PRINCIPAL TOWNS
(estimated population at mid-1999)

Bogotá, DC (capital)	6,260,862	Neiva	300,052
Cali	2,077,386	Soledad	295,058
Medellín	1,861,265	Armenia	281,422
Barranquilla	1,223,260	Villavicencio	273,140
Cartagena	805,757	Soacha	272,058
Cúcuta	606,932	Valledupar	263,247
Bucaramanga	515,555	Montería	248,245
Ibagué	393,664	Itagüí	228,985
Pereira	381,725	Palmira	226,509
Santa Marta	359,147	Buenaventura	224,336
Manizales	337,580	Floridablanca	221,913
Bello	333,470	Sincelejo	220,704
Pasto	332,396	Popayán	200,719

Mid-2010 (incl. suburbs, UN estimates): Bogotá, DC 8,499,820; Medellín 3,593,821; Cali 2,401,004; Barranquilla 1,866,711; Bucaramanga 1,091,819; Cartagena 962,321; Cúcuta 774,343; (Source: UN, *World Urbanization Prospects: The 2009 Revision*).

BIRTHS, MARRIAGES AND DEATHS*

	Registered live births	Registered deaths
2000	752,834	187,432
2001	724,319	191,513
2002	700,455	192,262
2003	710,702	192,121
2004	723,099	188,933
2005	719,968	189,022
2006	714,450	192,814
2007	709,253	193,936
2008†	715,453	196,943
2009†	699,775	196,933

* Data are tabulated by year of registration rather than by year of occurrence, although registration is incomplete. According to UN estimates, the average annual rates in 1995–2000 were: births 24.0 per 1,000, deaths 5.8 per 1,000; in 2000–05: births 22.0 per 1,000, deaths 5.6 per 1,000; and in 2005–10: births 20.6 per 1,000, deaths 5.5 per 1,000 (Source: UN, *World Population Prospects: The 2010 Revision*).

† Preliminary figures.

Registered marriages: 102,448 in 1980; 95,845 in 1981; 70,350 in 1986.

Life expectancy (years at birth, WHO estimates): 76 (males 73; females 80) in 2009 (Source: WHO, *World Health Statistics*).

ECONOMICALLY ACTIVE POPULATION
('000 persons aged 10 years and over)

	2006	2007	2008
Agriculture, hunting, forestry and fishing	2,059.2	3,035.0	3,054.5
Mining and quarrying	102.0	103.2	149.1
Manufacturing	1,998.0	2,361.4	2,335.6
Electricity, gas and water	62.9	83.7	78.7
Construction	755.2	905.1	878.5
Trade, restaurants and hotels	3,646.5	4,344.4	4,605.3
Transport, storage and communications	1,097.9	1,450.1	1,467.4
Financial intermediation	204.8	222.2	219.6
Real estate, renting and business activities	811.2	995.7	1,146.8
Community, social and personal services	3,183.0	3,567.3	3,463.3
Sub-total	13,920.8	17,068.0	17,398.8
Activities not adequately described	2,760.1	8.5	26.9
Total employed	16,680.9	17,076.5	17,425.7
Unemployed	2,424.8	2,089.2	2,245.7
Total labour force	19,105.7	19,165.7	19,671.4
Males	11,283.8	11,396.4	11,644.0
Females	7,821.9	7,769.3	8,027.4

Source: ILO.

Health and Welfare

KEY INDICATORS

Total fertility rate (children per woman, 2009)	2.4
Under-5 mortality rate (per 1,000 live births, 2009)	19
HIV/AIDS (% of persons aged 15–49, 2009)	0.5
Physicians (per 1,000 head, 2002)	1.4
Hospital beds (per 1,000 head, 2004)	1.2
Health expenditure (2008): US $ per head (PPP)	517
Health expenditure (2008): % of GDP	5.9
Health expenditure (2008): public (% of total)	83.9
Access to water (% of persons, 2008)	92
Access to sanitation (% of persons, 2008)	74
Total carbon dioxide emissions ('000 metric tons, 2007)	63,387.2
Carbon dioxide emissions per head (metric tons, 2007)	1.4
Human Development Index (2011): ranking	87
Human Development Index (2011): value	0.710

For sources and definitions, see explanatory note on p. vi.

Agriculture

PRINCIPAL CROPS
('000 metric tons)

	2008	2009	2010
Rice, paddy	2,792	2,985	2,412
Maize	1,727	1,637	1,536
Sorghum	134	97	99
Potatoes	2,373	2,273	2,122
Cassava (Manioc)	1,804	2,202	2,364
Yams	266	297	395
Sugar cane	38,500*	38,500*	20,273
Beans, dry	161	154	149
Soybeans (Soya beans)	56	59	54
Coconuts*	83	82	82
Oil palm fruit*	3,200	3,200	3,200
Cabbages and other brassicas*	159	156	150
Tomatoes	491	515	546
Chillies and peppers, green*	55	54	50
Onions, dry	308	311	330
Carrots and turnips	299	299	260
Watermelons	88	91	136
Bananas	1,988	2,020	2,034
Plantains	3,380	3,012	2,815
Oranges*	353	332	330
Mangoes, mangosteens and guavas	175	187	243
Avocados	184	165	202
Pineapples	436	428	398
Papayas	208	189	263
Coffee, green	689	888	514

* FAO estimate(s).

Aggregate production ('000 metric tons, may include official, semi-official or estimated data): Total cereals 4,707 in 2008, 4,765 in 2009, 4,080 in 2010; Total roots and tubers 4,534 in 2008, 4,870 in 2009, 4,981 in 2010; Total vegetables (incl. melons) 1,781 in 2008, 1,786 in 2009, 1,867 in 2010; Total fruits (excl. melons) 8,437 in 2008, 7,938 in 2009, 7,990 in 2010.

Source: FAO.

LIVESTOCK
('000 head, year ending September)

	2008	2009	2010
Horses	2,421	2,506	2,126
Asses	224	221	172
Mules	430	433	310
Cattle	26,878	27,359	27,754
Pigs*	1,830	1,850	1,850
Sheep*	3,400	3,400	3,400
Goats*	1,200	1,200	1,200
Chickens*	155,000	157,000	157

* FAO estimates.

Source: FAO.

LIVESTOCK PRODUCTS
('000 metric tons)

	2008	2009	2010
Cattle meat	917.4	936.3	930.0*
Sheep meat*	7.3	7.5	7.5
Goat meat*	7.2	7.4	7.4
Pig meat	169.8	179.5	180.0*
Horse meat*	6.6	6.8	6.7
Chicken meat	1,010.7	1,020.3	1,000.0*
Cows' milk	7,431	7,545	7,500*
Hen eggs	542	581	510

* FAO estimate(s).

Source: FAO.

Forestry

ROUNDWOOD REMOVALS
('000 cu metres, excl. bark)

	2007	2008	2009
Sawlogs, veneer logs and logs for sleepers	658	1,062	1,062*
Pulpwood	808	746	825
Other industrial wood	145	503	503*
Fuel wood	8,829	8,826	8,826
Total	10,440	11,137	11,216

* FAO estimate.

2010: Production assumed to be unchanged from 2009 (FAO estimates).

Source: FAO.

SAWNWOOD PRODUCTION
('000 cu metres, incl. railway sleepers)

	2008	2009*	2010†
Coniferous (softwood)	115	126	115
Broadleaved (hardwood)	366	399	366
Total	481	525	481

* Unofficial figures.
† FAO estimates.

Source: FAO.

Fishing

('000 metric tons, live weight)

	2007	2008	2009
Capture	124.1*	114.4*	106.6
Bigeye tuna	3.2	4.0	1.3
Characins	8.0*	8.7*	9.4
Freshwater siluroids	9.4*	10.5*	11.5
Other freshwater fishes	3.4*	2.5*	1.7
Pacific anchoveta	21.1*	22.1*	5.7
Skipjack tuna	17.9	22.1	14.1
Yellowfin tuna	20.8	21.6	31.5
Aquaculture*	66.6	68.2	85.3
Tilapias	18.3*	22.0*	28.2
Pirapatinga*	2.3	2.2	2.2
Rainbow trout	1.1	1.0*	5.7
Whiteleg shrimp	20.3	18.4	18.1
Total catch*	190.7	182.6	191.9

* FAO estimate(s).

Note: Figures exclude crocodiles, recorded by number rather than by weight. The number of spectacled caimans caught was: 673,062 in 2007; 532,394 in 2008; 405,772 in 2009. The number of American crocodiles caught was: 250 in 2007; 367 in 2008; 10 in 2009.

Source: FAO.

Mining

('000 metric tons unless otherwise indicated)

	2007	2008	2009
Gold (kg)	15,482	34,321	47,800
Silver (kg)	9,765	9,162	10,800*
Salt	514	632	612
Hard coal	69,902	73,502	72,800
Iron ore†	624	473	300
Crude petroleum ('000 barrels)	193,815	214,620	244,800

* Preliminary figure.
† Figures refer to the gross weight of ore. The estimated iron content was 46%.

Source: US Geological Survey.

Industry

SELECTED PRODUCTS
('000 metric tons unless otherwise indicated)

	2006	2007	2008
Sugar	2,415	2,277	2,036
Crude steel ingots (incl. steel for casting)*	1,221	1,260	1,125
Semi-manufactures of iron and steel (hot-rolled)*	1,598	1,598	1,435
Gas-diesel (distillate fuel) oils	4,456	4,395	4,395
Residual fuel oils	2,792	3,318	3,318
Motor spirit (petrol)	3,618	3,164	3,164

* Source: US Geological Survey.

Source: mostly UN Industrial Commodity Statistics Database.

2009 ('000 metric tons, preliminary): Cement 9,100; Crude steel ingots (incl. steel for casting) 1,100; Semi-manufactures of iron and steel (hot-rolled) 1,454 (Source: US Geological Survey).

Finance

CURRENCY AND EXCHANGE RATES

Monetary Units
100 centavos = 1 Colombian peso.

Sterling, Dollar and Euro Equivalents (30 December 2011)
£1 sterling = 3,003.6 pesos;
US $1 = 1,942.7 pesos;
€1 = 2,513.7 pesos;
10,000 Colombian pesos = £3.33 = $5.15 = €3.98.

Average Exchange Rate (pesos per US $)
2009 2,166.79
2010 1,898.57
2011 1,848.14

GOVERNMENT FINANCE
(budgetary central government transactions, non-cash basis, '000 million pesos, provisional figures)

Summary of Balances

	2007	2008	2009
Revenue	103,986	73,975	87,369
Less Expense	110,014	96,819	98,473
Net operating balance	–6,028	–22,844	–11,104
Less Net acquisition of non-financial assets	1,694	9,627	9,188
Net lending/borrowing	–7,722	–32,471	–20,292

Revenue

	2007	2008	2009
Taxes	58,644	59,245	60,164
Taxes on income, profits and capital gains	17,336	19,725	23,027
Individuals	17,336	19,725	23,027
Taxes on goods and services	27,181	29,684	28,157
Social contributions	4,273	5,002	5,329
Grants	170	220	1,386
Other revenue	40,899	9,508	20,490
Total	103,986	73,975	87,369

Expense/Outlays

Expense by economic type	2007	2008	2009
Compensation of employees	20,468	15,158	15,940
Use of goods and services	5,645	5,518	6,295
Consumption of fixed capital	914	1,056	1,186
Interest	27,562	14,985	16,509
Subsidies	273	7,166	5,442
Grants	41,689	23,335	26,410
Social benefits	6,221	9,906	13,147
Other expense	7,240	19,674	13,543
Total	110,014	96,798	98,472

Source: IMF, *Government Finance Statistics Yearbook*.

Public sector account ('000 million pesos): *Revenue:* 130,672.9 in 2008; 138,982.2 in 2009; 146,896.3 in 2010. *Expenditure (incl. interest payments):* 128,478.3 in 2008; 149,898.8 in 2009; 161,588.6 in 2010.

INTERNATIONAL RESERVES

(US $ million at 31 December)

	2008	2009	2010
Gold (national valuation)	191	243	311
IMF special drawing rights	229	1,184	1,157
Reserve position in IMF	440	406	260
Foreign exchange	22,810	23,158	26,349
Total	23,670	24,991	28,077

Source: IMF, *International Financial Statistics*.

MONEY SUPPLY

('000 million pesos at 31 December)

	2008	2009	2010
Currency outside banks	24,351.6	25,671.2	29,674.1
Transferable deposits	23,075.9	24,796.3	29,790.5
Other deposits	58,409.5	66,134.6	78,180.1
Securities other than shares	65,538.9	68,579.6	68,754.7
Broad money	171,375.9	185,181.8	206,399.3

Source: IMF, *International Financial Statistics*.

COST OF LIVING

(Consumer Price Index for low-income families; base: 2000 = 100)

	2006	2007	2008
Food and beverages	150.5	162.5	182.6
Clothing and footwear	109.7	111.4	112.0
Rent, fuel and light*	121.1	126.4	132.5
All items (incl. others)	145.2	153.4	166.0

* Including certain household equipment.

2009: Food and beverages 189.6; All items (incl. others) 173.2.

2010: Food and beverages 191.7; All items (incl. others) 177.4.

Source: ILO.

NATIONAL ACCOUNTS

('000 million pesos at current prices, provisional figures)

Expenditure on the Gross Domestic Product

	2008	2009	2010
Final consumption expenditure	379,201	404,299	434,030
Households*	304,703	322,147	345,269
General government	74,498	82,152	88,761
Gross capital formation	112,759	115,280	126,375
Total domestic expenditure	491,960	519,579	560,405
Exports of goods and services	86,355	81,165	86,164
Less Imports of goods and services	97,278	92,212	98,296
GDP in market prices	481,037	508,532	548,273
GDP at constant 2005 prices	401,744	407,577	425,063

* Including non-profit institutions serving households.

Gross Domestic Product by Economic Activity

	2008	2009	2010
Agriculture, hunting, forestry and fishing	32,964	34,352	35,552
Mining and quarrying	38,824	36,325	44,966
Manufacturing	66,689	70,442	74,936
Electricity, gas and water	17,714	20,485	21,956
Construction	33,379	39,203	40,639
Wholesale and retail trade; repair of motor vehicles, motorcycles, and personal and household goods; hotels and restaurants	55,803	58,638	64,417
Transport, storage and communications	31,847	33,044	34,770
Financial intermediation, insurance, real estate, renting and business activities	90,416	96,754	102,313
Other community, social and personal service activities	71,925	78,488	84,988
Gross value added in basic prices	439,561	467,731	504,537
Taxes on products	42,068	41,418	44,394
Less Subsidies on products	592	617	658
GDP in market prices	481,037	508,532	548,273

BALANCE OF PAYMENTS

(US $ million)

	2008	2009	2010
Exports of goods f.o.b.	38,534	34,026	40,777
Imports of goods f.o.b.	–37,563	–31,479	–38,628
Trade balance	971	2,546	2,150
Exports of services	4,137	4,202	4,446
Imports of services	–7,210	–7,030	–7,986
Balance on goods and services	–2,101	–281	–1,390
Other income received	1,745	1,289	1,370
Other income paid	–12,078	–10,777	–13,487
Balance on goods, services and income	–12,435	–9,770	–13,507
Current transfers received	5,898	5,253	5,343
Current transfers paid	–386	–640	–868
Current balance	–6,923	–5,157	–9,032
Direct investment abroad	–2,254	–3,088	–6,562
Direct investment from abroad	10,596	7,137	6,765
Portfolio investment assets	188	–2,802	–1,768
Portfolio investment liabilities	–1,195	4,668	3,263
Other investment assets	–173	–1,615	486
Other investment liabilities	2,262	2,052	9,759
Net errors and omissions	70	245	207
Overall balance	2,571	1,441	3,117

Source: IMF, *International Financial Statistics*.

External Trade

PRINCIPAL COMMODITIES
(US $ million)

Imports c.i.f.	2008	2009	2010
Agricultural, livestock, hunting and forestry products	2,217	1,733	2,000
Prepared foodstuffs, beverages and tobacco	2,057	1,859	2,236
Textiles, clothing and leather products	1,488	1,307	1,723
Chemical products	7,362	6,119	7,387
Rubber and plastic goods	1,277	1,157	1,406
Metals and metal manufactures	3,898	2,530	3,328
Mechanical, electrical, office, telecommunications and medical equipment	11,558	9,438	11,579
Vehicles and transport equipment	6,142	6,179	7,155
Total (incl. others)	39,669	32,898	40,683

Exports f.o.b.	2008	2009	2010
Coffee	1,883	1,543	1,884
Coal	5,043	5,416	6,015
Petroleum and its derivatives	12,213	10,268	16,485
Prepared foodstuffs, beverages and tobacco	2,627	2,330	1,708
Textiles, clothing and leather products	2,747	1,492	1,250
Paper and publishing	871	764	666
Chemicals	2,674	2,482	2,613
Metal manufactures	2,357	2,422	3,148
Mechanical, electrical and office equipment	1,101	987	633
Vehicles and transport equipment	1,224	698	920
Total (incl. others)	37,626	32,853	39,820

PRINCIPAL TRADING PARTNERS
(US $ million)

Imports c.i.f.	2008	2009	2010
Brazil	2,328	2,147	2,370
China, People's Republic	4,549	3,715	5,477
Ecuador	810	695	835
Germany	1,557	1,338	1,658
Japan	1,153	825	1,157
Mexico	3,126	2,298	3,857
Spain	568	442	502
USA	11,437	9,456	10,477
Venezuela	1,198	563	305
Total (incl. others)	39,669	32,898	40,683

Exports f.o.b.	2008	2009	2010
Belgium	460	409	450
Ecuador	1,500	1,257	1,825
Germany	638	365	250
Japan	372	336	511
Mexico	617	536	638
Peru	855	788	1,132
USA	14,053	12,879	16,764
Venezuela	6,092	4,050	1,423
Total (incl. others)	37,626	32,853	39,820

Transport

RAILWAYS
(traffic)

	1996	1997	1998
Freight ('000 metric tons)	321	348	281
Freight ton-km ('000)	746,544	736,427	657,585

Source: Sociedad de Transporte Ferroviario, SA.

ROAD TRAFFIC
(motor vehicles in use at 31 December)

	1997	1998	1999
Passenger cars	1,694,323	1,776,100	1,803,201
Buses	126,362	131,987	134,799
Goods vehicles	179,530	183,335	184,495
Motorcycles	385,378	450,283	479,073

2007: Passenger cars 1,674,441; Buses 148,537; Vans and lorries 1,064,513; Motorcycles and mopeds 1,930,978.

2008: Passenger cars 1,849,962; Buses 197,285; Vans and lorries 554,064; Motorcycles and mopeds 2,311,652.

Source: IRF, *World Road Statistics*.

SHIPPING

Merchant Fleet
(registered at 31 December)

	2007	2008	2009
Number of vessels	147	149	146
Total displacement ('000 grt)	90.8	91.4	89.7

Source: IHS Fairplay, *World Fleet Statistics*.

Domestic Sea-borne Freight Traffic
('000 metric tons)

	1987	1988	1989
Goods loaded and unloaded	772.1	944.8	464.6

International Sea-borne Freight Traffic
('000 metric tons)

	1999	2000	2001
Goods loaded	4,111	3,543	3,832
Goods unloaded	1,274	1,114	1,399

CIVIL AVIATION
(traffic)

	2007	2008	2009
Kilometres flown (million)	155	162	158
Passengers carried ('000)	11,631	12,339	12,115
Passenger-km (million)	12,114	14,025	14,534
Total ton-km (million)	2,457	2,524	2,530

Source: UN, *Statistical Yearbook*.

Tourism

TOURIST ARRIVALS

Country of origin	2007	2008	2009
Argentina	50,632	51,057	61,358
Brazil	41,145	45,506	47,493
Canada	28,279	27,632	28,157
Chile	29,371	29,716	36,168
Costa Rica	21,326	21,179	20,184
Ecuador	110,508	93,452	101,820
France	27,611	27,381	30,366
Germany	21,668	22,133	26,138
Italy	24,620	24,320	26,054
Mexico	60,340	59,107	57,474
Netherlands	17,104	20,576	23,621
Panama	31,459	28,379	30,956
Peru	58,332	66,313	77,733
Spain	66,748	62,176	77,913
United Kingdom	14,071	17,112	18,947
USA	265,651	264,453	314,858
Venezuela	196,863	237,329	238,078
Total (incl. others)	1,195,443	1,222,966	1,353,700

Tourism receipts (US $ million, excl. passenger transport): 1,669 in 2007; 1,844 in 2008; 1,999 in 2009; 2,083 in 2010 (provisional).

Source: World Tourism Organization.

Communications Media

	2008	2009	2010
Telephones ('000 main lines in use)	7,928.9	7,473.9	7,186.2
Mobile cellular telephones ('000 subscribers)	41,364.8	42,159.6	44,477.7
Internet subscribers ('000)	1,880.0	2,266.2	2,675.5
Broadband subscribers ('000)	1,473.1	2,012.5	2,594.1

Radio receivers ('000 in use): 21,000 in 1997.

Television receivers ('000 in use): 11,396 in 2000.

Personal computers: 5,062,885 (112.5 per 1,000 persons) in 2008.

Book production: 5,302 titles in 1997.

Daily newspapers: 23 titles in 2004 (total average circulation 1,004,000).

Non-daily newspapers: 5 titles in 2004 (total average circulation 289,000).
Sources: UN, *Statistical Yearbook*; UNESCO, *Statistical Yearbook*; International Telecommunication Union.

Education

(2009/10 unless otherwise indicated)

	Institutions*	Teachers	Students ('000) Males	Females	Total
Pre-primary	32,432	48,981	665.7	636.0	1,301.7
Primary	55,869	180,760	2,618.7	2,466.3	5,085.0
Secondary: general	12,921	155,129†	2,294.7	2,399.4	4,694.1
Secondary: technical/vocational		32,146†	176.3	209.3	385.6
Higher (incl. universities)	32	110,488†	811.1	863.3	1,674.4

* 2001/02.

† 2008/09.

Sources: Ministerio de Educación Nacional and UNESCO Institute for Statistics.

Pupil-teacher ratio (primary education, UNESCO estimate): 28.1 in 2009/10 (Source: UNESCO Institute for Statistics).

Adult literacy rate (UNESCO estimates): 93.2% (males 93.1%; females 93.4%) in 2009 (Source: UNESCO Institute for Statistics).

Directory

The Government

HEAD OF STATE

President: JUAN MANUEL SANTOS CALDERÓN (took office on 7 August 2010).

Vice-President: ANGELINO GARZÓN.

CABINET
(May 2012)

The Government is formed by a coalition led by the Partido Social de Unidad Nacional.

Minister of Foreign Affairs: MARÍA ANGELA HOLGUÍN.

Minister of Finance and Public Credit: JUAN CARLOS ECHEVERRY.

Minister of National Defence: JUAN CARLOS PINZÓN.

Minister of Justice and Law: JUAN CARLOS ESGUERRA PORTOCARRERO.

Minister of Agriculture and Rural Development: JUAN CAMILO RESTREPO SALAZAR.

Minister of Health and Social Protection: BEATRIZ LONDOÑO SOTO.

Minister of Mines and Energy: MAURICIO CARDENAS.

Minister of Trade, Industry and Tourism: SERGIO DÍAZ GRANADOS.

Minister of National Education: MARÍA FERNANDA CAMPO.

Minister of Housing, Cities and Territorial Development and Acting Minister of the Interior: GERMÁN VARGAS LLERAS.

Minister of the Environment and Sustainable Development: FRANK PEARL.

Minister of Information Technology and Communications: DIEGO MOLANO.

Minister of Transport: GERMÁN CARDONA GUTIÉRREZ.

Minister of Culture: MARIANA GARCÉS CÓRDOBA.

Minister of Labour: RAFAEL PARDO RUEDA.

MINISTRIES

Office of the President: Palacio de Nariño, Carrera 8, No 7-26, Bogotá, DC; tel. (1) 562-9300; fax (1) 286-8063; internet www.presidencia.gov.co.

Ministry of Agriculture and Rural Development: Avda Jiménez, No 7-65, Bogotá, DC; tel. (1) 334-1199; fax (1) 284-1775; e-mail contactenos@minagricultura.gov.co; internet www.minagricultura.gov.co.

Ministry of Culture: Carrera 8, No 8-43, Bogotá, DC; tel. (1) 342-4100; fax (1) 342-1721; e-mail servicioalcliente@mincultura.gov.co; internet www.mincultura.gov.co.

Ministry of the Environment and Sustainable Development: Calle 37, No 8-40, Bogotá, DC; tel. (1) 332-3434; e-mail correspondencia@minambiente.gov.co; internet www.minambiente.gov.co.

Ministry of Finance and Public Credit: Carrera 8, No 6-64, Of. 305, Bogotá, DC; tel. (1) 381-1700; fax (1) 350-9344; e-mail atencioncliente@minhacienda.gov.co; internet www.minhacienda.gov.co.

Ministry of Foreign Affairs: Palacio de San Carlos, Calle 10, No 5-51, Bogotá, DC; tel. (1) 381-4000; fax (1) 381-4747; e-mail cancilleria@cancilleria.gov.co; internet www.cancilleria.gov.co.

Ministry of Health and Social Protection: Carrera 13, No 32-76, Bogotá, DC; tel. (1) 330-5000; fax (1) 330-5050; e-mail atencionalciudadano@minproteccionsocial.gov.co; internet www.minproteccionsocial.gov.co.

Ministry of Housing, Cities and Territorial Development: Calle 37, No 8-40, Bogotá, DC; tel. (1) 332-3434; fax (1) 332-3400; e-mail correspondencia@minvivienda.gov.co; internet www.minvivienda.gov.co.

Ministry of Information Technology and Communications: Edif. Murillo Toro, Carrera 8A entre, Calle 12 y 13, Apdo Aéreo 14515, Bogotá, DC; tel. (1) 344-3460; fax (1) 344-3434; e-mail info@mintic.gov.co; internet www.mintic.gov.co.

Ministry of the Interior: Palacio Echeverry, Carrera 9, No 14-10, Bogotá, DC; tel. (1) 444-3100; fax (1) 341-9583; e-mail atencionalcliente@mij.gov.co; internet www.mij.gov.co.

Ministry of Justice and Law: Carrera 9, No 12C-10, Bogotá, DC; tel. (1) 444-3100; e-mail servicioalcliente@mij.gov.co; internet www.minjusticia.gov.co.

Ministry of Labour: Carrera 14, No 99-33, Bogotá, DC; tel. (1) 489-3900; e-mail contactenostlc@mintrabajo.gov.co; internet http:www.mintrabajo.gov.co.

Ministry of Mines and Energy: Calle 43, No 57-31, Centro Administrativo Nacional (CAN), Bogotá, DC; tel. (1) 220-0300; fax (1) 222-3651; e-mail menergia@minminas.gov.co; internet www.minminas.gov.co.

Ministry of National Defence: Carrera 54, No 26-25, Centro Administrativo Nacional (CAN), 2°, Bogotá, DC; tel. (1) 266-0296; fax (1) 315-0111; e-mail usuarios@mindefensa.gov.co; internet www.mindefensa.gov.co.

Ministry of National Education: Calle 43, No 57-14, Centro Administrativo Nacional (CAN), Bogotá, DC; tel. (1) 222-2800; fax (1) 222-4578; e-mail dci@mineducacion.gov.co; internet www.mineducacion.gov.co.

Ministry of Trade, Industry and Tourism: Edif. Centro de Comercio Internacional, Calle 28, No 13A-15, 18°, Bogotá, DC; tel. (1) 606-7676; fax (1) 606-7521; e-mail info@mincomercio.gov.co; internet www.mincomercio.gov.co.

Ministry of Transport: Centro Administrativo Nacional (CAN), Of. 409, Avda El Dorado, Bogotá, DC; tel. (1) 324-0800; e-mail mintrans@mintransporte.gov.co; internet www.mintransporte.gov.co.

President and Legislature

PRESIDENT

Presidential Election, First Round, 30 May 2010

	Valid votes	% of votes cast
Juan Manuel Santos Calderón (Partido de la U)	6,802,043	46.67
Antanas Mockus Šivickas (PV)	3,134,222	21.51
Germán Vargas Lleras (CR)	1,473,627	10.11
Gustavo Petro Urrego (PDA)	1,331,267	9.13
Noemí Sanín (PCC)	893,819	6.13
Rafael Pardo Rueda (PL)	638,302	4.38
Others	75,336	0.52
Votos en blanco*	223,977	1.53
Total†	14,573,593	100.00

* Blank, valid votes.
† In addition, there were 208,427 invalid votes.

Presidential Election, Second Round, 20 June 2010

	Valid votes	% of votes cast
Juan Manuel Santos Calderón (Partido de la U)	9,028,942	69.13
Antanas Mockus Šivickas (PV)	3,587,975	27.47
Votos en blanco*	444,274	3.40
Total valid votes†	13,061,192	100.00

* Blank, valid votes.
† In addition, there were 235,732 invalid votes.

CONGRESO

Senado
(Senate)

President: AMANDO BENEDETTI.

General Election, 14 March 2010

	Seats
Partido Social de la Unidad Nacional (Partido de la U)	28
Partido Conservador Colombiano (PCC)	22
Partido Liberal Colombiano (PL)	17
Partido de Integración Nacional (PIN)	9
Cambio Radical (CR)	8
Polo Democrático Alternativo (PDA)	8
Partido Verde (PV)	5
Movimiento MIRA	3
Indigenous groups*	2
Total	102

* Under the terms of the Constitution, at least two Senate seats are reserved for indigenous groups.

Cámara de Representantes
(House of Representatives)

President: SIMÓN GAVIRIA MUÑOZ.

General Election, 14 March 2010

	Seats
Partido Social de Unidad Nacional (Partido de la U)	47
Partido Conservador Colombiano (PCC)	37
Partido Liberal Colombiano (PL)	35
Cambio Radical (CR)	16
Partido de Integración Nacional (PIN)	11
Polo Democrático Alternativo (PDA)	4
Partido Verde (PV)	3
Movimiento MIRA	1
Others	10
Indigenous groups*	2
Total	166

* Under the terms of the Constitution, at least two lower house seats are reserved for indigenous groups.

Governors

DEPARTMENTS
(April 2012)

Amazonas: CARLOS ARTURO RODRÍGUEZ CELIS.
Antioquia: SERGIO FAJARDO VALDERRAMA.
Arauca: JOSÉ FACUNDO CASTILLO CISNERO.
Atlántico: JOSÉ ANTONIO SEGEBRE BERARDINELLI.
Bolívar: JUAN CARLOS GOSSAÍN ROGNINI.
Boyacá: JUAN CARLOS GRANADOS BECERRA.
Caldas: GUIDO ECHEVERRI PIEDRAHITA.
Caquetá: VÍCTOR ISIDRO RAMÍREZ LOAIZA.
Casanare: NELSON RICARDO MARINO VELANDIA.
Cauca: TEMÍSTOCLES ORTEGA NARVÁEZ.
Cesar: LUIS ALBERTO MONSALVO GNECCO.
Chocó: LUÍS GILBERTO MURILLO URRUTIA.
Córdoba: ALEJANDRO LYONS MUSKUS.
Cundinamarca: ALVARO CRÚZ VARGAS.
Guainía: OSCAR ARMANDO RODRÍGUEZ SÁNCHEZ.
Guaviare: JOSÉ OCTAVIANO RIVERA MONCADA.
Huila: CIELO GONZÁLEZ VILLA.
La Guajira: JUAN FRANCISCO GÓMEZ CERCHAR.
Magdalena: LUÍS MIGUEL COTES HABEYCH.
Meta: ALÁN JESÚS EDMUNDO JARA URZOLA.
Nariño: SEGUNDO RAÚL DELGADO GUERRERO.
Norte de Santander: EDGAR JESÚS DÍAZ CONTRERAS.
Putumayo: JIMMY HAROLD DÍAZ BURBANO.
Quindío: SANDRA PAOLA HURTADO PALACIO.
Risaralda: CARLOS ALBERTO BOTERO LÓPEZ.
San Andrés, Providencia y Santa Catalina: AURY SOCORRO GUERRERO.
Santander: RICHARD ALFONSO AGUILAR VILLA.
Sucre: JULIO CÉSAR GUERRA TULENA.
Tolima: LUÍS CARLOS DELGADO PEÑÓN.
Valle del Cauca: AURELIO IRRAGORI VALENCIA.
Vaupés: ROBERTO JARAMILLO GARCÍA.
Vichada: SERGIO ANDRÉS ESPINOSA FLORES.
Bogotá, DC: GUSTAVO FRANCISCO PETRO URREGO.

Election Commission

Consejo Nacional Electoral (CNE): Avda El Dorado 46-20, Centro Administrativo Nacional (CAN), 6°, Bogotá, DC; tel. (1) 220-0800; internet www.cne.gov.co; f. 1888 as Gran Consejo Electoral; refounded under current name in 1985; Pres. MARCO EMILIO HINCAPIÉ RAMÍREZ.

Political Organizations

Alianza Social Independiente: Calle 17, No 5-43, 8°, Bogotá, DC; tel. (1) 283-0616; fax (1) 282-7474; e-mail alianzasocialindependiente@gmail.com; internet www.asicolombia.com; f. 1991; fmrly Alianza Social Indígena; Leader ALONSO TOBON.

Cambio Radical (CR): Carrera 7, No 26-20, 26°, Bogotá, DC; tel. (1) 327-9696; fax (1) 210-6800; e-mail cambioradical@cable.net.co; internet www.partidocambioradical.org; f. 1998; Pres. ALEX CHAR; Sec.-Gen. ANTONIO ALVAREZ LLERAS.

Compromiso Ciudadano por Colombia: Carrera 36, 8A-46, Of. 201, Medellín; tel. (4) 448-6048; fax (4) 312-7014; e-mail info@sergiofajardo.com; internet www.sergiofajardo.com; f. 2008; contested the 2010 presidential campaign in alliance with the Partido Verde (q.v.); Leader SERGIO FAJARDO.

Movimiento Apertura Liberal: Avda 3B, 5-70B, Latino, Cúcuta, Norte de Santander; tel. (7) 571-3729; e-mail correo@aperturaliberal.com; internet www.aperturaliberal.com; f. 1993; Nat. Dir Dr MIGUEL ANGEL FLORES RIVERA.

Movimiento de Autoridades Indígenas de Colombia (AICO): Calle 23, No 7-61, Of. 302, Bogotá DC; tel. (1) 286-8233; fax (1) 341-8930; e-mail aico@aicocolombia.org; internet www.aicocolombia.org; f. 1990; Pres. LUIS ALBERTO CUACES.

Movimiento MIRA (Movimiento Independiente de Renovación Absoluta): Transversal 29, No 36-40, Bogotá, DC; tel. (1) 369-3222;

fax 369-3210; e-mail contacto@movimientomira.com; internet www.movimientomira.com; f. 2000; Pres. CARLOS ALBERTO BAENA LÓPEZ.

Movimiento Progresista Colombiano: Avda Caracas 4-07 Sur, Bogotá, DC; tel. (1) 289-7895; internet movimientoprogresistacol.blogspot.in; f. 2011; Leader GUSTAVO FRANCISCO PETRO URREGO.

Partido Colombia Democrática: Calle 41, No 13A-07, 2°, Bogotá, DC; tel. (1) 338-3624; fax (1) 338-2310; e-mail contactenos@colombiademocratica.com; internet www.colombiademocratica.com; f. 2003; conservative; Nat. Dir MARIO URIBE ESCOBAR; Sec.-Gen. GABRIEL SIERRA.

Partido Comunista Colombiano (PC): Calle 18A, No 14-56, Apdo Aéreo 2523, Bogotá, DC; tel. (1) 334-1947; fax (1) 281-8259; e-mail notipaco@pacocol.org; internet www.pacocol.org; f. 1930; Marxist-Leninist; Sec.-Gen. JAIME CAYCEDO TURRIAGO.

Partido Conservador Colombiano (PCC): Avda Carrera 24, No 37-09, La Soledad, Bogotá, DC; tel. (1) 597-9630; fax (1) 369-0053; e-mail presidencia@partidoconservador.com; internet www.partidoconservador.com; f. 1849; 2.9m. mems; Pres. EFRAÍN CEPEDA SARABIA; Sec.-Gen. JORGE HUMBERTO MANTILLA.

Partido de Integración Nacional (PIN): Calle 39, No 28A-26, Barrio La Soledad, Bogotá, DC; tel. (1) 608-8822; fax (1) 244-0189; e-mail convergencia@intercable.net.co; internet partidopin.org; f. 2009; pro-Govt party; Pres. ANGEL ALIRIO MORENO MATEUS; Leader ALVARO CAICEDO.

Partido Liberal Colombiano (PL): Avda Caracas, No 36-01, Bogotá, DC; tel. (1) 593-4500; fax (1) 323-1070; e-mail direcciondecomunicaciones@partidoliberal.org.co; internet www.partidoliberal.org.co; f. 1848; Pres. SIMON GAVIRIA MUÑOZ; Sec.-Gen. MAURICIO JARAMILLO MORALES.

Partido Social de la Unidad Nacional (Partido de la U): Carrera 7, No 32-16, 21°, Bogotá, DC; tel. and fax (1) 350-0215; internet www.partidodelau.com; f. 2005; conservative; Pres. JUAN LOZANO RAMÍREZ; Sec.-Gen. JUAN CAMILO RESTREPO.

Partido Verde (PV): Calle 66, No 7–69, Bogotá, DC; tel. (1) 606-7888; fax (1) 608-1312; e-mail movilizacion@partidoverde.org.co; internet www.partidoverde.org.co; Nat. Dir CARLOS RAMÓN GONZÁLEZ.

Polo Democrático Alternativo (PDA): Carrera 17A, No 37-27, Bogotá, DC; tel. (1) 288-6188; e-mail info@polodemocratico.net; internet www.polodemocratico.net; f. 2002 as electoral alliance, constituted as a political party in July 2003; founded by fmr mems of the Movimiento 19 de Abril; fmrly Polo Democrático Independiente; adopted current name 2006; left-wing; Pres. CLARA LÓPEZ OBREGÓN; Sec.-Gen. GERMÁN ÁVILA.

The following are the principal guerrilla groups in operation in Colombia:

Ejército de Liberación Nacional (ELN): internet www.eln-voces.com; Castroite guerrilla movt; f. 1964; 3,500 mems; political status recognized by the Govt in 1998; mem. of the Coordinadora Nacional Guerrilla Simón Bolívar; Leader NICOLÁS RODRÍGUEZ BAUTISTA.

Fuerzas Armadas Revolucionarias de Colombia—Ejército del Pueblo (FARC—EP): f. 1964, although mems active from 1949; name changed from Fuerzas Armadas Revolucionarias de Colombia to the above in 1982; fmrly military wing of the Communist Party; composed of 39 armed fronts and about 6,000–8,000 mems; political status recognized by the Govt in 1998; mem. of the Coordinadora Nacional Guerrilla Simón Bolívar; C-in-C RODRIGO LONDONO ECHEVERRI (alias Timochenko).

Diplomatic Representation

EMBASSIES IN COLOMBIA

Algeria: Carrera 11, No 93-53, Of. 302, Bogotá, DC; tel. (1) 635-0520; fax (1) 635-0531; e-mail ambalgbg@cable.net.co; internet www.embargelia-colombia.org; Ambassador MOHAMED ZIANE HASSENI.

Argentina: Avda 40A, No 13-09, 16°, Apdo Aéreo 53013, Bogotá, DC; tel. (1) 288-0900; fax (1) 288-8868; e-mail embargentina@etb.net.co; Ambassador CELSO ALEJANDRO JAQUE.

Austria: Edif. Fiducafé, 4°, Carrera 9, No 73-44, Bogotá, DC; tel. (1) 326-3680; fax (1) 317-7639; e-mail bogota-ob@bmeia.gv.at; internet www.embajadadeaustria.org.co; Ambassador ANDREAS LIEBMANN-HOLZMANN.

Belgium: Calle 26, No 4A-45, 7°, Apdo Aéreo 3564, Bogotá, DC; tel. (1) 380-0370; fax (1) 380-0340; e-mail bogota@diplobel.fed.be; internet www.diplomatie.be/bogota; Ambassador SADI PAUL BRANCART.

Bolivia: Calle 108A, No 21-42, Chicó Navarra, Bogotá, DC; tel. (1) 619-5509; fax (1) 619-6050; e-mail embolivia-bogota@rree.gov.bo; internet www.embajadaboliviacolombia.org; Ambassador MARÍO CARVAJAL LOZANO.

Brazil: Calle 93, No 14-20, 8°, Apdo 90540, Bogotá, DC; tel. (1) 218-0800; fax (1) 218-8393; e-mail embaixada@brasil.org.co; internet bogota.itamaraty.gov.br; Ambassador ANTONINO LISBOA MENA GONÇALVES.

Canada: Carretera 7, No 114-33, 14°, Apdo Aéreo 110067, Bogotá, DC; tel. (1) 657-9800; fax (1) 657-9912; e-mail bgota@international.gc.ca; internet www.canadainternational.gc.ca/colombia-colombie; Ambassador TIM MARTIN.

Chile: Calle 100, No 11B-44, Apdo Aéreo 90061, Bogotá, DC; tel. (1) 620-6613; fax (1) 744-1468; e-mail echile.colombia@minrel.gov.cl; internet chileabroad.gov.cl/colombia; Ambassador GUSTAVO AYARES OSSANDÓN.

China, People's Republic: Carrera 16, No 98-30, Bogotá, DC; tel. (1) 622-3215; fax (1) 622-3114; e-mail chinaemb_co@mfa.gov.cn; internet co.china-embassy.org; Ambassador WANG XIAOYUAN.

Costa Rica: Casa Barrio, Calle 118A, No 14-62, Santa Barbara, Bogotá, DC; tel. (1) 629-5095; fax (1) 691-8558; e-mail embacosta@etb.net.co; internet www.embajadadecostarica.org; Ambassador CIRCE MILENA VILLANUEVA MONGE.

Cuba: Carrera 9, No 92-54, Bogotá, DC; tel. (1) 621-7054; fax (1) 611-4382; e-mail embacuba@cable.net.co; internet www.cubadiplomatica.cu/colombia; Ambassador JORGE IVÁN MORA GODOY.

Dominican Republic: Carrera 18, No 123-43, Bogotá, DC; tel. (1) 601-1670; fax (1) 620-7597; e-mail embajado@cable.net.co; Ambassador HÉCTOR GALVÁN SUZAÑA.

Ecuador: Edif. Fernando Mazuera, 7°, Calle 72, No 6-30, Bogotá, DC; tel. (1) 212-6549; fax (1) 212-6536; e-mail eecucolombia@mmrree.gov.ec; Ambassador CÉSAR RAUL VALLEJO CORRAL.

Egypt: Carrera 16, No 101–51, Bogotá, DC; tel. (1) 236-9917; fax (1) 236-9914; e-mail embajadadeegipto@telmex.net.co; Ambassador TAREK ELKOUNY.

El Salvador: Edif. El Nogal, Of. 503, Carrera 9, No 80-15, Bogotá, DC; tel. (1) 349-6765; fax (1) 349-6670; e-mail elsalvador@supercable.net.co; Ambassador GUILLERMO RUBIO FUNES.

France: Carrera 11, No 93-12, Bogotá, DC; tel. (1) 638-1400; fax (1) 638-1430; e-mail amfrabog@andinet.com; internet www.ambafrance-co.org; Ambassador PIERRE-JEAN VANDOORRNE.

Germany: Avda El Dorado, Edif. World Business Port, 7°, Carrera 69, No 25B-44, Apdo 98833, Bogotá, DC; tel. (1) 423-2600; fax (1) 429-3145; e-mail info@bogota.diplo.de; internet www.bogota.diplo.de; Ambassador JÜRGEN CHRISTIAN MERTENS.

Guatemala: Calle 87, No 20-27, Of. 302, Bogotá, DC; tel. (1) 636-1724; fax (1) 610-1449; e-mail embcolombia@minex.gob.gt; Ambassador CARLOS RAMIRO SANTIAGO MORALES.

Holy See: Carrera 15, No 36-33, Apdo Aéreo 3740, Bogotá, DC (Apostolic Nunciature); tel. (1) 705-4545; fax (1) 285-1817; e-mail nunciatura@cable.net.co; Apostolic Nuncio Most Rev. ALDO CAVALLI (Titular Archbishop of Vibo).

Honduras: Calle 65, No 8-26, Of. 201, Bogotá, DC; tel. (1) 248-2195; fax (1) 217-1457; e-mail info@embajadadehonduras.org.co; internet www.embajadadehonduras.org.co; Ambassador CARLOS HUMBERTO RODRÍGUEZ.

India: Calle 116, No 301, Torre Cusezar, Bogotá, DC; tel. (1) 637-3259; fax (1) 637-3451; e-mail central@embajadaindia.org; internet www.embajadaindia.org; Ambassador RIEWARD W. WARJRI.

Indonesia: Carrera 11, No 75-27, Bogotá, DC; tel. (1) 217-2404; fax (1) 326-2165; e-mail eindones@colomsat.net.co; internet www.indonesiabogota.org.co; Ambassador MICHAEL MENUFANDU.

Iran: Calle 96, No 11A-20, Apdo 93854, Bogotá, DC; tel. (1) 610-3064; fax (1) 610-2556; e-mail embajadairan@andinet.com.co; internet bogota.mfa.ir; Ambassador AHMAD PABARJA.

Israel: Calle 35, No 7-25, 14°, Bogotá, DC; tel. (1) 327-7500; fax (1) 327-7555; e-mail info@bogota.mfa.gov.il; internet bogota.mfa.gov.il; Ambassador YOED MAGEN.

Italy: Calle 93B, No 9-92, Apdo Aéreo 50901, Bogotá, DC; tel. (1) 218-7206; fax (1) 610-5886; e-mail ambbogo.mail@esteri.it; internet www.ambbogota.esteri.it; Ambassador ELIO MENZIONE.

Jamaica: Avda 19, No 106A-83, Of. 304, Apdo Aéreo 102428, Bogotá, DC; tel. (1) 612-3389; fax (1) 612-3479; e-mail emjacol@cable.net.com; Chargé d'affaires ELAINE TOWNSEND DE SÁNCHEZ.

Japan: Carrera 7A, No 71-21, 11°, Torre B, Bogotá, DC; tel. (1) 317-5001; fax (1) 317-5007; e-mail info@embjp-colombia.com; internet www.colombia.emb-japan.go.jp; Ambassador KAZUMI SUZUKI.

Korea, Republic: Calle 94, No 9-39, Bogotá, DC; tel. (1) 616-7200; fax (1) 610-0338; e-mail embcorea@mofat.go.kr; internet col.mofat.go.kr/index.jsp; Ambassador CHOO JONG-YOUN.

Lebanon: Calle 74, No 11-88, CP 51084, Bogotá, DC; tel. (1) 348-1781; fax (1) 347-9106; e-mail info@embajadadellibano.org.co; internet www.embajadadellibano.org.co; Chargé d'affaires a.i. HADI JABER.

Mexico: Edif. Teleport Business Park, Calle 113, No 7-21, Of. 204, Torre A, Barrio Santa Ana, Bogotá, DC; tel. (1) 629-4989; fax (1) 629-5121; e-mail emcolmex@etb.net.co; internet www.sre.gob.mx/colombia; Ambassador FLORENCIO SALAZAR ADAME.

Morocco: Carrera 23, No 104A-34, Bogotá, DC; tel. (1) 619-3681; fax (1) 619-3685; e-mail embamarruecos@etb.net.co; internet www.embajadamarruecosbogota.com; Ambassador NOUREDDINE KHALIFA.

Netherlands: Carrera 13, No 93-40, 5°, Apdo Aéreo 43585, Bogotá, DC; tel. (1) 638-4200; fax (1) 623-3020; e-mail bog@minbuza.nl; internet www.mfa.nl/bog; Ambassador MARION S. KAPPEYNE VAN DE COPPELLO.

Nicaragua: Calle 108A, No 25-42, Bogotá, DC; tel. (1) 619-8911; fax (1) 612-6050; e-mail embnicaragua@007mundo.com; Ambassador JULIO JOSÉ CALERO REYES.

Panama: Calle 92, No 7A-40, Bogotá, DC; tel. (1) 257-5067; fax (1) 257-5068; e-mail embpacol@cable.net.co; internet www.empacol.org; Ambassador RICARDO ANGUIZOLA.

Paraguay: Calle 72, No 10-51, 10º, Of. 1001, Bogotá, DC; tel. (1) 235-6987; e-mail embparaguaycol@gmail.com; internet www.mre.gov.py/embaparcolombia; Ambassador WALTER DANIEL BIEDERMANN MONTANER.

Peru: Calle 80A, No 6-50, Bogotá, DC; tel. (1) 257-0505; fax (1) 249-8581; e-mail embaperu@embajadadelperu.org.co; internet www.embajadadelperu.org.co; Ambassador JORGE VOTO-BERNALES GATICA.

Poland: Carrera 21, Calle 104A, No 23-48, Apdó Aereo 101363, Bogotá, DC; tel. (1) 214-0400; fax (1) 214-0854; e-mail bogota.amb.sekretariat@msz.gov.pl; internet www.bogota.polemb.net; Ambassador JACEK PERLIN.

Portugal: Calle 98, No 9-03, Of. 906, Bogotá, DC; tel. (1) 622-1649; fax (1) 236-5269; e-mail embporbog@cable.net.co; Ambassador AUGUSTO JOSÉ PESTANA SARAIVA PEIXOTO.

Romania: Carrera 7A, No 92-58, Chico, Bogotá, DC; tel. (1) 256-6438; fax (1) 256-6158; e-mail ambrombogota@etb.net.co; internet bogota.mae.ro; Ambassador MARÍA SIPOȘ.

Russia: Carrera 4, No 75-02, Apdo Aéreo 90600, Bogotá, DC; tel. (1) 212-1881; fax (1) 210-4694; e-mail embajadarusia@cable.net.co; internet www.colombia.mid.ru; Ambassador PÁVEL SÉRGIEV.

Spain: Calle 92, No 12-68, Apdo 90355, Bogotá, DC; tel. (1) 622-0090; fax (1) 621-0809; e-mail bogota@maec.es; internet www.mae.es/embajadas/bogota; Ambassador NICOLÁS MARTIN CINTO.

Sweden: Edif. Avenida Chile, 8°, Calle 72, No 5-83, Apdo Aéreo 52966, Bogotá, DC; tel. (1) 325-6180; fax (1) 325-6181; e-mail embsueca@cable.net.co; internet www.swedenabroad.com/bogota; Ambassador MARIE ANDERSSON DE FRUTOS.

Switzerland: Carrera 9, No 74-08, Of. 1101, 11°, Apdo Aéreo 251957, Bogotá, DC; tel. (1) 349-7230; fax (1) 349-7195; e-mail bog.vertretung@eda.admin.ch; internet www.eda.admin.ch/bogota; Ambassador DIDIER DIETER ULRICH PFIRTER.

Turkey: Calle 76, No 8-47, Bogotá, DC; tel. (1) 321-0070; fax (1) 321-0076; e-mail turkemb.bogota@hotmail.com; Ambassador CEMIL FERHAT KARAMAN.

United Kingdom: Edif. ING Barings, Carrera 9, No 76-49, 9°, Bogotá, DC; tel. (1) 326-8300; fax (1) 326-8302; e-mail ppa.bogota@fco.gov.uk; internet ukincolombia.fco.gov.uk; Ambassador JOHN DEW.

USA: Calle 24-bis, No 48-50, Apdo Aéreo 3831, Bogotá, DC; tel. (1) 315-0811; fax (1) 315-2197; e-mail AmbassadorB@state.gov; internet bogota.usembassy.gov; Ambassador PETER MICHAEL MCKINLEY.

Uruguay: Edif. El Nogal, Carrera 9A, No 80-15, 11°, Apdo Aéreo 101466, Bogotá, DC; tel. (1) 235-2748; fax (1) 248-3734; e-mail urucolom@etb.net.co; Ambassador HUGO ARTURO CAYRÚS MAURIN.

Venezuela: Edif. Horizonte, 5°, Carrera 11, No 87-51, 5°, Bogotá, DC; tel. (1) 644-5555; fax (1) 640-1242; e-mail correspondencia.colombia@mppre.gob.ve; internet colombia.embajada.gob.ve; Ambassador IVÁN GUILLERMO RINCÓN URDANETA.

Judicial System

CONSTITUTIONAL COURT

The constitutional integrity of the State is ensured by the Constitutional Court. The Constitutional Court is composed of nine judges who are elected by the Senate for eight years. Judges of the Constitutional Court are not eligible for re-election.

Corte Constitucional

Edif. del Palacio de Justicia, Calle 12, No 7-65, Bogotá, DC; tel. (1) 350-6200; fax (1) 336-8759; internet www.corteconstitucional.gov.co.

President: GABRIEL EDUARDO MENDOZA MARTELO.

Judges: JORGE IVAN PALACIO PALACIO (Vice-Pres.), JUAN CARLOS HENAO PÉREZ, MARÍA VICTORIA CALLE CORREA, MAURICIO GONZÁLEZ CUERVO, NILSON PINILLA PINILLA, JORGE IGNACIO PRETELT CHALJUB, HUMBERTO ANTONIO SIERRA PORTO, LUIS ERNESTO VARGAS SILVA.

SUPREME COURT OF JUSTICE

The ordinary judicial integrity of the State is ensured by the Supreme Court of Justice. The Supreme Court of Justice is composed of the Courts of Civil and Agrarian, Penal, and Laboral Cassation. Judges of the Supreme Court of Justice, of which there are 23, are selected from the nominees of the Higher Council of Justice and serve an eight-year term of office, which is not renewable.

Corte Suprema de Justicia

Edif. de Palacio de Justicia, Calle 12, No 7-65, Bogotá, DC; tel. (1) 562-2000; internet www.cortesuprema.gov.co.

President: Dr JAVIER ZAPATA ORTIZ.

Attorney-General: EDUARDO MONTEALEGRE LYNETT.

Court of Civil and Agrarian Cassation (seven judges): Pres. Dr FERNANDO GIRALDO GUTIÉRREZ.

Court of Penal Cassation (nine judges): Pres. Dr JOSÉ LEONIDAS BUSTOS MARTÍNEZ.

Court of Laboral Cassation (seven judges): Pres. Dr LUIS GABRIEL MIRANDA BUELVAS.

COUNCIL OF STATE

The Council of State serves as the supreme consultative body to the Government in matters of legislation and administration. It also serves as the supreme tribunal for administrative litigation (*Contencioso Administrativo*). It is composed of 27 magistrates, including a President.

Council of State

Edif. del Palacio de Justicia, 7-65 Calle 12, Bogotá, DC; tel. (1) 350-6700; internet www.consejodeestado.gov.co

President: Dr GUSTAVO EDUARDO GÓMEZ ARANGUREN.

Religion

CHRISTIANITY

The Roman Catholic Church

Colombia comprises 13 archdioceses, 52 dioceses and 10 apostolic vicariates. Some 87% of the population are Roman Catholics.

Bishops' Conference

Conferencia Episcopal de Colombia, Carrera 47, No 84-85, Apdo Aéreo 7448, Bogotá, DC; tel. (1) 311-4277; fax (1) 311-5575; e-mail colcec@cec.org.co; internet www.cec.org.co.

f. 1978; statutes approved 1996; Pres. Rt Rev. JESÚS RUBÉN SALAZAR GÓMEZ (Archbishop of Bogotá).

Archbishop of Barranquilla: JAIRO JARAMILLO MONSALVE, Carrera 45, No 53-122, Apdo Aéreo 1160, Barranquilla 4, Atlántico; tel. (5) 349-1145; fax (5) 349-1530; e-mail arquidio@arquidiocesibaq.org.co.

Archbishop of Bogotá: JESÚS RUBÉN SALAZAR GÓMEZ, Carrera 7A, No 10-20, Bogotá, DC; tel. (1) 350-5511; fax (1) 350-7290; e-mail cancilleria@arquidiocesisbogota.org.co.

Archbishop of Bucaramanga: ISMAEL RUEDA SIERRA, Calle 33, No 21-18, Bucaramanga, Santander del Sur; tel. (7) 642-4387; fax (7) 642-1361; e-mail sarqdbu@col1.telecom.com.

Archbishop of Cali: DARJÍO DE JESÚS MONSALVE MEJÍA, Carrera 4, No 7-17, Apdo Aéreo 8924, Cali, Valle del Cauca; tel. (2) 889-0562; fax (2) 883-7980; e-mail jsarasti@andinet.com.

Archbishop of Cartagena: JOSÉ ENRIQUE JIMÉNEZ CARVAJAL, Apdo Aéreo 400, Cartagena; tel. (5) 664-5308; fax (5) 664-4974; e-mail arzoctg@telecartagena.com.

Archbishop of Ibagué: FLAVIO CALLE ZAPATA, Calle 10, No 2-58, Ibagué, Tolima; tel. (8) 261-1680; fax (8) 263-2681; e-mail arguibague@hotmail.com.

Archbishop of Manizales: GONZALO RESTREPO RESTREPO, Carrera 23, No 19-22, Manizales, Caldas; tel. (6) 884-0114; fax (6) 882-1853; e-mail arquiman@epm.net.co.

Archbishop of Medellín: RICARDO ANTONIO TOBÓN RESTREPO, Calle 57, No 49-44, 3°, Medellín; tel. (4) 251-7700; fax (4) 251-9395; e-mail arquidiomed@epm.net.co.

Archbishop of Nueva Pamplona: (vacant), Carrera 5, No 4-87, Nueva Pamplona; tel. (7) 568-1329; fax (7) 568-4540; e-mail gumafri@hotmail.com.

Archbishop of Popayán: IVÁN ANTONIO MARÍN LÓPEZ, Calle 5, No 6-71, Apdo Aéreo 593, Popayán; tel. (2) 824-1710; fax (2) 824-0101; e-mail ivanarzo@emtel.net.co.

Archbishop of Santa Fe de Antioquia: ORLANDO ANTONIO CORRALES GARCÍA, Plazuela Martínez Pardo, No 12-11, Santa Fe de

Antioquia; tel. (4) 853-1155; fax (4) 853-1596; e-mail arquistafe@edatel.net.co.

Archbishop of Tunja: Luis Augusto Castro Quiroga, Calle 17, No 9-85, Apdo Aéreo 1019, Tunja, Boyacá; tel. (8) 742-2093; fax (8) 743-3130; e-mail arquidio@telecom.com.co.

Archbishop of Villavicencio: Oscar Urbina Ortega, Carrera 39, No 34-19, Apdo Aéreo 2401, Villavicencio, Meta; tel. (8) 663-0337; fax (8) 665-3200; e-mail diocesisvillavicencio@andinet.com.

The Anglican Communion

Anglicans in Colombia are members of the Episcopal Church in the USA.

Bishop of Colombia: Rt Rev. Francisco José Duque Gómez, Carrera 6, No 49-85, Apdo Aéreo 52964, Bogotá, DC; tel. (1) 288-3167; fax (1) 288-3248; e-mail iec@iglesiaepiscopal.org.co; internet www.iglesiaepiscopal.org.co.

Protestant Church

Iglesia Evangélica Luterana de Colombia: Calle 75, No 20-54, Apdo Aéreo 51538, Bogotá, DC; tel. (1) 212-5735; fax (1) 212-5714; e-mail ofcentral@ielco.org; internet www.ielco.org; 1,519 mems; Pres. Bishop Eduardo Martinez.

BAHÁ'Í FAITH

National Spiritual Assembly of the Bahá'ís of Colombia: Apdo Aéreo 51387, Bogotá, DC; tel. and fax (1) 268-1658; e-mail bahaicol@colombianet.net; internet www.bahaicol.org; Gen. Sec. Ximena Osorio V.; adherents in 1,013 localities.

JUDAISM

There is a community of about 4,200 Jews.

The Press

DAILIES

Bogotá, DC

El Espacio: Carrera 61, No 45-35, Avda El Dorado, Apdo Aéreo 80111, Bogotá, DC; tel. (1) 425-1570; fax (1) 410-4595; internet www.elespacio.com.co; f. 1965; evening; Dir Jaime Ardila Casamitjana; Editor Edgar Sierra Anaya; circ. 159,000.

El Espectador: Avda El Dorado 69-76, Bogotá, DC; tel. and fax (1) 423-2300; e-mail editorweb@elespectador.com.co; internet www.elespectador.com; f. 1887; Editor Leonardo Rodríguez.

El Nuevo Siglo: Calle 45A, No 102-02, Apdo Aéreo 5452, Bogotá, DC; tel. (1) 413-9200; fax (1) 413-8547; e-mail contacto@elnuevosiglo.com.co; internet www.elnuevosiglo.com.co; f. 1936; conservative; Dir Juan Gabriel Uribe; Editor Alberto Abello; circ. 68,000.

Portafolio: Avda El Dorado, No 59-70, Apdo Aéreo 3633, Bogotá, DC; internet www.portafolio.com.co; f. 1993; economics and business; Dir Ricardo Avila Pinto.

La República: Calle 25 Bis, 102A-63, Bogotá, DC; tel. (1) 413-5077; fax (1) 413-3725; e-mail diario@larepublica.com.co; internet www.larepublica.com.co; f. 1954; morning; finance and economics; Editor Jorge Emilio Sierra M.; circ. 55,000.

El Tiempo: Avda El Dorado, No 59-70, Apdo Aéreo 3633, Bogotá, DC; tel. (1) 294-0100; fax (1) 410-5088; e-mail julguz@eltiempo.com.co; internet www.eltiempo.com; f. 1911; morning; liberal; Dir Enrique Santos Calderón; circ. 265,118 (weekdays), 536,377 (Sun.).

Barranquilla, Atlántico

El Heraldo: Calle 53B, No 46-25, Barranquilla, Atlántico; tel. (5) 371-5000; fax (5) 371-5091; internet www.elheraldo.com.co; f. 1933; morning; liberal; Dir Gustavo Bell Lemus; circ. 70,000.

La Libertad: Carrera 53, No 55-166, Barranquilla, Atlántico; tel. (5) 349-1175; fax (5) 349-1298; e-mail libertad@lalibertad.com.co; internet www.lalibertad.com.co; f. 1979; liberal; Dir Roberto Esper Rebaje; Editor Luz Marina Esper Fayad; circ. 25,000.

Bucaramanga, Santander del Sur

Vanguardia Liberal: Calle 34, No 13-42, Bucaramanga, Santander del Sur; tel. (7) 680-0700; fax (7) 630-2443; e-mail erodriguez@vanguardialiberal.com.co; internet www.vanguardia.com; f. 1919; morning; liberal; Sunday illustrated literary supplement and women's supplement; Dir Sebastián Hiller Galvis; circ. 48,000.

Cali, Valle del Cauca

Diario Occidente: Centro Comercial Chipichape, Bodega 2, 2°, Of. 220, Cali, Valle del Cauca; tel. (2) 680-2002; e-mail direccion@diariooccidente.com.co; internet www.diariooccidente.com.co; f. 1961; morning; conservative; Editor Rosa María Agudelo Ayerbe; circ. 25,000.

El País: Carrera 2A, No 24-46, Apdo Aéreo 4766, Cali, Valle del Cauca; tel. (2) 898-7000; e-mail diario@elpais.com.co; internet www.elpais.com.co; f. 1950; conservative; Dir and Gen. Man. María Elvira Domínguez; circ. 60,000 (weekdays), 120,000 (Sat.), 108,304 (Sun.).

Cartagena, Bolívar

El Universal: Pie del Cerro Calle 30, No 17-36, Cartagena, Bolívar; tel. (5) 650-1050; fax (5) 650-1057; e-mail director@eluniversal.com.co; internet www.eluniversal.com.co; f. 1948; daily; liberal; Editor-in-Chief Ledis Calo; Dir Pedro Luis Mogollón Vélez; circ. 167,000.

Cúcuta, Norte de Santander

La Opinión: Avda 4, No 16-12, Cúcuta, Norte de Santander; tel. (7) 582-9999; fax (7) 571-7869; e-mail gerencia@laopinion.com.co; internet www.laopinion.com.co; f. 1960; morning; liberal; Dir Dr José Eustorgio Colmenares Ossa; circ. 27,000.

Manizales, Caldas

La Patria: Carrera 20, No 46-35, Manizales, Caldas; tel. (6) 878-1700; e-mail lapatria@lapatria.com; internet www.lapatria.com; f. 1921; morning; independent; Dir Nicolás Restrepo Escobar; circ. 22,000.

Medellín, Antioquia

El Colombiano: Carrera 48, No 30 sur-119, Apdo Aéreo 80636, Medellín, Antioquia; tel. (4) 331-5252; fax (4) 331-4858; e-mail elcolombiano@elcolombiano.com.co; internet www.elcolombiano.com; f. 1912; morning; conservative; Dir Ana Mercedes Gómez Martínez; circ. 90,000.

El Mundo: Calle 53, No 74-50, Apdo Aéreo 53874, Medellín, Antioquia; tel. (4) 264-2800; fax (4) 264-3729; e-mail direccion@elmundo.com; internet www.elmundo.com; f. 1979; Dir Guillermo Gaviria Echeverri; Editor Irene Gaviria Correa; circ. 37,200 (Mon.–Sat.), 55,000 (Sun.).

Neiva, Huila

Diario del Huila: Calle 8A, No 6-30, Neiva, Huila; tel. (8) 871-2458; fax (8) 871-2543; e-mail prensa@diariodelhuila.com; internet www.diariodelhuila.com; f. 1966; Dir Javier Cabrera Padrón; circ. 12,000.

Pasto, Nariño

Diario del Sur: Calle 18, No 47-160, Torobajo, San Juan de Pasto, Nariño; tel. (2) 731-0048; e-mail diariodelsur@diariodelsur.com.co; internet www.diariodelsur.com.co; f. 1983; Dir Hernando Suárez Burgos.

Pereira, Risaralda

El Diario del Otún: Carrera 8A, No 22-75, Apdo Aéreo 2533, Pereira, Risaralda; tel. (6) 335-1313; fax (6) 325-4878; e-mail luiscramirez@eldiario.com.co; internet www.eldiario.com.co; f. 1982; Administrative Dir Javier Ignacio Ramírez Múnera; Editor-in-Chief Martha Lucía Monsalve Trujillo; circ. 30,000.

La Tarde: Carrera 9A, No 20-54, Pereira, Risaralda; tel. (6) 313-7676; fax (6) 335-5187; internet www.latarde.com; f. 1975; evening; Dir Sonia Díaz Mantilla; circ. 30,000.

Popayán, Cauca

El Liberal: Carrera 3, No 2-60, Apdo Aéreo 538, Popayán, Cauca; tel. (28) 24-2418; fax (28) 23-3888; e-mail gerencia@elliberal.com.co; internet www.elliberal.com.co; f. 1938; Man. Ana Maria Londoño R.; Dir Ismenia Ardila Díaz; circ. 6,500.

Santa Marta, Magdalena

El Informador: Avda Libertador 12A-37, Santa Marta, Magdalena; tel. (5) 421-7736; e-mail mensajes@elinformador.com.co; internet www.elinformador.com.co; f. 1958; liberal; Dir Alfonso Vives Campo; circ. 26,000.

PERIODICALS

ART NEXUS/Arte en Colombia: Carrera 5, No 67-19, Apdo Aéreo 90193, Bogotá, DC; tel. (1) 312-9435; fax (1) 312-9252; e-mail info@artnexus.com; internet www.artnexus.com; f. 1976; quarterly; Latin American art, photography, visual arts; editions in English and Spanish; Pres. and Chief Editor Celia Sredni de Birbragher; CEO Susanne Birbragher; circ. 26,000.

Cambio: Avda El Dorado No 59-70, 2°, Bogotá, DC; tel. (1) 294-0100; fax (1) 416-5643; internet www.cambio.com.co; weekly; current affairs; Dir RODRIGO PARDO.

Cromos Magazine: Avda El Dorado 69-76, Bogotá, DC; tel. (1) 423-2300; fax (1) 423-7641; e-mail internet@cromos.com.co; internet www.cromos.com.co; f. 1916; weekly; illustrated; general news; Dir ALBERTO ZALAMEA; circ. 102,000.

Dinero: Calle 93B, No 13-47, Bogotá, DC; tel. (1) 646-8400; fax (1) 621-9526; e-mail correo@dinero.com; internet www.dinero.com; f. 1993; fortnightly; economics and business; Dir ROSARIO CÓRDOBA GARCÉS.

El Malpensante: Calle 35, No 14-27, Bogotá, DC; tel. (1) 320-0120; fax (1) 340-2808; e-mail contacto@elmalpensante.com; internet www.elmalpensante.com; f. 1996; monthly; literature; Dir MARIO JURSICH DURÁN.

Revista Escala: Calle 30, No 17-752, Bogotá, DC; tel. (1) 287-8200; fax (1) 285-9882; e-mail escala@revistaescala.com; internet www.revistaescala.com; f. 1962; fortnightly; architecture; Dir DAVID SERNA CÁRDENAS; circ. 18,000.

Revista Fucsia: Calle 93B, No 13-47, Bogotá, DC; tel. (1) 646-8400; fax (1) 621-9526; e-mail correo@fucsia.com; internet www.revistafucsia.com; fortnightly; women's interest; Dir LILA OCHOA.

Semana: Calle 93B, No 13-47, Bogotá, DC; tel. (1) 646-8400; fax (1) 621-9526; e-mail director@semana.com; internet www.semana.com; f. 1982; general; weekly; Dir ALEJANDRO SANTOS RUBINO.

Tribuna Médica: Calle 8B, No 68A-41, y Calle 123, No 8-20, Bogotá, DC; tel. (1) 262-6085; fax (1) 262-4459; internet www.tribunamedica.com; f. 1961; monthly; medical and scientific; Editor JACK ALBERTO GRIMBERG; circ. 50,000.

Tribuna Roja: Calle 39, No 21-30, Bogotá, DC; tel. (1) 245-9647; e-mail tribojar@moir.org.co; internet tribunaroja.moir.org.co; f. 1971; quarterly; organ of the MOIR (pro-Maoist Communist party); Dir CARLOS NARANJO; circ. 300,000.

PRESS ASSOCIATIONS

Asociación Nacional de Diarios Colombianos (ANDIARIOS): Calle 61, No 5-20, Apdo Aéreo 13663, Bogotá, DC; tel. (1) 212-8694; fax (1) 212-7894; internet www.andiarios.com; f. 1962; 32 affiliated newspapers; Pres. LUIS MIGUEL DE BEDOUT; Exec. Dir NORA SANÍN DE SAFFON.

Asociación Nacional de Medios de Comunicación (ASOMEDIOS): see Broadcasting and Communications.

Círculo de Periodistas de Bogotá (CPB): Calle 26, No 13A-15, Bogotá, DC; tel. (1) 282-5573; e-mail escribanos@cpb.org.co; internet www.cpb.org.co; f. 1946; Pres. MAURA ACHURY RAMÍREZ.

Publishers

Cengage Learning de Colombia, SA: Edif. Seguros Aurora, 8°, Carrera 7, No 74-21, Bogotá, DC; tel. (1) 212-3340; fax (1) 211-3995; e-mail clientes.pactoandino@cengage.com; internet www.cengage.com.co; Country Man. LILIANA GUTIERREZ.

Ecoe Ediciones Ltda: Carrera 19, No 63C-32, Bogotá, DC; tel. (1) 248-1449; fax (1) 346-1741; e-mail oswaldo@ecoeediciones.com; internet www.ecoeediciones.com; science, medical and general interest; Gen. Man. OSWALDO PEÑUELA CARRIÓN.

Ediciones Gaviota: Carrera 62, No 98B-13, Bogotá, DC; tel. (1) 613-6650; fax (1) 613-9117; e-mail gaviotalibros@edicionesgaviota.com.co; internet www.edicionesgaviota.com.co; Rep. FABIOLA RAMOS MONDRAGÓN.

Ediciones Modernas: Carrera 41A, No 22F-22, Bogotá, DC; tel. (1) 269-0072; fax (1) 244-0706; e-mail edimodernas@edimodernas.com.co; internet www.empresario.com.co/edimodernas; f. 1991; juvenile; Gen. Man. JORGE SERRANO GARCES.

Editorial Cypres Ltda: Carrera 15, No 80-36, Of. 301, Bogotá, DC; tel. (1) 618-0657; fax (1) 691-0578; e-mail cypresad@etb.net.co; general interest and educational; Gen. Man. JOHANNA VALENZUELA GONZÁLEZ.

Editorial El Globo, SA: Calle 25D, Bis 102A-63, Bogotá, DC; tel. (1) 606-1290; fax (1) 210-4900; e-mail rhumanos@larepublica.com.co; Gen. Man. OLGA LUCIA LONDOÑO M.

Editorial Kinesis: Carrera 25, No 18-12, Armenia; tel. (6) 740-9155; fax (6) 740-1584; e-mail informacion@kinesis.com.co; internet www.kinesis.com.co; physical education, recreation and sport; Dir DIÓGENES VERGARA LARA.

Editorial Leyer Ltda: Carrera 4, No 16-51, Bogotá, DC; tel. (1) 282-1903; fax (1) 282-2373; e-mail contacto@edileyer.com; internet www.edileyer.com; f. 1991; law; Dir HILDEBRANDO LEAL PÉREZ.

Editorial Paulinas: Calle 161A, No 15-50, Bogotá, DC; tel. (1) 528-7444; fax (1) 671-0992; e-mail comunicaciones@paulinas.org.co; internet www.paulinas.org.co; Christian and self-help.

Editorial San Pablo (Sociedad de San Pablo): Carrera 46, No 22A-90, Quintaparedes, Apdo Aéreo 080152, Bogotá, DC; tel. (1) 368-2099; fax (1) 244-4383; e-mail editorial@sanpablo.com.co; internet www.sanpablo.com.co; f. 1914; religion (Catholic); Editorial Dir Fr VICENTE MIOTTO; Editor AMPARO MAHECHA.

Editorial Temis, SA: Calle 17, No 68D, Apdo Aéreo 46, Bogotá, DC; tel. (1) 424-7855; fax (1) 292-5801; e-mail editorial@editorialtemis.com; internet www.editorialtemis.com; f. 1951; law, sociology, politics; Gen. Man. ERWIN GUERRERO PINZÓN.

Editorial Voluntad, SA: Avda El Dorado, No 90-10, Bogotá, DC; tel. (1) 410-6355; fax (1) 295-2994; e-mail voluntad@voluntad.com.co; internet www.voluntad.com.co; f. 1930; school books; Pres. GASTÓN DE BEDOUT.

Fondo de Cultura Económica: Calle de la Enseñanza 11, No 5–60, La Candelaria, Zona C, Bogotá, DC; tel. (1) 283-2200; fax (1) 337-4289; e-mail caguilar@fce.com.co; internet www.fce.com.co; f. 1934; academic; Gen. Man. CÉSAR ANGEL AGUILAR ASIAIN.

Fundación Centro de Investigación y Educación Popular (CINEP): Carrera 5A, No 33A-08, Apdo Aéreo 25916, Bogotá, DC; tel. (1) 245-6181; fax (1) 287-9089; e-mail cinep@cinep.org.co; internet www.cinep.org.co; f. 1972; education and social sciences; Exec. Dir MAURICIO GARCÍA-DURÁN.

Instituto Caro y Cuervo: Calle 10, No 4-69, Bogotá, DC; tel. (1) 342-2121; fax (1) 284-1248; e-mail direcciongeneral@caroycuervo.gov.co; internet www.caroycuervo.gov.co; f. 1942; philology, general linguistics and reference; Dir-Gen. GENOVEVA IRIARTE.

Inversiones Cromos, SA: Avda El Dorado, No 69-76, Bogotá, DC; tel. (1) 423-2300; fax (1) 423-7641; e-mail jduenas@cromos.com.co; internet www.cromos.com.co; f. 1916; Dir JAIRO DUEÑAS VILLAMIL; Editor LEONARDO RODRÍGUEZ.

Legis, SA: Avda Calle 26, No 82–70, Apdo Aéreo 98888, Bogotá, DC; tel. (1) 425-5200; e-mail servicio@legis.com.co; internet www.legis.com.co; f. 1952; economics, law, general; Pres. LUIS ALFREDO MOTTA VENEGAS.

McGraw Hill Interamericana, SA: Carrera 85D, No 46A–65, Bodegas 9, 10 y 11, Complejo Logístico San Cayetano, Urb. San Cayetano Norte, Bogotá, DC; tel. (1) 600-3800; fax (1) 600-3855; e-mail info_colombia@mcgraw-hill.com; internet www.mcgraw-hill.com.co; university textbooks; Dir-Gen. MARTÍN RENÉ CHUECO.

Publicar, SA: Avda 68, No 75A-50, 2°, 3° y 4°, Centro Comercial Metrópolis, Apdo Aéreo 8010, Bogotá, DC; tel. (1) 646-5555; fax (1) 646-5523; e-mail e-hamburger@publicar.com; internet www.publicar.com; f. 1959; owned by the Carvajal Group; directories; Pres. ERIC HAMBURGER.

Siglo del Hombre Editores, SA: Carrera 31A, No 25B-50, Bogotá, DC; tel. (1) 337-7700; fax (1) 337-7665; e-mail info@siglodelhombre.com; internet www.siglodelhombre.com; f. 1992; arts, politics, anthropology, history, humanities; Gen. Man. EMILIA FRANCO DE ARCILA.

Tercer Mundo Editores, SA: Grupo TM, SA, Calle 25B, No 31A-34, Bogotá, DC; tel. (1) 368-8645; e-mail grupotmsa@etb.net.co; internet grupotmsa.blogspot.com; f. 1963; social sciences.

Thomson PLM: Calle 106, No 54–81, Apdo Aéreo 52998, Barrio Puente Largo, Bogotá, DC; tel. (1) 613-1111; fax (1) 624-2335; e-mail contactoco@plmlatina.com; internet www.plmlatina.com; medical; Regional Dir CONSTANZA RIAÑO RODRÍGUEZ.

Tragaluz Editores: Edif. Lugo, Of. 108, Calle 6 Sur, No 43A-200, Medellín, Antioquia; tel. (4) 312-0295; fax (4) 268-4366; e-mail info@tragaluzeditores.com; internet tragaluzeditores.com; literature and graphics; Editorial Dir PILAR GUTIÉRREZ LLANO.

Villegas Editores: Avda 82, No 11-50, Interior 3, Bogotá, DC; tel. (1) 616-1788; fax (1) 616-0020; e-mail informacion@villegaseditores.com; internet www.villegaseditores.com; f. 1986; illustrated and scholarly; Pres. BENJAMÍN VILLEGAS JIMÉNEZ.

ASSOCIATIONS

Asociación de Editoriales Universitarias de Colombia (ASEUC): Carrera 13A, No 38-82, Of. 901, Bogotá, DC; tel. (1) 805-2357; fax (1) 287-9257; e-mail asistente@aseuc.org.co; internet www.aseuc.org.co; Pres. NICOLÁS MORALES THOMAS; Sec.-Gen. LORENA RUIZ SERNA.

Cámara Colombiana del Libro: Calle 35, No 5A-05, Bogotá, DC; tel. (1) 323-0111; fax (1) 285-1082; e-mail camlibro@camlibro.com.co; internet www.camlibro.com.co; f. 1951; Pres. GUSTAVO RODRÍGUEZ GARCÍA; Exec. Dir ENRIQUE GONZÁLEZ VILLA; 95 mems.

Fundalectura: Avda Diagonal 40A Bis, No 16-46, Bogotá, DC; tel. (1) 320-1511; fax (1) 287-7071; e-mail contactenos@fundalectura.org.co; internet www.fundalectura.org; f. 1990; Pres. ALFONSO OCAMPO GAVIRIA; Exec. Dir CARMEN BARVO.

Broadcasting and Communications

REGULATORY AUTHORITIES

Comisión de Regulación de Comunicaciones (CRC): No 28-01, Carrera 13, 8°, Bogotá, DC; tel. (1) 327-7000; fax (1) 327-7001; e-mail atencioncliente@crt.gov.co; internet www.crcom.gov.co; f. 2000; regulatory body; Exec. Dir CRISTHIAN OMAR LIZCANO ORTIZ.

Comisión Nacional de Televisión: Calle 72, No 12-77, Bogotá, DC; tel. (1) 595-3000; e-mail info@cntv.org.co; internet www.cntv.org.co; Dir JUAN ANDRÉS CARREÑO.

TELECOMMUNICATIONS

COMCEL: Bogotá, DC; internet www.comcel.com.co; f. 1994 as Occidente y Caribe Celular, SA (Occel); present name adopted in 2000; merged with Celcaribe in 2003; owned by América Móvil, SA de CV (Mexico); cellular mobile telephone operator.

Empresa de Telecomunicaciones de Bogotá, SA (ETB): Carrera 8, No 20-56, 3°–9°, Bogotá, DC; tel. (1) 242-3483; fax (1) 242-2127; e-mail adrimara@etb.com.co; internet www.etb.com.co; Bogotá telephone co; partially privatized in May 2003; Pres. FERNANDO CARRIZOSA RASCH-ISLA; Sec.-Gen. ANDRÉS PÉREZ VELASCO.

Telefónica Móviles Colombia (Movistar): Edif. Capital Tower, 17°, Calle 100, No 7-33, Bogotá, DC; tel. (1) 650-0000; fax (1) 650-1852; internet www.movistar.com.co; f. 2004 following acquisition of BellSouth's operations by Telefónica Móviles, a subsidiary of Telefónica, SA of Spain.

Telefónica Telecom: Carrera 70, No 108-84, Bogotá, DC; tel. (1) 593-5399; fax (1) 593-1252; internet www.telefonica.com.co; f. 2003 following dissolution of state-owned Empresa Nacional de Telecomunicaciones (TELECOM, f. 1947); subsidiary of Telefónica, SA (Spain); Pres. MAURICIO SANTAMARÍA.

BROADCASTING

Radio

Cadena Melodía de Colombia: Calle 45, No 13-70, Bogotá, DC; tel. (1) 323-1500; fax (1) 288-4020; e-mail presidencia@cadenamelodia.com; internet www.cadenamelodia.com; Pres. EFRAÍN PÁEZ ESPITIA; Gen. Man. ELVIRA MEJÍA DE PÁEZ.

CARACOL, SA (Primera Cadena Radial Colombiana, SA): Edif. Caracol Radio, Calle 67, No 7-37, Bogotá, DC; tel. (1) 348-7600; fax (1) 337-7126; internet www.caracol.com.co; f. 1948; 107 stations; Pres. JOSÉ MANUEL RESTREPO FERNÁNDEZ DE SOTO.

Circuito Todelar de Colombia: Avda 13, No 84-42, Apdo Aéreo 27344, Bogotá, DC; tel. (1) 616-1011; fax (1) 616-0056; e-mail dircomercial@todelar.com; internet www.todelar.com; f. 1953; 74 stations; Dir SANDRA PATRICIA BARBOSA.

Colmundo Radio, SA ('La Cadena de la Paz'): Diagonal 61D, No 26A-29, Apdo Aéreo 36750, Bogotá, DC; tel. (1) 217-9220; fax (1) 348-2746; e-mail direcciongeneral@colmundoradio.com.co; internet colmundoradio.com.co; f. 1989; Pres. ZAIDY MORA QUINTERO; Dir-Gen. MIRIAM QUINTERO.

Organización Radial Olímpica, SA (ORO, SA): Calle 72, No 48-37, 2°, Apdo Aéreo 51266, Barranquilla; tel. (5) 358-0500; fax (5) 345-9080; e-mail ventasbarranquila@oro.com.co; internet www.oro.com.co; programmes for the Antioquia and Atlantic coast regions; Pres. MIGUEL CHAR; Production Dir RAFAEL PÁEZ.

Radio Cadena Nacional, SA (RCN Radio): Calle 37, No 13A-19, Apdo Aéreo 4984, Bogotá, DC; tel. (1) 314-7070; fax (1) 288-6130; e-mail rcn@impsat.net.co; internet www.rcn.com.co; 116 stations; official network; Pres. FERNANDO MOLINA SOTO.

Radio Nacional de Colombia: Carrera 45, No 26-33, Bogotá, DC; tel. (1) 597-8111; fax (1) 597-8011; e-mail contactoradionacional@rtvc.gov.co; internet www.radionacionaldecolombia.gov.co; f. 1940; national public radio; Dir GABRIEL GÓMEZ MEJÍA.

Radio Regional Independiente: Carrera 19A, No 98-12, Of. 801, Bogotá, DC; tel. (1) 691-9724; fax (1) 691-9725; e-mail info@reiltda.com; internet www.reiltda.com; f. 1995; Gen. Man. JUAN MANUEL ORTIZ NOGUERA.

Sistema Super de Columbia: Calle 39A, No 18-12, Bogotá, DC; tel. (1) 234-7777; fax (1) 287-8678; e-mail gerencia@cadenasuper.com; internet www.cadenasuper.com; f. 1971; stations include Radio Super and Super Stereo FM; Gen. Man. JUAN CARLOS PAVA CAMELO.

Television

Canal Institutional: Avda El Dorado, Carrera 45, No 26-33, Bogotá, DC; tel. (1) 597-8000; fax (1) 597-8011; e-mail contactoinstitucional@rtvc.gov.co; internet www.institucional.gov.co; f. 2004; govt-owned; Co-ordinator LENNART RODRÍGUEZ.

Canal RCN Televisión: Avda Américas, No 65-82, Bogotá, DC; tel. (1) 426-9292; e-mail quienessomos@canalrcn.com; internet www.canalrcnmsn.com; f. 1998; Pres. GABRIEL REYES.

Caracol Televisión, SA: Calle 103, No 69B-43, Apdo Aéreo 26484, Bogotá, DC; tel. (1) 643-0430; fax (1) 643-0444; internet www.caracoltv.com; f. 1969; Pres. PAULO LASERNA PHILLIPS.

Fox Telecolombia: Carrera 50, No 17–77, Bogotá, DC; tel. (1) 417-4200; fax (1) 341-6198; e-mail john.ahumada@foxtelecolombia.com; internet www.foxtelecolombia.com; formerly Cadena Uno; f. 1992; acquired by Fox International Channels and changed name as above in 2007; Pres. SAMUEL DUQUE ROZO.

Señal Colombia: Avda El Dorado, Carrera 45, No 26-33, Bogotá, DC; tel. (1) 597-8132; fax (1) 597-8062; e-mail senalencontacto@rtvc.gov.co; internet www.senalcolombia.tv; govt-owned; Co-ordinator ADRIAN FRANCISCO COMAS.

Teleantioquia: Calle 44, No 53A–11, Apdo Aéreo 8183, Medellín, Antioquia; tel. (4) 356-9900; fax (4) 356-9909; e-mail comunicaciones@teleantioquia.com.co; internet www.teleantioquia.com.co; f. 1985; Gen. Man. SELENE BOTERO GIRALDO.

Telecafé: Carrera 19A, Calle 43, Barrio Sacatín contiguo Universidad Autónoma, Manizales, Caldas; tel. (6) 872-7100; fax (6) 872-7610; e-mail info@telecafe.tv; internet www.telecafe.tv; f. 1986; govt-owned; broadcasts to the 'Eje Cafetero' (departments of Caldas, Quindío and Risaralda); Gen. Man. JORGE EDUARDO URREA GIRALDO.

TeleCaribe: Carrera 54, No 72-142, 4°, Barranquilla, Atlántico; tel. (5) 368-0184; fax (5) 360-7300; e-mail info@telecaribe.com.co; internet www.telecaribe.com.co; f. 1986; Pres. ARTURO SARMIENTO; Gen. Man. IVÁN GUILLERMO BARRIOS MASS.

Telepacífico (Sociedad de Televisión del Pacifico Ltda): Calle 5, No 38A-14, 3°, esq. Centro Comercial Imbanaco, Cali, Valle del Cauca; tel. (2) 518-4000; fax (2) 588-281; e-mail gerenciatp@telepacifico.com; internet www.telepacifico.com; Gen. Man. LORENA IVETTE MENDOZA MARMOLEJO.

TV Cúcuta: tel. (7) 574-7874; fax (7) 575-2922; f. 1992; Pres. JOSÉ A. ARMELLA.

ASSOCIATION

Asociación Nacional de Medios de Comunicación (ASOMEDIOS): Carrera 19C, No 85-72, Bogotá, DC; tel. (1) 611-1300; fax (1) 621-6292; e-mail asomedios@asomedios.com; internet www.asomedios.com; f. 1978; Exec. Pres. TITULO ANGEL ARBELAEZ.

Finance

(cap. = capital; res = reserves; dep. = deposits; m. = million; brs = branches; amounts in pesos)

Contraloría General de la República: Carrera 10, No 17-18, Torre Colseguros, 27°, Bogotá, DC; tel. (1) 353-7700; fax (1) 353-7616; e-mail mesaportal@contraloriagen.gov.co; internet www.contraloriagen.gov.co; f. 1923; Comptroller-Gen. JULIO CÉSAR TURBAY QUINTERO.

BANKING

Supervisory Authority

Superintendencia Financiera de Colombia: Calle 7, No 4-49, 11°, Apdo Aéreo 3460, Bogotá, DC; tel. (1) 594-0200; fax (1) 350-7999; e-mail super@superfinanciera.gov.co; internet www.superfinanciera.gov.co; f. 2006 following merger of the Superintendencia Bancaria and the Superintendencia de Valores; Supt GERARDO HERNÁNDEZ CORREA.

Central Bank

Banco de la República: Carrera 7A, No 14-78, 5°, Apdo Aéreo 3551, Bogotá, DC; tel. (1) 343-1111; fax (1) 286-1686; e-mail wbanco@banrep.gov.co; internet www.banrep.gov.co; f. 1923; sole bank of issue; cap. 12,711m., res 13,671,591.5m., dep. 11,092,426.6m. (Dec. 2009); Gov. JOSÉ DARÍO URIBE ESCOBAR; 17 brs.

Commercial Banks

Banco Agrario de Colombia (Banagrario): Carrera 8, No 15-43, Bogotá, DC; tel. (1) 382-1400; fax (1) 599-5509; e-mail presidencia@bancoagrario.gov.co; internet www.bancoagrario.gov.co; f. 1999; state-owned; Pres. DAVID GUERRERO PÉREZ; 732 brs.

Banco de Bogotá: Calle 36, No 7-47, 15°, Apdo Aéreo 3436, Bogotá, DC; tel. (1) 332-0032; fax (1) 338-3302; internet www.bancodebogota.com.co; f. 1870; cap. 2,382m., res 3,595,606m., dep. 24,455,660m. (Dec. 2009); Pres. Dr ALEJANDRO FIGUEROA JARAMILLO; 556 brs.

Banco Colpatria: Torre Colpatria, Carrera 7A, No 24-89, Bogotá, DC; tel. (1) 756-1616; e-mail serviciocliente@colpatria.com; internet www.colpatria.com; f. 1969; 51% owned by Scotiabank (Canada) from 2012.

Banco de Comercio Exterior de Colombia, SA (BANCOLDEX): Calle 28, No 13A-15, 40°, Apdo Aéreo 240092, Bogotá, DC; tel. (1) 382-

1515; fax (1) 286-2451; internet www.bancoldex.com; f. 1992; provides financing alternatives for Colombian exporters; affiliate trust co FIDUCOLDEX, SA, manages PROEXPORT (Export Promotion Trust); cap. 855,669.6m., res 427,846.9m., dep. 1,292,963.4m. (Dec. 2010); Pres. SANTIAGO ROJAS ARROYO.

Banco Davivienda, SA: Edif. Torre Bolívar, 68B-31, 1°, Avda El Dorado, Bogotá, DC; tel. (1) 338-3838; e-mail contactenos@davivienda.com; internet www.davivienda.com; f. 1972 as Corporación Colombiana de Ahorro y Vivienda (Coldeahorro), current name adopted in 1997; merged with Banco Superior in 2006, with Bancafé in 2010; Pres. EFRAÍN ENRIQUE FORERO FONSECA.

Banco GNB Sudameris, SA: Carrera 7, No 71-52, 19°, Torre B, Bogotá, DC; tel. (1) 325-5000; fax (1) 313-3259; internet www.sudameris.com.co; f. 2005 following merger of Banco Sudameris Colombia, SA and Banco Tequendama; cap. 44,649.4m., res 445,474.6m., dep. 4,953,116.9m. (Dec. 2010); Pres. and Chair. CAMILO VERÁSTEGUI CARVAJAL; 6 brs.

Banco de Occidente: Carrera 4, No 7-61, 12°, Apdo Aéreo 7607, Cali, Valle del Cauca; tel. (2) 886-1111; fax (2) 886-1298; e-mail dinternacional@bancodeoccidente.com.co; internet www.bancodeoccidente.com.co; f. 1965; cap. 4,110.8m., res 1,758,718.2m., dep. 11,982,296.2m. (Dec. 2009); 78.2% owned by Grupo Aval Acciones y Valores; Pres. EFRAÍN OTERO ÁLVAREZ; 194 brs.

Banco Popular, SA: Calle 17, No 7-43, 3°, Bogotá, DC; tel. (1) 339-5449; fax (1) 281-9448; e-mail vpinternacional@bancopopular.com.co; internet www.bancopopular.com.co; f. 1950; cap. 77,253m., res 1,249,901m., dep. 8,348,174m. (Dec. 2010); Pres. HERNÁN RINCÓN GÓMEZ; 216 brs.

Banco Santander: Carrera 7, No 99-53, Bogotá, DC; tel. (1) 284-3100; fax (1) 281-0311; e-mail comex@santander.com.co; internet www.santander.com.co; f. 1961; fmrly Banco Comercial Antioqueño, SA; subsidiary of Banco Santander (Spain); cap. 218,731m., res 345,013m., dep. 4,695,712m. (Dec. 2009); Pres. ROMÁN BLANCO REINOSA; 74 brs.

Bancolombia, SA: Carrera 52, No 50-20, Medellín, Antioquia; tel. (4) 576-6060; fax (4) 513-4827; e-mail comunica@bancolombia.com.co; internet www.grupobancolombia.com; f. 1998 by merger of Banco Industrial Colombiano and Banco de Colombia; cap. 393,914m., res 5,205,456m., dep. 43,538,967m. (Dec. 2010); Pres. CARLOS RAÚL YEPES JIMÉNEZ; Chair. DAVID EMILIO BOJANINI GARCÍA; 727 brs.

BBVA Colombia: Carrera 9, No 72-21, 11°, Bogotá, DC; tel. (1) 312-4666; fax (1) 347-1600; internet www.bbva.com.co; f. 1956 as Banco Ganadero; assumed current name 2004; 95.2% owned by Banco Bilbao Vizcaya Argentaria, SA (Spain); cap. 89,779m., res 271,955m., dep. 16,522,016m. (Dec. 2010); Exec. Pres. OSCAR CABRERA IZQUIERDO; 279 brs.

Citibank Colombia, SA: Carrera 9A, No 99-02, 3°, Bogotá, DC; tel. (1) 638-2420; fax (1) 618-2606; internet www.citibank.com.co; wholly owned subsidiary of Citibank (USA); cap. 144,123m., res 891,786m., dep. 5,811,626m. (Dec. 2009); Chair. and CEO MANUEL MEDINA-MORA; 23 brs.

Helm Bank SA: Carrera 7, No 27-18, 19°, Bogotá, DC; tel. (1) 581-8181; e-mail servicio.empresarial@grupohelm.com; internet www.grupohelm.com; f. 1963 as Banco de Crédito; renamed Banco de Credito—Helm Financial Services in 2000; present name adopted in 2009; cap. 201,608m., res 768,039m., dep. 5,478,185m. (Dec. 2009); Pres. CARMIÑA FERRO IRIARTE; 26 brs.

HSBC Colombia, SA: Carrera 7, No 71-21, Of. 1601, Torre B, 16°, Apdo Aéreo 3532, Bogotá, DC; tel. (1) 334-5088; fax (1) 341-9433; e-mail columbia.contactenos@hsbc.com.co; internet www.hsbc.com.co; f. 1976 as Banco Anglo Colombiano; present name adopted in 2007; bought by HSBC Bank PLC (United Kingdom) in 2006; cap. 316,230m., res –86,919m., dep. 1,228,903m. (Dec. 2009); Pres. HANS JUERGEN THEILKUHL; 52 brs.

Development Bank

BCSC: Carrera 7, No 77-65, 11°, Bogotá, DC; tel. (1) 313-8000; fax (1) 321-6912; e-mail csgarzon@fundacion-social.com.co; internet www.bcsc.com.co; f. 1911 as Banco Caja Social; adopted current name 2005; cap. 185,392m., dep. 4,420,000m. (Dec. 2006); Pres. CARLOS UPEGUI CUARTAS; 260 brs.

Banking Associations

Asociación Bancaria y de Entidades Financieras de Colombia (Asobancaria): Carrera 9A, No 74-08, 9°, Bogotá, DC; tel. (1) 326-6612; fax (1) 326-6600; e-mail info@asobancaria.com; internet www.asobancaria.com; f. 1936; 56 mem. banks; Pres. MARÍA MERCEDES CUÉLLAR LÓPEZ.

Asociación Nacional de Instituciones Financieras (ANIF): Calle 70A, No 7-86, Bogotá, DC; tel. (1) 310-1500; fax (1) 235-5947; internet www.anif.org; f. 1974; Pres. Dr SERGIO CLAVIJO.

STOCK EXCHANGE

Bolsa de Valores de Colombia: Carrera 7, No 71-21, Edif. Bancafé, Torre B, Of. 1201, Bogotá, DC; tel. (1) 313-9800; fax (1) 313-9766; internet www.bvc.com.co; f. 2001 following merger of stock exchanges of Bogotá, Medellín and Occidente; Pres. JUAN PABLO CÓRDOBA GARCÉS; Sec.-Gen. ANGEL ALBERTO VELANDIA RODRÍGUEZ.

INSURANCE

Principal Companies

ACE Seguros, SA: Calle 72, No 10-51, 7°, Apdo Aéreo 29782, Bogotá, DC; tel. (1) 319-0300; fax (1) 319-0304; e-mail ace.servicioalcliente@acegroup.com; internet www.acelatinamerica.com; fmrly Cigna Seguros de Colombia, SA; Pres. PILAR LOZANO.

Aseguradora Colseguros, SA: Carrera 13A, No 29-24, Parque Central Bavaria, Apdo Aéreo 3537, Bogotá, DC; tel. (1) 560-0600; fax (1) 561-6695; internet www.colseguros.com; subsidiary of Allianz AG, Germany; f. 1874; Pres. ALBA LUCIA GALLEGO NIETO.

Aseguradora Solidaria de Colombia: Calle 100, No 9A-45, 8° y 12°, Bogotá, DC; tel. (1) 646-4330; fax (1) 296-1527; e-mail eguzman@solidaria.com.co; internet www.aseguradorasolidaria.com.co; Pres. CARLOS ARTURO GUZMÁN PÉREZ.

BBVA Seguros: Carrera 11, No 87-51, Bogotá, DC; tel. (1) 219-1100; fax (1) 640-7995; internet www.bbvaseguros.com.co; f. 1994; Pres. JORGE MANUEL SEIJAS RUMBRO; Sec.-Gen. HERNÁN FELIPE GUZMÁN ALDANA.

Chartis Seguros Colombia, SA: Calle 78, No 9–57, Apdo Aéreo 9281, Bogotá, DC; tel. (1) 317-2193; fax (1) 310-1014; e-mail servicioal.cliente@chartisinsurance.com; internet www.chartisinsurance.com; fmrly AIG Colombia Seguros Generales, SA; Pres. ANDRES HÉCTOR BOULLÓN.

Chubb de Colombia Cía de Seguros, SA: Carrera 7A, No 71-52, Torre B, 10°, Bogotá, DC; tel. (1) 326-6200; fax (1) 326-6210; e-mail informaciongeneral@chubb.com; internet www.chubb.com.co; f. 1972; Pres. MANUEL OBREGÓN; 4 brs.

Cía Aseguradora de Fianzas, SA (Confianza): Calle 82, No 11-37, 7°, Apdo Aéreo 056965, Bogotá, DC; tel. (1) 644-4690; fax (1) 610-8866; e-mail correos@confianza.com.co; internet www.confianza.com.co; f. 1979; Pres. LUIS ALEJANDRO RUEDA RODRÍGUEZ; Exec. Vice-Pres. ANDRÉS EDUARDO MONTOYA SOTO.

Cía Mundial de Seguros, SA: Calle 33, No 6B-24, 2° y 3°, Bogotá, DC; tel. (1) 285-5600; fax (1) 285-1220; e-mail mundial@mundialseguros.com.co; internet www.mundialseguros.com.co; f. 1995; Pres. JUAN ENRIQUE BUSTAMANTE MOLINA.

Cía de Seguros Bolívar, SA: Avda El Dorado, No 68B-31, 10°, Casilla 4421 y 6406, Bogotá, DC; tel. (1) 341-0077; fax (1) 283-0799; internet www.segurosbolivar.com.co; f. 1939; Pres. JORGE ENRIQUE URIBE MONTAÑO.

Cía de Seguros Colmena, SA: Calle 26, No 69C-03, Torre A, 4°–6°, Apdo Aéreo 5050, Bogotá, DC; tel. (1) 324-1111; fax (1) 324-0866; internet www.colmena-arp.com.co; Pres. SILVIA CAMARGO.

Cía de Seguros de Vida Aurora, SA: Carrera 7, No 74-21, 1°–3°, Bogotá, DC; tel. (1) 319-2930; fax (1) 345-5980; e-mail soporte@segurosaurora.com; internet www.segurosaurora.com; f. 1967; Pres. EUDORO CARVAJAL IBAÑEZ; Sec.-Gen. ANDREA MORA SÁNCHEZ.

Condor, SA, Cía de Seguros Generales: Carrera 7, No 74-21, 2°, Bogotá, DC; tel. (1) 319-2930; fax (1) 345-4980; e-mail orlandolugo@condorsa.com.co; internet www.seguroscondor.com.co; f. 1957 as Cía de Seguros del Pacífico, SA; changed name as above as above 1983; Pres. JOSÉ ANCÍZAR JIMÉNEZ GUITÍERREZ.

La Equidad Seguros, Organización Cooperativa: Edif. Torre La Equidad Seguros, 13° y 14°, Carrera 9A, 99-07, Apdo Aéreo 30261, Bogotá, DC; tel. (1) 592-2929; fax (1) 520-0169; e-mail equidad@laequidadseguros.coop; internet www.laequidadseguros.coop; Exec. Pres. Dr CLEMENTE AUGUSTO JAIMES PUENTES.

Generali Colombia—Seguros Generales, SA: Edif. Generali, Carrera 7A, No 72-13, 8°, Apdo Aéreo 076478, Bogotá, DC; tel. (1) 346-8888; fax (1) 319-8280; e-mail generali_colombia@generali.com.co; internet www.generali.com.co; f. 1937; Pres. EDUARDO SARMIENTO PULIDO.

Global Seguros, SA: Carrera 9, No 74-62, Bogotá, DC; tel. (1) 313-9200; fax (1) 317-5376; e-mail rodrigo.uribe@globalseguroscolombia.com; internet www.globalseguroscolombia.com; Pres. RODRIGO URIBE BERNAL.

Liberty Seguros, SA: Calle 72, No 10-07, 6°–8°, Apdo Aéreo 57227 y 57243, Bogotá, DC; tel. (1) 376-5330; fax (1) 217-9917; e-mail lhernandez@impsat.net.co; internet www.libertycolombia.com.co; f. 1954; fmrly Latinoamericana de Seguros, SA; Pres. MAURICIO GARCÍA ORTIZ.

Mapfre Seguros de Crédito, SA (Mapfre Crediseguro, SA): Edif. Forum II, 8°, Calle 7 Sur, No 42-70, Antioquia; tel. (4) 444-0145; fax (4) 314-1990; e-mail adritoac@crediseguro.com.co; internet www

.crediseguro.com.co; f. 1999; subsidiary of Mapfre; Pres. ALEJANDRO CALCEDO.

Mapfre Seguros Generales de Colombia, SA: Carrera 14, No 96-34, Bogotá, DC; tel. (1) 650-3300; fax (1) 650-3400; e-mail mapfre@mapfre.com.co; internet www.mapfre.com.co; f. 1995; Pres. VICTORIA EUGENIA BEJARANO DE LA TORRE.

Metlife Colombia Seguros de Vida, SA: Carrera 7, No 99-53, 17°, Bogotá, DC; tel. (14) 358-1258; fax (14) 638-1299; e-mail cliente@metlife.com.co; internet www.metlife.com.co; fmrly American Life Insurance Co (Alico); sold to MetLife in 2010; Pres. SANTIAGO OSORIO; Sec.-Gen. CONSUELO GONZÁLEZ.

Pan American de Colombia Cía de Seguros de Vida, SA: Carrera 7A, No 75-09, Apdo Aéreo 76000, Bogotá, DC; tel. (1) 326-7400; fax (1) 326-7390; e-mail servicioalclienteco@panamericanlife.com; internet www.panamericanlife.com; f. 1974; Gen. Man. MANUEL LEMUS.

La Previsora, SA, Cía de Seguros: Calle 57, No 9-07, Apdo Aéreo 52946, Bogotá, DC; tel. (1) 348-5757; fax (1) 540-5294; e-mail contactenos@previsora.gov.co; internet www.previsora.gov.co; f. 1914; Exec. Pres. DIEGO BARRAGÁN CORREA.

QBE Seguros, SA: Carrera 7, No 76-35, 7°–9°, Apdo Aéreo 265063, Bogotá, DC; tel. (1) 319-0730; fax (1) 319-0749; e-mail sylvia.rincon@qbe.com.co; internet www.qbe.com.co; subsidiary of QBE Insurance Group, Australia; Pres. SYLVIA LUZ RINCÓN LEMA.

RSA Colombia: Edif. Royal & Sun Alliance, Avda 19, No 104-37, Apdo Aéreo 4225, Bogotá, DC; tel. (1) 488-1000; fax (1) 214-0440; e-mail servicioalcliente@co.rsagroup.com; internet www.rsagroup.com.co; fmrly Seguros Fénix, SA, then Royal and Sun Alliance Seguros; Pres. LILIAN PEREA RONCO.

Segurexpo de Colombia, SA: Calle 72, No 6-44, 12°, Apdo Aéreo 75140, Bogotá, DC; tel. (1) 326-6969; fax (1) 211-0218; e-mail segurexpo@segurexpo.com; internet www.segurexpo.com; f. 1993; Gen. Man. JESÚS URDANGARAY LÓPEZ.

Seguros Alfa, SA: Carrera 13, No 27-47, 22° y 23°, Apdo Aéreo 27718, Bogotá, DC; tel. (1) 743-5333; fax (1) 344-6770; e-mail presidencia@segurosalfa.com.co; internet www.segurosalfa.com.co; Pres. ROBERTO VERGARA ORTIZ.

Seguros Colpatria, SA: Carrera 7A, No 24-89, 27°, Apdo Aéreo 7762, Bogotá, DC; tel. (1) 336-4677; fax (1) 286-9998; e-mail servicioalcliente@ui.colpatria.com; internet www.seguroscolpatria.com; f. 1955; Pres. FERNANDO QUINTERO ARTURO.

Seguros del Estado, SA: Carrera 13, No 96-66, Apdo Aéreo 6810, Bogotá, DC; tel. (1) 218-0903; fax (1) 218-0913; e-mail luis.correa@segurosdelestado.com; internet www.segurosdelestado.com; f. 1956 as Cía Aliadas de Seguros, SA; changed name as above in 1973; Pres. JORGE MORA SÁNCHEZ.

Seguros Generales Suramericana, SA (Sura): Centro Suramericana, Carrera 64B, No 49A-30, Apdo Aéreo 780, Medellín, Antioquia; tel. (4) 260-2100; fax (4) 260-3194; e-mail contactenos@suramericana.com; internet www.sura.com; f. 1944; Pres. GONZALO ALBERTO PÉREZ ROJAS.

Seguros de Riesgos Profesionales Suramericana, SA (ARP Sura): Centro Suramericana, Edif. Torre Suramericana, 7°, Calle 49A, No 63-55, Medellín, Antioquia; tel. (4) 430-7100; fax (4) 231-8080; e-mail scliente@sura.com.co; internet www.arpsura.com; f. 1996; fmrly SURATEP; name changed as above in 2009; subsidiary of Cía Suramericana de Seguros (Sura); Gen. Man. IVÁN IGNACIO ZULUAGA LATORRE.

Skandia Seguros de Vida, SA: Avda 19, No 109A-30, Apdo Aéreo 100327, Bogotá, DC; tel. (1) 658-4000; fax (1) 658-4123; e-mail servicioempresa@skandia.com.co; internet www.skandia.com.co; Pres. MARÍA CLAUDIA CORREA ORDÓÑEZ.

Insurance Association

Federación de Aseguradores Colombianos (FASECOLDA): Carrera 7A, No 26-20, 11° y 12°, Apdo Aéreo 5233, Bogotá, DC; tel. (1) 344-3080; fax (1) 210-7041; e-mail fasecolda@fasecolda.com; internet www.fasecolda.com; f. 1976; 32 mems; Chair. FERNANDO QUINTERO ARTURO; Exec. Pres. ROBERTO JUNGUITO BONNET.

Trade and Industry

GOVERNMENT AGENCIES

Agencia Nacional de Hidrocarburos (ANH): Calle 26, No 59, 2°, Bogotá, DC; tel. (1) 593-1717; fax (1) 593-1718; e-mail info@anh.gov.co; internet www.anh.gov.co; f. 2003; govt agency responsible for regulation of the petroleum industry; Dir-Gen. JOSÉ ARMANDO ZAMORA REYES.

Departamento Nacional de Planeación: Edif. Fonade, Calle 26, No 13-19, 14°, Bogotá, DC; tel. (1) 381-5000; fax (1) 281-3348; e-mail vgonzalez@dnp.gov.co; internet www.dnp.gov.co; f. 1958; supervises and administers devt projects; approves foreign investments; Dir-Gen. HERNANDO JOSÉ GÓMEZ RESTREPO.

Superintendencia de Industria y Comercio (SUPERINDUSTRIA): Carrera 13, No 27-00, 5°, Bogotá, DC; tel. (1) 382-0840; fax (1) 382-2696; e-mail contactenos@sic.gov.co; internet www.sic.gov.co; supervises chambers of commerce; controls standards and prices; Supt JOSÉ MIGUEL DE LA CALLE.

Superintendencia de Sociedades (SUPERSOCIEDADES): Avda El Dorado, No 51-80, Apdo Aéreo 4188, Bogotá, DC; tel. (1) 324-5777; fax (1) 324-5000; e-mail webmaster@supersociedades.gov.co; internet www.supersociedades.gov.co; f. 1931; oversees activities of local and foreign corpns; Supt LUIS GUILLERMO VÉLEZ CABRERA.

DEVELOPMENT AGENCIES

Agencia Presidencial para la Acción Social y la Cooperación Internacional: Calle 7, No 6-54, Bogotá, DC; tel. (1) 352-6666; fax (1) 284-4120; internet www.accionsocial.gov.co; f. 2005 following merger of Red de Solidaridad Social (RSS) and Agencia Colombiana de Cooperación Internacional (ACCI); govt agency intended to channel domestic and international funds into social programmes; Dir DIEGO ANDRÉS MOLANO APONTE.

Asociación Colombiana de Ingeniería Sanitaria y Ambiental (ACODAL): Calle 39, No 14-75, Bogotá, DC; tel. (1) 245-9539; fax (1) 323-1408; e-mail gerencia@acodal.org.co; internet www.acodal.org.co; f. 1956 as Asociación Colombiana de Acueductos y Alcantarillados; asscn promoting sanitary and environmental engineering projects; Pres. MARYLUZ MEJÍA DE PUMAREJO; Man. ALBERTO VALENCIA MONSALVE.

Asociación Colombiana de las Micro, Pequeñas y Medianas Empresas (ACOPI): Carrera 15, No 36-70, Bogotá, DC; tel. and fax (1) 320-4783; e-mail prensa@acopi.org.co; internet www.acopi.org.co; f. 1951; promotes small and medium-sized industries; Pres. MAURICIO RAMÍREZ MALAVER.

Centro Internacional de Educación y Desarrollo Humano (CINDE): Calle 77, Sur 43A-27 Sabaneta, Antioquia, Medellín; tel. (4) 444-8424; fax (4) 288-3991; e-mail cinde@cinde.org.co; internet www.cinde.org.co; education and social devt; f. 1977; Dir-Gen. MARTA ARANGO MONTOYA.

Corporación para la Investigación Socioeconómica y Tecnológica de Colombia (CINSET): Carrera 48, No 91-94, La Castellana, Bogotá, DC; tel. (1) 256-0961; fax (1) 218-6416; e-mail cinset@cinset.org.co; internet www.cinset.org.co; f. 1987; social, economic and technical devt projects; Pres. ENRIQUE DARÍO JIMÉNEZ; Exec. Dir JUAN CARLOS GUTIÉRREZ ARIAS.

Corporación Región: Calle 55, No 41-10, Medellín; tel. (4) 216-6822; fax (4) 239-5544; e-mail coregion@region.org.co; internet www.region.org.co; f. 1989; environmental, political and social devt; Pres. MAX YURI GIL RAMÍREZ; Dir-Gen. RUBÉN HERNANDO FERNÁNDEZ ANDRADE.

Fondo Financiero de Proyectos de Desarrollo (FONADE): Calle 26, No 13-19, 19°-22°, Apdo Aéreo 24110, Bogotá, DC; tel. (1) 594-0407; fax (1) 282-6018; e-mail fonade@colomsat.net.co; internet www.fonade.gov.co; f. 1968; responsible for channelling loans towards economic devt projects; administered by a cttee under the head of the Departamento Nacional de Planeación; FONADE works in close asscn with other official planning orgs; Gen. Man. Dr ALBERTO CARDONA BOTERO.

Instituto Colombiano de Desarrollo Rural: Centro Administrativo Nacional (CAN), Avda Eldorado, Calle 43, No 57-41, Bogotá, DC; tel. (1) 383-0444; e-mail buzonciudadano@incoder.gov.co; internet www.incoder.gov.co; rural devt agency; Gen. Man. JUAN MANUEL OSPINA RESTREPO.

CHAMBERS OF COMMERCE

Confederación Colombiana de Cámaras de Comercio (CONFECAMARAS): Edif. Banco de Occidente, Of. 502, Carrera 13, No 27-47, Apdo Aéreo 29750, Bogotá, DC; tel. (1) 381-4100; fax (1) 346-7026; e-mail confecamaras@confecamaras.org.co; internet www.confecamaras.org.co; f. 1969; 56 mem. orgs; Exec. Pres. JULIÁN DOMÍNGUEZ RIVERA.

Cámara Colombo Japonesa de Comercio e Industria: Calle 72, No 7-82, 7°, Bogotá, DC; tel. (1) 210-0383; fax (1) 349-0736; e-mail camcoljapon@etb.net.co; internet www.ccjci.com.co; f. 1988; Colombian-Japanese trade asscn; Pres. JUAN CARLOS MONDRAGÓN A.

Cámara Colombo Venezolana: Edif. Suramericana, Of. 503, Calle 72, No 8-24, Bogotá, DC; tel. (1) 211-6224; fax (1) 211-6089; e-mail info@comvenezuela.com; internet www.comvenezuela.com; f. 1977; Colombian-Venezuelan trade asscn; 19 mem. cos; Pres. MAGDALENA PARDO DE SERRANO.

Cámara de Comercio de Bogotá: Avda Eldorado, 68D-35, Bogotá, DC; tel. (1) 383-0300; fax (1) 284-7735; e-mail webmaster@ccb.org.co;

internet www.ccb.org.co; f. 1878; 3,650 mem. orgs; Pres. Juan Diego Trujillo Mejía.

Cámara de Comercio Colombo Americano: Of. 1209, Calle 98, No 22-64, Bogotá, DC; tel. (1) 587-7828; fax (1) 621-6838; e-mail website@amchamcolombia.com.co; internet www.amchamcolombia.com.co; f. 1955; Colombian-US trade asscn; Exec. Dir Camilo Reyes Rodríguez.

Cámara de Comercio Colombo Británica: Of. 301, Calle 104, No 14a-45, Bogotá, DC; tel. (1) 256-2833; fax (1) 256-3026; e-mail comunicaciones@colombobritanica.com; internet www.colombobritanica.com; Colombian-British trade asscn; Pres. Santiago Echavarria; Dir Patricia Tovar.

INDUSTRIAL AND TRADE ASSOCIATIONS

Corporación de la Industria Aeronáutica Colombiana, SA (CIAC SA): Avda Calle 26, No 103-08, Entrada 1, Bogotá, DC; tel. (1) 413-8312; e-mail atencion@ciac.gov.co; internet www.ciac.gov.co; Gen. Man. Hugo Enrique Acosta Tellez.

Industria Militar (INDUMIL): Calle 44, No 51-11, Apdo Aéreo 7272, Bogotá, DC; tel. (1) 220-7800; fax (1) 222-4889; internet www.indumil.gov.co; attached to Ministry of National Defence; Gen. Man. Col (retd) César José Fernández Barreto.

Instituto Colombiano Agropecuario (ICA): Calle 37, No 8-43, 5°, Bogotá, DC; tel. (1) 332-3700; fax (1) 232-4689; e-mail info@ica.gov.co; internet www.ica.gov.co; f. 1962; attached to the Ministry of Agriculture and Rural Devt; institute for promotion, co-ordination and implementation of research into and teaching and devt of agriculture and animal husbandry; Gen. Man. Teresita Beltrán Ospina.

Instituto Colombiano de Geología y Minería (INGEOMINAS): Diagonal 53, No 34-53, Apdo Aéreo 4865, Bogotá, DC; tel. (1) 222-1811; fax (1) 220-0797; e-mail henciso@ingeominas.gov.co; internet www.ingeominas.gov.co; f. 1968; responsible for mineral research, geological mapping and research including hydrogeology, remote sensing, geochemistry, geophysics and geological hazards; attached to the Ministry of Mines and Energy; Dir Oscar Paredes Zapata.

EMPLOYERS' AND PRODUCERS' ORGANIZATIONS

Asociación Colombiana de Cooperativos (ASCOOP): Transversal 29, No 36-29, Bogotá, DC; tel. (1) 368-3500; fax (1) 369-5475; e-mail ascoop@ascoop.coop; internet www.ascoop.coop; promotes co-operatives; Exec. Dir Carlos E. Acero.

Asociación de Cultivadores de Caña de Azúcar de Colombia (ASOCAÑA): Calle 58n, No 3n-15, Apdo Aéreo 4448, Cali, Valle del Cauca; tel. (2) 664-7902; fax (2) 664-5888; internet www.asocana.com.co; f. 1959; sugar planters' asscn; Pres. Luis Fernando Londoño Capurro.

Asociación Nacional de Comercio Exterior (ANALDEX): Edif. UGI, Calle 40, No 13-09, 10°, Bogotá, DC; tel. (1) 570-0600; fax (1) 284-6911; e-mail analdex@analdex.org; internet www.analdex.org; exporters' asscn; Pres. Javier Díaz Molina.

Asociación Nacional de Empresarios de Colombia (ANDI): Carrera 43a, No 1-50, San Fernando Plaza, Torre 2, 9º, Apdo Aéreo 997, Medellín, Antioquia; tel. (4) 326-5100; fax (4) 326-0068; e-mail comercial@andi.com.co; internet www.andi.com.co; f. 1944; Pres. Luis Carlos Villegas Echeverri; 9 brs; 756 mems.

Asociación Nacional de Exportadores de Café de Colombia: Calle 72, No 10-07, Of. 1101, Bogotá, DC; tel. (1) 347-8419; fax (1) 347-9523; e-mail asoexport@asoexport.org; internet www.asoexport.org; f. 1933; private asscn of coffee exporters; Pres. Mauricio Bernal Londoño.

Federación Colombiana de Ganaderos (FEDEGAN): Calle 37, No 14-31, Apdo Aéreo 9709, Bogotá, DC; tel. (1) 245-3041; fax (1) 578-2020; e-mail fedegan@fedegan.org.co; internet www.fedegan.org.co; f. 1963; cattle raisers' asscn; about 350,000 affiliates; Exec. Pres. José Félix Lafaurie Rivera.

Federación Nacional de Cacaoteros: Carrera 17, No 30-39, Apdo Aéreo 17736, Bogotá, DC; tel. (1) 327-3000; fax (1) 288-4424; e-mail presidencia@fedecacao.com.co; internet www.fedecacao.com.co; fed. of cocoa growers; Gen. Man. Dr José Omar Pinzón Useche.

Federación Nacional de Cafeteros de Colombia (FEDERACAFE) (National Federation of Coffee Growers): Calle 73, No 8-13, Apdo Aéreo 57534, Bogotá, DC; tel. (1) 217-0600; fax (1) 217-1021; internet www.federaciondecafeteros.org; f. 1927; totally responsible for fostering and regulating the coffee economy; Gen. Man. Luis Genaro Muñoz Ortega; 203,000 mems.

Federación Nacional de Comerciantes (FENALCO): Carrera 4, No 19-85, 7°, Bogotá, DC; tel. (1) 350-0600; fax (1) 350-9424; e-mail fenalco@fenalco.com.co; internet www.fenalco.com.co; Pres. Guillermo Botero Nieto.

Federación Nacional de Cultivadores de Cereales y Leguminosas (FENALCE): Carrera 14, No 97-62, Apdo Aéreo 8694, Bogotá, DC; tel. (1) 218-2114; fax (1) 218-9463; e-mail fenalce@cable.net.co; internet www.fenalce.org; f. 1960; fed. of grain growers; Gen. Man. Henry Vanegas Anagarita; 30,000 mems.

Sociedad de Agricultores de Colombia (SAC) (Colombian Farmers' Society): Carrera 7, No 24-89, Of. 4402, Bogotá, DC; tel. (1) 281-0263; fax (1) 284-4572; e-mail prensa@sac.org.co; internet www.sac.org.co; f. 1871; Pres. Rafael Mejía López.

There are several other organizations, including those for rice growers, engineers and financiers.

UTILITIES

Electricity

Corporación Eléctrica de la Costa Atlántica, SA ESP (Corelca): Centro Ejecutivo II, 5°, Calle 55, No 72-109, 9°, Barranquilla, Atlántico; tel. (5) 330-3000; fax (5) 330-3011; e-mail presidencia@corelca.com.co; internet www.corelca.com.co; responsible for supplying electricity to the Atlantic departments; generates more than 2,000m. kWh annually from thermal power stations; Gen. Man. Daniel Alsina Galofre.

Empresa de Energía de Bogotá, SA ESP (EEB): Of. Principal, 6°, Carrera 9a, No 73-44, Bogotá, DC; tel. (1) 326-8000; fax (1) 226-8010; e-mail webmaster@eeb.com.co; internet www.eeb.com.co; provides electricity for Bogotá area by generating capacity of 680 MW, mainly hydroelectric; Pres. Mónica de Greiff; Man. Dir Astrid Martínez Ortiz.

Instituto de Planificación y Promoción de Soluciones Energéticas para las Zonas No Interconectadas (IPSE): Carrera 12, No 84-12, 8°, Bogotá, DC; tel. (1) 644-9300; fax (1) 622-3461; e-mail ipse@ipse.gov.co; internet www.ipse.gov.co; f. 1999; attached to the Ministry of Mines and Energy; co-ordinates and develops energy supply in rural areas; Dir-Gen. Juan Carlos Caiza Rosero.

Interconexión Eléctrica, SA (ISA): Calle 12 Sur, No 18-168, El Poblado, Apdo Aéreo 8915, Medellín, Antioquia; tel. (4) 325-2270; fax (4) 317-0848; e-mail isa@isa.com.co; internet www.isa.com.co; f. 1967; created by Colombia's principal electricity production and distribution cos to form a national network; operations in Brazil, Ecuador, Peru, Bolivia and Central America; 52.9% state-owned; Pres. Orlando Cabrales Martínez; Gen. Man. Luis Fernando Alarcón Mantilla.

Isagen: Avda El Poblado, Carrera 43a, No 11a-80, Apdo Aereo 8762, Medellín, Antioquia; tel. (4) 316-5000; fax (4) 268-4646; e-mail isagen@isagen.com.co; internet www.isagen.com.co; f. 1995 following division of ISA (q.v.); 57.7% state-owned; generates electricity from 3 hydraulic and 2 thermal power plants; Gen. Man. Luis Fernando Rico Pinzón.

Gas

Empresa Colombiana de Gas (Ecogás): Of. 209, Centro Internacional de Negocios La Triada, Calle 35, No 19-41, Bucaramanga, Santander del Sur; tel. (7) 642-1000; fax (7) 642-6446; e-mail correspondencia@ecogas.com.co; internet www.ecogas.com.co; f. 1997; operation and maintenance of gas distribution network; sold in 2006 to Empresa de Energía de Bogotá, SA; Dir Geronimo Manuel Guerra Cárdenas.

Gas Natural, SA ESP: Calle 71a, No 5-38, Bogotá, DC; tel. (1) 338-1199; fax (1) 288-0807; internet portal.gasnatural.com; f. 1987; owned by Gas Natural of Spain; distributes natural gas in Bogotá and Soacha; Dir-Gen. (Latin America) Sergio Aranda Moreno; Pres. María Eugenia Coronado.

TRADE UNIONS

Central Unitaria de Trabajadores de Colombia (CUT): Calle 35, No 7-25, 9°, Apdo Aéreo 221, Bogotá, DC; tel. and fax (1) 323-7550; e-mail comunicaciones@cut.org.co; internet www.cut.org.co; f. 1986; comprises 50 feds and 80% of all trade union members; Pres. Tarcisio Hora Godoy; Sec.-Gen. Domingo Tovar Arrieta.

Federación Colombiana de Educadores (FECODE): Carrera 13a, No 34-54, Bogotá, DC; tel. (1) 338-1711; fax (1) 285-3245; internet fecode.edu.co; Pres. Senén Niño Avendaño; Sec.-Gen. Luis Eduardo Varela.

Federación de Loterías de Colombia (FEDELCO): Carrera 6, No 26–85, 8°, Bogotá, DC; tel. (1) 282-5874; fax (1) 282-5894; e-mail info@fedelco.com.co; internet www.fedelco.com.co; f. 1970; lottery ticket sellers' union; Pres. Luz Stella Cardona Meza.

Federación Nacional Sindical Unitaria Agropecuaria (FENSUAGRO): Calle 17, No 10-16, Of. 104, Bogotá, DC; tel. (1) 286-7794; fax (1) 282-8871; e-mail fensuagro@hotmail.com; internet www.fensuagro.org; f. 1976 as Federación Nacional Sindical Agropecuaria (FENSA); comprises 37 unions, 7 peasant asscns, with 80,000 mems; Pres. Eberto Díaz Montes; Sec.-Gen. Parmenio Poveda.

Federación Nacional Sindicatos Bancarios Colombianos (FENASIBANCOL): Calle 30A, No 6-22, Of. 1601, Bogotá, DC; tel. (1) 287-5728; fax (1) 288-0235; e-mail fenasibancol@telecom.com.co; internet www.fenasibancol.org; Pres. ROBERTO MORENO SERNA; Sec.-Gen. CESAR AUGUSTO CÁRDENAS.

Federación Nacional de Trabajadores de Alimentación, Bebidas, Afines y Similar (Fentralimentación): Calle 8 sur, 68B-60, Bogotá, DC; tel. (1) 414-6505; fax (1) 290-0390; e-mail fentralimentacion@hotmail.com; represents the food and drink industry; Pres. ALFONSO LÓPEZ FREYLE.

Federación Nacional de Trabajadores al Servicio del Estado (FENALTRASE): Calle 17, No 5-21, Of. 502, Bogotá, DC; tel. (1) 334-4815; e-mail fenaltrese@hotmail.com; f. 1960; Pres. ROBERTO CHAMUCERO.

FUNTRAENERGETICA: Calle 16, No 13-49, Of. 201, Bogotá, DC; tel. (1) 334-0447; fax (1) 286-5259; e-mail funtraenergetica@colombia.com; f. 2001 following merger of Funtrammetal and Fedepetrol; represents workers in the energy sector; Pres. JOAQUÍN ROMERO.

Unión Sindical Obrera de la Indústria del Petróleo (USO): Calle 38, No 13-37, Of. 302, Bogotá, DC; tel. (1) 234-4074; fax (1) 234-4399; e-mail prensa@usofrenteobrero.org; internet www.usofrenteobrero.org; f. 1922; petroleum workers' union; affiliated to CUT; Pres. RODOLFO VECINO ACEVEDO; Sec.-Gen. ISNARDO LOZANO GÓMEZ; 3,200 mems.

Confederación General del Trabajo (CGT): Calle 39A, No 14-52, Bogotá, DC; tel. (1) 288-1504; fax (1) 573-4021; e-mail cgtprensa2010@gmail.com; internet www.cgtcolombia.org; Pres. JULIO ROBERTO GÓMEZ ESGUERRA; Sec.-Gen. MIRYAM LUZ TRIANA ALVIS.

Confederación de Trabajadores de Colombia (CTC) (Colombian Confederation of Workers): Calle 39, No 26A-23, Barrio La Soledad, Apdo Aéreo 4780, Bogotá, DC; tel. (1) 269-7117; fax (7) 268-8576; e-mail ctc1@etb.net.co; internet www.ctc-colombia.com.co; f. 1934; mainly liberal; 600 affiliates, including 6 national orgs and 20 regional feds; admitted to the International Trade Union Confederation; Pres. LUIS MIGUEL MORANTES ALFONSO; Sec.-Gen. ROSA ELENA FLÉREZ; 400,000 mems.

Transport

Land transport in Colombia is rendered difficult by high mountains, so the principal means of long-distance transport is by air.

Superintendencia de Puertos y Transporte: Ministerio de Transporte, Edif. Estación de la Sabana, 2° y 3°, Calle 63, No 9A–45, Bogotá, DC; tel. and fax (2) 352-6700; e-mail atencionciudadano@supertransporte.gov.co; internet www.supertransporte.gov.co; f. 1992 as Superintendencia General de Puertos, present name adopted in 1998; part of the Ministry of Transport; oversees transport sector; Supt Dr JUAN MIGUEL DURÁN PRIETO.

Agencia Nacional de Infraestructura (ANI): Edif. Ministerio de Transporte, Centro Administrativo Nacional (CAN), 3°, Avda El Dorado, Bogotá, DC; tel. (1) 379-1720; fax (1) 324-0800; e-mail contactenos@ani.gov.co; internet www.ani.gov.co; fmrly Instituto Nacional de Concesiones; changed name as above in 2011; govt agency charged with contracting devt of transport infrastructure to private operators; part of the Ministry of Transport; Pres. LUIS FERNANDO ANDRADE MORENO.

Instituto Nacional de Vías (INVIAS): Edif. INVIAS, Centro Administrativo Nacional (CAN), Carrera 59, No 26-60, Bogotá, DC; tel. and fax (1) 705-6000; e-mail atencionciudadano@invias.gov.co; internet www.invias.gov.co; govt agency responsible for non-contracted transport infrastructure; Dir-Gen. CARLOS ALBERTO ROSADO ZÚÑIGA.

RAILWAYS

In 2008 there were 1,663 km of track. The Agencia Nacional de Infraestructura (q.v.) operates the Red Ferrea del Atlántico and the Red Ferrea del Pacífico. Construction of Ferrocarril del Carare, which would connect mining sites in the departments of Santander, Boyacá and Cundinamarca with ports on the Atlantic coast, was expected to begin in late 2012. The cost of the proposed project was US $2,700m.

El Cerrejón Mine Railway: Cerrejón, Calle 100, No 19-54, Bogotá, DC; tel. (1) 595-5555; e-mail comunica@cerrejon.com; internet www.cerrejon.com; f. 1989 to link the mine and the port at Puerto Bolívar; 150 km.

Ferrocarriles del Norte de Colombia, SA (FENOCO, SA): Calle 94A, No 11A-27, 3°, Bogotá, DC; tel. (1) 622-0505; fax (1) 622-0440; e-mail contactenos@fenoco.com.co; internet www.fenoco.com.co; f. 1999; operates the Concesión de la Red Férrea del Atlántico; 226 kms; Pres. PETER BURROWES.

Metro de Medellín (Empresa de Transporte Masivo del Valle de Aburrá Ltda): Calle 44, No 46-001, Apdo Aéreo 9128, Bello, Medellín, Antioquia; tel. (4) 444-9598; fax (4) 452-4450; e-mail contactenos@metrodemedellin.gov.co; internet www.metrodemedellin.gov.co; f. 1995; 5-line metro system; Gen. Man. RAMIRO MÁRQUEZ RAMÍREZ.

Tren de Occidente, SA: Avda Vásquez Cobo, No 23N-27, Of. 308, Santiago de Cali, Valle del Cauca; tel. (2) 667-7733; e-mail contacto.cali@trendeoccidente.com; internet www.trendeoccidente.com; f. 1998; operates the Concesión de la Red Férrea del Pacífico; Gen. Man. ALFONSO PATIÑO FAJARDO.

ROADS

In 2008 there were 164,183 km of roads.

Transmilenio: Edif. Ministerio de Transporte, Centro Administrativo Nacional (CAN), 3°, Avda El Dorado, No 66-63, Bogotá, DC; tel. (1) 220-3000; fax (1) 324-9870; e-mail marthal.gutierrez@transmilenio.gov.co; internet www.transmilenio.gov.co; f. 2000; bus-based mass transit system in Bogotá; Gen. Man. JAIRO FERNANDO PAÉZ MENDIETA.

INLAND WATERWAYS

The Magdalena–Cauca river system is the centre of river traffic and is navigable for 1,500 km, while the Atrato is navigable for 687 km. The Orinoco system has more than five navigable rivers, which total more than 4,000 km of potential navigation (mainly through Venezuela); the Amazon system has four main rivers, which total 3,000 navigable km (mainly through Brazil).

SHIPPING

The four most important ocean terminals are Buenaventura on the Pacific coast and Santa Marta, Barranquilla and Cartagena on the Atlantic coast. The port of Tumaco on the Pacific coast is gaining in importance and there are plans for construction of a deep-water port at Bahía Solano. In December 2009 Colombia's merchant fleet comprised of 146 vessels, with a total displacement of some 89,745 grt.

Port Authorities

Sociedad Portuaria Regional de Barranquilla: Carrera 38, Calle 1A, Barranquilla, Atlántico; tel. (5) 371-6200; fax (5) 371-6310; e-mail servicioalcliente@sprb.com.co; internet www.sprb.com.co; privatized in 1993; Man. ENRIQUE CARVAJALES MARULANDA.

Sociedad Portuaria Regional de Buenaventura: Edif. de Administración, Avda Portuaria, Apdo 478-10765, Buenaventura; tel. 241-0700; fax 242-2700; e-mail servicioalaccionista@sprbun.com; internet www.puertobuenaventura.com; Pres. PEDRO JOSÉ GUTIÉRREZ HELO; Gen. Man. DOMINGO CHINEA BARRERA.

Sociedad Portuaria Regional de Cartagena: Manga, Terminal Marítimo, Cartagena, Bolívar; tel. (5) 660-7781; fax (5) 650-2239; e-mail comercial@sprc.com.co; internet www.puertocartagena.com; f. 1993; Gen. Man. ALFONSO SALAS TRUJILLO.

Sociedad Portuaria de Santa Marta: Carrera 1, 10A-12, Apdo 655, Santa Marta; tel. (5) 421-7970; fax (5) 421-2161; e-mail spsm@spsm.com.co; internet www.spsm.com.co; Dir ARMANDO DUARTE-PELÁEZ; Gen. Man. MAURICIO SUÁREZ.

Private shipping companies include the following:

NAVESCO, SA: Torre Cusezar, No 7-15, 17°, Avda Calle 116, Bogotá, DC; tel. (1) 657-5868; fax (1) 657-5869; e-mail gsolano@navesco.com.co; internet www.navesco.com.co; f. 1980; Pres. RUBEN ESCOBAR; Gen. Man. GUILLERMO SOLANO.

CIVIL AVIATION

Colombia has more than 100 airports, including 11 international airports: Bogotá, DC (El Dorado International Airport), Medellín, Cali, Barranquilla, Bucaramanga, Cartagena, Cúcuta, Leticia, Pereira, San Andrés and Santa Marta.

Airports Authority

Aeronaútica Civil (Aerocivil): Nuevo Edif. Aerocivil, Avda El Dorado 103–15, 4°, Bogotá, DC; tel. (1) 425-1000; fax (1) 413-5000; e-mail quejasyreclamos@aerocivil.gov.co; internet www.aerocivil.gov.co; f. 1967 as Departamento Administrativo de Aeronáutica Civil, reorganized in 1992; part of the Ministry of Transport; develops and regulates the civil aviation industry; Dir-Gen. SANTIAGO CASTRO.

National Airlines

Avianca (Aerovías Nacionales de Colombia, SA): Avda El Dorado, No 93-30, 5°, Bogotá, DC; tel. (1) 413-9862; fax (1) 413-8716; internet www.avianca.com; f. 1919; operates domestic services to all cities in Colombia and international services to the USA, France, Spain, and throughout Central and Southern America; allied with TACA of El Salvador (q.v.) in 2009; Exec. Pres. FABIO VILLEGAS RAMÍREZ.

Copa Airlines Colombia: Edif. Citibank, Calle 100, Carrera 9A, No 99–02, Bogotá, DC; tel. (1) 320-9090; fax (1) 320-9095; internet www.copaair.com; f. 1992 as Aero República; changed name as above in 2010; subsidiary of Copa Holdings (Panama); Pres. ROBERTO JUNGUITO POMBO.

LAN Colombia (Aires Colombia): El Dorado International Airport, Bogotá, DC; internet www.lan.com; f. 1980 as Aerovías de Integración Regional (AIRES); acquired by LAN Airlines, SA (Chile) and rebranded as above in 2010; domestic and international passenger services, domestic cargo services; CEO HERNÁN PASMAN.

Líneas Aéreas Suramericanas (LAS): Avda El Dorado, No 103-22, Entrada 2, Interior 7, Bogotá, DC; tel. (1) 413-9515; fax (1) 413-5356; internet www.lascargo.com; f. 1972 as AeroNorte, present name adopted 1986; charter cargo services.

Satena (Servicio de Aeronavegación a Territorios Nacionales): Avda El Dorado, No 103-08, Apdo Aéreo 11163, Bogotá, DC; tel. (1) 423-8530; e-mail info@satena.com; internet www.satena.com; f. 1962; commercial enterprise attached to the Ministry of National Defence; internal services; Pres. Brig.-Gen. CARLOS EDUARDO MONTEALEGRE RODRIGUEZ.

Tampa Cargo, SA: Aeropuerto José María Córdova, Terminal Internacional de Carga, Rionegro, Medellín, Antioquia; tel. (4) 569-9200; fax (4) 562-2847; e-mail laura.herzberg@aviancataca.com; internet www.tampacargo.com.co; f. 1973; operates international cargo services to destinations throughout the Americas; acquired by AviancaTaca Holdings in 2010; Dir LUÍS FELIPE GOMÉZ TORO.

Tourism

The principal tourist attractions are the Caribbean coast (including the island of San Andrés), the 16th-century walled city of Cartagena, the Amazonian town of Leticia, the Andes mountains, the extensive forests and jungles, pre-Columbian relics and monuments of colonial art. In 2009 there were 1,353,700 visitors, most of whom came from the USA and Venezuela. In 2010 tourism receipts were a provisional US $2,083m.

Ministry of Trade, Industry and Tourism: Edif. Centro de Comercio Internacional, Calle 28, No 13A-15, 18°, Bogotá, DC; tel. (1) 606-7676; fax (1) 696-7521; internet www.mincomercio.gov.co; Vice-Minister responsible for Tourism OSCAR RUEDA GARCÍA.

Asociación Colombiana de Agencias de Viajes y Turismo (ANATO): Carrera 19B, No 83-49, 4°, Apdo Aéreo 7088, Bogotá, DC; tel. (1) 610-7099; fax (1) 236-2424; e-mail anato@anato.org; internet www.anato.org; f. 1949; Pres. PAULA CORTÉS CALLE; Exec. Dir ISMAEL ENRIQUE RAMIREZ.

Defence

As assessed at November 2011, Colombia's armed forces numbered 283,004, of whom the army comprised 235,798, the navy 33,138 (including 14,000 marines and 7,200 conscripts) and the air force 13,758. In addition, there were some 61,900 reservists, of whom 54,700 were in the army, 4,800 in the navy, 1,200 in the air force and 1,200 in the joint services. There was also a paramilitary National Police Force numbering 158,824. Military service is compulsory for men (except for students) and lasts for 12–24 months.

Defence Budget: 10,300,000m. pesos in 2011.

Commander of the Armed Forces: Gen. ALEJANDRO NAVAS RAMOS.

Chief of Staff of the Armed Forces: Gen. JOSÉ JAVIER PÉREZ.

Commander of the Army: Gen. SERGIO MANTILLA SANMIGUEL.

Commander of the Navy: Rear-Adm. ROBERTO GARCÍA MÁRQUEZ.

Commander of the Air Force: Gen. TITO SAÚL PINILLA.

Education

Education in Colombia commences at nursery level for children under six years of age. Primary education is free and compulsory for five years. Admission to secondary school is conditional upon the successful completion of these five years. Secondary education is for four years. Following completion of this period, pupils may pursue a further two years of vocational study, leading to the *Bachiller* examination. In 2009/10 a total of 5,085,000 students were in primary education and in 2008 4,617,900 attended secondary schools. In 2008/09 enrolment at primary and secondary schools included 90% and 74% of the school-age population, respectively. In 2009/10 there were an estimated 55,869 primary schools and and in 2008 there were 13,280 secondary schools. In 2007 there were 32 public universities in Colombia. The proposed central Government expenditure on education for 2012 is 23m. pesos.

THE COMOROS*

Introductory Survey

LOCATION, CLIMATE, LANGUAGE, RELIGION, FLAG, CAPITAL

The Union of the Comoros (formerly the Federal Islamic Republic of the Comoros) is an archipelago in the Mozambique Channel, between the island of Madagascar and the east coast of the African mainland. The group comprises four main islands (Ngazidja, Nzwani and Mwali—formerly Grande-Comore, Anjouan and Mohéli, respectively—and Mayotte, which is a French overseas possession) and numerous islets and coral reefs. The climate is tropical, with average temperatures ranging from 23°C (73.4°F) to 28°C (82.4°F). Average annual rainfall is between 1,500 mm (59 ins) and 5,000 mm (197 ins). The official languages are Comorian (a blend of Swahili and Arabic), French and Arabic. Islam is the state religion. The flag (proportions 2 by 3) has four equal horizontal stripes, of yellow, white, red and blue, with a green triangle at the hoist depicting a white crescent moon and a vertical row of four five-pointed white stars. The capital, which is situated on Ngazidja, is Moroni.

CONTEMPORARY POLITICAL HISTORY

Historical Context

Formerly attached to Madagascar, the Comoros became a separate French Overseas Territory in 1947. The islands achieved internal self-government in December 1961, with a Chambre des députés and a Government Council responsible for local administration.

On 6 July 1975 the Chambre des députés voted for immediate independence, elected the President of the Government Council, Ahmed Abdallah, to be first President of the Comoros and reconstituted itself as the Assemblée nationale. Although France made no attempt to intervene, it maintained control of the island of Mayotte. Abdallah was deposed in August, and the Assemblée nationale was abolished. A National Executive Council was established, with Prince Saïd Mohammed Jaffar, leader of the opposition party, the Front national uni, as its head, and Ali Soilih, leader of the coup, among its members. In November the Comoros was admitted to the UN, as a unified state comprising the whole archipelago. In December France officially recognized the independence of Ngazidja, Nzwani and Mwali, but relations between France and the Comoros were effectively suspended. In February 1976 Mayotte voted overwhelmingly to retain its links with France.

Soilih, who had been elected Head of State in January 1976, was killed in May 1978, following a coup by a group of European mercenaries, led by a Frenchman, Col Robert Denard, on behalf of Abdallah. The Comoros was proclaimed a Federal Islamic Republic and diplomatic relations with France were restored. In October a new Constitution was approved in a referendum, on the three islands excluding Mayotte, by 99.3% of the votes cast. Abdallah was elected President in the same month, and in December elections for a new legislature, the Assemblée fédérale, took place. In January 1979 the Assemblée fédérale approved the formation of a one-party state (unofficial opposition groups, however, continued to exist). In September 1984 Abdallah was re-elected President.

Domestic Political Affairs

In November 1989 a constitutional amendment permitting Abdallah to remain in office for a third six-year term was approved by 92.5% of votes cast in a popular referendum. The result of the referendum, however, was disputed by the President's opponents. Violent demonstrations followed, and opposition leaders were detained. On the night of 26–27 November Abdallah was assassinated by members of the presidential guard, under the command of Denard. The President of the Supreme Court, Saïd Mohamed Djohar, was appointed interim Head of State; however, Denard and his supporters defeated the regular army in a coup. The mercenaries' action provoked international condemnation, despite denials by Denard of complicity in Abdallah's death. (In May 1999 Denard stood trial in Paris, France, in connection with the assassination. Both Denard and his co-defendant, Dominique Malacrino, were acquitted of the murder charge.) In mid-December Denard agreed to relinquish power and, following the arrival of French paratroops in Moroni, was transported to South Africa, together with the remaining mercenaries.

At the end of December 1989 the main political groups formed a provisional Government of National Unity. An amnesty for all political prisoners was proclaimed, and an inquiry into the death of Abdallah was instigated. In March 1990 Djohar, the official candidate for the Union comorienne pour le progrès (Udzima), secured victory at a multi-candidate presidential election, taking 55.3% of the votes cast and defeating Mohamed Taki Abdulkarim, the leader of the Union nationale pour la démocratie aux Comores (UNDC).

In November 1991 agreement was reached between Djohar and the principal opposition leaders to initiate a process of national reconciliation, which would include the formation of a government of national unity and the convening of a constitutional conference. The accord also guaranteed the legitimacy of Djohar's election as President. In January 1992 a new transitional Government of National Unity was formed, pending legislative elections.

At a constitutional referendum, held on 7 June 1992, reform proposals, which had been submitted in April, were approved by 74.3% of the votes cast. The new Constitution limited the presidential tenure to a maximum of two five-year terms of office and provided for a bicameral legislature, comprising an Assemblée fédérale, elected for a term of four years, and a 15-member Sénat, selected for a six-year term by the regional Councils.

The first round of voting in legislative elections, which had originally been scheduled to take place in October 1992, took place on 22 November. Numerous electoral irregularities and violent incidents were reported and several opposition parties demanded that the results be declared invalid. Election results in six constituencies were subsequently annulled, while the second round of voting on 29 November took place in only 34 of the 42 constituencies. Following partial elections on 13 and 30 December, reports indicated that candidates supporting Djohar—including seven members of the Union des démocrates pour la démocratie (UDD), a pro-Government organization based on Nzwani—had secured a narrow majority in the Assemblée fédérale. The leader of the UDD, Ibrahim Abdérémane Halidi, was appointed Prime Minister on 1 January 1993 and formed a new Council of Ministers.

In May 1993 eight supporters of the Minister of Finance, Commerce and Planning (and Djohar's son-in-law), Mohamed Saïd Abdallah M'Changama, allied with a number of opposition deputies, proposed a motion of no confidence in the Government (apparently with the tacit support of Djohar), which was approved by 23 of the 42 deputies. Shortly afterwards, Djohar appointed an associate of M'Changama, Saïd Ali Mohamed, as Prime Minister, and a new Council of Ministers was formed. In June, in view of the continued absence of a viable parliamentary majority, Djohar dissolved the Assemblée fédérale and announced legislative elections. He subsequently dismissed Mohamed and appointed a former presidential adviser, Ahmed Ben Cheikh Attoumane, as Prime Minister. Shortly afterwards an interim Council of Ministers was formed (although two of the newly appointed ministers immediately resigned).

Following the dissolution of the Assemblée fédérale, opposition parties declared Djohar unfit to hold office, in view of the increasing political confusion, and demanded that legislative elections take place within the period of 40 days stipulated in the Constitution. In July 1993, however, Djohar announced that the legislative elections (which were to take place concurrently with local elections) were to be postponed until October—they were later postponed until November. In October Djohar established a political organization, the Rassemblement pour la démocratie et

*Some of the information contained in this chapter refers to the whole Comoros archipelago, which the independent Comoran state claims as its national territory. However, the island of Mayotte (Mahoré) is, in fact, administered by France. Separate information on Mayotte may be found in the chapter on French Overseas Possessions.

le renouveau (RDR), principally comprising supporters of M'Changama and several prominent members of the Government. In November the legislative elections were rescheduled for December, while the local elections were postponed indefinitely. Later in November Djohar reorganized the Council of Ministers and established a new national electoral commission, in response to opposition demands.

At the first round of the legislative elections, which took place on 12 December 1993, four opposition candidates secured seats in the Assemblée fédérale. Following a second round of voting on 20 December, the electoral commission declared the results in several constituencies to be invalid. Opposition candidates refused to participate in further elections in these constituencies, on the grounds that voting was again to be conducted under the supervision of the authorities, rather than that of the commission; RDR candidates consequently won all 10 contested seats, and 22 seats overall, thereby securing a narrow majority in the Assemblée fédérale.

In September 1995 about 30 European mercenaries, led by Denard, staged a military coup, seizing control of the garrison at Kandani and capturing Djohar. The mercenaries, who were joined by some 300 members of the Comoran armed forces, released a number of prisoners and installed a former associate of Denard, Capt. Ayouba Combo, as leader of a Transitional Military Committee. The French Government denounced the coup and suspended economic aid to the Comoros, but initially refused to take military action, despite requests for assistance from the Comoran Prime Minister Mohamed Caabi El Yachroutu, who had taken refuge in the French embassy. In October Combo announced that he had transferred authority to Taki and the leader of CHUMA (Islands' Fraternity and Unity Party), Saïd Ali Kemal, (who had both welcomed the coup) as joint civilian Presidents, apparently in an attempt to avert military repercussions by the French Government. An alliance of opposition parties, however, rejected the new leadership and entered into negotiations with El Yachroutu. Following a further appeal for intervention from El Yachroutu, who invoked a defence co-operation agreement that had been established between the two countries in 1978, some 900 French military personnel landed on the Comoros and surrounded the mercenaries at Kandani. Shortly afterwards Denard and his associates, together with the disaffected members of the Comoran armed forces, surrendered to the French troops. (In October 1996, following his release from imprisonment in France in July, Denard claimed that the coup attempt had been planned at the request of several Comoran officials, including Taki. In mid-2006 Denard was given a suspended sentence of five years by a French court for his involvement in the coup. Denard died in France in October 2007.)

Following the French military intervention, El Yachroutu declared himself interim President, in accordance with the Constitution, and formed a Government of National Unity. Djohar (who had been transported to Réunion by the French in order to receive medical treatment) rejected El Yachroutu's assumption of power and announced the reappointment of Mohamed as Prime Minister. Later in October 1995 a National Reconciliation Conference decided that El Yachroutu would remain interim President, pending the forthcoming election, which was provisionally scheduled for early 1996. The incumbent administration opposed Djohar's stated intention to return to the Comoros and announced that measures would be taken to prevent him from entering the country. At the end of October 1995 El Yachroutu granted an amnesty to all Comorans involved in the coup attempt and appointed representatives of the UNDC and Udzima (which had supported the coup) to the new Council of Ministers. In November Djohar announced the formation of a rival government, headed by Mohamed. El Yachroutu, who was supported by the Comoran armed forces, refused to recognize the legitimacy of Djohar's appointments, while opposition parties equally opposed his return to power; only elements of the RDR continued to support Djohar's authority. There was also widespread speculation that the French Government had believed Djohar's authority to be untenable and had tacitly supported his removal from power. Political leaders on Mwali rejected the authority of both rival governments, urged a campaign of civil disobedience and established a 'citizens' committee' to govern the island; discontent with the central administration also emerged on Nzwani.

A presidential election took place in March 1996 in which Taki was elected to the presidency. He appointed a new Council of Ministers, which included five of the presidential candidates who had supported him in the second round of the election, and in April he dissolved the Assemblée fédérale. New Governors, all belonging to the UNDC, were appointed to each of the three islands. In August Taki issued a decree awarding himself absolute powers. This measure was widely criticized in the media and by opposition groups as being in violation of the Constitution.

In September 1996 Taki established a constitutional consultative committee, comprising 42 representatives of political parties and other organizations, which was to provide advice concerning the drafting of a new constitution. Also in that month the legislative elections were postponed until November. A national referendum to endorse a new draft Constitution was scheduled for 20 October. In order to comply with a constitutional proposal, which effectively restricted the number of political parties to a maximum of three, 24 pro-Taki political organizations merged to form one presidential party, the Rassemblement national pour le développement (RND). The new Constitution, which was approved by 85% of votes cast, vested legislative power in a unicameral parliament, the Assemblée fédérale, and extended the presidential term to six years, with an unrestricted number of consecutive mandates. Political parties were required to have two parliamentary deputies from each island (following legislative elections) to be considered legal; organizations that did not fulfil these stipulations were to be dissolved. Extensive executive powers were vested in the President, who was to appoint the Governors of the islands and who acquired the right to initiate constitutional amendments.

Following unsuccessful negotiations with the Government, the opposition parties (having formed a new alliance) refused to participate in the electoral process. Consequently, the legislative elections, which took place in two rounds in December 1996, were only contested by the RND and the Front national pour la justice (FNJ), a fundamentalist Islamist organization, together with 23 independent candidates (in apparent contravention of a stipulation in the new Constitution that only legally created political parties were entitled to participate in national elections). The RND secured 36 of the 43 seats in the expanded Assemblée fédérale, while the FNJ won three, with four seats taken by independent candidates. Taki nominated Ahmed Abdou, who had served in the administration of former President Ahmed Abdallah, as Prime Minister to head a new Council of Ministers.

The separatist movement

During early 1996 separatist leaders declared their intention to seek the restoration of French rule and in March established a 'political directorate' on Nzwani, chaired by Abdallah Ibrahim, the leader of the Mouvement populaire anjouanais, a grouping of separatist movements on Nzwani. (The relative prosperity of neighbouring Mayotte appeared to have prompted the demand for a return to French rule; it was reported that up to 200 illegal migrants a day attempted to enter Mayotte from Nzwani.) Military reinforcements were sent to Nzwani and the Governor of the island was replaced once again.

On 3 August 1997 the 'political directorate' unilaterally declared Nzwani's secession from the Comoros. The separatists subsequently elected Ibrahim as president of a 13-member 'politico-administrative co-ordination', which included Abdou Madi as spokesperson. France, while denouncing the secession, refused to mediate in the crisis and declared itself in favour of the intervention of the Organization of African Unity (OAU, now the African Union—AU, see p. 189), which dispatched a special envoy to the Comoros. Meanwhile, separatist agitation intensified on Mwali, culminating on 11 August, when secessionists declared Mwali's independence from the Comoros, appointed a president and a prime minister to head a 12-member government, and called for re-attachment to France.

As OAU mediation efforts proceeded, Taki dispatched some 300 troops to Nzwani in early September 1997 in an attempt forcibly to suppress the separatist insurrection. The Government claimed that the separatists had been aided by foreign elements and expressed regret at France's refusal to support the military operation. As it emerged that some 40 Comoran soldiers and 16 Nzwani residents had been killed in the fighting, with many more injured, demonstrators demanding Taki's resignation clashed violently with the security forces in Moroni. The separatists on Nzwani reaffirmed their independence and empowered Ibrahim to rule by decree. Taki subsequently declared a state of emergency, assumed absolute power and dismissed the Government of Ahmed Abdou and his military and civilian advisers. (Abdou had reportedly resigned from his position in late August, although this had not been announced publicly.) Shortly afterwards, Taki established a State

Transition Commission, which included representatives from Nzwani and Mwali. The reconciliation conference was postponed indefinitely by the OAU. The League of Arab States (Arab League, see p. 364) agreed to a request from Taki for assistance, and following talks with the OAU regarding the co-ordination of the mediation effort, all three islands hosted discussions in late September, which were convened by envoys from both organizations.

In September 1997 Ibrahim announced his decision to hold a referendum on self-determination for Nzwani on 26 October, prior to a reconciliation conference sponsored by both the OAU and the Arab League. Despite international opposition, the referendum was conducted as scheduled; according to separatist officials, 99.9% of the electorate voted in favour of independence for Nzwani. The following day Ibrahim dissolved the 'politico-administrative co-ordination' and appointed a temporary government, which was charged with preparing a constitution and organizing a presidential election. Taki responded by severing Nzwani's telephone lines and suspending air and maritime links. In November the OAU announced plans to deploy a force of military observers in the Comoros, despite the separatists' insistence that the force would not be allowed to land on Nzwani; an initial eight-member contingent, which arrived that month, was subsequently to be increased to 25 and was to receive logistical support from France.

In early December 1997 Taki formed a new Council of Ministers, appointing Nourdine Bourhane as Prime Minister. An inter-Comoran reconciliation conference was held later that month; some agreement was reached on proposals for the establishment of an international commission of inquiry to investigate September's military intervention and on the holding of a Comoran inter-island conference to discuss institutional reform. In January 1998 the OAU announced that both the Comoran Government and the Nzwani separatists had agreed to a number of conciliatory measures, including the restoration of air and maritime links and the release of federal soldiers still detained on Nzwani.

In July 1998, as social unrest on Nzwani escalated, a dispute over the future aims of the secessionist movement led to the dismissal of the island's government, provoking violent clashes between islanders loyal to Ibrahim, who favoured independence within the framework of an association of the Comoran islands, and supporters of the outgoing prime minister of the island, Chamassi Saïd Omar, who continued to advocate re-attachment to France. Meanwhile, as social and economic conditions deteriorated further, with salaries still unpaid and strike action ongoing, Taki sought overseas assistance in resolving the crisis. In August 1998 the Government provisionally suspended transport links with both Nzwani and Mayotte. France later refused the Government's request for a suspension of links between Mayotte and Nzwani, thus worsening the already fragile relations between the two countries.

On 6 November 1998 President Taki died unexpectedly, reportedly having suffered a heart attack, although several senior officials expressed serious doubts about the cause of death. Tadjidine Ben Saïd Massoundi, the President of the High Council of the Republic and a former Prime Minister, was designated acting President, in accordance with the Constitution, pending an election which would be held after 30–90 days. Massoundi immediately revoked the ban on the movement of people and goods to Nzwani and proceeded with the formation of a government. In January 1999 Massoundi extended his presidential mandate, which was soon to expire, pending a resolution of the crisis dividing the islands. Also in that month Ibrahim agreed to relinquish some of his powers to a five-member 'politico-administrative directorate', as meetings commenced between the rival separatist factions. No consensus was reached in the following months, however, and when Ibrahim replaced the directorate with a 'committee of national security' in March, the new administration was immediately rejected by rival leaders.

At an OAU-sponsored inter-island conference, held in Antananarivo, Madagascar, in April 1999, an agreement was reached that envisaged substantial autonomy for Nzwani and Mwali, the changing of the country's name to the Union of the Comoran Islands and the rotation of the presidency among the three islands. However, the delegates from Nzwani refused to sign the agreement, insisting on the need to consult the Nzwani population prior to a full endorsement. On 30 April the Chief of Staff of the Comoran armed forces, Col Assoumani Azali, seized power in a bloodless coup, deposing Massoundi and dissolving the Government, the Assemblée fédérale and all other constitutional institutions. Azali promulgated a new constitutional charter and proclaimed himself head of state and of government and Commander-in-Chief of the armed forces. Full legislative functions were also vested in Azali, who announced his intention to stay in power for one year only, during which time he pledged to oversee the creation of the new institutions envisaged in the Antananarivo accord. The appointment of a State Committee (composed of six members from Ngazidja, four from Mwali and two from Nzwani) was followed by that of a State Council, which was to supervise the activities of the State Committee and comprised eight civilians and 11 army officers. The coup was condemned by the OAU; the UN, however, sent representatives to Azali's inauguration.

In June 1999 Lt-Col Saïd Abeid Abdérémane, who had previously held the role of 'national mediator' on Nzwani, formed a government of national unity on the island and assumed the role of 'national co-ordinator'. In July delegates from the three islands, including Azali and Abeid, met on Mwali for talks aimed at resolving the political crisis. The negotiations represented the most senior-level contact between the islands since the secessions of August 1997.

In December 1999 the OAU threatened to impose sanctions on Nzwani should its leaders not have signed the peace accord by 1 February 2000. In response, Abeid announced that a referendum would be held on Nzwani in January 2000 regarding the signing of the Antananarivo accord. According to the separatist authorities of Nzwani, the results of the referendum revealed an overwhelming majority (94.5%) in favour of full independence for the island; the OAU, however, announced that it did not recognize the outcome of the ballot, following allegations of intimidation and repression of those in favour of reconciliation. Meanwhile, following a series of meetings between Azali and a number of political parties from all three islands regarding the establishment of a more representative and decentralized government in Moroni, the State Committee underwent an extensive reorganization in December 1999, including the appointment of a Prime Minister, Bianrifi Tarmidi (from Mwali).

In February 2000, as threatened, the OAU imposed economic sanctions on Nzwani; the overseas assets of the separatist leaders were frozen and they themselves were confined to the island. Furthermore, as part of the OAU sanctions, the federal Government suspended sea and air transport links, as well as telephone communications, with Nzwani. In May the OAU announced that the lifting of sanctions against Nzwanian separatists was dependent on a return to constitutional order on the Comoros; it advocated the restoration of the October 1996 Constitution and the reinstatement of Massoundi as Head of State, as well as the appointment of an interim government and Prime Minister. The possibility of armed intervention on Nzwani was rejected at an OAU summit, held in July, although it was agreed to establish a total maritime blockade of the island.

Towards a new constitution

In August 2000 an agreement, known as the Fomboni Accord, was reached by Azali and Abeid following negotiations on Mwali. The agreement provided for the establishment of a new Comoran entity and granted the three islands considerable control over internal matters. A new constitution was to be drafted and approved, by referendum, within 12 months. Moreover, Abeid and Azali appealed for the sanctions imposed on Nzwani to be lifted. The declaration was rejected by the OAU, however, on the grounds that it contravened the Antananarivo accord and threatened the integrity of the Comoros. Nevertheless, a tripartite commission, comprising delegates from Ngazidja, Nzwani and Mwali, was established to define the terms of the new constitution. In November Bianrifi Tarmidi was replaced as Prime Minister by Hamada Madi 'Boléro', who subsequently formed a new Government. Despite attempts to include them in the new Government and the tripartite commission, opposition members refused to participate, instead presenting to international mediators their own proposals for a resolution to the crisis.

With the mediation of the OAU and the Organisation internationale de la francophonie (OIF), negotiations between opposition and government members continued throughout late 2000 and early 2001. In February the Framework Agreement for Reconciliation in the Comoros was signed in Fomboni by representatives of the Comoran Government, the Nzwani administration, opposition parties and civil society. The OAU, the OIF and the European Union (EU, see p. 276) were to be guarantors of the peace accord, which provided for the establishment of a new Comoran entity. Under the provisions of the agreement, an independent tripartite commission (comprising equal numbers of delegates from each of the islands, representing all the signatory groups) was to draft a new constitution, which would be subject to approval in a national referendum. The new constitution was to define the areas of jurisdiction of the new entity and the individual islands, although the central administration would retain control over religion, nationality, currency, foreign affairs and defence. An independent national electoral commission was also to be created. Following the constitutional referendum, a transitional government of national union was to be formed and charged with creating the new institutions by 31 December. However, in March, following disagreements over the composition of a follow-up committee intended to monitor the implementation of the Fomboni Accord, the opposition withdrew from the reconciliation process. Despite this, the OAU suspended sanctions against Nzwani in May.

On 8–9 August 2001 a bloodless military coup on Nzwani resulted in the removal from power of Abeid, who was replaced by a collective presidency, comprising Maj. Mohamed Bacar, Maj. Hassane Ali Toihili and Maj. Charif Halidi; a government of eight civilian commissioners (none of whom had been members of the previous administration) was appointed. The new leadership stated its commitment to the Fomboni Accord. However, on 24 September a further bloodless military coup was instigated by the deputy head of the Comoran army and close ally of Col Azali, Maj. Ayouba Combo. Although Combo was initially declared leader of the army, and Ahmed Aboubakar Foundi was installed as leader of Nzwani, they were captured the following day, before subsequently escaping the island. In November Abeid attempted unsuccessfully to regain control of Nzwani, but was defeated by forces loyal to Bacar and fled the island; the attempted coup was strongly condemned by the Government, which reaffirmed its support for the island's authorities.

At the constitutional referendum, which took place on 23 December 2001, 76.4% of the electorate voted in favour of the proposed new constitution. The country, which was to change its name to the Union of the Comoros, was to be led by the President of the Union, at the head of a Council of the Union, and governed by a legislative assembly, the Assemblée de l'Union. The position of President was to rotate between the islands, while the Vice-Presidents, who were also members of the Council of the Union, were to be inhabitants of the two remaining islands; the first President was to come from Ngazidja. Each of the three islands was to become financially autonomous and was to be ruled by its own local government and institutions. The Union was to be responsible for matters of religion, nationality, currency, foreign affairs and external defence, while shared responsibilities between the Union and the islands were to be determined at a later date. A transitional government was to be established to monitor the installation of the new institutions.

In January 2002 a transitional Government of National Unity (GNU) was installed, with 'Boléro' reappointed as Prime Minister; the new administration included members of the former Government, opposition representatives and two of Nzwani's separatist leaders. However, on the following day the GNU collapsed, after the withdrawal of the opposition representatives, as a result of a disagreement over the allocation of ministerial portfolios. Meanwhile, Col Azali resigned as Head of State and announced his intention to stand as an independent candidate in the forthcoming presidential election; 'Boléro' was to serve as acting President. In February the GNU was re-established.

Azali elected Federal President

In March and April 2002 voters on Nzwani, Mwali and Ngazidja approved new local Constitutions. In a first round of voting in the federal presidential election on 17 March, contested by nine candidates, Col Azali secured 39.8% of the vote. Mahamoud Mradabi won 15.7% and Saïd Ali Kemal 10.7%; however, both Mradabi and Kemal boycotted the second round. Consequently, on 14 April Col Azali was elected unopposed as Federal President of the Union of the Comoros, reportedly securing more than 75% of the votes cast. Although the result was declared invalid by the electoral commission, on the grounds that the election had not been free and fair, following the dissolution of the electoral commission and the appointment of an independent electoral body, Col Azali was declared Federal President. Meanwhile, in late March and early April, Maj. Mohamed Bacar and Mohamed Saïd Fazul were elected as regional Presidents of Nzwani and Mwali, respectively; on 19 May Abdou Soulé Elbak was elected regional President of Ngazidja. The regional Presidents subsequently formed local Governments. Col Azali appointed a new federal Government in early June.

In August 2003, at an AU-sponsored meeting in Pretoria, South Africa, representatives of the federal and island governments signed a memorandum, according to which the federal Government would retain control of the army, but the administration of the police force would be devolved to the island Governments. Agreement was also reached that, during a transitional period leading to legislative elections, the customs services would be managed by a joint board, with taxes shared between the federal and island administrations. In December, following further mediation by the AU, the agreement reached in August was ratified by Azali and the three island Presidents at a ceremony in Moroni. A follow-up committee was appointed to monitor the implementation of the accord.

Elections to the three island assemblies were held on 14 and 21 March 2004. Pro-Azali candidates won an overall total of only 12 seats in the assemblies, while candidates allied to Elbak secured 14 of the 20 seats in the Ngazidja assembly, supporters of Bacar were reported to have won 19 of the 25 seats available on Nzwani, and nine allies of Fazul were elected to the 10-member assembly on Mwali. Elections to the Assemblée de l'Union took place on 18 and 25 April. According to final results, declared on 28 April, Azali's party, the Convention pour le renouveau des Comores (CRC) won only six of the 18 directly elected seats, while a loose coalition supporting the three island Presidents secured 11 seats and CHUMA took one seat. The rate of participation by eligible voters at the second round was 68.5%. The remaining 15 seats in the 33-member federal assembly were taken by five nominees from each of the island legislatures. The inauguration of the Assemblée, at which Saïd Dhiuffur Bounou was elected Speaker, took place on 4 June. In mid-July President Azali announced his new ministerial team, granting responsibility for co-ordinating Union affairs on their home islands to the two Vice-Presidents. The new cabinet comprised the two Vice-Presidents, seven ministers of state and two secretaries of state, and included a member of CHUMA, and representatives nominated by the island Presidents of Nzwani and Mwali. President Bacar declined to participate in the creation of the Government.

Despite the submission of draft legislation in April 2005 that would have permitted President Azali to stand for a second term as President of the Union, in June the Assemblée de l'Union officially approved a rotating presidency among the three islands, thus ensuring that the next President of the Union would be from Nzwani. In October the Assemblée de l'Union approved legislation granting Comorans living abroad the right to vote. It was estimated that some 200,000 Comorans were resident in France. In early 2006 the Commission nationale des élections aux Comores announced that the presidential elections would be held on 14 May.

The 2006 presidential elections were the first in which the principle of the office rotating between alternating islands of the Union was enacted. In the first round of the elections, held on 16 April 2006, three of the 13 candidates from the island of Nzwani received sufficient votes cast to proceed to the nationwide second ballot; this took place on 14 May and resulted in Ahmed Abdallah Sambi, a businessman and the founder of the Islamist FNJ, securing 99,112 (58.0%) of the votes cast. The elections were observed to have been free, fair and credible by international monitors. The former Prime Minister, Ibrahim Halidi, was placed second with 48,378 (28.3%) of the votes, while Mohammad Djaanfari received 23,322 votes (13.7%). Sambi officially assumed the presidency on 26 May and a new Government was appointed within three days, considerably reduced in size, and consisting of two Vice-Presidents and six ministers. Notably, the defence portfolio was allocated to the President's office and the army was to be re-unified under single command. National troops were confined to barracks for the duration of the elections and the AU contributed over 400 troops to ensure the first peaceful transition of power since independence.

The new Government was swift to pursue corruption charges against former officials, to recommence the payment of salaries to civil servants (which had been suspended from the beginning of the year), and to reduce the price of rice—a staple food. Economic issues were paramount on the agenda of the new administration. However, conflicts over the competencies of the Union and island Governments persisted, with negotiations over legislation on the division of powers regarding justice, internal security and management of state companies (including ports and airports) reaching stalemate in early December 2006. Later in that month President Sambi flew to Nzwani with the aim of installing a regional branch of the Armée nationale de développement (AND) and ensuring its representation at the island's port and airport. However, he was obstructed in the latter goal by the island Government's own armed forces. Negotiations resumed in early 2007, following international mediation.

In March 2007 President Sambi carried out a reorganization of the Government and created four new portfolios, increasing the number of ministers to 12. Most notably, Mohamed Ali Solihi was appointed Minister of Finance, Budget and Planning, while the newly created departments included the Ministry of Energy, headed by Houmadi Abdallah, and the Ministry of Islamic Affairs, Human Rights and Information.

Instability on Nzwani

The period prior to the island presidential elections in mid-2007 was marred by violence and allegations of corruption and intimidation. Elections took place on Ngazidja and Mwali on 10 June as scheduled, while the election on Nzwani was postponed until 17 June at the request of President Sambi and the AU. However, Bacar proceeded to hold the election despite its rescheduling and subsequently claimed victory with 73.2% of the vote, declaring himself President of Nzwani for a second term. Both the AU and the Union Government announced that the election was null and void. While unrest continued on Nzwani, a second round of voting took place on Ngazidja and Mwali on 25 June. Mohamed Abdouloihabi was elected to the presidency on Ngazidja and Mohamed Ali Said secured victory on Mwali in what were largely deemed to be free and fair elections. Meanwhile, a meeting between President Sambi and the AU was convened on 24 June in an attempt to resolve the issue on Nzwani; a statement was subsequently released demanding that a new election be held on the island.

The impasse persisted, however, and in October 2007 the AU imposed sanctions on Nzwani, including restrictions on the movements of the self-proclaimed President and his supporters and the freezing of their assets. These attempts to regain control of the island and restore peace failed and Bacar dismissed threats of military force. The Union Government conceded that a military intervention by the AND would be unlikely to succeed given the limited strength of the Union's armed forces compared to the contingent of armed militia on Nzwani.

Following the failure of further negotiations aimed at breaking the deadlock, in mid-February 2008 the AU Peace and Security Council mandated the deployment of a Mission d'assistance électorale et sécuritaire (MAES) to 'facilitate the restoration of the authority of the Union' on Nzwani by use of military force. The MAES was to comprise some 1,500 members, including troops from Senegal, Sudan and Tanzania, as well as logistical support staff from Libya, and represented the first occasion that the AU had approved military intervention to enforce peace in a member country. On 25 March some 450 Sudanese, Tanzanian and Comoran troops landed on Nzwani and succeeded in regaining control of the island. The following day President Sambi announced that Union Vice-President Ikililou Dhoinine had been appointed interim President of Nzwani, pending the formation of a transitional regional government, and confirmed that the presidential election on the island would be re-held within two months. On 31 March Laili Zamane Abdou, hitherto President of the Nzwani Court of Appeal, was sworn in as interim President. In the mean time, Bacar was reported to have fled Nzwani, initially taking refuge on Mayotte from where the Comoran authorities immediately sought his extradition; however, on 28 March Bacar was transported by the French military to Réunion where he was, according to French officials, to be investigated for landing illegally on Mayotte in possession of weapons. Initially that charge was dismissed, although Bacar and 22 of his supporters remained in custody on Réunion, and in June the Réunion Cour d'Appel sentenced Bacar to a three-month suspended prison term for importing weapons. Bacar's application for political asylum in France had been rejected in May, but that country also ruled that he could not be sent back to the Comoros. In July the Beninois Government agreed to a request by the French authorities that Bacar be transported to Benin, where in early 2012 he remained in exile.

Meanwhile, in June 2008 presidential elections were held in Nzwani to establish a permanent replacement for Bacar. Five candidates contested the first round on 15 June, including Djaanfari, who had unsuccessfully challenged for the Union presidency in May 2006, and Moussa Toybou, a former minister under Djohar. Toybou and Djaanfari won 42.5% and 42.3% of the votes, respectively, and contested a second round of voting on 29 June, at which Toybou secured 52.4% of the votes cast. Local and international monitors declared the elections to have been free and fair.

In July 2008 President Sambi announced a reorganization of the Union Government: Anissi Chamsidine was appointed Minister for Agriculture, Fisheries and the Environment, replacing Siti Kassim, who became Secretary of State at the Vice-Presidency, with responsibility for Solidarity and the Promotion of Gender. A total of five new ministers were appointed, including Mohamed Larif Oukacha as Minister of Territorial Management, Infrastructure, Urban Planning and Housing. In December further governmental changes were made and the number of ministries was reduced from 15 to 10. The reduction in cabinet posts was a condition imposed by the IMF mission as part of the Emergency Post-conflict Assistance Programme.

In mid-April 2009 Sambi declared that a constitutional referendum was to be held on 17 May, the aim of which was to 'harmonize' the Comoran Constitution: Sambi's term of office was to be extended by one year, the mandates of the Ngazidja and Mwali Presidents were to be reduced by one year and that of the President of Nzwani by two years. Although Sambi had declared that opposition parties were free to campaign against the plan, the security forces prevented the holding of an opposition rally in Moroni and arrested a number of protesters. Despite a low rate of participation in the referendum, which opposition parties claimed to be a consequence of their call to boycott the vote, the right to reduce the size of the Government and the powers of the three autonomous island Presidents by restyling them as Governors was approved by 92.3% of those who voted, according to official figures. These stated that the rate of voter participation was 44.8%; however, opposition estimates claimed that less than 20% of the electorate voted. In a joint declaration at the end of May, a coalition of 20 opposition parties announced that they would present single candidates in each constituency in the legislative elections scheduled for 2 August, in order to increase the chances of defeating Sambi's Mouvance présidentielle. In late July Sambi effected a minor reorganization of the Union Government.

The legislative elections were postponed until 29 November 2009 and were subsequently delayed by a further week. The first round of voting took place on 6 December, with a second round held on 20 December. Of the 33 seats available in the Assemblée de l'Union, 24 were to be decided by direct universal suffrage, while the remaining nine were to be allocated by the island assemblies at a rate of three per island. On 12 November the Constitutional Court had rejected the candidature of former Prime Minister, Ibrahim Halidi, due to his failure to produce his police record, and on 17 November the leader of the opposition party, the Rassemblement pour une initiative de développement avec une jeunesse avertie (RIDJA), was arrested and put on trial for 'insulting the head of state' at a political meeting. Results of the first round of voting were announced on 13 December: the Mouvance présidentielle secured three seats but no seats were won by opposition parties. In the second round the Mouvance présidentielle took a further 14 seats, while three seats were won by allies of the President and four by opposition candidates.

Recent developments: the 2010 presidential and gubernatorial elections

Under the rotating presidential system, Sambi (from Nzwani) was to hand over power to a leader from Mwali upon the expiry of his term on 26 May 2010. However, legislation approved on 1 March by the Assemblée de l'Union provided for the postponement of the presidential election until November 2011, thus effectively extending Sambi's tenure by 18 months and depriving Mwali of its turn to hold the presidency. The opposition denounced such a major reform being passed without consultation and protests took place in the town of Fomboni, the administrative centre of Mwali, where army reinforcements had been put in place under orders to disperse any public gathering. Libyan troops were also dispatched to bolster local forces, and several people were arrested, accused of pouring sand onto the landing strip of the island's airport to prevent the landing of a Qatari delegation making an official visit. On 8 May 2010 the Constitutional Court ruled the extension of Sambi's presidential mandate as illegal; however, on 25 May, the eve of the formal expiration of his mandate, Sambi announced the appointment of an interim administration, prompting only days later the formation of a national Union Government-in-exile in France with the stated aim of expediting Sambi's deposition. In mid-June Sambi announced a further reorganization and tasked the new Government with the planning of fresh Union elections within six months. Presidential and gubernatorial elections were subsequently scheduled to take place on 7 November, with a second round due to be held on 26 December.

Meanwhile, there were conflicting reports concerning events relating to the Comoran army; a state-owned newspaper reported that an internal disagreement had been officially ended in the presence of Sambi with the signing of a reconciliation accord between Chief of General Staff Gen. Salimou Mohamed Amiri and head of the military cabinet in the Office of the President Col Ahmed Abdoulbastoi, while a number of French media outlets claimed that the President had dismissed Gen. Amiri, and the recently appointed Minister of Defence, the Interior and Information, Mohamed Bacar, to end the feuding. In June 2010 Lt-Col Ayouba Combo, Chief of Staff of the Comoran Defence Force and one of the army's most senior officers, was assassinated outside his home; Gen. Amiri was subsequently arrested in connection with the incident (he was replaced as Chief of General Staff by Lt-Col Abdallah Gamil Solihi). In April 2011 charges of rebellion held against Gen. Amiri were dropped, although accusations of his complicity in Combo's murder were upheld and he remained under house arrest.

A total of 10 candidates contested the first round of the presidential election, which was held as scheduled on 7 November 2010. According to results confirmed by the Constitutional Court on 13 November, Dhoinine, the Union Vice-President with responsibility for Land Settlement, Infrastructure, Town Planning and Housing, secured 28.2% of the votes cast, while Mohamed Saïd Fazul and Dr Abdou Djabir took 22.9% and 9.9% of the votes, respectively. The three candidates contested a run-off on 26 December at which Dhoinine was returned the victor having won 60.9% of the votes cast. The rate of voter participation was recorded by the Commission électorale nationale indépendante at 52.8%. Gubernatorial polls held concurrently with the presidential ballots resulted in the re-election of Ali Said to the governorship of Mwali, while Anissi Chamsidine and Mouigni Baraka Saïd Soilih became Governors of Nzwani and Ngazidja, respectively.

On 13 January 2011 the Constitutional Court confirmed the election of Dhoinine (and those of the three island Governors). On 26 May Dhoinine was officially inugurated as President—the country's first Head of State from the island of Mwali. On 31 May Dhoinine's 10-member Government was announced, including seven new ministers, six of whom had never before held office. A shortage of petroleum products and a government decision to increase massively the market price of the commodity led to social unrest in September. The protests, which were supported by the political opposition, employers' and consumer associations and trade unions, culminated in the shutting down of all businesses and transport services in Moroni for two days at the beginning of October. The Government responded promptly by setting up a commission to consider a new price structure for petroleum products and by dismissing the Director-General of the Société Comorienne des Hydrocarbures.

Foreign Affairs

Diplomatic relations between the Comoros and France, suspended in December 1975, were restored in July 1978; in November of that year the two countries signed agreements on military and economic co-operation, apparently deferring any decision on the future of Mayotte. In subsequent years, however, member countries of the UN General Assembly repeatedly voted in favour of a resolution affirming the Comoros' sovereignty over Mayotte, with only France dissenting. In November 2008 the Comoran authorities objected strongly to the announcement by the French Government that it intended to hold a referendum over the future status of Mayotte. At the referendum, which was held on 29 March 2009, 95.2% of voters approved of Mayotte attaining the status of an Overseas Department within the French Republic (in contradiction to the AU's and the Comoran Government's recognition of the island as an inseparable part of the Comoran state). Some 61% of those eligible to vote cast their ballots. The Comoran Government denounced the referendum and declared it 'null, void and without effect'. None the less, on 31 March 2011 Mayotte was officially granted departmental status.

Relations between the Comoros and France had significantly worsened following Bacar's removal as President of Nzwani in March 2008 (see above). Many Comorans believed that the French Government had helped Bacar to escape from Nzwani, leading to widespread anti-French sentiment and the staging of demonstrations outside the French embassy in Moroni. Nevertheless, the French Government played an important role in securing the IMF's allocation of US $5.1m. to the Comoros, in a combination of its Exogenous Shocks Facility and Emergency Post-conflict Assistance Programme, which was approved in December.

Following Djohar's accession to power, diplomatic relations were established with the USA in June 1990. In September 1993 the Comoros' application was accepted and it became a member of the Arab League. In mid-1999, following the military coup headed by Col Azali, France and the USA suspended all military co-operation with the Comoros; France resumed military co-operation in September 2002. In September 2004 the USA claimed that the Comoros was harbouring members of a militant Islamist group, Al Haramain. In mid-2004 a joint commission with Sudan was created, and in early 2005 the Franco-Comoran commission resumed, after a hiatus of 10 years. In November 2006 a framework partnership agreement was signed by the French Minister-Delegate for Co-operation, Development and La Francophonie, allocating a grant of €88m. to the Union for 2006–10. Following the accession of President Sambi, relations with and funding from Iran increased significantly, owing to the Comoran Head of State's personal historical connections with that country.

CONSTITUTION AND GOVERNMENT

Under the Constitution of 23 December 2001 (and as amended on 23 May 2009), each of the islands in the Union of the Comoros is headed by a local government and is partially autonomous. The Head of State of the Union of the Comoros is the President, who appoints the members of the Government and heads the Council of the Union, which also includes the Vice-Presidents. The President is elected for a five-year term, and the position of President rotates between the islands, while the Vice-Presidents are inhabitants of the two remaining islands. The President appoints the members of the Government (ministers of the Union) and determines their respective portfolios. The composition of the Government must represent all of the islands equally. Federal legislative power is vested in the Assemblée de l'Union, which serves a five-year term and is composed of 33 deputies, 24 of whom are directly elected, with the remaining 9 seats divided equally among representatives of the three islands. Each island also elects its own legislative local assembly and Governor.

REGIONAL AND INTERNATIONAL CO-OPERATION

In 1985 the Comoros joined the Indian Ocean Commission (IOC, see p. 450). The country is also a member of the Common Market for Eastern and Southern Africa (COMESA, see p. 237), of the Franc Zone (see p. 332) and the African Union (see p. 189).

The Comoros became a member of the UN in 1975, and a Working Party was established in 2007 to examine the country's application to join the World Trade Organization (WTO, see p. 433).

ECONOMIC AFFAIRS

In 2010, according to estimates from the World Bank, the gross national income (GNI) of the Comoros (excluding Mayotte), measured at average 2008–10 prices, was US $550m., equivalent to $750 per head (or $1,080 per head on an international purchasing-power parity basis). During 2001–10, it was estimated, the population increased at an average annual rate of 2.7%, while gross domestic product (GDP) per head decreased, in real terms, by an average of 0.8% per year. Overall GDP grew, in real terms, at an average annual rate of 1.9% in 2001–10; it increased by 2.1% in 2010.

Agriculture (including hunting, forestry and fishing) contributed an estimated 42.9% of GDP in 2010, according to the African Development Bank (AfDB). Approximately 68.6% of the labour force, according to FAO estimates, were employed in the agricultural sector in mid-2012. In 2004 the sector accounted for some 98% of export earnings. The principal cash crops are vanilla, ylang ylang and cloves. In 2009 export earnings for vanilla totalled 726m. Comoros francs, a significant decline from the early 2000s. The Comoros produces an estimated 80% of the ylang ylang consumed globally. Cassava, taro, rice, maize, pulses, coconuts and bananas are also cultivated. In late 2005 an agreement on fishing rights in Comoran waters, which would extend until 2010, was reached with the European Union (EU). The agreement was renewed for a further three years in late 2010. (Moroni was selected to host a new Indian Ocean Commission Centre for Fishing Surveillance, largely funded by the EU.) According to the World Bank, the real GDP of the agricultural sector increased at an average annual rate of 1.7% in 2001–09; agricultural GDP grew by 4.5% in 2009.

According to the AfDB, industry (including manufacturing, construction and power) contributed an estimated 10.5% of GDP in 2010. Some 9.4% of the labour force were employed in the industrial sector in 1990. According to the World Bank, the Comoros' industrial GDP increased at an average annual rate of 3.1% in 2001–09; industrial GDP grew by 4.4% in 2009.

The manufacturing sector contributed an estimated 3.7% of GDP in 2010, according to the AfDB. The sector consists primarily of the processing of agricultural produce, particularly of vanilla and essential oils. Manufacturing GDP increased at an average annual rate of 1.8% in 2001–09, according to the World Bank; manufacturing GDP expanded by 3.8% in 2009.

The construction sector contributed an estimated 5.4% of GDP in 2010, according to estimates by the AfDB. According to the AfDB, the sector's GDP increased by 1.8% in 2010.

Electrical energy is derived from wood (some 80%) and from thermal installations. Imports of petroleum products comprised only 0.1% of the total cost of imports in 2009 and approximately 54m. kWh of electricity were produced in the Comoros in 2008.

The services sector contributed an estimated 46.6% of GDP in 2010, according to the AfDB. Strong growth in tourism from 1991 led to a significant expansion in trade, restaurant and hotel activities, although political instability inhibited subsequent growth and there remained much potential for development. In 2007 a new facility at Moroni airport was completed; the project was financed by the Government of the People's Republic of China and was expected to precipitate a three-fold increase in annual passenger turnover. However, in 2009 Comoro Islands Airline closed its operations after only five months, and although Air Mohéli International made its first flight in July 2011 it failed to comply with government regulations and by September it also was no longer flying. According to the World Bank, the GDP of the services sector increased at an average rate of 3.8% per year in 2000–06. It grew by 14.5% in 2006.

In 2009 the Comoros recorded an estimated trade deficit of 54,427m. Comoros francs and there was a deficit of 18,411m. Comoros francs on the current account of the balance of payments. In 2008, according to the AfDB, the principal source of imports was the United Arab Emirates (accounting for some 12.2% of the total); the other major sources were France, China and Pakistan. France was the principal market for exports (14.3%) in that year; the other major purchaser was Turkey. The leading exports in 2009 were cloves and vanilla. The principal imports in that year were iron and steel, rice, and meat and meat products.

The Comoran budget registered an estimated surplus of 8,701m. Comoros francs in 2010, equivalent to 4.5% of GDP. The Comoros' general government gross debt was 104,296m. Comoros francs in 2010, equivalent to 51.8% of GDP. The Comoros' external public debt at the end of 2009 totalled US $279m., of which $264m. was public and publicly guaranteed debt. The annual rate of inflation averaged 4.2% during 2000–09. In 2009 consumer prices rose by 4.6%. According to the IMF, an estimated 13.3% of the labour force were unemployed in 2005.

The Comoros has a relatively undeveloped economy, with high unemployment, a limited transport system, a severe shortage of natural resources and heavy dependence on foreign aid. Although membership of the Franc Zone was credited with maintaining relatively low levels of inflation and fiscal deficit, the large public wage bill (the cost of maintaining the complex political system within the islands was estimated at 80% of GDP) and weak institutional capacity inhibited fiscal progress and the financial conditions were discouraging to private sector investment. In 2009, in an attempt to improve the performance of the Comoran economy, President Sambi implemented a number of structural reforms requested by the IMF and constitutional changes aimed at reducing annual government expenditure by 15%. In 2010 the IMF praised the largely encouraging macroeconomic measures that had resulted in a rise in the rate of GDP growth, from 1.0% in 2008 to 1.8% in 2009. However, 2011 proved to be a testing year for private investment in the state enterprises. A contract issued by governmental decree in January to a private British-based telecommunications firm encountered resistance from employees in the state-owned telecommunications company Comores Télécom (Comtel), who refused to allow access to documents and equipment. Likewise, Société d'Electricité d'Anjouan was in conflict with its Belgian private partner, Semlex. A contract for the management of Moroni Port was open to tender in 2011, and despite the dock workers' trade union favouring the generous bid of a family-owned Tanzanian company, the Government granted the contract to a French company in partnership with a multinational. Also in 2011, India granted the Comoros a loan of US $41.6m. to construct a number of power stations, rehabilitate the electricity distribution network and supply technicians, while the AfDB pledged a further €13.4m. to increase the electrification of the islands from 35% to 60%. The end-of-year IMF review was optimistic and projected economic growth above 2% for 2011; at the same time, however, the IMF called for a redoubling of efforts to restructure public utilities and for greater reform in the telecommunications sector.

PUBLIC HOLIDAYS

2013: 1 January (New Year's Day), 24 January* (Mouloud, Birth of the Prophet), 1 May (International Labour Day), 6 June* (Leilat al-Meiraj, Ascension of the Prophet), 6 July (Independence Day), 8 August* (Id al-Fitr, end of Ramadan), 15 October* (Id al-Adha, Feast of the Sacrifice), 4 November (Muharram, Islamic New Year), 13 November (Ashoura), 27 November (Anniversary of President Abdallah's assassination).

* These holidays are dependent on the Islamic lunar calendar and may differ by one or two days from the dates given.

Statistical Survey

Sources (unless otherwise stated): *Rapport Annuel*, Banque Centrale des Comores, place de France, BP 405, Moroni; tel. 7731814; fax 7730349; e-mail bancecom@comorestelecom.km; internet www.bancecom.com.

Note: Unless otherwise indicated, figures in this Statistical Survey exclude data for Mayotte.

AREA AND POPULATION

Area: 1,862 sq km (719 sq miles). *By Island*: Ngazidja (Grande-Comore) 1,146 sq km, Nzwani (Anjouan) 424 sq km, Mwali (Mohéli) 290 sq km.

Population: 446,817, at census of 15 September 1991; 575,660, at census of 1 September 2003. *Mid-2012* (UN estimate): 773,346 (Source: UN, *World Population Prospects: The 2010 Revision*). *By Island* (1991 census): Ngazidja (Grande-Comore) 233,533; Nzwani (Anjouan) 188,953; Mwali (Mohéli) 24,331.

Density (at mid-2012): 415.3 per sq km.

Population by Age and Sex (UN estimates at mid-2012): *0–14:* 329,501 (males 167,797, females 161,704); *15–64:* 423,200 (males 212,546, females 210,654); *65 and over:* 20,645 (males 9,275, females 11,370); *Total* 773,346 (males 389,618, females 383,728) (Source: UN, *World Population Prospects: The 2010 Revision*).

Principal Towns (incl. suburbs, mid-2009, UN estimate): Moroni (capital) 48,629. Source: UN, *World Urbanization Prospects: The 2009 Revision*.

Births and Deaths (incl. figures for Mayotte, UN estimates, 2005–10): Average annual birth rate 39.0 per 1,000; average annual death rate 9.4 per 1,000. Source: UN, *World Population Prospects: The 2010 Revision*.

Life Expectancy (years at birth, including Mayotte, WHO estimates): 60 (males 58; females 62) in 2009. Source: WHO, *World Health Statistics*.

Economically Active Population (ILO estimates, '000 persons at mid-1980, including figures for Mayotte): Agriculture, forestry and fishing 150; Industry 10; Services 20; Total 181 (males 104, females 77) (Source: ILO, *Economically Active Population Estimates and Projections, 1950–2025*). *1991 Census* (persons aged 12 years and over, excluding Mayotte): Total labour force 126,510 (males 88,034, females 38,476) (Source: UN, *Demographic Yearbook*). *Mid-2012* (official estimates in '000): Agriculture, etc. 234; Total labour force 341 (Source: FAO).

HEALTH AND WELFARE

Key Indicators

Total Fertility Rate (children per woman, 2009): 3.9.

Under-5 Mortality Rate (per 1,000 live births, 2009): 104.

HIV/AIDS (% of persons aged 15–49, 2009): 0.1.

Physicians (per 1,000 head, 2004): 0.15.

Hospital Beds (per 1,000 head, 2006): 1.70.

Health Expenditure (2008): US $ per head (PPP): 39.

Health Expenditure (2008): % of GDP: 3.5.

Health Expenditure (2008): public (% of total): 60.4.

Access to Water (% of persons, 2008): 95.

Access to Sanitation (% of persons, 2008): 36.

Total Carbon Dioxide Emissions ('000 metric tons, 2007): 120.9.

Carbon Dioxide Emissions Per Head (metric tons, 2007): 0.2.

Human Development Index (2011): ranking: 163.

Human Development Index (2011): value: 0.433.

For sources and definitions, see explanatory note on p. vi.

AGRICULTURE, ETC.

Principal Crops ('000 metric tons, unless otherwise indicated, 2010, FAO estimates): Rice, paddy 19.4; Maize 6.4; Potatoes 0.8; Sweet potatoes 5.4; Cassava (Manioc) 57.0; Taro 10.6; Yams 4.2; Pulses 17.4; Groundnuts, with shell 1.0; Coconuts 88.2; Tomatoes 0.7; Bananas 44.4; Vanilla (dried, metric tons) 66; Cloves 2.8. *Aggregate Production* ('000 metric tons, may include official, semi-official or estimated data): Total vegetables (incl. melons) 6.0; Total fruits (excl. melons) 47.8.

Livestock ('000 head, year ending September 2010, FAO estimates): Asses 5.0; Cattle 50.0; Sheep 23.0; Goats 118.0; Chickens 520.

Livestock Products (metric tons, 2010, FAO estimates): Cattle meat 1,243; Sheep and goat meat 469; Chicken meat 536; Cows' milk 5,200; Hen eggs 784.

Fishing ('000 metric tons, live weight, 2009, FAO estimates): Total catch 20.5 (Sardinellas 1.2; Anchovies, etc. 1.1; Seerfishes 0.8; Skipjack tuna 4.5; Yellowfin tuna 8.0; Carangids 0.7; Indian mackerels 0.3).

Source: FAO.

INDUSTRY

Electric Energy (million kWh): 51.0 in 2006; 53.0 in 2007; 54.0 in 2008 (Source: UN Industrial Commodity Statistics Database).

FINANCE

Currency and Exchange Rates: 100 centimes = 1 Comoros franc. *Sterling, Dollar and Euro Equivalents* (30 December 2011): £1 sterling = 587.860 Comoros francs; US $1 = 380.221 Comoros francs; €1 = 491.968 Comoros francs; 1,000 Comoros francs = £1.70 = $2.63 = €2.03. *Average Exchange Rate* (Comoros francs per US $): 354.140 in 2009; 371.458 in 2010; 353.900 in 2011. Note: The Comoros franc was introduced in 1981, replacing (at par) the CFA franc. The fixed link to French currency was retained, with the exchange rate set at 1 French franc = 50 Comoros francs. This remained in effect until January 1994, when the Comoros franc was devalued by 33.3%, with the exchange rate adjusted to 1 French franc = 75 Comoros francs. This relationship to French currency remained in effect with the introduction of the euro on 1 January 1999. From that date, accordingly, a fixed exchange rate of €1 = 491.968 Comoros francs has been in operation.

Budget (million Comoros francs, 2009): *Revenue:* Tax revenue 21,089; Non-tax revenue 5,313; Total 26,402 (excluding grants received 18,374). *Expenditure:* Current expenditure 35,971 (Wages and salaries 16,932); Capital expenditure 8,939; Total 44,910. *2010:* Total revenues (incl. grants) 56,951; Total expenditures (incl. net lending) 48,250. Source: African Development Bank.

International Reserves (US $ million at 31 December 2010): Gold (national valuation) 0.82; Reserve position in IMF 0.84; Foreign exchange 131.76; Total 133.42. Source: IMF, *International Financial Statistics*.

Money Supply (million Comoros francs at 31 December 2010): Currency outside depository corporations 18,115; Transferable deposits 24,534; Other deposits 26,097; *Broad money* 68,747. Source: IMF, *International Financial Statistics*.

Cost of Living (Consumer Price Index; base: 2000 = 100): All items 131.8 in 2007; 138.2 in 2008; 144.5 in 2009. Source: African Development Bank.

Expenditure on the Gross Domestic Product (million Comoros francs at current prices, 2010, estimates): Government final consumption expenditure 22,597; Private final consumption expenditure 197,553; Gross fixed capital formation 23,485; Changes in inventories 3,380; *Total domestic expenditure* 247,015; Exports of goods and services 5,922; *Less* Imports of goods and services 58,609; *GDP in purchasers' values* 194,329. Source: African Development Bank.

Gross Domestic Product by Economic Activity (million Comoros francs at current prices, 2010, estimates): Agriculture, hunting, forestry and fishing 85,351; Manufacturing 7,398; Electricity, gas and water 2,774; Construction 10,782; Wholesale and retail trade, restaurants and hotels 50,740; Transport and communications 9,067; Finance, insurance, real estate and business services 8,366; Public administration and defence 23,686; Other services 996; *Sub-total* 199,160; Indirect taxes –4,832; *GDP in purchasers' values* 194,329. Source: African Development Bank.

Balance of Payments (million Comoros francs, 2009, provisional): Exports of goods f.o.b. 5,618; Imports of goods f.o.b. –60,045; *Trade balance* –54,427; Services (net) –9,947; *Balance on goods and services* –64,374; Income (net) –4; *Balance on goods, services and income* –64,378; Current transfers (net) 45,967; *Current balance* –18,411; Capital and financial account 16,198; Net errors and omissions 4,959; *Overall balance* 2,746.

EXTERNAL TRADE

Principal Commodities (million Comoros francs, 2009): *Imports c.i.f.:* Rice 3,747; Meat and meat products 1,846; Petroleum products 78; Iron and steel 4,266; Total (incl. others) 74,532. *Exports f.o.b.:* Vanilla 726; Cloves 766; Total (incl. others) 5,618. Source: African Development Bank.

Principal Trading Partners (million Comoros francs, 2008): *Imports:* China, People's Republic 8,562; France (incl. Monaco) 9,684; Pakistan 4,286; South Africa 2,226; United Arab Emirates 10,381; Total (incl. others) 85,406. *Exports:* France (incl. Monaco) 3,573; Germany 486; Singapore 931; Turkey 2,027; USA 327; Total (incl. others) 25,001. Source: African Development Bank.

TRANSPORT

Road Traffic (motor vehicles in use, 2007): Passenger cars 19,245; Vans and lorries 1,790; Motorcycles and mopeds 1,343; Total 22,378. Source: International Road Federation, *World Road Statistics*.

Shipping: *Merchant Fleet* (registered at 31 December 2009): Number of vessels 312; Total displacement (grt) 905,214 (Source: IHS Fairplay, *World Fleet Statistics*). *International Sea-borne Freight Traffic* (estimates, '000 metric tons, 1991): Goods loaded 12; Goods unloaded 107 (Source: UN Economic Commission for Africa, *African Statistical Yearbook*).

Civil Aviation (traffic at Prince Said Ibrahim international airport, 1999): Passengers carried ('000) 130.4; Freight handled 1,183 metric tons.

TOURISM

Tourist Arrivals (2007): France 8,975; Madagascar 818; Réunion 1,286; South Africa 409; Total (incl. others) 14,582.

Receipts from Tourism (US $ million, incl. passenger transport): 21.4 in 2004; 23.6 in 2005; 26.8 in 2006.

Source: World Tourism Organization.

COMMUNICATIONS MEDIA

Radio Receivers (1997): 90,000 in use. Source: UNESCO, *Statistical Yearbook*.

Television Receivers (1997): 1,000 in use. Source: UNESCO, *Statistical Yearbook*.

Telephones (2010): 21,000 main lines in use. Source: International Telecommunication Union.

Mobile Cellular Telephones (2010): 165,300 in use. Source: International Telecommunication Union.

Personal Computers: 5,400 (9.0 per 1,000 persons) in 2005. Source: International Telecommunication Union.

Internet Subscribers (2009): 1,600. Source: International Telecommunication Union.

EDUCATION

Pre-primary (2007/08, unless otherwise indicated): 483 teachers (2004/05); 14,058 pupils (males 7,280, females 6,778). Source: UNESCO Institute for Statistics.

Primary (2007/08, unless otherwise indicated): 348 schools (1998); 3,685 teachers (males 2,326, females 1,359); 111,115 pupils (males 58,775; females 52,340). Sources: UNESCO Institute for Statistics and IMF, *Comoros: Statistical Appendix* (August 2005).

Secondary (2004/05, unless otherwise indicated): Teachers: general education 2,812 (2006/07); teacher training 11 (1991/92); vocational 20. Pupils: 43,349 (males 24,921, females 18,428). Sources: UNESCO Institute for Statistics and IMF, *Comoros: Statistical Appendix* (August 2005).

Post-secondary Vocational (2004/05): 51 teachers (males 41, females 10); 734 pupils (males 399, females 335). Source: UNESCO Institute for Statistics.

Tertiary (2003/04): 130 teachers (males 111, females 19); 1,779 pupils (males 1,011, females 768). *2008/09:* 5,091 pupils. Source: UNESCO Institute for Statistics.

Pupil-teacher Ratio (primary education, UNESCO estimate): 30.2 in 2007/08. Source: UNESCO Institute for Statistics.

Adult Literacy Rate: 74.2% (males 79.7%; females 68.7%) in 2009. Source: UNESCO Institute for Statistics.

Directory

The Government

HEAD OF STATE

Federal President: Dr IKILILOU DHOININE (elected 26 December 2010).

REGIONAL GOVERNORS

Mwali: MOHAMED ALI SAID.

Ngazidja: MOUIGNI BARAKA SAÏD SOILIH.

Nzwani: ANISSI CHAMSIDINE.

GOVERNMENT OF THE UNION OF THE COMOROS
(May 2012)

Vice-President, with responsibility for Production, the Environment, Energy, Industry and Crafts: Dr FOUAD MOHADJI.

Vice-President, with responsibility for Finance, the Economy, the Budget and Investments and External Trading (Privatization): MOHAMED ALI SOILIHI.

Vice-President, with responsibility for Land Settlement, Town Planning and Housing: NOURDINE BOURHANE.

Minister of External Relations and Co-operation, with responsibility for the Diaspora, and for Francophone and Arab Relations: MOHAMED BAKRI BEN ABDOULFATAH CHARIF.

Minister of Post and Telecommunications, Communication and the Promotion of New Information Technology, with responsibility for Transport and Tourism: MOUHIDINE RASTAMI.

Keeper of the Seals, Minister of Justice, the Civil Service, Administrative Reforms, Human Rights and Islamic Affairs: Dr AHMED ANLIANE.

Minister of National Education, Research, Culture and the Arts, with responsibility for Youth and Sports: MOHAMED ISSIMAILA.

Minister of Health, Solidarity, Social Cohesion and Gender Empowerment: Dr MOINAFOURAHA AHMED.

Minister of Employment, Professional Training, Labour and Female Entrepreneurship, Government Spokesperson: SITI KASSIM.

Minister of the Interior, Information and Decentralization, with responsibility for Relations with the Institutions: ABDALLAH HAMADA.

MINISTRIES

Office of the Head of State: Palais de Beit Salam, BP 521, Moroni; tel. 7744808; fax 7744829; e-mail presidence@comorestelecom.km; internet www.beit-salam.km.

Ministry of Agriculture, Fisheries, the Environment, Energy, Industry and Crafts: Moroni.

Ministry of the Civil Service, Administrative and Institutional Reforms, Decentralization and Human Rights: Moroni.

Ministry of Defence, the Interior and Information: Moroni.

Ministry of External Relations and Co-operation: BP 428, Moroni; tel. 7732306; fax 7732108; e-mail mirex@snpt.km.

Ministry of Finance, the Budget and Investments: BP 324, Moroni; tel. 7744140; fax 7744141.

Ministry of Health, Solidarity and Gender Empowerment: Moroni.

Ministry of Industry, Labour, Employment, Female Entrepreneurship and External Trade: Moroni.

Ministry of Justice, Penitentiary Administration, Islamic Affairs and Relations with Parliament: BP 2028, Moroni; tel. 7744040; fax 7734045.

Ministry of Land Settlement, Infrastructure, Town Planning and Housing: BP 12, Moroni; tel. 7744500; fax 7732222.

Ministry of National Education, Research, Culture and the Arts: BP 73, Moroni; tel. 7744180; fax 7744181.

Ministry of Post and Telecommunications, Communication and the Promotion of New Information Technology: BP 1315, Moroni; tel. 7734266; fax 7732222.

Ministry of Transport and Tourism: Moroni; tel. 7732098.

President and Legislature

PRESIDENT

Presidential Election, First Round, 7 November 2010

Candidate	Votes	% of votes
Dr Ikililou Dhoinine	3,785	28.19
Mohamed Saïd Fazul	3,080	22.94
Dr Abdou Djabir	1,327	9.88
Bianrifi Tarmidi	1,250	9.31
Saïd Dhiuffur Bounou	1,154	8.59
Hamada Madi Boléro	1,060	7.89
Mohamed Larif Oukacha	977	7.28
Mohamed Hassanaly	523	3.90
Abdoulhakime Said Allaoui	208	1.55
Zahariat Said Ahmed	63	0.47
Total	13,427	100.00

Presidential Election, Second Round, 26 December 2010

Candidate	Votes	% of votes
Dr Ikililou Dhoinine	106,890	60.91
Mohamed Saïd Fazul	57,587	32.81
Dr Abdou Djabir	11,018	6.28
Total	175,495	100.00

LEGISLATURE

Assemblée de l'Union: BP 447, Moroni; tel. 7744000; fax 7744011.

President: BOURHANE HAMIDOU.

Elections, 6 and 20 December 2009

Party	Seats
Mouvance présidentielle	17
Opposition candidates	4
Allies of the Mouvance présidentielle	3
Total	33*

* The remaining nine seats were filled by nominees from the islands' local assemblies, each of which selected three members.

Election Commission

Commission électorale nationale indépendante aux Comores (CENI): Moroni; f. 2007 to succeed the Commission nationale des élections aux Comores; 10–13 mems; each island has a Commission électorale insulaire, consisting of 7 mems; Pres. MMADI LAGUERA.

Political Organizations

CHUMA (Islands' Fraternity and Unity Party): Moroni; e-mail chuma@pourlescomores.com; f. 1985; Leader SAÏD ALI KEMAL.

Convention pour le renouveau des Comores (CRC): f. 2002; Leader Col ASSOUMANI AZALI; Sec.-Gen. HOUMED M'SAIDIE.

Djawabu: Leader YOUSSOUF SAÏD SOILIHI.

Forces pour l'action républicaine (FAR): Leader Col ABDOURAZAK ABDULHAMID.

Front de l'action pour la démocratie et le développment (FADD): Nzwani; main opposition party on Nzwani.

Front démocratique (FD): BP 758, Moroni; tel. 7733603; e-mail idriss@snpt.km; f. 1982; Chair. MOUSTOIFA SAÏD CHEIKH; Sec.-Gen. ABDALLAH HALIFA.

Front national pour la justice (FNJ): Islamist fundamentalist orientation; Leader AHMED RACHID.

Mouvement des citoyens pour la République (MCR): f. 1998; Leader MAHAMOUD MRADABI.

Mouvement populaire anjouanais (MPA): f. 1997 by merger of Organisation pour l'indépendance d'Anjouan and Mouvement séparatiste anjouanais; principal separatist movement on Nzwani (Anjouan).

Mouvement pour la démocratie et le progrès (MDP—NGDC): Moroni; Leader ABBAS DJOUSSOUF.

Mouvement pour la République, l'ouverture et l'unité de l'archipel des Comores (Mouroua) (Movement for the Republic, Openness and the Unity of the Comoran Archipelago): Moroni; f. 2005; advocates institutional reform; Pres. SAÏD ABBAS DAHALANI.

Mouvement pour le socialisme et la démocratie (MSD): Moroni; f. 2000 by splinter group of the FD; Leader ABDOU SOEFOU.

Parti comorien pour la démocratie et le progrès (PCDP): route Djivani, BP 179, Moroni; tel. 7731733; fax 7730650; Leader ALI MROUDJAÉ.

Parti républicain des Comores (PRC): BP 665, Moroni; tel. 7733489; fax 7733329; e-mail prc@online.fr; internet www.chez.com/prc; f. 1998; Leader MOHAMED SAÏD ABDALLAH M'CHANGAMA.

Parti social démocrate des Comores (PSDC-Dudja): Ngazidja; f. 2008; Leader ABDOU SOULÉ ELBAK; Sec.-Gen. Dr SOULE AHAMADA.

Parti socialiste des Comores (Pasoco): tel. 7731328; Leader AHMED AFFANDI ALI.

Rassemblement pour une initiative de développement avec une jeunesse avertie (RIDJA): BP 1905, Moroni; tel. and fax 7733356; f. 1999; Leader SAÏD LARIFOU; Sec.-Gen. AHAMED ACHIRAFI.

Rassemblement national pour le développement (RND): f. 1996; Chair. OMAR TAMOU; Sec. Gen. ABDOULHAMID AFFRAITANE.

Shawiri: Moroni; Leader Col MAHAMOUD MRADABI.

Shawiri—Unafasiya (SU): Moroni; f. 2003 following a split in Shawiri; Sec.-Gen. HADJI BEN SAÏD.

Union nationale pour la démocratie aux Comores (UNDC): Moroni; f. 1986; Pres. KAMAR EZZAMANE MOHAMED.

There are also a number of Islamist groups.

Diplomatic Representation

EMBASSIES IN THE COMOROS

China, People's Republic: Coulée de Lave, C109, BP 442, Moroni; tel. 7732521; fax 7732866; e-mail ambassadechine@snpt.km; Ambassador WANG LEYOU.

France: blvd de Strasbourg, BP 465, Moroni; tel. 7730615; fax 7730922; e-mail cad.moroni-ambassade@diplomatie.gouv.fr; internet www.ambafrance-km.org; Ambassador LUC HALLADE.

Libya: Moroni; Chargé d'affaires HUSSEIN ALI AL-MIZDAWI.

South Africa: BP 2589, Moroni; tel. 7734783; fax 7734786; e-mail moroni@foreign.gov.za; Ambassador MASILO MABETA.

Judicial System

Under the terms of the Constitution, the President is the guarantor of the independence of the judicial system, and is assisted by the Higher Council of the Magistracy (Conseil Supérieur de la Magistrature). The highest ruling authority in judicial, administrative and fiscal matters is the Supreme Court (Cour Suprême), which comprises a President, a Vice-President, an Attorney-General, at least nine councillors, at least one law commissioner, a general advocate, a chief clerk and other clerks. The High Council considers constitutional matters. A Constitutional Court (Cour Constitutionelle), comprising eight members—appointed by the President of the Union of the Comoros, the Vice-Presidents and the three regional Governors, was established in 2004.

Cour Constitutionelle (Constitutional Court): Moroni; e-mail mohamedyoussouf@hotmail.com; 8 mems.

Cour Suprême: Moroni; f. 2011.

Religion

The majority of the population are Muslims, mostly Sunni.

ISLAM

Organisation Islamique des Comores: BP 596, Coulée, Moroni; tel. 7732071.

CHRISTIANITY

The Roman Catholic Church

Adherents comprise just 1% of the total population.

Office of Vicariate Apostolic of the Comoros: Mission Catholique, BP 46, Moroni; tel. and fax 7631996; fax 7730503; e-mail mcatholique@comorestelecom.km; f. 1975; Vicar Apostolic Bishop CHARLES MAHUZA YAVA.

The Press

Albalad: Bacha ancien SOCOCOM, route Asgaraly, BP 7702, Moroni; tel. 7739471; e-mail amoindjie@albaladcomores.com; internet www.albaladcomores.com; daily; Dir of Publication ALI MOINDJIÉ.

Al Watwan: Nagoudjou, BP 984, Moroni-Coulée; tel. and fax 7734448; fax 7733340; e-mail contact@alwatwan.net; internet www.alwatwan.net; f. 1985; weekly; state-owned; Dir-Gen. HASSANE MOINDJIÉ (acting); Editor-in-Chief MOHAMED SOILIHI AHMED; circ. 1,500.

Comores Aujourd'hui: Moroni; Dir HAMADA MADI.

La Gazette des Comores: BP 2216, Moroni; tel. 7735234; e-mail la_gazette@snpt.km; weekly; Publication Dir ALLAOUI SAÏD OMAR.

Kashkazi: BP 5311, Moroni; internet www.kashkazi.com; f. 2005; weekly; French.

Le Matin des Comores: BP 1040, Moroni; tel. 7732995; fax 7732939; daily; Dir ALILOIAFA MOHAMED SAÏD.

NEWS AGENCY

Agence comorienne de presse (HZK-Presse): BP 2216, Moroni; tel. and fax 7632620; e-mail hzk_presse2@yahoo.fr; internet www.hzkpresse.com; f. 2004; Dir EL-HAD SAID OMAR.

PRESS ASSOCIATION

Organisation comorienne de la presse écrite (OCPE): Moroni; f. 2004; Pres. ABOUBACAR MCHANGAMA.

Publisher

KomÉdit: BP 535, Moroni; e-mail edition@komedit.com; f. 2000; general.

Broadcasting and Communications

TELECOMMUNICATIONS

Autorité Nationale de Régulation des TIC (ANRTIC): Moroni; tel. 7634595; e-mail ibrahim.mzemohamed@gmail.com; f. 2009; Dir-Gen. MOHAMED HASSANE ALFEINE.

Comores Télécom (Comtel): BP 7000, Moroni; tel. 7631031; fax 7732222; e-mail marketing@comorestelecom.km; internet www

.comorestelecom.km; formerly Société Nationale des Postes et des Télécommunications; post and telecommunications operations separated in 2004; scheduled for privatization; also operates mobile cellular telephone network (HURI); Dir-Gen. MAHAMOUDOU ABIAMRI.

BROADCASTING

Transmissions to the Comoros from Radio France Internationale commenced in early 1994. A number of privately owned radio and television stations also broadcast in the Comoros.

Office de la Radio Télévision des Comores (ORTC): Moroni; internet www.radiocomores.km; Comoran state broadcasting company; broadcasts Radio Comoros (f. 1960) and Télévision Nationale Comorienne (TNC, f. 2006); Dir-Gen. SOILIH MOHAMED SOILIH.

Radio-Télévision Anjouanaise (RTA): Mbouyoujou-Ouani, Nzwani; tel. 7710124; e-mail contact@rtanjouan.org; internet www .rtanjouan.org; f. 1997; television station f. 2003; owned by the Nzwani regional government; Dir (Radio) FAHARDINE ABDOULBAY; Dir (Television) AMIR ABDALLAH.

Radio

Radio-Comoro: BP 250, Moroni; tel. 7732531; fax 7730303; govt-controlled; domestic programmes in Comoran and French; international broadcasts in Swahili, Arabic and French; Dir-Gen. ISMAIL IBOUROI; Tech. Dir ABDULLAH RADJAB.

Radio Dzialandzé Mutsamudu (RDM): Mutsamudu, Nzwani; f. 1992; broadcasts on Nzwani; Co-ordinator SAÏD ALI DACAR MGAZI.

Radio KAZ: Mkazi, BP 1933; tel. 7735201.

Radio Ngazidja: Moroni; broadcasts on Ngazidja; also known as Radio Mdjidjengo; represents Ngazidja regional government; Man. MOHAMED ABDELKADER.

Television

Djabal TV: Iconi, BP 675, Moroni; tel. 7736767.

Mtsangani Television (MTV): Mtsangani, BP 845, Moroni; tel. 7733316; f. 1996; owned by Centre d'Animation Socio-culturelle de Matsangani; cultural and educational programmes.

TV—SHA: Shashagnogo; tel. 7733636.

Finance

In 2010 there were four banking institutions in the Comoros: one central bank, one commercial bank, one development bank and one savings bank.

BANKING

(cap. = capital; res = reserves; dep. = deposits; m. = million; brs = branches; amounts in Comoros francs)

Central Bank

Banque Centrale des Comores: pl. de France, BP 405, Moroni; tel. 7731814; fax 7730349; e-mail bancecom@comorestelecom.com; internet www.bancecom.com; f. 1981; bank of issue; cap. 1,100m., res 10,305m., dep. 17,606m. (Dec. 2006); Gov. MZÉ ABOUDOU MOHAMED CHANFIOU.

Commercial Bank

Banque pour l'Industrie et le Commerce—Comores (BIC): pl. de France, BP 175, Moroni; tel. 7730243; fax 7731229; e-mail bic@ bnpparibas.com; f. 1990; 51% owned by BNP Paribas-BDDI Participations (France); 34% state-owned; cap. 300.0m., res 1,690.2m., dep. 16,263.3m. (Dec. 2009); Dir-Gen. CHRISTIAN GOULT; 6 brs.

There are a number of offshore financial institutions based in the Comoros. In 2005 the Madagascar-based bank BNI–Crédit Lyonnais announced plans to open a branch in the Comoros. In 2006 it was announced that EXIM Bank (Tanzania) would open a subsidiary in Moroni and that a merchant bank would open during that year.

Savings Bank

Société Nationale de la Poste et des Services Financiers (SNPSF): BP 5000, Moroni; tel. 734327; fax 730304; internet www.lapostecomores.com; f. 2005; Dir-Gen. IBRAHIM ABDALLAH.

Development Bank

Banque de Développement des Comores: pl. de France, BP 298, Moroni; tel. 7720818; fax 7730397; e-mail info@bdevcom.net; internet www.bdevcom.net; f. 1982; provides loans, guarantees and equity participation for small- and medium-scale projects; 50% state-owned; cap. and res 1,242.0m., total assets 3,470.5m. (Dec. 2002); Pres. MZE CHEI OUBEIDI; Gen. Man. SAÏD ABDILLAHI.

Trade and Industry

GOVERNMENT AGENCIES

Office National du Commerce: Moroni; state-operated agency for the promotion and development of domestic and external trade.

Office National d'Importation et de Commercialisation du Riz (ONICOR): BP 748, Itsambouni, Moroni; tel. 7735566; fax 7730144; e-mail onicor_moroni@snpt.km; Dir-Gen. ALADINE DAROUMI.

Société de Développement de la Pêche Artisanale des Comores (SODEPAC): Moroni; state-operated agency overseeing fisheries development programme.

DEVELOPMENT ORGANIZATION

Centre Fédéral d'Appui au Développement Rural (CEFADER): Moroni; rural development org. with branches on each island.

CHAMBERS OF COMMERCE

Union des Chambres de Commerce, d'Industrie et d'Agriculture des Comores: BP 763, Moroni; tel. 7730958; fax 7731983; e-mail secretariat@uccia.km; internet www.uccia-comores.com; privatized in 1995; Pres. AHMED ALI BAZI.

TRADE ASSOCIATIONS

Organisation Comorienne de la Vanille (OCOVA): BP 472, Moroni; tel. 7732709; fax 7732719.

There is a further association, the **Fédération du secteur privé comorien** (FSPC).

EMPLOYERS' ORGANIZATIONS

Club d'Actions des Promoteurs Economiques: Moroni; f. 1999; Head SAÏD HASSANE DINI.

Organisation Patronale des Comores (OPACO): Oasis, BP 981, Moroni; tel. 7730848; internet www.opaco.km; f. 1991; Pres. MOHAMED ABDALLAH HALIFA.

UTILITIES

MA-MWE—Gestion de l'Eau et de l'Electricité aux Comores: BP 1762, Moroni; tel. 7733130; fax 7732359; e-mail cee@snpt.km; f. as Electricité et Eau des Comores; transferred to private management and renamed Comorienne de l'Eau et de l'Electricité in 1997; renationalized and renamed Service Public de l'Eau et de l'Electricité in 2001; reprivatized in Jan. 2002 and renamed as above; responsible for the production and distribution of electricity and water; Dir-Gen. HENRI MLANAO ALPHONSE.

Société d'Electricité d'Anjouan (EDA): Nzwani; Technical Dir YOUSSOUF ALI OICHEH.

STATE-OWNED ENTERPRISE

Societé Comorienne des Hydrocarbures (SCH): BP 28, Moroni; tel. 7730486; fax 7731883; imports petroleum products; Dir-Gen. HOUSSEINE CHEIKH SOILIH.

TRADE UNION

Confédération des Travailleurs des Comores (CTC): BP 1199, Moroni; tel. and fax 7633439; e-mail syndicatctcomores@yahoo.fr; f. 1996; Sec.-Gen. IBOUROI ALI TABIBOU; 5,000 mems.

Transport

ROADS

In 2000 there were an estimated 880 km of classified roads. About 76.5% of the network was paved in that year.

SHIPPING

The port of Mutsamudu, on Nzwani, can accommodate vessels of up to 11 m draught. Goods from Europe are routed via Madagascar, and coastal vessels connect the Comoros with the east coast of Africa. The country's registered merchant fleet at 31 December 2009 numbered 312 vessels, totalling 905,214 grt.

Autorité Portuaire des Comores (APC): Moroni; f. 2001.

Société de Représentation et de Navigation (SORNAV): M.Z.I. Mavouna, BP 2493, Moroni; tel. 7730590; fax 7730377; e-mail sornav .moroni@comorestelecom.km; internet www.sornav.com; f. 1996; shipping agents; responsible for handling, unloading and shipping of goods; Dir-Gen. Capt. MANSOUR IBRAHIM.

CIVIL AVIATION

The international airport is at Moroni-Hahaya on Ngazidja. Work began on the upgrading of the airport in late 2004. Each of the other islands has a small airfield. International services are operated by Air Austral (Réunion), Air Mayotte, Air Tanzania, Sudan Airways, Precision Air (Tanzania) and Yemenia. Kenya Airways commenced flying to the Comoros and Mayotte in November 2006.

Agence Nationale de l'Aviation Civile et de la Météorologie (ANACM): Moroni; tel. 7730948; e-mail transport@anacm-comores.com; internet www.anacm-comores.com; f. 2008; Dir-Gen. MOHAMED ATTOUMANE (acting).

AB Aviation: Hadoudja, Moroni; tel. and fax 7732714; internet www.flyabaviation.com; f. 2010.

Air Service Comores (ASC): Moroni; tel. 7733366; internet www.airservicecomores.com; internal services and international flights to Madagascar.

Comores Aviation International: route Corniche, Moroni; tel. 7733400; fax 7733401; internet www.comoresaviation.com; f. 1999; twice-weekly charter flights between Moroni and Mayotte; Dir JEAN-MARC HEINTZ.

Tourism

The principal tourist attractions are the beaches, underwater fishing and mountain scenery. Increasing numbers of Comorans resident abroad are choosing to visit the archipelago; in 2004 it was estimated that 58.3% of visitors to the Comoros were former Comoran residents. In 2005 hotel capacity amounted to an estimated 836 beds. Tourist arrivals increased to 27,474 in 1998, but had decreased to 14,582 by 2007. Receipts from tourism totalled US $26.8m. in 2006.

Defence

The national army, the Armée nationale de développement, comprised about 1,100 men in early 2009. In December 1996 an agreement was ratified with France, which provided for the permanent presence of a French military contingent in the Comoros. Following the military coup in April 1999, French military co-operation with the Comoros was suspended, but resumed in September 2002.

Defence Expenditure: Estimated at US $3m. in 1994.

Chief of General Staff of the Comoran Armed Forces: Lt-Col ABDALLAH GAMIL SOLIHI.

Education

Education is officially compulsory for 10 years between six and 16 years of age. Primary education begins at the age of six and lasts for six years. Secondary education, beginning at 12 years of age, lasts for seven years, comprising a first cycle of four years and a second of three years. According to UNESCO estimates, enrolment at primary schools in 2006/07 included 78% of children in the relevant age-group (males 81%; females 75%), while enrolment at secondary schools in 2004/05 was equivalent to 46% of children in the relevant age-group (males 52%; females 40%). In 2003/04 a total of 5,091 pupils were enrolled in tertiary education. Children may also receive a basic education through traditional Koranic schools, which are staffed by Comoran teachers. The Comoros' first university opened in December 2003, and in 2004/05 there were 2,187 students enrolled at that institution. In 2008 spending on education was equivalent to 7.6% of GDP.

THE DEMOCRATIC REPUBLIC OF THE CONGO

Introductory Survey

LOCATION, CLIMATE, LANGUAGE, RELIGION, FLAG, CAPITAL

The Democratic Republic of the Congo (formerly Zaire) lies in central Africa, bordered by the Republic of the Congo to the north-west, by the Central African Republic and South Sudan to the north, by Uganda, Rwanda, Burundi and Tanzania to the east and by Zambia and Angola to the south. There is a short coastline at the outlet of the River Congo. The climate is tropical, with an average temperature of 27°C (80°F) and an annual rainfall of 150 cm–200 cm (59 ins–97 ins). French is the official language. More than 400 Sudanese and Bantu dialects are spoken; Kiswahili, Kiluba, Kikongo and Lingala being the most widespread. An estimated 50% of the population is Roman Catholic, and there is a smaller Protestant community. Many inhabitants follow traditional (mostly animist) beliefs. The national flag (proportions 2 by 3) is light blue, with a yellow star in the upper left corner and a diagonal red stripe edged in yellow. The capital is Kinshasa.

CONTEMPORARY POLITICAL HISTORY

Historical Context

The Democratic Republic of the Congo (DRC), formerly the Belgian Congo, became independent from Belgium as the Republic of the Congo on 30 June 1960. Five days later the armed forces mutinied, and the UN subsequently dispatched troops to the region to maintain order. In July 1964 President Joseph Kasavubu appointed Moïse Tshombe, the former leader of a group supporting the secession of the Katanga region, as interim Prime Minister, pending elections, and in August the country was renamed the Democratic Republic of the Congo. In November 1965 Col (subsequently Marshal) Joseph-Désiré Mobutu seized power and proclaimed himself head of the 'Second Republic'. In late 1970 Mobutu, as sole candidate, was elected President. (From January 1972, as part of a national policy of 'authenticity', he became known as Mobutu Sese Seko.) In October 1971 the DRC was renamed the Republic of Zaire, and one year later the Government of Zaire and the Executive Committee of the Mouvement populaire de la révolution (MPR), the sole legal political party, merged into the National Executive Council (NEC).

Legislative elections took place in October 1977, and, at a presidential election in December, Mobutu (again the sole candidate) was re-elected for a further seven-year term. In early 1982 opponents of Zaire's one-party system of government formed the Union pour la démocratie et le progrès social (UDPS). This was followed by the formation of the Front congolais pour le rétablissement de la démocratie (FCD), a coalition of opposition parties.

In April 1990 Mobutu declared the inauguration of the 'Third Republic' and announced that a plural political system, initially to comprise three parties, would be introduced after a transitional period of one year; the UDPS was immediately granted legal status. The NEC was dissolved and Prof. Lunda Bululu, previously an adviser to Mobutu, was appointed First State Commissioner (Prime Minister). In May 1990 a new, smaller, transitional NEC was formed, and in June Mobutu relinquished presidential control of the NEC and of foreign policy and authorized the formation of independent trade unions. Legislation permitting the establishment of a full multi-party political system was introduced in November.

Domestic Political Affairs

By early 1991 a large number of new parties had emerged. However, none of the major opposition parties agreed to join the new Government installed in March and which was headed by Prof. Mulumba Lukoji, an economist who had served in previous administrations, as First State Commissioner.

A National Conference, initially convened in August 1991, reopened in April 1992 and in August it elected Etienne Tshisekedi Wa Mulumba, the leader of the UDPS, as First State Commissioner, following the resignation of Nguza Karl-I-Bond. A 'transition act', adopted by the Conference in early August, afforded Tshisekedi a mandate to govern, pending the promulgation of a new constitution that would curtail the powers of the President. Later that month Tshisekedi appointed a transitional 'Government of National Union', which included opponents of Mobutu.

In November 1992 the National Conference adopted a draft Constitution, providing for the establishment of a 'Federal Republic of the Congo', the introduction of a bicameral legislature and the election of a President (who would fulfil a largely ceremonial function) by universal suffrage. In early December the Conference dissolved itself and was succeeded by a 453-member High Council of the Republic (HCR), headed by Archbishop Laurent Monsengwo Pasinya and empowered to amend and adopt the new Constitution and to organize elections. Attempts by the presidential guard to obstruct the convening of the HCR ended, following the organization of a public rally in Kinshasa by Monsengwo and other members of the HCR. With support from the USA, Belgium and France, Monsengwo reiterated the HCR's recognition of Tshisekedi as head of Zaire's Government.

In mid-January 1993 the HCR declared Mobutu to be guilty of treason, on account of his mismanagement of state affairs, and threatened impeachment proceedings unless he recognized the legitimacy of the 'Government of National Union'. In March Mobutu convened a special 'conclave' of political forces to debate the country's future, which appointed Faustin Birindwa, a former UDPS member and adviser to Tshisekedi, as Prime Minister, charged with the formation of a 'Government of National Salvation'. Birindwa's Cabinet, appointed in April, included Karl-I-Bond as First Deputy Prime Minister in charge of Defence but was denied widespread official international recognition.

In early January 1994 an agreement to form a government of national reconciliation was signed by all major political parties, with the notable exception of Tshisekedi's own UDPS. Encouraged by the unexpected level of political support for the initiative, in mid-January Mobutu announced the dissolution of the HCR, the dismissal of the Government of National Salvation and the candidacy for the premiership of two contestants, Tshisekedi and Lukoji, to be decided by the transitional legislature (to be known as the Haut Conseil de la République—Parlement de Transition, HCR—PT). The HCR—PT promptly rejected Mobutu's procedure for the selection of a new Prime Minister.

In April 1994 the HCR—PT endorsed a new Transitional Constitution Act, reiterating the provisions of previous accords for the organization of a constitutional referendum and presidential and legislative elections, and defining the functions of transitional institutions during a 15-month period. The Government, to be accountable to the HCR—PT, was to assume some former powers of the President, including the control of the Central Bank and the security forces.

In June 1995 the HCR—PT adopted a constitutional amendment (approved by Mobutu), whereby the period of national transition (due to end on 9 July) was to be extended by two years, owing to a shortage of government resources. A draft of the new Constitution, which provided for a federal state with a parliamentary system of government and a president with limited powers, was approved by the Government in late May 1996.

In the mid-1990s existing ethnic tensions in eastern Zaire were heightened by the inflow of an estimated 1m. Hutu refugees from Rwanda. The plight of the region's Zairean Tutsis (Banyamulenge) aroused international concern in late 1996, following reports of the organized persecution of Banyamulenge communities by elements of the Zairean security forces and by extremist Hutu refugees. In October the Sud-Kivu regional administration ordered all Banyamulenge to leave the area within one week or risk internment or forced expulsion. Although the order was subsequently rescinded, this threat provoked the mobilization of armed Banyamulenge rebels, who launched a violent counter-offensive, allegedly supported by the Tutsi-dominated authorities in Rwanda and Burundi. Support for the rebels from dissidents of diverse ethnic origin (including Shaba and Kasaï secessionists, and local Mai-Mai warriors) increased, and later in October the rebels announced the formation of the Alliance des forces démocratiques pour la libération du Congo-Zaïre (AFDL), under the leadership of Laurent-Désiré Kabila (hitherto leader of the Parti de la révolution populaire, and a known opponent of the Mobutu regime since the 1960s). AFDL forces made rapid territorial gains, and the movement soon gathered momentum, emerging as a national rebellion aimed at overthrowing Mobutu. In March 1997 the AFDL entered the strategically important northern town of Kisangani (which had served as the centre of military operations for the Government), and in early April Mbuji-Mayi fell to the rebels. AFDL troops, entering Lubumbashi on 9 April, were welcomed as liberators, while government troops withdrew from the city. The Zairean Government continued to make allegations that the AFDL offensive was being supported by government troops from Rwanda, Uganda, Burundi and Angola, while the AFDL, in turn, claimed that the Zairean army had been reinforced by forces of the União Nacional para a Independência Total de Angola (UNITA).

Meanwhile, in August 1996 Mobutu had travelled to Switzerland to receive medical treatment. His absence, and uncertainties as to the state of his health, contributed to the poor co-ordination of the Zairean Government's response to the AFDL, which by the end of November was in control of most of Kivu. In that month the HCR—PT urged the expulsion of all Tutsis from Zairean territory; following attacks on Tutsis and their property, many Tutsi residents of Kinshasa fled to Brazzaville (Republic of the Congo). In December Mobutu returned to Zaire, appointed Gen. Mahele Bokungu as Chief of General Staff and reorganized the Government.

The continued exclusion of Tshisekedi from the Government prompted his supporters to mount a campaign of civil disobedience, and in January 1997 his faction of the UDPS announced its support for the AFDL. On 8 April Mobutu declared a national state of emergency, dissolving the Government and ordering the deployment of security forces throughout Kinshasa. Gen. Likulia Bolongo was appointed Prime Minister at the head of a 'Government of National Salvation'.

Kabila assumes power

Peace talks between Mobutu and Kabila ended in failure in early May 1997, and on 16 May Mobutu left Kinshasa (travelling to Togo, and then to Morocco, where he died in September), while many of his supporters and family fled across the border to Brazzaville. On 17 May AFDL troops entered Kinshasa and Kabila declared himself President of the DRC (the name in use during 1964–71), which swiftly gained international recognition. On 23 May 1997 Kabila formed a transitional Government, which, while dominated by members of the AFDL, also included members of the UDPS and of the Front patriotique. All political parties and public demonstrations were banned and on 28 May Kabila issued a temporary constitutional decree (pending the adoption of a new constitution), investing the President with virtually absolute legislative and executive power, as well as control over the armed forces and the treasury. Of the previously existing state institutions, only the judiciary was not dissolved.

On 29 May 1997 Kabila was inaugurated as President of the DRC, assuming full executive, legislative and military powers. In October Kabila appointed a 42-member Constitutional Commission, which was to draft a new constitution by March 1998. In the following month Kabila reaffirmed that the activities of political parties were suspended, pending presidential and legislative elections, scheduled to take place in 1999.

In July 1998 Kabila issued a decree expelling Rwandan troops from the country. In August an armed insurrection was launched in Nord-Kivu province, in the east of the DRC, reportedly with Rwandan and French support. The rebels advanced quickly in the east of the country and were soon reported to have captured Bukavu and Goma. Shortly afterwards a second front was opened from Kitona, in the west of the country, where further advances resulted in the rebels gaining control of Boma, Banana and Matadi. The Inga Dam, which supplies both electricity and water to Kinshasa and the Katanga mining region, was also captured, enabling the rebels to interrupt power supplies. At that time the rebel forces announced that they had formed a political organization, the Rassemblement congolais démocratique (RCD), with the aim of introducing political democracy in the DRC.

Other countries in the region were, meanwhile, becoming involved in the conflict. While Rwanda had initially denied accusations that it was supporting the rebels, it quickly became evident that the anti-Kabila insurgents had the support of both Rwanda and Uganda, and that Kabila was receiving support from Angola, Namibia and Zimbabwe. Regional divisions were clearly evident in August 1998 at a meeting of Ministers of Defence of the Southern African Development Community (SADC, see p. 423) to mobilize support for Kabila; only one-half of the participating delegates favoured intervention in the conflict. Regional efforts to reach a political solution to the civil conflict continued in September. The Government refused to negotiate with the RCD and a newly formed rebel grouping, the Mouvement de libération du Congo (MLC), however, on the grounds that their activities were supported by Rwanda and Uganda, respectively. Although their advance had been halted in the west, the rebels continued to make progress in the east, capturing towns in Kasaï Oriental and Katanga.

In May 1999 the RCD announced changes to its executive committee; Wamba dia Wamba was replaced as President by Dr Emile Ilunga. However, a number of the RCD's founding members opposed this move, and dia Wamba denounced it as a coup. Following clashes in Kisangani between supporters of dia Wamba and those of Ilunga, two factions emerged; one of these, led by Ilunga, was based in Goma, with the support of Rwanda, while the other, led by dia Wamba, was based in Kisangani and supported by Uganda.

Cease-fire agreement

Despite a number of regional initiatives to end the civil war in late 1998 and early 1999, no lasting cease-fire agreement was negotiated, largely owing to Kabila's continued insistence that the rebels were supported by Rwanda and Uganda, and that they, therefore, be excluded from any talks. Although Col Muammar al-Qaddafi, the Libyan leader, hosted two rounds of regional talks in Sirte (Libya), it was in Lusaka, Zambia, under the mediation of Zambia's President Frederick Chiluba, that the rebels were first accorded a place at the negotiations, during a summit held in late June. Following this meeting, a cease-fire agreement was signed by the Heads of State of the DRC, Angola, Namibia, Zimbabwe, Rwanda and Uganda on 10 July, by the leader of the MLC, Jean-Pierre Bemba Gombo, on 1 August and eventually by the RCD on 31 August. The agreement provided for an immediate cease-fire, the establishment of a Joint Military Commission (JMC) and the deployment of a UN peace-keeping force. In July a general amnesty for rebels within the DRC was announced, and in that month the JMC was formed, comprising representatives of the rebel groups and the six Lusaka signatory states (the DRC, Angola, Namibia, Rwanda, Uganda and Zimbabwe). In mid-August the UN military liaison mission received official approval.

In August 1999 further fighting erupted in Kisangani between forces from Rwanda and Uganda and their respective factions of the RCD. A cease-fire was negotiated in late August, and at the end of the month the Ilunga faction of the RCD (known as RCD—Goma) announced a new executive committee. An investigation into the causes of the fighting recommended that all fighting forces be removed from Kisangani; as a result, the MLC transferred its headquarters to Gbadolite, while the dia Wamba faction of the RCD, known as the RCD—Mouvement de libération (RCD—ML), withdrew from Bunia.

In November 1999 both factions of the RCD announced that they no longer respected the cease-fire (having previously denied violations), and RCD—Goma accused the Government of openly breaching the agreement. In that month the UN Security Council voted to extend the mandate of the military liaison mission until mid-January 2000, owing to the difficulties experienced in obtaining security assurances and permission to deploy throughout the DRC. On 30 November 1999 the Council approved the establishment of a UN Mission in the Democratic Republic of the Congo (MONUC), to comprise some 5,000 troops, together with up to 500 military observers and liaison and technical assessment officers, with an initial mandate until March 2000. At a meeting of the UN Security Council concerning the conflict in the DRC, which took place in New York, USA, in January 2000, regional Heads of State expressed support for the rapid deployment of MONUC forces to support the Lusaka peace accord. In February the UN Security Council authorized the expansion of MONUC to number 5,537 and the extension of its mandate to the end of August.

In July 2000 240 deputies of a new 300-member transitional Parliament were elected by a commission under the supervision of the Ministry of Internal Affairs, while the remaining 60 were nominated by Kabila. A presidential decree, adopted in that month, provided for the decentralization of the Government, with the transferral of the legislature to Lubumbashi. On 22 August the new transitional Parliament was inaugurated in Lubumbashi, despite criticism from the international community, which accused Kabila of acting in contravention of the Lusaka accord.

In August 2000 the UN Security Council adopted a resolution extending the mandate of MONUC until mid-October to allow further time for the implementation of a cease-fire agreement. In October, in a reorganization of the RCD—Goma leadership, Ilunga was replaced by Adolphe Onusumba. In the same month an attempt to oust dia Wamba from the leadership of the RCD—ML was suppressed by Ugandan troops. The RCD—ML subsequently divided, following the establishment of a dissident breakaway faction, led by Roger Lumbala, which became known as RCD—National (RCD—N). In December the six countries and three rebel groups involved in the conflict signed an agreement in Harare, Zimbabwe, pledging to withdraw forces 15 km from positions of military engagement, prior to the deployment of MONUC troops (which was scheduled to take place within 45 days). Nevertheless, hostilities continued at Pweto, and in other eastern regions, while RCD—Goma refused to withdraw its forces in accordance with the agreement until the Government entered into bilateral discussions with the rebels and permitted the complete deployment of MONUC troops. In mid-December the UN Security Council adopted a resolution in favour of extending the mandate of MONUC to mid-June 2001.

Assassination of Kabila

On 16 January 2001 Kabila was assassinated by a member of his presidential guard at his private residence in Kinshasa. The transitional Parliament approved the nomination by the political leadership of his son, Maj.-Gen. Joseph Kabila Kabange (hitherto Chief of Staff), as interim President. Following his inauguration on 26 January, Joseph Kabila immediately engaged in international diplomatic efforts to resolve the conflict and urged rebel leaders to attend peace discussions with him. At a meeting of the UN Security Council in February, attended by representatives of the six countries and three rebel factions involved in the conflict, it was agreed that the 15 km withdrawal of forces was to commence by mid-March.

The withdrawal from positions of military engagement duly commenced in mid-March 2001, in accordance with the UN-sponsored agreement, with the retreat from Pweto of the RCD—Goma and allied Rwandan troops. The first contingents of MONUC troops arrived in the DRC, and by the end of the month were stationed in the north-east of the country. At the beginning of April, however, the Ugandan-supported Forces pour la libération du Congo (FLC, which had been formed earlier that year by breakaway members of the MLC and the RCD—ML) refused to proceed with the withdrawal from military positions near Kisangani until MONUC guaranteed security in the region. The deployment of MONUC troops in the east of the country was delayed, after RCD forces initially prevented the peace-keeping forces from entering Kisangani.

In May 2001 representatives of the DRC Government and the rebel factions, meeting in Lusaka, under the aegis of the Organization of African Unity (OAU, now the African Union, see p. 189), SADC and the UN, signed a declaration establishing the principles for an 'Inter-Congolese National Dialogue' (a formal process of national consultation, with the aim of reaching a permanent peace settlement). Later that month Kabila ended the remaining restrictions on political activity and ordered the release of a number of detained human rights activists.

In late May 2001 a report by the state prosecutor claimed that forces opposing the Government (the RCD factions, and Rwandan and Ugandan troops) had conspired in the assassination of Laurent-Désiré Kabila, with the aim of seizing power. In June the UN Security Council approved a resolution extending the mandate of MONUC until mid-2002; the Council welcomed the progress towards negotiating a peace settlement, but reiterated demands that all foreign forces complete their withdrawal from the country. In early August, however, the President of Rwanda, Maj.-Gen. Paul Kagame insisted that Kabila fulfil pledges to demobilize Rwandan Hutu militia, known as Interahamwe (who had become allied with DRC government forces, after participating in the genocide in Rwanda in 1994), as a precondition to withdrawing the Rwandan troops deployed in the country. Also in August dia Wamba was ousted as the RCD—ML leader by Mbusa Nyamwisi.

Preparatory discussions between Kabila and the leaders of the FLC and the RCD factions, which were for the first time attended by unarmed opposition groups and civic associations, were conducted in Gaborone, Botswana, in August 2001. The Inter-Congolese National Dialogue commenced in the Ethiopian capital, Addis Ababa, in October, and, having been suspended in late 2001, was reconvened in Sun City, South Africa, in February 2002. In April it was announced that the Government and the MLC had reached a compromise agreement, providing for the establishment of an administration of national unity: Kabila was to remain President and Bemba became Prime Minister for a transitional period, prior to general elections. Signatories to the agreement commenced discussions in Matadi in May to draft a new constitution, while RCD—Goma and the UDPS announced their intention to form a political alliance to oppose the accord between Kabila and Bemba. At the end of July a peace agreement was signed by Kabila and President Kagame in Pretoria, South Africa. Under the accord, Kabila pledged to arrest and disarm the Interahamwe militia in the DRC, while the Rwandan Government was to withdraw all troops from the country (thereby also providing for the integration of RCD—Goma into the peace process). President Robert Mugabe of Zimbabwe subsequently announced his intention of withdrawing the remaining Zimbabwean troops supporting the DRC Government. In early September the DRC and Uganda reached an accord in the Angolan capital, Luanda, providing for the normalization of relations between the two countries, and the full withdrawal of Ugandan troops in the DRC. The Ugandan and Zimbabwean Governments subsequently commenced the withdrawal of forces from the DRC (although the UN permitted some Ugandan troops provisionally to remain near Bunia to assist in the maintenance of security). At the end of September the withdrawal of Rwandan forces commenced, and it was announced that all 23,400 Rwandan troops had left the country by early October.

Following the convening of a peace conference in early December 2002 in Pretoria, the Government and rebels signed an extensive power-sharing agreement later that month. Under the terms of this accord, Kabila was to remain as President, while four vice-presidential posts were to be allocated, respectively, to the incumbent Government, opposition parties, RCD—Goma and the MLC. The new 36-member transitional administration, to remain in power for a two-year period, was to comprise representatives of the Government, all three RCD factions, the MLC, the opposition and civil society. At the end of December the MLC and the RCD factions signed a cease-fire agreement in Gbadolite, which was to allow the transportation of humanitarian assistance in the region. (However, all rebel factions subsequently failed to observe the cease-fire, and continued hostilities near the border with Uganda were reported.)

Transitional government

Further discussions on constitutional and security issues for the transitional period were conducted in Pretoria in early 2003; agreement was reached on the adoption of a draft constitution and the deployment of a neutral international force in the country, pending the establishment of a new national army (which would include former rebel combatants). On 20 March, in response to continuing violence near Bunia, in contravention of the cease-fire agreement, the UN Security Council adopted a resolution urging an increase in the number of military and humanitarian observers stationed in the DRC under the MONUC mandate, and an immediate withdrawal of the Ugandan troops. At the final peace conference, which was convened at Sun City on 2 April, government and rebel representatives endorsed the establishment of the two-year transitional administration. The official adoption of the Constitution on 4 April was followed by Kabila's inauguration as interim Head of State on 7 April. Despite the deployment of some 700 (mainly Uruguayan) MONUC troops at Bunia to compensate for the Ugandan withdrawal, Hema militia forces recaptured the town following intensive fighting, during which large numbers of civilians were massacred. On 30 May, in response to the developing humanitarian crisis, the UN Security Council authorized the establishment of a 1,500-member Interim Emergency Multinational Force, with a three-month mandate to restore order. Deployment of the contingent (which comprised troops from several European Union—EU, see p. 276—nations, principally France) commenced in early June despite protests from the various factions at French involvement in the conflict.

In May 2003 the nomination of the four Vice-Presidents to the new transitional Government was announced: these included Bemba and the new leader of RCD—Goma, Azarias Ruberwa. On 29 June all former combatant groups finally signed an agreement on power-sharing in the future integrated transitional armed forces. On the following day Kabila nominated a transitional

Government, in which portfolios were divided between representatives of the former rebel factions, the incumbent administration, political opposition and civil society organizations. While Kabila's Government, RCD—Goma, and the MLC were allocated the most significant portfolios, the new administration also included Nyamwisi (representing the RCD—ML), and Lumbala (representing RCD—N). The four Vice-Presidents were inaugurated on 17 July and the new power-sharing Government was installed on 24 July. At the end of that month the UN Security Council approved a one-year extension of MONUC's mandate, and increased the contingent's military strength significantly; it was envisaged that these MONUC reinforcements would replace the Interim Emergency Multinational Force at the beginning of September. The new International Criminal Court (ICC, see p. 342), which had been established on 1 July 2002 in The Hague, Netherlands, announced that it was to initiate investigations into alleged atrocities committed in the Ituri region. On 20 August 2003 Kabila announced nominations to the military leadership of the new unified armed forces, which was to incorporate elements of all the former rebel groups and the Mai-Mai militia; former RCD—Goma and MLC commanders were appointed to senior posts. On 22 August the inaugural session of the new bicameral transitional Parliament was conducted in Kinshasa; representation in the 500-member Assemblée nationale and 120-member Sénat was likewise divided between the former rebel groups, the Mai-Mai, the incumbent Government, political opposition and civil society. At the beginning of September the Interim Emergency Multinational Force officially transferred control of the Ituri region to MONUC reinforcements; the remaining French troops belonging to the contingent were finally withdrawn by the end of that month. In November, following the final report by the Panel of Experts, the UN Security Council issued a statement condemning the widespread illicit exploitation of the DRC's natural resources, which had financed the activities of former combatant groups, and urged the imposition of state authority throughout the country.

At the end of May 2004 some 2,000 dissident troops, led by Banyamulenge former RCD—Goma commanders who had been integrated into the national army, Brig.-Gen. Laurent Nkunda and Col Jules Mutebutsi, attacked forces loyal to the Government deployed in Bukavu, and by 2 June had seized control of the town. Rebel forces began to withdraw about two days later, and troops loyal to Kabila succeeded in regaining control of the town by 9 June. Nkunda, together with some 300 supporters, fled to Rwanda, and was subsequently disarmed. In mid-June Kabila dispatched some 10,000 troop reinforcements to the eastern border with Rwanda, prompting Kagame to warn that Rwanda would take any necessary measures to protect national security. (Later in June, however, the two Heads of State reached agreement to abide by the 2002 peace agreement.)

Following the massacre of some 160 Banyamulenge in August 2004, Nkunda warned that he would take retaliatory action if the DRC Government failed to protect the refugees. (Some 20,000 Banyamulenge had fled from Bakavu to Burundi in June.) Ruberwa announced that RCD—Goma, in view of the collapse of the peace process, was to suspend participation in the transitional Government. At the end of August the Governments of the DRC, Uganda and Rwanda agreed to co-operate in the disarmament of the militia continuing to operate in the country, including the Interahamwe and members of the Ugandan rebel organization, the Alliance of Democratic Forces. At the beginning of September, following a visit by the South African President, Thabo Mbeki, to Kinshasa for mediation, Ruberwa announced that RCD—Goma had rejoined the Government. During that month the UN Security Council authorized the expansion of MONUC to 16,700, while renewing the contingent's mandate for a further six months.

At the beginning of December 2004, after MONUC troops confirmed the presence of Rwandan forces in the DRC, Kabila requested that the UN Security Council impose sanctions against Rwanda. Kagame protested that Rwandan forces had responded to rebel bombardments launched from DRC territory. Heavy fighting continued in Nord-Kivu between government forces and dissident army units reportedly supported by Rwanda, and later in December MONUC announced that its troops were to establish a temporary 'buffer zone' between the factions engaged in conflict.

At the end of March 2005 the mandate of MONUC was extended for a further six months, while in April the UN Security Council voted to adopt the recommendation of the UN panel of experts investigating implementation of the armaments embargo in eastern DRC, that the embargo be extended to the entire country, and provided for the imposition of a travel ban and 'freeze' of assets on those who violated the sanctions. On 13 May the transitional Assemblée nationale finally approved a new Constitution, which was to be submitted for endorsement at a national referendum. The new Constitution provided for the election of a President by popular vote for a maximum of two five-year terms, a balanced distribution of power between the executive and legislature and the granting of citizenship to members of all ethnic groups resident in the country since 1960. In June Parliament approved the extension of the transitional period for six months (in accordance with the provisions of the April 2003 Constitution). In September 2005, in response to the continuing instability in eastern DRC, the UN Security Council authorized the temporary reinforcement of MONUC by 841 mainly police personnel; on 28 October a further increase in military strength of 300 for the period of the elections was approved and the mandate of the contingent was extended until the end of September 2006.

According to official results of the national referendum, which was conducted on 18 December 2005, the draft Constitution was adopted by 84.3% of votes cast, subject to its approval by the country's Supreme Court. The minimum age for a presidential candidate was reduced from 35 to 30 years, thereby allowing Kabila to contest the forthcoming elections. (Kabila was subsequently officially nominated as the candidate of the Parti du peuple pour la reconstruction et la démocratie—PPRD, which he had formed in 2002.) The new Constitution also provided for an increase in the number of provinces from 11 to 26 (including Kinshasa), and granted them significant powers of self-government. The Supreme Court endorsed the results of the referendum on 3 February 2005, having rejected a number of legal challenges by opposition parties and non-governmental organizations. The new Constitution was signed into effect by Kabila on 18 February. (A new national flag was adopted at the same time.) New electoral legislation was approved by Parliament on 21 February, when the Commission électorale indépendante (CEI) also announced that the presidential and legislative elections were again to be postponed, to 18 June, to allow the completion of preparations, including voter registration, throughout the country. In March Thomas Lubanga of the Union des patriotes congolais was transferred from MONUC custody to the ICC on charges of war crimes, becoming the first indictee to be extradited to the Court.

In May 2006 government and MONUC troops intensified operations in Ituri, in an effort to ensure that elections there were conducted peacefully and in mid-July the Government announced that it would integrate FNI units into its forces. Also in July a militia group engaged in hostilities in the Ituri region, known as the Mouvement Révolutionnaire Congolais (MRC), agreed to end hostilities in return for integration into the armed forces. In an attempt to ensure peaceful elections in the capital, on 26 April the UN Security Council authorized the temporary deployment of an EU military force (EUFOR RD Congo). The European Council of Ministers gave its approval in mid-June and the troops began arriving shortly afterwards. On 27 July the Government reached a UN-mediated peace agreement with the MRC, whereby the militia coalition, in return for an amnesty from prosecution, undertook to end hostilities in the Ituri region, to allow the free movement of displaced civilians for the elections and to become integrated into the armed forces.

The July 2006 elections

The presidential and legislative elections finally took place on 30 July 2006. Although a South African observer mission announced that the elections had been conducted fairly, a number of presidential candidates subsequently accused the authorities of perpetrating mass falsification of the results, and in early August six poll officials were arrested on suspicion of malpractice. According to the CEI, Kabila secured 44.8% and Bemba 20.0% of votes cast; about 70.5% of the electorate had participated in the ballot. Consequently, a second round of the presidential election was scheduled for 29 October (when deputies were also to be elected to the provincial Assemblies).

Results of the legislative elections were released in early September 2006; the PPRD secured 111 seats, Bemba's MLC won 64, the revived Parti lumumbiste unifié (PALU) 34, the Mouvement social pour le renouveau 27, the Forces du renouveau (FR) 26 and the RCD 15. More than 70 other parties also secured parliamentary representation. The new Assemblée nationale was officially inaugurated on 22 September; however, in December petitions were raised against the election of 18 deputies and in July 2007 the results of those seats were annulled. Meanwhile, Kabila conclusively won the second presidential round on 29 October 2006 by 58.1% of votes cast, according to official results.

Kabila was inaugurated as President on 6 December 2006. At the end of that month the leader of PALU, Antoine Gizenga, was nominated Prime Minister-Designate. Meanwhile, following negotiations mediated by the Rwandan Government, the DRC authorities reached a peace agreement with Nkunda, whereby his forces, now grouped together as the Congrès national pour la défense du peuple (CNDP), were to be integrated into the national army. On 19 January 2007 the provincial Assemblies elected the 108-member Sénat. According to official results, the PPRD secured 22 seats in the chamber, the MLC 14, while the FR and the RCD each received seven seats. A further 22 parties were represented in the Sénat, while Bemba himself became one of eight senators representing the capital. Gubernatorial elections took place later in January. The Sénat was installed on 3 February and two days later the establishment of a 60-member coalition Government was announced.

The uneasy peace accords signed in early 2007 were short-lived. In mid-February the holding of local elections precipitated violent clashes in the west of the country. Bemba was threatened with an arrest warrant for failing to command his troops to withdraw from the capital and he subsequently sought refuge in the South African embassy in Kinshasa. In April he was granted permission to leave the country to receive medical treatment in Portugal. (In May 2008 Bemba was arrested and detained in Brussels, Belgium, on charges of war crimes, and in July he was transferred to the ICC to await trial.)

Fighting escalated in Nord-Kivu in mid-2007, prompting the UN to extend the mandate of MONUC until the end of that year. Nkunda had consolidated his influence over the region and withdrew his forces from the national army just months after they had been integrated into it. In August, under pressure from Rwandan officials, the DRC Government announced that it would deploy troops to Nord-Kivu. In September the UN brokered a fragile cease-fire under which Nkunda ordered the withdrawal of CNDP troops to areas outside Kivu, while President Kabila entered into talks with Nkunda to negotiate the reintegration of his fighters into the national army. Nkunda subsequently declared that his forces would only integrate when his demands for Rwandan rebel forces to be removed from the DRC were met. Just weeks after the cease-fire was agreed Nkunda claimed that his troops had been attacked by Interahamwe and Hutu militia groups and fighting resumed.

At a meeting on 9 November 2007 in Nairobi, Kenya, mediated by the UN, the USA and the EU, the Governments of the DRC and Rwanda reached a mutual agreement on their commitments to ending the violence in eastern DRC. The DRC Government pledged to develop a detailed plan for the disarmament of militia groups in Kivu to be presented in December. In response, Rwanda agreed that no support would be given to armed rebels and controls would be enforced to prevent the groups crossing the border in either direction. However, renewed attacks by Nkunda's forces on the national army were launched just days after the agreement; in December the UN Security Council extended MONUC's mandate for a further year. Meanwhile, in late November Kabila announced a major government reorganization, in which the number of ministers was reduced from 60 to 32, and the number of ministers of state from six to three.

Renewed hostilities and overthrow of Nkunda

Following a peace conference, which was convened in early January 2008, an official cease-fire was signed on 23 January; under the peace accord, the DRC Government pledged not to renew an arrest warrant for war crimes charges against Nkunda. In February, however, Nkunda announced that the CNDP was to withdraw from the cease-fire agreement, reportedly in protest against UN accusations of his faction's involvement in the killing of some 30 Hutu civilians during the peace negotiations the previous month. Although he declared his intention to co-operate with international mediators to restore peace, Nkunda's forces continued to clash with rival militia, and in April humanitarian agencies were obliged to suspend aid supplies. Meanwhile, in March one of the principal rebel factions to sign the January cease-fire agreement also withdrew from the accord, amid complaints over the composition of monitoring bodies to be established to oversee the implementation of the peace process.

In September 2008 Prime Minister Gizenga announced his resignation citing health concerns, although there had been reports of a planned vote of no confidence in his administration in the Parlement. In October President Kabila named Adolphe Muzito, hitherto Minister of the Budget, as Gizenga's successor, and a new Cabinet was appointed. In late October heavy fighting resumed when Nkunda's CNDP advanced within Nord-Kivu to Goma, gaining control of a large part of the province from government forces and precipitating the displacement of some 150,000 civilians, before declaring a cease-fire. The DRC Government accused Rwanda of deploying troops in Nord-Kivu to support Nkunda's forces. Former Nigerian President Gen. (retd) Olusegun Obasanjo was appointed the UN Secretary-General's Special Envoy to the eastern DRC, and on 7 November he mediated an emergency summit meeting in Nairobi. On 9 November SADC leaders, meeting at a summit in Sandton, South Africa, endorsed a joint statement on an immediate cease-fire in Nord-Kivu, the guarantee of safe passage for international humanitarian personnel and the implementation of the previous peace agreements. However, later in November the CNDP violated the cease-fire and continued to advance; the UN approved the deployment of further MONUC troops, bringing the strength of the peace-keeping mission to some 20,000, and in December renewed its mandate for a further year. In December Ugandan government troops, supported by DRC and southern Sudanese forces, launched an offensive against bases of Ugandan rebel movement the Lord's Resistance Army (LRA) in northern DRC; it was reported that more than 600 Congolese civilians were subsequently killed in reprisal attacks by LRA combatants.

Divisions within the CNDP emerged in January 2009 when a breakaway faction, led by the movement's military commander, Bosco Ntaganda, announced Nkunda's dismissal and support for the Governments of the DRC and Rwanda, which had unexpectedly formed an alliance and agreed to conduct a joint operation to suppress rebel activity in the Kivu provinces (principally involving Rwandan rebel group the Forces démocratiques de libération du Rwanda—FDLR). Nkunda denied that he had been removed from the leadership of the CNDP; however, in late January, after refusing to support the operation by DRC and Rwandan troops, he sought to escape arrest and fled to Rwanda where he was captured and detained. In February 2009 it was announced that a five-week joint operation conducted by DRC and Rwandan troops against the FDLR and forces loyal to Nkunda in Nord-Kivu had severely weakened the rebels; Rwandan troops commenced withdrawal from the country. Former CNDP combatants under the command of Ntaganda became integrated into the DRC armed forces, and in March it was reported that an agreement had been reached with the Government whereby the CNDP was to be reconstituted as a political party, chaired by Desiré Kamanzi, while prisoners belonging to the former rebel movement were to be released. The President of the Assemblée nationale, Vital Kamerhe, resigned in March, owing to pressure from supporters of Kabila, after he criticized the agreement between the DRC and Rwandan Governments; Evariste Boshab of the PPRD was elected as the new parliamentary President in April. In May both chambers of the Parlement approved legislation providing for the amnesty of rebel combatants (excluding those suspected of acts of genocide or other war crimes). Following the opening of Lubanga's trial at the ICC (on charges relating to the conscription and use of child soldiers during 2002 and 2003) in January, the trial of two militia leaders, Germain Katanga and Mathieu Ngudjolo Chui, began in November. In December the UN Security Council extended the mandate of MONUC for only five months, envisaging a reconfiguration of the mission, while Kabila favoured a full withdrawal.

In February 2010 Kabila effected a major reorganization of the Government, reducing it in size. Muzito was retained as Prime Minister, but two new Deputy Prime Ministers were appointed and new ministers of finance, of energy and of international and regional co-operation were notably installed; no members of the CNDP received ministerial portfolios. In accordance with a UN Security Council resolution on 28 May, MONUC was reconstituted as the UN Organization Stabilization Mission in the Democratic Republic of Congo (MONUSCO), with a maximum authorized strength of about 22,000 personnel, which had a mandate to remain in the country until the end of June 2011. In addition to stabilization and peace consolidation in the DRC, MONUSCO was tasked with monitoring the implementation of the UN armaments embargo, and providing technical and logistical support in the organization of forthcoming elections. In June 2010 a prominent human rights activist, Floribert Chebeya, was found dead in Kinshasa after he had been summoned to a meeting with police. Following widespread allegations of police involvement in Chebeya's death, the Inspector-General of the police, John Numbi, was suspended from his post shortly afterwards. As a result of an investigation, eight police officers (but not Numbi) were subsequently placed on trial at a military court on charges relating to the killing of Chebeya.

In October 2010 the appeals chamber of the ICC reversed an earlier decision by the Court that proceedings against Lubanga be abandoned (after the prosecution failed to disclose information identifying witnesses), and his trial resumed. The trial of Bemba, in connection with atrocities allegedly perpetrated by the MLC in the Central African Republic during 2002 and 2003, began at the ICC in November 2010 (representing the first to be heard at the Court in which a military commander was charged with responsibility for crimes committed by his troops). At the end of November the UN Security Council renewed the armament sanction and other sanctions in force against the DRC, and the mandate of a Group of Experts tasked with monitoring the measures, for a further year. (A report by the Group of Experts had noted the involvement of the DRC armed forces with criminal networks in the illegal exploitation of natural resources.) In December the Assemblée nationale approved legislation that was designed to reform the country's police force (largely comprising former combatants).

On 15 January 2011 the Assemblée nationale and the Sénat approved a number of significant amendments to the Constitution. The amendments, inter alia, stipulated that the presidential election be conducted in just one round, granted the President the right to dissolve provincial assemblies and remove provincial governors, provided for the enlargement of the number of provinces (from 11 to 26), and transferred authority over judicial prosecutors from the judiciary to the Ministry of Justice and Human Rights. The parliamentary vote was boycotted by over 100 opposition members, and the constitutional amendments were widely denounced as undemocratic. On 27 February an attack by armed combatants against Kabila's presidential palace in Kinshasa was repelled by the Republican Guard. The Government subsequently accused Gen. Faustin Munene, a former army chief of staff, who had established a rebel movement, the Armée de Résistance Populaire, of involvement in the attack, and requested his extradition from Brazzaville, where he had been detained in January. (However, the authorities of the Republic of the Congo refused to extradite Munene.) In March Kabila removed François Joseph Mobutu Nzanga Ngbangawe (the son of the former President), from his government post as Deputy Prime Minister, owing to his absence from the country since November 2010. Mobutu's party, the Union des démocrates mobutistes, subsequently withdrew from Kabila's presidential alliance. In April 2011 a new Commission électorale nationale indépendante (CENI), headed by Daniel Ngoy Mulunda, a pastor with close ties to Kabila, announced that the presidential and legislative elections would be conducted on 28 November. In June MONUSCO's mandate was extended for a further year.

Recent developments: presidential and legislative elections

The pre-election period in November 2011 was marred by violent incidents, which included clashes between supporters of rival political parties (resulting in the death of at least eight people) and the shooting of a prominent MLC politician. In early November the UN Security Council denounced human rights violations committed by the police. The presidential and legislative elections were conducted on 28 November, as scheduled, but were disrupted by continuing violent incidents and by rioting at polling centres; voting was extended for a further day in some regions, owing to severe logistical difficulties, including shortages of voting materials. An EU monitoring mission and US observers reported widespread electoral irregularities, and three opposition presidential candidates demanded that the elections be annulled on the grounds of malpractice. On 9 December the CENI declared that Kabila (under the amended system) had been re-elected with about 49% of the votes cast, while Tshisekedi had received 32.3% of the votes; the participation rate was estimated at 58% of the electorate. The announcement of the results prompted further rioting in Kinshasa and the official figures were strongly rejected by Tshisekedi's UDPS. On 16 December, however, the Supreme Court dismissed an opposition appeal against the official electoral results. The US Administration criticized the Supreme Court's ruling and described the conduct of the elections as severely flawed. Kabila was inaugurated for a new term on 20 December. Tshisekedi, who continued to contest the legitimacy of Kabila's election, was prevented by police from publicly conducting his own 'swearing-in' ceremony, which instead took place at his residence, amid protests by his supporters. Later in December the Government pledged to order an investigation into post-election killings (which were reported to number at least 24) by security forces. Following delays in the vote-counting process for the legislative elections, on 1 February 2012 the CENI announced provisional results for 162 of the 169 electoral districts, recommending that the results for the remaining seven electoral districts be annulled: the PPRD won 62 seats in the 500-seat Assemblée nationale, while the UDPS received about 41 seats. The provisional results represented a significant decline in support for the PPRD; opposition parties, however, demanded a full recount of the presidential and parliamentary votes. On 12 February a senior presidential aide was killed and the Minister of Finance severely injured in an aircraft crash near Bukavu.

By mid-April 2012 no further update had been made to the legislative election results released by the CENI in February. However, in early March Muzito resigned from his position as Prime Minister and was replaced on an interim basis by Louis Alphonse Koyagialo Gbase te Gerengbo, hitherto Deputy Prime Minister, Minister of Posts, Telephones and Telecommunications. A total of 22 ministers in the outgoing Muzito Government had been elected to the Assemblée nationale and thus were to be replaced in the new administration. In mid-April Aubin Minaku was elected President of the Assemblée nationale. Meanwhile, in mid-March the ICC found Lubanga guilty on charges relating to the conscription and use of child soldiers during 2002 and 2003, thereby becoming the first person to be convicted by the Court since its inception in 2002. He was expected to be sentenced later in 2012.

In late April 2012 Augustin Matata Ponyo, hitherto Minister of Finance, was appointed Prime Minister and days later the composition of the new Government was finally announced. The new administration was reduced in size from 46 ministers to 36; Ponyo retained the finance portfolio, while Daniel Mukoko Samba was appointed Deputy Prime Minister, Minister of the Budget, and Alexandre Luba Ntambo became Deputy Prime Minister, Minister of National Defence and War Veterans.

Foreign Affairs

The DRC Government has maintained strong relations with its former allies in the civil conflict, Zimbabwe, Angola and Namibia, but Zimbabwe's political and economic influence has been overtaken by that of South Africa, owing to former President Mbeki's strong involvement in the domestic and regional peace process. Following Kabila's agreement with Kagame in Pretoria in July 2002, relations improved between the Rwandan and DRC Governments, although the two continued to support opposing forces engaged in hostilities in Nord-Kivu. The DRC Government's relations with Uganda also improved, despite ongoing tensions between Kabila and Uganda's main ally in the DRC, the MLC. The occupation of Bukavu by dissident troops in mid-2004 again increased concerns of conflict between the DRC and Rwanda and prompted the mass flight of civilians to neighbouring countries. Following the massacre of Banyamulenge refugees from the DRC in Burundi in August, MONUC confirmed later that year that Rwandan troops had re-engaged in hostilities in DRC territory. In December 2005 the International Court of Justice (ICJ, see p. 25) upheld an appeal by the DRC against Uganda, submitted in April, and ordered the Ugandan Government to pay reparations for violations of international law perpetrated by its forces deployed in the country during 1998–2003. In February 2006, however, the ICJ ruled that it was unable to issue a decision in a similar case brought by the DRC against the Rwandan Government (which had refused to accept the jurisdiction of the Court). The renewal of hostilities in Nord-Kivu in October 2008 (see above) prompted further accusations by the DRC that Rwandan government troops were supporting rebel activity, and international diplomatic efforts to ease tensions ensued. Intensive ministerial negotiations resulted in an agreement between the DRC and Rwandan Governments in December, whereby Kabila officially permitted Rwandan troops to enter the country in a counter-rebel action. In early 2009 the DRC and Rwandan Governments conducted an unprecedented joint operation to suppress rebel activity in Nord-Kivu. In October 2010 the DRC Minister of Defence and his Rwandan counterpart, in a joint statement following a meeting in Kinshasa, claimed that progress had been made in the gradual eradication of armed groups in the region through collaborative efforts of the two countries' armed forces.

In October 2009 it was reported that Kabila had ordered the expulsion of some 30,000 Angolans, in response to Angola's deportation campaign of economic migrants from the DRC (under which some 160,000 DRC nationals had been expelled since December 2008); both Governments subsequently agreed to suspend forcible expulsions, pending a formal agreement. However, in 2010 the deportation of migrants from Angola resumed on a smaller scale, and tensions between the two countries increased; the UN Office for the Coordination of Humanitarian Affairs estimated that 20,000 migrants had been expelled from Angola during January–September. According to the Office of the UN High Commissioner for Refugees, the total number of refugees in the DRC at the beginning of 2011 was estimated at 166,336. Following continued repatriation to Angola in 2011, the number of Angolan refugees in the DRC was projected to have fallen to 59,620 by January 2012.

CONSTITUTION AND GOVERNMENT

According to the new Constitution, which entered into effect in February 2006, the President is the Head of State and Commander-in-Chief of the armed forces and is elected by direct universal suffrage for a term of five years, which is renewable once. Legislative power is vested in a bicameral Parlement, comprising a lower chamber, the Assemblée nationale, and an upper chamber, the Sénat. The 500 members of the Assemblée nationale are elected by direct universal suffrage for a renewable term of five years, while the 108 members of the Sénat are indirectly elected by the Assemblies of each of the country's 26 provinces for a renewable term of five years.

REGIONAL AND INTERNATIONAL CO-OPERATION

The DRC maintains economic co-operation agreements with neighbouring states, Burundi and Rwanda, through the Economic Community of the Great Lakes Countries (see p. 449). The DRC is a member of the Common Market for Eastern and Southern Africa (COMESA, see p. 237), and in September 1997 the DRC became a member of the Southern African Development Community (SADC, see p. 423). In September 2009 Kabila became Chairman of SADC for a one-year term.

The DRC joined the UN in 1960, and was admitted to the World Trade Organization (WTO, see p. 433) in 1997. The DRC is also a member of the International Coffee Organization (see p. 445).

ECONOMIC AFFAIRS

In 2010, according to estimates by the World Bank, the gross national income (GNI) of the DRC, measured at average 2008–10 prices, was US $11,951m., equivalent to $180 per head (or $320 per head on an international purchasing-power parity basis). During 2001–10, it was estimated, the population increased at an average annual rate of 2.9%, while gross domestic product (GDP) per head grew, in real terms, by an average of 2.5% per year. Overall GDP increased, in real terms, at an average annual rate of 5.5% in 2001–10; it rose by an estimated 2.7% in 2009 and by 7.2% in 2010.

According to the African Development Bank (AfDB), agriculture (including forestry, livestock, hunting and fishing) contributed an estimated 16.6% of GDP in 2009. According to FAO estimates, about 56.2% of the working population were projected to be employed in agriculture in mid-2012. The principal cash crops are coffee (which accounted for 8.8% of export earnings in 1999, although its contribution declined to an estimated 0.9% in 2008, owing largely to the dramatic increase in exports of copper and cobalt), palm oil and palm kernels, sugar, tea, cocoa, rubber and cotton. According to World Bank estimates, agricultural GDP increased at an average annual rate of 2.1% in 2001–09; the sector's GDP grew by 3.0% in 2009.

According to the AfDB, industry (including mining, manufacturing, construction and public works, and power) contributed an estimated 29.9% of GDP in 2009. Some 15.9% of the working population were employed in industry in 1991. According to World Bank estimates, industrial GDP increased at an average annual rate of 8.2% in 2001–10. The sector's GDP expanded by 7.1% in 2008, but declined by 4.2% in 2009.

According to the AfDB, mining (including mineral processing) contributed an estimated 3.6% of GDP in 2009. Diamonds, of which the DRC has rich deposits, are an important source of foreign exchange, accounting for an estimated 10.7% of export earnings in 2008. Other important minerals are copper, cobalt (of which the country has 65% of the world's reserves) and zinc. Cadmium, cassiterite, gold and silver are also mined on a small scale. Columbite-tantalite (coltan) has become a principal export in eastern regions previously under rebel control. By the mid-2000s the partial restoration of peace and the adoption of new mining and investment codes had prompted renewed investment interest in the sector. There are extensive offshore reserves of petroleum (revenue from petroleum accounted for an estimated 11.9% of export earnings in 2008). According to the IMF, the GDP of the mining sector grew at an average annual rate of 8.8% during 2003–08. The sector's GDP increased by 11.4% in 2008, but declined by 0.2% in 2009, according to the AfDB.

According to the AfDB, manufacturing contributed an estimated 21.8% of GDP in 2009. The most important sectors are textiles, building materials, agricultural processing and industrial chemicals. According to World Bank estimates, manufacturing GDP increased at an average annual rate of 8.5% in 2001–07. According to the AfDB, it grew by 2.5% in 2009.

According to the AfDB, construction contributed an estimated 3.8% of GDP in 2009. the IMF estimated that the GDP of the construction sector increased at an average annual rate of 13.5% in 2003–08. However, the sector's GDP decreased by 1.6% in 2008 before expanding again, by 1.8%, in 2009, according to the AfDB.

Energy is derived principally from hydroelectric power. In 2008 an estimated 99.4% of electricity production was generated by hydroelectric plants. In 2008 imports of petroleum comprised an estimated 11.6% of the value of total merchandise imports.

According to the AfDB, the services sector contributed an estimated 53.5% of GDP in 2009. Some 19.0% of the working population were engaged in the sector in 1991. The GDP of the services sector increased at an average annual rate of 11.1% in 2001–09, and grew by an estimated 5.9% in 2009, according to World Bank estimates.

In 2009 the DRC recorded an estimated trade deficit of US $578m., while there was a deficit of $1,166m. on the current account of the balance of payments. In 1995 the principal source of imports (an estimated 16.6%) was Belgium-Luxembourg; other major suppliers were South Africa, Nigeria, Ecuador, the United Kingdom and Germany. In that year South Africa was the principal market for exports (taking an estimated 29.6% of the total); the USA, Belgium-Luxembourg and Angola were also important markets for exports. According to estimates, the principal exports in 2008 were cobalt (38.3%), copper, crude petroleum and diamonds. The principal import was petroleum.

In 2009 the estimated overall budget deficit was 379,000m. new Congolese francs, equivalent to 2.8% of GDP. The DRC's general government gross debt was 4,014.250m. new Congolese francs in 2010, equivalent to 33.8% of GDP. In 2009 external debt totalled US $12,183m., of which $10,788m. was public and publicly guaranteed debt. In that year the cost of servicing long-term public and publicly guaranteed debt and repayments to the IMF was equivalent to 8.7% of the value of exports of goods, services and income (excluding workers' remittances). According to the IMF, consumer prices increased at an average annual rate of 14.1% during 2002–08. Consumer prices expanded by 17.3% in 2008.

Potentially one of Africa's richest states, the DRC has extensive agricultural, mineral and energy resources. However, the outbreak of civil war in August 1997 resulted in a serious deterioration in the financial situation, and rebel factions systematically exploited mineral resources. Following the succession to the presidency of Joseph Kabila in 2001, significant progress in peace negotiations was achieved, and a UN embargo on trade in unlicensed diamonds was imposed. The Kabila Government's economic plan for 2005–07 received considerable pledges of financial support. In March 2009 the IMF approved a disbursement of some US $195.5m. to the DRC under an Exogenous Shocks Facility, in an effort to counteract the adverse effects of the international financial crisis, which (together with the resumption of fighting) had resulted in a severe decline in the country's terms of trade and in foreign direct investment. In December, following a favourable assessment, the IMF approved a three-year Poverty Reduction and Growth Facility (PRGF) arrangement (totalling $551m.), and $73m. in interim assistance under the Heavily Indebted Poor Countries (HIPC) Initiative for the DRC. In June 2010 the IMF issued a commendatory review of the DRC's economic performance under the Extended Credit Facility (ECF) arrangement (which had replaced the PRGF) and approved a $73m. disbursement. The IMF and World Bank subsequently stated that the DRC had implemented the measures required to reach completion point under the HIPC Initiative, allowing substantial HIPC debt relief and additional bilateral assistance. Accordingly, the institutions announced the approval of debt relief totalling $12,300m., thereby significantly reducing the country's external debt burden. In November the Paris Club of creditor nations, in accordance with IMF and World Bank recommendations, cancelled a large part of the DRC's foreign debt. In April 2011 the IMF approved a disbursement of $80m. for the DRC under the ECF arrangement, following its assessment that implementation of required transparency reforms in the extractive industry had proceeded satisfactorily. Later that year, however, the release of a $90m. tranche was suspended by the IMF, after state-owned mining company GÉCAMINES failed to publish contracts relating to joint ventures with international partners in accordance with the stipulated transparency programme. Nevertheless, the IMF projected continued growth of some 7% for 2011. The introduction of a 16% value-added tax at the beginning of 2012 resulted in a sharp rise in the inflation rate; the country's business federation stated that the measure had caused confusion and demanded a one-year postponement in its implementation. The conduct of elections in November 2011 (see Domestic Political Affairs) was widely criticized by international observers and described by the US Administration as severely flawed; in early 2012 protracted delays in the official confirmation of the legislative election results presented a further potential obstacle to international funding.

PUBLIC HOLIDAYS

2013: 1 January (New Year's Day), 4 January (Commemoration of the Martyrs of Independence), 17 January (National Hero's Day), 1 May (Labour Day), 17 May (National Liberation Day), 30 June (Independence Day), 1 August (Parents' Day), 14 October (Youth Day), 17 November (Army Day), 24 November (Anniversary of the Second Republic), 25 December (Christmas Day).

Statistical Survey

Sources (unless otherwise stated): Département de l'Economie Nationale, Kinshasa; Institut National de la Statistique, Office Nationale de la Recherche et du Développement, BP 20, Kinshasa; tel. (12) 31401.

Area and Population

AREA, POPULATION AND DENSITY

Area (sq km)	2,344,885*
Population (census result)	
1 July 1984	
Males	14,543,800
Females	15,373,000
Total	29,916,800
Population (UN estimates at mid-year)†	
2010	65,965,795
2011	67,757,576
2012	69,575,391
Density (per sq km) at mid-2012	29.7

* 905,365 sq miles.

† Source: UN, *World Population Prospects: The 2010 Revision*.

POPULATION BY AGE AND SEX

(UN estimates at mid-2012)

	Males	Females	Total
0–14	15,943,014	15,850,142	31,793,156
15–64	17,850,149	18,073,590	35,923,739
65 and over	812,430	1,046,066	1,858,496
Total	34,605,593	34,969,798	69,575,391

Source: UN, *World Population Prospects: The 2010 Revision*.

REGIONS*

	Area (sq km)	Population (31 Dec. 1985)†
Bandundu	295,658	4,644,758
Bas-Zaïre	53,920	2,158,595
Equateur	403,293	3,960,187
Haut-Zaïre	503,239	5,119,750
Kasaï Occidental	156,967	3,465,756
Kasaï Oriental	168,216	2,859,220
Kivu	256,662	5,232,442
Shaba (formerly Katanga)	496,965	4,452,618
Kinshasa (city)‡	9,965	2,778,281
Total	2,344,885	34,671,607

* In October 1997 a statutory order redesignated the regions as provinces. Kivu was divided into three separate provinces, and several of the other provinces were renamed. The Constitution of February 2006 increased the existing 11 provinces to 26: Bas-Uele, Équateur, Haut-Lomami, Haut-Katanga, Haut-Uele, Ituri, Kasaï, Kasaï Oriental, Kongo Central, Kwango, Kwilu, Lomami, Lualaba, Lulua, Mai-Ndombe, Maniema, Mongala, Nord-Kivu, Nord-Ubangi, Sankuru, Sud-Kivu, Sud-Ubangi, Tanganyika, Tshopo, Tshuapa and Kinshasa (city).

† Provisional.

‡ Including the commune of Maluku.

Source: Département de l'Administration du Territoire.

PRINCIPAL TOWNS

(population at census of July 1984)

Kinshasa (capital)	2,664,309	Likasi	213,862
Lubumbashi	564,830	Boma	197,617
Mbuji-Mayi	486,235	Bukavu	167,950
Kolwezi	416,122	Kikwit	149,296
Kisangani	317,581	Matadi	138,798
Kananga	298,693	Mbandaka	137,291

Source: UN, *Demographic Yearbook*.

Mid-2010: (incl. suburbs, UN estimates) Kinshasa (capital) 8,753,869; Lubumbashi 1,542,945; Mbuji-Mayi 1,488,468; Kisangani 812,489; Kananga 878,263 (Source: UN, *World Urbanization Prospects: The 2009 Revision*).

BIRTHS AND DEATHS

(annual averages, UN estimates)

	1995–2000	2000–05	2005–10
Birth rate (per 1,000)	49.8	48.2	44.9
Death rate (per 1,000)	19.7	18.2	17.2

Source: UN, *World Population Prospects: The 2010 Revision*.

Life expectancy (years at birth, WHO estimates): 49 (males 47; females 51) in 2009 (Source: WHO, *World Health Statistics*).

Economically Active Population (mid-2012, estimates in '000): Agriculture, etc. 14,684; Total labour force 26,115 (Source: FAO).

Health and Welfare

KEY INDICATORS

Total fertility rate (children per woman, 2009)	5.9
Under-5 mortality rate (per 1,000 live births, 2009)	199
HIV/AIDS (% of persons aged 15–49, 2005)	3.2
Physicians (per 1,000 head, 2004)	0.1
Hospital beds (per 1,000 head, 2005)	1.1
Health expenditure (2008): US $ per head (PPP)	23
Health expenditure (2008): % of GDP	7.3
Health expenditure (2008): public (% of total)	54.2
Access to water (% of persons, 2008)	46
Access to sanitation (% of persons, 2008)	23
Total carbon dioxide emissions ('000 metric tons, 2007)	2,432.9
Carbon dioxide emissions per head (metric tons, 2007)	<0.1
Human Development Index (2011): ranking	187
Human Development Index (2011): value	0.286

For sources and definitions, see explanatory note on p. vi.

Agriculture

PRINCIPAL CROPS

('000 metric tons)

	2008	2009	2010
Rice, paddy	317	317	317
Maize	1,156	1,156	1,156
Millet	38	38	38
Sorghum	6	6	6
Potatoes	94	94	95
Sweet potatoes	240	243	247
Cassava (Manioc)	15,014	15,034	15,050
Taro (Cocoyam)	66	66	67
Yams	88	89	90
Sugar cane	1,793*	1,827*	1,827†
Beans, dry	113	114	115
Peas, dry	1	1	1
Groundnuts, with shell	370	371	371
Oil palm fruit	1,135	1,150	1,164
Melonseed†	51	51	52
Cabbages and other brassicas†	25	25	26
Tomatoes	47*	49*	50†
Onions, dry†	55	56	60
Pumpkins, squash and gourds	31	30†	31†
Bananas	315	316	316
Plantains	1,207	1,200†	1,250†
Oranges	181	181	181
Avocados	65	66	67
Mangoes, mangosteens and guavas	208	210	212
Pineapples	198	199	201
Papayas	222	224	226
Coffee, green	32	32	32

* Unofficial figure.
† FAO estimate(s).

Aggregate production ('000 metric tons, may include official, semi-official or estimated data): Total cereals 1,526 in 2008, 1,527 in 2009, 1,528 in 2010; Total roots and tubers 15,572 in 2008, 15,618 in 2009, 15,643 in 2010; Total vegetables (incl. melons) 536 in 2008, 545 in 2009, 557 in 2010; Total fruits (excl. melons) 2,480 in 2008, 2,483 in 2009, 2,541 in 2010.

Source: FAO.

LIVESTOCK

('000 head, year ending September)

	2008	2009	2010*
Cattle	753	751†	755
Sheep	902	903†	905
Goats	4,046	4,100*	4,150
Pigs	965	967†	967
Chickens	19,948†	20,007†	20,500

* FAO estimate(s).
† Unofficial figure.

Source: FAO.

LIVESTOCK PRODUCTS

('000 metric tons)

	2008	2009*	2010*
Cattle meat	12.3	12.0	12.5
Goat meat	17.8	17.8	17.8
Pig meat	24.0	24.0	26.0
Chicken meat	10.7	10.8	10.8
Game meat	89.1	89.0	101.1
Sheep meat	2.8	2.8	2.8
Cows' milk*	6.8	6.9	8.0
Hen eggs*	8.7	8.7	8.9

* FAO estimates.

Source: FAO.

Forestry

ROUNDWOOD REMOVALS

('000 cubic metres, excl. bark, FAO estimates)

	2007	2008	2009
Sawlogs, veneer logs and logs for sleepers	205	205	205
Other industrial wood	4,282	4,282	4,282
Fuel wood	73,209	74,315	75,446
Total	77,696	78,802	79,933

2010: Production assumed to be unchanged from 2009 (FAO estimates).

Source: FAO.

SAWNWOOD PRODUCTION

('000 cubic metres, incl. railway sleepers)

	2003	2004	2005
Total (all broadleaved)	15	15	15

2006–10: Production assumed to be unchanged from 2005 (FAO estimates).

Source: FAO.

Fishing

('000 metric tons, live weight, FAO estimates)

	2005	2006	2007
Capture	236.6	236.6	236.0
Aquaculture	3.0	3.0	3.0
Total catch	239.6	239.6	239.0

2008–09: Catch assumed to be unchanged from 2007 (FAO estimates).

Source: FAO.

Mining

(metric tons, unless otherwise indicated)

	2007	2008	2009
Hard coal	128,000	116,000	120,000*
Crude petroleum ('000 barrels)	8,816	8,365	9,382
Copper ore†*	146,000	238,000	295,000*
Tantalum and niobium (columbium) concentrates	267	509	490*
Cobalt concentrates†	25,300	31,000	29,000*
Gold (kg)	5,100	3,300	3,500*
Silver (kg)	76,242	34,083	n.a.
Germanium (kg)	2,500	2,500*	2,500*
Diamonds ('000 carats)‡	28,265	20,947	18,275

* Estimated production.
† Figures refer to the metal content of mine output.
‡ An estimated 20% of the diamond output is gem quality; the majority of production is from artisanal mining.

Source: US Geological Survey.

Industry

SELECTED PRODUCTS
('000 metric tons, unless otherwise indicated)

	2006	2007	2008*
Maize flour	14	15	15
Wheat flour	186	179	184
Sugar	91	94	96
Cigarettes ('000 cartons)	3,048	3,433	3,536
Beer (million litres)	301	295	304
Soft drinks (million litres)	162	130	140
Soaps	24	8	25
Acetylene	10	7	19
Tyres ('000 units)	53	55	56
Cement	530	539	411
Steel	104	110	113
Explosives	26	27	—
Bottles ('000 units)	18	19	21
Cotton fabrics ('000 sq m)	852	267	—
Printed fabrics ('000 sq m)	6,411	5,616	—
Footwear ('000 pairs)	1,432	21,178	21,814
Blankets ('000 units)	12	12	13
Electric energy (million kWh)	7,633	7,543	7,495

* Estimates.

Source: IMF, *Democratic Republic of the Congo: Statistical Appendix* (January 2010).

Finance

CURRENCY AND EXCHANGE RATES

Monetary Units
100 centimes = 1 new Congolese franc.

Sterling, Dollar and Euro Equivalents (30 December 2011)
£1 sterling = 1,407.96 new Congolese francs;
US $1 = 910.65 new Congolese francs;
€1 = 1,178.29 new Congolese francs;
10,000 new Congolese francs = £7.10 = $10.98 = €8.49.

Average Exchange Rate (new Congolese francs per US $)
2009 809.786
2010 905.914
2011 919.492

Note: In June 1967 the zaire was introduced, replacing the Congolese franc (CF) at an exchange rate of 1 zaire = CF 1,000. In October 1993 the zaire was replaced by the new zaire (NZ), equivalent to 3m. old zaires. On 30 June 1998 a new Congolese franc, equivalent to NZ 100,000, was introduced. The NZ was withdrawn from circulation on 30 June 1999. Some of the figures in this survey are still given in terms of a previous currency.

BUDGET
('000 million new Congolese francs)*

Revenue†	2006	2007	2008‡
Taxes on income and profits	128,774	161,371	253,100
Corporations and enterprises	79,076	89,408	147,790
Individuals	40,756	58,107	85,601
Taxes on goods and services	146,301	192,774	282,866
Turnover taxes	110,056	150,917	221,628
Selective excises	35,543	40,406	59,431
Beer	13,804	16,911	26,771
Tobacco	11,040	11,985	20,146
Taxes on international trade	163,805	239,333	342,528
Import duties and taxes	154,045	230,596	326,240
Export duties and taxes	9,630	8,679	16,288
Others	129	58	0
Other revenue	89,818	167,509	326,795
Total	528,698	760,987	1,205,289

Expenditure	2006	2007	2008‡
Wages and salaries	218,898	300,984	452,220
Goods and services (incl. off-budget)	133,194	203,685	277,694
Interest on domestic debt	22,921	28,721	34,225
Interest on external debt	72,995	155,413	169,550
Transfers and subsidies	87,102	111,730	226,871
Exceptional expenditure	171,706	45,034	74,417
Investment	134,050	121,085	243,706
Total	840,866	966,653	1,478,682

* Figures refer to the consolidated accounts of the central Government.
† Excluding grants received ('000 million new Congolese francs): 328,507 in 2006; 76,014 in 2007; 121,484 in 2008 (estimate).
‡ Estimates.

Source: IMF, *Democratic Republic of the Congo: Statistical Appendix* (January 2010).

2009 ('000 million new Congolese francs, preliminary): *Revenue:* Customs and excise 560; Direct and indirect taxes 565; Petroleum royalties and taxes 132; Non-tax revenue 271; Total revenue 1,528 (excl. grants 679). *Expenditure:* Current expenditure 1,652; Capital expenditure 704; Exceptional expenditure 231; Total expenditure 2,586 (Source: IMF, *Democratic Republic of the Congo: Third Review of the Three-Year Arrangement Under the Extended Credit Facility, Financing Assurances Review, and Request for Modification of Performance Criteria—Staff Report and Press Release on the Executive Board Discussion*—July 2011).

2010 ('000 million new Congolese francs, estimates): *Revenue:* Customs and excise 754; Direct and indirect taxes 778; Petroleum royalties and taxes 266; Non—tax revenues 455; Total revenue 2,253 (excl. grants 1,676). *Expenditure:* Current expenditure 1,724; Capital expenditure 1,678; Exceptional expenditure 245; Total expenditure 3,647 (Source: IMF, *Democratic Republic of the Congo: Third Review of the Three-Year Arrangement Under the Extended Credit Facility, Financing Assurances Review, and Request for Modification of Performance Criteria—Staff Report and Press Release on the Executive Board Discussion*—July 2011).

2011 ('000 million new Congolese francs, projections): *Revenue:* Customs and excise 949; Direct and indirect taxes 1,048; Petroleum royalties and taxes 415; Non—tax revenues 594; Total revenue 3,006 (excl. grants 1,268). *Expenditure:* Current expenditure 2,525; Capital expenditure 2,421; Exceptional expenditure 322; Budget reserve 39; Total expenditure 5,308 (Source: IMF, *Democratic Republic of the Congo: Third Review of the Three-Year Arrangement Under the Extended Credit Facility, Financing Assurances Review, and Request for Modification of Performance Criteria—Staff Report and Press Release on the Executive Board Discussion*—July 2011).

INTERNATIONAL RESERVES
(excluding gold, US $ million at 31 December)

	2008	2009	2010
IMF special drawing rights	5.98	612.58	543.93
Foreign exchange	71.75	422.80	755.72
Total	77.73	1,035.38	1,299.65

Source: IMF, *International Financial Statistics*.

MONEY SUPPLY
(million new Congolese francs at 31 December)

	2008	2009	2010
Currency outside banks	304,568	381,486	489,377
Demand deposits at deposit money banks	86,324	91,037	212,909
Total money (incl. others)	392,484	479,875	706,164

Source: IMF, *International Financial Statistics*.

COST OF LIVING
(Consumer Price Index for Kinshasa at 31 December; base: August 1995 = 100)

	2005	2006	2007
Food	546,165	697,790	762,946
Rent	622,109	736,670	817,241
Clothing	930,811	1,077,902	1,128,393
All items (incl. others)	644,137	798,297	877,842

Source: IMF, *Democratic Republic of the Congo: Statistical Appendix* (January 2010).

Cost of living (Consumer Price Index; base: 2005 = 100): 113.1 in 2006; 132.2 in 2007; 155.1 in 2008 (Source: IMF, *International Financial Statistics*).

NATIONAL ACCOUNTS
('000 million new Congolese francs at current prices)

Expenditure on the Gross Domestic Product

	2007	2008	2009
Government final consumption expenditure	658	758	846
Private final consumption expenditure	7,139	7,304	7,887
Gross fixed capital formation	1,969	3,169	4,290
Change in inventories	5	5	6
Total domestic expenditure	9,771	11,236	13,029
Exports of goods and services	1,982	3,658	4,602
Less Imports of goods and services	3,377	4,274	4,277
GDP in purchasers' values	8,376	10,621	13,355

Gross Domestic Product by Economic Activity

	2007	2008	2009
Agriculture, forestry, livestock, hunting, and fishing	1,684	1,919	2,126
Mining	484	555	462
Manufacturing	1,654	2,150	2,795
Construction and public works	417	407	482
Electricity and water	85	89	96
Wholesale and retail trade; restaurants and hotels	1,457	1,980	2,690
Transport and telecommunications	1,253	1,664	2,210
Public administration, defence and other services	544	817	990
Other services	464	514	978
Sub-total	8,042	10,094	12,828
Taxes, less subsidies, on imports	362	557	557
Less Imputed bank service charge	29	30	31
GDP at market prices	8,376	10,621	13,355

Source: African Development Bank.

2010 ('000 million new Congolese francs at current prices, preliminary): GDP at market prices 11,908 (Source: IMF, *Democratic Republic of the Congo: Third Review of the Three-Year Arrangement Under the Extended Credit Facility, Financing Assurances Review, and Request for Modification of Performance Criteria—Staff Report and Press Release on the Executive Board Discussion*—July 2011).

BALANCE OF PAYMENTS
(US $ million)

	2007	2008	2009
Exports of goods f.o.b.	6,143	6,585	4,370
Imports of goods f.o.b.	−5,257	−6,711	−4,949
Trade balance	886	−125	−578
Exports of services	392	522	651
Imports of services	−1,618	−2,146	−1,817
Balance on goods and services	−340	−1,749	−1,745
Other income received	26	27	26
Other income paid	−661	−1,348	−805
Balance on goods, services and income	−975	−3,070	−2,524
Current transfers (net)	821	1,231	1,357
Current balance	−153	−1,839	−1,166
Capital and financial account (net)	66	1,007	198
Net errors and omissions	−262	−115	81
Overall balance	−349	−946	−888

* Preliminary figures.

Source: IMF, *Democratic Republic of the Congo: Third Review of the Three-Year Arrangement Under the Extended Credit Facility, Financing Assurances Review, and Request for Modification of Performance Criteria—Staff Report and Press Release on the Executive Board Discussion* (July 2011).

External Trade

PRINCIPAL COMMODITIES
(US $ million)

Imports c.i.f.	2006	2007	2008*
Petroleum	486	571	778
Non-petroleum	2,405	4,686	5,933
Total	2,892	5,257	6,711

Exports f.o.b.†	2006	2007	2008*
Copper	869	2,040	2,333
Cobalt	373	2,310	2,523
Diamonds	884	836	702
Crude petroleum	579	612	783
Coffee	46	52	59
Total (incl. others)	2,931	6,143	6,585

* Estimates.

† Including 'parallel' exports (US $ million): 221 in 2006; 248 in 2007; 207 in 2008 (estimate).

Source: IMF, *Democratic Republic of the Congo: Statistical Appendix* (January 2010).

SELECTED TRADING PARTNERS
(US $ million)

Imports c.i.f.	1995
Belgium-Luxembourg	147.2
Canada	9.8
China, People's Repub.	26.8
Côte d'Ivoire	35.5
Ecuador	65.1
Germany	48.2
India	9.9
Iran	10.3
Italy	26.5
Japan	11.8
Kenya	22.5
Morocco	9.2
Netherlands	36.5
Nigeria	72.5
South Africa	89.3
Togo	22.5
United Kingdom	50.2
Zambia	9.4
Total (incl. others)	889.2

Exports f.o.b.	1995
Angola	51.0
Belgium-Luxembourg	90.9
Canada	11.6
Germany	8.7
Israel	17.2
Italy	29.6
Philippines	30.2
Senegal	9.5
South Africa	219.7
Switzerland	29.7
United Kingdom	29.7
USA	107.6
Total (incl. others)	742.8

Source: UN, *International Trade Statistics Yearbook*.

Transport

RAILWAYS
(traffic)*

	1999	2000	2001†
Passenger-km (million)	145.2	187.9	222.1
Freight (million ton-km)	386.5	429.3	459.1

* Figures refer to Société Nationale des Chemins de Fer du Congo (SNCC) services only.
† Estimates.

Source: IMF, *Democratic Republic of the Congo: Selected Issues and Statistical Appendix* (June 2003).

ROAD TRAFFIC
(motor vehicles in use at 31 December)

	1994	1995*	1996*
Passenger cars	698,672	762,000	787,000
Buses and coaches	51,578	55,000	60,000
Lorries and vans	464,205	495,000	538,000
Total vehicles	1,214,455	1,312,000	1,384,000

* Estimates.

2007: Total vehicles 311,781.

Source: IRF, *World Road Statistics*.

1999: Passenger cars 172,600; Commercial vehicles 34,600 (Source: UN, *Statistical Yearbook*).

SHIPPING

Merchant Fleet
(registered at 31 December)

	2007	2008	2009
Number of vessels	21	21	21
Total displacement ('000 grt)	13.9	13.9	13.9

Source: IHS Fairplay, *World Fleet Statistics*.

International Sea-borne Freight Traffic
(estimates, '000 metric tons)

	1988	1989	1990
Goods loaded	2,500	2,440	2,395
Goods unloaded	1,400	1,483	1,453

Source: UN, *Monthly Bulletin of Statistics*.

CIVIL AVIATION
(traffic on scheduled services)

	1992	1993	1994
Kilometres flown (million)	4	4	6
Passengers carried ('000)	116	84	178
Passenger-km (million)	295	218	480
Total ton-km (million)	56	42	87

Source: UN, *Statistical Yearbook*.

2001: Passengers carried ('000) 95.2; Total ton-km (million) 7.4 (Source: World Bank, World Development Indicators database).

Tourism

FOREIGN TOURIST ARRIVALS BY ORIGIN

	2007	2008	2009
Africa	27,767	27,969	31,328
Congo, Republic	666	n.a.	1,916
East Asia	5,478	5,233	5,540
Europe	11,314	13,104	13,101
Belgium	3,033	4,159	4,087
France	2,992	2,793	2,654
Germany	843	1,266	1,424
Italy	609	1,102	1,182
Central America, North America, South America	2,933	3,665	3,433
Total	47,492	49,971	53,402

Tourism receipts (US $ million): 2 in 1998.

Source: World Tourism Organization.

Communications Media

	2008	2009	2010
Telephones ('000 main lines in use)	37.3	42.3	42.0
Mobile cellular telephones ('000 subscribers)	9,937.6	9,458.6	11,820.3
Internet subscribers ('000)	67.0	73.4	75.7
Broadband subscribers ('000)	1.5	6.8	8.7

Radio receivers ('000 in use): 18,030 in 1997.

Television receivers ('000 in use): 100 in 1998.

Personal computers: 500,000 in 1999.

Book production (titles published): 112 in 1996.

Daily newspapers: 12 in 2004 (estimated average circulation 129,000 in 1998).

Non-daily newspapers: 164 in 2004.

Sources: International Telecommunication Union; UNESCO Institute for Statistics.

Education

(2008/09 unless otherwise indicated)

		Students		
	Teachers	Males	Females	Total
Pre-primary	10,139	121,649	127,677	249,326
Primary	274,453	5,537,072	4,707,014	10,244,086
General secondary	212,273	1,774,852	1,006,706	2,781,558
Technical and vocational		407,521	209,471	616,992
Tertiary	23,009	288,657	89,210	377,867

Institutions (1998/99): Primary 17,585; Secondary 6,007.

Source: UNESCO Institute for Statistics.

Pupil-teacher ratio (primary education, UNESCO estimate): 37.3 in 2008/09 (Source: UNESCO Institute for Statistics).

Adult literacy rate (UNESCO estimates): 66.8% (males 77.4%; females 56.6%) in 2009 (Source: UNESCO Institute for Statistics).

Directory

The Government

HEAD OF STATE

President: Maj.-Gen. JOSEPH KABILA KABANGE (inaugurated 26 January 2001, 7 April 2003, 6 December 2006 and 28 November 2011).

CABINET
(May 2012)

Prime Minister: AUGUSTIN MATATA PONYO.

Deputy Prime Minister, Minister of the Budget: DANIEL MUKOKO SAMBA.

Deputy Prime Minister, Minister of National Defence and War Veterans: ALEXANDRE LUBA NTAMBO.

Minister of Foreign Affairs, International Co-operation and the Francophonie: RAYMOND TSHIBANDA N'TUNGAMULONGO.

Minister of the Interior, Security, Decentralization and Traditional Affairs: RICHARD MUYEJ MANGEZ.

Minister of Justice and Human Rights: WIVINE MUMBA MATIPA.

Minister of Media, in charge of Relations with Parliament and Initiation of New Citizenship: LAMBERT MENDE OMALANGA.

Minister of Planning, Implementation and Modernization: CÉLESTIN VUNABANDI KANYAMIHIGO.

Minister of Portfolio: LOUISE MUNGA MESOZI.

Minister of the Economy and Commerce: JEAN PAUL NEMOYATO BEGEPOLE.

Minister of Land Settlement, Town Planning, Housing, Infrastructure, Public Works and Reconstruction: FRIDOLIN KASWESHI MUSOKA.

Minister of Transport and Communication Routes: JUSTIN KALUMBA MWANA NGONGO.

Minister of the Environment, Conservation of Nature and Tourism: BAVON N'SA MPUTU ELIMA.

Minister of Mines: MARTIN KABWELULU.

Minister of Water Resources and Electricity: BRUNO KAPANJI KALALA.

Minister of Hydrocarbons: CRISPIN ATAMA TABE.

Minister of Industry and Small and Medium-sized Enterprises: REMY MUSUNGAYI BAMPALE.

Minister of Posts, Telecommunications and New Information and Communication Technologies: TRIPHON KIN KIEY MULUMBA.

Minister of Employment, Labour and Social Security: MODESTE BAHATI LUKWEBO.

Minister of Public Health: FÉLIX KABANGE NUMBI MUKWAMPA.

Minister of Higher and University Education and Scientific Research: CHELO LOTSIMA.

Minister of Primary and Secondary Education and Professional Training: MAKER MWANGU FAMBA.

Minister of Agriculture and Rural Development: JEAN CHRISOSTOME VAHAMWITI MUKESYAYIRA.

Minister of Land Affairs: ROBERT MBWINGA BILA.

Minister of Social Affairs, Humanitarian Action and National Solidarity: CHARLES NAWEJ MUNDELE.

Minister of Gender Equality, the Family and Children: GENEVIÈVE INAGOSI.

Minister of the Civil Service: JEAN CLAUDE KIBALA.

Minister of Youth, Sport, Culture and the Arts: BANZA MUKALAYI NSUNGU.

Minister-delegate to the Prime Minister, in charge of Finance: PATRICE KITEBI KIBOL MVUL.

There were also eight deputy ministers.

MINISTRIES

Office of the President: Hôtel du Conseil Exécutif, ave de Lemera, Kinshasa-Gombe; tel. (12) 30892; internet www.presidentrdc.cd.

Office of the Prime Minister: Kinshasa.

Ministry of Agriculture and Rural Development: Kinshasa.

Ministry of the Budget: blvd du 30 juin, Immeuble Alhadeff, Kinshasa; internet www.ministeredubudget.cd.

Ministry of the Civil Service: Kinshasa.

Ministry of Employment, Labour and Social Security: blvd du 30 juin, BP 3840, Kinshasa-Gombe.

Ministry of the Environment, Conservation of Nature and Tourism: 76 ave des Cliniques, Kinshasa-Gombe; tel. 8802401; internet www.minenv.itgo.com.

Ministry of Finance: blvd du 30 juin, BP 12998 KIN I, Kinshasa-Gombe; tel. (12) 33232; internet www.minfinrdc.cd.

Ministry of Foreign Affairs, International Co-operation and the Francophonie: Kinshasa.

Ministry of Gender Equality, the Family and Children: Kinshasa.

Ministry of Higher and University Education and Scientific Research: Kinshasa.

Ministry of Hydrocarbons: Kinshasa.

Ministry of Industry and Small and Medium-sized Enterprises: Kinshasa.

Ministry of the Interior, Security, Decentralization and Traditional Affairs: ave de Lemera, Kinshasa-Gombe; tel. (12) 23171.

Ministry of Justice and Human Rights: 228 ave de Lemera, BP 3137, Kinshasa-Gombe; tel. (12) 32432.

Ministry of Land Affairs: Kinshasa.

Ministry of Land Settlement, Town Planning, Housing, Infrastructure, Public Works and Reconstruction: Kinshasa.

Ministry of Media: Immeuble RATELESCO, 83 ave Tombalbaye, Kinshasa; tel. 818134753; e-mail mincomedia.rdc@gmail.com; internet www.comediardc.org.

Ministry of Mines: Kinshasa; internet www.miningcongo.cd.

Ministry of National Defence and War Veterans: BP 4111, Kinshasa-Gombe; tel. (12) 59375.

Ministry of the Economy and Commerce: Kinshasa.

Ministry of Planning, Implementation and of Modernization: 4155 ave des Côteaux, BP 9378, Kinshasa-Gombe 1; tel. 810306644; e-mail miniplan@micronet.cd; internet www.ministereduplan.cd.

Ministry of Posts, Telecommunications and New Information and Communication Technologies: Immeuble Kilou, 4484 ave des Huiles, BP 800 KIN I, Kinshasa-Gombe; tel. (12) 24854.

Ministry of Primary and Secondary Education and Professional Training: Enceinte de l'Institut de la Gombe, BP 3163, Kinshasa-Gombe; tel. (12) 30098; internet www.eduquepsp.org.

Ministry of Public Health: blvd du 30 juin, BP 3088 KIN I, Kinshasa-Gombe; tel. (12) 31750.

Ministry of Social Affairs, Humanitarian Action and National Solidarity: Kinshasa.

Ministry of Transport and Communication Routes: Immeuble ONATRA, blvd du 30 juin, BP 3304, Kinshasa-Gombe; tel. (12) 23660.

Ministry of Water Resources and Electricity: Immeuble SNEL, 239 ave de la Justice, BP 5137 KIN I, Kinshasa-Gombe; tel. (12) 22570.

Ministry of Youth, Sport, Culture and the Arts: 77 ave de la Justice, BP 8541 KIN I, Kinshasa-Gombe.

President and Legislature

PRESIDENT

Presidential Election, 28–29 November 2011, provisional results

Candidate	Votes	% of votes
Joseph Kabila Kabange (Ind.)	8,880,944	48.95
Etienne Tshisekedi Wa Mulumba (Union pour la démocratie et le progrès social)	5,864,775	32.33
Vital Kamerhe Lwa-Kanyiginyi (Union pour la nation congolaise)	1,403,372	7.74
Léon Kengo Wa Dondo (Union des forces du changement)	898,362	4.95
Antipas Mbusa Nyamwisi (Ind.)	311,787	1.72
François Joseph Mobutu Nzanga Ngbangawe (Union des démocrates mobutistes)	285,273	1.57

Candidate—*continued*	Votes	% of votes
Jean Andeka Djamba (Alliance des nationalistes croyants congolais)	128,820	0.71
Adam Bombole Intole (Ind.)	126,623	0.70
François Nicéphore Kakese Malela (Union pour le réveil et le développement du Congo)	92,737	0.51
Josué Alex Mukendi Kamama (Ind.)	78,151	0.43
Dr. Oscar Kashala Lukumuena (Union pour la réconstruction du Congo)	72,260	0.40
Total	18,143,104*	100.00

* In addition, there were 768,468 blank or invalid votes.

LEGISLATURE

The bicameral Parlement of the Democratic Republic of the Congo comprises a lower chamber, or Assemblée nationale, and an upper chamber, or Sénat, members of which are elected by the deputies of the provincial Assemblées.

Assemblée nationale

President: AUBIN MINAKU.

General Election, 28–29 November 2011, provisional results

Party	Seats
Parti du peuple pour la reconstruction et la démocratie (PPRD)	62
Union pour la démocratie et le progrès social (UDPS/ Tshisekedi)	41
Parti du peuple pour la paix et la démocratie (PPPD)	29
Mouvement social pour le renouveau (MSR)	27
Mouvement de libération du Congo (MLC)	22
Parti lumumbiste unifié (PALU)	19
Union pour la nation congolaise (UNC)	17
Alliance pour le renouveau au Congo (ARC)	16
Alliance des forces démocratiques du Congo (AFDC)	15
Eveil de la conscience pour le travail et le développement (ECT)	11
Rassemblement pour la reconstruction du Congo (RRC)	11
Mouvement pour l'intégrité du peuple (MIP)	10
Parti démocrate chrétien (PDC)	7
Union pour le développement du Congo (UDCO)	7
Rassemblement congolais pour la démocratie—kisangani mouvement de libération (RCD/K-ML)	6
Union nationale des démocrates féderalistes (UNADEF)	6
Union des nationalistes féderalistes du Congo (UNAFEC)	6
Others*	147
Independents	16
Total	475†

* Comprising political parties that won fewer than six seats.
† The results in 25 constituencies had yet to be declared.

Sénat

President: LÉON KENGO WA DONDO.

Election, 19 January 2007

Party	Seats
Parti du peuple pour la reconstruction et la démocratie	22
Mouvement de libération du Congo	14
Forces du renouveau	7
Rassemblement congolais pour la démocratie	7
Parti démocrate chrétien	6
Convention des démocrates chrétiens	3
Mouvement social pour le renouveau	3
Parti lumumbiste unifié	2
Others*	18
Independents	26
Total	108

* Comprising 18 political parties that each won one seat.

Election Commission

Commission électorale nationale indépendante (CENI): 4471 blvd du 30 juin, Kinshasa; tel. 818110613; e-mail info@cei-rdc.org; internet www.ceni.gouv.cd; f. 2010 to replace the Commission électorale indépendante; 7 mems; Pres. Rev. DANIEL NGOY MULUNDA.

Political Organizations

In January 1999 a ban on the formation of political associations was officially ended, and in May 2001 remaining restrictions on the registration and operation of political parties were removed. At August 2011 some 417 political parties were registered with the Ministry of the Interior.

Alliance des nationalistes croyants congolais (ANCC): Kinshasa; Pres. JEAN ANDEKA DJAMBA.

Alliance pour le développement et la République (ADR): Kinshasa; f. 2011; Pres. FRANÇOIS MUAMBA TSHISHIMBI.

Camp de la patrie: Kinshasa; Leader ARTHUR Z'AHIDI NGOMA.

Coalition des démocrates congolais (CODECO): f. 2006; Leader PIERRE WA SYAKASSIGHE PAY-PAY.

Congrès national pour la défense du peuple: Bukavu; tel. 993456427; e-mail cndpadmin@cndp-congo.org; internet www.cndp-congo.org; f. 2006; Pres. LAURENT NKUNDA MIHIGO; Sec. G. KAMBASU NGEVE.

Convention des démocrates chrétiens: Kinshasa; Leader FLORENTIN MOKONDA BONZA.

Démocratie chrétienne féderaliste—Convention des fédéralistes pour la démocratie chrétienne (DCF—COFEDEC): 2209 ave des Etoiles, Kinshasa-Gombe; Leader VENANT TSHIPASA VANGI.

Forces du renouveau: Kinshasa; Leader ANTIPAS MBUSA NYAMWISI.

Alliance pour le renouveau du Congo (ARC): 1165-1175 ave Tombalbaye, Kinshasa-Gombe; tel. 998911096 (mobile); fax 815947347 (mobile); e-mail arc_secgen@yahoo.fr; f. 2006; Leader OLIVIER KAMITATU ETSU.

Rassemblement congolais pour la démocratie—Mouvement de libération (RCD—ML): 290 ave Libenge, Lingwala; broke away from main RCD in 1999; supported by Uganda; Pres. ANTIPAS MBUSA NYAMWISI.

Forces novatrices pour l'union et la solidarité (FONUS): 13 ave de l'Enseignement, Kasa-Vubu, Kinshasa; f. 2004; advocates political pluralism; Pres. JOSEPH OLENGHANKOY; Sec.-Gen. JOHN KWET.

Front des nationalistes intégrationnistes (FNI): Bunia; f. 2003 in Uganda; ethnic Lendu rebel group, in conflict with Union des patriotes congolais in north-east; Leader FLORIBERT NDJABU NGABU.

Mouvement de libération du Congo (MLC): 6 ave du Port, Kinshasa-Gombe; f. 1998; fmr Ugandan-supported rebel movement; incl. in Govt in July 2003; Leader JEAN-PIERRE BEMBA GOMBO; Sec.-Gen. THOMAS LUHAKA.

Mouvement populaire de la révolution (MPR): 5448 ave de la Justice, Immeuble Yoko, Kinshasa-Gombe; f. 1966 by Pres. Mobutu; sole legal political party until Nov. 1990; advocates national unity and opposes tribalism; Leader Prof. VUNDWAWE TE PEMAKO; Sec.-Gen. KITHIMA BIN RAMAZANI.

Mouvement social pour le renouveau (MSR): Kinshasa; f. 2006; Leader YVES MOBANDO YOGO.

Parti démocrate chrétien: Leader JOSÉ ENDUNDO BONONGE.

Parti démocrate et social chrétien (PDSC): 3040 route de Matadi, C/Ngaliema, Kinshasa; tel. (12) 21211; f. 1990; centrist; Pres. ANDRÉ BOBOLIKO; Sec.-Gen. TUYABA LEWULA.

Parti lumumbiste unifié (PALU): 9 rue Cannas, C/Limete, Kinshasa; Leader ANTOINE GIZENGA.

Parti du peuple pour la reconstruction et la démocratie (PPRD): Croisement des aves Pumbu et Batetela, Kinshasa-Gombe; f. March 2002 by Pres. Joseph Kabila; Sec.-Gen. EVARISTE BOSHAB.

Parti pour l'unité et la sauvegarde de l'intégrité du Congo (PUSIC): Bunia; coalition of 4 tribal militia groups, led by Hema; Leader ROBERT PIMBU.

Rassemblement congolais pour la démocratie (RCD—Goma): 26 ave Lukusa, Kinshasa-Gombe; f. 1998; rebel movement until Dec. 2002 peace agreement; incl. in Govt July 2003; main Ilunga faction; supported by Rwanda; Leader AZARIAS RUBERWA; Sec.-Gen. FRANCIS BEDY MAKHUBU MABELE.

Rassemblement congolais pour la démocratie—National (RCD—N): blvd du 30 juin, S.V./64 Haut-Uélé (Isiro); broke away from RCD—ML in Oct. 2000; Leader ROGER LUMBALA.

Rassemblement des forces sociales et fédéralistes (RSF): 98 rue Poto-poto, Kimbanseke; Leader VINCENT DE PAUL LUNDA BULULU.

Rassemblement pour une nouvelle société (RNS): 1 bis rue Lufu, C/Bandalungwa; e-mail info@congozaire.org; Leader Dr ALAFUELE M. KALALA.

Union des démocrates mobutistes (UDEMO): f. by son of fmr Pres. Mobutu; Leader FRANÇOIS JOSEPH MOBUTU NZANGA NGBANGAWE.

Union des forces du changement (UFC): Kinshasa; Pres. LÉON KENGO WA DONDO.

Union des nationalistes fédéralistes du Congo (UNAFEC): 5 ave Citronniers, Kinshasa-Gombe; Leader GABRIEL KYUNGA WA KUMWANZA.

Union des patriotes congolais (UPC): 25 blvd de la Libération, Bunia; rebel group of Hema ethnic group, fmrly in conflict with Lendu in north-east; registered as political org. 2004, after peace agreement with Govt; Leader THOMAS LUBANGA.

Union pour la démocratie et le progrès social (UDPS): 546 ave Zinnia, Limete, Kinshasa; tel. 813140685 (mobile); e-mail udps@udps.net; internet www.udps.net; f. 1982; Leader Dr ETIENNE TSHISEKEDI WA MULUMBA; Sec.-Gen. RÉMY MASSAMBA.

Union pour la nation congolaise (UNC): ave Croix-Rouge 3, Commune de Barumbu, Kinshasa; tel. 999915385 (mobile); e-mail unc_sg@yahoo.fr; internet www.unc-rdc.com; Pres. VITAL KAMERHE LWA-KANYIGINYI.

Union pour la reconstruction du Congo (UREC): Leader OSCAR LUKUMWENA KASHALA.

Union pour la République (UPR): 622 ave Monts des Arts, Kinshasa-Gombe; f. 1997; by fmr mems of the MPR; Leader BOBOY NYABAKA.

Union pour la République—Mouvement National (UNIR—MN): Immeuble VeVe center, 2 rue de Bongandanga, c/Kasa-Vubu, Kinshasa; tel. 812431078 (mobile); e-mail info@unir-mn.org; internet www.unir-mn.org; f. 2001; officially registered as a political party in 2005; Pres. FRÉDÉRIC BOYENGA-BOFALA; Sec.-Gen. OLIVIER MESKENS NTAMBU KUFUANGA.

Diplomatic Representation

EMBASSIES IN THE DEMOCRATIC REPUBLIC OF THE CONGO

Algeria: 50–52 ave Col Ebeya, Gombe, Kinshasa; tel. 818803717 (mobile); fax 813010577 (mobile); Ambassador ABDELDJALIL BELALA.

Angola: 4413–4429 blvd du 30 juin, BP 8625, Kinshasa; tel. (12) 32415; fax (13) 98971; e-mail consangolakatanga@voila.fr; Ambassador EMILIO DE CARVALHO GUERRA.

Belgium: Immeuble Le Cinquantenaire, pl. du 27 octobre, BP 899, Kinshasa; tel. (12) 20110; fax (12) 21058; e-mail kinshasa@diplobel.fed.be; internet www.diplobel.org/congo; Ambassador DOMINIQUE STRUYE DE SWIELANDE.

Benin: 3990 ave des Cliniques, BP 3265, Kinshasa-Gombe; tel. 98128659; e-mail abkin@raga.net; Ambassador OUSSOU-EDOUARDS AHO-GLELE.

Cameroon: 171 blvd du 30 juin, BP 10998, Kinshasa; tel. (12) 34787; Ambassador MARTIN CHUNGONG AYAFOR.

Canada: 17 ave Pumbu, Commune de la Gombe, BP 8341, Kinshasa 1; tel. 898950310 (mobile); fax 999975403 (mobile); e-mail knsha@international.gc.ca; internet www.dfait-maeci.gc.ca/world/embassies/drc; Ambassador JEAN-CAROL PELLETIER.

Central African Republic: 11 ave Pumbu, BP 7769, Kinshasa; tel. (12) 30417; Ambassador JOB ISIMA.

Chad: 67–69 ave du Cercle, BP 9097, Kinshasa; tel. (12) 22358; Ambassador (vacant).

Congo, Republic: 179 blvd du 30 juin, BP 9516, Kinshasa; tel. (12) 34028; Ambassador GUSTAVE ZOULA.

Côte d'Ivoire: 68 ave de la Justice, BP 9197, Kinshasa; tel. (12) 21208; Ambassador GUILLAUME AHIPEAU.

Cuba: 4660 ave Cateam, BP 10699, Kinshasa; tel. (12) 8803823; Ambassador LUIS CASTILLO.

Egypt: 519 ave de l'Ouganda, BP 8838, Kinshasa; tel. (51) 10137; fax (88) 03728; Ambassador MUHAMMAD EZZELDIN FODA.

Ethiopia: BP 8435, Kinshasa; tel. (12) 23327; Ambassador DIEUDEONNE A. GANGA.

France: 97 ave de la République du Tchad, BP 3093, Kinshasa; tel. 815559999 (mobile); fax 815559937 (mobile); e-mail ambafrancerdc@gmail.com; internet www.ambafrance-cd.org; Ambassador PIERRE JACQUEMOT.

Gabon: ave du 24 novembre, BP 9592, Kinshasa; tel. (12) 68325; Ambassador CHRISTOPHE ELLA EKOGHA.

Germany: 82 ave Roi Baudouin, BP 8400, Kinshasa-Gombe; tel. 815561380 (mobile); e-mail amballemagne@ic.cd; internet www.kinshasa.diplo.de; Ambassador Dr AXEL WEISHAUPT.

Greece: Immeuble de la Communauté Hellénique, 3ème étage, blvd du 30 juin, BP 478, Kinshasa; tel. 815554941 (mobile); fax 815554945 (mobile); e-mail gremb.kin@mfa.gr; Ambassador KATRANIS ALEXANDROS.

Holy See: 81 ave Goma, BP 3091, Kinshasa; tel. (88) 08814; fax (88) 48483; e-mail nuntius@raga.net; Apostolic Nuncio Most Rev. ADOLFO TITO YLLANA (Titular Archbishop of Montecorvino).

India: 18B, ave Batetela, Commune de la Gombe, Kinshasa; tel. 815559770 (mobile); fax 815559774 (mobile); e-mail amb.indembkin@gbs.cd; Ambassador DEVENDRA NATH SRIVASTAVA.

Japan: Immeuble Citibank, 2ème étage, ave Colonel Lukusa, BP 1810, Kinshasa; tel. 818845305 (mobile); fax 870-7639-59668 (satellite); e-mail ambjaponrdc@yahoo.fr; internet www.rdc.emb-japan.go.jp; Ambassador TOMINAGA YOSHIMASA.

Kenya: 4002 ave de l'Ouganda, BP 9667, Kinshasa; tel. 815554797 (mobile); fax 815554805 (mobile); e-mail kinshasa@mfa.go.ke; Ambassador KARUCHU SYLVESTER GAKUMU.

Korea, Democratic People's Republic: 168 ave de l'Ouganda, BP 16597, Kinshasa; tel. 8801443 (mobile); fax 815300194 (mobile); e-mail kenem-drc@jobantech.cd; Ambassador RI MYONG-CHOL.

Korea, Republic: 65 blvd Tshatshi, BP 628, Kinshasa; tel. 819820302 (mobile); e-mail amb-rdc@mofat.go.kr; Ambassador LEE HO-SUNG.

Lebanon: 3 ave de l'Ouganda, Kinshasa; tel. (12) 82469; Ambassador SAAD ZAKHIA.

Liberia: 3 ave de l'Okapi, BP 8940, Kinshasa; tel. (12) 82289; Ambassador JALLA D. LANSANAH.

Mauritania: BP 16397, Kinshasa; tel. (12) 59575; Ambassador Lt-Col M'BARECK OULD BOUNA MOKHTAR.

Morocco: POB 912, ave Corteaux et Vallée No. 40, Kinshasa 1; tel. (12) 34794; Ambassador MOHAMED BEN KADDOUR.

Netherlands: 11 ave Zongontolo, 55 Immeuble Residence, BP 10299, Kinshasa; tel. 996050600 (mobile); fax 996050629 (mobile); e-mail kss@minbuza.nl; internet www.minbuza.nl/kss; Ambassador ROBERT VAN EMBDEN.

Nigeria: 141 blvd du 30 juin, BP 1700, Kinshasa; tel. 817005142 (mobile); fax 812616115 (mobile); e-mail nigemb@jobantech.cd; Ambassador HUSSEIN ABDULLAHI.

Portugal: 270 ave des Aviateurs, BP 7775, Kinshasa; tel. 815161277 (mobile); e-mail ambassadeportugal@micronet.net; Ambassador JOÃO PERESTRELLO.

Russia: 80 ave de la Justice, BP 1143, Kinshasa 1; tel. (12) 33157; fax (12) 45575; e-mail amrussie@ic.cd; Ambassador ANATOLII KLIMENKO.

Rwanda: Kinshasa; Ambassador AMANDIN RUGIRA.

South Africa: 77 ave Ngongo Lutete, BP 7829, Kinshasa-Gombe; tel. 814769100 (mobile); fax 815554322 (mobile); e-mail pearces@foreign.gov.za; Ambassador JOSEPH NTSHIKIWANE MASHIMBYE.

Spain: blvd du 30 juin, Bldg Communauté Hellénique, Commune de la Gombe, BP 8036, Kinshasa; tel. 818843195 (mobile); fax 813010396 (mobile); e-mail emb.kinshasa@mae.es; Ambassador Dr FÉLIX COSTALES ARTIEDA.

Sudan: 24 ave de l'Ouganda, Kinshasa; tel. 999937396 (mobile); Ambassador GAAFAR BABIKER EL-KHALIFA EL-TAYEB.

Sweden: 93 ave Roi Baudouin, Commune de la Gombe, BP 11096, Kinshasa; tel. 999301102 (mobile); fax 870-600-147849 (satellite); e-mail ambassaden.kinshasa@foreign.ministry.se; internet www.swedenabroad.com/kinshasa; Ambassador METTE SUNNERGREN.

Switzerland: 654 blvd Col Tshatshi, BP 8724, Gombe, Kinshasa; tel. 898946800 (mobile); e-mail kin.vertretung@eda.admin.ch; internet www.eda.admin.ch/kinshasa; Ambassador JACQUES GREMAND.

Tanzania: 142 blvd du 30 juin, BP 1612, Kinshasa; tel. 815565850 (mobile); fax 815565852 (mobile); e-mail tanzanrepkinshasa@yahoo.com; Ambassador GORDON LUHWANO NGILANGWA.

Togo: 3 ave de la Vallée, BP 10117, Kinshasa; tel. (12) 30666; Ambassador YAWO ADOMAYAKPOR.

Tunisia: 67–69 ave du Cercle, BP 1498, Kinshasa; tel. 818803901 (mobile); e-mail atkinshasa@yahoo.fr; Ambassador EZZEDDINE ZAYANI.

Uganda: ave des Cocotiers, Plot no. 15, Place Wenge, Commune de la Gombe, BP 8804, Kinshasa; tel. 810507179 (mobile); e-mail ugambassy@simbatel.com; Ambassador Maj. JAMES KINOBE.

United Kingdom: 83 ave Roi Baudouin, BP 8049, Kinshasa; tel. 817150761 (mobile); fax 813464291 (mobile); e-mail ambrit@ic.cd; Ambassador NEIL WIGAN.

USA: 310 ave des Aviateurs, BP 397, Kinshasa; tel. 815560151 (mobile); fax 815560173 (mobile); e-mail AEKinshasaConsular@state.gov; internet kinshasa.usembassy.gov; Ambassador JAMES FREDERICK ENTWISTLE.

Zambia: 54–58 ave de l'Ecole, BP 1144, Kinshasa; tel. 819999437 (mobile); fax (88) 45106; e-mail ambazambia@ic.cd; Ambassador MAYBIN KAMBAMBA MUBANGA.

Judicial System

Under the Constitution that entered into effect in February 2006, the judicial system is independent. Members of the judiciary are under the authority of the Conseil Supérieur de la Magistrature. The Cour de Cassation has jurisdiction over legal decisions and the Conseil d'État over administrative decisions. The Cour Constitutionnelle interprets the provisions of the Constitution and ensures the conformity of new legislation. The judicial system also comprises a Haute Cour Militaire, and lower civil and military courts and tribunals. The Conseil Supérieur de la Magistrature has 18 members, including the Presidents and Chief Prosecutors of the main courts. The Cour Constitutionnelle comprises nine members, who are appointed by the President (including three nominated by the legislature and three by the Conseil Supérieur de la Magistrature) for a term of nine years. The Head of State appoints and dismisses magistrates, on the proposal of the Conseil Supérieur de la Magistrature.

Cour de Cassation

cnr ave de la Justice and ave de Lemera, BP 3382, Kinshasa-Gombe; tel. (12) 25104.

President of the Cour de Cassation: LWAMBA BINDU.

Procurator-General of the Republic: KABANGE NUMBI.

Cour Suprême de Justice: ave de la Justice 2, BP 13, Kinshasa-Gombe; Pres. BENOÎT LWAMBA BINDU.

Religion

Many of the country's inhabitants follow traditional beliefs, which are mostly animistic. A large proportion of the population is Christian, predominantly Roman Catholic, and there are small Muslim, Jewish and Greek Orthodox communities.

CHRISTIANITY

The Roman Catholic Church

The Democratic Republic of the Congo comprises six archdioceses and 41 dioceses. Some 51% of the population are Roman Catholics.

Bishops' Conference

Conférence Episcopale Nationale du Congo, BP 3258, Kinshasa-Gombe; tel. (12) 34528; fax (88) 44948; e-mail conf.episc.rdc@ic.cd; internet www.cenco.cd.

f. 1981; Pres. Most Rev. NICOLAS DJOMO LOLA (Bishop of Tshumbe).

Archbishop of Bukavu: FRANÇOIS-XAVIER MAROY RUSENGO, Archevêché, ave Mbaki 18, BP 3324, Bukavu; tel. 813180621 (mobile); e-mail archevechebk@yahoo.fr.

Archbishop of Kananga: Most Rev. MARCEL MADILA BASANGUKA, Archevêché, BP 70, Kananga; tel. 815013942 (mobile); e-mail archidiocesekananga@yahoo.fr.

Archbishop of Kinshasa: Cardinal LAURENT MONSENGWO PASINYA, Archevêché, ave de l'Université, BP 8431, Kinshasa 1; tel. (12) 3723546; e-mail archikin@ic.cd.

Archbishop of Kisangani: Most Rev. LAURENT MONSENGWO PASINYA, Archevêché, ave Mpolo 10B, BP 505, Kisangani; tel. 812006715 (mobile); fax (761) 608336.

Archbishop of Lubumbashi: Most Rev. JEAN-PIERRE TAFUNGA MBAYO, Archevêché, BP 72, Lubumbashi; tel. 997031991 (mobile); e-mail archidiolub@mwangaza.cd.

Archbishop of Mbandaka-Bikoro: Most Rev. JOSEPH KUMUONDALA MBIMBA, Archevêché, BP 1064, Mbandaka; tel. 817301027 (mobile); e-mail mbandakabikoro@yahoo.fr.

The Anglican Communion

The Church of the Province of the Congo comprises eight dioceses.

Archbishop of the Province of the Congo and Bishop of Kinshasa: Most Rev. Dr DIROKPA BALUFUGA FIDÈLE, 11 Ave Basalakala, Quartier Immocongo, Commune de Kalamu, BP 16482, Kinshasa; tel. 998611180 (mobile); e-mail dirokpa1@hotmail.com.

Bishop of Arua: Rt Rev. Dr GEORGE TITRE ANDE, POB 226, Arua, Uganda; tel. 810393071 (mobile); e-mail revdande@yahoo.co.uk.

Bishop of Boga: Rt Rev. HENRY KAHWA ISINGOMA, CAC- Boga, Congo Liaison Office, POB 25586, Kampala, Uganda; e-mail peac_isingoma@yahoo.fr.

Bishop of Bukavu: Rt Rev. SYLVESTRE BALI-BUSANE BAHATI, CAC-Bukavu, POB 53435, Nairobi, Kenya.

Bishop of Katanga: Rt Rev. MUNO KASIMA, c/o UMM, POB 22037, Kitwe, Zambia; tel. 97047173 (mobile); fax (88) 46383; e-mail peac_isingoma@yahoo.fr.

Bishop of Kindu: Rt Rev. ZACHARIE MASIMANGO KATANDA, c/o ESCO Uganda, POB 7892, Kampala, Uganda; e-mail angkindu@yahoo.fr.

Bishop of Kisangani: Rt Rev. LAMBERT FUNGA BOTOLOME, c/o Congo Liaison Office, POB 25586, Kampala, Uganda; e-mail lambertfunga@hotmail.com.

Bishop of Nord Kivu: Rt Rev. METHUSELA MUSUBAHO MUNZENDA, CAZ-Butembo, POB 506, Bwera-Kasese, Uganda; fax 870-166-1121 (satellite); e-mail munzenda_eac@yahoo.fr.

Kimbanguist

Eglise de Jésus Christ sur la Terre par le Prophète Simon Kimbangu: BP 7069, Kinshasa; tel. (12) 68944; f. 1921; officially est. 1959; c. 5m. mems (1985); Spiritual Head HE SALOMON DIALUNGANA KIANGANI; Sec.-Gen. Rev. LUNTADILLA.

Protestant Churches

Eglise du Christ au Congo (ECC): ave de la Justice 75, BP 4938, Kinshasa-Gombe; internet congodisciples.org; f. 1902; a co-ordinating agency for all the Protestant churches, with the exception of the Kimbanguist Church; 62 mem. communities and a provincial org. in each province; Pres. Bishop MARINI BODHO; includes:

Communauté Baptiste du Congo-Ouest: BP 4728, Kinshasa 2; f. 1970; 450 parishes; Gen. Sec. Rev. LUSAKWENO-VANGU.

Communauté des Disciples du Christ: BP 178, Mbandaka; tel. 31062; f. 1964; 250 parishes; Gen. Sec. Rev. Dr ELONDA EFEFE.

Communauté Episcopale Baptiste en Afrique: 2 ave Jason Sendwe, BP 2809, Lubumbashi 1; tel. and fax (2) 348602; e-mail kitobokabwe@yahoo.fr; f. 1956; 1,300 episcopal communions and parishes; 150,000 mems (2001); Pres. Bishop KITOBO KABWEKA-LEZA.

Communauté Evangélique: BP 36, Luozi; f. 1961; 50 parishes; Pres. Rev. K. LUKOMBO NTONTOLO.

Communauté Lumière: BP 10498, Kinshasa 1; f. 1931; 150 parishes; Patriarch KAYUWA TSHIBUMBU WA KAHINGA.

Communauté Mennonite: BP 18, Tshikapa; f. 1960; Gen. Sec. Rev. KABANGY DJEKE SHAPASA.

Communauté Presbytérienne: BP 117, Kananga; f. 1959; Gen. Sec. Dr M. L. TSHIHAMBA.

Eglise Missionaire Apostolique: 375 ave Commerciale, BP 15859, Commune de N'Djili, Kinshasa 1; tel. 988165927; e-mail buzi4@hotmail.com; f. 1986; 5 parishes; 2,600 mems; Apostle for Africa Rev. LUFANGA-AYIMOU NANANDANA.

Evangelical Lutheran Church in Congo: 150 ave Kasaï, Lumbabashi; tel. (2) 22396; fax (2) 24098; e-mail bnationaleelco@yahoo.fr; 136,000 mems (2010); Pres. Bishop RENÉ MWAMBA SUMAILI.

The Press

DAILIES

L'Analyste: 129 ave du Bas-Congo, BP 91, Kinshasa-Gombe; tel. (12) 80987; Dir and Editor-in-Chief BONGOMA KONI BOTAHE.

L'Avenir: Immeuble Ruzizi, 873 ave Bas-Congo, Kinshasa-Gombe; tel. 999942485 (mobile); internet www.groupelavenir.cd; owned by Groupe de l'avenir; Chair. PIUS MUABILU.

Elima: 1 ave de la Révolution, BP 11498, Kinshasa; tel. (12) 77332; f. 1928; evening; Dir and Editor-in-Chief ESSOLOMWA NKOY EA LINGANGA.

Mjumbe: BP 2474, Lubumbashi; f. 1963; Dir and Editor TSHIMANGA KOYA KAKONA.

Le Phare: bldg du 29 juin, ave Col Lukusa 3392, BP 2481, Kinshasa; tel. 813330195 (mobile); e-mail info@le-phare.com; internet www.lepharerdc.com; f. 1983; Editor POLYDOR MUBOYAYI MUBANGA; circ. 4,000.

Le Potentiel: Immeuble Ruzizi, 873 ave du Bas-Congo, BP 11338, Kinshasa; tel. 98135483; e-mail lepotentiel@lepotentiel.com; internet www.lepotentiel.com; f. 1982; Editor MODESTE MUTINGA MUTUISHAYI; circ. 8,000.

La Prospérité: Kinshasa; tel. 818135157 (mobile); e-mail marcelngo@yahoo.fr; internet www.laprosperiteonline.net; f. 2001; Dir-Gen. MARCEL NGOYI.

Le Palmarès: Kinshasa.

La Référence Plus: BP 22520, Kinshasa; tel. (12) 45783; f. 1989; Dir ANDRÉ IPAKALA.

PERIODICALS

Afrique Editions: Kinshasa; tel. (88) 43202; e-mail bpongo@raga.net.

Allo Kinshasa: 3 rue Kayange, BP 20271, Kinshasa-Lemba; monthly; Editor MBUYU WA KABILA.

L'Aurore Protestante: Eglise du Christ au Congo, BP 4938, Kinshasa-Gombe; French; religion; monthly; circ. 10,000.

Cahiers Economiques et Sociaux: BP 257, Kinshasa XI, (National University of the Congo); sociological, political and economic review; quarterly; Dir Prof. NDONGALA TADI LEWA; circ. 2,000.

Cahiers des Religions Africaines: Faculté de Théologie Catholique de Kinshasa, BP 712, Kinshasa/Limete; tel. (12) 78476; f. 1967; English and French; religion; 2 a year; circ. 1,000.

Le Canard Libre: Kinshasa; f. 1991; Editor JOSEPH CASTRO MULEBE.

La Colombe: 32B ave Tombalbaye, Kinshasa-Gombe; tel. (12) 21211; organ of Parti démocrate et social chrétien; circ. 5,000.

Congo-Afrique: Centre d'Etudes pour l'Action Sociale, 9 ave Père Boka, BP 3375, Kinshasa-Gombe; tel. 898912981 (mobile); e-mail congoafrique@yahoo.fr; internet www.congo-afrique.org; f. 1961; economic, social and cultural; monthly; Editors FRANCIS KIKASSA MWANALESSA, RENÉ BEECKMANS; circ. 2,500.

Le Conseiller Comptable: 51 rue du Grand Séminaire, Quartier Nganda, BP 308, Kinshasa; tel. (88) 01216; fax (88) 00075; f. 1974; French; public finance and taxation; quarterly; Editor TOMENA FOKO; circ. 2,000.

Documentation et Information Protestante (DIP): Eglise du Christ au Congo, BP 4938, Kinshasa-Gombe; tel. and fax (88) 46387; e-mail eccm@ic.cd; French and English; religion.

Documentation et Informations Africaines (DIA): BP 2598, Kinshasa 1; tel. (12) 33197; fax (12) 33196; e-mail dia@ic.cd; internet www.peacelink.it/dia/index.html; Roman Catholic news agency reports; 3 a week; Dir Rev. Père VATA DIAMBANZA.

L'Entrepreneur Flash: Association Nationale des Entreprises du Congo, 10 ave des Aviateurs, BP 7247, Kinshasa 1; tel. (12) 22565; f. 1978; business news; monthly; circ. 1,000.

Etudes d'Histoire Africaine: National University of the Congo, BP 1825, Lubumbashi; f. 1970; French and English; history; annually; circ. 1,000.

KYA: 24 ave de l'Équateur, BP 7853, Kinshasa-Gombe; tel. (12) 27502; f. 1984; weekly for Bas-Congo; Editor (vacant).

Libération: Kinshasa; f. 1997; politics; supports the AFDL; weekly; Man. NGOYI KABUYA DIKATETA M'MIANA.

Mambenga 2000: BP 477, Mbandaka; Editor BOSANGE YEMA BOF.

Le Moniteur de l'Economie (Economic Monitor): Kinshasa; Man. Editor FÉLIX NZUZI.

Mwana Shaba: Générale des Carrières et des Mines, BP 450, Lubumbashi; monthly; circ. 25,000.

Njanja: Société Nationale des Chemins de Fer du Congo, 115 pl. de la Gare, BP 297, Lubumbashi; tel. (2) 23430; fax (2) 61321; railways and transportation; annually; circ. 10,000.

NUKTA: 14 chaussée de Kasenga, BP 3805, Lubumbashi; weekly; agriculture; Editor NGOY BUNDUKI.

Post: Immeuble Linzadi, 1538 ave de la Douane, Kinshasa-Gombe; e-mail thepostrdc@yahoo.com; internet www.congoonline.com/thepost; 2 a week; Editor-in-Chief MUKEBAYI NKOSO.

Problèmes Sociaux Zaïrois: Centre d'Exécution de Programmes Sociaux et Economiques, Université de Lubumbashi, 208 ave Kasavubu, BP 1873, Lubumbashi; f. 1946; quarterly; Editor N'KASHAMA KADIMA.

Promoteur Congolais: Centre du Commerce International du Congo, 119 ave Colonel Tshatshi, BP 13, Kinshasa; f. 1979; international trade news; 6 a year.

Sciences, Techniques, Informations: Centre de Recherches Industrielles en Afrique Centrale (CRIAC), BP 54, Lubumbashi.

Le Sport Africain: 13è niveau Tour adm., Cité de la Voix du Congo, BP 3356, Kinshasa-Gombe; monthly; Pres. TSHIMPUMPU WA TSHIMPUMPU.

Taifa: 536 ave Lubumba, BP 884, Lubumbashi; weekly; Editor LWAMBWA MILAMBU.

Telema: Faculté Canisius, Kimwenza, BP 3724, Kinshasa-Gombe; f. 1974; religious; quarterly; edited by the Central Africa Jesuits; circ. 1,200.

Vision: Kinshasa; 2 a week; independent; Man. Editor XAVIER BONANE YANGANZI.

La Voix des Sans-Voix: ave des Ecuries 3858, commune de Ngaliema, BP 11445, Kinshasa-Gombe; tel. (88) 40394; fax (88) 01826; e-mail vsv@ic.cd; internet www.congonline.com/vsv.

NEWS AGENCIES

Agence Congolaise de Presse (ACP): 44–48 ave Tombalbaye, BP 1595, Kinshasa 1; tel. 816573788 (mobile); e-mail info@acpcongo.cd; internet www.acpcongo.cd; f. 1957; state-controlled; Dir-Gen. JEAN-MARIE VIANNEY LONGONYA (acting).

Digital Congo: 21 ave Kabasele Tshiamala, Kinshasa-Gombe; tel. 8941010; e-mail lettres@digitalcongo.net; internet www.digitalcongo.net; news service owned by Multimedia Congo.

Documentation et Informations Africaines (DIA): BP 2598, Kinshasa 1; tel. (12) 34528; f. 1957; Roman Catholic news agency; Dir Rev. Père VATA DIAMBANZA.

Press Association

Union de la Presse du Congo: BP 4941, Kinshasa 1; tel. (12) 24437.

Publishers

Aequatoria Centre: BP 276, Mbandaka; f. 1980; anthropology, biography, ethnicity, history, language and linguistics, social sciences; Dir HONORÉ VINCK.

CEEBA Publications: BP 246, Bandundu; f. 1965; humanities, languages, fiction; Man. Dir (Editorial) Dr HERMANN HOCHEGGER.

Centre de Documentation Agricole: BP 7537, Kinshasa 1; tel. (12) 32498; agriculture, science; Dir PIERTE MBAYAKABUYI; Chief Editor J. MARCELLIN KAPUKUNGESA.

Centre de Linguistique Théorique et Appliquée (CELTA): BP 4956, Kinshasa-Gombe; tel. 818129998 (mobile); e-mail anyembwe@yahoo.fr; f. 1971; language, arts and linguistics; Dir-Gen. ANDRÉ NYEMBWE NTITA.

Centre de Recherches Pédagogiques: BP 8815, Kinshasa 1; f. 1959; accounting, education, geography, language, science; Dir P. DETIENNE.

Centre de Vulgarisation Agricole: BP 4008, Kinshasa 2; tel. (12) 71165; fax (12) 21351; agriculture, environment, health; Dir-Gen. KIMPIANGA MAHANIAH.

Centre International de Sémiologie: 109 ave Pruniers, BP 1825, Lubumbashi.

Centre Protestant d'Editions et de Diffusion (CEDI): 209 ave Kalémie, BP 11398, Kinshasa 1; tel. (12) 22202; fax (12) 26730; f. 1935; fiction, poetry, biography, religious, juvenile; Christian tracts, works in French, Lingala, Kikongo, etc.; Dir-Gen. HENRY DIRKS.

Commission de l'Education Chrétienne: BP 3258, Kinshasa-Gombe; tel. (12) 30086; education, religion; Man. Dir Abbé MUGADJA LEHANI.

Connaissance et Pratique du Droit Congolais Editions (CDPC): BP 5502, Kinshasa-Gombe; f. 1987; law; Editor DIBUNDA KABUINJI.

Editions Lokole: BP 5085, Kinshasa 10; state org. for the promotion of literature; Dir BOKEME SHANE MOLOBAY.

Editions Saint Paul: BP 8505, Kinshasa; tel. 994657188 (mobile); e-mail fspkin10@ic.cd; f. 1988; fiction, general non-fiction, poetry, religion; Dir Sister MASTAKI GODELIEVE; Sec. Sister M. ROSARIO ZAMBELLO.

Facultés Catholiques de Kinshasa: 2 ave de l'Université, Kinshasa-Limete; tel. and fax (12) 46965; e-mail facakin@ic.cd; f. 1957; anthropology, art, economics, history, politics, computer science; Rector Prof. Mgr HIPPOLYTE NGIMBI NSEKA.

Les Editions du Trottoir: BP 1800, Kinshasa; tel. (12) 9936043; e-mail smuyengo@yahoo.fr; f. 1989; communications, fiction, literature, drama; Pres. CHARLES DJUNJU-SIMBA.

Librairie les Volcans: 22 ave Pres. Mobutu, BP 400, Goma, Nord-Kivu; f. 1995; social sciences; Man. Dir RUHAMA MUKANDOLI.

Presses Universitaires du Congo (PUC): 290 rue d'Aketi, BP 1800, Kinshasa 1; tel. (12) 9936043; e-mail smuyengo@yahoo.fr; f. 1972; science, arts and communications; Dir Abbé SÉBASTIEN MUYENGO.

GOVERNMENT PUBLISHING HOUSE

Imprimerie du Gouvernement Central: BP 3021, Kinshasa-Kalina.

Broadcasting and Communications

REGULATORY AUTHORITY

Autorité de Régulation de la Poste et des Télécommunications du Congo (ARPTC): blvd du 30 juin, BP 3000, Kinshasa 1; tel. (13) 92491; e-mail info.arptc@arptc.cd; Pres. OSCAR MANIKUNDA.

Telecommunications

Airtel Congo: croisement des aves Tchad et Bas-Congo, Kinshasa; tel. 996000121 (mobile); e-mail info.airteldrc@cd.airtel.com; internet africa.airtel.com/drc; acquired by Bharti Airtel (India) in 2010; mobile cellular telephone network; fmrly Celtel Congo, subsequently Zain Congo, present name adopted in 2010; Dir-Gen. ANTOINE PAMBORO; 1.83m. subscribers (Dec. 2006).

Congo Chine Telecom (CCT): ave du Port, Kinshasa; tel. 8400085 (mobile); e-mail admin@cct.cd; internet www.cct.cd; mobile cellular telephone network; covers Kinshasa and Bas-Congo, Kasaï, Katanga and Oriental provinces; 100% owned by France Télécom; Dir-Gen. WANG XIANGGUO; 466,000 subscribers (Dec. 2006).

Oasis Telecom (Tigo): 372 ave Col Mondjiba, Kinshasa; tel. 898901000 (mobile); fax 898901001 (mobile); internet www.tigo.cd; 100% owned by Millicom; 50,000 subscribers (Dec. 2006).

Supercell: 99 ave des Tulipiers, BP 114, Goma; tel. 808313010 (mobile); e-mail rogern@supercell.cd; 69,000 subscribers.

Vodacom Congo: Immeuble Mobil–Oil, 2ème étage, 3157 blvd du 30 juin, BP 797, Kinshasa 1; tel. 813131000 (mobile); fax 813131351 (mobile); e-mail vodacom@vodacom.cd; internet www.vodacom.cd; 51% owned by Vodacom (South Africa); 2.33m. subscribers (Dec. 2006).

BROADCASTING

Radio-Télévision Nationale Congolaise (RTNC): ave Kabinda, Lingwala, Kinshasa; tel. 9999256200 (mobile); e-mail info@radiotele-rdc.net; internet www.radiotele-rdc.net; state radio, terrestrial and satellite television broadcasts; Dir-Gen. JOSE KAJANGUA.

Radio

Several private radio broadcasters operate in Kinshasa. Radio France Internationale broadcasts via FM in nine localities.

Radio Candip: Centre d'Animation et de Diffusion Pédagogique, BP 373, Bunia.

Radio Okapi: 12 ave des Aviateurs, Gombe, Kinshasa; tel. 818906747 (mobile); e-mail contact@radiookapi.net; internet radiookapi.net; f. 2002; owned by the Fondation Hirondelle (Switzerland).

La Voix du Congo: Station Nationale, BP 3164, Kinshasa-Gombe; tel. (12) 23175; state-controlled; operated by RTNC; broadcasts in French, Swahili, Lingala, Tshiluba, Kikongo; regional stations at Kisangani, Lubumbashi, Bukavu, Bandundu, Kananga, Mbuji-Mayi, Matadi, Mbandaka and Bunia.

Television

Several private television broadcasters operate in Kinshasa.

Antenne A: Immeuble Forescom, 2e étage, ave du Port 4, POB 2581, Kinshasa 1; tel. (12) 21736; private and commercial station; Dir-Gen. IGAL AVIVI NEIRSON.

Canal Z: ave du Port 6, POB 614, Kinshasa 1; tel. (12) 20239; commercial station; Dir-Gen. FRÉDÉRIC FLASSE.

Tele Kin Malebo (TKM): 32B route de Matadi, Ngaliema, Kinshasa; tel. (12) 2933338; e-mail malebokin@hotmail.com; private television station; nationalization announced 1997; Dir-Gen. NGONGO LUWOWO.

Télévision Congolaise: ave Kabinda, Lingwala, Kinshasa; tel. 9999256200 (mobile); e-mail info@radiotele-rdc.net; govt commercial station; operated by RTNC; broadcasts 2 channels.

Finance

(cap. = capital; res = reserves; dep. = deposits; m. = million; br(s). = branch(es); amounts in new Congolese francs unless otherwise indicated)

BANKING

The introduction as legal tender of a new currency unit, the new Congolese franc (CF), was completed on 30 June 1998. However, as a result of the civil conflict, its value immediately declined dramatically. In late 2003, following the restoration of relative peace and the installation of new transitional authorities, the Central Bank introduced new notes in an effort to revive the national currency and nation-wide operations were gradually restored. In 2010 there were 21 banks and 17 microfinance institutions.

Central Bank

Banque Centrale du Congo: 563 blvd Colonel Tshatshi au nord, BP 2697, Kinshasa; tel. (12) 20704; fax (12) 8805152; e-mail webmaster@bcc.cd; internet www.bcc.cd; f. 1964; dep. 254,133m., total assets 2,174,871m. (Dec. 2009); Gov. JEAN-MARIE EMUNGU EHUMBA; 8 brs.

Commercial Banks

Advans Banque Congo: ave du Bas Congo 4, Commune de la Gombe, Kinshasa; tel. 995904466 (mobile); internet www.advansgroup.com; f. 2008; Dir-Gen. BRUNO DEGOY; 2 brs.

Afriland First Bank: 767 blvd du 30 juin, BP 10470, Kinshasa-Gombe; tel. 810775359 (mobile); e-mail jtoubi@afrilandfirstbank.com; internet www.afrilandfirstbank.com; f. 2004; 2 brs.

Bank of Africa: 22 ave des Aviateurs, Kinshasa-Gombe; tel. 993004600 (mobile); e-mail infos@boa-rdc.com; internet www.bank-of-africa.net; f. 2010; Pres. PAUL DERREUMAUX.

Banque Commerciale du Congo SARL (BCDC): blvd du 30 juin, BP 2798, Kinshasa 1; tel. 818845704 (mobile); fax 99631048 (mobile); e-mail dir@bcdc.cd; internet www.bcdc.cd; f. 1952 as Banque du Congo Belge; name changed as above 1997; cap. 4,975.8m., res 18,143.6m., dep. 207,535.8m. (Dec. 2009); Pres. GUY-ROBERT LUKAMA NKUNZI; Man. Dir YVES CUYPERS; 16 brs.

Banque Congolaise SARL: Immeuble Flavica 14/16, ave du Port, BP 9497, Kinshasa 1; tel. 996050000 (mobile); fax (13) 98298; e-mail bank@rayventures.com; internet www.congobank.com; f. 1988; cap. 14,363.0m., res –1,335.7m., dep. 170,284.4m. (Dec. 2008); Pres. ROGER ALFRED YAGHI; Dir-Gen. GEORGES ABILLAMA; 17 brs.

Banque Internationale de Crédit SARL (BIC): 191 ave de l'Equateur, BP 1299, Kinshasa 1; tel. 999921624 (mobile); fax 812616000 (mobile); e-mail bic@ic.cd; internet www.bic.cd; f. 1994; cap. and res 946.2m., dep. 12,352.7m. (Dec. 2003); Pres. PASCAL KINDUELO LUMBU; Dir-Gen. FREDERIC PULULU MANGONDA; 23 brs.

Banque Internationale pour l'Afrique au Congo (BIAC): 87 blvd du 30 juin, BP 8725, Kinshasa; tel. 815554000 (mobile); fax 8153010681 (mobile); e-mail contact@biac.cd; internet www.biac.cd; f. 1970; cap. 6,140.5m., res 5,539.4m., dep. 176,546.5m. (Dec. 2009); Pres. CHARLES SANLAVILLE; 30 brs.

Citigroup (Congo) SARL Congo: 657 Immeuble Citibank Congo, angle aves Col Lukusa et Ngongo Lutete, BP 9999, Kinshasa 1; tel. 815554808 (mobile); fax 813017070 (mobile); e-mail singa.boyenge@citicorp.com; f. 1971; res 1,111.5m., dep. 14,691.4m. (Dec. 2005); Man. Dir MICHAEL LOSEMBE; 1 br.

La Cruche Banque: 37 rue Kinshasa, Ville de Butembo, Nord-Kivu; tel. 815203045 (mobile); e-mail lacruchebank@yahoo.fr; internet www.lacruchebank.com; Pres. KATEMBO MBANGA.

Ecobank DRC: Immeuble Future Tower, 3642 blvd du 30 Juin, BP 7515, Kinshasa; tel. 996016000 (mobile); fax 996016070 (mobile); internet www.ecobank.com; Pres. JEAN-PIERRE KIWAKANA KIMAYALA; Dir Gen. SERGE ACKRE; 14 brs.

Rawbank Sarl: 3487 blvd du 30 juin, Immeuble Concorde, POB 2499, Kinshasa; tel. 998320000 (mobile); fax 89240224 (mobile); e-mail contact@rawbank.cd; internet www.rawbank.cd; f. 2002; cap. 10,066.0m., res 12,982.6m., dep. 212,368.4m. (Dec. 2009); Pres. MAZHAR RAWJI; Dir-Gen. THIERRY TAEYMANS; 19 brs.

Société Financière de Développement SARL (SOFIDE): Immeuble SOFIDE, 9–11 angle aves Ngabu et Kisangani, BP 1148, Kinshasa 1; tel. 816601531 (mobile); e-mail sofide2001@yahoo.fr; f. 1970; partly state-owned; provides tech. and financial aid, primarily for agricultural devt; cap. and res 285.3m., total assets 1,202.0m. (Dec. 2003); Pres. and Dir-Gen. RAPHAËL SENGA KITENGE; 4 brs.

Standard Bank RDC: 12 ave de Mongala, BP 16297, Kinshasa 1; tel. 817006000 (mobile); fax 813013848 (mobile); e-mail stanbiccongoinfo@stanbic.com; internet www.standardbank.cd; f. 1973; subsidiary of Standard Bank Investment Corpn (South Africa); cap. 1,768.0m., res –1,163.6m., dep. 19,160.1m. (Dec. 2005); Chair. CLIVE TASKER; Man. Dir JEAN REY; 1 br.

INSURANCE

INTERAFF: Bldg Forescom, ave du Port 4, Kinshasa-Gombe; tel. (88) 01618; fax (320) 2091332; e-mail interaff@raga.net; internet www.ic.cd/interaff.

Société Nationale d'Assurances (SONAS): 3443 blvd du 30 juin, Kinshasa-Gombe; tel. (12) 5110503; e-mail sonask@hotmail.com; f. 1966; state-owned; cap. US $5m.; 9 brs.

Trade and Industry

GOVERNMENT AGENCY

Bureau Central de Coordination (BCECO): ave Colonel Mondjiba 372, Complexe Utex Africa, Kinshasa; tel. 815096430 (mobile); e-mail bceco@bceco.cd; internet www.bceco.cd; f. 2001; manages projects funded by the African Development Bank and the World Bank; Dir-Gen. MATONDO MBUNGU (acting).

DEVELOPMENT ORGANIZATIONS

Agence Congolaise des Grands Travaux: Kinshasa; tel. and fax 816909241 (mobile); e-mail contact@acgt.cd; internet acgt.cd; f. 2008; Dir-Gen. CHARLES MÉDARD ILUNGA MWAMBA.

Bureau pour le Développement Rural et Urbain: Mont Ngafula, Kinshasa; e-mail bdru_kin@yahoo.fr.

Caisse de Stabilisation Cotonnière (CSCo): BP 3058, Kinshasa-Gombe; tel. (12) 31206; f. 1978 to replace Office National des Fibres Textiles; acts as an intermediary between the Govt, cotton ginners and textile factories, and co-ordinates international financing of cotton sector.

La Générale des Carrières et des Mines (GÉCAMINES): 419 blvd Kamanyola, BP 450, Lubumbashi; tel. (2) 341105; fax (2) 341041; e-mail info@gecamines.cd; internet www.gecamines.cd; f. 1967 to acquire assets of Union Minière du Haut-Katanga; state-owned corpn engaged in mining and marketing of copper, cobalt, zinc and coal; also has interests in agriculture; Dir-Gen. AHMED KALEJ NKAND.

Institut National pour l'Etude et la Recherche Agronomiques (INERA): BP 1513, Kisangani; internet www.inera-rdc.org; f. 1933; agricultural research.

Office National du Café: ave Général Bobozo 1082, BP 8931, Kinshasa 1; tel. (12) 77144; internet www.onc-rdc.cd; f. 1979; state agency for coffee and also cocoa, tea, quinquina and pyrethrum; Dir-Gen. DAMAS EMMANUEL KANGWENYE.

Pêcherie Maritime Congolaise: Kinshasa; DRC's only sea-fishing enterprise.

CHAMBER OF COMMERCE

Chambre de Commerce, d'Industrie et d'Agriculture du Congo: 10 ave des Aviateurs, BP 7247, Kinshasa 1; tel. (12) 22286; Pres. ILUNGA KONYA.

EMPLOYERS' ASSOCIATION

Fédération des Entreprises du Congo: 10 ave des Aviateurs, BP 7247, Kinshasa; tel. 812488890 (mobile); fax 812488909 (mobile); e-mail fec@ckt.cd; internet www.fec.cd; f. 1972 as the Association Nationale des Entreprises du Zaïre; name changed as above in 1997; represents business interests for both domestic and foreign institutions; Pres. ALBERT YUMA MULIMBI.

UTILITIES

Electricity

Société Nationale d'Electricité (SNEL): 2831 ave de la Justice, BP 500, Kinshasa; tel. 815041639 (mobile); e-mail cco@snel.cd; internet www.snel.cd; f. 1970; state-owned; Pres. MAKOMBO MONGA MAWAWI; Dir-Gen. ERIC MBALA MUSANDA.

Water

Régie de Distribution d'Eau (REGIDESO): 59–63 blvd du 30 juin, BP 12599, Kinshasa; tel. (88) 45125; e-mail courrier@regidesordc.com; internet www.regidesordc.com; f. 1978; water supply admin; Pres. ROMBEAU FUMANI GIBANDI; Dir-Gen. JACQUES MUKALAY MWEMA.

TRADE UNIONS

The Union Nationale des Travailleurs du Congo was founded in 1967 as the sole organization. In 1990 the establishment of independent trade unions was legalized, and by early 1991 there were 12 officially recognized organizations.

Confédération Démocratique du Travail: BP 10897, Quartier Industriel, C/Limete, Kinshasa 1; tel. (88) 0457311; e-mail cdtcongo@yahoo.fr; Pres. LIÉVIN KALUBI.

Confédération Syndicale du Congo: 81 ave Tombalbaye, Kinshasa-Gombe; tel. 898922090 (mobile); fax (13) 98126; e-mail csc_congo@hotmail.com; internet www.csc.cd; f. 1991; Pres. SYMPHORIEN DUNIA.

Syndicat des Enseignants du Congo (SYECO): Kinshasa; Sec.-Gen. JEAN-PIERRE KIMBUYA.

Union Nationale des Travailleurs du Congo: Commune de la Gombe, BP 8814, 5 ave Mutombo Katshi, Kinshasa; tel. 998616193 (mobile); e-mail untcrdc@yahoo.fr; internet www.untc-congo.org; f. 1967; comprises 16 unions; Pres. MODESTE AMÉDÉ NDONGALA N'SIBU.

Transport

Compagnie des Transports du Congo: ave Muzu 52/75, Kinshasa; tel. (88) 46249; fax (322) 7065718; e-mail ros@ic.cd; road transport; Dir ROGER SENGER.

Office National des Transports (ONATRA): BP 98, Kinshasa 1; tel. (12) 21457; fax (12) 1398632; e-mail onatradf@ic.cd; f. 1935; operates 12,674 km of waterways, 366 km of railways and road and air transport; administers ports of Matadi, Boma and Banana; Man. Dir RAYMOND GEORGES.

RAILWAYS

In 2008 the rail network totalled 4,007 km, of which 858 km were electrified. The main line runs from Lubumbashi to Ilebo. International services run to Dar es Salaam (Tanzania) and Lobito (Angola), and also connect with the Zambian, Zimbabwean, Mozambican and South African systems. In May 1997 the railway system was nationalized. In late 2003, under a major government programme, the rehabilitation of 500 km of railway linking northern and southern regions of the country commenced. Work on the rehabilitation of railway lines in Kinshasa commenced in 2008 and was expected to be completed by 2012.

Kinshasa–Matadi Railway: BP 98, Kinshasa 1; 366 km operated by ONATRA; Pres. JACQUES MBELOLO BITWEMI.

Société Nationale des Chemins de Fer du Congo (SNCC): 115 pl. de la Gare, BP 297, Lubumbashi; tel. (2) 346306; fax (2) 342254; e-mail sncc01@ic-libum.cd; f. 1974; 3,641 km (including 858 km electrified); administers all internal railway sections as well as river transport and transport on Lakes Tanganyika and Kivu; management contract concluded with a Belgian-South African corpn, Sizarail, in 1995 for the management of the Office des Chemins de Fer du Sud (OCS) and the Société des Chemins de Fer de l'Est (SFE) subsidiaries, with rail networks of 2,835 km and 1,286 km, respectively; assets of Sizarail nationalized and returned to SNCC control in May 1997; CEO FREDDY STRUMANE.

ROADS

In 2004 there were an estimated 154,000 km of roads, of which some 42,000 km were highways. Following the installation of transitional authorities in July 2003, an extensive infrastructure rehabilitation programme, financed by external donors, including the World Bank, was initiated. Work on a principal road, connecting the south-western town of Moanda with Kinshasa and Lubumbashi, commenced late that year.

Office des Routes: Direction Générale, ave Ex-Descamp, BP 10899, Kinshasa-Gombe; tel. (12) 32036; construction and maintenance of roads; Man. Dir MUTIMA BATRIMU HERMAN.

INLAND WATERWAYS

The River Congo is navigable for more than 1,600 km. Above the Stanley Falls the Congo becomes the Lualaba, and is navigable along a 965-km stretch from Ubundu to Kindu and Kongolo to Bukama. The River Kasaï, a tributary of the River Congo, is navigable by shipping as far as Ilebo, at which the line from Lubumbashi terminates. The total length of inland waterways is 14,935 km.

Régie des voies fluviales: 109 ave Lumpungu, Kinshasa-Gombe, BP 11697, Kinshasa 1; tel. (12) 26526; fax (12) 42580; f. 1971; administers river navigation; Pres. BENJAMIN MUKULUNGU; Gen. Man. RUFFIN NGOMPER ILUNGA (acting).

Société Congolaise des Chemins de Fer des Grands Lacs: River Lualaba services: Bubundu–Kindu and Kongolo–Malemba N'kula; Lake Tanganyika services: Kamina–Kigoma–Kalundu–Moba–Mpulungu; Pres. and Gen. Man. KIBWE MBUYU KAKUDJI.

SHIPPING

The principal seaports are Matadi, Boma and Banana on the lower Congo. The port of Matadi has more than 1.6 km of quays and can accommodate up to 10 deep-water vessels. Matadi is linked by rail with Kinshasa. The country's merchant fleet numbered 21 vessels and amounted to 13,922 gross registered tons at 31 December 2009.

Compagnie Maritime du Congo SARL: Immeuble AMICONGO-CMDC, 6e étage, ave des Aviateurs 13, pl. de la Poste, Gombe, BP 9496, Kinshasa; tel. 898928782; e-mail info@cmdc.cd; internet www.cmdc.cd; f. 1974; services: North Africa, Europe, North America and Asia to West Africa, East Africa to North Africa; Pres. LAURE-MARIE KAWANDA KAYENA; Dir-Gen. CAROLINE MAWANDJI MASALA.

CIVIL AVIATION

International airports are located at Ndjili (for Kinshasa), Luano (for Lubumbashi), Bukavu, Goma and Kisangani. There are smaller airports and airstrips dispersed throughout the country.

Blue Airlines: BP 1115, Barumbu, Kinshasa 1; tel. (12) 20455; f. 1991; regional and domestic charter services for passengers and cargo; Man. T. Mayani.

Business Aviation: Aeroport Ndolo, Ndolo, Limete, Kinshasa; tel. 999942262 (mobile); fax 818142259 (mobile); e-mail businessaviation@gbs.cd; internet www.businessaviation.cd; regional services.

Compagnie Africaine d'Aviation: 6ème rue, Limete, Kinshasa; tel. (88) 43072; fax (88) 41048; e-mail ltadek@hotmail.com; f. 1992; Pres. David Blattner.

Congo Express: Kinshasa; f. 2010; operates from Kinshasa to Lubumbashi and Mbuji-Mayi; Man. Dir Didier Kindambu.

Fly Congo: 1928 ave Kabambare, BP 1284, Kinshasa; tel. 817005015 (mobile); f. 2012 to replace Hewa Bora Airways; international, regional and domestic scheduled services for passengers and cargo; Dir-Gen. Jean-Marc Pajot.

Korongo Airlines: Lubumbashi; internet www.flykorongo.com; f. 2010; expected to commence operations in April 2012; majority owned by Brussels Airlines; Dir-Gen. Christophe Allard.

Lignes Aériennes du Congo (LAC): 4 ave du Port, Kinshasa-Gombe, BP 8552, Kinshasa 1; tel. 819090001 (mobile); Pres. Louise L. Longange; Man. Dir Prosper Mazimpaka Faaty.

Malila Airlift: ave Basoko 188, BP 11526, Kinshasa-Gombe; tel. (88) 46428; fax 1-5304817707 (satellite); e-mail malila.airlift@ic.cd; internet malift.isuisse.com; f. 1996; regional services; Man. Véronique Malila.

Waltair Aviation: 9ème rue 206, Limete, Kinshasa; tel. (88) 48439; fax 1-3094162616 (satellite); e-mail waltair.rdc@ic.cd; regional services; Dir Vincent Gillet.

Tourism

The country offers extensive lake and mountain scenery, although tourism remains largely undeveloped. In 2009 tourist arrivals totalled 53,402. Receipts from tourism amounted to an estimated US $2m. in 1998.

Office National du Tourisme: 2A/2B ave des Orangers, BP 9502, Kinshasa-Gombe; tel. (12) 30070; f. 1959; Man. Dir Botolo Magoza.

Société Congolaise de l'Hôtellerie: Immeuble Memling, BP 1076, Kinshasa; tel. (12) 23260; Man. N'Joli Balanga.

Defence

The total strength of the armed forces of the Democratic Republic of the Congo, as assessed at November 2011, was estimated at between 144,000 and 159,000 (central staff 14,000; army 110,000–120,000; Republican Guard 6,000–8,000; navy 6,703; air force 2,548). The UN Organization Stabilization Mission in the Democratic Republic of Congo (MONUSCO) has a maximum authorized strength of about 22,000 personnel. MONUSCO had a mandate to remain in the country until the end of June 2011. In that month the mission's mandate was extended for a further year.

Defence Expenditure: Estimated at CF 213,000m. in 2012.

Commander-in-Chief: Maj.-Gen. Joseph Kabila Kabange.

Chief of Staff of the Armed Forces: Lt-Gen. Dieudonne Kayembe Mbandakulu.

Chief of Staff of the Army: Lt-Gen. Didier Etumba.

Chief of Staff of the Navy: Vice-Adm. Didier Etumba Longila.

Chief of Staff of the Air Force: Maj.-Gen. Rigobert Masamba Musungui.

Education

Primary education, beginning at six years of age and lasting for six years, is officially compulsory and is available free of charge in public institutions. Secondary education, which is not compulsory, begins at 12 years of age and lasts for up to six years, comprising a first cycle of two years and a second of four years. In 2008/09, according to UNESCO estimates, primary enrolment was equivalent to 93% of pupils (100% of boys; 86% of girls), while the comparable ratio for secondary enrolment was 38% (49% of boys; 27% of girls). There are four universities, located at Kinshasa, Kinshasa/Limete, Kisangani and Lubumbashi. In 2008/09 there were a total of 379,867 students enrolled in tertiary education. In 2010 spending on education represented 1.6% of total budgetary expenditure.

THE REPUBLIC OF THE CONGO

Introductory Survey

LOCATION, CLIMATE, LANGUAGE, RELIGION, FLAG, CAPITAL

The Republic of the Congo is an equatorial country on the west coast of Africa. It has a coastline of about 170 km on the Atlantic Ocean, from which the country extends northward to Cameroon and the Central African Republic. The Republic of the Congo is bordered by Gabon to the west and the Democratic Republic of the Congo to the east, while in the south there is a short frontier with the Cabinda exclave of Angola. The climate is tropical, with temperatures averaging 21°C–27°C (70°F–80°F) throughout the year. The average annual rainfall is about 1,200 mm (47 ins). The official language is French; Kituba, Lingala and other African languages are also used. Some 40% of the population follow traditional animist beliefs and about 57% are Roman Catholics. There are small Protestant and Muslim minorities. The national flag (proportions 2 by 3) comprises a yellow stripe running diagonally from lower hoist to upper fly, separating a green triangle at the hoist from a red triangle in the fly. The capital is Brazzaville.

CONTEMPORARY POLITICAL HISTORY

Historical Context

Formerly part of French Equatorial Africa, Middle Congo became the autonomous Republic of the Congo, within the French Community, in November 1958, with Abbé Fulbert Youlou as Prime Minister, and subsequently as President when the Congo became fully independent on 15 August 1960. Youlou relinquished office in August 1963, following a period of internal unrest, and was succeeded by Alphonse Massamba-Débat, initially as Prime Minister, and from December as President. In July 1964 the Mouvement national de la révolution (MNR) was established as the sole political party. In August 1968 Massamba-Débat was overthrown in a military coup, led by Capt. (later Maj.) Marien Ngouabi, who was proclaimed President in January 1969. A new Marxist-Leninist party, the Parti congolais du travail (PCT), replaced the MNR, and in January 1970 the country was renamed the People's Republic of the Congo. In March 1977 Ngouabi was assassinated, and in April Col (later Brig.-Gen.) Jacques-Joachim Yhombi-Opango, the head of the armed forces, became the new Head of State. In February 1979 Yhombi-Opango surrendered his powers to a Provisional Committee appointed by the PCT. In March the head of the Provisional Committee, Col (later Gen.) Denis Sassou-Nguesso, became Chairman of the PCT Central Committee and President of the Republic. In July 1989 Sassou-Nguesso, the sole candidate, was re-elected Chairman of the PCT and President of the Republic for a third five-year term. At legislative elections in September the PCT-approved single list of 133 candidates was endorsed by 99.2% of voters. The list included, for the first time, non-party candidates.

Progress towards political reform dominated the latter half of 1990. In August several political prisoners were released, among them Yhombi-Opango, and in September the Central Committee of the PCT agreed to the immediate registration of new political parties. During an extraordinary Congress of the PCT the party abandoned Marxism-Leninism as its official ideology and formulated constitutional amendments legalizing a multi-party system, which took effect in January 1991. Gen. Louis Sylvain Goma was appointed Prime Minister (a position he had held between 1975 and 1984), to lead an interim Government.

A National Conference, chaired by the Roman Catholic Bishop of Owando, Ernest N'Kombo, was convened in February 1991; opposition movements were allocated seven of the 11 seats on the Conference's governing body. Having voted to establish itself as a sovereign body, in April the Conference announced proposals to abrogate the Constitution and abolish the Assemblée nationale populaire. In June a 153-member legislative Haut conseil de la République (HCR) was established, chaired by N'Kombo; this was empowered to supervise the implementation of the resolutions made by the Conference. From June the Prime Minister replaced the President as Chairman of the Council of Ministers, and the country's official name reverted to the Republic of the Congo. A new Prime Minister, André Milongo (a former World Bank official), was appointed in June.

Domestic Political Affairs

In March 1992 a new Constitution, which provided for legislative power to be vested in an elected Assemblée nationale and Sénat and for executive power to be held by an elected President, was approved by 96.3% of voters at a national referendum. At elections to the Assemblée nationale, held in June and July, the Union panafricaine pour la démocratie sociale (UPADS) won 39 of the 125 seats, the Mouvement congolais pour la démocratie et le développement intégral (MCDDI) 29 seats and the PCT 18 seats. At indirect elections to the Sénat, held in July, the UPADS won the largest share (23) of the 60 seats, followed by the MCDDI, with 13 seats. At the first round of presidential voting, in August, Pascal Lissouba, the leader of the UPADS (and Prime Minister in 1963–66), won the largest share of the votes cast (35.9%); of the 15 other candidates, his closest rival was Bernard Kolélas of the MCDDI (22.9%). Sassou-Nguesso took 16.9% of the votes cast. At a second round of voting, two weeks later, Lissouba defeated Kolélas, with 61.3% of the votes cast.

Lissouba took office as President in August 1992. Maurice-Stéphane Bongho-Nouarra, of the UPADS, was appointed as Prime Minister. Meanwhile, the Union pour le renouveau démocratique (URD), a new alliance of seven parties, including the MCDDI, formed a coalition with the PCT (thereby establishing a parliamentary majority), which succeeded in winning a vote of no confidence against the Government in October. In November the Government resigned, and shortly afterwards Lissouba dissolved the Assemblée nationale and announced that fresh legislative elections would be held. In December Claude Antoine Dacosta, a former World Bank official, was appointed Prime Minister and formed a transitional Government, comprising members of all the main political parties.

At the first round of elections to the Assemblée nationale, which took place in May 1993, the Mouvance présidentielle (MP), an electoral coalition of the UPADS and its allies, won 62 of the 125 seats, while the URD-PCT coalition secured 49. Protesting that serious electoral irregularities had occurred, the URD-PCT refused to contest the second round of elections in June (for seats where a clear majority had not been achieved in the first round) and demanded the repetition of some of the first-round polls. After the second round the MP had secured an absolute majority (69) of seats in the legislature. In June President Lissouba appointed a new Council of Ministers, with Yhombi-Opango as Prime Minister. Later that month the Supreme Court ruled that electoral irregularities had occurred at the first round of elections, and in August, following external mediation, the Government and the opposition agreed to rerun the second round of elections.

Following the repeated elections, held in October 1993, the MP retained its majority in the Assemblée nationale, with 65 seats. In September six opposition parties formed an alliance, the Forces démocratiques unies (FDU), headed by Sassou-Nguesso and affiliated with the URD. In December Lissouba and the two main opposition leaders—Sassou-Nguesso and Kolélas—signed an agreement seeking a permanent end to hostilities between their supporters.

In February 1997 some 19 opposition parties issued a number of demands, including the expedited establishment of republican institutions, the creation of an independent electoral commission, the disarmament of civilians and the deployment of a multinational peace-keeping force. A fierce national conflict along ethnic and political lines developed and, despite mediation, none of the numerous cease-fire agreements signed during mid-1997 endured. In June French troops assisted in the evacuation of foreign residents from Brazzaville, and later in the month themselves departed. In September Lissouba appointed a Government of National Unity, under the premiership of Kolélas, thereby compromising the latter's role as a national mediator.

Sassou-Nguesso takes power

In October 1997 Sassou-Nguesso's forces, assisted by Angolan government troops, won control of Brazzaville and the strategic port of Pointe-Noire. Lissouba and Kolélas both found refuge abroad. Sassou-Nguesso was inaugurated as President on 25 October; he appointed a new transitional Government in November. It was later announced that a Conseil national de transition (CNT) was to hold legislative power, pending the approval of a new constitution by referendum (scheduled for 2001), and subsequent legislative elections. It was reported that some 10,000 people had been killed during the civil war.

Throughout 1998 clashes continued in the southern Pool region, a stronghold of the militia loyal to Kolélas, causing thousands to flee the area. In December a battle for control of Brazzaville broke out between forces loyal to Kolélas (who remained in exile), reputedly supported by Angolan rebel groups, and Congolese government forces, augmented by Sassou-Nguesso's militia and Angolan government troops. More than 8,000 refugees were reported to have fled into the neighbouring Democratic Republic of the Congo (DRC). In late December government forces, aided by Angolan troops, launched offensives against Kolélas' forces in the south and west of the country. By March 1999 the rebel militias had been obliged to withdraw to Pool, and by mid-1999 the further advance of government forces permitted residents to return to evacuated districts. In May 2000 Kolélas and his nephew, Col Philippe Bikinkita, the Minister of the Interior in the previous Lissouba administration, were convicted, *in absentia*, of operating personal prisons in Brazzaville and of mistreating prisoners and causing their deaths during the 1997 civil war. Kolélas and Bikinkita, both in exile abroad, were sentenced to death and ordered to pay compensation to their victims.

In December 1999 President Omar Bongo of Gabon was designated the official mediator in negotiations between the Government and the militias. Following discussions in Libreville, Gabon, representatives of the armed forces and of the rebel militias subsequently signed a peace agreement, in the presence of Bongo and Sassou-Nguesso. In February 2000 the committee in charge of observing the implementation of the peace process announced, at a meeting with Bongo, that the civil war was definitively over. By that month it was estimated that around one-half of the estimated 810,000 people displaced by the conflict had returned to their homes.

In November 2000 the Government adopted a draft Constitution, which included provisions for the institution of an executive presidency and a bicameral legislature. The Head of State would be elected for a term of seven years, renewable only once. In December it was announced that some 13,000 weapons had been surrendered and 12,000 militiamen disarmed in the past year, although UN sources suggested that this represented less than one-half of the total number of militiamen in the Congo.

Internal and exiled opposition groups boycotted the opening ceremony of a period of national dialogue in March 2001. Some 2,200 delegates from public institutions, civic associations and political parties attended a series of regional debates, reportedly reaching a consensus on the draft Constitution, despite concerns that the President would have the power to appoint and dismiss ministers at will, and that there would be no provision for a vote of censure against the Government.

A new Constitution was approved by 84.5% of votes cast at the referendum that took place on 20 January 2002, with a participation rate of 77.5% of the electorate. In February the Supreme Court approved 10 presidential candidates, including Sassou-Nguesso and Milongo. In March three opposition candidates, including Milongo, who had been widely regarded as the sole credible challenger to Sassou-Nguesso, and who now headed the Union pour la démocratie et la République (UDR—Mwinda), withdrew from the election. Milongo urged his supporters to boycott the poll, stating that his concerns about the transparency of electoral procedures and the impartiality of the Commission nationale d'organisation des élections (CONEL) remained unresolved. With all the major opposition candidates thereby excluded, Sassou-Nguesso won an overwhelming victory at the presidential election, which was held on 10 March, securing 89.4% of the votes cast. According to official figures, 69.4% of the electorate participated in the election.

Conflict in the Pool region

Meanwhile, in late March 2002 renewed violence erupted in the Pool region, apparently instigated by members of a 'Ninja' militia group, led by Rev. Frédéric Bitsangou Ntumi (who had been a co-signatory of the peace agreement reached in 1999), which attacked the town of Kindamba, prompting several thousand civilians to flee. By mid-April the unrest had spread to southern Brazzaville, and by late May some 50,000 people were reported to have been displaced. In late April government forces announced that they had regained control of the railway, facilitating a normalization in the supply of fuel and food to Brazzaville, although fighting continued in Pool. At the end of May government troops regained control of the rebel stronghold of Vindza, and in early June humanitarian assistance was finally permitted to reach the region.

The first round of elections to the 137-member Assemblée nationale took place on 26 May 2002. As a result of the unrest in Pool, voting was postponed indefinitely in eight constituencies, while disruption caused by protesters and administrative irregularities necessitated a rerun of polling in a further 12 constituencies on 28–29 May. Turn-out in the first round, at which the PCT and its allies in the FDU won 38 of the 51 seats decided, was around 65%. Prior to the second round, the security situation in Brazzaville deteriorated markedly. In mid-June, while Sassou-Nguesso was in Italy, Ninja troops attacked the capital's main military base resulting in the deaths of 72 rebels, three army officers and 15 civilians. Despite requests by the UDR—Mwinda for a postponement of the elections in those areas where fighting had occurred, voting went ahead on 23 June, although the rate of participation, at an estimated 30% nation-wide, was appreciably lower than in the first round, and was as low as 10% in some constituencies in Brazzaville and in Pointe-Noire. Following the polls, supporters of Sassou-Nguesso held an absolute majority in the new Assemblée; the PCT emerged as the largest party, with 53 seats, while the FDU alliance, by this stage comprising some 29 parties, held a total of 30 seats. The UDR—Mwinda became the largest opposition party, with six seats, while the UPADS held four seats. Notably, the MCDDI failed to secure representation in the Assemblée.

Following local and municipal elections, held on 30 June 2002, the Sénat comprised 56 supporters of the President (44 from the PCT and 12 from the FDU), two representatives of civil society organizations, one independent and one member of the opposition. In early August Jean-Pierre Thystère Tchicaya, the leader of the Rassemblement pour la démocratie et le progrès social, one of the constituent parties of the FDU, was elected as President of the Assemblée nationale, and the Secretary-General of the PCT, Ambroise-Edouard Noumazalay, was elected as President of the Sénat. Sassou-Nguesso was inaugurated as elected President on 14 August; later in the month he announced the formation of a new Government, which, notably, included no representatives of the opposition (although several representatives from civil society were appointed to ministerial positions).

During the second half of 2002 sporadic attacks by Ninja militias in the Pool region, in particular against freight trains on the Congo–Océan railway, continued. In October unrest intensified, and several deaths of civilians were reported in clashes; up to 10,000 civilians were reported to have fled Pool for Brazzaville, or the neighbouring Bouenza region, between early October and mid-November. In mid-November Sassou-Nguesso announced that a 'safe passage' would be provided from Pool to Brazzaville until mid-December for fighters who surrendered their arms, reiterating that the terms of the peace agreement concluded in 1999 remained valid. Fighting subsequently intensified, however, and despite an extension of the amnesty offered by Sassou-Nguesso, fewer than 500 rebels had surrendered by January 2003 (estimates of the number of rebels at large varied from 3,000–10,000), some 15 civilians were killed in an attack in Pool in January, and in February the first outbreak of violence in the Bouenza region since 1999 was reported. None the less, in March 2003 the Government and Ntumi's Ninja militia group signed a peace agreement. It was reported that at least 2,300 rebels had surrendered their weapons by April. In August the Assemblée nationale formally approved an amnesty for former Ninja fighters, to cover the period from January 2000. By September 2003 the situation in Pool had stabilized sufficiently to allow an electoral commission to be formed in the region; the delayed local and legislative elections were due to be held in 2005. None the less, in October 2003 renewed clashes between Ninja fighters and government forces near Mindouli, in Pool, resulted in at least 13 deaths.

In July 2004 the Congo was suspended from the Kimberley Process, an international initiative to eliminate the illegal trade in diamonds to fund conflicts, after a report identified irregularities in the country's diamond exports. Sassou-Nguesso subsequently pledged to halt diamond trading pending the implementation of reforms in the sector aimed at securing recertification by the Process.

In mid-October 2004 the rail service between Brazzaville and Pointe-Noire was suspended following a series of attacks on trains in the Pool region. Ntumi denied claims that the attacks had been perpetrated by his Ninja rebel group, by now also known as the Conseil national de la résistance (CNR), and demanded an independent inquiry into the incidents. Meanwhile, displaced persons who had fled hostilities in Pool continued to return gradually during 2004 with government assistance, although reports suggested that armed fighters continued to intimidate civilians, despite the peace agreement signed in March 2003. (It was estimated that between 100,000 and 147,000 people had fled Pool between 1998 and 2002, and that by late 2004 most towns and villages in the region had regained no more than two-thirds of their original populations.)

Towards conciliation

In January 2005 President Sassou-Nguesso effected a reorganization of the Council of Ministers. The new Government comprised 35 ministers, all of whom were members of the PCT. The post of Prime Minister was created, and awarded to Isidore Mvouba, hitherto Minister of State, Minister of Transport and Privatization, responsible for the Co-ordination of Government Action and a native of the Pool region. The hitherto deputy Governor of the Banque des états de l'Afrique centrale, Pacifique Issoïbeka, was appointed as Minister for the Economy, Finance and the Budget, while Bruno Itoua, hitherto Managing Director of the Société Nationale des Pétroles du Congo, was appointed Minister of Energy and Hydraulics. Opposition figures criticized the creation of the post of Prime Minister, claiming that it was in violation of the 2002 Constitution, which had enshrined presidential control over the executive.

During 2005 the Pool region continued to be a source of instability. In March the Government initiated a new programme for the disarmament, demobilization and reintegration of former combatants in Pool. In May it was announced that the Government had commenced power-sharing talks with the CNR with the aim of bringing members of the movement into 'all national institutions'. Meanwhile, the CNR also declared its intention of participating in future elections in the region (although it remained unclear as to when the holding of legislative elections in the region, postponed since 2002, would be feasible: the Government had intended that the polls be held in late 2005). The reintegration of some 30,000 former combatants of the civil war began in June 2008.

Indirect partial elections to renew one-half of the seats in the Sénat were held, as scheduled, on 2 October 2005, after which the PCT continued to hold an absolute majority of seats in the chamber, although its representation was reduced from 44 senators to 39. Most opposition parties boycotted these elections, and, partly in consequence, several independent representatives were elected.

In mid-October 2005 at least six people were killed in clashes in southern Brazzaville between Ninja fighters and pro-Government troops. The outbreak of violence followed the return of Kolélas to the Congo, to attend the funeral of his wife (who had died in Paris, France). President Sassou-Nguesso subsequently requested that the legislature grant amnesty to Kolélas, in the interests of national reconciliation; legislation to that end was duly approved on 6 December, and the death sentence issued *in absentia* against the former Prime Minister in May 2000 was overturned. The Minister of Justice and Human Rights, Gabriel Entcha Ebia, stated that private citizens would none the less retain the right to file lawsuits against Kolélas. Several days after the granting of amnesty, Kolélas issued an apology to the Congolese people for his role in instigating the 1997 civil conflict.

Unrest in the south of the country continued into 2006; in January the International Committee of the Red Cross (ICRC, see p. 350) and the international aid organization Médecins sans frontières suspended their operations after attacks on their staff by armed bandits. (The ICRC resumed its activities in the region in mid-February.) By this time some 43,000 members of rebel militias were thought to have been disarmed; however, in March Ntumi insisted on the creation of an agreement on 'political partnership' between the Government and the CNR as a condition for complete disarmament of his troops. In March the acting President of the UPADS, Pascal Gamassa, asked that the party be pardoned, in the name of former President Lissouba, for its role in the 1997 civil war.

The 2007 legislative elections

In January 2007 Sassou-Nguesso resigned from the presidency of the PCT, citing Article 72 of the Constitution which rendered incompatible the functions of the Head of State with those of a party leader. In February it was announced that the first and second rounds of legislative elections would be held on 24 June and 22 July, respectively.

Despite several opposition parties opting to boycott the ballot, the first round of legislative elections took place as scheduled on 24 June 2007, at which the PCT claimed 23 of the initial 44 seats available. However, allegations of widespread malpractice and procedural irregularities threatened to undermine the legitimacy of the poll and the results in 19 constituencies were annulled. A new ballot was held in those areas, although the announcement of the results was delayed until 19 July, prompting the postponement (until 5 August) of the second round of the elections. Following the second round of voting, official results indicated that the PCT had retained control of the Assemblée nationale, securing 46 of the 137 seats; the MCDDI and the UPADS each secured 11 seats. Observers from the African Union (AU, see p. 189) subsequently urged that a new independent electoral commission be established, following claims from opposition parties that the recently inaugurated supervisory body comprised a disproportionate number of government supporters.

In early December 2007 André Obami Itou was elected President of the Sénat, following the death the previous month of Noumazalay. In late December Sassou-Nguesso effected a minor reorganization of the Government; no changes were made to the key portfolios and Mvouba retained the premiership. Also in December 58 political parties loyal to the President formed an alliance, the Rassemblement de la majorité présidentielle (RMP), led by the PCT, to contest local and senatorial elections in 2008 and the presidential election in July 2009. At elections for 42 of the 72 seats in the enlarged Sénat (membership of that body had been increased from 66 following the creation of Pointe-Noire département), held on 5 August 2008, the RMP secured 33 seats, while independent candidates won seven seats and the UPADS two.

The 2009 presidential election

In December 2008 13 opposition parties, including the UPADS, signed a declaration requesting the suspension of the revision of electoral lists, and stating that dialogue regarding the organization of the presidential election planned for July 2009 had not been held prior to the revision of the lists. In April a 'Republican dialogue' between the Government, clergy, diplomatic corps and deputies of the ruling parties was boycotted by opposition parties which also demanded the dissolution of the CONEL (which had been mandated at the four-day meeting in Brazzaville to organize the elections) and the establishment of a joint and inclusive electoral commission. In a move described as 'provocative' by Guy Romain Kimfoussia, the presidential candidate for the UDR—Mwinda, a planned protest rally by the opposition alliance was banned by the authorities.

The presidential election, held on 12 July 2009, was contested by 13 candidates. (Former Prime Minister Ange Edouard Poungui had been selected as the presidential candidate of the UPADS, but his candidature was rejected by the Constitutional Court on the grounds that he had not been resident in the country for two years prior to the election.) According to provisional figures, Sassou-Nguesso was re-elected to the presidency with 78.6% of the votes, independent candidate Joseph Kignoumbi Kia Mbougou was placed second with 7.5% of the ballot, followed by Nicéphore Fylla de Saint-Eudes of the Parti républicain et libéral, who took 7.0% of the votes. Mathias Dzon, a former finance minister representing the opposition Alliance pour la république et la démocratie, who had been seen as Sassou-Nguesso's most serious contender, took only 2.3% of the votes. According to official figures, 66.4% of the registered electorate participated in the poll.

The AU issued a joint statement with the Communauté économique des états de l'Afrique centrale (CEEAC) that the elections had taken place 'in a calm and serene atmosphere'. However, a national human rights organization, the Observatoire congolais des droits humains, highlighted 'fraud and irregularities'. Independent observers claimed that the electoral register had been inflated by 458,000 'ghost' voters and that opposition press conferences had been prevented from taking place on the grounds that they were unauthorized public rallies. The election results were validated in late July 2009 by the Constitutional Court, which also rejected five applications from opposition candidates for the outcome to be annulled, judging that of Dzon as unfounded and that of Kimfoussia as inadmissible. In a further development, several opposition leaders, among them Dzon and Poungui, had their permission to travel restricted, due to their participation in post-election protest rallies, all of which had been banned by the authorities.

President Sassou-Nguesso carried out a major government reorganization in September 2009: the position of Prime Minister was abolished and Isidore Mvouba took over as Minister of State, Co-ordinator of Basic Infrastructures, and Minister of Civil Aviation and of Maritime Trade, the most senior position in the Government. In addition to that of basic infrastructures, a further three principal portfolios were created (economy, sovereignty and socio-cultural issues). Meanwhile, in Paris the Congolese opposition in exile formed a parallel 'government' led by Tony Gilbert Moudilou, a former adviser to Kolélas (who died in November), and appealed for the dismantling of the Sassou-Nguesso 'dictatorship'.

In October 2010 Congolese security forces commenced operations to restore civil order in the Pool region and to prepare for the rehabilitation of basic infrastructures, including the construction of a road linking the main town of Kinkala to Brazzaville. Police officers and members of the armed forces were initially to identify areas where they could safely establish bases, before taking steps to reduce incidences of banditry and disruption to the Brazzaville–Point Noire railway line.

Recent developments: senatorial elections

On 9 October 2011 the PCT and allied parties of the RMP overwhelmingly won partial elections to the Sénat that were held in six of the country's 12 départments, securing 33 of the 36 contested seats. (The UPADS held only four seats overall in the Sénat.) In November the Congolese Government announced that it had initiated a dialogue with opposition parties and civil society groups over the conduct of forthcoming legislative elections in 2012, with discussions focusing on revision of the electoral register and the restructuring of the electoral authority, the Commission nationale d'organisation des élections, following demands from opposition parties, civil society organizations and international observers for the adoption of reforms to address previous electoral shortcomings.

Foreign Affairs

Since the 1997 civil war the principal aims of Congolese foreign policy have been to gain international recognition for the legitimacy of the Sassou-Nguesso Government and to ensure the continued support of the country's bilateral and multilateral donors. During the 1997 civil war President Lissouba accused France of favouring the rebel forces of Sassou-Nguesso (who was reported to have allied himself with French petroleum interests) over the elected administration. In May 1998 France extended its formal recognition to the Sassou-Nguesso Government, and in June resumed aid payments that had been suspended since the 1997 conflict. Relations between France and the Congo deteriorated from mid-2002, as a result of an investigation by a French court into several Congolese officials, including Sassou-Nguesso, in connection with the reported disappearance of 353 Congolese citizens, following their return from asylum in the DRC to the Congo in 1999. In December 2002 the Congo filed a case against France at the International Court of Justice (ICJ) in The Hague, Netherlands, claiming that the investigations represented a violation of Congolese sovereignty and disregarded Sassou-Nguesso's immunity as a Head of State. In November 2010 the French Court of Cassation ruled that investigations into the financial transactions of Sassou-Nguesso in France could proceed. Charges had been brought by Transparency International, which maintained that Sassou-Nguesso and members of his family had used Congolese public funds in order to purchase property in France and had opened as many as 112 bank accounts in that country.

Relations between the Republic of the Congo and the DRC steadily improved from the late 1990s. In December 1998 the two countries signed a non-aggression pact and agreed to establish a joint force to guarantee border security. In December 1999 Sassou-Nguesso met President Laurent-Désiré Kabila in order to discuss bilateral co-operation and the implementation of the tripartite Luanda accord, and further discussion on issues of common interest subsequently took place regularly between the two countries. In May 2001 some 19 DRC nationals suspected of involvement in the assassination of Laurent-Désiré Kabila in January were extradited from the Republic of the Congo to Kinshasa. In September 2002 Congolese authorities announced that, in accordance with a programme established in association with the International Organization for Migration (see p. 347), up to 4,000 soldiers from the DRC who had sought refuge or deserted in the Congo were to be repatriated. In October a formal repatriation agreement for the 62,000 refugees from the DRC in the Congo was signed by representatives of both countries, in collaboration with the office of the UN High Commissioner for Refugees (UNHCR). Moreover, some 400 Congolese refugees were believed to have been repatriated from the Kimaza refugee camp in south-western DRC during 2004. In April 2005 the repatriation of some 57,000 refugees from the Congo to the DRC's Equateur province commenced under an agreement signed in September 2004 by officials from the two countries and UNHCR; by October 2007 a total of 36,000 refugees had returned to Equateur province since the programme began, including almost 18,000 since the beginning of 2007. However, in late 2009 it was estimated that a further 114,000 people fleeing renewed inter-ethnic violence in the Equateur province had taken refuge in the northern Congolese forests. In 2011 UNHCR estimated that a total of 139,000 refugees, mainly from the DRC, remained in the Congo.

By the mid-2000s Sassou-Nguesso's attempts to obtain international legitimacy for his regime had been largely successful. In 2003 Sassou-Nguesso served as President of the CEEAC (see p. 449) for the period of one year, and also became President of the Communauté économique et monétaire de l'Afrique centrale (see p. 333). In January 2006 Sassou-Nguesso was elected as head of the AU, following the withdrawal of the candidacy of President Lt-Gen. Omar Hassan Ahmad al-Bashir of Sudan, as a result of controversy regarding the support of that country's Government for *Janjaweed* militia in the conflict in the western region of Darfur.

CONSTITUTION AND GOVERNMENT

Under the terms of the 2002 Constitution, executive power is vested in a President, who is directly elected for a seven-year term, renewable only once. The President appoints a Council of Ministers. (The President appointed a Prime Minister in early 2005, although no explicit constitutional provision for such a post existed; in 2010 he abolished the role.) Legislative power is vested in a bicameral Parlement, comprising a 137-member Assemblée nationale, which is directly elected for a five-year term, and a 72-member Sénat, which is indirectly elected by local councils for a six-year term (with one-half of the membership renewable every three years).

For administrative purposes, the country is divided into 12 départments, consisting of 86 districts (sous-préfectures) and seven municipalities (communes urbaines).

REGIONAL AND INTERNATIONAL CO-OPERATION

The Republic of the Congo is a member of the African Union (see p. 189), the Central African organs of the Franc Zone (see p. 333) and of the CEEAC (see p. 449).

The Republic of the Congo became a member of the UN in 1960, and was admitted to the World Trade Organization (WTO, see p. 433) in 1997. The Republic of the Congo participates in the Group of 77 (G77, see p. 450) developing countries, and the country was also elected as a non-permanent member of the UN Security Council for a period of two years, with effect from September 2005.

ECONOMIC AFFAIRS

In 2010, according to estimates by the World Bank, the Congo's gross national income (GNI), measured at average 2008–10 prices, was US $8,698m., equivalent to $2,150 per head (or $3,050 on an international purchasing-power parity basis). During 2001–10, it was estimated, the population increased at an average annual rate of 2.6%, while gross domestic product (GDP) per head increased, in real terms, by an average of 2.1% per year. Overall GDP increased, in real terms, at an average annual rate of 4.7% in 2001–10; it grew by 8.8% in 2010.

Agriculture (including forestry and fishing) contributed an estimated 5.4% of GDP in 2009, according to the African Development Bank (AfDB), and employed about 30.4% of the total labour force in mid-2012, according to FAO estimates. The staple crops are cassava, bananas and plantains, while the major cash crops are sugar cane and oil palm and cocoa. In recent years cassava production has declined owing to the spread of the cassava mosaic disease, leading to fears of widespread hunger in the country. In 2008 the total production of cassava was estimated at 1m. metric tons. Thousands of varieties created by the International Institute of Agricultural Technologies to be resistant to the disease were brought in from the Democratic Republic of the Congo and distributed throughout five départements in an attempt to improve food security. Forests cover about 57% of the country's total land area, and forestry is a major economic activity. In 2008 exports of wood provided 3.8% of export earnings. In 2009 an accord was signed with the European Union, which provided for the strict control of timber exportation and the prevention of illegal logging. According to the AfDB, during 2000–07 agricultural GDP increased at an average annual rate of 5.9%; in 2008 agricultural GDP increased by 5.6%, but it declined by 4.6% in 2009.

Industry (including mining, manufacturing, construction and power) contributed an estimated 67.6% of GDP in 2009, according to the AfDB, and employed an estimated 14.7% of the labour force in 1990. During 2000–07, according to the AfDB, industrial GDP increased at an average annual rate of 1.5%; it increased by 6.9% in 2006, but contracted by 3.2% in 2007.

Mining contributed an estimated 57.1% of GDP in 2009, according to AfDB estimates. The hydrocarbons sector is the only significant mining activity. In 2007 sales of petroleum and petroleum products provided 92.8% of export earnings. Petroleum production (an estimated 292,000 barrels per day in 2010, according to the BP Statistical Review of World Energy) was expected to continue to increase, as a result of major exploration and development planned at various offshore deposits, in particular near to the maritime border with Angola. At the end of 2010 the Congo had estimated petroleum reserves of 1,900m. barrels, sufficient to sustain production at current levels for some 19 years. Deposits of natural gas are also exploited. Lead, zinc, gold and copper are produced in small quantities. There are also exploitable reserves of diamonds, phosphate, iron ore and bauxite. A joint venture with a Canadian company commenced in 2009 for the construction of a potash mining plant aimed at placing the Congo among the world's leading producers of that commodity and which would create some 4,000 jobs.

Manufacturing contributed 5.4% of GDP in 2009, according to AfDB estimates. The most important industries, the processing of agricultural and forest products, were adversely affected by the civil conflict in the late 1990s, but recovered in the early 2000s, as political stability was restored. The textile, chemical and construction materials industries are also significant. According to the AfDB, during 2000–07 manufacturing GDP increased at an average annual rate of 11.3%; growth of 5.5% was recorded in 2009.

The construction sector contributed 4.3% of GDP in 2009. According to the AfDB, the sector grew by 8.7% in 2009.

In 2008 81.3% of the country's electricity production was generated by hydroelectric plants, with the remainder generated by natural gas. The construction of a new hydroelectric dam at Imboulou, some 200 km north of Brazzaville, commenced in late 2003, with an anticipated completion date of 2010.

The services sector contributed 26.9% of GDP in 2009, according to AfDB estimates. During 2000–07, according to the AfDB, the GDP of the services sector increased at an average annual rate of 9.3%; the GDP of the sector increased by 4.2% in 2007.

In 2007 the Congo recorded a visible trade surplus of an estimated US $2,949.9m., when there was an estimated deficit of $2,181.0m. on the current account of the balance of payments. In 2003 the principal source of imports (37.6%) was the Netherlands. In that year the People's Republic of China was the principal market for exports (21.8%). France, the Republic of Korea, the USA, the Democratic People's Republic of Korea, Italy and Germany are also important export-trading partners. The principal exports in 2003 were petroleum and petroleum products, and wood. The principal imports in that year were machinery and transport equipment, food and live animals and basic manufactures.

According to IMF estimates, in 2009 there was a budget surplus of 313,000m. francs CFA, equivalent to 8.3% of GDP. Congo's general government gross debt was 1,417.315m. francs CFA in 2010, equivalent to 23.8% of GDP. The country's external debt totalled US $5,041m. in 2009, of which $4,785m. was public and publicly guaranteed debt. In that year, the cost of servicing long-term public and publicly guaranteed debt and repayments to the IMF was equivalent to 6.8% of the value of exports of goods, services and income (excluding workers' remittances). The average annual rate of inflation in Brazzaville during 2001–10 was 3.7%. Consumer prices increased by an average of 3.0% in 2010.

The Republic of the Congo is the fourth largest producer of petroleum in sub-Saharan Africa; nevertheless, the World Bank estimated that more than one-half of the 4.2m. Congolese lived under the poverty threshold, and other sources maintained that two-thirds of the population lived on less than one euro per day. Thus, the country continued to draw upon significant external assistance, including the initiative for heavily indebted poor countries (HIPC) debt relief scheme, under which the Congo had been able to achieve cancellation of a substantial proportion of its external debt (to the USA, Germany, Italy and Switzerland) and make use of further low interest loans. In July 2010 the USA agreed to cancel the entirety of the Congo's debt to that country, totalling some US $33.4m., after the 'Paris Club' of creditors agreed that the Congo had reached completion point on the HIPC initiative. In October a 'debt reduction and development contract' was signed with France allowing repaid debt, totalling an estimated €80m., to be redirected towards development projects. Furthermore, in August the IMF approved the disbursement of further funds amounting to $1.8m. under an Extended Credit Facility (ECF) totalling about $12.8m., which had been agreed in December 2008. In October 2010 the first of three new state-funded farming communities was established in Nkouo, north of Brazzaville, where some 40 families had been relocated in an attempt to counter food-security concerns Meanwhile, plans were announced in mid-2010 to develop the country's tourism industry, which at that time generated just 1% of GDP, initially through the development of the country's national parks. In January 2011 the IMF extended a tranche of $1.9m. under the ECF arrangement. In July a further disbursement of $3.9m. was approved, following the favourable conclusion of performance reviews of the supported economic programme. A government plan to improve the business environment as part of its poverty reduction strategy, in conjunction with continued public infrastructure investment, was particularly commended by the IMF. Increased GDP growth of 8.8% was estimated for 2010, while GDP was projected to rise by 5.3% in 2011 and by as much as 10% in 2012 (owing in part to the country's first stock market and a number of new industries under construction in Brazzaville, including an aluminium refinery, being scheduled to enter into operation in the second half of that year).

PUBLIC HOLIDAYS

2013: 1 January (New Year's Day), 29 March (Good Friday), 1 April (Easter Monday), 1 May (Labour Day), 20 May (Whit Monday), 15 August (Independence Day), 25 December (Christmas).

Statistical Survey

Source (unless otherwise stated): Direction Générale, Centre National de la Statistique et des Etudes Economiques, Immeuble du Plan, Rond point du Centre Culturel Français, BP 2031, Brazzaville; tel. and fax 22-281-59-09; e-mail cnsee@hotmail.com; internet www.cnsee.org.

Area and Population

AREA, POPULATION AND DENSITY

Area (sq km)	342,000*
Population (census results)	
30 July 1996	2,591,271
28 April 2007 (provisional)	3,697,487
Population (UN estimates at mid-year)†	
2010	4,042,899
2011	4,139,748
2012	4,233,062
Density (per sq km) at mid-2012	12.4

* 132,047 sq miles.

† Source: UN, *World Population Prospects: The 2010 Revision*.

POPULATION BY AGE AND SEX

(UN estimates at mid-2012)

	Males	Females	Total
0–14	862,464	848,902	1,711,366
15–64	1,185,630	1,180,647	2,366,277
65 and over	70,918	84,501	155,419
Total	2,119,012	2,114,050	4,233,062

Source: UN, *World Population Prospects: The 2010 Revision*.

ETHNIC GROUPS

1995 (percentages): Kongo 51.4; Téké 17.2; Mbochi 11.4; Mbédé 4.7; Punu 2.9; Sanga 2.5; Maka 1.8; Pygmy 1.4; Others 6.7 (Source: La Francophonie).

REGIONS

(population at 1996 census)

	Area (sq km)	Population	Capital
Bouenza	12,260	189,839	Madingou
Cuvette	74,850	112,946	Owando
Cuvette ouest		49,422	Ewo
Kouilou	13,650	77,048	Pointe-Noire
Lékoumou	20,950	75,734	Sibiti
Likouala	66,044	66,252	Impfondo
Niari	25,925	103,678	Loubomo (Dolisie)
Plateaux	38,400	139,371	Djambala
Pool	33,955	265,180	Kinkala
Sangha	55,795	39,439	Ouesso
Total*	341,829	1,118,909	

* Excluding the municipalities of Brazzaville (100 sq km, population 856,410), Pointe-Noire (45 sq km, population 455,131), Loubomo (Dolisie—18 sq km, population 79,852), Nkayi (8 sq km, population 46,727), Ouesso (population 17,784) and Mossendjo (population 16,458).

PRINCIPAL TOWNS

(population at 1996 census)

Brazzaville (capital)	856,410	Loubomo (Dolisie)	79,852
Pointe-Noire	455,131	Nkayi	46,727

Mid-2010 (incl. suburbs, UN estimate): Brazzaville 1,323,311 (Source: UN, *World Urbanization Prospects: The 2009 Revision*).

BIRTHS AND DEATHS

(annual averages, UN estimates)

	1995–2000	2000–05	2005–10
Birth rate (per 1,000)	37.7	37.2	36.0
Death rate (per 1,000)	12.6	12.5	11.7

Source: UN, *World Population Prospects: The 2010 Revision*.

Life expectancy (years at birth, WHO estimates): 55 (males 53; females 57) in 2009 (Source: WHO, *World Health Statistics*).

EMPLOYMENT

('000 persons at 1984 census)

	Males	Females	Total
Agriculture, etc.	105	186	291
Industry	61	8	69
Services	123	60	183
Total	289	254	543

Mid-2012 (estimates in '000): Agriculture, etc. 527; Total labour force 1,735 (Source: FAO).

Health and Welfare

KEY INDICATORS

Total fertility rate (children per woman, 2009)	4.3
Under-5 mortality rate (per 1,000 live births, 2009)	128
HIV/AIDS (% of persons aged 15–49, 2009)	3.4
Physicians (per 1,000 head, 2004)	0.2
Hospital beds (per 1,000 head, 2005)	1.6
Health expenditure (2008): US $ per head (PPP)	108
Health expenditure (2008): % of GDP	2.7
Health expenditure (2008): public (% of total)	49.9
Access to water (% of persons, 2008)	71
Access to sanitation (% of persons, 2008)	30
Total carbon dioxide emissions ('000 metric tons, 2007)	1,586.5
Carbon dioxide emissions per head (metric tons, 2007)	0.4
Human Development Index (2011): ranking	137
Human Development Index (2011): value	0.533

For sources and definitions, see explanatory note on p. vi.

Agriculture

PRINCIPAL CROPS

('000 metric tons)

	2008	2009	2010
Maize	9.9	10.2	10.5
Sweet potatoes*	6.0	7.2	7.7
Cassava (Manioc)	1,112.7	1,148.5	1,148.5
Yams*	12.0	15.4	16.5
Sugar cane*	565.0	600.0	650.0
Groundnuts, with shell	28.2	29.1	29.1
Oil palm fruit*	139.5	140.0	141.3
Bananas*	99.0	99.5	100.0
Plantains	78.6	80.4	81.1
Guavas, mangoes and mangosteens*	26.0	27.8	28.0
Avocados*	6.6	6.5	6.8

* FAO estimates.

Aggregate production ('000 metric tons, may include official, semi-official or estimated data): Total cereals 23.1 in 2008, 24.0 in 2009, 25.0 in 2010; Total roots and tubers 1,175.2 in 2008, 1,227.3 in 2009, 1,232.8 in 2010; Total vegetables (incl. melons) 118.8 in 2008, 125.4 in 2009, 114.4 in 2010; Total fruits (excl. melons) 254.6 in 2008, 260.7 in 2009, 263.8 in 2010.

Source: FAO.

LIVESTOCK
('000 head, year ending September)

	2008	2009	2010
Cattle*	325	310	330
Pigs	69	69*	70*
Sheep*	116	118	120
Goats*	295	315	320
Chickens*	2,450	2,500	2,600

* FAO estimate(s).

Source: FAO.

LIVESTOCK PRODUCTS
('000 metric tons)

	2008	2009	2010*
Cattle meat	6.1	5.6	6.2
Pig meat	1.7	1.8	1.9
Chicken meat	5.9*	6.0*	6.3
Game meat	30.0*	32.0*	39.6
Sheep and goat meat	1.3*	1.4*	1.5
Cows' milk	1.3*	1.3*	1.3
Hen eggs	1.5*	1.6*	1.6

* FAO estimate(s).

Source: FAO.

Forestry

ROUNDWOOD REMOVALS
('000 cubic metres, excluding bark, FAO estimates)

	2007	2008	2009
Sawlogs, veneer logs and logs for sleepers	1,700	1,700	1,700
Pulpwood	361	361	361
Other industrial wood	370	370	370
Fuel wood	1,275	1,295	1,315
Total	3,706	3,726	3,746

2010: Production assumed to be unchanged from 2009 (FAO estimates).

Source: FAO.

SAWNWOOD PRODUCTION
('000 cubic metres, including railway sleepers)

	2008	2009	2010
Total (all broadleaved)	369	369	268

Source: FAO.

Fishing

('000 metric tons, live weight)

	2007	2008	2009
Capture	59.2	54.1	61.2
Freshwater fishes	30.1	29.4	28.4
West African croakers	2.8	2.3	3.2
Sardinellas	6.9	9.6	12.2
Aquaculture	0.0	0.1	0.1*
Total catch	59.2	54.2	61.3*

* FAO estimate.

Source: FAO.

Mining

	2007	2008	2009
Crude petroleum ('000 barrels)	80,692	85,037	99,348
Gold (kg)*	100	100	100

* Estimated metal content of ore.

Source: US Geological Survey.

Industry

SELECTED PRODUCTS
('000 metric tons, unless otherwise indicated)

	2006	2007	2008
Raw sugar	65.0	56.0	67.0
Veneer sheets ('000 cu metres)	14	14	14
Jet fuels	53.0	55.0	31.0
Motor gasoline (petrol)	53.0	63.0	46.0
Kerosene	12	14	17
Distillate fuel oils	123	141	109
Residual fuel oils	377	437	327
Electric energy (million kWh)	453	407	461

Source: UN Industrial Commodity Statistics Database.

Finance

CURRENCY AND EXCHANGE RATES

Monetary Units
100 centimes = 1 franc de la Coopération financière en Afrique centrale (CFA).

Sterling, Dollar and Euro Equivalents (30 December 2011)
£1 sterling = 783.813 francs CFA;
US $1 = 506.961 francs CFA;
€1 = 655.957 francs CFA;
10,000 francs CFA = £12.76 = $19.73 = €15.24.

Average Exchange Rate (francs CFA per US $)
2009 472.186
2010 495.277
2011 471.866

Note: The exchange rate of 1 French franc = 50 francs CFA, established in 1948, remained in force until January 1994, when the CFA franc was devalued by 50%, with the exchange rate adjusted to 1 French franc = 100 francs CFA. The relationship to French currency remained in effect with the introduction of the euro on 1 January 1999. From that date, accordingly, a fixed exchange rate of €1 = 655.957 francs CFA has been in operation.

BUDGET
(central government operations, '000 million francs CFA)

Revenue*	2008	2009†	2010‡
Oil revenue	2,118	1,070	2,187
Non-oil revenue	324	372	422
Investment income	20	27	20
Total	2,462	1,469	2,629

Expenditure	2008	2009†	2010‡
Current expenditure	785	587	593
Wages and salaries	166	175	188
Materials and supplies	176	164	175
Transfers	228	172	153
Common charges	42	25	23
Budgetary reserves	—	15	10
Interest payments	150	10	8
External	140	3	2
Domestic	10	7	6
Local authorities	23	25	36
Capital expenditure	453	591	655
Externally financed	64	122	139
Domestically financed	390	469	516
Total	1,238	1,178	1,248

* Excluding grants received ('000 million francs CFA): 18 in 2008; 22 in 2009 (budgeted figure); 33 in 2010 (projection).

† Budgeted figures.

‡ Projections.

Source: IMF, *Republic of Congo: Second Review Under the Three-Year Arrangement Under the Poverty Reduction and Growth Facility—Staff Report; Press Release on the Executive Board Discussion; and Statement by the Executive Director for the Republic of Congo* (February 2010).

2011 ('000 million francs CFA, projections): *Revenue:* Oil revenue 2,627, Non-oil revenue 576, Investment income 36; Total 3,239 (excluding grants 35). *Expenditure:* Current expenditure 687, (Wages and salaries 225, Other current expenditure 411, Local authorities 40, Interest payments 11), Capital expenditure 981 (Externally financed 291, Domestically financed 690); Total 1,668 (Source: IMF, *Republic of Congo: Fifth and Sixth Reviews Under the Three-Year Arrangement Under the Extended Credit Facility and Financing Assurances Review—Staff Report; Staff Statement and Supplement; Press Release on the Executive Board Discussion; and Statement by the Executive Director for the Republic of Congo.*— August 2011).

INTERNATIONAL RESERVES

(US $ million at 31 December)

	2008	2009	2010
Gold (national valuation)	1.62	—	17.82
IMF special drawing rights	0.22	109.83	107.89
Reserve position in IMF	0.89	0.90	0.89
Foreign exchange	3,870.68	3,695.51	4,338.07
Total	3,873.41	3,806.25*	4,464.67

* Excluding gold.

Source: IMF, *International Financial Statistics*.

MONEY SUPPLY

('000 million francs CFA at 31 December)

	2008	2009	2010
Currency outside banks	347.34	342.22	408.44
Demand deposits at active commercial banks	447.04	484.54	755.28
Total money (incl. others)	853.40	891.17	1,251.79

Source: IMF, *International Financial Statistics*.

COST OF LIVING

(Consumer Price Index for Brazzaville; base: 2000 = 100)

	2007	2008	2009
Food	112.9	122.1	131.3
Clothing	96.0	97.3	100.0
Rent	130.9	137.3	144.7
Fuel and electricity	137.9	143.9	154.0
All items (incl. others)	119.9	128.7	135.1

2010: Food 143.3; All items (incl. others) 139.2.

Source: ILO.

NATIONAL ACCOUNTS

('000 million francs CFA at current prices)

Expenditure on the Gross Domestic Product

	2007	2008	2009
Government final consumption expenditure	412.8	448.1	468.9
Private final consumption expenditure	987.5	1,269.3	1,006.1
Gross fixed capital formation	1,426.6	1,775.6	1,928.7
Changes in inventories	20.4	12.5	9.5
Total domestic expenditure	2,847.3	3,505.5	3,413.2
Exports of goods and services	2,845.7	4,086.1	3,052.7
Less Imports of goods and services	2,129.4	3,155.9	2,707.5
GDP at purchasers' values	3,563.6	4,435.7	3,758.4

Gross Domestic Product by Economic Activity

	2007	2008	2009
Agriculture, hunting, forestry and fishing	173.9	192.3	200.0
Mining and quarrying	2,172.0	2,905.5	2,107.5
Manufacturing	162.2	181.4	199.2
Electricity, gas and water	28.8	31.1	32.9
Construction	124.2	139.4	158.0
Trade, restaurants and hotels	243.4	269.6	302.0
Transport and communications	180.9	201.9	223.2
Public administration and defence	181.4	191.5	205.3
Other services	222.5	242.0	264.3
GDP at factor cost	3,489.3	4,354.7	3,692.4
Indirect taxes	74.3	81.0	66.0
GDP in purchasers' values	3,563.6	4,435.7	3,758.4

Note: Deduction for imputed bank service charge assumed to be distributed at origin.

Source: African Development Bank.

BALANCE OF PAYMENTS

(US $ million)

	2005	2006	2007
Exports of goods f.o.b.	4,745.3	6,065.7	5,808.0
Imports of goods f.o.b.	–1,305.5	–2,003.5	–2,858.1
Trade balance	3,439.8	4,062.2	2,949.9
Exports of services	220.5	266.0	319.4
Imports of services	–1,417.1	–2,425.9	–3,527.7
Balance on goods and services	2,243.2	1,902.3	–258.3
Other income received	17.6	20.1	23.4
Other income paid	–1,595.5	–1,772.6	–1,908.1
Balance on goods, services and income	665.3	149.7	–2,143.1
Current transfers received	87.2	37.9	43.0
Current transfers paid	–56.9	–63.5	–81.0
Current balance	695.6	124.1	–2,181.0
Capital account (net)	11.2	9.6	31.7
Direct investment from abroad	513.6	1,487.7	2,638.4
Portfolio investment assets	–1.1	–1.3	–1.5
Other investment assets	–246.5	–228.9	266.2
Other investment liabilities	–492.7	–831.5	–356.4
Net errors and omissions	30.5	142.5	–201.1
Overall balance	510.5	702.1	196.4

Source: IMF, *International Financial Statistics*.

External Trade

PRINCIPAL COMMODITIES
(distribution by SITC, US $ million)

Imports c.i.f.	2001	2002	2003
Food and live animals	114.0	110.6	144.3
Meat and meat preparations	24.9	25.7	39.0
Fish, crustaceans, molluscs and preparations thereof	19.9	14.3	29.3
Cereals and cereal preparations	34.4	43.8	36.2
Chemicals and related products	52.9	20.8	97.2
Medicinal and pharmaceutical products	25.1	2.9	39.0
Basic manufactures	139.1	145.2	134.2
Non-metallic mineral manufactures	21.1	33.0	22.7
Iron and steel	6.2	7.1	47.6
Machinery and transport equipment	208.3	201.8	196.7
Road vehicles and parts*	38.0	32.6	41.5
Miscellaneous manufactured articles	49.3	69.8	62.7
Total (incl. others)	564.2	643.5	681.5

Exports f.o.b.	2001	2002	2003
Crude materials (inedible) except fuels	111.9	140.7	216.3
Cork and wood	111.9	140.7	216.3
Wood in the rough or roughly squared	71.7	108.8	167.6
Wood, simply worked and railway sleepers of wood	40.2	31.9	48.7
Mineral fuels, lubricants, etc.	1,177.4	2,252.6	1,465.2
Petroleum, petroleum products, etc.	1,177.4	2,148.8	1,418.3
Crude petroleum oils, etc.	1,129.9	2,102.6	1,418.3
Refined petroleum oils, etc.	47.5	46.2	n.a.
Total (incl. others)	1,313.1	2,423.2	1,722.0

* Data on parts exclude tyres, engines and electrical parts.

Source: UN, *International Trade Statistics Yearbook*.

PRINCIPAL TRADING PARTNERS
(US $ million)

Imports c.i.f.	2001	2002	2003
Belgium	24.3	31.8	30.5
Cameroon	22.2	23.0	29.7
China, People's Rep.	6.8	26.0	22.8
Congo, Democratic Rep.	3.0	5.5	5.6
Côte d'Ivoire	6.9	7.0	10.2
France (incl. Monaco)	127.2	166.4	191.3
Gabon	9.0	2.9	1.9
Germany	16.3	23.3	35.8
India	6.0	11.9	10.4
Indonesia	6.2	5.6	2.8
Ireland	4.1	5.4	8.6
Italy	79.7	53.2	43.2
Japan	27.6	21.4	23.3
Lebanon	0.6	38.1	2.3
Netherlands	29.2	29.0	256.5
Saudi Arabia	3.6	9.1	2.5
Senegal	5.1	5.7	9.2
South Africa	14.7	11.8	15.8
Thailand	7.2	7.5	6.0
United Kingdom	21.5	24.1	17.7
USA	59.2	66.4	69.9
Total (incl. others)	564.2	643.5	681.5

Exports f.o.b.	2001	2002	2003
Brazil	21.7	16.5	56.5
Cameroon	1.1	26.7	10.2
Chile	10.9	33.6	—
China, People's Rep.	78.0	168.8	375.8
France (incl. Monaco)	25.1	175.5	68.4
Germany	4.4	142.7	8.8
Iceland	1.5	63.0	47.5
India	20.6	18.8	—
Indonesia	—	21.3	24.9
Israel	0.8	36.7	2.9
Italy	38.0	39.3	21.9
Japan	1.7	97.1	0.4
Korea, Democratic People's Rep.	207.0	271.5	131.0
Korea, Rep.	20.6	174.7	239.1
Netherlands	21.2	35.3	8.6
Portugal	17.7	24.9	38.9
Singapore	0.3	44.3	0.1
Spain	15.8	18.2	26.7
USA	273.3	252.4	165.3
Total (incl. others)	1,313.1	2,423.2	1,722.0

Source: UN, *International Trade Statistics Yearbook*.

Transport

RAILWAYS
(traffic)

	1999	2000	2001
Passengers carried ('000)	56.5	546.0	742.0
Freight carried ('000 metric tons)	65.7	236.0	548.0

Passenger-km (million): 9 in 1999.

Freight ton-km (million): 21 in 1999.

Sources: UN, *Statistical Yearbook;* IMF, *Republic of Congo: Selected Issues and Statistical Appendix* (July 2004).

ROAD TRAFFIC
(estimates, '000 motor vehicles in use)

	1999	2000	2001
Passenger cars	26.2	29.7	29.7
Commercial vehicles	20.4	23.1	23.1

Source: UN, *Statistical Yearbook*.

2007 ('000 motor vehicles in use at 31 December): Passenger cars 56; Vans and lorries 36; Motorcycles and mopeds 3; Total (incl. others) 100 (Source: IRF, *World Road Statistics*).

SHIPPING

Merchant Fleet
(registered at 31 December)

	2007	2008	2009
Number of vessels	20	20	20
Total displacement ('000 grt)	3.8	3.8	3.8

Source: IHS Fairplay, *World Fleet Statistics*.

Freight Traffic at Pointe-Noire
(metric tons)

	1996	1997	1998
Goods loaded	670,150	708,203	n.a.
Goods unloaded	584,376	533,170	724,000*

* Rounded figure.

Source: mainly Banque des états de l'Afrique centrale, *Etudes et Statistiques*.

CIVIL AVIATION
(traffic on scheduled services)*

	2001	2002	2003
Kilometres flown (million)	3	1	1
Passengers carried ('000)	95	47	52
Passenger-km (million)	157	27	31
Total ton-km (million)	22	3	3

* Including an apportionment of the traffic of Air Afrique.

Source: UN, *Statistical Yearbook*.

Tourism

FOREIGN VISITORS BY COUNTRY OF RESIDENCE*

	2007	2008	2009
Angola	2,837	2,134	2,558
Belgium	1,266	1,056	1,516
Cameroon	2,136	2,792	3,688
Congo, Democratic Rep.	4,154	5,224	4,489
France	14,466	22,473	23,017
Gabon	1,689	1,629	1,773
Italy	999	1,617	2,747
United Kingdom	743	819	3,094
USA	612	1,218	n.a.
Total (incl. others)	54,260	63,343	85,000

* Arrivals at hotels and similar establishments.

Receipts from tourism (US $ million, excl. passenger transport): 40 in 2005; 45 in 2006; 54 in 2007.

Source: World Tourism Organization.

Communications Media

	2008	2009	2010
Telephones ('000 main lines in use)	9.0	9.5	9.8
Mobile cellular telephones ('000 subscribers)	1,807.0	2,171.0	3,798.6
Internet users ('000)	155	245	n.a.
Broadband subscribers	—	—	100

Source: International Telecommunication Union.

Personal computers: 19,000 (5.6 per 1,000 persons) in 2005 (Source: UNESCO Institute for Statistics).

Radio receivers ('000 in use): 341 in 1997 (Source: UNESCO Institute for Statistics).

Television receivers ('000 in use): 33 in 1997 (Source: UNESCO Institute for Statistics).

Daily newspapers (national estimates): 6 in 1997 (average circulation 20,500 copies) (Source: UNESCO, *Statistical Yearbook*).

Non-daily newspapers (national estimates): 15 in 1995 (average circulation 38,000 copies) (Source: UNESCO, *Statistical Yearbook*).

Education

(2009/10 except where otherwise indicated)

			Students		
	Institutions*	Teachers	Males	Females	Total
Pre-primary	95	1,868	21,169	22,303	43,472
Primary	1,168	14,347	364,335	340,758	705,093
Secondary	n.a.	9,915†	125,229‡	106,797‡	232,026‡
Tertiary	n.a.	1,170§	15,331	5,052	20,383

* 1998/99.
† 2004/05.
‡ 2003/04.
§ 2008/09.

Sources: mostly UNESCO Institute for Statistics.

Pupil-teacher ratio (primary education, UNESCO estimate): 49.1 in 2009/10 (Source: UNESCO Institute for Statistics).

Adult literacy rate (UNESCO estimates): 86.8% (males 92.1%; females 81.7%) in 2007 (Source: UNESCO Institute for Statistics).

Directory

The Government

HEAD OF STATE

President: Gen. Denis Sassou-Nguesso (assumed power 15 October 1997; inaugurated 25 October 1997; elected 10 March 2002; re-elected 12 July 2009).

COUNCIL OF MINISTERS
(May 2012)

Minister of State, Co-ordinator of Basic Infrastructures, and Minister of Transport, Civil Aviation and Maritime Trade: Isidore Mvouba.

Minister of State, Co-ordinator of the Economy, and Minister of Planning, Land Management and Integration: Pierre Moussa.

Minister of State, Co-ordinator of Sovereignty, and Keeper of the Seals, Minister of Justice and Human Rights: Aimé Emmanuel Yoka.

Minister of State, Co-ordinator of Socio-cultural Issues, and Minister of Labour and Social Security: Florent Tsiba.

Minister of State, Minister of Industrial Development and the Promotion of the Private Sector: Rodolphe Adada.

Minister of Finance, the Budget and of the Public Portfolio: Gilbert Ondongo.

Minister of Foreign Affairs and Co-operation: Basile Ikouébé.

Minister of the Interior and Decentralization: Raymond Zéphyrin Mboulou.

Minister of Mining and Geology: Gen. Pierre Oba.

Minister of Sustainable Development, the Forest Economy and the Environment: Henri Djombo.

Minister of the Civil Service and State Reform: Guy Brice Parfait Kolelas.

Minister of Equipment and Public Works: Emile Ouosso.

Minister of Construction, Town Planning and Housing: Claude Alphonse Nsilou.

Minister of Agriculture and Stockbreeding: Rigobert Maboundou.

Minister at the Presidency, responsible for National Defence: Charles Zacharie Bowao.

Minister of Small and Medium-sized Enterprises and Crafts: Adélaïde Moundélé-Ngollo.

Minister of Trade and Supplies: Claudine Mounari.

Minister of Technical Education, Vocational Training and Employment: André Okombi Salissa.

Minister of Primary and Secondary Education, responsible for Literacy: ROSALIE KAMA-NIAMAYOUA.

Minister of Higher Education: ANGE ANTOINE ABENA.

Minister of Fisheries and Aquaculture: HELLOT MAMPOUYA MATSON.

Minister of Health and Population: GEORGES MOYEN.

Minister of Energy and Water Resources: HENRI OSSEBI.

Minister of Hydrocarbons: ANDRÉ RAPHAËL LOEMBA.

Minister of Scientific Research: BRUNO JEAN-RICHARDS ITOUA.

Minister of Culture and the Arts: JEAN-CLAUDE GAKOSSO.

Minister of Social Affairs, Humanitarian Action and Solidarity: EMILIENNE RAOUL.

Minister of Sports: LÉON ALFRED OPIMBAT.

Minister at the Presidency, responsible for the Special Economic Zones: ALAIN AKOUALA ATIPAULT.

Minister of Posts, Telecommunications and ICT: THIERRY MOUNGALLA.

Minister of Tourism and Leisure: MATHIEU MARTIAL KANI.

Minister of Land Reform and the Preservation of the Public Domain: PIERRE MABIALA.

Minister of Communication and Relations with Parliament: BIENVENUE OKIEMY.

Minister of the Promotion of Women and the Integration of Women into Development: MADELEINE YILA BOUMPOTO.

Minister of Civic Education and Youth: ANATOLE COLLINET MAKOSSO.

Minister-delegate to the Minister of Transport, Civil Aviation and Maritime Trade, responsible for Maritime Trade: MARTIN PARFAIT AIMÉ COUSSOUD MAVOUNGOU.

Minister-delegate to the Minister of State, Minister of Economy, Planning and Land Management and Integration, responsible for Land Management and Integration: JOSUÉ RODRIGUE NGOUNIMBA.

MINISTRIES

Office of the President: Palais du Peuple, Brazzaville; tel. 22-281-17-11; internet www.presidence.cg.

Office of the Minister at the Presidency, responsible for National Defence: Brazzaville; tel. 22-281-22-31.

Office of the Minister at the Presidency, responsible for the Special Economic Zones: Brazzaville.

Ministry of Agriculture and Stockbreeding: BP 2453, Brazzaville; tel. 22-281-41-31; fax 22-281-19-29.

Ministry of Civic Education and Youth: Brazzaville.

Ministry of the Civil Service and State Reform: BP 12151, Brazzaville; tel. 22-281-41-68; fax 22-281-41-49.

Ministry of Communication, responsible for Relations with Parliament: BP 114, Brazzaville; tel. 22-281-41-29; fax 22-281-41-28; e-mail depcompt@congonet.cg.

Ministry of Construction, Town Planning and Housing: BP 1580, Brazzaville; tel. 22-281-34-48; fax 22-281-12-97.

Ministry of Culture and the Arts: BP 20480, Brazzaville; tel. 22-281-02-35; fax 22-281-40-25.

Ministry of the Economy, Planning, Land Management and Integration: BP 64, Brazzaville; tel. 22-281-06-56; fax 22-281-58-08.

Ministry of Energy and Water Resources: Brazzaville.

Ministry of Equipment and Public Works: BP 2099, Brazzaville; tel. 22-281-59-41; fax 22-281-59-07.

Ministry of Finance and the Budget and the Public Portfolio: ave de l'Indépendance, croisement ave Foch, BP 2083, Brazzaville; tel. 22-281-45-24; fax 22-281-43-69; e-mail mefb-cg@mefb-cg.net; internet www.mefb-cg.org.

Ministry of Fisheries and Aquaculture: Brazzaville.

Ministry of Foreign Affairs and Co-operation: BP 2070, Brazzaville; tel. 22-281-10-89; fax 22-281-41-61.

Ministry of Health and Population: BP 20101, Brazzaville; tel. 22-281-30-75; fax 22-281-14-33.

Ministry of Higher Education: Ancien Immeuble de la Radio, BP 169, Brazzaville; tel. 22-281-08-15; fax 22-281-52-65.

Ministry of Hydrocarbons: BP 2120, Brazzaville; tel. 22-281-10-86; fax 22-281-10-85.

Ministry of Industrial Development and the Promotion of the Private Sector: Centre Administratif, Quartier Plateau, BP 2117, Brazzaville; tel. 22-281-30-09; fax 22-281-06-43.

Ministry of the Interior and Decentralization: BP 880, Brazzaville; tel. 22-281-40-60; fax 22-281-33-17.

Ministry of Justice and Human Rights: BP 2497, Brazzaville; tel. and fax 22-281-41-49.

Ministry of Labour and Social Security: Immeuble de la BCC, ave Foch, BP 2075, Brazzaville; tel. 22-281-41-43; fax 22-281-05-50.

Ministry of Land Reform and the Preservation of the Public Domain: Brazzaville; tel. 22-281-34-48.

Ministry of Maritime Transport and the Merchant Navy: Brazzaville; tel. 22-281-10-67; fax 22-282-55-14.

Ministry of Mining and Geology: BP 2124, Brazzaville; tel. 22-281-02-64; fax 22-281-50-77.

Ministry of Posts and Telecommunications: BP 44, Brazzaville; tel. 22-281-41-18; fax 22-281-19-34.

Ministry of Primary and Secondary Education: BP 5253, Brazzaville; tel. 22-281-24-52; fax 22-281-25-39.

Ministry of the Promotion of Women and the Integration of Women into Development: Brazzaville; tel. 22-281-19-29.

Ministry of Scientific Research: Ancien Immeuble de la Radio, Brazzaville; tel. 22-281-03-59.

Ministry of Security and Public Order: BP 2474, Brazzaville; tel. 22-281-41-73; fax 22-281-34-04.

Ministry of Small and Medium-sized Enterprises and Crafts: Brazzaville.

Ministry of Social Affairs, Humanitarian Action and Solidarity: Brazzaville.

Ministry of Sports: BP 2061, Brazzaville; tel. 06-660-89-24 (mobile).

Ministry of Sustainable Development, the Forest Economy and the Environment: Immeuble de l'Agriculture, face à Blanche Gomez, BP 98, Brazzaville; tel. 22-281-41-37; fax 22-281-41-34; e-mail ajdbosseko@minifor.com.

Ministry of Technical Education, Vocational Training and Employment: BP 2076, Brazzaville; tel. 22-281-17-27; fax 22-281-56-82; e-mail metp_cab@yahoo.fr.

Ministry of Tourism and Leisure: Brazzaville.

Ministry of Trade and Supplies: BP 2965, Brazzaville; tel. 22-281-41-16; fax 22-281-41-57; e-mail mougany@yahoo.fr.

Ministry of Transport, Civil Aviation and Maritime Trade: Immeuble Mafoua Virgile, BP 2066, Brazzaville; tel. 22-281-53-39; fax 22-281-57-56.

President and Legislature

PRESIDENT

Presidential Election, 12 July 2009

Candidate	Votes	% of votes
Denis Sassou-Nguesso	1,055,117	78.61
Joseph Kignoumbi Kia Mbougou	100,181	7.46
Nicéphore Fylla de Saint-Eudes	93,749	6.98
Mathias Dzon	30,861	2.30
Joseph Hodjuila Miokono	27,060	2.02
Guy-Romain Kinfoussia	11,678	0.87
Jean François Tchibinda Kouangou	5,475	0.41
Anguios Nganguia-Engambé	4,064	0.30
Bonaventure Mizidy Bavouéza	3,594	0.27
Clément Miérassa	3,305	0.25
Bertin Pandi-Ngouari	2,749	0.20
Marion Michel Madzimba Ehouango	2,612	0.19
Jean Ebina	1,797	0.13
Total	1,342,242	100.00

LEGISLATURE

The legislature, Parlement, comprises two chambers: a directly elected lower house, the Assemblée nationale; and an indirectly elected upper house, the Sénat.

Assemblée nationale

Palais du Parlement, BP 2106, Brazzaville; tel. 22-281-11-12; fax 22-281-41-28; e-mail dsancongo@yahoo.fr.

President: JUSTIN KOUMBA.

General Election, 24 June and 5 August 2007

Party	Seats
Parti congolais du travail (PCT)	46
Mouvement congolais pour la démocratie et le développement intégral (MCDDI)	11
Union panafricaine pour la démocratie sociale (UPADS)	11
Mouvement d'action pour le renouveau (MAR)	5
Mouvement pour la solidarité et la démocratie (MSD)	5
Club 2002-Parti pour l'unité et la République (Club 2002 PUR)	3
Action pour le Congo (APC)	3
Forces démocratiques nouvelles (FDN)	2
Rassemblement pour la démocratie et le progrès social (RDPS)	2
Union pour la République (UR)	2
Union patriotique pour la démocratie et le progrès (UPDP)	2
Union pour le progrès (UP)	2
Jeunesse en mouvement (JEM)	1
Mouvement pour la démocratie et le progrès (MDP)	1
Parti la vie	1
Rassemblement citoyen (RC)	1
Union des forces démocratiques (UFD)	1
Union pour la démocratie et la République—Mwinda (UDR—Mwinda)	1
Independents	37
Total	137

Sénat

Palais du Parlement, Brazzaville; tel. and fax 22-281-18-34; internet www.senat.cg.

President: ANDRÉ OBAMI ITOU.

The upper chamber comprises 72 members, elected by representatives of local, regional and municipal authorities for a six-year term. After elections to the Sénat held on 9 October 2011 the strength of the parties was as follows:

Party	Seats
Rassemblement de la majorité présidentielle (RMP) *	38
Parti congolais du travail (PCT)	12
Union panafricaine pour la démocratie sociale (UPADS)	4
Club 2002 Parti pour l'unité et la République (Club 2002 PUR)	2
Mouvement congolais pour la démocratie et le développement intégral (MCDDI)	2
Mouvement pour la solidarité et le démocratie (MSD)	1
Parti républicain et libéral (PRL)	1
Independents	12
Total	72

* An alliance of parties and associations supporting Pres. Denis Sassou-Nguesso.

Elections to renew 36 seats were held on 9 October 2011, at which the PCT secured 12 seats, the RMP 11 seats, the UPADS two, the MCDDI two, the Club 2002 PUR two, the PRL and the MSD one seat each, and independent candidates won five seats.

Election Commission

Commission nationale d'organisation des élections (CONEL): Brazzaville; f. 2001; reorganized in 2007; mems appointed by President of the Republic; Pres. HENRI BOUKA.

Advisory Council

Conseil économique et social (Economic and Social Council): Brazzaville; f. 2003; 75 mems, appointed by the President of the Republic; Pres. AUGUSTE-CÉLESTIN GONGARAD NKOUA.

Political Organizations

In early 2004 there were more than 100 political parties and organizations in the Republic of the Congo. The following were among the most important of those believed to be active in 2011:

Action pour le Congo (APC): Brazzaville.

Alliance pour la démocratie et le développement national (ADDN): Brazzaville; f. 2005; supports Govt of Pres. Sassou-Nguesso; Pres. BRUNO MAZONGA.

Alliance pour la république et la démocratie (ARD): Brazzaville; internet www.alternance-congo.com; f. 2007.

Union patriotique pour le renouveau national (UPRN): Brazzaville; Leader MATHIAS DZON.

Club 2002 Parti pour l'unité et la République (Club 2002 PUR): Brazzaville; f. 2002; Pres. WILFRID NGUESSO.

Conseil national de la résistance (CNR): formed as political wing of 'Ninja' rebel group; Leader Rev. FRÉDÉRIC BITSANGOU (NTUMI).

Forces démocratiques nouvelles (FDN): Brazzaville.

Jeunesse en mouvement (JEM): Brazzaville; f. 2002.

Mouvement d'action pour le renouveau (MAR): BP 1287, Pointe-Noire; Leader (vacant).

Mouvement congolais pour la démocratie et le développement intégral (MCDDI): 744 route de Djoué, Brazzaville; e-mail info@mcddi.net; internet www.mcddi.org; f. 1990; Leader (vacant).

Mouvement pour la démocratie et le progrès (MDP): Brazzaville; f. 2007; Leader JEAN-CLAUDE IBOVI.

Mouvement pour la solidarité et la démocratie (MSD): Brazzaville; Leader RENÉ SERGE BLANCHARD OBA.

Parti congolais du travail (PCT): BP 80, Brazzaville; f. 1969; sole legal political party 1969–90; Pres. DENIS SASSOU-NGUESSO; Sec.-Gen. PIERRE NGOLO.

Parti républicain et libéral (PRL): Brazzaville; Pres. NYCÉPHORE FYLLA DE SAINT-EUDES.

Parti social démocrate congolais (PSDC): Brazzaville; Pres. CLÉMENT MIÉRASSA.

Parti pour l'unité et la République (PUR): Brazzaville.

Parti la vie: Brazzaville.

Rassemblement citoyen (RC): route du Djoué, face Centre Sportif de Bacongo, Brazzaville; Pres. CLAUDE ALPHONSE NSILOU.

Rassemblement pour la démocratie et le progrès social (RDPS): Pointe-Noire; f. 1990; Pres. BERNARD MBATCHI.

Rassemblement de la majorité présidentielle (RMP): Brazzaville; f. 2007; org. of some 100 political parties and associations supporting Pres. Sassou-Nguesso.

Union pour la démocratie et la République—Mwinda (UDR—Mwinda): Brazzaville; e-mail journalmwinda@presse-ecrite.com; f. 1992; Leader GUY ROMAIN KIMFOUSSIA.

Union des forces démocratiques (UFD): Brazzaville; supports Govt; Pres. DAVID CHARLES GANOU.

Union panafricaine pour la démocratie sociale (UPADS): BP 1370, Brazzaville; e-mail courrier@upads.org; internet www.upads.org; Pres. PASCAL LISSOUBA; Sec.-Gen. PASCAL TSATY MABIALA.

Union patriotique pour la démocratie et le progrès (UPDP): 112 rue Lamothe, Brazzaville; Pres. GONGARA KOUA.

Union pour le progrès (UP): 965 rue Sounda, pl. des 15 ans, Brazzaville; Pres. JEAN-MARTIN MBEMBA; Sec.-Gen. OMER DEFOUNDOUX.

Diplomatic Representation

EMBASSIES IN THE REPUBLIC OF THE CONGO

Algeria: rue Col Brisset, BP 2100, Brazzaville; tel. 22-281-17-37; fax 22-281-54-77; Ambassador AHMED ABDESSADOK.

Angola: ave Fourneau, BP 388, Brazzaville; tel. 22-281-47-21; fax 22-283-52-96; e-mail miranotom@yahoo.fr; Ambassador Dr PEDRO FERNANDO MAVUNZA.

Belgium: blvd Sassou Nguesso, BP 225, Brazzaville; tel. 22-281-07-65; e-mail brazzaville@diplobel.fed.be; internet www.diplomatie.be/brazzaville; Ambassador HERMAN MERCKX.

Cameroon: ave Bayardelles, Brazzaville; tel. 22-281-10-08; fax 22-281-56-75; Ambassador HAMIDOU KOMIDOR NJIMOLUH.

Central African Republic: BP 10, Brazzaville; tel. 05-526-75-55 (mobile); Ambassador MARIE-CHARLOTTE FAYANGA.

Chad: BP 386, Brazzaville; tel. 05-558-92-06 (mobile); Ambassador KALZEUBE KINGAR.

China, People's Republic: blvd du Marechal Lyauté, BP 213, Brazzaville; tel. 22-281-11-32; fax 22-281-11-35; e-mail amba_chine@yahoo.fr; internet cg.chineseembassy.org; Ambassador LI SHULI.

Congo, Democratic Republic: ave Nelson Mandela, Brazzaville; tel. 22-281-30-52; Ambassador CHRISTOPHE MUZUNGU.

Cuba: 28 rue Lacien Fourneaux, BP 80, Brazzaville; tel. 22-281-03-79; e-mail embacuba@congonet.cg; Ambassador MATIAS ELENO CHAPEUX SAN MIGUEL.

Egypt: 7 bis ave Bayardelle, BP 917, Brazzaville; tel. 22-281-07-94; fax 22-281-15-33; Ambassador KHALED EZZAT OMRAH.

Equatorial Guinea: Brazzaville; Ambassador ELA EBANG MBANG.

France: rue Alfassa, BP 2089, Brazzaville; tel. 22-281-55-41; e-mail webmestre@mail.com; internet www.ambafrance-cg.org; Ambassador JEAN-FRANÇOIS VALETTE.

Gabon: BP 20336, Brazzaville; tel. 22-281-56-20; Ambassador BARTHÉLEMY ONGAYE.

Holy See: rue Col Brisset, BP 1168, Brazzaville; tel. 06-950-56-66 (mobile); fax 22-281-55-81; e-mail nonapcg@yahoo.com; Apostolic Nuncio JAN ROMEO PAWLOWSKI.

Italy: 2 ave Auxence Ickonga, BP 2484, Brazzaville; tel. 22-281-58-41; fax 22-283-52-70; e-mail ambasciata.brazzaville@esteri.it; internet www.ambbrazzaville.esteri.it; Ambassador FRANCESCO PAOLO VENIER.

Libya: BP 920, Brazzaville; tel. 22-281-56-35; Chargé d'affaires a.i. IBRAHIM TAHAR EL-HAMALI.

Nigeria: 11 blvd Lyauté, BP 790, Brazzaville; tel. 22-281-10-22; fax 22-281-55-20; e-mail embnigbra@yahoo.co.uk; Ambassador SALEH MANU PISAGIH.

Russia: ave Félix Eboué, BP 2132, Brazzaville; tel. 22-281-19-23; fax 22-281-50-85; e-mail amrussie@ic.cd; internet www.congo.mid.ru; Ambassador YURII ALEKSANDROVICH.

Senegal: Brazzaville; Ambassador BATOURA KANE NIANG.

South Africa: 82 ave Marechal Lyautey, Brazzaville; tel. 22-281-08-49; e-mail brazzaville@foreign.gov.za; Ambassador W. G. MAKANDA.

USA: BP 1015, Brazzaville; tel. 22-281-33-68; e-mail BrazzavilleHR@state.gov; internet brazzaville.usembassy.gov; Ambassador CHRISTOPHER W. MURRAY.

Judicial System

The 2002 Constitution provides for the independence of the judiciary from the legislature. Judges are to be accountable to the Higher Council of Magistrates, under the chairmanship of the President of the Republic. The constituent bodies of the judiciary are the Supreme Court, the Revenue and Budgetary Discipline Court and the appeal courts. The High Court of Justice is chaired by the First President of the Supreme Court and is competent to try the President of the Republic in case of high treason, and to try members of the legislature, the Supreme Court, the Constitutional Court and government ministers for crimes or offences committed in the execution of their duties.

Cour suprême (Supreme Court): BP 597, Brazzaville; tel. 22-283-01-32; First Pres. PLACIDE LENGA.

Haute cour de justice (High Court of Justice): Brazzaville; f. 2003; Pres. PLACIDE LENGA (First Pres. of the Supreme Court); Chief Prosecutor GEORGES AKIERA.

Cour constitutionnelle (Constitutional Court): Brazzaville; Pres. GÉRARD BITSINDOU; Vice-Pres. AUGUSTE ILOKI; Mems SIMON-PIERRE NGOUONIMBA NCZARY, THOMAS DHELLO, MARC MASSAMBA-NDILOU, JACQUES BOMBÈTE, JEAN-PIERRE BERRI, DELPHINE-EMMANUELLE ADOUKI, JEAN-BERNARD ANAËL SAMORY.

Religion

More than 40% of the population follow traditional animist beliefs. Most of the remainder are Christians (of whom a majority are Roman Catholics).

CHRISTIANITY

The Roman Catholic Church

The Congo comprises one archdiocese, five dioceses and an apostolic prefecture. An estimated 57% of the population are Roman Catholics.

Bishops' Conference

Conférence Episcopale du Congo, BP 200, Brazzaville; tel. 06-663-83-91 (mobile); fax 22-281-18-28; e-mail confepiscongo@yahoo.fr.

f. 1992; Pres. Most Rev. LOUIS PORTELLA MBUYU (Bishop of Kinkala).

Archbishop of Brazzaville: Most Rev. ANATOLE MILANDOU, Archevêché, BP 2301, Brazzaville; tel. 05-538-20-84 (mobile); fax 22-281-26-15; e-mail archibrazza@yahoo.fr.

Protestant Church

Eglise Evangélique du Congo: BP 3205, Bacongo-Brazzaville; tel. and fax 22-281-04-54; internet www.eeccongo.org; f. 1909; Presbyterian; autonomous since 1961; 150,000 mems (2007); 120 parishes (2007); Pres. Rev. Dr PATRICE N'SOUAMI.

Eglise Evangélique Luthérienne du Congo: 137 rue Osséle-Mougali, BP 1456, 00242 Brazzaville; tel. 05-557-15-00 (mobile); e-mail evlcongo@yahoo.fr; Pres. Rev. JOSEPH TCHIBINDA MAVOUNGOU; 1,828 mems (2010).

ISLAM

In 1997 an estimated 2% of the population were Muslims.

Comité Islamique du Congo: 77 Makotipoko Moungali, BP 55, Brazzaville; tel. 22-282-87-45; f. 1988; Leaders HABIBOU SOUMARE, BACHIR GATSONGO, BOUILLA GUIBIDANESI.

BAHÁ'Í FAITH

Assemblée spirituelle nationale: BP 2094, Brazzaville; tel. 22-281-36-93; e-mail congolink1@aol.com.

The Press

In July 2000 legislation was adopted on the freedom of information and communication. The legislation, which confirmed the abolition of censorship and reduced the penalty for defamation from imprisonment to a fine, specified three types of punishable offence: the encouragement of social tension (including incitement to ethnic conflict), attacks on the authorities (including libels on the Head of State or on the judiciary) and libels against private individuals. The terms of the legislation were to be guaranteed by a regulatory body, the Higher Council for the Freedom of Communication.

DAILIES

ACI Actualité: BP 2144, Brazzaville; tel. and fax 22-281-01-98; publ. by Agence Congolaise d'Information; Dir-Gen. THÉODORE KIAMOSSI.

Les Dépêches de Brazzaville: 84 ave Denis Sassou N'Guesso, Immeuble Les Manguiers (Mpila), Brazzaville; tel. 05-532-01-09; internet www.brazzaville-adiac.com; Dir of Publication JEAN-PAUL PIGASSE.

PERIODICALS

L'Arroseur: Immeuble Boulangerie ex-Léon, BP 15021, Brazzaville; tel. 05-558-65-51 (mobile); fax 05-558-37-60 (mobile); e-mail larroseur@yahoo.fr; f. 2000; weekly; satirical; Dir GERRY-GÉRARD MANGONDO; Editor-in-Chief JEAN-MARIE KANGA.

L'Autre Vision: 48 rue Assiéné-Mikalou, BP 5255, Brazzaville; tel. 05-551-57-06 (mobile); e-mail lautrevision@yahoo.fr; 2 a month; Dir JEAN PAULIN ITOUA.

Capital: 3 ave Charles de Gaulle, Plateau Centre Ville, BP 541, Brazzaville; tel. 05-558-95-10 (mobile); fax 05-551-37-48 (mobile); e-mail capital@hotmail.com; 2 a month; economics and business; Dir SERGE-DENIS MATONDO; Editor-in-Chief HERVÉ SAMPA.

Le Choc: BP 1314, Brazzaville; tel. 06-666-42-96 (mobile); fax 22-282-04-25; e-mail groupejustinfo@yahoo.fr; internet www.lechoc.info; weekly; Dir-Gen. and Publr ASIE DOMINIQUE DE MARSEILLE; Dir of Publication MARIEN NGAPILI.

Le Coq: Brazzaville; e-mail sosolecoq@yahoo.fr; f. 2000; weekly; Editor-in-Chief MALONGA BOUKA.

Le Défi Africain: Brazzaville; f. 2002; Dir of Publication JEAN ROMUALD MBEPA.

Les Echos du Congo: Immeubles Fédéraux 036, Centre-ville, Brazzaville; tel. 05-551-57-09 (mobile); e-mail wayiadrien@yahoo.fr; weekly; pro-govt; Dir-Gen. ADRIEN WAYI-LEWY; Editor-in-Chief INNOCENT OLIVIER TATY.

Epanza Makita: Brazzaville; f. 2004.

Le Flambeau: BP 1198, Brazzaville; tel. 06-666-35-23(mobile); e-mail congolink1@aol.com; weekly; independent; supports Govt of Pres. Sassou-Nguesso; Dir and Man. Editor PRINCE-RICHARD NSANA.

La Lettre de Brazzaville: Résidence Méridien, BP 15457, Brazzaville; tel. and fax 22-281-28-13; e-mail redaction@adiac.com; f. 2000; weekly; publ. by Agence d'Information d'Afrique Centrale; Man. Dir JEAN-PAUL PIGASSE; Editor-in-Chief BELINDA AYESSA.

Le Nouveau Stade: BP 2159, Brazzaville; tel. 06-668-45-52 (mobile); 2 a month; sports; Dir-Gen. LOUIS NGAMI; Editor-in-Chief S. F. KIMINA MAKUMBU.

La Nouvelle République: 3 ave des Ambassadeurs, BP 991, Brazzaville; tel. 22-281-00-20; state-owned; weekly; Dir-Gen. GASPARD NWAN; Editorial Dir HENRI BOUKOULOU.

L'Observateur: 165 ave de l'Amitié, BP 13370, Brazzaville; tel. 06-666-33-37 (mobile); fax 22-281-11-81; e-mail lobservateur_2001@yahoo.fr; f. 1999; weekly; independent; opposes Govt of Pres. Sassou-Nguesso; Dir GISLIN SIMPLICE ONGOUYA; circ. 2,000 (2004).

Le Pays: BP 782, Brazzaville; tel. 06-661-06-11 (mobile); fax 22-282-44-50; e-mail heblepays@yahoo.fr; f. 1991; weekly; Editorial Dir SYLVÈRE-ARSÈNE SAMBA.

La Référence: BP 13778, Brazzaville; tel. 05-556-11-37 (mobile); fax 06-662-80-13 (mobile); 2 a month; supports Govt of Pres. Sassou-Nguesso; Dir PHILIPPE RICHET; Editor-in-Chief R. ASSEBAKO AMAID-JORE.

La Rue Meurt (Bala-Bala): BP 1258, Brazzaville; tel. 06-666-39-80 (mobile); fax 22-281-02-30; e-mail laruemeurt@yahoo.fr; f. 1991; weekly; satirical; opposes Govt of Pres. Sassou-Nguesso; Publr MATTHIEU GAYELE; Editorial Dir JEAN-CLAUDE BONGOLO; circ. 2,000 (2004).

La Semaine Africaine: blvd Lyautey, face Chu, BP 2080, Brazzaville; tel. 06-678-76-94 (mobile); e-mail contact@lasemaineafricaine.com; internet www.lasemaineafricaine.com; f. 1952; 2 a week; Roman Catholic; general news and social comment; circulates widely in francophone equatorial Africa; Editor-in-Chief JOACHIM MBANZA; circ. 7,500.

Le Stade: BP 114, Brazzaville; tel. 22-281-47-18; f. 1985; weekly; sports; Dir HUBERT-TRÉSOR MADOUABA-NTOUALANI; Editor-in-Chief LELAS PAUL NZOLANI; circ. 6,500.

Tam-Tam d'Afrique: 97 rue Moussana, Ouenzé, BP 1675, Brazzaville; tel. 05-551-03-95 (mobile); e-mail gouala@yahoo.fr; weekly; economics, finance; circ. 1,500 (2004).

Le Temps: BP 2104, Brazzaville; e-mail kiala_matouba@yahoo.fr; weekly; owned by supporters of former Pres. Lissouba; Editor-in-Chief HENRI BOUKOULOU.

Vision pour Demain: 109 rue Bakongo Poto-Poto, BP 650, Brazzaville; tel. 04-441-14-22 (mobile); 6 a year; Dir SAINT EUDES MFUMU FYLLA.

NEWS AGENCIES

Agence Congolaise d'Information (ACI): ave E. P. Lumumba, BP 2144, Brazzaville; tel. and fax 22-281-01-98; e-mail agencecongoinfo@yahoo.fr; f. 1961; Gen. Man. THÉODORE KIAMOSSI.

Agence d'Information d'Afrique Centrale (ADIAC): Les Manguiers, 76 ave Paul Doumer, Brazzaville; tel. 05-532-01-09 (mobile); fax 05-532-01-10 (mobile); e-mail belie@congonet.cg; internet www.brazzaville-adiac.com; f. 1997; Dirs JEAN-PAUL PIGASSE, BELINDA AYESSA; br. in Paris (France).

Publishers

Editions ADIAC—Agence d'Information d'Afrique Centrale: Hôtel Méridien, BP 15457, Brazzaville; tel. and fax 22-281-28-13; e-mail redaction@brazzaville-adiac.com; internet www.brazzaville-adiac.com; f. 1997; publishes chronicles of current affairs; Dirs JEAN-PAUL PIGASSE, BELINDA AYESSA.

Editions 'Héros dans l'Ombre': BP 1678, Brazzaville; e-mail leopold_mamo@yahoo.fr; f. 1980; literature, criticism, poetry, essays, politics, drama, research; Chair. LÉOPOLD PINDY MAMONSONO.

Editions Lemba: 20 ave des Emetteurs, Sangolo-OMS, Malèkélé, BP 2351, Brazzaville; tel. 06-667-65-58 (mobile); fax 22-281-00-17; e-mail editions_lemba@yahoo.fr; literature; Dir APOLLINAIRE SINGOU-BASSEHA.

Editions PAARI—Pan African Review of Innovation: BP 1622, Brazzaville; tel. 05-551-86-49 (mobile); e-mail edpaari@yahoo.fr; internet www.cafelitteraire.fr; f. 1991; social and human sciences, philosophy; Dir MÂWA-KIESE MAWAWA.

Imprimerie Centrale d'Afrique (ICA): ave du Gen. de Gaulle, BP 162, Pointe-Noire; f. 1949; Man. Dir M. SCHNEIDER.

Mokandart: BP 939, Brazzaville; tel. 06-668-46-69 (mobile); e-mail mokandart@yahoo.fr; adult and children's literature; Pres. ANNICK VEYRINAUD MAKONDA.

GOVERNMENT PUBLISHING HOUSE

Imprimerie Nationale du Congo (INC): BP 58, Brazzaville; Dir JULES ONDZEKI.

Broadcasting and Communications

REGULATORY AUTHORITIES

Agence de Régulation des Postes et des Communications Electroniques (ARPCE): Immeuble Socofran, ave du 5 juin, BP 2490, Mpila, Brazzaville; tel. 05-510-72-72 (mobile); e-mail contact@arpce.net; internet www.arpce.cg; f. 2009; regulatory authority; Dir-Gen. YVES CASTANOU.

Conseil supérieur de la liberté de la communication (Higher Council for the Freedom of Communication): Brazzaville; f. 2003; 11 mems, nominated by the President of the Republic; Pres. JACQUES BANANGANZALA.

TELECOMMUNICATIONS

In 2011 there were four providers of mobile cellular telecommunications services in the country.

Airtel Congo: blvd Charles de Gaulle, angle allée Makimba, BP 1267, Pointe-Noire; tel. 05-520-00-00 (mobile); fax 22-294-88-75; e-mail info.africa@airtel.com; internet africa.airtel.com/congob; f. 1999 as Celtel Congo and fmrly Zain Congo; acquired by Bharti Airtel (India) in 2010; mobile cellular telephone operator; network covers Brazzaville, Pointe-Noire, Loubomo (Dolisie), Ouesso, Owando and other urban areas; Dir-Gen. BESTON TSHINSELÉ.

Équateur Telecom Congo: 35 William Guynet, Poto-Poto, Brazzaville; e-mail info@azur-congo.com; internet www.azur-congo.com; f. 2010; provides mobile cellular telephone services under the brand name Azur; STÉPHANE BEUVELET.

MTN Congo: ave Foch, face a la Mairie Centrale, Brazzaville; tel. 06-669-15-40 (mobile); e-mail yellonews@mtncongo.net; internet www.mtncongo.net; f. 2000; mobile cellular telephone operator; Dir-Gen. MATHIEU FREDDY TCHALA ABINA.

Société des Télécommunications du Congo (SOTELCO): BP 39, Brazzaville; tel. 22-281-00-00; fax 22-281-19-35; e-mail sotelco@congonet.cg; f. 2001 by division of postal and telecommunications services of the fmr Office National des Postes et Télécommunications; mobile cellular telephone system introduced in 1996; operates under the brand name Congo Telecom; majority govt-owned, part-owned by Atlantic TeleNetwork; further transfer to private ownership pending; Dir-Gen. CÉDRIC BEN CABINE AKOUALA.

Warid Congo SA: 4th Floor, Tour ARC, BP 238, Brazzaville; tel. 04-400-01-23 (mobile); internet waridtel.cg; mobile cellular telephone operator; Pres. Sheikh NAHAYAN MABARAK AL NAHAYAN; Dir-Gen. MICHEL OLIVIER ELAMÉ.

RADIO AND TELEVISION

Canal FM: BP 60, Brazzaville; tel. 22-283-03-09; f. 1977 as Radio Rurales du Congo; present name adopted 2002; community stations established by the Agence de coopération culturelle et technique; transmitters in Brazzaville, Sembé, Nkayi, Etoumbi and Mossendjo; Dir ETIENNE EPAGNA-TOUA.

Digital Radio Télévision: BP 1974, Brazzaville; internet drtvcongo@drtvcongo.com; f. 2002; Dir-Gen. PAUL SONI-BENGA.

Radio Brazzaville: face Direction Générale, SOTELCO, Brazzaville; tel. 05-551-60-73 (mobile); f. 1999; official station; Man. JEAN-PASCAL MONGO SLYM.

Radio Liberté: BP 1660, Brazzaville; tel. 22-281-57-42; f. 1997; operated by supporters of Pres. Sassou-Nguesso.

Radio Magnificat: Centre Interdiocésain des Oeuvres (CIO), Brazzaville; tel. 05-531-12-60; e-mail radio.magnificat@yahoo.fr; f. 2006; Man. MAURICE MILANDOU.

Radiodiffusion-Télévision Congolaise (RTC): BP 2241, Brazzaville; tel. 22-281-24-73; state-owned; Pres. JEAN-GILBERT FOUTOU; Dir-Gen. GILBERT-DAVID MUTAKALA.

Radio Congo: BP 2241, Brazzaville; tel. 22-281-50-60; radio programmes in French, Lingala, Kikongo, Subia, English and Portuguese; transmitters at Brazzaville and Pointe-Noire; Gen. Man. ALPHONSE BOUYA DIMI; Dir of Broadcasting THÉOPHILE MIETE LIKIBI.

Télé Pointe-Noire: BP 769, Pointe-Noire; tel. 22-294-02-65; f. 1988.

Télé Congo: Brazzaville; f. 1960; operated by Radiodiffusion-Télévision Congolaise; Dir-Gen. JEAN OBAMBI.

Finance

(cap. = capital; res = reserves; dep. = deposits; m. = million; br(s). = branch(es); amounts in francs CFA)

BANKING

In 2008 there were seven commercial banks and one other financial institution in the Republic of the Congo.

Central Bank

Banque des Etats de l'Afrique Centrale (BEAC): BP 126, Brazzaville; tel. 22-281-10-73; fax 22-281-10-94; e-mail beacbzv@beac.int; internet www.beac.int; HQ in Yaoundé, Cameroon; f. 1973;

bank of issue for mem. states of the Communauté économique et monétaire en Afrique centrale (CEMAC, fmrly Union douanière et économique de l'Afrique centrale) comprising Cameroon, the Central African Repub., Chad, the Repub. of the Congo, Equatorial Guinea and Gabon; cap. 88,000m., res 227,843m., dep. 4,110,966m. (Dec. 2007); Gov. LUCAS ABAGA NCHAMA; Dir in Repub. of the Congo CÉDRIC JOVIAL ONDAYE EBAUH; br. at Pointe-Noire.

Commercial Banks

Banque Commerciale Internationale: ave Amílcar Cabral, BP 147, Brazzaville; tel. 22-281-58-34; fax 22-281-03-73; internet www.bci.banquepopulaire.com; f. 2001 on privatization of Union Congolaise de Banques; renamed as above in 2006; cap. and res 2,868.2m., total assets 57,523.9m. (Dec. 2003); Pres. DOMINIQUE MARTINIE; Dir-Gen. ALAIN MERLOT; 16 brs.

Banque Congolaise de l'Habitat (BCH): ave Amílcar Cabral, BP 987, Brazzaville; tel. 22-281-25-88; fax 22-281-33-56; e-mail audriche.elenga@bch.cg; internet www.bch.cg; f. 2008; Dir-Gen. FADHEL GUIZANI.

BGFI Bank Congo: angle rue Reims, face à paierie de France, BP 14579, Brazzaville; tel. 22-281-40-50; fax 22-281-50-89; e-mail agence_brazzaville@bgfi.com; internet www.bgfi.com; subsidiary of BGFIBANK Group (Gabon); cap. 5,000m. (2007); Dir-Gen. NARCISSE OBIANG ONDO; 2 brs.

La Congolaise de Banque (LCB): ave Amílcar Cabral, BP 2889, Brazzaville; tel. 22-281-09-79; fax 22-281-09-77; internet lacongolaisedebanque.com; f. 2004 on privatization of Crédit pour l'Agriculture, l'Industrie et le Commerce (CAIC); cap. 4,000m. (2005); Dir-Gen. YOUNÈS EL MASLOUMI; 17 brs.

Crédit du Congo (CDCo): ave Emmanuel Daddet, BP 1312, Pointe-Noire; tel. 22-294-24-00; fax 22-294-16-65; e-mail svpinfos@creditducongo.com; internet www.creditducongo.com; f. 2002 to replace Banque Internationale du Congo; fmrly Crédit Lyonnais Congo; name changed as above in 2007; 91% owned by Attijariwafa bank (Morocco), 9% state-owned; cap. and res 2,868.2m., total assets 116,550.0m. (Dec. 2007); Pres. BOUBKER JAÏ; Dir-Gen. ABDELAHAD KETTANI; 4 brs.

Ecobank Congo: rond point de la Coupole, BP 2485, Brazzaville; tel. 05-547-00-35 (mobile); e-mail ecobankcg@ecobank.com; internet www.ecobank.com; Pres. GERVAIS BOUITI-VIAUDO; Dir-Gen. LAZARE KOMI NOULEKOU.

Société Congolaise de Financement (SOCOFIN): BP 899, Pointe-Noire; tel. 06-667-10-44 (mobile); fax 22-294-37-93; e-mail socofin.pnr@celtelplus.com; f. 2001; acquired by BGFI Bank in 2008; cap. 1,000m., res 109.5m., total assets 6,434.3m. (Dec. 2005); Pres. PHILIPPE DE LAPLAGNOLLE; Dir-Gen. BONGO MAVOUNGOU.

Co-operative Banking Institution

Mutuelle Congolaise d'Epargne et de Crédit (MUCODEC): ave Paul Doumer, BP 13237, Brazzaville; tel. 22-281-07-57; fax 22-281-01-68; e-mail contact@mucodec.com; internet www.mucodec.com; f. 1994; cap. and res 2,080m., total assets 29,000m. (Dec. 2003); Pres. BIENVENU MAZIÉZOULA; Dir-Gen. GÉRARD LEGIER; 45 brs.

Development Bank

Banque de Développement des Etats de l'Afrique Centrale: BP 1177, Brazzaville; tel. 22-281-18-85; fax 22-281-18-80; e-mail bdeac@bdeac.org; internet www.bdeac.org; cap. 34,811.2m., res –1,316.0m., dep. 44,021.0m. (Dec. 2009); Pres. MICHAËL ANDADÉ.

Financial Institution

Caisse Congolaise d'Amortissement (CCA): ave Foch, BP 2090, Brazzaville; tel. 22-281-57-35; fax 22-281-52-36; f. 1971; management of state funds; Dir-Gen. GEORGES NGUEKOUMOU.

INSURANCE

Assurances Générales du Congo: Brazzaville; tel. 22-918-93-00; fax 22-281-55-57; e-mail agccongo@yahoo.fr; f. 1999; Dir-Gen. RAYMOND IBATA.

Assurances et Réassurances du Congo (ARC): ave du Camp, BP 14524, Brazzaville; tel. 22-281-35-08; f. 1973; 50% state-owned; privatization pending; Dir-Gen. RAYMOND IBATA; brs at Brazzaville, Loubomo and Ouesso.

Gras Savoye Congo: 13 rue Germain Bikouma, angle route de la Radio, Immeuble Guenin, BP 1901, Pointe-Noire; tel. 22-294-79-72; fax 22-294-79-74; e-mail grassavoye.congo@cg.celtelplus.com; affiliated to Gras Savoye (France); insurance brokers and risk managers; Man. PHILIPPE BAILLÉ.

Nouvelle Société Interafricaine d'Assurances: 1 ave Foch, angle rue Sergent Malamine, face hôtel de ville, BP 1151, Brazzaville; tel. 22-281-13-34; fax 22-281-21-70; f. 2004; Dir-Gen. ANGÉLIQUE DIARRASSOUBA.

Société de Courtage d'Assurances et de Réassurances (SCDE): Immeuble Foch, ave Foch, BP 13177, Brazzaville; tel. 22-281-17-63.

Trade and Industry

GOVERNMENT AGENCY

Comité des Privatisations et de Renforcement des Capacités Locales: Immeuble ex-SCBO, 7ème étage, BP 1176, Brazzaville; tel. 22-281-46-21; fax 22-281-46-09; e-mail privat@aol.com; oversees and co-ordinates transfer of state-owned enterprises to the private sector.

DEVELOPMENT ORGANIZATIONS

Agence Française de Développement (AFD): rue Béhagle, BP 96, Brazzaville; tel. 22-281-53-30; fax 22-281-29-42; e-mail afdbrazzaville@afd.fr; internet www.afd.fr; French fund for economic co-operation; Country Dir PATRICK DAL BELLO.

Service de Coopération et d'Action Culturelle: BP 2175, Brazzaville; tel. 22-283-15-03; f. 1959; administers bilateral aid from France; Dir DOMINIQUE RICHARD.

Société Nationale d'Elevage (SONEL): BP 81, Loutété, Massangui; f. 1964; development of semi-intensive stock-rearing; exploitation of cattle by-products; Man. Dir THÉOPHILE BIKAWA.

CHAMBERS OF COMMERCE

Chambre de Commerce, d'Industrie, d'Agriculture et des Métiers de Brazzaville (CCIAMB): ave Amílcar Cabral, Centre Ville, BP 92, Brazzaville; tel. 05-521-70-04; tel. 22-281-16-08; internet cciambrazza.com; f. 1935; Pres. PAUL OBAMBI; Sec.-Gen. FIDÈLE BOSSA.

Chambre de Commerce, d'Industrie, d'Agriculture et des Métiers de Pointe-Noire: 3 blvd Général Charles de Gaulle, BP 665, Pointe-Noire; tel. 22-294-12-80; fax 22-294-07-13; e-mail infos@cciampnr.org; internet www.cciampnr.com; f. 1948; Chair. SYLVESTRE DIDIER MAVOUENZELA; Sec.-Gen. JEAN-BAPTISTE SOUMBOU.

Chambre Nationale d'Industrie et d'Agriculture du Congo: BP 1119, Brazzaville; tel. 22-283-29-56; fmrly Conférence Permanente des Chambres de Commerce du Congo; Pres. PAUL OBAMBI.

EMPLOYERS' ORGANIZATIONS

Forum des Jeunes Entreprises du Congo (FJEC): Quartier Milice, Villa 43B, ave de l'OUA, BP 13700, Makélékélé, Brazzaville; tel. 22-281-56-34; e-mail fjecbrazza@fjec.org; internet www.fjec.org; f. 1990; Sec.-Gen. PAUL KAMPAKOL.

Union Nationale des Opérateurs Economiques du Congo (UNOC): BP 5187, Brazzaville; tel. 22-281-54-32; e-mail unoc_patronat@yahoo.fr; f. 1985; operates a professional training centre; Pres. El Hadj DJIBRIL ABDOULAYE BOPAKA.

Union Patronale et Interprofessionnelle du Congo (UNICONGO): Immeuble CAPINFO, 1er étage, ave Paul Doumer, BP 42, Brazzaville; tel. 06-629-79-06 (mobile); fax 22-281-47-66; e-mail unicongobvz@unicongo.net; internet www.unicongo.org; f. 1958; Nat. Pres. CHRISTIAN BARROS; Sec.-Gen. JEAN-JACQUES SAMBA; membership of 20 feds (2008).

UTILITIES

Electricity

Agence Nationale d'Électrification Rurale du Congo (ANER): BP 2120, Brazzaville; tel. 05-570-19-52 (mobile); fax 22-281-50-77; e-mail aner_congo@yahoo.fr; f. 2003.

Société Nationale d'Electricité (SNE): 95 ave Paul Doumer, BP 95, Brazzaville; tel. 22-281-05-66; fax 22-281-05-69; e-mail snecongo@caramail.com; f. 1967; transfer to private management proposed; operates hydroelectric plants at Bouenza and Djoué; Dir-Gen. ALBERT CAMILLE PELLA.

Water

Société Nationale de Distribution d'Eau (SNDE): rue du Sergent Malamine, BP 229, Brazzaville; tel. 22-294-22-16; fax 22-294-28-60; internet www.sndecongo.com; f. 1967; transferred to private sector management by Bi-Water (United Kingdom) in 2002; water supply and sewerage; holds monopoly over wells and import of mineral water; Dir-Gen. EMILE MOKOKO.

TRADE UNION FEDERATIONS

Independent trade unions were legalized in 1991.

Confédération Générale des Travailleurs du Congo (CGTC): Brazzaville; f. 1995; Chair. PAUL DOUNA.

Confédération Nationale des Syndicats Libres (CNASYL): Brazzaville; f. 1994; Sec.-Gen. MICHEL KABOUL MAOUTA.

Confédération Syndicale Congolaise (CSC): BP 2311, Brazzaville; tel. 22-283-19-23; f. 1964; 80,000 mems.

Confédération Syndicale des Travailleurs du Congo (CSTC): BP 14743, Brazzaville; tel. 06-661-47-35 (mobile); f. 1993; fed. of 13 trade unions; Chair. MICHEL SOUZA; 40,000 mems.

Confédération des Syndicats Libres Autonomes du Congo (COSYLAC): BP 14861, Brazzaville; tel. 22-282-42-65; fax 22-283-42-70; e-mail b.oba@congonet.cg; Pres. RENÉ BLANCHARD SERGE OBA.

Fédération nationale des travailleurs du Congo (FENATRAC): Brazzaville; f. 2001 by split from CSTC (q.v.); Sec. JULIEN NGOULOU.

Transport

RAILWAYS

In 2008 there were 795 km of railway track in the Congo. Rail traffic was severely disrupted by the 1997 civil war. The main line (of some 518 km) between Brazzaville and Pointe-Noire reopened briefly in November 1998 for freight traffic, but was subsequently closed following further unrest and sabotage. In early 2000 the Government signed two agreements with the Société Nationale des Chemins de Fer Français (France) relating to the repair of the line and associated infrastructure, and to the management of the network. Freight services resumed in August 2000, followed by passenger services in January 2001, although there was further disruption to the railways during unrest in mid-2002. In May 2004 the rail service linking Brazzaville to the Pool region resumed operations. In 2008 work started on a 1,000-km railway project to link Pointe-Noire with Ouesso, which was expected to be completed by 2013.

Chemin de Fer Congo-Océan (CFCO): ave Charles de Gaulle, BP 651, Pointe-Noire; tel. 05-559-91-24 (mobile); fax 22-294-04-47; internet www.cfco.cg; f. 1969; entered partnership with Rail Afrique International in June 1998; transfer to private management proposed; Dir-Gen. SAUVEUR JOSEPH EL BEZ.

ROADS

In 2004 there were an estimated 17,289 km of roads. Only about 5% of the total network was paved. The principal routes link Brazzaville with Pointe-Noire, in the south, and with Ouesso, in the north. A number of major construction projects initiated by President Sassou-Nguesso in 2000 and 2001 have involved the highways from Brazzaville to Kinkala, and from Brazzaville to the Pool region.

Régie Nationale des Transports et des Travaux Publics: BP 2073, Brazzaville; tel. 22-283-35-58; f. 1965; civil engineering, maintenance of roads and public works; Man. Dir HECTOR BIENVENU OUAMBA.

INLAND WATERWAYS

The Congo and Oubangui rivers form two axes of a highly developed inland waterway system. The Congo river and seven tributaries in the Congo basin provide 2,300 km of navigable river, and the Oubangui river, developed in co-operation with the Central African Republic, an additional 2,085 km.

Coordination Nationale des Transports Fluviaux: BP 2048, Brazzaville; tel. 22-283-06-27; Dir MÉDARD OKOUMOU.

Transcap—Congo: BP 1154, Pointe-Noire; tel. 22-294-01-46; f. 1962; Chair. J. DROUAULT.

SHIPPING

The deep-water Atlantic seaport at Pointe-Noire is the most important port in Central Africa, and Brazzaville is one of the principal ports on the Congo river. A major rehabilitation programme began in October 1999, with the aim of establishing Pointe-Noire as a regional centre for container traffic and as a logistics centre for offshore oil exploration.

La Congolaise de Transport Maritime (COTRAM): Pointe-Noire; f. 1984; national shipping co; state-owned.

Maersk Congo: 10 rue Massabi, Zone Portuaire, Pointe-Noire; tel. 22-294-21-41; fax 22-294-23-25; f. 1997; represents Maersk Sealand (Denmark).

Port Autonome de Brazzaville: BP 2048, Brazzaville; tel. 22-283-00-42; f. 2000; port authority; Dir JEAN-PAUL BOCKONDAS.

Port Autonome de Pointe-Noire (PAPN): BP 711, Pointe-Noire; tel. 22-294-00-52; fax 22-294-20-42; e-mail info@papn-cg.com; internet www.papn-cg.com; f. 2000; port authority; Dir-Gen. JEAN-MARIE ANIÉLÉ.

SAGA Congo: 18 rue du Prophète Lasse Zephirin, BP 674, Pointe-Noire; tel. 22-294-10-16; fax 22-294-34-04; e-mail emmanuelle.peillon@bollore.com.

Société Congolaise de Transports Maritimes (SOCOTRAM): BP 4922, Pointe-Noire; tel. 22-294-49-21; fax 22-294-49-22; e-mail info@socotram.com; internet www.socotram.fr; f. 1990; Dir JUSTE MONDELE.

CIVIL AVIATION

There are international airports at Brazzaville (Maya-Maya) and Pointe-Noire (Agostinho Neto). There are also five regional airports, at Loubomo (Dolisie, Ngot-Nzounzoungou), Nkayi, Owando, Ouesso and Impfondo, as well as 12 smaller airfields. In early 2001 the construction of a new international airport at Ollombo, some 500 km north of Brazzaville, began; the airport was inaugurated in late 2007.

Agence Nationale de l'Aviation Civile: rue de la Libération de Paris, Camp Clairon, BP 128, Brazzaville; e-mail courrier@anac-congo.org; internet anac-congo.org; MICHEL AMBENDÉ.

Aéro-Service: ave Charles de Gaulle, BP 1138, Pointe-Noire; tel. 05-556-41-41 (mobile); fax 22-294-14-41; e-mail info@aero-service.net; internet www.aero-service.net; f. 1967; scheduled and charter passenger and freight services; operates nationally and to regional destinations; Pres. and Dir-Gen. R. GRIESBAUM.

Trans Air Congo: Immeuble City Center, ave Amílcar Cabral, BP 2422, Brazzaville; tel. 22-281-10-46; fax 22-281-10-57; e-mail info@flytransaircongo.com; internet www.transaircongo.org; f. 1994; private airline operating internal scheduled and international charter flights; Pres. and Dir-Gen. BASSAM ELHAGE.

Tourism

Tourist visitors numbered 85,000 in 2009 (compared with tourist arrivals of 21,611 in 2002) and the industry has been identified as having considerable potential for growth by the Government. In 2007 earnings from tourism were estimated at US $54m.

Office National du Tourisme: BP 456, Brazzaville; tel. 22-283-09-53; f. 1980; Dir-Gen. ANTOINE KOUNKOU-KIBOUILOU.

Defence

As assessed at November 2011, the army numbered 8,000, the navy about 800 and the air force 1,200. In addition, there was a 2,000-strong gendarmerie. National service is voluntary for men and women, and lasts for two years.

Defence Expenditure: Estimated at 108,000m. francs CFA for 2010.

Supreme Commander of the Armed Forces: Gen. DENIS SASSOU-NGUESSO.

Chief of General Staff of the Congolese Armed Forces: Gen. NORBERT ROBERT MONDJO.

Chief of Staff of the Air Force: Col JEAN-BAPTISTE FÉLIX TCHIKAYA.

Chief of Staff of the Navy: Col FULGOR ONGOBE.

Commander of the Ground Forces: Gen. NOËL LEONARD ESSONGO.

Sec.-Gen. of the National Security Council: Col JEAN-DOMINIQUE OKEMBA.

Education

Education is officially compulsory for 10 years between six and 16 years of age and is provided free of charge in public institutions. Primary education begins at the age of six and lasts for six years. Secondary education, from 12 years of age, lasts for seven years, comprising a first cycle of four years and a second of three years. According to UNESCO estimates, in 2009/10 enrolment at primary schools included 91% of children in the relevant age-group (boys 92%; girls 89%). In 2003/04 enrolment at secondary schools was equivalent to 45% of children in the relevant age-group (boys 48%; girls 41%). In 2009/10 20,383 students were attending tertiary institutions. Some Congolese students also attend further education establishments abroad. In September 2004 the World Bank approved a grant of US $20m. to assist with the reconstruction of the country's educational sector, which had been severely damaged by years of civil conflict. In 2005 spending on education represented 8.1% of total budgetary expenditure.

COSTA RICA

Introductory Survey

LOCATION, CLIMATE, LANGUAGE, RELIGION, FLAG, CAPITAL

The Republic of Costa Rica lies in the Central American isthmus, with Nicaragua to the north, Panama to the south, the Caribbean Sea to the east and the Pacific Ocean to the west. The climate is warm and damp in the lowlands (average temperature 27°C (81°F)) and cooler on the Central Plateau (average temperature 22°C (72°F)), where two-thirds of the population live. The language spoken is Spanish. Almost all of the inhabitants profess Christianity, and the majority adhere to the Roman Catholic Church, the state religion. The national flag (proportions 3 by 5) has five horizontal stripes, of blue, white, red, white and blue, the red stripe being twice the width of the others. The state flag, in addition, has on the red stripe (to the left of centre) a white oval enclosing the national coat of arms, showing three volcanic peaks between the Caribbean and the Pacific. The capital is San José.

CONTEMPORARY POLITICAL HISTORY

Historical Context

Costa Rica was ruled by Spain from the 16th century until 1821, when independence was declared. The only significant interruption in the country's constitutional government since 1920 occurred in February 1948, when the victory of the opposition candidate, Otilio Ulate Blanco, in the presidential election was disputed. The legislature annulled the election but a civil war ensued. The anti-Government forces, led by José Figueres Ferrer, were successful, and a revolutionary junta took power in April. Costa Rica's army was abolished in December. After the preparation of a new Constitution, Ulate took office as President in January 1949.

Figueres, who founded the socialist Partido Liberación Nacional (PLN), dominated national politics for decades, holding presidential office in 1953–58 and 1970–74. Under his leadership, Costa Rica became one of the most democratic countries in Latin America. Since the 1948 revolution, there have been frequent changes of power, all achieved by constitutional means.

Domestic Political Affairs

Figueres's first Government nationalized the banks and instituted a comprehensive social security system. The presidential election of 1958, however, was won by a conservative, Mario Echandi Jiménez, who reversed many PLN policies. His successor, Francisco Orlich Bolmarich (President from 1962 to 1966), was supported by the PLN but continued the encouragement of private enterprise. Another conservative, José Joaquín Trejos Fernández, held power in 1966–70. In 1974 the PLN candidate, Daniel Oduber Quirós, was elected President. He continued the policies of extending the welfare state and of establishing amicable relations with communist states. Communist and other left-wing parties were legalized in 1975. In 1978 Rodrigo Carazo Odio of the conservative Partido Unidad Opositora coalition (subsequently the Coalición Unidad) was elected President. During Carazo's term of office increasing instability in Central America led to diplomatic tension, and the President was criticized for his alleged involvement in illegal arms-trafficking between Cuba and El Salvador.

At elections in February 1982, Luis Alberto Monge Alvarez and his party, the PLN, won a comfortable majority. Following his inauguration in May, President Monge announced a series of emergency economic measures, in an attempt to rescue the country from near-bankruptcy. A policy of neutrality towards the left-wing Sandinista Government of Nicaragua was continued. However, following a number of cross-border raids, a national alert was declared in May. The rebel Nicaraguan leader, Edén Pastora Gómez, was expelled in order to reduce Costa Rican involvement in the Nicaraguan conflict. Relations with Nicaragua deteriorated as guerrilla activity spread to San José. Three leading members of the anti-Sandinista (Contra) movement were expelled from Costa Rica in May 1983 and 80 of Pastora's supporters were arrested in September. In November Monge declared Costa Rica's neutrality in an attempt to elicit foreign support for his country. This declaration was opposed by the USA and led to the resignation of the Costa Rican Minister of Foreign Affairs.

In 1984 there were increasing reports of incursions into Costa Rica by the Sandinista forces. An attempt was made to defuse the tension with the establishment of a commission, supported by the Contadora group (Colombia, Mexico, Panama and Venezuela), to monitor events in the border area. In May, however, the attempted assassination of Pastora near the Costa Rican border exacerbated the inter-government differences on policy towards Nicaragua. Reports of clashes between Costa Rican Civil Guardsmen and Sandinista forces along the joint border became increasingly frequent and in 1985 the Government's commitment to neutrality was disputed when it decided to establish an anti-guerrilla battalion, trained by US military advisers.

At presidential and legislative elections in February 1986 Oscar Arias Sánchez, the PLN candidate, was elected President, with 52% of the votes cast. The PLN also obtained a clear majority in the Asamblea Legislativa. The new Government was committed to the development of a welfare state, the renegotiation of the country's external debt, and the conclusion of a social pact with the trade unions. Furthermore, Arias was resolved to reinforce Costa Rica's policy of neutrality. Diplomatic relations with Nicaragua were fully restored, and it was decided to establish a permanent inspection commission at the common border. The Government embarked on a series of arrests and expulsions of Contras resident in Costa Rica. A degree of Costa Rican complicity in anti-Sandinista activity became apparent, however, in 1986, when the existence of a secret airstrip in Costa Rica, which was used as a supply base for the Contras, was made public.

Throughout his presidency Arias became increasingly involved in the quest for peace in Central America. In August 1987 the Presidents of El Salvador, Nicaragua, Guatemala, Honduras and Costa Rica signed a peace agreement based on proposals presented by Arias, who was subsequently awarded the Nobel Peace Prize. In January 1988 Arias brought Nicaraguan government officials and Contra leaders together in San José for their first discussions concerning the implementation of a cease-fire.

Industrial unrest

At presidential and legislative elections in February 1990, Rafael Angel Calderón Fournier, the candidate of the Partido Unidad Social Cristiana (PUSC), was elected President. The PUSC also obtained a clear majority in the Asamblea Legislativa. The defeat of the PLN was widely attributed to popular dissatisfaction at the Government's economic policies, which appeared to have been designed to appease the IMF and World Bank. Calderón inherited a large fiscal deficit and was therefore forced to renege on his pre-election promise of improvements in welfare and income distribution. In an attempt to reduce the deficit, the Government introduced an adjustment programme of austerity measures. However, this austerity programme was abandoned in November 1991, in response to pressure from student and public sector unions. The decision prompted the resignation of the Minister of Finance, who claimed that the President's action would make it impossible to curb the rapidly increasing fiscal deficit.

Presidential and legislative elections were held in February 1994. The presidential ballot was narrowly won by José María Figueres Olsen, the PLN candidate. The PLN failed to obtain an outright majority in the Asamblea Legislativa, however.

Industrial unrest increased in 1994 and 1995. Growing dissatisfaction among teachers and other public sector employees at government economic policy, in particular proposals for the deregulation and privatization of state enterprises, culminated in a 100,000-strong demonstration in the capital in August 1994. Following the protest, the Government agreed to establish a commission, to include representatives of the teachers' unions, to debate proposed reforms of the pension system and other government policies.

The PUSC in power

At the presidential election of February 1998 Miguel Angel Rodríguez Echeverría, the candidate of the PUSC, secured a narrow victory over the PLN candidate, José Miguel Corrales Bolaños. The PUSC failed to obtain an outright majority in the concurrently held legislative election. The new President's attempts to alleviate the budget deficit through economic reform met with considerable opposition. In May 2000 the Government was forced to withdraw proposed legislation on the privatization of the telecommunications and energy sectors, after the largest popular protests in the country in 30 years.

Presidential and legislative elections were held in February 2002. As no candidate gained 40% of the votes cast, for the first time a further round of voting was held between the two leading candidates, Abel Pacheco de la Espriella of the ruling PUSC and Rolando Araya of the PLN. Pacheco won 58% of the votes cast in the second round ballot in April. Pacheco pledged to reform the tax system and to curb public sector expenditure in order to reduce the budget deficit. In the legislative election the recently formed Partido Acción Ciudadana (PAC) secured 14 seats at the expense of the two main parties.

In May 2003 employees at the state electricity and telecommunications company, the Instituto Costarricense de Electricidad (ICE), began industrial action in an attempt to force the Government to issue a US $100m. bond to finance the company, after that year's budget had reduced funding to the electricity and telecommunications sectors. In June ICE employees returned to work, having secured the Government's agreement on most demands. However, in October trade unions held a demonstration in the capital to voice concerns that the Government would end the ICE's monopoly in order to meet criteria for the proposed Central American Free Trade Agreement (CAFTA). Although Pacheco insisted his Government was opposed to such a move, in January 2004 the administration made certain concessions on liberalization of the sector. In August the deteriorating economic situation prompted public sector unions to organize a week-long general strike. The unrest escalated after drivers' associations also began protests against the monopoly on vehicle inspections held by the Spanish company Riteve SyC. At the end of the month the Government agreed to increase salaries and to review Riteve SyC's contract. The concessions provoked the resignation of the Minister of Finance and the Minister of the Presidency.

Throughout 2004 a series of disclosures of alleged corruption within the public sector tarnished the country's reputation for transparency. In May an investigation was begun into a loan in 2001 by the Government of Finland to the Costa Rican health service. The inquiry revealed that a number of executives at the social security institute, the Caja Costarricense de Seguro Social (CCSS), had received payments from the company contracted to supply the medical equipment. The former head of the CCSS and former PUSC deputy, Elisio Vargas, and the President of of the medical company were both subsequently imprisoned in connection with the case. In September former President Calderón was charged with accepting illegal payments and was placed under house arrest. His apprehension came just one week after another former PUSC President, Miguel Angel Rodríguez, had resigned as Secretary-General of the Organization of American States (OAS) after being accused of accepting payments from a French company in connection with a contract with the ICE; he was also placed under house arrest. Furthermore, in the same month President Pacheco admitted to having received an illegal campaign contribution of US $100,000. In the following month it was revealed that two Taiwanese firms had also donated $350,000 to the President's campaign (foreign contributions and those over $28,000 were prohibited). Pacheco was beleaguered by further accusations of corrupt practices in 2005: in June of that year he submitted to a parliamentary inquiry into a number of undisclosed gifts. The President declined to renounce his immunity from prosecution.

The corruption scandals prompted a protest march, attended by thousands of people, in the capital in October 2004. Later that month another former President, this time from the PLN, José María Figueres, was accused of receiving illegal payments totalling US $900,000. Figueres was subsequently expelled from the PLN and four other members of the PLN, including the Secretary-General, Carmen María Valverde Acosta, resigned from the party to avoid internal investigations. In October 2009 Calderón was convicted of embezzlement and sentenced to five years' imprisonment, while in April 2011 Rodríguez was found guilty of accepting bribes and also received a five-year prison sentence.

The PLN in power

Presidential and legislative elections were held on 5 February 2006. Former President Oscar Arias Sánchez, representing the PLN, secured the presidency with 41% of the votes cast, ahead of Ottón Solís Fallas of the PAC, who obtained 40% of the ballot. The PLN also performed well in the concurrently held legislative election, winning 25 of the 57 seats in the Asamblea Legislativa.

Arias was inaugurated as President in May 2006 and a new Cabinet installed. Upon assuming office, Arias negotiated an alliance with the Movimiento Libertario (ML) and the PAC to secure a legislative majority. In return for their support, the new President undertook to introduce legislation granting property rights to residents in marginal urban areas, and to restrict political patronage by abolishing the executive presidencies and the boards of directors of a number of public institutions.

Intermittent protests against the proposed DR-CAFTA (as CAFTA had been renamed following the inclusion of the Dominican Republic) continued in 2006 and 2007. In October 2006 ICE employees were joined by workers from the health, education and finance sectors to participate in two days of industrial action. Some 9,000 people gathered in San José to signal their opposition to the putative trade agreement with the USA. Protesters were particularly opposed to proposed legislation, necessary for DR-CAFTA to take effect, that would liberalize the telecommunications and insurance industries, as well as privatizing the ICE. Nevertheless, in December the legislative committee studying the accord voted to submit the bill for ratification to the Asamblea Legislativa. In April 2007, in what many viewed as a delaying tactic, the opposition submitted a request to the Tribunal Supremo de Elecciones that a referendum on implementation of DR-CAFTA be held; the request was granted, subject to the opposition providing 132,000 signatures (equivalent to 5% of the electorate) in favour of a vote. The time limit for the collection of signatures was 10 months, which would have made implementation of the accord almost impossible before the 1 March 2008 deadline. However, President Arias pre-empted the opposition tactic by asking the Asamblea to approve his request for a binding plebiscite on ratification to be held within 90 days instead. This was duly approved later in the month.

In July 2007 the Supreme Court ruled against an opposition claim that DR-CAFTA would be unconstitutional and set a date for the referendum of 7 October. The referendum campaign was bitterly fought: in September the Second Vice-President (and Minister of Planning), Kevin Casas Zamora, resigned after it was revealed he had written to the President recommending aggressive tactics be used by the 'yes' campaign to win the plebiscite. Supporters of the free trade agreement secured a narrow victory in the referendum, winning 51.6% of the total votes cast, compared with 48.4% garnered by the 'no' campaign, led by the PAC. Turn-out was estimated at 59.2% of the electorate. At the end of November President Arias signed into law the proposed DR-CAFTA. However, the legislature still had to approve the 13 measures necessary to implement the treaty by the March 2008 deadline. Although it agreed not to obstruct passage of the enabling laws, the PAC refused to attend congressional sessions to discuss the reforms, rendering many sessions inquorate. By February 2008 less than one-half of the necessary laws had been approved, forcing Arias to appeal to the DR-CAFTA signatories for an extension of the deadline, granted until 1 October. One of the most significant enabling laws was passed in May when the 50-year state monopoly on telecommunications by the ICE was ended. By September 12 of the enabling laws had been approved, but the final piece of legislation, concerning intellectual property and biodiversity, was rejected by the Constitutional Court. As a result, Arias was obliged to ask for a further extension of the deadline. The final law required for Costa Rica's implementation of DR-CAFTA was approved on 12 November, and the agreement took effect from 1 January 2009.

In December 2008 the Government indicated that it intended to seek a reform of the Constitution, in order to 'improve governability and to update the balance of powers'. The opposition claimed that the Government's true intention was to secure greater powers for itself. In March 2009 Arias proposed constitutional reforms, including plans to give presidential decrees priority over other legislation and a proposal to restrict the right of the Asamblea to amend government-sponsored legislation. The suggested reforms also included plans to allow the President to seek re-election for one term.

In 2009 the Organisation for Economic Co-operation and Development (OECD) moved Costa Rica from its 'black list' of unco-operative tax havens to its 'grey list' of jurisdictions that had 'committed to the international tax standard' but had 'not yet substantially implemented' it. The country was removed from the OECD 'grey list' in July 2011, after signing 12 tax information exchange agreements with other states.

Recent developments: the Chinchilla Government

A presidential election was held on 7 February 2010. The candidate of the ruling PLN, Laura Chinchilla Miranda, won with a substantial 46.9% of the votes cast, becoming Costa Rica's first female head of state. Ottón Solís Fallas of the PAC won 25.1% of the ballot, followed by the ML's Otto Guevara Guth, who received 20.9%, and the PUSC's nominee, Luis Fishman Zonzinski, with 3.9%. In concurrent legislative elections, the PLN remained the largest party with 24 of the 57 seats in the Asamblea Legislativa. The PAC and ML secured 11 and nine seats, respectively, while the PUSC won six seats and the Partido Accesibilidad sin Exclusión (PASE) four seats. The remaining three seats were distributed between the Frente Amplio (FA), the Partido Renovación Costarricense (PRC) and the Partido Restauración Nacional. Chinchilla was inaugurated on 8 May.

Rising crime rates had been a dominant theme of the electoral campaign and Chinchilla had pledged to increase spending on security by 50%. To this end, two days after taking office the new President instigated a consultation process on security reform. Following a public consultation, in February 2011 a 10-year security policy was announced; an additional 4,000 police officers were to be recruited by 2014, and there was also to be increased training, with an emphasis on narcotics-surveillance and anti-corruption. There was to be greater co-operation between security forces and local government and emphasis was to be placed on keeping young people within the education system. More prisons were also to be built, although it was unclear how this was to be financed. Chinchilla also took steps to address the growing problem of drugs-trafficking and in May 2010 issued a decree establishing an anti-narcotics commission. The USA provided US $1m. in funding for the national coastguard service and in July, in an attempt to strengthen counter-narcotics efforts, the Asamblea Legislativa approved the largest ever number of US vessels and personnel on Costa Rican territory. Despite these measures, in mid-September the USA included Costa Rica for the first time on its list of major illicit drugs-producing and -trafficking countries. Following widespread dissatisfaction with the Government's often vague security plans, in May 2011 Chinchilla appointed a new Minister of Governance, Police and Public Security, Mario Zamora Cordero, who pledged funds for additional vehicles to enhance police mobility. During a visit to Mexico in August Chinchilla signed multiple security co-operation accords with Mexican President Felipe Calderón. To finance further anti-crime measures, in December the Asamblea Legislativa authorized the imposition of a security levy on corporations; it was projected that the new tax would raise $70m. annually, while the 2012 budget allocated an extra $35m. to the security forces.

Besides addressing the country's crime problem, the Chinchilla administration's other main priority was fiscal reform. By introducing new taxes and increasing existing levies, Chinchilla planned to generate some US $900m. in additional annual revenues, which could then be used to lower the fiscal deficit and fund her policy agenda. However, the Government's attempts to restructure the tax system were repeatedly obstructed by the opposition parties, which in May 2011 had formed a fragile coalition (comprising the PAC, the ML, the PUSC, the PASE and the FA), giving them control over the Asamblea Legislativa. The ruling PLN had also been undermined by internal divisions between rival factions supporting, respectively, Chinchilla and Rodrigo Arias Sánchez (the brother of the former President); indeed, in April almost one-half of the PLN's deputies had briefly established a separate voting bloc in the Asamblea Legislativa. In September the PAC, the main opposition party, entered into negotiations with the Government regarding a compromise fiscal reform plan. However, in spite of this apparent breakthrough, the revised tax reform bill did not receive initial legislative approval until March 2012. The political deadlock also placed the Government's other policy pledges—including initiatives to reduce poverty and unemployment, as well as the implementation of Chinchilla's security strategy—in jeopardy: the financing underpinning these schemes was dependent upon the adoption of the fiscal reform legislation, which needed to secure approval of the Constitutional Court before it could be passed into law. However, in April this Court ruled the legislation unconstitutional.

Meanwhile, in July 2011 Chinchilla announced that René Castro would be replaced as Minister of Foreign Relations by Enrique Castillo Barrantes (who took office in September). Earlier in July the President had dismissed 27 diplomats following allegations that they had acquired their positions through nepotism, although Chinchilla denied that there was any connection between the two events; Castro's critics claimed that he had been replaced after being outmanoeuvred by the Nicaraguan authorities in relation to the San Juan territorial dispute (see Regional relations). Also in that month, the Minister of Public Health, María Luisa Ávila, resigned amid a funding crisis in the national social security scheme; she was replaced by Daisy Corrales Díaz in the following month. In an unprecedented move, in September a court ordered the eviction of all residents of an indigenous reserve in Limón not belonging to the BriBrí ethnic group, and authorized the restitution of the land to the former. The Minister of National Planning and Economic Policy, Laura Alfaro, stood down in March 2012; she was replaced by Roberto Gallardo. In the following month the Minister of Finance, Fernando Herrero, became the eighth minister to resign from the Chinchilla administration. He was replaced by Edgar Ayales.

Foreign Affairs

Regional relations

Relations with Nicaragua became strained in 1995 after a tightening of immigration policy in Costa Rica that led to the automatic expulsion of illegal immigrants who had previously been tolerated. In 1998 further antagonism developed between the two countries when Nicaragua prohibited Costa Rican civil guards from carrying arms while navigating the San Juan river, part of Nicaraguan territory, which forms the border between the two countries. In 2000 both Governments agreed a procedure that would allow armed Costa Rican police officers to patrol the river. In 2009 the International Court of Justice (ICJ) decreed that Costa Rica had navigational rights on the San Juan river for commercial purposes, but prohibited Costa Rica from policing the river and upheld Nicaragua's right to regulate its traffic. Tensions increased again in October 2010 after Costa Rica accused Nicaragua of violating Costa Rican territory during a dredging operation on the San Juan river. The Chinchilla Government dispatched police officers to the border area. Nicaraguan troops remained in the disputed area, despite an OAS resolution in November. In March 2011, pending a definitive ruling, the ICJ ordered military and civilian personnel from both sides to leave the disputed area (some Costa Rican workers were to remain to assess any environmental damage), although it did not halt Nicaraguan dredging. Relations remained tense throughout the second half of 2011: Costa Rica repeatedly protested to Nicaragua against alleged border infractions, while the Nicaraguan authorities expressed concern about the environmental impact of a planned Costa Rican road alongside the river. Nicaragua commenced legal proceedings, at the ICJ against Costa Rica over this matter in December. Meanwhile, in 2002 the two Governments came into conflict over a separate issue when Nicaragua announced that it was to award concessions for petroleum exploration in an area of the Caribbean Sea and Pacific Ocean claimed by Costa Rica. Failure to resolve the dispute prompted Costa Rica, in 2005, to refer the matter to the ICJ.

In March 2009 it was announced that the Government of Costa Rica would re-establish diplomatic ties with Cuba, 48 years after they were severed.

Other external relations

Costa Rica severed diplomatic relations with Taiwan in 2007 in favour of establishing relations with the People's Republic of China, which provided US $20m. in immediate aid for victims of severe floods that occurred in September, and a further $27m. for longer-term projects. In 2008 President Hu Jintao of China visited Costa Rica and signed a series of co-operation accords, which included assurances to invest in the state petroleum company, Refinadora Costarricense de Petróleo, and to fund a national stadium. In April 2010 a bilateral free trade agreement was signed by representatives of the two countries; Costa Rica ratified the agreement in June 2011.

CONSTITUTION AND GOVERNMENT

Under the Constitution of 1949, executive power is vested in the President, assisted by two Vice-Presidents (or, in exceptional circumstances, one Vice-President) and an appointed Cabinet. The President is elected for a four-year term by compulsory adult suffrage, and a successful candidate must receive at least 40% of the votes. The legislative organ is the unicameral Asamblea Legislativa, with 57 members who are similarly elected for four years. Judicial power is vested in the Supreme Court, the justices of which are elected by the Asamblea Legislativa for an initial term of eight years (a second eight-year term automatically follows, unless the legislature votes against it).

REGIONAL AND INTERNATIONAL CO-OPERATION

Costa Rica was a founder member of the UN. As a contracting party to the General Agreement on Tariffs and Trade, Costa Rica joined the World Trade Organization (see p. 433) on its establishment in 1995. Costa Rica is a member of the Organization of American States (see p. 394), the Central American Common Market (CACM, see p. 232), the Association of Caribbean States (see p. 448), the Inter-American Development Bank (see p. 334), and the Community of Latin American and Caribbean States (see p. 462), which was formally inaugurated in December 2011. The country is a member of the Group of 77 (see p. 450) developing states.

ECONOMIC AFFAIRS

In 2010, according to estimates by the World Bank, Costa Rica's gross national income (GNI), measured at average 2008–10 prices, was US $30,518m., equivalent to $6,550 per head (or $10,840 per head on an international purchasing-power parity basis). During 2001–10, it was estimated, the population increased by an average of 1.7% per year, while gross domestic product (GDP) per head increased, in real terms, by an average of 2.7% per year. According to official preliminary figures, overall GDP increased, in real terms, by an average annual rate of 4.5% in 2001–10; GDP decreased by an estimated 1.5% in 2009, but increased by an estimated 3.5% in 2010.

Agriculture (including hunting, forestry and fishing) contributed an estimated 6.6% of GDP and employed 15.1% of the economically active population in 2010. The principal cash crops are bananas (which accounted for 7.7% of export earnings in 2010), pineapples (7.4%) and coffee (2.9%). Sugar cane is also cultivated. According to official preliminary figures, the real GDP of the agricultural sector increased at an average annual rate of 2.9% during 2001–10; real agricultural GDP decreased by an estimated 3.2% in 2009, but increased by an estimated 6.5% in 2010.

Industry (including mining, manufacturing, construction and power) employed 19.6% of the economically active population and provided an estimated 24.9% of GDP in 2010. According to official preliminary figures, real industrial GDP increased at an average annual rate of 4.5% during 2001–10; the real GDP of the sector decreased by an estimated 3.2% in 2009, but increased by an estimated 1.7% in 2010.

Mining employed 0.1% of the economically active population and contributed an estimated 0.2% of GDP in 2010. According to official preliminary figures, real mining GDP increased at an estimated average annual rate of 1.1% during 2001–10; the sector's GDP decreased by an estimated 6.1% in 2010.

The manufacturing sector employed 12.1% of the employed work-force and contributed an estimated 16.5% of GDP in 2010. The principal branches of manufacturing were food products, chemical products, beverages, and paper and paper products. Production of computer components was also important. In 2010 the manufacturing sector accounted for some 23.3% of total export earnings. According to official preliminary figures, the real GDP of the manufacturing sector increased at an average annual rate of 4.3% during 2001–10; the sector's GDP decreased by an estimated 3.9% in 2009, but increased by an estimated 3.3% in 2010.

Construction employed 5.5% of the economically active population and provided an estimated 5.5% of GDP in 2010. According to official preliminary figures, the real GDP of the construction sector increased at an average annual rate of 5.7% during 2001–10; the sector's GDP decreased by an estimated 5.6% in 2010.

Energy is derived principally from petroleum and hydroelectric power. In 2009 China National Petroleum Corporation reached agreement with the state petroleum company, Refinadora Costarricense de Petróleo, to invest in an expansion of the refinery at Moín. Construction was expected to begin in early 2012. The Chinese firm was also scheduled to commence oil and gas exploration in areas off the country's Caribbean coast. In 2008 hydroelectric power accounted for 78.0% of total electrical energy generation. Imports of mineral products accounted for an estimated 12.4% of the total value of imports in 2010.

The services sector employed 65.3% of the economically active population and provided an estimated 68.5% of GDP in 2010. According to official preliminary figures, the real GDP of this sector increased at an average annual rate of 5.4% during 2001–10; sectoral GDP increased by an estimated 5.1% in 2010. Tourism is the country's most important source of foreign-exchange earnings. Receipts from tourism totalled an estimated US $2,111m. in 2010. Tourist arrivals reached 2,089,174 in 2008 before declining slightly in 2009, to 1,922,579. Tourist arrivals recovered to 2,099,829 in 2010, from 1,922,579 in 2009. Some 39.6% of the 2010 total came from the USA.

In 2010 Costa Rica recorded a visible trade deficit of US $3,467.9m. and there was a deficit of $1,438.7m. on the current account of the balance of payments. In 2010 the principal source of imports (46.5%) was the USA; other major suppliers were the People's Republic of China and Mexico. The USA was also the principal market for exports (36.1%); other significant purchasers were the Netherlands, Hong Kong and Panama. China became the second largest market for Costa Rican exports (mostly microprocessors) in 2007, and trade between the two countries was expected to increase further following the implementation of a free trade agreement in late 2010. The principal exports in 2010 were food and live animals (particularly bananas), machinery and electrical equipment (particularly computer components), optical and topographical equipment, and basic manufactures. The principal imports in that year were machinery and electrical equipment, mineral products, chemicals and related products, plastic materials and manufactures, common metals and manufactures, food and live animals, and transport equipment.

In 2007 there was an estimated budgetary surplus of 211,012.6m. colones (equivalent to some 1.6% of GDP). Costa Rica's general government gross debt was 5,562,340m. colones in 2010, equivalent to 29.6% of GDP. Costa Rica's estimated total external debt at the end of 2009 was US $8,070m., of which $3,190m. was long-term public debt. In that year, the cost of servicing long-term public and publicly guaranteed debt and repayments to the IMF was equivalent to 5.6% of the value of exports of goods, services and income (excluding workers' remittances). The annual rate of inflation averaged 10.2% in 2001–10. Consumer prices increased by.2% in 2011. Some 7.3% of the labour force were unemployed in 2010.

A free trade agreement, known as DR-CAFTA, between Costa Rica, the Dominican Republic, El Salvador, Guatemala, Honduras, Nicaragua and the USA, was implemented on 1 January 2009. Ratification of DR-CAFTA in the Costa Rican Asamblea had been delayed owing to opposition to US demands that Costa Rica liberalize its telecommunications industry. The sector was finally opened up to competition in mid-2010. The international economic downturn from 2008 and, particularly, recession in the USA, Costa Rica's principal trading partner, impeded Costa Rica's economic performance in 2009. Although the economy recovered in 2010 (growing by 3.5%), the incoming Government of Laura Chinchilla inherited a substantial fiscal deficit (relatively, the largest in the region, at 5.5% of GDP in 2010). The new administration's fiscal reform proposals were repeatedly rejected by the opposition during 2011, and the IMF reported that the deficit actually rose slightly in that year, to an estimated 5.6% of GDP. Nevertheless, economic growth remained strong in 2011 (4.3%, according to IMF estimates), and exports and foreign direct investment both increased markedly. These positive economic trends were expected to continue into 2012, with the IMF projecting real GDP growth of 4.4%.

PUBLIC HOLIDAYS

2013: 1 January (New Year's Day), 19 March (Feast of St Joseph, San José only), 28 March (Maundy Thursday), 29 March (Good Friday), 15 April (for Anniversary of the Battle of Rivas), 1 May (Labour Day), 29 July (for Anniversary of the Annexation of Guanacaste Province), 2 August (Our Lady of the Angels), 19 August (Mothers' Day), 15 September (Independence Day), 12 October (Columbus Day), 25 December (Christmas Day), 28–31 December (San José only).

Statistical Survey

Sources (unless otherwise stated): Instituto Nacional de Estadística y Censos, Edif. Ana Lorena, Calle Los Negritos, de la Rotonda de la Bandera 450 m oeste, Mercedes de Montes de Oca, San José; tel. 2280-9280; fax 2224-2221; e-mail informacion@inec.go.cr; internet www.inec.go.cr; Banco Central de Costa Rica, Avdas Central y Primera, Calles 2 y 4, Apdo 10058, 1000 San José; tel. 2233-4233; fax 2223-4658; internet www.bccr.fi.cr.

Area and Population

AREA, POPULATION AND DENSITY

Area (sq km)	
Land	51,060
Inland water	40
Total	51,100*
Population (census results)	
28 June 2000	3,810,179
30 May–3 June 2011	
Males	2,106,188
Females	2,195,524
Total	4,301,712
Density (per sq km) at 2011 census	84.2

* 19,730 sq miles.

POPULATION BY AGE AND SEX
(official estimates at mid-2012)

	Males	Females	Total
0–14	561,982	534,315	1,096,297
15–64	1,651,902	1,593,052	3,244,954
65 and over	151,541	174,304	325,845
Total	2,365,425	2,301,671	4,667,096

Note: Estimates not adjusted to take account of results of 2011 census.

PROVINCES
(population at 2011 census)

	Area (sq km)	Population	Density (per sq km)	Capital (with population)
Alajuela	9,757.5	847,660	86.9	Alajuela (254,567)
Cartago	3,124.7	491,425	157.3	Cartago (147,882)
Guanacaste	10,140.7	326,821	32.2	Liberia (62,987)
Heredia	2,657.0	433,975	163.3	Heredia (123,067)
Limón	9,188.5	386,954	42.1	Limón (94,420)
Puntarenas	11,265.7	410,914	36.5	Puntarenas (115,009)
San José	4,965.9	1,403,963	282.7	San José (287,619)
Total	51,100.0	4,301,712	84.2	—

PRINCIPAL TOWNS
(population at 2011 census)

San José	287,619	Pérez Zeledón	135,429
Alajuela	254,567	Pococí	125,847
Desamparados	207,082	Heredia	123,067
San Carlos	163,751	Puntarenas	115,009
Cartago	147,882	Goicoechea	114,736

BIRTHS, MARRIAGES AND DEATHS

	Registered live births		Registered marriages		Registered deaths	
	Number	Rate (per 1,000)	Number	Rate (per 1,000)	Number	Rate (per 1,000)
2003	72,938	17.6	24,448	5.9	15,800	3.8
2004	72,247	17.2	25,370	6.0	15,949	3.8
2005	71,548	16.8	25,631	6.0	16,139	3.8
2006	71,291	16.5	26,575	6.1	16,766	3.9
2007	73,144	16.7	26,010	5.9	17,071	3.9
2008	75,187	16.9	25,034	5.6	18,021	4.1
2009	75,000	16.6	23,920	5.3	18,560	4.1
2010	70,922	15.5	23,955	5.3	19,077	4.2

Life expectancy (years at birth, WHO estimates): 79 (males 77; females 81) in 2009 (Source: WHO, *World Health Statistics*).

ECONOMICALLY ACTIVE POPULATION*
('000 persons aged 12 years and over, household survey, July)

	2008	2009	2010
Agriculture, hunting and forestry	235.06	224.32	276.77
Fishing	6.57	7.27	8.31
Mining and quarrying	2.17	1.59	2.12
Manufacturing	239.54	232.92	227.74
Electricity, gas and water supply	27.95	27.09	35.68
Construction	152.45	128.39	104.58
Wholesale and retail trade	377.61	390.13	347.85
Hotels and restaurants	100.31	105.74	96.33
Transport, storage and communications	143.05	148.73	119.35
Financial intermediation	53.34	49.04	48.98
Real estate, renting and business activities	137.58	130.28	127.42
Public administration activities	93.76	112.74	92.82
Education	112.55	114.63	126.94
Health and social work	64.67	73.07	63.95
Other community, social and personal service activities	81.13	75.78	69.52
Private households with employed persons	118.96	123.17	135.51
Extra-territorial organizations and bodies	2.70	5.39	2.15
Sub-total	1,949.39	1,950.29	1,886.03
Not classifiable by economic activity	8.32	5.22	16.14
Total employed	1,957.71	1,955.51	1,902.16
Unemployed	101.91	165.94	149.53
Total labour force	2,059.61	2,121.45	2,051.70

* Figures for activities are rounded to the nearest 10 persons, and totals may not be equivalent to the sum of component parts as a result.

Health and Welfare

KEY INDICATORS

Total fertility rate (children per woman, 2009)	1.9
Under-5 mortality rate (per 1,000 live births, 2009)	11
HIV/AIDS (% of persons aged 15–49, 2009)	0.3
Physicians (per 1,000 head, 2000)	1.3
Hospital beds (per 1,000 head, 2006)	1.3
Health expenditure (2008): US $ per head (PPP)	1,059
Health expenditure (2008): % of GDP	9.4
Health expenditure (2008): public (% of total)	66.9
Access to water (% of persons, 2008)	97
Access to sanitation (% of persons, 2008)	95
Total carbon dioxide emissions ('000 metric tons, 2007)	8,112.1
Carbon dioxide emissions per head (metric tons, 2007)	1.8
Human Development Index (2011): ranking	69
Human Development Index (2011): value	0.744

For sources and definitions, see explanatory note on p. vi.

Agriculture

PRINCIPAL CROPS

('000 metric tons)

	2008	2009	2010
Rice, paddy	221.5	259.7	264.8
Potatoes	66.1	74.6	55.7
Cassava (Manioc)	97.8	189.4	144.7
Sugar cane	3,596.7	3,635.4	3,734.7
Watermelons	49.3	45.9	46.9
Cantaloupes and other melons	209.1	198.6	198.3
Oil palm fruit	863.2	897.8	897.8
Bananas	1,887	1,589	1,804
Plantains	85.2	60.0	90.0
Oranges	278	350	312.0
Pineapples	1,667.5	1,682.0	1,976.8
Coffee, green	112.0	91.4	97.3

Aggregate production ('000 metric tons, may include official, semi-official or estimated data): Total cereals 234.2 in 2008, 283.5 in 2009, 283.5 in 2010; Total roots and tubers 211.0 in 2008, 329.7 in 2009, 239.6 in 2010; Total vegetables (incl. melons) 412.6 in 2008, 399.5 in 2009, 392.8 in 2010; Total fruits (excl. melons) 4,318.2 in 2008, 4,115.2 in 2009, 4,620.4 in 2010.

Source: FAO.

LIVESTOCK

('000 head, year ending September, FAO estimates)

	2008	2009	2010
Horses	120	120	120
Asses	8	8	8
Cattle	1,287	1,287	1,287
Pigs	447	440	440
Sheep	3	3	3
Goats	5	5	5
Chickens	23,500	22,100	22,000

Source: FAO.

LIVESTOCK PRODUCTS

('000 metric tons)

	2008	2009	2010
Cattle meat	87.5	92.7	97.5
Pig meat	51.9	53.9	53.6
Chicken meat	106.6	110.5	105.1
Cows' milk	890.0	911.7	950.7
Hen eggs	52.2	51.7	53.5
Honey*	1.1	1.1	1.1

* FAO estimates.

Source: FAO.

Forestry

ROUNDWOOD REMOVALS

('000 cubic metres, excl. bark)

	2007	2008	2009
Sawlogs, veneer logs and logs for sleepers	1,339	1,229*	1,048*
Other industrial wood†	246	246	246
Fuel wood†	3,411	3,398	3,387
Total†	4,609	4,596	4,681

* Unofficial figure.
† FAO estimates.

2010: Production assumed to be unchanged from 2009 (FAO estimates).

Source: FAO.

SAWNWOOD PRODUCTION

('000 cubic metres, incl. railway sleepers, unofficial figures)

	2007	2008	2009
Broadleaved (hardwood)	670	615	524
Total	670	615	524

Source: FAO.

2010: Production assumed to be unchanged from 2009 (FAO estimates).

Fishing

('000 metric tons, live weight)

	2007	2008	2009
Capture*	21.7	21.8	21.8
Clupeoids	2.2	2.2*	2.2*
Marlins, sailfishes, etc.	0.9	0.9*	0.9*
Tuna-like fishes	1.4	1.4*	1.4*
Common dolphinfish	2.7	2.7	2.7
Sharks, rays, skates, etc.	3.9	3.9*	3.9*
Other marine fishes	4.5	4.5	4.5
Aquaculture	25.8	27.0	24.7
Tilapias	19.8	21.2	20.6
Whiteleg shrimp	5.3	5.3	3.5
Total catch*	47.5	48.8	46.5

* FAO estimate(s).

Source: FAO.

Industry

SELECTED PRODUCTS

('000 metric tons unless otherwise indicated)

	2006	2007	2008
Raw sugar	348	373	351
Kerosene	3	1	2
Distillate fuel oils	230	248	242
Residual fuel oils	295	328	207
Bitumen	26	22	9
Electric energy (million kWh)	8,697	9,050	9,475

Source: UN Industrial Commodity Statistics Database.

Cement ('000 metric tons): 2,300 in 2007; 2,500 in 2008–10 (estimates) (Source: US Geological Survey).

Finance

CURRENCY AND EXCHANGE RATES

Monetary Units

100 céntimos =1 Costa Rican colón.

Sterling, Dollar and Euro Equivalents (30 December 2011)

£1 sterling = 791.356 colones;
US $1 = 511.840 colones;
€1 = 662.270 colones;
10,000 Costa Rican colones = £12.64 = $19.54 = €15.10.

Average Exchange Rate (colones per US $)

2009 573.288
2010 525.829
2011 505.664

GENERAL BUDGET
(million colones)

Revenue	2005	2006	2007
Current revenue	2,218,904	2,754,039	3,370,533
Taxation	1,882,185	2,320,676	2,926,121
Income tax	324,224	394,095	531,552
Social security contributions	593,623	721,453	871,228
Taxes on property	48,751	62,860	83,478
Taxes on goods and services	797,608	1,006,111	1,269,413
Taxes on international trade	111,048	136,128	170,414
Other taxes	6,932	30	36
Other current revenue	105,802	193,845	166,625
Current transfers	–2,452	2,509	4,741
Operational surplus	233,369	237,010	273,046
Capital revenue	3,385	3,819	723
Total	2,222,288	2,757,859	3,371,257

Expenditure*	2005	2006	2007
Current expenditure	1,961,290	2,312,074	2,668,931
Wages and salaries	717,477	843,895	977,353
Social security contributions	4,399	4,958	5,807
Other purchases of goods and services	187,543	232,339	288,354
Interest payments	394,364	437,946	420,967
Internal	313,278	349,675	332,474
External	81,086	88,271	88,493
Current transfers	656,200	791,536	976,450
Operational deficit	1,307	1,401	—
Capital expenditure	342,705	361,115	495,165
Investment	230,897	227,311	312,749
Real sector	219,115	224,564	308,733
Financial sector	11,782	2,747	4,016
Capital transfers	111,808	133,803	182,417
Total	2,303,995	2,673,189	3,164,096

* Excluding lending minus repayments (million colones): 97 in 2005; –1,986.1 in 2006; –3,851.5 in 2007.

Note: Figures represent the consolidated accounts of central and local government activities.

Source: Ministerio de Haciendo, San José.

INTERNATIONAL RESERVES
(excl. gold, US $ million at 31 December)

	2008	2009	2010
IMF special drawing rights	0.30	208.30	204.20
Reserve position in IMF	30.83	31.38	30.83
Foreign exchange	3,767.53	3,826.49	4,392.20
Total	3,798.66	4,066.17	4,627.23

Source: IMF, *International Financial Statistics*.

MONEY SUPPLY
('000 million colones at 31 December)

	2008	2009	2010
Currency outside depository corporations	400.1	431.5	473.7
Transferable deposits	3,619.2	3,813.1	4,286.8
Other deposits	64.4	56.5	78.5
Securities other than shares	4,714.3	5,202.8	4,743.3
Broad money	8,798.0	9,504.0	9,582.3

Source: IMF, *International Financial Statistics*.

COST OF LIVING
(Consumer Price Index at July; base: July 2006 = 100)

	2009	2010	2011
Food and non-alcoholic beverages	152.7	162.4	170.5
Clothing and footwear	101.0	102.5	103.3
Housing	144.6	154.5	160.8
Medical care	136.7	147.8	156.1
Transport	117.9	128.9	140.3
Education	141.0	154.6	167.3
All items (incl. others)	132.7	140.3	147.6

NATIONAL ACCOUNTS
(million colones at current prices)

National Income and Product

	2008	2009*	2010*
GDP in purchasers' values	15,701,760.4	16,763,545.5	18,841,223.0
Net primary incomes from abroad	–396,443.5	–512,335.9	–492,034.7
Gross national income	15,305,317.0	16,251,209.6	18,349,188.3
Less consumption of fixed capital	896,869.8	1,029,027.8	1,156,565.8
Net national income	14,408,447.2	15,222,181.8	17,192,622.6
Net current transfers	233,097.8	205,769.6	194,626.8
Gross national disposable income	14,641,545.0	15,427,951.4	17,387,249.4

* Preliminary figures.

Expenditure on the Gross Domestic Product

	2008	2009*	2010*
Government final consumption expenditure	2,258,175.9	2,826,136.2	3,343,014.1
Private final consumption expenditure	10,645,096.8	11,179,071.4	12,317,715.9
Increase in stocks	625,785.4	–1,056,646.4	69,431.4
Gross fixed capital formation	3,704,619.0	3,716,906.8	3,694,233.8
Total domestic expenditure	17,233,677.1	16,665,468.0	19,424,395.2
Exports of goods and services	7,134,125.8	7,121,773.8	7,172,794.5
Less Imports of goods and services	8,666,042.5	7,023,696.2	7,755,966.7
GDP in purchasers' values	15,701,760.4	16,763,545.5	18,841,223.0
GDP at constant 1991 prices	2,097,395.1	2,070,319.9	2,157,839.6

* Preliminary figures.

Gross Domestic Product by Economic Activity

	2008	2009*	2010*
Agriculture, hunting, forestry and fishing	1,011,879.4	1,115,876.8	1,191,963.1
Mining and quarrying	35,406.6	29,690.5	28,284.0
Manufacturing	2,851,823.5	2,710,648.2	2,986,217.6
Electricity, gas and water	272,138.8	449,932.4	478,552.5
Construction	868,425.5	979,457.8	1,001,158.3
Trade, restaurants and hotels	2,816,097.9	2,753,948.2	3,000,505.1
Transport, storage and communications	1,423,571.0	1,429,626.6	1,696,289.2
Finance and insurance	948,195.4	1,090,548.6	1,217,767.3
Real estate	443,302.6	481,141.0	536,537.4
Other business services	800,097.8	978,118.1	1,172,296.7
Public administration	577,081.8	708,300.7	825,421.1
Other community, social and personal services	2,702,383.8	3,330,004.1	3,921,114.3
Sub-total	14,750,404.1	16,057,293.0	18,056,106.6
Less Imputed bank service charge	707,600.2	800,137.1	864,363.1
GDP at basic prices	14,042,803.8	15,257,155.8	17,191,743.5
Taxes on products	1,711,417.6	1,553,942.0	1,698,670.1
Less Subsidies	52,460.9	47,552.4	49,190.6
GDP in purchasers' values	15,701,760.4	16,763,545.5	18,841,223.0

* Preliminary figures.

BALANCE OF PAYMENTS
(US $ million)

	2008	2009	2010
Exports of goods f.o.b.	9,555.4	8,838.2	9,481.5
Imports of goods f.o.b.	–14,568.7	–10,877.3	–12,949.4
Trade balance	–5,013.3	–2,039.1	–3,467.9
Exports of services	4,083.3	3,592.9	4,180.2
Imports of services	–1,882.4	–1,404.8	–1,773.3
Balance on goods and services	–2,812.4	149.0	–1,061.0

—continued	2008	2009	2010
Other income received	696.8	219.3	199.3
Other income paid	–1,113.9	–1,303.0	–947.5
Balance on goods, services and income	–3,229.5	–934.7	–1,809.2
Current transfers received	706.6	593.3	609.7
Current transfers paid	–264.4	–234.6	–239.3
Current balance	–2,787.3	–576.0	–1,438.7
Capital account (net)	7.4	58.3	54.7
Direct investment abroad	–5.9	–7.5	–24.8
Direct investment from abroad	2,078.2	1,346.5	1,465.6
Portfolio investment assets	537.3	–321.7	218.6
Portfolio investment liabilities	–93.7	–105.7	—
Other investment assets	–684.6	332.2	–376.5
Other investment liabilities	690.2	–739.2	549.0
Net errors and omissions	–47.6	131.6	–41.2
Overall balance	–305.9	118.6	406.7

Source: IMF, *International Financial Statistics*.

External Trade

PRINCIPAL COMMODITIES
(US $ million)

Imports c.i.f.	2008	2009	2010
Food and live animals	832.7	617.9	736.0
Mineral products	2,263.6	1,328.7	1,733.2
Basic manufactures	511.9	484.0	554.7
Chemicals and related products	1,673.3	1,413.5	1,575.5
Plastic materials and manufactures	1,014.1	797.5	1,017.0
Leather, hides and furs	52.3	40.5	77.5
Paper, paperboard and manufactures	70.3	41.2	50.8
Wood pulp and other fibrous materials	608.1	507.4	597.4
Silk, cotton and textile fibres	549.4	431.7	512.2
Footwear, hats, umbrellas, etc.	113.3	97.3	118.5
Stone manufactures, etc.	195.5	131.3	144.4
Natural and cultured pearls	44.0	54.9	51.6
Common metals and manufactures	1,450.2	810.6	1,088.3
Machinery and electrical equipment	4,395.4	3,678.5	3,959.6
Transport equipment	958.9	540.9	733.5
Optical and topographical apparatus and instruments, etc.	318.6	321.2	365.2
Total (incl. others)	15,289.4	11,552.9	13,920.2

Exports f.o.b.	2008	2009	2010
Food and live animals	2,451.1	2,267.5	2,476.3
Mineral products	94.9	102.2	76.8
Basic manufactures	859.9	839.0	857.4
Chemicals and related products	599.4	588.8	573.8
Plastic materials and manufactures	430.9	373.7	443.2
Leather, hides and furs	45.8	27.5	27.6
Paper, paperboard and manufactures	53.2	46.9	45.4
Wood pulp and other fibrous materials	221.0	196.4	221.8
Silk, cotton and textile fibres	318.1	236.0	205.4
Stone manufactures, etc.	102.3	87.3	93.1
Natural and cultured pearls	49.6	65.3	68.3
Common metals and manufactures	406.8	278.5	318.1
Machinery and electrical equipment	2,857.1	2,585.0	2,380.2
Transport equipment	42.7	26.2	47.9
Optical and topographical apparatus and instruments, etc.	990.2	1,031.7	1,102.2
Total (incl. others)	9,606.0	8,836.4	9,044.8

PRINCIPAL TRADING PARTNERS
(US $ million)

Imports c.i.f.	2008	2009	2010
Aruba	491.1	13.0	0.0
Brazil	420.1	271.1	294.6
China, People's Rep.	865.4	699.6	990.7
Colombia	401.3	316.1	499.2
Germany	272.0	215.3	310.3
Guatemala	296.8	277.9	324.0
Ireland	439.4	55.1	30.4
Japan	822.7	657.8	499.5
Korea, Republic	279.0	145.5	152.2
Mexico	941.2	750.1	895.6
USA	5,812.4	5,261.0	6,477.1
Venezuela	692.3	103.9	47.0
Total (incl. others)	15,289.4	11,552.9	13,920.2

Exports f.o.b.	2008	2009	2010
China, People's Rep.	620.1	765.3	268.8
El Salvador	250.7	206.1	269.2
Germany	210.3	159.1	138.6
Guatemala	336.9	311.0	361.7
Honduras	293.5	263.8	292.2
Hong Kong	391.5	336.6	438.0
Mexico	264.9	212.8	254.4
Netherlands	488.9	619.2	633.7
Nicaragua	376.9	332.3	378.9
Panama	369.3	341.2	430.2
USA	3,480.5	3,041.7	3,269.0
Total (incl. others)	9,606.0	8,836.4	9,044.8

Transport

ROAD TRAFFIC
(motor vehicles in use at 31 December)

	2002	2003	2004
Private cars	367,832	581,247	620,992
Buses and coaches	12,891	18,516	20,950
Goods vehicles	191,315	195,449	199,506
Road tractors	25,842	n.a.	n.a.
Motorcycles and mopeds	91,883	61,273	64,947

2007: Passenger cars 525,376; Buses and coaches 12,345; Lorries and vans 139,588; Motorcycles and mopeds 100,083.

2008: Passenger cars 571,651; Buses and coaches 13,765; Lorries and vans 151,161; Motorcycles and mopeds 136,109.

Source: IRF, *World Road Statistics*.

SHIPPING

Merchant Fleet
(registered at 31 December)

	2007	2008	2009
Number of vessels	15	15	15
Total displacement ('000 grt)	3.6	3.6	3.6

Source: IHS Fairplay, *World Fleet Statistics*.

International Sea-borne Freight Traffic
('000 metric tons)

	1996	1997	1998
Goods loaded	3,017	3,421	3,721
Goods unloaded	3,972	4,522	5,188

Source: Ministry of Public Works and Transport.

CIVIL AVIATION
(scheduled services)

	2007	2008	2009
Kilometres flown (million)	28	28	27
Passengers carried ('000)	1,017	1,024	933
Passenger-km (million)	2,373	2,467	2,312
Total ton-km (million)	161	168	156

Source: UN, *Statistical Yearbook*.

Tourism

FOREIGN TOURIST ARRIVALS BY COUNTRY OF ORIGIN

	2008	2009	2010
Canada	109,854	102,471	119,654
Colombia	33,644	32,014	32,999
El Salvador	46,837	44,185	53,669
France	34,622	30,737	35,266
Germany	44,705	40,918	44,539
Guatemala	40,840	40,340	48,682
Honduras	31,714	31,324	34,043
Italy	18,994	18,497	19,658
Mexico	59,545	47,771	54,662
Netherlands	30,615	25,006	26,373
Nicaragua	455,412	413,713	427,362
Panama	72,855	58,202	77,918
Spain	54,029	46,457	48,492
United Kingdom	40,250	28,882	34,745
USA	807,162	770,129	830,993
Venezuela	20,506	21,138	24,586
Total (incl. others)	2,089,174	1,922,579	2,099,829

Tourism receipts (US $ million, excl. passenger transport): 2,283 in 2008; 1,815 in 2009; 2,111 in 2010 (provisional) (Source: World Tourism Organization).

Communications Media

	2008	2009	2010
Telephones ('000 main lines in use)	1,437.7	1,499.6	1,481.7
Mobile cellular telephones ('000 subscribers)	1,886.6	1,950.3	3,035.0
Internet subscribers ('000)	183.5	271.5	n.a.
Broadband subscribers ('000)	107.4	179.8	288.2

Personal computers: 1,000,000 (231.0 per 1,000 persons) in 2005.

Radio receivers ('000 in use): 3,045 in 1999.

Television receivers ('000 in use): 930 in 2000.

Daily newspapers: 7 in 2004.

Non-daily newspapers: 42 in 2004.

Book production: 1,464 titles (excluding pamphlets) in 1998.

Sources: UNESCO, *Statistical Yearbook*, UN, *Statistical Yearbook*, International Telecommunication Union.

Education

(2009/10 unless otherwise indicated)

	Institutions	Teachers	Students		
			Males	Females	Total
Pre-primary	2,705*	7,509	55,126	53,120	108,246
Primary	4,007*	29,163	268,750	251,859	520,609
Secondary	708*	26,676	207,042	206,644	413,686
General	n.a.	23,089	176,368	175,579	351,947
Vocational	n.a.	3,587	30,674	31,065	61,739
Tertiary	52†	4,494‡	50,573§	60,144§	110,717§

* 2005.
† 1999.
‡ 2002/03.
§ 2004/05.

Source: mainly UNESCO Institute for Statistics.

Pupil-teacher ratio (primary education, UNESCO estimate): 17.9 in 2009/10 (Source: UNESCO Institute for Statistics).

Adult literacy rate (UNESCO estimates): 96.1% (males 95.9%; females 96.3%) in 2009 (Source: UNESCO Institute for Statistics).

Directory

The Government

HEAD OF STATE

President: LAURA CHINCHILLA MIRANDA (took office 8 May 2010).

First Vice-President: ALFIO PIVA MESÉN.

Second Vice-President: LUIS LIBERMAN GINSBURG.

THE CABINET
(May 2012)

The Government was formed by the Partido Liberación Nacional (PLN).

Minister of the Presidency: CARLOS RICARDO BENAVIDES JIMÉNEZ.

Minister of Justice: HERNANDO PARÍS RODRÍGUEZ.

Minister of National Planning and Economic Policy: ROBERTO JAVIER GALLARDO NUÑEZ.

Minister of Finance: EDGAR AYALES ESNA.

Minister of Foreign Relations: ENRIQUE CASTILLO BARRANTES.

Minister of Foreign Trade: ANABEL GONZÁLEZ CAMPABADAL.

Minister of Governance, Police and Public Security: MARIO ZAMORA CORDERO.

Minister of Economy, Industry and Commerce: MAYI ANTILLÓN GUERRERO.

Minister of Decentralization and Local Government: JUAN MARÍN QUIRÓS.

Minister of Social Welfare: FERNANDO MARÍN ROJAS.

Minister of the Environment, Energy and Telecommunications: RENÉ CASTRO SALAZAR.

Minister of Labour and Social Security: SANDRA PISZK FEINZILBER.

Minister of Public Education: LEONARDO GARNIER RIMOLO.

Minister of Public Health: DAISY CORRALES DÍAZ.

Minister of Housing and Settlements: IRENE CAMPOS GÓMEZ.

Minister of Public Works and Transport: (vacant).

Minister of Science and Technology: ALEJANDRO CRUZ MOLINA.

Minister of Culture and Youth: MANUEL OBREGÓN LÓPEZ.

Minister of Tourism: ALLAN FLORES.

Minister of Agriculture and Livestock: GLORIA ABRAHAM PERALTA.

Minister of Communications and Public Relations: FRANCISCO CHACÓN GONZALEZ.

MINISTRIES

Ministry of Agriculture and Livestock: Antigüo Colegio La Salle, Sabana Sur, Apdo 10094, 1000 San José; tel. 2231-2344; fax 2232-2103; e-mail sunii@mag.go.cr; internet www.mag.go.cr.

Ministry of Communications and Public Relations: San José.

Ministry of Culture and Youth: Avdas 3 y 7, Calles 11 y 15, frente al parque España, San José; tel. 2255-3188; fax 2233-7066; e-mail mincjd@mcjd.go.cr; internet www.mcjdcr.go.cr.

Ministry of Decentralization and Local Government: San Vicente de Moravia, del antiguo Colegio Lincoln 200O este, 100 sur y 200 oeste, contiguo a Sinfónica Juvenil, San José; tel. 2507-1070; e-mail webmaster@ifam.go.cr; internet www.ifam.go.cr.

Ministry of Economy, Industry and Commerce: 400 m oeste de la Contraloría General de la República, Sabana Sur, Apdo 10216-1000, San José; tel. 2291-2115; fax 2291-2059; e-mail informacion@meic.go.cr; internet www.meic.go.cr.

Ministry of the Environment, Energy and Telecommunications: Avdas 8 y 10, Calle 25, Apdo 10104, 1000 San José; tel. 2233-4533; fax 2257-0697; e-mail prensa@minae.go.cr; internet www.minae.go.cr.

Ministry of Finance: Edif. Antigüo Banco Anglo, Avda 2a, Calle 3a, San José; tel. 2257-9333; fax 2255-4874; e-mail webmaster1@hacienda.go.cr; internet www.hacienda.go.cr.

Ministry of Foreign Relations: Avda 7 y 9, Calle 11 y 13, Apdo 10027, 1000 San José; tel. 2223-7555; fax 2257-6597; e-mail despacho.ministro@rree.go.cr; internet www.rree.go.cr.

Ministry of Foreign Trade: Apdo 2297, 1007 Centro Colón, San José; tel. 2299-4700; fax 2255-3281; e-mail pep@comex.go.cr; internet www.comex.go.cr.

Ministry of Governance, Police and Public Security: Apdo 55, 4874 San José; tel. 2227-4866; fax 2226-6581; internet www.msp.go.cr.

Ministry of Housing and Settlements: Of. Mall San Pedro, 7°, Costado Norte, Apdo 1753, 2050 San Pedro de Montes de Oca; tel. 2202-7900; fax 2202-7910; e-mail info@mivah.go.cr; internet www.mivah.go.cr.

Ministry of Justice: 50 m norte de la Clínica Bíblica, frente a la Escuela M. García Flamenco, 1000 San José; tel. 2256-6700; fax 2234-7959; e-mail justicia@gobnet.go.cr; internet www.mjp.go.cr.

Ministry of Labour and Social Security: Edif. Benjamín Núñez, 4°, Barrio Tournón, Apdo 10133, 1000 San José; tel. 2257-8211; internet www.ministrabajo.go.cr.

Ministry of National Planning and Economic Policy: De Autos Subarú 200 m al norte, Barrio Dent, San Pedro de Montes de Oca; tel. 2281-2700; fax 2253-6243; e-mail despacho@mideplan.go.cr; internet www.mideplan.go.cr.

Ministry of Presidency: Casa Presidencial, Zapote, Apdo 520, 2010 San José; tel. 2207-9100; fax 2253-9078; e-mail sugerencias@presidencia.go.cr; internet www.presidencia.go.cr.

Ministry of Public Education: Edif. Rofas, frente al Hospital San Juan de Dios, Apdo 10087, 1000 San José; tel. 2258-3745; fax 2248-1763; e-mail contraloriaservicios@mep.go.cr; internet www.mep.go.cr.

Ministry of Public Health: Calle 16, Avda 6 y 8, Apdo 10123, 1000 San José; tel. 2223-0333; fax 2255-2636; e-mail prensams@netsalud.sa.cr; internet www.ministeriodesalud.go.cr.

Ministry of Public Works and Transport: Plaza González Víquez, Calles 9 y 11, Avda 20 y 22, Apdo 10176, 1000 San José; tel. 2523-2000; fax 2257-7405; e-mail ofprensa@mopt.go.cr; internet www.mopt.go.cr.

Ministry of Science and Technology: 50 m Este del Museo Nacional, Avda Segunda, Calles 19 y 17, Apdo 5589, 1000 San José; tel. 2248-1515; fax 2257-8895; e-mail micit@micit.go.cr; internet www.micit.go.cr.

Ministry of Social Welfare: San José; tel. 2202-4000; fax 2202-4069; e-mail informatica@imas.go.cr; internet www.imas.go.cr.

Ministry of Tourism: Costado Este del Puente Juan Pablo II, sobre Autopista General Cañas, Apdo 777, 1000 San José; tel. 2299-5800; fax 2220-0243; internet www.ict.go.cr.

President and Legislature

PRESIDENT

Election, 7 February 2010

Candidate	Valid votes cast	% of valid votes
Laura Chinchilla Miranda (PLN)	896,516	46.91
Ottón Solís Fallas (PAC)	478,877	25.05
Otto Guevara Guth (ML)	399,788	20.92
Luis Fishman Zonzinski (PUSC)	74,114	3.88
Oscar López (PASE)	36,104	1.89
Mayra González (PRC)	13,945	0.73
Eugenio Trejo Benavides (Frente Amplio)	6,782	0.35
Rolando Araya (Alianza Patriótica)	3,158	0.16
Walter Muñoz (PIN)	2,049	0.11
Total (incl. others)	1,911,333	100.00

ASAMBLEA LEGISLATIVA

President: VICTOR EMILIO GRANADOS.

General Election, 7 February 2010

Party	% of votes cast	Seats
Partido Liberación Nacional (PLN)	37.16	24
Partido Acción Ciudadana (PAC)	17.68	11
Movimiento Libertario (ML)	14.48	9
Partido Unidad Social Cristiana (PUSC)	8.05	6
Partido Accesibilidad sin Exclusión (PASE)	9.17	4
Partido Renovación Costarricense (PRC)	3.77	1
Frente Amplio	3.66	1
Partido Restauración Nacional	1.62	1
Total (incl. others)	100.00	57

Election Commission

Tribunal Supremo de Elecciones (TSE): Avda 1 y 3, Calle 15, Apdo 2163, 1000 San José; tel. 2287-5555; e-mail secretariatse@tse.go.cr; internet www.tse.go.cr; f. 1949; independent; Pres. LUIS ANTONIO SOBRADO GONZÁLEZ; Exec. Dir FRANCISCO RODRÍGUEZ SILES.

Political Organizations

Alianza Patriótica: Edif. Rojo, 2°, de la esquina sureste del Museo Nacional, 1 cuadra este a mano derecha, San José; tel. 2223-9595; fax 2223-9596; e-mail info@ap.cr; internet www.ap.cr; Pres. MARIANO FIGUERES OLSEN; Sec.-Gen. ARNOLDO MORA VAGLIO.

Frente Amplio: Barrio Amón, costado suroeste del INVU, 25 m sur, Apdo 280, Moravia, San José; tel. and fax 2258-5641; e-mail info@frenteamplio.org; internet www.frenteamplio.org; Pres. JOSÉ MERINO DEL RÍO; Sec.-Gen. SONIA SOLÍS UMAÑA.

Movimiento Libertario (ML): Of. de Cabinas San Isidro, Barrio Los Yoses Sur, Apdo 4674, 1000 San José; tel. 2283-8600; fax 2283-9600; internet www.movimientolibertario.com; f. 1994; Pres. OTTO GUEVARA GUTH; Sec.-Gen. MIRNA PATRICIA PÉREZ HEGG.

Partido Accesibilidad sin Exclusión (PASE): San José; tel. 2214-6110; internet partidopase.blogspot.in; f. 2004; Leader OSCAR LÓPEZ ARIAS; Sec. HUGO NAVAS VARGAS.

Partido Acción Ciudadana (PAC): 25 San Pedro, 425 m sur del Templo Parroquial, San José; tel. 2281-2727; fax 2280-6640; e-mail accionciudadana@pac.or.cr; internet www.pac.or.cr; f. 2000; centre party; Pres. ELIZABETH FONSECA; Sec.-Gen. MARGARITA BOLAÑOS ARQUÍN.

Partido Integración Nacional (PIN): Edif. de Imágenes Médicas, 2°, Apdo 219, 2050 San Pedro de Montes de Oca, San José; tel. 2221-3300; fax 2500-0729; e-mail waltermunoz@costarricense.cr; internet www.pin.co.cr; f. 1996; Pres. Dr WALTER MUÑOZ CÉSPEDES; Sec.-Gen. HEINER ALBERTO LEMAITRE ZAMORA.

Partido Liberación Nacional (PLN): Mata Redonda, 125 m oeste del Ministerio de Agricultura y Ganadería, Casa Liberacionista José Figueres Ferrer, Apdo 10051, 1000 San José; tel. 2232-5133; fax 2231-4097; e-mail secregeneralpln@ice.co.cr; internet www.pln.or.cr; f. 1952; social democratic party; affiliated to the Socialist International; 500,000 mems; Pres. BERNAL JIMÉNEZ MONGE; Sec.-Gen. ANTONIO CALDERÓN CASTRO.

Partido Renovación Costarricense (PRC): Centro Educativo Instituto de Desarrollo de Inteligencia, Hatillo 1, Avda Villanea, Apdo 31, 1300 San José; tel. 2254-3651; fax 2252-3270; e-mail jimmysos@costarricense.cr; f. 1995; Pres. JUSTO OROZCO ALVAREZ; Sec. JIMMY SOTO SOLANO.

Partido Restauración Nacional: Del Restaurante la Princesa Marina, 75 m norte, portón amarillo, casa al fondo, contiguo al local de pinturas Protecto, Moravia, San Vicente; f. 2005; provincial party; Pres. CARLOS LUIS AVENDAÑO CALVO.

Partido Unidad Social Cristiana (PUSC): 100 m al oeste del Hospital de Niños, Paseo Colón, Apdo 10095, 1000 San José; tel. 2280-2920; fax 2248-3678; e-mail info@partidounidadsocialcristiana.com; internet www.partidounidadsocialcristiana.com; f. 1983; Pres. GERARDO VARGAS ROJAS; Sec.-Gen. WILLIAM ALVARADO BOGANTES.

Diplomatic Representation

EMBASSIES IN COSTA RICA

Argentina: McDonald's de Curridabat, 700 m sur y 25 m este, Apdo 1963, 1000 San José; tel. 2234-6520; fax 2283-9983; e-mail embarg@racsa.co.cr; Chargé d'affaires a.i. JULIO CÉSAR AYALA.

Belgium: Los Yoses, 4a entrada, 25 m sur de la Subaru, Apdo 3725, 1000 San José; tel. 2225-6633; fax 2225-0351; e-mail sanjose@diplobel.fed.be; internet www.diplomatie.be/sanjose; Ambassador GRÉGOIRE VARDAKIS.

Bolivia: Barrio Francisco Peralta, de la Casa Italia 100 m oeste, Apdo 84810, 1000 San José; tel. 2524-3491; fax 2280-0320; e-mail embocr@racsa.co.cr; Chargé d'affaires a.i. YOVANKA OLIDEN TAPIA.

Brazil: Edif. Torre Mercedes, 6°, Paseo Colón, Apdo 10132, 1000 San José; tel. 2295-6875; fax 2295-6874; e-mail brasemb.saojose@itamaraty.gov.br; internet www.brasilcostarica.tk; Ambassador MARIA DULCE SILVA BARROS.

Canada: Oficentro Ejecutivo La Sabana, Edif. 5, 3°, detrás de la Contraloría, Centro Colón, Apdo 351, 1007 San José; tel. 2242-4400; fax 2242-4410; e-mail sjcra@international.gc.ca; internet www.canadainternational.gc.ca/costa_rica; Ambassador CAMERON MACKAY.

Chile: Casa 225, Los Yoses, del Automercado Los Yoses 225 m sur, Calle 39, Avdas 10 y 12, Apdo 10102, 1000 San José; tel. 2280-0037; fax 2253-7016; e-mail info@embachile.co.cr; internet www.embachile.co.cr; Ambassador GONZALO MENDOZA NEGRI.

China, People's Republic: De la casa de D. Oscar Arias, 100 m sur y 50 m este, Rohrmoser, Pavas, Apdo 1518, 1200 San José; tel. 2291-4811; fax 2291-4820; e-mail embchina_costarica@yahoo.com.cn; internet cr.chineseembassy.org/esp; Ambassador LI CHANGHUA.

Colombia: Barrio Dent de Taco Bell, San Pedro, Apdo 3154, 1000 San José; tel. 2283-6871; fax 2283-6818; e-mail esanjose@cancilleria.gov.co; internet www.embajadaencostarica.gov.co; Ambassador HERNANDO HERRERA VERGARA.

Cuba: Sabana Norte, del restaurante El Chicote 100 norte, 50 este y 200 norte, Casa esquinera, costado izquierdo, San José; tel. 2231-6812; fax 2232-2985; e-mail oficinapolitica@consulcubacr.com; internet www.cubadiplomatica.cu/costarica; Ambassador ANTONIO MIGUEL PARDO SÁNCHEZ.

Czech Republic: 75 m oeste de la entrada principal del Colegio Humboldt, Apdo 12041, 1000 San José; tel. 2296-5671; fax 2296-5595; e-mail sanjose@embassy.mzv.cz; internet www.mzv.cz/sanjose; Ambassador PAVEL PROCHAZKA.

Dominican Republic: McDonald's de Curridabat 400 sur, 100 m este, Apdo 4746, 1000 San José; tel. 2283-8103; fax 2280-7604; e-mail embdominicanacr@ice.co.cr; Ambassador NESTOR JUAN CERON SUERO.

Ecuador: De la casa de Oscar Arias 100 m norte, Rohrmoser, Apdo 1374, 1000 San José; tel. and fax 2232-1503; e-mail eecucostarica@mmrree.gov.ec; internet www.consuladoecuadorsj.com; Ambassador DAISY TULA ESPINEL DE ALVARADO.

El Salvador: Paseo Colón, Calle 30, Avda 1, No 53, Apdo 1378, 1000 San José; tel. 2257-7855; fax 2258-1234; e-mail embasacr@amnet.co.cr; Ambassador SEBASTIÁN VAQUERANO LÓPEZ.

France: Carretera a Curridabat, de Mitsubishi 200 m sur y 25 m oeste, Apdo 10177, 1000 San José; tel. 2234-4167; fax 2234-4195; e-mail sjfrance@sol.racsa.co.cr; internet www.ambafrance-cr.org; Ambassador FABRICE DELLOYE.

Germany: Edif. Torre la Sabana, 8°, Sabana Norte, Apdo 4017, 1000 San José; tel. 2290-9091; fax 2231-6403; e-mail info@san-jose.diplo.de; internet www.san-jose.diplo.de; Ambassador Dr ERNST MARTENS.

Guatemala: De Sabana Sur, del Gimnasio Fitsimons 100 sur y 50 m oeste, Apdo 328, 1000 San José; tel. 2291-6172; fax 2290-4111; e-mail embaguat@ice.co.cr; Ambassador MANLIO FERNANDO SESENNA OLIVERO.

Holy See: Barrio Rohrmoser, Centro Colón, Apdo 992, 1007 San José (Apostolic Nunciature); tel. 2232-2128; fax 2231-2557; e-mail nuapcr@racsa.co.cr; Apostolic Nuncio Right Rev. PIERRE NGUYÊN VAN TOT (Titular Archbishop of Rusticiana).

Honduras: Rohrmoser, Pavas, Apdo 2239, 1000 San José; tel. 2231-1642; fax 2291-5147; e-mail embhoncr@embajadahonduras.co.cr; internet www.embajadahonduras.co.cr; Ambassador JAIME GÜELL BOGRÁN.

Israel: Edif. Centro Colón, 11°, Calle 38 Paseo Colón, Apdo 5147, 1000 San José; tel. 2221-6444; fax 2257-0867; e-mail info@sanjose.mfa.gov.il; internet sanjose.mfa.gov.il; Ambassador DANIEL SABAN.

Italy: Los Yoses, 5a entrada, Apdo 1729, 1000 San José; tel. 2224-6574; fax 2225-8200; e-mail ambasciata.sanjose@esteri.it; internet www.ambsanjose.esteri.it; Ambassador DIEGO UNGARO.

Japan: Edif. Torre La Sabana, 10°, Sabana Norte, Apdo 501, 1000 San José; tel. 2232-1255; fax 2231-3140; e-mail embjapon@racsa.co.cr; internet www.cr.emb-japan.go.jp; Ambassador YOSHIHARU NAMIKI.

Korea, Republic: 125 m norte del banco Cuscatlán, Rohrmoser, Paseo Colón, Apdo 838, 1007 San José; tel. 2220-3160; fax 2220-3168; e-mail koco@mofat.go.kr; internet cri.mofat.go.kr; Ambassador HONG JO CHUN.

Mexico: Avda 7A, No 1371, Apdo 10107, 1000 San José; tel. 2257-0633; fax 2258-2437; e-mail rmision@embamexico.or.cr; internet portal.sre.gob.mx/costarica; Chargé d'affaires a.i. MARTHA EUGENIA TAPIA BERMUDEZ.

Netherlands: Oficentro Ejecutivo La Sabana (detrás de la Contraloría), Edif. 3, 3°, Sabana Sur, Apdo 10285, 1000 San José; tel. 2296-1490; fax 2296-2933; e-mail sjo@minbuza.nl; internet costarica.nlembajada.org; Ambassador METTE GONGGRIJP.

Nicaragua: Avda Central 2540, Calle 25 bis, Barrio la California, Apdo 1382, 1000 San José; tel. 2221-2924; fax 2221-3036; e-mail embanic@racsa.co.cr; Ambassador HAROLD FERNANDO RIVAS REYES.

Panama: Del Antiguo Higuerón de San Pedro 200 m sur y 25 m este, Barrio La Granja, San Pedro de Montes de Oca, Apdo 103, 2050 San José; tel. 2280-1570; fax 2281-2161; e-mail panaembacr@racsa.co.cr; Ambassador JOSÉ JAVIER MULINO.

Paraguay: De la Kentucky de Plaza del Sol 600 m al sur y 50 m al este, 12 Curridabat, San Pedro de Montes de Oca, Apdo 2420, 2050 San José; tel. 2234-2932; fax 2234-0891; e-mail embapar@racsa.co.cr; Ambassador OSCAR BUENAVENTURA LLANES TORRES.

Peru: Del Colegio de Igenieros y Arquitectos, 350 m al norte, Urb. Freses, Curridabat, Apdo 4248, 1000 San José; tel. 2225-9145; fax 2253-0457; e-mail embaperu@amnet.co.cr; Chargé d'affaires a.i. GUSTAVO FELIPE JOSÉ LEMBCKE HOYLE.

Russia: Barrio Escalante, 100 m norte y 150 m este de la Iglesia Santa Teresita, Apdo 6340, 1000 San José; tel. 2256-9181; fax 2221-2054; e-mail emrusa@sol.racsa.co.cr; Ambassador VLADIMIR TIKHONOVICH KURAEV.

Spain: Calle 32, entre Paseo Colón y Avda 2, Apdo 10150, 1000 San José; tel. 2222-1933; fax 2222-4180; e-mail Emb.SanJose@maec.es; internet www.maec.es/subwebs/embajadas/sanjosecostarica; Ambassador ELENA MADRAZO HEGEWISCH.

Switzerland: Edif. Centro Colón, 10°, Paseo Colón, Apdo 895, 1007 San José; tel. 2221-4829; fax 2255-2831; e-mail sjc.vertretung@eda.admin.ch; internet www.eda.admin.ch/sanjose; Ambassador HANS-RUDOLF HODEL.

United Kingdom: Edif. Centro Colón, 11°, Paseo Colón, Apdo 815, 1007 San José; tel. 2258-2025; fax 2233-9938; e-mail britemb@racsa.co.cr; internet www.ukincostarica.fco.gov.uk; Ambassador SHARON ISABEL CAMPBELL.

Uruguay: Trejos Monte Alegre, Escazú, del Vivero Exótica 900 m oeste y 100 m sur, Apdo 3448, 1000 San José; tel. 2288-3424; fax 2288-3070; e-mail embajrou@sol.racsa.co.cr; Ambassador FERNANDO DANIEL ALEJANDRO MARR MERELLO.

USA: Calle 120, Avda 0, Pavas, Apdo 920, 1200 San José; tel. 2519-2000; fax 2220-2305; e-mail info@usembassy.or.cr; internet sanjose.usembassy.gov; Ambassador ANNE SLAUGHTER ANDREW.

Venezuela: De la Casa de Don Óscar Arias, 100 m al sur, 400 m al oeste y 25 m al sur, Barrio Rohrmoser, Apdo 10230, 1000 San José; tel. 2220-3102; fax 2290-3806; e-mail embve.crsjo@mre.gob.ve; internet embavenezuelacr.org; Ambassador AURA MAHUAMPI RODRÍGUEZ DE ORTIZ.

Judicial System

Ultimate judicial power is vested in the Supreme Court, the justices of which are elected by the Legislative Assembly for a term of eight years, and are automatically re-elected for an equal period, unless the Assembly decides to the contrary by a two-thirds' vote. The Supreme Court justices sit in four courts: the First Court (civil, administrative, agrarian and commercial matters), the Second Court (employment and family), the Third Court (penal) and the Constitutional Court. There are, in addition, appellate courts, criminal courts, civil courts and special courts. The jury system is not used.

The Supreme Court

Sala Constitucional de la Corte Suprema de Justicia, Apdo 5, 1003 San José; tel. 2295-3000; fax 2257-0801; e-mail sala4-informacion@poder-judicial.go.cr; internet www.poder-judicial.go.cr.

President of the Supreme Court: LUIS PAULINO MORA MORA.

Religion

Under the Constitution, all forms of worship are tolerated. Roman Catholicism is the official religion of the country. Various Protestant churches are also represented.

CHRISTIANITY

The Roman Catholic Church

Costa Rica comprises one archdiocese and seven dioceses. Roman Catholics represent some 82% of the total population.

Bishops' Conference

Conferencia Episcopal de Costa Rica, Apdo 7288, 1000 San José; tel. 2221-3053; fax 2221-6662; e-mail seccecor@racsa.co.cr; internet www.iglesiacr.org.

f. 1977; Pres. Most Rev. HUGO BARRANTES UREÑA (Archbishop of San José de Costa Rica).

Archbishop of San José de Costa Rica: Most Rev. HUGO BARRANTES UREÑA, Arzobispado, Apdo 497, 1000 San José; tel. 2258-1015; fax 2221-2427; e-mail arzobispo@arquisanjose.org; internet www.arquisanjose.org.

The Anglican Communion

Costa Rica comprises one of the five dioceses of the Iglesia Anglicana de la Región Central de América.

Bishop of Costa Rica: Rt Rev. HÉCTOR MONTERROSO, Apdo 10520, 1000 San José; tel. 2225-0790; fax 2253-8331; e-mail iarca@amnet.co.cr.

Other Churches

Federación de Asociaciones Bautistas de Costa Rica: Apdo 1631, 2100 Guadalupe; tel. 2253-5820; fax 2253-4723; e-mail fabcr2@icc.co.cr; internet www.fabcr.org; f. 1946; represents Baptist churches; Pres. JOSÉ ARMANDO SOTO VILLEGAS.

Iglesia Evangélica Luterana de Costa Rica (Evangelical Lutheran Church of Costa Rica): Apdo 1512, Pavas, 1200 San José; tel. 2231-3345; fax 2291-0986; e-mail evkirche@racsa.co.cr; f. 1955; German congregation; 220 mems; Pres. Rev. MATTHIAS VON WESTHERHOLT.

Iglesia Evangélica Metodista de Costa Rica (Evangelical Methodist Church of Costa Rica): Apdo 5481, 1000 San José; tel. 2236-2171; fax 2236-5921; e-mail iglesiametodistacr@yahoo.com; internet www.geocities.com/iglesiametodistacr; autonomous since 1973; affiliated to the United Methodist Church; 6,000 mems; Pres. Bishop LUIS F. PALOMO.

BAHÁ'Í FAITH

National Spiritual Assembly of the Bahá'ís of Costa Rica: Apdo 553, 1150 La Uruca; tel. 2520-2127; fax 2296-1033; e-mail info@bahaicr.org; internet www.bahaicr.org; f. 1942.

The Press

DAILIES

Al Día: Llorente de Tibás, Apdo 10138, 1000 San José; tel. 2247-4647; fax 2247-4665; e-mail mgomez@aldia.co.cr; internet www.aldia.co.cr; f. 1992; morning; independent; Dir EDGAR FONSECA; Editor MÓNICA GÓMEZ; circ. 60,000.

Diario Extra: Edif. de La Prensa Libre, Calle 4, Avda 4, Apdo 177, 1009 San José; tel. 2223-6666; fax 2223-6101; e-mail redaccion@diarioextra.com; internet www.diarioextra.com; f. 1978; morning; independent; Dir WILLIAM GÓMEZ VARGAS, IARY GOMÉZ; circ. 157,000.

El Heraldo: 400 m al este de las oficinas centrales, Apdo 1500, San José; tel. 2222-6665; fax 2222-3039; e-mail info@elheraldo.net; internet www.elheraldo.net; f. 1994; morning; independent; Chief Editor VANESSA ESQUIVEL S.; Dir ERWIN KNOHR; circ. 30,000.

La Nación: Llorente de Tibás, Apdo 10138, 1000 San José; tel. 2247-4747; fax 2247-5022; e-mail agonzales@nacion.com; internet www.nacion.com; f. 1946; morning; independent; Dir YANANCY NOGUERA; circ. 90,000.

La Prensa Libre: Calle 4, Avda 4, Apdo 10121, 1000 San José; tel. 2223-6666; fax 2223-4671; e-mail plibre@prensalibre.co.cr; internet www.prensalibre.co.cr; f. 1889; evening; independent; Dir WILLIAM GÓMEZ VARGAS; Editor MARÍA ELENA JIMÉNEZ VEGA; circ. 56,000.

La República: Barrio Tournón, Guadalupe, Apdo 2130, 1000 San José; tel. 2522-3300; fax 2257-0401; e-mail redaccion@larepublica.net; internet www.larepublica.net; f. 1950; reorganized 1967; morning; independent; Dir LUIS ALBERTO MUÑOZ; circ. 61,000.

PERIODICALS

Abanico: Calle 4, Avda 4, Apdo 10121, 1000 San José; tel. 2223-6666; fax 2223-4671; e-mail abanico@diarioextra.com; internet www.prensalibre.co.cr; weekly supplement of La Prensa Libre; women's interests; circ. 50,000.

Actualidad Económica: San José; tel. 2226-6483; fax 2224-1528; e-mail wordmagic@live.com; internet www.actualidad.co.cr; Dir NORA RUIZ.

Eco Católico: Calle 22, Avdas 3 y 5, Apdo 1064, San José; tel. 2222-8391; fax 2256-0407; e-mail info@elecocatolico.org; internet www.elecocatolico.org; f. 1931; Catholic weekly; Dir MARTÍN RODRÍGUEZ GONZÁLEZ; circ. 20,000.

El Financiero: Grupo Nación, Edif. Subsidiarias, Llorente de Tibás, 185-2120 Guadalupe; tel. 2247-5555; fax 2247-5177; e-mail redaccion@elfinancierocr.com; internet www.elfinancierocr.com; f. 1995; Dir JOSÉ DAVID GUEVARA MUÑOZ.

INCAE Business Review: Apdo 960-4050, Alajuela; tel. 2258-6834; fax 2258-2874; e-mail info@revistaincae.com; internet www.revistaincae.com; f. 1982; publ. by INCAE business school; Dir MARLENE DE ESTRELLA LÓPEZ; circ. 18,000.

Perfil: Llorente de Tibás, Apdo 1517, 1100 San José; tel. 2247-4345; fax 2247-5110; e-mail perfil@nacion.co.cr; internet www.perfilcr.com; f. 1984; fortnightly; women's interests; Dir ISABEL OVARES; Man. Editor THAIS AGUILAR ZÚÑIGA; circ. 16,000.

The Tico Times: Calle 15, Avda 8, Apdo 4632, 1000 San José; tel. 2258-1558; fax 2223-6378; e-mail info@ticotimes.net; internet www.ticotimes.net; f. 1956; weekly; in English; Editor STEVE MACK; circ. 15,210.

PRESS ASSOCIATIONS

Colegio de Periodistas de Costa Rica: Sabana Este, Calle 42, Avda 4, Apdo 5416, San José; tel. 2233-5850; fax 2278-4345; e-mail director@comunicacionefectiva.com; internet www.colper.or.cr; f. 1969; 1,447 mems; Pres. RAÚL SILESKY JIMÉNEZ.

Sindicato Nacional de Periodistas de Costa Rica: Edif. Colegio de Periodistas de Costa Rica, 2°, 50 m sur de la Soda Tapia, Calle 42, Avda 20 y 4,Sabana Este, San José; tel. 2222-7589; fax 2258-3229; e-mail sindicato@colper.or.cr; internet www.sindicatodeperiodistas.org; f. 1970; 220 mems; Sec.-Gen. CLAUDIA DURÁN CHACÓN.

Publishers

Caribe-Betania Editores: Apdo 1.307, San José; tel. 2222-7244; e-mail info@editorialcaribe.com; internet www.caribebetania.com; f. 1949 as Editorial Caribe; present name adopted 1992; division of Thomas Nelson Publrs; religious textbooks; Exec. Vice-Pres. TAMARA L. HEIM; Dir JOHN STROWEL.

Editorial Costa Rica: Calle 1, entre avda 8 y 10, esq. suroeste del Banco Popular, 250 m al sur, Apdo 10010-1000, San José; tel. 2233-0812; fax 2233-1949; e-mail difusion@editorialcostarica.com; internet www.editorialcostarica.com; f. 1959; govt-owned; cultural; Pres. LUIS ENRIQUE ARCE NAVARRO; Gen. Man. MARÍA ISABEL BRENES ALVARADO.

Editorial Fernández Arce: 50 este de Sterling Products, la Paulina de Montes de Oca, Apdo 2410, 1000 San José; tel. 2224-5201; fax 2225-6109; e-mail ventas@fernandez-arce.com; internet www.fernandez-arce.com; f. 1967; textbooks for primary, secondary and university education; Dir Dr MARIO FERNÁNDEZ ARCE.

Editorial INBio de Costa Rica: San José; tel. 2507-8183; e-mail editorial@inbio.ac.cr; internet www.inbio.ac.cr/editorial; f. 2000; part of Instituto Nacional de Biodiversidad; Man. FABIO ROJAS.

Editorial Legado: Apdo 2160, 2050 San José; tel. 2280-8007; fax 2280-0945; e-mail legado@editlegado.com; internet www.editlegado.com; f. 1976; Gen. Man. SEBASTIÁN VAQUERANO.

Editorial Tecnológica de Costa Rica: 1 km al sur de la Basílica de Los Angeles, Apdo 159-7050, Cartago; tel. 2550-2297; fax 2552-5354; e-mail editorial@tec.ac.cr; internet www.tec.ac.cr; f. 1978; Dir ANA RUTH VÍLCHEZ RODRÍGUEZ.

Editorial de la Universidad Autónoma de Centro América (UACA): Apdo 7637, 1000 San José; tel. 2272-9100; fax 2271-2046; e-mail info@uaca.ac.cr; internet www.uaca.ac.cr; f. 1981; Editor JULISSA MÉNDEZ MARÍN.

Editorial Universidad de Costa Rica: Ciudad Universitaria Rodrigo Facio, San Pedro, Montes de Oca, 2060 San José; tel. 2511-5310; fax 2511-5257; e-mail direccion.siedin@ucr.ac.cr; internet www.editorial.ucr.ac.cr; Dir FERNANDO DURÁN AYANEGUI.

Editorial de la Universidad Estatal a Distancia (EUNED): Mercedes de Montes de Oca, Apdo 474-2050, San José; tel. 2527-2440; fax 2234-9138; e-mail euned@uned.ac.cr; internet www.uned.ac.cr/

editorial; f. 1979; Pres. Dr LUIS ALBERTO CAÑAS ESCALANTE; Dir RENÉ MUIÑOS GUAL.

Editorial Universidad Nacional: Campus Universitario, Frente Escuela de Ciencias Ambientales, Apdo 86, 3000 Heredia; tel. 2277-3204; fax 2277-3825; e-mail editoria@una.ac.cr; internet www.una.ac.cr/euna; f. 1976; Pres. CARLOS FRANCISCO MONGE.

Grupo Editorial Norma: Zona Franca Metropolitana Local 7B, Barreal de Heredia, Heredia, Apdo 592, 1200 Pavas; tel. 2293-1333; fax 2239-3947; e-mail gerencia@farben.co.cr; internet www.norma.com; fmrly Ediciones Farben; Man. Editor ALEXANDER OBONAGA.

Grupo Santillana: La Uruca 78, 1150 San José; tel. 2220-4242; fax 2220-1320; e-mail santilla@santillana.co.cr; internet www.gruposantillana.co.cr; f. 1993; Editorial Dir ELSA MORALES CORDERO.

Imprenta Nacional: La Uruca, San José; tel. 2296-9570; e-mail direccion@imprenta.go.cr; internet www.imprentanacional.go.cr; Dir-Gen. JORGE VARGAS ESPINOZA.

Librería Lehmann, Imprenta y Litografía, Ltda: Calles 1 y 3, Avda Central, Apdo 10011, 1000 San José; tel. 2522-4848; fax 2233-0713; e-mail servicio@librerialehmann.com; internet www.librerialehmann.com; f. 1896; general fiction, educational, textbooks; Man. Dir ANTONIO LEHMANN GUTIÉRREZ.

Océcor de CR: Edif. Océano, Sabana Norte, del ICE 300m al Noreste, San José; tel. 2210-2000; fax 2210-2061; e-mail ocecor@racsa.co.cr; internet www.oceano.com; Gen. Man. JORGE ROJAS.

PUBLISHING ASSOCIATION

Cámara Costarricense del Libro: Paseo de los Estudiantes, Apdo 1571, 1002 San José; tel. 2225-1363; fax 2253-4297; e-mail ccl@libroscr.com; internet www.libroscr.com; f. 1978; Pres. DUNIA SOLANO AGUILAR.

Broadcasting and Communications

TELECOMMUNICATIONS

In June 2008 legislation was passed to end the monopoly over the telecommunications sector enjoyed by the Instituto Costarricense de Electricidad (ICE). Implementation of the reform was delayed until mid-2010, however.

Regulatory Bodies

Cámara Costarricense de Telecomunicaciones (CCTEL): Edif. Centro Colón, Apdo 591, 1007 San José; tel. and fax 2255-3422; e-mail cctel@cctel.org; internet cctel.org; Pres. MIGUEL LEÓN S.

Superintendencia de Telecomunicaciones (SUTEL): Edif. Tapantí, 3°, Complejo Multipark, 100 m norte Construplaza, Guachipelín de Escazú, San José; tel. 4000-0000; fax 2215-6821; e-mail info@sutel.go.cr; internet www.sutel.go.cr; f. 2008; regulatory body for the telecommunications sector; forms part of the Autoridad Reguladora de los Servicios Públicos (ARESEP—see Trade and Industry—Utilities); Pres. MARYLEANA MÉNDEZ; Vice-Pres. CARLOS RAÚL GUTIÉRREZ.

RADIO

Asociación Costarricense de Información y Cultura (ACIC): Apdo 365, 1009 San José; f. 1983; independent body; controls private radio stations; Pres. JUAN FEDERICO MONTEALEGRE MARTÍN.

Cámara Nacional de Radio (CANARA): Paseo de los Estudiantes, Apdo 1583, 1002 San José; tel. 2256-2338; fax 2255-4483; e-mail info@canara.org; internet www.canara.org; f. 1947; Pres. LUIS ENRIQUE ORTIZ VAGLIO; Sec. JUAN JOSÉ CHENG AZOFEIFA.

Control Nacional de Radio (CNR): Edif. García Pinto, 2°, Calle 33, Avdas Central y Primera, Barrio Escalante, Apdo 1344, 1011 San José; tel. 2524-0455; fax 2524-0454; e-mail controlderadio@ice.co.cr; internet www.controlderadio.go.cr; f. 1954; governmental supervisory department; Dir MELVIN MURILLO ALVAREZ.

Non-commercial

Faro del Caribe: Apdo 2710, 1000 San José; tel. 2286-1755; fax 2227-1725; e-mail info@farodelcaribe.org; internet www.farodelcaribe.org; f. 1948; religious and cultural programmes in Spanish and English; Dir LUIS SERRANO.

FCN Radio Internacional (Family Christian Network): Apdo 60-2020, Zapote, San José; tel. 2209-8000; fax 2293-7993; e-mail info@fcnradio.com; internet www.fcnradio.com; Dir Dr DECAROL WILLIAMSON.

Radio Fides: Avda 4, 2°, costado sur de la Catedral Metropolitana, Curia Metropolitana, Apdo 5079, 1000 San José; tel. 2258-1415; fax 2233-2387; e-mail programas@radiofides.co.cr; internet www.radiofides.co.cr; f. 1952; Roman Catholic station; Dir Fr MARIO SEGURA BONILLA.

Radio Nacional: 1 km oeste del Parque Nacional de Diversiones, La Uruca, Apdo 7, 1980 San José; tel. 2231-3331; fax 2220-0070; e-mail rnacional@sinart.go.cr; internet www.sinart.go.cr; f. 1978; Exec. Pres. ALFONSO ESTEVANOVICH GONZÁLEZ; Dir SYLVIA CAMAÑO RENCORET.

Radio Santa Clara: Edif. CENCO, Santa Clara, San Carlos, Apdo 221, Ciudad Quesada, Alajuela; tel. 2460-6666; fax 2460-2151; e-mail radio@radiosantaclara.org; internet www.radiosantaclara.org; f. 1984; Roman Catholic station; Dir Rev. MARCO ANTONIO SOLÍS V.

Radio Universidad: Ciudad Universitaria Rodrigo Facio, San Pedro, Montes de Oca, Apdo 2060, 1000 San José; tel. 2234-3233; fax 2511-4832; e-mail info@radiosucr.com; internet radiosucr.com/radiouniversidad; f. 1949; classical music; Dir GISELLE BOZA SOLANO.

Commercial

There are about 80 commercial radio stations, including:

Cadena Radial Costarricense: 100 m oeste de Taca, La Uruca, San José; tel. 2231-0455; fax 2255-4483; e-mail aguevara@crc.cr; internet www.crc.cr; operates nine AM and FM radio stations; Dir ANDRÉS QUINTANA CAVALLINI.

Grupo Centro: Tibás, 100 norte y 125 oeste de la Municipalidad, Apdo 6133, 1000 San José; tel. 2240-7591; fax 2236-3672; e-mail info@radiocentrocr.com; internet www.radiocentrocr.com; f. 1971; operates Radio Centro 96.3 FM, Radio 820 AM, Televisora Guanacasteca Channels 16 and 28; Dir ROBERTO HERNÁNDEZ RAMÍREZ.

Grupo Columbia: 200 m oeste de la Casa Presidencial, Zapote, Apdo 168-2020, San José; tel. 2224-7272; fax 2225-9275; e-mail columbia@columbia.co.cr; internet www.columbia.co.cr; operates Radio Columbia, Radio Dos, Radio 955 Jazz; Dir YASHÍN QUESADA ARAYA; Gen. Man. MIGUEL MONGE.

Radio 16: Centro Comercial San Francisco, Calle 5 y 6, Grecia 16-4100, Alajuela; tel. 2494-5356; fax 2494-2031; e-mail gerencia@radio16.com; internet www.radio16.com; Dir LUIS GUSTAVO JIMÉNEZ RAMÍREZ.

Radio América: Sociedad Periódistica Extra Ltda, Edif. Borrasé de la Prensa Libre, Calle 4, Avda 4, Fecosa 177, 1009 San José; tel. 2223-6666; fax 2255-3712; e-mail radioamerica@780am.com; internet www.780america.com; f. 1948 as Radio América Latina; changed name as above in 1996; Dir ADRIÁN MARRERO REDONDO.

Radio Chorotega: Conferencia Episcopal de Costa Rica, Casa Cural de Santa Cruz, Apdo 92, 5175 Guanacaste; tel. and fax 2680-0447; e-mail ugiocr@hotmail.com; f. 1983; Roman Catholic station; Dir Rev. HUGO BRENES VILLALOBOS.

Radio Eco: Apdo 585, 1007 Centro Colón, San José; tel. 2220-1001; fax 2290-0970; e-mail info@radioeco.com; internet www.radioeco.com; Dir RICARDO ZAMORA; Gen. Man. LUIS ENRIQUE ORTIZ VAGLIO.

Radio Emaús: San Vito, Coto Brus; tel. and fax 2773-3101; e-mail radioemaus@racsa.co.cr; f. 1962; Roman Catholic station; religious programmes; Dir Rev. MIGUEL ANGEL BERGANZA.

Radio Monumental: Avda Central y 2, Calle 2, Apdo 800, 1000 San José; tel. 2296-6093; fax 2296-0413; e-mail ventas@monumental.co.cr; internet www.monumental.co.cr; f. 1929; operates 8 radio stations: Radio Monumental, Radio ZFM, Radio Reloj, Punto Cinco, EXA FM, Radio Fabulosa, Radio Favorita and 670 AM; Gen. Man. TERESA MARÍA CHÁVES ZAMORA.

Radio Musical: 1 km al este Hipermás, Carretera a 3 Ríos, Apdo 854, 1000 San José; tel. 2518-2290; fax 2518-2270; e-mail info@radiomusical.com; internet www.radiomusical.com; f. 1951; Gen. Man. JAVIER CASTRO.

Radio Sendas de Vida: San José; tel. 2294-4622; fax 2294-4324; e-mail info@radiosendas.com; internet www.radiosendas.com; f. 1982; Christian station; Pres. DANNY STEED SEGURA.

TELEVISION

Government-owned

Sistema Nacional de Radio y Televisión Cultural (SINART): 1 km al oeste del Parque Nacional de Diversiones La Uruca, Apdo 7, 1980 San José; tel. 2231-6553; fax 2231-6604; e-mail sinart@racsa.co.cr; internet www.sinart.go.cr; f. 1977; cultural; Dir-Gen. RODRIGO ARIAS CAMACHO.

Commercial

Cablevision de Costa Rica, SA: Edif. CableVision, Calle Privada, esq. noreste del colegio San Francis, 75 m este y 25 m sur, Moravia, San José; tel. 2545-1111; fax 2236-8801; e-mail mbarboza@cablevision.co.cr; internet www.cablevision.co.cr; more than 100 channels; digital television; Gen. Man. LEYDA ELIZABETH LOMBANA.

Canal 54–Cable Mas: Detrás de la Iglesia Santa Marta, Carretera a Desamparados, San José; tel. 2286-3344; fax 2226-9092; e-mail canalcr@racsa.co.cr; internet www.teleplusdigital.com; f. 1996; Pres. ANTONIO ALEXANDRE GARCÍA.

Representaciones Televisivas Repretel (Canales 4, 6 y 11): Edif. Repretel, La Uruca del Hospital México, 300 m al oeste, Apdo 2860, 1000 San José; tel. 2299-7200; fax 2232-4203; e-mail info@repretel.com; internet www.repretel.com; f. 1993; Pres. FERNANDO CONTRERAS LÓPEZ; News Dir MARCELA ANGULO.

Telefides (Canal 40): detrás de la Imprenta Nacional, de La Kia Motors, 200 m sur y 200 m oeste, La Uruca, San José; tel. 2520-1112; fax 2290-5346; e-mail info@telefides.com; internet www.telefides.com; f. 1992; Man. SARAY AMADOR.

Televisora de Costa Rica (Canal 7), SA (Teletica): Costado oeste Estadio Nacional, Apdo 3876, San José; tel. 2290-6245; fax 2231-6258; e-mail escribanos@teletica.com; internet www.teletica.com; f. 1960; operates Channel 7; Pres. OLGA COZZA DE PICADO; Gen. Man. RENÉ PICADO COZZA.

Finance

(cap. = capital; res = reserves; dep. = deposits; m. = million; brs = branches; amounts in colones, unless otherwise indicated)

BANKING

Central Bank

Banco Central de Costa Rica: Avdas Central y Primera, Calles 2 y 4, Apdo 10058, 1000 San José; tel. 2243-3333; fax 2243-4566; internet www.bccr.fi.cr; f. 1950; cap. and res –1,276,176.5m., dep. 3,991,482.1m. (Dec. 2009); state-owned; Pres. Dr RODRIGO BOLAÑOS ZAMORA; Gen. Man. FÉLIX DELGADO QUESADA.

State-owned Banks

Banco de Costa Rica (BCR): Avdas Central y 2da, Calles 4 y 6, Apdo 10035,1000 San José; tel. 2287-9000; fax 2255-0911; e-mail ServiciosBancaElectronica@bancobcr.com; internet www.bancobcr.com; f. 1877; responsible for industry; cap. 96,571.5m., res 139,846.3m., dep. 1,766,243.4m. (Dec. 2009); Pres. LUIS CARLOS DELGADO MURILLO; Gen. Man. MARIO RIVERO TURCIOS; 260 brs.

Banco Crédito Agrícola de Cartago (BANCREDITO): Costado sur de la Catedral de Cartago (Iglesia del Carmen), 7050 Cartago; tel. 2550-0202; fax 2222-1911; e-mail zailyn.espinoza@bancreditocr.com; internet www.bancreditocr.com; f. 1918; cap. 14,039.1m., res 18,112.4m., dep. 515,392.3m. (Dec. 2010); Pres. ALVARO DENGO SOLERA (2012).

Banco Nacional de Costa Rica: Avda 1–3, Calle 4, Apdo 10015, 1000 San José; tel. 2212-2000; fax 2255-0270; e-mail bncr@bncr.fi.cr; internet www.bncr.fi.cr; f. 1914; responsible for the agricultural sector; cap. 67,384.4m., res 230,242.6m., dep. 2,806,756.5m. (Dec. 2009); Pres. ALFREDO VOLIO PÉREZ; Gen. Man. FERNANDO NARANJO VILLALOBOS; 150 brs.

Banco Popular y de Desarrollo Comunal: Calle 1, Avda 2, Apdo 10190, 1000 San José; tel. 2211-7000; fax 2258-5259; e-mail popularenlinea@bp.fi.cr; internet www.bancopopular.fi.cr; f. 1969; cap. 130,000m., res 54,225.5m., dep. 1,025,696.8m. (Dec. 2009); Pres. RODOLFO MADRIGAL SABORÍO; Gen. Man. GERARDOS PORRAS SANABRIA.

Private Banks

Banca Promérica, SA: El Cedral, Escazú Trejos Montealegre, Costado Oeste del Hipermás, Apdo 1289, 1200 San José; tel. 2505-7000; fax 2290-1991; e-mail solucion@promerica.fi.cr; internet www.promerica.fi.cr; cap. 18,688.6m., res 1,639.5m., dep.187,941m. (Dec. 2010); Pres. EDGAR ZURCHER; 21 brs.

Banco BAC San José, SA: Calle Central, Avdas 3 y 5, Apdo 5445, 1000 San José; tel. 295-9797; fax 256-7200; e-mail info@bacsanjose.com; internet www.bacsanjose.com; f. 1986; fmrly Bank of America, SA; cap. 77,200m., res 14,779.3m., dep. 890,256.1m. (Dec. 2010); Pres. ERNESTO CASTEGNARO ODIO; Gen. Man. GERARDO CORRALES BRENES; 38 brs.

Banco BCT, SA: 150 m norte de la Catedral Metropolitana, San José; tel. 2212-8000; fax 2222-3706; e-mail info@corporacionbct.com; internet www.bancobct.com; f. 1984; total assets 13,794m. (1999); merged with Banco del Comercio, SA, in 2000; Pres. LEONEL BARUCH.

Banco CMB (Costa Rica), SA: Oficentro Plaza Roble, Edif. El Patio, 4°, Guachipelín de Escazú; tel. 2201-0800; fax 2201-8311; e-mail citibab@sol.racsa.co.cr; internet www.latam.citibank.com/corporate/lacrco/spanish/index.htm; f. 1984 as Banco de Fomento Agrícola; changed name to Banco BFA in 1994 and became Cuscatlan in 2000; current name adopted in 2008 after acquisition by Citi.

Banco HSBC, SA: Barrio Tournón, Diagonal a Ulacit, Apdo 7983, 1000 San José; tel. 2257-1155; fax 2257-1167; e-mail interna@banex.com; internet www.hsbc.fi.cr; f. 1981 as Banco Agroindustrial y de Exportaciones, SA; became Banco Banex SA in 1987; incorporated Banco Metropolitano in 2001 and Banco Bancrecen in 2002; adopted present name in 2007; bought by Banco Davivienda (Colombia) in 2012; cap. 57,597.2m., res 7,649.6m., dep. 492,720.3m. (Dec. 2010); Pres. ALBERTO VALLARINO; Gen. Man. SERGIO RUIZ; 33 brs.

Banco Improsa, SA: Barrio Tournón, costado sur del Periódico La República, San José; tel. 2284-4000; fax 2284-4009; e-mail cramirez@improsa.com; internet www.improsa.com; Gen. Man. FRANCO NARANJO JIMÉNEZ.

Banco Lafise: Fuente de la Hispanidad 50 m este, San Pedro, Montes de Oca; tel. 2246-0800; fax 2280-5090; e-mail info@lafise.fi.cr; internet www.lafise.fi.cr; f. 1974; owned by Grupo Lafise; cap. 3,403.6m., res 258.0m., total assets 3,983.1m. (Dec. 2004); Pres. ROBERTO J. ZAMORA LLANES; Gen. Man. GILBERTO SERRANO.

Bansol (Banco de Soluciones de Costa Rica, SA): Montes de Oca, frente al costado norte del Mall San Pedro, Apdo 10882, 1000 San José; tel. 2528-1800; fax 2528-1880; e-mail info@bansol.fi.cr; internet www.bansol.fi.cr; f. 2010; owned by Grupo Financiera Acobo; internet banking; total assets 9,021.1m. (Dec. 2010); Pres. JACK LOEB; Gen. Man. CARLOS FERNÁNDEZ ROMÁN; 5 brs.

Scotiabank Costa Rica: Frente a la esquina noroeste de La Sabana, Edif. Scotiabank, Apdo 5395, 1000, San José; tel. 2210-4000; fax 2233-13766; e-mail scotiacr@scotiabank.com; internet www.scotiabankcr.com; f. 1995; Pres. CARLOS LOMELI ALONZO; Gen. Man. BRIAN W. BRADY; 13 brs.

Banking Associations

Asociación Bancaria Costarricense: Apdo 7-0810, 1000 San José; tel. 2253-2898; fax 2225-0987; e-mail ejecutiva@abc.fi.cr; internet www.abc.fi.cr; Pres. FRANCO NARANJO.

Cámara de Bancos e Instituciones Financieras de Costa Rica: Edif. Torre Mercedes, 2°, Paseo Colón, San José; tel. 2256-4652; fax 2221-9444; e-mail info@camaradebancos.fi.cr; internet www.camaradebancos.fi.cr; f. 1968; Pres. GUILLERMO QUESADA O.; Exec. Dir ANNABELLE ORTEGA A.

STOCK EXCHANGE

Bolsa Nacional de Valores, SA: Parque Empresarial FORUM (Autopista Próspero Fernández), Apdo 03-6155, 1000 San José; tel. 2204-4848; fax 2204-4749; e-mail servicioalcliente@bolsacr.com; internet www.bolsacr.com; f. 1976; Pres. Dr ORLANDO SOTO ENRÍQUEZ; Vice-Pres. THOMAS FREDERICK ALVARADO ACOSTA.

INSURANCE

State monopoly of the insurance sector was ended in 2008.

Supervisory Authorities

Instituto Nacional de Seguros: Avdas 7 y 9, Calles 9 y 9B, Apdo 10061, 1000 San José; tel. 2287-6000; fax 2255-3381; e-mail contactenos@ins-cr.com; internet www.ins-cr.com; f. 1924; Exec. Pres. Dr GUILLERMO CONSTENLA UMAÑA; Vice-Pres. LUIS ALBERTO CASAFONT FLORES.

Superintendencia General de Seguros (SUGESE): San José; tel. 2243-5151; e-mail sugese@sugese.fi.cr; internet www.sugese.fi.cr; f. 2010; regulates the insurance sector; Supt JAVIER CASCANTE.

Principal Companies

ALICO Costa Rica, SA (American Life Insurance Co): Oficentro Fuentes del Obelisco, 2°, Of. 18, San Rafael de Escazú, San José; tel. 2288-0960; fax 2288-0931; e-mail servicioalcliente@alico.co.cr; internet www.alico.co.cr; f. 2010; part of MetLife Inc; Pres. RICARDO RODOLFO GARCÍA HOLTZ; Gen. Man. LUIS YOUNG VIRZI.

Aseguradora del Istmo (ADISA), SA: Edif. Banco General, 4°, San Rafael de Escazú, San José; e-mail info@adisa.cr; internet www.adisa.cr; f. 2010; Gen. Man. KEVIN LUCAS HOLCOMBE.

ASSA Cía de Seguros, SA: Edif. F, Centro Empresarial Fórum I, 1°, Santa Ana, San José; tel. 2503-2700; fax 2503-2797; e-mail contacto@assanet.com; internet www.assanet.cr; f. 2009; subsidiary of Grupo ASSA, Argentina; Pres. STANLEY MOTTA; Gen. Man. SERGIO RUÍZ.

Caja Costarricense de Seguro Social: Avda 2da, entre calles 5 y 7, Apdo 10105, San José; tel. 2539-0000; fax 2222-1217; e-mail ibalmace@ccss.sa.cr; internet www.info.ccss.sa.cr; accident and health insurance; state-owned; Exec. Pres. Dr ILEANA BALMACEDA ARIAS.

Mapfre Seguros Costa Rica, SA: Edif. Alvasa, 2°, Barrio Tournón, Ruta 32, San José; tel. 2010-3000; e-mail servicioalcliente@mapfre.co.cr; internet www.mapfrecr.com; f. 2010; fmrly Aseguradora Mundial, SA; Pres. MANUEL JOSÉ PAREDES LEFEVRE; Gen. Man. CARLOS GRANGEL LOIRA.

Pan-American Life Insurance de Costa Rica, SA: Edif. Los Balcones B, 3°, Centro Corporativo Plaza Roble, Guachipelín de Escazú, San José; tel. 2505-3600; e-mail servicioalclientecr@

panamericanlife.com; internet www.panamericanlife.com; f. 2010; Country Man. ALFREDO RAMÍREZ.

Seguros del Magisterio, SA: Costado Sur de la Sociedad de Seguros del Vida del Magisterio Nacional, Calle 1, Avda 10, San José; tel. 2523-6704; fax 2222-5431; e-mail info@segurosdemagisterio.com; internet www.segurosdelmagisterio.com/index.htm; f. 2008; Pres. JOSÉ ANTONIO CASTILLO ARAYA; Gen. Man. RAFAEL MONGE CHINCHILLA.

Trade and Industry

GOVERNMENT AGENCIES

Instituto Nacional de Vivienda y Urbanismo (INVU): Avda 9, Calles 3 bis y 5, Apdo 2534-1000, San José; tel. 2256-5265; fax 2223-4006; internet www.invu.go.cr; housing and town planning institute; Exec. Pres. EUGENIA VARGAS GURDIÁN; Gen. Man. MARÍA DEL CARMEN REDONDO SOLÍS.

Promotora del Comercio Exterior de Costa Rica (PROCOMER): Edif. Centro de Comercio Exterior, Avdas 3, Calle 40, Centro Colón, Apdo 1278, 1007 San José; tel. 2299-4700; fax 2233-5755; e-mail info@procomer.com; internet www.procomer.com; f. 1997 to improve international competitiveness by providing services aimed at increasing, diversifying and expediting international trade; Pres. ANABEL GONZÁLEZ CAMPABADAL; Dir ROBERTO CALVO.

DEVELOPMENT ORGANIZATIONS

Cámara de Azucareros: Calle 3, Avda Fernández Güell, Apdo 1577, 1000 San José; tel. 2221-2103; fax 2222-1358; e-mail nalfaro@laica.co.cr; f. 1949; sugar growers; 16 mems; Pres. FEDERICO CHAVARRÍA K; Exec. Dir NIDIA ALFARO.

Cámara Nacional de Bananeros: Edif. Urcha, 3°, Calle 11, Avda 6, Apdo 10273, 1000 San José; tel. 2222-7891; fax 2233-1268; e-mail canaba@ice.co.cr; internet canabacr.com; f. 1967; banana growers; Pres. JORGE OSBORNE; Exec. Dir MARÍA DE LOS ANGELES VINDAS.

Cámara Nacional de Cafetaleros: Condominio Oroki 4D, La Uruca, Apdo 1310, San José; tel. and fax 2296-8334; e-mail camcafe@ice.co.cr; f. 1948; 30 mems; coffee millers and growers; Pres. RODRIGO VARGAS RUÍZ; Exec. Dir GABRIELA LOBO H.

Coalición Costarricense de Iniciativas de Desarrollo (CINDE) (Costa Rican Investment Promotion Agency): Edif. Los Balcones, Plaza Roble, 4°, Guachipelin, Ezcazú; tel. 2201-2800; fax 2201-2867; e-mail invest@cinde.org; internet www.cinde.org; f. 1983; coalition for development of initiatives to attract foreign investment for production and export of new products; Chair. ALBERTO TREJOS; CEO EDNA CAMACHO.

Corporación Bananera Nacional, SA (CORBANA): Zapote frente Casa Presidencial, Apdo 6504-1000 San José; tel. 2202-4700; fax 2234-9421; e-mail corbana@racsa.co.cr; internet www.corbana.co.cr; f. 1971; public co; cultivation and wholesale of agricultural produce, incl. bananas; Pres. JORGE SAUMA; Man. ROMANO ORLICH.

InfoAgro (Sistema de Información del Sector Agropecuario): Ministerio de Agricultura y Ganadería, Antigüo Colegio La Salle, Sabana Sur, San José; tel. 2296-2579; fax 2296-1652; e-mail infoagro@mag.go.cr; internet www.infoagro.go.cr; state agency; dissemination of information to promote the agricultural sector; Nat. Co-ordinator ANA ISABEL GÓMEZ DE MIGUEL.

Instituto del Café de Costa Rica: Calle 1, Avdas 18 y 20, Apdo 37, 1000 San José; tel. 2222-6411; fax 2222-2838; internet www.icafe.go.cr; e-mail promo@icafe.go.cr; f. 1933 to develop the coffee industry, to control production and to regulate marketing; Exec. Dir RONALD PETERS SEEVERS.

CHAMBERS OF COMMERCE

Cámara de Comercio de Costa Rica: Urb. Tournón, 125 m noroeste del parqueo del Centro Comercial El Pueblo, Goicochea, Apdo 1114, 1000 San José; tel. 2221-0005; fax 2223-1157; e-mail camara@camara-comercio.com; internet www.camara-comercio.com; f. 1915; 900 mems; Pres. ARNOLDO ANDRÉ TINOCO; Exec. Dir ALONSO ELIZONDO BOLAÑOS.

Cámara de Industrias de Costa Rica: 350 m sur de la Fuente de la Hispanidad, San Pedro de Montes de Oca, Apdo 10003, San José; tel. 2202-5600; fax 2234-6163; e-mail cicr@cicr.com; internet www.cicr.com; Pres. MARCO MENESES GRANADOS; Exec. Vice-Pres. MARTHA CASTILLO DÍAZ.

Unión Costarricense de Cámaras y Asociaciones de la Empresa Privada (UCCAEP): De McDonald's en Sabana Sur, 400 m al sur, 100 m al este, 25 m al sur, San José; tel. 2290-5595; fax 2290-5596; e-mail uccaep@uccaep.or.cr; internet www.uccaep.or.cr; f. 1974; business fed; Pres. MANUEL H. RODRÍGUEZ PEYTON; Exec. Dir SHIRLEY SABORÍO MARCHENA.

INDUSTRIAL AND TRADE ASSOCIATIONS

Asociación de Empresas de Zonas Francas (AZOFRAS): Plaza Mayor, 2°, Pavas, San José; tel. 2520-1635; fax 2520-1636; e-mail azofras@racsa.co.cr; internet www.azofras.com; f. 1990; Pres. JORGE BRENES; Exec. Dir ALVARO VALVERDE PALAVICINI.

Cámara Nacional de Agricultura y Agroindustria: 300 m sur y 50 m este de McDonald's, Plaza del Sol, Curridabat, Apdo 1671, 1000 San José; tel. 2280-0996; fax 2280-0969; e-mail camaradeagricultura@cnaacr.com; internet www.cnaacr.com; f. 1947; Pres. ALVARO SÁENZ SABORÍO; Exec. Dir MARTÍN CALDERÓN CHAVES.

Consejo Nacional de Producción: 125 m al sur de Yamuni La Sabana en Avda 10, Apdo 2205, San José; tel. 2257-9355; fax 2256-9625; e-mail sim@cnp.go.cr; internet www.cnp.go.cr; f. 1948 to encourage agricultural and fish production and to regulate production and distribution of basic commodities; state-run; Gen. Man. ZORAIDA FALLAS CORDERO.

Instituto de Desarrollo Agrario (IDA): Ofs Centrales IDA, Moravia, Residencial Los Colegios, frente al IFAM, Apdo 5054, 1000 San José; tel. 2247-7400; fax 2241-4891; internet www.ida.go.cr; Exec. Pres. ROLANDO BGONZÁLEZ ULLOA; Gen. Man. VÍCTOR JULIO CARVAJAL GARRO.

Instituto Mixto de Ayuda Social (IMAS): Calle 29, Avdas 2 y 4, Apdo 6213, San José; tel. 2202-4066; fax 2224-8930; e-mail gerencia_general@imas.go.cr; internet www.imas.go.cr; Exec. Pres. FERNANDO MARÍN ROJAS; Gen. Man. MARGARITA FERNÁNDEZ GARITA.

Instituto Nacional de Fomento Cooperativo: Avdas 5 y 7, Calle 20 Norte, Apdo 10103, 1000 San José; tel. 2256-2944; fax 2255-3835; e-mail info@infocoop.go.cr; internet www.infocoop.go.cr; f. 1973 to encourage the establishment of co-operatives and to provide technical assistance and credit facilities; Pres. FREDDY GONZÁLEZ ROJAS; Exec. Dir MARTÍN ROBLES ROBLES.

UTILITIES

Regulatory Body

Autoridad Reguladora de los Servicios Públicos (ARESEP): Edif. Turrubares, Complejo Multipark, 100 m norte Construplaza, Guachipelín de Escazú, Apdo 936, 1000 San José; tel. 2506-3200; fax 2215-6052; e-mail cmora@aresep.go.cr; internet www.aresep.go.cr; f. 1996; oversees telecommunications, public utilities and transport sectors; Regulator Gen. DENNIS MELÉNDEZ HOWELL.

Electricity

Instituto Costarricense de Electricidad (ICE): Apdo 10032, 1000 San José; tel. 2220-7720; fax 2220-1555; e-mail ice-si@ice.co.cr; internet www.ice.co.cr; f. 1949; govt agency for power and telecommunications; Exec. Pres. PEDRO PABLO QUIRÓS CORTÉZ; Dir TEÓFILO DE LA TORRE ARGUELLO.

Cía Nacional de Fuerza y Luz, SA (CNFL): Calle Central y 1, Avda 5, Apdo 10026, 1000 San José; tel. 2296-4608; fax 2296-3950; e-mail info@cnfl.go.cr; internet www.cnfl.go.cr; f. 1941; electricity co; mem. of ICE Group; Gen. Man. PABLO COB.

JASEC (Junta Administrativa del Servicio Eléctrico Municipal de Cartago): Apdo 179, 7050 Cartago; tel. 2550-6800; fax 2551-1683; e-mail agomez@jasec.co.cr; internet www.jasec.co.cr; f. 1964; Pres. ALFONSO VÍQUEZ SÁNCHEZ.

Water

Instituto Costarricense de Acueductos y Alcantarillados: Edif. Central, Pavas, 1000 San José; tel. 2242-5591; fax 2222-2259; e-mail centrodoc@aya.go.cr; internet www.aya.go.cr; water and sewerage; Pres. OSCAR NÚÑEZ CALVO.

TRADE UNIONS

Asociación Nacional de Empleados Públicos (ANEP): Casa Sindical, Calle 20 norte, 300 N Hospital Nacional de Niños, frente a Coopeservidores, Apdo 5152, 1000 San José; tel. 2257-8233; fax 2257-8859; e-mail info@anep.or.cr; internet www.anep.or.cr; f. 1958; Sec.-Gen. ALBINO VARGAS BARRANTES.

Central del Movimiento de Trabajadores Costarricenses (CMTC) (Costa Rican Workers' Union): Calle 20, 200 m norte del Hospital de Niños, 1000 San José; tel. 2221-7701; fax 2221-3353; e-mail info@cmtccr.org; internet www.cmtccr.org; f. 1994; Pres. OLMAN CHINCILLA; 108,000 mems (2011).

Confederación de Trabajadores Rerum Novarum (CTRN): Barrio Escalante, de la Rotonda el Farolito 250 m este, Apdo 31100, San José; tel. 2283-4244; fax 2234-2282; e-mail ctrn@ice.co.cr; internet www.rerumnovarum.or.cr; Pres. RODRIGO AGUILAR ARCE; Sec.-Gen. SERGIO SABORÍO BRENES.

Transport

Autoridad Reguladora de los Servicios Públicos (ARESEP): regulatory body for the telecommunications industry, public utilities and transport (see Trade and Industry—Utilities).

RAILWAYS

AmericaTravel: Edif. INCOFER, Estación al Pacífico, Avda 20, Calle 2, Apdo 246, 1009 San José; tel. 2233-3300; fax 2223-3311; e-mail americatravel@ice.co.cr; operates weekend tourist trains between San José and Caldera; Gen. Man. JUAN PANIAGUA ZELEDÓN.

Instituto Costarricense de Ferrocarriles (INCOFER): Calle Central, Avda 22 y 24, Apdo 1, 1009 San José; tel. 2222-8857; fax 2222-6998; e-mail incofer@sol.racsa.co.cr; f. 1985; govt-owned; 471 km, of which 388 km are electrified; in 1995 INCOFER suspended most operations, pending privatization, although some cargo transport continued; by mid-2009 a wide range of rail lines had reopened; Pres. MIGUEL CARABAGUÍAZ.

ROADS

In 2008 there were 38,049 km of roads, of which 25% were paved. In 2009 the Government and the Andean Promotion Corporation signed a US $60m. loan agreement for the Atlantic Corridor Investment Program. The project included construction of a new highway between the Atlantic ports of Costa Rica and Nicaragua, as well as a new bridge over the Sixaola river on the border with Panama. In October 2010 the Central American Bank for Economic Integration approved a loan of US $140m. for the San José–San Carlos highway. This was expected to improve access between the capital and the north of the country.

Consejo Nacional de Vialidad (CONAVI): 50 m este y 10 m norte de la Rotonda Betania, Apdo 616, Zapote, 2010 San José; tel. 2202-5300; e-mail contraloria@conavi.go.cr; internet www.conavi.go.cr; f. 1998; Exec. Dir CARLOS ACOSTA MONGE.

SHIPPING

Local services operate between the Costa Rican ports of Puntarenas and Limón and those of Colón and Cristóbal in Panama and other Central American ports. Caldera on the Gulf of Nicoya is the main Pacific port. The Caribbean coast is served by the port complex of Limón/Moín.

Instituto Costarricense de Puertos del Pacífico (INCOP): Calle 36, Avda 3, Apdo 543, 1000 San José; tel. 2634-9100; fax 2634-9105; e-mail info@incop.go.cr; internet www.incop.go.cr; f. 1972; state agency for the development of Pacific ports; Exec. Pres. URIAS UGALDE VARELA; Gen. Man. WITMAN CRUZ MÉNDEZ.

Junta de Administración Portuaria y de Desarrollo Económico de la Vertiente Atlántica (JAPDEVA): Calle 17, Avda 7, Apdo 5.330, 1000 San José; tel. 2795-4747; fax 2795-0728; e-mail cthomas@japdeva.go.cr; internet www.japdeva.go.cr; f. 1963; state agency for the devt of Atlantic ports; Exec. Pres. ALLAN HIDALGO CAMPOS; Gen. Man. CARLOS THOMAS ARROYO.

Principal Shipping Companies

Inter-Moves SG Global de Costa Rica: Apdo 11990, 1000 San Jose; tel. 2241-2147; fax 2241-2260; e-mail info@intermoves-sgcr.com; internet www.intermoves-sgcr.com; shipping, freight forwarding and logistics; Gen. Man. JOSÉ ANTONIO SUEIRAS.

Maersk Costa Rica, SA: San José; tel. 2543-5100; fax 2543-5150; e-mail crics@maersk.com; internet www.maerskline.com; f. 1994; subsidiary of Maersk Line (Denmark); Man. PAOLO JIMENEZ.

Puerto Limon Agency: 800 este y 100 sur Plaza del Sol, San José; tel. 2758-2062; fax 2758-2022; e-mail info@limonagency.com; internet www.limonagency.com.

CIVIL AVIATION

Costa Rica has four international airports: Juan Santamaría Airport, the largest, 16 km from San José at El Coco, Tobías Bolaños Airport in Pavas, Daniel Oduber Quirós Airport, at Liberia, and Limón International.

Fly Latin America: San José; tel. 2256-3222; e-mail info@flylatinamerica.net; internet www.flylatinamerica.com; operates services to 9 destinations in Central and South America; Pres. CHARLES STRATFORD; Man. RICHARD KRUG.

Nature Air: Tobías Bolaños Airport, Hangar 27, San José; tel. 2299-6000; fax 2232-2516; e-mail info@natureair.com; internet www.natureair.com; f. 2000; flights from San José to 15 domestic destinations; international destinations include Nicaragua and Panama; carbon-neutral airline; CEO ALEX KHAJAVI.

Servicios Aéreos Nacionales, SA (SANSA): Edif. TACA, La Uruca, San José; tel. 2290-3543; fax 2290-3538; e-mail infosansa@taca.com; internet www.flysansa.com; subsidiary of TACA; international, regional and domestic scheduled passenger and cargo services; Man. Dir CARLOS MANUEL DELGADO AGUILAR.

Tourism

Costa Rica boasts a system of nature reserves and national parks unique in the world, covering one-third of the country. Some 2,099,829 tourists visited Costa Rica in 2010, while tourism receipts totalled a provisional US $2,111m. Most visitors came from the USA (40%).

Cámara Nacional de Turismo de Costa Rica (CANATUR): Zapote, de la Universidad Veritas, 200 m hacia el este, San José; tel. 2234-6222; fax 2253-8102; e-mail supervisor@canatur.org; internet www.canatur.org; f. 1974; Pres. JUAN CARLOS RAMOS TORRES; Exec. Dir MAURICIO CÉSPEDES.

Instituto Costarricense de Turismo (ICT): La Uruca, Costado Este del Puente Juan Pablo II, Apdo 777, 1000 San José; tel. 2299-5876; fax 2220-3559; e-mail info@visitcostarica.com; internet www.visitcostarica.com; f. 1931; Exec. Pres. ALLAN RENE FLORES MOYA; Gen. Man. JUAN CARLOS BORBON MARKS.

Defence

Costa Rica has had no armed forces since 1948. As assessed at November 2011, Rural and Civil Guards totalled 2,000 and 4,500 men and women, respectively. In addition, there were 2,500 Border Security Police. There was also a Coast Guard Unit numbering 400 and an Air Surveillance Unit of 400.

Security Budget: an estimated 175,000m. colones in 2012.

Minister of Governance, Police and Public Security: MARIO ZAMORA CORDERO.

Education

Education in Costa Rica is free, and is compulsory between six and 13 years of age. Primary education begins at the age of six and lasts for six years. Official secondary education consists of a three-year basic course, followed by a more specialized course lasting two years in academic schools and three years in technical schools. In 2009/10 a total of 520,609 students attended primary schools. In 2008/09 secondary enrolment was equivalent to 96% of children in the relevant age-group. In 2009 there were 4,071 primary schools and 59 universities. There were 708 secondary schools in 2005. The provision for education in the 2010 government budget was 1,200m. colones, equivalent to 6.9% of total government spending.

CÔTE D'IVOIRE

(THE IVORY COAST)

Introductory Survey

LOCATION, CLIMATE, LANGUAGE, RELIGION, FLAG, CAPITAL

The Republic of Côte d'Ivoire lies on the west coast of Africa, between Ghana to the east and Liberia to the west, with Guinea, Mali and Burkina Faso to the north. Average temperatures vary between 21°C and 30°C (70°F and 86°F). The main rainy season, May–July, is followed by a shorter wet season in October–November. The official language is French, and a large number of African languages are also spoken. At the time of the 1998 census it was estimated that some 34% of the population were Christians (mainly Roman Catholics), 27% Muslims, 15% followed traditional indigenous beliefs, and 3% practised other religions, while 21% had no religious affiliation. (However, it was thought that the proportion of Muslims was, in fact, significantly higher, as the majority of unregistered foreign workers in Côte d'Ivoire were believed to be Muslims.) The national flag (proportions 2 by 3) has three equal vertical stripes, of orange, white and green. The political and administrative capital is Yamoussoukro, although most government ministries and offices remain in the former capital, Abidjan, which is the major centre for economic activity.

CONTEMPORARY POLITICAL HISTORY

Historical Context

Formerly a province of French West Africa, Côte d'Ivoire achieved self-government, within the French Community, in December 1958. Dr Félix Houphouët-Boigny, leader of the Parti démocratique de la Côte d'Ivoire—Rassemblement démocratique africain (PDCI—RDA), became Prime Minister in 1959. The country became fully independent on 7 August 1960; a new Constitution was adopted in October 1960, and Houphouët-Boigny became President in November.

Until 1990 the PDCI—RDA was Côte d'Ivoire's only legal political party, despite constitutional provision for the existence of other political organizations. A high rate of economic growth, together with strong support from France, contributed, until the late 1980s, to the stability of the regime. However, the announcement in early 1990 of austerity measures precipitated an unprecedented level of unrest. In April Houphouët-Boigny appointed Alassane Ouattara, the Governor of the Banque centrale des états de l'Afrique de l'ouest (BCEAO, the regional central bank), to chair a special commission to formulate economic and political reforms. From May it was announced that hitherto unofficial political organizations were to be formally recognized.

Domestic Political Affairs

Côte d'Ivoire's first contested presidential election was held on 28 October 1990. Houphouët-Boigny—challenged by Laurent Gbagbo, the candidate of the socialist Front populaire ivoirien (FPI)—was re-elected for a seventh term with the support of 81.7% of votes cast. In November the legislature, the Assemblée nationale, approved two constitutional amendments. The first authorized the President of the legislature to assume the functions of the President of the Republic, in the event of the presidency becoming vacant, until the expiry of the previous incumbent's mandate (an arrangement that had existed, on an interim basis, since October 1985, following the abolition of the post of Vice-President of the Republic). The second amendment provided for the appointment of a Prime Minister, who would be accountable to the President; Ouattara was subsequently designated premier. At legislative elections that month the PDCI—RDA returned 163 deputies to the 175-member Assemblée nationale; the FPI won nine seats, the Parti ivoirien des travailleurs (PIT) one, and two independent candidates were elected. Henri Konan Bédié, who had held the presidency of the legislature since 1980, was re-elected to that post.

The Government's response to the report of a commission of inquiry into student disturbances in May–June 1991, in which one student died, provoked renewed violence in early 1992, led by the outlawed Fédération estudiantine et scolaire de Côte d'Ivoire (FESCI). Houphouët-Boigny refused to subject the armed forces Chief of General Staff, Brig.-Gen. Robert Gueï, to disciplinary proceedings, despite the commission's conclusion that Gueï was ultimately responsible for violent acts perpetrated by forces under his command. In February Gbagbo was among more than 100 people arrested during a violent anti-Government demonstration in Abidjan, and in March was one of nine opposition leaders imprisoned under a new presidential ordinance that rendered political leaders responsible for violent acts committed by their supporters.

Houphouët-Boigny left Côte d'Ivoire in May 1993 to receive medical treatment in Europe. As the President's health failed, controversy arose over the issue of succession. Many senior politicians, including Ouattara and Gbagbo (both of whom were known to have presidential aspirations), asserted that the process defined in the Constitution effectively endorsed an 'hereditary presidency', since Bédié, like Houphouët-Boigny, was a member of the Akan ethnic group. Houphouët-Boigny died on 7 December and Bédié assumed the duties of President of the Republic with immediate effect. Ouattara refused to recognize Bédié's right of succession and tendered his resignation two days later. Bédié's position was consolidated by his election to the chairmanship of the PDCI—RDA in April 1994. Disaffected members of the PDCI—RDA left the party in June to form what they termed a moderate, centrist organization, the Rassemblement des républicains (RDR); Ouattara formally announced his membership of the RDR in early 1995.

A new electoral code, adopted in December 1994, imposed new restrictions on eligibility for public office, notably stipulating that candidates for the presidency or for the Assemblée nationale be of direct Ivorian descent. The RDR protested that these restrictions would prevent Ouattara from contesting the presidency, since the former Prime Minister was of Burkinabè descent and would also be affected by the code's requirement that candidates had been continuously resident in Côte d'Ivoire for five years prior to seeking election.

In October 1995 the FPI (which was to have been represented by Gbagbo) and the RDR (whose Secretary-General, Djény Kobina, was to have replaced Ouattara as the party's candidate) announced their boycott of the forthcoming presidential election as long as the conditions were not 'clear and open'. Subsequent negotiations involving Bédié and opposition groups made no effective progress, and the presidential election took place, as scheduled, on 22 October 1995, following a week of violence in several towns. Bédié, with 95.3% of the valid votes cast, secured an overwhelming victory.

In December 1999 a mutiny by soldiers demanding salary increases, the payment of outstanding arrears and the reinstatement of Gueï as armed forces Chief of General Staff rapidly escalated into a *coup d'état*. (Gueï had been replaced in this position in October 1995.) On 24 December 1999 Gueï announced that he had assumed power at the head of a Comité national de salut public (CNSP), and that the Constitution and its institutions had been suspended. In January 2000 Bédié left Côte d'Ivoire; he subsequently sought refuge in France. A controversial draft Constitution, presented in May, demanded that presidential candidates be of only Ivorian nationality and parentage. The revised Constitution was endorsed by 86.5% of votes cast in a referendum on 23–24 July, with turn-out estimated at 56%. Notably, all those involved in the *coup d'état* and members of the CNSP were granted immunity from prosecution.

Gbagbo becomes President

Preliminary results of the presidential election held on 22 October 2000 indicated that Gbagbo had received a greater percentage of votes cast than Gueï; however, on 24 October the Ministry of the Interior and Decentralization dissolved the national electoral commission and declared Gueï the winner of the election. The Government claimed that certain, unspecified, political parties had perpetrated electoral fraud, and announced that, following the readjustment of the results, Gueï, with 52.7% of the votes cast, had defeated Gbagbo, with 41.0%. Following clashes between rival army factions in the military barracks in Abidjan, and a declaration of support for Gbagbo by the Chief of Staff of the Armed Forces, Gueï fled, and Gbagbo declared himself President.

According to official figures released by the electoral commission, and confirmed by the Supreme Court, Gbagbo had secured 59.4% of the valid votes cast, while Gueï had received 32.7%. However, a low rate of participation (an estimated 33.2% overall, but markedly lower in the largely Muslim and RDR-supporting regions in the north, as well as in Yamoussoukro and other strongholds of the PDCI—RDA) cast doubt on the legitimacy of Gbagbo's victory. Concern was raised that Gbagbo had voiced support, during his campaign, for the notion of strengthening national identity, or '*ivoirité*', in potentially inflammatory terms, similar to those used previously by Bédié. Gbagbo was inaugurated as President on 26 October 2000. The following day Gbagbo appointed a new Council of Ministers, comprising members of the FPI, the PDCI—RDA and the PIT. (The RDR stated that it would await legislative elections before participating in a coalition government.) Pascal Affi N'Guessan, the manager of Gbagbo's electoral campaign and a minister in the outgoing Government, was named as Prime Minister.

Legislative elections proceeded on 10 December 2000, although violent clashes between RDR supporters and the security forces prevented voting in 28 northern constituencies. Electoral turn-out was low, at 31.5%. The FPI won 96 of the 225 seats in the Assemblée nationale, the PDCI—RDA 77, the PIT four, and independent candidates 17, while a 'moderate' faction of the RDR secured one seat.

At the remaining legislative elections, held in mid-January 2001, the PDCI—RDA secured 17 of the 26 contested seats, increasing its overall representation in the Assemblée nationale to 94 seats, only two less than the FPI. Independent candidates won five seats and the RDR faction four. Only 13.3% of eligible voters participated in the elections. The legislative balance of power remained unclear, and it soon emerged that seven of the 22 nominally independent deputies had been financed by the PDCI—RDA and were to return to that party. A further 14 independents formed a parliamentary alliance with the FPI and, in February, created a new centre-right party with some 50 other former members of the PDCI—RDA, the Union pour la démocratie et pour la paix de la Côte d'Ivoire (UDPCI).

Attempted coup

On 19 September 2002, while Gbagbo was on a state visit to Italy, a co-ordinated armed rebellion broke out, almost simultaneously, in Bouaké, Korhogo and Abidjan. The unrest in Abidjan culminated in an attack on a military barracks and the assassination of Emile Boga Doudou, the Minister of State, Minister of the Interior and Decentralization. Gueï, who had recently gained in prominence as a critic of the Government, was also killed. Although some 300 people were killed in the city, government troops rapidly regained control of Abidjan. However, two ministers were held hostage for several days in the north, which remained under rebel control. Gbagbo, following his return to Côte d'Ivoire on 20 September, implied that an unnamed foreign country (widely understood to refer to Burkina Faso) was implicated in the insurgency, which he described as an attempted *coup d'état*.

Continuing unrest in the north prompted widespread concern across West Africa. In late September 2002 an emergency summit of the Economic Community of West African States (ECOWAS, see p. 264) resolved to dispatch a military mission to act as a 'buffer' between government and rebel troops, and mandated a 'contact group', comprising six Heads of State, to undertake negotiations between Gbagbo and the insurgents. In early October Master-Sgt Tuo Fozié emerged as a spokesman for the rebels, who identified themselves as the Mouvement patriotique de la Côte d'Ivoire (MPCI) and stated as their principal demand the removal of Gbagbo from the presidency and the holding of fresh elections. By late October demands for a rejection of any compromise with rebel groups were being expressed by the Coordination des jeunes patriotes (CJP), a movement led by Charles Blé Goudé, a former leader of the FESCI and an ally of Gbagbo. Nevertheless, at the end of October the Government and the MPCI entered into negotiations in Lomé, Togo, under the aegis of ECOWAS; another former leader of the FESCI, Guillaume Kigbafori Soro, now the Secretary-General of the recently formed political wing of the MPCI, led the rebel delegation.

In November 2002 national security deteriorated further, with the emergence of two new rebel groups, apparently unconnected to the MPCI, in western regions. The Mouvement populaire ivoirien du grand ouest (MPIGO) and the Mouvement pour la justice et la paix (MJP) both announced their intention of taking vengeance for Gueï's death, and by the end of the month had gained control of the cities of Man and Danane, near the border with Liberia. In December the French Minister of Defence announced that French troops in Côte d'Ivoire were henceforth to be permitted to use force to maintain the cease-fire; France was to increase its contingent of troops in the country to number some 2,500, while the deployment of the ECOWAS mission remained in abeyance.

Representatives of the Ivorian Government, seven political parties and the three rebel groups attended the Marcoussis summit (in France), which commenced on 15 January 2003. On 18 January the first contingent of the ECOWAS military mission (ECOMICI) arrived in Côte d'Ivoire. Although unrest continued, on 24 January unanimous agreement on a peace plan was reached by all parties involved in the negotiations. In accordance with this plan, Gbagbo was to remain as President until the expiry of his term of office in 2005, but was to share power with a new Prime Minister, appointed by consensus, at the head of a government of national reconciliation; the premier was to be forbidden from contesting the subsequent presidential election. Rebel groups and opposition parties were to receive government posts.

Further delays in the formation of the proposed government of national reconciliation resulted from the deteriorating security situation, although on 8 March 2003 an ECOWAS summit in Accra, Ghana, resulted in an agreement on the allocation of ministerial portfolios; the FPI was to be given 10 posts, the PDCI—RDA eight, the RDR and the MPCI seven each, and the MJP and the MPIGO one each, while four smaller parties were to receive a total of six posts. The defence and security portfolios were to be excluded from these arrangements. Instead, a 15-member Conseil de la securité nationale (CSN), comprising the President, the Prime Minister, the Chief of Staff of the Armed Forces, the leaders of the gendarmerie and the police force, and representatives of the political parties and groups in the Government of National Reconciliation, was to be established to monitor the operations of these ministries, and to approve Prime Minister Seydou Diarra's nominees to these posts.

Further difficulties were encountered prior to the inaugural session of the Council of Ministers on 13 March 2003 with the MPCI, the MPIGO and the MJP refusing to attend meetings at which ministerial posts were to be allocated and later that month Gbagbo issued a decree confirming a CSN decision that two existing ministers, from the FPI and the RDR, were to assume additional responsibilities for the security and defence ministries, on an interim basis. These interim appointments were denounced by the MPCI, which denied that its representative on the CSN had consented to the measures. In mid-April the first full meeting of the Council of Ministers was held; among the former rebels appointed to the Government were Soro, as Minister of State, Minister of Communication, and Fozié, as Minister of Youth and Public Service, while the military leader of the MPCI, Col Michel Gueu, was appointed as Minister of Sports and Leisure.

In early May 2003 the Chief of Staff of the Armed Forces, Gen. Mathias Doué, and Gueu signed a cease-fire agreement, which was intended to apply to all rebel groups operating within the country. In mid-June the national army and rebel forces agreed to the eventual confinement of troops, and by the end of the month it was reported that order had been restored in western regions. In late June the UN Mission in Côte d'Ivoire (MINUCI), authorized by the UN Security Council in May and charged with overseeing the implementation of the Marcoussis Accords, commenced operations in Abidjan, and on 4 July MPCI leaders formally announced the end of the conflict. In August the Assemblée nationale approved legislation providing for an amnesty for those involved in political unrest between 17 September 2000 and 19 September 2002, excluding those involved in abuses of human rights or violations of international humanitarian law. By the end of August 2003 more than 50 political prisoners had been released. Meanwhile, the MPCI effectively absorbed the MPIGO and MJP, and announced that the organization was henceforth to be known as the Forces nouvelles (FN).

Effective division of the country

In early December 2003 Gbagbo announced that the former rebel forces in the north of the country would commence disarmament later that month, several months later than had been initially planned. In the event the disarmament process was further delayed, although some 40 government soldiers that had been held as prisoners-of-war in FN-controlled areas were, none the less, released. Also that month the Council of Ministers approved legislation that permitted presidential candidates to have only one parent of Ivorian origin, rather than two.

In February 2003 the UN Security Council established the UN Operation in Côte d'Ivoire (UNOCI, see p. 96); with an authorized military strength of 6,240, the peace-keeping operation was deployed for an initial period of 12 months from early April, when authority was transferred from MINUCI and ECOMICI to UNOCI. Nevertheless, the process of national reconciliation appeared to be stalling, with Soro's announcement that former rebel fighters would not disarm prior to legislative and presidential elections scheduled for 2005.

In March 2004 clashes occurred between members of the security forces and protesters following a demonstration in Abidjan, organized by seven of the 10 signatory parties of the Marcoussis Accords (known collectively as the G7). According to official figures, 37 people were killed, although opposition sources estimated the number of deaths at more than 300. An inquiry, conducted by the office of the UN High Commissioner for Human Rights (see p. 15), concluded that the security forces had been responsible for the killings of at least 120 civilians in a 'carefully planned operation' organized by 'the highest authorities of the state'. Following the outbreak of violence, the RDR, the FN and the Mouvement des forces d'avenir (MFA) announced that they were to suspend their participation in the Government.

In mid-April 2004 President Gbagbo acceded to the G7's principal demands in an attempt to restore some stability, agreeing to allow equal access to the state media to all political organizations, to respect the right to demonstrate and to ensure the security of the people. The peace process remained stalled, however, and in mid-May Gbagbo dismissed three opposition ministers from the Government, including Soro, replacing them, in an acting capacity, with members of the FPI. Soro had previously urged FN ministers to return to Bouaké from Abidjan, after Gbagbo had threatened to suspend their salaries and restrict their freedom to travel in response to their boycott of government meetings.

All parties to the conflict attended a meeting of West African heads of state in Accra in July 2004, convened by the UN Secretary-General and the President of Ghana, at which they signed an agreement on means of implementing the Marcoussis Accords. The agreement, which was to be monitored by UNOCI, ECOWAS and the African Union (AU, see p. 189), stated that disarmament of the rebels was to commence by 15 October. In mid-August, in accordance with the agreement, Gbagbo reinstated the three government ministers dismissed in May, and all ministers from opposition parties and rebel groups resumed participation in the Government. Shortly afterwards Gbagbo delegated some of his powers to the Prime Minister pending a presidential election scheduled for October 2005. However, the disarmament deadline was not observed by the former rebels, who declared that insufficient progress had been made towards the realization of the proposed political reforms.

In early November 2004 the 18-month cease-fire was broken when the Ivorian air force launched bombing raids on Bouaké and other targets in the north of the country, reportedly resulting in the deaths of nine French peace-keeping troops, together with a US aid consultant. In retaliation, French forces, acting on the direct orders of President Jacques Chirac, destroyed the Ivorian air force on the ground. This precipitated several days of violence in Abidjan and elsewhere, with thousands of Ivorians, in particular members of Blé Goudé's CJP, rioting, looting and attacking French and other foreign targets. French troops intervened to take control of Abidjan's airport and major thoroughfares and to protect French and other foreign nationals, clashing with rioters and protesters in the process (see below). On 15 November the UN Security Council voted unanimously in favour of imposing a 13-month arms embargo, drafted by France, on Côte d'Ivoire (the embargo was reinforced by a further Security Council resolution in February 2005, although additional sanctions regarding the assets and travel movements of specific political figures were not enforced). Meanwhile, Soro and eight other opposition ministers announced that they would not attend meetings of the Government, claiming that their security in Abidjan could not be guaranteed.

Towards rebel disarmament

In November and December 2004 the South African President, Thabo Mbeki, designated as mediator by the AU, held talks with both the Ivorian Government and the FN aimed at re-establishing the Marcoussis Accords as the basis for solution of the crisis. Despite a number of concessions made by Gbagbo, unrest intensified in February–March 2005 and on 4 April the mandate of the UNOCI and French peace-keeping troops was extended for one month. (The mandate was extended for a further month on 4 May, and for an interim period of 21 days on 3 June, pending a reassessment of the mandate of UNOCI.)

In early April 2005 Mbeki hosted a summit in Pretoria, South Africa, attended by Bédié, Diarra, Gbagbo, Ouattara and Soro, as a result of which an agreement was signed, on 6 April, committing all parties to the disbandment of militia groups and to the disarmament of the former rebel troops. Conditions for eligibility of presidential candidates at the election due to be held in October were to be decided separately by Mbeki, following consultation with the UN Secretary-General, Kofi Annan, and the Chairman of the AU, the President of Nigeria, Olusegun Obasanjo. One week later, in a letter to the signatories of the Pretoria agreement, Mbeki ruled that the Ivorian Constitutional Council should confirm the candidates of those parties that signed the Marcoussis Accords; this was interpreted as permitting Ouattara's eventual candidacy. Two of the FN ministers subsequently resumed participation in the Government. Later that month Gbagbo declared that he would accept Ouattara as a legitimate candidate at the presidential election.

In mid-May 2005 the FN and the Ivorian armed forces agreed that disarmament of the former rebel forces would commence on 27 June and be completed by 10 August, and that a new republican army would be established to incorporate members of the existing armed forces and former rebel fighters. Later that month the PDCI—RDA, the RDR, the MFA and the UDPCI formed a new alliance, known as the Rassemblement des Houphouëtistes pour la démocratie et la paix (RHDP), and agreed that, in the event of the presidential election progressing to a second round (which would occur if no candidate received an absolute majority of votes cast in the first round), all four parties would support a common candidate in opposition to Gbagbo.

On 24 June 2005 the UN Security Council extended the mandate of UNOCI and the French peace-keeping forces for a further seven months, until January 2006, broadening the mandate granted to UNOCI to include an active role in disarmament, support for the organization of elections and the establishment of the rule of law and increasing its authorized military strength to 7,090. At the end of June 2005, following two days of talks in Pretoria, it was agreed that the dismantling of pro-Government militias would commence immediately and be completed by 20 August, while legislation providing for the establishment of an independent electoral commission would be approved by mid-July. Following further negotiations, the timetable for disarmament was revised again: some 40,500 former rebels and 15,000 pro-Government troops were to assemble at cantonment sites from 31 July and surrender their weapons between 26 September and 3 October. Later that month Gbagbo approved a number of legislative reforms, notably concerning nationality, citizenship rights and the establishment of an independent electoral commission, using his exceptional constitutional powers to override the requirement for parliamentary approval.

The FN refused to begin the disarmament process on 31 July 2005, stating that the terms of the legislation recently adopted by decree by Gbagbo differed from those that had been agreed at Pretoria in April. The G7 had also criticized the new legislation, claiming that the proposed electoral commission had not been provided with sufficient powers and that the amended law on nationality would restrict the number of people eligible to vote. However, in August South African mediators judged that the legislation conformed to the provisions of the peace agreement, prompting the FN to express doubts about the impartiality of Mbeki. Later that month the FN and the main opposition parties declared that it would be impossible for a free and fair election to be held within two months and called for Gbagbo's resignation to allow a transitional administration to organize the poll at a later date. At the beginning of September the FN rejected South Africa's mediation, after the South African Government blamed the movement for hindering the peace process in a briefing to the UN Security Council, and urged the AU and ECOWAS to assume control of efforts to resolve the crisis. Later that month Annan acknowledged that it was no longer feasible to hold the presidential election on 30 October, given that the electoral commission had still to be established and the voters' register updated.

The Peace and Security Council (PSC) of the AU proposed the extension by up to 12 months of President Gbagbo's term of office following its expiry at the end of October 2005, and the appointment of a new Prime Minister with more extensive powers, acceptable to all signatories of the Marcoussis Accords. The Council supported the continued involvement of South Africa in mediation efforts, and also recommended the establishment of an international working group to monitor the implementation of the peace plan. Chaired by the Nigerian Minister of Foreign Affairs, the working group was to comprise high-ranking officials from Benin, Ghana, Guinea, Niger, Nigeria, South Africa, France, the United Kingdom, the USA, the UN, the AU, ECOWAS, the European Union (see p. 276), La Francophonie, the World Bank and the IMF. The UN Security Council adopted a resolution endorsing the AU proposals later that month, despite calls from the RHDP and the FN for Gbagbo's removal from the presidency.

Banny appointed Prime Minister

In November 2005 Obasanjo led efforts to reach a consensus on the nomination of a new Prime Minister, holding talks with all sides. IIowever, the FN repeatedly insisted that, if Gbagbo were to remain in office, Soro or one of his deputies should assume the premiership on the grounds that the FN controlled one-half of the country. Nevertheless, on 4 December Charles Konan Banny, hitherto Governor of the BCEAO, was designated as interim Prime Minister. The appointment of Banny, who was sworn in to replace Diarra on 7 December, was broadly welcomed; the new Prime Minister was to be responsible for ensuring the disarmament of former rebel fighters and pro-Gbagbo militias and organizing a presidential election (which he would not be permitted to contest) by October 2006.

On 15 December 2005 the UN Security Council unanimously adopted a resolution to ban imports of rough diamonds from Côte d'Ivoire and to renew for a further year the arms embargo and the possibility of imposing sanctions on individuals deemed to have impeded the peace process. Later that month, after three weeks of negotiations, Banny announced the formation of a 32-member transitional Council of Ministers, which comprised seven ministers from the FPI, six from the FN, five each from the PDCI—RDA and the RDR and one each from the MFA, the PIT, the UDPCI and the Union démocratique citoyenne, as well as four representatives of civil society. Banny assumed personal responsibility for the economy and finance (as well as communication), while Soro was appointed as Minister of State for the Programme of Reconstruction and Reintegration, the most senior position in the Government after that of Prime Minister. Antoine Bohoun Bouabré of the FPI, an ally of Gbagbo and hitherto Minister of State, Minister of the Economy and Finance, became Minister of State for Planning and Development. The portfolios of defence and the interior were, notably, allocated to independents.

After three days of protests held in front of the UN's headquarters in Abidjan in January 2006, Obasanjo, Banny and Gbagbo issued a joint statement urging an end to the unrest and insisting that the working group did not have the power itself to dissolve the legislature. On the following day Blé Goudé called on the demonstrators to dismantle their barricades and disperse, and relative calm returned to Abidjan. UN officials warned that the provision of humanitarian assistance to refugees and displaced persons in western Côte d'Ivoire had been severely disrupted owing to damage to UN facilities (estimated at US $3.5m.) and the evacuation of staff.

On 24 January 2006 the UN Security Council extended the mandate of UNOCI and the French troops until 15 December and in early February approved the imposition of sanctions against three individuals: Blé Goudé, Eugène Djué, also a leader of the CJP, and Martin Kouakou Fofié, an FN commander accused of human rights abuses, were to be subject to a 12-month travel ban and a freeze on their assets. In late February negotiations were held, chaired by Banny, between Gbagbo, Soro, Bédié and Ouattara, in Yamoussoukro, representing the first occasion on which the four leaders had met in Côte d'Ivoire since the de facto division of the country between opposing forces in late 2002. It was agreed, in principle, that further discussions between the parties would take place, with a particular view to establishing a new schedule for the disbanding of the rival militia and paramilitary groups. In March Soro returned to Abidjan after more than one year, to assume his ministerial responsibilities.

In May 2006, despite strong opposition from Gbagbo, Banny announced that a one-week pilot phase of voter identification would begin in seven areas across the country on 18 May, to be followed by a national programme of identification and disarmament. Meanwhile, the military authorities on both sides took the first steps towards redeploying their forces in preparation for disarmament. This was followed in late May by the resumption of talks between government and FN forces on the sequencing of the disarmament process. However, the disarmament, initially scheduled to take place in early June, was delayed until mid-July.

In early September 2006 a further meeting between Banny, Gbagbo, Soro, Bédié and Ouattara took place, although no agreement could be reached on the issues of disarmament, the elections and voter identification. The following day the entire Ivorian Government resigned after three people were killed and some 1,500 others were taken ill as a result of the illegal unloading of toxic waste from a Panamanian-registered vessel at Abidjan port in mid-August; the waste was subsequently deposited at numerous sites around the city. Gbagbo requested that Banny form a new administration and in mid-September, by which time a further four people had died and some 30,000 people had reportedly sought medical attention, Banny unveiled a new Council of Ministers. The key positions remained unaltered, but the Minister of Transport and the Minister of the Environment, Water and Forestry were both replaced. (In October 2008 the Nigerian head of the company responsible for dumping the toxic waste was sentenced to 20 years' imprisonment and an Ivorian shipping agent received a five-year term for their respective roles in the incident.) Also in September 2006 the UN confirmed that the presidential election would not take place in October after a meeting in New York, USA, between a number of African mediators and the main parties involved in the crisis ended in deadlock. Gbagbo had refused to attend the talks and subsequently stated that he intended to remain as President, despite the expiry of his mandate at the end of October.

Following a meeting in Addis Ababa, Ethiopia, on 17 October 2006, the PSC recommended that a new transitional period, with a maximum duration of 12 months, commence on 1 November. The mandates of Gbagbo and Banny were to be extended until 31 October 2007 and the Prime Minister was to assume 'all the necessary powers, and all appropriate financial, material and human resources' to ensure, *inter alia*, that credible electoral rolls were compiled, and that the disarmament, demobilization and reintegration (DDR) programme was carried out, with a view to holding transparent elections by the expiry of his mandate. The granting to the Prime Minister of the power to introduce legislation by decree was contrary to the 2000 Constitution, which vested legislative authority in the President, and Banny was also to take control of the country's defence and security forces. The FN stated that it would refuse to recognize any arrangement whereby Gbagbo remained head of state, while Gbagbo, for his part, was reported to have maintained that any recommendations that did not comply with the Ivorian Constitution would not be applied. Nevertheless, on 1 November 2006 the UN Security Council adopted a resolution (No. 1721) endorsing the PSC's decision. On 15 December the Security Council extended the mandate of UNOCI until 10 January 2007 and on that date UNOCI's mandate was further extended until 30 June.

The Ouagadougou Agreement

Meanwhile, in December 2006 the President unveiled a new initiative aimed at resolving the stalled peace process and offered to commence direct dialogue with the FN. Under Gbagbo's proposals the 'buffer zone' dividing the country would be removed and a new amnesty law would be enacted. At an ECOWAS summit held in Ouagadougou, Burkina Faso, in mid-January 2007 the Burkinabè President and newly appointed Chairman of ECOWAS, Blaise Compaoré, was entrusted with facilitating dialogue between Gbagbo and the FN. Both Soro, on behalf of the FN, and Gbagbo attended separate meetings with Compaoré in Burkina Faso later that month and representatives from both sides attended discussions with the Burkinabè President in early February. Ouattara, on behalf of the RDR, and Alphonse Djédjé Mady, the Secretary-General of the PDCI—RDA, met with Compaoré later that month.

On 4 March 2007 Gbagbo and Soro signed an agreement in Ouagadougou, which provided a detailed timetable for the resolution of the ongoing political crisis in Côte d'Ivoire. According to the schedule, a joint armed forces command, the Centre de commandement integré (CCI), was to be established within two weeks, and was to comprise an equal number of troops from both sides, while a power-sharing government was to be formed by mid-April. The signatories to the accord also agreed to undertake a nation-wide identification programme, scheduled to last for up to three months, which would result in the issuing of identity cards and the compilation of a definitive electoral list to replace the 2000 register. The DDR programme was scheduled to commence two weeks after the formation of the new administration. In mid-March President Gbagbo announced the creation of the CCI, and on 29 March Soro was appointed Prime Minister. A 33-member Government, which featured six new appointees, was installed on 7 April. On 16 April the 'buffer zone' was officially abolished.

The reconciliation and disarmament process continued to progress at a slow pace, owing to ongoing disagreements between the signatories to the Ouagadougou Agreement. In August 2007 it was announced that elections, previously scheduled to be held in January 2008, were to be postponed until later that year. In September 2007 the much-delayed process of issuing identification papers to Ivorians without documents was officially launched, thus granting all citizens the right to enrol on the electoral register. This was deemed the precursor to establishing a full electoral list ahead of the planned legislative and presidential elections the following year. In November the country's major political parties adopted an electoral code, under the aegis of the Commission électorale indépendant (CEI), which aimed to ensure the free and fair conduct of future polls. Although Gbagbo had abandoned talks with the FN at the end of that month, at which a draft agreement aimed at accelerating the reconciliation process and scheduling elections for mid-2008 had been presented, he subsequently agreed to hold elections in June 2008. In December 2007 the disarmament of former rebel forces began. It was anticipated that some 5,000 government soldiers and 33,000 members of the rebel forces were to assemble at disarmament sites and barracks by the end of March 2008. In January the UN Security Council had approved the extension of UNOCI's mandate until 30 July and the mandate was subsequently extended on two further occasions and was due to expire on 31 July 2009. In view of the improving conditions in Côte d'Ivoire the Security Council also agreed in January to reduce the level of authorized military personnel in UNOCI from 8,115 to 7,450. The mandate was subsequently extended until December 2010, although by late 2010 the number of military personnel had been reduced further to 6,240.

Repeated electoral delays

In March 2008 it became apparent that preparations for the forthcoming presidential election, including the provision of identification documents, would not be completed in time for the ballot to take place as planned in June. Acting upon recommendations made by the CEI in April, a new date was set for the election to be held on 30 November. Legislative elections were to be held at a later, unspecified date. Registration for the postponed presidential election began in mid-September; however, in October the UN issued a report stating that the process of disarming former rebels had stalled and that unrest in Bouaké in June had presented a renewed threat to national security. Earlier, in April, the UN accused the Ivorian armed forces and the FN of engaging in military training that contravened the arms embargo imposed in 2004. The UN asserted that inspection officials were denied access to several bases; both the armed forces and the FN denied the allegations. Following a meeting of the main political parties, convened in Burkina Faso in November 2008 to discuss security concerns and delays to voter registration, the presidential election was again postponed and the CEI was instructed to draw up a new electoral schedule by the end of December.

Meanwhile, in July 2008 it was announced that the members of the Ivorian Government had agreed a reduction, of 50%, to their salaries, in order to fund a nation-wide decrease in the cost of fuel. Escalating food costs had provoked violent protests in Abidjan in March and April and public transport workers had threatened to commence industrial action, in response to recent increases in the cost of diesel and petrol. Prime Minister Soro also stated that running costs and investments in government departments would be cut, while overseas visits by government members would be reduced to a 'bare minimum'.

On 24 December 2008 Gbagbo and Soro signed a fourth complementary peace accord to the Ouagadougou Agreement, known as 'Ouaga IV', under Compaoré's mediation. The agreement created the framework for demobilizing 36,000 FN troops and an unspecified number of militia forces, integrating 9,000 of them into the national army and police force, and extending the central government administration into rebel-held areas. The agreement also proposed a timetable for disarming an estimated 70 militias.

In April 2009 the CCI announced that a mixed force of 8,000 troops would redeploy into the north of the country as part of the process of reunification agreed under Ouaga IV. The force would comprise 2,000 troops from the national army, 2,000 gendarmes and 4,000 FN troops, with a mandate to re-establish the Government's authority across the national territory and provide security for the electoral process. The first contingents of this force were deployed to Bouaké in May and late that month a ceremony was held there marking the transfer of power from the FN's ten regional commanders—'com-zones'—to central government *préfets*, in accordance with Ouaga IV. However, the deployment of the CCI's security force was slow, with only 500 FN troops deploying to Bouaké by the end of May.

Following repeated demands to maintain the momentum of the peace process from UN Secretary-General Ban Ki-Moon, who again reiterated the urgency for credible and transparent elections, in April 2009 the FN asked Prime Minister Soro to resign from a government that they considered to be deliberately delaying progress. Nevertheless, in May Soro announced that the presidential election would take place on 29 November 2009; compilation of the electoral lists was to be completed by 30 June and publication of the provisional electoral list was scheduled for September. Owing to logistical problems (most notably industrial action by electoral agents who demanded payment of salary arrears) it was not until October that the provisional list of 6.3m. electors was delivered to Soro, after which it was handed over to Gbagbo for approval. By mid-October the CEI announced that it had received 20 candidatures for the presidential elections, among them the country's first female candidate, Jaqueline Lohoues-Oble, Dean of the Faculty of Law at the Université de Cocody and a former minister of justice. In early November the CEI validated 5,300,586 out of 6,384,253 electors who had registered; however, on 11 November it announced that there would be a 'slight delay' in the electoral timetable. In early December, following a meeting of mediators in Ouagadougou, Compaoré, in his capacity as 'facilitator' of the inter-Ivorian dialogue, stated that it was intended to hold the presidential election in late February or early March 2010. However, he also expressed concern about the delay encountered by the CCI in establishing the mixed units responsible for election security—at this time less than one-half of the proposed force had been assembled—and requested the provision of further security reinforcements.

In September 2010 the FN marked the completion of the demobilization process in a ceremony in Dabakala. Reports claimed that 5,000 fighters had been reintegrated into the national armed forces with a further 5,000 scheduled to return to barracks before being reintegrated.

The disputed 2010 presidential election

Meanwhile, in January 2010 Gbagbo accused the President of the CEI, Robert Mambé, of having allowed as many as 429,000 ineligible voters to register to participate in the election, and on 12 February, following violent protests across the country, most notably in Man, Divo and Katiola, Gbagbo dissolved both the Government and the CEI, describing the peace process as 'broken'. The examination of the appeals for the voter registration lists, which had originally been scheduled to proceed until 14 February, was immediately suspended, resulting in renewed demonstrations, and a further delay to the electoral schedule appeared inevitable. Soro was reappointed to the premiership and was tasked with forming a new administration. Opposition parties denounced Gbagbo's decision as anti-democratic and anti-constitutional, and the RHDP coalition urged the population to mobilize against the President, who they maintained they no longer recognized as the legitimate head of the country. Two weeks of predominantly non-violent protests followed; however, police were reported to have fired on protesters in Gagnoa, killing five and wounding several others, while two people were killed during demonstrations in the western town of Daloa.

On 23 February 2010 Soro appointed the members of his new Government; however, only 16 of the 27 ministerial posts were confirmed as both the RDR and the PDCI—RDA refused to join the Government until the CEI had been reconstituted. Three days later Youssouf Bakayoko of the PDCI—RDA, and a former foreign minister, was sworn in as President of the CEI and Ouattara announced that the RDR would end its protests and take up its positions in the Government. On 4 March Soro duly presented the new Government, which included members of the PIT, the RDR, the PDCI—RDA, the UDPCI and the MFA.

A new electoral list was published on 12 July 2010 by the authorities and the verification thereof was completed on 2 August. Three days later the Ivorian Council of Ministers announced that the presidential election would take place on 31 October; on that date a total of 14 candidates contested the elections. According to results released by the CEI on 3 November, and which were confirmed by the Constitutional Council on 6 November, no candidate succeeded in securing a majority of the votes cast and thus a second round of voting, to be held on 21 November, was scheduled. The run-off was to be contested by Gbagbo and Ouattara who had, respectively, received 38.0% and 32.1% of the votes cast. Bédié had been placed third, having taken 25.2%. The rate of voter participation was officially recorded at 83.7%.

A number of additional security measures, including the deployment of supplementary UN peace-keepers and the imposition of a night-time curfew, were enforced in Côte d'Ivoire prior to the run-off, which was postponed by one week and thus took place on 28 November 2010. On 1 December a spokesperson for the CEI was prevented from announcing initial results of the second round by a supporter of Gbagbo, who destroyed the documents the spokesperson was preparing to read to members of the press. The following day the CEI proclaimed Ouattara, who it maintained had secured 54.1% of the votes cast, the victor of the run-off. However, on 2 December the President of the Constitutional Council, Paul Yao N'Dré, declared the CEI's announcement null and void and the following day released results indicating that Gbagbo had won the election, having received 51.5% of votes cast. The Special Representative of the UN Secretary-General for Côte d'Ivoire, Choi Young-Jin, described N'Dré's decision as 'having no factual basis'; furthermore, in his role as certifier of the Ivorian elections Choi declared Ouattara the winner of the poll. Ouattara was also recognized as the legitimate head of state by, *inter alia*, US President Barack Obama, the European Union, France, the IMF and ECOWAS—the latter announced the suspension of Côte d'Ivoire from that organization on 7 December. Shortly thereafter the AU also announced that Côte d'Ivoire's participation in AU activities had been suspended. Nevertheless, in separate ceremonies on 4 December both Gbagbo and Ouattara were sworn in to the presidency and subsequently named governments. (Ouattara's administration, which rapidly gained legitimacy, was headed by Soro as Prime Minister and Minister of Defence and retained a number of senior ministers from the cabinet appointed in March.) The armed forces announced the closure of Côte d'Ivoire's borders and violent clashes ensued in numerous parts of the country.

Both presidents subsequently retrenched in their positions in Abidjan, with Ouattara blockaded in a hotel under protection from assault by troops loyal to Gbagbo by UN peace-keepers and members of the FN. In December 2010 Gbagbo demanded that all UN and French troops leave the country; however, his appeals were rejected by UN Secretary-General Ban; UNOCI's mandate was extended by six months later in December. Also in late December the BCEAO announced that it would deny Gbagbo access to Ivorian funds at the bank and that only officials designated by the legitimate Government (the BCEAO also recognized Ouattara as the elected President) could access the country's deposits and represent it within the Union économique et monétaire ouest-africaine (UEMOA, see p. 333). A delegation of West African leaders, comprising the Presidents of Cape Verde, Benin and Sierra Leone, subsequently held a series of meetings with Gbagbo in Abidjan on behalf of ECOWAS, but by early January 2011 they had been unable to secure a suitable solution to the crisis, despite reports that ECOWAS was considering the use of force to remove Gbagbo. A number of major international banking groups suspended their operations in Côte d'Ivoire in February, while further economic disruption was encountered after Ouattara appealed for a ban on the export of cocoa and requested that Ivorian companies withhold the payment of taxes. There were violent clashes in the suburbs of Abidjan in late February and early March, most notably in the northern Abobo district where it was reported that soldiers had shot and killed six Ouattara supporters. In retaliation four vehicles of the security forces were ambushed and their occupants killed. Meanwhile, Gbagbo began to use the state media as a propaganda tool, accusing the UN and French forces of plotting to depose him, and on 16 March 2011 Ouattara's supporters marched on the national broadcasting headquarters. The march was violently suppressed by troops loyal to Gbagbo and there were conflicting reports of between 30 and 48 deaths. By this time, the office of the UN High Commissioner for Refugees (UNHCR) estimated that as many as 450,000 Ivorians had fled their homes.

By late March 2011 Ouattara's forces had captured Yamoussoukro and were reported to have reached Abidjan and surrounded Gbagbo. A number of heavy assaults were carried out on Gbagbo's residence and violence was reported across the country: the International Committee of the Red Cross stated that at least 800 people had been killed in the western town of Duékoué. (There were contrasting reports regarding who had been responsible for the deaths and the UN subsequently confirmed that the total number of those killed was 536.) On 4 April it was confirmed that UN and French forces had fired upon on military camps operated by Gbagbo, although Ban maintained that these actions had been carried out in order to prevent attacks on civilians by Gbagbo loyalists. On 11 April forces loyal to Ouattara, with the assistance of French troops and UN peace-keepers, captured Gbagbo. Ouattara pledged to put in place a commission of truth and reconciliation, which would investigate any crimes committed in the post-election period. The UN welcomed the detention of Gbagbo, and offered its support to the new Government.

By early May 2011 Ouattara announced that government forces had regained control of Abidjan and on 5 May the Constitutional Council confirmed Ouattara as the winner of the presidential election. On the following day he was officially sworn in as President. (An inauguration ceremony attended by many heads of state, including French President Nicolas Sarkozy, followed in Yamoussoukro on 21 May.) Ouattara requested that the International Criminal Court (ICC) investigate allegations of serious human rights crimes committed during the fighting; ICC prosecutors subsequently reported that at least 3,000 people had been killed. On 1 June Ouattara appointed a new Government, which was again under the premiership of Soro and retained several senior ministers of the previous administration.

Recent developments: the 2011 legislative elections

In early July 2011 Gen. Soumaila Bakayoko, a former rebel commander loyal to President Ouattara, was appointed as the Chief of Staff of the Armed Forces. On 27 July the UN Security Council adopted a resolution extending the mandate of UNOCI until the end of July 2012. In August 2011 it was reported that 12 associates of former President Gbagbo, including his son, Michel, and former Prime Minister Pascal Affi N'Guessan, hitherto under house arrest, had been formally charged in connection with the violence. Later that month Gbagbo and his wife were also charged with involvement in a series of economic crimes, including looting, armed robbery and embezzlement. It was announced in September that legislative elections would be held on 11 December. On 28 September President Ouattara formally established a Commission on Dialogue, Truth and Reconciliation, headed by former Prime Minister Banny and including one Christian member and one Muslim religious leader, as well as five representatives of the country's major regions; the Commission was to present recommendations to him following an investigation into the post-election violence. Meanwhile, although the humanitarian situation had improved significantly, 247,000 civilians remained internally displaced in Côte d'Ivoire at September, according to UNHCR.

On 29 November 2011 Gbagbo, who had remained under house arrest since April, was extradited to the ICC on four counts of crimes against humanity in connection with the atrocities committed during the post-election violence (becoming the first former head of state to be taken into custody by the ICC); he appeared before the Court in early December. In response, three pro-Gbagbo parties announced their withdrawal from the forthcoming elections; the FPI had already announced an electoral boycott in protest at Gbagbo's detention. Only about 36.6% of the electorate participated in the legislative elections, which took place on 11 December. Following complaints that troops had intimidated FPI supporters during pre-election rallies, the authorities announced that 19 members of the armed forces had been detained. According to provisional results, which were announced by the CEI on 16 December, Ouattara's RDR won 127 of the 255 seats contested in the Assemblée nationale, while the PDCI—RDA received 77. It was subsequently reported that several independent candidates had also joined the RDR-led alliance. In early February 2012, however, the Constitutional Council upheld complaints of irregularities in 11 constituencies, in which the results were annulled; polls were to be repeated for those seats (and held in a further constituency where the vote had been postponed due to the death of a candidate) on 26 February. Of the 13 seats contested on that date, the RDR won four, the UDPCI two and the PDCI—RDA one, while four independent candidates secured seats. The results in the remaining two constituencies remained undeclared. According to final results published by the CEI on 8 March, the RDR held 138 of the 253 declared seats, the PDCI—RDA held 86, independent candidates held 17 seats and the UDPCI held eight seats. Other party representations remained unchanged.

Also on 8 March 2012 Soro announced his resignation and that of his Government. Soro was elected President of the Assemblée nationale on 12 March and on the following day Jeannot Kouadio Ahoussou of the PDCI, and hitherto Minister of State, Keeper of the Seals, Minister of Justice, was appointed Prime Minister, while retaining the justice portfolio. All other members of the outgoing administration were reappointed to the positions that they had held in the Soro Government.

Foreign Affairs

Regional relations

The emphasis on '*ivoirité*', or national identity, in the domestic policies of Bédié, Gueï and Gbagbo, has strained Côte d'Ivoire's relations with other West African states, particularly Burkina Faso; Burkinabè migrants in Côte d'Ivoire increasingly suffered from discrimination and became the victims of inter-ethnic violence, causing several thousand to flee the country in early 2001. As the process of national reconciliation advanced, tensions eased somewhat, and Gbagbo made his first visit as President to Burkina in December. However, following the onset of widespread civil unrest in Côte d'Ivoire in September 2002, thousands of citizens of Burkina and Mali left the country, and the common border of Côte d'Ivoire and Burkina Faso was closed until early September 2003, when stability appeared to be returning to the region. In July 2004, at a meeting in Abidjan, representatives of the two countries pledged to combat 'destabilizing acts' against their respective countries and agreed to increase co-operation in security and defence matters, and in July 2008, on his first state visit to Burkina, Gbagbo signed a treaty of friendship and co-operation with President Compaoré. In early 2010 the Ivorian Minister of Economy and Finance pledged to pay an outstanding debt to the Burkinabè Post Office of 3,200m. francs CFA, non-payment of which had caused the suspension of transactions between the countries since 2000 and had adversely affected the 3m. Burkinabè citizens working in the Ivorian cocoa plantations.

The protracted civil war in neighbouring Liberia resulted in the presence of large numbers of Liberian refugees in Côte d'Ivoire in the 1990s; UNHCR estimated the total number at 327,288 at the end of 1996. The possible infiltration of refugee groups by Liberian fighters, together with sporadic incursions into eastern Côte d'Ivoire by Liberian armed factions, proved a significant security concern of the Ivorian authorities at this time. By 2002, following the installation of elected organs of state in Liberia in 1997, and the outbreak of civil conflict in Côte d'Ivoire in September 2002, the number of Liberian refugees in the country registered with UNHCR had declined to 43,000, although it rose again to 74,180 over the course of 2003, following the deterioration of the security situation in eastern Liberia. Conversely, some 25,000 Ivorian nationals were thought by UNHCR to have fled to Liberia in 2002 to escape fighting in western Côte d'Ivoire, while in 2004 some 10,000 Ivorians were reported to have sought refuge in Liberia following the renewed outbreak of violence in Côte d'Ivoire in November. During the political crisis which followed the 2010 presidential election in Côte d'Ivoire, it was claimed that Gbagbo had recruited Liberian mercenaries to abduct adversaries and carry out extrajudicial executions, while UNHCR estimated that some 180,000 Ivorians had crossed into Liberia. In August 2011 UNHCR signed an agreement with the Governments of Côte d'Ivoire and Liberia to facilitate the voluntary repatriation of Ivorian refugees from Liberia. (In October a similar agreement was signed with the Government of Ghana.)

Other external relations

Relations with France, the country's principal trading partner and provider of bilateral assistance, have generally been close since independence. In January 2001 France announced that full co-operation with Côte d'Ivoire, which had been suspended following the December 1999 *coup d'état*, would be restored. From late 2002 France dispatched additional troops to Côte d'Ivoire to supplement the 550 already stationed in the country and by late 2004 there were some 4,000 French troops stationed in Côte d'Ivoire, independent of the 6,000 UNOCI troops also deployed there. The French Government also played an active role in the diplomatic efforts that led to the signature of the Marcoussis Accords in late January 2003 (see above). However, France stated that it regarded the civil conflict as an internal Ivorian matter, disregarding Gbagbo's statements relating to the alleged involvement of external forces in the rebellion; such involvement would have resulted in the invocation of a clause in a defence treaty between the two countries, necessitating the active military support of France for the Ivorian authorities. None the less, there was widespread anti-French feeling, particularly in Abidjan, following the conclusion of the Marcoussis Accords, and several thousand French citizens resident in Côte d'Ivoire reportedly left the country.

Following the destruction of the Ivorian air force by the French military on 6 November 2004, in retaliation for an Ivorian bombing raid that had resulted in the deaths of nine French peace-keeping troops, numerous French targets in Abidjan, including schools, businesses and homes, were attacked. French troops entered Abidjan to secure the international airport and protect French citizens, airlifting many of them out of the city. (In total it was estimated that 9,000 foreign citizens, the majority of them French, were evacuated from Abidjan during the crisis; the embassies of several European countries in the city suspended their operations in subsequent months.) Some 600 French troops were dispatched to reinforce that country's military presence in Côte d'Ivoire, while diplomatic relations between the two countries remained tense. The French Government subsequently admitted that its forces had killed some 20 Ivorian civilians during clashes with rioters in Abidjan; the Ivorian authorities claimed the number was significantly higher. In early 2008 the French President, Nicolas Sarkozy, announced plans to reduce the French military presence in a number of African countries, including Côte d'Ivoire. Accordingly, the number of French troops in Côte d'Ivoire (excluding the 181 French members of UNOCI) decreased from 2,400 to 1,800 by late 2008. Bases at Abidjan and Bouaké were to remain operational, although the operations centre at Tombokro was closed. By November 2009 the number of French troops in Côte d'Ivoire had been further reduced to just 900. In February 2011, in view of the political stalemate in the country, the French force (Licorne) was strengthened to 1,100 soldiers (and subsequently to 1,600). French forces played a significant role in the capture of Gbagbo in April, and French advisers supported the country's economic reconstruction following the installation of a new Government, headed by President Alassane Ouattara, in June. In January 2012 Ouattara made his first state visit to France, where he signed a new security agreement with President Sarkozy; by that time French forces in Côte d'Ivoire had again been reduced, to just 450.

CONSTITUTION AND GOVERNMENT

Under the terms of the Constitution of July 2000, executive power is vested in the President, as Head of State, who is appointed by direct universal suffrage for a term of five years, renewable only once. (The mandate of former President Laurent Gbagbo expired in October 2005, but was periodically extended as a result of the failure of the Côte d'Ivoire authorities to hold presidential elections.) The President appoints a Prime Minister, and on the latter's recommendation, a Council of Ministers. Legislative power is held by the Assemblée nationale, which is elected for a term of five years. The country is divided into 19 regions, and further sub-divided into 57 departments and 197 communes, each with its own elected council.

REGIONAL AND INTERNATIONAL CO-OPERATION

Côte d'Ivoire is a member of numerous regional organizations, including the West African organs of the Franc Zone (see p. 333) and the African Petroleum Producers' Association (APPA, see p. 444). Côte d'Ivoire is also a member of the Economic Community of West African States (ECOWAS, see p. 264) and the African Union (see p. 189) but membership of both organizations was suspended in December 2010 following the disputed results of the presidential election (see above). The African Development Bank (see p. 186) has its headquarters in Abidjan; however, in February 2003 the bank temporarily relocated to Tunis, Tunisia, as a result of heightened instability in Côte d'Ivoire.

Côte d'Ivoire became a member of the UN in 1960. As a contracting party to the General Agreement on Tariffs and

Trade, Côte d'Ivoire joined the World Trade Organization (WTO, see p. 433) on its establishment in 1995. Côte d'Ivoire participates in the Group of 77 (G77, see p. 450) developing countries. Côte d'Ivoire is also a member of the International Cocoa Organization (ICCO, see p. 445), the International Coffee Organization (see p. 445) and the Conseil de l'Entente (see p. 449).

ECONOMIC AFFAIRS

In 2010, according to estimates by the World Bank, Côte d'Ivoire's gross national income (GNI), measured at average 2008–10 prices, was US $22,976m., equivalent to $1,160 per head (or $1,800 on an international purchasing-power parity basis). During 2001–10, it was estimated, the population increased at an average annual rate of 1.7%, while gross domestic product (GDP) per head declined, in real terms, by an average of 0.5% per year. Overall GDP increased, in real terms, by an average annual rate of 1.3% in 2001–10; real GDP grew by 3.0% in 2010.

Agriculture (including forestry and fishing) contributed 22.9% of GDP in 2010, according to the World Bank. The sector employed about 35.8% of the labour force in mid-2012, according to FAO estimates. Côte d'Ivoire is the world's foremost producer of cocoa, responsible for some 38% of global cocoa bean production in 2005/06. In 2009 cocoa and related products contributed 35.1% of the country's total export earnings. In 2008 speculation over low yields, at 40% below the average of the previous four years, caused a 70% increase in cocoa prices; political instability in early 2011 further increased cocoa prices to their highest level in 32 years. Côte d'Ivoire also produces and exports coffee, although output declined markedly during the early 2000s, and sales of coffee in 2010 declined by 34% due to a decrease in market prices. Other major cash crops include cotton, rubber, bananas and pineapples. The principal subsistence crops are yams, cassava, plantains, rice (although large quantities of the last are still imported) and maize. Poultry production has seen strong growth since 2005 (when taxes were introduced on imported poultry and by-products) rising from 9,000 metric tons to 23,000 tons in 2009 and creating 39,000 new jobs. Excessive exploitation of the country's forest resources has led to a decline in the importance of this sector. Abidjan is among sub-Saharan Africa's principal fishing ports; however, the participation of Ivorian fishing fleets is minimal. According to World Bank estimates, during 2001–10 agricultural GDP increased at an average annual rate of 1.8%. Agricultural GDP grew by 4.7% in 2010.

Industry (including mining, manufacturing, construction and power) contributed 27.4% of GDP in 2010, according to the World Bank. According to UN estimates, 11.5% of the labour force were employed in the sector in 1994. During 2001–10 industrial GDP declined by an average annual rate of 0.6%, according to World Bank estimates; however, industrial GDP increased by 5.2% in 2010.

Mining and quarrying contributed only 4.0% of GDP in 2009, according to the African Development Bank (AfDB). Commercial exploitation of important offshore reserves of petroleum and natural gas commenced in the mid-1990s, and output of crude petroleum amounted to some 21.5m. barrels in 2009. Gold and diamonds are also mined, although illicit production of the latter has greatly exceeded commercial output. There is believed to be significant potential for the development of nickel deposits, and there are also notable reserves of manganese, iron ore and bauxite. By the end of 2009 there were at least five major mining operations in progress throughout the country.

The manufacturing sector, which, according to the World Bank contributed 19.2% of GDP in 2010, is dominated by agro-industrial activities (such as the processing of cocoa, coffee, cotton, palm kernels, pineapples and fish). Crude petroleum is refined at Abidjan, while the tobacco industry uses mostly imported tobacco. According to World Bank estimates, during 2001–10 manufacturing GDP decreased by an average of 0.7% per year. However, the GDP of the sector increased by 4.9% in 2010.

Construction contributed 2.2% of GDP in 2009, according to the AfDB. According to 1988 census figures, the sector employed 7.6% of the labour force.

Some 65.1% of Côte d'Ivoire's electricity generation in 2008 was derived from natural gas, while 32.7% was derived from hydroelectric installations, and a negligible portion from petroleum (a major decline from 1994, when 50.3% of the country's electricity had been generated from petroleum combustion). Since 1995 the country has exploited indigenous reserves of natural gas, with the intention of becoming not only self-sufficient in energy, but also a regional exporter; the first stage of a major gas-powered turbine and power station in Abidjan commenced operations in 1999. Imports of petroleum and petroleum products accounted for 25.0% of the value of total merchandise imports in 2009.

According to the World Bank, the services sector contributed 49.7% of GDP in 2010, and (according to UN estimates) employed 37.4% of the labour force in 1994. The transformation of Abidjan's stock market into a regional exchange for the member states of the Union économique et monétaire ouest-africaine was expected to enhance the city's status as a centre for financial services. However, Abidjan's position as a major hub of regional communications and trade has been threatened by political unrest since the late 1990s, particularly following the rebel uprising of 2002–03 and violence that followed the presidential election of November 2010. According to World Bank estimates, the GDP of the services sector increased by an average of 1.3% per year in 2001–10. The GDP of the sector increased by 1.5% in 2010.

In 2009 Côte d'Ivoire recorded a visible trade surplus of US $4,185.2m., and there was a surplus of $1,670.2m. on the current account of the balance of payments. In 2009 the principal source of imports was Nigeria (which supplied 20.6% of total imports); France, the People's Republic of China and Thailand were also notable suppliers. The Netherlands was the principal market for exports in 2009 (taking 13.8% of total exports), followed by France, the USA, Germany, Nigeria and Ghana. The principal exports in 2009 were cocoa (amounting to 35.1% of total exports) and petroleum and petroleum products. The principal imports in the same year were petroleum and petroleum products (representing 24.6% of total imports), machinery and transport equipment, basic manufactures, cereals and cereal preparations, and road vehicles.

According to IMF estimates, Côte d'Ivoire recorded an estimated overall budget deficit of 261,200m. francs CFA in 2010. Côte d'Ivoire's general government gross debt was 7,286.2m. francs CFA in 2009, equivalent to 67.0% of GDP. The country's total external debt was US $11,701m. at the end of 2009, of which $10,979m. was public and publicly guaranteed debt. In that year, the cost of servicing long-term public and publicly guaranteed debt and repayments to the IMF was equivalent to 4.4% of the value of exports of goods, services and income (excluding workers' remittances). The annual rate of inflation averaged 2.7% in 2001–10. Consumer prices increased by 1.2% in 2010. An estimated 216,158 persons were registered as unemployed in 2006, representing 2.7% of the labour force.

Since the late 1990s political instability and civil strife in Côte d'Ivoire have resulted in an economic decline that has reduced living standards and increased poverty. The division of the country occasioned by the 2002 rebellion inhibited economic growth and international trade was disrupted, particularly as a result of the closure of the border with Burkina Faso for a period of 12 months. However, following the signing of the Ouagadougou Agreement in March 2007, international donor confidence increased. In March 2009 the country reached the completion point under the Heavily Indebted Poor Countries (HIPC) Initiative allowing it debt relief from the majority of its creditors, and a three-year Poverty Reduction and Growth Facility (PRGF) arrangement was signed with the IMF (the first review in November allowing an immediate disbursement of US $57.3m.). In April 2010 the IMF approved the Economic Governance & Recovery Grant III, which was to support public expenditure, financial management and procurement; state enterprise and banking reform and privatization; and the improvement of corporate governance. However, after the disputed presidential election of November 2010, the refusal of Laurent Gbagbo to relinquish the presidency resulted in economic disruption (most notably to the country's cocoa sector and banking operations), which was compounded by the negative impact of sanctions that had been imposed on him. Following the removal of Gbagbo in April and the installation of President Alassane Ouattara in May, the new Government initiated a programme of recovery, together with a number of measures to restore social order. The Government received emergency assistance of $128m. under the IMF's Rapid Credit Facility in July, and business activity rapidly normalized. In November the IMF approved a new, three-year Extended Credit Facility (ECF) arrangement for Côte d'Ivoire totalling $615.9m., immediately disbursing the first tranche of $128.3m., and also released about $8m. under the HIPC Initiative. Although GDP was estimated to have contracted by about 5.8% in 2011, the IMF projected resumed growth of 8.5% for 2012 (with French support for economic reconstruction and owing in part to a large cocoa harvest anticipated in that year). In January 2012 it was reported that UN agencies sought relief aid of more than $173m. for over 3m. people during that year.

PUBLIC HOLIDAYS

2013: 1 January (New Year's Day), 29 March (Good Friday), 1 April (Easter Monday), 1 May (Labour Day), 9 May (Ascension Day), 20 May (Whit Monday), 7 August (National Day and Id al-Fitr, end of Ramadan*), 15 August (Assumption), 14 October* (Id al-Adha, Feast of the Sacrifice), 1 November (All Saints' Day), 7 December (Félix Houphouët-Boigny Remembrance Day), 25 December (Christmas).

* These holidays are dependent on the Islamic lunar calendar and may vary by one or two days from the dates given.

Statistical Survey

Source (unless otherwise stated): Institut National de la Statistique, BP V55, Abidjan; tel. 20-21-05-38; fax 20-21-44-01; e-mail site-ins@globeaccess.net; internet www.ins.ci.

Area and Population

AREA, POPULATION AND DENSITY

Area (sq km)	322,462*
Population (census results)	
1 March 1988	10,815,694
20 December 1998	
Males	7,844,621
Females	7,522,050
Total	15,366,671
Population (official estimates at December)	
2007	20,227,876
2008	20,807,216
2009	21,395,198
Density (per sq km) at December 2009	66.3

* 124,503 sq miles.

ETHNIC GROUPS

1998 census (percentages, residents born in Côte d'Ivoire): Akan 42*; Voltaïque 18†; Mandé du nord 17‡; Krou 11; Mandé du sud 10§; Naturalized Ivorians 1; Others 1.

* Comprising the Baoulé, Agni, Abrou, Ebrié, Abouré, Adioukrou and Appollonien groupings.

† Comprising the Sénoufo, Lobi and Koulango groupings.

‡ Comprising the Malinké and Dioula groupings.

§ Comprising the Yacouba and Gouro groupings.

POPULATION BY AGE AND SEX

(UN estimates at mid-2012)

	Males	Females	Total
0–14	4,169,878	4,143,809	8,313,687
15–64	5,874,588	5,607,578	11,482,166
65 and over	428,633	370,131	798,764
Total	10,473,099	10,121,518	20,594,617

Source: UN, *World Population Prospects: The 2010 Revision*.

NATIONALITY OF POPULATION

(numbers resident in Côte d'Ivoire at 1998 census)

Country of citizenship	Population	%
Côte d'Ivoire	11,366,625	73.97
Burkina Faso	2,238,548	14.57
Mali	792,258	5.16
Guinea	230,387	1.50
Ghana	133,221	0.87
Liberia	78,258	0.51
Other	527,375	3.43
Total	15,366,672	100.00

POPULATION BY REGION

(1998 census)

Region	Population
Centre	1,001,264
Centre-Est	394,758
Centre-Nord	1,189,424
Centre-Ouest	2,169,826
Nord	929,686
Nord-Est	696,292
Nord-Ouest	740,175
Ouest	1,445,279
Sud	5,399,220
Sud-Ouest	1,400,748
Total	15,366,672

Note: In January 1997 the Government adopted legislation whereby Côte d'Ivoire's regions were to be reorganized. Further minor reorganizations were effected in April and July 2000. The new regions (with their regional capitals) are: Agnéby (Agboville), Bas-Sassandra (San-Pédro), Bafing (Touba), Denguélé (Odienné), 18 Montagnes (Man), Fromager (Gagnoa), Haut-Sassandra (Daloa), Lacs (Yamoussoukro), Lagunes (Abidjan), Marahoué (Bouaflé), Moyen-Cavally (Guiglo), Moyen-Comoé (Abengourou), N'zi-Comoé (Dimbokro), Savanes (Korhogo), Sud-Bandama (Divo), Sud-Comoé (Aboisso), Vallée du Bandama (Bouaké), Worodougou (Mankono) and Zanzan (Bondoukou).

PRINCIPAL TOWNS

(population at 1998 census)

Abidjan*	2,877,948	Korhogo	142,093
Bouaké	461,618	San-Pédro	131,800
Yamoussoukro*	299,243	Man	116,657
Daloa	173,107	Gagnoa	107,124

* The process of transferring the official capital from Abidjan to Yamoussoukro began in 1983.

2008 ('000 at December, official estimate): Abidjan 3,899.

Mid-2010 (incl. suburbs, UN estimates): Abidjan 4,125,174; Yamoussoukro 885,267 (Source: UN, *World Urbanization Prospects: The 2009 Revision*).

BIRTHS AND DEATHS

(annual averages, official estimates)

	2007	2008	2009
Birth rate (per 1,000)	37.5	37.1	36.7
Death rate (per 1,000)	13.8	13.6	13.3

Life expectancy (years at birth, WHO estimates): 50 (males 49; females 52) in 2009 (Source: WHO, *World Health Statistics*).

ECONOMICALLY ACTIVE POPULATION*
(persons aged 6 years and over, 1988 census)

	Males	Females	Total
Agriculture, hunting, forestry and fishing	1,791,101	836,574	2,627,675
Mining and quarrying Manufacturing	78,768	6,283	85,051
Electricity, gas and water	13,573	1,092	14,665
Construction	82,203	2,313	84,516
Trade, restaurants and hotels	227,873	302,486	530,359
Transport, storage and communications	114,396	3,120	117,516
Other services	434,782	156,444	591,226
Sub-total	2,742,696	1,308,312	4,051,008
Activities not adequately defined	998	297	1,295
Total labour force	2,743,694	1,308,609	4,052,303

* Figures exclude persons seeking work for the first time, totalling 210,450 (males 142,688; females 67,762).

Source: UN, *Demographic Yearbook*.

1988 census (revised figures): Total employed 4,025,478; Unemployed 237,275; Total labour force 4,262,753.

1998 census: Total employed 6,084,487; Unemployed 163,647; Total labour force 6,248,134.

2006 (official estimates): Total employed 7,787,952; Unemployed 216,158; Total labour force 8,004,110.

Mid-2012 ('000, estimates): Agriculture, etc. 2,811; Total labour force 7,846 (Source: FAO).

Health and Welfare

KEY INDICATORS

Total fertility rate (children per woman, 2009)	4.5
Under-5 mortality rate (per 1,000 live births, 2009)	118
HIV/AIDS (% of persons aged 15–49, 2009)	3.4
Physicians (per 1,000 head, 2004)	0.10
Hospital beds (per 1,000 head, 2006)	0.40
Health expenditure (2008): US $ per head (PPP)	67
Health expenditure (2008): % of GDP	5.4
Health expenditure (2008): public (% of total)	16.9
Access to water (% of persons, 2008)	88
Access to sanitation (% of persons, 2008)	23
Total carbon dioxide emissions ('000 metric tons, 2007)	6,379.0
Carbon dioxide emissions per head (metric tons, 2007)	0.3
Human Development Index (2011): ranking	170
Human Development Index (2011): value	0.400

For sources and definitions, see explanatory note on p. vi.

Agriculture

PRINCIPAL CROPS
('000 metric tons)

	2008	2009	2010
Rice, paddy	679.0	687.7	650.0*
Maize	630.2	637.4	700.0†
Millet	40.8	45.6	48.0*
Sorghum	40.8	41.3	43.0*
Sweet potatoes	51.0	45.6	52.0*
Cassava (Manioc)	2,531	2,262	2,450*
Taro (Cocoyam)	76.5	68.4	70.0*
Yams	5,945.4	5,313.4	5,700.0*
Sugar cane	1,660.1	1,578.6	1,650.0*
Cashew nuts, with shell	330	350	370*
Kolanuts	65.4	64.9	67.0*
Groundnuts, with shell	81.0	85.0	85.0*
Coconuts*	220.0	213.3	249.2
Oil palm fruit	1,424.0	1,748.8	1,500.0*
Cottonseed†	65.0	95.0	94.0
Tomatoes	28.8	30.2	33.2*
Aubergines (Eggplants)	77.7	81.5	82.0*
—continued			
Chillies and peppers, green*	31.0	19.3	25.0
Maize, green*	202.5	161.0	185.0
Bananas	249.2	255.0	265.0*
Plantains	1,674.7	1,496.7	1,600.0*
Oranges*	36.0	40.0	40.0
Pineapples	86.1	66.7	65.0*
Guavas, mangoes and mangosteens	39.8	42.2	42.5*
Coffee, green	173.1	142.9	100.0†
Cocoa beans	1,382	1,223	1,242†
Natural rubber (dry weight)	203.0	209.5	215.0*

* FAO estimate(s).
† Unofficial figure(s).

Aggregate production ('000 metric tons, may include official, semi-official or estimated data): Total cereals 1,408.4 in 2008, 1,429.9 in 2009, 1,461.0 in 2010; Total roots and tubers 8,618.1 in 2008, 7,701.8 in 2009, 8,284.0 in 2010; Total vegetables (incl. melons) 628.6 in 2008, 561.4 in 2009, 619.4 in 2010; Total fruits (excl. melons) 2,241.0 in 2008, 2,072.7 in 2009, 2,187.0 in 2010.

Source: FAO.

LIVESTOCK
('000 head, year ending September)

	2008	2009	2010*
Cattle	1,538	1,573	1,550
Pigs	330	344	350
Sheep	1,631	1,670	1,700
Goats	1,282	1,307	1,325
Poultry	32,561	33,359	34,000

* FAO estimates.

Source: FAO.

LIVESTOCK PRODUCTS
('000 metric tons)

	2008	2009	2010*
Cattle meat	30.8	33.6	35.0
Sheep meat	8.2	8.2*	8.3
Goat meat	3.5	3.5*	3.7
Pig meat	6.9	7.1	7.3
Chicken meat	22.8	23.4	24.0
Game meat	135.0*	137.0*	140.4
Cows' milk	30.4	31.1	32.0
Hen eggs	30.4	30.0	32.0

* FAO estimate(s).

Source: FAO.

Forestry

ROUNDWOOD REMOVALS
('000 cubic metres, excluding bark, FAO estimates)

	2007	2008	2009
Sawlogs, veneer logs and logs for sleepers	1,469	1,469	1,469
Fuel wood	8,785	8,835	8,889
Total	10,254	10,304	10,358

2010: Production assumed to be unchanged from 2009 (FAO estimates).

Source: FAO.

SAWNWOOD PRODUCTION
('000 cubic metres, including railway sleepers, FAO estimates)

	2008	2009	2010
Total (all broadleaved)	471	471	456

Source: FAO.

Fishing

('000 metric tons, live weight)

	2007	2008	2009
Capture*	47.3	58.0	48.0
Freshwater fishes	3.2	3.2*	3.2*
Bigeye grunt	2.2	2.2*	2.2*
Round sardinella	8.4	8.4*	8.4*
Skipjack tuna	1.8	9.0	2.8
Aquaculture*	1.3	1.3	1.3
Total catch*	48.6	59.3	49.3

* FAO estimate(s).

Source: FAO.

Mining

(estimates)

	2007	2008	2009
Gold (kg)	1,243	4,205	6,947
Natural gas (million cubic metres)	1,574	1,600	1,600
Crude petroleum ('000 barrels)	17,727	22,000	21,500
Manganese ore (metric tons)	94,618	176,561	177,000

Source: US Geological Survey.

Industry

SELECTED PRODUCTS

('000 metric tons unless otherwise indicated)

	2006	2007	2008
Beer of barley*†	287	267	306
Palm oil—unrefined*	281	289	285
Raw sugar	145	145	150
Plywood ('000 cubic metres)*	88	82	81§
Jet fuel	88	47	53
Motor gasoline (petrol)	605	564	466
Kerosene	976	933	750
Gas-diesel (distillate fuel) oils	1,269	1,089	1,174
Residual fuel oils	521	500	657
Cement‡	360	469	360
Electric energy (million kWh)	5,535	5,631	5,800

Cotton yarn (pure and mixed, '000 metric tons): 24.7† in 1989.

Canned fish ('000 metric tons): 121.8 in 2002 (Source: FAO).

Beer of barley ('000 metric tons, FAO estimate): 315 in 2009 (estimate), 344 in 2010 (estimate) (Source: FAO).

Palm oil—unrefined ('000 metric tons): 345.0 in 2009 (unofficial figure), 300.0 in 2010 (unofficial figure) (Source: FAO).

Plywood ('000 cubic metres): 81.0 in 2009 (estimate), 82.1 in 2010 (estimate) (Source: FAO).

Cement ('000 metric tons): 283 in 2009 (Source: US Geological Survey).

* Data from FAO.

† Estimated figures.

‡ Data from the US Geological Survey.

§ Unofficial figure.

Source: mainly UN Industrial Commodity Statistics Database.

Finance

CURRENCY AND EXCHANGE RATES

Monetary Units

100 centimes = 1 franc de la Communauté financière africaine (CFA).

Sterling, Dollar and Euro Equivalents (30 December 2011)

£1 sterling = 783.813 francs CFA;
US $1 = 506.961 francs CFA;
€1 = 655.957 francs CFA;
10,000 francs CFA = £12.76 = $19.73 = €15.24.

Average Exchange Rate (francs CFA per US $)

2009 472.19
2010 495.28
2011 471.87

Note: An exchange rate of 1 French franc = 50 francs CFA, established in 1948, remained in force until January 1994, when the CFA franc was devalued by 50%, with the exchange rate adjusted to 1 French franc = 100 francs CFA. This relationship to French currency remained in effect with the introduction of the euro on 1 January 1999. From that date, accordingly, a fixed exchange rate of €1 = 655.957 francs CFA has been in operation.

BUDGET

('000 million francs CFA)

Revenue*	2008	2009	2010†
Tax revenue	1,638.0	1,795.6	1,971.0
Direct taxes	541.7	542.9	598.1
Indirect taxes‡	1,096.3	1,252.7	1,372.9
Social security contributions	141.4	151.2	177.7
Oil and gas revenue	138.6	0.0	0.0
Other	58.8	110.9	97.8
Total	1,976.8	2,057.7	2,246.6

Expenditure§	2008	2009	2010†
Current expenditure	1,879.9	1,945.2	2,124.6
Wages and salaries	711.7	745.0	814.1
Social security benefits	188.6	203.4	217.1
Subsidies and other current transfers	164.7	216.1	281.5
Crisis-related expenditure	122.5	128.5	145.5
Other current expenditure	504.3	483.7	482.3
Interest due	188.1	168.5	184.2
Internal	64.5	42.0	52.5
External	123.6	126.5	131.7
Capital expenditure	319.6	334.3	355.4
Domestically funded	230.3	217.4	254.8
Funded from abroad	77.7	102.8	85.7
Total	2,199.5	2,279.5	2,480.0

* Excluding grants received ('000 million francs CFA): 179.5 in 2008; 63.1 in 2009; 35.8 in 2010 (programmed figure).

† Programmed figures.

‡ Excluding taxes on petroleum products.

§ Excluding net lending ('000 million francs CFA): 17.7 in 2008; 12.4 in 2009; 31.7 in 2010 (programmed figure).

Source: IMF, *Côte d'Ivoire: Second Review Under the Three-Year Arrangement Under the Extended Credit Facility, Request for Waivers of Non-observance of Performance Criteria, and Financing Assurances Review—Staff Report; Staff Statement; Press Release on the Executive Board Discussion; and Statement by the Executive Director for Côte d'Ivoire* (July 2010).

2010 ('000 million francs CFA): *Revenue:* Tax revenue 1,928.5 (Direct taxes 551.1, Indirect taxes 1,377.4); Social security contributions 162.8; Other revenue 84.9; Total 2,176.2 (excl. grants received 60.4). *Expenditure:* Current expenditure 2,115.8 (Wages and salaries 800.4, Social security benefits 212.6, Subsidies and other current transfers 272.5, Crisis-related expenditure 144.2, Other current expenditure 491.6, Interest due 194.5); Capital expenditure 348.6 (Domestically funded 259.2, Funded from abroad 89.4); Total 2,464.4 (excl. net lending 33.4) (Source: *Côte d'Ivoire: 2011 Article IV Consultation and Requests for a Three-Year Arrangement Under the Extended Credit Facility and for Additional Interim Assistance Under the Enhanced Initiative for Heavily Indebted Poor Countries—Staff Report; Public Information Notice and Press Release on the Executive Board Discussion; and Statement by the Executive Director for Côte d'Ivoire.*—November 2011).

INTERNATIONAL RESERVES
(excluding gold, US $ million at 31 December)

	2008	2009	2010
IMF special drawing rights	1.2	427.5	420.5
Reserve position in IMF	1.2	1.3	1.3
Foreign exchange	2,250.3	2,838.1	3,202.6
Total	2,252.7	3,266.8	3,624.4

Source: IMF, *International Financial Statistics*.

MONEY SUPPLY
('000 million francs CFA at 31 December)

	2008	2009	2010
Currency outside banks	1,078.7	1,343.2	1,638.2
Demand deposits at deposit money banks*	894.3	967.6	1,091.1
Total money (incl. others)	1,999.5	2,341.7	2,736.6

* Excluding the deposits of public establishments of an administrative or social nature.

Source: IMF, *International Financial Statistics*.

COST OF LIVING
(Consumer Price Index for African households in Abidjan; base: 2000 = 100)

	2006	2007	2008
Food, beverages and tobacco	117.5	123.8	137.8
Clothing and footwear	101.4	100.9	100.2
Rent and utilities	128.3	127.7	133.5
All items (incl. others)	119.9	122.2	130.0

2009: Food, beverages and tobacco 142.3; All items (incl. others) 131.3.

2010: All items 132.9.

Source: ILO.

NATIONAL ACCOUNTS
(million francs CFA at current prices)

Expenditure on the Gross Domestic Product

	2007	2008	2009
Government final consumption expenditure	1,298,823	1,466,813	1,527,992
Private final consumption expenditure	6,995,110	7,507,222	7,544,758
Change in inventories	−166,093	−197,315	−323,940
Gross fixed capital formation	1,132,444	1,297,781	1,493,746
Total domestic expenditure	9,260,284	10,074,501	10,242,556
Exports of goods and services	4,604,547	5,212,347	5,259,258
Less Imports of goods and services	4,115,648	4,514,866	4,216,885
GDP in purchasers' values	9,749,183	10,771,983	11,284,929

Gross Domestic Product by Economic Activity

	2007	2008	2009
Agriculture, forestry and fishing	2,144,500	2,408,072	2,605,113
Mining and quarrying	409,707	498,204	411,516
Manufacturing	1,523,119	1,742,047	1,776,299
Electricity, gas and water	125,496	135,410	143,399
Construction	210,677	238,908	231,502
Wholesale and retail trade, restaurants and hotels	1,138,852	1,228,821	1,292,597
Finance, insurance, real estate and business services	1,552,347	1,703,496	1,823,481
Transport and communications	827,777	912,590	968,492
Public administration and defence	646,359	658,404	633,205
Other services	448,640	452,759	513,881
Sub-total	9,027,474	9,978,711	10,399,485
Indirect taxes	1,073,428	1,165,743	1,277,654
Less Imputed bank service charge	351,719	372,470	392,211
GDP in purchasers' values	9,749,183	10,771,983	11,284,929

Source: African Development Bank.

BALANCE OF PAYMENTS
(US $ million)

	2007	2008	2009
Exports of goods f.o.b.	8,668.8	10,390.1	10,503.3
Imports of goods f.o.b.	−6,104.4	−7,068.6	−6,318.1
Trade balance	2,564.4	3,321.5	4,185.2
Exports of services	933.0	1,024.5	975.0
Imports of services	−2,483.7	−2,659.9	−2,485.0
Balance on goods and services	1,013.7	1,686.1	2,675.2
Other income received	218.1	236.6	223.9
Other income paid	−1,027.5	−1,138.7	−1,114.0
Balance on goods, services and income	204.3	784.0	1,785.1
Current transfers received	476.6	582.3	760.9
Current transfers paid	−819.9	−914.8	−875.8
Current balance	−139.0	451.6	1,670.2
Capital account (net)	92.9	89.3	103.8
Direct investment from abroad	426.8	446.1	380.9
Portfolio investment assets	−42.9	−28.6	−42.1
Portfolio investment liabilities	145.6	76.6	−8.8
Financial derivatives (net)	−7.0	−6.2	—
Other investment assets	−377.1	−369.9	−1,432.0
Other investment liabilities	181.6	−322.0	295.1
Net errors and omissions	39.9	−106.5	0.8
Overall balance	320.7	230.5	967.8

Source: IMF, *International Financial Statistics*.

External Trade

PRINCIPAL COMMODITIES
(distribution by SITC, US $ million)

Imports c.i.f.	2007	2008	2009
Food and live animals	1,025.5	1,376.8	1,442.3
Fish, crustaceans and molluscs, and preparations thereof	277.8	394.0	360.6
Fish, frozen, excl. fillets	270.9	385.9	353.5
Cereals and cereal preparations	484.3	657.8	787.0
Rice	326.1	468.3	597.3
Rice, semi-milled or wholly milled	325.0	468.3	597.3
Rice, semi-milled or wholly milled (unbroken)	251.7	332.0	458.7
Mineral fuels, lubricants, etc.	2,016.3	2,815.2	1,739.7
Petroleum, petroleum products, etc.	2,005.0	2,806.4	1,712.2
Crude petroleum and oils obtained from bituminous materials	1,887.6	2,669.0	1,622.9
Petroleum products, refined	102.8	119.1	76.5
Chemicals and related products	735.4	898.0	916.3
Medical and pharmaceutical products	178.9	228.5	251.2
Medicaments (incl. veterinary medicaments)	164.9	209.8	213.9
Basic manufactures	740.5	886.6	816.2
Iron and steel	200.0	259.3	207.0
Non-metallic mineral manufactures	149.7	191.1	162.2
Machinery and transport equipment	1,315.1	1,317.6	1,442.9
Road vehicles	463.0	404.4	341.3
Other transport equipment	93.2	25.4	55.3
Miscellaneous manufactured articles	350.0	107.1	129.3
Total (incl. others)*	6,683.1	7,883.7	6,959.9

Exports f.o.b.	2007	2008	2009
Food and live animals	3,041.2	3,715.2	4,646.5
Fish, crustaceans and molluscs, and preparations thereof	172.0	196.5	170.2
Fish, prepared or preserved	155.8	174.8	135.7
Vegetables and fruit	291.3	344.7	335.3
Fruit and nuts, fresh, dried	287.2	338.0	321.9
Coffee, tea, cocoa, spices and manufactures thereof	2,460.8	3,016.0	3,944.5
Coffee and coffee substitutes	252.4	204.5	217.3
Coffee, not roasted; coffee husks and skins	181.0	132.5	134.4
Cocoa	2,131.0	2,644.1	3,606.1
Cocoa beans, raw, roasted	1,438.4	1,754.1	2,596.1
Cocoa butter and paste	214.2	282.5	323.3
Crude materials (inedible) except fuels	740.8	910.9	609.2
Cork and wood	246.3	260.6	148.6
Wood, simply worked and railway sleepers of wood	211.3	220.6	109.1
Wood, non-coniferous species, sawn, planed, tongued, grooved, etc.	181.5	193.5	90.0
Textile fibres (not wool tops) and their wastes (not in yarn)	98.7	80.7	68.8
Raw cotton, excl. linters, not carded or combed	98.0	79.7	68.1
Mineral fuels, lubricants, etc.	2,629.3	3,627.9	3,019.2
Petroleum, petroleum products, etc.	2,627.7	3,625.4	3,016.7
Crude petroleum and oils obtained from bituminous materials	1,035.4	1,524.5	1,141.1
Petroleum products, refined	1,552.9	2,036.4	1,409.3
Chemicals and related products	305.5	369.7	405.2
Basic manufactures	345.9	376.3	346.8
Machinery and transport equipment	391.7	315.8	630.0
Road vehicles	198.3	41.4	86.5
Other transport equipment	96.7	194.4	423.3
Ships, boats and floating structures	4.3	96.8	338.8
Total (incl. others)†	8,067.7	9,778.8	10,280.1

* Including commodities and transactions not classified elsewhere in SITC (US $ million): 107.6 in 2007; 33.6 in 2008; 47.8 in 2009.

† Including commodities and transactions not classified elsewhere in SITC (US $ million): 50.6 in 2007; 94.9 in 2008; 220.7 in 2009.

Source: UN, *International Trade Statistics Yearbook*.

PRINCIPAL TRADING PARTNERS
(US $ million)

Imports c.i.f.	2007	2008	2009
Belgium	98.3	75.9	96.9
Brazil	89.3	86.4	67.7
China, People's Republic	438.2	542.1	501.0
France (incl. Monaco)	1,451.8	999.6	991.5
Germany	181.0	224.5	205.2
India	169.8	131.5	127.7
Italy	138.8	160.9	152.7
Japan	163.9	204.6	146.7
Korea, Republic	97.5	108.9	99.3
Mauritania	76.7	114.7	117.2
Morocco	39.8	85.0	62.7
Netherlands	120.5	155.8	163.5
Nigeria	1,607.7	2,313.4	1,434.8
South Africa	75.3	89.3	98.9
Spain	102.4	193.9	182.3
Thailand	185.8	356.2	355.2
United Kingdom	146.5	158.8	103.1
USA	180.0	209.1	228.3
Venezuela	213.5	284.2	126.5
Viet Nam	49.6	82.0	144.6
Total (incl. others)	6,683.1	7,883.7	6,959.9

Exports f.o.b.	2007	2008	2009
Algeria	117.5	103.3	97.3
Belgium	179.5	204.6	238.6
Benin	106.1	104.2	96.9
Burkina Faso	340.3	412.0	381.4
Canada	117.9	36.6	144.8
Equatorial Guinea	104.9	148.4	112.6
France (incl. Monaco)	1,650.7	1,357.8	1,123.1
Germany	251.5	694.6	738.0
Ghana	162.4	450.9	563.9
India	196.3	178.3	281.4
Italy	280.5	380.5	328.1
Mali	297.3	326.0	267.0
Netherlands	737.1	1,100.3	1,428.2
Nigeria	644.2	625.2	715.6
Panama	7.4	7.4	0.6
Poland	77.1	95.7	97.0
Senegal	127.1	163.8	146.3
Spain	292.8	223.6	191.1
Togo	77.4	138.5	70.4
United Kingdom	300.3	278.1	259.3
USA	547.2	945.1	800.3
Total (incl. others)	8,067.7	9,778.8	10,280.1

Source: UN, *International Trade Statistics Yearbook*.

Transport

RAILWAYS
(traffic)

	2001	2002	2003
Passengers ('000)	399.5	320.0	87.5
Freight carried ('000 metric tons)	1,016.3	900.7	149.7

Passenger-km (million): 93.1 in 1999 (Source: SITARAIL—Transport Ferroviaire de Personnel et de Marchandises, Abidjan).

Freight ton-km (million): 537.6 in 1999 (Source: SITARAIL—Transport Ferroviaire de Personnel et de Marchandises, Abidjan).

ROAD TRAFFIC
('000 motor vehicles in use)

	1998	1999	2000
Passenger cars	98.4	109.6	113.9
Commercial vehicles	45.4	54.1	54.9

2001–02 ('000 motor vehicles in use): Figures assumed to be unchanged from 2000.

Source: UN, *Statistical Yearbook*.

2007 (motor vehicles in use): Passenger cars 314,165; Buses and coaches 17,512; Vans and lorries 78,575; Motorcycles and mopeds 38,105 (Source: IRF, *World Road Statistics*).

SHIPPING

Merchant Fleet
(registered at 31 December)

	2007	2008	2009
Number of vessels	35	35	35
Total displacement ('000 grt)	9.2	9.2	9.2

Source: IHS Fairplay, *World Fleet Statistics*.

International Sea-borne Freight Traffic
(freight traffic at Abidjan, '000 metric tons)

	2001	2002	2003
Goods loaded	5,787	5,710	6,108
Goods unloaded	9,858	9,018	8,353

Source: Port Autonome d'Abidjan.

Freight traffic at San-Pédro ('000 metric tons, 2000): Goods loaded 1,102; Goods unloaded 251.

CIVIL AVIATION
(traffic on scheduled services)*

	1999	2000	2001
Kilometres flown (million)	6	3	1
Passengers carried ('000)	260	108	46
Passenger-km (million)	381	242	130
Total ton-km (million)	50	34	19

* Including an apportionment of the traffic of Air Afrique.

Source: UN, *Statistical Yearbook*.

Tourism

ARRIVALS BY COUNTRY OF RESIDENCE
('000)

	1996*	1997†	1998†
Belgium	4.3	4.2	4.5
Benin	12.5	11.1	14.3
Burkina Faso	11.0	11.9	17.1
Congo, Repub.	6.0	n.a.	7.6
France	66.7	69.0	73.2
Gabon	3.0	n.a.	5.4
Germany	3.2	3.8	3.9
Ghana	5.4	n.a.	6.7
Guinea	8.1	n.a.	12.5
Italy	5.0	14.0	7.6
Mali	10.7	n.a.	15.2
Niger	5.0	n.a.	5.4
Nigeria	7.9	n.a.	14.1
Senegal	13.0	12.1	16.6
Togo	8.7	8.2	10.8
United Kingdom	5.1	4.5	5.6
USA	15.3	17.0	18.8
Total (incl. others)	236.9	274.1	301.0

* Figures refer only to air arrivals at Abidjan—Félix Houphouët-Boigny airport.

† Figures refer to air arrivals at Abidjan—Félix Houphouët-Boigny airport and to arrivals at land frontiers.

Receipts from tourism (US $ million, excl. passenger transport): 317 in 1997; 331 in 1998; 337 in 1999; 291 in 2000; 289 in 2001; 490 in 2002.

Source: World Tourism Organization.

Communications Media

	2008	2009	2010
Telephones ('000 main lines in use)	356.5	282.1	283.3
Mobile cellular telephones ('000 subscribers)	10,449.0	13,184.3	15,026.8
Internet users ('000)	660	967	n.a.
Broadband subscribers ('000)	10.0	10.0	7.9

Personal computers: 323,000 (16.8 per 1,000 persons) in 2005.

Source: International Telecommunication Union.

Television receivers ('000 in use): 887 in 2000 (Source: UNESCO, *Statistical Yearbook*).

Radio receivers ('000 in use): 2,260 in 1997 (Source: UNESCO, *Statistical Yearbook*).

Daily Newspapers (national estimates): 12 (average circulation 235,000 copies) in 1997; 12 (average circulation 238,000 copies) in 1998; 21 in 2004 (Source: UNESCO Institute for Statistics).

Non-daily Newspapers: 15 in 1996 (average circulation 251,000 copies) (Source: UNESCO, *Statistical Yearbook*).

Education

(2008/09, unless otherwise indicated)

	Teachers	Students		
		Males	Females	Total
Pre-primary	3,697	32,574	31,562	64,136
Primary	56,575	1,317,988	1,065,371	2,383,359
Secondary	20,124*	474,203†	262,446†	736,649†
Tertiary‡	n.a.	104,571	52,201	156,772

* 1998/99.
† 2001/02.
‡ 2006/07.

Institutions: 207 pre-primary in 1995/96; 7,599 primary in 1996/97.

Source: mostly UNESCO Institute for Statistics.

Pupil-teacher ratio (primary education, UNESCO estimate): 42.1 in 2008/09 (Source: UNESCO Institute for Statistics).

Adult literacy rate (UNESCO estimates): 55.3% (males 64.7%; females 45.3%) in 2009 (Source: UNESCO Institute for Statistics).

Directory

The Government

HEAD OF STATE

President of the Republic, Minister of Defence: ALASSANE DRAMANE OUATTARA (elected 28 November 2010; sworn in 6 May 2011).

COUNCIL OF MINISTERS
(May 2012)

Prime Minister and Keeper of the Seals, Minister of Justice: JEANNOT KOUADIO AHOUSSOU.

Minister of State, Minister of the Interior: HAMED BAKAYOKO.

Minister of State, Minister of Foreign Affairs: DANIEL KABLAN DUNCAN.

Minister of State, Minister of Employment, Social Affairs and Solidarity: GILBERT KAFANA KONÉ.

Minister of State, Minister of Planning and Development: ALBERT TOIKESSE MABRI.

Minister of State, Minister of Industry: MOUSSA DOSSO.

Minister of the Economy and Finance: CHARLES KOFFI DIBY.

Minister of Economic Infrastructure: PATRICK ACHI.

Minister of Mines, Petroleum and Energy: ADAMA TOUNGARA.

Minister of Health and the Fight Against AIDS: Prof. THÉRÈSE AYA N'DRI YOMAN.

Minister of National Education: KANDIA KAMISSOKO CAMARA.

Minister of the Civil Service and Administrative Reform: KONAN GNAMIEN.

Minister of Handicrafts and the Promotion of Small and Medium-sized Enterprises: SIDIKI KONATÉ.

Minister of Higher Education and Scientific Research: IBRAHIMA CISSÉ BACONGO.

Minister of Animal and Fishing Resources: KOBENA KOUASSI ADJOUMANI.

Minister of Agriculture: MAMADOU SANGAFOWA COULIBALY.

Minister of Trade: DAGOBERT BANZIO.

Minister of Technical Education and Professional Training: ALBERT FLINDÉ.

Minister in charge of Human Rights and Civil Liberties: GNÉNÉMA COULIBALY.

Minister of Culture and Francophone Affairs: MAURICE KOUAKOU BANDAMA.

Minister of the Family, Women and Children: RAYMONDE GOUDOU COFFIE.

Minister of Communication: SOULEYMANE COTY DIAKITÉ.

Minister of the Environment and Sustainable Developmen RÉMI ALLAH KOUADIO.

Minister of Tourism: CHARLES AKÉ ATCHIMON.

Minister of Construction, Sanitation and Town Planning: MAMADOU SANOGO.

Minister of Sport and Leisure: PHILIPPE LÉGRÉ.

Minister of Posts and Information and Communication Technologies: BRUNO NABAGNÉ KONÉ.

Minister of Transport: GAOUSSOU TOURÉ.

Minister of Water and Forests: CLÉMENT BOUEKA NABO.

Minister in charge of African Integration: ADAMA BICTOGO.

Minister of the Promotion of Youth and Social Services: ALAIN MICHEL LOBOGNON.

Minister of the Promotion of Housing: NIALÉ KABA.

Minister in charge of War Veterans and War Victims: MATHIEU BABAUD DARRET.

Minister of Urban Health: ANNE DÉSIRÉE OULOTO.

Minister-delegate to the Prime Minister, with responsibility for Justice: LOMA CISSÉ MATTO.

Minister of State, Secretary-General of the Presidency: AMADOU GON COULIBALY.

Minister, Director of the Presidential Cabinet: MARCEL AMON-TANOH.

Minister in charge of Presidential Affairs: TENÉ BIRAHIMA OUATTARA.

Minister at the Presidency, in charge of Defence: PAUL KOFFI KOFFI.

Minister at the Presidency, in charge of Relations with the Institutions: ALBERT AGGREY.

MINISTRIES

Office of the President: 01 BP 1354, Abidjan 01; tel. 20-22-02-22; fax 20-21-14-25; internet www.cotedivoirepr.ci.

Office of the Prime Minister: blvd Angoulvant, 01 BP 1533, Abidjan 01; tel. 20-31-50-00; fax 20-22-18-33; internet www.premierministre.ci.

Ministry of Agriculture: 25e étage, Immeuble Caisse de Stabilisation, BP V82, Abidjan; tel. 20-21-38-58; fax 20-21-46-18; e-mail minagra@cimail.net.

Ministry of Animal and Fishing Resources: 11e étage, Immeuble Caisse de Stabilisation, Plateau, Abidjan; tel. 20-21-33-94.

Ministry of the Civil Service and Administrative Reform: Immeuble Fonction Public, blvd Angoulvand, BP V93, Abidjan; tel. 20-21-42-90; fax 20-21-12-86; internet www.emploi.gouv.ci.

Ministry of Communication: 22e étage, Tour C, Tours Administratives, Plateau, Abidjan; tel. 20-21-07-84; internet www.communication.gouv.ci.

Ministry of Construction, Sanitation and Town Planning: 26e étage, Tour D, Tours Administratives, 20 BP 650, Abidjan; tel. 20-21-82-35; fax 20-21-35-68.

Ministry of Culture and Francophone Affairs: 22e étage, Tour E, Tours Administratives, BP V39, Abidjan; tel. 20-21-40-34; fax 20-21-33-59; e-mail culture.ci@ci.refer.org; internet www.mcf-culture.ci.

Ministry of Defence: Camp Galliéni, côté Bibliothèque nationale, BP V241, Abidjan; tel. 20-21-02-88; fax 20-22-41-75.

Ministry of Economic Infrastructure: 23e étage, Immeuble Postel 2001, BP V6, Plateau, Abidjan; tel. 20-34-73-01; fax 20-21-20-43; e-mail minie@aviso.ci.

Ministry of the Economy and Finance: 16e étage, Immeuble SCIAM, ave Marchand, BP V163, Abidjan; tel. 20-20-08-42; fax 20-21-32-08; internet www.finances.gouv.ci.

Ministry of Employment, Social Affairs and Solidarity: Abidjan.

inistry of the Environment and Sustainable Development: étage, Tour D, Tours Administratives, BP V06, Abidjan; tel. 20-1-35; fax 20-22-20-50.

stry of the Family, Women and Children: Tour E, Tours istratives, BP V200, Abidjan; tel. 20-21-76-26; fax 20-21-44-

of Foreign Affairs and African Integration: Bloc l, blvd Angoulvant, BP V109, Abidjan; tel. 20-22-71-50; 3-08; e-mail infos@mae.ci; internet www.mae.ci.

Handicrafts and the Promotion of Small and d Enterprises: Abidjan.

alth and the Fight Against AIDS: 16e étage, Tour istratives, Plateau, Abidjan; tel. 20-21-52-40.

her Education and Scientific Research: 20e s Administratives, BP V151, Abidjan; tel. 20-21-25.

Ministry of Industry: 15e étage, Immeuble CCIA, rue Jean-Paul II, BP V65, Abidjan; tel. 20-21-64-73.

Ministry of Information and Communication Technology: 21e étage, Immeuble Postel 2001, BP V138, Abidjan; tel. 22-34-73-65; fax 22-44-78-47.

Ministry of the Interior: Immeuble SETU, en face de la préfecture, BP V241, Abidjan; tel. 20-22-38-16; fax 20-22-36-48.

Ministry of Justice and Human Rights: Bloc Ministériel, blvd Angoulvand A-17, BP V107, Plateau, Abidjan; tel. 20-21-17-27; fax 20-33-12-59; internet www.justice.gouv.ci.

Ministry of Mines, Petroleum and Energy: 15e étage, Immeuble SCIAM, ave Marchand, BP V40, Abidjan; tel. 20-21-66-17; fax 20-21-37-30.

Ministry of National Education: 28e étage, Tour D, Tours Administratives, BP V120, Abidjan; tel. 20-21-85-27; fax 20-22-93-22; e-mail menfb@ci.refer.org.

Ministry of Planning and Development: 16eme étage, Immeuble SCIAM, Plateau, Abidjan; tel. 20-20-08-42; fax 20-20-08-65; e-mail gvode@plan.gouv.ci.

Ministry of the Promotion of Housing: Abidjan.

Ministry of the Promotion of Youth and Social Services: 8e étage, Tour B, Tours Administratives, BP V136, Abidjan; tel. 20-21-92-64; fax 20-22-48-21.

Ministry of Sport and Leisure: Abidjan.

Ministry of the Struggle against AIDS: 7e étage, Immeuble Caisse de Stabilisation, Plateau, Abidjan; tel. 20-21-08-46.

Ministry of Technical Education and Professional Training: 10e étage, Tour C, Tours Administratives, Plateau, Abidjan; tel. 20-21-17-02.

Ministry of Tourism: 15e étage, Tour D, Tours Administratives, BP V184, Abidjan 01; tel. 20-34-79-13; fax 20-44-55-80; internet www.tourisme.gouv.ci.

Ministry of Trade: 26e étage, Immeuble CCIA, rue Jean-Paul II, BP V65, Abidjan; tel. 20-21-76-35; fax 20-21-64-74.

Ministry of Transport: 14e étage, Immeuble Postel 2001, BP V06, Abidjan; tel. 20-34-48-58; fax 20-34-48-54.

Ministry of Urban Health: Abidjan.

Ministry of Water and Forests: Abidjan.

President and Legislature

PRESIDENT

Presidential Election, First Round, 31 October 2010

Candidate	Votes	% of votes
Laurent Gbagbo (FPI)	1,756,504	38.04
Alassane Dramane Ouattara (RDR)	1,481,091	32.07
Henri Konan Bédié (PDCI—RDA)	1,165,532	25.24
Albert Toikesse Mabri (UDPCI)	118,671	2.57
Others*	96,023	2.08
Total†	4,617,821	100.00

* There were 10 other candidates.
† Excluding invalid votes (225,624).

Presidential Election, Second Round, 28 November 2010

Candidate	Votes	% of votes
Alassane Dramane Ouattara (RDR)	2,483,164	54.10
Laurent Gbagbo (FPI)	2,107,055	45.90
Total	4,590,219	100.00

The above results were released by the Commission électorale indépendant (CEI) on 2 December 2010. However, later on 2 December the President of the Conseil constitutionnel, Paul Yao N'Dré, declared the CEI's announcement null and void and the following day released results indicating that Gbagbo had won the election, having received 51.45% of votes cast to Ouattara's 48.55%. The Special Representative of the UN Secretary-General for Côte d'Ivoire, Choi Young-Jin, described N'Dré's decision as 'having no factual basis'; furthermore, in his role as certifier of the Ivorian elections Choi declared Ouattara the winner. On 8 December the UN Security Council released a statement confirming its endorsement of Ouattara as the President-elect of Côte d'Ivoire.

LEGISLATURE

Assemblée nationale

01 BP 1381, Abidjan 01; tel. 20-20-82-00; fax 20-20-82-33; e-mail admin@anci.ci; internet www.anci.ci.

President: GUILLAUME SORO.

General Election, 11 December 2011*

Party	Seats
Rassemblement des républicains (RDR)	127
Parti démocratique de la Côte d'Ivoire—Rassemblement démocratique africain (PDCI—RDA)	77
Union pour la démocratie et la paix de la Côte d'Ivoire (UDPCI)	7
Rassemblement des Houphouëtistes pour la démocratie et la paix (RHDP)	4
Mouvement des forces d'avenir (MFA)	3
Union pour la Côte d'Ivoire (UPCI)	1
Independents	35
Total	254‡

* The election was boycotted by the Front populaire ivoirien (FPI).

‡ Voting in one constituency did not take place owing to the death of a candidate. On 31 January 2012 the Constitutional Council annulled the results of voting in 12 constituencies owing to irregularities. Subsequently, by-elections were held on 26 February in the 13 constituencies, at which the RDR won four seats, the UDPCI two seats, the PDCI—RDA one seat and independent candidates secured four seats. The results in the remaining two constituencies remained undeclared. According to final results published by the CEI on 8 March, the RDR held 138 of the 253 declared seats, the PDCI—RDA held 86 seats, independent candidates held 17 seats and the UDPCI held eight seats. Other party representations remained unchanged.

Election Commission

Commission électorale indépendant: 08 BP 2648, Abidjan; tel. 21-30-58-01; internet www.ceici.org; f. 2001; 30 mems; Pres. YOUSSOUF BAKAYOKO.

Advisory Councils

Constitutional Council: 22 blvd Carde, BP 4642, Abidjan 01; tel. 20-21-31-64; fax 20-21-21-68; internet www.gouv.ci/conconst.php; f. 2000; Pres. FRANCIS WODIÉ.

Economic and Social Council: blvd Carde, angle ave Terrasson de Fougère, 04 BP 304, Abidjan 04; tel. 20-21-14-54; internet ces-ci.org; f. 1961; Pres. MARCEL ZADI KESSY; 120 mems.

Political Organizations

In mid-2007 there were more than 100 registered political organizations.

Alliance pour la nouvelle Côte d'Ivoire (ANCI): Cocody II Plateaux, 06 BP 677, Abidjan 06; tel. 22-41-56-45; fax 21-24-37-97; e-mail info@an-ci.org; internet www.an-ci.org; f. 2007 by fmr mems of Rassemblement des républicains; Pres. ZEMOGO FOFANA; Sec.-Gen. JEAN-JACQUES BÉCHIO.

Alliance pour la paix, le progrès et la souveraineté (APS): Abidjan; f. 2003 by fmr members of the UDPCI (q.v.); Pres. HILAIRE DIGBEU ANI.

Forces nouvelles (FN): Bouaké; tel. 20-20-04-04; e-mail senacom@fnci.info; internet www.fnci.info; f. 2003 by the Mouvement patriotique de Côte d'Ivoire (MPCI), following its absorption of the Mouvement populaire ivoirien du grand ouest (MPIGO) and the Mouvement pour la justice et la paix (MJP), both of which were based in Man, in the west of Côte d'Ivoire; representatives of these three 'politico-military' groups, which had emerged following the outbreak of civil conflict in September 2002, were included in the Government of National Reconciliation formed in March 2003.

Front populaire ivoirien (FPI): Marcory Zone 4C, 22 BP 302, Abidjan 22; tel. 21-24-36-76; fax 21-35-35-50; internet www.fpi.ci; f. 1990; socialist; Sec.-Gen. SYLVAIN MIAKA OURETO.

Liberté et démocratie pour la République (Lider): Abidjan; f. 2011; Leader MAMADOU COULIBALY.

Mouvement des forces d'avenir (MFA): 15 BP 794, Abidjan 15; tel. 21-24-42-02; e-mail contact@mfa-ci.com; internet www.mfa-ci.com; f. 1995; mem. of alliance, Rassemblement des Houphouëtistes pour la démocratie et la paix, formed in advance of proposed (but subsequently postponed) presidential elections in 2005; Pres. INNOCENT KOBENA ANAKY; Sec.-Gen. DAKPA PHILIPPE LEGRE.

Parti africain pour la renaissance ivoirienne (PARI): Abidjan; f. 1991; Sec.-Gen. DANIEL ANIKPO.

Parti démocratique de la Côte d'Ivoire—Rassemblement démocratique africain (PDCI—RDA): 05 BP 36, Abidjan 05; e-mail sg@pdcirda.org; internet www.pdcirda.org; f. 1946; mem. of alliance, Rassemblement des Houphouëtistes pour la démocratie et la paix, formed in advance of proposed (but subsequently postponed) presidential elections in 2005; Pres. HENRI KONAN BÉDIÉ; Sec.-Gen. ALPHONSE DJÉDJÉ MADY.

Parti ivoirien des travailleurs (PIT): Adjamé 220 logements, face Cinéma Liberté, Immeuble Mistral Appartement 602, 20 BP 43, Abidjan 20; tel. 20-37-79-42; fax 20-37-29-00; e-mail pit.ci@aviso.ci; internet www.pit-ci.org; social-democratic; f. 1990; First Nat. Sec. FRANCIS WODIÉ.

Rassemblement du peuple de Côte d'Ivoire (RPCI): Abidjan; f. 2012; Pres. MORIFERÉ BAMBA.

Parti pour le progrès et le socialisme (PPS): Abidjan; f. 1993; Sec.-Gen. Prof. MORIFÉRÉ BAMBA.

Union des sociaux-démocrates (USD): 08 BP 1866, Abidjan 08; tel. 22-44-06-70; Pres. BERNARD ZADI ZAOUROU; Sec.-Gen. Me JÉRÔME CLIMANLO COULIBALY.

Rassemblement des républicains (RDR): 8 rue Lepic, Cocody, 06 BP 111, Abidjan 06; tel. 22-44-33-51; fax 22-41-55-73; e-mail le-rdr@yahoo.fr; internet www.le-rdr.org; f. 1994 following split from PDCI—RDA (q.v.); officially boycotted the general election of Dec. 2000, except for a faction of some 60 candidates, led by ALPHONSE OULAÏ TOUSSÉA; mem. of alliance, Rassemblement des Houphouëtistes pour la démocratie et la paix, formed in advance of proposed (but subsequently postponed) presidential elections in 2005; Pres. Dr ALASSANE DRAMANE OUATTARA; Sec.-Gen. HENRIETTE DAGRI-DIABATÉ.

Union démocratique citoyenne (UDCY): 37 bis rue de la Canebière—PISAM, 01 BP 1410, Abidjan 01; tel. 22-47-12-94; e-mail udcy_ci@hotmail.com; internet www.udcy.com; f. 2000 following split from PDCI—RDA (q.v.); Pres. THÉODORE MEL-EG.

Union pour la démocratie et pour la paix de la Côte d'Ivoire (UDPCI): 06 BP 1481, Abidjan 06; tel. 22-41-60-94; e-mail info@udpci.org; internet www.udpci.org; f. 2001 following split from PDCI—RDA by supporters of fmr Head of State Gen. Robert Gueï; mem. of alliance, Rassemblement des Houphouëtistes pour la démocratie et la paix, formed in advance of proposed (but subsequently postponed) presidential elections in 2005; Pres. ALBERT TOIKESSE MABRI; Sec.-Gen. ALASSANE SALIF N'DIAYE.

Diplomatic Representation

EMBASSIES IN CÔTE D'IVOIRE

Algeria: 53 blvd Clozel, 01 BP 1015, Abidjan 01; tel. 20-21-23-40; fax 20-22-37-12; Ambassador (vacant).

Angola: Lot 2461, rue des Jardins, Cocody-les-Deux-Plateaux, 01 BP 1734, Abidjan 01; tel. 22-44-45-91; fax 22-44-46-52; Ambassador GILBERTO BUTA LUTUKUTA.

Belgium: Cocody Ambassades, angle rue de Bélier et rue A56, 01 BP 1800, Abidjan 01; tel. 22-48-33-60; fax 22-44-16-40; e-mail abidjan@diplobel.fed.be; internet www.diplomatie.be/abidjan; Ambassador PETER HUYGHEBAERT.

Benin: rue des Jasmins, Lot 1610, Cocody-les-Deux-Plateaux, 09 BP 283, Abidjan 09; tel. 22-41-44-13; fax 22-41-27-89; e-mail ambabenin@aviso.ci; Ambassador ANTOINE DIMON AFOUDA.

Burkina Faso: Immeuble SIDAM, 5e étage, 34 ave Houdaille, 01 BP 908, Plateau, Abidjan 01; tel. 20-21-15-01; fax 20-21-66-41; e-mail amba.bf@africaonline.ci; Ambassador JUSTIN KOUTABA.

Cameroon: Immeuble le Général, blvd Botreau Roussel, 06 BP 326, Abidjan 06; tel. 20-21-33-31; fax 20-21-66-11; Ambassador (vacant).

Canada: Immeuble Trade Center, 23 ave Noguès, 01 BP 4104, Abidjan 01; tel. 20-30-07-00; fax 20-30-07-20; e-mail abdjn@international.gc.ca; internet www.canadainternational.gc.ca/cotedivoire; Ambassador CHANTAL DE VARENNES.

Central African Republic: 9 rue des Jasmins, Cocody Danga Nord 01 BP 3387, Abidjan 01; tel. 20-21-36-46; fax 22-44-85-16; Ambassador YAGAO-N'GAMA LAZARE.

China, People's Republic: Lot 45, ave Jacques Aka, Cocody, 01 BP 3691, Abidjan 01; tel. 22-44-59-00; fax 22-44-67-81; e-mail ambchine@aviso.ci; Ambassador WEI WENHUA.

Congo, Democratic Republic: Carrefour France-Amérique, RAN Treichville, ave 21, 01 BP 541, Abidjan 01; tel. 21-24-69-06; Ambassador Isabelle I. Ngangelli.

Egypt: Immeuble El Nasr, 17e étage, rue du Commerce, 01 BP 2104, Abidjan 01; tel. 20-22-62-31; fax 20-22-30-53; e-mail amegypteci@afnet.net; Ambassador Tareq Ibrahim Maaty.

Ethiopia: Immeuble Nour Al-Hayat, 8e étage, 01 BP 3712, Abidjan 01; tel. 20-21-33-65; fax 20-21-37-09; e-mail ambethio@gmail.com; Ambassador Abdulaziz Ahmed Adem.

France: 17 rue Lecoeur, 17 BP 175, Abidjan 17; tel. 20-20-04-04; fax 20-20-04-47; e-mail scac.abidjan-amba@diplomatie.gouv.fr; internet www.ambafrance-ci.org; Ambassador George Serre.

Gabon: Immeuble Les Heveas, blvd Carde, 01 BP 3765, Abidjan 01; tel. 22-44-51-54; fax 22-44-75-05; Ambassador Faustin Mounguengui Nzigou.

Germany: 39 blvd Hassan II, Cocody, 01 BP 1900, Abidjan 01; tel. and fax 22-44-20-30; fax 22-44-20-41; e-mail info@abidjan.diplo.de; internet www.abidjan.diplo.de; Ambassador Karl Prinz.

Ghana: Lot 2393, rue J 95, Cocody-les-Deux-Plateaux, 01 BP 1871, Abidjan 01; tel. 20-33-11-24; fax 20-22-33-57; Ambassador Lt-Col (retd) Enoch Kwame Tweneboah Donkor.

Guinea: Immeuble Duplessis, 08 BP 2280, Abidjan 08; tel. 20-22-25-20; fax 20-32-82-45; Ambassador (vacant).

Holy See: Apostolic Nunciature, rue Mgr. René Kouassi 18, 08 BP 1347, Abidjan 08; tel. 22-40-17-70; fax 22-40-17-74; e-mail nuntius.ci@gmail.com; Apostolic Nuncio Most Rev. Ambrose Madtha.

India: Cocody Danga Nord, 06 BP 318, Abidjan 06; tel. 22-42-37-69; fax 22-42-66-49; e-mail indemabj@afnet.net; Ambassador Shamma Jain.

Iran: blvd de France, en Face de Campus Université de Cocody, rue Belier, Villa No. 1, Abidjan; tel. 22-48-75-48; fax 22-48-75-47; Ambassador Nobakhti Seyed Reza.

Israel: Immeuble Nour Al-Hayat, 9th Floor, ave Chardy, 01 BP 1877, Abidjan 01; tel. 20-21-31-78; fax 20-21-87-04; e-mail info@abidjan.mfa.gov.il; internet abidjan.mfa.gov.il; Ambassador Daniel Kedem.

Italy: 16 rue de la Canebière, Cocody, 01 BP 1905, Abidjan 01; tel. 22-44-61-70; fax 22-44-35-87; e-mail ambasciata.abidjan@esteri.it; internet www.ambabidjan.esteri.it; Ambassador Giancarlo Izzo.

Japan: Immeuble Alpha 2000, ave Chardy, 01 BP 1329, Abidjan 01; tel. 20-21-28-63; fax 20-21-30-51; Ambassador Susumu Inoue.

Korea, Democratic People's Republic: Abidjan; Ambassador Jong Hake.

Korea, Republic: Immeuble le Mans, 8e étage, 01 BP 3950, Abidjan 01; tel. 20-32-22-90; fax 20-22-22-74; e-mail ambcoabj@mofat.go.kr; Ambassador Park Yoon-june.

Lebanon: Immeuble Trade Center, ave Noguès, 01 BP 2227, Abidjan 01; tel. 20-33-28-24; fax 20-32-11-37; e-mail ambliban@hotmail.com; Ambassador Dr Ali Ajami.

Liberia: Immeuble La Symphonie, ave Général de Gaulle, 01 BP 2514, Abidjan 01; tel. 20-22-23-59; fax 22-44-14-75; Ambassador Vivienne Titi Wreh.

Libya: Immeuble Shell, 01 BP 5725, Abidjan 01; tel. 20-22-01-27; fax 20-22-01-30; Chargé d'affaires Taher A. S. Bakir.

Mali: 46 blvd Lagunaire, 01 BP 2746, Abidjan 01; tel. 20-32-31-47; fax 20-21-55-14; Ambassador Amadou Ousmane Touré.

Mauritania: rue Pierre et Marie Curie, 01 BP 2275, Abidjan 01; tel. 22-41-16-43; fax 22-41-05-77; Ambassador Sidi Mohamed Ould Sidaty.

Morocco: 24 rue de la Canebière, 01 BP 146, Cocody, Abidjan 01; tel. 22-44-58-73; fax 22-44-60-58; e-mail sifmaabj@aviso.ci; Ambassador Ahmed Faouzi.

Niger: 23 ave Angoulvant, 01 BP 2743, Abidjan 01; tel. 21-26-28-14; fax 21-26-41-88; Ambassador Moussa Aloua.

igeria: Immeuble Maison du Nigéria, 35 blvd de la République, 01 1906, Abidjan 01; tel. 20-22-30-82; fax 20-21-30-83; e-mail info@ riaembassyci.org; internet www.nigeriaembassyci.org; Ambas- Kayodé Olajuluwa.

a: BP 583, Riviera, Abidjan 01; tel. 22-43-09-59; fax 22-43-11- ail ambrus@globeaccess.net; Ambassador Leonid Rogod.

rabia: Plateau, Abidjan; Ambassador Jamal Bakr Abdul- YOOR.

mmeuble Nabil Choucair, 6 rue du Commerce, 08 BP n 08; tel. 20-33-28-76; fax 20-32-50-39; Ambassador GA.

Villa Marc André, rue Mgr René Kouassi, Cocody, 08 ian 08; tel. 22-44-59-63; fax 22-44-74-50; e-mail iso.ci; Ambassador (vacant).

la Pokou, Cocody Danga Nord, 08 BP 876, Abidjan ; fax 22-44-71-22; e-mail embespci@correo.mae NANDO Moran Calvo-Sotelo.

Switzerland: Immeuble Botreau Roussel, 28 ave Delafosse, Plateau, 01 BP 1914, Abidjan 01; tel. 20-21-17-21; fax 20-21-27-70; e-mail abi.vertretung@eda.admin.ch; Ambassador (vacant).

Tunisia: Immeuble Shell, ave Lamblin, 01 BP 3906, Abidjan 01; tel. 20-22-61-23; fax 20-22-61-24; Ambassador Naceur Bou Ali.

USA: Cocody Riviera Golf, 01 BP 1712, Abidjan 01; tel. 22-49-40-00; fax 22-49-43-23; e-mail abjpress@state.gov; internet abidjan.usembassy.gov; Ambassador Phillip Carter, III.

Judicial System

Since 1964 all civil, criminal, commercial and administrative cases have come under the jurisdiction of the courts of first instance, the assize courts and the Courts of Appeal, with the Supreme Court (referred to in the Constitution of 2000 as the Court of Cassation) as the highest court of appeal.

Supreme Court: rue Gourgas, Cocody, BP V30, Abidjan; tel. 20-22-73-72; fax 20-21-63-04; internet www.gouv.ci/coursupreme.php; comprises three chambers: judicial, administrative and auditing; Pres. Mamadou Koné; Pres. of the Judicial Chamber Kama Yao; Pres. of the Administrative Chamber Georges Amangoua.

Courts of Appeal: Abidjan: First Pres. Marie-Félicité Arkhust Homa Yao; Bouaké: First Pres. Christian Anibié Kakré Zéphirin; Daloa: First Pres. Gonhi Sahi.

Courts of First Instance: Abidjan: Pres. Antoinette Marsouin; Bouaké: Pres. Kablan Aka Edoukou; Daloa: Pres. Woune Bleka; there are a further 25 courts in the principal centres.

High Court of Justice: composed of deputies elected from and by the Assemblée nationale; has jurisdiction to impeach the President or other mems of the Govt.

Constitutional Council: 22 blvd Carde, BP 4642, Abidjan 01; tel. 20-21-31-64; fax 20-21-21-68; internet www.gouv.ci/conconst.php; f. 2000 to replace certain functions of the fmr Constitutional Chamber of the Supreme Court; Pres. Francis Wodié.

Religion

The Constitution guarantees religious freedom, and this right is generally respected. Religious groups are required to register with the authorities, although no penalties are imposed on a group that fails to register. At the 1998 census it was estimated that about 34% of the population were Christians (mainly Roman Catholics), 27% of the population were Muslims, 15% followed traditional indigenous beliefs, 3% practised other religions, while 21% had no religious affiliation. It is, however, estimated that the proportion of Muslims is in fact significantly higher, as the majority of unregistered foreign workers are Muslims. Muslims are found in greatest numbers in the north of the country, while Christians are found mostly in the southern, central, western and eastern regions. Traditional indigenous beliefs are generally prevalent in rural areas.

ISLAM

Conseil National Islamique (CNI): Mosquée d'Aghien les deux Plateaux, BP 174 Cédex 03, Abidjan 08; tel. and fax 22-42-67-79; e-mail infos@cnicosim.org; f. 1993; groups more than 5,000 local communities organized in 13 regional and 78 local organizations; Chair. Imam El Hadj Idriss Koudouss Koné.

Conseil Supérieur des Imams (COSIM): 05 BP 2092, Abidjan 08; tel. 21-35-87-51; fax 05-79-61-04; e-mail contact@cosim-ci.org; internet www.cosim-ci.org; Pres. Cheick Boikary Fofana.

Conseil Supérieur Islamique (CSI): 11 BP 71, Abidjan 11; tel. 21-25-24-70; fax 21-24-28-04; f. 1978; Pres. Moustapha Sy Fadiga.

Other Islamic organizations include the Association des Musulmans Sunnites, Conseil des Imams Sunnites, Front de la Oummat Islamique and Haut Conseil des Imamats et Oulémas.

CHRISTIANITY

The Roman Catholic Church

Côte d'Ivoire comprises four archdioceses and 11 dioceses. An estimated 20% of the total population are Roman Catholics.

Bishops' Conference

Conférence Episcopale de la Côte d'Ivoire, BP 713 Cédex 03, Abidjan-Riviera; tel. 22-47-20-00; fax 22-47-60-65.

f. 1973; Pres. Most Rev. Joseph Yapo Aké (Archbishop of Gagnoa).

Archbishop of Abidjan: Most Rev. Jean-Pierre Kutwa, Archevêché, ave Jean-Paul II, 01 BP 1287, Abidjan 01; tel. 20-21-23-08; fax 20-21-40-22.

Archbishop of Bouaké: Most Rev. PAUL-SIMÉON AHOUANAN DJRO, Archevêché, 01 BP 649, Bouaké 01; tel. and fax 31-63-24-59; e-mail archebke@aviso.ci.

Archbishop of Gagnoa: Most Rev. JOSEPH YAPO AKÉ, Archevêché, BP 527, Gagnoa; tel. and fax 32-77-25-68; e-mail evechegagnoa@aviso.ci.

Archbishop of Korhogo: Most Rev. MARIE-DANIEL DADIET, BP 1581, Yamoussoukro; tel. 36-86-01-18; fax 36-86-08-31; e-mail dieulesauve@yahoo.fr.

Protestant Churches

Conseil National des Eglises protestantes et évangéliques de Côte d'Ivoire (CNEPECI): Abidjan; Pres. PAUL AYOH.

Eglise Evangélique des Assemblées de Dieu de Côte d'Ivoire: 26 BP 1396, Abidjan 26; tel. 21-35-55-48; fax 21-24-94-65; e-mail itpk2006@yahoo.fr; internet www.eeadci.org; f. 1960; Pres. BÉCHIÉ DÉSIRÉ GNANCHOU; Sec.-Gen. CHARLES ATTOUA GBANDA.

Eglise Harriste: 01 BP 3620, Abidjan 01; tel. 22-42-31-03; internet egliseharriste.org; f. 1913 by William Wadé Harris; affiliated to World Council of Churches 1998; allows polygamous new converts; 100,000 mems, 1,400 preachers, 7,000 apostles; Sec.-Gen. DOGBO JULES.

Eglise Méthodiste Unie de Côte d'Ivoire: 41 blvd de la République, 01 BP 1282, Abidjan 01; tel. 20-21-17-97; fax 20-22-52-03; e-mail emuciconf@yahoo.fr; internet www.emu-ci.org; f. 1924; publ. Le Méthodiste (monthly); autonomous since 1985; c. 800,000 mems; Pres. BENJAMIN BONI.

Eglise du Nazaréen (Church of the Nazarene): 22 BP 623, Abidjan 22; tel. 22-41-07-80; fax 22-41-07-81; e-mail awfcon@compuserve.com; internet www.nazarenemissions.org; f. 1987; active in evangelism, ministerial training and medical work; 4,429 mems; Dir JOHN SEAMAN.

Eglise Protestante Baptiste Oeuvres et Mission Internationale: 03 BP 1032, Abidjan 03; tel. 23-45-20-18; fax 23-45-56-41; e-mail epbomi@yahoo.com; internet www.epbomi.net; f. 1975; active in evangelism, teaching and social work; medical centre, 6,000 places of worship, 400 missionaries and 193,000 mems; Pres. Rev. Dr YAYE ROBERT DION.

Eglise Protestante Evangélique CMA de Côte d'Ivoire: BP 585, Bouaké 01; tel. 22-49-07-96; fax 31-63-54-12; e-mail contact@eglisecma-ci.org; internet www.eglisecma-ci.org; f. 1930; 300,000 mems; Nat. Pres. Rev. KOUAKOU CÉLESTIN KOFFI; Sec.-Gen AMANI N'GUESSAN.

Mission Evangélique de l'Afrique Occidentale (MEAO): 08 BP 1873, Abidjan 08; tel. and fax 22-47-59-95; e-mail hebohl@gmx.net; f. 1934; Team Leaders BRUCE PINKE, CAROLYN PINKE; affiliated church: Alliance des Eglises Evangéliques de Côte d'Ivoire (AEECI); 3 MEAO missionaries, 4 AEECI missionaries, 400 churches, 104 full-time pastors; Pres. ALAINGBRÉ PASCAL KOUASSI.

Mission Evangélique Luthérienne en Côte d'Ivoire (MELCI): BP 196, Touba; tel. 33-70-77-11; e-mail melci@aviso.ci; f. 1984; active in evangelism and social work; Dir GJERMUND VISTE.

Union des Eglises Evangéliques, Services et Œuvres de Côte d'Ivoire: 08 BP 20, Abidjan 08; tel. 40-22-75-00; e-mail ueesoci63@yahoo.fr; internet www.ueeso-ci.org; f. 1927; c. 250 places of worship; Pres. GILBERT GOUENTOUEU; Sec.-Gen. MICHEL LOH.

WorldVenture: BP 109, Korhogo; tel. 36-86-01-07; fax 36-86-11-50; internet www.worldventure.com; f. 1947; fmrly Conservative Baptist Foreign Mission Society, subsequently CB International; active in evangelism, medical work, translation, literacy and theological education in the northern area and in Abidjan.

The Press

Conseil National de la Presse (CNP): Cocody-les-Deux-Plateaux, 1ère tranche, Villa 224 bis, BP V 106, Abidjan; tel. 22-40-53-53; fax 22-41-27-90; e-mail info@lecnp.ci; internet www.lecnp.com; f. 1991; Pres. DÉBY DALLI GBALAWOULOU; Sec.-Gen. RENÉ BOURGOIN.

DAILIES

24 Heures: rue St Jean, duplex 65, Cocody–Val Doyen I, 10 BP 3302, Abidjan 10; tel. 22-41-29-53; fax 22-41-37-82; e-mail infos@24heures.net; internet www.24heuresci.com; f. 2002; Dir-Gen. ABDOULAYE SANGARÉ; Dir of Publication and Editor-in-Chief JOACHIM BEUGRÉ; circ. 21,000 (2005).

Côte d'Ivoire Economie: Cocody-les-Deux-Plateaux, rue K24, 28 BP 1473, Abidjan 28; tel. 22-41-77-50; fax 22-41-76-16; e-mail info@cotedivoire-economie.com; internet www.cotedivoire-economie.com; f. 2010; Dir-Gen. and Dir of Publication MARION N'GOUAN EZZEDINE; Editor-in-Chief JEAN-PIERRE PONT.

Le Courrier d'Abidjan: Riviera Bonoumin, 25 BP 1682, Abidjan 25; tel. 22-43-38-22; fax 22-43-30-46; internet www.lecourrierdabidjan.info; f. 2003.

Douze: rue Louis Lumière, Zone 4C, 10 BP 2462, Abidjan 10; tel. 21-25-54-00; fax 21-24-47-27; e-mail douze@afnet.net; publ. by Editions Olympe; f. 1994; sport; Dir MAZÉ SOUMAHORO; Editor-in-Chief FRANÇOIS BINI.

Fraternité Matin: blvd du Général de Gaulle, 01 BP 1807, Abidjan 01; tel. 20-37-06-66; fax 20-37-25-45; e-mail contact@fratmat.info; internet www.fratmat.info; f. 1964; official newspaper; state-owned; Dir-Gen. JEAN-BAPTISTE AKROU; Editorial Dir ALFRED DAN MOUSSA; circ. 26,000 (2011).

L'Intelligent d'Abidjan: Villa 12S, Bâtiment Star 4, 19 BP 1534, Abidjan 19; tel. 22-42-71-61; fax 22-42-11-70; e-mail Editeur@lintelligentdabidjan.org; internet www.lintelligentdabidjan.org; f. 2003; Dir-Gen. W. ALAFÉ ASSÉ.

L'Inter: 10 BP 2462, Abidjan 10; tel. 21-21-28-00; fax 21-21-28-05; e-mail linter@linter-ci.com; internet www.linter-ci.com; f. 1998; publ. by Editions Olympe; national and international politics and economics; Dir RAYMOND N'CHO NIMBA; Editor-in-Chief CHARLES A. D'ALMÉIDA; circ. 18,000 (2002).

Le JD (Jeune Démocrate): 23 BP 3842, Abidjan 23; tel. 23-51-62-45; fax 23-51-63-75; f. 1999; Dir IGNACE DASSOHIRI; Editor-in-Chief OCTAVE BOYOU.

Le Jour Plus: 26 Cocody-les-Deux-Plateau, 25 BP 1082, Abidjan 25; tel. 20-21-95-78; fax 20-21-95-80; f. 1994; publ. by Editions Le Nere; independent; Dir of Publication COULIBALY SEYDOU; Editor-in-Chief FRÉDÉRIC KOFFI; circ. 15,000 (2002).

Le Libéral: 01 BP 6938, Abidjan 01; tel. and fax 22-52-21-41; e-mail leliberal@aviso.ci; f. 1997; Dir YORO KONÉ; Editor-in-Chief BAKARY NIMAGA; circ. 15,000.

Le Matin d'Abidjan: 2 Plateaux Vallon 06, BP 2853, Abidjan 06; tel. 22-42-74-57; fax 22-42-59-06; e-mail info@lematindabidjan.com; internet www.lematindabidjan.com; Dir KOUAMENAN G. LAURENT.

Le National: Angré, Cocody, 16 BP 165, Abidjan 16; tel. 22-52-27-43; fax 22-52-27-42; f. 1999; nationalist; Publr LAURENT TAPÉ KOULOU; Editor-in-Chief (vacant); circ. 20,000 (2002).

Nord-Sud: Abidjan; internet nordsudquotidien.net; f. 2005; Dir TOURÉ MOUSSA; circ. 18,000 (2005).

Notr'Aurore: Immeuble SICOGI, Bâtiment K, Appt 124, Deux-Plateaux Aghien, blvd Latrille, Abidjan; tel. 22-42-08-21; fax 22-42-08-24; f. 2002; nationalist; Editor-in-Chief EMMANUEL GRIÉ.

Notre Voie: Cocody-les-Deux-Plateaux, 06 BP 2868, Abidjan 06; tel. 22-42-63-31; fax 22-42-63-32; e-mail gnh@africaonline.co.ci; internet www.notrevoie.com; f. 1978; organ of the FPI; Dir and Editor-in-Chief LAHOUA SOUANGA ETIENNE; circ. 20,000 (2002).

Le Nouveau Courrier: Abidjan; Editor-in-Chief SAINT-CLAVER OULA.

Le Nouveau Réveil: Adjamé Sud 80 Logements, Tours SICOGI, face Frat-Mat, Bâtiment A, 2e étage, porte 6, 01 BP 10684, Abidjan 01; tel. 20-38-42-00; fax 20-38-67-91; e-mail lenouveaureveil@yahoo.fr; internet www.lenouveaureveil.com; f. 2001 to replace weekly *Le Réveil-Hebdo*; supports PDCI—RDA; Dir-Gen. DENIS KAH ZION; Dir of Publication PATRICE YAO; circ. 18,000 (2005).

Le Patriote: 23 rue Paul Langevin, Zone 4C, 22 BP 509, Abidjan 22; tel. 21-21-19-45; fax 21-35-11-83; e-mail info@lepatriote.net; internet www.lepatriote.net; organ of the RDR; Dir of Publication CHARLES SANGA; Editor-in-Chief KORÉ EMMANUEL; circ. 40,000 (2002).

Le Populaire: 19 blvd Angoulvant, résidence Neuilly, Plateau, 01 BP 5496, Abidjan 01; tel. 21-36-34-15; fax 21-36-43-28; Dir RAPHAËL ORE LAKPÉ.

Soir Info: 10 BP 2462, Abidjan 10; tel. 21-21-28-00; fax 21-21-28-06; e-mail soirinfo@soirinfo.com; internet www.soirinfo.com; f. 1994; publ. by Editions Olympe; independent; Dir MAURICE FERRO BI BALI; Editor-in-Chief ZOROMÉ LOSS; circ. 22,000 (2002).

Le Sport: Cocody Attoban, face au Groupe Scolaire Jules Ferry, 09 BP 3685, Abidjan 09; tel. 22-43-92-54; fax 22-43-01-90; internet www.lesport.ci; Dir of Publication ASSI ADON AMÉDÉE.

Supersport: Abidjan; internet www.supersport.ci; f. 2006; Dir-Gen. HAMIDOU FOMBA.

La Voie: face Institut Marie-Thérèse Houphouët-Boigny, 17 BP 65(Abidjan 17; tel. 20-37-68-23; fax 20-37-74-76; organ of the FPI; D ABOU DRAHAMANE SANGARÉ; Man. MAURICE LURIGNAN.

SELECTED BI-WEEKLIES AND WEEKLIES

L'Agora: Immeuble Nana Yamoussou, ave 13, rue 38, Treichvil' BP 5326, Abidjan 01; tel. 21-34-11-72; f. 1997; weekly; Dir FEF DÉDÉ; Editor-in-Chief BAMBA ALEX SOULEYMANE.

Le Démocrate: Maison du Congrès, ave 2, Treichville, 01 B Abidjan 01; tel. 21-24-45-88; fax 21-24-25-61; f. 1991; weekly; the PDCI—RDA; Dir NOËL YAO.

Le Front: Immeuble Mistral, 3e étage, 220 Logements, 11 BP 11 2678, Abidjan 11; tel. 20-38-13-24; fax 20-38-70-83; e-mail quotidienlefront@yahoo.fr; internet www.lefront.com; two a week; Editorial Dir FATOUMATA COULIBALY; Editor KPOKPA BLÉ.

Gbich!: 10 BP 399, Abidjan 10; tel. and fax 21-26-31-94; e-mail gbich@assistweb.net; internet www.gbichonline.com; weekly; satirical; Editor-in-Chief MATHIEU BLEDOU.

Le Nouvel Horizon: 220 Logements, blvd du Général de Gaulle, Adjamé, 17 BP 656, Abidjan 17; tel. 20-37-68-23; f. 1990; weekly; organ of the FPI; Dir ABOU DRAHAMANE SANGARÉ; circ. 15,000.

La Nouvelle Presse: rue des Jardins, Cocody-les-Deux-Plateaux, 01 BP 8534, Abidjan 01; tel. 22-41-04-76; fax 22-41-04-15; e-mail jvieyra@africaonline.co.ci; f. 1992; weekly; publ. by Centre Africain de Presse et d'Edition; current affairs; Editors JUSTIN VIEYRA, JÉRÔME CARLOS; circ. 10,000.

Le Repère: 220 Logements, Adjamé Sud-Tours SICOGI, face Frat-Mat, Bâtiment A, 2e étage P6, 04 BP 1947, Abidjan 04; tel. and fax 20-38-67-91; supports PDCI—RDA; two a week; Dir of Publication DENIS KAH ZION; circ. 10,000 (2004).

Sports Magazine: Yopougon-SOGEFIHA, 01 BP 4030, Abidjan 01; tel. 23-45-14-02; f. 1997; weekly; Dir JOSEPH ABLE.

Téré: 220 Logements, blvd du Général de Gaulle, Adjamé-Liberté, 20 BP 43, Abidjan 20; tel. and fax 20-37-79-42; weekly; organ of the PIT; Dir ANGÈLE GNONSOA.

Top-Visages: rue du Commerce, 23 BP 892, Abidjan 23; tel. 20-33-72-10; fax 20-32-81-05; e-mail contact@topvisages.net; internet www.topvisages.net; weekly; Editor-in-Chief E. TONGA BÉHI; circ. 40,000 (2004).

La Voie du Compatriote: Adjamé St-Michel, 09 BP 2008, Abidjan 09; tel. 20-37-50-13; f. 1998; weekly; Dir SINARI KAL.

SELECTED PERIODICALS

Côte d'Ivoire Magazine: Présidence de la République, 01 BP 1354, Abidjan 01; tel. 20-22-02-22; f. 1998; quarterly; Dir JEAN-NOËL LOUKO.

Juris-Social: Centre National de Documentation Juridique (CNDJ), Villa 381, ilôt 43, face Polyclinique Saint Jacques, blvd Latrille, Cocody-les-Deux-Plateaux, 01 BP 2757, Abidjan 01; tel. 20-22-74-85; fax 20-22-74-86; e-mail cndj@aviso.ci; internet www.cndj.ci; monthly; jurisprudence; CNDJ also publishes quarterly periodical *Juris OHADA*.

La Lettre de l'Afrique de l'Ouest: rue des Jardins, Cocody-les-Deux-Plateaux, 01 BP 8534, Abidjan 01; tel. 22-41-04-76; fax 22-41-04-15; f. 1995; publ. by Centre Africain de Presse et d'Edition; six a year; politics, economics, regional integration; Editors JUSTIN VIEYRA, JÉRÔME CARLOS.

Maisons et Matériaux: 08 BP 2150, Abidjan 08; tel. 22-42-92-17; monthly; Dir THIAM T. DJENEBOU.

Roots-Rock Magazine: Abidjan; tel. 22-42-84-74; f. 1998; monthly; music; Dir DIOMANDÉ DAVID.

RTI-Mag: 08 BP 663, Abidjan 08; tel. 20-33-14-46; fax 20-32-12-06; publ. by Radiodiffusion-Télévision Ivoirienne; listings magazine.

Sentiers: 26 ave Chardy, 01 BP 2432, Abidjan 01; tel. 20-21-95-68; fax 20-21-95-80; e-mail redaction@aviso.ci; Editor-in-Chief DIÉGOU BAILLY.

Stades d'Afrique: blvd du Général de Gaulle, 01 BP 1807, Abidjan 01; tel. 20-37-06-66; fax 20-37-25-45; f. 2000; sports; monthly; Dir-Gen. EMMANUEL KOUASSI KOKORÉ; Editor-in-Chief HÉGAUD OUATTARA.

... Succès: 21 BP 3748, Abidjan 21; tel. 20-37-71-64; monthly; Dir ...LA PLAKATOU.

...ers jeunes: 01 BP 3713, Abidjan 01; tel. 20-21-20-00; fax 21-35-... monthly; Editor-in-Chief MOUSSA SY SAVANÉ.

... d'Afrique: rue des Jardins, Cocody-les-Deux-Plateaux, 01 ... Abidjan 01; tel. 22-41-04-76; fax 22-41-04-15; publ. by ...icain de Presse et d'Edition; monthly; Editor-in-Chief ...AMISSOKO.

NEWS AGENCY

...ne de Presse (AIP): ave Chardy, 04 BP 312, ...-22-64-13; fax 20-21-35-99; e-mail aip@aip.ci; f. 1961; Dir DALLI DEBY.

...ESS ASSOCIATIONS

...se Démocratique Ivoirienne (APDI): ... 1994; Chair. JEAN-BAPTISTE AKROU.

...alistes de Côte d'Ivoire (UNJCI): 06 ... tel. 20-21-61-07; e-mail prunjci@unjci ...ARA.

Publishers

Centre Africain de Presse et d'Edition (CAPE): rue des Jardins, Cocody-les-Deux-Plateaux, 01 BP 8534, Abidjan 01; tel. 22-41-04-76; fax 22-41-04-15; Man. JUSTIN VIEYRA.

Centre d'Edition et de Diffusion Africaines (CEDA): 17 rue des Carrossiers, 04 BP 541, Abidjan 04; tel. 20-24-65-10; fax 21-25-05-67; e-mail infos@ceda-ci.com; internet www.ceda-ci.com; f. 1961; 20% state-owned; general non-fiction, school and children's books, literary fiction; Pres. and Dir-Gen. VENANCE KACOU.

Centre de Publications Evangéliques: 08 BP 900, Abidjan 08; tel. 22-44-48-05; fax 22-44-58-17; e-mail cpe@aviso.ci; internet www.editionscpe.com; f. 1967; evangelical Christian; Dir JULES OUOBA.

Editions Bognini: 06 BP 1254, Abidjan 06; tel. 20-41-16-86; social sciences, literary fiction.

Editions Eburnie: 01 BP 1984, 01 Abidjan; tel. 20-21-64-65; fax 20-21-45-46; e-mail eburnie@aviso.ci; f. 2001; illustrated books for children, social sciences, poetry.

Editions Neter: 01 BP 7370, Abidjan 01; tel. 22-52-52-68; f. 1992; politics, culture, history, literary fiction; Dir RICHARD TA BI SENIN.

Nouvelles Editions Ivoiriennes: 1 blvd de Marseille, 01 BP 1818, Abidjan 01; tel. 21-24-07-66; fax 21-24-24-56; e-mail edition@nei-ci.com; internet www.nei-ci.com; f. 1972; literature, criticism, essays, drama, social sciences, history, in French and English; Dir GUY LAMBIN.

Presses Universitaires et Scolaires d'Afrique (PUSAF—Editions Cissé): 08 BP 177, Abidjan 08; tel. 22-41-12-71; mathematics, economics, medicine.

Université Nationale de Côte d'Ivoire: 01 BP V34, Abidjan 01; tel. 22-44-08-59; f. 1964; academic and general non-fiction and periodicals; Publications Dir GILLES VILASCO.

GOVERNMENT PUBLISHING HOUSE

Imprimerie Nationale: BP V87, Abidjan; tel. 20-21-76-11; fax 20-21-68-68.

Broadcasting and Communications

TELECOMMUNICATIONS

In 2011 there were six operators in the Côte d'Ivoire telecommunications market. Four of these provided mobile cellular telephone services, one provided fixed-line services and one provided both mobile and fixed-line services. A new mobile company, Aircom, was to commence operations in early 2012 under the brand name Café Mobile.

Regulatory Authorities

Agence des Télécommunications de Côte d'Ivoire (ATCI): Immeuble Postel 2001, 4e étage, rue Lecoeur, 18 BP 2203, Abidjan 18; tel. 20-34-43-74; fax 20-34-43-75; e-mail courrier@atci.ci; internet www.atci.ci; f. 1995; Pres. LASSINA KONÉ; Dir-Gen. ARTHUR ALLOCO KOUASSI.

Conseil des Télécommunications de Côte d'Ivoire (CTCI): 17 BP 110, Abidjan 17; tel. 20-34-43-04; f. 1995; deals with issues of arbitration; Pres. LEMASSOU FOFANA.

Service Providers

Atlantique Telecom—Moov (Moov): Immeuble Karrat, rue du Commerce, 01 BP 2347, Abidjan 01; tel. 20-25-01-01; fax 20-25-26-62; e-mail moovcontact@moov.com; internet www.moov.com; f. 2005 as jt venture by Atlantique Télécom (Côte d'Ivoire) and Etisalat (United Arab Emirates); 80% owned by Etisalat (United Arab Emirates); mobile cellular telecommunications; CEO NAGI ABBOUD; 4m. subscribers (March 2009).

Comium: Blvd VGE Marcory, cnr rue Lumière, 4106444W 11, BP 2591, Abidjan 11; tel. 21-35-90-41; internet www.koz.ci; f. 2009; Pres. NIZAR DALLOUL; Dir-Gen MICHEL HEBERT.

Côte d'Ivoire-Télécom (CI-Télécom): Immeuble Postel 2001, rue Lecoeur, 17 BP 275, Abidjan 17; tel. 20-34-40-00; fax 20-21-28-28; internet www.citelecom.ci; f. 1991; 51% owned by France Télécom, 49% state-owned; Pres. YAYA OUATTARA; Man. Dir MAMADOU BAMBA; 327,000 subscribers (June 2002).

Green Network (GreenN): Abidjan; tel. 60-00-60-60; internet www.greenn.ci; f. 2009; owned by Libya Africa Portfolio; Dir-Gen. ABDULGHANI RAMADAN.

MTN Côte d'Ivoire: Immeuble Loteny, 12 rue Crossons Duplessis, 01 BP 3685, Abidjan 01; tel. 20-31-63-16; fax 20-31-84-50; internet www.mtn.ci; f. 1996 as Loteny Télécom-Télécel; present name adopted 2005; mobile cellular telephone operator in more than 110 urban centres and on principal highway routes; 51% owned by Mobile

Telephone Network International (South Africa); Chief Exec. WIM VAN HELLEPUTTE; 1.63m. subscribers (Dec. 2006).

Orange Côte d'Ivoire: Immeuble Saha, blvd Valéry Giscard d'Estaing, Zone 4C, 11 BP 202, Abidjan 11; tel. 21-23-90-07; fax 21-23-90-11; internet www.orange.ci; f. 1996 as Ivoiris, present name adopted 2002; mobile cellular telephone operator in more than 60 urban centres; 85% owned by France Télécom; Man. Dir MAMADOU BAMBA; 1.75m. subscribers (Dec. 2006).

BROADCASTING

Regulatory Authority

Haute Autorité de la Communication Audiovisuelle: Pl. de la République, 05 BP 56, Abidjan; tel. 20-31-15-80; internet www.haca.ci; f. 2011 to replace Conseil National de la Communication Audiovisuelle (CNCA); Pres. IBRAHIM SY SAVANÉ.

Radio

In 1993 the Government permitted the first commercial radio stations to broadcast in Côte d'Ivoire; of the five licences initially granted, four were to foreign stations. Between 1998 and early 2001, a further 52 licences were granted.

Radiodiffusion-Télévision Ivoirienne (RTI): blvd des Martyrs, Cocody, 08 BP883, Abidjan 08; tel. 22-48-61-62; fax 22-44-78-23; e-mail info.rti@rti.ci; internet www.rti.ci; f. 1962; state-owned; two national TV channels, La Première and TV2, and two national radio channels, La Nationale and Fréquence II; Pres. PASCAL BROU AKA; Dir-Gen. LAZARE AKA SAYÉ (acting); Dir, La Première VICTOR DEBASS KPAN; Dir, TV2 ADÈLE DJEDJE; Dir, Radiodiffusion ELOI OULAÏ.

Abidjan 1: Deux Plateaux Hayat, au dessus de la pharcie des jardins, Abidjan; tel. 22-41-29-03; e-mail info@radioabidjan1.com; internet www.radioabidjan1.com; Dir JULIEN ADAYE.

City FM: Immeuble Alpha Cissé, avant la piscine d'Etat, Treichville, 01 BP 7207, Abidjan 01; tel. 21-25-10-28; f. 1999; Pres. and Man. Dir Me ALIOU SIBI.

Radio Espoir: 12 BP 27, Abidjan 12; tel. 21-75-68-01; fax 21-75-68-04; e-mail respoir@aviso.ci; internet www.radioespoir.ci; f. 1990; Roman Catholic; broadcasts in French, local and sub-regional languages; Dir Fr BASILE DIANÉ KOGNAN.

Radio JAM: Abidjan; tel. 21-25-08-73; e-mail radiojamofficiel@yahoo.fr; internet www.radiojam.biz; Dir FRANÇOIS KONIAN.

Radio Nostalgie: Immeuble Le Paris, ave Chardy, 01 BP 157, Abidjan 01; tel. 20-21-10-52; fax 20-21-85-53; e-mail contact@nostalgie.ci; internet www.nostalgie.ci; f. 1993; Dir-Gen. HERVÉ CORNUEL.

Radio Notre Dame: BP 1555, Yamoussoukro; tel. 30-64-41-55; e-mail nfo@radionotredame-yakro.com; internet www.radionotredame-yakro.com; broadcasts religious programmes; Dir-Gen. JEAN-CLAUDE ATSAIN.

Radio Peleforo Gbon: route Ferké km 2, BP 841, Korhogo; tel. 21-86-22-62; fax 21-86-20-33.

Radio Soleil: 16 BP 1179, Abidjan 16; tel. 21-99-17-64; fax 21-79-12-48; e-mail badouel_jeannette@yahoo.fr; f. 2001; Dir JEANNETTE BADOUEL.

Côte d'Ivoire also receives broadcasts from the Gabon-based Africa No 1 radio station, from the French-language Africa service of the BBC (United Kingdom), and from Radio France Internationale.

Television

Radiodiffusion-Télévision Ivoirienne (RTI): see Radio section.

Canal+ Côte d'Ivoire: Immeuble Alpha 2000, 01 BP 1132, Abidjan 01; tel. 20-31-99-97; fax 20-22-72-22; e-mail abonne@canalhorizons.ci; internet www.canalplus-afrique.com; broadcasts commenced 1994; subsidiary of Canal Plus (France); Dir-Gen. SERGE AGNÉRO.

Finance

(cap. = capital; res = reserves; dep. = deposits; m. = million; br(s). = branch(es); amounts in francs CFA, unless otherwise indicated)

BANKING

In 2009 there were 20 commercial banks and three financial institutions in Côte d'Ivoire. Following the disputed presidential election of 28 November 2010, a number of commercial banking institutions announced the suspension of their operations. Of these, the Banque Internationale pour le Commerce et l'Industrie de la Côte d'Ivoire, Citibank, the Société Générale de Banques en Côte d'Ivoire and the Standard Chartered Bank Côte d'Ivoire were later forcibly nationalized by Laurent Gbagbo, who refused to relinquish the presidency. The Bourse Régionale des Valeurs Mobilières also suspended its operations, but subsequently resumed them from a new base in Bamako, Mali. Gbagbo was detained in April 2011, and in early May the legitimately elected President, Alassane Ouattara, confirmed that banking operations in the country would recommence.

Central Bank

Banque centrale des états de l'Afrique de l'ouest (BCEAO): blvd Botreau-Roussel, angle ave Delafosse, 01 BP 1769, Abidjan 01; tel. 20-20-85-00; fax 20-22-28-52; e-mail webmaster@bceao.int; internet www.bceao.int; f. 1962; HQ in Dakar, Senegal; bank of issue for the mem. states of the Union économique et monétaire ouest-africaine (UEMOA, comprising Benin, Burkina Faso, Côte d'Ivoire, Guinea-Bissau, Mali, Niger, Senegal and Togo); cap. 134,120m., res 1,474,195m., dep. 2,124,051m. (Dec. 2009); Gov. KONÉ TIÉMOKO MEYLIET; Dir in Côte d'Ivoire JEAN-BAPTISTE AMAN AYAYE; 7 brs in Côte d'Ivoire.

Commercial Banks

Access Bank Cote d'Ivoire: 6e étage, Immeuble Alliance, 17 ave Terrasson de Fougères, 01 BP 6928, Abidjan 01; tel. 20-31-58-30; fax 20-21-42-58; e-mail info.cotedivoire@accessbankplc.com; internet subs.accessbankplc.com; f. 1996; name changed as above in 2008; 88% owned by Access Bank (Nigeria); cap. 3,000m. (Dec. 2005); Pres. JACOB AWUKU AMEMATEKPO; Dir-Gen. AMADOU LY.

Bank of Africa—Côte d'Ivoire (BOA—CI): ave Terrasson de Fougères, angle Rue Gourgas, 01 BP 4132, Abidjan 01; tel. 20-30-34-00; fax 20-30-34-01; e-mail boaci@bkofafrica.com; internet www.boacoteivoire.com; f. 1996; 68.1% owned by BOA Group (Luxembourg); cap. 4,500m., res 3,343m., dep. 189,765m., total assets 208,647m. (Dec. 2008); Dir-Gen. LALA MOULAYE; 18 brs.

Banque Atlantique Côte d'Ivoire (BACI): Immeuble Atlantique, ave Noguès, Plateau, 04 BP 1036, Abidjan 04; tel. 20-31-59-50; fax 20-21-68-52; e-mail kone.dossongui@banqueatlantique.net; internet www.banqueatlantique.net; f. 1979; merged with Compagnie Bancaire de l'Atlantique Côte d'Ivoire in 2009; cap. and res 13,230m., dep. 224,832m. (Dec. 2007); Pres. KONE DOSSONGUI; Dir-Gen. SOULEYMANE DIARRASSOUBA; 3 brs.

Banque de l'Habitat de Côte d'Ivoire (BHCI): 22 ave Joseph Anoma, 01 BP 2325, Abidjan 01; tel. 20-25-39-39; fax 20-22-58-18; e-mail info@bhci.ci; internet www.bhci.ci; f. 1993; cap. and res 1,755m., total assets 16,834m. (Dec. 1999); Chair. DAVID AMUAH; Man. Dir SOULEYMANE DOGONI; 3 brs.

Banque pour le Financement de l'Agriculture (BFA): Immeuble Alliance B, 2e étage, rue Lecoeur, BP 103 Poste Entreprise, Cedex 1, Abidjan; tel. 20-25-61-61; fax 20-25-61-99; e-mail info@bfa.ci; internet www.bfa.ci; Dir-Gen. WENCESLAS APPIA; 4 brs.

Banque Internationale pour le Commerce et l'Industrie de la Côte d'Ivoire SA (BICI-CI): ave Franchet d'Espérey, 01 BP 1298, Abidjan 01; tel. 20-20-16-00; fax 20-20-17-00; e-mail michel.lafont@africa.bnpparibas.com; internet www.bicicinet.net; f. 1962; 67.5% owned by BNP Paribas (France); absorbed BICI Bail de Côte d'Ivoire in 2003 and Compagnie Financière de la Côte d'Ivoire in 2004; cap. and res 38,436.7m., total assets 276,432.1m. (Dec. 2004); Chair. ANGE KOFFY; 39 brs.

Banque Nationale d'Investissement (BNI): Immeuble SCIAM, ave Marchand, Plateau, 01 BP 670, Abidjan 01; tel. 20-31-51-00; fax 20-22-92-33; e-mail info@bni-ci.net; internet www.bni.ci; f. 1959 as Caisse Autonome d'Amortissement de Côte d'Ivoire (CAA); name and operations changed as above in 2004; cap. and res 28,408m., total assets 253,668m. (Dec. 2003); Dir-Gen. EUGÈNE NDA KASSI.

BIAO—Côte d'Ivoire (BIAO—CI): 8–10 ave Joseph Anoma, 01 BP 1274, Abidjan 01; tel. 20-20-07-20; fax 20-20-07-00; e-mail info@biao.co.ci; internet www.biao.co.ci; f. 1980; fmrly Banque Internationale pour l'Afrique de l'Ouest—Côte d'Ivoire; 20% state-owned; cap. 10,000.0m., res 173.0m., dep. 163,501.m. (Dec. 2005); Pres. SEYDOU ELIMANE DIARRA; Dir-Gen. MARTIN DJEDJES; 31 brs.

La Caisse d'Épargne de Côte d'Ivoire: 11 ave Joseph Anoma, 01 BP 6889, Abidjan 01; tel. 20-25-43-00; fax 20-25-53-11; e-mail info@caissepargne.ci; internet www.caissepargne.ci; f. 1998; Dir-Gen. MAMAH DIABAGATÉ.

Citibank Côte d'Ivoire: Immeuble Botreau-Roussel, 28 ave Delafosse, 01 BP 3698, Abidjan 01; tel. 20-20-90-00; fax 20-21-76-85 e-mail citibank@odaci.net; f. 1976; total assets US $198.7m. (2003 Dir-Gen. CHARLES KIE.

COFIPA Investment Bank CI: Immeuble Botreau Roussel, étage, ave Delafosse, 04 BP 411, Abidjan 04; tel. 20-30-23-00; fax 30-23-01; e-mail Info@cofipa.ci; internet www.cofipa.ci; cap. anc 2,382.5m., total assets 19,171.2m. (Dec. 2002); Chair. MACA OVIA; Man. Dir and CEO GUY KOIZAN; 49 brs.

Ecobank Côte d'Ivoire: Immeuble Alliance, 1 ave Terras Fougères, 01 BP 4107, Abidjan 01; tel. 20-31-92-00; fax 20-21 e-mail ecobankci@ecobank.com; internet www.ecobank.com; 94% owned by Ecobank Transnational Inc (Togo); cap. 22,25

296,326m, total assets 341,666m. (Dec. 2009); Chair. AKA AOUÉLÉ; Dir-Gen. CHARLES DABOIKO; 16 brs.

Société Générale de Banques en Côte d'Ivoire (SGBCI): 5–7 ave Joseph Anoma, 01 BP 1355, Abidjan 01; tel. 20-20-10-10; fax 20-20-14-92; e-mail info.sgbci@socgen.com; internet www.sgbci.ci; f. 1962; 66.8% owned by Société Générale (France); cap. 15,556m., res 25,298m., dep. 429,765m. (Dec. 2007); Pres. TIÉMOKO YADÉ COULIBALY; Dir-Gen. BERNARD LABADENS; 41 brs.

Société Ivoirienne de Banque (SIB): Immeuble Alpha 2000, 34 blvd de la République, 01 BP 1300, Abidjan 01; tel. 20-20-00-00; fax 20-20-01-19; e-mail info@sib.ci; internet www.sib.ci; f. 1962; 51% owned by Calyon, Paris La Défense (France), 49% state-owned; reduction of state holding to 19% proposed; cap. 4,000m., res 10,710m., total assets 148,340m. (Dec. 2006); Pres. LAMBERT FEH KESSE; Administrator and Dir-Gen. MOUNIR OUDGHIRI; 15 brs.

Standard Chartered Bank Côte d'Ivoire (SCBCI): 23 blvd de la République, face Commissariat du 1er arrondissement, 17 BP 1141, Abidjan 17; tel. 20-30-32-00; fax 20-30-32-01; e-mail info.CDI@sc.com; internet www.standardchartered.com/ci; f. 2001; subsidiary of Standard Chartered Bank (United Kingdom); cap. and res 9,218m., total assets 76,289m. (Dec. 2003); Pres. EBENEZER ESSOKA; CEO SERGES BAILLY; 4 brs.

United Bank for Africa Côte d'Ivoire: blvd Botreau-Roussel, Plateau, Abidjan; tel. 20-31-22-22; fax 20-31-22-26; e-mail ubacotedivoire@ubagroup.com; internet www.ubagroup.com/ubacotedivoire; f. 2008; Dir-Gen. GUILLAUME LIBY.

Versus Bank: Immeuble CRAAE-UMOA, blvd Botreau Roussel, angle ave Joseph Anoma, 01 BP 1874, Abidjan 01; tel. 20-25-60-60; fax 20-25-60-99; e-mail infos@versusbank.com; internet www.versusbank.com; f. 2004; cap. 3,000m.; Pres. DANO DJÉDJÉ; Dir-Gen. GUY KOIZAN.

Credit Institutions

Afribail—Côte d'Ivoire (Afribail—CI): 8–10 ave Joseph Anoma, 01 BP 1274, Abidjan 01; tel. 20-20-07-20; fax 20-20-07-00; 95% owned by BIAO—CI; cap. and res 334m., total assets 2,651m. (Dec. 2002); Chair. RENÉ AMANY; Pres. and Dir-Gen. ERNEST ALLOU TOGNAN.

Coopérative Ivoirienne d'Epargne et de Crédit Automobile (CIECA): 04 BP 2084, Abidjan 04; tel. 20-22-77-13; fax 20-22-77-35; cap. and res 805m. (Dec. 1998), total assets 1,169m. (Dec. 1999); Dir-Gen. DALLY ZABO.

Société Africaine de Crédit Automobilier (SAFCA): 1 rue des Carrossiers, Zone 3, 04 BP 27, Abidjan 04; tel. 21-21-07-07; fax 21-21-07-00; e-mail safca@afnet.net; f. 1956; cap. and res 5,681.8m., total assets 22,511.1m. (Dec. 2001); Pres. and Dir-Gen. THIERRY PAPILLION.

Société Africaine de Crédit-Bail (SAFBAIL): Immeuble SAFCA, 1 rue des Carrossiers, Zone 3, 04 BP 27, Abidjan 04; tel. 21-24-91-77; fax 21-35-77-90; e-mail safca@aviso.ci; f. 1971; cap. and res 2,922m., total assets 13,414m. (Dec. 1999); Chair. and Man. Dir DIACK DIAWAR.

SOGEFIBAIL—CI: 26 ave Delafosse, 01 BP 1355, Abidjan 01; tel. 20-32-85-15; fax 20-33-14-93; 35% owned by GENEFITEC, 35% by SOGEFINANCE, 25% by SGBCI; cap. and res 2,560.2m., total assets 4,452.3m. (Dec. 2003); Pres. JEAN-LOUIS MATTEI.

Bankers' Association

Association Professionnelle des Banques et Etablissements Financiers de Côte d'Ivoire (APBEFCI): Immeuble Aniaman, ave Lamblin, 01 BP 3810, Abidjan 01; tel. 20-32-20-08; fax 20-32-69-60; internet www.apbef-ci.org; affiliated to Confédération Générale des Entreprises de Côte d'Ivoire (q.v.); Pres. JACOB ANEMATEKPO.

STOCK EXCHANGE

…urse Régionale des Valeurs Mobilières (BRVM): 18 ave …h Anoma, 01 BP 3802, Abidjan 01; tel. 20-32-66-85; fax 20-…84; e-mail brvm@brvm.org; internet www.brvm.org; f. 1998 to … Bourse des Valeurs d'Abidjan; regional stock exchange …nem. states of UEMOA; Dir-Gen. JEAN-PAUL GILLET.

INSURANCE

… were 34 insurance companies in Côte d'Ivoire.

…'Assurances: Immeuble Woodin Center, ave No-… Abidjan 01; tel. 20-22-46-96; fax 20-22-64-81; Dir-…OND.

… Insurance Co (AFRAM): Immeuble ex-Mono-… BP 7124, Abidjan 01; tel. 20-31-30-44; fax 20-… …ISTIAN CASEL.

…ssurances (3A): Immeuble Le Mans, 6e …l, 01 BP 11944, Abidjan 01; tel. 20-33-85-… …aavie@aaavie.com; internet www.3a-vie …E.

… d'Ivoire: Immeuble MACI, 2e étage, …1 BP 1841, Abidjan 01; tel. 20-31-78-00; fax 20-33-18-37; e-mail atlantiqueassurances@atlantiqueassurances.net; f. 1956; Dir-Gen. PIERRE MAGNE.

AXA Assurances Côte d'Ivoire: ave Delafosse Prolongée, 01 BP 378, Abidjan 01; tel. 20-31-88-88; fax 20-31-88-00; e-mail axarci@africaonline.co.ci; f. 1981; fmrly l'Union Africaine—IARD; insurance and reinsurance; Dir-Gen. ROGER BOA.

AXA Vie Côte d'Ivoire: 9 ave Houdaille, 01 BP 2016, Abidjan 01; tel. 20-22-25-15; fax 20-22-37-60; e-mail info@axa-vie.ci; f. 1985; fmrly Union Africaine Vie; life assurance and capitalization; Chair. JOACHIM RICHMOND; Dir PATRICE DESGRANGES.

Colina: Immeuble Colina, blvd Roume 3, 01 BP 3832, Abidjan 01; tel. 20-25-36-00; fax 20-22-59-05; e-mail colinaci@groupecolina.com; internet www.colina-sa.com; f. 1980; Chair. MICHEL PHARAON; Dir-Gen. M. J. ACKAH.

Compagnie Nationale d'Assurances (CNA): Immeuble Symphonie, 30 ave du Général de Gaulle, 01 BP 1333, Abidjan 01; tel. 20-21-49-19; fax 20-22-49-06; f. 1972; cap. 400m.; insurance and reinsurance; transfer to private ownership pending; Chair. SOUNKALO DJIBO; Man. Dir RICHARD COULIBALY.

Génération Nouvelle d'Assurances Côte d'Ivoire (GNA-CI): Ground Floor, Immeuble l'Ebrien, rue du commerce, Abidjan; tel. 20-25-98-00; fax 20-33-60-65; internet www.gnassurances.com; f. 2006; Pres. BARTHÉLEMY VIDJANNANGNI; Dir-Gen. FÉLIX KOUAME ZEGBE N'GUESSAN.

Gras Savoye Côte d'Ivoire: Immeuble Trade Center, ave Noguès, 01 BP 5675, Abidjan 01; tel. 20-25-25-00; fax 20-25-25-25; e-mail grassavoyeci@ci.grassavoye.com; affiliated to Gras Savoye (France); Man. JEAN-FRANÇOIS ALAUZE.

Mutuelle Centrale d'Assurances: 15 Immeuble Ebrien, 01 BP 12724, Abidjan 01; tel. 20-31-11-30; fax 20-31-11-32; e-mail mca@mca.ci; Administrator ANOKOI KODJO.

Nouvelle Société Africaine d'Assurances (NSIA AGCI): Immeuble Manci, rue A43, 01 BP 1571, Abidjan 01; tel. 20-31-75-00; fax 20-31-98-00; f. 1995; Pres. and Dir-Gen. JEAN KACOU DIAGOU.

NSIA-Vie: Immeuble Zandaman, ave Noguès, 01 BP 4092, Abidjan 01; tel. 20-31-98-00; fax 20-33-25-79; f. 1988; fmrly Assurances Générales de Côte d'Ivoire—Vie (AGCI-Vie); life; Pres. and Dir-Gen. JEAN KACOU DIAGOU.

Serenity: 41 blvd Général de Gaulle (face gare sud), Immeuble Ex-Monoprix, 01 BP 10244, Abidjan 01; tel. 20-32-16-52; fax 20-32-16-63; internet www.serenity-sa.com; f. 2009; Dir-Gen. MAURICE KIPRÉ DIGBEU.

Société Africaine d'Assurances et de Réassurances en République de Côte d'Ivoire (SAFARRIV): Immeuble SAFARRIV, 2, blvd Roume, 01 BP 1741, Abidjan 01; tel. 20-30-40-00; fax 20-30-40-01; e-mail groupe-safarriv@safarriv.ci; internet www.agf-ci.com; f. 1975; affiliated to AGF Afrique; Pres. TIÉMOKO YADÉ COULIBALY; Man. Dir CHRISTIAN ARRAULT.

Trade and Industry

GOVERNMENT AGENCIES

Autorité pour la Régulation du Café et du Cacao (ARCC): blvd Botreau Roussel, Immeuble Caistab 17ème–19ème étages, Plateau, 25 BP 1501, Abidjan 25; tel. 20-20-29-87; fax 20-20-27-05; e-mail courrier@arcc.ci; internet www.arcc.ci; f. 2000; implements regulatory framework for coffee and cocoa trade; Pres. GILBERT N'GUESSAN.

Bureau National d'Etudes Techniques et de Développement (BNETD): ancien hôtel 'Le Relais', blvd Hassan II, Cocody, 04 BP 945, Abidjan 04; tel. 22-48-34-00; fax 22-44-56-66; e-mail info@bnetd.ci; internet www.bnetd.ci; f. 1978 as Direction et Contrôle des Grands Travaux; management and supervision of major public works projects; Dir-Gen. KRA KOFFI PASCAL.

Comité de Privatisation: 6 blvd de l'Indénié, 01 BP 1141, Abidjan 01; tel. 20-22-22-31; fax 20-22-22-35; f. 1990; state privatization authority; Pres. PAUL AGODIO; Dir-Gen. AHOUA DON MELLO.

Conseil du Café-Cacao (CCC): 04 BP 2576, Abidjan 04; tel. 20-25-69-69; fax 20-21-83-30; e-mail info@cgfcc.ci; internet www.frc.ci; f. 2012 to replace the Comite de Gestion de la Filière Café-Cacao; comprises the Autorité pour la Régulation du Café et du Cacao (ARCC), the Bourse du Café et du Cacao (BCC), the Fonds de Régulation et de Contrôle du Café et du Cacao (FRCC) and the Fonds de Développement et de Promotion des Activités des Producteurs de Café et de Cacao (FDPCC); Pres. LAMBERT KOUASSI KONAN; Dir-Gen. MASSANDJÉ TOURÉ-LITSE.

Conseil Économique et Social: angle blvd Carde et ave Terrason de Fougère, 04 BP 304, Abidjan 04; tel. 20-21-14-54; internet ces-ci.org; f. 1961; Pres. MARCEL ZADI KESSY.

Fonds de Régulation et de Contrôle du Café et du Cacao (FRCC): Immeuble Caistab, 17 BP 797, Abidjan 17; tel. 20-20-27-11;

fax 20-21-83-30; e-mail frc@frc.ci; internet www.frc.ci; f. 2002; assists small-scale producers and exporters of coffee and cocoa; administrative bd comprises five representatives of producers, two of exporters, three of banks and insurance cos, two of the state; Pres. ANGELINE KILI; Dir-Gen. FIRMIN KOUAKOU.

PETROCI: Immeuble les Hévéas, 14 blvd Carde, BP V194, Abidjan 01; tel. 20-20-25-00; fax 20-21-68-24; e-mail info@petroci.ci; internet www.petroci.ci; f. 1975 as Société Nationale d'Opérations Pétrolières de la Côte d'Ivoire (PETROCI); restructured 2000 to comprise three companies—Petroci Exploration Production, SA, Petroci Gaz and Petroci Industries Services; all aspects of hydrocarbons devt; Pres. PAUL GUI DIBO; Dir-Gen. DANIEL GNAGNI.

Société de Développement des Forêts (SODEFOR): blvd François Mitterrand, 01 BP 3770, Abidjan 01; tel. 22-48-30-00; fax 22-44-02-40; e-mail info@sodefor.ci; internet www.sodefor.ci; f. 1966; establishment and management of tree plantations, sustainable management of state forests, marketing of timber products; Dir-Gen. SANGARÉ MAMADOU.

Société pour le Développement Minier de la Côte d'Ivoire (SODEMI): 31 blvd des Martyrs, 01 BP 2816, Abidjan 01; tel. 22-44-29-94; fax 22-44-08-21; e-mail sodemidg@aviso.cg; f. 1962; geological and mineral research; Pres. NICOLAS KOUANDI ANGBA; Man. Dir KOUAMÉ KADIO.

Société pour le Développement des Productions Animales (SODEPRA): 01 BP 1249, Abidjan 01; tel. 20-21-13-10; f. 1970; rearing of livestock; Man. Dir (vacant).

DEVELOPMENT AGENCIES

Agence Française de Développement (AFD): blvd François Mitterrand, 01 BP 1814, Abidjan 01; tel. 22-40-70-40; fax 22-44-21-78; e-mail afdabidjan@afd.fr; internet www.afd.fr; Country Dir PHILIPPE-CYRILLE BERTON.

Association pour la Promotion des Exportations de Côte d'Ivoire (Apex-CI): 01 BP 3485, Abidjan 01; tel. 20-30-25-30; fax 20-21-75-76; e-mail marketing@apexci.org; internet www.apexci.org; Dir-Gen. GUY M'BENGUE.

Centre de Promotion des Investissements en Côte d'Ivoire (CEPICI): Quartier des Ambassades, angle rue Booker Washington et ave Jacques AKA, BP V152, Abidjan 01; tel. 22-44-45-35; fax 22-44-28-22; e-mail infos-cepici@cepici.ci; f. 1993; investment promotion authority; Dir-Gen. EMMANUEL ESSIS ESMEL.

France Volontaires: 01 BP 2532, Abidjan; tel. 20-22-85-09; fax 20-22-05-96; internet www.france-volontaires.org; f. 1965; name changed as above in 2009; Nat. Delegate JEAN-PIERRE JUIF.

Institut de Recherche pour le Développement: Quartier Marcory Zone 4C, rue Dr Alexander Fleming, 15 BP 917, Abidjan 15; tel. 21-35-96-03; fax 21-35-40-15; e-mail cote-ivoire@ird.fr; internet www.ird.ci; Admin. SÉKOU YEO.

CHAMBERS OF COMMERCE

Chambre d'Agriculture de la Côte d'Ivoire: 11 ave Lamblin, 01 BP 1291, Abidjan 01; tel. 20-32-92-13; fax 20-32-92-20; Sec.-Gen. GAUTHIER N'ZI.

Chambre de Commerce et d'Industrie de Côte d'Ivoire: 6 ave Joseph Anoma, 01 BP 1399, Abidjan 01; tel. 20-33-16-00; fax 20-30-97-35; e-mail info@chamco-ci.org; internet www.chamco-ci.org; f. 1992; Pres. JEAN-LOUIS BILLON; Dir-Gen. MAMADOU SARR.

TRADE ASSOCIATIONS

Association Nationale des Organisations Professionnelles Agricoles de Côte d'Ivoire (ANOPACI): Cocody Cité des Arts, Derrière la Cité BAD, rue C7, 20 BP 937, Abidjan 20; tel. 22-44-11-76; e-mail anopaci@yahoo.fr; internet www.anopaci.org; f. 1998; Pres. MATHIAS N'GOAN.

Bourse du Café et du Cacao (BCC): 04 BP 2576, Abidjan 04; tel. 20-20-27-20; fax 20-20-28-14; e-mail info@bcc.ci; internet www.bcc.ci; f. 2001 to replace marketing, purchasing and certain other functions of La Nouvelle Caistab (Caisse de Stabilisation et de Soutien des Prix des Productions Agricoles); Pres. LUCIEN TAPÉ DOH; Dir-Gen. TANO KASSI KADIO.

Fédération Ivoirienne des Producteurs de Café et de Cacao (FIPCC): Yamoussoukro; f. 1998; coffee and cocoa growers' asscn; Chair. CISSÉ LOCINÉ; c. 3,000 mems.

Organisation de Commercialisation de l'Ananas et de la Banane (OCAB): Abidjan; pineapple and banana growers' asscn; Pres. MICHEL GNUI; Exec. Sec. EMMANUEL DOLI.

EMPLOYERS' ORGANIZATIONS

Association Nationale des Paysans de Côte d'Ivoire (ANAPACI): Bouaké; Pres. KONÉ WAYARAGA.

Association Nationale des Producteurs de Café-Cacao de Côte d'Ivoire (ANAPROCI): BP 840, San-Pédro; tel. 34-71-20-98; fax 34-71-14-65; Pres. BOTI BI ZOUA; Sec.-Gen. THOMAS EYIMIN.

Confédération Générale des Entreprises de Côte d'Ivoire: 01 BP 8666, Abidjan 01; tel. 20-30-08-21; fax 20-22-28-25; e-mail cgeci@cgeci.org; internet www.cgeci.org; f. 1993 as Conseil National du Patronat Ivoirien; current name adopted 2005; Pres. JEAN KACOU DIAGOU; Dir-Gen. LAKOUN OUATTARA; nine affiliated federations, including the following:

Fédération Maritime de Côte d'Ivoire (FEDERMAR): Treichville, ave Christiani, 01 BP 4082, Abidjan 01; tel. 21-22-08-09; fax 21-22-07-90; e-mail issouf.fadika@ci.dti.bollore.com; f. 1958; Pres. ISSOUF FADIKA; Sec.-Gen. VACABA TOURÉ DE MOVALY.

Fédération Nationale des Industries et Services de Côte d'Ivoire (FNISCI): Immeuble Les Harmonies, Plateau, Abidjan 01; tel. 20-31-90-70; fax 20-21-53-52; e-mail infos@fnisci.net; internet siege.fnisci.net; f. 1993; Pres. JOSEPH-DESIRÉ BILEY; Dir-Gen. ADAMA COULIBALY; 180 mems.

Groupement Ivoirien du Bâtiment et des Travaux Publics (GIBTP): 25 rue des Carrossiers, Concession SIDELAF, zone 3, 01 BP 464, Abidjan 01; tel. 21-25-29-46; fax 21-25-29-57; f. 1934 as Syndicat des Entrepreneurs et des Industriels de la Côte d'Ivoire; present name adopted 1997; Pres. KONGO KOUADIO KOUASSI.

Syndicat des Commerçants Importateurs et Exportateurs (SCIMPEX): 01 BP 3792, Abidjan 01; tel. 20-21-54-27; fax 20-32-56-52; Pres. JACQUES ROSSIGNOL; Sec.-Gen. M. KOFFI.

Syndicat Autonome des Producteurs de Café-Cacao de Côte d'Ivoire (SYNAPROCI): Abidjan; f. 2003; Pres. BANNY KOFFI GERMAIN (acting).

Syndicat des Exportateurs et Négociants en Bois de Côte d'Ivoire: route du Lycée Technique, Cocody Danga, Villa No. 4, 01 BP 1979, Abidjan 01; tel. 22-44-44-80; fax 22-44-44-74; e-mail unemaf@africaonline.co.ci; f. 1960; Pres. SOULEYMANE COULIBALY.

Syndicat des Producteurs Industriels du Bois (SPIB): route du Lycée Technique, Cocody Danga, Villa No. 4, 01 BP 318, Abidjan; tel. 22-44-44-80; fax 22-44-44-74; e-mail unemaf@africaonline.co.ci; f. 1943; Pres. WILFRIED BIRKENMAIER.

Union des Entreprises Agricoles et Forestières: route du Lycée Technique, Cocody Danga, Villa No. 4, 01 BP 2300, Abidjan 01; tel. 22-44-44-80; fax 22-44-44-74; e-mail unemaf@africaonline.co.ci; f. 1952; Pres. YORO BI TRAZIÉ.

UTILITIES

Electricity

Compagnie Ivoirienne d'Electricité (CIE): 1 ave Christiani, 01 BP 6932, Abidjan 01; tel. 21-23-33-00; fax 21-23-63-22; e-mail info@cie.ci; internet www.groupecie.net; f. 1990; 71% controlled by Société Bouygues group (France); Pres. OUSMANE DIARRA; Dir-Gen. DOMINIQUE KACOU.

Compagnie Ivoirienne de Production d'Electricité (CIPREL): Tour Sidom, 12e étage, ave Houdaille, 01 BP 4039, Abidjan 01; tel. 20-22-60-97; independent power production; Dir-Gen. N'GUESSAN KOUASSI.

Gas

Gaz de Côte d'Ivoire (GDCI): 01 BP 1351, Abidjan; tel. 22-44-49-55; f. 1961; transfer to majority private ownership pending; gas distributor; Man. Dir LAMBERT KONAN.

Water

Société de Distribution d'Eau de la Côte d'Ivoire (SODECI): 1 ave Christiani, Treichville, 01 BP 1843, Abidjan 01; tel. 21-23-30-00; fax 21-24-30-06; e-mail sodeci@sodeci.ci; internet www.sodeci.com; f. 1959; production, treatment and distribution of drinking water; 46% owned by Groupe Bouygues (France), 51% owned by employees; Pres. FIRMIN AHOUNÉ; Dir-Gen. BASILE EBAH.

TRADE UNIONS

Dignité: 03 BP 2031, Abidjan 03; tel. 21-37-74-89; fax 20-37-85-00; e-mail dignite@aviso.ci; Sec.-Gen. BASILE MAHAN-GAHE; 10,000 mems (2001).

Fédération des Syndicats Autonomes de la Côte d'Ivoire (FESACI): Abidjan; breakaway group from the Union Générale des Travailleurs de Côte d'Ivoire; Sec.-Gen. TRAORÉ DOHIA MAMADOU.

Union Générale des Travailleurs de Côte d'Ivoire (UGTCI): 05 BP 1203, Abidjan 05; tel. and fax 21-24-09-78; fax 20-24-08-83; e-mail ugtcisg@yahoo.fr; internet www.ugtci.org; f. 1962; Sec.-Gen. FRANÇOIS ADE MENSAH; 100,000 individual mems; 157 affiliated unions.

Transport

RAILWAYS

The rail network in Côte d'Ivoire totalled 1,316 km in 2000, including 660 km of track from Abidjan to Niangoloko, on the border with Burkina Faso; from there, the railway extends to Kaya, via the Burkinabè capital, Ouagadougou. Work on a 737-km railway project linking San-Pédro with the western parts of the country was expected to begin in 2014.

SITARAIL—Transport Ferroviaire de Personnel et de Marchandises: Résidence Memanou, blvd Clozel, Plateau, 16 BP 1216, Abidjan 16; tel. 20-20-80-00; fax 20-22-48-47; f. 1995 to operate services on Abidjan–Ouagadougou–Kaya (Burkina Faso) line; Man. Dir PIERRE MARTINEAU.

ROADS

In 2004 there were about 80,000 km of roads, of which some 6,500 km were paved. Some 68,000m. francs CFA was invested in the road network in 1994–98; projects included the upgrading of 3,000 km of roads and 30,000 km of tracks. Tolls were introduced on some roads in the mid-1990s, to assist in funding the maintenance of the network.

Fonds d'Entretien Routier (FER): 04 BP 3089, Abidjan 04; tel. 20-31-13-05; e-mail fer@aviso.ci; f. 2001; Dir-Gen. PHILIPPE GOTH.

Société des Transports Abidjanais (SOTRA): 01 BP 2009, Abidjan 01; tel. 21-24-90-80; fax 21-25-97-21; e-mail infos@sotra.ci; internet www.sotra.ci; f. 1960; 60% state-owned; urban transport; Dir-Gen. BOUAKÉ MÉITÉ.

SHIPPING

Côte d'Ivoire has two major ports, Abidjan and San-Pédro, both of which are industrial and commercial establishments with financial autonomy. Abidjan, which handled some 14.5m. metric tons of goods in 2003, is the largest container and trading port in West Africa. Access to the port is via the 2.7-km Vridi Canal. The port at San-Pédro, which handled 1.2m. tons of goods in 1999, remains the main gateway to the south-western region of Côte d'Ivoire. As a result of widespread civil unrest from September 2002, much international freight transport that formerly left or entered the West African region through ports in Côte d'Ivoire was transferred to neighbouring countries. At 31 December 2009 the country's merchant fleet comprised 35 vessels, with a total displacement of 9,200 grt.

Port Autonome d'Abidjan (PAA): BP V85, Abidjan; tel. 21-23-80-00; fax 21-23-80-80; e-mail info@paa-ci.org; internet www.paa-ci.org; f. 1992; transferred to private ownership in 1999; Pres. ANGE-FRANÇOIS BARRY-BATTESTI; Man. Dir HIEN SIÉ.

Port Autonome de San-Pédro (PASP): BP 339/340, San-Pédro; tel. 34-71-72-00; fax 34-71-72-15; e-mail pasp@pasp.ci; internet addns3@gmail.com; f. 1971; Pres. YÉBARTH LUCIEN; Man. Dir HILAIRE MARCEL LAMIZANA.

AMICI: Km 1, blvd de Marseille, 16 BP 643, Abidjan 16; tel. 21-35-28-50; fax 21-35-28-53; e-mail amici.abj@aviso.ci; f. 1998; 45% owned by Ivorian interests, 25% by Danish interests, 20% by German interests and 10% by French interests.

Compagnie Maritime Africaine—Côte d'Ivoire (COMAF—CI): rond-point du Nouveau Port, 08 BP 867, Abidjan 08; tel. 20-32-40-77; f. 1973; navigation and management of ships; Dir FRANCO BERNARDINI.

SAGA Côte d'Ivoire: rond-point du Nouveau Port, 01 BP 1727, Abidjan 01; tel. 21-23-23-23; fax 21-24-25-06; f. 1959; merchandise handling, transit and storage; privately owned; Pres. M. GEORGES; Dir-Gen. DAVID CHARRIER.

SDV—Côte d'Ivoire (SDV—CI): 01 BP 4082, Abidjan 01; tel. 20-20-20-20; fax 20-20-21-20; f. 1943; sea and air transport; storage and warehousing; affiliated to Groupe Bolloré (France); Pres. GILLES CUCHE.

Société Agence Maritime de l'Ouest Africain—Côte d'Ivoire (SAMOA—CI): rue des Gallions, 01 BP 1611, Abidjan 01; tel. 20-21-29-65; f. 1955; shipping agents; Man. Dir CLAUDE PERDRIAUD.

Société Ivoirienne de Navigation Maritime (SIVOMAR): 5 rue Charpentier, Zone 2B, Treichville, 01 BP 1395, Abidjan 01; tel. 20-21-73-23; fax 20-32-38-53; f. 1977; shipments to ports in Africa, the Mediterranean and the Far East; Dir SIMPLISSE DE MESSE ZINSOU.

Société Ouest-Africaine d'Entreprises Maritimes en Côte d'Ivoire (SOAEM–CI): 01 BP 1727, Abidjan 01; tel. 20-21-59-69; fax 20-32-24-67; f. 1978; merchandise handling, transit and storage; Chair. JACQUES PELTIER; Dir JACQUES COLOMBANI.

SOCOPAO-Côte d'Ivoire: Km 1, blvd de la République, 01 BP 1297, Abidjan 01; tel. 21-24-13-14; fax 21-24-21-30; shipping agents; Shipping Dir OLIVIER RANJARD.

CIVIL AVIATION

There are three international airports: Abidjan–Félix Houphouët-Boigny, Bouaké and Yamoussoukro. In addition, there are 25 domestic and regional airports, including those at Bouna, Korhogo, Man, Odienné and San-Pédro.

Autorité Nationale de l'Aviation Civile: 07 BP 148, Abidjan 07; tel. 21-27-74-24; fax 21-27-63-46; internet www.anac.ci; civil aviation authority; Dir JEAN KOUASSI ABONOUAN.

Air Inter Ivoire: Aéroport de Port Boüet, 07 BP 62, Abidjan 07; tel. 21-27-84-65; internal flights.

Société Nouvelle Air Ivoire: Immeuble République, pl. de la République, 01 BP 7782, Abidjan 01; tel. 20-25-15-61; fax 20-32-04-90; e-mail info@airivoire.com; internet www.airivoire.com; f. 2000 to replace Air Ivoire (f. 1960); privatized in 2001; 76.42% owned by All Africa Airways, 23.58% state-owned; internal and regional flights.

Tourism

The game reserves, forests, lagoons, coastal resorts, rich ethnic folklore and the lively city of Abidjan are tourist attractions; Côte d'Ivoire also has well-developed facilities for business visitors, including golfing centres. Some 301,000 tourists visited Côte d'Ivoire in 1998; receipts from tourism in that year totalled US $331m. In 2002 receipts from tourism totalled $490m. Tourism was negatively affected by instability from the late 1990s, most recently as a result of the violence that followed the disputed presidential run-off election of November 2010.

Office Ivoirien du Tourisme et de l'Hôtellerie: Immeuble ex-EECI, pl. de la République, 01 BP 8538, Abidjan 01; tel. 20-25-16-00; fax 20-32-03-88; internet oith@tourismeci.org; internet tourismeci.org; f. 1992; Dir CAMILLE KOUASSI.

Defence

As assessed at November 2010, Côte d'Ivoire's active armed forces comprised an army of 6,500 men, a navy of about 900, an air force of 700, a paramilitary presidential guard of 1,350 and a gendarmerie of 7,600. There was also a 1,500-strong militia, and reserve forces numbered 10,000 men. Military service is by selective conscription and lasts for 18 months. In late February 2004 the UN Security Council established the UN Operation in Côte d'Ivoire (UNOCI) for an initial period of 12 months from early April, with an authorized military strength of 6,240. In June 2005 the strength of UNOCI was increased to 7,090 troops, and in January 2006 the mandate of the operation was extended until December of that year. The mandate was periodically extended until July 2009, although in January that year the Security Council also agreed, in view of the improved security situation in Côte d'Ivoire, to reduce the authorized military strength of UNOCI from 8,115 to 7,450. However, following the disputed presidential election of November 2010 and a subsequent increase in violence in the country, the mandate of UNOCI was extended until 30 June 2011 and in January the Security Council approved the deployment of an additional 2,000 military personnel to UNOCI, bringing the total authorized strength to 10,650.

Defence Expenditure: Estimated at 152,000m. francs CFA in 2011.

Chief of Staff of the Armed Forces: Gen. SOUMAILA BAKAYOKO.

Commander of Land-based Forces: Col SÉKOU TOURÉ.

Commander of the Navy: Frigate Capt. DJAKARIDJA KONATÉ.

Commander of the Air Force: Maj.-Col JEAN-JACQUES RÉNÉ OUEGNIN.

Education

Education at all levels is available free of charge. Primary education, which is officially compulsory for six years between the ages of seven and 13 years, begins at six years of age and lasts for six years. According to UNESCO estimates, enrolment at primary schools in 2008/09 included 61% of children in the relevant age-group (males 67%; females 56%). Secondary education, from the age of 12, lasts for up to seven years, comprising a first cycle of four years and a second cycle of three years. In 2001/02 total enrolment at secondary level was equivalent to 27% of children in the relevant age-group (males 35%; females 19%), according to UNESCO estimates. The Université de Cocody (formerly the Université Nationale de Côte d'Ivoire), in Abidjan, has six faculties, and there are two other universities, at Abodo-Adjamé (also in Abidjan) and at Bouaké. In 2006 there were 18 private universities and 120 private grande écoles in the country. The country's first Islamic university, Université Musulmane de Côte d'Ivoire (UMCI), was opened in 2009. Some 156,772 students were enrolled at tertiary-level institutions in 2006/07. In 2008 spending on education represented 24.6% of total budgetary expenditure.

CROATIA

Introductory Survey

LOCATION, CLIMATE, LANGUAGE, RELIGION, FLAG, CAPITAL

The Republic of Croatia is situated in south-eastern Europe and has a long western coastline on the Adriatic Sea. It is bordered to the north-west by Slovenia, to the north-east by Hungary and to the east by Serbia (the province of Vojvodina). Bosnia and Herzegovina abuts into Croatia, forming a southern border along the Sava river and an eastern border within the Dinaric Alps. The Croatian territory of Dubrovnik, which is situated at the southern tip of the narrowing stretch of Croatia (beyond a short coastal strip of Bosnia and Herzegovina), has a short border with Montenegro. The climate is continental in the hilly interior and Mediterranean on the coast. There is steady rainfall throughout the year, although summer is the wettest season. The average annual rainfall in Zagreb is 890 mm (35 ins). Both the ethnic Croats (who comprised 89.6% of the total population according to the 2001 census) and the Serb minority (4.5%) speak closely related languages of the Southern Slavonic group formerly referred to as variants of Serbo-Croat, but known, since the early 1990s, as Croatian and Serbian. Croatian is written in the Latin script, while Serbian is more commonly written in the Cyrillic script. There are, in addition, a number of small minority communities in Croatia, notably the Slav Muslim (Bosniak) community (which comprised 0.5% of the total population in 2001). The national flag (proportions 1 by 2) consists of three horizontal stripes, of red, white and dark blue, with the arms of Croatia (a shield of 25 squares, alternately red and white, below a blue crown composed of five shields) fimbriated in red and white and set in the centre of the flag, overlapping all three stripes. The capital is Zagreb.

CONTEMPORARY POLITICAL HISTORY

Historical Context

From the 16th century the territory of what is now Croatia was divided between the Osmanlı (Ottoman—Turkish) and Habsburg (Austrian) Empires (although Dalmatia and Istria were dominated at different times by Venice and by France, while Ragusa—Dubrovnik—was formerly an independent republic). After the Hungarian revolution of 1848–49, Croatia and Slavonia (the north-eastern region of present-day Croatia) were made Austrian crown-lands. The Habsburg Empire became the Dual Monarchy of Austria-Hungary in 1867, and the territories were restored to the Hungarian Crown in the following year. Croatia gained its autonomy and was formally joined with Slavonia in 1881. However, Hungarian nationalism transformed traditional Croat–Serb rivalries into Southern Slav (Yugoslav) solidarity. Following the collapse of the Austro-Hungarian Empire at the end of the First World War in October 1918, a Kingdom of Serbs, Croats and Slovenes (under the Serbian monarchy) was proclaimed on 4 December. The new Kingdom united Serbia, including Macedonia and Kosovo, with Montenegro and the Habsburg lands (modern Croatia, Slovenia and Vojvodina). The Kingdom was, however, dominated by the Serbs. Increasing unrest within the Kingdom culminated in the meeting of a separatist Croat assembly in Zagreb in 1928. King Aleksandar imposed a royal dictatorship in January 1929, formally renaming the country Yugoslavia in October. In 1934 the King was assassinated in France by Croat extremists.

Meanwhile, the Fascist Ustaša (Rebel) movement was gaining support among the discontented Croat peasantry. When German and Italian forces invaded Yugoslavia in 1941, many Croats welcomed the Axis powers' support for the establishment, on 9 April, of the Independent State of Croatia (NDH), incorporating all of Bosnia and Herzegovina and parts of Serbia and Slovenia as well as much of modern-day Croatia. The NDH was led by the leader of the Ustaša, Ante Pavelić. During the Ustaša regime political dissidents, hundreds of thousands of Serbs, and thousands of Roma (Gypsies) and Jews were murdered in extermination camps. At the same time fierce armed resistance was being waged by the Partisans, who were led by Josip Broz (Tito), the Croat-Slovene leader of the Communist Party of Yugoslavia (CPY). By 1943 Tito's forces were able to proclaim a provisional government in a number of areas. The NDH collapsed in 1945, and Croatia was restored to Yugoslavia as one unit of a federal communist republic, which became the Socialist Federal Republic of Yugoslavia (SFRY) in 1963.

During the 1960s there was an increase in nationalism in Croatia, both among non-communists and among Croatian members of the ruling League of Communists (as the CPY had been renamed). In December 1971 the Croatian communist leaders were obliged to resign. Together with other prominent nationalists they were arrested, and a purge of the League of Communists of Croatia (LCC) followed. In 1974, however, Tito introduced a new Constitution, which enshrined the federal and collective nature of the Yugoslav state.

When the power of the LCC began to decline, particularly from 1989, Croatian nationalism re-emerged as a significant force. Dr Franjo Tuđman, who had twice been imprisoned for publicly criticizing repression in Croatia, formed the Croatian Democratic Union (CDU) in 1990, which rapidly became the main challenger to the ruling party, by then called the League of Communists of Croatia—Party of Democratic Reform (LCC—PDR). Tuđman campaigned as a nationalist for multi-party elections to the republican legislature, and advocated a 'Greater Croatia' (to include Bosnia).

At the elections to the tricameral republican Sabor (Assembly), which took place on 24 April and 6–7 May 1990, the CDU obtained an absolute majority of seats in each of the three chambers, with 205 out of 351 seats in total. The next largest party was the LCC—PDR, with 73 seats. (Both the CDU and LCC—PDR won further seats in alliance with other parties.) Tuđman was elected President of Croatia. Although he offered the vice-presidency of the Sabor to a Serb, Serb-dominated areas remained alienated by Tuđman's nationalism. A 'Serb National Council', based at Knin (in the south-western Krajina region), formed in July, organized a referendum on autonomy for the Croatian Serbs. Despite attempts by the Croatian authorities to prohibit the referendum, it took place, amid virtual insurrection in some areas, in late August–early September. In October the 'Serb National Council', announcing the results of the referendum, declared autonomy for the Krajina areas as the 'Serb Autonomous Region (SAR) of Krajina'.

Meanwhile, in August 1990 the Socialist Republic of Croatia was renamed the Republic of Croatia. In that month the Sabor voted to dismiss the republican member of the federal State Presidency, Dr Stjepan Šuvar, and replace him with Stjepan (Stipe) Mesić, then President of the Government (premier) of Croatia. His appointment was confirmed in October. In December the Sabor enacted a new republican Constitution, which declared Croatia's sovereignty, its authority over its own armed forces and its right to secede from the SFRY. Tensions increased when, in January 1991, the Croatian authorities refused to comply with an order by the federal State Presidency to disarm all paramilitary groups, and subsequently boycotted negotiations on the future of the federation. On 21 February Croatia asserted the primacy of its Constitution and laws over those of the SFRY. Later that month the self-proclaimed SAR of Krajina declared its separation from Croatia and its intention of uniting with Serbia. In April a Croatian National Guard was formed, replacing the Territorial Defence Force. On 19 May some 94% of the voters participating in a referendum (largely boycotted by the Serb population) favoured Croatia's becoming a sovereign entity, while 92% rejected a federal Yugoslavia.

On 25 June 1991 Croatia and Slovenia declared independence, beginning the process of dissociation from the SFRY. Two days later the SAR of Krajina declared its unification with the self-proclaimed Serb 'Community of Municipalities of Bosnian Krajina', based in Banja Luka, in Bosnia and Herzegovina. During July war effectively began between the Croat and Serb communities in Croatia. In August an SAR of West Slavonia (in north-eastern Croatia) was declared; the SAR of Slavonia, Baranja and Western Srem (Sirmium) also proclaimed its autonomy later that month. In the same month Tuđman appointed a coalition Government, dominated by the CDU. In September the UN placed an embargo on the delivery of all military equipment to the territories formerly comprising the SFRY. In October the Croatian Government refused to extend the three-month moratorium on the process of dissociation from the SFRY that had been agreed during peace negotiations sponsored by the European Community (EC—later European Union, EU, see p. 276) in The Hague, Netherlands, in July. By November the Yugoslav People's Army (JNA), supported by Serbian irregular troops, had secured about one-third of Croatian territory. The main area of conflict was Slavonia, although Serbian and JNA attacks were also concentrated on the port of Zadar, in central Dalmatia. In November, in accordance with the principles formulated at The Hague, the Sabor declared its readiness to enact legislation guaranteeing minority rights. However, there were increasing allegations of atrocities on both sides. The CDU came under pressure from more extreme nationalist elements to make no concessions. Meanwhile, in October principally Montenegrin units of the JNA attacked and besieged Dubrovnik. The eastern Slavonian town of Vukovar (where particularly intense fighting had taken place) finally surrendered on 18 November, after the 13th cease-fire agreement negotiated by the EC, which supervised the subsequent civilian evacuation. (At least 260 civilians were massacred by JNA troops during the evacuation.) Both parties indicated readiness to accept a UN peace-keeping force. The 14th cease-fire agreement, therefore, involved the UN, although it did not bring an end to the fighting. In December UN Security Council Resolution 724 provided for observers to be sent to the SFRY, in addition to a small team of civilian and military personnel to prepare for a possible peace-keeping force. In the same month a 'Republic of Serb Krajina' (RSK), formed by the union of the three SARs, was proclaimed.

Domestic Political Affairs

In November 1991 the Supreme Council (a special war cabinet, chaired by Tuđman) ordered all Croats to vacate any federal posts that they held and to place their services at the disposal of Croatia. On 5 December Mesić resigned as Yugoslavia's nominal head of state; the federal Prime Minister, Ante Marković, resigned on 19 December. On 23 December Germany announced its recognition of Croatia, and on 15 January 1992 the other members of the EC initiated general international recognition of Croatia, which culminated in its accession to the UN in May.

Unconditional cease-fire and the re-election of Franjo Tuđman

With more than 6,000 dead and 400,000 internally displaced in Croatia, the Croatian National Guard and the JNA signed a UN-sponsored, unconditional cease-fire on 2 January 1992. In February a 14,000-strong UN Protection Force (UNPROFOR) was entrusted with ensuring the withdrawal of the JNA from Croatia and the demilitarization of the three Serb-held enclaves, which were designated UN Protected Areas (UNPAs). In the same month UNPROFOR's mandate in Croatia was extended to cover those areas occupied by JNA troops and with majority Serb populations, but outside the official UNPAs. In May the JNA began to withdraw from Croatia. Sporadic shelling continued, however, and UNPROFOR failed to prevent the expulsion of over 1,000 Croats by Serbian forces from East Slavonia. In June Croat forces launched a series of offensives in Serb-held areas. This development provoked UN Security Council Resolution 762, adopted on 30 June, which required the Croatian forces to withdraw to the positions that they had held prior to 21 June and to refrain from entering Serb-controlled areas.

In late July 1992 a military court in Split convicted 19 leading figures from the RSK of threatening the territorial integrity of Croatia. Shortly afterwards, the leaders of the RSK renounced their claims to independence. In early September the Prime Minister of the Federal Republic of Yugoslavia (now comprising Serbia and Montenegro), Milan Panić, announced Yugoslavia's willingness to recognize Croatia within its pre-1991 borders, so long as the Serb enclaves be granted special status. During an EC/UN peace conference convened in London, United Kingdom, in August, agreement was reached on economic co-operation between representatives of Croatia and the RSK, and in late September Presidents Tuđman of Croatia and Dobrica Ćosić of Yugoslavia agreed to work towards a normalization of relations between the two countries.

Presidential and legislative elections (the latter to a new bicameral legislature comprising a directly elected Zastupnički dom—Chamber of Representatives—and an indirectly elected Županijski dom—Chamber of Counties) were held in Croatia on 2 August 1992. Tuđman was re-elected President, with 56% of the votes cast, more than twice the proportion obtained by his nearest rival, Dražen Budiša of the Croatian Social Liberal Party (CSLP), while at the legislative elections the ruling CDU obtained a majority, securing 85 of the 138 seats contested in the lower Zastupnički dom. A new Government, under the premiership of Hrvoje Šarinić, was appointed shortly thereafter. Elections to the Županijski dom were held on 7 February. The CDU won 37 of the elective 63 seats, while the CSLP, together with allied parties, obtained 16 seats.

Meanwhile, in late January 1993 Croatian troops launched an offensive across UN peace-keeping lines into the Serb-held Krajina, in an effort to gain control of the Maslenica bridge, a vital communications link between northern Croatia and the Dalmatian coast. The Serb forces in Krajina reclaimed weapons that they had earlier surrendered to UNPROFOR. The UN responded by ordering Croatia to withdraw its troops and the Serb forces to return their weapons. On 26 January Ćosić warned the UN that, if UNPROFOR did not intervene, Yugoslavia would dispatch troops to defend the Serbs in Croatia. Two members of UNPROFOR were killed in fighting around Zadar on the following day. The Croats regained control of the Maslenica bridge and Zemunik airport, although extensive political unrest in Croatia continued. At local elections in Istria in February, the Istrian Democratic Assembly (IDA), a party advocating Istrian autonomy—a proposal strongly opposed by the Government—obtained 72% of the total votes cast. In March Šarinić's Government resigned. A former executive of the Croatian state petroleum company, Nikica Valentić, was appointed Prime Minister.

In early April 1993 a UN-sponsored agreement guaranteed the reconstruction and reopening of the Maslenica bridge, Zemunik airport and the Peruca hydroelectric plant, under UNPROFOR supervision. After the Croats reconstructed the bridge themselves, Tuđman reopened it in July, in which month Serb troops launched an attack on Croatian forces. Also in July the UN successfully negotiated the Erdut Agreement between the leaders of Croatia and Serbia, whereby Croat forces were to leave the Maslenica area by the end of the month, which would be returned to UNPROFOR administration. However, the Croats failed to withdraw and fighting resumed. In August the Croatian Minister of Foreign Affairs, Dr Mate Granić, declared the Erdut Agreement invalid. In September a full-scale mobilization was undertaken among the Serbs of East Slavonia, Baranja and West Sirmium. Serb–Croat hostilities extended to Zagreb by mid-September. By this time most of the JNA had withdrawn from Croatia, and some Serb artillery had been placed under UN control, but UNPROFOR forces were not in effective control of Croatia's borders.

On 4 October 1993 the UN Security Council voted unanimously to extend UNPROFOR's mandate by Resolution 871, which also required the return to Croatian sovereignty of all remaining areas occupied by JNA troops outside the UNPAs, and the disarmament of Serb paramilitary groups. The UNPROFOR forces were empowered to act in self-defence. The Croatian administration accepted the Resolution, but it was rejected by the assembly of the RSK, which proceeded to order the mobilization of all Serb conscripts in Krajina. Multi-party elections held in the RSK in December were declared illegal by the Constitutional Court of Croatia. In January 1994 Milan Martić, a candidate supported by President Slobodan Milošević of Serbia, was elected 'President' of the RSK.

In mid-January 1994 Croatia and Yugoslavia announced their intention to begin the normalization of relations, including the establishment of representative offices in their respective capitals. (A parallel agreement was also signed between representatives of the Croat and Serb communities in Bosnia and Herzegovina.) In the same month the Croatian Government indicated the possibility of direct Croatian intervention in central Bosnia and Herzegovina, prompting the US Permanent Representative to the UN, Madeleine Albright, to threaten the imposition of international sanctions against Croatia. (Croatian army units had from 1992 supported the self-styled breakaway Croat state in western Bosnia and Herzegovina, the 'Croat Community of Herzeg-Bosna'.) In February Tuđman approved proposals, advanced by the USA, for a Bosniak (Muslim)-Croat federation within Bosnia and Herzegovina, known as the Federation of Bosnia and Herzegovina. In the RSK, meanwhile, a cease-fire, agreed in December 1993, was extended for a third time, until 31 March 1994. On 30 March a further cease-fire provided for the establishment of a 'buffer' zone, to be monitored by UNPROFOR.

In April 1994 a long-standing public dispute between Tuđman and Josip Manolić, the President of the Županijski dom and a leading member of the CDU, led to a division in the party. Manolić and other prominent liberals objected to Tuđman's collusion with Gojko Šušak, the Minister of Defence, who was widely considered responsible for Croatia's actions against the Bosniaks in the Bosnian conflict. After Tuđman suspended Manolić from his position within the CDU, the latter, together with Mesić (by this time the President of the Zastupnički dom), left the CDU to form a new party, the Croatian Independent Democrats (CID). The CID, led by Mesić, became the largest opposition party in the Sabor, with 18 deputies. In June the principal opposition parties commenced a boycott of the Sabor, in protest at the appointment of two CDU deputies as Presidents of the parliamentary chambers (Manolić and Mesić having agreed to resign from their posts in mid-May); opposition deputies returned to the Sabor in September.

Meanwhile, the cease-fire in the RSK continued precariously. In September 1994 the UN Security Council renewed the UNPROFOR mandate in Croatia for a further six months. In October a new negotiating forum, the Zagreb Group, was established with the aim of resolving the Krajina question; it comprised two representatives of the EU and the US and Russian ambassadors to Croatia. The RSK rejected the group's initial proposal that it be reintegrated into Croatia, with extensive autonomy. In January 1995 President Tuđman announced that the Government would not renew the UNPROFOR mandate in Croatia upon its expiry in March, claiming that its presence had reinforced the Serbs' position. In late January the Zagreb Group presented a fresh peace plan, which envisaged the return of one-half of Serb-controlled territory to Croatia, in exchange for extensive regional autonomy for the Krajina Serbs. (The areas to be reintegrated would be demilitarized, and administered by the UN for a minimum of five years.) In February the RSK suspended an economic accord concluded with Croatia in December 1994. In March Tuđman reversed his decision to expel UNPROFOR from Croatian territory, two weeks before the UN troops were due to begin their withdrawal. Croatia had agreed to a revised peace-keeping plan, following intensive diplomatic negotiations conducted by the international community (in particular, the USA), as a result of which a compromise UN mandate was to provide for a reduced peace-keeping force (to be known as the UN Confidence Restoration Operation—UNCRO) until October, including several hundred troops to be deployed along Croatia's frontiers with Bosnia and Herzegovina and Yugoslavia (effectively isolating Serb-occupied territory in Croatia from sources of military aid).

In early March 1995 a formal military alliance was announced between the Herzeg-Bosna and the (by that time predominantly Bosniak) Bosnian government armies. (A similar agreement establishing a military alliance between the Croatian Serbs and the Bosnian Serbs had been drawn up in February.) In mid-April Bosnian Serb artillery attacked Dubrovnik and its airport. On 1–2 May Croatian government forces regained control of West Slavonia; large numbers of Serb troops fled the area. The Croatian Serbs launched artillery attacks on Zagreb (where six civilians were killed), Karlovac and Sisak. On 3 May, under the mediation of the UN Special Envoy, the warring parties agreed a cease-fire, according to which Serb artillery was to be surrendered to the UN, in exchange for the safe passage of all Serb civilians and troops from West Slavonia into Bosnia and Herzegovina.

'Operation Storm' and the reintegration of East Slavonia

In June 1995 Tuđman threatened further offensives to seize Serb-held territories. In July a joint offensive by Croatian government forces and Herzeg-Bosna troops resulted in the seizure of the Serb-held town of Bosansko Grahovo, in western Bosnia and Herzegovina, thereby blocking the principal supply route from Serb-held areas of northern Bosnia and Herzegovina to Serb-held Krajina. On 4 August Croatian government troops launched a massive military operation ('Operation Storm') and rapidly recaptured the Krajina enclave, as a result of which about 150,000 Croatian Serbs fled or were expelled to Serb-held areas in Bosnia and Herzegovina or to Serbia. In early September the UN announced that some 10,500 peace-keeping troops were to be withdrawn from Croatia, in view of the restoration of government authority over Krajina. On 20 September the Zastupnički dom voted to suspend sections of the law on minorities, which had provided the Krajina Serbs with special rights in areas where they had been a majority; this decision had been preceded two days earlier by a new electoral law reducing the reserved representation of the Serb minority in the Croatian legislature from 13 seats to three. The law also provided for 12 seats in the Zastupnički dom to represent some 470,000 Croatian emigrés, thus giving the right to vote to some 291,000 Bosnian Croats (many of whom supported the CDU's associated party in Bosnia and Herzegovina).

In early October 1995, despite the cease-fire, heavy clashes were reported between Croatian troops and Serb forces in East Slavonia. On 3 October, however, Croatian government officials and Serb leaders in East Slavonia signed an 'agreement on basic principles', following talks in the Serb-held town of Erdut. The 11-point agreement provided for a 'transitional period', during which authority over the enclave would be invested in an interim administration established by the UN, demilitarization of the area and creation of a joint Serb-Croat police force, and the safe return of refugees.

Following a campaign that was marred by widespread allegations of state media bias, the CDU secured about 45% of votes cast in elections to the Zastupnični dom on 29 October 1995. A new Government was appointed in early November, headed by the erstwhile Minister of the Economy, Zlatko Matesa.

In November 1995 representatives of Croatia and the East Slavonian Serbs signed an agreement on the reintegration of the East Slavonian enclave. Under the terms of the accord, East Slavonia was to be placed under the authority of a UN-appointed transitional administration for a period of up to two years prior to its full reintegration into Croatia. The interim administration and UN peace-keeping forces would supervise the demilitarization of the area and the return of refugees and displaced persons. In January 1996, under Resolution 1037, the UN Security Council established the UN Transitional Administration for Eastern Slavonia, Baranja and Western Sirmium (UNTAES), with an initial one-year mandate. The UN Security Council also authorized the establishment of a UN Mission of Observers in Prevlaka (UNMOP), comprising 28 military observers, to assume responsibility for monitoring the demilitarization of the Prevlaka peninsula, south-east of Dubrovnik, which was claimed by Yugoslavia, on the grounds of its proximity to a naval base in Montenegro.

In April 1996 the Regional Executive Council of East Slavonia appointed a former RSK 'President' (1992–94), Goran Hadžić, as President of the region. A new Regional Assembly (comprising representatives of Krajina and the five East Slavonian municipalities) and Executive Council were subsequently established. In the same month the Zastupnički dom approved legislation on co-operation between Croatia and the UN International Criminal Tribunal for the Former Yugoslavia (ICTY—based in The Hague), which provided for the transfer of authority to conduct criminal proceedings to the Tribunal and the extradition of the accused. In May the Zastupnički dom adopted legislation granting amnesty for crimes (but not war crimes) committed during the civil conflict in East Slavonia from August 1990. Later in May 1996 a 30-day process for the demilitarization of East Slavonia commenced, and was completed as scheduled. In July an international security force was installed in East Slavonia for the transitional period.

In August 1996, following a meeting between Tuđman and Milošević in Athens, Greece, an agreement was signed, providing for the establishment of full diplomatic relations between Croatia and Yugoslavia; remaining issues of contention, most notably the territorial dispute over Prevlaka, were to be resolved by further negotiations. In October the Council of Europe (see p. 256) agreed to accept Croatia's application for membership, after the Government undertook to ratify the European Convention on Human Rights within one year of admission.

In early April 1997 Serb officials in East Slavonia conducted a referendum (which the Croatian Government and UN officials declared to be illegitimate) regarding the future of the enclave; about 99.5% of the participating electorate voted in favour of East Slavonia remaining a single administrative unit under Serb control after its return to Croatia. In mid-April elections to the Županijski dom and to a number of municipal and regional councils took place. Election monitors from the Organization for Security and Co-operation in Europe (OSCE, see p. 388) declared that the elections had been largely free and fair. The CDU secured 42 of the 63 elective seats in the Županijski dom, while the Croatian Peasants' Party took nine, the CSLP six, the Social Democratic Party of Croatia (SDP, which had been constituted from the former LCC–PDR) four, and the IDA two seats. (A further five deputies were to be nominated by Tuđman, of whom two were to be members of the Serb community in East Slavonia.)

During a visit to East Slavonia in early June 1997 Tuđman publicly offered reconciliation to all Serbs who were willing to accept Croatian citizenship, following continued pressure from Albright (by this time US Secretary of State), who had met Tuđman in May. On 15 June Tuđman was re-elected as President, obtaining 61.4% of the votes cast. Although OSCE monitors declared that the election had not been conducted fairly, on the grounds that opposition parties had not been permitted coverage in the state-controlled media, the Constitutional Court endorsed the results of the election later in the month. Tuđman was officially inaugurated for a second term on 5 August. In November the legislature approved constitutional amendments, proposed by Tuđman, which, notably, prohibited the re-establishment of a union of Yugoslav states.

Meanwhile, in July 1997 the Government had announced the initiation of the programme for the return of some 80,000 Croat refugees to East Slavonia. In the same month, despite previous objections from the Croatian Government, the UN Security Council had adopted a resolution extending the mandate of UNTAES (which had already been renewed for an additional six months) until January 1998, owing to UN concern over the continued stability of East Slavonia. After East Slavonia was returned to Croatian authority in January, an increase in the number of Serbs leaving the region was reported. In May the Government announced a programme that relaxed conditions for the return of Serb refugees to Croatia, following pressure from the international community.

In May 1998 Šušak died; Andrija Hebrang succeeded him as Minister of Defence. In June Croatia submitted to the UN a proposal for a settlement of the status of the Prevlaka peninsula; it was envisaged that a joint Croatian-Yugoslav commission would demarcate the borders between the two countries and that a demilitarized zone would be established for a period of five years. In October, following a disagreement with Tuđman, Hebrang resigned as Minister of Defence and Vice-President of the CDU.

In January 1999 the UN Security Council adopted a resolution on UNMOP, stating that violations of the Prevlaka demilitarized zone had continued and that negotiations on the normalization of relations between Yugoslavia and Croatia had not resulted in any significant progress. In July Croatia submitted an application at the International Court of Justice (ICJ, see p. 25) to institute legal proceedings against Yugoslavia for crimes of genocide allegedly committed by Yugoslav forces in Croatia in 1991–95. In August the Croatian Government complied with a request by the ICTY for the extradition of Vinko Martinović, who had been indicted for crimes committed during the Croat–Muslim conflict in Bosnia and Herzegovina. However, the authorities' reluctance to extradite Mladen Naletilić, who had been indicted on similar charges, prompted severe criticism from the ICTY. (Naletilić's extradition was facilitated in March 2000.)

The death of Tuđman and the defeat of the CDU

On 26 November 1999 the Sabor provisionally transferred the powers of Head of State to the parliamentary Speaker, Vlatko Pavletić, after Tuđman underwent emergency medical treatment. Pavletić rescheduled elections to the Zastupnički dom, due to take place on 22 December, for 3 January 2000. An alliance of six opposition parties—the Croatian Peasants' Party (CPP), the Croatian People's Party, the CSLP, the IDA, the Liberal Party and the SDP—known as the Opposition Six, pledged to establish a coalition government in the event that the parties of the coalition won the parliamentary elections. Meanwhile, Tuđman's medical condition deteriorated, and he died on 10 December 1999. Later that month the Government announced that the election for his successor would take place on 24 January 2000.

Meanwhile, some 55 political associations contested the elections to the Zastupnički dom, held on 3 January 2000. A coalition of the SDP and the CSLP (together with two minor parties) secured 47.0% of the votes cast and 71 of the 151 seats, followed by the CDU, which obtained 30.5% of the votes cast and 45 seats; the alliance of the four other Opposition Six parties, together with the Croatian Social Democrats' Action, won 15.9% of the total votes cast and 25 seats. The Chairman of the SDP, Ivica Račan, was subsequently designated as Prime Minister. Later in January nine candidates emerged to contest the presidential election, including the CSLP leader, Budiša (who was to represent the SDP-CSLP alliance), and Mesić, who was the joint candidate of the four other principal opposition parties. The CDU selected Mate Granić, hitherto Deputy Prime Minister and Minister of Foreign Affairs, as its presidential candidate. In the first round of the election, held on 24 January, Mesić secured 41.1% of the votes cast, while Budiša won 27.7% and Granić 22.5%. On 27 January Pavletić formally appointed Račan as Prime Minister. Račan announced the establishment of a coalition Government, comprising members of the Opposition Six parties. In the second round of voting in the presidential election, on 7 February, Mesić secured 56.2% of the votes cast. On 9 February the Sabor adopted a motion expressing confidence in Račan's Government. Following his inauguration as President on 18 February, Mesić pledged to support the return of Serb refugees to Croatia.

In March 2000 the Government established a council for co-operation with the ICTY. In April Granić left the CDU to form a new party, the Democratic Centre (DC). In that month Ivo Sanader was elected as leader of the CDU at a party congress. In May the Zastupnički dom approved constitutional amendments guaranteeing representation in the legislature for those ethnic groups constituting more than 8% of the total population. On 25 May Croatia officially joined the 'Partnership for Peace' (PfP) programme of the North Atlantic Treaty Organization (NATO, see p. 370).

In November 2000 the Zastupnički dom adopted constitutional amendments reducing the powers of the President and increasing those of the legislature, which, henceforth, was to appoint the Government. In March 2001 the Government submitted a proposal to the Zastupnički dom for the abolition of the Županijski dom. Despite the strenuous opposition of the CDU, which held a majority of seats in the upper house, the Zastupnički dom accordingly approved a constitutional amendment converting the Sabor into a unicameral legislature. At local government elections on 20 May the SDP-led coalition obtained control of 14 of the 21 County Assemblies. The CDU secured a majority in only four County Assemblies (compared with the 16 it controlled after the 1997 elections). In early June the IDA (which had held the European integration portfolio) withdrew from the Government.

In June 2001 the County Court in Rijeka indicted a prominent former rebel Bosniak, Fikret Abdić, for crimes against humanity, including the killing of civilians in a detention camp in 1993. In accordance with a bilateral agreement between Croatia and Bosnia and Herzegovina, the trial of Abdić, who had obtained Croatian citizenship in 1995, commenced in the Croatian town of Karlovac in July 2001. (He was sentenced to 20 years' imprisonment in July 2002.) In July 2001 the Government voted to extradite two Croat generals suspected of war crimes to the ICTY, precipitating the resignation in protest of four CSLP ministers. In mid-July Račan's administration won a motion of confidence in the Sabor, which also approved a statement reaffirming the Government's policy of co-operation with the ICTY. Following the forced resignation of Budiša (who had strongly opposed the extradition) from the leadership of the CSLP, the four representatives of that party rejoined the Government. Later in July one of the indicted suspects, Gen. (retd) Rahim Ademi, surrendered to the ICTY. The other suspect, Gen. (retd) Ante Gotovina, who had been indicted on similar charges, pertaining to having led 'Operation Storm' in 1995, remained at large.

In September 2001 Milošević, who had been extradited to the ICTY in June on charges relating to the province of Kosovo (see the chapter on Serbia), was formally indicted for crimes against humanity and violations of the Geneva Convention; he was held responsible for the killing of Croat civilians and the expulsion of 170,000 non-Serbs from Croatian territory by Serb forces in 1991–92. (Milošević died in March 2006, while on trial at the ICTY.) In October 2001 Croatia (following its co-operation with the ICTY) signed a Stabilization and Association Agreement with the EU, with the ultimate aim of securing membership of the organization; the Sabor ratified this Agreement on 5 December.

In February 2002 Budiša was re-elected to the presidency of the CSLP. At the end of the month the CSLP leadership decided to remove the First Deputy Prime Minister, Goran Granić, and a further two of its ministers from the Government, reportedly owing to their failure to support Budiša in opposing co-operation with the ICTY. The remaining three CSLP members in the Government subsequently tendered their resignations to demonstrate disagreement with the party leadership. In early March the governing coalition parties agreed on a cabinet reorganization. Budiša became First Deputy Prime Minister, while Granić (henceforth an independent) and three of the CSLP representatives were reappointed to the Government.

In May 2002 Milan Martić, the former 'President' of the RSK, who had been indicted in 1996 for war crimes, in particular his alleged responsibility for the bombardment of Zagreb in 1995, surrendered to the ICTY. In early July 2002 Budiša finally withdrew the CSLP from the government coalition, after an agreement on Croatian-Slovenian joint ownership of the Krško nuclear power installation in Slovenia (see the chapter on Slovenia) was ratified in the Sabor, despite the opposition of 17 of the CSLP's 23 deputies. On 5 July Račan submitted his resignation to Mesić, following the collapse of his administration. Five days later, however, Račan was returned to the office of Prime Minister, after his nomination by Mesić was supported by 84 deputies in the Sabor. On 28 July Račan and the leaders of the other political parties belonging to the ruling coalition reached agreement on a new Council of Ministers, which was approved by the Sabor two days later.

In July 2002 the Presidents of Croatia and Yugoslavia met the members of the collective State Presidency of Bosnia and Herzegovina in Sarajevo (the first such trilateral summit meeting since the dissolution of the SFRY). In December the Ministers of Foreign Affairs of Croatia and Yugoslavia reached a provisional accord on Prevlaka, thereby allowing the UN Security Council to end the mandate of UNMOP; the peninsula was to remain demilitarized and joint maritime patrols were to be introduced. In early 2003 the Government declared its commitment to full co-operation with the ICTY, and in February Croatia submitted a formal application for membership of the EU. In March a former army commander, Gen. (retd) Mirko Norac (the most senior officer to be convicted by a Croatian court), was sentenced to 12 years' imprisonment for his involvement in the killing of some 50 Croatian Serb civilians in 1991; a further two defendants received terms of 15 years and 10 years, respectively. (In May 2004 the ICTY issued an indictment against Norac on a further five charges relating to an attack by Croatian troops in 1993.) During an official visit to Belgrade in September 2003 (the first to be made by a Croatian head of state since 1991), Mesić and Svetozar Marović, the President of the State Union of Serbia and Montenegro (which had been reconstituted from Yugoslavia in February 2003), exchanged formal apologies for war crimes perpetrated against the citizens of the two states. In November the former leader of the self-proclaimed SAR of Krajina, Milan Babić, appearing before the ICTY, was charged with war crimes and crimes against humanity in connection with the 'ethnic cleansing' of Croats from regions under his control in 1991–92.

The CDU regains power

Legislative elections were conducted on 23 November 2003. The CDU obtained 66 of the 152 elective seats in the Sabor, while the SDP, led by Račan, won a total of 43 seats, including 28 in coalition with other parties, among them the IDA. The CDU negotiated coalition agreements with the CSLP and the DC (which, in coalition, had received three seats) and the CPP (which held 10 seats), and obtained the support of several other deputies, in order to command a narrow parliamentary majority. On 23 December a new Government, headed by Sanader and principally comprising members of his CDU, was approved by 88 votes in the Sabor. The administration included former members of the Tuđman administration, notably Hebrang, as Deputy Prime Minister and Minister of Health and Social Welfare; and a former ambassador to the USA, Miomir Žužul, as Minister of Foreign Affairs. The newly elected President of the DC, Vesna Škare-Ožbolt, was appointed Minister of Justice.

In March 2004, following continued international pressure on Croatia, two retired generals, Ivan Čermak and Mladen Markač, surrendered to the ICTY, which had charged them with crimes relating to the seizure of Krajina by Croatian government forces in 1995. In April 2004 the European Commission announced that it favoured the opening of accession negotiations with Croatia, subject to the Government's continued compliance with the ICTY. In June Croatia was awarded the official status of EU candidate country. At the end of June the ICTY imposed a custodial term of 13 years on Babić (he committed suicide in detention in March 2006).

In early January 2005 Žužul, who had been implicated by media reports concerning corrupt financial practices during the Tuđman regime, announced his resignation. Meanwhile, candidates contested the first round of the presidential election on 2 January; Mesić, supported by an alliance of centre-left parties led by the SDP, secured 48.9% of the votes cast. His principal opponent, Jadranka Kosor, a Deputy Prime Minister and the CDU representative, won 20.3% of the votes, and an independent candidate, Boris Mikšić, won 17.8%. At the second round on 16 January, Mesić was re-elected to the presidency, receiving 65.9% of the votes cast.

In January 2005 Lt-Gen. (retd) Pavle Strugar, a former commander of the Yugoslav navy, was sentenced by the ICTY to eight years' imprisonment for his involvement in the military campaign by the JNA against the Dubrovnik region in 1991. (Strugar was released in February 2009, after his sentence was commuted on grounds of his deteriorating health.) In February 2005 Sanader reorganized the Government, after Hebrang resigned from the Council of Ministers. A prominent business executive, Damir Polančec, replaced Hebrang as Deputy Prime Minister, while the Ministries of Foreign Affairs and of European Integration were merged. Mesić was inaugurated as President on 18 February. In March, following an official report by the ICTY Prosecutor, Carla Del Ponte, stating that the Croatian authorities had failed to demonstrate full co-operation with the ICTY (with regard to Gotovina), the EU announced the postponement of accession negotiations, which had been scheduled to begin in that month. In mid-May elections for local and regional governments were conducted throughout the country; the CDU lost significant support to centre-left coalitions led by the SDP and to the extreme nationalist Croatian Party of Rights. On 3 October Croatia was unexpectedly declared eligible to enter into accession negotiations with the EU (which were officially opened on the following day), after Del Ponte, despite reiterating dissatisfaction at the end of September, issued an assessment stating that the Government's co-operation with the ICTY had improved.

In December 2005 Gotovina was apprehended in the Canary Islands, Spain, reportedly as a result of information received by ICTY investigators from the Croatian authorities; his arrest was perceived as removing the main obstacle to the country's NATO and EU membership. On 10 December Gotovina was extradited to the Tribunal, where he pleaded not guilty to charges relating to the killing and forcible expulsion of Serbs from the Krajina region in August–November 1995. Several thousand nationalist supporters of Gotovina staged demonstrations in Zagreb and Split, to demand the transfer of his trial to Croatian jurisdiction.

In February 2006 Sanader announced that Škare-Ožbolt had been removed from the post of Minister of Justice, following which the DC withdrew from the Government. In October a CDU parliamentary deputy, Branimir Glavaš, who had been charged with involvement in the killing of Serbs in Slavonia in 1991, surrendered to the Croatian authorities, following the removal of his parliamentary immunity. (His trial commenced in 2007.)

In January 2007 Račan resigned as SDP Chairman. (Račan died in April, and Zoran Milanović was elected Chairman of the party in June.) In June Martić, the former 'President' of the RSK, was sentenced to 35 years' imprisonment at the ICTY on 16 charges of war crimes. In the same month the trial of Norac and Ademi (who had both been transferred to Croatia by the ICTY in November 2005) began at Zagreb County Court.

On 25 November 2007 elections to the Sabor took place. The CDU secured 66 of the 153 seats, and the SDP obtained 56. Glavaš, of the Croatian Democratic Alliance of Slavonia and Baranja, secured one of the eight seats reserved for representatives of national minorities; the party claimed that his parliamentary immunity had been reinstated. In December Sanader received a mandate from Mesić to form a new administration. Later that month the Minister of the Interior, Ivica Kirin, tendered his resignation, after it emerged that he and other senior government officials had participated in a hunting expedition with Mladen Markač (in violation of the conditions for Markač's provisional pre-trial release from the ICTY); Markač was subsequently returned to The Hague. In January 2008, following lengthy negotiations, the CDU signed an official coalition agreement with the CPP and CSLP (which, as part of an electoral alliance, had won eight seats in the Sabor), and seven of the eight parliamentary parties representing minority ethnic groups. On 12 January the Sabor voted to approve a new Government, comprising representatives of the CDU, the CPP, the CSLP and the Independent Democratic Serb Party (IDSP).

The trial of Gotovina, together with those of Markač and Čermak, commenced at the ICTY in March 2008. In May, following the conclusion of their trial at Zagreb County Court, Norac was sentenced to seven years' imprisonment, while Ademi was acquitted of all charges. In October, after the daughter of a prominent lawyer was shot dead in Zagreb, Sanader dismissed the Minister of the Interior, Berislav Rončević, and the Minister of Justice, Ana Lovrin, together with the national chief of police. Tomislav Karamarko, hitherto the head of the Security and

Intelligence Agency, received the interior portfolio, while Ivan Šimonović, an independent former Deputy Minister of Foreign Affairs, was appointed to succeed Lovrin. Later that month the editor of independent newspaper *Nacional*, Ivo Pukanić, and another journalist were killed by a car bomb in Zagreb. Following renewed pledges of efforts to combat organized crime, in November the authorities announced the establishment of four special courts for cases of corruption and organized crime. In May 2009 Glavaš fled to Bosnia and Herzegovina, after being convicted by a Zagreb court of atrocities against Serb civilians in Osijek in 1991 and sentenced to 10 years' imprisonment.

The presidency of Ivo Josipović

On 1 July 2009 Sanader announced his resignation as Prime Minister, citing personal reasons, and stated that he was to withdraw from political life; he named the Deputy Prime Minister and Minister of the Family, Veterans' Affairs and Intergenerational Solidarity, Jadranka Kosor, as his successor to the premiership and to the chairmanship of the CDU. The nomination of Kosor (the country's first female Prime Minister) was officially approved by the Sabor on 6 July. A reorganized Government, with four new ministers, was subsequently formed. Following her appointment, Kosor, as part of her stated commitment to suppress corruption, encouraged investigations into the suspected involvement of senior CDU members in corrupt practices within state-controlled enterprises. In October the Deputy Prime Minister and Minister of Economy, Labour and Entrepreneurship, Damir Polančec, tendered his resignation, following allegations of corruption relating to fraudulent transactions by managers of a local food producer, Podravka. In mid-November Đuro Popijač, hitherto the President of the Croatian Employers' Association, became Minister of Economy, Labour and Entrepreneurship; the Minister of Health and Social Welfare, Darko Milinović, and the Minister of Finance, Ivan Šuker, were appointed by Kosor as deputy premiers (while retaining their portfolios).

The first round of a presidential election was conducted on 27 December 2009; of the 12 candidates contesting the ballot, Ivo Josipović of the SDP, a university professor, secured 32.4% of the votes cast, the mayor of Zagreb and independent candidate Milan Bandić, obtained 14.8% of the votes, and former member of the Tuđman administration and Deputy Prime Minister Andrija Hebrang of the CDU, 12.1% of the votes. On 3 January 2010 Sanader announced his intention to return to active politics, criticizing the poor performance of the CDU in the presidential election. On the following day, however, he was expelled from the CDU, following his criticism of Kosor's administration and consequent concern at the prospect of divisions within the party. In the second round of the presidential election, which took place on 10 January, Josipović was elected to the presidency, with 60.3% of the votes cast, according to official results. Josipović was inaugurated on 18 February. On 16 June Croatia approved constitutional amendments that allowed the implementation of a number of EU regulations and facilitated the organization of a referendum on accession to the Union; the amendments also enabled Croatia, *inter alia*, to extradite its nationals abroad to stand trial. On 10 July the CSLP withdrew from the ruling coalition, which, however, retained sufficient parliamentary support for stability.

In September 2010 Glavaš was detained in Bosnia and Herzegovina at the request of the Croatian authorities after his conviction had been confirmed, with a reduced sentence of eight years, by the Croatian Supreme Court in July. In late September the head of the Customs Administration and close associate of Sanader, Mladen Barišić, was arrested on suspicion of corrupt practices. In early October Polančec (who in March had been arrested over the allegations relating to Podravka) was sentenced to 15 months' imprisonment on further charges of abuse of office. Also in October a parliamentary motion of no confidence submitted against Kosor's Government by the SDP (which had cited a deterioration in the economy) was defeated. In early November six men were sentenced by a court in Zagreb, one *in absentia*, to terms of imprisonment ranging from 15 to 40 years, after being convicted of the killing of Pukanić in October 2008. In early December 2010 Berislav Rončević was sentenced to four years' imprisonment, after being convicted on charges of abuse of office while Minister of Defence in Sanader's administration. On 9 December Sanader (who in October had been permitted to return to the Sabor as an independent deputy) left the country shortly before his parliamentary immunity from prosecution was suspended. He was subsequently detained in Austria, following an arrest warrant issued by Croatia relating to corruption charges against him.

In late December 2010 the Sabor approved an extensive government reorganization, which was effected by Kosor with the intention of assisting economic recovery efforts; Domagoj Milošević was appointed to a newly created post of Deputy Prime Minister in charge of investments, while a further four new government members included Martina Dalić as Minister of Finance. In February 2011 a number of anti-Government demonstrations were organized, in protest at a deterioration in living standards; protesters demanded the nationalization of foreign-owned banks, salary increases and the resignation of Kosor's administration. In late February some 60 protesters were arrested in Zagreb, following clashes with police, and further demonstrations were staged in March.

On 15 April 2011 the ICTY convicted Gotovina and Markač of war crimes against the Serb population of the Krajina region in 1995, sentencing them to 24 years' and 18 years' imprisonment, respectively. (Čermak was acquitted of the charges at the same time.) The announcement of their sentences precipitated large protests in Zagreb and other main towns. On 20 July 2011 the arrest of Goran Hadžić, the final indicted war crimes suspect to remain at large, was announced by the Serbian authorities; two days later he was extradited to the ICTY to be brought to trial on 14 charges of war crimes and crimes against humanity. Later that month the Constitutional Court reversed an amendment approved in June 2010, under which Serbs, as representatives of the only minority ethnic group constituting more than 1.5% of the total population, had been allocated at least three seats in the Sabor. Meanwhile, in July 2011 Sanader was extradited by the Austrian authorities in compliance with Croatia's arrest warrant. Sanader's parliamentary immunity was formally removed in September, and his trial on charges of corruption began on 3 November.

Recent developments: centre-left coalition is elected

In October 2011 Prime Minister Kosor pledged that the CU would co-operate with an official inquiry into allegations that the party had raised illicit funds to finance undisclosed activities. In legislative elections, which took place on 4 December, the centre-left Kukuriku coalition, comprising the SDP, the Croatian People's Party, the IDA and the Croatian Pensioners' Party, secured about 45.7% of votes cast and 80 of the 151 seats in the Sabor, decisively defeating the CDU, which obtained 18.4% of votes and 47 seats. Josipović appointed SDP and Kukuriku leader Milanović as Prime Minister; his new Government, comprising members of the four coalition parties, was approved in the Sabor on 23 December. In early April 2012 Zlatko Komadina resigned as Minister of Maritime Affairs, Transport and Infrastructure, on grounds of ill health; he was succeeded by the hitherto Župan (Governor) of Krapina-Zagorje County, Siniša Hajdaš Dončić.

Regional Affairs

In early 2007 a longstanding dispute between Croatia and Slovenia over their joint maritime boundary was revived with a diplomatic protest by Slovenia that the Croatian Government had pre-empted a border demarcation by extending concessions for petroleum exploration in the disputed region. The Croatian Government demanded that the dispute be referred to international arbitration (a measure that the Slovenian Government strongly opposed). In early 2008 Croatia implemented legislation enforcing an environmental fishing zone in the Adriatic Sea, which the Government had declared in 2003; Italy and Slovenia opposed the measure, which would result in significant financial damage for their fleets, and the EU repeatedly expressed concern that the legislation would adversely affect Croatia's application for entry. In March, following continued pressure from the EU, the Government agreed to postpone the implementation of the environmental fishing zone until Croatia's entry into the Union, a decision that was subsequently approved in the Sabor.

In October 2007 NATO member states adopted a resolution supporting the accession application of Croatia (together with those of Albania and the former Yugoslav republic of Macedonia—FYRM). At a NATO summit meeting, convened in Bucharest, Romania, on 2 April 2008, it was announced that official invitations to begin accession negotiations were to be extended to Croatia and Albania. Shortly afterwards, US President George W. Bush made an official two-day visit to Croatia. The accession protocols of Croatia (and Albania) to NATO were officially signed on 9 July, and were submitted for ratification by the legislatures of NATO member countries. In December 2008 the Slovenian

Government announced that it would veto Croatia's EU accession process, after Croatia presented documentation to the European Commission, which was considered by Slovenia to predetermine the common maritime border that remained under dispute. In February 2009 Slovenia's legislature ratified the protocols for Croatia's accession to NATO. By early March all NATO member states had ratified Croatia's accession protocols, and on 1 April Croatia was admitted as a member of the Alliance. Later in April the EU cancelled a round of entry negotiations with Croatia, owing to the continued dispute with Slovenia. Following discussions between new Prime Minister Jadranka Kosor and her Slovenian counterpart, Borut Pahor, it was finally agreed in September that the border dispute should not present an obstacle to the resumption of Croatia's EU accession negotiations, and that the dispute would be resolved through international arbitration. Croatia resumed negotiations with the EU in early October. On 4 November the Governments of Croatia and Slovenia signed an agreement whereby international arbitrators were to delineate the joint border, and the agreement was ratified by the Sabor on 20 November. In June 2010 a legally binding national referendum was held in Slovenia to confirm support for the arbitration agreement with Croatia; some 51.5% of the participating electorate voted in support of the initiative. The agreement officially became binding in November. In the same month the EU issued a favourable report on Croatia's progress in meeting membership criteria, with stipulations that further efforts were necessary to combat corruption, to strengthen the independence of the media and to co-operate fully with the ICTY. On 30 June 2011 the EU confirmed that Croatia had complied with the requirements of the final outstanding negotiating chapters of the *acquis communautaire*, the EU's body of law, thereby allowing the country's accession to the Union, which was expected to take effect on 1 July 2013. The Croatian Government officially signed the EU Accession Treaty on 9 December 2011. Croatia's membership of the EU was submitted for approval at a national referendum on 22 January 2012, when it was endorsed by about 66.3% of votes cast (with a participation rate of only about 44%).

During a visit to Zagreb in June 2007, the President of Serbia, Boris Tadić, issued an unprecedented apology to the Croatian people for atrocities committed by Serbs during the war. However, Croatia's relations with Serbia became increasingly strained after the Croatian Government recognized Kosovo's independence in March 2008. In November the ICJ ruled that it had jurisdiction to hear Croatia's case of genocide against Serbia (as the successor state to the State Union of Serbia and Montenegro, and Yugoslavia), pertaining to crimes allegedly committed by Yugoslav forces in Croatia in 1991–95, which had been submitted to the Court in 1999. (In February 2007 the ICJ had ruled that Serbia was not directly responsible for genocide in Bosnia and Herzegovina in 1992–95.) In January 2010 Serbia submitted a genocide counter-case against Croatia for alleged war crimes committed during Operation Storm in 1995. In April 2009 the Bosnian presidency threatened to institute legal proceedings against Croatia unless a settlement was negotiated on a continued dispute over the delineation of a small border area on the Adriatic Sea, including the status of Neum, in Bosnian territory, and the Croatian port of Ploče. In June 2010 the Croatian and Serbian Ministers of Defence signed a military co-operation agreement between the two countries in Zagreb, and in July Josipović met Tadić in Belgrade to discuss outstanding issues of contention. In August 2011 Tadić issued a critical statement of Prime Minister Kosor for sending greetings to imprisoned war criminals Gotovina and Markač on the anniversary of Operation Storm. Following the election of a centre-left Government in December, the new Minister of Foreign Affairs indicated that Croatia might abandon its ongoing genocide case against Serbia at the ICJ, but later stipulated that the Serbian Government would first be required to meet conditions on missing persons, looted property and war crimes.

CONSTITUTION AND GOVERNMENT

According to the 1990 Constitution (as subsequently amended), legislative power is vested in the unicameral Sabor (Assembly), which has between 100 and 160 members and is elected for a four-year term. Executive power is held by the President, who is elected by universal adult suffrage for a period of five years. The Sabor appoints the Prime Minister and (upon the recommendation of the Prime Minister) the ministers. Judicial power is vested in the courts and is autonomous and independent. Croatia is divided, for administrative purposes, into 20 counties and the City of Zagreb, 424 municipalities and 123 towns.

REGIONAL AND INTERNATIONAL CO-OPERATION

Croatia was admitted to the Organization for Security and Co-operation in Europe (OSCE, see p. 388) in 1992, and became a member of the Council of Europe (see p. 256) in 1996. Croatia joined the Central European Free Trade Agreement (CEFTA, see p. 448) in 2003. In February 2003 Croatia made a formal application for membership of the European Union (EU, see p. 276), following the signature of a Stabilization and Association Agreement in 2001, and EU entry negotiations officially opened in October 2005. Croatia formally acceded to the North Atlantic Treaty Organization (NATO, see p. 370) on 1 April 2009.

Croatia was admitted to the UN in 1992, and became a member of the World Trade Organization (see p. 433) in 2000.

ECONOMIC AFFAIRS

In 2010, according to estimates by the World Bank, Croatia's gross national income (GNI), measured at average 2008–10 prices, was US $60,965m., equivalent to $13,780 per head (or $18,730 per head on an international purchasing-power parity basis). During 2001–10, it was estimated, while the population remained constant, gross domestic product (GDP) per head increased, in real terms, by an average of 2.6% per year. Overall GDP increased, in real terms, at an average annual rate of 2.6% in 2001–10; real GDP decreased by 1.2% in 2010.

Agriculture (including hunting, forestry and fishing) contributed 5.5% of GDP and engaged 4.6% of the employed labour force in 2010. The principal crops are sugar beet, maize, wheat, potatoes and barley. According to World Bank estimates, the GDP of the agricultural sector increased by 1.7%, in real terms, during 2001–10; real agricultural GDP increased by 0.1% in 2010.

Industry (including mining, manufacturing, construction and power) contributed 25.7% of GDP in 2010, when it engaged 29.6% of the employed labour force. According to World Bank estimates, industrial GDP increased, in real terms, at an average annual rate of 3.1% during 2001–10; real GDP in the industrial sector decreased by 2.4% in 2010.

The mining sector contributed 5.5% of GDP in 1998, and engaged only 0.5% of the employed labour force in 2010. Croatia has many exploitable mineral resources, including petroleum, coal and natural gas. In March 2010 Croatia signed an agreement with Russia, according to which it was to join the proposed South Stream project, which was intended to carry natural gas under the Black Sea from Russia to Western Europe.

According to World Bank estimates, the manufacturing sector contributed 17.4% of GDP in 2010. The sector, along with mining and utilities, engaged 19.0% of the employed labour force in 2010. The GDP of the manufacturing sector increased, in real terms, at an average annual rate of 2.7% during 2001–10; real manufacturing GDP decreased by 9.4% in 2009, but increased by 0.6% in 2010.

The construction sector contributed 6.7% of GDP in 2010, when it engaged 8.4% of the employed labour force.

Of total electricity production in 2008, some 42.7% was provided by hydroelectric power, 20.4% by coal, 16.2% by petroleum and 20.1% by natural gas. However, the country remains dependent on imported fuel. In 2010 mineral fuels accounted for 18.8% of total imports, according to official figures.

Services provided 68.8% of GDP in 2010, and the sector engaged 65.9% of the employed labour force in the same year. According to World Bank estimates, the GDP of the services sector increased, in real terms, at an average annual rate of 2.9% in 2001–10; real GDP in the sector declined by 1.2% in 2010.

In 2010 Croatia recorded a visible trade deficit of US $7,877.2m., while there was a deficit of $900.7m. on the current account of the balance of payments. In 2010 the principal source of imports was Italy (supplying 15.2% of total imports); other major sources were Germany, Russia, the People's Republic of China and Slovenia. Italy was also Croatia's principal market for exports (accounting for 18.6% of the total); other important purchasers were Bosnia and Herzegovina, Germany, Slovenia and Austria. The main imports in 2010 were machinery and transport equipment, which accounted for 25.6% of all imports. Other significant imports were basic manufactures, mineral fuels and lubricants (particularly petroleum and petroleum products), chemical products, miscellaneous manufactured articles, and food and live animals. The principal exports in that year were machinery and transport equipment, which accounted for 31.7% of all exports. Other important exports were basic manufactures, miscellaneous manufactured articles, mineral fuels and lubricants, chemical products, and food and live animals.

According to the IMF, Croatia's overall budgetary deficit for 2009 was 4,363.0m. kuna. Croatia's general government gross debt was 135,757m. in 2010, equivalent to 40.6% of GDP. The country's total external debt at the end of 2007 amounted to US $48,584m., of which $14,212m. was public and publicly guaranteed debt. In that year the cost of servicing long-term public and publicly guaranteed debt and repayments to the IMF was equivalent to 33.0% of the value of exports of goods, services and income (excluding workers' remittances). Consumer prices increased at an average annual rate of 2.7% in 2001–10. Consumer price inflation in 2010 was 1.0%. In that year 17.4% of the labour force were registered as unemployed.

Relations with the international community improved markedly following the installation of a pro-reform Government in early 2000, and financial aid increased. Croatia again became a popular tourist destination (as it had been prior to the conflict of the early 1990s), and the tourism sector an increasingly significant source of income. The quantity of international tourist arrivals increased from 3,805,000 in 1999 to 9,111,000 in 2010, in which year receipts from tourism amounted to US $8,268m., according to provisional figures. A European Union (EU, see p. 276) Stabilization and Association Agreement for Croatia was signed in 2001 and entered into force in February 2005 as a framework for the country's progress towards EU integration; accession negotiations officially opened in October. Following a steady economic expansion until 2007, the onset of the international financial crisis from late 2008 caused a severe deceleration in Croatia's GDP growth. Despite reform efforts by the Government during 2009, which included measures to modernize the civil service, to reduce subsidies and to privatize loss-making state enterprises, domestic consumption and investment failed to recover. Nevertheless, the Government insisted that it would not request IMF assistance but would continue to implement its economic recovery programme. Meanwhile, the deterioration in economic conditions, particularly the sharp rise in unemployment and decline in living standards, prompted a series of anti-Government demonstrations from early 2011. The IMF projected resumed GDP growth, of around only 1%, for 2011. At the end of June the EU declared that Croatia had fulfilled the final requirements for accession to the Union. Having been endorsed by a national referendum held on 22 January 2012, the country's membership was expected to enter into effect from 1 July 2013. The new, centre-left Government that was installed in December 2011 (see Domestic Political Affairs) inherited high levels of foreign debt and budget deficits, and announced that further austerity measures, amounting to a €1,200m. reduction in expenditure for 2012, would be necessary to avert a domestic debt crisis and a downgrade in the country's international credit rating. Proposed retrenchment measures included a one-third reduction of state officials, an increase in value-added tax and the reintroduction of a levy on mobile-phone services.

PUBLIC HOLIDAYS

2013: 1 January (New Year's Day), 6 January (Epiphany), 1 April (Easter Monday), 1 May (Labour Day), 30 May (Corpus Christi), 22 June (Anti-Fascism Day), 25 June (Statehood Day), 5 August (National Day), 15 August (Assumption), 8 October (Independence Day), 1 November (All Saints' Day), 25–26 December (Christmas).

Statistical Survey

Source (unless otherwise stated): Central Bureau of Statistics of the Republic of Croatia, 10000 Zagreb, Ilica 3; tel. (1) 4806111; fax (1) 4806148; e-mail stat.info@dzs.hr; internet www.dzs.hr.

Area and Population

AREA, POPULATION AND DENSITY

Area (sq km)	56,594*
Population (census results)	
31 March 2001†	
Males	2,135,900
Females	2,301,560
Total	4,437,460
1–28 April 2011 (preliminary)	4,456,096
Density (per sq km) at 2011 census	78.7

* 21,851 sq miles.

† Data are not directly comparable to those from the 1991 census, owing to a change in the definition used to calculate total population.

POPULATION BY AGE AND SEX

(official estimates at mid-2010)

	Males	Females	Total
0–14	344,500	326,800	671,300
15–64	1,489,800	1,494,400	2,984,200
65 and over	297,500	464,800	762,300
Total	2,131,800	2,286,000	4,417,800

Note: Estimates are rounded to nearest 100 persons and have not been adjusted to take account of the results of the 2011 census.

POPULATION BY ETHNIC GROUP

(census of 31 March 2001)

	Number ('000)	% of total population
Croat	3,977.2	89.6
Serb	201.6	4.5
Muslim	20.8	0.5
Italian	19.6	0.4
Hungarian	16.6	0.4
Albanian	15.1	0.3
Slovene	13.2	0.3
Czech	10.5	0.2
Roma	9.5	0.2
Others*	153.4	3.5
Total	4,437.5	100.0

* Including other groups, ethnically non-declared persons and those of unknown ethnicity.

ADMINISTRATIVE DIVISIONS

(population at 2011 census, preliminary)

	Area (sq km)	Population	Density (per sq km)
Counties (Županije)			
Bjelovar-Bilogora	2,640	123,390	46.7
Dubrovnik-Neretva	1,781	125,589	70.5
Istria	2,813	213,891	76.0
Karlovac	3,626	134,153	37.0
Koprivnica-Križevci	1,748	118,261	67.7
Krapina-Zagorje	1,229	134,936	109.8
Lika-Senj	5,353	53,099	9.9
Međimurje	729	118,476	162.5
Osijek-Baranja	4,155	319,245	76.8
Požega-Slavonia	1,823	82,375	45.2
Primorje-Gorski kotar	3,588	307,852	85.8
Sisak-Moslavina	4,468	179,087	40.1
Slavonski Brod-Posavina	2,030	166,731	82.1

—continued	Area (sq km)	Population	Density (per sq km)
Split-Dalmatia	4,540	471,278	103.8
Šibenik-Knin	2,984	114,935	38.5
Varaždin	1,262	180,423	143.0
Virovitica-Podravina	2,024	87,125	43.0
Vukovar-Sirmium	2,454	190,404	77.6
Zadar	3,646	179,186	49.1
Zagreb	3,060	327,039	106.9
Capital City			
Zagreb	641	828,621	1,292.7
Total	56,594	4,456,096	78.7

PRINCIPAL TOWNS
(population at 2011 census, preliminary)

Zagreb (capital)	828,621	Karlovac	58,095
Split	183,796	Sesvete	56,707
Rijeka	135,385	Sisak	48,632
Osijek	115,441	Varaždin	48,568
Zadar	78,135	Šibenik	47,274
Velika Gorica	64,773	Dubrovnik	43,481
Slavonski Brod	62,770	Vinkovci	36,487
Pula	59,286	Vukovar	29,425

BIRTHS, MARRIAGES AND DEATHS

	Registered live births		Registered marriages		Registered deaths	
	Number	Rate (per 1,000)	Number	Rate (per 1,000)	Number	Rate (per 1,000)
2003	39,668	8.9	22,337	5.0	52,575	11.8
2004	40,307	9.1	22,700	5.1	49,756	11.2
2005	42,492	9.6	22,138	5.0	51,790	11.7
2006	41,446	9.3	22,092	5.0	50,378	11.3
2007	41,910	9.4	23,140	5.2	52,367	11.8
2008	43,753	9.9	23,373	5.3	52,151	11.8
2009	44,577	10.1	22,382	5.1	52,414	11.8
2010	43,361	9.8	21,294	4.8	52,096	11.8

Life expectancy (years at birth, official estimates): 76.6 (males 73.5; females 79.6) in 2010.

IMMIGRATION AND EMIGRATION

	2008	2009	2010
Immigrants	14,541	8,468	4,985
Emigrants	7,488	9,940	9,860

ECONOMICALLY ACTIVE POPULATION
(annual averages, '000 persons)

	2008	2009	2010
Agriculture, hunting and forestry	70.2	69.6	65.5
Fishing	4.7	n.a.	n.a.
Mining and quarrying	9.3	8.8	7.5
Manufacturing	302.1	272.8	256.8
Electricity, gas and water supply	26.8	38.3	38.8
Construction	145.7	140.7	120.0
Wholesale and retail trade; repair of motor vehicles, motorcycles and personal and household goods	269.9	243.3	225.0
Hotels and restaurants	90.7	85.9	83.5
Transport, storage and communications	99.1	114.0	110.1
Financial intermediation	38.4	39.0	37.7
Real estate, renting and business activities	116.4	113.6	113.3
Public administration and defence; compulsory social security	110.1	113.5	115.5
Education	100.9	103.7	105.4
Health and social work	94.1	93.3	94.0
Other community, social and personal service activities	65.2	53.7	52.2
Private households with employed persons	8.3	7.0	5.9
Sub-total	1,551.8	1,497.3	1,431.2
Activities not classified	3.0	1.5	1.2
Total employed	1,554.8	1,498.8	1,432.5
Registered unemployed	236.7	263.2	302.4
Total labour force	1,791.5	1,762.0	1,734.9

Health and Welfare

KEY INDICATORS

Total fertility rate (children per woman, 2009)	1.4
Under-5 mortality rate (per 1,000 live births, 2009)	6
HIV/AIDS (% of persons aged 15–49, 2009)	<0.1
Physicians (per 1,000 head, 2006)	2.5
Hospital beds (per 1,000 head, 2006)	5.5
Health expenditure (2008): US $ per head (PPP)	1,553
Health expenditure (2008): % of GDP	7.8
Health expenditure (2008): public (% of total)	84.9
Access to water (% of total population, 2008)	99
Access to sanitation (% of total population, 2008)	99
Total carbon dioxide emissions ('000 metric tons, 2007)	24,819.9
Carbon dioxide emissions per head (metric tons, 2007)	5.6
Human Development Index (2011): ranking	46
Human Development Index (2011): value	0.796

For sources and definitions, see explanatory note on p. vi.

Agriculture

PRINCIPAL CROPS
('000 metric tons)

	2008	2009	2010
Wheat	858.3	936.1	681.0
Barley	279.1	243.6	172.4
Maize	2,504.9	2,182.5	2,067.8
Oats	65.3	62.3	48.2
Potatoes	255.6	270.3	178.6
Sugar beet	1,269.5	1,217.0	1,249.2
Beans, dry	3.3	2.5	1.6
Soybeans (Soya beans)	107.6	115.2	153.6
Sunflower seed	119.9	82.1	61.8
Rapeseed	62.9	80.4	33.0
Cabbages and other brassicas	50.6	66.8	37.0
Tomatoes	32.4	37.4	33.6
Cucumbers and gherkins	14.8	14.5	10.9
Chillies and peppers, green	34.8	36.0	18.6
Onions, dry	30.6*	36.6	30.4
Garlic*	5.1	5.1	4.2
Beans, green	7.7	9.3	5.3
Peas, green	14.0	4.7	3.7
Carrots and turnips	7.6	11.0	13.0
Watermelons	32.0	44.2	19.3
Apples	80.2	93.4	106.9
Pears	8.8	10.0	8.7
Peaches and nectarines	7.3	10.1	8.9
Plums and sloes	48.6	38.4	49.9
Grapes	185.3	206.4	207.7
Tobacco, unmanufactured	12.9	13.3	8.5

* Unofficial figure(s).

Aggregate production ('000 metric tons, may include official, semi-official or estimated data): Total cereals 3,725.5 in 2008, 3,441.8 in 2009, 3,017.1 in 2010; Total roots and tubers 255.6 in 2008, 270.3 in 2009, 178.6 in 2010; Total vegetables (incl. melons) 261.8 in 2008, 305.5 in 2009, 209.3 in 2010; Total fruits (excl. melons) 404.3 in 2008, 413.4 in 2009, 458.2 in 2010.

Source: FAO.

LIVESTOCK
('000 head at 31 December)

	2008	2009	2010
Horses	16	17	17*
Cattle	454	447	444
Pigs	1,104	1,250	1,231
Sheep	643	619	630
Goats	84	76	75
Chickens	6,727	6,707	5,041
Ducks	184	187	201
Geese and guinea fowls	57	62	46
Turkeys	577	584	726

* FAO estimate.

Source: FAO.

LIVESTOCK PRODUCTS
('000 metric tons)

	2008	2009	2010
Cattle meat*	35.7	36.8	37.5
Sheep meat*	2.4	2.3	2.2
Pig meat*	121.0	131.0	121.0
Chicken meat*	31.1	29.0	22.4
Cows' milk	825.7	817.8	760.0*
Sheep's milk	7.8	7.2	7.0†
Hen eggs	47.2	48.3	42.1
Honey	2.7	2.9	2.8†

* Unofficial figures.
† FAO estimate.

Source: FAO.

Forestry

ROUNDWOOD REMOVALS
('000 cubic metres)

	2008	2009	2010
Sawlogs and veneer logs	2,496	2,212	2,068
Pulpwood	766	758	1,205
Other industrial wood	444	410	148
Fuel wood	763	862	1,056
Total	4,469	4,242	4,477

Source: FAO.

SAWNWOOD PRODUCTION
('000 cubic metres)

	2008	2009	2010
Coniferous (softwood)	91	100	93
Broadleaved (hardwood)	630	553	584
Total	721	653	677

Source: FAO.

Fishing

(metric tons, live weight)

	2007	2008	2009
Capture	40,199	49,024	55,750
European pilchard (sardine)	16,900	21,194	32,191
European anchovy	13,200	13,054	15,456
Atlantic bluefin tuna	825	833	619
Cephalopods	1,215	640	n.a.
Aquaculture	12,884	12,017	13,371
Common carp	1,503	1,546	2,058
Rainbow trout	2,031	2,058	1,982
European seabass	2,800	2,700	2,800
Mediterranean mussel	3,000	2,800	2,000
Total catch	53,083	61,041	69,121

Mining

('000 metric tons unless otherwise indicated)

	2007	2008	2009
Crude petroleum*	652	620	576
Natural gas (million cu m)	2,892	2,729	2,717
Bentonite	19.6	19.8	19.0*
Ceramic clay*	300.0	300.0	300.0
Salt (unrefined)	32.5	32.5*	32.5*
Gypsum (crude)	335.0	329.6	234.3

* Estimate(s).

Source: US Geological Survey.

Industry

SELECTED PRODUCTS
('000 metric tons unless otherwise indicated)

	2006	2007	2008
Beer ('000 hectolitres)	3,689	3,810	3,880
Spirits ('000 hectolitres)	133	136	53
Cigarettes (million)	14,457	14,415	15,586
Leather footwear ('000 pairs)	3,805	4,026	3,713
Motor spirit (petrol)	1,083	1,202	1,001
Gas-diesel oil (distillate fuel oil)	1,565	1,676	1,395
Cement	3,622	3,587	3,636
Tractors (number)	12,616	12,645	15,136
Tankers ('000 gross registered tons)	378	476	377
Electric energy (million kWh)	12,430	12,245	12,326

2003: Cotton fabrics and blankets ('000 sq metres) 12,321; Ready-to-wear clothing ('000 sq metres) 17,710; Tankers ('000 gross registered tons) 262; Cargo ships ('000 gross registered tons) 83; Chairs ('000) 2,059.

Source: UN Industrial Commodity Statistics Database.

Finance

CURRENCY AND EXCHANGE RATES

Monetary Unit
100 lipa = 1 kuna.

Sterling, Dollar and Euro Equivalents (30 December 2011)
£1 sterling = 8.998 kuna;
US $1 = 5.820 kuna;
€1 = 7.530 kuna;
100 kuna = £11.11 = $17.18 = €13.28.

Average Exchange Rate (kuna per US $)
2009 5.284
2010 5.498
2011 5.344

Note: The Croatian dinar was introduced on 23 December 1991, replacing (and initially at par with) the Yugoslav dinar. On 30 May 1994 the kuna, equivalent to 1,000 dinars, was introduced.

GOVERNMENT FINANCE
(general government operations, cash basis, million kuna)

Summary of Balances

	2007	2008	2009
Revenue	126,716	134,738	128,087
Less Expense	118,770	130,259	132,450
Net cash inflow from operating activities	7,946	4,479	–4,363
Less Purchase of non-financial assets	12,320	8,877	7,132
Sales of non-financial assets	1,305	1,533	775
Cash surplus/deficit	–3,069	–2,865	–10,720

Revenue

	2007	2008	2009
Taxes	73,392	79,670	73,571
Taxes on income, profits and capital gains	18,763	21,326	19,801
Taxes on property	1,155	1,231	1,045
Taxes on goods and services	51,491	54,895	49,645
General taxes on goods and services	37,972	41,533	37,227
Excises	12,169	11,875	10,999
Social contributions	37,204	40,704	39,995
Grants	446	499	624
Other revenue	15,674	13,866	13,898
Total	126,716	134,738	128,087

Expense/Outlays

Expense by economic type	2007	2008	2009
Compensation of employees	31,112	33,621	35,240
Use of goods and services	15,196	16,548	15,012
Interest	5,555	5,035	5,625
Subsidies	7,504	8,130	8,075
Grants	1,702	2,305	2,384
Social benefits	48,731	53,282	56,928
Other expense	8,971	11,338	9,186
Total	118,770	130,259	132,450

Source: IMF, *Government Finance Statistics Yearbook*.

INTERNATIONAL RESERVES

(US $ million at 31 December)

	2008	2009	2010
IMF special drawing rights	0.2	475.2	466.9
Reserve position in IMF	0.2	0.2	0.2
Foreign exchange	12,956.8	14,419.0	13,665.4
Total	12,957.3	14,894.5	14,132.5

Source: IMF, *International Financial Statistics*.

MONEY SUPPLY

(million kuna at 31 December)

	2008	2009	2010
Currency outside depository corporations	17,051.0	15,282.1	15,262.7
Transferable deposits	38,953.6	32,901.4	35,325.3
Other deposits	170,411.3	176,750.3	183,755.5
Securities other than shares	611.9	768.0	1,018.7
Broad money	227,027.8	225,701.9	235,362.2

Source: IMF, *International Financial Statistics*.

COST OF LIVING

(Consumer Price Index; base: 2000 = 100)

	2006	2007	2008
Food	113.1	116.9	128.6
Fuel and light	132.5	132.1	141.1
Clothing (incl. footwear)	108.0	113.6	116.6
Housing	146.6	161.9	184.2
All items (incl. others)	117.7	121.1	128.4

2009: Food 130.6; All items (incl. others) 131.5.

2010: Food 128.7; All items (incl. others) 132.9.

Source: ILO.

NATIONAL ACCOUNTS

(million kuna at current prices)

Expenditure on the Gross Domestic Product

	2008	2009	2010
Government final consumption expenditure	69,701	72,041	71,935
Private final consumption expenditure	197,943	185,651	186,098
Change in inventories*	10,357	7,299	5,862
Gross fixed capital formation	95,572	83,386	72,373
Total domestic expenditure	373,573	348,377	336,268
Exports of goods and services	143,738	118,748	128,214
Less Imports of goods and services	172,296	131,935	129,919
GDP in purchasers' values	345,015	335,189	334,564

* Including statistical discrepancy.

Gross Domestic Product by Economic Activity

	2008	2009	2010
Agriculture, hunting, forestry and fishing	15,333	15,745	15,902
Mining and quarrying; manufacturing; electricity, gas and water supply	57,855	53,337	54,791
Construction	24,716	23,241	19,268
Wholesale and retail trade; repair of motor vehicles, motorcycles and personal and household goods	36,626	32,136	31,939
Hotels and restaurants	12,562	12,619	12,868
Transport, storage and communications	22,639	21,484	21,034
Financial intermediation; real estate, renting and business activities	74,682	77,980	78,720
Public administration and defence; compulsory social security; education; health and social work; other community, social and personal services; private households with employed persons	51,673	54,107	53,834
Gross value added in basic prices *	296,086	290,647	288,356
Taxes, *less* subsidies, on products	48,928	44,542	46,207
GDP in market prices	345,015	335,189	334,564

* Deduction for financial intermediation services indirectly measured assumed to be distributed by sector.

BALANCE OF PAYMENTS

(US $ million)

	2008	2009	2010
Exports of goods f.o.b.	14,460.4	10,735.8	12,066.6
Imports of goods f.o.b.	–30,416.0	–21,025.5	–19,943.8
Trade balance	–15,955.6	–10,289.7	–7,877.2
Exports of services	15,162.2	11,890.0	11,020.6
Imports of services	–4,419.8	–3,743.0	–3,452.1
Balance on goods and services	–5,213.2	–2,142.7	–308.7
Other income received	2,060.8	1,116.2	1,203.2
Other income paid	–4,452.2	–3,591.4	–3,249.1
Balance on goods, services and income	–7,604.5	–4,617.9	–2,354.6
Current transfers received	2,468.2	2,247.9	2,246.4
Current transfers paid	–892.0	–797.6	–792.5
Current balance	–6,028.3	–3,167.8	–900.7
Capital account (net)	23.3	61.1	45.5
Direct investment abroad	–1,317.2	–1,244.5	147.1
Direct investment from abroad	6,023.3	2,861.5	334.2
Portfolio investment assets	–306.7	–891.8	–437.4
Portfolio investment liabilities	–707.8	1,579.8	907.3
Financial derivatives (net)	—	—	–333.6
Other investment assets	–2,250.4	901.1	965.1
Other investment liabilities	6,496.4	3,276.7	97.2
Net errors and omissions	–2,323.9	–1,540.0	–816.9
Overall balance	–391.3	1,836.3	7.7

Source: IMF, *International Financial Statistics*.

External Trade

PRINCIPAL COMMODITIES
(distribution by SITC, € million)

Imports c.i.f.	2009	2010
Food and live animals	1,341.9	1,360.0
Mineral fuels, lubricants, etc.	2,566.0	2,843.5
Petroleum and petroleum products	1,763.9	2,211.9
Chemicals and related products	1,885.2	2,137.2
Basic manufactures	2,761.5	2,725.0
Machinery and transport equipment	4,337.2	3,880.4
Electrical machinery, apparatus etc. (excl. telecommunications and sound equipment)	713.6	709.0
Road vehicles and parts*	909.3	737.7
Other transport equipment and parts*	355.6	357.0
Miscellaneous manufactured articles	1,878.2	1,736.1
Clothing and accessories (excl. footwear)	461.3	435.2
Total (incl. others)	15,220.1	15,137.0

Exports f.o.b.	2009	2010
Food and live animals	740.6	760.3
Crude materials (inedible) except fuels	459.8	601.5
Cork and wood	235.7	277.0
Mineral fuels, lubricants, etc.	977.5	1,113.1
Petroleum and petroleum products	638.4	865.4
Chemicals and related products	726.4	1,013.5
Medicinal and pharmaceutical products	241.1	328.2
Plastics in primary forms	154.1	235.8
Basic manufactures	1,133.3	1,260.8
Non-metallic mineral manufactures	298.1	306.8
Machinery and transport equipment	2,233.8	2,819.5
Electrical machinery, apparatus etc. (excl. telecommunications and sound equipment)	704.0	732.1
Transport equipment and parts (excl. road vehicles)*	623.8	1,143.6
Miscellaneous manufactured articles	1,073.3	1,120.1
Clothing and accessories (excl. footwear)	364.9	368.1
Total (incl. others)	7,529.4	8,905.2

* Data on parts exclude tyres, engines and electrical parts.

PRINCIPAL TRADING PARTNERS
(€ million)

Imports c.i.f.	2009	2010
Austria	764.3	720.9
Belgium	221.5	204.8
Bosnia and Herzegovina	406.5	461.7
China, People's Republic	1,036.3	1,085.0
Czech Republic	303.3	288.7
France	455.6	409.7
Germany	2,059.6	1,893.1
Hungary	492.6	421.6
Italy	2,342.6	2,308.2
Japan	207.3	184.4
Korea, Republic	102.0	128.2
Netherlands	305.4	325.3
Russia	1,448.4	1,365.8
Slovenia	871.1	886.0
Spain	246.4	226.8
Sweden	141.5	128.7
Switzerland	338.6	260.0
United Kingdom	265.8	241.9
USA	385.5	327.2
Total (incl. others)	15,220.1	15,137.0

Exports f.o.b.	2009	2010
Austria	405.3	471.4
Bosnia and Herzegovina	965.9	1,033.9
France	149.9	121.7
Germany	827.5	922.7
Greece	37.8	66.7
Hungary	132.5	199.8
Italy	1,432.2	1,660.4
Liberia	45.7	36.4
Macedonia, former Yugoslav republic	86.8	84.7
Malta	156.7	154.6
Netherlands	99.7	128.3
Poland	81.6	89.7
Russia	110.1	175.0
Serbia	400.8	349.2
Slovenia	557.1	697.1
United Kingdom	158.9	132.2
USA	168.9	222.0
Total (incl. others)	7,529.4	8,905.2

Transport

RAILWAYS
(traffic)

	2008	2009	2010
Passenger journeys ('000)	70,961	73,545	69,564
Passenger-kilometres (million)	1,810	1,835	1,742
Freight carried ('000 metric tons)	14,851	11,651	12,203
Freight net ton-km (million)	3,312	2,641	2,618

ROAD TRAFFIC
(registered motor vehicles at 30 September)

	2008	2009	2010
Passenger cars	1,535,280	1,532,549	1,515,449
Buses	5,099	5,071	4,877
Registered goods vehicles	170,704	164,761	157,731
Motorcycles and mopeds	183,814	184,483	176,773

INLAND WATERWAYS
(vessels and traffic)

	2008	2009	2010
Tugs	24	24	n.a.
Barges, tanker and cargo vessels	74	72	45
Goods unloaded (million metric tons)	0.3	0.3	0.2

SHIPPING

Merchant Fleet
(registered at 31 December)

	2007	2008	2009
Number of vessels	299	300	314
Total displacement ('000 grt)	1,373.5	1,444.6	1,389.7

Source: IHS Fairplay, *World Fleet Statistics*.

International Sea-borne Freight Traffic

	2002	2003	2004
Vessels entered (million grt)	33.1	43.1	51.5
Goods loaded ('000 metric tons)	4,597	4,053	4,809
Goods unloaded ('000 metric tons)	6,705	7,364	7,757
Goods in transit ('000 metric tons)	4,443	5,618	7,582

CIVIL AVIATION

	2008	2009	2010
Kilometres flown ('000)	22,307	19,932	19,058
Passengers carried ('000)	2,329	2,053	1,861
Passenger-km (million)	1,945	1,636	1,510
Freight carried (metric tons)	5,136	3,828	3,197
Ton-km ('000)	3,038	2,621	2,167

Tourism

FOREIGN TOURIST ARRIVALS BY COUNTRY OF ORIGIN
('000)

	2008	2009	2010
Austria	814	882	810
Bosnia and Herzegovina	240	213	217
Czech Republic	623	607	606
France	439	406	388
Germany	1,546	1,580	1,525
Hungary	370	323	298
Italy	1,168	1,200	1,018
Poland	417	454	454
Slovakia	299	307	310
Slovenia	1,043	1,013	1,017
United Kingdom	261	249	241
USA	158	124	133
Total (incl. others)	9,415	9,335	9,111

Receipts from tourism (US $ million, incl. passenger transport, unless otherwise indicated): 11,681 in 2008; 9,224 in 2009; 8,268 in 2010 (excl. passenger transport, provisional) (Sources: World Tourism Organization).

Communications Media

	2008	2009	2010
Telephones ('000 main lines in use)	1,878.1	1,859.2	1,865.7
Mobile cellular telephones ('000 subscribers)	5,879.8	6,035.1	6,362.1
Internet subscribers ('000)	1,360.6	1,498.3	n.a.
Broadband subscribers ('000)	524.7	685.0	803.8

Personal computers: 800,000 (180.2 per 1,000 persons) in 2003.

Source: International Telecommunication Union.

2003: Radio licences ('000) 1,168; Television licences ('000) 1,095; Telephone licences ('000) 1,853; Book production (titles) 6,447; Daily newspapers (number) 12; Non-daily newspapers 269; Periodicals 2,422.

Education

(2010/11 unless otherwise indicated)

	Institutions	Teachers	Students
Pre-primary	1,495	10,046	125,166
Primary schools	2,130	32,213	351,345
Secondary schools	711	24,223	180,158
Higher education	133	16,319	148,616

Pupil-teacher ratio (primary education, UNESCO estimate): 14.8 in 2008/09 (Source: UNESCO Institute for Statistics).

Adult literacy rate (UNESCO estimates): 98.8% (males 99.5%; females 98.1%) in 2009 (Source: UNESCO Institute for Statistics).

Directory

The Government

HEAD OF STATE

President of the Republic: Ivo Josipović (elected 10 January 2010; inaugurated 18 February 2010).

GOVERNMENT
(May 2012)

A coalition comprising representatives of the Social Democratic Party of Croatia (SDP), the Croatian People's Party—Liberal Democrats (HNS), the Istrian Democratic Assembly (IDA) and the Croatian Pensioners' Party (HSU).

Prime Minister: Zoran Milanović (SDP).

Deputy Prime Minister and Minister of the Economy: Radimir Čačić (HNS).

Deputy Prime Minister and Minister of Social Policy and Youth: Milanka Opačić (SDP).

Deputy Prime Minister, responsible for Interior, Foreign and European Policy: Neven Mimica (SDP).

Deputy Prime Minister and Minister of Regional Development and EU Funds: Branko Grčić (SDP).

Minister of Finance: Slavko Linić (SDP).

Minister of Defence: Ante Kotromanović (SDP).

Minister of Foreign and European Affairs: Vesna Pusić (HNS).

Minister of Internal Affairs: Ranko Ostojić (SDP).

Minister of Justice: Orsat Miljenić (Independent).

Minister of Public Administration: Arsen Bauk (SDP).

Minister of Entrepreneurship and Trade: Gordan Maras (SDP).

Minister of Labour and Pensions: Mirando Mrsić (SDP).

Minister of Maritime Affairs, Transport and Infrastructure: Siniša Hajdaš Dončić (SDP).

Minister of Agriculture: Tihomir Jakovina (SDP).

Minister of Tourism: Veljko Ostojić (IDA).

Minister of Environmental Protection and Nature: Mirela Holy (SDP).

Minister of Construction and Physical Planning: Ivan Vrdoljak (HNS).

Minister of Veterans: Predrag Matić (Independent).

Minister of Health: Rajko Ostojić (SDP).

Minister of Science, Education and Sport: Željko Jovanović (SDP).

Minister of Culture: Andrea Zlatar Violić (HNS).

MINISTRIES

Office of the President: 10000 Zagreb, Pantovčak 241; tel. (1) 4565191; fax (1) 4565299; e-mail ured@predsjednik.hr; internet www.predsjednik.hr.

Office of the Prime Minister: 10000 Zagreb, trg sv. Marka 2; tel. (1) 4569239; fax (1) 6303022; e-mail press@vlada.hr; internet www.vlada.hr.

Ministry of Agriculture: 10000 Zagreb, ul. grada Vukovara 78; tel. (1) 6106111; fax (1) 6109201; e-mail office@mps.hr; internet www.mps.hr.

Ministry of Construction and Physical Planning: 10000 Zagreb, ul. Republike Austrije 20; tel. (1) 3782143; fax (1) 3772822; internet : www.mgipu.hr.

Ministry of Culture: 10000 Zagreb, Runjaninova 2; tel. (1) 4866666; fax (1) 4816755; e-mail kabinet@min-kulture.hr; internet www.min-kulture.hr.

Ministry of Defence: 10000 Zagreb, Sarajevska cesta 7; tel. (1) 4567111; fax (1) 4832905; e-mail infor@morh.hr; internet www.morh.hr.

Ministry of the Economy: 10000 Zagreb, ul. grada Vukovara 78; tel. (1) 6106111; fax (1) 6106282; e-mail info@mingorp.hr; internet www.mingorp.hr.

Ministry of Entrepreneurship and Trade: 10000 Zagreb, ul. grada Vukovara 78; tel. (1) 6106111.

Ministry of Environmental Protection and Nature: 10000 Zagreb, ul. Republike Austrije 14; tel. (1) 3782413; fax (1) 3717149; e-mail pr@mzopu.hr; internet www.mzopu.hr.

Ministry of Finance: 10000 Zagreb, ul. Katančićeva 5; tel. (1) 4591333; fax (1) 4922583; e-mail kabinet@mfin.hr; internet www.mfin.hr.

Ministry of Foreign and European Affairs: 10000 Zagreb, trg Nikole Šubića Zrinskog 7–8; tel. (1) 4569800; fax (1) 4551795; e-mail kabinet.ministrice@mvep.hr; internet www.mvpei.hr.

Ministry of Health: 10000 Zagreb, Ksaver 200A; tel. (1) 4607555; fax (1) 4677076; internet www.miz.hr.

Ministry of the Interior: 10000 Zagreb, ul. grada Vukovara 33; tel. (1) 6122111; fax (1) 6122452; e-mail pitanja@mup.hr; internet www.mup.hr.

Ministry of Justice: 10000 Zagreb, ul. Dežmanova 10; tel. (1) 3710666; fax (1) 3710602; e-mail minister@pravosudje.hr; internet www.mprh.hr.

Ministry of Labour and Pensions: 10000 Zagreb, ul. grada Vukovara 78; tel. (1) 6106111.

Ministry of Maritime Affairs, Transport and Infrastructure: 10000 Zagreb, Prisavlje 14; tel. (1) 3784520; fax (1) 3784580; e-mail ministar@mmpi.hr; internet www.mmpi.hr.

Ministry of Public Administration: 10000 Zagreb, Maksimirska 63; tel. (1) 2357555; fax (1) 2357607; internet www.uprava.hr.

Minister of Regional Development and EU Funds: 10000 Zagreb, Kralja Petra Krešimira IV 1; tel. (1) 6400660; fax (1) 6400644; e-mail ivanka.drmic@mrrfeu.hr; internet www.mrrfeu.hr.

Ministry of Science, Education and Sport: 10000 Zagreb, Donje Svetice 38; tel. (1) 4569000; fax (1) 4594301; e-mail ured@mzos.hr; internet www.public.mzos.hr.

Ministry of Social Policy and Youth: 10000 Zagreb, trg Hrvatskih velikana 6; tel. (1) 2308888.

Ministry of Tourism: 10000 Zagreb, Prisavlje 14; tel. (1) 6169111; fax (1) 6169181; e-mail ministar@mint.hr; internet www.mint.hr.

Ministry of Veterans: 10000 Zagreb, trg Hrvatskih velikana 6; tel. (1) 2308888; e-mail ministarstvo@branitelji.hr.

President

Presidential Election, First Ballot, 27 December 2009

	Votes	% of votes
Ivo Josipović (Social Democratic Party of Croatia)	640,594	32.43
Milan Bandić (Independent)	293,068	14.84
Andrija Hebrang (Croatian Democratic Union)	237,998	12.05
Nadan Vidošević (Independent)	223,892	11.33
Vesna Pusić (Croatian People's Party—Liberal Democrats)	143,190	7.25
Dragan Primorac (Independent)	117,154	5.93
Others	298,545	15.11
Total*	1,975,331	100.00

* Including 20,890 invalid votes (1.06% of the total).

Second Ballot, 10 January 2010

	Votes	% of votes
Ivo Josipović (Social Democratic Party of Croatia)	1,339,385	60.26
Milan Bandić (Independent)	883,222	39.74
Total*	2,222,607	100.00

* Excluding 30,547 invalid votes.

Legislature

Sabor
(Assembly)

10000 Zagreb, trg sv. Marka 6; tel. (1) 4569222; fax (1) 4569611; e-mail assembly@assembly.hr; internet www.sabor.hr.

The unicameral Sabor comprises a minimum of 100 and a maximum of 160 members, who are elected directly for a term of four years. Eight seats are reserved for representatives of minority ethnic groups. Of these, three seats are elected by Serbs, one by Hungarians and one by Italians. One representative is elected by Czechs and Slovaks; one by a constituency comprising Austrians, Bulgarians, Germans, Jews, Poles, Roma, Romanians, Russians, Ruthenians, Turks, Ukrainians and Vlachs; and one by Albanians, Bosniaks, Macedonians, Montenegrins and Slovenes.

President: Boris Šprem.

General Election, 4 December 2011

Parties/coalitions	% of votes	Seats
Kukuriku*	45.65	80
Croatian Democratic Union†	18.39	47
Croatian Labourists–Party of Labour	7.68	6
Croatian Democratic Alliance of Slavonia and Baranja	4.45	6
Independent List–Ivan Grubišić	2.35	2
Croatian Party of Rights–Dr Ante Starčević‡	2.86	1
Croatian Peasants' Party‖	1.24	1
Others	17.38	0
Total	100.00	151§

* Coalition comprising the Social Democratic Party of Croatia, the Croatian People's Party—Liberal Democrats, the Istrian Democratic Assembly and the Croatian Pensioners' Party.

† In coalition with the Croatian Civic Party and Democratic Centre.

‡ In coalition with the Croatian Pure Party of Rights.

‖ In coalition with the Green Party and Pensioners' Party.

§ Including eight seats reserved for representatives of minority ethnic groups.

Election Commission

Državno izborno povjerenstvo Republike Hrvatske (State Electoral Commission of the Republic of Croatia): 10000 Zagreb, Visoka 15; tel. (1) 4569712; fax (1) 6303509; e-mail dip@izbori.hr; internet www.izbori.hr; Pres. Branko Hrvatin.

Political Organizations

Croatian Civic Party (Hrvatska građanska stranka—HGS): 21000 Split, Zrinsko frankopanska 68; tel. and fax (21) 381023; e-mail hgs@hgs.com.hr; internet www.hgs.com.hr; f. 2009; Pres. Željko Kerum.

Croatian Democratic Alliance of Slavonia and Baranja (CDASB) (Hrvatski demokratski savez Slavonije i Baranje): 31000 Osijek, trg Lava Mirskog 1; tel. (31) 250910; fax (31) 250919; e-mail info@hdssb.hr; internet www.hdssb.hr; f. 2006; Pres. Vladimir Šišljagić.

Croatian Democratic Union (CDU) (Hrvatska demokratska zajednica—HDZ): 10000 Zagreb, trg Žrtava fašizma 4; tel. (1) 4553000; fax (1) 4552600; e-mail hdz@hdz.hr; internet www.hdz.hr; f. 1989; Christian Democrat; Chair. Jadranka Kosor; 220,000 mems (2005).

Croatian Labourists—Party of Labour (Hrvatski Laburisti—Stranka Rada): 1000 Zagreb, Ilica 108; tel. (1) 8890750; e-mail info@laburisti.com; internet www.laburisti.hr; f. 2010; left-wing; Leader Dragutin Lesar.

Croatian Party of Rights (CPR) (Hrvatska stranka prava—HSP): 10000 Zagreb, Primorska 5; tel. (1) 3778016; fax (1) 3778736; e-mail hsp@hsp.hr; internet www.hsp.hr; f. 1990 as revival of group originally founded in 1861; extreme right-wing nationalist; armed br. was the Croatian Defence Asscn or Hrvatske Obrambene Snage (HOS); Pres. Daniel Srb; 30,979 mems (2006).

Croatian Party of Rights—Dr Ante Starčević (Hrvatska stranka prava—dr Ante Starčević): 10000 Zagreb, Čulinečka 119; tel. (1) 2865261; fax (1) 2865264; e-mail hsp@hsp-ante-starcevic.hr; internet www.hsp-ante-starcevic.hr; f. 2009 as splinter group from the Croatian Party of Rights; Pres. Ruža Tomašić.

Croatian Peasants' Party (CPP) (Hrvatska seljačka stranka—HSS): 10000 Zagreb, ul. Kralja Zvonimira 17; tel. (1) 4553624; fax (1) 4553631; e-mail hss@hss.hr; internet www.hss.hr; f. 1989; Pres. Josip Friščić; 43,000 mems (2005).

Croatian Pensioners' Party (Hrvatska stranka umirovljenika—HSU): 10000 Zagreb, Frankopanska 7/1; tel. (1) 4840058; fax (1) 4815324; e-mail strankahsu@hsu.hr; internet www.hsu.hr; f. 1996; Pres. Silvano Hrelja.

Croatian People's Party—Liberal Democrats (Hrvatska narodna stranka—Liberalni demokrati—HNS): 10000 Zagreb, Kneza Mislava 8; tel. (1) 4629111; fax (1) 4629110; e-mail hns@hns.hr; internet www.hns.hr; f. 1990; fmrly Croatian People's Party; Pres. Radimir Čačić; 31,500 mems (2006).

Croatian Popular Party (Hrvatska pučka stranka): 10000 Zagreb, Ozaljska 93/2; tel. (1) 3633569; fax (1) 3633749; e-mail hps@hps.hr; f. 1997; Pres. TOMISLAV MERČEP; 23,700 mems (2006).

Croatian Pure Party of Rights (Hrvatska čista stranka prava—HČSP): 10000 Zagreb, Tratinska 2; tel. and fax (1) 3864059; e-mail hcsp.hr@gmail.com; internet www.hcsp.hr; f. 1992; Pres. JOSIP MILJAK.

Croatian Social Liberal Party (CSLP) (Hrvatska socijalno-liberalna stranka—HSLS): 10000 Zagreb, trg N. Š. Zrinskog 17/1; tel. (1) 4810401; fax (1) 4810404; e-mail hsls@hsls.hr; internet www.hsls.hr; f. 1989; Pres. DARINKO KOSOR; 25,000 mems (2011).

Democratic Centre (DC) (Demokratski Centar): 10000 Zagreb, Ilica 48/1; tel. (1) 4831111; fax (1) 4831045; e-mail tajnistvo@demokratski-centar.hr; internet www.demokratski-centar.hr; f. 2000 by mems of Croatian Democratic Union; pro-European, moderate; Pres. VESNA ŠKARE OŽBOLT; 14,000 mems (2004).

Democratic Party of Zagorje (DPZ) (Zagorska demokratska stranka): 49210 Zabok, Matije Gupce 53/1; tel. and fax (49) 222359; e-mail zagorska-demokratska-stranka@kr.htnet.hr; internet www.zds.hr; f. 1997; Pres. Dr STANKO BELINA; 5,500 mems (2002).

Independent Democratic Serb Party (IDSP) (Samostalna demokratska srpska stranka): 32000 Vukovar, trg Drvena Pijaca 28; tel. (32) 423211; fax (32) 424606; e-mail sdss@vk.t-com.hr; internet www.sdss.hr; f. 1995 by Serbs in Eastern Slavonia; liberal, social democratic; Pres. Dr VOJISLAV STANIMIROVIĆ; 8,000 mems (2009).

Istrian Democratic Assembly (IDA) (Istarski demokratski sabor): 52000 Pula, Splitska 3; tel. (52) 210588; fax (52) 223316; e-mail info@ids-ddi.com; internet www.ids-ddi.com; f. 1990; Pres. IVAN JAKOVČIĆ; 5,000 mems (2011).

Party of Democratic Action of Croatia (Stranka demokratske akcije Hrvatske): 10000 Zagreb, Mandaličina 17; tel. (1) 4569472; fax (1) 3771288; e-mail sdah@sdah.hr; internet www.sdah.hr; f. 1990; represents interests of Bosniaks and Muslims; Pres. Prof. ŠEMSO TANKOVIĆ; 4,850 mems (2006).

Primorje-Gorski kotar Alliance (Primorsko Goranski Savez): 51000 Rijeka, Ciottina 19; tel. (51) 335418; fax (51) 335359; e-mail pgs@pgs.hr; internet www.pgs.hr; f. 1990; regionalist; Chair. DARIJE VASILIĆ; 5,077 mems (2004).

Social Democratic Party of Croatia (SDP) (Socijaldemokratska partija Hrvatske): 10000 Zagreb, Iblerov trg 9; tel. (1) 4552055; fax (1) 4557509; e-mail sdp@sdp.hr; internet www.sdp.hr; f. 1990; fmrly the ruling League of Communists of Croatia (Party of Democratic Reform), renamed as above in 1993; Chair. ZORAN MILANOVIĆ; 25,000 mems (2004).

Zagorje Party (Zagorska Stranka): 49210 Zabok, M. Gupca 53; tel. and fax (49) 221224; e-mail info@zagorskastranka.hr; internet www.zagorskastranka.hr; f. 2004; Pres. MILJENKO JERNEIĆ.

Diplomatic Representation

EMBASSIES IN CROATIA

Albania: 10000 Zagreb, Boškovićeva 7A; tel. (1) 4810679; fax (1) 4810682; e-mail embassy.zagreb@mfa.gov.al; Ambassador PËLLUMB QAZIMI.

Algeria: 10000 Zagreb, Bosanska 26; tel. (1) 3780333; fax (1) 3780344; e-mail info@ambalgzagreb.com; internet www.ambalgzagreb.com; Ambassador FARIDA AÏOUAZE.

Australia: 10000 Zagreb, Nova Ves 11/III; tel. (1) 4891200; fax (1) 4891216; e-mail australian.embassy@zg.t-com.hr; internet www.croatia.embassy.gov.au; Ambassador BEVERLY MERCER.

Austria: 10000 Zagreb, Radnička cesta 80/IX; tel. (1) 4881050; fax (1) 4834461; e-mail agram-ob@bmaa.gv.at; Ambassador JAN KICKERT.

Belgium: 10000 Zagreb, Pantovčak 125/B1; tel. (1) 4578901; fax (1) 4578902; e-mail zagreb@diplobel.fed.be; internet www.diplomatie.be/zagreb; Ambassador NANCY ROSSIGNOL.

Bosnia and Herzegovina: 10000 Zagreb, Josipa Torbara 9; tel. (1) 4501070; fax (1) 4501071; e-mail amb.zagreb@mvp.gov.ba; Ambassador VLADIMIR RASPUDIĆ.

Brazil: 10000 Zagreb, Trg Nikole Šubića Zrinskog 10/I; tel. (1) 4002250; fax (1) 4002266; e-mail info@brazilembassy.hr; internet www.brazilembassy.hr; Ambassador LUIZ FERNANDO GOUVÊA DE ATHAYDE.

Bulgaria: 10000 Zagreb, Nike Grškovića 31; tel. (1) 4646609; fax (1) 46446625; e-mail veleposlanstvo.republike.bugarske@zg.t-com.hr; Ambassador IVAN SIRAKOV.

Canada: 10000 Zagreb, prilaz Gjure Deželića 4; tel. (1) 4881200; fax (1) 4881230; e-mail zagrb@international.gc.ca; internet www.canadainternational.gc.ca/croatia-croatie; Ambassador EDWIN LOUGHLIN.

Chile: 10000 Zagreb, Smičiklasova 23/II; tel. (1) 4611958; fax (1) 4610328; e-mail embajada@echile.hr; Chargé d'affaires a.i. ALBERTO SEPÚLVEDA.

China, People's Republic: 10000 Zagreb, Mlinovi 132; tel. (1) 4637011; fax (1) 4637012; e-mail chnemb@zg.tel.hr; internet hr.china-embassy.org; Ambassador SHEN ZHIFEI.

Czech Republic: 10000 Zagreb, Radnička cesta 47/6, Romeo Tower; tel. (1) 6177246; fax (1) 6176630; e-mail zagreb@embassy.mzv.cz; internet www.mzv.cz/zagreb; Ambassador KAREL KÜHNL.

Denmark: 10000 Zagreb, Trg Nikole Šubića Zrinskog 10; tel. (1) 4924530; fax (1) 4924554; e-mail zagreb@um.dk; Ambassador BO ERIC WEBER.

Egypt: 10000 Zagreb, Petrova 51B; tel. (1) 2310781; fax (1) 2310619; e-mail embassy.zagreb@mfa.gov.eg; Ambassador EMAN MOHAMED ZAKI MOHARRAM.

Finland: 10000 Zagreb, Miramarska 23; tel. (1) 6312080; fax (1) 6312090; e-mail sanomat.zag@formin.fi; internet www.finland.hr; Ambassador JUHA OTTMAN.

France: 10000 Zagreb, Hebrangova 2; tel. (1) 4893600; fax (1) 4893660; e-mail presse@ambafrance.hr; internet www.ambafrance.hr; Ambassador JÉRÔME PASQUIER.

Germany: 10000 Zagreb, ul. grada Vukovara 64; tel. (1) 6300100; fax (1) 6155536; e-mail info@zagreb.diplo.de; internet www.zagreb.diplo.de; Ambassador BERND FISCHER.

Greece: 10000 Zagreb, Opatička 12; tel. (1) 4810444; fax (1) 4810419; e-mail greece-embassy@grembassy.hr; internet www.grembassy.hr; Ambassador OURANIA ARVANITI.

Holy See: 10000 Zagreb, Ksaverska cesta 10 A; tel. (1) 4673996; fax (1) 4673997; e-mail apostolska.nuncijatura.rh@inet.hr; Apostolic Nuncio H. E. Mgr. MARIO ROBERTO CASSARI (Titular Archbishop of Truentum).

Hungary: 10000 Zagreb, Pantovčak 255–257; tel. (1) 4890900; fax (1) 4579301; e-mail mission.zgb@mfa.gov.hu; internet www.mfa.gov.hu/emb/zagreb; Ambassador GÁBOR IVÁN.

India: 10000 Zagreb, ul. Kulmerska 23A; tel. (1) 4873239; fax (1) 4817907; e-mail embassy.india@zg.htnet.hr; internet www.indianembassy.hr; Ambassador PRADEEP SINGH.

Iran: 10000 Zagreb, Pantovčak 125C; tel. (1) 4578980; fax (1) 4578987; e-mail iran.embassy@zg.t-com.hr; Ambassador MOHSEN SHARIF KHODAEI.

Israel: 10000 Zagreb, ul. grada Vukovara 271/11; tel. (1) 6169500; fax (1) 6169555; e-mail info@zagreb.mfa.gov.il; Ambassador YOSEF AMRANI.

Italy: 10000 Zagreb, Medulićeva 22; tel. (1) 4846386; fax (1) 4846384; e-mail amb.zagabria@esteri.it; internet www.ambzagabria.esteri.it; Ambassador ALESSANDRO PIGNATTI MORANO DI CUSTOZA.

Japan: 10000 Zagreb, Boškovićeva 2; tel. (1) 4870650; fax (1) 4667334; e-mail politics_economy@japan.t-com.hr; internet www.hr.emb-japan.go.jp; Ambassador (vacant).

Korea, Republic: 10000 Zagreb, Ksaverska cesta 111A–B; tel. (1) 4821282; fax (1) 4821274; e-mail croatia@mofat.go.kr; internet hrv.mofat.go.kr; Ambassador PARK SEONG-UNG.

Kosovo: 10001 Zagreb, Hotel Dubrovnik, Gajeva 1, PP 246; tel. (1) 4863555; fax (1) 4863952; Ambassador VALDET SADIKU.

Libya: 10000 Zagreb, Gornje Prekrižje 51B; tel. (1) 4629250; fax (1) 4629279; e-mail lnb@zg.htnet.hr; Ambassador (vacant).

Macedonia, former Yugoslav republic: 10000 Zagreb, Kralja Zvonimira 6/1; tel. (1) 4620261; fax (1) 4617369; e-mail zagreb@mfa.gov.mk; Ambassador DANČO MARKOVSKI.

Malaysia: 10000 Zagreb, Slavujevac 4A; tel. (1) 4834346; fax (1) 4834348; e-mail malzagreb@kln.gov.my; Ambassador YEAN YOKE HENG.

Montenegro: 10000 Zagreb, Trg Nikole Šubića Zrinskog 1/IV; tel. (1) 4573362; fax (1) 4573423; e-mail ambacrnegore@rcg.hr; Ambassador GORAN RAKOČEVIĆ.

Netherlands: 10000 Zagreb, Medveščak 56; tel. (1) 4642200; fax (1) 4642211; e-mail zag@minbuza.nl; internet www.netherlandsembassy.hr; Ambassador STELLA RONNER-GRUBAČIĆ.

Norway: 10000 Zagreb, Hektorovićeva 2/3; tel. (1) 6273800; fax (1) 6273899; e-mail emb.zagreb@mfa.no; internet www.norwegianembassy.hr; Ambassador HENRIK OFSTAD.

Poland: 10000 Zagreb, Krležin Gvozd 3; tel. (1) 4899444; fax (1) 4834577; e-mail ambasada-polska@zg.t-com.hr; internet www.zagrzeb.polemb.net; Ambassador WIESŁAW TARKA.

Portugal: 10000 Zagreb, Trg ban J. Jelačića 5/2; tel. (1) 4882210; fax (1) 4920663; e-mail emb.port.zagreb@zg.htnet.hr; Ambassador PAULO TIAGO FERNANDES JERÓNIMO DA SILVA.

Romania: 10000 Zagreb, Mlinarska 43; tel. (1) 4677550; fax (1) 4677854; e-mail veleposlanstvo.rumunjske@zg.t-com.hr; internet zagreb.mae.ro; Ambassador COSMIN-GEORGE DINESCU.

Russia: 10000 Zagreb, Bosanska 44; tel. (1) 3755038; fax (1) 3755040; e-mail veleposlanstvo-ruske-federacije@zg.htnet.hr; internet www.zagreb.mid.ru; Ambassador ROBERT MARKARIAN.

Serbia: 10000 Zagreb, Pantovčak 245; tel. (1) 4579067; fax (1) 4573338; e-mail ambasada@ambasada-srbije.hr; internet www.ambasada-srbije.hr; Ambassador STANIMIR VUKIĆEVIĆ.

Slovakia: 10000 Zagreb, prilaz Gjure Deželića 10; tel. (1) 4877070; fax (1) 4877078; e-mail emb.zagreb@mzv.sk; internet www.mzv.sk/zahreb; Ambassador ROMAN SUPEK.

Slovenia: 10000 Zagreb, Alagovićeva 30; tel. (1) 6311000; fax (1) 6177236; e-mail vzg@gov.si; internet www.zagreb.embassy.si; Ambassador VOJKO VOLK.

Spain: 10000 Zagreb, Tuškanac 21A; tel. (1) 4848950; fax (1) 4848711; e-mail emb.zagreb@mae.es; Ambassador RODRIGO AGUIRRE DE CÁRCER.

Sweden: 10000 Zagreb, Frankopanska 22; tel. (1) 4925100; fax (1) 4925125; e-mail ambassaden.zagreb@foreign.ministry.se; internet www.swedenabroad.com/zagreb; Ambassador FREDRIK VAHLQUIST.

Switzerland: 10000 Zagreb, Bogovićeva 3; tel. (1) 4810800; fax (1) 4810890; e-mail zag.vertretung@eda.admin.ch; internet www.eda.admin.ch/zagreb; Ambassador DENIS KNOBEL.

Turkey: 10000 Zagreb, Masarykova 3/II; tel. (1) 4864660; fax (1) 4864670; e-mail turkishemb@zg.t-com.hr; internet zagreb.emb.mfa.gov.tr; Ambassador BURAK ÖZÜGERGIN.

Ukraine: 10000 Zagreb, Voćarska 52; tel. (1) 4616296; fax (1) 4633726; e-mail emb_hr@mfa.gov.ua; internet www.mfa.gov.ua/croatia; Ambassador OLEKSANDR M. LEVCHENKO.

United Kingdom: 10000 Zagreb, Ivana Lučića 4; tel. (1) 6009100; fax (1) 6009111; e-mail british.embassyzagreb@fco.gov.uk; internet ukincroatia.fco.gov.uk; Ambassador DAVID ARTHUR SLINN.

USA: 10010 Zagreb, Thomasa Jeffersona 2; tel. (1) 6612200; fax (1) 6658936; e-mail irc@usembassy.hr; internet zagreb.usembassy.gov; Ambassador JAMES B. FOLEY.

Judicial System

The Supreme Court is the highest judicial body in the country, comprising 26 judges, elected for a period of eight years. The Constitutional Court consists of 11 judges, elected by the Sabor for a period of eight years.

Supreme Court: 10000 Zagreb, trg Nikole Šubića Zrinskog 3; tel. (1) 4862222; fax (1) 4810035; e-mail vsrh@vsrh.hr; internet www.vsrh.hr; Pres. BRANKO HRVATIN.

Constitutional Court: 10000 Zagreb, Marka trg 4; tel. (1) 6400251; fax (1) 4551055; e-mail ustavni_sud@usud.hr; internet www.usud.hr; f. 1991; Pres. Prof. JASNA OMEJEC.

State Judicial Council: 10000 Zagreb, trg Nikole Šubića Zrinskog 3; tel. and fax (1) 4811501; Pres. MILAN GUDELJ.

Office of the Public Prosecutor: 10000 Zagreb, Gajeva 30A; tel. (1) 4591888; fax (1) 4591854; e-mail dorh@zg.htnet.hr; Public Prosecutor MLADEN BAJIĆ.

Religion

Most of the population are Christian, the largest denomination being the Roman Catholic Church, of which most ethnic Croats are adherents. The Archbishop of Zagreb is the most senior Roman Catholic prelate in Croatia. There is a significant Orthodox minority. According to the 2001 census, 87.8% of the population of Croatia were Roman Catholics, 4.4% were Eastern Orthodox, 1.3% Muslim, and there were small communities of Protestants and Jews.

CHRISTIANITY

The Roman Catholic Church

For ecclesiastical purposes, Croatia comprises five archdioceses (including one, Zadar, directly responsible to the Holy See) and 12 dioceses, including one for Catholics of the Byzantine rite. The dioceses of Srijem, in Serbia, and Kotor, in Montenegro, are also suffragan to the Croatian hierarchy. There are an estimated 4.1m. adherents, equivalent to 91.5% of the total population.

Bishops' Conference: 10000 Zagreb, Kaptol 22; tel. (1) 4811893; fax (1) 4811894; e-mail tanjnistvo@hbk.hr; Pres. Most Rev. MARIN SRAKIĆ (Archbishop of Đakovo-Osijek).

Latin Rite

Archbishop of Đakovo-Osijek: Most Rev. MARIN SRAKIĆ, 31400 Đakovo, Strossmayerov trg 6; tel. (31) 802200; fax (31) 812310; e-mail biskupski-ordinarijat-djakovo@os.t-com.hr.

Archbishop of Split-Makarska: Most Rev. MARIN BARIŠIĆ, 21000 Split, Poljana kneza Trpimira 7, POB 328; tel. (21) 407501; fax (21) 407538; e-mail marin.barisic@hbk.hr.

Archbishop of Zadar: Most Rev. ŽELIMIR PULJIĆ, 23000 Zadar, trg Jurja Bijankinija 2; tel. (23) 208650; fax (23) 208640; e-mail nadbiskupija.zadarska@zd.htnet.hr.

Archbishop of Zagreb: Cardinal JOSIP BOZANIĆ, 10001 Zagreb, Kaptol 31; tel. (1) 4894808; fax (1) 4816104; e-mail kancelar@zg-nadbiskupija.hr.

Byzantine Rite

Bishop of Križevci: Most Rev. SLAVOMIR MIKLOVŠ, 10000 Zagreb, Kaptol 20; tel. (1) 4811872; fax (1) 4811873; 21,467 adherents (2004).

Serbian Orthodox Church

Metropolitan of Zagreb and Ljubljana: Bishop JOVAN, 10000 Zagreb, Srpska Biskupija.

The Press

In 2007 16 daily newspapers and 27 weekly periodicals were published in Croatia.

PRINCIPAL NEWSPAPERS

24 Sata (24 Hours): 10000 Zagreb, Oreškovićeva 3D; tel. (1) 6069500; fax (1) 6069660; e-mail redakcija@24sata.hr; internet www.24sata.hr; f. 2005; Editor-in-Chief RENATO IVANUŠ; circ. 163,505 (2009).

Business.hr: 10000 Zagreb, Slavonska Ave. 2/9; tel. (1) 5551600; fax (1) 5551678; e-mail redakcija@business.hr; internet www.business.hr; f. 2005 as weekly; published daily since 2008; Editor-in-Chief ŽELJKO ŠOJER (acting).

Glas Istre (Voice of Istria): 52100 Pula, Riva 10; tel. (52) 591500; fax (52) 591555; e-mail redakcija@glasistre.hr; internet www.glasistre.hr; morning; Dir ŽELJKO ŽMAK; Editor-in-Chief RANKO BOROVČKI; circ. 20,000.

Glas Slavonije (Voice of Slavonia): 31000 Osijek, Hrvatske Republike 20; tel. (31) 223200; fax (31) 223203; e-mail glas@glas-slavonije.t-com.hr; internet www.glas-slavonije.hr; f. 1920; morning; independent; Editor-in-Chief DAMIR GREGOROVIĆ; circ. 25,000 (2009).

Jutarnji list: 10000 Zagreb, Koranska 2; tel. (1) 6103100; e-mail redakcija@jutarnji.hr; internet www.jutarnji.hr; Editor-in-Chief MLADEN PLEŠE.

Novi List (New Paper): 51001 Rijeka, Zvonimirova 20A, POB 130; tel. (51) 650011; fax (51) 672114; e-mail redakcija@novilist.hr; internet www.novilist.hr; morning; Editor-in-Chief BRANKO MIJIĆ; circ. 60,000.

Poslovni Dnevnik (Business News): 10000 Zagreb, Savska 66/10; tel. (1) 6326000; fax (1) 6326060; e-mail redakcija@poslovni.hr; internet www.poslovni.hr; Editor-in-Chief DARKO MARKUŠIĆ.

Slobodna Dalmacija (Free Dalmatia): 21000 Split, ul. Hrvatske mornarice 4; tel. (21) 352888; fax (21) 383102; e-mail redakcija@slobodnadalmacija.hr; internet www.slobodnadalmacija.com; morning; Editor-in-Chief KRUNOSLAV KLJAKOVIĆ; circ. 102,000 .

Sportske novosti (Sports News): 10000 Zagreb, Koranska 2; tel. (1) 6173500; fax (1) 6173567; internet www.sportske.jutarnji.hr; morning; Editor-in-Chief DANIJET BRAČUN; circ. 55,000.

Večernji list (Evening Paper): 10000 Zagreb, Slavonska Ave. 4; tel. (1) 6500944; fax (1) 6300676; e-mail gl.urednik@vecernji.net; internet www.vecernji.hr; evening; Editor-in-Chief GORAN OGURLIĆ; circ. 200,000.

Vjesnik (Herald): 10000 Zagreb, Slavonska Ave. 4, POB 104; tel. (1) 6161662; fax (1) 6161650; e-mail vjesnik@vjesnik.hr; internet www.vjesnik.com; morning; Editor DARKO ĐURETEK; circ. 8,000.

La Voce del Popolo (Voice of the People): 51000 Rijeka, Zvonimirova 20A; tel. (51) 672119; fax (51) 672112; e-mail lavoce@edit.hr; internet www.edit.hr/lavoce; f. 1944; morning; Italian; Editor-in-Chief ERROL SUPERINA; circ. 4,000.

PERIODICALS

Arena: 10000 Zagreb, Koranska 2; tel. (1) 6103400; fax (1) 6103404; e-mail arena@eph.hr; f. 1957; illustrated weekly; Editor MARK CIGOJ; circ. 135,000.

Dubrovački list (Dubrovnik News): 20000 Dubrovnik, Ćira Carića 3; tel. (20) 350670; fax (20) 350675; e-mail info@dulist.hr; internet www.dulist.hr; weekly; Editor BARBARA DJURASOVIĆ.

Eukonomist: 10000 Zagreb, Savska 28; tel. (1) 4882582; fax (1) 4843860; e-mail veceslav.kocijan@eukonomist.com; internet www.eukonomist.com; monthly; business and economy; Editor-in-Chief VEĆESLAV KOCIJAN.

Feral Tribune: 21000 Split, Šetalište Bačvice 10; tel. (21) 488949; fax (21) 488941; e-mail info@feral.hr; internet www.feral.hr; f. 1984; weekly; satirical; Editor-in-Chief HENI ERCEG.

Glas Koncila (The Voice of the Council): 10000 Zagreb, Kaptol 8/216; tel. (1) 4874300; fax (1) 4874303; e-mail redakcija@glas-koncila.hr; internet www.glas-koncila.hr; f. 1962; weekly; Catholic; Editor-in-Chief NEDJELJKO PINTARIĆ.

Globus: 10000 Zagreb, Koranska 2; tel. (1) 6103200; fax (1) 6103204; e-mail globus@eph.hr; internet www.globus.jutarnji.hr; f. 1990; political weekly; Editor-in-Chief NINO ĐULA; circ. 110,000.

Gloria: 10000 Zagreb, Koranska 2; tel. (1) 6103250; fax (1) 6103252; e-mail gloria@eph.hr; internet www.gloria.com.hr; f. 1994; weekly; popular culture; Editor DUBRAVKA TOMEKOVIĆ ARALICA; circ. 110,000.

Hrvatsko slovo (Croatian Letter): 10000 Zagreb, Hrvatske bratske zajednice 4; tel. (1) 4814965; fax (1) 6190111; e-mail hkz@zg.htnet.hr; internet www.hkz.hr; f. 1995; weekly; culture; Editor NENAD PISKAČ.

Informator: 10000 Zagreb, ul. Pavla Hatza 26; tel. (1) 5612295; fax (1) 5604440; e-mail informator@informator.hr; internet www.informator.hr; f. 1952; economic and legal matters; Dir and Editor NATAŠA HREN.

Karlovački tjednik (The Karlovac Weekly): 47000 Karlovac, ul. J. Križanića 30; tel. (47) 611855; fax (47) 615011; e-mail zdenko@karlovacki-tjednik.hr; internet www.karlovacki-tjednik.hr; f. 1944; weekly; news from Karlovac County; Editor-in-Chief ZDENKO ŽIVČIĆ.

Lider (The Leader): 10144 Zagreb, Savska cesta 41; tel. (1) 6333500; fax (1) 6333599; e-mail webredakcija@liderpress.hr; internet www.liderpress.hr; f. 2005; weekly; business; Man. Editor MIODRAG ŠAJATOVIĆ.

Majstor: 10000 Zagreb, Ivanićgradska 64; tel. (1) 6055777; fax (1) 2450163; e-mail ttoth@majstor.hr; internet www.majstor.hr; f. 1992; monthly; trade-related technology; Editor-in-Chief TOMISLAV TOTH.

Međimurje: 40000 Čakovec, Zrinsko frankopanska 10/75; tel. (40) 310822; fax (40) 638995; e-mail urednik@medjimurje.hr; internet www.medjimurje.hr; weekly, Tuesdays; regional; Editor-in-Chief IVICA JURGEC.

Nacional (The National): 10000 Zagreb, Vlaška 40; tel. (1) 5555000; fax (1) 4814393; e-mail nacional@nacional.hr; internet www.nacional.hr; f. 1995; independent weekly; also daily online edn, in Croatian and English; Chief Editor MISLAV ŠIMATOVIĆ.

Narodni list (The People's Paper): 23000 Zadar, Poljana Zemaljskog odbora 2; tel. (23) 224835; fax (23) 224824; e-mail redakcija@narodni-list.hr; internet www.narodni-list.hr; f. 1862; weekly; Editor-in-Chief SIMEONA PANCIROV.

Novi Plamen (The New Flame): 10000 Zagreb, Pavla Hatza 14; tel. (1) 4835340; fax (1) 6679518; e-mail redakcija@noviplamen.org; internet www.noviplamen.org; f. 2007; every four months; democratic socialist; Editors-in-Chief FILIP ERCEG, MLADEN JAKOPOVIĆ, GORAN MARKOVIĆ.

Privredni vjesnik (Economic Herald): 10000 Zagreb, Kačićeva 9; tel. (1) 4846233; fax (1) 4846232; e-mail redakcija@privredni.hr; internet www.privredni.hr; f. 1953; weekly; economics, finance; Chief Editor DARKO BUKOVIĆ.

Republika: 10000 Zagreb, trg bana Josipa Jelačića 7; tel. (1) 4816931; fax (1) 4816959; e-mail dhk@dhk.hr; internet www.dhk.hr; f. 1945; monthly; published by Društvo hrvatskih književnika; literary review; Editor-in-Chief ANTE STAMAĆ.

Školske Novine: 10000 Zagreb, Andrije Hebranga 40; tel. (1) 4855720; fax (1) 4855712; e-mail info@skolskenovine.hr; internet www.skolskenovine.hr; educational weekly; Gen. Man. IVAN RODIĆ.

NEWS AGENCIES

HINA News Agency—Hrvatska izvještajna novinska agencija (Croatian Information and News Agency): 10000 Zagreb, trg Marulidev 16; tel. (1) 4808700; fax (1) 4808820; e-mail newsline@hina.hr; internet websrv2.hina.hr; f. 1990; Dir SMILJANKA ŠKUGOR-HRNČEVIĆ.

IKA—Informativna katolička agencija (Catholic Press Agency): 10000 Zagreb, Kaptol 4; tel. (1) 4814951; fax (1) 4814957; e-mail ika-zg@zg.htnet.hr; internet www.ika.hr; f. 1993; Man. Editor SUZANA VRHOVSKI PERAN.

STINA: 21000 Split, Šetaliste Bačvice 10; tel. (21) 488945; fax (21) 321421; e-mail stina@st.htnet.hr; internet www.stina.hr; f. 1991; Dir GORAN VEŽIĆ; Editor-in-Chief STOJAN OBRADOVIĆ.

Publishers

AGM Publisher: 10000 Zagreb, Mihanovićeva 28; tel. (1) 4856307; fax (1) 4856316; e-mail agm@agm.hr; internet www.agm.hr; Croatian and foreign literature, arts, economics, science; Gen. Dir BOŽE ČOVIĆ.

Algoritam: 10000 Zagreb, Harambašićeva 19; tel. (1) 2359333; fax (1) 2335956; e-mail info@algoritam.hr; internet www.algoritam.hr; international bestsellers; Pres. NEVEN ANTIČEVIĆ.

August Cesarec: 10000 Zagreb, prilaz Đure Deželića 57; tel. (1) 171071; fax (1) 573695; Croatian and foreign literature.

Ceres: 10000 Zagreb, Tomašićeva 13; tel. (1) 4558501; fax (1) 4550387; e-mail ceres@zg.tel.hr; poetry, fiction, and philosophical and scientific writings; Gen. Dir DRAGUTIN DUMANČIĆ.

Croatian Academy of Sciences and Arts Publishing Dept (Hrvatska akademija znanosti i umjetnosti, Odjel za izdavačku djelatnost): 10000 Zagreb, Zrinski trg 11; tel. (1) 4895111; fax (1) 4819979; e-mail naklada@hazu.hr; internet info.hazu.hr; f. 1861; Sec.-Gen. SLAVKO CVETIĆ.

Egmont: 10000 Zagreb, Višnjevac 3; tel. (1) 3040555; fax (1) 3091713; e-mail info@cro.egmont.com; internet www.egmont.hr; f. 1995; children's books.

Erasmus Publishing: 10000 Zagreb, Rakušina 4; tel. and fax (1) 433114; Croatian literature; Gen. Dir SREĆKO LIPOVČAN.

Europa Press: 10000 Zagreb, Koranska 2; tel. (1) 6173760; fax (1) 6173704; f. 1990; Pres. NINOSLAV PAVIĆ.

Fraktura: 10290 Zaprešić, Gorica 30; tel. (1) 3357863; fax (1) 3358320; e-mail fraktura@fraktura.hr; internet www.fraktura.hr; f. 2002; literary fiction.

Golden Marketing-Tehnička Knjiga: 10000 Zagreb, Jurišičeva 10; tel. (1) 4810820; fax (1) 4810821; e-mail gmtk@gmtk.net; tel. www.gmtk.net; f. 1947; academic publisher; Dir ANA REŠETAR.

Hena Com: 10000 Zagreb, Gospsvetska 28; tel. and fax (1) 3750206; fax (1) 3756037; e-mail hena-com@hena-com.hr; internet www.hena-com.hr; children's books; Gen. Man. UZEIR HUSKOVIĆ.

Izvori: 10000 Zagreb, Trnjanska 64; tel. (1) 6112576; fax (1) 6112321; e-mail info@izvori.com; internet www.izvori.com; f. 1990; scientific journalism, literature, classics, popular fiction, comic books.

Kršćanska Sadašnjost: 10000 Zagreb, ul. Vukovara 271/XI; tel. (1) 6349010; fax (1) 4666815; e-mail uprava@ks.hr; internet www.ks.hr; theological publications.

Masmedia: 10000 Zagreb, ul. Baruna Trenka 11–13; tel. (1) 4577400; fax (1) 4577769; e-mail mm@masmedia.hr; internet www.masmedia.hr; f. 1990; business and professional literature; Gen. Dir STJEPAN ANDRAŠIĆ.

Matica Hrvatska: 10000 Zagreb, trg Strossmayerov 4; tel. (1) 4878360; fax (1) 4819319; e-mail matica@matica.hr; internet www.matica.hr; f. 1842; arts and science, fiction, popular science, politics, economics, sociology, history; Chair. Prof. IGOR ZIDIĆ.

Miroslav Krleža Lexicographic Institute (Leksikografski zavod Miroslav Krleža): 10000 Zagreb, Frankopanska 26; tel. (1) 4800333; fax (1) 4800399; e-mail lzmk@lzmk.hr; internet www.lzmk.hr; f. 1950; encyclopedias, lexicons, bibliographies and dictionaries; Pres. VLAHO BOGIŠIĆ.

Mozaik Knjiga: 10000 Zagreb, Sauska 66/IV; tel. (1) 6315101; fax (1) 6315222; e-mail info@mozaik-knjiga.hr; internet www.mozaik-knjiga.hr; f. 1991; educational books; Gen. Dir BOJAN VIDMAR.

Naprijed-Ljevak: 10000 Zagreb, trg Josipa Jelačića 17; tel. (1) 4812992; fax (1) 3887886; e-mail ljevak@ljevak.hr; internet www.naklada-ljevak.hr; f. 1957; philosophy, psychology, religion, sociology, medicine, dictionaries, children's books, art, politics, economics, tourist guides; Exec. Dir PETRA LJEVAK.

Školska Knjiga (Schoolbooks): 10001 Zagreb, Masarykova 28, POB 1039; tel. (1) 4830511; fax (1) 4830505; e-mail ante.zuzul@skolskaknjiga.hr; internet www.skolskaknjiga.hr; education, textbooks, art; Dir Prof. ANTE ŽUŽUL.

SysPrint: 10020 Zagreb, Medarska 69; tel. (1) 6558740; fax (1) 6558741; e-mail info@sysprint.hr; internet www.sysprint.hr; fiction, textbooks, journals and manuals; Dir ROBERT ŠIPEK.

Verbum: 21000 Split, Trumbićeva obala 12; tel. (21) 340260; fax (21) 340270; e-mail naklada@verbum.hr; internet www.verbum.hr; f. 1992; religion, philosophy and humanism; Gen. Man. MIRO RADALJ.

Znanje (Knowledge): 10000 Zagreb, Mandićeva 2; tel. (1) 3689534; fax (1) 3689531; e-mail znanje@znanje.hr; internet www.znanje.hr; f. 1958; popular science, agriculture, fiction, poetry, essays; Dir ZVONIMIR ĆIMIĆ.

PUBLISHERS' ASSOCIATION

Croatian Publishers' and Booksellers' Asscn (Poslovna Zajednica Izdavača i Knjižara Hrvatske): 10000 Zagreb, Klaićeva 7; fax (1) 171624; f. 1996; Pres. ZDENKO LJEVAK; 187 mem orgs.

Broadcasting and Communications

TELECOMMUNICATIONS

The mobile cellular communications sector in Croatia was liberalized in 1998, and competition in fixed telephony has been permitted since 2005.

T-Hrvatski Telekom (T-HT): 10000 Zagreb, Savska cesta 32; tel. (1) 4911000; fax (1) 4911011; e-mail kontakt@t-com.hr; internet www.t.ht.hr; f. 1999; 51% owned by Deutsche Telekom (Germany); offers services under two brands: T-Com (fixed network telephony and online services) and T-Mobile (mobile cellular telecommunications); Pres. IVICA MUDRINIĆ.

Tele2 Croatia: 10000 Zagreb, ul. grada Vukovara 269D; internet www.tele2.com.hr; f. 2005; wholly owned by Tele2 AB (Sweden); mobile cellular telecommunications and internet services; CEO JULIAN OGRIN.

VIPnet: 10000 Zagreb, Put Vrtni 1; tel. (1) 4691091; fax (1) 4691099; e-mail communications@vipnet.hr; internet www.vipnet.hr; wholly owned by Mobilkom Austria; f. 1998; provides mobile cellular telecommunications services; CEO MLADEN PEJKOVIĆ.

BROADCASTING

In 2007, in addition to the publicly owned broadcaster Croatian Television (HRT), which operated two terrestrial television networks, a satellite channel and a radio station, there were two private broadcasters operating national terrestrial networks and 15 private regional television stations. There were additionally two private national radio stations and numerous regional, country and community radio stations at that time.

Radio

Croatian Radio (HRT): 10000 Zagreb, Prisavlje 3; tel. (1) 6343258; fax (1) 6343936; internet www.hrt.hr; f. 1926; 3 radio stations; 8 regional stations (Sljeme, Osijek, Pula, Rijeka, Split, Zadar, Dubrovnik and Knin); broadcasts in Croatian, English and Spanish; Dir-Gen. JOSIP POPOVAC (acting).

Otvoreni Radio: 10010 Zagreb, Cebini 28; tel. (1) 6623700; fax (1) 6623800; e-mail otvoreni@otvoreni.hr; internet www.otvoreni.hr; broadcasts popular music and entertainment programmes nationwide; Dirs ROBERT MILIČEVIĆ, DANIEL BERDAIS.

Radio 101: 10000 Zagreb, Teslina 7; tel. (1) 4891101; e-mail studio1@radio101.hr; internet www.radio101.hr; independent radio station; Editor-in-Chief ŽELJKO MATIĆ.

Radio Baranja: 31300 Beli Manastir, trg Slobode 32/3; e-mail radio-baranja@zg.tel.hr; internet www.radio-baranja.hr; f. 1992; independent; Dir ZLATA MARŠIĆ.

Television

Croatian Television (HRT): 10000 Zagreb, Prisavlje 3; tel. (1) 6342634; fax (1) 6343712; e-mail program@hrt.hr; internet www.hrt.hr; f. 1956; 2 channels; Dir-Gen. JOSIP POPOVAC (acting); Dir MARIJA NEMČIĆ.

Finance

(cap. = capital; res = reserves; dep. = deposits; m. = million; amounts in kuna; brs = branches)

BANKING

In early 2010 some 32 commercial banks, two savings banks, and five building societies were operating in Croatia.

Central Bank

Croatian National Bank (HNB) (Hrvatska Narodna Banka): 10002 Zagreb, trg Hrvatskih velikana 3; tel. (1) 4564555; fax (1) 4550726; e-mail info@hnb.hr; internet www.hnb.hr; in 1991 assumed the responsibilities of a central bank empowered as the republic's bank of issue; cap. 2,500.0m., res 5,846.5m., dep. 46,470.8m. (Dec. 2009); Gov. ŽELJKO ROHATINSKI.

Selected Banks

Croatian Bank for Reconstruction and Development (Hrvatska Banka za Obnovu i Razvoj—HBOR): 10000 Zagreb, Strossmayerov trg 9; tel. (1) 4591666; fax (1) 4591721; e-mail office-management@hbor.hr; internet www.hbor.hr; f. 1992; name changed in 1995; cap. 4,943.7m., res 1,563.6m., dep. 7,730.0m. (Dec. 2009); CEO ANTON KOVAČEV.

Erste & Steiermärkische Bank d.d.: 51000 Rijeka, Jadranski trg 3A; tel. (62) 371371; fax (62) 371981; e-mail erstebank@erstebank.hr; internet www.erstebank.hr; f. 2000 by merger of Bjelovarska Banka, Cakoveka Banka and Trgovačka Banka; cap. 1,698m., res 2,014m., dep. 31,826m. (Dec. 2009); CEO PETAR RADAKOVIĆ.

Hrvatska Poštanska Banka (Croatian Post Bank): 10000 Zagreb, Jurišićeva 4; tel. (1) 4804615; fax (1) 4804522; e-mail hpb@hpb.hr; internet www.hpb.hr; f. 1991; 29.08% state owned, 27.49% Croatian Post, 22.38% Croatian Privatization Fund; cap. 654.3m., res 282.0m., dep. 10,586.1m. (Dec. 2009); Chair. ČEDO MALETIĆ.

Hypo Alpe-Adria-Bank d.d.: 10000 Zagreb, Slavonska Ave. 6; tel. (1) 6030976; fax (1) 6007000; e-mail bank@hypo.hr; internet www.hypo-alpe-adria.hr; f. 1996; cap. 5,959.8m., res 248.1m., dep. 29,526.4m. (Dec. 2009); CEO MARKUS FERSTI.

Istarska Kreditna Banka Umag (Istria Credit Bank Umag): 52470 Umag, Ernesta Miloša 1; tel. (52) 702300; fax (52) 702388; e-mail callcentar@ikb.hr; internet www.ikb.hr; f. 1956; commercial and joint-stock bank; cap. 163.0m., res 37.7m., dep. 2,186.8m. (Dec. 2011); Chair. MIRO DODIĆ; 25 brs.

Međimurska Banka Čakovec: 40000 Čakovec, Valenta Morandinija 37; tel. (40) 340000; fax (40) 340010; e-mail info@mb.hr; internet www.mb.hr; f. 1954; cap. 127.9m., res 14.6m., dep. 2,152.5m. (Dec. 2009); Pres. NENAD JEĐUD.

OTP Banka Hrvatska d.d.: 23000 Zadar, Domovinskog rata 3; tel. (62) 201555; fax (62) 201950; e-mail info@otpbanka.hr; internet www.otpbanka.hr; f. 1957 as Komunalna Banka Zadar; merged with Dubrovačka Banka Dubrovnik in 2004; acquired by OTP Bank (Hungary) (q.v.) and name changed from Nova Banka in 2005; cap. 822.2m., res 442.0m., dep. 9,256.1m. (Dec. 2009); Pres. DAMIR ODAK; 6 brs.

Podravska Banka d.d.: 48000 Koprivnica, Opatička 3; tel. (62) 655000; fax (62) 655200; e-mail info@poba.hr; internet www.poba.hr; cap. 267.5m., res 84.0m., dep. 2,179.3m. (Dec. 2009); Pres. JULIO KURUC; 35 brs.

Privredna Banka Zagreb d.d.: 10000 Zagreb, Račkoga 6, POB 1032; tel. (1) 6360000; fax (1) 6360063; e-mail pbz@pbz.hr; internet www.pbz.hr; f. 1966; commercial bank; cap. 1,907m., res 7,733m., dep. 48,287m. (Dec. 2009); Pres. and CEO BOŽO PRKA; 18 brs.

Raiffeisenbank Austria d.d.: 10000 Zagreb, ul. Petrinjska 59; tel. (1) 4566466; fax (1) 4811624; e-mail info@rba.hr; internet www.rba.hr; f. 1994; cap. 3,699m., res 557m., dep. 22,375m. (Dec. 2009); Chair. ZDENKO ADROVIĆ.

Slavonska Banka d.d. Osijek (Slavonian Bank): 31000 Osijek, Kapucinska 29, POB 108; tel. (31) 231231; fax (31) 201039; e-mail info@slavonska-banka.hr; f. 1989; cap. 1,490.9m., res 311.8m., dep. 7,828.6m. (Dec. 2007); Pres. IVAN MIHALJEVIĆ; 11 brs.

Société Générale-Splitska Banka d.d.: 21000 Split, Ruđera Boškovića 16; tel. (21) 304304; fax (21) 304034; e-mail info@splitskabanka.hr; internet www.splitskabanka.hr; f. 1966; cap. 491m., res 724m., dep. 15,373m. (Dec. 2009); Pres. PIERRE BOURSOT; 130 brs.

Štedbanka d.d.: 10000 Zagreb, Slavonska Ave. 3; tel. (1) 6306666; fax (1) 6187015; e-mail stedbanka@stedbanka.hr; internet www.stedbanka.hr; f. 1994; cap. 250.0m., res 43.2m., dep. 794.9m. (Dec. 2009); Pres. ANTE BABIĆ.

Volksbank: 10000 Zagreb, Varšavska 9; tel. (1) 4801300; fax (1) 4801365; e-mail info@volksbank.hr; internet www.volksbank.hr; f. 1997; cap. 615.6m., res 1,003.5m., dep. 5,474.2m. (Dec. 2009); Chair. TOMASZ TARABA.

Zagrebačka Banka d.d. (Bank of Zagreb): 10000 Zagreb, Paromlinska 2; tel. (1) 3773333; fax (1) 3789764; e-mail zaba@zaba.hr; internet www.zaba.hr; f. 1914; cap. 1,281m., res 4,110m., dep. 69,313m. (Dec. 2009); Chair. FRANJO LUKOVIĆ; 136 brs.

Bankers' Organization

Croatian Banking Asscn (Hrvatska udruga banaka): 10000 Zagreb, Centar Kaptol, Nova Ves 17; tel. (1) 4860080; fax (1) 4860081; e-mail info@hub.hr; internet www.hub.hr; Man. Dir Dr ZORAN BOHACEK.

Supervisory Authority

Croatian Agency for Supervision of Financial Services (HANFA) (Hrvatska Agencija za Nadzor Financijskih Usluga): 10000 Zagreb, Miramarska 24B; tel. (1) 6173200; fax (1) 4811406; e-mail info@hanfa.hr; internet www.hanfa.hr.

STOCK EXCHANGE

Zagreb Stock Exchange (Zagrebačka Burza): 10000 Zagreb, Ivana Lučića 2A; tel. (1) 4686800; fax (1) 4677680; e-mail pitanja@zse.hr; internet www.zse.hr; f. 1990; Gen. Man. IVANA GAŽIĆ.

INSURANCE

In mid-2009 there were 29 licensed insurance companies operating in Croatia; of these, eight specialized in life insurance, 10 in non-life insurance and the remainder covered both life and non-life insurance.

Agram životno osiguranje d.d.: 10000 Zagreb, Trnjanska cesta 108; tel. (1) 6004400; fax (1) 6004940; e-mail zagreb@agramlife.hr; internet www.agramlife.hr; f. 1997; CEO TOMISLAV NOVAČIĆ.

Allianz: 10000 Zagreb, Selska 136–138; tel. (1) 3670367; fax (1) 3670411; e-mail osiguranje@allianz.hr; internet www.allianz.hr; life insurance, annuity, property, motor vehicle and transport insurance, personal accident insurance, health insurance, liability insurance; CEO and Chair. of Bd BORIS GALIĆ.

Basler Osiguranje Zagreb: 10000 Zagreb, Radnička cesta 37B,; tel. (1) 6405000; fax (1) 6405003; e-mail info@basler-oz.hr; internet www.basler-oz.hr; CEO DARKO CESAR.

Croatia Osiguranje: 10000 Zagreb, Miramarska 22; tel. (1) 6332000; fax (1) 6332020; e-mail info@crosig.hr; internet www.crosig.hr; f. 1884; privatized in 2002; Chair. of Bd ZDRAVKO ZRINUŠIĆ.

Erste Osiguranje: 10000 Zagreb, Miramarska 23; tel. (62) 372700; fax (62) 372710; e-mail kontakt@erste-osiguranje.hr; internet www.erste-osiguranje.hr; mem. of Vienna Insurance Group (Austria); CEO SNJEŽANA BERTONCELJ; 10 mems.

Euroherc Osiguranje: 10000 Zagreb, ul. grada Vukovara 282; tel. (1) 6004601; fax (1) 6004999; e-mail euroherc@euroherc.hr; internet www.euroherc.hr; f. 1992; CEO DAMIR ZORIĆ; 14 brs.

Grawe Hrvatska d.d.: 10000 Zagreb, ul. grada Vukovara 5; tel. (1) 3034000; fax (1) 3034500; e-mail info@grawe.hr; internet www.grawe.hr; CEO IGOR PURETA.

Helios VIG: 10000 Zagreb, Poljička 5; tel. (1) 7899000; fax (1) 7899001; e-mail osiguranje@helios.hr; internet www.helios.hr; f. 2008; by merger of Osiguranje Helios and Wiener Städtische Versicherung AG (Austria); Pres. WALTER LEONHARTSBERGER; 32 brs.

Jadransko Osiguranje: 10000 Zagreb, Listopadska 2; tel. (1) 3036666; fax (1) 3036000; e-mail zg@jadransko.hr; internet www.jadransko.hr; Chair. of Bd ŽARKO BUBALO.

Kvarner Vienna Insurance Group: 10000 Zagreb, ul. Slovenska 24; tel. (1) 3718600; fax (1) 3718601; e-mail kontakt@kvarner-vig.hr; internet www.kvarner-vig.hr; CEO LUKA MATOŠIĆ.

Merkur Osiguranje: 10000 Zagreb, ul. grada Vukovara 237; tel. (1) 6308333; fax (1) 6157130; e-mail info@merkur.hr; internet www.merkur.hr; f. 1996; Exec. Dir MILAN KRIZMANIĆ.

Triglav Osiguranje d.d.: 10000 Zagreb, Antuna Heinza 4; tel. (1) 5632777; fax (1) 5632799; e-mail centrala@triglav-osiguranje.hr; internet www.triglav-osiguranje.hr; subsidiary of Triglav Insurance Co (Slovenia); CEO MARIN MATIJACA.

Trade and Industry

GOVERNMENT AGENCIES

Croatian Agency for Small Business (Hrvatska agencija za malo gospodarstvo): 10000 Zagreb, Prilaz Gjure Deželića 7; tel. (1) 4881003; fax (1) 4881009; e-mail hamag@hamag.hr; internet www.hamag.hr; Pres. of Man. Bd TOMISLAV KOVAČEVIĆ.

Croatian Competition Agency (Agencija za zaštitu tržišnog natjecanja): 10000 Zagreb, Savska cesta 41/XIV; tel. (1) 6176448; fax (1) 6176450; e-mail agencija.ztn@aztn.hr; internet www.aztn.hr; Pres. OLGICA SPEVEC.

Croatian Privatization Fund (Hrvatski fond za privatizaciju): 10000 Zagreb, Ivana Lučića 6; tel. (1) 6346111; fax (1) 6346224; e-mail investcroatia@hfp.hr; internet www.hfp.hr; f. 1994; Pres. IVA GALIĆ (acting).

Trade and Investment Promotion Agency (Agencija za promicanje izvoza i ulaganja): 10000 Zagreb, Andrije Hebranga 34/II; tel. (1) 4866000; fax (1) 4866008; Man. Dir SANI LJUBUNČIĆ.

CHAMBERS OF COMMERCE

Croatian Chamber of Economy (Hrvatska Gospodarska Komora): 10000 Zagreb, trg Rooseveltov 2; tel. (1) 4561555; fax (1) 4828380; e-mail hgk@hgk.hr; internet www.hgk.hr; Pres. NADAN VIDOŠEVIĆ.

Croatian Chamber of Economy—Zagreb Chamber: 10000 Zagreb, Draškovićeva 45, POB 238; tel. (1) 4606777; fax (1) 4606813; e-mail hgkzg@hgk.hr; internet www.zg.hgk.hr; f. 1852; Pres. Dr ZLATAN FRÖHLICH.

Croatian Chamber of Trades and Crafts (Hrvatska obrtnička komora—HOK): 10000 Zagreb, Ilica 49/2, POB 166; tel. (1) 4806666; fax (1) 4846610; e-mail hok@hok.hr; internet www.hok.hr; Pres. DRAGUTIN RANOGAJEC.

EMPLOYERS' ASSOCIATION

Croatian Employers' Association (Hrvatska udruga poslodavaca—HUP): 10000 Zagreb, Pavla Hatza 12; tel. (1) 4897555; fax (1) 4897556; e-mail hup@hup.hr; internet www.hup.hr; Gen. Dir DAVOR MAJETIĆ.

UTILITIES

Regulatory Authority

Croatian Energy Regulatory Agency (Hrvatska energetska regulatorna agencija—HERA): 10000 Zagreb, ul. grada Vukovara 14; tel. (1) 6323777; fax (1) 6115344; e-mail hera@hera.hr; internet www.hera.hr; Pres. DANIJEL ŽAMBOKI.

Electricity

HEP—Hrvatska Elektroprivreda (Croatian Electricity): 10000 Zagreb, ul. grada Vukovara 37; tel. (1) 6322111; fax (1) 6170430; e-mail leo.begovic@hep.hr; internet www.hep.hr; f. 1990; production and distribution of electricity; Dir LEO BEGOVIĆ.

Gas

Gradska Plinara d.o.o.: 10000 Zagreb, Radnička cesta 1; tel. (1) 6302333; fax (1) 6302587; e-mail info@plinara-zagreb.hr; internet www.plinara-zagreb.hr; f. 1862; municipal and regional distribution of natural gas; Dir MLADEN PEJNOVIĆ.

Plinacro Ltd: 10000 Zagreb, Savska cesta 88 A; tel. (1) 6301777; fax (1) 6301787; e-mail plinacro@plinacro.hr; internet www.plinacro.hr; f. 2001; gas transmission system operator; 100% state-owned; Pres. JERKO JELIĆ-BALTA.

Water

Hrvatske Vode (Croatian Water): 10000 Zagreb, ul. grada Vukovara 220; tel. (1) 6307333; fax (1) 6155910; e-mail voda@voda.hr; internet www.voda.hr; f. 1995; state water management organization; Dir-Gen. JADRANKO HUSARIĆ.

TRADE UNIONS

Independent Trade Unions of Croatia (Nezavisni Hrvatski Sindikati—NHS): 10000 Zagreb, trg Francuske Republike 9/V; tel. (1) 3908620; fax (1) 3908621; e-mail nhs@nhs.hr; internet www.nhs.hr; f. 1992; 87,313 mems (2007); Pres. KREŠIMIR SEVER.

Union of Autonomous Trade Unions of Croatia—UATUC (Savez samosalnih sindikata hrvatske—SSSH): 10000 Zagreb, trg kralja Petra Krešimira IV 2; tel. (1) 4655013; fax (1) 4655040; e-mail sssh@sssh.hr; internet www.sssh.hr; f. 1990; 17 br. unions with 100,000 mems (2010); Pres. MLADEN NOVOSEL.

Workers' Trade Union Assen of Croatia (Udruga radničkih sindikata Hrvatske—URSH): 10000 Zagreb, ul. Kralja Držislava 4/1; tel. (1) 4617791; fax (1) 4612896; e-mail ursh@inet.hr; internet www.ursh.hr; 45 affiliated member unions; Pres. DAMIR JAKUŠ.

Transport

RAILWAYS

In 2009 there were an estimated 2,723 km of railway lines in Croatia.

Croatian Railways (Hrvatske Željeznice): 10000 Zagreb, Mihanovićeva 12; tel. (1) 4577111; fax (1) 4577730; e-mail hrvatske.zeljeznice@hznet.hr; internet www.hznet.hr; f. 1990; state-owned; public railway transport, construction, modernization and maintenance of railway vehicles; Pres. RENÉ VALČIĆ.

ROADS

In 2008 there were an estimated 29,248 km of roads in Croatia, of which 1,043 km were motorways.

SHIPPING

The principal ports are located at Rijeka, Šibenek, Split, Ploče, Omišalj, Dubrovnik and Zadar. At the end of 2009 Croatia's merchant fleet had 314 vessels, with a total displacement of 1.39m. grt.

Atlantska Plovidba: 20000 Dubrovnik, od sv. Mihajla 1; tel. (20) 352333; fax (20) 356148; e-mail atlant@atlant.hr; internet www.atlant.hr; f. 1974; Dir ANTE JERKOVIĆ.

Jadrolinija Adriatic Shipping Line: 51000 Rijeka, Riva 16; tel. (51) 666111; fax (51) 213116; e-mail jadrolinija@jadrolinija.hr; internet www.jadrolinija.hr; f. 1872; regular passenger and car-ferry services between Croatian and Italian ports, and along the Adriatic coast of Dalmatia; Pres. SLAVKO LONČAR.

Jadroplov: 21000 Split, Obala kneza Branimira 16; tel. (21) 302666; fax (21) 342198; e-mail jadroplov@jadroplov.com; internet www.jadroplov.com; f. 1984; fleet of 17 vessels and 1,500 containers engaged in linear and tramping service; Gen. Man. NIKŠA GIOVANELLI.

Tankerska Plovidba: 23000 Zadar, Božidara Petranovića 4; tel. (23) 202202; fax (23) 202375; e-mail info@tankerska.hr; internet www.tankerska.hr; f. 1976; Gen. Dir IVE MUSTAĆ.

CIVIL AVIATION

There are 10 international airports in Croatia.

Croatia Airlines: 10000 Zagreb, Savska cesta 41; tel. (1) 6160066; fax (1) 6176845; e-mail pr@ctn.tel.hr; internet www.croatiaairlines.com; f. 1989 as Zagreb Airlines; name changed 1990; operates domestic and international services; Pres. IVAN MIŠETIĆ.

Tourism

The attractive Adriatic coast and the country's 1,185 islands make Croatia a popular tourist destination. In 2010 the number of foreign tourist arrivals numbered 9.1m., and revenue from tourism (excluding passenger transport) totalled US $8,268m., according to provisional figures.

Croatian Tourist Board (Hrvatska turistička zajednica): 10000 Zagreb, Ilberov trg 10/4; tel. (1) 4699333; fax (1) 4557827; e-mail info@htz.hr; internet www.croatia.hr; Pres. DAMIR BAJS.

Defence

As assessed at November 2011, the estimated total strength of the armed forces was 18,600, comprising an army of 11,390, a navy of 1,850 and an air force of 3,500, and 1,860 general staff. There were, in addition, 3,000 armed military police, and a total of 21,000 reservists. In May 2000 Croatia was admitted to the 'Partnership for Peace' programme of the North Atlantic Treaty Organization (NATO), and it acceded to NATO in April 2009. Compulsory military service was abolished from the beginning of 2008.

Defence Expenditure: Budgeted at 4,960m. kuna in 2011.

Commander of the Army: DRAGUTIN REPINC.

Chief of the General Staff: Lt-Gen. DRAGO LOVRIĆ.

Commander of the Navy: Rear Adm. ANTE URLIĆ.

Education

Pre-school education, for children aged from three to six years, is available free of charge. Education is compulsory for eight years, between seven and 15 years of age. Primary education continues for four years. Secondary education lasts for up to eight years, comprising two cycles of four years each. There are various types of secondary school: grammar, technical and specialized schools and mixed-curriculum schools. In 2008/09 the pre-primary education enrolment ratio included 57% of children in the relevant age-group. In the same year 89% of children in the relevant age-group were enrolled at primary schools, while the equivalent rate for secondary education was 92% of children in the appropriate age-group. In 2010/11 a total of 148,616 students were enrolled at 133 institutions of higher education. Government expenditure on education totalled 7,244.7m. kuna (8.5% of total spending) in 2004.

CUBA

Introductory Survey

LOCATION, CLIMATE, LANGUAGE, RELIGION, FLAG, CAPITAL

The Republic of Cuba is an archipelago of two main islands, Cuba and the Isla de la Juventud (Isle of Youth), formerly the Isla dc Pinos (Isle of Pines), and about 1,600 keys and islets. It lies in the Caribbean Sea, 145 km (90 miles) south of Florida, USA. Other nearby countries are the Bahamas, Mexico, Jamaica and Haiti. The climate is tropical, with the annual rainy season from May to October. The average annual temperature is 25°C (77°F) and hurricanes are frequent. The language spoken is Spanish. Most of the inhabitants are Christians, of whom the great majority are Roman Catholics. The national flag (proportions 1 by 2) has five equal horizontal stripes, of blue, white, blue, white and blue, with a red triangle, enclosing a five-pointed white star, at the hoist. The capital is Havana (La Habana).

CONTEMPORARY POLITICAL HISTORY

Historical Context

Cuba was ruled by Spain from the 16th century until 1898, when the island was ceded to the USA following Spain's defeat in the Spanish–American War. Cuba became an independent republic on 20 May 1902, but the USA retained its naval bases on the island and, until 1934, reserved the right to intervene in Cuba's internal affairs. In 1933 an army sergeant, Fulgencio Batista Zaldívar, came to power at the head of a military revolt. Batista ruled the country until 1944, when he retired after serving a four-year term as elected President.

Domestic Political Affairs

In March 1952, however, Gen. Batista (as he had become) seized power again, deposing President Carlos Prío Socarrás in a bloodless coup. Batista's new regime soon proved to be unpopular and became harshly repressive. In July 1953 a radical opposition group, led by Dr Fidel Castro Ruz, attacked the Moncada army barracks in Santiago de Cuba. Castro was captured, with many of his supporters, but was later released. He went into exile and formed a revolutionary movement committed to Batista's overthrow. In December 1956 Castro landed in Cuba with a small group of followers, most of whom were captured or killed. However, 12 survivors, including Castro and the Argentine-born Dr Ernesto ('Che') Guevara, escaped into the hills of the Sierra Maestra, where they formed the nucleus of the guerrilla forces which, after a prolonged struggle, forced Batista to flee from Cuba on 1 January 1959. The Batista regime collapsed, and Castro's forces occupied Havana.

The assumption of power by the victorious rebels was initially met with great popular acclaim. The 1940 Constitution was suspended in January 1959 and replaced by a new 'Fundamental Law'. Executive and legislative power was vested in the Council of Ministers, with Fidel Castro as Prime Minister and his brother Raúl as his deputy and Minister of the Revolutionary Armed Forces. The new regime ruled by decree but promised to hold elections within 18 months. When it was firmly established, the Castro Government adopted a radical economic programme, including agrarian reform and the nationalization of industrial and commercial enterprises. These drastic reforms, combined with the regime's authoritarian nature, provoked opposition from some sectors of the population, including former supporters of Castro, and many Cubans went into exile.

All US business interests in Cuba were expropriated, without compensation, in October 1960, and the USA severed diplomatic relations in January 1961. A US-sponsored force of anti-Castro Cuban émigrés landed in April 1961 at the Bahía de Cochinos (Bay of Pigs), in southern Cuba, but the invasion was thwarted by Castro's troops. Later in the year, all pro-Government groups were merged to form the Organizaciones Revolucionarias Integradas (ORI). In December 1961 Fidel Castro announced that Cuba had become a communist state, and he proclaimed a 'Marxist-Leninist' programme for the country's future development. In January 1962 Cuba was excluded from active participation in the Organization of American States (OAS). The USA instituted a full economic and political embargo against Cuba. Hostility to the USA was accompanied by increasingly close relations between Cuba and the USSR. In October the USA revealed the presence of Soviet missiles in Cuba but, after the imposition of a US naval blockade, the weapons were withdrawn. The missile bases, capable of launching nuclear weapons against the USA, were dismantled, thus resolving one of the most serious international crises since the Second World War. In 1964 the OAS imposed diplomatic and commercial sanctions against Cuba.

The ORI was replaced in 1962 by a new Partido Unido de la Revolución Socialista Cubana (PURSC), the country's sole legal party. In October 1965 the PURSC was renamed the Partido Comunista de Cuba (PCC). Although ostracized by most other Latin American countries, the PCC Government consolidated its internal authority. Supported by considerable aid from the USSR, the regime made significant progress in social and economic development, including improvements in education and public health. At the same time, Cuba continued to give active support to left-wing revolutionary movements in Latin America and elsewhere. Guevara was killed in Bolivia, following an unsuccessful guerrilla uprising under his leadership, in October 1967. In 1972 Cuba's links with the Eastern bloc were strengthened when the country became a full member of the Council for Mutual Economic Assistance (dissolved in 1991), a Moscow-based organization linking the USSR and other communist states, receiving preferential trade terms from these countries as a result.

In June 1974 the country's first elections since the revolution were held for municipal offices in Matanzas province. Cuba's first 'socialist' Constitution was submitted to the First Congress of the PCC, held in December 1975, and came into force in 1976, after being approved by popular referendum. As envisaged by the new Constitution, elections for 169 municipal assemblies were held in October. These assemblies later elected delegates to provincial assemblies and deputies to the Asamblea Nacional del Poder Popular (National Assembly of People's Power), 'the supreme organ of state'. The National Assembly chose the members of a new Council of State, with Fidel Castro as President.

Cuba continued to be excluded from the activities of the OAS, although the Organization voted in favour of allowing members to normalize their relations with Cuba in 1975. The relaxation of restrictions on emigration in 1980 resulted in the departure of more than 125,000 Cubans for Florida, USA. Antagonism continued as Cuba's presence abroad increased, threatening US spheres of influence. High-level talks between Cuba and the USA took place in November 1981, but US hostility increased. Economic sanctions were strengthened, the major air link was closed, and tourism and investment by US nationals was prohibited in 1982. Cuba's support of Argentina during the 1982 crisis concerning the Falkland Islands improved relations with the rest of Latin America, and the country's legitimacy was finally acknowledged when it was elected to the chair of the UN General Assembly Committee on Decolonization in September of that year.

An increase in US military activity in Honduras and the Caribbean region led President Castro to declare a 'state of national alert' in August 1983. The US invasion of Grenada in October, and the ensuing short-lived confrontation between US forces and Cuban personnel on the island, severely damaged relations, and left Cuba isolated in the Caribbean, following the weakening of its ties with Suriname in November.

In July 1984 official negotiations were begun with the USA on the issues of immigration and repatriation, and in December agreement was reached on the resumption of Cuban immigration to the USA. The repatriation of Cuban 'undesirables' began in February 1985, but, following the inauguration of Radio Martí (a radio station sponsored by the 'Voice of America' radio network, which began to broadcast Western-style news and other programmes to Cuba from Florida), the Cuban Government suspended its immigration accord with the USA. Subsequently, all visits to Cuba by US residents of Cuban origin were banned. In September 1986, as a result of mediation by the

Roman Catholic Church, more than 100 political prisoners and their families were permitted to leave Cuba for the USA.

Relations with the USA continued to deteriorate in 1987 when the US Government launched a campaign to direct public attention to human rights violations in Cuba. In 1988 the Cuban Government released some 250 political prisoners, and in the following January President Castro pledged to release the remaining 225 political prisoners acknowledged by the regime.

President Castro was confronted by Cuba's most serious political crisis since the 1959 Revolution in June 1989. It was discovered that a number of senior military personnel were not only involved in smuggling operations in Angola but were also aiding Colombian drugs-traffickers by enabling them to use Cuban airstrips. Gen. Arnaldo Ochoa Sánchez, who had led the military campaign in Angola, as well as three other officers, were found guilty of high treason and were executed. A further purge led to the imposition of harsh sentences on 14 senior officials. The scandal undermined the regime's credibility at the international, as well as the domestic, level.

Post-Cold War Cuba

In September 1991 the USSR announced that it intended to withdraw the majority of its military personnel (some 3,000 troops and advisers) from Cuba. The decision, condemned by Cuba as a threat to its national security, came as the result of US demands that the USSR reduce its aid to Cuba as a precondition to the provision of US aid to the USSR. Cuba's subsequent demands that the USA withdraw its troops from the naval base at Guantánamo were rejected. The withdrawal of Russian troops was completed in June 1993. Meanwhile, the collapse of the USSR in late 1991, and the resulting termination of Soviet subsidies to Cuba, initiated a period of severe economic decline.

In 1992 President Castro's efforts to quiet internal dissent and bolster the country against the perceived US threat revealed an increasingly militant attitude, as several death sentences were imposed on Cuban dissidents. In the same year the USA began to implement a series of measures strengthening its economic blockade against Cuba. In April US President George Bush barred ships that were engaged in trade with Cuba from entering US ports. In October the Cuban Democracy Act, also known as the 'Torricelli Law', was adopted, making it illegal for foreign subsidiaries of US companies to trade with Cuba. These measures encountered widespread international criticism and in November the UN General Assembly adopted a non-binding resolution demanding the cessation of the trade embargo. The General Assembly continued to adopt similar resolutions on an annual basis, most recently in October 2011.

In July 1992 the National Assembly approved a number of amendments to the Constitution: President Castro was granted the authority to declare a state of emergency and, in such an event, to assume full control of the armed forces. The constitutional revisions also legitimized foreign investment in approved state enterprises and recognized foreign ownership of property in joint ventures. Elections to the National Assembly were also to be conducted by direct vote. The first such elections were held in 1993. Only candidates nominated by the PCC were permitted to contest the elections. According to official results, 87% of the electorate cast a 'united' ballot (a vote for the entire list of candidates). In the following month Fidel Castro and Raúl Castro were unanimously re-elected by the National Assembly to their respective posts as President and First Vice-President of the Council of State.

In July 1993, with the economic crisis deepening and international reserves exhausted, Castro announced that a 30-year ban on Cuban citizens possessing foreign currency was to be lifted. The measure, which represented a significant departure from the country's centrally planned socialist economy, was intended to attract the large sums of foreign currency (principally US dollars) in circulation on the black market into the economy, and to encourage remittances from Cuban exiles. Restrictions on Cuban exiles travelling to Cuba were also to be relaxed. Later in the year the Government authorized limited individual private enterprise in a range of occupations. Plans were announced for the introduction of agricultural reforms allowing for the decentralization and reorganization of state farms into 'Units of Basic Co-operative Production', to be managed and financed by the workers themselves.

In April 1994 four new ministries were created and a number of state committees and institutes dissolved. In August, however, increasing discontent at deteriorating economic conditions resulted in rioting in the capital. The surge of Cubans attempting to reach the USA by sea reached crisis proportions, and the US President, Bill Clinton, was forced to revoke the automatic refugee status conferred on Cubans under the 1966 Cuban Adjustment Act to deter them; in addition, cash remittances from Cuban exiles in the USA were halted. However, these measures failed to stem the flow of Cubans seeking refuge in the USA, and in September 1994 the US and Cuban Governments held bilateral talks to resolve the crisis. The USA promised to grant visas allowing for the migration of a minimum of 20,000 Cubans annually; in return, Cuba reintroduced border restrictions. A further immigration accord was signed in 1995, bringing to an official end the automatic refugee status that had been revoked in the previous August. The accord also stated that all Cuban refugees intercepted at sea by the USA would thenceforth be repatriated. In addition, the USA agreed to grant visas to the majority of the approximately 20,000 Cuban refugees detained at Guantánamo, although the figure was to be deducted from the annual quota of visas granted under the 1994 accord.

The Helms-Burton bill

In early 1995 legislative proposals seeking to tighten the US embargo against Cuba were introduced to the US Congress. The proposals, referred to as the Helms-Burton bill after its proposers, sought to impose sanctions on countries trading with or investing in Cuba, and threatened to reduce US aid to countries providing Cuba with financial assistance, notably Russia. The proposed law provoked international criticism, and a formal complaint was registered by the European Union (EU, see p. 276), which claimed that the legislation would be in violation of international law and the rules of the World Trade Organization (WTO, see p. 433). The bill was approved by the House of Representatives in September but was considerably modified by the Senate.

In February 1996 Cuban MiG fighters shot down two US light aircraft piloted by members of the Cuban-American exile group Brothers to the Rescue, killing all four crew members. The action was vigorously condemned by the USA, which rejected Cuban claims that the aircraft had violated Cuban airspace. Further US sanctions were immediately implemented, including the indefinite suspension of charter flights to Cuba. As a result of the incident, President Clinton reversed his previous opposition to certain controversial elements of the Helms-Burton bill, and in March he signed the legislation, officially entitled the Cuban Liberty and Democratic Solidarity (LIBERTAD) Act. However, Clinton was empowered to issue executive orders postponing the implementation of a section of the law, Title III, which allowed US citizens, including naturalized Cuban exiles, to prosecute through US courts any foreign corporation or investor with business dealings involving property that had been expropriated during the Castro regime. Approval of the Helms-Burton Act prompted strenuous criticism from Cuba's major trading partners and Canada, Mexico and the EU adopted legislation to protect companies against the Act.

In December 1996 agreement was reached by the members of the EU to make the extent of economic co-operation with Cuba contingent upon progress towards democracy in the country. In that month the Cuban Government adopted legislation to counteract the application of the Helms-Burton Act in an attempt to protect foreign investment in the country. The Government also expressed its readiness to negotiate with the USA regarding the compensation of US citizens with property claims in Cuba. In April 1997 the EU and the USA reached an agreement on a resolution of the dispute whereby the USA was to continue deferring the implementation of Title III indefinitely, while negotiations continued towards a multilateral accord defining investment principles. In March 1998 it was agreed that shipments of food and medicines from the USA to Cuba were to be permitted. In addition, the USA ended the ban on direct flights between the two countries and on the transfer of cash remittances from the USA to Cuba. However, the Cuban Government was extremely critical of a further outline agreement on extra-territorial legislation drafted by the US Government and the EU in May, which it considered to be highly concessionary on the part of the EU, at the expense of Cuban interests. Under the terms of the agreement, in return for a commitment from the US President to seek congressional consensus for a relaxation of the application of the Helms-Burton Act, EU member states would participate in the compilation of a register of former US assets in Cuba (considered to have been illegally expropriated) and would observe firm US recommendations regarding their exclusivity. The USA continued to suspend the implementation of Title III at six-monthly intervals.

Strained Cuban–US relations

Despite a further easing of restrictions relating to the US embargo in August 1999, attempts by the US Government to appease the increasingly influential anti-embargo lobby were largely frustrated by an exchange of legal challenges. In March a US judge ruled that payments owed to the Cuban national telecommunications company, withheld by a number of US telecommunications companies by judicial request, could be used to help honour a compensation award of US $187m. against the Cuban authorities, made in the USA in 1997 to benefit relatives of the four pilots shot down by the Cuban air force in 1996. The US Government had made known its objection to the ruling, claiming that the decision amounted to interference in foreign policy. In October 2000 legislation was passed by the US Congress easing some aspects of the trade embargo, including the export of food and medicine. However, the Cuban Government declared that the conditions attached to the lifting of the restrictions were such that the legislation would tighten, rather than ease, the US embargo. In response, Cuba imposed a 10% tax on all telephone calls between the two countries and, in December, suspended telephone links with the USA, following the refusal of US telecommunications companies to pay the levy.

An alleged plot to assassinate President Castro in Panama was uncovered in November 2000. Anti-Castro activist Luis Posada Carriles was arrested, along with three others. Posada Carriles had escaped from custody in Venezuela, where he was indicted for the bombing of a Cuban aeroplane near Barbados in 1976, and was also implicated in a series of hotel bombings in Havana in 1997. In April 2004 Posada Carriles was sentenced in Panama to an eight-year prison term. However, in August of that year, having been pardoned by the Panamanian President, Posada Carriles fled the country. In the following year Posada Carriles filed a request for political asylum in the USA and was subsequently arrested on the charge of illegal entry into the USA. Both the Cuban and Venezuelan Governments demanded his extradition and Castro conceded that extradition to Venezuela would be acceptable—while Venezuela had an extradition treaty with the USA, Cuba did not. However, the US Government refused to co-operate, citing the threat posed to, and lack of evidence against, Posada Carriles, prompting both the Cuban and Venezuelan Governments to accuse the USA of hypocrisy in its 'war on terror'. In April 2009 an indictment was filed against Posada Carriles in the USA for allegedly lying when questioned about the 1997 Havana hotel bombings. In April 2011 Posada Carriles was acquitted of all charges by a court in Texas, and released. The Cuban Government condemned the verdict.

In May 2002 US President George W. Bush affirmed that the embargo and travel restrictions would remain in place until Cuba installed a government that would respect political and civil rights. Cuban–US relations were further strained when, in the same month, the US Administration added Cuba to the list of states it claimed formed an 'axis of evil' that supported international terrorism. In November Cuba finally acceded to the Treaty on the Non-Proliferation of Nuclear Weapons (see p. 125).

Continuing repression

In May 2002 an 11,000-signature petition—part of a dissident initiative known as the 'Varela Project'—was submitted to the National Assembly; it called for a referendum on basic civil and political liberties. (The Constitution allowed legislative proposals that were supported by at least 10,000 registered voters to be submitted to the National Assembly for consideration.) In the following month the Government responded by initiating a drive to mobilize popular support for an amendment to the Constitution, declaring the socialist system to be 'untouchable' and ratifying that 'economic, diplomatic and political relations with any other state can never be negotiated in the face of aggression, threat or pressure from a foreign power'. The National Assembly subsequently voted unanimously to adopt a constitutional amendment declaring socialism in Cuba to be permanent and 'irrevocable'.

Relations with the USA worsened in March 2003 when James Cason, Principal Officer of the US Interests Section in Havana, was accused by the Cuban Government of attempting to incite a counter-revolution, having met with opponents of Fidel Castro and, allegedly, disseminated anti-Government propaganda. Castro subsequently ordered that all those dissidents who had met with Cason be arrested, and imposed strict travel restrictions on all US diplomatic personnel resident in Cuba. The arrests provoked condemnation from international organizations and human rights groups. In April 75 of the dissidents (who included many of the leaders of the Varela Project) were found guilty of charges of subversion and treason and sentenced to prison terms of up to 28 years. Meanwhile, bilateral tensions were heightened further by government accusations that the USA was encouraging a spate of aeroplane hijackings by Cubans seeking asylum in the USA, owing to its lenient treatment of Cuban emigrants. In the same month, as the Government continued to adopt a more repressive stance towards the opposition, three men found guilty of hijacking a ferry in an attempt to reach the USA were convicted of terrorism and executed. In July, after the EU suspended Cuba's application to join its Cotonou Agreement (see below) in protest at the country's recent human rights record, President Castro announced that his Government would reject any aid offered by the EU and would terminate all political contact with the organization. Meanwhile, the EU imposed 'diplomatic sanctions' on Cuba, announcing that its member states would officially welcome Cuban dissidents into their embassies while restricting contact with the Government.

The Government continued to operate in an increasingly repressive manner. In January 2004 new regulations concerning internet usage were announced, further enforcing state control over access to information. In April the UN Commission on Human Rights adopted a motion condemning human rights violations in Cuba and mandating the Commission to send a mission to the country. In response, the Cuban Government declared that it would not permit any human rights monitors to enter the country. In May the USA announced further restrictions on remittances into the country and that US military aircraft would be used to prevent Cuban radio stations from blocking pro-democracy broadcasts. In addition, Cuban Americans resident in the USA were only to be permitted to visit their relatives in Cuba once every three years. In response, President Castro orchestrated a protest march in Havana and restricted the quantity of goods available for purchase in US dollars within Cuba. In October the Government announced that circulation of the US dollar in Cuba would not be permitted from the following month; a commission of 10% would also be imposed henceforth when changing US dollars into Cuban convertible pesos.

In April 2005 the UN Human Rights Commission approved a resolution condemning the imprisonment of political dissidents and journalists in Cuba and calling for the renewal of the mandate of a UN envoy to investigate alleged human rights abuses in the country. In the following month the Assembly for the Promotion of Civil Society in Cuba took place in Havana. Castro denounced all attendees of the gathering as 'counter-revolutionaries'. Two Polish members of the European Parliament were prohibited from entering Cuba prior to the Assembly, while the ejection of a German and a Czech parliamentarian from the island on the eve of the gathering prompted official complaints from both the Czech and German Governments. The Assembly itself went ahead without incident; those in attendance demanded the immediate release of imprisoned dissidents, economic freedom and the return of a multi-party democracy.

In July 2005, in the largest crackdown on dissidents since March 2003, 26 people were arrested during a protest outside the French embassy in Havana. The demonstrators were opposed to France's decision to normalize relations with Cuba. In the same month the USA appointed Caleb McCarry to be Cuba Transition Co-ordinator, a position charged with directing the US Government's actions 'in support of a free Cuba' and hastening the end to President Castro's premiership.

After Hurricane Dennis struck the island in July 2005, killing 16 Cubans and causing damage estimated at US $1,400m., the US Government offered financial aid of $50,000 for emergency supplies; in a state television broadcast President Castro expressed gratitude but refused the offer, insisting that Cuba would not accept any assistance from the USA while the US trade embargo remained in place. In the wake of Hurricane Wilma, which caused serious flooding in Havana and forced the evacuation of over 250,000 Cubans resident across the west of the island in October, Cuba did accept a US offer of an assessment team from the Office of US Foreign Disaster Assistance. However, in November the US Department of State withdrew the offer after Castro announced he wanted to discuss regional co-operation with the team, although a US donation of $100,000 to non-governmental organizations working within Cuba was to proceed. The Cuban Government dismissed the aid as a veiled method of funding 'the mercenary groups that the US Government organizes and directs in Cuba'. In September President Bush had rejected an offer by the Cuban Government to send doctors, medical supplies and field hospitals to the US city of New Orleans following its destruction by Hurricane Katrina.

In April 2006 the PCC announced a structural reorganization that included the re-establishment of the party Secretariat, which had been dissolved in 1991; the 12-member body was charged with ensuring adherence to the party line and eradicating insubordination and misconduct. In the same month Juan Carlos Robinson was dismissed from the PCC's Political Bureau (Politburo) amid allegations of corruption; he was sentenced to 12 years' imprisonment in June.

Raúl Castro assumes power

In July 2006 it was announced that, owing to ill health, President Castro was temporarily to cede power to his brother, Raúl. A recurrent theme in Raúl Castro's early public addresses was the need to engage in more open discussion of the seminal challenges facing Cuba. At the National Assembly's end-of-year session in December, from which Fidel Castro was conspicuously absent, the acting President urged the legislature to strive for greater transparency, encouraging Assembly members publicly to accept responsibility for its failings where appropriate. Earlier in December, in an apparent manifestation of a more pragmatic approach to relations with the USA, Castro expressed his amenability to negotiations in order to resolve the protracted dispute. In July 2007 Castro acknowledged Cuba's severe economic difficulties, including under-production, low wages and high prices, and declared that 'structural and conceptual changes' were necessary to overcome them.

In December 2007 it was announced that Cuba would subscribe to two of the UN's seven conventions on human rights, as well as allowing the recently constituted UN Human Rights Council to scrutinize the status of human rights in the country. Cuba had previously opposed any monitoring of its affairs by the UN. The conventions, which were signed by Cuba in February 2008, covered civil and political and social, economic and cultural rights, respectively, including freedom of expression and association and the right to travel. Dissident groups expressed scepticism of the Government's commitment to the accords.

Elections to the National Assembly (enlarged from 609 to 614 seats) were held on 20 January 2008. All of the 614 candidates were elected with the requisite 50% of valid votes. The participation rate was 96.9%, of whom some 4.8% cast blank or spoiled ballots. Despite continuing uncertainty as to his health, Fidel Castro was re-elected to the National Assembly, a necessary condition to his remaining as Head of State. However, in mid-February Castro announced that he would not aspire to nor accept re-election to the presidency of the Council of State. On 24 February the Assembly unanimously elected Raúl Castro to succeed his brother as President of the Council of State and of the Council of Ministers. Raúl Castro was replaced as First Vice-President by José Ramón Machado Ventura, a senior member of the PCC's Politburo and a veteran of the Revolution; Machado Ventura's election surprised many observers, who had expected a younger member of the Government to accede to the position. The new President obtained the Assembly's approval to consult his brother on major issues of state.

In his inaugural address to the National Assembly, Raúl Castro indicated an imminent relaxation of some of the island's more restrictive economic and social policies. Accordingly, it was announced in March 2008 that restrictions on the sale of computers and various other electronic appliances would be removed from April, while the sale of mobile telephones to the public would also be permitted. It was also revealed that Cubans would be permitted to stay in hotels hitherto restricted to foreign tourists and to hire cars. Reforms of the agricultural sector were announced in March, which were to include the distribution of unused state-owned land to private farmers. (By late 2011 1.6m. ha of land had been leased to some 143,000 farmers under this programme, although there were concerns that the redistributed land was being underutilized, partly owing to a lack of resources and drought conditions.) Wage reform was announced in June, whereby upper limits on salaries were abolished and employees would be able to earn bonuses for meeting production quotas.

In March 2009 President Castro carried out an extensive government reorganization affecting some 11 ministerial posts. Most notably, Felipe Pérez Roque and Carlos Lage Dávila, both regarded as close allies of Fidel Castro and possible candidates to succeed Raúl Castro as Head of State, were unexpectedly dismissed from their roles as Minister of Foreign Relations and Secretary of the Council of Ministers, respectively; it later emerged that both men had been secretly recorded making derogatory remarks about the Castro brothers. Brig.-Gen. José Amado Ricardo Guerra replaced Lage as cabinet secretary, and Bruno Rodríguez Parrilla was awarded the foreign relations portfolio. Among other changes, Dr José M. Miyar Barruecos, hitherto Secretary of the Council of State, became Minister of Science, Technology and the Environment, the Ministry of Foreign Trade was merged with that of Foreign Investment and Economic Co-operation, while the Ministry of the Fishing Industry was abolished.

Relations between Castro and Obama

In April 2009 the new US President, Barack Obama, relaxed restrictions on US residents making family visits to Cuba, introduced under the Bush Administration in 2004, and limitations on the transfer of remittances to family members in Cuba were also revoked. Furthermore, Obama removed the existing constraints preventing US telecommunications companies from operating within Cuba, although this also required the approval of the Cuban Government. Castro described these measures as 'positive but minimal'. As a further sign of US attempts to improve relations with Cuba, Obama expressed his willingness to talk to the Cuban Government but emphasized that the trade embargo, which was renewed for another year in September 2009 (and again in September 2010 and 2011), would remain in place and would only be eased following democratic reform and an improvement in human rights. The Cuban response to these developments was lukewarm: Castro announced that he was open to fresh dialogue with the Obama Administration, but stressed that talks would only take place if there were no preconditions attached and that the Cuban political system was non-negotiable. In July migration talks between Cuba and the USA, suspended since 2003, resumed. However, this amelioration in bilateral relations began to falter in November following a report by Human Rights Watch critical of human rights abuses in Cuba. The report, *New Castro, Same Cuba*, censured the ongoing repression of dissenters by the Cuban leadership, including the use of violence and imprisonment. Cuban–US relations were further strained in December when a US government contractor, Alan Gross, was arrested in Havana for allegedly supplying computers and mobile telephones to dissident organizations; these accusations were vehemently denied by the US Government. In March 2011 Gross was convicted of committing acts against 'the integrity and territorial independence' of the state and sentenced to 15 years' imprisonment. The case remained an obstacle to initiatives aimed at improving bilateral relations. Nevertheless, in January Obama further eased restrictions on travel and the transfer of remittances to Cuba by US residents, notably allowing religious organizations and higher education institutions to sponsor visits to the country. The Ministry of Foreign Relations described the changes as being 'positive' but of 'limited reach' and condemned US officials participating in a fourth round of migrations talks in Havana that month for meeting Cuban opposition figures. In March the USA increased the number of US airports permitted to operate charter flights to Cuba from three to 11; further authorizations followed.

Recent developments: economic crisis and reforms

In response to a growing liquidity crisis that had left the country struggling to pay for its energy imports, emergency restrictions on electricity usage were announced in June 2009. This was followed by the rationing of several staple food items and the closure of some subsidized workers' canteens, while in August the Government revealed that there would be a decrease in public spending on health and education, sectors that the Cuban leadership had previously regarded as immune from spending reductions.

In July 2010 the Roman Catholic Church announced that, following negotiations also involving the Spanish Government, President Castro had agreed to release 52 of the 75 political dissidents detained in March 2003 (the other 23 having been previously freed). Pressure for their release had intensified after the death in February of one of the detainees, who had been on hunger strike for nearly three months. All 52 had been freed by the end of March 2011, together with a number of additional prisoners not included in the agreement with the Church, most going into exile in Spain.

Amid continuing economic difficulties, during the second half of 2010 the Government announced a series of reforms aimed at increasing productivity and reducing the size of the public sector. In an attempt to improve agricultural production, farmers were allowed to purchase a limited range of supplies directly from local shops, rather than being allocated such resources centrally by the state. Moreover, under new legislation adopted in July and specifically aimed at facilitating foreign participation in the development of the tourism sector, foreign investors were permitted to lease state-owned land for a period of up to 99 years (compared with 50 years previously); in the following month the Minister of Tourism, Manuel Marrero Cruz, revealed that the Government had approved several projects for the construction of golf resorts by foreign companies. Addressing the National Assembly at the beginning of August, President Castro pledged to reduce the role of the state in some areas of the economy, to cut the state payroll and to ease restrictions on self-employment and the creation of small businesses, but ruled out major market reforms. A decree taking effect later that month legalized the sale at unregulated prices of agricultural produce from roadside stands, subject to a 5% sales tax, while the development of co-operatives to operate small manufacturing and retail businesses was also to be encouraged. In September it was confirmed that 500,000 people would be removed from the state payroll by March 2011, followed by a further 500,000 at a later date. The Government hoped that 465,000 non-state jobs would be created in 2011, with 250,000 new licences for self-employment to be issued (143,800 people were self-employed in 2009). The self-employed would be permitted to hire employees but would be obliged to pay a range of taxes. It was also suggested that the pay of those workers remaining in the public sector would be related to their productivity. The number of products available to Cubans at subsidized prices would also be gradually reduced. Meanwhile, Fidel Castro had made a number of public appearances since July, notably giving a speech in the legislature in August (for the first time since June 2006, the month before he ceded power to his brother). However, he refrained from commenting on domestic political affairs, opting instead to criticize US policy on Iran's nuclear ambitions.

In November 2010 President Raúl Castro announced that the long-delayed sixth congress of the PCC, which would determine government policy for the forthcoming years, would be held in April 2011. (The fifth congress had taken place in 1997.) The Government subsequently distributed a 32-page consultation document, *Draft Guidelines for the Economic and Social Policy of the Party*, and a three-month national debate on the proposals commenced in December 2010. The guidelines reaffirmed the Government's commitment to retaining a centrally planned socialist economic model, but defined socialism as equality of rights and of opportunity for all citizens rather than egalitarianism, and emphasized that the focus of central planning would be on regulating and taxing state businesses rather than administering them. Foreign investment would be encouraged, while the two Cuban currencies would eventually be unified. A minor government reorganization in January 2011 included the appointment of René Mesa Villafaña to replace Fidel Figueroa de la Paz as Minister of Construction. In March Adel Izquierdo Rodríguez was appointed as Minister of Economy and Planning, succeeding Marino Murillo Jorge, who was designated Chairman of the Economic Policy Commission of the Sixth Party Congress, responsible for supervising the implementation of the ongoing economic reforms.

The changes to the economic system proposed by President Castro were approved at the sixth congress of the PCC, which was held, as scheduled, in April 2011. In addition to the measures aimed at expanding the private sector, the reforms—which numbered more than 300 and were expected to be implemented over a period of at least five years—included the granting of more autonomy to state enterprises and the introduction of the right to buy and sell houses and cars. In late March Fidel Castro had announced that he had relinquished the post of First Secretary of the Central Committee of the PCC in favour of his brother when he fell ill in July 2006. President Raúl Castro was thus confirmed as First Secretary at the congress, while First Vice-President José Ramón Machado Ventura became Second Secretary, and three new members were elected to the Politburo: Adel Izquierdo, Marino Murillo and Mercedes López Acea, the head of the party in Havana. In addition, President Castro notably proposed a limit of two consecutive five-year terms for senior political and state officials. Significant progress in the implementation of some of the economic reforms had already been achieved, with more than 200,000 licences for the establishment of privately run businesses having been issued since October 2010, although the process of reducing the public sector workforce had suffered delays, partly as a result of disagreements between trade unions and administrators at the state-run bodies affected.

In May 2011, as part of wider efforts by the Cuban authorities to curb corruption, a former Minister of the Food Industry, Alejandro Francisco Roca Iglesias, who had been dismissed from the Council of Ministers in March 2009, was sentenced to 15 years' imprisonment after being found guilty of accepting bribes for the awarding of government contracts. His erstwhile deputy, Celio Hernández, and 10 other senior officials were convicted on similar charges in June and received prison sentences of between three and five years.

The economic reforms approved by the sixth congress of the PCC in April 2011 were endorsed by the National Assembly in August. Their introduction was to be monitored by an Implementation and Development Permanent Commission. Meanwhile, President Castro announced plans to ease foreign travel restrictions imposed on Cuban citizens. The Minister of the Revolutionary Armed Forces, Gen. Julio Casas Regueiro, who was also a member of the Politburo and a close ally of the President, died in September; he was succeeded in the Council of Ministers by his deputy, Lt-Gen. Leopoldo Cintra Frías. Also in September, reflecting the Government's policy of decentralizing economic power, it was decided that the Ministry of Sugar would be replaced by the Grupo Empresarial de la Agroindustria Azucarera, a public holding company comprising 13 provincial state-owned enterprises. Legislation allowing and regulating the sale and purchase of cars and property by Cuban residents entered into force in October and November, respectively. Under further reforms announced in November, moreover, from December farmers were permitted to sell their produce directly to state-run hotels and restaurants, rather than through government agencies, while bank loans were made available to self-employed people (now estimated to number some 364,000). In late December President Castro announced that 2,900 prisoners, including some convicted of crimes against 'the security of the state', would be pardoned for humanitarian reasons. At a PCC conference held in January 2012, Castro reaffirmed his plan to limit the mandates of senior officials to two five-year terms, but defended the one-party political sytem.

Foreign Affairs

Regional relations

Since 1985 Cuba has succeeded in establishing strong ties throughout Latin America and the Caribbean. Full diplomatic relations were restored with Colombia in 1993, with Chile in 1995, with Guatemala and the Dominican Republic in 1998, and with Honduras in 2002. By 2009, with both Costa Rica and El Salvador re-establishing ties in that year, every country in the region had diplomatic relations with Cuba. In October 2010 the President of El Salvador, Carlos Mauricio Funes, became the first head of state from that country to visit Cuba in more than 50 years. In October 2011, after 15 years of negotiations, Cuba and the Bahamas reached agreement on the delimitation of their maritime border.

On 3 June 2009 the OAS voted overwhelmingly to abolish its 1962 suspension of Cuba's membership. Although the Cuban Government announced that it had no intention of rejoining the organization, which was viewed with suspicion in Cuba, it expressed satisfaction with this diplomatic victory. The USA, the only OAS member without diplomatic relations with Cuba, had pressed for Cuban membership to be contingent upon political reform and an improvement in human rights, but was forced to compromise; a 'process of dialogue', conforming to the OAS's democratic values, was agreed as a less stringent precondition to Cuban re-entry.

Cuba traditionally enjoyed good relations with Mexico (which was the only Latin American country not to suspend diplomatic relations with the Castro regime in 1961). However, in 2002 bilateral relations were strained when Mexico lent its support to a resolution sponsored by Uruguay condemning Cuba's human rights record at a meeting of the UN Human Rights Commission. Cuban-Mexican relations subsequently improved somewhat, but in May 2004 Mexico recalled its ambassador and expelled the Cuban ambassador to Mexico after President Castro criticized Mexican policy towards Cuba. Peru also withdrew its ambassador from Cuba at the same time. Diplomatic relations were restored in July. Meanwhile, diplomatic relations with Argentina, severed in 2001 following Argentina's support of a UN vote condemning Cuba's human rights record, were restored in October 2003. In August 2004 Cuba broke off diplomatic relations with Panama following that country's pardon of four

Cuban exiles suspected of involvement in an attempt to assassinate President Castro in 2000 (see above). The two countries restored diplomatic links in August 2005. A bilateral co-operation agreement with Bolivia came into effect in January 2006, with the accession of Evo Morales to the Bolivian presidency.

Relations between Cuba and Venezuela were bolstered considerably subsequent to Hugo Chávez's accession to the Venezuelan presidency in 1999. Venezuelan aid was crucial in allowing the Cuban economy to recover from its post-Soviet era economic depression, and numerous military exchanges were conducted between the two countries. In December 2004 Presidents Castro and Chávez signed the Bolivarian Alternative for the Americas (Alternativa Bolivariana para las Américas—ALBA, see p. 462), which was intended as an alternative to the US-supported proposed Free Trade Area of the Americas, from which Cuba had been excluded. Cuba agreed to provide skilled workers, particularly doctors, to Venezuela, in return for oil at preferential rates. In 2005 some 182 new co-operative agreements were signed between Cuba and Venezuela, including deals pertaining to education, health, energy and petroleum. Raúl Castro visited Chávez in Venezuela in December 2008 at the start of his first foreign tour since taking office. On the same tour Castro travelled to Brazil to take part in the inaugural Latin America and the Caribbean Integration and Development Summit in Sauípe, an initiative organized by Brazilian President Lula da Silva. The summit was the first meeting of all of the region's heads of government without the presence of the USA or members of the EU, and was regarded as an important step in Cuba's reintegration with other Latin American and Caribbean states. Meanwhile, in December 2009 Castro and Chávez concluded a significant trade agreement worth some US $3,200m., confirming Venezuela's position as Cuba's principal commercial partner. The deal also granted Venezuela further petroleum exploration rights in Cuban waters. In November 2010, during a meeting in Havana, Castro and Chávez renewed a bilateral economic co-operation agreement first signed in 2000 for a further 10-year period. Chávez travelled to Cuba several times in 2011 and 2012 to undergo treatment for cancer.

Other external relations

In 1998 Cuba was afforded observer status to the Lomé Convention co-operation accord between the EU and the African, Caribbean and Pacific countries (which expired in February 2000 and was replaced in June by the Cotonou Agreement, see p. 328). In 2001 Cuba signed an agreement with the Caribbean Community and Common Market (CARICOM, see p. 227) designed to promote trade and co-operation, and the country hosted a CARICOM summit meeting for the first time in the following year. In March 2003 the EU opened a legation office in Havana. The EU initially declared its support for Cuba's application to join the Cotonou Agreement; however, following the Government's imprisonment of a large number of dissidents in the following month, it subsequently downgraded relations with Cuba and indefinitely postponed the country's application to join the Agreement. Following the release of some of the dissidents, the EU ended its 'diplomatic sanctions' in June 2008. In October co-operation between Cuba and the EU was formally revived when the EU agreed to provide financial assistance towards reconstruction efforts following a series of hurricanes.

Cuba strengthened its relations with the Far East in the 2000s. Several bilateral agreements were signed between Cuba and Viet Nam in 2005, including a memorandum of understanding on health care co-operation and a co-operation agreement on science, technology and the environment. A further memorandum, on marine biodiversity, was signed between Cuba and the People's Republic of China in November; furthermore, the commencement in the latter half of 2006 of Sino-Cuban joint oil and gas explorations, following the signing of a bilateral energy accord in 2005, heightened already sizeable US concerns about the burgeoning relationship between the two communist states. Sino-Cuban relations were further strengthened by the signature of a bilateral economic and technical co-operation agreement during a visit to Havana by the Chinese Minister of Foreign Affairs in July 2010 and by the conclusion of several further co-operation agreements during a visit by the Chinese Vice-President, Xi Jinping, in June 2011. China notably pledged to invest some US $6,000m. in the expansion of Cuba's Cienfuegos oil refinery and the construction of a new liquefied natural gas plant, while a new accord on joint oil and gas explorations in Cuban waters was also signed.

Relations with Russia, which went into sharp decline after the collapse of the USSR in 1991, were strengthened following President Raúl Castro's assumption of office in 2008. The Deputy Chairman of the Russian Government, Igor I. Sechin, visited Cuba three times in that year, and signed 10 economic co-operation agreements. Russian President Dmitrii A. Medvedev visited Cuba in November, and in January–February 2009 Castro paid a return visit to Russia as part of his second foreign tour as President. Sechin visited Cuba again in July 2009 and signed an agreement granting the Russian oil company Zarubezhneft petroleum exploration rights in the Gulf of Mexico. As part of the deal, Cuba secured a US $150m. loan for the purchase of Russian agricultural and construction supplies.

CONSTITUTION AND GOVERNMENT

Under the 1976 Constitution (the first since the 1959 Revolution, amended in July 1992), the supreme organ of state, and the sole legislative authority, is the Asamblea Nacional del Poder Popular (National Assembly of People's Power), with deputies (614 following the general election of 2008) elected for five years by direct vote. The National Assembly elects 31 of its members to form the Council of State, the Assembly's permanent organ. The Council of State is the highest representative of the State, and its President is both Head of State and Head of Government. Executive and administrative authority is vested in the Council of Ministers, appointed by the National Assembly on the proposal of the Head of State. Municipal, regional and provincial assemblies have also been established. The Partido Comunista de Cuba (PCC), the only authorized political party, is 'the leading force of society and the State'. The PCC's highest authority is the Party Congress, which elects a Central Committee and a Secretariat to supervise the Party's work. To direct its policy, the Central Committee elects a Politburo.

REGIONAL AND INTERNATIONAL CO-OPERATION

Cuba has been a member of the UN since its inception in 1945. The country acceded to the World Trade Organization (see p. 433) in April 1995. Cuba is a member of the Latin American Economic System (see p. 451), the Association of Caribbean States (see p. 448), and of the Community of Latin American and Caribbean States (see p. 462), which was formally inaugurated in December 2011. In 1998 Cuba became the 12th full member of the Latin American Integration Association (LAIA, see p. 362), having enjoyed observer status since 1986. Cuba was afforded observer status to the European Union's (EU) Lomé Convention (which expired in February 2000 and was replaced in June by the Cotonou Agreement, see p. 328) in 1998, which guaranteed access to EU markets. Cuba became a member of Venezuela's Bolivarian Alternative for the Americas (Alternativa Bolivariana para las Américas—ALBA, see p. 462) in 2004. The country is a member of the Group of 77 (see p. 450) developing states.

ECONOMIC AFFAIRS

In 2009 Cuba's gross domestic product (GDP), measured at current prices, was an estimated 62,278.6m. pesos. During 2001–09, GDP increased, in real terms, at an average annual rate of 5.8%. During 2001–10 the population increased by an average of 0.1% per year. According to official figures, GDP increased by 2.1% in 2010.

Agriculture (including hunting, forestry and fishing) contributed 4.0% of GDP and employed 18.5% of the employed labour force in 2009. The principal cash crop has traditionally been sugar cane; however, as the industry became increasingly unprofitable, the Government closed many sugar mills in the 2000s. By 2009 sugar and its derivatives accounted for 7.8% of export earnings, compared with 27.4% in 2000. In 2010 sugar production was estimated at just 1.0m. metric tons, the worst harvest for over a century. In that year Cuba produced some 20,500 tons of tobacco, when 357.6m. cigars were made. Other important crops are rice (an estimated 454,400 tons in 2010), citrus fruits (an estimated 345,100 tons in 2010), plantains and bananas. Fishing exports contributed 1.6% of the value of total exports in 2009. In real terms, the GDP of the agricultural sector declined at an average rate of 0.2% per year during 2001–09. However, agricultural GDP increased by 3.4% in 2009.

Industry (including mining, manufacturing, construction and power) contributed 22.8% of GDP and employed 17.5% of the employed labour force in 2009. Industrial GDP increased, in real terms, at an average rate of 3.7% per year in 2001–09. Sectoral growth of 4.1% was recorded in 2008, but the sector remained stagnant in 2009.

Mining contributed 1.0% of GDP and employed 0.5% of the employed labour force in 2009. Nickel is the principal mineral export. Production totalled an estimated 2.5m metric tons in 2010. Cuba also produces considerable amounts of chromium and copper, some iron and manganese, and there are workable deposits of gold and silver. The GDP of the mining sector increased by an average of 3.6% per year in 2001–09; sectoral GDP increased by 3.2% in 2008, but declined by 3.3% in 2009.

Manufacturing contributed 14.7% of GDP in 2009. In that year the sector engaged 10.5% of the employed labour force. The principal branches of manufacturing were food products, beverages and tobacco, machinery and industrial chemicals. During 2001–09 manufacturing GDP increased, in real terms, at an average annual rate of 3.8%. The sector's GDP increased by 4.9% in 2008, but decreased by 0.1% in 2009.

Construction contributed 5.5% of GDP and engaged 4.7% of the employed labour force in 2009. During 2001–09 construction GDP increased, in real terms, at an average annual rate of 7.1%. The sector's GDP increased by 0.6% in 2009.

Energy is derived principally from petroleum and natural gas. In 2010 Cuba produced approximately 3.0m. metric tons of crude petroleum and 1,072.5m. cu m of natural gas. Imports of mineral fuels accounted for 29.7% of the total cost of imports in 2009. In 2005 Cuba was one of the signatories to the PetroCaribe accord, under which Caribbean nations could purchase petroleum from Venezuela at reduced prices. In 2008 the country generated 97% of its electricity requirement from petroleum. In early 2012 exploratory drilling for petroleum began at a site off the north coast of the island. The operation was led by Spanish company Repsol YPF, using a rig built in the People's Republic of China. The consortium also included the Russian state company Gazpromneft and Norway's Statoil.

Services accounted for 73.3% of GDP in 2009 when the sector engaged 63.9% of the total employed force. Tourism is one of the country's principal sources of foreign exchange, earning an estimated US $2,080m. in 2009, and development of the sector remained a priority of the Government. In 2010 tourist arrivals reached 2.5m., a slight increase on the 2.4m. recorded in the previous year. In real terms, the GDP of the services sector increased at an average rate of 7.0% per year during 2001–09. The GDP of the services sector increased by 2.6% in 2009.

In 2007 Cuba recorded a trade deficit of 6,252.7m. pesos, and a surplus of 488.5m. pesos on the current account of the balance of payments. In 2009 the principal source of imports was Venezuela (29.2%), followed by China and Spain. Venezuela was also the principal market for exports, accounting for 18.5% of the total, followed by China, Canada and the Netherlands. The principal imports in 2009 were mineral fuels, lubricants and related products and machinery and transport equipment. The principal exports in that year were metalliferous ores and metal scrap (mainly nickel) and chemicals and related products.

In 2010 Cuba recorded a budget deficit of 2,202.7m. pesos. The country's external debt totalled US $19,440m. at the end of 2009, according to media reports. In 2007 an accord was reached between Cuba and Russia on the restructuring of Cuba's post-Soviet debt to Russia, estimated at $166m.; however, the agreement did not cover Cuba's debt to the USSR, which was put at $26,000m. In 2004 a deal signed between the Governments of Cuba and China provided for a 10-year postponement of payments on the debt owed by the former to the latter. According to official figures, 1.7% of the labour force were unemployed in 2009. Although no index of consumer prices is published, official estimates put inflation at 0.3% in 1999.

The accession of Raúl Castro to the presidency in 2008 precipitated a number of significant economic reforms. Residents were also permitted access to tourist facilities. However, as all such non-essential goods and services were priced in convertible pesos, they generally remained affordable only to Cubans with access to foreign currency. To improve productivity salary controls were removed and performance-related bonuses were instigated. Elsewhere, the authorities sought to reduce the dependence of the economy on food imports by allocating unused arable land to private farmers. In the second half of 2010 Castro announced a series of measures aimed at improving productivity, reducing the role of the state and expanding the private sector (see Contemporary Political History): 500,000 public sector employees were redundant, while self-employment and the creation of small businesses and co-operations were encouraged. Although the implementation of the reforms progressed more slowly than anticipated, the number of self-employed people increased to some 364,000 in late 2011, compared with 143,800 in 2009. Further reforms took effect in late 2011, including the legalization of trade in cars and property, the provision of loans to privately run businesses and, with the aim of increasing domestic agricultural production, amid a sharp rise in the cost of food imports, a further easing of restrictions on farmers. According to official figures, GDP growth increased to an estimated 2.7% in 2011.

PUBLIC HOLIDAYS

2013: 1 January (Liberation Day), 2 January (Armed Forces' Victory Day), 1 May (Labour Day), 25–27 July (Anniversary of the 1953 Revolution), 10 October (Wars of Independence Day), 25 December (Christmas Day), 31 December (New Year's Eve).

Statistical Survey

Sources (unless otherwise stated): Cámara de Comercio de la República de Cuba, Calle 21, No 661/701, esq. Calle A, Apdo 4237, Vedado, Havana; tel. (7) 830-4436; fax (7) 833-3042; e-mail pdcia@camara.com.cu; internet www.camaracuba.cu; Oficina Nacional de Estadísticas, Calle Paseo 60, entre 3 y 5, Plaza de la Revolución, Vedado, Havana, CP 10400; tel. (7) 830-0053; fax (7) 833-3083; e-mail oneweb@one.gov.cu; internet www.one.cu.

Area and Population

AREA, POPULATION AND DENSITY

Area (sq km)	109,886*
Population (census results)	
11 September 1981	9,723,605
7–16 September 2002	
Males	5,597,233
Females	5,580,510
Total	11,177,743
Population (official estimates at 31 December)	
2008	11,236,099
2009	11,242,628
2010	11,241,161
Density (per sq km) at 31 December 2010	102.3

* 42,427 sq miles.

POPULATION BY AGE AND SEX

(official estimates at 31 December 2010)

	Males	Females	Total
0–14	1,003,575	942,867	1,946,442
15–64	3,853,804	3,905,884	7,859,688
65 and over	671,617	763,414	1,435,031
Total	5,628,996	5,612,165	11,241,161

PROVINCES

(official population estimates at 31 December 2010)

	Area (sq km)	Population	Density (per sq km)	Capital (population)
Camagüey	15,615.0	780,598	50.7	Camagüey (305,845)
Ciego de Avila	6,783.1	424,245	60.9	Ciego de Avila (110,422)

—continued	Area (sq km)	Population	Density (per sq km)	Capital (population)
Cienfuegos	4,180.0	407,189	97.2	Cienfuegos (144,207)
Ciudad de la Habana*	721.0	2,135,498	2,932.3	—
Granma	8,375.5	836,366	99.9	Bayamo (147,563)
Guantánamo	6,168.0	511,116	82.9	Guantánamo (207,857)
La Habana*	5,731.6	749,289	130.9	—
Holguín	9,292.8	1,037,573	112.6	Holguín (277,050)
Isla de la Juventud	2,419.3	86,420	35.7	Nueva Gerona (47,070)
Matanzas	11,802.7	692,536	58.7	Matanzas (132,665)
Pinar del Río	10,904.0	728,297	66.8	Pinar del Río (137,523)
Sancti Spíritus	6,736.5	465,674	68.7	Sancti Spíritus (98,794)
Santiago de Cuba	6,156.4	1,047,963	168.3	Santiago de Cuba (425,851)
Las Tunas	6,587.8	538,062	81.6	Las Tunas (153, 982)
Villa Clara	8,412.4	800,335	95.1	Santa Clara (205,812)
Total	109,886.2	11,241,161	102.3	—

* Ciudad de la Habana is the capital of La Habana province, but also a province in its own right.

From 1 January 2011 La Habana province was divided into two new provinces, Artemisa and Mayabeque, and Ciudad de la Habana province was renamed La Habana.

PRINCIPAL TOWNS

(estimated population at 31 December 2010)

La Habana (Havana, the capital)	2,135,498	Las Tunas	153,982
Santiago de Cuba	425,851	Bayamo	147,563
Camagüey	305,845	Cienfuegos	144,207
Holguín	277,050	Pinar del Río	137,523
Guantánamo	207,857	Matanzas	132,665
Santa Clara	205,812	Ciego de Avila	110,422

Note: Havana contained 12 municipalities with populations exceeding 100,000 at 31 December 2008; other highly populated municipalities included Cárdenas (109,097, Province of Matanzas), Manzanillo (131,425, Province of Granma), Palma Soriano and Contramaestre (123,064 and 104,575, respectively, Province of Santiago de Cuba) and Mayarí (103,884, Province of Holguín).

BIRTHS, MARRIAGES AND DEATHS*

	Registered live births†		Registered marriages‡		Registered deaths	
	Number	Rate (per 1,000)	Number	Rate (per 1,000)	Number	Rate (per 1,000)
2003	136,795	12.2	54,739	4.9	78,434	7.0
2004	127,192	11.3	50,878	4.5	81,110	7.2
2005	120,716	10.7	51,831	4.6	84,824	7.5
2006	111,323	9.9	56,377	5.0	80,831	7.2
2007	112,472	10.0	56,781	5.1	81,927	7.3
2008	122,569	10.9	61,852	5.5	86,423	7.7
2009	130,036	11.6	54,969	4.9	86,940	7.7
2010	127,746	11.4	58,490	5.2	91,048	8.1

* Data are tabulated by year of registration rather than by year of occurrence.

† Births registered in the National Consumers Register, established on 31 December 1964.

‡ Including consensual unions formalized in response to special legislation.

Life expectancy (years at birth, WHO estimates): 78 (males 76; females 80) in 2009 (Source: WHO, *World Health Statistics*).

ECONOMICALLY ACTIVE POPULATION

('000 persons aged 15 years and over, official estimates)

	2008	2009	2010
Agriculture, hunting, forestry and fishing	919.1	945.6	921.5
Mining and quarrying	26.7	27.0	33.7
Manufacturing	543.1	530.8	486.6
Electricity, gas and water	79.8	90.3	101.6
Construction	245.2	239.1	224.5
Trade, restaurants and hotels	610.2	628.2	641.9
Transport, storage and communications	301.4	297.1	304.5
Financing, insurance, real estate and business services	123.0	118.5	116.2
Community, social and personal services	2,099.7	2,195.8	2,154.0
Total employed	4,948.2	5,072.4	4,984.5
Unemployed	79.7	86.1	81.0
Total labour force	5,027.9	5,158.5	5,065.5

CIVILIAN EMPLOYMENT IN THE STATE SECTOR

('000 persons)

	1998	1999	2000
Agriculture, hunting, forestry and fishing	733.1	714.4	714.2
Mining and quarrying	47.3	20.8	20.8
Manufacturing	458.9	512.7	512.6
Electricity, gas and water	46.0	51.0	51.0
Construction	178.9	167.1	167.8
Trade, restaurants and hotels	355.2	375.2	375.2
Transport, storage and communications	175.2	157.4	157.4
Financing, insurance, real estate and business services	47.6	54.3	54.3
Community, social and personal services	964.5	952.1	951.8
Total	3,006.7	3,005.0	3,005.1

Health and Welfare

KEY INDICATORS

Total fertility rate (children per woman, 2009)	1.5
Under-5 mortality rate (per 1,000 live births, 2009)	6
HIV/AIDS (% of persons aged 15–49, 2009)	0.1
Physicians (per 1,000 head, 2002)	5.9
Hospital beds (per 1,000 head, 2006)	4.9
Health expenditure (2008): US $ per head (PPP)	495
Health expenditure (2008): % of GDP	12.0
Health expenditure (2008): public (% of total)	95.5
Access to water (% of persons, 2008)	94
Access to sanitation (% of persons, 2008)	91
Total carbon dioxide emissions ('000 metric tons, 2007)	27,033.0
Carbon dioxide emissions per head (metric tons, 2007)	2.4
Human Development Index (2011): ranking	51
Human Development Index (2011): value	0.776

For sources and definitions, see explanatory note on p. vi.

Agriculture

PRINCIPAL CROPS

('000 metric tons)

	2008	2009	2010
Rice, paddy	436.0	563.6	454.4
Maize	325.7	304.8	324.5
Potatoes	196.1	278.6	191.5
Sweet potatoes	375.0	437.1	384.7
Cassava (Manioc)	339.6	315.8	405.6
Yautia (Cocoyam)	240.0	199.4	137.4

—continued	2008	2009	2010
Sugar cane	15,700.0	14,900.0	11,300.0
Beans, dry	97.2	110.8	80.4
Groundnuts, in shell*	8.5	6.3	5.8
Coconuts	105.6	78.1	72.1
Cabbages and other brassicas	186.7	160.3	134.6
Tomatoes	575.9	750.0	517.0
Pumpkins, squash and gourds	422.5	413.2	347.1
Cucumbers and gherkins	139.3	110.4	92.7
Chillies and peppers, green	63.7	56.7	47.6
Onions, dry	128.1	131.3	111.7
Garlic	34.8	40.2	33.8
Watermelons	60.4	61.9	52.0
Cantaloupes and other melons*	53.3	55.7	46.8
Bananas	280.8	245.4	249.2
Plantains	477.4	425.0	485.8
Oranges	200.4	261.0	178.3
Tangerines, mandarins, clementines and satsumas	19.9	27.2	23.0
Lemons and limes	5.4	8.3	6.1
Grapefruit and pomelos	166.1	121.5	137.7
Guavas, mangoes and mangosteens	228.7	269.3	203.6
Pineapples	55.4	70.9	64.8
Papayas	89.4	95.7	135.7
Coffee, green†	6.2	8.0	9.8
Tobacco, unmanufactured	21.5	25.2	20.5

* FAO estimates.

† Unofficial figures.

Aggregate production ('000 metric tons, may include official, semi-official or estimated data): Total cereals 762.2 in 2008, 868.7 in 2009, 779.1 in 2010; Total roots and tubers 1,392.5 in 2008, 1,565.6 in 2009, 1,515.0 in 2010; Total vegetables (incl. melons) 2,492.6 in 2008, 2,604.5 in 2009, 2,187.8 in 2010; Total fruits (excl. melons) 1,809.3 in 2008, 1,784.5 in 2009, 1,794.7 in 2010.

Source: FAO.

LIVESTOCK

('000 head, year ending September)

	2008	2009	2010
Cattle	3,821.3	3,892.8	3,992.5
Horses	534.0	573.8	613.6
Mules	20.5	20.3	20.3
Pigs	1,878.6	1,767.8	1,591.0
Sheep	2,675.0	2,584.1	2,361.9
Goats	1,134.0	1,110.2	938.1
Chickens	29,201	30,817	30,950

Source: FAO.

LIVESTOCK PRODUCTS

('000 metric tons)

	2008	2009	2010
Cattle meat	62.0	65.0	63.5
Pig meat	192.7	178.9	172.3
Chicken meat	33.1	33.2	33.6
Cows' milk	545.5	600.3	629.5
Hen eggs	102.4	106.8	106.9
Honey	5.1	5.2	4.7

Source: FAO.

Forestry

ROUNDWOOD REMOVALS

('000 cubic metres, excl. bark, FAO estimates)

	2006	2007	2008
Sawlogs, veneer logs and logs for sleepers	400	400	400
Other industrial wood	361	361	361
Fuel wood	1,818	1,413	1,273
Total	2,579	2,174	2,034

2009–10: Production assumed to be unchanged from 2008 (FAO estimates).

Source: FAO.

SAWNWOOD PRODUCTION

('000 cubic metres, incl. railway sleepers)

	2007	2008	2009
Coniferous (softwood)	135	115	119
Broadleaved (hardwood)	60	51	52
Total	195	166	171

2010: Production assumed to be unchanged from 2009 (FAO estimates).

Source: FAO.

Fishing

('000 metric tons, live weight)

	2007	2008	2009
Capture	33.7	30.7	28.9
Blue tilapia	3.1	2.8	2.5
Lane snapper	1.3	1.6	1.3
Caribbean spiny lobster	4.8	5.7	4.1
Aquaculture*	33.2	34.5	36.2
Silver carp	19.9	20.2	17.4
Total catch*	66.9	65.2	65.1

* FAO estimates.

Note: Figures exclude sponges (metric tons): 38 in 2007; 46 in 2008; 46 in 2009.

Source: FAO.

Mining

('000 metric tons unless otherwise indicated)

	2008	2009	2010
Crude petroleum	3,003.1	2,731.3	3,024.8
Natural gas (million cu metres)	1,161.0	1,155.3	1,072.5
Nickel (metal content)	3,289.5	3,949.0	2,511.0

Chromite: 27.9 in 2006.

Industry

SELECTED PRODUCTS

('000 metric tons unless otherwise indicated)

	2008	2009	2010
Crude steel	273.8	265.8	277.6
Grey cement	1,705.2	1,625.7	1,631.4
Corrugated asbestos-cement tiles	5,660.2	5,948.7	5,430.8
Colour television sets ('000)	94.2	79.4	46.5
Fuel oil	2,667.8	2,629.3	2,435.9
New tyres ('000)	66.4	42.8	57.4
Recapped tyres ('000)	67.6	56.9	90.2
Woven textile fabrics (million sq metres)	31.6	28.1	25.6
Cigarettes ('000 million)	14.2	13.4	13.1
Cigars (million)	386.7	375.2	375.6
Alcoholic beverages (excl. wines, '000 litres)	1,100.1	990.2	1,102.8
Beer ('000 hectolitres)	2,508.2	2,474.4	2,586.3
Soft drinks ('000 hectolitres)	3,713.3	3,747.5	3,669.9
Bicycles ('000)	53.3	36.4	28.2
Fishing vessels	927	263	14
Electric energy (million kWh)	17,681.3	17,727.1	17,395.5

Finance

CURRENCY AND EXCHANGE RATES

Monetary Units
100 centavos = 1 Cuban peso.
1 Cuban peso = 1 convertible peso (official rate).

Sterling, Dollar and Euro Equivalents (30 December 2011)
£1 sterling = 1.432 convertible pesos;
US $1 = 0.926 convertible pesos;
€1 = 1.198 convertible pesos;
100 convertible pesos = £69.86 = $108.00 = €83.47.

Note: The foregoing information relates to official exchange rates. For the purposes of foreign trade, the peso was at par with the US dollar during each of the 10 years 1987–96. In addition, a 'convertible peso' was introduced in December 1994. Although officially at par with the Cuban peso, in March 2005 the 'unofficial' exchange rate prevailing in domestic exchange houses was adjusted to 24 pesos per convertible peso.

STATE BUDGET
(million pesos)

Revenue	2008	2009	2010*
Tax revenue	25,847.0	25,447.7	24,835.0
Road and sales tax	13,219.9	12,791.0	11,342.4
Taxes on services	1,460.4	1,543.2	1,647.0
Taxes on utilities	2,950.0	2,660.7	2,811.5
Taxes on labour	3,956.2	4,267.7	4,593.0
Personal income tax	453.4	465.4	508.7
Other taxes	1,216.5	956.7	951.3
Social security contributions	2,590.6	2,763.0	2,981.1
Non-tax revenue	16,535.6	18,468.2	18,550.5
Transfers from state enterprises	3,240.0	3,100.4	3,256.9
Other non-tax revenue	13,295.6	15,367.8	15,293.6
Restitution payments	–327.0	–320.4	–320.4
Total	42,055.6	43,595.5	43,065.1

Expenditure	2008	2009	2010*
Current expenditure	41,755.5	41,800.0	41,770.8
Education	7,503.4	9,030.6	9,904.0
Public health	7,188.6	6,610.3	6,823.7
Defence and public order	2,036.8	2,126.2	2,206.1
Social security	4,400.0	4,704.0	4,900.0
Administration	1,456.5	1,525.9	1,522.3
Community services	1,688.8	1,717.2	1,664.6
Industry	2,108.5	2,157.3	801.7
Art and culture	1,314.9	1,327.2	1,321.5
Science and technology	570.3	603.6	663.6
Sport	547.2	617.9	717.8
Social assistance	940.2	934.0	885.8
Other activities	1,910.1	1,675.3	1,609.0
Subsidies, etc. to state enterprises	8,632.0	7,462.1	7,150.7
Subsidy for losses	1,053.0	n.a.	n.a.
Subsidy for price differentials	2,212.0	n.a.	n.a.
Others	5,367.0	n.a.	n.a.
Financial operations	1,300.0	1,308.4	1,400.0
Adjustment	158.0	—	200.0
Investment expenditure	4,500.0	4,811.2	3,237.0
Reserves	—	—	260.0
Total	46,255.6	46,611.2	45,267.8

* Approved budgetary proposal.

INTERNATIONAL RESERVES
(million pesos at 31 December)

	1987	1988
Gold and other precious metals	17.5	19.5
Cash and deposits in foreign banks (convertible currency)	36.5	78.0
Sub-total	54.0	97.5
Deposits in foreign banks (in transferable roubles)	142.5	137.0
Total	196.5	234.5

MONEY SUPPLY
(million pesos)

	2007	2008	2009
Currency in circulation	10,566.2	11,579.7	10,874.7
Savings	11,293.4	13,946.6	15,186.2
Total	21,859.6	25,526.3	26,060.9

NATIONAL ACCOUNTS
(million pesos at current prices)

Composition of Gross National Product

	2007	2008	2009
Compensation of employees	20,385.7	21,729.1	23,006.1
Operating surplus / Consumption of fixed capital	24,295.1	25,077.8	24,263.8
Gross domestic product (GDP) at factor cost	44,680.8	46,806.9	47,269.9
Indirect taxes, less subsidies	13,923.1	13,999.4	15,008.7
GDP in purchasers' values	58,603.9	60,806.3	62,278.6
Less Factor income paid abroad (net)	959.7	1,055.2	1,643.0
Gross national product	57,644.2	59,751.1	60,635.6

Expenditure on the Gross Domestic Product

	2007	2008	2009
Government final consumption expenditure	20,751.5	24,250.0	23,957.1
Private final consumption expenditure	30,299.4	29,829.5	30,009.3
Increase in stocks	289.7	2,443.0	652.2
Gross fixed capital formation	5,678.0	6,583.5	5,772.9
Total domestic expenditure	57,018.6	63,106.0	60,391.5
Exports of goods and services	11,917.9	12,506.4	11,170.6
Less Imports of goods and services	10,332.6	14,806.1	9,283.5
GDP in purchasers' values	58,603.9	60,806.3	62,278.6
GDP at constant 1997 prices	43,883.3	45,689.9	46,352.0

Gross Domestic Product by Economic Activity

	2007	2008	2009
Agriculture, hunting, forestry and fishing	2,290.3	2,321.0	2,439.5
Mining and quarrying	539.3	596.6	594.1
Manufacturing	8,307.9	8,682.7	9,060.5
Electricity, gas and water	1,137.3	1,029.7	1,000.3
Construction	3,217.2	3,303.4	3,377.0
Wholesale and retail trade, restaurants and hotels	14,989.5	14,457.8	14,432.8
Transport, storage and communications	4,562.6	4,927.4	5,150.6
Finance, insurance, real estate and business services	2,659.7	2,763.9	2,798.3
Community, social and personal services	20,239.9	21,827.9	22,797.5
Sub-total	57,943.7	59,910.4	61,650.6
Import duties	660.2	895.9	628.0
Total	58,603.9	60,806.3	62,278.6

BALANCE OF PAYMENTS
(million pesos)

	1999	2000	2001
Exports of goods	1,456.1	1,676.8	1,661.5
Imports of goods	–4,365.4	–4,876.7	–4,838.3
Trade balance	–2,909.3	–3,117.2	–3,076.2
Services (net)	2,162.7	2,223.0	2,212.8
Balance on goods and services	–746.6	–894.2	–863.4
Other income (net)	–514.1	–622.2	–502.2
Balance on goods, services and income	–1,260.7	–1,516.4	–1,365.6
Current transfers (net)	798.9	740.4	812.9
Current balance	–461.8	–776.0	–552.7
Direct investment (net)	178.2	448.1	38.9
Other long-term capital (net)	31.7	570.3	328.3
Other capital (net)	275.0	–213.0	227.3
Overall balance	23.1	29.4	41.8

2005 (million pesos): Exports of goods 2,159.4; Imports of goods –7,604.3; Goods acquired at seaports and airports 210.2; *Trade balance* –5,234.7; Services (net) 6,375.2; *Balance on goods and services* 1,140.5; Income (net) –633.2; Current transfers (net) –367.2; *Current balance* –140.1.

2006 (million pesos): Exports of goods 2,924.6; Imports of goods –9,497.9; Goods acquired at seaports and airports 243.0; *Trade balance* –6,330.3; Services (net) 6,456.0; *Balance on goods and services* 125.7; Income (net) –618.0; Current transfers (net) 277.7; *Current balance* –214.6.

2007 (million pesos): Exports of goods 3,701.4; Imports of goods –10,082.6; Goods acquired at seaports and airports 128.5; *Trade balance* –6,252.7; Services (net) 7,899.9; *Balance on goods and services* 1,647.2; Income (net) –959.7; Current transfers (net) –199.0; *Current balance* 488.5.

External Trade

PRINCIPAL COMMODITIES
('000 pesos)

Imports c.i.f.	2007	2008	2009
Food and live animals	1,548,923	2,205,342	1,494,102
Cereals and cereal preparations	671,795	1,128,738	647,682
Wheat and meslin (unmilled)	164,256	272,702	189,806
Rice	229,239	478,830	238,411
Mineral fuels, lubricants, etc.	2,382,884	4,561,798	2,648,703
Chemicals and related products	825,901	1,179,997	817,956
Basic manufactures	1,101,795	1,548,650	1,049,942
Iron and steel	223,017	318,408	264,254
Manufactures of metal	293,134	399,335	282,463
Machinery and transport equipment	3,005,681	3,154,618	1,784,808
Power-generating machinery and equipment	546,495	538,726	211,395
General industrial machinery and equipment and machine parts	487,243	686,096	423,087
Total (incl. others)	10,082,557	14,234,094	8,909,541

Exports f.o.b.	2007	2008	2009
Food and live animals	325,794	340,067	306,711
Fish, crustaceans and molluscs and preparations thereof	83,389	73,758	46,573
Fresh, chilled or frozen fish	82,363	73,620	46,471
Fruit and vegetables	32,011	26,271	27,881
Sugar, sugar preparations and honey	200,861	233,425	225,057
Beverages and tobacco	288,671	318,000	281,872
Crude materials (inedible) except fuels	2,143,823	1,483,700	880,434
Metalliferous ores and metal scrap	2,140,044	1,479,917	873,777
Chemicals and related products	332,286	347,929	567,775
Basic manufactures	117,162	137,887	100,518
Iron and steel	56,901	76,905	44,942
Machinery and transport equipment	171,714	164,454	169,362
Miscellaneous manufactured articles	139,433	58,417	61,312
Total (incl. others)	3,685,665	3,664,157	2,879,036

PRINCIPAL TRADING PARTNERS
('000 pesos)

Imports c.i.f.	2007	2008	2009
Algeria	225,469	243,698	169,163
Argentina	146,036	125,305	117,599
Brazil	382,087	600,141	508,913
Canada	436,723	655,778	291,834
Chile	74,522	73,990	52,999
China, People's Republic	1,518,084	1,480,791	1,171,485
Colombia	71,674	69,005	49,790
France	166,659	226,737	139,678
Germany	371,730	377,617	275,306
Italy	391,063	488,408	323,651
Japan	224,428	153,304	88,506
Mexico	204,703	369,144	303,485
Netherlands Antilles	882	698	249
Russia	291,788	268,745	195,406
Spain	982,305	1,232,473	752,536
Venezuela	2,243,242	4,473,223	2,604,988
Viet Nam	281,430	514,342	276,117
Total (incl. others)	10,079,210	14,234,094	8,909,541

Exports f.o.b.	2007	2008	2009
Belgium	17,253	10,849	8,218
Brazil	64,293	41,679	69,356
Canada	962,966	756,622	434,396
China, People's Republic	928,320	677,107	516,504
Dominican Republic	32,757	46,061	21,578
France	68,461	45,897	45,472
Germany	24,259	27,041	29,440
Japan	12,467	9,289	5,691
Mexico	14,975	14,160	14,502
Netherlands	435,514	288,599	236,853
Portugal	24,143	47,534	21,335
Russia	70,570	55,961	87,683
Spain	172,533	194,802	154,664
Switzerland	12,472	15,235	14,506
Venezuela	450,397	413,781	533,148
Total (incl. others)	3,685,665	3,664,157	2,879,036

Transport

RAILWAYS

	2008	2009	2010
Passenger-kilometres (million)	1,057	980	892
Freight ton-kilometres (million)	1,388	2,791	1,852

ROAD TRAFFIC
(motor vehicles in use at 31 December)

	1996	1997
Passenger cars	216,575	172,574
Buses and coaches	28,089	28,861
Lorries and vans	246,105	156,634

2007–08: Passenger cars 236,881; Buses and coaches 19,740; Lorries and vans 171,081; Motorcycles and mopeds 217,141.

Source: IRF, *World Road Statistics*.

SHIPPING

Merchant Fleet
(registered at 31 December)

	2007	2008	2009
Number of vessels	68	67	65
Total displacement ('000 grt)	61	60	44

Source: IHS Fairplay, *World Fleet Statistics*.

International Sea-borne Freight Traffic
('000 metric tons)

	2008	2009	2010
Goods loaded	2,556	2,376	2,520
Goods unloaded	10,188	8,724	9,252

Source: UN, *Monthly Bulletin of Statistics*.

CIVIL AVIATION
(traffic on scheduled services)

	2004	2005	2006
Kilometres flown (million)	21	22	22
Passengers carried ('000)	743	813	812
Passenger-kilometres (million)	2,241	2,422	2,337
Total ton-kilometres (million)	246	263	254

Source: UN, *Statistical Yearbook*.

2007: Passengers carried ('000) 857.2 (Source: World Bank, World Development Indicators database).

2008: Passengers carried ('000) 861.4 (Source: World Bank, World Development Indicators database).

2009: Passengers carried ('000) 780.5 (Source: World Bank, World Development Indicators database).

Tourism

ARRIVALS BY COUNTRY OF RESIDENCE*

	2008	2009	2010
Canada	818,246	914,884	945,248
France	90,731	83,478	80,470
Germany	100,964	93,437	93,136
Italy	126,042	118,347	112,298
Mexico	84,052	61,487	66,650
Spain	121,166	129,224	104,948
United Kingdom	193,932	172,318	174,343
USA	41,904	52,455	63,046
Venezuela	31,931	28,657	30,965
Total (incl. others)	2,348,340	2,429,809	2,531,745

* Figures include same-day visitors (excursionists).

Tourism receipts (US $ million, excl. passenger transport): 2,141 in 2007; 2,258 in 2008; 2,080 in 2009 (provisional) (Source: World Tourism Organization).

Communications Media

	2008	2009	2010
Telephones ('000 main lines in use)	1,088.1	1,119.8	1,163.6
Mobile cellular telephones ('000 subscribers)	331.7	621.2	1,003.0
Internet subscribers ('000)	n.a.	39.9	40.1
Broadband subscribers ('000)	2.2	2.9	3.7

Radio receivers ('000 in use): 3,900 in 1997.

Television receivers ('000 in use): 2,800 in 2000.

Book production: 1,004 titles published in 2001.

Daily newspapers: 2 in 2004 (average estimated circulation 727,600 copies).

Personal computers: 630,000 (56.2 per 1,000 persons) in 2008.

Sources: UNESCO, *Statistical Yearbook*; UN, *Statistical Yearbook*; International Telecommunication Union.

Education

(2010/11)

	Institutions	Teachers	Students
Pre-primary	1,110*	9,417	113,659
Primary	7,244	115,494	788,117
Secondary	1,840	102,091	834,307
Tertiary	64	65,489	473,309

* 2008/09 figure.

Pupil-teacher ratio (primary education, UNESCO estimate): 9.1 in 2009/10 (Source: UNESCO Institute for Statistics).

Adult literacy rate (UNESCO estimates): 99.8% (males 99.8%; females 99.8%) in 2009 (Source: UNESCO Institute for Statistics).

Directory

The Government

Head of State: Gen. Raúl Castro Ruz (took office 24 February 2008).

COUNCIL OF STATE

President: Gen. Raúl Castro Ruz.

First Vice-President: José Ramón Machado Ventura.

Vice-Presidents: Juan Esteban Lazo Hernández, Lt-Gen. Abelardo Colomé Ibarra, Ramiro Valdes Menéndez, Gladys Bejerano Portela.

Secretary: Homero Acosta Alvarez.

Members: José Ramón Balaguer Cabrera, Roberto Fernández Retamar, Lt-Gen. Leopoldo Cintra Frías, Orlando Lugo Fonte, Tania León Silveira, Lt-Gen. Álvaro López Miera, Inés María Chapman Waugh, Iris Betancourt Téllez, Guillermo García Frías, María Yolanda Ferrer Gómez, Regla Dayamí Armenteros Mesa, Dignora Montano Perdomo, Salvador Antonio Valdés Mesa, María del Carmen Concepción González, Juan José Rabilero Fonseca, Surina Acosta Brook, Liudmila Alamo Dueñas, Isis Angelina Diez Duardo, Kirenia Díaz Burke, Marino Alberto Murillo Jorge, Sergio Juan Rodrígiez Morales.

COUNCIL OF MINISTERS
(May 2012)

The Government is formed by the Partido Comunista de Cuba.

President: Gen. Raúl Castro Ruz.

Secretary: Brig.-Gen. José Amado Ricardo Guerra.

First Vice-President: José Ramón Machado Ventura.

The Gambia: Calle 24, No 307, entre 3 y 5, Miramar, Havana; tel. and fax (7) 204-9242; e-mail mofacuba@ceniai.inf.cu; Ambassador YUSUPHA BABOUCARR DIBBA.

Germany: Calle 13, No 652, esq. B, Vedado, Havana; tel. (7) 833-2569; fax (7) 833-1586; e-mail info@havanna.diplo.de; internet www.havanna.diplo.de; Ambassador WOLF DAERR.

Ghana: Avda 5, No 1808, esq. 20, Miramar, Havana; tel. (7) 204-2153; fax (7) 204-2317; e-mail chancery@ghanaembassy.cu; internet www.ghanaembassy.cu; Ambassador DAVID SARPONG BOTENG.

Greece: Avda 5, No 7802, esq. 78, Miramar, Havana; tel. (7) 204-2995; fax (7) 204-9770; e-mail gremb@enet.cu; Ambassador PANTELIS CARCABASSIS.

Grenada: Avda 5, No 2006, entre 20 y 22, Miramar, Havana; tel. (7) 204-6764; fax (7) 204-6765; e-mail embgranada@enet.cu; Ambassador RAPHAEL JOSEPH.

Guatemala: Calle 20, No 301, entre 3 y 5, Miramar, Havana; tel. (7) 204-3417; fax (7) 204-8173; e-mail embagucu@ceniai.inf.cu; Ambassador HERBERT ESTUARDO MENECES CORONADO.

Guinea: Calle 20, No 504, entre 5 y 7, Miramar, Havana; tel. (7) 292-9212; fax (7) 204-1894; e-mail ambaguineehav@yahoo.com; Ambassador HADIATOU SOW.

Guinea-Bissau: Avda 5, No 8203, entre 82 y 84, Miramar, Havana; tel. (7) 204-5742; fax (7) 204-2794; e-mail embaguib@enet.cu; Ambassador ABEL COELHO MENDONÇA.

Guyana: Calle 18, No 506, entre 5 y 7, Miramar, Havana; tel. (7) 204-2094; fax (7) 204-2867; e-mail embguyana@enet.cu; Ambassador Dr MITRADEVI ALI.

Haiti: Avda 7, No 4402, esq. 44, Miramar, Havana; tel. (7) 204-5421; fax (7) 204-5423; e-mail embhaiti@enet.cu; internet www.embhaiti.cu; Ambassador JEAN VICTOR GENEUS.

Holy See: Calle 12, No 514, entre 5 y 7, Miramar, Havana (Apostolic Nunciature); tel. (7) 204-2700; fax (7) 204-2257; e-mail csa@pcn.net; Apostolic Nuncio BRUNO MUSARÒ (Titular Archbishop of Abari).

Honduras: Edif. Santa Clara, 1°, Of. 121 Centro de Negocios Miramar, Calle 3a No 123, entre 78 y 80 Calles, Miramar, Havana; tel. (7) 204-5496; fax (7) 204-5497; e-mail embhocu@enet.cu; Ambassador ALAMS ARMANDO ESPINAL ZUNIGA.

Hungary: Calle G, No 458, entre 19 y 21, Vedado, Havana; tel. (7) 833-3365; fax (7) 833-3286; e-mail mission.hav@kum.hu; internet www.mfa.gov.hu/kulkepviselet/cu/hu; Ambassador MIKLÓS DEÁK.

India: Calle 21, No 202, esq. K, Vedado, Havana; tel. (7) 833-3777; fax (7) 833-3287; e-mail hoc@indembassyhavana.cu; internet www.indembassyhavana.cu; Ambassador DEEPAK KISHINCHAND BHOJWANI.

Indonesia: Avda 5, No 1607, esq. 18, Miramar, Havana; tel. (7) 204-9618; fax (7) 204-9617; e-mail indonhav@ceniai.inf.cu; internet www.indohav.cu; Ambassador TEISERAN FOUN CORNELIS.

Iran: Avda 5, No 3002, esq. 30, Miramar, Havana; tel. (7) 204-2675; fax (7) 204-2770; e-mail embairan@enet.cu; Ambassador ALI CHEGENI.

Italy: Avda 5, No 402, esq. 4, Miramar, Havana; tel. (7) 204-5615; fax (7) 204-5659; e-mail ambasciata.avana@esteri.it; internet www.amblavana.esteri.it; Ambassador MARCO BACCIN.

Jamaica: Calle 22, No 503, entre 5 y 7, Miramar, Havana; tel. (7) 204-2908; fax (7) 204-2531; e-mail embjmcub@enet.cu; Ambassador A'DALE GEORGE ROBINSON.

Japan: Centro de Negocios Miramar, Avda 3, Edif. 1, 5°, esq. 80, Miramar, Havana; tel. (7) 204-3355; fax (7) 204-8902; e-mail taisi@ceniai.inf.cu; internet www.cu.emb-japan.go.jp; Ambassador MASUO NISHIBAYASHI.

Korea, Democratic People's Republic: Calle 17 y Paseo, No 752, Vedado, Havana; tel. (7) 833-2313; fax (7) 833-3073; e-mail dprkorcuba@enet.cu; Ambassador JON YONG JIN.

Laos: Avda 5, No 2808, esq. 30, Miramar, Havana; tel. (7) 204-1057; fax (7) 204-9622; e-mail embalao@enet.cu; Ambassador KHAMPO KYAKHAMPHITOUNE.

Lebanon: Calle 17A, No 16403, entre 164 y 174, Siboney, Havana; tel. (7) 208-6220; fax (7) 208-6432; e-mail lbcunet@ceniai.inf.cu; Ambassador JEAN MACARON.

Libya: Avda 7, No 1402, esq. 14, Miramar, Havana; tel. (7) 204-2192; fax (7) 204-2991; e-mail oficinalibia@ip.etecsa.cu; Ambassador ALI MOHAMED AHMED AJEILI.

Malaysia: Avda 5, No 6612, entre 66 y 68, Miramar, Havana; tel. (7) 204-8883; fax (7) 204-6888; e-mail malhavana@kln.gov.my; internet www.kln.gov.my/perwakilan/havana; Ambassador JOJIE SAMUEL.

Mali: Calle 36A, No 704, entre 7 y 42, Miramar, Havana; tel. (7) 204-5321; fax (7) 204-5320; e-mail ambamali@ceniai.inf.cu; Ambassador MODIBO DIARRA.

Mexico: Calle 12, No 518, esq. Avda 7, Miramar, Playa, Havana; tel. (7) 204-2553; fax (7) 204-2717; e-mail embamex@embamexcuba.org; internet www.sre.gob.mx/cuba; Ambassador ENRIQUE GABRIEL JIMÉNEZ REMUS.

Mongolia: Calle 66, No 505, esq. 5A, Miramar, Havana; tel. (7) 204-2763; fax (7) 204-0639; e-mail embahavana@ceniai.inf.cu; Ambassador OTGONBAYARYN DAVAASAMBUU.

Mozambique: Avda 7, No 2203, entre 22 y 24, Miramar, Havana; tel. (7) 204-2443; fax (7) 204-2232; e-mail embamoc@ceniai.inf.cu; Ambassador MIGUEL COSTA MKAIMA.

Namibia: Calle 36, No 504, entre 5 y 5A, Miramar, Havana; tel. (7) 204-1430; fax (7) 204-1431; e-mail embnamibia@embnam.co.cu; Ambassador HOPELONG UUSHONA IPINGE.

Netherlands: Calle 8, No 307, entre 3 y 5, Miramar, Havana; tel. (7) 204-2511; fax (7) 204-2059; e-mail hav@minbuza.nl; internet cuba.nlambassade.org; Ambassador RONALD MUYZERT.

Nicaragua: Calle 20, No 709, entre 7 y 9, Miramar, Havana; tel. (7) 204-1025; fax (7) 204-5387; e-mail nicaragua@embnicc.co.cu; Ambassador LUIS CABRERA GONZÁLEZ.

Nigeria: Avda 5, No 1401, entre 14 y 16, Miramar, Havana; tel. (7) 204-2898; fax (7) 204-2202; e-mail chancery@nigeria-havana.com; Ambassador LARABA ELSIE BINTA BHUTTO.

Norway: Calle 30, No 315, entre 3 y 5, Miramar, Havana; tel. (7) 204-0696; fax (7) 204-0699; e-mail emb.havana@mfa.no; internet www.noruega-cuba.org; Ambassador JOHN PETTER OPDAHL.

Panama: Calle 26, No 109, entre 1 y 3, Miramar, Havana; tel. (7) 204-0858; fax (7) 204-1674; e-mail panaemba_cuba@panaemba.co.cu; Ambassador MARIO RAFAEL GÁLVEZ EVERS.

Paraguay: Calle 34, No 503, entre 5 y 7, Miramar, Havana; tel. (7) 204-0884; fax (7) 204-0883; e-mail cgphav@enet.cu; Ambassador LUIS DOMINGO LAINO GUANES.

Peru: Calle 30, No 107, entre 1 y 3, Miramar, Havana; tel. (7) 204-2632; fax (7) 204-2636; e-mail embaperu@embaperu.org; Ambassador VÍCTOR RICARDO MAYORGA MIRANDA.

Philippines: Avda 5, No 2207, esq. 24, Miramar, Havana; tel. (7) 204-1372; fax (7) 204-2915; e-mail philhavpe@enet.cu; Ambassador Dr WILFREDO D. MAXIMO.

Poland: Calle G, No 452, esq. 19, Vedado, Havana; tel. (7) 833-2439; fax (7) 833-2442; e-mail hawana.amb.sekretariat@msz.gov.pl; Ambassador MALGORZATA GALINSKA-TOMASZEWSKA.

Portugal: Avda 7, No 2207, esq. 24, Miramar, Havana; tel. (7) 204-0149; fax (7) 204-2593; e-mail embpthav@embporthavana.org; Ambassador LUIS JOSÉ MOREIRA DA SILVA BARREIROS.

Qatar: Avda 3, No 3407, entre 34 y 36, Miramar, Havana; tel. (7) 204-0587; fax (7) 204-0003; e-mail embajada@qatar.co.cu; Ambassador ALI BIN SAAD AL-KHARJI.

Romania: Calle 21, No 307, entre H y I, Vedado, Havana; tel. (7) 833-3325; fax (7) 833-3324; e-mail erumania@ceniai.inf.cu; Ambassador DUMITRU PREDA.

Russia: Avda 5, No 6402, entre 62 y 66, Miramar, Havana; tel. (7) 204-2686; fax (7) 204-1038; e-mail embrusia@newmail.cu; internet www.cuba.mid.ru; Ambassador MIKHAIL L. KAMYNIN.

Saint Lucia: Centro de Negocios Miramar, Edif. Jerusalen, Calle 3, No 403, entre 78 y 80, Miramar, Havana; tel. (7) 206-9609; fax (7) 206-9610; Ambassador Dr JOVITA ST. MARTHE.

Saint Vincent and the Grenadines: Centro de Negocios Miramar, Edif. Jerusalén, Of. 403, Avda 3 y Calle 80, Miramar, Havana; tel. (7) 206-9783; fax (7) 206-9782; e-mail embsvg@mtc.co.cu; Ambassador DEXTER E. M. ROSE.

Serbia: Avda 5, No 4406, entre 44 y 46, Miramar, Havana; tel. (7) 204-2488; fax (7) 204-2982; e-mail ambsrbhav@embajadaserbia.co.cu; Ambassador MARINA PEROVIĆ PETROVIĆ.

Slovakia: Calle 66, No 521, entre 5B y 7, Miramar, Havana; tel. (7) 204-1884; fax (7) 204-1883; e-mail embeslovaca@mzv.sk; Ambassador ZDENEK ROZHOLD.

South Africa: Avda 5, No 4201, esq. 42, Miramar, Havana; tel. (7) 204-9671; fax (7) 204-1101; e-mail mision@sudafrica.cu; Ambassador PHATSE JUSTICE PIITSO.

Spain: Cárcel No 51, esq. Zulueta, Havana; tel. (7) 866-8025; fax (7) 866-8006; e-mail emb.lahabana@maec.es; Ambassador MANUEL CACHO QUESADA.

Sri Lanka: Avda 5, No 3004, entre 30 y 32, Miramar, Havana; tel. (7) 204-2562; fax (7) 204-2183; e-mail sri.lanka@enet.cu; Charge d'affaires a.i. WARUNA WILPATHA.

Suriname: Edif. Jerusalén, Of. 106, Centro de Negocios de Miramar, Calle 3, entre 78 y 80, Playa, Miramar, Havana; tel. (7) 207-9559; fax (7) 207-9561; e-mail secembsur@mtc.co.cu; Ambassador IKE DESMOND ANTONIUS.

Sweden: Calle 34, No 510, entre 5 y 7, Miramar, Havana; tel. (7) 204-2831; fax (7) 204-1194; e-mail ambassaden.havanna@foreign.ministry.se; internet www.swedenabroad.com/havanna; Ambassador CAROLINE FLEETWOOD.

Switzerland: Avda 5, No 2005, entre 20 y 22, Miramar, Havana; tel. (7) 204-2611; fax (7) 204-1148; e-mail hav.vertretung@eda.admin.ch; internet www.eda.admin.ch/havana; Ambassador PETER BURKHARD.

Syria: Calle 20, No 514, entre 5 y 7, Miramar, Havana; tel. (7) 204-2266; fax (7) 204-9754; e-mail embsiria@ceniai.inf.cu; Ambassador (vacant).

Timor-Leste: Calle 40A, No 301, esq. 3, Miramar, Havana; tel. (7) 206-9911; e-mail embtimor@enet.cu; Ambassador OLIMPIO BRANCO.

Trinidad and Tobago: Avda 5, No 6603, entre 66 y 68, Miramar, Havana; tel. (7) 207-9603; fax (7) 207-9604; e-mail ttmissionscuba@enet.cu; Ambassador JENNIFER JONES-KERNAHAN.

Turkey: Avda 5, No 3805, entre 36 y 40, Miramar, Havana; tel. (7) 204-1204; fax (7) 204-2899; e-mail turkemb@gmail.com; Ambassador INCY TUMAY.

Ukraine: Avda 5, No 4405, entre 44 y 46, Miramar, Havana; tel. (7) 204-2586; fax (7) 204-2341; e-mail emb_cu@mfa.gov.ua; internet www.mfa.gov.ua/cuba; Ambassador TETIANA G. SAIENKO.

United Kingdom: Calle 34, No 702/4, esq. 7 y 17, Miramar, Havana; tel. (7) 214-2200; fax (7) 214-2218; e-mail embrit@ceniai.inf.cu; internet ukincuba.fco.gov.uk; Ambassador DIANNA MELROSE.

USA (Relations severed in 1961): Interests Section in the Embassy of Switzerland: Calzada, entre L y M, Vedado, Havana; tel. (7) 833-3551; fax (7) 833-1084; e-mail irchavana@state.org; internet havana.usinterestsection.gov; Principal Officer JOHN CAULFIELD.

Uruguay: Calle 36, No 716, entre 7 y 17, Miramar, Havana; tel. (7) 204-2311; fax (7) 206-9683; e-mail urucub@rou.co.cu; Ambassador ARIEL BERGAMINO.

Venezuela: Edif. Beijing, 2°, Centro de Negocios Miramar, Avda 3, entre 74 y 76, Miramar, Havana; tel. (7) 204-2612; fax (7) 204-9790; e-mail embajada@venezuela.co.cu; internet www.venezuelaencuba.co.cu; Ambassador RONALDO BLANCO LA CRUZ.

Viet Nam: Avda 5, No 1802, esq. 18, Miramar, Havana; tel. (7) 204-1525; fax (7) 204-5333; e-mail embavina@embavicu.org; internet www.vietnamembassy-cuba.org; Ambassador VU CHI CONG.

Yemen: Avda 5, No 8201, entre 82 y 84, Miramar, Havana; tel. (7) 204-1506; fax (7) 204-1131; e-mail gamdan-hav@enet.cu; Ambassador YAHYA MOHAMED AHMED AL-SYAGHI.

Zimbabwe: Avda 3, No 1001, entre 10 y 12, Miramar, Havana; tel. (7) 204-2857; fax (7) 204-2720; e-mail zimhavan@enet.cu; Ambassador JOHN SHUMBA MVUNDURA.

Judicial System

The judicial system comprises the People's Supreme Court, the People's Provincial Courts and the People's Municipal Courts. The People's Supreme Court exercises the highest judicial authority.

Public Prosecutor: JUAN ESCALONA REGUERA.

PEOPLE'S SUPREME COURT

The People's Supreme Court comprises the Plenum, the six Courts of Justice in joint session and the Council of Government. When the Courts of Justice are in joint session they comprise all the professional and lay judges, the Attorney-General, and the Minister of Justice. The Council of Government comprises the President and Vice-Presidents of the People's Supreme Court, the Presidents of each Court of Justice, and the Attorney-General of the Republic. The Minister of Justice may participate in its meetings.

President: Dr RUBÉN REMIGIO FERRO.

Vice-Presidents: OSVALDO SÁNCHEZ MARTÍN, EMILIA GONZÁLEZ PÉREZ, EDUARDO RODRÍGUEZ GONZÁLEZ.

Criminal Court

President: CARLOS ZARAGOZA PUPO.

Civil and Administrative Court

President: CARLOS M. DÍAZ TENREIRO.

Labour Court

President: Dr ANTONIO RAUDILLO MARTÍN SÁNCHEZ.

Court for State Security

President: PLÁCIDO BATISTA VERANES.

Economic Court

President: NARCISO COBO ROURA.

Military Court

President: Col JUAN MARINO FUENTES CALZADO.

Religion

There is no established Church, and all religions are permitted, though Roman Catholicism predominates. The Afro-Cuban religions of Regla de Ocha (Santería) and Regla Conga (Palo Monte) also have numerous adherents.

CHRISTIANITY

Consejo de Iglesias de Cuba (CIC) (Cuban Council of Churches): Calle 14, No 304, entre 3 y 5, Miramar, Playa, Havana; tel. (7) 204-2878; fax (7) 204-1755; e-mail iglesias@enet.cu; f. 1941; 25 mem. churches; Pres. Rev. MARCIAL MIGUEL HERNÁNDEZ SALAZAR.

The Roman Catholic Church

Cuba comprises three archdioceses and eight dioceses. Adherents represent some 53% of the total population.

Conferencia de Obispos Católicos de Cuba (COCC) (Bishops' Conference)

Calle 26, No 314, entre 3 y 5, Miramar, Apdo 635, 11300 Havana; tel. (7) 29-2298; fax (7) 24-2168; e-mail cocc@iglesiacatolica.cu; internet www.iglesiacubana.org.

f. 1983; Pres. DIONISIO GUILLERMO GARCÍA IBÁÑEZ (Archbishop of Santiago de Cuba).

Archbishop of Camagüey: JUAN GARCÍA RODRÍGUEZ, Calle Luaces, No 55, Apdo 105, 70100 Camagüey; tel. (32) 229-2268; fax (32) 228-7143; e-mail arzcam@cocc.co.cu.

Archbishop of San Cristóbal de la Habana: Cardinal JAIME LUCAS ORTEGA Y ALAMINO, Calle Habana No 152, esq. a Chacón, Apdo 594, 10100 Havana; tel. (7) 862-4000; fax (7) 866-8109; e-mail cocc@brigadoo.com.

Archbishop of Santiago de Cuba: DIONISIO GUILLERMO GARCÍA IBÁÑEZ, Sánchez Hechevarría No 607, Apdo 26, 90100 Santiago de Cuba; tel. (226) 25480; fax (226) 86186.

The Anglican Communion

Anglicans are adherents of the Iglesia Episcopal de Cuba (Episcopal Church of Cuba).

Bishop of Cuba: Rt Rev. MIGUEL TAMAYO ZALDÍVAR, Calle 6, No 273, Vedado, 10400 Havana; tel. (7) 832-1120; fax (7) 334-3293; e-mail episcopal@ip.etecsa.cu; internet www.cuba.anglican.org.

Other Christian Churches

Iglesia Metodista en Cuba (Methodist Church in Cuba): Calle K, No 502, 25 y 27, Vedado, 10400 Havana; tel. (7) 832-2991; fax (7) 832-0770; e-mail imecu@enet.cu; internet www.imecu.com; autonomous since 1968; 215 churches, 17,000 mems (2005); Bishop RICARDO PEREIRA DÍAZ.

Iglesia Presbiteriana Reformada en Cuba (Presbyterian-Reformed Church in Cuba): Salud 222, entre Lealtad y Campanario, 10200 Havana; tel. (7) 862-1219; fax (7) 866-8819; e-mail presbit@enet.cu; internet www.prccuba.org; f. 1890; 8,000 mems; Moderator Rev. Dr HÉCTOR MÉNDEZ.

Other denominations active in Cuba include the Apostolic Church of Jesus Christ, the Bethel Evangelical Church, the Christian Pentecostal Church, the Church of God, the Church of the Nazarene, the Free Baptist Convention, the Holy Pentecost Church, the Pentecostal Congregational Church and the Salvation Army. Membership of evangelical churches increased from the late 20th century—in 2010 there were an estimated 800,000 adherents, according to the Consejo de Iglesias de Cuba.

The Press

DAILIES

Granma: Avda Gen. Suárez y Territorial, Plaza de la Revolución, Apdo 6187, CP 10699, Havana; tel. (7) 881-3333; fax (7) 881-9854; e-mail english@granma.cip.cu; internet www.granma.cubaweb.cu; f. 1965, to replace *Hoy* and *Revolución*; official Communist Party organ; Dir-Gen. LÁZARO BARREDO MEDINA; Editor-in-Chief OSCAR SÁNCHEZ SERRA; circ. 400,000.

Juventud Rebelde: Avda Territorial y Gen. Suárez, Plaza de la Revolución, Apdo 6344, CP 10600, Havana; tel. (7) 882-0155; fax (7) 883-8959; e-mail lectores@juventudrebelde.cu; internet www.juventudrebelde.cu; f. 1965; organ of the Young Communist League; Dir PELAYO TERRY CUERVO; circ. 250,000.

PERIODICALS

Adelante: Salvador Cisneros Betancourt 306, Camagüey; e-mail cip222@cip.enet.cu; internet www.adelante.cu; f. 1959; Dir Dr C. SANTIAGO LAJES CHOY; Editor JORGE LUIS PEIX AGÜERO; circ. 42,000.

Ahora: Salida a San Germán y Circunvalación, Holguín; e-mail director@ahora.cu; internet www.ahora.cu; f. 1962; Dir RODOBALDO MARTÍNEZ PÉREZ; Chief Editor JORGE L. CRUZ BERMÚDEZ; circ. 50,000.

Alma Mater: Prado 553, esq. Teniente Rey, Habana Vieja, Havana; e-mail almamater@editoraabril.co.cu; internet www.almamater.cu; f. 1922; aimed at a student readership; Chief Editor MIRIAM ANCÍZAR.

ANAP: Calle I, No 206, entre Línea y 13, Vedado, Havana; e-mail revista@anap.org.cu; internet www.campesinocubano.anap.cu; f. 1961; 6 a year; organ of the Asociación Nacional de Agricultores Pequeños; information for small farmers; Dir FÉLIX SIMÓN SANTA CRUZ; circ. 90,000.

Bohemia: Avda Independencia y San Pedro, Apdo 6000, Havana; tel. (7) 81-9213; fax (7) 33-5511; e-mail bohemia@bohemia.co.cu; internet www.bohemia.cu; f. 1908; fortnightly; politics; Dir JOSÉ FERNÁNDEZ VEGA; circ. 100,000.

El Caimán Barbudo: Casa Editora Abril, Prado 553, entre Dragones y Teniente Rey, Vedado, Havana; e-mail caimanbarbudo@editoraabril.co.cu; internet www.caimanbarbudo.cu; f. 1966; monthly; cultural; Dir FIDEL DÍAZ CASTRO; Editor RAFAEL GRILLO; circ. 47,000.

Cinco de Septiembre: Avda 54, No 3516, entre 35 y 37, CP 55100, Cienfuegos; tel. (43) 52-2144; e-mail admin@gmail.com; internet www.5septiembre.cu; f. 1980; Dir ALINA ROSELL CHONG; circ. 18,000.

Dedeté: Territorial y Gen. Suárez, Plaza de la Revolución, Apdo 6344, Havana; tel. (7) 82-0134; fax (7) 81-8621; e-mail contacto@dedete.cu; internet www.dedete.cu; f. 1969; weekly; humorous supplementary publ. of Juventud Rebelde; Dir ADÁN IGLESIAS TOLEDO; circ. 70,000.

La Demajagua: Amado Estévez, esq. Calle 10, Rpto R. Reyes, Bayamo; tel. (23) 42-4221; e-mail cip225@cip.enet.cu; internet www.lademajagua.co.cu; f. 1977; Dir LUIS CARLOS FRÓMETA AGÜERO; Editor GISLANIA TAMAYO CEDEÑO; circ. 21,000.

El Deporte, Derecho del Pueblo: Vía Blanca y Boyeros, Havana; tel. (7) 40-6838; f. 1968; monthly; sports supplement of *Granma*; Dir MANUEL VAILLANT CARPENTE; circ. 15,000.

El Economista de Cuba: Asociación Nacional de Economistas y Contadores de Cuba, Calle 22, No 901 esq. a 901, Miramar, Havana; tel. (7) 209-3303; fax (7) 202-3456; e-mail presidencia@anec.co.cu; internet www.eleconomista.cubaweb.cu; monthly; business; Dir-Gen. ROBERTO VERRIER CASTRO; Editor MAGALY GARCÍA MORÉ.

Escambray: Adolfo del Castillo 10, Sancti Spíritus; tel. (41) 32-3003; e-mail cip220@cip.enet.cu; internet www.escambray.cu; f. 1979 as daily; weekly from 1992; serves Sancti Spíritus province; Dir JUAN ANTONIO BORREGO DÍAZ; circ. 21,000.

Girón: Avda Camilo Cienfuegos No 10505, P. Nuero, Matanzas; e-mail cip217@cip.enet.cu; internet www.giron.co.cu; f. 1960; organ of the Communist Party in Matanzas province; Dir CLOVIS ORTEGA CASTAÑEDA; circ. 25,000.

Guerrillero: Colón 12 entre Juan Gualberto Gómez y Adela Azcuy, CP 20100, Pinar del Río; e-mail cip216@cip.enet.cu; internet www.guerrillero.co.cu; f. 1969; organ of Communist Party in Pinar del Río province; Dir ERNESTO OSORIO ROQUE; Editor MARLON RODRÍGUEZ ESTUPIÑÁN; circ. 33,000.

El Habanero: Gen. Suárez y Territorial, Plaza de la Revolución, Apdo 6187, Havana; e-mail internet@habanero.cip.cu; internet www.elhabanero.cubaweb.cu; f. 1987; Dir ANDRÉS HERNÁNDEZ RIVERO; circ. 21,000.

Invasor: Avda de los Deportes s/n, Ciego de Avila; e-mail cip221@cip.enet.cu; internet www.invasor.cu; f. 1979; provincial periodical; Dir MIGDALIA UTRERA PEÑA; Editor ROBERTO CARLOS DELGADO BURGOS; circ. 10,500.

Juventud Técnica: Prado 553, esq. Teniente Rey, Habana Vieja, Havana; tel. (7) 62-4330; e-mail jtecnica@editoraabril.co.cu; internet www.juventudtecnica.cu; f. 1965; every 2 months; scientific-technical; Dir IRAMIS ALONSO PORRO; Editor DANIA RAMOS; circ. 20,000.

Mar y Pesca: San Ignacio 303, entre Amargura y Teniente Rey, Habana Vieja, 10100 Havana; tel. (7) 861-5518; fax (7) 861-6280; e-mail revist@marypesca.cu; internet www.marypesca.cu; f. 1965; quarterly; fishing; Dir PEDRO PÉREZ BORDÓN; circ. 20,000.

Muchacha: Galiano 264, entre Neptuno y Concordia, CP 10200, Havana; tel. (7) 861-5919; f. 1980; monthly; young women's magazine; published by the Cuban Women's Federation; Dir IVETTE VEGA; circ. 120,000.

Mujeres: Galiano 264, entre Neptuno y Concordia, CP 10200, Havana; tel. (7) 861-5919; e-mail mujeres@enet.cu; internet www.mujeres.cubaweb.cu; f. 1961; weekly; organ of the Cuban Women's Fed; Dir-Gen. ISABEL MOYA RICHARD; circ. 270,000.

El Nuevo Fenix: Independencia 52, esq. Honorato del Castillo, Sancti Spíritus; tel. (41) 327902; e-mail plss@ip.etecsa.cu; internet www.fenix.co.cu; f. 1999; published by Sancti Spíritus bureau of Prensa Latina (see News Agencies); Editor-in-Chief RAÚL I. GARCÍA ALVAREZ.

Opciones: Territorial esq. Gen. Suárez, Plaza de la Revolucíon, Havana; tel. (7) 881-8934; fax (7) 881-8621; e-mail opciones@jrebelde.cip.cu; internet www.opciones.cu; f. 1994; weekly; finance, commerce and tourism; Chief Editor ISABEL FERNÁNDEZ GARRIDO.

Palante: Calle 21, No 954, entre 8 y 10, Vedado, Havana; e-mail cip319@cip.enet.cu; internet www.palante.co.cu; f. 1961; weekly; humorous; Dir PEDRO EMIGDIO VIÑAS ALFONSO; circ. 235,000.

Periódico 26: Avda Carlos J. Finlay s/n, CP 75100, Las Tunas; e-mail cip224@cip.enet.cu; internet www.periodico26.cu; f. 2000; provincial periodical; Dir RAMIRO SEGURA GARCÍA; Chief Editor OSCAR GÓNGORA JORGE.

Pionero: Calle 17, No 354, Havana; tel. (7) 32-4571; e-mail pionero@editoraabril.co.cu; internet www.pionero.cu; f. 1961; monthly; children's magazine; Dir LUCÍA SANZ ARAUJO; circ. 210,000.

Revista Casa: 3 y G, Vedado, CP 10400, Havana; tel. (7) 838-2706; fax (7) 834-4554; e-mail revista@casa.cult.cu; internet www.casadelasamericas.com; f. 1959; 6 a year; Latin American theatre; Dir ROBERTO FERNÁNDEZ RETAMAR.

Sierra Maestra: Avda de Los Desfiles, Santiago de Cuba; e-mail cip226@cip.enet.cu; internet www.sierramaestra.cu; f. 1957; weekly; organ of the PCC in Santiago de Cuba; Dir ARNALDO CLAVEL CARMENATY; circ. 45,000.

Somos Jóvenes: Calle Prado, esq. a Teniente Rey, Havana; tel. (7) 862-5031; e-mail abadell@gmail.com; internet www.somosjovenes.cu; f. 1977; weekly; Dir MARIETTA MANSO MARTÍN; Editor ALICIA CENTELLES; circ. 200,000.

Temas: Calle 23, No 1155, 5º entre 10 y 12, CP 10400, El Vedado, Havana; tel. and fax (7) 838-3010; e-mail temas@iciaic.cu; internet www.temas.cult.cu; f. 1995; quarterly; cultural, political; Dir RAFAEL HERNÁNDEZ; Chief Editor ALFREDO PRIETO.

Trabajadores: Territorial esq. Gen. Suárez, Plaza de la Revolución, CP 10698, Havana; tel. (7) 79-0819; fax (7) 55-5927; e-mail editor@trabaja.cip.cu; internet www.trabajadores.cu; f. 1970; organ of the trade union movt; Dir ALBERTO NÚÑEZ BETANCOURT; Chief Editor RAFAELQ HOJAS MARTÍNEZ; circ. 150,000.

Tribuna de la Habana: Territorial esq. Gen. Suárez, Plaza de la Revolución, Havana; tel. (7) 881-8021; e-mail redac@tribuna.cip.cu; internet www.tribuna.co.cu; f. 1980; weekly; Dir JESÚS ALVAREZ FERRER; circ. 90,000.

Vanguardia: Calle Céspedes 5, esq. Plácido, Santa Clara, CP 50100, Matanzas; e-mail cip218@cip.enet.cu; internet www.vanguardia.co.cu; f. 1962; weekly; Dir F. A. CHANG L.; circ. 45,000.

Venceremos: Avda Ernesto Che Guevara, Km $1\frac{1}{2}$, CP 95400, Guantánamo; tel. (7) 32-7398; e-mail cip227@cip.enet.cu; internet www.venceremos.co.cu; f. 1962; economic, political and social publ. for Guantánamo province; Dir YAMILKA ALVAREZ RAMOS; Editor-in-Chief JORGE CANTALAPIEDRA LUQUE; circ. 33,500.

Victoria: Carretera de la Fe, Km $1\frac{1}{2}$, Plaza de la Revolución, Nueva Gerona, Isla de la Juventud; tel. (46) 32-4210; e-mail cip228@cip.enet.cu; internet www.victoria.co.cu; f. 1967; Dir SERGIO RIVERO CARRASCO; Chief Editor MATILDE CAMPOS JOA; circ. 9,200.

Zunzún: Prado 553, CP 10500, Havana; e-mail zunzun@eabril.jovenclub.cu; internet www.zunzun.cu; f. 1980; children's magazine; Dir ADELA MORO; Chief Editor HÉCTOR QUINTERO.

PRESS ASSOCIATIONS

Unión de Escritores y Artistas de Cuba: Calle 17, No 354, entre G y H, Vedado, Havana; tel. (7) 838-3158; e-mail presidencia@uneac.co.cu; internet www.uneac.org.cu; f. 1961; Pres. MIGUEL BARNET LANZA.

Unión de Periodistas de Cuba (UPEC): Avda 23, No 452, esq. a I, Vedado, CP 10400, Havana; tel. (7) 832-4550; fax (7) 33-3079; e-mail vpetica@upec.co.cu; internet www.cubaperiodistas.cu; f. 1963; Pres. TUBAL PÁEZ HERNÁNDEZ.

NEWS AGENCIES

Agencia de Información Nacional (AIN): Calle 23, No 358, esq. J, Vedado, Havana; tel. (7) 881-6423; fax (7) 66-2049; e-mail igg@ain.cu; internet www.ain.cu; f. 1974; national news agency; Gen. Dir ESTEBAN RAMÍREZ ALONSO.

Prensa Latina (Agencia Informativa Latinoamericana, SA): Calle 23, No 201, esq. N, Vedado, Havana; tel. (7) 838-3496; fax (7) 33-3068; e-mail difusion@prensa-latina.cu; internet www.prensa-latina.cu; f. 1959; Pres. FRANCISCO GONZÁLEZ.

Publishers

Artecubano Ediciones: Calle 3, No 1205, entre 12 y 14, Playa, Havana; tel. (7) 203-8581; fax (7) 204-2744; e-mail cnap@cubarte.cult.cu; attached to the Ministry of Culture; Dir RAFAEL ACOSTA DE ARRIBA.

Casa de las Américas: Calle 3 y Avda G, Plaza de la Revolución, Vedado, 10400 Havana; tel. (7) 838-2706; fax (7) 834-4554; e-mail presidencia@casa.cult.cu; internet www.casadelasamericas.com; f. 1959; Latin American literature and social sciences; Dir ROBERTO FERNÁNDEZ RETAMAR.

Casa Editora Abril: Prado 553, esq. Teniente Rey y Dragones, Habana Vieja, 10200 Havana; tel. (7) 862-5031; fax (7) 862-4330; e-mail webeditora@editoraabril.co.cu; internet www.editoraabril.cu/editora; f. 1980; attached to the Union of Young Communists; cultural, children's literature; Dir NIURKA DUMÉNIGO GARCÍA.

Ediciones Creart: Calle 4, No 205, entre Línea y 11, Plaza de la Revolución, Vedado, Havana; tel. (7) 55-3496; fax (7) 33-3069; e-mail creart@cubarte.cult.cu; f. 1994; Dir TOMÁS VALDÉS BECERRA.

Ediciones Unión: Calle 17, No 354, entre G y H, Plaza de la Revolución, Vedado, 10400 Havana; tel. (7) 55-3112; fax (7) 33-3158; e-mail editora@uneac.co.cu; internet www.uneac.org.cu; f. 1962; publishing arm of the Unión Nacional de Escritores y Artistas de Cuba; Cuban literature, art; Dir OLGA MARTA PÉREZ RODRÍGUEZ.

Ediciones Vigía: Magdalena 1, Plaza de la Vigía, 40100 Matanzas; tel. (452) 44845; e-mail vigia@cult.cu; internet www.atenas.cult.cu/?q=editorialedicionesvigia; f. 1985; Dir AGUSTINA PONCE.

Editora Atril (Ediciones Musicales—ABDALA): Producciones Abdala, SA, Calle 32, No 318, esq. 5 Avda, Miramar, Playa, Havana; tel. (7) 204-5213; fax (7) 204-4006; e-mail atril.abdalal@cimex.com.cu; internet www.abdala.cu; Dir TERESA TORRES PÁEZ.

Editora Política: Belascoaín No 864, esq. Desagüe, Centro Habana, 10300 Havana; tel. (7) 879-8553; fax (7) 55-6836; e-mail editora@epol.cc.cu; internet www.editpolitica.cu; f. 1963; publishing institution of the Communist Party of Cuba; Dir SANTIAGO DÓRQUEZ PÉREZ.

Editorial Academia: Industria y Barcelona, Capitolio Nacional, 4°, Centro Habana, 10200 Havana; tel. and fax (7) 863-0315; e-mail editorial@gecyt.cu; f. 1962; attached to the Ministry of Science, Technology and the Environment; scientific and technical; Dir GLADYS HERNÁNDEZ HERRERA.

Editorial Arte y Literatura: Calle O'Reilly, No 4, esq. Tacón, Habana Vieja, 10100 Havana; tel. (7) 862-4326; fax (7) 833-8187; e-mail publicaciones@icl.cult.cu; internet www.cubaliteraria.cu/editorial/Arte_y_Literatura; f. 1967; traditional Cuban literature and arts; Dir LOURDES GONZÁLEZ CASAS.

Editorial Ciencias Médicas: Edif. Soto, 2°, Calle 23, No 177, entre N y O, Plaza de la Revolución, Vedado, 10400 Havana; tel. (7) 833-0311; fax (7) 33-3063; e-mail ecimed@infomed.sld.cu; internet www.sld.cu/sitios/ecimed; f. 1988; publishing arm of the Centro Nacional de Información de Ciencias Médicas de Cuba; attached to the Ministry of Public Health; books and magazines specializing in the medical sciences; Dir DAMIANA MARTÍN LAURENCIO.

Editorial Félix Varela: San Miguel No 1011, entre Mazón y Basarrate, Plaza de la Revolución, Vedado, 10400 Havana; tel. (7) 877-5617; fax (7) 73-5419; e-mail elsa@enpses.co.cu; Dir ELSA RODRÍGUEZ.

Editorial Gente Nueva: Calle 2, No 58, entre 3 y 5, Plaza de la Revolución, Vedado, 10400 Havana; tel. (7) 833-7676; fax (7) 33-8187; e-mail gentenueva@icl.cult.cu; f. 1967; books for children; Dir ENRIQUE PÉREZ DÍAZ.

Editorial José Martí: Calzada 259, entre I y J, Apdo 4208, Plaza de la Revolución, Vedado, 10400 Havana; tel. (7) 835-1921; fax (7) 33-3441; e-mail editjmal@icl.cult.cu; internet www.cubaliteraria.cu/editorial/editora_marti; f. 1982; attached to the Ministry of Culture; foreign-language publishing; Dir ANA MARÍA DÍAZ CANALS.

Editorial Letras Cubanas: Calle O'Reilly, No 4, esq. Tacón, Habana Vieja, 10100 Havana; tel. (7) 862-4378; fax (7) 66-8187; e-mail elc@icl.cult.cu; internet www.letrascubanas.cult.cu; f. 1977; attached to the Ministry of Culture; general, particularly classic and contemporary Cuban literature and arts; Dir ROGELIO RIVERÓN.

Editorial de la Mujer: Calle Galiano, No 264, esq. Neptuno, Havana; tel. (7) 862-4905; e-mail mujeres@enet.cu; f. 1995; female literature; publishing house of the Cuban Women's Fed; Dir-Gen. ISABEL MOYA RICHARD.

Editorial Nuevo Milenio: Calle 14, No 4104, entre 41 y 43, Playa, Havana; tel. (7) 203-6090; fax (7) 833-3441; e-mail nuevomil@cubarte.cult.cu; internet www.cubaliteraria.cu/editorial/Nuevo Milenio; f. 1967 as Editorial de Ciencias Sociales and Editorial Científico-Técnica; merged and name changed as above in 1999; attached to the Ministry of Culture; technical, scientific and social sciences literature; Dir SONIA ALMAGUER DARNA.

Editorial Oriente: Santa Lucía 356, 90100 Santiago de Cuba; tel. (226) 22496; fax (226) 86111; e-mail edoriente@cultstgo.cult.cu; internet www.cubaliteraria.cu/editorial/editorial_oriente; f. 1971; publishes works from the Eastern provinces; fiction, history, female literature and studies, art and culture, practical books, and books for children; Dir AIDA BAHR.

Editorial Pablo de la Torriente Brau: Calle 11, No 160, entre K y L, Plaza de la Revolución, Vedado, 10400 Havana; tel. (7) 832-7581; fax (7) 33-3079; e-mail pbagenda@ip.etecsa.cu; f. 1985; publishing arm of the Unión de Periodistas de Cuba; Dir IRMA DE ARMAS FONSECA.

Editorial Pueblo y Educación: Avda 3A, No 4601, entre 46 y 60, Playa, Havana; tel. (7) 202-1490; fax (7) 204-0844; e-mail epe@ceniai.inf.cu; f. 1971; textbooks and educational publs; publishes Revista Educación (3 a year, circ. 2,200); Dir CATALINA LAJUD HERRERO.

Editorial Sanlope: Calle Gonzalo de Quesada, No 121, entre Lico Cruz y Lucas Ortiz, Las Tunas; tel. (31) 48191; fax (31) 47380; e-mail librolt@tunet.cult.cu; internet www.tunet.cult.cu/pagsec/institut/sanlope/index.html; f. 1991; attached to the Ministry of Culture; Dir VERENA GARCÍA MIRABAL.

GOVERNMENT PUBLISHING HOUSES

Instituto Cubano del Libro: Palacio del Segundo Cabo, Calle O'Reilly, No 4, esq. Tacón, Habana Vieja, Havana; tel. (7) 862-8091; fax (7) 33-8187; e-mail promocion@icl.cult.cu; internet www.cubaliteraria.cu; f. 1967; printing and publishing org. attached to the Ministry of Culture, which combines several publishing houses and has direct links with others; presides over the National Editorial Council (CEN); organizes the annual Havana International Book Fair; Pres. ZULEICA ROMAY GUERRA.

Oficina Publicaciones del Consejo de Estado: Calle 17, No 552, esq. D, Plaza de la Revolución, Vedado, 10400 Havana; tel. (7) 55-1406; fax (7) 57-5258; e-mail palvarez@ip.etecsa.cu; f. 1972; attached to the Council of State; books, pamphlets and other printed media on historical and political matters; Dir PEDRO ALVAREZ TABÍO.

Broadcasting and Communications

TELECOMMUNICATIONS

Empresa de Telecomunicaciones de Cuba, SA (ETECSA): Edif. Beijing, 5°, Avda 3, entre 76 y 78, Centro de Negocios Miramar, 11300 Havana; tel. (7) 266-8500; fax (7) 860-5144; e-mail atencion_usuarios@etecsa.cu; internet www.etecsa.cu; f. 1991; merged with Empresa de Telecomunicaciones Celulares del Caribe, SA (C-Com) and Teléfonos Celulares de Cuba, SA (CUBACEL) in 2003; Exec. Pres. MAIMIR MESA RAMOS.

Empresa de Transporte de Señales de Telecomunicaciones (Transbit): Havana; state-owned; Pres. WALDO REBOREDO ARROYO.

Instituto de Investigación y Desarrollo de Comunicaciones (LACETEL): Avda Independencia, No 34515, Km 14½, Reparto 1 de Mayo, Rancho Boyeros, CP 19210, Havana; tel. (7) 683-9180; fax (7) 649-5828; e-mail glauco@lacetel.cu; internet www.lacetel.cu; Dir-Gen. GLAUCO GUILLÉN NIETO.

Ministerio de la Informática y las Comunicaciones (Dirección de Regulaciones y Normas): Avda Independencia y 19 de Mayo, Plaza de la Revolución, Havana; tel. (7) 81-7654; e-mail infosoc@mic.cu; internet www.mic.gov.cu; regulatory authority; Dir WILFREDO LÓPEZ.

Telecomunicaciones Móviles, SA (MOVITEL): Avda 47, No 3405, Reparto Kohly, Playa, Havana; tel. (7) 204-8400; fax (7) 204-4264; e-mail movitel@movitel.co.cu; internet www.movitel.co.cu; mobile telecommunications; Dir-Gen. ASELA FERNÁNDEZ LORENZO.

BROADCASTING

Empresa de Radiocomunicación y Difusión de Cuba (RADIOCUBA): Calle Habana 406, entre Obispo y Obrapía, Habana Vieja, Havana; tel. (7) 860-0796; fax (7) 860-3107; e-mail radiocuba@radiocuba.cu; f. 1995; controls the domestic and international broadcast transmission networks; Dir-Gen. JUSTO GERVACIO MORENO GARCÍA.

Instituto Cubano de Radio y Televisión (ICRT): Edif. Radiocentro, Avda 23, No 258, entre L y M, Vedado, Havana 4; tel. (7) 32-1568; fax (7) 33-3107; e-mail icrt@cecm.get.tur.cu; internet www.cubagob.cu/des_soc/icrt; f. 1962; Pres. DANIEL SIRIO.

Radio

In 2009 there were seven national networks and one international network, 18 provincial radio stations and 25 municipal radio stations.

Habana Radio: Edif. Lonja del Comercio, Lamparilla 2, Plaza de San Francisco de Asís, Habana Vieja, Havana; tel. (7) 866-2706; e-mail sitioweb@habradio.ohc.cu; internet www.habanaradio.cu; f. 1999; run by the Oficina del Historiador de la Ciudad de La Habana; cultural and factual programmes; Dir MAGDA RESIK.

Radio Cadena Agramonte: Calle Cisneros, No 310, entre Ignacio Agramonte y General Gómez, 70100 Camagüey; tel. (322) 29-8673;

e-mail cip240@cip.enet.cu; internet www.cadenagramonte.cu; f. 1957; serves Camagüey; Dir ONELIO CASTILLO CORDERÍ.

Radio Enciclopedia: Edif. N, Calle N, No 266, entre 21 y 23, Vedado, 10400 Havana; tel. (7) 838-4586; e-mail lmarquez@renciclopedia.icrt.cu; internet www.radioenciclopedia.cu; f. 1962; national network; instrumental music programmes; 24 hours daily; Dir-Gen. LUISA MÇARQUEZ ECHEVARRIA.

Radio Habana Cuba: Infanta 105, Apdo 6240, Havana; tel. (7) 877-6628; fax (7) 881-2927; e-mail radiohc@enet.cu; internet www.radiohc.cu; f. 1961; shortwave station; broadcasts in Spanish, English, French, Portuguese, Arabic, Esperanto, Quechua, Guaraní and Creole; Dir-Gen. ISIDRO BETANCOURT SILVA.

Radio Musical Nacional (CBMF): Edif. N, Calle N, No 266, entre 21 y 23, Vedado, 10400 Havana; tel. (7) 832-8893; e-mail rmusical@cmbf.icrt.cu; internet www.cmbfradio.cu; f. 1948; national network; classical music programmes; 17 hours daily; Dir OTTO BRAÑA GONZÁLEZ.

Radio Progreso: Infanta 105, esq. a 25, 6°, Apdo 3042, Havana; tel. (7) 877-5519; e-mail paginaweb@rprogreso.icrt.cu; internet www.radioprogreso.cu; f. 1929; national network; mainly entertainment and music; 24 hours daily; Dir-Gen. JOSÉ ANTONIO GUERRA GARCÍA.

Radio Rebelde: Calle 23, No 258, entre L y M, Plaza de la Revolución, Vedado, Apdo 6277, 10400 Havana; tel. (7) 838-4365; fax (7) 33-4270; e-mail smabel@radiorebelde.icrt.cu; internet www.radiorebelde.com.cu; f. 1958; merged with Radio Liberación in 1984; national network; 24-hour news and cultural programmes, music and sports; Dir-Gen. SOFÍA MABEL MANSO DELGADO.

Radio Reloj: Edif. Radiocentro, Calle 23, No 258, entre L y M, Plaza de la Revolución, Vedado, 10400 Havana; tel. (7) 838-4185; fax (7) 838-4225; e-mail relojmailj@rreloj.icrt.cu; internet www.radioreloj.cu; f. 1947; national network; 24-hour news service; Dir OMAIDA ALONSO DIEZCABEZA.

Radio Revolución: Aguilera No 554, entre San Agustín y Barnada, 90100 Santiago de Cuba; tel. (226) 28038; e-mail cip233@cip.enet.cu; internet www.cmkc.cu; serves Santiago de Cuba; Dir ROSA ILEANA NAVARRO PUPO.

Radio Taino: Edif. Radiocentro, Calle 23, No 258, Plaza de la Revolución, entre L y M, Vedado, 10400 Havana; tel. (7) 838-4157; fax (7) 55-4490; e-mail sitioweb@rtaino.icrt.cu; internet www.radiotaino.cu; f. 1985; broadcasts in English and Spanish; Dir MARICELA ESCOTO CAYUSO.

Television

The Cuban Government holds a 19% stake in the regional television channel Telesur (q.v.), based in Caracas, Venezuela.

Instituto Cubano de Radio y Televisión—TV Cubana: Avda 23, No 258, entre L y M, Vedado, 10400 Havana; tel. (7) 55-4059; fax (7) 33-3107; e-mail tvcubana@icrt.cu; internet www.tvcubana.icrt.cu; f. 1950; broadcasts through five national channels—Canal Educativo, Canal Educativo 2, Cubavisión, Multivisión, Tele Rebelde—and 15 provincial channels; Pres. DANIEL SIRIO.

Canal Educativo: Calle P, entre Humbolt y 23, Plaza de la Revolución, Vedado, 10400 Havana; tel. (7) 831-4653; fax (7) 831-4654; e-mail canaleducativo@cedu.icrt.cu; internet www.canaleducativo.cu; f. 2002; broadcasts on channel 13; educational; Dir IVÁN BARRETO.

Cubavisión: Calle M, No 313, Vedado, Havana; e-mail info@cubavision.icrt.cu; internet www.cubavision.cubaweb.cu; broadcasts on channel 6.

Multivisión: f. 2008; broadcasts programmes from foreign networks.

Tele Rebelde: Mazón, No 52, Vedado, Havana; tel. (7) 32-3369; broadcasts on channel 2; Dir MAURICIO NÚÑEZ RODRÍGUEZ.

Finance

(cap. = capital; res = reserves; dep. = deposits; m. = million; brs = branches)

BANKING

All banks were nationalized in 1960. Legislation establishing the national banking system was approved by the Council of State in 1984. A restructuring of the banking system, initiated in 1995, to accommodate Cuba's transformation to a more market-orientated economy, was proceeding. A new central bank, the Banco Central de Cuba (BCC), was created in 1997 to supersede the Banco Nacional de Cuba (BNC). The BCC was to be responsible for issuing currency, proposing and implementing monetary policy, and the regulation of financial institutions. The BNC was to continue functioning as a commercial bank and servicing the country's foreign debt. The restructuring of the banking system also allowed for the creation of an investment bank, the Banco de Inversiones, to provide medium- and long-term financing for investment, and the Banco Financiero Internacional, SA, to offer short-term financing. A new agro-industrial and commercial bank was also to be created to provide services for farmers and co-operatives. The new banking system is under the control of Grupo Nueva Banca, which holds a majority share in each institution. In 2010 there were nine commercial banks, 12 non-banking financial institutions, nine representative offices of foreign banks and two representative offices of non-banking financial institutions operating in Cuba.

Central Bank

Banco Central de Cuba (BCC): Calle Cuba, No 402, Aguiar 411, Apdo 746, Habana Vieja, Havana; tel. (7) 860-4811; fax (7) 863-4061; e-mail webmaster@bc.gov.cu; internet www.bc.gov.cu; f. 1997; sole bank of issue; Pres. ERNESTO MEDINA VILLAVEIRÁN.

Commercial Banks

Banco de Crédito y Comercio (BANDEC): Amargura 158, entre Cuba y Aguiar, Habana Vieja, Havana; tel. (7) 861-4533; fax (7) 866-8968; e-mail ileana@oc.bandec.cu; f. 1997; cap. 740.8m., res 765.7m., dep. 15,140.2m. (Dec. 2009); Pres. ILEANA ESTÉVEZ.

Banco Exterior de Cuba: Calle 23, No 55, esq. P, Vedado, Municipio Plaza, Havana; tel. (7) 55-0795; fax (7) 55-0794; e-mail bec@bec.co.cu; f. 1999; cap. 431.1m. pesos and 18.9m. convertible pesos, total assets 431.4m. pesos and 333.8m. convertible pesos (Dec. 2006); Pres. JACOBO PEISON WEINER.

Banco Financiero Internacional, SA: Avda 5, No 9009, esq. 92, Miramar, Municipio Playa, Havana; tel. (7) 267-5000; fax (7) 267-5002; e-mail bfi@bfi.com.cu; f. 1984; autonomous; finances Cuba's foreign trade; Pres. (vacant); 29 brs.

Banco Industrial de Venezuela-Cuba, SA (BIVC): Edif. Jerusalem, 2°, Of. 201, Centro de Negocios Miramar, Sector Miramar, Havana; tel. (7) 206-9650; f. 2005 as a subsidiary of state-owned Banco Industrial de Venezuela, SA.

Banco Internacional de Comercio, SA: 20 de Mayo y Ayestarán, Apdo 6113, 10600 Havana; tel. (7) 883-6038; fax (7) 883-6028; e-mail bicsa@bicsa.co.cu; f. 1993; cap. 198.7m. convertible pesos, res 24.2m. convertible pesos, dep. 1,877.1m. convertible pesos (Dec. 2006); Chair. and Pres. JOSE JULIO RODRÍGUEZ FALCÓN.

Banco Metropolitano, SA: Avda 5 y Calle 112, Miramar, Municipio Habana Vieja, 11600 Havana; tel. (7) 204-3869; fax (7) 204-9193; e-mail bm@banco-metropolitano.com; internet www.banco-metropolitano.com; f. 1996; offers foreign currency and deposit account facilities; cap. 254.3m., res 36.3m., dep. 11,857.8m. (Dec. 2008); Pres. MANUEL VALE; Dir-Gen. PEDRO DE LA ROSA GONZÁLEZ.

Banco Nacional de Cuba (BNC): Aguiar 456, entre Amargura y Lamparilla, Habana Vieja, Havana; tel. (7) 862-8896; fax (7) 866-9390; e-mail bancuba@bnc.cu; f. 1950; reorganized 1997; Pres. ILEANA MARTÍNEZ.

Savings Bank

Banco Popular de Ahorro: Calle 16, No 306, entre 3ra y 5ta, Playa, Miramar, Havana; tel. (7) 204-2545; fax (7) 204-1180; e-mail presidencia@mail.bpa.cu; f. 1983; savings bank; Pres. JOSÉ LÁZARO ALARI MARTÍNEZ; 520 brs.

Investment Bank

Banco de Inversiones, SA: Avda 5, No 6802 esq. a 68, Miramar, Havana; tel. (7) 204-3374; fax (7) 204-3377; e-mail inversiones@bdi.cu; internet www.bdi.cu; f. 1996; cap. 39.9m., dep. 158.6m. (Dec. 2009), res 5.7m. (Dec. 2008); Exec. Pres. RAÚL E. RANGEL.

INSURANCE

The Superintendencia de Seguros (f. 1997) is the regulatory authority supervising the entities engaged in insurance, reinsurance and auxiliary services of brokers and insurance agents. The insurance market consists of two direct insurance companies, two auxiliary service agencies, two insurance brokers and over 2,000 individuals agents.

State Organizations

Grupo Caudal, SA (Grupo de Seguros y Servicios Financieros de Cuba): Calle 43, No 2210, entre 22 y 24, Playa, Havana; tel. (7) 204-8822; fax (7) 204-8813; e-mail caudal@caudal.cu; management and development of insurance, brokerage and insurance auxiliary services; includes Agencia Internacional de Inspección, Ajuste de Averías y Otros Servicios Conexos (INTERMAR, SA), Asistencia al Turista (ASISTUR), Consultorías y Avalúos (CONAVANA, SA), Empresa Grafica de Finanzas y Precios (EGRAFIP) and INTER-AUDIT, SA; Pres. JOSÉ M. ESCANDELL CÁMBARA.

Empresa del Seguro Estatal Nacional (ESEN): Calle 5, No 306, entre C y D, Vedado, Havana; tel. (7) 832-2500; fax (7) 833-8717; e-mail rfo@esen.com.cu; internet www.ain.cu/publicidad/sitio esen/index.htm; f. 1978; motor and agricultural insurance; Dir-Gen. RAFAEL J. GONZÁLEZ PÉREZ.

Seguros Internacionales de Cuba, SA (Esicuba): Cuba No 314, entre Obispo y Obrapía, Habana Vieja, Havana; tel. (7) 862-8031; fax (7) 866-8038; e-mail esicuba.clientes@esicuba.cu; internet www.esicuba.cu; f. 1963; reorganized 1986; all classes of insurance except life; Dir-Gen. JOSÉ CARLOS MEIJIDES ALFONSO.

Trade and Industry

GOVERNMENT AGENCIES

Ministry of Foreign Trade and Investment: see Ministries.

Centro para la Promoción del Comercio Exterior de Cuba (CEPEC): Infanta 16, esq. 23, 2°, Vedado, Municipio Plaza, Havana; tel. (7) 838-0428; fax (7) 833-2220; e-mail cepecdir@mincex.cu; internet www.cepec.cu; f. 1995; Dir-Gen. RAYSA COSTA BLANCO.

Grupo Empresarial de la Agroindustria Azucarera (AZCUBA): Of. de Comunicación Institucional, Calle 23, No 171, entre N y O, Vedado, Havana; tel. (7) 832-9356; e-mail liobel@ocentral.minaz.cu; f. 2011 to replace the Ministry of Sugar; 13 provincial brs managing 56 sugar mills.

CHAMBER OF COMMERCE

Cámara de Comercio de la República de Cuba: Calle 21, No 661/701, esq. Calle A, Apdo 4237, Vedado, Havana; tel. (7) 830-4436; fax (7) 833-3042; e-mail camaracuba@camara.com.cu; internet www.camaracuba.cu; f. 1963; mems include all Cuban foreign trade enterprises and the most important agricultural and industrial enterprises; Pres. PEDRO ALVAREZ BORREGO; Sec.-Gen. IVÁN MARICHAL AGUILERA.

AGRICULTURAL ORGANIZATION

Asociación Nacional de Agricultores Pequeños (ANAP) (National Association of Small Farmers): Calle I, No 206, entre Linea y 13, Vedado, Havana; tel. (7) 32-4541; fax (7) 33-4244; internet www.campesinocubano.anap.cu; f. 1961; 331,874 mems; Pres. ORLANDO LUGO FONTE; Vice-Pres. EVELIO PAUSA BELLO.

STATE IMPORT-EXPORT BOARDS

Alimport (Empresa Cubana Importadora de Alimentos): Infanta 16, 3°, Apdo 7006, Havana; tel. (7) 54-2501; fax (7) 33-3151; e-mail precios@alimport.com.cu; f. 1962; controls import of foodstuffs and liquors; CEO PEDRO ALVAREZ BORREGO.

Autoimport (Empresa Central de Abastecimiento y Venta de Equipos de Transporte Ligero): Galiano 213, entre Concordia y Virtudes, Habana Vieja, Havana; tel. (7) 61-5322; fax (7) 66-6549; e-mail magda@autoimport.com.cu; imports cars, light vehicles, motor cycles and spare parts; Dir JOSÉ ARAÑABURU.

Aviaimport (Empresa Cubana Importadora y Exportadora de Aviación): Calle 182, No 126, entre 1 y 5, Rpto Flores, Playa, Havana; tel. (7) 273-0077; fax (7) 273-6365; e-mail dcom@aviaimport.avianet.cu; import and export of aircraft and components; Man. Dir MARCOS LAGO MARTÍNEZ.

Caribex (Empresa Comercial Caribe): Avda La Pesquera y Atarés, Puerto Pesquero de La Habana, 3°, Habana Vieja, Havana; tel. (7) 864-4135; fax (7) 864-4144; e-mail caribex@caribex.cu; internet www.caribex.cu; export of seafood and marine products; Dir D. RENÉ BESTEIRO.

Catec (Empresa Cubana Exportadora y Comercializadora de Productos y Servicios de la Ciencia y la Técnica Agraria): Calle 148, No 905, entre 9 y 9A, Rpto Cubanacán, Playa, Havana; tel. (7) 208-2164; fax (7) 204-6071; e-mail alina@catec.co.cu; internet www.catec.cu; exports, imports and markets scientific and technical products relating to the farming and forestry industries; Dir-Gen. OSVALDO CARVEJAL GABELA.

Construimport (Empresa Exportadora e Importadora de Equipos de Construcción): Carretera de Varona, Km 1½, Capdevila, Havana; tel. (7) 645-2567; fax (7) 646-8943; e-mail equipo@construimport.co.cu; internet www.construimport.cubaindustria.cu; f. 1969; controls the import and export of construction machinery and equipment; Gen. Dir DEYSI ROMAY.

Consumimport (Empresa Cubana Importadora de Artículos de Consumo General): Calle 23, No 55, 9°, Apdo 6427, Vedado, Plaza de Revolución, Havana; tel. (8) 36-7717; fax (8) 33-3847; e-mail comer@consumimport.infocex.cu; f. 1962; imports and exports general consumer goods; Dir MERCEDES REY HECHAVARRÍA.

Copextel (Corporación Productora y Exportadora de Tecnología Electrónica): Avda 11, entre 222B y 222C, Siboney, Playa, Havana; tel. (7) 273-0820; fax (7) 273-6540; e-mail copextel@copextel.com.cu; internet www.copextel.com.cu; f. 1985; exports LTEL personal computers and micro-computer software; Dir CIRO MURO.

Coprefil (Empresa Comercial y de Producciones Filatélicas): Avda 49, No 2831, esq. 49A, Rpto Kohly, Playa, Havana; tel. (7) 204-9668; fax (7) 204-5077; e-mail coprefil@coprefil.cu; imports and exports postage stamps, postcards, calendars, handicrafts, communications equipment, electronics, watches, etc.; Dir NELSON IGLESIAS FERNÁNDEZ.

Cubaelectrónica (Empresa Importadora y Exportadora de Productos de la Electrónica): Calle 22, No 510, entre 5 y 7, Miramar, Havana; tel. (7) 204-0178; fax (7) 204-1233; e-mail mariaisabel@columbus.cu; f. 1986; imports and exports electronic equipment and devices; Dir GERARDO LÓPEZ BRITO.

Cubaexport (Empresa Cubana Exportadora de Alimentos y Productos Varios): Calle 23, No 55, entre Infanta y P, 8°, Vedado, Apdo 6719, Havana; tel. (7) 838-0595; fax (7) 833-3587; e-mail cubaexport@cexport.mincex.cu; f. 1965; export of foodstuffs and industrial products; Man. Dir FRANCISCO SANTIAGO PICHARDO.

Cubahidráulica (Empresa Central de Equipos Hidráulicos): Carretera Vieja de Guanabacoa y Linea de Ferrocarril, Rpto Mañana, Guanabacoa, Havana; tel. (7) 797-0821; fax (7) 797-1627; e-mail cubahidraulica@enet.cu; internet www.cubahidraulica.com; f. 1995; imports and exports hydraulic and mechanical equipment, parts and accessories; Dir-Gen. OSMUNDO PAZ PAZ.

Cubametales (Empresa Cubana Importadora de Metales, Combustibles y Lubricantes): Infanta 16, 4°, entre 23 y Humboldt, Apdo 6917, Vedado, Havana; tel. (7) 838-0531; fax (7) 838-0530; e-mail mcarmen@cubametal.mincex.cu; f. 1962; controls import of metals (ferrous and non-ferrous), crude petroleum and petroleum products; also engaged in the export of petroleum products and ferrous and non-ferrous scrap; Dir-Gen. MARY CARMEN ARENCIBIA VÁZQUEZ.

Cubaniquel (Empresa Cubana Exportadora de Minerales y Metales): Carretera Moa, Sagua Km 1½, Moa, CP 83330, Holguín; tel. (24) 60-8283; fax (24) 60-2156; e-mail cceac@cubaniquel.moa.minbas.cu; f. 1961; sole exporter of minerals and metals; Man. Dir ANGEL ROBERTO HERNÁNDEZ.

Cubatabaco (Empresa Cubana del Tabaco): Calle Nueva 75, entre Universidad y Pedroso, Cerro, Havana; tel. (7) 879-0253; fax (7) 33-8214; e-mail cubatabaco@cubatabaco.cu; internet www.cubatabaco.cu; f. 1962; controls export of leaf tobacco, cigars and cigarettes to France; Dir ALFREDO S. CALERO ACOSTA.

Cubazúcar (Empresa Cubana Exportadora de Azúcar y sus Derivados): Calle 23, No 55, 7°, Vedado, Apdo 6647, Havana; tel. (7) 54-2275; fax (7) 33-3482; e-mail producer@cubazucar.com; internet www.cubazucar.com; f. 1962; controls export of sugar, molasses and alcohol; Pres. JOSÉ LÓPEZ SILVERO.

Ecimetal (Empresa Importadora y Exportadora de Objetivos Industriales): Calle 23, No 55, 2°, esq. Plaza, Vedado, Havana; tel. (7) 55-0548; fax (7) 33-4737; e-mail ecimetal@infocex.cu; f. 1977; controls import and export of plant, equipment and raw materials for all major industrial sectors; Dir CONCEPCIÓN BUENO.

Ediciones Cubanas (Empresa de Comercio Exterior de Publicaciones): Obispo 527, esq. Bernaza, Apdo 47, Habana Vieja, Havana; tel. (7) 863-1989; fax (7) 33-8943; e-mail edicuba@cubarte.cult.cu; controls import and export of books and periodicals; Dir ROLANDO VERDÉS PINEDA.

Egrem (Estudios de Grabaciones y Ediciones Musicales): Calle 3, No 1008, entre 10 y 12, Miramar, Playa, Havana; tel. (7) 204-1925; fax (7) 204-2519; e-mail director@egrem.co.cu; internet www.egrem.com.cu; f. 1964; controls the import and export of records, tapes, printed music and musical instruments; Gen. Dir MARIO ESCALONA SERRANO.

Emiat (Empresa Importadora y Exportadora de Suministros Técnicos): Avda 47, No 2828, entre 28 y 34, Rpto Kohly, Havana; tel. (7) 203-0345; fax (7) 204-9353; e-mail emiat@enet.cu; f. 1983; imports technical materials, equipment and special products; exports furniture, kitchen utensils and accessories; Man. FIDEL GARCÍA HERNÁNDEZ.

Emidict (Empresa Especializada Importadora, Exportadora y Distribuidora para la Ciencia y la Técnica): Calle 16, No 102, esq. Avda 1, Miramar, Playa, 13000 Havana; tel. (7) 203-5316; fax (7) 204-1768; e-mail emidict@ceniai.inf.cu; internet www.emidict.com.cu; f. 1982; controls import and export of scientific and technical products and equipment, live animals; scientific information; Dir-Gen. CARLOS CANALES ENRÍQUEZ.

Energoimport (Empresa Importadora de Objetivos Electro-energéticos): Amenidad No 124, entre Nueva y 20 de Mayo, Municipio Cerro, 10600 Havana; tel. (7) 70-2501; fax (7) 66-6079; f. 1977; controls import of equipment for electricity generation; Dir-Gen. ANDRÉS MONTES PEREA.

Eprob (Empresa de Proyectos para las Industrias de la Básica): Avda 31A, No 1805, entre 18 y 20, Edif. Las Ursulinas, Miramar, Playa, Apdo 12100, Havana; tel. (7) 202-5562; fax (7) 204-2146; e-mail direccion@eprob.cu; f. 1967; exports consulting services, processing of engineering construction projects and supplies of complete industrial plants and turnkey projects; Man. Dir GLORIA EXPÓSITO DÍAZ.

Eproyiv (Empresa de Proyectos para Industrias Varias): Calle 31A, No 1815, entre 18 y 20, Playa, Havana; tel. (7) 202-7097; fax (7) 204-2149; e-mail dg-eproyiv@eproyiv.cu; internet www.eproyiv.cu; f. 1967; consulting services, feasibility studies, devt of basic and detailed engineering models, project management and turnkey projects; Dir MARTA ELENA HERNÁNDEZ DÍAZ.

Esi (Empresa de Suministros Industriales): Calle Aguiar, No 556, entre Teniente Rey y Muralla, Habana Vieja, Havana; tel. (7) 62-0696; fax (7) 33-8951; f. 1985; imports machinery, equipment and components for industrial plants; Dir-Gen. FRANCISCO DÍAZ CABRERA.

Fondo Cubano de Bienes Culturales: Calle 36, No 4702, esq. Avda 47, Rpto Kohly, Playa, Havana; tel. (7) 204-6428; fax (7) 204-0391; e-mail fcbc@fcbc.cult.cu; f. 1978; controls export of fine handicrafts and works of art; Dir-Gen. GUILLERMO SOLENZAL MORALES.

Habanos, SA: Avda 3, No 2006, entre 20 y 22, Miramar, Havana; tel. (7) 204-0524; fax (7) 204-0491; e-mail habanos@habanos.cu; internet www.habanos.com; f. 1994; controls export of leaf and pipe tobacco, cigars and cigarettes to all markets; jt venture with Altadis, SA (Spain); Pres. JORGE LUIS FERNÁNDEZ MAIQUE.

ICAIC (Instituto Cubano del Arte e Industria Cinematográficos): Calle 23, No 1155, Vedado, Havana 4; tel. (7) 55-3128; fax (7) 33-3032; e-mail webmaster@icaic.cu; internet www.cubacine.cu; f. 1959; production, import and export of films and newsreel; Dir CAMILO VIVES PALLÉS.

Maprinter (Empresa Cubana Importadora y Exportadora de Materias Primas y Productos Intermedios): Edif. MINCEX, Calle 23, No 55, entre P e Infanta, 8°, Plaza de la Revolución, Vedado, Havana; tel. (7) 878-0711; fax (7) 833-3535; e-mail direccion@maprinter.mincex.cu; internet www.maprinter.cu; f. 1962; controls import and export of raw materials and intermediate products; Dir-Gen. ODALYS ALDAMA VALDÉS.

Maquimport (Empresa Comercializadora de Objetivos Industriales, Maquinarias, Equipos y Artículos de Ferretería): Calle 23, No 55, 6°, entre P e Infanta, Vedado, Apdo 6052, Havana; tel. (7) 838-0635; fax (7) 838-0632; e-mail direccion@maquimport.mincex.cu; imports industrial goods and equipment; Dir ESTHER VERA GONZALEZ.

Medicuba (Empresa Cubana Importadora y Exportadora de Productos Médicos): Máximo Gómez 1, esq. Egido, Habana Vieja, Havana; tel. (7) 862-4061; fax (7) 866-8516; e-mail dirgeneral@medicuba.sld.cu; f. 1962; enterprise for the export and import of medical and pharmaceutical products; Dir-Gen. JORGE LUIS MECÍAS CUBILLA.

Produimport (Empresa Central de Abastecimiento y Venta de Productos Químicos y de la Goma): Calle Consulado 262, entre Animas y Virtudes, Havana; tel. (7) 62-0581; fax (7) 62-9588; f. 1977; imports and exports spare parts for motor vehicles; Dir ARTURO J. CINTRA GÓNGORA.

Propes (Empresa Importadoro y Proveedora de Productos para la Pesca): Calle 22, No 2, esq. Calzada, Vedado, Havana; tel. (7) 830-3770; fax (7) 55-1729; e-mail pesmar@apropes.fishnavy.inf.cu; importer and distributor of a wide variety of equipment and accessories pertaining to the fishing industry; Dir-Gen. PEDRO BLAS ARTEAGA.

Quimimport (Empresa Cubana Importadora y Exportadora de Productos Químicos): Calle 23, No 55, entre Infanta y P, Apdo 6088, Vedado, Havana; tel. (7) 33-3394; fax (7) 33-3190; e-mail global@quimimport.infocex.cu; internet www.quimimport.cu; controls import and export of chemical products; Dir ARMANDO BARRERA MARTÍNEZ.

Suchel (Empresa de Jabonería y Perfumería): Calzada de Buenos Aires 353, esq. a Durege, Apdo 6359, Havana; tel. (7) 649-8008; fax (7) 649-5311; e-mail direccion@suchel.co.cu; f. 1977; imports materials for the detergent, perfumery and cosmetics industry, exports cosmetics, perfumes, hotel amenities and household products; Dir JOSÉ GARCÍA DÍAZ.

Tecnoazúcar (Empresa de Servicios Técnicos e Ingeniería para la Agro-industria Azucarera): Calle 12, No 310, entre 3 y 5, Miramar, Playa, Havana; tel. (7) 29-5441; fax (7) 33-1218; e-mail tecno@tecnoazucar.cu; internet www.tecnoazucar.cu; imports machinery and equipment for the sugar industry; provides technical and engineering assistance for the sugar industry; exports equipment and spare parts for sugar machinery; provides engineering and technical assistance services for sugar-cane by-product industry; Dir-Gen. HÉCTOR COMPANIONI ECHEMENDÍA.

Tecnoimport (Empresa Importadora y Exportadora de Productos Técnicos): Edif. La Marina, Avda del Puerto 102, entre Justiz y Obrapía, Habana Vieja, Havana; tel. (7) 861-5552; fax (7) 66-9777; e-mail celeste@ti.gae.com.cu; f. 1968; imports technical products; Dir ADEL IZQUIERDO RODRÍGUEZ.

Tecnotex (Empresa Cubana Exportadora e Importadora de Servicios, Artículos y Productos Técnicos Especializados): Avda 47, No 3419, Playa, Havana; tel. (7) 861-3536; fax (7) 66-6270; e-mail ailede@tecnotex.qae.com.cu; f. 1983; imports specialized technical and radiocommunications equipment, exports outdoor equipment and geodetic networks; Dir RENÉ ROJAS RODRÍGUEZ.

Tractoimport (Empresa Central de Abastecimiento y Venta de Maquinaria Agrícola y sus Piezas de Repuesto): Avda Rancho Boyeros y Calle 100, Apdo 7007, Havana; tel. (7) 45-2166; fax (7) 267-0786; e-mail direccion@tractoimport.co.cu; f. 1962; import of tractors and agricultural equipment; also exports pumps and agricultural implements; Dir-Gen. ABDEL GARCÍA GONZÁLEZ.

Transimport (Empresa Central de Abastecimiento y Venta de Equipos de Transporte Pesados y sus Piezas): Calle 102 y Avda 63, Marianao, Apdo 6665, 11500 Havana; tel. (7) 260-0329; fax (7) 267-9050; e-mail direccion@transimport.co.cu; internet www.transimport.co.cu; f. 1968; controls import and export of vehicles and transportation equipment; Dir-Gen. JUAN CARLOS TASSÉ BELLOT.

UTILITIES

Electricity

Unión Nacional Eléctrica (UNE): Havana; public utility; Dir-Gen. VICENTE LEVY.

Water

Aguas de la Habana: Fomento y Recreo, Rpto Palatino, Cerro, Havana; tel. and fax (7) 642-4901; e-mail jmtura@ahabana.co.cu; water supplier; Dir-Gen. JOSEP OLLER HERNÁNDEZ.

Instituto Nacional de Recursos Hidráulicos (INRH) (National Water Resources Institute): Calle Humbolt, No 106, esq. a P, Plaza de la Revolución, Vedado, Havana; tel. (7) 836-5571; e-mail gisel@hidro.cu; internet www.hidro.cu; regulatory body; Pres. INÉS MARÍA CHAPMAN WAUGH.

TRADE UNIONS

All workers have the right to become members of a national trade union according to their industry and economic branch.

The following industries and labour branches have their own unions: Agriculture, Chemistry and Energetics, Civil Workers of the Revolutionary Armed Forces, Commerce and Gastronomy, Communications, Construction, Culture, Defence, Education and Science, Food, Forestry, Health, Light Industry, Merchant Marine, Mining and Metallurgy, Ports and Fishing, Public Administration, Sugar, Tobacco, and Transport.

Central de Trabajadores de Cuba (CTC) (Confederation of Cuban Workers): Palacio de los Trabajadores, San Carlos y Peñalver, Havana; tel. (7) 78-4901; fax (7) 55-5927; e-mail cubasindical@ctc.cu; internet www.cubasindical.cu; f. 1939; affiliated to WFTU and CPUSTAL; official organ *Trabajadores*; 19 national trade unions affiliated; Gen. Sec. SALVADOR ANTONIO VALDÉS MESA.

Transport

The Ministry of Transportation controls all public transport.

RAILWAYS

The total length of railways in 2008 was 5,076 km. All railways were nationalized in 1960.

Ferrocarriles de Cuba: Edif. Estación Central, Egido y Arsenal, Havana; tel. (7) 70-1076; fax (7) 33-1489; f. 1960; operates public services; Dir-Gen. MIGUEL ACUÑA FERNÁNDEZ; divided as follows:

División Camilo Cienfuegos: serves part of Havana province and Matanzas.

División Centro: serves Villa Clara, Cienfuegos and Sancti Spíritus.

División Centro-Este: serves Camagüey, Ciego de Avila and Las Tunas.

División Occidente: serves Pinar del Río, Ciudad de la Habana, Havana province and Matanzas.

División Oriente: serves Santiago de Cuba, Granma, Guantánamo and Holguín.

ROADS

In 2001 there were an estimated 60,856 km of roads, of which 4,353 km were highways or main roads. Nearly 50% of the total road network is paved. The Central Highway runs from Pinar del Río in the west to Santiago de Cuba, for a length of 1,144 km. In addition to this highway, there are a number of secondary and 'farm-to-market' roads. A small proportion of these secondary roads is paved, but many can be used by motor vehicles only during the dry season.

SHIPPING

Cuba's principal ports are Havana (which handles 60% of all cargo), Santiago de Cuba, Cienfuegos, Nuevitas, Matanzas, Antilla, Guayabal and Mariel. Maritime transport has developed rapidly since 1959, and at 31 December 2009 Cuba had a merchant fleet of 65 ships (with a combined total displacement of some 43,719 grt). In late 2010 a project to expand the port of Cienfuegos, including the construction of a super-freighter terminal, was announced. In 2012 a US $800m. expansion of the Port of Mariel was under way, funded by a loan from the Brazilian Government. The project, which included expansion of the container and oil logistics port west of Havana, was scheduled to be completed in 2014.

Regulatory Authority

Administración Portuaria Nacional (APN): Calle Oficios 170, entre Teniente Rey y Amargura, Habana Vieja, Havana; tel. (7) 860-5383; internet www.apn.transnet.cu; f. 2005; Dir LUIS MEDINA SOÑARA.

Principal Companies

Consignataria Marítima Caribeña, SA: Quinta Avda, No. 4001, entre 40 y 42, Miramar, Playa, Havana; tel. (7) 204-1226; fax (7) 204-1227; e-mail info@cmc.com.cu; internet www.cmc.com.cu; f. 1996; Pres. ALEJANDRO GONZÁLEZ NEIRA.

Coral Container Lines, SA: Of. 170, 1°, POB 6755, Habana Vieja, Havana; tel. (7) 33-8261; fax (7) 33-8970; e-mail info@coral.com.cu; internet fis.com/coralcontainer; f. 1994; liner services to Europe, Canada, Brazil and Mexico; 11 containers; Dir LUIS RODRÍGUEZ HERNÁNDEZ.

Empresa Consignataria Mambisa: San José No 65, entre Prado y Zulueta, Habana Vieja, Havana; tel. (7) 862-2061; fax (7) 66-8111; e-mail mercedes@mambisa.transnet.cu; shipping agent, bunker suppliers; Man. Dir MERCEDES PÉREZ NEWHALL.

Empresa de Navegación Caribe (Navecaribe): Calle San Martín, No 65, 4°, entre Agramonte y Pasco de Martí, Habana Vieja, Havana; tel. (7) 861-8611; fax (7) 866-8564; e-mail navcar@transnet.cu; f. 1966; operates Cuban coastal fleet; Dir LUIS IRENE RODRÍGUEZ HERNÁNDEZ.

Expedimar, SA: Avda 1, no 1404, entre Calle 14 y 16, 3°, Playa, Havana; tel. (7) 204-2440; fax (7) 204-0080; e-mail expedimar@expedimar.cu; Dir JOSÉ ANTONIO FERNÁNDEZ ESTEVES.

Waterfront AUSA: Centro de Negocios AUSA, Of. 513, Desamparados 166, entre Habana y Compostela, Habana Vieja, Havana; tel. (7) 866-4976; fax (7) 863-5814; e-mail ariel@waterfrontshipping.com; internet www.waterfrontshipping.com; joint venture between Waterfront Shipping Ltd and Almacenes Universales SA.

CIVIL AVIATION

There are a total of 21 civilian airports, with 11 international airports, including Havana, Santiago de Cuba, Camagüey, Varadero and Holguín. Abel Santamaría International Airport opened in Villa Clara in 2001. In 2003 the King's Gardens International Airport in Cayo Coco was opened. The airport formed part of a new tourist 'offshore' centre. The international airports were all upgraded and expanded during the 1990s and a third terminal was constructed at the José Martí International Airport in Havana. In 2001 three North American airlines were permitted to commence direct flights from Miami, FL, and New York, USA, to Havana.

Instituto de Aeronáutica Civil de Cuba (IACC): Calle 23, No 64, Plaza de la Revolución, Vedado, Havana; tel. (7) 834-4949; fax (7) 834-4553; e-mail webmaster@iacc.gov.cu; internet www.iacc.gov.cu; f. 1985; responsible for directing, implementing and monitoring air transport and other related services; Pres. RAMÓN MARTÍNEZ ECHEVARRÍA.

Aero Caribbean: Calle 23, No 64, esq. P, Vedado, Havana; tel. (7) 832-7584; fax (7) 336-5016; e-mail reserva@cacsa.avianet.cu; f. 1982; international and domestic scheduled and charter services; state-owned; Chair. JULIÁN ALVAREZ INFIESTA.

Aerogaviota: Aeropuerto de Playa Baracoa, Carretera Panamericana. Km. 15 ½, Caimito, Artemisa; tel. (7) 203-0668; fax (7) 204-2621; e-mail vpcom@aerogaviota.avianet.cu; internet www.aerogaviota.com; f. 1994; Exec. Pres. VÍCTOR MANUEL AGUILAR OSORIA.

Empresa Consolidada Cubana de Aviación (Cubana): Aeropuerto Internacional José Martí, Terminal 1, Avda Rancho Boyeros, Havana; tel. (7) 266-4644; fax (7) 33-4056; e-mail comunicacion@cubana.avianet.cu; internet www.cubana.cu; f. 1929; international services to North America, Central America, the Caribbean, South America and Europe; internal services from Havana to 14 other cities; Pres. RICARDO SANTILLÁN MIRANDA.

Tourism

Tourism began to develop after 1977, with the easing of travel restrictions by the USA, and Cuba subsequently attracted European tourists. In 2010 the number of hotel rooms had reached 65,031. In 2009 receipts from tourism totalled an estimated US $2,080m. Tourist arrivals stood at an estimated 2,531,745 in 2010, compared with 2,429,809 in 2009.

Cubanacán: Calle 23, No 156, entre O y P, Vedado, 10400 Havana; tel. (7) 833-4090; fax (7) 22-8382; e-mail com_electronic@cubanacan.cyt.cu; internet www.cubanacan.cu; f. 1987; Pres. JUAN JOSÉ VEGA.

Empresa de Turismo Internacional (Cubatur): Calle 15, No 410, entre F y G, Plaza, Vedado, Havana; tel. (7) 836-2076; fax (7) 836-3170; e-mail casamatriz@cubatur.cu; internet www.cubatur.cu; f. 1963 as Empresa de Turismo Nacional e Internacional; changed name as above in 1969; Dir BÁRBARA CRUZ.

Defence

As assessed at November 2011, according to Western estimates, Cuba's Revolutionary Armed Forces numbered 49,000 (including ready reserves, serving 45 days a year to complete active and reserve units): Army 38,000, Navy 3,000 and Air Force 8,000. There were an additional 39,000 army reserves. Cuba's paramilitary forces included 20,000 State Security troops, 6,500 border guards, a civil defence force of 50,000 and a Youth Labour Army of some 70,000. There was also a Territorial Militia, comprising an estimated 1m. men and women. Conscription for military service is for a two-year period from 17 years of age, and conscripts also work on the land. Despite Cuban hostility, the USA maintains a base at Guantánamo Bay, which comprised 482 naval, 127 marine and 293 army personnel as assessed at November 2010.

Defence Expenditure: The state budget for 2010 allocated 1,960m. pesos to defence and public order.

Minister of the Revolutionary Armed Forces: Lt-Gen. LEOPOLDO CINTRA FRÍAS.

Head of the Joint Chiefs of Staff: Lt-Gen. ALVARO LÓPEZ MIERA.

Education

Education is universal and free at all levels. Education is based on Marxist-Leninist principles and combines study with manual work. Day nurseries are available for all children after their 45th day, and national schools at the pre-primary level are operated by the State for children of five years of age. Primary education, from six to 11 years of age, is compulsory, and secondary education lasts from 12 to 17 years of age, comprising two cycles of three years each. In 2010/11 an estimated 788,117 children were enrolled in primary schools, while 834,307 pupils were enrolled in secondary schools. There were an estimated 473,309 students in higher education in the same year. Workers attending university courses receive a state subsidy to provide for their dependants. Courses at intermediate and higher levels lay an emphasis on technology, agriculture and teacher training. A Latin American School of Medicine opened in Havana in 1999. In 2009 budgetary expenditure on education was 9,624.2m. pesos (22.7% of total spending).

CYPRUS

Introductory Survey

LOCATION, CLIMATE, LANGUAGE, RELIGION, FLAG, CAPITAL

The Republic of Cyprus is an island in the eastern Mediterranean Sea, about 100 km south of Turkey. The climate is mild, although snow falls in the mountainous south-west between December and March. Temperatures in Nicosia are generally between 5°C (41°F) and 36°C (97°F). About 75% of the population speak Greek and almost all of the remainder Turkish. The Greek-speaking community is overwhelmingly Christian, and nearly all Greek Cypriots adhere to the Orthodox Church of Cyprus, while most of the Turkish Cypriots are Muslims. The national flag of the Republic of Cyprus (proportions 3 by 5) is white, with a gold map of Cyprus, above two crossed green olive branches, in the centre. The flag of the 'Turkish Republic of Northern Cyprus' (proportions 2 by 3) has a white field, with a red crescent and star to the left of centre between two narrow horizontal bands of red towards the upper and lower edges. The capital is Nicosia.

CONTEMPORARY POLITICAL HISTORY

Historical Context

A guerrilla war against British rule in Cyprus was begun in 1955 by Greek Cypriots seeking unification (*Enosis*) with Greece. Their movement, the National Organization of Cypriot Combatants (EOKA), was led politically by Archbishop Makarios III, the head of the Greek Orthodox Church in Cyprus, and militarily by Gen. George Grivas. Archbishop Makarios was suspected by the British authorities of being involved in EOKA's campaign of violence, and in March 1956 he and three other *Enosis* leaders were deported. After a compromise agreement between the Greek and Turkish communities, a Constitution for an independent Cyprus was finalized in 1959. Makarios returned from exile and was elected the country's first President in December 1959. Cyprus became independent on 16 August 1960, although the United Kingdom retained sovereignty over two military base areas.

A constitutional dispute resulted in the withdrawal of the Turks from the central Government in December 1963 and serious intercommunal violence. In March 1964 a UN Peacekeeping Force in Cyprus (UNFICYP, see p. 98) was established to prevent a recurrence of fighting between the Greek and Turkish Cypriot communities. The effective exclusion of the Turks from political power led to the creation of separate administrative, judicial and legislative organs for the Turkish community. Discussions with a view to establishing a more equitable constitutional arrangement began in 1968; these continued intermittently for six years without achieving any agreement.

In 1971 Gen. Grivas returned to Cyprus, revived EOKA and began a terrorist campaign for *Enosis*, directed against the Makarios Government and apparently supported by the military regime in Greece. Grivas died in January 1974, and in June Makarios ordered a purge of EOKA sympathizers from the police, National Guard and civil service, accusing the Greek regime of subversion. On 15 July Makarios was deposed in a military coup led by Greek officers of the National Guard, who appointed as President Nikos Sampson, an extremist Greek Cypriot politician and former EOKA militant. Makarios escaped from the island the following day and travelled to the United Kingdom. At the request of Rauf Denktaş, the Turkish Cypriot leader, the Turkish army intervened to protect the Turkish community and to prevent Greece from using its control of the National Guard to take over Cyprus. Turkish troops landed on 20 July and rapidly occupied the northern third of Cyprus, dividing the island along what became the Green Line (also known as the Attila Line), which runs from Morphou through Nicosia to Famagusta. Sampson resigned on 23 July, and Glavkos Klerides, the President of the House of Representatives, became acting Head of State. The military regime in Greece collapsed the same day. In December Makarios returned to Cyprus and resumed the presidency. However, the Turkish Cypriots established a de facto Government in the north, and in February 1975 declared a 'Turkish Federated State of Cyprus' ('TFSC'), with Denktaş as President.

Domestic Political Affairs

Makarios died in August 1977. He was succeeded as President by Spyros Kyprianou. Following a government reorganization in September 1980, the powerful communist party, the Anorthotiko Komma Ergazomenou Laou (AKEL—Progressive Party of the Working People), withdrew its support from the ruling Dimokratiko Komma (DIKO—Democratic Party), and Kyprianou lost his overall majority in the legislature. At the next general election, held in May 1981, AKEL and the Dimokratikos Synagermos (DISY—Democratic Rally) each won 12 seats in the House. DIKO, however, won only eight seats, so the President remained dependent on the support of AKEL.

In the 'TFSC' a new Council of Ministers was formed in December 1978, under Mustafa Çağatay, of the Ulusal Bırlık Partisi (UBP—National Unity Party). At elections held in June 1981 President Denktaş was returned to office, but his party, the UBP, lost its legislative majority, and the Government that was subsequently formed by Çağatay was defeated in December. In March 1982 Çağatay formed a coalition Government, comprising the UBP, the Demokratik Halk Partisi (Democratic People's Party) and the Türkiye Bırlık Partisi (Turkish Unity Party).

In September 1980 UN-sponsored intercommunal peace talks resumed. The constitutional issue remained the main problem: the Turkish Cypriots demanded equal status for the two communities, with equal representation in government, while the Greek Cypriots, although accepting the principle of an alternating presidency, favoured a strong central government and objected to any disproportionate representation for the Turkish Cypriot community, which constituted less than 20% of the population. Discussions on a UN plan involving a federal council, an alternating presidency and the allocation of 70% of the island to the Greek Cypriot community faltered in February 1982, when the Greek Prime Minister, Andreas Papandreou, proposed the withdrawal of all Greek and Turkish troops and the convening of an international conference rather than the continuation of intercommunal talks. Meanwhile, in April 1981 it was agreed to establish a Committee on Missing Persons in Cyprus, comprising one representative of each community and a representative of the International Committee of the Red Cross, to investigate the fate of 1,619 Greek Cypriots and 803 Turkish Cypriots listed as missing since the 1974 invasion. In May 1983 the UN General Assembly voted in favour of the withdrawal of Turkish troops from Cyprus, whereupon Denktaş threatened to boycott any further intercommunal talks and to seek recognition for the 'TFSC' as a sovereign state; simultaneously it was announced that the Turkish lira was to replace the Cyprus pound as legal tender in the 'TFSC'.

Declaration of independence of the 'Turkish Republic of Northern Cyprus'

On 15 November 1983 the 'TFSC' made a unilateral declaration of independence as the 'Turkish Republic of Northern Cyprus' ('TRNC'), with Denktaş as President. Çağatay subsequently resigned the premiership and as leader of the UBP, and an interim Government was formed in December under Nejat Konuk. Like the 'TFSC', the 'TRNC' was recognized only by Turkey, and the declaration of independence was condemned by the UN Security Council. The 'TRNC' and Turkey established diplomatic relations in April 1984, and the 'TRNC' formally rejected UN proposals for a suspension of its declaration of independence prior to further talks.

During 1984 a 'TRNC' Constituent Assembly drafted a new Constitution, which was approved by 70% of voters at a referendum in May 1985. At a presidential election in the 'TRNC' on 9 June Denktaş was returned to office, with more than 70% of votes cast. A general election followed on 23 June, at which the UBP, led by Dr Derviş Eroğlu, won 24 of the 50 seats in the Legislative Assembly. In July Eroğlu became 'TRNC' Prime Minister, leading a coalition Government comprising the UBP and the Toplumcu Kurtuluş Partisi (TKP—Communal Liberation Party).

In February 1983 Kyprianou was returned to the Greek Cypriot presidency for a second term, taking 56.5% of the votes. In November 1985, following a debate on his leadership, the House of Representatives was dissolved. Legislative elections proceeded in December: Kyprianou's DIKO secured 16 seats in the chamber (which, under a constitutional amendment, had been enlarged to 56 Greek Cypriot deputies), while DISY, which won 19 seats, and AKEL, with 15, failed to reach the two-thirds' majority required to amend the Constitution and thus challenge the President's tenure of power. Kyprianou failed to secure a third presidential term in February 1988; the election was won at a second round of voting by Georghios Vassiliou, an independent candidate who nevertheless enjoyed unofficial support from AKEL and the Socialistiko Komma Kyprou EDEK (EDEK—EDEK Socialist Party of Cyprus). Vassiliou undertook to restore a multi-party National Council (originally convened by President Makarios) to address the Cyprus issue.

Settlement plans proposed by the UN Secretary-General in July 1985 and in April 1986 were rejected by the Turkish Cypriots and the Greek Cypriots, respectively. Further measures concerning the demilitarization of the island, reportedly proposed by the Greek Cypriot Government, were rejected by Denktaş, who maintained that negotiations on the establishment of a two-zone, federal republic should precede any demilitarization. In March 1988 the new Greek Cypriot President rejected various proposals submitted by Denktaş, via the UN, including a plan to form committees to study the possibilities of intercommunal co-operation. Following a meeting with the revived National Council in June, however, Vassiliou agreed to a proposal by the UN Secretary-General that he and Denktaş should resume intercommunal talks, without pre-conditions, in their capacity as leaders of the two communities. Denktaş also approved the proposal, and a UN-sponsored summit meeting between the Greek and Turkish Cypriot leaders took place in Geneva, Switzerland, in August. Vassiliou and Denktaş subsequently began direct negotiations, under UN auspices, in September. Despite resuming negotiations at the UN in February 1990, these were abandoned in March, chiefly because Denktaş demanded recognition of the right to self-determination for Turkish Cypriots.

In April 1988 Eroğlu resigned as 'TRNC' Prime Minister, following a disagreement between the UBP and its coalition partner since September 1986, the Yeni Doğuş Partisi (New Dawn Party), which was demanding greater representation in the Government. At the request of Denktaş, Eroğlu formed a new Council of Ministers in May, comprising mainly UBP members but also including independents. In April 1990 Denktaş secured nearly 67% of the votes cast in an early presidential election. Eroğlu retained the office of Prime Minister, after the UBP won 34 of the 50 seats in the 'TRNC' Legislative Assembly at elections in May. (Following by-elections for 12 seats in October 1991, the UBP increased its representation in the Assembly to 45 members.)

Initiatives for reconciliation following Cyprus's application for European Community membership

In July 1990 the Government of Cyprus formally applied to join the European Community (EC, now European Union—EU, see p. 276). Denktaş condemned the application, on the grounds that the Turkish Cypriots had not been consulted, and stated that the action would prevent the resumption of intercommunal talks. In June 1993, none the less, the European Commission approved the eligibility of Cyprus for EC membership, although it insisted that the application should be linked to progress in the latest UN-sponsored talks concerning the island.

At the May 1991 elections for the Greek Cypriot seats in the House of Representatives, the conservative DISY, in alliance with the Komma Phileleftheron (Liberal Party), received 35.8% of the votes cast, thereby securing 20 of the 56 seats in the legislature. AKEL unexpectedly made the most significant gains, obtaining 30.6% of the votes and 18 seats.

Following unsuccessful attempts to promote the resumption of discussions between Vassiliou and Denktaş by the UN, the EC and the USA during 1990–91, the new UN Secretary-General, Dr Boutros Boutros-Ghali, made the resolution of the Cyprus problem a priority. However, despite Boutros-Ghali holding separate meetings in New York, USA, with Vassiliou and Denktaş, and UN envoys visiting Cyprus, Turkey and Greece, no progress was achieved in the early part of 1992. The UN Secretary-General conducted a second round of talks with the two leaders in mid-1992, which subsequently involved direct discussions. The talks aimed to arrive at a draft settlement based on his proposals and endorsed by UN Security Council Resolution 750, advocating 'uninterrupted negotiations' until a settlement was reached. The UN proposals centred on the demarcation of Greek Cypriot and Turkish Cypriot areas of administration under a federal structure. However, following a disclosure to the Turkish Cypriot press that the proposed area of Turkish administration was some 25% smaller than the 'TRNC', Denktaş asserted that the UN's territorial proposals were totally unacceptable to the 'TRNC' Government, and the discussions ended in August. Political opinion in the Greek Cypriot area was also divided.

At an election to the Greek Cypriot presidency in February 1993 the DISY leader, Glavkos Klerides, narrowly defeated the incumbent Vassiliou at a second round of voting. Vassiliou subsequently formed a new party, the Kinema ton Eleftheron Dimokraton (KED—Movement of Free Democrats). UN-sponsored negotiations were reconvened in New York in May, focusing on the Secretary-General's plan to introduce a series of what were termed 'confidence-building measures', which included the proposed reopening, under UN administration, of the international airport at Nicosia. However, the talks were abandoned in June, when the Turkish Cypriot negotiators declined to respond to the proposals.

An early general election was held in the 'TRNC' in December 1993, partly in response to increasing disagreement between President Denktaş and Prime Minister Eroğlu over the handling of the UN-sponsored peace talks. The UBP lost its majority in the Legislative Assembly, retaining only 17 of the 50 seats, and at the end of the month a coalition Government was formed by the Demokrat Parti (DP—Democrat Party), which had been supported by Denktaş, and the left-wing Cumhuriyetçi Türk Partisi (CTP—Republican Turkish Party). Together the DP and the CTP won 53.4% of the votes cast and 28 seats. The leader of the DP, Hakkı Atun, was appointed as Prime Minister of the new administration.

In July 1994 the UN Security Council adopted Resolution 939, advocating a new initiative on the part of the Secretary-General to formulate a solution for peace, based on a single nationality, international identity and sovereignty. In response, in the following month the 'TRNC' Legislative Assembly approved measures seeking to co-ordinate future foreign and defence policies with those of Turkey, asserting that no peace solution based on the concept of a federation would be acceptable, and demanding political and sovereign status equal to that of Greek Cyprus. The issue of Cyprus's bid to accede to the EU had greatly disrupted the progress of negotiations. In June EU Heads of Government, meeting in Corfu, Greece, had confirmed that Cyprus would be included in the next round of expansion of the Union. Denktaş remained adamant that any approach by the Greek Cypriots to the EU would prompt the 'TRNC' to seek further integration with Turkey.

At a presidential election held on 15 April 1995, Denktaş received a mere 40.4% of votes cast in the first poll, only securing a conclusive victory against Eroğlu, with 62.5% of the votes, at a second round on 22 April. Following protracted inter-party negotiations, a new coalition of the DP and the CTP, under Atun's premiership, took office in June. In August the 'TRNC' Legislative Assembly adopted legislation concerning compensation for Greek-owned property in the north. However, in November Atun submitted the resignation of his entire Government, after Denktaş rejected a new list of CTP ministers. A new DP-CTP coalition, again under Atun's leadership and with Mehmet Ali Talat (of the CTP) as Deputy Prime Minister, took office in December.

Elections for the Greek Cypriot seats in the House of Representatives on 26 May 1996 produced little change in the composition of the legislature. DISY retained 20 seats, with 34.5% of the votes cast; AKEL took 19 seats, an increase of one, with 33.0% of the votes, while DIKO secured 10 seats, a loss of one, with 16.4%. Persistent policy differences within the 'TRNC' coalition caused the Government to resign in July, and in August the DP and the UBP signed a coalition agreement whereby UBP leader Eroğlu became Prime Minister of a new administration.

Meanwhile, in April 1996 the UN Security Council endorsed a US initiative to promote a federal-based settlement for Cyprus. In June, in advance of a visit to the island by the UN Secretary-General's newly appointed Special Representative in Cyprus, Han Sung-Joo, Boutros-Ghali held discussions, separately, with Denktaş and Klerides. In October a UN-mediated military dialogue, involving senior commanders of the Greek and Turkish Cypriot armed forces, was initiated to consider proposals for reducing intercommunal tension. However, further mediation efforts were undermined in November by alleged violations of Greek Cypriot airspace by Turkish military aircraft, as well as by Greek Cypriot efforts to prevent tourists from visiting the 'TRNC' and the continued opposition of the 'TRNC' to Cyprus's application to join the EU. In December the European Court of Human Rights (ECHR) ruled that Turkey was in breach of the European Convention on Human Rights by denying a woman access to her property as a result of its occupation in the north. The ruling implicated Turkey as fully responsible for activities in the 'TRNC' and for the consequences of the military action in 1974.

In January 1997 an agreement signed by the Greek Cypriot Government and Russia regarding the purchase of an advanced anti-aircraft missile system became the focus of political hostilities between the Greek and Turkish Cypriots. The purchase agreement was condemned by the 'TRNC' as an 'act of aggression', and the potential for conflict over the issue increased when Turkey declared its willingness to use military force to prevent the deployment of the system. Greece in turn reiterated that it would defend Cyprus against any Turkish attack. US mediators sought urgent meetings with the Cypriot leaders, and were assured by the Greek Cypriot Government that deployment would not take place until at least May 1998 and would be dependent upon the progress made in talks. In addition, both sides approved UN-supported measures to reduce tension in the border area, although the Greek Cypriots rejected a US proposal for a ban on all military flights over the island. Later in January 1997 Turkey threatened to establish air and naval bases in the 'TRNC' if Greece continued to promote plans for the establishment of military facilities in the Greek Cypriot zone, and at the end of the month Turkish military vessels arrived in the 'TRNC' port of Famagusta. Turkey and the 'TRNC' also declared their commitment to a joint military concept whereby any attack on the 'TRNC' would be deemed a violation against Turkey.

In July 1997 Klerides and Denktaş took part in direct UN-sponsored negotiations in the USA, under the chairmanship of the UN Special Envoy for Cyprus, Dr Diego Córdovez. The discussions took place under the auspices of the new UN Secretary-General, Kofi Annan, and with the participation of Richard Holbrooke, the newly appointed US Special Envoy to Cyprus. Further private direct talks took place in Nicosia at the end of July, when agreement was reached to co-operate in efforts to trace persons missing since the hostilities in 1974. However, a second formal round of UN-sponsored negotiations, convened in Switzerland in August 1997, collapsed without agreement, after Denktaş demanded the suspension of Cyprus's application for EU membership, to which he remained opposed on the grounds that accession negotiations, scheduled to begin in 1998, were to be conducted with the Greek Cypriot Government, ignoring the issue of Turkish Cypriot sovereignty.

On 15 February 1998, at the second round of voting in the Greek Cypriot presidential election, Klerides defeated Georghios Iacovou, an independent candidate supported by AKEL and DIKO, securing 50.8% of the votes cast. A new coalition Government, composed of members of DISY, EDEK, the Enomeni Dimokrates (EDI—United Democrats—formed in 1996 by a merger of the KED and the Ananeotiko Dimokratiko Socialistiko Kinima) and independents, was sworn in at the end of the month.

The Greek Cypriot Government began accession talks with the EU in March 1998. In May Holbrooke visited Cyprus and held discussions with Klerides and Denktaş, although no progress was made. In August Denktaş rejected a UN plan for the reunification of Cyprus, proposing instead a confederation of equal status; this was deemed unacceptable by Klerides on the grounds that it would legitimize the status of the 'TRNC'.

In June 1998 a number of Greek military aircraft landed at the Paphos airfield in southern Cyprus for the first time since the airfield's completion in January. Shortly afterwards Turkish military aircraft made reciprocal landings in the 'TRNC'. In July the Greek Cypriot Government condemned the arrival of Turkish military naval vessels and aircraft in the 'TRNC' to mark the anniversary of the Turkish invasion of the island. During the course of the year Turkish aircraft were accused of violating Greek Cypriot airspace on a number of occasions. However, in October Denktaş proposed a non-aggression treaty between the two sides.

It was formally announced in December 1998 that the contentious Russian missile system would not be deployed in Cyprus, following diplomatic pressure from Greece, the EU (which threatened to suspend Cypriot accession talks if the deployment proceeded), the USA and the UN. The missiles were reportedly deployed in Crete, Greece, in March 1999, following the signature in February of an agreement by the Greek and Greek Cypriot Governments to the effect that Cyprus would own the missiles although they would be under Greek operational control. Klerides's reversal of policy regarding the missiles' deployment provoked intense domestic criticism, and prompted the withdrawal of EDEK (to which party the Minister of Defence belonged) from the Greek Cypriot governing coalition. (In 2000 Kinima Sosialdimokraton EDEK, KISOS—Movement of Social Democrats, was established as a successor movement to EDEK.)

Meanwhile, at legislative elections held in the 'TRNC' on 6 December 1998 the UBP increased its representation to 24 seats (from 16 in 1993), while the DP held only 13 seats. The TKP won seven seats and the CTP the remaining six. At the end of the month a new UBP-TKP Council of Ministers received presidential approval. Eroğlu remained as Prime Minister, and the TKP leader, Mustafa Akıncı, became Minister of State and Deputy Prime Minister.

In December 1999 Denktaş and Klerides attended proximity talks in New York under the auspices of the UN, at which Annan acted as a mediator; however, the indirect talks were undermined by a decision taken that month at a summit meeting of EU Heads of State and Government in Helsinki, Finland, that a political settlement for Cyprus was not a precondition to the accession of the Greek Cypriot Government to the EU. This decision was widely acknowledged to be a response to Greece's reversal of its opposition to Turkey's EU membership application, and the summit thus accorded Turkey formal status as a candidate for EU membership.

A first round of presidential voting in the 'TRNC', conducted on 15 April 2000, was contested by eight candidates. Denktaş won 43.7% of the votes cast, thus failing to secure the majority necessary for outright victory, but on 19 April his closest contender, Eroğlu, announced his withdrawal from the process and Denktaş was consequently proclaimed President.

Resolution 1303, which was adopted by the UN Security Council in mid-June 2000 and extended the mandate of UNFICYP for a further six months, notably excluded any reference to the authority of the 'TRNC', citing only the Government of Cyprus, and at the end of the month the 'TRNC' instituted a number of retaliatory measures against UNFICYP, including measures to impede the movement of UN forces and new tariffs for UN vehicles and for the use of utilities supplied by the north. 'TRNC' and Turkish forces also crossed into the buffer zone and established a checkpoint at a village inhabited by Greek Cypriots.

A third round of proximity talks, mediated by the UN Special Adviser on Cyprus, Alvaro de Soto, took place in Geneva in July–August 2000. Again, there were no direct exchanges between the Greek Cypriot and Turkish Cypriot representatives, and the talks ended without progress. A further round of indirect negotiations began in New York in September. Klerides boycotted the early stages of the talks, in protest at a statement in which Annan had, in the view of the Greek Cypriots, implied that the 'TRNC' was equal in authority to the internationally recognized Cypriot Government; however, the Greek Cypriot leader resumed attendance after receiving assurances that the UN would act in accordance with earlier Security Council resolutions on the Cyprus issue. Nevertheless, the Greek and Turkish Cypriots remained apparently irreconcilable on the issue of a future structure for Cyprus, with the former advocating a reunified, bicommunal federation and the latter a looser confederation based on equal sovereignty. A fifth round of UN-sponsored proximity talks was convened in Geneva in November. After separate meetings with both Klerides and Denktaş, Annan expressed his view that the negotiations had progressed, and both leaders were invited to further discussions in January 2001. Later in November 2000, however, Denktaş stated that he would not return to the talks until such time as the 'TRNC' was accorded international recognition. His decision, taken with the support of the Government of Turkey, apparently reflected anger in the 'TRNC' that the UN Secretary-General had emphasized that any agreement on Cyprus must be based on the premise of a single sovereign entity, and in Turkey that the European Commission had, in a draft partnership agreement published earlier in November, stipulated among preconditions for Turkish admission to the EU Turkey's willingness to promote a settlement for Cyprus based on UN resolutions. De Soto visited Cyprus in December in an effort to foster a resumption of dialogue, but Denktaş reiterated that the 'TRNC' would not take part in any further talks unless its sovereignty was recognized; he warned, furthermore, that in the absence of such recognition UNFICYP would no longer be welcome in the 'TRNC'. In the same month the UN Security Council adopted Resolution 1331, which urged the 'TRNC' to revoke the restrictive measures imposed against UNFICYP in June, noting that these had undermined the operational effectiveness of the peacekeeping force.

At elections for the Greek Cypriot members of the House of Representatives on 27 May 2001, AKEL secured a narrow victory over DISY, taking 20 seats (with 34.7% of the votes cast), compared with the latter's 19 (34.0%). DIKO held nine seats (14.8%), one fewer than in 1996. In June the AKEL leader, Demetris Christofias, was elected as the new President of the legislature, defeating the DISY leader, Nicos Anastasiades, with support from the DIKO deputies.

The governing coalition of the 'TRNC' collapsed in late May 2001, following disagreement between the UBP and the TKP on the issue of whether to rejoin talks on the future status of the island. In June the UBP and the DP agreed to form a new coalition administration, with Eroğlu continuing as Prime Minister. The new Government was expected to be more supportive than its predecessor of President Denktaş's policy on the Cyprus question.

EU accession and the 'Annan Plan'

In early December 2001 Presidents Klerides and Denktaş met briefly for the first time in four years; following the meeting, Álvaro de Soto stated that the two leaders had agreed to recommence direct talks on the future of the island in January 2002 'without preconditions'. On 5 December 2001 Klerides became the first Greek Cypriot leader to visit the Turkish Cypriot northern sector since the island's partition, when he travelled to the 'TRNC' to meet with Denktaş. The resumption of contacts was broadly welcomed in the 'TRNC', but Greek Cypriot opposition parties and representatives of Greek Cypriots whose relatives had been 'missing' since the invasion, or who had been forced from their homes in the north, were critical of Klerides's visit. Denktaş made a reciprocal visit to meet with his Greek Cypriot counterpart at the end of December. Formal direct negotiations, mediated by de Soto, commenced on 21 January 2002, with a view to reaching agreement by the end of June.

In September 2002 Kofi Annan hosted talks between Klerides and Denktaş in Paris, France, with de Soto in attendance. On 11 November the UN presented a comprehensive new peace plan (which became known as the 'Annan Plan') to Klerides and Denktaş. The plan envisaged the creation of a common federal state with two equal components, but a single international legal personality. The state would have a joint six-member presidential council, with members holding a 10-month rotating presidency, and a bicameral legislature, comprising a 48-member senate with an equal number of deputies from both sides, and a 48-member proportionally composed chamber of deputies. A common supreme court would have three judges from both sides, and three non-Cypriots. Dispossessed property owners would receive compensation, and the 'TRNC' would return territory to the Greek side, reducing the former's share of the island from 36% to 28.5%. Cyprus would be demilitarized, but Greece and Turkey would each be permitted to station up to 9,999 troops on the island, and UNFICYP would retain its presence. The two leaders initially agreed to use the plan as a basis for future negotiations, but in early December Denktaş rejected a revised version of it.

The progress of EU accession talks meant that the need for a settlement to the Cyprus problem was increasingly urgent. At the EU summit held in Copenhagen, Denmark, in December 2002, Cyprus was formally invited to join the EU in 2004. However, it was reiterated that in the absence of a peace agreement, only the Greek part of the island would be admitted. Meanwhile, Greece, which assumed the presidency of the EU in January 2003, had earlier emphasized that it would veto the admission of other EU candidate countries if Cyprus was not admitted at the next round of expansion. Turkey, for its part, had warned in November 2001 that it might annex northern Cyprus if a divided island under a Greek Cypriot government was admitted to the EU.

In the Greek Cypriot presidential election held on 16 February 2003 the DIKO leader, Tassos Papadopoulos (who was also supported by AKEL), was elected outright, with 51.5% of the votes cast. Klerides won 38.8% of the votes. Papadopoulos appointed a new Government, which for the first time included four AKEL representatives. There were concerns that Papadopoulos's victory would delay the implementation of the UN peace plan, as he was widely believed to favour a less compromising approach towards the Turkish Cypriots than his predecessor. The new President immediately demanded changes to the Annan Plan that would allow all Greek Cypriot refugees to return to the north. Annan extended, to 10 March, a deadline previously set at 28 February for agreement on the island's future, which would thus allow a unified Cyprus to accede to the EU, and Papadopoulos and Denktaş held discussions in The Hague, Netherlands. However, the new deadline passed without agreement: Denktaş denounced the Annan Plan as unacceptable, and refused to continue discussions. The office of the UN Secretary-General's Special Adviser on Cyprus was subsequently closed down. In early April the Greek Cypriot Government rejected an offer by Denktaş to return the eastern town of Varosha, stating that the UN plan should be the principal basis for negotiation.

On 16 April 2003 President Papadopoulos signed Cyprus's Treaty of Accession to the EU in Athens, Greece, thereby confirming that Cyprus would join the organization on 1 May 2004. On 23 April 2003 the Turkish Cypriot authorities announced that they would open the 'TRNC' border to the Greek part of the island for the first time in 30 years, allowing Turkish Cypriots to visit that area for one-day trips and permitting Greek Cypriots to visit the north for up to three nights. The Greek Cypriot Government stated that the opening of the border should not be regarded as a substitute for a settlement in accordance with UN resolutions. However, popular approval of the decision in both the north and south of the island was evident, and by July more than 900,000 people were reported to have crossed the border. The Treaty of Accession was unanimously approved by the Greek Cypriot House of Representatives on 14 July and ratified by Papadopoulos on 28 July.

Legislative elections held in the 'TRNC' on 14 December 2003 proved inconclusive with regard to the issue of EU accession: the pro-EU CTP narrowly defeated the ruling UBP; however, parliamentary seats were distributed equally between pro-EU parties and parties that remained opposed to the reunification of Cyprus under the terms of the Annan Plan. On 16 December Eroğlu resigned and Talat was appointed as the new Turkish Cypriot Prime Minister. At the beginning of January 2004 Talat agreed to enter into a coalition with the DP (led by the President's son, Serdar Denktaş), despite differences of opinion between the CTP and the DP over the reunification issue. On 13 January President Denktaş approved a new coalition Government nominated by Talat, comprising six CTP ministers and four DP ministers. Serdar Denktaş was appointed Deputy Prime Minister and Minister of Foreign Affairs in the new administration.

The formation of a new Turkish Cypriot Government gave renewed impetus to the search for a political settlement. In early February 2004, under the aegis of UN Secretary-General Annan, Denktaş and Papadopoulos attended a further round of discussions in New York. On 13 February agreement was reached for the resumption of bilateral negotiations based on the Annan Plan (providing for a federation of two politically equal states), with a schedule for reaching a settlement prior to the island's accession to the EU on 1 May. In late February Papadopoulos and Denktaş resumed UN-sponsored negotiations in Nicosia, in an effort to finalize the details of a settlement, which was to be submitted for approval by both the Greek and Turkish Cypriot communities at concurrent referendums scheduled for 24 April. However, intensive discussions between the two leaders failed to resolve the remaining issues of disagreement and were relocated to Bürgenstock, Switzerland, in late March (where the Greek and Turkish Prime Ministers also joined the process). Denktaş, who continued to reject the UN plan, refused to continue his participation in the negotiations and was replaced by Talat as head of the Turkish Cypriot delegation. At the end of March Annan presented a finalized version of the peace plan, which was accepted by the 'TRNC' leadership and by the Greek and Turkish Governments; however, Papadopoulos (in a reversal of previous Greek Cypriot government policy) campaigned against this final settlement, which he strongly opposed on the grounds that it provided for the establishment of a recognized Turkish Cypriot state. At the referendums held on 24 April the Annan Plan was endorsed by Turkish Cypriots by 64.9% of votes cast, but rejected by Greek Cypriots by 75.8% of the votes. Consequently, only the Greek Cypriot-administered part of the island was admitted to the EU on 1 May; the *acquis communautaire* (the body of EU legislation, treaties and case law) was suspended in the 'TRNC', pending a future political settlement. Following appeals by Talat, the EU proposed measures for the resumption of direct trade between the two sides of the island, and consequently for the export of commodities produced in the 'TRNC' to EU member states.

The Cyprus question after EU accession

At the end of April 2004 the 'TRNC' coalition Government lost its parliamentary majority, after two DP deputies withdrew their support and resigned from the Legislative Assembly. In October the UN Security Council renewed the mandate of UNFICYP until June 2005, but significantly reduced the size of the contingent. On 20 October 2004 Talat tendered his resignation, following the failure of his efforts to form a new 'TRNC' coalition administration. On the following day Denktaş invited Eroğlu (as leader of the UBP, the strongest party in the Legislative Assembly) to nominate a new government; at the end of the month, however, Eroğlu returned the mandate to the President, after being unable to secure sufficient support from other parliamentary parties. In November Denktaş redesignated Talat as Prime Minister, but he again failed to reach a coalition agreement and also returned the mandate later that month. Denktaş subsequently announced that early legislative elections would be conducted in the 'TRNC' on 20 February 2005, while Talat's incumbent Government remained in office in an interim capacity.

At the elections to the 'TRNC' Legislative Assembly on 20 February 2005 Talat's CTP secured 44.5% of votes cast and 24 of the 50 seats in the chamber (a gain of seven seats), while the UBP won 31.6% of the votes (19 seats). The CTP was thus obliged to seek a renewed parliamentary alliance with Serdar Denktaş's anti-reunification DP, which had secured 13.4% of the vote (six seats), to enable Talat to command a parliamentary majority. On 8 March President Denktaş approved a new 'TRNC' coalition Government (the composition of which was effectively unchanged from the previous administration), formed by Talat under a slightly amended power-sharing arrangement. On 9 March Talat met with the Secretary-General of AKEL, Demetris Christofias, in the first discussions between 'TRNC' and Greek Cypriot leaders since the April 2004 referendums.

Nine candidates contested the 'TRNC' presidential election, held on 17 April 2005: Mehmet Ali Talat was elected outright, with 55.6% of votes cast, while Eroğlu, his closest rival, secured 22.7%. Talat, who pledged his commitment to achieving reunification of Cyprus, was inaugurated on 24 April. He duly nominated the Secretary-General of the CTP, Ferdi Sabit Soyer, as Prime Minister, and a new CTP-DP coalition Government was approved by the Legislative Assembly on 28 April.

In April 2005 the ECHR issued a significant decision upholding a Greek Cypriot property claim against Turkey and rejecting the contention that the 'TRNC' authorities had provided adequate restitution for such claims by establishing a property commission. The case reflected Greek Cypriot concerns over increasing sales of property in the 'TRNC' involving houses and land owned legally by Greek Cypriots. The Greek Cypriot House of Representatives ratified the EU constitutional treaty in June.

Meanwhile, the EU's provisional invitation to Turkey, issued on 17 December 2004, to open accession negotiations in October 2005 again focused international attention on the necessity of reaching a political settlement in Cyprus. The Turkish Prime Minister, Recep Tayyip Erdoğan, accepted a condition to extend Turkey's customs accord with the EU to cover the 10 new member states that had joined the organization in May 2004, including Cyprus; however, Erdoğan insisted that the protocol would not constitute official Turkish recognition of the authorities of Greek Cypriot-administered Cyprus, instead agreeing to a compromise arrangement whereby Turkey made a commitment for future recognition. The Turkish Government signed the requisite customs protocol in July 2005. In September EU member states adopted a draft declaration stating that Turkish recognition of Cyprus was necessary to the accession process, but without stipulating a date for this, thus posing no obstacle to the beginning of accession negotiations, which were officially approved on 3 October (see the chapter on Turkey).

Eroğlu resigned from the leadership of the UBP in November 2005, and in February 2006 Hüseyın Özgürgün was elected as his successor. Meanwhile, in January 2006 the Turkish Government proposed a resumption of dialogue concerning reunification, and presented an 'action plan' to the UN Secretary-General, under which Turkish ports and airports would be opened to Cypriot traffic in exchange for the ending of trade restrictions against the 'TRNC'. The Greek Cypriot Government immediately rejected the Turkish proposals, emphasizing that the Turkish authorities were required to open ports and airports to all EU member states by the end of 2006 as a condition to progress in the accession negotiations. In February the EU approved an aid disbursement of €139m. for the 'TRNC', after agreeing to a Greek Cypriot demand that the financial assistance be addressed separately to the proposed trade measures, eliciting strong protests by the Turkish Government (which had insisted that the provisions for direct trade be included). Following a UN-mediated meeting in July, Papadopoulos and Talat reached a framework agreement on an initiative—known as 'the 8 July process'—to resolve technical issues between the two communities, with the objective of resuming the formal peace process.

Elections conducted to the Greek Cypriot House of Representatives on 21 May 2006 resulted in no major changes to its composition. AKEL and DISY both won 18 seats, attracting 31.1% and 30.3% of the votes cast, respectively, while DIKO secured 11 seats, with 17.9% of the ballot. Also securing representation were KISOS, with five seats (8.9%), the Evropaiko Komma (Evro.Ko—European Party—which contested an election for the first time), with three seats (5.8%), and the Kinima Oikologon Perivallontiston (KOP—Cyprus Green Party), with one seat (2.0%).

Following the onset of hostilities between the militant Shi'a organization Hezbollah and Israeli armed forces in July 2006 (see the chapter on Lebanon), Cyprus became the main transit point for refugees fleeing southern Lebanon by sea, and applied to the EU for financial assistance in managing the influx. By 14 August, upon which date a UN-imposed cease-fire agreement entered into effect, some 60,000 civilians (mainly foreign nationals) fleeing the fighting in Lebanon had been evacuated through Cyprus, although most had stayed on the island only briefly. The Greek Cypriot Minister of Finance announced that the cost to the authorities had been equivalent to US $223,000 per day, and the EU pledged some $8.9m. towards meeting the expense. Following the implementation of the cease-fire, Cyprus made available Larnaca and Limassol ports, and a military air base at Paphos, for the transportation of international peace-keeping troops and humanitarian aid to Lebanon.

In the 'TRNC', three parliamentary deputies resigned from the UBP and one from the DP in early September 2006, and collectively established a new organization, the Özgürlük ve Reform Partisi (ORP—Freedom and Reform Party). Soyer subsequently dissolved the Government, citing prolonged disagreements within the coalition over a reallocation of ministerial positions and policy regarding the reunification of Cyprus. Having received the necessary mandate, on 13 September Soyer formed a new coalition administration with the ORP, which was approved by Talat on 25 September. Three ORP representatives were included within the administration, including the party leader, Turgay Avcı, who became Deputy Prime Minister and Minister of Foreign Affairs. On 5 October the new Government secured a motion of confidence in the Legislative Assembly by 28 of the 50 deputies; however, the DP and the UBP refused to recognize its legitimacy.

In November 2006 the European Commission published a critical report on Turkey's accession progress, in which it issued an ultimatum demanding that the Turkish Government open ports and airports in accordance with the 2005 customs protocol by early December 2006, prior to a meeting of EU foreign ministers. In early December, following indications that the continuing impasse would result in the partial suspension of Turkey's accession negotiations, the Turkish Government offered to open one port and one airport to Greek Cyprus, in exchange for the resumption of international flights to the 'TRNC' airport of Ercan and direct trade to the port of Famagusta. The Greek Cypriot Government immediately rejected the proposal and, together with Greece and Austria, continued to demand a total cessation of EU discussions with Turkey. In mid-December EU ministers of foreign affairs agreed to a suspension of negotiations on eight of the 35 policy areas (concerning trade and external relations).

At the end of December 2006, following a meeting between Demetris Christofias and Soyer in the northern part of Nicosia, it was announced that both sides had expressed willingness to enter into further dialogue concerning a resolution for Cyprus. On 22 January 2007 a meeting of EU foreign ministers issued a statement urging immediate action towards the ending of trade restrictions against the 'TRNC', in accordance with the EU's commitment made in 2004. In February 2007 Archbishop Chrysostomos of the Greek Orthodox Church of Cyprus and Ahmet Yonluer, head of the 'TRNC' Religious Affairs Directorate, met for the first time since 1974, and discussed methods of fostering dialogue between the two communities with a view to increasing inter-religious tolerance. In the following month the Greek Cypriot Government orchestrated the demolition of a wall at Ledra Street in Nicosia, which formed part of the barrier that had divided the city into Greek and Turkish sectors for more than four decades and which had come to symbolize the wider divisions and conflict within Cyprus. Since 2004 five crossing-points had been opened along the Green Line, although, thus far, none had been opened in the capital. However, the dismantling of the barrier subsequently led to the establishment of an official crossing-point in central Nicosia (see The election of Demetris Christofias as Greek Cypriot President and the resumption of reunification talks).

In July 2007 AKEL announced its decision to withdraw from the Greek Cypriot governing coalition, thereby enabling party leader Christofias to stand in the presidential election scheduled to take place in early 2008. The four government portfolios relinquished by AKEL were awarded later that month to independents, including Eratou Kozakou-Marcoullis as the Minister of Foreign Affairs.

The election of Demetris Christofias as Greek Cypriot President and the resumption of reunification talks

In the first round of the presidential election, held on 17 February 2008, Papadopoulos was unexpectedly eliminated from the running, a result attributed by many to increasing levels of popular frustration at his perceived intractability with regard to the Cyprus problem. The DISY-backed independent Ioannis Kasoulides, a former Minister of Foreign Affairs, garnered 33.5% of the ballot, and Demetris Christofias secured 33.4%, relegating Papadopoulos, with 31.8% of the vote, into third place among a total of nine candidates; voter turn-out was 89.6% of the registered electorate. The run-off election between the two highest-polling candidates, held on 24 February, was a relatively close contest, from which Christofias emerged victorious, with 240,604 votes (53.4% of the ballot), compared with 210,195 votes cast in favour of Kasoulides (46.6%); turn-out was again high, at 90.8%. DIKO had transferred its backing from Papadopoulos to Christofias before the second round of voting, although the former President remained officially neutral. During his electoral campaign Christofias had expressed a desire to 'reunite the state, the people, the institutions and the economy', and pledged his firm commitment to the holding of reunification negotiations with the 'TRNC'.

Christofias was formally inaugurated as President on 28 February 2008, and a new Council of Ministers was sworn in on the following day. The allocation of portfolios effectively, though unofficially, restored the tripartite coalition that had been in power prior to AKEL's withdrawal in July 2007: four ministries were headed by AKEL, and two each by DIKO and KISOS, with responsibility for the remaining two being awarded to AKEL-backed independents. Notable appointments included those of Markos Kyprianou (DIKO—hitherto EU Commissioner for Health) as Minister of Foreign Affairs and Charilaos Stavrakis (independent—Chief Executive of the Bank of Cyprus) as Minister of Finance.

During discussions between Christofias and Talat in Nicosia in March 2008, the two leaders agreed to: open the Ledra Street crossing in central Nicosia as a symbol of reconciliation between their two communities (this occurred in early April); devise a precise agenda for the reunification negotiations to take place; and establish a number of working groups and technical committees. This latter objective was achieved in mid-April, when six bicommunal working groups and seven technical committees were set up to consider a number of issues pertinent to the success of further talks. The working groups were to consider: governance and power-sharing; EU matters; security and guarantees; territory; property; and economic matters; while the technical committees would oversee: crime/criminal matters; economic and commercial matters; cultural heritage; crisis management; humanitarian matters; health; and the environment.

In May 2008 Christofias and Talat conducted a second meeting in Nicosia, hosted by the UN Secretary-General's newly appointed Special Representative in Cyprus and head of UNFICYP, Tayé-Brook Zerihoun of Ethiopia. At the close of the meeting, which focused primarily on the progress achieved thus far by the working groups and technical committees, the Greek and Turkish Cypriot leaders reiterated their 'commitment to a bizonal, bicommunal federation with political equality, as defined by relevant Security Council resolutions'. A third bilateral meeting was held in early July, and later that month it was announced that Alexander Downer, hitherto the Australian Minister for Foreign Affairs, had been appointed as the UN Secretary-General's Special Adviser on Cyprus. The Greek and Turkish Cypriot leaders subsequently reconvened in Nicosia in late July, where they conducted a final review of the working groups and technical committees. They met again in September, where the foundations were laid for the start of more substantive negotiations. In the mean time, Christofias and Talat agreed to conduct weekly talks, in a development seen as indicative of the continued desire by both parties to achieve a comprehensive solution to the Cyprus problem.

The Greek and Turkish Cypriot Presidents reconvened in Nicosia in mid-September 2008, in the presence of Zerihoun and Downer. This marked the first of a series of meetings held between the two leaders over successive months, which were intended to facilitate consensus on matters ranging from power-sharing and governance to security, property and the environment. In spite of the considerable optimism generated by the commencement of these long-awaited, fully fledged negotiations, familiar tensions—principally with regard to issues of power-sharing—soon began to hamper the progress of the meetings. At the close of their first meeting of 2009, held in January, Christofias and Talat acknowledged that, while progress so far had been insufficient, they remained fully committed to finding a lasting settlement to the island's problems.

Christofias had previously stated his intention to step down as Secretary-General of AKEL following his election to the Greek Cypriot presidency, and he officially announced his resignation from the post in December 2008. At the elections to the party leadership, held by secret ballot on 21 January 2009, AKEL political bureau member (in charge of international relations) Andros Kyprianou defeated AKEL parliamentary spokesperson Nicos Katsourides, with 57 of the 105 votes (54.3%). Upon assuming the post of Secretary-General, Kyprianou emphasized his support for the ongoing reunification negotiations.

Elections in the 'TRNC' and the withdrawal of KISOS from the Greek Cypriot Government

It was announced in February 2009 that the 'TRNC' would hold an early parliamentary election in April—a year ahead of schedule. The proposal for an early election was reportedly an effort by the 'TRNC' Government to ensure that the Legislative Assembly was able to offer adequate support to the Turkish Cypriot community in ongoing reunification talks with Greek Cypriots. At the election held on 19 April, the UBP secured 44.0% of the votes cast, increasing its representation to 26 seats (from 19 in 2005) and securing an overall majority in the legislature, while President Talat's CTP garnered only 15 seats (a loss of nine) and 29.3% of the votes. The DP won five seats (compared with six in 2005), and the ORP and Toplumcu Demokrasi Partisi each secured two seats. A new 'TRNC' Council of Ministers was approved by Talat in May. Derviş Eroğlu, who had been re-elected as leader of the UBP in November 2008, reassumed the post of Prime Minister; Hüseyın Özgürgün was accorded the foreign affairs portfolio. Eroğlu pledged his Government's support for the reunification talks between Talat and Christofias. None the less, it was widely felt that the election victory by the UBP, which had long been an exponent of the 'TRNC' as an independent nation, would almost certainly undermine negotiations with the Greek Cypriots.

Meanwhile, in April 2009 a judgment at the European Court of Justice (ECJ) threatened further to undermine the reunification talks. The ECJ upheld a ruling, first issued by a Greek Cypriot court in 2004, that ordered the restoration of a property in the 'TRNC' to its original Greek Cypriot owner. The property in question, which had been vacated following the 1974 invasion, had subsequently been sold to a British couple who had constructed a holiday villa on the site. The couple were ordered to relinquish their claim on the land, restore the site to its original state, and pay rent and damages to the owner. Owing to the Cypriot court's lack of jurisdiction in northern Cyprus, the original verdict had not been enforced. However, the plaintiff's legal team subsequently petitioned the High Court of Justice in the United Kingdom, from where the case was referred to the ECJ. The latter concluded that, as the defendants were EU citizens, the ruling could be enforced by EU law, raising fears that the judgment could form a legal precedent for similar cases. The Turkish Cypriot authorities stated that all property disputes should be resolved solely through the ongoing political negotiations and warned that the decision could seriously disrupt the reunification process. They declared that they would not enforce the decision, despite an appeal by the defendants being rejected by the British Court of Appeal in January 2010.

By early June 2009 Christofias and Talat had held over 30 meetings since their first substantive negotiations on reunification in September of the previous year. At the 32nd meeting, in mid-June, discussions on economic matters—at least at the presidential level—were concluded and talks on territorial issues commenced. In late June it was announced that agreement had been reached on the opening of an additional crossing-point at Limnitis (Yeşilırmak), near the island's north-eastern coast; this finally occurred on 14 October 2010. Meanwhile, following a 40th meeting on 6 August 2009, the first round of negotiations was concluded. A second round of talks, encompassing power-sharing, property rights, economic affairs and the EU, began on 10 September. Many observers believed that the talks were entering a critical period, as both leaders were confronting increasing domestic pressure over their handling of the negotiations, with hardline elements on both sides opposed to the granting of concessions. In late September, in recognition of the urgency of the political situation, the two leaders agreed to intensify negotiations, with meetings scheduled to take place twice weekly from October. In November British Prime Minister Gordon Brown promised to transfer into Cypriot control around one-half of the territory currently under British military jurisdiction, upon the successful conclusion of a settlement. On 14 December the UN Security Council adopted Resolution 1898, which urged the leaders to redouble their efforts to exploit the existing opportunity to reach a settlement and extended the mandate of the UN force until June 2010. (UNFICYP's mandate had been consistently renewed at six-monthly intervals since its inception in 1964.)

Following the conclusion of the second round of talks on 29 January 2010, Downer announced that 'significant progress' had been made in the negotiations concerning governance. In an attempt to bolster the protracted negotiations, UN Secretary-General Ban Ki-Moon arrived in Cyprus on 30 January for his first official visit. The Secretary-General held separate talks with the Greek and Turkish Cypriot leaders. However, his meeting with Talat resulted in criticism from numerous Greek Cypriot politicians, who maintained that the decision to hold the meeting at Talat's presidential office was tantamount to UN recognition of the Turkish Cypriot state. Four parties, including DIKO and KISOS, subsequently boycotted an official reception in honour of the Secretary-General. At a joint press conference on 1 February Ban praised the efforts of Christofias and Talat, and appealed for renewed 'commitment, vision and flexibility'; however, there was a notable absence of any announcement on new initiatives or a further round of negotiations. Meanwhile, in late January 'TRNC' Prime Minister Eroğlu officially declared his candidacy for the April presidential election.

In February 2010 KISOS announced its withdrawal from the Greek Cypriot governing coalition, citing its dissatisfaction with the strategy implemented by President Christofias in the reconciliation talks. However, the party's two ministers agreed to remain in their respective posts until a new government could be formed. The leader of DIKO, Marios Karoyian, subsequently held discussions with Christofias regarding his party's continued participation in the Council of Ministers. Following a meeting of its Central Committee later in February, DIKO announced that it would remain in the Government, having obtained greater representation within the Greek Cypriot negotiating party. In March President Christofias announced the appointment of two independents to the Council of Ministers, in place of the two outgoing KISOS representatives: former Minister of Foreign Affairs Kozakou-Marcoullis became the Minister of Communications and Works, and Demetris Eliades was appointed Minister of Agriculture, Natural Resources and the Environment.

The 'TRNC' presidential election took place as scheduled on 18 April 2010. According to results published by the 'TRNC' Higher Council of Elections, the UBP's Derviş Eroğlu emerged victorious, having secured 50.4% of the valid votes cast. The incumbent, Mehmet Ali Talat, received 42.9% of the votes cast, while five other independent candidates all achieved less than 4.0%. The rate of participation by voters was recorded at 76.4%. Following the announcement of the results, Eroğlu stated his commitment to continuing the reconciliation talks begun by his predecessor. However, it was widely believed that his victory, which reinforced the nationalist UBP's dominance of Turkish Cypriot politics, would not give any new impetus to the stalled discussions. Eroğlu was sworn in as President on 23 April, and on 10 May he nominated the new leader of the UBP, İrsen Küçük, as Prime Minister. A new, minority 'TRNC' Government—in which the main portfolios remained unchanged—was endorsed by President Eroğlu on 17 May and won a vote of confidence in the Legislative Assembly on 27 May, having obtained the support of DP and ORP deputies.

UN efforts to accelerate the reunification talks

After a two-month break, the UN-led reunification talks resumed in May 2010, with newly elected 'TRNC' President Eroğlu leading the Turkish Cypriot negotiating team. In June Lisa Buttenheim of the USA was appointed to succeed Zerihoun as the UN Secretary-General's Special Representative in Cyprus and head of UNFICYP. In mid-June the UN Security Council extended UNFICYP's mandate until December, and commended the Greek and Turkish Cypriot leaders for the progress made thus far in the reconciliation talks. Both the Secretary-General and the Security Council assessed that a settlement of the Cyprus issue was now 'well within reach', and the UN resolution urged the two sides to seize the opportunity and accelerate the peace process, citing in particular the need to introduce further confidence-building measures. Hopes that the Greek and Turkish Cypriots would agree a settlement by the end of 2010—the target date outlined by the two leaders at their 59th meeting on 21 December 2009—proved fruitless. The discussions since the resumption of negotiations had focused on the controversial issue of property rights, which the UN Secretary-General described as 'seemingly irreconcilable' and which was frequently the subject of court hearings. In late June 2010 a ruling by the ECHR had condemned the Turkish authorities for having denied nine Greek Cypriots access to the properties that they had owned in northern Cyprus prior to the 1974 invasion; Turkey was reportedly required to pay between €10,000 and €400,000 in compensation to the claimants.

Ban Ki-Moon invited Christofias and Eroğlu to hold a further meeting in New York in November 2010, amid concern that the negotiations towards a settlement of the Cyprus issue were losing momentum. The UN Secretary-General urged the Greek and Turkish Cypriot leaders to identify the core issues in all of the chapters yet to be resolved and to formulate a practical plan to overcome these differences. In December the UN Security Council approved Resolution 1953, which renewed the UNFICYP mandate until June 2011. In this resolution the UN was far more critical of the way in which the fully fledged negotiations were being conducted, noting the recent lack of progress in the discussions and reiterating the need for a practical plan to be agreed by Christofias and Eroğlu prior to a scheduled meeting with the UN Secretary-General in January 2011. Ban emphasized his view that the reunification talks could not be open-ended and that a settlement based on a bicommunal, bizonal federation with political equality must be reached in the coming months. The leaders of Cyprus's two communities were also urged to adopt a more 'constructive and open' approach both in their dealings with each other and in the manner in which they relayed details of the negotiations to their respective populations.

Christofias held further discussions with Eroğlu in Geneva in January 2011, in the presence of the UN Secretary-General, after which Ban Ki-Moon expressed his satisfaction at the efforts made by both leaders to formulate a practical plan for resolving specific issues and asserted that progress had been made on several chapters, particularly those concerning the economy, the EU, and governance and power-sharing. Nevertheless, he urged the Greek and Turkish Cypriot leaders to do more to resolve outstanding differences, while the UN was to provide technical expertise to assist in resolving the fundamental differences regarding property ownership. In June the UN Security Council adopted Resolution 1986, extending the mandate of UNFICYP for a further six months, until December; in the resolution the UN again noted with concern the continued slow pace of progress arising from reunification talks, and urged them to accelerate the negotiations and also to implement confidence-building measures, including the opening of more crossing points between the Greek- and Turkish-controlled areas of the island.

Meanwhile, in January 2011 tens of thousands of Turkish Cypriot public sector workers went on strike and staged a mass protest in Nicosia against the package of economic austerity measures that the Government had imposed at the beginning of the month. These measures included significant reductions in the salaries of civil servants and the divestment to private Turkish companies of several public sector institutions in the 'TRNC', notably in the electricity, telecommunications and education sectors. There were fears that a further reduction in the availability of public sector jobs might encourage an even greater number of Turkish Cypriots to emigrate. The protesters also claimed that the austerity measures were in fact being imposed by Turkey, which was seeking to reduce its expenditure on financing the budget deficit of the 'TRNC'. Further general strikes and rallies against the austerity measures took place in March and April. In the latter month Küçük effected a extensive reorganization of the Government, although no official explanation for the changes was given; most notably, Nazım Çavuşoğlu (hitherto Minister of National Education, Youth and Sport) replaced İrkay Kamil as Minister of Interior Affairs and Local Administrations.

Recent developments: Greek Cypriot parliamentary elections

Elections to the 56-seat Greek Cypriot House of Representatives were held on 22 May 2011. The opposition DISY increased its parliamentary representation from 18 to 20 seats (securing 34.3% of the votes cast), while AKEL increased its own representation from 18 to 19 seats (with 32.7% of the ballot); AKEL's coalition partner, DIKO, secured nine seats (15.8%), which represented a loss of two seats from 2006, while KISOS won five seats (8.9%) and Evro.Ko two (3.9%), with the remaining seat secured by KOP (2.2%). Turn-out was recorded at 78.7% of the registered electorate.

A series of explosions at a naval base in southern Cyprus in July 2011 resulted in the deaths of 13 people—including the head of the Cypriot naval force, Andreas Ioannides, and the base commander, Lambros Lambrou—while more than 60 others were injured. The incident, which caused severe damage to the nearby Vassiliko power station (which provided more than one-half of Cyprus's electricity), prompted the resignations of both the Minister of Defence, Costas Papacostas, and the commander of the National Guard, Brig.-Gen. Petros Tsaliklides. The explosions were later found to have been caused by a small fire igniting improperly stored containers of Iranian munitions that had been confiscated from a Syrian-bound vessel in 2009. Public anger in response to the Government's failure adequately to dispose of the munitions precipitated the staging of popular protests in the capital, with an estimated 10,000 people amassing outside the presidential palace in mid-July 2011 to demand the resignation of President Christofias. In an apparent attempt to deflect the mounting criticism, the Government claimed that it had requested several times that the UN remove the munitions from Cyprus but that the organization had declined. A few days later Minister of Foreign Affairs Kyprianou tendered his resignation from the Council of Ministers, and, with anti-Government sentiment running at a high, in late July the entire cabinet resigned at the request of President Christofias to facilitate an extensive government reorganization.

A new Council of Ministers, comprising members of AKEL and independents, was inaugurated in early August 2011. Eratou Kozakou-Marcoullis (hitherto Minister of Communications and Works) was appointed Minister of Foreign Affairs, while the incumbent Minister of Agriculture, Demetris Eliades, was transferred to the defence portfolio. Kikis Kazamias joined the Government as Minister of Finance. Other notable appointees included Efthymios Flourentzos, who was awarded the communication and works portfolio, and Praxoulla Antoniadou, who became Minister of Commerce, Industry and Tourism. The Ministers of the Interior, of Justice and Public Order, and of Labour and Social Insurance all retained their portfolios. Two days previously, DIKO had announced that it was to withdraw from the ruling coalition, citing irreconcilable differences with Christofias and AKEL regarding the ongoing reunification talks. DIKO's withdrawal left Christofias even more isolated in the House of Representatives, and threatened to undermine the Government's efforts to pass key austerity measures and economic reforms intended to address the country's increasingly precarious economic situation as a result of the ongoing financial crisis within the euro area (see Economic Affairs.)

In early October 2011 the findings of an inquiry into the munitions explosion in July were published in a report by Polys Polyviou, a lawyer appointed by the Government to investigate the incident. In a press conference following the report's publication, Polyviou concluded that President Christofias bore 'a serious and very heavy personal responsibility' for the disaster, having ignored warnings prior to the explosion that the confiscated munitions were in an unstable condition. Nevertheless, the President dismissed the report's findings, insisting that he remained in no way culpable.

Following a break in negotiations owing to the elections in May 2011, together with those in Turkey (q.v.) in June, the UN-led reunification talks between the Greek and Turkish Cypriot leaders were resumed at the end of October 2011, when Christofias and Eroğlu held discussions in Manhasset, New York, under the auspices of the UN Secretary-General. The focus of the meeting was reported to have been issues concerning the executive branch of government and citizenship within a reunified Cyprus. In a report published in the same month, the European Commission urged the 'TRNC' to do more to normalize relations with the Greek Cypriot administration, noting with concern that the 'TRNC's EU accession negotiations had 'regrettably not moved into any new areas for a year'. Following a further meeting at the end of January 2012 between the two leaders and Ban, little progress was reported, with Christofias noting that 'significant differences on governance, property and territory as well as details of other issues that may prove significant are still pending'. The resignation in mid-March of Minister of Finance Kazamias on grounds of ill health prompted a reorganization of the Government. AKEL's Eleni Mavrou, a former mayor of Nicosia, took office as Minister of the Interior on 21 March, while her immediate predecessor, Neoklis Sylikiotis became Minister of Commerce, Industry and Tourism. Two days later Vasos Shiarlis, an independent, was sworn in as Minister of Finance.

CONSTITUTION AND GOVERNMENT

The 1960 Constitution provided for a system of government in which power would be shared by the Greek and Turkish communities in proportion to their numbers. This Constitution officially remains in force, but since the ending of Turkish participation in the Government in 1963, and particularly since the creation of a separate Turkish area in northern Cyprus in 1974, each community has administered its own affairs, refusing to recognize the authority of the other's Government. The Greek Cypriot administration claims to be the Government of all Cyprus, and (apart from by Turkey) is internationally recognized as such, although it has no Turkish participation. The northern area is under the de facto control of the 'Turkish Republic of Northern Cyprus' ('TRNC'—for which a new Constitution was approved by a referendum in May 1985). The 'TRNC' is recognized only by Turkey. The Greek Cypriot President is elected for a term of five years and appoints a Council of Ministers. (Under the 1960 Constitution, the position of Vice-President and three posts in the Council of Ministers were reserved for Turkish Cypriots.) The Greek Cypriot House of Representatives comprises 56 deputies, who are elected for a five-year term (under the Constitution, as amended in 1985, the House of Representatives officially comprised 80 seats, of which 24 were allocated to Turkish Cypriots). The 'TRNC' elects its own 50-member Legislative Assembly for a term of five years and has an independent judicial system. The President of the 'TRNC' is elected for a term of five years and appoints a Prime Minister, who forms a 10-member Council of Ministers.

REGIONAL AND INTERNATIONAL CO-OPERATION

Following an application by the Greek Cypriot Government in July 1990, the Greek Cypriot area of Cyprus officially acceded to the European Union (EU, see p. 276) on 1 May 2004 (see Contemporary Political History). Cyprus also participates in the Council of Europe (see p. 256) and the Organization for Security and Co-operation in Europe (OSCE, see p. 388).

Cyprus became a member of the UN on 20 September 1960 and, as a contracting party to the General Agreement on Tariffs and Trade, it joined the World Trade Organization (WTO, see p. 433) on its establishment in 1995. Cyprus is also a member of The Commonwealth (see p. 239). The 'Turkish Republic of Northern Cyprus' has been granted special guest status at the Economic Cooperation Organization (ECO, see p. 269).

ECONOMIC AFFAIRS

In 2009, according to estimates by the World Bank, Cyprus's gross national income (GNI), measured at average 2007–09 prices, was US $24,383m., equivalent to $30,480 per head (or $30,180 per head on an international purchasing-power parity basis). During 2001–10, it was estimated, the population increased at an average annual rate of 1.5%, while in 2001–09 gross domestic product (GDP) per head increased, in real terms, by an average of 1.2% per year. Overall GDP increased, in real terms, at an average annual rate of 2.9% in 2001–09; it grew by an estimated 3.6% in 2008, but decreased by an estimated 1.0% in 2009. In the 'TRNC' gross national product (GNP) was officially estimated at $5,649.5m., or $14,703 per head, in 2010. Real GDP increased at an average annual rate of 2.0% in 2005–10. GDP declined by 5.5% in 2009, before increasing by 3.7% in 2010, according to the State Planning Organization.

In the Greek Cypriot area, agriculture (including hunting, forestry and fishing) contributed 2.4% of GDP in 2010, according to provisional figures. An estimated 7.4% of the employed labour force were engaged in the sector in that year. The principal crops of the area are citrus fruit, potatoes and vegetables; grapes are cultivated notably for the wine industry, and barley is the principal cereal crop. Food and live animals contributed 17.0% of total export earnings in 2009. In an effort to offset the island's vulnerability to drought, during the 1990s the Greek Cypriot Government granted concessions for the construction and operation of several desalination plants. According to the World Bank, the GDP of the area's agricultural sector declined by an average of 3.4% per year in 2001–08; agricultural GDP decreased by an estimated 1.9% in 2008. In the 'TRNC' the agricultural sector contributed 6.5% of GDP in 2010, and engaged 4.8% of the employed labour force in 2009. The principal crops of the 'TRNC' are citrus fruit, vegetables, potatoes, barley and wheat. The 'TRNC' imports water from Turkey in order to address the problem of drought. The GDP of the agricultural sector declined by an average of 1.1% per year in 2005–10. Agricultural GDP increased by 10.0% in 2010.

Industry (comprising mining, manufacturing, construction and power) accounted for 18.8% of GDP in 2010, according to provisional figures, and engaged an estimated 19.2% of the employed labour force in the Greek Cypriot area. According to the World Bank, industrial GDP increased by an average of 3.2% per year in 2001–08; growth in the sector was estimated at 4.1% in 2008. In the 'TRNC' the industrial sector contributed 17.0% of GDP in 2010, and engaged 19.2% of the employed labour force in 2009. Industrial GDP in the 'TRNC' increased at an average annual rate of 3.0% in 2005–10. The GDP of the industrial sector declined by some 14.6% in 2009, before increasing by 2.0% in 2010.

In the Greek Cypriot area mining and quarrying, principally the extraction of material for the construction industry, provided only 0.3% of GDP in 2010, according to provisional figures, and engaged about 0.2% of the employed labour force in the same year. In 2001 it was announced that 25 foreign oil companies had expressed interest in acquiring exploration rights for potential petroleum and gas deposits in the eastern Mediterranean within Cyprus's economic zone. The Greek Cypriot Government signed respective agreements with Egypt and Lebanon in 2006 and 2007 concerning the joint exploration of potential offshore oil- and gasfields, and a similar deal with Israel in 2010 to develop natural gas reserves; these agreements have provoked a strong response from the Turkish authorities. Mining GDP rose by an estimated 7.7% in 2008. In the 'TRNC' mining and quarrying contributed 0.7% of GDP in 2010, and engaged 0.1% of the employed labour force in 2009. The GDP of the 'TRNC' mining sector increased by an average of 2.7% per year in 2005–10; however, mining GDP declined by 15.6% in 2009, and remained constant in 2010.

In the Greek Cypriot area manufacturing accounted for 6.4% of GDP in 2010, according to provisional figures, and engaged about 9.4% of the employed labour force. The GDP of the manufacturing sector increased by an average of 0.5% per year in 2001–08, increasing by an estimated 3.3% in 2008, according to the World Bank. In the 'TRNC' the manufacturing sector provided 2.6% of GDP in 2010, and engaged 8.0% of the employed labour force in 2009. The GDP of the 'TRNC' manufacturing sector declined at an average annual rate of 2.2% in 2005–10; manufacturing GDP decreased by 1.6% in 2010.

In the Greek Cypriot area, construction accounted for 9.5% of GDP in 2010, and engaged about 9.1% of the employed labour force in that year, according to provisional figures. Construction GDP increased by an estimated 4.5% in 2008. In the 'TRNC' the construction sector provided 6.1% of GDP in 2010, and engaged 10.1% of the employed labour force in 2009. The GDP of the 'TRNC' construction sector increased at an average annual rate of 6.7% in 2005–10; sectoral GDP declined by some 18.5% in 2009, before increasing by 3.8% in 2010.

Energy is derived almost entirely from imported petroleum, and mineral fuels and lubricants comprised 17.5% of total imports (including goods for re-export) in the Greek Cypriot area in 2009. The Greek Cypriot Government is encouraging the development of renewable energy sources, including solar, wind and hydroelectric power. Mineral fuels and lubricants comprised 19.7% of total imports in the 'TRNC' in 2008.

The services sector in the Greek Cypriot area contributed 78.8% of GDP in 2010, according to provisional figures, and engaged 73.4% of the employed labour force. Within the sector, financial and business services provided 25.7% of total GDP in 2010, according to provisional figures, and generated 10.9% of employment. The Greek Cypriot authorities have also attempted to enhance the island's status as an entrepôt for shipping and trade throughout the Eastern Mediterranean. In 2010 tourism arrivals were recorded at 2.17m., while receipts from tourism in that year amounted to an estimated €1,549.8m. In the Greek Cypriot zone the GDP of the services sector increased at an average annual rate of 3.8% in 2001–08; the sector recorded growth of 3.7% in 2008, according to the World Bank. In the 'TRNC' the services sector contributed 76.5% of GDP in 2010, and engaged 76.0% of the employed labour force in 2009. In 2009 a total of 800,376 tourists (638,700 of whom were from Turkey) visited the 'TRNC', and net tourism receipts were estimated at US $390.7m. Services GDP in the 'TRNC' increased by an average of 1.7% per year in 2005–10; sectoral GDP declined by 3.1% in 2009, before increasing by 1.0% in 2010.

According to the IMF, in 2010 the Greek Cypriot area recorded a visible trade deficit of US $6,514m. and a deficit of $2,803m. on the current account of the balance of payments. In 2009 the principal source of imports to the Greek Cypriot area was Greece (20.0%), followed by Italy, the United Kingdom, Germany, Israel and the People's Republic of China. Greece was also the principal purchaser of Greek Cypriot exports in that year, taking 22.7% of the total; Germany and the United Kingdom were also important markets. The principal exports from the Greek Cypriot zone in 2009 were machinery and transport equipment, chemicals and related products, and food and live animals. Among the principal imports in that year were machinery and transport equipment, mineral fuels and lubricants, miscellaneous manufactured products, and basic manufactures. The 'TRNC' recorded a visible trade deficit in 2009 of $1,255.1m., and there was a deficit of $65.4m. on the current account of the balance of payments. In 2009 the principal imports to the 'TRNC' were machinery and transport equipment (23.2%), basic manufactures (20.2%), mineral fuels and lubricants (17.0%), and food and live animals (12.9%); the principal exports were industrial products (63.8%), agricultural products, and minerals. Turkey is by far the principal trading partner of the 'TRNC', supplying 69.6% of imports and taking 54.1% of exports in 2009.

In 2010 the Greek Cypriot Government recorded a budget deficit of an estimated C£850.3m., equivalent to 4.9% of GDP. The Greek Cypriot's general government gross debt was C£10.619m. in 2010, equivalent to 60.8% of GDP. The annual rate of inflation averaged 2.5% in 2001–10, with consumer prices increasing by only 0.3% in 2009 and by 2.5% in 2010. The rate of unemployment in the Greek Cypriot area was some 6.3% of the labour force in 2010. A budgetary deficit of 724.5m. Turkish lira was estimated in the 'TRNC' in 2009, equivalent to 13.5% of GDP. In the 'TRNC' the average increase in prices for the 12 months to December averaged 18.2% in 2000–09; the end-of-year rate of inflation was 5.7% in 2009 and 3.3% in 2010. The unemployment rate was recorded at 12.4% in 2009.

The economy of Cyprus and its future development are inextricably linked to the continuing division of the island, which intensive efforts by the UN and the European Union (EU) have failed to resolve. The Turkish Cypriot economy has continued to suffer from its international isolation and has consequently remained heavily dependent on financial aid from Turkey; the proposed ending of international trade restrictions against the 'TRNC' was not realized, owing to continued opposition from the Greek Cypriot Government, while goods produced in the north must also be re-exported via Turkey, making them more costly and therefore less competitive in global markets. Owing to financial turmoil in the global credit markets the Greek Cypriot economy experienced a slowdown in late 2008, and negative growth was recorded, for the first time in some 30 years, in mid-2009, with GDP contracting by an estimated 1.7% in 2009 as a whole. The downturn was attributed principally to declining activity in the important construction, tourism and financial services sectors. Following the onset of recession in most EU countries, including the United Kingdom (which contributes the largest percentage of tourists to Cyprus), tourism receipts declined by almost 17% in 2009. None the less, observers noted that the negative effects of the financial crisis on the Greek Cypriot economy were mitigated by the adoption of the European single currency, the euro, on 1 January 2008 and the strict regulatory environment in the banking sector. Following a sharp increase in the Greek Cypriot budget deficit, to 6.1% of GDP, in 2009, and an anticipated rise in public debt to 62.3% of GDP in 2010, the country was placed under the EU's excessive deficit procedure in July 2010; the authorities—whose target was to reduce the fiscal deficit gradually to below 3% by 2012—were subsequently commended for their stabilization efforts. GDP in the Greek Cypriot-administered area returned to positive growth in 2010, expanding by an estimated 0.9%, according to the Greek Cypriot Ministry of Finance; growth was projected to increase to 1.5% in 2011 and further to 2.5% in 2012. Austerity measures introduced by the 'TRNC' Government in January 2011 led to mass protests by state employees in Nicosia (see Contemporary Political History). Amid the ongoing financial crisis within the euro area, and following a report published by the IMF in October in which it had cautioned that a strong and immediate policy response was required to address the urgent risks confronting the Cypriot economy, new economic legislation was approved by the Greek Cypriot House of Representatives in December. Among the adopted measures was an increase, from 15% to 17%, in the standard rate of value-added tax (VAT), which was to be implemented from 1 March 2012, while public sector salaries were to be frozen until the end of 2013. Legislation was also approved providing for the establishment of an independent, self-funded financial stability fund intended to support and finance the resolution of ailing credit institutions without recourse to public funds, and to restore and maintain public confidence in the financial system, which would be essential in order to regain access to capital markets. However, a special levy introduced by the Government in April 2011, under which financial institutions operating in Cyprus were required to pay a fee of 0.095% of their total deposits at the end of each calendar year (up to a maximum of 20% of the institution's total taxable profits), was repealed, with effect from 2013. Meanwhile, in July 2010 a long-awaited agreement was signed providing for the funding by Turkey of the construction of a US $450m. undersea pipeline capable of transporting 75m. cu m of fresh water annually to northern Cyprus, where water shortages are frequent, and—if the political situation improved—possibly also to the Greek Cypriot-controlled area. It was hoped that renewed reconciliation talks between the Greek and Turkish Cypriot leaders, initiated in 2008 and ongoing in early 2012, would yield results, although there remained significant obstacles to the achievement of a lasting settlement for the island.

PUBLIC HOLIDAYS

2013: 1 January (New Year's Day), 6 January (Epiphany)*, 23 January (Birth of the Prophet)†, 18 March (Green Monday)*, 25 March (Greek Independence Day)*, 1 April (Anniversary of Cyprus Liberation Struggle), 23 April (National Sovereignty and Children's Day)†, 1 May (May Day), 3–6 May (Easter)*, 19 May (Youth and Sports Day)†, 24 June (Pentecost)*, 20 July (Peace and Freedom Day, anniversary of the Turkish invasion in 1974)†, 1 August (Communal Resistance Day)†, 7 August (Ramazam Bayram—end of Ramadan)†, 15 August (Assumption)*, 30 August (Victory Day)†, 1 October (Independence Day)*, 14 October (Kurban Bayram—Feast of the Sacrifice)†, 28 October (Greek National Day)*, 29 October (Turkish Republic Day)†, 15 November ('TRNC' Day)†, 24–26 December (Christmas)*.

* Greek and Greek Orthodox.

† Turkish and Turkish Muslim.

Statistical Survey

Source (unless otherwise indicated): Statistical Service of Cyprus (CYSTAT), Ministry of Finance, Michalakis Karaolis St, 1444 Nicosia; tel. 22602102; fax 22661313; e-mail enquiries@cystat.mof.gov.cy; internet www.cystat.gov.cy.

Note: Since July 1974 the northern part of Cyprus has been under Turkish occupation. As a result, some of the statistics relating to subsequent periods do not cover the whole island. Some separate figures for the 'TRNC' are also given.

AREA AND POPULATION

Area: 9,251 sq km (3,572 sq miles), incl. Turkish-occupied region; 5,896 sq km (2,276 sq miles), government-controlled area only.

Population: 703,529 (males 345,322, females 358,207), excl. Turkish-occupied region, at census of 1 October 2001 (adjusted figures); 867,600, incl. 88,900 in Turkish-occupied region, at 31 December 2006 (official estimate); 803,200 (government-controlled area only) at 31 December 2009. Note: Figures for the Turkish-occupied region exclude settlers from Turkey, estimated at 115,000 in 2001.

Density (at 31 December 2009): 86.8 per sq km.

Population by Age and Sex (official estimates at 31 December 2009, govt-controlled area only): *0–14:* 135,700 (males 69,800, females 65,900); *15–64:* 562,800 (males 280,800, females 282,000); *65 and over:* 104,700 (males 47,500, females 57,200); *Total* 803,200 (males 398,100, females 405,100).

Ethnic Groups (31 December 2001, estimates): Greeks 639,400 (80.6%), Turks 87,600 (11.1%), Others 66,100 (8.3%); Total 793,100.

Districts (population at 31 December 2009, government-controlled area only): Ammochostos 44,800; Larnaka (Larnaca) 134,400; Lefkosia 315,400; Lemesos (Limassol) 230,800; Pafos (Paphos) 77,800; *Total* 803,200.

Principal Towns (population at 31 December 2009): Nicosia (capital) 236,200 (excl. Turkish-occupied portion); Limassol 187,100; Larnaca 83,500; Paphos 56,700.

Births, Marriages and Deaths (government-controlled area, 2009): Registered live births 9,608 (birth rate 12.0 per 1,000); Registered marriages 12,769 (incl. 6,327 residents of Cyprus); Registered deaths 5,182 (death rate 6.5 per 1,000).

Life Expectancy (years at birth, WHO estimates): 81 (males 78; females 83) in 2009. Source: WHO, *World Health Statistics*.

Economically Active Population (government-controlled area, '000 persons aged 15 years and over, excl. armed forces, 2010, provisional figures): Agriculture, hunting and forestry 26.6; Fishing 1.3; Mining and quarrying 0.7; Manufacturing 35.5; Electricity, gas and water 2.0; Construction 34.6; Wholesale and retail trade; repair of motor vehicles, motor cycles and personal and household goods 67.2; Restaurants and hotels 34.8; Transport, storage and communications 23.4; Financial intermediation 17.6; Real estate, renting and business activities 23.9; Public administration and defence 28.8; Education 21.6; Health and social work 16.0; Other community, social and personal service activities 17.5; Private households 24.8; Extra-territorial organizations 2.7; *Total* 379.0; Unemployed 25.4; *Total labour force* 404.4.

HEALTH AND WELFARE

Key Indicators

Total Fertility Rate (children per woman, 2009): 1.5.

Under-5 Mortality Rate (per 1,000 live births, 2009): 3.

HIV/AIDS (% of persons aged 15–49, 2007): 0.25.

Physicians (per 1,000 head, 2006): 2.3.

Hospital Beds (per 1,000 head, 2006): 3.8.

Health Expenditure (2008): US $ per head (PPP): 1,838.

Health Expenditure (2008): % of GDP: 6.0.

Health Expenditure (2008): public (% of total): 41.0.

Total Carbon Dioxide Emissions ('000 metric tons, 2007): 8,192.7.

Carbon Dioxide Emissions Per Head (metric tons, 2007): 9.6.

Human Development Index (2011): ranking: 31.

Human Development Index (2011): index: 0.840.

For sources and definitions, see explanatory note on p. vi.

AGRICULTURE

Principal Crops (government-controlled area, '000 metric tons, 2009): Wheat 8.0; Barley 30.0; Potatoes 131.8; Olives 13.7; Cabbages and other brassicas 4.4; Tomatoes 26.5; Cucumbers and gherkins 15.7; Onions, dry 6.4; Bananas 5.8; Oranges 42.1; Tangerines, mandarins, etc. 33.4; Lemons and limes 14.2; Grapefruit and pomelos 26.7; Apples 6.6; Grapes 27.5; Cantaloupes and other melons 10.2.

Livestock (government-controlled area, '000 head, 2009): Cattle 55.6; Sheep 267.3; Goats 318.4; Pigs 464.9; Chickens 2,904.0.

Livestock Products (government-controlled area, '000 metric tons, 2009): Sheep meat 2.7; Goat meat 2.7; Pig meat 58.1; Chicken meat 26.9; Cows' milk 148.5; Hen eggs 9.9.

Forestry (government-controlled area, '000 cubic metres, 2009): Roundwood removals (excl. bark) 9.9; Sawnwood production (incl. railway sleepers) 4.6.

Fishing (government-controlled area, metric tons, live weight, 2009): Capture 1,405 (FAO estimate—Bogue 253; Picarels 211); Aquaculture 3,346 (European seabass 703; Gilthead seabream 2,552); *Total catch* 4,751 (FAO estimate).

Source: FAO.

MINING

Selected Products (government-controlled area, '000 metric tons, 2008): Sand and gravel 15,151.0; Gypsum 283.1; Bentonite 114.5; Umber 7.6.

INDUSTRY

Selected Products (government-controlled area, 2010 unless otherwise indicated): Wine 15.4m. litres (2008); Beer 34.2m. litres; Soft drinks 55.0m. litres; Cigarettes 3,803m. (2001); Footwear 272,844 pairs (2007); Bricks 103.3m (2008); Floor and wall tiles 320,000 sq m (2004); Cement 1,328,763 metric tons; Electric energy 4,786 million kWh (2009).

FINANCE

Currency and Exchange Rates: 100 cent = 1 euro (€). *Sterling and Dollar Equivalents* (30 December 2011): £1 sterling = €1.195; US $1 = €0.773; €10 = £8.37 = US $12.94. *Average Exchange Rate* (euros per US dollar): 0.7198 in 2009; 0.7550 in 2010; 0.7194 in 2011. Note: The Cyprus pound (C£) was formerly in use. The government-controlled area of Cyprus adopted the euro on 1 January 2008, and this became the sole legal tender in these areas from the end of the same month.

Budget (government-controlled area, € million, 2010): *Revenue:* Taxation 5,415.5 (Direct taxes 1,876.3, Indirect taxes 2,496.8, Social security contributions 1,042.4); Other current revenue 944.1; Total 6,359.6, excl. grants from abroad (101.7). *Expenditure:* Current expenditure 6,741.6 (Wages and salaries 1,876.2, Other goods and services 529.7, Social security payments 1,264.7, Subsidies 81.3, Interest payments 453.9, Pensions and gratuities 493.4, Social pension 59.8, Other current transfers 1,877.0, Unallocated 105.5); Capital expenditure (investments) 570.0; Total 7,311.6. Source: Budgets and Fiscal Control Directorate, Ministry of Finance, Nicosia.

International Reserves (government-controlled area, US $ million at 31 December 2010): Gold (national valuation) 629.0; IMF special drawing rights 188.0; Reserve position in IMF 49.1; Foreign exchange 276.2; Other reserve assets 1.6; Total 1,143.9. Source: IMF, *International Financial Statistics*.

Money Supply (incl. shares, government-controlled area, € million at 31 December 2010): Currency issued 1,607 (Currency issued by the Central Bank of Cyprus 1,607); Demand deposits 9,319; Other deposits 36,005; Securities other than shares 2,564; Shares and other equity 13,440; Other items (net) –1,360; Total 61,575. Source: IMF, *International Financial Statistics*.

Cost of Living (government-controlled area, Retail Price Index; base: 2005 = 100): 109.8 in 2008; 110.2 in 2009; 112.9 in 2010. Source: IMF, *International Financial Statistics*.

Gross Domestic Product (government-controlled area, € million at current prices): 17,157.1 in 2008; 16,853.5 in 2009; 17,333.6 in 2010 (provisional figure).

Expenditure on the Gross Domestic Product (government-controlled area, € million at current prices, 2010, provisional figures): Government final consumption expenditure 3,367.2; Private final consumption expenditure 11,667.9; Increase in stocks 25.5; Gross fixed capital formation 3,228.0; *Total domestic expenditure* 18,288.6; Exports of goods and services 7,457.1; *Less* Imports of goods and services 8,412.1; *GDP in market prices* 17,333.6.

Gross Domestic Product by Economic Activity (government-controlled area, € million at current prices, 2010, provisional figures): Agriculture, forestry and fishing 381.4; Mining and quarrying 53.4; Manufacturing 1,003.6; Electricity, gas and water supply 398.2; Construction 1,479.0; Wholesale and retail trade 1,879.8; Restaurants and hotels 967.4; Transport, storage and communications 1,440.5; Financial intermediation 1,263.6; Real estate, renting and business activities 2,751.0; Public administration and defence 1,721.9; Education 1,020.9; Health and social work 636.9; Other community, social and personal services 450.7; Private households with employed persons 170.3; *Sub-total* 15,618.5; Import duties 135.7; Value-added tax 1,579.4; *GDP in market prices* 17,333.6.

Balance of Payments (government-controlled area, US $ million, 2010): Exports of goods f.o.b. 1,518; Imports of goods f.o.b. –8,032; *Trade balance* –6,514; Exports of services 8,226; Imports of services –3,203; *Balance on goods and services* –1,491; Other income received 3,235; Other income paid –4,502; *Balance on goods, services and income* –2,758; Current transfers received 1,134; Current transfers paid –1,179; *Current balance* –2,803; Capital account (net) 38; Direct investment abroad –1,004; Direct investment from abroad 1,886; Portfolio investment assets –3,115; Portfolio investment liabilities 162; Financial derivatives assets 302; Financial derivatives liabilities –478; Other investment assets 20,885; Other investment liabilities –15,978; Net errors and omissions –152; *Overall balance* –258. Source: IMF, *International Financial Statistics*.

EXTERNAL TRADE

Principal Commodities (government-controlled area, US $ million, distribution by SITC, 2009): *Imports c.i.f.:* Food and live animals 893.1; Mineral fuels and lubricants 1,391.8 (Petroleum and products 1,353.7); Chemicals and related products 824.8; Basic manufactures 1,027.9 (Iron and steel 190.5); Machinery and transport equipment 2,073.0 (Passenger cars 425.6); Miscellaneous manufactured articles 1,293.0 (Clothing and accessories 395.4); Total (incl. others) 7,933.4. *Exports f.o.b.:* Food and live animals 229.5 (Vegetables and fruit 119.5); Beverages and tobacco 89.3; Mineral fuels and lubricants 188.1; Chemicals and related products 265.5 (Medicinal and pharmaceutical products 198.7); Machinery and transport equipment 266.0 (Road vehicles 33.0); Miscellaneous manufactured articles 196.1; Total (incl. others) 1,350.9. Source: UN, *International Trade Statistics Yearbook*.

Principal Trading Partners (government-controlled area, US $ million, distribution by SITC, 2009): *Imports c.i.f.:* Belgium 254.9; Brazil 17.3; China, People's Repub. 432.7; Egypt 79.8; France (incl. Monaco) 312.6; Germany 684.0; Greece 1,586.6; Israel 542.4; Italy 849.5; Japan 153.9; Netherlands 378.3; Spain 284.7; United Kingdom 721.5; USA 128.3; Total (incl. others) 7,933.4. *Exports f.o.b.* (incl. re-exports): Belgium 14.1; Egypt 34.5; Germany 113.4; Greece 306.9; Ireland 6.1; Italy 25.5; Japan 0.8; Jordan 17.2; Lebanon 45.5; Netherlands 17.8; Romania 13.3; Russia 19.2; Syria 26.3; United Arab Emirates 24.5; United Kingdom 111.0; Total (incl. others) 1,350.9. Source: UN, *International Trade Statistics Yearbook*.

TRANSPORT

Road Traffic (government-controlled area, licensed motor vehicles, 31 December 2010): Private passenger cars 453,432; Taxis and self-drive cars 9,220; Buses and coaches 3,403; Lorries and vans 120,690; Motorcycles 40,727; Total (incl. others) 648,143.

Shipping (government-controlled area, freight traffic, '000 metric tons, 2010): Goods loaded 1,375, Goods unloaded 6,474. *Merchant Fleet:* At 31 December 2009 a total of 1,026 merchant vessels (combined displacement 20,168,906 grt) were registered in Cyprus (Source: IHS Fairplay, *World Fleet Statistics*).

Civil Aviation (government-controlled area, 2009): Overall passenger traffic 6,817,491; Total freight transported 35,777 metric tons.

TOURISM

Foreign Tourist Arrivals (government-controlled area, '000): 2,403.8 in 2008; 2,141.2 in 2009; 2,173.0 in 2010.

Arrivals by Country of Residence (government-controlled area, '000, 2010): France 28.7; Germany 139.2; Greece 127.7; Norway 63.3; Russia 223.9; Sweden 109.7; Switzerland 41.7; United Kingdom 996.0; Total (incl. others) 2,173.0.

Tourism Receipts (government-controlled area, € million): 1,792.8 in 2008; 1,493.2 in 2009; 1,549.8 in 2010.

COMMUNICATIONS MEDIA

Radio Receivers (government-controlled area, 1997): 310,000 in use.

Television Receivers (government-controlled area, 2000): 122,000 in use.

Telephones (main lines in use, 2010): 413,200.

Mobile Cellular Telephones (subscribers, 2010): 1,034,100.

Personal Computers: 324,000 (383.4 per 1,000 persons) in 2006.

Internet Subscribers (2010): 206,600.

Broadband Subscribers (2010): 194,500.

Book Production (government-controlled area, 1999): 931 titles.

Newspapers (2004, unless otherwise indicated): 8 daily (circulation 87,000 copies in 2000); 22 non-daily (circulation 200,000 copies in 2000).

Periodicals (2000): 50 daily (circulation 372,000 copies).

Sources: mainly UNESCO, *Statistical Yearbook*, UN, *Statistical Yearbook*, and International Telecommunication Union.

EDUCATION

2009/10 (government-controlled area): Pre-primary: 682 institutions, 2,269 teachers, 27,985 pupils; Primary: 370 institutions, 4,754 teachers, 54,522 pupils; Secondary (Gymnasiums and Lyceums): 165 institutions, 7,692 teachers, 64,611 pupils; Tertiary (incl. University of Cyprus): 42 institutions, 1,778 teachers, 32,233 students (of whom 11,138 were foreign students). Note: 20,051 Cypriot students were studying abroad.

Pupil-teacher Ratio (primary education, UNESCO estimate): 14.2 in 2008/09 (Source: UNESCO Institute for Statistics).

Adult Literacy Rate (UNESCO estimates): 97.9% (males 99.1%; females 96.9%) in 2009. Source: UNESCO Institute for Statistics.

'Turkish Republic of Northern Cyprus'

Source: Statistics and Research Dept, State Planning Organization, Prime Ministry, Lefkoşa (Nicosia), Mersin 10, Turkey; tel. (22) 83141; fax (22) 85988; e-mail trnc-spo@management.emu.edu.tr; internet www.devplan.org.

AREA AND POPULATION

Area: 3,242 sq km (1,251 sq miles).

Population: 256,644 (males 138,568, females 118,076) at census of 30 April 2006. *Mid-2009:* 283,736.

Density (at mid-2009): 87.5 per sq km.

Population by Country of Nationality (self-declaration at census of 30 April 2006): 'TRNC' 135,106; Joint 'TRNC' and other 42,925 (with Turkey 34,370, with United Kingdom 3,854, with Other 4,701); Turkey 70,525; United Kingdom 2,729; Bulgaria 797; Iran 759; Pakistan 475; Moldova 354; Germany 181; Other 2,793; *Total* 256,644.

Districts (population at census of 30 April 2006): Lefkoşa 84,776; Mağusa 63,603; Girne 57,902; Güzelyurt 29,264; İskele 21,099.

Principal Towns (population within the municipal boundary at census of 30 April 2006): Lefkoşa (Nicosia) 49,868 (Turkish-occupied area only); Gazi Mağusa (Famagusta) 35,381; Girne (Kyrenia) 23,839; Güzelyurt 12,391.

Births, Marriages and Deaths (registered, 2001): Live births 2,550 (birth rate 15.0 per 1,000); Marriages 1,090 (marriage rate 5.2 per 1,000); Deaths 781 (death rate 8.0 per 1,000). *2009:* Birth rate 15.4 per 1,000; Death rate 6.9 per 1,000.

Life Expectancy (years at birth, 2009): Males 71.8; Females 76.5.

Employment (labour force survey, October 2009): Agriculture, forestry and fishing 4,432; Mining and quarrying 106; Manufacturing 7,312; Construction 9,204; Electricity, gas and water 952; Wholesale and retail trade 15,609; Hotels and restaurants 7,316; Transport, storage and communications 4,872; Financial institutions 3,777; Real estate and renting 4,180; Public administration 15,417; Education 10,182; Health 2,533; Other community services 5,658; *Total employed* 91,550. *2009:* Total unemployed 12,941.

HEALTH AND WELFARE

Key Indicators

Total Fertility Rate (children per woman, 2009): 1.9.

Under-5 Mortality Rate (per 1,000 live births, 2006): 13.9.

Physicians (per 1,000 head, 2009): 2.1.

Hospital Beds (per 1,000 head, 2009): 4.6.

AGRICULTURE

Principal Crops ('000 metric tons, 2001): Wheat 7.6; Barley 102.1; Potatoes 14.0; Legumes 2.5; Tomatoes 8.3; Onions 1.7; Artichokes 1.2; Watermelons 9.7; Melons 3.0; Cucumbers 2.1; Carobs 2.8; Olives 3.1; Lemons 10.7; Grapefruit 15.8; Oranges 61.6; Tangerines 2.0.

Livestock ('000 head, 2001): Cattle 34.2; Sheep 202.7; Goats 54.8; Chickens 4,238.

Livestock Products ('000 metric tons, unless otherwise indicated, 2001): Sheep's and goats' milk 11.4; Cows' milk 66.5; Sheep meat 3.3; Goat meat 0.8; Cattle meat 2.1; Chicken meat 6.8; Wool 0.2; Eggs (million) 13.4.

Fishing (metric tons, 2001): Total catch 400.

FINANCE

Currency and Exchange Rates: Turkish currency: 100 kuruş = 1 Turkish lira. *Sterling, Dollar and Euro Equivalents* (30 December 2011): £1 sterling = 2.955 liras; US $1 = 1.911 liras; €1 = 2.473 liras; 100 Turkish liras = £33.84 = $52.33 = €40.44. Note: A new currency, the new Turkish lira, equivalent to 1,000,000 of the former units, was introduced on 1 January 2005. Figures in this survey have been converted retrospectively to reflect this development. (The name of the currency reverted to Turkish lira on 1 January 2009, although new Turkish lira banknotes and coins were to remain in circulation for a further year.) *Average Exchange Rate* (liras per US dollar): 1.550 in 2009; 1.503 in 2010; 1.675 in 2011.

Budget ('000 Turkish liras, 2009): *Revenue:* Local revenue 1,577,760.0 (Direct taxes 554,007.8, Indirect taxes 591,153.8, Other income 148,866.9, Fund revenues 283,731.6); Foreign aid 272,819.9; Total 1,850,580.0. *Expenditure:* Personnel 936,237.8; Other goods and services 167,177.6; Transfers 1,154,300.9; Investments 149,996.5; Defence 167,395.6; Total 2,575,108.3.

Cost of Living (Consumer Price Index, annual averages; base: 2008 = 100): 105.8 in 2009; 110.3 in 2010; 120.9 in 2011.

Expenditure on the Gross Domestic Product ('000 Turkish liras at current prices, 2003, provisional figures): Government final consumption expenditure 482,674; Private final consumption expenditure 1,071,916; Increase in stocks 30,900; Gross fixed capital formation 300,218; *Total domestic expenditure* 1,885,707; Net exports of goods and services −56,763; *GDP in purchasers' values* 1,828,944; *GDP at constant 1977 prices* (million liras) 9,523.6.

Gross Domestic Product by Economic Activity ('000 Turkish liras, 2010): Agriculture, forestry and fishing 330,292.7; Mining and quarrying 35,628.4; Manufacturing 130,888.7; Electricity and water 386,319.1; Construction 312,118.7; Wholesale and retail trade 598,030.0; Restaurants and hotels 302,003.6; Transport and communications 525,213.2; Finance 404,371.0; Ownership of dwellings 220,581.2; Business and personal services 652,317.3; Government services 1,180,064.6; *Sub-total* 5,077,828.4; Import duties 536,308.5; *GDP in purchasers' values* 5,614,136.9.

Balance of Payments (US $ million, 2008): Merchandise exports f.o.b. 83.7; Merchandise imports c.i.f. −1,680.7; *Trade balance* −1,597.0; Services and unrequited transfers (net) 1,206.7; *Current balance* −390.3; Foreign aid and loans from Turkey 337.1; Other short-term capital movements 73.4; Net errors and omissions −289.7; *Overall balance* −269.5.

EXTERNAL TRADE

Principal Commodities (US $ million, 2009): *Imports c.i.f.:* Food and live animals 171.4; Beverages and tobacco 80.1; Mineral fuels, lubricants, etc. 225.8; Basic manufactures 268.1; Machinery and transport equipment 308.0; Miscellaneous manufactured articles 122.8; Total (incl. others) 1,326.2. *Exports f.o.b.:* Food and live animals 20.9; Industrial products 45.4; Minerals 4.8; Total 71.1.

Principal Trading Partners (US $ million, 2009): *Imports c.i.f.:* Turkey 923.4; United Kingdom 61.8; USA 11.6; Total (incl. others) 1,326.2. *Exports f.o.b.:* Turkey 38.5; United Kingdom 2.8; Total (incl. others) 71.1.

TRANSPORT

Road Traffic (registered motor vehicles, 2001): Saloon cars 76,850; Estate cars 9,168; Pick-ups 3,825; Vans 9,131; Buses 2,077; Trucks 1,593; Lorries 6,335; Motorcycles 16,424; Agricultural tractors 6,594; Total (incl. others) 134,454.

Shipping (2001): Freight traffic ('000 metric tons): Goods loaded 247.2, Goods unloaded 898.1; Vessels entered 3,220.

Civil Aviation (2001): Passenger arrivals and departures 691,431; Freight landed and cleared (metric tons) 4,297.

TOURISM

Visitors (2009): 800,376 (including 638,700 Turkish visitors).

Tourism Receipts (US $ million, 2009): 390.7.

COMMUNICATIONS MEDIA

Radio Receivers (2001, provisional): 82,364 in use.

Television Receivers (2001, provisional): 70,960 in use.

Telephones (31 December 2002): 87,745 subscribers.

Mobile Cellular Telephones (31 December 2002): 147,522 subscribers.

EDUCATION

2009/10: *Pre-primary schools:* 143 institutions, 416 teachers, 5,784 pupils; *Primary schools:* 93 institutions, 1,547 teachers, 17,725 pupils; *Secondary Schools:* 34 institutions, 1,082 teachers, 10,484 students; *General High Schools:* 25 institutions, 919 teachers, 7,449 students; *Vocational Schools:* 11 institutions, 559 teachers, 3,315 students; *Universities:* 8 institutions, 40,431 students (of which 8,356 Turkish Cypriots, 29,191 from Turkey, 2,884 from other countries). Note: 1,214 'TRNC' students were studying abroad.

Adult Literacy Rate (at census of 15 December 1996): 93.5%.

Directory

The Government

HEAD OF STATE

President: DEMETRIS CHRISTOFIAS (took office 28 February 2008).

COUNCIL OF MINISTERS
(May 2012)

The executive is formed by the Anorthotiko Komma Ergazomenou Laou (AKEL) and independents (Ind.).

Minister of Foreign Affairs: ERATOU KOZAKOU-MARCOULLIS (Ind.).

Minister of Defence: DEMETRIS ELIADES (Ind.).

Minister of Finance: VASOS SHIARLIS (Ind.).

Minister of the Interior: ELENI MAVROU (AKEL).

Minister of Justice and Public Order: LOUCAS LOUCA (Ind.).

Minister of Commerce, Industry and Tourism: NEOKLIS SYLIKIOTIS (AKEL).

Minister of Education and Culture: GIORGOS DEMOSTHENOUS (Ind.).

Minister of Health: STAVROS MALAS (Ind.).

Minister of Labour and Social Insurance: SOTIROULLA CHARALAMBOUS (AKEL).

Minister of Communications and Works: EFTHYMIOS FLOURENTZOS (Ind.).

Minister of Agriculture, Natural Resources and the Environment: SOFOCLIS ALETRARIS (Ind.).

Government Spokesman: STEPHANOS STEPHANOU (AKEL).

Note: Under the Constitution of 1960, the position of Vice-President and three posts in the Council of Ministers are reserved for Turkish Cypriots. However, there has been no Turkish Cypriot participation in the Government since December 1963.

MINISTRIES

Office of the President: Presidential Palace, Demosthenis Severis Ave, 1400 Nicosia; tel. 22867400; fax 22663799; e-mail info@presidency.gov.cy; internet www.presidency.gov.cy.

Ministry of Agriculture, Natural Resources and the Environment: Loukis Akritas Ave, 1411 Nicosia; tel. 22408307; fax 22781156; e-mail registry@moa.gov.cy; internet www.moa.gov.cy.

Ministry of Commerce, Industry and Tourism: 6 Andreas Araouzos St, 1421 Nicosia; tel. 22867100; fax 22375120; e-mail perm.sec@mcit.gov.cy; internet www.mcit.gov.cy.

Ministry of Communications and Works: 28 Achaeon St, Agios Andreas, 1424 Nicosia; tel. 22800288; fax 22776266; e-mail ipiresia.politi@mcw.gov.cy; internet www.mcw.gov.cy.

Ministry of Defence: 4 Emmanuel Roides Ave, 1432 Nicosia; tel. 22807622; fax 22676182; e-mail defence@mod.gov.cy; internet www.mod.gov.cy.

Ministry of Education and Culture: Kimonos and Thoukididis, 1434 Nicosia; tel. 22800600; fax 22426349; e-mail minister@moec.gov.cy; internet www.moec.gov.cy.

Ministry of Finance: Cnr Michalakis Karaolis St and Gregoriou Afxentiou St, 1439 Nicosia; tel. 22601104; fax 22602741; e-mail registry@mof.gov.cy; internet www.mof.gov.cy.

Ministry of Foreign Affairs: Presidential Palace Ave, 1447 Nicosia; tel. 22401000; fax 22661881; e-mail minforeign1@mfa.gov.cy; internet www.mfa.gov.cy.

Ministry of Health: 1 Prodomou and 17 Chilonos, 1448 Nicosia; tel. 22605300; fax 22305803; e-mail ministryofhealth@cytanet.com.cy; internet www.moh.gov.cy.

Ministry of the Interior: Demosthenis Severis Ave, Ex Secretariat Compound, 1453 Nicosia; tel. 22867800; fax 22671465; e-mail info@moi.gov.cy; internet www.moi.gov.cy.

Ministry of Justice and Public Order: 125 Athalassa Ave, 1461 Nicosia; tel. 22805955; fax 22518356; e-mail registry@mjpo.gov.cy; internet www.mjpo.gov.cy.

Ministry of Labour and Social Insurance: 7 Byron Ave, 1463 Nicosia; tel. 22401600; fax 22670993; e-mail administration@mlsi.gov.cy; internet www.mlsi.gov.cy.

President and Legislature

PRESIDENT

Presidential Election, First Ballot, 17 February 2008

Candidate	Valid votes	%
Ioannis Kasoulides (Ind., with DISY support)	150,996	33.51
Demetris Christofias (AKEL)	150,016	33.29
Tassos Papadopoulos (DIKO)	143,249	31.79
Marios Matsakis (DIKO)	3,460	0.77
Costas Kyriacou (Ind.)	1,092	0.24
Costas Themistocleous (Ind.)	753	0.17
Andreas Efstratiou (Ind.)	713	0.16
Christodoulos Neophytou (Ind.)	243	0.05
Anastasis Michael (Ind.)	117	0.03
Total	462,847*	100.00

* Including 12,208 blank or invalid votes (2.64% of total votes cast).

Presidential Election, Second Ballot, 24 February 2008

Candidate	Votes	%
Demetris Christofias (AKEL)	240,604	53.37
Ioannis Kasoulides (Ind., with DISY support)	210,195	46.63
Total*	469,143	100.00

* Including 18,344 blank or invalid votes (3.91% of total votes cast).

House of Representatives

1402 Nicosia; tel. 22407300; fax 22668611; e-mail vouli@parliament.cy; internet www.parliament.cy.

The House of Representatives originally consisted of 50 members, 35 from the Greek community and 15 from the Turkish community, elected for a term of five years. In January 1964 the Turkish members withdrew and set up the 'Turkish Legislative Assembly of the Turkish Cypriot Administration'. At the 1985 elections the membership of the House was expanded to 80 members, of whom 56 were to be from the Greek community and 24 from the Turkish community (according to the ratio of representation specified in the Constitution).

President: YIANNAKIS OMIROU.

Elections for the Greek Representatives, 22 May 2011

Party	Votes	% of Votes	Seats
Dimokratikos Synagermos (DISY)	138,682	34.28	20
Anorthotiko Komma Ergazomenou Laou (AKEL)	132,171	32.67	19
Dimokratiko Komma (DIKO)	63,763	15.76	9
Kinima Sosialdimokraton EDEK (KISOS)	36,113	8.93	5
Evropaiko Komma (Evro.Ko)	15,711	3.88	2
Kinima Oikologon Perivallontiston (KOP)	8,960	2.21	1
Others	9,177	2.27	—
Total*	404,577	100.0	56

* Excluding 8,701 invalid votes and 4,969 blank votes.

Political Organizations

Agonistiko Dimokratiko Kinima (ADIK) (Fighting Democratic Movement): POB 216095, 80 Archbishop Makarios III Ave, 2085 Nicosia; tel. 22765353; fax 22375737; e-mail info@adik.org.cy; internet www.adik.org.cy; f. 1999; centre-right; supports independent and united Cyprus and a settlement based on UN resolutions; Pres. DINOS MICHAELIDES; Gen. Sec. SPYROS STEFOU.

Anorthotiko Komma Ergazomenou Laou (AKEL) (Progressive Party of the Working People): POB 21827, 4 E. Papaioannou St, 1075 Nicosia; tel. 22761121; fax 22761574; e-mail k.e.akel@cytanet.com.cy; internet www.akel.org.cy; f. 1941; successor to the Communist Party of Cyprus (f. 1926); Marxist-Leninist; supports united, sovereign, independent, federal and demilitarized Cyprus; over 14,000 mems; Sec.-Gen. ANDROS KYPRIANOU.

Dimokratiko Komma (DIKO) (Democratic Party): POB 23979, 50 Grivas Dhigenis Ave, 1080 Nicosia; tel. 22873800; fax 22873801; e-mail diko@diko.org.cy; internet www.diko.org.cy; f. 1976; absorbed Enosi Kentrou (Centre Union, f. 1981) in 1989; supports settlement of the Cyprus problem based on UN resolutions; Pres. MARIOS KAROYIAN; Gen. Sec. KYRIAKOS KENEVEZOS.

Dimokratikos Synagermos (DISY) (Democratic Rally): POB 25305, 25 Pindarou St, 1308 Nicosia; tel. 22883000; fax 22753821; e-mail disy@disy.org.cy; internet www.disy.org.cy; f. 1976; absorbed Democratic National Party (DEK) in 1977, New Democratic Front (NEDIPA) in 1988 and Liberal Party in 1998; advocates the reunification of Cyprus on the basis of a bizonal federation; also advocates market economy with restricted state intervention and increased state social role; 35,000 mems; Pres. NIKOS ANASTASIADES; Dir-Gen. PANAYIOTIS ANTONIOU.

Enomeni Dimokrates (EDI) (United Democrats): POB 23494, 1683 Nicosia; tel. 22663030; fax 22664747; e-mail info@edi.org.cy; internet www.edi.org.cy; f. 1996 by merger of Ananeotiko Dimokratiko Socialistiko Kinima (ADISOK—Democratic Socialist Reform Movement) and Kinima ton Eleftheron Dimokraton (KED—Movement of Free Democrats); Pres. PRAXOULA ANTONIADOU KYRIAKOU; Gen. Sec. COSTAS MELANIDES.

Epalxi Anasygrotisis Kentrou (EPALXI) (Political Forum for the Restructuring of the Centre): 1 Lambousa St, 1095 Nicosia; POB 22119, 1517 Nicosia; tel. 22777000; fax 22779939; e-mail info@epalxi.com; internet www.epalxi.com; f. 1998; aims to achieve a wider grouping of all centrist social-democratic movements; supports a settlement to the Cyprus problem based on the principles of the Rule of Law, international law and respect for human rights for all citizens, and the establishment of a democratic federal system of govt.

Ethniko Laiko Metopo (ELAM) (National People's Front): Nicosia; e-mail ethnikolaikometwpo@gmail.com; internet www.elamcy.com; right-wing, nationalist; Leader CHRISTOS CHRISTOU.

Evropaiko Komma (Evro.Ko) (European Party): POB 22496, 1522 Nicosia; tel. 22460033; fax 22761144; e-mail evropaiko.komma@cytanet.com.cy; internet www.evropaikokomma.org; f. 2005 by fmr mems of Neoi Orizontes (NEO) and other political orgs; Pres. DEMETRIS SYLLOURIS.

Kinima Oikologon Perivallontiston (KOP) (Cyprus Green Party): POB 29682, 169 Athalassas Ave, Strovolos, 2024 Nicosia; tel. 22518787; fax 22512710; e-mail greenparty@cytanet.com.cy; internet www.greenpartycy.com; f. 1996; advocates the reunification of Cyprus; promotes the principles of sustainable devt; Sec.-Gen. IOANNA PANAYIOTOU.

Kinima Sosialdimokraton EDEK (KISOS) (Movement of Social Democrats): POB 21064, 40 Byron Ave, 1096 Nicosia; tel. 22670121; fax 22678894; e-mail socialdimokratestypos@cytanet.com.cy; internet www.edek.org.cy; f. 2000 as successor to Socialistico Komma Kyprou (EDEK—Socialist Party of Cyprus, f. 1969); supports independent, non-aligned, unitary, demilitarized Cyprus; Pres. YIANNAKIS OMIROU; Hon. Pres. Dr VASSOS LYSSARIDES.

Diplomatic Representation

EMBASSIES AND HIGH COMMISSIONS IN CYPRUS

Australia: 4 Annis Komninis St, 2nd Floor, 1060 Nicosia; tel. 22753001; fax 22766486; e-mail auscomm@logos.cy.net; internet www.cyprus.embassy.gov.au; High Commr TREVOR PEACOCK.

Austria: POB 23961, 34 Demosthenis Severis Ave, 1687 Nicosia; tel. 22410151; fax 22680099; e-mail nicosia-ob@bmeia.gv.at; internet www.bmeia.gv.at/botschaft/nikosia; Ambassador MARTIN WEISS.

Belgium: 2A Chilonos St, Office 102, 1101 Nicosia; tel. 22449020; fax 22774717; e-mail nicosia@diplobel.fed.be; internet www.diplomatie.be/nicosia; Ambassador GUY SEVRIN.

Bulgaria: POB 24029, 13 Konst. Paleologos St, 2406 Engomi, Nicosia; tel. 22672486; fax 22676598; e-mail bulgaria@cytanet.com.cy; internet www.mfa.bg/nicosia; Ambassador VESSELIN VALCHEV.

China, People's Republic: POB 24531, 30 Archimedes St, 2411 Engomi, Nicosia; tel. 22352182; fax 22353530; e-mail chinaemb_cy@mfa.gov.cn; internet cy.china-embassy.org; Ambassador LI GUOBANG.

Cuba: POB 28173, 51-A Kratinou St, 2040 Strovolos, Nicosia; tel. 22769743; fax 22753820; e-mail embacuba@spidernet.com.cy; internet emba.cubaminrex.cu; Ambassador FIDEL EMILIO VASCÓS GONZÁLEZ.

Czech Republic: POB 5202, 48 Arsinois St, 1307 Nicosia; tel. 22421118; fax 22421059; e-mail nicosia@embassy.mzv.cz; internet www.mzv.cz/nicosia; Ambassador LADISLAV ŠKEŘÍK.

Denmark: POB 20995, 7 Dositheou St, Parabldg Block C, 4th Floor, 1071 Nicosia; tel. 22377417; fax 22377472; e-mail nicamb@um.dk; internet www.ambnicosia.um.dk; Ambassador KIRSTEN ROSENVOLD GEELAN.

Egypt: POB 21752, 14 Ayios Prokopios St, Engomi, 2406 Nicosia; tel. 22449050; fax 22449081; e-mail info@egyptianembassy.org.cy; internet www.egyptianembassy.org.cy; Ambassador MENHA MAHROUS BAKHOUM.

Finland: POB 21438, 9 Arch. Makarios III Ave, 1508 Nicosia; tel. 22458020; fax 22477880; e-mail sanomat.nic@formin.fi; internet www.finland.org.cy; Ambassador RIITTA RESCH.

France: 14–16 Saktouri St, 2nd Floor, Agioi Omologitai, 1080 Nicosia; tel. 22585300; fax 22585335; e-mail ambafrance@cytanet.com.cy; internet www.ambafrance-cy.org; Ambassador JEAN-MARC RIVES.

Georgia: 46 Themistocles Dervis St, Medcon Tower, 5th Floor, 1066 Nicosia; tel. 22357327; fax 22357307; e-mail geoembassy@cytanet.com.cy; Ambassador VLADIMER KONSTANTINIDI.

Germany: 10 Nikitaras St, Ay. Omoloyitae, 1080 Nicosia; POB 25705, 1311 Nicosia; tel. 22451145; fax 22665694; e-mail info@nikosia.diplo.de; internet www.nikosia.diplo.de; Ambassador Dr GABRIELA GUELLIL.

Greece: POB 21799, 8–10 Byron Ave, 1096 Nicosia; tel. 22445111; fax 22680649; e-mail info@greekembassy-cy.org; internet www.greekembassy-cy.org; Ambassador VASSILIS PAPAIOANNOU.

Holy See: POB 21964, Holy Cross Catholic Church, Paphos Gate, 1010 Nicosia (Apostolic Nunciature); tel. 22662132; fax 22660767; e-mail holcross@logos.cy.net; Apostolic Nuncio Most Rev. ANTONIO FRANCO (Titular Archbishop of Gallese—resident in Jerusalem).

Hungary: 2 Prodromou and Demetrakopoulou, Zenios Tower, 3rd Floor, 1090 Nicosia; tel. 22459130; fax 22459134; e-mail huembnic@cytanet.com.cy; Ambassador BALAAZS BOTOS.

India: POB 25544, 3 Indira Gandhi St, Engomi, 2413 Nicosia; tel. 22351741; fax 22352062; e-mail hicomind@spidernet.com.cy; internet www.hcinicosia.org.cy; High Commr ASHOK KUMAR.

Iran: POB 8145, 42 Armenias St, Acropolis, Nicosia; tel. 22314459; fax 22315446; e-mail iranemb@cytanet.com.cy; Ambassador Dr ALI AKBAR REZAEI.

Ireland: 7 Aiantas St, Ayios Omoloyites, 1082 Nicosia; POB 23848, 1686 Nicosia; tel. 22818183; fax 22660050; e-mail nicosiaembassy@dfa.ie; internet www.embassyofireland.com.cy; Ambassador PATRICK SCULLION.

Israel: POB 25159, 4 Ioanni Grypari St, 1090 Nicosia; tel. 22369500; fax 22666338; e-mail ambass-sec@nicosia.mfa.gov.il; internet nicosia.mfa.gov.il; Ambassador MICHAEL HARARI.

Italy: POB 27695, 11 25th March St, Engomi, 2408 Nicosia; tel. 22357635; fax 22357616; e-mail ambnico.mail@esteri.it; internet www.ambnicosia.esteri.it; Ambassador ALFREDO BASTIANELLI.

Lebanon: POB 21924, 6 Chiou St, Ayios Dhometios, 1515 Nicosia; tel. 22878282; fax 22878293; e-mail lebanon.emb@cytanet.com.cy; Ambassador (vacant).

Libya: POB 22487, 7 Stassinos Ave, 1060 Nicosia; tel. 22460055; fax 22452710; e-mail info@libyanpeoplebureau.com.cy; Ambassador MUSTAFA A. ALMGHERBI.

Netherlands: POB 23835, 34 Demosthenis Severis Ave, 1080 Nicosia; tel. 22873666; fax 22872399; e-mail nic@minbuza.nl; internet www.nlembassy.org.cy; Ambassador BRECHJE SCHWACHÖFER.

Poland: POB 22743, 12–14 Kennedy Ave, 1087 Nicosia; tel. 22753517; fax 22751981; e-mail nikozja.amb.sekretariat@msz.gov.pl; internet www.nikozja.polemb.net; Ambassador PAWEŁ DOBROWOLSKI.

Portugal: 9 Arch. Makarios III Ave, Severis Bldg, 5th Floor, POB 27407, 1645 Nicosia; tel. 22375131; fax 22756456; e-mail embportugal@nicosia.dgaccp.pt; Chargé d'affaires a.i. JOÃO BERNARDO WEINSTEIN.

Qatar: POB 22023, 1516 Nicosia; tel. 22466864; fax 22466893; e-mail qatarembassy@cytanet.com.cy; Ambassador MUBARAK ABD AL-RAHMAN MUBARAK AL-NASSER.

Romania: POB 22210, 27 Pireos St, Strovolos, 2023 Nicosia; tel. 22495333; fax 22517383; e-mail embrom@cytanet.com.cy; internet www.nicosia.mae.ro; Ambassador ION PASCU.

Russia: POB 21845, Ayios Prokopias St and Archbishop Makarios III Ave, Engomi, 2406 Nicosia; tel. 22774622; fax 22774854; e-mail russia1@cytanet.com.cy; internet www.cyprus.mid.ru; Ambassador VYACHESLAV SHUMSKIY.

Serbia: 2 Vasilissis Olgas St, Engomi, 1903 Nicosia; tel. 22777511; fax 22775910; e-mail nicosia@serbia.org.cy; internet www.serbia.org.cy; Ambassador SAVO DJURICA.

Slovakia: POB 21165, 4 Kalamatas St, 2002 Strovolos, Nicosia; tel. 22879681; fax 22311715; e-mail skembassy@cytanet.com.cy; Ambassador ANNA TURENIČOVA.

Spain: POB 28349, 32 Strovolos Ave, 2018 Strovolos, Nicosia; tel. 22450410; fax 22491291; e-mail emb.nicosia@maec.es; Ambassador ANA MARÍA SÁLOMON PÉREZ.

Sweden: POB 21621, 9 Archbishop Makarios Ave, Severis Bldg, Second Floor, 1065 Nicosia; tel. 22458088; fax 22374522; e-mail ambassaden.nicosia@foreign.ministry.se; internet www.swedenabroad.se/nicosia; Ambassador KLAS GIEROW.

Switzerland: 46 Themistocles Dervis St, Medcon Tower, 1066 Nicosia; POB 20729, 1663 Nicosia; tel. 22466800; fax 22766008; e-mail nic.vertretung@eda.admin.ch; internet www.eda.admin.ch/nicosia; Chargé d'affaires a.i. FRANK NOHL.

Syria: POB 21892, 24 Nikodimos Mylona St, Ayios Antonios, 1071 Nicosia; tel. 22817333; fax 22756963; e-mail syremb@cytanet.com.cy; Chargé d'affaires LAMIA AL-HARIRI.

Ukraine: 10 Andrea Miaouli St, Makedonitissa, Engomi, 2415 Nicosia; tel. 22464380; fax 22464381; e-mail emb_cy@mfa.gov.ua; internet www.mfa.gov.ua/cyprus; Ambassador BORYS HUMENIUK.

United Kingdom: POB 21978, Alexander Pallis St, 1587 Nicosia; tel. 22861100; fax 22861125; e-mail brithc.2@cytanet.com.cy; internet ukincyprus.fco.gov.uk; High Commr MATTHEW KIDD.

USA: Metochiou and Ploutarchou, Engomi, 2407 Nicosia; POB 24536, 1385 Nicosia; tel. 22393939; fax 22780944; e-mail info@americanembassy.org.cy; internet cyprus.usembassy.gov; Chargé d'affaires a.i. ANDREW JAMES SCHOFER.

Venezuela: POB 23367, 12 Andrea Zakou St, Engomi, 2402 Nicosia; tel. 22445332; fax 22662975; e-mail embaven_chipre@hotmail.com; Ambassador Dr ANGEL RAFAEL TORTOLERO.

Judicial System

Supreme Council of Judicature: Nicosia; tel. 22865716; fax 22304500; The Supreme Council of Judicature is composed of the President and Judges of the Supreme Court. It is responsible for the appointment, promotion, transfer, etc., of the judges exercising civil and criminal jurisdiction in the District Courts, the Assize Courts, the Family Courts, the Military Court, the Rent Control Courts and the Industrial Dispute Court.

SUPREME COURT

The Constitution of 1960 provided for a separate Supreme Constitutional Court and High Court, but in 1964, in view of the resignation of their neutral presidents, these were amalgamated to form a single Supreme Court. The Supreme Court is the final appellate court in the Republic and the final adjudicator in matters of constitutional and administrative law, including recourses on conflict of competence between state organs on questions of the constitutionality of laws, etc. It deals with appeals from Assize Courts, District Courts and other inferior courts as well as from the decisions of its own judges when exercising original jurisdiction in certain matters such as prerogative orders of *habeas corpus, mandamus, certiorari*, etc., and in admiralty cases.

Supreme Court: Charalambos Mouskos St, 1404 Nicosia; tel. 22865741; fax 22304500; e-mail chief.reg@sc.judicial.gov.cy; internet www.supremecourt.gov.cy.

President: PETROS ARTEMIS.

Judges: IOANNIS CONSTANTINIDES, FRIXOS NICOLAIDES, ANDREAS KRAMVIS, DEMETRIOS H. HADJIHAMBIS, EFFIE PAPADOPOULOU, MICHAEL PHOTIOU, MYRON NICOLATOS, GEORGE EROTOKRITOU, STELIOS NATHANAEL, COSTAS CLERIDES, COSTAS PAMBALLIS, ANDREAS PASCHALIDES.

Attorney-General: PETROS CLERIDES.

OTHER COURTS

As required by the Constitution, a law was adopted in 1960 providing for the establishment, jurisdiction and powers of courts of civil and criminal jurisdiction, i.e. of six District Courts and six Assize Courts. In accordance with the provisions of new legislation, approved in 1991, a permanent Assize Court, with powers of jurisdiction in all districts, was established.

In addition to a single Military Court, there are specialized courts concerned with cases relating to industrial disputes, rent control and family law.

'Turkish Republic of Northern Cyprus'

The Turkish intervention in Cyprus in July 1974 resulted in the establishment of a separate area in northern Cyprus under the control of the Autonomous Turkish Cypriot Administration, with a Council of Ministers and separate judicial, financial, police, military and educational machinery serving the Turkish community.

On 13 February 1975 the Turkish-occupied zone of Cyprus was declared the 'Turkish Federated State of Cyprus', and Rauf Denktaş declared President. At the second joint meeting held by the Executive Council and Legislative Assembly of the Autonomous Turkish Cypriot Administration, it was decided to set up a Constituent Assembly, which would prepare a constitution for the 'Turkish Federated State of Cyprus' within 45 days. This Constitution, which was approved by the Turkish Cypriot population in a referendum held on 8 June 1975, was regarded by the Turkish Cypriots as a first step towards a federal republic of Cyprus. The main provisions of the Constitution are summarized below:

The 'Turkish Federated State of Cyprus' is a democratic, secular republic based on the principles of social justice and the rule of law. It shall exercise only those functions that fall outside the powers and functions expressly given to the (proposed) Federal Republic of Cyprus. Necessary amendments shall be made to the Constitution of the 'Turkish Federated State of Cyprus' when the Constitution of the Federal Republic comes into force. The official language is Turkish.

Legislative power is vested in a Legislative Assembly, composed of 40 deputies, elected by universal suffrage for a period of five years. The President is Head of State and is elected by universal suffrage for a period of five years. No person may be elected President for more than two consecutive terms. The Council of Ministers shall be composed of a prime minister and 10 ministers. Judicial power is exercised through independent courts.

Other provisions cover such matters as the rehabilitation of refugees, property rights outside the 'Turkish Federated State', protection of coasts, social insurance, the rights and duties of citizens, etc.

On 15 November 1983 a unilateral declaration of independence brought into being the 'Turkish Republic of Northern Cyprus', which, like the 'Turkish Federated State of Cyprus', was not granted international recognition.

The Constituent Assembly, established after the declaration of independence, prepared a new Constitution, which was approved by the Turkish Cypriot electorate on 5 May 1985. The new Constitution is very similar to the old one, but the number of deputies in the Legislative Assembly was increased to 50.

HEAD OF STATE

President of the 'Turkish Republic of Northern Cyprus': Dr DERVIŞ EROĞLU (inaugurated 23 April 2010).

COUNCIL OF MINISTERS

(May 2012)

The executive is formed by members of the Ulusal Bırlık Partisi (UBP).

Prime Minister: İRSEN KÜÇÜK.

Minister of Foreign Affairs: HÜSEYIN ÖZGÜRGÜN.

Minister of Interior Affairs and Local Administrations: NAZIM ÇAVUŞOĞLU.

Minister of Finance: ERSIN TATAR.

Minister of National Education, Youth and Sport: KEMAL DÜRÜST.

Minister of Health: Dr AHMET KAŞIF.

Minister of Agriculture and Natural Resources: ALI ÇETIN AMCAOĞLU.

Minister of Public Works and Communications: HAMZA ERSAN SANER.

Minister of Tourism, Environment and Culture: ÜNAL ÜSTEL.

Minister of Labour and Social Security: ŞERIFE ÜNVERDI.

Minister of Economy and Energy: SUNAT ATUN.

MINISTRIES

Office of the President: Şht Selahattin Sonat Sok., Lefkoşa (Nicosia), Mersin 10, Turkey; tel. 2283444; fax 2272252; internet www.kktcb.eu.

Prime Minister's Office: Selçuklu Rd, Lefkoşa (Nicosia), Mersin 10, Turkey; tel. 2283141; fax 2287280; e-mail info@kktcbasbakanlik.org; internet www.kktcbasbakanlik.org.

Ministry of Agriculture and Natural Resources: Salih Mecit Sok. 16, Lefkoşa (Nicosia), Mersin 10, Turkey; tel. 2283735; fax 2286945; e-mail info@kktob.org; internet www.kktob.org.

Ministry of Economy and Energy: Lefkoşa (Nicosia), Mersin 10, Turkey; tel. 2289629; fax 2273976.

Ministry of Finance: Lefkoşa (Nicosia), Mersin 10, Turkey; tel. 2283116; fax 2278230; e-mail bim@kktcmaliye.com; internet www.kktcmaliye.com.

Ministry of Foreign Affairs: Selçuklu Rd, Lefkoşa (Nicosia), Mersin 10, Turkey; tel. 2283241; fax 2284290; e-mail bakanlik@trncinfo.org; internet www.trncinfo.org.

Ministry of Health: Lefkoşa (Nicosia), Mersin 10, Turkey; tel. 2283173; fax 2283893; e-mail saglik@kktc.net; internet www.saglikbakanligi.com.

Ministry of Interior Affairs and Local Administrations: Lefkoşa (Nicosia), Mersin 10, Turkey; tel. 2283344; fax 2283043.

Ministry of Labour and Social Security: 7 İplik Pazarı Sok., Lefkoşa (Nicosia), Mersin 10, Turkey; tel. 2273643; fax 2283776; e-mail info@csgb.eu; internet www.csgb.eu.

Ministry of National Education, Youth and Sport: Lefkoşa (Nicosia), Mersin 10, Turkey; tel. 2284505; fax 2282334; e-mail info@mebnet.net; internet www.mebnet.net.

Ministry of Public Works and Communications: Lefkoşa (Nicosia), Mersin 10, Turkey; tel. 2283666; fax 2281981; e-mail info@kktculastirma.com; internet www.kktculastirma.com.

Ministry of Tourism, Environment and Culture: Selçuklu Rd, Lefkoşa (Nicosia), Mersin 10, Turkey; tel. 2289629; fax 2285625; internet www.turizmcevrekultur.org.

PRESIDENT

Election, 18 April 2010

Candidates	Votes	%
Dr Derviş Eroğlu (Ulusal Bırlık Partisi)	61,422	50.35
Mehmet Ali Talat (Ind.)	52,294	42.87
Tahsin Ertuğruloğlu (Ind.)	4,647	3.81
Zeki Besiktepeli (Ind.)	1,967	1.61
Mustafa Kemal Tümkan (Ind.)	964	0.79
Arif Salih Kirdag (Ind.)	520	0.43
Ayhan Kaymak (Ind.)	168	0.14
Total*	121,982	100.00

* Excluding 3,312 invalid votes.

LEGISLATIVE ASSEMBLY

Speaker: HASAN BOZER (UBP).

General Election, 19 April 2009

Party	Votes	% of votes	Seats
Ulusal Bırlık Partisi	620,354	44.02	26
Cumhuriyetçi Türk Partisi	412,710	29.29	15
Demokrat Parti	150,023	10.65	5
Toplumcu Demokrasi Partisi	96,583	6.85	2
Özgürlük ve Reform Partisi	87,657	6.22	2
Others	41,959	2.98	—
Total	1,409,286	100.00	50

ELECTORAL COMMISSION

Yüksek Seçim Kurulu (YSK) (Higher Council of Elections): Lefkoşa (Nicosia), Mersin 10, Turkey; internet ysk.makhemeler.net; Pres. METIN A. HAKKI.

POLITICAL ORGANIZATIONS

Birleşik Kıbrıs Partisi (BKP) (United Cyprus Party): Ali Paşa Sok. 4, Çağlayan, Lefkoşa (Nicosia), Mersin 10, Turkey; tel. 2281845; fax 2281617; e-mail bkp@birlesikkibris.com; internet www.birlesikkibrispartisi.org; f. 2002; Marxist-Leninist; Sec.-Gen. İZZET İZCAN.

Cumhuriyetçi Türk Partisi (CTP) (Republican Turkish Party): 99 Şehit Salahi, Şevket Sok., Lefkoşa (Nicosia), Mersin 10, Turkey; tel. 2273300; fax 2281914; e-mail ctp@defne.net; internet www.ctp-bg.org; f. 1970 by mems of the Turkish community in Cyprus; district orgs at Gazi Mağusa (Famagusta), Girne (Kyrenia), Güzelyurt (Morphou) and Lefkoşa (Nicosia); Leader ÖZKAN YORGANCIOĞLU; Gen. Sec. ASIM AKANSOY.

Demokrat Parti (DP) (Democrat Party): Hasane Ilgaz Sok. 13A, Lefkoşa (Nicosia), Mersin 10, Turkey; tel. 2283795; fax 2287130; e-mail basin@demokratparti.net; internet www.demokratparti.net; f. 1992 by disaffected representatives of the Ulusal Bırlık Partisi; merged with the Yeni Doğuş Partisi (New Dawn Party; f. 1984) and Sosyal Demokrat Partisi (Social Democrat Party) in May 1993; Leader SERDAR DENKTAŞ; Gen. Sec. ERTUĞRUL HASIPOĞLU.

Kıbrıs Adalet Partisi (KAP) (Cyprus Justice Party): 1 Osman Paşa Ave, Köşklüçiftlik, Lefkoşa (Nicosia), Mersin 10, Turkey; tel. 2270274; fax 2289938; Leader OĞUZ KALEIOĞLU.

Kıbrıs Sosyalist Partisi (KSP) (Cyprus Socialist Party): Lefkoşa (Nicosia), Mersin 10, Turkey; e-mail ksp@kibrissosyalistpartisi.org; internet www.kibrissosyalistpartisi.org; Gen. Sec. MEHMET BIRINCI.

Milliyetçi Bariş Partisi (MBP) (National Peace Party): Lefkoşa (Nicosia), Mersin 10, Turkey; f. 2003; Leader ERTUĞRUL HASIPOĞLU.

Özgürlük ve Reform Partisi (ORP) (Özgür Parti—Freedom and Reform Party): Lala Mustafa Paşa Sok. 18, Köşklüçiftlik, Lefkoşa (Nicosia), Mersin 10, Turkey; tel. 2290593; fax 2270537; f. 2006 by breakaway parliamentary deputies; Leader Dr TURGAY AVCI.

Toplumcu Demokrasi Partisi (TDP) (Communal Democracy Party): 33A 11 Selim Cad., Lefkoşa (Nicosia), Mersin 10, Turkey; tel. 2272555; fax 2287539; e-mail tdp@kktc.net; internet www.toplumcudemokrasipartisi.com; f. 2007, by merger between the Bariş ve Demokrasi Hareketi (Peace and Democracy Movement) and the Toplumcu Kurtuluş Partisi (Communal Liberation Party); Pres. MEHMET ÇAKICI.

Ulusal Bırlık Partisi (UBP) (National Unity Party): 9 Atatürk Meydanı, Lefkoşa (Nicosia), Mersin 10, Turkey; tel. 2273972; fax 2288732; e-mail ubp@kibris.net; internet www.ubp-kktc.org; f. 1975; right of centre; opposes reunification of Cyprus; Pres. DERVIŞ EROĞLU; Sec.-Gen. NAZIM ÇAVUŞOĞLU.

Yeni Partisi (New Party): Lefkoşa (Nicosia), Mersin 10, Turkey; f. 2004; Leader NURI ÇEVIKEL.

Yeni Kıbrıs Partisi (YKP) (New Cyprus Party): Tahir Hussain Bldg, Lefkoşa (Nicosia), Mersin 10, Turkey; tel. 2274917; fax 2288931; e-mail ykp@ykp.org.cy; internet www.ykp.org.cy; f. 1989; operated as Yurtsever Bırlık Hareketi (YBH) between 1998–2004; publishes weekly newsletter *Yeniçag*; Gen. Sec. MURAT KANATLI.

DIPLOMATIC REPRESENTATION

Embassy in the 'TRNC'

Turkey: Bedrettin Demirel Cad., T. C. Lefkoşa Büyükelçisi, Lefkoşa (Nicosia), Mersin 10, Turkey; tel. 2272314; fax 2282209; e-mail turkemb.lefkose@mfa.gov.tr; internet www.tclefkosabe.org; Ambassador HALIL İBRAHIM AKÇA.

Turkey is the only country officially to have recognized the 'Turkish Republic of Northern Cyprus'.

JUDICIAL SYSTEM

Supreme Court: Lefkoşa (Nicosia), Mersin 10, Turkey; tel. 2287535; fax 2285265; e-mail erkancoskun@kamunet.net; internet www.mahkemeler.net; The Supreme Court is the highest court in the 'TRNC', and functions as the Constitutional Court, the Court of Appeal and the High Administrative Court. The Supreme Court, sitting as the Constitutional Court, has exclusive jurisdiction to adjudicate finally on all matters prescribed by the Constitution. The Supreme Court, sitting as the Court of Appeal, is the highest appellate court in the 'TRNC' in both civil and criminal cases. It also has original jurisdiction in certain matters of judicial review. The Supreme Court, sitting as the High Administrative Court, has exclusive jurisdiction on matters relating to administrative law.

The Supreme Court is composed of a President and seven judges.

President: NEVVAR NOLAN.

Judges: TALAT D. REFIKER, NECMETTIN BOSTANCI, NARIN FERDI ŞEFIK, HÜSEYIN BESIMOĞLU, AHMET KALKAN, MEHMET TÜRKER, ŞAFAK ÖNERI.

Subordinate Courts: Judicial power other than that exercised by the Supreme Court is exercised by the Assize Courts, District Courts and Family Courts.

Supreme Council of Judicature

The Supreme Council of Judicature, composed of the president and judges of the Supreme Court, a member appointed by the President of the 'TRNC', a member appointed by the Legislative Assembly, the Attorney-General and a member elected by the Bar Association, is responsible for the appointment, promotion, transfer and matters relating to the discipline of all judges. The appointments of the president and judges of the Supreme Court are subject to the approval of the President of the 'TRNC'.

Attorney-General: ASKAN ILGEN.

Religion

Greeks form 77% of the population, and most of them belong to the Orthodox Church, although there are also adherents of the Armenian Apostolic Church, the Anglican Communion and the Roman Catholic Church (including Maronites). Most Turks (about 18% of the population) are Muslims.

CHRISTIANITY

The Orthodox Church of Cyprus

The Autocephalous Orthodox Church of Cyprus, founded in AD 45, is part of the Eastern Orthodox Church; the Church is independent, and the Archbishop, who is also the Ethnarch (national leader of the Greek community), is elected by representatives of the towns and villages of Cyprus. The Church comprises 16 dioceses, and in 1995 had an estimated 600,000 members.

Archbishop of Nova Justiniana and all Cyprus: Archbishop CHRYSOSTOMOS II, POB 1130, Archbishop Kyprianos St, Nicosia; tel. 22554600; fax 22431796; e-mail office@churchofcyprus.org.cy; internet www.churchofcyprus.org.cy.

Metropolitan of Kitium: Bishop CHRYSOSTOMOS.

Metropolitan of Kyrenia: Bishop KYKKOTIS.

Metropolitan of Limassol: Bishop ATHANASIOS.

Metropolitan of Morphou: Bishop NEOPHYTOS.

Metropolitan of Paphos: Bishop GEORGIOS.

The Roman Catholic Church

Latin Rite

The Patriarchate of Jerusalem covers Israel, Jordan and Cyprus. The Patriarch is resident in Jerusalem (see the chapter on Israel).

Vicar Patriarchal for Cyprus: Fr UMBERTO BARATO, Holy Cross Catholic Church, Paphos Gate, POB 21964, 1010 Nicosia; tel. 22662132; fax 22660767; e-mail holcross@logos.cy.net.

Maronite Rite

Most of the Roman Catholics in Cyprus are adherents of the Maronite rite. Prior to June 1988 the Archdiocese of Cyprus included part of Lebanon. At 31 December 2006 the archdiocese contained an estimated 10,000 Maronite Catholics.

Archbishop of Cyprus: Most Rev. JOSEPH SOUEIF, POB 22249, Maronite Archbishop's House, 8 Ayios Maronas St, Nicosia; tel. 22678877; fax 22668260; e-mail archmar@cytanet.com.cy.

The Anglican Communion

Anglicans in Cyprus are adherents of the Episcopal Church in Jerusalem and the Middle East, officially inaugurated in January 1976. The Church has four dioceses. The diocese of Cyprus and the Gulf includes Cyprus, Iraq and the countries of the Arabian peninsula.

Bishop in Cyprus and the Gulf, President Bishop of the Episcopal Church in Jerusalem and the Middle East: Right Rev. MICHAEL LEWIS, c/o POB 22075, Diocesan Office, 2 Grigoris Afxentiou St, 1516 Nicosia; tel. 22671220; fax 22674553; e-mail cygulf@spidernet.com.cy; internet www.cypgulf.org; Archdeacon in Cyprus Very Rev. STEPHEN COLLIS.

Other Christian Churches

Among other denominations active in Cyprus are the Armenian Apostolic Church and the Greek Evangelical Church.

ISLAM

Most adherents of Islam in Cyprus, of whom the majority reside in the 'TRNC', are Sunni Muslims of the Hanafi sect. In 2006 an estimated 99% of Turkish Cypriots were Muslims, compared with less than 3% of Greek Cypriots. The religious head of the Muslim community in the 'TRNC' is the Grand Mufti.

Grand Mufti of the 'TRNC': Sheikh AL-SAYYID MUHAMMAD NAZIM ADIL AL-QUBRUSI AL-HAQQANI, PK 142, Lefkoşa (Nicosia), Mersin 10, Turkey.

The Press

GREEK CYPRIOT DAILIES

Alithia (Truth): 26A Pindaros and Androklis St, 1060 Nicosia; POB 21695, 1512 Nicosia; tel. 22763040; fax 22763945; e-mail news@alithia-news.com; internet www.alithia.com.cy; f. 1952 as a weekly, 1982 as a daily; morning; Greek; right-wing; Man. Dir FRIXOS N. KOULERMOS; Editor-in-Chief PAMBOS CHARALAMBOUS; circ. 11,000.

Cyprus Mail: 24 Vassilios Voulgaroktonos St, 1010 Nicosia; POB 21144, 1502 Nicosia; tel. 22818585; fax 22676385; e-mail mail@cyprus-mail.com; internet www.cyprus-mail.com; f. 1945; morning; English; independent; Man. Dir KYRIACOS IAKOVIDES; Editor JEAN CHRISTOU; circ. 6,000.

Haravgi (Dawn): ETAK Bldg, 6 Ezekia Papaioannou St, 1075 Nicosia; POB 21556, 1510 Nicosia; tel. 22766666; fax 22765154; e-mail haravgi@spidernet.com.cy; internet www.haravgi.com.cy; f. 1956; morning; Greek; organ of AKEL; Dir and Chief Editor ANDROULLA GIOUROV; Publr KYPROS KOURTELLARIS; circ. 10,000.

MAXH (Combat): POB 27628, 1st Floor, Block D, 109 office, 2113 Engomi, Nicosia; tel. 22356676; fax 22356701; e-mail newsmaxi@spidernet.com.cy; internet www.maxhnews.com; f. 1960; weekly; Greek; right-wing; Gen. Man. MINA SAMPSON; Chief Editor FROSSO GEORGIOU; circ. 5,000.

O Phileleftheros (Liberal): POB 21094, 1501 Nicosia; tel. 22744000; fax 22590122; e-mail mailbox@phileleftheros.com; internet www.phileleftheros.com.cy; f. 1955; morning; Greek; independent; moderate; Exec. Dir MYRTO MARKIDOU-SELIPA; Sr Editor ARISTOS MICHAELIDES; circ. 28,000.

Politis (Citizen): 8 Vassilios Voulgaroktonos St, 1010 Nicosia; POB 22894, 1524 Nicosia; tel. 22861861; fax 22861871; e-mail info@politis-news.com; internet www.politis.com.cy; f. 1999; morning; Greek; independent; Publr YIANNIS PAPADOPOULOS; Chief Editors GEORGE KASKANIS, SOTIRIS PAROUTIS.

Simerini (Today): POB 21836, 31 Archangelos Ave, Strovolos, 2054 Nicosia; tel. 22580580; fax 22580570; e-mail mail@simerini.com; internet www.simerini.com; f. 1976; morning; Greek; right-wing; supports DISY; Pres. KOSTAS HADJIKOSTIS; Publr PETROS ZACHARIADES; circ. 17,000.

TURKISH CYPRIOT DAILIES

Afrika: Lefkoşa (Nicosia), Mersin 10, Turkey; tel. 2271338; fax 2274585; e-mail avrupa@kktc.net; internet www.afrikagazetesi.net; fmrly Avrupa; Turkish; independent; Editor ŞENER LEVENT; circ. 3,000.

Halkın Sesi (Voice of the People): 172 Girne Cad., Lefkoşa (Nicosia), Mersin 10, Turkey; tel. 22856453141; fax 2272612; e-mail halkinsesi@superonline.com; internet www.halkinsesi.org; f. 1942; morning; Turkish; independent Turkish nationalist; Editor SEFA KARAHASAN.

Kıbrıs (Cyprus): Dr Fazil Küçük Bul., Yeni Sanayi Bölgesi, Lefkoşa (Nicosia), Mersin 10, Turkey; tel. 2252555; fax 2255176; e-mail kibris@kibrisgazetesi.com; internet www.kibrisgazetesi.com; Turkish; Editor BAŞARAN DÜZGÜN; circ. 13,000.

Ortam (Political Conditions): 7 Cengiz Han Sok, Kösklüciflik, Lefkoşa (Nicosia), Mersin 10, Turkey; tel. 2280852; fax 2283784; e-mail ortam@north-cyprus.net; internet www.ortamgazetesi.com; f. 1981; Turkish; organ of the TDP; Editor-in-Chief MEHMET DAVULCU; circ. 1,250.

Vatan (Homeland): 46 Müftü Ziyai Sok., PK 842, Lefkoşa (Nicosia), Mersin 10, Turkey; tel. 2277557; fax 2277558; e-mail atekman@vatangazetesi.net; internet www.vatangazetesi.com; f. 1991; Turkish; Editor ALI TEKMAN.

Yeni Düzen (New System): Organize Sanayi Bölgesi, Lefkoşa (Nicosia), Mersin 10, Turkey; tel. 2256658; fax 2253240; e-mail yeniduzen@defne.net; internet www.yeniduzengazetesi.com; f. 1975; Turkish; organ of the CTP; Chief Editor CENK MUTLUYAKALI; circ. 1,250.

GREEK CYPRIOT WEEKLIES

Athlitiki tis Kyriakis (Sunday Sports News): 53 Demosthenis Severis Ave, 9th Floor, 1080 Nicosia; tel. 22664344; fax 22664543; e-mail fellouka@cytanet.com.cy; f. 1996; Greek; athletics; Dir PANAYIOTIS FELLOUKAS; Chief Editor NICOS NICOLAOU; circ. 4,000.

Cyprus Weekly: POB 24977, 1 Diogenous St, Engomi, 2404 Nicosia; tel. 22744400; fax 22744440; e-mail info@cyprusweekly.com.cy; internet www.cyprusweekly.com.cy; f. 1979; English; independent; Publishing Dirs ALEX EFTHYVOULOS, ANDREAS HADJIPAPAS; Chief Editor MARTYN HENRY; circ. 17,000.

Dimosios Ypallilos (Civil Servant): 3 Demosthenis Severis Ave, 1066 Nicosia; tel. 22844445; fax 22668639; e-mail pasydy@spidernet.com.cy; internet www.pasydy.org; f. 1927; Greek; publ. by the Cyprus Civil Servants' Trade Union (PASYDY); circ. 15,000.

Ergatiki Phoni (Workers' Voice): POB 25018, SEK Bldg, 23 Alkeou St, Engomi, 2018 Nicosia; tel. 22849849; fax 228498508; e-mail sekxenis@cytanet.com.cy; f. 1947; Greek; organ of SEK trade union; Dir NICOS MOYSEOS; Chief Editor XENIS XENOFONTOS; circ. 10,000.

Ergatiko Vima (Workers' Tribune): POB 21185, 1514 Nicosia; tel. 22866400; fax 22349381; e-mail ergatiko-vima@peo.org.cy; f. 1956; Greek; organ of PEO trade union; Chief Editor LEFTERIS GEORGIADIS; circ. 14,000.

Financial Mirror: POB 16077, 2085 Nicosia; tel. 22678666; fax 22678664; e-mail info@financialmirror.com; internet www.financialmirror.com; f. 1993; English (with Greek-language supplement); independent; Publr and Dir MASIS DER PARTHOGH; circ. 4,000.

Official Gazette: Printing Office of the Republic of Cyprus, 1445 Nicosia; tel. 22405811; fax 22303175; e-mail entorzi@gpo.mof.gov.cy; internet www.mof.gov.cy/gpo; f. 1960; Greek; publ. by the Govt of the Republic of Cyprus; circ. 5,000.

Selides (Pages): POB 21094, 1 Diogenous St, Engomi, 2404 Nicosia; POB 21094, 1501 Nicosia; tel. 22744000; fax 22590516; e-mail mailbox@phileleftheros.com; internet www.phileleftheros.com; f. 1991; Greek; Exec. Dir MYRTO MARKIDOU-SELIPA; Chief Editor MARIA MENIKOU; circ. 16,500.

Tharros (Courage): POB 27628, 14A Danaes St, Engomi, Nicosia; tel. 22356676; fax 22356701; e-mail newsmaxi@spidernet.com.cy; internet www.maxinewspaper.com; f. 1961; Greek; right-wing; Gen. Man. MINA SAMSON; circ. 5,500.

To Periodiko: POB 21836, 23 Alkeou St, 4th Floor, 2404 Nicosia; tel. 22580670; fax 22662247; e-mail psillidesc@toperiodiko.com; f. 1986; Greek; general interest; Dir ANTIS HADJIKOSTIS; Chief Editor POPI VAKI; circ. 16,000.

TURKISH CYPRIOT WEEKLIES

Cyprus Observer: 18 Aytekin Zekai Sok., Kyrenia (Girne), Mersin 10, Turkey; POB 29085, Nicosia; tel. 8155387; fax 8155585; e-mail news@observercyprus.com; internet www.observercyprus.com; f. 2005; English; Exec. Editor HASAN ERCAKICA; Editor UMUT URAS.

Cyprus Today: Dr Fazil Küçük Bul., PK 831, Lefkoşa (Nicosia), Mersin 10, Turkey; tel. 2252555; fax 2253708; e-mail cyprustoday@yahoo.com; f. 1991; English; political, social, cultural and economic; Editor GILL FRASER; circ. 6,000.

Ekonomi (The Economy): 90 Bedrettin Demirel Cad., Lefkoşa (Nicosia), Mersin 10, Turkey; tel. 2283760; fax 2283089; f. 1958; Turkish; publ. by the Turkish Cypriot Chamber of Commerce; Editor-in-Chief SAMI TAŞARKAN; circ. 3,000.

Safak: PK 228, Lefkoşa (Nicosia), Mersin 10, Turkey; tel. 2271472; fax 2287910; f. 1992; Turkish; circ. 1,000.

Yeniçağ: 28 Ramadan Cad., Lefkoşa (Nicosia), Mersin 10, Turkey; tel. 2274917; fax 2271476; e-mail irtibat@yenicaggazetesi.com.tr; internet www.yenicaggazetesi.com.tr; f. 1990; Turkish; organ of the YKP; Editor MURAT KANATLI; circ. 600.

OTHER WEEKLIES

The Blue Beret: POB 21642, HQ UNFICYP, 1590 Nicosia; tel. 22614550; fax 22614461; e-mail unficyp-blue-beret@un.org; internet www.unficyp.org; bi-monthly journal of the UN Peace-keeping Force in Cyprus (UNFICYP); English; f. 1965; circ. 1,500; Editor JOSÉ DIAZ.

The Cyprus Lion: 55 AEC Episkopi, BFPO 53; tel. 25962052; fax 25963181; e-mail lioncy@cytanet.com.cy; distributed to British Sovereign Base Areas, UN Forces and principal Cypriot towns; includes British Forces Broadcasting Services programme guide; Editor LOUISE CARRIGAN; circ. 5,000.

Middle East Economic Survey: Middle East Petroleum and Economic Publications (Cyprus), POB 24940, 23 Alkeos St, Politica Business Centre, 1355 Nicosia; tel. 22665431; fax 22671988; e-mail info@mees.com; internet www.mees.com; f. 1957 (in Beirut, Lebanon); review and analysis of petroleum, finance and banking, and political devts; Publr Dr SALEH S. JALLAD; Editor-in-Chief DAVID KNOTT.

GREEK CYPRIOT PERIODICALS

Cool: POB 8205, 86 Iphigenias St, 2091 Nicosia; tel. 22378900; fax 22378916; f. 1994; Greek; youth magazine; Chief Editor PROMETHEAS CHRISTOPHIDES; circ. 4,000.

Cypria (Cypriot Woman): POB 28506, 56 Kennedy Ave, 11th Floor, Strovolos, 2080 Nicosia; tel. 22494907; fax 22427051; e-mail pogo@spidernet.com.cy; f. 1983; every 2 months; Greek; Owner MARO KARAYIANNI; circ. 7,000.

Cyprus P.C.: POB 24989, 6th Floor, 1 Kyriakou Matsi St, 1306 Nicosia; tel. 22765999; fax 22765909; e-mail pc@infomedia.cy.net; f. 1990; monthly; Greek; computing magazine; Dir LAKIS VARNAVA; circ. 5,000.

Cyprus Time Out: POB 3697, 4 Pygmalionos St, 1010 Nicosia; tel. 22472949; fax 22360668; f. 1978; monthly; English; Dir ELLADA SOPHOCLEOUS; Chief Editor LYN HAVILAND; circ. 8,000.

Cyprus Today: c/o Ministry of Education and Culture, Cultural Services, Ifighenias 27, 2007 Strovolos, Nicosia; tel. 22809845; fax 22809876; e-mail plyssioti@pio.moi.gov.cy; f. 1963; quarterly; English; cultural and information review; publ. and distributed by Press and Information Office; Chair. PAVLOS PARASKEVAS; circ. 15,000.

Cyprus Tourism: POB 51697, Limassol; tel. 25337377; fax 25337374; f. 1989; bi-monthly; Greek and English; tourism and travel; Man. Dir G. EROTOKRITOU; circ. 250,000.

Enosis (Union): 71 Piraeus & Tombazis, Nicosia; tel. 22756862; fax 22757268; f. 1996; monthly; Greek; satirical; Chief Editor VASOS FTOCHOPOLILOS; circ. 2,000.

Eva: 6 Psichikou St, Strovolos, Nicosia; tel. 22322959; fax 22322940; f. 1996; Greek; Dir DINOS MICHAEL; Chief Editors CHARIS PONTIKIS, KATIA SAVVIDOU; circ. 4,000.

Hermes International: POB 24512, Nicosia; tel. 22570570; fax 22581617; f. 1992; quarterly; English; lifestyle, business, finance, management; Chief Editor JOHN VICKERS; circ. 8,500.

I Kypros Simera (Present Day Cyprus): 1 Apellis St, 1456 Nicosia; tel. 22801186; fax 22666123; e-mail kvrahimis@pio.moi.gov.cy; f. 1983; fortnightly; Greek; publ. by the Press and Information Office of the Ministry of the Interior; Principal Officers MILTOS MILTIADOU, MICHALAKIS CHRISTODOULIDES; circ. 3,500.

Nicosia This Month: POB 20365, 2 Agathokleous St, Strovolos, Nicosia; tel. 22441922; fax 22519743; e-mail info@gnora.com; internet www.gnora.com; f. 1984; monthly; English; Publr MARINOS MOUSHIOTTAS; Man. Dir ANDREAS HADJKYRIACOS; circ. 4,000.

Omicron: POB 21094,1 Diogenous St, Engomi, 1501 Nicosia; tel. 22744000; fax 22590516; f. 1996; Greek; Dir NIKOS CHR. PATTICHIS; Chief Editor MARIANNA KARAVALI; circ. 10,000.

Paediki Chara (Children's Joy): POB 136, 18 Archbishop Makarios III Ave, 1065 Nicosia; tel. 22817585; fax 22817599; e-mail poed@cytanet.com.cy; f. 1962; monthly; for pupils; publ. by the Pancyprian Union of Greek Teachers; Dir FILIOS FILAKTOU; circ. 15,000.

Synergatiko Vima (The Co-operative Tribune): Kosti Palama 5, 1096 Nicosia; tel. 22680757; fax 22660833; e-mail coop.confeder@cytanet.com.cy; internet confederation.coop.com.cy; f. 1983; monthly; Greek; official organ of Pancyprian Co-operative Confed. Ltd; circ. 5,000; Sec. PAVLOS THEODOTOU.

Synthesis (Composition): 6 Psichikou St, Strovolos, Nicosia; tel. 22322959; fax 22322940; f. 1988; every 2 months; Greek; interior decorating; Dir DINOS MICHAEL; circ. 6,000.

Tele Ores: POB 28205, 4 Acropoleos St, 1st Floor, 2091 Nicosia; tel. 22513300; fax 22513363; f. 1993; fortnightly; Greek; television guide; Chief Editor PROMETHEAS CHRISTOPHIDES; circ. 17,000.

TV Kanali (TV Channel): POB 25603, 5 Aegaleo St, Strovolos, Nicosia; tel. 22353603; fax 22353223; f. 1993; Greek; Dirs A. STAVRIDES, E. HADJIEFTHYMIOU; Chief Editor CHARIS TOMAZOS; circ. 13,000.

TURKISH CYPRIOT PERIODICALS

Güvenlik Kuvvetleri Magazine: Lefkoşa (Nicosia), Mersin 10, Turkey; tel. 2275880; publ. by the Security Forces of the 'TRNC'.

Halkbilimi (Folklore): Hasder, PK 199, Lefkoşa (Nicosia), Mersin 10, Turkey; tel. 8534983; fax 2287798; e-mail hasder@hasder.org;

internet www.hasder.org; f. 1986; annual; publ. of Hasder Folk Arts Foundation; academic, folkloric; Turkish, with a short summary in English; Chief Editor ALI NEBIH; circ. 750.

Kıbrıs—Northern Cyprus Monthly: Ministry of Foreign Affairs, Lefkoşa (Nicosia), Mersin 10, Turkey; tel. 2283365; fax 2287641; e-mail pio@trncpio.org; internet www.trncpio.org; f. 1963; Editor GÖNÜL ATANER.

Kıbrıslı Türkün Sesi: 44 Mecidiye St, Lefkoşa (Nicosia), Mersin 10, Turkey; tel. 2278520; fax 2287966; monthly; political; Exec. Dir DOGAN HARMAN; Gen. Co-ordinator CEVDET ALPARSLAN.

Kuzey Kıbrıs Kültür Dergisi (North Cyprus Cultural Journal): PK 157, Lefkoşa (Nicosia), Mersin 10, Turkey; tel. 2231298; f. 1987; monthly; Turkish; Chief Editor GÜNSEL DOĞASAL.

NEWS AGENCIES

Cyprus News Agency: 7 Kastorias St, Strovolos, 2002 Nicosia; tel. 22556009; fax 22556103; e-mail news@cna.org.cy; internet www.cna.org.cy; f. 1976; Greek, Turkish and English; Dir and Editor-in-Chief GEORGE PENINTAEX (acting); Chair. of Bd LARKOS LARKOU.

Kuzey Kıbrıs Haber Ajansı (Northern Cyprus News Agency): Alirizin Efendi Cad., Vakiflar Işhani, Kat 2, No. 3, Ortaköy, Lefkoşa (Nicosia), Mersin 10, Turkey; tel. 2281922; fax 2281934; f. 1977; Dir-Gen. M. ALI AKPINAR.

TürkAjansı-Kıbrıs (TAK) (Turkish News Agency of Cyprus): PK 355, 30 Mehmet Akif Cad., Lefkoşa (Nicosia), Mersin 10, Turkey; tel. 2282773; fax 2271213; e-mail tak@emu.edu.tr; internet kktc.gov.nc.tr/tak; f. 1973; Dir EMIR HÜSEYN ERSOY.

Publishers

GREEK CYPRIOT PUBLISHERS

Andreou Chr. Publishers: POB 22298, 67A Regenis St, 1520 Nicosia; tel. 22666877; fax 22666878; e-mail andreou2@cytanet.com.cy; f. 1979; biography, literature, history, regional interest.

Costas Epiphaniou: Ekdoseis Antiprosopies Ltd, POB 2451, 1521 Nicosia; tel. 22750873; fax 22759266; f. 1973; Dir COSTAS EPIPHANIOU.

KY KE M (Cyprus Research Centre): POB 22687, 1523 Nicosia; tel. 22668848; fax 22667816; e-mail kykem@cytanet.com.cy; Pres. KOSTA GOULIAMOS.

Anastasios G. Leventis Foundation: 40 Gladstonos St, POB 22543, 1095 Nicosia; tel. 22667706; fax 22675002; e-mail leventcy@zenon.logos.cy.net; internet www.leventisfoundation.org; f. 1980; Dir VASSOS KARAGEORGHIS.

MAM Ltd (The House of Cyprus and Cyprological Publications): POB 21722, 1512 Nicosia; tel. 22753536; fax 22375802; e-mail mam@mam.com.cy; internet www.mam.com.cy; f. 1965.

Nikoklis Publishing House: POB 20300, 2150 Nicosia; tel. 22334918; fax 22330218; history, geography, culture, travel; Man. Dr ANDREAS SOPHOCLEOUS.

Omilos Pnevmatikis Ananeoseos: 1 Omirou St, 2407 Engomi, Nicosia; tel. 22775854; literature.

Pierides Foundation: POB 40025, 6300 Larnaca; tel. 24814555; fax 24817868; e-mail centrart@spidernet.com.cy; internet www.pieridesfoundation.com.cy; f. 1974.

TURKISH CYPRIOT PUBLISHERS

Action Global Communications: 6 Kondilaki St, 1090 Lefkoşa (Nicosia), Mersin 10, Turkey; tel. 22818884; fax 22873633; e-mail action@actionprgroup.com; internet www.actionprgroup.com; f. 1971; affiliate of Weber Shandwick; has 44 offices in the emerging markets; travel, aviation and hospitality; Man. Dir TONY CHRISTODOULOU.

Bolan Matbaası: 35 Pençizade Sok., Lefkoşa (Nicosia), Mersin 10, Turkey; tel. 2274802.

Devlet Basımevi (Turkish Cypriot Government Printing House): Şerif Arzik Sok., Lefkoşa (Nicosia), Mersin 10, Turkey; tel. 2272010; Dir SONGUC KÜRŞAD.

Güneş Gazetesi: Yediler Sok., Lefkoşa (Nicosia), Mersin 10, Turkey; tel. and fax 2272959; e-mail gunesgazetesi@kibris.net; f. 1980; Dir EROL ÖNEY.

Halkın Sesi Ltd: 172 Girne Cad., Lefkoşa (Nicosia), Mersin 10, Turkey; tel. 2285645; fax 2272612; e-mail halkinsesi@superonline.com; internet www.halkinsesi.org.

Kema Matbaası: 1 Tabak Hilmi Sok., Lefkoşa (Nicosia), Mersin 10, Turkey; tel. 2272785.

Kıbrıs Araştırma ve Yayın Merkezi (North Cyprus Research and Publishing Centre—CYREP): PK 327, Lefkoşa (Nicosia), Mersin 10, Turkey; tel. 8555179; fax 2272592; e-mail gazioglu@kktc.net; Dir AHMET C. GAZIOĞLU.

K. Rüstem & Bro.: 22–24 Girne Cad., Lefkoşa (Nicosia), Mersin 10, Turkey; tel. 2271418; fax 2283641.

Tezel Matbaası: 35 Şinasi Sok., Lefkoşa (Nicosia), Mersin 10, Turkey; tel. 2271022.

Broadcasting and Communications

TELECOMMUNICATIONS

Greek Cypriot Operators

Cyprus Telecommunications Authority (CYTA): POB 24929, Telecommunications St, Strovolos, 1396 Nicosia; tel. 22701000; fax 22494940; e-mail enquiries@cyta.com.cy; internet www.cyta.com.cy; provides fixed-line telecommunications services and broadband internet access; signed partnership agreement with Vodafone PLC (United Kingdom) in 2004 to offer mobile cellular telecommunications services under brand name *Cytamobile-Vodafone*; Chair. STATHIS KITTIS; CEO PHOTIOS SAVVIDES.

MTN Cyprus: Nicosia; e-mail contactus@mtn.com.cy; internet www.mtn.com.cy; f. 2004 as Areeba; 51% owned by MTN Group, 49% by Amaracos Holding; provides mobile cellular telecommunications services; Group Pres. and CEO PHUTHUMA NHLEKO.

PrimeTel PLC: POB 51490, The Maritime Center, 141 Omonia Ave, 3506 Limassol; tel. 22027300; fax 22102211; e-mail info@prime-tel.com; internet www.prime-tel.com; f. 2003; provides fixed-line telecommunications services, broadband internet access and cable television to domestic customers under brand name *PrimeHome*; Man. Dir HERMES N. STEPHANOU.

Turkish Cypriot Operators

KKTC Telsim: Girne Cad. 81, Lefkoşa (Nicosia), Mersin 10, Turkey; tel. 4440542; fax 2280181; e-mail info@kktctelsim.com; internet www.kktctelsim.com; f. 1995; provides mobile cellular telecommunications services; subsidiary of Vodafone Turkey.

Kuzey Kıbrıs TURKCELL (KKTCell): Bedrettin Demirel Cad., Salih Mecit Sok. 1, Kızılay, Lefkoşa (Nicosia), Mersin 10, Turkey; tel. 6001030; internet www.kktcell.com; f. 1999; subsidiary of Turkcell; provides mobile cellular telecommunications services; 318,000 subscribers (March 2009).

Telekomünikasyon Dairesi Müdürlüğü (Directorate of Telecommunications): Lefkoşa (Nicosia), Mersin 10, Turkey; tel. 2281888; fax 2288666; f. 1963; state-owned; admin. and operation of telecommunications services; Gen. Man. MUSTAFA BERKTUĞ.

BROADCASTING

Radio

British Forces Broadcasting Service, Cyprus: Akrotiri, BFPO 57; tel. 25278518; fax 25278580; e-mail cyprus@bfbs.com; internet www.ssvc.com/bfbs/radio/cyprus; f. 1948; broadcasts daily radio and television services in English; Station Man. CHRIS PEARSON; Engineering Man. GEORGE MATSANGOS.

Cyprus Broadcasting Corporation (CyBC): POB 24824, CyBC St, 2120 Nicosia; tel. 22862000; fax 22314050; e-mail rik@cybc.com.cy; internet www.cybc.com.cy; f. 1952; four 24-hour radio channels, two of which are mainly Greek; channel 2 broadcasts programmes in Turkish, English and Armenian; Pres. MAKIS SYMEOU; Dir-Gen. THEMIS THEMISTOCLEOUS.

Kanali Exi: POB 54845, 69 Irinis St, 3041 Limassol; tel. 25820500; fax 25820550; e-mail info@kanali6.com; internet www.kanali6.com.cy; Dir MICHALIS PAPAEVAGOROU.

Logos: Church of Cyprus, POB 27400, 1644 Nicosia; tel. 22477965; fax 22352349; e-mail a.lambrou@logosradio.com.cy; internet www.logosradio.com.cy; Pres. PANIKOS HADJIPANTELI; Dir-Gen. LOUCAS A. PANAYIOTOU.

Radio Astra: Arch. Makarios III Ave 33, 2220 Latsia, Nicosia; tel. 22368888; fax 22319262; e-mail astra@cytanet.com.cy; internet www.astra.com.cy; Chair. YIANNAKIS KOLOKASIDES; Dir GEORGE PAVLIDES.

Radio Proto: POB 21836, 31 Archangelos St, Parissinos, 2057 Nicosia; tel. 22580400; fax 22580425; e-mail web@radioproto.com; internet www.radioproto.com; Chair. KOSTAS HADJIKOSTIS; Gen. Man. MANOS MOYSEOS.

Super FM: POB 22795, 4 Annis Komninis St, Solea Court, 6th Floor, 1060 Nicosia; tel. 22460150; fax 22769516; e-mail studio@superfmradio.com; internet www.superfmradio.com; Gen. Man. MANOS MOYSEOS.

Bayrak Radio and TV Corpn (BRTK): BRTK Sitesi, Dr Fazıl Kucuk Bul., Lefkoşa (Nicosia), Mersin 10, Turkey; tel. 2255555; fax 2254581; e-mail info@brtk.net; internet www.brtk.net; f. 1963 as Bayrak Radio; became independent Turkish Cypriot corpn, partly financed by the 'TRNC' Govt, in July 1983; now has five radio stations on air: Radio Bayrak, Bayrak International (international music, 24-hour, and news in English, Greek, Russian, Arabic and German), Bayrak FM (popular music, 24-hour), Bayrak Classic (classical music, 24-hour) and Bayrak Turkish Music (Turkish classical and folk music, 18-hour); Chair. YILMAZ BAŞKAYA; Gen. Man. ÖZER KANLI.

First FM and Interfirst FM: Lefkoşa (Nicosia), Mersin 10, Turkey; tel. 2289308; fax 2276363; f. 1996.

Kıbrıs FM / Kıbrıs TV: Dr Fazil Küçük Blvd, Yeni Sanayi Bolgesi, Lefkoşa (Nicosia), Mersin 10, Turkey; tel. 2252555; fax 2253707; e-mail kibris@kibrisgazetesi.com; Dir ERDINCH GUNDUZ.

Radio Emu: Eastern Mediterranean University, Gazi Mağusa (Famagusta), Mersin 10, Turkey; e-mail radio@emu.edu.tr; internet www.emu.edu.tr.

Television

Greek Cypriot viewers have access to Greek television channels via satellite. Several Turkish channels are transmitted to the 'TRNC'. Digital Video Broadcasting is expected fully to replace analogue transmission networks in Cyprus by 2011.

Antenna TV Cyprus (ANT1 Cyprus): POB 20923, 1665 Nicosia; tel. 22200200; fax 22200210; e-mail infowebsite@antenna.com.cy; internet www.antenna.com.cy; f. 1983; Chair. LOUKIS PAPAPHILIPPOU; Gen. Man. STELIOS MALEKOS.

British Forces Broadcasting Service, Cyprus: BFPO 57, Akrotiri; tel. 25952009; fax 25278580; e-mail dusty.miller@bfbs.com; internet www.bfbs.com/tv; f. 1948; broadcasts a daily TV service; Station Man. IAN NOAKES; Engineering Man. ADRIAN ALMOND.

Cyprus Broadcasting Corporation (CyBC): POB 24824, CyBC St, 1397 Nicosia; tel. 22862000; fax 22314050; e-mail rik@cybc.com.cy; internet www.cybc.com.cy; f. 1957; Pik 1 (CyBC 1) one Band III 100/10-kW transmitter on Mount Olympus; Pik 2 (CyBC 2) one Band IV 100/10-kW ERP transmitter on Mount Olympus; ET1 one Band IV 100/10-kW ERP transmitter on Mount Olympus for transmission of the ETI Programme received, via satellite, from Greece; the above three TV channels are also transmitted from 80 transposer stations; Pres. MAKIS SYMEOU; Dir-Gen. THEMIS THEMISTOCLEOUS; Dir of Television GREGORIS MALIOTIS.

Lumiere TV Public Co Ltd: POB 25614, 1311 Nicosia; tel. 22357272; fax 22354638; e-mail administration@ltv.com.cy; internet www.ltv.tv; f. 1992; encoded signal; Exec. Chair. AKIS AVRAAMIDES; Man. Dir GEORGE XINARIS.

MEGA TV: POB 27400, 1644 Nicosia; tel. 22477777; fax 22477737; e-mail newsdpt@megatv.com.cy; internet www.megatv.com; Gen. Man. GEORGE CHOULIARAS.

Sigma Radio TV Ltd: POB 21836, 2054 Nicosia; tel. 22580100; fax 22358645; e-mail programme@sigmatv.com; internet www.sigmatv.com; f. 1995; island-wide coverage; Chair. and Dir KOSTAS HADJICOSTIS.

Bayrak Radio and TV Corpn (BRTK): BRTK Sitesi, Dr Fazıl Kucuk Bul., Lefkoşa (Nicosia), Mersin 10, Turkey; tel. 2255555; fax 2254581; e-mail info@brtk.net; internet www.brtk.cc; f. 1976; in July 1983 it became an independent Turkish Cypriot corpn, partly financed by the 'TRNC' Govt; Bayrak TV; transmits programmes in Turkish, Greek and English; Chair. of Bd YILMAZ BAŞKAYA; Dir-Gen. ÖZER KANLI.

Kanal T: Üsteğmen Mustafa Orhan Sok., Lefkoşa (Nicosia), Mersin 10, Turkey; tel. 2271666; fax 2234979; e-mail kanalt@kibris.net; internet www.kanaltkibris.net; Owner ERSIN TATAR.

Kıbrıs Genç TV: Şehit Ecvet Yusuf Cad. 8, Yenişehir, Lefkoşa (Nicosia), Mersin 10, Turkey; tel. 2280790; fax 2276363; e-mail iletisim@kibrisgenctv.com; internet www.kibrisgenctv.com; Dir ERTAN BIRINCI.

Finance

(br.(s) = branches; cap. = capital; res = reserves; dep. = deposits; m. = million; amounts in euros unless otherwise indicated, except for Turkish Cypriot banks)

BANKING

Central Banks

Central Bank of Cyprus: POB 25529, 80 Kennedy Ave, 1076 Nicosia; tel. 22714100; fax 22714959; e-mail cbcinfo@centralbank.gov.cy; internet www.centralbank.gov.cy; f. 1963; became fully independent from govt control in July 2002; cap. 30m., res 33m., dep. 3,713m. (Dec. 2009); Gov. PANICOS DEMETRIADES.

Central Bank of the 'Turkish Republic of Northern Cyprus': POB 857, Bedreddin Demirel Ave, Lefkoşa (Nicosia), Mersin 10, Turkey; tel. 2283216; fax 2285240; e-mail ileti@kktcmb.trnc.net; internet www.kktcmb.trnc.net; f. 1984; Pres. AHMET TUGAY.

Greek Cypriot Banks

Alpha Bank Cyprus Ltd: POB 21661, 3 Lemesos Ave, 1596 Nicosia; tel. 22888888; fax 22334868; e-mail secretariat@alphabank.com.cy; internet www.alphabank.com.cy; f. 1960 as Lombard Banking (Cyprus) Ltd; name changed to Lombard NatWest Banking Ltd in 1989 and as above in 1998; locally incorporated although foreign-controlled; 100% owned by Alpha Bank (Greece); cap. 118m., res 354m., dep. 7,734m. (Dec. 2009); Chair. SPYROS N. FILARETOS; Man. Dir CONSTANTINOS KOKKINOS; 35 brs and three international units.

Bank of Cyprus Public Company Ltd: POB 21472, 51 Stassinos St, Ayia Paraskevi, 2002 Strovolos 140, 1599 Nicosia; tel. 22842100; fax 22378111; e-mail info@cy.bankofcyprus.com; internet www.bankofcyprus.com; f. 1899; reconstituted 1943 by the amalgamation of Bank of Cyprus, Larnaca Bank Ltd and Famagusta Bank Ltd; cap. 586.6m., res 577.1m., dep. 32,032.2m. (Dec. 2008); Chair. THEODOROS ARISTODEMOU; Vice-Chair. ANDREAS ARTEMIS; 143 brs in Cyprus, 452 brs abroad.

Co-operative Central Bank Ltd: POB 24537, 8 Gregoris Afxentiou St, 1096 Nicosia; tel. 22743097; fax 22670261; e-mail coopbank.gm@ccb.com.cy; internet www.coopbank.com.cy; f. 1937 under the Co-operative Societies Law; banking and credit facilities to mem. societies, importer and distributor of agricultural requisites, insurance agent; cap. 78m., res 27m., dep. 4,413m. (Dec. 2009); Chair. D. STAVROU; CEO and Gen. Man. EROTOKRITOS CHLORAKIOTIS; 4 brs.

Hellenic Bank Public Company Ltd: 200 cnr Limassol and Athalassa Ave, 2025 Nicosia; tel. 22500000; fax 22500050; e-mail hellenic@hellenicbank.com; internet www.hellenicbank.com; f. 1974; financial services group; cap. 127.8m., res 312.6m., dep. 6,811.3m. (Dec. 2008); Chair. Dr ANDREAS P. PANAYIOTOU; CEO MAKIS KERAVNOS; 70 brs in Cyprus, 27 abroad.

Marfin Popular Bank Public Co Ltd (Laiki Bank): POB 22032, Laiki Bank Bldg, 154 Limassol Ave, 1598 Nicosia; tel. 22552000; fax 22811496; e-mail laiki.telebank@laiki.com; internet www.laiki.com; f. 1901 as People's Savings Bank of Limassol; operated under several subsequent names, incl. The Cyprus Popular Bank Public Co Ltd, before adopting present name in Dec. 2006; full commercial banking; cap. 721.0m., res 2,915.0m., dep. 35,755.1m. (Dec. 2009); Chair. MICHALIS SARRIS; Group CEO CHRISTOS STYLIANIDIS; 114 brs in Cyprus, 5 brs abroad.

National Bank of Greece (Cyprus) Ltd: 15 Arch. Makarios III Ave, 1597 Nicosia; tel. 22840000; fax 22840010; e-mail cloizou@nbg.com.cy; internet www.nbg.com.cy; f. 1994 by incorporating all local business of the National Bank of Greece SA; full commercial banking; Chair. ALEXANDROS TOURKOLIAS; Man. Dir M. KOKKINOS; 24 brs.

USB Bank PLC: 83 Dhigenis Akritas Ave, 1070 Nicosia; tel. 22883333; fax 22875899; e-mail usbmail@usb.com.cy; internet www.usbbank.com.cy; f. 1925 as Yialousa Savings Ltd (closed 1974, reopened 1990), renamed Universal Savings Bank Ltd 2001, became Universal Bank Public Ltd 2004, restyled as above 2009; cap. 25m., res 24m., dep. 477m. (Dec. 2009); Chair. MAURICE SEHNAOUI; 16 brs.

Turkish Cypriot Banks

(amounts in Turkish liras)

Asbank Ltd: 8 Mecidiye Sok., PK 448, Lefkoşa (Nicosia), Mersin 10, Turkey; tel. 2283023; fax 2287790; e-mail info@asbank.com.tr; internet www.asbank.com.tr; f. 1986; cap. 17m., res 2m., dep. 301m. (Dec. 2009); Chair. ALTAY ADADEMIR; Gen. Man. TASTAN M. ALTUNER; 8 brs.

CreditWest Bank Ltd: Şehit Mustafa A. Ruso Cad. No. 27, Lefkoşa (Nicosia), Mersin 10, Turkey; tel. 6780000; fax 6780026; e-mail pazarlama@creditwestbank.com; internet www.creditwestbank.com; f. 1993 as Kıbrıs Altinbaş Bank Ltd; name changed as above Oct. 2006; cap. 10m., res 16m., dep. 369m. (Dec. 2009); Pres. SOFU ALTINBAŞ; CEO SÜLEYMAN EROL; 13 brs.

Kıbrıs Continental Bank Ltd: 35–37 Girne Cad., Lefkoşa (Nicosia), Mersin 10, Turkey; tel. 2273220; fax 2286334; e-mail info@kibriscontinentalbank.net; internet www.kibriscontinentalbank.net; f. 1998; cap. 10m., res –5m., dep. 47m. (Dec. 2009); Chair. OSMAN KARAISMAILOĞLU; Gen. Man. SERACETTIN BAKTAY.

Kıbrıs Iktisat Bankasi Ltd (Cyprus Economy Bank Ltd): 151 Bedreddin Demiral Cad., Lefkoşa (Nicosia), Mersin 10, Turkey; tel. 6004000; fax 2281311; e-mail info@iktisatbank.com; internet www.iktisatbank.com; f. 1990; cap. 18m., res 6m., dep. 550m. (Dec. 2009); Chair. METE OZMERTER; 17 brs.

Kıbrıs Türk Kooperatif Merkez Bankası Ltd (Cyprus Turkish Co-operative Central Bank): PK 823, 49–55 Mahmut Paşa Sok., Lefkoşa (Nicosia), Mersin 10, Turkey; tel. 2273398; fax 2276787; e-mail info@koopbank.com; internet www.koopbank.com; f. 1959; cap. 18m., res 121m., dep. 1,870m. (Dec. 2009); banking and credit facilities to mem. societies and individuals; Chair. ÜSTÜN TURAN; Gen. Man. GÜLHAN ALP; 20 brs.

Kıbrıs Vakiflar Bankası Ltd (Cyprus Vakiflar Bank Ltd): PK 212, 66 Atatürk Cad., Yenisehir, Lefkoşa (Nicosia), Mersin 10, Turkey;

tel. 2275169; fax 2285872; e-mail kvb@kktc.net; internet www.vakiflarbankasi.com; f. 1982; cap. 26m., res 13m., dep. 574m. (Dec. 2009); Chair. MEHMET SALIH YILDIRIR; 13 brs.

Limassol Turkish Co-operative Bank Ltd: 10 Orhaneli Sok., Kyrenia, PK 247, Mersin 10, Turkey; tel. 2280333; fax 2281350; e-mail info@limasolbank.com.tr; internet www.limasolbank.com; f. 1939; cap. 11m., res -2m., dep. 196m. (Dec. 2009); Chair. HÜSEYIN KEMALER; Gen. Man. AHMET GÜNDÜZ.

Türk Bankası Ltd (Turkish Bank Ltd): 92 Girne Cad., PK 242, Lefkoşa (Nicosia), Mersin 10, Turkey; tel. 2283313; fax 2282432; e-mail info@turkishbank.net; internet www.turkishbank.com; f. 1901; cap. 56m., res 25m., dep. 659m. (Dec. 2009); Chair. M. TANJU ÖZYOL; Man. Dir İ. HAKAN BÖRTEÇENE; 21 brs.

Viyabank Ltd: Atatürk Cad., 16 Muhtar Yusuf Galleria, Lefkoşa (Nicosia), Mersin 10, Turkey; tel. 2285286; fax 2285878; e-mail gm@viyabank.com; internet www.viyabank.com; f. 1998; cap. 40m., res 6m., dep. 16m. (Dec. 2009); Pres. SALVO TARAGANO; Chair. ERDOĞAN SEVINÇ; 1 br.

Yakin Dogu Bank Ltd (Near East Bank Ltd): POB 47, 1 Girne Cad., Lefkoşa (Nicosia), Mersin 10, Turkey; tel. 2283834; fax 2284180; e-mail ydbank@kktc.net; internet www.yakindogubank.com; cap. 17m., res 1m., dep. 170m. (Dec. 2009); Chair. Dr SUAT I. GÜNSEL; Gen. Man. SELCUK BURAT; 7 brs.

Yeşilada Bank Ltd: POB 626, 11 Atatürk Ave, Lefkoşa (Nicosia), Mersin 10, Turkey; tel. 2281789; fax 2277106; e-mail info@yesilada-bank.com; internet www.yesilada-bank.com; cap. 8m., res –8m., dep. 28m. (Dec. 2009); Chair. and Pres. ISMET KOTAK; Gen. Man. MUSTAFA UZUN.

Investment Organization

The Cyprus Investment and Securities Corpn Ltd: POB 20597, 1660 Nicosia; tel. 22881700; fax 22338488; e-mail info@cisco.bankofcyprus.com; internet www.cisco-online.com.cy; f. 1982 to promote the devt of capital market; brokerage services, fund management, investment banking; mem. of Bank of Cyprus Group; issued cap. 22m. (2004); Chair. DEMETRIS IOANNOU; Gen. Man. ANNA SOFRONIOU.

Development Bank

The Cyprus Development Bank Public Company Ltd: POB 21415, Alpha House, 50 Archbishop Makarios III Ave, 1065 Nicosia; tel. 22846500; fax 22846600; internet www.cyprusdevelopmentbank.com; f. 1963; cap. 21m., res 19m., dep. 304m. (Dec. 2009); aims to accelerate the economic devt of Cyprus by providing medium- and long-term loans for productive projects, developing the capital market, encouraging jt ventures, and providing technical and managerial advice to productive private enterprises; Chair. RENA ROUVITHA PANOU; CEO KYRIACOS IACOVIDES; 1 br.

STOCK EXCHANGE

Cyprus Stock Exchange: POB 25427, 71–73 Lordou Vyronos Ave, 1309 Nicosia; tel. 22712300; fax 22570308; e-mail info@cse.com.cy; internet www.cse.com.cy; f. 1996; official trading commenced in March 1996; 135 cos listed in Feb. 2009; Chair. GIORGOS KOUFARIS; Dir-Gen. NONDAS METAXAS.

INSURANCE

Insurance Companies Control Service: Ministry of Finance, POB 23364, 1682 Nicosia; tel. 22602952; fax 22660135; e-mail insurance@mof.gov.cy; internet www.mof.gov.cy; f. 1969 to control insurance cos, insurance agents, brokers and agents for brokers in Cyprus; Superintendent VICTORIA NATAR.

Greek Cypriot Insurance Companies

Atlantic Insurance Co Public Ltd: POB 24579, 15 Espiridon St, 1301 Nicosia; tel. 22886000; fax 22886111; e-mail atlantic@atlantic.com.cy; internet www.atlantic.com.cy; f. 1983; general, non-life; Chair. and Man. Dir EMILIOS PYRISHIS.

Cosmos Insurance Co Public Ltd: Cosmos Tower, 46 Griva Digeni St, 1080 Nicosia; POB 21770, 1513 Nicosia; tel. 22796000; fax 22022000; e-mail info@cosmosinsurance.com.cy; internet www.cosmosinsurance.com.cy; f. 1981; present name adopted 2004; general; Pres. ANDREAS P. EROTOKRITOU; Man. Dir ANDREAS K. TYLLIS.

Eurolife Ltd: POB 21655, Eurolife House, 4 Evrou, 1511 Nicosia; tel. 22474000; fax 22341090; e-mail info@eurolife.bankofcyprus.com; internet www.eurolife.com.cy; wholly owned subsidiary of Bank of Cyprus; life, accident and health; CEO ARTEMIS PANTELIDOU.

General Insurance of Cyprus Ltd: POB 21668, 2–4 Themistoklis Dervis St, 1511 Nicosia; tel. 22848700; fax 22676682; e-mail general@gic.bankofcyprus.com; internet www.gic.com.cy; f. 1951; wholly owned subsidiary of Bank of Cyprus; general, non-life; CEO STELIOS CHRISTODOULOU.

Hellenic Alico Life Insurance Ltd: POB 20672, 38 Kennedy Ave, 1662 Nicosia; tel. 22450650; fax 22450750; e-mail life@hellenicalico.com; internet www.hellenicbank.com; f. by merger of Hellenic Bank PCL and Alico AIG Life; 72.5% stake owned by Hellenic Bank PCL; Chair. and Man. Dir CHRISTOS A. ANTONIOU.

Laiki Cyprialife Ltd: POB 20819, 64 Archbishop Makarios III Ave and 1 Karpenisiou St, 1077 Nicosia; tel. 22887300; fax 22374460; e-mail pmichaelides@laiki.com; internet www.laiki.com; f. 1995; wholly owned subsidiary of Marfin Popular Bank; life, accident and health; CEO POLIS MICHAELIDES.

Laiki Insurance Co Ltd: POB 25218, 45 Vyzantiou St, Strovolos, 1307 Nicosia; tel. 22887600; fax 22887501; e-mail anstylianou@cnpmarfin.com; internet www.laiki.com; f. 1981; subsidiary of Marfin Popular Bank and CNP Assurances; general; Gen. Man. ANDREAS STYLIANOU.

Minerva Insurance Co Public Ltd: POB 23544, 1684 Nicosia; tel. 22551616; fax 22551717; e-mail minerva@minerva.com.cy; f. 1970; general and life; CEO COSTAKIS KOUTSOKOUMNIS.

Pancyprian Insurance Ltd: POB 21352, Pancyprian Tower, 66 Grivas Dhigenis Ave, 1095 Nicosia; tel. 22743743; fax 22677656; e-mail pancyprian@hellenicbank.com; internet www.pancyprianinsurance.com; f. 1992; wholly owned subsidiary of Hellenic Bank PCL; general, non-life; CEO SOCRATES DEMETRIOU.

Prime Insurance Co Ltd: POB 22475, 1522 Nicosia; tel. 22896000; fax 22767768; e-mail info@primeinsurance.eu; internet www.primeinsurance.eu; acquired by Demco Insurance Ltd (Greece) May 2011; fmrly Interlife Insurance Co; present name adopted Sept. 2011; life and general; Man. Dir MICHALIS MICHAELIDES.

Universal Life Insurance Public Company Ltd: POB 21270, Universal Tower, 85 Dhigenis Akritas Ave, 1505 Nicosia; tel. 22882222; fax 22882200; e-mail info@unilife.com.cy; internet www.universallife.com.cy; f. 1970; life, accident, health and general; Chair. PHOTOS PHOTIADES; CEO and Man. Dir ANDREAS GEORGHIOU.

Greek Cypriot Insurance Association

Insurance Association of Cyprus: POB 22030, Insurance Centre, 23 Zenon Sozos St, 1st Floor, 1516 Nicosia; tel. 22452990; fax 22374288; e-mail info@iac.org.cy; internet www.iac.org.cy; 29 mem. cos; Chair. PHILIOS ZACHARIADES; Dir-Gen. STEPHIE DRACOS.

Turkish Cypriot Insurance Companies

Akfinans Sigorta Insurance Ltd: 16 Osman Paşa Cad., Lefkoşa (Nicosia), POB 451, Mersin 10, Turkey; tel. 2284506; fax 2285713; e-mail akfinans@akfinans.com; internet www.akfinans.com; f. 1996; Gen. Man. MEHMET KADER.

Anadolu Anonim: Memduh Asaf Sokak 8, Lefkoşa (Nicosia), Mersin 10, Turkey; tel. 2279595; fax 2279596; e-mail bolge50@anadolusigorta.com.tr; internet www.anadolusigorta.com.tr.

Ankara Sigorta: PK 551, Bedrettin Demirel Cad., Lefkoşa (Nicosia), Mersin 10, Turkey; tel. 2285815; fax 2283099; internet www.ankarasigorta.com.tr.

ERGOİSVİÇRE Sigorta AŞ: Şehit Mustafa Ahmet Ruso Cad. Küçükkaymaklı, Lefkoşa (Nicosia), Mersin 10, Turkey; tel. 2282125; fax 2288236; internet www.ergoisvicre.com.tr; acquired by ERGO Versicherungsgruppe AG (Germany) in 2008.

Gold Insurance Ltd: Salih Mecit Sok. 9, Lefkoşa (Nicosia), Mersin 10, Turkey; tel. and fax 2286500; e-mail info@gold-insurance.com; internet www.gold-insurance.com; f. 1996; Man. Dir ULKER FAHRI.

Groupama Sigorta: Mehmet Akif Cad. 95, Lefkoşa (Nicosia), Mersin 10, Turkey; tel. 2280208; fax 2286160; e-mail n.kural@groupama.com.tr; internet www.groupama.com.tr; Man. NAMIK KEMAL KURAL.

Güneş Sigorta AŞ: Şehit Mustafa Ahmet Ruso Cad., Küçükkaymaklı, Galeria Muhtar İş Merkezi 218, Lefkoşa (Nicosia), Mersin 10, Turkey; tel. 2286690; fax 2292657; internet www.gunessigorta.com.tr.

Kıbrıs Sigorta STI Ltd (Cyprus Insurance Co Ltd): Abdi İpekçi Cad., Eti Binaları, Lefkoşa (Nicosia), Mersin 10, Turkey; tel. 2283022; fax 2279277; e-mail info@kibris-sigorta.com; internet www.kibris-sigorta.com; Man. Dir MEHMET UĞUR KIRAZ.

Ray Sigorta AŞ: Bedrettin Demirel Cad., Arabacıoğlu Apt 7, Lefkoşa (Nicosia), Mersin 10, Turkey; tel. 2270380; fax 2270383; internet www.raysigorta.com.tr.

Şeker Sigorta (Kıbrıs) Ltd: Mahmut Paşa Sok. 14/A, PK 664, Lefkoşa (Nicosia), Mersin 10, Turkey; tel. 2285883; fax 2274074; e-mail bilgi@sekersigorta-kibris.com; internet www.sekersigorta-kibris.com; Man. Dir AHMET ERASLAN.

Turkish Cypriot Insurance Association

Kuzey Kıbrıs Sigorta ve Reasürans Şirketleri Birliği (Insurance and Reinsurance Association of Northern Cyprus): Selim Cad.

49, Arca Apartment No. 3, Lefkoşa (Nicosia), Mersin 10, Turkey; tel. 2280937; fax 2286483; e-mail info@kksrsb.org; internet www.kksrsb.org; 32 mem. cos; Pres. ÜLKER FAHRI.

Trade and Industry

GREEK CYPRIOT CHAMBERS OF COMMERCE AND INDUSTRY

Cyprus Chamber of Commerce and Industry: POB 21455, 38 Grivas Dhigenis Ave, 1509 Nicosia; tel. 22889800; fax 22669048; e-mail chamber@ccci.org.cy; internet www.ccci.org.cy; f. 1927; Pres. MANTHOS MAVROMMATIS; Sec.-Gen. PANAYIOTIS LOIZIDES; 8,000 mems, 120 affiliated trade asscns.

Famagusta Chamber of Commerce and Industry: POB 53124, 339 Ayiou Andreou St, Andrea Chambers Bldg, 2nd Floor, Office No. 201, 3300 Limassol; tel. 25370165; fax 25370291; e-mail chamberf@cytanet.com.cy; internet www.fcci.org.cy; f. 1952; Pres. ANDREAS MATSIS; Sec. and Dir IACOVOS HADJIVARNAVAS; 400 mems and 20 assoc. mems.

Larnaca Chamber of Commerce and Industry: POB 40287, 12 Gregoriou Afxentiou St, Skouros Bldg, Apt 43, 4th Floor, 6302 Larnaca; tel. 24655051; fax 24628281; e-mail lcci@spidernet.com.cy; f. 1954; Pres. ANDREAS LOUROUTZIATIS; Sec. GEORGE PSARAS; 600 mems and 25 assoc. mems.

Limassol Chamber of Commerce and Industry: 170 Franklin Roosevelt Ave, 3045 Limassol; POB 55699, 3781 Limassol; tel. 25877350; fax 25661655; e-mail info@limassolchamber.eu; internet www.limassolchamber.eu; f. 1962; Pres. PHILOKYPROS ANDREOU; Sec. and Dir CHRISTOS ANASTASSIADES; 800 mems.

Nicosia Chamber of Commerce and Industry: POB 21455, 38 Grivas Dhigenis Ave, Chamber Bldg, 1509 Nicosia; tel. 22889600; fax 22667433; e-mail reception@ncci.org.cy; internet www.ncci.org.cy; f. 1952; Pres. CHRISTODOULOS ANGASTINIOTIS; Dir SOCRATES HERACLEOUS; 1,520 mems.

Paphos Chamber of Commerce and Industry: POB 82, Tolmi Court, 1st Floor, cnr Athinon Ave and Alexandrou Papayou Ave, 8100 Paphos; tel. 26818173; fax 26944602; e-mail evepafos@cytanet.com.cy; internet www.pcci.org.cy; Pres. THEODOROS ARISTODEMOU; Sec. KENDEAS ZAMPIRINIS; 530 mems and 6 assoc. mems.

TURKISH CYPRIOT CHAMBERS OF COMMERCE AND INDUSTRY

Turkish Cypriot Chamber of Commerce: 90 Bedrettin Demirel Cad., PK 718, Lefkoşa (Nicosia), Mersin 10, Turkey; tel. 2283645; fax 2283089; e-mail ktto@ktto.net; internet www.ktto.net; f. 1958; Pres. GÜNAY ÇERKEZ; Sec.-Gen. JANEL BURCAN; more than 9,000 mems.

Turkish Cypriot Chamber of Industry: 126 Mehmet Akif Cad., Lefkoşa (Nicosia), Mersin 10, Turkey; tel. 2258131; fax 2258130; e-mail info@kibso.org; internet www.kibso.org; f. 1977; Pres. ALI ÇIRALI; Sec.-Gen. DOĞA DÖNMEZER; 600 mems.

GREEK CYPRIOT EMPLOYERS' ORGANIZATION

Cyprus Employers' & Industrialists' Federation: POB 21657, 2 Acropoleos Ave, 1511 Nicosia; tel. 22665102; fax 22669459; e-mail info@oeb.org.cy; internet www.oeb.org.cy; f. 1960; 64 mem. trade asscns, 500 direct and 4,500 indirect mems; Chair. PHILIOS ZACHARIADES; Dir-Gen. MICHAEL PILIKOS; the largest of the trade asscn mems are: Cyprus Building Contractors' Asscn; Land and Building Developers' Asscn; Asscn of Cyprus Tourist Enterprises; Cyprus Shipping Asscn; Cyprus Footwear Mfrs' Asscn; Cyprus Metal Industries Asscn; Cyprus Bankers Employers' Asscn; Cyprus Asscn of Business Consultants; Mechanical Contractors Asscn of Cyprus; Union of Solar Energy Industries of Cyprus.

TURKISH CYPRIOT EMPLOYERS' ORGANIZATION

Kıbrıs Türk İşverenler Sendikası (Turkish Cypriot Employers' Association): PK 674, Lefkoşa (Nicosia), Mersin 10, Turkey; tel. 2273673; fax 2277479; Chair. HASAN SUNGUR.

GREEK CYPRIOT UTILITIES

Electricity

Electricity Authority of Cyprus (EAC): POB 24506, 1399 Nicosia; tel. 22201000; fax 22201020; e-mail eac@eac.com.cy; internet www.eac.com.cy; generation, transmission and distribution of electric energy in govt-controlled area; also licensed to install and commercially exploit wired telecommunication network; total installed capacity 1,118 MW in 2008; Chair. HARRIS THRASSOU; Gen. Man. STELIOS STYLIANOU.

Water

Water Development Department: 100–110 Kennenty Ave, 1047 Pallouriotissa, Nicosia; tel. 22609000; fax 22675019; e-mail eioannou@wdd.moa.gov.cy; internet www.moa.gov.cy/wdd; f. 1939; owned by Ministry of Agriculture, Natural Resources and the Environment; dam storage capacity 327.5m. cu m; Dir SOFOCLIS ALETRARIS.

TURKISH CYPRIOT UTILITIES

Electricity

Cyprus Turkish Electricity Corpn: Lefkoşa (Nicosia), Mersin 10, Turkey; tel. 2283730; fax 2286945; e-mail info@kibtek.com; internet www.kibtek.com; Chair. AHMET HÜDAOĞLU; Gen. Man. FUAT MERTAY.

TRADE UNIONS

Greek Cypriot Trade Unions

Cyprus Civil Servants' Trade Union (PASYDY): 3 Demosthenis Severis Ave, 1066 Nicosia; tel. 22844445; fax 22668639; e-mail pasydy@spidernet.com.cy; internet www.pasydy.org; f. 1927; regd 1966; restricted to persons in the civil employment of the Govt and public authorities; 6 brs with a total membership of 15,383; Pres. ANDREAS CHRISTODOULOU; Gen. Sec. GLAFKOS HADJIPETROU.

Dimokratiki Ergatiki Omospondia Kyprou (DEOK) (Democratic Labour Federation of Cyprus): POB 21625, 40 Byron Ave, 1511 Nicosia; tel. 22872177; fax 22670494; e-mail deok@cytanet.com.cy; internet www.deok.org.cy; f. 1962; 5 workers' unions with a total membership of 9,220; Gen. Sec. DIOMEDES DIOMEDOUS.

Pankypria Ergatiki Omospondia (PEO) (Pancyprian Federation of Labour): POB 21885, 31–35 Archermos St, Nicosia 1045; tel. 22886400; fax 22349382; e-mail peo@peo.org.cy; internet www.peo.org.cy; f. 1946; regd 1947; previously the Pancyprian Trade Union Cttee (f. 1941, dissolved 1946); 8 unions and 176 brs with a total membership of 75,000; affiliated to WFTU; Gen. Sec. PAMBIS KYRITSIS.

Pankypria Omospondia Anexartition Syntechnion (Pancyprian Federation of Independent Trade Unions): 168 Athalassa Ave, Apt 401, Minos Court; 2025 Nicosia; tel. and fax 22516600; fax 22516717; e-mail info@poas.org.cy; f. 1957; regd 1957; has no political orientation; 10 unions with a total membership of 1842; Gen. Sec. GREGORY KATSELLIS.

Synomospondia Ergazomenon Kyprou (SEK) (Cyprus Workers' Confederation): POB 25018, 11 Strovolos Ave, 2018 Strovolos, 1306 Nicosia; tel. 22849849; fax 22849850; e-mail sek@sek.org.cy; internet www.sek.org.cy; f. 1944; regd 1950; 7 federations, 5 labour centres, 47 unions, 12 brs with a total membership of 65,000; affiliated to ITUC and the European Trade Union Confed.; Gen. Sec. NIKOS MOYSEOS.

Union of Cyprus Journalists: POB 23495, Rik Ave 12, 1683 Nicosia; tel. 22446090; fax 22446095; e-mail cyjourun@logosnet.cy.net; internet www.esk.org.cy; f. 1959; Chair. ANDREAS KANNAOUROS.

Turkish Cypriot Trade Unions

Devrimci İşçi Sendikaları Federasyonu (Dev-İş) (Revolutionary Trade Unions' Federation): 6 Serabioğlu Sok., 748 Lefkoşa (Nicosia), Mersin 10, Turkey; tel. 2286462; fax 2286463; e-mail devis@defne.net; f. 1976; 4 unions with a total membership of 1,850 (2002); affiliated to WFTU; Pres. ALI GULLE; Gen. Sec. MEHMET SEYIS.

Kıbrıs Türk İşçi Sendikaları Federasyonu (TÜRK-SEN) (Turkish Cypriot Trade Union Federation): POB 829, 7–7A Şehit Mehmet R. Hüseyin Sok., Lefkoşa (Nicosia), Mersin 10, Turkey; tel. 2272444; fax 2287831; e-mail erkan.birer@turk-sen.org; internet www.turk-sen.org; f. 1954; regd 1955; affiliated to ITUC, the European Trade Union Confed., the Commonwealth Trade Union Council and the Confed. of Trade Unions of Turkey (Türk-İş); Pres. ARSLAN BIÇAKLI; Gen. Sec. ERKAN BIRER.

Transport

RAILWAYS

There are no railways in Cyprus.

ROADS

According to the International Road Federation, in 2008 there were 12,321 km of roads in the government-controlled areas, of which 2,131 km were motorways; some 64.6% of the road network was paved. The Nicosia–Limassol four-lane dual carriageway, which was completed in 1985, was subsequently extended with the completion of the Limassol and Larnaca bypasses. Highways also connect Nicosia and Larnaca, Nicosia and Anthoupolis-Kokkinotrimithia, Larnaca and Kophinou, Aradippo and Dhekelia, Limassol and

Paphos, and Dhekelia and Ammochostos (Famagusta). The north and south are now served by separate transport systems, and there are no services linking the two sectors.

SHIPPING

Until 1974 Famagusta, a natural port, was the island's most important harbour, handling about 83% of the country's cargo. Since its capture by the Turkish army in August of that year the port has been officially declared closed to international traffic. However, it continues to serve the Turkish-occupied region.

The main ports that serve the island's maritime trade at present are Larnaca and Limassol. There is also an industrial port at Vassiliko, and there are three specialized petroleum terminals, at Larnaca, Dhekelia and Moni. Bids were tendered in September 2009 for the redevelopment (on a build-operate-transfer basis) of Larnaca port. Construction was expected to commence in 2012, and to cost an estimated €200m.

In addition to serving local traffic, Limassol and Larnaca ports act as transshipment load centres and as regional warehouse and assembly bases. Both Kyrenia and Karavostassi are under Turkish occupation and have been declared closed to international traffic. A hydrofoil service operates between Kyrenia and Mersin on the Turkish mainland.

At 31 December 2009 the Greek Cypriot shipping registry comprised 1,026 merchant vessels, with an aggregate displacement of 20.2m. grt.

Port and Regulatory Authorities

Department of Merchant Shipping: POB 56193, Kylinis St, Mesa Geitonia, 4007 Limassol; tel. 25848100; fax 25848200; e-mail maritimeadmin@dms.mcw.gov.cy; internet www.shipping.gov.cy; f. 1977; Dir Serghios S. Serghiou.

Cyprus Ports Authority: POB 22007, 23 Crete St, 1516 Nicosia; tel. 22817200; fax 22765420; e-mail cpa@cpa.gov.cy; internet www.cpa.gov.cy; f. 1973; Chair. Chrysis Prentzas.

Greek Cypriot Shipping Companies

Ahrenkiel Shipmanagement (Cyprus) Ltd: POB 53594, 4th Floor, O & A Tower, 25 Olympion St, 3033 Limassol; tel. 25854000; fax 25854001; e-mail infocy@ahrenkiel.net; internet www.ahrenkiel.net; f. 1977; Man. Dir Vassos Stavrou.

Amer Shipping Ltd: POB 27363, 701 Ghinis Bldg, 58–60 Dhigenis Akritas Ave, 1644 Nicosia; tel. 22875188; fax 22756556; e-mail ateam@amershipping.com; internet www.amershipping.com; f. 1989; Man. Dir Anil Deshpande.

Bernhard Schulte Shipmanagement (Cyprus) Ltd: Hanseatic House, 111 Spyrou Araouzou St, POB 50127, 3036 Limassol; tel. 25846400; fax 25745245; e-mail cy-sdc-man@bs-shipmanagement.com; internet www.bs-shipmanagement.com; f. 1972; CEO Andreas J. Droussiotis.

Columbia Shipmanagement Ltd: Dodekanissou St, 4043 Limassol; tel. 25843100; fax 25320325; e-mail marketing@csmcy.com; internet www.columbia.com.cy; f. 1978; Man. Dir Dirk Fry.

Cyprus Shipping Chamber: POB 56607, City Chambers, 1st Floor, 6 Regas Fereos St, 3309 Limassol; tel. 25360717; fax 25358642; e-mail csc@csc-cy.org; internet www.csc-cy.org; f. 1989; Dir-Gen. Thomas A. Kazakos.

Interorient Navigation Co Ltd: POB 51309, 142 Franklin Roosevelt Ave, 3504 Limassol; tel. 25840300; fax 25575895; e-mail management@interorient.com.cy; internet www.interorient.com; Man. Dir Jan Lissow.

Louis Cruise Lines: Louis House, 20 Amphipoleos St, 2025 Strovolos; tel. 22588168; fax 22442957; e-mail investors@louisgroup.com; internet www.louisgroup.com; f. 1935; Exec. Chair. Costakis Loizou.

Marlow Navigation Co Ltd: POB 54077, 13 Alexandrias St, 3720 Limassol; tel. 25882588; fax 25882599; e-mail marlow@marlow.com.cy; internet www.marlownavigation.com.cy; f. 1982; Chair. Hermann Eden; Man. Dirs Andreas Neophytou, Jan Meyering.

Oldendorff Ltd, Reederei 'Nord' Klaus E: POB 56345, Libra Tower, 23 Olympion St, 3306 Limassol; tel. 25841400; fax 25345077; e-mail mail@rnkeo.com.cy; internet www.rnkeo.com; f. 1964; Chair. and Man. Dir Christiane E. Oldendorff; Gen. Man. Capt. Keith V. Obeyesekera.

Turkish Cypriot Shipping Companies

Ak-Günler Co Ltd: Girne (Kyrenia), Mersin 10, Turkey; tel. 8156002; fax 8153268; e-mail denizcilik@akgunler.com.tr; internet www.akgunler.com.tr; f. 1978; operates a fleet of 8 passenger and cargo vessels; Man. Dir İçim Kavuklu; Gen. Man. Hamit Görgün.

Armen Shipping Ltd: Altun Tabya, St 10/1, Gazi Mağusa (Famagusta), Mersin 10, Turkey; tel. 3664086; fax 3665860; e-mail armen@armenshipping.com; internet www.armenshipping.com; provides transportation services, shipping agency services and customer clearance facilities; Dir Vargin Varer.

Fergün Shipping Co: Girne Yeni Liman Yolu, Fergün Apt 1, Girne (Kyrenia), Mersin 10, Turkey; tel. 8151770; fax 8151989; e-mail info@fergun.ne; internet www.fergun.net; ferries to Turkish ports; Owner Fehim Küçük.

Kıbrıs Türk Denizcilik Ltd, Şti (Turkish Cypriot Maritime Co Ltd): 3 Bülent Ecevit Bul., Gazi Mağusa (Famagusta), Mersin 10, Turkey; tel. 3665995; fax 3667840; e-mail cypship@superonline.com.

Tahsin Transtürk ve Oğlu Ltd: 11 Kizilkule Yolu, Gazi Mağusa (Famagusta), Mersin 10, Turkey; tel. 3665409; fax 3660330.

CIVIL AVIATION

There is an international airport at Nicosia, which has been closed since 1974, following the Turkish invasion. A new international airport was constructed at Larnaca, from which flights operate to Europe, the USA, the Middle East and Asia. Another international airport at Paphos began operations in 1983. A project to expand and modernize Larnaca and Paphos airports commenced in June 2006; by mid-November 2008 the new terminal at Paphos airport was fully operational, and the new Larnaca airport, with an annual capacity of 7.5m. passengers, was inaugurated in November 2009.

In 1975 the Turkish authorities opened Ercan (fmrly Tymbou) airport, and a second airport was opened at Geçitkale (Lefkoniko) in 1986. However, only Turkey and Azerbaijan recognize the airports as legitimate points of entry; flights from all other countries involve a preliminary stopover at one of Turkey's airports.

Cyprus Airways: POB 21903, 21 Alkeou St, Engomi, 2404 Nicosia; tel. 22661800; fax 22663167; e-mail webcenter@cyprusairways.com; internet www.cyprusairways.com; f. 1947; jointly owned by Cyprus Govt (69.62%) and local interests; services throughout Europe and the Middle East; restructuring plan announced Oct. 2005; Exec. Chair. George Mavrocostas.

Eurocypria Airlines (ECA): POB 40970, 97 Artemidos Ave, Artemis Bldg, 6308 Larnaca; tel. 24658005; fax 24658573; e-mail eurocypria@cytanet.com.cy; internet www.eurocypria.com; f. 1991; services to European destinations from Larnaca and Paphos; Chair. Dr Lazaros S. Savvides.

Tourism

In 2010 an estimated 2.2m. foreign tourists visited the Greek Cypriot area (compared with 2.4m. in 2008), while receipts from tourism amounted to some €1,549.8m. In that year there were 88,234 hotel beds in the Greek Cypriot zone.

In 2008 421,162 tourists (excluding Turkish Cypriot citizens and excursionists), 317,529 of whom were from Turkey, visited the Turkish Cypriot area, while revenue from tourism amounted to US $383.7m. There were 15,784 hotel beds in the Turkish Cypriot zone in 2008.

Cyprus Tourism Organisation (CTO): POB 24535, 19 Leoforos Lemesou, Aglantzia, 1390 Nicosia; tel. 22691100; fax 22334696; e-mail cytour@visitcyprus.com; internet www.visitcyprus.com; Chair. Alecos Orountiotis.

North Cyprus Tourism Centre: Ministry of Tourism, Environment and Culture, Selçuklu Rd, Lefkoşa (Nicosia), Mersin 10, Turkey; tel. 2289629; fax 2285625; e-mail info@northcyprus.cc; internet www.northcyprus.cc; headquarters based in London, United Kingdom.

Defence

The House of Representatives authorized the formation of the National Guard in 1964, after the withdrawal of the Turkish members. Men aged between 18 and 50 years are liable to 24 months' conscription. As assessed at November 2011, the National Guard comprised an army of 12,000 regulars, mainly composed of Cypriot conscripts (some 9,100) but with an estimated 200 seconded Greek Army officers and NCOs, and 50,000 reserves. A further 950 Greek army personnel were stationed in Cyprus at that time. There is also a Greek Cypriot paramilitary police force of some 750. In 2010 the defence budget for the Greek Cypriot area was some €376m. As assessed at November 2011, the 'TRNC' had an army of an estimated 5,000 regulars and 26,000 reserves. There was also a paramilitary armed police force of about 150. Men between 18 and 50 years of age are liable to 24 months' conscription. The 'TRNC' forces were being supported by an estimated 36,000 Turkish troops. In 2009 the defence budget for the 'TRNC' was TL 167.4m. A UN peace-keeping force is also based in Cyprus, and there are British military bases at Akrotiri, Episkopi, Ayios Nikolaos and Dhekelia.

Commander of the Greek Cypriot National Guard: Lt-Gen. Nasis Stylianos.

Commander of 'TRNC' Security Forces: Maj.-Gen. Mehmet Daysal.

UNITED NATIONS PEACE-KEEPING FORCE IN CYPRUS (UNFICYP)

POB 21642, 1590 Nicosia; tel. 22464000; email unficyp-public-information-office@un.org; internet www.unficyp.org.

UNFICYP was established for a three-month period in March 1964 by a UN Security Council resolution (subsequently extended at intervals of three or six months by successive resolutions) to keep the peace between the Greek and Turkish communities and help to solve outstanding issues between them. In mid-1993, following an announcement by troop-providing countries that they were to withdraw a substantial number of troops, the Security Council introduced a system of financing UNFICYP by voluntary and assessed contributions. Following a significant reduction in the size of UNFICYP, as prescribed by a UN Security Council resolution adopted in October 2004, the contingent numbered 932 uniformed personnel (864 troops, 68 police), supported by 148 local and international civilian staff, at the end of March 2012.

Commander: Maj.-Gen. Chao Liu (People's Republic of China).

Special Representative of the UN Secretary-General and Head of Mission: Lisa M. Buttenheim (USA).

See also the section on UN Peace-keeping Operations in the Regional Organizations section of Part Three.

BRITISH SOVEREIGN BASE AREAS

Akrotiri and Dhekelia

Headquarters British Forces Cyprus, Episkopi 3370, BFPO 53; tel. 25967295; fax 25963521; e-mail cosba@cytanet.com.cy; internet www.sba.mod.uk.

Under the Cyprus Act 1960, the United Kingdom retained sovereignty in two base areas and this was recognized in the Treaty of Establishment signed between the United Kingdom, Greece, Turkey and the Republic of Cyprus in August 1960. The base areas cover 99 sq miles. The Treaty also conferred on Britain certain rights within the Republic, including rights of movement and the use of specified training areas. As assessed at November 2011, military personnel in the sovereign base areas numbered 2,791.

Administrator: Air Vice-Marshal Graham Stacey.

Education

Until 1965 each community in Cyprus managed its own schooling through a Communal Chamber. In March, however, the Greek Communal Chamber was dissolved and a Ministry of Education was established to take its place. Intercommunal education has been placed under this Ministry. Public expenditure on education by the central Government in the Greek Cypriot area was €1.329.1m. (equivalent to 7.8% of GDP) in 2009, according to provisional official figures.

GREEK CYPRIOT EDUCATION

Primary education is compulsory and is provided free in six grades to children between five-and-a-half and 12 years of age. In some towns and large villages there are separate junior schools consisting of the first three grades. Apart from schools for the deaf and blind, there are also seven schools for handicapped children. In 2009/10 there were 682 kindergartens, with 2,269 teachers and 27,985 pupils. There were 370 primary schools, with 4,754 teachers and 54,522 pupils in that year. According to UNESCO estimates, enrolment in primary education in 2008/09 included 99% of children in the relevant age-group.

Secondary education is also free for all years of study and lasts for six years, with three compulsory years at a general secondary school (gymnasium) being followed by three non-compulsory years at a technical school or lyceum. Pupils at the lyceums may choose one of five main fields of specialization: humanities, science, economics, commercial/secretarial and foreign languages. At technical schools students may undertake one of several specializations offered within two categories of courses—technician and craft; the school-leaving certificate awarded at the end of the course is equivalent to that of the lyceums. In 2009/10 there were 165 secondary schools (gymnasiums and lyceums), with 7,692 teachers and 64,611 pupils. In addition, there were numerous privately operated secondary schools, where instruction is in English. According to UNESCO estimates, in 2008/09 enrolment in secondary education included 96% of children in the relevant age-group.

Post-secondary education is provided at a total of 42 tertiary institutions in 2009/10, including schools in the humanities and social sciences, pure and applied sciences, and economics and management. The University of Cyprus was established in September 1992. The Higher Technical Institute offers sub-degree courses, leading to a diploma, in civil, electrical, mechanical and marine engineering and in computer studies. Other specialized training is provided at the Cyprus Forestry College, the Higher Hotel Institute, the Mediterranean Institute of Management and the School of Nursing. In 2009/10 32,233 students (including 11,138 foreign pupils) were enrolled in tertiary education, while a total of 20,051 students from the Greek Cypriot area were studying at universities abroad, mainly in Greece, the USA and the United Kingdom.

TURKISH CYPRIOT EDUCATION

With the exception of private kindergartens, a vocational school of agriculture attached to the Ministry of Agriculture and Natural Resources, a training school for nursing and midwifery attached to the Ministry of Health, and a school for hotel catering attached to the Ministry of Tourism, Environment and Culture, all schools and educational institutes are administered by the Ministry of National Education, Youth and Sport.

Education in the Turkish Cypriot zone is divided into two sections, formal and adult (informal) education. Formal education covers nursery, primary, secondary and higher education. Adult education caters for special training outside the school system.

Formal education is organized into four categories: pre-primary, primary, secondary and higher education. Pre-primary education is provided by kindergartens for children between the ages of 5 and 6. Primary education lasts for five years and caters for children aged 7–11. In 2008/09 there were 288 pre-primary and primary schools, with 1,972 teachers and 23,400 pupils. Secondary education is provided in two stages. The first stage (junior), lasting three years, is intended for pupils aged 12–14. In 2008/09 there were 33 secondary schools, with 1,106 teachers and 10,571 pupils. The second stage consists of a three-year programme of instruction for pupils aged 15–17. Pupils elect either to prepare for higher education, to prepare for higher education with vocational training, or to prepare for vocational training only. This stage of education is free, but not compulsory. In 2008/09 there were 24 general high schools, with 925 teachers and 7,141 pupils. There were also 11 vocational schools, with 550 teachers and 3,362 pupils.

Cyprus's first university, The Eastern Mediterranean University, which is located near Gazi Mağusa (Famagusta), was opened in October 1986. A total of 13,255 students attended the university in 2008/09. Other institutions providing higher education in the Turkish Cypriot zone are: the Near East University in Lefkoşa (Nicosia); the Girne (Kyrenia) American University; the Anadolu University; the European University of Lefke (Levka); the International American University; the Cyprus International University; and the Teachers' Training College in Lefkoşa (Nicosia), which trains teachers for the elementary school stage. In 1982 an International Institute of Islamic Banking and Economics was opened to provide postgraduate training. In 2008/09 45,634 students were studying at universities in the 'TRNC', while 2,245 students were pursuing higher education studies abroad, mainly in Turkey, the USA and the United Kingdom.

THE CZECH REPUBLIC

Introductory Survey

LOCATION, CLIMATE, LANGUAGE, RELIGION, FLAG, CAPITAL

The Czech Republic lies in central Europe and comprises the Czech Lands of Bohemia and Moravia, and part of Silesia. Its neighbours are Poland to the north, Germany to the north-west and west, Austria to the south, and Slovakia to the east. The climate is continental, with warm summers and cold winters. The average mean temperature is 9°C (49°F). Czech, a member of the west Slavonic group, is the official language. There is a sizeable Slovak minority and also small Polish, German, Silesian, Roma, Hungarian and other minorities. The major religion is Christianity. The national flag (proportions 2 by 3) has two equal horizontal stripes, of white and red, on which is superimposed a blue triangle (half the length) at the hoist. The capital is Prague (Praha).

CONTEMPORARY POLITICAL HISTORY

Historical Context

In October 1918, following the collapse of the Austro-Hungarian Empire at the end of the First World War, the Republic of Czechoslovakia was established. The new state united the Czech Lands of Bohemia and Moravia, which had been incorporated into the Austrian Empire in the 16th and 17th centuries, and Slovakia, which had been under Hungarian rule for almost 1,000 years. After the Nazis came to power in Germany in 1933, there was increased agitation in the Sudetenland (an area in northern Bohemia that was inhabited by about 3m. German-speaking people) for autonomy within, and later secession from, Czechoslovakia. In 1938, to appease German demands, the British, French and Italian Prime Ministers concluded an agreement with the German leader, Adolf Hitler, whereby the Sudetenland was ceded to Germany, and other parts of Czechoslovakia were transferred to Hungary and Poland. The remainder of Czechoslovakia was invaded and occupied by Nazi armed forces in March 1939, and a German protectorate was established in Bohemia and Moravia. In Slovakia, which had been granted self-government in late 1938, a separate state was formed, under the pro-Nazi regime of Jozef Tiso.

After Germany's defeat in the Second World War, the pre-1938 frontiers of Czechoslovakia were restored, although a small area in eastern Slovakia was ceded to the USSR in June 1945. Almost all of the German-speaking inhabitants were expelled, and the Sudetenland was settled by Czechs from other parts of Bohemia. In response to Slovakian demands for greater autonomy, a legislature (the Slovenská národná rada—Slovakian National Council) and an executive Board of Commissioners were established in Bratislava, the Slovakian capital. At elections in 1946, the Communist Party of Czechoslovakia (KSČ) emerged as the leading party, winning 38% of the votes cast. The party's leader, Klement Gottwald, became Prime Minister in a coalition Government. After ministers of other parties resigned, communist control became complete on 25 February 1948. A People's Republic was established on 9 June. Gottwald replaced Eduard Beneš as President, a position that he held until his death in 1953. The country aligned itself with the Soviet-led Eastern European bloc, joining the Council for Mutual Economic Assistance and the Warsaw Pact. Government followed a rigid Stalinist pattern, and in the early 1950s there were many political trials. Although these ended under Gottwald's successors, Antonín Zápotocký and, from 1956, Antonín Novotný, there was no relaxation of policy until 1963, when a new Government, with Jozef Lenárt as Prime Minister, was formed. Meanwhile, the country was renamed the Czechoslovak Socialist Republic, under a new Constitution, proclaimed in July 1960.

In January 1968 Alexander Dubček succeeded Novotný as First Secretary of the KSČ, and in March Gen. Ludvík Svoboda succeeded Novotný as President. Oldřich Černík became Prime Minister in April. The new Government envisaged widespread reforms, including the introduction of a federal system of government, a more democratic electoral system, and a greater degree of separation between party and state. In August Warsaw Pact forces (numbering an estimated 600,000) invaded Czechoslovakia, occupying Prague and other major cities. Mass demonstrations in protest at the invasion were held throughout the country, and many people were killed in clashes with occupation troops. The Soviet Government exerted heavy pressure on the Czechoslovak leaders to suppress their reformist policies, and in April 1969 Dubček was replaced by a fellow Slovak, Dr Gustáv Husák, as First (subsequently General) Secretary of the KSČ. Under Husák's leadership, there was a severe purge of the KSČ membership and most of Dubček's supporters were removed from the Government. All the reforms of 1968 were duly abandoned, with the exception of the federalization programme. This was implemented in January 1969, when the unitary Czechoslovak state was transformed into a federation, with separate Czech and Slovakian Republics, each having its own legislature and government. A Federal Government was established as the supreme executive organ of state power, and the legislature was transformed into a bicameral Federální shromáždění (Federal Assembly). The first legislative elections since 1964 were held in November 1971, and 99.8% of the votes cast were in favour of candidates of the National Front (the communist-dominated organization embracing all the legal political parties in Czechoslovakia).

In May 1975 Husák was appointed to the largely ceremonial post of President of Czechoslovakia, retaining his positions of Chairman of the National Front and General Secretary of the KSČ. He held the latter post until December 1987, when he was replaced by Miloš Jakeš, an economist and member of the Presidium of the party's Central Committee. However, Husák remained as President of the Republic.

Although Jakeš affirmed his commitment to the moderate programme of reform initiated by Husák, repressive measures continued against the Catholic Church and dissident groups, such as Charter 77, which had been established in January 1977 by intellectuals and former politicians to campaign for the observance of civil and political rights. Despite continued attempts to suppress the movement, it played a leading role in anti-Government demonstrations, which began in 1988. In February 1989, following one such demonstration, the Czech playwright Václav Havel (a leader of Charter 77) was sentenced to nine months' imprisonment. (He was released in May, following international condemnation.) Anti-Government demonstrations followed in May, August and October.

In November 1989 the protest actions evolved into a process of largely peaceful political change, which subsequently became known as the 'velvet revolution'. On 17 November an anti-Government demonstration in Prague, the largest public protest for 20 years, was violently dispersed by the police; large numbers of demonstrators (mainly students) were injured. Large-scale protests continued in Prague and in other towns. Later that month several opposition and human rights organizations, including Charter 77, were united in an informal alliance, Civic Forum, which rapidly attracted widespread popular support. On 24 November it was announced that Jakeš and the entire membership of the Presidium of the Central Committee had resigned. Karel Urbánek, a member of the Presidium, replaced Jakeš as General Secretary of the party, and a new Presidium was elected. Opposition demands for the ending of censorship and the release of all political prisoners were accepted by the authorities, and at the end of November the articles guaranteeing the KSČ's predominance were deleted from the Constitution.

In December 1989 Civic Forum and its Slovakian counterpart, Public Against Violence (VPN), denounced the composition of a reorganized Government, which included only five non-communists. Ladislav Adamec subsequently resigned as Prime Minister, and was replaced by Marián Čalfa. In the following week a new interim Federal Government was formed, with a majority of non-communist members, including seven non-party supporters of Civic Forum. Husák resigned from the office of President of the Republic and, at the end of December, was replaced by Havel. Dubček was elected Chairman of the Federální shromáždění. At an emergency congress of the KSČ, held in December, the position of General Secretary of the Central

Committee was abolished. Adamec was appointed to the new post of Chairman of the party.

In April 1990 the Federální shromáždění voted to rename the country the Czech and Slovak Federative Republic (CzSFR). The decision, which followed intense controversy, satisfied Slovakian demands that the new title should reflect the equal status of Slovakia within the federation. On 8–9 June the first democratic legislative elections since 1946 were held in Czechoslovakia. A total of 27 political associations contested representation to the Federální shromáždění and to each republican legislature, with the participation of some 97% of the electorate. In the elections at federal level, the highest proportion of the total votes cast (about 46%) was secured by Civic Forum, in the Czech Lands, and by VPN in Slovakia. The KSČ won a greater than expected proportion of the votes (about 14%), obtaining the second highest representation in the Federální shromáždění. The Christian Democratic Union (a coalition of the Czechoslovak People's Party, the Christian Democratic Party—KDS—and the Slovakian-based Christian Democratic Movement—KDH) obtained some 12% of the votes cast. Two parties that had campaigned for regional autonomy or secession secured more than the 5% minimum required for representation in the legislature: the Movement for Autonomous Democracy–Society for Moravia and Silesia (HSD–SMS) and the separatist Slovak National Party (SNS). The newly elected Federální shromáždění was to serve a transitional two-year term, during which time it was to draft new federal and republican constitutions and elect a new President of the Republic. In late June Dubček was re-elected Chairman of the Federální shromáždění. A new Federal Government, announced in that month, comprised 16 members: four from Civic Forum, three from VPN, one from the KDH and eight independents. In early July Havel was re-elected to the post of President.

In the latter half of 1990 there was increasing support in Slovakia for autonomy. A widening division emerged between the more moderate Slovakian movements, such as VPN and the KDH, and a minority of more radical parties, which campaigned for full independence. In early March 1991 Vladimír Mečiar, the Slovakian Prime Minister and a founding member of VPN, announced the formation of a minority faction within VPN (the Movement for a Democratic Slovakia—HZDS), in support of greater autonomy. Meanwhile, disagreement over the direction of post-communist politics and economic management had led to a split within Civic Forum, with conservatives and economic liberals forming the Civic Democratic Party (ODS), led by Václav Klaus. Mečiar's policies and aggressive style of leadership were seen by many as detrimental to the future of Czech-Slovakian relations, and in April the Slovenská národná rada voted to remove him from the Slovakian premiership. Following this, the HZDS was established as a separate political group. The constitutional debate in the Federální shromážděn continued in the first half of 1992, with increasing Slovakian support for the loosest possible confederation, comprising two nominally independent states. The majority of Czech politicians, however, were in favour of preserving the existing state structure, and rejected such proposals. In March it was agreed that the constitutional talks would be postponed until after the legislative elections due to take place in mid-1992.

The legislative elections of 5–6 June 1992 proved to be decisive in the eventual dismantling of Czechoslovakia, particularly as Mečiar's HZDS emerged as the dominant political force in Slovakia. With about 34% of the total votes cast in Slovakia, the party obtained 57 seats (the second largest representation) in the 300-member Federální shromáždění. The leading party in the Slovakian Government, the KDH (which advocated a continued federation), won only 9% of the votes cast in Slovakia, securing 14 seats in the Federální shromáždění, one seat fewer than the separatist SNS. Václav Klaus's party, the ODS (in coalition with the KDS), won the largest proportion (about 34%) of the total votes cast in the Czech Lands. The ODS was one of only two parties to contest the elections in both republics, and in Slovakia it received 4% of the votes cast. In total, the ODS won 85 seats in the Federální shromáždění, thus becoming the largest party in the legislature. Two other splinter groups of the former Civic Forum, including the Civic Democratic Alliance (ODA), failed to win representation in the Federální shromáždění, as did the Civic Democratic Union (formerly VPN), in Slovakia. The successor organizations to the communist parties of the two republics achieved considerable success: the Left Bloc (which included the Communist Party of Bohemia and Moravia—KSČM) won a total of 34 seats in the Federální shromáždění, while the Slovakian-based Party of the Democratic Left secured 23 seats. The representation of parties in the new republican legislatures did not differ greatly from that of the Federální shromáždění, although the ODA and the HSD–SMS succeeded in winning seats in the Česká národní rada (Czech National Council).

A transitional Federal Government, dominated by members of the ODS and the HZDS, was appointed in early July 1992. The new Prime Minister was Jan Stráský of the ODS, who had served as a Deputy Prime Minister in the outgoing Czech Government. There was increasing recognition by Czech politicians that the constitutional talks on the future of Czechoslovakia were no longer viable and that a complete separation was preferable to the compromise measures that most Slovakian parties favoured. Meanwhile, in late June the new Slovakian Government was announced, with Mečiar as Prime Minister. All but one of the ministers were members of the HZDS. A new coalition Czech Government, dominated by the ODS and with Klaus as Prime Minister, was appointed in early July. In the same month the Federální shromáždění failed to elect a new president in three rounds of voting. Havel's re-election as President had been blocked by the HZDS and the SNS, and in mid-July he resigned.

The events of June and July 1992 had ensured that the emergence of two independent states was inevitable. On 17 July the Slovenská národná rada approved a (symbolic) declaration of Slovakian sovereignty, and in the following week the Czech and Slovakian Prime Ministers agreed, in principle, to the dissolution of the CzSFR. In the following months extensive negotiations were conducted to determine the modalities of the division, which was to take effect from 1 January 1993. While many Czechs and Slovakians (more than 60%, according to public opinion polls) remained opposed to the country's division, the two republican Prime Ministers, supported by their respective Governments, stressed that the process of partition was irreversible. In late October 1992 the Czech and Slovakian Governments ratified a number of accords, including a customs union treaty to abolish trade restrictions between the two republics following their independence. Finally, on 25 November the Federální shromáždění adopted legislation providing for the constitutional disbanding of the federation, having secured the necessary three-fifths' majority by a margin of only three votes. Accordingly, the Federal Government accelerated the process of dividing the country's assets and liabilities as well as its armed forces (mainly in the ratio 2 to 1—the proportion of the Czech and Slovak populations within Czechoslovakia).

Domestic Political Affairs

In anticipation of the establishment of the Czech Republic as an independent state, the existing legislature was replaced by a bicameral body under a new Constitution, which was adopted on 16 December 1992; the 200-member Česká národní rada was transformed into a Poslanecká sněmovna (Chamber of Deputies—lower house), while an upper house, the Senát (Senate), was to be elected at a later date. On 17 December a treaty pledging cordial relations and co-operation was signed, followed by the establishment of diplomatic relations between the two republics. At midnight on 31 December all federal structures were dissolved and the Czech Republic and the Slovak Republic were officially established. The dissolution of the CzSFR had thus been entirely peaceful. The two republics were quickly recognized by the states that had maintained diplomatic relations with the CzSFR, as well as by those international bodies of which the CzSFR had been a member. Existing treaties and agreements to which the CzSFR had been a party were to be honoured by both republics.

The Presidency of Václav Havel

On 26 January 1993 the Poslanecká sněmovna elected Havel as the Czech Republic's first President. The composition of the Government remained largely unchanged. It included among its principal objectives the pursuance of the former Federal Government's economic reforms, including its programme of large-scale privatization. Central banks for each state were established, and in February two separate currencies were introduced.

Relations between the Czech Republic and Slovakia were troubled in early 1993 by disagreements over former Czechoslovak assets and property that still remained to be divided. In April 1994 the Poslanecká sněmovna adopted legislation permitting the restitution of property expropriated from Czech Jews during the period of Nazi occupation (1938–45). At local elections in November, the ODS was confirmed as the party with the broadest support (receiving some 31% of the total votes cast). Renewed controversy emerged in 1995 over the so-called 'lustration', or screening, law, which had been adopted by the Czechoslovak Federální shromáždění in October 1991. The law effectively banned former communist functionaries, as well as members of the former state security service and the People's Militia (the KSČ's paramilitary force), from holding senior political, economic and judicial posts. In September 1995 the Poslanecká sněmovna voted to extend until 2000 the legislation on screening (which had been due to expire in late 1996). In the following month Havel rejected the decision, but the Chamber approved it for a second time, and the extension of the law entered into force.

The first general election since the dissolution of the CzSFR took place on 31 May and 1 June 1996. The ODS (which had merged with the KDS in April) won 68 of the 200 seats in the Poslanecká sněmovna (with 29.6% of the total votes cast), while the Czech Social Democratic Party (ČSSD), which had become a major force of the centre-left under the leadership of Miloš Zeman, greatly increased its parliamentary representation, winning 61 seats (26.4%). As a result, the coalition of the ODS, the Christian Democratic Union-Czechoslovak People's Party (KDU-ČSL, which obtained 18 seats) and the ODA (13 seats) lost its overall majority, achieving a total of 99 seats. The KSČM and the Association for the Republic—Republican Party of Czechoslovakia secured 22 and 18 seats, respectively. Despite losing its parliamentary majority, the governing coalition remained intact. The ČSSD refused to join the coalition, but agreed to give tacit support on most issues to a minority government. In July Klaus formed a new Government; in a major concession to the ČSSD, Zeman was appointed Chairman of the Poslanecká sněmovna. The ruling coalition won 52 of the 81 seats in elections to the Senát, held in November.

Tension within the ODS and between the ruling coalition parties intensified in October 1997, and Josef Zieleniec resigned from his position as Minister of Foreign Relations and as Deputy Chairman of the ODS. In November allegations of impropriety in the funding of the ODS led to the resignation of the Klaus administration (which denied the accusations), following the withdrawal of the KDU-ČSL and the ODA from the coalition. Josef Tošovský, hitherto Governor of the Czech National Bank, was designated Prime Minister in December, and a new interim Government, comprising seven non-partisan ministers, four ODS members, three KDU-ČSL members and three ODA members, was appointed in January 1998. The ODS was divided over its participation in the new administration, and the party's ministers subsequently defected to the Freedom Union (US), a newly established breakaway party, which held 31 seats in the Poslanecká sněmovna by mid-February.

On 20 January 1998 Havel was narrowly re-elected to the presidency. At the end of that month the Government won a vote of confidence in the Poslanecká sněmovna. In April the Czech Republic's proposed membership of the North Atlantic Treaty Organization (NATO, see p. 370) was formally approved by the legislature, after the ČSSD withdrew its demand for a referendum on the issue.

Early elections to the Poslanecká sněmovna were held on 19–20 June 1998. The ČSSD retained its position (held since the earlier defection of the ODS deputies to the US) as the largest party in the Poslanecká sněmovna, winning 74 seats (with 32.3% of the votes cast), while the ODS secured 63 seats (with 27.7% of the votes). The remaining seats were divided between the KSČM (with 24 seats), the KDU-ČSL (20) and the US (19). The rate of voter participation was 74%. In July Zeman and Klaus signed an agreement whereby the ODS pledged not to initiate or support a motion expressing no confidence in a minority ČSSD government, in exchange for a number of senior parliamentary posts, including the chairmanship of the Poslanecká sněmovna (to which Klaus was later elected), and a commitment to early constitutional reform. On 17 July Zeman was formally appointed Prime Minister, and a new Council of Ministers was subsequently formed. Elections to renew one-third of the seats in the Senát were held in two rounds in November. The ČSSD won only three of the 27 seats contested, while the ODS secured nine seats, and an informal alliance, comprising the KDU-ČSL, the ODA, the Democratic Union (DEU) and the US, won 13 seats.

In July 1999 Ivo Svoboda was dismissed from the post of Minister of Finance. (In May 2002 he was charged with embezzlement during his term in office, and he was sentenced to five years' imprisonment in March 2004.) In September 1999 the Council of Ministers approved a number of proposals for constitutional change, which had been drafted by a joint ČSSD-ODS commission. The amendments aimed to restrict presidential powers, including the right to appoint the Prime Minister and the heads of principal state institutions, and the right to grant amnesty. (The Poslanecká sněmovna approved the changes in January 2000, despite an opposition boycott of the vote.) In November 1999 celebrations commemorating the 10th anniversary of the 'velvet revolution' coincided with a protest against the existing political system, organized by a group of former student leaders who had participated in the events of November 1989. Their appeal had been signed by some 150,000 supporters by early December 1999, when a large rally was staged in Prague.

In elections to one-third of the seats in the Senát in November 2000, the alliance of the KDU-ČSL, the ODA, the DEU and the US secured 16 seats, thereby increasing its overall representation to 39 seats (although narrowly failing to obtain a majority in the chamber). In early April 2001 Vladimír Špidla, the Deputy Prime Minister and Minister of Labour and Social Affairs, was elected unopposed to the chairmanship of the ČSSD; Zeman had agreed to relinquish the party leadership (although he was to remain Prime Minister pending legislative elections).

In late 2001 the US and DEU merged to form a single organization. In February 2002 it was announced that the electoral alliance of the KDU-ČSL, ODA and US-DEU had been dissolved, owing to inter-party disagreement; however, the KDU-ČSL and US-DEU subsequently formed a further grouping, the Coalition. At elections to the Poslanecká sněmovna on 14–15 June, the ČSSD was the most successful party (with 30.2% of the votes cast). President Havel invited Špidla to form a government, and on 9 July an agreement establishing a new administration was signed by the leaders of the ČSSD and the Coalition. A new coalition Government, headed by Špidla and dominated by the ČSSD, was appointed by Havel in mid-July, and approved by 101 votes in the Poslanecká sněmovna in early August.

Václav Klaus elected President

Prior to the expiry of Havel's second term on 2 February 2003, voting took place in both legislative chambers to select a successor. Following several inconclusive rounds of voting, Klaus (who had relinquished the chairmanship of the ODS) was finally elected President on 28 February, defeating the candidate of the ruling coalition, Jan Sokol, with 142 of the 281 votes cast in both chambers. Klaus was inaugurated on 7 March. Four days later the Government won a vote of confidence in the Poslanecká sněmovna (which had been requested by the Prime Minister) by one vote. In mid-June the results of a referendum approved the Czech Republic's proposed accession to the European Union—EU (see p. 276). Klaus, notably, did not urge voters to support accession. In September, after the Government narrowly survived a vote of no confidence, the Poslanecká sněmovna adopted its reform proposals. In the following month the Minister of Finance, Bohuslav Sobotka, was also appointed Deputy Prime Minister, with responsibility for implementing the public finance reform programme.

In June 2004 a new political party, the Democratic Union of the Czech Republic, was founded by members of the former DEU. At the end of June Špidla resigned as head of the Government and as leader of the ČSSD, after narrowly surviving a vote of confidence in his leadership of the ČSSD. Of 181 delegates, 103 voted against Špidla; although it fell short of the three-fifths' majority needed to remove him, the result indicated that Špidla had lost the support of the majority of his party. The vote followed a defeat for the ČSSD in the Czech Republic's first elections to the European Parliament earlier in the month (following the country's accession to the EU on 1 May), in which the ČSSD had obtained only two of the 24 seats contested. Špidla's resignation was formally accepted at the beginning of July. In August Stanislav Gross, the acting leader of the ČSSD and hitherto the First Deputy Prime Minister and Minister of the Interior, formed a new Government, which included six new ministers and again comprised members of the KDU-ČSL and the US-DEU, as well as members of the ČSSD. Later in August it narrowly won a vote of confidence in the Poslanecká sněmovna, with 101 of the 200 deputies voting in favour. In October–November an election for one-third of the seats in the Senát was conducted; the ČSSD won no seats, while the number of seats held by the opposition ODS increased substantially. In local elections held concurrently, the ODS won the largest proportion of votes cast (36.4%).

In early 2005 Prime Minister Gross was the subject of allegations of financial impropriety. Nevertheless, he was re-elected as Chairman of the ČSSD in late March. At the end of that month the KDU-ČSL (which demanded Gross's resignation) withdrew from the governing coalition, causing the Government to lose its majority in the Poslanecká sněmovna. Gross resigned on 25 April; on the same day Klaus appointed the Minister of Regional Development, Jiří Paroubek, the deputy leader of the ČSSD, as Prime Minister. The new, largely unchanged Council of Ministers formed by Paroubek (with the renewed participation of the KDU-ČSL) was confirmed in office on 13 May by a vote of confidence in the Poslanecká sněmovna. In late September Gross resigned as leader of the ČSSD. In January 2006 Klaus appointed Jiří Havel as Deputy Prime Minister, responsible for the Economy, replacing Milan Jahn.

In May 2006 Paroubek was elected Chairman of the ČSSD. Later that month he took legal action for defamation against the Chairman of the ODS, Mirek Topolánek, who had accused him of having connections with organized crime. Legislative elections took place on 2–3 June. The ODS won 81 of the 200 seats in the Poslanecká sněmovna, with 35.4% of the votes cast; the ČSSD secured 74 seats, with 32.3% of the votes, the KSČM obtained 26 seats (12.8%), the KDU-ČSL 13 seats (7.2%) and the Green Party (SZ) six (6.3%). Some 64% of the electorate participated in the elections. Paroubek accused the ODS of perpetrating malpractice in the electoral campaign by instigating the publication of claims that government members were implicated in organized crime. Topolánek was invited by Klaus to form a new administration, and a coalition agreement between the ODS, the KDU-ČSL and the SZ was signed on 26 June.

The ČSSD, however, refused to support Topolánek's proposed coalition government, which, with 100 seats in the Poslanecká sněmovna, had the support of one deputy fewer than the 101 required to hold a majority. A protracted impasse ensued, with six failed attempts to elect a new Chairman of the Poslanecká sněmovna. Finally, on 14 August 2006 a member of the ČSSD, Miloslav Vlček, was elected provisionally as Chairman. Two days later Klaus accepted the resignation of Paroubek's Government and officially appointed Topolánek as Prime Minister. However, Topolánek's proposed coalition government again failed to secure support, and attempts by the ČSSD to form an alliance with the KDU-ČSL also proved unsuccessful. A minority ODS-led administration was consequently formed by Topolánek and, after approval by Klaus, was installed on 4 September. In early October, however, the Government lost a vote of confidence in the Poslanecká sněmovna, and Topolánek subsequently tendered his resignation. Elections to one-third of the seats in the Senát took place in two rounds on 20–21 October and 27–28 October; the ODS secured 12 seats, the ČSSD six seats and the KDU-ČSL four seats. The ODS was the most successful party in local elections held concurrently with the first round of senatorial polling. In November Klaus redesignated Topolánek as Prime Minister, with a mandate to form a new coalition administration.

Political uncertainty

On 9 January 2007 Klaus officially appointed a coalition administration formed by Topolánek, which comprised eight members of the ODS, five of the KDU-ČSL and four of the SZ. The new Government was narrowly endorsed by a motion of confidence in the Poslanecká sněmovna on 19 January, receiving 100 votes, after two ČSSD deputies agreed to abstain from voting. Jiří Čunek (who had been elected Chairman of the KDU-ČSL) received the post of Deputy Prime Minister and Minister of Regional Development, while the leader of the SZ, Martin Bursík, became Deputy Prime Minister and Minister of the Environment. In August Topolánek narrowly succeeded in securing approval in the Poslanecká sněmovna for an extensive programme of fiscal reforms, although the plan was less stringent than originally proposed. Nevertheless, divisions between the ODS and other parties in the ruling coalition increased, and public dissatisfaction with the Government became more widespread, as a result of the adoption of the reforms and opposition to US plans to establish a military base near Prague (see Foreign Affairs). Controversy over Čunek, who was subject to a criminal investigation into his alleged acceptance of a bribe from a real estate company in 2002, was also perceived to be damaging to the Government; Čunek resigned in early November 2007.

An inconclusive presidential ballot was conducted in both legislative chambers on 8–9 February 2008. Klaus, representing the ODS, was opposed by Jan Švejnar, an economics professor with joint US-Czech nationality, who was supported by the ČSSD. In a further ballot on 15 February, again contested by Klaus and Švejnar, Klaus was narrowly elected in a third round of voting, with 141 votes. On 7 March Klaus was inaugurated for a second term. In early April Čunek, who had been cleared of the charges against him, was reappointed to the Government, assuming his former position as Deputy Prime Minister and Minister of Regional Development. Prior to senatorial and local elections, divisions emerged within the ODS owing to policy differences between Klaus and Topolánek with regard to the EU and the planned US military base. Elections to one-third of the seats in the Senát, conducted in two rounds on 17–18 October and 24–25 October, resulted in significant gains for the ČSSD, which increased its representation to 23 of the 81 seats, although the ODS remained the largest faction in the chamber, with 33 seats. In local elections, which also took place on 17–18 October, the ČSSD secured control of all 13 regional assemblies, with 35.9% of the votes cast; the ODS (which had previously held 12 of the regional assemblies) received 23.6% of votes. Paroubek subsequently demanded that Topolánek resign from office. However, later that month the Government narrowly survived a motion of no confidence in the Poslanecká sněmovna.

In January 2009, following controversy over a planned ministerial reorganization, Čunek announced his resignation from the Government, stating that he wished to protect the reputation of the KDU-ČSL; he and three other ministers were subsequently replaced. The incumbent Minister of Defence, Vlasta Parkanová, also of the KDU-ČSL, also became Deputy Prime Minister. On 26 March Topolánek's Government submitted its resignation, after a motion of no confidence was adopted in the Poslanecká sněmovna. On 9 April President Klaus nominated Jan Fischer, a non-partisan candidate and hitherto the head of the Czech Statistical Office, as Prime Minister, with a mandate to form an interim administration.

On 9 May 2009 a new Government, headed by Fischer and comprising new, mainly technocratic ministers nominated by the principal parties, was installed on an interim basis, with the intention that early legislative elections would be held. At elections to the European Parliament on 5–6 June, the ODS secured 31.5% of votes cast and nine seats, the ČSSD 22.4% of votes and seven seats, the KSČM 14.2% of votes and four seats, and the KDU-ČSL 7.6% of votes and two seats; voter turn-out was estimated at some 28.2% of the electorate. Also in June a former Chairman of the KDU-ČSL, Miroslav Kalousek, established a breakaway party, Traditions, Responsibility, Prosperity 09 (TOP 09), headed by former Minister of Foreign Affairs Karel Schwarzenberg, which subsequently gained support at the expense of the KDU-ČSL. At the beginning of July the presidential office announced that the early elections to the Poslanecká sněmovna were to be conducted on 9–10 October. In early September 2009 the Constitutional Court, upholding a legal challenge by an independent deputy previously a member of the ČSSD, declared the legislation allowing early elections to be invalid. President Klaus subsequently endorsed a constitutional amendment providing for the dissolution of the Poslanecká sněmovna and an amendment to the electoral code that permitted the shortening of election terms. However, in mid-September the ČSSD, in a reversal of its previous stance, refused to vote in favour of the self-dissolution of the chamber and the KSČM also withdrew its support, with the consequence that early elections were effectively cancelled; Fischer's Government was to remain in place until the parliamentary term ended when it was originally due to expire.

The 2010 legislative elections

In February 2010 Klaus announced that the elections to the Poslanecká sněmovna would be conducted on 28–29 May. In March Jan Dusík of the SZ resigned as Minister of the Environment, in protest at government proposals concerning the modernization of the Prunéřov coal-fired power station. The other representative of the SZ in the Council of Ministers, Michael Kocáb, resigned as Minister, responsible for Human Rights later in March, after the party announced that it had withdrawn its support for the Government. In April Rut Bízková of the ODS (who had previously been employed at the České energetické závody Skupina—ČEZ—company that owned the power station at Prunéřov) was appointed as the new Minister of the Environment. In the same month Topalánek announced his resignation as Chairman of the ODS, following the publication, in the previous month, of an interview in which he had made various controversial remarks. His hitherto deputy, Petr Nečas, was appointed to lead the party's election campaign. At the end of April the Chairman of the Poslanecká sněmovna, Miloslav Vlček of the ODS, also resigned, after the publication of allegations suggesting that he had misused public funds.

At the elections to the Poslanecká sněmovna on 28–29 May 2010, the ČSSD obtained the largest share of the votes, with 22.1% and 56 seats, while the ODS was placed second, with 20.2% and 53 seats, followed by TOP 09 (16.7% and 41 seats), the KSČM (11.3% and 26 seats) and the anti-corruption Public Affairs (VV—10.9% and 24 seats). The KDU-ČSL, which obtained only 4.4% of the votes cast, failed to obtain representation in the chamber for the first time since the restoration of democracy. On 29 May Paroubek resigned as Chairman of the ČSSD, acknowledging that the party would be unable to form a governing coalition. He was replaced in an interim capacity by Sobotka. On 24 June Miroslava Němcová of the ODS, who had served as acting Chairman of the lower legislative chamber after the resignation of Vlček, was formally elected to that position. On 28 June President Klaus nominated Nečas (who had been elected as ODS Chairman earlier in the month) as Prime Minister. Following lengthy negotiations, an agreement was signed between the ODS, TOP 09 and VV, which together held 118 of the 200 legislative seats, and a new coalition Government, headed by Nečas, was appointed on 13 July. Among the principal appointments were Schwarzenberg as Deputy Prime Minister and Minister of Foreign Affairs; Radek John, the leader of VV, as Deputy Prime Minister and Minister of the Interior; and Alexandr Vondra of the ODS as Minister of Defence. On 10 August the new administration won a vote of confidence in the Poslanecká sněmovna.

Partial elections to the Senát were conducted in two rounds, on 15–16 October and 22–23 October 2010: the ČSSD, winning 12 of the 27 contested seats, gained the highest representation in the chamber, with 41 seats overall, while the ODS took eight seats, its total representation falling to 25 seats. In concurrent local elections on 15–16 October, the ODS secured 18.8% of votes cast and 5,181 seats; the ČSSD, with 19.7% of the votes, won 4,633 seats. In Prague TOP 09 was successful in elections to the city assembly, receiving 30.2% of the votes. On 20 December Pavel Drobil resigned as Minister of the Environment, after concerns about alleged corruption within the State Environmental Fund had led the ČSSD to demand a vote of no confidence in the Government; the parliamentary motion was defeated by 113 votes to 80. Tomáš Chalupa, like his predecessor a member of the ODS, was appointed Minister of the Environment in January 2011.

Recent developments: concerns about corruption

In April 2011 a former director of the police organized crime division, Jan Kubice (an independent candidate), was appointed as Minister of the Interior. His predecessor, John, retained his position as a Deputy Prime Minister, and was additionally appointed to head a new anti-corruption committee. Also in April Vít Bárta of VV resigned as Minister of Transport, after it was alleged that he had bribed parliamentary deputies of the party. He was succeeded by an independent, Radek Šmerda. On 20 May Nečas accepted John's resignation as Deputy Prime Minister, which he had tendered earlier in the month expressing discontent with the level of support shown towards his anti-corruption policies by the Government. John also announced that he was to seek re-election to the post of Chairman of VV, in the hope of strengthening his mandate within the party. At a congress of the party, held later in May, John was duly endorsed as Chairman. On 1 July two new appointments of VV representatives were made to the Government, including that of Karolína Peake, who succeeded John as Deputy Prime Minister (and additionally assumed the office of Chairman of the Government Legislative Council). The Minister of Agriculture, Ivan Fuksa, was dismissed by Klaus in October, after Nečas expressed dissatisfaction at his forest-management policy; he was replaced by Petr Bendl. (Fuksa, an ODS member, attributed his removal to disagreements within the party.) In November the Minister of Industry and Trade, Martin Kocourek of the ODS, was obliged to tender his resignation, owing to the revelation of fraudulent transactions in his personal finances. In early December the Minister of Culture, Jiři Besser of TOP 09, also resigned his post, after it emerged that he had failed to list his partial ownership of a US company in asset declarations. Later that month the death of former President Havel prompted tributes to his leadership from international heads of state. In early February 2012 the Senát approved draft legislation providing for the introduction of direct popular elections to the presidency, although the legislation would require final approval by October 2012 in order to have entered into effect by the end of Klaus's mandate in February 2013. In mid-April 2012 Bárta was found guilty of bribery, and given an 18 month suspended sentence (Bárta announced that he would appeal against the court ruling.) In response to the ruling, Peake announced her resignation from VV, and announced that she would form a new parliamentary faction, encouraging other VV deputies to join her; by late April six other VV deputies had announced that they were to do so. Meanwhile, Nečas announced his unwillingness to continue leading a coalition government with VV so long as Bárta remained a member of its parliamentary faction. Nečas also spoke of the need to continue governing with a stable legislative majority, rather than with a notional majority of a small number of deputies. On 27 April Nečas called for a vote of confidence in the Government's austerity measures; although the Government won this vote, with the support of 105 deputies, it remained unclear whether a stable parliamentary majority supportive of the Prime Minister could be maintained.

Roma Affairs

In August 1997 the Government began to address the issues affecting the Roma population (unofficially estimated at some 300,000), after hundreds of Roma, claiming to have suffered persecution in the Czech Republic, attempted to obtain political asylum in Canada and the United Kingdom. The Government established an interministerial commission for Roma community affairs in October and outlined further measures aimed at improving the situation of Roma in the Czech Republic. In early 1998 the Government formed a second commission, headed by Roma, to address issues affecting the Roma population, and a 40-year law restricting their nomadic way of life was revoked. None the less, a large number of Roma continued to seek political asylum abroad. In November 2007 the European Court of Human Rights found the Czech Republic to be in breach of the European convention on human rights for educational discrimination against the Roma population; Roma children were believed to be often segregated and placed in 'special schools' for children with learning difficulties.

In late 2008 increasing activity by extreme nationalist groups was reported; the most significant of these was the Workers' Party (DS). In March 2009 the Supreme Administrative Court rejected a request by the Ministry of the Interior that the DS be prohibited, on grounds of insufficient evidence. In May a political broadcast by the National Party (NS) prior to the elections to the European Parliament, which advocated the expulsion of the country's Roma population, was withdrawn; it was subsequently condemned by Prime Minister Fischer and the Minister responsible for Human Rights as incitement to racial hatred (many of the senior members of the party left the NS later in the year). In February 2010 the Supreme Administrative Court upheld a further appeal by the Government and imposed a ban on the DS, ruling that it posed a threat to democracy. Following the proscription of the party, some of its former members joined an existing nationalist grouping, the Workers' Party for Social Justice.

Foreign Affairs

Regional relations

The Czech Republic is a member, with Slovakia, Hungary and Poland, of the Visegrad Group (established, following the collapse of communist rule, to promote economic, defence and other co-operation in the region). Relations with Slovakia were strained in the 1990s, mainly because of disagreements over the division of former federal property. In mid-September 1998, however, following talks between Miloš Zeman and Vladimír Mečiar, the Slovakian Prime Minister, it was announced that a joint Czech-Slovakian committee would meet in an attempt to further discussions on unresolved issues. The success of opposition parties in Slovakian legislative elections held at the end of that month, and the subsequent change of government, led to a further improvement in bilateral relations. Measures providing for dual Czech-Slovakian citizenship became fully effective in October 1999, and in November an agreement on the division of former federal property was signed in Bratislava by Zeman and Mikuláš Dzurinda, Mečiar's successor. The agreement provided for the exchange of shares between the Czech Republic's Komerční banka and Slovakia's Všeobecná úverová banka, and the restitution of gold reserves to Slovakia, which had been held by the Czech National Bank as collateral for debts owed by Slovakia. The Czech Government consequently opted effectively to relieve Slovakia of its debts by buying the National Bank's claim for a symbolic one koruna, despite the opposition of several Czech politicians. In May 2000 Zeman and Dzurinda signed an agreement that resolved the remaining problems associated with the division of jointly held assets.

Since the end of the Second World War Czech-German relations have been dominated by two issues: the question of compensation for Czech victims of Nazism, and demands for the restitution of property to the Sudeten Germans who were driven from Czechoslovakia in 1945–46. A joint declaration was finally signed by the Czech and German Ministers of Foreign Affairs in December 1996, and by Prime Minister Klaus of the Czech Republic and Federal Chancellor Helmut Kohl of Germany in January 1997. In the declaration, Germany admitted that it was to blame for the Nazi occupation and the partition of Czechoslovakia in 1938–39, while the Czech Republic apologized for the abuses of human rights that were committed during the deportation of ethnic Germans. The declaration did not, however, entitle the expelled Sudeten Germans to make claims for compensation. A Czech-German fund was established in January 1998 to finance joint projects, in particular benefiting victims of the Nazis. Relations were strained somewhat later that year, however, when the nomination of Sudeten Germans to a Czech-German advisory council was rejected by Zeman, who claimed that the nominees had opposed the January 1997 declaration that had provided for the establishment of the council.

In February 2002 Zeman and Dzurinda announced that they would not be attending a summit meeting of the Visegrad countries, scheduled to take place on 1 March, following a demand by their Hungarian counterpart, Viktor Orbán, for the abolition of the Beneš Decrees, which had provided for the expulsion of ethnic Germans, as well as Hungarians, from the Sudetenland. In April the Poslanecká sněmovna unanimously approved a resolution stipulating the inviolability of the Beneš Decrees. In August 2005 the Czech Government formally apologized to Sudeten Germans actively opposed to Nazism who had experienced persecution after the Second World War. In July 2009 Liechtenstein agreed to establish diplomatic relations with the Czech Republic, having failed to recognize it after independence, in protest at the seizure of land belonging to Liechtenstein citizens in the former Czechoslavakia under the Beneš Decrees. The two countries formally established diplomatic relations in September, also deciding to create a commission of historians in an effort to resolve outstanding matters of concern.

The question of the nuclear power installation at Temelín, in southern Bohemia, has impeded good relations between the Czech Republic and Austria. Despite pressure from the Austrian Government, which suspended imports of Czech electricity, the nuclear power plant began production in October 2000. In December the Czech Republic and Austria signed an agreement, whereby the plant was not to operate at commercial capacity until its safety and its environmental impact had been fully evaluated. In August 2001 the European Commission issued a controversial report: the Czech authorities maintained that the report demonstrated the safety of the plant and immediately commenced its reconnection with the national power network; however, Austrian anti-nuclear organizations announced that they were to submit a legal challenge to the resumption of operations at the plant, which was also strongly criticized by the Austrian authorities. Further safety issues were eventually agreed, and in April 2003 the Temelín installation began production at full capacity, following the commencement of operations of a second reactor. In late 2011 the Czech Government formally announced a tender for the construction of a further two nuclear reactors at the Temelín installation.

The Czech Republic was one of a number of central and eastern European states invited to commence negotiations in March 1998 on possible entry to the EU. In December 2002, at a summit meeting in Copenhagen, Denmark, the Czech Republic was one of 10 nations formally invited to join the EU in May 2004. A plebiscite on EU membership was held in the Czech Republic on 13–14 June 2003. Of the 55.2% of the electorate who took part in the referendum, 77.3% voted in support of Czech membership of the EU. The Czech Republic became a full member on 1 May 2004. In December 2007 the Czech Republic, together with eight other nations, implemented the EU's Schengen Agreement, enabling its citizens to travel to and from other member states without border restrictions. In February 2009 President Klaus, who had attracted further controversy for refusing to allow the EU flag to be hoisted above Prague Castle (the Czech presidential office) during the Czech Republic's tenure of the Presidency of the EU Council in the first half of the year, as was customary, at a session of the European Parliament, criticized the bureaucratization of EU decision-making and reiterated his opposition to the institutional Lisbon Treaty. On 18 February the Lisbon Treaty was approved in the Poslanecká sněmovna (by 125 deputies, with 61 opposing). The Lisbon Treaty was approved in the Senát on 6 May; however, 17 members of the Senát subsequently submitted a legal challenge against it at the Constitutional Court. On 3 November the Court rejected the appeal; the Lisbon Treaty was signed by Klaus on the same day (although he continued to express opposition to it), the Czech Republic becoming the last EU member state to ratify the treaty. Amid an ongoing debt crisis in the euro area, in early 2012 the Czech Republic and the United Kingdom were the only member states of the Union that refused to enter into a new treaty, the European Fiscal Compact, committing them to fiscal discipline measures, although the decision of Prime Minister Nečas, which was strongly supported by Klaus, drew criticism from Minister of Foreign Affairs Schwarzenberg.

Other external relations

In August 1993 the Czech Republic and Russia signed a treaty of friendship and co-operation (replacing the Russian-Czechoslovak treaty of 1992). In March 1994 the Czech Republic joined NATO's 'Partnership for Peace' programme of military co-operation. In 1996 the Poslanecká sněmovna approved legislation prohibiting the storage of nuclear weapons on Czech territory, except where international treaties are concerned, thereby allowing for full membership of NATO. In July 1997 the Czech Republic, together with Hungary and Poland, was invited to commence membership negotiations. A protocol providing for the accession of the three states to NATO was signed in December, and in March 1999 the Czech Republic, Hungary and Poland became full members of the alliance.

In January 2007 Prime Minister Topolánek entered into negotiations with the USA regarding the establishment of a military base in the Czech Republic as part of the proposed US National Missile Defence programme. Domestic opposition to the plans had resulted in the establishment of a group comprising some 40 Czech and international civic organizations, which organized protests in Prague at the end of January. (Russia strenuously opposed the proposed installation of military bases in the Czech Republic and Poland as part of the US missile defence system.) At a NATO summit meeting, which took place in Bucharest, Romania, in early April 2008, member states endorsed US plans to position missile defence bases in the Czech Republic and Poland; coinciding with the meeting, the Czech Government announced that it had reached agreement with the USA on establishing a US anti-missile radar station in the region of Brdy, near Prague. On 8 July an accord providing for the installation of the radar system in the Czech Republic was officially signed in Prague.

Following the election of US President Barack Obama in November 2008, however, the US Administration announced in September 2009 that the plans for the deployment of part of a long-range missile defence system on Czech Republic and Polish territory had been abandoned. The declaration was welcomed by Russia but prompted criticism from politicians in Central Europe who had supported the system. In response to concerns expressed by the Czech Republic and Polish Governments, the USA indicated that both countries would continue to be involved in revised defence plans. Nevertheless, in June 2011 the Czech Minister of Defence, Alexandr Vondra, announced the Czech Republic's withdrawal from the US missile defence system, owing to dissatisfaction with the country's downgraded participation under the revised proposals.

In July 2009 Canada reintroduced visa requirements for Czech citizens, following a dramatic increase in asylum applications from members of the Czech Roma community since visa restrictions were ended in 2007; the Czech Government responded by reimposing visa requirements for Canadian citizens and recalling its ambassador to Canada for consultations. In September 2009 a Canadian-Czech Working Group was established and convened in Ottawa, Canada, to examine the issue. Although the EU Justice and Home Affairs Council urged the restoration of visa-free travel for Czech nationals to Canada, the visa requirements remained in force at early 2012.

CONSTITUTION AND GOVERNMENT

Under the Constitution, which entered into force on 1 January 1993, legislative power is vested in the 200-member Poslanecká sněmovna (Chamber of Deputies) and the 81-member Senát (Senate). Members of the Poslanecká sněmovna and the Senát are elected for terms of four and six years, respectively, by universal adult suffrage. (One-third of the seats in the Senát are renewable every two years.) The President of the Republic (Head of State) is elected for a term of five years by a joint session of the legislature. The President, who is also Commander of the Armed Forces, may not be elected for more than two consecutive terms. He appoints the Prime Minister and, on the latter's recommendation, the other members of the Council of Ministers (the highest organ of executive power). The judiciary consists of the Supreme Court, the Supreme Administrative Court, and high, regional and district courts. For administrative purposes, the Czech Republic is divided into 14 self-governing regions.

REGIONAL AND INTERNATIONAL CO-OPERATION

The Czech Republic became a member of the Council of Europe (see p. 256) in 1993. In 1995 the Czech Republic became the first post-communist state in Eastern Europe to be admitted to the Organisation for Economic Co-operation and Development (OECD, see p. 379). The Czech Republic was admitted to the North Atlantic Treaty Organization (NATO, see p. 370) in 1999. In 2004 the country became a full member of the European Union (EU, see p. 276).

The Czech Republic was admitted to the UN following independence in 1993 and, as a contracting party to the General Agreement on Tariffs and Trade, joined the World Trade Organization (WTO, see p. 433) on its establishment in 1995.

ECONOMIC AFFAIRS

In 2010, according to estimates by the World Bank, the Czech Republic's gross national income (GNI), measured at average 2008–10 prices, was US $188,269m., equivalent to $17,890 per head (or $23,640 per head on an international purchasing-power parity basis). During 2001–10, it was estimated, the population increased at an average annual rate of 0.3%, while gross domestic product (GDP) per head increased, in real terms, by an average of 2.9% per year. According to official figures, overall GDP increased, in real terms, at an average annual rate of 3.4% in 2001–10. Real GDP declined by 4.7% in 2009, but grew by 2.7% in 2010.

Agriculture (including hunting, forestry and fishing) contributed 1.7% of GDP in 2010 and engaged 3.3% of the employed labour force in 2008. The principal crops are wheat, sugar beet, barley, rapeseed, potatoes, maize, hops (the Czech Republic is a major producer and exporter of beer) and apples. According to official estimates, the GDP of the agricultural sector decreased, in real terms, at an average annual rate of 1.9% in 2001–10. Agricultural GDP increased by 13.4% in 2009, but decreased by 22.1% in 2010.

Industry (including manufacturing, mining, construction and power) contributed 37.5% of GDP in 2010 and engaged 40.6% of the employed labour force in 2008. According to official estimates, the GDP of the industrial sector increased, in real terms, at an average annual rate of 5.9% in 2001–10. Real industrial GDP declined by 8.8% in 2009, as a result of the global economic downturn but it increased by 9.1% in 2010.

Mining and quarrying contributed 7.0% of GDP in 2010 and engaged 1.1% of the employed labour force in 2008. The principal minerals extracted are coal and lignite. According to official estimates, the GDP of the mining and quarrying sector decreased, in real terms, at an average annual rate of 3.1% in 2001–10. Mining and quarrying GDP decreased by 4.1% in 2010.

The manufacturing sector contributed 23.3% of GDP in 2010 and engaged 28.6% of the employed labour force in 2008. According to official estimates, the GDP of the manufacturing sector increased at an average annual rate of 8.2%, in real terms, in 2001–10. Sectoral GDP decreased by 10.8% in 2009 but increased by 13.8% in 2010.

The construction sector contributed 7.2% of GDP in 2010 and engaged 9.2% of the employed labour force in 2008. According to official estimates, the GDP of the construction sector increased at an average annual rate of 2.5%, in real terms, in 2001–10. Sectoral GDP increased by 3.8% in 2010.

In 2008 coal provided 59.9% of total electricity production and nuclear power 31.9%. In 2010 the Czech Republic's proven coal reserves were estimated at about 1,100m. metric tons. Production of coal amounted to 50.6m. metric tons in 2010. Imports of mineral fuels comprised 9.6% of the value of total imports in 2010.

The services sector contributed 60.8% of GDP in 2010 and engaged 56.1% of the employed labour force in 2008. Tourism is an important source of revenue, providing receipts of US $6,671m. in 2010, according to provisional figures. According to official estimates, the GDP of the services sector increased, in real terms, at an average annual rate of 2.2% in 2001–10. Real GDP in the services sector decreased by 4.1% in 2009 but increased by 1.9% in 2010.

In 2010 the Czech Republic recorded a visible trade surplus of US $2,804m., but there was a deficit of $5,992m. on the current account of the balance of payments. In 2011, the principal source of imports (accounting for 25.6% of the total) was Germany; other major sources were the People's Republic of China, Poland, Slovakia and Russia. Germany was also the principal market for exports (taking 32.2% of the total) in that year; other important purchasers were Slovakia, Poland and France. The principal imports in 2011 were machinery and transport equipment (accounting for 41.8% of imports), basic manufactures, chemical products, mineral fuels and miscellaneous manufactured articles. The principal exports in that year were machinery and transport equipment (accounting for 54.4% of exports), basic manufactures, miscellaneous manufactured articles, and chemical products.

In 2010 there was a budgetary deficit of 156,416m. koruna (equivalent to 4.1% of GDP). The Czech Republic's general government gross debt was 1,282,291m. koruna in 2009, equivalent to 35.3% of GDP. The Czech Republic's total external debt was US $45,561m. at the end of 2004, of which $12,020m. was long-term public debt. In that year, the cost of debt-servicing long-term public and publicly guaranteed debt and repayments to the IMF was equivalent to 10.5% of the value of exports of goods, services and income (excluding workers' remittances). According to IMF estimates, the country's gross external debt was equivalent to 40.3% of GDP in 2008. The annual rate of inflation averaged 2.3% in 2001–10 and consumer prices increased by 1.5% in 2010, according to ILO. The official rate of unemployment was 4.4% in 2008, the lowest rate for 10 years.

In 1992–95 the Czech Republic's programme of liberal economic reform attracted widespread foreign investment, and GDP growth was recorded from 2000. The Czech Republic's integration with the EU, following its accession to full membership of the Union in May 2004, resulted in a period of export-generated expansion. Following the negative impact of the international financial crisis, which included a sharp contraction of GDP, a programme of austerity measures was formally adopted in October 2009. In March 2010 the IMF and the Czech National Bank signed an agreement to provide the Fund with up to €1,030m., as part of a commitment made by the EU to contribute up to €75,000m. to support the IMF's lending capacity during the international financial crisis. In an assessment in early 2011, the IMF confirmed the Czech Republic's recovery from the economic downturn, with a return to positive GDP growth, estimated at more than 2%, in 2010, and a reduction in the budgetary deficit (which had remained persistently high) to below 5% of GDP, but also emphasized the necessity for further pension and health care reforms. Growth of 1.0% was projected by the IMF for 2011. In October the Government's National Economic Council recommended that the planned adoption of the euro (which would require the country to maintain a budgetary deficit of less than 3% of GDP in two consecutive years) should be suspended for the duration of the ongoing debt crisis in the euro area, and that the authorities instead implement further reforms intended to ensure financial stabilization. In December the Government expressed concern at EU plans to establish common corporation and financial transaction taxes between member states, considering that any such system should apply only to states that had joined the euro zone. In January 2012 it was reported that the ruling coalition was divided over whether to participate in an IMF emergency stabilization fund for the euro area. On 2 March the Czech Republic (together with the United Kingdom) declined to sign the European Fiscal Compact, committing EU member states to fiscal discipline measures.

PUBLIC HOLIDAYS

2013: 1 January (New Year's Day), 1 April (Easter Monday), 1 May (Labour Day), 8 May (Liberation Day), 5 July (Day of the Apostles SS Cyril and Methodius), 6 July (Anniversary of the Martyrdom of Jan Hus), 28 September (Czech Statehood Day), 28 October (Independence Day), 17 November (Freedom and Democracy Day), 24–25 December (Christmas), 26 December (St Stephen's Day).

Statistical Survey

Source: mainly Czech Statistical Office, Na padesátém 81, 100 82 Prague 10; tel. 274051111; internet www.czso.cz.

Area and Population

AREA, POPULATION AND DENSITY

Area (sq km)	78,867*
Population (census results)	
1 March 2001	10,230,060
25 March 2011 (preliminary)	
Males	5,188,188
Females	5,374,026
Total	10,562,214
Density (per sq km) at 2011 census	133.9

* 30,451 sq miles.

POPULATION BY AGE AND SEX

(UN estimates at mid-2012)

	Males	Females	Total
0–14	772,320	731,834	1,504,154
15–64	3,747,176	3,654,120	7,401,296
65 and over	669,273	990,956	1,660,229
Total	5,188,769	5,376,910	10,565,679

Note: Estimates not adjusted to take account of results of the 2011 census.

Source: UN, *World Population Prospects: The 2010 Revision*.

POPULATION BY ETHNIC GROUP

(census of 1 March 2001)

	Number	%
Czech (Bohemian)	9,249,777	90.4
Moravian	380,474	3.7
Slovak	193,190	1.9
Polish	51,968	0.5
German	39,106	0.4
Roma (Gypsy)	11,746	0.1
Silesian	10,878	0.1
Others and unknown	292,921	2.9
Total	10,230,060	100.0

REGIONS

(population at 2011 census, preliminary)

	Area (sq km)	Population	Density (per sq km)
Central Bohemia (Středočeský)	11,014	1,274,633	115.7
Highlands (Vysočina)	6,796	512,727	75.4
Hradec Králové (Královéhradecký)	4,758	555,683	116.8
Karlovy Vary (Karlovarský)	3,315	310,245	93.6
Liberec (Liberecký)	3,163	439,262	138.9
Moravia-Silesia (Moravskoslezský)	5,427	1,236,028	227.8
Olomouc (Olomoucký)	5,267	639,946	121.5
Pardubice (Pardubický)	4,519	518,228	114.7
Plzeň (Plzeňský)	7,561	574,694	76.0
Prague City (Pražský)	496	1,272,690	2,565.9
South Bohemia (Jihočeský)	10,057	637,460	63.4
South Moravia (Jihomoravský)	7,196	1,169,788	162.6
Ústí nad Labem (Ústecký)	5,335	830,371	155.6
Zlín (Zlínský)	3,964	590,459	149.0
Total	78,868	10,562,214	133.9

PRINCIPAL TOWNS

(population at December 2010)

Praha (Prague, capital)	1,257,158	Pardubice	90,401
Brno	371,371	Havířov	82,022
Ostrava	303,609	Zlín	75,469
Plzeň (Pilsen)	168,808	Kladno	70,665
Liberec	101,865	Most	67,466
Olomouc	100,233	Karviná	60,679
Ústí nad Labem	95,464	Opava	58,274
České Budějovice (Budweis)	94,754	Frýdek-Místek	58,200
Hradec Králové	94,318		

BIRTHS, MARRIAGES AND DEATHS

	Registered live births		Registered marriages		Registered deaths	
	Number	Rate (per 1,000)	Number	Rate (per 1,000)	Number	Rate (per 1,000)
2003	93,685	9.2	48,943	4.8	111,288	10.9
2004	97,664	9.6	51,447	5.0	107,177	10.5
2005	102,211	10.0	51,829	5.1	107,938	10.5
2006	105,831	10.3	52,860	5.1	104,441	10.2
2007	114,632	11.1	57,157	5.5	104,636	10.1
2008	119,570	11.5	52,457	5.0	104,948	10.1
2009	118,348	11.3	47,862	4.6	107,421	10.2
2010	117,153	11.1	46,746	4.4	106,844	10.2

Life expectancy (years at birth, WHO estimates): 77 (males 74; females 80) in 2009 (Source: WHO, *World Health Statistics*).

IMMIGRATION AND EMIGRATION

	2008	2009	2010
Immigrants	77,817	39,973	30,515
Emigrants	6,027	11,629	14,867

ECONOMICALLY ACTIVE POPULATION

('000 persons aged 15 years and over)

	2006	2007	2008
Agriculture, hunting, forestry and fishing	182	176	166
Mining and quarrying	55	54	56
Manufacturing	1,362	1,406	1,433
Electricity, gas and water	77	73	78
Construction	436	447	462
Wholesale and retail trade, repair of motor vehicles, motorcycles and personal household goods	614	613	633
Hotels and restaurants	187	181	177
Transport, storage and communications	361	364	375
Financial intermediation	92	102	115
Real estate, renting and business activities	321	353	370
Public administration, defence and compulsory social security	326	326	327

—continued	2006	2007	2008
Education	288	290	282
Health and social welfare	330	338	328
Other community, social and personal services	193	194	199
Households with employed persons	3	3	3
Extraterritorial organizations	1	1	—
Sub-total	4,827	4,921	5,002
Not classifiable by economic activity	1	1	—
Total employed	4,828	4,922	5,002
Registered unemployed	371	276	230
Total labour force	5,199	5,198	5,232

Source: ILO.

Health and Welfare

KEY INDICATORS

Total fertility rate (children per woman, 2009)	1.5
Under-5 mortality rate (per 1,000 live births, 2009)	4.0
HIV/AIDS (% of persons aged 15–49, 2009)	0.1
Physicians (per 1,000 head, 2006)	3.6
Hospital beds (per 1,000 head, 2006)	8.4
Health expenditure (2008): US $ per head (PPP)	1,830
Health expenditure (2008): % of GDP	7.1
Health expenditure (2008): public (% of total)	80.1
Access to sanitation (% of total population, 2008)	98
Total carbon dioxide emissions ('000 metric tons, 2007)	124,861.8
Carbon dioxide emissions per head (metric tons, 2007)	12.1
Human Development Index (2011): ranking	27
Human Development Index (2011): value	0.865

For sources and definitions, see explanatory note on p. vi.

Agriculture

PRINCIPAL CROPS

('000 metric tons)

	2008	2009	2010
Wheat	4,632	4,358	4,162
Barley	2,244	2,003	1,585
Maize	858	890	693
Rye*	210	178	118
Oats	156	166	138
Potatoes	770	753	665
Sugar beet	2,885	3,038	3,065
Peas, dry	41	52	48
Rapeseed	1,049	1,128	1,042
Cabbages and other brassicas	51	50	36
Tomatoes	28	29	7
Cauliflowers and broccoli	8	6	5
Cucumbers and gherkins	29	24	11
Onions, dry	42	46	35
Carrots and turnips	34	32	19
Apples	158	170	100
Pears	2	4	4
Peaches and nectarines	4	3	2
Plums and sloes	6	6	4
Grapes	98	69	46
Hops	7	7	8

* Including mixed crops of wheat and rye.

Aggregate production ('000 metric tons, may include official, semi-official or estimated data): Total cereals 8,374 in 2008, 7,836 in 2009, 6,883.1 in 2010; Total roots and tubers 770 in 2008, 753 in 2009, 665 in 2010; Total vegetables (incl. melons) 244 in 2008, 238 in 2009, 149 in 2010; Total fruits (excl. melons) 318 in 2008, 301 in 2009, 181 in 2010.

LIVESTOCK

('000 head at 1 March)

	2008	2009	2010
Horses	28	30	31
Cattle	1,363	1,349	1,329
Pigs	1,917	1,909	1,908
Sheep	183	197	206
Goats	17	22	22
Chickens	25,488	24,042	24,284
Ducks	504	402	374
Turkeys	478	376	389

Source: FAO.

LIVESTOCK PRODUCTS

('000 metric tons unless otherwise indicated)

	2008	2009	2010
Cattle meat	80	77	74
Pig meat	336	300	291
Chicken meat	195	188	185
Cows' milk (million litres)	2,801	2,781	2,683
Hen eggs	99	98*	122

* Unofficial figure.

Source: FAO.

Forestry

ROUNDWOOD REMOVALS

('000 cubic metres)

	2008	2009	2010
Sawlogs, veneer logs and logs for sleepers	8,928	8,852	9,302
Pulpwood	5,280	4,827	5,501
Other industrial wood	99	90	103
Fuel wood	1,880	1,733	2,115
Total	16,187	15,502	17,022

Source: FAO.

SAWNWOOD PRODUCTION

('000 cubic metres)

	2008	2009	2010*
Coniferous (softwood)	4,409	3,800	4,400
Broadleaved (hardwood)	227	248	254
Total	4,636	4,048	4,654

* Unofficial figures.

Source: FAO.

Fishing

(metric tons)

	2007	2008	2009
Common carp	21,288	20,764	20,472
Others	3,435	3,795	3,711
Total catch	24,723	24,559	24,183

Source: FAO.

Mining

('000 metric tons unless otherwise indicated)

	2007	2008	2009
Hard coal	12,462	12,197	10,631
Brown coal and lignite	49,571	47,872	45,616
Crude petroleum ('000 barrels)	1,600	1,600	1,500
Kaolin	3,604	3,833	2,886

Source: US Geological Survey.

Industry

SELECTED PRODUCTS

('000 metric tons unless otherwise indicated)

	2008	2009	2010
Wheat flour	720	713	735
Refined sugar	418	444	446
Wine ('000 hectolitres)	497	480	463
Beer ('000 hectolitres)	19,213	18,053	16,738
Cotton yarn (metric tons)	29,940	14,297	12,535
Woven cotton fabrics ('000 metres)	94,191	67,931	51,683
Woollen fabrics ('000 metres)	14,013	n.a.	n.a.
Woven flax fabrics ('000 metres)	5,450	655	638
Paper and paperboard	198	153	118
Footwear ('000 pairs)	997	1,017	911
Nitrogenous fertilizers*†‡	200	200	n.a.
Soap	32	33	26
Cement	4,805	3,851	3,559
Pig-iron†	4,737	3,483	n.a.
Crude steel†	6,387	4,594	n.a.
Electric energy (million kWh)	83,518	82,250	85,910§
Motor spirit (petrol)	1,601	n.a.	n.a.
Gas-diesel (distillate fuel) oil	3,460.	n.a.	n.a.
Residual fuel oils	335	n.a.	n.a.
Coke	3,645	n.a.	n.a.
Bicycles (number)	304,630	n.a.	n.a.

* Estimated.

† Source: US Geological Survey.

‡ Production in terms of nitrogen.

§ Preliminary.

Source: partly UN Industrial Commodity Statistics Database.

Finance

CURRENCY AND EXCHANGE RATES

Monetary Units

100 haléřů (singular: haléř—heller) = 1 Czech koruna (Czech crown or Kč.).

Sterling, Dollar and Euro Equivalents (30 December 2011)

£1 sterling = 30.829 koruna;
US $1 = 19.940 koruna;
€1 = 24.800 koruna;
1,000 koruna = £32.44 = $50.15 = €38.76.

Average Exchange Rate (koruna per US $)

2009 19.063
2010 19.098
2011 17.696

Note: In February 1993 the Czech Republic introduced its own currency, the Czech koruna, to replace (at par) the Czechoslovak koruna.

STATE BUDGET

(million koruna)

Revenue	2008	2009	2010
Tax revenue	929,895	833,221	863,859
Income tax	222,131	168,989	173,794
Value-added tax	177,816	176,717	187,821
Consumption tax	125,538	123,836	130,859
Social security and employment insurance premiums and contributions	385,504	347,841	355,835
Pension insurance premiums	319,947	310,208	317,772
Non-tax revenue, capital revenue and subsidies received	134,046	141,393	136,518
Total	1,063,941	974,615	1,000,377

Expenditure	2008	2009	2010
Non-investment purchases and related expenses	119,591	125,836	118,646
Social security benefits	400,917	429,330	430,907
Pensions	312,532	339,788	346,213
Capital expenditure	105,034	133,164	130,224
Total (incl. others)	1,083,944	1,167,009	1,156,793

INTERNATIONAL RESERVES

(US $ million at 31 December)

	2008	2009	2010
Gold (national value)	358	454	584
IMF special drawing rights	21	1,245	1,224
Reserve position in IMF	162	241	349
Foreign exchange	36,472	39,670	40,335
Total	37,013	41,610	42,492

Source: IMF, *International Financial Statistics*.

MONEY SUPPLY

('000 million koruna at 31 December)

	2008	2009	2010
Currency outside depository corporations	365.6	353.6	357.5
Transferable deposits	1,309.5	1,418.3	1,664.2
Other deposits	980.8	892.0	698.7
Securities other than shares	47.6	45.3	39.6
Broad money	2,703.4	2,709.1	2,760.0

Source: IMF, *International Financial Statistics*.

COST OF LIVING

(Consumer Price Index; base: 2000 = 100)

	2006	2007	2008
Food	111.5	118.0	127.9
Clothing	78.1	77.5	76.6
Fuel and light	146.9	151.6	172.6
Rent	135.7	142.5	153.9
All items (incl. others)	114.6	117.9	125.4

2009: Food 126.7; All items (incl. others) 126.7.

2010: Food 115.7; All items (incl. others) 128.6.

Source: ILO.

NATIONAL ACCOUNTS
('000 million koruna at current prices)

Expenditure on the Gross Domestic Product

	2008	2009	2010
Final consumption expenditure	2,642.6	2,689.4	2,707.6
Households	1,856.7	1,852.5	1,871.8
General government	759.4	809.6	808.0
Non-profit institutions serving households	26.6	27.3	27.8
Gross capital formation	1,113.8	898.4	947.1
Gross fixed capital formation	1,031.2	927.5	923.0
Changes in inventories	79.1	−33.0	20.1
Net acquisition of valuables	3.6	3.9	4.0
Total domestic expenditure	3,756.4	3,587.8	3,654.7
Exports of goods and services	2,480.2	2,233.0	2,561.9
Less Imports of goods and services	2,388.3	2,081.5	2,441.4
GDP in purchasers' values	3,848.4	3,739.2	3,775.2
GDP at constant 2005 prices	3,635.3	3,464.7	3,559.6

Gross Domestic Product by Economic Activity

	2008	2009	2010
Agriculture, forestry and fishing	80.3	64.2	57.1
Mining and quarrying	239.2	253.4	237.7
Manufacturing	846.3	765.1	794.1
Construction	235.7	238.4	245.8
Trade, transport and restaurants and hotels	701.9	648.1	656.5
Information and communications	177.2	176.3	174.0
Financial intermediation	139.3	149.2	159.0
Real estate, renting and business activities	230.5	235.6	237.0
Public administration and defence; compulsory social security	249.0	233.9	238.1
Education, health and social work	502.6	527.2	524.3
Other community, social and personal service activities	78.0	79.0	81.0
Sub-total	3,479.9	3,370.5	3,404.7
Taxes on products	405.0	410.8	417.5
Less Subsidies on products	36.5	42.1	46.9
GDP in purchasers' values	3,848.4	3,739.2	3,775.2

BALANCE OF PAYMENTS
(US $ million)

	2008	2009	2010
Exports of goods f.o.b.	125,066	99,111	116,723
Imports of goods f.o.b.	−123,359	−94,534	−113,919
Trade balance	1,706	4,577	2,804
Exports of services	21,879	19,445	20,942
Imports of services	−17,509	−15,536	−17,013
Balance on goods and services	6,076	8,486	6,733
Other income received	10,212	5,167	4,895
Other income paid	−20,756	−18,349	−18,093
Balance on goods, services and income	−4,467	−4,696	−6,465
Current transfers received	3,894	3,711	4,618
Current transfers paid	−4,201	−3,864	−4,145
Current balance	−4,774	−4,849	−5,992
Capital account (net)	1,620	2,731	1,680
Direct investment abroad	−4,315	−917	−1,758
Direct investment from abroad	6,573	2,869	6,720
Portfolio investment assets	−498	3,419	705
Portfolio investment liabilities	458	5,169	7,371
Financial derivatives assets	3,505	2,528	3,497
Financial derivatives liabilities	−3,495	−2,493	−3,660
Other investment assets	−5,339	777	−4,512
Other investment liabilities	8,536	−2,301	1,124
Net errors and omissions	169	−2,646	−3,099
Overall balance	2,420	4,285	2,076

Source: IMF, *International Financial Statistics*.

External Trade

COMMODITY GROUPS
(distribution by SITC, million koruna)

Imports f.o.b.	2009	2010	2011
Food and live animals	106,901	112,559	122,255
Beverages and tobacco	13,452	14,373	16,377
Crude materials (inedible) except fuels	44,790	64,648	80,322
Mineral fuels, lubricants, etc.	183,966	231,447	283,162
Chemicals and related products	222,618	257,351	292,746
Basic manufactures	350,998	430,281	486,089
Machinery and transport equipment	821,223	1,046,030	1,118,667
Miscellaneous manufactured articles	237,305	247,443	263,847
Total (incl. others)	1,989,036	2,411,556	2,674,696

Exports f.o.b.	2009	2010	2011
Food and live animals	73,908	76,266	91,426
Beverages and tobacco	16,156	16,781	17,272
Crude materials (inedible) except fuels	57,539	75,908	80,919
Mineral fuels, lubricants, etc.	77,571	93,874	107,419
Chemicals and related products	136,420	164,213	180,784
Basic manufactures	376,391	435,348	507,616
Machinery and transport equipment	1,145,473	1,382,306	1,560,253
Miscellaneous manufactured articles	250,201	280,531	312,178
Total (incl. others)	2,138,623	2,532,797	2,866,123

PRINCIPAL TRADING PARTNERS
(million koruna)

Imports f.o.b.	2009	2010	2011
Austria	72,472	81,227	89,461
Belgium	41,282	44,013	47,771
China, People's Republic	199,939	295,799	333,343
France	76,782	79,800	87,067
Germany	528,649	613,698	684,310
Hungary	45,429	52,342	58,539
Italy	86,206	94,228	104,478
Japan	62,447	58,667	54,539
Netherlands	67,039	77,764	87,364
Poland	126,644	154,241	175,018
Russia	102,604	130,121	142,707
Slovakia	108,623	125,944	151,804
Spain	37,898	43,919	43,881
Sweden	18,519	22,285	24,515
Switzerland	23,632	25,656	28,511
United Kingdom	42,936	49,152	50,514
USA	41,889	54,000	52,267
Total (incl. others)	1,989,036	2,411,556	2,674,696

Exports f.o.b.	2009	2010	2011
Austria	100,007	119,667	131,402
Belgium	55,351	62,587	68,513
France	122,810	135,194	156,585
Germany	694,482	819,245	921,994
Hungary	54,589	58,266	65,041
Italy	94,407	112,244	118,691
Netherlands	83,260	93,354	100,445
Poland	123,064	154,644	179,553
Romania	24,212	28,565	31,647
Russia	49,618	67,337	92,626
Slovakia	186,946	217,292	257,109
Spain	50,818	60,495	61,201
Sweden	33,215	41,163	46,921
Switzerland	34,250	41,812	48,620
United Kingdom	105,875	124,923	129,608
USA	34,299	44,269	55,839
Total (incl. others)	2,138,623	2,523,797	2,866,123

Transport

RAILWAYS
(traffic)

	2008	2009	2010*
Passengers carried ('000)	177,424	164,958	164,801
Passenger-km (million)	6,803	6,503	6,591
Freight carried ('000 metric tons)	95,074	76,715	82,900
Freight net ton-km (million)	15,437	12,791	13,770

* Preliminary figures.

ROAD TRAFFIC
(motor vehicles in use at 31 December)

	2008	2009	2010
Passenger cars*	4,423,370	4,435,052	4,496,232
Buses and coaches	20,375	19,943	19,653
Commercial vehicles	589,598	587,032	584,921
Trailers	229,039	248,355	266,866
Motorcycles	892,564	903,175	924,178

* Including vans.

INLAND WATERWAYS
(freight carried, '000 metric tons)

	2008	2009	2010*
Imports	173	130	167
Exports	182	324	276
Internal	388	335	371
Total (incl. others)	1,905	1,647	1,642

* Preliminary figures.

CIVIL AVIATION

	2007	2008	2009
Kilometres flown ('000)	104,626	111,024	110,729
Passengers carried ('000)	6,977	7,158	7,354
Freight carried (metric tons)	21,596	20,438	15,044
Passenger-km ('000)	10,477	10,749	11,330
Freight ton-km ('000)	40,760	37,086	28,718

* Preliminary.

2010 (preliminary figures): Passengers carried ('000) 7,466; Passenger-km ('000) 10,902.

Tourism

FOREIGN TOURIST ARRIVALS*

Country of origin	2008	2009	2010
Austria	170,663	177,715	189,886
Denmark	108,552	99,563	109,292
France	235,654	223,901	251,468
Germany	1,475,858	1,393,112	1,348,482
Italy	374,632	357,492	332,551
Japan	123,275	114,777	133,052
Netherlands	236,193	203,764	194,138
Poland	376,592	341,136	350,637
Russia	418,184	326,895	414,671
Slovakia	299,278	287,810	307,192
Spain	247,240	194,406	196,011
United Kingdom	484,279	371,346	368,643
USA	305,057	274,311	312,883
Total (incl. others)	6,649,410	6,032,370	6,333,996

* Figures refer to visitors staying for at least one night at registered accommodation facilities.

Tourism receipts (US $ million, excl. passenger transport): 7,207 in 2008; 6,478 in 2009; 6,671 in 2010 (provisional) (Source: World Tourism Organization).

Communications Media

	2008	2009	2010
Radio transmitters	522*	n.a.	n.a.
Television transmitters	1,720*	n.a.	n.a.
Telephones ('000 main lines in use)†	2,477.9	2,526.9	2,405.5
Mobile cellular telephones ('000 subscribers)†	13,780.2	14,258.4	14,393.0
Internet subscribers ('000)†	1,794.1	1,369.5	1,529.1
Broadband subscribers ('000)†	1,759.6	1,355.0	1,521.0
Book production (titles)	18,520	17,598	17,054
Other periodicals (number)	5,687	5,481	5,265

* Preliminary figure.
† Source: International Telecommunication Union.

2005 (number): Daily newspapers 116.

Personal computers: 2,800,000 (273.5 per 1,000 persons) in 2005 (Source: International Telecommunication Union).

Education

(2010/11 unless otherwise indicated)

	Institutions	Teachers	Students
Pre-primary	4,880	25,737	328,612
Basic (primary and lower secondary)	4,123	58,023	789,486
Upper secondary:			
general	372	10,980*	139,066
technical and vocational	1,107	36,372*	393,852
Tertiary:			
higher professional schools	182	1,841	29,800
universities	72	16,504	396,307

* 2005/06.

Pupil-teacher ratio (primary education, UNESCO estimate): 18.5 in 2008/09 (Source: UNESCO Institute for Statistics).

Directory

The Government

HEAD OF STATE

President: VÁCLAV KLAUS (inaugurated 7 March 2008).

COUNCIL OF MINISTERS
(May 2012)

A coalition, principally comprising nominees of the Civic Democratic Party (ODS), Traditions, Responsibility, Prosperity 09 (TOP 09) and Public Affairs (VV).

Prime Minister: PETR NEČAS (ODS).

Deputy Prime Minister and Minister of Foreign Affairs: KAREL SCHWARZENBERG (TOP 09).

Deputy Prime Minister, Chairman of the Government Legislative Council: KAROLÍNA PEAKE (Independent).

Minister of the Interior: JAN KUBICE (Independent).

Minister of Defence: ALEXANDR VONDRA (ODS).

Minister of Regional Development: KAMIL JANKOVSKÝ (VV).

Minister of Industry and Trade: Dr MARTIN KUBA (ODS).

Minister of Agriculture: PETR BENDL (ODS).

Minister of Health Care: Dr LEOŠ HEGER (TOP 09).

Minister of Justice: Dr JIŘÍ POSPÍŠIL (ODS).

Minister of Labour and Social Affairs: JAROMÍR DRÁBEK (TOP 09).

Minister of Finance: MIROSLAV KALOUSEK (TOP 09).

Minister of Education: PETR FIALA (Independent).

Minister of the Environment: TOMÁŠ CHALUPA (ODS).

Minister of Culture: ALENA HANÁKOVÁ (TOP 09).

Minister of Transport: PAVEL DOBEŠ (VV).

MINISTRIES

Office of the President: Pražský hrad, 119 08 Prague 1; tel. 224371111; fax 224373300; e-mail ladislav.jakl@hrad.cz; internet www.hrad.cz.

Office of the Government: náb. E. Beneše 4, 118 01 Prague 1; tel. 224002111; fax 257531283; e-mail posta@vlada.cz; internet www.vlada.cz.

Ministry of Agriculture: Těšnov 17, 117 05 Prague 1; tel. 221811111; fax 224810478; e-mail info@mze.cz; internet www.eagri.cz.

Ministry of Culture: Maltéské nám. 471/1, 118 11 Prague 1; tel. 257085111; fax 224318155; e-mail epodatelna@mkcr.cz; internet www.mkcr.cz.

Ministry of Defence: Tychonova 1, 160 01 Prague 6; tel. 973201111; fax 973200149; e-mail info@army.cz; internet www.army.cz.

Ministry of Education: Karmelitská 7, 118 12 Prague 1; tel. 234811111; fax 234811753; e-mail posta@msmt.cz; internet www.msmt.cz.

Ministry of the Environment: Vršovická 1442/65, 100 10 Prague 10; tel. 267121111; fax 267310308; e-mail info@mzp.cz; internet www.env.cz.

Ministry of Finance: Letenská 15, 118 00 Prague 1; tel. 257041111; fax 257042788; e-mail podatelna@mfcr.cz; internet www.mfcr.cz.

Ministry of Foreign Affairs: Loretánské nám. 101/5, 118 00 Prague 1; tel. 224181111; fax 224182031; e-mail podatelna@mzv.cz; internet www.mzv.cz.

Ministry of Health Care: Palackého nám. 4, 128 01 Prague 2; tel. 224971111; fax 224972111; e-mail mzcr@mzcr.cz; internet www.mzcr.cz.

Ministry of Industry and Trade: Na Františku 32, 110 15 Prague 1; tel. 224851111; fax 224811089; e-mail posta@mpo.cz; internet www.mpo.cz.

Ministry of the Interior: Nad Štolou 3, POB 21, 170 34 Prague 7; tel. 974811111; fax 974833582; e-mail posta@mvcr.cz; internet www.mvcr.cz.

Ministry of Justice: Vyšehradská 16, 128 10 Prague 2; tel. 221997111; fax 224919927; e-mail posta@msp.justice.cz; internet www.justice.cz.

Ministry of Labour and Social Affairs: Na poříčním právu 1/376, 128 01 Prague 2; tel. 221921111; fax 224918391; e-mail posta@mpsv.cz; internet www.mpsv.cz.

Ministry of Regional Development: Staroměstské nám. 6, 110 15 Prague 1; tel. 224861111; fax 224861333; e-mail info@mmr.cz; internet www.mmr.cz.

Ministry of Transport: nábř. L. Svobody 12/1222, POB 9, 110 15 Prague 1; tel. 225131184; fax 225131112; e-mail posta@mdcr.cz; internet www.mdcr.cz.

President

Following voting in both legislative chambers, VÁCLAV KLAUS was elected to a second five-year presidential term on 15 February 2008. Klaus secured 141 of the votes cast, defeating JAN ŠVEJNAR, who received 111 votes. Klaus was inaugurated on 7 March.

Legislature

The Czech Constitution, which was adopted in December 1992, provides for a bicameral legislature as the highest organ of state authority in the Czech Republic (which was established as an independent state on 1 January 1993, following the dissolution of the Czech and Slovak Federative Republic). The lower house, the Poslanecká sněmovna (Chamber of Deputies), retained the structure of the Czech National Council (the former republican legislature). The upper chamber, the Senát (Senate), was first elected in November 1996.

Poslanecká sněmovna (Chamber of Deputies)

Sněmovní 4, 118 26 Prague 1; tel. 257171111; fax 257534469; e-mail posta@psp.cz; internet www.psp.cz.

Chairman: MIROSLAVA NĚMCOVÁ.

General Election, 28–29 May 2010

Party	Votes	% of votes	Seats
Czech Social Democratic Party	1,155,267	22.09	56
Civic Democratic Party	1,057,792	20.22	53
Traditions, Responsibility, Prosperity 09	873,833	16.71	41
Communist Party of Bohemia and Moravia	589,765	11.27	26
Public Affairs	569,127	10.88	24
Others	985,075	18.83	—
Total	5,230,859	100.00	200

Senát (Senate)

Valdštejnské nám. 4, 118 01 Prague 1; tel. 257071111; fax 257075700; e-mail epodatelna@senat.cz; internet www.senat.cz.

Chairman: MILAN ŠTĚCH.

One-third of the 81 seats of the Senát are renewed every two years. Following a partial election, which was conducted in two rounds on 15–16 October and 22–23 October 2010, the strength of the parties was as follows:

Party	Seats
Czech Social Democratic Party	41
Civic Democratic Party	25
Christian Democratic Union-Czechoslovak People's Party	6
Traditions, Responsibility, Prosperity 09 (TOP 09)-Mayors and Independents	2
Communist Party of Bohemia and Moravia	2
NorthBohemians.cz	2
Others	3
Total	81

Election Commission

Státní volební komise, Český statistický úřad (State Electoral Commission, Czech Statistical Office): Na padesátém 81, 100 82 Prague 10; tel. 274051111; e-mail krausova@mvcr.cz; internet www.volby.cz; Chair. Minister of the Interior.

Political Organizations

In early March 2012 some 79 active political parties and 55 active political movements were officially registered with the Ministry of the Interior. The following are among the most significant:

Christian Democratic Union-Czechoslovak People's Party (KDU-ČSL) (Křesťanská a demokratická unie-Československá strana lidová): Palác Charitas, Karlovo nám. 5, 128 01 Prague 2; tel. 226205111; fax 226205333; e-mail info@kdu.cz; internet www.kdu.cz; f. 1991; Chair. PAVEL BĚLOBRÁDEK.

Civic Democratic Party (ODS) (Občanská demokratická strana): Polygon House, Doudlebská 1699/5, 140 00 Prague 4; tel. 234707111; fax 234707103; e-mail hk@ods.cz; internet www.ods.cz; f. 1991 following a split in Civic Forum (f. 1989); merged with Christian Democratic Party in 1996; 33,916 mems (April 2009); liberal-conservative; Chair. PETR NEČAS.

Communist Party of Bohemia and Moravia (KSČM) (Komunistická strana Čech a Moravy): Politických vězňů 9, 111 21 Prague 1; tel. 222897111; fax 222897207; e-mail info@kscm.cz; internet www.kscm.cz; f. 1990 as a result of the reorganization of the fmr Communist Party of Czechoslovakia; c. 66,627 mems (2010); Chair. VOJTĚCH FILIP.

Czech Social Democratic Party (ČSSD) (Česká strana sociálně demokratická): Lidový dům, Hybernská 7, 110 00 Prague 1; tel. 296522111; fax 224222190; e-mail info@socdem.cz; internet www.socdem.cz; f. 1878; prohibited 1948; re-established 1990; fmrly the Czechoslovak Social Democratic Party; Chair. BOHUSLAV SOBOTKA.

Green Party (SZ) (Strana zelených): Nové Město, 110 00 Prague 1; tel. and fax 734388936; e-mail info@zeleni.cz; internet www.zeleni.cz; f. 1990; Pres. ONDŘEJ LIŠKA.

Mayors and Independents (STAN) (Starostové a nezávislí): V Rovinách 40, 140 00 Prague 4; tel. 241412091; e-mail info@starostove-nezavisli.cz; internet www.starostove-nezavisli.cz; f. 2004; localism; Pres. PETR GAZDÍK.

NorthBohemians.cz (Severočeši.cz): tř. Čs. armády 1766, 434 01 Most; tel. 476146187; e-mail sekretariat@severocesi.cz; internet www.severocesi.cz; Chair. RYBA FRANTIŠEK.

Public Affairs (Věci veřejné—VV): Štefánikova 23/203, 150 00 Prague 5; tel. 800879709; e-mail info@veciverejne.cz; internet www.veciverejne.cz; f. 2002; supports the use of referendums and other forms of direct democracy to increase public involvement in politics; Pres. RADEK JOHN.

Traditions, Responsibility, Prosperity 09 (TOP 09) (Tradice, Odpovědnost, Prosperita 09): Michnův palác, budova č. 2, Újezd 450/40, Malá Strana, 118 00 Prague 1; tel. 255790999; fax 255790899; e-mail info@top99.cz; internet www.top09.cz; conservative; f. 2009; Chair. KAREL SCHWARZENBERG.

Diplomatic Representation

EMBASSIES IN THE CZECH REPUBLIC

Afghanistan: Komornická 1852/25, Dejvice, 160 00 Prague 6; tel. 233544228; fax 233542009; e-mail afg.prague@centrum.cz; Ambassador MOHAMMAD KABIR FARAHI.

Albania: Nad Šárkou 1514/59, 160 00 Prague 6; tel. 233370594; fax 233313654; e-mail alembprg@mbox.vol.cz; Chargé d'affaires a.i. GENC PECANI.

Algeria: V Tišině 10/483, POB 204, 160 41 Prague 6; tel. 233371142; fax 233371144; e-mail ambalger@mbox.vol.cz; internet www.algerie.cz; Ambassador BELAID HADJEM.

Argentina: Panská 6, 110 00 Prague 1; tel. 224212448; fax 222241246; e-mail eches@mrecic.gov.ar; Ambassador VICENTE ESPECHE GIL.

Armenia: Na Pískách 1411/95, Dejvice, 160 00 Prague 6; tel. 220518175; fax 220517686; e-mail armembassy.cz@mfa.am; internet www.cz.mfa.am; Ambassador TIGRAN SEYRANIAN.

Austria: Viktora Huga 10, Smíchov, 151 15 Prague 5; tel. 257090511; fax 257316045; e-mail prag-ob@bmeia.gv.at; internet www.bmeia.gv.at/prag; Ambassador FERDINAND TRAUTTSMANDORFF.

Azerbaijan: Na Míčánce 32, Hanspaulka, 160 00 Prague 6; tel. 246032422; fax 246032423; e-mail prague@mission.mfa.gov.az; internet www.azembassyprague.az; Ambassador TAHIR TAGHIZADE.

Belarus: Sádky 626, 171 00 Prague 7; tel. 233540899; fax 233540925; e-mail czech@belembassy.org; internet www.czech.belembassy.org; Chargé d'affaires a.i. VASIL MARKOVICH.

Belgium: Valdštejnská 6, Malá Strana, 118 01 Prague 1; tel. 257533524; fax 257533750; e-mail prague@diplobel.fed.be; internet www.diplomatie.be/prague; Ambassador RENILDE LEOCKX.

Bosnia and Herzegovina: Opletalova 27, 110 00 Prague 1; tel. 224422510; fax 222210183; e-mail embbh@iol.cz; Ambassador NEDILJKO BILIĆ.

Brazil: Panská 5, 110 00 Prague 1; tel. 224321910; fax 224312901; e-mail brazil@brazil.cz; internet www.brazil.cz; Ambassador GEORGE MONTEIRO PRATA.

Bulgaria: Krakovská 6, 110 00 Prague 1; tel. 222211258; fax 222211728; e-mail bulvelv@volny.cz; Chargé d'affaires a.i. ELEONORA DIMITROVA.

Canada: Muchova 6/240, 160 00 Prague 6; tel. 272101800; fax 272101890; e-mail canada@canada.cz; internet www.canada.cz; Ambassador VALERIE RAYMOND.

Chile: U Vorlíků 4/623, Bubeneč, 160 00 Prague 6; tel. 224315064; fax 224316069; e-mail embachile@embachile.cz; Ambassador JOSÉ MANUEL LIRA.

China, People's Republic: Pelléova 18, Bubeneč, 160 00 Prague 6; tel. 224311323; fax 224319888; e-mail chinaembassy@seznam.cz; internet www.chinaembassy.cz; Ambassador YU QINGTAI.

Congo, Democratic Republic: Soukenická 34, 110 00 Prague 1; tel. 222316762; fax 224829302; e-mail ambardcprague@yahoo.fr; Chargé d'affaires a.i. CATHY MULAMBA MUHOMA.

Croatia: V Průhledu 9, 162 00 Prague 6; tel. 235090801; fax 233343464; e-mail velrhprag@vol.cz; internet cz.mvp.hr; Ambassador FRANE KRNIĆ.

Cuba: Sibiřské nám. 1, 160 00 Prague 6; tel. 224311253; fax 233341029; e-mail embacubapraga@embacuba.cz; internet www.embacuba.cz; Chargé d'affaires a.i. NELSON TAMAYO CARO.

Cyprus: Pod Hradbami 9, 160 00 Prague 6; tel. 224316833; fax 224317529; e-mail embassy@kypros.cz; internet www.mfa.gov.cy/embassyprague; Ambassador PHAEDON ANASTASIOU.

Denmark: Maltézské nám. 5, POB 25, Malá Strana, 118 01 Prague 1; tel. 257531600; fax 257531410; e-mail prgamb@um.dk; internet www.ambprag.um.dk; Ambassador OLE EMIL MOESBY.

Egypt: Pelléova 14, Bubeneč, 160 00 Prague 6; tel. 224311506; fax 224311157; e-mail embassyegypt@centrum.cz; Ambassador AMAL MOSTAFA K. MOURAD.

Estonia: Na Kampě 1, 118 00 Prague 1; tel. 257011180; fax 257011181; e-mail embassy.prague@estemb.cz; internet www.estemb.cz; Ambassador LAMBIT UIBO.

Finland: Hellichova 1, 118 00 Prague 1; tel. 251177251; fax 251177241; e-mail sanomat.pra@formin.fi; internet www.finland.cz; Ambassador PÄIVI HILTUNEN-TOIVIO.

France: Velkopřevorské nám. 2, 118 00 Prague 1; tel. 251171711; fax 251171720; e-mail ambapresse@france.cz; internet www.france.cz; Ambassador PIERRE LÉVY.

Georgia: Malostranské náměstí 5/28, 118 00 Prague 1; tel. 233311749; fax 233311752; e-mail prague.emb@mfa.gov.ge; internet www.czech.mfa.gov.ge; Ambassador NINO NAKASHIDZE.

Germany: Vlašská 19, 118 01 Prague 1; tel. 257113111; fax 257113318; e-mail zreg@prag.diplo.de; internet www.prag.diplo.de; Ambassador JOHANNES HAINDL.

Ghana: V Tišině 4, Bubeneč, 160 00 Prague 6; tel. 233377236; fax 233375647; e-mail ghanaemb@gmail.com; Ambassador VICTOR SMITH.

Greece: Na Ořechovce 19, Střešovice, 162 00 Prague 2; tel. 222250943; fax 222253686; e-mail gremb.pra@mfa.gr; Ambassador CONSTANTINOS KOKOSSIS.

Holy See: Voršilská 12, 110 00 Prague 1; tel. 224999811; fax 224999833; e-mail nunciatgc@mbox.vol.cz; Apostolic Nuncio Most Rev. GIUSEPPE LEANZA (Titular Archbishop of Lilybaeum).

Hungary: Pod Hradbami 17, Střešovice, 160 00 Prague 6; tel. 220317200; fax 233322104; e-mail mission.prg@kum.hu; internet www.mfa.gov.hu/emb/prague; Ambassador LÁSZLÓ SZÖKE.

India: Milady Horákové 60/93, 170 00 Prague 7; tel. 257533490; fax 257533378; e-mail india@india.cz; internet www.india.cz; Ambassador DINKAR PRAKASH SRIVASTAVA.

Indonesia: Nad Buďánkami II/7, 150 21 Prague 5; tel. 257214388; fax 257212105; e-mail informace@indonesian-embassy.cz; internet www.indonesia.cz; Ambassador EMERIA WILUJENG AMIR SIREGAR.

Iran: Na Zátorce 18, 160 00 Prague 6; tel. 220570454; fax 233380255; e-mail iranemb_sec@volny.cz; Chargé d'affaires a.i. MAJID RAMEZANI.

Iraq: Mongolská 607/3, 160 00 Prague 6; tel. 224326976; fax 224321715; e-mail iraqembassy@post.cz; Ambassador HUSSAIN SALEH MAJEED MUALLA.

Ireland: Tržiště 13, 118 00 Prague 1; tel. 257530061; fax 257531387; e-mail pragueembassy@dfa.ie; internet www.embassyofireland.cz; Ambassador ALISON KELLY.

Israel: Badeniho 2, 170 06 Prague 7; tel. 233097500; fax 233097519; e-mail info@prague.mfa.gov.il; internet prague.mfa.gov.il; Ambassador YAAKOV LEVY.

Italy: Nerudova 20, Malá Strana, 118 00 Prague 1; tel. 233080111; fax 257531522; e-mail ambasciata.praga@esteri.it; internet www.ambpraga.esteri.it; Ambassador PASQUALE D'AVINO.

Japan: Maltézské nám. 6, Malá Strana, 118 01 Prague 1; tel. 257533546; fax 257532377; e-mail ryoji@japanembassy.cz; internet www.cz.emb-japan.go.jp; Ambassador TOSHIO KUNIKATA.

Kazakhstan: Romaina Rollanda 12, 160 00 Prague 6; tel. 233375642; fax 233371019; e-mail kzembas@bon.cz; internet www.kazembassy.cz; Ambassador ANARBEK B. KARASHEV.

Korea, Democratic People's Republic: Na Větru 395/18, 162 00 Prague 6; tel. 235362210; fax 235355000; e-mail vel.kldr@seznam.cz; Ambassador KWANG II RI.

Korea, Republic: Slavíčkova 5, Bubeneč, 160 00 Prague 6; tel. 2234090411; fax 2234090450; e-mail czech@mofat.go.kr; internet cze.mofat.go.kr; Ambassador OH GABRIEL.

Kosovo: Tržiště 366/13, 118 00 Prague 1; tel. 257217775; fax 257310229; e-mail embassy.cz.republic@ks-gov.net; Chargé d'affaires a.i. HILMI ZOGJANI.

Kuwait: Na Zátorce 26, 160 00 Prague 6; tel. 220570781; fax 220570787; e-mail kuwaiti@volny.cz; Ambassador AYMAN MOHAMED YOUSSEF AL-ADSSANI.

Latvia: Hradešínská 3, POB 54, 101 00 Prague 10; tel. 255700881; fax 255700880; e-mail embassy.czech@mfa.gov.lv; internet www.latvia.cz; Ambassador KASPARS OZOLIŅŠ.

Lebanon: Lazarská 6, 120 00 Prague 2; tel. 224930495; fax 224934534; e-mail czklebemb@vol.cz; Chargé d'affaires a.i. NADIM SOURATY.

Lithuania: Pod Klikovkou 1916/2, 150 00 Prague 5; tel. 257210122; fax 257210124; e-mail amb.cz@urm.lt; internet cz.mfa.lt; Ambassador AURIMAS TAURANTAS.

Luxembourg: Apolinářská 439/9, 128 00 Prague 2; tel. 257181800; fax 257532537; e-mail prague.amb@mae.etat.lu; internet www.ambalux.cz; Ambassador JEAN FALTZ.

Macedonia, former Yugoslav republic: Balbínova 392/4, Vinohrady, 120 00 Prague 2; tel. 222521093; fax 222521108; e-mail prague@mfa.gov.mk; Ambassador IGOR ILIEVSKI.

Malaysia: Na Zátorce 675/30, Bubeneč, 160 00 Prague 6; tel. 234706611; fax 296326192; e-mail mwprague@mwprague.cz; internet www.kln.gov.my/perwakilan/prague; Ambassador ZAINAL ABIDIN BAKAR.

Mexico: V Jirchářích 151/10, 110 00 Prague 1; tel. 283061530; fax 233550477; e-mail embamex@rep-checa.cz; internet www.rep-checa.cz; Ambassador JOSÉ LUIS BERNAL RODRÍGUEZ.

Moldova: Na Juárezova 14, Bubeneč, 160 00 Prague 6; tel. 233323762; fax 233323765; e-mail praga@mfa.md; internet www.ambasadamoldova.cz; Ambassador. STEFAN GORDA.

Mongolia: Na Marně 5, 160 00 Prague 6; tel. 224311198; fax 224314827; e-mail monemb@bohem-net.cz; Ambassador NAMNANGIIN NYAMJAV.

Morocco: Mickiewiczova 254/6, Dejvice, 160 00 Prague 6; tel. 233325656; fax 233322634; e-mail sifamapragu@iol.cz; Ambassador SORAYA OTHMANI.

Netherlands: Gotthardská 6/27, Bubeneč, 160 00 Prague 6; tel. 233015200; fax 233015254; e-mail pra@minbuza.nl; internet www.netherlandsembassy.cz; Ambassador JAN CORNELIS HENNEMAN.

Norway: Hellichova 1/458, Malá Strana, 118 00 Prague 1; tel. 257323737; fax 257326827; e-mail emb.prague@mfa.no; internet www.noramb.cz; Ambassador JENS EIKAAS.

Pakistan: U Páté Baterie 7/761, Střešovice, 162 00 Prague 6; tel. 233312868; fax 233312885; e-mail pareppprague@gmail.com; Ambassador AITZAZ AHMED.

Peru: Muchova 9, Dejvice, 160 00 Prague 6; tel. 224316210; fax 224314749; e-mail embajada@peru-embajada.cz; internet www.peru-embajada.cz; Ambassador MARÍA SUSANA LANDAVERI PORTURAS.

Philippines: Senovážné nám. 8, 110 00 Prague 1; tel. 224216397; fax 224216390; e-mail praguepe@gmail.com; internet www.praguepe.cz; Ambassador EVELYN D. AUSTRIA-GARCIA.

Poland: Valdštejnská 8, 118 01 Prague 1; tel. 257099500; fax 257530399; e-mail praga.amb.sekretariat@msz.gov.pl; internet www.prague.polemb.net; Ambassador JAN PASTWA.

Portugal: Pevnostní 9, 160 00 Prague 6; tel. 257311230; fax 257311234; e-mail embport@mbox.vol.cz; internet www.embportugal.cz; Ambassador JOSÉ JÚLIO PEREIRA GOMES.

Romania: Nerudova 5, POB 87, 118 01 Prague 1; tel. 257534210; fax 257531017; e-mail embroprg@mbox.vol.cz; internet www.rouemb.cz; Ambassador DANIELA ANDA GRIGORE-GITMAN.

Russia: nám. Pod Kaštany 1, Bubeneč, 160 00 Prague 6; tel. 233374100; fax 233377235; e-mail embrus@bluetone.cz; internet www.czech.mid.ru; Ambassador SERGEI KISELEV.

Saudi Arabia: Na Hřebenkách 70, 150 00 Prague 5; tel. 257316606; fax 257316593; e-mail resa@saudiembassy.cz; Ambassador ABDULLAH A. AL-ALSHEIKH.

Serbia: Mostecká 15, 118 00 Prague 1; tel. 257532075; fax 257533948; e-mail yuambacz@mbox.vol.cz; Ambassador MAJA MITROVIĆ.

Slovakia: Pelléova 87/12, 160 00 Prague 6; tel. 233113051; fax 233113054; e-mail emb.prague@mzv.sk; internet www.mzv.sk/praha; Ambassador PETER BRŇO.

Slovenia: Pod Hradbami 15, 160 41 Prague 6; tel. 233081211; fax 224314106; e-mail vpr@gov.si; internet praga.veleposlanistvo.si; Ambassador SMILJANA KNEZ.

South Africa: Ruská 65, POB 133, Vršovice, 100 00 Prague 10; tel. 267311114; fax 267311395; e-mail prague.ambassador@foreign.gov.za; internet www.saprague.cz; Ambassador CELIA-SANDRA BOTHA.

Spain: Badeniho 401/4, 170 00 Prague 7; tel. 233097211; fax 233341770; e-mail emb.praga@maec.es; internet www.embajada-esp-praga.cz; Ambassador D. ARTURO LACLAUSTRA BELTRÁN.

Sweden: Úvoz 13, POB 35, 160 12 Prague 612; tel. 220313200; fax 220313240; e-mail ambassaden.prag@foreign.ministry.se; internet www.swedenabroad.com/prague; Ambassador ANNIKA JAGANDER.

Switzerland: Pevnostní 588/7, POB 84, Střešovice, 162 01 Prague 6; tel. 220400611; fax 224311312; e-mail pra.vertretung@eda.admin.ch; internet www.eda.admin.ch/prag; Ambassador ANDRÉ REGLI.

Syria: Českomalínská 20/7, 160 00 Prague 6; tel. 224310952; fax 224317911; e-mail souria@volny.cz; internet www.syrianembassy.cz; Ambassador NADRA FAYEZ SAYAF.

Thailand: Romaina Rollanda 3, Bubeneč, 160 00 Prague 6; tel. 220571435; fax 220570049; e-mail thaiemb@volny.cz; internet www.thaiembassy.cz; Ambassador KRISANA CHANDRAPRABHA.

Tunisia: Nad Kostelem 8, Bráník, 147 00 Prague 4; tel. 244460652; fax 244460825; e-mail at.prague@vol.cz; Ambassador BADII ELKEDIDI.

Turkey: Na Ořechovce 69, 162 00 Prague 616; tel. 224311402; fax 224311279; e-mail tr1@telecom.cz; Ambassador CIHAD ERGINAY.

Ukraine: Charlese de Gaulla 29, 160 00 Prague 6; tel. 233342000; fax 233344366; e-mail emb_cz@mfa.gov.ua; internet www.mfa.gov.ua/czechia; Ambassador IVAN HRYTSAK.

United Kingdom: Thunovská 14, 118 00 Prague 1; tel. 257402111; fax 257402296; e-mail info@britain.cz; internet ukinczechrepublic.fco.gov.uk; Ambassador SIAN CHRISTINA MACLEOD.

Uruguay: Muchova 9, 160 00 Prague 6; tel. 224314755; fax 224313780; e-mail urupra@urupra.cz; Ambassador DIANA MAGDALENA ESPINO PUGLIESE DE PAPANTONAKIS.

USA: Tržiště 15, 118 01 Prague 1; tel. 257022000; fax 257022809; e-mail consprague@state.gov; internet prague.usembassy.gov; Ambassador NORMAN EISEN.

Venezuela: Sněmovní 9, 118 00 Prague 1; tel. 257534253; fax 257534257; e-mail embaven@vol.cz; internet www.embajada-venezuela.cz; Ambassador VÍCTOR JULIÁN HERNÁNDEZ LEÓN.

Viet Nam: Plzeňská 214/2578, 150 00 Prague 5; tel. 257211540; fax 257211792; e-mail dsqvietnamcz@yahoo.com; internet www.vietnamembassy-czech.org; Ambassador DO XUAN DONG.

Yemen: Pod Hradbami 5, 160 00 Prague 6; tel. 233331568; fax 233332204; e-mail yemb-prague@mofa.gov.ye; Ambassador ABDULRAHMAN MOHAMED AL-HAMDI.

Judicial System

The judicial system comprises the Supreme Court, the Supreme Administrative Court, and high, regional and district courts. There is also a 15-member Constitutional Court.

Supreme Court (Nejvyšší soud): Burešova 20, 657 37 Brno; tel. 541593111; fax 541213493; e-mail podatelna@nsoud.cz; internet www.nsoud.cz; Chair. IVA BROŽOVÁ.

Supreme Administrative Court (Nejvyšší správní soud): Moravské nám. 6, 657 40 Brno; tel. 542532311; fax 542532361; e-mail podatelna@nssoud.cz; internet www.nssoud.cz; Pres. JOSEF BAXA.

Office of the Chief Prosecutor: Náměstí Hrdinů 1300, 140 65 Prague 4; tel. 261196111; fax 261196550; e-mail podatelna@vsz.pha.justice.cz; internet portal.justice.cz; Chief Prosecutor RENÁTA VESECKÁ.

Constitutional Court (Ústavní soud): Joštova 8, 660 83 Brno 2; tel. 542162111; fax 542161309; e-mail podani@usoud.cz; internet www.concourt.cz; Chair. PAVEL RYCHETSKÝ.

Religion

According to the results of the March 2001 national census, about 60% of the population profess no religious belief. Among believers, the principal religion is Christianity, and the largest denomination is Latin-rite Catholicism.

CHRISTIANITY

Ecumenical Council of Churches in the Czech Republic (Ekumenická rada církví v České republice): Donská 5/370, 101 00 Prague 10; tel. and fax 271742326; e-mail erc@ekumenickarada.cz; internet www.ekumenickarada.cz; f. 1955; 11 mem. churches; Pres. Mgr. JOEL RUML; Gen. Sec. SANDRA ZÁLABOVÁ.

The Roman Catholic Church

The Czech Republic comprises two archdioceses and six dioceses. There is also an Apostolic Exarchate for Catholics of the Byzantine Rite. The Catholic Church estimated a total of3,289,836 adherents in the country at 31 December 2008, equivalent to 32.0% of the total population. Of this number, some 178,150 were adherents of the Byzantine Rite.

Latin Rite

Bishops' Conference: Thákurova 3, 160 00 Prague 6; tel. 223315421; fax 224310144; e-mail cbk2@ktf.cuni.cz; Pres. Most Rev. JAN GRAUBNER (Archbishop of Olomouc).

Archbishop of Olomouc: Most Rev. JAN GRAUBNER, Archibiskupský Ordinát, Biskupské nám. 2, POB 193, 771 01 Olomouc; tel. 587405111; fax 585222244; e-mail arcibol@arcibol.cz; internet www.ado.cz.

Archbishop of Prague: Most Rev. DOMINIK DUKA, Hradčanské nám. 56/16, 119 02 Prague 1; tel. 220392123; fax 220515396; e-mail apha@apha.cz; internet www.apha.cz.

Byzantine Rite

Apostolic Exarch for Catholics of the Byzantine Rite Resident in the Czech Republic: Most Rev. Dr LADISLAV HUČKO (Titular Bishop of Orea), Haštalské nám. 4, 110 00 Prague 1; tel. 221778491; fax 222312817; e-mail exarchat@volny.cz; internet www.exarchat.cz.

The Eastern Orthodox Church

Orthodox Church in the Czech Lands and Slovakia (Pravoslavná církev v Českých zemích a na Slovensku): Resslova 9A, 120 00 Prague 2; tel. 224920686; fax 224916100; e-mail cilova@pravoslavnacirkev.cz; internet www.pravoslavnacirkev.cz; divided into two eparchies in the Czech Republic: Prague and Olomouc-Brno; and two eparchies in Slovakia: Prešov and Michalovce; Archbishop of Prague, Metropolitan of the Czech Lands and Slovakia His Beatitude Dr KRYŠTOF.

Protestant Churches

Brethren Evangelical Free Church (Církev bratrská): Soukenická 15, 110 00 Prague 1; tel. and fax 222318131; e-mail sekretariat@cb.cz; internet www.cb.cz; f. 1880; 10,000 mems, 76 churches; mem. of the Ecumenical Council of Churches in the Czech Republic and the International Federation of Free Evangelical Churches; Pres. DANIEL FAJFR; Sec. PETR GRULICH.

Evangelical Church of Czech Brethren (Českobratrská církev evangelická): Jungmannova 9, 111 21 Prague 1; tel. 224999211; fax 224999219; e-mail e-cirkev@e-cirkev.cz; internet www.e-cirkev.cz; f. 1781; united since 1918; Presbyterian; active in Bohemia, Moravia and Silesia; 94 000 adherents and 256 parishes (2010); Pres. JOEL RUML; Moderator LIA VALKOVÁ.

Silesian Evangelical Church of the Augsburg Confession (Slezská církev evangelická a.v.): Na nivách 7, 737 01 Český Těšín; tel. 558764200; fax 558764201; e-mail sekretariat@sceav.cz; internet www.sceav.cz; Lutheran; 15,572 mems (2010); Bishop JAN WACŁAWEK.

Unity of Brethren of the Czech Republic—Unitas Fratrum (Jednota bratrská v České republice): B. Němcové 54/9, 460 05 Liberec; tel. 484847916; e-mail jbcr@jbcr.info; internet www.jbcr.info; f. 1457, reorganized 1862; widely known as the 'Moravian Church'; 4,243 mems in 27 parishes (2011); Pres. Rev. Mgr EVALD RUCKÝ.

Other Christian Churches

Apostolic Church in the Czech Republic (Apoštolská církev ČR): V Zídkách 402, 280 02 Kolín; tel. 321720457; fax 321727668; e-mail ustredi.kolin@apostolskacirkev.cz; internet www.apostolskacirkev.cz; f. 1989; 5,634 mems; Bishop RUDOLF BUBIK.

Church of the Seventh-day Adventists—Czech and Slovak Union (Církev adventistů sedmého dne—Česko-Slovenská Unie): Londýnská 30, 120 00 Prague 2; tel. 241471939; fax 244471863; e-mail unie@casd.cz; internet www.casd.cz; f. 1919; 9,638 mems; 185 congregations; Pres. MIKULÁŠ PAVLÍK.

Czechoslovak Hussite Church (Církev československá husitská): Wuchterlova 5, 166 26 Prague 6; tel. 220398114; fax 220398123; e-mail external.affairs@ccsh.cz; internet www.ccsh.cz; f. 1920; 99,103 mems (2006); six dioceses, 292 parishes; Chair. Patriarch TOMÁŠ BUTTA.

JUDAISM

Federation of Jewish Communities in the Czech Republic (Federace židovských obcí v ČR): Maiselova 18, 110 00 Prague 1; tel. 224800824; fax 224810912; e-mail sekretariat@fzo.cz; internet www.fzo.cz; 3,000 mems in 10 registered communities; Pres. JIŘÍ DANÍČEK; Chief Rabbi EPHRAIM KAROL SIDON.

The Press

PRINCIPAL DAILIES

There were 116 national and regional daily newspapers published in 2005.

Blesk (Lightning): Komunardů 1548/42, 170 00 Prague 7; tel. 225977478; fax 225977473; e-mail blesk@blesk.cz; internet www.blesk.cz; popular; Editor-in-Chief VLADIMÍR MUŽÍK; circ. 394,225 (Nov. 2010).

Brněnský deník—Rovnost (Brno Daily—Equality): Milady Horákové 9, 602 00 Brno; tel. 545212884; fax 545212873; e-mail tomas.herman@denik.cz; internet brnensky.denik.cz; f. 1885; fmrly *Rovnost* (Equality); morning; Editor-in-Chief TOMÁŠ HERMAN; circ. 62,000.

České noviny/Czech Happenings: Neris s.r.o. Opletalova 5, 110 00 Prague 1; tel. 222098439; fax 222098113; e-mail cn@ctk.cz; internet www.ceskenoviny.cz; f. 1996; online only; in Czech and English; also produces *Finanční noviny* (Financial News) and *Sportovní noviny* (Sport News); Editor-in-Chief KAREL PETRÁK.

Českobudějovický deník (České Budějovice Daily): Přemysla Otakara II 8/5, 370 01 České Budějovice; tel. 386100721; fax 386100770; e-mail redakce.ceskobudejovicky@denik.cz; internet ceskobudejovicky.denik.cz; f. 1992; morning; Editor-in-Chief HANA SVÍTILOVÁ; circ. 53,000.

Českokrumlovský denik: Zámek 57, 381 01 Český Krumlov; tel. 380709211; fax 380711265; e-mail redakce.ceskokrumlovsky@denik.cz; internet www.ceskokrumlovsky.denik.cz; f. 1994; Chief Editor ZUZANA KYSELOVÁ.

Haló noviny: Politických vězňů 9, 111 21 Prague 1; tel. 222897111; e-mail halonoviny@halonoviny.cz; internet www3.halonoviny.cz; f. 1991; communist; published by Futura; Editor-in-Chief PAVEL ŠAFRÁNEK.

Hospodářské noviny (Economic News): Dobrovského 25, 170 55 Prague 7; tel. 233073001; fax 233072009; e-mail petr.simunek@economia.cz; internet www.hn.ihned.cz; f. 1957; morning; Editor-in-Chief PETR ŠIMŮNEK; circ. 44,340 (Nov. 2010).

Hradecký deník (Hradec Králové Daily): Kladská 17, 500 03 Hradec Králové; tel. 495800838; fax 495800875; e-mail jitka.hodasova@denik.cz; internet hradecky.denik.cz; f. 1992; fmrly *Hradecké noviny* (Hradec Králové News); Editor-in-Chief JITKA HODASOVÁ; circ. 30,000.

Lidové noviny (People's News): Karla Engliše 519/11, 150 00 Prague 5; tel. 225067111; fax 225067399; e-mail redakce@lidovky.cz; internet www.lidovky.cz; f. 1893, re-established 1988; morning; Man. Editor DALIBOR BALŠÍNEK; circ. 47,002 (Nov. 2010).

Mladá fronta Dnes (The Youth Front Today): Anděl Media Centrum, POB 43, Karla Engliše 519/11, 150 00 Prague 5; tel. 225061111; fax 225066229; e-mail mfdnes@mfdnes.cz; internet www.zpravy.idnes.cz/mfdnes.asp; f. 1990; morning; independent; Editor-in-Chief ROBERT ČÁSENSKÝ; circ. 245,862 (Nov. 2010).

Moravskoslezský deník (Moravia-Silesia Daily): Mlýnská 10, 701 11 Ostrava; tel. 596176311; fax 596176312; e-mail redakce.moravskoslezsky@denik.cz; internet www.msdenik.cz; f. 1991; Editor-in-Chief TOMÁŠ ŠIŘINA; circ. 130,000.

Plzeňský deník (Plzeň Daily): Kovářská 4, 301 00 Plzeň; tel. 3377168321; fax 377221875; e-mail redakce.plzensky@denik.cz; internet www.plzensky.denik.cz; f. 1992; Editor-in-Chief EVA PLEVKOVÁ; circ. 50,000.

Prague Daily Monitor: Laubova 6, 130 00 Prague 3; tel. 222365216; e-mail info@praguemonitor.com; internet www.praguemonitor.com; Man. Editor KRISTINA ALDA.

Právo (Right): Slezská 2127/13, 121 50 Prague 2; tel. 221001111; fax 541616160; e-mail redakce@pravo.cz; internet pravo.novinky.cz; f. 1920 as *Rudé právo*; present name adopted 1995; morning; Editor-in-Chief ZDENĚK PORYBNÝ; circ. 124,151 (Nov. 2010).

Šíp (The Arrow): Přátelství 986, 104 00 Prague 10; tel. 221999303; fax 221999304; e-mail redakce@sipplus.cz; internet www.sip.denik .cz; f. 2005 to replace *Večerník Praha* (Evening Prague); popular; also weekly edn, *Šíp Plus* (f. 2009); Editor-in-Chief MICHAL BROŽ; circ. 130,000.

Ústecký deník (Ústí nad Labem Daily): Klíšská 25, 400 01 Ústí nad Labem; tel. 475212022; fax 475246814; e-mail ustecky@denik.cz; internet www.usteckydenik.cz; f. 1993; Editor-in-Chief HANA VOJTOVÁ; circ. 95,000.

PRINCIPAL PERIODICALS

21. Století (The 21st Century): Bohdalecká 6/1420, 101 00 Prague 10; tel. 281090610; fax 281090623; e-mail 21.stoleti@rf-hobby.cz; internet www.21stoleti.cz; science and technology; monthly; Editor PAVEL PŘEUČIL; circ. 60,251 (2009).

100+1 (Sto plus jedna) ZZ–Zahraniční zajímavost (100+1 ZZ–Foreign Interest): Karlovo nám. 5, 120 00 Prague 2; tel. 224914793; fax 224916922; f. 1964; every two weeks; foreign press digest incl. culture, politics, history, sport, health, etc.; Man. Editor MARIE KYSILKOVÁ; circ. 28,712 (2009).

Agris online: Kamýcká 129, 165 21 Prague 6; tel. 224382050; e-mail agrisonline@pef.czu.cz; internet online.agris.cz; f. 2009; economics and informatics; quarterly; published by the Faculty of Economics and Management, Czech University of Life Sciences, Prague; Editor-in-Chief MIROSLAV SVATOŠ.

Ateliér (Studio): třída Národní 9, 110 00 Prague 1; tel. and fax 222322316; e-mail atelier.art@volny.cz; internet www .atelier-journal.cz; f. 1988; contemporary fine arts; fortnightly; Editor-in-Chief BLANKA JIRÁČKOVÁ.

Divadelní noviny (Theatre News): Celetná 17, 110 00 Prague 1; tel. 224809114; fax 222315912; e-mail divadelni.noviny@divadlo.cz; internet www.divadlo.cz/noviny; fortnightly; Editor-in-Chief JAN KOLÁŘ.

Ekonom (Economist): Dobrovského 25, 170 55 Prague 7; tel. 233071301; fax 233072002; e-mail ekonom@economia.cz; internet ekonom.ihned.cz; weekly; Editor-in-Chief EVA HANÁKOVÁ; circ. 19,682 (2009).

Euro: Holečkova 103/31, 150 00 Prague 5; tel. 251026107; fax 257325905; e-mail vydavatelstvi@euro.cz; internet www.euro.cz; weekly; finance, business, economics; f. 1999; Editor PAVEL PÁRAL; circ. 22,567 (Nov. 2010).

History Revue: Bohdalecká 6/1420, 101 00 Prague 10; tel. 281090610; fax 281090623; e-mail sekretariat@rf-hobby.cz; internet www.historyrevue.cz; history magazine; monthly; Editor-in-Chief ILONA KUČEROVÁ; circ. 65,370 (2009).

Instinkt (Instinct): Panská 7/890, 110 00 Prague 1; tel. 827110112; fax 296827292; e-mail instinkt@instinkt-online.cz; internet www .instinkt-online.cz; fmrly *Mladý svět* (The Young World); illustrated weekly; Man. Editor PETR SKOČDOPOLE; circ. 24,509 (Nov. 2010).

Katolický týdeník (Catholic Weekly): Londýnská 44, 120 00 Prague 2; tel. 224250395; fax 224257041; e-mail sekretariat@katyd.cz; internet www.katyd.cz; f. 1989; weekly; Editor-in-Chief ANTONÍN RANDA; circ. 70,000.

Landeszeitung: Na dlouhém lánu 67, 160 00 Prague 6; tel. 235365903; fax 233344372; e-mail landeszeitung@centrum.cz; internet www.landeszeitung.cz; German; expressing the interests of the German minority in the Czech Republic; fortnightly; Man. Editor JAN BARTOŠ.

Pestrý Svět (Colourful World): Viktora Huga 6, 150 00 Prague 5; tel. 225008366; fax 257327103; e-mail pestrysvet@bauermedia.cz; internet www.bauermedia.cz/casopisy/pestry-svet; f. 2004; weekly; women, social; Editor-in-Chief BARBORA ŠTENGLOVÁ; circ. 262,104 (2009).

Prager Zeitung: Orlická 9, 130 00 Prague 3; tel. 222250125; fax 222253379; e-mail info@pragerzeitung.cz; internet www .pragerzeitung.cz; in German; politics, economy, culture and sport; weekly; Editor-in-Chief MARCUS HUNDT.

Prague Post: Štěpánská 616/20, 110 00 Prague 1; tel. 296334400; fax 296334450; e-mail info@praguepost.com; internet www .praguepost.com; f. 1991; political, economic and cultural weekly in English; Man. Editor BENJAMIN CUNNINGHAM; circ. 15,000.

Prague Tribune: Na Maninách 876/7, 170 00 Prague 7; tel. 220400121; fax 220400123; e-mail praguetribune@explorer.cz; internet www.prague-tribune.cz; in English; business and lifestyle; monthly; Gen. Man. GIRGIT RECHBERGEROVÁ; circ. 22,800.

Profit: Francouzská 94, 110 00 Prague 10; tel. 234071377; fax 225010377; e-mail redakce@profit.cz; internet www.profit.cz; business, investment; weekly; f. 1990; Man. Dir TOMÁŠ VYŠOHLÍD; Editor-in-Chief PETR KORBEL; circ. 19,184 (2009).

Raport: Ottova 418, 269 01 Rakovník; tel. 313512601; fax 313512992; e-mail raport@raport.cz; internet www.raport.cz; f. 1991; focus on people and events of Central Bohemia; weekly; Editor PAVEL SKLENIČKA.

Reflex: Komunardů 1584/42, 170 00 Prague 7; tel. 225977458; fax 225977470; e-mail reflex@ringier.cz; internet www.reflex.cz; f. 1990; general; weekly; Thursdays; Editor-in-Chief PAVEL ŠAFR; circ. 60,571 (Oct. 2010).

Respekt (Respect): Dobrovskèho 25, 170 00 Prague 1; tel. 22493441; fax 224930792; e-mail redakce@respekt.cz; internet www.respekt .ihned.cz; f. 1990; political and cultural weekly; Editor-in-Chief ERIK TABERY; circ. 27,267 (Nov. 2010).

Revue Sondy (Revue Soundings): W. Churchilla 2, 113 59 Prague 3; tel. 234462328; fax 224462313; e-mail sondy@cmkos.cz; internet www.e-sondy.cz; f. 2008 to replace *Sondy* (weekly); 18 a year; journal of the Czech (Bohemian)-Moravian Confederation of Trade Unions; Chief Editor JANA KAŠPAROVÁ; circ. 30,000 (2009).

Romano Hangos/Romský hlas (Romany Voice): Bratislavsá 65A, 602 00 Brno; tel. 728916007; fax 545246674; e-mail rhangos@volny .vz; internet www.srnm.cz/cz/romanohangos.htm; f. 1999; every two weeks; in Romany and Czech; Editor-in-Chief PAVEL PEČÍNKA.

Rytmus života (Rhythm of Life): Viktora Huga 6, 150 00 Prague 5; tel. 225008303; fax 257327103; e-mail rytmuszivota@bauermedia.cz; internet www.bauermedia.cz/casopisy/7-rytmus-zivota; f. 1996; weekly; Mondays; social; Editor-in-Chief VERONIKA HRACHOVCOVÁ; circ. 257,116 (Nov. 2010).

Týden (The Week): Panská 7, 110 00 Prague 1; tel. 296827110; fax 224239408; e-mail dopisy@tyden.cz; internet www.tyden.cz; f. 1994; general; Editor-in-Chief FRANTIŠEK NACHTIGALL; circ. 39,417 (Nov. 2010).

Týdeník Rozhlas (Radio Weekly): Jeseniova 36, 130 00 Prague 3; tel. 272096302; fax 272096303; e-mail tydenik.rozhlas@rozhlas.cz; internet www.radioservis-as.cz/tydenik; f. 1923; Editor-in-Chief MILAN POKORNÝ.

Žena a Život (Woman and Life): Viktora Huga 6, 150 00 Prague 5; tel. 225008260; fax 257323287; e-mail zenaazivot@bauermedia.cz; internet www.zenaazivot.cz; f. 1994; fortnightly; lifestyle, women; Editor-in-Chief MICHAELA KRAMÁROVÁ; circ. 70,434 (2009).

NEWS AGENCY

Česká tisková kancelář (ČTK) (Czech News Agency): Opletalova 5/7, 111 44 Prague 1; tel. 222098111; fax 224225376; e-mail ctk@ctk .cz; internet www.ctk.cz; f. Nov. 1992, assuming control of all property and activities (in the Czech Lands) of the former Czechoslovak News Agency; news and photo-exchange service with all international and many national news agencies; maintains network of foreign correspondents; Czech and English general and economic news service; publishes daily bulletins in English; Gen. Dir Dr MILAN STIBRAL.

PRESS ASSOCIATION

Syndicate of Journalists of the Czech Republic (Syndikát novinářů České republiky): Senovážné náměstí 23, 110 00 Prague 1; tel. 224142455; fax 224142458; e-mail kancelar@ syndikat-novinaru.cz; internet www.syndikat-novinaru.cz; f. 1877; reorganized 1990; 5,000 mems; Chair. ADAM ČERNÝ.

Publishers

Academia: Vodičkova 40, 110 00 Prague 1; tel. 221403820; fax 224941982; e-mail padevet@academia.cz; internet www.academia .cz; f. 1953; scientific books, periodicals; Dir JIŘÍ PADEVĚT.

Akropolis: Na Bělidle 1, 150 00 Prague 5; tel. 251560234; e-mail tomas.akropolis@worldonline.cz; internet www.akropolis.info; f. 1990; Dir JIŘÍ TOMÁŠ.

Albatros: Na Pankráci 30, 140 00 Prague 4; tel. 234633260; fax 234633262; e-mail albatros@albatrosmedia.cz; internet www .albatros.cz; f. 1949; literature for children and young people, encyclopedias; Chair. and CEO MICHAL KREJČÍ.

Argo: Milíčova 13, 130 00 Prague 3; tel. 222781601; fax 222780184; e-mail argo@argo.cz; internet www.argo.cz; f. 1992; literature, translations, history, social sciences; Dir MILAN GELNAR.

BB Art: Bořivojova 85, 130 00 Prague 3; tel. 222721538; fax 222720525; e-mail info@bbart.cz; internet www.bbart.cz; fiction, history, biography, poetry, children's books.

Brána: Jankovcova 18/938, 170 37 Prague 7; tel. and fax 220191313; e-mail info@brana-knihy.cz; internet www.brana-knihy.cz; fiction; Asst Publr JAROSLAVA FEJFAROVÁ.

Brio: Osadní 12A, 170 00 Prague 7; tel. 224236286; fax 224228533; e-mail jiri.stepan@briopublishing.cz; internet www.briopublishing.cz; children's; Man. Dir JIŘÍ ŠTĚPÁN.

Ekopress: U Líhní 100, 142 01 Prague 4; tel. and fax 244471676; e-mail nakladatelstvi@ekopress.cz; internet www.ekopress.cz; f. 1992; economics, information technology, languages.

Epocha: Kaprova 12/40, 110 00 Prague 1; tel. 224810353; e-mail epocha@epocha.cz; internet www.epocha.cz; non-fiction, military and other history, biography, fiction; f. 1996.

Fragment: Radiová 1122/1, 102 27 Prague 10; tel. 267008272; fax 267008273; e-mail prijmeni@fragment.cz; internet www.fragment.cz; children's; f. 1991; Dirs JAN EISLER, PAVEL NÝČ.

Fraus: Edvarda Beneše 72, 301 00 Plzeň; tel. 377226102; fax 377224594; e-mail info@fraus.cz; internet www.fraus.cz; f. 1991; textbooks, languages and dictionaries; Dir and CEO JIŘÍ FRAUS.

Grada Publishing: U Průhonu 22, 170 00 Prague 7; tel. 234264411; fax 220386400; e-mail info@gradapublishing.cz; internet www.gradapublishing.cz; f. 1991; Dir MILAN BRUNÁT.

Host: Radlas 5, 602 00 Brno; tel. 545214468; fax 545212747; e-mail redakce@hostbrno.cz; internet www.hostbrno.cz; f. 1990; fiction, literary criticism and theory; Editor-in-Chief MIROSLAV BALAŠTÍK.

Karolinum: Ovocný trh 3/5, 116 36 Prague 1; tel. 224491276; fax 224212041; e-mail cupress@cuni.cz; internet cupress.cuni.cz; f. 1990; publishing house of the Charles University in Prague; Dir PETR VALO.

Labyrint (Labyrinth): Jablonecká 715, POB 52, 190 00 Prague 9; tel. and fax 224922422; e-mail labyrint@labyrint.net; internet www.labyrint.net; publishing house and cultural magazine; prose, poetry, the arts, children's illustrated books and comics; f. 1991; Dir and Editor-in-Chief JOACHIM DVOŘÁK.

Levné knihy: Do Čertous 2660/16, 193 00 Prague 9; tel. 226253515; e-mail info@levneknihy.cz; internet www.levneknihy.cz; mainly classic Czech and international fiction at discounted prices; f. 2000; Man. JAN MAIVALD.

Libri: Neklanova 109/27, 128 00 Prague 2; tel. 252541632; e-mail libri@libri.cz; internet www.libri.cz; f. 1992; encyclopedias, specialist literature; Editor-in-Chief FRANTIŠEK HONZÁK.

Mladá fronta (The Youth Front): Mezi Vodami 1952/9, 143 00 Prague 4; tel. 225276411; fax 225276222; e-mail mf@mf.cz; internet www.mf.cz; f. 1945; science fiction and fantasy literature, philosophy, sociology; CEO DAVID HURTA.

Motto: Na Pankráci 30, 140 00 Prague 4; tel. 234633288; fax 234633262; e-mail miluse.krejcova@albatrosmedia.cz; internet www.motto.cz.

Nakladatelství Lidové noviny: Dykova 15, 101 00 Prague 10; tel. 222522350; fax 222514012; e-mail nln@nln.cz; internet www.nln.cz; fiction, history, languages, guide-books, popular science; Dir EVA PLEŠKOVÁ.

Olympia: Vaničkova 2D, 160 17 Prague 6; tel. 602394610; fax 274821530; e-mail olympia@mbox.vol.cz; internet www.iolympia.cz; f. 1954; sports, tourism, encyclopedias, fiction, illustrated books; Dir Dr VLADIMÍR TIKAL.

Panton: Radlická 99, 150 00 Prague 5; tel. 251553952; fax 251555994; e-mail panton@panton.cz; tel. www.panton.cz; f. 1958; publishing house of the Czech Musical Fund; books on music, sheet music, records; CEO MARIE KARLICKÁ.

Paseka: Chopinova 4, 120 00 Prague 2; tel. 222710751; fax 222718886; e-mail paseka@paseka.cz; internet www.paseka.cz; f. 1989; Owner LADISLAV HORÁČEK.

SPN pedagogické nakladatelství (SPN Pedagogical Publishing House): Ostrovní 30, 110 00 Prague 1; tel. and fax 224931447; e-mail spn@spn.cz; internet www.spn.cz; f. 1775; fmrly Státní pedagogické nakladatelství (State Pedagogical Publishing House); school and university textbooks, dictionaries, literature; Dir VÁCLAV HOLICKÝ.

Vyšehrad: Víta Nejedlého 15, 130 00 Prague 3; tel. and fax 224221703; e-mail info@vysehrad.cz; internet www.ivysehrad.cz; f. 1934; religion, philosophy, history, fiction; Dir PRAVOMIL NOVÁK.

PUBLISHERS' ASSOCIATION

Association of Czech Booksellers and Publishers (Svaz českých knihkupců a nakladatelů): POB 117, Klementinum 190, 110 01 Prague 1; tel. and fax 224219944; e-mail sckn@sckn.cz; internet www.sckn.cz; f. 1879; Sec. MARCELA TUREČKOVÁ.

Broadcasting and Communications

TELECOMMUNICATIONS

In 2009 24 telecommunications services providers were active in the Czech Republic.

České Radiokomunikace: U Nákladového nádraži 3144, 130 00 Prague 3; tel. 242411111; e-mail spolecnost@radiokomunikace.cz; internet www.radiokomunikace.cz; f. 1963; privatized 2000; owned Macquarie Infrastructure and Real Assets (United Kingdom); CEO JANE HANNAH.

T-Mobile Czech Republic: Tomíčkova 2144/1, 149 00 Prague 4; tel. 603603603; fax 603604606; e-mail info@t-mobile.cz; internet www.t-mobile.cz; fmrly RadioMobil; 60.8% owned by C-Mobil, 39.2% by České Radiokomunikace, a.s.; f. 1996; Gen. Dir ROLAND MAHLER.

Telefónica Czech Republic: Brumlovkou 266/2, 140 22 Prague 4; tel. 840114114; fax 266316666; e-mail jobs.cz@o2.com; internet www.o2.cz; f. 1992; fmrly Český Telecom; present name adopted 2011; monopoly operator of long-distance and international services; 51.1% owned by Telefónica (Spain); CEO LUIS A. MALVIDO.

Vodafone Czech Republic: Vinohradská 167, 100 00 Prague 10; tel. 775011288; fax 776971960; e-mail miroslav.cepicky@vodafone.com; internet www.vodafone.cz; f. 2000; CEO MURIEL ANTON.

RADIO

The Czech Republic has a dual state and private broadcasting system, with one publicly owned radio broadcaster, Český rozhlas (Czech Radio), and two private, nation-wide radio broadcasters, Frekvence 1 and Rádio Impuls.

Local stations broadcast from Prague, Brno, České Budějovice, Hradec Králové, Ostrava, Plzeň, Ústí nad Labem and other towns. By the end of 2003 74 licences for local terrestrial radio-broadcasting had been granted.

Český rozhlas (Czech Radio): Vinohradská 12, 120 99 Prague 2; tel. 221551111; fax 221551342; e-mail info@rozhlas.cz; internet www.rozhlas.cz; broadcasts nation-wide programmes (incl. ČRo 1 Radiožurnál, ČRo 2 Praha, ČRo 3 Vlava) and Radio Praha's programme to foreign countries (ČRo 7); Dir-Gen. PETER DUHAN (acting).

Country Radio: Říčanská 3, 101 00 Prague 10; tel. 251024111; fax 251024224; e-mail info@countryradio.cz; internet www.countryradio.cz; f. 1991; commercial station; Dir RADEK VELECHOVSKÝ.

Evropa 2: Wenzigova 4, 120 00 Prague 2; tel. 257001111; fax 257001807; e-mail info@evropa2.cz; internet www.evropa2.cz; commercial station; Pres. MICHAEL FLEISCHMANN.

Frekvence 1: Wenzigova 4, 120 00 Prague 2; tel. 257001111; fax 257001150; e-mail info@frekvence1.cz; internet www.frekvence1.cz; commercial station; Pres. MICHAEL FLEISCHMANN.

Hitrádio FM Plus: Zikmunda Wintra 21, 301 01 Plzeň; tel. 377422222; fax 377422221; e-mail redakce.fmplus@hitradio.cz; internet www.hitradiofmplus.cz; commercial station; Dir VÁCLAV JEŽEK.

Radio Free Europe/Radio Liberty: Vinohradská 159A, 110 00 Prague 10; tel. 221121111; fax 221123010; e-mail hokuvovaj@rferl.org; internet www.rferl.org; non-profit corpn financed by the federal Govt of the USA; broadcasts c. 1,000 hours weekly in 28 languages to Eastern Europe, Eurasia and the Middle East; Chair. KENNETH Y. TOMLINSON; Dir of Broadcasting JEFF TRIMBLE.

Rádio Impuls: Ortenovo nám. 15A, 170 00 Prague 7; tel. 255700700; fax 255700721; e-mail impuls@impuls.cz; internet www.impuls.cz; f. 1999; Man. Dir JIŘÍ HRABÁK.

TELEVISION

The gradual transition from terrestrial analogue broadcasting to terrestrial digital broadcasting commenced in the second half of 2008, and the process was completed in Prague and Plzeň in 2009. At the end of 2009 the two state-run channels, ČT1 and ČT2, reached 89.1% and 46.4% of the population, respectively, while two private commercial stations, Nova TV and Prima TV, were received by 92.0% and 47.2%, respectively.

Česká televize (Czech Television): Kavčí hory, 140 70 Prague 4; tel. 261131111; fax 26927202; e-mail info@ceskatelevize.cz; internet www.ceskatelevize.cz; f. 1992; state-owned; five channels (ČT1, ČT2, ČT4, ČT24, ČT HD); studios in Prague, Brno and Ostrava; Dir (vacant).

Nova TV: Kříženeckého nám. 1078/5, 152 00 Prague 5; tel. 242464517; e-mail dopisove@nova.cz; internet tv.nova.cz; f. 1994, through a joint venture with Central European Media Enterprises Ltd (CME—of the USA) as the Czech Republic's first independent commercial station; majority owned by CME; Gen. Dir JAN ANDRUŠKO.

Prima TV: Na Žertvách 24/132, 180 00 Prague 8; tel. 266700111; fax 266700111; e-mail informace@iprima.cz; internet www.iprima.cz; f. 1993; CEO MAREK SINGER.

Finance

(cap. = capital; res = reserves; dep. = deposits; m. = million; brs = branches; amounts in Czech koruna)

BANKING

With the establishment of independent Czech and Slovak Republics on 1 January 1993, the State Bank of Czechoslovakia was divided and its functions were transferred to the newly created Czech National Bank and National Bank of Slovakia. The Czech National Bank is independent of the Government. At 30 June 2008 35 banks were operating in the Czech Republic, 13 of which were branches of foreign banks.

Central Bank

Czech National Bank (Česká národní banka): Na Příkopě 28, 115 03 Prague 1; tel. 224411111; fax 224412404; e-mail monestat@cnb.cz; internet www.cnb.cz; f. 1993; bank of issue, the central authority of the Czech Republic in the monetary sphere, legislation and foreign exchange permission; central bank for directing and securing monetary policy, supervision of the financial market; cap. 1,400.0m., res –155,872m., dep. 491,213m. (Dec. 2009); Gov. MIROSLAV SINGER; 7 brs.

Commercial Banks

Česká exportní banka, a.s. (Czech Export Bank): Vodičkova 34, POB 870, 111 21 Prague 1; tel. 222843111; fax 224226162; e-mail ceb@ceb.cz; internet www.ceb.cz; f. 1995; cap. 2,950m., res –91m., dep. 46,533m. (Dec. 2009); Chair. and CEO TOMÁŠ UVÍRA.

Česká spořitelna, a.s. (Czech Savings Bank): Olbrachtova 1929/62, 140 00 Prague 4; tel. 844117118; fax 224640663; e-mail csas@csas.cz; internet www.csas.cz; f. 1825; 98% holding owned by Erste Bank AG (Austria–q.v.); dep. 758,514m., total assets 855,137m. (Dec. 2009); Chair. and CEO PAVEL KYSILKA; 637 brs.

Československá obchodní banka, a.s. (CSOB) (Czechoslovak Commercial Bank): Radlická 333/150, 150 57 Prague 5; tel. 224111111; fax 495819531; e-mail info@csob.cz; internet www.csob.cz; f. 1965; owned by KBC Bank NV (Belgium); commercial and foreign trade transactions; cap. 5,855m., res 28,618m., dep. 778,233m. (Dec. 2009); Chair. and CEO PAVEL KAVÁNEK; 220 brs.

GE Money Bank, a.s.: Vyskočilova 1422/1A, BB Centrum, 140 28 Prague 4; tel. 224441111; fax 224448199; internet www.gemoney.cz; f. 1998; present name adopted 2005; 100% owned by GE Capital International Holdings Corpn (USA); cap. 510.0m., res 20,093.7m., dep. 109,492.8m. (Dec. 2009); Chair. PETER RONALD HERBERT; 201 brs.

J&T Banka, a.s.: Pobřežní 14/297, 186 00 Prague 8; tel. and fax 221710211; e-mail cleardeal@jtbank.cz; internet www.jtbank.cz; f. 1998; cap. 1,838.1m., dep. 35,134m., total assets 39,644.4m. (Dec. 2009); Chair. PATRIK TKÁČ.

Komerční banka, a.s.: Na Příkopě 33, POB 839, 114 07 Prague 1; tel. 955512230; fax 955534300; e-mail mojebanka@kb.cz; internet www.kb.cz; f. 1990; 60.4% owned by Société Générale (France); cap. 19,005m., res 48,529m., dep. 607,534m. (Dec. 2009); Chair. and CEO HENRI BONNET; 398 brs (2009).

LBBW Bank CZ: Vitězná 1/126, 150 00 Prague 5; tel. 233233233; fax 233233299; e-mail info@lbbw.cz; internet www.lbbw.cz; 100% owned by LBBW—Landesbank Baden-Württemberg (Germany) (q.v.); fmrly BAWAG Bank CZ; present name adopted 2008; cap. 1,708.7m., res 1,830.9m., dep. 25,300.5m. (Dec. 2009); Chair. of Bd GERNOT DAUMANN.

Raiffeisenbank, a.s.: Hvězdova 1716/2B, City Tower, 140 78 Prague 4; tel. 225541111; fax 225542111; e-mail info@rb.cz; internet www.rb.cz; f. 1993; 51% owned by Raiffeisenbank (Austria–q.v.); merged with eBanka 2008; cap. 6,564m., res 4,609.2m., dep. 173,056.3m. (Dec. 2009); Chair. LUBOR ŽALMAN.

UniCredit Bank Czech Republic, a.s.: Na Příkopě 858/20, POB 421, 113 80 Prague 1; tel. 955911111; fax 224121666; e-mail info@unicreditgroup.cz; internet www.unicreditbank.cz; f. 2007 by merger of HVB Bank Czech Republic and Živnostenská banka; owned by Bank Austria Creditanstalt AG; cap. 5,125m., res 6,427m., dep. 230,529m. (Dec. 2009); Chair. and CEO JIŘÍ KUNERT.

Volksbank CZ, a.s.: Na Pankráci 1724/129, 140 00 Prague 4; tel. 800133444; fax 221584219; e-mail mail@volksbank.cz; internet www.volksbank.cz; f. 1993; 98.14% owned by Volksbank International AG (Austria); cap. 2,005m., res 267m., dep. 41,467m. (Dec. 2009); f. 1993; Chair. LIBOR HOLUB; 20 brs.

Bankers' Organization

Czech Bankers' Association (Česká bankovní asociace): Vodičkova 30, 110 00 Prague 1; tel. 224422080; fax 224422090; e-mail cba@czech-ba.cz; internet www.czech-ba.cz; f. 1990; current name adopted in 1992; Pres. JIŘÍ KUNERT; 33 mem. banks.

STOCK EXCHANGE

Prague Stock Exchange (Burza cenných papírů Praha): Rybná 14, 110 05 Prague 1; tel. 221832204; fax 224814193; e-mail info@pse.cz; internet www.pse.cz; f. 1992; Chair. PETR KOBLIC.

INSURANCE

There were 52 companies providing insurance services in the Czech Republic in 2009, including seven foreign-owned institutions. Of these, 29 provided non-life insurance, seven provided life insurance and 16 provided universal insurance.

Allianz pojišťovna, a.s.: Ke Štvanici 656/3, 186 00 Prague 8; tel. 224405111; fax 242455555; e-mail klient@allianz.cz; internet www.allianz.cz; f. 1993; owned by Allianz AG (Germany—q.v.).

Česká pojišťovna a.s. (Czech Insurance Corpn): Na Pankráci 123, 140 21 Prague 4; tel. 224550444; fax 224552200; internet www.ceskapojistovna.cz; f. 1827; mem. of financial group PPF Group; issues life, accident, fire, aviation, industrial and marine insurance and all classes of reinsurance; CEO and Chair. of Bd LADISLAV BARTONÍČEK.

ČSOB pojišťovna (ČSOB Insurance): Masarykovo nám. 1458, 532 18 Pardubice; tel. 467007111; fax 467007444; e-mail info@csobpoj.cz; internet www.csobpoj.cz; life and non-life; Chair. and Gen. Dir JEROEN VAN LEEUWEN.

Generali pojišťovna a.s. (Generali Insurance): Bělehradská 132, 120 84 Prague 2; tel. 221091575; fax 221099904; e-mail libuse.kaprova@generali.cz; internet www.generali.cz; f. 1832; life and non-life; Chair. of Bd and Gen. Dir PETR KOPECKÝ.

ING pojišťovna: Nádražní 25, 150 00 Prague 5; tel. 257471111; fax 257473555; e-mail klient@ing.cz; internet www.ing.cz; f. 1992; owned by ING (Netherlands); financial and investment insurance, life and health insurance; Gen. Dir DICK OKHUIJSEN.

Kooperativa pojišťovna (Co-operative Insurance Co): Templová 747, 110 01 Prague 1; tel. 221000111; fax 222322633; e-mail info@koop.cz; internet www.koop.cz; f. 1993; 96.32% owned by Wiener Städtische Versicherung AG (Austria–q.v.); life and non-life insurance; Chair. and CEO MARTIN DIVIŠ.

Uniqa pojišťovna, a.s.: Evropská 136, 160 12 Prague 6; tel. 225393111; fax 225393777; e-mail info@uniqa.cz; internet www.uniqa.cz/uniqa_cz; owned by Uniqa Versicherungen AG (Austria–q.v.); Chair. MARTIN ŽÁČEK.

Trade and Industry

GOVERNMENT AGENCIES

CzechInvest—Investment and Business Development (Agentura pro podporu podnikání a investic): Štěpánská 15, 120 00 Prague 2; tel. 296342500; fax 296342502; e-mail info@czechinvest.org; internet www.czechinvest.org; f. 1992; foreign investment agency; incorporates fmr Agency for the Development of Industry (CzechIndustry); Dir-Gen. ALEXANDRA RUDYŠAROVÁ.

Czech Trade Promotion Agency (Česká agentura na podporu obchodu): Dittrichova 21, POB 76, 128 01 Prague 2; tel. 224907820; fax 224913440; e-mail info@czechtrade.cz; internet www.czechtrade.cz; Gen. Dir IVAN JUKL.

CHAMBER OF COMMERCE

Economic Chamber of the Czech Republic (Hospodářská komora ČR): Freyova 27, 190 00 Prague 9; tel. 266721300; fax 266721690; e-mail office@komora.cz; internet www.komora.cz; f. 1850; has almost 15,000 members (trading corpns, industrial enterprises, banks and private enterprises); Pres. PETR KUŽEL.

EMPLOYERS' ORGANIZATIONS

Association of Entrepreneurs of the Czech Republic (Sdružení podnikatelů ČR): Na strži 1837/9, 140 00 Prague 2; tel. 733669180; fax 261104262; e-mail info@sppz.cz; internet www.sdruzenispcr.cz; Chair. BEDŘICH DANDA.

Confederation of Industry of the Czech Republic (Svaz průmyslu a dopravy ČR): Freyova 948/11, 190 05 Prague 9; tel. 225279111; fax 225279100; e-mail spcr@spcr.cz; internet www.spcr.cz; f. 1990; Pres. JAROSLAV MÍL.

UTILITIES

Electricity

České energetické závody Skupina (ČEZ) (Czech Power Co Group): Duhová 2/1444, 140 53 Prague 4; tel. 211041111; fax 211042001; e-mail cez@cez.cz; internet www.cez.cz; f. 1992; production and distribution co; 69.37% owned by National Property Fund; merged with five regional distribution cos in 2003; also operates two nuclear energy plants at Dukovany and Temelín; Gen. Dir Dr MARTIN ROMAN; 8,770 employees.

Dalkia Česká republika: 28 října 3123/152, 709 74 Ostrava; tel. 596609111; fax 596609300; e-mail info@dalkia.cz; internet www.dalkia.cz; f. 1992; Chair. of Bd ZDENĚK DUBA; CEO LAURENT BARRIEUX; 2,500 employees (2010).

E.ON Česká republika: F. A. Gerstnera 2151/6, 370 49 České Budějovice; tel. 387861111; fax 545142584; e-mail info@eon.cz; internet www.eon.cz; f. 2005; comprises three subsidiary cos: E.ON Energie; E.ON Distribuce; and E.ON Trend; Chair. of Management and Chair. of Supervisory Bd MICHAEL FEHN.

International Power Opatovice: Pardubice 2, 532 13 Opatovice nad; tel. 466843111; fax 466536030; e-mail info@ipplc.cz; internet www.eop.cz; f. 1992; fmrly Opatovice Electricity (Elektrarny Opatovice); present name adopted 2005; generation and distribution co; 100% owned by East Bohemia Energy Holding Ltd; Chair. of Bd JAN ŠPRINGL.

Pražská energetika (Prague Energy Co): Na Hroudě 1492/4, 100 05 Prague 10; tel. 267051111; fax 267310817; e-mail pre@pre.cz; internet www.pre.cz; distribution co to Prague city and surrounding area; Chair. and Man. Dir PAVEL ELIS.

Gas

RWE Transgas (Czech Republic): Limuzská 12, 100 98 Prague 10; tel. 267971111; fax 267976965; e-mail info@rwe.cz; internet www.rwe.cz; majority-owned by RWE Energie AG (Germany); subsidiaries incl. 4 regional distribution cos, 4 trading cos, transmission, storage, and import and distribution cos; Chair. of Bd. MARTIN SCHMITZ.

Water

Pražské vodovody a kanalizace (PVK) (Prague Water Supply and Sewerage Co): Pařížská 11, 110 00 Prague 1; tel. 840111112; fax 272172379; e-mail info@pvk.cz; internet www.pvk.cz; f. 1998; owned by Veolia Voda (France); CEO MILAN KUCHAR.

TRADE UNIONS

Czech (Bohemian)-Moravian Confederation of Trade Unions (Českomoravská konfederace odborových svazů): W. Churchilla nám. 2, 113 59 Prague 3; tel. 224461111; fax 222718994; e-mail info@cmkos.cz; internet www.cmkos.cz; f. 1990; 32 affiliated unions (2011); Pres. JAROSLAV ZAVADIL.

Transport

RAILWAYS

In 2009 the total length of the Czech railway network was 9,539 km.

ČD Cargo: Jankovcova 1569/2C, 170 00 Prague 7; tel. 972242255; fax 972242103; e-mail info@cdcargo.cz; internet www.cdcargo.cz; f. 2007; freight transportation co; merger with Železničná spoločnost Cargo Slovakia, a.s. (Slovakia) announced 2008; Chair. of Bd of Dirs and Dir-Gen. JOSEF BAZALA.

České dráhy (Czech Railways): nábř. L. Svobody 1222/12, 110 15 Prague 1; tel. 972211111; fax 222328784; e-mail infoservis@gr.cdrail.cz; internet www.cdrail.cz; f. 1993; Gen. Dir JOSEF BAZALA.

Prague Public Transport Co (Dopravní podnik hl. m. Prahy): Sokolovska 217/42, 190 22 Prague 9; tel. 296192011; fax 296192019; e-mail tiskoveoddeleni@dpp.cz; internet www.dpp.cz; f. 1974; operates public transport services in Prague, including buses, trams, funicular cars, suburban train services and Prague underground railway (55 km and 54 stations operational in 2006); Gen. Dir MARTIN DVOŘÁK.

ROADS

In 2008 there were an estimated 130,573 km of roads in the Czech Republic, including 691 km of motorways and 6,210 km of national roads.

INLAND WATERWAYS

The total length of navigable waterways in the Czech Republic is 663.6 km. The Elbe (Labe) and its tributary, the Vltava, connect the Czech Republic with the North Sea via the port of Hamburg (Germany). The Oder provides a connection with the Baltic Sea and the port of Szczecin (Poland). There are river ports at Prague-Holešovice, Prague-Radotín, Kolín, Mělník, Ústí nad Labem and Děčín.

ČSPL Děčín: K. Čapka 211/1, 405 91 Děčín; tel. 412561111; fax 412510140; e-mail info@cspl.cz; internet www.cspl.cz; f. 1922; fmrly Czechoslovak Elbe Navigation Co (Československá plavba labská); river transport of goods to Germany, Poland, the Netherlands, Belgium, Luxembourg, France and Switzerland; Chair. of Bd JIŘÍ KRATOCHVIL.

CIVIL AVIATION

There are main civil airports at Prague (Ruzyně), Brno, Karlovy Vary and Ostrava, operated by the Czech Airport Administration.

ČSA—České aerolinie (Czech Airlines): Ruzyně Airport, 160 08 Prague 6; tel. 239007007; fax 224314273; e-mail call.centre@csa.cz; internet www.csa.cz; f. 1923; services to destinations in Europe, the Near, Middle and Far East, North Africa and North America; Pres. and Chair. RADOMÍR LAŠÁK.

Smart Wings: K letišti 1068/30, 160 08 Prague 6; tel. 255700827; internet www.smartwings.net; f. 2005; low-cost airline to various European destinations.

Tourism

The Czech Republic has magnificent scenery, with summer and winter sports facilities. Prague, Kutna Hora, Olomouc, Český Krumlov and Telč are among the best-known of the historic towns, and there are famous castles and cathedrals, and numerous resorts, as well as spas with natural mineral springs at Karlovy Vary (Carlsbad) and Mariánské Lázně (Marienbad). In 2010 a total of 6,333,996 tourist arrivals were recorded, and receipts from tourism (excluding passenger transport) totalled US $6,671m., according to provisional figures

CzechTourism: Vinohradská 46, POB 32, 120 41 Prague 2; tel. 221580111; fax 224247516; e-mail info@czechtourism.cz; internet www.czechtourism.com; f. 1993; Dir ROSTISLAV VONDRUSKA.

Defence

As assessed at November 2011, the total active armed forces numbered 25,421, including an army of 12,833 and an air force of 4,804. There were additionally 8,177 civilian Ministry of Defence staff. Paramilitary forces totalled 3,100. In March 1994 the Czech Republic joined the North Atlantic Treaty Organization's (NATO) 'Partnership for Peace' programme of military co-operation, and it was formally admitted to the Alliance in March 1999.

Defence Expenditure: Budgeted at 43,600m. koruna in 2012.

Chief of the General Staff of the Armed Forces: Lt-Gen. VLASTIMIL PICEK.

Education

Pre-school education is available for children aged between three and six years. In 2007/08 291,194 children attended kindergarten (mateřská škola). Education is compulsory for children aged six to 15 years, who attend basic school, covering both primary and lower secondary levels. There are three types of upper secondary schools: gymnasia (academic); vocational; and technical. In 2008/09 enrolment in secondary education was equivalent to 95% of children in the relevant age-group (94% males; 96% females). The combined enrolment in primary and secondary education in the same year was equivalent to 98% of children in the relevant age-group. Tertiary education comprises higher professional schools and universities. In 2010/11 some 789,486 children attended basic schools and 532,918 attended upper secondary schools. In that year 396,307 students attended 72 universities. In 2004 total budgetary expenditure on education was 116,359m. koruna, 10.0% of total budgetary expenditure.

DENMARK

Introductory Survey

LOCATION, CLIMATE, LANGUAGE, RELIGION, FLAG, CAPITAL

The Kingdom of Denmark is situated in northern Europe. Metropolitan Denmark consists of the peninsula of Jutland, the islands of Zealand, Funen, Lolland, Falster and Bornholm, and 401 smaller islands. The country lies between the North Sea, to the west, and the Baltic Sea, to the east. Denmark's only land frontier is with Germany, to the south. Norway lies to the north of Denmark, across the Skagerrak, while Sweden, the most southerly region of which is separated from Zealand by the narrow Øresund strait, lies to the north-east. The Kingdom of Denmark also includes the self-governing territories of Greenland and the Faroe Islands, both of which are situated in the North Atlantic Ocean. Denmark is low-lying and the climate is temperate, with mild summers and cold, rainy winters. The language is Danish. Almost all of the inhabitants profess Christianity: the Evangelical Lutheran Church, to which some 81% of the population belong, is the established Church, and there are also small communities of other Protestant groups and of Roman Catholics. The national flag (proportions 28 by 37) displays a white cross on a red background, the upright of the cross being to the left of centre. The capital is Copenhagen (København).

CONTEMPORARY POLITICAL HISTORY

Historical Context

In 1945, following the end of German wartime occupation, Denmark recognized the independence of Iceland, which had been declared in the previous year. Home rule was granted to the Faroe Islands in 1948 and to Greenland in 1979. Denmark was a founder member of the North Atlantic Treaty Organization (NATO, see p. 370) in 1949 and of the Nordic Council (see p. 464) in 1952. In January 1973, following a referendum, Denmark entered the European Community (EC), now European Union (EU, see p. 276).

In 1947 King Frederik IX succeeded to the throne on the death of his father, Christian X. Denmark's Constitution was radically revised in 1953: new provisions allowed for female succession to the throne, abolished the upper house of the Folketing (parliament) and amended the franchise. King Frederik died in January 1972, and his eldest daughter, Margrethe II, became the first queen to rule Denmark for nearly 600 years.

Domestic Political Affairs

The system of proportional representation, which is embodied in the 1953 Constitution, makes it difficult for a single party to gain a majority in the Folketing. The minority Government of Venstre (Liberals), formed in 1973 and led by Poul Hartling, was followed in 1975 by a minority Government of the Socialdemokraterne (Social Democrats) under Anker Jørgensen. Jørgensen led various coalitions and minority Governments until 1982. General elections in 1977, 1979 and 1981 were held against a background of growing unemployment and attempts to tighten control of the economy.

In September 1982 divisions within the Cabinet over Jørgensen's economic policy led the Government to resign. Det Konservative Folkeparti (the Conservative People's Party), which had been absent from Danish coalitions since 1971, formed a centre-right four-party Government—with Venstre, the Centrum-Demokraterne (Centre Democrats) and the Kristeligt Folkeparti (Christian People's Party)—led by Poul Schlüter, who became Denmark's first Conservative Prime Minister since 1894. Holding only 66 of the Folketing's 179 seats, the coalition narrowly avoided defeat over its economic programme in October 1982 and September 1983, when larger reductions in public spending were proposed. In December the right-wing Fremskridtspartiet (Progress Party) withdrew its support for further cuts in expenditure, and the Government was defeated. Following a general election in January 1984, Schlüter's Government remained in office, with its component parties holding a total of 77 seats, and relying on the support of members of Det Radikale Venstre (Social Liberals).

At a general election held in September 1987 Schlüter's coalition retained 70 seats in the Folketing, while the opposition Socialdemokraterne lost two of their 56 seats. Jørgensen later resigned as leader of the latter party. Several smaller and extremist parties made considerable gains, thus weakening the outgoing coalition, while the main opposition parties were unable to command a working majority. Schlüter eventually formed a new Cabinet comprising representatives of the former governing coalition. However, Det Radikale Venstre had earlier declared that they would not support any administration that depended on the support of the Fremskridtspartiet.

In April 1988 the Folketing adopted an opposition-sponsored resolution requiring the Government to inform visiting warships of the country's ban on nuclear weapons. The British and US Governments were highly critical of the resolution. Schlüter consequently announced an early general election for May 1988, on the issue of Denmark's membership of NATO and defence policy. In June a new minority coalition, comprising members of Det Konservative Folkeparti, Venstre and Det Radikale Venstre, formed a Cabinet under Schlüter. The new Government restored good relations with its NATO allies by adopting a formula that requested all visiting warships to respect Danish law in its territorial waters, while making no specific reference to nuclear weapons.

The Government proposed large reductions in social welfare provision for 1989, and attacked demands by the Fremskridtspartiet for less taxation as unrealistic. The Fremskridtspartiet, however, continued to increase in popularity, and in November 1989 its share of the vote rose significantly in municipal elections, while Det Konservative Folkeparti lost support. An early general election was organized for December 1990. Although the Socialdemokraterne retained the largest share of the vote (winning 69 seats), Schlüter formed a minority coalition Government, comprising Det Konservative Folkeparti, which had lost five seats in the election, and Venstre, which had gained an additional seven seats. As expected, Det Radikale Venstre, while no longer part of the Government, continued to support the majority of the new coalition Government's policies.

In January 1993 Schlüter resigned from the premiership after a judicial inquiry found that he had misled the Folketing in April 1989 over a scandal that had its origin in 1987, when the Minister of Justice had illegally ordered civil servants to delay issuing entry visas to the families of Tamil refugees from Sri Lanka. In late January 1993 the leader of the Socialdemokraterne, Poul Nyrup Rasmussen, formed a majority, four-party coalition Government with Det Radikale Venstre, the Centrum-Demokraterne and the Kristeligt Folkeparti.

At an early general election held in September 1994 the Socialdemokraterne won a reduced number of seats, although they retained the largest share of the vote. Venstre gained an additional 13 seats, but the Kristeligt Folkeparti, a member of the outgoing coalition, failed to secure representation in the new legislature. None the less, Nyrup Rasmussen was able to form a minority Government with Det Radikale Venstre and the Centrum-Demokraterne, and denied that the Government would be dependent for support on the left-wing Socialistisk Folkeparti (Socialist People's Party). In December 1996, however, the Centrum-Demokraterne withdrew from the coalition, following the Government's decision to seek support from left-wing parties in order to achieve parliamentary approval for legislation relating to the 1997 budget.

An early general election was conducted on 11 March 1998. Nyrup Rasmussen's Government was returned to office with a narrow majority in the Folketing: the Socialdemokraterne, together with their coalition partner Det Radikale Venstre and other informal allies, secured a total of 90 seats, compared with 89 seats won by the centre-right opposition. The right-wing Dansk Folkeparti (Danish People's Party), which campaigned for stricter immigration controls, won 13 seats.

At a general election held on 20 November 2001, four months earlier than scheduled, the Socialdemokraterne won 52 seats in the Folketing, compared with 56 seats for Venstre; thus, for the first time since 1920, the Socialdemokraterne was no longer the party with the largest representation in the legislature. Venstre, led by Anders Fogh Rasmussen, formed a minority coalition Government with Det Konservative Folkeparti, which had won 16 seats. The Dansk Folkeparti performed well, winning 22 seats; the leaders of Venstre stressed, however, that the far-right, anti-immigration party would not exert any influence over government policy. Nevertheless, by the end of November 2001 the Government had announced its intention to remove the legal right of refugees to bring their families to Denmark, to extend the period of residence required to obtain a residence permit from three to seven years, and to deport immediately all immigrants convicted of crimes. A new Ministry of Refugee, Immigration and Integration Affairs was also created. The proposed legislation came into force, with the support of the Dansk Folkeparti, in July 2002. Divisions within the Socialdemokraterne following the 2001 election culminated in Nyrup Rasmussen's resignation as party leader in November 2002 and his replacement by Mogens Lykketoft.

The Government, with the support of the Dansk Folkeparti, proposed controversial legislation in June 2004 to replace the 14 county authorities with five new administrative regions and to reduce the number of municipalities from 271 to 98. The new regions were to have responsibility for hospital administration, general urban planning, collective transportation and several social welfare institutions. Most of the remaining policy areas currently handled by counties were to be dealt with by municipal authorities. Despite the defeat of an opposition motion that the general election due to be held in 2005 take place prior to the parliamentary vote on the proposed reforms, in January 2005 Fogh Rasmussen announced that the general election would indeed be held early, on 8 February, to precede the ballot on the municipal reforms. Both Venstre and the Socialdemokraterne lost support to the other, smaller parties. Nevertheless, with 52 seats, Venstre remained the largest party in the Folketing; Fogh Rasmussen thus became the first Venstre Prime Minister to win a second term, and renewed his party's governing coalition with Det Konservative Folkeparti (which won 18 seats). The Socialdemokraterne won 47 seats; Lykketoft subsequently resigned as party leader and was replaced by Helle Thorning-Schmidt. The Dansk Folkeparti increased its representation in the legislature to 24 seats, while Det Radikale Venstre made the largest gain, winning 17 seats. The legislation on municipal reform was adopted during the first half of 2005, and entered into force on 1 January 2007.

Controversy over press freedom

In September 2005 one of Denmark's principal newspapers, *Jyllands-Posten*, provoked considerable anger among Muslim communities by printing 12 cartoons depicting the Prophet Muhammad, in order to draw attention to perceived self-censorship in the Danish press. Protests against the publication of the caricatures took place in Denmark and a number of predominantly Muslim countries. Despite receiving death threats against its staff, the editors of the newspaper refused to issue an apology. Tensions were heightened when a radical Islamist cleric, who had been granted asylum in Denmark, led a delegation to the Middle East in December, in an attempt to widen support for the protests. Included in the documents that he showed to delegates at a meeting of the Organization of the Islamic Conference (OIC), and which provoked further condemnation of the cartoons, were three offensive images that had not been published by the press in Denmark. During January and February 2006 Iran, Libya, Saudi Arabia and Syria temporarily withdrew their ambassadors from Copenhagen. At the end of January the editors of *Jyllands-Posten* finally apologized for causing offence (although not for publishing the caricatures). Fogh Rasmussen welcomed the apology, but defended the freedom of the press, repudiating demands by Islamic states that the Danish Government should punish those responsible for the cartoons and their publication. Muslim outrage over the images continued to escalate in February, as they were reprinted by publications in several other European countries to show solidarity with *Jyllands-Posten*. Many Muslims boycotted Danish goods and violent anti-Danish protests took place in several countries, and in mid-February the Danish embassies in Indonesia, Iran, Lebanon, Pakistan and Syria were temporarily closed owing to security concerns. In February 2008 three people were arrested on charges of planning to murder one of the cartoonists, Kurt Westergaard, who had contributed arguably the most contentious cartoon to *Jyllands-Posten*, which depicted the Prophet Muhammad wearing a bomb as a turban. On the following day several of Denmark's major daily newspapers, including *Jyllands-Posten*, reprinted his cartoon, as a gesture of support for freedom of expression, prompting further protests. In January 2010 an intruder at Westergaard's home was arrested; he was convicted of attempted murder and terrorism in February 2011, and sentenced to nine (later increased to 10) years' imprisonment. An apology issued by the newspaper *Politiken* in February 2010, for offence caused by its republication of Westergaard's cartoon two years earlier, was criticized by *Jyllands-Posten* and other newspapers that had reprinted the cartoon and had united to reject demands by Muslim groups that they apologize. The offices of *Jyllands-Posten* were believed to have been the intended target of two planned attacks that were discovered in the second half of 2010. In September a man was arrested in Copenhagen following the premature explosion of a letter bomb he was allegedly preparing; he was convicted on charges of terrorism and illegal weapons possession in June 2011, and sentenced to 12 years' imprisonment. In the second case, in December 2010, three suspected Islamist militants were charged by a Danish court with attempting to carry out an act of terrorism against the newspaper.

Events following the 2005 election

As a minority coalition, the Government continued to rely on the parliamentary support of the populist, anti-immigrant Dansk Folkeparti. In May 2007 a prominent member of the Folketing for Det Radikale Venstre, Naser Khader, resigned from that party and announced the formation of a new party, the Ny Alliance (New Alliance), which was intended to reduce the influence of the Dansk Folkeparti on government policy. Following a period of internal conflict within Det Radikale Venstre, in June the party leader, Marianne Jelved, resigned. She was replaced by Margrethe Vestager. In October Fogh Rasmussen announced that legislative elections were to take place in November, some two years before the scheduled end of the parliamentary term, in order to facilitate forthcoming cross-party negotiations over welfare reform.

At the general election, which took place on 13 November 2007, the two main parties again lost support to smaller rivals. None the less, Venstre remained the strongest party in the Folketing, winning 46 seats, while its partner in the outgoing coalition Government, Det Konservative Folkeparti, retained its 18 seats in the legislature. The Socialdemokraterne lost one seat, winning 45 seats. The Dansk Folkeparti increased its representation in the Folketing to 25 seats, while the Socialistisk Folkeparti made the most significant gains of any party, winning 23 seats. However, the Ny Alliance won only five seats, and was outperformed by Det Radikale Venstre, which nevertheless lost almost one-half of its seats, winning only nine. In late November Fogh Rasmussen announced the renewal of the minority coalition between Venstre and Det Konservative Folkeparti and reorganized the Cabinet. Among the most notable changes was the appointment of Venstre's Lars Løkke Rasmussen (hitherto Minister of the Interior and Health) as Minister of Finance.

The coalition parties' failure to increase their representation at the general election required the Government to continue to rely upon parliamentary support from the Dansk Folkeparti. The decision of a member of Det Konservative Folkeparti to leave that party in December 2007 and to remain in the Folketing as an independent increased the Government's reliance on the smaller parties, prompting concern that no agreement would be reached with regard to the Government's programme, particularly over asylum and immigration. In January 2008 the coalition Government concluded an agreement with the Dansk Folkeparti over a reform of asylum policy that would allow a small number of unsuccessful asylum seekers, who had so far been unable to return to their countries of origin, to live in private accommodation. Opposition parties were excluded from the talks and subsequently accused the Government of reneging on a promise to hold cross-party talks after the election. Nevertheless, later in that month Khader announced that his party would vote in favour of the proposals, stating that the Ny Alliance was a centre-right party and would thus support the governing coalition. This statement prompted one of the party's co-founders to resign from the party at the end of that month, citing her opposition to the Ny Alliance's implicit co-operation with the Dansk Folkeparti. In February another of its parliamentarians left the Ny Alliance to join Venstre. In August the party was renamed the Liberal Alliance. In January 2009 Khader resigned from the Liberal Alliance, citing declining support for the party and personal disillusionment with its failure effectively to counter the Dansk Folkeparti; Leif Mikkelsen was appointed as party leader.

Following the resignation of Bendt Bendtsen as leader of Det Konservative Folkeparti in early September 2008, the government portfolios allocated to members of that party were reorganized. Lene Espersen (hitherto Minister of Justice), who had succeeded Bendtsen as party leader, replaced him as Deputy Prime Minister and Minister of Economic and Business Affairs.

Lars Løkke Rasmussen's Premiership

On 5 April 2009 Fogh Rasmussen resigned both as Prime Minister and leader of Venstre after his official nomination as Secretary-General of NATO. Lars Løkke Rasmussen, the deputy leader of Venstre, was sworn in as Prime Minister later that day, following pledges of continued parliamentary support for the coalition Government from the Dansk Folkeparti and the Liberal Alliance. Two days later Løkke Rasmussen effected a reorganization of the Cabinet, in which Claus Hjort Frederiksen (hitherto the Minister of Employment) succeeded Løkke Rasmussen as Minister of Finance. Meanwhile, Løkke Rasmussen was also appointed as acting leader of Venstre; he was formally confirmed in office at a special party congress in the following month.

In June 2009 a national referendum (held concurrently with the election to the European Parliament) approved a constitutional amendment allowing the monarch's eldest child, regardless of gender, to inherit the throne. The amendment was supported by 85.4% of valid votes cast; however, due to the low participation rate (58.3%), the votes in favour represented only 45.1% of registered voters.

In November 2009 Connie Hedegaard of the Det Konservative Folkeparti resigned as Minister of Climate and Energy, having been nominated for membership of the European Commission. She was replaced by Lykke Friis, a politically independent academic, who subsequently announced that she was to join Venstre. Hedegaard remained a member of the Government until December in order to chair the UN Climate Change Conference, which was held in Copenhagen. Despite high international expectations, the conference failed to reach a legally binding international agreement on limiting the emission of gases thought to cause global warming. Løkke Rasmussen carried out a wider ranging cabinet reorganization in February 2010. Most of the ministers belonging to Det Konservative Folkeparti received new portfolios: notably, Espersen was appointed Minister of Foreign Affairs, replacing Per Stig Møller (who became Minister of Culture), while Brian Mikkelsen succeeded Espersen as Minister of Economics and Business Affairs and was replaced as Minister of Justice by Lars Barfoed (hitherto Minister of Transport). Meanwhile, Bertel Haarder of Venstre became Minister of the Interior and Health, Friis added responsibility for gender equality to her existing portfolio, and Gitte Lillelund Bech replaced Søren Gade as Minister of Defence; Gade had resigned following a series of political controversies involving his ministry in previous months.

In order to secure the Dansk Folkeparti's support, in May 2010, for a fiscal consolidation agreement and, later that year, for the 2011 budget, the Government agreed to a further tightening of immigration regulations, including the introduction of a points-based system for those seeking to be reunited with family members already resident in Denmark.

Opinion polls from late 2009 consistently indicated that the opposition Socialdemokraterne had become the most popular of Denmark's political parties. Support for the party was briefly undermined in mid-2010 by allegations of tax evasion by the husband of the party leader, Helle Thorning-Schmidt, who admitted mistakenly giving incorrect information to the Danish authorities, but recovered after the couple were absolved of any wrongdoing in September. Following a marked decline in support for Det Konservative Folkeparti during 2010, according to opinion poll ratings, Espersen resigned as party leader in January 2011, although she remained Minister of Foreign Affairs, despite some criticism of her performance in this post; she was succeeded as party leader by the Minister of Justice, Lars Barfoed.

The Minister of Refugee, Immigration and Integration Affairs, Birthe Rønn Hornbech, was dismissed in March 2011, following a report about the ministry's failure to grant citizenship to stateless Danish-born Palestinians, which was in violation of UN conventions. Hornbech had originally denied responsibility for the rejections on the grounds that they had begun in 2002 and she had taken office in 2007. However, it was later disclosed by officials that she had been aware of the issue in 2008. Hornbech was replaced by the Minister of Development Co-operation, Søren Pind, who also retained his previous portfolio. Hornbech's responsibility for ecclesiastical affairs was transferred to the Minister of Culture, Møller. The Minister for Education, Tina Nedergaard, resigned for personal reasons and was replaced by Troels Lund Poulsen, hitherto the Minister of Taxation; Peter Christensen of Venstre joined the Cabinet to replace Poulsen in this role.

Political agreement was reached in May 2011 on a series of economic reforms aimed at achieving a balanced budget by 2020, with the Government notably securing the approval of the opposition Det Radikale Venstre for its proposed changes to the pensions system, including a phasing out of the early retirement benefit and an accelerated increase in the retirement age. However, a concession made to the Dansk Folkeparti in return for its support, to reintroduce permanent customs inspections at Denmark's borders with Germany and Sweden, provoked considerable controversy. Although the Government insisted that the controls, which were ostensibly aimed at countering rising cross-border crime, would not contravene its commitments under the EU's Schengen Agreement on internal borders, the European Commission questioned their compatibility with EU law, as did Germany. Despite this opposition, the enhanced customs checks commenced in July, having been approved by the Folketing. Following a visit to inspect the checkpoints, the Commission continued to express concern regarding their legality.

Recent developments: the 2011 general election

In late August 2011 Prime Minister Løkke Rasmussen announced that the general election, due to be held by November, would take place in September. Economic concerns dominated the electoral campaign, amid stagnant growth, a rising budget deficit and difficulties in the banking sector. Rasmussen pledged to continue with the implementation of his Government's planned reductions in public expenditure if re-elected, while his rival for the premiership, Thorning-Schmidt, proposed raising taxes on the financial services sector and high earners, increasing spending on health, education and infrastructure, and lengthening the working week by one hour with the aim of boosting productivity and reviving growth.

At the general election, which was conducted on 15 September 2011, the four centre-left opposition parties, the Socialdemokraterne, the Socialistisk Folkeparti, Det Radikale Venstre and the far-left Enhedslisten—de Rød-Grønne (Red-Green Alliance), won a narrow majority of seats in the Folketing, ending 10 years of minority government by the centre-right parties supported by the Dansk Folkeparti. However, the legislative representation of both the Socialdemokraterne and the Socialistisk Folkeparti actually declined (although only marginally so for the former), to 44 seats (24.8% of the votes cast) and 16 seats (9.2%), respectively, while support rose strongly for the Det Radikale Venstre, which secured 17 seats (9.5%), and for the Enhedslisten—de Rød-Grønne, which tripled its number of seats to 12 (6.7%). Of the parties in the outgoing coalition Government, Venstre retained its position as the largest single party in the legislature, obtaining 47 seats (26.7%), but its partner, Det Konservative Folkeparti, performed particularly poorly, securing only eight seats (4.9%), constituting a loss of 10 seats, and the representation of their ally, the Dansk Folkeparti, also decreased, to 22 seats (12.3%). The only other party to win parliamentary representation was the Liberal Alliance, with nine seats (5.0%). An electoral turn-out of 87.7% was recorded.

A minority coalition Government of the Socialdemokraterne, Det Radikale Venstre and the Socialistisk Folkeparti took office on 3 October 2011, with Thorning-Schmidt as Denmark's first female Prime Minister. Margrethe Vestager, the leader of Det Radikale Venstre, was appointed as Minister of Economics and of the Interior and Villy Søvndal, the leader of the Socialistisk Folkeparti, was allocated the foreign affairs portfolio. The minority Government would require the support of the Enhedslisten—de Rød-Grønne to secure the approval of legislation, while three of the four deputies elected to represent the Faroe Islands and the Greenland were also allied to the new administration, which thus held a five-seat majority in the Folketing. The new Prime Minister announced her Government's intention to create at least 135,000 jobs by 2020 and to invest some 10,750m. kroner in 2012 in upgrading transport infrastructure, schools, hospitals and housing. In addition, the previous Government's restoration of border controls was to be reversed, although its plan to phase out the early retirement benefit would be retained, at the insistence of Det Radikale Venstre, as would its target of achieving a balanced budget by 2020. In the area of immigration policy, many of the restrictions introduced during the previous decade, largely at the behest of the Dansk Folkeparti, were to be removed or eased, and the Ministry of Refugee, Immigration and Integration Affairs was abolished.

Foreign Affairs

Regional relations

The extent of Denmark's commitment to its membership of the EU has frequently been a matter of debate within the country. In January 1986 the left-wing parties in the Folketing combined to reject the ratification by Denmark of the Single European Act (which amended the Treaty of Rome—the agreement that founded the EC—in order to establish the EC's single market and allow the EC Council of Ministers to take decisions by a qualified majority vote if unanimity was not achieved). Opponents of ratification argued that it would lead to a diminution of Denmark's power to maintain strict environmental controls. In a national referendum in February, however, 56.2% of the votes cast were in favour of ratification of the Act, and the Folketing formally approved it in May.

In May 1992 the Folketing voted, by 130 votes to 25, to approve the Treaty on European Union (the Maastricht Treaty), which further expanded the scope of the Treaty of Rome. In a national referendum held in June, however, 50.7% of the votes cast were against ratification of the Treaty. In December EC heads of government agreed that Denmark should be allowed exemption from certain provisions of the Treaty, namely the final stage of European Monetary Union (including the adoption of a single currency); participation in a common defence policy; common European citizenship; and co-operation in legal and home affairs. The agreement was endorsed by seven of the eight parties represented in the Folketing (the exception being the Fremskridtspartiet), and in a second referendum, held in May 1993, 56.7% of the votes cast were in favour of ratification.

In May 1998 Danish voters narrowly endorsed the ratification of the Amsterdam Treaty on European integration. In September 2000 the Government held a national referendum regarding adoption of the single European currency, the euro. Approval for the euro had been strong when the referendum was called in May, but had declined throughout the months preceding the vote, despite the support of the Government, the majority of the major political parties, the industrial sector, banks, trade unions and the media. In the event, 53.1% of the votes cast were opposed to membership of the single currency; the rate of participation was 87.5%.

In February 2005 Fogh Rasmussen, following Venstre's re-election to office, announced that a draft treaty outlining a constitution of the EU would be ratified by public referendum. However, the referendum, which was scheduled for September 2005, was postponed following the treaty's rejection by voters in France and the Netherlands in May and June, respectively. A new treaty to replace the rejected constitutional treaty was signed by the heads of state and of government of the 27 EU member states during a summit meeting held in Lisbon, Portugal, on 13 December. The Folketing ratified the Treaty of Lisbon in May 2008, a referendum having been deemed unnecessary by the Government in a decision supported both by the Socialdemokraterne and by Det Radikale Venstre. The treaty entered into force in December 2009, following its ratification by all 27 member states.

Meanwhile, in November 2007, following the general election, Fogh Rasmussen, confirmed his intention to hold a referendum during the next parliamentary term over the four exemptions from the provisions of the Maastricht Treaty—the adoption of the euro, participation in a common defence policy, common European citizenship and co-operation in legal and home affairs—that had been negotiated in 1992 to secure the ratification of the Treaty. Shortly after his inauguration as Prime Minister in April 2009, Lars Løkke Rasmussen declared that a referendum on the exemptions would be held 'when the time is right'. In 2010–11, however, Danish public support for euro adoption, in particular, weakened, amid instability in the euro zone, and the referendum had not been held by September 2011, when Løkke Rasmussen's Government was defeated in the election. The new Government of Helle Thorning-Schmidt announced its intention to conduct referendums during the next parliamentary term on abolishing two of the exemptions: participation in a common defence policy and co-operation in legal and home affairs. Denmark assumed the six-month rotating Presidency of the Council of the EU in January 2012.

Other external relations

The Danish Government contributed a warship, a submarine and 160 troops to the US-led military operation in Iraq to remove the regime of Saddam Hussain in early 2003. Deep public divisions over the Government's support for the invasion were reflected in the Folketing: only 93 members voted to approve the deployment of troops. Following the collapse of Saddam Hussain's regime in April, a 410-strong Danish peace-keeping force was dispatched to Iraq and was stationed near Basra (in southern Iraq) under British command. The Government was also involved in plans for the post-war redevelopment of Iraq. In April 2004 the Minister of Defence, Svend Aage Jensby, resigned amid allegations made by the opposition that the Danish military authorities had exaggerated the threat posed by Saddam Hussain in an attempt to justify the military action in Iraq. In January 2006 the Folketing approved a government proposal to send an additional 200 soldiers to participate in the NATO-led International Security Assistance Force (ISAF) in Afghanistan, bringing the number of Danish troops deployed in that country to some 360.

In February 2007 the Prime Minister announced that all Danish troops were to be withdrawn from Iraq by August of that year. However, a replacement contingent of around 50 troops and advisers would undertake an observer mission in that country. (The withdrawal of troops from Iraq was completed as planned on 1 August, although six officers remained in Iraq until January 2009.) On 1 June 2007 the Folketing approved a two-stage deployment of Danish troops that increased the size of the Danish contingent in Afghanistan to 520 by October. In June 2008 the Folketing approved the extension of the mandate of Danish forces in Afghanistan to 2012, and in July the Government won approval for its strategy for Danish involvement in Afghanistan from 2008–12, which included proposals to increase the number of troops deployed in that country to 750. In January 2012 the 750 Danish military personnel in Afghanistan were mostly deployed in Helmand province. NATO combat forces were scheduled to be withdrawn from Afghanistan by the end of 2014. Meanwhile, following the outbreak of civil conflict in Libya in early 2011, and the UN Security Council's adoption in March of Resolution 1973, permitting UN member states to take 'all necessary measures' (short of military occupation) to protect civilians in that country, Danish military forces participated in the enforcement of an air exclusion zone over Libya. NATO military action in Libya ended in October, following the death of the Libyan leader, Col Muammar al-Qaddafi.

In October 2004 the Minister of Science, Technology and Innovation, Helge Sander, announced that Denmark, in co-operation with the Governments of the Faroe Islands and Greenland, would attempt to prove that the seabed beneath the North Pole (the Polar Basin) was a natural continuation of Greenland and that Denmark could thus claim legal ownership of any natural resources discovered there. Other claimants to the Pole (currently considered international territory) included Canada, Norway, Russia and the USA. In July 2005 the Danish Government made a formal protest to the Canadian ambassador after the Canadian Minister of National Defence landed on Hans Island without first notifying the Danish Government. The sovereignty of the small uninhabited island, in the Nares Strait between Ellesmere Island (Canada) and north-west Greenland, had been in dispute for more than 30 years, and would affect Denmark's claim for ownership of the North Pole. In September the ministers responsible for foreign affairs of both countries agreed to hold talks on sovereignty and to inform each other of any activities around the island. In May 2008 the Danish Minister of Foreign Affairs and the Prime Minister of Greenland co-hosted a meeting in Ilulissat, Greenland, of the countries bordering the Arctic Ocean in an attempt to address issues arising from conflicting territorial interests and increased use of Arctic waters, notably for tourism and shipping, as a result of diminishing sea ice. The ensuing Ilulissat Declaration, which was agreed by Canada, Denmark, Norway, Russia and the USA, confirmed the five nations' commitment to compliance with the UN's Convention on the Law of the Sea and ruled out the creation of any new comprehensive legal framework for the governance of the Arctic region. The signatories also committed those countries to 'the orderly settlement' of any disputes over the delineation of borders along the continental shelf. At a ministerial meeting held in Nuuk, the capital of Greenland, in May 2011, Denmark and the seven other states comprising the Arctic Council (see p. 448) (Canada, Finland, Iceland, Norway, Russia, Sweden and the USA) notably signed their first legally binding agreement, which concerned co-operation in search and rescue efforts in the Arctic. In August, in a joint document detailing their strategy for the Arctic during 2011–20, the Governments of Denmark, Greenland and the Faroes stated that, as the Kingdom of Denmark, they had already submitted evidence to the UN Commission on the Limits of the Continental Shelf for their claim to sovereignty over two areas near the Faroes and, by 2014, planned to do the same for three areas near Greenland, one of which included the North Pole. As regards defence, the document also confirmed plans to establish a non-permanent Arctic Response Force from existing armed forces units and to merge the Greenland and Faroe military commands to form a joint service Arctic Command.

CONSTITUTION AND GOVERNMENT

The Constitutional Act (*Grundlov*) was adopted on 5 June 1953, replacing the Constitutional Acts of 1849, 1866 and 1915. Denmark is a constitutional monarchy. Legislative power is held jointly by the hereditary monarch (who has no personal political power) and the unicameral Folketing (parliament), which has 179 members, including 175 from metropolitan Denmark and two each from the Faroe Islands and Greenland. Members are elected for four years (subject to dissolution) on the basis of proportional representation. Executive power is exercised by the monarch through a Cabinet, which is led by the Prime Minister and is responsible to the Folketing. Following municipal reforms which came into effect on 1 January 2007, Denmark comprises five administrative regions, one city and one borough, all with elected regional councils, and 98 municipalities.

REGIONAL AND INTERNATIONAL CO-OPERATION

Denmark is a member of the European Union (EU, see p. 276), although it did not participate in Economic and Monetary Union and thus remains outside of the single currency. Denmark is a member of the Nordic Council (see p. 464) and the Nordic Council of Ministers (see p. 464), which are based in Copenhagen. It is member of the Arctic Council (see p. 448), and was a founder member of both the Council of Europe (see p. 256) and the Council of the Baltic Sea States (see p. 254).

Denmark was a founder member of the UN in 1945. As a contracting party to the General Agreement on Tariffs and Trade, Denmark joined the World Trade Organization (WTO, see p. 433) on its establishment in 1995. It is a member of the North Atlantic Treaty Organization (NATO, see p. 370), and participates in the Organization for Security and Co-operation in Europe (OSCE, see p. 388). Denmark is a member of the Organisation for Economic Co-operation and Development (OECD, see p. 379).

ECONOMIC AFFAIRS

In 2010, according to estimates by the World Bank, Denmark's gross national income (GNI), measured at average 2008–10 prices, was US $328,252m., equivalent to $59,210 per head (or $40,290 per head on an international purchasing-power parity basis). During 2001–10 Denmark's population grew at an average annual rate of 0.4%, while gross domestic product (GDP) per head increased, in real terms, at an average rate of 0.3% per year. According to World Bank figures, overall GDP increased, in real terms, at an average annual rate of 0.7% in 2001–10; real GDP decreased by 5.2% in 2009 but increased by 2.1% in 2010.

Agriculture (including forestry and fishing) contributed 1.3% of GDP in 2010 and employed 2.6% of the economically active population in 2008. The principal activities are pig farming and dairy farming; Denmark is a major exporter of pork products, and exports of meat and meat preparations accounted for 5.2% of total export revenue in 2010. Most of Denmark's agricultural production is exported, and the sector accounted for more than 16% of total exports in 2010. The fishing industry accounted for 2.8% of total export earnings in 2010. According to World Bank estimates, agricultural GDP decreased, in real terms, at an average annual rate of 0.7% in 2001–09; the GDP of the sector declined by 3.7% in 2008, but increased by 19.7% in 2009.

Industry (including mining, manufacturing, construction, power and water) provided 22.2% of GDP in 2010, and employed 22.7% of the working population in 2008. According to World Bank estimates, industrial GDP, in real terms, declined by 1.4% during 2001–09; the sector's GDP contracted by 0.3% in 2008, followed by a sharp decline of 11.1% in 2009.

Mining provided 3.4% of GDP in 2010 and accounted for only 0.1% of employment in 2008. Denmark has few natural resources, but exploration for petroleum reserves in the Danish sector of the North Sea in the 1970s proved successful. Natural gas has also been extensively exploited. There is a significant reserve of sand in north-western Jutland which could potentially be exploited for rich yields of titanium, zirconium and yttrium. The GDP of the mining sector increased, in real terms, at an average annual rate of 1.0% in 2002–05; the sector's GDP grew by 0.5% in 2005.

Manufacturing contributed 11.5% of GDP in 2010 and employed 15.1% of the working population in 2008. Measured by value of turnover, in 2006 the most important manufacturing industries were food products (accounting for 22.3% of the total), non-electric machinery and equipment (12.5%), electronic components (12.5%), chemicals and pharmaceuticals (10.5%), metal products (8.4%) and computers and electric motors (7.5%). According to World Bank estimates, manufacturing GDP declined, in real terms, at an average annual rate of 0.7% in 2001–09; it increased by 3.7% in 2008 but decreased by 12.1% in 2009.

The construction sector contributed 4.7% of GDP in 2010 and employed 6.8% of the working population in 2008.

Energy is derived principally from petroleum and natural gas. Since 1997 Denmark has produced enough energy to satisfy its domestic consumption. In 2010 crude petroleum production amounted to 249m. barrels and total gas output was 8,173m. cu m. In 2010, according to official figures, imports of mineral fuels accounted for 8.2% of the total cost of imports, while exports of mineral fuels contributed 9.7% of total export revenue. In 2008 48.0% of electricity was produced from coal, 19.0% from natural gas and 3.1% from petroleum. At the end of 2010 Denmark's proven oil reserves stood at 900m. barrels, while natural gas reserves were 52,000m. cu m in that year. The use of renewable sources of energy (including wind power) has been encouraged. In 2009 Denmark derived about 20% of its electricity consumption from renewable sources (mostly wind turbines), and planned to increase the share to 50% by 2020.

Services provided 76.5% of GDP in 2010 and engaged 74.7% of the employed population in 2008. Shipping is an important sector in Denmark. According to World Bank estimates, in real terms, the combined GDP of the service sectors increased at an average rate of 1.0% per year in 2001–09; it declined by 3.0% in 2009.

In 2010, according to the IMF, Denmark recorded a visible trade surplus of US $8,696m. and a surplus of $16,210m. on the current account of the balance of payments. Most Danish trade is with the other member states of the European Union (EU, see p. 276), which accounted for 69.3% of imports and 61.5% of exports in 2010. The principal source of imports in 2010 was Germany (contributing 20.7% of the total); other major suppliers were Sweden (13.4%), the People's Republic of China (7.6%), the Netherlands (7.0%) and the United Kingdom (6.0%). Germany was also the principal market for exports (accounting for 15.0% of the total); other major purchasers included Sweden (12.7%), the United Kingdom (7.6%), Norway (6.1%) and the USA (5.2%). The principal exports in 2010 were machinery and transport equipment (accounting for 25.1% of total export revenue), food and live animals, chemicals and related products and miscellaneous manufactured articles. Pork, pharmaceutical products, gas, petroleum and wind turbines are among the key exports. The principal imports in 2010 were machinery and transport equipment (accounting for 31.4% of total import costs), miscellaneous manufactured articles, basic manufactures, and chemicals and related products.

In 2010 there was a general government deficit of an estimated 50,805m. kroner, equivalent to 2.3% of GDP. Denmark's general government gross debt was 76,074m. kroner in 2010, equivalent to 43.7% of GDP. The average annual rate of inflation was 2.0% in 2000–10. Consumer prices increased by 2.3% in 2010. The rate of unemployment was 3.4% in 2008.

Denmark is a small open economy, which is highly dependent on trade with other countries. Denmark did not participate in the EU's programme of Economic and Monetary Union (EMU), although it has maintained a stable rate of exchange with the common European currency, the euro. As a result of reforms introduced in the 1980s, Denmark enjoyed a long period of sustained economic growth, low unemployment and generous social welfare provisions. A system known as flexicurity emphasized both flexibility for employers, allowing them to hire or dismiss workers easily while keeping labour costs low, and security for employees, by providing for government-subsidized retraining programmes and generous unemployment benefits. As in many other EU countries, however, demographic changes posed a challenge to Denmark's economy, resulting in a smaller labour force and a larger elderly population. An agreement to reform the welfare system was reached in June 2006, which included the gradual increase in the retirement and early retirement ages to 67 and 62 years, respectively. In May 2011, moreover, it was agreed to bring forward the increase in the retirement age and to phase out the early retirement benefit. The economy began to decelerate in 2007 as a result of the slowing of the housing market and declining investment. This coincided with the effects of the global financial crisis, causing Denmark to be the first country in the EU to fall into recession. Despite government initiatives to improve liquidity and stability in the banking sector, a total of nine banks were taken into state control in 2008–11. The recession worsened in 2009, with GDP contracting by 5.2%. Exports and imports declined, and there was an increase in business bankruptcies and in the unemployment rate, which reached 5.1% in January 2010 (compared with 1.6% in September 2008) and remained relatively high, at 3.9%, in December 2011. The economy began to recover gradually in the second half of 2009, and GDP increased by 2.1% in 2010 (although World Bank estimates were subsequently revised from 2.1% to just 1.3% for 2010). However, quarter-on-quarter contractions were recorded in the final quarter of 2010 and the first quarter of 2011, technically signifying a return to recession, and overall annual growth in 2011 slowed to a projected 1.0%, amid declining private consumption, continued difficulties in the banking sector and a stagnant property market. Rather than focusing solely on austerity, the new centre-left Government that took office in October 2011 announced measures designed to stimulate growth and create employment, including investment of 18,750m. kroner in 2012–13 in public works projects. In December 2011 the Government reduced its growth forecast for 2012 from 1.8% to 1.0%, in view of a weaker global economic outlook and, in particular, the ongoing debt crisis in several European countries (although Denmark's own government debt was notably relatively low). The budget deficit was projected to widen to 4.0% of GDP in 2011 and to 5.5% of GDP in 2012, partly owing to the planned stimulus measures and the need to repay early retirement contributions, before narrowing to 2.6% of GDP in 2013 (within the 3% limit mandated by the EU's Stability and Growth Pact).

PUBLIC HOLIDAYS

2013: 1 January (New Year's Day), 28 March (Maundy Thursday), 1 April (Easter Monday), 26 April (General Prayer Day), 9 May (Ascension Day), 19 May (Whit Monday), 5 June (Constitution Day), 24–26 December (Christmas).

Statistical Survey

Source (unless otherwise stated): Danmarks Statistik, Sejrøgade 11, POB 2550, 2100 Copenhagen Ø; tel. 39-17-39-17; fax 39-17-39-99; e-mail dst@dst.dk; internet www.dst.dk.

Note: The figures in this survey relate only to metropolitan Denmark, excluding the Faroe Islands (see p. 1552) and Greenland (see p. 1559), figures for which are dealt with in separate chapters.

Area and Population

AREA, POPULATION AND DENSITY

Area (sq km)	43,098*
Population (census results)	
1 January 2001	5,349,212
1 January 2011	
Males	2,756,582
Females	2,804,046
Total	5,560,628
Density (per sq km) at 1 January 2011	129.0

* 16,640 sq miles.

POPULATION BY AGE AND SEX
(at 2011 census)

	Males	Females	Total
0–14	509,707	485,380	995,087
15–64	1,830,091	1,801,669	3,631,760
65 and over	416,784	516,997	933,781
Total	2,756,582	2,804,046	5,560,628

ADMINISTRATIVE DIVISIONS
(population at 2011 census)

Region	Area (sq km)	Population	Density (per sq km)
Hovedstaden	2,561.3	1,699,387	663.5
Midtjylland	13,124.3	1,260,993	96.1
Nordjylland	7,933.3	579,829	73.1
Sjælland	7,273.2	819,763	112.7
Syddanmark	12,206.2	1,200,656	98.4
Total	43,098.3	5,560,628	129.0

PRINCIPAL MUNICIPALITIES
(population at 2011 census)

København (Copenhagen, the capital)	539,542	Horsens	82,835
Århus (Aarhus)	310,956	Roskilde	82,542
Ålborg (Aalborg)	199,188	Næstved	80,963
Odense	190,245	Slagelse	77,442
Esbjerg	115,184	Sønderborg	76,193
Vejle	107,218	Gentofte	71,714
Frederiksborg (Frederiksberg)	98,782	Holbæk	69,521
Randers	95,318	Hjørring	66,473
Viborg	93,498	Gladsaxe	64,951
Kolding	89,210	Guldborgsund	62,583
Silkeborg	88,913	Frederikshavn	61,576
Herning	85,852	Helsingør	61,368

BIRTHS, MARRIAGES AND DEATHS

	Registered live births		Registered marriages		Registered deaths	
	Number	Rate (per 1,000)	Number	Rate (per 1,000)	Number	Rate (per 1,000)
2003	64,599	12.0	35,041	6.5	57,574	10.7
2004	64,609	11.9	37,711	7.0	55,806	10.3
2005	64,282	11.9	36,148	6.7	54,962	10.1
2006	64,984	12.0	36,452	6.7	55,477	10.2
2007	64,082	11.8	36,576	6.7	55,604	10.2
2008	65,038	11.8	37,376	6.8	54,591	9.9
2009	62,818	11.4	32,934	6.0	54,872	9.9
2010	63,411	11.5	30,949	5.6	54,368	9.8

Life expectancy (years at birth, WHO estimates): 79 (males 77; females 81) in 2009 (Source: WHO, *World Health Statistics*).

ECONOMICALLY ACTIVE POPULATION
(sample surveys, '000 persons aged 15–66 years, April–June)

	2006	2007	2008
Agriculture, hunting and forestry	79.4	79.7	73.8
Mining and quarrying	5.6	5.2	3.6
Manufacturing	427.6	432.9	426.0
Electricity, gas and water supply	16.6	16.5	17.6
Construction	201.2	192.9	193.0
Wholesale and retail trade; repair of motor vehicles, motorcycles and personal and household goods	409.1	412.1	430.5
Hotels and restaurants	76.7	81.1	82.0
Transport, storage and communications	176.1	173.1	158.9
Financial intermediation	93.0	85.9	86.9
Real estate, renting and business activities	275.9	268.4	292.2
Public administration and defence; compulsory social security	168.2	164.2	177.6
Education	211.1	215.2	210.6
Health and social work	486.9	499.9	516.2
Other community, social and personal service activities	150.7	145.7	148.8
Private households with employed persons	—	3.9	—
Extra-territorial organizations and bodies	—	1.9	—
Sub-total	2,786.6	2,778.6	2,823.7
Activities not adequately defined	—	—	3.7
Total employed	2,786.6	2,778.6	2,827.4
Unemployed	117.9	114.5	98.4
Total labour force	2,904.5	2,893.1	2,925.8
Males	1,600.2	1,531.2	1,544.4
Females	1,304.3	1,362.1	1,381.4

Source: ILO.

Health and Welfare

KEY INDICATORS

Total fertility rate (children per woman, 2009)	1.8
Under-5 mortality rate (per 1,000 live births, 2009)	4
HIV/AIDS (% of persons aged 15–49, 2009)	0.2
Physicians (per 1,000 head, 2004)	3.6
Hospital beds (per 1,000 head, 2004)	3.8
Health expenditure (2008): US $ per head (PPP)	3,814
Health expenditure (2008): % of GDP	9.9
Health expenditure (2008): public (% of total)	80.1
Total carbon dioxide emissions ('000 metric tons, 2007)	49,955.0
Carbon dioxide emissions per head (metric tons, 2007)	9.1
Human Development Index (2011): ranking	16
Human Development Index (2011): value	0.895

For sources and definitions, see explanatory note on p. vi.

Agriculture

PRINCIPAL CROPS
('000 metric tons)

	2008	2009	2010
Wheat	5,018.7	5,940.4	5,059.9
Barley	3,396.0	3,393.8	2,981.3
Rye	151.5	238.1	254.7
Oats	322.1	315.2	274.4
Triticale (wheat-rye hybrid)	185.3	229.3	177.4
Potatoes	1,705.4	1,617.7	1,357.8
Sugar beet	2,187.2	1,898.2	2,356.0
Peas, dry	10.6	18.9	28.0
Other pulses	3.4	3.5	5.8
Rapeseed	629.2	634.8	579.8
Cabbages and other brassicas	25.3*	27.6	30.6*

—continued	2008	2009	2010
Lettuce and chicory	10.5*	9.8	11.5
Tomatoes*	20.0	19.8	20.3
Cucumbers and gherkins*	18.5	19.0	21.0
Onions, dry*	63.6	54.6	52.3
Peas, green*	10.0	8.7	10.1
Carrots and turnips	67.3*	91.6	107.8
Apples*	33.5	30.3	28.4

* FAO estimate(s).

Aggregate production ('000 metric tons, may include official, semi-official or estimated data): Total cereals 9,106 in 2008, 10,164 in 2009, 8,772 in 2010; Total roots and tubers 1,705 in 2008, 1,618 in 2009, 1,358 in 2010; Total vegetables (incl. melons) 255 in 2008, 275 in 2009, 306 in 2010; Total fruits (excl. melons) 73 in 2008, 70 in 2009, 69 in 2010.

Source: FAO.

LIVESTOCK
(at May)

	2008	2009	2010
Horses	60,029	57,981	60,000
Cattle	1,564,390	1,540,340	1,571,050
Pigs	12,737,600	12,369,100	13,173,100
Sheep	136,049	103,977	159,626
Chickens ('000 head)	14,710	19,224	14,114
Turkeys ('000 head)	169	165	201
Ducks ('000 head)	214	208	224
Geese ('000 head)	14	10	7

Source: FAO.

LIVESTOCK PRODUCTS
('000 metric tons)

	2008	2009	2010
Cattle meat	129	128	133
Pig meat	1,707	1,585	1,668
Chicken meat	176	169	186
Cows' milk	4,720	4,814	4,909
Butter*	38	37	34
Cheese*	332	321	292
Hen eggs	81	74	76

* FAO estimates.

Source: FAO.

Forestry

ROUNDWOOD REMOVALS
('000 cu m, excl. bark)

	2008	2009*	2010*
Sawlogs, veneer logs and logs for sleepers	891	906	844
Pulpwood	694	705	656
Other industrial wood	95	96	90
Fuel wood	1,106	1,106	1,080
Total	2,786	2,813	2,669

* FAO estimates.

Source: FAO.

SAWNWOOD PRODUCTION
('000 cu m, incl. railway sleepers)

	2007	2008	2009*
Coniferous (softwood)	250	250	239
Broadleaved (hardwood)	50	191*	209
Total	300	441	448

* Unofficial figure(s).

Source: FAO.

Fishing

('000 metric tons, live weight)

	2007	2008	2009
Capture	652.9	690.2	777.8
Norway pout	0.0	32.6	19.8
Blue whiting (Poutassou)	52.7	18.0	0.2
Sandeels (Sandlances)	167.3	255.6	305.6
Atlantic herring	120.7	105.5	92.0
European sprat	140.9	126.7	195.2
Blue mussel	57.3	35.1	37.4
Aquaculture	31.2	35.3	34.1
Rainbow trout	27.7	31.4	29.4
Total catch	684.1	725.5	811.9

Source: FAO.

Mining

('000 metric tons, unless otherwise indicated)

	2007	2008	2009
Crude petroleum	15,168	14,035	12,903
Natural gas (million cu m)	9,223	10,091	8,428
Limestone (agricultural)	700	700	700
Limestone (industrial)	250	250	250
Chalk	1,950	1,900	446
Salt	600	600	600
Peat	242	145	145

2010: Crude petroleum ('000 metric tons) 12,157; Natural gas (million cu m) 8,173.

Source: BP, *Statistical Review of World Energy*; US Geological Survey.

Industry

SELECTED PRODUCTS

('000 metric tons, unless otherwise indicated)

	2003	2004	2005
Pig meat:			
Fresh, chilled or frozen	1,216	1,274	1,240
Salted, dried or smoked	127	105	266
Poultry meat and offal	199	192	173
Fish fillets, etc.: fresh, chilled, frozen	65	61	61
Salami, sausages, etc.	85	74	67
Beet and cane sugar (solid)	512	453	509
Beer ('000 hectolitres)	8,352	8,550	8,493
Flours, meals and pastes of fish	258	302	320
Oil cake and meal	160	249	291
Cigarettes (million)	12,897	13,459	14,867
Cement	2,642	2,946	2,923
Motor spirit (petrol) (million litres)	2,461	2,231	2,526
Gas oils	3,544	3,146	3,253
Motor and fuel oils	1,709	1,857	1,567
Asphalt for road surfaces	2,656	3,706	3,869
Washing powders, softeners, etc.	150	141	134
Refrigerators for household use ('000)	42	35	30

Finance

CURRENCY AND EXCHANGE RATES

Monetary Units

100 øre = 1 Danish krone (plural: kroner).

Sterling, Dollar and Euro Equivalents (30 December 2011)

£1 sterling = 8.883 kroner;
US $1 = 5.746 kroner;
€1 = 7.434 kroner;
100 Danish kroner = £11.26 = $17.40 = €13.45.

Average Exchange Rate (kroner per US $)

2009 5.3609
2010 5.6241
2011 5.3687

GENERAL BUDGET

(million kroner, estimates)

Revenue	2010	2011	2012
Current taxes on income and wealth	524,553	501,571	524,521
Taxes on production and imports	292,747	304,288	315,638
Social security contributions	17,437	18,153	18,072
Interest and dividends	29,430	28,025	28,410
Other current revenue	88,347	83,918	85,049
Capital revenue (incl. taxes)	9,431	9,147	8,735
Total	961,945	945,102	980,425

Expenditure	2010	2011	2012
General public services	135,440	132,011	133,361
Defence	25,312	26,468	26,687
Public order and safety	19,480	19,148	19,183
Education	142,561	140,167	143,801
Health	144,958	149,028	148,760
Social protection	447,582	456,808	488,137
Housing and community amenities	5,616	7,872	6,788
Religious, recreational and cultural services	28,850	28,046	28,009
Economic services	54,606	55,830	61,483
Environmental protection	8,345	9,130	8,724
Total	1,012,750	1,024,508	1,064,933

INTERNATIONAL RESERVES

(US $ million at 31 December)*

	2008	2009	2010
Gold (national valuation)	1,851	2,362	3,017
IMF special drawing rights	320	2,384	2,343
Reserve position in IMF	323	648	826
Foreign exchange	39,823	71,259	70,334
Total	42,317	76,653	76,520

* Data referring to holdings of gold and foreign exchange exclude deposits made with the European Monetary Institute.

Source: IMF, *International Financial Statistics*.

MONEY SUPPLY

('000 million kroner at 31 December)

	2008	2009	2010
Currency outside depository corporations	50.43	48.51	52.81
Transferable deposits	704.83	772.09	771.60
Other deposits	308.83	213.68	216.02
Securities other than shares	379.33	510.29	457.02
Broad money	1,443.43	1,544.56	1,497.45

Source: IMF, *International Financial Statistics*.

COST OF LIVING

(Consumer Price Index; base: 2000 = 100)

	2008	2009	2010
Food and non-alcoholic beverages	123.8	123.7	124.2
Alcoholic beverages and tobacco	105.5	107.8	115.9
Clothing and footwear	96.9	98.1	98.0
Housing, water, electricity, gas and other fuels	125.3	127.8	132.5
Furnishings, household, etc.	113.1	116.4	116.8
Health	110.2	113.7	115.2
Transport	123.5	121.4	125.3
Communications	87.7	85.2	82.7
Recreation and culture	103.4	104.2	104.4
Education	159.1	166.4	173.6
Restaurants and hotels	124.6	127.3	129.4
Miscellaneous goods and services	125.5	129.8	134.5
All items	118.1	119.7	122.4

NATIONAL ACCOUNTS

National Income and Product

(million kroner at current prices)

	2008	2009	2010
Compensation of employees	979,286	972,335	974,249
Gross operating surplus and mixed income	517,838	464,851	536,564
Gross domestic income at factor cost	1,497,124	1,437,186	1,510,814
Taxes, less subsidies, on production	1,612	−2,844	−443
Gross value added	1,498,736	1,434,342	1,510,371
Taxes on products	269,382	249,036	260,034
Less Subsidies on products	14,966	15,539	15,757
GDP in purchasers' values	1,753,152	1,667,839	1,754,648
Factor income from abroad	200,889	143,170	157,258
Less Factor income paid abroad	173,154	116,376	116,302
Gross national income	1,780,887	1,694,633	1,795,606
Current taxes on income, wealth, etc. abroad (net)	4,131	3,498	3,361
Other current transfers to and from abroad (net)	−36,966	−38257	−39,855
Gross national disposable income	1,748,052	1,659,874	1,759,111

Expenditure on the Gross Domestic Product

('000 million kroner at current prices)

	2008	2009	2010
Government final consumption expenditure	465.4	497.0	510.2
Private final consumption expenditure	840.0	814.9	850.9
Changes in inventories	20.4	−20.1	−4.0
Gross fixed capital formation	371.7	313.5	305.1
Total domestic expenditure	1,697.5	1,605.2	1,662.3
Exports of goods and services	959.6	793.7	883.0
Less Imports of goods and services	904.0	731.1	790.7
GDP in purchasers' values	1,753.2	1,667.8	1,754.6

Gross Domestic Product by Economic Activity

(million kroner at current prices)

	2008	2009	2010
Agriculture, horticulture and forestry	12,425	11,970	17,166
Fishing	1,832	1,594	2,453
Mining and quarrying	62,589	36,071	52,103
Manufacturing	192,448	176,286	174,063
Electricity, gas and water supply	37,471	33,457	38,043
Construction	89,639	76,854	70,684
Wholesale and retail trade, restaurants and hotels	208,937	189,055	196,716
Transport, post and telecommunications	151,236	130,387	161,304
Finance and insurance	91,257	93,450	94,496
Real estate and renting activities	148,829	159,081	164,861
Business services	116,041	113,357	112,804
Public administration and defence; compulsory social security	92,997	92,707	95,119
Education	82,515	93,551	97,531
Health care activities	69,504	76,112	78,795
Social work activities	91,893	98,253	100,699
Other community, social and personal service activities	49,123	52,157	53,535
Gross value added at basic prices	1,498,736	1,434,342	1,510,371
Taxes on products	269,382	249,036	260,034
Less Subsidies on products	14,966	15,539	15,757
GDP in purchasers' values	1,753,152	1,667,839	1,754,648

BALANCE OF PAYMENTS

(US $ million)

	2008	2009	2010
Exports of goods f.o.b.	115,135	91,930	96,044
Imports of goods f.o.b.	−114,216	−83,826	−87,348
Trade balance	919	8,103	8,696
Exports of services	72,661	55,346	60,388
Imports of services	−62,561	−50,912	−52,086
Balance on goods and services	11,020	12,538	16,998
Other income received	37,395	26,102	27,527
Other income paid	−33,823	−22,170	−22,549
Balance on goods, services and income	14,592	16,470	21,976
Current transfers received	4,650	4,622	4,070
Current transfers paid	−10,147	−9,871	−9,836
Current balance	9,095	11,222	16,210
Capital account (net)	75	−45	116
Direct investment abroad	−15,241	−6,436	−2,971
Direct investment from abroad	2,606	2,905	−680
Portfolio investment assets	−8,634	−23,339	−17,186
Portfolio investment liabilities	17,900	35,655	15,907
Financial derivatives assets	2,843	2,985	4,805
Other investment assets	−22,412	35,942	−7,698
Other investment liabilities	29,902	−21,784	15,912
Net errors and omissions	−8,711	−3,436	−20,136
Overall balance	7,423	33,670	4,279

Source: IMF, *International Financial Statistics*.

External Trade

PRINCIPAL COMMODITIES

(distribution by SITC, million kroner)

Imports c.i.f.	2008	2009	2010
Food and live animals	54,342.8	48,012.6	53,214.2
Crude materials (inedible) except fuels	15,472.1	12,178.0	14,717.5
Mineral fuels, lubricants, etc.	46,538.9	31,306.1	38,767.8
Petroleum, petroleum products, etc.	36,936.8	25,499.0	32,719.5
Chemicals and related products	60,038.1	51,283.0	55,327.9
Medical and pharmaceutical products	17,118.6	17,736.5	19,302.3
Basic manufactures	92,624.0	61,802.4	68,078.8
Iron and steel	24,082.9	11,345.2	13,872.3
Machinery and transport equipment	186,290.7	148,353.1	149,257.6
Machinery specialized for particular industries	17,642.1	9,820.5	9,910.9
General industrial machinery, equipment and parts	30,686.9	22,947.3	23,582.6
Office machines and automatic data-processing equipment	18,320.9	15,925.8	17,620.8
Telecommunications and sound equipment	19,769.6	17,390.0	18,412.5
Road vehicles (incl. air-cushion vehicles) and parts	40,811.2	23,778.4	28,911.1
Miscellaneous manufactured articles	82,547.1	72,312.5	79,949.7
Clothing and accessories (excl. footwear)	24,131.5	21,326.0	23,915.9
Total (incl. others)	553,294.5	440,196.5	475,117.1

Exports f.o.b.	2008	2009	2010
Food and live animals	91,229.2	85,006.8	91,429.6
Meat and meat preparations	29,587.4	26,913.8	28,412.2
Fish (not marine mammals), crustaceans, molluscs and aquatic invertebrates	16,330.9	14,186.3	15,356.4
Crude materials (inedible) except fuels	21,872.2	18,022.9	24,035.3
Mineral fuels, lubricants, etc.	69,439.8	45,199.6	52,406.3
Petroleum, petroleum products, etc.	51,876.7	35,440.2	41,120.0
Chemicals and related products	76,894.9	76,664.1	88,000.5
Medicinal and pharmaceutical products	40,630.0	42,507.7	51,209.8
Basic manufactures	65,005.7	50,338.8	49,630.9
Machinery and transport equipment	156,569.4	127,421.1	135,971.1
Power-generating machinery and equipment	27,925.8	23,358.7	21,781.0
Machinery specialized for particular industries	21,558.0	16,738.0	18,301.1
General industrial machinery, equipment and parts	42,807.4	33,696.7	36,723.5
Miscellaneous manufactured articles	87,276.9	78,370.9	85,069.5
Clothing and accessories (excl. footwear)	20,883.7	19,042.8	21,686.1
Total (incl. others)	587,601.8	496,903.4	542,483.8

PRINCIPAL TRADING PARTNERS

(million kroner)

Imports c.i.f.	2008	2009	2010
Austria	5,914.5	4,191.4	4,598.8
Belgium	19,070.4	15,234.4	15,917.7
China, People's Republic	32,875.8	28,487.9	35,999.6
Finland	12,635.1	7,286.8	8,125.9
France (incl. Monaco)	20,342.5	15,047.4	15,823.7
Germany	115,680.3	92,532.5	98,442.5
Ireland	5,309.4	4,982.4	5,814.2
Italy	21,516.0	15,062.3	16,023.4
Netherlands	37,139.4	30,789.7	33,755.1
Norway	26,445.1	23,197.8	18,489.7
Poland	15,007.5	11,655.1	13,538.7
Russia	10,865.2	4,629.5	5,732.0
Spain	9,119.3	6,353.9	6,923.3
Sweden	76,603.1	57,502.1	63,431.5
Turkey	5,313.5	3,958.2	4,432.7
United Kingdom	27,963.0	25,194.0	28,557.7
USA	17,630.1	14,912.6	14,837.7
Total (incl. others)	553,294.5	440,196.5	475,117.1

Exports f.o.b.	2008	2009	2010
Belgium	7,503.4	7,159.5	6,867.0
Canada	5,437.8	4,641.7	6,236.6
China, People's Republic	10,355.4	10,350.6	12,105.1
Czech Republic	3,268.6	2,815.7	3,109.7
Finland	13,836.0	10,784.4	12,314.5
France (incl. Monaco)	23,243.7	18,967.0	20,281.6
Germany	95,958.5	79,583.1	81,245.3
Hong Kong	5,201.0	4,778.6	7,976.8
Ireland	6,994.7	5,672.9	5,740.3
Italy	16,218.6	13,052.1	14,229.1
Japan	8,958.4	7,439.7	8,081.2
Netherlands	25,224.4	21,448.1	22,740.8
Norway	34,992.9	30,606.2	33,177.2
Poland	13,037.3	10,990.8	11,993.5
Russia	9,486.1	6,950.1	8,358.9
Spain	14,308.5	11,729.5	11,908.4
Sweden	82,593.9	61,624.5	69,007.4
United Kingdom	45,426.1	39,770.4	41,131.8
USA	29,521.3	27,407.8	28,451.3
Total (incl. others)	587,601.8	496,903.4	542,483.8

Transport

RAILWAYS

(traffic)

	2008	2009	2010
Passengers carried ('000)	226,250	233,029	238,447
Passenger-km (million)	6,475	6,367	6,587
Goods carried ('000 tons)	7,198	6,163	8,121
Ton-km (million)	1,867	1,698	2,240

ROAD TRAFFIC

(motor vehicles in use at 1 January)

	2009	2010	2011
Private cars	2,099,090	2,120,322	2,163,676
Vans	481,887	462,359	441,455
Buses, coaches	14,452	14,509	14,496
Lorries	34,629	32,300	30,820
Tractors	14,887	13,202	12,891
Motorcycles and mopeds	204,770	205,239	203,608

SHIPPING

Merchant Fleet
(registered at 31 December)

	2007	2008	2009
Number of vessels	782	802	807
Total displacement ('000 grt)	9,230.6	10,352.2	11,057.0

Source: IHS Fairplay, *World Fleet Statistics*.

Sea-borne Freight Traffic at Danish Ports*
('000 metric tons loaded and unloaded)

	2001	2002	2003
Aalborg	2,581	2,652	2,756
Aarhus	9,980	9,621	9,983
Copenhagen	6,688	5,996	6,769
Fredericia	15,763	16,585	16,513
Kalundborg	8,530	7,613	8,342
Skaelskør	645	132	445
Others	49,785	51,684	59,146
Total	93,972	94,283	103,954

* Including domestic traffic and ferry traffic.

International Sea-borne Shipping*
(freight traffic, '000 metric tons)

	2008	2009	2010
Goods loaded	21,830	20,831	20,574
Goods unloaded	34,451	28,893	26,591

* Excluding international ferry traffic.

CIVIL AVIATION

(traffic on scheduled services)*

	2007	2008	2009
Kilometres flown (million)	42	110	97
Passengers carried ('000)	2,624	10,398	8,880
Passenger-km (million)	4,314	10,222	8,781
Total ton-km (million)	569	1,169	960

* Including an apportionment (2/7) of international operations by Scandinavian Airlines System (SAS).

Source: UN, *Statistical Yearbook*.

Tourism

FOREIGN TOURIST ARRIVALS

(at accommodation establishments)

Country of residence	2007	2008	2009
Germany	2,723,110	2,593,135	2,538,209
Netherlands	341,116	344,607	319,267
Norway	1,728,419	1,693,932	1,628,381
Sweden	1,489,141	1,433,781	1,241,798
United Kingdom	763,082	740,361	711,362
USA	478,262	474,373	512,034
Total (incl. others)	9,832,042	9,563,857	9,264,870

Tourism receipts (US $ million, excl. passenger transport): 5,976 in 2007; 6,242 in 2008; 5,679 in 2009.

Source: World Tourism Organization.

Communications Media

	2008	2009	2010
Book production: titles*	12,354	13,667	12,593
Daily newspapers:			
number	37	37	35
average circulation ('000 copies)†	1,843	1,660	1,471
Telephones ('000 main lines in use)	2,975.0	2,774.3	2,629.0
Mobile cellular telephones ('000 subscribers)	6,557.0	6,833.7	6,922.5
Internet subscribers ('000)	2,113.2	2,131.1	2,167.0
Broadband subscribers ('000)	1,984.9	2,040.9	2,092.4

* Including pamphlets.
† On weekdays.

Television receivers ('000 in use, estimate): 4,600 in 2001.

Personal computers: 3,000,000 (549.3 per 1,000 persons) in 2007.

Sources: partly International Telecommunication Union; UN, *Statistical Yearbook*.

Education

(2009)

	Institutions	Students		
		Males	Females	Total
General schools	2,848	400,702	403,759	804,461
Basic schools, public	1,899	305,207	287,535	592,742
Basic schools, private	519	47,444	48,800	96,244
Continuation schools	261	13,406	13,449	26,855
Upper secondary schools	169	34,645	53,975	88,620
Vocational institutions of education	121	24,748	63,573	88,321
Social and health schools	36	3,507	30,705	34,212
Schools of teacher training and education science	13	7,942	23,408	31,350
Transport and navigation schools	9	1,047	79	1,126
Institutions of education within police and defence	6	1,620	416	2,036
Academies of fine art and music, library schools etc.	26	2,411	3,006	5,417
Institutions of education within agriculture and food science	14	2,573	855	3,428
Colleges of social work	6	816	3,275	4,091
Engineering colleges and schools of architecture	11	4,832	1,829	6,661
Universities	13	60,184	68,192	128,376
Other schools	85	100,039	61,851	161,890
Total	3,067	585,673	597,375	1,183,048

Teachers (1994/95): Pre-primary 19,200; Primary 33,100; General secondary 37,000; Vocational secondary 13,100; Higher 9,600.

Directory

The Government

HEAD OF STATE

Queen of Denmark: HM Queen MARGRETHE II (succeeded to the throne 14 January 1972).

THE CABINET

(April 2012)

A coalition of the Socialdemokraterne (SD—Social Democrats), Det Radikale Venstre (DRV—Social Liberals) and the Socialistisk Folkeparti (SF—Socialist People's Party).

Prime Minister: HELLE THORNING-SCHMIDT (SD).

Minister of Economics and of the Interior: MARGRETHE VESTAGER (DRV).

Minister of Foreign Affairs: VILLY SØVNDAL (SF).

Minister of Finance: BJARNE CORYDON (SD).

Minister of Justice: MORTEN BØDSKOV (SD).

Minister of Science, Innovation and Higher Education: MORTEN ØSTERGAARD (DRV).

Minister of Taxation: THOR MÖGER PEDERSEN (SF).

Minister of Transport: HENRIK DAM KRISTENSEN (SD).

Minister of Business Affairs and Growth: OLE SOHN (SF).

Minister of City, Housing and Rural Affairs: CARSTEN HANSEN (SD).

Minister of Employment: METTE FREDERIKSEN (SD).

Minister of Children and Education: CHRISTINE ANTORINI (SD).

Minister of Social Affairs and Integration: KAREN HÆKKERUP (SD).

Minister of Food, Agriculture and Fisheries: METTE GJERSKOV (SD).

Minister of Climate, Energy and Building: MARTIN LIDEGAARD (DRV).

Minister of Trade and Investments: PIA OLSEN DYHR (SF).

Minister of Health and Prevention: ASTRID KRAG (SF).

Minister of Defence: NICK HÆKKERUP (SD).

Minister of the Environment: IDA AUKEN (SF).

Minister of European Affairs: NICOLAI WAMMEN (SD).

Minister of Gender Equality, Ecclesiastical Affairs and Nordic Co-operation: MANU SAREEN (DRV).

Minister of Development Co-operation: CHRISTIAN FRIIS BACH (DRV).

Minister of Culture: UFFE ELBÆK (DRV).

MINISTRIES

Prime Minister's Office: Christiansborg, Prins Jørgens Gård 11, 1218 Copenhagen K; tel. 33-92-33-00; fax 33-11-16-65; e-mail stm@stm.dk; internet www.stm.dk.

Ministry of Climate and Energy: Stormgade 2–6, 1470 Copenhagen K; tel. 33-92-28-00; fax 33-92-28-01; e-mail kemin@kemin.dk; internet www.kemin.dk.

Ministry of Culture: Nybrogade 2, 1203 Copenhagen K; tel. 33-92-33-70; fax 33-91-33-88; e-mail kum@kum.dk; internet www.kum.dk.

Ministry of Defence: Holmens Kanal 42, 1060 Copenhagen K; tel. 33-92-33-20; fax 33-32-06-55; e-mail fmn@fmn.dk; internet www.fmn.dk.

Ministry of Ecclesiastical Affairs: Frederiksholms Kanal 21, POB 2123, 1015 Copenhagen K; tel. 33-92-33-90; fax 33-92-39-13; e-mail km@km.dk; internet www.km.dk.

Ministry of Business and Growth: Slotsholmsgade 10–12, 1216 Copenhagen K; tel. 33-92-33-50; fax 33-12-37-78; e-mail oem@oem.dk; internet www.oem.dk.

Ministry of Children and Education: Frederiksholms Kanal 21, 1220 Copenhagen K; tel. 33-92-50-00; fax 33-92-55-67; e-mail uvm@uvm.dk; internet www.uvm.dk.

Ministry of Economics and the Interior: Slotsholmsgade 10–12, 1216 Copenhagen K; tel. 72-28-24-00; fax 72-28-24-01; e-mail im@im.dk; internet www.oeim.dk.

Ministry of Employment: Ved Stranden 8, 1061 Copenhagen K; tel. 72-20-50-00; fax 33-12-13-78; e-mail bm@bm.dk; internet www.bm.dk.

Ministry of the Environment: Højbro Pl. 4, 1200 Copenhagen K; tel. 72-54-60-00; fax 33-32-22-27; e-mail mim@mim.dk; internet www.mim.dk.

Ministry of Finance: Christiansborg Slotspl. 1, 1218 Copenhagen K; tel. 33-92-33-33; fax 33-32-80-30; e-mail fm@fm.dk; internet www.fm.dk.

Ministry of Food, Agriculture and Fisheries: Slotsholmsgade 12, 1216 Copenhagen K; tel. 33-92-33-01; fax 33-14-50-42; e-mail fvm@fvm.dk; internet www.fvm.dk.

Ministry of Foreign Affairs: Asiatisk Pl. 2, 1448 Copenhagen K; tel. 33-92-00-00; fax 32-54-05-33; e-mail eup@um.dk; internet www.um.dk; incorporates Development Co-operation.

Ministry of Health: Holbergsgade 6, 1057 Copenhagen K; tel. 72-26-90-00; fax 72-26-90-01; e-mail sum@sum.dk; internet www.sum.dk.

Ministry of Justice: Slotsholmsgade 10, 1216 Copenhagen K; tel. 72-26-84-00; fax 33-93-35-10; e-mail jm@jm.dk; internet www.jm.dk.

Ministry of Science, Innovation and Higher Education: Bredgade 43, 1260 Copenhagen K; tel. 33-92-97-00; fax 33-32-35-01; e-mail vtu@vtu.dk; internet fivu.dk.

Ministry of Social Affairs and Integration: Holmens Kanal 22, 1060 Copenhagen K; tel. 33-92-93-00; fax 33-93-25-18; e-mail sm@sm.dk; internet www.sm.dk.

Ministry of Taxation: Nicolai Eigtveds Gade 28, 1402 Copenhagen K; tel. 33-92-33-92; fax 33-14-91-05; e-mail skm@skm.dk; internet www.skm.dk.

Ministry of Transport: Frederiksholms Kanal 27, 1220 Copenhagen K; tel. 33-92-33-55; fax 33-12-38-93; e-mail trm@trm.dk; internet www.trm.dk.

Legislature

Folketing

Christiansborg, 1240 Copenhagen K; tel. 33-37-55-00; fax 33-32-85-36; e-mail folketinget@folketinget.dk; internet www.folketinget.dk.

President of the Folketing: MOGENS LYKKETOFT.

General Election, 15 September 2011

Party	Votes	% of votes	Seats
Venstre (Liberals)	947,725	26.73	47
Socialdemokraterne (Social Democrats)	879,615	24.81	44
Dansk Folkeparti (Danish People's Party)	436,726	12.32	22
Det Radikale Venstre (Social Liberals)	336,698	9.50	17
Socialistisk Folkeparti (Socialist People's Party)	326,192	9.20	16
Enhedslisten—de Rød-Grønne (Red-Green Alliance)	236,860	6.68	12
Liberal Alliance	176,585	4.98	9
Det Konservative Folkeparti (Conservative People's Party)	175,047	4.94	8
Kristendemokraterne (Christian Democrats)	28,070	0.79	—
Total (incl. others)	3,545,368*	100.00	179†

* Metropolitan Denmark only.

† Includes two members from the Faroe Islands and two from Greenland.

Political Organizations

Dansk Folkeparti (Danish People's Party): Christiansborg, 1240 Copenhagen K; tel. 33-37-51-99; fax 33-37-51-91; e-mail df@ft.dk; internet www.danskfolkeparti.dk; f. 1995 by defectors from the Progress Party; right-wing, populist; Leader PIA KJÆRSGAARD.

Enhedslisten—de Rød-Grønne (Red-Green Alliance): Studiestræde 24, 1, 1455 Copenhagen K; tel. 33-93-33-24; fax 33-32-03-72; e-mail landskontoret@enhedslisten.dk; internet www.enhedslisten.dk; f. 1989 as an alliance of 3 left-wing parties: Danmarks Kommunistiske Parti, Socialistisk Arbejderparti and Venstresocialisterne; 25-mem. collective leadership; Spokesperson JOHANNE SCHMIDT-NIELSEN; 5,500 mems (2011).

Folkebevægelsen mod EU (People's Movement Against the European Union): Tordenskjoldsgade 21, 1055 Copenhagen K; tel. 35-36-37-40; fax 35-82-18-06; e-mail fb@folkebevaegelsen.dk; internet www.folkebevaegelsen.dk; f. 1972; opposes membership of the EU, in favour of democracy and co-operation in Nordic and European regions, and world-wide; 21-mem. collective leadership; Sec.-Gen. POUL GERHARD KRISTIANSEN; 3,500 mems (2011).

Fremskridtspartiet (Progress Party): Stationsmestervej 11, 9200 Aalborg SV; tel. 70-26-20-27; fax 70-26-23-27; e-mail frp@frp.dk; internet www.frp.dk; f. 1972; right-wing; advocates deportation of Muslims from Denmark, gradual abolition of income tax, disbandment of most of the civil service, and abolition of diplomatic service and about 90% of all legislation; Leader NIELS HØJLAND.

Det Konservative Folkeparti (Conservative People's Party): Nyhavn 4, 1051 Copenhagen K; tel. 33-13-41-40; fax 33-93-37-73; e-mail info@konservative.dk; internet www.konservative.dk; f. 1916; advocates free initiative and the maintenance of private property, but recognizes the right of the state to take action to keep the economic and social balance; Leader LARS BARFOED.

Kristendemokraterne (Christian Democrats): Allégade 24A, 2000 Frederiksberg; tel. 33-27-78-10; fax 33-21-31-16; e-mail kd@kd.dk; internet www.kd.dk; f. 1970 as Kristeligt Folkeparti (Christian People's Party); present name adopted 2003; emphasizes the need for political decisions based on Christian ethics; Chair. PER ØRUM JØRGENSEN.

Liberal Alliance: Christiansborg, 1240 Copenhagen K; tel. 33-37-49-95; e-mail amalie.lyhne@ft.dk; internet liberalalliance.dk; f. 2007 as Ny Alliance by former members of Det Radikale Venstre and Det Konservative Folkeparti; present name adopted 2008; centrist, advocates liberalization of immigration policy and is pro-EU; Chair. LEIF MIKKELSEN.

Det Radikale Venstre (Social Liberals): Christiansborg, 1240 Copenhagen K; tel. 33-37-47-47; fax 33-13-72-51; e-mail radikale@radikale.dk; internet www.radikale.dk; f. 1905; supports international détente and co-operation within regional and world orgs, social reforms without socialism, income policy, workers' participation in industry, state intervention in industrial disputes, state control of trusts and monopolies, strengthening private enterprise; Nat. Chair. KLAUS FRANDSEN; Parliamentary Leader MARGRETHE VESTAGER.

Schleswigsche Partei/Slesvigsk Parti (SP) (Schleswig Party): Vestergade 30, 6200 Aabenraa; tel. 74-62-38-33; fax 74-62-79-39; e-mail sp@bdn.dk; internet www.schleswigsche-partei.dk; f. 1920; represents the German minority in North Schleswig; Chair. GERHARD D. MAMMEN.

Socialdemokraterne (Social Democrats): Danasvej 7, 1910 Frederiksberg C; tel. 72-30-08-00; fax 72-30-08-50; e-mail annesofie@socdem.dk; internet www.socialdemokraterne.dk; f. 1871; finds its chief adherents among workers, employees and public servants; c. 55,000 mems; Leader HELLE THORNING-SCHMIDT; Party Sec. LARS MIDTIBY.

Socialistisk Folkeparti (SF) (Socialist People's Party): Christiansborg, 1240 Copenhagen K; tel. 33-37-44-44; fax 33-32-72-48; e-mail sf@sf.dk; internet www.sf.dk; f. 1959; Chair. VILLY SØVNDAL; Parliamentary Leader OLE SOHN.

Venstre, Danmarks Liberale Parti (V) (Liberals): Søllerødvej 30, 2840 Holte; tel. 45-80-22-33; fax 45-80-38-30; e-mail venstre@venstre.dk; internet www.venstre.dk; f. 1870; supports free trade, a minimum of state interference, and the adoption, in matters of social expenditure, of a modern general social security system; Pres. LARS LØKKE RASMUSSEN; Sec.-Gen. JENS SKIPPER RASMUSSEN; 50,356 mems (Dec. 2009).

Diplomatic Representation

EMBASSIES IN DENMARK

Albania: Fredriksholms Kanal 4, 1220 Copenhagen K; tel. 33-91-79-79; fax 33-91-79-69; e-mail embassy.copenhagen@mfa.gov.al; internet www.albanian-embassy.dk; Ambassador ARBEN CICI.

Algeria: Hellerupvej 66, 2900 Hellerup; tel. 33-11-94-40; fax 33-11-58-50; e-mail ambalda@mail.tele.dk; internet www.algerianembassy.dk; Ambassador ABDELHAMID BOUBAZINE.

Argentina: Borgergade 16, 4th Floor, 1300 Copenhagen K; tel. 33-15-80-82; fax 33-15-55-74; e-mail edina@mrecic.gov.ar; internet www.embargentina.dk; Ambassador RAÚL ALBERTO RICARDES.

Armenia: Ryvangs Allé 50, 2900 Hellerup; Ambassador HRACHYA AGHAJANYAN.

Australia: Dampfærgevej 26, 2100 Copenhagen Ø; tel. 70-26-36-76; fax 70-26-36-86; e-mail genen.cpgn@dfat.gov.au; internet www.denmark.embassy.gov.au; Ambassador JAMES CHOI.

Austria: Sølundsvej 1, 2100 Copenhagen Ø; tel. 39-29-41-41; fax 39-29-20-86; e-mail kopenhagen-ob@bmeia.gv.at; Ambassador Dr DANIEL KRUMHOLZ.

Belgium: Øster Allé 7, 2100 Copenhagen Ø; tel. 35-25-02-00; fax 35-25-02-11; e-mail copenhagen@diplobel.fed.be; internet www.diplomatie.be/copenhagen; Ambassador JEAN-FRANÇOIS BRANDERS.

Benin: Skelvej 2, 2900 Hellerup; tel. 39-68-10-30; fax 39-68-10-32; e-mail ambabenin@c.dk; internet www.ambabenin.dk; Ambassador ARLETTE DAGNON VIGNIKIN.

Bolivia: Store Kongensgade 81, 2nd Floor, 1264 Copenhagen K; tel. 33-12-49-00; fax 33-12-49-03; e-mail embocopenhagen@mail.dk; Ambassador EUGENIO POMA AÑAGUAYA.

Bosnia and Herzegovina: H. C. Andersens Blvd 48, 2nd Floor, 1553 Copenhagen V; tel. 33-33-80-40; fax 33-33-80-17; e-mail info@embassybh.dk; internet www.embassybh.dk; Ambassador KEMAL MUFTIĆ.

Brazil: Chr. IX's Gade 2, 1st Floor, 1111 Copenhagen K; tel. 39-20-64-78; fax 39-27-36-07; e-mail brasemb.copenhague@itamaraty.gov.br; internet www.brazil.dk; Ambassador GONÇALO MELLO MOURÃO.

Bulgaria: Gamlehave Allé 7, 2920 Charlottenlund; tel. 39-64-24-84; fax 39-63-49-23; e-mail embassy@bgemb.dk; Ambassador VALENTIN DELCHEV PORIAZOV.

Burkina Faso: Svanemøllevej 20, 2100 Copenhagen Ø; tel. 39-18-40-22; fax 39-27-18-86; e-mail mail@ambaburkina.dk; internet www.ambaburkina.dk; Ambassador MONIQUE ILBOUDO.

Canada: Kr. Bernikowsgade 1, 1105 Copenhagen K; tel. 33-48-32-00; fax 33-48-32-20; e-mail copen@international.gc.ca; internet www.canadainternational.gc.ca; Ambassador PETER LUNDY.

Chile: Kastelsvej 15, 3rd Floor, 2100 Copenhagen Ø; tel. 35-38-58-34; fax 35-38-42-01; e-mail embassy@chiledk.dk; internet www.chiledk.dk; Ambassador RICARDO CONCHA.

China, People's Republic: Øregårds Allé 25, 2900 Hellerup; tel. 39-46-08-89; fax 39-62-54-84; e-mail mail@chinaembassy.dk; internet www.chinaembassy.dk; Ambassador LI RUIYU.

Côte d'Ivoire: Gersonsvej 8, 2900 Hellerup; tel. 39-62-88-22; fax 39-62-01-62; e-mail ambaivoire@mail.tele.dk; internet www.ambacotedivoire.org; Ambassador MINA MARIA LAURENT BALDÉ.

Croatia: Frederiksgade 19, 1st Floor, 1265 Copenhagen K; tel. 33-91-90-95; fax 33-91-71-31; e-mail denmark@mvpei.hr; Ambassador LADISLAV PIVČEVIĆ.

Cuba: Kastelsvej 19, 3rd Floor, 2100 Copenhagen Ø; tel. and fax 39-40-15-06; e-mail embacuba@dk.embacuba.cu; internet www.cubaembassy.dk; Ambassador CARIDAD YAMIRA CUETO MILIÁN.

Cyprus: Borgergade 28, 1st Floor, 1300 Copenhagen K; tel. 33-91-58-88; fax 33-91-58-77; e-mail copenhagenembassy@mfa.gov.cy; internet www.mfa.gov.cy/embassycopenhagen; Ambassador GEORGE C. KASOULIDES.

Czech Republic: Ryvangs Allé 14–16, 2100 Copenhagen Ø; tel. 39-10-18-10; fax 39-29-09-30; e-mail copenhagen@embassy.mzv.cz; internet www.mfa.cz/copenhagen; Ambassador ZDENĚK LYČKA.

Egypt: Kristianiagade 19, 2100 Copenhagen Ø; tel. 35-43-70-70; fax 35-25-32-62; e-mail egyptembassydenmark@yahoo.com; Ambassador NABIL RIAD HABASHI.

Estonia: Aurehøjvej 19, 2900 Hellerup; tel. 39-46-30-70; fax 39-46-30-76; e-mail embassy.copenhagen@mfa.ee; internet www.estemb.dk; Ambassador KATRIN KIVI.

Finland: Skt Annæ Pl. 24, 1250 Copenhagen K; tel. 33-13-42-14; fax 33-32-47-10; e-mail sanomat.kob@formin.fi; internet www.finlandsambassade.dk; Ambassador RITVA MAARIT KRISTIINA JALAVA.

France: Kongens Nytorv 4, 1050 Copenhagen K; tel. 33-67-01-00; fax 33-93-97-52; e-mail cad.copenhague-amba@diplomatie.gouv.fr; internet www.ambafrance-dk.org; Ambassador VÉRONIQUE BUJON-BARRÉ.

Georgia: Nybrogade 10, 1st Floor, 1203 Copenhagen K; tel. 39-11-00-00; fax 39-11-00-01; e-mail copenhagen.emb@mfa.gov.ge; internet www.denmark.mfa.gov.ge; Ambassador NIKOLOZ RTVELIASHVILI.

Germany: Stockholmsgade 57, POB 2712, 2100 Copenhagen Ø; tel. 35-45-99-00; fax 35-26-71-05; e-mail info@kope.diplo.de; internet www.kopenhagen.diplo.de; Ambassador MICHAEL ZENNER.

Ghana: Egebjerg Allé 13, 2900 Hellerup; tel. 39-62-82-22; fax 39-62-16-52; e-mail ghana@mail.dk; internet www.ghanaembassy.dk; Ambassador HAJIA FATI HABIB-JAWULAA.

Greece: Hammerensgade 4, 3rd Floor, 1267 Copenhagen K; tel. 33-11-45-33; fax 33-93-16-46; e-mail gremb.cop@mfa.gr; internet www.greekembassy.dk; Ambassador ALEXANDROS COUYOU.

Hungary: Strandvejen 170, 2920 Charlottenlund; tel. 39-63-16-88; fax 39-63-00-52; e-mail mission.cph@kum.hu; internet mission.cph@mfa.gov.hu; Ambassador Dr FERENC SZEBÉNYI.

Iceland: Strandgade 89, 1401 Copenhagen K; tel. 33-18-10-50; fax 33-18-10-59; e-mail icemb.coph@utn.stjr.is; internet www.iceland.org/dk; Ambassador STURLA SIGURJÓNSSON.

India: Vangehusvej 15, 2100 Copenhagen Ø; tel. 39-18-28-88; fax 39-27-02-18; e-mail hoc.copenhagen@mea.gov.in; internet www.indian-embassy.dk; Ambassador Ashok Kumar Attri.

Indonesia: Ørehøj Allé 1, 2900 Hellerup; tel. 39-62-44-22; fax 39-62-44-83; e-mail unitkomkph@kbricph.dk; internet www.kbricph.dk; Ambassador Bomer Pasaribu.

Iran: Svanemøllevej 48, 2100 Copenhagen Ø; tel. 39-16-00-03; fax 39-16-00-01; e-mail info@iran-embassy.dk; internet www.iran-embassy.dk; Ambassador Morteza Damanpak Jami.

Iraq: Granhøjen 18, 2900 Hellerup; tel. 39-45-02-70; fax 39-40-69-97; e-mail kbnemb@iraqmofamail.net; Ambassador Dr Albert Issa Nadhar.

Ireland: Østbanegade 21, 2100 Copenhagen Ø; tel. 35-47-32-00; fax 35-43-18-58; e-mail copenhagenembassy@dfa.ie; internet www.embassyofireland.dk; Ambassador Brendan Scannell.

Israel: Lundevangsvej 4, 2900 Hellerup; tel. 88-15-55-00; fax 88-15-55-55; e-mail administration@copenhagen.mfa.gov.il; internet copenhagen.mfa.gov.il; Ambassador Arthur Avnon.

Italy: Gammel Vartov Vej 7, 2900 Hellerup; tel. 39-62-68-77; fax 39-62-25-99; e-mail info.copenaghen@esteri.it; internet www.ambcopenaghen.esteri.it; Ambassador Carlo Tripepi.

Japan: Pilestræde 61, 1112 Copenhagen K; tel. 33-11-33-44; fax 33-11-33-77; e-mail amb@embjapan.dk; internet www.dk.emb-japan.go.jp; Ambassador Toshio Sano.

Korea, Republic: Svanemøllevej 104, 2900 Hellerup; tel. 39-46-04-00; fax 39-46-04-22; e-mail korembdk@mofat.go.kr; internet dnk.mofat.go.kr; Ambassador Byung-Ho Kim.

Latvia: Rosbæksvej 17, 2100 Copenhagen Ø; tel. 39-27-60-00; fax 39-27-61-73; e-mail embassy.denmark@mfa.gov.lv; internet www.am.gov.lv/copenhagen; Ambassador Gints Jegermanis.

Lithuania: Bernstorffsvej 214, 2920 Charlottenlund; tel. 39-63-62-07; fax 39-63-65-32; e-mail amb.dk@urm.lt; internet dk.mfa.lt; Ambassador Vytautas Pinkus.

Luxembourg: Fridtjof Nansens Pl. 5, 1st Floor, 2100 Copenhagen Ø; tel. 35-26-82-00; fax 35-26-82-08; e-mail copenhague.amb@mae.etat.lu; internet www.luxembourgembassy.dk; Ambassador Pierre-Louis Lorenz.

Macedonia, former Yugoslav republic: Skindergade 28a, 1st Floor, 1159 Copenhagen K; tel. 39-76-69-20; fax 39-76-69-23; e-mail copenhagen@mfa.gov.mk; Ambassador Asaf Ademi.

Malta: Lille Strandstræde 14b, 1254 Copenhagen K; tel. 33-15-30-90; fax 33-15-30-91; e-mail maltaembassy.copenhagen@gov.mt; Chargé d'affaires a.i. Deborah Attard Montalto.

Mexico: Bredgade 65, 1st Floor, 1260 Copenhagen K; tel. 39-61-05-00; fax 39-61-05-12; e-mail info@mexican-embassy.dk; internet www.sre.gob.mx/dinamarca; Ambassador Martha Elena Federica Bárcena Coqui.

Morocco: Øregårds Allé 19, 2900 Hellerup; tel. 39-62-45-11; fax 39-62-24-49; e-mail sifamaeco@yahoo.fr; Ambassador Raja Ghannam.

Nepal: Svanemøllervej 92, 2900 Hellerup; tel. 44-44-40-26; fax 44-44-40-27; e-mail embdenmark@gmail.com; internet www.nepalembassydenmark.org; Ambassador Vijaykant Lal Karna.

Netherlands: Toldbodgade 33, 1253 Copenhagen K; tel. 33-70-72-00; fax 33-14-03-50; e-mail kop@minbuza.nl; internet denmark.nlembassy.org; Ambassador Eduard Johannes Maria Middeldorp.

Norway: Amaliegade 39, 1256 Copenhagen K; tel. 33-14-01-24; fax 33-14-06-24; e-mail emb.copenhagen@mfa.no; internet www.norsk.dk; Ambassador Jørg Willy Bronebakk.

Pakistan: Valeursvej 17, 2900 Hellerup; tel. 39-62-11-88; fax 39-40-10-70; e-mail parepcopenhagen@pakistanembassy.dk; internet www.pakistanembassy.dk; Ambassador Fauzia Mufti Abbas.

Poland: Richelieus Allé 12, 2900 Hellerup; tel. 39-46-77-00; fax 39-46-77-66; e-mail copenhagen.info@msz.gov.pl; internet www.copenhagen.polemb.net; Ambassador Rafał Wiśniewski.

Portugal: Toldbodgade 31, 1st Floor, 1253 Copenhagen K; tel. 33-13-13-01; fax 33-14-92-14; e-mail embport@get2net.dk; Ambassador João Pedro da Silveira Carvalho.

Romania: Strandagervej 27, 2900 Hellerup; tel. 39-40-71-77; fax 39-62-78-99; e-mail roemb@mail.tele.dk; internet copenhaga.mae.ro; Chargé d'Affaires Cristian Negrilă.

Russia: Kristianiagade 5, 2100 Copenhagen Ø; tel. 35-42-55-85; fax 35-42-37-41; e-mail embrus@mail.dk; internet www.denmark.mid.ru; Ambassador Teimuraz O. Ramishvili.

Saudi Arabia: Strandvej 162, 2920 Charlottenlund; tel. 39-62-12-00; fax 39-62-60-09; e-mail embassy@saudiemb.dk; internet www.saudiembassy.dk; Ambassador Abd al-Rahman Saad al-Hadlaq.

Serbia: Svanevænget 36, 2100 Copenhagen Ø; tel. 39-29-77-84; fax 39-29-79-19; e-mail serbianemb@city.dk; internet www.serbianembassy.dk; Ambassador Vida Ognjenović.

Slovakia: Vesterled 26–28, 2100 Copenhagen Ø; tel. 39-20-99-11; fax 39-20-99-13; e-mail emb.copenhagen@mzv.sk; internet www.mzv.sk/copenhagen; Ambassador Radomír Boháč.

Slovenia: Amaliegade 6, 2nd Floor, 1256 Copenhagen K; tel. 33-73-01-20; fax 33-15-06-07; e-mail vkh@gov.si; internet kopenhagen.veleposlanistvo.si; Ambassador Bogdan Benko.

South Africa: Gammel Vartov Vej 8, POB 128, 2900 Hellerup; tel. 39-18-01-55; fax 39-18-40-06; e-mail sa.embassy@southafrica.dk; internet www.southafrica.dk; Ambassador Samkelisiwe Mhlanga.

Spain: Kristianiagade 21, 2100 Copenhagen Ø; tel. 35-42-47-00; fax 35-42-47-26; e-mail emb.copenhague@maec.es; internet www.maec.es/embajadas/copenhague; Ambassador Diego Muñiz Lovelace.

Sweden: Skt Annæ Pl. 15b, 1250 Copenhagen K; tel. 33-36-03-70; fax 33-36-03-95; e-mail ambassaden.kopenhamn@foreign.ministry.se; internet www.swedenabroad.com/copenhagen; Ambassador Inga Eriksson Fogh.

Switzerland: Amaliegade 14, 1256 Copenhagen K; tel. 33-14-17-96; fax 33-33-75-51; e-mail cop.vertretung@eda.admin.ch; internet www.eda.admin.ch/copenhagen; Ambassador Paul Viktor Christen.

Thailand: Norgesmindevej 18, 2900 Hellerup; tel. 39-62-50-10; fax 39-62-50-59; e-mail mail@thaiembassy.dk; internet www.thaiembassy.dk; Ambassador Piyawat Niyomrerks.

Turkey: Rosbæksvej 15, 2100 Copenhagen Ø; tel. 39-20-27-88; fax 39-20-51-66; e-mail turkembassy@internet.dk; internet www.turkishembassy.dk; Ambassador Ahmet Berki Dibek.

Uganda: Sofievej 15, 2900 Hellerup; tel. 39-62-09-66; fax 39-61-01-48; e-mail info@ugandaembassy.dk; internet www.ugandaembassy.dk; Ambassador Joseph Tomusange.

Ukraine: Toldbodgade 37a, 1st Floor, 1253 Copenhagen K; tel. 33-18-56-20; fax 33-16-00-74; e-mail embassy.ua@mail.tele.dk; internet www.mfa.gov.ua/denmark; Ambassador Mykhajlo V. Skuratovskyi.

United Kingdom: Kastelsvej 36–40, 2100 Copenhagen Ø; tel. 35-44-52-00; fax 35-44-52-93; e-mail enquiry.copenhagen@fco.gov.uk; internet ukindenmark.fco.gov.uk; Ambassador Nicholas Archer.

USA: Dag Hammarskjölds Allé 24, 2100 Copenhagen Ø; tel. 33-41-71-00; fax 35-43-02-23; e-mail usembassycopenhagen@state.gov; internet denmark.usembassy.gov; Ambassador Laurie Susan Fulton.

Venezuela: Toldbodgade 31, 3rd Floor, 1253 Copenhagen K; tel. 33-93-63-11; fax 33-37-76-59; e-mail emvendk@mail.dk; internet www.ve-ambassade.dk; Chargé d'affaires a.i. Dr Roger Corbacho Moreno.

Viet Nam: Bernstorffsvej 30c, 2900 Hellerup; tel. 39-18-39-32; fax 39-18-41-71; e-mail embvndk@hotmail.com; internet www.vietnamemb.dk; Ambassador Vu Van Luu.

Judicial System

In Denmark the judiciary is independent of the Government. Judges are appointed by the Crown on the recommendation of the Minister of Justice and cannot be dismissed except by judicial sentence.

The ordinary courts are divided into three instances, the District Courts, the High Courts and the Supreme Court. There is one District Court for each of the 24 judicial districts in the country. These courts must have at least one judge trained in law and they hear all criminal and civil cases. The two High Courts serve Jutland (West High Court) and the islands (East High Court), respectively. They serve as appeal courts for cases from the District Courts. Each case must be heard by at least three judges. The Supreme Court, at which at least five judges must sit, is the court of appeal for cases from the High Courts. Usually only one appeal is allowed from either court, but in special instances the Appeals Permission Board may give leave for a second appeal, to the Supreme Court, from a case that started in a District Court. Furthermore, in certain minor cases, appeal from the District Courts to the High Courts is allowed only by leave of appeal from the Appeals Permission Board.

There is a special Maritime and Commercial Court in Copenhagen, consisting of a President and two Vice-Presidents with legal training and a number of commercial and nautical assessors. The Land Registration Court, which was established in 2007, deals with disputes regarding the registration of titles to land, marriage settlements and mortgage payments. The West High Court serves as the appeal court for cases from the Land Registration Court.

An ombudsman is appointed by the Folketing (parliament) after each general election, and is concerned with the quality and legality of the administration of the laws and administrative provisions. Although the ombudsman holds no formal power to change decisions taken by the administration, he may, on a legal basis, express criticism of acts and decisions of administrative bodies. He is obliged to present an annual report to the Folketing.

Supreme Court
Prins Jørgens Gård 13, 1218 Copenhagen K; tel. 33-63-27-50; fax 33-15-00-10; e-mail post@hoejesteret.dk; internet www.domstol.dk/hojesteret.

President of the Supreme Court: TORBEN MELCHIOR.

Judges: PETER BLOK, JENS PETER CHRISTENSEN, BØRGE DAHL, NIELS GRUBBE, ASBJØRN JENSEN, POUL DAHL JENSEN, LENE PAGTER KRISTENSEN, MARIANNE HØJGAARD PEDERSEN, MICHAEL REKLING, VIBEKE RØNNE, THOMAS RØRDAM, JYTTE SCHARLING, HANNE SCHMIDT, JON STOKHOLM, POUL SØGAARD, PER SØRENSEN, HENRIK WAABEN, PER WALSØE.

President of the East High Court: BENT CARLSEN.

President of the West High Court: BJARNE CHRISTENSEN.

President of the Maritime and Commercial Court: HENRIK ROTHE.

President of the Land Registration Court: SØRUP HANSEN.

Ombudsman: HANS GAMMELTOFT-HANSEN.

Religion

At 1 January 2010 some 80.9% of the population belonged to the Evangelical Lutheran Church in Denmark. In 2002 the second largest religion was Islam, constituting approximately 3% of the population (170,000 persons), followed by communities of Roman Catholics (36,000), Jehovah's Witnesses (15,000), Jews (7,000), Baptists (5,500), Pentecostalists (5,000) and the Church of Jesus Christ of Latter-day Saints (Mormons—4,500). The German minority in South Jutland and other non-Danish communities (particularly Scandinavian groups) have their own religious communities.

CHRISTIANITY

National Council of Churches in Denmark (Danske Kirkers Råd): Peter Bangs Vej 1D, 2000 Frederiksberg; tel. 35-43-29-43; fax 38-87-14-93; e-mail dkr@danskekirkersraad.dk; internet www.danskekirkersraad.dk; f. 1939; associate council of the World Council of Churches; 15 mem. churches; Chair. ANDERS GADEGAARD; Gen. Sec. MADS CHRISTOFFERSEN.

The National Church

Evangelical Lutheran Church in Denmark (Den evangelisk-lutherske Folkekirke i Danmark)
Nørregade 11, 1165 Copenhagen K; tel. 33-47-65-00; fax 33-14-39-69; e-mail folkekirken@folkekirken.dk; internet www.folkekirken.dk.

The established Church of Denmark, supported by the state; no bishop exercises a presiding role, but the Bishop of Copenhagen is responsible for certain co-ordinating roles. The Council on International Relations of the Evangelical Lutheran Church in Denmark (Peter Bangs Vej 1D, 2000 Frederiksberg; e-mail interchurch@interchurch.dk; internet www.interchurch.dk) is responsible for ecumenical relations. Membership at 1 January 2010 was 4,479,214 (80.9% of the population).

Bishop of København (Copenhagen): PETER SKOV-JAKOBSEN.

Bishop of Helsingør: LISE LOTTE REBEL.

Bishop of Roskilde: PETER FISCHER-MØLLER.

Bishop of Lolland-Falster: STEEN SKOVSGAARD.

Bishop of Odense: KRESTEN DREJERGAARD.

Bishop of Ålborg (Aalborg): HENNING TOFT BRO.

Bishop of Viborg: KARSTEN NISSEN.

Bishop of Århus (Aarhus): KJELD HOLM.

Bishop of Ribe: ELISABETH DONS CHRISTENSEN.

Bishop of Haderslev: NIELS HENRIK ARENDT.

The Roman Catholic Church

Denmark comprises a single diocese, directly responsible to the Holy See. At 31 December 2006 there were an estimated 36,707 adherents in the country (around 0.7% of the population). The Bishop participates in the Scandinavian Episcopal Conference (based in Sweden).

Bishop of København (Copenhagen): Rt Rev. CZESLAW KOZON, Katolsk Bispekontor, Gl. Kongevej 15, 1610 Copenhagen V; tel. 33-55-60-80; fax 33-55-60-18; e-mail biskop@katolsk.dk; internet www.katolsk.dk.

Other Churches

Apostolic Church in Denmark: Holbergsvej 45, 6000 Kolding; tel. 79-32-16-00; fax 79-32-16-01; e-mail servicecenter@apostolic.dk; internet www.apostolskkirke.dk; f. 1924; Nat. Leader JACOB VIFTRUP.

Baptistkirken i Danmark (Baptist Union of Denmark): Købnerhus, Lærdalsgade 7, 2300 Copenhagen S; tel. 32-59-07-08; fax 98-11-68-50; e-mail info@baptist.dk; internet www.baptistkirken.dk; f. 1839; 5,100 mems; Pres. MOGENS ANDERSEN.

Church of England: St Alban's Church, Churchill Parken 6, 1263 Copenhagen K; tel. 39-62-77-36; fax 39-62-77-35; e-mail chaplain@st-albans.dk; internet www.st-albans.dk; f. 1728; Chaplain Rev. JONATHAN LLOYD.

Church of Jesus Christ of Latter-day Saints (Mormons): Borups Allé 128, 2000 Frederiksberg; tel. 38-11-18-50; e-mail martin@wpmail.dk; internet www.mormon.dk; f. in Denmark 1850; c. 4,500 mems in 22 congregations; Dir, Public Affairs MARTIN STOKHOLM.

Danish Mission Covenant Church (Det Danske Missionsforbund): Rosenlunden 17, 5000 Odense C; tel. 66-14-83-31; fax 66-14-83-00; e-mail ddm@email.dk; internet www.missionsforbundet.dk; Sec. PALLE BYG.

Methodist Church: Frederikshaldsgade 7, 8200 Århus N; tel. 86-16-69-16; internet www.metodistkirken.dk; f. 1910; Chair. CHRISTIAN ALSTED.

Moravian Brethren: The Moravian Church, Lindegade 26, 6070 Christiansfeld; tel. 74-56-14-20; fax 74-56-14-21; e-mail boeytler@post7.tele.dk; f. in Denmark 1773; Pastor Rev. Dr JØRGEN BØYTLER.

Reformed Church: Reformed Synod of Denmark, Dronningensgade 87, 7000 Fredericia; tel. and fax 75-92-05-51; e-mail s.hofmeister@reformert.dk; internet www.reformert.dk; Moderator Rev. SABINE HOFMEISTER.

Religious Society of Friends (Quakers): Danish Quaker Centre, Drejervej 15, 4th Floor, 2400 Copenhagen NV; tel. and fax 36-47-00-95; e-mail post@kvaekerne.dk; internet www.kvaekerne.dk; Clerk HJERRE F. HVIID.

Russian Orthodox Church: Alexander Nevski Church, Bredgade 53, 1260 Copenhagen K; tel. 33-13-60-46; fax 33-13-28-85; e-mail ruskirke@ruskirke.dk; internet www.ruskirke.dk; f. 1883; Rector Fr SERGY PLEKHOV.

Seventh-day Adventists: Syvende Dags Adventistkirken, Concordiavej 16, POB 15, 2850 Nærum; tel. 45-58-77-77; fax 45-58-77-78; e-mail adventistkirken@adventist.dk; internet www.adventist.dk; f. 1863; Pres. BJØRN OTTESEN.

ISLAM

The Muslim Faith Society (Det Islamiske Trossamfund i Danmark): Dortheavej 45–47, 2400 Copenhagen NV; tel. 38-11-22-25; fax 38-11-22-26; e-mail wakf@wakf.com; internet www.wakf.com; f. 1995; Chair. BILAL ASSAAD.

JUDAISM

The Jewish Community (Det Mosaiske Troessamfund): Krystalgade 12, 1st Floor, 1172 Copenhagen K; tel. 33-12-88-68; fax 33-12-33-57; e-mail mt@mosaiske.dk; internet www.mosaiske.dk; Chief Rabbi BENT LEXNER; Pres. FINN SCHWARZ; c. 2,300 mems.

The Press

There are more than 220 separate newspapers, including some 35 principal dailies. The average total circulation of daily newspapers in 2010 was 1,471,000 on weekdays.

Most newspapers and magazines are privately owned and published by joint concerns, co-operatives or limited liability companies. The main concentration of papers is held by the Berlingske Group, which owns *Berlingske Tidende*, *B.T.* and *Weekendavisen*, and the provincial *Jydskevestkysten* and *Århus Stiftstidende*.

The largest-selling newspaper in Denmark is *Jyllands-Posten*, published in Viby, a suburb of Århus. Its main competitors are *Berlingske Tidende* and *Politiken*, both published in Copenhagen, but there is no truly national press. Copenhagen accounts for 20% of the national dailies and about one-half of the total circulation.

PRINCIPAL DAILIES

(circulation figures refer to Jan.–June 2011, unless otherwise indicated)

Aabenraa

Der Nordschleswiger: Skibbroen 4, POB 1041, 6200 Aabenraa; tel. 74-62-38-80; fax 74-62-94-30; e-mail redaktion@nordschleswiger.dk; internet www.nordschleswiger.dk; f. 1946; German; Editor-in-Chief SIEGFRIED MATLOK; circ. 2,230.

Ålborg
(Aalborg)

Nordjyske Stiftstidende: Langagervej 1, POB 8000, 9220 Ålborg Øst; tel. 99-35-33-00; fax 99-35-33-75; e-mail redaktion@nordjyske.dk; internet www.nordjyske.dk; f. 1767; adopted present name in 1999, following the merger of six regional dailies; mornings; Publr and Editor-in-Chief PER LYNGBY; circ. weekdays 51,980, Sundays 57,312.

Århus
(Aarhus)

Århus Stiftstidende: Banegårdspladsen 11, POB 3, 8000 Århus C; tel. 87-40-10-10; fax 87-40-13-21; e-mail red@stiften.dk; internet www.stiften.dk; f. 1794; evening and weekend mornings; Editor-in-Chief TURID FENNEFOSS NIELSEN; circ. weekdays 20,329, Sundays 24,754.

Esbjerg

Jydskevestkysten: Norgesgade 1, 6700 Esbjerg; tel. 79-12-45-00; fax 75-13-22-07; e-mail jydskevestkysten@jv.dk; internet www.jv.dk; f. 1917 as *Vestkysten*; merged with *Jydske Tidende* in 1991 to form present daily; morning; Editor-in-Chief MIKAEL KAMBER; circ. weekdays 60,312, Sundays 67,044 (2011).

Helsingør

Helsingør Dagblad: Klostermosevej 101, 3000 Helsingør; tel. 49-22-21-10; fax 49-26-65-05; e-mail redaktionen@hdnet.dk; internet www.helsingordagblad.dk; f. 1867; Editor-in-Chief KLAUS DALGAS; circ. 5,625.

Herning

Herning Folkeblad: Østergade 21, 7400 Herning; tel. 96-26-37-00; fax 97-22-36-00; e-mail hk@herningfolkeblad.dk; internet www.aoh.dk; f. 1869; evening; Editor-in-Chief VIBEKE LARSEN; circ. 11,880.

Hillerød

Dagbladet/Frederiksborg Amts Avis: Slotsgade 1, 3400 Hillerød; tel. 48-24-41-00; fax 48-25-48-40; e-mail frederiksborg@sn.dk; internet www.sn.dk; f. 1874; morning; Editor TORBEN DALBY LARSEN; circ. weekdays 39,025.

Holbæk

Holbæk Amts Venstreblad: Ahlgade 1C, 4300 Holbæk; tel. 88-88-43-03; fax 59-44-50-34; e-mail red.hol@nordvest.dk; internet www.nordvestnyt.dk; f. 1905; evening; Editor-in-Chief MOGENS FLYVHOLM; circ. 13,288 (2009).

Holstebro

Dagbladet Holstebro-Struer: Lægårdvej 86, 7500 Holstebro; tel. 99-12-83-00; fax 97-42-62-94; e-mail holstebro@bergske.dk; internet www.dagbladet-holstebro-struer.dk; evening; Editor-in-Chief HANS KRABBE; circ. 12,230.

Horsens

Horsens Folkeblad: Søndergade 47, 8700 Horsens; tel. 76-27-20-00; fax 75-61-07-97; e-mail redaktionen@hsfo.dk; internet hsfo.dk; f. 1866; evening; Editor ALEX PEDERSEN; circ. 13,571.

Kalundborg

Kalundborg Folkeblad: Skibbrogade 40–42, 4400 Kalundborg; tel. 88-88-44-00; fax 59-51-02-80; e-mail red.kf@nordvest.dk; internet www.nordvestnyt.dk; circ. 5,602.

København
(Copenhagen)

Berlingske Tidende: Pilestræde 34, 1147 Copenhagen K; tel. 33-75-75-75; fax 33-75-20-20; e-mail redaktionen@berlingske.dk; internet www.berlingske.dk; f. 1749; morning; Editor-in-Chief LISBETH KNUDSEN; circ. weekdays 100,811, Sundays 118,309.

Børsen: Møntergade 19, 1140 Copenhagen K; tel. 33-32-01-02; fax 33-12-24-45; e-mail redaktionen@borsen.dk; internet www.borsen.dk; f. 1896; morning; business news; Editor-in-Chief ANDERS KRAB-JOHANSEN; circ. 73,330.

B.T.: Pilestræde 34, 1147 Copenhagen; tel. 33-75-75-33; fax 33-75-20-33; e-mail pbr@bt.dk; internet www.bt.dk; f. 1916; morning; independent; Editor-in-Chief OLAV ANDERSEN; circ. weekdays 66,547, Sundays 88,898.

Dagbladet Arbejderen: Ryesgade 3F,2200 Copenhagen N; tel. 35-35-21-93; fax 35-37-20-39; e-mail redaktion@arbejderen.dk; internet www.arbejderen.dk; Editor-in-Chief BIRTHE SØRENSEN.

Dagbladet Information: Store Kongensgade 40C, POB 188, 1264 Copenhagen K; tel. 33-69-60-00; fax 33-69-60-79; e-mail inf-dk@information.dk; internet www.information.dk; f. 1943 (illicitly during occupation by Nazi Germany and then legally in 1945); morning; independent; Editor-in-Chief CHRISTIAN JENSEN; circ. 21,763.

Ekstra Bladet: Rådhuspladsen 37, 1785 Copenhagen V; tel. 33-11-13-13; fax 33-14-10-00; e-mail redaktionen@eb.dk; internet www.eb.dk; f. 1904; evening; Editor-in-Chief POUL MADSEN; circ. weekdays 66,764, Sundays 94,370.

Kristeligt Dagblad: Vimmelskaftet 47, 1161 Copenhagen K; tel. 33-48-05-00; fax 33-48-05-01; e-mail kristeligt-dagblad@kristeligt-dagblad.dk; internet www.kristeligt-dagblad.dk; f. 1896; morning; independent; Editor-in-Chief ERIK BJERAGER; circ. 26,952.

Politiken: Politikens Hus, Rådhuspladsen 37, 1785 Copenhagen V; tel. 33-11-85-11; fax 33-15-41-17; e-mail politiken.dk@pol.dk; internet www.politiken.dk; f. 1884; morning; Editor-in-Chief BO LIDEGAARD; circ. weekdays 98,973, Sundays 124,603.

Næstved

Sjællandske: Dania 38, 4700 Næstved; tel. 72-45-11-00; fax 72-45-11-17; e-mail red@sn.dk; internet www.sn.dk; f. 2005 by merger of *Næstved Tidende* (f. 1866) and *Sjællands Tidende* (f. 1815); Editor HELJE WEDEL; circ. 16,308.

Nykøbing

Lolland-Falsters Folketidende: Tværgade 14, 4800 Nykøbing F; tel. 54-88-02-00; fax 54-88-02-96; e-mail redaktion@folketidende.dk; internet www.folketidende.dk; f. 1873; evening; Editor LARS HOVGAARDHOV; circ. 17,072.

Morsø Folkeblad: Elsøvej 105, 7900 Nykøbing M; tel. 97-72-10-00; fax 97-72-10-10; e-mail mf@mf.dk; internet www.mf.dk; f. 1877; daily except Sun; Senior Editor LEIF KRISTIANSEN; circ. 4,936.

Odense

Fyens Stiftstidende: Banegårdspladsen, 5100 Odense C; tel. 66-11-11-11; fax 65-45-52-88; e-mail redaktion@fyens.dk; internet www.fyens.dk; f. 1772; adopted current name in 1852; morning; independent; Editor-in-Chief PER WESTERGÅRD; circ. weekdays 45,516, Sundays 53,452.

Randers

Randers Amtsavis: Nørregade 7, 8900 Randers; tel. 87-12-20-00; fax 87-12-21-21; e-mail redaktion@amtsavisen.dk; internet www.amtsavisen.dk; f. 1810; evening; independent; Editor-in-Chief TURID FENNEFOSS NIELSEN; circ. 8,211.

Ringkøbing

Dagbladet Ringkøbing-Skjern: Sankt Blichersvej 5, POB 146, 6950 Ringkøbing; tel. 99-75-73-00; fax 99-75-74-30; e-mail ringkoebing@bergske.dk; internet www.dagbladetringskjern.dk; evening; Editor SØREN CHRISTENSEN; circ. 8,488.

Rønne

Bornholms Tidende: Nørregade 11–19, 3700 Rønne; tel. 56-90-30-00; fax 56-90-30-91; e-mail redaktion@bornholmstidende.dk; internet www.bornholmstidende.dk; f. 1866; evening; Editor-in-Chief DAN QVITZAU; circ. 9,960.

Silkeborg

Midtjyllands Avis: Papirfabrikken 18, 8600 Silkeborg; tel. 86-82-13-00; fax 86-81-35-77; e-mail slang@mja.dk; internet www.midtjyllandsavis.dk; f. 1857; daily except Sun.; Editor-in-Chief STEFFEN LANGE; circ. 12,364.

Skive

Skive Folkeblad: Gemsevej 7, 7800 Skive; tel. 97-51-34-11; fax 97-51-28-35; e-mail redaktion@skivefolkeblad.dk; internet www.skivefolkeblad.dk; f. 1880; Editor OLE DALL; circ. 10,268.

Svendborg

Fyns Amts Avis: Skt Nicolai Gade 3, POB 40, 5700 Svendborg; tel. 62-21-46-21; fax 62-22-06-10; e-mail post@faa.dk; internet www.fynsamtsavis.dk; f. 1863; Editor-in-Chief TROELS MYLENBERG; circ. weekdays 12,253, Sundays 12,544.

Vejle

Vejle Amts Folkeblad: Bugattivej 8, 7100 Vejle; tel. 75-85-77-88; fax 76-41-48-82; e-mail vaf@vejleamtsfolkeblad.dk; internet www.vejleamtsfolkeblad.dk; f. 1865; evening; Editor ALEX PEDERSON; circ. 12,547.

Viborg

Viborg Stifts Folkeblad: Vesterbrogade 8, 8800 Viborg; tel. 89-27-63-00; fax 89-27-64-80; e-mail viborg@bergske.dk; internet www.viborg-folkeblad.dk; f. 1877; evening; also publishes: *Viborg Nyt* (weekly); Editor LARS NORUP; circ. 9,084.

Viby

Jyllands-Posten: Grøndalsvej 3, 8260 Viby J; tel. 87-38-38-38; fax 87-38-31-99; internet www.jp.dk; f. 1871; independent; Editor-in-Chief JØRN MIKKELSEN; circ. weekdays 104,195, Sundays 135,038.

OTHER NEWSPAPERS

Den Blå Avis (East edition): Generatorvej 8D, 2730 Herlev; tel. 44-85-44-44; fax 44-85-44-15; e-mail rubrik.ost@dba.dk; internet www.dba.dk; 2 a week; circ. 73,000 (July–Dec. 2007).

Den Blå Avis (West edition): Axel Kiers Vej 11, 8270 Højbjerg; tel. 87-31-31-31; fax 86-20-20-02; e-mail rubrik.vest@dba.dk; internet www.dba.dk; Thur.; circ. 46,160 (July–Dec. 2007).

Weekendavisen: Pilestræde 34, 1147 Copenhagen K; tel. 33-75-25-33; fax 33-75-20-50; e-mail bwa@weekendavisen.dk; internet www.weekendavisen.dk; f. 1749; present name adopted in 1972; Fri.; Editor-in-Chief ANNE KNUDSEN; circ. 56,625.

POPULAR PERIODICALS

(circulation figures refer to Jan.–June 2010, unless otherwise indicated)

Ældre Sagen NU: Nørregade 49, 1165 Copenhagen K; tel. 33-96-86-86; fax 33-96-86-87; e-mail aeldresagen@aeldresagen.dk; internet www.aeldresagen.dk; 6 a year; members' magazine for senior citizens; Editor–in–chief SANNA KJÆR HANSEN; circ. 440,000 (2012).

Alt for damerne: Hellerupvej 51, 2900 Hellerup; tel. 39-45-75-00; fax 39-45-74-80; e-mail alt@altfordamerne.dk; internet www.altfordamerne.dk; f. 1946; weekly; publ. by Egmont Magasiner A/S; women's magazine; Editor-in-Chief CAMILLA FRANK; circ. 60,884.

Anders And & Co: Vognmagergade 11, 1148 Copenhagen K; tel. 70-20-50-35; fax 33-30-57-60; e-mail redaktion@andeby.dk; internet www.andeby.dk; weekly; children's magazine; Man. Editor FRANK KNAU; circ. 38,896.

Basserne: Vognmagergade 11, 1148 Copenhagen K; tel. 70-20-50-35; fax 33-30-57-60; e-mail basserne@tsf.egmont.com; internet www.basserne.dk; f. 1972; fortnightly; children and youth; circ. 14,327.

Billed-Bladet: Havneholmen 33, 1561 Copenhagen V; tel. 72-34-20-00; e-mail bb@billed-bladet.dk; internet www.billedbladet.dk; f. 1938; weekly; publ. by Aller Press A/S; royal family and celebrity pictures; Editor-in-Chief ANNEMETTE KRAKAU; circ. 185,757.

Bo Bedre: Strandboulevarden 130, 2100 Copenhagen Ø; tel. 39-17-20-00; fax 39-29-01-99; e-mail bobedre@bobedre.dk; internet www.bobedre.dk; monthly; publ. by Bonnier Pub. A/S; homes and gardens; Editor-in-Chief ERIK RIMMER; circ. 78,072.

Familie Journal: Havneholmen 33, 1561 Copenhagen V; tel. 72-34-22-22; e-mail redaktionen@familiejournal.dk; internet www.familiejournal.dk; f. 1877; weekly; publ. by Aller Press A/S; Editor-in-Chief ANETTE KOKHOLM; circ. 182,520.

Femina: Havneholmen 33, 1561 Copenhagen V; tel. 70-20-75-92; e-mail redaktionen@femina.dk; internet www.femina.dk; f. 1873; weekly; publ. by Aller Press A/S; Editor-in-Chief CAMILLA LINDEMANN; circ. 62,623.

Gør Det Selv: Strandboulevarden 130, 2100 Copenhagen Ø; tel. 39-17-20-00; fax 39-21-23-07; e-mail gds@bonnier.dk; internet www.goerdetselv.dk; f. 1975; every 3 weeks; publ. by Bonnier Pub. A/S; home improvements; Editor RUNE MICHAELSEN; circ. 28,454.

Helse: Frederiksberg Runddel 1, 2000 Frederiksberg; tel. 35-25-05-25; fax 35-26-87-60; e-mail helse@helse.dk; internet www.helse.dk; f. 1955; 10 a year; social, mental and physiological health; Editor-in-Chief JESPER BO BENDTSEN; circ. 102,630.

Hendes Verden: Hellerupvej 51, 2900 Hellerup; tel. 39-45-75-00; fax 39-45-75-99; e-mail hv@hendesverden.dk; internet www.hendesverden.dk; f. 1937; weekly; publ. by Egmont Magasiner A/S; for women; Editor IBEN NIELSEN; circ. 38,617.

Her & Nu: Hellerupvej 51, 2900 Hellerup; tel. 39-45-77-00; fax 39-45-77-17; e-mail herognu@herognu.com; internet www.herognu.com; weekly (Thur.); publ. by Egmont Magasiner A/S; illustrated television and film guide; news about the royal family and celebrities; Editor-in-Chief MICHAEL RASMUSSEN; circ. 107,823.

Hjemmet (The Home): Hellerupvej 51, 2900 Hellerup; tel. 39-45-76-00; fax 39-45-76-60; e-mail red@hjemmet.dk; internet www.hjemmet.dk; weekly; publ. by Egmont Magasiner A/S; Editor-in-Chief BJARNE RAVNSTED; circ. 132,063.

I form: Strandboulevarden 130, 2100 Copenhagen Ø; tel. 39-17-20-00; fax 39-17-23-11; e-mail iform@iform.dk; internet www.iform.dk; f. 1987; 17 a year; publ. by Bonnier Pub. A/S; sport, health, nutrition, sex, psychology; Editor KAREN LYAGER HORVE; circ. 39,491.

Idé-nyt: Gl. Klausdalsbrovej 495, 2730 Herlev; tel. 44-53-40-00; fax 44-92-11-21; e-mail idenyt@idenyt.dk; internet www.idenyt.dk; f. 1973; 10 a year; free magazine (regional editions); homes and gardens; Editor-in-Chief ANNA-LISE AAEN; circ. 1,666,339.

Illustreret Videnskab: Strandboulevarden 130, 2100 Copenhagen Ø; tel. 39-17-20-00; fax 39-17-23-12; e-mail sebastian.relster@illvid.dk; internet www.illvid.dk; f. 1984; 15 a year; publ. by Bonnier Pub. A/S; popular science; Chief Editor SEBASTIAN RELSTER; circ. 53,724.

Kig Ind: Havneholmen 33, 1561 Copenhagen V; tel. 72-34-20-00; e-mail redaktionen@ki.aller.dk; internet www.kigind.com; weekly (Wed.); publ. by Aller Press A/S; fashion and celebrity news; Editor-in-Chief MICHAEL HANSEN; circ. 52,549.

Mad og Bolig: Havneholmen 33, 1561 Copenhagen V; tel. 72-34-27-61; e-mail mb@madogbolig.dk; internet www.madogbolig.dk; f. 1991; 10 a year; publ. by Aller Press A/S; gastronomy, wine, interiors and travel; Editor SØREN ANKER MADSEN; circ. 37,062.

Modemagasinet IN: Havneholmen 33, 1561 Copenhagen V; tel. 72-34-20-50; fax 72-34-20-03; e-mail redaktionen@in.dk; internet www.in.dk; monthly; publ. by Aller Press A/S; fashion; Editor-in-Chief CAMILLA LINDEMANN; circ. 32,614.

Motor: Firskovvej 32, 2800 Kgs Lyngby; tel. 45-27-07-07; fax 45-27-09-89; e-mail fdm@fdm.dk; internet www.fdm.dk; f. 1906; monthly; cars and motoring; Editor-in-Chief BO CHRISTIAN KOCH; circ. 236,888.

Samvirke: FDB, Ragnesminde, Vallensbæk Torvevej 9, 2620 Albertslund; tel. 39-47-00-00; fax 39-47-00-01; e-mail samvirke.redaktionen@fdb.dk; internet www.samvirke.dk; f. 1928; consumer monthly; Editor-in-Chief PIA THORSEN JACOBSEN; circ. 488,267 (2008/09).

Se og Hør: Havneholmen 33, 1561 Copenhagen V; tel. 72-34-20-00; e-mail redaktionen@seoghoer.dk; internet www.seoghoer.dk; f. 1940; weekly (Thur.); publ. by Aller Press A/S; news and TV; Editor-in-Chief KIM HENNINGSEN; circ. 158,875.

Søndag: Havneholmen 33, 1561 Copenhagen V; tel. 72-34-20-00; fax 72-34-20-05; e-mail soendag@soendag.dk; internet www.soendag.dk; f. 1921; weekly; publ. by Aller Press A/S; family magazine; Editor JOHNNY JOHANSEN; circ. 80,852.

Tipsbladet: Tomsgårdsvej 19, st. tv., 2400 Copenhagen NV; tel. 49-70-89-00; fax 49-70-88-30; e-mail redaktion@tipsbladet.dk; internet www.tipsbladet.dk; f. 1948; twice weekly; comprises *Tipsbladet Update* (Tues.) and *Tipsbladet Insigt* (Fri.); sport; Editor-in-Chief THOMAS FÆRCH KVIST; circ. 4,339 (*Tipsbladet Update*), 7,670 (*Tipsbladet Insigt*).

Ud og Se: DSB, Sølvgade 40, 1349 København K; tel. 70-13-14-15; e-mail udogse@dsb.dk; internet www.dsb.dk/Om-DSB/DSB-i-medierne/Ud-og-Se; monthly; travel; publ. by DSB (Danish State Railways); circ. 183,394.

Ude og Hjemme: Havneholmen 33, 1561 Copenhagen V; tel. 72-34-20-00; e-mail redaktionen@udeoghjemme.dk; internet www.udeoghjemme.dk; f. 1926; family weekly; publ. by Aller Press A/S; Editor-in-Chief KAJ ELGAARD; circ. 142,862.

Vi Unge: Havneholmen 33, 1561 Copenhagen V; tel. 72-34-20-00; e-mail redaktionen@viunge.dk; internet www.viunge.dk; 14 a year; publ. by Aller Press A/S; for teenage girls; Editor-in-Chief KATRINE MEMBORG; circ. 40,100.

SPECIALIST PERIODICALS

ABF-Nyt: Vester Farimagsgade 1, 8 sal, POB 239, 1501 Copenhagen V; tel. 33-86-28-30; fax 33-86-28-55; e-mail abf@abf-rep.dk; internet www.abf-rep.dk; for members of Andelsboligforeningernes Fællesrepræsentation (ABF, Co-operative Housing Association); 4 a year; Editor JAN HANSEN; circ. 92,931 (2009/10).

Aktuel Elektronik: Naverland 35, 2600 Glostrup; tel. 43-24-26-28; fax 43-24-26-26; e-mail rsh@techmedia.dk; internet www.techmedia.dk; 22 a year; computing and information technology; Editor-in-Chief ROLF SYLVESTER-HVID; circ. 6,502 (July–Dec. 2007).

Alt om Data: Sejrøgade 7-9, 2100 Copenhagen Ø; tel. 33-74-71-03; fax 33-74-71-91; e-mail redaktion@altomdata.dk; internet www.altomdata.dk; f. 1983; monthly; Editor-in-Chief LARS BENNETZEN; circ. 7,054.

Automatik: Glostrup Torv 6, 2600 Glostrup; tel. 43-46-67-00; fax 43-43-15-13; e-mail elo@folkebladet.dk; internet www.automatik.nu; engineering; 10 a year; Editor ELO THORNDAHL; circ. 20,901 (April–June 2010).

Bådnyt: Dortheavej 59, 2400 Copenhagen NV; tel. 32-71-12-00; e-mail redaktionen@baadnyt.dk; internet www.baadnyt.dk; monthly; boats and sailing; Editor MORTEN BRANDT; circ. 10,381 (July–Dec. 2008).

Beboerbladet: Studiestræde 50, 1554 København V; tel. 33-76-20-00; e-mail beboerbladet@bl.dk; internet www.beboerbladet.dk; quarterly; for tenants in public housing; Man. Editor BENT MADSEN; circ. 556,205 (2009/10).

Beredskab: Hedelykken 10, 2640 Hedehusene; tel. 35-24-00-00; fax 35-24-00-01; e-mail bf@beredskab.dk; internet www.beredskab.dk; f. 1934; 6 a year; civil protection and preparedness; publ. by the Danish Civil Protection League; circ. 13,059 (2009/10).

Bilsnak: Park Allé 355, 2605 Brøndby; tel. 43-28-82-00; fax 43-63-27-22; e-mail redaktion@bilsnak.dk; internet www.bilsnak.dk; f. 1976; 4 a year; cars; Editor SØS RIGHOLT ILUM; circ. 170,000 (2012).

Boligen: Studiestræde 50, 1554 Copenhagen V; tel. 33-76-20-00; fax 33-76-20-01; e-mail bl@bl.dk; internet www.bl.dk; 12 a year; publ. by Boligselskabernes Landsforening; housing asscns, architects; Editor GERT NIELSEN; circ. 30,714 (2009/10).

BygTek: Stationsparken 25, 2600 Glostrup; tel. 45-43-29-00; fax 45-43-13-28; e-mail redaktion@odsgard.dk; internet www.odsgard.dk; monthly; building and construction; Editor-in-Chief PETER ODSGARD; circ. 21,396 (2009/10).

Computerworld: IDG Danmark A/S, Hørkær 18, 2730 Herlev; tel. 77-30-03-00; fax 77-30-03-01; e-mail redaktionen@computerworld .dk; internet www.cw.dk; f. 1981; 22 a year; computing; Editor-in-Chief LINE ØRSKOV; circ. 9,097.

Cyklister: Dansk Cyklist Forbund, Rømersgade 5, 1362 Copenhagen K; tel. 33-32-31-21; fax 33-32-76-83; e-mail dcf@dcf.dk; internet www.dcf.dk; f. 1905; 6 a year; organ of Danish Cyclist Federation; Editor LOTTE MALENE RUBY; circ. 12,250.

DLG Nyt: Axelborg, Vesterbrogade 4A, 1503 Copenhagen V; tel. 33-69-87-00; fax 33-69-87-28; e-mail information@dlg.dk; internet www .dlg.dk; 11 a year; farming; Editor-in-Chief ELSE DAMSGAARD.

Diabetes: Rytterkasernen 1, 5000 Odense C; tel. 66-12-90-06; fax 65-91-49-08; e-mail df@diabetes.dk; internet www.diabetes.dk; f. 1940; 4 a year; diabetes; Editor HELEN H. HEIDEMANN; circ. 71,000 (2010/11).

Effektivt Landbrug: Odensevej 29, 5550 Langeskov; tel. 70-15-12-37; fax 70-15-12-47; e-mail redaktion@effektivtlandbrug.dk; internet www.landbrugnet.dk; 21 a year; farming; Editor BØJE ØSTERLUND; circ. 31,407 (July–Dec. 2006).

Finans: Applebys Pl. 5, POB 1960, 1411 Copenhagen K; tel. 32-96-46-00; e-mail cjo@finansforbundet.dk; internet www .finansforbundet.dk; 11 a year; for employees in the financial sector; Editor-in-Chief CARSTEN JØRGENSEN; circ. 54,731 (Jan.–June 2010).

Folkeskolen: Undervisere, Vandkunsten 12, POB 2139, 1015 Copenhagen K; tel. 33-69-63-00; fax 33-69-64-26; e-mail folkeskolen@dlf.org; internet www.folkeskolen.dk; f. 1883; 40 a year; teaching; publ. by Danish Teachers' Union; Editor HANNE B. JØRGENSEN; circ. 86,661 (Jan.–June 2010).

Havebladet: Frederikssundsvej 304A, 2700 Brønshøj; tel. 38-28-87-50; fax 32-28-83-50; e-mail info@kolonihave.dk; internet www .kolonihave.dk; 5 a year; publ. by Kolonihaveforbundet for Danmark; gardening; Editor PREBEN JACOBSEN; circ. 39,774 (2009/10).

Hunden: Parkvej 1, 2680 Solrød; tel. 56-18-81-00; fax 56-18-81-91; e-mail post@dansk-kennel-klub.dk; internet www .dansk-kennel-klub.dk; 10 a year; organ of Dansk Kennel Klub.

Ingelise's STRIKKE Magasin: Ved Søen 1, Jels, 6630 Rødding; tel. 70-11-70-80; fax 73-99-66-22; internet www.ingelise.dk; knitting; Editor-in-Chief INGELISE BJERRE.

Ingeniøren: Skelbækgade 4, POB 373, 1503 Copenhagen V; tel. 33-26-53-00; fax 33-26-53-01; e-mail redaktion@ing.dk; internet www .ing.dk; f. 1892; weekly engineers' magazine; Editor-in-Chief ARNE R. STEINMARK; circ. 72,049.

Jaeger: Hojnæsvej 56, 2610 Rødovre; tel. 88-88-75-00; fax 36-72-09-11; e-mail post@jaegerne.dk; internet www.jaegerforbundet.dk; monthly except July; hunting; Editor STIG TJELLEGAARD MØLLER; circ. 74,918.

Jern og Maskinindustrien: Marielundvej 46E, POB 358, 2730 Herlev; tel. 70-11-37-00; fax 44-85-10-13; e-mail jm@jernindustri.dk; internet www.jernindustri.dk; 36 a year; iron and metallic industries; owned by Ofin A/S; Editor-in-Chief HENRIK FOUGT; circ. 23,237 (2008/09).

Kommunalbladet: Weidekampsgade 8, 0900 Copenhagen C; tel. 33-30-49-00; fax 33-30-44-49; e-mail kommunalbladet@hk.dk; internet www.hk.dk/kommunal/kommunalbladet; 21 a year; municipal administration, civil servants; Editor LENE LUNDGAARD; circ. 59,864 (2008/09).

Komputer for Alle: Strandboulevarden 130, 2100 Copenhagen Ø; tel. 39-17-20-00; e-mail red@komputer.dk; internet www.komputer .dk; 18 a year; publ. by Bonnier Publications A/S; computers; Editor-in-Chief LEIF JONASSON; circ. 33,698.

Kvæg: Vesterbrogade 6D, 2. sal, 1620 Copenhagen V; tel. 33-39-47-00; fax 33-39-47-49; e-mail kvaeg@dlmedier.dk; monthly; for cattle breeders and dairy farmers; Editor HENNING LAEN SØRENSEN; circ. 4,675 (2009/10).

Lederne: Vermlandsgade 65, 2300 Copenhagen S; tel. 32-83-32-83; fax 32-83-32-84; e-mail lh@lederne.dk; internet www.lederne.dk; 11 a year; for managers; Editor-in-Chief ULLA BECHSGAARD; circ. 93,650 (2009/10).

Metal: Nyropsgade 38, 1602 Copenhagen V; tel. 33-63-20-00; fax 33-63-21-51; e-mail metal@danskmetal.dk; internet www.danskmetal .dk; 6 a year; metal industries; Editor-in-Chief MARINA HOFFMANN; circ. 135,902 (2009/10).

Spejdersnus: Det Danske Spejderkorps, Arsenalvej 10, 1436 Copenhagen K; tel. 32-64-00-50; fax 32-64-00-75; e-mail dds@dds .dk; internet www.dds.dk; 7 a year; organ of the Danish Guide and Scout Association; circ. 38,900.

Stat & Kommune Indkøb: Rundforbivej 2, 2950 Vedbæk; tel. 43-43-31-21; fax 45-65-05-99; e-mail saki@saki.dk; internet www.saki .dk; monthly; public works and administration; Editor DAN MORRISON; circ. 7,196 (2008/09).

Sygeplejersken: Skt Annæ Pl. 30, POB 1084, 1008 Copenhagen K; tel. 33-15-15-55; e-mail redaktionen@dsr.dk; internet www .sygeplejersken.dk; 14 a year; nursing; Editor-in-Chief SIGURD NISSEN-PETERSEN; circ.73,367.

Ugeskrift for Læger: Kristianiagade 12, 2100 Copenhagen Ø; tel. 35-44-85-00; fax 35-44-85-02; e-mail ufl@dadl.dk; internet www .ugeskriftet.dk; weekly; medical; Editor-in-Chief TORBEN KITAJ; circ. 24,373.

NEWS AGENCY

Ritzaus Bureau I/S: Store Kongensgade 14, 1264 Copenhagen K; tel. 33-30-00-00; fax 33-30-00-01; e-mail ritzau@ritzau.dk; internet www.ritzau.dk; f. 1866; general, financial and commercial news; owned by all Danish newspapers; Chair. ERIK BJERAGER; Man. Editor LARS VESTERLØKKE.

PRESS ASSOCIATIONS

Danske Dagblades Forening (Danish Newspaper Publishers' Association): Pressens Hus, Skindergade 7, 1159 Copenhagen K; tel. 33-97-40-00; fax 33-14-23-25; e-mail ddf@danskedagblade.dk; internet www.danskedagblade.dk; f. 1968; comprises managers and editors-in-chief of all newspapers; general representative for the Danish press; CEO EBBE DAL.

Danske Specialmedier (Association of the Danish Specialized Press): Pressens Hus, Skindergade 7, 1159 Copenhagen K; tel. 33-97-40-00; fax 33-91-26-70; e-mail specialmedierne@specialmedierne .dk; internet www.specialmedierne.dk; f. 1905; fmrly Dansk Fagpresse; 362 mems; Chair. CHRISTIAN KIERKEGAARD.

Dansk Magasinpresses Udgiverforening (Danish Magazine Publishers' Association): Pressens Hus, Skindergrade 7, 1159 Copenhagen K; tel. 33-11-88-44; fax 33-15-01-86; e-mail dmu-mags@ internet.dk; internet www.dmu-mags.dk; f. 1949; represents 90% of magazine publishers; Chair. PÅL THORE KROSBY; Dir JOHN KRISTENSEN.

Publishers

Aarhus Universitetsforlag: Langelandsgade 177, 8200 Aarhus N; tel. 87-15-39-63; fax 87-15-38-75; e-mail unipress@au.dk; internet www.unipress.dk; reference, non-fiction and educational; Man. Dir CLAES HVIDBAK.

Forlaget åløkke A/S: Porskærvej 15, Nim, 8740 Brædstrup; tel. 75-67-11-19; fax 75-67-10-74; e-mail alokke@get2net.dk; internet www .alokke.dk; f. 1977; educational, children's books, audio-visual and other study aids; Man. Dir BERTIL TOFT HANSEN.

Alrune A/S: Søndergade 31, 5620 Glamsbjerg; tel. 64-72-27-50; fax 64-72-28-50; e-mail alrune@alrune.com; internet www.alrune.com; textbooks; Dir GORM NIELSEN.

Akademisk Forlag A/S (Danish University Press): Vognmagergade 11, 2. sal, 1148 Copenhagen K; tel. 33-43-40-80; fax 33-43-40-99; e-mail info@akademisk.dk; internet www.akademisk.dk; f. 1962; history, health, linguistics, university textbooks, educational materials; Dir EBBE DAM NIELSEN.

Forlaget Apostrof ApS: Berggreensgade 24, POB 2580, 2100 Copenhagen Ø; tel. 39-20-84-20; fax 39-20-84-53; e-mail apostrof@ apostrof.dk; internet www.apostrof.dk; f. 1980; psychotherapy and contemporary psychology, fiction and non-fiction for children; Publrs MIA THESTRUP, OLE THESTRUP.

Arkitektens Forlag: Pasteursvej 14, 6. sal, 1799 Copenhagen K; tel. 32-83-69-70; fax 32-83-69-41; e-mail arkfo@arkfo.dk; internet www.arkfo.dk; f. 1949; architecture, planning; Man. Dir SANNE WALL-GREMSTRUP.

Peter Asschenfeldt's nye Forlag A/S: Ny Adelgade 6–10, 1104 Copenhagen K; tel. 33-37-07-60; fax 33-91-03-04; e-mail asschenfeldt@dk-online.dk; fiction; Publr PETER ASSCHENFELDT.

Thomas Bloms Forlag ApS: Skovenggaardsvej 8, 9490 Pandrup; tel. 98-24-85-25; fax 98-24-80-60; e-mail thomas@thomasblom.dk; internet www.thomasblom.dk; fiction, non-fiction, children's books, talking books; Publrs CONNIE BLOM, THOMAS BLOM.

Bogans Forlag: Stenvej 25 A, 8270 Højbjerg; tel. 86-27-65-00; fax 86-27-65-37; e-mail bogan@post.tele.dk; internet bogan.dk; f. 1974; imprint of Forlaget Hovedland; general paperbacks, popular science, non-fiction, humour, health; Publr EVAN BOGAN.

Borgens Forlag A/S: Mosedalvej 15, 3. sal, 2500 Valby, Copenhagen; tel. 36-15-36-15; fax 36-15-36-16; e-mail post@borgen.dk; internet www.borgen.dk; f. 1948; fiction, poetry, children's books, humour, general non-fiction; Man. Dir NIELS BORGEN.

Carit Andersens Forlag A/S: Kirke Værløsevej 38, 3500 Værløse; tel. 35-43-62-22; fax 35-43-51-51; e-mail info@caritandersen.dk; internet www.caritandersen.dk; Publr ERIK ALBRECHTSEN.

Forlaget Carlsen A/S: Vognmagergade 11, 1148 Copenhagen K; tel. 33-69-50-00; fax 36-16-04-27; e-mail carlsen@carlsen.dk; internet www.carlsen.dk; children's books; Man. Dir JENS TRASBORG.

Cicero (Chr. Erichsens Forlag A/S): Ørnevej 45, 2400 Copenhagen NV; tel. 33-16-03-08; fax 33-16-03-07; e-mail niels@cicero.dk; internet www.cicero.dk; f. 1902; fiction, non-fiction, art, culture; Publr ANNE SØNDERGAARD.

DA-Forlag/Dansk Arbejdsgiverforening: Vester Voldgade 113, 1790 Copenhagen V; tel. 33-38-92-24; fax 33-91-09-32; e-mail ehj@da.dk; internet www.daforlag.dk; non-fiction and reference; Dir. ELVIND HOLCK JENSEN.

Dafolo A/S: Suderbovej 22–24, 9900 Frederikshavn; tel. 96-20-66-66; fax 98-42-97-11; e-mail dafolo@dafolo.dk; internet www.dafolo.dk; educational books; Publr MICHAEL SCHELDE.

Dansk BiblioteksCenter A/S (DBC): Tempovej 7–11, 2750 Ballerup; tel. 44-86-77-77; fax 44-86-76-93; e-mail dbc@dbc.dk; internet www.dbc.dk; f. 1991; bibliographic data, information services; CEO MOGENS BRABRAND JENSEN.

Dansk Psykologisk Forlag: Knabrostraede 3, 1st Floor, 2830 Virum; tel. 45-46-00-50; e-mail info@dpf.dk; internet www.dpf.dk; educational books, health, psychology; Man. Dir HENRIK SKOVDAHL.

Det Danske Bibelselskab/Det Kongelige Vajsenhus' Forlag: Frederiksborggade 50, 1360 Copenhagen K; tel. 33-12-78-35; fax 33-93-21-50; e-mail bibelselskabet@bibelselskabet.dk; internet www.bibelselskabet.dk; bibles, religious and liturgical books, children's books; Dir TINE LINDHARDT.

Dansklæreforeningens: Rathsacksvej 7, 1862 Frederiksberg C; tel. 33-79-00-11; fax 33-27-60-79; e-mail dansklf@dansklf.dk; internet www.dansklf.dk; art, culture, school books, non-fiction; Editorial Dir CHARLOTTE SVENDSTRUP.

Forlaget Flachs: Holte Midtpunkt 20, 2. sal, 2840 Holte; tel. 45-42-48-30; fax 45-42-48-29; e-mail flachs@flachs.dk; internet www.flachs.dk; f. 1986; fiction, non-fiction, reference, educational and children's books; Publrs ALLAN FLACHS, ANETTE FLACHS.

Forlaget Palle Fogtdal A/S: Østergade 22, 1100 Copenhagen K; tel. 33-15-39-15; fax 33-93-35-05; e-mail pallefogtdal@pallefogtdal.dk; Danish history, photography; Man. Dir PALLE FOGTDAL.

Forum: Købmagergade 62, 1019 Copenhagen K; tel. 33-41-18-00; fax 33-41-18-01; f. 1940; history, fiction, biographies, quality paperbacks and children's books; Man. Dir TORBEN MADSEN.

Fremad: Købmagergade 62, POB 2252, 1150 Copenhagen K; tel. 33-41-18-00; fax 33-41-18-01; e-mail bogsalg@rosinante-co.dk; f. 1912; general trade, fiction, non-fiction, juveniles, reference, children's books.

G.E.C. Gad Forlag A/S: Klosterstræde 9, 1157 Copenhagen K; tel. 77-66-60-00; fax 77-66-60-01; e-mail reception@gads-forlag.dk; internet www.gads-forlag.dk; f. 1855; biographies, history, reference, educational materials; Publ. Dir ULRIK HVILSHØJ.

Gyldendalske Boghandel, Nordisk Forlag A/S (Gyldendal): Klareboderne 3, 1001 Copenhagen K; tel. 33-75-55-55; fax 33-75-55-56; e-mail gyldendal@gyldendal.dk; internet www.gyldendal.dk; f. 1770; fiction, non-fiction, reference books, paperbacks, children's books, textbooks; Man. Dir STIG ANDERSEN.

Haase & Søns Forlag A/S: Løvstræde 8, 2nd Floor, 1152 Copenhagen K; tel. 33-14-41-75; fax 33-11-59-59; e-mail haase@haase.dk; internet www.haase.dk; f. 1877; educational books, audio-visual aids, non-fiction; imprints: Natur og Harmoni, Rasmus Navers Forlag; Man. Dir MICHAEL HAASE.

Edition Wilhelm Hansen A/S: Bornholmsgade 1, 1266 Copenhagen K; tel. 33-11-78-88; fax 33-14-81-78; e-mail ewh@ewh.dk; internet www.ewh.dk; f. 1857; music books, school and educational books; Man. Dir TINE BIRGER CHRISTENSEN.

Hernovs Forlag: Nørrebakken 25, 2820 Gentofte; tel. 32-96-33-14; fax 32-96-04-46; e-mail admin@hernov.dk; internet www.hernov.dk; f. 1941; fiction, non-fiction, classic literature and children's; Man. Dir ELSE HERNOV.

Holkenfeldt 3: Fuglevadsvej 71, 2800 Lyngby; tel. 45-93-12-21; fax 45-93-82-41; fiction, non-fiction, reference, sport, humour; Publr KAY HOLKENFELDT.

Høst & Søns Forlag: Købmagergade 62, POB 2252, 1019 Copenhagen K; tel. 33-41-18-00; fax 33-41-18-01; e-mail info@rosinante-co.dk; internet www.hoest.dk; f. 1836; fiction, crafts and hobbies, languages, books on Denmark, children's books; Man. Dir TINE SMEDEGAARD ANDERSEN.

Forlaget Hovedland: Stenvej 25A, 8270 Højbjerg; tel. 86-27-65-00; fax 86-27-65-37; e-mail mail@hovedland.dk; internet www.hovedland.dk; fiction, non-fiction, environment, sport, health, crafts; Publr STEEN PIPER.

Karnov Group Denmark A/S: Nytorv 5, 1450 Copenhagen K; tel. 33-74-07-00; fax 33-12-16-36; e-mail post.dk@karnovgroup.com; internet www.karnovgroup.dk; print and online publications for legal, auditing and accounting professionals; Man. Dir NEIL STORY.

Forlaget Klematis A/S: Østre Skovvej 1, 8240 Risskov; tel. 86-17-54-55; fax 86-17-59-59; e-mail klematis@klematis.dk; internet www.klematis.dk; f. 1987; fiction, non-fiction, crafts, children's books; Dir CLAUS DALBY.

Forlaget Per Kofod ApS: Strandgade 32A, 3000 Helsingør; tel. 33-32-70-27; e-mail info@per-kofod.com; internet www.per-kofod.com; f. 1986; fiction, non-fiction, art and culture; Publr PER KOFOD.

Krak: Sydmarken 44A, 2860 Søborg; tel. 88-38-38-00; fax 88-38-38-10; e-mail krak@krak.dk; internet www.krak.dk; f. 1770; business information, maps and yearbooks; Dir OVE LETH-SØRENSEN.

Egmont Lademann A/S: Gerdasgade 37, 2500 Valby; tel. 36-15-66-00; fax 36-44-11-62; f. 1954; non-fiction, reference.

Lindhardt og Ringhof A/S: Vognmagergade 11, 1148 Copenhagen K; tel. 33-69-50-00; fax 33-69-50-01; e-mail info@lindhardtogringhof.dk; internet www.lindhardtogringhof.dk; f. 1971; merged with Aschehoug Dansk Forlag A/S in 2007; general fiction and non-fiction; imprints: Akademisk Forlag, Børsens Forlag, Sesam, Athene, Alinea, Forlag Malling Beck, Alfabeta, Carlsen, Aschehoug; Man. Dir ANNETTE WAD.

Forlagsgruppen Lohse: Korskærvej 25, 7000 Fredericia; tel. 75-93-44-55; fax 75-92-42-75; e-mail info@lohse.dk; internet www.lohse.dk; f. 1868; imprints: Credo, Fokal, Kolon, Korskær, Lohse; religion, children's books, biographies, devotional novels; Dir THORKILD HØJVIG; Editorial Dir THOMAS B. MIKKELSEN.

Forlaget Lotus: Bryggervangen 76, 2100 Copenhagen Ø; tel. 29-61-20-01; e-mail fialotus@post7.tele.dk; internet www.forlagetlotus.dk; management, health, religion, the occult, educational; Publr FINN ANDERSEN.

Magnus Informatik A/S: Palægade 4, POB 9026, 1022 Copenhagen K; tel. 70-20-33-14; fax 33-96-01-01; e-mail magnus@magnus.dk; internet www.magnus.dk; f. 1962; guidebooks, journals, law; Man. Dir MORTEN ARNBERG.

Medicinsk Forlag ApS: Rønnebærvej 20, 4500 Nykøbing Sj; tel. and fax 47-17-65-92; e-mail anni@medicinskforlag.dk; internet www.medicinskforlag.dk; astrology, medical and scientific books; Man. Dir ANNI LINDELØV.

Forlaget Modtryk: Anholtsgade 4–6, 8000 Århus C; tel. 87-31-76-00; fax 87-31-76-01; e-mail forlaget@modtryk.dk; internet www.modtryk.dk; f. 1972; children's and school books, fiction, thrillers and non-fiction; Man. Dir ILSE NØRR.

Nyt Nordisk Forlag-Arnold Busck A/S: Landemærket 11, 5. sal, 1119 Copenhagen K; tel. 33-73-35-75; fax 33-73-35-85; e-mail nnf@nytnordiskforlag.dk; internet www.nytnordiskforlag.dk; f. 1896; textbooks, school books, guidebooks, fiction and non-fiction; Man. Dir JESPER T. FENSVIG; Dir JOAKIM WERNER.

Nyt Teknisk Forlag A/S: Vigerslev Allé 18, 2500 Valby; tel. 63-15-17-00; fax 63-15-17-33; e-mail info@nyttf.dk; internet www.nyttf.dk; f. 1948; owned by Erhvervsskolernes Forlag; technical books, reference, educational, science, popular science; Publr HENRIK LARSEN.

Hans Reitzels Forlag A/S: Sjæleboderne 2, 1122 Copenhagen K; tel. 33-38-28-00; fax 33-38-28-08; e-mail hrf@hansreitzel.dk; internet www.hansreitzel.dk; f. 1949; education, philosophy, psychology, sociology; Publ. Dir HANNE SALOMONSEN.

Forlaget Rhodos: Holtegaard, Hørsholmvej 17, 3050 Humlebæk; tel. 32-54-30-20; fax 32-54-30-22; e-mail rhodos@rhodos.dk; internet www.rhodos.dk; f. 1959; university books, art, science, fiction, poetry; Dir RUBEN BLAEDEL.

Samlerens Forlag A/S: Købmagergade 62, POB 2252, 1019 Copenhagen K; tel. 33-41-18-00; fax 33-41-18-01; e-mail samleren@samleren.dk; internet www.samleren.dk; Danish and foreign fiction, contemporary history and politics, biographies; Man. Dir TORBEN MADSEN.

Scandinavia: Drejervej 15, 3. sal, 2400 Copenhagen NV; tel. 35-31-03-30; fax 35-31-03-34; e-mail knud@scanpublishing.dk; internet www.scanpublishing.dk; f. 1973; children's books, religion, Hans Christian Andersen; Dir JØRGEN VIUM OLESEN.

Det Schønbergske Forlag A/S: Landemærket 5, 1119 Copenhagen K; tel. 33-73-35-85; fax 33-73-35-86; e-mail schoenberg@nytnordiskforlag.dk; f. 1857; division of Nyt Nordisk Forlag-Arnold Busck A/S; fiction, humour, psychology, biography, children's books, paperbacks, textbooks.

Strandbergs Forlag ApS: Skodsborgparken 12, 2942 Skodsborg; tel. 45-89-47-60; fax 45-89-47-01; e-mail niels@strandbergsforlag.dk; internet www.strandbergsforlag.dk; f. 1861; cultural history, travel; Publr NIELS NØRGAARD.

Tiderne Skifter: Læderstræde 5, 1. sal, 1201 Copenhagen K; tel. 33-18-63-90; fax 33-18-63-91; e-mail tiderneskifter@tiderneskifter.dk; internet www.tiderneskifter.dk; f. 1973; fiction, sexual and cultural politics, psychology, science, religion, arts; Man. Dir CLAUS CLAUSEN.

Unitas Forlag: Peter Bangs Vej 1D, 2000 Frederiksberg; tel. 36-16-64-81; fax 38-11-64-81; e-mail info@unitasforlag.dk; internet www.unitasforlag.dk; religion, fiction, education, children's books; Man. HENRIK NIELSEN.

Forlaget Vindrose A/S: Valbygaardsvej 33, 2500 Valby; tel. 36-15-36-15; fax 36-15-36-16; e-mail post@borgen.dk; internet www.borgen.dk; f. 1980; acquired by Borgens Forlag in 1989; general trade, fiction and non-fiction; Man. Dir NIELS BORGEN.

Forlag Wiboltts: POB 2587, 2100 Copenhagen Ø; tel. 31-39-11-21; e-mail info@wiboltt.com; internet wiboltt.com; spirituality.

Wisby & Wilkens og Mikro: Vesterled 45, 8300 Odder; tel. 70-23-46-22; fax 70-23-47-22; e-mail mikro@wisby-wilkens.com; f. 1986; children's books, crafts, fiction, health, humour, science, religion; imprint: Mikro (drama, poetry, humour); Publr JACOB WISBY.

PUBLISHERS' ASSOCIATION

Forlæggerforeningen: Børsen, 1217 Copenhagen K; tel. 33-15-66-88; fax 33-15-65-88; e-mail danishpublishers@danishpublishers.dk; internet www.danskeforlag.dk; f. 1837; formerly Den danske Forlæggerforening; 64 mems, 3 associate mems; Chair. PER HEDEMAN; Man. Dir CHRISTINE BØDTCHER-HANSEN.

Broadcasting and Communications

TELECOMMUNICATIONS

Major Service Providers

Hi3G Denmark ApS (3 DK): Scandiagade 8, 2450 Copenhagen SV; tel. 33-33-01-35; fax 33-33-01-55; internet www.3.dk; f. 2003; mobile cellular and other telecommunications services; 60% owned by Hutchison Whampoa Ltd (Hong Kong) and 40% owned by Investor AB (Sweden); CEO MORTEN CHRISTIANSEN.

TDC A/S: Teglholmsgade 1–3, 0900 Copenhagen; tel. 66-63-76-80; fax 33-15-75-70; e-mail investorrelations@tdc.dk; internet www.tdc.dk; f. 1995 as Tele Danmark A/S; present name adopted 2000; fixed-line and mobile cellular telecommunications, digital television and broadband internet access; fmrly state-owned telecommunications co; transferred to private ownership 1998; Chair. VAGN OVE SØRENSEN; Pres. and CEO HENRIK POULSEN.

Telenor A/S: Frederikskaj, 1780 Copenhagen V; tel. 72-10-01-00; fax 72-12-70-70; internet www.telenor.dk; f. 2009 following the merger of Sonofon (f. 1991) and Cybercity (f. 1995); subsidiary of Telenor ASA (Norway); mobile cellular telecommunications services; Man. Dir JON ERIK HAUG; 1.7m. subscribers (2008).

Telia Nattjanster Norden A/B (Telia DK): Holmbladsgade 139, 2300 Copenhagen S; tel. 82-33-70-00; fax 82-33-70-09; internet www.telia.dk; subsidiary of Telia Sonera AB (Sweden); f. 1995; fixed-line and mobile cellular telecommunications, broadband internet access; Man. Dir SØREN ABILDGAARD.

BROADCASTING

Regulatory Authority

Kulturstyrelsen (Danish Agency for Culture): H. C. Andersens Blvd 2, 1553 Copenhagen V; tel. 33-73-33-73; fax 33-73-33-72; e-mail post@kulturstyrelsen.dk; internet www.kulturstyrelsen.dk; f. 2012 by merger of the Danish Arts Agency, the Heritage Agency of Denmark and the Danish Agency for Libraries and Media; under Ministry of Culture; Dir JENS THORHAUGE.

Radio

Digital audio broadcasting (DAB) began in Denmark in 2002, with 10 transmitters in operation covering the main cities of Copenhagen, Aarhus, Odense and Aalborg. The transmitter network has since expanded to cover 90% of the population. The main DAB operator is DR RADIO, which offers eight music channels (DR Boogieradio, DR Dansktop, DR Hit, DR Jazz, DR Klassisk, DR Pop DK, DR Rock and P5000), two news channels (DR Erhverv, DR Nyheder and DR Politik) and a dedicated children's channel (DR Oline), as well as simulcasts of P1, P2, P3, P4 and P5). The private operators, Radio 100FM, Radio Soft and Nova FM, also offer DAB services.

DR RADIO: DR Byen, Emil Holms Kanal 20, 0999 Copenhagen C; tel. 35-20-30-40; fax 35-20-26-44; e-mail drkommunikation@dr.dk; internet www.dr.dk; fmrly Danmarks Radio; independent statutory corpn; Dir-Gen. MARIA RØRBYE RØNN; Exec. Dir of DR Media MIKAEL KAMBER; operates 4 FM stations, 17 DAB stations and nearly 30 channels on the internet

The four FM stations are as follows:

P1: broadcasts for 110 hours per week on FM, in Danish (Greenlandic programmes weekly); simulcast on DAB; Head FINN SLUMSTRUP.

P2: specializes in classical music, jazz, opera and culture, broadcasts on FM for 45 hours per week nationally, in Danish, as well as regional and special (for foreign workers) programmes; Head OLE DAMGAARD.

P3: popular music channel, broadcasts on FM for 24 hours per day, in Danish; also broadcasts news in Greenlandic, Faroese and English; simulcast on DAB; Head OLE DAMGAARD.

P4: popular music, news and regional programmes; 11 regional stations; broadcasts on FM for about 97 hours per week; simulcast on DAB; Head OLE DAMGAARD.

Radio 100: Rådhuspladsen 45, 1550 Copenhagen V; tel. 33-37-89-00; fax 33-37-89-67; e-mail info@radio100.dk; internet www.radio100.dk; f. 2003; commercial channel, specializing in popular music; owned by Talpa Radio International (Netherlands); Dir BJØRN KRISTENSEN.

There are also some 250 operators licensed for low-power FM transmissions of local and community radio, etc.

Television

Digital transmission in Denmark began in March 2006, and the analogue network ceased transmission in November 2009.

Canal Digital Danmark: Stationsparken 25, 2600 Glostrup; tel. 70-13-19-19; fax 70-27-27-61; e-mail cma@canaldigital.dk; internet www.canaldigital.dk; f. 1997; owned by Telenor ASA (Norway); operates 11 TV channels; Man. Dir JARL SØRDERMAN.

DR TV: DR Byen, Emil Holms Kanal 20, 0999 Copenhagen C; tel. 35-20-30-40; fax 35-20-26-44; e-mail dr-kommunikation@dr.dk; internet www.dr.dk; operates 2 services, DR 1 and DR 2; operates 4 more TV channels; Dir-Gen. MARIA RØRBYE RØNN; Dir of Programmes MIKAEL KAMBER; Exec. Dir of DR Media MIKAEL KAMBER.

DR 1: terrestrial television channel; Controller (vacant).

DR 2: satellite television channel; Controller (vacant).

TV 2 | DANMARK A/S: Rugaardsvej 25, 5100 Odense C; tel. 65-91-91-91; fax 65-91-33-22; e-mail tv2@tv2.dk; internet www.tv2.dk; began broadcasts in 1988; Denmark's first national commercial and public service TV station; changed to a state share co in 2003; part-privatization pending; Dir-Gen. MERETE ELDRUP; Dir of Programmes PALLE STRØM.

TV3 Viasat: Wildersgade 8, 1408 Copenhagen K; tel. 77-30-55-00; fax 77-30-55-10; e-mail tv3@viasat.dk; internet www.tv3.dk; began broadcasts in 1987; reaches 71% of the country via cable and satellite; Man. Dir LARS BO ANDERSEN; Dir of Programmes HENRIK RAVN.

Broadcasting Association

Forenede Danske Antenneanlæg (FDA) (Danish Cable Television Asscn): Bøgehus, Annebergparken 21, POB 151, 4500 Nykøbing Sjælland; tel. 59-96-17-00; fax 59-96-17-17; e-mail fda@fda.dk; internet www.fda.dk; f. 1983; organizes 310 local networks, representing c. 400,000 connected households; Chair. CARSTEN KARLSEN.

Finance

(cap. = capital; res = reserves; dep. = deposits; m. = million; brs = branches; amounts in kroner, unless otherwise indicated)

BANKING

The first Danish commercial bank was founded in 1846. In 1975 restrictions on savings banks were lifted, giving commercial and savings banks equal rights and status, and restrictions on the establishment of full branches of foreign banks were removed. In 1988 all remaining restrictions on capital movements were ended. In 2009 there were 132 banks and savings banks in operation. All banks are under government supervision, and public representation is obligatory on all bank supervisory boards.

Supervisory Authority

Finanstilsynet (Danish Financial Supervisory Authority): Århusgade 110 2100, Copenhagen Ø; tel. 33-55-82-82; fax 33-55-82-00; e-mail finanstilsynet@ftnet.dk; internet www.ftnet.dk; f. 1988; agency of the Ministry of Business and Growth; Man. Dir ULRIK NØDGAARD.

Central Bank

Danmarks Nationalbank: Havnegade 5, 1093 Copenhagen K; tel. 33-63-63-63; fax 33-63-71-03; e-mail nationalbanken@nationalbanken.dk; internet www.nationalbanken.dk; f. 1818; name changed as above 1936; self-governing; sole right of issue; conducts monetary policy; administers reserves of foreign exchange; cap. 50m., res 60,425.6m., dep. 410,247.1m. (Dec. 2009); Chair. of the Bd of Govs NILS BERNSTEIN; Govs TORBEN NIELSEN, JENS THOMSEN.

Commercial Banks

Alm. Brand Bank: Midtermolen 7, 2100 Copenhagen Ø; tel. 35-47-47-47; fax 35-47-47-35; e-mail bank@almbrand.dk; internet www.almbrand.dk; f. 1983; present name adopted 2003; cap. 1,021m., dep. 15,140.2m. (Dec. 2010); Chair. JØRGEN HESSELBJERG MIKKELSEN; Pres. and CEO SØREN BOE MORTENSEN; 25 brs.

Amagerbanken: Amagerbrogade 25, 2300 Copenhagen S; tel. 32-66-66-66; fax 32-54-45-34; e-mail international@amagerbanken.dk; internet www.amagerbanken.dk; f. 1903; part of BankNordik; owned by the Danish Financial Stability Company; cap. 665m., res 2m., dep. 28,144m. (Dec. 2009); Chair. N. E. NIELSEN; CEO and Man. Dir JØRGEN BRÆNDSTRUP; 25 brs.

Arbejdernes Landsbank A/S: Vesterbrogade 5, 1502 Copenhagen V; tel. 38-48-48-48; fax 38-48-50-50; e-mail info@al-bank.dk; internet www.al-bank.dk; f. 1919; present name acquired 1938; cap. 300m., res 445.2m., dep. 23,823.3m. (Dec. 2010); Chair. POUL ERIK SKOV CHRISTENSEN; Man. Dir GERT R. JONASSEN; 66 brs.

Danske Andelskassers Bank A/S: Baneskellet 1, Hammershøj, 8830 Tjele; tel. 87-99-30-00; fax 87-99-30-98; e-mail foreign@dabank.dk; internet www.dabank.dk; f. 1970; owned by 22 co-operative banks; cap. 125m., res 113.6m., dep. 4,224.9m. (Dec. 2010); Chair. JAKOB FASTRUP; CEO JAN PEDERSEN; 20 brs.

Danske Bank A/S: Holmens Kanal 2–12, 1092 Copenhagen K; tel. 33-44-00-00; fax 70-12-10-80; e-mail danskebank@danskebank.com; internet www.danskebank.com; f. 1871 as Danske Landmandsbank; merged with Copenhagen Handelsbank and Provinsbanken in 1990 to form Den Danske Bank A/S; present name adopted 2000; cap. 6,988m., res –1,466m., dep. 1,613,330m. (Dec. 2010); Chair. OLE ANDERSEN; CEO EIVIND KOLDING.

Jyske Bank A/S: Vestergade 8–16, 8600 Silkeborg; tel. 89-89-89-89; fax 89-89-19-99; e-mail jyskebank@jyskebank.dk; internet www.jyskebank.dk; f. 1967 by merger of Silkeborg Bank, Kjellerup Bank, Kjellerup Handels- og Landbrugsbank and Handels- og Landbrugsbanken i Silkeborg; cap. 648m., res 299.3m., dep. 175,960.3m. (Dec. 2010); Chair. SVEN BUHRKALL RØDDING; CEO ANDERS DAM; 124 brs.

Nordea Bank Danmark A/S: Christiansbro, Strandgade 3, 0900 Copenhagen C; tel. 33-33-33-33; fax 33-33-63-63; internet www.nordea.dk; f. 1990 as Unibank A/S by merger of Andelsbanken, Privatbanken and SDS; in 1999 the bank merged with the insurance co Tryg-Baltica Forsikring A/S, but remained part of the Unidanmark A/S group, which became part of Nordea Group (Finland) in 2000; acquired Fionia Bank A/S in 2010; cap. 5,000m., res 3,342m., dep. 669,135m. (Dec. 2010); Chair. ARI KAPERI; 344 brs.

Nordjyske Bank A/S: Jernbanegade 4–8, POB 701, 9900 Frederikshavn; tel. 96-33-50-00; fax 96-33-50-03; e-mail email@nordjyskebank.dk; internet www.nordjyskebank.dk; f. 2002 by merger of Egnsbank Nord A/S and Vendsyssel Bank A/S; cap. 80.4m., res 37.3m., dep. 8,204.2m. (Dec. 2010); Chair. HANS JØRGEN KAPTAIN; Dirs CLAUS ANDERSEN, MIKAEL JAKOBSEN; 17 brs.

Nørresundby Bank A/S: Torvet 4, 9400 Nørresundby; tel. 98-70-37-00; fax 98-70-37-19; e-mail post@nrsbank.dk; internet www.nrsbank.dk; f. 1898 as Banken for Nörresundby og Omegn A.S.; name changed as above 1976; cap. 46m., res 33.4m., dep. 8,300.9m. (Dec. 2010); Chair. MADS HVOLBY; Man. Dirs ANDREAS RASMUSSEN, FINN ØST ANDERSSON; 19 brs.

Nykredit Bank A/S: Kalvebod Brygge 1–3, 1780 Copenhagen V; tel. 70-10-90-00; fax 70-10-90-01; e-mail kundeservice@nykredit.dk; internet www.nykreditbank.dk; f. 1986 as Sankt Annae Bank A/S; present name adopted 1994; mem. of Nykredit Group; cap. 6,045m., dep. 149,489m. (Dec. 2010); Chair. STEEN E. CHRISTENSEN; Group Chief Exec. PETER ENGBERG JENSEN.

Ringkjøbing Landbobank A/S: Torvet 1, 6950 Ringkøbing; tel. 97-32-11-66; fax 97-32-18-18; e-mail post@landbobanken.dk; internet www.landbobanken.dk; f. 1886; cap. 25.2m., res 61.2m., dep. 11,661.7m. (Dec. 2010); Chair. JENS KJELDSEN; Gen. Mans BENT NAUR KRISTENSEN, JOHN BULL FISKER; 16 brs.

Sparbank A/S: Adelgade 8, POB 505, 7800 Skive; tel. 96-16-16-16; fax 96-16-16-15; e-mail info@sparbank.dk; internet www.sparbank.dk; f. 1857; fmrly Sparbank Vest, present name adopted 2007; cap. 120.5m., dep. 8,346m. (Dec. 2010); Chair. ALEX NIELSEN; CEO KARL THOLSTRUP; 22 brs.

Sydbank A/S: Peberlyk 4, POB 169, 6200 Aabenraa; tel. 74-37-37-37; fax 74-36-35-49; e-mail info@sydbank.dk; internet www.sydbank.com; f. 1970 by merger of 4 regional banks in southern Jutland; cap. 742m., res 643m., dep. 116,060m. (Dec. 2010); Chair. ANDERS THOUSTRUP; CEO CARSTEN ANDERSEN; 112 brs.

vestjyskBANK A/S: Torvet 4–5, 7620 Lemvig; tel. 96-63-20-00; fax 96-63-21-39; internet www.vestjyskbank.dk; f. 2008 by merger of vestjyskBANK A/S and Ringkjøbing Bank A/S; cap. 125m., res 31m., dep. 27,323m. (Dec. 2009); Chair. ANDERS BECH; Man. Dir FRANK KRISTENSEN; 18 brs.

Savings Banks

Lån & Spar Bank A/S: Højbro Pl. 9–11, POB 2117, 1014 Copenhagen K; tel. 33-78-20-00; fax 33-78-23-09; e-mail lsb@lsb.dk; internet www.lsb.dk; f. 1880; present name adopted 1990; cap. 271m., res 60.7m., dep. 8,614.6m. (Dec. 2010); Chair. ANDERS BECH; Man. Dir and CEO FRANK KRISTENSEN; 16 brs.

Spar Nord Bank A/S: Skelagervej 15, POB 162, 9100 Ålborg; tel. 96-34-40-00; fax 96-34-45-60; e-mail sparnord@sparnord.dk; internet www.sparnord.dk; f. 1967; name changed as above 1998 following merger; cap. 570.7m., res 504.7m., dep. 46,188.6m. (Dec. 2010); Chair. STEFFEN NØRGAARD; CEO BJARNE DAMM JOHANSEN; 80 brs.

Bankers' Organization

Finansrådet: Finansrådets Hus, Amaliegade 7, 1256 Copenhagen K; tel. 33-70-10-00; fax 33-93-02-60; e-mail mail@finansraadet.dk; internet www.finansraadet.dk; f. 1990; 130 mems; Chair. PETER STRAARUP; Man. Dir JØRGEN A. HORWITZ.

STOCK EXCHANGE

NASDAQ OMX Nordic Exchange Copenhagen: Nikolaj Pl. 6, POB 1040, 1007 Copenhagen K; tel. 33-93-33-66; fax 33-12-86-13; internet www.nasdaqomx.com; f. 2005 by merger of Københavns Fondsbørs and OMX (Sweden); became part of OMX Nordic Exchange with Helsinki (Finland) and Stockholm (Sweden) exchanges in 2006; acquired by NASDAQ Stock Market, Inc (USA) in 2008; Group CEO ROBERT GREIFELD; Group Pres. MAGNUS BÖCKER.

INSURANCE

In 2009 there were 100 non-life insurance companies in operation and 33 companies offering life insurance.

Principal Companies

Alm. Brand Forsikring A/S: Midtermolen 7, 2100 Copenhagen Ø; tel. 35-47-47-47; fax 35-47-35-47; e-mail almbrand@almbrand.dk; internet www.almbrand.dk; f. 1792; life, non-life and pensions; Chief Exec. SØREN BOE MORTENSEN.

AP Pension Liv: Østbanegade 135, 2100 Copenhagen Ø; tel. 39-16-50-00; e-mail email@appension.dk; internet www.appension.dk; f. 1919; as Cooperative Pension asscn; name changed as above in 1989; pensions, life; Chair. HOLGER DAMGAARD.

Codan A/S: Codanhus, Gl. Kongevej 60, 1790 Copenhagen V; tel. 33-55-55-50; fax 33-55-21-22; internet www.codan.dk; f. 1915 as Forsikringsselskabet Codan A/S; adopted present name 2000; mem. of RSA Insurance Group PLC (UK); accident, life; Chair. SIMON LEE; CEO MIKE HOLLIDAY-WILLIAMS.

Danica Pension: Parallelvej 17, 2800 Lyngby; tel. 70-11-25-25; fax 45-14-96-16; e-mail kontakt@danicapension.dk; internet www.danicapension.dk; f. 1842 as state insurance co; privatized 1991; acquired by Danske Bank 1995; pensions, life; CEO PER KLITGÅRD.

If: Stamholmen 159, 2650 Hvidovre; tel. 70-12-24-24; fax 70-12-24-25; e-mail carsten.muller@if.dk; internet www.if.dk; f. 1999; property and accident; subsidiary of Sampo PLC (Finland); Man. Dir TORBJÖRN MAGNUSSON.

Industriens Pensionsforsikring: Nørre Farimagsgade 3, Copenhagen K; tel. 70-33-70-70; fax 33-66-80-90; e-mail kundeservice@industrienspension.dk; internet www.industrienspension.dk; f. 1992; by Confed. of Danish Industries (DI) and CO, representing 7 unions, with 35% and 65% ownership respectively; life; CEO LAILA MORTENSEN.

Lærestandens Brandforsikring G/S (LB): Farvergade 17, 1463 Copenhagen K; tel. 33-11-77-55; fax 33-15-77-55; e-mail annm@lb.dk; internet www.lb.dk; f. 1880; specializes in vehicle, home and accident insurance; Man. Dir JØRN ANKER-SVENDSEN.

Nordea Liv & Pension: Klausdalsbrovej 615, 2750 Ballerup; tel. 43-33-99-99; fax 43-33-98-98; e-mail Nordealivogpension@nordea

.dk; internet www.nordealivogpension.dk; life; CEO STEEN MICHAEL ERICHSEN.

Pension Denmark: Kongens Vænge 8, 3400 Hillerød; tel. 70-12-13-30; e-mail service@pension.dk; internet www.pension.dk; f. 1993; owned by the Pension Denmark Holding A/S; life, health, pensions; Chair. POUL ERIK SKOV CHRISTENSEN.

PFA Pension: Marina Park, Sundkrogsgade 4, 2100 Copenhagen Ø; tel. 39-17-50-00; fax 39-17-59-50; e-mail pension@pfa.dk; internet www.pfa.dk; f. 1917 as Pensionsforsikringsanstalten; present name adopted 1987; life, health, pensions; Chair. SVEND ASKÆR; CEO HENRIK HEIDEBY.

Topdanmark Forsikring A/S: Borupvang 4, 2750 Ballerup; tel. 44-68-33-11; fax 44-74-46-50; e-mail kundeservice@topdanmark.dk; internet www.topdanmark.dk; f. 1985; all classes, with subsidiaries; CEO CHRISTIAN SAGILD.

Tryg A/S: Klausdalsbrovej 601, 2750 Ballerup; tel. 70-11-20-20; fax 44-20-66-00; e-mail tryg@tryg.com; internet www.tryg.com; f. 1995 by merger of Tryg Forsikring A/S and Baltica Forsikring A/S; general; CEO MORTEN HÜBBE.

Insurance Association

Forsikring & Pension: Philip Heymans Allé 1, 2900 Hellerup; tel. 41-91-91-91; e-mail fp@forsikringogpension.dk; internet www.forsikringogpension.dk; f. 1918 as Assurandør-Societetet; present name adopted 1999; Man. Dir PER BREMER RASMUSSEN; 200 mems.

Trade and Industry

DEVELOPMENT ORGANIZATION

Det Økonomiske Råd (Danish Economic Council): Amaliegade 44, 1256 Copenhagen K; tel. 33-44-58-00; fax 33-32-90-29; e-mail dors@dors.dk; internet www.dors.dk; f. 1962; supervises national economic development and helps to co-ordinate the actions of economic interest groups; 26 members representing both sides of industry, the Government and independent economic experts; Co-Chairs Prof. PETER BIRCH SØRENSEN, Prof. JAN ROSE SKAKSEN, Prof. MICHAEL ROSHOLM, Prof. EIRIK SCHRØDER AMUNDSEN.

CHAMBER OF COMMERCE

Dansk Erhverv (Danish Chamber of Commerce): Børsen, 1217 Copenhagen K; tel. 33-74-60-00; fax 33-74-60-80; e-mail info@danskerhverv.dk; internet www.danskerhverv.dk; f. 1742; Pres. POUL-ERIK PEDERSEN; Man. Dir JENS KLARSKOV; approx. 20,000 mem. cos.

INDUSTRIAL AND TRADE ASSOCIATIONS

Bryggeriforeningen (Danish Brewers' Asscn): Faxehus, Gamle Carlsberg Vej 16, 2500 Valby; tel. 72-16-24-24; fax 72-16-24-44; e-mail contact@bryggeriforeningen.dk; internet www.bryggeriforeningen.dk; f. 1899; Chair. JESPER B. JØRGENSEN; Dir NIELS HALD; 44 mems.

Dansk Energi: Rosenørns Allé 9, 1970 Frederiksberg C; tel. 35-30-04-00; fax 35-30-04-01; e-mail they@danskenergi.dk; internet www.danskenergi.dk; f. 1923; fmrly Dansk Elvaerkers Forening (Asscn of Danish Energy Cos); promotes the interests of Danish producers and suppliers of electricity; Chair. LARS AGAART; 100 mem. cos.

Danske Maritime (Danish Maritime): Amaliegade 33B, 4th Floor, 1256 Copenhagen K; tel. 33-13-24-16; fax 33-11-10-96; e-mail mail@danishmaritime.org; internet www.danskemaritime.dk; f. 1919; fmrly Skibsværftsforeningen (Asscn of Danish Shipbuilders); meeting place for Danish producers of maritime equipment and ships; Pres. THOMAS S. KNUDSEN; Man. Dir THORKIL H. CHRISTENSEN.

Energi- og olieforum (EOF) (Danish Petroleum Asscn): Landemærket 10, 5th Floor, POB 120, 1004 Copenhagen K; tel. 33-45-65-10; fax 33-45-65-11; e-mail eof@eof.dk; internet www.eof.dk; representative org. for petroleum industry; Pres. STEFFEN PEDERSEN; Dir PETER STIGSGAARD.

Kopenhagen Fur: Langagervej 60, 2600 Glostrup; tel. 43-26-10-00; fax 43-26-11-26; e-mail mail@kopenhagenfur.com; internet www.kopenhagenfur.com; fmrly Dansk Pelsdyravlerforening (Danish Fur Breeders' Asscn); co-operative of 2,300 mems; Man. Dir TORBEN NIELSEN.

Landbrug & Fødevarer (Danish Agriculture & Food Council): Axeltorv 3, 1609 Copenhagen V; tel. 33-39-40-00; fax 33-39-41-41; e-mail info@lf.dk; internet www.lf.dk; f. 2009 by merger of 5 agricultural and food orgs; Pres. MICHAEL BROCKENHUUS-SCHACK; CEO. CARL AAGE DAHL.

Mejeriforeningen (Danish Dairy Board): Sønderhøj 1, 8260 Viby J; tel. 87-31-20-00; fax 87-31-20-01; e-mail info@mejeri.dk; internet www.mejeri.dk; f. 1912; Chair. STEEN NØRGAARD MADSEN; Man. Dir JØRGEN HALD CHRISTENSEN; 33 mems.

Vindmølleindustrien (Danish Wind Energy Association): Rosenørns Allé 9, 1970 Frederiksberg C; tel. 33-73-03-30; fax 33-73-03-33; e-mail danish@windpower.org; internet www.windpower.org/da/; CEO JAN HYLLEBERG.

EMPLOYERS' ORGANIZATIONS

Dansk Arbejdsgiverforening (DA) (Confederation of Danish Employers): Vester Voldgade 113, 1790 Copenhagen V; tel. 33-38-90-00; fax 33-12-29-76; e-mail da@da.dk; internet www.da.dk; f. 1896; Chair. TORBEN DALBY LARSEN; 14 mem. orgs.

Dansk Industri (DI) (Confederation of Danish Industries): H. C. Andersens Blvd 18, 1787 Copenhagen V; tel. 33-77-33-77; fax 33-77-33-00; e-mail di@di.dk; internet www.di.dk; f. 1992; Dir-Gen. and CEO HANS SKOV CHRISTENSEN.

Håndværksrådet (Danish Federation of Small and Medium-sized Enterprises): Islands Brygge 26, POB 1990, 2300 Copenhagen S; tel. 33-93-20-00; fax 33-32-01-74; e-mail hvr@hvr.dk; internet www.hvr.dk; f. 1879; Chair. NIELS TECHEN; Man. Dir ANE BUCH; 110 asscns with 23,000 mems.

Industriens Arbejdsgivere i København (The Copenhagen Employers' Federation): 1787 Copenhagen V; tel. 33-77-39-16; fax 33-77-33-00; e-mail iak@di.dk; mem. of Confed. of Dansk Industri; Chair. NIELS JACOBSEN; Sec. SUSANNE ANDERSEN; 370 mems.

Provinsindustriens Arbejdsgiverforening (Federation of Employers in Provincial Industry): 1787 Copenhagen V; tel. 33-77-33-77; fax 33-77-33-00; e-mail pfo@di.dk; internet foreninger.di.dk/pa; f. 1895; mem. of Dansk Industri (q.v.); Chair. BO STÆRMOSE; Sec. PETER FOSDAL; 558 mem. orgs.

Sammenslutningen af Landbrugets Arbejdsgiverforeninger (SALA) (Danish Confederation of Employers' Asscns in Agriculture): Vester Farimagsgade 1, 5. sal, POB 367, 1504 Copenhagen V; tel. 33-13-46-55; fax 33-11-89-53; e-mail info@sala.dk; internet www.sala.dk; 4 mem. orgs; Chair. PEJTER SØNDERGAARD.

UTILITIES

Energistyrelsen (Danish Energy Agency): Amaliegade 44, 1256 Copenhagen K; tel. 33-92-67-00; fax 33-11-47-43; e-mail ens@ens.dk; internet www.ens.dk; f. 1976; govt agency under Ministry of Climate and Energy; Dir-Gen. IB LARSEN.

Energitilsynet (Danish Energy Regulatory Authority): Nyropsgade 30, 1780 Copenhagen V; tel. 72-26-80-70; fax 33-18-14-27; e-mail et@dera.dk; internet www.energitilsynet.dk; f. 2000; independent authority; regulates prices and access to transmission networks for electricity, gas and heating supply cos; bd mems appointed by Minister of Climate,Energy and Building; Chair. UFFE BUNDGAARD-JØRGENSEN.

Electricity

DONG Energy A/S: Kraftværksvej 53, Skærbæk, 7000 Fredericia; tel. 99-55-11-11; e-mail info@dongenergy.com; internet www.dongenergy.com; f. 2006 by merger of 6 energy cos: DONG, Elsam, E2, Nesa, Copenhagen Energy's power activities and Frederiksberg Forsyning; petroleum and natural gas exploration, production, storage and distribution; production and sale of electricity, wind power and geothermal energy; CEO CARSTEN KROGSGAARD THOMSEN (acting).

EnergiMidt A/S: Tietgensvej 2–4, 8600 Silkeborg; tel. 70-15-15-60; fax 87-22-87-11; internet www.energimidt.dk; co-operative society; 176,000 customers; energy supplier; Chair. JENS JØRN JUSTESEN; Man. Dir HOLGER BLOK.

Energinet.dk: Tonne Kjærsvej 65, 7000 Fredericia; tel. 70-10-22-44; fax 76-24-51-80; e-mail info@energinet.dk; internet www.energinet.dk; f. 2005 by merger of Eltra, Elkraft System, Elkraft Transmission and Gastra; state-owned; co-ordinates supply of electricity, gas and co-generated heat; Chair. NIELS FOG.

Vattenfall A/S: Støberigade 14, 2450 Copenhagen SV; tel. 88-27-50-00; e-mail marianne.grydgaard@vattenfall.com; internet www.vattenfall.dk; f. 1996; owned by Vattenfall AB (Sweden); generation and supply of thermal and wind energy; acquired assets of Elsam and E2 in 2006; Group CEO LARS G. JOSEFSSON.

Gas

Dansk Gas Forening (Danish Gas Asscn): c/o Dansk Gasteknisk Center a/s, Dr Neergaards Vej 5B, 2970 Hørsholm; tel. 20-16-96-00; fax 45-16-11-99; e-mail dgf@dgc.dk; internet www.gasteknik.dk; f. 1911; promotes the use of gas; Sec. PETER I. HINSTRUP; 450 mems.

DONG Energy A/S: see Electricity.

Hovedstadsregionens Naturgas I/S (HNG): Gladsaxe Ringvej 11, 2860 Søborg; tel. 39-54-70-00; fax 39-67-23-98; e-mail ks@hng.dk; internet www.hng.dk; f. 1979; distribution and sale of gas in Greater

Copenhagen region; Chair. OLE BJØRSTORP; Man. Dir. NIELS ERIK ANDERSEN.

Københavns Energi A/S (Copenhagen Energy): Ørestads Blvd 35, 2300 Copenhagen S; tel. 33-95-33-95; fax 33-95-20-20; e-mail ke@ke.dk; internet www.ke.dk; f. 1857 as Københavns Belysningsvæsen; present name adopted 1999; merger with Københavns Vand 2001; supplier of gas, heating and water in Copenhagen and surrounding area; Chair. LEO LARSEN; Man. Dir LARS THERKILDSEN.

Naturgas Fyn A/S: Ørbækvej 260, 5220 Odense SØ; tel. 63-15-64-15; fax 66-15-51-27; e-mail ngf@ngf.dk; internet www.ngf.dk; distribution of gas on island of Funen; Chair. LARS ERIK HORNEMANN; Man. Dir BJARKE PÅLSSON.

Water

Water provision in Denmark is highly decentralized. Local councils are responsible for the maintenance of water supply infrastructure and the supervision of suppliers. Water supply utilities, of which there were some 2,740 in 2001, are owned either by municipal administrations or by local consumer co-operative organizations.

CO-OPERATIVE

Co-op Danmark A/S (Co-operative of Denmark): Roskildevej 65, 2620 Albertslund; tel. 43-86-43-86; fax 43-86-33-86; e-mail coop@coop.dk; internet www.coop.dk; f. 1896; owned by Fællesforeningen for Danmarks Brugsforeninger (FDB); CEO JESPER LIEN; c. 1.6m. mems.

TRADE UNIONS

National Confederations

Akademikernes Centralorganisation (AC) (Danish Confederation of Professional Asscns): Nørre Voldgade 29, POB 2192, 1017 Copenhagen K; tel. 33-69-40-40; fax 33-93-85-40; e-mail ac@ac.dk; internet www.ac.dk; f. 1972; Pres. ERIK JYLLING; 23 affiliated unions, with a total of 197,900 mems (2011).

FTF (Confederation of Professionals in Denmark): Niels Hemmingsens Gade 12, POB 1169, 1100 Copenhagen K; tel. 33-36-88-00; fax 33-36-88-80; e-mail ftf@ftf.dk; internet www.ftf.dk; f. 1952; affiliated to ITUC and ETUC; Pres. BENTE SORGENFREY; 90 affiliated unions, with c. 450,000 mems.

Landsorganisationen i Danmark (LO) (Danish Confederation of Trade Unions): Islands Brygge 32D, 2300 Copenhagen S; tel. 35-24-60-00; fax 35-24-63-00; e-mail lo@lo.dk; internet www.lo.dk; Pres. HARALD BØRSTING; Vice-Pres. LIZETTE RISGAARD; 17 affiliated unions, with a total of 1.2 m. mems (2007).

Principal Unions

BUPL—Børne- og Ungdomspædagogernes Landsforbund (National Federation of Early Childhood Teachers and Youth Workers): Blegdamsvej 124, 2100 Copenhagen Ø; tel. 35-46-50-00; fax 35-46-50-39; e-mail bupl@bupl.dk; internet www.bupl.dk; f. 1973; affiliated to FTF; Pres. HENNING PEDERSEN; 65,115 mems (2012).

C3, ledelse og økonomi (Asscn of Danish Business Economists): Søtorvet 5, POB 2043, 1012 Copenhagen K; tel. 33-14-14-46; fax 33-14-14-49; e-mail info@c3.dk; internet www.c3.dk; f. 2005 by merger of Yngre Civiløkonomerne, Civiløkonomerne, KARRYERE and CA, økonomernes a-kasse; affiliated to AC; Pres. MADS HENRIKSEN; 15,000 mems (2009).

Danmarks Jurist- og Økonomforbund (DJØF) (Asscn of Danish Lawyers and Economists): Gothersgade 133, POB 2126, 1015 Copenhagen K; tel. 33-95-97-00; fax 33-95-99-99; e-mail djoef@djoef.dk; internet www.djoef.dk; affiliated to AC; Pres. FINN BORCH ANDERSEN; 54,183 mems (2009).

Danmarks Lærerforening (Danish Union of Teachers): Vandkunsten 12, 1467 Copenhagen K; tel. 33-69-63-00; fax 33-69-63-33; e-mail dlf@dlf.org; internet www.dlf.org; affiliated to FTF; Pres. ANDERS BONDO CHRISTENSEN; c. 90,000 mems.

Dansk El-Forbund (Electricians' Union): Vodroffsvej 26, 1900 Frederiksberg C; tel. 33-29-70-00; fax 33-29-70-70; e-mail def@def.dk; internet www.def.dk; affiliated to LO; Pres. JÖRGEN JUUL RASMUSSEN; 29,769 mems (2007).

Dansk Jernbaneforbund (Railway Workers): Søndermarksvej 16, 2500 Valby; tel. 36-13-25-00; fax 36-13-25-01; e-mail dj@djf.dk; internet www.djf.dk; f. 2002; affiliated to LO; Pres. ULRIK SALMONSEN; 5,492 mems (2007).

Dansk Metal (Metalworkers): Nyropsgade 38, POB 308, 1780 Copenhagen V; tel. 33-63-20-00; fax 33-63-21-00; e-mail metal@danskmetal.dk; internet www.danskmetal.dk; f. 1888; affiliated to LO; Pres. THORKILD E. JENSEN; 130,000 mems (2008).

Dansk Sygeplejeråd (Danish Nurses' Org.): Sankt Annæ Pl. 30, POB 1084, 1008 Copenhagen K; tel. 33-15-15-55; fax 33-15-24-55; e-mail dsr@dsr.dk; internet www.dsr.dk; f. 1899; affiliated to FTF; Pres. GRETE CHRISTENSEN; 75,066 mems (2008).

Fag og Arbejde (FOA) (Trade and Labour): Stauningspl. 1–3, 1790 Copenhagen V; tel. 46-97-26-26; fax 46-97-23-00; e-mail foa@foa.dk; internet www.foa.dk; f. 2005 by merger of Forbundet af Offentligt Ansatte and Pædagogisk Medhjælper Forbund; affiliated to LO; Pres. DENNIS KRISTENSEN; 194,000 mems (March 2012).

Fagligt Fælles Forbund (3F) (United Federation of Danish Workers): Kampmannsgade 4, 1790 Copenhagen V; tel. 70-30-03-00; fax 70-30-03-01; e-mail 3f@3f.dk; internet www.3f.dk; f. 2005 by merger of Kvindeligt Arbejderforbund and Specialarbejderforbundet; affiliated to LO; Pres. POUL ERIK SKOV CHRISTENSEN; 319,380 mems (2010).

Finansforbundet (Financial Services Union): Applebys Pl. 5, POB 1960, 1411 Copenhagen K; tel. 32-96-46-00; fax 32-96-12-25; e-mail post@finansforbundet.dk; internet www.finansforbundet.dk; affiliated to FTF; Pres. KENT PETERSEN; 54,700 mems (Nov. 2009).

Forbundet Trae-Industri-Byg i Danmark (TIB) (Timber Industry and Construction Workers): Mimersgade 41, 2200 Copenhagen N; tel. 88-18-70-00; fax 88-18-71-10; e-mail tib@tib.dk; internet www.tib.dk; affiliated to LO; Pres. JOHNNY SKOVENGAARD; 65,000 mems (2007).

Gymnasieskolernes Lærerforening (GL) (Danish National Union of Upper Secondary School Teachers): Vesterbrogade 16, 1620 Copenhagen V; tel. 33-29-09-00; fax 33-29-09-01; e-mail gl@gl.org; internet www.gl.org; f. 1890; affiliated to AC; Pres. GORM LESCHLY; 13,000 mems (2012).

HK Danmark (Union of Commercial and Clerical Employees in Denmark): Weidekampsgade 8, POB 470, 0900 Copenhagen C; tel. 70-11-45-45; fax 33-30-40-99; e-mail hk@hk.dk; internet www.hk.dk; f. 1900; affiliated to LO; Pres. KIM SIMONSEN; 329,679 mems (2007).

Ingeniørforeningen i Danmark (IDA) (Danish Society of Engineers): Ingeniørhuset, Kalvebod Brygge 31–33, 1780 Copenhagen V; tel. 33-18-48-48; fax 33-18-48-99; e-mail ida@ida.dk; internet www.ida.dk; affiliated to AC; Pres. FRIDA FROST; 80,000 mems (2010).

Lægeforeningen (Danish Medical Asscn): Kristianiagade 12, 2100 Copenhagen Ø; tel. 35-44-85-00; fax 35-44-85-05; e-mail dadl@dadl.dk; internet www.laeger.dk; affiliated to AC; Pres. MADS KOCH HANSEN; 25,666 mems (2011, incl. Yngre Læger, Foreningen af Speciallæger and Praktiserende Lægers Organisation).

Malerforbundet i Danmark (Painters): Lersø Parkallé 109, 2100 Copenhagen Ø; tel. 39-16-79-00; fax 39-16-79-10; e-mail maler@maler.dk; internet www.maler.dk; f. 1890; affiliated to LO; Pres. JØRN ERIK NIELSEN; 12,666 mems (2007).

Nærings- og Nydelsesmiddelarbejder Forbundet (NNF) (Food, Sugar Confectionery, Chocolate, Dairy Produce and Tobacco Workers): C. F. Richs Vej 103, POB 1479, 2000 Frederiksberg; tel. 38-18-72-72; fax 38-18-72-00; e-mail nnf@nnf.dk; internet www.nnf.dk; f. 1980; affiliated to LO; Pres. OLE WEHLAST; 27,000 mems.

Serviceforbundet (Federation of Employees in the Service Trade): Upsalagade 20, 2100 Copenhagen Ø; tel. 70-15-04-00; fax 70-15-04-05; e-mail dservice@forbundet.dk; internet www.forbundet.dk; affiliated to LO; Pres. KARSTEN HANSEN; 18,000 mems (2010).

Socialpædagogernes Landsforbund (National Federation of Social Educators in Denmark): Brolæggerstræde 9, 1211 Copenhagen K; tel. 72-48-60-00; fax 72-48-60-01; e-mail sl@sl.dk; internet www.sl.dk; affiliated to LO; Pres. KIRSTEN NISSEN; 35,345 mems (2009).

Teknisk Landsforbund (Professional Technicians): Nørre Voldgade 12, 1358 Copenhagen K; tel. 33-43-65-00; fax 33-43-66-77; e-mail tl@tl.dk; internet www.tl.dk; f. 1919; Pres. GITA ALICE GRÜNING; c. 30,000 mems (2007).

Transport

In June 1998 an 18-km combined tunnel-and-bridge road and rail link between the islands of Zealand and Funen was completed; the project incorporated the world's second longest suspension bridge. A 16-km road and rail link (incorporating a 4-km tunnel, an artificial island and an 8-km suspension bridge) across the Øresund strait, between Copenhagen and Malmö, Sweden, was completed in July 2000. Construction of a road and rail tunnel across the 19 km Fehmarn Belt, linking eastern Denmark with Germany, was expected to be completed by 2020.

DANISH TRANSPORT AUTHORITY

Danish Transport Authority: Gammel Mønt 4, 1117 Copenhagen K; tel. 72-26-70-00; fax 33-69-05-48; e-mail info@trafikstyrelsen.dk; internet www.trafikstyrelsen.dk; f. 2010 following merger of the Public Transport Authority (Trafikstyrelsen) and the Civil Aviation Administration (Statens Luftfartsvæsen); Dir-Gen. CARSTEN FALK HANSEN.

RAILWAYS

Banedanmark (Rail Net Denmark): Amerika Pl. 15, 2100 Copenhagen Ø; tel. 82-34-00-00; fax 82-34-45-72; e-mail banedanmark@bane.dk; internet www.banedanmark.dk; f. 1997 as Banestyrelsen to assume, from the DSB (see below), responsibility for the maintenance and development of the national rail network; controls 2,349 km of line, of which 602 km are electrified; also manages signalling and train control; CEO JESPER HANSEN.

DSB (Danish State Railways): Sølvgade 40, 1349 Copenhagen K; tel. 70-13-14-15; fax 33-51-41-20; e-mail dsb@dsb.dk; internet www.dsb.dk; wholly owned by Ministry of Transport and Energy; became an independent public corpn in Jan. 1999; privatization pending; operates passenger services; Chair. PETER SCHÜTZE; CEO JESPER T. LOK.

A total of 495 km, mostly branch lines, is run by 15 private companies.

METROPOLITAN TRANSPORT

Metroselskabet I/S: Metrovej 5, 2300 Copenhagen S; tel. 33-11-17-00; fax 33-11-23-01; e-mail m@m.dk; internet www.m.dk; f. 2002; operates 21-km, 22-station underground light rail network in Copenhagen; construction of 2 new lines due to be completed in 2018; 50% owned by Copenhagen city council, 41.7% by Ministry of Transport and 8.3% by Frederiksberg city council; Chair. HENNING CHRISTOPHERSEN; Man. Dir HENRIK PLOUGMANN OLSEN.

ROADS

In 2008, according to the International Road Federation, Denmark had an estimated 69,399 km of paved roads, including 1,103 km of motorways and 2,755 km of national roads. A 3-km road connecting Nordhavn in Copenhagen with Helsingørmotorvejen (the Elsinore Highway) to the north of the city was expected to be completed by 2015. This new link was expected to ease the flow of traffic in densely populated city areas.

SHIPPING

The Port of Copenhagen is the largest port in Denmark and the only one to incorporate a Free Port Zone. The other major ports are Aarhus, Fredericia, Aalborg, Hirtshals, and Esbjerg, all situated in Jutland. There are petroleum terminals, with adjacent refineries, at Kalundborg, Stigsnæs and Fredericia. Ferry services are provided by Scandlines (see below) and by various private companies. At 31 December 2009 the merchant fleet numbered 807 vessels, with a combined displacement of 11.1m. grt.

Port Authorities

Århus: Port Authority of Århus, Mindet 2, POB 130, 8100 Århus C; tel. 86-13-32-66; fax 86-12-76-62; e-mail port@aarhus.dk; internet www.aarhushavn.dk; Port Dir BJARNE MATHIESEN.

Associated Danish Ports A/S (ADP): Vesthavnsvej 33, 7000 Fredericia; tel. 79-21-50-00; fax 79-21-50-05; e-mail post@adp-as.dk; internet www.adp-as.dk; has authority for ports of Middelfart, Fredericia and Nyborg; Man. Dir JENS PETER PETERS.

Copenhagen: Copenhagen Malmö Port AB, Containervej 9, POB 900, 2100 Copenhagen Ø; tel. 35-46-11-11; fax 35-46-11-64; e-mail cmport@cmport.com; internet www.cmport.com; f. 2001 by merger of ports of Copenhagen and Malmö; owned by Malmö Municipality (27%), City & Port Development (50%) and pvt. investors (23%); CEO JOHAN RÖSTIN; Port Capt. SØREN F. ANDERSEN.

Esbjerg: Port of Esbjerg, Hulvejen 1, 6700 Esbjerg; tel. 75-12-40-00; fax 75-13-40-50; e-mail adm@portesbjerg.dk; internet www.portesbjerg.dk; Port Dir OLE INGRISCH; Head of Maritime Dept TORBEN JENSEN.

Frederikshavn Havn A/S: Oliepieren 7, POB 129, 9900 Frederikshavn; tel. 96-20-47-00; fax 96-20-47-11; e-mail info@frederikshavnhavn.dk; internet www.frederikshavnhavn.dk; Man. Dir MIKKEL SEEDORFF SØRENSEN; Harbour Capt. JESPER G. THOMSEN.

Kalundborg: Kalundborg Port Authority, Baltic Pl., POB 54, 4400 Kalundborg; tel. 59-53-40-00; fax 59-53-40-03; e-mail info@portofkalundborg.dk; internet www.portofkalundborg.dk; Harbour Dir BENT RASMUSSEN.

Sønderborg: Sønderborg Havn, Nørrebro 1, 6400 Sønderborg; tel. 74-42-27-65; fax 74-43-30-19; e-mail havnen@sonderborg.dk; internet www.sonderborg.dk/havn; Port Controller FINN HANSEN.

Principal Shipping Companies

Corral Line A/S: Havnevej 18, 6320 Egernsund; tel. 74-44-14-35; fax 74-44-14-75; e-mail info@corralline.com; fmrly Sønderborg Rederiaktieselskab; 8 livestock carriers of 19,302 grt; shipowners, managers, chartering agents; world-wide; Man. Dir B. CLAUSEN.

Rederiet Otto Danielsen: Kongevejen 272A, 2830 Virum; tel. 45-83-25-55; fax 45-83-17-07; e-mail od@ottodanielsen.com; internet www.ottodanielsen.com; f. 1944; 7 general cargo vessels, totalling 20,793 grt, under foreign flags; general tramp trade, chartering, ship sales; Man. Dir SØREN ANDERS; Fleet Man. JØRN STAUREBY.

Dannebrog Rederi A/S: Rungsted Strandvej 113, 2960 Rungsted Kyst; tel. 45-17-77-77; fax 45-17-77-70; e-mail blu@dannebrog.com; internet www.dannebrog.com; f. 1883; 3 ro-ro vessels, product chemical tanker services; liner service USA–Europe, US Gulf–Caribbean, Mediterranean–Caribbean; Man. Dir JOHAN WEDELL-WEDELLSBORG.

DFDS A/S: Sundkrogsgade 11, 2100 Copenhagen Ø; tel. 33-42-33-42; fax 33-42-33-41; e-mail dfds@dfds.com; internet www.dfds.com; f. 1866; 5 car/passenger ships and 60 freight vessels; passenger and car ferry services between Denmark, Belgium, Finland, France, Germany, Ireland, Latvia, Lithuania, the Netherlands, Norway, Poland, Sweden and the United Kingdom; Pres. and CEO NIELS SMEDEGAARD.

H. Folmer & Co: Fredericiagade 57, 1310 Copenhagen K; tel. 33-36-09-00; fax 33-13-54-64; e-mail folmer@folmer.dk; internet www.folmer.dk; f. 1955; 13 general cargo vessels of 14,100 grt; world-wide tramping; Man. Owners J. J. FOLMER, UFFE MARTIN JENSEN.

J. Lauritzen A/S: Sankt Annæ Pl. 28, POB 2147, 1291 Copenhagen K; tel. 33-96-80-00; fax 33-96-80-01; e-mail tni@j-l.com; internet www.j-lauritzen.com; f. 1884; operates reefer ships, LPG/C carriers and bulk ships; Pres. and CEO TORBEN JANHOLT.

A. P. Møller—Mærsk A/S: Esplanaden 50, 1098 Copenhagen K; tel. 33-63-33-63; fax 33-63-41-08; e-mail cphinfo@maersk.com; internet www.maersk.com; f. 1904; fleet of 113 container vessels, 19 products tankers, 3 crude petroleum tankers, 5 gas carriers, 10 car carriers, 59 offshore vessels and 22 drilling rigs; further tonnage owned by subsidiary cos in Singapore and the UK; world-wide liner and feeder services under the name of Maersk Line, and world-wide tanker, bulk, offshore and rig services; CEO NILS SMEDEGAARD ANDERSEN.

Dampskibsselskabet Norden A/S: 52 Strandvejen, 2900 Hellerup; tel. 33-15-04-51; fax 33-15-61-99; e-mail direktion@ds-norden.com; internet www.ds-norden.com; f. 1871; operates about 45 tankers and bulk carriers; world-wide tramping; Pres. and CEO CARSTEN MORTENSEN.

Scandlines Danmark A/S: Havneholmen 29, 1561 Copenhagen V; tel. 33-15-15-15; fax 72-68-60-58; e-mail scandlines@scandlines.dk; internet www.scandlines.dk; f. 1998 by merger of Scandlines A/S and Deutsche Fährgesellschaft Ostsee GmbH (Germany); maintains offices in Germany and Sweden; acquired by Deutsche Seereederei GmbH in 2007; operates 12 ferry routes around Denmark and throughout the Baltic; Dirs STEEN WÆVERTAGE REINERT.

Svitzer A/S: Pakhus 48, Sundkaj 9, 2100 Copenhagen Ø; tel. 39-19-39-19; fax 39-19-39-09; e-mail info@svitzer.dk; internet www.svitzer.com; f. 1833; wholly owned subsidiary of A. P. Møller—Mærsk Group; 22 tugs and salvage vessels and a barge fleet; salvage, towage and barge services; Gen. Man. KELD BALLE MORTENSEN.

Torm A/S: Tuborg Havnevej 18, 2900 Hellerup; tel. 39-17-92-00; fax 39-17-93-93; e-mail mail@torm.com; internet www.torm.com; f. 1889; more than 140 tankers and bulk carriers; operator of a time-chartered fleet; Chair. NIELS ERIK NIELSEN; CEO JACOB MELDGAARD.

Shipping Association

Danmarks Rederiforening (Danish Shipowners' Asscn): Amaliegade 33, 1256 Copenhagen K; tel. 33-11-40-88; fax 33-11-62-10; e-mail info@shipowners.dk; internet www.shipowners.dk; f. 1884; 49 mems (2010); Chair. of the Bd LARS VANG CHRISTENSEN; Man. Dir PETER BJERREGAARD.

CIVIL AVIATION

The main international airport is Copenhagen Airport, situated about 10 km from the centre of the capital. The following domestic airports have scheduled flights to European and Scandinavian destinations: Ålborg, Århus and Billund in Jutland. Other domestic airports include: Roskilde (30 km south-west of Copenhagen); Esbjerg, Karup, Skrydstrup, Stauning, Sønderborg and Thisted in Jutland; Odense in Funen; and Bornholm Airport on the island of Bornholm.

Statens Luftfartsvæsen (SLV) (Civil Aviation Administration): Luftfartshuset, Ellebjergvej 50, POB 744, 2450 Copenhagen SV; tel. 36-18-60-00; fax 36-18-60-01; e-mail dcaa@slv.dk; internet www.slv.dk; Dir-Gen. KURT LYKSTOFT LARSEN.

Airlines

Scandinavian Airlines System (SAS): SAS Huset, Lufthavnsboulevarden 10, POB 150, 2770 Kastrup; tel. 32-32-00-00; fax 32-32-21-49; internet www.sas.dk; f. 1946; the national carrier of Denmark, Norway and Sweden. It is a consortium owned two-sevenths by SAS Danmark A/S, two-sevenths by SAS Norge ASA and three-sevenths by SAS Sverige AB. Each parent org. is a limited co owned 50% by its respective govt and 50% by private shareholders. The SAS group includes the consortium and the subsidiaries in which the consortium has a majority or otherwise controlling interest; the Board consists of 2 members from each of the parent cos and the chairmanship rotates among the 3 national chairmen on an annual basis; strategic alliance with Lufthansa (Germany) formed in 1995; Chair. FRITZ H. SCHUR; Pres. and CEO RICKARD GUSTAFSON.

Cimber Sterling: Sønderborg Airport, Lufthavnsvej 2, 6400 Sønderborg; tel. 74-42-22-77; fax 74-42-65-11; e-mail management@cimber.dk; internet www.cimber.com; f. 2008, following acquisition of Sterling Airlines brand by Cimber Air Denmark; operates flights to 33 destinations in Denmark and throughout Europe; CEO JAN PALMER.

SUN-AIR of Scandinavia A/S: Cumulusvej 10, 7190 Billund; tel. 76-50-01-00; fax 75-33-86-18; e-mail info@sunair.dk; internet www.sunair.dk; f. 1978; also maintains offices at Ålborg, Århus, Billund and Thisted Airports; operates charter flights, sells and leases aircraft and operates aircraft maintenance services, operates a franchise of scheduled flights throughout northern Europe in co-operation with British Airways since 1996; CEO NIELS SUNDBERG.

Thomas Cook Airlines Scandinavia A/S: Copenhagen Airport South, Hangar 276, 2791 Dragør; tel. 32-47-72-00; fax 32-45-12-20; e-mail thomascookairlines@thomascook.dk; internet www.thomascookairlines.dk; f. 2008 by merger of MyTravel Airways A/S and Premiair; part of the Thomas Cook Group PLC; flights to major destinations in Europe; Man. Dir TORBEN ØSTERGAARD.

Tourism

In 2009 foreign tourist arrivals in Denmark totalled some 9.3m.; receipts from tourism totalled US $5,679m. in that year.

VisitDenmark: Islands Brygge 43, 2300 Copenhagen S; tel. 32-88-99-00; fax 32-88-99-01; e-mail contact@visitdenmark.com; internet www.visitdenmark.com; f. 1967; fmrly Danmarks Turistråd (Danish Tourist Board); Dirs LARS ERIK JØNSSON, FLEMMING BRUHN.

Defence

As assessed at November 2011, Denmark maintained total armed forces of 18,628, comprising an army of 9,925 (including 1,770 conscripts), a navy of 2,880 (150 conscripts), an air force of 3,358 (100 conscripts), and joint forces of 2,465. There was, in addition, a volunteer Home Guard (Hjemmeværnet) numbering some 40,800. Military service is compulsory and lasts for 4–12 months. Denmark abandoned its neutrality after the Second World War and has been a member of the North Atlantic Treaty Organization (NATO) since 1949.

Defence Expenditure: Budget estimated at 25,900m. kroner for 2012.

Chief of Defence: Brig. Gen. PETER BARTRAM.

Education

Primary and lower secondary education at *Folkeskole* is the joint responsibility of the Ministry of Education and the municipal councils. The Ministry of Education, the Ministry of Culture and the Ministry of Science, Technology and Innovation are collectively responsible for providing higher education. Education is compulsory for ten years between six and 16 years of age. The state is obliged to offer a pre-school class and an 11th voluntary year. State-subsidized private schools are available, but in 2008/09 81.6% of pupils attended municipal schools. Pre-primary education between the ages of three and seven years at a *Børnehave* (Kindergarten) is optional, except for the compulsory pre-primary class, *Børnehaveklasse*, for children aged six to seven years. In 2006/07 enrolment at pre-primary level included 92% of children in the relevant age-group. Primary and lower secondary education begins at seven years of age and lasts for nine years (with the option of an additional year). This includes at least six years at primary school. Enrolment at primary level was equivalent to 99% of children in the relevant age-group in 2006/07. Secondary education is divided into two cycles of three years, the first beginning at 13 years of age, the second at the age of 16 or 17. At the end of the lower secondary cycle students must take a final exam in seven subjects. Students then progress to one of four options, all of which may lead to higher education: an academically orientated three-year course, *Studentereksamen* (STX), at a *Gymnasium*; a two-year course at a *Højere Forberedelseseksamen* (HF), which follows the voluntary 10th year of the *Folkeskole*; a three-year higher commercial examination course, *Højere Handelseksamen* (HHX), or a higher technical examination course, *Højere Teknisk Eksamen* (HTX). Alternatively students may transfer to vocational courses at this stage. A new vocational programme at the upper secondary level named *Eksamen i Forbindelse med en Erhvervsuddannelse* (EUX) was launched in August 2010. This programme is combined with an upper secondary education examination to give access to higher education. Total enrolment at secondary level in 2007/08 was equivalent to 96% of those in the relevant age-group. There are eight universities or *Lange Videregående Uddannelser* (long-cycle education) and other institutions of further and higher education: university colleges, *Mellemlange Videregäende Uddannelser* (medium-cycle non-university education), and academies of higher education, *Korte Videregäende Uddannelser* (short-cycle non-university education). The first degree course in the university sector is the Bachelor of Arts or Science (BA or BSc) and lasts for three years. In 2005/06 enrolment at tertiary level was equivalent to 81% of those in the relevant age-group (males 68%; females 94%). The government budget for 2010 allocated an estimated 146,281m. kroner to education, representing 14.5% of total budgeted spending.

DANISH EXTERNAL TERRITORIES

THE FAROE ISLANDS

Introductory Survey

LOCATION, CLIMATE, LANGUAGE, RELIGION, FLAG, CAPITAL

The Faroe Islands are a group of 18 islands (of which 17 are inhabited) in the Atlantic Ocean, between the United Kingdom and Iceland. The main island is Streymoy, where more than one-third of the population resides. The climate is mild in winter and cool in summer, with a mean temperature of 7°C (45°F). Most of the inhabitants profess Christianity: 83.1% of Faroese were Lutherans belonging to the Faroes National Church in 2008. The principal language is Faroese, but Danish is a compulsory subject in all schools. The flag (proportions 16 by 22) displays a red cross, bordered with blue, on a white background, the upright of the cross being to the left of centre. The capital is Tórshavn, which is situated on Streymoy.

CONTEMPORARY POLITICAL HISTORY

The Faroe Islands have been under Danish administration since Queen Margrethe I of Denmark inherited Norway in 1380. The islands were occupied by the United Kingdom while Denmark was under German occupation during the Second World War, but they were restored to Danish control immediately after the war. The Home Rule Act of 1948 gave the Faroese control over all their internal affairs. The Faroe Islands did not join the European Community (now European Union—EU, see p. 276) with Denmark in 1973. There is a local parliament (the Løgting—Lagting in Danish), but the Danish Folketing (parliament), to which the Faroese send two members, is responsible for defence and foreign policy, constitutional matters, and the judicial and monetary systems. The transfer of competency in some areas from Denmark to the Faroe Islands began in 2005. The Faroes control fishing resources within their fisheries zone, and in September 1992 a long-standing dispute between Denmark and the Faroes was settled when the Danish Government agreed to give the Faroese authorities legislative and administrative power over mineral resources, including those beneath the seabed in the area adjacent to the islands. This agreement removed one of the major obstacles to exploration for hydrocarbons off the Faroe Islands, where geologists considered that prospects for discovering reserves of petroleum and natural gas were favourable. In 1994 the Faroe Islands accordingly awarded a US company a licence to begin exploratory surveys, despite the existence of a long-standing dispute between Denmark and the United Kingdom over the demarcation of the continental shelf west of the Shetland Islands and south-east of the Faroe Islands, which had threatened to delay prospecting. This dispute was resolved in mid-1999, however, when representatives of the Faroese Government (the Landsstýri) signed an agreement with the Danish and British Governments regarding the location of the boundaries of the area concerned.

Following the general election of November 1990, in January 1991 a centre-left coalition Government was formed between the Social Democratic Party (SDP) and the conservative People's Party, with the SDP's Atli Dam as Prime Minister (Løgmaður). Dam was replaced in January 1993 by Marita Petersen (also of the SDP). In April the People's Party withdrew from the coalition, and was replaced by the Republican Party and the Home Rule Party. At a general election held in July 1994, the Union Party became the largest party in the Løgting, winning eight seats, while the SDP's allocation of seats was reduced from 10 to five. In September a coalition of the Union Party, the SDP, the Home Rule Party and the newly formed Labour Front took office. The Union Party's Edmund Joensen became Prime Minister.

At a general election held in April 1998, both the Republican Party and the People's Party increased their representation to eight seats, while the number of seats secured by the SDP rose to seven; the representation of the Union Party was reduced to six seats. In May a coalition Government was formed by members of the People's Party, the Republican Party and the Home Rule Party, with Anfinn Kallsberg of the People's Party as Prime Minister.

Tensions with the Danish Government in the early 1990s, the nationalistic persuasion of the new Government and the prospect of offshore petroleum discoveries revived Faroese ambitions for political and economic independence. (The Faroese had narrowly favoured independence from Denmark in a referendum in 1946, but the decision had been overturned by the Danish Folketing.) In October 1998 the Løgting adopted a resolution in support of the Government's intention to seek status for the Faroe Islands as a 'sovereign nation' under the Danish monarchy, having a common monetary system with Denmark. The Faroese Government considered that sovereignty for the islands would be most appropriately achieved through continued co-operation with Denmark within a new constitutional framework, based on a bilateral treaty between the two countries as equal, independent partners. A commission charged with the development of a proposal for a Faroese constitution was established by the Government in February 1999, and submitted its conclusions to the Løgting in June 2000. The Faroese envisaged retaining Queen Margrethe II of Denmark as their Head of State and maintaining the link between their local currency and the Danish krone. The islands would seek to continue to co-operate with Denmark in social affairs, justice, health and air traffic control, and would also maintain present arrangements such as mutual rights of residence, employment and education. The Faroes would also seek to join the North Atlantic Treaty Organization (NATO, see p. 370) and the UN.

Negotiations between the Danish and Faroese administrations concerning the future independence of the Faroe Islands began in March 2000, but swiftly stalled after the Danish Government confirmed that, although it would not oppose Faroese independence, it would terminate annual subsidies (of about 1,000m. kroner) to the Faroes in four years should secession take place, compared with the 15 years proposed by the Faroese. The Danish Prime Minister, Poul Nyrup Rasmussen, rejected an offer of mediation from the Icelandic premier, Davíð Oddsson. Discussions were resumed later in the year, but finally collapsed in October, prompting Kallsberg to announce a plan to hold a referendum on independence in 2001. The Faroese had initially envisaged the successful negotiation of a treaty with the Danish Government prior to a referendum. The referendum, which was scheduled to be held on 26 May, was to include four issues: the full transfer of authority to the Faroese by 2012; the establishment of an economic fund to guarantee financial security during the transitional period; the gradual elimination of subsidies from Denmark; and the holding of a further referendum establishing the Faroe Islands as an independent state by 2012. However, the Danish Government stated that Denmark would regard it as a de facto referendum on sovereignty and that a vote in favour of the proposals for independence would result in the halting of Danish aid within four years. The reluctance of the Faroese population to lose Danish subsidies and disagreement within the Faroese coalition Government resulted in the cancellation of the referendum in March 2001.

At the general election, held on 30 April 2002, the People's Party won seven seats in the Løgting; it subsequently formed a coalition Government with the Republican Party (which had secured eight seats), the Home Rule Party and the Centre Party (one seat apiece); the Union Party secured eight seats in the Løgting, and the SDP won seven seats.

In June 2003 the Danish Prime Minister, Anders Fogh Rasmussen, made an official visit to the Faroe Islands. During his visit he and Kallsberg signed a bill providing a legal basis for the transfer of competencies from the Danish to the Faroese Governments. The legislation did not in itself transfer any powers (this was to be done subsequently, with a separate resolution required in the Løgting for each power to be transferred), but it did detail those powers that would remain with the Danish Folketing, namely: the Danish Constitution; Danish citizenship; the Danish Supreme Court; currency and monetary policy; and foreign, security and defence policy. As with other bilateral agreements, identical versions of the bill, in both Faroese and Danish, were to pass before the Løgting and the Folketing, respectively.

In December 2003 the Republican Party withdrew from the ruling coalition, causing the collapse of the Government. The crisis was precipitated by the publication of a book that alluded to Kallsberg's past involvement in accounting fraud; he was accused of misappropriating 912,000 kroner between 1977 and 1981. Claiming that the money had subsequently been repaid and that he had not personally gained from the affair, Kallsberg rejected demands by the Republican Party to issue a public apology or to resign. At an ensuing early election, held on 20 January 2004, the Republican Party won eight seats, while the Union Party, the SDP and the People's Party each won seven seats. A new coalition Government was formed in February, with Jóannes Eidesgaard of the SDP as Prime Minister. Whereas the previous coalition had been composed of only pro-independence parties, the new administration comprised the People's Party, which supported independence, and the Union Party and the SDP, which both favoured continued union with Denmark.

In March 2004 the Government proposed a resolution recognizing that, despite the Faroes' long-standing policy of neutrality, they were a de facto member of NATO and had been so for some 50 years. In August the Danish Minister of Foreign Affairs, Per Stig Møller, paid a one-day visit to the Faroes, during which he promised the islanders greater influence over Faroese foreign policy issues and stated that the islands would be given 'full insight' into any issues affecting Faroese defence policy. Faroese representatives would also be permitted to attend NATO meetings whenever relevant issues were under discussion.

The legislation on the transfer of competencies was enacted on 29 July 2005 (the Faroese National Day). Following its enactment the Faroese Government intended to transfer to its control powers covering civil emergency preparedness, company law, copyright law and industrial property rights, and the established church—all before its mandate expired in 2008. Areas that remained to be transferred at a later stage were the regulation of immigration and border control; criminal law; legislation and administration of the financial sector; health care; the judicial courts (excluding the Danish Supreme Court); the issuing of passports; the police and prosecution service; the prison service; and public pensions. Adopted and enacted concurrently with the transfer of competencies bill was an additional piece of new legislation, which granted the Faroese Government authority to negotiate and conclude agreements under international law with other states and international organizations, and allowed (under certain circumstances) the Faroe Islands to become a member of international organizations in their own right. In July 2006 Eidesgaard and Fogh Rasmussen signed an agreement for the Faroese Government to assume ownership of Vágar Airport from Denmark.

At the general election held on 19 January 2008 the Republican Party retained its eight seats in the Løgting, while the Union Party and People's Party each won seven seats. The SDP won just six seats, prompting speculation over the continuation of Eidesgaard's premiership. In February a new coalition Government, comprising the SDP, the Republican Party and the Centre Party (which had won three seats at the election), took office. Eidesgaard remained as Prime Minister, while Høgni Hoydal assumed the newly created role of Minister of Foreign Affairs.

In September 2008 the coalition Government collapsed, following the resignation of Eidesgaard as a result of a series of disagreements with Hoydal. A new coalition administration, comprising the Union Party, the People's Party and the SDP, took office later that month. The Chairman of the Union Party, Kaj Leo Johannesen, was appointed Prime Minister, while Eidesgaard became Minister of Finance. Each party was allocated three portfolios.

In March 2010 a committee of the Løgting agreed on the text of a draft constitution for the Faroe Islands, concluding a process that had been under way for some eight years. The text aroused controversy in Denmark, particularly owing to its assertion that 'all power' in the Faroes resided with the Faroese people and the absence of any reference to the Islands' status within the Danish Kingdom. In June the Danish Ministry of Justice declared that the text was contrary to the Danish Constitution and that it would place the Islands' constitutional status in doubt. A revised version of the draft constitution, which addressed some of the Danish Government's concerns, was approved by the Løgting in May 2011. However, Denmark maintained that the revised document could still be interpreted as a de facto declaration of independence from the Kingdom, and in June the Danish Prime Minister, Lars Løkke Rasmussen, warned Johannesen that, were the constitution to be promulgated in its current form, Denmark would expect the Faroe Islands formally to declare their independence. In response, Johannesen stated that the Islands had no intention of seeking immediate independence, and that he would seek to resolve the Danish Government's concerns before the Løgting began further work on the document.

Meanwhile, in January 2011 Jørgen Niclasen resigned as Minister of Foreign Affairs, a post that he had held since September 2008, citing his desire to focus on his role as Chairman of the People's Party ahead of the next general election, which was due to be held by January 2012. The Minister of Fisheries, Jacob Vestergaard, also of the People's Party, was subsequently allocated additional responsibility for the foreign affairs portfolio. However, the People's Party withdrew its support from the coalition in April 2011; the portfolios previously held by members of the People's Party were redistributed between ministers from the other two parties.

A general election was held on 29 October 2011, some three months early. The Union Party and the People's Party both increased their representation in the Løgting to eight seats, while the Republican Party and the SDP each secured six seats, the former losing its position as the largest parliamentary party. The newly formed pro-independence Progress Party won two seats, as did the Centre Party, with the remaining seat taken by the Home Rule Party. An electoral turn-out of 86.6% was recorded. A new centre-right coalition Government, comprising the Union Party, the People's Party, the Centre Party and the Home Rule Party, took office on 14 November, again headed by Johannesen, who also became Minister of Foreign Affairs. Annika Olsen of the People's Party was appointed as Deputy Prime Minister and Minister of Social Affairs, while the party's leader, Niclasen, assumed responsibility for the finance portfolio.

In international affairs, the Faroe Islanders attracted opprobrium for their traditional slaughter of pilot whales, an important source of food. After foreign journalists publicized the whaling in 1986, stricter regulations were imposed on whaling operations. In July 1992 the Faroese Government threatened to leave the International Whaling Commission (IWC, see p. 442), following the latter's criticism of whaling methods practised in the Faroe Islands. It was, however, claimed that the Faroese did not have the legal right to withdraw from the Commission independently of Denmark. In September the Faroe Islands, Greenland, Norway and Iceland agreed to establish the North Atlantic Marine Mammal Commission, in protest at what they viewed as the IWC's preoccupation with conservation. The Faroe Islands resumed commercial hunting of the minke whale in 1993 and began trading in whale meat in 2002 after a halt of 14 years.

Agreements on free trade were concluded between the Faroe Islands and Iceland, Norway, Sweden, Finland and Austria in 1992–93 and between the Faroe Islands and the EU in January 2004. A new free trade agreement between the Faroe Islands and Iceland, known as the Hoyvík Agreement, was signed in August 2005. The agreement, which received legislative approval in April 2006, allowed for the free movement of all goods, services, capital and persons—effectively creating a common market between the two countries. A trade delegation led by the Icelandic Prime Minister, Halldór Asgrímsson, visited the Faroe Islands in that month in order to explore new business opportunities made possible by the agreement. Eidesgaard and Ásgrímsson discussed the two countries' relations with the EU and the possibility of the Faroe Islands joining the European Free Trade Association (EFTA, see p. 450), for which Ásgrímsson pledged Iceland's support. In May Eidesgaard sought and obtained the Løgting's approval for the initiation of membership negotiations with EFTA. The Faroe Islands were granted observer status in the EFTA Committee of Origin and Customs Experts in July. An agreement on research co-operation between the Faroe Islands and the EU was signed in June 2010, with the Faroe Islands becoming an associate member of the EU's Seventh Framework Programme for research and technological development.

In September 2006 the Government signed an interim agreement with Denmark, Iceland and Norway regarding the demarcation of the continental shelf north of the Faroe Islands. In February 2007 Eidesgaard and the Icelandic Minister of Foreign Affairs, Valgerður Sverrisdóttir, signed a bilateral agreement delimiting the maritime boundary between their respective territories, thereby ending a dispute lasting for three decades regarding overlapping claims to an area of around 3,650 sq km.

Faroese relations with the EU and Norway were strained during the second half of 2010 and early 2011 by a dispute over fishing quotas in the north-east Atlantic Ocean, amid concerns regarding the sustainability of the mackerel stock. In July 2010 the Faroe Islands unilaterally increased its mackerel quota for 2010 from 25,000 metric tons to 85,000 tons, in the absence of an agreement on the issue between the interested states. (Iceland had similarly decided to raise its quota, also leading to tensions in its relations with Norway and the EU.) The Faroe Islands and Iceland maintained that they had been forced to take this action having been excluded from a bilateral quota arrangement between the EU and Norway and that stocks of mackerel had become more plentiful in their waters as a result of changing migration patterns. Seven rounds of negotiations between officials from the four parties, held between October 2010 and March 2011, ended without agreement on quotas for 2011. Following the failure of the discussions in March, the Faroe Islands unilaterally announced that its mackerel quota for 2011 would be 150,000 tons. Several further rounds of negotiations, concerning quotas for 2012, took place between October 2011 and February 2012, but again ended without agreement. Meanwhile, as a result of the ongoing dispute, the EU was considering the adoption of a regulation to restrict imports of fish from countries deemed to be engaging in unsustainable fishing practices.

GOVERNMENT

Under the Home Rule Act of 1948 the Faroe Islands became a self-governing community in the Kingdom of Denmark. Under the Act, so-called Joint Matters (the judiciary, defence and foreign affairs) are under the authority of the Danish Government, whereas Special Matters (financial, economic and cultural matters, industry, foreign trade, natural resources in the subsoil) are under the control of the Faroese Government. A new Act in 2005 increased the areas of unilateral competence for the Faroese Government (see Contemporary Political History).

The legislative body is the Løgting (Lagting in Danish), which consists of 33 members, who are elected for four years on a basis of proportional representation. Following reforms implemented in 2007, the seven electoral constituencies that comprised the Faroe Islands were merged into a single constituency. All Faroese over the age of 18 years have the right to vote. Based on the strength of the parties in the Løgting, a Government (Landsstýri) is formed. This is the administrative body in certain spheres, chiefly relating to

Faroese economic affairs. The Prime Minister (Løgmaður) has to ratify all laws approved by the Løgting. Power is decentralized and there are about 50 local authorities. The High Commissioner (Ríkisumboðsmaður) represents the Danish Government, and has the right to address the Løgting and to advise on joint affairs. All Danish legislation must be submitted to the Landsstýri before becoming law in the Faroe Islands. The Faroese send two members to the Danish Folketing (parliament).

The Faroe Islands have 30 municipal councils.

REGIONAL CO-OPERATION

The Faroe Islands did not join the European Community (now the European Union—EU, see p. 276) with Denmark in 1973, but did secure favourable terms of trade with Community members and special concessions in Denmark and the United Kingdom. The Faroe Islands and Iceland form a free trade area under the Hoyvík Agreement. In international fisheries organizations, where Denmark is represented by the EU, the Kingdom maintains separate membership in respect of the Faroe Islands (and Greenland). The Faroe Islands are also a member of the Nordic Council (see p. 464).

ECONOMIC AFFAIRS

In 2009, according to official figures, gross national income (GNI) was 12,011m. kroner (at current prices). Between 1989 and 1993 gross national product (GNP) decreased dramatically, at an average rate, in real terms, of 9.4% per year. During 1994–95, however, real GNP increased by 4.2%. The population increased at an average annual rate of 0.6% per year in 2001–10. Gross domestic product (GDP) increased, in real terms, by an estimated 9.3% in 2007.

According to preliminary official figures, agriculture (principally sheep farming) and fishing contributed 15.1% of GDP in 2010. In July 2011 the sector provided 10.2% of employment. Potatoes and other vegetables are the main crops. Only about 6% of the land surface is cultivated.

Fishing is the dominant industry. In 1999 fishing, aquaculture and fish-processing accounted for 25.1% of GDP; the sector (excluding fish-processing) engaged 9.9% of the employed labour force in July 2011. Fish products accounted for 85.4% of exports in 2010. Most fishing takes place within the 200-nautical-mile (370-km) fisheries zone imposed around the Faroes in 1977. Fish farming, principally of salmon and trout, began in the 1980s. The traditional hunting of pilot whales continues to provide an important source of meat for the Faroese. The Faroe Islands resumed commercial hunting of the minke whale in 1993 and began trading in whale meat in 2002 after a halt of 14 years.

Industry (including mining, manufacturing, construction and power) contributed 16.0% of GDP in 2010, according to preliminary official figures. In July 2011 the sector provided 18.9% of employment. The dominant sectors are fishing-related industries, such as fish-drying and -freezing, and ship maintenance and repairs.

Mining and quarrying contributed only 0.3% of GDP in 2000 and engaged 0.4% of the employed labour force in July 2011. 'Brown coal' (lignite) is mined on Suðuroy. The potential for petroleum production around the islands was initially believed to be significant. However, drilling between 2000 and 2010 did not uncover hydrocarbons on a commercial scale and thus expectations became more moderate.

Manufacturing contributed 6.0% of GDP in 2010, according to preliminary official figures. It provided 11.3% of employment in July 2011, while technical repairs and shipyards are also significant: exports of vessels accounted for 4.7% of exports in 2010. A small textile industry exports traditional Faroese woollens.

According to preliminary official figures, the construction sector contributed 6.0% of GDP in 2010. The sector engaged 6.9% of the employed labour force in July 2011.

In 2007 55% of the islands' electricity production was provided by thermal energy, 39% by hydroelectric power and 6% by wind power. Imports of fuels and related products accounted for 15.8% of imports in 2009.

The services sector accounted for 68.9% of GDP in 2010, according to preliminary official figures. In July 2011 the sector provided almost 70.9% of employment. In November 2003 an independent Faroese securities market was launched in co-operation with the Icelandic stock market.

In 2010 the Faroe Islands recorded a trade surplus of 459.7m. kroner, and there was a surplus of 784.7m. kroner on the current account of the balance of payments. Denmark was the Faroes' principal source of imports (34.2%) in 2010; other major suppliers were Norway, Sweden and Germany. The United Kingdom was the principal market for exports (16.2%) in that year; other major purchasers were Germany, Denmark and France (including Monaco). In 2008 the European Union (EU, see p. 276) as a whole took 65.6% of exports and supplied 62.7% of imports. The principal import in 2010 was machinery and transport equipment (accounting for 23.2% of the total cost of imports), followed by mineral fuels and lubricants and food and live animals. Fish and fish products accounted for 85.4% of total exports in the same year; other important exports were ships.

Danish subsidies are an important source of income to the islands, and accounted for 12.2% of total government revenue in 2008. In 2010 the Faroese Government recorded a budget deficit of 452m. kroner, equivalent to 3.6% of GDP. In 2006 the public sector debt was 405m. kroner. The average annual rate of inflation was 1.7% in 2001–11; consumer prices rose by 1.9% in 2011. Unemployment was 7.4% of the labour force in July 2011.

The Faroe Islands' economy is dependent on the fishing industry for its principal source of income. Depletion of stocks and the resulting decline in catches, together with a fall in export prices, led to a reduction in export earnings and a financial crisis in the early 1990s. From the end of the 1990s until the mid-2000s the Faroe Islands experienced a period of economic prosperity, with high levels of growth and low unemployment. Increases in private consumption and investment in 2006–07 accounted for the rapid expansion of the economy, following a period of slower growth as a result of a decline in the fishing catch and aquaculture production. Despite public sector investment and tax cuts in 2008, the Faroes were affected by the global financial crisis, which had an adverse impact on the cost and availability of borrowing, and thus on investment, as well as on consumer confidence. There was also a decline in the volume and value of the fishing catch in 2009, although fish farming continued to expand. These factors were responsible for an estimated total contraction in real GDP of some 8% in 2008–09. The economy returned to growth in 2010, according to the Government Bank, and was forecast to expand further in 2011, mainly as a result of an improved outlook for the fisheries sector, particularly salmon farming and mackerel fisheries. However, the unemployment rate increased significantly in 2008–11, from a low of 1.1% in June 2008 to a peak of 7.9% in February 2011, partly owing to significant job losses resulting from the bankruptcy of Faroe Seafood in late 2010, and remained high in December 2011, at 6.5%.

PUBLIC HOLIDAYS

Public holidays in the Faroe Islands are the same as those for Denmark. In addition, the Faroese also celebrate Flag Day on 25 April and Ólavsøka (St Olav's Day) on 28–29 July each year. Various regional holidays are also observed in May–July.

Statistical Survey

Sources (unless otherwise stated): Statistics Faroe Islands, Traðagøta 39, POB 2068, 165 Argir; tel. 352028; fax 352038; e-mail hagstova@hagstova.fo; internet www.hagstova.fo; Faroese Government Office, Hovedvagtsgade 8, 2, 1103 Copenhagen K; tel. 33-14-08-66; fax 33-93-85-75; Landsbanki Føroya (Faroese Government Bank), Staravegur 5, POB 229, 110 Tórshavn; tel. 308120; fax 318537; e-mail landsbank@landsbank.fo; internet landsbankin.fo.

AREA AND POPULATION

Area: 1,396 sq km (539 sq miles).

Population: 48,574 at 1 January 2011 (males 25,227, females 23,347).

Density (1 January 2011): 34.8 per sq km.

Population by Age and Sex (official estimates at 1 January 2011): *0–14:* 10,521 (males 5,436, females 5,085); *15–64:* 30,777 (males 16,370, females 14,407); *65 and over:* 7,276 (males 3,421, females 3,855); *Total* 48,574 (males 25,227, females 23,347).

Principal Towns (population at 1 January 2011): Tórshavn (capital) 12,333; Klaksvík 4,565; Hoyvík 3,635; Argir 2,043; Fuglafjørður 1,511; Vágur 1,377; Vestmanna 1,206; Miðvágur 1,059; Tvøroyri 809.

Births, Marriages and Deaths (2010): Registered live births 635 (birth rate 13.1 per 1,000); Registered marriages 232 (marriage rate 4.8 per 1,000); Registered deaths 348 (death rate 7.2 per 1,000).

Life Expectancy (years at birth, 2010): 80 (males 77; females 83).

Immigration and Emigration (2011): *Immigration:* Denmark 975; Greenland 28; Iceland 71; Norway 30; Sweden 22; Total (incl. others) 1,351. *Emigration:* Denmark 1,334; Greenland 16; Iceland 55; Norway 49; Sweden 25; Total (incl. others) 1,678.

Economically Active Population (persons aged 16–74 years with at least seven hours' paid work per month, at July 2011): Agriculture 70; Fishing 1,727; Aquaculture 669; Mining 89; Fish-processing 1,384; Shipyards and machine shops 525; Other production 816; Construction 1,672; Energy supply 163; Wholesale and retail trade 2,953; Restaurants and hotels 592; Sea transport 890; Other transport 601; Communication 519; Finance and insurance 855; Business services 706; Household services 328; Public administration (incl.

municipal services) 3,883; Education 1,557; Health and social work 3,570; Other services 583; *Total employed* 24,152; Registered unemployed 1,923; *Total labour force* 26,075 (males 13,367, females 12,708).

HEALTH AND WELFARE

Key Indicators

Physicians (per 1,000 head, 2008): 1.3.

Hospital Beds (per 1,000 head, 2007): 7.7.

Total Carbon Dioxide Emissions ('000 metric tons, 2007): 696.2.

Carbon Dioxide Emissions Per Head (metric tons, 2007): 14.4.

AGRICULTURE, ETC.

Principal Crop (2010, FAO estimate): Potatoes 1,400 metric tons. Source: FAO.

Livestock ('000 head, year ending September 2010, FAO estimates): Cattle 2; Sheep 68. Source: FAO.

Livestock Products (metric tons, 2010, FAO estimates): Cattle meat 78; Sheep meat 528. Source: FAO.

Fishing ('000 metric tons, live weight, 2010): Capture 393.9 (Argentines 18.6; Atlantic cod 33.0; Atlantic horse mackerel 11.9; Atlantic mackerel 71.6; Saithe—Pollock 49.0; Blue whiting—Poutassou 52.3; Atlantic herring 87.6); Aquaculture 39.0 (Atlantic salmon 37.2); *Total catch* 432.9.

INDUSTRY

Selected Products ('000 metric tons, 1996): Frozen or chilled fish 123; Salted and processed fish products 15; Aquaculture products 13; Oils, fats and meal of aquatic animals 124; *2006:* Soft drinks ('000 litres) 1,974; Beer ('000 litres) 2,326. *2010:* Electric energy (million kWh) 280.4.

FINANCE

(Danish currency is in use)

Budget (general government budget, million kroner, 2006): *Revenue:* Taxes and duties 3,482; Interest, dividends 156; Transfers from the Danish Government 658; Loan repayments 101; Total (incl. others) 4,088. *Expenditure:* Salaries 1,775; Purchase of goods and services 874; Construction and fixed assets production 238; Transfers to households 1,164; Total (incl. others) 3,946. *2010:* Total revenue 6,867 (Taxes 5,719, Interest and dividends 215, Other current transfers 926, Capital revenue 7); Total expenditure 7,319 (Interest and other property expenditure 149, Subsidies 173, Other current transfers 2,032, Final consumption expenditure 4,096, Capital expenditure 868).

Cost of Living (Consumer Price Index at July–Sept.; base: 2001 = 100): All items 115.4 in 2009; 116.2 in 2010; 118.4 in 2011.

Gross Domestic Product (million kroner at current prices): 12,303 in 2008; 12,100 in 2009; 12,504 in 2010 (provisional).

Expenditure on the Gross Domestic Product (million kroner at current prices, 2009): Government final consumption expenditure 3,952; Private final consumption expenditure 6,905; Gross capital formation 2,148; *Total domestic expenditure* 13,005; Exports of goods and services 5,220; *Less* Imports of goods and services 6,125; *GDP in purchasers' values* 12,100.

Gross Domestic Product by Sector (million kroner at current prices, 2010, provisional): Agriculture, hunting, forestry and fishing 1,632; Manufacture of food products and beverages 652; Electricity, gas and water supply 88; Construction 652; Other industry 345; Wholesale and retail trade, hotels and restaurants 1,069; Transport and communications 1,065; Financial intermediation, insurance and pension funding 452; Real estate and business activities 1,310; Public administration 693; Education 736; Health and social work 1,371; Other service activities 775; *Gross value added in basic prices* 10,840; Taxes on products (net) 1,664; *GDP in market prices* 12,504. Note: Financial intermediation services indirectly measured assumed to be distributed at source.

Balance of Payments (million kroner, 2010): Exports of goods f.o.b. 4,643.3; Imports of goods c.i.f. –4,183.5; *Trade balance* 459.7; Exports of services 1,072.4; Imports of services –2,059.1; *Balance on goods and services* –526.9; Net transfers and income 1,311.6; *Current balance* 784.7.

EXTERNAL TRADE

Principal Commodities (million kroner, 2010): *Imports c.i.f.:* Food and live animals 637.0; Mineral fuels, lubricants and related materials 962.6 (Petroleum and petroleum products 960.3); Chemicals and related products 372.8; Manufactured goods classified chiefly by material 541.0; Machinery and transport equipment 1,010.7 (General industrial machinery and equipment 110.7; Road vehicles 172.8; Other transport equipment 302.6); Miscellaneous manufactured articles 523.4; Total (incl. others) 4,364.7. *Exports f.o.b.:* Fish products (chilled, frozen and salted) 3,960.9 (Cod 525.4, Haddock 102.0, Saithe 550.7, Salmon 1,338.1, Trout 70.0, Blue whiting 115.4, Herring 229.0, Atlantic mackerel 309.8, Prawns 94.9, Other fish products 905.3); Vessels 217.0; Other products 181.7; Total 4,639.3.

Principal Trading Partners (million kroner, 2010): *Imports c.i.f.:* China, People's Rep. 191.9; Denmark 1,492.9; France 73.2; Germany 274.9; Iceland 121.1; Norway 773.4; Spain 30.3; Sweden 304.5; United Kingdom 152.4; Total (incl. others) 4,364.7. *Exports f.o.b.:* Canada 43.0; China, People's Rep. 63.6; Denmark 480.9; France 414.6; Germany 530.7; Greenland 23.5; Iceland 77.0; Italy 148.7; Japan 53.3; Nigeria 351.9; Norway 243.2; Russia 150.8; Spain 203.5; United Kingdom 753.8; Total (incl. others) 4,639.3.

TRANSPORT

Road Traffic (registered motor vehicles, 1 January 2011): Private motor cars 19,897 (incl. 99 taxis); Buses 223; Lorries and vans 4,337; Motorcycles 899; Mopeds 1,663.

Shipping: *Merchant Fleet* (31 December 2009): 152 vessels, Total displacement 231,467 grt (Source: IHS Fairplay, *World Fleet Statistics*). *International Sea-borne Freight Traffic* (1996, '000 metric tons): Goods loaded 223, Goods unloaded 443.

TOURISM

Nationality of Overnight Guests at Guesthouses (2006): Faroe Islands 30,383; Denmark 44,147; Iceland 7,793; Norway 11,423; Sweden 2,249; Finland 1,285; United Kingdom and Ireland 4,842; Germany 3,922; USA and Canada 1,583; Austria and Switzerland 906; Total (incl. others) 116,236.

COMMUNICATIONS MEDIA

Radio Receivers (1997): 26,000 in use (Source: UNESCO, *Statistical Yearbook*).

Television Receivers (1997): 15,000 in use (Source: UNESCO, *Statistical Yearbook*).

Book Production (2010): 209 titles.

Newspapers (2010): 10 titles per week (circulation 26,400).

Telephones ('000 main lines in use, 2010): 20.2 (Source: International Telecommunication Union).

Mobile Cellular Telephones ('000 subscribers, 2010): 59.4 (Source: International Telecommunication Union).

Internet Subscribers ('000, 2010): 16.4 (Source: International Telecommunication Union).

Broadband Subscribers ('000, 2010): 16.3 (Source: International Telecommunication Union).

EDUCATION

Institutions (2000/01): Basic schools 61 (Secondary schools 21); Upper secondary schools 3; Higher preparatory institutions 3.

Teachers (2002/03): 697 (full-time equivalent) in primary and secondary schools.

Students (2002/03, unless otherwise indicated): Pre-primary (1998/99) 59; Primary 5,567; Secondary 2,131; Upper secondary 600; Higher preparatory 165; Business schools 351; Fishery college 31; Social and health care school 60; Technical schools 108; University 154; Total further education (1996/97) 2,166.

Directory

The Government

The legislative body is the Løgting (Lagting in Danish), which consists of 33 members, who are elected for four years on a basis of proportional representation. Following reforms implemented in 2007, the seven electoral constituencies that comprised the Faroe Islands were merged into a single constituency. All Faroese over the age of 18 years have the right to vote. Based on the strength of the parties in the Løgting, a Government (Landsstýri) is formed. This is the administrative body in certain spheres, chiefly relating to Faroese economic affairs. The Prime Minister (Løgmaður) has to ratify all laws approved by the Løgting. Power is decentralized and there are about 50 local authorities. The High Commissioner (Ríkisumboðsmaður) represents the Danish Government, and has the right to address the Løgting and to advise on joint affairs. All Danish legislation must be submitted to the Landsstýri before becoming law in the Faroe Islands.

The Danish Folketing (parliament), to which the Faroese send two members, is responsible for defence and foreign policy, constitutional matters and the judicial and monetary systems.

HEAD OF STATE

Queen of Denmark: HM Queen MARGRETHE II.

LANDSSTÝRI

(May 2012)

A coalition of the Union Party (UP), the People's Party (PP), the Centre Party and the Home Rule Party.

Prime Minister: KAJ LEO JOHANNESEN.

Minister of Social Affairs: ANNIKA OLSEN.

Minister of Finance: JØRGEN NICLASEN.

Minister of Health: KARSTEN HANSEN.

Minister of Education, Research and Culture: BJØRN KALSØ.

Minister of Trade, Industry and Fisheries: JOHAN DAHL.

Minister of the Interior: KÁRI P. HØJGAARD.

Minister of Fisheries: JACOB VESTERGAARD.

Government Offices

Ríkisumboðsmaðurin (Danish High Commission): Amtmansbrekkan 6, POB 12, 110 Tórshavn; tel. 351200; fax 310864; e-mail riomfr@fo.stm.dk; internet www.rigsombudsmanden.fo; High Commissioner DAN MICHAEL KNUDSEN.

Løgmansskrivstovan (Prime Minister's Office): Tinganes, POB 64, 110 Tórshavn; tel. 306000; fax 351015; e-mail info@tinganes.fo; internet www.tinganes.fo.

Ministry of Education, Research and Culture: Hoyvíksvegur 72, POB 3279, 110 Tórshavn; tel. 306500; fax 306555; e-mail mmr@mmr.fo; internet www.mmr.fo.

Ministry of Finance: Kvíggjartún 1, POB 2039, 165 Argir; tel. 352020; fax 352025; e-mail fmr@fmr.fo; internet www.fmr.fo.

Ministry of Fisheries: Bókbindaragøata 8, POB 347, 110 Tórshavn; tel. 353030; fax 353035; e-mail fisk@fisk.fo; internet www.fisk.fo.

Ministry of Foreign Affairs: Tinganes, 110 Tórshavn; tel. 306100; fax 306105; e-mail mfa@mfa.fo; internet www.mfa.fo.

Ministry of Health: Eirargarður 2, 100 Tórshavn; tel. 304050; fax 304025; e-mail hmr@hmr.fo; internet www.hmr.fo.

Ministry of the Interior: POB 159, 110 Tórshavn; tel. 306800; fax 306885; e-mail imr@imr.fo; internet www.imr.fo.

Ministry of Trade and Industry: Tinganes, POB 377, 110 Tórshavn; tel. 306600; fax 306665; e-mail vmr@vmr.fo; internet www.vmr.fo.

Representation of the Faroes in Copenhagen: North Atlantic House, Strandgade 91, 4th Floor, 1401 Copenhagen K, Denmark; tel. 32-83-37-70; fax 32-83-37-75; e-mail mfa@mfa.fo; internet www.faroes.dk.

LØGTING

The Løgting has 33 members, elected by universal adult suffrage.

Løgtingsskrivstovan (Parliament Office): Tinghúsvegur 1–3, POB 208, 110 Tórshavn; tel. 363900; fax 363901; e-mail logting@logting.fo; internet www.logting.fo.

Speaker: HERGEIR NIELSEN.

Election, 29 October 2011

Party	Votes	% of votes	Seats
Sambandsflokkurin (Union Party)	7,545	24.71	8
Fólkaflokkurin (People's Party)	6,882	22.54	8
Tjóðveldi (Republican Party)	5,584	18.29	6
Javnaðarflokkurin (Social Democratic Party)	5,417	17.74	6
Framsókn (Progress Party)	1,933	6.33	2
Miðflokkurin (Centre Party)	1,882	6.16	2
Sjálvstýrisflokkurin (Home Rule Party)	1,289	4.22	1
Total	30,532	100.00	33

Political Organizations

Fólkaflokkurin (People's Party): Jónas Broncksgøta 29, 100 Tórshavn; tel. 312491; fax 322091; e-mail folkaflokkurin@logting.fo; internet folkaflokkurin.fo; f. 1940; conservative-liberal party, favours free enterprise and wider political and economic autonomy for the Faroes; Chair. JØRGEN NICLASEN.

Framsókn (Progress Party): Tórshavn; e-mail framsokn@framsokn.fo; internet www.framsokn.fo; centre-right, liberal, separatist party.

Javnaðarflokkurin (Social Democratic Party—SDP): Áarvegur 2, POB 208, 100 Tórshavn; tel. 312493; fax 319397; e-mail javnadarflokkarin@logting.fo; internet www.j.fo; f. 1925; Chair. JÓANNES EIDESGAARD.

Miðflokkurin (Centre Party): Áarvegur 2, POB 3237, 110 Tórshavn; tel. 310599; fax 312206; e-mail midflokkurin@olivant.fo; internet www.midflokkurin.fo; f. 1992; Christian principles; Chair. JENIS AV RANA.

Sambandsflokkurin (Union Party): Áarvegur 2, POB 208, 110 Tórshavn; tel. 318870; fax 312496; e-mail sambandsflokkurin@logting.fo; internet www.samband.fo; f. 1906; favours the maintenance of close relations between the Faroes and the Kingdom of Denmark; conservative in internal affairs; Chair. KAJ LEO JOHANNESEN.

Sjálvstýrisflokkurin (Home Rule Party): POB 141, 600 Saltangará; tel. 312494; e-mail post@sjalvstyrisflokkurin.fo; internet www.sjalvstyri.fo; f. 1906; social-liberal; advocates eventual political independence for the Faroes within the Kingdom of Denmark; Chair. KÁRI P. HØJGAARD.

Tjóðveldi (Republican Party): POB 143, 110 Tórshavn; tel. 312200; fax 312262; e-mail loysing@post.olivant.fo; internet www.tjodveldi.fo; f. 1948 as Tjóðveldisflokkurin; adopted current name 2007; left-wing, advocates the secession of the Faroes from Denmark; Chair. HØGNI HOYDAL.

Religion

CHRISTIANITY

The Faroes National Church (Fólkakirkjan) is the established church in the islands. Formerly a diocese of the Evangelical Lutheran Church of Denmark, it gained independence in July 2007 as part of an agreement signed in 2005 between the Faroese and Danish authorities regarding the transfer of competencies to the Faroese Government. The Church had 40,065 members in 2010, accounting for 82.5% of the population. The largest independent group is the Plymouth Brethren. There is also a small Roman Catholic community.

Evangelical Lutheran Church

Føroyska Fólkakirkjan (Faroes National Church): Føroya Stiftsstjórn, J. Paturssonargøta 20, 100 Tórshavn; tel. 311995; fax 315889; e-mail tacks@folkakirkjan.fo; internet www.folkakirkjan.fo; f. 2007; 40,065 mems (2010); Bishop JÓGVAN FRÍÐRIKSSON.

Christian Brethren Assemblies (Plymouth Brethren)

Around 10% of the population of the Faroe Islands are adherents of the Christian Brethren Assemblies, of which there are 35 in total. The first assembly on the Islands was established in 1878 by a Scottish missionary.

Ebenezer Samkoman (Ebenezer Evangelical Church): N. Finsensgøta, 100 Tórshavn; tel. 311804; e-mail ebenezer@ebenezer.fo; internet www.ebenezer.fo; f. 1879.

The Roman Catholic Church

The Catholic Church in the Faroe Islands: Mariukirkjan (St Mary's Church), Mariugøta 4, 100 Tórshavn; tel. and fax 310380; e-mail sktmaria@post.olivant.fo; internet www.katolsk.fo; 150 adherents; Parish Priest Fr PAUL MARX.

The Press

In 2010 there were two daily newspapers in the Faroe Islands, *Dimmalætting* and *Sosialurin*, with a combined circulation of 16,500.

Dimmalætting: Staravegur 5, POB 3019, 110 Tórshavn; tel. 790200; fax 790201; e-mail redaktion@dimma.fo; internet www.dimma.fo; f. 1878; 5 a week; Tues. edn distributed free of charge; Editor BRYNHILD THOMSEN; circ. 8,500 (18,500 on Tues.).

Norðlýsið: Rygsvegur 3, POB 58, 700 Klaksvík; tel. 456285; fax 456498; e-mail info@nordlysid.fo; internet www.nordlysid.fo; f. 1915; weekly; Editor JOHN WILLIAM JOENSEN; circ. 6,400.

Oyggjatíðindi: Lýðarsvegur 19, POB 3312, 110 Tórshavn; tel. 314411; fax 316411; e-mail oyggjat@post.olivant.fo; internet www.oyggjatidindi.com; 2 a week; circ. 3,500.

Sosialurin: Tórsgøta 1, 110 Tórshavn; tel. 341800; fax 341801; e-mail post@sosialurin.fo; internet www.sosialurin.fo; f. 1927; 5 a week; 34% owned by Føroya Tele; Editor EIRIKUR LINDENSKOV; circ. 8,000.

Vikublaðið: Niels Winthersgøta 5, 110 Tórshavn; tel. 321000; fax 321005; e-mail vikublad@vikublad.fo; internet www.vikublad.fo; f. 2001; weekly; distributed free of charge; acquired by Dimmalætting P/F in 2008; Editor ERNST S. OLSEN; circ. 20,000.

Vinnuvitan: Smyrilsvegur 13, POB 3202, 110 Tórshavn; tel. 541200; fax 541201; e-mail info@vinnuvitan.fo; internet www.vinnuvitan.biz; f. 2004; weekly; business issues; acquired by Dimmalætting P/F in 2008; Editor (vacant); circ. 2,300.

Publishers

Bókadeild Føroya Lærarafelags: Pedda við Steinsgøta 9, 100 Tórshavn; tel. 317644; fax 319644; e-mail bfl@bfl.fo; internet www.bfl.fo; division of Faroese Teachers Assen; run on a commercial basis, but receives govt grants; children's books, a children's magazine (*Strok*) and a teachers' magazine (*Skúlablaðið*); Dir NIELS JÁKUP THOMSEN; Editors MARNA JACOBSEN, TURIÐ KJØLBRO.

Føroya Skúlabókagrunnur: Lützenstrøð 4, 100 Tórshavn; tel. 316100; fax 318726; e-mail snar@snar.fo; internet www.fsg.fo; educational; Chair. ÁRNI DAHL.

Broadcasting and Communications

TELECOMMUNICATIONS

The Faroese telecommunications industry, formerly a monopoly under Føroya Tele, was opened to competition in the early 2000s.

Fjarskiftiseftirlitið (Telecommunications Authority of the Faroe Islands): Skálatrøð 20, POB 73, 110 Tórshavn; tel. 356020; fax 356035; e-mail fjarskiftiseftirlitid@fjarskiftiseftirlitid.fo; internet www.fjarskiftiseftirlitid.fo; f. 1997; independent govt agency with regulatory powers; Dir JÓGVAN THOMSEN.

Føroya Tele (Faroese Telecom): Klingran 3, POB 27, 110 Tórshavn; tel. 303030; fax 303031; e-mail ft@ft.fo; internet www.tele.fo; f. 1906; owned by Faroese Govt; fixed-line and mobile cellular telecommunications, broadband internet services; Chair. KLAUS PEDERSEN; CEO KRISTIAN R. DAVIDSEN.

Vodafone: Óðinshædd 2, POB 3299, 110 Tórshavn; tel. 202020; fax 202021; e-mail vodafone@vodafone.fo; internet www.vodafone.fo; f. 1999 as Kall P/F; name changed as above 2008; offers mobile cellular telecommunications and broadband internet access; CEO GUDNY LANGGAARD.

BROADCASTING

Radio

Kringvarp Føroya (Faroese Broadcasting Corpn): Norðari Ringvegur 20, Postboks 1299, 110 Tórshavn; tel. 347500; fax 347501; e-mail netvarp@kringvarp.fo; internet www.kringvarp.fo; f. 2005 by merger of Sjónvarp Føroya (Faroese Television) and Útvarp Føroya (Radio Faroe Islands); Man. ANNIKA MITTÚN JACOBSEN.

Television

P/F Televarpið: Klingran 1, POB 3128, 110 Tórshavn; tel. 340340; fax 340341; e-mail televarp@televarp.fo; internet www.televarp.fo; f. 2002; digital terrestrial broadcaster; provides 28 channels; subsidiary of Føroya Tele; Man. Dir LAILA HENTZE.

Finance

BANKS

(cap. = capital; res = reserves; dep. = deposits; m. = million; brs = branches; amounts in kroner)

Bank Nordik P/F (Faroese Bank): Húsagøta 3, POB 3048, 110 Tórshavn; tel. 330330; fax 330001; e-mail info@foroya.fo; internet www.foroya.fo/ir; f. 1994 as Føroya Banki P/F following merger of Føroya Banki (f. 1906) and Sjóvinnubankin (f. 1932); name changed as above 2010; 33.3% owned by Faroese Govt through Finansieringsfonden af 1992 following privatization in June 2007; cap. 200m., res 58.5m., dep. 9,089.2m. (Dec. 2010); Chair. KLAUS RASMUSSEN; CEO JANUS PETERSEN; 9 brs.

Landsbanki Føroya (Faroese Government Bank): Yviri við Strond 15, POB 229, 110 Tórshavn; tel. 350300; fax 350301; e-mail landsbankin@landsbankin.fo; internet landsbankin.fo; financial administrator for the Faroe Islands, primarily with respect to the national treasury, but also acts as financial adviser/administrator for public bodies and agencies; Man. Dir SIGURÐ POULSEN.

Eik Banki P/F: Yviri við Strond 2, POB 34, 110 Tórshavn; tel. 348000; fax 348800; e-mail eik@eik.fo; internet www.eik.fo; f. 1832; Bank's activities transferred to Eik Banki Foroya P/F in 2010; cap. 813m., res 764m., dep. 6,429m. (Sept. 2009); Chair. TORBEN NIELSEN; CEO SÚNI SCHWARTZ JACOBSEN; 15 brs.

Norðoya Sparikassi: Ósávegur 1, POB 149, 700 Klaksvík; tel. 475000; fax 476000; e-mail ns@ns.fo; internet www.ns.fo; savings bank; Man. Dir EYÐFINN REYÐBERG.

Suðuroyar Sparikassi P/F: POB 2, 900 Vágur; tel. 359870; fax 359871; e-mail sparsu@sparsu.fo; internet www.sparsu.fo; savings bank; Man. Dir SØREN L. BRUHN.

STOCK EXCHANGE

Virðisbrævamarknaður Føroya P/F (VMF) (Faroese Securities Market): c/o Landsbanki Føroya, Yviri við Strond 15, POB 229, 110 Tórshavn; tel. 350300; fax 350301; internet vmf.fo; f. 2000; lists Faroese securities in co-operation with Nasdaq OMX Iceland; Chair. STEFÁN HALLDÓRSSON; CEO SIGURÐ POULSEN.

INSURANCE

Tryggingareftirlitið (Insurance Authority): Skálatrøð 20, POB 73, 110 Tórshavn; tel. 356020; fax 356035; e-mail tryggingareftirlitid@tryggingareftirlitid.fo; internet www.tryggingareftirlitid.fo; nat. financial supervisory authority with jurisdiction over insurance, pension funds and one mortgage credit institution; Dir JÓGVAN THOMSEN.

Føroya Lívstrygging P/F (Lív) (Faroese Life Assurance Co): Kopargøta, POB 206, 110 Tórshavn; tel. 311111; fax 351110; e-mail liv@liv.fo; internet www.liv.fo; f. 1967; reorg. 2000; owned by Faroese Govt; partial privatization pending; life insurance; Man. Dir POUL CHRISTOFFUR THOMASSEN.

Trygd P/F: Gongin 7, POB 44, 110 Tórshavn; tel. 358100; fax 317211; e-mail trygd@trygd.fo; internet www.trygd.fo; f. 1932; activities suspended 1940–97; owned by Føroya Banki P/F; all types of insurance, both marine and non-marine; Man. Dir JANUS THOMSEN.

Tryggingarfelagið Føroyar P/F: Kongabrúgvin, POB 329, 110 Tórshavn; tel. 345600; fax 345601; e-mail tf@trygging.fo; internet www.trygging.fo; f. 1998; all types of insurance, both marine and non-marine; Man. Dir REGIN HAMMER.

Trade and Industry

GOVERNMENT AGENCIES

Jarðfeingi (Faroese Earth and Energy Directorate): Brekkutún 1, POB 3059, 110 Tórshavn; tel. 357000; fax 357001; e-mail jardfeingi@jardfeingi.fo; internet www.jardfeingi.fo; f. 2006 by merger of Oljufyrisitingin (Faroese Petroleum Administration) and Jarðfrøðisavnið (Faroese Geological Survey); responsible for the administration and responsible utilization of all Faroese earth and energy resources, including hydrocarbons; Dir PETUR JOENSEN.

Kappingarráðið (Competition Council): Skálatrøð 20, POB 73, 110 Tórshavn; tel. 356040; fax 356055; e-mail terje@kapping.fo; internet www.kapping.fo; f. 1997; consists of a chairman and 3 members, appointed by the Minister of Trade and Industry for a 4-year term; Chair. JÓGVAN THOMSEN.

INDUSTRIAL AND TRADE ASSOCIATIONS

L/F Føroya Fiskasøla—Faroe Seafood P/F: Vestara Bryggja, POB 68, 110 Tórshavn; tel. 355555; fax 355550; e-mail meinhard@faroe.com; internet www.faroe.com; f. 1948; restructured 1995; jt stock co of fish producers; exports all seafood products; Chair. ANFINNUR OLSEN; CEO MEINHARD JACOBSEN.

Føroya Reiðarafelag (Faroe Shipowners' Assen): Gongin 10, POB 361, 110 Tórshavn; tel. 311800; fax 320380; e-mail shipown@olivant.fo; internet www.shipowner-fo.com; f. 1908; Chair. VIBERG SØRENSEN.

SamVit (Faroe Islands Enterprise): Bryggjubakki 12, POB 259, 110 Tórshavn; tel. 353100; fax 353101; e-mail samvit@samvit.fo; internet www.samvit.fo; f. 2006 by merger of Faroe Islands Trade Council and Faroe Islands Tourist Board; Man. Dir ELIN HEINESEN.

Vinnuhúsið (House of Industry): Smærugøta 9A, POB 1038, 100 Tórshavn; tel. 309900; fax 309901; e-mail industry@industry.fo; internet www.industry.fo; confed. of industrial orgs; 15 branches representing all areas of Faroese industry; Dir MARITA RASMUSSEN.

UTILITIES

Electricity

Elfelagið SEV: Landavegur 92, POB 319, 110 Tórshavn; tel. 346800; fax 346801; e-mail sev@sev.fo; internet www.sev.fo; owned by Faroese Govt; Man. Dir HÁKUN DJURHUUS.

Gas

AGA Føroyar Sp/f (Føroya Gassøla): Akranesgøta 2, POB 1088, 110 Tórshavn; tel. 315544; fax 311706; e-mail gassola@gassola.fo; internet gassola.fo; subsidiary of AGA A/S (Denmark); Dir ANNFINN HANNSON.

Water

Local councils are responsible for the provision of water.

EMPLOYERS' ORGANIZATION

Føroya Arbeiðsgevarafelag (Faroese Employers' Asscn): Vinnuhúsið, Smærugøta 9A, POB 1038, 110 Tórshavn; tel. 311864; fax 317278; e-mail industry@industry.fo; internet www.industry.fo; more than 550 mem. cos; owns and manages House of Industry (see above); organized in 15 sectoral asscns, including Faroe Trade Masters Asscn, Faroe Fish Producers' Asscn, Faroe Fish Farming Asscn, Fed. of Faroes Industries, Faroe Merchant and Shopkeepers Asscn and Faroe Oil Industries Asscn; Chair. JÓHAN PÁLL JOENSEN.

TRADE UNION

Føroya Arbeiðarafelag (Faroese Labour Organization): Tjarnardeild 5–7, POB 56, 110 Tórshavn; tel. 312101; fax 315374; e-mail fafelag@fafelag.fo; internet www.fafelag.fo; Chair. INGEBORG VINTHER.

Transport

There are about 458 km of roads in the Faroe Islands. A 4.9-km tunnel running under the sea, linking Vágur to Streymoy, was opened in December 2002. A second tunnel, linking Borðoy with Eysturoy, was opened in 2006. Three further tunnels are under construction, one joining Eysturoy with Streymoy (due for completion in 2013), another linking Sandoy with southern Streymoy (due for completion in 2014), and the third joining Runavík with Tórshavn (due for completion in 2016).

The main harbour is at Tórshavn; the other ports are at Fuglafjørður, Klaksvík, Skálafjørður, Tvøroyri, Vágur and Vestmanna. Between mid-May and mid-September a ferry service links the Faroe Islands with Iceland, Denmark and Norway.

There is an airport on Vágur. There are no railway lines in the Faroe Islands.

Atlantic Airways P/F: Vágur Airport, 380 Sørvágur; tel. 341000; fax 341001; e-mail info@atlantic.fo; internet www.atlantic.fo; f. 1987; 67% owned by Faroese Govt; part privatized 2007; scheduled and charter passenger and cargo services to Denmark (Copenhagen, Billund and Aalborg), Greenland, Iceland (Reykjavík), Norway (Stavanger and Oslo), Sweden (Stockholm) and the United Kingdom (London, the Shetland Islands and Aberdeen); CEO MAGNI ARGE.

Smyril Line P/F: Yviri við Strond 1, POB 370, 110 Tórshavn; tel. 345900; fax 345901; e-mail office@smyril-line.fo; internet www.smyril-line.com; f. 1982; ferry services to Denmark, Iceland and Norway; Man. Dir RÚNI VANG POULSEN.

Tourism

Tourism is the Islands' second largest industry after fishing. In 2006 there were 116,236 tourist arrivals.

SamVit (Faroe Islands Enterprise): Bryggjubakka 17, POB 118, 100 Tórshavn; tel. 355800; fax 355801; e-mail tourist@tourist.fo; internet www.faroeislands.com; f. 2006 by merger of Faroe Islands Tourist Board and Faroe Islands Trade Council; Dir ELIN HEINESEN.

Defence

See the chapter on Denmark.

Education

The education system is similar to that of Denmark, except that Faroese is the language of instruction. Danish is, however, a compulsory subject in all schools. Education is compulsory for nine years between seven and 16 years of age. There is one University in the Faroe Islands.

In 2008 government expenditure on education, research and culture was budgeted at 833.6m. kroner (representing 17.6% of total budgetary spending).

GREENLAND

Introductory Survey

LOCATION, CLIMATE, LANGUAGE, RELIGION, FLAG, CAPITAL

Greenland (Kalaallit Nunaat) is the world's largest island, with a total area of 2,166,086 sq km, and lies in the North Atlantic Ocean, east of Canada. Most of the territory is permanently covered by ice, but 410,449 sq km of coastland are habitable. Greenlandic (Kakaallisut), an Inuit language, is the official language, although Danish is also widely spoken. The majority of the population profess Christianity and belong mainly to the Evangelical Lutheran Church of Denmark. There are also small communities of other Protestant groups and of Roman Catholics. The flag (proportions 2 by 3) consists of two equal horizontal stripes (white above red), on which is superimposed a representation of the rising sun (a disc divided horizontally, red above white) to the left of centre. Nuuk (Godthåb) is the capital.

CONTEMPORARY POLITICAL HISTORY

Domestic Political Affairs

Greenland first came under Danish rule in 1380. In the revision of the Danish Constitution in 1953, Greenland became part of the Kingdom and acquired the representation of two members in the Danish Folketing (parliament). In October 1972 the Greenlanders voted, by 9,658 to 3,990, against joining the European Community (EC, now European Union—EU, see p. 276) but, as part of Denmark, were bound by the Danish decision to join. Resentment of Danish domination of the economy, education and the professions continued, taking expression when, in 1977, the nationalist Siumut (Forward) movement formed a left-wing party. In 1975 the Minister for Greenland appointed a commission to devise terms for Greenland home rule, and its proposals were approved, by 73.1% to 26.9%, in a referendum among the Greenland electorate in January 1979. Siumut, led by a Lutheran pastor, Jonathan Motzfeldt, secured 13 seats in the 21-member Landsting (parliament—known as Inatsisartut in Greenlandic) at a general election in April, and a five-member Landsstyre (Home Rule Government), with Motzfeldt as Prime Minister, took office in May. From 1979 the island gradually assumed full administration of its internal affairs.

In February 1982 a referendum was held to decide Greenland's continued membership of the EC. This resulted in a 53% majority in favour of withdrawal. In May the Danish Government commenced negotiations on Greenland's behalf, and from February 1985 Greenland was accorded the status of an overseas territory in association with the Community, with preferential access to EC markets.

At the April 1983 general election to the Landsting (enlarged, by measures adopted in 1982, to between 23 and 26 seats, depending on the proportion of votes cast), Siumut and the conservative Atassut (Solidarity) party won 12 seats each, while the Inuit Ataqatigiit (Inuit Brotherhood—IA) obtained two seats. Siumut once again formed a Government, led by Motzfeldt, dependent on the support of the IA members in the Landsting: this support was withdrawn in March 1984, when the IA members voted against the terms of withdrawal from the EC, and Motzfeldt resigned. In the ensuing general election, held in June, Siumut and Atassut won 11 seats each, while the IA took three seats. Motzfeldt formed a coalition Government, comprising Siumut and the IA.

In March 1987 the coalition Government collapsed, following a dispute between Siumut and the IA over policy towards the modernization of the US radar facility at Thule, which was claimed by the IA to be in breach of the 1972 US-Soviet Anti-Ballistic Missile Treaty. A general election was held in May. Siumut and Atassut retained 11 seats each in the Landsting (which had been enlarged to 27 seats, 23 of which were to be obtained by election in multi-member constituencies, while four were to be supplementary seats); the IA won four seats, and the remaining seat was secured by the newly formed Issittup Partiia. Motzfeldt eventually formed a new coalition Government with the IA. In June 1988 the coalition between Siumut and the IA collapsed, and Motzfeldt formed a new Siumut Government, with support from Atassut. In December 1990, when Atassut withdrew its support (following allegations that government ministers had misused public funds), Motzfeldt organized an early general election for March 1991. Siumut retained 11 seats in the Landsting, while Atassut's representation decreased to eight seats and the IA's increased to five. A new party, the liberal Akulliit Partiiaat, won two seats, and the remaining place was taken by the Issittup Partiia. Siumut and the IA formed a coalition Government, with the Chairman of Siumut, Lars Emil Johansen, as Prime Minister.

At the general election held in March 1995 Siumut increased its representation in the Landsting (enlarged to 31 seats) to 12 seats, while Atassut won 10 seats and the IA obtained six. A coalition

Government was formed between Siumut and Atassut, following the withdrawal from negotiations of the IA, owing to disagreements regarding the question of independence. Johansen retained the premiership. In September 1997 Johansen resigned from the Landsstyre and was replaced as Prime Minister by Motzfeldt.

At the general election held in February 1999 Siumut remained the largest party in the Landsting, winning 11 seats. Atassut obtained eight seats, while the IA won seven. On 22 February a coalition Government was formed between Siumut and the IA. Jonathan Motzfeldt retained the premiership, while Josef Motzfeldt, the Chairman of the IA, was appointed Minister of Economy, Trade and Taxation.

In September 2001 Jonathan Motzfeldt was forced to resign as leader of Siumut, after he was held responsible for a deficit of 3,000m. kroner on the part of Royal Greenland (the island's main fish and seafood export company); however, he retained the post of Prime Minister. In December the IA withdrew from the coalition Government, accusing Siumut of lacking direction in its policies. Siumut subsequently formed a new coalition Government with Atassut.

At the general election held on 3 December 2002 Siumut won 10 seats in the Landsting, compared with eight for the IA and seven for Atassut. Demokraatit (the Democrats, a new party formed in October 2002) won five seats and Kattusseqatigiit (Alliance of Independent Candidates) one seat. Later that month Siumut and the IA formed a coalition Government, viewed by many as being strongly pro-independence, under Hans Enoksen of Siumut as Prime Minister. The Government was, however, extremely short-lived: the appointment to the most senior post of the civil service of Jens Lybeth, Enoksen's electoral campaign manager and close personal friend, prompted accusations of favouritism. Lybeth then engaged the services of an Inuit 'healer' to 'chase away evil spirits' from government offices, urging some 600 civil servants to use similar methods to promote harmony between Greenlanders and Danes. In the ensuing furore, Enoksen was obliged to dismiss Lybeth. Josef Motzfeldt, the Deputy Prime Minister and Chairman of the IA, remained dissatisfied with the situation, and approached Demokraatit to discuss ousting Enoksen and forming a new Government. Enoksen, again compelled to act, dissolved the coalition in January 2003 and formed a new Government in coalition with Atassut.

The new Government was dogged by political controversy, most notably the discord between the coalition partners concerning the revision of a commercial fishing agreement with the EU. In early September 2003 the leaders of Siumut called for a formal investigation into allegations that Augusta Salling, the Minister of Finance and Chairperson of Atassut, was involved in an accounting discrepancy amounting to some 97m. kroner. Salling threatened to withdraw Atassut from the coalition unless she received a guarantee that she would not face a motion of no confidence when the Landsting assembled later that month. Siumut was unwilling to give her such a guarantee, and the governing coalition was consequently dissolved on 9 September. Siumut and the IA formed a new coalition Government, with Enoksen as Prime Minister, on 13 September.

In January 2004, following negotiations between Enoksen and the Danish Prime Minister, Anders Fogh Rasmussen, it was announced that the Danish Government and the Landsstyre were to appoint a joint commission in early 2004 to explore ways of granting greater devolution to Greenland, after civil servants had presented their recommendations. Greenland was to remain within the Kingdom of Denmark, however, and would continue receiving grants from Denmark. In March 2005, following a request by the joint commission to the Danish Ministry of Justice, Greenlanders were granted recognition as a separate people under international law. Whether this required recognition by the UN, and whether it granted Greenlanders sovereign rights, remained unresolved.

In June 2005 Jens Napãtôk, the Minister of Infrastructure, Housing and the Environment, resigned following revelations that he had used public funds for personal expenses. Tension in the ruling coalition intensified in August, when an audit report showed that Rasmus Frederiksen, the Minister of Fisheries and Hunting, had also misused public funds, prompting his resignation from the Landsstyre. A further four members of the Government could not provide sufficient documentation for their spending. The governing coalition finally collapsed in September, when Siumut and the IA failed to reach an agreement on the budget. Enoksen called an early election, which was held on 15 November 2005. Siumut retained 10 seats in the Landsting, while Demokraatit and the IA each took seven seats. Atassut secured six seats, and the remaining seat was won by Kattusseqatigiit Partiiat (as the alliance had been restyled). Siumut, Atassut and the IA formed a coalition Government, with Enoksen as Prime Minister. Jørgen Wæver Johansen, who had been the Minister of Social Affairs and Labour in 1999–2001, returned to the Landsstyre as Minister of Housing, Infrastructure, Minerals and Petroleum.

In late April 2007 the governing coalition collapsed, marking the culmination of an ongoing dispute between the IA and Siumut regarding government policy on the regulation of the prawn fishing industry. In May a new coalition comprising Siumut and Atassut took office. Enoksen remained as Prime Minister and Finn Karlsen of Atassut became Deputy Prime Minister, while regaining his previous role as Minister for Fisheries, Hunting and Agriculture. The appointment of Lars Emil Johansen as Minister of Finance and Foreign Affairs proved controversial, owing to his role as one of Greenland's two representatives in the Danish Folketing and later in May he resigned from the Government. In July Enoksen effected a government reorganization, in which the Minister for Family Affairs and Justice, Aleqa Hammond of Siumut, was appointed to replace Johansen. The family affairs and justice portfolio was divided and its responsibilities were allocated to other members of the Landsstyre. In January 2008 a minor reshuffle of ministerial responsibilities took place. Arkalo Abelsen relinquished the environment portfolio, while gaining that of family affairs (and thus became Minister for Family Affairs and Health), and Kim Kielsen took the title of Minister for Infrastructure, the Environment, Minerals and Petroleum.

Following extensive negotiations, in May 2008 the Danish-Greenlandic Self-rule Commission on autonomy presented its final report to the Danish and Greenlandic premiers. Most notably, the report recommended the division of all future revenues from the exploitation of petroleum reserves in Greenland's waters. Under the proposals, up to 75m. kroner in annual revenue would be allocated solely to Greenland; any further revenue would be divided equally between Denmark and the Self-rule Government (Naalakkersuisut—as the Home Rule Government was henceforth to be known), and the annual block-grant paid by Denmark would be reduced annually by an amount equivalent to the revenues allocated to Denmark. The proposed reforms also included the establishment of Greenlandic as the sole official language and the assumption of policing and judicial powers by the Greenlandic authorities. Foreign affairs, defence, rulings by the Danish Supreme Court and policies regarding currency remained outside of the self-rule agreement. The proposals were welcomed by both Enoksen and Fogh Rasmussen and were incorporated in the draft Act on Greenland Self-rule. At a referendum held in Greenland on 25 November, at which 72.0% of the electorate participated, the new Act was approved by 75.5% of voters.

Meanwhile, in September 2008 Hammond resigned as Minister of Finance and Foreign Affairs, citing her disapproval of the Government's economic policies. She was replaced by the former leader of Demokraatit, Per Berthelsen, who had defected to Siumut earlier that month. In November Abelsen was forced to resign as Minister of Family Affairs and Health, following accusations that he had breached legislation regarding ministerial accountability. Abelsen, who had been criticized by both opposition and government representatives for withholding information from a parliamentary committee, tendered his resignation following demands for a vote of no confidence in him by the opposition; Naja Petersen of Atassut was appointed to replace him.

An early general election was held on 2 June 2009, in advance of the entry into effect of the self-rule agreement scheduled for 21 June. The election resulted in a defeat for the ruling coalition and a strong performance from the IA, which became the largest party in the Landsting for the first time, taking 44.0% of votes cast and doubling its representation to 14 seats (two short of an overall majority). Siumut won 26.8% of votes and nine seats, Demokraatit 12.8% and four seats, and Atassut 10.9% and three seats. The IA subsequently formed a coalition with Demokraatit and Kattusseqatigiit Partiiat, which held the one remaining seat. Kuupik Kleist, the leader of the IA, became the first Prime Minister from a party other than Siumut in the new administration, which took office on 12 June. Kleist also took responsibility for foreign affairs, while other appointments included Jens B. Frederiksen of Demokraatit as Deputy Prime Minister and Minister for Housing, Infrastructure and Transport, and Anthon Frederiksen of Kattusseqatigiit Partiiat as Minister of Domestic Affairs, Nature and the Environment. The self-rule arrangements duly entered into force on 21 June at a ceremony in Nuuk attended by Queen Margrethe II.

In March 2011 a cabinet reorganization and a reconfiguration of portfolios took place: Mimi Karlsen of the IA, hitherto the Minister for Culture, Education, Research and Church Affairs became the Minister for Social Affairs, Culture, Church Affairs and Gender Equality; Palle Christiansen of Demokraatit, who had been the Minister for Finance, assumed responsibility for education and research, while remaining the Member of the Greenland Government for Nordic Co-operation; and Maliina Abelsen, previously Minister for Family Affairs, was appointed Minister for Finance.

Foreign Affairs

Denmark remains ultimately responsible for Greenland's foreign relations. Greenland does, however, have separate representation on the Nordic Council (see p. 464), and is a member of the Inuit Circumpolar Council (see p. 451). Denmark, a member of the North Atlantic Treaty Organization (NATO, see p. 370), retains its responsibility for defence. Danish-US military co-operation in Greenland began in 1951, when Denmark signed a defence agreement with the US Government to allow four US bases in Greenland, including the Thule airbase, near the Uummannaq Inuit settlement. Two years after the establishment of the base the indigenous Inuits, whose hunting grounds had been severely diminished by the development of the base, were forcibly resettled further north in Qaanaaq. Under a 1981 agreement on the defence of Greenland, two US radar bases were established on the island, at Thule and at Kangerlussuaq (Søndre Strømfjord). An agreement between the USA and Denmark for the reduction of the size of the bases from 325,000 ha to 160,000 ha took effect from October 1986, and the land thus available was returned to the Inuit. In March 1991 the USA agreed to transfer ownership and control of the base at Kangerlussuaq to the Landsstyre in September 1992, in exchange for the right to use it again in the future. In August 1999 the Danish High Court ordered the Danish Government to pay compensation of 500,000 kroner to Inuits who had been forced to leave their land in 1953 to allow for the expansion of the base at Thule; a subsequent appeal against the ruling was rejected by the Danish Supreme Court in November 2003.

Jonathan Motzfeldt and the Danish Minister of Foreign Affairs, Mogens Lykketoft, agreed in February 2001 not to adopt an official policy on the proposed US missile defence system, which would involve the upgrading of the early-warning radar station at the Thule base, pending an official request by the USA. Motzfeldt did, however, express personal concern at the plans, and called on the USA to discuss the proposals with its NATO allies. He added that Greenland would not accept the plans if they proved to be in breach of the 1972 Anti-Ballistic Missile Treaty, or if Russia opposed them. Josef Motzfeldt and the opposition parties of the Folketing had expressed strong opposition to the proposals, claiming that they risked provoking another 'arms race'. Public opinion in Greenland was also strongly opposed to the plans; many feared that they would place Greenland at the centre of potential future conflicts.

In September 2002 the USA returned the town of Dundas (also known as Uummannaq in Greenlandic) and its surroundings to Greenland; the USA had incorporated it into the Thule base some 50 years earlier. The US Administration formally submitted a request to upgrade the facilities at the Thule base in December 2002. In May 2003 Enoksen and the Danish Minister of Foreign Affairs, Dr Per Stig Møller, signed a Danish-Greenlandic principle agreement under which Greenland was to gain greater influence in foreign policy relating to the island, in return for its support for the modernization of the Thule base as part of the US missile defence programme. Henceforth, Denmark was to consult Greenland on foreign policy matters in which Greenland was directly involved; the Landsstyre was to participate in future negotiations with Denmark on Greenland's foreign policy. Greenland was to be a co-signatory to future international agreements, provided they did not compromise local rights.

In May 2004 Greenland, Denmark and the USA reached an agreement on the upgrading of radar facilities at the Thule base as part of the US missile defence programme. The Landsstyre, the Foreign and Security Policy Committee of the Landsting and the Danish Folketing all approved the agreement unanimously, and it was signed in August by the Deputy Prime Minister, Josef Motzfeldt, the US Secretary of State, Colin Powell, and Møller. Under the agreement both Greenland and Denmark were to have representatives at the base, and Greenland's flag was to be flown there alongside those of the USA and Denmark. The USA was required both to consult with Greenland and Denmark on any further developments at the base and henceforth to notify the Landsstyre of any US aircraft landing outside the regular airports in Greenland. Agreements were also concluded on wider co-operation between Greenland and the USA, in areas such as research, energy, the environment and education.

In June 1980 the Danish Government declared an economic zone extending 200 nautical miles (370 km) off the east coast of Greenland. This, however, caused a dispute with Norway over territorial waters, owing to the existence of the small Norwegian island of Jan Mayen, 460 km off the east coast of Greenland. In 1988 Denmark requested the International Court of Justice (ICJ), based in The Hague, Netherlands, to arbitrate on the issue of conflicting economic zones. A delimitation line was established by the ICJ in June 1993. A subsequent accord on maritime delimitation, agreed between the Governments of Norway, Greenland and Iceland in November 1997, established the boundaries of a 1,934-sq km area of Arctic sea that had been excluded from the terms of the 1993 settlement. In January 2002 Greenland and the Faroe Islands renewed an agreement granting the mutual right to fish in each other's waters.

Greenland hosted a ministerial meeting of the Arctic Council (see p. 448) in Nuuk in May 2011, at which the eight member states agreed to increase co-operation in search and rescue efforts in the Arctic. A document issued jointly by the Governments of Denmark, Greenland and the Faroes in August, detailing their strategy for the Arctic during 2011–20, notably stated that, by 2014, they planned to submit evidence to the UN Commission on the Limits of the Continental Shelf supporting their claim to sovereignty three areas near Greenland, one of which included the North Pole. Meanwhile, the Greenland and Faroe military commands were to be merged to form a joint service Arctic Command.

In June 2008 the International Whaling Commission (IWC), in which Greenland is represented by Denmark, rejected a request on behalf of Greenland to be allowed to hunt humpback whales during the following year. Following the decision, the Deputy Prime Minister and Minister for Fisheries, Hunting and Agriculture, Finn Karlsen, advocated the withdrawal of Greenland from the IWC in a letter to the Danish Minister of Foreign Affairs. In June 2010, however, the IWC agreed to allow Greenland to hunt humpback whales for the first time since 1986, setting a quota of nine per year during 2010–12.

GOVERNMENT

Greenland is part of the Kingdom of Denmark. Since 1979 the Greenlandic authorities have gradually assumed control of the administration of Greenland's internal affairs. At a referendum held in Greenland on 25 November 2008 the Act on Greenlandic Self-rule was adopted. The reforms, which included the establishment of Greenlandic as the sole official language and the assumption of policing and judicial powers by the Greenlandic authorities, entered into effect from 21 June 2009. Foreign affairs, defence, rulings by the Danish Supreme Court and policies regarding currency remain with the Danish Government, the highest representative of which, in Greenland, is the High Commissioner (Rigsombudsmand). Members are elected for a maximum term of four years to the legislature, Inatsisartut (Landsting in Danish), on a basis of proportional representation. Based on the strength of the parties in the legislature, an executive, the Self-rule Government (Naalakkersuisut, or Landsstyre in Danish), is formed. Greenland sends two representatives to the Danish legislature, the Folketing.

For administration purposes, Greenland is divided into four municipalities, of which the largest is Qaasuitsup (which, by area, is also the largest municipality in the world). The merger of the previous 18 municipalities into just four took effect on 1 January 2009.

REGIONAL CO-OPERATION

Greenland, although a part of the Kingdom of Denmark, withdrew from the European Community (now the European Union—EU, see p. 276) in 1985. It remains a territory in association with the EU, however, and has preferential access to European markets. Greenland, the EU and Denmark signed a new partnership agreement in June 2006, allowing Greenland to continue to receive its EU subsidy in return for EU control over policies such as scientific research and climate change. Greenland is a member of the Nordic Council (see p. 464) and the Inuit Circumpolar Council (see p. 451).

ECONOMIC AFFAIRS

In 2006, according to official figures, Greenland's gross national income (GNI) was 10,394m. kroner, equivalent to 182,450 kroner per head. In 2007 the gross national income was 10,821m. kroner. The population remained almost constant in 2001–10. The economy enjoyed overall growth during the 1970s and 1980s, but gross domestic product (GDP) declined by 11.7%, in real terms, in 1990, according to the World Bank, and continued to decline (owing to depleted fish stocks and the discontinuation of lead and zinc mining) until 1994, when a real growth rate of 5.9% was recorded. Positive growth was maintained until 2008, with the exception of small contractions in 2002 and 2003: GDP increased, in real terms, by 5.5% in 2007 and by 0.3% in 2008, but decreased by 5.4% in 2009.

Agriculture (including animal husbandry, fishing and hunting) employed 3.8% of those in paid employment in 2009. Fishing dominates the commercial economy, as well as being important to the traditional way of life. In 2006 the fishing industry accounted for a provisional 88.0% of Greenland's total export revenue. In 2006 216,300 metric tons of fish (excluding aquatic mammals) were landed in Greenland. The traditional occupation of the Greenlanders is seal-hunting (for meat and fur), which remains important in the north. The most feasible agricultural activity in the harsh climate is livestock-rearing, and only sheep-farming has proved to be of any commercial significance. There are also herds of domesticated reindeer. However, owing to the effects of global warming, in the 2000s some farmers began to cultivate crops, including barley and vegetables.

Industry (including mining, manufacturing, construction and public works) employed some 14.1% of those in paid employment in 2009. Mining earned 13.0% of total export revenue in 1990, but in 2009 employed only 0.2% of the working population. Lead, zinc and some silver were extracted from the Black Angel mine at Marmorilik in the north-west until its closure in 1990. In May 2008 a British company, Angus & Ross (subsequently renamed Angel Mining), was granted a licence to reopen the mine; the company began the construction of a cable car to provide access to the mine in 2011. In December 2010 Angel Mining also began full production of gold at the Nalunaq mine at Kirkspirdalen, in southern Greenland, which it had purchased the previous year. Mineral deposits in Greenland also include diamonds, uranium and large reserves of rare earth elements (used in the manufacture of electronic components). Seismic analyses have indicated that there are significant reserves of petroleum and natural gas beneath the sea off the western coast of Greenland, and petroleum traces have been discovered in rocks in Disko Bay. In July 2010 a British company, Cairn Energy, commenced the first exploratory drilling operations in Baffin Bay since 2000; although the presence of traces of both natural gas and petroleum was discovered in one well, no commercially viable discoveries had been made by the end of 2011. Seven new licences for petroleum and gas exploration in Baffin Bay were awarded in December 2010, bringing the total number of hydrocarbon licences awarded in Greenland to 20, covering an area of some 200,000 sq km. In addition, licensing rounds for exploration in the Greenland Sea were scheduled for 2012–13. Global warming has facilitated access to deposits through the melting of sheet ice.

Manufacturing is mainly dependent upon the fishing industry and is dominated by processing plants for the shrimp industry. Water power (meltwater from the ice cap and glaciers) is an important potential source of electricity. All mineral fuels are imported. In 2007 crude petroleum accounted for a provisional 14.3% of total imports. Manufacturing employed only 2.4% of those in paid employment in 2009.

The services sector employed 82.1% of the working population in 2009; it is dominated by public administration, which alone employed 47.0% of the working population in that year. Tourism is increasingly important, but the sector is limited by the short season and high costs.

In 2010 Greenland recorded a trade deficit of 2,387m. kroner. Its principal trading partner remains Denmark, although its monopoly on trade ceased in 1950. Denmark supplied 66.5% of imports and received 86.8% of exports in 2009. Trade is still dominated by companies owned by the Self-rule Government. The principal export is food and live animals (accounting for a provisional 89.8% of total exports in 2010), mainly comprising fish and fish products. The principal imports in 2010 were machinery and transport equipment (accounting for 24.2% of total imports), petroleum oils and lubricants (accounting for 21.5% of total imports) and food and live animals (16.8% of total imports).

Greenland is dependent upon large grants from the central Danish Government. In 2010 central government expenditure on Greenland included some 4,227m. kroner in the form of a direct grant to the Greenlandic Government. Greenland has few debts, and also receives valuable revenue from the European Union (EU, see p. 276), for fishing licences. The 2010 budget recorded a surplus of 220m. kroner. The annual rate of inflation averaged 2.8% in 2001–10; consumer prices increased by 1.9% in 2010. In 2010 4.2% of the labour force were unemployed.

Greenland's economy has traditionally been dominated by the fishing industry. Migration to the towns and the rejection of a traditional lifestyle by many young people have, however, created new social and economic problems, while dependence on a single commodity has left the economy vulnerable to the effects of depletion of fish stocks and fluctuating international prices. After significant expansion in the late 1990s, the economy slowed in 2001 and contracted in both 2002 and 2003, owing to a decline in shrimp prices and high oil prices. Economic conditions began to improve in 2004 and 2005, with a rise in shrimp prices, and strong growth was recorded in 2006 and 2007. Following a deceleration in 2008, real GDP contracted by 5.4% in 2009, largely as a result of the impact of the global economic slowdown, with the value of exports declining by a provisional 22.4% in that year. Exports reportedly recorded strong growth in 2011, however, mainly owing to high fish prices. The annual Danish subsidy is fundamental to Greenlandic finances. However, it was hoped that exploitation of Greenland's mineral resources would provide a significant new source of income and lessen the reliance on Danish aid, with the eventual aim of achieving financial independence. The Act on Greenland Self-rule, which took effect in June 2009, provided for the allocation of state revenues from future mineral and petroleum exploitation to the Self-rule Government, together with a corresponding reduction in the Danish state subsidy. Tourism was also being promoted. The melting of the ice sheets due to global warming, while threatening the traditional way of life, was also expected to yield new economic opportunities, including the development of hydroelectric power and the discovery of further mineral deposits.

PUBLIC HOLIDAYS

Public holidays are the same as those for Denmark, with the exception of Constitution Day, which is not celebrated in Greenland. In addition, Greenlanders celebrate Mitaartut on 6 January, and Ullortuneq (Greenland's national day—literally, 'the longest day') on 21 June. Various regional holidays are also held to celebrate the return of the sun following the end of the long polar night; the timing of these vary according to latitude.

Statistical Survey

Sources: Statistics Greenland, *Statistical Yearbook;* Greenland Home Rule Government—Representation in Denmark, Strandgade 91, 3rd Floor, POB 2151, 1016 Copenhagen K; tel. 33-13-42-24; fax 33-13-49-71; Statistics Greenland, Manutooq 1, POB 1025, 3900 Nuuk; tel. 362366; fax 362361; e-mail stat@gh.gl; internet www.stat.gl.

AREA, POPULATION AND DENSITY

Area: Total 2,166,086 sq km (836,330 sq miles); ice-free portion 410,449 sq km (158,475 sq miles).

Population (official figures): 56,615 (males 29,942, females 26,673) at 1 January 2011.

Density (1 January 2011, ice-free portion): 0.14 per sq km.

Population by Age and Sex (official figures at 1 January 2011): *0–14:* 12,690 (males 6,465, females 6,225); *15–66:* 39,978 (males 21,491, females 18,487); *67 and over:* 3,947 (males 1,986, females 1,961); *Total* 56,615 (males 29,942, females 26,673).

Principal Towns (population at 1 January 2011): Nuuk (Godthåb, the capital) 15,862; Sisimiut 5,498; Ilulissat 4,606; Qaqortoq 3,230; Aasiaat 3,113.

Births, Marriages and Deaths (2010 unless otherwise indicated): Registered live births 868 (birth rate 15.4 per 1,000); Registered marriages (1999) 253 (marriage rate 4.5 per 1,000); Registered deaths 504 (death rate 8.9 per 1,000). Source: mainly UN, *Population and Vital Statistics Report*.

Life expectancy (years at birth, 2008): Males 66.6; Females 71.6.

Immigration and Emigration (2010): Immigrants 2,491 (persons born in Greenland 1,043, persons born outside Greenland 1,448); Emigrants 2,651 (persons born in Greenland 1,334, persons born outside Greenland 1,317).

Employment (employed persons with annual income exceeding 40,000 kroner, 2009): Agriculture, fishing and hunting 1,114; Quarrying 61; Manufacturing 698; Energy supply 417; Construction 2,986; Trade and repairs 4,469; Hotels and restaurants 914; Transportation and tourism 2,801; Financial and insurance services 177; Real estate and rental 1,210; Public administration services 13,881; Education 145; Health and social affairs 132; Other collective and social services 509; Activities not classified (incl. statistical discrepancy) 8; Total 29,522. *2010:* Total employed 32,263; Total unemployed 1,406; Total labour force 33,669.

HEALTH AND WELFARE

Key Indicators

Total Fertility Rate (children per woman, 2009): 2.4.

Physicians (per 1,000 head, 2000): 1.6.

Health Expenditure (general government, million kronor, 2008): 1,116.

Total Carbon Dioxide Emissions ('000 metric tons, 2007): 520.3.

Carbon Dioxide Emissions Per Head (metric tons, 2007): 9.2.

AGRICULTURE, ETC.

Livestock (2008): Sheep 20,494, Horses 203, Beehives 10, Poultry 148, Cattle 49, Reindeer 2,500.

Livestock Products (metric tons, 2010, FAO estimate): Sheep meat 340 (Source: FAO).

Hunting (2009): Musk ox 2,331; Polar bears 124; Polar fox 1,263; Polar hare 1,826; Reindeer 10,620.

Fishing ('000 metric tons, live weight, 2009): Greenland halibut 29.2; Lumpfish (Lumpsucker) 6.9; Capelin 0.2; Northern prawn 131.5; Total catch (incl. others) 197.9. The total excludes aquatic mammals, which are recorded by number rather than by weight. In 2009, unless otherwise indicated, the number of aquatic mammals caught was: Minke whale 169; Fin whale (2008) 14; Humpback whale 3; Long-finned pilot whale 107 (2008); Harbour porpoise 1,403 (2008); White whale 126 (2008); Narwhal 360 (2008); Walrus 94 (2008); Harp seal 80,037 (2008); Harbour seal 79 (2008); Ringed seal 68,876 (2008); Bearded seal 1,393 (2008); Hooded seal 723 (2008). Source: FAO.

INDUSTRY

Selected Products: Frozen fish 21,700 metric tons (2001); Electric energy 376 million kWh (2009); Dwellings completed 364 (2008). Source: partly UN, *Industrial Commodity Statistics Yearbook*.

FINANCE

(Danish currency is in use)

Central Government Current Expenditure (by Ministry, million kroner, 2000): Finance 2,725 (Grant to Home Rule Government 2,725), Defence (incl. Fisheries Inspection) 268, Justice 165, Environment and Energy 58, Transport 38, Research 7, Prime Minister's Office 8, Labour 3, Agriculture and Fisheries 1, Business and Industry 2, Total 3,274. *2003:* Grant to Home Rule Government 2,952m. kroner.

Budget (general government, million kroner, 2010): *Revenue:* Gross operating surplus 508; Interest, etc. 303; Taxes on production and imports 703 (Taxes on imports 526); Taxes on income, wealth, etc. 3,438; Transfers 4,545 (from Danish state 4,227); Total (incl. others) 9,606; *Expenditure:* Final consumption expenditure 6,638 (Compensation of employees 3,871); Income transfers 1,962 (Households 1,261); Non-financial capital accumulation 636; Investment grants and capital transfers 150 (Households 106); Total 9,386.

Cost of Living (Consumer Price Index; at July each year; base: 2000 = 100): All items 126.3 in 2008; 129.2 in 2009; 131.7 in 2010 (Source: ILO).

Gross Domestic Product (million kroner at current market prices): 10,112 in 2005; 10,636 in 2006; 11,063 in 2007 (provisional).

National Income and Product (million kroner at current prices, 2007, provisional): Compensation of employees 8,752; Gross operating surplus 2,172; *GDP at factor cost* 10,924; Indirect taxes 692; *Less* Subsidies 553; *GDP at market prices* 11,063; Net salary transfers –242; *Gross national income* 10,821; Expenditure of Danish Government 3,866; *Gross disposable national income* 14,687.

EXTERNAL TRADE

Principal Commodities (million kroner, 2010): *Imports c.i.f.:* Food and live animals 759.9; Beverages and tobacco 138.4; Raw materials, inedible 58.3; Petroleum oils and lubricants 973.1; Chemicals and chemical products 268.8; Manufactured goods and products thereof 576.2; Machinery and transport equipment 1,098.4; Manufactured products 535.1; Total (incl. others) 4,531.8. *Exports f.o.b.:* Food and live animals 1,925.8; Raw materials, inedible 19.4; Machinery and transport equipment 80.7; Manufactured products 20.7; Miscellaneous articles and transactions 91.6; Total exports (incl. others) 2,144.5.

Principal Trading Partners (million kroner, 2009): *Imports c.i.f.:* China, People's Republic 73.2; Denmark 2,440.1; Germany 98.5; Japan 34.5; Norway 51.2; Sweden 630.8; USA 49.5; Total (incl. others) 3,668.8. *Exports f.o.b.:* Canada 74.5; Denmark 1,669.7; Iceland 20.0; Japan 835.0; Norway 32.7; Portugal 71.3; United Kingdom 15.3; Total (incl. others) 1,923.4. *2010:* Total imports 4,531.8; Total exports 2,144.5.

TRANSPORT

Road Traffic (registered motor vehicles excl. emergency services, 2008): Private cars 5,036; Taxis 89; Buses 80; Lorries 355; Motorcycles 6.

Shipping (2000): Number of vessels 162 (passenger ships 7, dry cargo ships 39, fishing vessels 110, others 6); Total displacement 59,938 grt (passenger ships 5,780 grt, dry cargo ships 6,411 grt, fishing vessels 47,046 grt, others 701 grt).

International Sea-borne Freight Traffic ('000 cubic metres, 2003): Goods loaded 357; Goods unloaded 350.

International Transport (passengers conveyed between Greenland, Denmark and Iceland): Ship (1983) 94; Aircraft (2002) 103,562.

TOURISM

Occupancy of Registered Hotel Accommodation (nights, 2010): 216,141.

COMMUNICATIONS MEDIA

Radio Receivers (1997): 27,000 in use.

Television Receivers (1997): 22,000 in use.

Telephones ('000 main lines in use, 2010): 21.8.

Mobile Cellular Telephones ('000 subscribers, 2010): 57.3.

Internet Subscribers ('000, 2009): 12.2.

Broadband Subscribers ('000, 2010): 12.0.

Book Publishing (titles, 2008): 126.

Sources: UNESCO, *Statistical Yearbook,* International Telecommunication Union and UN, *Statistical Yearbook*.

EDUCATION

(municipal primary and lower secondary schools only, 2001/02)

Institutions: 87.

Teachers: 1,191 in 2000/01 (incl. 380 temporarily employed teachers and 202 non-Greenlandic-speaking teachers).

Students: 11,368.

2007/08 (Primary schools only): Teachers 1,189; Students 10,255.

Pupil-teacher Ratio (primary education, official estimate): 8.6 in 2007/08.

Directory

The Government

Since 1979 the Greenlandic authorities have gradually assumed control of the administration of Greenland's internal affairs. At a referendum held in Greenland on 25 November 2008 the Act on Greenlandic Self-rule was adopted. The reforms, which included the establishment of Greenlandic as the sole official language and the assumption of policing and judicial powers by the Greenlandic authorities, entered into effect from 21 June 2009. Foreign affairs, defence, rulings by the Danish Supreme Court and policies regarding currency remain with the Danish Government, the highest representative of which, in Greenland, is the High Commissioner (Rigsombudsmand). Based on the strength of the parties in the legislature, an executive, known as Naalakkersuisut (Landsstyre in Danish), is formed. Greenland sends two representatives to the Danish legislature, the Folketing.

HEAD OF STATE

Queen of Denmark: HM Queen MARGRETHE II.

NAALAKKERSUISUT

(Self-rule Government)
(May 2012)

A coalition of Inuit Ataqatigiit (IA), Demokraatit (D) and Kattusseqatigiit Partiiat (KP).

Prime Minister, responsible for Foreign Affairs: KUUPIK KLEIST (IA).

Deputy Prime Minister and Minister for Housing, Infrastructure and Transport: JENS B. FREDERIKSEN (D).

Minister for Finance: MALIINA ABELSEN (IA).

Minister for Fisheries, Hunting and Agriculture: ANE HANSEN (IA).

Minister for Industry and Mineral Resources: OVE KARL BERTHELSEN (IA).

Minister for Social Affairs, Culture, Church Affairs and Gender Equality: MIMI KARLSEN (IA).

Minister for Health: AGATHE FONTAIN (IA).

Minister for Education and Research, and Member of the Greenland Government for Nordic Co-operation: PALLE CHRISTIANSEN (D).

Minister for Domestic Affairs, Nature and the Environment: ANTHON FREDERIKSEN (KP).

Government Offices

Rigsombudsmanden i Grønland (High Commission of Greenland): Indaleeqqap Aqq. 3, POB 1030, 3900 Nuuk; tel. 321001; fax 324171; e-mail riomgr@gl.stm.dk; internet www.rigsombudsmanden.gl; High Commissioner SØREN HALD MØLLER.

Grønlands Selvstyre (Naalakkersuisut—Greenland Self-rule Government): Imaneq 4, POB 1015, 3900 Nuuk; tel. 345000; fax 325002; e-mail info@gh.gl; internet www.nanoq.gl.

Representation of Greenland in Copenhagen: Strandgade 91, 3rd Floor, POB 2151, 1016 Copenhagen K; tel. 32-83-38-00; fax 32-83-38-01; e-mail journal@ghsdk.dk.

Legislature

The legislative body, Inatsisartut (Landsting in Danish), has 31 members elected for four years, on a basis of proportional representation. Greenlanders and Danes resident in Greenland for at least six months prior to an election and over the age of 18 years have the right to vote.

Inatsisartut (Landsting)

POB 1060, 3900 Nuuk; tel. 345000; fax 324606; e-mail inatsisartut@inatsisartut.gl; internet www.inatsisartut.gl.

Chairman: JOSEF (TUUSI) MOTZFELDT.

General Election, 2 June 2009

	Votes	% of votes	Seats
Inuit Ataqatigiit (Inuit Brotherhood)	12,457	44.01	14
Siumut (Forward)	7,567	26.76	9
Demokraatit (Democrats)	3,620	12.80	4
Atassut (Solidarity)	3,094	10.94	3
Kattusseqatigiit Partiiat (Alliance of Independent Candidates)	1,084	3.83	1
Sorlaat Partiiat	383	1.35	—
Total (incl. others)	28,275	100.00	31

Political Organizations

Atassut (Solidarity): POB 399, 3900 Nuuk; tel. 323366; fax 325840; e-mail atassut@greennet.gl; internet www.atassut.gl; f. 1978 and became political party in 1981; supports close links with Denmark and favours EU membership for Greenland; Chair. GERHARDT PETERSEN.

Demokraatit (Democrats): POB 132, 3900 Nuuk; tel. 346281; fax 311084; e-mail demokrat@demokrat.gl; internet www.demokrat.gl; f. 2002; Chair. JENS B. FREDERIKSEN.

Inuit Ataqatigiit (Inuit Brotherhood—IA): POB 321, 3900 Nuuk; tel. 323702; fax 323232; e-mail ia@greennet.gl; internet www.ia.gl; f. 1978; socialist party, demanding that Greenland citizenship be restricted to those of Inuit parentage; advocates Greenland's eventual independence from Denmark; Leader KUUPIK KLEIST.

Kattusseqatigiit Partiiat (Alliance of Independent Candidates): POB 74, 3952 Ilulissat; tel. 944653; fax 944753; e-mail afr@ilulissat.gl; internet www.kattusseqatigiit.gl; Chair. ANTHON FREDERIKSEN.

Siumut (Forward): POB 357, 3900 Nuuk; tel. 322077; fax 322319; e-mail siumut@greennet.gl; internet www.siumut.gl; f. 1971 and became political party in 1977; aims to promote collective ownership and co-operation, and to develop greater reliance on Greenland's own resources; favours greatest possible autonomy within the Kingdom of Denmark; social democratic party; Chair. ALEQA HAMMOND.

Judicial System

The island is divided into 18 court districts and these courts all use lay assessors. For most cases these lower courts are for the first instance and appeal is to the Landsret, the higher court in Nuuk, which is the only one with a professional judge. This court hears the more serious cases in the first instance and appeal in these cases is to the East High Court (Østre Landsret) in Copenhagen.

Landsret (High Court): POB 1040, 3900 Nuuk; tel. 363800; fax 323975; e-mail landsret@lkr.gl; internet www.domstol.dk/gronland.

Religion

CHRISTIANITY

The Greenlandic Church, of which most of the population are adherents, forms an independent diocese of the Evangelical Lutheran Church in Denmark and comes under the jurisdiction of the Self-rule Government and of the Bishop of Greenland. There are 17 parishes and in 2007 there were 26 ministers serving in Greenland.

Biskoppen over Grønlands Stift (Bishop of Greenland): SOFIE PETERSEN, Evangelical Lutheran Church, Hans Egedesvej 9, POB 90, 3900 Nuuk; tel. 321312; fax 321061; e-mail bispekontor@gh.gl; internet www.groenlandsstift.dk.

There are also small groups of other Protestant churches and of Roman Catholics.

The Press

There are no daily newspapers in Greenland.

Arnanut: Spindlersbakke 10B, POB 150, 3900 Nuuk; tel. 343570; fax 322499; e-mail arnanut@sermitsiaq.gl; internet www.arnanut.gl; f. 2003; quarterly; women's magazine; Editor IRENE JEPPSON.

Atuagagdliutit (AG): Sipisaq Avannarleq 10, POB 39, 3900 Nuuk; tel. 383950; fax 322499; e-mail administration@sermitsiaq.ag; internet www.sermitsiaq.gl; f. 1861; weekly; Editor-in-Chief HEIDI MØLLER.

Niviarsiaq: POB 357, 3900 Nuuk; tel. 322077; fax 322319; e-mail contact@niviarsiaq.net; organ of Siumut; monthly; Editor MIKAEL PETERSEN.

Sermitsiaq: Sipisaq Avannarleq 10B, POB 150, 3900 Nuuk; tel. 383940; fax 322499; e-mail redaktion@sermitsiaq.gl; internet www.sermitsiaq.gl; f. 1958; weekly; published by Mediahouse Sermitsiaq; Editor POUL KRARUP.

Publishers

Ilinniusiorfik Undervisningsmiddelforlag: H. J. Rinksvej 35, 1st Floor, POB 1610, 3900 Nuuk; tel. 349889; fax 326236; e-mail ilinniusiorfik@ilinniusiorfik.gl; internet www.ilinniusiorfik.gl; Govt-owned; textbooks and teaching materials; non-profit-making org.; Man. ABIA ABELSEN.

Milik Publishing: POB 7017, 3905 Nuussuaq; tel. 322602; e-mail milik@greennet.gl; internet www.milik.gl; f. 2003; children's, culture and society; Publr LENE THERKILDSEN.

Broadcasting and Communications

TELECOMMUNICATIONS

TELE Greenland A/S: Farip Aqqutaa 8, POB 1002, 3900 Nuuk; tel. 341255; fax 325955; e-mail tele@tele.gl; internet www.tele.gl; f. 1994; Govt-owned; also owner of Greenland's postal service; Chair. AGNER MARK; Man. Dir SØREN ERIKSEN.

BROADCASTING

Radio

Kalaallit Nunaata Radioa: Kissarneqqortuunnguaq 15, POB 1007, 3900 Nuuk; tel. 361500; fax 361502; e-mail info@knr.gl; internet www.knr.gl; f. 1958; 5 AM stations, 45 FM stations; bilingual programmes in Greenlandic and Danish, 17 hours a day; Chair. HANS-PETER POULSEN.

Avannaata Radioa: POB 223, 3952 Ilulissat; tel. 943633; fax 943618; e-mail avannaata@radio.knr.gl; regional station in north Greenland.

Kujataata Radioa: POB 158, 3920 Qaqortoq; tel. 642234; fax 641334; e-mail kujataataradioa@knr.gl; regional station in south Greenland.

Radio—5 OZ 20: SPE BOX 139, 3970 Pituffik; tel. and fax 976680; FM/stereo, non-commercial station; broadcasts 21 hours a day; news, music, etc.; Station Man. INGRID KRISTENSEN.

Television

Kalaallit Nunaata Radioa—Greenlandic Broadcasting Corporation: see Radio section; broadcasts by VHF transmitter to all of Greenland; public service; most programmes in Danish.

Finance

BANK

(cap. = capital; res = reserves; dep. = deposits; m. = million; brs = branches; amounts in kroner)

Bank of Greenland—GrønlandsBANKEN A/S: Imaneq 33, POB 1033, 3900 Nuuk; tel. 701234; fax 347706; e-mail banken@banken.gl; internet www.banken.gl; f. 1967 as Bank of Greenland A/S; present name adopted following merger with Nuna Bank A/S in 1997; cap. 180m., res 24.4m., dep. 3,540.9m. (Dec. 2010); Chair. GUNNAR Í LIÐA; Gen. Man. MARTIN KVIESGAARD; 5 brs.

Trade and Industry

GOVERNMENT AGENCY

Råstofdirektoratet (Bureau of Minerals and Petroleum): POB 930, 3900 Nuuk; tel. 346800; fax 324302; e-mail bmp@gh.gl; internet www.bmp.gl; f. 1998; performs the central administrative co-ordinating and regulatory tasks regarding exploration and production of mineral resources in Greenland; Dep. Min. JØRN SKOV NIELSEN.

GOVERNMENT-OWNED COMPANIES

KNI A/S (Greenland Trade Service): J. M. Jensenip Aqq. 2, POB 319, 3911 Sisimiut; tel. 862444; fax 866263; internet www.pilersuisoq.gl; f. 1992; statutory wholesale and retail trading co, petroleum and fuel supply; Chair. MICHAEL MIKKILI SKOURUP; Man. Dir SØREN LENNERT MORTENSEN.

Pisiffik A/S: POB 1009, 3911 Sisimiut; tel. 862900; fax 864171; e-mail mos@pisiffik.gl; internet www.pisiffik.gl; f. 1993; statutory wholesale and retail trading co; co-owned by Dagrofa A/S (Denmark) and Greenlandic Govt; Chair. HENRIK GUNDELACH; Man. MICHAEL ØSTERGAARD.

Royal Greenland A/S: POB 1073, 3900 Nuuk; tel. 361300; fax 323349; e-mail info@royalgreenland.com; internet www.royalgreenland.com; f. 1774; trade monopoly ended 1950; Govt assumed control 1986; established as share co 1990 (all shares owned by Govt); fishing group based in Greenland with subsidiaries in Japan, the United Kingdom, Scandinavia, the USA, Italy, France and Germany; main products are coldwater prawns and halibut; 5 trawlers; factories in Greenland, China, Denmark, Germany and Poland; Chair. PETER GRØNVOLD SAMUELSEN; CEO FLEMMING KNUDSEN.

EMPLOYERS' ASSOCIATION

Grønlands Arbejdsgiveforening (GA) (Greenland Employers' Assen): Jens Kreutzmannip Aqq. 3, POB 73, 3900 Nuuk; tel. 321500; fax 324340; e-mail ga@ga.gl; internet www.ga.gl; f. 1966; c. 400 mem. orgs; Chair. HENRIK SØRENSEN; Dir HENRIK LETH.

TRADE UNION

Sulinermik Inuussutissarsiuteqartut Kattuffiat (SIK) (Greenland Workers' Union): POB 9, 3900 Nuuk; tel. 322133; fax 324939; e-mail sik@sik.gl; internet www.sik.gl; f. 1956 as Grønlands Arbejeder Sammenslutning (GAS); Pres. JESS G. BERTHELSEN; c. 6,000 mems.

Transport

Owing to the long distances and harsh conditions there are no railways, inland waterways or roads connecting towns in Greenland. Domestic traffic is mainly by aircraft (fixed-wing and helicopter) for long distances, and by boat, snowmobile and dog-sled for shorter distances. There are airports or heliports in all towns for domestic flights. The main international airport is located on a former US military base at Kangerlussuaq (Søndre Strømfjord). There are smaller international airports at Narsarsuaq and Kulusuk. Scandinavian Airlines System (SAS) offers direct flights from Aalborg, Aarhus and Copenhagen (all Denmark) to Kangerlussuaq airport, which operate during May–September. Air Iceland also offers year-round flights from Keflavík (Iceland) to Kulusuk and Nerlerit Inaat in eastern Greenland.

The main port is at Nuuk; there are also all-year ports at Paamiut (Frederikshåb), Maniitsoq (Sukkertoppen) and Sisimiut (Holsteinsborg). In addition, there are shipyards at Nuuk, Qaqortoq, Paamiut, Maniitsoq, Sisimiut and Aasiaat. Coastal motor vessels operate passenger services along the west coast from Upernavik to Nanortalik.

SHIPPING COMPANY

Royal Arctic Line A/S: Aqqusinersuaq 52, POB 1580, 3900 Nuuk; tel. 349100; fax 322450; e-mail marketing@ral.dk; internet www.ral.gl; f. 1993; Govt-owned; 5 container vessels of 49,230 grt and 1 general cargo vessel of 1,171 grt; Chair. MARTHA LABANSEN; Man. Dir JENS ANDERSEN.

AIRLINE

Air Greenland: POB 1012, Nuuk Airport, 3900 Nuuk; tel. 343434; fax 327288; e-mail info@airgreenland.gl; internet www.airgreenland.gl; f. 1960 as Grønlandsfly A/S; air services to the 24 principal centres in Greenland, and to Copenhagen (Denmark); supply, survey, ice-reconnaissance services and helicopter/fixed-wing charters; owned by Danish Govt, Greenlandic Govt and SAS; Chair. JENS WITTRUP WILLUMSEN; CEO MICHAEL BINZER.

Tourism

The national tourist board of Greenland, Greenland Tourism, was established in 1992 in order to develop tourism in Greenland, and concentrates primarily on developing sustainable tourism projects. In 2010 a total of 216,141 accommodation nights were recorded at registered hotels.

Greenland Tourism and Business Council: Hans Egedesvej 29, POB 1615, 3900 Nuuk; tel. 342820; fax 322877; e-mail info@greenland.com; internet www.greenland.com; f. 1992; Chair. BJARNE EKLUND; Man. Dir ANDERS STENBAKKEN.

Defence

The Danish Government, which is responsible for Greenland's defence, co-ordinates military activities through its Greenland Command. The Greenland Command, which also undertakes fisheries control and sea rescues, is based at the Grønnedal naval base, in south-west Greenland. Greenlanders are not liable for military service. As part of the Kingdom of Denmark, Greenland belongs to the North Atlantic Treaty Organization (NATO). The USA operates an airbase at Thule. In 2009 the Government spent 262.0m. kroner on the territory's defence.

Education

The education system is based on that of Denmark, except that the main language of instruction is Greenlandic. Danish is, however, widely used. There is a school in every settlement. In 2001/02 there were 87 municipal primary and lower-secondary schools, with 11,368 pupils and 1,191 teachers (including 380 temporarily employed teachers). In 2006/07 there were 10,688 pupils at primary schools. In 1999/2000 there were three secondary schools with 571 pupils. There is a teacher-training college in Nuuk, and a university centre opened in 1987. In 2005 the Greenlandic Parliament adopted the Greenland Education Program (GEP), in order to improve levels of academic attainment in Greenland. The GEP aimed to ensure that two-thirds of the working population had academic qualifications or vocational skills by 2020. Expenditure on the GEP was projected at €51.5m. in 2009. In 2008 current expenditure on education by the Government amounted to 1,659m. kroner (representing 18.9% of total current budget spending).

DJIBOUTI

Introductory Survey

LOCATION, CLIMATE, LANGUAGE, RELIGION, FLAG, CAPITAL

The Republic of Djibouti is in the Horn of Africa, at the southern entrance to the Red Sea. It is bounded on the north by Eritrea, on the north, west and south-west by Ethiopia, and on the south-east by Somalia. The land is mainly volcanic desert, and the climate hot and arid. There are two main ethnic groups, the Issa, who are of Somali origin and comprise 50% of the population, and the Afar, who comprise 40% of the population and are of Ethiopian origin. Both groups are Muslims, and they speak related Cushitic languages. The official languages are Arabic and French. The flag has two equal horizontal stripes, of light blue and light green, with a white triangle, enclosing a five-pointed red star, at the hoist. The capital is Djibouti.

CONTEMPORARY POLITICAL HISTORY

Historical Context

In 1945 the area now comprising the Republic of Djibouti (then known as French Somaliland) was proclaimed an overseas territory of France, and in 1967 was renamed the French Territory of the Afars and the Issas. The Afar and the Issa have strong connections with Ethiopia and Somalia, respectively. Until the 1960s ethnic divisions were not marked; subsequently, however, internal tensions arose. Demands for independence were led by the Issa community, and, under pressure from the Organization of African Unity (OAU, now the African Union—AU, see p. 189) to grant full independence to the territory, France acted to improve relations between the two communities. Following a referendum in May 1977, the territory became independent on 27 June. Hassan Gouled Aptidon, a senior Issa politician, became the first President of the Republic of Djibouti.

Domestic Political Affairs

In March 1979 Gouled formed a new political party, the Rassemblement populaire pour le progrès (RPP), which was declared the sole legal party in October 1981. In June 1981 Gouled had been elected to a further six-year term as President. Legislative elections were held in May 1982, when candidates were chosen from a single list approved by the RPP. At the next presidential and legislative elections, held in April 1987, Gouled was re-elected, while RPP-sponsored candidates for all 65 seats in the legislature were elected unopposed.

In November 1991 the Front pour la restauration de l'unité et de la démocratie (FRUD), formed by a merger of three insurgent Afar movements, launched a full-scale insurrection against the Government and by the end of that month controlled many towns and villages in the north of the country. The Government introduced mass conscription and requested military assistance from France (see below) to repel what it described as 'external aggression' by soldiers loyal to the deposed President Mengistu Haile Mariam of Ethiopia. The FRUD denied that it constituted a foreign aggressor, claiming that its aim was to secure fair political representation for all ethnic groups in Djibouti.

In January 1992, under pressure from France to accommodate opposition demands for democratic reform, President Gouled appointed a commission to draft a new constitution, which was to restore the multi-party system and provide for free elections. The FRUD stated its willingness to negotiate with Gouled and undertook to observe a cease-fire, subject to satisfactory progress on democratic reforms. Gouled, however, reasserted that the FRUD was controlled by 'foreign interests' and accused France of failing to honour its defence agreement. By late January most of northern Djibouti was under FRUD control, although armed conflict between the FRUD and the Government continued. In June Ahmed Dini Ahmed, who had been Djibouti's first Prime Minister after independence, assumed the leadership of the FRUD.

President Gouled's constitutional plan, which was announced in April 1992, conceded the principle of political pluralism, but proposed few other changes and retained a strong executive presidency. The plan was rejected by the opposition parties and by the FRUD, although cautiously welcomed by France. A constitutional referendum, which was held in September, was boycotted by all the opposition groups; the Government, however, stated that, with 75.2% of the electorate participating, 96.8% of voters had endorsed the new Constitution. At the 30 September deadline for party registration, only the RPP and the Parti du renouveau démocratique (PRD), an opposition group formed earlier in 1992 under the leadership of Mohamed Djama Elabe, were granted legal status. The application for registration by the opposition Parti national démocratique (PND) was initially rejected, although it was allowed in October. Elections to the Assemblée nationale were held on 18 December, and all 65 seats were won by the RPP. However, turn-out was less than 50%, leading to charges from the PND that the legislature was unrepresentative.

Five candidates stood in Djibouti's first contested presidential election, which was held on 7 May 1993: Gouled, Elabe, Aden Robleh Awalleh (for the PND) and two independents. The election was again notable for a low turn-out (49.9%), but resulted in a clear victory for Gouled, who, according to official results, obtained 60.8% of the valid votes cast.

In March 1994 serious divisions emerged within the FRUD leadership. It was reported that the political bureau, led by Ahmed Dini, had been dissolved and that dissident members had formed an 'executive council', headed by Ougoureh Kifleh Ahmed. This dissident leadership (Ali Mohamed Daoud was subsequently declared President) sought support within the movement for a negotiated political settlement of the conflict. In June Kifleh Ahmed and the Government agreed terms for a cease-fire, and formal negotiations for a peace settlement began in July. Executive bodies of both FRUD factions continued to operate during the latter half of 1994, and parallel national congresses rejected the legitimacy of the opposing faction's leadership. In December an agreement signed by Kifleh Ahmed and the Minister of the Interior, Idris Harbi Farah, provided for a permanent cessation of hostilities, the incorporation of FRUD armed forces into the national force, the recognition of the FRUD as a legal political party, the multi-ethnic composition of a new council of ministers and the reform of electoral procedures prior to the next legislative elections. In accordance with the peace agreement, 300 members of the FRUD armed forces were integrated into the national army in March 1995. However, there was little further implementation of the accord, and there was considerable criticism of the agreement by the radical faction of the FRUD (which, under the leadership of Ahmed Dini, favoured a continuation of military operations and launched a number of small-scale attacks against government targets in late 1995) and other opposition groups. Nevertheless, Ali Mohamed Daoud and Kifleh Ahmed were appointed to posts in the Government in June. In March 1996 the Government granted legal recognition to the FRUD, which became the country's fourth and largest political party. However, Ibrahim Chehem Daoud, a former high-ranking official in the FRUD, who opposed reconciliation with the Government, formed a new group, FRUD-Renaissance.

In early 1996 President Gouled's prolonged hospitalization in France prompted a succession crisis within the RPP, between the President's nephew and principal adviser, Ismaïl Omar Guelleh, and his private secretary, Ismaël Guedi Hared. In March the Minister of Justice and Islamic Affairs, Bahdon Farah, who was opposed to Guelleh, was dismissed from the Council of Ministers, together with Ahmed Bulaleh Barreh, the Minister of Defence. In April Bahdon Farah established a splinter group of the RPP, the Groupe pour la démocratie de la république (RPP—GDR), which included 13 of the 65 members of the Assemblée nationale. The President of the Assemblée subsequently claimed that the RPP—GDR would remain banned while Bahdon Farah continued to hold his position as Secretary-General of the RPP. In May Gouled expelled Guedi Hared from the RPP's executive committee, together with Bahdon Farah and former ministers Barreh and Ali Mahamade Houmed, all of whom opposed Guelleh. In June Guedi Hared formed an opposition alliance, the Coordination de l'opposition djiboutienne, embracing the PND, the Front uni de l'opposition djiboutienne (a coalition of internal opposition groups) and the RPP—GDR.

In April 1997 the FRUD faction led by Ali Mohamed Daoud announced its intention to participate in the forthcoming legislative elections and to present joint electoral lists with the RPP. At the legislative elections, held on 19 December, the RPP-FRUD alliance won all the seats in the Assemblée nationale. The rate of voter participation was officially recorded at 63.8%. In late December President Gouled formed a new Council of Ministers.

The Guelleh presidency

In February 1999 President Gouled confirmed that he would not stand in the forthcoming presidential election and the RPP named Guelleh as its presidential candidate. At the election, held on 9 April, Guelleh won 74.4% of the votes cast, convincingly defeating his sole opponent, Moussa Ahmed Idris, who represented an opposition coalition, the Opposition djiboutienne unifiée (ODU), including the PND, the PRD and the Dini wing of the FRUD. Electoral participation was estimated at 60%. Following his inauguration as President on 7 May, Guelleh reappointed Barkad Gourad Hamadou as Prime Minister, at the head of a new Council of Ministers.

In February 2000 the Government and the Dini wing of the FRUD signed a peace agreement in Paris, France. The accord provided for an end to hostilities, the reciprocal release of prisoners, the return of military units to positions held before the conflict, freedom of movement for persons and goods, the reintegration of FRUD insurgents into their previous positions of employment, and an amnesty for the rebels. In late March Ahmed Dini returned to Djibouti from a self-imposed nine-year exile and announced his intention to assist in the implementation of the peace agreement. Meanwhile, earlier that month the RPP had convened its eighth congress, at which Gouled officially announced his retirement from active politics. Guelleh was elected to succeed him as party President.

In February 2001 Hamadou resigned as Prime Minister on the grounds of ill health, after some 22 years in office. Dileita Mohamed Dileita was appointed as Hamadou's replacement in March.

In May 2001 it was announced that an agreement bringing an official end to hostilities between the Government and the FRUD had been signed. The Government, for its part, pledged to establish a number of more representative local bodies and to introduce an 'unrestricted multi-party system' by September 2002. In early July 2001 President Guelleh effected a minor reorganization of the Council of Ministers, with moderate FRUD members allocated two portfolios.

On 4 September 2002, to coincide with the 10th anniversary of the approval of the new Constitution, the limit on the number of permitted political parties (previously fixed at four) was lifted. Henceforth, all parties would be recognized, subject to approval by the Ministry of the Interior and Decentralization, and, during the following months, a number of new parties registered with the intention of participating in the forthcoming legislative elections. At the elections, held on 10 January 2003, the Union pour la majorité présidentielle (UMP), a coalition comprising the RPP, the FRUD, the PND and the Parti populaire social démocrate, won 62.7% of the total votes cast; in accordance with the electoral laws, as it had won the majority of votes in each of the five constituencies, the UMP secured all 65 seats in the Assemblée nationale. Therefore, despite receiving 37.3% of votes cast, the opposition coalition, the Union pour l'alternance démocratique (UAD), comprising the Alliance républicaine pour le développement (ARD), the PRD (which in November was renamed the Mouvement pour le renouveau démocratique et développement), the Parti djiboutien pour la démocratie and the Union djiboutienne pour la démocratie et la justice, failed to attain any legislative representation. According to official figures, the rate of voter participation was 48.4%.

In late July 2003 the Djibouti Government announced that owing to 'security and economic' reasons all illegal immigrants would be required to leave Djibouti by the end of August. The deadline was subsequently extended until mid-September, by which time more than 80,000 immigrants, predominantly from Ethiopia and Somalia, had voluntarily left the country. The USA, which in August had warned of the possibility of terrorist attacks against Western targets in Djibouti, denied allegations that it had exerted pressure on the Government to expel the illegal immigrants. Following the expiry of the deadline, security forces commenced operations to arrest and expel any remaining immigrants not in possession of identity papers.

At the presidential election held on 8 April 2005 Guelleh, who was unopposed following the withdrawal of the sole challenger, the Parti djiboutien pour le développement (PDD) President Mohamed Daoud Chehem, was returned for a second term of office. Numerous opposition groups had appealed for a boycott of the election; however, official figures put the rate of voter participation at 78.9% and confirmed that Guelleh had received 100% of the votes cast. Guelleh reorganized the Government in mid-May, most notably appointing Ali Farah Assoweh as Minister of the Economy, Finance and Planning, in charge of Privatization.

Legislative elections were held on 8 February 2008. The opposition parties had announced their intention to boycott the ballot, and thus the elections were contested solely by candidates from the UMP, which, according to official results, took 94.1% of the total votes cast and secured all 65 seats in the Assemblée nationale. The rate of voter participation was estimated at 72.6%. President Guelleh named a new, 21-member Council of Ministers in late March. Dileita was reappointed as Prime Minister.

Recent developments: the 2011 presidential election

In March 2009 delegates at the RPP's annual national conference adopted a resolution requesting constitutional changes that would allow Guelleh to stand for a third term of office. On 19 April 2010, as expected, the Assemblée nationale unanimously approved an amendment to the Constitution removing the presidential two-term limit, thereby permitting Guelleh to contest the presidential election scheduled to be held on 8 April 2011. Other constitutional revisions included the imposition of a 75-year age limit for an incoming President, the reduction of the presidential mandate by one year (to five years), the establishment of an upper legislative chamber (the Senate) and the abolition of the death penalty.

In May 2010 there were reports of renewed fighting in northern regions of the country between government troops and armed FRUD rebels, who claimed to have killed three soldiers. Further small-scale clashes were subsequently reported, with some commentators linking the unrest to the abolition of presidential term limits in the previous month.

Conflicting reports emerged in February 2011 regarding the number of participants in demonstrations against Guelleh's candidature in the presidential election. Opposition sources claimed that at least 30,000 people took part in the protests, while the Government maintained that the number of people involved totalled less than 1,000. The security forces were reported to have forcibly dispersed the protesters, resulting in the deaths of at least two people, and following the protests three opposition leaders, Daoud Chehem of the PDD, Robleh Awalleh of the PND and Guedi Hared of the Union djiboutienne pour la démocratie et la justice were briefly detained.

The presidential election was held as scheduled on 8 April 2011, but was boycotted by the main opposition parties. According to results released by the Minister of the Interior and Decentralization, Guelleh was re-elected having secured 80.6% of the votes cast. His only challenger, the independent candidate Mohamed Warsama Ragueh, received 19.4%. The rate of voter participation was officially recorded at 69.7% of the registered electorate and international observers described the elections as free, fair and transparent. In mid-May Guelleh announced a new Government comprising 22 ministers, 11 of whom were new appointments, under the leadership of the incumbent Prime Minister Dileita. In October the Minister of National Education and Professional Training, Adawa Hassan Ali, was dismissed, reportedly as a result of having held talks with an opposition movement based in Canada. Local elections, which were also boycotted by the political opposition, were held on 20 January and 10 February 2012.

Foreign Affairs

Regional relations

Separate treaties of friendship and co-operation were signed in 1981 with Ethiopia, Somalia, Kenya and Sudan, with the aim of resolving regional conflicts. Djibouti's interest in promoting regional co-operation was exemplified by the creation, in February 1985, of the Intergovernmental Authority on Drought and Development (now the Intergovernmental Authority on Development, see p. 338), with six (now seven) member states; Djibouti was chosen as the site of its permanent secretariat, and President Gouled became the first Chairman.

In November 1997 Djibouti granted official recognition to the self-proclaimed 'Republic of Somaliland', which declared independence in 1991. In late 1999 President Guelleh drafted a peace plan aimed at reunifying Somali territory, to which the leaders of

'Somaliland' expressed their vehement opposition. Relations deteriorated further in April 2000 when the 'Somaliland' authorities closed the common border with Djibouti, claiming that Djibouti was encouraging ethnic violence and had been responsible for a series of bomb attacks in Hargeisa. In response, Djibouti expelled three 'Somaliland' diplomats and closed the 'Somaliland' liaison office in Djibouti town. Furthermore, in May the 'Somaliland' authorities issued a ban on all flights from Djibouti to its territory; the Djibouti Government responded by prohibiting all flights to and from 'Somaliland'. The Djibouti-sponsored Somali national reconciliation conference, chaired by Guelleh, opened in May in Arta, about 40 km south-west of Djibouti town. The conference was attended by 810 representatives of Somali clans and political and armed groups, and in August, following three months of extensive negotiations, the newly created Somali Transitional National Assembly elected Abdulkasim Salad Hasan President of Somalia. Relations between Djibouti and 'Somaliland' were further strained in April 2001 after the Djibouti authorities closed the common border and outlawed the transport of all goods and people between the two territories. In October a delegation from 'Somaliland', led by its minister responsible for foreign affairs, held talks with Djibouti officials in an attempt to improve relations; although several bilateral agreements were concluded, the common border remained closed. Following the death of President Mohamed Ibrahim Egal in May 2002, Guelleh moved swiftly to establish cordial relations with the new President of 'Somaliland', Dahir Riyale Kahin.

In December 1995 the Djibouti Government protested to the Eritrean authorities about alleged incursions by Eritrean troops into north-eastern Djibouti. These allegations were vehemently denied by Eritrea. Relations between the two countries were strained in April 1996, when President Gouled rejected a map of Eritrea submitted by the Eritrean Minister of Foreign Affairs, which reportedly included a 20-km strip of territory belonging to Djibouti. In November 1998 Djibouti suspended diplomatic relations with Eritrea, following accusations by that country that it was supporting Ethiopia in the Eritrea–Ethiopia border dispute. Gouled had been actively involved in an OAU committee mediating on the dispute, which earlier in the month had proposed a peace plan that was accepted by Ethiopia, but not by Eritrea. In November 1999 President Guelleh was praised by the Ethiopian President for his efforts in promoting a peace settlement in Somalia and in December the Djibouti and Ethiopian Governments signed a protocol of understanding on military co-operation, with the aim of establishing a further mutual defence pact. In March 2000, following Libyan mediation, Djibouti and Eritrea announced that they had resumed diplomatic relations. Nevertheless, the border dispute between the two countries remained unresolved, and tensions escalated in early 2008 when Eritrean forces began to mobilize and prepare military positions in the disputed Ras Doumeira region of the common border. In April President Guelleh accused Eritrea of incursions into Djiboutian territory, although the Eritrean Government denied this. Djibouti dispatched troops to the area in response, and, despite diplomatic efforts to settle the dispute, including appeals for restraint from the AU and the League of Arab States (Arab League), fighting broke out in June after Djibouti refused to hand over Eritrean soldiers who had deserted and crossed into Djiboutian territory. Several deaths were reported on both sides and the hostilities elicited strong international condemnation. The UN Security Council launched an investigation into the clashes, and appealed for a normalization in relations between the two countries, warning that further hostility could result in a wider regional conflict. In October Guelleh appealed to the Security Council for mediation, requesting joint demilitarization in the border region, and in January 2009 the Security Council adopted a resolution ordering Eritrea to withdraw its forces from the area, as Djibouti had done following the fighting in June 2008. However, Eritrea refused to comply with this demand and furthermore issued a strongly worded statement to the Security Council in May 2009 denying any involvement in the destabilization of either Djibouti or Somalia. In October the Djibouti Minister of Foreign Affairs and Co-operation accused Eritrea of arming and training militias to carry out acts of sabotage in Djibouti, and of fomenting chaos in the region. Following increasing pressure for the imposition of sanctions from numerous East African governments, in December the UN Security Council placed an arms embargo on Eritrea, imposed travel restrictions on political and military leaders and also froze the overseas funds and financial assets of those individuals. An unexpected breakthrough in the Djibouti–Eritrea border dispute was achieved on 6 June 2010, when both sides signed an accord committing themselves to a peaceful solution, with Qatar acting as mediator. As part of the agreement, Eritrea finally withdrew its troops from the disputed areas, while Qatar deployed a peacekeeping force to patrol the border. It was anticipated that future negotiations would concentrate on the exchange of prisoners and the delineation of the border, paving the way for the re-establishment of cordial relations. The sanctions imposed upon Eritrea remained in place despite UN acknowledgement of the progress made by both nations.

Following the overthrow of the Ethiopian President, Mengistu Haile Mariam, in May 1991, Djibouti established good relations with the successor transitional Government in that country. However, in December 2000 relations between Djibouti and Ethiopia temporarily deteriorated after plans were announced to increase handling charges at Djibouti port by more than 150%, which the Ethiopian authorities maintained violated a 1999 trade agreement between the two countries. In February 2001 the Dubai Port Authority, which had assumed control of Djibouti port in May 2000, agreed to reduce the tariffs, and bilateral relations subsequently improved. Following lengthy negotiations, in mid-November 2006 Djibouti and Ethiopia signed an agreement allowing for goods imported by Ethiopia to be transported via Djibouti port over the following 20 years. Nevertheless, relations between the two countries deteriorated somewhat in late December owing to Djibouti's alleged support for the Islamist Supreme Somali Islamic Courts' Council organization (see Somalia).

Djibouti re-established an embassy in Somalia in December 2010 and appealed to other nations to do the same. Somalian Prime Minister Mohamed Abdullahi Mohamed travelled to Djibouti shortly afterwards, his first official trip as premier. In 2011 some 300 Somalian military personnel were given training by military experts in Djibouti, and in December of that year Djibouti dispatched a contingent of troops to strengthen the African Union Mission in Somalia which was engaged in fighting the al-Shabaab militia; a second contingent was sent in January 2012. It was estimated that Djibouti was host to 14,500 Somalian refugees fleeing worsening violence in that country.

Other external relations

Djibouti's stance during the Gulf War of January–February 1991 strengthened its ties with France, and in February the Djibouti and French Governments signed defence treaties, extending military co-operation, although France refused to intervene militarily in the conflict between the Government and the FRUD. In July 2002, as part of a restructuring of the French forces in Djibouti, a new French army base was inaugurated, and in May 2003 the French Government agreed to provide Djibouti with up to €30m. per year of development aid over a 10-year period. However, in late January 2005 relations between the two countries became strained when Djibouti expelled six French aid workers and closed the Radio France Internationale transmitter in the country, apparently in response to France's summoning on 10 January of the Djiboutian chief of security services to appear before an inquiry into the death of Bernard Borrel, a French judge attached to the Djibouti Ministry of Justice, in Djibouti in 1995. (An inquiry conducted by French officials in Djibouti later that year had concluded that Borrel had committed suicide; however, his family had never accepted this verdict.) Relations appeared to have improved by May 2005 when President Guelleh made an official visit to Paris to meet with President Jacques Chirac. In mid-January 2006, however, Djibouti requested that the International Court of Justice (ICJ) in The Hague, Netherlands, intervene in the case after French investigators indicated that Borrel could have been assassinated. Relations further deteriorated in early October when French magistrates issued arrest warrants for the head of Djibouti's security services, Hassan Said, and Chief Prosecutor Djama Souleiman Ali on suspicion of deliberately obstructing the investigation into Borrel's death. Djibouti reacted angrily and refused to accept the warrants. Ali and Said were sentenced *in absentia* to terms of imprisonment of 18 months and one year, respectively, in March 2008 after a French court found them guilty of interfering with witnesses in the Borrel case. In June the ICJ ruled that the French Government's refusal to hand over information from its investigation into the killing of Borrel constituted a violation of its international obligations of co-operation. However, cordial relations between the two countries appeared to have been restored by the decision of a French court in May 2009 to quash the convictions handed down to Said and Ali and to cancel their international arrest warrants.

The attacks on the World Trade Center in New York and the Pentagon in Washington, DC, on 11 September 2001 resulted in a significant enhancement of Djibouti's strategic importance to the USA and its allies. In early October Djibouti demonstrated its support for the US-led coalition against terrorism by establishing a seven-member Comité national de lutte contre le terrorisme to monitor domestic security conditions. Djibouti agreed to grant access to its port and airfields, and coalition members stated their intention to use Djibouti as a base from which to monitor developments in Somalia, Sudan and other countries in the region. In January 2002 Djibouti and Germany signed a memorandum of understanding on the status of German military and civilian personnel in Djibouti. The accord granted German military personnel access to Djibouti's port and airfields to conduct surveillance missions in the region, and some 1,200 German naval personnel were subsequently stationed in Djibouti, although this number had been reduced to 320 by early 2005. In December 2002 the US Secretary of Defense, Donald Rumsfeld, visited the 1,500 US troops based off the coast of Djibouti who formed the Combined Joint Task Force-Horn of Africa (CJTF-HOA), which was to monitor ship movements in the Red Sea and along the East African coast. In February 2003 Djibouti and the USA concluded an agreement that allowed US forces to use Djiboutian military installations, and in May CJTF-HOA moved its headquarters onshore to a base in Djibouti. Throughout 2004 the US military presence in Djibouti increased further with the construction of a new port at Doraleh. The USA also doubled its budget for training the Djibouti military to US $325,000 in 2004. In April 2006 a report published by the human rights organization Amnesty International accused Djibouti of collaborating with US authorities in a practice known as 'rendition'. The report alleged that terrorist suspects detained by the US intelligence services had been held in secret prisons in Djibouti and later transferred to countries where torture was tolerated. In early January 2007 Djibouti criticized the USA after US forces based in Djibouti launched a series of air-strikes against suspected members of the radical Islamist al-Qa'ida (Base) organization in southern Somalia. In 2009 the USA announced a major increase in funding for US arms sales to Djibouti through the Foreign Military Financing programme, while also budgeting $60m. to fund CJTF-HOA operations in 2010 and $249m. towards the operation of the 500-acre base at Camp Lemonier.

CONSTITUTION AND GOVERNMENT

The Djibouti Constitution was approved by national referendum on 4 September 1992 and entered into force on 15 September. Executive power is vested in the President, who is directly elected by universal adult suffrage for a six-year term, initially renewable only once. In April 2010, however, the Assemblée nationale removed the limit on terms served. Legislative power is held by the Assemblée nationale, consisting of 65 members elected for five years. The Council of Ministers, presided over by a Prime Minister, is responsible to the President. The Republic comprises five electoral districts.

REGIONAL AND INTERNATIONAL CO-OPERATION

Djibouti is a member of the African Union (see p. 189), the Intergovernmental Authority on Development (see p. 338) and the Arab Fund for Economic and Social Development (see p. 201).

Djibouti became a member of the UN in 1977, and was admitted to the World Trade Organization (WTO, see p. 433) in 1995. Djibouti participates in the Group of 77 (G77, see p. 450) developing countries.

ECONOMIC AFFAIRS

In 2009, according to estimates by the World Bank, Djibouti's gross national income (GNI), measured at average 2007–09 prices, was US $1,105m., equivalent to $1,270 per head (or $2,440 on an international purchasing-power parity basis). During 2001–10, it was estimated, the population increased at an average annual rate of 1.9%, while gross domestic product (GDP) per head increased, in real terms, by an average of 2.2% per year during 2001–09. Overall GDP increased, in real terms, at an average annual rate of 4.2% during 2001–09; growth of 5.0% was recorded in 2009.

Agriculture (including hunting, forestry and fishing) provided only 3.9% of GDP in 2010, according to the African Development bank (AfDB), although some 73.0% of the labour force were estimated to be engaged in the sector in mid-2012, according to FAO. There is little arable farming, owing to Djibouti's unproductive terrain, and the country is able to produce only about 3% of its total food requirements. More than one-half of the population are pastoral nomads, herding goats, sheep and camels. During 2001–06, according to the World Bank, the real GDP of the agricultural sector increased at an average annual rate of 3.5%; agricultural GDP increased by 7.0% in 2009, according to the AfDB.

Industry (comprising manufacturing, construction and utilities) provided 19.6% of GDP in 2010, according to the AfDB, and engaged 11.0% of the employed labour force in 1991. Industrial activity is mainly limited to a few small-scale enterprises. During 2001–06 industrial GDP increased at an average annual rate of 4.7%, according to the World Bank; it increased by 3.7% in 2006.

The manufacturing sector contributed 2.3% of GDP in 2010, according to the AfDB. Almost all consumer goods have to be imported. According to the World Bank, manufacturing GDP increased by an average of 2.9% per year in 2001–06. According to the AfDB, the GDP of the sector increased by 7.0% in 2009.

According to the AfDB, the construction sector contributed 12.1% of GDP in 2010, and the sector grew by 10.0% in 2009, according to the AfDB.

Total electricity generating capacity rose from 40 MW to 80 MW in 1988, when the second part of the Boulaos power station became operative; this figure continued to rise during the 1990s, and in 2009 Djibouti produced 342.7m. kWh of electricity. Nevertheless, imported fuels continued to satisfy a large proportion of Djibouti's energy requirements. Imports of mineral fuels and lubricants accounted for 6.5% of the value of total imports in 2009. In December 2004 Djibouti and Ethiopia agreed to connect their power generating facilities in an attempt to increase access to electricity.

Djibouti's economic viability is based on trade through the international port of Djibouti, and on the developing service sector, which accounted for 76.5% of GDP in 2010, according to the AfDB, and engaged 13.8% of the employed labour force in 1991. In May 2000 the Government and Dubai Ports International (DPI—now DP World) signed an agreement providing DPI with a 20-year contract to manage the port of Djibouti. During 2000–05 the GDP of the services sector increased at an average annual rate of 3.0%. Services GDP increased by 2.5% in 2005.

In 2010 Djibouti recorded a visible trade deficit of US $278.6m., but there was a surplus of $50.5m. on the current account of the balance of payments. According to the UN, the principal sources of imports in 2009 were France (30.5%), the United Arab Emirates, Saudi Arabia Japan and Ethiopia. The principal markets for exports in that year were Ethiopia (35.4%), France, Somalia, Brazil and Qatar. The principal imports in 2009 were machinery and electrical appliances, food and beverages, vehicles and transport equipment and telecommunication and sound equipment. In that year, the country's principal exports were machinery and transport equipment, and food and live animals.

Djibouti recorded a budget deficit of 9,067m. Djibouti francs in 2009, equal to some 4.9% of GDP in that year. The country's general government gross debt was 112,611m. Djibouti francs in 2010, equivalent to 56.1% of GDP. The country's total external debt was US $752m. at the end of 2009, of which $732m. was public and publicly guaranteed debt. In that year, the cost of servicing long-term public and publicly guaranteed debt and repayments to the IMF was equivalent to 6.7% of the value of exports of goods, services and income (excluding workers' remittances). According to the IMF, the annual rate of inflation averaged 4.8% during 2004–10. Consumer prices increased by 4.0% in 2010. In 1996 unemployment was estimated to affect some 58% of the labour force.

Djibouti has traditionally relied heavily on foreign assistance, and recent significant investment in the country's economy has been made by the USA and France, both of which wished to take advantage of Djibouti's strategic location to secure bases for their respective militaries. In May 2003 France agreed to contribute €30m. per year over a 10-year period in order to maintain its military presence in the country, while the USA was to pay Djibouti US $31m. for hosting its military base. In September 2008 the IMF approved a three-year Poverty Reduction and Growth Facility valued at some $20m. to support the Government's economic programme and poverty alleviation strategy. The Fund welcomed the reform of Djibouti's labour code in 2006 and, after its fourth review in 2011, the Government's continued commitment to fiscal discipline and structural reforms in tax revenue. The services sector continues to dominate the country's economy and growing demand for berths at the port of Djibouti resulted in the construction of a new container terminal by DP World that opened in early 2009, with the aim of establishing Djibouti as the leading shipping hub for East Africa and land-locked countries. such as Ethiopia, which, in 2011, launched a new railway line between the two countries' capitals. However, the rapid rise in global food and petroleum prices in the late 2000s adversely affected the country, and in November 2010 the UN Office for the Co-ordination of Humanitarian Affairs initiated a $39m. aid appeal as a result of successive droughts and persistently high prices for foodstuffs. In early 2012 the Ministry of Agriculture, Fishing and Stockbreeding accepted grain, veterinary products, and irrigation and agricultural equipment to the value of 179m. Djibouti francs from FAO to help pastoralists affected by drought. Furthermore, the World Bank approved an IDA grant of $5.83m for a project aimed at increasing rural communities' access to water, and a subsidiary of a French engineering company was awarded the contract to build and manage a wastewater treatment plant at Doudah. Additional aid was provided by the AfDB, which, in its strategy for the years 2011–15, highlighted the public sector as the main cause of the country's poverty, and pledged €4m. towards strengthening institutional capacity, €4.8m for access to water and wastewater treatment, and €6.4m for developing agricultural and fisheries infrastructure. GDP growth of 5.1% was forecast for 2012.

PUBLIC HOLIDAYS

2013: 1 January (New Year's Day), 23 January* (Mouloud, Birth of the Prophet), 1 May (Workers' Day), 27 June (Independence Day), 7 August* (Id al-Fitr, end of Ramadan), 14 October* (Id al-Adha, Feast of the Sacrifice), 4 November (Muharram, Islamic New Year), 25 December (Christmas Day).

* These holidays are dependent on the Islamic lunar calendar and may vary by one or two days from the dates given.

Statistical Survey

Source (unless otherwise stated): Ministère de l'Economie, des Finances et de la Planification, chargé de la Privatisation, Cité Ministérielle, BP 13, Djibouti; tel. 21353331; fax 21356501; e-mail cabmefpp@intnet.dj; internet www.ministere-finances.dj.

AREA AND POPULATION

Area: 23,200 sq km (8,958 sq miles).

Population: 519,900 (including refugees and resident foreigners) at 31 December 1990 (official estimate); 818,159 at the census of 29 May 2009 (official figure). *2012* (UN estimate at mid-year): 922,709 (Sources: UN, *Population and Vital Statistics Report* and *World Population Prospects: The 2010 Revision*).

Density (mid-2012): 39.8 per sq km.

Population by Age and Sex (UN estimates at mid-2012): *0–14:* 323,712 (males 163,421, females 160,291); *15–64:* 567,122 (males 283,984, females 283,138); *65 and over:* 31,875 (males 14,229, females 17,646); *Total* 922,709 (males 461,634, females 461,075) (Source: UN, *World Population Prospects: The 2010 Revision*).

Regions (population at 2009 census): Ali-Sabieh 86,949; Arta 42,380; Dikhil 88,948; Djibouti (ville) 475,322; Obock 37,856; Tadjourah 86,704; *Total* 818,159.

Principal Town (population at 2009 census): Djibouti (capital) 475,322.

Births, Marriages and Deaths (2005–10, UN estimates): Average annual birth rate 29.4 per 1,000; Average annual death rate 10.5 per 1,000 (Source: UN, *World Population Prospects: The 2010 Revision*). *1999* (capital district only): Births 7,898; Marriages 3,808. *2009:* Crude birth rate 28.0 per 1,000; Crude death rate 10.9 per 1,000 (Source: African Development Bank).

Life Expectancy (years at birth, WHO estimates): 60 (males 58; females 62) in 2009. Source: WHO, *World Health Statistics*.

Economically Active Population (estimates, '000 persons, 1991): Agriculture, etc. 212; Industries 31; Services 39; *Total* 282 (males 167, females 115) (Source: UN Economic Commission for Africa, *African Statistical Yearbook*). *Mid-2012* ('000 persons, estimates): Agriculture, etc. 297; Total labour force 407 (Source: FAO).

HEALTH AND WELFARE

Key Indicators

Total Fertility Rate (children per woman, 2008): 3.9.

Under-5 Mortality Rate (per 1,000 live births, 2009): 93.

HIV/AIDS (% of persons aged 15–49, 2009): 2.5.

Physicians (per 1,000 head, 2005): 0.2.

Hospital Beds (per 1,000 head, 2000): 1.6.

Health Expenditure (2008): US $ per head (PPP): 153.

Health Expenditure (2008): % of GDP: 6.9.

Health Expenditure (2008): public (% of total): 76.5.

Access to Water (% of persons, 2008): 92.

Access to Sanitation (% of persons, 2008): 56.

Total Carbon Dioxide Emissions ('000 metric tons, 2007): 487.3.

Carbon Dioxide Emissions Per Head (metric tons, 2007): 0.6.

Human Development Index (2011): ranking: 165.

Human Development Index (2011): value: 0.430.

For sources and definitions, see explanatory note on p. vi.

AGRICULTURE, ETC.

Principal Crops ('000 metric tons, 2010, FAO estimates): Beans, dry 1.5; Tomatoes 1.2; Lemons and limes 1.6. *Aggregate Production* ('000 metric tons, may include official, semi-official or estimated data): Vegetables (incl. melons) 32.2; Fruits (excl. melons) 3.2.

Livestock ('000 head, 2010, FAO estimates): Cattle 297; Sheep 466; Goats 512; Asses 8; Camels 70.

Livestock Products ('000 metric tons, 2010, FAO estimates): Cattle meat 6.1; Sheep meat 2.2; Goat meat 2.4; Camel meat 0.7; Cows' milk 9.2; Camels' milk 6.6.

Fishing (metric tons, live weight, 2009, FAO estimates): Groupers 133; Snappers and jobfishes 179; Barracudas 120; Carangids 204; Seerfishes 82; Other tuna-like fishes 100; Total catch (incl. others) 1,058.

Source: FAO.

INDUSTRY

Electric Energy (million kWh): 321.2 in 2007; 325.9 in 2008; 342.7 in 2009. Source: Banque Centrale de Djibouti, *Rapport Annuel 2009*.

FINANCE

Currency and Exchange Rates: 100 centimes = 1 Djibouti franc. *Sterling, Dollar and Euro Equivalents* (30 December 2011): £1 sterling = 274.774 Djibouti francs; US $1 = 177.721 Djibouti francs; €1 = 229.953 Djibouti francs; 1,000 Djibouti francs = £3.64 = $5.63 = €4.35. *Exchange Rate:* Fixed at US $1 = 177.721 Djibouti francs since February 1973.

Budget (million Djibouti francs, 2009): *Revenue:* Tax revenue 37,449 (Direct taxes 17,229, Indirect taxes 18,330, Other taxes 1,890); Other revenue (incl. property sales) 19,519; Total 56,968 (excl. official grants 11,948). *Expenditure:* Current expenditure 45,862 (Salaries and wages 24,058); Capital expenditure 32,121; Total 77,983. Source: Banque Centrale de Djibouti, *Rapport Annuel 2009*.

International Reserves (US $ million at 31 December 2010, excl. gold): IMF special drawing rights 16.73; Reserve position in IMF 1.69; Foreign exchange 230.57; Total 249.0. Source: IMF, *International Financial Statistics*.

Money Supply (million Djibouti francs at 31 December 2010): Currency outside banks 20,085; Demand deposits at commercial banks 107,207; *Total money* 127,292. Source: IMF, *International Financial Statistics*.

Cost of Living (Consumer Price Index; base: 2005 = 100): All items 121.6 in 2008; 123.6 in 2009; 128.5 in 2010. Source: IMF, *International Financial Statistics*.

Expenditure on the Gross Domestic Product (million Djibouti francs at current prices, 2010): Government final consumption expenditure 37,758; Private final consumption expenditure 156,753; Gross capital formation 34,994; *Total domestic expenditure* 229,505; Exports of goods and services 66,435; *Less* Imports of goods and services 109,470; *GDP in purchasers' values* 186,471. Source: African Development Bank.

Gross Domestic Product by Economic Activity (million Djibouti francs at current prices, 2010): Agriculture 6,537; Mining and quarrying 266; Manufacturing 3,951; Electricity, gas and water 8,559; Construction 20,326; Wholesale and retail trade, restaurants and hotels 31,512; Transport and communications 47,772; Finance, insurance and real estate 23,273; Public administration and defence 23,457; Other services 2,824; *GDP at factor cost* 168,477; Indirect taxes 17,994; *GDP in purchasers' values* 186,471. Note: Deduction for imputed bank service charge assumed to be distributed at origin. Source: African Development Bank.

Balance of Payments (US $ million, 2010): Exports of goods f.o.b. 85.1; Imports of goods f.o.b. –363.8; *Trade balance* –278.6; Exports of services 335.7; Imports of services –119.1; *Balance on goods and services* –62.0; Other income received 32.8; Other income paid –15.4; *Balance on goods, services and income* –44.7; Current transfers received 108.7; Current transfers paid –13.5; *Current balance* 50.5; Capital account (net) 55.3; Direct investment from abroad 36.5; Other investment assets –87.8; Other investment liabilities 55.5; Net errors and omissions –112.9; *Overall balance* –2.8. Source: IMF, *International Financial Statistics*.

EXTERNAL TRADE

Principal Commodities: *Imports c.i.f.* (US $ million, 2009): Food and beverages 173.0; Mineral fuels and lubricants 41.8; Chemical products 50.3; Basic manufactures 73.6; Telecommunications and sound equipment 57.9; Machinery and electrical appliances 211.2; Vehicles and transport equipment 66.6; Total (incl. others) 647.6. *Exports f.o.b.:* Food and live animals 69.9 (Milk products 29.4; Cereals 10.0); Basic manufactures 61.3; Machinery and transport equipment 177.2 (Road vehicles and parts 105.1); Commodities not classified according to kind 20.7; Total (incl. others) 363.7. Source: UN, *International Trade Statistics Yearbook*.

Principal Trading Partners (US $ million, 2009): *Imports c.i.f.:* Belgium 12.7; China, People's Republic 20.7; Egypt 10.5; Ethiopia 32.5; France 197.5; India 20.6; Italy 18.6; Japan 35.4; Netherlands 4.4; Pakistan 16.7; Saudi Arabia 38.7; Singapore 2.2; Ukraine 13.8; United Arab Emirates 119.7; United Kingdom 3.3; USA 25.6; Yemen 22.2; Total (incl. others) 647.6. *Exports f.o.b.:* Brazil 31.5; Ethiopia 128.6; France 73.0; Pakistan 15.2; Qatar 22.9; Somalia 43.2; Yemen 12.3; Total (incl. others) 363.7. Source: UN, *International Trade Statistics Yearbook*.

TRANSPORT

Railways (traffic, 2002): Passengers ('000) 570; Freight ton-km (million) 201. Source: IMF, *Djibouti: Statistical Appendix* (March 2004).

Road Traffic (motor vehicles in use, 1996, estimates): Passenger cars 9,200; Lorries and vans 2,040. Source: IRF, *World Road Statistics*.

Shipping: *Merchant Fleet* (registered at 31 December 2009): 12 vessels (displacement 3,018 grt) (Source: IHS Fairplay, *World Fleet Statistics*). *Freight Traffic* ('000 metric tons, 2009): Goods 9,011.9; Fuels 2,269.3 (Source: Banque Centrale de Djibouti, *Rapport Annuel 2009*).

Civil Aviation (international traffic, 2009): *Passengers:* 259,811; *Freight:* 7,524 metric tons. Source: Banque Centrale de Djibouti, *Rapport Annuel 2009*.

TOURISM

Tourist Arrivals ('000): 20 in 1996; 20 in 1997; 20 in 1998.

Receipts from Tourism (excl. passenger transport, US $ million): 6.8 in 2007; 7.8 in 2008; 16.0 in 2009.

Source: World Tourism Organization.

COMMUNICATIONS MEDIA

Newspapers (1995): 1 non-daily (estimated circulation 1,000).

Periodicals (1989): 7 (estimated combined circulation 6,000).

Radio Receivers (1997): 52,000 in use.

Television Receivers (2000): 45,000 in use.

Telephones (2010): 18,500 main lines in use.

Mobile Cellular Telephones (2010): 165,600 subscribers.

Personal Computers: 32,000 (37.7 per 1,000 persons) in 2008.

Internet Subscribers (2010): 11,900.

Broadband Subscribers (2010): 8,100.

Sources: mainly UNESCO, *Statistical Yearbook;* UN, *Statistical Yearbook;* International Telecommunication Union.

EDUCATION

Pre-primary (2008/09, unless otherwise indicated): 2 schools (2004/05); 1,228 pupils (males 634, females 594); 75 teaching staff.

Primary (2008/09, unless otherwise indicated): 82 schools (2004/05); 55,546 pupils (males 29,589, females 25,957); 1,627 teaching staff.

Secondary (2008/09): 42,690 pupils (males 24,764, females 17,926); 1,497 teaching staff.

Higher (2008/09): 3,159 students (males 1,875, females 1,284); 157 teaching staff.

Sources: UNESCO Institute for Statistics; Ministère de l'éducation nationale et de l'enseignement supérieur; Université de Djibouti.

Pupil-teacher Ratio (primary education, UNESCO estimate): 34.1 in 2008/09. Source: UNESCO Institute for Statistics.

Adult Literacy Rate (UNESCO estimate): 65.5% in 2003. Source: UN Development Programme, *Human Development Report*.

Directory

The Government

HEAD OF STATE

President and Commander-in-Chief of the Armed Forces: Ismaïl Omar Guelleh (inaugurated 7 May 1999, re-elected 8 April 2005 and 8 April 2011).

COUNCIL OF MINISTERS
(May 2012)

The Government is formed by the Rassemblement populaire pour le progrès.

Prime Minister: Dileita Mohamed Dileita.

Minister of Justice and Penal Affairs, in charge of Human Rights: Ali Farah Assoweh.

Minister of the Economy and Finance, in charge of Industry and Planning: Ilyas Moussa Dawaleh.

Minister of Defence: Abdoulkader Kamil Mohamed.

Minister of Foreign Affairs and International Co-operation: Mahamoud Ali Youssouf.

Minister of the Interior: Hassan Darar Houffaneh.

Minister of Health: Ali Yacoub Mahamoud.

Minister of National Education and Professional Training: Moussa Ahmed Hassan.

Minister of Higher Education and Research: Dr Nabil Mohammed Ahmed.

Minister of Agriculture, Fishing and Stockbreeding: Mohamed Ahmed Awaleh.

Minister of Equipment and Transport: Mohamed Moussa Ibrahim Balala.

Minister of Muslim Affairs and Endowments: Dr Hamoud Adbi Sultan.

Minister of Energy and Water, in charge of Natural Resources: Dr Fouad Ahmed Aye.

Minister of Communication and Culture, in charge of Post and Telecommunications, and Government Spokesperson: Abdi Hussain Ahmed.

Minister of Labour, in charge of Administrative Reform: Hassan Ali Bahdon.

Minister of Housing, Urban Planning and the Environment: Hassan Omar Mohamed Bourhan.

Minister of the Promotion of Women and Family Planning, in charge of Relations with Parliament: Hasna Barkat Daoud.

Minister-delegate to the Minister of Foreign Affairs, in charge of International Co-operation: AHMED ALI SILAY.

Minister-delegate to the Minister of the Economy and Finance, in charge of the Budget: AMAREH ALI SAID.

Minister-delegate to the Minister of the Economy and Finance, in charge of Trade, Small and Medium-sized Enterprises, Handicrafts and Tourism: ABDI ELMI ACHKIR.

Secretary of State in the Office of the Prime Minister, in charge of National Solidarity: ZAHRA YOUSSOUF KAYAD.

Secretary of State to the Minister of Housing, Urban Planning and the Environment, in charge of Accommodation: AMINA ABDI ADEN.

Secretary of State for Youth and Sports: Dr DJAMA ELMI OKIEH.

MINISTRIES

Office of the President: Djibouti; e-mail sggpr@intnet.dj; internet www.presidence.dj.

Office of the Prime Minister: BP 2086, Djibouti; tel. 21351494; fax 21355049.

Ministry of Agriculture, Fishing and Stockbreeding: BP 453, Djibouti; tel. 21351297.

Ministry of Communication and Culture: BP 32, 1 rue de Moscou, Djibouti; tel. 21355672; fax 21353957; e-mail mccpt@intnet.dj; internet www.mccpt.dj.

Ministry of Defence: BP 42, Djibouti; tel. 21352034.

Ministry of the Economy, Finance and Planning: BP 13, Djibouti; tel. 21353331; fax 21356501; e-mail sg_mefpp@intnet.dj; internet www.ministere-finances.dj.

Ministry of Employment, Integration and Professional Training: Djibouti; tel. 21351838; fax 21357268; e-mail adetip@intnet.dj.

Ministry of Energy and Natural Resources: BP 175, Djibouti; tel. 21350340.

Ministry of Equipment and Transport: Palais du Peuple, BP 2501, Djibouti; tel. 21350990; fax 21355975.

Ministry of Foreign Affairs and International Co-operation: blvd Cheik Osman, BP 1863, Djibouti; tel. 21352471; fax 21353049; internet www.djibdiplomatie.dj.

Ministry of Health: BP 296, Djibouti; tel. 21353331; fax 21356300.

Ministry of Higher Education and Research: Djibouti.

Ministry of Housing, Urban Planning and the Environment: BP 11, Djibouti; tel. 21350006; fax 21351618.

Ministry of the Interior: BP 33, Djibouti; tel. 21352542; fax 21354862.

Ministry of Justice and Penal Affairs: BP 12, Djibouti; tel. 21351506; fax 21354012.

Ministry of Labour: Djibouti.

Ministry of Muslim Affairs and Endowments: Djibouti.

Ministry of National Education and Professional Training: BP 16, Cité Ministérielle, Djibouti; tel. 21350997; fax 21354234; e-mail education.gov@intnet.dj; internet www.education.gov.dj.

Ministry of the Promotion of Women and Family Planning: BP 458, Djibouti; tel. 21353409; fax 21350439; e-mail minfemme@intnet.dj; internet www.ministere-femme.dj.

Ministry of Trade and Industry: BP 1846, Djibouti; tel. 21351682.

Ministry of Youth, Sports, Leisure and Tourism: BP 2506, Djibouti; tel. 21355886; fax 21356830.

President and Legislature

PRESIDENT

Presidential Election, 8 April 2011

Candidate	% of votes
Ismaïl Omar Guelleh	80.63
Mohamed Warsama Ragueh	19.37
Total	100.00

ASSEMBLÉE NATIONALE

Assemblée nationale: BP 138, pl. Lagarde, Djibouti; tel. 21350172; internet www.assemblee-nationale.dj.

Speaker: IDRISS ARNAOUD ALI.

Elections to the Assemblée nationale were held on 8 February 2008. The 65 seats were contested solely by candidates from the Union pour la majorité présidentielle (UMP) after opposition parties boycotted the ballot. According to official results, the UMP received 103,463 (94.1%) of the 109,999 votes cast; the remaining 6,536 votes were invalid. Voter turn-out was estimated at 72.6%.

Election Commission

Commission électorale nationale indépendante: Djibouti; f. 2002; President ADEN AHMED DOUALEH.

Political Organizations

On 4 September 2002, to coincide with the 10th anniversary of the approval of the Constitution, restrictions on the number of legally permitted political parties (hitherto four) were formally removed.

Union pour l'alternance démocratique (UAD): 2 rue de Pékin, Héron, Djibouti; tel. 21341822; fax 77829999 (mobile); e-mail realite_djibouti@yahoo.fr; coalition of major opposition parties; Pres. ISMAËL GUEDI HARED.

Alliance républicaine pour le développement (ARD): BP 1074, Marabout, Djibouti; tel. 21341822; e-mail realite_djibouti@yahoo.fr; internet www.ard-djibouti.org; f. 2002; Leader AHMAD YOUSSOUF HOUMED; Sec.-Gen. KASSIM ALI DINI.

Mouvement pour le renouveau démocratique et le développement (MRD): BP 3570, ave Nasser, Djibouti; e-mail lerenouveau@mrd-djibouti.org; internet www.mrd-djibouti.org; f. 1992 as the Parti du renouveau démocratique; renamed as above in 2002; Pres. DAHER AHMED FARAH; Sec.-Gen. SOULEIMAN HASSAN FAIDAL.

Parti djiboutien pour le développement (PDD): BP 892, Djibouti; tel. 77822860 (mobile); f. 2002; Pres. MOHAMED DAOUD CHEHEM; Sec.-Gen. ABDOULFATAH HASSAN IBRAHIM.

Union djiboutienne pour la démocratie et la justice (UDJ): Djibouti; Chair. ISMAËL GUEDI HARED.

Union pour la majorité présidentielle (UMP): Djibouti; internet www.ump.dj; coalition of major parties in support of Pres. Guelleh; Pres. DILEITA MOHAMED DILEITA.

Front pour la restauration de l'unité et de la démocratie (FRUD): Djibouti; tel. 21250279; f. 1991 by merger of 3 militant Afar groups; advocates fair representation in govt for all ethnic groups; commenced armed insurgency in Nov. 1991; split into 2 factions in March 1994; the dissident group, which negotiated a settlement with the Govt, obtained legal recognition in March 1996 and recognizes the following leaders; Pres. ALI MOHAMED DAOUD; Sec.-Gen. OUGOUREH KIFLEH AHMED; a dissident group, FRUD-Renaissance (led by IBRAHIM CHEHEM DAOUD), was formed in 1996.

Parti national démocratique (PND): BP 10204, Djibouti; tel. 21342194; f. 1992; Pres. ADEN ROBLEH AWALLEH.

Parti social démocrate (PSD): BP 434, route Nelson Mandela, Djibouti; f. 2002; Pres. HASNA MOUMIN BAHDON; Sec.-Gen. HASSAN IDRISS AHMED.

Rassemblement populaire pour le progrès (RPP): Djibouti; e-mail rpp@intnet.dj; internet www.rpp.dj; f. 1979; sole legal party 1981–92; Pres. ISMAÏL OMAR GUELLEH; Sec.-Gen. IDRISS ARNAOUD ALI.

Union pour la réforme (UPR): Djibouti; f. 2006; Pres. IBRAHIM CHEHEM DAOUD.

Diplomatic Representation

EMBASSIES IN DJIBOUTI

China, People's Republic: BP 2021, rue Addis Ababa, Lotissement Heron, Djibouti; tel. 21352247; fax 21354833; e-mail chinaemb_dj@mfa.gov.cn; internet dj.chineseembassy.org; Ambassador ZHANG GUOQING.

Egypt: BP 1989, Djibouti; tel. 21351231; fax 21356657; e-mail ambegypte2004@gawab.com; Ambassador FARGHALI ABDEL HALIM TAHA.

Eritrea: BP 1944, Djibouti; tel. 21354961; fax 21351831; Ambassador MOHAMED SAÏD MANTAY (recalled in June 2008).

Ethiopia: rue Clochette, BP 230, Djibouti; tel. 21350718; fax 21354803; e-mail ethemb@intnet.dj; Ambassador KHALED AHMED TAHA.

France: 45 blvd du Maréchal Foch, BP 2039, Djibouti; tel. 21350963; fax 21350272; e-mail ambfrdj@intnet.dj; internet www.ambafrance-dj.org; Ambassador RENÉ FORCEVILLE.

Libya: BP 2073, Djibouti; tel. 21350202; Chargé d'affaires HADI WAHECHI.

Qatar: Ambassador ALI BIN MUBARAK AL-MOHANNADI.

Russia: BP 1913, Plateau du Marabout, Djibouti; tel. 21350740; fax 21355990; e-mail russiaemb@intnet.dj; internet www.djibouti.mid.ru; Ambassador VALERII ORLOV.

Saudi Arabia: BP 1921, Djibouti; tel. 21351645; fax 21352284; Ambassador IBRAHIM ABD AL-AZIZ AN-NAOUFAL.

Somalia: BP 549, Djibouti; tel. 21353521; internet www.djibouti.somaligov.net; Chargé d'affaires a.i. ABDURRAHMAN ABDI HUSSEIN.

Sudan: BP 4259, Djibouti; tel. 21356404; fax 21356662; Ambassador HASSAN EL-TALIB.

United Arab Emirates: Djibouti; Ambassador SAÏD BEN HAMDAM BEN MUHAMMAD AN-NAGHI.

USA: Lot No. 350-B, Haramous, Djibouti; tel. 21353995; fax 21353940; e-mail amembadm@bow.intnet.dj; internet djibouti.usembassy.gov; Ambassador JAMES C. SWAN.

Yemen: BP 194, Djibouti; tel. 352975; Ambassador MOHAMMED ABDULLAH HAJAR.

Judicial System

The Supreme Court was established in 1979. There is a high court of appeal and a court of first instance in Djibouti; each of the six administrative districts has a 'tribunal coutumier'.

President of the Court of Appeal: KADIDJA ABEBA.

Conseil Constitutionnel: Plateau du Serpent, blvd Foch, BP 4081, Djibouti; tel. 21358662; fax 21358663; e-mail conseil@intnet.dj; f. 1992; Pres. AHMED IBRAHIM ABDI; six mems.

Religion

ISLAM

Almost the entire population are Muslims.

Qadi of Djibouti: MOGUE HASSAN DIRIR, BP 168, Djibouti; tel. 21352669.

Haut Conseil Islamique (High Islamic Council): Djibouti; f. 2004; 7 mems; Pres. Dr CHIKH BOUAMRANE; Sec.-Gen. ALI MOUSSA OKIEH.

CHRISTIANITY

The Roman Catholic Church

Djibouti comprises a single diocese, directly responsible to the Holy See. There were some 7,000 adherents in the country.

Bishop of Djibouti: GIORGIO BERTIN, Evêché, blvd de la République, BP 94, Djibouti; tel. and fax 21350140; e-mail evechcat@intnet.dj.

The Anglican Communion

Within the Episcopal Church in Jerusalem and the Middle East, Djibouti lies within the jurisdiction of the Bishop in Egypt.

Other Christian Churches

Eglise Protestante: blvd de la République, BP 416, Djibouti; tel. 21351820; fax 21350706; e-mail eped@intnet.dj; internet membres.lycos.fr/missiondjibouti; f. 1957; Pastor NATHALIE PAQUEREAU.

Greek Orthodox Church: blvd de la République, Djibouti; tel. 21351325; c. 350 adherents; Archimandrite STAVROS GEORGANAS.

The Ethiopian Orthodox Church is also active in Djibouti.

The Press

Al Qarn: angle rue de Moscou, blvd Cheick Osman, Djibouti; tel. 21355193; fax 21353310; e-mail alqarn@intnet.dj; internet www.alqarn.dj; biweekly; Arabic; Dir YASSIN ABDULLAH BOUH.

Carrefour Africain: BP 393, Djibouti; fax 21354916; fortnightly; publ. by the Roman Catholic mission; circ. 500.

Djibouti Post: blvd Bonhoure, près de l'IGAD, BP 32, Djibouti; tel. 21352201; fax 21353937; internet www.lanation.dj/djibpost; fortnightly; English; circ. 500.

La Nation de Djibouti: blvd Bonhoure, près de l'IGAD, BP 32, Djibouti; tel. 21352201; fax 21353937; e-mail lanation@intnet.dj; internet www.lanation.dj; daily; Dir MOHAMED GASS BARKHADLEH; circ. 4,300.

Le Progrès: Djibouti; weekly; publ. by the RPP; Publr ALI MOHAMED HUMAD.

Le Renouveau: BP 3570, ave Nasser, Djibouti; tel. 21351474; weekly; independent; publ. by the MRD; Editor-in-Chief DAHER AHMED FARAH.

La République: Djibouti; weekly; independent; Editor-in-Chief AMIR ADAWEH.

Revue de l'ISERT: BP 486, Djibouti; tel. 21352795; twice a year; publ. by the Institut Supérieur d'Etudes et de Recherches Scientifiques et Techniques (ISERT).

Le Temps: Djibouti; opposition newspaper; Owners MOUSSA AHMED IDRIS, ALI MEIDAL WAIS.

NEWS AGENCY

Agence Djiboutienne d'Information (ADI): 1 rue de Moscou, BP 32, Djibouti; tel. 21354013; fax 21354037; e-mail adi@intent.dj; internet www.adi.dj; f. 1978.

Broadcasting and Communications

TELECOMMUNICATIONS

Djibouti Télécom: 3 blvd G. Pompidou, BP 2105, Djibouti; tel. 21352777; fax 21359200; e-mail adjib@intnet.dj; internet www.adjib.dj; f. 1999 to replace Société des Télécommunications Internationales; 100% state-owned; Dir-Gen. ABDIRAHMAN MOHAMED HASSAN.

BROADCASTING

Radio and Television

Djibnet: BP 1409, Djibouti; tel. 21354288; e-mail webmaster@djibnet.com; internet www.djibnet.com.

Radiodiffusion-Télévision de Djibouti (RTD): BP 97, 1 ave St Laurent du Var, Djibouti; tel. 21352294; fax 21356502; e-mail rtd@intnet.dj; internet www.rtd.dj; f. 1967; state-controlled; programmes in French, Afar, Somali and Arabic; 17 hours radio and 5 hours television daily; Dir-Gen. Dr KADAR ALI DIRANEH.

Telesat Djibouti: route de l'Aéroport, BP 3760, Djibouti; tel. 21353457.

In 2010 a private television operator Djibsat provided a number of foreign channels, including Horn Cable Television (Somalia), TV5, TF1, M6, Canal+, Medsat and BBC.

Finance

(cap. = capital; res = reserves; dep. = deposits; m. = million; brs = branches; amounts in Djibouti francs)

BANKING

In 2010 there were 10 banks operating in Djibouti, of which four were Islamic banks.

Central Bank

Banque Centrale de Djibouti: BP 2118, ave St Laurent du Var, Djibouti; tel. 21352751; fax 21356288; e-mail bndj@intnet.dj; internet www.banque-centrale.dj; f. 1977 as Banque Nationale de Djibouti; present name adopted 2002; bank of issue; cap. and res 6,056m. (Feb. 2005); Gov. DJAMA MAHAMOUD HAID; Gen. Man. AHMED OSMAN.

Commercial Banks

Bank of Africa—Mer Rouge (BOA—MR): 10 pl. Lagarde, BP 88, Djibouti; tel. 21353016; fax 21351638; e-mail secretariat@bimr-banque.com; f. 1908 as Banque de l'Indochine; present name adopted 2010; cap. 1,500.0m., res 1,041.0m., dep. 60,594.3m. (Dec. 2009); Chair. and CEO PHILIPPE BOUYAUD; 3 brs.

Banque pour le Commerce et l'Industrie—Mer Rouge (BCI—MR): pl. Lagarde, BP 2122, Djibouti; tel. 21350857; fax 21354260; e-mail contact@bcimr.dj; f. 1977; 51% owned by BRED Banque Populaire (France); cap. 2,092.5m., res 209.3m., dep. 82,428.6m. (Dec. 2009); Pres. ERIC MONTAGNE; Dir-Gen. YAHYA OULD AMAR; 6 brs.

International Commercial Bank (Djibouti) SA: Immeuble 15, pl. du 27 juin, rue d'Ethiopie, Djibouti; tel. 21355006; fax 21355003; e-mail info@icbank-djibouti.com; f. 2007; 1 br.

Warka Bank: Djibouti; tel. 21311611; fax 21353693; f. 2010.

Development Bank

Fonds de Développement Economique de Djibouti (FDED): angle ave Georges Clemenceau et rue Pierre Curie, BP 520, Djibouti; tel. 21353391; fax 21355022; f. 2004; Dir-Gen. HIBA AHMED HIBA.

Islamic Banks

Dahabshil Bank International SA: pl. du 27 Juin, BP 2022, Djibouti; tel. 21352233; fax 21355322; e-mail info@dahabshilbank.com; internet www.dahabshilbank.com; f. 2009; Pres. MOHAMED SAID DUALEH.

Saba Islamic Bank (SIB): Immeuble Yassin Yabeh, pl. du 27 juin, BP 1972, Djibouti; tel. 21355777; fax 21357770; e-mail djSaba@SabaBank.com; f. 2006; Dir-Gen. JAMEEL M. ALANSY.

Salaam African Bank (SAB): ave Pierre Pascal, BP 2550, Djibouti; tel. 21351544; fax 21351534; e-mail info@banksalaam.com; internet www.banksalaam.com; f. 2008; Pres. OMAR ISMAÏL EGUEH; Dir-Gen. MOHAMED YUSUF AHMED.

Shoura Bank: Djibouti; tel. 21343892; fax 21343896; e-mail info@shoura-bank.com; f. 2010.

Banking Association

Association Professionnelle des Banques: c/o Banque pour le Commerce et l'Industrie—Mer Rouge, pl. Lagarde, BP 2122, Djibouti; tel. 21350857; fax 21354260; Pres. YAHYA OULD AMAR.

INSURANCE

In 2009 there were two insurance companies in Djibouti.

Les Assureurs de la Mer Rouge et du Golfe Arabe (AMERGA): 8 rue Marchand, BP 2653, Djibouti; tel. 21352510; fax 21355623; e-mail courrier@amerga.com; internet www.amerga.com; f. 2000; Dirs THIERRY MARILL, LUC MARILL, ABDOURAHMAN BARKAT ABDILLAHI, MOHAMED ADEN ABOUBAKER.

GXA Assurances: 3 rue Marchand, BP 200, Djibouti; tel. 21353636; fax 21353056; e-mail accueil@gxaonline.com; internet www.gxaonline.com; Country Man. CHRISTIAN BOUCHER.

Trade and Industry

CHAMBER OF COMMERCE

Chambre de Commerce de Djibouti: pl. Lagarde, BP 84, Djibouti; tel. 21351070; fax 21350096; e-mail ccd@intnet.dj; f. 1906; 24 mems, 12 assoc. mems; Pres. SAÏD OMAR MOUSSA; First Vice-Pres. ABDOURAHMAN MAHAMOUD BOREH.

TRADE ASSOCIATION

Office National d'Approvisionnement et de Commercialisation (ONAC): BP 79, Djibouti; tel. 21350327; fax 21356701; Chair. MOHAMED ABDOULKADER.

UTILITIES

Electricity

Electricité de Djibouti (EdD): blvd de la République, BP 175, Djibouti; tel. 21352851; fax 21354396; e-mail clientele@edd.dj; internet www.edd.dj; Dir-Gen. DJAMA ALI GELLEH.

Water

Office National de l'Eau et de l'Assainissement de Djibouti (ONEAD): blvd de la République, BP 1914, Djibouti; tel. 21351159; fax 21354423; e-mail oneadinfo@intnet.dj; f. 2006; Dir-Gen. M. YOUSSOUF MIRGAN BARKATH.

TRADE UNIONS

Union Djiboutienne pour les Droits Economiques Sociaux et Culturels & Civils et Politiques: rue Pierre Pascal, BP 2767, Djibouti; tel. 77823979 (mobile); e-mail uddesc@yahoo.fr; internet www.uddesc.org; f. 2005; confed. of 21 trade unions; Sec.-Gen. HASSAN CHER HARED.

Union Générale des Travailleurs Djiboutiens (UGTD): Sec.-Gen. ABDO SIKIEH.

Transport

RAILWAYS

In 2011 the Indian Government announced its intention to provide US $300m. towards the construction of a new railway line connecting Ethiopia and Djibouti.

Chemin de Fer Djibouti–Ethiopien (CDE): BP 2116, Djibouti; tel. 21350280; fax 21351256; e-mail adoches@hotmail.com; f. 1909; adopted present name in 1981; jtly owned by govts of Djibouti and Ethiopia; 781 km of track (121 km in Djibouti) linking Djibouti with Addis Ababa; Pres. ALI HASSAN BAHDON.

ROADS

In 2000 there were an estimated 3,065 km of roads; in 2009 it was estimated that 16% of Djibouti's roads were paved. About one-half of the roads are usable only by heavy vehicles. In 1981 the 40-km Grand Bara road was opened, linking the capital with the south. In 1986 the Djibouti–Tadjoura road, the construction of which was financed by Saudi Arabia, was opened, linking the capital with the north. In May 2004 the European Development Fund approved a US $38.4m. road construction project between Djibouti and Addis Ababa, and in October the Kuwait Fund for Arabic Economic Development approved a $20m. loan to build a road between Tadjourah and Obock.

SHIPPING

Djibouti, which was established as a free port in 1981, handled 11.3m. metric tons of freight in 2009.

Djibouti Maritime Management Investment Company (DMMI): BP 1812, Djibouti; f. 2004 to manage Djibouti's fishing port.

Port Autonome International de Djibouti (PAID): BP 2107, Djibouti; tel. 21357372; fax 21355476; e-mail customer.care@port.dj; internet www.dpworld-djiboutiport.com; managed by DP World, UAE, since 2000; Gen. Man. JOHANNES DE JONG.

Principal Shipping Agents

Almis Shipping Line & Transport Co: BP 85, Djibouti; tel. 21356998; fax 21356996; Man. Dir MOHAMED NOOR.

Cie Maritime et de Manutention de Djibouti (COMAD): ave des Messageries Maritimes, BP 89, Djibouti; tel. 21351028; fax 21350466; e-mail hettam@intnet.dj; f. 1990; stevedoring; Man. Dir ALI A. HETTAM.

Global Logistics Services Djibouti: rue Clemenceau, POB 3239, Djibouti; tel. 77839000 (mobile); fax 21352283; e-mail gls.djibouti@gls-logistics.tk; shipping, clearing and freight-forwarding agent; Gen. Man. MOHAMED A. ELMI.

Global Shipping Services (GSS): POB 2666, Djibouti; tel. 21251302; fax 21353395; e-mail gss@intnet.dj; shipping agents; Man. Dir ALI A. HETTAM.

Inchcape Shipping Services & Co (Djibouti) SA: 9–11 rue de Genève, BP 81, Djibouti; tel. 21353844; fax 21353294; e-mail portagencydjibouti@iss-shipping.com; internet www.iss-shipping.com; f. 1942; Man. Dir AHMED OSMAN GELLEH.

International Transit Services: POB 1177, Djibouti; tel. 21251155; fax 21353258; e-mail its02@intnet.dj; Man. Dir ROBLEH MOHAMED.

J. J. Kothari & Co Ltd: rue d'Athens, BP 171, Djibouti; tel. 21350219; fax 21351778; e-mail ops@kothari.dj; internet www.kotharishipping.net; f. 1957; LLC; shipping agents; also ship managers, stevedores, freight forwarders, project cargo movers; Man. Dir NALIN KOTHARI; Dep. Man. Dir PIERRE VINCIGUERRA.

Smart Logistic Services: BP 1579, Djibouti; tel. 21343950; fax 21340523; e-mail sls@intnet.dj; internet www.smartforwarders.com; f. 2010; Man. Dir FAHMI A. HETTAM.

Société Djiboutienne de Trafic Maritime (SDTM): blvd Cheik Osman, BP 640, Djibouti; tel. 21352351; fax 21351103.

Société Maritime L. Savon et Ries: blvd Cheik Osman, BP 2125, Djibouti; tel. 21352352; fax 21351103; e-mail smsr@intnet.dj; Gen. Man. JEAN-PHILIPPE DELARUE.

CIVIL AVIATION

The international airport is at Ambouli, 6 km from Djibouti. There are six other airports providing domestic services. In late 2009 the European Union banned all Djibouti airlines from flying in its airspace.

Daallo Airlines: BP 2565, Djibouti; tel. 21353401; fax 21351765; e-mail daallo@intnet.dj; internet www.daallo.com; f. 1991; operates services to Somalia, Saudi Arabia, the United Arab Emirates, France, the United Kingdom, Kenya and Ethiopia; CEO MOHAMED IBRAHIM YASSIN.

Djibouti Airlines (Puntavia Airline de Djibouti): BP 2240, pl. Lagarde, Djibouti; tel. 21351006; fax 21352429; e-mail djibouti-airlines@intnet.dj; internet www.djiboutiairlines.com; f. 1996; scheduled and charter regional and domestic flights; Man. Dir Capt. MOUSSA RAYALEH WABERI.

Tourism

Djibouti offers desert scenery in its interior and watersport facilities on its coast. A casino operates in the capital. There were about 20,000 tourist arrivals in 1998. Receipts from tourism totalled US $16.0m. in 2009.

Office National du Tourisme de Djibouti (ONTD): pl. du 27 juin, BP 1938, Djibouti; tel. 21353790; fax 21356322; e-mail onta@intnet.dj; internet www.office-tourisme.dj; Dir MOHAMED ABDILLAHI WAIS.

Defence

Arrangements for military co-operation exist between Djibouti and France, and in November 2011 there were about 1,500 French military personnel stationed in Djibouti, while the US-led Combined Joint Task Force-Horn of Africa also had its headquarters in the country. Around 1,285 US military, naval and air force personnel were stationed there. In January 2010 Djibouti announced that it would contribute some 450 troops to the African Union Mission in Somalia. As assessed at November 2011, the total armed forces of Djibouti itself, in which all services form part of the army, numbered some 8,450 (including 200 naval and 250 air force personnel). There were also paramilitary forces numbering 2,000 gendarmes, as well as a 2,500-strong national security force. Conscription of all men between 18 and 25 years of age was introduced in 1992.

Defence Expenditure: Budgeted at 1,720m. Djibouti francs in 2010.

Commander-in-Chief of the Armed Forces: Pres. ISMAÏL OMAR GUELLEH.

Chief of Staff of the Army: Gen. ZAKARIA CHEIK IBRAHIM.

Education

The Government has overall responsibility for education. Primary education generally begins at six years of age and lasts for six years. Secondary education, usually starting at the age of 12, lasts for seven years, comprising a first cycle of four years and a second of three years. In 2008/09 primary enrolment included 44% of pupils in the relevant age-group (47% of boys; 42% of girls), and secondary enrolment was equivalent to 30% of pupils in the relevant age-group (35% of boys; 26% of girls). In 2007 spending on education represented 22.8% of total government expenditure. In 2008/09, according to UNESCO estimates, there were 55,546 primary school pupils and 42,690 pupils receiving general secondary and vocational education. Djibouti's sole university, the Université de Djibouti, was formed in January 2006 as a replacement for the Pôle Universitaire de Djibouti, which opened in 2000 and had 3,159 students in 2008/09.

DOMINICA

Introductory Survey

LOCATION, CLIMATE, LANGUAGE, RELIGION, FLAG, CAPITAL

The Commonwealth of Dominica is situated in the Windward Islands group of the West Indies, lying between Guadeloupe, to the north, and Martinique, to the south. The climate is tropical, though tempered by sea winds, which sometimes reach hurricane force, especially from July to September. The average temperature is about 27°C (80°F), with little seasonal variation. Rainfall is heavy, especially in the mountainous areas, where the annual average is 6,350 mm (250 ins), compared with 1,800 mm (70 ins) along the coast. English is the official language, but a local French patois, or Creole, is widely spoken. In parts of the north-east an English dialect, Cocoy, is spoken by the descendants of Antiguan settlers. There is a small community of Carib Indians on the east coast. Almost all of the inhabitants profess Christianity, and about 62% are Roman Catholics. The national flag (proportions 1 by 2) has a green field, with equal stripes of yellow, white and black forming an upright cross, on the centre of which is superimposed a red disc containing a parrot surrounded by 10 five-pointed green stars (one for each of the island's parishes). The capital is Roseau.

CONTEMPORARY POLITICAL HISTORY

Historical Context

Dominica was first settled by Arawaks and then Caribs. Control of the island was fiercely contested by the Caribs, British and French during the 17th and 18th centuries. The British eventually prevailed and Dominica formed part of the Leeward Islands federation until 1939. In 1940 it was transferred to the Windward Islands and remained attached to that group until the federal arrangement was ended in December 1959. Under a new Constitution, effective from January 1960, Dominica (like each other member of the group) achieved a separate status, with its own Administrator and an enlarged Legislative Council.

Domestic Political Affairs

At the January 1961 elections to the Legislative Council, the ruling Dominica United People's Party was defeated by the Dominica Labour Party (DLP). Edward LeBlanc, leader of the DLP, became Chief Minister. In March 1967 Dominica became one of the West Indies Associated States, gaining full autonomy in internal affairs, with the United Kingdom retaining responsibility for defence and foreign relations. The House of Assembly replaced the Legislative Council, the Administrator became Governor and the Chief Minister was restyled Premier. At elections to the House in October 1970, LeBlanc was returned to power as Premier.

In July 1974 LeBlanc retired, and was replaced as DLP leader and Premier by Patrick John. At elections to the enlarged House of Assembly in March 1975 the DLP was returned to power. Following a decision in 1975 by the Associated States to seek independence separately, Dominica became an independent republic within the Commonwealth on 3 November 1978. John became Prime Minister, and Frederick Degazon was eventually elected President.

In May 1979 two people were killed by the Defence Force at a demonstration against the Government's attempts to introduce legislation that would restrict the freedom of trade unions and the press. The deaths fuelled increasing popular opposition to the Government, and a pressure group, the Committee for National Salvation (CNS), was formed to campaign for John's resignation. Government opponents organized a general strike that lasted 25 days, with John relinquishing power only after all his cabinet ministers had resigned and President Degazon had gone into hiding abroad (there was a succession of Acting Presidents; Degazon finally resigned in February 1980). Oliver Seraphin, the candidate proposed by the CNS, was elected Prime Minister, and an interim Government was formed to prepare for a general election after six months.

The Dominica Freedom Party (DFP) achieved a convincing victory in the general election of July 1980. Eugenia Charles, the party's leader, became the Caribbean's first female Prime Minister.

In January 1981 the Government disarmed the Defence Force following reports that weapons were being traded for marijuana. Against a background of increasing violence and the declaration of a state of emergency, however, there were two coup attempts involving former Defence Force members. John, the former Prime Minister, was also implicated and imprisoned. In June 1982 John and his fellow prisoners were tried and acquitted, but the Government secured a retrial in October 1985. John and the former Deputy Commander of the Defence Force each received a prison sentence of 12 years. In 1986 the former Commander of the Defence Force was hanged for the murder of a police officer during the second coup attempt. The death sentences on five other soldiers were commuted to life imprisonment.

By 1985 the DLP, the Democratic Labour Party, the United Dominica Labour Party and the Dominica Liberation Movement had united to form a new left-wing grouping, the Labour Party of Dominica, although in practice the party continued to be known as the DLP. At a general election in July 1985 the DFP was returned to power. Following the election, the DLP began an 18-month boycott of the House, in protest against the Government's decision to curtail live broadcasts of parliamentary proceedings.

Dissatisfaction at continued government austerity measures was offset by the success of the land reform programme. Since independence, the Government had acquired nearly all the large estates, often in an attempt to forestall violence. In 1986 the first of the estates was divided, and tenure granted to the former workers. The DFP was returned for a third term in government at a general election in May 1990.

A programme, introduced in 1991, granting Dominican citizenship to foreigners in return for a minimum investment of US $35,000 in the country caused considerable controversy. The Dominica United Workers' Party (UWP—formed in 1988) expressed opposition to the policy, and in 1992 a pressure group, 'Concerned Citizens', organized protests demanding that the programme be modified. In response, the Government announced in July that the minimum investment was to be increased substantially, the number of applications was to be limited to 800 and restrictions were to be placed on the investors' right to vote in Dominica.

At a general election in June 1995 the DFP's 15-year tenure was finally ended as the UWP secured a narrow victory. The UWP leader, Edison James, was subsequently appointed Prime Minister, and the DLP and DFP leaders agreed to occupy the position of Leader of the Opposition in alternate years.

In December 1997 the Government's citizenship programme again provoked controversy. It was alleged that, under the scheme, passports were being sold by agents for between US $15,000 and $20,000. The opposition DLP accused the Government of undermining the credibility of Dominican citizenship. In late 1999 it was announced that the Government had stopped granting citizenship to Russians, following reports that up to 300 Russians had paid $50,000 each to obtain a Dominican passport. In addition, there were complaints from the US Government that the trade in passports had increased 'suspicions of money-laundering' in Dominica.

The rise of the DLP

A general election was held on 31 January 2000. The DLP was returned to power after two decades in opposition, albeit one seat short of a majority. Douglas was named as Prime Minister and formed a coalition Government with the DFP (which was allocated two ministerial portfolios). On taking office, the new Government immediately suspended the controversial citizenship programme; however, following changes to ensure that passports would not be granted to those with a criminal record, the programme was relaunched in June 2002, with a fee of US $100,000 for individual applicants.

In October 2000 Prime Minister Douglas died suddenly of a heart attack. Pierre Charles, previously the Minister of Communications and Works, succeeded him as premier. In November

Charles placed Ambrose George, the Minister of Finance, on two weeks' leave of absence following the arrest on money-laundering charges of a businessman with whom he was travelling in Puerto Rico. Upon his return to government George was stripped of the finance portfolio, which passed to Charles, and given the post of Minister of Industry, Physical Planning and Enterprise Development.

Meanwhile, in December 2000 legislation was approved in the House of Assembly making the crime of money-laundering punishable by up to seven years' imprisonment and a fine of EC $1m. At the same time, the Government introduced stricter regulations governing its 'offshore' banking sector, following Dominica's inclusion on a 'black list' published by the Financial Action Task Force earlier in the year. Dominica was removed from the black list in 2002 after the Government made progress in improving its anti-money-laundering measures. Part of these measures was the approval, in December 2001, of the Exchange of Information Bill, designed to give foreign authorities greater access to information about Dominica's 'offshore' banks.

In February 2003 the Public Service Union (PSU), objecting to government proposals to reduce the size of the public sector work-force and to compel workers to take two days of unpaid leave every month, organized a six-day strike. The strike ended after the Government agreed to review its proposal to reduce the public sector wage bill. However, between 2004 and 2005 the Government enforced a 5% reduction in public sector salaries, attracting criticism from the PSU, but approval from the IMF.

Charles died of a heart attack in January 2004. Roosevelt Skerrit, hitherto Minister of Education, Youth and Sports, was sworn in as Prime Minister after his nomination had been endorsed by the coalition's other member, the DFP. On the same day, Skerrit appointed his first Cabinet; notable appointments included the return of Ambrose George (who had left the Cabinet in 2002), as Minister of Agriculture and the Environment. In the following month Skerrit was elected leader of the DLP; George was appointed deputy leader.

In spite of the country's economic difficulties, at the general election on 5 May 2005 the DLP was re-elected with an overall majority of seats (12 of the 21) in the House of Assembly. The UWP secured eight seats, while a close ally of the DLP, standing as an independent candidate, won the remaining seat. The junior coalition partner, the DFP, was defeated in the two constituencies in which it competed; however, its leader, Charles Savarin, was appointed as a senator and retained his place in Skerrit's new administration as Minister of Foreign Affairs, Trade, Labour and the Public Service. In December Earl Williams, a former cabinet minister, succeeded Edison James as leader of the UWP, and proceeded to replace him as Leader of the Opposition in July 2007 when James resigned from office. In September 2006 the former deputy leader of the party, Julius Timothy, defected to the DLP in acceptance of Prime Minister Skerrit's invitation to the Cabinet as Minister for Economic Development and Planning.

In July 2008 Williams was forced to resign as Leader of the Opposition and of the UWP following allegations that he had mishandled clients' money in his capacity as a lawyer. He was succeeded by the party's Deputy Leader, Ron Green. In October Nicholas Liverpool secured a second term as President after receiving the nomination of both the DLP and the UWP. Prime Minister Skerrit reorganized his Cabinet in November 2008, removing Ambrose George from his post as Minister of Public Works following accusations of corruption that included his alleged involvement in an internet fraud operation. His position was reallocated to the hitherto Minister of National Security, Immigration and Labour, Rayburn Blackmoore, while Vince Henderson became Minister of Foreign Affairs, Immigration and Labour. The office of Minister of National Security was assumed by the Prime Minister.

Recent developments: the re-election of Skerrit's DLP

In the general election, held on 18 December 2009, the DLP increased its majority in the House of Assembly, securing 18 of the 21 elective seats, while the UWP won the remaining three. Among those to lose their seats were UWP leader Ron Green, who lost to the DLP candidate by two votes, and his deputy, Claudius Sanford. The rate of participation by the electorate was recorded at 59.1%. In the months preceding the election, campaign financing had been a prominent issue: it was alleged that the DLP campaign had been funded by the People's Republic of China and Venezuela, while the UWP was accused of accepting funds from Taiwan. Both parties denied the charges.

Shortly after the release of the election results, Green alleged that the DLP had used bribery to manipulate the outcome of the ballot, which he described as 'fraudulent, unfair and unlawful'. He also criticized the DLP's disproportionate access to the state-controlled media. Green announced that the three UWP deputies would boycott the House of Assembly in protest, and appealed to the High Court for a recount in his closely contested constituency. He also demanded that a fresh election be convened within 18 months, despite the fact that monitors from the Caribbean Community and the Organization of American States had declared the ballot to be free and fair. In February 2010, with the parliamentary boycott continuing, the UWP announced that it would instead participate in a separate 'People's Parliament'. Nevertheless, Skerrit's new Cabinet was sworn in on 4 January, which, controversially, included Ambrose George as Minister of Information, Telecommunication and Constituency Empowerment. Skerrit appointed Charles Savarin as Minister of National Security, Labour and Immigration, but retained responsibility for the key portfolios of finance and foreign affairs.

The continuing boycott by two of the three UWP deputies, former Prime Minister Edison James and Hector John, prompted the Speaker of the House of Assembly to designate their seats as vacant in May 2010. By-elections to fill the seats were conducted on 9 July and the two UWP members were re-elected. John became Leader of the Opposition later that month, although by early 2012 the UWP was still maintaining its parliamentary boycott. The opposition party declared that it would not participate in the legislature until the Government introduced electoral reforms, including the allocation of voter identification cards; Skerrit argued that such a scheme would be too expensive to implement.

Meanwhile, in August 2010 the High Court, responding to a UWP petition, announced that Skerrit and Minister of Education and Human Resource Development Peter Saint Jean would be required to stand trial to defend themselves against dual-citizenship charges. According to Dominican law, persons maintaining allegiance to a non-Commonwealth country are not permitted to contest elections. Therefore, Skerrit's joint French-Dominican nationality brought into question his eligibility to govern. The Prime Minister asserted that his French citizenship had been attained while he was a child, thereby exempting him from the electoral regulation in question, although the UWP claimed that he had acquired French nationality during 2007. The trial took place in September 2011, and in January 2012 the High Court exonerated Skerrit and Saint Jean of any wrongdoing, declaring that there was insufficient evidence to uphold the UWP petition. Following this defeat, Green declined to stand in the UWP leadership election later that month, and Edison James was selected as the party's new leader. Several prominent UWP members, including James, Green, Stanford and John, were due to stand trial in February on charges of organizing an illegal protest in November 2010.

Amid concerns about the levels of violent crime on the island, in March 2011 the House of Assembly approved new anti-firearms legislation, which increased sentences for offences involving guns. Also in that month, the United Kingdom provided Dominica with surveillance equipment to combat illegal drugs-smuggling operations, while in January the Dominican Government had concluded an anti-narcotics-trafficking agreement with the USA.

Foreign Affairs

Regional relations

In 2005 the Government became one of 13 Caribbean administrations to sign the PetroCaribe accord, under which Dominica would be allowed to purchase petroleum from Venezuela at reduced prices. Owing to insufficient existing petroleum storage and refining capacity on the island, an agreement was signed in mid-2006 between the Government and PDVSA, the state-managed Venezuelan oil company, for the construction of a fuel storage and distribution plant to assist in dissemination of oil under the PetroCaribe initiative. The Venezuelan President, Hugo Chávez, visited Dominica in June 2009 to attend the official opening ceremony of the fuel plant, which had an oil storage capacity of 35,000 barrels. During his visit Chávez also announced plans to fund the construction of a coffee-processing plant on the island and to establish a local office of the

Venezuelan-led Bolivarian Alternative for the Americas (Alternativa Bolivariana para las Américas—ALBA) group. Dominica had joined ALBA in 2008, which was intended to be an alternative to the proposed Free Trade Area of the Americas advanced by the USA.

Other external relations

Dominica has close links with France and the USA. France helped in suppressing the coup attempts against the DFP Government in 1981, and Dominica was the first Commonwealth country to benefit from the French aid agency Fonds d'aide et de coopération. In October 2005 the USA announced a US $2m. per year aid programme, to help improve Dominica's international competitiveness.

In 2001 Libya granted Dominica, in common with other eastern Caribbean islands, access to a US $2,000m. development fund. In 2005 the Government announced that Libya was paying for the construction of two schools on the island and for 15 scholarships for Dominican students to attend university courses in Libya. The Government refused to sever diplomatic ties with the Libyan regime of Col Muammar al-Qaddafi in early 2011 despite the increasingly violent attempts by the Libyan authorities to suppress a popular domestic uprising. Dominica also declined to participate in a UN vote in September that granted recognition to the rebel 'National Transitional Council of Libya'.

In 2004 Skerrit announced that Dominica would establish diplomatic relations with the People's Republic of China in place of Taiwan. (China agreed to provide an estimated US $111m. in budgetary support, infrastructure grants and education exchanges.) A Chinese embassy was duly opened in Roseau in June. Skerrit was heavily criticized by the opposition over the severing of relations with Taiwan. In January 2005 Skerrit accused the UWP of jeopardizing Dominica's nascent relations with China by accepting campaign funds from Taiwan. The Chinese embassy in Roseau condemned the display of Taiwanese flags by UWP supporters and expressed strongly worded dismay at local opposition to the 'one China' principle. In August 2009 the Government negotiated a EC $35m. low-interest loan with China to fund a new college on the island. The Chinese Government also agreed to a concessionary loan to finance road rehabilitation and housing development projects.

Dominica's perceived attachment to so-called 'chequebook diplomacy' was criticized again in December 2004 when Japan provided funding of some EC $33m. for the construction of a fisheries complex on the island, allegedly in return for supporting the Japanese Government's pro-whaling stance at the annual meeting of the International Whaling Commission (IWC) in June 2006. In April 2007 Prime Minister Skerrit made an official visit to Japan, following which he announced that Japanese funding for a further fisheries facility had been secured. Skerrit also stated his intention to renew Dominica's support for the Japanese Government's bid to resume commercial whaling. The President of the Caribbean Conservation Association and former Minister of the Environment in the Dominican Government, Atherton Martin, accused his country of behaving like 'an international prostitute' for agreeing to support Japan at the IWC while accepting financial assistance from the Japanese Government. In June 2008 Skerrit reversed his decision and withdrew his support for the overturning of the whaling ban, citing the island's strict environmental commitments and the importance of its abundant sealife for the tourism industry.

CONSTITUTION AND GOVERNMENT

The Constitution came into effect at the independence of Dominica in November 1978. Legislative power is vested in the unicameral House of Assembly, comprising 30 members (nine nominated and 21 elected for five years by universal adult suffrage). Executive authority is vested in the President, who is elected by the House, but in most matters the President is guided by the advice of the Cabinet and acts as the constitutional Head of State. He appoints the Prime Minister, who must be able to command a majority in the House, and (on the Prime Minister's recommendation) other ministers. The Cabinet is responsible to the House. Justice is administered by the Eastern Caribbean Supreme Court (based in Saint Lucia), although further appeal can, in certain cases, be made to the Privy Council in the United Kingdom. The island is divided into 10 administrative divisions, known as parishes, and there is limited local government in Roseau, the capital, and in the Carib Territory.

REGIONAL AND INTERNATIONAL CO-OPERATION

Dominica is a member of the Organization of American States (see p. 394), the Caribbean Community and Common Market (CARICOM, see p. 227), the Association of Caribbean States (see p. 448), the Organisation of Eastern Caribbean States (OECS, see p. 465), and of the Community of Latin American and Caribbean States (see p. 462), which was formally inaugurated in December 2011. Dominica is also a member of the Eastern Caribbean Central Bank (see p. 453) and the Eastern Caribbean Securities Exchange (both based in Saint Christopher and Nevis). On 18 June 2010 Dominica was a signatory to the Revised Treaty of Basseterre, establishing an Economic Union among OECS member states. The Cabinet ratified the Treaty in January 2011, and the Economic Union, which involved the removal of barriers to trade and the movement of labour as a step towards a single financial and economic market, came into effect on 21 January. Freedom of movement between the signatory states was granted to OECS nationals on 1 August.

Dominica became a member of the UN when it became independent in 1978. As a contracting party to the General Agreement on Tariffs and Trade, Dominica joined the World Trade Organization (see p. 433) on its establishment in 1995. The country joined the Commonwealth (see p. 239) upon independence. The country is a signatory of the Cotonou Agreement, the successor arrangement to the Lomé Conventions between the African, Caribbean and Pacific (ACP) countries and the European Union (see p. 276). Dominica is also a member of the Group of 77 (see p. 450) organization of developing states.

ECONOMIC AFFAIRS

In 2010, according to estimates by the World Bank, Dominica's gross national income (GNI), measured at average 2008–10 prices, was US $367m., equivalent to $5,410 per head (or $9,370 per head on an international purchasing-power parity basis). Between 2000 and 2010 the population decreased at an average annual rate of 0.3%, while gross domestic product (GDP) per head increased, in real terms, by an average of 2.8% per year. According to the Eastern Caribbean Central Bank (ECCB, see p. 453), overall GDP increased, in real terms, by an average of 2.5% per year in 2001–10; GDP declined by 0.7% in 2009 and increased only marginally, by 0.3%, in 2010.

Agriculture (including forestry and fishing) is the principal economic activity, accounting for 12.2% of GDP in 2010. In mid-2012 the sector was expected to engage an estimated 20.0% of the employed labour force, according to FAO estimates. The principal cash crop is bananas, although the industry was adversely affected by the ending of Dominica's preferential access to the European (particularly the British) market from 2010. In 2010 banana output totalled an estimated 21,000 metric tons. In 2008 receipts from banana exports amounted to an estimated US $8.0m. (some 20.0% of total domestic exports). Other important crops include coconuts (which provide copra for export as well as edible oil and soap), mangoes, avocados, papayas, ginger, citrus fruits and, mainly for domestic consumption, vegetables. Non-banana crops have rapidly grown in significance during recent years, from one-half of total crop production before 2000 to four-fifths by the late 2000s. Livestock-rearing and fishing are also practised for local purposes. Numerous Japanese-funded fisheries projects have been donated to Dominica in recent years. Dominica has extensive timber reserves (more than 40% of the island's total land area is forest and woodland), and international aid agencies are encouraging the development of a balanced timber industry. According to the Eastern Caribbean Central Bank (ECCB, see p. 453), the GDP of the agricultural sector declined at an average annual rate of 1.3% in 2001–10; agricultural GDP decreased by 10.6% in 2010.

Industry (comprising mining, manufacturing, construction and utilities) provided 14.5% of GDP in 2010, and employed an estimated 22.0% of the employed labour force in 2001. According to the ECCB, real industrial GDP decreased at an average rate of 3.5% per year during 2001–10; the sector declined by 6.6% in 2009, but increased by 6.1% in 2010.

The mining sector contributed only 1.5% of GDP in 2010. There is some quarrying of pumice, and there are extensive reserves of limestone and clay. According to the ECCB, the sector increased at an annual average rate of 1.8% in 2001–10; after two years of impressive growth, in 2009 mining GDP declined massively, by 47.2%, before increasing by 3.0% in 2010.

In 2010 manufacturing contributed 2.7% of GDP and, in 2001, an estimated 10.6% of the employed work-force were engaged in manufacturing, mining and quarrying activities. The Government has encouraged the manufacturing sector, which is mainly small-scale and dependent upon agriculture, in an attempt to diversify the economy. According to the ECCB, real manufacturing GDP decreased at an average rate of 0.4% per year during 2001–10; the sector decreased by 12.2% in 2008, following the closure of part of Dominica Coconut Products in 2007. The sector declined further, by 2.6% in 2009, and there was negligible growth (0.4%) in 2010. There is a banana-packaging plant, a brewery and factories for the manufacturing and refining of crude and edible vegetable oils and for the production of soap, canned juices and cigarettes. Furniture, paint, cardboard boxes and candles are also produced.

The construction industry accounted for 5.6% of GDP in 2010, and employed 9.8% of the employed labour force in 2001. Extensive infrastructure development by the Government has maintained high levels of activity in the construction sector in recent years. According to the ECCB, the sector's GDP increased at an average annual rate of 9.4%, in real terms, during 2001–10; following annual growth of over 30% in 2007 and 2008, sectoral GDP declined by 7.3% in 2009, although an increase of 10.2% was recorded in 2010.

In 2000 some 70% of Dominica's energy requirements were supplied by hydroelectric power. Investment in a hydroelectric development scheme and in the water supply system has been partially financed by the export of water, from Dominica's extensive reserves, to drier Caribbean islands such as Aruba. In 2008 Dominica's imports of mineral fuels totalled 15.6% of the cost of total imports. The state-owned Dominica Electricity Services (Domlec) was privatized in 1996. Construction of a new 20-MW electric power plant, at an estimated cost of EC $80m., was completed in 2001. New electricity supply legislation, instituted in November 2006, was to establish an independent regulatory commission to oversee the sector and, in a repeal of the Electricity Supply Act (1996), would foreshorten Domlec's monopoly licence by 10 years, effectively liberalizing the market by 2015. The Government had plans in 2011 to build a 120-MW geothermal power plant in Wotten Waven, in order to reduce reliance on imported energy.

Services engaged an estimated 58.8% of the employed labour force in 2001, and provided 73.3% of GDP in 2010. According to the ECCB, the combined GDP of the services sector increased at an average rate of 2.4% per year during 2001–10; the sector expanded by 1.4% in 2010. The tourism industry, which directly contributed an estimated 7.5% of GDP and 6.9% of employment in 2011, according to the World Travel and Tourism Council, is of increasing importance to the economy, and exploits Dominica's natural history and scenery. Successive governments have placed considerable emphasis on the country's potential as an 'eco-tourism' destination. The majority of tourists are cruise ship passengers. Total visitor arrivals stood at 603,227 in 2010, a 0.6% decrease over the previous year (606,578 visitors). Tourism receipts totalled EC $268.3m. in 2010, compared with $232.6m. in the previous year.

In 2010 Dominica recorded an estimated visible trade deficit of US $159.3m. and a deficit of $96.8m. on the current account of the balance of payments. The principal source of imports in 2008 was the USA, which accounted for 39.7% of total imports, followed by Trinidad and Tobago (21.3%) and the United Kingdom (4.6%). The principal market for exports in 2008 was Jamaica, with 16.3% of the total. The United Kingdom, which receives a large proportion of Dominica's banana production, was the second largest market, receiving 13.3% of total domestic exports in that year. The principal imports in 2010 were machinery and transport equipment, and food and live animals. The principal exports in the same year were chemicals and related products and food and live animals.

In 2010, according to the ECCB, there was an estimated budget surplus of EC $15.5m., equivalent to 2.1% of GDP. Dominica's general government gross debt was EC $693,000 in 2009, equivalent to 53.7% of GDP. At the end of 2009 Dominica's total external debt was US $252m., of which 193m. was public and publicly guaranteed debt. In that year, the cost of servicing long-term public and publicly guaranteed debt and repayments to the IMF was equivalent to 11.6% of the value of exports of goods, services and income (excluding workers' remittances). According to the IMF, the annual rate of inflation averaged 1.9% in 2004–10; consumer prices increased by an average of 3.2% in 2010. An estimated 10.9% of the labour force were unemployed in 2001.

The Dominican economy is heavily dependent on the production of bananas, and is thus vulnerable to adverse weather conditions and price fluctuations. Efforts to expand the country's economic base have been impeded by poor infrastructure and, in terms of tourism, a paucity of desirable beaches. The gradual elimination of the European Union's (see p. 276) tariff system from 2010 brought further insecurity for the banana sector following several years of decline. Although Dominica was not as badly affected by the global financial crisis as many other nations in the region, the economy contracted slightly (by 0.7%) in 2009, owing to a fall in tourist receipts, a decline in foreign direct investment and reduced remittances from Dominicans working abroad. Expansionary spending policies throughout 2009, and the receipt of a US $5m. IMF grant in July, cushioned the country from the worst effects of the economic crisis. Although banana production declined as a result of disease and drought in 2010, increased activity in the construction sector supported a fragile economic recovery, with real GDP rising by 0.3% in that year, according to the IMF. However, the tourism sector was expected to contract in 2011 after a major cruise line removed Dominica from its itinerary in late 2010. There were indications of an upturn in the agricultural sector in 2011, but the construction industry, which had previously been bolstered by various public works programmes, was negatively affected by the reduction of spending from mid-2011. The IMF estimated that real GDP expansion accelerated slightly, to 0.9%, in 2011 and forecast growth of 1.5% in 2012. In January 2012 the IMF dispensed $3.1m. to Dominica to assist the Government's reconstruction efforts following severe flooding during mid-2011. Meanwhile, drilling to assess Dominica's geothermal energy potential was due to commence in 2012. The Government had plans to establish a 120-MW geothermal power station on the island, with excess electricity to be exported to Guadeloupe and Martinique, although the construction of an initial 15-MW plant was the main priority.

PUBLIC HOLIDAYS

2013: 1 January (New Year's Day), 11–12 February (Masquerade, Carnival), 29 March (Good Friday), 1 April (Easter Monday), 6 May (May or Labour Day), 20 May (Whit Monday), 5 August (Emancipation, August Monday), 4 November (Independence Day and Community Service Day), 25–26 December (Christmas).

Statistical Survey

Source (unless otherwise stated): Eastern Caribbean Central Bank; internet www.eccb-centralbank.org.

AREA AND POPULATION

Area: 751 sq km (290 sq miles).

Population: 71,727 (males 36,434, females 35,293) at census of 12 May 2001. *Mid-2010* (estimate): 73,724.

Density (mid-2010): 98.2 per sq km.

Population by Age and Sex (31 December 2006): *0–14:* 20,976 (males 10,759, females 10,217); *15–64:* 42,979 (males 22,280, females 20,699); *65 and over:* 7,226 (males 3,200, females 4,026); *Total* 71,180 (males 36,238, females 34,942) (Source: UN, *Demographic Yearbook*).

Population by Ethnic Group (*de jure* population, excl. those resident in institutions, 1981): Negro 67,272; Mixed race 4,433; Amerindian (Carib) 1,111; White 341; Total (incl. others) 73,795 (males 36,754, females 37,041). Source: UN, *Demographic Yearbook*.

Principal Town (population at 1991 census): Roseau (capital) 15,853. *Mid-2009* (UN estimate): Roseau 14,266 (Source: UN, *World Urbanization Prospects: The 2009 Revision*).

Births, Marriages and Deaths (registrations, 2002 unless otherwise indicated): Live births 1,081 (birth rate 15.4 per 1,000); Marriages (1998) 336 (marriage rate 4.4 per 1,000); Deaths 594 (death rate 8.4 per 1,000) (Source: UN, *Demographic Yearbook*). *2006:* Live births 1,058 (birth rate 14.9 per 1,000); Deaths 536 (death rate 7.5 per 1,000) (Source: UN, *Population and Vital Statistics Report*).

Life Expectancy (years at birth, WHO estimates): 74 (males 72; females 76) in 2009. Source: WHO, *World Health Statistics*.

Economically Active Population ('000 persons aged 15 years and over, 2001): Agriculture, hunting, forestry and fishing 5.22; Manufacturing (incl. mining and quarrying) 2.10; Utilities 0.41; Construction 2.42; Wholesale and retail trade, restaurants and hotels 5.12; Transport, storage and communications 1.56; Financing, insurance, real estate and business services 1.14; Community, social and personal services 6.77; *Sub-total* 24.73; Activities not adequately defined 0.08; *Total employed* 24.81; Unemployed 3.05; *Total labour force* 27.86 (males 17.03, females 10.83) (Source: ILO). *Mid-2012* (estimates): Agriculture, etc. 6,000; Total labour force 30,000 (Source: FAO).

HEALTH AND WELFARE

Key Indicators

Total Fertility Rate (children per woman, 2009): 2.1.

Under-5 Mortality Rate (per 1,000 live births, 2009): 10.

Physicians (per 1,000 head, 1997): 0.5.

Hospital Beds (per 1,000 head, 2005): 3.9.

Health Expenditure (2008): US $ per head (PPP): 584.

Health Expenditure (2008): % of GDP: 6.0.

Health Expenditure (2008): public (% of total): 62.5.

Access to Water (% of persons, 2004): 97.

Access to Sanitation (% of persons, 2004): 84.

Total Carbon Dioxide Emissions ('000 metric tons, 2007): 120.9.

Total Carbon Dioxide Emissions Per Head (metric tons, 2007): 1.7.

Human Development Index (2011): ranking: 81.

Human Development Index (2011): value: 0.724.

For sources and definitions, see explanatory note on p. vi.

AGRICULTURE, ETC.

Principal Crops ('000 metric tons, 2010, FAO estimates): Sweet potatoes 2.5; Cassava 1.0; Yautia (Cocoyam) 3.3; Taro (Cocoyam) 17.1; Yams 15.3; Sugar cane 4.8; Coconuts 9.0; Cabbages 0.7; Pumpkins 0.9; Cucumbers 1.3; Carrots 0.7; Bananas 21.0; Plantains 5.0; Oranges 7.3; Lemons and limes 1.1; Grapefruit (incl. pomelos) 16.0; Guavas, mangoes and mangosteens 2.2; Avocados 0.4. *Aggregate Production* ('000 metric tons, may include official, semi-official or estimated data, 2010): Fruits (excl. melons) 53.8.

Livestock ('000 head, year ending September 2010, FAO estimates): Cattle 13.5; Pigs 5.0; Sheep 7.6; Goats 9.7; Chickens 190.

Livestock Products ('000 metric tons, 2010, FAO estimates): Cattle meat 0.5; Pig meat 0.4; Chicken meat 0.3; Cows' milk 7.5; Hen eggs 0.2.

Fishing (metric tons, live weight, 2009): Capture 790 (Skipjack tuna 28; Yellowfin tuna 112; Marlins, sailfishes, etc. 84; Common dolphinfish 201); Aquaculture 0; *Total catch* 790.

Source: FAO.

MINING

Pumice ('000 metric tons, incl. volcanic ash): Estimated production 100 per year in 1988–2004. Source: US Geological Survey.

INDUSTRY

Production (2006, metric tons, unless otherwise indicated, preliminary): Laundry soap 3,605; Toilet soap 4,296; Dental cream 1,376; Liquid disinfectant 1,861; Crude coconut oil 855 (2001); Coconut meal 331 (2001); Electricity 87.0 million kWh (2008). Sources: IMF, *Dominica: Statistical Appendix* (September 2007), and UN Industrial Commodity Statistics Database.

FINANCE

Currency and Exchange Rates: 100 cents = 1 Eastern Caribbean dollar (EC $). *Sterling, US Dollar and Euro Equivalents* (30 December 2011): £1 sterling = EC $4.174; US $1 = EC $2.700; €1 = EC $3.494; EC $100 = £24.00 = US $37.04 = €28.62. *Exchange Rate:* Fixed at US $1 = EC $2.70 since July 1976.

Budget (EC $ million, 2010): *Revenue:* Tax revenue 327.9 (Taxes on income and profits 62.4, Taxes on property 8.7, Taxes on domestic goods and services 184.0, Taxes on international trade and transactions 72.9); Other current revenue 23.9; Total 351.8, excl. grants received 58.3. *Expenditure:* Current expenditure 306.4 (Wages and salaries 127.5, Goods and services 89.0, Interest payments 21.0, Transfers and subsidies 68.8); Capital expenditure and net lending 88.2; Total 394.6.

International Reserves (US $ million at 31 December 2010): IMF special drawing rights 9.67; Reserve position in IMF 0.01; Foreign exchange 66.41; Total 76.10. Source: IMF, *International Financial Statistics*.

Money Supply (EC $ million at 31 December 2010): Currency outside depository corporations 46.46; Transferable deposits 182.85; Other deposits 874.99; *Broad money* 1,104.31. Source: IMF, *International Financial Statistics*.

Cost of Living (Retail Price Index, base: 2005 = 100): All items 112.6 in 2008; 112.7 in 2009, 116.3 in 2010. Source: IMF, *International Financial Statistics*.

Gross Domestic Product (EC $ million at constant 1990 prices): 643.2 in 2008; 638.0 in 2009; 634.8 in 2010. Source: IMF, *International Financial Statistics*.

Expenditure on the Gross Domestic Product (EC $ million at current prices, 2010): Government final consumption expenditure 193.2; Private final consumption expenditure 930.9; Gross fixed capital formation 247.4; *Total domestic expenditure* 1,371.5; Exports of goods and services 413.7; *Less* Imports of goods and services 754.6 *GDP in purchasers' values* 1,030.7. Source: IMF, *International Financial Statistics*.

Gross Domestic Product by Economic Activity (EC $ million at current prices, 2010, preliminary): Agriculture, hunting, forestry and fishing 131.85; Mining and quarrying 15.79; Manufacturing 28.83; Electricity and water 51.34; Construction 60.65; Wholesale and retail trade 146.94; Restaurants and hotels 20.60; Transport, storage; and communications 154.45; Finance and insurance 77.18; Real estate, housing and business activities 104.68; Government services 275.15; Other services 14.73; *Sub-total* 1,082.19; *Less* Financial intermediation services indirectly measured (FISIM) 60.28; *Gross value added in basic prices* 1,021.91; Taxes, less subsidies, on products 252.09; *GDP in market prices* 1,274.00.

Balance of Payments (US $ million, 2010): Exports of goods f.o.b. 34.35; Imports of goods f.o.b. –193.65; *Trade balance* –159.31; Services (net) 54.83; *Balance on goods and services* –104.48; Other income (net) –12.24; *Balance on goods, services and income* –116.73; Current transfers (net) 19.90; *Current balance* –96.83; Capital transfers 29.11; Direct investment from abroad 30.82; Portfolio investment (net) 2.84; Other investment (net) 40.72; Net errors and omissions –1.91; *Overall balance* 4.76. Source: IMF, *International Financial Statistics*.

EXTERNAL TRADE

Principal Commodities (US $ million, 2008): *Imports c.i.f.:* Food and live animals 37.1 (Meat and meat preparations 8.1; Cereals and cereal preparations 8.3); Mineral fuels and lubricants 36.3 (Petroleum and petroleum products 33.8); Animal and vegetable oils 7.3; Chemicals, etc. 20.3; Basic manufactures 39.0 (Paper products 6.8; Iron and steel 8.1); Machinery and transport equipment 56.3 (Telecommunications and sound equipment 4.4; Road vehicles 14.5); Miscellaneous manufactured articles 23.2; Total (incl. others) 232.4. *Exports f.o.b.:* Food and live animals 14.9 (Vegetables and roots and tubers 2.8; Bananas 8.0); Stone, sand and gravel 5.4; Chemicals, etc. 17.7 (Perfumes, cosmetics, toilet products, etc. 0.9; Soap 13.3; Disinfectants 0.1); Total (incl. others) 40.0. Source: UN, *International Trade Statistics Yearbook*.

Principal Trading Partners (US $ million, 2008): *Imports c.i.f.:* Barbados 4.2; Brazil 2.8; Canada 6.3; China, People's Republic 4.6; Colombia 2.5; Dominican Republic 5.0; France (incl. Monaco) 3.7; Grenada 3.5; Guyana 3.5; Jamaica 2.3; Japan 10.0; Netherlands 2.9; Saint Lucia 4.1; Saint Vincent and the Grenadines 2.6; Trinidad and Tobago 49.6; United Kingdom 10.7; USA 92.3; Venezuela 4.1; Total (incl. others) 232.4. *Exports f.o.b.:* Anguilla 1.0; Antigua and Barbuda 6.1; Barbados 1.1; France (incl. Monaco) 5.5; Guyana 2.1; Jamaica 6.5; Saint Christopher and Nevis 1.8; Saint Lucia 0.9; Saint Vincent and the Grenadines 1.0; Suriname 0.5; Trinidad and Tobago 3.5; United Kingdom 5.3; USA 1.2; Total (incl. others) 40.0. Source: UN, *International Trade Statistics Yearbook*.

TRANSPORT

Road Traffic (motor vehicles licensed in 1994): Private cars 6,491; Taxis 90; Buses 559; Motorcycles 94; Trucks 2,266; Jeeps 461; Tractors 24; Total 9,985. *2000* (motor vehicles in use): Passenger cars

8,700; Commercial vehicles 3,400. Source: partly UN, *Statistical Yearbook*.

Shipping: *Merchant Fleet* (registered at 31 December 2009): 102 vessels (total displacement 913,090 grt) (Source: IHS Fairplay, *World Fleet Statistics*); *International Freight Traffic* ('000 metric tons, estimates, 1993): Goods loaded 103.2; Goods unloaded 181.2.

Civil Aviation (1997): Aircraft arrivals and departures 18,672; Freight loaded 363 metric tons; Freight unloaded 575 metric tons.

TOURISM

Visitor Arrivals: 443,486 (88,035 stop-over visitors, 936 excursionists, 354,515 cruise ship passengers) in 2007; 470,332 (88,725 stop-over visitors, 936 excursionists, 380,671 cruise ship passengers) in 2008; 571,881 (85,271 stop-over visitors, 842 excursionists, 485,768 cruise ship passengers) in 2009.

Tourism Receipts (EC $ million): 201.1 in 2007; 193.2 in 2008; 183.3 in 2009.

COMMUNICATIONS MEDIA

Radio Receivers (1997): 46,000 in use.

Television Receivers (1999): 17,000 in use.

Telephones (2010): 15,500 main lines in use.

Mobile Cellular Telephones (2010, estimate): 105,600 subscribers.

Personal Computers: 13,000 (181.9 per 1,000 persons) in 2004.

Internet Subscribers (2010): 9,500.

Broadband Subscribers (2010): 9,400.

Non-daily Newspapers (2004): 3.

Sources: mainly UNESCO, *Statistical Yearbook*, International Telecommunication Union and UN, *Statistical Yearbook*.

EDUCATION

Institutions (1994/95 unless otherwise indicated): Pre-primary 72 (1992/93); Primary 64; Secondary 14; Tertiary 2.

Teachers (2009/10 unless otherwise indicated): Pre-primary 137; Primary 508; General secondary 491; Secondary vocational 20; Tertiary 34 (1992/93).

Pupils (2009/10 unless otherwise indicated): Pre-primary 1,891 (males 955, females 936); Primary 8,138 (males 4,156, females 3,982); General secondary 6,581 (males 3,263, females 3,318); Secondary vocational 185; Tertiary 461 (1995/96).

Sources: UNESCO, *Statistical Yearbook*, Institute for Statistics; Caribbean Development Bank, *Social and Economic Indicators*; UN Economic Commission for Latin America and the Caribbean, *Statistical Yearbook*.

Pupil-teacher Ratio (primary education, UNESCO estimate): 16.0 in 2009/10 (Source: UNESCO Institute for Statistics).

Adult Literacy Rate (2004): 88.0%. Source: UN Development Programme, *Human Development Report*.

Directory

The Government

HEAD OF STATE

President: Dr NICHOLAS LIVERPOOL (assumed office 1 October 2003; began a second term 2 October 2008).

CABINET
(May 2012)

The Government is formed by the Dominica Labour Party.

Prime Minister and Minister of Finance, Foreign Affairs and Information Technology: ROOSEVELT SKERRIT.

Attorney-General: LEVI PETER.

Minister of Housing, Lands, Settlement and Water Resources: REGINALD AUSTRIE.

Minister of Agriculture and Forestry: MATTHEW WALTER.

Minister of Employment, Trade, Industry and Diaspora Affairs: Dr JOHN COLIN MCINTYRE.

Minister of the Environment, Natural Resources, Physical Planning and Fisheries: Dr KENNETH DARROUX.

Minister of Education and Human Resource Development: PETER SAINT JEAN.

Minister of Social Services, Community Development and Gender Affairs: GLORIA SHILLINGFORD.

Minister of Culture, Youth and Sports: JUSTINA CHARLES.

Minister of Tourism and Legal Affairs: IAN DOUGLAS.

Minister of Information, Telecommunication and Constituency Empowerment: AMBROSE GEORGE.

Minister of Health: JULIUS TIMOTHY.

Minister of Public Works, Energy and Ports: RAYBURN BLACKMORE.

Minister of Carib Affairs: ASHTON GRANEAU.

Minister of National Security, Labour and Immigration: CHARLES SAVARIN.

Minister of State in the Ministry of Foreign Affairs: ALVIN BERNARD.

Parliamentary Secretary in the Office of the Prime Minister, responsible for Information Technology: KELVAR DARROUX.

Parliamentary Secretary in the Ministry of Public Works: JOHNSON DRIGO.

Parliamentary Secretary in the Ministry of Housing, Lands, Settlement and Water Resources: IVOR STEPHENSON.

MINISTRIES

Office of the President: Morne Bruce, Roseau; tel. 4482054; fax 4498366; e-mail presidentoffice@cwdom.dm; internet presidentoffice.gov.dm.

Office of the Prime Minister: 6th Floor, Financial Centre, Roseau; tel. 2663300; fax 4488960; e-mail pmoffice@cwdom.dm.

All other ministries are at Government Headquarters, Kennedy Ave, Roseau; tel. 4482401.

CARIB TERRITORY

This reserve of the remaining Amerindian population is located on the central east coast of the island. The Caribs enjoy a measure of local government and elect their chief.

Chief: GARNET JOSEPH.

Waitukubuli Karifuna Development Committee (WAIKADA): Salybia, Carib Territory; tel. 4457336; e-mail waikada@cwdom.dm.

Legislature

HOUSE OF ASSEMBLY

Speaker: ALIX BOYD-KNIGHT.

Clerk: VERNANDA RAYMOND.

Senators: 9.

Elected Members: 21.

General Election, 18 December 2009

Party	% of votes	Seats
Dominica Labour Party (DLP)	61.2	18
Dominica United Workers' Party (UWP)	34.9	3
Dominica Freedom Party (DFP)	2.4	—
Others	1.5	—
Total	100.0	21

Election Commission

Electoral Office: Cnr Turkey Lane and Independence St, Roseau; tel. 2663336; fax 4483399; e-mail elections@cwdom.dm; internet electoraloffice.gov.dm; Chief Elections Officer MERINA WILLIAMS.

Political Organizations

Dominica Freedom Party (DFP): 37 Great George St, Roseau; tel. 4482104; fax 4481795; e-mail freedompar2@yahoo.com; internet www.thedominicafreedomparty.com; f. 1968; Leader JUDITH PESTAINA.

Dominica Labour Party (DLP): 18 Hanover St, Roseau; tel. 4488511; e-mail dlp@cwdom.dm; internet www.togetherwemust.net; f. 1985 as a merger and reunification of left-wing groups, incl. the Dominica Labour Party (f. 1961); Leader ROOSEVELT SKERRIT; Deputy Leader AMBROSE GEORGE.

Dominica Progressive Party: Roseau; Leader ERNEST TAVERNIER.

Dominica United Workers' Party (UWP): 37 Cork St, POB 00152, Roseau; tel. 6134508; fax 4498448; e-mail secretariat@uwpdm.com; internet www.uwpdm.com; f. 1988; Leader EDISON JAMES.

People's Democratic Movement (PDM): 22 Upper Lane, POB 2248, Roseau; tel. 2354171; e-mail para@cwdom.dm; internet www.dapdm.org; f. 2006; Leader Dr WILLIAM E. 'PARA' RIVIERE.

Real Labour Party (RLP): Roseau; f. 2009 by mems of Labour Party of Dominica; Leader Dr SAM CHRISTIAN; Co-ordinator ADENAUER WARSHWOA DOUGLAS.

Diplomatic Representation

EMBASSIES IN DOMINICA

China, People's Republic: Ceckhall, Morne Daniel, POB 2247, Roseau; tel. 4490198; fax 4400088; e-mail chinaemb_dm@mfa.gov.cn; internet dm.chineseembassy.org; Ambassador WANG ZONGLAI.

Cuba: Morne Daniel, Canefield, POB 1170, Roseau; tel. 4490727; e-mail cubanembassy@cwdom.dm; internet www.cubadiplomatica.cu/dominica; Ambassador JUANA ELENA RAMOS RODRÍGUEZ.

Venezuela: 20 Bath Rd, 3rd Floor, POB 770, Roseau; tel. 4483348; fax 4486198; e-mail embven@cwdom.dm; Ambassador CARMEN MARTÍNEZ DE GRIJALVA.

Judicial System

Justice is administered by the Eastern Caribbean Supreme Court (based in Saint Lucia), consisting of the Court of Appeal and the High Court. Two of the High Court Judges are resident in Dominica and preside over the Court of Summary Jurisdiction. The District Magistrate Courts deal with summary offences and civil offences involving limited sums of money (specified by law).

High Court Judges: BRIAN COTTLE, M. E. BIRNIE STEPHENSON-BROOKS.

Registrar: REGINALD WINSTON.

Religion

Most of the population profess Christianity, but there are some Muslims, Bahá'ís and Jews. The largest denomination is the Roman Catholic Church.

CHRISTIANITY

The Roman Catholic Church

Dominica comprises the single diocese of Roseau, suffragan to the archdiocese of Castries (Saint Lucia). According to official figures from 2001, 62% of the population are Roman Catholics. The Bishop participates in the Antilles Episcopal Conference (currently based in Port of Spain, Trinidad and Tobago).

Bishop of Roseau: Rt Rev. GABRIEL MALZAIRE, Bishop Arnold Boghaert Catholic Centre, Turkey Lane, POB 790, Roseau; tel. 4482837; fax 4483404; e-mail bishop@cwdom.dm; internet www.dioceseofroseau.org.

The Anglican Communion

Anglicans in Dominica, representing less than 1% of the population in 2001, are adherents of the Church in the Province of the West Indies. The country forms part of the diocese of the North Eastern Caribbean and Aruba. The Bishop is resident in Antigua, and the Archbishop of the Province is the Bishop of the Bahamas and the Turks and Caicos Islands.

Other Christian Churches

According to official figures from 2001, 6% of the population are Seventh-day Adventists, 6% are Pentecostalists, 4% are Baptists and 4% are Methodists. In addition to the Christian Union Church, other denominations include Church of God, Presbyterian, the Assemblies of Brethren and Moravian groups, and the Jehovah's Witnesses.

BAHÁ'Í FAITH

National Spiritual Assembly: 79 Victoria St, POB 136, Roseau; tel. 4483881; fax 4488460.

The Press

The Chronicle: Wallhouse, Loubiere, POB 1764, Roseau; tel. 4487887; fax 4480047; e-mail thechronicle@cwdom.dm; f. 1909; Friday; progressive independent; Chair. FRANKLIN A. BARON; Editor GWENDOLYN EVELYN (acting); circ. 4,500.

Official Gazette: Office of the Prime Minister, Financial Centre, 6th Floor, Kennedy Ave, Roseau; tel. 2363300; fax 4488960; e-mail cabsec@cwdom.dm; weekly; circ. 550.

The Sun: Sun Inc, 50 Independence St, POB 2255, Roseau; tel. 4484744; fax 4484764; e-mail acsun@cwdom.dm; f. 1998; weekly; Editor CHARLES JAMES.

The Times: 15 Kennedy Ave, Roseau; tel. 4403949; fax 4404056; e-mail timesnews@cwdom.dm; f. 2004; Friday; Editor MATT PELTIER.

The Tropical Star: Canefield, Roseau; tel. 4484634; fax 4485984; e-mail tpl@cwdom.dm; weekly; Editor NIGEL LAWRENCE; circ. 3,000.

Broadcasting and Communications

TELECOMMUNICATIONS

Regulatory Authority

National Telecommunications Regulatory Commission of Dominica (NTRC Dominica): 42-2 Kennedy Ave, POB 649, Roseau; tel. 4400627; fax 4400835; e-mail secretariat@ntrcdm.org; internet www.ectel.int/ntrcdm; f. 2000 as the Dominican subsidiary of the Eastern Caribbean Telecommunications Authority (ECTEL)—established simultaneously in Castries, St Lucia, to regulate telecommunications in Dominica, Grenada, St Christopher and Nevis, St Lucia and St Vincent and the Grenadines; Chair. JULIAN JOHNSON.

Major Service Providers

Digicel Dominica: Wireless Ventures (Dominica) Ltd, POB 2236, Roseau; tel. 6161500; fax 4403189; e-mail customercare.dominica@digicelgroup.com; internet www.digiceldominica.com; acquired Cingular Wireless's Caribbean operations and licences in 2005; owned by an Irish consortium; acquired Orange Dominica in 2009; Chair. DENIS O'BRIEN; Country Man. RICHARD STANTON.

LIME: Hanover St, POB 6, Roseau; tel. 2551000; fax 2551111; e-mail pr@cwdom.dm; internet www.time4lime.com; fmrly Cable & Wireless Dominica; name changed as above 2008; Caribbean CEO RICHARD DODD.

Marpin 2K4: 5–7 Great Marlborough St, POB 2381, Roseau; tel. 5004107; fax 5002965; e-mail manager@mtb.dm; internet www.marpin.dm; f. 1982, present name adopted in 1996; commercial; cable telephone, television and internet services.

BROADCASTING

Radio

Dominica Broadcasting Corporation: Victoria St, POB 148, Roseau; tel. 4483283; fax 4482918; e-mail dbsmanager@dbcradio.net; internet www.dbcradio.net; f. 1971; govt station; daily broadcasts in English; 2 hrs daily in French patois; 10 kW transmitter on the medium wave band; FM service; programmes received throughout Caribbean excluding Jamaica and Guyana; Chair. IAN MUNRO.

Kairi FM: 42 Independence St, POB 931, Roseau; tel. 4487331; fax 4487332; e-mail hello@kairifmonline.com; internet www.kairifm.com; f. 1994; CEO FRANKIE BELLOT; Gen. Man. STEVE VIDAL.

Voice of Life Radio (ZGBC): Gospel Broadcasting Corpn, Loubiere, POB 205, Roseau; tel. 4487017; fax 4400551; e-mail volradio@cwdom.dm; internet www.voiceofliferadio.dm; f. 1975; 24 hrs daily FM; Gen. Man. CLEMENTINA MUNRO.

Television

There is no national television service, although there is a cable television network serving 95% of the island.

Finance

(cap. = capital; res = reserves; dep. = deposits; m. = million; brs = branches; amounts in East Caribbean dollars)

The Eastern Caribbean Central Bank, based in Saint Christopher, is the central issuing and monetary authority for Dominica.

Eastern Caribbean Central Bank—Dominica Office: Financial Centre, 3rd Floor, Kennedy Ave, POB 23, Roseau; tel. 4488001; fax 4488002; e-mail eccbdom@cwdom.dm; internet www.eccb-centralbank.org; Country Dir EDMUND ROBINSON.

Financial Services Unit: Ministry of Finance and Planning, Kennedy Ave, Roseau; tel. 2663559; fax 4480054; e-mail fsu@cwdom.dm; regulatory authority for banks and insurance cos; Man. AL MONELLE.

BANKS

FirstCaribbean International Bank (Barbados) Ltd: Old St, POB 4, Roseau; tel. 4482571; fax 4483471; internet www.firstcaribbeanbank.com; f. 2002 following merger of Caribbean operations of Barclays Bank PLC and CIBC; Barclays relinquished its stake to CIBC in 2006; Exec. Chair. MICHAEL MANSOOR; CEO JOHN D. ORR; Country Dir PAUL FRAMPTON.

National Bank of Dominica: 64 Hillsborough St, POB 271, Roseau; tel. 2552300; fax 4483982; e-mail customersupport@nbd.dm; internet www.nbdominica.com; f. 1976 as the National Commercial Bank of Dominica; name changed as above following privatization in 2003; cap. 11.0m., res 21.8m., dep. 716.3m. (June 2010); 49% govt-owned; Chair. PATRICK PEMBERTON; Gen. Man. MICHAEL BIRD; 6 brs.

DEVELOPMENT BANK

Dominica Agricultural, Industrial and Development Bank (AID Bank): cnr Charles Ave and Rawles Lane, Goodwill, POB 215, Roseau; tel. 4482853; fax 4484903; e-mail aidbank@cwdom.dm; internet www.aidbank.com; f. 1971; responsible to Ministry of Finance, Foreign Affairs and Information Technology; provides finance for the agriculture, tourism, housing, education and manufacturing sectors; total assets 125.3m. (June 2006); Chair. AMBROSE SYLVESTER; Gen. Man. KINGSLEY THOMAS.

STOCK EXCHANGE

Eastern Caribbean Securities Exchange: Bird Rock, Basseterre, Saint Christopher and Nevis; tel. (869) 466-7192; fax (869) 465-3798; e-mail info@ecseonline.com; internet www.ecseonline.com; f. 2001; regional securities market designed to facilitate the buying and selling of financial products for the eight member territories—Anguilla, Antigua and Barbuda, Dominica, Grenada, Montserrat, St Christopher and Nevis, St Lucia and St Vincent and the Grenadines; Chair. Sir K. DWIGHT VENNER; Gen. Man. TREVOR E. BLAKE.

INSURANCE

First Domestic Insurance Co Ltd: 19–21 King George V St, POB 1931, Roseau; tel. 4498202; fax 4485778; e-mail insurance@cwdom.dm; internet www.firstdomestic.dm; f. 1993; privately owned; Chair. CURTIS TONGE; Man. Dir and CEO ROBERT TONGE.

Windward Islands Crop Insurance Co (Wincrop): Vanoulst House, Goodwill, POB 469, Roseau; tel. 4483955; fax 4484197; f. 1987; regional; coverage for weather destruction of, mainly, banana crops; Man. HERNICA FERREIRA; brs in Grenada, Saint Lucia and Saint Vincent.

Trade and Industry

DEVELOPMENT ORGANIZATIONS

Invest Dominica Authority: Financial Centre, 1st Floor, Roseau; tel. 4482045; fax 4485840; e-mail investdominica@investdominica.dm; internet www.investdominica.dm; f. 1988 as National Development Corpn (NDC) by merger of Industrial Development Corpn (f. 1974) and Tourist Board; NDC disbanded in 2007 by act of parliament and replaced by two separate entities, Invest Dominica and Discover Dominica Authority (q.v.); promotes local and foreign investment to increase employment, production and exports; Chair. YVOR NASSIEF; Exec. Dir RHODA LETANG.

Organisation of the Eastern Caribbean States Export Development Unit (OECS–EDU): Financial Centre, 4th Floor, Kennedy Ave, POB 769, Roseau; tel. 4482240; fax 4485554; e-mail eduinfocenter@oecs.org; internet www.oecs.org/edu; f. 1997 as Eastern Caribbean States Export Devt Agency and Agricultural Diversification Unit; reformed as above in 2000; OECS regional devt org.; Exec. Dir VINCENT PHILBERT.

INDUSTRIAL AND TRADE ASSOCIATIONS

Dominica Agricultural Producers and Exporters Ltd (DAPEX): Fond Cole Hwy, Fond Cole, POB 1620, Roseau; tel. 4482671; fax 4486445; e-mail dapex@cwdom.dm; f. 1934 as Dominica Banana Growers' Asscn; restructured 1984 as the Dominica Banana Marketing Corpn; renamed Dominica Banana Producers Ltd in 2003; present name adopted in 2010; privatized; Chair. LUKE PREVOST; Gen. Man. ERROL EMANUEL.

Dominica Association of Industry and Commerce (DAIC): 14 Church St, POB 85, Roseau; tel. and fax 4491962; e-mail daic@cwdom.dm; internet www.daic.dm; f. 1972 by a merger of the Manufacturers' Asscn and the Chamber of Commerce; represents the business sector, liaises with the Govt, and stimulates commerce and industry; 100 mems; Pres. GENEVIEVE ASTAPHAN; CEO ACHILLE CHRIS JOSEPH.

Dominica Export-Import Agency (DEXIA): Bay Front, POB 173, Roseau; tel. 4482780; fax 4486308; e-mail info@dexia.dm; internet www.dexia.dm; f. 1986; replaced the Dominica Agricultural Marketing Board and the External Trade Bureau; exporter of Dominican agricultural products, trade facilitator and importer of bulk rice and sugar; Chair. MARGARET GEORGE.

EMPLOYERS' ORGANIZATION

Dominica Employers' Federation: 14 Church St, POB 1783, Roseau; tel. 4482314; fax 4484474; e-mail def@cwdom.dm; f. 1966; Pres. CLEMENT CARTY.

UTILITIES

Regulatory Body

Independent Regulatory Commission (IRC): 42-2 Kennedy Ave, 3rd Floor, Roseau; tel. 4406634; fax 4406635; e-mail admin@ircdominica.org; internet www.ircdominica.org; f. 2006 to oversee the electricity sector; Exec. Dir LANCELOT McCARSKY.

Electricity

Dominica Electricity Services Ltd (Domlec): 18 Castle St, POB 1593, Roseau; tel. 2256000; fax 4485397; e-mail support@domleconline.com; internet www.domlec.dm; national electricity service; 72% owned by WRB Enterprises Ltd (USA) since takeover of the Commonwealth Devt Corpn's (United Kingdom) stake in 2004; Chair. ROBERT BLANCHARD, Jr; Gen. Man. COLLIN GROVER.

Water

Dominica Water and Sewerage Co Ltd (DOWASCO): 3 High St, POB 185, Roseau; tel. 4484811; fax 4485813; e-mail dowasco@cwdom.dm; internet www.dowasco.com; state-owned; Chair. LARRY BARDOUILLE; Gen. Man. BERNARD ETTINOFFE.

TRADE UNIONS

Dominica Amalgamated Workers' Union (DAWU): 43 Hillsborough St, POB 137, Roseau; tel. 4482343; fax 4480086; e-mail wawuunion@hotmail.com; f. 1960; Gen. Sec. ELIAS LEAH SHILLINGFORD (acting); 500 mems (1996).

Dominica Association of Teachers: 7 Boyd's Ave, POB 341, Roseau; tel. and fax 4488177; e-mail dat@cwdom.dm; internet dateachers.org; f. 1990; Pres. CELIA NICHOLAS; Gen. Sec. ISABELLA PRENTICE; 670 mems (2012).

Dominica Public Service Union (DPSU): cnr Valley Rd and Windsor Lane, POB 182, Roseau; tel. 4482102; fax 4488060; e-mail dcs@cwdom.dm; internet dpsu.org; f. 1940; registered as a trade union in 1960; representing all grades of civil servants, including firemen, prison officers, nurses, teachers and postal workers; Pres. STEVE JOSEPH; Gen. Sec. THOMAS LETANG; 1,400 mems.

Dominica Trade Union: 70–71 Independence St, Roseau; tel. 4498139; fax 4499060; e-mail domtradun@hotmail.com; f. 1945; Pres. HAROLD SEALEY; Gen. Sec. LEO J. BERNARD NICHOLAS; 400 mems (1995).

National Workers' Union: 102 Independence St, POB 387, Roseau; tel. 4485209; fax 4481934; e-mail icss@cwdom.dm; f. 1977; Pres.-Gen. RAWLINS JEMMOTT; Gen. Sec. FRANKLIN FABIEN; 450 mems (1996).

Waterfront and Allied Workers' Union: 43 Hillsborough St, POB 181, Roseau; tel. 4482343; fax 4480086; e-mail wawuunion@hotmail.com; f. 1965; Sec.-Treas. KERTISTE AUGUSTUS; 1,500 mems.

Transport

ROADS

In 2001 there were an estimated 780 km (485 miles) of roads, of which about 50.4% was paved; there were also numerous tracks. In 2010 work began on construction and improvement of the road from

Roseau to Portsmouth. The West Coast Road Project was estimated to cost some EC $100m. and was to be partly financed by the Government of the People's Republic of China. There were also plans to improve the Wotten Waven Road, to be financed by the Caribbean Development Bank.

SHIPPING

A deep-water harbour at Woodbridge Bay serves Roseau, which is the principal port. Several foreign shipping lines call at Roseau, and there is a high-speed ferry service between Martinique and Guadeloupe, which calls at Roseau eight times a week. A ferry service between Dominica and Guadeloupe, Martinique and Saint Lucia was scheduled to begin operations in October 2011. Ships of the Geest Line call at Prince Rupert's Bay, Portsmouth, to collect bananas, and there are also cruise ship facilities there. There are other specialized berthing facilities on the west coast.

Dominica Air and Seaport Authority (DASPA): Woodbridge Bay, Fond Cole, POB 243, Roseau; tel. 4484131; fax 4486131; e-mail daspa@cwdom.dm; f. 1972; air transit, pilotage and cargo handling; Chair. Dermot Southwell; Gen. Man. Benoit Bardouille.

CIVIL AVIATION

Melville Hall Airport, 64 km (40 miles) from Roseau, and Canefield Airport, 5 km (3 miles) from Roseau, are the two airports on the island.The first phase of a scheme to rebuild the road from Roseau to Melville Hall Airport at a cost of EC $54m., funded by the French Government, was completed in 2010, and work on the second phase, valued at EC $52m. and also funded by France, was agreed in the same year. The regional airline LIAT (based in Antigua and Barbuda, and in which Dominica is a shareholder) acquired its troubled rival, Caribbean Star Airline (also headquartered in Antigua and Barbuda), in late 2007. The two airlines had separately offered almost identical schedules, which, now consolidated, provide daily services and, together with Air Caraïbes, connect Dominica with all the islands of the Eastern Caribbean, including the international airports of Puerto Rico, Antigua, Guadeloupe and Martinique.

Tourism

The Government has designated areas of the island as nature reserves, to preserve the beautiful, lush scenery and the rich, natural heritage that constitute Dominica's main tourist attractions. Birdlife is particularly prolific, and includes several rare and endangered species, such as the Imperial parrot. There are also two marine reserves. Tourism is not as developed as it is among Dominica's neighbours, but the country is being promoted as an 'eco-tourism' and cruise destination. There were an estimated 603,227 visitors in 2010 (of whom 517,979 were cruise ship passengers). Receipts from tourism totalled an estimated EC $268.3m. in 2010.

Discover Dominica Authority: Financial Centre, 1st Floor, Roseau; tel. 4482045; fax 4485840; e-mail tourism@dominica.dm; internet www.discoverdominica.com; f. 1988 following merger of Tourist Board with Industrial Devt Corpn; CEO and Dir of Tourism Colin Piper.

Dominica Hotel and Tourism Association (DHTA): 17 Castle St, POB 384, Roseau; tel. 4403430; fax 4403433; e-mail dhta@cwdom.dm; internet www.dhta.org; Pres. Yvonne Armour; 98 mems.

Defence

The Dominican Defence Force was officially disbanded in 1981. There is a police force of about 325, which includes a coastguard service. The country participates in the US-sponsored Regional Security System.

Education

Education is free and is provided by both government and denominational schools. There are also a number of schools for the mentally and physically handicapped. Education is compulsory for 10 years between five and 15 years of age. Primary education begins at the age of five and lasts for seven years. Enrolment at primary schools during the academic year 2008/09 included an estimated 93% of children in the relevant age-group. Secondary education, beginning at 12 years of age, lasts for five years. In 2007/08, according to UNESCO estimates, enrolment at secondary schools included 68% of pupils in the relevant age-group. The Dominica State College, established in 2002 by merging four publicly owned tertiary education institutions, is the main provider of higher education. There is also a teacher-training college, a nursing school and a branch of the University of the West Indies on the island. The 2010/11 budget allocated EC $18.6m. for educational assistance.

THE DOMINICAN REPUBLIC

Introductory Survey

LOCATION, CLIMATE, LANGUAGE, RELIGION, FLAG, CAPITAL

The Dominican Republic occupies the eastern part of the island of Hispaniola, which lies between Cuba and Puerto Rico in the Caribbean Sea. The country's only international frontier is with Haiti, to the west. The climate is sub-tropical, with an average annual temperature of 27°C (80°F). In Santo Domingo temperatures are generally between 19°C (66°F) and 31°C (88°F). The west and south-west of the country are arid. Hispaniola lies in the path of tropical cyclones. The official language is Spanish. Almost all of the inhabitants profess Christianity, and some 87% are Roman Catholics. There are small Protestant and Jewish communities. The national flag (proportions 5 by 8) is blue (upper hoist and lower fly) and red (lower hoist and upper fly), quartered by a white cross, with the national coat of arms, showing a quartered shield in the colours of the flag (on which are superimposed national banners, a cross and an open Bible) between scrolls above and below, at the centre of the cross. The capital is Santo Domingo.

CONTEMPORARY POLITICAL HISTORY

Historical Context

The Dominican Republic became independent in 1844, although it was occupied by US military forces between 1916 and 1924. General Rafael Leónidas Trujillo Molina overthrew the elected President, Horacio Vázquez, in 1930 and dominated the country until his assassination in 1961. The dictator ruled personally from 1930 to 1947 and indirectly thereafter. His brother, Héctor Trujillo, was President from 1947 until August 1960, when he was replaced by Dr Joaquín Balaguer Ricardo, hitherto Vice-President. After Rafael Trujillo's death, Balaguer remained in office, but in December 1961 he permitted moderate opposition groups to participate in a Council of State, which exercised legislative and executive powers. Balaguer resigned in January 1962, when the Council of State became the Provisional Government. A presidential election in December, the country's first free election for 38 years, was won by Dr Juan Bosch Gaviño, the founder and leader of the Partido Revolucionario Dominicano (PRD), who had been in exile since 1930. President Bosch, a left-of-centre democrat, was overthrown in September 1963 by a military coup. The leaders of the armed forces transferred power to a civilian triumvirate, led by Emilio de los Santos. In April 1965 a revolt by supporters of ex-President Bosch overthrew the triumvirate. Civil war broke out between pro-Bosch forces and military units headed by Gen. Elías Wessin y Wessin, who had played a leading role in the 1963 coup. The violence was eventually suppressed by the intervention of US troops, who were incorporated into an Inter-American peace force by the Organization of American States (OAS).

Domestic Political Affairs

Following a period of provisional government under Héctor García Godoy, a presidential election in 1966 was won by Balaguer, the candidate of the Partido Reformista Social Cristiano (PRSC). The PRSC also won a majority of seats in both houses of the new Congreso Nacional (National Congress). A new Constitution was promulgated in November. Despite his association with the Trujillo dictatorship, Balaguer initially proved to be a popular leader, and in 1970 he was re-elected for a further four years. In February 1973 a state of emergency was declared when guerrilla forces landed on the coast. Captain Francisco Caamaño Deño, the leader of the 1965 revolt, and his followers were killed. Bosch and other opposition figures went into hiding. Bosch later resigned as leader of the PRD (founding the Partido de la Liberación Dominicana—PLD), undermining hopes of a united opposition in the 1974 elections, when Balaguer was re-elected with a large majority.

In the 1978 presidential election Balaguer was defeated by the PRD candidate, Silvestre Antonio Guzmán Fernández. This was the first occasion in the country's history when an elected President yielded power to an elected successor. President Guzmán undertook to professionalize the armed forces by removing politically ambitious high-ranking officers. In 1981 he declared his support for Jacobo Majluta Azar, his Vice-President, as his successor, but the PRD rejected Majluta's candidacy in favour of Dr Salvador Jorge Blanco, a left-wing senator, who was elected President in 1982. In the concurrent congressional election the PRD secured a majority in both the Senado (Senate) and the Cámara de Diputados (Chamber of Deputies). Although a member of the Socialist International, Blanco maintained good relations with the USA (on which the country is economically dependent).

Substantial price increases in 1985 led to violent clashes between demonstrators and the security forces. Public unrest was exacerbated by the Government's decision to accept the IMF's terms for financial aid. More violence preceded the presidential and legislative elections of May 1986. Balaguer of the PRSC was declared the winner of the presidential election by a narrow margin.

Upon taking office as President for the fifth time in August 1986, Balaguer initiated an investigation into alleged corrupt practices by members of the outgoing administration. Blanco was charged with embezzlement and the illegal purchase of military vehicles. (In 1991 he was convicted of abuse of power and misappropriation of public funds, and sentenced to 20 years' imprisonment, although in 1994 he was granted an amnesty.) The financial accounts of the armed forces were examined, and the former Secretary of State for the Armed Forces was subsequently imprisoned. Some 35,000 government posts were abolished; expenditure was to be redirected to a programme of public works projects, which were expected to create almost 100,000 new jobs. Nevertheless, the civil unrest continued in the remainder of the decade.

Balaguer's prospects for re-election in 1990 were impeded considerably by the continuing deterioration of the economy. His principal contender was the PLD candidate, Bosch, who concentrated his election campaign on seeking support from the private sector, promising privatization of state-owned companies. When the initial results indicated a narrow victory for Balaguer, Bosch accused the ruling PRSC and the Junta Central Electoral (JCE—Central Electoral Board) of fraud, necessitating a recount, supervised by monitors from the OAS. Balaguer was eventually declared the official winner. The PRSC also secured a narrow majority in the Senado. No party won an outright majority in the Cámara de Diputados, although this did not threaten seriously to impede government policies, in view of Balaguer's extensive powers to govern by decree.

In August 1990, in an attempt to reduce inflation, the Government announced a programme of austerity measures, almost doubling the price of petrol and essential foodstuffs. In response, the trade unions called a 48-hour general strike and in the ensuing conflict with the security forces some 14 people were killed. The price increases were partially offset by an increase of 30% in the salaries of army personnel and civil servants. A stand-by agreement was concluded with the IMF in 1991, in spite of trade union and public opposition.

The interim results of the presidential election of May 1994 indicated a narrow victory for Balaguer. Following a full recount, an investigative commission confirmed that, as a result of serious irregularities, some 73,000 of the registered electorate had been denied a vote. Nevertheless, in August the JCE, having apparently overlooked the commission's findings, proclaimed Balaguer the winner by a margin of less than 1% of the votes cast. Talks aimed at ending the political crisis, mediated by the OAS and the Roman Catholic Church, resulted in the signing of the Pact for Democracy. Under the terms of the accord (agreed by all the major parties), a fresh presidential election was to be held in November 1995 and a series of constitutional reforms would be adopted, providing for the prohibition of the re-election of a president to a consecutive term, a new electoral system for the head of state (see below), and the reorganization of the judiciary. Additionally, the legislative and municipal elections were to be held midway through the presidential term. Nevertheless, in the same month the Congreso Nacional voted to extend Balaguer's mandate from 18 months to two years. The PRD withdrew from the legislature in protest, and the OAS criticized the Congreso for violating the terms of the Pact for Democracy. The constitutional amendments that the Pact envisaged were, however, approved by the Congreso. On 16 August Balaguer was inaugurated as President for a seventh term.

A post-Balaguer era

The May 1996 presidential election, the first for some 30 years in which Balaguer was not a candidate, was conducted according to a new system, whereby a second round of voting would be conducted between the two leading candidates should nobody secure an absolute majority in the initial ballot. In the event, a second round of voting—between José Francisco Peña Gómez of the PRD and Leonel Fernández Reyna of the PLD—was held at the end of June. Fernández won 51% of the votes to Peña Gómez's 49%. Fernández was inaugurated in August, and the Cabinet, consisting almost exclusively of PLD members, was sworn in.

In 1997, as part of a campaign to eliminate deep-seated corruption in the country's institutions, Fernández restructured both the police and the judiciary. He also oversaw a restructuring of the Supreme Court, including the appointment of 15 new judges. Responsibility for appointing judges at all other levels of the judicial system was transferred from the Senado to the Supreme Court, to avoid political appointments. Nevertheless, growing dissatisfaction with the continuing deterioration of public services and Fernández's failure to honour election promises provoked widespread disturbances and strike action in 1997 and 1998, with violent confrontations between demonstrators and the security forces resulting in several deaths. In October, in an effort to defuse the volatile social and political climate, Fernández introduced a recovery plan aimed at overcoming electricity and food shortages. However, in the following month another general strike was organized. The PRD won a majority of seats in the enlarged 149-seat Cámara de Diputados at legislative elections in 1998.

In the first round of the May 2000 presidential election, Rafael Hipólito Mejía Domínguez, the PRD candidate, narrowly failed to secure the 50% of the ballot required to avoid a second round of voting. Nevertheless, a second ballot was not held and the JCE allowed Mejía to declare himself the winner. He was inaugurated as President in August and a new Cabinet was officially appointed. The PRD campaign against the previous PLD administration's alleged corruption proved controversial, creating open hostility between the two parties. In November former President Fernández led a protest, following the arrest of various former senior government officials on corruption charges. Fernández himself was later similarly accused and arrested; however, all were subsequently released, owing to lack of evidence. With only 73 PRD deputies in the 149-seat lower house (10 of the 83 elected in May 1998 had been expelled from the party), Mejía lacked a parliamentary majority, and was dependent for support on the PRSC.

In early 2001 President Mejía initiated a series of fiscal measures to increase tax revenues. The Government also introduced a poverty mitigation programme, including training, infrastructural programmes and education, social security, health and housing reforms. The political programme also included decentralization of power and the restructuring of the public sector.

The Senado approved constitutional amendments in late 2000 to extend the presidential term to five years and the congressional term to six years, and to lower the minimum requirement of votes in a presidential election. In order to appease opposition to the bill, Mejía appointed a Committee on Constitutional Reform to assess the situation. In October 2001 the Committee submitted legislation to the Congreso, the principal provision of which was to reduce the proportion of votes needed to win a presidential election to 45% (or 40% if the leading candidate had at least a 10% majority). The Senado subsequently voted to include in the constitutional amendments a clause permitting the re-election of a President. Mejía opposed the inclusion of this reform, and in December the Supreme Court ruled the proposed legislation to be unconstitutional. However, in January 2002 the Cámara de Diputados approved the formation of a National Constituent Assembly and in July, following re-examination, a bill of amendment permitting presidential re-election received assent from the National Assembly.

Legislative elections were held in May 2002. The PRD won a majority in the Senado, although its failure to secure a majority in the lower house ensured its continued dependence upon the support of the PRSC for the passage of legislation.

In May 2003 the dissolution of the commercial bank Banco Intercontinental, SA (Baninter), following the exposure of huge losses at the bank owing to fraud, had serious political, as well as economic, implications. The President of Baninter, Ramón Báez Figueroa, allegedly had links to the PLD, thus damaging the reputation of that party as well as the Government. Figueroa and two other bank officials were later arrested on fraud charges (2007 Figueroa was sentenced to 10 years' imprisonment). The Government's subsequent decision to guarantee all the deposits held at Baninter, at a cost of approximately US $2,200m., resulted in the onset of an economic crisis so severe that the Government was forced to request IMF assistance; in August a $618m. stand-by arrangement with the IMF was concluded.

In November 2003 a 24-hour general strike took place, during which violent clashes occurred between the security forces and anti-Government protesters in several cities, resulting in the deaths of at least seven people. The strike was in protest against governmental mismanagement of the economy and, in particular, the failure to resolve the ongoing, and increasingly severe, power shortages (the partially privatized electricity company, Corporación Dominicana de Electricidad, had been renationalized in that year). In January 2004 a 48-hour general strike was held, during which at least nine people were killed and many more injured.

At the presidential election in May 2004, former President Fernández of the PLD defeated the incumbent Mejía by a decisive margin, securing 57% of the votes cast. Mejía attracted 34% of the ballot. On taking office in August, President Fernández pledged to alleviate the chronic power shortages in the country. Although power supplies initially improved, following the Government's payment of US $50m. towards the debt owed to electricity suppliers, by 2005 the electricity shortages had returned to pre-election levels.

The PLD in power

Legislative and municipal elections were held on 16 May 2006. For the first time in its history, the PLD secured a congressional majority in both legislative chambers, winning 96 seats in the Cámara de Diputados (which had been increased from 150 to 178 seats) and 22 seats in the Senado. The PRD's representation was reduced to 60 seats in the Cámara de Diputados and just six seats in the Senado, while the PRSC won 22 in the former and four in the latter.

A series of corruption scandals and continuing labour unrest in early 2008 presented considerable difficulties for the Government in the months preceding the presidential election. However, a programme of state spending, including increased subsidies, and major public works (including the hastily completed Santo Domingo metro) attracted support for Fernández, who won a third term with 53.8% of the vote on 16 May. His main rival, Miguel Vargas Maldonado of the PRD, took 40.5% of the valid votes cast.

In October 2009 the Cámara de Diputados approved changes to more than 40 articles of the Constitution, despite public protests and opposition from civil society groups who were against the more socially conservative provisions. The amendments stipulated a complete ban on abortion and defined marriage as solely between a man and woman. Other measures included making administrative corruption of public officials a constitutional offence and establishing trade unionism, strikes, public education and swift justice with the presumption of innocence as constitutional rights. The new Constitution came into force on 26 January 2010.

The PLD secured a resounding victory in legislative elections held on 16 May 2010. To facilitate a joint presidential and legislative ballot in 2016, congressional members were elected to an extended six-year term. The ruling party increased its representation in both legislative chambers, winning 105 of the 183 seats in the enlarged Cámara de Diputados and 31 of the 32 Senado seats. The PRD improved its position in the lower house, obtaining 75 seats, but failed to gain representation in the upper chamber. Support for the PRSC, which had organized an electoral pact with the PLD in April 2010, declined dramatically compared with the 2006 election, and the party only managed to win three lower house seats and the remaining Senado seat. The rate of participation by the electorate was a disappointing 56.4%. In concurrent municipal elections, the PLD emerged victorious in 92 of the 155 contested municipalities, while the PRD won 57 and the PRSC four. The PLD argued that the results were a reflection of voter satisfaction with the Government's economic and social policies. However, OAS monitors and the JCE expressed concern regarding the PLD's alleged misuse of public funds to subsidize its election campaign, and the PRD claimed that there had been irregularities in the ballot. The elections were further tarnished by sporadic violence, which left five people dead.

President Fernández reorganized the Cabinet in March 2011. José Ramón Fadul was appointed as Secretary of State for the Interior and Police, Daniel Toribio received the finance portfolio, and Josefina Pimentel became the new Secretary of State for Education. This latter appointment was seemingly made in response to public dissatisfaction with the country's underperforming educational system.

Recent developments: 2012 election

In March 2011 former President Mejía was elected as the PRD's candidate to stand in the upcoming presidential ballot, scheduled for 20 May 2012. President Fernández announced in April 2011 that he would not seek re-election, which would have required further amendment of the Constitution and, according to the President, may have increased tensions in the country. His wife, Margarita María Cedeño de Fernández, announced shortly thereafter that she would compete in the primary election to select the PLD's presidential candidate. However, she withdrew from the contest later that month, reportedly because of disquiet among factions within the party. In the event, Danilo Medina (who had been defeated by Mejía in the 2000 presidential election) won the primary vote in June and was formally named as the ruling party's presidential nominee in August. Despite earlier tensions with Fernández, Medina selected Cedeño to be his vice-presidential candidate in November.

Foreign Affairs

Regional relations

The continuing illegal import of plantation labour into the Dominican Republic from Haiti was a major issue for successive Governments. Following the army coup in 1991 in Haiti, tens of thousands of Haitians fled to the Dominican Republic. However, few were granted refugee status. In 1997 the Dominican and Haitian Presidents agreed to put an immediate end to large-scale repatriations and for the repatriation process to be monitored by an international body to ensure the observance of human rights. In 1998 agreement was reached on the establishment of joint border patrols to combat the traffic of drugs, arms and other contraband across the countries' border. In 1999, following the summary deportation of some 8,000 Haitians, the two Governments signed a protocol limiting the repatriations.

Following the murder of a Dominican woman in May 2005, allegedly carried out by two Haitian men, the Dominican army forcibly repatriated thousands of Haitians resident in the Dominican Republic. The army insisted that only illegal immigrants had been targeted, but human rights organizations accused the army of acting indiscriminately. In December, in response to another murder, residents in the northern town of Villa Trina set fire to settlements housing Haitian immigrants. Later that month President Fernández made an official visit to Haiti; however, hopes that the visit would ease tensions were quashed when violent demonstrations erupted outside the presidential palace, in protest at the treatment of Haitians in the Dominican Republic. Human rights groups were becoming increasingly outspoken about the Dominican mistreatment of illegal immigrants, and in December a US congressional delegation strongly criticized treatment of Haitian workers on Dominican sugar farms, prompting the Dominican Government to respond angrily to what it perceived to be unwarranted intervention in its domestic affairs. In September 2007 a new military border security force, the Cuerpo Especializado de Seguridad Fronteriza (Cesfront), began patrolling the frontier; however, in November 2010 the Border Affairs Commission of the Congreso Nacional asserted that Cesfront was corrupt and that border trafficking had increased since its inception.

In January 2010, following a devastating earthquake in Haiti, the Dominican Government waived visa restrictions for Haitians seeking emergency medical care, authorized nearly 300 flights carrying aid, donated US $11m. and despatched more than 100 soldiers to aid UN forces in stabilizing the country. In an attempt to prevent a cholera outbreak in Haiti from spreading into the Dominican Republic, in October the Government introduced limitations on cross-border travel. However, this failed to prevent the dissemination of the disease, and occurrences of cholera were reported in the Dominican Republic in November. With thousands of cholera deaths documented in Haiti and anti-Haitian attitudes hardening within the Dominican Republic, in January 2011 the Government restarted the process of deporting illegal Haitian immigrants. Human rights organization Amnesty International criticized the move, but the Government argued that it was necessary in order to prevent the further proliferation of the disease. In March 2012 the two countries signed several co-operation agreements aimed at improving bilateral relations.

Other external relations

In 2006 President Fernández expended considerable energy in efforts to strengthen relations with the Dominican Republic's Asian allies. In April he hosted an official visit by Taiwanese President Chen Shui-bian, during which a possible bilateral free trade agreement was discussed. Further dialogue was held during the President's visit to Taiwan in June. The first round of negotiations were held in Santo Domingo in October. The Taiwanese Government pledged aid to the value of US $50m. over a four-year period to assist with the construction of a national science and industrial technology park in Santo Domingo. President Fernández also visited Japan and the Republic of Korea in 2006, where he met with the Japanese Prime Minister and the South Korean President, respectively. In September the Dominican Government announced that it had established formal diplomatic relations with Viet Nam, following discussions between President Fernández and Vietnamese President Nguyen Minh Triet during the summit meeting of the Non-aligned Movement held earlier that month in Havana, Cuba.

CONSTITUTION AND GOVERNMENT

Under the Constitution that was introduced in January 2010, legislative power is exercised by the bicameral Congreso Nacional (National Congress), with a Senado (Senate) of 32 members and a Cámara de Diputados (Chamber of Deputies) comprising 183 members. Members of both houses are elected for four years by universal adult suffrage. Executive power lies with the President, who is also elected by direct popular vote for four years. He is assisted by a Vice-President and a Cabinet comprising Secretaries of State. Judicial power is exercised by the Supreme Court of Justice and the other Tribunals. The Dominican Republic comprises 31 provinces, each administered by an appointed governor, and a Distrito Nacional (DN) containing the capital.

REGIONAL AND INTERNATIONAL CO-OPERATION

The Dominican Republic was granted observer status in the Caribbean Community and Common Market (CARICOM, see p. 227) in 1984. An agreement, originally signed in August 1998, establishing a free trade area between CARICOM countries and the Dominican Republic, came into effect on 1 December 2001. In September 2005 the Congreso Nacional approved the country's membership of the proposed Dominican Republic-Central American Free Trade Agreement (DR-CAFTA) with the USA. Implementation of the accord took place in March 2007. The Dominican Republic is a member of the Association of Caribbean States (see p. 448), and of the Community of Latin American and Caribbean States (see p. 462), which was formally inaugurated in December 2011.

The Dominican Republic was a founder member of the UN. The country acceded to the World Trade Organization (see p. 433) in March 1995. The country was one of the African, Caribbean and Pacific nations covered by the European Union's (EU) Cotonou Agreement (see p. 328), which guaranteed access to EU markets. The Dominican Republic is a member of the Group of 77 (see p. 450) developing states.

ECONOMIC AFFAIRS

In 2010, according to estimates by the World Bank, the Dominican Republic's gross national income (GNI), measured at average 2008–10 prices, was US $49,662m., equivalent to $5,000 per head (or $8,960 per head on an international purchasing-power parity basis). During 2001–10, it was estimated, the population increased by an average of 1.4% per year, while gross domestic product (GDP) per head increased, in real terms, by an average of 4.2% per year. Overall GDP increased, in real terms, by an average of 5.7% per year in 2001–10; real GDP increased by 7.8% in 2010.

According to official data, agriculture, including hunting, forestry and fishing, contributed 6.0% of GDP in 2010 and employed an estimated 14.7% of the employed labour force in April 2011. The principal cash crops are sugar cane (sugar and sugar derivatives accounted for an estimated 7.1% of total export earnings in 2010), coffee, cocoa beans and tobacco. According to the World Bank, agricultural GDP increased, in real terms, by an average of 1.1% per year during 2001–10; real agricultural GDP increased by 12.5% in 2009, but decreased by 14.1% in 2010.

Industry (including mining, manufacturing, construction and power) employed an estimated 17.7% of the economically active population in April 2011 and contributed 31.0% of GDP in 2010. According to the World Bank, industrial GDP increased, in real terms, by an average of 1.8% per year during 2001–10; real industrial GDP declined by 2.2% in 2009 and by a further 1.8% in 2010.

Mining contributed just 0.1% of GDP in 2010, and employed 0.5% of the economically active population in April 2011. The major mineral export is ferro-nickel. Export earnings from ferro-nickel (excluding exports to free trade zones) contributed 46.5% of the total value of exports in 2008; however, the closure of the Falconbridge Dominicana complex in late 2008, owing to falling nickel prices, meant that earnings in 2009 fell dramatically, to just 0.2% of total earnings. The mine's owners, Xstrata, reopened the complex in February 2011. Gold and silver are also exploited, and there are workable deposits of gypsum, limestone and mercury. Real mining GDP decreased by an annual average of 2.5% during 2000–08. The GDP of the mining sector declined by 30.0% in 2008.

Manufacturing contributed 23.3% of GDP in 2010 and employed an estimated 10.1% of the economically active population in April 2011. Important branches of manufacturing included beer, cigarettes and cement. At the end of 2010, according to the Consejo Nacional de Zonas Francas de Exportación, there were 555 companies operating in 48 free trade zones in the Dominican Republic, employing some 121,001 people. According to the World Bank, the GDP of the manufacturing sector increased, in real terms, at an average rate of 3.0% per year during 2001–10; sectoral GDP increased by 5.5% in 2010.

Construction employed an estimated 6.2% of the economically active population in April 2011 and contributed 5.4% of GDP in 2010. Construction GDP increased, in real terms, by an average of 1.6% per year during 2000–08. Construction GDP increased by 3.2% in 2007, but decreased by 0.4% in 2008.

Energy is derived principally from petroleum; however, there is no domestic petroleum production. Imports of crude petroleum and related products accounted for an estimated 26.6% of the total cost of imports in 2010. As part of the PetroCaribe agreement signed in 2005, the Dominican Republic could purchase petroleum from Venezuela at reduced prices. Petroleum provided 61.8% of total energy requirements in 2008, while coal provided a further 13.8% and hydroelectricity 11.2%. In 2009 a hydroelectric plant in Monseñor Nouel province began operations and a further plant, Palomino in San Juan, was scheduled to begin operating in July 2012.

The services sector contributed 63.0% of GDP in 2010, and employed an estimated 67.7% of the economically active population in April 2011. The tourism sector was the country's primary source of foreign exchange earnings. In 2010 an estimated 4,414,756 tourists visited the Dominican Republic; receipts from tourism, excluding passenger transport, totalled US $4,051m. in 2009. According to the World Bank, the GDP of the services sector expanded at an average annual rate of 8.3% during 2001–10; real services GDP increased by 19.7% in 2010.

In 2010 the Dominican Republic recorded a visible trade deficit of US $8,700.8m., and there was a deficit of $4,434.9m. on the current account of the balance of payments. In 2010 the principal source of imports was the USA (33.0%); other major suppliers were the People's Republic of China, Venezuela and Mexico. In the same year the Haiti was the principal market for exports (27.7% of the total); other significant purchasers were the USA and United Kingdom. The principal exports in 2010 were petroleum products, cocoa beans and sugar and sugar cane derivatives; exports from the free trade zones in that year amounted to $4,080.0m. The principal imports in 2010 were petroleum and petroleum products and durable goods.

In 2010 there was an estimated budgetary deficit of RD $55,276.2m. (equivalent to 2.9% of GDP). The Dominican Republic's general government gross debt was RD $545,879m. in 2010, equivalent to 28.7% of GDP. The Dominican Republic's total external debt at the end of 2009 was estimated at US $11,003m., of which $4,434.9m. was public and publicly guaranteed debt. In that year, the cost of debt-servicing long-term public and publicly guaranteed debt and repayments to the IMF was equivalent to 10.5% of value of exports of goods, services and income (excluding workers' remittances). In 2001–10 the average annual rate of inflation was 12.5%. Consumer prices increased by 6.3% in 2010. An estimated 14.6% of the total labour force was unemployed in April 2011.

Tourism revenues, remittances from abroad and the value of exports all declined in 2009 as a consequence of the global economic crisis. In November the IMF approved a 28-month stand-by arrangement, worth approximately US $1,700m., to support the Government's strategy to stabilize the economy. Expansionary government spending continued into 2010, precipitating renewed growth in virtually all sectors of the economy. With the recovery under way, the Government began to reduce spending from mid-2010 in order to stabilize the fiscal position. The Government initiated reforms to the unprofitable, state-owned electricity sector in 2010. Investment to upgrade the power grid and create extra generating capacity was also announced to address the long-standing problem of power cuts. The Government increased electricity rates in December 2010 and June 2011 as part of a gradual process to fund the withdrawal of costly power subsidies. The restructuring of electricity tariffs formed a central component of the Government's strategy to eliminate the fiscal deficit. In a complementary move, in mid-2011 the Congreso Nacional approved a number of fiscal reforms, including tax increases and the imposition of new levies, while in March substantial reductions in public expenditure had been announced. In spite of these measures, the country's financial position remained under pressure during 2011 owing to increases in the price of imported petroleum, which necessitated the commitment of additional government funds to cover the resultant rise in the electricity subsidy. Moreover, elevated commodity prices also led to higher levels of inflation. Nevertheless, the IMF reported that real GDP expanded by approximately 4.5% in 2011 and projected growth of 5.5% in 2012, underlining the strength of the country's ongoing economic recovery amid challenging external conditions.

PUBLIC HOLIDAYS

2013: 1 January (New Year's Day), 6 January (Epiphany), 21 January (Our Lady of Altagracia), 26 January (Birth of Juan Pablo Duarte), 27 February (Independence Day), 29 March (Good Friday), 29 April (for Labour Day), 30 May (Corpus Christi), 16 August (Restoration Day), 24 September (Our Lady of Mercedes), 4 November (for Constitution Day), 25 December (Christmas Day).

Statistical Survey

Sources (unless otherwise stated): Oficina Nacional de Estadística, Edif. de Oficinas Gubernamentales, 9°, Avda México, esq. Leopoldo Navarro, Santo Domingo, DN; tel. 682-7777; fax 685-4424; e-mail info@one.gob.do; internet www.one.gob.do; Banco Central de la República Dominicana, Calle Pedro Henríquez Ureña, esq. Leopoldo Navarro, Apdo 1347, Santo Domingo, DN; tel. 221-9111; fax 686-7488; e-mail info@bancentral.gov.do; internet www.bancentral.gov.do.

Area and Population

AREA, POPULATION AND DENSITY

Area (sq km)	
Land	48,137
Inland water	597
Total	48,734*
Population (census results)	
18–20 October 2002	8,562,541
1–7 December 2010†	
Males	4,707,921
Females	4,670,898
Total	9,378,819
Population (official projections)‡	
2011	10,010,590
2012	10,135,105
Density (per sq km) at 2012	208.0

* 18,816 sq miles.

† Preliminary figures.

‡ Not adjusted to take account of results of 2010 census.

POPULATION BY AGE AND SEX

(official projections, 2012)

	Males	Females	Total
0–14	1,591,202	1,534,907	3,126,109
15–64	3,167,330	3,219,165	6,386,495
65 and over	298,385	324,116	622,501
Total	5,056,917	5,078,188	10,135,105

PROVINCES

(official population projections, 2012)

	Area (sq km)	Population	Density (per sq km)
Distrito Nacional Region			
Distrito Nacional	104.4	1,140,605	10925.3
Santo Domingo	1,296.4	2,274,110	1754.2
Valdesia Region			
Peravia	997.6	208,101	208.6
Monte Plata	2,632.1	215,346	81.8
San Cristóbal	1,265.8	685,768	541.8
San José de Ocoa	650.2	69,312	106.6
Norcentral Region			
Espaillat	839.0	240,389	286.5
Puerto Plata	1,856.9	332,295	179.0
Santiago	2,839.0	1,074,950	378.6
Nordeste Region			
Duarte	1,605.4	302,405	188.4
Hermanas Mirabal	440.4	103,775	235.6
María Trinidad Sánchez	1,271.7	143,008	112.5
Samaná	853.7	100,690	117.9
Enriquillo Region			
Baoruco	1,282.2	117,889	91.9
Barahona	1,739.4	203,861	117.2
Independencia	2,006.4	56,836	28.3
Pedernales	2,074.5	26,239	12.6
Este Region			
El Seibo	1,786.8	108,492	60.7
Hato Mayor	1,329.3	91,718	69.0
La Altagracia	2,474.3	240,108	97.0
La Romana	654.0	252,558	386.2
San Pedro de Macorís	1,255.5	346,513	276.0
El Valle Region			
Azua	2,531.8	247,435	97.7
Elías Piña	1,426.2	73,351	51.4
San Juan	3,569.4	244,539	68.5
—continued			
Noroeste Region			
Dajabón	1,020.7	67,762	66.4
Monte Cristi	1,924.4	123,100	64.0
Santiago Rodríguez	1,111.1	54,576	49.1
Valverde	823.4	195,239	237.1
Cibao Central Region			
La Vega	2,287.0	437,691	191.4
Monseñor Nouel	992.4	199,405	200.9
Sánchez Ramírez	1,196.1	157,039	131.3
Total	48,137.0*	10,135,105	210.5*

* Land area only.

PRINCIPAL TOWNS

(population at census of October 2002)

Santo Domingo DN (capital)	2,302,759	San Felipe de Puerto Plata	146,882
Santiago de los Caballeros	622,101	Higuey	141,751
San Cristóbal	220,767	Moca	131,733
Concepción de la Vega	220,279	San Juan de la Maguana	129,224
San Pedro de Macorís	217,141	Monseñor Nouel	115,743
La Romana	202,488	Baní	107,926
San Francisco de Macorís	156,267	Bajos de Haina	80,835

Mid-2010 (incl. suburbs, UN estimate): Santo Domingo DN 2,180,150 (Source: UN, *World Urbanization Prospects: The 2009 Revision*).

BIRTHS, MARRIAGES AND DEATHS

(year of registration)

	Registered live births		Registered marriages		Registered deaths	
	Number	Rate (per 1,000)	Number	Rate (per 1,000)	Number	Rate (per 1,000)
2003	209,069	23.4	37,225	4.2	29,821	3.3
2004	198,304	21.8	38,642	4.3	34,325	3.8
2005	183,819	19.9	39,439	4.3	33,949	3.7
2006	174,393	18.3	42,375	4.5	33,060	3.5
2007	193,817	20.4	39,993	4.2	33,842	3.6

2008: Registered marriages 38,310 (4.0 per 1,000 persons).

2009: Registered marriages 40,040 (4.1 per 1,000 persons).

2010: Registered marriages 43,797 (4.7 per 1,000 persons).

Life expectancy (years at birth, WHO estimates): 71 (males 71; females 72) in 2009 (Source: WHO, *World Health Statistics*).

ECONOMICALLY ACTIVE POPULATION
('000 persons aged 10 years and over, official estimates at April 2011)

	Males	Females	Total
Agriculture, hunting, forestry and fishing	535.3	35.3	570.6
Mining and quarrying	17.8	0.6	18.4
Manufacturing	287.6	107.5	395.1
Electricity, gas and water supply	27.3	6.7	34.0
Construction	228.3	12.0	240.2
Wholesale and retail trade	558.9	297.7	856.5
Hotels and restaurants	100.6	130.1	230.7
Transport, storage and communications	265.0	22.2	287.2
Financial intermediation; Real estate, renting and business activities	48.1	46.8	94.9
Public administration and defence	126.6	60.1	186.7
Education; Health and social work; Other community, social and personal service activities	317.3	661.9	979.3
Total employed	2,512.7	1,380.9	3,893.6
Unemployed	270.2	395.6	665.8
Total labour force	2,782.9	1,776.5	4,559.5

Health and Welfare

KEY INDICATORS

Total fertility rate (children per woman, 2009)	2.6
Under-5 mortality rate (per 1,000 live births, 2009)	32
HIV/AIDS (% of persons aged 15–49, 2009)	0.9
Physicians (per 1,000 head, 2000)	1.88
Hospital beds (per 1,000 head, 2005)	2.0
Health expenditure (2008): US $ per head (PPP)	465
Health expenditure (2008): % of GDP	5.7
Health expenditure (2008): public (% of total)	37.1
Access to water (% of persons, 2008)	86
Access to sanitation (% of persons, 2008)	83
Total carbon dioxide emissions ('000 metric tons, 2007)	20,741.9
Carbon dioxide emissions per head (metric tons, 2007)	2.1
Human Development Index (2011): ranking	98
Human Development Index (2011): value	0.689

For sources and definitions, see explanatory note on p. vi.

Agriculture

PRINCIPAL CROPS
('000 metric tons)

	2008	2009	2010
Rice, paddy	778.5	848.3	916.8
Maize	27.5	35.0	36.7
Potatoes	34.1	43.5	51.4
Sweet potatoes	38.3	47.1	53.6
Cassava (Manioc)	106.3	165.7	211.1
Yautia (Cocoyam)	24.4	29.0	30.3
Sugar cane	4,741.8	4,716.2	4,781.4
Beans, dry	21.3	30.6	33.0
Coconuts	94.5	84.0	95.0*
Oil palm fruit*	188.8	188.8	188.8
Tomatoes	243.0	234.5	240.3
Pumpkins, squash and gourds	41.0	42.1	40.6
Chillies and peppers, green	32.9	37.8	37.2
Onions, dry	51.2	47.3	48.4
Garlic	2.6	1.1	2.0
Carrots and turnips	19.7	20.0*	20.3*
Cantaloupes and other melons*	17.0	16.7	17.0
Bananas	439.6	589.5	734.9
Plantains	352.0	517.3	491.5
Oranges	90.3	128.8	138.0
Guavas, mangoes and mangosteens*	195.0	257.9	299.6
Avocados	187.4	184.4	275.6
Pineapples	100.5	127.2	157.4
Papayas*	23.0	23.5	27.3
Coffee, green	47.6	39.9	32.6
Cocoa beans	45.5	50.2	53.0
Tobacco, unmanufactured	9.1	11.7	7.0

* FAO estimate(s).

Aggregate production ('000 metric tons, may include official, semi-official or estimated data): Total cereals 806.6 in 2008, 884.1 in 2009, 954.3 in 2010; Total roots and tubers 232.0 in 2008, 312.8 in 2009, 374.1 in 2010; Total vegetables (incl. melons) 462.1 in 2008, 456.6 in 2009, 463.6 in 2010; Total fruits (excl. melons) 1,437.1 in 2008, 1,890.2 in 2009, 2,196.1 in 2010.

Source: FAO.

LIVESTOCK
('000 head, year ending September, estimates)

	2005	2006	2007
Horses	345	348	350
Asses	151	151	151
Cattle	2,200.0	2,228.1	2,652.6
Pigs	580.0	580.0	580.0
Sheep	123.0	123.0	123.0
Goats	190.0	190.0	190.0
Chickens	86,000	91,000	100,500

2008–10: Production assumed to be unchanged from 2007 (FAO estimates).

Source: FAO.

LIVESTOCK PRODUCTS
('000 metric tons)

	2008	2009	2010
Cattle meat	99.3	101.8	100.0*
Pig meat	90.5	82.0	87.0*
Chicken meat	299.5	315.0	315.0*
Cows' milk	610.2	649.9	701.2
Hen eggs†	87.2	91.9	105.7
Honey*	4.7	4.9	4.9

* FAO estimate(s).
† Unofficial figures.

Source: FAO.

Forestry

ROUNDWOOD REMOVALS
('000 cubic metres, excl. bark)

	2007	2008	2009
Sawlogs, veneer logs and logs for sleepers	14	7	7
Other industrial wood*	3	3	3
Fuel wood*	887	895	904
Total*	904	905	914

* FAO estimates.

2010: Production assumed to be unchanged from 2009 (FAO estimates).

Source: FAO.

Fishing

('000 metric tons, live weight)

	2007	2008	2009
Capture	13.7	15.4	14.2
Tilapia	0.8	0.7	0.3
Groupers, seabasses	0.6	0.7	1.4
Common carp	0.4	0.5	0.3
Snappers and jobfishes	1.3	1.2	1.2
King mackerel	0.1	0.3	0.3
Blackfin tuna	n.a.	0.3	0.9
Caribbean spiny lobster	1.1	1.3	1.4
Stromboid conchs	1.3	1.6	2.3
Aquaculture*	1.0	1.0	1.0
Penaeus shrimps*	0.5	0.5	0.5
Total catch*	14.7	16.4	15.2

* FAO estimates.

Source: FAO.

Mining

('000 metric tons)

	2008	2009	2010
Ferro-nickel*	84.0	84.0	84.0
Nickel (metal content of laterite ore)	31.3	0.5	0
Gypsum	350.0	175.0	195.0

* Estimated production.

Source: US Geological Survey.

Industry

SELECTED PRODUCTS
('000 metric tons, unless otherwise indicated)

	2004	2005	2006*
Flour and derivatives ('000 quintales†)	2,516.4	2,543.2	1,581.5
Refined sugar	124.0	140.1	132.2
Cement	2,653.6	2,778.7	1,888.4
Beer ('000 hl)	3,546.1	4,408.1	2,133.7
Cigarettes (million)	3,445.9	3,300.3	1,415.8

* Preliminary figures.

† 1 quintale is equivalent to 46 kg.

2009 ('000 barrels, estimates): Motor spirit (petrol) 3,000; Jet fuel 1,900; Distillate fuel oil 2,900; Residual fuel oil 4,600 (Sources: US Geological Survey).

2010 ('000 barrels, estimates): Motor spirit (petrol) 3,000; Jet fuel 1,900; Distillate fuel oil 2,900; Residual fuel oil 4,600 (Sources: US Geological Survey).

Electric energy (million kWh): 12,899 in 2005; 14,150 in 2006; 14,839 in 2007; 15,414 in 2008 (Source: UN Industrial Commodity Statistics Database).

Finance

CURRENCY AND EXCHANGE RATES

Monetary Units
100 centavos = 1 Dominican Republic peso (RD $ or peso oro).

Sterling, Dollar and Euro Equivalents (30 December 2011)
£1 sterling = 59.976 pesos;
US $1 = 38.792 pesos;
€1 = 50.192 pesos;
1,000 Dominican Republic pesos = £16.67 = $25.78 = €19.92.

Average Exchange Rate (RD $ per US $)
2009 36.027
2010 36.876
2011 38.109

BUDGET
(RD $ million)

Revenue	2008	2009	2010*
Tax revenue	236,166.1	220,373.6	243,942.9
Taxes on income and profits	58,534.7	54,127.7	53,643.5
Taxes on goods and services	139,766.7	132,411.8	151,802.4
Taxes on international trade and transactions	24,829.9	21,942.4	23,408.4
Other current revenue	10,744.2	5,830.3	11,128.1
Capital revenue	0.1	9.2	14.2
Total	246,910.4	226,213.2	255,085.2

Expenditure	2008	2009	2010*
Current expenditure	228,478.2	222,336.3	239,988.3
Wages and salaries	58,787.3	68,495.1	72,254.3
Other services; Materials and supplies	32,085.3	30,335.6	34,401.1
Current transfers	111,426.7	92,958.8	96,100.5
Interest payments	26,179.0	30,546.9	37,232.5
Capital expenditure	80,849.4	60,032.5	70,373.1
Machines and equipment; Construction of works and agricultural plantations	53,930.2	37,950.9	51,542.9
Capital transfers	26,333.5	21,321.4	18,127.9
Total	309,327.6	282,368.8	310,361.4

* Preliminary figures.

INTERNATIONAL RESERVES
(US $ million at 31 December)

	2008	2009	2010
Gold*	15.9	19.9	25.7
IMF special drawing rights	36.0	275.6	117.7
Foreign exchange	2,235.6	2,609.5	3,358.0
Total	2,287.5	2,905.0	3,501.4

* Valued at market-related prices.

Source: IMF, *International Financial Statistics*.

MONEY SUPPLY
(RD $ million at 31 December)

	2008	2009	2010
Currency outside depository corporations	50,478	55,413	59,559
Transferable deposits	77,867	96,981	106,880
Other deposits	209,302	232,630	279,729
Securities other than shares	156,728	175,672	183,091
Broad money	494,376	560,695	629,259

Source: IMF, *International Financial Statistics*.

COST OF LIVING
(Consumer Price Index including direct taxes; base: 2000 = 100)

	2008	2009	2010
Food, beverages and tobacco	295.7	307.3	320.4
Clothing	219.1	232.5	n.a.
Rent	277.1	299.3	n.a.
All items (incl. others)	291.1	295.3	314.0

Source: ILO.

NATIONAL ACCOUNTS
(RD $ million at current prices)

Expenditure on the Gross Domestic Product

	2008	2009	2010
Final consumption expenditure	1,504,352.5	1,564,274.5	1,811,935.3
Households Non-profit institutions serving households	1,383,957.8	1,432,777.4	1,666,249.9
General government	120,394.7	131,497.1	145,685.4
Gross capital formation	288,574.0	248,858.8	313,355.6
Gross fixed capital formation	286,457.4	246,585.6	310,784.7
Changes in inventories Acquisitions, less disposals, of valuables	2,116.6	2,273.2	2,570.9
Total domestic expenditure	1,792,926.5	1,813,133.3	2,125,290.9
Exports of goods and services	401,703.0	373,490.8	423,402.2
Less Imports of goods and services	618,466.8	507,861.5	646,796.5
GDP in market prices	1,576,162.8	1,678,762.6	1,901,896.7
GDP at constant 1991 prices	331,126.8	342,564.1	369,117.0

Gross Domestic Product by Economic Activity

	2008	2009	2010
Agriculture, hunting, forestry and fishing	92,297.4	96,366.8	109,084.9
Mining and quarrying	5,415.1	2,184.3	2,698.4
Manufacturing	338,745.0	379,489.7	422,135.1
Local manufacturing	282,660.4	328,550.6	365,955.7
Free trade zones	56,084.6	50,939.1	56,179.4
Electricity and water	33,988.2	35,993.7	39,596.4
Construction	92,737.3	85,596.0	97,324.1
Wholesale and retail trade	148,069.5	142,390.8	171,968.3
Restaurants and hotels	159,793.5	158,984.5	175,214.7
Transport and storage	136,157.4	125,373.3	149,553.7
Communications	42,438.9	49,654.4	54,340.7
Finance, insurance and business activities	90,494.5	102,545.6	120,542.7
Real estate	125,698.3	139,676.2	156,624.2
General government services (incl. defence)	51,775.3	57,707.1	58,504.0
Education	50,135.9	61,309.1	69,759.2
Health	30,271.7	33,127.1	37,812.2
Other services	111,356.2	134,047.9	147,925.4
Sub-total	1,509,374.2	1,604,446.5	1,813,084.0
Less Financial intermediation services indirectly measured	46,440.4	53,727.1	59,567.2
Gross value added in basic prices	1,462,933.8	1,550,719.4	1,753,516.9
Taxes, *less* subsidies	113,229.0	128,043.2	148,379.7
GDP in market prices	1,576,162.8	1,678,762.6	1,901,896.7

BALANCE OF PAYMENTS
(US $ million)

	2008	2009	2010
Exports of goods f.o.b.	6,747.5	5,482.9	6,598.1
Imports of goods f.o.b.	–15,992.9	–12,295.9	–15,298.9
Trade balance	–9,245.4	–6,813.0	–8,700.8
Exports of services	4,951.2	4,835.9	5,098.7
Imports of services	–1,989.4	–1,848.6	–2,162.8
Balance on goods and services	–6,283.6	–3,825.7	–5,764.9
Other income received	728.7	461.1	499.6
Other income paid	–2,476.6	–2,181.9	–2,287.8
Balance on goods, services and income	–8,031.5	–5,546.5	–7,553.1
Current transfers received	3,789.1	3,499.4	3,473.3
Current transfers paid	–276.2	–283.8	–355.1
Current balance	–4,518.6	–2,330.9	–4,434.9
Capital account (net)	135.0	106.5	81.9
Direct investment from abroad	2,870.0	2,165.4	1,625.8
Portfolio investment assets	107.7	46.8	–10.3
Portfolio investment liabilities	–483.5	–496.3	535.2
Other investment assets	541.3	255.4	352.3
Other investment liabilities	1,038.0	789.6	1,903.8
Net errors and omissions	–14.6	–125.3	10.9
Overall balance	–324.7	411.2	64.7

Source: IMF, *International Financial Statistics*.

External Trade

PRINCIPAL COMMODITIES
(US $ million)*

Imports f.o.b.	2008	2009	2010†
Consumer goods	6,857.0	5,327.4	6,640.8
Durable goods	946.6	641.9	942.9
Foodstuffs	619.4	625.6	697.9
Petroleum products	2,999.8	2,048.3	2,649.8
Raw materials	4,574.7	3,026.2	4,054.3
Artificial plastic materials	326.1	264.4	334.9
Petroleum and petroleum products	1,241.5	592.7	777.7
Cast iron and steel	751.3	360.4	606.2
Capital goods	2,132.2	1,592.6	2,190.1
For transport	329.9	148.3	237.3
For industry	409.1	339.9	526.7
Machinery	427.8	413.7	514.9
Total	13,564.0	9,946.1	12,885.2

Exports f.o.b.	2008	2009	2010†
Sugar and sugar cane derivatives	108.5	121.1	177.6
Raw cane sugar	77.3	91.4	145.2
Cocoa and cocoa manufactures	106.7	164.0	187.0
Cocoa beans	92.6	153.0	173.6
Tobacco and tobacco manufactures	13.6	11.9	12.5
Ferro-nickel	492.3	4.1	n.a.
Other goods	1,113.3	1,030.0	1,710.0
Petroleum products	522.3	315.6	398.4
Total (incl. others)	2,394.0	1,689.7	2,518.3

* Figures exclude imports into free trade zones (US $ million): 2,428.9 in 2008; 2,349.8 in 2009; 2,413.7 in 2010 (preliminary). Also excluded are exports from free trade zones (US $ million): 4,354.1 in 2008; 3,793.6 in 2009; 4,080.0 in 2010 (preliminary).

† Preliminary figures.

PRINCIPAL TRADING PARTNERS
(excl. free trade zones, US $ '000)

Imports c.i.f.	2008	2009*	2010*
Argentina	153,463.5	179,431.2	153,392.3
Brazil	385,351.9	270,222.1	327,249.2
Canada	146,213.5	134,209.8	188,383.6
China, People's Republic	1,201,628.1	1,114,179.3	1,503,598.2
Colombia	738,856.0	504,796.3	560,197.1
Costa Rica	186,260.4	158,911.3	206,569.7
Denmark	100,254.9	67,444.5	80,735.4
France	122,197.0	83,259.9	107,825.6
Germany	205,349.0	215,427.4	236,304.9
Guatemala	103,254.5	97,586.8	124,766.6
Italy	141,461.4	139,241.3	173,621.8
Japan	314,129.1	160,091.1	306,047.2
Mexico	828,697.4	512,986.9	880,149.6
Panama	186,571.7	116,085.3	107,070.6
Spain	397,022.9	248,298.9	267,575.6
Trinidad and Tobago	356,059.0	361,804.8	468,149.2
USA	4,296,734.0	3,220,239.4	4,261,844.5
Venezuela	1,242,097.9	654,000.2	1,083,434.2
Total (incl. others)	13,342,736.0	9,603,051.0	12,925,939.0

Exports f.o.b.	2008	2009*	2010*
Canada	29,416.0	10,738.8	12,573.3
China, People's Republic	51,690.7	50,820.5	58,230.7
Cuba	55,348.4	22,854.4	32,577.4
Germany	16,536.5	11,739.3	16,688.4
Haiti	239,996.2	266,905.2	491,373.2
Italy	25,516.5	10,332.4	27,596.5
Jamaica	54,330.2	37,217.9	46,344.1
Japan	28,858.3	1,834.6	2,190.0
Korea, Democratic People's Republic	18,785.5	9,215.7	18,785.4
Netherlands	106,587.7	28,559.8	41,160.5
Spain	156,541.8	73,714.8	87,474.1
United Kingdom	57,286.4	77,964.8	92,321.5
USA	393,592.4	304,075.3	340,154.9
Total (incl. others)	2,431,500.9	1,300,036.5	1,772,588.2

* Preliminary figures.

Transport

ROAD TRAFFIC
(motor vehicles in use)

	2003	2004	2005
Passenger cars ('000)	638.0	662.0	721.0
Commercial vehicles ('000)	320.0	329.0	351.0

Source: UN, *Statistical Yearbook*.

2007 (motor vehicles in use at 31 December): Passenger cars 602,671; Buses and coaches 64,236; Vans and Lorries 525,391; Motorcycles and mopeds 1,044,510 (Source: IRF, *World Road Statistics*).

SHIPPING

Merchant Fleet
(registered at 31 December)

	2007	2008	2009
Number of vessels	23	25	25
Total displacement ('000 grt)	9.7	10.1	9.7

Source: IHS Fairplay, *World Fleet Statistics*.

International Sea-borne Freight Traffic
('000 metric tons)

	2006	2007	2008
Goods loaded	3,036	3,000	3,768
Goods unloaded	12,504	13,236	14,724

Source: UN, *Monthly Bulletin of Statistics*.

CIVIL AVIATION
(traffic on scheduled services)

	1997	1998	1999
Kilometres flown (million)	1	1	0
Passengers carried ('000)	34	34	10
Passenger-km (million)	16	16	5
Total ton-km (million)	1	1	0

Source: UN, *Statistical Yearbook*.

Tourism

ARRIVALS BY NATIONALITY

	2008	2009	2010
Canada	591,871	639,796	650,111
France	287,147	279,408	247,038
Germany	214,942	206,940	178,533
Italy	140,423	127,383	115,775
Puerto Rico	104,227	97,592	107,610
Spain	267,365	239,638	231,275
United Kingdom*	217,490	206,372	176,180
USA	1,099,906	1,107,898	1,150,875
Total (incl. others)	4,428,005	4,398,743	4,414,756

* Includes arrivals from England and Scotland only.

Tourism receipts (US $ million, excl. passenger transport): 3,917 in 2006; 4,064 in 2007; 4,166 in 2008; 4,051 in 2009 (Source: World Tourism Organization).

Communications Media

	2008	2009	2010
Telephones ('000 main lines in use)	985.7	965.4	1,000.9
Mobile cellular telephones ('000 subscribers)	7,210.5	8,629.8	8,892.8
Internet subscribers ('000)	320.9	328.2	379.3
Broadband subscribers ('000)	226.0	294.5	360.0

Daily newspapers: 11 in 2004 (average circulation 365,000 copies).

Non-daily newspapers: 8 in 2000 (average circulation 215,000 copies).

Radio receivers ('000 in use): 1,440 in 1997.

Television receivers ('000 in use): 790 in 1998.

Personal computers: 200,000 (21.3 per 1,000 persons) in 2004.

Sources: UNESCO, *Statistical Yearbook*; UN, *Statistical Yearbook*; International Telecommunication Union.

Education

(2009/10 unless otherwise indicated)

		Students		
	Teachers	Males	Females	Total
Pre-primary	10,260	123,550	118,131	241,681
Primary	51,615	711,838	605,964	1,317,802
Secondary	32,084	430,969	473,558	904,527
General	28,042	416,451	450,074	866,525
Vocational	4,042	14,518	23,484	38,002
Higher*	11,367	113,520	180,045	293,565

* Estimates for 2003/04.

Institutions: Primary 4,001 (1997/98); General secondary 1,737 (1996/97).

Source: UNESCO, mostly Institute for Statistics.

Pupil-teacher ratio (primary education, estimate): 25.5 in 2009/10 (Source: UNESCO Institute for Statistics).

Adult literacy rate (estimates): 88.2% (males 88.2%; females 88.3%) in 2007 (Source: UNESCO Institute for Statistics).

Directory

The Government

HEAD OF STATE

President: LEONEL FERNÁNDEZ REYNA (took office 16 August 2004; re-elected 16 May 2008).

Vice-President: Dr RAFAEL FRANCISCO ALBURQUERQUE DE CASTRO.

CABINET
(May 2012)

The Government is formed by the Partido de la Liberación Dominicana.

Secretary of State for the Presidency: Dr CÉSAR PINA TORIBIO.

Secretary of State for Foreign Affairs: CARLOS MORALES TRONCOSO.

Secretary of State for the Interior and Police: JOSÉ RAMÓN FADUL.

Secretary of State for the Armed Forces: Lt-Gen. JOAQUÍN VIRGILIO PERÉZ FELIZ.

Secretary of State for Finance: DANIEL TORIBIO.

Secretary of State for Education: JOSEFINA PIMENTEL.

Secretary of State for Agriculture: SALVADOR JIMÉNEZ.

Secretary of State for Public Works and Communications: VÍCTOR JOSÉ DÍAZ RÚA.

Secretary of State for Public Health and Social Welfare: Dr BAUTISTA ROJAS GÓMEZ.

Secretary of State for Industry and Commerce: MANUEL GARCÍA ARÉVALO.

Secretary of State for Labour: FRANCISCO DOMÍNGUEZ BRITO.

Secretary of State for Tourism: FRANCISCO JAVIER GARCÍA.

Secretary of State for Sport and Recreation: FELIPE (JAY) PAYANO.

Secretary of State for Culture: JOSÉ RAFAEL LANTIGUA.

Secretary of State for Higher Education, Science and Technology: LIGIA AMADA DE MELO.

Secretary of State for Women: ALEJANDRINA GERMÁN.

Secretary of State for Youth: FRANKLIN RODRÍGUEZ.

Secretary of State for the Environment and Natural Resources: Dr ERNESTO REYNA ALCÁNTARA.

Secretary of State for the Economy, Planning and Development: JUAN TEMÍSTOCLES MONTÁS.

Secretary of State for Public Administration: RAMÓN VENTURA CAMEJO.

Administrative Secretary to the Presidency: LUIS MANUEL BONETTI.

SECRETARIATS OF STATE

Office of the President: Palacio Nacional, Avda México, esq. Dr Delgado, Gazcue, Santo Domingo, DN; tel. 695-8000; fax 682-4558; internet www.presidencia.gob.do.

Secretariat of State for Agriculture: Autopista Duarte, Km 6.5, Los Jardines del Norte, Santo Domingo, DN; tel. 547-3888; fax 227-1268; e-mail agricultura@agricultura.gob.do; internet www.agricultura.gob.do.

Secretariat of State for the Armed Forces: Plaza de la Bandera, Avda 27 de Febrero, esq. Avda Luperón, Santo Domingo, DN; tel. 530-5149; fax 531-0461; e-mail directorrev@j2.mil.do; internet www.fuerzasarmadas.mil.do.

Secretariat of State for Culture: Centro de Eventos y Exposiciones, Avda George Washington, esq. Presidente Vicini Burgos, Santo Domingo, DN; tel. 221-4141; fax 688-2908; e-mail contacto@cultura.gob.do; internet www.cultura.gob.do.

Secretariat of State for the Economy, Planning and Development: Palacio Nacional, Avda México, esq. Dr Delgado, Bloque B, 2°, Santo Domingo, DN; tel. 221-5140; fax 221-8627; e-mail informacion@economia.gob.do; internet www.economia.gob.do.

Secretariat of State for Education: Avda Máximo Gómez, esq. Santiago 2, Gazcue, Santo Domingo, DN; tel. 688-9700; fax 689-8688; e-mail mlibreacceso@see.gob.do; internet www.see.gob.do.

Secretariat of State for the Environment and Natural Resources: Plaza Naco 28, Avda Tiradentes, esq. Fantico Falco, Ensanche Naco, Santo Domingo, DN; tel. 567-4300; fax 683-4774; e-mail contacto@medioambiente.gob.do; internet www.ambiente.gob.do.

Secretariat of State for Finance: Avda México 45, esq. Leopoldo Navarro, Apdo 1478, Santo Domingo, DN; tel. 687-5131; fax 682-0498; e-mail info@hacienda.gov.do; internet www.hacienda.gov.do.

Secretariat of State for Foreign Affairs: Avda Independencia 752, Estancia San Gerónimo, Santo Domingo, DN; tel. 987-7001; fax 987-7002; e-mail relexteriores@serex.gob.do; internet www.serex.gov.do.

Secretariat of State for Higher Education, Science and Technology: Avda Máximo Gómez 31, esq. Pedro Henríquez Ureña, Santo Domingo, DN; tel. 731-1100; fax 535-4694; e-mail info@seescyt.gob.do; internet www.seescyt.gov.do.

Secretariat of State for Industry and Commerce: Edif. de Ofs Gubernamentales Juan Pablo Duarte, 7°, Avda México, esq. Leopoldo Navarro, Apdo 9876, Santo Domingo, DN; tel. 685-5171; fax 686-1973; e-mail info@seic.gob.do; internet www.seic.gov.do.

Secretariat of State for the Interior and Police: Edif. de Ofs Gubernamentales Juan Pablo Duarte, 13°, Avda México, esq. Leopoldo Navarro, Santo Domingo, DN; tel. 686-6251; fax 689-6599; e-mail info@seip.gob.do; internet www.seip.gob.do.

Secretariat of State for Labour: Centro de los Héroes, Avda Jiménez Moya 9, La Feria, Santo Domingo, DN; tel. 535-4404; fax 535-4833; e-mail oai@set.gob.do; internet www.set.gob.do.

Secretariat of State for Public Administration: Edif. de Ofs. Gubernamentales Juan Pablo Duarte, 12°, Avda México, esq. Leopoldo Navarro, Apdo 20031, Santo Domingo, DN; tel. 682-3298; fax 686-6652; e-mail seap@seap.gob.do; internet www.seap.gob.do.

Secretariat of State for Public Health and Social Welfare: Avda San Cristóbal, esq. Tiradentes, Ensanche La Fe, Santo Domingo, DN; tel. 541-3121; fax 540-6445; e-mail correo@sespas.gob.do; internet www.sespas.gov.do.

Secretariat of State for Public Works and Communications: Avda San Cristóbal, esq. Avda Tiradentes, Ensanche La Fe, Santo Domingo, DN; tel. 565-2811; fax 562-3382; e-mail info@seopc.gob.do; internet www.seopc.gov.do.

Secretariat of State for Sport and Recreation: Avda Correa y Cidrón, esq. John F. Kennedy, Estadio Olímpico, Centro Olímpico Juan Pablo Duarte, Santo Domingo, DN; tel. 565-3325; fax 563-6586; e-mail juliomonnadal@miderec.gov.do; internet www.miderec.gov.do.

Secretariat of State for Tourism: Edif. de Ofs Gubernamentales, Bloque D, Avda México, esq. 30 de Marzo, Apdo 497, Santo Domingo, DN; tel. 221-4660; fax 682-3806; e-mail info@sectur.gob.do; internet www.sectur.gob.do.

Secretariat of State for Women: Edif. de Ofs. Gubernamentales, Bloque D, 2°, Avda México, esq. 30 de Marzo, Santo Domingo, DN; tel. 685-3755; fax 686-0911; e-mail info@mujer.gob.do; internet www.mujer.gob.do.

Secretariat of State for Youth: Avda Jiménez de Moya 71, esq. Calle Desiderio Arias, Ensanche La Julia, Santo Domingo, DN; tel. 508-7227; fax 508-6686; e-mail info@juventud.gob.do; internet www.juventud.gob.do.

President and Legislature

PRESIDENT

Election, 16 May 2008

Candidate	Votes	% of valid votes cast
Leonel Fernández Reyna (PLD)	2,199,734	53.83
Miguel Vargas Maldonado (PRD)	1,654,066	40.48
Amable Aristy Castro (PRSC)	187,645	4.59
Others	45,096	1.10
Total	4,086,541	100.00

CONGRESO NACIONAL

The Congreso Nacional comprises a Senado and a Cámara de Diputados.

President of the Senado: Dr REINALDO PARED PÉREZ (PLD).

President of the Cámara de Diputados: JULIO CÉSAR VALENTÍN JIMINIÁN (PLD).

General Election, 16 May 2010

	Seats	
	Senate	Chamber of Deputies
Partido de la Liberación Dominicana (PLD)	31	105
Partido Revolucionario Dominicano (PRD)	—	75
Partido Reformista Social Cristiano (PRSC)	1	3
Total	32	183

Election Commission

Junta Central Electoral (JCE): Avda 27 de Febrero, esq. Gregorio Luperón, Santo Domingo, DN; tel. 539-5419; e-mail webmaster@jce.do; internet www.jce.do; f. 1923; govt-appointed body; Pres. Dr ROBERTO ROSARIO MÁRQUEZ.

Political Organizations

Alianza por la Democracia (APD): Benito Mención 10, Gazcue, Santo Domingo, DN; tel. 687-0337; fax 687-0360; f. 1992 by breakaway group of the PLD; Pres. MAXIMILIANO PUIG; Sec.-Gen. CARLOS LUIS SÁNCHEZ S.

Bloque Institucional Socialdemócrata (BIS): Avda Bolívar 24, esq. Uruguay, Ensanche Lugo, Apdo 5413, Santo Domingo, DN; tel. 682-3232; fax 682-3375; e-mail adm@bis.org.do; internet bis.org.do; f. 1989 by breakaway group of PRD under Dr José Francisco Peña Gómez; Pres. JOSÉ FRANCISCO PEÑA GUABA.

Fuerza Nacional Progresista (FNP): Calle Emilio A. Morel 17, Ensanche La Fe, Santo Domingo, DN; tel. 732-0849; e-mail fuerza_nacional_progresista@hotmail.com; internet fuerzanacionalprogresista.blogspot.com; right-wing; Pres. MARINO VINICIO CASTILLO (alias Vincho); Sec.-Gen. JOSÉ RICARDO TAVERAS BLANCO.

Partido de la Liberación Dominicana (PLD): Avda Independencia 401, Santo Domingo, DN; tel. 685-3540; fax 687-5569; e-mail pldorg@pld.org.do; internet www.pld.org.do; f. 1973 by breakaway group of PRD; left-wing; Leader LEONEL FERNÁNDEZ REYNA; Sec.-Gen. REINALDO PARED PÉREZ.

Partido Reformista Social Cristiano (PRSC): Avda Tiradentes, esq. San Cristóbal, Ensanche La Fe, Apdo 1332, Santo Domingo, DN; tel. 621-7772; fax 476-9361; e-mail s.seliman@codetel.net.do; internet www.prsc.com.do; f. 1964; centre-right party; Pres. CARLOS MORALES TRONCOSO; Sec.-Gen. RAMÓN ROGELIO GENAO.

Partido Revolucionario Dominicano (PRD): Avda Dr Comandante Enrique Jiménez Moya 14, Bella Vista, Santo Domingo, DN; tel. 687-2193; e-mail prensa_tribunalp.r.d@hotmail.com; internet www.prd.org.do; f. 1939; democratic socialist; Pres. MIGUEL VARGAS MALDONADO; Sec.-Gen. ORLANDO JORGE MERA.

Partido Revolucionario Independiente (PRI): Edif. Galerías Comerciales, Avda 57, Apdo 509, Santo Domingo, DN; tel. 221-8286; e-mail Trajano.S@codetel.net.do; f. 1985 after split by the PRD's right-wing faction; Pres. Dr TRAJANO SANTANA; Sec.-Gen. DR JORGE MONTES DE OCA.

Partido de los Trabajadores Dominicanos (PTD): Avda Bolívar 101, esq. Dr Báez, Gazcue, Santo Domingo, DN; tel. 685-7705; fax 333-6443; e-mail contacto@ptd.org.do; internet www.ptd.org.do; f. 1979; Communist; Pres. JOSÉ GONZÁLEZ ESPINOZA; Sec.-Gen. ANTONIO FLORIÁN.

Diplomatic Representation

EMBASSIES IN THE DOMINICAN REPUBLIC

Argentina: Avda Máximo Gómez 10, Apdo 1302, Santo Domingo, DN; tel. 682-2977; fax 221-2206; e-mail edomi@mreic.gov.ar; Ambassador NOEMI MARCÍA GOMEZ.

Belize: Carretera La Isabela, Calle Proyecto 3, Arroyo Manzano 1, Santo Domingo, DN; tel. 567-7146; fax 567-7159; e-mail domrep@embelize.org; internet www.embelize.org; Ambassador R. EDUARDO LAMA S.

Brazil: Eduardo Vicioso 46A, esq. Avda Winston Churchill, Ensanche Bella Vista, Apdo 1655, Santo Domingo, DN; tel. 532-0868; fax 532-0917; e-mail contato@embajadadebrasil.org.do; internet www.embajadadebrasil.org.do; Ambassador JOÃO SOLANO CARNEIRO DA CUNHA.

Canada: Avda Winston Churchill 1099, Torre Citigroup en Acrópolis Center, 18°, Ensanche Piantini, Apdo 2054, Santo Domingo, DN; tel. 262-3100; fax 262-3108; e-mail sdmgo@international.gc.ca; internet www.canadainternational.gc.ca/dominican_republic-republique_dominicaine; Ambassador TODD KUIACK.

Chile: Avda Anacaona 11, Mirador del Sur, Santo Domingo, DN; tel. 532-7800; fax 530-8310; e-mail embaj.chile@verizon.net.do; Ambassador MANUEL ENRIQUE HINOJOSA MUÑOZ.

Colombia: Fernando Escobar 8, Ensanche Serralles, Santo Domingo, DN; tel. 562-5282; fax 562-3253; e-mail erdomini@cancilleria.gov.co; internet www.embajadaenrepublicadominicana.gov.co; Chargé d'affaires a.i. MARÍA FERNANDA POTES PAIER.

Costa Rica: Calle Malaquías Gil 11 Altos, entre Abraham Lincoln y Lope de Vega, Ensanche Serralles, Santo Domingo, DN; tel. 683-7209; fax 565-6467; e-mail emb.costarica@codetel.net; Ambassador JOSÉ RAFAEL TORRES CASTRO.

Cuba: Francisco Prats Ramírez 808, El Millón, Santo Domingo, DN; tel. 537-2113; fax 537-9820; e-mail embadom@verizon.net.do; internet embacu.cubaminrex.cu/dominicana; Ambassador ALEXIS BANDRICH VEGA.

Ecuador: Edif. Optica Félix, Penthouse 601, Avda Abraham Lincoln 1007, Ensanche Piantini, Santo Domingo, DN; tel. 563-8363; fax 563-8153; e-mail mecuador@verizon.net.do; Ambassador CARLOS LÓPEZ DAMM.

El Salvador: Edif. Odontología Dominicana, 4°, Calle Haim López Penha 32, Ensanche Piantini, Santo Domingo, DN; tel. 565-4311; fax 541-7503; e-mail emb.salvador@codetel.net.do; Ambassador AMERICA MAURO ARAUJO.

France: Calle Las Damas 42, esq. El Conde, Zona Colonial, Santo Domingo, DN; tel. 695-4300; fax 695-4311; e-mail ambafrance@ambafrance-do.org; internet www.ambafrance.org.do; Ambassador BLANDINE KREISS.

Germany: Edif. Torre Piantini, 16° y 17°, Calle Gustavo Mejía Ricart 196, esq. Avda Abraham Lincoln, Ensanche Piantini, Santo Domingo, DN; tel. 542-8949; fax 542-8955; e-mail info@santo-domingo.diplo.de; internet www.santo-domingo.diplo.de; Ambassador THOMAS C. BRUNS.

Guatemala: Edif. Corominas Pepín, 9°, Avda 27 de Febrero 233, Santo Domingo, DN; tel. 381-0249; fax 381-0278; e-mail embrepdominicana@minex.gob.gt; Ambassador GIOVANNI RENÉ CASTILLO POLANCO.

Haiti: Calle Juan Sánchez Ramírez 33, esq. Desiderio Valdez 33, Zona Universitaria, Santo Domingo, DN; tel. 686-8185; fax 686-6096; e-mail embajadahaiti@yahoo.com; Ambassador Dr FRITZ N. CINEAS.

Holy See: Avda Máximo Gómez 27, esq. César Nicolás Penson, Apdo 312, Santo Domingo, DN (Apostolic Nunciature); tel. 682-3773; fax 687-0287; Apostolic Nuncio Most Rev. JÓZEF WESOŁOWSKI (Titular Archbishop of Slebte).

Honduras: Calle Arístides García Mella, esq. Rodríguez Objío, Edif. El Buen Pastor VI, Apt 1B, 1°, Mirador del Sur, Santo Domingo, DN; tel. 482-7992; fax 482-7505; e-mail e.honduras@codetel.net.do; Ambassador MARÍA EUGENIA BARRIOS ALEMÁN.

Israel: Calle Pedro Henríquez Ureña 80, La Esperilla, Santo Domingo, DN; tel. 472-0774; fax 472-1785; e-mail info@santodomingo.mfa.gov.il; internet santodomingo.mfa.gov.il; Ambassador MOSHE SERMONETTA.

Italy: Calle Rodríguez Objío 4, Gazcue, Santo Domingo, DN; tel. 682-0830; fax 682-8296; e-mail ambsdom.mail@esteri.it; internet www.ambsantodomingo.esteri.it; Ambassador ARTURO OLIVIERI.

Jamaica: Avda Sarasota 36, Bella Vista, Plaza Kury, Suite 304, Santo Domingo, DN; tel. 567-7770; fax 620-2497; e-mail emb.jamaica@codetel.net.do; internet www.embajadadejamaica-rd.com; Chargé d'affaires a.i. THOMAS F. ALLAN MARLEY.

Japan: Torre BHD, 8°, Avda Winston Churchill, esq. Luis F. Thomén, Ensanche Evaristo Morales, Apdo 9825, Santo Domingo, DN; tel. 567-3365; fax 566-8013; e-mail embjpn@codetel.net.do; internet www.do.emb-japan.go.jp; Ambassador SOICHI SATO.

Korea, Republic: Calle Maney 13, Los Cacicazgos, Santo Domingo, DN; tel. 482-6505; fax 482-6504; e-mail embcod@mofat.go.kr; internet dom.mofat.go.kr; Ambassador PARK DONG-SIL.

Mexico: Arzobispo Meriño 265, esq. Las Mercedes, Zona Colonial, Santo Domingo, DN; tel. 687-7793; fax 687-7872; e-mail embamex@codetel.net.do; Ambassador JOSÉ IGNACIO PIÑA ROJAS.

Morocco: Avda Abraham Lincoln 1009, Edif. Profesional EFA, 6°, Ensanche Piantini, Santo Domingo, DN; tel. 732-0409; fax 732-1703; e-mail sifamasdomingo@codetel.net.do; Ambassador IBRAHIM HOUSSEIN MOUSSA.

Netherlands: Max Henríquez Ureña 50, entre Avda Winston Churchill y Abraham Lincoln, Ensanche Piantini, Apdo 855, Santo

Domingo, DN; tel. 262-0320; fax 565-4685; e-mail std@minbuza.nl; internet www.holanda.org.do; Ambassador Rita D. Rahman.

Nicaragua: Avda Helios, Calle Corozal, No 6, Bella Vista, Santo Domingo, DN; tel. 535-1120; fax 535-1230; e-mail embanic-rd@codetel.net.do; Ambassador Rosa Adilia Vizcaya Briones.

Panama: Benito Monción 255, Gazcue, Santo Domingo, DN; tel. 688-3789; fax 685-3665; e-mail emb.panam@codetel.net.do; Chargé d'affaires a.i. Alberto Magno Castillero Pinilla.

Peru: Calle Mayreni 31, Urb. Los Cacicazgos, Santo Domingo, DN; tel. 482-3300; fax 482-3334; e-mail embaperu@verizon.net.do; Ambassador Vicente Azula de la Guerra.

Qatar: Avda Sarasota 7, Santo Domingo, DN; tel. 533-7526; fax 532-8974; Ambassador Saud Abd al-Aziz al-Sowaidi.

Spain: Avda Independencia 1205, Apdo 1468, Santo Domingo, DN; tel. 535-6500; fax 535-1595; e-mail embespdo@correo.mae.es; internet www.mae.es/embajadas/santodomingo; Ambassador Jaume Segura Socias.

Switzerland: Edif. Aeromar, 2°, Avda Winston Churchill 71, esq. Desiderio Arias, Bella Vista, Apdo 3626, Santo Domingo, DN; tel. 533-3781; fax 532-3781; e-mail sdd.vertretung@eda.admin.ch; internet www.eda.admin.ch/santodomingo; Ambassador Jacques Gremaud.

Taiwan (Republic of China): Avda Rómulo Betancourt 1360, Secto Bella Vista, Santo Domingo, DN; tel. 508-6200; fax 508-6335; e-mail dom@mofa.gov.tw; internet www.taiwanembassy.org/DO; Ambassador Tomás Ping Fu Hou.

United Kingdom: Edif. Corominas Pepin, 7°, Avda 27 de Febrero 233, Santo Domingo, DN; tel. 472-7111; fax 472-7574; e-mail brit.emb.sadom@codetel.net.do; internet ukindominicanrepublic.fco.gov.uk; Ambassador Steven Fisher.

USA: Avda César Nicolás Pensón, esq. Leopoldo Navarro, Santo Domingo, DN; tel. 221-2171; fax 686-7437; e-mail irc@usemb.gov.do; internet santodomingo.usembassy.gov; Ambassador Raul H. Yzaguirre.

Uruguay: Edif. Gapo, Local 401, Avda Luis F. Thomen 110, Ensanche Evaristo Morales, Santo Domingo, DN; tel. 227-3475; fax 472-4231; e-mail embur@codetel.net.do; Ambassador Luis Alberto Carrese Prieto.

Venezuela: Avda Anacoana 7, Mirador del Sur, Santo Domingo, DN; tel. 537-8882; fax 537-8780; e-mail embvenezuela@codetel.net.do; internet www.embavenezdominicana.org; Ambassador Eduardo Alfredo Murga.

Judicial System

The Judicial Power resides in the Suprema Corte de Justicia (Supreme Court of Justice), the Cortes de Apelación (Courts of Appeal), the Juzgados de Primera Instancia (Tribunals of First Instance), the municipal courts and the other judicial authorities provided by law. The Supreme Court is composed of 16 judges and the Attorney-General, and exercises disciplinary authority over all the members of the judiciary. The Attorney-General of the Republic is the Chief of Judicial Police and of the Public Ministry, which he or she represents before the Supreme Court of Justice. The Consejo Nacional de la Magistratura (National Judiciary Council) appoints the members of the Supreme Court, which in turn appoints judges at all other levels of the judicial system.

Suprema Corte de Justicia

Centro de los Héroes, Calle Juan de Dios Ventura Simó, esq. Enrique Jiménez Moya, Apdo 1485, Santo Domingo, DN; tel. 533-3191; fax 532-2906; e-mail suprema.corte@verizon.net.do; internet www.suprema.gov.do.

President: Dr Jorge A. Subero Isa.

Vice-President and President of First Court: Dr Rafael Luciano Pichardo.

Second Vice-President: Dra Eglys Margarita Esmurdoc Castellanos.

President of Second Court: Dr Hugo Álvarez Valencia.

Justices: Dra Margarita A. Tavares, Víctor José Castellanos Estrella, Dr Julio Ibarra Ríos, Dr Edgar Hernández Mejía, Dra Dulce M. Rodríguez de Goris, Dra Ana Rosa Bergés Dreyfous, Dr Juan Luperón Vásquez, Dr Julio Aníbal Suárez, Dra Enilda Reyes Pérez, Dr José Enrique Hernández Machado, Dr Pedro Romero Confesor, Dr Darío Octavio Fernández Espinal.

Attorney-General: Dr Radhamés Jiménez Peña.

Religion

The majority of the inhabitants belong to the Roman Catholic Church, but freedom of worship exists for all denominations. The Baptist, Evangelist and Seventh-day Adventist churches and the Jewish faith are also represented.

CHRISTIANITY

The Roman Catholic Church

The Dominican Republic comprises two archdioceses and nine dioceses. Roman Catholics represent about 87% of the population.

Bishops' Conference

Conferencia del Episcopado Dominicano, Apdo 186, Calle Isabel la Católica 55, Santo Domingo, DN; tel. 685-3141; fax 685-0227; e-mail nicolas.clr@codetel.net.do; internet www.ced.org.do.

f. 1985; Pres. Cardinal Nicolás de Jesús López Rodríguez (Archbishop of Santo Domingo).

Archbishop of Santiago de los Caballeros: Most Rev. Ramón Benito de la Rosa y Carpio, Arzobispado, Duvergé 14, Apdo 679, Santiago de los Caballeros; tel. 582-2094; fax 581-3580; e-mail arzobisp.stgo@verizon.net.do.

Archbishop of Santo Domingo: Cardinal Nicolás de Jesús López Rodríguez, Arzobispado, Isabel la Católica 55, Apdo 186, Santo Domingo, DN; tel. 685-3141; fax 688-7270; e-mail nicolas.clr@codetel.net.do.

The Anglican Communion

Anglicans in the Dominican Republic are under the jurisdiction of the Episcopal Church in the USA. The country is classified as a missionary diocese, in Province IX.

Bishop of the Dominican Republic: Rt Rev. Julio César Holguín Khoury, Santiago 114, Apdo 764, Santo Domingo, DN; tel. 688-6016; fax 686-6364; e-mail iglepidom@verizon.net.do; internet www.dominicanepiscopalchurch.org.

BAHÁ'Í FAITH

National Spiritual Assembly of the Bahá'ís of the Dominican Republic: Cambronal 152, esq. Beller, Santo Domingo, DN; tel. 687-1726; fax 687-7606; e-mail bahai.rd.aen@verizon.net.do; internet www.bahai.org.do; f. 1961; 402 localities.

The Press

Dirección General de Información, Publicidad y Prensa: Palacio Nacional, Santo Domingo, DN; f. 1983; govt supervisory body; Dir Rafael Núñez.

DAILIES

El Caribe: Calle Doctor Defilló 4, Los Prados, Apdo 416, Santo Domingo, DN; tel. 683-8100; fax 544-4003; e-mail editora@elcaribe.com.do; internet www.elcaribe.com.do; f. 1948; morning; Pres. Félix M. García; Dir Manuel A. Quiroz; circ. 32,000.

El Día: Avda San Martín 236, Santo Domingo, DN; tel. 565-5581; fax 540-1697; e-mail eldia@eldia.com.do; internet www.eldia.com.do; f. 2002; Dir Rafael Molina Morillo; Editor Franklin Puello.

Diario Libre: Avda Abraham Lincoln, esq. Max Henríquez Ureña, Santo Domingo, DN; tel. 476-7200; fax 616-1520; internet www.diariolibre.com; Dir Adriano Miguel Tejada; Editor Eli Heiliger.

Hoy: Avda San Martín 236, Santo Domingo, DN; tel. 565-5581; fax 567-2424; e-mail hoydigital@hoy.com.do; internet www.hoy.com.do; f. 1981; morning; Dir Alvarez Vega; Man. Editors Claudio Acosta, Marien Capitán; circ. 40,000.

La Información: Carretera Licey, Km 3, Santiago de los Caballeros; tel. 581-1915; fax 581-7770; e-mail e.informacion@codetel.net.do; internet lainformacion.com.do; f. 1915; morning; Dir Fernando A. Pérez Memén; circ. 15,000.

Listín Diario: Paseo de los Periodistas 52, Ensanche Miraflores, Santo Domingo, DN; tel. 686-6688; fax 686-6595; e-mail info@listindiario.com.do; internet www2.listindiario.com; f. 1889; morning; bought in mid-2010; Dir-Gen. Miguel Franjul; Editor-in-Chief Fabio Cabral; circ. 60,000.

El Nacional: Avda San Martín 236, Santo Domingo, DN; tel. 565-5581; fax 565-4190; e-mail elnacional@elnacional.com.do; internet www.elnacional.com.do; f. 1966; evening and Sun.; Dir Radhamés Gómez Pepín; circ. 45,000.

El Nuevo Diario: Avda Francia 41, Santo Domingo, DN; tel. 687-7450; fax 687-3205; e-mail redaccionnd@gmail.com; internet www.elnuevodiario.com.do; f. 1981; morning; Exec. Dir Cosette Bonnelly; Editor Luis Brito.

PERIODICALS

¡Ahora!: San Martín 236, Apdo 1402, Santo Domingo, DN; tel. 565-5581; e-mail revistaahora@internet.net.do; internet www.ahora.com.do; f. 1962; weekly; Editor RAFAEL MOLINA MORILLO.

Arquitexto: Gustavo Mejía Ricart 37, 6°, Ensanche Naco, Apdo 560, Santo Domingo, DN; tel. 732-7674; e-mail arquitexto@arquitexto.com; internet arquitexto.com; f. 1985; 4 a year; architecture; Editor CARMEN ORTEGA.

Gestión: Torre Piantini, Suite 903, Avda Abraham Lincoln, esq. Gustavo Mejía Ricart, Santo Domingo, DN; tel. 542-0126; fax 540-1982; internet www.gestion.com.do; f. 2008; Editor NEY DIAZ.

Novus Dominicana: Progreso Business Center, 8°, Avda Lope de Vega 13, Ensanche Naco, Santo Domingo, DN; tel. 289-2022; fax 341-8877; e-mail info@novusdominicana.com; internet www.novusdominicana.com; Gen. Man DAVIDE VIANELLO.

Pandora: Calle Doctor Defilló 4, Los Prados, Apdo 416, Santo Domingo, DN; tel. 683-8504; fax 544-4003; e-mail pandora@elcaribe.com.do; internet www.pandora.com.do; f. 2003; 2 a month; Editor AIRAM TORIBIO.

Refugios: Edif. Tres Robles, Calle Freddy Prestol Castillo 23, Apto 1-C, Piantini, Santo Domingo, DN; tel. and fax 732-0421; e-mail info@coralcomunicaciones.com; internet www.refugiosmagazine.com; f. 2007; 6 a year; travel; Pres. LAURA DE LA NUEZ.

Revista Social Sports: Avda José Horacio Rodriguez, La Vega; tel. 977-0117; internet www.revistasocialsports.com; monthly; Pres. JULIO ALBERTO SUÁREZ.

Visión Agropecuaria: Autopista Duarte, Km 6.5, Los Jardines del Norte, Santo Domingo, DN; tel. 547-1193; e-mail visionagropecuaria27@gmail.com; newsletter of the Secretariat of State for Agriculture; 6 a year; Dir WILFREDO POLANCO; Editor ANTONIO CÁCERES.

NEWS AGENCY

La Noticia: Julio Verne 14, Santo Domingo, DN; tel. 535-0815; f. 1973; evening; Pres. JOSÉ A. BREA PEÑA; Dir BOLÍVAR BELLO.

Publishers

Editora Alfa y Omega: José Contreras 69, Santo Domingo, DN; tel. 532-5578; e-mail alpha.omgea@codetel.net.do.

Editora El Caribe, C por A: Calle Doctor Defilló 4, Los Prados, Apdo 416, Santo Domingo, DN; tel. 683-8100; fax 544-4003; e-mail editora@elcaribe.com.do; internet www.elcaribe.com.do; f. 1948; Pres. FÉLIX GARCÍA.

Editora Hoy, C por A: Avda San Martín 436, Santo Domingo, DN; tel. 566-1147.

Editora Listín Diario, C por A: P. A. Lluberes 182, La Romana; tel. 550-6688; f. 1889.

Editorama, SA: Calle Eugenio Contreras, No 54, Los Trinitarios, Apdo 2074, Santo Domingo, DN; tel. 596-6669; fax 594-1421; e-mail editorama@editorama.com; internet www.editorama.com; f. 1970; Pres. JUAN ANTONIO QUIÑONES MARTE.

Grupo Editorial Norma: Calle D, Zona Industrial de Herrera, Santo Domingo, DN; tel. 274-3333; e-mail editoranorma@codetel.net.do; internet www.norma.com.do.

Grupo Editorial Oceano: Edif. Calidad a Tiempo, 2°, Calle J, esq. Calle L, Zona Industrial de Herrera, Santo Domingo, DN; tel. 537-0832; fax 537-5187; e-mail info@oceano.com.do; internet www.oceano.com.

Publicaciones Ahora, C por A: Avda San Martín 236, Apdo 1402, Santo Domingo, DN; tel. 565-5580; fax 565-4190; Pres. JULIO A. MORENO.

ASSOCIATIONS

Asociación Dominicana de Libreros y Afines (Asodolibro): Calle Espaillat 201, entre El Conde y Arzobispo Nou, Santo Domingo, DN; tel. 688-8425; fax 689-3865; e-mail asodolibro@codetel.net.do; Pres. DENNIS PEÑA.

Cámara Dominicana del Libro, Inc: Arzobispo Nouel 160, Santo Domingo, DN; tel. 682-1032; fax 686-6110; e-mail camaradominicanadellibro@hotmail.com; internet www.camaradominicanadellibro.com; f. 1970; Pres. DENNIS PEÑA; Sec. JACQUELINE DÍAZ.

Broadcasting and Communications

Instituto Dominicano de las Telecomunicaciones (INDOTEL): Avda Abraham Lincoln, No 962, Edif. Osiris, CP 10148, Santo Domingo, DN; tel. 732-5555; fax 732-3904; e-mail centrodeasistencia@indotel.org.do; internet www.indotel.org.do; f. 1998; Pres. Dr DAVID PÉREZ TAVERAS; Exec. Dir Dr JOELLE EXARHAKOS.

TELECOMMUNICATIONS

Compañía Dominicana de Teléfonos, C por A (Claro—Codetel): Avda John F. Kennedy 54, Apdo 1377, Santo Domingo, DN; tel. 220-1111; fax 543-1301; e-mail servicioalcliente@codetel.net.do; internet www.codetel.net.do; f. 1930; owned by América Móvil, SA de CV (Mexico); operates mobile services as Claro and fixed-line services as Codetel; Pres. OSCAR PEÑA CHACÓN.

Ericsson República Dominicana: Edif. Empresarial Hylsa, 2°, Avda Winston Churchill, esq. Víctor Garrido Puello, Santo Domingo, DN; tel. 683-7701; fax 616-0962; e-mail media.relations@ericsson.com; internet www.ericsson.com/do; f. 2000; mobile cellular telephone network provider; subsidiary of Telefon AB LM Ericsson (Sweden); Country Man. PETER FÄLLMAN.

Orange Dominicana, SA: Calle Víctor Garrido Puello 23, Edif. Orange, Ensanche Piantini, Santo Domingo, DN; tel. 859-1000; fax 539-8454; e-mail servicio.cliente@orange.com.do; internet www.orange.com.do; f. 2000; mobile cellular telephone operator, providing GSM network coverage to 89% of the Dominican Republic population; subsidiary of Orange, SA (France); Pres. JEAN MARC HARION.

Tricom Telecomunicaciones de Voz, Data y Video: Avda Lope de Vega 95, Ensanche Naco, Santo Domingo, DN; tel. 476-6000; fax 476-6700; e-mail sc@tricom.com.do; internet www.tricom.net; f. 1992; Pres. and CEO HÉCTOR CASTRO NOBOA; Gen. Man. CARLOS ESCOBAR.

BROADCASTING

Radio

There were some 130 commercial stations in the Dominican Republic. The government-owned broadcasting network, Corporación Estatal de Radio y Televisión (see Television), operates three radio stations.

Asociación Dominicana de Radiodifusoras Inc (ADORA): Calle Paul Harris 3, Centro de los Héroes, Santo Domingo, DN; tel. 535-4057; fax 535-4058; e-mail adora.org.do@gmail.com; internet adora-do.blogspot.com; f. 1967; Pres. SANDRA PONS.

Cadena de Noticias (CDN) Radio: Calle Doctor Defilló 4, Los Prados, Apdo 416, Santo Domingo, DN; tel. 683-8100; fax 544-4003; e-mail inforadio@cdn.com.do; internet www.cdn.com.do.

Television

Antena Latina, Canal 7: Avda Gustavo Mejía Ricart 45, Ensanche Naco, Santo Domingo, DN; tel. 412-0707; fax 333-0707; e-mail contacto@antenalatina7.com; internet www.antenalatina7.com; f. 1999; Pres. JOSÉ MIGUEL BONETTI.

Cadena de Noticias (CDN) Televisión: Calle Doctor Defilló 4, Los Prados, Apdo 416, Santo Domingo, DN; tel. 262-2100; fax 567-2671; e-mail direccion@cdn.com.do; internet www.cdn.com.do; broadcasts news on Channel 37; Dir FERNANDO HASBÚN.

Color Visión, Canal 9: Emilio A. Morel, esq. Luis Pérez, Ensanche La Fe, Apdo 30043, Santo Domingo, DN; tel. 566-5875; fax 732-9347; e-mail color.vision@colorvision.com.do; internet www.colorvision.com.do; f. 1969; majority-owned by Corporación Dominicana de Radio y Televisión; commercial station; Dir-Gen. MANUEL ANTONIO QUIROZ MIRANDA.

Corporación Estatal de Radio y Televisión (CERTV): Dr Tejada Florentino 8, Apdo 869, Santo Domingo, DN; tel. 689-2120; e-mail rm.colombo@codetel.net.do; internet www.certvdominicana.com; f. 1952; fmrly Radio Televisión Dominicana, Canal 4; changed name as above in 2003; govt station; Channel 4; Pres. ELISEO PÉREZ; Dir-Gen. PEDRO J. BATISTA CABA.

Teleantillas, Canal 2: Autopista Duarte, Km 7½, Los Prados, Apdo 30404, Santo Domingo, DN; tel. 567-7751; fax 540-4912; e-mail webmaster@tele-antillas.tv; internet www.tele-antillas.tv; f. 1979; Gen. Man. HÉCTOR VALENTÍN BÁEZ.

Telecentro, Canal 13: Avda Luperón 25, Herrera, Santo Domingo, DN; tel. 334-3040; fax 274-0599; e-mail tele.centro@telecentro.com.do; internet www.telecentro.com.do; f. 1986; Santo Domingo and east region; Pres. NELSON GUILLÉN.

Telemedios Dominicanos, Canal 25: 16 de Agosto, Santo Domingo, DN; tel. 583-2525; internet www.canal25net.tv; f. 1999; Dir CÉSAR HERNÁNDEZ.

Telemicro, Canal 5: Edif. Telemicro, Calle Mariano Cestero, esq. Enrique Henríquez 1, Gazcue, Santo Domingo, DN; tel. 689-0555; fax 686-6528; e-mail programacion@telemicro.com.do; internet www.telemicro.com.do; f. 1982; Dir DOMINGO DEL PILLAR.

Telesistema, Canal 11: Avda 27 de Febrero 52, esq. Máximo Gómez, Sector Bergel, Santo Domingo, DN; tel. 563-6661; fax 472-1754; e-mail info@telesistema11.tv; internet www.telesistema11.tv; Pres. José L. Correpio.

Finance

(cap. = capital; res = reserves; dep. = deposits; m. = million; brs = branches; amounts in pesos)

BANKING

Supervisory Body

Superintendencia de Bancos: 52 Avda México, esq. Leopoldo Navarro, Apdo 1326, Santo Domingo, DN; tel. 685-8141; fax 685-0859; e-mail nmolina@supbanco.gov.do; internet www.supbanco.gov.do; f. 1947; Supt Haivanjoe Ng Cortiñas.

Central Bank

Banco Central de la República Dominicana: Calle Pedro Henríquez Ureña, esq. Leopoldo Navarro, Apdo 1347, Santo Domingo, DN; tel. 221-9111; fax 687-7488; e-mail info@bancentral.gov.do; internet www.bancentral.gov.do; f. 1947; cap. 2,371.3m., res 1.0m., dep. 312,156.4m. (Dec. 2009); Gov. Héctor Valdez Albizu; Man. Pedro Silverio Alvarez.

Commercial Banks

Banco BHD, SA: Avda 27 de Febrero, esq. Avda Winston Churchill, Santo Domingo, DN; tel. 243-3232; fax 541-4949; e-mail servicio@bhd.com.do; internet www.bhd.com.do; f. 1972; cap. 5,658.9m., res 1,241.5m., dep. 71,427.1m. (Dec. 2010); Pres. Luis Eugenio Molina Achécar; 80 brs.

Banco Dominicano del Progreso, SA (Progreso): Avda John F. Kennedy 3, Apdo 1329, Santo Domingo, DN; tel. 378-3201; fax 227-3137; e-mail informacion@progreso.com.do; internet www.progreso.com.do; f. 1974; merged with Banco Metropolitano, SA, and Banco de Desarrollo Dominicano, SA, in 2000; cap. 4,228.6m., res –2,543.9m., dep. 21,884.8m. (Dec. 2009); Pres. Juan B. Vicini Lluberes; 20 brs.

Banco Múltiple Leon, SA: Avda John F. Kennedy 135, esq. Tiradentes, Apdo 1502, Santo Domingo, DN; tel. 476-2000; fax 473-2050; e-mail info@leon.com.do; internet www.leon.com.do; f. 1981; fmrly Banco Nacional de Crédito, SA; became Bancrédito, SA, in 2002; adopted current name Dec. 2003; cap. 2,620.3m., res 373.2m., dep. 33,506m. (Dec. 2010); Pres. and CEO Manuel Peña-Morros; 56 brs.

Banco Popular Dominicano: Avda John F. Kennedy 20, Torre Popular, Apdo 1441, Santo Domingo, DN; tel. 544-5555; fax 544-5899; e-mail contactenos@bpd.com.do; internet www.bpd.com.do; f. 1963; cap. 9,317.3m., res 3,312.8m., dep. 153,494.4m. (Dec. 2010); Pres., Chair. and Gen. Man. Manuel Alejandro Grullón; 187 brs.

Banco de Reservas de la República Dominicana (Banreservas): Isabel la Católica 201, Apdo 1353, Santo Domingo, DN; tel. 960-2000; fax 685-0602; e-mail mensajeadministrador@banreservas.com; internet www.banreservas.com.do; f. 1941; state-owned; cap. 3,500.0m., res 6,678.5m., dep. 96,012m. (Dec. 2009); Pres. Daniel Toribio (Secretary of State for Finance); Administrator Vicente Bengoa Albizu; 195 brs.

Development Banks

Banco ADEMI, SA: Avda Pedro Henríquez Ureña 78, La Esperilla, Santo Domingo, DN; tel. 683-0853; internet www.bancoademi.com.do; f. 1998; Pres. Manuel Arsenio Ureña.

Banco Agrícola de la República Dominicana: Avda G. Washington 601, Apdo 1057, Santo Domingo, DN; tel. 535-8088; fax 535-8022; e-mail bagricola@bagricola.gov.do; internet www.bagricola.gov.do; f. 1945; govt agricultural devt bank; Gen. Man. and Chair. Paíno Abreu Collado.

Banco BDI, SA: Avda Sarasota 27, esq. La Julia, Santo Domingo, DN; tel. 535-8586; fax 508-4390; internet www.bdi.com.do; f. 1974; Contact Jorge Abreu.

STOCK EXCHANGE

Bolsa de Valores de la República Dominicana, SA: Edif. Empresarial, 1°, Avda John F. Kennedy 16, Apdo 25144, Santo Domingo, DN; tel. 567-6694; fax 567-6697; e-mail info@bolsard.com; internet www.bolsard.com; Pres. María Antonia Esteva de Bisono; Gen. Man. Darys Estrella.

INSURANCE

Supervisory Body

Superintendencia de Seguros: Secretaría de Estado de Finanzas, Avda México 54, esq. Leopoldo Navarro, Apdo 2207, Santo Domingo, DN; tel. 221-2606; fax 685-5096; e-mail info@superseguros.gob.do; internet www.superseguros.gob.do; f. 1969; Supt Euclides Gutiérrez Félix.

Insurance Companies

Angloamericana de Seguros, SA: Avda Gustavo Mejía Ricard 8, esq. Hermanos Roque Martínez, Ensanche El Millón, Santo Domingo, DN; tel. 227-1002; fax 227-6005; e-mail angloseguros@angloamericana.com.do; internet www.angloamericana.com.do; f. 1996; Pres. Nelson Hedi Hernández P.; Vice-Pres. Esteban Betances Fabré.

ARS Palic Salud: Edif. ARS Palic Salud, Avda 27 de Febrero 50, Urb. El Vergel, Santo Domingo, DN; tel. 381-5000; fax 381-4646; e-mail servicios@arspalic.com.do; internet www.arspalic.com.do; fmrly Cía de Seguros Palic, SA; acquired by Centro Financiero BHD in 1998; changed name as above in 2003; Exec. Vice-Pres. Andrés Mejía.

Aseguradora Agropecuaria Dominicana, SA (AGRODOSA): Avda Independencia 455, Gazcue, Santo Domingo, DN; tel. 562-6849; fax 687-4790; e-mail agrodosa@claro.net.do; agricultural sector; Exec. Dir Agron Emilio Olivo Toribio.

Atlántica Insurance, SA: Avda 27 de Febrero 365a, 2°, Apdo 826, Santo Domingo, DN; tel. 565-5591; fax 565-4343; e-mail atlanticains@codetel.net.do; Pres. Rhina Ramirez; Gen. Man. Lic. Gerardo Peralta.

BMI Compañía de Seguros, SA: Edif. Alfonso Comercial, Avda Tiradentes 14, Apdo 916, Ensanche Naco, Santo Domingo, DN; tel. 562-6660; fax 562-6849; e-mail reclamos@bmi.com.do; internet www.bmi.com.do; f. 1998; Exec. Vice-Pres. Hubert Weichselbaumer; Gen. Man. Efrén Ortiz.

Bupa Dominicana,SA: Avda Lope de Vega 13, casi esq. Avda Roberto Pastoriza, Plaza Progreso Business Center, Suite 310, Santo Domingo, DN; tel. 566-7759; fax 565-6451; e-mail dr@bupalatinamerica.com; internet www.bupalatinamerica.com; fmrly Amedex Insurance Co; Gen. Man. Ingrid Reynoso.

Caribbean American Life and General Insurance Co, C por A: Edif. ALICO, 5°, Avda Abraham Lincoln, Apdo 131, Santo Domingo, DN; tel. 533-7131; fax 535-0362; e-mail caribalico@codetel.net.do; general; Gen. Man. Francisco Cabreja.

Cía Dominicana De Seguros, C por A: Avda 27 de Febrero 302, Bella Vista, Santo Domingo, DN; tel. 535-1030; fax 533-2576; e-mail dominicana.seg@codetel.net.do; internet www.dominicanadeseguros.com; f. 1960; Pres. Ramón Molina; CEO Víctor J. Rojas.

La Colonial, SA: Avda Sarasota 75, Bella Vista, Santo Domingo, DN; tel. 508-8000; fax 508-0608; e-mail luis.guerrero@lacolonial.com.do; internet www.lacolonial.com.do; f. 1971; general; Pres. Dr Miguel Feris Iglesias; Exec. Vice-Pres. Luis Eduardo Guerrero Román.

Confederación del Canadá Dominicana: Calle Salvador Sturla 17, Ensanche Naco, Apdo 30088, Santo Domingo, DN; tel. 544-4144; fax 540-4740; e-mail confedom@codetel.net.do; internet www.confedom.com; f. 1988; Pres. Lic. Moises A. Franco Llenas.

Cooperativa Nacional De Seguros, Inc (COOP-SEGUROS): Calle Hermanos Deligne 156, Gazcue, Santo Domingo, DN; tel. 682-6118; fax 682-6313; e-mail contacto@coopseguros.coop; internet coopseguros.coop; f. 1990; functions as a co-operative; general and life; Pres. Dr Ignacion Valenzuela.

Cuna Mutual Insurance Society Dominicana, C. por A: Edif. AIRAC, Avda Aristides Fiallo Cabral 258, Zona Universitaria, Santo Domingo, DN; tel. 682-2862; fax 687-2862; internet www.cunamutual.com.do/RepDom; f. 2010; Regional Man. Francisco Antonio Estepan Grisanty.

General de Seguros, SA: Avda Sarasota 55, esq. Pedro A. Bobea, Apdo 2183, Santo Domingo, DN; tel. 535-8888; fax 532-4451; e-mail info@gs.com.do; internet www.lageneraldeseguros.com; f. 1981; general; Pres. Dr Fernando A. Ballista Díaz.

Progreso Compañía de Seguros, SA (PROSEGUROS): Avda John F. Kennedy 1, Ensanche Miraflores, Santo Domingo, DN; tel. 985-5000; fax 985-5187; e-mail carlosro@progreso.com.do; internet www.proseguros.com.do; Pres. Gonzalo Alberto Pérez Rojas; CEO Carlos Romero.

REHSA Compañía de Seguros y Reaseguros: Avda Gustavo Mejía Ricart, esq. Hermanas Roques Martínez, Ensanche El Millón, Santo Domingo, DN; tel. 548-7171; fax 584-7222; e-mail info@rehsa.com.do; internet www.rehsa.com.do; Pres. Nelson Hernández.

Scotia Seguros: Avda Francia No 141, esq. Máximo Gómez, 3°, Sección 2, Gazcue, Santo Domingo, DN; tel. 730-4031; fax 686-2165; e-mail info@scotiaseguros.com.do; internet www.scotiaseguros.com.do; f. 2006; fmrly BBVA Seguros; Gen. Man. DENIS LISANDRO BERROCAL.

Seguros BanReservas: Avda Jiménez Moya, esq. Calle 4, Centro Technológico Banreservas, Ensanche La Paz, Santo Domingo, DN; tel. 960-7200; fax 960-5148; e-mail serviseguros@segbanreservas.com; internet www.segurosbanreservas.com; Pres. VICENTE BENGOA ALBIZU; Exec. Vice-Pres. HÉCTOR SABA PANTALEÓN.

Seguros Constitución: Calle Seminario 55, Ensanche Piantini, Santo Domingo, DN; tel. 620-0765; fax 412-8358; e-mail info@segurosconstitucion.com.do; internet www.segurosconstitucion.com.do; fmrly El Sol de Seguros; changed name as above in 2008; Gen. Man. JUAN JOSÉ GUERRERO GRILLASCA.

Seguros Pepín, SA: Edif. Corp. Corominas Pepín, Avda 27 de Febrero 233, Ensanche Naco, Santo Domingo, DN; tel. 472-1006; fax 565-9176; e-mail info@segurospepin.com; internet www.segurospepin.com; general; Pres. Dr BIENVENIDO COROMINAS PEPÍN; Exec. Vice-Pres. HÉCTOR COROMINAS PEÑA.

Seguros Universal: Avda Winston Churchill 1100, Evaristo Morales, Apdo 1242, Santo Domingo, DN; tel. 544-7200; fax 544-7999; e-mail eizquierda@segurospopular.com.do; internet www.universal.com.do; f. 1964 as La Universal de Seguros; merged with Grupo Asegurador América in 2000; name changed as above in 2006; general; Pres. ERNESTO IZQUIERDO; Exec. Vice-Pres. RAFAEL E. IZQUIERDO.

Unión de Seguros, C por A: Edif. B 101, Avda John F. Kennedy, Apartamental Proesa, Santo Domingo, DN; tel. 566-2191; fax 542-0065; e-mail a.cortina@codetel.net.do; internet uniondeseguros.com; f. 1964; Exec. Vice-Pres. ANGEL CORTINA.

Insurance Association

Cámara Dominicana de Aseguradores y Reaseguradores, Inc: Edif. Torre BHD, 5°, Luis F. Thomen, esq. Winston Churchill, Apdo 601, Santo Domingo, DN; tel. 566-0014; fax 566-2600; e-mail cadoar@codetel.net.do; internet www.cadoar.org.do; f. 1972; Pres. Dr LUIS EDUARDO GUERRERO; Exec. Vice-Pres. MIGUEL VILLAMÁN.

Trade and Industry

GOVERNMENT AGENCIES

Comisión Nacional de Energía (CNE): Calle Gustavo Mejía Ricart 73, esq. Agustín Lara, 3°, Ensanche Serralles, Santo Domingo, DN; tel. 732-2000; fax 547-2073; e-mail info@cne.gov.do; internet www.cne.gov.do; f. 2001; responsible for regulation and devt of energy sector; Pres. ENRIQUE RAMIREZ.

Comisión para la Reforma de la Empresa Pública: Edif. Gubernamental Dr Rafael Kasse Acta, 6°, Gustavo Mejía Ricart 73, esq. Agustín Lara, Ensanche Serrallés, Santo Domingo, DN; tel. 683-3591; fax 683-3114; e-mail Info@fonper.gov.do; internet www.fonper.gov.do; commission charged with divestment and restructuring of state enterprises; Pres. JOSÉ AUGUSTO IZQUIERDO.

Consejo Estatal del Azúcar (CEA) (State Sugar Council): Calle Fray Cipriano de Utrera, Centro de los Héroes, Apdo 1256/1258, Santo Domingo, DN; tel. 533-1161; fax 533-1305; internet www.cea.gov.do; f. 1966; management of operations contracted to private consortiums in 1999 and 2000; Dir-Gen. JUAN FRANCISCO MATOS CASTAÑO.

Instituto de Estabilización de Precios (INESPRE): Plaza de la Bandera, Apdo 86-2, Santo Domingo, DN; tel. 621-0020; fax 620-2588; e-mail informacion@inespre.gov.do; internet www.inespre.gov.do; f. 1969; price commission; Exec. Dir RICARDO JACOBO CABRERA.

Instituto Nacional de la Vivienda: Avda Pedro Henríquez Ureña, esq. Avda Alma Mater, Santo Domingo, DN; tel. 732-0600; fax 227-5803; e-mail invi@verizon.net.do; internet www.invi.gob.do; f. 1962; low-cost housing institute; Dir-Gen. ALMA FERNÁNADEZ DURÁN.

DEVELOPMENT ORGANIZATIONS

Centro para el Desarrollo Agropecuario y Forestal, Inc (CEDAF): Calle José Amado Soler 50, Ensanche Paraíso, CP 567-2, Santo Domingo, DN; tel. 565-5603; fax 544-4727; e-mail cedaf@cedaf.org.do; internet www.cedaf.org.do; f. 1987 to encourage the devt of agriculture, livestock and forestry; fmrly Fundación de Desarrollo Agropecuario, Inc; Pres. MARCIAL NAJRI; Exec. Dir JUAN JOSÉ ESPINAL.

Centro de Desarrollo y Competitividad Industrial (PROINDUSTRIA): Avda 27 de Febrero, esq. Avda Luperón, Plaza de las Banderas, Apdo 1462, Santo Domingo, DN; tel. 530-0010; fax 530-1303; e-mail info@proindustria.gov.do; internet www.proindustria.gov.do; f. 1962 as Corporación de Fomento Industrial; restructured and name changed as above in 2007; industrial sector regulator; Dir-Gen. ANGEL ROSARIO VIÑAS.

Fundación Dominicana de Desarrollo (Dominican Development Foundation): Mercedes No 4, Apdo 857, Santo Domingo, DN; tel. 688-8101; fax 686-0430; e-mail info@fdd.org.do; internet fdd.org.do; f. 1962 to mobilize private resources for collaboration in financing small-scale devt programmes; 384 mems; Pres. (2011–12) PEDRO GAMUNDI; Exec. Dir FRANCISCO J. ABATE.

Instituto de Desarrollo y Crédito Cooperativo (IDECOOP): Avda Héroes de Luperón 1, Centro de los Héroes, Apdo 1371, Santo Domingo, DN; tel. 533-8131; fax 533-5149; e-mail idecoop@codetel.net.do; internet idecoop.gov.do; f. 1963 to encourage the devt of co-operatives; Pres. PEDRO CORPORÁN CABRERA; Dir CARLOS JUNIOR ESPINAL.

CHAMBERS OF COMMERCE

Cámara Americana de Comercio de la República Dominicana: Torre Empresarial, 6°, Avda Sarasota 20, Apdo 99999, Santo Domingo, DN; tel. 381-0777; fax 381-0286; e-mail amcham@codetel.net.do; internet www.amcham.org.do; Pres. JULIO V. BRACHE ALVAREZ; Exec. Vice-Pres. WILLIAM M. MALAMUD.

Cámara de Comercio y Producción de Santo Domingo: Arzobispo Nouel 206, Zona Colonial, Apdo 815, Santo Domingo, DN; tel. 682-2688; fax 685-2228; e-mail ccpsd@camarasantodomingo.org.do; internet www.camarasantodomingo.org.do; f. 1910; 1,500 active mems; Pres. MARÍA ISABEL GASSÓ; Exec. Vice-Pres. MILAGROS J. PUELLO.

INDUSTRIAL AND TRADE ASSOCIATIONS

Asociación Dominicana de Hacendados y Agricultores (ADHA): 265 Avda 27 de Febrero, al lado de Plaza Central, Santo Domingo, DN; tel. 565-0542; fax 565-8696; farming and agricultural org.; Pres. RICARDO BARCELÓ.

Asociación Dominicana de la Industria Eléctrica (ADIE): Calle Gustavo Mejía Ricart, esq. Avda Abraham Lincoln, Torre Piantini, 5°, Local 502-B, Ensanche Piantini, Santo Domingo, DN; tel. 547-2109; e-mail info@adie.org.do; internet www.adie.org.do; f. 2009; electrical industry asscn; Pres. TITO SANJURJO.

Asociación Dominicana de Zonas Francas Inc (ADOZONA): Avda Sarasota 20, 4°, Torre Empresarial AIRD, Apdo 3184, Santo Domingo, DN; tel. 472-0251; fax 472-0256; e-mail info@adozona.org; internet www.adozona.org; f. 1988; Pres. AQUÍLES BERMÚDEZ; Exec. Vice-Pres. JOSÉ MANUEL TORRES.

Asociación de Industrias de la República Dominicana, Inc: Avda Sarasota 20, Torre Empresarial AIRD, 12°, Santo Domingo, DN; tel. 472-0000; fax 472-0303; e-mail aird@verizon.net.do; internet www.aird.org.do; f. 1962; industrial org.; Pres. LIGIA BONETTI DE VALIENTE; Exec. Vice-Pres. CIRCE ALMÁNZAR MELGÉN.

Centro de Exportacióne e Inversión de la República Dominicana (CEI-RD): Avda 27 de Febrero, esq. Avda Gregorio Luperón, Los Restauradores, Apdo 199-2, Santo Domingo, DN; tel. 530-5505; fax 530-8208; e-mail webmaster@cei-rd.gov.do; internet www.cei-rd.gov.do; fmrly Centro Dominicano de Promoción de Exportaciones (CEDOPEX); merged with Oficina para la Promoción de Inversiónes de la República Dominicana (OPI-RD) and changed name as above in 2003; promotion of exports and investments; Exec. Dir EDDY M. MARTÍNEZ MANZUETA.

Consejo Nacional de la Empresa Privada (CONEP): Avda Sarasota 20, Torre Empresarial, 12°, Ensanche La Julia, Santo Domingo, DN; tel. 472-7101; fax 472-7850; e-mail conep@conep.org.do; internet www.conep.org.do; Pres. MANUEL DIEZ CABRAL; Exec. Vice-Pres. FRANCISCO JOSÉ CASTILLO.

Consejo Nacional de Zonas Francas de Exportación (CNZFE): Edif. San Rafael, 5°, Avda Leopoldo Navarro 61, Apdo 21430, Santo Domingo, DN; tel. 686-8077; fax 686-8079; e-mail e.castillo@cnzfe.gob.do; internet www.cnzfe.gov.do; co-ordinating body for the free trade zones; Exec. Dir LUISA FERNÁNDEZ DURÁN.

Dirección General de Minería: Edif. de Ofs Gubernamentales, 10°, Avda México, esq. Leopoldo Navarro, Santo Domingo, DN; tel. 685-8191; fax 686-8327; e-mail direc.mineria@verizon.net.do; internet www.dgm.gov.do; f. 1947; govt mining and hydrocarbon org.; Dir-Gen. OCTAVIO LÓPEZ.

Instituto Agrario Dominicano (IAD): Avda 27 de Febrero, Plaza la Bandera, Santo Domingo, DN; tel. 620-6585; fax 620-1537; e-mail info@iad.gob.do; internet www.iad.gob.do; Exec. Dir JUAN RODRÍGUEZ RAMÍREZ.

Instituto Azúcarero Dominicano (INAZUCAR): Avda Jiménez Moya, Apdo 667, Santo Domingo, DN; tel. 532-5571; fax 533-2402; e-mail inst.azucar2@codetel.net.do; internet www.inazucar.gov.do; f. 1965; sugar institute; Exec. Dir FAUSTINO JIMÉNEZ.

Instituto de Innovación en Biotecnología e Industria (INDOTEC): Calle Olof Palme, esq. Núñez de Cáceres, San Gerónimo, Apdo

392-2, Santo Domingo, DN; tel. 566-8121; fax 227-8808; e-mail sugerencias@iibi.gov.do; internet www.iibi.gov.do; fmrly Instituto Dominicano de Tecnología Industrial (INDOTEC); name changed as above in 2005; Pres. FRANCISCO JAVIER GARCÍA; Exec. Dir Dra BERNARDA A. CASTILLO.

EMPLOYERS' ORGANIZATIONS

Confederación Patronal de la República Dominicana (COPARDOM): Torre Empresarial AIRD, Suite 207, Avda Sarasota 20, Santo Domingo, DN; tel. 381-4233; fax 381-4266; internet www.copardom.org; f. 1946; Pres. JAIME O. GONZÁLEZ.

Federación Dominicana de Comerciantes: Carretera Sánchez Km 10, Santo Domingo, DN; tel. 533-2666; Pres. IVAN GARCÍA.

UTILITIES

Regulatory Authority

Superintendencia de Electricidad: Edif. CREP, 5°, Avda Gustavo Mejía Ricart 73, esq. Agustín Lara, Ensanche Serrallés, Apdo 1725, Santo Domingo, DN; tel. 683-2500; fax 544-1637; e-mail sie@sie.gov.do; internet www.sie.gov.do; f. 2001; Pres. JUAN BAUTISTA GÓMEZ.

Electricity

AES Dominicana: Torre Acrópolis, 23°, Santo Domingo, DN; tel. 955–2223; e-mail infoaesdominicana@aes.com; internet www.aesdominicana.com.do; f. 1997; subsidiary of AES Corpn, USA; largest private electricity generator in the Dominican Republic (300 MW); Pres. MARCO DE LA ROSA.

Corporación Dominicana de Empresas Eléctricas Estatales (CDEEE): Edif. Principal CDE, Centro de los Héroes, Avda Independencia, esq. Fray C. de Utrera, Apdo 1428, Santo Domingo, DN; tel. 535-9098; fax 533-7204; e-mail info@cdeee.gov.do; internet www.cdeee.gov.do; f. 1955; state electricity co; partially privatized in 1999, renationalized in 2003; Pres. ARMANDO PEÑA CASTILLO; Exec. Vice-Pres. CELSO MARRANZINI.

EDE Este, SA (Empresa Distribuidora de Electricidad del Este): Avda Sábana Larga 1, esq. San Lorenzo, Los Mina, Santo Domingo, DN; tel. 788-2373; fax 788-2595; e-mail infoedeeste@edeeste.com.do; internet www.edeeste.com.do; f. 1999; state-owned electricity distributor; Gen. Man. FRANCISCO LEIVA LANDABUR.

EDENORTE Dominicana, SA (Empresa Distribuidora de Electricidad del Norte): internet www.edenorte.com.do; f. 1999; state-owned electricity distributor; Gen. Man. EDUARDO SAAVEDRA PIZARRO.

EDESUR Dominicana, SA (Empresa Distribuidora de Electricidad del Sur): Calle Carlos Sánchez y Sánchez, esq. Avda Tiradentes, Torre Serrano, Santo Domingo, DN; tel. 683-9292; internet www.edesur.com.do; f. 1999; state-owned electricity distributor; Man. MARCELO ROGELIO SILVA IRIBARNE.

Empresa de Generación Hidroeléctrica Dominicana (EGE-HID): Avda Rómulo Betancourt 303, Bella Vista, Santo Domingo, DN; tel. 533-5555; fax 535-7472; e-mail administrador@hidroelectrica.gob.do; internet www.hidroelectrica.gob.do; distributor of hydroelectricity; Pres. JOHNNY JONES; Dir VICTOR G. VENTURA HERNÁNDEZ.

Unidad de Electrificación Rural y Suburbana (UERS): Avda José Andrés Aybar Castellanos 136, Ensanche La Esperilla, Santo Domingo, DN; tel. 227-7666; e-mail info@uers.gov.do; internet www.uers.gov.do; f. 2006; manages supply of electricity to rural areas; Pres. JULIO CÉSAR BERROA ESPAILLAT; Dir-Gen. THELMA MARÍA EUSEBIO.

Gas

AES Andrés: Santo Domingo, DN; internet www.aes.com; f. 2003; subsidiary of AES Corpn (USA); 3 generation facilities; 2 gas-fired plant and liquefied natural gas terminal, 319-MW in Andrés and 236-MW in Los Mina; 1 coal-fired plant in Itabo; Pres. ANDREW VESEY.

Water

Corporación del Acueducto y Alcantarillado de Santo Domingo: Calle Euclides Morillo 65, Arroyo Hondo, Santo Domingo, DN; tel. 562-3500; fax 541-4121; e-mail info@caasd.gov.do; internet www.caasd.gov.do; f. 1973; Dir FREDDY PÉREZ.

Instituto Nacional de Aguas Potables y Alcantarillado (INAPA): Edif. Inapa, Centro Comercial El Millón, Calle Guarocuya, Apdo 1503, Santo Domingo, DN; tel. 567-1241; fax 567-8972; e-mail info@inapa.gob.do; internet www.inapa.gob.do; Exec. Dir MARIANO GERMÁN.

Instituto Nacional de Recursos Hidráulicos: Avda Jiménez de Moya, Centro de los Héroes, Santo Domingo, DN; tel. 532-3271; fax 532-2321; internet www.indrhi.gov.do; f. 1965; Exec. Dir FRANCISCO TOMAS RODRÍGUEZ.

TRADE UNIONS

Asociación Dominicana de Profesores (ADP): Avda Cervantes 57, Gazcue, Santo Domingo, DN; tel. 687-3268; fax 687-5800; e-mail adpinstitucion@gmail.com; internet adpmagisterio.org; f. 1972; Pres. RADHAMÉS CAMACHO.

Confederación Autónoma de Sindicatos Clasistas (CASC) (Autonomous Confederation of Trade Unions): Juan Erazo 14, Villa Juana, 4°, Santo Domingo, DN; tel. 687-8533; fax 689-1439; e-mail cascnacional@codetel.net.do; f. 1962; supports PRSC; Sec.-Gen. GABRIEL DEL RÍO.

Confederación Nacional de Trabajadores Dominicanos (CNTD) (National Confederation of Dominican Workers): Calle José de Jesús Ravelo 56, Villa Juana, 2°, Santo Domingo, DN; tel. 221-2117; fax 221-3217; e-mail cntd@codetel.net.do; f. 1988 by merger; 11 provincial federations totalling 150 unions are affiliated; Sec.-Gen. JACOBO RAMOS; c. 188,000 mems.

Confederación Nacional de Unidad Sindical (CNUS): Edif. Centrales Sindicales, Calle Juan Erazo 14, Villa Juana, Santo Domingo, DN; tel. 221-2158; fax 689-1248; e-mail cnus@verizon.net.do; internet www.cnus.org.do; Pres. RAFAEL (PEPE) ABREAU.

Federación Dominicana de Trabajadores de Zona Francas, Industrias Diversas y de Servicios (FEDOTRAZONAS): Edif. Centrales Sindicales, 1°, Calle Juan Erazo 14, Villa Juana, Santo Domingo, DN; tel. 686-8140; fax 685-2476; e-mail info@fedotrazonas.org; internet fedotrazonas.org; f. 2002; 10 affiliate trade unions; Sec.-Gen. YGNACIO HERNÁNDEZ HICIANO.

Confederación de Trabajadores Unitaria (CTU) (United Workers' Confederation): Edif. de las Centrales Sindicales, Luis Manuel Caceres (Tunti) 222, 3°, Villa Juana, Santo Domingo, DN; tel. 565-0881; e-mail ctu01@codetel.net.do; internet ctu.com.do; f. 1991; Sec.-Gen. EUGENIO PÉREZ CÉSPEDES.

Unión General de Trabajadores Dominicanos (UGTD): Santo Domingo, DN; e-mail uniongeneraldetrabajadores dominicanosugtd@hotmail.com; Pres. CRISTÓBAL MANZANILLO.

Transport

Oficina por la Reordenamiento de Transporte (OPRET): Avda Maximo Gomez esq. Reyes Católicos, Antigua Cementera, Santo Domingo, DN; tel. 732-2670; fax 563-0199; internet www.opret.gov.do; f. 2005 to oversee devt and modernization of the transport system.

RAILWAYS

The Government invested US $50m.–$100m. in the installation of an underground railway system in Santo Domingo. The first line—14 km in length, between Villa Mella and Centro de los Héroes—entered into service in 2009. Two further lines were planned, and the completed network was to have a total length of some 60 km. In 2011 the legislature approved funding for the second line, to run for 32 km between Los Alcarrizos and the Francisco del Rosario Sánchez bridge.

ROADS

In 2005 there were an estimated 17,000 km of roads, of which about 6,225 km were paved. There is a direct route from Santo Domingo to Port-au-Prince in Haiti. In 2008 the Government announced the construction of the Coral Highway to improve road connectivity to the east coast. The work was to be carried out in two phases, with the first stage costing US $272.3m. In 2010 a further $54m. was approved. The project was scheduled to be inaugurated in July 2012.

Autoridad Metropolitana de Transporte (AMET): Avda Expreso V Centenario, esq. Avda San Martín, Santo Domingo, DN; tel. 686-8469; fax 686-6766; e-mail info@amet.gov.do; internet www.amet.gov.do; Dir-Gen. Maj.-Gen. JOSÉ ANIBAL SANZ JIMINIAN.

Dirección General de Carreteras y Caminos Vecinales: Avda San Cristóbal, esq. Avda Tiradentes, Ensanche la Fe, Santo Domingo, DN; tel. 565-2811; fax 567-5470; f. 1987; operated by the Secretary of State for Public Works and Communications.

SHIPPING

The Dominican Republic has 14 ports, of which Río Haina is by far the largest, handling about 80% of imports in 2005. Other important ports are Boca Chica, Santo Domingo and San Pedro de Macorís on the south coast, and Puerto Plata in the north. The Caucedo port and transshipment centre, near the Las Américas international airport, opened in 2003 and was destined specifically for use by free trade zone businesses.

Agencias Navieras B&R, SA: Avda Abraham Lincoln 504, Apdo 1221, Santo Domingo, DN; tel. 544-2200; fax 562-3383; e-mail ops@navierasbr.com; internet www.navierasbr.com; f. 1919; shipping agents and export services; Man. HUMBERTO SOSA.

Autoridad Portuaria Dominicana: Avda Máximo Gómez, Santo Domingo, DN; tel. 687-4772; fax 687-2661; internet www.apordom.gov.do; Pres. VÍCTOR DÍAZ RÚA; Exec. Dir RAMÓN RIVAS.

Frederic Schad, Inc: José Gabriel García 26, Apdo 941, Santo Domingo, DN; tel. 221-8000; fax 688-7696; e-mail mail@fschad.com; internet www.fschad.com; f. 1922; logistics and shipping agent; Pres. FEDERICO SCHAD.

Maersk Dominicana, SA: Calle J. A. Soler 49, Santo Domingo, DN; tel. 732-1234; fax 566-5950; e-mail crbcsegen@maersk.com; internet www.maerskline.com; f. 1995; Gen. Man. MANUEL ALEJANDRO TERRERO.

Naviera Ebenezer, C por A: Los Charamicos, Sosua, Puerto Plata; tel. 875-9704; fax 571-4258; e-mail navieraebenezer@hotmail.com; Pres. MIGUEL A. DÍAZ.

CIVIL AVIATION

There are nine international airports, two at Santo Domingo, and one each at Puerto Plata, Punta Cana, Santiago, La Romana, Samaná, Sánchez and Barahona. The international airport, Aeropuerto Internacional La Isabela, at El Higuero, near Santo Domingo, replaced the Aeropuerto Internacional de Herrera, which was closed in 2006. The newest airport, President Juan Bosch International Airport, in El Catey, in the north of the country, was inaugurated in 2007. Most main cities have domestic airports including a military air base in San Isidro. The regional airline LIAT (see Antigua and Barbuda) provides scheduled passenger and cargo services.

Instituto Dominicano de Aviación Civil: Avda México, esq. Avda 30 de Marzo, Apdo 1180, Santo Domingo, DN; tel. 221-7909; fax 221-6220; e-mail info@idac.gov.do; internet www.idac.gov.do; f. 1955; fmrly Dirección General de Aeronáutica Civil; adopted current name 2007; govt supervisory body; Dir-Gen. Dr ALEJANDRO HERRERA RODRIGUEZ.

Aerodomca (Aeronaves Dominicanas): Joaquin Balaguer Int. Airport, El Higuero La Isabela, Santo Domingo, DN; tel. 826-4141; fax 826-4065; e-mail ventas@aerodomca.com; internet www.aerodomca.com; f. 1980; operates charter flights to the Caribbean.

Caribair (Caribbean Atlantic Airlines): Aeropuerto Internacional La Isabela, Santo Domingo, DN; tel. 826-4444; fax 826-4063; e-mail info@caribair.com.do; internet www.caribair.com.do; f. 1983; licence temporarily suspended in 2009; operates scheduled flights to Aruba, Haiti, and domestic and regional charter flights; CEO RAFAEL ROSADO FERMIN.

Servicios Aéreos Profesionales (SAP): Dr Joaquín Balaguer International Airport, La Isabela, Santo Domingo, DN; tel. 858-000; fax 372-8817; e-mail hheyer@sapair.com; internet www.sapair.com; f. 1981; operates charter flights to Central America, the Caribbean and the USA; Pres. JOSE MIGUEL PATIN.

VOLAIR Líneas Aéreas del Caribe, SA: Dr Joaquín Balaguer International Airport, Santo Domingo, DN; tel. 826-4068; fax 826-4071; e-mail info@govolair.com; internet www.govolair.com; f. 2004; operates charter flights to domestic destinations and the Caribbean.

Tourism

The total number of visitors to the Dominican Republic in 2010 was 4,414,756. In 2009 receipts from tourism, excluding passenger transport, totalled US $4,051m. There were 67,197 hotel rooms in the Dominican Republic in 2009.

Secretaría de Estado de Turismo: See the Government—Ministries.

Asociación Dominicana de Agencias de Viajes y Turismo (ADAVIT): Calle Padre Billini 263, Apdo 2097, Santo Domingo, DN; tel. 221-4343; fax 685-2577; e-mail adavit@codetel.net.do; f. 1963; Pres. EDISON UREÑA; Sec. ANA KATINGO SANTELISES DE LATOUR; 126 mems.

Asociación de Hoteles y Turismo de la República Dominicana, Inc (ASONAHORES): Edif. La Cumbre, 8°, Calle Presidente González, esq. Avda Tiradentes, Ensanche Naco, Santo Domingo, DN; tel. 368-4676; fax 368-5566; e-mail asonahores@asonahores.com; internet www.asonahores.com; f. 1962; asscn of private orgs; includes the Consejo de Promoción Turística; Pres. JULIO LIBRE.

Corporación de Fomento de la Industria Hotelera y Desarrollo del Turismo (CORPHOTELS): Avda México, esq. 30 de Marzo, Ofs Gubernamentales, Santo Domingo, DN; tel. 688-3417; fax 689-3907; internet corphotels.com; f. 1969; promotes the hotel industry and tourism in general; state-run; Dir BIENVENIDO PÉREZ.

Defence

As assessed at November 2011, the Dominican Republic's armed forces numbered an estimated 24,500: army 15,000, navy 4,000 (including naval infantry), air force 5,500. There were also paramilitary forces numbering 15,000. Military service is voluntary and lasts for four years. In February 2012 it was announced that a US naval station was to be constructed on the island of Saona.

Defence Expenditure: The budget allocation for 2012 was an estimated RD $9,600m.

Secretary of State for the Armed Forces and General Chief of Staff: Lt-Gen. JOAQUÍN VIRGILIO PERÉZ FELIZ.

Army Chief of Staff: Maj.-Gen. PEDRO ANTONIO CÁCERES CHESTARO.

Navy Chief of Staff: Vice-Adm. NICOLAS CABRERA ARIAS.

Air Force Chief of Staff: Maj.-Gen. GILBERTO SANTIAGO DELGADO VALDEZ.

Education

Education is, where possible, compulsory for children between the ages of six and 14 years. Primary education commences at the age of six and lasts for eight years. Secondary education, starting at 14 years of age, lasts for four years. In 2008 enrolment at primary level included 80% of children in the relevant age-group, while secondary enrolment included 58% of children in the relevant age-group (males 52%, females 63%). In 1997/98 there were 4,001 primary schools and in 1996/97 there were an estimated 1,737 secondary schools. There were eight universities. Budgetary expenditure on education in 2012 was estimated at RD $46,236m. In 2010 the Government agreed a US $100m. loan with the Inter-American Development Bank for school improvements, as part of its 10-Year Plan for Education.

ECUADOR

Introductory Survey

LOCATION, CLIMATE, LANGUAGE, RELIGION, FLAG, CAPITAL

The Republic of Ecuador lies on the west coast of South America. It is bordered by Colombia to the north, by Peru to the east and south, and by the Pacific Ocean to the west. The Galápagos Islands, about 960 km (600 miles) off shore, form part of Ecuador. The climate is affected by the Andes mountains, and the topography ranges from the tropical rainforest on the coast and in the Oriente (the eastern region) to the tropical grasslands of the central valley and the permanent snowfields of the highlands. The official language is Spanish, but Quechua, Shuar and other indigenous languages are very common. Almost all of the inhabitants profess Christianity, and some 90% are Roman Catholics. The national flag (proportions 1 by 2) has three horizontal stripes, of yellow (one-half of the depth), blue and red. The state flag has, in addition, the national emblem (an oval cartouche, showing Mount Chimborazo and a steamer on a lake, surmounted by a condor) in the centre. The capital is Quito.

CONTEMPORARY POLITICAL HISTORY

Historical Context

Ecuador was ruled by Spain from the 16th century until 1822, when it achieved independence as part of Gran Colombia. In 1830 Ecuador seceded and became a separate republic. A longstanding division between Conservatives (Partido Conservador), whose support was generally strongest in the highlands, and Liberals (Partido Liberal, subsequently Partido Liberal Radical), based in the coastal region, began in the 19th century. Until 1948 Ecuador's political life was characterized by a rapid succession of presidents, dictators and juntas. Between 1830 and 1925 the country was governed by 40 different regimes. From 1925 to 1948 there was even greater instability, with a total of 22 heads of state.

Domestic Political Affairs

Dr Galo Plaza Lasso, who was elected in 1948 and remained in power until 1952, was the first President since 1924 to complete his term of office. He created a climate of stability and economic progress. Dr José María Velasco Ibarra, who had previously been President in 1934–35 and 1944–47, was elected again in 1952 and held office until 1956. A 61-year history of Liberal Presidents was broken in 1956, when a Conservative candidate, Dr Camilo Ponce Enríquez, took office. He was succeeded in 1960 by Velasco, who campaigned as a non-party Liberal. In the following year, however, Velasco was deposed by a coup, and was succeeded by his Vice-President, Dr Carlos Julio Arosemena Monroy. The latter was himself deposed in 1963 by a military junta, led by Capt. (later Rear-Adm.) Ramón Castro Jijón, the Commander-in-Chief of the Navy, who assumed the office of President. In 1966 the High Command of the Armed Forces dismissed the junta and installed Clemente Yerovi Indaburu, a wealthy business executive and a former Minister of Economics, as acting President. Yerovi was forced to resign when the Constituent Assembly proposed a new constitution that prohibited the intervention of the armed forces in politics. In November he was replaced as provisional President by Dr Otto Arosemena Gómez, who held office until the elections of 1968, when Velasco returned from exile to win the presidency for the fifth time.

In 1970 Velasco, with the support of the army, suspended the Constitution and assumed dictatorial powers to confront a financial emergency. In 1972 he was overthrown for the fourth time by a military coup, led by Brig.-Gen. Guillermo Rodríguez Lara, the Commander-in-Chief of the Army, who proclaimed himself Head of State. In 1976 President Rodríguez resigned, and power was assumed by a three-man military junta, led by Vice-Adm. Alfredo Poveda Burbano. The new junta announced its intention to lead the country to a truly representative democracy. A national referendum approved a newly drafted Constitution in January 1978 and a presidential election took place in July. No candidate achieved an overall majority, and a second round of voting was held in April 1979, when a new legislature was also elected. Jaime Roldós Aguilera of the Concentración de Fuerzas Populares was elected President and he took office in August, when the Congreso was inaugurated and the new Constitution came into force. Roldós encountered antagonism from both the conservative sections of the Congreso Nacional and the trade unions. In 1981 Roldós died and was replaced by the Vice-President, Dr Osvaldo Hurtado Larrea. Hurtado faced opposition from left-wing politicians and trade unions for his efforts to reduce government spending and from right-wing and commercial interests, which feared encroaching state intervention in the private economic sector. In 1982 the heads of the armed forces resigned and the Minister of Defence was dismissed, when they opposed Hurtado's attempts to settle amicably the border dispute with Peru (see below).

In 1983 the Government introduced a series of austerity measures, which met with immediate opposition from the trade unions and private sector employees. Discontent with the Government's performance was reflected in the results of the January 1984 elections, when the ruling party, Democracia Popular-Unión Demócrata Cristiana (DP-UDC), lost support. At a second round of voting in May León Febres Cordero, leader of the Partido Social Cristiano (PSC) and presidential candidate of the conservative Frente de Reconstrucción Nacional, unexpectedly defeated Dr Rodrigo Borja Cevallos of the left-wing Izquierda Democrática (ID).

The dismissal of the Chief of Staff of the Armed Forces, Lt-Gen. Frank Vargas Pazzos, brought about a military crisis in 1986. Vargas and his supporters barricaded themselves inside the Manta military base until they had forced the resignation of both the Minister of Defence and the army commander, who had been accused by Vargas of embezzlement. Vargas then staged a second rebellion at the military base where he had been detained. Troops loyal to the President made an assault on the base, captured Vargas and arrested his supporters. In January 1987 President Febres Cordero was abducted and, after being held for 11 hours, was released in exchange for Vargas, who was granted an amnesty. In July 58 members of the air force were sentenced to up to 16 years' imprisonment for involvement in the abduction of the President.

Borja of the ID won the 1988 presidential election, defeating Abdalá Bucaram Ortiz of the Partido Roldosista Ecuatoriano (PRE). Borja promised to act promptly to address Ecuador's increasing economic problems; however, large demonstrations in protest against the consequent economic austerity measures swiftly followed.

In May 1990 about 1,000 indigenous Indians marched into Quito to demand official recognition of the land rights and languages of the indigenous population and compensation from petroleum companies for environmental damage. In the following month the Confederación de Nacionalidades Indígenas del Ecuador (CONAIE) organized an uprising in seven Andean provinces. Roads were blockaded, *haciendas* occupied, and supplies to the cities interrupted. Following the arrest of 30 Indians by the army, the rebels took military hostages. Negotiations between CONAIE and President Borja collapsed in August but were resumed in February 1991, following the seizure by Indian groups in the Oriente of eight oil wells. As a result, the Government promised to consider the Indians' demands for stricter controls on the operations of the petroleum industry, and for financial compensation. In April 1992 several thousand Amazon Indians marched from the Oriente to Quito to demand that their historical rights to their homelands be recognized. In May President Borja agreed to grant legal title to more than 1m. ha of land in the province of Pastaza to the Indians.

At legislative elections in May 1992 the PSC gained the highest number of seats in the enlarged Congreso Nacional. The Partido Unidad Republicano (PUR), formed prior to the elections by the former PSC presidential candidate, Sexto Durán Ballén, won the second highest number of seats, and was to govern with its ally, the Partido Conservador (PC). However, as the two parties' seats did not constitute a majority in the Congreso, support from other centre-right parties, particularly the PSC, was sought. In the second round of the presidential election, Durán defeated Jaime Nebot Saadi of the PSC.

In September 1992 the Government's announcement of a programme of economic austerity measures prompted violent demonstrations and several bomb attacks in Quito and Guayaquil, as well as a general strike in May 1993. Legislation to provide for the privatization of some 160 state-owned companies and a reduction in the number of employees in the public sector by 100,000 was approved by the Congreso in August. The Government's decision in January 1994 to increase the price of fuel by more than 70% provoked violent demonstrations throughout the country and a general strike. The unpopularity of Durán's PUR-PC governing alliance was demonstrated at mid-term congressional elections in May, when it won only nine of the 77 seats.

Environmental concerns regarding the exploitation of the Oriente by the petroleum industry continued to be expressed during 1993. In November five Amazon Indian tribes began legal proceedings against the international company Texaco to claim compensation totalling US $1,500m. for its part in polluting the rainforest—see below. (It was estimated that some 17m. barrels of oil had been spilled during the company's 25 years of operations in the region.) In June 1994 the increasingly vociferous indigenous movement organized large-scale demonstrations across the country, in protest at a recently approved Land Development Law. The law, which allowed for the commercialization of Amerindian lands for farming and resource extraction, provoked serious unrest and a general strike, during which a state of emergency was declared and the army mobilized. The law was subsequently judged to be unconstitutional.

In August 1994 a national referendum on constitutional reform took place, following much disagreement between the Government and the judiciary and opposition parties. All but one of the eight proposed reforms (which included measures to alter the electoral system and the role of the Congreso Nacional, and the establishment of a bicameral legislature) were approved; however, only some 50% of eligible voters participated, of whom some 20% returned void ballot papers. A further referendum was held in November 1995, when all of the proposed changes were rejected; the result was widely regarded as a reflection of the Government's continued unpopularity.

In July 1995 the country was plunged into a serious political crisis when Vice-President Alberto Dahik admitted giving budgetary funds to opposition deputies (allegedly for use in local public works projects) in return for their support for the economic reform programme. Dahik resigned following the initiation of impeachment proceedings in October.

In September 1995 troops were dispatched to the Galápagos Islands, following disturbances among the islanders, who were demanding the Government's acceptance of a special law granting increased political and financial autonomy to the islands, in addition to some US $16m. in priority economic aid. Concerned about the potentially disastrous effect of the protests on the country's important tourism industry, the Government quickly withdrew its opposition to the proposed legislation and agreed to establish a specialist commission to draft a new law acceptable to all parties.

A presidential election in May 1996 failed to produce an outright winner, necessitating a second round of voting for the two leading contenders, Nebot of the PSC and Abdalá Bucaram Ortiz of the PRE. An increasingly vocal and politically organized indigenous movement resulted in the strong performance of Freddy Ehlers, the candidate for the newly formed Movimiento Nuevo País—Pachakútik (MNPP), a coalition of Amerindian and labour groups. The MNPP also emerged as a significant new force in the legislature, with a total of eight seats, at a concurrent legislative election. At the second round presidential ballot in July Bucaram was the unexpected victor. His success was widely interpreted as an expression of disenchantment with established party politics.

A 48-hour general strike began in January 1997, prompted by increases of up to 600% in the price of certain commodities and a climate of considerable dissatisfaction with the President's leadership. Protests intensified in February and troops were deployed in the capital. Violent clashes erupted between protesters and security personnel, and Bucaram was barricaded inside the presidential palace. On 6 February, at an emergency session, the Congreso Nacional voted to dismiss the President on the grounds of mental incapacity (thus evading the normal impeachment requirements of a two-thirds' majority). A state of emergency was declared, and the erstwhile Speaker, Fabián Alarcón Rivera, assumed the presidency in an acting capacity, despite the claim by Vice-President Rosalia Arteaga to be the legitimate constitutional successor to Bucaram. Confusion over the correct procedure led to fears of a military coup, despite a declaration of neutrality by the armed forces. Bucaram fled from the presidential palace on 9 February, and on the following day Arteaga was declared interim President. However, by 11 February Arteaga had resigned amid continued constitutional uncertainty, and Alarcón was reinstated as President. Alarcón announced a reorganization of cabinet portfolios (which included no members of the two largest parties in the Congreso, the PSC and the PRE) and the creation of a commission to investigate allegations of corruption against Bucaram's administration. In March Bucaram's extradition from Panama (where he had been granted political asylum) was requested in order that he face charges of misappropriating some US $90m. of government funds. In May, in response to Bucaram's declaration that he intended to contest Ecuador's next presidential election, the legislature approved a motion to impose an indefinite ban on Bucaram's candidacy in any future ballot. (In 1998 the Supreme Court issued a four-year prison sentence, *in absentia*, to Bucaram for libel, and in 2001 he was indicted on corruption charges.)

At a national referendum in May 1997 the most notable results were that 76% supported the decision to remove Bucaram from office and 68% supported the appointment of Alarcón as interim President. However, Alarcón's apparent success in the referendum was undermined by high voter absenteeism (41%) and by the launch, in June, of an official congressional inquiry into allegations that leading drugs-traffickers in the country had contributed to political party funds, and, particularly, to Alarcón's Frente Radical Alfarista.

In January 1998, following persistent pleas from international environmental and scientific organizations for greater protection of the Galápagos Islands, the Congreso Nacional approved a law that aimed to preserve the islands' unique environment more effectively. An element of the law, providing for an extension of the marine reserve around the islands from 15 to 40 nautical miles, attracted intense criticism from powerful fishing interests in the country and was vetoed by Alarcón, prompting condemnation by environmentalists and small-scale fishing concerns.

At a presidential election in May 1998 the DP candidate and mayor of Quito, Jamil Mahuad Witt, emerged as the strongest contender. At the second round of voting in July, between Mahuad and his closest rival, Alvaro Noboa Pontón of the PRE, Mahuad narrowly defeated Noboa. Mahuad took office in August and appointed a Cabinet consisting predominantly of independent members.

A programme of severe adjustment measures, which included huge rises in the cost of domestic gas and electricity, as well as substantial increases in public transport fares and fuel prices, was introduced in September 1998, prompting a general strike in the following month. Clashes between demonstrators and security personnel resulted in the deaths of four people. In February 1999 disagreement over economic policy and severe disruption arising from extensive fuel shortages prompted the respective resignation of the Ministers of Finance and of Energy and Mines.

In March 1999 a substantial decrease in the value of the sucre led President Mahuad to declare a week-long bank holiday in an attempt to prevent the withdrawal of deposits and reduce the pressure on the currency. In addition, the Government announced an economic retrenchment programme to restore investor confidence and prevent economic collapse. Measures included an increase in fuel prices of up to 160%, tax rises, the partial freezing of bank accounts, and the planned privatization of certain state-owned companies. These prompted further protests and the resignation of the majority of the board of the Central Bank. The main opposition party, the PSC, refused to endorse the austerity programme, thus compelling the President to dilute the measures. In April the Government announced an economic revival plan, which included a number of measures demanded by the IMF. Some US $400m. in initial financing was to be provided by the IMF. In In response to further industrial unrest, the Government imposed a further state of emergency in July.

In early January 2000, in an attempt to curb increasing unrest, President Mahuad imposed another state of emergency. However, on 21 January he was forced to flee from the presidential palace following large-scale protests in Quito by thousands of mainly Indian demonstrators, who were supported by sections of the armed forces, over the President's perceived mismanagement of the economic crisis (especially his controversial decision to replace the sucre with the US dollar). A three-man council was established to oversee the country. However, Gen. Carlos Mendoza, the Chief of Staff of the Armed Forces, swiftly disbanded the council, and announced the appointment of former Vice-President Gustavo Noboa Bejerano as President. This move followed talks with US officials, who had warned that foreign aid to Ecuador would be curtailed if power was not restored to the elected Government. Noboa, whose appointment as Head of State was endorsed by the Congreso Nacional, promised to restore economic stability to the country. However, Indian activists who had supported the short-lived council continued to demonstrate against the assumption of the presidency by Noboa, whom they viewed as ideologically similar to Mahuad. In February four members of the armed forces, who allegedly participated in the events leading to Mahuad's removal from office, were charged with insurrection. The entire military high command was replaced in May, even though later that month the Congreso approved an amnesty for military officers and civilians arrested in connection with the coup.

In August 2000 the governing coalition lost its majority in the Congreso, endangering the proposed reform (also known as Trole 11) of the labour and petroleum sectors, as well as the privatization process. President Noboa resorted to presidential decree to promulgate the proposed Trole 11 legislation, prompting CONAIE and trade unions to claim that the move was illegal. In January 2001 the Constitutional Tribunal upheld almost one-third of the objections against Trole 11, most notably declaring unconstitutional the clause concerning the proposed privatization of state-owned companies.

Popular resentment against the Government erupted in early 2001 following significant increases in fuel prices and transport costs. Thousands of Indian protesters occupied Quito and roadblocks were erected across the Andean highlands and the Amazon lowlands. In early 2002 indigenous and civic groups in the north-east of the country occupied petroleum refineries, halted construction of a new oil pipeline and blocked major roads, prompting President Noboa once again to declare a state of emergency.

No party won an overall majority in the legislative elections of 20 October 2002. In the concurrent presidential ballot, none of the 11 candidates obtained sufficient votes to secure election, and a second round of voting was held between Lucio Gutiérrez Borbua (a former colonel who had been imprisoned for participating in the coup against President Mahuad in 2000) and Alvaro Noboa Pontón (the defeated candidate in the 1998 presidential election and founder of the right-wing Partido Renovador Institucional de Acción Nacional—PRIAN). Gutiérrez, who campaigned on a populist, anti-corruption platform, and whose own party (the Partido Sociedad Patriótica 21 de Enero—PSP) was supported by the MNPP, secured the presidency.

During 2003 the new Government continuously failed to gain approval for its proposed reforms in the opposition-dominated legislature. In September President Gutiérrez secured a legislative alliance with the PSC, which resulted in the approval of far-reaching reforms to labour practices within the civil service. Meanwhile, trade unions and indigenous groups continued to protest at the Government's decision to reduce fuel subsidies.

In December 2004 the Congreso voted to replace 27 of the 31 members of the Supreme Court, in which, President Gutiérrez alleged, the PSC exerted undue influence. Most of the new judges were allied with, or were sympathetic to, the pro-Government parties. The replacement of the Supreme Court judges was condemned by opposition groups and foreign governments as unconstitutional. The dismissed judges subsequently established a 'Supreme Court-in-exile' in protest. In April Bucaram returned to Ecuador after the new President of the Supreme Court, Guillermo Castro, a co-founder of the PRE, annulled his 1998 conviction. Castro claimed that Bucaram had been denied due process during his trial. Proceedings were also suspended against former President Noboa and former Vice-President Dahik on the same grounds.

In early 2005 opposition parties organized a series of marches in protest at the Government's increasingly authoritarian measures. In response, on 15 April Gutiérrez announced the dissolution of the Supreme Court. None the less, on 19 April some 30,000 demonstrators surrounded the presidential palace to demand the President's resignation. On the following day the Congreso voted almost unanimously to dismiss Gutiérrez from office (Gutiérrez claimed asylum in Brazil). Alfredo Palacio Gonzales, hitherto Vice-President, was subsequently appointed head of state. Palacio appointed a Cabinet composed largely of independent technocrats, which included Rafael Correa Delgado as Minister of Economy and Finance. In late April the Congreso voted to dismiss the judges of the Constitutional and Electoral Courts and in November new judges were appointed to the Supreme Court by an ostensibly independent selection panel.

During its first 10 months in office, Palacio's Government was extremely unstable, with 34 ministerial changes. Most notably, in September 2005 Mauricio Gándara resigned as Minister of Government and Police following criticism of his response to the occupation the previous month of petroleum production facilities in the provinces of Sucumbíos and Orellana. Protesters, demanding greater state control over the oil industry and more equitable distribution of its revenues, effectively suspended Ecuador's crude petroleum exports, leading to a state of emergency being declared in the two provinces and the deployment of troops to quell disorder. The occupations ceased at the end of August after Palacio pledged to revise contracts with foreign energy companies in order to increase the state's share of revenue and to allocate more petroleum revenue to social services in the two provinces.

Further unrest affected the petroleum sector in 2006. In March employees at refineries in Napo, Orellana and Sucumbíos began a strike over non-payment of their salaries and reiterated their demands for greater state control of the industry. In response, CONAIE organized a widely supported nation-wide protest in solidarity with the oil workers and also to demand a referendum on government plans to negotiate a free trade agreement (FTA) with the USA. The unrest prompted the resignation of the new Minister of Government and Police, Alfredo Castillo Bujase, who declared himself to be in sympathy with the protesters. Negotiations on the FTA with the USA were suspended in May after the Government revoked the contract of Occidental Petroleum of the USA and announced that it would confiscate its assets in Ecuador. The company announced its intention to seek US $1,000m. in damages by taking the matter to arbitration at the International Center for the Settlement of Investment Disputes in Washington, DC, USA.

The election of Rafael Correa

Presidential and legislative elections were held on 15 October 2006. Alvaro Noboa of the PRIAN, whose electoral pledges included increasing foreign investment and employment, won the largest share of the votes in the first round presidential ballot, followed by former finance minister Rafael Correa. Correa, who had pledged to dissolve the Congreso and to rewrite the Constitution, as well as to sever Ecuador's ties with the IMF and the World Bank and renegotiate its contracts with foreign petroleum companies, had been widely expected to win the first round of voting. PRIAN also won the most seats in the congressional ballot. Correa's Alianza País, contesting the elections in alliance with the Partido Socialista—Frente Amplio coalition, failed to win any seats. In the second round of the presidential election in November, Correa emerged victorious, with 57% of the votes. The new President expressed his commitment to investing in Ecuador's social sector and to strengthening the country's ties with its neighbours, at the expense of its proposed FTA with the USA. He declared that his first act as President would be to promulgate a referendum on the creation of a constituent assembly.

Tension between the newly elected Congreso and the President emerged in January 2007, principally over Correa's campaign for a constituent assembly. The decision on whether to hold a referendum on the new institution rested with the election commission (Tribunal Supremo Electoral—TSE), which comprised seven members from the main parties in the Congreso. However, following a series of protests by government supporters, the TSE handed responsibility for the decision over to the Congreso. At the end of January thousands of demonstrators surrounded the legislature to demand that the deputies approve the referendum; some entered the building, forcing the deputies to evacuate. In February, after a series of nation-wide pro-Government demonstrations, the Congreso finally approved Correa's proposal for a referendum. The plebiscite was approved by the TSE at the beginning of March but without an amendment protecting the position of the Congreso and the President demanded by parliament. Four days later the Congreso filed a lawsuit against the referendum with the Constitutional Court, and voted to remove the President of the TSE, Jorge Acosta, from his post. The TSE immediately retaliated by suspending the rights of the 57 deputies who supported the lawsuit, all from the four opposition parties, for one year; as a result, the Congreso, which was now inquorate, was forced to suspend its session. In mid-March violent clashes occurred outside the parliament building between the barred deputies and their supporters and the police. On 20 March, however, 21 alternates of the suspended deputies attended the congressional session, giving it a quorum and ending the impasse. None the less, at the end of March the Congreso was again suspended after a provincial judge issued an injunction reinstating the suspended deputies; he, in turn, was dismissed by the TSE. In the referendum of 15 April an overwhelming majority of those voting, some 81.7%, were in favour of the establishment of a constituent assembly.

A series of demonstrations took place in early 2007 at petroleum installations in the Oriente by community and indigenous groups demanding a greater share of the profits from foreign companies operating in the region. The protesters disrupted production at the facilities, and, consequently, in April Correa granted increased powers to the security forces to suppress further demonstrations around the country's oil installations. The protests continued, however, and in November the Minister of Government, Worship, Police and Municipalities, Gustavo Larrea, and President of PETROECUADOR, Carlos Pareja, were dismissed for failing to prevent further demonstrations, which had resulted in a 20% decrease in daily oil output. A state of emergency was introduced in the province of Orellana in order to safeguard oil production, which was responsible for generating some 35% of government revenue.

Meanwhile, in mid-2007 the Government announced its intention to seek compensation for leaving its petroleum reserves (estimated at some 920m. barrels) in the country's northern Amazonian region untouched. Several concerns, including the state oil companies of Venezuela, Brazil, Chile and the People's Republic of China, had been hoping to secure operating contracts in the Ishpingo-Tiputini-Tambococha (ITT) oil fields, which lie beneath the Yasuní national park, believed by scientists to have the highest biodiversity of any area in the world. Correa expressed the view that, in the interests of the environment and the indigenous communities inhabiting the area, his Government would prefer to leave the reserves unexploited. Under the Yasuní-ITT Initiative, as it was called, Correa's Government requested a total of US $350m. per year (equivalent to some 50% of the estimated revenue of the oil) from the international community as compensation for leaving the oil, which was estimated at 20% of Ecuador's total petroleum reserves, in the ground. However, in January 2010 Correa made a statement in which he accused those organizing the project of mismanagement and expressed frustration at its slow progress. The Minister of Foreign Affairs, Fander Falconí, who had been managing the scheme, resigned in protest at the President's comments, as did two of the five members of the government committee established to oversee the Yasuní fund. In August Falconí's replacement, Ricardo Patiño, signed an agreement with the UN Development Programme on the establishment of a trust fund for contributions from donor countries. The Government was by this stage seeking a total of $3,600m. over a 13-year period, with Patiño indicating that it would consider exploiting the reserves if an initial funding target of $100m. had not been met within 18 months. By the deadline of December 2011 the initial target had been met, with a total of $116m. received from regional and national governments in Spain, Belgium, France, Turkey, Georgia, Australia, Chile, Colombia and Peru, as well as from individuals.

In early 2007 UNESCO added the Galápagos Islands to its 'in danger' list, stating that the World Heritage Site was seriously threatened by invasive species, growing tourism and associated immigration. Correa signed an emergency decree aimed at tackling the crisis, which included the expulsion of illegal workers from the islands. By June, however, Correa admitted that Ecuador had failed to protect the Galápagos; his statement followed the discovery of the shells of eight endangered Galápagos giant tortoises, killed by poachers. This event, together with other similar incidents, led many environmental experts and other observers to question the Government's ability to protect the islands adequately.

Elections to the Constituent Assembly took place on 30 September 2007, and resulted in a significant majority for Correa's Movimiento País. Correa subsequently reiterated his determination to disband the depleted Congreso and establish the new Assembly as the sole legislative authority. A draft constitution was approved by the Assembly in July 2008. The proposed constitution increased the executive power of the President, who was granted the ability to dissolve the legislature (which was to be renamed the Asamblea Nacional—National Assembly) and call new elections under specified circumstances; conversely, the Asamblea Nacional was given similar powers to dismiss the President. The judicial system was to be reformed, with the Supreme Court refounded as the National Court of Justice (Corte Nacional de Justicia—CNJ) and a new Constitutional Court founded as the supreme judicial authority; moreover, the TSE was to be replaced by two bodies, namely a commission in charge of organizing elections and a court responsible for resolving electoral disputes. Substantial portions of the 444-article draft constitution were dedicated to defining civil rights and shaping economic and social policies; notably, state control of the economy was to be increased, with responsibility for setting monetary policy transferred from the Central Bank to the President. In addition, protection of the environment and natural resources was declared mandatory.

In a referendum on the proposed constitution held on 28 September 2008, in which 75.8% of registered voters participated, the text was approved by 63.9% of the votes cast. The new Constitution duly entered into force on 20 October. In accordance with the Constitution's transition regime, on 25 October the Constituent Assembly elected 76 of its members to a Legislative and Supervisory Commission, which was to act as an interim legislature until elections to the new Asamblea Nacional (later scheduled, together with a presidential election, for 26 April 2009) were held; the Constituent Assembly subsequently disbanded. The Supreme Court was also dissolved in October 2008.

In November 2008 a government commission, established to audit the foreign debt incurred by Ecuador between 1976 and 2006 (reported to total US $10,000m.), published a report that found that a large proportion of the debt had been contracted illegally. The commission's report recommended that the Government halt interest payments on three bond issues worth some $3,860m. issued between 2002 and 2005. In December 2008 Correa announced that the Government would not make a payment of $30.6m. that had become due on one of the three bond issues in the previous month; defaults on the other two issues occurred in early 2009. It was widely reported that Ecuador did not lack the ability to meet its payment obligations, and that this was therefore the first time in recent history that a country had defaulted on its debt for political, rather than fiscal, reasons.

Recent developments: Correa's second term

President Correa won a second term of office at elections in April 2009. In a comfortable first round victory, Correa attracted 52.0% of the votes, while his nearest rival, former President Lucio Gutiérrez, polled 28.2%. Correa's victory was the first time since the restoration of civilian democracy in 1979 that a second round had not been required in a presidential contest. Correa also became the first incumbent President to win re-election (President Velasco Ibarra was elected five times between 1934–68, but failed to complete his term on each occasion).

President Correa benefited from a particularly weak and fragmented opposition. As well as Gutiérrez, another conservative populist candidate, Alvaro Noboa, a third-time losing presidential nominee, polled poorly, winning just 11.4% of the votes. A third candidate, Martha Roldós Bucaram, attracted just 4.3% of the votes from supporters of Amerindian groups dissatisfied with the Government's support for large mining projects. Neither of the traditionally powerful parties, the PSC from the right nor the ID from the left, put forward candidates. Correa enjoyed broad popular support for his spending increases on health, education, pensions and infrastructure. His defiance in the face of the perceived influence of the USA and international financial institutions garnered further support. The concurrent legislative elections gave the Alianza País 59 seats in the 124-seat Asamblea Nacional, while the PSP and PSC secured 19 and 11, respectively.

The Government's efforts to secure the passage of its legislative proposals through the Asamblea Nacional were hampered in the first half of 2010 by the Alianza País's lack of a majority, as well as by the divisions within the party. Notably, in May a controversial bill aimed at introducing greater centralization within the water sector, by creating a single water authority appointed by the President, was effectively abandoned when it became clear that it would not be approved. The draft legislation had provoked large-scale protests organized by the indigenous organization CONAIE, which feared that it would lead to the privatization of water provision and demanded indigenous and consumer representation in the planned authority. Other major reforms for which the Government struggled to muster sufficient legislative support concerned the regulation of the media and higher education sectors. In July Correa threatened to call new elections if the legislature continued to impede the approval of major reforms, and used his constitutional right to promulgate by decree a bill of 'economic urgency', relating to the renegotiation of contracts with foreign companies operating in the oil sector (see Economic Affairs), after the Asamblea failed to approve it within a 30-day deadline.

Meanwhile, a truth commission appointed by Correa to investigate government-sponsored human rights violations in Ecuador during 1983–2008 presented its report in June 2010: 457 officials were found to have participated in the perpetration of abuses against 456 people, 310 of whom had suffered under the presidency of Febres Cordero (1984–88) and 17 during Correa's first term in office.

On 30 September 2010 some 800 police officers staged a protest against newly approved legislation that included a reduction in police bonuses. The protest escalated after Correa went to address the disaffected officers at the main police barracks in Quito, where they had congregated. As he was leaving the building two hours later, the President was attacked with tear gas. He was taken for treatment to a nearby police hospital, which the mutinous officers then surrounded, demanding the annulment of the legislation and refusing to allow Correa to leave. After more than 10 hours, during which he claimed that a coup attempt had been made against him and declared a nationwide state of emergency, the President was finally rescued from the hospital, amid gunfire, by a special army unit. Five people were reportedly killed and more than 16 others seriously injured in the violence. Several days after the uprising, which was condemned by the UN and the Organization of American States (OAS, see p. 394), the Government announced a substantial increase in the salaries of a number of ranks of officers in the police and armed forces. Some 13 police officers were arrested in connection with the uprising, while Correa continued to insist that he had been the victim of a coup plot, planned by an alleged paramilitary police unit and supported by Gutiérrez's PSP. Gutiérrez, who had been in Brazil at the time of the police revolt, denied any involvement. In June 2011 six police officers were found guilty of conspiring against state security during the uprising and were sentenced to between one and three years' imprisonment. The Government's decision to create a 1,000-strong unit of military police within the armed forces, announced that month, was widely interpreted as an official lack of confidence in the security services.

Correa's authority appeared to have been strengthened by the police mutiny. In mid-October 2010 the Asamblea Nacional approved controversial public finance legislation that allowed the Government to increase or reduce budget spending by up to 15% without seeking legislative approval and raised the maximum limit of the level of public debt from 40% of GDP to 50%. Correa appointed a new Minister of Government, Worship, Police and Municipalities, Alfredo Vera Arrata, and issued a decree giving the ministry full administrative control over the police force. Meanwhile, the President submitted a proposal for a referendum to the Constitutional Court, comprising the 10 questions that Correa wished to pose to the electorate. These covered a number of areas, including major reforms to the penal code and the judiciary and restrictions on the media and financial institutions. The proposed judicial reforms, provoked particular controversy, prompting criticism from former allies of Correa, including Alberto Acosta and Gustavo Larrea (former Minister of Government, Worship, Police and Municipalities), who accused Correa of jeopardizing the autonomy of the judiciary. The President, however, maintained that the reforms were necessary to rid the country of corrupt and inefficient judges and to tackle increasing crime rates. Correa's position was further weakened by the withdrawal from the Alianza País of the Ruptura de los 25 movement, which held four seats in the legislature and two government posts.

The referendum took place on 7 May 2011. Allegations by the opposition parties of voting irregularities delayed the release of official results by several weeks. When the results were published they showed a narrow victory for Correa, with an average of 47.1% of the votes in favour of the proposed reforms (between 45.0% and 50.5% depending on the proposal) and an average of 41.1% against (between 39.3% and 42.6%). Although Correa hailed the result as an emphatic success, many observers believed that this latest move to extend executive power was further evidence of an increasingly authoritarian style of leadership that was undermining his support among some sections of the electorate. In September the Government began to implement some of the reforms approved in the referendum, including the closure of all casinos in the country and a ban on entertainment that involves the death of an animal, particularly cockfighting and bullfighting. In addition, the practice of cross-shareholding between financial and media organizations was outlawed. This measure, which the Government had claimed was necessary in order to prevent conflicts of interest, together with a number of regulations governing the way in which elections are reported in the media, proved highly controversial and attracted widespread criticism for eroding the freedom of the press. Meanwhile, in October an international advisory commission, composed of senior, well-respected public figures including Spanish judge Baltazar Garzón, former President of Chile Ricardo Lagos, the secretary-general of UNASUR (q.v.), and a former adviser to the Argentine Government, arrived in the country in order to evaluate the judicial reforms approved in the referendum prior to their implementation.

In February 2012 the newly appointed Corte Nacional de Justicia (National Court of Justice) upheld a ruling made under the new media laws against a journalist and three directors from the newspaper *El Universo*. The defendants, who were charged with defamation of Correa in a report on his handling of the police revolt in 2010, were fined US $40m. and each sentenced to three years' imprisonment. The case attracted international condemnation from media organizations who saw it as an attack on the freedom of the press and damaging to Ecuador's reputation as a democracy.

In a reorganization of government portfolios in November 2011 Correa nominated a new head of the Central Bank and appointed Jeannette Sánchez Zurita and Doris Solíz Carrión as Co-ordinating Ministers for Economic Policy and for Social Development, respectively. His decision to appoint Betty Tola Bermeo, a former Vice-President of Pachakútik, as Co-ordinating Minister for Policy and Autonomous Governance was widely seen as an attempt by Correa to improve relations with the indigenous community. Moreover, his appointment of Mireya Cárdenas, a former AVC activist, as National Secretary of the People, Social Movements and Citizen Participation, was expected to find favour with his more left-wing supporters. Most significant of all, however, was the return to the Government of Fander Falconí, the former Minister of Foreign Affairs who resigned in 2010 following a disagreement over the Yasuní-ITT Initiative (see above). Falconí, a senior ally of Correa, whose presence was likely to strengthen the Government in preparation for the legislative and presidential elections of 2013, assumed the position of National Secretary of Planning and Development. In a further reshuffle in April 2012, Javier Ponce Cevallos was succeeded by Miguel Carvajal at the defence ministry while Doris Solis was moved to the Ministry of Economic and Social Inclusion.

Legal proceedings begun in 1993 against the US oil company Texaco (later acquired by Chevron) had been expected to reach a conclusion in 2011, although the corporation's refusal to accept the judgment meant that the case remained unresolved in mid-2012. The case, believed to be the largest environmental lawsuit of its kind, had been brought by some 30,000 indigenous people living in the Oriente region of Ecuador who had suffered from large-scale pollution caused by the dumping of toxic waste products and crude oil in the river systems and unlined ground pits in that area of the Amazon. Correa had supported the indigenous people in bringing the case for compensation and decontamination, describing Texaco's actions as 'a crime against humanity'. Chevron countered that any decontamination of the area was the responsibility of the Ecuadorean Government. In February 2011 an international arbitration tribunal ordered Ecuador to suspend enforcement of any judgment against Chevron in the case. In that month Chevron was ordered to pay US $18,000m. in compensation by the National Court of Justice in Ecuador. Further appeals by Chevron against the ruling were rejected in September 2011 and January 2012. However, Chevron continued to refuse to accept the ruling. In February 2012 an arbitration panel in The Hague, Netherlands, granted Chevron temporary protection against international legal action to enforce the payment.

Foreign Affairs

Regional relations

In April 1999 the World Trade Organization (WTO) upheld a complaint, put forward by the USA, Ecuador and four other Latin American countries, that the European Union (EU) unfairly favoured Caribbean banana producers. A two-tier tariff rate quota arrangement was agreed between Ecuadorean government officials and leaders of Caribbean banana-producing countries in November, easing restrictions on Latin American banana exporters and consequently assisting Ecuadorean producers. Furthermore, EU quotas for Latin American producers were to be phased out by 2006 and replaced by a uniform tariff system. However, in 2005 the Government expressed its strong opposition to the EU's successive proposals of tariff levels of €230 and €187 per metric ton on Latin American banana imports, both of which the WTO subsequently rejected. A challenge to the EU's third proposal, of a tariff of €176 per ton, was initiated by Ecuador in November 2006 and upheld by the WTO in April 2008. The dispute was finally resolved in December 2009, when representatives from the EU, Ecuador and 10 other Latin American countries signed an agreement that provided for a gradual reduction in the tariff level from €176 per ton to €114 per ton by 2017.

The long-standing border dispute with Peru over the Cordillera del Cóndor erupted into war in January 1981. A cease-fire was declared a few days later under the auspices of the guarantors of the Rio Protocol of 1942 (Argentina, Brazil, Chile and the USA). The Protocol was not recognized by Ecuador, as it awarded the area, which affords access to the Amazon river system, to Peru. In 1992 discussions on the border dispute were resumed. However, in January 1995 serious fighting broke out between the two sides. Representatives of the two Governments met for negotiations in Rio de Janeiro, Brazil, and a cease-fire agreement was concluded in February. An observer mission, representing the four guarantor nations of the Rio Protocol, was dispatched to the border, to oversee the separation of forces and demilitarization of the border area. Following intensive negotiations, agreement on the delimitation of the demilitarized zone was reached in July, and in October Ecuador finally repealed the state of emergency. A resumption of negotiations in 1996 resulted in the signing of the Santiago Agreement, which was to provide a framework for a definitive solution to the issue. Talks culminated in the signing of an accord confirming Peru's claim on the delineation of the border, but granting Ecuador navigation and trading rights on the Amazon and its tributaries and the opportunity to establish two trading centres in Peru (although this was not to constitute sovereign access). Both countries confirmed that two ecological parks were to be created along the common border, where military personnel would not be allowed access.

Following the suspected involvement of Colombian paramilitaries in the murder of an Ecuadorean politician in Quito in 1999 and reports of the presence of these troops in the country, Ecuador's military presence was strengthened at its border with Colombia. Nevertheless, criminal and military activities attributed to Colombian combatants continued on Ecuadorean territory and the number of Colombian refugees in Ecuador increased steadily. In 2003 bilateral relations suffered after the new Government of Lucio Gutiérrez ruled out the possibility of formally classifying the Fuerzas Armadas Revolucionarias de Colombia—Ejército del Pueblo (FARC—EP) as a terrorist organization. In October, however, allegations emerged that members of the Ecuadorean army had supplied a rocket used by the FARC in an attack in the Colombian capital, Bogotá. The Ecuadorean military protested the allegations and deployed some 7,000 troops to patrol the joint border. In November the Ecuadorean Government cancelled plans to allow the USA to construct three logistical centres in the country's northern provinces.

Following the initiation in April 2004 of the so-called 'Plan Patriota' offensive by the Colombian military against the FARC, the Ecuadorean Government again expressed concern at an increase in illegal incursions into its territory by Colombian combatants and increased its troop numbers on its border with Colombia. Relations improved in November after the Colombian Government agreed temporarily to halt aerial fumigation of coca crops in border areas from 2006, but the resumption of the practice, which the Government described as a 'hostile act', led President Correa to cancel a trip to Colombia in 2007. Following intervention by the OAS, an agreement was reached whereby Colombia was to notify Ecuador in advance of any plans to spray the border area and the OAS was to conduct a full investigation into the effects of the herbicide glyphosate on the local population; however, the Ecuadorean authorities accused Colombia of continuing to spray without notification. In February Correa announced the implementation of 'Plan Ecuador', which was intended to counteract the effects of 'Plan Colombia', a US-backed operation by that country to eliminate the FARC and its source of funding, the coca crops. As part of Plan Ecuador, Correa declared that the 500,000 Colombian refugees residing in Ecuador would be granted formal asylum status. Relations between the two countries deteriorated significantly following a military incursion by Colombian forces into Ecuadorean territory in March 2008, during which a FARC leader, Raúl Reyes, was killed along with 16 other rebels. The Colombian Government claimed that documents seized during the raid proved that Correa was interested in establishing official relations with the FARC. (Correa dismissed the claims, countering that his Government's involvement had been solely on humanitarian grounds as part of efforts to secure the release of hostages; his claim was supported by the French ambassador in Quito.) The Ecuadorean Government responded to the incident by expelling Colombia's ambassador in Quito, withdrawing its own ambassador from Bogotá and sending troops to the border. Relations continued to be strained during 2009. In July the Colombian Government made allegations (refuted by Correa) that Correa's election campaign had received funding from the FARC. A slight *rapprochement*, during which diplomatic relations at chargé d'affaires level were restored, was jeopardized in April 2010 by an Ecuadorean court's decision to uphold an arrest warrant issued for Colombia's former Minister of National Defence and a candidate in that country's forthcoming presidential election, Juan Manuel Santos Calderón, in connection with the 2008 raid. However, following his victory in the election in June, Santos swiftly sought to improve bilateral relations. Correa and Santos (the warrant for whose arrest had been revoked in August) announced that full diplomatic relations had been restored in late November, a week after the Colombian Government had provided Ecuador with information on the 2008 raid.

In June 2006 the heads of PETROECUADOR and PDVSA, the Venezuelan state petroleum company, and President Palacio signed an agreement under which 65,000 barrels per day of Ecuadorean oil would be refined in Venezuela in return for refined products of an equivalent value. The deal was to last for five years. Following his inauguration, President Correa also stressed his commitment to strengthening Ecuador's relations with Venezuela and to regional integration.

Other external relations

In November 1999 Ecuador and the USA signed an agreement allowing the USA to establish an air base at Manta, for a period of 10 years, for the purpose of counter-narcotics surveillance operations in the Andean region. In July 2008 the Correa Government gave the USA formal notice to vacate the base by November 2009. Moreover, the 2008 Constitution contained a clause prohibiting the establishment of military installations by foreign states in Ecuadorean territory. Ecuador did sign a new counter-narcotics agreement with the USA in 2009, under which two new élite police units would be created. These units, the Unidades de Investigaciones Anti-Drogas Sensitivas, were to be established with US assistance and charged with combating illegal drugs and contraband activities in Ecuador. Bilateral relations were further strengthened in June 2010, when the US Secretary of State, Hillary Clinton, made her first visit to Ecuador. The USA's Andean Trade Promotion and Drug Eradication Act (ATPDEA) with Ecuador was finally renewed in October 2011, eight months after its expiry.

In April 2011 the US ambassador Heather Hodges was expelled from Quito following the publication of leaked diplomatic correspondence in which she claimed that corruption was endemic at all levels of government in Ecuador. In the communication the ambassador specifically accused former police chief Gen. Jaime Aquilino Hurtado Vaca of a range of corrupt practices, including bribery, human trafficking and the misappropriation of public funds. Relations with the USA were further strained in May 2011 when Jay Bergman, the Andean regional director of the US Drug Enforcement Agency (DEA), stated that Ecuador had become a 'United Nations of organized crime' and was being used by drugs-traffickers from across the world. His comments coincided with the publication of figures in the World Drug Report 2011 (compiled by the UN Office on Drugs and Crime) that showed record seizures of cocaine in the country in 2009 and increases of up to 50% in some provinces in violent crime.

In 2007 President Correa made an official state visit to China to sign an agreement aimed at enhancing bilateral relations, particularly with regard to energy, agriculture, technology and infrastructure. Bilateral economic co-operation increased further in 2010. An Ecuadorean ministerial delegation secured Chinese funding for two hydroelectric projects in Ecuador during a visit to China in June, and in August an agreement was signed whereby China would provide Ecuador with a loan of US $1,000m. in exchange for the supply of 36,000 barrels per day of crude petroleum over a four-year period. Further loans of $2,000m. and $1,700m. were approved in 2011 and 2012, respectively. It was estimated that Ecuador had accepted a total of $7,000m. in financial assistance from China between 2008 and early 2012. Since the Government's decision in 2008 to default on its foreign debt and the subsequent withdrawal of substantial amounts of international finance, China had become Ecuador's most important creditor.

President Correa attracted international attention for his outspoken criticism of the World Bank at an Ibero-America summit meeting in Asunción, Paraguay, in October 2011. Correa refused to listen to a speech by Pamela Cox, the World Bank's Vice-President for Latin America, declaring to the gathered delegates that she should apologize 'for the damage the World Bank has inflicted upon Latin America and the planet'. He went to accuse the institution, which he claimed had withheld financial assistance to Ecuador on political grounds, of 'ideological fundamentalism [defending]...big capital and the interests of hegemonic countries'.

CONSTITUTION AND GOVERNMENT

The Constitution of the Republic of Ecuador—the country's 20th—was promulgated on 20 October 2008 following its approval in a referendum in September. Under the terms of the Constitution, executive power is vested in the President, who is directly elected by universal adult suffrage for a four-year term (starting from 24 May following his or her election). The President may be re-elected once only. Legislative power is held by the unicameral Asamblea Nacional (National Assembly), which is also directly elected for a four-year term. For administrative purposes Ecuador is divided into provinces, cantons and parishes. Each province has a Governor, who is appointed by the President.

REGIONAL AND INTERNATIONAL CO-OPERATION

Ecuador became a member of the UN in 1945. Ecuador is a member of the Andean Community (see p. 197), the Organization of American States (OAS, see p. 394), the Asociación Latinoamericana de Integración (ALADI, see p. 362), and of the Community of Latin American and Caribbean States (see p. 462), which was formally inaugurated in December 2011. In 2007 Ecuador rejoined the Organization of the Petroleum Exporting Countries (OPEC, see p. 408), having previously given up membership in 1992. In 1996 Ecuador joined the World Trade Organization (WTO, see p. 433). In December 2004 Ecuador was one of 12 countries that were signatories to the agreement, signed in Cusco, Peru, creating the South American Community of Nations (Comunidad Sudamericana de Naciones, which was renamed the Union of South American Nations—Unión de Naciones Suramericanas, UNASUR—in April 2007), intended to promote greater regional economic integration. In December 2011 Ecuador formally presented a request for membership of Mercosur (Mercado Común del Sur, see p. 428), claiming that its links with the Andean countries could be an advantage to the trade bloc.

ECONOMIC AFFAIRS

In 2010, according to estimates by the World Bank, Ecuador's gross national income (GNI), measured at average 2008–10 prices, was US $62,106m., equivalent to $4,290 per head (or $8,830 per head on an international purchasing-power parity basis). During 2001–10, it was estimated, the population increased at an average annual rate of 1.6%, while gross domestic product (GDP) per head increased, in real terms, at an average annual rate of 2.9%. According to estimates by the World Bank, overall GDP increased, in real terms, at an average annual rate of 4.5% in 2001–10; GDP increased by 3.6% in 2010.

Agriculture (including hunting, forestry and fishing) contributed 6.8% of GDP in 2010. According to FAO, some 17.5% of the active labour force were estimated to be employed in the agricultural sector in mid-2012. Ecuador is the world's leading exporter of bananas, and coffee and cocoa are also important cash crops. The seafood sector, particularly the shrimp industry, was also a significant contributor to the economy. Ecuador's extensive forests yield valuable hardwoods, and the country is a leading producer of balsawood. Exports of cut flowers were also important, and generated US $611.3m. in earnings in 2010 (equivalent to 3.5% of the total value of exports). According to the World Bank, during 2001–10 agricultural GDP increased at an average annual rate of 1.9%. Sectoral GDP contracted by 16.1% in 2009, but grew by a meagre 0.3% in 2010.

Industry (including mining, manufacturing, construction and power) employed 21.8% of the active urban labour force in 2006, and provided 37.8% of GDP in 2010. According to the World Bank, during 2001–10 industrial GDP increased at an average annual rate of 3.1%. The sector decreased by 4.1% in 2009 and increased by only a negligible 0.3% in 2010.

Mining contributed an estimated 15.4% of GDP in 2010, although the mining sector employed only 0.4% of the urban labour force in 2006. Petroleum and its derivatives remained the major exports in the early 21st century. Earnings from petroleum exports amounted to US $8,951.9m. in 2010, equivalent to 51% of the total value of exports. According to the US Energy Information Administration, production averaged 487,292 barrels per day (b/d) in 2010. In January of that year proven petroleum reserves were estimated at 6,500m. barrels. Natural gas is extracted, but only a small proportion is retained. In 2011 proven reserves of natural gas were 282,000m. cu ft, according to the *Oil and Gas Journal*. Gold, silver, copper, antimony and zinc are also mined. In real terms, according to the Central Bank, the GDP of the mining sector increased at an average rate of 3.3% per year during 2001–10; mining GDP decreased by 3.3% in 2009, but increased by 0.2% in 2010.

Manufacturing (excluding petroleum refining) contributed 9.6% of GDP in 2010 and employed 13.8% of the active labour force in urban areas in 2006. During 2001–10 manufacturing GDP increased at an average annual rate of 4.2%, according to the World Bank. Sectoral GDP decreased by 1.5% in 2009, before increasing by 0.3% in 2010.

The construction sector contributed 10.6% of GDP in 2010 and engaged some 7.2% of the employed labour force in 2006. According to the Central Bank, during 2001–10 construction GDP increased at an average annual rate of 6.5%; sectoral GDP increased by 6.7% in 2010.

Energy is derived principally from hydroelectric plants, responsible for 60.7% of total production in 2008, with petroleum accounting for most of the remainder. The country had an estimated installed capacity of 4.9m. MW in 2009, of which about one-half was produced domestically, mostly from the 1,075-MW Paute hydroelectric plant. A 160-MW hydroelectric station at Mazar, south of Paute, was officially inaugurated in January 2011 with the aim of alleviating the effects of the frequent power shortages, especially in the dry season. Imports of mineral fuels and oils, etc., comprised 21.3% of the value of total imports in 2010.

The services sector contributed an estimated 55.4% of GDP in 2010. Some 69.9% of the active urban labour force were employed in services in 2006. The sector's GDP increased at an average annual rate of 4.2% during 2001–10, according to World Bank figures; services GDP increased by 9.2% in 2010.

In 2010 Ecuador recorded a visible trade deficit of US $1,504m., and there was a deficit of $1,785m. on the current account of the balance of payments. In 2010 the principal source of imports was the USA (accounting for 27.9% of the total); that country was also the principal market for exports (34.7%). Other major trading partners were Colombia, the People's Republic of China, Panama and Peru for imports and exports. In addition to petroleum and derivatives, the principal exports in 2010 were edible fruit nuts and fish, crustaceans, molluscs, aquatic invertebrates. The principal imports in 2010 were mineral products (21.3%), machinery and apparatus, vehicles and, electrical and electronic equipment.

In 2010 there was a provisional budgetary deficit of about US $1,131.4m., equivalent to 2.0% of GDP. In that year some 27.2% of government expenditure was financed by revenue from petroleum. Ecuador's general government gross debt was US $12,011m. in 2010, equivalent to 20.7% of GDP. Ecuador's total external debt was US $12,930m. at the end of 2009, of which $6,910m. was public and publicly guaranteed debt. In that year, the cost of servicing long-term public and publicly guaranteed debt and repayments to the IMF was equivalent to 24.7% of the value of exports of goods, services and income (excluding workers' remittances). The average annual rate of inflation in 2001–10 was 5.3%; the rate averaged 3.5% in 2010. The average rate of unemployment in urban areas stood at 9.1% in 2010.

Although Ecuador's proven petroleum reserves almost tripled in the 1990s following discoveries in the Amazon region, the country's limited refining capacity meant it relied on other countries to benefit from its reserves. The administration of Rafael Correa, which took office in 2007, strengthened state intervention in the oil sector: private oil firms operating in Ecuador were, henceforth, required to pay 99% of 'windfall' profits from rising oil prices to the Government, which was then channelled into budgetary operations. In 2010, with the aim of increasing productivity and state revenue, Correa enacted legislation requiring foreign companies operating in Ecuador's oil sector to move from production-sharing agreements to service-provision contracts with fixed tariffs; contracts with foreign oil companies were consequently renegotiated. After slowing sharply to 0.4% in 2009, largely owing to low world oil prices, GDP grew by 3.6% in 2010 and by 8.4% in 2011; the rate was forecast to slow to 4.6% in 2012. A moderation in world food prices was expected to reduce inflation to 3.0% by the end of 2012. The budget for 2012 envisaged a 9% increase in expenditure compared with the previous year, prompting concerns about fiscal sustainability. Under legislation approved in October 2010, the Government had been permitted to increase spending by up to a further 15% without seeking legislative approval. Correa's decision to enact a series of tax increases in early 2012 to fund record budgetary expenditure, despite the measures having been rejected by the legislature, proved controversial and led to accusations that his Government was becoming increasingly authoritarian. Moreover, the Government's mounting reliance on financial support from China (see Recent History) was thought likely to have serious implications for the country's future stability and independence.

PUBLIC HOLIDAYS

2013: 1 January (New Year's Day), 11–12 February (Carnival), 29 March (Good Friday), 1 May (Labour Day), 24 May (Battle of Pichincha), 10 August (Independence of Quito), 9 October (Independence of Guayaquil), 2 November (All Souls' Day), 3 November (Independence of Cuenca), 6 December (Foundation of Quito), 25 December (Christmas Day), 31 December (New Year's Eve).

Statistical Survey

Sources (unless otherwise stated): Instituto Nacional de Estadística y Censos, Juan Larrea 534 y Riofrío, Quito; tel. (2) 252-9858; e-mail inec1@ecnet.ec; internet www.inec.gov.ec; Banco Central del Ecuador, Casilla 339, Quito; tel. (2) 257-2522; fax (2) 295-5458; internet www.bce.fin.ec; Ministerio de Industrias y Competitividad, Avda Eloy Alfaro y Amazonas, Quito; tel. (2) 254-6690; fax (2) 250-3818; e-mail info@mic.gov.ec; internet www.mic.gov.ec.

Area and Population

AREA, POPULATION AND DENSITY

Area (sq km)	272,045*
Population (census results)	
25 November 2001	
Males	6,018,353
Females	6,138,255
Total	12,156,608
28 November 2010	14,483,499
Population (UN estimates at mid-year)†	
2011	14,666,053
2012	14,864,987
Density (per sq km) at mid-2012	54.6

* 105,037 sq miles.

† Source: UN, *World Population Prospects: The 2010 Revision*, estimates not adjusted to take account of 2010 census.

POPULATION BY AGE AND SEX

(UN estimates at mid-2012)

	Males	Females	Total
0–14	2,239,352	2,151,178	4,390,530
15–64	4,754,747	4,754,586	9,509,333
65 and over	447,319	517,805	965,124
Total	7,441,418	7,423,569	14,864,987

Source: UN, *World Population Prospects: The 2010 Revision*.

Note: Estimates not adjusted to take account of results of 2010 census.

REGIONS AND PROVINCES

(projected population estimates at mid-2007)

	Area (sq km)	Population	Density (per sq km)	Capital
Sierra	63,269	6,111,542	96.6	—
Azuay	8,125	678,746	83.5	Cuenca
Bolívar	3,940	180,293	45.8	Guaranda
Cañar	3,122	226,021	72.4	Azogues
Carchi	3,605	166,116	46.1	Tulcán
Chimborazo	6,072	443,522	73.0	Riobamba
Cotopaxi	6,569	400,411	61.0	Latacunga
Imbabura	4,559	397,704	87.2	Ibarra
Loja	11,027	434,020	39.4	Loja
Pichincha	12,915	2,683,272	207.8	Quito
Tungurahua	3,335	501,437	150.4	Ambato
Costa	67,646	6,720,798	99.4	—
El Oro	5,850	608,032	103.9	Machala
Esmeraldas	15,239	438,576	28.8	Esmeraldas
Guayas	20,503	3,617,504	176.4	Guayaquil
Los Ríos	7,175	742,241	103.4	Babahoyo
Manabí	18,879	1,314,445	69.6	Portoviejo
Amazónica	130,834	662,948	5.1	—
Morona Santiago	25,690	131,337	5.1	Macas
Napo	11,431	96,029	8.4	Tena
Orellana	22,500	110,782	4.9	Puerto Francisco de Orellana (Coca)
Pastaza	29,774	75,782	2.5	Puyo
Sucumbíos	18,328	163,447	8.9	Nueva Loja
Zamora Chinchipe	23,111	85,571	3.7	Zamora
Insular	8,010	22,678	2.8	—
Archipiélago de Colón (Galápagos)	8,010	22,678	2.8	Puerto Baquerizo (Isla San Cristóbal)
Uncharted areas	2,289	87,519	38.2	—
Total	272,045	13,605,485	50.0	

Note: Two new provinces, Santo Domingo de los Tsáchilas and Santa Elena, were created in late 2007.

Source: partly Stefan Helders, *World Gazetteer*.

PRINCIPAL TOWNS

(2001 census)

Guayaquil	1,985,379	Ambato	154,095
Quito (capital)	1,399,378	Riobamba	124,807
Cuenca	277,374	Quevedo	120,379
Machala	204,578	Loja	118,532
Santo Domingo de los Colorados	199,827	Milagro	113,440
Manta	183,105	Ibarra	108,535
Portoviejo	171,847	Esmeraldas	95,124

Mid-2010 ('000, incl. suburbs, estimates): Guayaquil 2,690; Quito 1,846 (Source: UN, *World Urbanization Prospects: The 2009 Revision*).

BIRTHS, MARRIAGES AND DEATHS
(excluding nomadic Indian tribes)*

	Registered live births†		Registered marriages		Registered deaths	
	Number	Rate (per 1,000)	Number	Rate (per 1,000)	Number	Rate (per 1,000)
2003	262,004	20.4	65,393	5.1	53,521	4.2
2004	254,362	19.5	63,299	4.9	54,729	4.2
2005	252,725	19.1	66,612	5.0	56,825	4.3
2006	278,591	20.8	74,036	5.5	57,940	4.3
2007	283,984	20.9	76,154	5.6	58,016	4.3
2008	291,055	21.1	76,354	5.5	60,023	4.3
2009	298,337	21.3	76,892	5.5	59,714	4.3
2010	n.a.	n.a.	74,800	5.3	61,681	4.3

* Registrations incomplete.

† Figures include registrations of large numbers of births occurring in previous years. The number of births registered in the year of occurrence was: 178,549 in 2003, 168,893 in 2004, 168,324 in 2005, 185,056 in 2006, 195,051 in 2007, 206,215 in 2008; 215,906 in 2009; 219,162 in 2010.

Life expectancy (years at birth, estimates): 75 (males 73; females 78) in 2009 (Source: WHO, *World Health Statistics*).

ECONOMICALLY ACTIVE POPULATION
(ISIC major divisions, urban areas only, '000 persons aged 10 years and over, at November of each year, unless otherwise indicated)

	2004	2005	2006
Agriculture, hunting and forestry	320.8	273.5	285.0
Fishing	37.5	51.1	48.9
Mining and quarrying	16.1	10.7	15.8
Manufacturing	539.0	537.2	555.5
Electricity, gas and water	22.9	18.8	19.4
Construction	248.7	258.7	290.1
Wholesale and retail trade; repair of motor vehicles, motorcycles and personal and household goods	1,096.2	1,099.0	1,151.8
Hotels and restaurants	171.1	190.8	225.4
Transport, storage and communications	264.7	280.1	292.3
Financial intermediation	49.1	51.9	47.9
Real estate, renting and business activities	189.8	199.7	200.7
Public administration and defence; compulsory social security	173.9	168.2	170.3
Education	263.0	258.9	281.0
Health and social work	137.8	132.0	116.0
Other community, social and personal service activities	176.1	158.7	162.9
Private households with employed persons	150.4	201.7	167.7
Extra-territorial organizations and bodies	1.4	0.7	0.9
Total employed	3,858.5	3,891.9	4,031.6
Unemployed	362.1	333.6	341.8
Total labour force	4,220.6	4,225.5	4,373.4
Males	2,449.2	2,471.1	2,559.9
Females	1,771.5	1,754.3	1,813.5

2010 (urban areas only, '000 persons aged 10 years and over, at March): Total employed 4,182,798; Unemployed 418,367; Total labour force 4,601,165 (males 2,601,602, females 1,999,563).

Source: ILO.

Mid-2012 (estimates in '000): Agriculture, etc. 1,219; Total labour force 6,953 (Source: FAO).

Health and Welfare

KEY INDICATORS

Total fertility rate (children per woman, 2009)	2.5
Under-5 mortality rate (per 1,000 live births, 2009)	24
HIV/AIDS (% of persons aged 15–49, 2009)	0.4
Physicians (per 1,000 head, 2000)	1.5
Hospital beds (per 1,000 head, 2003)	1.7
Health expenditure (2008): US $ per head (PPP)	466
Health expenditure (2008): % of GDP	5.7
Health expenditure (2008): public (% of total)	39.5
Access to water (% of persons, 2008)	94
Access to sanitation (% of persons, 2008)	92
Total carbon dioxide emissions ('000 metric tons, 2007)	29,964.2
Carbon dioxide emissions per head (metric tons, 2007)	2.2
Human Development Index (2011): ranking	83
Human Development Index (2011): value	0.720

For sources and definitions, see explanatory note on p. vi.

Agriculture

PRINCIPAL CROPS
('000 metric tons)

	2008	2009	2010
Rice, paddy	1,442	1,579	1,706
Barley	18	21	19
Maize	805	811	984
Potatoes	267	287	387
Cassava (Manioc)	102	66	54
Sugar cane	9,341	8,473	8,347
Beans, dry	15	11	15
Soybeans (Soya beans)*	64	68	70
Oil palm fruit†	2,100	2,100	2,100
Tomatoes	51	47	54
Onions and shallots, green†	94	81	95
Carrots and turnips†	28	27	28
Watermelons†	27	35	41
Bananas	6,701	7,637	7,931
Plantains	506	549	547
Oranges	55	49	47
Mangoes†	160	182	188
Pineapples†	100	110	114
Papayas†	43	37	39
Coffee, green	32	34	31
Cocoa beans	94	121	132
Abaca (Manila hemp)†	31	25	27

* Unofficial figures.

† FAO estimates.

Aggregate production ('000 metric tons, may include official, semi-official or estimated data): Total cereals 2,284 in 2008, 2,435 in 2009, 2,730 in 2010; Total roots and tubers 386 in 2008, 370 in 2009, 462 in 2010; Total vegetables (incl. melons) 413 in 2008, 385 in 2009, 429 in 2010; Total fruits (excl. melons) 7,931 in 2008, 8,976 in 2009, 9,292 in 2010.

Source: FAO.

LIVESTOCK
('000 head, year ending September)

	2008	2009	2010
Cattle	4,892	5,195	5,254
Sheep*	1,860	1,950	1,900
Pigs	1,097	1,406	1,490
Horses	364	360	367
Goats	150	158	135
Asses	145	134	139
Mules	120	120	125
Chickens	141,962	149,872	152,926

* FAO estimates.

Source: FAO.

LIVESTOCK PRODUCTS
('000 metric tons)

	2008	2009	2010
Cattle meat	248.1	244.8*	237.8*
Sheep meat	8.4	8.4*	8.4*
Pig meat	212.5	180.0*	184.7*
Goat meat	1.3	1.3*	1.3*
Chicken meat*	330.0	329.5	186.0
Cows' milk	5,325.7	5,228.7	5,709.5
Sheep's milk*	6.8	7.0	7.1
Goats' milk*	3.1	3.0	2.9
Hen eggs*	91.1	93.6	93.3
Wool, greasy*	1.7	1.5	1.4

* FAO estimate(s).

Source: FAO.

Forestry

ROUNDWOOD REMOVALS
('000 cubic metres, excluding bark, FAO estimates)

	2007	2008	2009
Sawlogs, veneer logs and logs for sleepers	1,198	1,280	1,280
Pulpwood	476	364	364
Other industrial wood	296	296	296
Fuel wood	4,112	4,076	4,090
Total	6,082	6,016	6,030

2010: Production assumed to be unchanged from 2009 (FAO estimates).

Source: FAO.

SAWNWOOD PRODUCTION
('000 cubic metres, including railway sleepers)

	2008	2009*	2010*
Coniferous (softwood)	107*	118	107
Broadleaved (hardwood)	310	310	310
Total	417	428	417

* Estimate(s).

Source: FAO.

Fishing

('000 metric tons, live weight)

	2007	2008	2009
Capture	389.9*	469.7*	478.4
Pacific thread herring	14.2	25.3	22.5
Anchoveta (Peruvian anchovy)	58.3	44.6	20.2
Pacific anchoveta	1.1	26.9	7.6
Frigate and bullet tunas	21.8	19.3	35.0
Skipjack tuna	100.0	143.0	129.0
Yellowfin tuna	22.3	21.0	22.8
Bigeye tuna	30.7	39.8	33.5
Chub mackerel	43.2	21.8	36.7
Aquaculture	171.0*	172.1*	218.4
Whiteleg shrimp	150.0*	150.0*	179.1
Nile tilapia	20.0*	21.0*	37.5
Total catch	560.9*	641.8*	696.8

* Estimate.

Source: FAO.

Mining

	2007	2008	2009*
Crude petroleum ('000 barrels)	186,669	184,780	177,620
Natural gas (gross, million cu m)	1,196	1,200	1,200
Gold (kg)†	3,186	800	—

* Preliminary.

† Metal content of ore only.

Source: US Geological Survey.

Industry

SELECTED PRODUCTS
('000 barrels unless otherwise indicated)

	2007	2008	2009*
Jet fuels	2,913	n.a.	n.a.
Motor spirit (gasoline)	7,311	17,090	18,600
Distillate fuel oils	11,789	8,561	8,000
Residual fuel oils	23,052	13,251	10,400
Liquefied petroleum gas	1,614	1,924	2,200
Crude steel ('000 metric tons)	87	85	85
Cement ('000 metric tons)	4,420	5,493	5,000

* Preliminary estimates.

Source: US Geological Survey.

Electric energy (million kWh): 13,929 in 2006; 16,154 in 2007; 18,609 in 2008 (Source: UN Industrial Commodity Statistics Database).

Finance

CURRENCY AND EXCHANGE RATES

Monetary Units

United States currency is used: 100 cents = 1 US dollar ($).

Sterling and Euro Equivalents (30 December 2011)

£1 sterling = US $1.546;
€1 = US $1.294;
US $100 = £64.68 = €77.29.

Note: Ecuador's national currency was formerly the sucre. From 13 March 2000 the sucre was replaced by the US dollar, at an exchange rate of $1 = 25,000 sucres. Both currencies were officially in use for a transitional period of 180 days, but from 9 September sucres were withdrawn from circulation and the dollar became the sole legal tender.

BUDGET
(consolidated central government accounts, US $ million)

Revenue	2007	2008*	2009*
Petroleum revenue	1,764.3	4,641.7	2,298.2
Non-petroleum revenue	6,725.9	9,157.2	9,284.8
Taxation	4,749.4	6,569.8	7,256.7
Taxes on goods and services	2,728.6	3,298.5	3,466.7
Value-added tax	2,508.8	2,824.9	3,018.5
Taxes on income	1,268.0	2,338.6	2,517.5
Import duties	678.6	789.3	923.4
Other non-petroleum revenue	505.3	969.3	752.4
Transfers	1,471.2	1,618.2	1,275.6
Total	8,490.2	13,799.0	11,582.9

Expenditure	2007	2008*	2009*
Wages and salaries	2,913.9	3,928.6	4,707.8
Purchases of goods and services	537.4	844.6	824.0
Interest payments	915.3	796.9	474.1
Transfers	800.0	1,880.6	1,962.1
Other current expenditure	833.3	1,034.6	966.0
Capital expenditure	2,627.5	5,928.6	5,283.9
Total	8,627.3	14,413.9	14,217.9

* Provisional figures.

Note: Data exclude adjustment in treasury accounts for expenditure (US $ million): –73.4 in 2007; 0.0 in 2008–09.

2010 (US$ million, provisional): Total revenue 15,075.7 (Petroleum revenue 4,411.0, Non-petroleum revenue 10,664.7); Total expenditure 16,207.1 (Current expenditure 9,775.4, Capital expenditure 6,431.7).

INTERNATIONAL RESERVES
(US$ million at 31 December)

	2008	2009	2010
Gold (national valuation)	734.7	918.6	1,187.3
IMF special drawing rights	26.2	26.5	24.9
Reserve position in IMF	26.4	26.9	26.4
Foreign exchange	3,685.5	2,819.8	1,383.5
Total	4,472.8	3,791.8	2,622.1

Source: IMF, *International Financial Statistics*.

MONEY SUPPLY
(US$ million at 31 December)

	2008	2009	2010
Currency outside depository corporations	77.3	77.4	82.4
Transferable deposits	5,829.7	6,255.5	7,657.2
Other deposits	9,383.4	10,506.4	12,232.2
Broad money	15,290.4	16,839.3	19,971.8

Source: IMF, *International Financial Statistics*.

COST OF LIVING
(Consumer Price Index; base: 2005 = 100)

	2007	2008	2009
Food (incl. non-alcoholic beverages)	109.1	127.5	135.0
Fuel (excl. light)	100.2	100.3	98.4
Clothing	101.5	107.9	114.5
Rent	114.5	119.7	123.7

2010: Food (incl. non-alcoholic beverages) 141.5.

All items (base: 2000 = 100): 185.4 in 2007; 200.9 in 2008; 211.3 in 2009; 218.8 in 2010.

Source: ILO.

NATIONAL ACCOUNTS
(US $ million at current prices)

Expenditure on the Gross Domestic Product

	2008	2009	2010
Government final consumption expenditure	5,959.9	6,395.1	6,807.3
Private final consumption expenditure	33,091.9	34,750.4	39,281.1
Changes in stocks	2,095.4	–456.9	589.1
Gross fixed capital formation	13,022.4	12,599.1	14,587.5
Total domestic expenditure	54,169.6	53,287.8	61,264.9
Exports of goods and services	20,524.5	15,368.1	19,103.4
Less Imports of goods and services	20,485.5	16,633.9	22,390.3
GDP in market prices	54,208.5	52,021.9	57,978.1
GDP in constant 2000 prices	24,032.5	24,119.5	24,983.3

Gross Domestic Product by Economic Activity

	2008	2009	2010
Agriculture, hunting, forestry and fishing	3,478.2	3,524.8	3,824.3
Petroleum and other mining	9,979.8	6,254.2	8,679.2
Manufacturing (excl. petroleum-refining)	5,004.0	4,792.9	5,406.7
Manufacture of petroleum derivatives	1,262.4	1,157.7	849.6
Electricity, gas and water	666.9	547.5	460.4
—continued			
Construction	5,344.2	5,498.2	5,973.0
Wholesale and retail trade	6,359.5	5,925.3	6,837.1
Transport, storage and communications	3,306.8	3,456.2	3,583.5
Financial intermediation	1,290.5	1,361.9	1,618.5
Public administration, defence and other social services	2,773.2	3,002.7	3,118.1
Other services	13,827.9	14,684.9	16,058.7
Private households with domestic services	61.1	65.1	72.9
Sub-total	53,354.5	50,271.3	56,482.0
Less Financial intermediation services indirectly measured	1,316.7	1,381.8	1,625.6
Gross value added in basic prices	52,037.8	48,889.4	54,856.4
Taxes, less subsidies, on products	2,170.8	3,132.4	3,121.7
GDP in market prices	54,208.5	52,021.9	57,978.1

BALANCE OF PAYMENTS
(US$ million)

	2008	2009	2010
Exports of goods f.o.b.	19,461	14,412	18,137
Imports of goods f.o.b.	–17,912	–14,268	–19,641
Trade balance	1,549	144	–1,504
Exports of services	1,442	1,337	1,473
Imports of services	–3,013	–2,618	–3,010
Balance on goods and services	–23	–1,138	–3,040
Other income received	315	106	76
Other income paid	–1,771	–1,490	–1,130
Balance on goods, services and income	–1,479	–2,522	–4,095
Current transfers received	3,107	2,719	2,654
Current transfers paid	–162	–287	–345
Current balance	1,467	–90	–1,785
Capital account (net)	20	18	23
Direct investment from abroad	1,006	319	167
Portfolio investment assets	217	–152	–721
Portfolio investment liabilities	–4	–2,989	–10
Other investment assets	–1,398	–1,095	582
Other investment liabilities	–189	1,867	652
Net errors and omissions	–183	–660	–119
Overall balance	935	–2,783	–1,211

Source: IMF, *International Financial Statistics*.

External Trade

PRINCIPAL COMMODITIES
(distribution by HS, US$ million)

Imports f.o.b.	2008	2009	2010
Mineral fuels, oils, distillation products, etc.	3,443.1	2,670.6	4,380.4
Pharmaceutical products	615.4	683.4	791.6
Plastics and articles thereof	839.2	646.8	865.2
Iron and steel	1,224.0	526.6	680.9
Articles of iron or steel	395.9	447.7	475.4
Nuclear reactors, boilers, machinery, etc	2,078.1	2,006.4	2,459.5
Electrical, electronic equipment	1,793.6	1,320.4	1,986.0
Vehicles other than railway, tramway	2,007.3	1,590.7	2,360.9
Total (incl. others)	18,685.5	15,093.3	20,590.8

Exports f.o.b.	2008	2009	2010
Fish, crustaceans, molluscs, aquatic invertebrates	868.9	886.8	1,094.1
Live trees, plants, bulbs, roots, cut flowers, etc.	566.7	510.1	611.3
Edible fruit, nuts, peel of citrus fruit, melons	1,716.9	2,086.6	2,119.2
Food preparations of meat, fish and seafood	815.4	630.8	603.8
Mineral fuels, oils, distillation products, etc.	11,672.3	6,963.9	9,672.5
Crude petroleum oils, etc.	10,568.3	6,284.1	8,951.9
Total (incl. others)	18,510.6	13,724.3	17,489.9

Source: Trade Map-Trade Competitiveness Map, International Trade Centre, www.intracen.org/marketanalysis.

PRINCIPAL TRADING PARTNERS
(US $ million)

Imports c.i.f.	2008	2009	2010
Argentina	580.3	482.9	584.9
Brazil	913.1	690.2	853.8
Canada	259.1	209.6	265.2
Chile	553.3	446.9	564.3
China, People's Republic	2,320.5	1,722.8	1,606.6
Colombia	1,714.3	1,452.6	2,022.3
Germany	403.4	414.3	475.6
Italy	235.4	225.1	274.6
Japan	935.3	766.9	692.7
Korea, Republic	650.1	504.6	896.9
Mexico	811.1	660.1	727.6
Netherlands	113.0	109.2	133.9
Panama	47.3	55.3	1,027.2
Peru	462.6	564.9	1,035.6
Spain	203.5	174.5	268.8
Thailand	325.0	171.3	311.5
USA	2,792.8	2,495.9	5,736.4
Venezuela	488.7	226.5	549.8
Total (incl. others)	18,685.5	15,093.3	20,590.8

Exports f.o.b.	2008	2009	2010
Belgium and Luxembourg	196.2	189.1	244.4
Chile	1,503.4	897.8	846.6
China, People's Republic	384.7	122.5	328.7
Colombia	775.3	673.1	793.1
El Salvador	309.1	156.4	183.8
France	156.1	155.7	206.4
Germany	300.0	323.1	320.3
Guatemala	170.5	224.3	104.0
Italy	510.3	575.0	582.4
Korea, Republic	19.6	6.2	9.2
Malaysia	1.0	1.2	124.4
Netherlands	250.4	294.8	331.6
Netherlands Antilles	2.8	30.7	131.2
Panama	897.6	1,963.4	2,139.2
Peru	1,702.4	932.1	1,335.6
Russia	548.6	603.9	596.7
Spain	418.4	314.4	354.2
USA	8,379.6	4,582.5	6,077.5
Venezuela	698.4	535.3	974.0
Total (incl. others)	18,510.6	13,724.3	17,489.9

Source: Trade Map-Trade Competitiveness Map, International Trade Centre, www.intracen.org/marketanalysis.

Transport

RAILWAYS
(traffic)

	2002	2003	2004
Passenger-km (million)	33	4	2

Source: UN, *Statistical Yearbook*.

ROAD TRAFFIC
(motor vehicles in use at 31 December)

	2005	2006	2007
Passenger cars	462,175	519,041	507,469
Buses and coaches	10,349	11,164	10,925
Lorries and vans	334,998	346,350	323,480
Motorcycles and mopeds	60,144	85,001	78,323

Source: IRF, *World Road Statistics*.

SHIPPING

Merchant Fleet
(registered at 31 December)

	2007	2008	2009
Number of vessels	243	258	262
Total displacement ('000 grt)	300.0	318.3	321.6

Source: IHS Fairplay, *World Fleet Statistics*.

International Sea-borne Freight Traffic
('000 metric tons; estimates derived from monthly averages)

	2005	2006	2007
Goods loaded	24,636	26,736	24,612
Goods unloaded	5,484	8,832	10,332

Note: For goods unloaded, data include freight movement at ports of El Salitral, Esmeraldas, Guayaquil, La Libertad, Manta and Puerto Bolívar; data for goods loaded also include movements at the port of Balao.

Source: UN, *Monthly Bulletin of Statistics*.

CIVIL AVIATION
(traffic on scheduled services)

	2007	2008	2009
Kilometres flown (million)	34.4	33.0	35.3
Passenger-km (million)	3,692.9	3,772.4	4,247.9
Total ton-km (million)	139.4	114.4	103.4

Passengers carried ('000): 1,123 in 2003.

Source: UN, *Statistical Yearbook for Latin America and the Caribbean*.

Tourism

FOREIGN VISITOR ARRIVALS*

Country of residence	2007	2008	2009
Argentina	19,226	21,718	22,675
Canada	21,571	22,839	22,489
Chile	21,674	24,212	25,195
Colombia	203,326	200,487	160,116
France	16,856	18,876	19,810
Germany	23,302	24,227	24,841
Peru	150,439	147,420	150,548
Spain	46,358	49,937	56,400
United Kingdom	27,014	25,223	25,030
USA	241,018	244,406	242,096
Venezuela	21,110	26,771	29,416
Total (incl. others)	937,487	1,005,297	968,499

* Figures refer to total arrivals (including same-day visitors), except those of Ecuadorean nationals residing abroad.

Tourism receipts (US $ million, incl. passenger transport): 626 in 2007; 745 in 2008; 674 in 2009.

Source: World Tourism Organization.

Communications Media

	2008	2009	2010
Telephones ('000 main lines in use)	1,906.5	2,013.2	2,085.7
Mobile cellular telephones ('000 subscribers)	11,684.5	13,241.8	14,780.7
Internet subscribers ('000)	305.8	349.2	485.1
Broadband subscribers ('000)	156.0	241.2	197.9

Personal computers: 1,710,000 (129.5 per 1,000 persons) in 2006.

Radio receivers ('000 in use): 5,040 in 1999.

Daily newspapers: 36 in 2000 (average circulation 1,220,000).

Sources: UNESCO, *Statistical Yearbook*; UN, *Statistical Yearbook*; International Telecommunication Union.

Education

(2008/09 unless otherwise indicated)

		Students ('000)		
	Teachers	Males	Females	Total
Pre-primary	20,011	182.7	190.3	373.0
Primary	120,064	1,016.2	991.8	2,008.0
Secondary	60,032	667.8	676.6	1,344.3
general	47,357	526.4	524.4	1,050.8
technical/vocational	12,675	141.4	152.1	293.4
Tertiary*	26,910	251.9	282.6	534.5

* 2007/08.

Institutions (2002/03): Pre-primary 5,244; Primary 18,203; Secondary 3,486.

Sources: UNESCO Institute for Statistics; Ministerio de Educación y Cultura.

Pupil-teacher ratio (primary education, UNESCO estimate): 16.7 in 2008/09 (Source: UNESCO Institute for Statistics).

Adult literacy rate: 84.2% (males 87.1%; females 81.5%) in 2009 (Source: UNESCO Institute for Statistics).

Directory

The Government

HEAD OF STATE

President: RAFAEL CORREA DELGADO (took office 15 January 2007; re-elected 26 April 2009).

Vice-President: LENÍN MORENO GARCÉS.

CABINET
(May 2012)

The electoral alliance Alianza País formed a Government following the election of April 2009.

Co-ordinating Ministers

Co-ordinating Minister for Social Development: Dr RICHARD ESPINOSA GUZMÁN.

Co-ordinating Minister for Cultural and Natural Heritage: MARÍA FERNANDA ESPINOSA GARCÉS.

Co-ordinating Minister for Strategic Sectors: JORGE GLAS ESPINEL.

Co-ordinating Minister for Policy and Autonomous Governance: BETTY TOLA BERMEO.

Co-ordinating Minister for Economic Policy: JEANNETTE SÁNCHEZ ZURITA.

Co-ordinating Minister for Security: HOMERO ARELLANO.

Co-ordinating Minister for Production, Competitiveness and Commercialization: SANTIAGO LEÓN.

Co-ordinating Minister for Human Resources: AUGUSTO ESPINOSA.

Ministers

Minister of Foreign Relations, Trade and Integration: RICARDO ARMANDO PATIÑO AROCA.

Minister of Finance: PATRICIO RIVERA.

Minister of the Interior: JOSÉ SERRANO.

Minister of National Defence: MIGUEL CARVAJAL.

Minister of Electricity and Renewable Energy: ESTEBAN ALBORNOZ.

Minister of Transport and Public Works: MARÍA DE LOS ÁNGELES DUARTE.

Minister of Information and Telecommunications: JAIME RUÍZ GUERRERO.

Minister of Agriculture, Livestock, Aquaculture and Fishing: JAVIER PONCE CEVALLOS.

Minister of Education: GLORIA VIDAL ILLINGWORTH.

Minister of Justice, Human Rights and Worship: JOHANNA PESÁNTEZ.

Minister of Labour Relations: Dr JUAN JOSÉ FRANCISCO VACAS.

Minister of Economic and Social Inclusion: DORIS SOLIS CARRIÓN.

Minister of Public Health: Dr CARINA VANCE MAFLA.

Minister of Urban Development and Housing: PEDRO JARAMILLO CASTILLO.

Minister of Culture: ÉRIKA SYLVA CHARVET.

Minister of Sport: JOSÉ FRANCISCO CEVALLOS VILLAVICENCIO.

Minister of the Environment: MARCELA AGUIÑAGA VALLEJO.

Minister of Tourism: FREDDY EHLERS.

Minister of Non-Renewable Natural Resources: WILSON PÁSTOR MORRIS.

Minister of Industry and Productivity: VERÓNICA SIÓN.

National Secretaries

National Secretary of Public Administration: VINICIO ALVARADO ESPINEL.

National Secretary of Communication: FERNANDO ALVARADO ESPINEL.

National Secretary of Risk Management: MARÍA DEL PILAR CORNEJO.

National Secretary of Management Transparency: EDWIN JARRÍN.

National Secretary of Water: WALTER SOLÍS.

National Secretary of Planning and Development: FANDER FALCONÍ.

National Secretary of Migrants: FRANCISCO HAGÓ.

National Secretary of the People, Social Movements and Citizen Participation: MIREYA CÁRDENAS.

National Secretary of Science and Technology: RENÉ RAMÍREZ.

National Secretary of Intelligence: RAÚL PATIÑO AROCA.

MINISTRIES

Office of the President: Palacio Nacional, García Moreno 1043, Quito; tel. (2) 382-7000; internet www.presidencia.gob.ec.

Office of the Vice-President: Calle Benalcázar N4-40, entre Calles Espejo y Chile, Quito; tel. and fax (2) 258-4574; internet www.vicepresidencia.gob.ec.

Ministry of Agriculture, Livestock, Aquaculture and Fishing: Avda Eloy Alfaro y Amazonas, Quito; tel. (2) 396-0100; fax (2) 396-0200; e-mail webmaster@magap.gob.ec; internet www.magap.gob.ec.

Ministry of Culture: Avda Colón E5-34 y Juan León Mera, Quito; tel. (2) 381-4550; e-mail comunicacion@ministeriodecultura.gob.ec; internet www.ministeriodecultura.gob.ec.

Ministry of Economic and Social Inclusion: Edif. Matríz, Robles 850 y Páez, Quito; tel. (2) 398-3000; fax (2) 250-9850; e-mail ris@mies.gob.ec; internet www.mies.gob.ec.

Ministry of Education: Avda Amazonas N34-451, entre Avda Atahualpa y Juan Pablo Sánz, Quito; tel. (2) 396-1300; e-mail info@educacion.gob.ec; internet www.educacion.gob.ec.

Ministry of Electricity and Renewable Energy: Edif. Correos del Ecuador, 6°, Eloy Alfaro N29-50 y 9 de Octubre, Edif. Correos del Ecuador, Quito; tel. (2) 397-6000; e-mail info@mer.gov.ec; internet www.mer.gob.ec.

Ministry of the Environment: Calle Madrid 1159 y Andalusía, Quito; tel. (2) 398-7600; fax (2) 256-3462; e-mail mma@ambiente.gob.ec; internet www.ambiente.gob.ec.

Ministry of Finance: Avda 10 de Agosto 1661 y Bolivia, Quito; tel. (2) 399-8300; fax (2) 250-5256; e-mail mefecuador@finanzas.gob.ec; internet finanzas.gob.ec.

Ministry of Foreign Relations, Trade and Integration: Avda 10 de Agosto y Carrión E1-76, Quito; tel. (2) 299-3200; fax (2) 299-3273; e-mail gabminis@mmrree.gob.ec; internet www.mmrree.gob.ec.

Ministry of Industry and Productivity: Avda Eloy Alfaro y Amazonas, Quito; tel. (2) 254-6690; fax (2) 250-3818; e-mail info@mic.gov.ec; internet www.mipro.gob.ec.

Ministry of Information and Telecommunications: Avda 6 de Diciembre N25-75 y Avda Colón, Quito; tel. (2) 220-0200; fax (2) 222-8950; e-mail info@mintel.gob.ec; internet www.mintel.gob.ec.

Ministry of the Interior: Espejo y Benalcázar N4-24, Quito; tel. (2) 295-5666; fax (2) 295-8360; e-mail informacion@ministeriodelinterior.gob.ec; internet www.ministeriodelinterior.gob.ec.

Ministry of Justice, Human Rights and Worship: Avda Amazonas N34-451 y Atahualpa, Quito; tel. (2) 246-3083; fax (2) 246-4914; e-mail webmaster@minjusticia-ddhh.gov.ec; internet www.minjusticia-ddhh.gob.ec.

Ministry of Labour Relations: Clemente Ponce N15-59 y Piedrahita, Quito; tel. (2) 254-8900; fax (2) 254-2580; e-mail comunicacion_social@mrl.gov.ec; internet www.mrl.gob.ec.

Ministry of National Defence: Calle Exposición 208, La Recoleta, Quito; tel. (2) 295-1951; fax (2) 258-0941; e-mail comunicacion@midena.gob.ec; internet www.midena.gob.ec.

Ministry of Non-Renewable Natural Resources: Edif. MOP, Avda Orellana 26-220 y Juan León Mera (esq.), Quito; tel. (2) 297-7000; e-mail info@minasypetroleos.gov.ec; internet www.mrnnr.gob.ec.

Ministry of Public Health: República de El Salvador 950, entre Suecia y Naciones Unidas, Quito; tel. and fax (2) 381-4400; e-mail comunicacion.social@msp.gob.ec; internet www.msp.gob.ec.

Ministry of Sport: Avda Gaspar de Villaroel E10-122 y 6 de Diciembre, Quito; tel. (2) 396-9200; fax (2) 245-4418; e-mail storres@deporte.gob.ec; internet www.deporte.gob.ec.

Ministry of Tourism: Avda Eloy Alfaro N32-300 y Carlos Tobar, 2°, Quito; tel. and fax (2) 399-9333; e-mail contactenos@turismo.gob.ec; internet www.turismo.gob.ec.

Ministry of Transport and Public Works: Avda Juan León Mera N26-220 y Orellana, Quito; tel. (2) 397-4600; e-mail comunicacion@mtop.gov.ec; internet www.mtop.gob.ec.

Ministry of Urban Development and Housing: Avda 10 de Agosto 2270 y Corotero, 6°, Quito; tel. (2) 223-8060; fax (2) 256-6785; e-mail despacho@miduvi.gob.ec; internet www.miduvi.gob.ec.

President and Legislature

PRESIDENT

Election, 26 April 2009

Candidate	Valid votes	% of valid votes
Rafael Correa Delgado (Alianza País)	3,586,439	51.99
Lucio Gutiérrez Borbua (PSP)	1,947,830	28.24
Alvaro Fernando Noboa Pontón (PRIAN)	786,718	11.40
Martha Roldós Bucaram (RED/MPD)	298,765	4.33
Others	278,160	4.04
Total*	6,897,912	100.00

* In addition, there were 534,149 blank and 496,687 invalid ballots.

ASAMBLEA NACIONAL

President: FERNANDO CORDERO.

Election, 26 April 2009

Political parties	Seats
Alianza País	59
Partido Sociedad Patriótica 21 de Enero (PSP)	18
Partido Social Cristiano (PSC)	11
Partido Renovador Institucional de Acción Nacional (PRIAN)	7
Movimiento Municipalista por la Integridad Nacional	4
Movimiento Popular Democrático (MPD)	5
Movimiento de Unidad Pluriacional Pachakútik—Nuevo País (MUPP—NP)	4
Partido Roldosista Ecuatoriano (PRE)	3
Izquierda Democrática (ID)	1
Others	12
Total	124

Election Commission

Consejo Nacional Electoral (CNE): Avda 6 de Diciembre N33-122 y Bosmediano, Quito; tel. (2) 381-5410; internet www.cne.gob.ec; f. 2008 to replace the Tribunal Supremo Electoral; independent; Pres. OMAR SIMÓN CAMPAÑA.

Political Organizations

Alianza País (Patria Altiva i Soberana): Of. 501, Edif. Torres Whimper, Diego de Almagro 32-27 y Whimper, Quito; tel. (2) 600-0630; fax (2) 600-1029; e-mail galoisho57@yahoo.com; internet movimientoalianzapais.com.ec; f. 2006; electoral alliance mainly comprising the Movimiento País; left-wing; Pres. RAFAEL CORREA DELGADO; Exec. Sec. GALO MORA WITT.

Izquierda Democrática (ID): Polonia N30-83 y Vancouver, Quito; tel. (2) 256-4436; fax (2) 256-4860; e-mail webmaster@partidoizquierdademocratica.org; internet www.partidoizquierdademocratica.org; f. 1977; absorbed Fuerzas Armadas Populares Eloy Alfaro—Alfaro Vive ¡Carajo! in 1991; Pres. DALTÓN EMORY BACIGALUPO BUENAVENTURA.

Movimiento Municipalista por la Integridad Nacional (MMIN): Quito; tel. (2) 246-9683; fax (2) 246-9769; internet www.movimientomunicipalista.com; f. 2008; left-wing; advocated further provincial autonomy; Leader PACO MONCAYO GALLEGOS; Sec.-Gen. CARLOS VILLALBA.

Movimiento Popular Democrático (MPD): Manuel Larrea N14-70 y Rio Frío, Quito; tel. (2) 250-3580; fax (2) 252-6111; e-mail info@mpd15.org.ec; internet www.mpd15.org.ec; f. 1978; attached to the PCMLE (q.v.); Dir LUIS VILLACÍS; Sec. MARCO CADENA.

Movimiento de Unidad Pluriacional Pachakútik—Nuevo País (MUPP—NP): Calle Lugo 13-04 y Avda Ladrón de Guevara, La Floresta, Quito; tel. (2) 322-7259; fax (2) 256-0422; e-mail info@pachakutik.org.ec; internet www.pachakutik.org.ec; f. 1995 as Movimiento Nuevo País—Pachakútik (MNPP); represents indigenous, environmental and social groups; Nat. Co-ordinator RAFAEL ANTUNÍ; Sec. PATRICIO QUEZADA ORTEGA.

Participación: Quito; f. 2011; Pres. GUSTAVO LARREA.

Partido Comunista Marxista-Leninista de Ecuador (PCMLE): e-mail pcmle@bigfoot.com; internet www.pcmle.org; f. 1964; contests elections as the MPD (q.v.).

Partido Renovador Institucional Acción Nacional (PRIAN): Quito; internet www.prian.org.ec; right-wing, populist; Leader ALVARO FERNANDO NOBOA PONTÓN.

Partido Roldosista Ecuatoriano (PRE): 1 de Mayo 912 y Tulcán, Quito; tel. (2) 229-0542; fax (2) 269-0250; e-mail dalo-por-hecho@hotmail.com; internet www.dalo10.com; f. 1982; populist; Nat. Dir ABDALÁ BUCARAM PULLEY.

Partido Social Cristiano (PSC): Carrión 548 y Reina Victoria, Casilla 9454, Quito; tel. (2) 254-4536; fax (2) 256-8562; e-mail sugerencias@partidosocialcristiano.org; internet www.partidosocialcristiano.org; f. 1951; centre-right; Pres. PASCUAL EUGENIO DEL CIOPPO ARAGUNDI; Sec. XAVIER EDUARDO BUITRÓN CARRERA.

Partido Socialista—Frente Amplio (PS—FA): Avda Gran Colombia N15-201 y Yaguachi, Quito; tel. (2) 232-4417; fax (2) 222-2184; e-mail psecuador@andinanet.net; internet psfaecuador.org; f. 1926; Pres. RAFAEL QUINTERO; Sec.-Gen. JOSÉ ROBAYO ZAPATA.

Partido Sociedad Patriótica 21 de Enero (PSP): Quito; internet www.sociedadpatriotica.com; contested the 2002 elections in alliance with the MUPP—NP; Leader GILMAR GUTIÉRREZ.

Red Etica y Democracia (RED): Edif. Alemania, 1°, Alemania y Guayanas, Quito; tel. (2) 222-3348; e-mail info@redeticaydemocracia.com; Leader MARTHA ROLDÓS.

Unión Demócrata Cristiana (UDC): Pradera N30-58 y San Salvador, Quito; tel. (2) 250-2995; e-mail cbonilla@udc.com.ec; internet www.udc.com.ec; f. 1978 as Democracia Popular—Unión Demócrata Cristiana (DP—UDC); adopted current name 2006; Christian democrat; Pres. SANDRA ALARCÓN; Sec. MARCO BENAVIDES.

OTHER ORGANIZATIONS

Confederación de las Nacionalidades Indígenas de la Amazonia Ecuatoriana (CONFENIAE): Union Base, Apdo 17-01-4180, Puyo; tel. (3) 227-644; fax (3) 227-644; e-mail info_confel@confeniae.org.ec; represents indigenous peoples; mem. of CONAIE (q.v.); Pres. TITO PUANCHIR.

Confederación de Nacionalidades Indígenas del Ecuador (CONAIE): Avda Los Granados 2553 y 6 de Diciembre, Quito; tel. (2) 245-2335; fax (2) 244-4991; e-mail info@conaie.org; internet www.conaie.org; f. 1986; represents indigenous peoples; MUPP—NP (q.v.) represents CONAIE and related orgs in the legislature; Pres. HUMBERTO CHOLANGO; Vice-Pres. MIGUEL GUATEMAL.

Confederación de los Pueblos de Nacionalidad Kichua del Ecuador (Ecuarunari): Edif. El Conquistador, 1°, Julio Matovelle 128, entre Vargas y Pasaje San Luis, Quito; tel. (2) 258-0700; fax (2) 258-0713; e-mail ecuarunari@ecuarunari.org; internet www.ecuarunari.org; f. 1972; indigenous movt; Pres. DELFÍN TENESACA.

Coordinadora de las Organizaciones Indígenas de la Cuenca Amazónica (COICA): Sevilla N24-358 y Guipuzcoa, La Floresta, Quito; tel. (2) 322-6744; e-mail com@coica.org.ec; internet www.coica.org.ec; f. 1984 in Lima, Peru; moved to Quito in 1993; umbrella group of 9 orgs representing indigenous peoples of the Amazon Basin in Bolivia, Brazil, Colombia, Ecuador, French Guiana, Guyana, Suriname and Venezuela; Gen. Co-ordinator EGBERTO TABO CHIPUNAVI; Vice-Co-ordinator ROSA ALVORADO.

ARMED GROUPS

The following guerrilla organizations were reported to be active in the 2000s.

Ejército de Liberación Alfarista (ELA): f. 2001; extreme left-wing insurrectionist group; formed by fmr mems of disbanded armed groups Alfaro Vive ¡Carajo!, Montoneros Patria Libre and Sol Rojo; Spokesperson SEBASTIÁN SÁNCHEZ.

Grupos de Combatientes Populares (GCP): Cuenca; internet gcp-ecuador.blogspot.com; communist guerrilla grouping; active since 2000.

Izquierda Revolucionaria Armada (IRA): extreme left-wing revolutionary group opposed to international capitalism.

Milicias Revolucionarias del Pueblo (MRP): extreme left-wing grouping opposed to international capitalism.

Diplomatic Representation

EMBASSIES IN ECUADOR

Argentina: Avda Amazonas 21-147 y Roca, 8°, Of. 812 a la 820, Apdo 17-12-937, Quito; tel. (2) 256-2292; fax (2) 256-8177; e-mail embarge2@uio.satnet.net; Ambassador ALBERTO ÁLVAREZ TUFILLO.

Bolivia: Avda Eloy Alfaro 2432 y Fernando Ayarza, Apdo 17-210003, Quito; tel. (2) 244-4830; fax (2) 224-4833; e-mail emboliviaquito@andinanet.net; Chargé d'affaires a.i. MANUEL MONROY.

Brazil: Edif. España, Avda Amazonas 1429 y Colón, 9° y 10°, Apdo 17-01-231, Quito; tel. (2) 256-3142; fax (2) 250-4468; e-mail ebrasil@embajadadelbrasil.org.ec; internet www.embajadadelbrasil.org.ec; Ambassador FERNANDO SIMAS MAGALHÃES.

Canada: Edif. Eurocenter, 3°, Avda Amazonas 4153 y Unión Nacional de Periodistas, Apdo 17-11-6512, Quito; tel. (2) 245-5499; fax (2) 227-7672; e-mail quito@international.gc.ca; internet www.canadainternational.gc.ca/ecuador-equateur; Ambassador ANDREW SHISKO.

Chile: Edif. Xerox, 4°, Juan Pablo Sanz 3617 y Amazonas, Apdo 17-17-206, Quito; tel. (2) 224-9403; fax (2) 244-4470; e-mail embachileecu@uio.satnet.net; Ambassador JUAN PABLO LIRA BIANCHI.

China, People's Republic: Avda Atahualpa 349 y Amazonas, Quito; tel. (2) 243-3337; fax (2) 244-4364; e-mail embchina@uio.telconet.net; Ambassador YUAN GUISEN.

Colombia: Edif. Arista, 7°, Avda Colón 1133 y Amazonas, Quito; tel. (2) 222-2486; fax (2) 222-8296; e-mail equito@cancilleria.gov.co; internet www.embajadaenecuador.gov.co; Ambassador FERNANDO ENRIQUE ARBOLEDA RIPOLL.

Costa Rica: Javier Aráuz 111 y Germán Alemán, Apdo 17-03-301, Quito; tel. (2) 225-2330; fax (2) 225-4087; e-mail embajcr@uio.satnet.net; Ambassador GERARDO LIZANO VINDAS.

Cuba: Mercurio 365, entre La Razón y El Vengador, Quito; tel. (2) 245-6936; fax (2) 243-0594; e-mail embajada@embacuba.ec; internet www.cubadiplomatica.cu/ecuador; Ambassador JORGE RODRIGUEZ HERNÁNDEZ.

Dominican Republic: German Alemán E12-80 y Juan Ramírez, Sector Megamaxi, Batan Alto, Quito; tel. (2) 243-4232; fax (2) 243-4275; e-mail info@embajadadominicanaecuador.com; internet www.embajadadominicanaecuador.com; Ambassador VÍCTOR REINALDO LORA DÍAZ.

Egypt: Avda Tarqui E4-56 y Avda 6 de Diciembre, Apdo 17-7-9355, Quito; tel. (2) 222-5240; fax (2) 256-3521; e-mail embassy.quito@mfa.gov.eg; Ambassador MEDHAT K. EL-MELIGY.

El Salvador: Edif. Gabriela III, 3°, Avda República de El Salvador 733 y Portugal, Quito; tel. (2) 243-3070; fax (2) 224-2829; e-mail embajada@elsalvador.com.ec; internet www.elsalvador.com.ec; Ambassador MARIO JOSÉ AVILA ROMERO.

France: Calle Leonidas Plaza 107 y Avda Patria, Apdo 19-13-536, Quito; tel. (2) 294-3800; fax (2) 294-3809; e-mail chancellerie.quito@ifrance.com; internet www.ambafrance-ec.org; Ambassador JEAN-BAPTISTE MAIN DE BOISSIÈRE.

Germany: Edif. Citiplaza, 13° y 14°, Avda Naciones Unidas E10-44 y República de El Salvador, Apdo 17-17-536, Quito; tel. (2) 297-0820; fax (2) 297-0815; e-mail info@quito.diplo.de; internet www.quito.diplo.de; Ambassador PETER LINDER.

Guatemala: Edif. Gabriela III, 3°, Of. 301, Avda República de El Salvador 733 y Portugal, Apdo 17-03-294, Quito; tel. (2) 245-9700; fax (2) 226-4228; e-mail embecuador@minex.gob.gt; Chargé d'affaires a.i. FLORIDALMA FRANCO PAIZ.

Holy See: Avda Orellana 692 E10-03, Apdo 17-07-8980, Quito; tel. (2) 250-5200; fax (2) 256-4810; e-mail nunzec@uio.satnet.net; Apostolic Nuncio Most Rev. GIACOMO GUIDO OTTONELLO (Titular Archbishop of Sasabe).

Honduras: Edif. Suecia, Avda Shyris y calle Suecia 277, 5° Norte, Apdo 17-03-4753, Quito; tel. (2) 243-8820; fax (2) 244-2476; e-mail embhquito@yahoo.com; Ambassador RAFAEL MURILLO SELVA.

Indonesia: Avda Portugal y Francisco Cazanova, Quito; tel. (2) 245-3260; fax (2) 256-9226; e-mail lopezmar_indos@yahoo.com; Ambassador SAUT MARULI TUA GULTOM.

Iran: José Queri E14-43 y Avda Los Granados, Quito; tel. (2) 334-3450; fax (2) 245-2824; e-mail embiranecuador@gmail.com; Ambassador MAJID SALEHI.

Israel: Edif. Altana Plaza, 5°, Avda Coruña E26-48 y San Ignacio, Apdo 17-21-038, Quito; tel. (2) 397-1500; fax (2) 397-1555; e-mail info@quito.mfa.gov.il; internet www.quito.mfa.gov.il; Ambassador EYAL SELA.

Italy: Calle La Isla 111 y Humberto Alborñoz, Apdo 17-03-72, Quito; tel. (2) 256-1077; fax (2) 250-2818; e-mail archivio.quito@esteri.it; internet www.ambquito.esteri.it; Ambassador GIANNI MICHELE PICCATO.

Japan: Edif. Amazonas Plaza, 11° y 12°, Avda Amazonas N39-123 y Arízaga, Apdo 17-21-01518, Quito; tel. (2) 227-8700; fax (2) 244-9399; e-mail embapon@embajadadeljapon.org.ec; internet www.ec.emb-japan.go.jp; Ambassador OSAMU IMAI.

Korea, Republic: Edif. World Trade Center, Avda 12 de Octubre 1942 y Cordero, Torre B, 3°, Apdo 17-03-626, Quito; tel. (2) 290-9227; fax (2) 250-1190; e-mail ecuador@mofat.go.kr; internet ecu.mofat.go.kr; Ambassador IN GYUN CHUNG.

Mexico: Avda 6 de Diciembre N36-165 y Naciones Unidas, Apdo 17-11-6371, Quito; tel. (2) 292-3770; fax (2) 244-8245; e-mail embajadamexico@embamex.org.ec; internet www.sre.gob.mx/ecuador; Ambassador ERNESTO CAMPOS TENORIO.

Panama: Edif. Maria Gabriela, 5°, Avda Coruña 601 y Orellana (esq.), Quito; tel. (2) 256-6449; fax (2) 250-8837; e-mail panaembaecuador@hotmail.com; internet www.embajadadepanamaecuador.com; Ambassador JOSÉ NORIEL ACOSTA RODRÍQUEZ.

Paraguay: Edif. Torre Sol Verde, 8°, Avda 12 de Octubre, esq. Salazar, Apdo 17-03-139, Quito; tel. (2) 290-9005; fax (2) 290-9006; e-mail embapar@uio.satnet.net; Ambassador ANTONIO RIVAS PALACIOS.

Peru: Avda República de El Salvador N34-361 e Irlanda, Apdo 17-07-9380, Quito; tel. (2) 246-8410; fax (2) 225-2560; e-mail embaperu-quito@rree.gob.pe; internet www.embajadadelperu.org.ec; Ambassador JAVIER LEÓN OLAVARRÍA.

Russia: Reina Victoria 462 y Ramón Roca, Apdo 17-01-3868, Quito; tel. (2) 252-6361; fax (2) 256-5531; e-mail embrusia_ecuador@mail.ru; internet www.ecuador.mid.ru; Ambassador YAN A. BURLIAY.

Spain: General Francisco Salazar E12-73 y Toledo (Sector La Floresta), Apdo 17-01-9322, Quito; tel. (2) 322-6296; fax (2) 322-7805; e-mail emb.quito@mae.es; internet www.maec.es/embajadas/quito; Ambassador FEDERICO TORRES MURO.

Switzerland: Edif. Xerox, 2°, Avda Amazonas 3617 y Juan Pablo Sanz, Apdo 17-11-4815, Quito; tel. (2) 243-4949; fax (2) 244-9314; e-mail qui.vertretung@eda.admin.ch; internet www.eda.admin.ch/quito; Ambassador ROLAND FISCHER.

United Kingdom: Edif. Citiplaza, 14°, Avda Naciones Unidas y República de El Salvador, Apdo 17-17-830, Quito; tel. (2) 297-0800; fax (2) 297-0809; e-mail britembq@uio.satnet.net; internet ukinecuador.fco.gov.uk; Ambassador LINDA CROSS.

USA: Avigiras 12-170 y Eloy Alfaro, Apdo 17-17-1538, Quito; tel. (2) 398-5000; fax (2) 398-5100; e-mail contacto.usembuio@state.gov; internet ecuador.usembassy.gov; Ambassador ADAM E. NAMM.

Uruguay: Edif. Josueth González, 9°, Avda 6 de Diciembre 2816 y Paul Rivet, Apdo 17-12-282, Quito; tel. (2) 256-3762; fax (2) 256-3763; e-mail uruguay@embajadauruguay.com.ec; Ambassador ENRIQUE DELGADO GENTA.

Venezuela: Edif. COMONSA, 8° y 9°, Avda Amazonas N30-240 y Eloy Alfaro, Apdo 17-01-688, Quito; tel. (2) 255-4032; fax (2) 252-0306; e-mail embve.ecqto@mre.gob.ve; internet www.venezuela.org.ec; Ambassador RODOLFO EDUARDO SANZ.

Judicial System

CONSTITUTIONAL COURT

Tribunal Contencioso Electoral: José Manuel Abascal N37-499 y Portete, Apdo 17-17-949, Quito; tel. (2) 381-5000; e-mail servicio.ciudadano@tce.gob.ec; internet www.tce.gob.ec; f. 2008 by reform of fmr Tribunal Constitucional; Pres. Dr XIMENA ENDARA OSEJO; Sec.-Gen. Dr FABIÁN HARO ASPIAZU.

NATIONAL COURT OF JUSTICE

The former Supreme Court of Justice was reconstituted as the National Court of Justice in 2008 under the terms of the new Constitution. It is composed of 21 Justices, including the President. Three Justices sit in each of its seven chambers, which comprise two penal law courts, one administrative litigation court, one fiscal law court, one civil law court and two employment law courts.

Corte Nacional de Justicia: Avda Amazonas N37-101, esq. Unión Nacional de Periodistas, Quito; tel. (2) 227-8396; e-mail ramaguai@funcionjudicial-pichincha.gov.ec; internet www.cortesuprema.gov.ec; f. 1830; scheduled for restructuring under the Consejo de la Judicatura de Transición; Pres. Dr CARLOS RAMIREZ ROMERO.

Attorney-General: Dr DIEGO GARCÍA CARRIÓN.

OTHER COURTS

Other courts include Higher or Divisional Courts and Provincial Courts.

TRANSITIONAL COUNCIL OF THE JUDICIARY

Consejo de la Judicatura de Transición: Jorge Washington E4-157, entre Juan León Mera y Avda Río Amazonas, Quito; e-mail webadmin@funcionjudicial.gob.ec; internet www.funcionjudicial.gob.ec; f. 1998; transitional council created by July 2011 referendum; operational for a maximum period of 18 months; Pres. PAULO RODRÍGUEZ.

Religion

There is no state religion, but the vast majority of the population are Roman Catholics. There are representatives of various Protestant Churches and of the Jewish faith in Quito and Guayaquil.

CHRISTIANITY

The Roman Catholic Church

Ecuador comprises four archdioceses, 12 dioceses and eight Apostolic Vicariates. Some 90% of the population are Roman Catholics.

Bishops' Conference

Conferencia Episcopal Ecuatoriana, Avda América 24-59 y La Gasca, Apdo 17-01-1081, Quito; tel. (2) 222-3137; fax (2) 250-1429; e-mail confepec@uio.satnet.net.

f. 1939 statutes approved 1999; Pres. Most Rev. ANTONIO ARREGUI YARZA (Archbishop of Guayaquil).

Archbishop of Cuenca: LUIS GERARDO CABRERA HERRERA, Arzobispado, Manuel Vega 8-66 y Calle Bolívar, Apdo 01-01-0046, Cuenca; tel. (7) 847-234; fax (7) 844-436; e-mail dicuenca@etapaonline.ne.ec.

Archbishop of Guayaquil: ANTONIO ARREGUI YARZA, Arzobispado, Calle Clemente Ballén 501 y Chimborazo, Apdo 09-01-0254, Guayaquil; tel. (4) 232-2778; fax (4) 232-9695; e-mail marregui@q.ecua.net.ec; internet www.iglesiacatolicaguayaquil.org.

Archbishop of Portoviejo: LORENZO VOLTOLINI ESTI, Arzobispado, Avda Universitaria s/n, Entre Alajuela y Ramos y Duarte, Apdo 13-01-0024, Portoviejo; tel. (5) 263-0404; fax (5) 263-4428; e-mail arzobis@ecua.net.ec.

Archbishop of Quito: FAUSTO GABRIEL TRÁVEZ TRÁVEZ, Arzobispado, Calle Chile 1140 y Venezuela, Apdo 17-01-00106, Quito; tel. (2) 228-4429; fax (2) 258-0973; e-mail raul.vela@andinanet.net; internet www.arquidiocesisdequito.org.

The Anglican Communion

Anglicans in Ecuador are under the jurisdiction of Province IX of the Episcopal Church in the USA. The country is divided into two dioceses, one of which, Central Ecuador, is a missionary diocese.

Bishop of Central Ecuador: Rt Rev. WILFRIDO RAMOS-ORENCH, Avda Amazonas 4430 y Villalengua, 7°, Of. 708, Quito.

Bishop of Littoral Ecuador: Rt Rev. ALFREDO MORANTE, Calle Bogotá 1010, Barrio Centenario, Apdo 5250, Guayaquil; tel. (2) 443-3050; e-mail iedl@gu.pro.ec.

Other Churches

Convención Bautista Ecuatoriana: Casilla 3236, Guayaquil; tel. (4) 237-5673; fax 245-2319; e-mail cbe@telconet.net; f. 1950; Baptist; Pres. Rev. JULIO XAVIER ALVARADO SILVA.

Iglesia Evangélica Metodista del Ecuador: Rumipamba 915, Apdo 17-03-236, Quito; tel. (2) 226-5158; fax (2) 243-9576; Methodist; 800 mems, 2,000 adherents.

BAHÁ'Í FAITH

National Spiritual Assembly of the Bahá'ís: Apdo 869A, Quito; tel. (2) 256-3484; fax (2) 252-3192; e-mail ecua9nsa@uio.satnet.net; mems resident in 1,121 localities.

The Press

PRINCIPAL DAILIES

Quito

El Comercio: Avda Pedro Vicente Maldonado 11515 y el Tablón, Apdo 17-01-57, Quito; tel. (2) 267-0999; fax (2) 267-0214; e-mail contactenos@elcomercio.com; internet www.elcomercio.com; f. 1906; morning; independent; Proprs Compañía Anónima El Comercio; Pres. FABRIZIO ACQUAVIVA MANTILLA; Dir-Gen. GUADALUPE MANTILLA DE ACQUAVIVA; circ. 160,000.

La Hora: Panamericana Norte km 3½, Quito; tel. (2) 247-3724; fax (2) 247-5086; e-mail lahora@uio.satnet.net; internet www.lahora.com.ec; f. 1982; 12 regional edns; Pres. Dr FRANCISCO VIVANCO RIOFRÍO; Gen. Editor JUANA LÓPEZ SARMIENTO.

Hoy: Avda Mariscal Sucre Of. 6-116, Apdo 17-07-09069, Quito; tel. (2) 249-0888; fax (2) 249-1881; e-mail hoy@hoy.com.ec; internet www.hoy.com.ec; f. 1982; morning; independent; Dir JAIME MANTILLA ANDERSON; Editor JUAN TIBANLOMBO; circ. 72,000.

Ultimas Noticias: Avda Pedro Vicente Maldonado 11515 y el Tablón, Apdo 17-01-57, Quito; tel. (2) 267-0999; fax (2) 267-4923; e-mail mivoz@ultimasnoticias.ec; internet www.ultimasnoticias.ec; f. 1938; evening; independent; commercial; Proprs Compañía Anónima El Comercio; Dir JORGE RIBADENEIRA ARAUJO; circ. 60,000.

Guayaquil

Expreso: Avda Carlos Julio Arosemena km 2½, Casilla 5890, Guayaquil; tel. (4) 220-1100; fax (4) 220-0291; e-mail editorgeneral@granasa.com.ec; internet www.diario-expreso.com; f. 1973; morning; independent; Gen. Editor EDWIN ULLOA ARELLANO; circ. 60,000.

Extra: Avda Carlos Julio Arosemena km 2½, Casilla 5890, Guayaquil; tel. (4) 220-1100; fax (4) 220-0291; e-mail matriz@granasa.com.ec; internet www.diario-extra.com; f. 1974; morning; popular; Dir NICOLÁS ULLOA FIGUEROA; Editor HENRY HOLGUÍN; circ. 200,000.

La Razón: Avda Constitución y las Américas, Guayaquil; tel. (4) 228-0100; fax (4) 228-5110; e-mail cartas@larazonecuador.com; internet www.larazonecuador.com; f. 1965; morning; independent; Propr ROBERTO ISAÍAS DASSUM; circ. 35,000.

El Telégrafo: Avda 10 de Agosto 601 y Boyacá, Casilla 415, Guayaquil; tel. (4) 232-6500; fax (4) 232-3265; e-mail contacto@telegrafo.com.ec; internet www.telegrafo.com.ec; f. 1884; acquired by the state in 2008 and refounded; morning; Dir RUBÉN MONTOYA VEGA; Chief Editor PATRICIO GONZÁLEZ.

El Universo: Avda Domingo Comín y Alban, Casilla 09-01-531, Guayaquil; tel. (4) 249-0000; fax (4) 249-1034; e-mail pocha@eluniverso.com; internet www.eluniverso.com; f. 1921; morning; independent; Pres. NICOLÁS PÉREZ LAPENTTI; Dir CARLOS PÉREZ BARRIGA; circ. 174,000 (weekdays), 290,000 (Sundays).

Cuenca

El Mercurio: Avda las Américas Sur y N. Aguilar, Sector El Arenal, Casilla 01-60, Cuenca; tel. (7) 409-5682; fax (7) 409-5685; e-mail redaccion1@elmercurio.com.ec; internet www.elmercurio.com.ec; f. 1924; morning; Dir NICANOR MERCHÁN LUCO.

El Tiempo: Avda Loja y Rodrigo de Triana, Cuenca; tel. (7) 288-2551; fax (7) 288-2555; e-mail redaccion@eltiempo.com.ec; internet www.eltiempo.com.ec; f. 1955; morning; independent; Dir Dr RENÉ TORAL CALLE; circ. 35,000.

PERIODICALS

Quito

Chasqui: Avda Diego de Almagro 32-133 y Andrade Marín, Apdo 17-01-584, Quito; tel. (2) 254-8011; fax (2) 250-2487; e-mail chasqui@ciespal.net; internet chasqui.comunica.org; f. 1997; quarterly; media studies; publ. of the Centro Internacional de Estudios Superiores de Comunicación para América Latina (CIESPAL); Dir EDGAR JARAMILLO; Editor LUIS ELADIO PROAÑO.

Cosas: Avda 12 de Octubre N26-14 y Coruña, Quito; tel. and fax (2) 250-2444; e-mail redaccion@cosas.com.ec; internet www.cosas.com.ec; f. 1994; women's interest; Dir CLAUDIA GONZÁLEZ DE RIZZI; Editor MARTHA DUBRAVCIC.

Criterios: Edif. Las Cámaras, 4°, Avda Amazonas y República, Casilla 17-01-202, Quito; tel. (2) 244-3787; fax (2) 243-5862; e-mail criterios@lacamaradequito.com; internet www.lacamaradequito.com; f. 1996; monthly; organ of the Cámara de Comercio de Quito; commerce; Dir-Gen. LOLO ECHEVERRÍA; Gen. Editor MARÍA UTRERAS.

Gestión: Avda González Suárez 335 y San Ignacio, 2°, Quito; tel. (2) 223-6848; fax (2) 255-9930; e-mail info@dinediciones.com; internet www.gestion.dinediciones.com; f. 1994; monthly; economy and society; Gen. Man. HERNÁN ALTAMIRANO; Editor JUANITA ORDÓÑEZ; circ. 15,000.

Mundo Diners: Avda 12 de Octubre N25-32 y Coruña, Quito; tel. (2) 254-5209; fax (2) 254-5188; e-mail jortiz@dinediciones.com; internet www.dinediciones.com/diners; f. 1986; monthly; culture, politics, society, etc.; Pres. FIDEL EGAS GRIJALVA.

Guayaquil

El Agro: Avda Constitución y Avda de las Américas 11 y Calle A, Casilla 09-01-9686, Guayaquil; tel. (4) 269-0019; fax (4) 269-0555; e-mail elagro@uminasa.com; internet www.elagro.com.ec; f. 1991; monthly; agriculture; Pres. EDUARDO PEÑA; Gen. Editor ALEXANDRA ZAMBRANO DE ANDRIUOLI.

Análisis Semanal: Edif. La Previsora, 30°, Of. 3005, Avda 9 de Octubre 100 y Malecón Simón Bolívar, Guayaquil; tel. (4) 230-7371; fax (4) 232-6842; e-mail wspurrier@ecuadoranalysis.com; internet www.ecuadoranalysis.com; weekly; economic and political affairs; Editor WALTER SPURRIER BAQUERIZO.

El Financiero: Avda Jorge Pérez Concha (Circunvalación Sur) 201 y Única, Casilla 6666, Guayaquil; tel. (4) 261-1000; fax (4) 288-2950; e-mail redacciong@elfinanciero.com; internet www.elfinanciero.com; weekly; business and economic news; f. 1990; Dir XAVIER PÉREZ MACCOLLUM.

Generación XXI: Aguirre 734 y García Avilés, Guayaquil; tel. (4) 232-7200; fax (4) 232-4870; e-mail g21@vistazo.com; internet www.generacion21.com; f. 1996; youth; Dir SEBASTIAN MÉLIÈRES; Editor CHRISTIAN KALIL CARTER.

Revista Estadio: Aguirre 734 y García Avilés, Casilla 09-01-1239, Guayaquil; tel. (4) 232-7200; fax (4) 232-0499; e-mail estadio@vistazo.com; internet www.revistaestadio.com; f. 1962; fortnightly; sport; Dir-Gen. SEBASTIAN MÉLIÈRES; Editor FABRICIO ZAVALA GARCÍA; circ. 40,000.

Revista Hogar: Aguirre 724 y Boyacá, Apdo 09-01-1239, Guayaquil; tel. (4) 232-7200; fax (4) 232-4870; e-mail rbustap@vistazo.com; internet www.revistahogar.com; f. 1964; monthly; women's interest; Dir-Gen. MARÍA GABRIELA GÁLVEZ VERA; Chief Editor ALEXANDRA ZURITA ANDRADE; circ. 47,000.

La Verdad: Malecón 502 y Tomás Martínez, Guayaquil; e-mail laverdad@telconet.net; internet www.revista-laverdad.com; f. 1988; monthly; politics and economics; associated with the Partido Renovador Institucional de Acción Nacional; Pres. ALVARO FERNANDO NOBOA PONTÓN; Dir RODOLFO BAQUERIZO BLUM.

Vistazo: Aguirre 734 y García Avilés, Casilla 09-01-1239, Guayaquil; tel. (4) 232-7200; fax (4) 232-4870; e-mail vistazo@vistazo.com; internet www.vistazo.com; f. 1957; fortnightly; general; Gen. Editor PATRICIA ESTUPIÑÁN DE BURBANO; circ. 85,000.

PRESS ASSOCIATION

Asociación Ecuatoriana de Editores de Periódicos (AEDEP): Edif. World Trade Center, 14°, Of. 14-01, Avda 12 de Octubre y Cordero, Quito; tel. (2) 254-7457; fax (2) 254-7404; e-mail aedep@aedep.org.ec; internet www.aedep.org.ec; f. 1985; Exec. Dir DIEGO CORNEJO.

Publishers

Casa de la Cultura Ecuatoriana: Avdas 6 de Diciembre 16–224 y Patria, El Ejido, Quito; tel. (2) 290-2272; e-mail info@cce.org.ec; internet www.cce.org.ec; Pres. MARCO ANTONIO RODRÍGUEZ.

Centro de Planificación y Estudios Sociales (CEPLAES): Sarmiento N39-198 y Hugo Moncayo, Apdo 17-11-6127, Quito; tel. (2) 225-0659; fax (2) 245-9417; e-mail ceplaes@andinanet.net; internet www.ceplaes.org.ec; f. 1978; agriculture, anthropology, education, health, social sciences, women's studies; Exec. Dir GLORIA CAMACHO.

Centro Interamericano de Artesanías y Artes Populares (CIDAP): Hermano Miguel 3-23, Casilla 01-011-943, Cuenca; tel. (7) 282-9451; fax (7) 283-1450; e-mail cidapl@cidap.org.ec; internet www.cidap.org.ec; art, crafts, games, hobbies; Dir CLAUDIO MALO GONZÁLEZ.

Centro Internacional de Estudios Superiores de Comunicación para América Latina (CIESPAL): Avda Diego de Almagro 32-133 y Andrade Marín, Apdo 17-01-584, Quito; tel. (2) 254-8011; fax (2) 250-2487; e-mail ciespal@ciespal.net; internet www.ciespal.net; f. 1959; communications, technology; Dir FERNANDO CHECA MONTÚFAR.

Corporación Editora Nacional: Roca E9–59 y Tamayo, Apdo 17-12-886, Quito; tel. (2) 255-4358; fax (2) 256-6340; e-mail cen@cenlibrosecuador.org; internet www.cenlibrosecuador.org; f. 1977; archaeology, economics, education, geography, political science, history, law, literature, management, philosophy, social sciences; Pres. HERNÁN MALO GONZÁLEZ.

Corporación de Estudios y Publicaciones: Acuna E2-02 y Juan Agama, entre 10 de Agosto e Inglaterra, Casilla 17-21-00186, Quito; tel. (2) 222-1711; fax (2) 222-6256; e-mail editorial@cep.org.ec; internet www.cep.org.ec; f. 1963; law, public administration; Dir MAURICIO TROYA MENA.

Dinediciones: Avda 12 de Octubre N25-32 y Coruña, esq., Quito; tel. (2) 254-5209; fax (2) 254-5188; e-mail info@dinediciones.com; internet www.portal.dinediciones.com; magazines; Dir HERNÁN ALTAMIRANO.

Ediciones Abya-Yala: Avda 12 de Octubre 1430 y Wilson, Apdo 17-12-719, Quito; tel. (2) 250-6251; fax (2) 250-6255; e-mail editorial@abyayala.org; internet www.abyayala.org; f. 1975; anthropology, environmental studies, languages, education, theology; Pres. Fr JUAN BOTTASSO; Dir-Gen. P. XAVIER HERRÁN.

Edinun: Avda Occidental 10-65 y Manuel Valdivieso, Sector Pinar Alto, Quito; tel. (2) 227-0316; fax (2) 227-0699; e-mail edinun@edinun.com; internet www.edinun.com; f. 1982; Gen. Man. VICENTE VELÁSQUEZ.

Editorial Don Bosco: Vega Muñoz 10-68 y General Torres, Cuenca; tel. (7) 283-1745; fax (7) 284-2722; e-mail edibosco@bosco.org.ec; internet www.lns.com.ec; f. 1920; Gen. Man. MARCELO MEJIA MORALES.

Editorial El Conejo: Edif. Brother, 3°, Avda 6 de Diciembre N26-97 y La Niña, Apdo 17-03-4629, Quito; tel. (2) 222-7948; fax (2) 250-1066; e-mail info@editorialelconejo.com; internet www.editorialelconejo.com; f. 1979; non-profit publr of educational and literary texts; Dir ABDÓN UBIDIA.

Editorial Santillana: Avda Eloy Alfaro N33-347 y Avda 6 de Diciembre, Pichincha, Quito; tel. (2) 244-6656; fax (2) 244-8791; e-mail comunicaciones@santillana.com.ec; internet www.santillana.com.ec; f. 1994; part of Grupo Santillana, Spain; Gen. Man. FERNANDO REVILLA.

Eskeletra Editorial: Edif. Gayal, 1°, Of. 102, Roca 130 y 12 de Octubre, Quito; tel. (2) 255-6691; e-mail eskeletra@hotmail.com; internet www.eskeletra.com; f. 1990; Gen. Man. AZUCENA ROSERO JÁCOME.

Libresa, SA: Murgeón Oe 3–10 y Ulloa, Apdo 17-01-456, Quito; tel. (2) 223-0925; fax (2) 250-2992; e-mail libresa@libresa.com; internet www.libresa.com; f. 1979; education, literature, philosophy; Pres. FAUSTO COBA ESTRELLA; Man. JAIME PEÑA NOVOA.

Manthra Editores: Cádiz N24-309 y Guipúzcoa, Quito; tel. (2) 600-0998; fax (2) 255-8264; e-mail info@manthra.net; internet www.manthra.net; Gen. Man. ANDRÉS DUEÑAS.

Maya Ediciones: Avda 6 de Diciembre N40-34 y Los Granados, Quito; tel. (2) 510-2447; e-mail servicioalcliente@mayaediciones.com; internet www.mayaediciones.com; f. 1992; children's books; Gen. Man. FANNY BUSTOS PEÑAHERRERA.

Pontificia Universidad Católica del Ecuador, Centro de Publicaciones: Avda 12 de Octubre, entre Patria y Veintimilla, Apdo 17-01-2184, Quito; tel. (2) 299-1700; fax (2) 256-7117; e-mail puce@edu.ec; internet www.puce.edu.ec; f. 1974; literature, natural science, law, anthropology, sociology, politics, economics, theology, philosophy, history, archaeology, linguistics, languages, business; Dir Dr PATRICIA CARRERA.

Trama Ediciones: Juan de Dios Martínez N34-367 y Portugal, El Batán, Quito; tel. (2) 224-6315; fax (2) 224-6317; e-mail info@trama.ec; internet www.trama.com.ec; f. 1977; architecture, design, art, tourism; Dir-Gen. ROLANDO MOYA TASQUER.

ASSOCIATIONS

Asociación Ecuatoriana de Editores de Libros de Texto: Quito; tel. (2) 227-0285; e-mail revistadidactica@gmail.com; internet www.revistadidactica.blogspot.com; f. 2004; publ. *Revista Didáctica*; Pres. VICENTE VELÁSQUEZ GUZMÁN.

Cámara Ecuatoriana del Libro: Edif. Eloy Alfaro, 9°, entre Inglaterra, Avda Eloy Alfaro 29-61, Quito; tel. (2) 255-3311; fax (2) 222-2150; e-mail celnp@uio.satnet.net; internet www.celibro.org.ec; f. 1978; Pres. FABIÁN LUZURIAGA.

Broadcasting and Communications

TELECOMMUNICATIONS

Regulatory Authorities

Consejo Nacional de Telecomunicaciones (CONATEL): Avda Diego de Almagro 31-95, entre Whymper y Alpallana, Casilla 17-07-9777, Quito; tel. (2) 294-7800; fax (2) 250-5119; e-mail contactanos@conatel.gob.ec; internet www.conatel.gob.ec; f. 1942 as Instituto Ecuatoriano de Telecomunicaciones (IETEL); Pres. JAIME GUERRERO RUIZ; Sec. EDUARDO AGUIRRE VALLADAREZ.

Secretaría Nacional de Telecomunicaciones (SENATEL): Edif. SENATEL, Avda Diego de Almagro 31-95, entre Whymper y Alpallana, Casilla 17-07-9777, Quito; tel. (2) 294-7800; fax (2) 290-1010; e-mail comunicacion@conatel.gob.ec; internet www.conatel.gob.ec; Nat. Sec. RUBÉN LEÓN.

Superintendencia de Telecomunicaciones (SUPERTEL): Edif. Matriz, Avda 9 de Octubre 1645 (N27-75) y Berlín, Casilla 17-21-1797, Quito; tel. (2) 294-6400; fax (2) 223-2115; e-mail info@supertel.gob.ec; internet www.supertel.gob.ec; f. 1992; Supt FABIÁN LEONARDO JARAMILLO PALACIOS.

Major Service Providers

Alegro (Telecomunicaciones Móviles del Ecuador, SA—Telecsa): Edif. Vivaldi, Amazonas 3837 y Corea, Quito; tel. and fax (2) 299-0000; e-mail info@alegro.com.ec; internet www.alegro.com.ec; state-owned; cellular telephone provider; Gen. Man. AUGUSTO ESPÍN.

Claro (CONECEL, SA): Edif. Centrum, Avda Francisco de Orellana y Alberto Borgues, Guayaquil; tel. (4) 269-3693; e-mail callcenter@conecel.com; internet www.claro.com.ec; f. 1993; fmrly Porta; subsidiary of América Móvil group (Mexico); mobile telecommunications provider; Pres. ALFREDO ESCOBAR SAN LUCAS.

Corporación Nacional de Telecomunicaciones: Edif. Estudio Zeta, Avda Veintimilla 1149 y Amazonas, Quito; tel. (2) 297-7100; fax (2) 256-2240; e-mail servicioalcliente@cnt.com.ec; internet www.cnt.com.ec; f. 2008 by merger of Andinatel and Pacifictel; state-owned; Pres. RODRIGO LÓPEZ; Gen. Man. CÉSAR REGALADO IGLESIAS.

Movistar Ecuador: Avda República y esq. La Pradera, Quito; tel. (2) 222-7700; fax (2) 222-7597; internet www.movistar.com.ec; f. 1997; name changed from BellSouth Ecuador to above in 2004; owned by Telefónica Móviles, SA (Spain); mobile telephone services; CEO JUAN FEDERICO GOULU.

Otecel, SA: f. 2004; subsidiary of Movistar Ecuador; mobile cellular telephone network provider.

Telmex Ecuador: Edif. Plaza 2000, 2°, Avda Gen. Salazar y 12 de Octubre, Quito; tel. (2) 223-0093; fax (2) 224-0494; e-mail servicios.ec@telmex.com; internet www.telmex.com/ec; fmrly Ecuador Telecom (Ecutel); part of Teléfonos de México, SA de CV (Mexico); Gen. Man. JOSÉ VÉDOVA.

BROADCASTING

Radio

There are nearly 300 commercial stations, 10 cultural stations and 10 religious stations. The following are among the most important stations:

Radio Católica Nacional: Avda América 1830 y Mercadillo, Casilla 17-03-540, Quito; tel. (2) 254-1557; fax (2) 256-7309; e-mail social@radiocatolica.org.ec; internet www.radiocatolica.org.ec; f. 1985; Dir-Gen. P. FRANCISCO SOJOS.

Radio Centro: Avda República de El Salvador 836 y Portugal, Quito; tel. and fax (2) 288-0500; e-mail censt@gye.satnet.net; internet www.radiocentro.com.ec; f. 1977; Dir HERNÁN OVIEDO GUTIERREZ; Gen. Man. JUAN XAVIER BENEDETTI RIPALDA.

Radio Colón: Avda Juan Tanca Marengo Km 1, entre Honda Motos y Cerámica Grayman, Guayaquil; tel. (4) 268-2279; fax (4) 268-2272; e-mail escucha@radiocolon.ec; f. 1935; Pres. Dr GERARDO CASTRO.

Radio CRE Satelital (CORTEL, SA): Edif. El Torreón, 8°, Avda Boyacá 642 y Padre Solano, Apdo 4144, Guayaquil; tel. (4) 256-4290; fax (4) 256-0386; e-mail cre@cre.com.ec; internet www.cre.com.ec; Pres. RAFAEL GUERRERO VALENZUELA; Gen. Man. ANTONIO GUERRERO GÓMEZ.

Radio Latina: Quito; internet www.radiolatina.com.ec; f. 1990; Pres. ROBERTO OMAR MACHADO.

Radio La Luna: Quito; internet www.radiolaluna.com; Owner PACO VELASCO; Gen. Man. ATAÚLFO TOBAR.

Radio Quito: Edif. Aragones, 9°, Avda Coruña 2104 y Whimper, Quito; tel. (2) 250-8301; fax (2) 250-3311; e-mail info@ecuadoradio.com; internet www.ecuadoradio.ec; f. 1940; owned by *El Comercio* newspaper.

Radio Sonorama (RDSR): Moscú 378 y República del Salvador, Quito; tel. (2) 243-5355; fax (2) 227-1555; internet www.sonorama.com.ec; f. 1975; Gen. Man. MAURICIO RIVAS.

Radio Sucre: Avda Joaquín Orrantia y Miguel H. Alcivar (Casa de las Américas Kennedy Norte), Guayaquil; tel. (4) 268-0301; fax (4) 268-0592; e-mail info@radiosucre.com.ec; internet www.radiosucre.com.ec; f. 1983; Dir GABRIEL ARROBA.

La Voz de los Andes (HCJB): Villalengua OE2-52 y Avda 10 de Agosto, Casilla 17-17-691, Quito; tel. (2) 226-6808; fax (2) 226-4765; e-mail radio@hcjb.org.ec; internet www.radiohcjb.org; f. 1931; operated by World Radio Missionary Fellowship; programmes in 11 languages (including Spanish and English) and 22 Quechua dialects; Evangelical; Dir TATIANA DE LA TORRE; Production Dir DUVAL RUEDA.

Television

EcuadorTV: Edif. Medios Públicos, San Salvador E6-49 y Eloy Alfaro, Quito; tel. (2) 397-0800; internet www.ecuadortv.ec; f. 2007; public service broadcaster; br. in Guayaquil.

Ecuavisa Guayaquil: Cerro El Carmen, Casilla 1239, Guayaquil; tel. (4) 256-2444; fax (4) 256-2432; e-mail contacto@ecuavisa.com; internet www.ecuavisa.com; f. 1967; Pres. XAVIER ALVARADO ROCA; Gen. Man. FRANCISCO AROSEMENA ROBLES.

Ecuavisa Quito: Bosmediano 447 y José Carbo, Bellavista, Quito; tel. (2) 244-8101; fax (2) 244-5488; internet www.ecuavisa.com; commercial; f. 1970; Pres. PATRICIO JARAMILLO; Editor-in-Chief FREDDY BARROS.

TC Televisión: Avda de las Américas, frente al Aeropuerto, Casilla 09-01-673, Guayaquil; tel. (4) 239-7664; fax (4) 228-7544; internet www.tctelevision.com; f. 1969; commercial; seized by the Govt in 2008; Gen. Man. CARLOS COELLO BECEKE.

Teleamazonas Cratel, CA: Granda Centeno Oeste 4–29 y Brasil, Casilla 17-11-04844, Quito; tel. (2) 397-4444; fax (2) 244-1620; e-mail abravo@teleamazonas.com; internet www.teleamazonas.com; f. 1974; commercial; Exec. Dir LUIS CUCALÓN; Gen. Man. SEBASTIÁN CORRAL.

Association

Asociación Ecuatoriana de Radiodifusión (AER): Edif. Atlas, 8°, Of. 802, Calle Justino Cornejo con Francisco de Orellana, Guayaquil; tel. and fax (4) 229-1783; internet www.aer.com; ind. asscn; Pres. ROBERTO MANCIATI ALARCÓN.

Finance

(cap. = capital; res = reserves; dep. = deposits; m. = million; brs = branches; amounts in US dollars unless otherwise indicated)

SUPERVISORY AUTHORITY

Superintendencia de Bancos y Seguros: Avda 12 de Octubre 1561 y Madrid, Casilla 17-17-770, Quito; tel. (2) 255-4225; fax (2) 250-6812; e-mail webmaster@sbs.gob.ec; internet www.sbs.gob.ec;

f. 1927; supervises national banking system, including state and private banks and other financial institutions; Supt PEDRO SOLINES.

BANKING

Central Bank

Banco Central del Ecuador: Avda 10 de Agosto N11-409 y Briceño, Casilla 339, Quito; tel. (2) 257-2522; fax (2) 295-5458; internet www.bce.fin.ec; f. 1927; cap. 2.4m., res 724.9m., dep. 5,300m. (Dec. 2009); Pres. PEDRO DELGADO; Gen. Man. CHRISTIAN RUIZ; 2 brs.

Other State Banks

Banco Ecuatoriano de la Vivienda: Avda 10 de Agosto 2270 y Luis Cordero, Casilla 3244, Quito; tel. and fax (2) 396-3300; e-mail bevinfo@bevecuador.com; internet www.bevecuador.com; f. 1961; Pres. WALTER SOLÍS VALAREZO; Gen. Man. RODRIGO GONZÁLEZ KELZ.

Banco del Estado (BDE): Avda Atahualpa OE1-109 y Avda 10 de Agosto, Casilla 17-17-1728, Quito; tel. (2) 299-9600; fax (2) 225-0320; e-mail secretaria@bancoestado.com; internet www.bancoestado.com; f. 1979 as Banco de Desarrollo del Ecuador (BEDE); Pres. PATRICIO RIVERA (Minister of Finance); Gen. Man. DIEGO AULESTIA VALENCIA.

Banco Nacional de Fomento: Ante 107 y Avda 10 de Agosto, Casilla 685, Quito; tel. (2) 257-2049; fax (2) 257-0286; e-mail judithcevallos@bnf.fin.ec; internet www.bnf.fin.ec; f. 1928; cap. 254.2m., res 144.1m., dep. 621.9m. (Dec. 2009); Pres. RAMON ESPINEL; Gen. Man. ROBERTO BARRIGA AYALA; 70 brs.

Corporación Financiera Nacional (CFN): Avda Juan León Mera 130 y Avda Patria, Casilla 17-21-01924, Quito; tel. (2) 256-4900; fax (2) 222-3823; e-mail informatica@q.cfn.fin.ec; internet www.cfn.fin.ec; f. 1964; state-owned bank providing export credits, etc.; Pres. CAMILO SAMÁN SALEM; Gen. Man. JORGE WATED.

Commercial Banks

Banco Amazonas, SA: Avda Francisco Orellana 238, Guayaquil; tel. (4) 268-3600; fax (4) 268-3400; e-mail storassa@bancoamazonas.com; internet www.bancoamazonas.com; f. 1976; cap. 14.5m., res 1.4m., dep. 122.6m. (Dec. 2010); affiliated to Banque Paribas; CEO SERGIO R. TORASSA; CFO JOSÉ PONCE.

Banco del Austro: Sucre y Borrero (esq.), Casilla 01-01-0167, Cuenca; tel. (7) 283-1646; fax (7) 283-2633; internet www.bancodelaustro.com; f. 1977; cap. 44.4m., res 11.9m., dep. 614.7m. (Dec. 2009); Pres. JUAN ELJURI ANTÓN; Gen. Man. GUILLERMO TÁLBOT DUEÑAS; 19 brs.

Banco Bolivariano, CA: Junín 200 y Panamá, Casilla 09-01-10184, Guayaquil; tel. (4) 230-5000; fax (4) 256-6707; e-mail info@bolivariano.com; internet www.bolivariano.com; f. 1978; cap. 102.5m., res 17.7m., dep. 1,402.3m. (Dec. 2010); Pres. JOSÉ SALAZAR BARRAGÁN; CEO MIGUEL BABRA LEÓN; 53 brs.

Banco Comercial de Manabí, SA: Avda 10 de Agosto 600 y 18 de Octubre, Portoviejo; tel. and fax (5) 263-2222; e-mail info@bcmanabi.com; internet www.bcmanabi.com; f. 1980; Gen. Man. ARISTO ANDRADE DÍAZ.

Banco General Rumiñahui: Avda República E6-573 y Avda Eloy Alfaro, Quito; tel. (2) 250-9929; fax (2) 256-3786; e-mail mrodas@bgr.com.ec; internet www.bgr.com.ec; cap. 19.4m., res 2.0m., dep. 324.4m. (Dec. 2009); Gen. Man. ALEJANDRO RIBADENEIRA JARAMILLO.

Banco de Guayaquil, SA: Plaza Ycaza 105 y Pichincha, Casilla 09-01-1300, Guayaquil; tel. (4) 251-7100; fax (4) 251-4406; e-mail servicios@bankguay.com; internet www.bancoguayaquil.com; f. 1923; cap. 135m., res 30.2m., dep. 1,796.9m. (Dec. 2009); Pres. DANILO CARRERA DROUET; Exec. Pres. GUILLERMO LASSO MENDOZA; 50 brs.

Banco Internacional, SA: Avda Patria E-421 y 9 de Octubre, Casilla 17-01-2114, Quito; tel. (2) 256-5547; fax (2) 256-5758; e-mail baninteronline@bancointernacional.com.ec; internet www.bancointernacional.com.ec; f. 1973; cap. 8,600m. (Dec. 2000); Pres. JOSÉ ENRIQUE FUSTER CAMPS; CEO ENRIQUE BELTRÁN MATA; 58 brs.

Banco de Loja: esq. Bolívar y Rocafuerte, Casilla 11-01-300, Loja; tel. (7) 257-1682; fax (7) 257-3019; internet www.bancodeloja.fin.ec; f. 1968; cap. 15m., res 3.8m., dep. 204.3m. (Dec. 2009); Pres. STEVE BROWN HIDALGO; Man. LEONARDO BURNEO MULLER.

Banco de Machala, SA: Avda 9 de Mayo y Rocafuerte, Casilla 711, Machala; tel. (7) 293-0100; fax (7) 292-2744; e-mail jorejuela@bmachala.com; internet www.bmachala.com; f. 1962; cap. 27m., res 5m., dep. 336.6m. (Dec. 2009); Pres. Dr ESTEBAN QUIROLA FIGUEROA; 2 brs.

Banco del Pacífico: Francisco de P. Ycaza 200, entre Pichincha y Pedro Carbo, Casilla 09-01-988, Guayaquil; tel. (4) 256-6010; fax (4) 232-8333; e-mail webadmin@pacifico.fin.ec; internet www.bp.fin.ec; f. 2000 by merger of Banco del Pacífico and Banco Continental; 100% owned by Banco Central del Ecuador; cap. 151.7m., res 112.3m., dep. 1,545.3m. (Dec. 2009); Exec. Pres. ANDRÉS BAQUERIZO; 227 brs.

Banco del Pichincha, CA: Avda Amazonas 4560 y Pereira, Casilla 261, Quito; tel. (2) 298-0980; fax (2) 298-1226; e-mail sugerencias@pichincha.com; internet www.pichincha.com; f. 1906; cap. 358m., res 121.1m., dep. 4,808.6m. (Dec. 2010); 61.82% owned by Exec. Pres. and Chair.; Exec. Pres. and Chair. Dr FIDEL EGAS GRIJALVA; Gen. Man. FERNANDO POZO CRESPO; 267 brs.

Banco Territorial, SA: P. Icaza 115, entre Malecón y Pichincha, Guayaquil; tel. (4) 256-1950; e-mail informacion@grupozunino.com; internet www.bancoterritorial.com; f. 1886; Gen. Man. JUAN CARLOS CASTAÑEDA ARCHILA.

Produbanco (Banco de la Producción, SA): Avda Amazonas N35-211 y Japón, Quito; tel. (2) 299-9000; fax (2) 244-7319; e-mail bancaenlinea@produbanco.com; internet www.produbanco.com; f. 1978 as Banco de la Producción; adopted current name in 1996; cap. 124m., res 23.8m., dep. 1,438.7m. (Dec. 2009); part of Grupo Financiero Producción; Exec. Pres. ABELARDO PACHANO BERTERO; Chair. RODRIGO PAZ DELGADO; 75 brs.

UniBanco (Banco Universal, SA): Avda 10 de Agosto 937 y Buenos Aires, Quito; tel. (2) 290-6555; fax (2) 222-7898; internet unibanco.ec; f. 1964 as Banco de Cooperativas del Ecuador; adopted current name 1994; Pres. ANDRÉS JERVIS GONZÁLEZ.

Associations

Asociación de Bancos Privados del Ecuador: Edif. Delta 890, 7°, Avda República de El Salvador y Suecia, Casilla 17-11-6708, Quito; tel. (2) 246-6670; fax (2) 246-6702; e-mail abpe1@asobancos.org.ec; internet www.asobancos.org.ec; f. 1965; 36 mems; Pres. RICARDO CUESTA DELGADO; Exec. Pres. CÉSAR ROBALINO GONZAGA.

Asociación de Instituciones Financieras del Ecuador (AIFE): Edif. La Previsora, Torre B, 3°, Of. 308, Avda Naciones Unidas 1084 y Amazonas, Quito; tel. and fax (2) 246-6560; e-mail aife1@punto.net.ec; internet www.aife.com.ec; Pres. GIANNI GARIBALDI; Exec. Dir JULIO DOBRONSKY NAVARRO.

STOCK EXCHANGES

Bolsa de Valores de Guayaquil: 9 de Octubre 110 y Pichincha, Guayaquil; tel. (4) 256-1519; fax (4) 256-1871; e-mail rgallegos@bvg.fin.ec; internet www.mundobvg.com; Pres. RODOLFO KRONFLE AKEL; Dir-Gen. ARTURO BEJARANO ICAZA.

Bolsa de Valores de Quito: Edif. Londres, 8°, Avda Amazonas 21–252 y Carrión, Casilla 17-01-3772, Quito; tel. (2) 222-1333; fax (2) 250-0942; e-mail informacion@bolsadequito.com; internet www.bolsadequito.com; f. 1969; Chair. PATRICIO PEÑA ROMERO; Exec. Pres. MÓNICA VILLAGÓMEZ DE ANDERSON.

INSURANCE

Instituto Ecuatoriano de Seguridad Social: Edif. Zarzuela, 6°, Avda 9 de Octubre 20–68 y Jorge Washington, Quito; tel. (2) 396-9300; fax (2) 256-3917; e-mail cdirectivo@iess.gob.ec; internet www.iess.gob.ec; f. 1928; directs the Ecuadorean social insurance system; provides social benefits and medical service; Pres. RAMIRO GONZÁLEZ JARAMILLO; Dir-Gen. FERNANDO GUIJARRO CABEZAS.

Principal Companies

Ace Seguros, SA: Edif. Antisana, 4°, Avdas Amazonas 3655 y Juan Pablo Sanz, Quito; tel. (2) 292-0555; fax (2) 244-5817; e-mail serviciocliente@ace-ina.com; internet www.acelatinamerica.com; Exec. Pres. EDWIN ASTUDILLO.

AIG Metropolitana Cía de Seguros y Reaseguros, SA: Edifc. IACA, 5°, Avda Brasil 293 y Antonio Granda Centeno, Quito; tel. (2) 246-6955; fax (2) 292-4434; e-mail servicio.cliente@aig.com; internet www.aig.com.ec; part of American International Group, Inc (USA); Exec. Pres. DIANA PINILLA ROJAS.

Alianza Cía de Seguros y Reaseguros, SA: Avdas 12 de Octubre 24-359 y Baquerizo Moreno, Apdo 17-17-041, Quito; tel. (2) 256-6143; fax (2) 256-4059; e-mail alianzauio@segurosalianza.com; internet www.segurosalianza.com; f. 1982; Gen. Man. EDUARDO BARQUET PENDÓN.

Bolívar Cía de Seguros del Ecuador, SA: Edif. Centro Empresarial Las Cámaras, Torre B, 3° y 12°, Planta Baja, Avda Francisco de Orellana, Calle Kennedy Norte, Guayaquil; tel. (2) 602-0700; fax (2) 268-3363; e-mail ssanmiguel@seguros-bolivar.com; internet www.seguros-bolivar.com; f. 1957; Pres. FABIÁN ORTEGA TRUJILLO.

Cía de Seguros Ecuatoriano Suiza, SA: Avda 9 de Octubre 2101 y Tulcán, Apdo 09-01-397, Guayaquil; tel. (4) 373-1515; fax (4) 245-3229; e-mail ecuasuiza@ecuasuiza.com; internet www.ecuasuiza.com; f. 1954; Pres. JOSÉ SALAZAR BARRAGÁN; Gen. Man. LUIS FERNANDO SALAS RUBIO.

Cía Seguros Unidos, SA: Edif. Metrocar, 3°, Avda 10 de Agosto 31–162 y Avda Mariana de Jesús, Quito; tel. (2) 252-6466; fax (2) 245-0920; e-mail quito@sunidos.fin.ec; internet www.segurosunidos.ec; Gen. Man. JUAN XAVIER RIBAS DOMÉNECH.

Cóndor Cía de Seguros, SA: Edif. Seguros Cóndor, 6°, Francisco de Plaza Ycaza 302, Apdo 09-01-5007, Guayaquil; tel. (4) 256-5300; fax (4) 256-5041; e-mail ochavez@seguroscondor.com; internet www.seguroscondor.com; f. 1966; Gen. Man. OTÓN CHÁVEZ TORRES.

Coopseguros del Ecuador, SA: Edif. Coopseguros, Avda Noruega 210 y Suiza, Casilla 17-15-0084-B, Quito; tel. (2) 292-1669; fax (2) 292-1666; internet www.coopseguros.com; f. 1970; Gen. Man. JUÁN ENRIQUE BUSTAMENTE.

Mapfre Atlas Cía de Seguros, SA: Edif. Torre Atlas, 11°, Kennedy Norte, Justino Cornejo, entre Avda Francisco de Orellana y Avda Luis Orrantia, Casilla 09-04-491, Guayaquil; tel. (4) 269-0430; fax (4) 228-3099; e-mail noticiascorporativas@mapfreatlas.com.ec; internet www.mapfreatlas.com.ec; f. 1984; Gen. Man. RAFAEL SUÁREZ LÓPEZ.

Panamericana del Ecuador, SA: Edif. Panamericana, Calle Portugal E-12-72 y Avda Eloy Alfaro, Quito; tel. (2) 298-9600; fax (2) 246-9650; e-mail larango@panamericana.com.ec; internet www.panamericana.com.ec; f. 1973; Gen. Man. FRANCISCO PROAÑO SALVADOR.

QBE Seguros Colonial: Avda. Eloy Alfaro 40-270 y José Queri, Quito; tel. (2) 399-0500; e-mail info@qbe.com.ec; internet www.qbe.com.ec; f. 1992 as Seguros Colonial, SA; acquired by Grupo QBE (Australia) and changed name as above in 2010; Exec. Pres. FERNANDO MANTILLA.

Seguros Rocafuerte, SA: Edif. Filanbanco, 14°–16°, Plaza Carbo 505 y Avda 9 de Octubre, Apdo 09-04-6491, Guayaquil; tel. (4) 232-6125; fax (4) 232-9353; e-mail segroca@gye.satnet.net; internet www.rocafuerte.com; f. 1967; life and medical; Exec. Pres. PEDRO PICHARDO ZAPAC QUEVEDO.

Seguros Sucre, SA: Edif. San Francisco 300, 6°, Pedro Carbo 422 y Avda 9 de Octubre, Apdo 09-01-480, Guayaquil; tel. (4) 256-3399; fax (4) 231-4163; e-mail pespinel@segurossucre.fin.ec; internet www.segurossucre.fin.ec; f. 1944; part of Grupo Banco del Pacífico; Gen. Man. MAXÍMILIANO DONOSO VALLEJO.

La Unión Cía Nacional de Seguros: Urb. Los Cedros Solares 1–2, Km 5½, Vía a la Costa, Apdo 09-01-1294, Guayaquil; tel. (4) 285-1500; fax (4) 285-1700; e-mail rgoldbaum@seguroslaunion.com; internet www.seguroslaunion.com; f. 1943; state-owned; Pres. ROBERTO GOLDBAUM; Gen. Man. LUIS AGUIRRE.

ASSOCIATIONS

Asociación de Compañías de Seguros del Ecuador (ACOSE): Edif. Carolina Park, 2°, Calle Japón 230 y Avda Amazonas, Quito; tel. (2) 225-6182; fax (2) 246-3057; internet www.acose.org; f. 1978; affiliated to FEDESEG (q.v.); 15 mems; Pres. RODRIGO CEVALLOS BREIHL; Gen. Man. PATRICIO SALAS GUZMÁN.

Federación Ecuatoriana de Empresas de Seguros (FEDESEG): Edif. Intercambio, 1°, Junín y Malecón Simón Bolivar 105, Guayaquil; tel. (4) 456-5340; fax (4) 430-6208; affiliated to Federación Interamericana de Empresas de Seguros (FIDES); Pres. JOSÉ CÚCALON DE YCAZA; Exec. Sec. LUIS LARREA BENALCÁZAR.

Trade and Industry

GOVERNMENT AGENCIES

Secretaría Nacional de Planificación y Desarrollo (SENPLADES): Edif. CFN, 8°, Avda Juan León Mera 130 y Avda Patria, Quito; tel. (2) 397-8900; e-mail senplades@senplades.gob.ec; internet www.senplades.gob.ec; f. 1954 as Junta Nacional de Planificación y Coordinación Económica (JUNAPLA); changed name as above 1979; decentralized planning and policy-making; Nat. Sec. FANDER FALCONÍ BENÍTEZ.

Superintendencia de Compañías del Ecuador: Roca 660 y Amazonas, Casilla 687, Quito; tel. (2) 252-9960; fax (2) 256-6685; e-mail comunicacionuio@supercias.gob.ec; internet www.supercias.gob.ec; f. 1964; responsible for the legal and accounting control of commercial enterprises; Supt SUAD RAQUEL MANSSUR VILLAGRÁN; Sec.-Gen. VÍCTOR CEVALLOS VÁSQUEZ.

CHAMBERS OF COMMERCE AND INDUSTRY

Cámara de Comercio de Ambato: Edif. Las Cámaras, Montalvo 03-31, entre Bolívar y Rocafuerte, Ambato; tel. (3) 242-4773; fax (3) 242-1930; e-mail webmaster@ccomercioambato.org.ec; internet www.ccomercioambato.org.ec; Pres. MIGUEL SUÁREZ JARAMILLO.

Cámara de Comercio de Cuenca: Edif. Cámara de Industrias de Cuenca, 12° y 13°, Avda Florencia Astudillo y Alfonso Cordero, Casilla 4929, Cuenca; tel. (7) 288-5070; fax (7) 281-3100; e-mail cccuenca@etapa.com.ec; internet www.industriascuenca.org.ec; f. 1936; 5,329 mems; Pres. AUGUSTO TOSI LEÓN.

Cámara de Comercio Ecuatoriano-Americana (Amcham Quito-Ecuador): Edif. Multicentro, 4°, Avda 6 de Diciembre y la Niña, Quito; tel. (2) 250-7450; fax (2) 250-4571; e-mail info@ecamcham.com; internet www.ecamcham.com; f. 1974; promotes bilateral trade and investment between Ecuador and the USA; brs in Ambato, Cuenca and Manabí; Pres. XAVIER PONCE VILLAGOMEZ; Gen. Man. JOSÉ RUMAZO.

Cámara de Comercio Ecuatoriano Canadiense (Ecuadorean-Canadian Chamber of Commerce): Torre Centro Ejecutivo, Of. 201, 2°, Inglaterra 1373 y Avda Amazonas, Quito; tel. (2) 244-5972; fax (2) 246-8598; e-mail camara.canadiense@ecucanchamber.org; internet www.ecucanchamber.org; Pres. PAUL HARRIS; Exec. Dir CECILIA PEÑA ODE.

Cámara de Comercio de Guayaquil: Edif. Centro Empresarial 'Las Cámaras', 2° y 3°, Avda Francisco de Orellana y Miguel H. Alcívar, Guayaquil; tel. (4) 268-2771; fax (4) 268-2766; e-mail info@lacamara.org; internet www.lacamara.org; f. 1889; 31,000 affiliates; Pres. EDUARDO PEÑA HURTADO; Sec. JUAN ESTANISLAO LUTYK.

Cámara de Comercio de Machala: Edif. Cámara de Comercio, 2°, Rocafuerte y Buenavista, CP 825, Machala, Cuenca; tel. (7) 293-0640; fax (7) 293-4454; e-mail ccomach@ecua.net.ec; Pres. CÉSAR CHÁVEZ VELASCO.

Cámara de Comercio de Manta: Edif. Cámara de Comercio, Avda 2, entre Calles 10 y 11, Apdo 13-05-477, Manta; tel. and fax (5) 262-1306; e-mail direccion@ccm.org.ec; internet www.ccm.org.ec; f. 1927; Pres. LUCÍA FERNÁNDEZ DE DEGENNA; Exec. Dir EMILIA RIVADENEIRA.

Cámara de Comercio de Quito: Edif. Las Cámaras, 6°, Avda República y Amazonas, Casilla 17-01-202, Quito; tel. (2) 244-3787; fax (2) 243-5862; e-mail ccq@ccq.org.ec; internet www.ccq.org.ec; f. 1906; 12,000 mems; Pres. BLASCO PEÑAHERRERA SOLAH; Exec. Dir GUIDO TOLEDO ANDRADE.

Cámara de Industrias de Cuenca: Edif. Cámara de Industrias de Cuenca, 12° y 13°, Avda Florencia Astudillo y Alfonso Cordero, Cuenca; tel. (7) 284-5053; fax (7) 284-0107; internet www.industriascuenca.org.ec; f. 1936; Pres. AUGUSTO TOSI LEÓN; Exec. Vice-Pres. CAROLA RÍOS DE ANDRADE.

Cámara de Industrias de Guayaquil: Centro Empresarial Las Cámaras, Torre Institucional, 4° y 5°, Avda Francisco de Orellana y M. Alcívar, Casilla 09-01-4007, Guayaquil; tel. (4) 268-2618; fax (4) 268-2680; e-mail caindgye@cig.org.ec; internet www.cig.ec; f. 1936; Pres. HENRY KRONFLE KOZHAYA.

Federación Nacional de Cámaras de Comercio del Ecuador: Avda Amazonas y República, Edif. Las Cámaras, Quito; tel. (2) 244-3787; fax (2) 292-2084; Pres. BLASCO PEÑAHERRERA SOLAH; Vice-Pres. MARÍA GLORIA ALARCÓN.

Federación Nacional de Cámaras de Industrias del Ecuador: Avda República y Amazonas, 10°, Casilla 2438, Quito; tel. (2) 245-2994; fax (2) 244-8118; e-mail fedin@cip.org.ec; internet www.camindustriales.org.ec; f. 1974; Pres. Dr PABLO DÁVILA JARAMILLO.

INDUSTRIAL AND TRADE ASSOCIATIONS

Asociación de la Industria Hidrocarburífera del Ecuador (AIHE): Edif. Puerta del Sol, 8°, Avda Amazonas 4080 y Calle UNP, Quito; tel. (2) 226-1270; fax (2) 226-1272; e-mail aihe@aihe.org.ec; internet www.aihe.org.ec; f. 1997 as Asociación de Compañías Petroleras de Exploración y Explotación de Hidrocarburos del Ecuador (ASOPEC); name changed as above in 2002; asscn of 24 int. and domestic hydrocarbon cos; Exec. Pres. JOSÉ LUIS ZIRITT.

Corporación de Promoción de Exportaciones e Inversiones (CORPEI): Centro de Convenciones Simón Bolivar, 1°, Avda de las Américas 406, Guayaquil; tel. (4) 228-7123; fax (4) 229-2910; internet www.corpei.org; f. 1997 to promote exports and investment; CEO RICARDO ALFREDO ESTRADA.

EMPLOYERS' ORGANIZATIONS

Asociación de Atuneros: Malecón s/n, Muelle Portuario de Manta 1, Manta; tel. and fax (5) 262-6467; e-mail atunec@manta.ecua.net.ec; asscn of tuna producers; Pres. PATRICIO VELÁSQUEZ.

Asociación de Compañías Consultoras del Ecuador: Edif. Delta, 4°, Avda República de El Salvador 890 y Suecia, Quito; tel. (2) 246-5048; fax (2) 245-1171; e-mail acce@acce.com.ec; internet www.acce.com.ec; asscn of consulting cos; Pres. FERNANDO AGUILAR GARCÍA.

Asociación Ecuatoriana de Industriales de la Madera: Edif. de las Cámaras, 7°, República y Amazonas, Quito; tel. (2) 226-0980; fax (2) 243-9560; e-mail secre@aima.org.ec; internet www.aima.org.ec; wood mfrs' asscn; Pres. SEBASTIÁN ZUQUILANDA.

Asociación de Exportadores de Banano del Ecuador (AEBE): Edif. World Trade Center, Torre A, 9°, Of. 904, Avda Francisco de Orellana, Calle Kennedy Norte, Guayaquil; tel. (4) 263-1419; fax (4) 263-1485; e-mail eledesma@aebe.com.ec; internet www.aebe.com.ec; banana exporters' asscn; Pres. JORGE ALEX SERRANO; Exec. Dir EDUARDO LEDESMA.

Asociación de Industriales Gráficos de Pichincha: Edif. de las Cámaras, 8°, Amazonas y República, Quito; tel. (2) 292-3141; fax (2)

245-6664; e-mail aigquito@aig.org.ec; internet www.aig.org.ec; asscn of the graphic industry; Pres. MAURICIO MIRANDA.

Asociación de Industriales Textiles del Ecuador (AITE): Edif. Las Cámaras, 8°, Avda República y Amazonas, Casilla 2893, Quito; tel. (2) 224-9434; fax (2) 244-5159; e-mail aite@aite.org.ec; internet www.aite.com.ec; f. 1938; textile mfrs' asscn; 40 mems; Pres. JOSÉ MARÍA PONCE; CEO JAVIER DÍAZ CRESPO.

Asociación Nacional de Empresarios (ANDE): Edif. España, 6°, Of. 67, Avda Amazonas 25–23 y Colón, Casilla 17-01-3489, Quito; tel. (2) 290-2545; fax (2) 223-8507; e-mail info@ande.org.ec; internet www.ande.org.ec; national employers' asscn; Pres. PATRICIO DONOSO CHIRIBOGA; Vice-Pres. ALEJANDRO RIBADENEIRA.

Asociación Nacional de Exportadores de Cacao y Café (ANECAFE): Edif. Banco Pichincha, 10°, Of. 1001, Avda 2da entre calles 11 y 12, Manta; tel. (5) 261-3337; fax (5) 262-3315; e-mail info@anecafe.org.ec; internet www.anecafe.org.ec; f. 1983; cocoa and coffee exporters' asscn; Pres. ASKLEY DELGADO.

Asociación Nacional de Molineros: 6 de Diciembre 3470 e Ignacio Bossano, Quito; tel. (2) 246-5597; fax (2) 246-4754; Exec. Dir RAFAÉL SERRANO.

Cámara de Agricultura: Edif. La Previsora, Torre B, 8°, Of. 805, Avda Naciones Unidas 1084 y Amazonas, Casilla 17-21-322, Quito; tel. (2) 225-7618; fax (2) 227-4187; e-mail gremios@caiz.org.ec; internet www.agroecuador.com; Pres. MAURICIO BUSTAMENTE.

STATE HYDROCARBON COMPANY

EP PETROECUADOR (Empresa Pública de Hidrocarburos del Ecuador): Alpallana E8-86 y Avda 6 de Diciembre, Casilla 17-11-5007, Quito; tel. (2) 256-3060; fax (2) 250-3571; e-mail rin@petroecuador.com.ec; internet www.eppetroecuador.ec; f. 1989; state petroleum co; Exec. Pres. Rear-Adm. MANUEL E. ZAPATER RAMOS.

UTILITIES

Regulatory Authorities

Agencia de Control y Regulación Hidrocarburífera (ARCH): Quito; f. 2010; responsible for the regulation and control of the hydrocarbons sector; Dir CARLOS LOOR.

Centro Nacional de Control de Energía (CENACE): Panamericana Sur Km 17.5, Sector Santa Rosa de Cutuglagua, Casilla 17-21-1991, Quito; tel. (2) 299-2001; fax (2) 299-2031; e-mail pcorporativo@cenace.org.ec; internet www.cenace.org.ec; f. 1999; co-ordinates and oversees national energy system; Exec. Dir GABRIEL ARGÜELLO RÍOS.

Consejo Nacional de Electricidad (CONELEC): Avda Naciones Unidas E7-71 y Avda De Los Shyris, Apdo 17-17-817, Quito; tel. (2) 226-8746; fax (2) 226-8737; e-mail conelec@conelec.gob.ec; internet www.conelec.gob.ec; f. 1999; supervises electricity industry following transfer of assets of the former Instituto Ecuatoriano de Electrificación (INECEL) to the Fondo de Solidaridad; pending privatization as 6 generating cos, 1 transmission co and 19 distribution cos; Exec. Dir FRANCISCO VERGARA ORTÍZ.

Secretaría de Hidrocarburos: Ministerio de Recursos Norenovables, Juan León Mera y Orellana, Quito; f. 2010, fmrly known as the Dirección Nacional de Hidrocarburos; part of the Ministry of Non-Renewable Natural Resources; supervision of the enforcement of laws regarding the exploration and devt of petroleum; also responsible for dispute resolution and imposition of sanctions against oil cos failing industry standards; Dir RAMIRO CAZAR.

Secretaría Nacional del Agua (SENAGUA): Edif. MAGAP, 3°, Avda Amazonas y Avda Eloy Alfaro, Quito; tel. (2) 381-5640; fax (2) 255-4251; e-mail secretarionacional@senagua.gob.ec; internet www.senagua.gob.ec; Nat. Sec. WALTER SOLÍS VALAREZO.

Electricity

Eléctrica de Guayaquil: Urb. La Garzota, Sector 3, Manzana 47; tel. (4) 224-8006; fax (4) 224-8040; internet www.electricaguayaquil.gov.ec; f. 2003, as Corporación para la Administración Temporal Eléctrica de Guayaquil (Categ) to administer activities of fmr state-owned Empresa Eléctrica del Ecuador (EMELEC); privatized and changed name as above in 2009; major producer and distributor of electricity, mostly using oil-fired or diesel generating capacity; Admin. OSCAR ARMIJOS GONZÁLEZ-RUBIO.

Empresa Eléctrica Quito, SA (EEQ): Avda 10 de Agosto y Las Casas, Casilla 17-01-473, Quito; tel. (2) 396-4700; fax (2) 250-3817; e-mail asoeeq@eeq.com.ec; internet www.eeq.com.ec; f. 1955; produces electricity for the region around Quito, mostly from hydroelectric plants; Gen. Man. CARLOS ANDRADE FAINI.

Empresa Eléctrica Regional El Oro, SA (EMELORO): Dir Arízaga 1810 y Santa Rosa, esq. Machala, El Oro; tel. (7) 293-0500; e-mail emeloro@emeloro.gov.ec; internet www.emeloro.gov.ec; electricity production and generation in El Oro province; Chair. GONZALO QUINTANA GALVEZ; Exec. Pres. WASHINGTON MORENO BENITEZ.

Empresa Eléctrica Regional del Sur, SA (EERSSA): internet www.eerssa.com; f. 1973; electricity production and generation in Loja and Zamora Chinchipe provinces; Exec. Pres. WILSON VIVANCO ARIAS.

Empresa Eléctrica Riobamba, SA: Larrea 2260 y Primera Constituyente, Riobamba; tel. (3) 296-0283; fax (3) 296-5257; e-mail e-mail@eersa.com.ec; internet www.eersa.com.ec/eersa.php; state-owned utility; Pres. MARIANO CURICAMA; Gen. Man. JOE RUALES.

TRADE UNIONS

Central Ecuatoriana de Organizaciones Clasistas (CEDOC-CLAT): Avda 24 de Mayo 344, Quito; tel. (2) 221-3704; internet www.cedoc-clat.org; f. 1938 as Confederación Ecuatoriana de Obreros Católicos (CEDOC); changed name as above in 2000; humanist; craft and manual workers, and intellectuals; affiliated to Confederación Sindical de Trabajadores y Trabajadoras de las Américas; Pres. FERNANDO IBARRA.

Confederación Sindical de Trabajadoras y Trabajadores del Ecuador (CSE): Pasaje Fray Gerundio E7-19 y el Tiempo (Tras Hotel Crown Plaza), Quito; tel. (2) 246-9547; e-mail cseecuador@cse-ec.org; internet www.gye.cse-ec.org; f. 2010; formed by dissident members of Confederación Ecuatoriana de Organizaciones Sindicales Libres (CEOSL); Pres. JAIME ARCINIEGA.

Frente Unitario de los Trabajadores (FUT): f. 1971; left-wing; 300,000 mems; Pres. MESÍAS TATAMUEZ; comprises:

Confederación Ecuatoriana de Organizaciones Clasistas Unitarias de Trabajo (CEDOCUT): Edif. Cedocut, 5°, Flores 846 y Manabí, Quito; tel. (2) 295-4551; fax 295-4013; e-mail presicdocut@cedocut.org; internet www.cedocut.org.ec; f. 1938; humanist; Pres. MESÍAS TATAMUEZ MORENO; 1,065 mem. orgs, 86,416 individual mems.

Confederación Ecuatoriana de Organizaciones Sindicales Libres (CEOSL): Avda Tarqui 15-26 (785) y Estrada, 6°, Casilla 17-11-373, Quito; tel. (2) 252-2511; fax (2) 250-0836; e-mail presidencia@ceosl.net; internet ceosl.net; f. 1962; Pres. EDUARDO VALDEZ CUÑAS; 110,000 mems (2007).

Confederación de Trabajadores del Ecuador (CTE) (Confederation of Ecuadorean Workers): Avda 9 de Octubre 1248 y Marieta de Veintimilla, Casilla 17-01-4166, Quito; tel. (2) 252-0456; fax (2) 252-0446; e-mail presidencia@cte-ecuador.org; internet www.cte-ecuador.org; f. 1944; Pres. SANTIAGO YAGUAL YAGUAL; Vice-Pres. EDGAR SARANGO CORREA.

Unión General de Trabajadores del Ecuador (UGTE): Avda Arenas 3-22 y Juan Larrea, Quito; tel. (2) 254-8915; e-mail info@ugtecuador.com; internet www.ugtecuador.com; f. 1982; Pres. NELSON ERAZO H.; Sec. LUIS DUTÁN.

Transport

RAILWAYS

All railways are government controlled. In 2000 the total length of track was 960 km. A programme for the rehabilitation of 456 km of disused lines was begun in 2008. By 2011 nine sections had been reopened.

Ferrocarriles del Ecuador Empresa Publica (FEEP): Quilotoa y Sangay, estación Eloy Alfaro (Chimbacalle), Quito; tel. (2) 399-2100; e-mail info@ferrocarrilesdelecuador.gob.ec; internet www.ferrocarrilesdelecuador.gob.ec; fmrly Empresa de Ferrocarriles Ecuatorianos (EFE); Pres. MARÍA FERNANDA ESPINOSA GARCÉS (Co-ordinating Minister for Cultural and Natural Heritage); Gen. Man. JORGE EDUARDO CARRERA SÁNCHEZ.

ROADS

There were 43,670 km of roads in 2007, of which 15.0% were paved. The Pan-American Highway runs north from Ambato to Quito and to the Colombian border at Tulcán, and south to Cuenca and Loja.

SHIPPING

Port Authorities

Autoridad Portuaria de Esmeraldas: Avda Jaime Roldós Aguilera (Recinto Portuario), Esmeraldas; tel. (6) 272-1352; fax (6) 272-1354; e-mail ape@puertoesmeraldas.gob.ec; internet www.puertoesmeraldas.gob.ec; f. 1970; 25-year operating concession awarded to private consortium in 2004; renationalized in 2010; Gen. Man. RAFAEL PLAZA PERDOMO.

Autoridad Portuaria de Guayaquil: Avda de la Marina, Vía Puerto Marítimo, Guayaquil; tel. (4) 248-0120; fax (4) 248-4728; internet www.apg.gob.ec; f. 1958; Pres. RUBÉN MORÁN CASTRO; Man. PUBLIO FRANCISCO FARFÁN BLACIO.

Autoridad Portuaria de Manta: Avda Malecón s/n, Manta; tel. (5) 262-7161; fax (5) 262-1861; e-mail info@puertodemanta.gob.ec; internet www.puertodemanta.gob.ec; Pres. ROBERTO SALAZAR BRACCO.

Autoridad Portuaria de Puerto Bolívar: Avda Bolívar Madero Vargas, Puerto Bolívar; tel. (7) 292-9999; e-mail appb@appb.gob.ec; internet www.appb.gob.ec; f. 1970; Pres. MONTGOMERY SÁNCHEZ REYES; Gen. Man. WILMER ENCALADA LUDEÑA.

Principal Shipping Companies

Andinave, SA: Edif. Previsora, 29°, Of. 2901, Avda 9 de Octubre 100 y Malecon Simon Bolivar, Guayaquil; tel. (4) 232-5555; fax (4) 232-5957; e-mail info@andinave.com; internet www.andinave.com; f. 1983; shipping and port agents, stevedoring and logistics; Gen. Man. RODRIGO VITERI.

BBC Ecuador Andino Cía Ltda: Edif. San Luis, 3°, Suite 6, Avda Tulcan 809 y Hurtado, Casilla 3338, Guayaquil; tel. (4) 236-5585; fax (4) 604-1898; e-mail guayaquil@bbc-chartering.com; internet www.bbc-chartering.com; subsidiary of BBC Chartering & Logistic (Germany); Gen. Man. FEDERICO FERBER.

CMA CGM Ecuador, SA: Parque Empresarial Colon, Corporativo 2, Ofs 501 y 503, Avda Rodrigo Chàvez s/n, Guayaquil; tel. (4) 213-6500; fax (4) 336-5626; e-mail gql.genmbox@cma-cgm.com; internet www.cma-cgm.com; Gen. Man. ANNY BARRET VALDIVIEZO.

Flota Petrolera Ecuatoriana (FLOPEC): Edif. FLOPEC, Avda Amazonas No 24–196 y Cordero, Casilla 535-A, Quito; tel. (2) 398-3600; fax (2) 250-1428; e-mail planificacion@flopec.com.ec; internet www.flopec.com.ec; f. 1972; Gen. Man. Capt. RAÚL SAMANIEGO GRANJA.

Investamar, SA: Edif. Berlín, 4°, Las Monjas 10 y C. J. Arosemena, Guayaquil; tel. (4) 220-4000; fax (4) 220-6646; e-mail investamar@grupoberlin.com; internet www.investamar.com.ec; Gen. Man. Capt. ROLF BENZ.

J. M. Palau Agencia de Vapores: Edif. Plaza, 6°, Of. 603-604, Baquierzo Moreno 1119 y Avda 9 de Octubre, POB 09019108, Guayaquil; tel. (4) 256-2178; fax (4) 256-3473; e-mail jmpav@ecua.net.ec; internet www.jmpalau-shipagency.com; f. 1956; Gen. Man. MAURICE PALAU VELÁSQUEZ.

Naviera Marnizam, SA: Edif. El Navio, Avda Malecon y Calle 19, Manta; tel. (5) 262-6445; fax (5) 262-4414; e-mail info@marzam-online.com; internet www.marzam-online.com; f. 1985; Gen. Man. LUCÍA ZAMBRANO SEGOVIA.

CIVIL AVIATION

There are four international airports: Mariscal Sucre in Quito, José Joaquín de Olmedo in Guayaquil, Eloy Alfaro in Manta (Manabí) and Cotopaxi Internacional in Latacunga. In 2009 the total number of airports in Ecuador was 402, of which 103 had paved runways.

Dirección General de Aviación Civil: Avda Buenos Aires Oeste 1-53 y 10 de Agosto, Quito; tel. (2) 223-2184; fax (2) 255-2987; e-mail subdirector.subdac@dgac.gov.ec; internet www.dgac.gob.ec; f. 1946; Dir-Gen. FERNANDO GUERRERO LÓPEZ.

Aerogal (Aerolíneas Galápagos): Amazonas 7797 y Juan Holguín, Quito; tel. (2) 396-0600; fax (2) 243-0487; e-mail customerservice@aerogal.com.ec; internet www.aerogal.com.ec; f. 1985; owned by Avianca (Colombia); domestic flights and also flights to Colombia and USA; Exec. Pres. JULIO GAMERO.

LAN Ecuador, SA: Avda de las Américas s/n, Guayaquil; tel. (4) 269-2850; fax (4) 228-5433; internet www.lan.com; f. 2002; commenced operations in 2003 following acquisition of assets of Ecuatoriana by LAN Chile; scheduled daily flights to Quito, Guayaquil, and the USA; Gen. Man. MAXIMILIANO NARANJO ITURRALDE.

TAME Línea Aérea del Ecuador: Edif. TAME, Avda Amazonas No 24–260 y Avda Colón, 6°, Casilla 17-07-8736, Sucursal Almagro, Quito; tel. (2) 396-6300; fax (2) 255-4907; e-mail tamejefv@impsat.net.ec; internet www.tame.com.ec; f. 1962; fmrly Transportes Aéreos Mercantiles Ecuatorianos, SA; removed from military control in 1990; state-owned; domestic scheduled and charter services for passengers and freight; Pres. FERNANDO MARTÍNEZ DE LA VEGA.

Tourism

Tourism has become an increasingly important industry in Ecuador, with a wide variety of heritage sites, beaches, rainforest reserves and national parks. The main attractions include the Galapagos Islands and the Yasuní National Park. In 2009 foreign arrivals (including same-day visitors) numbered 968,499. In the same year receipts from the tourism industry amounted to a provisional US $674m.

Asociación Ecuatoriana de Agencias de Viajes, Operadores de Turismo y Mayoristas (ASECUT): Caldas 340 y Guayaquil, Edif. San Blas, 6°, Ofs 61–62, Quito; tel. (2) 250-0759; fax (2) 250-3669; e-mail asecut@pi.pro.ec; f. 1953; Pres. ALFONSO SEVILLA.

Federación Hotelera del Ecuador (AHOTEC): América No 38–80 y Diguja, Quito; tel. (2) 244-3425; fax (2) 245-3942; e-mail ahotec@interactive.net.ec; internet www.hotelesecuador.com.ec; Pres. JOSÉ OCHOA GARCÍA; Exec. Dir DIEGO UTRERAS.

Defence

As assessed at November 2011, Ecuador's armed forces numbered 57,983: army 46,500, navy 7,283 (including 2,160 marines and 375 in the naval air force) and air force 4,200. Paramilitary forces included 500 coastguards. Military service lasts for one year and is selective for men at the age of 20.

Defence Budget: an estimated US $1,510m. in 2010.

Chief of the Joint Command of the Armed Forces: Gen. LUIS ERNESTO GONZÁLEZ VILLARREAL.

Chief of Staff of the Army: MARCO AURELIO VERA.

Chief of Staff of the Navy: Vice-Adm. JORGE GROSS ALBORNOZ.

Chief of Staff of the Air Force: LEONARDO BARREIRO MUÑOZ.

Education

Education in Ecuador is officially compulsory for 10 years, to be undertaken between five and 15 years of age. All public schools are free. Private schools feature prominently in the educational system. Primary education begins at six years of age and lasts for six years. Secondary education, in general and specialized technical or humanities schools, begins at the age of 12 and lasts for up to six years, comprising two equal cycles of three years each. In 2007/08 enrolment at primary schools included 95% of pupils in the relevant age-group, while the comparable ratio for secondary schools in 2007/08, according to UNESCO estimates, was 62%. A 10-year plan to make education universal at primary and secondary levels was begun in 2006. University courses last for up to six years, and include programmes for teacher training. In many rural areas, Quechua and other indigenous Amerindian languages are used in education. The total government expenditure on education was estimated at US $23.9m. for 2012.

EGYPT

Introductory Survey

LOCATION, CLIMATE, LANGUAGE, RELIGION, FLAG, CAPITAL

The Arab Republic of Egypt occupies the north-eastern corner of Africa, with an extension across the Gulf of Suez into the Sinai Peninsula, sometimes regarded as lying within Asia. Egypt is bounded to the north by the Mediterranean Sea, to the north-east by Israel, to the east by the Red Sea, to the south by Sudan, and to the west by Libya. The climate is arid, with a maximum annual rainfall of only 200 mm around Alexandria. More than 90% of the country is desert, and some 99% of the population live in the valley and delta of the River Nile. Summer temperatures reach a maximum of 43°C (110°F) and winters are mild, with an average day temperature of about 18°C (65°F). Arabic is the official language. More than 90% of the population are Muslims, mainly of the Sunni sect. The remainder are mostly Christians, principally Copts. The national flag (proportions 2 by 3) has three equal horizontal stripes, of red, white and black; the white stripe has, in the centre, the national emblem (a striped shield superimposed on an eagle, with a cartouche beneath bearing the inscription, in Kufic script, 'Arab Republic of Egypt') in gold. The capital is Cairo (al-Qahirah).

CONTEMPORARY POLITICAL HISTORY

Historical Context

Egypt, a province of Turkey's Ottoman Empire from the 16th century, was occupied by British forces in 1882. The administration was controlled by British officials, although Egypt remained nominally an Ottoman province until 1914, when a British protectorate was declared. The country was granted titular independence on 28 February 1922. Fuad I, the reigning Sultan, became King. He was succeeded in 1936 by his son, King Faruq (Farouk). The Anglo-Egyptian Treaty of 1936 recognized full Egyptian sovereignty, and after the Second World War (1939–45) British forces withdrew from Egypt, although a military presence was maintained in the Suez Canal Zone. When the British mandate in Palestine was ended in 1948, Arab armies intervened to oppose the newly proclaimed State of Israel. A cease-fire was agreed in 1949, leaving Egyptian forces occupying the Gaza Strip.

On 23 July 1952 power was seized by a group of young army officers in a bloodless coup led by Lt-Col (later Col) Gamal Abd al-Nasir (Nasser). Farouk abdicated in favour of his infant son, Ahmad Fuad II, and went into exile. Gen. Muhammad Nagib (Neguib) was appointed Commander-in-Chief of the army and Chairman of the Revolution Command Council (RCC). In September Neguib was appointed Prime Minister and Military Governor, with Nasser as Deputy Prime Minister. In December the 1923 Constitution was abolished, and in January 1953 all political parties were dissolved. The monarchy was abolished on 18 June 1953, and Egypt was proclaimed a republic, with Neguib as President and Prime Minister. In April 1954 Neguib was succeeded as Prime Minister by Nasser. In October Egypt and the United Kingdom signed an agreement providing for the withdrawal of all British forces from the Suez Canal by June 1956. President Neguib was relieved of all his remaining posts in November 1954, whereupon Nasser became acting head of state.

The establishment of military rule was accompanied by wide-ranging reforms, including the redistribution of land, the promotion of industrial development and the expansion of social welfare services. In foreign affairs, the new regime was strongly committed to Arab unity, and Egypt played a prominent part in the Non-aligned Movement. In 1955, having failed to secure Western armaments on satisfactory terms, Egypt accepted military assistance from the USSR.

A new Constitution was approved by a national referendum in June 1956; Nasser was elected President unopposed, and the RCC was dissolved. In July, following the departure of British forces, the US and British Governments withdrew their offers of financial assistance for Egypt's construction of the Aswan High Dam. Nasser responded by announcing the nationalization of the Suez Canal Company, so that revenue from Canal tolls could be used to finance the dam's construction. The takeover of the Canal was a catalyst for Israel's invasion of the Sinai Peninsula on 29 October. British and French forces launched military operations against Egypt two days later. Intense pressure from the UN and the USA resulted in a cease-fire on 6 November and supervision by the UN of the invaders' withdrawal.

Egypt and Syria merged in February 1958 to form the United Arab Republic (UAR), with Nasser as President. The new state strengthened earlier ties with the USSR and other countries of the communist bloc. In September 1961 Syria seceded from the UAR, but Egypt retained this title for a further decade. In December 1962 Nasser established the Arab Socialist Union (ASU) as the country's only recognized political organization. In May 1967 he secured the withdrawal of the UN Emergency Force from Egyptian territory. Egypt subsequently reoccupied Sharm el-Sheikh, on the Sinai Peninsula, and closed the Straits of Tiran to Israeli shipping. This precipitated the so-called Six-Day War, or June War, when Israel quickly defeated neighbouring Arab states, including Egypt. The war left Israel in control of the Gaza Strip and a large area of Egyptian territory, including the whole of the Sinai Peninsula. The Suez Canal was blocked, and remained closed until June 1975.

Nasser died suddenly in September 1970, and was succeeded by his Vice-President, Col Anwar Sadat. In September 1971 the UAR was renamed the Arab Republic of Egypt, and a new Constitution took effect. In 1976 Egypt terminated its Treaty of Friendship with the USSR. Relations with the USA developed meanwhile, as President Sadat came to rely increasingly on US aid.

In October 1973 Egyptian troops crossed the Suez Canal to recover territory lost to Israel in 1967. After 18 days of fighting a cease-fire was achieved. In 1974–75 the US Secretary of State, Dr Henry Kissinger, negotiated disengagement agreements whereby Israel evacuated territory in Sinai and Israeli and Egyptian forces were separated by a UN-controlled buffer zone. In a dramatic peace-making initiative, opposed by many Arab countries, Sadat visited Israel in 1977 and addressed the Knesset (parliament). In September 1978, following talks held at the US presidential retreat at Camp David, Maryland, Sadat and the Israeli Prime Minister, Menachem Begin, signed two agreements: the first provided for a five-year transitional period during which the inhabitants of the Israeli-occupied West Bank of Jordan and the Gaza Strip would obtain full autonomy and self-government; the second provided for a peace treaty between Egypt and Israel. The latter was signed in March 1979, whereafter Israel made phased withdrawals from the Sinai Peninsula, the last taking place in April 1982. The League of Arab States (the Arab League, see p. 364) expelled Egypt following the signing of the peace treaty, and imposed political and economic sanctions. Nevertheless, Egypt continued to forge relations with Israel, and in February 1980 the two countries exchanged ambassadors for the first time.

Domestic Political Affairs

In 1974 Sadat began to introduce a more liberal political and economic regime. Political parties (banned since 1953) were allowed to participate in the 1976 elections for the Majlis al-Sha'ab (People's Assembly), and in July 1978 Sadat formed the National Democratic Party (NDP), with himself as leader. In 1979 the special constitutional status of the ASU was ended. In October 1981 Sadat was assassinated by members of Islamic Jihad, a group of militant, fundamentalist Islamists. He was succeeded by Lt-Gen. Muhammad Hosni Mubarak, his Vice-President and a former Commander-in-Chief of the air force. Immediately following Sadat's assassination a national state of emergency was declared. A new electoral law required parties to receive a minimum of 8% of the total vote in order to secure representation in the People's Assembly. This prompted opposition parties to boycott elections to local councils and to the Majlis al-Shura (Advisory Council). At legislative elections in May 1984 the ruling NDP won 72.9% of the total vote. Of the four other participating parties, only the New Wafd Party (or New Delegation Party), in alliance with the Muslim Brotherhood, achieved representation, with 15.1%.

Meanwhile, a division in the Arab world between a 'moderate' grouping (including Jordan, Iraq and the Gulf states), which viewed the participation of Egypt as indispensable to any diplomatic moves towards solving the problems of the region, and a 'radical' grouping, led by Syria, became increasingly evident. The leader of the Palestinian Liberation Organization (PLO), Yasser Arafat, visited President Mubarak for discussions in December 1983, signifying the end of estrangement between Egypt and the PLO, and in 1984 Jordan resumed diplomatic relations with Egypt. These two developments led to the profound involvement of Egypt in the pursuit of a negotiated settlement of the Palestinian question. In November 1987, at a summit conference in Jordan attended by the majority of Arab leaders, President Hafiz Assad of Syria obstructed proposals to readmit Egypt to the Arab League. However, recognizing Egypt's support for Iraq in the Iran–Iraq War (1980–88) and acknowledging the influence that Egypt could exercise on the problems of the region, the conference approved a resolution placing the establishment of diplomatic links with Egypt at the discretion of member states. Egypt was readmitted to the Arab League in May 1989.

At the general election held in April 1987 the ruling NDP won 346 of the 448 elective seats in the People's Assembly, the opposition parties together won 95, and independents seven. The Muslim Brotherhood took 37 seats, to become the largest single opposition group in the legislature. At a referendum held in October Mubarak was confirmed as President for a second six-year term of office by 97.1% of voters. In March 1988 the Government renewed the national state of emergency for a further three years, citing a continued threat of internal and external subversion. The legislation was subsequently extended at regular intervals, most recently in May 2010 for a further two years, although the Supreme Council of the Armed Forces (SCAF), which assumed power following Mubarak's resignation as President in February 2011 (see The ouster of President Mubarak), indicated its intention to rescind the legislation.

Following Iraq's invasion and annexation of Kuwait in August 1990, Egypt convened an emergency summit meeting of Arab leaders at which 12 of the 20 Arab League states supported a resolution demanding the withdrawal of Iraqi forces from Kuwait and, in response to Saudi Arabia's request for international assistance to deter potential aggression by Iraq, voted to send an Arab force to the Persian (Arabian) Gulf region. The Egyptian contingent within the multinational force eventually amounted to 35,000 troops. Egypt emerged from the Gulf conflict with its international reputation enhanced, largely as a result of what was regarded as Mubarak's firm leadership of 'moderate' Arab opinion.

Legislative elections in November and December 1990 were boycotted by the principal opposition parties, in protest at the Government's refusal to concede to demands that the elections be removed from the supervision of the Ministry of the Interior and that the state of emergency be repealed. Of the 444 elective seats in the new Assembly, the NDP won 348, the National Progressive Unionist Party (NPUP or Tagammu) six, and independent candidates (the majority of whom were affiliated to the NDP) 83. Voting for the remaining seven seats was suspended.

At a national referendum in October 1993, Mubarak was confirmed as President for a third term of office by some 96.3% of the valid votes cast. The opposition parties, none of which had endorsed Mubarak's candidature, demanded reforms including the amendment of the Constitution to allow direct presidential elections, the unrestricted formation of political parties and the introduction of a two-term limit to the presidency.

During the early 1990s the Government's attempts to suppress Islamist fundamentalism dominated the domestic political agenda, as fundamentalist violence increasingly targeted foreign interests in Egypt, and there were frequent confrontations between Islamist militants and the security forces. There were, however, regular reports of successful action by the Egyptian security forces against militants, including a large number of arrests. In March 1994 nine members of the Vanguards of Conquest (a faction of Islamic Jihad) were sentenced to death, having been convicted of conspiring to assassinate the Prime Minister in November 1993. In July 1994 a further five members of the militant group received death sentences for the attempted assassination of the Minister of the Interior in August 1993. Meanwhile, in April 1994 the chief of the anti-terrorist branch of the State Security Investigation Section was assassinated by members of Gama'ah al-Islamiyah (one of Egypt's principal militant Islamist groups), prompting retaliatory security operations. By the mid-1990s the Government began to take steps to isolate the Muslim Brotherhood and to weaken its political influence. Several leading members of the Brotherhood were arrested, and it was claimed by the Government that there was evidence of links between the movement and Islamist extremists. In June 1995 Mubarak escaped an assassination attempt, apparently carried out by Islamist militants, while he was travelling to a summit meeting of the Organization of African Unity (OAU, now African Union—AU) in Addis Ababa, Ethiopia. (In September 1996 three Egyptians were sentenced to death by the Ethiopian Supreme Court for their involvement in the attempted assassination.)

Legislative elections were held in November–December 1995, at which candidates of the NDP won 316 seats, thus retaining a decisive (albeit reduced) majority in the People's Assembly. The opposition parties collectively secured just 13 seats. Of the 115 independent candidates elected, 99 were reported to have immediately joined or rejoined the NDP. Allegations of electoral malpractices on the part of agents acting for the NDP were widespread. A new Council of Ministers was appointed in January 1996, with Dr Kamal Ahmad al-Ganzouri, hitherto Minister of Planning, appointed Prime Minister (in place of Dr Atif Sidqi, who had held the post since 1986).

In November 1997 the massacre near Luxor of 70 people, including 58 foreign tourists, by members of Gama'ah al-Islamiyah severely undermined both the tourism sector and the claims of the Government to have suppressed Islamist violence. Mubarak criticized the security forces' failure to protect tourists, and dismissed the Minister of the Interior. In December a number of Gama'ah al-Islamiyah's exiled leaders claimed that the Luxor massacre had been perpetrated by a 'rogue' element acting independently of the group's leadership; furthermore, the leaders in exile announced that Gama'ah al-Islamiyah (at least, those members under their specific authority) would no longer target tourists in their conflict with the Government. In March 1998 Gama'ah al-Islamiyah declared a unilateral cease-fire. Although the Government gave no formal acknowledgement to the declaration, the process of releasing imprisoned Islamist militants was subsequently accelerated. In April some 1,200 Gama'ah al-Islamiyah detainees were freed, and a further 1,200 left prison in December.

In September 1999 Mubarak's nomination for a fourth presidential term was approved by 93.8% of the valid votes cast in a national referendum. Of the four main legal opposition parties, only the Nasserist Party had refused to endorse Mubarak's candidature. In October Dr Atif Muhammad Obeid, previously Minister of the Public Enterprise Sector and responsible for the Government's privatization programme, succeeded al-Ganzouri as Prime Minister.

The Supreme Constitutional Court issued a judgment in July 2000 that the People's Assembly elected in 1995 was illegitimate (as was the Assembly elected in 1990), and that the existing electoral system was invalid since the constitutional requirement that the judiciary have sole responsibility for the supervision of elections had not been observed. President Mubarak subsequently convened an extraordinary session of the Assembly, at which amendments to the existing electoral legislation were unanimously approved: these provided for judges to monitor voting at both the main and auxiliary polling stations in the impending general election.

Almost 4,000 candidates contested the 444 elective seats in the People's Assembly at polls conducted in three separate rounds, each of two stages, in October–November 2000. The NDP increased its majority, taking 353 seats. Independent candidates secured 72 seats, but 35 of these were reported either to have joined or rejoined the NDP shortly after the elections. The opposition garnered 17 seats between them. Voting for the two seats in one constituency in Alexandria was postponed following the arrest of some 20 Muslim Brotherhood activists. At least 14 people were killed during the polls.

Meanwhile, in January 2000 three days of violent clashes between Muslims and Copts in the southern village of el-Kosheh resulted in the deaths of an estimated 20 Christians and one Muslim. A subsequent inquiry conducted by the Egyptian Organization for Human Rights inferred that the primary cause of the violence was the 'economic inequalities' between the relatively prosperous Coptic majority and the poorer Muslim minority. In February 2001 four Muslims were sentenced to custodial terms of up to 10 years for their part in the violence, while a further 92 defendants were acquitted. However, after a retrial of all 96 defendants, in February 2003 two men were sentenced to prison terms of 15 years and three-and-a-half years, respectively; the remainder were again acquitted. In June 2004 these sentences were again reviewed, with three men receiving one- and two-year prison terms, and the fourth man's 15-year sentence being reduced to 13 years. Once again, the other 92 defendants were acquitted. In April 2006 two Coptic Christians were killed in attacks against Coptic churches in Alexandria.

President Mubarak was swift to condemn the suicide attacks on New York and Washington, DC, USA, of 11 September 2001. Several members of Islamic Jihad were alleged to have assumed significant roles in the suicide attacks, held to have been perpetrated by the militant Islamist al-Qa'ida network then under the leadership of Osama bin Laden. Dr Ayman al-Zawahiri, the head of Islamic Jihad and current al-Qa'ida leader (following bin Laden's death in a US military raid in Pakistan in May 2011), was presumed responsible for the organization of the attacks. Another Egyptian, Muhammad Atef, who was reportedly killed by US forces in Afghanistan in November 2001, was, according to US intelligence, believed to have been al-Qa'ida's chief military planner. Furthermore, an Egyptian national was suspected of having piloted one of the hijacked aircraft that hit the World Trade Center in New York. Following the events of 11 September, more than 260 suspected Islamists were detained in Egypt, and arrests of Islamists continued on a large scale during 2002. In August 16 members of the Muslim Brotherhood were sentenced to terms of imprisonment ranging from three to five years after being convicted of inciting anti-Government demonstrations. In the following month 51 militants, who had initially been arrested in May 2001, were sentenced to up to 15 years' imprisonment for conspiring to overthrow the Government. In August 2002, meanwhile, a number of imprisoned senior members of Gama'ah al-Islamiyah reiterated their commitment to the cease-fire declared in 1998 and announced their complete renunciation of violence. Some 900 members of the organization were released from prison in October 2003.

Limited reform in the early 2000s

At the eighth congress of the NDP in September 2002, Mubarak's second son, Gamal, was elected Secretary-General for Policy, effectively making him the third most senior figure in the party and further fuelling speculation that he was being groomed eventually to succeed his father. The Minister of Information, Muhammad Safwat el-Sherif, became the party's Secretary-General.

During 2003 the NDP appeared to acquiesce to demands for greater political liberalization. In June the People's Assembly approved the creation of a National Council for Human Rights, as well as the closure of a number of the State Security Courts; the punishment of hard labour was also abolished. At the NDP's first annual party conference, held in September, President Mubarak announced that all military orders issued under the emergency laws, which had been in place since the assassination of President Sadat in 1981, would be abolished, except those that were 'necessary to maintain public order and security'. However, a committee established by the Prime Minister to review the existing emergency powers recommended that only six of the 13 military orders could be withdrawn. Nevertheless, restrictions and limitations pertaining to the formation of new political parties and the activities of existing political organizations were also to be reviewed, and Gamal Mubarak pledged to take steps to ensure that all Egyptians would receive the fundamental rights of participatory democracy and equality.

The Egyptian authorities instigated the largest crackdown on the activities of the Muslim Brotherhood for many years in May 2004: in a series of raids some 54 members of the Muslim Brotherhood were arrested, and shops and publishing houses were closed down. Protests by Muslim Brotherhood activists increased in early 2005, as they demanded political reforms in advance of the elections scheduled to take place that year. Round-ups of Brotherhood members thus continued, with hundreds of activists—including the group's Secretary-General, Mahmoud Izzat—being arrested in May.

Meanwhile, at partial elections to the 264-member Advisory Council in May and June 2004, the NDP won 70 of the 88 seats contested, while 17 seats were secured by NDP members who had stood as independents, and one seat was taken by the NPUP. A further 44 members of the Council were appointed by the President. In late June el-Sherif was elected Speaker of the Advisory Council. In July Prime Minister Obeid announced the resignation of his entire administration, precipitating a long-anticipated reorganization of the Council of Ministers. Dr Ahmad Mahmoud Muhammad Nazif, the former Minister of Communications and Information Technology, was appointed Prime Minister. The new Government, which was also reported to be of a technocratic, reformist nature, included several appointees regarded as having close links with Gamal Mubarak, among them Ahmad Aboul Gheit, hitherto Egypt's Permanent Representative to the UN, who became Minister of Foreign Affairs.

In October 2004 a new political party, Al-Ghad (Tomorrow), was approved after its fourth application. This decision was apparently prompted by criticism from the USA regarding the slow pace of democratic reform in Egypt, which had seen only two new political parties being licensed since 1977. Under the leadership of former New Wafd Party deputy Ayman Abd al-Aziz al-Nour, Al-Ghad brought to 18 the number of officially recognized parties. In January 2005 al-Nour was arrested and charged with having forged signatures required in order to secure his party's registration. After being released on bail in March, al-Nour announced that he intended to contest the presidential election scheduled for later that year. His trial commenced in Cairo in June, but was subsequently postponed until late September, thus permitting the Al-Ghad leader to contest the presidential election (see below). In December al-Nour was given a five-year prison sentence, having been found guilty of forgery; he began an appeal against the sentence in February 2006, citing violations of his rights during detention and serious flaws in the original trial. However, in May the Court of Cassation upheld the original sentence, a decision that was strongly criticized by the USA, the European Union (EU), and domestic and international human rights organizations. Despite a further appeal against his sentence on medical grounds, in early 2007 al-Nour was deemed by the Egyptian authorities to be in sufficient health to serve his full prison term; the same ruling was issued by a Cairo court in March 2008. Al-Nour was finally released from prison on medical grounds in February 2009, after serving a little over three years of his sentence; observers suggested that his release was intended to allow Egypt to forge stronger ties with the USA (see Relations with the USA).

Egypt's first terrorist attack for seven years occurred in early October 2004, at the height of the Jewish holiday season, when three bombs exploded in the resorts of Taba, Ras Shitan and Nuweiba on the Sinai Peninsula, killing 34 people—many of whom were Israelis. In late October five Egyptians suspected of involvement in the bombings were arrested and the blame for the attacks was placed upon a Palestinian, Ayad Said Salah, who had been living in Egypt and who had died in the explosion in Taba. The Ministry of the Interior announced that Salah had acted to highlight the deteriorating situation in the Gaza Strip. In March 2005 three Egyptians were charged—one *in absentia*—in connection with the bombings, while it was reported that two others suspected of involvement in the attacks had been killed by security forces in the previous month.

In October 2004 more than 650 Egyptian activists, politicians and intellectuals released a statement urging a constitutional amendment to prevent President Mubarak from standing for another term in office. In February 2005 Mubarak did propose altering the Constitution to allow for direct, contested presidential elections. The constitutional amendment was drafted by a parliamentary committee in early May; however, many opposition parties argued that the proposed changes, which stated that a presidential candidate would need the support of at least 65 members of the People's Assembly, would prevent candidates from outside the ruling party from standing. Nevertheless, the amendment, which also stipulated that political parties required 5% of parliamentary seats in order to field a presidential candidate, was overwhelmingly approved by the People's Assembly on 10 May. At a referendum held on 25 May, some 82.9% of the electorate voted in favour of the changes. Participation was officially recorded at 53.6%; however, opposition figures claimed that actual turn-out was as low as 5%.

Egypt was the target of terrorist attacks twice in 2005. In April three foreign tourists were killed in a bomb attack in Cairo, and in July at least 60 people, some of them foreigners, were killed and around 200 injured following three bomb attacks at hotels in the Red Sea resort of Sharm el-Sheikh. In October it was announced that a security fence would be erected around the resort in order to prevent further attacks. In August 2007 four Egyptian nationals were sentenced to life imprisonment, having been convicted of involvement in the Cairo bombing of April 2005; a further five defendants received terms of between one and 10 years, and four were acquitted.

The 2005 presidential and legislative elections

At the first ever multi-candidate presidential election, held on 7 September 2005, President Mubarak was re-elected for a fifth consecutive six-year term. Mubarak won 88.6% of the vote, while Ayman al-Nour of Al-Ghad came second, with 7.6%, and No'man Khalil Gomaa of the New Wafd Party secured third place, with 2.9%. Seven other candidates all received less than 0.5% of the vote. Turn-out was registered at only 23.0%, attributed in part to an appeal by several opposition parties for a boycott of the poll. The election was marred by opposition protests in Cairo, accusations of a media bias towards Mubarak and controversy surrounding the newly established Presidential Election Commission's decision to ban independent groups from monitoring the ballot. Mubarak was sworn in on 27 September.

Elections to contest the 444 elective seats in the People's Assembly were conducted in three rounds on 9 November, 20 November and 1 December 2005 (with run-off elections held on 15 and 26 November and 7 December). Prior to the elections the Muslim Brotherhood announced that it would be presenting a list of 150 members as independent candidates, after the Egyptian authorities for the first time allowed the party to campaign freely. Both prior to and during the elections, however, more than 850 members of the Muslim Brotherhood were arrested amid reports of clashes between NDP and Brotherhood supporters. More than 10 people were killed in rioting during the ballot. Official results issued in mid-December revealed that the NDP had won 311 of the 432 decided seats (with 71.9% of the vote). The most notable gains, however, were made by the Muslim Brotherhood, which increased its representation from 17 seats to 88. Other independent candidates won 24 seats, while the remaining 12 seats were won by the New Wafd Party (six), the NPUP (two) and Al-Ghad (one). Turn-out was low (at only 26.2% of the electorate) and voting had to be postponed for 12 seats in six constituencies owing to violence. On 12 December Mubarak appointed five women and five Coptic Christians to the 10 presidentially appointed seats in the People's Assembly in order to increase their level of parliamentary representation. Mubarak retained Nazif as Prime Minister and asked him to form a new government. Observers commented that the new ministerial appointments, which included several businessmen, would accelerate the pace of reform in the country and reinforce the position of Gamal Mubarak, who was named as one of three Deputy Secretary-Generals of the NDP in January 2006.

President Mubarak's decision, in February 2006, to postpone local elections scheduled for April of that year until 2008 attracted criticism both externally, in particular from the USA, and internally from the Muslim Brotherhood. The amended Constitution required independent candidates standing for the presidency to obtain the support of at least 10 local councillors, and Egyptian Islamists claimed that the delay in holding the polls would thus ensure that the NDP retained control over nominations for the presidency. Meanwhile, four senior judges who had persistently criticized government interference in judicial matters and made allegations of vote-rigging in the legislative elections of 2005 were stripped of their immunity and were to face an investigation by a state security court. In April–May 2006 the Government's decision to prosecute two of the judges provoked angry demonstrations in Cairo, which were forcibly dispersed by the security forces; hundreds of protesters were arrested for their roles in the demonstrations, including an estimated 400 members of the Muslim Brotherhood.

On 24 April 2006 a total of 23 people were killed, and around 150 injured, following three co-ordinated explosions in the Red Sea resort of Dahab. Days later the People's Assembly voted to approve a two-year extension to the national state of emergency, despite earlier indications from Prime Minister Nazif that new anti-terrorism legislation would be implemented in its place.

The 2007 referendum on constitutional reform

In December 2006 the President proposed a total of 34 amendments to the Constitution, including a reduction of presidential powers in favour of the People's Assembly and the Council of Ministers, and steps to ease restrictions on political parties' candidates for presidential elections. However, opposition figures criticized a number of the proposals, in particular the reversal of earlier legislation providing for full judicial supervision of elections. Instead, an 11-member Higher Election Commission (HEC), to be appointed by the Government and chaired by the Minister of Justice, was henceforth to monitor the legislative election process. In addition to substituting a reference in the Constitution to the 'socialist character of the state' with the fact that Egypt's economy was now based on 'market principles', one of the most significant changes was an increase in the powers of the security forces to monitor, detain and imprison citizens suspected of involvement in terrorist activities. Mubarak also proposed a formal ban on the establishment of political parties based on religion, one of a number of changes aimed at curbing the growing influence of the Muslim Brotherhood. A national referendum on the constitutional amendments, which—despite a boycott of the proceedings by members and affiliates of the Brotherhood—were approved by a significant majority of deputies in the People's Assembly in mid-March 2007, took place on 26 March. According to official figures, the 34 constitutional amendments were endorsed by 75.9% of voters, although turn-out was estimated by the Ministry of Justice at only 27.1%. Opposition parties, including the Muslim Brotherhood, immediately contested the outcome of the poll.

Concerns about the extent of freedom of expression in Egypt again came to the fore in the early part of 2007, particularly as increasing numbers of dissidents were using blogs to publish articles critical of the Mubarak regime. A new liberal political grouping, the Democratic Front Party, was registered by the authorities in May, under the leadership of Dr Osama al-Ghazali Harb, a former member of the NDP and editor-in-chief of the political journal *Al-Siyassa al-Dawliya*, and former cabinet minister Dr Yahia el-Gamal. By mid-2007 the number of legalized political organizations in Egypt had increased to 24. In August there was a renewed crackdown on the activities of the Muslim Brotherhood, amid reports that the group was preparing to establish a political party and to publish full details of its agenda. In the following month the editors of four independent newspapers were given one-year prison sentences and also fined, after they had been found guilty by a court in Cairo of defamation against President Mubarak and his son, Gamal.

Partial elections to select 88 members of the Advisory Council were held on 11 and 18 June 2007; 84 seats were secured by the NDP, three by independents aligned to the NDP and one by the NPUP. The Muslim Brotherhood thus failed to win a seat, despite having fielded candidates who stood as independents. A further 44 members of the Council were appointed by President Mubarak. In November Mubarak was re-elected unchallenged as leader of the NDP at the party's ninth congress; it was the first time since the President assumed the NDP leadership in 1981 that members had voted by secret ballot. There was renewed speculation concerning the likelihood of Gamal Mubarak succeeding his father as President after it was revealed that the party's Politburo and Secretariat-General had been merged to form a new Supreme Council. This meant that Gamal now belonged to the NDP's governing body (he had not been a member of the Politburo), and thus met the constitutional requirement that presidential candidates must either stand as independents or be members of the governing body of a legal political party. However, party officials denied that this had been the reason for the reform. In April 2008 President Mubarak announced an administrative reorganization, appointing 12 new governors and creating two new governorates (Helwan and Sixth of October). Despite protests from human rights organizations and political parties, in May the People's Assembly voted to extend until 2010 the state of emergency in place since President Sadat's assassination in 1981. The decision was particularly controversial given that Mubarak had pledged to abolish the emergency law during his 2005 presidential campaign.

Meanwhile, in April 2008 a series of strikes were organized by workers seeking to make public sector salaries more commensurate with soaring food and commodity prices. Rioting broke out in the city of Mahalla al-Kobra after police prevented industrial action by textile workers; two people died in the clashes and more than 100 were injured. In a move indicative of the wider sense of economic unrest felt by many Egyptians, students and professionals across the country staged demonstrations in solidarity with the protesters. By the end of April President Mubarak, keen to avert the possibility of a nation-wide strike, capitulated to public pressure and proposed a 30% increase in the salaries of public sector employees. However, given the steep rate of inflation in Egypt, scepticism remained about whether the measure was sufficient to address the growing problem of economic and social polarization in the country.

Increasing political tensions and civil unrest

In June 2009 the People's Assembly approved controversial legislation that increased the number of seats in the People's Assembly from 454 to 518, with all of the 64 additional seats reserved for female candidates. The changes were to take effect following the legislative elections scheduled for late 2010 and were intended to remain in place for at least two legislative terms. It was declared that the legislation—intended to promote the empowerment of women—represented the implementation of the constitutional amendments approved in 2007. However, opposition groups insisted that the changes were not sufficiently far-reaching.

During 2009 reports emerged of a rift in the Muslim Brotherhood between the conservative branch of the group and the so-called reformists, who favoured greater engagement in politics. In December internal elections were held for the party's governing body, with the majority of the 16 members elected being aligned with the conservative group. The party's deputy leader, Muhammad Habib, was not elected, and, following his subsequent omission from the list of candidates to succeed Muhammad Mahdi Akif as the group's Supreme Leader, stepped down from his post at the end of December. Akif had previously announced his intention to stand down at the end of his term in January 2010. In mid-January it was announced that Muhammad Badie—an academic with little political experience, who was regarded as a supporter of Akif's policies and was thought to be strongly opposed to reform—had been elected to replace Akif.

Meanwhile, in October 2009 opposition groups began a campaign against the possible candidacy of Gamal Mubarak to succeed his father at the end of the latter's presidential term in 2011. A new opposition movement, Mayihkomsh ('he will not rule'), was formed under the leadership of Ayman al-Nour. Its first conference was held in Cairo on 14 October 2009 and was attended by, among others, representatives of the Muslim Brotherhood, the Democratic Front Party and the Egyptian Movement for Change, also known as Kefaya (Enough). The campaign gained further prominence in February 2010, following an announcement by the former Secretary-General of the International Atomic Energy Agency, Mohammed el-Baradei, that he would be prepared to contest the presidential election. Upon his arrival in Cairo later that month, el-Baradei was greeted by opposition activists professing support for his possible candidacy. However, state-run media attempted to portray him as an outsider with little knowledge of contemporary Egyptian society. Moreover, the prospect of el-Baradei contesting the election remained uncertain, as the terms of the Constitution require non-affiliated candidates to obtain the support of at least 250 members of parliament or local officials before seeking the presidency.

In January 2010 six Coptic Christians and a security guard were shot dead outside a church in the town of Nag Hammadi, near Qena. The trial of three Muslims on charges of premeditated murder, endangering the life of citizens, and damage to public and private property in relation to the attack began at a court in Qena the following month. In January 2011 the main perpetrator of the attack was convicted and sentenced to death, pending confirmation from Egypt's Grand Mufti, Sheikh Ali Gomaa. However, in February two men accused of acting as accomplices were acquitted of all charges. Tensions between Egypt's Muslim and Coptic Christian communities escalated following a bomb attack outside a Coptic Christian church in Alexandria at the end of December 2010 while a New Year's Eve service was in progress; 21 people were killed. The authorities subsequently stated that the explosion had been carried out by a lone suicide bomber among the crowd. President Mubarak appealed to Muslims and Christians alike to unite against the common threat of terrorism, and alleged that the attack had been orchestrated by 'foreign hands' aiming to destabilize Egypt. Although senior Muslim leaders in Egypt expressed their sorrow at the attack, hundreds of Coptic Christians continued to clash angrily with the authorities. Many were incensed by the security forces' perceived failure properly to address threats against Egypt's Copts that had been issued several weeks previously by the Islamic State of Iraq, an organization comprising a number of Sunni Muslim insurgent groups.

In May 2010 the People's Assembly voted, by 305 votes to 103, to approve President Mubarak's request to extend the state of emergency for a further two years. Although new limits to the legislation were introduced, the extension of the emergency law elicited widespread condemnation from both campaigners for political reform and human rights organizations. Despite Prime Minister Nazif's insistence that the emergency law would 'not be used to undermine freedoms or infringe upon rights if these two threats [of terrorism and the supply of narcotics] are not involved', critics of the legislation argued that, even in its new, diluted form—whereby the state would no longer have such wide-ranging powers to monitor communications, confiscate property and censor publications—it could be used to stifle opposition to the Government.

At partial elections to the Advisory Council held on 1 June and 8 June 2010, the NDP secured 80 of the 88 contested seats; Al-Ghad, the NPUP, the Arab Democratic Nasserist Party and the Democratic Generation Party each won one seat, with the remaining four seats taken by independent candidates. As in 2007, affiliates of the Muslim Brotherhood, standing as independents, failed to secure a single seat. The Brotherhood subsequently pledged its support to a campaign for political reform that had been launched by el-Baradei, stating that it would help the potential presidential candidate in his efforts to collect 1m. signatures on a petition demanding, *inter alia*, constitutional reform and a revocation of the state of emergency. El-Baradei stated that he would contest the presidential election then scheduled for 2011 only if constitutional amendments were implemented so as to ensure a 'free and fair election'; el-Baradei's proposed reforms included full judicial supervision of elections and independent candidates being allowed to stand for President.

Meanwhile, extensive protests against alleged police brutality were sparked by the death, reportedly at the hands of police officers, of an activist in Alexandria in early June 2010. Witnesses had claimed that Khalid Said, who had posted a video recording on the internet that purported to show police officers misappropriating narcotics confiscated during a police raid, had been forcibly removed from a café and beaten by members of the police force. Human Rights Watch alleged that the authorities' response to the protests had been excessive, and that many demonstrators had been arrested arbitrarily. Meanwhile, state autopsies on Said's body determined that he had died of asphyxiation, sustained while attempting to swallow a plastic bag containing illicit drugs, and that his body showed no signs of having sustained any sort of violence. However, images posted on the internet that appeared to show Said's body covered in heavy bruising and other substantial injuries were widely believed to cast considerable doubt on these findings. Two police officers were arrested in connection with Said's death later in June. Their trial, on charges of 'illegal arrest, using physical torture and brutality', commenced in July; both men denied any wrongdoing. After court proceedings were adjourned several times during 2011, in late October both police officers were found guilty of the charges and sentenced to seven years' imprisonment.

The 2010 legislative elections

In October 2010 President Mubarak announced that elections to the People's Assembly were to be held on 28 November, with run-off elections scheduled for 5 December. In the previous month el-Baradei had urged an electoral boycott, claiming that the ballot was certain to be rigged by the Government. However, the outlawed Muslim Brotherhood subsequently announced its intention to field candidates as independents. On 25 November the NDP announced that it had filed complaints against 52 nominally independent candidates whom it believed to be affiliated to the Muslim Brotherhood; dozens of Brotherhood-affiliated candidates had already been disqualified and more than 1,000 of the group's supporters were reported to have been arrested in the weeks preceding the poll. On 26 November administrative courts ordered the cancellation of the elections in 24 districts after the HEC had ignored previous court orders demanding the reinstatement of disqualified opposition and independent candidates; however, the cancellation orders appeared to go similarly unheeded.

In the first round of voting, held as scheduled on 28 November 2010, the NDP was reported to have won the vast majority of seats, with independent candidates affiliated to the Muslim Brotherhood failing to secure a single seat. The second round of voting was boycotted by the New Wafd Party and the Brotherhood, both of which alleged widespread voting irregularities during the first round. According to final results released by the HEC, the NDP secured 420 seats (86.4% of the 508 contested seats in the People's Assembly), the New Wafd Party six, the NPUP five, and the Democratic Generation Party, Al-Ghad, Al-Salam and the Social Justice Party each garnered one seat; independent candidates won 69 seats, of which just one was taken by an affiliate of the Muslim Brotherhood (compared with 88 in 2005). The results appeared to preclude the possibility of any of the opposition parties fielding a candidate at the 2011 presidential election; according to the terms of the Constitution, in order to field a candidate, a political party had to have obtained 3% of the total number of seats in the People's Assembly and 5%

of seats in the Advisory Council; the chances of an independent candidate being able to stand also appeared remote, with such candidates being required to attain the endorsement of 250 elected members from Egypt's representative bodies. The New Wafd Party ordered its six elected legislators to resign from parliament, while the Brotherhood pledged to withdraw its support for Magdi Ashour, the sole affiliate of the organization to win a seat. The Government, meanwhile, continued to deny any allegations of vote-rigging, acknowledging only 'minor irregularities' that it claimed had no bearing on any results. However, election monitors reported widespread electoral violations, while two people were killed during violent clashes between the supporters of rival candidates.

In mid-December 2010 a group of about 20 opposition party members who had failed to secure election, including members of the Muslim Brotherhood and the New Wafd Party, announced the formation of a shadow parliament, pledging allegiance to the Constitution and 'the will of the people'. There were also widespread popular protests against the perceived fraudulent nature of the elections. While the Muslim Brotherhood remained ambivalent to the protests, in a video recording posted on the internet el-Baradei offered implicit approval of the demonstrators' actions and warned of potential violence if their demands were not heeded. In mid-January 2011 el-Baradei announced that he would not be seeking election in the presidential poll due later in the year, contending that it would be 'meaningless under current circumstances'; el-Baradei appealed for a boycott of the poll in an attempt to 'erode the regime's legitimacy'. He repeated in January 2012, by which time the ballot had been scheduled for June (see Recent developments) that he would not stand for the presidency until such an election was being organized 'within a democratic framework'.

The ouster of President Mubarak

Seemingly inspired by the overthrow of the Tunisian President, Zine al-Abidine Ben Ali, in mid-January 2011 (see the chapter on Tunisia), activists in Egypt called for a 'day of revolt' across the country on 25 January, in protest at state corruption, the alleged practice of torture by state security forces, poverty and unemployment. Thousands of demonstrators gathered in Cairo, Alexandria and other cities, demanding Mubarak's resignation as President and expressing their opposition to the possible candidacy of Gamal Mubarak as his successor. Three protesters were reported to have been killed in clashes with the authorities in Suez, while state television reported that a police officer had died in Cairo. Although foreign governments, including the US Administration, urged the Egyptian authorities to allow peaceful demonstrations, on 26 January the Government stated that anyone engaging in public gatherings, protests and marches would be prosecuted, and access to internet sites which had been used by activists to plan many of the protests was blocked. Nevertheless, demonstrators returned to the streets on 26–27 January, during which time a further two people were reported to have been killed and more than 800 people arrested. In anticipation of further mass protests planned for 28 January, the authorities detained a number of senior Muslim Brotherhood members, imposed a total block on internet access across the country and disrupted mobile telephone services. During the protests, which were staged across Cairo, Alexandria, Suez and other major cities, 18 people were reported to have been killed and more than 1,000 people injured. A nation-wide evening curfew was imposed in an attempt to defuse the situation. Mubarak issued a statement live on television in which he appealed to the protesters to desist, announcing his intention to replace the cabinet and to introduce political and economic reforms. However, the demonstrators intensified their protests overnight, and continued to demand the resignation of the President and other key officials.

On 29 January 2011 Mubarak appointed the chief of the General Intelligence Service, Omar Suleiman, as Vice-President, and announced the dismissal of Prime Minister Nazif and his administration. Later that day Gen. Ahmad Muhammad Shafiq, who had served as Minister of Civil Aviation under Nazif, was named as premier and on 31 January a new Council of Ministers was sworn in, most notably including Gen. Mahmoud Wagdi as Minister of the Interior, in place of Habib el-Adli, and the replacement of Minister of Information Anas Ahmad el-Fiki. However, demonstrations in Cairo and other cities across Egypt continued, with protesters denouncing the new Government as 'illegitimate', particularly citing the reappointment of several unpopular members of the previous administration. On 1 February President Mubarak announced in a televised address that neither he nor his son, Gamal, would contest the presidential election then scheduled for September, but that he would remain in office until the election was concluded. A televised statement earlier that day by a spokesman for the armed forces had indicated that troops would not obey orders to use military force to quell the protests. However, these announcements appeared not to have placated the protesters as violent confrontations between pro- and anti-Government groups erupted on 2 February in Cairo's Tahrir (Independence) Square, which had become the focal point of the demonstrations; the Ministry of Health reported that at least eight people had been killed and up to 900 injured in the clashes, which continued into the following day.

On 5 February 2011 Vice-President Suleiman began talks on constitutional reform with representatives of opposition groups, including the Muslim Brotherhood, which on 21 February announced its intention to establish a political party, the Freedom and Justice Party (FJP). The new party, officially founded on 30 April, declared that it would put forward candidates for some 50% of seats in the forthcoming elections to the People's Assembly, and that it would not be contesting the presidential poll. In June the FJP entered into a coalition, the Democratic Alliance, with a diverse group of Islamist and secular parties, including the New Wafd Party, the NPUP and the Al-Nour (Light) Party—an ultra-conservative Salafi Islamist organization established in January. (However, amid political disagreements, some members of the alliance subsequently withdrew in order to contest the legislative ballot independently.) In late February a moderate Islamist party, the Hizb al-Wasat al-Jadid (New Centre Party, or Al-Wasat)—established in 1996 by breakaway members of the Muslim Brotherhood—also achieved legal status. Despite the constitutional talks, demands for Mubarak's resignation increased as crowds of demonstrators returned to Tahrir Square. In a second televised address on 10 February 2011, Mubarak promised to transfer unspecified powers to Vice-President Suleiman. However, he insisted that he would remain in office until September's presidential election, citing concern over Egypt's national security if he were to depart immediately. Earlier that day a communiqué by a group of senior military officials, the Supreme Council of the Armed Forces (SCAF), had been broadcast on state television, in which the group, led by the Commander-in-Chief of the Armed Forces, Deputy Prime Minister and Minister of Defence Field Marshal Muhammad Hussein Tantawi, pledged the army's 'support for the legitimate demands of the people'.

Suleiman appeared on state television on 11 February 2011 to announce that Mubarak had resigned as President and transferred his powers to the SCAF. In a further communiqué issued on 13 February, the SCAF announced the dissolution of parliament, suspended the Constitution and declared that it would 'run the affairs of the country on a temporary basis for six months or until the end of parliamentary and presidential elections'. A judicial committee was instructed to formulate amendments to the Constitution in preparation for a national referendum in March. The communiqué also confirmed that Tantawi, as Chairman of the SCAF, was to act as de facto head of state, while the Government of Ahmad Shafiq was requested to remain in office, pending the conclusion of elections. However, protests against Shafiq's participation in the Government continued in Cairo, while police officers and other workers began a series of separate demonstrations, demanding wage increases. A minor cabinet reorganization was effected on 22 February, in which Yahia el-Gamal was appointed as Deputy Prime Minister for National Dialogue. In late February it was reported that the public prosecution service had begun an investigation into allegations of corruption and money-laundering against a number of senior members of the former governing regime, including el-Fiki, el-Adli and the businessman Ahmed Ezz, who had been an NDP member of the People's Assembly and was regarded as a close associate of Gamal Mubarak. The judicial committee on constitutional reform published its draft amendments on 28 February, including revisions to those articles regarding political parties and the criteria of eligibility for presidential candidates; on 4 March the SCAF decreed that a referendum was to take place on 19 March. Meanwhile, on 3 March it was announced that Shafiq had resigned as Prime Minister; former Minister of Transport Dr Essam Sharaf was subsequently appointed to replace him. Sharaf's new Council of Ministers was sworn in on 7 March. Most notably, Nabil al-Arabi, hitherto Egypt's ambassador to the UN, was appointed as Minister of Foreign Affairs, while Muhammad Abd al-Aziz al-Gendi became Minister of Justice and Gen. Mansour al-Essawi Minister of the Interior.

Also that day the trial of former Minister of the Interior el-Adli on separate charges of money-laundering and unlawful acquisition of public funds began at a court in Cairo. However, the proceedings were adjourned until early April.

On 19 March 2011, despite opposition from prominent figures in the anti-Mubarak protest movement, including el-Baradei, the constitutional amendments (which were supported by both the NDP and the Muslim Brotherhood) were approved by some 77.3% of voters; voter turn-out was recorded at 41.2%. Accordingly, on 23 March the SCAF issued a Constitutional Declaration —including the amendments approved at the referendum— which was to usurp the former Constitution until a new document could be formulated. Legislative elections were scheduled for September, although they did not in fact take place until November (see Recent developments). Also included in the draft amendments was the introduction of a two-term limit to the presidency, the judicial monitoring of future polls, and the stipulation that a President must henceforth name a Vice-President.

Former President Mubarak and his family were placed under house arrest at their residence in Sharm el-Sheikh at the end of March 2011, and in early April the Prosecutor-General requested that Mubarak and his sons Gamal and Alaa be questioned regarding allegations of corruption and the deaths of protesters during the February uprising. Renewed protests began in Tahrir Square by activists demanding that the former head of state be put on trial, and days later both his sons were detained for an initial 15-day period at a gaol in Cairo, while Mubarak was also under police custody at a hospital in Sharm el-Sheikh, having reportedly suffered from heart problems. On 17 April the High Administrative Court approved the dissolution of the NDP and the return of its assets to the state, while two days later the Prosecutor-General announced that former Prime Minister Nazif and former Minister of Finance Yousuf Boutros-Ghali had been charged with corruption and misuse of public funds. On 19 April a government committee formed to investigate the deaths of protesters revealed that a total of 846 people had been killed and at least 6,400 injured during the unrest of early 2011. In its report, the committee also accused the security forces of using 'excessive' force in their attempts to quell the protests. On 5 May el-Adli became the first senior member of the Mubarak regime to be convicted on charges relating to his time in office and was sentenced to 12 years' imprisonment and fined some £E14m., having been found guilty of money-laundering and of illicitly procuring public funds. El-Adli was expected to stand trial again later that month on charges of murder and attempted murder (he was accused of ordering police to shoot demonstrators during the anti-Mubarak uprising). When, on 26 June, it was announced that el-Adli's second trial had been postponed, protesters again took to the streets of the capital, demanding that Egypt's new authorities accelerate the pace of change and prosecute former officials accused of wrongdoing. On 24 May it had been officially announced that Hosni, Alaa and Gamal Mubarak would all face trial proceedings over their alleged crimes; the former leader's wife, Suzanne, was required to return to the state a list of illegally acquired personal belongings. Meanwhile, on 30 April 2011 Muhammad Mursi was appointed as President of the newly formed FJP by the Muslim Brotherhood leadership, while Muhammad Saad el-Katatni became the party's Secretary-General. (El-Katatni resigned his post on becoming parliamentary Speaker in January 2012.) On 10 May the former Minister of Tourism Zuhair Garranah was handed down a five-year prison term, having been found guilty of the illegal provision of tourism licences to private developers in a Red Sea resort; Garranah was given a further three-year sentence for engaging in corruption in mid-September (he was to serve the five-year term), while Ahmed Ezz was also imprisoned, having been found guilty of the corruption allegations. On 4 June Boutros-Ghali was sentenced to 30 years' imprisonment, *in absentia*, for corruption, including the use of public funds for personal gain, while serving as Minister of Finance. On 25 June Rachid Muhammad Rachid, a Minister of Industry and Foreign Trade under Mubarak, was convicted, also *in absentia*, and sentenced to five years in gaol for the embezzlement of state funds.

There was a notable increase in sectarian violence during 2011. In early March violence between Coptic Christians and Muslims in a district of Cairo led to more than 13 deaths; a further 140 people were wounded in the clashes, which erupted when Copts initiated protests against the burning down of a local church by hardline Muslims. Further clashes between members of the two communities in the capital in early May led to another 12 people being killed and around 200 injured; the latest incidents arose after rumours spread that a female Copt who had married a Muslim man was being forcibly prevented from converting to Islam. In early October 25 people (mostly Copts) were reported to have died as a result of renewed fighting between Copts and security forces who, joined by militant Salafi Islamists, reacted forcefully when Coptic protesters held a rally outside the headquarters of Egypt's state television corporation in Cairo against systematic discrimination of their religious community.

Recent developments: the trial of Mubarak and Islamist successes in legislative elections

On 15 May 2011 Egypt's newly appointed Minister of Foreign Affairs, Nabil al-Arabi, was appointed as Secretary-General of the Arab League, a post he assumed formally on 3 July. Muhammad al-Orabi was sworn in as al-Arabi's successor on 26 June. However, in anticipation of an expected government reorganization, in a further attempt by the SCAF to placate its opponents— who held rallies in Cairo's Tahrir Square throughout July in a demonstration of growing public discontent regarding the progress of political and economic reforms—al-Orabi resigned on 16 July, and on the following day was replaced by Muhammad Kamel Amr. Also on 17 July Hazem al-Beblawi (one of two Deputy Prime Ministers) succeeded Samir Radwan as the Minister of Finance; the revised Council of Ministers took office under Prime Minister Sharaf on 21 July. The outgoing Ministers of the Interior and of Justice retained their posts, as did 11 other members of the previous administration. Meanwhile, the continuing arrest and imprisonment of many pro-reform activists under Egypt's emergency laws continued to provoke considerable anger among the population. On 28 June 2011, two months after the NDP was disbanded, it was announced that 1,750 municipal councils formed under Mubarak's rule would be dissolved. On 13 July the interim Government also declared that up to 700 police officers would be dismissed from their posts for their alleged role in the deaths of protesters earlier in the year. On 19 July the SCAF stated that a new electoral commission, to be presided over by senior judge Abd al-Moez Ibrahim, would monitor both the legislative polls—registration for which was to commence in mid-September—and the subsequent presidential election.

The trial of Hosni Mubarak, together with his sons Gamal and Alaa, el-Adli and six other senior officials of the former regime, commenced at a court in Cairo on 3 August 2011; all the defendants pleaded not guilty to the charges of the unlawful killing of protesters, profiteering and conducting illegal business transactions. The start of the trial proceedings again precipitated a number of violent incidents between supporters and opponents of the former President. On 28 September the former Minister of Information, Anas el-Fiki, was convicted of the misuse of public funds in relation to the purchase of television programmes and given a seven-year prison sentence; Osama el-Sheikh, a former director of Egypt's state television corporation, received a five-year sentence, having been found guilty of similar charges.

In response to the deaths of three protesters at the Israeli embassy in Cairo in early September 2011 (see Egypt and the Middle East peace process), the SCAF announced that, in order to maintain national security, it would be required to reintroduce the emergency legislation that had been in force under President Mubarak; this action led to further protests by activists in Tahrir Square. On 20 November the Minister of Culture, Dr Emad Abu Ghazi, resigned in protest at the authorities' response to the latest demonstrations. Renewed clashes in Cairo and other major cities across Egypt between security forces and protesters demanding the replacement of the SCAF with a civilian administration had intensified on the previous day. On 22 November Tantawi accepted the resignation of Prime Minister Sharaf and his Council of Ministers, although they were requested to remain in office pending the formation of a new government. According to the Ministry of Health, at least 40 protesters died in the week prior to 23 November and some 3,500 were wounded. On 25 November Kamal al-Ganzouri, who had served as Prime Minister in 1996–99, was instructed to form a new 'national unity' government; he was also given the SCAF's presidential powers, with the exception of those relating to military and judicial matters. A new Council of Ministers was duly sworn in on 7 December; notable appointments included Mumtaz Said Abu el-Nour and Gen. Muhammad Youssuf Ibrahim Ahmad (a former

Cairo chief of police) as the Ministers of Finance and of the Interior, respectively. In November 2011 Tantawi had pledged that a presidential election would take place by the end of June 2012, and that the SCAF would order an independent inquiry into alleged violations by Egypt's security forces against pro-reform activists. In mid-December 2011 thousands of Egyptians again took to the streets of Cairo to protest against the harsh treatment of protesters by the police and security forces; recent evidence that female demonstrators had been beaten for participating in rallies prompted an apology from military officials. Some 18 people were reportedly killed in clashes outside the cabinet building and, in an effort to calm the situation, the SCAF suggested an acceleration of the process to elect members of the committee tasked with formulating a new constitution.

Although the pro-democracy protesters who took to the streets from early 2011 did not take an overtly Islamist stance, it was undoubtedly the Islamist parties, and in particular the Muslim Brotherhood, which benefited most from the downfall of the Mubarak regime. Egypt's various Islamist movements were by far the most successful at the first legislative elections to take place in the post-Mubarak era—the first polls which they were legally entitled to contest. Elections to the 508-member People's Assembly were held in three stages, each of two rounds: on 28–29 November and 5–6 December 2011, on 14–15 December and 21–22 December, and on 3–4 January and 10–11 January 2012. Official results issued by the electoral commission on 21 January 2012 revealed that the FJP (the political wing of the Muslim Brotherhood) had won 235 of the 498 elective seats (47.2% of the vote) and the Salafist Al-Nour Party 123 seats (24.7%); Islamist parties had thus garnered at least 70% of the votes. The New Wafd Party secured 38 seats, the Egyptian Bloc (a secular alliance of liberal or left-wing groups formed in August) 34 and the Al-Wasat Party 10; independent candidates won 23 seats, while the remaining seats were won by the Reformation and Development Party (nine), The Revolution Continues (seven), the National Party of Egypt (five), the Egypt Freedom Party and the Egyptian Citizen Party (both four), the Union Party (two) and other parties (four). In addition, 10 seats were appointed by the SCAF.

At the first session of the newly elected People's Assembly, held on 23 January 2012, Muhammad Saad el-Katatni, Secretary-General of the FJP, was elected as Speaker. It was of huge significance that a member of the Muslim Brotherhood, which had been officially proscribed under the Mubarak regime, had assumed the role. The new chamber's principal task was to select members of a committee to draft Egypt's new constitution, to be voted on in a national referendum before the SCAF was due to transfer power to a government of 'national salvation' after the forthcoming presidential election. On 24 January Tantawi announced that the state of emergency was to be partially lifted on the following day; however, details regarding the changes remained imprecise and pro-democracy activists were largely sceptical about the announcement. At elections to the Advisory Council, which took place in two stages on 29 January and 22 February, the Islamist parties again secured an overwhelming representation: the FJP took 105 of the 180 elective seats, while the Al-Nour Party garnered 45 seats. Most notably among other parties, the New Wafd Party won 14 seats and the Egyptian Bloc eight seats; four seats were taken by independents. A further 90 members were due to be appointed by the SCAF. The Council held its inaugural session on 29 February, at which the FJP's Ahmad Fahmi was elected as Speaker. Also that day it was announced by the electoral commission that the first round of the presidential poll would take place on 23–24 May. If required, a second round 'run-off' contest would be held on 16–17 June. At the deadline for nominations on 8 April, a total of 23 people had submitted their candidacy to the electoral commission. Most notably, these included former Secretary-General of the Arab League Amr Moussa, former Vice-President and head of General Intelligence Omar Suleiman, Ahmad Shafiq and the Salafist Hazem Abu Ismail. Controversially, having previously stated that it would not seek to contest the elections, the Muslim Brotherhood nominated two candidates: deputy Supreme Guide Khairat al-Shater and FJP leader Muhammad Mursi. However, the final list published by the electoral commission on 26 April included only 13 of the original 23 nominees. It had previously been announced that 10 candidates were to be disqualified, including al-Shater and Nour, owing to previous criminal convictions, and Abu Ismail, following claims that his mother had held dual US and Egyptian citizenship, thus contravening the legal requirement that a candidate be solely of Egyptian parentage. Suleiman was also prevented from contesting the poll, under legislation approved by the People's Assembly in mid-April designed to disbar anyone who had held the roles of Vice-President or Prime Minister during the last 10 years of the Mubarak regime. Nevertheless, an appeal by Shafiq (who had briefly acted as Prime Minister in January–March 2011) against his disqualification was upheld by the commission, and he was duly included in the list of approved candidates. The results of the election were expected to be announced on 21 June.

Foreign Affairs

Egypt and the Middle East peace process

Egypt played an important role in the efforts leading to the convening of a Middle East peace conference in Madrid, Spain, in October 1991, and an Egyptian delegation attended the first, symbolic session of the conference. Egyptian mediators were also influential in the secret negotiations between Israel and the PLO that led to the signing of the Declaration of Principles on Palestinian Self-Rule in September 1993. In May 1994 an agreement on Palestinian self-rule in the Gaza Strip and the Jericho area (see the chapter on Israel) was signed in Cairo by the Israeli Prime Minister, Itzhak Rabin, and the PLO Chairman, Yasser Arafat, at a ceremony presided over by President Mubarak. However, despite an official visit to Egypt by President Ezer Weizman in December (the first such visit by an Israeli head of state), relations between Egypt and Israel began to deteriorate. Egypt hosted summit meetings of Arab leaders in December 1994 and February 1995, prompting censure from the Israeli Government, and further tension arose when Mubarak reiterated his warning that Egypt would not sign the Treaty on the Non-Proliferation of Nuclear Weapons (or Non-Proliferation Treaty—NPT), which was due for renewal in April 1995, unless Israel also agreed to sign it.

Egypt continued its mediatory role in the complex negotiations that eventually led to the signing, in Washington, DC, of the Israeli-Palestinian Interim Agreement on the West Bank and the Gaza Strip in September 1995. In November Mubarak made his first presidential visit to Israel to attend the funeral of the assassinated Israeli Prime Minister, Itzhak Rabin. Egypt's relations with Israel deteriorated again in April 1996, as a consequence of Israeli military operations in Lebanon (q.v.). In June, in response to the apparently rejectionist stance of the new Israeli administration of Binyamin Netanyahu with regard to the exchange of land for peace, Mubarak convened an emergency summit meeting of the Arab League in Cairo—the first such meeting for six years. The summit's final communiqué reaffirmed the Arab states' commitment to peace, but warned that any further rapprochement between them and Israel depended on Israel's returning all the Arab land that it occupied in 1967.

President Mubarak cautiously welcomed the Wye River Memorandum signed by Netanyahu and Arafat in October 1998 (see the chapter on Israel). However, in January 1999 Egypt suspended all contacts with the Israeli Government in protest against its decision to suspend implementation of the agreement. The election, in May, of the leader of the One Israel alliance, Ehud Barak, to the Israeli premiership was generally welcomed in Egypt, but in July the Egyptian Minister of Foreign Affairs emphasized that there could be no normalization of Egyptian-Israeli relations prior to the resumption of comprehensive peace talks. Egyptian mediation was subsequently influential in discussions between Israeli and Palestinian negotiators that led to the signing of the Sharm el-Sheikh Memorandum by Barak and Arafat in September (see the chapter on Israel). Both the Israeli and Palestinian leaders made brief visits to Cairo prior to the US-hosted summit at the US presidential retreat at Camp David, Maryland, in July 2000. After the failure of the summit, Mubarak emphasized that he would not put pressure on Arafat to make concessions regarding the central issue of the status of Jerusalem, and urged all Arab states to unite in support of the Palestinians until they regained all their legitimate rights in accordance with the pertinent UN resolutions.

Following the outbreak in September 2000 of violent clashes between Palestinians and Israeli security forces in Jerusalem, which swiftly spread throughout the West Bank and Gaza, President Mubarak assumed an important role in attempting to prevent the violence from escalating into a major regional crisis. Most notably, a summit meeting held in mid-October at Sharm el-Sheikh, which was attended by Barak and Arafat and brokered by US President Bill Clinton, resulted in an agreement on the establishment of a fact-finding committee to investigate the causes of what had become known as the al-Aqsa *intifada* (uprising), although a tentative truce proved unviable. Later that month an emergency meeting of Arab League heads of state was convened in Cairo, at which Arab leaders held Israel solely to blame for the continuing violence. In November Egypt recalled its ambassador to Tel-Aviv, denouncing Israel's 'escalation of aggression and deliberate use of force against the Palestinian people'.

Following his election to the Israeli premiership in February 2001, it was alleged that the Likud leader, Ariel Sharon, had requested that the USA decrease military assistance to Egypt. Mubarak subsequently warned Sharon that he would interpret any such demand as a 'hostile action'. Nevertheless, at an Arab League summit on the Palestinian situation, held in Jordan in March, Mubarak deflected demands from more radical Arab states that Egypt and Jordan should sever diplomatic relations with Israel entirely. In April a joint Egyptian-Jordanian peace plan urged an immediate halt to Israeli construction of settlements and a withdrawal of Israeli forces to pre-*intifada* positions. The plan was supported by the new US Administration of President George W. Bush, the EU and Arab leaders; however, diplomatic progress subsequently stalled as violence continued to escalate. At an emergency meeting of Arab League ministers of foreign affairs in Cairo in May, it was agreed to suspend all political contacts with Israel until its attacks on Palestinians were halted; Egypt suspended all non-diplomatic contacts with Israel in April 2002.

Although President Mubarak strongly welcomed the publication, in April 2003, of the 'roadmap' peace plan drafted by the Quartet group (comprising the UN, the USA, the EU and Russia—see the chapter on Israel), Egyptian efforts to secure a cease-fire by armed Palestinian factions made no further progress. In December the Israeli Deputy Prime Minister and Minister of Foreign Affairs, Silvan Shalom, met with President Mubarak in Geneva, Switzerland, and the following week Egypt's Minister of Foreign Affairs, Ahmad Maher, travelled to Israel for discussions with Sharon and Shalom. The meeting was overshadowed, however, by an attack on Maher, perpetrated by Palestinian extremists, while he was visiting the al-Aqsa Mosque in Jerusalem. In April 2004 Mubarak travelled to the USA to discuss the roadmap with President Bush; the US President also met with Sharon and endorsed Sharon's proposals for an Israeli 'disengagement' from Gaza, which also involved the consolidation of six Jewish settlements in the West Bank. It was envisaged that Egyptian forces would assume responsibility for border security in Gaza after Israel's unilateral withdrawal, which Sharon maintained would be completed by the end of 2005 (although in the event it was completed by September). In December 2004, after talks held in Jerusalem between the Israeli Minister of Defence, Lt-Gen. Shaul Mofaz, and the Egyptian intelligence chief, Omar Suleiman, it was agreed that 750 Egyptian troops would be stationed on the border with Gaza ahead of the Israeli withdrawal, in a bid to prevent arms from being smuggled into the territory for use by Palestinian militants.

Following the terrorist attacks in the Sinai region in October 2004 (see above), Egypt made clear its wish to send troops into the demilitarized buffer zone along the border with Israel, claiming that a military presence there could prevent further attacks. In December a new trade deal between Egypt and Israel was signed allowing duty-free export between three newly established 'qualified industrial zones' and the USA, provided that at least 11.7% of the goods were manufactured in Israel. Despite being positively received within many Egyptian business circles, the protocol triggered angry demonstrations in Cairo among those who believed it would give Israel too much economic power over the country. In March 2005 Muhammad Asim Ibrahim assumed the role of ambassador to Israel (the post having been vacant since November 2000).

In the months prior to the Israeli withdrawal from the Gaza Strip in August–September 2005 (see the chapter on Israel) Israel and Egypt held official talks regarding the deployment of Egyptian forces along the border with Gaza. A deal confirming that 750 Egyptian border guards would police the southern border was approved by the Israeli Knesset on 31 August. In October it was announced that the border with Gaza would be reopened at the Rafah checkpoint to allow key crossings, and on 26 November some 1,500 Palestinians passed into Egypt. In February 2006, following Hamas's decisive victory in the first Palestinian legislative elections since 1996, leaders of the organization held discussions in Cairo regarding the formation of a new administration. Egypt subsequently began to exert pressure on Hamas to reconsider its position regarding Israel's right to existence, while urging Israel not to impose sanctions on the Hamas-led administration formed in the West Bank and Gaza in March 2006.

The election of a new Israeli Government under Prime Minister Ehud Olmert in March 2006 led to renewed Egyptian efforts to revive the Middle East peace process. In early June Mubarak and Olmert held their first summit meeting in Sharm el-Sheikh, during which Olmert agreed to meet with Palestinian President Mahmud Abbas for talks later in that month. In July Mubarak expressed Egypt's solidarity with Lebanon after Israel launched a large-scale offensive against positions held by the Shi'ite fundamentalist group Hezbollah in southern Lebanon in response to the kidnapping by Hezbollah militants of two Israeli soldiers and the killing of several others in a cross-border raid, and amid a series of missile attacks on northern Israel (see the chapters on Israel and Lebanon).

After the commencement of serious factional fighting between militias of the rival Hamas and Fatah factions in the Gaza Strip following the formation of the new Palestinian administration in March 2006, Egyptian officials were involved in diplomatic efforts, led principally by Saudi Arabia, to secure a lasting cease-fire between the two sides and establish a Palestinian national unity cabinet. Although a power-sharing administration was formed in March 2007, Hamas militants seized control of Gaza in June, effectively dividing the Palestinian territories into two separate entities (see the chapter on the Palestinian Autonomous Areas). In June President Mubarak hosted a summit meeting of regional leaders in Sharm el-Sheikh, with a view to restarting Middle East peace negotiations based on the 'land-for-peace' plan proposed by Saudi Arabia in 2002.

Despite initial hopes for an improvement in the regional situation following the international peace conference held in Annapolis, Maryland, USA, in November 2007, Mubarak was highly critical of Israel's continued expansion of Jewish settlements in the West Bank, which he said would seriously hinder the prospects of a comprehensive peace deal being achieved by the US Administration's intended deadline of the end of 2008. The Israeli Deputy Prime Minister and Minister of Defence, Ehud Barak, ordered virtually a complete blockade on the Gaza Strip in mid-January 2008, in an attempt to counter the growing number of rockets being launched onto Israeli border towns from the Strip by Hamas militants. In late January Palestinian fighters succeeded in breaching the Rafah crossing that divides Gaza from Egypt, and hundreds of thousands of Palestinians entered Egypt in search of food, fuel and medical supplies. The crossing had been almost permanently closed since Hamas's takeover of the Strip in June 2007 because the Egyptian Government, as did Israel, refused to recognize Hamas as the legitimate administration there. Egyptian officials responded by offering their backing to a plan proposed by President Abbas that would allow for the Palestinian (National) Authority (PA), rather than Hamas, to assume control of the Egypt–Gaza border. The breaches in the border were repaired in February 2008; however, there were reports of exchanges of gunfire between Egyptian security forces and Palestinian militants as tensions continued.

Following several months of negotiations mediated by Egyptian officials, in June 2008 a cease-fire was agreed between Israel and representatives of Hamas in the Gaza Strip, which was to remain in place for at least six months. On 19 December 2008 Hamas formally declared an end to the cease-fire agreement with Israel. In the following days Palestinian militants launched rocket and mortar attacks on northern Israel, while Israel conducted air-strikes against Gaza. Following Israel's military response, code-named 'Operation Cast Lead' (see the chapter on the Palestinian Autonomous Areas), Egypt continued to be involved in international diplomatic efforts to secure a formal, more durable cease-fire between Israel and Hamas.

The appointment of the Likud leader, Binyamin Netanyahu, as Israeli Prime Minister in March 2009, threatened to strain relations between Israel and Egypt. In May 2009, however, Netanyahu paid an official visit to Sharm el-Sheikh to discuss the Israeli–Palestinian situation with Mubarak and declared his country's desire to recommence peace talks. In December Netanyahu met with Mubarak in Cairo to outline proposals for the next stage of talks and, upon returning to Israel, proposed a summit meeting hosted by Egypt as a means to achieve this aim. Bilateral relations were threatened by the arrest in December 2010 of two Israeli citizens and one Egyptian citizen by the Egyptian authorities on suspicion of spying for Israel between May 2008 and August 2010. The three suspects were convicted of the charges of espionage and endangering Egyptian national interests in late June 2011, and were each sentenced to 25 years in gaol (the Israelis *in absentia*).

Meanwhile, Egypt hosted negotiations between representatives of Hamas and Fatah, and in September 2009 drafted a reconciliation agreement, which was subsequently accepted by Fatah; negotiations broke down, however, after Hamas refused to sign the agreement. Following further Egyptian-brokered negotiations between the two factions in September 2010, Hamas and Fatah published a joint communiqué confirming their intention to adopt practical measures to end the protracted impasse. An unsuccessful second round of talks was held in Damascus, Syria, in November. Following the appointment, in early March 2011, of Essam Sharaf as Prime Minister (see The ouster of President Mubarak), his Government placed a renewed emphasis on the reconciliation talks between Hamas and Fatah, and on 3 May representatives of 13 Palestinian factions signed a so-called 'unity' agreement following a round of talks in Cairo; on 4 May President Abbas and Hamas's political leader, Khalid Meshaal, travelled to the Egyptian capital for a ceremony to mark the agreement, which was expected to result in the formation of a joint administration for the West Bank and Gaza (see the chapter on the Palestinian Autonomous Areas). This 'national unity' administration was to take charge of the Palestinian territories pending the outcome of legislative and presidential elections, which were due to be held within one year; however, the new cabinet had not been formed by the start of 2012, talks between Fatah and Hamas having stalled in June 2011, amid ongoing disagreements between the two sides.

Although the SCAF declared after the overthrow of President Mubarak in February 2011 that it would honour Egypt's peace treaty with Israel, many Israelis feared the implications for their country's long-term security of a victory in Egypt's first post-revolution legislative polls of Islamist parties. Israeli officials claimed to have evidence that Hamas was already benefiting from the change of Egyptian regime, with reports that militant Islamist groups there were increasingly involved in the smuggling of arms to Hamas fighters in the Gaza Strip. On 28 May, despite Israeli objections, the Egyptian Government allowed the Rafah border crossing with Gaza to reopen for Palestinians, with certain restrictions on those using the crossing to be imposed for security reasons; cross-border trade remained prohibited. It was reported on 9 September that three Egyptian protesters had died as violence broke out between Egyptian security forces and militant demonstrators who forced their way into the Israeli embassy in Cairo, prompting Israel to evacuate its ambassador and most diplomatic staff the following day. The protests followed the accidental killing by the Israeli military of five Egyptian security officials in mid-August, as Israeli forces responded to the deaths of eight Israelis in gun and bomb attacks carried out by suspected Palestinian militants in southern Israel, close to the border with Egypt, by launching attacks against Palestinian militants in the Gaza border area (Israel claimed that the attackers had entered Israel from Gaza via Egypt's Sinai Peninsula). The Israeli Deputy Prime Minister and Minister of Defence, Ehud Barak, expressed regret over the incident, and pledged to hold a joint investigation with Egypt into the circumstances of the Egyptians' deaths. In mid-October, following an agreement reached between Israel and Hamas in Cairo earlier that month as a result of German- and Egyptian-sponsored negotiations, the Israeli soldier kidnapped by Hamas militants in Gaza in June 2006 was returned to Israel via Egypt. Under the terms of the deal, Israel freed 477 Palestinian prisoners initially to Egypt, with the release of a further 550 to take place two months later. In late October 2011 the Egyptian and Israeli authorities exchanged 25 Egyptians who had been held in Israeli detention for a US-Israeli citizen who had been held by Egypt on charges of spying for Israel.

Other regional relations

In October 2008 the Egyptian Minister of Foreign Affairs, Ahmad Aboul Gheit, visited Iraq—the first such trip to be undertaken since 1990—in an effort to renew Iraqi-Egyptian relations. In July 2009 Aboul Gheit and al-Zibari signed a memorandum of understanding covering bilateral co-operation in security and commerce, following a meeting in Cairo. In November Sharif Kamal Shahin arrived in Baghdad to take up appointment as Egypt's ambassador to Iraq (which role had been vacant since the abduction and murder in 2005 of the previous ambassador, Ihab al-Sherif, by a militant Islamist group claiming to represent al-Qa'ida in Iraq), and in December Iraqi Prime Minister Nuri Kamal (Jawad) al-Maliki arrived in Cairo for a two-day official visit, during which he held talks with President Mubarak on increased Egyptian investment in Iraq's reconstruction effort.

In December 2003 President Mubarak held talks with the Iranian President, Dr Sayed Muhammad Khatami, in Geneva—the first meeting between the leaders of the two countries since bilateral diplomatic relations were severed following the Islamic Revolution in Iran of 1979. In December 2004 Iran handed over to Egypt Moustafa Hamzah, a leader of Gama'ah al-Islamiyah and the alleged mastermind of a 1995 assassination attempt on President Mubarak (see Domestic Political Affairs), representing a significant step towards improving bilateral relations. After Khatami's successor, President Mahmoud Ahmadinejad, declared in May 2007 that Iran was prepared to resume diplomatic ties with Egypt and to open an embassy in Cairo, senior officials from the respective countries held what were said to have been 'constructive' discussions, which included a visit by the Speaker of the Iranian Majlis (parliament) to Cairo in January 2008. Despite the evident thaw in bilateral relations, however, it appeared that the Egyptian leadership was reluctant to proceed with the normalization until Iran first ended what it deemed to be its interference in the internal affairs of several Arab countries, notably Iraq, Lebanon and the Palestinian territories. In mid-February 2011 Egypt's new caretaker Government after the overthrow of President Mubarak's regime provoked serious concern in Israel by allowing two Iranian naval ships to pass through the Suez Canal for the first time since 1979.

Egypt has a long-standing border dispute with Sudan concerning the so-called Halaib triangle. Relations deteriorated sharply in mid-1995, after Egypt accused Sudan of complicity in the attempted assassination of President Mubarak in Addis Ababa (see above). Egypt strengthened its control of the Halaib triangle, and subsequently (in contravention of a bilateral agreement concluded in 1978) imposed visa and permit requirements on Sudanese nationals visiting or resident in Egypt. In February 1996 the Sudanese authorities introduced permit requirements for Egyptian nationals resident in Sudan. In July Egypt accused Sudan of harbouring Egyptian terrorists. None the less, Egypt opposed the imposition by the UN of more stringent economic sanctions against Sudan (q.v.), on the grounds that they would harm the Sudanese people more than the regime.

Following the resumption of bilateral security talks in August 1997, in December 1999 Egypt and Sudan agreed to a full normalization of relations, and resolved to co-operate in addressing their border dispute. The new Egyptian ambassador to Sudan assumed his post in Khartoum in March 2000, and in September a number of bilateral co-operation accords were signed. In January 2004 Mubarak and his Sudanese counterpart, Lt-Gen. Omar Hassan Ahmad al-Bashir, signed what was termed the 'four freedoms' agreement, which allowed for freedom of movement, residence, work and property ownership between the two countries; the agreement came into effect in September. During 2006–07 Egyptian officials were involved in mediation efforts to find a regional solution to the conflict in Sudan's Darfur region, and in January 2008 the country deployed 1,200 troops to Darfur as part of a joint African Union-UN peace-keeping force. Egypt, like many other African and Arab states, rejected the International Criminal Court's decision, in March 2009, to issue a warrant for the arrest of al-Bashir for alleged war crimes in Darfur, suggesting that it would serve only to exacerbate the already volatile situation in the Darfur region.

Meanwhile, in 2004 disputes over the Nile began to escalate as Tanzania confirmed that it intended to build a 170-km pipeline to draw water from Lake Victoria. This decision contravened the Nile Water Agreement drawn up in 1929 between Egypt and the United Kingdom, which states that Egypt has the right to veto any work that might threaten the flow of the river and allows the country to inspect the entire length of the Nile. Talks began in Uganda in March 2004 between the 10 countries that share the Nile's waters, and an agreement was reached in April 2006 whereby a permanent commission was to be established to oversee management, planning and use of the river. In May 2010 Ethiopia, Kenya, Rwanda, Tanzania and Uganda signed a Nile River Basin Co-operative Framework Agreement, which, upon ratification, would create the Nile Basin Commission; Burundi followed suit in February 2011. However, an Egyptian government spokesperson stated that Egypt 'will not join or sign any agreement that affects its share'; Sudan was also not expected to sign the agreement. (The agreement had initially been due to be signed in 2007, but, at the request of Egypt, the opening of the agreement to signatures had been delayed.)

Relations with the USA

Although in March 1999 an agreement was made for the USA to supply Egypt with US $3,200m. of defence equipment, bilateral relations have remained tense. During a visit to the USA in April 2001 President Mubarak met with President George W. Bush for the first time and urged the USA actively to support the Egyptian-Jordanian peace plan (see above). Meanwhile, Bush, who had indicated that Iraq would be his Administration's priority in terms of Middle East policy, expressed his unease at Egypt's lack of support for international sanctions against the Iraqi President, Saddam Hussain. Relations between Egypt and the USA deteriorated in mid-2002 following the announcement by the Bush Administration that it would suspend any additional foreign aid to Egypt in protest at what it considered to be the country's poor treatment of pro-democracy campaigners and human rights organizations. It was emphasized, however, that existing aid programmes would not be affected (the USA provides Egypt with annual assistance worth some US $1,700m.).

As the likelihood of a US-led military campaign to oust the Iraqi regime of Saddam Hussain increased during late 2002, President Mubarak was one of a number of Arab leaders who expressed their concern at the effects of military intervention in Iraq on the Middle East as a whole, as well as its implications for the unity of Iraq. In September Mubarak received the Iraqi Minister of Foreign Affairs and requested that Iraq comply with pertinent UN resolutions and allow UN weapons inspectors to operate freely within the country. Following the commencement of US-led hostilities against the Iraqi regime in mid-March 2003, there were a number of anti-war demonstrations in Cairo, resulting in the arrest of some 800 protesters. At the end of March Mubarak warned that the conflict would ignite Islamist fanaticism and create '100 new bin Ladens'. None the less, the ouster of Saddam Hussain in early April was met with ambivalence by Egypt. In May 2006 a proposal to reduce US aid to Egypt, in response to the recent stalling on political and economic reform, was defeated in the US House of Representatives; the initiative, none the less, demonstrated the growing frustration on the part of the USA over the issue of reform.

The waning importance of US-Egyptian relations to both countries again became apparent in January 2008, when President Bush visited Egypt only briefly at the end of an eight-day tour of the Middle East. The US leadership had been strongly critical of Egypt for its failure to secure its border with the Gaza Strip following the takeover of the territory by Hamas militants in June 2007 and to prevent Palestinian militants from smuggling weapons into Gaza for use in attacks against Israeli targets. In December of that year the US Congress voted to withhold US $100m. in aid to Egypt until the USA had received assurances that the authorities in Cairo had imposed sufficient measures to bring to an end the cross-border arms-smuggling and had also taken steps to improve the country's human rights record. Ayman al-Nour's release from prison on medical grounds in February 2009 (see Domestic Political Affairs) was considered by many commentators to be an effort by Mubarak to improve bilateral relations with the USA. The fact that several prior appeals for al-Nour to be freed because of his poor health had been rejected suggested that the decision to release him at this time represented an overture to the recently inaugurated US President, Barack Obama, whose Administration had reportedly stated its reluctance to engage fully with Mubarak while al-Nour remained imprisoned.

In June 2009 President Obama arrived in Cairo on an official visit, during which he gave a speech that was broadcast via television to much of the Arab world. In the speech Obama pledged a new beginning in relations between the USA and Muslim countries, and emphasized the importance of a solution to the Israeli–Palestinian conflict. In August Mubarak paid a return visit to Washington, DC, where he held talks with Obama on proposals to revive peace talks between Israel and the PA. However, many analysts commented that Gamal Mubarak's presence on this visit indicated that the President was using the trip as an opportunity to introduce his son to an international audience prior to the Egyptian presidential election scheduled for 2011. Relations were strained following widespread allegations of voting irregularities during Egypt's legislative elections in November–December 2010 (see Domestic Political Affairs); a spokesperson for the US Department of State stated that the Obama Administration was 'disappointed' by the reports of a pre-election clampdown on opposition candidates, and was 'dismayed by reports of election-day interference and intimidation by security forces'. Egypt's Government dismissed such comments as 'unacceptable interference' in Egyptian internal affairs. Following Mubarak's first televised address in response to the protests of January 2011, Obama stated that he had urged the Egyptian authorities to desist from violence and allow the Egyptian people to 'determine their own destiny'. In mid-March, after the resignation of President Mubarak (see Domestic Political Affairs), the US Secretary of State, Hillary Clinton, visited Cairo for talks with leading Egyptian officials and pro-democracy campaigners; during the visit Clinton offered political and economic support to the new Government, including some US $90m. in emergency assistance.

CONSTITUTION AND GOVERNMENT

A new Constitution for the Arab Republic of Egypt was approved by referendum on 11 September 1971. Amendments to the Constitution were endorsed by the People's Assembly on 30 April 1980, 10 May 2005 and 19 March 2007, and subsequently approved at national referendums. Following the ouster of former President Muhammad Hosni Mubarak in early February 2011, further amendments to the Constitution were approved by some 77.3% of voters at a national referendum held on 19 March (see Contemporary Political History).

Legislative power is held by the unicameral Majlis al-Sha'ab (People's Assembly), which has 508 members: 10 nominated by the President (in 2012, by the head of the Supreme Council of the Armed Forces) and 498 directly elected for five years from 222 constituencies. There is also a 264-member advisory body, the Majlis al-Shura (Advisory Council), which ratifies amendments to the Constitution and treaties affecting Egypt's territorial integrity or sovereignty. The Council advises on draft legislation pertaining to social and economic development. Two-thirds of the members of the Advisory Council are elected by direct suffrage; the remainder are appointed by the President. The Council's term in office is six years, with one-half of its members being replaced every three years. In May 2005 a constitutional amendment was approved by national referendum to introduce a system of direct, contested presidential elections. The President, who is the head of state, has executive powers and is required to appoint at least one Vice-President. According to the terms of the constitutional amendments promulgated in March 2011, the President may serve no more than two consecutive terms of four years. The country is divided into 29 governorates.

REGIONAL AND INTERNATIONAL CO-OPERATION

Egypt is a member of the African Union (AU, see p. 189), the Common Market for Eastern and Southern Africa (COMESA, see p. 237), the Community of Sahel-Saharan States (CEN-SAD, see p. 449) and the Organization of Arab Petroleum Exporting Countries (OAPEC, see p. 401). The League of Arab States (Arab League, see p. 364) has its permanent headquarters in the Egyptian capital, Cairo.

Egypt has been a member of the UN since its foundation in 1945, and, as a contracting party to the General Agreement on Tariffs and Trade, joined the World Trade Organization (WTO) on its establishment in 1995. The country also participates in the Organization of Islamic Cooperation (OIC, see p. 404) and the Group of 77 developing countries (G77, see p. 450).

ECONOMIC AFFAIRS

In 2010, according to estimates by the World Bank, Egypt's gross national income (GNI), measured at average 2008–10 prices, was US $197,922m., equivalent to $2,440 per head (or $6,160 per head on an international purchasing-power parity basis). During 2001–10, it was estimated, the population increased at an average annual rate of 1.8%, while gross domestic product (GDP) per head increased, in real terms, by 3.4% per year. Overall GDP increased, in real terms, at an average annual rate of 5.3% in 2001–10; according to Central Bank of Egypt (CBE) figures, real GDP increased by 1.9% in 2010/11.

Agriculture (including forestry and fishing) contributed 14.5% of GDP in 2010/11, and employed an estimated 31.7% of the economically active population in 2008. The principal crops include sugar cane, wheat, maize, rice, and fruit and vegetables (particularly tomatoes). Cotton is the principal cash crop. According to the World Bank, during 2001–10 agricultural GDP increased at an average annual rate of 3.3%. Agricultural GDP grew by 2.7% in 2010/11, according to the CBE.

Industry (including mining, manufacturing, construction and power) provided 37.6% of GDP in 2010/11, and engaged about 23.0% of the employed labour force in 2008. According to the World Bank, during 2001–10 industrial GDP expanded at an average annual rate of 5.7%. Industrial GDP increased by 0.5% in 2010/11, according to CBE data.

Mining contributed 14.9% of GDP in 2010/11. Egypt's mineral resources include petroleum, natural gas, phosphates, manganese, uranium, coal, iron ore and gold. Although the mining sector employed only 0.2% of the working population in 2008, petroleum and petroleum products accounted for 28.8% of total export earnings in 2010. Petroleum production averaged an estimated 736,000 barrels per day in 2010, and at the end of that year Egypt's oil reserves were estimated to total 4,500m. barrels (sufficient to sustain production at 2010 levels for just over 16 years). At the end of 2010 Egypt's proven natural gas reserves totalled 2,210,000m. cu m, sustainable for almost 36 years at constant production levels (totalling 61,300m. cu m in 2010). Until the early part of this century all the natural gas produced was consumed domestically, but the Government began exporting the commodity in 2003. In mid-2003 BP Egypt announced the largest petroleum discovery in the country for 14 years, and there were also major discoveries of natural gas and condensate during the decade. Mining GDP increased by 0.6% in 2010/11, according to the CBE.

Manufacturing contributed 16.5% of GDP in 2010/11, and engaged some 11.4% of the employed labour force in 2008. Based on the value of output, the main branches of manufacturing are food products, petroleum-refining, chemicals, textiles, metals and metal products, and non-metallic mineral manufactures. In 2005 the Government initiated a 20-year plan to invest US $10m. in the construction of 14 new petrochemical complexes. Plans to build a $2,000m. petroleum refinery with two Chinese companies were agreed in May 2010; the refinery was expected to have an initial annual capacity of 15m. metric tons, with capacity projected ultimately to increase to 30m. tons. According to the World Bank, the real GDP of the manufacturing sector increased by an average of 5.2% per year during 2001–10. Manufacturing GDP declined by 0.9% in 2010/11, according to the CBE.

The construction sector contributed 4.6% of GDP in 2010/11, and engaged some 10.1% of the employed labour force in 2008. Construction GDP increased by 3.7% in 2010/11, according to CBE figures.

Energy is derived principally from natural gas (which provided 68.4% of total electricity output in 2008), petroleum (19.7%) and hydroelectric power (11.2%). In 2010 imports of mineral fuels accounted for 13.5% of the total value of merchandise imports. In 2006 the Government announced that the programme to develop peaceful nuclear technology, which had been suspended in the mid-1980s, was to recommence. A project to construct a 1,000-MW nuclear plant on the Mediterranean coast at Dabaa was proposed as part of a plan to increase capacity by 5,000 MW through the development of four civil nuclear energy plants by 2025. In August 2010 the Government formally announced that Dabaa was to be the site for the first such plant, with a contract for the US $4,000m. project expected to be awarded in 2011 and completion tentatively scheduled for 2019; however, the award of the contract was subsequently delayed, following the ouster of President Hosni Mubarak in February 2011 (see Contemporary Political History). Egypt's first solar energy plant, located in Kuraymat, south of Cairo, commenced operations in December 2010.

Services contributed 47.9% of GDP in 2010/11, and employed about 45.4% of the working population in 2008. Following the campaign of violence aimed by militant Islamists at tourist targets during the 1990s, a recovery in the tourism sector was again hindered by the regional insecurity arising from the Israeli–Palestinian violence from late 2000, the terrorist attacks against the USA in September 2001 and the US-led intervention in Iraq in early 2003. Despite the Sinai bombings in 2004–06, however, the number of visitors to Egypt increased each year in 2005–08. According to preliminary figures for 2011 from the Ministry of Tourism, visitor numbers fell by 33% as a result of the political unrest, to some 9.8m. According to the World Bank, in 2000–10 the real GDP of the services sector increased by an average of 5.1% per year. Services GDP increased by 2.8% in 2010/11, according to CBE figures.

In 2010 Egypt recorded a visible trade deficit of US $20,120m., and there was a deficit of $4,504m. on the current account of the balance of payments. In 2010 the principal source of imports (9.4%) was the USA; other major suppliers were the People's Republic of China, Germany and Italy. The principal market for exports was Italy (8.0%), followed by Spain, Saudi Arabia and the USA. Egypt's principal exports in 2010 were mineral fuels and lubricants, fertilizers, and pearls and precious stones. The principal imports were mineral fuels and lubricants, machinery, nuclear reactors and boilers, vehicles (excluding railway and tramway), cereals, electronic equipment, and iron and steel.

For the financial year 2010/11 there was a deficit of £E53,583m. in the central government budget (equivalent to 4.1% of GDP). Egypt's general government gross debt was £E890,211m. in 2010, equivalent to 73.8% of GDP. Egypt's external debt totalled US $33,257m. at the end of 2009, of which $30,622m. was public and publicly guaranteed debt. In that year, the cost of servicing long-term public and publicly guaranteed debt and repayments to the IMF was equivalent to 6.2% of the value of exports of goods, services and income (excluding workers' remittances). The annual rate of inflation averaged 5.5% in 2001–10. Consumer prices increased by an average of 11.8% in 2009, but declined by 22.6% in 2010. An estimated 9.0% of the total labour force were unemployed at the end of 2010.

Following an impressive macroeconomic performance during much of the 1990s, characterized by strong GDP growth and low inflation, Egypt's economy suffered a series of major reverses from the end of that decade. However, a series of fiscal reforms introduced from 2004 stimulated inflows of foreign direct investment, leading to impressive rates of economic growth. Despite the difficult economic conditions brought about by the global economic slowdown from late 2008, and partly owing to the Government's investment in infrastructure projects and policies designed to protect Egyptian companies from exposure to the crisis, GDP growth was recorded at 4.7% in 2008/09. A slight recovery, to 5.1%, occurred in 2009/10, with a further acceleration in growth—to 5.5%—projected for 2010/11, according to the IMF. A non-budgetary stimulus plan announced by the Government in December 2010 was projected to inject US $3,440m. into the economy during 2011; a further development plan worth £E230,000m. was launched in April. However, as a result of the political uprising that toppled the regime of President Mubarak in February 2011, GDP contracted by 4.2% in the first quarter, and in mid-2011 the Government predicted growth for the year to fall to 2.5%. Amid continuing demonstrations during 2011, the protesters' economic grievances included unemployment (estimated at 11.9% in mid-2011), poverty, rising food prices and official corruption. In November interim Prime Minister Kamal al-Ganzouri announced a range of austerity measures to tackle Egypt's chronic budget deficit, which had worsened following Mubarak's overthrow. In June 2011 the Council of Ministers had approved a draft budget for 2011/12, which projected a 25% increase in public expenditure (focusing on social security provision and job creation) and a deficit of 10.9%; this was, however, later revised to 8.6%. In 2011 the tourism industry (which contributes around 11% of GDP) was seriously affected by the political instability; the sector's decline had a major impact on Egypt's dwindling foreign exchange reserves. Furthermore, the stock exchange (which ceased trading between January and March) lost more than 40% of its value during 2011, owing to fears over Egypt's future political direction and a possible devaluation of the pound. In early February 2012 it was reported that the Egyptian authorities had requested a loan of $1,000m. from the World Bank to support the country's economic reform programme, and were also discussing a $3,200m. loan package with the IMF. In 2011 the World Bank had pledged some $4,500m. in assistance over a two-year period, while Egypt had also accepted additional financial support from the African Development Bank and from Saudi Arabia and Qatar. During this current period of uncertainty, the success of the Egyptian Government's austerity measures and the long-term prospects for economic growth will depend to a large extent on the political landscape that emerges after the recent legislative elections and the presidential poll scheduled for May 2012.

PUBLIC HOLIDAYS

2013: 1 January (New Year), 23 January* (Mouloud/Yum al-Nabi, Birth of Muhammad), 25 April (Sinai Day), 6 May (Sham al-Nessim, Coptic Easter Monday), 5 June* (Leilat al-Meiraj, Ascension of Muhammad), 23 July (Revolution Day), 7 August* (Id al-Fitr, end of Ramadan), 6 October (Armed Forces Day), 14 October* (Id al-Adha, Feast of the Sacrifice), 24 October (Popular Resistance Day), 4 November* (Muharram, Islamic New Year), 23 December (Victory Day).

* These holidays are dependent on the Islamic lunar calendar and may vary by one or two days from the dates given.

Coptic Christian holidays include: Christmas (7 January), Palm Sunday (28 April) and Easter Sunday (5 May).

Statistical Survey

Sources (unless otherwise stated): Central Agency for Public Mobilization and Statistics, POB 2086, Cairo (Nasr City); tel. (2) 4020574; fax (2) 4024099; e-mail misr@capmas.gov.eg; internet www.capmas.gov.eg; Research Department, National Bank of Egypt, Cairo.

Area and Population

AREA, POPULATION AND DENSITY

Area (sq km)	1,009,450*
Population (census results)†	
31 December 1996	59,312,914
21 November 2006	
Males	37,219,056
Females	35,578,975
Total	72,798,031
Population (official estimates at 1 January, preliminary)	
2009	76,054,112
2010	77,775,247
2011‡	79,602,000
Density (per sq km) at 1 January 2011	78.9

* 389,751 sq miles.

† Excluding Egyptian nationals abroad, totalling an estimated 2,180,000 in 1996 and an estimated 3,901,396 in 2006.

‡ Rounded figure.

POPULATION BY AGE AND SEX

(official estimates at 1 January 2010, preliminary)

	Males	Females	Total
0–14	12,719,852	11,957,732	24,677,584
15–64	25,520,411	24,664,695	50,190,106
65 and over	1,516,657	1,390,900	2,907,557
Total	39,756,920	38,013,327	77,775,247

GOVERNORATES

(population at 2006 census)

	Area (sq km)	Population	Density (per sq km)	Capital
Cairo*	214.20	6,758,581	31,552.7	Cairo
Alexandria	2,679.36	4,123,869	1,539.1	Alexandria
Port Said	72.07	570,603	7,917.3	Port Said
Ismailia	1,441.59	953,006	661.1	Ismailia
Suez	17,840.42	512,135	28.7	Suez
Damietta	589.17	1,097,339	1,862.5	Damietta
Dakahlia	3,470.90	4,989,997	1,437.7	El-Mansoura
Sharkia	4,179.55	5,354,041	1,281.0	Zagazig
Kalyoubia	1,001.09	4,251,672	4,247.0	Banha
Kafr el-Sheikh	3,437.12	2,620,208	762.3	Kafr el-Sheikh
Gharbia	1,942.21	4,011,320	2,065.3	Tanta
Menoufia	1,532.13	3,270,431	2,134.6	Shebien el-Kom
Behera	10,129.48	4,747,283	468.7	Damanhour
Giza†	85,153.56	3,143,486	36.9	Giza
Beni-Suef	1,321.50	2,291,618	1,734.1	Beni-Suef
Fayoum	1,827.10	2,511,027	1,374.3	El-Fayoum
Menia	2,261.70	4,166,299	1,842.1	El-Menia
Asyout	1,553.00	3,444,967	2,218.3	Asyout
Suhag	1,547.20	3,747,289	2,422.0	Suhag
Qena	1,795.60	3,001,681	1,671.7	Qena
Luxor	55.00	457,286	8,314.3	Luxor
Aswan	678.45	1,186,482	1,748.8	Aswan
Red Sea	203,685.00	288,661	1.4	Hurghada
El-Wadi el-Gidid	376,505.00	187,263	0.5	El-Kharga
Matruh	212,112.00	323,381	1.5	Matruh
North Sinai	27,574.00	343,681	12.5	El-Areesh
South Sinai	33,140.00	150,088	4.5	El-Tour
Total	997,738.40‡	72,798,031	72.1‡	—

* Including territory designated as the governorate of Helwan in April 2008 and consisting of 1,713,278 persons at the time of the census.

† Including territory designated as the governorate of Sixth of October in April 2008 and consisting of 2,581,059 persons at the time of the census.

‡ The official, rounded national total is 1,009,450 sq km.

PRINCIPAL TOWNS

(population at 1996 census)*

Cairo (Al-Qahirah, the capital)	6,789,479	Zagazig (Al-Zaqaziq)	267,351
Alexandria (Al-Iskandariyah)	3,328,196	El Fayoum (Al-Fayyum)	260,964
Giza (Al-Jizah)	2,221,868	Ismailia (Al-Ismailiyah)	254,477
Shoubra el-Kheima (Shubra al-Khaymah)	870,716	Kafr el-Dawar (Kafr al-Dawwar)	231,978
Port Said (Bur Sa'id)	469,533	Aswan	219,017
Suez (Al-Suways)	417,610	Damanhour (Damanhur)	212,203
El-Mahalla el-Koubra (Al-Mahallah al-Kubra)	395,402	El-Menia (Al-Minya)	201,360
Tanta	371,010	Beni-Suef (Bani-Suwayf)	172,032
El-Mansoura (Al-Mansurah)	369,621	Qena (Qina)	171,275
Luxor (Al-Uqsor)	360,503	Suhag (Sawhaj)	170,125
Asyout (Asyut)	343,498	Shebien el-Kom (Shibin al-Kawn)	159,909

* Figures refer to provisional population. Revised figures include: Cairo 6,800,992; Alexandria 3,339,076; Port Said 472,335; Suez 417,527.

Mid-2010 ('000, incl. suburbs, UN estimates): Cairo 11,001; Alexandria 4,387 (Source: UN, *World Urbanization Prospects: The 2007 Revision*).

BIRTHS, MARRIAGES AND DEATHS

	Registered live births		Registered marriages		Registered deaths	
	Number ('000)	Rate (per 1,000)	Number	Rate (per 1,000)	Number ('000)	Rate (per 1,000)
2002	1,767	26.5	510,518	7.7	424	6.4
2003	1,777	26.2	537,092	7.9	440	6.5
2004	1,780	25.7	550,709	7.9	442	6.4
2005	1,801	25.5	522,751	7.4	451	6.4
2006	1,854	25.7	522,887	7.3	452	6.3
2007	1,950	26.5	614,848	8.5	451	6.1
2008	2,051	27.3	660,000	8.8	462	6.1
2009	2,217	28.8	759,004	9.9	477	6.2

Life expectancy (years at birth, WHO estimates): 71 (males 69; females 73) in 2009 (Source: WHO, *World Health Statistics*).

ECONOMICALLY ACTIVE POPULATION

(sample surveys at May and November, '000 persons aged 15–64 years)

	2006	2007	2008
Agriculture, hunting and forestry	6,208.9	6,744.2	6,965.0
Fishing	161.8	144.8	151.0
Mining and quarrying	53.3	35.5	37.0
Manufacturing	2,380.8	2,412.2	2,567.0
Electricity, gas and water supply	250.4	282.3	297.0
Construction	1,822.9	2,078.1	2,268.0
Wholesale and retail trade; repair of motor vehicles, motorcycles, and personal and household goods	2,171.9	2,307.0	2,387.0
Hotels and restaurants	411.4	370.8	462.0
Transport, storage and communications	1,357.3	1,452.4	1,575.0
Financial intermediation	175.0	194.9	166.0
Real estate, renting and business activities	431.8	451.7	448.0
Public administration and defence; compulsory social security	1,901.7	1,974.5	1,890.0
Education	1,969.9	2,079.8	2,042.0
Health and social work	545.5	573.1	583.0

—continued	2006	2007	2008
Other community, social and personal service activities	507.5	538.8	574.0
Private households with employed persons	45.0	51.6	66.0
Extra-territorial organizations and bodies	2.5	1.0	3.0
Sub-total	20,397.4	21,689.7	22,481.0
Activities not adequately defined	46.2	34.1	26.0
Total employed	20,443.6	21,723.8	22,507.0
Unemployed	2,434.5	2,135.1	2,143.0
Total labour force	22,878.1	23,858.9	24,651.0
Males	17,767.1	18,167.1	19,120.0
Females	5,111.0	5,691.8	5,531.0

Source: ILO.

2009 (annual estimates, '000 persons aged 15–64 years): Total employed 22,975; Unemployed 2,378; Total labour force 25,353 (males 19,410, females 5,943).

2010 (annual estimates, '000 persons aged 15–64 years, preliminary): Total employed 23,829; Unemployed 2,350; Total labour force 26,180 (males 20,140, females 6,040).

Health and Welfare

KEY INDICATORS

Total fertility rate (children per woman, 2009)	2.8
Under-5 mortality rate (per 1,000 live births, 2009)	21
HIV/AIDS (% of persons aged 15–49, 2009)	<0.1
Physicians (per 1,000 head, 2005)	2.4
Hospital beds (per 1,000 head, 2005)	2.2
Health expenditure (2008): US $ per head (PPP)	261
Health expenditure (2008): % of GDP	4.8
Health expenditure (2008): public (% of total)	42.2
Access to water (% of persons, 2008)	99
Access to sanitation (% of persons, 2008)	94
Total carbon dioxide emissions ('000 metric tons, 2007)	184,508.0
Carbon dioxide emissions per head (metric tons, 2007)	2.3
Human Development Index (2011): ranking	113
Human Development Index (2011): value	0.644

For sources and definitions, see explanatory note on p. vi.

Agriculture

PRINCIPAL CROPS
('000 metric tons)

	2008	2009	2010
Wheat	7,977.1	8,523.0	7,177.4
Rice, paddy	7,253.4	5,520.5	4,329.5
Barley	149.2	148.4	117.1
Maize, green	7,401.4	7,686.1	7,041.1
Sorghum	866.9	780.9	701.6
Potatoes	3,567.1	3,659.3	3,643.2
Sweet potatoes	259.0	357.3	370.9
Taro (Coco yam)	152.0	114.3	119.4
Sugar cane	16,470.2	15,482.2	15,708.9
Sugar beet	5,132.6	5,333.5	7,840.3
Broad beans, horse beans, dry	244.1	297.6	233.5
Groundnuts, with shell	208.8	198.0	202.9
Olives	480.1	500.0*	611.9*
Cabbages and other brassicas	638.7	740.4	690.6
Artichokes	176.4	209.6	215.5
Lettuce and chicory	111.7	80.1	97.7
Tomatoes	9,204.1	10,278.5*	8,545.0
Cauliflowers and broccoli	124.7	99.5	117.9
Pumpkins, squash and gourds	651.9	624.9	658.2
Cucumbers and gherkins	595.7	600.0	631.4
Aubergines (Eggplants)	1,242.7	1,290.2	1,229.8
Chillies and peppers, green	703.4	792.8	655.8
Onions, dry	1,948.9	2,128.6	2,208.1
Garlic	339.6	195.7	244.6
Beans, green	247.3	282.3	270.7
Peas, green	285.1	330.0†	300.0†
Carrots and turnips	185.8	175.9	139.0
Okra	104.7	134.7	86.2
Bananas	1,062.5	1,120.5	1,029.0
Oranges	2,138.4	2,372.3	2,401.0
Tangerines, mandarins, clementines and satsumas	758.1	809.8	796.9
Lemons and limes	329.7	809.8	318.1
Apples	550.7	508.8	493.1
Peaches and nectarines	399.4	363.2	273.3
Strawberries	200.3	242.8	238.4
Grapes	1,531.4	1,370.2	1,360.3
Watermelons	1,485.9	1,653.2	1,637.1
Cantaloupes and other melons	923.7	918.4	1,076.8
Figs	304.1	286.7	185.0
Guavas, mangoes and mangosteens	466.4	534.4	505.7
Dates	1,326.1	1,270.5	1,353.0

* FAO estimate.

† Unofficial estimate.

Aggregate production ('000 metric tons, may include official, semi-official or estimated data): Total cereals 23,693.0 in 2008, 22,706.9 in 2009, 19,407.7 in 2010; Total roots and tubers 3,982.0 in 2008, 4,135.1 in 2009, 4,137.7 in 2010; Total vegetables (incl. melons) 19,707.2 in 2008, 21,397.6 in 2009, 19,516.4 in 2010; Total fruits (excl. melons) 9,617.0 in 2008, 10,298.6 in 2009, 9,581.1 in 2010.

Source: FAO.

LIVESTOCK
('000 head, year ending September)

	2008	2009	2010*
Cattle	5,023	4,525	4,525
Buffaloes	4,053	3,839	3,839
Sheep	5,498	5,592	5,592
Goats	4,473	4,139	4,200
Pigs*	36	38	38
Horses	66	66	65
Asses	3,363	3,350*	3,350
Camels	107	137	140
Chickens*	96,000	98,000	100,000
Ducks*	9,500	9,500	9,500
Geese and guinea fowls*	9,200	9,200	9,200
Turkeys*	1,850	1,850	1,850

* FAO estimate(s).

Source: FAO.

LIVESTOCK PRODUCTS
('000 metric tons)

	2008	2009	2010*
Cattle meat	430.0	447.0	415.0
Buffalo meat*	297.0	295.0	327.5
Sheep meat*	44.2	44.8	47.5
Goat meat*	20.9	21.3	20.8
Pig meat	2.2	1.0	1.0
Camel meat	45.3	45.0*	46.0
Rabbit meat*	69.8	69.8	69.8
Chicken meat	628.8	671.1	685.0
Cows' milk	3,211.4	2,803.3	2,901.6
Buffaloes' milk	2,640.6	2,696.7	2,725.0
Sheep's milk*	110.9	107.9	97.7
Goats' milk*	16.8	16.1	18.1
Hen eggs	355.5	333.3	335.8
Honey	7.0	7.0	7.2
Wool, greasy	11.0	11.2	12.0

* FAO estimate(s).

Source: FAO.

Forestry

ROUNDWOOD REMOVALS
('000 cubic metres, excluding bark, FAO estimates)

	2007	2008	2009
Sawlogs, veneer logs and logs for sleepers	134	134	134
Other industrial roundwood	134	134	134
Fuel wood	17,170	17,283	17,397
Total	17,438	17,551	17,665

2010: Production assumed to be unchanged from 2009 (FAO estimates).

Source: FAO.

SAWNWOOD PRODUCTION
('000 cubic metres, incl. railway sleepers)

	2002	2003	2004
Total (all broadleaved)	3	3	2

2005–10: Output assumed to be unchanged from 2004 (FAO estimates).

Source: FAO.

Fishing

('000 metric tons, live weight)

	2007	2008	2009*
Capture	372.5	373.8	374.0
Grass carp	26.2	21.2	21.2
Nile tilapia	102.6	91.3	91.3
Mudfish	31.2	32.4	32.4
Mullets	27.7	24.6	24.6
Aquaculture	635.5	693.8	705.5
Cyprinids	109.7	61.8	62.0
Nile tilapia	265.9	386.2	390.3
Flathead grey mullet	252.5	209.3	210.0
Total catch	1,008.0	1,067.6	1,079.5

* FAO estimates.

Note: Figures exclude capture data for sponges, estimated by FAO at 1 metric ton per year.

Source: FAO.

Mining

('000 metric tons, unless otherwise indicated, year ending 30 June)

	2007	2008	2009
Crude petroleum	34,110	34,640	35,261
Natural gas (million cu m)	55,690	58,970	62,690
Aluminium	220	220	220
Iron ore*	665	773	1,780
Salt (unrefined)	1,214	1,879	2,952
Phosphate rock	3,890	5,523	6,227
Gypsum (crude)	94	95	456
Kaolin	332	523	295
Granite (cu m)	8,651	19,461	22,155
Marble (cu m)	427,000	420,000	401,000

* Figures refer to gross weight. The estimated iron content is 50%.

2010: Crude petroleum ('000 metric tons) 35,040; Natural gas (million cu m) 61,330.

Sources: US Geological Survey; BP, *Statistical Review of World Energy 2011*.

Industry

SELECTED PRODUCTS
('000 metric tons, unless otherwise indicated)

	2006	2007	2008
Cigarettes (million)	55,123	n.a.	n.a.
Mineral water ('000 hectolitres)	6,164	n.a.	n.a.
Caustic soda	95	n.a.	n.a.
Jet fuels	2,033	2,422	2,319
Kerosene	167	143	133
Distillate fuel oils	8,440	8,803	8,666
Motor spirit (gasoline)	3,659	4,195	4,240
Residual fuel oil (mazout)	10,653	10,989	9,529
Petroleum bitumen (asphalt)	815	831	783
Electric energy (million kWh)	118,407	128,129	134,565

Source: UN Industrial Commodity Statistics Database.

Cement ('000 metric tons, estimates): 38,469 in 2007; 39,800 in 2008; 46,500 in 2009 (Source: US Geological Survey).

Finance

CURRENCY AND EXCHANGE RATES

Monetary Units

1,000 millièmes = 100 piastres = 5 tallaris = 1 Egyptian pound (£E).

Sterling, Dollar and Euro Equivalents (31 October 2011)

£1 sterling = £E9.544;
US $1 = £E5.956;
€1 = £E8.339;
£E100 = £10.48 sterling = $16.79 = €11.99.

Note: From February 1991 foreign exchange transactions were conducted through only two markets, the primary market and the free market. With effect from 8 October 1991, the primary market was eliminated, and all foreign exchange transactions are effected through the free market. In January 2001 a new exchange rate mechanism was introduced, whereby the value of the Egyptian pound would be allowed to fluctuate within narrow limits: initially, as much as 1% above or below a rate that was set by the Central Bank of Egypt, but would be adjusted periodically in response to market conditions. The trading band was widened to 3% in August, and in January 2003 the Government adopted a floating exchange rate.

Average Exchange Rate (Egyptian pound per US $)

2008 5.433
2009 5.545
2010 5.622

GOVERNMENT FINANCE
(budgetary central government operations, cash basis, £E million, year ending 30 June, preliminary)

Summary of Balances

	2006/07	2007/08	2008/09
Revenue	205,655	248,836	288,545
Less Expense	218,489	271,500	313,464
Net cash inflow from operating activities	–12,834	–22,664	–24,919
Less Purchases of non-financial assets	21,114	34,297	43,480
Cash surplus/deficit	–33,948	–56,961	–68,399

Revenue

	2006/07	2007/08	2008/09
Taxes	114,326	137,195	163,223
Taxes on income, profits and capital gains	58,535	67,058	80,255
Individuals	9,720	11,495	14,284
Corporations and other enterprises	48,815	55,563	65,971
Taxes on goods and services	39,436	49,747	62,650
Taxes on international trade and transactions	10,370	14,021	14,091
Grants	3,687	1,463	7,984
Other revenue	87,642	110,177	117,338
Total	205,655	248,836	288,545

Expense/Outlays

Expense by economic type	2006/07	2007/08	2008/09
Compensation of employees	52,746	63,531	76,967
Use of goods and services	17,121	18,790	25,203
Subsidies	54,231	84,431	94,113
Other payments	38,367	40,957	43,755
Total (incl. others)	218,489	271,500	313,464

Outlays by function of government	2006/07	2007/08	2008/09
General public services	58,354	62,291	73,968
Defence	17,922	20,050	22,531
Public order and safety	11,129	13,139	16,170
Economic affairs	13,914	18,592	23,002
Environmental protection	828	912	1,259
Housing and community amenities	9,248	13,865	18,200
Health	10,434	13,162	15,783
Recreation, culture and religion	8,729	10,974	13,807
Education	27,761	33,678	39,880
Social protection	85,701	119,133	132,344
Statistical discrepancy	–4,417	—	—
Total	239,602	305,795	356,944

Source: IMF, *Government Finance Statistics Yearbook*.

INTERNATIONAL RESERVES

(US $ million at 31 December)

	2008	2009	2010
Gold (national valuation)	1,633	1,680	2,180
IMF special drawing rights	108	1,306	1,261
Foreign exchange	32,108	30,947	32,351
Total	33,849	33,933	35,792

Source: IMF, *International Financial Statistics*.

MONEY SUPPLY

(£E million at 31 December)

	2008	2009	2010
Currency outside depository corporations	114,036	126,666	143,632
Transferable deposits	86,313	99,431	113,895
Other deposits	591,029	640,257	716,434
Broad money	791,378	866,354	973,962

Source: IMF, *International Financial Statistics*.

COST OF LIVING

(Consumer Price Index; base: 2004 = 100, unless otherwise indicated)

	2007	2008	2009
Food and beverages	130.6	162.0	188.1
Clothing and footwear	n.a.	121.2	131.9
Rent, fuel and light	n.a.	121.7	126.7

All items (base: 2000 = 100): 157.6 in 2007; 186.4 in 2008; 208.4 in 2009; 161.3 in 2010.

Source: ILO.

NATIONAL ACCOUNTS

(£E million at current prices, year ending 30 June)

Expenditure on the Gross Domestic Product

	2007/08	2008/09	2009/10
Government final consumption expenditure	97,500	118,300	134,700
Private final consumption expenditure	647,600	793,200	901,700
Changes in inventories	1,000	2,900	3,500
Gross fixed capital formation	199,500	197,100	224,400
Total domestic expenditure	945,600	1,111,500	1,264,300
Exports of goods and services	295,900	260,100	257,600
Less Imports of goods and services	346,000	329,300	315,300
GDP in purchasers' values	895,500	1,042,300	1,206,600

Gross Domestic Product by Economic Activity

	2007/08	2008/09	2009/10
Agriculture, hunting, forestry and fishing	113,104	135,465	160,970
Mining and quarrying	133,674	147,966	165,747
Manufacturing	139,003	164,523	194,290
Electricity, gas and water	14,166	16,020	18,287
Construction	36,780	44,026	52,609
Wholesale and retail trade, restaurants and hotels	125,806	147,780	173,802
Transport, storage and communications	90,669	98,973	108,021
Suez Canal	29,421	n.a.	n.a.
Finance, insurance, real estate and business services	86,465	98,389	112,957
Public administration and defence	79,737	98,575	114,974
Other services	35,898	39,466	45,694
GDP at factor cost	855,302	991,183	1,147,350
Indirect taxes, *less* subsidies	40,198	51,117	59,250
GDP in purchasers' values	895,500	1,042,300	1,206,600

Note: Deduction for imputed bank service charge assumed to be distributed at origin.

Source: mainly African Development Bank.

BALANCE OF PAYMENTS

(US $ million)

	2008	2009	2010
Exports of goods f.o.b.	29,849	23,089	25,024
Imports of goods f.o.b.	–49,608	–39,907	–45,145
Trade balance	–19,759	–16,818	–20,120
Exports of services	24,912	21,520	23,807
Imports of services	–17,615	–13,935	–14,718
Balance on goods and services	–12,462	–9,233	–11,031
Other income received	3,065	992	534
Other income paid	–1,776	–3,068	–6,446
Balance on goods, services and income	–11,173	–11,309	–16,943
Current transfers received	10,072	8,305	12,836
Current transfers paid	–314	–345	–397
Current balance	–1,415	–3,349	–4,504
Capital account (net)	–1	–19	–39
Direct investment abroad	–1,920	–571	–1,176
Direct investment from abroad	9,495	6,712	6,386
Portfolio investment assets	–623	–267	–445
Portfolio investment liabilities	–7,027	–260	10,887
Other investment assets	4,633	–5,879	–11,185
Other investment liabilities	717	1,601	2,003
Net errors and omissions	–2,928	398	–2,145
Overall balance	931	–1,635	–218

Source: IMF, *International Financial Statistics*.

External Trade

Note: Figures exclude trade in military goods.

PRINCIPAL COMMODITIES

(distribution by HS, US $ million)

Imports c.i.f.	2008	2009	2010
Cereals	3,103.8	2,434.0	3,483.9
Wheat and meslin	2,110.9	1,576.1	2,181.9
Mineral fuels, oils, distillation products, etc.	5,766.3	4,466.0	7,130.7
Crude petroleum oils	1,595.3	1,079.0	1,321.2
Non-crude petroleum oils	2,249.0	1,888.9	3,656.7
Petroleum gases	1,514.3	1,287.2	1,806.2
Plastics and articles thereof	2,322.0	1,890.6	2,296.1
Iron and steel	4,945.7	3,563.6	3,125.8
Iron ingots, wastes and scraps	1,608.5	474.1	669.4
Articles of iron or steel	2,727.2	2,630.9	2,787.1
Machinery, nuclear reactors, boilers, etc.	6,172.3	5,823.4	5,613.3
Electrical, electronic equipment	3,249.8	2,923.7	3,376.1
Vehicles other than railway, tramway	3,040.8	2,648.6	3,768.2
Total (incl. others)	52,751.0	44,912.5	53,003.4

Exports f.o.b.	2008	2009	2010
Vegetables, roots and tubers	663.6	805.9	834.3
Fruit, nuts, peel of citrus fruit and melons	708.1	1,005.8	955.1
Mineral fuels, oils, distillation products, etc.	11,604.7	6,935.2	7,593.9
Crude petroleum oils	2,194.9	1,568.3	1,777.5
Non-crude petroleum oils	4,945.9	2,064.0	2,962.0
Petroleum gases	3,989.7	2,414.2	2,266.6
Fertilizers	678.3	1,143.2	1,152.3
Nitrogenous fertilizers	432.2	1,081.9	1,080.8
Chemical products	781.8	325.8	502.3
Plastics and articles thereof	869.2	754.6	886.5
Non-knitted articles of apparel and accessories	254.3	811.4	821.0
Pearls, precious stones, metals, coins, etc.	17.3	918.4	1,037.4
Gold, unwrought or semi-manufactured	14.9	906.3	1,033.8
Iron and steel	1,222.2	556.7	872.9
Electrical and electronic equipment	791.6	637.6	816.4
Total (incl. others)	25,966.8	24,182.3	26,331.8

Source: Trade Map-Trade Competitiveness Map, International Trade Centre, www.intracen.org/marketanalysis.

PRINCIPAL TRADING PARTNERS

(US $ million)*

Imports c.i.f.	2008	2009	2010
Argentina	1,014.8	459.5	888.2
Australia	284.4	305.1	538.5
Belgium	797.0	661.6	861.6
Brazil	1,444.0	1,235.0	1,736.2
China, People's Republic	4,432.0	3,910.9	4,901.8
France (incl. Monaco)	1,335.8	1,597.9	1,886.1
Germany	3,262.0	3,602.2	4,023.9
India	1,758.3	1,258.0	1,557.8
Indonesia	759.8	532.9	532.6
Italy	3,023.3	2,652.3	2,962.6
Japan	1,841.8	1,436.0	1,440.2
Korea, Republic	1,058.8	1,239.9	1,906.0
Kuwait	1,595.6	1,151.0	1,524.1
Malaysia	559.8	518.1	784.6
Malta	197.4	352.3	1,053.8
Netherlands	729.5	900.4	831.5
Russia	2,247.1	1,549.3	1,835.1
Saudi Arabia	3,102.1	2,015.0	2,120.1
Spain	679.6	821.5	847.9
Sweden	757.0	585.8	623.3
Switzerland	839.4	459.7	542.4
Thailand	629.2	555.6	749.1
Turkey	1,174.8	2,347.2	1,880.0
Ukraine	2,009.8	1,338.5	1,624.8
United Arab Emirates	879.0	435.9	730.2
United Kingdom	1,379.3	962.7	1,269.0
USA	5,673.1	4,744.2	4,961.9
Zambia	600.5	194.3	260.5
Total (incl. others)	52,751.0	44,912.5	53,003.4

Exports f.o.b.	2008	2009	2010
Algeria	181.2	381.0	262.4
Belgium	490.0	388.8	351.2
China, People's Republic	341.5	975.1	431.6
France (incl. Monaco)	779.0	664.0	924.1
Germany	438.1	461.3	573.4
Greece	323.6	249.9	271.9
India	1,658.8	1,455.2	1,227.9
Iraq	334.9	387.6	382.9
Italy	2,700.5	1,585.5	2,199.2
Japan	873.2	104.5	188.9
Jordan	712.8	930.9	711.8
Korea, Republic	630.9	127.5	531.3
Lebanon	411.8	450.2	523.9
Libya	773.6	1,008.3	1,220.4
Mexico	278.4	65.1	30.8
Morocco	335.2	360.1	402.1
Netherlands	1,493.3	498.9	558.8
Nigeria	467.8	90.9	142.6
Qatar	147.7	275.4	227.0
Saudi Arabia	1,239.4	1,381.6	1,549.0
Singapore	285.8	65.7	112.8
South Africa	54.4	29.0	395.6
Spain	1,483.4	1,588.5	1,621.4
Sudan	530.9	560.4	559.2
Switzerland	23.6	736.0	398.1
Syria	547.1	843.4	800.5
Turkey	770.3	704.8	985.3
United Arab Emirates	516.7	578.6	613.4
United Kingdom	910.8	868.0	813.4
USA	1,255.0	1,633.9	1,547.1
Total (incl. others)†	25,966.8	24,182.3	26,331.8

* Imports by country of consignment, exports by country of destination. Totals include trade in free zones, not classifiable by country.

† Including bunkers and ships' stores (US $ million): 1,302.9 in 2008; 653.0 in 2009; 948.2 in 2010.

Source: Trade Map-Trade Competitiveness Map, International Trade Centre, www.intracen.org/marketanalysis.

Transport

RAILWAYS

(traffic, year ending 30 June)

	2001/02	2002/03	2003/04
Passenger-km (million)	39,083	46,185	52,682
Net ton-km (million)	4,188	4,104	4,663

Source: UN, *Statistical Yearbook*.

2005 (million): Passengers carried 451.1; Freight carried (metric tons) 10.1; Passenger-km 40,837; Freight ton-km 3,917 (Source: World Bank, World Development Indicators database).

ROAD TRAFFIC
(licensed motor vehicles in use at 31 December)

	1995*	1996	1997
Passenger cars	1,280,000	1,099,583	1,154,753
Buses and coaches	36,630	39,781	43,740
Lorries and vans	387,000	489,542	510,766
Motorcycles and mopeds	397,000	427,864	439,756

* Estimates from IRF, *World Road Statistics*.

2002: Passenger cars ('000): 1,847.0; Commercial vehicles ('000): 650.0 (Source: UN, *Statistical Yearbook*).

2008 (licensed motor vehicles in use at 31 December): Passenger cars 2,545,758; Buses and coaches 92,625; Vans and lorries 838,781; Motorcycles and mopeds 995,781 (Source: IRF, *World Road Statistics*).

SHIPPING

Merchant Fleet
(registered at 31 December)

	2007	2008	2009
Number of vessels	344	349	357
Displacement ('000 grt)	1,113.3	1,070.1	1,070.0

Source: IHS Fairplay, *World Fleet Statistics*.

International sea-borne freight traffic ('000 metric tons, incl. ships' stores, 2005, figures are rounded): Goods loaded 21,230; Goods unloaded 42,410 (Source: UN, *Monthly Bulletin of Statistics*).

SUEZ CANAL TRAFFIC

	2008	2009	2010
Transits (number)	21,415	17,228	17,993
Displacement ('000 net tons)	910,100	734,500	846,400
Total cargo volume ('000 metric tons)	723,000	559,200	646,100

Source: Egyptian Maritime Data Bank, Alexandria.

CIVIL AVIATION
(traffic on scheduled services)

	2007	2008	2009
Kilometres flown (million)	90	110	113
Passengers carried ('000)	5,829	6,689	6,216
Passenger-km (million)	12,001	14,266	14,801
Total ton-km (million)	1,429	1,631	1,670

Source: UN, *Statistical Yearbook*.

Tourism

ARRIVALS BY NATIONALITY
('000)

	2007	2008	2009
France	464.2	586.9	551.7
Germany	1,085.9	1,202.5	1,202.3
Israel	234.5	213.1	203.3
Italy	983.3	1,073.2	1,048.0
Libya	439.5	481.5	410.2
Netherlands	232.3	279.8	249.0
Palestinian Autonomous Areas	118.4	68.4	104.7
Russia	1,516.6	1,825.3	2,035.3
Saudi Arabia	412.5	402.3	348.0
United Kingdom	1,055.0	1,201.9	1,346.7
USA	272.5	319.1	321.3
Total (incl. others)	11,090.9	12,835.4	12,535.9

2010: Total tourist arrivals ('000) 14,051 (provisional).

Tourism receipts (US $ million, incl. passenger transport unless otherwise indicated): 10,327 in 2008; 12,104 in 2009; 12,528 (excl. passenger transport, provisional) in 2010.

Source: World Tourism Organization.

Communications Media

	2008	2009	2010
Telephones ('000 main lines in use)	11,852.5	10,312.6	9,618.1
Mobile cellular telephones ('000 subscribers)	41,286.7	55,352.2	70,661.0
Internet subscribers ('000)	2,504.8	2,346.5	n.a.
Broadband subscribers ('000)	769.7	1,101.6	1,476.5

Personal computers: 3,197,036 (39.2 per 1,000 persons) in 2008.

1997: Radio receivers ('000 in use) 20,500.

1998: Book production 1,410 titles.

1999: Daily newspapers 16 (average circulation 2,080,000 copies); Other periodicals 45 (average circulation 1,371,000 copies).

2000: Television receivers ('000 in use) 12,000.

Sources: UNESCO, *Statistical Yearbook*; International Telecommunication Union.

Education

(2008/09, unless otherwise indicated, estimates)

	Schools	Teachers	Students
Pre-primary	3,172*	32,809	813,934
Primary	15,533†	382,488	10,407,187
Preparatory	7,544†	193,469*	4,345,356†
Secondary:			
general	1,595†	322,040‡	5,804,507‡
technical	1,826†	165,669‡	1,311,831
Higher	356*	80,658‡	2,488,434§

* 1998/99 figure.
† 1999/2000 figure.
‡ 2003/04 figure.
§ 2007/08 figure.

Sources: UNESCO Institute for Statistics; Ministry of Education.

Al-Azhar (1999/2000, provisional figures): Primary: 2,631 schools; 707,633 students. Preparatory: 1,805 schools; 316,108 students. Secondary: 1,081 schools; 269,469 students.

Pupil-teacher ratio (primary education, UNESCO estimate): 27.2 in 2008/09 (Source: UNESCO Institute for Statistics).

Adult literacy rate (UNESCO estimates): 72.0% (males 83.6%; females 60.7%) in 2007 (Source: UNESCO Institute for Statistics).

Directory

The Government

HEAD OF STATE

Chairman of the Supreme Council of the Armed Forces: Field Marshal MUHAMMAD HUSSEIN TANTAWI (became de facto head of state on 11 February 2011, following the resignation of former President Muhammad Hosni Mubarak).

COUNCIL OF MINISTERS
(May 2012)

Prime Minister: Dr KAMAL AL-GANZOURI.

Minister of Finance: MUMTAZ SAID ABU EL-NOUR.

Minister of Electricity and Energy: Dr HASSAN AHMAD YOUNES.

Minister of Planning and International Co-operation: FAIZA MUHAMMAD ABOULNAGA.

Minister of Housing, Utilities and Urban Planning: Dr MUHAMMAD FATHI AL-BARADEI.

Minister of Education: GAMAL MUHAMMAD EL-ARABI AHMAD.

Minister of State for Antiquities: MUHAMMAD IBRAHIM ALI SAID.

Minister of Insurance and Social Affairs: Dr NAGWA HUSSEIN AHMAD KHALIL.

Minister of Tourism: MOUNIR FAKHRI ABD AL-NOUR.

Minister of Supplies and Domestic Trade: Dr GAWDA ABD AL-KHALEK SAYID MUHAMMAD.

Minister of Justice: ADEL ABD AL-HAMID ABDALLAH.

Minister of the Interior: Gen. MUHAMMAD YOUSSUF IBRAHIM AHMAD.

Minister of Manpower and Immigration: RIFAAT MUHAMMAD HASSAN.

Minister of Culture: Dr MUHAMMAD SABIR ARAB.

Minister of Petroleum: MUHAMMAD ABDALLA MUHAMMAD ABD AL-MENIM GHORAB.

Minister of Information: AHMAD MAHMOUD ISMAIL ANIS.

Minister of Scientific Research: Dr NADIA ISKANDAR ZAKHARI.

Minister of Awqaf (Islamic Endowments): MUHAMMAD ABD-AL FADIL MUHAMMAD ABD-AL AZIZ AL-QOUSI.

Minister of Foreign Affairs: MUHAMMAD KAMEL AMR.

Minister of Civil Aviation: Eng. HUSSEIN HASSAN AHMAD MASSOUD.

Minister of Higher Education: MUHAMMAD ABD AL-HAMID AL-NASHAR.

Minister of Agriculture and Land Cultivation: MUHAMMAD REDA ISMAIL ABD AL-HADI GOMAA.

Minister of Water Resources and Irrigation: Dr HISHAM MUHAMMAD QANDIL.

Minister of Health and Population: Dr FOUAD ALI FAHMI SALEH AL-NAWAWI.

Minister of Transport: Dr GALAL MOUSTAFA MUHAMMAD AL-SAID.

Minister of Industry and Foreign Trade: MAHMOUD ABD AL-RAHMAN AL-SAID EISSA.

Minister of Communications and Information Technology: Dr MUHAMMAD ABD AL-QADER MUHAMMAD SALIM.

Minister of State for Local Development: MUHAMMAD AHMAD ATYIA IBRAHIM.

Minister of State for Military Production: Dr ALI IBRAHIM SABRI.

Minister of State for Environmental Affairs: Prof. MUSTAFA HUSSEIN KAMEL.

Minister of Parliamentary Affairs: AMR MUHAMMAD SALIM.

MINISTRIES

Office of the Prime Minister: 2 Sharia Majlis al-Sha'ab, Cairo; tel. (2) 27935000; fax (2) 27958048; e-mail questions@cabinet.gov.eg; internet www.cabinet.gov.eg.

Ministry of Agriculture and Land Cultivation: 1 Sharia Nadi el-Seid, Cairo (Dokki); tel. (2) 33372970; fax (2) 33372435; e-mail info@agr-egypt.gov.eg; internet www.agr-egypt.gov.eg.

Ministry of Awqaf (Islamic Endowments): Sharia Sabri Abu Alam, Bab el-Louk, Cairo; tel. (2) 23929403; fax (2) 23929828; e-mail awkafministry@yahoo.com; internet www.awkaf.org.

Ministry of Civil Aviation: Sharia Cairo Airport, Cairo; tel. (2) 22688342; fax (2) 22688341; e-mail info@civilaviation.gov.eg; internet www.civilaviation.gov.eg.

Ministry of Communications and Information Technology: Smart Village, km 28, Sharia Cairo–Alexandria, Cairo; tel. (2) 35341300; fax (2) 35341111; e-mail info@mcit.gov.eg; internet www.mcit.gov.eg.

Ministry of Culture: 2 Sharia Shagaret el-Dor, Cairo (Zamalek); tel. (2) 27380761; fax (2) 27353947; e-mail ecm@idsc.net.eg; internet www.ecm.gov.eg.

Ministry of Defence and Military Production: Sharia 23 July, Kobri el-Kobba, Cairo; tel. (2) 4032159; fax (2) 2906004; e-mail mod@afmic.gov.eg.

Ministry of Education: 12 Sharia el-Falaky, Cairo; tel. (2) 27947363; fax (2) 27947502; e-mail info@mail.emoe.org; internet www.emoe.org.

Ministry of Electricity and Energy: POB 222, 8 Sharia Ramses, Abbassia Sq., Cairo (Nasr City); tel. (2) 22616317; fax (2) 22616302; e-mail info@moee.gov.eg; internet www.moee.gov.eg.

Ministry of Finance: Ministry of Finance Towers, Cairo (Nasr City); tel. (2) 23428886; fax (2) 26861561; e-mail finance@mof.gov.eg; internet www.mof.gov.eg.

Ministry of Foreign Affairs: Corniche el-Nil, Cairo (Maspiro); tel. (2) 25749820; fax (2) 25748822; e-mail info@mfa.gov.eg; internet www.mfa.gov.eg.

Ministry of Health: 3 Sharia Majlis al-Sha'ab, Lazoughli Sq., Cairo; tel. (2) 27942865; fax (2) 27953966; e-mail webmaster@mohp.gov.eg; internet www.mohp.gov.eg.

Ministry of Higher Education and Scientific Research: 101 Sharia Qasr el-Eini, Cairo; tel. (2) 27920323; fax (2) 27941005; e-mail mohe.info@gmail.com; internet www.egy-mhe.gov.eg.

Ministry of Housing, Utilities and Urban Development: 1 Sharia Ismail Abaza, 3rd Floor, Qasr el-Eini, Cairo; tel. (2) 27921440; fax (2) 27957836; internet www.moh.gov.eg.

Ministry of Industry and Foreign Trade: 2 Sharia Latin America, Cairo (Garden City); tel. (2) 27921167; fax (2) 27955025; e-mail inquiry@mti.gov.eg; internet www.mti.gov.eg.

Ministry of Information: Radio and TV Bldg, Corniche el-Nil, Cairo (Maspiro); tel. (2) 25757164; fax (2) 25746928; e-mail info@moinfo.gov.eg; internet www.minfo.gov.eg.

Ministry of Insurance and Social Affairs: 19 Sharia Maraghi, Cairo; tel. (2) 27947315; fax (2) 33375390.

Ministry of the Interior: 25 Sharia Sheikh Rihan, Bab el-Louk, Cairo; tel. (2) 27955005; fax (2) 27960682; e-mail center@iscmi.gov.eg; internet www.moiegypt.gov.eg.

Ministry of International Co-operation: 8 Sharia Adly, Cairo; tel. (2) 23910008; fax (2) 23908159; e-mail webmaster@mic.gov.eg; internet www.mic.gov.eg.

Ministry of Justice: Justice and Finance Bldg, Sharia Majlis al-Sha'ab, Lazoughli Sq., Cairo; tel. (2) 27922263; fax (2) 27958103; e-mail mojeb@idsc.gov.eg.

Ministry of Local Development: Sharia Nadi el-Seid, Cairo (Dokki); tel. (2) 37497470; fax (2) 37497788; internet www.mld.gov.eg.

Ministry of Manpower and Immigration: 3 Sharia Yousuf Abbas, Cairo (Nasr City); tel. (2) 22609359; fax (2) 23035332; e-mail manpower@mome.gov.eg; internet www.manpower.gov.eg.

Ministry of Petroleum: 1 Sharia Ahmad el-Zomor, Cairo (Nasr City); tel. (2) 26706401; fax (2) 26706419; e-mail contactus@petroleum.gov.eg; internet www.petroleum.gov.eg.

Ministry of Planning: POB 11765, Sharia Salah Salem, Cairo (Nasr City); tel. (2) 24014526; fax (2) 24014732; e-mail moed.egypt@gmail.com; internet www.mop.gov.eg.

Ministry of Supplies and Domestic Trade: 99 Sharia Qasr el-Eini, Cairo; tel. (2) 27958481; e-mail info@mss.gov.eg; internet www.mss.gov.eg.

Ministry of State for Antiquities: Cairo; tel. (2) 27358761; fax (2) 27357239.

Ministry of State for Environmental Affairs: 30 Sharia Misr Helwan el-Zirai, Maadi, Cairo; tel. (2) 25256452; fax (2) 25256490; e-mail eeaa@eeaa.gov.eg; internet www.eeaa.gov.eg.

Ministry of State for Military Production: 5 Sharia Ismail Abaza, Qasr el-Eini, Cairo; tel. (2) 27948739; fax (2) 27953063; e-mail mmpisscc@idsc.gov.eg.

Ministry of Tourism: Cairo International Conferences Center, Cairo (Nasr City); tel. (2) 22611732; fax (2) 26859551; e-mail mot@idsc.gov.eg; internet www.visitegypt.gov.eg.

Ministry of Transport: 105 Sharia Qasr el-Eini, Cairo; tel. (2) 27955562; fax (2) 27955564; e-mail info@mot.gov.eg; internet www.mot.gov.eg.

Ministry of Water Resources and Irrigation: Sharia Gamal Abd al-Nasser, Corniche el-Nil, Imbaba, Cairo; tel. (2) 35449420; fax (2) 35449470; e-mail minister@mwri.gov.eg; internet www.mwri.gov.eg.

President and Legislature

Following the resignation from office of former President Muhammad Hosni Mubarak on 11 February 2011, the Supreme Council of the Armed Forces (SCAF), under the chairmanship of Field Marshal Muhammad Hussein Tantawi, assumed the president's powers on an interim basis. The Constitution was suspended and both the Majlis al-Sha'ab (People's Assembly) and the Majlis al-Shura (Advisory Council) dissolved. Elections to the People's Assembly were held in three stages, from 28 November–11 January 2012, while elections to a new Advisory Council took place on 29 January–22 February. A presidential election was expected to take place on 23–24 May.

PRESIDENT

Presidential Election, 7 September 2005

Candidates	Votes	%
Muhammad Hosni Mubarak	6,316,784	88.57
Ayman Abd al-Aziz al-Nour	540,405	7.58
No'man Khalil Gomaa	208,891	2.93
Dr Osama Abd al-Shafi Shaltout	29,857	0.42
Wahid Fakhry al-Uqsuri	11,881	0.17
Ibrahim Muhammad Abd al-Moneim Turk	5,831	0.08
Mamdouh Qenawi	5,481	0.08
Ahmad al-Sabahi Khalil	4,393	0.06
Fawzi Khalil Ghazal	4,222	0.06
Dr Rifaat al-Agroudy	4,106	0.06
Total*	7,131,851	100.00

* Excluding 173,685 invalid votes (2.4% of total votes cast).

LEGISLATURE

Majlis al-Sha'ab (People's Assembly)

Cairo; tel. (2) 27945000; fax (2) 27943130; e-mail contact-us@parliament.gov.eg; internet www.parliament.gov.eg.

Speaker: MUHAMMAD SAAD EL-KATATNI.

Elections, 28–29 November and 5–6 December 2011, 14–15 December and 21–22 December 2011, 3–4 January and 10–11 January 2012

	Seats
The Freedom and Justice Party (FJP)	235
Al-Nour Party	123
New Wafd Party	38
Egyptian Bloc	34
Al-Wasat Party	10
The Reform and Development Party	9
The Revolution Continues Alliance	7
National Party of Egypt	5
Freedom Party	4
Egyptian Citizen Party	4
Union Party	2
Others	4
Independents	23
Total*	508†

* There are, in addition, 10 representatives appointed by the Supreme Council of the Armed Forces.

† Of the 498 elective seats, 332 seats are allocated to party lists under a system of proportional representation, while the remaining 166 seats are allocated to individual candidates who may or may not be affiliated to political organizations. (List candidates are elected from 46 constituencies and individual candidates from 83 constituencies.).

Majlis al-Shura (Advisory Council)

Cairo; tel. (2) 27955492; fax (2) 27941980; e-mail gsecretariat@parliament.gov; internet www.shoura.gov.eg.

In September 1980 elections were held for an advisory body, the **Shura (Advisory) Council**, which replaced the former Central Committee of the Arab Socialist Union. Two-thirds of the 270 members of the Advisory Council are elected by direct suffrage; the remainder are appointed by the Head of State (in 2012, by the Supreme Council of the Armed Forces). The Council's term in office is six years, with one-half of its members being replaced every three years. At a two-stage election held from 29 January to 22 February 2012 the Muslim Brotherhood's Freedom and Justice Party secured 105 of the 180 contested seats, while the Al-Nour Party took 45 seats. The New Wafd Party secured 14 seats and the Egyptian Bloc eight seats. The Freedom Party and the Democratic Peace Party, both offshoots of the defunct National Democratic Party, won three seats and one seat, respectively, while the remaining four seats went to independent candidates.

Speaker: AHMAD FAHMI.

Election Commissions

Higher Election Commission (HEC): Cairo; tel. (2) 4142613; fax (2) 4142615; e-mail info@elections.gov.eg; internet www.elections.gov.eg; regulates legislative elections; comprises 11 mems; Chair. AL-SAYED ABD AL-AZIZ OMAR; Sec.-Gen. MAHFOUZ SABER ABD AL-KADER.

Supreme Presidential Election Commission (PEC): 3rd Floor, 117 Sharia Abd al-Aziz Fahmy, Cairo (Heliopolis); f. 2005; independent; comprises 10 mems, presided over by the Chief Justice of the Supreme Constitutional Court and four other ex officio mems of the judiciary; of the remaining five mems (who are independent, public figures), three are appointed by the People's Assembly and two by the Advisory Council; Chair. Hon. FAROUK AHMED SULTAN.

Political Organizations

Following the removal from office of President Muhammad Hosni Mubarak in February 2011, new legislation governing the licensing of political organizations was promulgated in late March. A number of new parties were granted official recognition—including the Freedom and Justice Party (see below), which was founded in April by the Muslim Brotherhood—and participated in legislative elections held from November. Meanwhile, in mid-April the National Democratic Party of former President Mubarak was dissolved, following a ruling by the High Administrative Court.

Arab Democratic Nasserist Party: 8 Sharia Talaat Harb, Cairo; f. 1992; advocates maintaining the principles of the 1952 Revolution, achieving a strong national economy and protecting human rights; Chair. DIAA EL-DIN DAOUD; Sec.-Gen. AHMED HASSAN.

Democratic Front Party (Hizb al-Gabha al-Dimuqrati): 14 el-Muhammad Shafiq, Nile Valley, Cairo; tel. (3) 3050552; fax (3) 33050547; e-mail info@democraticfront.org; internet www.democraticfront.org; f. 2007 by fmr mems of the National Democratic Party; seeks to promote liberal democracy, the rule of law and a civil society; Founder and Chair. Dr OSAMA AL-GHAZALI HARB.

Democratic Generation Party (Hizb al-Geel al-Dimuqrati): f. 2002; advocates improvements in education and youth-based policies; Chair. NAGUI EL-SHEHABY.

Democratic Peace Party: Cairo; f. 2005; Chair. AHMAD MUHAMMAD BAYOUMI AL-FADALI.

The Egyptian Arab Association Party: Cairo.

Egyptian Arab Socialist Party (Hizb Misr al-Arabi al-Ishtiraki): f. 1976; seeks to maintain principles of the 1952 Revolution and to preserve Egypt's Islamic identity; f. 1985; Leader WAHID FAKHRY AL-UQSURI.

The Egyptian Bloc: e-mail kotla-masreya@info.com; internet www.elkotlaelmasreya.com; f. 2011; originally formed as a coalition of 15 political parties; secular, liberal; currently comprises the Free Egyptians Party, the Egyptian Social Democratic Party and the National Progressive Unionist Party—Tagammu.

Egyptian Citizen Party (Hizb al-Mowaten al-Masri): f. 2011; offshoot of the former National Democratic Party; Leader ALAA HASABALLAH.

Egyptian Green Party (Hizb al-Khudr al-Misri): 9 Sharia al-Tahrir, Cairo (Dokki); tel. and fax (2) 33364748; e-mail awad@egyptiangreens.com; internet www.egyptiangreens.com; f. 1990; Leader MUHAMMAD AWAD.

Egyptian Islamic Labour Party: 12 Sharia Awali el-Ahd, Cairo; e-mail magdyahmedhussein@gmail.com; internet www.el3amal.net; f. 1978; official opposition party; pro-Islamist; seeks establishment of economic system based on *Shari'a* (Islamic) law, unity between Egypt, Sudan and Libya, and the liberation of occupied Palestinian territory; Leader MAHFOUZ AZZAM; Sec.-Gen. MAGDY HUSSEIN.

Freedom Party (Hizb al-Horreya): f. 2011; offshoot of the former National Democratic Party; Chair. MAMDOUH HASSAN; Sec.-Gen MOATAZ HASSAN.

Free Social Constitutional Party: f. 2004; seeks introduction of further political, social and economic reforms; Leader MAMDOUH QENAWI.

Al-Ghad (Tomorrow) Party: Cairo; e-mail info@elghad.org; internet www.elghad.org; f. 2004; aims to combat poverty and to improve the living conditions of Egypt's citizens; Chair. AYMAN ABD AL-AZIZ AL-NOUR; Sec.-Gen. WAEL NAWARA.

Liberal Party (Hizb al-Ahrar): Cairo; f. 1976; advocates expansion of 'open door' economic policy and greater freedom for private enterprise and the press; Chair. MUHAMMAD FARID ZAKARIA.

Misr el-Fatah (Young Egypt Party): f. 1990; pursues a socialist, nationalist and reformist agenda.

Muslim Brotherhood (Al-Ikhwan al-Muslimun): internet www.ikhwanonline.com; f. 1928, with the aim of establishing an Islamic society; banned in 1954; transnational org.; moderate; advocates the adoption of *Shari'a* law as the sole basis of the Egyptian legal system; founded Freedom and Justice Party to contest at least one-half of the seats at 2011–12 legislative elections; Supreme Guide MUHAMMAD BADIE; Sec.-Gen. MAHMOUD IZZAT.

Freedom & Justice Party (FJP): Cairo; internet www.fjponline.com; f. 2011; Islamist party committed to democracy and social equality; member of the Democratic Alliance for Egypt; Chair Dr MUHAMMAD MURSI.

National Party of Egypt (Hizb Masr al-Qawmi): f. 2011; offshoot of the former National Democratic Party.

National Progressive Unionist Party (NPUP) (Hizb al-Tagammu' al-Watani al-Taqadomi al-Wahdawi—Tagammu): 1 Sharia Karim el-Dawlah, Cairo; tel. (2) 5791629; fax (2) 5784867; e-mail khaled@al-ahaly.com; internet www.al-ahaly.com; f. 1976; left-wing; seeks to defend the principles of the 1952 Revolution; Founder KHALED MOHI EL-DIN; Chair. Dr MUHAMMAD RIFA'AT EL-SAID; 160,000 mems.

New Wafd Party (New Delegation Party): POB 357, 1 Boulos Hanna St, Cairo (Dokki); tel. (2) 3383111; fax (2) 3359135; e-mail info@alwafdparty.com; internet www.alwafd.org; f. 1919 as Wafd Party; banned 1952; re-formed as New Wafd Party Feb. 1978; disbanded June 1978; re-formed 1983; seeks further political, economic and social reforms, greater democracy, the abolition of emergency legislation, and improvements to the health and education sectors; Chair. SAYED EL-BADAWI.

Al-Nour Party: Zezenia, Alexandria; tel. (3) 5741310; fax (3) 5741317; e-mail info@alnourparty.org; internet www.alnourparty.org; f. 2011; Chair EMAD ABD AL-GHAFOUR.

The Reform and Development Party (al-Islah wa al-Tanmiya): 2 El Khalil Agha, Garden City, Cairo; e-mail info@rdpegypt.org; internet www.rdpegypt.org; f. 2009; was denied licence in 2010; formed by merger of the Reformation and Development Party with the Masrena Party; Chair. MUHAMMAD ANWAR ESMAT AL-SADAT.

The Revolution Continues Alliance (RCA): Cairo; f. 2011; comprises the Socialist Popular Alliance Party, the Egyptian Current Party, the Revolution Youth Coalition, the Egyptian Socialist Party, the Egyptian Alliance Party, the Freedom Egypt Party and the Equality and Development Party.

Solidarity Party (Hizb al-Takaful): f. 1995; advocates imposition of 'solidarity' tax on the rich in order to provide for the needs of the poor; Chair. Dr OSAMA ABD AL-SHAFI SHALTOUT.

Ummah (People's) Party (Hizb al-Umma): f. 1983; social democratic party; Leader AHMAD AL-SABAHI KHALIL.

Union Party (Hizb al-Ittihad): f. 2011; offshoot of the former National Democratic Party; Leader HOSSAM BADRAWI.

Al-Wasat Party: 8 Pearl St, Mokattam, Cairo; tel. (2) 5044151; internet www.alwasatparty.com; f. 2011; originally formed in 1996 but denied licence under rule of former President Hosni Mubarak; Pres. ABUL ELA MADI.

Diplomatic Representation

EMBASSIES IN EGYPT

Afghanistan: 59 Sharia el-Orouba, Cairo (Heliopolis); tel. (2) 4177236; fax (2) 4177238; e-mail ambassador@afghanembassy-egypt.com; internet www.afghanembassy-egypt.com; Ambassador HAFIZULLAH AYUBI.

Albania: Ground Floor, 27 Sharia Gezira al-Wissta, Cairo (Zamalek); tel. (2) 27361815; fax (2) 27356966; e-mail embassy.cairo@mfa.gov.al; Ambassador NURI DOMI.

Algeria: 14 Sharia Bresil, Cairo (Zamalek); tel. (2) 7368527; fax (2) 7364158; e-mail nov54@link.net; Ambassador ABD AL-QADER HAGGAR.

Angola: 12 Midan Fouad Mohi ed-Din, Mohandessin, Cairo; tel. (2) 3377602; fax (2) 708683; e-mail angola@access.com.eg; Ambassador ANTÓNIO DA COSTA FERNANDES.

Argentina: 1st Floor, 8 Sharia el-Saleh Ayoub, Cairo (Zamalek); tel. (2) 27351501; fax (2) 27364533; e-mail eegip@mrecic.gov.ar; Ambassador LUIS ENRIQUE CAPPAGLI.

Armenia: 20 Sharia Muhammad Mazhar, Cairo (Zamalek); tel. (2) 27374157; fax (2) 27374158; e-mail armegyptembassy@mfa.am; internet www.armembegypt.com; Ambassador Dr ARMEN MELKONIAN.

Australia: 11th Floor, World Trade Centre, Corniche el-Nil, Cairo 11111 (Boulac); tel. (2) 25750444; fax (2) 25781638; e-mail cairo.austremb@dfat.gov.au; internet www.egypt.embassy.gov.au; Ambassador Dr RALPH KING.

Austria: 5th Floor, Riyadh Tower, 5 Sharia Wissa Wassef, cnr of Sharia el-Nil, Cairo 11111 (Giza); tel. (2) 35702975; fax (2) 35702979; e-mail kairo-ob@bmeia.gv.at; internet www.austriaegypt.org; Ambassador Dr THOMAS NADER.

Azerbaijan: Villa 16/24, Sharia 10, Maadi Sarayat, Cairo; tel. (2) 23583761; fax (2) 23583725; e-mail azsefqahira@link.net; internet www.azembassy.org.eg; Ambassador SHAHIN ABDULLAYEV.

Bahrain: 15 Sharia Bresil, Cairo (Zamalek); tel. (2) 27350642; fax (2) 27366609; e-mail cairo.mission@mofa.gov.bh; Ambassador Sheikh RASHID BIN ABD AL-RAHMAN AL KHALIFA.

Bangladesh: POB 136, 20 Sharia Geziret el-Arab, Mohandessin, Cairo; tel. (2) 33462003; fax (2) 33462008; e-mail bdoot@link.net; Ambassador MIZANUR RAHMAN (designate).

Belarus: 26 Sharia Gaber Ibn Hayan, Cairo (Dokki); tel. (2) 37499171; fax (2) 33389545; e-mail egypt@belembassy.org; internet www.egypt.belembassy.org; Ambassador IGOR FISSENKO.

Belgium: POB 37, 20 Sharia Kamal el-Shennawi, Cairo 11511 (Garden City); tel. (2) 27947494; fax (2) 27943147; e-mail cairo@diplobel.fed.be; internet www.diplomatie.be/cairo; Ambassador BRUNO NEVE DE MEVERGNIES.

Bolivia: 21 New Ramses Centre, Sharia B. Oman, Cairo 11794 (Dokki); tel. (2) 37624362; fax (2) 37624360; e-mail embolivia_egipto@yahoo.com; Chargé d'affaires a.i. RAÚL PALZA ZEBALLOS.

Bosnia and Herzegovina: 42 Sharia al-Sawra, Cairo (Dokki); tel. (2) 37499191; fax (2) 37499190; e-mail ambbih@link.net; Ambassador SLOBODAN ŠOJA.

Brazil: 1125 Corniche el-Nil Ave, Cairo 11561 (Maspiro); tel. (2) 25773013; fax (2) 25774860; e-mail brasemb@soficom.com.eg; Ambassador CESARIO MELANTONIO NETO.

Brunei: 14 Sharia Sri Lanka, Cairo (Zamalek); tel. (2) 27366651; fax (2) 27360240; e-mail cairo.egypt@mfa.gov.bn; Ambassador Dato Paduka Haji ISHAAQ Haji ABDULLAH.

Bulgaria: 6 Sharia el-Malek el-Ajdal, Cairo (Zamalek); tel. (2) 27363025; fax (2) 27363826; e-mail bulembcai@link.net; internet www.mfa.bg/en/28/; Ambassador RUMEN PETROV.

Burkina Faso: POB 306, Ramses Centre, 22 Sharia Wadi el-Nil, Mohandessin, Cairo 11794; tel. (2) 23898056; fax (2) 23806974; Ambassador MOUSSA B. NEBIE.

Burundi: 27 Sharia el-Ryad, Mohandessin, Cairo; tel. (2) 33024301; fax (2) 33441997; Ambassador GERVAIS NDIKUMAGNEGE.

Cambodia: 2 Sharia Tahawia, Cairo (Giza); tel. (2) 3489966; Ambassador IN SOPHEAP.

Cameroon: POB 2061, 15 Sharia Muhammad Sedki Soliman, Mohandessin, Cairo; tel. (2) 3441101; fax (2) 3459208; e-mail ambcam@link.net; Ambassador Dr MOHAMADOU LABARANG.

Canada: POB 1667, 26 Kamel el-Shenawy, Cairo (Garden City); tel. (2) 27918700; fax (2) 27918860; e-mail cairo@dfait-maeci.gc.ca; internet www.canadainternational.gc.ca/egypt-egypte; Ambassador FERRY DE KERCKHOVE.

Central African Republic: 41 Sharia Mahmoud Azmy, Mohandessin, Cairo (Dokki); tel. and fax (2) 33445942; Ambassador HENRY KOBA.

Chad: POB 1869, 12 Midan al-Refaï, Cairo 11511 (Dokki); tel. (2) 3373379; fax (2) 3373232; Ambassador EL HADJ MAHMOUD ADJI.

Chile: 19 Sharia Gabalaya, Apt 92, Cairo (Zamalek); tel. (2) 27358711; fax (2) 27353716; e-mail embchile.eg@gmail.com; Ambassador ALEX GEIGER SOFFIA.

China, People's Republic: 14 Sharia Bahgat Ali, Cairo (Zamalek); tel. (2) 2738046; fax (2) 27359459; e-mail webmaster_eg@mfa.gov.cn; internet eg.china-embassy.org/eng; Ambassador SONG AIGUO.

Colombia: 6 Sharia Gueriza, Cairo (Zamalek); tel. (2) 27364203; fax (2) 27357429; e-mail eelcairo@cancilleria.gov.co; Ambassador MARIO GERMÁN IGUARÁN ARANA.

Congo, Democratic Republic: 5 Sharia Mansour Muhammad, Cairo (Zamalek); tel. (2) 3403662; fax (2) 3404342; Ambassador RAFAEL MALONGA.

Côte d'Ivoire: 9 Sharia Shehab, Mohandessin, Cairo; tel. (2) 33034373; fax (2) 33050148; e-mail acieg@ambaci-egypte.org; internet www.ambaci-egypte.org; Ambassador TANOH BOUTCHOUE BERNARD.

Croatia: 3 Sharia Abou el-Feda, Cairo (Zamalek); tel. (2) 27383155; fax (2) 27355812; e-mail croemb.cairo@mvpei.hr; internet eg.mfa.hr; Ambassador DARKO JAVORSKI.

Cuba: Apartment 1, 13th Floor, 10 Sharia Kamel Muhammad, Cairo (Zamalek); tel. (2) 7360651; fax (2) 7360656; e-mail cubaemb@link .net; Ambassador OTTO VAILLANT FRÍAS.

Cyprus: 17 Sharia Omar Tosson, Ahmed Orabi, Mohandessin, Cairo; tel. (2) 33455967; fax (2) 33455969; e-mail kyproscai1@ access.com.eg; Ambassador SOTOS A. LIASIDES.

Czech Republic: 1st Floor, 4 Sharia Dokki, Cairo 12511 (Giza); tel. (2) 33339700; fax (2) 37485892; e-mail cairo@embassy.mzv.cz; internet www.mfa.cz/cairo; Ambassador PAVEL KAFKA.

Denmark: 12 Sharia Hassan Sabri, Cairo 11211 (Zamalek); tel. (2) 27396500; fax (2) 27396588; e-mail caiamb@um.dk; internet www .ambkairo.um.dk; Ambassador CHRISTIAN HOPPE.

Djibouti: 11 Sharia el-Gazaer, Aswan Sq., Cairo (Agouza); tel. (2) 3456546; fax (2) 3456549; Ambassador Sheikh MOUSSA MOHAMED AHMED.

Ecuador: 33 Sharia Ismail Muhammad, Cairo (Zamalek); tel. (2) 27372776; fax (2) 27361841; e-mail ecuademb@link.net; Ambassador EDWIN JOHNSON.

Eritrea: 6 Sharia el-Fallah, Mohandessin, Cairo; tel. (2) 3033503; fax (2) 3030516; e-mail eritembe@yahoo.com; Ambassador MAHMOUD OMAR CHIRUM.

Estonia: 8th Floor, Abou el-Feda Bldg, 3 Sharia Abou el-Feda, Cairo 11211 (Zamalek); tel. (2) 27384190; fax (2) 27384189; e-mail embassy .cairo@mfa.ee; internet www.kairo.vm.ee; Ambassador PAUL TEESALU.

Ethiopia: Mesaha Sq., Villa 11, Cairo (Dokki); tel. (2) 3353693; fax (2) 3353699; e-mail ethio@ethioembassy.org.eg; Ambassador MAHMOUD DRIR.

Finland: 13th Floor, 3 Sharia Abou el-Feda, Cairo 11211 (Zamalek); tel. (2) 27363722; fax (2) 27371376; e-mail sanomat.kai@formin.fi; internet www.finland.org.eg; Ambassador ROBERTO TANZI-ALBI.

France: POB 1777, 29 Sharia Charles de Gaulle, Cairo (Giza); tel. (2) 35673200; fax (2) 35718498; e-mail questions@ambafrance-eg.org; internet www.ambafrance-eg.org; Ambassador JEAN-FÉLIX PAGANON.

Gabon: 17 Sharia Mecca el-Moukarama, Cairo (Dokki); tel. (2) 3379699; Ambassador JOSEPH MAMBOUNGOU.

Georgia: 11 Sharia Tanta, Aswan Sq., Mohandessin, Cairo; tel. (2) 33044798; fax (2) 33044778; e-mail cairo.emb@mfa.gov.ge; internet www.egypt.mfa.gov.ge; Ambassador ARCHIL DZULIASHVILI.

Germany: 2 Sharia Berlin (off Sharia Hassan Sabri), Cairo (Zamalek); tel. (2) 27282000; fax (2) 27282159; internet www.kairo.diplo.de; Ambassador MICHAEL BOCK.

Ghana: 1 Sharia 26 July, Cairo (Zamalek); tel. (2) 3444455; fax (2) 3032292; Ambassador Alhaji SAID SINARE (designate).

Greece: 18 Sharia Aicha al-Taimouria, Cairo 11451 (Garden City); tel. (2) 27950443; fax (2) 27963903; e-mail gremb.cai@mfa.gr; internet www.hellas.org.eg; Ambassador CHRISTODOULOS LAZARIS.

Guatemala: 5th Floor, 17 Sharia Port Said, Maadi, Cairo; tel. (2) 23802914; fax (2) 23802915; e-mail embegipto@minex.gob.gt; internet www.embaguategypt.com; Ambassador ANTONIO MALOUF GABRIEL.

Guinea: 46 Sharia Muhammad Mazhar, Cairo (Zamalek); tel. (2) 7358109; fax (2) 7361446; Ambassador El Hadj IBRAHIMA SORI TRAORÉ.

Holy See: Apostolic Nunciature, Safarat al-Vatican, 5 Sharia Muhammad Mazhar, Cairo (Zamalek); tel. (2) 7352250; fax (2) 7356152; e-mail nunteg@yahoo.com; Apostolic Nuncio Most Rev. MICHAEL LOUIS FITZGERALD (Titular Archbishop of Nepte).

Honduras: 8th Floor, 5 Sharia el-Israa, Mohandessin, Cairo; tel. (2) 3441337; fax (2) 3441338; e-mail hondemb@idsc.net.eg; Ambassador NELSON VALENCIA.

Hungary: 29 Sharia Muhammad Mazhar, Cairo 11211 (Zamalek); tel. (2) 27358659; fax (2) 27358648; e-mail mission.cai@kum.hu; internet mfa.gov.hu/emb/cairo; Ambassador Dr PÉTER KVECK.

India: 5 Sharia Aziz Abaza, Cairo (Zamalek); tel. (2) 27363051; fax (2) 27364038; e-mail embassy@indembcairo.com; internet www .indembcairo.com; Ambassador R. SWAMINATHAN.

Indonesia: POB 1661, 13 Sharia Aicha al-Taimouria, Cairo (Garden City); tel. (2) 27947200; fax (2) 27962495; e-mail pwkcairo@access .com.eg; internet www.indonesiacairo.org; Ambassador Dr NURFAIZI SUWANDI.

Iraq: Cairo; tel. (2) 7358087; fax (2) 7366956; e-mail caiemb@ iraqmofamail.net; Ambassador NEZAR EISSA AL-KHAIRALLAH.

Ireland: 22 Sharia Hassan Assem, Cairo (Zamalek); tel. (2) 27358264; fax (2) 27362863; e-mail cairoembassy@dfa.ie; internet www.embassyofireland.org.eg; Ambassador ISOLDE MOYLAN.

Israel: 6 Sharia Ibn el-Malek, Cairo (Giza); tel. (2) 33321500; fax (2) 33321555; e-mail info@cairo.mfa.gov.il; Ambassador YAAKOV AMITAI.

Italy: 15 Sharia Abd al-Rahman Fahmi, Cairo (Garden City); tel. (2) 27943194; fax (2) 27940657; e-mail ambasciata.cairo@esteri.it; internet www.ambilcairo.esteri.it; Ambassador CLAUDIO PACIFICO.

Japan: 2nd Floor, 81 Sharia Corniche el-Nil, Maadi, Cairo; tel. (2) 25285903; fax (2) 25285906; e-mail culture@ca.mofa.go.jp; internet www.eg.emb-japan.go.jp; Ambassador NORIHIRO OKUDA.

Jordan: 6 Sharia Juhaini, Cairo; tel. (2) 37485566; fax (2) 37601027; e-mail jocairo2@ie-eg.com; internet www.jordanembassycairo.gov .jo; Ambassador Dr BISHR KHASAWNEH.

Kazakhstan: 9 Wahib Doss St, Maadi, Cairo; tel. (2) 23809804; fax (2) 23586546; e-mail cairo@mfa.kz; Ambassador BERIK ARYN.

Kenya: POB 362, 29 Sharia al-Quds al-Sharif, Mohandessin, Cairo (Giza); tel. (2) 33453907; fax (2) 33026979; e-mail info@kenemb-cairo .com; internet kenemb-cairo.com; Ambassador DAVE ARUNGA.

Korea, Democratic People's Republic: 6 Sharia al-Saleh Ayoub, Cairo (Zamalek); tel. (2) 3408219; fax (2) 3414615; Ambassador RI HYOK-CHOL.

Korea, Republic: 3 Sharia Boulos Hanna, Cairo (Dokki); tel. (2) 3611234; fax (2) 3611238; internet egy.mofat.go.kr; Ambassador YOON JONG-KON.

Kuwait: 12 Sharia Nabil el-Wakkad, Cairo (Dokki); tel. (2) 3602661; fax (2) 3602657; Ambassador Dr RASHID AL-HAMAD.

Latvia: 8th Floor, Abou el-Feda Bldg, 3 Sharia Abou el-Feda, Cairo (Zamalek); tel. (2) 27384188; fax (2) 27384189; e-mail embassy .egypt@mfa.gov.lv; Ambassador MARIS SELGA.

Lebanon: 22 Sharia Mansour Muhammad, Cairo (Zamalek); tel. (2) 7382823; fax (2) 7382818; Ambassador KHALED ZIADEH.

Lesotho: 5 Sharia Ahmed el-Meleby, Cairo (Dokki); tel. (2) 33369161; fax (2) 25211437; e-mail lesotho-cairo@foreign.gov.ls; Ambassador THABO KHASIPE.

Liberia: 4th Floor, 9 Ahmad Samy el-Sayeh Sq., Mohandessin, Cairo; tel. (2) 37626794; fax (2) 37627194; e-mail liberiaembassy1@yahoo.com; Ambassador ALEXANDER WALLACE.

Libya: 4 Sharia Patrice Lumumba, Cairo; tel. (2) 4940286; fax 3934643; Ambassador AHMAD IBRAHIM AL-FAQIH.

Lithuania: 23 Muhammad Mazhar, Cairo (Zamalek); tel. (2) 27366461; fax (2) 27365130; e-mail amb.eg@mfa.lt; internet eg.mfa .lt; Ambassador DAINIUS JUNEVIČIUS.

Malaysia: 21 Sharia el-Aanab, Mohandessin, Cairo (Giza); tel. (2) 37610013; fax (2) 37610216; e-mail mwcairo@soficom.com.eg; internet www.kln.gov.my/web/egy_cairo; Ambassador MUHAMMAD FAKHRUDIN ABDUL MUKTI.

Mali: POB 844, 3 Sharia al-Kansar, Cairo (Dokki); tel. and fax (2) 3371841; e-mail mali.eg@ie.eg.com; Ambassador MAMADOU KABA.

Malta: 1 Sharia el-Saleh Ayoub, Cairo (Zamalek); tel. (2) 27362368; fax (2) 27362371; e-mail maltaembassy.cairo@gov.mt; Ambassador GEORGE CASSAR.

Mauritania: 114 Mohi el-Din, Abou-el Ezz, Mohandessin, Cairo; tel. (2) 37490671; fax (2) 37491048; Ambassador MOHAMED WELD AL-TALBA.

Mauritius: 156 Sharia el-Sudan, Mohandessin, Cairo; tel. (2) 7618102; fax (2) 7618101; e-mail embamaur@thewayout.net; Ambassador D. I. FAKIM.

Mexico: 5th Floor, Apt 502–503, 17 Sharia Port Said, Maadi, 11431 Cairo; tel. (2) 23580256; fax (2) 23591887; e-mail oficial@ embamexcairo.com; internet www.sre.gob.mx/egipto; Ambassador MARÍA CARMEN OÑATE MUÑOZ.

Mongolia: 14 Sharia 152, Maadi, Cairo; tel. and fax (2) 3586012; Ambassador BANZRAGCH ODONJIL.

Morocco: 10 Sharia Salah el-Din, Cairo (Zamalek); tel. (2) 27359849; fax (2) 27361937; e-mail morocemb@link.net; Ambassador MUHAMMAD FARAG AL-DOKALI.

Mozambique: 2 Sharia Tahran, Cairo (Dokki); tel. (2) 7605505; fax (2) 7486378; e-mail tombolane2000@yahoo.com; Ambassador ARTUR JOSEFA JAMO.

Myanmar: 24 Sharia Muhammad Mazhar, Cairo (Zamalek); tel. (2) 27362644; fax (2) 27366793; Ambassador TIN YU.

Nepal: 23 Sharia al-Hassan, Mohandessin, Cairo (Dokki); tel. (2) 37612311; fax (2) 33374447; Ambassador SHYAM LAL TABDAR.

Netherlands: 18 Sharia Hassan Sabri, Cairo (Zamalek); tel. (2) 27395500; fax (2) 27365249; e-mail kai@minbuza.nl; internet www.hollandembassy.org.eg; Ambassador SUSAN BLANKHART.

New Zealand: North Tower, 8th Floor, Nile City Bldg, Sharia Corniche el-Nil, Cairo (Boulac); tel. (2) 24616000; fax (2) 24616099; e-mail enquiries@nzembassy.org.eg; internet www.nzembassy.com/egypt; Ambassador DAVID STRACHAN.

Niger: 101 Sharia Pyramids, Cairo (Giza); tel. (2) 3865607; Ambassador MOULOUD AL-HOUSSEINI.

Nigeria: 13 Sharia Gabalaya, Cairo (Zamalek); tel. (2) 3406042; fax (2) 3403907; internet www.nigeriaembassycairo.org; Ambassador B. G. WAKIL.

Norway: 8 Sharia el-Gezirah, Cairo (Zamalek); tel. (2) 27358046; fax (2) 27370709; e-mail emb.cairo@mfa.no; internet www.norway-egypt.org; Ambassador TOR WENNESLAND.

Oman: 52 Sharia el-Higaz, Mohandessin, Cairo; tel. (2) 27350792; fax (2) 27373188; e-mail cairo@mofa.gov.om; Ambassador Sheikh KHALIFA BIN ALI BIN ISSA AL-HARTHY.

Pakistan: 8 Sharia l-Salouli, Cairo (Dokki); tel. (2) 37487806; fax (2) 37480310; e-mail parepcairo@hotmail.com; internet www.mofa.gov.pk/egypt; Ambassador SEEMA NAQVI.

Panama: POB 62, 4A Sharia Ibn Zanki, Cairo 11211 (Zamalek); tel. (2) 3400784; fax (2) 3411092; Chargé d'affaires a.i. ROY FRANCISCO LUNA GONZÁLEZ.

Peru: 8 Sharia Kamel el-Shenawi, Cairo (Garden City); tel. (2) 3562973; fax (2) 3557985; Ambassador MANUEL VERAMENDI I. SERRA.

Philippines: Villa 28, Sharia 200, Cairo (Degla Maadi); tel. (2) 25213062; fax (2) 25213048; e-mail pe.cairo@dfa.gov.ph; Ambassador CLARO S. CRISTOBAL.

Poland: 5 Sharia el-Aziz Osman, Cairo (Zamalek); tel. (2) 27367456; fax (2) 27355427; e-mail secretary@kair.polemb.net; internet www.kair.polemb.net; Ambassador PIOTR PUCHTA.

Portugal: 1 Sharia el-Saleh Ayoub, Cairo (Zamalek); tel. (2) 27350779; fax (2) 27350790; e-mail embpcai@link.net; Ambassador ANTÓNIO CARLOS CARVALHO DE ALMEIDA RIBEIRO.

Qatar: 10 Sharia al-Thamar, Midan al-Nasr, Madinet al-Mohandessin, Cairo; tel. (2) 7604693; fax (2) 7603618; e-mail qa.emb.cai@gmail.com; internet www.qatarembassyegypt.com; Ambassador SALEH ABDULLAH AL-BUAINAIN.

Romania: 6 Sharia el-Kamel Muhammad, Cairo (Zamalek); tel. (2) 27360107; fax (2) 27360851; e-mail roembegy@link.net; internet www.cairo.mae.ro; Ambassador GHEORGHE DUMITRU.

Russia: 95 Sharia Giza, Cairo (Giza); tel. (2) 37489353; fax (2) 37609074; e-mail ruemeg@tedata.net.eg; internet www.egypt.mid.ru; Ambassador SERGEI KIRPICHENKO.

Rwanda: 23 Sharia Babel, Mohandessin, Cairo (Dokki); tel. (2) 3350532; fax (2) 3351479; Ambassador CÉLESTIN KABANDA.

Senegal: 46 Sharia Abd al-Moneim Riad, Mohandessin, Cairo (Dokki); tel. (2) 3460946; fax (2) 3461039; e-mail mamadousow@hotmail.com; Ambassador MAMADOU SOW.

Serbia: 33 Sharia Mansour Muhammad, Cairo (Zamalek); tel. (2) 27354061; fax (2) 27353913; e-mail serbia@serbiaeg.com; Ambassador DEJAN VASILJEVIĆ.

Singapore: 40 Sharia Babel, Cairo 11511 (Dokki); tel. (2) 37490468; fax (2) 37480562; e-mail singemb_cai@sgmfa.gov.sg; internet www.mfa.gov.sg/cairo; Ambassador TAN HUNG SENG.

Slovakia: 3 Sharia Adel Hussein Rostom, Dokki, Cairo (Giza); tel. (2) 33358240; fax (2) 33355810; e-mail zukahira@tedata.net.eg; Ambassador PETER ZSOLDOS.

Slovenia: 6th Floor, 21 Sharia Soliman Abaza, Mohandessin, Cairo; tel. (2) 37499878; fax (2) 37497141; e-mail vka@gov.si; internet cairo.embassy.si/en; Ambassador Dr ROBERT KOKALJ.

Somalia: 27 Sharia el-Somal, Cairo (Dokki), Giza; tel. (2) 3374577; Ambassador ABDULLAH HASSAN MAHMOUD.

South Africa: 6th Floor, 55 Rd 18, Maadi, Cairo; tel. (2) 23594365; fax (2) 23595015; e-mail saembcai@tedata.net.eg; internet saembassyinegypt.com; Ambassador NOLUTHANDO MAYENDE-SIBIYA.

Spain: 41 Sharia Ismail Muhammad, Cairo (Zamalek); tel. (2) 27356462; fax (2) 27352132; e-mail emb.elcairo@maec.es; internet www.maec.es/subwebs/embajadas/elcairo; Ambassador FIDEL SENDAGORTA GÓMEZ DEL CAMPILLO.

Sri Lanka: POB 1157, 8 Sharia Sri Lanka, Cairo (Zamalek); tel. (2) 27350047; fax (2) 27367138; e-mail slembare@menanet.net; Ambassador (vacant).

Sudan: 4 Sharia el-Ibrahimi, Cairo (Garden City); tel. (2) 3545043; fax (2) 3542693; Ambassador KAMAL HASSAN ALI.

Sweden: POB 131, 13 Sharia Muhammad Mazhar, Cairo (Zamalek); tel. (2) 27289200; fax (2) 27354357; e-mail ambassaden.kairo@foreign.ministry.se; internet www.swedenabroad.com/cairo; Ambassador MALIN KÄRRE.

Switzerland: POB 633, 10 Sharia Abd al-Khalek Sarwat, Cairo; tel. (2) 25758284; fax (2) 25745236; e-mail cai.vertretung@eda.admin.ch; internet www.eda.admin.ch/cairo; Ambassador DOMINIK FURGLER.

Syria: 18 Sharia Abd al-Rehim Sabry, POB 435, Cairo (Dokki); tel. (2) 3358806; fax (2) 3358232; Ambassador YOUSUF AL-AHMAD.

Tanzania: 10 Anas Ibn Malek St, Mohandessin, Cairo; tel. (2) 3374155; fax (2) 3374446; Ambassador ALI SHAURI HAJI.

Thailand: 9 Tiba St, Cairo (Dokki); tel. (2) 37603553; fax (2) 37605076; e-mail royalthai@link.net; internet www.thaiembassy.org/cairo; Ambassador CHALIT MANITYAKUL.

Tunisia: 26 Sharia el-Jazirah, Cairo (Zamalek); tel. (2) 27352032; fax 27362479; e-mail tunisiacairo@link.net; Ambassador MONGI BEDAOUI.

Turkey: 25 Sharia Felaki, Cairo (Bab el-Louk); tel. (2) 27978400; fax (2) 27978477; e-mail turkemb.cairo@mfa.gov.tr; internet cairo.emb.mfa.gov.tr; Ambassador HÜSEYIN AVNI BOTSALI.

Uganda: 66 Rd 10, Maadi, Cairo; tel. (2) 3802514; fax (2) 3802504; e-mail ugembco@link.net; Ambassador UMAR LUBUULWA.

Ukraine: 50 Sharia 83, Maadi, Cairo; tel. (2) 23786871; fax (2) 23786873; e-mail emb_eg@mfa.gov.ua; internet mfa.gov.ua/egypt/en; Ambassador YEVHEN MYKYTENKO.

United Arab Emirates: 4 Sharia Ibn Sina, Cairo (Giza); tel. (2) 7609723; fax 5700844; e-mail uae@intouch.com; Ambassador MUHAMMAD AL-ZAHIRI.

United Kingdom: 7 Sharia Ahmad Ragheb, Cairo (Garden City); tel. (2) 27916000; fax (2) 27916135; e-mail information.cairo@fco.gov.uk; internet ukinegypt.fco.gov.uk; Ambassador JAMES WATT.

USA: 8 Sharia Kamal el-Din Salah, Cairo (Garden City); tel. (2) 27973300; fax (2) 27973200; e-mail PressInfoEgypt@state.gov; internet cairo.usembassy.gov; Ambassador ANNE W. PATTERSON.

Uruguay: 6 Sharia Lotfallah, Cairo (Zamalek); tel. (2) 7353589; fax (2) 7368123; e-mail urugemb@idsc.gov.eg; Ambassador CÉSAR WALTER FERRER BURLE.

Uzbekistan: 18 Sharia Sad el-Aali, Cairo (Dokki); tel. (2) 3361723; fax (2) 3361722; Ambassador MINOVAROV SHAAZIM SHAISLAMOVICH.

Venezuela: POB 1217, 15A Sharia Mansour Muhammad, Cairo (Zamalek); tel. (2) 7363517; fax (2) 7367373; e-mail embvenez@tedata.net.eg; Ambassador VÍCTOR R. CARAZO.

Viet Nam: 8 Sharia Madina el-Monawara, Cairo (Dokki); tel. (2) 7617309; fax (2) 7617324; e-mail vinaemb@link.net; internet www.vietnamembassy-egypt.org; Ambassador PHAM SY TAM.

Yemen: 28 Sharia Amean al-Rafai, Cairo (Dokki); tel. (2) 3614224; fax (2) 3604815; e-mail info@yemenembassy-cairo.com; internet www.yemen-embassy-egy.com; Ambassador ABD AL-WALI ABD AL-WALITH AL-SHAMIRI.

Zimbabwe: 40 Sharia Ghaza, Mohandessin, Cairo; tel. (2) 3030404; fax (2) 3059741; e-mail zimcairo@thewayout.net; Ambassador MARGARET MUSKWE (designate).

Judicial System

The Courts of Law in Egypt are principally divided into two juridical court systems: Courts of General Jurisdiction and Administrative Courts. Since 1969 the Supreme Constitutional Court has been at the top of the Egyptian judicial structure.

THE SUPREME CONSTITUTIONAL COURT

Supreme Constitutional Court: Corniche el-Nil, Maadi, Cairo; tel. (2) 5246323; fax (2) 7958048; e-mail info@sccourt.gov.eg; internet www.sccourt.gov.eg; has specific jurisdiction over: (i) judicial review of the constitutionality of laws and regulations; (ii) resolution of positive and negative jurisdictional conflicts and determination of the competent court between the different juridical court systems, e.g. Courts of General Jurisdiction and Administrative Courts, as well as other bodies exercising judicial competence; (iii) determination of disputes over the enforcement of two final but contradictory judgments rendered by two courts each belonging to a different juridical court system; (iv) rendering binding interpretation of laws or decree laws in the event of a dispute in the application of said laws or decree laws, always provided that such a dispute is of a gravity requiring conformity of interpretation under the Constitution.

President: Hon. FAROUK AHMED SULTAN.

COURTS OF GENERAL JURISDICTION

The Courts of General Jurisdiction in Egypt are effectively divided into four categories, as follows: (i) the Court of Cassation; (ii) the

Courts of Appeal; (iii) the Tribunals of First Instance; (iv) the District Tribunals; each of the above courts is divided into Civil and Criminal Chambers.

Court of Cassation

The Court of Cassation is the highest court of general jurisdiction in Egypt. Its sessions are held in Cairo. Final judgments rendered by Courts of Appeal in criminal and civil litigation may be petitioned to the Court of Cassation by the Defendant or the Public Prosecutor in criminal litigation and by any of the parties in interest in civil litigation on grounds of defective application or interpretation of the law as stated in the challenged judgment, on grounds of irregularity of form or procedure, or violation of due process, and on grounds of defective reasoning of judgment rendered. The Court of Cassation is composed of the President, 41 Vice-Presidents and 92 Justices.

President and Chairman of the Supreme Judicial Council: Hon. ADEL ABD EL-HAMID.

Courts of Appeal: Each Court of Appeal has geographical jurisdiction over one or more of the governorates of Egypt, and is divided into Criminal and Civil Chambers. The Criminal Chambers try felonies, and the Civil Chambers hear appeals filed against such judgment rendered by the Tribunals of First Instance where the law so stipulates. Each Chamber is composed of three Superior Judges. Each Court of Appeal is composed of the President, and sufficient numbers of Vice-Presidents and Superior Judges.

Tribunals of First Instance: In each governorate there are one or more Tribunals of First Instance, each of which is divided into several Chambers for criminal and civil litigations. Each Chamber is composed of: (a) a presiding judge, and (b) two sitting judges. A Tribunal of First Instance hears, as an Appellate Court, certain litigations as provided under the law.

District Tribunals: Each is a one-judge ancillary Chamber of a Tribunal of First Instance, having jurisdiction over minor civil and criminal litigations in smaller districts within the jurisdiction of such a Tribunal of First Instance.

PUBLIC PROSECUTION

Public prosecution is headed by the Prosecutor-General, assisted by a number of deputies, and a sufficient number of chief prosecutors, prosecutors and assistant prosecutors. Public prosecution is represented at all levels of the Courts of General Jurisdiction in all criminal litigations and also in certain civil litigations as required by the law. Public prosecution controls and supervises enforcement of criminal law judgments.

Prosecutor-General: ABD AL-MAGID MAHMOUD ABD AL-MAGID.

ADMINISTRATIVE COURTS SYSTEM (CONSEIL D'ETAT)

The Administrative Courts have jurisdiction over litigations involving the State or any of its governmental agencies. The Administrative Courts system is divided into two courts: the Administrative Courts and the Judicial Administrative Courts, at the top of which is the High Administrative Court. The Administrative Prosecutor investigates administrative crimes committed by government officials and civil servants.

President of Conseil d'Etat: Hon. SAMIR ABD AL-HALIM AHMAD AL-BADAWY.

THE STATE COUNCIL

The State Council is an independent judicial body, which has the authority to make decisions in administrative disputes and disciplinary cases within the judicial system.

Chairman: Hon. MUHAMMAD AHMAD EL-HUSSEINI.

THE SUPREME JUDICIAL COUNCIL

The Supreme Judicial Council was reinstituted in 1984, having been abolished in 1969. It exists to guarantee the independence of the judicial system from outside interference and is consulted with regard to draft laws organizing the affairs of the judicial bodies.

Religion

According to the 1986 census, some 94% of Egyptians are Muslims (and almost all of these follow Sunni tenets). According to government figures published in the same year, there are about 2m. Copts (a figure contested by Coptic sources, whose estimates range between 6m. and 7m.), forming the largest religious minority, and about 1m. members of other Christian groups. There is also a small Jewish minority.

ISLAM

There is a Higher Council for the Islamic Call, on which sit: the Grand Sheikh of al-Azhar (Chair.); the Minister of Awqaf (Islamic Endowments); the President and Vice-President of Al-Azhar University; the Grand Mufti of Egypt; and the Secretary-General of the Higher Council for Islamic Affairs.

Grand Sheikh of Al-Azhar: Sheikh AHMED MUHAMMAD EL-TAYEB.

Grand Mufti of Egypt: Sheikh ALI GOMAA.

CHRISTIANITY

Orthodox Churches

Armenian Apostolic Orthodox Church: POB 48, 179 Sharia Ramses, Faggalah, Cairo; tel. (2) 25901385; fax (2) 25906671; e-mail armpatrcai@yahoo.com; Prelate Bishop ASHOT MNATSAKANIAN; 7,000 mems.

Coptic Orthodox Church: St Mark Cathedral, POB 9035, Anba Ruess, 222 Sharia Ramses, Abbassia, Cairo; tel. (2) 2857889; fax (2) 2825683; e-mail coptpope@copticpope.org; internet www.copticpope.org; f. AD 61; Patriarch Bishop PACHOMIOUS (ad interim); c. 13m. followers in Egypt, Sudan, other African countries, the USA, Canada, Australia, Europe and the Middle East.

Greek Orthodox Patriarchate: POB 2006, Alexandria; tel. (3) 4868595; fax (3) 4875684; e-mail patriarchate@greekorthodox-alexandria.org; internet www.greekorthodox-alexandria.org; f. AD 43; Pope and Patriarch of Alexandria and All Africa THEODOROS II; 3m. mems.

The Roman Catholic Church

Armenian Rite

The Armenian Catholic diocese of Alexandria, with an estimated 6,500 adherents at 31 December 2007, is suffragan to the Patriarchate of Cilicia. The Patriarch is resident in Beirut, Lebanon.

Bishop of Alexandria: Rt Rev. KRIKOR-OKOSDINOS COUSSA, Patriarcat Arménien Catholique, 36 Sharia Muhammad Sabri Abou Alam, 11121 Cairo; tel. (2) 23938429; fax (2) 23932025; e-mail pacal@tedata.net.eg.

Chaldean Rite

The Chaldean Catholic diocese of Cairo had an estimated 500 adherents at 31 December 2007.

Bishop of Cairo: Rt Rev. YOUSUF IBRAHIM SARRAF, Evêché Chaldéen, Basilique-Sanctuaire Notre Dame de Fatima, 141 Sharia Nouzha, 11316 Cairo (Heliopolis); tel. and fax (2) 26355718; e-mail fatimasarraf@yahoo.com.

Coptic Rite

Egypt comprises the Coptic Catholic Patriarchate of Alexandria and five dioceses. At 31 December 2007 there were an estimated 166,096 adherents in the country.

Patriarch of Alexandria: Cardinal ANTONIOS NAGUIB, Patriarcat Copte Catholique, POB 69, 34 Sharia Ibn Sandar, Koubbeh Bridge, 11712 Cairo; tel. (2) 22571740; fax (2) 24545766; e-mail p_coptocattolico@yahoo.it.

Latin Rite

Egypt comprises the Apostolic Vicariate of Alexandria (incorporating Heliopolis and Port Said), containing an estimated 14,298 adherents at 31 December 2007.

Vicar Apostolic: Rt Rev. ADEL ZAKY, 10 Sharia Sidi el-Metwalli, Alexandria; tel. (3) 4876065; fax (3) 4878169; e-mail latinvic@link.net.

Maronite Rite

The Maronite diocese of Cairo had an estimated 5,430 adherents at 31 December 2007.

Bishop of Cairo: Rt Rev. FRANÇOIS EID, Evêché Maronite, 15 Sharia Hamdi, Daher, 11271 Cairo; tel. (2) 26137373; fax (2) 25939610; e-mail feid43@yahoo.com.

Melkite Rite

His Beatitude Grégoire III Laham (resident in Damascus, Syria) is the Greek-Melkite Patriarch of Antioch and all the East, of Alexandria, and of Jerusalem.

Patriarchal Exarchate of Egypt and Sudan: Greek Melkite Catholic Patriarchate, 16 Sharia Daher, 11271 Cairo; tel. (2) 25905790; fax (2) 25935398; e-mail grecmelkitecath_egy@hotmail.com; 6,200 adherents (31 December 2007); General Patriarchal Vicar for Egypt and Sudan Most Rev. Archbishop GEORGES BAKAR (Titular Archbishop of Pelusium).

Syrian Rite

The Syrian Catholic diocese of Cairo had an estimated 1,632 adherents at 31 December 2007.

Bishop of Cairo: Rt Rev. CLÉMENT-JOSEPH HANNOUCHE, Evêché Syrien Catholique, 46 Sharia Daher, 11271 Cairo; tel. (2) 25901234; fax (2) 25923932.

The Anglican Communion

The Anglican diocese of Egypt, suspended in 1958, was revived in 1974 and became part of the Episcopal Church in Jerusalem and the Middle East, formally inaugurated in January 1976. The Province has four dioceses: Jerusalem, Egypt, Cyprus and the Gulf, and Iran, and its President is the Bishop in Egypt. The Bishop in Egypt has jurisdiction also over the Anglican chaplaincies in Algeria, Djibouti, Eritrea, Ethiopia, Libya, Somalia and Tunisia.

Bishop in Egypt: Rt Rev. Dr MOUNEER HANNA ANIS, Diocesan Office, POB 87, 5 Sharia Michel Lutfalla, 11211 Cairo (Zamalek); tel. (2) 7380829; fax (2) 7358941; e-mail diocese@link.net; internet www.dioceseofegypt.org.

Other Christian Churches

Coptic Evangelical Organization for Social Services: POB 162, 11811 El Panorama, Cairo; tel. (2) 26221425; fax (2) 26221434; e-mail gm@ceoss.org.eg; internet www.ceoss.org.eg; Chair. Dr MERVAT AKHNOUKH ABSAKHROUN; Dir-Gen. Dr NABIL SAMUEL ABADIR.

Other denominations active in Egypt include the Coptic Evangelical Church (Synod of the Nile) and the Union of the Armenian Evangelical Churches in the Near East.

JUDAISM

The 1986 census recorded 794 Jews in Egypt, and there were reported to be fewer than 100 by the mid-2000s.

Jewish Community: Main Synagogue, Shaar Hashamayim 17, Adly St, Cairo; tel. (2) 4824613; fax (2) 7369639; e-mail bassatine@yahoo.com; f. 19th century; Pres. CARMEN WEINSTEIN.

The Press

Despite a fairly high illiteracy rate in Egypt, the country's press is well developed. Cairo is one of the region's largest publishing centres.

All newspapers and magazines are supervised, according to law, by the Supreme Press Council. The four major state-owned publishing houses of Al-Ahram Establishment, Dar al-Hilal, Dar Akhbar el-Yom and El-Tahrir Printing and Publishing House operate as separate entities and compete with each other commercially.

DAILIES

Al-Ahram (The Pyramids): Sharia al-Galaa, Cairo 11511; tel. (2) 5801600; fax (2) 5786023; e-mail ahramdaily@ahram.org.eg; internet www.ahram.org.eg; f. 1875; morning, incl. Sun.; Arabic; international edn publ. in London, United Kingdom; North American edn publ. in New York, USA; Chair. ABD EL-MONEIM SAÏD; Chief Editor OSAMA SARAYA; circ. 900,000 (weekdays), 1.1m. (Fri.).

Al-Ahram al-Massa'i (The Evening Al-Ahram): Sharia al-Galaa, Cairo 11511; e-mail massai@ahram.org.eg; internet massai.ahram.org.eg; f. 1990; evening; Arabic; Editor-in-Chief MURSI ATALLAH.

Al-Ahrar: 58 Manshyet al-Sadr, Kobry al-Kobba, Cairo; tel. (2) 4823046; fax (2) 4823027; e-mail sawtalahrar@hotmail.com; internet www.sawt-alahrar.net; f. 1977; organ of Liberal Party; Editor-in-Chief SALAH QABADAYA.

Al-Akhbar (The News): Dar Akhbar el-Yom, 6 Sharia al-Sahafa, Cairo; tel. (2) 25782600; fax (2) 25782530; e-mail akhbarelyom@akhbarelyom.org; internet www.elakhbar.org.eg; f. 1952; Arabic; Chair. MUHAMMAD MAHDI FADLI; Editor-in-Chief MUHAMMAD BARAKAT; circ. 850,000.

Arev: 3 Sharia Sulayman Halabi, Cairo; tel. (2) 25754703; e-mail arev@intouch.com; f. 1915; evening; Armenian; official organ of the Armenian Liberal Democratic Party; Editor ASSBED ARTINIAN.

Al-Dustour (The Constitution): nr Kobri al-Gamaa, Cairo (Giza); tel. (2) 33379008; fax (2) 33379766; internet www.dostor.org; f. 1995; banned by the authorities in 1998; relaunched in 2005; daily and weekly edns; independent; Editor-in-Chief IBRAHIM ISSA.

The Egyptian Gazette: 111–115 Sharia Ramses, Cairo; tel. (2) 5783333; fax (2) 5784646; e-mail ask@egyptiangazette.net.eg; internet www.egyptiangazette.net.eg; f. 1880; morning; English; Chair. MUHAMMAD ABD AL-HADEED; Editor-in-Chief RAMADAN A. KADER; circ. 90,000.

Al-Gomhouriya (The Republic): 24 Sharia Zakaria Ahmad, Cairo; tel. (2) 25781515; fax (2) 25781717; e-mail eltahrir@eltahrir.net; internet www.algomhuria.net.eg; f. 1953; morning; Arabic; mainly economic affairs; Chair. MUHAMMAD ABU HADID; Editor-in-Chief MUHAMMAD ALI IBRAHIM; circ. 800,000.

Al-Masry al-Youm: Cairo; tel. (2) 27980100; fax (2) 27926331; e-mail admin@almasry-alyoum.com; internet www.almasry-alyoum.com; f. 2003; Arabic; independent, privately owned; Editor-in-Chief MAGDY AL-GALAD; circ. 100,000.

Al-Misaa' (The Evening): 24 Sharia Zakaria Ahmad, Cairo; tel. (2) 5781010; fax (2) 5784747; e-mail eltahrir@eltahrir.net; internet www.almessa.net.eg; f. 1956; evening; Arabic; political, social and sport; Editor-in-Chief MUHAMMAD FOUDAH; Man. Dir ABD AL-HAMROSE; circ. 450,000.

Le Progrès Egyptien: 24 Sharia Zakaria Ahmad, Cairo; tel. (2) 5783333; fax (2) 5781110; e-mail ask@progres.net.eg; internet www.progres.net.eg; f. 1893; morning incl. Sun.; French; Chair. ALI HACHEM; Editor-in-Chief AHMED AL-BARDISSI; circ. 60,000.

La Réforme: 8 Passage Sherif, Alexandria; French.

Al-Wafd: 1 Sharia Boulos Hanna, Cairo (Dokki); tel. (2) 33383111; fax (2) 33359135; e-mail contact@alwafd.org; internet www.alwafd.org; f. 1984; organ of the New Wafd Party; Editor-in-Chief ABBAS AT-TARABILI; circ. 220,000.

PERIODICALS

Al-Ahaly (The People): Sharia Kareem al-Dawli, Tala'at Harb Sq., Cairo; tel. (2) 7786583; fax (2) 3900412; internet www.al-ahaly.com; f. 1978; weekly; publ. by Nat. Progressive Unionist Party; Chair. LOTFI WAKID; Editor-in-Chief ABD AL-BAKOURY.

Al-Ahram al-Arabi: Sharia al-Galaa, Cairo 11511; tel. (2) 5786100; e-mail arabi@ahram.org.eg; internet arabi.ahram.org.eg; f. 1997; weekly (Sat.); Arabic; political, social and economic affairs; Editor-in-Chief ABD EL-ATTI MUHAMMAD.

Al-Ahram al-Dimouqratiyah (Democracy Review): Sharia al-Galaa, Cairo 11511; tel. (2) 25786960; fax (2) 27705238; e-mail democracy@ahram.org.eg; internet democracy.ahram.org.eg; f. 2001; quarterly; politics; Arabic and English; publ. by Al-Ahram Establishment; Editor-in-Chief HALA MUSTAFA.

Al-Ahram Hebdo: POB 1057, Sharia al-Galaa, Cairo 11511; tel. (2) 27703100; fax (2) 27703314; e-mail hebdo@ahram.org.eg; internet hebdo.ahram.org.eg; f. 1993; weekly (Wed.); French; publ. by Al-Ahram Establishment; Editor-in-Chief MUHAMMAD SALMAWI.

Al-Ahram al-Iqtisadi (The Economic Al-Ahram): Sharia al-Galaa, Cairo 11511; tel. (2) 25786100; fax (2) 25786833; e-mail ik@ahram.org.eg; internet ik.ahram.org.eg; Arabic; weekly (Mon.); economic and political affairs; publ. by Al-Ahram Establishment; Chief Editor ISSAM RIFA'AT; circ. 10,000.

Al-Ahram Weekly (The Pyramids): Al-Ahram Bldg, Sharia al-Galaa, Cairo 11511; tel. (2) 5786100; fax (2) 5786833; e-mail weeklyweb@ahram.org.eg; internet weekly.ahram.org.eg; f. 1989; English; weekly; publ. by Al-Ahram Establishment; Man. Editor GALAL NASSER; Editor-in-Chief ASSEM EL-KERSH; circ. 150,000.

Akhbar al-Adab: 6 Sharia al-Sahafa, Cairo; tel. (2) 5795620; fax (2) 5782510; e-mail akhbarelyom@akhbarelyom.org; internet www.akhbarelyom.org.eg/adab; f. 1993; literature and arts for young people; Editor-in-Chief ABLA AL-RUWAYNI.

Akhbar al-Hawadith: 6 Sharia al-Sahafa, Cairo; tel. (2) 5782600; fax (2) 5782510; e-mail akhbarelyom@akhbarelyom.org; internet www.akhbarelyom.org.eg/hawadeth; f. 1993; weekly; crime reports; Editor-in-Chief MUHAMMAD BARAKAT.

Akhbar al-Nogoom: 6 Sharia al-Sahafa, Cairo; tel. (2) 5782600; fax (2) 5782510; e-mail akhbarelyom@akhbarelyom.org; internet www.akhbarelyom.org.eg/nogoom; f. 1991; weekly; theatre and film news; Editor-in-Chief AMAL OSMAN.

Akhbar al-Riadah: 6 Sharia al-Sahafa, Cairo; tel. (2) 5782600; fax (2) 5782510; e-mail akhbarelyom@akhbarelyom.org; internet www.akhbarelyom.org.eg/riada; f. 1990; weekly; sport; Editor-in-Chief IBRAHIM HEGAZY.

Akhbar al-Sayarat: 6 Sharia al-Sahafa, Cairo; e-mail akhbarelyom@akhbarelyom.org; internet www.akhbarelyom.org.eg/sayarat; f. 1998; car magazine; Editor-in-Chief SOLIMAN QENAWI.

Akhbar el-Yom (Daily News): 6 Sharia al-Sahafa, Cairo; tel. (2) 25782600; fax (2) 25782520; e-mail akhbarelyom@akhbarelyom.org; internet www.akhbarelyom.org.eg; f. 1944; weekly (Sat.); Arabic; Chair. MUHAMMAD MAHDI FADLI; Editor-in-Chief MOMTAZ AL-QUT; circ. 1,184,611.

Akher Sa'a (Last Hour): Dar Akhbar el-Yom, Sharia al-Sahafa, Cairo; tel. (2) 5782600; fax (2) 5782530; e-mail akhbarelyom@akhbarelyom.org; internet www.akhbarelyom.org.eg/akhersaa; f. 1934; weekly (Sun.); Arabic; independent; consumer and news magazine; Editor-in-Chief MAHMOUD SALAH; circ. 150,000.

Aqidaty (My Faith): 24–26 Sharia Zakaria Ahmad, Cairo; tel. (2) 5783333; fax (2) 5781110; e-mail eltahrir@eltahrir.net; internet www.aqidati.net.eg; weekly; Arabic; Islamic newspaper; Editor-in-Chief ABD AL-RAOUF EL-SAYED; circ. 300,000.

Business Monthly: 33 Soliman Abaza St, Cairo (Giza); tel. (2) 33381050; fax (2) 33381060; e-mail publications@amcham.org.eg;

internet www.amcham.org.eg/resources_publications/publications/business_monthly; f. 1985; English; monthly; business; publ. by the American Chamber of Commerce in Egypt; Editor-in-Chief BERTIL G. PETERSON; circ. 9,000.

Business Today Egypt: 3A Sharia 199, IBA Media Bldg, Degla, Maadi, Cairo; tel. (2) 27555000; fax (2) 27555050; e-mail editor@businesstodayegypt.com; internet www.businesstodayegypt.com; f. 1994; English; monthly; business, economics and politics; publ. by IBA Media Group; Editor PATRICK FITZPATRICK.

Al-Da'wa (The Call): Cairo; monthly; Arabic; organ of the Muslim Brotherhood.

Egypt Today: 3A Sharia 199, IBA Media Bldg, Degla, Maadi, Cairo; tel. (2) 27555000; fax (2) 27555050; e-mail editor@egypttoday.com; internet www.egypttoday.com; f. 1979; monthly; English; current affairs; publ. by IBA Media Group; Editor-in-Chief Dr MURSI SAAD EL-DIN; circ. 11,500–14,500.

Egyptian Cotton Gazette: POB 1772, 12 Muhammad Talaat Nooman St, Ramel Station, Alexandria; tel. (3) 4806971; fax (3) 4873002; e-mail alcotexa@tedata.net.eg; internet www.alcotexa.org; f. 1947; 2 a year; English; organ of the Alexandria Cotton Exporters' Asscn; Chief Editor GALAL AL-REFAI.

El-Elm Magazine (Sciences): 24 Sharia Zakaria Ahmad, Cairo; tel. (2) 5781010; fax (2) 5784747; e-mail ask@elm.net.eg; internet www.elm.net.eg; f. 1976; monthly; Arabic; publ. with the Academy of Scientific Research in Egypt; circ. 70,000.

The Employer: 4 el-Marwa Bldgs, blk 2, Ahmad Taysir St, Heliopolis, Cairo; tel. and fax (2) 24189939; e-mail info@the-employer.com; internet www.the-employer.net; English; bi-monthly; employment; Man. Dir DINA MAKKAWI.

El-Fagr (The Dawn): Cairo; tel. (2) 33442306; fax (2) 33032344; e-mail info@elfagr.net; internet www.elfagr.org; f. 2005; Arabic; weekly; independent; Editor-in-Chief ADEL HAMMOUDA.

El Gouna Magazine: 66 Abu el-Mahasen el-Shazli St, 4th Floor, Agouza, Cairo; tel. (2) 33034654; e-mail editor@elgounamag.com; internet www.elgounamag.com; English; quarterly; lifestyle; Gen. Man. MARYSE RAAD.

Hawa'a (Eve): Dar al-Hilal, 16 Sharia Muhammad Ezz el-Arab, Cairo 11511; tel. (2) 3625450; fax (2) 3625469; f. 1892; weekly (Sat.); Arabic; women's magazine; Chief Editor EKBAL BARAKA; circ. 210,502.

Al-Hilal: Dar al-Hilal, 16 Sharia Muhammad Ezz el-Arab, Cairo 11511; tel. (2) 3625450; fax (2) 3625469; f. 1895; monthly; Arabic; literary; Editor MAIDI AL-SAYID AL-DAQAQ.

Horreyati: 24 Sharia Zakaria Ahmad, Cairo; tel. (2) 5781010; fax (2) 5784747; e-mail eltahrir@eltahrir.net; internet www.horreyati.net.eg; f. 1990; weekly; social, cultural and sport; Editor-in-Chief MUHAMMAD NOUR EL-DIN; circ. 250,000.

Al-Kawakeb (The Stars): Dar al-Hilal, 16 Sharia Muhammad Ezz el-Arab, Cairo 11511; tel. (2) 3625450; fax (2) 3625469; f. 1952; weekly; Arabic; film magazine; Editor-in-Chief FAWZI MUHAMMAD IBRAHIM; circ. 86,381.

El-Keraza (The Sermon): St Mark Cathedral, POB 9035, Anba Ruess, 222 Sharia Ramses, Abbassia, Cairo; e-mail coptpope@tecmina.com; internet www.copticpope.org; fortnightly newspaper of the Coptic Orthodox Church; Arabic and English; Editor-in-Chief (vacant).

Al-Kora wal-Malaeb (Football and Playgrounds): 24 Sharia Zakaria Ahmad, Cairo; tel. (2) 5783333; fax (2) 5784747; internet www.koura.net.eg; f. 1976; weekly; Arabic; sport; circ. 150,000.

Al-Liwa' al-Islami (Islamic Standard): 11 Sharia Sherif Pasha, Cairo; f. 1982; weekly; Arabic; govt paper to promote official view of Islamic revivalism; Propr AHMAD HAMZA; Editor MUHAMMAD ALI SHETA; circ. 30,000.

Magallat al-Mohandessin (The Engineer's Magazine): 30 Sharia Ramses, Cairo; e-mail info@eea.org.eg; internet www.eea.org.eg; f. 1945; publ. by The Engineers' Syndicate; 10 a year; Arabic and English; Editor and Sec. MAHMOUD SAMI ABD AL-KAWI.

Medical Journal of Cairo University: Qasr el-Eini Hospital, Sharia Qasr el-Eini, Cairo; tel. and fax (2) 3655768; internet www.medicaljournalofcairouniversity.com; f. 1933; Qasr el-Eini Clinical Society; quarterly; English; Editor-in-Chief AHMAD SAMEH FARID.

The Middle East Observer: 41 Sharia Sherif, Cairo; tel. and fax (2) 3939732; e-mail info@meobserver.com; internet middleeastobserver.com; f. 1954; weekly; English; specializes in economics of Middle East and African markets; also publishes supplements on law, foreign trade and tenders; agent for IMF, UN and IDRC publs, distributor of World Bank publs; Publr AHMAD FODA; Chief Editor HESHAM A. RAOUF; circ. 20,000.

Al-Mussawar: Dar al-Hilal, 16 Sharia Muhammad Ezz el-Arab, Cairo 11511; tel. (2) 3625450; fax (2) 3625469; f. 1924; weekly; Arabic; news; Chair. and Editor-in-Chief ABD AL-KADER SHUHAYIB; circ. 130,423.

Nesf al-Donia: Sharia al-Galaa, Cairo 11511; tel. (2) 5786100; internet www.ahram.org.eg; f. 1990; weekly; Arabic; women's magazine; publ. by Al-Ahram Establishment; Editor-in-Chief AFKAR EL-KHARADLI.

October: Dar al-Maaref, 1119 Sharia Corniche el-Nil, Cairo; tel. (2) 25777077; fax (2) 25744999; internet www.octobermag.com; f. 1976; weekly; Arabic; Chair. and Editor-in-Chief ISMAIL MUNTASSIR; circ. 140,500.

Al-Omal (The Workers): 90 Sharia al-Galaa, Cairo; internet www.etufegypt.com; weekly; Arabic; publ. by the Egyptian Trade Union Federation; Chief Editor AHMAD HARAK.

Le Progrès Dimanche: 24 Sharia al-Galaa, Cairo; tel. (2) 5781010; fax (2) 5784747; e-mail ask@progres.net.eg; internet leprogresdimanche.newspaperdirect.com; weekly; French; Sun. edition of *Le Progrès Egyptien*; Editor-in-Chief KHALED ANWAR BAKIR; circ. 35,000.

La Revue d'Egypte: 3A Sharia 199, IBA Media Bldg, Degla, Maadi, Cairo; tel. (2) 27555000; fax (2) 27555050; e-mail courrier@iba-media.com; internet www.larevuedegypte.com; f. 2002; monthly; French; current affairs, culture, lifestyle; publ. by IBA Media Group; Editor-in-Chief FRÉDÉRIC MIGEON.

Rose al-Yousuf: 89A Sharia Qasr el-Eini, Cairo; tel. (2) 7923514; fax (2) 7925540; e-mail info@rosaonline.net; internet www.rosaonline.net; f. 1925; weekly; Arabic; political; circulates throughout all Arab countries; Editor-in-Chief ABDULLAH KAMAL EL-SAYED; circ. 35,000.

Sabah al-Kheir (Good Morning): 89A Sharia Qasr el-Eini, Cairo; tel. (2) 27950367; fax (2) 27923509; e-mail noor@rosaonline.net; internet www.rosaonline.net/Sabah; f. 1956; weekly (Tue.); Arabic; light entertainment; Chief Editor MUHAMMAD ABD AL-NOUR; circ. 70,000.

Al-Shaab (The People): 313 Sharia Port Said, Sayeda Zeinab, Cairo; tel. (2) 3909716; fax (2) 3900283; e-mail elshaab@idsc.gov.eg; internet www.alshaab.com; f. 1979; bi-weekly (Tue. and Fri.); organ of Socialist Labour Party; pro-Islamist; Editor-in-Chief MAGDI AHMAD HUSSEIN; circ. 130,000.

Shashati (My Screen): 24 Sharia Zakaria Ahmad, Cairo; tel. (2) 5781010; fax (2) 5784747; e-mail eltahrir@eltahrir.net; internet www.shashati.net.eg; weekly; art, culture, fashion and television news.

Al-Siyassa al-Dawliya: Al-Ahram Bldg, 12th Floor, Sharia al-Galaa, Cairo 11511; tel. (2) 25786071; fax (2) 25792899; e-mail siyassa@ahram.org.eg; internet www.siyassa.org.eg; f. 1965; quarterly; politics and foreign affairs; publ. by Al-Ahram Establishment; Man. Editor KAREN ABOUL KHEIR; Editor-in-Chief MUHAMMAD ABD EL-SALAM.

Tabibak al-Khass (Family Doctor): Dar al-Hilal, 16 Sharia Muhammad Ezz el-Arab, Cairo; tel. (2) 3625473; fax (2) 3625442; monthly; Arabic.

Watani (My Country): 27 Sharia Abd al-Khalek Sarwat, Cairo; tel. (2) 23927201; fax (2) 23935946; e-mail watani@watani.com.eg; internet www.wataninet.com; f. 1958; weekly (Sun.); Arabic and English, with French supplement; independent newspaper addressing Egyptians in general and the Christian Copts in particular; Editor-in-Chief YOUSSEF SIDHOM; circ. 60,000–100,000.

NEWS AGENCY

Middle East News Agency (MENA): POB 1165, 17 Sharia Hoda Sharawi, Cairo; tel. (2) 3933000; fax (2) 3935055; e-mail newsroom@mena.org.eg; internet www.mena.org.eg; f. 1955; regular service in Arabic, English and French; Chair. and Editor-in-Chief ABDULLAH HASSAN ABD AL-FATTAH.

PRESS ASSOCIATIONS

Egyptian Press Syndicate: Cairo; Chair. MAKRAM MUHAMMAD AHMED.

Foreign Press Association: 2 Sharia Ahmad Ragheb, Cairo (Garden City); tel. (2) 27943727; fax (2) 27943747; e-mail info@fpaegypt.net; internet www.fpaegypt.net; f. 1972; Chair. VOLKHARD WINDFUHR.

Publishers

The General Egyptian Book Organization: POB 235, Sharia Corniche el-Nil, Cairo (Boulac) 11221; tel. (2) 25779283; fax (2) 25789316; e-mail info@egyptianbook.org.eg; internet www.egyptianbook.org.eg; f. 1961; affiliated to the Ministry of Culture; editing, publishing and distribution; organizer of Cairo International Book Fair; Chair. Dr NASSER AL-ANSARY; Gen. Dir AHMAD SALAH ZAKI.

Al-Ahram Establishment: Al-Ahram Bldg, 6 Sharia al-Galaa, Cairo 11511; tel. (2) 5786100; fax (2) 5786023; e-mail ahram@ahram.org.eg; internet www.ahram.org.eg; f. 1875; state-owned; publishes newspapers, magazines and books, incl. *Al-Ahram*; Chair. ABD EL-MONEIM SAÏD; Dep. Chair. and Gen. Man. ALI GHONEIM.

Dar Akhbar el-Yom: 6 Sharia al-Sahafa, Cairo; tel. (2) 5748100; fax (2) 5748895; e-mail akhbarelyom@akhbarelyom.org; internet www.akhbarelyom.org.eg; f. 1944; state-owned; publs include *Al-Akhbar* (daily), *Akhbar el-Yom* (weekly) and *Akher Sa'a* (weekly); Chair. MUHAMMAD MAHDI FADLI.

American University in Cairo Press: 113 Sharia Qasr el-Eini, POB 2511, Cairo 11511; tel. (2) 27976926; fax (2) 27941440; e-mail aucpress@aucegypt.edu; internet aucpress.com; political history, economics, Egyptology and Arabic literature in English translation; Dir MARK LINZ.

Boustany's Publishing House: 4 Sharia Aly Tawfik Shousha, Cairo (Nasr City) 11371; tel. and fax (2) 2623085; e-mail boustany@link.net; internet www.boustanys.com; f. 1900; fiction, poetry, history, biography, philosophy, language, literature, politics, religion, archaeology and Egyptology; Chief Exec. FADWA BOUSTANY.

Elias Modern Publishing House: 1 Sharia Kenisset al-Rum El-Kathulik, Daher, Cairo 11271; tel. (2) 25903756; fax (2) 25880091; e-mail info@eliaspublishing.com; internet www.eliaspublishing.com; f. 1913; publishing, printing and distribution; publ. dictionaries, children's books, and books on linguistics, poetry and arts; Chair. NADIM ELIAS; Man. Dir LAURA KFOURY.

Dar al-Farouk: 12 Sharia Dokki, 6th Floor, Cairo (Giza); tel. (2) 37622830; fax (2) 33380474; e-mail support@darelfarouk.com.eg; internet www.darelfarouk.com.eg; wide range of books incl. educational, history, science and business; Chair. FAROUK M. AL-AMARY; Gen. Man. Dr KHALED F. AL-AMARY.

Dar al-Gomhouriya: 24 Sharia Zakaria Ahmad, Cairo; tel. (2) 5781010; fax (2) 5784747; e-mail eltahrir@eltahrir.net; internet www.algomhuria.net.eg; state-owned; affiliate of El-Tahrir Printing and Publishing House; publs include the dailies *Al-Gomhouriya*, *Al-Misaa'*, *The Egyptian Gazette* and *Le Progrès Egyptien*; Pres. MUHAMMAD ABOUL HADID.

Dar al-Hilal: 16 Sharia Muhammad Ezz el-Arab, Cairo 11511; tel. (2) 3625450; fax (2) 3625469; f. 1892; state-owned; publs include *Al-Hilal*, *Kitab al-Hilal*, *Tabibak al-Khass* (monthlies); *Al-Mussawar*, *Al-Kawakeb*, *Hawa'a* (weeklies); Chair. ABD AL-KADER SHUHAYIB.

Dar al-Kitab al-Masri: POB 156, 33 Sharia Qasr el-Nil, Cairo 11511; tel. (2) 3922168; fax (2) 3924657; e-mail info@daralkitabalmasri.com; internet www.daralkitabalmasri.com; f. 1929; publishing, printing and distribution; publrs of books on Islam and history, as well as dictionaries, encyclopaedias, textbooks, children's and general interest books; Pres. and Dir-Gen. Dr HASSAN EL-ZEIN.

Dar al-Maaref: 1119 Sharia Corniche el-Nil, Cairo; tel. (2) 25777077; fax (2) 25744999; e-mail maaref@idselgov.eg; internet www.octobermag.com; f. 1890; publishing, printing and distribution of wide variety of books in Arabic and other languages; publrs of *October* magazine; Chair. ISMAIL MUNTASSIR.

Maktab al-Misri al-Hadith li-t-Tiba wan-Nashr: 7 Sharia Noubar, Alexandria; also at 2 Sharia Sherif, Cairo; Man. AHMAD YEHIA.

Maktabet Misr: POB 16, 3 Sharia Kamal Sidki, Cairo; tel. (2) 5898553; fax (2) 7870051; e-mail info@misrbookshop.com; f. 1932; fiction, biographies and textbooks for schools and universities; Man. AMIR SAID GOUDA EL-SAHHAR.

Dar al-Masri al-Lubnani: 16 Sharia Abd al-Khalek Sarwat, Cairo; tel. (2) 3910250; fax (2) 3909618; e-mail info@almasriah.com; internet www.almasriah.com; Arabic literature, history, sciences, textbooks and children's books; Chair. MUHAMMAD RASHED.

Nahdet Misr Group: al-Nahda Tower, 21 Sharia Ahmad Orabi, Sphinx Sq., Mohandessin, Cairo (Giza); tel. (2) 33464903; fax (2) 33462576; e-mail publishing@nahdetmisr.com; internet www.nahdetmisr.com; f. 1938; fiction, children's literature and educational books; also publishes magazines, incl. *Mickey* (weekly); Chair. MUHAMMAD AHMAD IBRAHIM.

Dar al-Nashr (fmrly Les Editions Universitaires d'Egypte): POB 1347, 41 Sharia Sherif, Cairo 11511; tel. (2) 3934606; fax (2) 3921997; f. 1947; university textbooks, academic works and encyclopaedias.

National Centre for Educational Research and Development: 12 Sharia Waked, el-Borg el-Faddy, POB 836, Cairo; tel. (2) 3930981; f. 1956; fmrly Documentation and Research Centre for Education (Ministry of Education); bibliographies, directories, information and education bulletins; Dir Prof. ABD EL-FATTAH GALAL.

National Library Press (Dar al-Kutub): POB 11638, 8 Sharia al-Sabtteya, Cairo; tel. (2) 5750886; fax (2) 5765634; e-mail info@darelkotob.org; internet www.darelkotob.org; bibliographic works; Pres. and Dir-Gen. SAMIR GHARIB.

Safeer Publishing: POB 425, Cairo (Dokki); tel. (2) 25329902; fax (2) 25329505; internet www.safeer.com.eg; f. 1982; children's books; Pres. MUHAMMAD ABD EL-LATIF.

Dar al-Shorouk: 8 Sibaweh al-Masri, Cairo (Nasr City) 11371; tel. (2) 24023399; fax (2) 24037567; e-mail dar@shorouk.com; internet www.shorouk.com; f. 1968; publishing, printing and distribution; publrs of books on current affairs, history, Islamic studies, literature, art and children's books; Chair. IBRAHIM EL-MOALLEM.

El-Tahrir Printing and Publishing House: 24 Sharia Zakaria Ahmad, Cairo; tel. (2) 5781222; fax (2) 2784747; e-mail eltahrir@eltahrir.net; internet www.eltahrir.net; f. 1953; state-owned; Pres. and Chair. of Bd ALI HASHIM.

Dar el-Thaqafa: Coptic Evangelical Organization for Social Services, Sharia Dr Ahmed Zaki, Cairo; tel. (2) 6221425; internet www.darelthaqafa.com; publishing dept of the Coptic Evangelical Org. for Social Services; publishes books on social issues as well as on spiritual and theological topics; Dir Rev. Dr ANDREA ZAKI STEPHANOUS.

Broadcasting and Communications

TELECOMMUNICATIONS

Regulatory Authority

National Telecommunications Regulatory Authority (NTRA): Smart Village, Bldg No. 4, km 28, Sharia Cairo–Alexandria, Cairo; tel. (2) 35344000; fax (2) 35344155; e-mail info@tra.gov.eg; internet www.ntra.gov.eg; f. 2000; Chair. Dr MUHAMMAD ABD AL-QADER MUHAMMAD SALIM (Minister of Communications and Information Technology); Exec. Pres. Dr AMR BADAWI.

Principal Operators

Egyptian Company for Mobile Services (MobiNil): The World Trade Center, 2005C, Corniche el-Nil, Boulaq, Cairo; tel. (2) 25747000; fax (2) 25747111; e-mail customercare@mobinil.com; internet www.mobinil.com; began operation of the existing state-controlled mobile telecommunications network in 1998; owned by France Télécom and Orascom Telecom; 13.7m. subscribers (Sept. 2007); Chair. ALEX SHALABY; CEO HASSAN KABBANI.

Etisalat Misr: POB 11, S4 Down Town, Sharia 90, 5th Compound, New Cairo; tel. (2) 35346333; internet www.etisalat.com.eg; f. 2007 as Egypt's third mobile telephone service provider; subsidiary of Etisalat (United Arab Emirates); Chair. GAMAL EL-SADAT; CEO SALEH EL-ABDOULI.

Orascom Telecom: 2005A Nile City Towers, South Tower, Corniche el-Nil, Ramlet Beaulac, 11221 Cairo; tel. (2) 24615050; fax (2) 24615054; e-mail info@orascom.com; internet www.orascomtelecom.com; Chair. JO LUNDER; Group CEO AHMED ABU DOMA.

Telecom Egypt: POB 2271, Sharia Ramses, Cairo 11511; tel. (2) 25793444; fax (2) 25744244; e-mail telecomegypt@telecomegypt.com.eg; internet www.telecomegypt.com.eg; f. 1957; provider of fixed-line telephone services; CEO and Man. Dir TAREK ABOU ALAM; Chair. AKIL HAMED BESHIR.

Vodafone Egypt: 7A Corniche el-Nil, Maadi, 11431 Cairo; tel. (2) 25292000; e-mail public.relations@vodafone.com; internet www.vodafone.com.eg; f. 1998 by the MisrFone consortium; mobile telephone service provider; majority-owned by Vodafone Int. (United Kingdom); 12.2m. subscribers (Sept. 2007); Chair. IAN GRAY; CEO HATEM DOWIDAR.

BROADCASTING

Radio and Television

Egyptian Radio and Television Union (ERTU): POB 11511, Cairo 1186; tel. (2) 5787120; fax (2) 746989; e-mail info@ertu.org; internet www.ertu.org; f. 1928; home service radio programmes in Arabic, English and French; foreign services in Arabic, English, French, German, Spanish, Portuguese, Italian, Swahili, Hausa, Urdu, Indonesian, Pashtu, Farsi, Turkish, Somali, Uzbek, Albanian, Afar, Amharic; operates 2 national and 6 regional television channels; also owns the satellite television network Nile TV, which offers 12 specialized channels; Pres. AHMAD ANIS.

Dreams TV: 23 Polis Hana St, Cairo (Giza); tel. (2) 7492817; fax (2) 7410949; e-mail urquestions@dreams.tv; internet www.dreams.tv; f. 2001; privately owned satellite television station; broadcasts on Dream 1 and Dream 2 networks, providing sports, music and entertainment programmes; Chair. Dr AHMAD BAHGAT.

El-Mehwar TV: Cairo; e-mail ElMehwar@ElMehwar.tv; internet www.elmehwar.tv; f. 2001; privately owned; entertainment and current affairs programmes; Founder Dr HASSAN RATEB.

Middle East Radio: Société Egyptienne de Publicité, 24–26 Sharia Zakaria Ahmad, Cairo; tel. (2) 5781010; fax (2) 5784747; e-mail radioinfo@ertu.org; internet ertu.org/radio/mideast.html.

Finance

(cap. = capital; res = reserves; dep. = deposits; m. = million; brs = branches; amounts in Egyptian pounds, unless otherwise stated)

BANKING

Central Bank

Central Bank of Egypt (CBE): 31 Sharia Qasr el-Nil, Cairo; tel. (2) 27702770; fax (2) 23925045; e-mail info@cbe.org.eg; internet www.cbe.org.eg; f. 1961; controls Egypt's monetary policy and supervises the banking sector; cap. 1,000m., res 1,543.7m., dep. 211,861.5m. (June 2007); Gov. and Chair. Dr Farouk Abd el-Baky el-Okdah; 4 brs.

Commercial and Specialized Banks

Bank of Alexandria: 49 Sharia Qasr el-Nil, Cairo; tel. (2) 23913822; fax (2) 23919805; e-mail info@alexbank.com; internet www.alexbank.com; f. 1957; 80% stake acquired by Gruppo Sanpaolo IMI (Italy) in Oct. 2006; cap. 800m., res 1,548m., dep. 27,801m. (Dec. 2009); Chair. and Man. Dir Bruno Gamba; 196 brs.

Banque du Caire, SAE: POB 9022, Banque du Caire Tower, 6 Sharia Dr Moustafa Abu Zahra, Nasr City, Cairo 11371; tel. (2) 2647400; fax (2) 403725; e-mail intl.division@bdc.com.eg; internet www.bdc.com.eg; f. 1952; state-owned; privatization pending; cap. 1,600.0m., res 1,187.6m., dep. 35,621.7m. (June 2009); Chair. Muhammad Kamal el-Din Barakat; CEO Muhammad Kafafi; 216 brs.

Banque Misr, SAE: 151 Sharia Muhammad Farid, Cairo; tel. (2) 3912711; fax (2) 3919779; e-mail staff@banquemisr.com.eg; internet www.banquemisr.com.eg; f. 1920; merger with Misr Exterior Bank in 2004; privatization pending; cap. 3,400m., res 3,425m., dep. 142,494m. (June 2009); Chair. Muhammad Kamal al-Din Barakat; Gen. Man. Amr Muhammad el-Mahdy Yousuf; 438 brs.

Commercial International Bank (Egypt), SAE: POB 2430, Nile Tower Bldg, 21–23 Sharia Charles de Gaulle, Cairo (Giza); tel. (2) 37472000; fax (2) 25701945; e-mail info@cibeg.com; internet www.cibeg.com; f. 1975 as Chase Nat. Bank (Egypt), SAE; adopted present name 1987; Nat. Bank of Egypt has 19.91% interest, Bankers Trust Co (USA) 18.76%, Int. Finance Corpn 5%; cap. 2,925m., res 2,362m., dep. 55,106m. (Dec. 2009); Chair. and Man. Dir Hisham Ezz al-Arab; 112 brs.

Egyptian Arab Land Bank: 78 Sharia Gameat al-Dowal al-Arabia, Mohandessin, Cairo 12311; tel. (2) 33368075; fax 33389218; e-mail foreign@eal-bank.com; internet www.eal-bank.com; f. 1880; state-owned; Chair. Muhammad Fathy el-Sebai; 26 brs in Egypt, 15 abroad.

Export Development Bank of Egypt (EDBE): 108 Mohi el-Din Abou al-Ezz, Cairo 12311 (Dokki); tel. (2) 7619006; fax (2) 3385938; e-mail info@edbebank.com; internet www.edbebank.com; f. 1983 to replace Nat. Import-Export Bank; cap. 1,200.0m., res –9.4m., dep. 9,610.7m. (June 2009); Chair. Hisham Ahmad Hassan; 15 brs.

HSBC Bank Egypt, SAE: POB 126, Abou el-Feda Bldg, 3 Sharia Abou el-Feda, Cairo (Zamalek); tel. (2) 27396001; fax (2) 27364010; e-mail hsbcegypt@hsbc.com; internet www.egypt.hsbc.com; f. 1982 as Hong Kong Egyptian Bank; name changed to Egyptian British Bank in 1994, and as above in 2001; 94.5% owned by Hongkong and Shanghai Banking Corpn; cap. 1,508m., res 731m., dep. 32,000m. (Dec. 2009); Chair. Abd al-Salam el-Anwar; CEO Andrew Long; 78 brs.

National Bank for Development (NBD): POB 647, 5 Sharia el-Borsa el-Gedida, Cairo 11511; tel. (2) 23959291; fax (2) 23936039; e-mail nbd@internetegypt.com; internet www.nbdegypt.com; f. 1980; 16 affiliated Nat. Banks for Devt merged with NBD in 1992; 51% share bought by Abu Dhabi Islamic Bank in 2007; cap. 1,750m., res 246m., dep. 9,409m. (Dec. 2009); Chair. Muhammad Taymour; Man. Dir and CEO Nevine Loutfy; 70 brs.

National Bank of Egypt (NBE): POB 11611, National Bank of Egypt Tower, 1187 Corniche el-Nil, Cairo; tel. (2) 25749101; fax (2) 25762672; e-mail nbe@nbe.com.eg; internet www.nbe.com.eg; f. 1898; merged with Mohandes Bank and Bank of Commerce and Devt in 2005; privatization pending; handles all commercial banking operations; cap. 2,250m., res 5,589m., dep. 231,692m. (June 2009); Chair. Hussein Abdel Aziz Hussein; 401 brs.

Principal Bank for Development and Agricultural Credit (PBDAC): 110 Sharia Qasr el-Eini, 11623 Cairo; tel. (2) 27951229; fax (2) 27948337; e-mail pbdac@pbdac.com.eg; internet www.pbdac.com.eg; f. 1976 to succeed former credit orgs; state-owned; cap. 1,500m., res 311m., dep. 22,074m. (June 2009); Chair. Ali Ismael Shaker; 172 brs.

Société Arabe Internationale de Banque (SAIB): 56 Sharia Gamet el-Dowal al-Arabia, Mohandessin, Cairo (Giza); tel. (2) 37499464; fax (2) 37603497; f. 1976; 46% owned by Arab Int. Bank; cap. US $150m., res $52m., dep. $1,431m. (Dec. 2009); Chair. Dr Hassan Abbas Zaki; Man. Dir Hassan Abd al-Meguid; 20 brs.

Union National Bank-Egypt SAE: el-Gamaa Bldg, 57 Sharia el-Giza, Alexandria 21519; tel. (2) 33385073; fax (2) 33384983; e-mail foreign@acmb.com.eg; internet www.acmb.com.eg; f. 1981 as Alexandria Commercial and Maritime Bank, SAE; adopted present name Dec. 2007; 94.8% owned by Union Nat. (United Arab Emirates); cap. 591m., res 83m., dep. 3,620m. (Dec. 2009); Chair. Sheikh Nahayan Mubarak Al Nahayan; Man. Dir Ramadan Anwar; 25 brs.

The United Bank (UBE): Cairo Center, 106 Sharia Qasr el-Eini, Cairo; tel. (2) 33326010; fax (2) 27920153; e-mail info@ube.net; internet www.theubeg.com; f. 1981 as Dakahlia Nat. Bank for Devt; renamed United Bank of Egypt 1997; current name adopted 2006, when merged with Nile Bank and Islamic Int. Bank for Investment and Devt; privatization mooted in 2008; cap. 1,000.0m., res –11.0m., dep. 10,390.8m. (Dec. 2008); Chair. and Man. Dir Muhammad Ashmawy; 41 brs.

Social Bank

Nasser Social Bank: POB 2552, 35 Sharia Qasr el-Nil, Cairo; tel. (2) 3924484; fax (2) 3921930; f. 1971; state-owned; interest-free savings and investment bank for social and economic activities, participating in social insurance, specializing in financing co-operatives, craftsmen and social institutions; cap. 20m.; Chair. Nassif Tahoon.

Multinational Banks

Arab African International Bank: 5 Midan al-Saray al-Koubra, POB 60, Majlis el-Sha'ab, Cairo 11516 (Garden City); tel. (2) 27924770; fax (2) 27925599; internet www.aaib.com; f. 1964 as Arab African Bank; renamed 1978; acquired Misr-America Int. Bank in 2005; cap. US $100m., res $512m., dep. $7,103m. (Dec. 2009); commercial investments and retail banking; shareholders are Central Bank of Egypt, Kuwait Investment Authority (49.37% each), and individuals and Arab institutions; Chair. Mahmoud A. al-Nouri; Vice-Chair. and Man. Dir Hassan E. Abdalla; 27 brs in Egypt, 3 abroad.

Arab International Bank: POB 1563, 35 Sharia Abd al-Khalek Sarwat, Cairo; tel. (2) 23918794; fax (2) 23916233; internet www.aib.com.eg; f. 1971 as Egyptian Int. Bank for Foreign Trade and Investment; renamed 1974; owned by Egypt, Libya, Oman, Qatar, the United Arab Emirates and private Arab shareholders; cap. US $450m., res $234m., dep. $3,431m. (Dec. 2009); 'offshore' bank; aims to promote trade and investment in shareholders' countries and other Arab countries; Chair. and Man. Dir Dr Atif Muhammad Obeid; 7 brs.

Commercial Foreign Venture Banks

Ahli United Bank (Egypt): POB 1159, 9th Floor, World Trade Center, 1191 Corniche el-Nil; tel. (2) 25801200; fax (2) 25757052; e-mail info@deltabank-egypt.com; internet www.ahliunited.com; f. 1978 as Delta Int. Bank; name changed as above in 2007; 89.3% stake owned by Ahli United Bank BSC (Bahrain) and other Gulf-based financial institutions; cap. 600m., res 200m., dep. 6,456m. (Dec. 2009); Chair. Fahad al-Rajaan; CEO and Man. Dir Nevine el-Messeery; 28 brs.

alBaraka Bank Egypt, SAE: POB 455, 60 Sharia Mohi el-Din Abu al-Ezz, Cairo (Dokki); tel. (2) 37481777; fax (2) 37611436; e-mail centeral@esf-bank.com; internet www.albaraka-bank.com.eg; f. 1980 as Pyramids Bank; renamed Egyptian-Saudi Finance Bank 1988; current name adopted April 2010; 73.7% owned by Al-Baraka Banking Group (Bahrain); cap. 500.0m., res 2.7m., dep. 9,467.8m. (Dec. 2008); Chair. Adnan Ahmad Yousuf; Man. Dir Ashraf Ahmad Moustafa el-Ghamrawy; 23 brs.

Bank Audi SAE: Pyramid Heights Office Park, km 22, Cairo–Alexandria Desert Rd, Cairo; tel. (2) 35343300; fax (2) 35362120; e-mail contactus.egypt@banqueaudi.com; f. 1978 as Cairo Far East Bank SAE; name changed as above in 2006, when acquired by Bank Audi SAL (Lebanon); cap. 1,123m., res –14m., dep. 9,700m. (Dec. 2009); Chair., Man. Dir and Pres. Hatem A. Sadek; 34 brs.

Barclays Bank Egypt, SAE: POB 110, 12 Midan el-Sheikh Yousuf, Cairo (Garden City); tel. (2) 23662600; fax (2) 23662810; internet www.barclays.com.eg; f. 1975 as Cairo Barclays Int. Bank; renamed Banque du Caire Barclays Int. in 1983 and Cairo Barclays Bank in 1999; name changed as above in 2004; wholly owned by Barclays Bank; acquired 40% stake held by Banque du Caire in 2004; cap. 995.1m., res 358.2m., dep. 13,560.7m. (Dec. 2008); Man. Dir Khalid el-Gibaly; 65 brs.

Blom Bank Egypt: 64 Sharia Mohi el-Din Abou al-Ezz, Cairo (Dokki); tel. (2) 33039825; fax (2) 33039804; e-mail mail@blombankegypt.com; internet www.blombankegypt.com; f. 1977 as Misr Romanian Bank, name changed as above in 2006; 99.7% owned by Blom Bank SAL (Lebanon); cap. 750m., res 58m., dep. 6,962m.

(Dec. 2009); Chair. SAAD AZHARI; CEO and Man. Dir MUHAMMAD OZALP; 25 brs.

BNP Paribas SAE: POB 2441, 3 Latin America St, Cairo (Garden City); tel. (2) 27948323; fax (2) 27942218; e-mail bnppegypt@bnpparibas.com; internet www.egypt.bnpparibas.com; f. 1977 as Banque du Caire et de Paris SAE, name changed to BNP Paribas Le Caire in 2001 and as above in 2006; BNP Paribas (France) has 95.2% interest and Banque du Caire 4.8%; cap. 1,700.0m., res –2.0m., dep. 17,655.3m. (Dec. 2007); Chair. JEAN THOMAZEAU; Man. Dir JANY GEROMETTA; 8 brs.

Crédit Agricole Egypt, SAE: POB 1825, 4 Hassan Sabri St, Cairo 11511 (Zamalek); tel. (2) 27382661; fax (2) 27380450; internet www.ca-egypt.com; f. 2006 by merger of Calyon Bank Egypt (Egyptian affiliate of Crédit Agricole Group—France) and Egyptian American Bank; owned by Crédit Agricole Groupe, Mansour and Maghrabi Investment and Devt, and Egyptian investors; cap. 1,148.0m., res 538.8m., dep. 20,107.7m. (Dec. 2009); Chair. MUHAMMAD MANSOUR; Man. Dir FRANÇOIS EDOUARD DRION; 44 brs.

Egyptian Gulf Bank: POB 56, El-Orman Plaza Bldg, 8–10 Sharia Ahmad Nessim, Cairo (Giza); tel. (2) 33368357; fax (2) 37490002; e-mail h.r.egb@mst1.mist.com.eg; internet www.egbbank.com.eg; f. 1981; Misr Insurance Co has 19.3% interest; cap. 906m., res 38m., dep. 4,987m. (Dec. 2009); Chair. MUHAMMAD GAMAL EL-DIN MAHMOUD; Exec. Man. Dir SAID ZAKY; 16 brs.

Faisal Islamic Bank of Egypt, SAE: POB 2446, 149 Sharia el-Tahrir, Galaa Sq., Cairo (Dokki); tel. (2) 37621285; fax (2) 37621281; e-mail foreigndept@faisalbank.com.eg; internet www.faisalbank.com.eg; f. 1979; all banking operations conducted according to Islamic principles; cap. 1,059.3m., res 391.2m., dep. 25,559.8m. (Dec. 2009); Chair. Prince MUHAMMAD AL-FAISAL AL-SAOUD; Gov. ABD AL-HAMID ABU MOUSSA; 24 brs.

Piraeus Bank Egypt SAE: POB 92, 4th Floor, Evergreen Bldg, 10 Sharia Talaat Harb, Majlis al-Sha'ab, Cairo; tel. (2) 25764644; fax (2) 25799862; internet www.ecb.com.eg; f. Jan. 2006, following acquisition of Egyptian Commercial Bank by Piraeus Bank Group (Greece) in June 2005; cap. 1,000m., res 36m., dep. 8,733m. (Dec. 2009); Chair. ILIAS MILIS; CEO and Man. Dir NAYERA AMIN; 49 brs.

Suez Canal Bank, SAE: POB 2620, 7 Abd el-Kader Hamza St, Cairo (Garden City); tel. (2) 27943433; fax (2) 27926476; e-mail info@scbank.com.eg; f. 1978; cap. 2,000m., res 109m., dep. 13,320m. (Dec. 2009); Chair. and Man. Dir TAREQ KANDIL; 29 brs.

Al-Watany Bank of Egypt: POB 63, 13 Sharia Semar, Dr Fouad Mohi el-Din Sq., Gameat el-Dewal al-Arabia, Mohandessin, Cairo 12655; tel. (2) 33388816; fax (2) 33362763; internet www.alwatany.net; f. 1980; 51% owned by Nat. Bank of Kuwait; cap. 1,000.0m., res 293.0m., dep. 12,558.6m. (Dec. 2009); Chair. SHEIKHA KHALED EL-BAHR; Man. Dir Dr YASSER ISMAIL HASSAN; 39 brs.

Non-Commercial Banks

Arab Banking Corporation—Egypt: 1 Sharia el-Saleh Ayoub, Cairo (Zamalek); tel. (2) 27362684; fax (2) 27363643; e-mail abcegypt@arabbanking.com.eg; internet www.arabbanking.com.eg; f. 1982 as Egypt Arab African Bank; acquired by Arab Banking Corpn (Bahrain) in 1999; Arab Banking Corpn has 93% interest, other interests 7%; cap. 600m., res 171m., dep. 3,976m. (Dec. 2009); commercial and investment bank; Chair. HASSAN ALI JUMA; Man. Dir and CEO AKRAM TINAWI; 28 brs.

Arab Investment Bank (Federal Arab Bank for Development and Investment): POB 826, Cairo Sky Center Bldg, 8 Sharia Abd al-Khalek Sarwat, Cairo; tel. (2) 5768097; fax (2) 5770329; e-mail arinbank@mst1.mist.com.eg; internet arab-investment-bank.egypt.com/index.asp; f. 1978 as Union Arab Bank for Devt and Investment; Egyptian/Syrian/Libyan jt venture; cap. 500m., res –5m., dep. 2,275m. (Dec. 2009); Chief Gen. Man. MUHAMMAD KHALED ABDEL ALIM MAKHLOUF; 13 brs.

EFG-Hermes: 58 Sharia el-Tahrir, Cairo 12311 (Dokki); tel. (2) 33383626; fax (2) 33383616; e-mail corporate@efg-hermes.com; internet www.efg-hermes.com; f. 1984; offices in Cairo, Alexandria and Mansoura; cap. 405.4m., res 109.0m., dep. 1,166.6m. (Dec. 2005); Chair. MONA ZULFICAR; CEO YASSER EL-MALLAWANY; 11 brs.

Housing and Development Bank, SAE: POB 234, 12 Sharia Syria, Mohandessin, Cairo (Giza); tel. (2) 37492013; fax (2) 37600712; e-mail hdbank@hdb-egy.com; internet www.hdb-egy.com; f. 1979; cap. 670m., res 164m., dep. 6,568m. (Dec. 2009); Chair. and Man. Dir FATHY EL-SEBAIE MANSOUR; 40 brs.

Industrial Development and Workers Bank of Egypt (IDWBE): 110 Sharia al-Galaa, Cairo 11511; tel. (2) 25772468; fax (2) 25751227; e-mail cs@idbe-egypt.com; internet www.idbe-egypt.com; f. 1947 as Industrial Bank; re-established as above in 1976; cap. 500.0m., res 419.1m., dep. 1,481.2m. (June 2008); Chair. and Man. Dir SHAHIN SERAGELDIN; 19 brs.

Misr Iran Development Bank: POB 219, Nile Tower Bldg, 21 Charles de Gaulle Ave, Cairo 12612 (Giza); tel. (2) 35727311; fax (2) 35701185; e-mail midb@mst1.mist.com.eg; internet www.midb.com.eg; f. 1975; Iran Foreign Investment Co has 40.14% interest, Bank of Alexandria and Misr Insurance Co each have 29.93% interest; cap. 714m., res 375m., dep. 7,690m. (Dec. 2009); Chair. and Man. Dir ISMAIL HASSAN MUHAMMAD; Gen. Man. HAMDY HASSAN MOUSSA HASSAN; 12 brs.

National Société Générale Bank, SAE (NSGB): POB 2664, 5 Sharia Champollion, 11111 Cairo; tel. (2) 27707000; fax (2) 27707799; e-mail info@nsgb.com.eg; internet www.nsgb.com.eg; f. 1978; Société Générale (France) has 78.38% interest, other interests 21.62%; merged with Misr Int. Bank SAE in 2006; cap. 3,332m., res 979m., dep. 44,440m. (Dec. 2009); Chair. and Man. Dir MUHAMMAD OSMAN EL-DIB; Vice-Chair. and Man. Dir JEAN-PHILLIPPE COULIER; 138 brs.

REGULATORY AUTHORITY

Egyptian Financial Supervisory Authority (EFSA): Unit 84B, Bldg 5A, Alexandria Desert Rd, km 28, Cairo 12577; tel. (2) 35370040; fax (2) 35370041; e-mail info@efsa.gov.eg; internet www.efsa.gov.eg; f. 2009, following the merger of the Capital Market Authority, the Egyptian Insurance Supervisory Authority and the Mortgage Finance Authority; also assumed the regulatory functions of the General Authority for Investment and Free Zones, and the Egyptian Exchange; supervision of all non-banking financial markets and institutions, incl. the stock exchange, the capital market, and the insurance and mortgage sectors; Chair. Dr ASHRAF EL-SHARKAWY.

STOCK EXCHANGE

Egyptian Exchange (EGX): 4A Sharia el-Sherifein, Cairo 11513; tel. (2) 23921447; fax (2) 23924214; e-mail webmaster@egyptse.com; internet www.egyptse.com; f. 1883 as the Cairo and Alexandria Stock Exchanges; present name adopted 2008; Chair. Dr MUHAMMAD OMRAN.

INSURANCE

Allianz Egypt: POB 266, Saridar Bldg, 92 Sharia el-Tahrir, Cairo (Dokki); tel. (2) 37605445; fax (2) 37605446; e-mail info@allianz.com.eg; internet www.allianz.com.eg; f. 1976 as Arab Int. Insurance Co; Allianz AG (Germany) purchased 80% stake in 2000; name changed as above in 2004; general and life insurance; Chair. RAYMOND SEMAAN EL-CHAM.

MetLife Alico: 28th Floor, Nile City Bldg, North Tower, Ramlet Beualac, Cairo; tel. (2) 4619020; fax (2) 4619015; e-mail service-egypt@metlifealico.com; internet www.eg.alico.com; f. 1997; first multinational insurance company to be granted licence to offer life insurance service in Egypt; CEO MICHEL KHALAF.

Misr Insurance Co: POB 950, 7 Sharia Abd al-Latif Boltia, Cairo; tel. (2) 7918300; fax (2) 797041; e-mail quality@misrins.com.eg; internet www.misrins.com.eg; f. 1934; merged with Al-Chark Insurance Co and Egyptian Reinsurance Co in Dec. 2007; scheduled for privatization; all classes of insurance and reinsurance; Chair. Prof. ADEL HAMMAD.

Mohandes Insurance Co: POB 62, 3 el-Mesaha Sq., Cairo (Dokki); tel. (2) 3352547; fax (2) 3361365; e-mail chairman@mohandes-ins.com; internet www.mohandes-ins.com; f. 1980; privately owned; insurance and reinsurance; Chair. and Man. Dir MUHAMMAD AHMED BARAKA.

Al-Mottahida: POB 804, 9 Sharia Sulayman Pasha, Cairo; f. 1957.

National Insurance Co of Egypt, SAE: POB 592, 41 Sharia Qasr el-Nil, Cairo; tel. (2) 3910731; fax (2) 3933051; internet www.ahlya.com; f. 1900; cap. 100m.; scheduled for privatization; Chair. SADEK HASSAN SADEK.

Provident Association of Egypt, SAE: POB 390, 9 Sharia Sherif Pasha, Alexandria; f. 1936; Man. Dir G. C. VORLOOU.

Trade and Industry

GOVERNMENT AGENCIES

Egyptian Mineral Resource Authority (EMRA): 3 Sharia Salah Salem, Abbassia, 11517 Cairo; tel. (2) 6828013; fax (2) 4820128; e-mail info@egsma.gov.eg; f. 1896 as the Egyptian Geological Survey and Mining Authority; state supervisory authority concerned with geological mapping, mineral exploration and other mining activities; Chair. HUSSEIN HAMOUDA.

General Authority for Investment (GAFI): Sharia Salah Salem, 11562 Cairo (Nasr City); tel. (2) 24055452; fax (2) 24055425; e-mail investorcare@gafinet.org; internet www.gafinet.org; Chair. OSAMA SALEH.

CHAMBERS OF COMMERCE

Federation of Egyptian Chambers of Commerce (FEDCOC): 4 el-Falaki Sq., Cairo; tel. (2) 7951136; fax (2) 7951164; e-mail fedcoc@menanet.net; internet www.fedcoc.org.eg; f. 1955; Chair. MUHAMMAD EL-MASRY.

Alexandria

Alexandria Chamber of Commerce: 31 Sharia el-Ghorfa Altogariya, Alexandria; tel. (3) 4837808; fax (3) 4837806; e-mail acc@alexcham.org; internet www.alexcham.org; f. 1922; Chair. AHMAD EL-WAKIL.

Cairo

American Chamber of Commerce in Egypt: 33 Sharia Sulayman Abaza, Cairo (Dokki) 12311; tel. (2) 33381050; fax (2) 33381060; e-mail info@amcham.org.eg; internet www.amcham.org.eg; f. 1981; Pres. OMAR MOHANNA; Exec. Dir HISHAM A. FAHMY.

Cairo Chamber of Commerce: 4 el-Falaki Sq., Cairo; tel. and fax (2) 27962091; f. 1913; Pres. MAHMOUD EL-ARABY; Sec.-Gen. MOSTAFA ZAKI TAHA.

In addition, there are 24 local chambers of commerce.

EMPLOYERS' ORGANIZATION

Federation of Egyptian Industries: 1195 Corniche el-Nil, Ramlet Boulal, Cairo; and 65 Gamal Abd al-Nasir Ave, Alexandria; tel. (2) 25796950; fax (2) 25796953 (Cairo); tel. and fax (3) 34916121 (Alexandria); e-mail info@fei.org.eg; internet www.fei.org.eg; f. 1922; Chair. GALAL ABD AL-MAKSOOD EL-ZORBA.

STATE HYDROCARBONS COMPANIES

Egyptian General Petroleum Corpn (EGPC): POB 2130, 4th Sector, Sharia Palestine, New Maadi, Cairo; tel. (2) 7065358; fax (2) 7028813; e-mail info@egpc.com.eg; state supervisory authority generally concerned with the planning of policies relating to petroleum activities in Egypt with the object of securing the devt of the petroleum industry and ensuring its effective administration; Chair. Eng. ABDALLAH GHORAB.

Arab Petroleum Pipelines Co (SUMED): POB 158, el-Saray, 431 el-Geish Ave, Louran, Alexandria; tel. (3) 5835152; fax (3) 5831295; internet www.sumed.org; f. 1974; EGPC has 50% interest, Saudi Arabian Oil Co 15%, Int. Petroleum Investment Co (United Arab Emirates) 15%, Kuwait Real Estate Investment Consortium 14.22%, Qatar Petroleum 5%, other Kuwaiti cos 0.78%; Suez–Mediterranean crude oil transportation pipeline (capacity: 117m. metric tons per year) and petroleum terminal operators; Chair. and Man. Dir Eng. SHAMEL HAMDI.

Belayim Petroleum Co (PETROBEL): POB 7074, Sharia el-Mokhayam, Cairo (Nasr City); tel. (2) 2621738; fax (2) 2609792; f. 1977; capital equally shared between EGPC and Int. Egyptian Oil Co, which is a subsidiary of Eni of Italy; petroleum and gas exploration, drilling and production; Chair. and Man. Dir MEDHAT EL-SAYED.

Egyptian Natural Gas Co (GASCO): Ring Rd, Exit 12, Sharia el-Tesien, 5th Settlement, Cairo; tel. (2) 6171911; fax (2) 6172824; e-mail gassupplyaffairs@gasco.com.eg; internet www.gasco.com.eg; f. 1997; 70% owned by EGPC, 15% by Petroleum Projects and Technical Consultations Co (PETROJET), 15% by Egypt Gas; transmission and processing of natural gas; operation of the national gas distribution network; Chair. and Man. Dir Eng. YAHIA AL-RIDI.

General Petroleum Co (GPC): POB 743, 8 Sharia Dr Moustafa Abou Zahra, Cairo (Nasr City); tel. (2) 4030975; fax (2) 4037602; f. 1957; wholly owned subsidiary of EGPC; operates mainly in Eastern Desert; Chair. HUSSEIN KAMAL.

Gulf of Suez Petroleum Co (GUPCO): POB 2400, 4th Sector, Sharia Palestine, New Maadi, Cairo 11511; tel. (2) 3520985; fax (2) 3531286; f. 1965; jt venture between EGPC and BP Egypt (United Kingdom/USA); developed the el-Morgan oilfield in the Gulf of Suez, also holds other exploration concessions in the Gulf of Suez and the Western Desert; Chair. Eng. MUHAMMAD ABOUL WAFA; Man. Dir L. D. MCVAY.

Middle East Oil Refinery (MIDOR): POB 2233, 22 Sharia el-Badeya, Cairo (Heliopolis) 11361; tel. (2) 24195501; fax (2) 24145936; e-mail info@midor.com.eg; internet www.midor.com.eg; f. 1994; 78% owned by EGPC, 10% by Engineering for the Petroleum and Process Industries (Enppi), 10% by Petroleum Projects and Technical Consultations Co (PETROJET), 2% by Suez Canal Bank; operation of oil-refining facilities at Ameriya, Alexandria; capacity 100,000 b/d; Chair. and CEO MEDHAT YOUSUF MAHMOUD.

Western Desert Petroleum Co (WEPCO): POB 412, Borg el-Thagr Bldg, Sharia Safia Zagloul, Alexandria; tel. (3) 4928710; fax (3) 4934016; f. 1967 as partnership between EGPC (50% interest) and Phillips Petroleum (35%) and later Hispanoil (15%); developed Alamein, Yidma and Umbarka fields in the Western Desert and later Abu Qir offshore gasfield in 1978, followed by NAF gasfield in 1987; Chair. MUHAMMAD MOHI EL-DIN BAHGAT.

Egyptian Natural Gas Holding Co (EGAS): POB 8064, 85C Sharia Nasr, 11371 Cairo (Nasr City); tel. (2) 24055845; fax (2) 24055876; e-mail egas@egas.com.eg; internet www.egas.com.eg; f. 2001 as part of a restructuring of the natural gas sector; strategic planning and promotion of investment in the natural gas industry; Chair. (vacant).

UTILITIES

Electricity

In 1998 seven new electricity generation and distribution companies were created, under the direct ownership of the Egyptian Electricity Authority (EEA). In 2000 the EEA was restructured into a holding company (the Egyptian Electricity Holding Co—see below) controlling five generation and seven distribution companies. A specialized grid company was to manage electricity transmission. The Government commenced partial privatizations of the generation and distribution companies in 2001–02, while retaining control of the hydroelectric generation and grid management companies. In 2006 the Ministry of Electricity and Energy announced a five-year plan to add 7,800 MW of capacity to the national grid by 2012. Nine electricity distribution companies, six generation companies and a transmission company were administered by the Egyptian Electricity Holding Co in 2008.

Egyptian Electricity Holding Co: Sharia Ramses, Cairo (Nasr City); tel. (2) 24030681; fax (2) 24031871; e-mail info@egelec.com; internet www.egelec.com; fmrly Egyptian Electricity Authority; renamed as above 2000; Chair. MUHAMMAD MUHAMMAD AWAD.

Gas

Egypt Gas: Corniche el-Nil, Warak-Imbaba, Cairo; tel. and fax (2) 5408882; e-mail info@egyptgas.com.eg; internet www.egyptgas.com.eg; f. 1983; Chair. and Man. Dir NABIL HASHEM.

Water

Holding Co for Water and Wastewater: Corniche el-Nil, Cairo; tel. (2) 24583590; fax (2) 24583884; e-mail hcww@hcww.com.eg; internet www.hcww.com.eg; f. 2004; operation, maintenance and devt of water and wastewater facilities; oversees the operations of 20 affiliated regional water cos; Chair. Dr ABD EL-KAWI KHALIFA.

National Organization for Potable Water and Sanitary Drainage (NOPWASD): 6th Floor, Mogamma Bldg, el-Tahrir Sq., Cairo; tel. (2) 3557664; fax (2) 3562869; f. 1981; water and sewerage authority; Chair. MUHAMMAD KHALED MOUSTAFA.

TRADE UNIONS

The Egyptian Trade Union Federation, which had been closely affiliated with the National Democratic Party of former President Muhammad Hosni Mubarak, was dissolved in August 2011.

Transport

RAILWAYS

The area of the Nile Delta is well served by railways. Lines also run from Cairo southward along the Nile to Aswan, and westward along the coast to Salloum. As part of an integrated transport strategy being developed by the Government, up to US $1,500m. was allocated for the upgrading of Egypt's ageing railway infrastructure from 2007. A feasibility study into construction of a high-speed rail connection between Cairo and Alexandria was initiated in mid-2009.

Egyptian National Railways: Station Bldg, Midan Ramses, Cairo 11794; tel. (2) 5751000; fax (2) 5740000; e-mail enr@egyptrail.gov.eg; internet www.egyptrail.gov.eg; f. 1852; length over 5,000 km; 42 km electrified; a 346-km line to carry phosphate and iron ore from the Bahariya mines, in the Western Desert, to the Helwan iron and steel works in south Cairo, was opened in 1973, and the Qena–Safaga line (length 223 km) came into operation in 1989; Chair. MUSTAFA QENAWI.

Alexandria Passenger Transport Authority: POB 466, Aflaton, el-Shatby, Alexandria 21111; tel. (3) 5975223; fax (3) 5971187; e-mail apta@link.net; internet www.alexapta.org; f. 1860; controls City Tramways (28 km), Ramleh Electric Railway (16 km), suburban buses and minibuses (1,688 km); 119 tram cars, 519 suburban buses and minibuses; 362 suburban buses and minibuses from private sector; Chair. and Tech. Dir Eng. SHERINE KASSEM.

Cairo Metro: National Authority for Tunnels, POB 466, Ramses Bldg, Midan Ramses, Cairo 11794; tel. (2) 5742968; fax (2) 5742950;

e-mail chairman@nat.org.eg; internet www.nat.org.eg; construction of the first electrified, 1,435-mm gauge underground transport system in Africa and the Middle East began in Cairo in 1982; Line 1, which opened to the public in 1987, has a total of 35 stations (5 underground), connects el-Marg el-Gedida with Helwan and is 44 km long with a 4.7-km tunnel beneath central Cairo; Line 2 links Shoubra el-Kheima with Giza, at el-Monib station, totalling 21.6 km (13 km in tunnel), and with 20 stations (12 underground), two of which interconnect with Line 1; the first section of Line 3, which will connect Imbaba and Mohandessin with Cairo International Airport and will total 34.2 km (30.3 km in tunnel) with 29 stations (27 underground), opened in early 2012, with completion of the line scheduled for 2013; Chair. Eng. ATTA A. R. EL-SHERBINY.

Cairo Transport Authority: Sharia Ramses, el-Gabal el-Ahmar, Cairo (Nasr City); tel. (2) 6845712; fax (2) 8654858; owned by the Governorate of Cairo; provider of public transport services in Greater Cairo, incl. tram, surface metro, bus and ferry services; rail system length 78 km (electrified); gauge 1,000 mm; operates 16 tram routes and 24 km of light railway; 720 cars; Chair. SALAH FARAG.

ROADS

The estimated total length of the road network in 2008 was 104,918 km, of which 86.9% was paved. There are good metalled main roads as follows: Cairo–Alexandria (desert road); Cairo–Banha–Tanta–Damanhour–Alexandria; Cairo–Suez (desert road); Cairo–Ismailia–Port Said or Suez; and Cairo–Fayoum (desert road). The Ahmad Hamdi road tunnel (1.64 km) beneath the Suez Canal was opened in 1980. A second bridge over the Suez Canal was completed in 2001. A project to develop the Cairo–Alexandria highway into a 231-km motorway was under way in 2012. Other road projects at the planning or construction stage in 2012 included the Mediterranean coastal highway, linking Port Said with Mersa Matruh, and the Shoubra el-Kheima–Banha and Kafr el-Zayat–Alexandria highways.

General Authority for Roads, Bridges and Land Transport—Ministry of Transport (GARBLT): 105 Sharia Qasr el-Eini, Cairo; tel. (2) 7957429; fax (2) 7950591; e-mail garblt@idsc.gov.eg; Chair. Eng. TAREK EL-ATTAR.

SHIPPING

Egypt's principal ports are Alexandria, Port Said and Suez. A port constructed at a cost of £E315m., and designed to handle up to 16m. metric tons of cargo per year in its first stage of development, was opened at Damietta in 1986. By mid-2008 handling capacity at Damietta had increased to 19.7m. tons. Egypt's first privately operated port was opened in 2002 at Ain Sokhna on the Red Sea coast, near the southern entrance of the Suez Canal. Sokhna's capacity was projected to increase from 6m. tons in 2005 to 90m. tons by 2020. The modernization of the quays at Alexandria port and the construction of two new container terminals at the adjacent Dakahlia port were completed during the first half of 2007. The first phase of a major expansion of the Suez Canal Container Terminal at Port Said, which envisaged a new container terminal with a total capacity of 5.4m. 20-foot equivalent units per year, was inaugurated in August 2010; the second phase was expected to be completed in 2012.

Port and Regulatory Authorities

Maritime Transport Sector: Ministry of Transport, 4 Sharia Ptolemy, Bab Sharqi, 21514 Alexandria; tel. (3) 4869836; fax (3) 4874674; e-mail mmt@idsc.net.eg; internet www.mts.gov.eg; supervision of the maritime sector; Dir-Gen. Rear-Adm. MUHAMMAD ABD AL-MENEM.

Alexandria Port Authority: 106 Sharia el-Hourriya, Alexandria 26514; tel. (3) 4800359; fax (3) 4807098; e-mail info@apa.gov.eg; internet www.apa.gov.eg; f. 1966; management of Alexandria and Dakahlia ports; Chair. Rear-Adm. AL-SAYED HAMAD SHAKER HEDAYA; Vice-Chair. Rear-Adm. ADEL YASSIN HAMAD.

Damietta Port Authority: POB 13, Damietta; tel. (57) 2290006; fax (57) 2290930; e-mail chairman@damietta-port.gov.eg; internet www.damietta-port.gov.eg; Chair. Adm. IBRAHIM FLAIFEL.

Port Said Port Authority: Intersection Sharia Moustafa Kamel and Sharia Azmy, Port Said; tel. (66) 3348270; fax (66) 3348262; e-mail info@psdports.org; internet www.psdports.org; Chair. Adm. IBRAHIM MUHAMMAD SADEK.

Red Sea Ports Authority: POB 1, Port Tawfik, Suez; tel. (62) 3190731; fax (62) 3191117; e-mail rspsite@emdb.gov.eg; responsible for ports incl. Suez, Sokhna and Hurghada; Chair. Gen. MUHAMMAD ABD EL-KADER.

Principal Shipping Companies

Arab Maritime Petroleum Transport Co (AMPTC): POB 143, 9th Floor, Nile Tower Bldg, 21 Sharia Giza, 12211 Giza; tel. (2) 35701311; fax (2) 33378080; e-mail amptc.cairo@amptc.net; internet www.amptc.net; f. 1973; affiliated to the Org. of Arab Petroleum Exporting Countries (OAPEC); 11 vessels; Gen. Man. SULAYMAN AL-BASSAM.

Canal Shipping Agencies Co: 26 Sharia Palestine, Port Said; tel. (66) 3227500; fax (66) 3239896; e-mail csaagencies@canalshipping.net; internet www.canalshipping.net; f. 1965; shipping agency, cargo and forwarding services; affiliated cos: Assuit Shipping Agency, Aswan Shipping Agency, Damanhour Shipping Agency, El-Menia Shipping Agency; Chair. FOUAD EL-SAYED EL-MULLA.

Egyptian Navigation Co (ENC): 2 el-Nasr St, el-Gomrok, Alexandria; tel. (3) 4800050; fax (3) 4871345; e-mail enc@dataxprs.com.eg; internet www.enc.com.eg; f. 1961; owners and operators of Egypt's mercantile marine; international trade transportation; 12 vessels; Chair. and Man. Dir AMR GAMAL EL-DIN ROUSHDY.

Holding Co for Maritime and Land Transport: POB 3005, Alexandria; tel. (3) 4865547; fax (3) 4872647; e-mail holding@hcmlt.com; internet www.hcmlt.gov.eg; govt-owned; 17 affiliated cos, incl. General Co for River Nile Transportation, Port Said Container and Cargo Handling Co, General Egyptian Warehouses Co; Chair. Adm. MUHAMMAD YOUSUF.

International Maritime Services Co: 20 Sharia Salah Salem, Alexandria; tel. (3) 4840817; fax (3) 4869177; e-mail agency@imsalex.com; internet www.imsalex.com; f. 1986; shipping agency, freight-forwarding, transshipment contractor, marine surveyor; subsidiary: Egyptian Register of Shipping Co; Chair. Capt. MONTASSER EL-SOKKARY.

National Navigation Co: 4 Sharia El-Hegaz, Cairo (Heliopolis); tel. (2) 24525575; fax (2) 24526171; e-mail nnc@nnc.com.eg; internet www.nnc.com.eg; f. 1981; specializes in bulk cargoes; operates passenger services between Egypt and Saudi Arabia; 18 vessels; Chair. and Man. Dir TAMER ABD EL-ALIM.

Pan-Arab Shipping Co: POB 39, 404 ave el-Hourriya, Rushdi, Alexandria; tel. (3) 5468835; fax (3) 5469533; internet www.pan-arab.org; f. 1974; Arab League Co; bulk handling, forwarding and warehousing services; 5 vessels; Chair. Adm. MUHAMMAD SHERIF EL-SADEK; Gen. Man. Capt. MAMDOUH EL-GUINDY.

Red Sea Navigation Co: 10 Gowhar el-Khaled St, Port Tawfik, Suez; tel. (62) 3196971; fax (62) 9136915; e-mail suez@rdnav.com; internet www.rdnav.com; f. 1986; operates a fleet of eight cargo vessels; shipping agency, Suez Canal transit and stevedoring; Chair. ABD EL-MAJID MATAR.

THE SUEZ CANAL

In 2010 a total of 17,993 vessels, with a net displacement of 846.4m. tons, used the Suez Canal, linking the Mediterranean and Red Seas.

Length of canal: 190 km; maximum permissible draught: 20.73 m (68 ft); breadth of canal at water level and breadth between buoys defining the navigable channel at −11 m: 365 m and 225 m, respectively, in the northern section, and 305 m and 205 m in the southern section.

Suez Canal Authority (Hay'at Canal al-Suways): Irshad Bldg, Ismailia; Cairo Office: 6 Sharia Lazoughli, Cairo (Garden City); tel. (64) 3392010; fax (64) 3392834; e-mail info@suezcanal.gov.eg; internet www.suezcanal.gov.eg; f. 1956; govt-owned; Chair. and CEO Adm. AHMAD ALI FADEL.

Suez Canal Container Terminal: POB 247, Port Said; tel. (66) 3254960; fax (66) 3254970; e-mail scct@scctportsaid.com; internet www.scctportsaid.com; f. 2000, with 30-year concession to operate the East Port Said container terminal; Man. Dir KLAUS HOLM LAURSEN.

CIVIL AVIATION

The main international airports are at Cairo (located at Heliopolis, 23 km from the centre of the city), Sharm el-Sheikh and Hurghada. A major programme of expansion at Cairo International Airport commenced in 2004: a third terminal was formally inaugurated in December 2008 and became fully operational in June 2009, while a fourth runway was completed in October 2010. Meanwhile, Cairo's Terminal Two was closed in April 2010 in preparation for the commencement of a US $400m. expansion project to increase the terminal's annual capacity to 7.5m. passengers; construction was expected to be completed by 2013. Construction work on a new international airport at Borg el-Arab (40 km south-west of Alexandria) was inaugurated in November 2010. The completion of a second terminal at Sharm el-Sheikh airport in 2007 increased capacity from 3m. to 7.5m. passengers per year; construction of a third terminal, which would increase annual passenger-handling capacity to 15m., was scheduled for completion in 2012.

EgyptAir: Administration Complex, Cairo International Airport, Cairo (Heliopolis); tel. (2) 22674700; fax (2) 22663773; e-mail callcenter@egyptair.com; internet www.egyptair.com.eg; f. 1932 as Misr Airwork; known as United Arab Airlines 1960–71; restructured as a holding co with nine subsidiaries 2002; operates internal services in Egypt and external services throughout the Middle East, Far East, Africa, Europe and the USA; Chair. and CEO HUSSEIN

MASSOUD (EgyptAir Holding Co); Chair. and CEO Capt. ALAA ASHOUR (EgyptAir Airlines).

Egyptian Civil Aviation Authority: ECAA Complex, Sharia Airport, Cairo 11776; tel. (2) 2677610; fax (2) 2470351; e-mail info@civilaviation.gov.eg; internet www.civilaviation.gov.eg; f. 2000; Pres. Capt. SAMEH EL-HEFNI.

Egyptian Holding Co for Airports and Air Navigation (EHCAAN): EHCAAN Bldg, Airport Rd, Cairo; tel. (2) 6352442; fax (2) 2663440; e-mail info@ehcaan.com; internet www.ehcaan.com; f. 2001; responsible for management and devt of all Egyptian airports; Chair. MUHAMMAD FATHALLAH REFAAT.

Cairo Airport Company: Cairo International Airport, 11776 Cairo (Heliopolis); tel. (2) 2474245; fax (2) 2432522; e-mail cac@cairo-airport.com; internet www.cairo-airport.com; under management of Egyptian Holding Co since 2003; Chair. Dr AHMAD HAFIZ; Exec. Dir PETER DIENSTBACH.

Egyptian Airports Co: Cairo; tel. (2) 22739417; fax (2) 22739416; e-mail info@eac-airports.com; internet www.eac-airports.com; f. 2001; management and devt of 19 regional airports; Chair. and Man. Dir YUSRI GAMAL EL-DIN.

Tourism

Tourism is currently Egypt's second largest source of revenue, generating an estimated US $12,528m. (excluding passenger transport) in 2010. The industry was adversely affected in the mid-1990s by the campaign of violence by militant Islamists; although some recovery in tourist numbers was recorded by the end of the decade, the sector was again affected by the crisis in Israeli–Palestinian relations from late 2000, the repercussions of the suicide attacks on the USA in September 2001 and the US-led intervention in Iraq in early 2003. Nevertheless, 8.1m. tourists visited Egypt in 2004 (compared with 5.2m. in 2002) and, despite further terrorist attacks in the Sinai region during 2004–06, the number of tourists visiting the country increased significantly in the following years. However, the industry was severely affected by the political unrest of 2011; according to official estimates, 9.8m. tourists visited Egypt in that year, compared with 14.1m. in 2010.

Egyptian Tourist Authority: Misr Travel Tower, 32 Sharia Emtidad Ramses, Abbassia Sq., Cairo; tel. (2) 2854509; fax (2) 2854363; e-mail user@egypt.travel; internet www.egypt.travel; f. 1965; brs at Alexandria, Port Said, Suez, Luxor and Aswan; Chair. AMR EL-EZABI.

Egyptian General Co for Tourism and Hotels (EGOTH): 4 Sharia Latin America, 11519 Cairo (Garden City); tel. (2) 27942914; fax (2) 27943531; e-mail info@egoth.com.eg; internet www.egoth.com.eg; f. 1961; affiliated to the Holding Co for Tourism, Hotels and Cinema; Chair. and Man. Dir NABIL SELIM.

Defence

Commander-in-Chief of the Armed Forces: Field Marshal MUHAMMAD HUSSEIN TANTAWI.

Chief of Staff of the Armed Forces: Lt-Gen. SAMI HAFEZ ENAN.

Commander of the Air Force: Air Marshal REDA MAHMOUD HAFEZ MUHAMMAD.

Commander of Air Defence Forces: Maj.-Gen. ABD AL-AZIZ MUHAMMAD SEIF EL-DIN.

Commander-in-Chief of the Navy: Vice-Adm. MOHAB MAMISH.

Budgeted Defence Expenditure (2012): £E25,300m.

Military service: one–three years, selective.

Total armed forces (as assessed at November 2011): 438,500: army 310,000; air defence command 80,000; navy 18,500 (10,000 conscripts); air force 30,000 (10,000 conscripts). Reserves 479,000.

Paramilitary Forces (as assessed at November 2011): est. 397,000 (Central Security Forces 325,000; National Guard 60,000 and Border Guard 12,000).

Education

Education is compulsory for eight years between six and 14 years of age. Primary education, beginning at six years of age, lasts for five years. Secondary education, beginning at 11 years of age, lasts for a further six years, comprising two cycles (the first being preparatory) of three years each. In 2008/09, according to UNESCO estimates, primary enrolment included an estimated 93% of children in the relevant age-group, while the comparable ratio for secondary enrolment was estimated at 65%. In 2007/08 there were an estimated 2,488,434 students enrolled at higher education institutions. The Al-Azhar University and its various preparatory and associated institutes provide instruction and training in several disciplines, with emphasis on adherence to Islamic principles and teachings. Education is free at all levels. In 2008/09 a total of £E39,880m. (some 11.2% of total expenditure) was allocated to education by the central Government.

EL SALVADOR

Introductory Survey

LOCATION, CLIMATE, LANGUAGE, RELIGION, FLAG, CAPITAL

The Republic of El Salvador lies on the Pacific coast of Central America. It is bounded by Guatemala to the west and by Honduras to the north and east. The climate varies from tropical on the coastal plain to temperate in the uplands. The language is Spanish. About 76% of the population are Roman Catholics, and other Christian churches are represented. The civil flag (proportions 2 by 3) consists of three equal horizontal stripes, of blue, over white, over blue. The state flag differs by the addition, in the centre of the white stripe, of the national coat of arms. The capital is San Salvador.

CONTEMPORARY POLITICAL HISTORY

Historical Context

El Salvador was ruled by Spain until 1821, and became independent in 1839. Since then the country's history has been one of frequent coups and outbursts of political violence. Gen. Maximiliano Hernández Martínez became President in 1931, and ruthlessly suppressed a peasant uprising, with an alleged 30,000 killings (including that of Farabundo Martí, the leader of the rebel peasants), in 1932. Hernández was deposed in 1944, and the next elected President, Gen. Salvador Castañeda Castro, was overthrown in 1948. His successor, Lt-Col Oscar Osorio (1950–56), relinquished power to Lt-Col José María Lemus, who was replaced by a military junta in 1960, which was itself supplanted by another junta in 1961. Under this Junta, the conservative Partido de Conciliación Nacional (PCN) was established and won all 54 seats in elections to the Asamblea Legislativa (Legislative Assembly). Lt-Col Julio Adalberto Rivera, was elected unopposed to the presidency in 1962. He was succeeded by Gen. Fidel Sánchez Hernández in 1967.

Domestic Political Affairs

In the 1972 presidential election Col Arturo Armando Molina Barraza, candidate of the ruling PCN, was elected, despite allegations of massive electoral fraud. Similar allegations were made during the 1977 presidential election, after which the PCN candidate, Gen. Carlos Humberto Romero Mena, took office.

Reports of violations of human rights by the Government were widespread. The polarization of left and right after 1972 was characterized by an increase in guerrilla activity. In 1979 President Romero was overthrown and replaced by a Junta of civilians and army officers. The Junta, which promised to install a democratic system and to organize elections, declared a political amnesty and invited participation from the guerrilla groups, but violence continued between government troops and guerrilla forces, and elections were postponed. In January 1980 an ultimatum from progressive members of the Government resulted in the formation of a new Government, a coalition of military officers and the Partido Demócrata Cristiano (PDC). In March the country moved closer to full-scale civil war following the assassination of the Roman Catholic Archbishop of San Salvador, Oscar Romero, an outspoken supporter of human rights.

In December 1980 José Napoleón Duarte, a member of the Junta, was sworn in as President. In 1981 the guerrillas launched their 'final offensive' and, after initial gains, the opposition front, Frente Democrático Revolucionario—FDR (allied with the guerrilla front, the Frente Farabundo Martí para la Liberación Nacional—FMLN), proposed negotiations with the USA. The US authorities referred them to the Salvadorean Government, which refused to recognize the FDR while it was linked with the guerrillas. The USA affirmed its support for the Duarte Government and provided civilian and military aid. During 1981 the guerrilla forces unified and strengthened their control over the north and east of the country. Attacks on economic targets continued, while the army retaliated by acting indiscriminately against the local population in guerrilla-controlled areas. By December there were an estimated 300,000 Salvadorean refugees, many of whom had fled to neighbouring countries.

At elections to a National Constituent Assembly in March 1982 the PDC failed to win an absolute majority against the five right-wing parties, which formed a Government of National Unity. Major Roberto D'Aubuisson Arrieta, leader of the extreme right-wing Alianza Republicana Nacionalista (ARENA), became President of the National Constituent Assembly. In April a political independent, Alvaro Magaña Borja, was elected interim President. However, the Assembly voted to award itself considerable power over the President.

Following a period of intense activity by 'death squads' in 1983, the US Government urged the removal of several high-level officials. In 1984, following a number of strategic territorial advances, the FDR-FMLN proposed the formation of a broadly based provisional government, as part of a peace plan without preconditions. The plan was rejected by the Government. The guerrillas refused to participate in the 1984 presidential election. As no candidate emerged with a clear majority, a second round of voting was held, when the PDC's José Napoleón Duarte emerged victorious.

Duarte instituted a purge of the armed forces and the disbanding of the notorious Treasury Police. Both the FDR-FMLN and the President expressed their willingness to commence peace negotiations, and the Government opened discussions with guerrilla leaders in Chalatenango in October 1984. A second round of negotiations ended amid accusations of intransigence from both sides. The PDC won a clear majority in the general election of March 1985.

In 1987 the Salvadorean Government's participation in a peace plan for Central America, which was signed in August in Guatemala City, encouraged hopes that a peaceful solution could be found to the conflict. Agreement was reached in October between the Government and the FDR-FMLN on the formation of two committees to study the possibility of a cease-fire and an amnesty. However, no long-term cessation of hostilities was maintained by either side. The political situation deteriorated further in late 1987, following President Duarte's public denunciation of D'Aubuisson's complicity in the murder of Archbishop Romero in 1980. Furthermore, in 1988 there were increasing reports of the resurgence of 'death squads', and it was suggested that abuses of human rights were rapidly returning to the level reached at the beginning of the internal conflict.

The peace process

By the end of 1988 it was estimated that as many as 70,000 Salvadoreans had died in the course of the civil war, while the US Administration had provided some US $3,000m. in aid to the Government. Moreover, by early 1989 many areas appeared to be without government, following the resignations of some 75 mayors, following death threats by the FMLN. In January, however, radical new peace proposals were announced by the FMLN, which, for the first time, expressed its willingness to participate in the electoral process. However, cease-fire negotiations failed to produce agreement. The FMLN advocated a boycott of the March presidential election, and intensified its campaign of violence. The ballot resulted in victory for the ARENA candidate, Alfredo Cristiani Burkard.

In August 1989 the Heads of State of five Central American countries signed an agreement in Tela, Honduras. The accord included an appeal to the FMLN to abandon its military campaign and to initiate dialogue with the Salvadorean Government. In November the UN Security Council authorized the creation of the UN Observer Group for Central America (ONUCA), a multinational military force, to monitor developments in the region. In the same month the FMLN launched a military offensive, resulting in the fiercest fighting for nine years. The Government declared a state of siege, and stability was further undermined when, on 16 November, gunmen murdered the head of a San Salvador Jesuit university and five other Jesuit priests, along with the Jesuits' housekeeper and her daughter. In January 1990, however, the FMLN announced that it would accept an offer to attend peace talks arranged by the UN Secretary-General, Javier Pérez de Cuéllar. In March President Cristiani announced that he was willing to offer a comprehensive amnesty, territorial concessions and the opportunity to participate fully in political processes to members of the FMLN, as part of a broad-based peace proposal. However, hopes for the successful negotiation of a peaceful settlement proved fruitless.

Negotiations between the Government and the FMLN continued throughout 1991. In March a new initiative for the negotiation of a peace settlement was presented by the FMLN in Managua, Nicaragua. This new proposal dispensed with previous stipulations put forward by the guerrillas that military and constitutional reforms should be effected prior to any cease-fire. The constitutional requirement that amendments to the Constitution be ratified by two successive legislative assemblies lent impetus to negotiations. An agreement on human rights (including the creation of a three-member truth commission, to be appointed by the UN Secretary-General) and on judicial and electoral reform was reached, and was swiftly approved by the Asamblea. The working structure of a cease-fire and the detailed reform and purge of the armed forces were set aside for negotiation at a later date.

In May 1991 the UN Security Council voted to create an observer mission to El Salvador (ONUSAL), to be charged with the verification of accords reached between the Government and the FMLN, despite protests by right-wing groups. In August both sides attended discussions in New York, USA, where a new framework for peace was agreed. A National Commission for the Consolidation of Peace (COPAZ) was to be created, which would supervise the enforcement of guarantees for the political integration of the guerrillas. The FMLN also secured guaranteed territorial rights for peasants settled in guerrilla-controlled areas, and the participation of former FMLN members in a National Civilian Police (Policía Nacional Civil—PNC).

In December 1991 a new peace initiative was announced. Under the terms of the agreement, a formal cease-fire was to be implemented on 1 February 1992, under the supervision of some 1,000 UN personnel. The FMLN was to begin a process of disarmament, to be completed by 31 October. The success of the cease-fire agreement was expected to be dependent upon the adequate implementation, by the Government, of previously agreed reforms to the judiciary, the electoral system, guarantees of territorial rights, human rights, and guerrilla participation in civil defence, and of newly agreed reforms to the armed forces. On 16 January 1992, at Chapultepec Castle in Mexico City, Mexico, the formal peace accord was ratified. In San Salvador on 15 December (declared National Reconciliation Day) the conflict was formally concluded. On the same day the FMLN was officially registered and recognized as a legitimate political party.

The Truth Commission

In November 1992, in accordance with the terms of the December 1991 peace accord, the Comisión de la Verdad (Truth Commission) announced the names of more than 200 military personnel alleged to have participated in abuses of human rights during the civil war. The reluctance of the Government to remove those personnel threatened the further successful implementation of the peace process, and prompted the FMLN to delay the demobilization of its forces and the destruction of its remaining arsenals. The situation was exacerbated in March 1993 by the publication of the Commission's report, which attributed responsibility for the vast majority of the war's 75,000 fatalities to the counter-insurgency measures of the armed forces, including the systematic eradication of civilians thought to harbour left-wing sympathies. Some 400 murders were attributed to the FMLN. Among those accused of human rights atrocities was the late ARENA founder Roberto D'Aubuisson Arrieta, who was identified as the authority behind the murder of Archbishop Romero; also implicated were the Minister of Defence and Public Security, Gen. René Emilio Ponce, his deputy, Gen. Orlando Zepeda, and the former air force chief, Gen. Juan Rafael Bustillo, who were believed to have ordered the murder of the six Jesuits in 1989. (In 1991 Col Guillermo Benavides and an army lieutenant were found guilty of murder and sentenced to 30 years' imprisonment; they were controversially released after just two years, however, following the declaration of an amnesty by President Cristiani. In 2004 Captain Alvaro Rafael Saravia was found guilty of planning and facilitating the murder of Archbishop Romero in a civil case brought in a US court. He was ordered, *in absentia*, to pay US $2.5m. in compensation and $7.5m. in punitive damages.) The report recommended that the judiciary should be reorganized, and that all individuals identified by the report should be permanently excluded from all institutions of national defence and public security, and should be barred from holding public office for a period of 10 years.

Representatives of the Government and the armed forces challenged the legal validity of the Commission's report, despite the UN's insistence that its recommendations were mandatory under the terms of the peace accord. Nevertheless, the strength of ARENA's representation in the Asamblea overcame opposition from the PDC, the Convergencia Democrática (CD, a left-wing alliance comprising two of the leading groups within the FDR-FMLN and the Partido Social Demócrata) and the Movimiento Nacional Revolucionario (MNR), and later in March 1993 secured the approval of an amnesty law to extend to all political crimes committed before 1992, prompting widespread public outrage. In June the Government announced the compulsory retirement of several veteran military officers, including Gen. Ponce, although their immunity from prosecution was still guaranteed.

The findings of the Truth Commission—together with declassified documents relating to the Administrations of former US Presidents Ronald Reagan and George Bush, Sr—suggested that detailed knowledge of abuses of human rights was suppressed by US officials in order to continue to secure congressional funding for the Government in El Salvador in the 1980s. Evidence also emerged that US military training had been provided, in at least one instance, for an El Salvadorean 'death squad'.

The continuing dominance of ARENA

Presidential and legislative elections took place in 1994. ARENA's presidential candidate, Armando Calderón Sol, emerged victorious following two rounds of voting. ARENA candidates also achieved considerable success in the legislative elections. FMLN candidates were also considered to have performed well in the party's first electoral contest, winning 21 seats in the Asamblea.

Meanwhile, serious divisions emerged within the FMLN during 1994, and in December two constituent parties, the Resistencia Nacional (RN) and the Expresión Renovadora del Pueblo (ERP—formerly the Fuerzas Armadas de la Resistencia Nacional and the Ejército Revolucionario Popular guerrilla groups, respectively) announced their withdrawal from the party. In 1995 the Secretary-General of the ERP, Joaquín Villalobos, announced the formation of a new centre-left political force, the Partido Demócrata (PD), comprising the ERP, the RN, the MNR and a dissident faction of the PDC.

In May 1994 the UN Security Council voted to extend the ONUSAL mandate for a further six months; two further extensions to the mandate were subsequently approved. A small contingent of UN observers, MINUSAL, was mandated to remain in El Salvador until April 1996, the revised deadline for the fulfilment of the outstanding terms of the peace accord. By this date, however, full implementation of those terms of the accord relating to land allocation for refugees and former combatants, and to the reform of the judiciary and the electoral code, had yet to be achieved. A reduced MINUSAL contingent was further mandated to oversee Government efforts to fulfil the outstanding terms of the agreement, and the mission was formally terminated on 31 December.

The results of the congressional and municipal elections of 1997 demonstrated a significant increase in support for the FMLN and a considerable erosion of ARENA's predominance, with the party securing 29 seats in the Asamblea, just one more than the FMLN. Nevertheless, the presidential election of 1999 was won by Francisco Flores Pérez, the candidate of ARENA. The Government was subsequently embarrassed by allegations that foreign funds, donated for disaster relief following the impact of Hurricane Mitch in 1998, had been diverted by ARENA to former paramilitaries in an attempt to buy votes for Flores.

Dissatisfaction with the ARENA Government was demonstrated in the results of the legislative elections of March 2000, in which the FMLN became the largest single party in the Asamblea. Nevertheless, during 2001 internal divisions deepened between the more orthodox and the reformist elements of the FMLN, culminating in the expulsion of the reformist leader Facundo Guardado. Salvador Sánchez Cerén, from the party's orthodox wing, was elected leader. Following Sánchez's election, in January 2002 six reformist FMLN deputies left the party, thus reducing the FMLN's legislative representation. ARENA became the largest parliamentary bloc.

In a general election held in March 2003 the FMLN garnered 31 seats in the Asamblea Legislativa. ARENA secured an unexpectedly low 27 seats. Following the election, President Flores announced an initiative, named 'Mano Dura' (Firm Hand), to combat the rising violent crime in the country, particularly that attributed to street gangs, or *maras*.

A presidential election was held in March 2004. In spite of the party's poor electoral performance in the previous year, the ARENA candidate, businessman Elías Antonio (Tony) Saca, secured an overwhelming victory. Upon taking office President Saca undertook to reduce gang-related crime. The 'Súper Mano Dura' initiative, launched in September as an extension of President Flores's 'Mano Dura' campaign (which the Supreme Court had ruled unconstitutional), gained widespread support. The renewed campaign included proposals to appoint prosecutors dedicated to bringing charges against members of the *maras* and to rehabilitate gang members. By mid-2005 an estimated 9,000 gang members had been arrested, of whom some 4,000 remained imprisoned. In May Saca introduced extensive house-to-house searches with the stated aims of confiscating illegal firearms and drugs and arresting known murderers; the preventive searches were widely criticized as unconstitutional. In July Saca announced the creation of a new task force, the Fuerza de Tarea Conjunta, intended to reinforce the police presence in the five departments with the highest rates of violent crime.

The FMLN increased its parliamentary representation to 32 seats in the general election of March 2006, although ARENA still held the largest number of seats, 34. The right-wing parties secured a working majority in the Asamblea, although the FMLN regained its power to veto proposals that required a two-thirds' majority. The FMLN also won the politically important mayoralty of San Salvador.

Domestic security remained a priority for the Saca Government. In June 2006 a new strategy to combat violent crime was proposed. The so-called Plan Maestro de Seguridad (Security Master Plan) was designed to increase the judicial conviction rate by improving the quality of evidence submitted by the police to public prosecutors. Gangs were to be considered as organized crime syndicates. The Government in July also overcame opposition from the FMLN to secure legislative approval of reforms to restrict the legal possession of firearms. In November President Saca announced that the Fuerza de Tarea Conjunta and the PNC were each to be strengthened by an additional 2,000 recruits. In 2007 the Government announced a joint initiative with the US Department of State to combat the *maras*: the US Federal Bureau of Intelligence (FBI) was to assist with the establishment of a Transnational Anti-Gang unit to identify and prosecute gang members.

The FMLN in power

In legislative elections held on 18 January 2009 ARENA lost two seats in congress, reducing its representation to 32 seats, while the FMLN secured 35 seats, an increase of three. The PCN and PDC took 11 and five seats, respectively. Shortly after the legislative elections, both the PDC and the PCN announced their withdrawal from the March presidential election. With only the FMLN and ARENA candidates remaining in the presidential contest, it was confirmed in February that the election on 15 March would not go to a second round of voting. An estimated 60% of the electorate participated in the ballot, in which Carlos Mauricio Funes Cartagena, from the moderate wing of the FMLN, secured 51.3% and Rodrigo Avila Avilez, a former Director-General of the national police force, representing ARENA, attracted 48.7% of votes, marking the first time that ARENA had lost control of the presidency since the end of the civil war in 1992.

Funes took office on 1 June 2009 and was immediately confronted with a hostile legislature. ARENA, the PCN and the PDC had formed an opposition coalition in May, allowing them to block Funes' proposed legislation. In July the new President was forced to compromise over the composition of the Supreme Court and the appointment of the Procurator-General, which preserved ARENA's domination of the judiciary, thereby undermining Funes' pledge to prosecute members of the previous administration for corruption. However, in a dramatic manifestation of the growing disharmony within ARENA, in October 12 deputies announced their withdrawal from the party and formed a new legislative bloc, the Gran Alianza por la Unidad Nacional (GANA). With the loss of its majority in the legislature, the right-wing coalition collapsed. The effects of this upheaval were observed in the following month when GANA, the PCN and the PDC voted with the FMLN to approve Funes' budget, which allocated additional funding for health and education, leaving ARENA politically isolated. Also approved with the help of the GANA deputies, in December, was a fiscal reform bill, intended to increase the low levels of tax collection. As an indication of the continuing discord within ARENA, former President Saca was expelled from the party in the same month; party officials blamed him for the defection of the 12 deputies and the party's lacklustre performance in the presidential election. (Saca was subsequently replaced as ARENA leader by former President Cristiani.)

Meanwhile, official crime figures released in mid-2009 indicated that extortion and murder were on the rise. Funes had espoused the benefits of focusing on the causes of crime, such as poverty and unemployment, but his security strategy, which involved the deployment of the army in high-crime areas to assist police operations, seemed to be a continuation of his right-wing predecessors' 'Mano Dura' campaigns and, although popular with the public, had little effect on crime.

Although Funes had taken advantage of ARENA's internal divisions, tensions within the FMLN also grew steadily throughout 2009. The party was still dominated by hard-liners from the civil war, such as Salvador Sánchez Cerén, the Vice-President. In November, during a visit to Venezuela, Sánchez declared his support for the socialism propounded by Venezuelan head of state Hugo Chávez, and criticized the USA; in December, while visiting Cuba, a country with which Funes had restored diplomatic relations in June, Sánchez proclaimed El Salvador's interest in joining the Venezuelan-led Bolivarian Alliance for the Americas (Alianza Bolivariana para las Américas—ALBA) grouping. Funes, a moderate, swiftly dismissed Sánchez's remarks and reaffirmed that there would be no radical left-wing shift in El Salvador, a stance that he had painstakingly maintained throughout the year in order to reassure the electorate and business interests. In a further challenge to Funes' authority, in January 2010 the Asamblea Legislativa adopted populist, FMLN-led legislation that removed telephone tariffs, undermining the President's efforts to develop a business environment attractive to investors.

In January 2010 Funes made the country's first official apology for the human rights violations perpetrated by the right-wing Governments that were in power throughout the civil war period. In a further unprecedented move, Funes issued a similar formal apology in March for the state's role in the murder of Archbishop Romero.

The continuing high levels of violent crime in the country—mainly blamed on the *maras*, but also related to a rise in vigilantism—prompted the Government to take further action in 2010. A new security strategy was announced in February to bolster the police force and increase co-operation with the military. Investment was directed towards upgrading police computer systems and purchasing new vehicles. Some 250 extra officers were also to be deployed. In the same month, the Asamblea adopted legislation permitting investigative teams to monitor telephone calls and increasing prison terms for juveniles. In May the Government revealed that further military troops would be deployed to assist in police operations and to maintain order in the country's gaols. However, armed attacks on two buses in the capital in June, thought to have been carried out by gang members, resulted in the deaths of 17 people. The brutality of the attacks provoked nation-wide outrage. Under intense pressure to address decisively the escalating crime problem, Funes submitted to the Asamblea a bill outlawing the *maras* and gang membership, which was approved in early September. However, the new law failed to establish the criteria for proving membership, and it was feared that the overcrowded prison system would not be able to cope with the expected upsurge in inmates. Shortly afterwards, in retaliation for the approval of the gang criminalization legislation, the major *maras* used the threat of violent reprisals to coerce bus operators throughout the country to observe a three-day strike, damaging the economy, generating transport chaos nation-wide and prompting the Government to deploy additional military troops onto the streets. None the less, Funes refused to soften his security strategy: a further anti-crime bill was adopted by the legislature in September, lengthening gaol sentences for weapons dealers, while later in the month the Government introduced new restrictions on prisoners, in an attempt to prevent inmates from organizing criminal acts from behind bars.

The strained relationship between Funes and the FMLN continued during 2010, forcing the President to seek the co-operation of the right-wing blocs in the Asamblea Legislativa. The Minister of Agriculture and Livestock, Manuel Sevilla, resigned in May, claiming that Funes had instructed him to divert ministry resources to members of GANA and the PCN in order to secure their legislative support. Funes denied the allegation, but the affair exacerbated the existing intra-party tensions. In a further demonstration of Funes' independence from the FMLN, and political parties in general, in May the President established a new grouping, the Movimiento Ciudadano por el Cambio (Citizens' Movement for Change). Nevertheless, there was evidence of a rapprochement with the FMLN in October. The improvement of ties with Cuba and Russia and the submission to the Asamblea of a proposal to increase pensions and raise the minimum wage for public sector workers were warmly welcomed by left-wing deputies.

In July 2010 the Supreme Court ruled as unconstitutional the requirement that legislative and municipal election candidates must belong to a political party. The Court also eliminated the controversial 'closed list' voting system, whereby the electorate could only vote for parties rather than designated candidates, which placed excessive power in the hands of those political leaders who created the party lists, encouraging parliamentarians to prioritize party interests over those of their constituents. Just before the Court made its announcement, the deputies in the Asamblea (all of whom belonged to political parties) attempted to undermine the ruling by pre-emptively adopting a constitutional amendment making party membership compulsory for election candidates; however, the amendment still required the approval of the incoming deputies in the 2012 Asamblea. Nevertheless, in accordance with the Court's judgment, in December the legislature voted in favour of permitting independents to compete in legislative and municipal ballots, although such candidates, unlike their counterparts standing for political parties, would have to finance their campaigns solely from private sources.

The Supreme Court, overruling an earlier decision by the legislature, announced the deregistration of the PCN and the PDC in April 2011, on the grounds that during the 2004 presidential poll they had not secured the constitutionally required 3% of the ballot. This judgment was endorsed by the Supreme Electoral Tribunal in October, although both parties initiated a legal challenge against the ruling. In the mean time, in order to compete in the legislative elections scheduled for March 2012, the PCN and the PDC were reconstituted as the Concertación Nacional (CN) and the Partido de la Esperanza (PES), respectively.

In May 2011 a Spanish court accused 20 former Salvadorean soldiers of perpetrating the 1989 Jesuit massacre in San Salvador, most of the victims of which were Spanish nationals. Nine of the accused, including former Minister of Defence Rafael Humberto Larios, surrendered themselves to the Salvadorean authorities in August. However, since Spain had neglected to submit an official extradition order, the Supreme Court authorized their release later that month, prompting criticism from human rights groups. The Spanish authorities formally requested the extradition of 15 of the accused in December. In the following month Funes notably urged the legislature to abrogate the amnesty law, an unprecedented appeal from a Salvadorean head of state.

Funes ratified a controversial legislative decree in June 2011 temporarily requiring Constitutional Court decisions to be endorsed by all of the serving judges rather than by a majority. This effectively granted the sole right-wing judge the power of veto over the remaining non-partisan judges, thereby rendering the Court largely inoperable and undermining its independence. The Court regarded this move as an unconstitutional overextension of the legislature's authority and rejected the decree, which had attracted widespread censure. However, the Asamblea Legislativa appeared reluctant to revoke the decree, ostensibly owing to concerns about the Court's growing assertiveness with respect to party political matters and a consequent desire to exert greater control over the judiciary. This institutional impasse was resolved in July, when the legislature, under intense public pressure, finally abrogated the decree; nevertheless, the affair had seriously damaged the Asamblea's reputation.

Funes announced further anti-crime measures in mid-2011, including a one-year extension of the military's involvement in civil policing activities, the enrolment of additional police recruits, the provision of extra financing for the security forces and the creation of two new gaols. Nevertheless, with the murder rate reaching a record high in 2011, Minister of Justice and Public Security Manuel Melgar submitted his resignation in November; he was succeeded later that month by Gen. (retd) David Victoriano Munguía Payés, who was replaced as Minister of National Defence by Gen. José Atilio Benítez. Some FMLN members expressed disapproval at Munguía's appointment due to his military background, while the appointment of another former general as chief of police generated further controversy in January 2012.

Recent developments: the 2012 legislative elections

ARENA secured a narrow victory in the legislative elections conducted on 11 March 2012, gaining control of 33 of the 84 seats in the Asamblea Legislativa. The FMLN won 31 seats, while GANA obtained 11, the CN six, and the PES, the Cambio Democrático (CD) and the CN-PES (the two parties formed a coalition in one department) each received one; independent candidates failed to gain legislative representation. Turn-out was recorded at approximately 55%. According to provisional results from the concurrent municipal polls, ARENA won 115 mayoralties, including San Salvador, and the FMLN secured 92. Analysts suggested that the FMLN had lost votes because of the country's ongoing economic problems and persistently high crime rates. None the less, Funes was expected to be able to advance his legislative agenda with continuing informal support from GANA and some of the smaller parties in the Asamblea.

Foreign Affairs

In an attempt to resolve a territorial dispute between El Salvador and Honduras over three islands in the Gulf of Fonseca and a small area of land on the joint border, President Duarte and President Azcona of Honduras submitted the dispute to the International Court of Justice (ICJ) for arbitration in 1986. In 1992 both countries accepted the ruling of the ICJ, which awarded one-third of the disputed mainland and two of the three disputed islands to El Salvador. Following prolonged negotiations, the two parties signed a convention in 1998 specifying the rights and obligations of those affected, including the right to choose between Honduran and Salvadorean citizenship. In 2001 El Salvador and Honduras signed a development plan for the border area between the two countries. In April 2006 the long-standing dispute was ended when the Presidents of both countries met to complete the formal ratification of the border demarcation.

During a visit to El Salvador in March 2011 US President Barack Obama pledged US $200m. of funding for a new regional security initiative, although in September, in an unprecedented move, the country was added to the USA's black list of significant drugs-producing and -trafficking nations. Seemingly as a concession to the USA, in August El Salvador agreed to send a small military detachment to Afghanistan as part of a training mission. El Salvador signed a Partnership for Growth agreement with the USA in November; the five-year programme was intended to boost El Salvador's slow rate of economic development.

CONSTITUTION AND GOVERNMENT

The Constitution came into effect in 1983. Executive power is held by the President, assisted by the Vice-President and the Cabinet. The President is elected for a five-year term beginning and ending on 1 June by universal adult suffrage. Legislative power is vested in the Asamblea Legislativa (Legislative Assembly), with 84 members elected by universal adult suffrage for a three-year term beginning on 1 May. Judicial power is exercised by the Supreme Court and other competent tribunals. Supreme Court judges are elected by the Asamblea.

REGIONAL AND INTERNATIONAL CO-OPERATION

El Salvador is a member of the Central American Common Market (CACM, see p. 232), which aims to increase trade within the region and to encourage monetary and industrial co-operation, the Inter-American Development Bank (see p. 334), the Organization of American States (see p. 394), the Association of Caribbean States (see p. 448), the Community of Latin American and Caribbean States (see p. 462), which was formally inaugurated in December 2011, and the Central American Integration System (SICA), which has its headquarters in El Salvador. El Salvador was a founder member of the UN in 1945. It acceded to the World Trade Organization (see p. 433) in 1995. The country is also a member of the Group of 77 (see p. 450) organization of developing states.

ECONOMIC AFFAIRS

In 2010, according to estimates by the World Bank, El Salvador's gross national income (GNI), measured at average 2008–10 prices, was US $20,820m., equivalent to $3,360 per head (or $6,390 per head on an international purchasing-power parity basis). In 2001–10 the population increased at an average annual rate of 0.4%, while gross domestic product (GDP) per head increased, in real terms, by an average of 1.6% per year. Overall GDP increased, in real terms, at an average annual rate of 1.9% in 2001–10. GDP declined by 3.1% in 2009, but grew by 1.4% in 2010.

Agriculture (including hunting, forestry and fishing) contributed an estimated 12.2% of GDP in 2010 and employed some 16.6% of the employed labour force in 2007. The principal cash crops are coffee and sugar cane. Maize, beans, rice and millet are the major subsistence crops. In 2010 coffee output stood at 97,300 metric tons, an increase on the 76,600 tons recorded in the previous year. Nevertheless, coffee's share of export earnings decreased in the 2000s: in 2000 coffee accounted for 22.4% of export earnings, excluding *maquila* (or assembly sector) zones, but this had fallen to 6.3% in 2010. The fishing catch stood at 35,900 metric tons in 2009, a decrease from the 52,400 tons recorded in 2007. During 2001–10 agricultural GDP increased at an average annual rate of 2.9%. The sector's GDP decreased by 2.9% in 2009, but increased by an estimated 3.3% in 2010.

Industry (including mining, manufacturing, construction and power) contributed an estimated 23.8% of GDP in 2010 and engaged 23.8% of the employed labour force in 2007. During 2001–10 industrial GDP increased at an average annual rate of 1.5%. The sector's GDP declined by 3.1% in 2009, but increased by an estimated 1.9% in 2010.

El Salvador has no significant mineral resources, and the mining sector employed less than 0.1% of the economically active population in 2007 and contributed only 0.3% of GDP in 2010. Small quantities of gold, silver, sea-salt and limestone are mined or quarried. During 2001–10 the GDP of the mining sector decreased at an average annual rate of 4.7%; mining GDP contracted by an estimated 16.7% in 2010.

Manufacturing contributed an estimated 19.8% of GDP in 2010 and employed 15.7% of the active labour force in 2007. The most important branches of manufacturing (excluding the *maquila* industry) were food products, chemical products, petroleum products, textiles, apparel (excluding footwear) and beverages. During 2001–10 manufacturing GDP increased at an average annual rate of 1.6%. The sector's GDP decreased by 3.0% in 2009, but increased by an estimated 2.2% in 2010. There is an important *maquila* sector, which in 2010 generated just over one-third (an estimated 33.7%) of the country's total exports. *Maquila* exports increased by 20.0% in 2010, according to the central bank.

Construction contributed an estimated 3.8% of GDP in 2010 and engaged 7.6% of the employed labour force in 2007. In 2001–10 the sector decreased at an average annual rate of 1.4%; construction contracted by an estimated 6.3% in 2010.

Energy is derived principally from imported fuel. Imports of mineral products accounted for an estimated 18.1% of the cost of merchandise imports in 2010. In 2008 El Salvador derived an estimated 38.6% of its electricity from petroleum. An estimated further 34.2% of total electricity production in 2008 was contributed by hydroelectric installations.

The services sector contributed an estimated 64.0% of GDP in 2010 and employed 59.6% of the economically active population in 2007. The GDP of the services sector increased by an average of 2.0% per year in 2001–10. The sector declined by 3.2% in 2010, but grew by an estimated 1.4% in 2010. Receipts from tourism stood at US $390m. in 2010.

In 2010 El Salvador recorded a visible trade deficit of US $3,612.0m., while there was a deficit of $488.3m. on the current account of the balance of payments. Remittances from workers abroad were an important source of income to the Salvadorean economy, contributing about 17% of GDP, according to IMF estimates. Remittances in 2011 totalled $3,648.8m. The Dominican Republic-Central American Free Trade Agreement (DR-CAFTA) with the USA came into effect in 2006. DR-CAFTA entailed the gradual elimination of tariffs on most industrial and agricultural products over 10 and 20 years, respectively. In 2010 just over 40% of total imports (including imports into *maquila* zones) was provided by the USA; other major suppliers were Guatemala, Mexico and Honduras. The USA was the principal market for exports (taking an estimated 64.2% of exports, including exports from the *maquila* sector); other significant purchasers were Guatemala, Honduras and Nicaragua. In 2010 the main exports were food, beverages and tobacco manufactures, chemicals products and vegetables and crops (particularly coffee). In the same year the principal imports were mineral products, mechanical and electrical machinery and apparatus, chemicals and related products and live animals and vegetables.

In 2010 there was an estimated budgetary deficit of US $726.7m., equivalent to some 3.4% of GDP. El Salvador's general government gross debt was US $10.667m. in 2010, equivalent to 50.3% of GDP. El Salvador's external debt totalled US $11,384m. at the end of 2009, of which $6,131m. was public and publicly guaranteed debt. In that year, the cost of debt-servicing long-term public and publicly guaranteed debt and repayments to the IMF was equivalent to 19.2% of the value of exports of goods, services and income (excluding workers' remittances). The average annual rate of inflation was 3.4% in 2001–10; consumer prices rose by 0.9% in 2010. Some 9.5% of the labour force were unemployed in 2007.

While remittances were a valuable means by which to stimulate domestic expenditure, there were concerns that large inflows of US dollars increased dependency on the US market. These concerns were qualified in late 2008, when the USA entered recession: remittances declined, while reduced US demand for Salvadorean exports precipitated a contraction in industrial output. In January 2009 the IMF approved a US $800m. stand-by arrangement to help the country withstand the effects of the global financial crisis. (This arrangement was replaced by a $790m. stand-by arrangement in March 2010.) The economy entered recession in 2009, but there was a resumption of real GDP growth in 2010, albeit of just 1.4%. Exports recovered in 2010, although the industrial sector remained sluggish and the continuing high levels of unemployment in the USA resulted in only a slight increase in remittances. Foreign direct investment decreased sharply in that year, lending credence to claims that El Salvador's high crime rates were discouraging investors. Fiscal reform precipitated a rise in tax receipts in 2010, and the Government's countercyclical spending strategy reinforced domestic demand. The 2011 budget allocated significant funding to social programmes and poverty alleviation, although expansionary spending policies had led to increasing levels of public debt. Exports and remittance inflows continued to rise during 2011, but the economy was negatively affected by severe flooding in October, which caused extensive damage to crops and infrastructure, and by the weak economic recovery in the USA. In an attempt to boost tax revenues further, legislation was approved in December raising corporate and personal income tax rates. The IMF estimated that real GDP expanded by 2.0% in 2011 and forecast further growth, of 2.5%, for 2012, but there were concerns that the economy could falter if global conditions deteriorated or if legislative approval for the Government's economic proposals were withdrawn.

PUBLIC HOLIDAYS

2013: 1 January (New Year's Day), 28 March–1 April (Easter), 1 May (Labour Day), 2–4 August (El Salvador del Mundo Festival), 15 September (Independence Day), 12 October (Discovery of America), 2 November (All Souls' Day), 5 November (Cry of Independence), 25 December (Christmas Day), 31 December (New Year's Eve).

Statistical Survey

Sources (unless otherwise stated): Banco Central de Reserva de El Salvador, Alameda Juan Pablo II y 17 Avda Norte, Apdo 01-106, San Salvador; tel. 2281-8000; fax 2281-8011; internet www.bcr.gob.sv; Dirección General de Estadística y Censos, Edif. Centro de Gobierno, Alameda Juan Pablo II y Calle Guadalupe, San Salvador; tel. 2286-4260; fax 2286-2505; internet www.digestyc.gob.sv.

Area and Population

AREA, POPULATION AND DENSITY

Area (sq km)	
Land	20,721
Inland water	320
Total	21,041*
Population (census results)†	
27 September 1992	5,118,599
12 May 2007	
Males	2,719,371
Females	3,024,742
Total	5,744,113
Population (official estimates)	
2010	6,183,002
2011	6,216,143
2012	6,251,494
Density (per sq km) at 2012	297.1

* 8,124 sq miles.

† Excluding adjustments for underenumeration.

POPULATION BY AGE AND SEX

(official estimates at 2012)

	Males	Females	Total
0–14	963,052	922,530	1,885,582
15–64	1,771,942	2,128,986	3,900,929
65 and over	203,327	261,857	464,984
Total	2,938,321	3,313,373	6,251,494

DEPARTMENTS

(official estimates at 2012)

	Area (sq km)	Population	Density (per sq km)
Ahuachapán	1,239.6	331,395	267.3
Santa Ana	2,023.2	567,768	280.6
Sonsonate	1,225.8	461,474	376.5
Chalatenango	2,016.6	203,873	101.1
La Libertad	1,652.9	738,843	447.0
San Salvador	886.2	1,738,668	1,961.9
Cuscatlán	756.2	248,414	328.5
La Paz	1,223.6	325,967	266.4
Cabañas	1,103.5	164,877	149.4
San Vicente	1,184.0	172,544	145.7
Usulután	2,130.4	363,198	170.5
San Miguel	2,077.1	475,713	229.0
Morazán	1,447.4	198,341	137.0
La Unión	2,074.3	260,419	125.5
Total	21,040.8	6,251,494	297.1

PRINCIPAL TOWNS

(official population projections at mid-2009)*

San Salvador (capital)	513,487	Mejicanos	215,528
San Miguel	308,635	Santa Tecla†	208,226
Soyapango	305,729	Ciudad Delgado	178,808
Santa Ana	288,588	Ilopango	165,452
Apopa	229,580	San Martín	155,396

* Figures refer to municipios, which may each contain rural areas as well as an urban centre.

† Formerly Nueva San Salvador.

BIRTHS, MARRIAGES AND DEATHS

	Registered live births		Registered marriages		Registered deaths	
	Number	Rate (per 1,000)	Number	Rate (per 1,000)	Number	Rate (per 1,000)
2001	138,354	21.6	29,216	4.6	29,559	4.6
2002	129,363	19.9	26,077	4.0	27,458	4.2
2003	124,476	18.7	25,071	3.8	29,377	4.4
2004	119,710	17.7	25,240	3.7	30,058	4.4
2005	112,769	16.4	24,475	3.6	30,933	4.5
2006	107,111	15.3	24,500	3.5	31,453	4.5
2007	106,471	15.0	28,675	4.0	31,349	4.4
2008	112,049	15.3	27,714	3.8	31,594	4.4

Life expectancy (years at birth, estimates): 72 (males 68; females 76) in 2009 (Source: WHO, *World Health Statistics*).

ECONOMICALLY ACTIVE POPULATION

(persons aged 16 years and over at 2007 census)

	Males	Females	Total
Agriculture and hunting	251,960	23,496	275,456
Forestry	1,208	74	1,282
Fishing	8,776	987	9,763
Mining and quarrying	1,202	70	1,272
Manufacturing	145,586	126,083	271,669
Electricity, gas and water	6,039	762	6,801
Construction	127,887	3,068	130,955
Wholesale and retail trade; repair of motor vehicles	200,442	185,397	385,839
Hotels and restaurants	17,393	51,666	69,059
Transport, storage and communications	82,070	8,719	90,789
Financing, insurance, real estate and business services	83,089	47,206	130,295
Public administration, defence and social security	53,488	23,656	77,144
Education	25,421	45,143	70,564
Health	18,348	34,580	52,928
Other community, social and personal services	18,640	15,118	33,758
Private households with employed persons	5,580	113,286	118,866
Extra-territorial organizations and bodies	395	319	714
Total employed	1,047,524	679,630	1,727,154
Unemployed	96,916	85,186	182,102
Total labour force	1,144,440	764,816	1,909,256

Health and Welfare

KEY INDICATORS

Total fertility rate (children per woman, 2009)	2.3
Under-5 mortality rate (per 1,000 live births, 2009)	17
HIV/AIDS (% of persons aged 15–49, 2009)	0.8
Physicians (per 1,000 head, 2002)	1.2
Hospital beds (per 1,000 head, 2005)	0.9
Health expenditure (2008): US $ per head (PPP)	410
Health expenditure (2008): % of GDP	6.0
Health expenditure (2008): public (% of total)	59.6
Access to water (% of persons, 2008)	87
Access to sanitation (% of persons, 2008)	87
Total carbon dioxide emissions ('000 metric tons, 2007)	6,694.1
Carbon dioxide emissions per head (metric tons, 2007)	1.1
Human Development Index (2011): ranking	105
Human Development Index (2011): value	0.674

For sources and definitions, see explanatory note on p. vi.

Agriculture

PRINCIPAL CROPS
('000 metric tons)

	2008	2009	2010
Rice, paddy	35.2	40.2	30.3
Maize	868.3	786.0	798.0
Sorghum	134.2	163.7	166.0
Yautia (Cocoyam)*	43.2	39.5	40.0
Sugar cane	5,249.9	5,736.1	5,126.7
Beans, dry	95.3	80.1	87.5
Coconuts	68.7	68.8	68.8*
Watermelons	98.3	49.3	49.3
Bananas*	75.3	78.1	86.7
Plantains	96.5	96.5	96.5*
Oranges	73.0	73.1	45.7
Coffee, green	89.8	76.6	97.3

* FAO estimate(s).

Aggregate production ('000 metric tons, may include official, semi-official or estimated data): Total cereals 1,037.7 in 2008, 989.9 in 2009, 994.3 in 2010; Total vegetables (incl. melons) 255.9 in 2008, 147.4 in 2009, 149.4 in 2010; Total fruits (excl. melons) 484.2 in 2008, 487.3 in 2009, 439.3 in 2010.

Source: FAO.

LIVESTOCK
('000 head, year ending September)

	2008	2009	2010
Horses*	96	96	96
Asses*	32	32	32
Mules*	24	24	24
Cattle	1,397	1,343	1,343*
Pigs	467	423†	423
Sheep*	5	5	5
Goats*	15	15	15
Chickens*	14,000	13,800	13,500

* FAO estimate(s).
† Unofficial figure.

Source: FAO.

LIVESTOCK PRODUCTS
('000 metric tons)

	2008	2009	2010
Cattle meat	32.1	31.1	33.0
Pig meat	8.8	8.3	8.3
Chicken meat	96.1	97.7	104.5
Cows' milk	494.1	541.6	556.6
Hen eggs	66.3	64.3	64.7

Source: FAO.

Forestry

ROUNDWOOD REMOVALS
('000 cubic metres, excl. bark, estimates)

	2007	2008	2009
Sawlogs, veneer logs and logs for sleepers	682	682	682
Fuel wood	4,210	4,217	4,223
Total	4,892	4,899	4,905

2010: Figures assumed to be unchanged from 2009 (estimates).

Source: FAO.

SAWNWOOD PRODUCTION
('000 cubic metres, incl. railway sleepers, estimates)

	2002	2003	2004
Total (all broadleaved, hardwood)	68.0	68.0	16.3

2005–10: Figures assumed to be unchanged from 2004 (estimates).

Source: FAO.

Fishing

('000 metric tons, live weight)

	2007	2008	2009
Capture	48.6	32.3	31.5*
Nile tilapia	0.8	4.0	4.0*
Other freshwater fishes	0.9	—	—
Croakers and drums	1.8	n.a.	n.a.
Skipjack tuna	11.1	13.5	12.6
Yellowfin tuna	4.4	5.9	5.7
Bigeye tuna	2.3	3.2	3.9
Sharks, rays, skates, etc.	0.7	—	—
Other marine fishes	7.8	0.4	0.6
Pacific seabobs	0.6	0.9	0.8
Marine molluscs	0.5	—	—
Aquaculture	3.7	3.8*	4.3
Total catch	52.4	36.1*	35.9*

* FAO estimate.

Source: FAO.

Mining

(metric tons, unless otherwise indicated)

	2005	2006	2007
Gypsum*	5,600	5,500	5,500
Steel (crude)	48,000*	72,000	73,000
Limestone ('000 metric tons)*	1,150	1,200	1,200
Salt (marine)*	31,400	30,000	30,000

* Estimate(s).

2008: Figures assumed to be unchanged from 2007 (estimates).

2009–10: Steel (crude) 56,000.

Source: US Geological Survey.

Industry

SELECTED PRODUCTS
('000 metric tons, unless otherwise indicated)

	2006	2007	2008
Raw sugar	542	560	597
Motor gasoline (petrol)	108	117	111
Kerosene	16	2	2
Distillate fuel oil	172	229	186
Residual fuel oil	463	477	410
Liquefied petroleum gas (refined)	17	20	14
Cement	1,311	1,300	1,300
Electric energy (million kWh)	5,597	5,807	5,960

Cement ('000 metric tons): 1,212 in 2009; 1,200 in 2010.

Source: US Geological Survey and UN Industrial Commodity Statistics Database.

Finance

CURRENCY AND EXCHANGE RATES

Monetary Units
100 centavos = 1 Salvadorean colón.

Sterling, Dollar and Euro Equivalents (30 December 2011)
£1 sterling = 13.528 colones;
US $1 = 8.750 colones;
€1 = 11.322 colones;
100 Salvadorean colones = £7.39 = $11.43 = €8.83.

Note: The foregoing information refers to the principal exchange rate, applicable to official receipts and payments, imports of petroleum and exports of coffee. In addition, there is a market exchange rate, applicable to other transactions. The principal rate was maintained at 8.755 colones per US dollar from May 1995 to December 2000. However, in January 2001, with the introduction of legislation making the US dollar legal tender, the rate was adjusted to $1 = 8.750 colones; both currencies have circulated freely as parallel legal currencies since that date.

CENTRAL GOVERNMENT BUDGET
(US $ million)

Revenue*	2008	2009	2010
Current revenue	3,190.7	2,773.8	3,070.2
Tax revenue	2,885.8	2,609.4	2,881.6
Taxes on earnings	1,004.1	949.2	994.8
Import duties	178.8	138.0	151.0
Value-added tax	1,460.7	1,251.2	1,432.8
Non-tax revenue	304.9	164.4	188.6
Public enterprise transfers	5.3	25.3	24.7
Financial public enterprise transfers	29.6	28.6	28.7
Capital revenue	0.1	0.1	0.2
Total	3,190.7	2,773.8	3,070.5

Expenditure†	2008	2009	2010
Current expenditure	2,778.9	3,031.4	3,114.3
Remunerations	973.0	1,069.8	1,109.0
Goods and services	516.5	538.5	587.0
Interest payments	509.4	518.0	496.3
Transfers	779.9	905.2	922.0
To other government bodies	407.1	448.9	469.6
To the private sector	357.9	444.3	439.6
Capital expenditure	603.3	602.6	682.9
Gross investment	305.4	305.3	392.2
Total	3,382.2	3,634.0	3,797.2

* Excluding grants received (US $ million): 52.2 in 2008; 83.5 in 2009; 142.8 in 2010.

† Excluding lending minus repayments (US $ million): –6.3 in 2008; –4.6 in 2009; –2.8 in 2010.

INTERNATIONAL RESERVES
(US $ million at 31 December)

	2008	2009	2010
Gold (national valuation)	101.9	117.5	313.6
IMF special drawing rights	38.5	256.8	252.3
Foreign exchange	2,404.6	2,612.0	2,317.4
Total	2,545.0	2,986.3	2,883.2

Source: IMF, *International Financial Statistics*.

MONEY SUPPLY
(US $ million at 31 December)

	2008	2009	2010
Currency outside depository corporations	33.0	32.8	4.7
Transferable deposits	1,837.0	2,120.4	2,522.5
Other deposits	6,901.0	6,858.0	6,860.8
Securities other than shares	1,432.4	1,405.7	1,023.6
Broad money	10,203.3	10,417.0	10,411.5

Source: IMF, *International Financial Statistics*.

COST OF LIVING
(Consumer Price Index; annual averages; base: December 1992 = 100)

	2007	2008	2009
Food and non-alcoholic beverages	214.9	240.6	231.5
Clothing and footwear	111.7	113.4	115.0
Rent, water, electricity, gas and other fuels	205.9	207.2	224.5
Health	224.5	229.2	237.2
Transport	164.4	178.2	168.2
All items (incl. others)	202.1	216.8	218.0

2010 (annual averages; base: December 2009 = 100): Food and non-alcoholic beverages 104.4; Clothing and footwear 100.0; Rent, water, electricity, gas and other fuels 98.7; Health 100.5; Transport 101.8; All items (incl. others) 101.1.

NATIONAL ACCOUNTS
(US $ million at current prices, preliminary)

Expenditure on the Gross Domestic Product

	2008	2009	2010
Final consumption expenditure	23,063.1	21,083.4	22,100.8
Households	21,096.8	18,887.3	19,789.1
General government	1,966.3	2,196.1	2,311.7
Gross capital formation	3,257.7	2,775.6	2,819.9
Total domestic expenditure	26,320.8	23,859.0	24,920.7
Exports of goods and services	5,761.0	4,792.7	5,552.6
Less Imports of goods and services	10,650.9	7,990.6	9,258.5
GDP in purchasers' values	21,431.0	20,661.0	21,214.7
GDP at constant 1990 prices	9,243.4	8,953.8	9,081.5

Gross Domestic Product by Economic Activity

	2008	2009	2010
Agriculture, hunting, forestry and fishing	2,465.0	2,367.7	2,486.9
Mining and quarrying	70.8	60.0	54.5
Manufacturing	4,233.5	3,924.8	4,039.7
Construction	807.4	803.7	771.0
Electricity, gas and water	382.3	417.6	435.0
Transport, storage and communications	1,816.9	1,656.8	1,699.1
Wholesale and retail trade, restaurants and hotels	4,354.6	4,141.1	4,253.7
Finance and insurance	968.7	921.3	973.2
Real estate and business services	899.6	926.2	969.7
Owner-occupied dwellings	1,382.2	1,414.1	1,438.2
Community, social, domestic and personal services	1,621.6	1,706.7	1,750.9
Government services	1,422.1	1,554.4	1,566.4
Sub-total	20,424.7	19,894.4	20,438.3
Import duties and value-added tax	1,774.3	1,518.7	1,578.4
Less Imputed bank service charge	768.0	752.0	802.0
GDP in purchasers' values	21,431.0	20,661.0	21,214.7

BALANCE OF PAYMENTS
(US $ million)

	2008	2009	2010
Exports of goods f.o.b.	4,702.6	3,929.8	4,576.7
Imports of goods f.o.b.	–9,379.4	–7,037.7	–8,188.7
Trade balance	–4,676.8	–3,107.9	–3,612.0
Exports of services	1,058.1	862.9	976.0
Imports of services	–1,271.0	–953.1	–1,069.9
Balance on goods and services	–4,889.7	–3,198.0	–3,705.9
Other income received	179.3	76.6	119.6
Other income paid	–568.3	–624.5	–500.6
Balance on goods, services and income	–5,278.8	–3,746.0	–4,086.9
Current transfers received	3,846.7	3,558.9	3,670.2
Current transfers paid	–100.1	–117.1	–71.6
Current balance	–1,532.2	–304.2	–488.3

—continued	2008	2009	2010
Capital account (net)	79.8	131.2	232.0
Direct investment abroad	–79.4	–1.8	–61.3
Direct investment from abroad	371.2	231.0	–5.6
Portfolio investment assets	195.7	350.2	–117.4
Portfolio investment liabilities	–74.3	7.2	31.0
Other investment assets	25.7	–629.1	235.7
Other investment liabilities	641.8	–554.5	–267.7
Net errors and omissions	164.1	659.5	–15.3
Overall balance	–207.6	–110.4	–456.8

Source: IMF, *International Financial Statistics*.

External Trade

PRINCIPAL COMMODITIES
(US $ million, preliminary)

Imports c.i.f.*	2008	2009	2010
Live animals and animal products; vegetables, crops and related products, primary	731.9	684.1	660.3
Food, beverages (incl. alcoholic) and tobacco manufactures	587.6	581.0	603.4
Mineral products	1,853.6	1,135.7	1,404.2
Crude petroleum oils	572.9	367.7	473.3
Light oils (gasoline, etc.)	288.3	193.9	209.3
Heavy oils (gas oil, diesel oil, fuel oil, etc.)	616.4	309.7	375.3
Chemicals and related products	1,043.8	872.9	971.5
Therapeutic and preventative medicines	256.0	252.9	272.4
Plastics, artificial resins, rubbers, and articles thereof	525.7	412.2	537.4
Plastics, artificial resins, and articles thereof	453.4	346.5	462.2
Wood pulp, paper, paperboard and articles thereof	360.3	294.2	348.2
Textile materials and articles thereof	702.0	614.2	779.8
Base metals and manufactures thereof	715.0	359.8	478.3
Cast iron and steel	397.1	142.4	226.0
Mechanical and electrical machinery and apparatus	1,264.5	1,001.2	1,103.0
Mechanical machinery and apparatus	628.6	499.2	549.8
Electrical machinery and appliances	635.9	502.0	553.1
Radio and television transmitters and receivers, and parts thereof	222.5	189.3	230.7
Transport equipment	348.5	242.5	243.7
Total (incl. others)	8,812.6	6,720.7	7,745.3

* Excluding imports into *maquila* zones (US $ million, preliminary): 1,005.1 in 2008; 604.7 in 2009; 752.9 in 2010.

Exports f.o.b.*	2008	2009	2010
Vegetables, crops and related products, primary	332.4	299.3	286.2
Coffee, including roasted and decaffeinated	258.7	230.3	213.2
Food, beverages (incl. alcoholic) and tobacco manufactures	516.7	513.0	616.5
Unrefined sugar	75.5	88.2	127.7
Mineral products	190.7	118.2	144.3
Chemical products	308.3	242.3	225.1
Therapeutic and preventative medicines	108.7	97.8	105.0
Plastics, rubber, and articles thereof	215.3	193.9	240.9
Boxes, bags, bottles, stoppers and other plastic containers	89.1	89.4	117.0
Wood pulp, paper, paperboard and articles thereof	227.1	228.0	232.9
Toilet paper for domestic use	97.5	96.9	90.6
Textile materials and articles thereof	868.0	822.8	1,009.7
Base metals and manufactures thereof	285.8	181.2	225.9
Iron and steel products, laminated	88.3	42.7	59.4
Other iron and steel products	122.4	81.8	96.6
Electrical machinery, appliances and associated products	87.3	63.1	76.7
Total (incl. others)	3,272.6	2,920.8	3,364.8

* Excluding exports from *maquila* zones (US $ million, preliminary): 1,368.5 in 2008; 945.2 in 2009; 1,134.4 in 2010.

PRINCIPAL TRADING PARTNERS
(US $ million, preliminary)

Imports c.i.f.*	2008	2009	2010
Argentina	78.4	40.8	35.6
Brazil	343.8	177.3	121.7
Chile	163.8	66.0	43.6
Colombia	137.0	94.2	85.7
Costa Rica	261.3	225.2	261.3
Ecuador	327.1	223.2	254.1
Germany	161.4	110.6	136.9
Guatemala	830.4	752.6	806.6
Honduras	377.5	351.8	374.1
Hong Kong	75.9	38.8	54.8
Italy	78.5	65.6	61.3
Japan	191.9	102.7	151.6
Korea, Republic	119.3	61.1	87.5
Mexico	895.1	546.3	752.3
Netherlands Antilles	117.0	90.1	158.4
Nicaragua	197.9	195.6	182.0
Panama	202.1	179.7	227.1
Spain	96.2	72.5	76.0
Taiwan	119.2	87.5	98.4
USA	3,365.9	2,636.0	3,127.5
Venezuela	197.8	97.5	132.2
Total (incl. others)	8,812.6	6,720.7	7,745.3

* Including imports into *maquila* zones (mostly from USA) (US$ million, preliminary): 1,005.1 in 2008; 604.7 in 2009; 752.9 in 2010.

Exports f.o.b.*	2008	2009	2010
Costa Rica	169.5	137.1	161.4
Dominican Republic	62.9	67.4	84.2
Germany	123.1	89.8	81.9
Guatemala	630.3	541.5	628.9
Honduras	600.2	519.5	579.4
Mexico	51.9	59.2	76.2
Nicaragua	255.7	213.0	244.0
Panama	125.4	110.9	102.4
Spain	105.7	65.3	51.7
USA	2,240.3	1,796.1	2,161.1
Total (incl. others)	3,272.6	2,920.8	3,364.8

* Including exports from *maquila* zones (mostly to USA) (US$ million, preliminary): 1,368.5 in 2008; 945.2 in 2009; 1,134.4 in 2010.

Transport

RAILWAYS
(traffic)

	1999	2000
Number of passengers ('000)	543.3	687.3
Passenger-km (million)	8.4	10.7
Freight ('000 metric tons)	188.6	136.2
Freight ton-km (million)	19.4	13.1

Source: Ferrocarriles Nacionales de El Salvador.

ROAD TRAFFIC
(motor vehicles in use at 31 December)

	1998	1999	2000
Passenger cars	187,440	197,374	207,259
Buses and coaches	34,784	36,204	37,554
Lorries and vans	166,065	177,741	189,812
Motorcycles and mopeds	32,271	35,021	37,139

Source: Servicio de Tránsito Centroamericano (SERTRACEN).

2007 (motor vehicles in use at 31 December): Passenger cars 283,787; Buses and coaches 6,306; Vans and lorries 283,787; Motorcycles and mopeds 44,145 (Sources: IRF, *International Road Statistics*).

SHIPPING

Merchant Fleet
(registered at 31 December)

	2007	2008	2009
Number of vessels	14	14	16
Total displacement ('000 grt)	6.6	6.6	10.8

Source: IHS Fairplay, *World Fleet Statistics*.

CIVIL AVIATION
(traffic on scheduled services)

	2007	2008	2009
Kilometres flown (million)	37	33	29
Passengers carried ('000)	2,537	2,280	1,997
Passenger-km (million)	4,282	3,775	3,516
Total ton-km (million)	407	358	332

Source: UN, *Statistical Yearbook*.

Tourism

TOURIST ARRIVALS BY NATIONALITY
(arrivals of non-resident tourists at national borders)

	2007	2008	2009
Canada	33,827	32,050	26,333
Costa Rica	44,782	27,668	17,714
Guatemala	488,453	537,578	462,944
Honduras	189,453	213,075	138,104
Mexico	32,418	28,999	17,633
Nicaragua	113,883	96,956	42,844
Panama	13,319	11,912	10,107
Spain	12,003	8,543	5,496
USA	320,298	361,858	327,314
Total (incl. others)	1,338,543	1,384,773	1,090,926

Receipts from tourism (US $ million, excl. passenger transport): 482 in 2007; 425 in 2008; 319 in 2009; 390 in 2010 (provisional).

Source: World Tourism Organization.

Communications Media

	2008	2009	2010*
Telephones ('000 main lines in use)	1,077.2	1,099.1	1,000.9
Mobile cellular telephones ('000 subscribers)	6,950.7	7,566.2	7,700.3
Internet subscribers ('000)	126.0	150.5	n.a.
Broadband subscribers ('000)	123.5	149.4	175.3

* Estimates.

Radio receivers ('000 in use): 2,940 in 1999.

Television receivers ('000 in use): 1,260 in 2000.

Daily newspapers: 5 in 2004 (circulation 250,000).

Non-daily newspapers: 6 in 1996 (circulation 52,000).

Book production: 663 in 1998.

Personal computers: 350,000 (57.8 per 1,000 persons) in 2005.

Sources: UNESCO, *Statistical Yearbook*, International Telecommunication Union.

Education

(2008/09)

	Teachers	Students		
		Males	Females	Total
Pre-primary	9,422	109,232	106,604	215,836
Primary	31,077	500,125	463,399	963,524
Secondary	22,807	279,206	276,439	555,645
Tertiary	8,893	65,648	78,201	143,849

Institutions (2001/02): Pre-primary 4,838; Primary 5,414; Secondary 757; Tertiary 43.

Sources: Ministry of Education and UNESCO Institute for Statistics.

Pupil-teacher ratio (primary education, UNESCO estimate): 31.0 in 2008/09 (Source: UNESCO Institute for Statistics).

Adult literacy rate (UNESCO estimates): 84.1% (males 86.8%; females 81.8%) in 2009 (Source: UNESCO Institute for Statistics).

Directory

The Government

HEAD OF STATE

President: CARLOS MAURICIO FUNES CARTAGENA (assumed office 1 June 2009).

Vice-President: SALVADOR SÁNCHEZ CERÉN.

CABINET
(May 2012)

The Government is formed by the Frente Farabundo Martí para la Liberación Nacional.

Minister of Finance: JUAN RAMÓN CARLOS ENRIQUE CÁCERES CHÁVEZ.

Minister of Foreign Affairs: HUGO ROGER MARTÍNEZ BONILLA.

Minister of Internal Affairs: GREGORIO ERNESTO ZELAYANDIA CISNEROS.

Minister of Justice and Public Security: Gen. (retd) DAVID VICTORIANO MUNGUÍA PAYÉS.

Minister of the Economy: ARMANDO FLORES.

Minister of Education: SALVADOR SÁNCHEZ CERÉN.

Minister of National Defence: Gen. JOSÉ ATILIO BENÍTEZ.

Minister of Labour and Social Security: HUMBERTO CENTENO NAJARRO.

Minister of Public Health and Social Welfare: Dra MARÍA ISABEL RODRÍGUEZ.

Minister of Agriculture and Livestock: GUILLERMO LÓPEZ SUÁREZ.

Minister of Public Works, Transport, Housing and Urban Development: MANUEL ORLANDO QUINTEROS A. (alias Gerson Martínez).

Minister of the Environment and Natural Resources: HERMÁN HUMBERTO ROSA CHÁVEZ.

Minister of Tourism: JOSÉ NAPOLEÓN DUARTE DURÁN.

MINISTRIES

Ministry for the Presidency: Alameda Dr Manuel Enrique Araujo 5500, San Salvador; tel. 2248-9000; fax 2248-9370; internet www.presidencia.gob.sv.

Ministry of Agriculture and Livestock: Final 1a, Avda Norte y Avda Manuel Gallardo, Santa Tecla; tel. 2241-1700; fax 2229-9271; e-mail info@mag.gob.sv; internet www.mag.gob.sv.

Ministry of the Economy: Edif. C1–C2, Centro de Gobierno, Alameda Juan Pablo II y Calle Guadalupe, San Salvador; tel. 2231-5600; fax 2221-5446; e-mail info@minec.gob.sv; internet www.minec.gob.sv.

Ministry of Education: Edif. A, Centro de Gobierno, Alameda Juan Pablo II y Calle Guadalupe, San Salvador; tel. 2281-0044; fax 2281-0077; e-mail educacion@mined.gob.sv; internet www.mined.gob.sv.

Ministry of the Environment and Natural Resources: Edif. MARN 2, Calle y Col. Las Mercedes, Carretera a Santa Tecla, Km 5.5, San Salvador; tel. 2267-6276; fax 2267-9420; e-mail medioambiente@marn.gob.sv; internet www.marn.gob.sv.

Ministry of Finance: Blvd Los Héroes 1231, San Salvador; tel. 2244-3000; fax 2244-6408; e-mail webmaster@mh.gob.sv; internet www.mh.gob.sv.

Ministry of Foreign Affairs: Calle El Pedregal, Blvd Cancillería, Ciudad Merliot, Antiguo Cuscatlán; tel. 2231-1000; fax 2289-8016; e-mail webmaster@rree.gob.sv; internet www.rree.gob.sv.

Ministry of Internal Affairs: Centro de Gobierno, Calle Oriente 9 y Avda Norte 15, San Salvador; tel. 2527-7000; fax 2527-7972; e-mail info@gobernacion.gob.sv; internet www.gobernacion.gob.sv.

Ministry of Justice and Public Security: Centro de Gobierno, Complejo Plan Maestro, Edifs B1, B2 y B3, Alameda Juan Pablo II y 17 Avda Norte, San Salvador; tel. 2526-3000; fax 2526-3105; internet www.seguridad.gob.sv.

Ministry of Labour and Social Security: Centro de Gobierno, Complejo Plan Maestro, Edifs 2 y 3, Alameda Juan Pablo II y 17 Avda Norte, San Salvador; tel. 2209-3700; fax 2209-3756; e-mail informacion@mtps.gob.sv; internet www.mtps.gob.sv.

Ministry of National Defence: Alameda Dr Manuel E. Araújo, Km 5, Carretera a Santa Tecla, San Salvador; tel. 2250-0100; e-mail fuerzaarmada@faes.gob.sv; internet www.fuerzaarmada.gob.sv/index.html.

Ministry of Public Health and Social Welfare: Calle Arce 827, San Salvador; tel. 2221-0966; fax 2221-0991; e-mail webmaster@mspas.gob.sv; internet www.mspas.gob.sv.

Ministry of Public Works, Transport, Housing and Urban Development: Plantel la Lechuza, Carretera a Santa Tecla Km 5.5, San Salvador; tel. 2528-3000; fax 2279-3723; e-mail info@mop.gob.sv; internet www.mop.gob.sv.

Ministry of Tourism: Edif. Carbonel 1, Alameda Dr Manuel Enrique Araujo y Pasaje Carbonel, Col. Roma, San Salvador; tel. 2243-7835; fax 2223-6120; e-mail info@corsatur.gob.sv; internet www.elsalvador.travel.

President and Legislature

PRESIDENT

Election, 15 March 2009

Candidates	Valid votes	% of valid votes
Carlos Mauricio Funes Cartagena (FMLN)	1,354,000	51.32
Rodrigo Avila Avilez (ARENA)	1,284,588	48.68
Total*	2,638,588	100.00

* In addition, there were 20,550 blank or invalid ballots.

ASAMBLEA LEGISLATIVA

President: OTHON SIGFRIDO REYES MORALES (FMLN).

General Election, 11 March 2012

Party	Valid votes cast	% of valid votes	Seats
Alianza Republicana Nacionalista (ARENA)	892,688	39.84	33
Frente Farabundo Martí para la Liberación Nacional (FMLN)	824,686	36.80	31
Gran Alianza por la Unidad Nacional (GANA)	214,498	9.57	11
Concertación Nacional (CN)	162,083	7.23	6
Partido de la Esperanza (PES)	60,641	2.71	1
Cambio Democrático (CD)	47,797	2.13	1
Coalición CN-PES*	17,580	0.78	1
Others	20,945	0.93	—
Total	2,240,918	100.00	84

* The Concertación Nacional (CN) and the Partido de la Esperanza (PES) formed a coalition in Chalatenango department.

Election Commission

Tribunal Supremo Electoral (TSE): 15a Calle Poniente 4223, Col. Escalón, San Salvador; tel. 2263-4641; fax 2263-4678; e-mail info@tse.gob.sv; internet www.tse.gob.sv; f. 1992; Pres. EUGENIO CHICAS.

Political Organizations

Alianza Republicana Nacionalista (ARENA): Prolongación Calle Arce 2426, Col. Flor Banca, San Salvador; tel. 2260-4400; fax 2260-6260; e-mail infoparena@gmail.com; internet www.arena.com.sv; f. 1981; right-wing; Pres. ALFREDO FÉLIX CRISTIANI BURKARD; Exec. Dir ORLANDO CABRERA CANDRAY.

Cambio Democrático (CD): Casa 197, Calle Héctor Silva, Col. Médica, San Salvador; tel. 2225-5978; fax 2281-9636; e-mail comunicaciones@cambiodemocraticosv.org; internet www.cambiodemocraticosv.org; f. 1987 as Convergencia Democrática (CD); changed name as above in 2005; Sec.-Gen. HÉCTOR DADA HIREZI; Dep. Sec. JUAN JOSÉ MARTEL.

Concertación Nacional (CN): 15 Avda Norte y 3a Calle Poniente 244, San Salvador; tel. 2221-3752; fax 2281-9272; f. 2011 as successor party to the Partido de Conciliación Nacional (f. 1961); right-wing; Sec.-Gen. CIRO CRUZ ZEPEDA.

Frente Democrático Revolucionario (FDR): Avda Sierra Nevada 926, Col. Miramonte, San Salvador; tel. 2237-8844; fax 2260-1547; e-mail info@fdr.org.sv; internet www.fdr.org.sv;

f. 2005; left-wing, reformist; breakaway faction of FMLN; Co-ordinator-Gen. JULIO HERNÁNDEZ.

Frente Farabundo Martí para la Liberación Nacional (FMLN): 27 Calle Poniente, Col. Layco 1316, San Salvador; tel. 2226-7183; e-mail comision.politica@fmln.org.sv; internet www.fmln.org.sv; f. 1980 as the FDR (Frente Democrático Revolucionario—FMLN) as a left-wing opposition front to the Govt; the FDR was the political wing and the FMLN was the guerrilla front; achieved legal recognition 1992; comprised various factions, including Communist (Leader SALVADOR SÁNCHEZ CERÉN), Renewalist (Leader OSCAR ORTIZ) and Terceristas (Leader GERSON MARTÍNEZ); Co-ordinator-Gen. MEDARDO GONZÁLEZ.

Gran Alianza por la Unidad Nacional (GANA): 41 Avda Sur y 16 Calle Poniente 2143, Col. Flor Blanca, San Salvador; tel. 2279-0254; internet www.gana.org.sv; f. 2009 by fmr mems of ARENA (q.v.); Pres. JOSÉ ANDRÉS ROVIRA CANALES.

Partido de la Esperanza (PES): Centro de Gobierno, Alameda Juan Pablo II y 11 Avda Norte bis 507, San Salvador; tel. 2281-5498; fax 7998-1526; e-mail pdcsal@navegante.com.sv; f. 2011; successor to the disbanded Partido Demócrata Cristiano (f. 1960); 150,000 mems; advocates self-determination and Latin American integration; Sec.-Gen. RODOLFO ANTONIO PARKER SOTO.

Diplomatic Representation

EMBASSIES IN EL SALVADOR

Argentina: Calle La Sierra 3-I-B, Col. Escalón, San Salvador; tel. 2263-3638; fax 2263-3687; e-mail esalv@mrecic.gov.ar; Ambassador RUBÉN NÉSTOR PATTO.

Belize: Plaza Viscaya, Final Calle La Mascota, 1015 Col. Maquilishuat, San Salvador; tel. and fax 2264-8024; e-mail embsalbel@yahoo.com; Ambassador CELIE PAZ MARIN.

Brazil: Blvd Sérgio Vieira de Mello 132, Col. San Benito, San Salvador; tel. 2298-3286; fax 2279-3934; e-mail embajada@brasil.org.sv; internet www.brasil.org.sv; Ambassador LUIZ FELIPE MENDONÇA FILHO.

Canada: Centro Financiero Gigante, Torre A, Lobby 2, Alameda Roosevelt y 65 Avda Sur, Col. Escalón, San Salvador; tel. 2279-4655; fax 2279-0765; e-mail ssal@international.gc.ca; internet www.canadainternational.gc.ca/el_salvador-salvador; Ambassador MARIANICK TREMBLAY.

Chile: Pasaje Bellavista 121, 9a Calle Poniente, Col. Escalón, San Salvador; tel. 2263-4285; fax 2263-4308; e-mail embachile@embachile.org.sv; internet www.conchileelsalvador.com.sv; Ambassador MANUEL MATTA ARAGAY.

Colombia: Calle El Mirador 5120, Col. Escalón, San Salvador; tel. 2263-1936; fax 2263-1942; e-mail elsalvador@minrelext.gov.co; Ambassador CARLOS ALBERTO GAMBA.

Costa Rica: 85 Avda Sur y Calle Cuscatlán 4415, Col. Escalón, San Salvador; tel. 2264-3863; fax 2264-3866; e-mail embajada@embajadacostarica.org.sv; internet www.embajadacostarica.org.sv; Ambassador INGRID HERRMANN ESCRIBANO.

Cuba: Calle Arturo Ambrogui 530, esq. Avda el Mirador, Col. Escalón, San Salvador; tel. 2508-0446; Ambassador PEDRO PABLO PRADA QUINTERO.

Dominican Republic: Edif. Colinas, 1°, Blvd El Hipódromo 253, Zona Rosa, Col. San Benito, San Salvador; tel. 2223-4036; fax 2223-3109; e-mail endosal@saltel.net; Ambassador ROBERTO VICTORIA.

Ecuador: Pasaje Los Pinos 241, entre 77 y 79 Avda Norte, Col. Escalón, San Salvador; tel. 2263-5258; fax 2264-2973; e-mail ecuador@integra.com.sv; Ambassador SEGUNDO ANDRANGO.

France: 1a Calle Poniente 3718, Col. Escalón, Apdo 474, San Salvador; tel. 2279-4016; fax 2298-1536; e-mail info@embafrancia.com.sv; internet www.embafrancia.com.sv; Ambassador BLANDINE KREISS.

Germany: 7a Calle Poniente 3972, esq. 77a Avda Norte, Col. Escalón, Apdo 693, San Salvador; tel. 2247-0000; fax 2247-0099; e-mail info@san-salvador.diplo.de; internet www.san-salvador.diplo.de; Ambassador Dr CHRISTIAN STOCKS.

Guatemala: 15 Avda Norte 135, entre Calle Arce y 1a Calle Poniente, San Salvador; tel. 2271-2225; fax 2221-3019; e-mail embelsalvador@minex.gob.gt; Ambassador SILVIA ELIZABETH CÁCERES VETTORAZZI DE ALEMÁN.

Holy See: 87 Avda Norte y 7a Calle Poniente, Col. Escalón, Apdo 01-95, San Salvador (Apostolic Nunciature); tel. 2263-2931; fax 2263-3010; e-mail nunels@telesal.net; Apostolic Nuncio Most Rev. LUIGI PEZZUTO (Titular Archbishop of Torre di Proconsolare).

Honduras: 89 Avda Norte 561, entre 7a y 9a Calle Poniente, Col. Escalón, San Salvador; tel. 2263-2808; fax 2263-2296; e-mail embhon@integra.com.sv; internet www.sre.hn/elsalvador.html; Ambassador CÉSAR PINTO.

Israel: Centro Financiero Gigante, Torre B, 11°, Alameda Roosevelt y Avda Sur 63, San Salvador; tel. 2211-3434; fax 2211-3443; e-mail info@sansalvador.mfa.gov.il; internet sansalvador.mfa.gov.il; Ambassador MATTANYA COHEN.

Italy: Calle la Reforma 158, Col. San Benito, Apdo 0199, San Salvador; tel. 2223-5184; fax 2298-3050; e-mail ambasciatore.sansalvador@esteri.it; internet www.ambsansalvador.esteri.it; Ambassador CATERINA BERTOLINI.

Japan: World Trade Center, Torre 1, 6°, 89 Avda Norte y Calle El Mirador, Col. Escalón, Apdo 115, San Salvador; tel. 2528-1111; fax 2528-1110; internet www.sv.emb-japan.go.jp; Ambassador YASUO MINEMURA.

Korea, Republic: 5a Calle Poniente 3970, entre 75 y 77 Avda Norte, Col. Escalón, San Salvador; tel. 2263-9145; fax 2263-0783; e-mail embcorea@mofat.go.kr; internet slv.mofat.go.kr; Ambassador MAENG DAL-YOUNG.

Mexico: Calle Circunvalación y Pasaje 12, Col. San Benito, Apdo 432, San Salvador; tel. 2248-9900; fax 2248-9906; e-mail embamex@intercom.com.sv; internet portal.sre.gob.mx/elsalvador; Ambassador LEANDRO ARELLANO RESÉNDIZ.

Nicaragua: Calle El Mirador y 93 Avda Norte 4814, Col. Escalón, San Salvador; tel. 2263-8770; fax 2263-2292; e-mail embanic@integra.com.sv; Ambassador GILDA MARÍA BOLT GONZÁLEZ.

Panama: Calle los Bambúes, Avda las Bugambilías 21, Col. San Francisco, San Salvador; tel. 2536-0601; fax 2536-0602; e-mail embpan@telesat.net; Ambassador ENRIQUE BERMÚDEZ MARTINELLI.

Peru: Avda Masferrer Norte 17P, Cumbres de la Escalafón, Col. Escalón, San Salvador; tel. 2275-5566; fax 2275-5569; e-mail embperu@telesal.net; internet www.embajadaperu.com.sv; Ambassador ERIC EDGARDO ANDERSON.

Qatar: Avda Boquerón, Lote 21, Poligono L, Urb. Cumbre de la Escalón, San Salvador; tel. 2562-1480; fax 2562-1883; e-mail eqatar.salvador@gmail.com; Ambassador ABDULRAHMAN MOHAMED HAMDAN AL-DOUSSARI.

Spain: Calle La Reforma 164 bis, Col. San Benito, San Salvador; tel. 2257-5700; fax 2257-5712; e-mail emb.sansalvador@mae.es; internet www.maec.es/embajadas/sansalvador; Ambassador ENRIQUE OJEDA VILA.

Taiwan (Republic of China): Avda La Capilla 716, Blvd. del Hipódromo, Col. San Benito, Apdo 956, San Salvador; tel. 2263-1330; fax 2263-1329; e-mail sinoemb3@intercom.com.sv; internet www.taiwanembassy.org/sv; Ambassador JAIME CHEN.

United Kingdom: (from Sept. 2012) Torre Futura, 14°, Plaza Futura, Calle El Mirador, Col. Escalón, San Salvador; e-mail britishembassy.elsalvador@fco.gov.uk; Ambassador LINDA MARY CROSS.

USA: Blvd Santa Elena Sur, Antiguo Cuscatlán, San Salvador; tel. 2501-2999; fax 2501-2150; internet sansalvador.usembassy.gov; Chargé d'affaires a.i. SEAN MURPHY.

Uruguay: Edif. Gran Plaza 405, Blvd del Hipódromo 111, Col. San Benito, San Salvador; tel. 2279-1626; fax 2279-1627; e-mail urusalva@telesal.net; Ambassador MARÍA CRISTINA FIGUEROA URSI.

Venezuela: 7a Calle Poniente 3921, entre 75 y 77 Avda Norte, Col. Escalón, San Salvador; tel. 2263-3977; fax 2211-0027; e-mail embajadadevenezuela@telesal.net; internet embavenez-elsalvador.com.sv; Ambassador NORA MARGARITA URIBE TRUJILLO.

Judicial System

Supreme Court of Justice

Frente a Plaza José Simeón Cañas, Centro de Gobierno, San Salvador; tel. 2271-8888; fax 2271-3767; internet www.csj.gob.sv.

f. 1824; composed of 15 Magistrates, one of whom is its President; the Court is divided into four chambers: Constitutional Law, Civil Law, Criminal Law and Litigation; Pres. Dr OVIDIO BONILLA.

Courts of First Instance: 201 courts throughout the country.

Courts of Appeal: 26 chambers composed of two Magistrates.

Courts of Peace: 322 courts throughout the country.

Attorney-General: ROMEO BENJAMÍN BARAHONA MELÉNDEZ (until Sept. 2012), ASTOR ESCALANTE (from Sept. 2012).

Procurator-General for the Defence of Human Rights: OSCAR HUMBERTO LUNA.

Religion

Roman Catholicism is the dominant religion, but other denominations are also permitted. The Baptist Church, Seventh-day Adventists, Jehovah's Witnesses, and the Church of Jesus Christ of Latter-day Saints (Mormons) are represented.

CHRISTIANITY

The Roman Catholic Church

El Salvador comprises one archdiocese and seven dioceses. Roman Catholics represent some 76% of the total population.

Bishops' Conference

Conferencia Episcopal de El Salvador, 15 Avda Norte 1420, Col. Layco, Apdo 1310, San Salvador; tel. 2225-8997; fax 2226-5330; e-mail cedes.casa@telesal.net; internet www.iglesia.org.sv.

f. 1974; Pres. Most Rev. JOSÉ LUIS ESCOBAR ALAS (Archbishop of San Salvador).

Archbishop of San Salvador: Most Rev. JOSÉ LUIS ESCOBAR ALAS, Arzobispado, Col. Médica, Avda Dr Emilio Alvarez y Avda Dr Max Bloch, Apdo 2253, San Salvador; tel. 2226-0501; fax 2226-4979; e-mail info@arzobispadosansalvador.org; internet www.arzobispadosansalvador.org.

The Anglican Communion

El Salvador comprises one of the five dioceses of the Iglesia Anglicana de la Región Central de América. The Iglesia Anglicana has some 5,000 members.

Bishop of El Salvador: Rt Rev. MARTÍN DE JESÚS BARAHONA PASCACIO, 47 Avda Sur, 723 Col. Flor Blanca, Apdo 01-274, San Salvador; tel. 2223-2252; fax 2223-7952; e-mail martinba@gbm.net; internet www.cristosal.org.

The Baptist Church

Baptist Association of El Salvador: Avda Sierra Nevada 922, Col. Miramonte, Apdo 347, San Salvador; tel. 2226-6287; e-mail asociacionbautistaabes@hotmail.com; internet www.ublaonline.org/paises/elsalvador.htm; f. 1933; Pres. MANUEL ENRIQUE RIVAS; 4,427 mems.

Other Churches

Sínodo Luterano Salvadoreño (Salvadorean Lutheran Synod): Final 49 Avda Sur, Calle Paralela al Bulevar de los Próceres, San Salvador; tel. 2225-2843; fax 2248-3451; e-mail lutomg@sls.org.sv; internet sls.org.sv; Pres. Bishop MEDARDO E. GÓMEZ SOTO; 20,000 mems.

The Press

DAILY NEWSPAPERS

San Miguel

Diario de Oriente: Avda Gerardo Barrios 406, San Miguel; internet www.elsalvador.com/diarios/oriente; Editor ROBERTO VALENCIA.

San Salvador

Co Latino: 23a Avda Sur 225, Apdo 96, San Salvador; tel. 2271-1303; fax 2271-0822; e-mail info@diariocolatino.com; internet www.diariocolatino.com; f. 1890; evening; Editor FRANCISCO ELÍAS VALENCIA SORIANO; circ. 15,000.

El Diario de Hoy: 11 Calle Oriente 271, Apdo 495, San Salvador; tel. 2231-7777; fax 2231-7869; e-mail redaccion@elsalvador.com; internet www.elsalvador.com; f. 1936; morning; independent; Dir ENRIQUE ALTAMIRANO MADRIZ; circ. 115,000.

Diario Oficial: 4a Calle Poniente y 15a, Avda Sur 829, San Salvador; tel. 2555-7829; fax 2222-4936; e-mail diariooficial@imprentanacional.gob.sv; internet www.imprentanacional.gob.sv; f. 1875; govt publ; Dir LUIS ERNESTO FLORES LÓPEZ; circ. 1,000.

El Mundo: 15 Calle Poniente y 7a Avda Norte 521, San Salvador; tel. 2234-8000; fax 2222-8190; e-mail mercadeo@elmundo.com.sv; internet www.elmundo.com.sv; f. 1967; morning; Exec. Dir ONNO WUELFERS; circ. 40,215.

La Prensa Gráfica: 3a Calle Poniente 130, San Salvador; tel. 2241-2000; fax 2271-4242; e-mail lpg@laprensa.com.sv; internet www.laprensagrafica.com; f. 1915; general information; conservative, independent; Editor RODOLFO DUTRIZ; circ. 97,312 (weekdays), 115,564 (Sundays).

Santa Ana

Diario de Occidente: 1a Avda Sur 3, Santa Ana; tel. 2441-2931; internet www.elsalvador.com/diarios/occidente; f. 1910; circ. 6,000.

PERIODICALS

Cultura: Dirección de Publicaciones e Impresos, 17 Avda Sur 430, San Salvador; tel. 2510-5318; fax 2221-4415; e-mail revistacultura@concultura.gob.sv; internet www.dpi.gob.sv/Revista_Cultura.htm; f. 1955; 3 a year; publ. by the National Council for Culture and the Arts; Pres. LUIS FEDERICO HERNÁNDEZ AGUILAR; circ. 1,000.

El Economista: Grupo Dutriz, Blvd Santa Elena, Antiguo Cuscatlán, La Libertad; tel. 2241-2677; e-mail eleconomista@eleconomista.net; internet www.eleconomista.net; f. 2005; owned by Grupo Dutriz; monthly; business and economics; Chairman JOSÉ ROBERTO DUTRIZ.

Ella: Final blvd Santa Elena, frente a embajada de EUA, Antiguo Cuscatlán, La Libertad; tel. 2241-2000; e-mail ella@laprensa.com.sv; internet www.laprensagrafica.com; publ. by La Prensa Gráfica.

El Salvador Investiga: Proyección de Investigaciones, Edif. A5, 2°, Centro de Gobierno, San Salvador; tel. 2221-4439; e-mail direccion.investigaciones@concultura.gob.sv; internet www.concultura.gob.sv/revistainvestiga.htm; f. 2005; 2 a year; publ. by the National Council for Culture and the Arts; historical and cultural research; Editor MARIO COLORADO.

Motor Magazine: Final blvd Santa Elena, frente a embajada de EUA, Antiguo Cuscatlán, La Libertad; tel. 2241-2000; e-mail motor@laprensa.com.sv; internet www.laprensagrafica.com; publ. by La Prensa Gráfica; Editor ROBERTO FLORES PINTO.

PRESS ASSOCIATION

Asociación de Periodistas de El Salvador (Press Association of El Salvador): Edif. Casa del Periodista, Paseo Gen. Escalón 4130, San Salvador; tel. 2263-5335; e-mail info@apes.org.sv; internet www.apes.org.sv; Pres. RAFAEL DOMÍNGUEZ.

Publishers

Clásicos Roxsil, SA de CV: 4a Avda Sur 2–3, Nueva San Salvador; tel. 2228-1832; fax 2228-1212; e-mail roxanabe@navegante.com.sv; f. 1976; textbooks, literature; Dir ROSA VICTORIA SERRANO DE LÓPEZ; Editorial Dir ROXANA BEATRIZ LOPEZ.

Dirección de Publicaciones e Impresos: Concultura, 17a Avda Sur 430, San Salvador; tel. 2271-1806; fax 2271-1071; e-mail publicaciones.direccion@concultura.gob.sv; internet www.dpi.gob.sv; f. 1953; literary and general; Dir JASMINE CAMPOS.

Editorial Delgado: Universidad 'Dr José Matías Delgado', Km 8.5, Carretera Santa Tecla; tel. 2278-1011; fax 2289-5314; e-mail boculin@yahoo.es; internet www.ujmd.edu.sv; f. 1984; Dir CLAUDIA HÉRODIER.

Editorial Universidad Don Bosco: Calle Plan del Pino, Ciudadela Don Bosco, Soyapango, San Salvador; tel. 2251-8212; e-mail hflores@udb.edu.sv; internet www.udb.edu.sv/editorial; f. 2005; academic periodicals and texts; Pres. Dr JOSÉ HUMBERTO FLORES.

UCA Editores: Blvd Los Próceres, Apdo 01-575, San Salvador; tel. 2210-6600; fax 2210-6650; e-mail ucaeditores@gmail.com; internet www.ucaeditores.com.sv/uca; f. 1975; social science, religion, economy, literature and textbooks; Dir ANDREU OLIVA.

PUBLISHERS' ASSOCIATION

Cámara Salvadoreña del Libro: Edif. Forty Seven, Local 4, Col. Flor Blanca, 47 Avda Norte y 1a Calle Poniente, Apdo 3384, San Salvador; tel. 2275-0293; fax 2261-2231; e-mail camsalibro@terra.com.sv; internet www.camsalibro.com; f. 1974; Pres. ANA DOLORES MOLINA DE FAUVET; Exec. Dir AMÉRICA DOMÍNGUEZ.

Broadcasting and Communications

TELECOMMUNICATIONS

Regulatory Authority

Superintendencia General de Electricidad y Telecomunicaciones (SIGET): 16a Calle Poniente y 37 Avda Sur 2001, Col. Flor Blanca, San Salvador; tel. 2257-4438; fax 2257-4498; e-mail info@siget.gob.sv; internet www.siget.gob.sv; f. 1996; Supt LUIS MÉNDEZ MENÉNDEZ.

Major Service Providers

Claro: Edif. F, 1°, Complejo Telecom Roma, Calle Liverpool y Final Calle El Progreso, Col. Roma, San Salvador; tel. 2250-5555; fax 2221-

4849; e-mail clientes@claro.com.sv; internet www.claro.com.sv; telecommunications network, fmrly part of Administración Nacional de Telecomunicaciones (ANTEL), which was divested in 1998; changed name from CTE Antel Telecom in 1999; acquired by América Móvil, SA de CV (Mexico) in 2003; fixed line and mobile cellular operations; Exec. Pres. ERIC BEHNER.

Digicel: Edif. Palic, 5°, Alameda Dr Manuel Enrique Araujo y Calle Nueva No 1, Col. Escalón, San Salvador; tel. 2285-5100; fax 2285-5585; e-mail servicioalcliente.sv@digicelgroup.com; internet www.digicel.com.sv; owned by Digicel (USA); negotiations under way in Aug. 2011 to sell Digicel to América Móvil, SA de CV (Mexico); mobile telecommunications; CEO JOSÉ ANTONIO RODRÍGUEZ.

Telefónica Móviles El Salvador, SA de CV (Movistar): Torre Telefónica (Torre B de Centro Financiero Gigante), Alameda Roosevelt y 63 Avda Sur, Col. Escalón, San Salvador; tel. 2244-0144; e-mail telefonica.empresas@telefonica.com.sv; internet www.movistar.com.sv; mobile telecommunications; 92% owned by Telefónica Móviles, SA (Spain); Exec. Dir HERNÁN OZÓN.

Tigo El Salvador: Centro Financiero, Gigante Torre D, 9°, Avda Roosevelt, San Salvador; tel. 2246-9977; fax 2246-9999; e-mail servicioalcliente@tigo.com.sv; internet www.tigo.com.sv; mobile telecommunications and internet services; subsidiary of Millicom International Cellular (Luxembourg); CEO GLORIA ORTEGA DE ARZA.

RADIO

Radio Nacional de El Salvador: Edif. Ministerio de Gobernación, Cto. de Gobierno, 7°, Alameda Juan Pablo II, San Salvador; tel. 2248-9000; e-mail radio.elsalvador@gobernacion.gob.sv; internet www.radioelsalvador.com.sv; f. 1926; non-commercial cultural station; Dir-Gen. ALBERTO BARRERA.

TELEVISION

Canal 8 (Agape TV): Centro Comunicaciones AGAPE, 1511 Calle Gerardo Barrios, Col. Cucumacuyán, San Salvador; tel. 2281-2828; fax 2211-0799; e-mail info@agapetv8.com; internet www.agapetv8.com; Catholic, family channel; Pres. FLAVIÁN MUCCI.

Canal 12: Blvd Santa Elena Sur 12, Antiguo Cuscatlán, La Libertad; tel. 2535-1212; fax 2278-0722; internet www.canal12.com.sv; f. 1984; Dir ALEJANDRO GONZÁLEZ.

Grupo Megavisión: Calle Poniente entre 85 y 86 Avda Norte, Apdo 2789, San Salvador; tel. 2283-2121; e-mail serviciosmegavision@salnet.net; internet www.megavision.com.sv; operates Canal 21.

Grupo Televisivo Cuscatleco: 6a–10a Calle Poniente 2323, Col. Flor Blanca, San Salvador; tel. 2559-8326; fax 2245-6142; e-mail info.sv@tecoloco.com; internet www.tecoloco.com.sv; operates Canal 23, 25, 67 and 69 (in the West only).

Tecnovisión Canal 33: entre 75 y 77 Avda Nte, Istmania No 262, San Salvador; tel. 2559-3333; e-mail info@canal33.tv; internet www.canal33.tv; Pres. JOSÉ MAURICIO LOUCEL.

Finance

(cap. = capital; res = reserves; dep. = deposits; m. = million; brs = branches; amounts in colones unless otherwise stated)

BANKING

Supervisory Bodies

Superintendencia del Sistema Financiero: 7a Avda Norte 240, Apdo 2942, San Salvador; tel. 2281-2444; fax 2281-1621; e-mail webmaster@ssf.gob.sv; internet www.ssf.gob.sv; Pres. VÍCTOR ANTONIO RAMÍREZ NAJARRO.

Superintendencia de Valores: Antiguo Edif. BCR, 2°, 1a Calle Poniente y 7a Avda Norte, San Salvador; tel. 2281-8900; fax 2221-3404; e-mail info@superval.gob.sv; internet www.superval.gob.sv; Supt RENÉ MAURICIO GUARDADO RODRÍGUEZ.

Central Bank

Banco Central de Reserva de El Salvador: Alameda Juan Pablo II, entre 15 y 17 Avda Norte, Apdo 01-106, San Salvador; tel. 2281-8000; fax 2281-8011; e-mail info@bcr.gob.sv; internet www.bcr.gob.sv; f. 1934; nationalized Dec. 1961; entered monetary integration process 1 Jan. 2001; cap. US $115.0m., res $171.2m., dep. $2,017.3m. (Dec. 2009); Pres. CARLOS ACEVEDO; Vice-Pres. MARTA EVELYN DE RIVERA.

Commercial and Mortgage Banks

Banco Agrícola: Blvd Constitución 100, San Salvador; tel. 2267-5000; fax 2267-5930; e-mail info@bancoagricola.com; internet www.bancoagricola.com; f. 1955; merged with Banco Desarrollo in 2000; acquired Banco Capital in Nov. 2001; cap. US $297.5m., res $218.7m., dep. $2,719m. (Dec. 2010); Pres. SERGIO RESTREPO ISAZA; 8 brs.

Banco Citibank de El Salvador, SA: Edif. Pirámide Cuscatlán, Km 10, Carretera a Santa Tecla, Apdo 626, San Salvador; tel. 2212-2000; fax 2228-5700; e-mail info@bancocuscatlan.com; internet www.bancocuscatlan.com/elsalvador; f. 1972; acquired by Citi (USA) in 2008; cap. US $155.7m., res $168.9m., dep. $2,011.3m. (Dec. 2008); Pres. JOSÉ MAURICIO SAMAYOA RIVAS; 31 brs.

Banco Hipotecario de El Salvador: Pasaje Senda Florida Sur, Col. Escalón, Apdo 999, San Salvador; tel. 2223-7713; fax 2298-2071; internet www.bancohipotecario.com.sv; f. 1935; cap. US $19.5m., res $21.1m., dep. $355.3m. (Dec. 2009); Pres. CARLOS ALBERTO ORTIZ; 16 brs.

Banco HSBC Salvadoreño, SA (Bancosal): Edif. Centro Financiero, Avda Manuel E. Araujo y Avda Olímpica 3550, Apdo 0673, San Salvador; tel. 2214-2000; fax 2214-2755; e-mail info@bancosal.com; internet www.hsbc.com.sv; f. 1885 as Banco Salvadoreño, SA; adopted current name 2007; bought by Banco Davivienda (Colombia) in 2012; cap. US $150m., res $83.1m., dep. $1,369.7m. (Dec. 2009); CEO GERARDO JOSÉ SIMÁN SIRI; 74 brs.

Banco Promérica: Edif. Promérica, Centro Comercial La Gran Vía, Antiguo Cuscatlán; tel. 2513-5000; e-mail soluciones@promerica.com.sv; internet www.promerica.com.sv; f. 1996; privately owned; cap. US $21.7m., res $338.5m. (Dec. 2009); Chair. RAMIRO ORTIZ GURDÍAN; Exec. Pres. EDUARDO A. QUEVEDO MORENO.

Public Institutions

Banco de Fomento Agropecuario: Km 10.5, Carretera al Puerto de la Libertad, Santa Tecla, La Libertad, Nueva San Salvador; tel. 2241-0966; fax 2241-0800; internet www.bfa.gob.sv; f. 1973; state-owned; cap. US $17.8m., res $6.3m., dep. $176.9m. (Dec. 2009); Pres. NORA MIRANDA DE LÓPEZ; Gen. Man. JOSÉ ANTONIO PEÑATE; 27 brs.

Banco Multisectorial de Inversiones: Edif. World Trade Center II, 4°, San Salvador; tel. 2267-0000; fax 2267-0011; e-mail servicio.cliente@bmi.gob.sv; internet www.bmi.gob.sv; f. 1994; Pres. RICARDO MORA.

Federación de Cajas de Crédito (FEDECREDITO): 25 Avda Norte y 23 Calle Poniente, San Salvador; tel. 2209-9696; fax 2226-7161; e-mail informacion@fedecredito.com.sv; internet www.fedecredito.com.sv; f. 1943; Pres. MACARIO ARMANDO ROSALES ROSA.

Fondo Social para la Vivienda (FSV): Calle Rubén Darío 901, entre 15 y 17 Avda Sur, Apdo 2179, San Salvador; tel. 2231-2000; fax 2271-4011; e-mail comunicaciones@fsv.gob.sv; internet www.fsv.gob.sv; f. 1973; provides loans to workers for house purchases; Pres. JOSÉ TOMÁS CHÉVEZ RUIZ; Gen. Man. FRANCISCO ANTONIO GUEVARA.

Banking Association

Asociación Bancaria Salvadoreña (ABANSA): Pasaje Senda, Florida Norte 140, Col. Escalón, San Salvador; tel. 2298-6959; fax 2223-1079; e-mail info@abansa.net; internet www.abansa.org.sv; f. 1965; Pres. ARMANDO ARIAS; Exec. Dir MARCELA DE JIMÉNEZ.

STOCK EXCHANGE

Mercado de Valores de El Salvador, SA de CV (Bolsa de Valores): Urb. Jardines de la Hacienda, Blvd Merliot y Avda Las Carretas, Antiguo Cuscatlán, La Libertad, San Salvador; tel. 2212-6400; fax 2278-4377; e-mail info@bves.com.sv; internet www.bves.com.sv; f. 1992; Pres. ROLANDO ARTURO DUARTE SCHLAGETER.

INSURANCE

Aseguradora Agrícola Comercial, SA: Alameda Roosevelt 3104, Apdo 1855, San Salvador; tel. 2261-8200; fax 2260-5592; e-mail informacion@acsasal.com.sv; internet www.acsasal.com.sv; f. 1973; Pres. LUIS ALFREDO ESCALANTE SOL; Gen. Man. RAÚL ANTONIO GUEVARA.

Aseguradora Popular, SA: Paseo Gen. Escalón 5338, Col. Escalón, San Salvador; tel. 2263-0700; fax 2263-1246; e-mail info@aseguradorapopular.com; internet aseguradorapopular.com; f. 1975; Pres. Dr CARLOS ARMANDO LAHÚD; Gen. Man. HERIBERTO PÉREZ AGUIRRE.

Aseguradora Suiza Salvadoreña, SA (ASESUISA): Alameda Dr Manuel Enrique Araujo, Plaza Suiza, Apdo 1490, Col. San Benito, San Salvador; tel. 2209-5000; fax 2209-5001; e-mail info@asesuisa.com; internet www.asesuisa.com; f. 1969; acquired in 2001 by Inversiones Financieras Banco Agrícola (Panama); Pres. Dr SERGIO RESTREPO ISAZA; Exec. Dir RICARDO COHEN.

La Central de Seguros y Fianzas, SA: Avda Olímpica 3333, Apdo 01-255, San Salvador; tel. 2268-6000; fax 2223-7647; e-mail gerenciaseguros@lacentral.com.sv; internet www.lacentral.com.sv; f. 1983; Pres. EDUARDO ENRIQUE CHACÓN BORJA; Man. (Insurance) MAURICIO E. ULLOA MORAZÁN.

Chartis Seguros El Salvador, SA: Calle Loma Linda 265, Col. San Benito, Apdo 92, San Salvador; tel. 2250-3200; fax 2250-3201; e-mail chartis.elsalvador@chartisinsurance.com; internet www.chartisinsurance.com; f. 1998 as AIG Unión y Desarrollo, SA; following merger of Unión y Desarrollo, SA and AIG; changed name as above in 2009; Gen. Man. PEDRO ARTANA.

Internacional de Seguros, SA (Interseguros): Edif. Plaza Credicorp Bank, Calle 50, 19°, 20° y 21°, San Salvador; tel. 2206-4000; fax 2210-1900; e-mail interseguros@interseguros.com.sv; internet isweb.iseguros.com/iseguros; f. 1910; merged with Seguros Universales in 2004; Pres. ROY ICAZA JIMÉNEZ; Exec. Vice-Pres. MAURICIO DE LA GUARDIA.

Mapfre La Centro Americana, SA: Alameda Roosevelt 3107, Apdo 527, San Salvador; tel. 2257-6666; fax 2223-2687; e-mail lacentro@lacentro.com; internet www.lacentro.com; f. 1915; acquired by Mapfre, SA in 2000; Pres. ANTONIO PENEDO CASMARTIÑO; Gen. Man. GILMAR NAVARRETE CASTAÑEDA.

Pan-American Life Insurance Co: Edif. PALIC, Alameda Dr Manuel Enrique Araujo y Calle Nueva 1, Col. Escalón, Apdo 255, San Salvador; tel. 2209-2700; fax 2245-2792; e-mail servicioalclientesv@panamericanlife.com; internet www.palig.com/Regions/el_salvador.aspx; f. 1928; Country Man. JEAN CARLO CALDERÓN.

Scotia Seguros, SA: Calle Loma Linda 223, Col. San Benito, Apdo 1004, San Salvador; tel. 2209-7000; fax 2223-0734; e-mail contactenos@scotiaseguros.com.sv; internet www.scotiaseguros.com.sv; f. 1955; fmrly Compañía General de Seguros, SA; changed name as above in 2005; Pres. JUAN CARLOS GARCÍA VIZCAÍNO; Gen. Man. PEDRO GEOFFROY.

Seguros e Inversiones, SA (SISA): Carretera Panamericana, 10.5 Km, Santa Tecla, La Libertad; tel. 2241-0000; fax 2241-1213; e-mail servicioalcliente@sisa.com.sv; internet www.sisa.com.sv; f. 1962; Pres. JOSÉ EDUARDO MONTENEGRO PALOMO.

Association

Asociación Salvadoreña de Empresas de Seguros (ASES): Calle Los Castaños 120, Col. San Francisco, San Salvador; tel. 2223-7169; fax 2223-8901; e-mail asesgeneral@ases.com.sv; internet www.ases.com.sv; f. 1970; Pres. GILMAR NAVARRETE CASTAÑEDA; Exec. Dir Dr RAÚL BETANCOURT MENÉNDEZ.

Trade and Industry

GOVERNMENT AGENCIES AND DEVELOPMENT ORGANIZATIONS

Comisión Nacional de la Micro y Pequeña Empresa (CONAMYPE): Of. 41, 1°, Avda Norte y Avda Scout de El Salvador, No 115, San Salvador; tel. 2521-2200; fax 2521-2274; e-mail conamype@conamype.gob.sv; internet www.conamype.gob.sv; f. 1996; micro and small industrial devt; Pres. ARMANDO FLORES (Minister of the Economy); Exec. Dir ILEANA ROGEL.

Consejo Nacional de Ciencia y Tecnología (CONACYT): Avda Dr Emilio Alvarez, Pasaje Dr Guillermo Rodríguez Pacas 51, Col. Médica, San Salvador; tel. 2234-8400; fax 2225-6255; e-mail cit@conacyt.gob.sv; internet www.conacyt.gob.sv/drupal; f. 1992; formulation and guidance of national policy on science and technology; Exec. Dir CARLOS ROBERTO OCHOA CÓRDOBA.

Corporación de Exportadores de El Salvador (COEXPORT): Avda La Capilla 359A, Col. San Benito, San Salvador; tel. 2212-0200; fax 2243-3159; e-mail info@coexport.com.sv; internet www.coexport.com.sv; f. 1973 to promote Salvadorean exports; Pres. FRANCISCO BOLAÑOS; Exec. Dir SILVIA M. CUÉLLAR DE PAREDES.

Corporación Salvadoreña de Inversiones (CORSAIN): Avda Bunganbilias, Casa 14, Col. San Francisco, San Salvador; tel. 2224-6070; fax 2224-6877; e-mail info@corsain.gob.sv; internet www.corsain.gob.sv; Pres. JOSÉ LEOPOLDO SAMOUR GÓMEZ.

Fondo de Inversión Social para el Desarrollo Local (FISDL): Avda Sur y Calle México, No 10, Barrio San Jacinto, San Salvador; tel. 2505-1200; fax 2505-1370; e-mail webmaster@fisdl.gob.sv; internet www.fisdl.gob.sv; f. 1990; poverty alleviation and development; Pres. HÉCTOR SILVA ARGÜELLO.

Instituto Salvadoreño de Fomento Cooperativo (INSAFOCOOP): Edif. Urrutia Abrego 2, Frente a INPEP, 15 Calle Poniente, No 402, San Salvador; tel. 2222-2563; fax 2222-4119; e-mail insafocoop@insafocoop.gob.sv; internet www.insafocoop.gob.sv; f. 1971; devt of co-operatives; Pres. FÉLIX CÁRCAMO.

Instituto Salvadoreño de Transformación Agraria (ISTA): Final Col. Las Mercedes, Km 5.5, Carretera a Santa Tecla, San Salvador; tel. 2527-2600; fax 2224-0259; e-mail info@ista.gob.sv; internet www.ista.gob.sv; f. 1976 to promote rural devt; empowered to buy inefficiently cultivated land; Pres. PABLO ALCIDES OCHOA.

CHAMBER OF COMMERCE

Cámara de Comercio e Industria de El Salvador: 9a Avda Norte y 5a Calle Poniente, Apdo 1640, San Salvador; tel. 2231-3000; fax 2271-4461; e-mail camara@camarasal.com; internet www.camarasal.com; f. 1915; 2,000 mems; Pres. LUIS CARDENAL; brs in San Miguel, Santa Ana, Sonsonate and La Unión.

INDUSTRIAL AND TRADE ASSOCIATIONS

Asociación Azúcarera de El Salvador (AAES): 103 Avda Norte y Calle Arturo Ambrogi 145, Col. Escalón, San Salvador; tel. 2264-1226; fax 2263-0361; e-mail asosugar@sal.gbm.net; internet www.asociacionazucarera.com; national sugar asscn, fmrly Instituto Nacional del Azúcar; Pres. MARIO SALAVERRÍA; Dir JULIO ARROYO.

Asociación Cafetalera de El Salvador (ACES): 67 Avda Norte 116, Col. Escalón, San Salvador; tel. 2223-3024; fax 2298-6261; e-mail ascafes@telesal.net; f. 1930; coffee growers' asscn; Pres. JOSÉ ROBERTO INCLÁN ROBREDO; Exec. Dir AMIR SALVADOR ALABÍ.

Asociación Salvadoreña de Beneficiadores y Exportadores de Café (ABECAFE): 87 Avda Norte, Condominio Fountainblue 4, Col. Escalón, San Salvador; tel. 2263-2834; fax 2263-2833; e-mail abecafe@telesal.net; coffee producers' and exporters' asscn; Pres. CARLOS BORGONOVO.

Asociación Salvadoreña de Industriales: Calles Roma y Liverpool, Col. Roma, Apdo 48, San Salvador; tel. 2279-2488; fax 2267-9253; e-mail medios@asi.com.sv; internet www.industriaelsalvador.com; f. 1958; 400 mems; manufacturers' asscn; Pres. JAVIER ERNESTO SIMAN; Exec. Dir JORGE ARRIAZA.

Cámara Agropecuaria y Agroindustrial de El Salvador (CAMAGRO): Calle El Lirio 19, Col. Maquilishuat, San Salvador; tel. 2264-4622; fax 2263-9448; e-mail contactenos@camagro.com; internet www.camagro.com; Pres. AGUSTÍN MARTÍNEZ.

Consejo Salvadoreño del Café (CSC) (Salvadorean Coffee Council): 1 Avda Norte y 13 Calle Poniente, Nueva San Salvador, La Libertad; tel. 2267-6600; fax 2267-6650; e-mail csc@consejocafe.org.sv; internet www.consejocafe.org; f. 1989 as successor to the Instituto Nacional del Café; formulates policy and oversees the coffee industry; Exec. Dir ANA ELENA ESCALANTE.

Unión de Cooperativas de Cafetaleras de El Salvador de RL (UCAFES): Avda Río Lempa, Calle Adriático 44, Jardines de Guadalupe, San Salvador; tel. 2243-2238; fax 2298-1504; union of coffee-growing co-operatives; Pres. ERNESTO LIMA.

EMPLOYERS' ORGANIZATION

Asociación Nacional de Empresa Privada (ANEP) (National Private Enterprise Association): 1 Calle Poniente y 71 Avda Norte 204, Col. Escalón, Apdo 1204, San Salvador; tel. 2209-8300; fax 2209-8317; e-mail communicaciones@anep.org.sv; internet www.anep.org.sv; national private enterprise asscn; Pres. JORGE DABOUB; Exec. Dir ARNOLDO JIMÉNEZ.

UTILITIES

Electricity

Comisión Ejecutiva Hidroeléctrica del Río Lempa (CEL): 9 Calle Poniente 950, entre 15 y 17 Avda Norte, Centro de Gobierno, San Salvador; tel. 2211-6000; fax 2207-1302; e-mail naguilar@cel.gob.sv; internet www.cel.gob.sv; f. 1948; hydroelectric electricity generation; Pres. IRVING PABEL TÓCHEZ MARAVILLA; Exec. Dir JAIME CONTRERAS.

Superintendencia General de Electricidad y Telecomunicaciones (SIGET): see Broadcasting and Communications—Telecommunications; regulatory authority.

Electricity Companies

AES El Salvador: e-mail consultas@aes.com; internet www.aeselsalvador.com; Exec. Pres. ABRAHAM BICHARA; operates four distribution cos in El Salvador:

CLESA: 23 Avda Sur y 5a Calle Oriente, Barrio San Rafael, Santa Ana; tel. 2429-4000; f. 1892.

Compañía de Alumbrado Electric (CAESS): Calle El Bambú, Col. San Antonio, Ayutuxtepeque, San Salvador; tel. 2529-9999; f. 1890.

Distribuidora Eléctrica de Usulután (DEUSEM): Centro Comercial Puerta de Oriente Local 2, Usulután; tel. 2622-4000; f. 1957.

EEO: Final 8, Calle Poniente, Calle a Ciudad Pacífico, Plantel Jalacatal, San Miguel; tel. 2606-8000; f. 1995.

Distribuidora de Electricidad del Sur (DELSUR): Edif. Corporativo DELSUR, Unidad de Comunicaciones, Final 17 Avda Norte y Calle El Boquerón, Santa Tecla, La Libertad; tel. 2233-5700; fax 2243-8662; e-mail comunicaciones@delsur.com.sv; internet www.delsur.com.sv; Pres. IVÁN DÍAZ MOLINA; Gen. Man. ALEXIS BUTTO.

La Geo: Final 15, Avda Sur y Blvd Sur, Col. Utila, Santa Tecla, La Libertad; tel. 2211-6700; fax 2211-6746; e-mail info@lageo.com.sv; internet www.lageo.com.sv; f. 1999; jt venture between state and ENEL Latin America; operates Ahuachapán and Berlin geothermal fields; Dir JORGE JOSÉ SIMÁN.

Water

Administración Nacional de Acueductos y Alcantarillados (ANDA): Edif. ANDA, Final Avda Don Bosco, Col. Libertad, San Salvador; tel. 2247-2700; fax 2225-3152; e-mail sugerencias@anda.gob.sv; internet www.anda.gob.sv; f. 1961; maintenance of water supply and sewerage systems; Pres. MARCO ANTONIO FORTÍN; Exec. Dir CARLOS MANUEL DERAS BARILLAS.

TRADE UNIONS

Central Autónoma de Trabajadores Salvadoreños (CATS): Calle Los Pinares 17, Col. Centroamérica, San Salvador; tel. 2211-2570; e-mail cats@integra.com.sv; internet www.catssal.com; Sec.-Gen. FRANCISCO QUIJANO; 30,000 mems (2010).

Central de Trabajadores Democráticos de El Salvador (CTD) (Democratic Workers' Confederation): Avda Norte 19 y Calle Poniente 17, No 135, Barrio San Miguelito, San Salvador; tel. and fax 2235-8043; e-mail ctdelsalv_orit@navegante.com.sv; Sec.-Gen. JOSÉ MARÍA AMAYA; 50,000 mems (2007).

Central de Trabajadores Salvadoreños (CTS) (Salvadorean Workers' Confederation): Calle Darío González 616, San Jacinto, San Salvador; tel. 2237-2315; fax 2270-1703; e-mail felixblancocts@hotmail.com; f. 1966; Christian Democratic; Pres. FÉLIX BLANCO; 30,000 mems (2007).

Confederación General de Sindicatos (CGS) (General Confederation of Unions): Edif. Kury, 3a Calle Oriente 226, San Salvador; tel. and fax 2222-3527; f. 1958; admitted to ITUC/ORIT; Sec.-Gen. JOSÉ ISRAEL HUIZA CISNEROS; 27,000 mems.

Confederación Sindical de Trabajadoras y Trabajadores Salvadoreños (CSTS) (Salvadorean Workers' Union Federation): Blvd Universitario 2226, Col. San José, San Salvador; tel. 2225-2315; fax 225-5936; e-mail confederacioncsts@gmail.com; internet www.cstsconfederacion.org; f. 2005; conglomerate of independent left-wing trade unions; Sec.-Gen. JOSÉ MARTIN JIMÉNEZ RAMÍREZ.

Confederación Unitaria de Trabajadores Salvadoreños (CUTS) (United Salvadorean Workers' Federation): 141 Avda A, Col. San José, San Salvador; tel. and fax 2226-2100; e-mail proyectocuts@salnet.net; internet www.cutselsalvador.org; left-wing; Sec.-Gen. JUAN EDITO GENOVES.

Federación Nacional Sindical de Trabajadores Salvadoreños (FENASTRAS) (Salvadorean Workers' National Union Federation): 4 Calle Poniente, No 2438A, Col. Flor Blanca, San Salvador; tel. 2298-2954; fax 2298-2953; e-mail fenastras@hotmail.com; internet www.fenastras.org; f. 1972; left-wing; 35,000 mems in 16 affiliates; Sec.-Gen. JUAN JOSÉ HUEZO.

Transport

Comisión Ejecutiva Portuaria Autónoma (CEPA): Edif. Torre Roble, Blvd de Los Héroes, Col. Miramonte, Centro Comercial Metrocentro, San Salvador; tel. 2218-1300; fax 2121-1212; e-mail info@cepa.gob.sv; internet www.cepa.gob.sv; f. 1952; operates and administers the ports of Acajutla and Cutuco and the El Salvador International Airport, as well as Ferrocarriles Nacionales de El Salvador; Pres. ALBERTO ARENE; Gen. Man. SALVADOR VILLALOBOS.

RAILWAYS

In 2005 there were 554.8 km of railway track in the country. The main track linked San Salvador with the ports of Acajutla and Cutuco (also known as La Unión) and with Santa Ana. Operation of the railway network was suspended in 2005; however, a passenger service between San Salvador and Apopa (a distance of 12.5 km) resumed in 2007, and the rehabilitation of further sections of track was planned.

Ferrocarriles Nacionales de El Salvador (FENADESAL): Final Avda Peralta 903, Apdo 2292, San Salvador; tel. 2530-1700; e-mail salvador.sanabria@cepa.gob.sv; internet www.fenadesal.gob.sv; 555 km of track; administered by CEPA (q.v.); Gen. Man. SALVADOR SANABRIA.

ROADS

There were some 10,886 km of roads in 2000, including the Pan-American Highway (306 km). In 2011 the first 44 km of the 178-km Carretera Longitudinal del Norte was inaugurated. The US $248m. project would connect the north of El Salvador with the rest of the country and was scheduled to be completed by September 2012.

Fondo de Conservación Vial (FOVIAL): Carretera a La Libertad, Km 10.5, Antiguo Cuscatlán, San Salvador; tel. 2257-8300; e-mail info@fovial.com; internet www.fovial.com; f. 2000; responsible for maintaining the road network; Exec. Dir ELIUD ULISES AYALA.

SHIPPING

The port of Acajutla is administered by CEPA (see above). Services are also provided by foreign lines. An expansion of the port of Cutuco (Puerto La Unión Centroamericana) was completed in 2009.

Autoridad Portuaria de La Unión: Depto de La Unión; tel. 2623-6100; e-mail info@launion.gob.sv; internet www.puertolaunion.gob.sv; Gen. Man. MILTON LACAYO.

CIVIL AVIATION

The El Salvador International Airport is located 40 km (25 miles) from San Salvador in Comalapa. The former international airport at Ilopango is used for military and private civilian aircraft; there are an additional 88 private airports.

TACA International Airlines: Santa Elena, Antiguo Cuscatlán, San Salvador; tel. 2267-8888; internet www.taca.com; f. 1931; allied with Avianca of Colombia in 2009; passenger and cargo services to Central America and the USA; Exec. Pres. FABIO VILLEGAS RAMÍREZ.

Tourism

In 2009 a total of 1,090,926 tourists visited the country. Tourism receipts, excluding passenger transport, stood at US $390m. in 2010, according to provisional figures.

Asociación Salvadoreña de Hoteles: Hotel Suites Las Palmas, Blvd del Hipódromo, Col. San Benito, San Salvador; tel. 2298-5383; fax 2298-5382; e-mail info@hoteles-elsalvador.com; internet www.hoteles-elsalvador.com; f. 1996; Pres. ALBERTO ASCENCIO; Exec. Dir MORENA TORRES; 33 mems.

Cámara Salvadoreña de Turismo (CASATUR): 63 Avda Sur, Pasaje y Urb., Santa Mónica 12-A, Col. Escalón, San Salvador; tel. 2298-6011; fax 2279-2156; e-mail info@casatur.org; internet www.casatur.org; f. 1978; non-profit org. concerned with promotion of tourism in El Salvador; Pres. RAFAEL LARET CASTILLO; Gen. Man. DALILA URRITIA.

Corporación Salvadoreña de Turismo (CORSATUR): Edif. Carbonel 1, Pasaje Carbonel, Alameda Doctor Manuel Enrique Araujo, Col. Roma, San Salvador; tel. 2241-3200; fax 2223-6120; e-mail info@corsatur.gob.sv; internet www.elsalvador.travel; f. 1996; Dir-Gen. ROBERTO VIERA.

Instituto Salvadoreño de Turismo (ISTU) (National Tourism Institute): 41 Avda Norte y Alameda Roosvelt 115, San Salvador; tel. 2260-9249; fax 2260-9254; e-mail informacion@istu.gob.sv; internet www.istu.gob.sv; f. 1950; Pres. MANUEL AVILÉS; Exec. Dir DOLORES EDUVIGES HENRÍQUEZ DE FUNES.

Defence

As assessed at November 2011, the armed forces totalled 15,500, of whom an estimated 13,850 (including 4,000 conscripts) were in the army, 700 were in the navy and 771 (including some 200 conscripts) were in the air force. There were also some 9,900 joint reserves. The Policía Nacional Civil numbered some 17,000. Military service is by compulsory selective conscription of 18–30 year old males and lasts for one year.

Defence Budget: an estimated US $141m. in 2012.

Chief of the Joint Command of the Armed Forces: Maj.-Gen. JAIME LEONARDO PARADA GONZÁLEZ.

Chief of Staff of the Army: Col CARLOS ANTONIO ZALDÍVAR AGUILAR.

Chief of Staff of the Navy: Capt. GUILLERMO JIMÉNEZ VÁSQUEZ.

Chief of Staff of the Air Force: Col NELSON EDGARDO HERNÁNDEZ DÍAZ.

Education

Education in El Salvador is provided free of charge in state schools and there are also numerous private schools. Pre-primary education, beginning at four years of age and lasting for three years, and primary education, beginning at the age of seven years and lasting for nine years, are officially compulsory. In 2007/08 enrolment at primary schools included 94% of children in the relevant age-group. Secondary education, from the age of 16, lasts for two years for an academic diploma or three years for a vocational one. In 2007/08 enrolment at secondary schools included 55% of students in the relevant age-group. Budget allocation for education was US $827m. in 2012.

EQUATORIAL GUINEA

Introductory Survey

LOCATION, CLIMATE, LANGUAGE, RELIGION, FLAG, CAPITAL

The Republic of Equatorial Guinea consists of the islands of Bioko (formerly Fernando Póo and subsequently renamed Macías Nguema Biyogo under the regime of President Francisco Macías Nguema), Corisco, Great Elobey, Little Elobey and Annobón (previously known also as Pagalu), and the mainland region of Río Muni (previously known also as Mbini) on the west coast of Africa. Cameroon lies to the north and Gabon to the east and south of Río Muni, while Bioko lies off shore from Cameroon and Nigeria. The small island of Annobón lies far to the south, beyond the islands of São Tomé and Príncipe. The climate is hot and humid, with average temperatures higher than 26°C (80°F). The official languages are Spanish, French and Portuguese. In Río Muni the Fang language is spoken, as well as those of coastal tribes such as the Combe, Balemke and Bujeba. Bubi is the indigenous language on Bioko, although Fang is also widely used, and Ibo is spoken by the resident Nigerian population. An estimated 90% of the population are adherents of the Roman Catholic Church, although traditional forms of worship are also followed. The national flag (proportions 2 by 3) has three equal horizontal stripes, of green, white and red, with a blue triangle at the hoist and the national coat of arms (a silver shield, containing a tree, with six yellow stars above and a scroll beneath) in the centre of the white stripe. The capital is Malabo (formerly Santa Isabel).

CONTEMPORARY POLITICAL HISTORY

Historical Context

In December 1963 the two provinces of Spanish Guinea (Río Muni, on the African mainland, and Fernando Póo—now Bioko—with other nearby islands) were merged to form Equatorial Guinea, with a limited measure of self-government. After 190 years of Spanish rule, independence was declared on 12 October 1968. Francisco Macías Nguema, Equatorial Guinea's first President, formed a coalition Government. In February 1970 Macías outlawed all existing political parties and formed the Partido Unico Nacional (PUN), which later became the Partido Unico Nacional de los Trabajadores (PUNT). A new Constitution, giving absolute powers to the President, was adopted in July 1973.

In August 1979 President Macías was overthrown in a coup led by his nephew, Lt-Col (later Gen.) Teodoro Obiang Nguema Mbasogo, hitherto the Deputy Minister of Defence. (Obiang Nguema subsequently ceased to use his forename.) Macías was found guilty of treason, genocide, embezzlement and violation of human rights, and was executed in September. The Spanish Government, which admitted prior knowledge of the coup, was the first to recognize the new regime, and remained a major supplier of financial and technical aid. In August 1982 Obiang Nguema was reappointed President for a further seven years, and later that month a new Constitution, which provided for an eventual return to civilian government, was approved by 95% of voters in a referendum.

The imposition, from 1979 to 1991, of a ban on organized political activity within Equatorial Guinea, and persistent allegations against the Obiang Nguema regime of human rights abuses and corruption, resulted in the development of a substantial opposition-in-exile. A series of attempted coups were reported during the 1980s, and in January 1986 the President reinforced his control by assuming the post of Minister of Defence. In August 1987 Obiang Nguema announced the establishment of a 'governmental party', the Partido Democrático de Guinea Ecuatorial (PDGE), while continuing to reject demands for the legalization of opposition parties. At legislative elections held in July 1988, 99.2% of voters endorsed a single list of candidates who had been nominated by the President.

Domestic Political Affairs

In June 1989, at the first presidential election to be held since independence, Obiang Nguema, the sole candidate, reportedly received the support of more than 99% of the electorate. Opposition groupings criticized the conduct of the election and declared the result invalid. Following his success, the President appealed to dissidents to return to Equatorial Guinea and declared an amnesty for political prisoners. However, Obiang Nguema reiterated his opposition to the establishment of a multi-party system, and in December 1990 it was reported that about 30 advocates of the introduction of a plural political system had been imprisoned.

A new Constitution, containing provisions for a multi-party political system, was approved by an overwhelming majority of voters at a national referendum in November 1991. However, opposition movements rejected the Constitution, owing to the inclusion of clauses exempting the President from any judicial procedures arising from his tenure of office and prohibiting citizens who had not been continuously resident in Equatorial Guinea for 10 years from standing as election candidates, while requiring all political parties to submit a large deposit (which could not be provided by funds from abroad) as a condition of registration. In January 1992 a transitional Government (comprising only members of the PDGE) was formed, and a general amnesty was extended to all political exiles. The UN published a report in January that criticized the human rights record of the Equato-Guinean authorities and some of the provisions incorporated in the new Constitution.

Multi-party legislative elections held in November 1993 were boycotted by most of the opposition parties in protest at Obiang Nguema's refusal to review contentious clauses of the electoral law promulgated in January 1993 or to permit impartial international observers to inspect the electoral register. The UN declined a request by the Equato-Guinean authorities to monitor the elections, contending that correct electoral procedures were evidently being infringed. Representatives of the Organization of African Unity (OAU—now the African Union—AU, see p. 189) were present and estimated that 50% of the electorate participated. The PDGE won 68 of the 80 seats in the House of Representatives, while, of the six opposition parties that presented candidates, the Convención Socialdemocrática Popular obtained six seats, the Unión Democrática y Social de Guinea Ecuatorial (UDS) won five seats and the Convención Liberal Democrática (CLD) secured one. Widespread electoral irregularities were alleged to have occurred. In December Silvestre Siale Bileka, hitherto Prime Minister of the interim Government, was appointed Prime Minister of the new administration, which included no opposition representatives.

In April 1994 Severo Moto Nsa, the founding leader of one of the most influential exiled opposition parties, the Partido del Progreso de Guinea Ecuatorial (PPGE), based in Spain, returned to Equatorial Guinea. In early 1995 the Constitution and electoral law were amended to reduce from 10 to five the minimum number of years required for candidates to have been resident in Equatorial Guinea.

At a presidential election held in February 1996 Obiang Nguema was returned to office, reportedly securing more than 90% of the votes cast. However, influential opposition leaders boycotted the contest, in protest at alleged electoral irregularities and official intimidation. In March Obiang Nguema appointed a new Prime Minister, Angel Serafin Seriche Dougan (hitherto a Deputy Minister).

In May 1997 Moto Nsa was arrested by the Angolan authorities with a consignment of arms, which were reportedly intended for use in a planned coup. Following his release in June, Moto Nsa was granted refuge in Spain. Meanwhile, the PPGE was banned and the party subsequently divided into two factions. In August Moto Nsa and 11 others were convicted *in absentia* of treason; Moto Nsa was sentenced to 101 years' imprisonment. In September the Government protested strongly to Spain for granting political asylum to Moto Nsa. Shortly afterwards French was declared the second official national language.

The 1999 legislative elections

Equatorial Guinea's second multi-party legislative elections took place in March 1999, amid allegations of electoral malpractice and of the systematic intimidation of opposition candidates by the security forces. The elections were contested by 13 parties, and some 99% of the electorate was estimated to have voted. According to the official results, the ruling PDGE obtained more than 90% of the votes, increasing its representation from 68 to 75 of the 80 seats in the House of Representatives. Two opposition parties, the Unión Popular (UP) and the Convergencia para la Democracia Social (CPDS), secured four seats and one seat, respectively. Both parties, however, refused to participate in the new administration, in protest at alleged violations of the electoral law. Following the election, Seriche Dougan was reappointed to the premiership, and in late July a new Council of Ministers was announced.

The new administration dismissed hundreds of civil servants, including a number of high-ranking officials, during its first three months in office, as part of efforts to eradicate corruption. Furthermore, in January 2000 a number of judicial officials, including the President of the Supreme Tribunal and the President of the Constitutional Court, were dismissed. Former Prime Minister Silvestre Siale Bileka was appointed to the presidency of the Supreme Tribunal. Nevertheless, in March the new Special Representative for Equatorial Guinea at the UN Human Rights Commission condemned the Equato-Guinean authorities for systematic and serious human rights violations and accused the Government of refusing to authorize the formation of human rights non-governmental organizations. Following intense lobbying by several African countries, the mandate of the Special Representative was terminated in April 2002. However, in December a new UN Human Rights Rapporteur arrived in Equatorial Guinea, with a mandate to investigate claims of human rights violations.

In late February 2001 Seriche Dougan announced the resignation of his Government, in response to further pressure from the President and the legislature. Cándido Muatetema Rivas, formerly Deputy Secretary-General of the PDGE, was subsequently appointed as Prime Minister and formed a new Council of Ministers. Five members of the opposition were appointed to the new Government, including Jeremías Ondo Ngomo, the President of the UP, as Minister-delegate for Communications and Transport. In July Obiang Nguema was nominated as the PDGE candidate for the 2003 presidential election.

In late 2002 a National Electoral Council was created, although international bodies were unwilling to monitor voting in view of the apparent weakness of the country's electoral institutions. Nevertheless, several leading members of both the exiled and resident opposition—including Celestino Bonifacio Bacale Obiang of the CPDS and Tomás Mecheba Fernández of the Partido Socialista de Guinea Ecuatorial—declared their intention to contest the forthcoming election. Alfonso Nsué Mokuy of the CLD also agreed to participate in the election, as did the Deputy Minister of Public Works, Housing and Urban Affairs, Carmelo Modú Acusé Bindang (the President of the UDS), and the Deputy Minister of Communications and Transport, Ondo Ngomo (of the UP).

On 15 December 2002, with voting already under way, Bacale Obiang and other opposition candidates announced their withdrawal from the election, alleging widespread irregularities in voting procedures. Their claims related to the apparent lack of secrecy in voting, the insufficient number of ballot papers for opposition candidates and voter intimidation. According to the official results, Obiang Nguema was re-elected to the presidency, with 97.1% of the votes cast. The conduct of the election was condemned by the European Union (EU, see p. 276). Despite the newly re-elected President's appeal for the opposition leaders to join the PDGE in a government of national unity, 'radical' opposition parties continued to refuse to participate in Obiang Nguema's administration. In February 2003 a new Government was formed, again headed by Prime Minister Rivas.

Attempted coup

In mid-March 2004 the Government announced that a group of 15 suspected mercenaries had been arrested on suspicion of planning a *coup d'état*, which President Obiang Nguema subsequently claimed had been funded by multinational companies and organized by Moto Nsa with the collusion of the Spanish Government. Following the death in custody of one of the accused, in November the remaining 14 defendants were found guilty of involvement in the coup attempt and received lengthy custodial sentences. Although Moto Nsa denied any involvement in the affair, he was sentenced *in absentia* by the court in Malabo to 63 years' imprisonment, while Nick du Toit, a former South African special forces officer alleged to have been the operational leader of the group in Equatorial Guinea, was sentenced to 34 years' imprisonment. Human rights organizations condemned the trial for grave abuses of procedure. Simon Mann, a South African-based British security consultant and the alleged leader of the coup plot, had been convicted in September of attempting illegally to procure weapons and was sentenced to seven years' imprisonment (subsequently reduced to four) in Zimbabwe, where he had been arrested. At the completion of that sentence in 2007, the Equato-Guinean authorities sought to extradite Mann in order to undergo further legal proceedings. That request was granted by a judge in Zimbabwe in May and in early February 2008 Mann was transported to custody in Equatorial Guinea. His trial began in June, along with that of the Lebanese business executive Mohamed Salaam and six Equato-Guinean nationals (all former members of the proscribed PPGE) who faced charges relating to the arrest of Moto Nsa in Spain in April, when weapons were discovered in a vehicle that was being exported to Equatorial Guinea, in a separate apparent coup plot. (The man who police claimed was to take delivery of the car in Malabo had been arrested earlier and died in custody.) In July Mann was sentenced to 34 years in prison, while Salaam received an 18-year sentence and four of the Equato-Guineans were imprisoned for six year terms. Of the remaining two defendants one was given a one-year sentence and the other was acquitted.

In August 2004 Sir Mark Thatcher (a businessman and son of the former British Prime Minister Baroness Thatcher) had been arrested in Cape Town, South Africa, on suspicion of having provided financial support for the alleged coup attempt. Thatcher initially denied any involvement in the affair; however, in January 2005 he admitted contravening South African anti-mercenary legislation and was fined R3m. (more than US $500,000) and given a four-year suspended sentence. None the less, in March 2008 it was reported that the Government of Equatorial Guinea had issued an arrest warrant for Thatcher, after the Attorney-General, José Olo Obono, claimed that Mann had provided new evidence regarding Thatcher's involvement in the coup plot. Subsequently, at his trial in June, Mann told the court that Thatcher had been part of the 'management team' for the attempted coup, and that Ely Calil, a Lebanese businessman, had masterminded the plot; Mann also claimed that both the Spanish and South African Governments were involved. In September 2005, following investigations into another alleged coup plot in October 2004, 23 members of the armed forces were convicted of treason and handed down lengthy gaol sentences. A further six senior members of the armed forces were sentenced to terms of imprisonment in the following month. Human rights groups claimed that confessions had been extracted under torture from those convicted.

Meanwhile, legislative and municipal elections were held concurrently on 25 April 2004. The PDGE won 68 of the 100 seats in an expanded House of Representatives, while a coalition of eight parties allied to Obiang Nguema, styled the 'democratic opposition', secured a further 30 seats. International observers and the CPDS, which took the remaining two seats, denounced the results as fraudulent. The rate of participation by eligible voters was estimated at 97%. In June Prime Minister Rivas announced the resignation of his Government and Obiang Nguema subsequently appointed a new PDGE-dominated Council of Ministers, headed by Miguel Abia Biteo Boricó, hitherto Minister of State for Parliamentary Relations and Judicial Affairs.

In August 2006 the Government resigned, following accusations of corruption and ineptitude from President Obiang Nguema. None the less, many previous members of the Council of Ministers were reappointed to the new administration, including the President's son, Teodoro (Teodorín) Nguema Obiang Mangue, as Minister of Agriculture and Forestry. Ricardo Mangué Obama Nfubea succeeded Miguel Abia Biteo Borico as Prime Minister; it was notable that the new incumbent was the first premier of Fang ethnicity to hold the office since independence.

In February 2008 Obiang Nguema dissolved the House of Representatives and announced that legislative elections, originally planned for May 2009, would be brought forward by one year, and held along with municipal elections on 4 May 2008. The ruling PDGE won 99 of the 100 seats in the legislature, while the one remaining seat was obtained by the opposition CPDS. In the concurrent municipal elections, the PDGE and its allies won 319 seats and the CPDS 13. The CPDS condemned the conduct of the poll, citing irregularities at many polling stations, and alleging harassment of CPDS representatives. Nevertheless, on 21 May it was reported that the Constitutional Court had confirmed the PDGE's overwhelming victory. Obama Nfubea resigned from his position as Prime Minister in July. A new Government was subsequently named by Obiang Nguema and was headed by Ignacio Milam Tang, hitherto the country's ambassador to Spain.

In February 2009 it was reported that there had been an attack on the presidential palace in Malabo for which the Equato-Guinean authorities initially held the Nigerian armed group Movement for the Emancipation of the Niger Delta (MEND) responsible. MEND denied any involvement in the incident, and the Government subsequently accused Equatorial Guineans of organizing, financing and participating in the attack, which, according to the authorities, aimed to effect the overthrow of the President. Some 10 members of the UP were detained, while a number of foreign nationals were also arrested in the aftermath of the alleged attack and were later expelled from the country. Following the attack, several members of the Government, including the Minister of National Security, were dismissed.

In November 2009 Mann, du Toit and three others who had been sentenced to terms of imprisonment for their roles in the 2004 coup attempt (see above) were pardoned by President Obiang Nguema and released from gaol. A government spokesperson stated that the decision to release Mann had been made on humanitarian and medical grounds.

Obiang Nguema's fourth term

At the presidential election held on 29 November 2009 Obiang Nguema secured a further term of office with 95.4% of the votes cast. The CPDS candidate Plácido Micó Abogo, Obiang Nguema's closest rival with just 3.6% of the vote, announced shortly after voting closed that the ballot had not been conducted fairly and that he would not accept the results of the election. Micó Abogo stated that the electoral register was not expected to be published and, with allies of the President occupying senior roles at the electoral authority, human rights organizations concurred that the ballot was unlikely to have been free and fair. Nevertheless, Obiang Nguema was inaugurated as President on 8 December. In mid-January 2010 Milam Tang was reappointed to the premiership and he subsequently named a new Government. Ebiaca Moheete was promoted to the position of First Deputy Prime Minister, in charge of the Economic and Financial Sector, while Obiang Mangue retained responsibility for the agriculture and forestry portfolio, but was nominated as Minister of State. The following month Lucas Nguema Esono was appointed Secretary-General of the PDGE, replacing Filiberto Ntutumu Nguema, who had been awarded the position of Minister of State, in charge of Education, Science and Sports in the new Government.

In early April 2010 seven Nigerians were sentenced to 12 years in gaol for their roles in the attack on the presidential palace in February 2009, although a number of Equato-Guinean citizens who had been accused of assisting the Nigerians were acquitted of any involvement in the incident. However, in mid-August 2010 four former military and government officials, including a former member of the President's personal security force, were convicted by a military court in Malabo of terrorism, treason and of carrying out an assault against the head of state, and were sentenced to death. The execution of the four men was confirmed by the Equato-Guinean Government later in August and was widely criticized by human rights organizations. Nevertheless, the Equato-Guinean authorities maintained that the trial had been conducted 'in public' and that the country's Constitution provided for the application of the death penalty for such crimes.

Recent developments: political reforms

I late June 2010 President Obiang Nguema announced his intention to carry out a series of wide-ranging reforms, pledging to ensure peace, political stability and transparency in the country. Addressing criticism of his Government and apologizing for previous shortcomings under his presidency, he unveiled a five-point programme, which would be carried out over 10 years in close co-operation with international institutions—notably the African Union—and non-governmental organizations, and which he hoped would encourage foreign investment in Equatorial Guinea. First, he promised reform of the petroleum sector with the aim of securing Equatorial Guinea's membership of the Extractive Industries Transparency Initiative. Second, the Government was to expand the current Social Development Fund by investing substantial resources from oil exploration revenues and other natural resources into, *inter alia*, education, health care, tourism, housing and infrastructure projects. Furthermore, he also pledged to promote human and civil rights (the International Committee of the Red Cross would be invited to establish an office in Equatorial Guinea and to assist in reviewing and assessing all allegations of human rights violations in the country, while the country's press organization was to be allowed to act with independence and freedom); to improve the criminal justice system; and to seek to enhance the protection of the environment. Opponents of the Obiang Nguema regime rejected the reform package and claimed that it lacked credibility.

Obiang Nguema effected a reorganization of the Government in January 2011; most notably Bacale Obiang of the CPDS was appointed Minister-delegate to the Minister of the Economy, Trade and Business Development, while Francisco Mbá Olú Bahamonde, the President of the opposition Alianza Democrática Progresista, also joined the Council of Ministers. Further minor changes were made in April, primarily among the Secretaries of State, bringing more members of Obiang Nguema's family into the Government and raising concerns over the dynastic nature of his control of power.

In May 2011 Obiang Nguema announced the establishment of the Comisión Nacional para el Estudio de la Reforma de la Ley Fundamental de Guinea Ecuatorial (National Commission for the Study of the Reform of the Equatorial Guinean Constitution). Its members comprised primarily PDGE representatives, although other parties were also included. The CPDS, the UP and the Acción Popular de Guinea Ecuatorial (APGE) objected to Obiang Nguema's control of the allocation of the membership and his failure to consider their proposals, therefore declining the invitation to participate. They also raised concerns that the proposed schedule for implementing the reforms did not allow for sufficient open discussions. The Commission's report was submitted to parliament on 15 July and included proposals on the creation of a new Council of the Republic, and Economic and Social Council and the post of Ombudsman. On 13 November the public voted in a referendum on constitutional reform, which provided for the creation of the post of Vice-President, and would limit the presidential term of office to two seven-year terms. Concerns were raised, however, that the text did not clarify whether Obiang Nguema would be required to step down at the end of his current term in 2016. It was also thought that his son, Obiang Mangue, was being lined up to assume the new vice-presidency, and ultimately the presidency, thus consolidating the familial role in governance. The results reported that 97.7% of votes cast were in favour of the new Constitution; voter turnout was estimated at 91.8%. The constitutional amendments were promulgated on 16 February 2012.

Meanwhile, in November 2011 a senior CPDS member, Marcial Abaga Barril, was arrested as part of an ongoing murder investigation. The CPDS was a vociferous opponent of the proposed Constitution and claimed that the Government was known to carry out arbitrary arrests, that this was politically motivated, and that there were no grounds for detaining Barril. In April two other senior CPDS officials were arrested, but were later released without charge.

Allegations of Corruption

Equatorial Guinea enjoyed exceptionally high revenues from petroleum exports from the late 1990s; allegations emerged, however, that members of the Obiang Nguema regime were accruing private profits from national petroleum exports. In May 2003 controversy arose when the US-based Riggs Bank acknowledged that some US $500m. had been paid into an account to which President Obiang Nguema was the sole signatory; international petroleum companies were alleged to be the source of the funds, which were 'frozen' by the US Senate in July 2004 pending further investigations. In January 2005 Riggs Bank admitted criminal liability in assisting Obiang Nguema in improper financial transactions. It was subsequently estimated that the funds totalled $700m., all of which were released by the US Senate, reportedly after appeals by the Obiang Nguema Government that the money was required to combat a cholera epidemic in the country. However, upon their release the funds were allegedly transferred to accounts in foreign countries. Meanwhile, in February 2004 Obiang Nguema issued a decree providing for the creation of a National Commission for Personal Ethics, which would oblige all public employees to declare their assets. However, in July a US Senate report concluded that to secure contracts and co-operation petroleum companies made substantial payments to government officials, their families or entities owned by them. In late January 2005 the Equato-Guinean authorities announced the discovery of chronic and systematic fraud in several government ministries. Controversy arose in November 2006, following reports that the President's son Teodorín had purchased a property for $35m. in the USA (in addition to two luxury homes in South Africa, with regard to which he was embroiled already in legal proceedings).

Foreign Affairs

Regional relations

In March 2003 relations between Equatorial Guinea and Gabon were strained following the occupation of the small island of Mbagne (Mbañé, Mbanie) by a contingent of Gabonese troops. Both countries had long claimed ownership of Mbagne and two smaller islands, which lie in potentially oil-rich waters in Corisco Bay, north of the Gabonese capital, Libreville, and south-west of the Equato-Guinean mainland. In June Equatorial Guinea rejected a Gabonese proposal to share any petroleum revenues from the island, and discussions between the two sides ended without agreement in December. However, in January 2004 Equatorial Guinea and Gabon issued a joint communiqué, accepting the appointment of a UN mediator in the dispute. In July a provisional agreement was reached to explore jointly for petroleum in the disputed territories. At a meeting in Libreville in January 2005 the Presidents of both countries expressed optimism that an amicable agreement would soon be finalized. However, in late 2006 negotiations were suspended indefinitely, potentially to be pursued at the International Court of Justice (ICJ, see p. 25). In 2008, following UN mediation, progress was made towards the referral of the case to the ICJ: in September the UN Secretary-General, Ban Ki-Moon, appointed Nicolas Michel, a Swiss legal expert, as a special adviser to assist in resolving the dispute. At a meeting of the two countries' leaders, convened by the UN Secretary-General in February 2011, Gabon and Equatorial Guinea reiterated their commitment to submitting their border dispute for ruling at the ICJ.

President Jacob Zuma of South Africa visited Equatorial Guinea in November 2009 to promote stronger economic relations between the two countries. Immediately prior to Zuma's visit four South Africans were pardoned and released from prison where they had been detained for their alleged involvement in the attempted coup in 2004 (see above). Representatives of the two countries met in November 2011 to discuss closer co-operation on trade and industry, transport, energy, agriculture and defence.

Equatorial Guinea has assumed a greater role at a regional level in recent years and in January 2010 Lucas Abaga Nchama, an Equato-Guinean, was appointed a governor of the Banque des états de l'Afrique centrale. In February Equatorial Guinea was elected to the AU's 15-member Peace and Security Council, to serve a three-year term and in April the Parlement of the Communauté économique et monétaire de l'Afrique centrale was inaugurated in Malabo. In late January 2011 Obiang Nguema was elected Chairperson of the Assembly of the AU. In November Equatorial Guinea hosted the third South America-Africa Summit meeting in Malabo.

Other external relations

While Spain (the former colonial power) has traditionally been a major trading partner and aid donor, Equatorial Guinea's entry in 1983 into the Customs and Economic Union of Central Africa (replaced in 1999 by the Communauté économique et monétaire de l'Afrique centrale, see p. 333) represented a significant move towards a greater integration with neighbouring francophone countries. In 1985 Equatorial Guinea joined the Franc Zone (see p. 332), with financial assistance from France. Obiang Nguema has regularly attended Franco-African summit meetings. From mid-1993 Equato-Guinean-Spanish relations deteriorated, and in January 1994 the Spanish Government withdrew one-half of its aid to Equatorial Guinea in retaliation for the expulsion in December 1993 of a Spanish diplomat whom the Equato-Guinean authorities had accused of interfering in the country's internal affairs. In October 1999 the Spanish Government agreed to resume full assistance to its former colony, and during a visit to Madrid in March 2001 President Obiang Nguema held talks with Spanish Prime Minister José María Aznar, who agreed to normalize relations with Equatorial Guinea in the economic field. In 2003 relations improved further following Spain's support for Equatorial Guinea's territorial claims to the island of Mbagne (Mbañé, Mbanie, see above), and the Spanish Ministers of Health and Consumer Affairs and of Foreign Affairs visited Malabo in November. In February 2004 the two Governments signed a new two-year agreement on development co-operation, worth some €34m. In April the Spanish Government cancelled 50% of Equatorial Guinea's debt, estimated at some €70m.

In late February 2005 Obiang Nguema held talks in Bata with the Spanish Minister of Foreign Affairs and Co-operation, Miguel Ángel Moratinos Cuyaubé, during which both parties expressed their desire to maintain cordial relations and high levels of co-operation between the two countries. Although Moratinos reassured Obiang Nguema that the Spanish Government would act forcefully to prevent any preparations being made in Spanish territory to destabilize or overthrow the Obiang Nguema administration, he reiterated that the extradition of opposition leader Severo Moto Nsa (see above) was a judicial matter, in which the Spanish Government would not intervene. However, in December the Spanish Government announced that Moto Nsa's asylum was to be revoked in the light of evidence that he had conspired to overthrow the Obiang Nguema regime. Moto Nsa announced his intention to return to Equatorial Guinea to demand the immediate holding of fair elections. Meanwhile, in June Moto Nsa had participated in a demonstration by exiled opposition groups at the Equato-Guinean embassy in Spain, which resulted in damage to embassy property (leading to the embassy's closure) and minor injuries to some of its staff. The Spanish and Equato-Guinean Governments condemned the demonstrators' actions. None the less, in March 2008 the Spanish Supreme Court accepted an appeal from Moto Nsa and ruled to uphold his asylum status, declaring that he did not pose a threat to Spain. In April Moto Nsa was arrested for arms trafficking, after weapons were discovered at a Spanish port in a car bound for Equatorial Guinea (see above), although he was released in August.

Relations with Spain once again improved in July 2009 when Obiang Nguema approved the re-entry of Spanish firms to the Equato-Guinean market and the ministers responsible for foreign affairs from Spain and Equatorial Guinea signed an agreement pledging the mutual protection of investments. Future projects in the construction and tourism sectors were to be discussed. Two Spanish firms, Repsol and Union Fenosa, had been contracted earlier in the year to operate in Equatorial Guinea exploiting gas and oil reserves.

Since 2006 Equatorial Guinea has held observer status within, but not full membership of, the Comunidade de Países de Língua Oficial Portuguesa (CPLP). President Obiang Nguema announced in 2008 that Portuguese was to be adopted as Equatorial Guinea's third official language and in 2009 strong ties were formed with CPLP member states, particularly Brazil, which opened an embassy in Malabo, and Portugal. In March 2010 a Portuguese delegation of government officials and businessmen visited Equatorial Guinea, and several trade agreements were signed. Equatorial Guinea was scheduled to be admitted to the CPLP as a full member later that year but as of November membership still had not been granted.

In 2011 Equatorial Guinea established diplomatic ties with Germany and in July that country opened an embassy in Malabo.

CONSTITUTION AND GOVERNMENT

The present Constitution was approved by a national referendum on 16 November 1991 and amended in January 1995, providing for the introduction of multi-party democracy. Further amendments were adopted in February 2012. Executive power is vested in the President, whose seven-year term of office is renewable twice. The President is immune from prosecution for offences committed before, during or after his tenure of the post. Legislative power is held by a 100-member House of Representatives, which serves for a term of five years. Both the President and the House of Representatives are directly elected by universal adult suffrage. The President appoints a Council of Ministers, headed by a Prime Minister, from among the members of the House of Representatives.

REGIONAL AND INTERNATIONAL CO-OPERATION

Equatorial Guinea is a member of the African Union (see p. 189) and of the Central African organs of the Franc Zone (see p. 333), including the Communauté économique et monétaire de l'Afrique centrale (CEMAC, see p. 333).

Equatorial Guinea became a member of the UN in 1976 and participates in the Group of 77 (see p. 450) developing countries.

ECONOMIC AFFAIRS

In 2010, according to estimates by the World Bank, Equatorial Guinea's gross national income (GNI), measured at average

2008–10 prices, was US $10,182m., equivalent to $14,540 per head (or $23,570 per head on an international purchasing-power parity basis). During 2001–10, it was estimated, the population increased at an average annual rate of 3.0%, while gross domestic product (GDP) per head increased, in real terms, by an average of 9.6% per year. Overall GDP increased, in real terms, at an average annual rate of 12.9% in 2001–10. Real GDP increased by 0.9% in 2010.

Agriculture (including hunting, forestry and fishing) contributed 64.6% of GDP in 2010, according to African Development Bank (AfDB) figures. The sector employed an estimated 63.2% of the labour force in mid-2012, according to FAO estimates. The principal cash crop is cocoa, which, according to the Banque de France, provided an estimated 1.2% of total export earnings in 2007. The Government is encouraging the production of bananas, spices (vanilla, black pepper and coriander) and medicinal plants for export. The main subsistence crops are cassava and sweet potatoes. Exploitation of the country's vast, but rapidly diminishing, forest resources (principally of okoumé and akoga timber) provided an estimated 0.7% (or 34,000m. francs CFA) of export revenue in 2007, according to the Banque de France. Almost all industrial fishing activity is practised by foreign fleets, notably by those of countries of the European Union. During 2001–09, according to the World Bank, the real GDP of the agricultural sector increased at an average annual rate of 4.7%; it declined by 1.3% in 2008, but grew by 3.0% in 2009.

According to the AfDB, industry (including mining, manufacturing, construction and power) contributed 31.1% of GDP in 2010. During 2001–09, according to the World Bank, industrial GDP increased at an average annual rate of 15.1%. Industrial GDP increased by 4.9% in 2009.

Extractive activities were minimal during the 1980s, and the mining sector employed less than 0.2% of the working population in 1983. However, the exploitation of onshore and offshore reserves of petroleum and of offshore deposits of natural gas led to unprecedented economic growth during the 1990s. Exports of petroleum commenced in 1992 and provided an estimated 82.5% of total export earnings in 2008, according to the IMF. Mining contributed 24.8% of GDP in 2010, according to the AfDB. Petroleum production increased from 91,000 barrels per day (b/d) in 2000 to an estimated 274,000 b/d in 2010, according to the BP Statistical Review of World Energy published in June 2011. Proven reserves of petroleum were some 1,700m. barrels at the end of 2010. Natural gas extraction also increased rapidly from the 1990s. Proven reserves at the country's largest gas field, Alba, were some 1,300,000m. cu ft in early 2006, although in 2010 the Equato-Guinean Government announced that it had raised the figure of its estimated reserves to around 4,500,000m. cu ft. The existence of deposits of gold, uranium, iron ore, titanium, tantalum and manganese has also been confirmed. During 2001–06 the GDP of the petroleum sector increased at an average annual rate of 32.3%, according to the IMF; growth in 2006 was 9.9%.

The manufacturing sector contributed 0.2% of GDP in 2010, according to the AfDB. Wood-processing constitutes the main commercial manufacturing activity. During 2001–09, according to the World Bank, manufacturing GDP increased at an average annual rate of 29.8%; the sector expanded by 8.8% in 2009.

According to the AfDB, construction contributed an estimated 5.4% of GDP in 2010. Construction GDP increased by 26.6% in 2008 mainly due to government investment in major infrastructures made possible by the rapidly increasing oil revenues. The sector's growth was recorded at 27.6% in 2009, but the sector contracted by 9.1% in 2010.

An estimated total of 31m. kWh of electric energy was generated in 2007. According to the EIA, in 2004 Equatorial Guinea had 15.4 MW of proven installed capacity and 5 MW–30 MW of estimated additional capacity and in 2009, its proven installed capacity increased to 31.0 MW. There was about 4 MW of oil-fired thermal capacity and 1 MW of hydroelectric capacity on the mainland. Bioko was supplied by one hydroelectric plant (on the Riaba river) with an estimated capacity of 3.6 MW and two thermal plants, including the 10.4-MW Punta Europa gas-fired plant located at the northern end of the island. In 2004 there was a further 4 MW–6 MW of generation capacity at the AMPCO complex on Bioko. Imports of fuel products comprised 25.2% of the value of total imports in 2008.

According to the AfDB, the services sector contributed only 4.2% of GDP in 2010. The dominant services are public administration and defence, and trade, restaurants and hotels. During 2001–09, according to the World Bank, the GDP of the services sector increased at an average annual rate of 15.1%; it grew by 19.9% in 2009.

In 2008, according to IMF estimates, there was a visible trade surplus of US $10,555.2m., while the surplus on the current account of the balance of payments was $1,673m. In 2003 the USA was the principal source of imports (40.6%), and exports (33.2%). Other major trading partners were Spain, the People's Republic of China, the United Kingdom, France and Italy. In 2008 crude petroleum and methanol constituted the principal sources of export revenue (with timber, cocoa and coffee the most significant non-hydrocarbon exports), while in 1990 the principal imports were ships and boats, petroleum and related products, and food and live animals.

In 2009 there was a budget deficit of 459.4m. francs CFA (equivalent to 10.1% of GDP). The country's general government gross debt was 541,152m. francs CFA in 2010, equivalent to 7.5% of GDP. Equatorial Guinea's external debt was US $278.1m. at the end of 2006, of which $224.6m. was long-term public debt. According to AfDB estimates, the rate of inflation averaged 5.3% per year in 2001–10: the annual average rate of inflation was 4.7% in 2010.

The production and export of petroleum led to exceptional economic growth from the late 1990s and economic relations with the USA have strengthened in recent years as a result of major investments in the development of Equato-Guinean oilfields by US energy companies. Furthermore, in late 2005 President Obiang Nguema signed an agreement to co-operate on hydrocarbon development with the People's Republic of China. Equatorial Guinea was therefore expected to benefit from the competition between the USA and China for stakes in the hydrocarbons sector, while there were also proposals to establish a new Joint Development Zone between Equatorial Guinea and Gabon in the disputed Corisco Bay, a region rich in petroleum and gas reserves. In 2004 rapid expansion of the hydrocarbon industry led to spectacular GDP growth of 31.7% and although the economy expanded by just 1.2% in 2010—the rate lowest since the commencement of petroleum exploitation—it was swift to recover, recording estimated growth of 5.0% in 2011. Furthermore, GDP growth of 7.5% was forecast for 2012, underpinned by an anticipated increase in petroleum production. Recovering oil prices had a beneficial effect on the national accounts, with the budgetary deficit declining to 2.6% of GDP in 2010, while the current account was estimated to have shown a surplus of 2.9% in 2011 and was expected to remain in surplus, at 3.8%, in 2012. However, the absence of any visible improvement in living standards among the general population since the early 1990s (in January 2006 the UN Development Programme announced that more than 70% of Equato-Guineans subsisted in poverty on less than $2 per day) has been variously attributed to corruption, the disadvantageous terms of many contracts negotiated by the state petroleum company, and reduced international aid. There also remained concerns that the country's petroleum revenues would be squandered as a result of senior level graft—a Transparency International report in 2008 ranked Equatorial Guinea as the ninth most corrupt country in the world—although in mid-2010 President Obiang Nguema announced a 10-year plan that would, *inter alia*, improve transparency with regard to oil revenues (see Recent developments: Obiang Nguema's fourth term).

PUBLIC HOLIDAYS

2013: 1 January (New Year's Day), 29 March–1 April (Easter), 1 May (Labour Day), 25 May (AU Day), 12 October (Independence Day), 10 December (Human Rights Day), 25 December (Christmas).

Statistical Survey

Source (unless otherwise stated): Dirección General de Estadística y Cuentas Nacionales, Ministerio de Planificación, Desarrollo Económico e Inversiones Públicas, Malabo; tel. 333093352; internet www.dgecnstat-ge.org.

AREA AND POPULATION

Area: 28,051 sq km (10,831 sq miles): Río Muni 26,017 sq km, Bioko 2,017 sq km, Annobón 17 sq km.

Population: 300,000 (Río Muni 240,804, Bioko 57,190, Annobón 2,006), comprising 144,268 males and 155,732 females, at census of 4–17 July 1983 (Source: Ministerio de Asuntos Exteriores, Madrid); 406,151 at census of 4 July 1994 (provisional). *Mid-2012* (UN estimate): 740,469 (Source: UN, *World Population Prospects: The 2010 Revision*).

Density (mid-2012): 26.4 per sq km.

Population by Age and Sex (UN estimates at mid-2012): *0–14:* 288,125 (males 144,761, females 143,364); *15–64:* 431,650 (males 224,121, females 207,529); *65 and over:* 20,694 (males 10,470, females 10,224); *Total* 740,469 (males 379,352, females 361,117) (Source: UN, *World Population Prospects: The 2010 Revision*).

Provinces (population, census of July 1994): Kié-Ntem 92,779; Litoral 100,047; Centro-Sur 60,341; Wele-Nzas 62,458; Bioko Norte 75,137; Bioko Sur 12,569; Annobón 2,820.

Principal Town (incl. suburbs, UN estimate): Malabo 127,743 (Source: UN, *World Urbanization Prospects: The 2009 Revision*).

Births and Deaths (UN estimates, annual averages): Birth rate 37.3 per 1,000 in 2005–10; Death rate 15.1 per 1,000 in 2005–10. Source: UN, *World Population Prospects: The 2010 Revision*.

Life Expectancy (years at birth, WHO estimates): 53 (males 53; females 54) in 2009. Source: WHO, *World Health Statistics*.

Economically Active Population (persons aged 6 years and over, 1983 census): Agriculture, hunting, forestry and fishing 59,390; Mining and quarrying 126; Manufacturing 1,490; Electricity, gas and water 224; Construction 1,929; Trade, restaurants and hotels 3,059; Transport, storage and communications 1,752; Financing, insurance, real estate and business services 409; Community, social and personal services 8,377; *Sub-total* 76,756; Activities not adequately defined 984; *Total employed* 77,740 (males 47,893, females 29,847); Unemployed 24,825 (males 18,040, females 6,785); *Total labour force* 102,565 (males 65,933, females 36,632). Note: Figures are based on unadjusted census data, indicating a total population of 261,779. The adjusted total is 300,000 (Source: ILO, *Yearbook of Labour Statistics*). *Mid-2012* ('000 persons, official estimates): Agriculture, etc. 184; Total labour force 291 (Source: FAO).

HEALTH AND WELFARE

Key Indicators

Total Fertility Rate (children per woman, 2009): 5.3.

Under-5 Mortality Rate (per 1,000 live births, 2009): 145.

HIV/AIDS (% of persons aged 15–49, 2009): 5.0.

Physicians (per 1,000 head, 2004): 0.3.

Hospital Beds (per 1,000 head, 2005): 2.2.

Health Expenditure (2008): US $ per head (PPP): 658.

Health Expenditure (2008): % of GDP: 1.9.

Health Expenditure (2008): public (% of total): 77.2.

Access to Water (% of persons, 2006): 43.

Access to Sanitation (% of persons, 2006): 51.

Total Carbon Dioxide Emissions ('000 metric tons, 2007): 4792.5.

Carbon Dioxide Emissions Per Head (metric tons, 2007): 7.5.

Human Development Index (2011): ranking: 136.

Human Development Index (2011): value: 0.537.

For sources and definitions, see explanatory note on p. vi.

AGRICULTURE, ETC.

Principal Crops ('000 metric tons, 2010, FAO estimates): Sweet potatoes 90; Cassava 64; Coconuts 7; Oil palm fruit 35; Bananas 27; Plantains 42; Cocoa beans 1 (unofficial figure); Coffee, green 3. *Aggregate Production* ('000 metric tons, may include official, semi-official or estimated data): Total roots and tubers 188; Total fruits (excl. melons) 69.

Livestock ('000 head, year ending September 2010, FAO estimates): Cattle 5; Pigs 6; Sheep 38; Goats 9; Chickens 340; Ducks 30.

Livestock Products (2010, FAO estimates): Meat 566 metric tons; Hen eggs 490 metric tons.

Forestry ('000 cubic metres, 2010, FAO estimates): *Roundwood Removals:* Fuel wood 447; Sawlogs, veneer logs and logs for sleepers 525; Total 972. *Sawnwood:* 4 (all broadleaved).

Fishing (metric tons, live weight, 2009): Freshwater fishes 1,000; Clupeoids 3,000; Sharks, rays, skates, etc. 200 (FAO estimate); Marine fishes 500; Total catch (incl. others) 7,719 (FAO estimate).

Source: FAO.

MINING

Production (2010): Crude petroleum 74m. barrels; Natural gas 6,500m. cu m (Source: US Geological Survey).

INDUSTRY

Palm Oil ('000 metric tons, FAO estimate): 3.7 in 2010. Source: FAO.

Veneer Sheets ('000 cubic metres, FAO estimate): 28.0 in 2010. Source: FAO.

Electric Energy (million kWh): 95 in 2006; 100 in 2007; 100 in 2008. Source: UN Industrial Commodity Statistics Database.

FINANCE

Currency and Exchange Rates: 100 centimes = 1 franc de la Coopération financière en Afrique centrale (CFA). *Sterling, Dollar and Euro Equivalents* (30 December 2011): £1 sterling = 783.813 francs CFA; US $1 = 506.961 francs CFA; €1 = 655.957 francs CFA; 10,000 francs CFA = £12.76 = $19.73 = €15.24. *Average Exchange Rate* (francs CFA per US dollar): 472.186 in 2009; 495.277 in 2010; 471.866 in 2011. *Note:* An exchange rate of 1 French franc = 50 francs CFA, established in 1948, remained in force until January 1994, when the CFA franc was devalued by 50%, with the exchange rate adjusted to 1 French franc = 100 francs CFA. This relationship to French currency remained in effect with the introduction of the euro on 1 January 1999. From that date, accordingly, a fixed exchange rate of €1 = 655.957 francs CFA has been in operation.

Budget ('000 million francs CFA, 2009): *Revenue:* Tax revenue 905.7 (Tax on income profits and capital gains 847.4, Domestic taxes on goods and services 44.0, Taxes on international trade and transactions 10.1, Other taxes 4.2); Non-tax revenue 1,462.4; Total revenue 2,368.1. *Expenditure:* Current expenditure 345.3 (Interest payments 3.4, Wages and salaries 70.7, Goods and services 154.2, Transfers and subsidies 117.0); Capital expenditure 2,482.3; Total expenditure 2,827.5. Source: IMF, *Republic of Equatorial Guinea: 2010 Article IV Consultation* (May 2010).

International Reserves (excl. gold, US $ million at 31 December 2010): IMF special drawing rights 39.95; Foreign exchange 2,306.41; Total 2,346.36. Source: IMF, *International Financial Statistics*.

Money Supply ('000 million francs CFA at 31 December 2010): Currency outside deposit money banks 168.61; Demand deposits at deposit money banks 758.13; *Total money* (incl. others) 927.45. Source: IMF, *International Financial Statistics*.

Cost of Living (Consumer Price Index; base: 2000 = 100): All items 155.0 in 2008; 166.1 in 2009; 173.9 in 2010. Source: African Development Bank.

Expenditure on the Gross Domestic Product ('000 million francs CFA in current prices, 2010): Government final consumption expenditure 268.8; Private final consumption expenditure 530.7; Gross capital formation 3,004.0; Change in inventories 0.2; *Total domestic expenditure* 3,803.7; Exports of goods and non-factor services 5,569.1; *Less* Imports of goods and services 3,238.1; *GDP at purchasers' values* 6,134.6. Source: African Development Bank.

Gross Domestic Product by Economic Activity ('000 million francs CFA in current prices, 2010): Agriculture, hunting, forestry and fishing 3,906.2; Mining and quarrying 1,500.6; Manufacturing 10.9; Electricity, gas and water 43.8; Construction 326.3; Trade, restaurants and hotels 53.0; Finance, insurance and real estate 43.2; Transport and communications 8.0; Public administration and defence 129.3; Other services 23.1; *GDP at factor cost* 6,044.4; Indirect taxes 90.3; *GDP at purchasers' values* 6,134.6. Note: Deduction for imputed bank service charge assumed to be distributed at origin. Source: African Development Bank.

Balance of Payments (US $ million, 2008): Exports of goods f.o.b. 14,465; Imports of goods c.i.f. –3,909; *Trade balance* 10,555; Services (net) –1,849; Net other income –6,953; *Balance on goods, services and income* 1,753; Current transfers (net) –81; *Current balance* 1,673; Direct investment (net) –570; Other investment (net) –693; Errors and omissions 424; *Overall balance* 834. Source: IMF, *Republic of Equatorial Guinea: 2010 Article IV Consultation* (May 2010).

EXTERNAL TRADE

Principal Commodities (distribution by SITC, US $ '000, 1990): *Imports c.i.f.:* Food and live animals 4,340; Beverages and tobacco 3,198 (Alcoholic beverages 2,393); Crude materials (inedible) except fuels 2,589 (Crude fertilizers and crude minerals 2,102); Petroleum and petroleum products 4,738; Chemicals and related products 2,378; Basic manufactures 3,931; Machinery and transport equipment 35,880 (Road vehicles and parts 3,764, Ships, boats and floating structures 24,715); Miscellaneous manufactured articles 2,725; Total (incl. others) 61,601. *Exports f.o.b.:* Food and live animals 6,742 (Cocoa 6,372); Beverages and tobacco 3,217 (Tobacco and tobacco manufactures 2,321); Crude materials (inedible) except fuels 20,017 (Sawlogs and veneer logs 12,839, Textile fibres and waste 7,078); Machinery and transport equipment 24,574 (Ships, boats and floating structures 23,852); Total (incl. others) 61,705 (Source: UN, *International Trade Statistics Yearbook*). *2008* (US $ million, estimates): Total imports f.o.b. 3,909.5 (Public sector equipment 2,485.9, Petroleum sector 733.4, Petroleum products 252.7, Other 437.4); Total exports f.o.b. 14,464.7 (Crude petroleum 11,929.0, Petroleum derivatives 2,436.6, Others 99.0) (Source: IMF, *Republic of Equatorial Guinea: Statistical Appendix*—April 2010).

Principal Trading Partners (US $ million, 2003): *Imports c.i.f.:* Belgium 14.6; France 87.0; Italy 58.0; Netherlands 20.4; United Kingdom 175.9; USA 336.3; Total (incl. others) 828.8. *Exports f.o.b.:* Canada 334.1; China, People's Repub. 411.9; Italy 182.6; Netherlands 43.6; Spain 739.3; Taiwan 53.4; USA 903.5; Total (incl. others) 2,721.8.

TRANSPORT

Road Traffic (estimates, motor vehicles in use at 31 December 2002): Passenger cars 1,811; Lorries and vans 727; Buses 302; Motorcycles 17.

Shipping: *Merchant Fleet* (at 31 December 2009): Vessels 39; Total displacement 27,194 grt (Source: IHS Fairplay, *World Fleet Statistics*). *International Sea-borne Freight Traffic* ('000 metric tons, 1990): Goods loaded 110; Goods unloaded 64 (Source: UN, *Monthly Bulletin of Statistics*).

Civil Aviation (traffic on scheduled services, 1998): Passengers carried ('000) 21; Passenger-km (million) 4. Source: UN, *Statistical Yearbook*.

COMMUNICATIONS MEDIA

Radio Receivers: 180,000 in use in 1997.

Television Receivers: 4,000 in use in 1997.

Newspaper: 1 daily (estimated circulation 2,000) in 1996.

Book Production: 17 titles in 1998.

Telephones: 13,500 main lines in use in 2010.

Mobile Cellular Telephones: 399,300 subscribers in 2010.

Personal Computers: 9,000 (14.8 per 1,000 persons) in 2005.

Internet Users: 14,400 in 2009.

Broadband Subscribers: 1,200 in 2010.

Sources: UNESCO, *Statistical Yearbook;* UN, *Statistical Yearbook;* International Telecommunication Union.

EDUCATION

Pre-primary (2007/08, unless otherwise indicated): Schools 180*; Teachers 1,655 (males 208, females 1,447); Students 39,551 (males 17,065, females 22,486).

Primary (2009/10, unless otherwise indicated): Schools 483*; Teachers 3,131 (males 2,011, females 1,120); Students 85,061 (males 43,294, females 41,767).

Secondary (2001/02, estimates, unless otherwise indicated): Schools 59; Teachers 894 (males 855, females 39)†; Students 21,173 (males 13,463, females 7,710).

Higher (1999/2000, unless otherwise indicated): Teachers 206 (males 174, females 32)‡; Students 1,003 (males 699, females 304).

* 1998 figure.

† 1999/2000 figure.

‡ 1999/2000 figure.

Pupil-teacher Ratio (primary education, UNESCO estimate): 27.2 in 2009/10.

Adult Literacy Rate: 93.3% (males 97.0%; females 89.8%) in 2009.

Source: UNESCO Institute for Statistics.

Directory

The Government

HEAD OF STATE

President and Supreme Commander of the Armed Forces: Gen. (retd) OBIANG NGUEMA MBASOGO (assumed office 25 August 1979; elected President 25 June 1989; re-elected 25 February 1996, 15 December 2002 and 29 November 2009).

COUNCIL OF MINISTERS

(May 2012)

The Government is formed predominantly by members of the Partido Democrático de Guinea Ecuatorial, with a small number of representatives from allied parties.

Prime Minister and Head of Government: IGNACIO MILAM TANG.

First Deputy Prime Minister, in charge of the Economic and Financial Sector: ANICETO EBIACA MOHETE.

Second Deputy Prime Minister, in charge of the Political and Democratic Sector, and Minister of Public Works and Infrastructure: DEMETRIO ELO NDONG NSEFUMU.

Third Deputy Prime Minister, in charge of the Social Sector and Human Rights, and Minister of Health and Social Welfare: SALOMÓN NGUEMA OWONO.

Minister of State at the Presidency of the Republic, in charge of Missions: ALEJANDRO EVUNA OWONO ASANGONO.

Minister of State at the Prime Minister's Office, in charge of Relations with Parliament and Legal Affairs of the Government: ÁNGEL MASIE MIBUY.

Minister of State, in charge of the Interior and Local Government: CLEMENTE ENGOGA NGUEMA ONGUENE.

Minister of State, in charge of Education, Science and Sports: JOAQUÍN MBAMA NCHAMA.

Minister of State, in charge of Agriculture and Forestry: TEODORO (TEODORÍN) NGUEMA OBIANG MANGUE.

Minister at the Presidency of the Republic, in charge of Cabinet Affairs: BRAULIO NCOGO ABEGUE.

Minister and Secretary-General to the Prime Minister, in charge of Administrative Co-ordination: VICENTE EHATE TOMI.

Minister at the Presidency of the Republic, in charge of Regional Integration: BALTASAR ENGOGA EDJO.

Minister of External Relations, International Co-operation and Francophone Affairs: PASTOR MICHA ONDO BILE.

Minister of Justice, Religion and Penitentiary Institutions: FRANCISCO JAVIER NGOMO MBENONO.

Minister of National Defence: ANTONIO MBA NGUEMA.

Minister of National Security: NICOLÁS OBAMA NCHAMA.

Minister of Transport, Technology, Post and Telecommunications and Minister of Labour and Social Security: MAURICIO BOKUNG ASUMU.

Minister of the Economy, Trade and Business Development: FRANCISCA TATCHOUP BELOPE.

Minister of Planning, Economic Development and Public Investment: JOSÉ ELA OYANA.

Minister of Finance and the Budget: ESTANISLAO DON MALABO.

Minister of Mines, Industry and Energy: MARCELINO OWONO EDU.

Minister of Social Affairs and Women's Advancement: EULALIA ENVO BELA.

Minister of Fisheries and the Environment: ANASTÁSIO ASUMU MUM MUÑOZ.

Minister of Information, Culture and Tourism and Government Spokesperson: JERÓNIMO OSA OSA EKORO.

Minister of the Civil Service and Administrative Planning: SALVADOR MANGUE NGONO.

Minister-delegate to the Minister of Planning, Economic Development and Public Investment: PEDRO ONDO NGUEMA.

Minister-delegate to Minister of Finance and the Budget: MARTÍN CRISANTOS EBE MBA.

Minister-delegate to the Minister of Mines, Industry and Energy: GABRIEL MBEGA OBIANG LIMA.

Minister-delegate to the Minister of External Relations, International Co-operation and Francophone Affairs: EUSTAQUIO NSENG ESONO.

Minister-delegate to the Minister of the Economy, Trade and Business Development: CELESTINO BONIFACIO BACALE OBIANG.

Minister-delegate, in charge of the State Treasury: MONSERRAT AFANG ONDO.

Minister-delegate, in charge of Posts and Transport: FRANCISCO MBÁ OLÚ BAHAMONDE.

Minister-delegate of Health and Social Welfare: TOMÁS MECHEBA FERNÁNDEZ GALILEA.

Minister-delegate of Information, Culture and Tourism: ALFONSO NSUY MOKUY.

In addition there were 16 Deputy Ministers and 20 Secretaries of State.

MINISTRIES

Ministry of Agriculture and Forestry: Apdo 504, Malabo.

Ministry of the Economy, Trade and Business Development: Apdo 404, Malabo; tel. 333093105; fax 333092043.

Ministry of External Relations, International Co-operation and Francophone Affairs: Malabo; tel. 333093220; fax 333093132.

Ministry of Finance and the Budget: Malabo; internet www.ceiba-guinea-ecuatorial.org/guineees/indexbienv1.htm.

Ministry of the Interior and Local Corporations: Malabo; fax 333092683.

Ministry of Justice, Religion and Penitentiary Institutions: Malabo; fax 333092115.

Ministry of Mines, Industry and Energy: Calle 12 de Octubre s/n, Malabo; tel. 333093567; fax 333093353; e-mail d.shaw@ecqc.com; internet www.equatorialoil.com.

Ministry of National Defence: Malabo; tel. 333092794.

Ministry of National Security: Malabo; tel. 333093469.

Ministry of Social Affairs and Women's Advancement: Malabo; tel. 333093469.

Ministry of Transport, Technology, Post and Telecommunications: Malabo; internet www.ceiba-guinea-ecuatorial.org/guineees/transport.htm.

President and Legislature

PRESIDENT

Presidential Election, 29 November 2009

Candidate	Votes	% of votes
Obiang Nguema Mbasogo (PDGE)	260,462	95.76
Plácido Micó Abogo (CPDS)	9,700	3.57
Archivaldo Montero (UP)	931	0.34
Bonaventura Monsuy Asumu (PCSD)	462	0.17
Carmelo Mba Bacale (APGE)	437	0.16
Total	271,992*	100.00

* The total number of votes officially attributed to candidates by the Constitutional Court amounted to 271,992. However, that body declared the total number of valid votes cast to be 271,964, and the percentage of votes awarded to Obiang Nguema Mbasogo to be 95.37%. According to the Constitutional Court, there were 1,167 invalid votes.

CÁMARA DE REPRESENTANTES
(House of Representatives)

Speaker: Dr ÁNGEL SERAFÍN SERICHE.

General Election, 4 May 2008

Party	Seats
Partido Democrático de Guinea Ecuatorial (PDGE)	99*
Convergencia para la Democracia Social (CPDS)	1
Total	100

* Including nine seats won by members of the coalition allied to the PDGE.

Election Commission

Constitutional Court: Malabo; Pres. SALVADOR ONDO NKUMU.

Political Organizations

Alianza Democrática Progresista (ADP): pro-Govt party; Pres. FRANCISCO MBÁ OLÚ BAHAMONDE.

Acción Popular de Guinea Ecuatorial (APGE): pro-Govt party; Pres. CARMELO MBA BACALE; Sec.-Gen. MIGUEL ESONO.

Convención Liberal Democrática (CLD): pro-Govt party; Pres. ALFONSO NSUE MOKUY.

Convención Socialdemocrática Popular (CSDP): pro-Govt party; Leader SECUNDINO OYONO.

Convergencia para la Democracia Social (CPDS): Calle Tres de Agosto, Apdo 72, 2º, 1 Malabo; tel. 333092013; e-mail cpds@intnet.gq; internet www.cpds-gq.org; Pres. SANTIAGO OBAMA NDONG; Sec.-Gen. PLÁCIDO MICÓ ABOGO.

Demócratas por el Cambio (DECAM): coalition based in Madrid, Spain; e-mail press@guinea-ecuatorial.org; internet www.guinea-ecuatorial.org; f. 2005; 16 mem. orgs; Gen. Co-ordinator DANIEL OYONO.

Fuerza Demócrata Republicana (FDR): f. 1995; Pres. FELIPE ONDO OBIANG; Sec.-Gen. GUILLERMO NGUEMA ELA.

Movimiento para la Autodeterminación de la Isla de Bioko (MAIB): e-mail info@maib.org; internet www.maib.org; f. 1993 by Bubi interests seeking independence of Bioko; clandestine; Gen. Co-ordinator WEJA CHICAMPO.

Partido de la Convergencia Social Demócrata (PCSD): pro-Govt party; Pres. BUENAVENTURA MONSUY ASUMU.

Partido Democrático de Guinea Ecuatorial (PDGE): Malabo; internet www.pdge-ge.org; f. 1987; sole legal party 1987–92; Chair. Gen. (TEODORO) OBIANG NGUEMA MBASOGO; Sec.-Gen. LUCAS NGUEMA ESONO.

Partido del Progreso de Guinea Ecuatorial (PPGE): Madrid, Spain; e-mail ppge@telepolis.com; internet www.guinea-ecuatorial.org; f. 1983; Christian Democrat faction led by SEVERO MOTO NSA.

Partido Socialista de Guinea Ecuatorial (PSGE): pro-Govt party; Sec.-Gen. TOMÁS MECHEBA FERNÁNDEZ-GALILEA.

Unión para la Democracia y el Desarrollo Social (UDDS): f. 1990; Sec.-Gen. AQUILINO NGUEMA ONA NCHAMA; in Cameroon.

Unión Democrática Independiente (UDI): Leader DANIEL M. OYONO (in Spain).

Unión Democrática Nacional (UDENA): Pres. JOSÉ MECHEBA.

Unión Democrática y Social de Guinea Ecuatorial (UDS): pro-Govt party; Pres. CARMELO MODÚ ACUSÉ BINDANG.

Unión Popular (UP): f. 1992; conservative; divided into two factions, one led by DANIEL DARÍO MARTÍNEZ AYACABA and another led by FAUSTINO ONDO in Madrid.

Diplomatic Representation

EMBASSIES IN EQUATORIAL GUINEA

Angola: Malabo; Ambassador ARMANDO MATEUS CADETE.

Brazil: Avda Parques de África, Carocolas, Apdo 119, Malabo; tel. 333099986; fax 333099987; Ambassador ELIANA DA COSTA Y SILVA.

Cameroon: 37 Calle Rey Boncoro, Apdo 292, Malabo; tel. and fax 333092263; Ambassador JOHN MPOUEL BALA LAZARE.

China, People's Republic: Carretera del Aeropuerto, Apdo 44, Malabo; tel. 333093505; fax 3330923-81; e-mail chinaemb_gq@mfa.gov.cn; Ambassador WANG SHIXIONG.

Congo, Republic: Malabo; Ambassador CÉLESTINE KOUAKOUA.

Cuba: Carretera de Luba y Cruce de Dragas s/n, Malabo; tel. and fax 333094793; e-mail embacubage@orange.gq; Ambassador VÍCTOR EMILIO DREKE CRUZ.

France: Carretera del Aeropuerto, Apdo 326, Malabo; tel. 333092005; fax 333092305; e-mail chancellerie.malabo-amba@diplomatie.gouv.fr; internet www.ambafrance-gq.org; Ambassador FRANÇOIS BARATEAU.

Gabon: Calle de Argelia, Apdo 18, Malabo; Ambassador JANVIER OBIANG ALLOGHO.

Germany: Edificio Venus, 4º.Piso, Carretera del Aeropuerto, Km 4, Malabo; e-mail embajada.alemana.malabo@diplo.de; Ambassador MICHAEL OTTO KLEPSCH.

Guinea: Malabo.

Korea, Democratic People's Republic: Malabo; tel. 333092047; Ambassador KWAK JI HWAN.

Morocco: Avda Enrique Nvo, Apdo 329, Malabo; tel. 333092650; fax 333092655; Ambassador JILALI HILAL.

Nigeria: 4 Paseo de los Cocoteros, Apdo 78, Malabo; tel. and fax 333093385; Ambassador JOHN SHINKAME.

South Africa: Parque de las Avenidas de Africa s/n, Apdo 5, Malabo; tel. 333207737; fax 333092746; e-mail malabo@foreign.gov.za; Ambassador PAKAMISA AUGUSTINE SIFUBA.

Spain: Parque de las Avenidas de África s/n, Malabo; tel. 333092020; fax 333092611; e-mail emb.malabo@maec.es; Ambassador MANUEL GÓMEZ-ACEBO RODRIGUEZ.

USA: K-3, Carretera de Aeropuerto, Malabo; tel. 333098895; fax 333098894; e-mail usembassymalabo@yahoo.com; internet malabo.usembassy.gov; Ambassador ALBERTO M. FERNANDEZ.

Judicial System

The Supreme Court of Justice and the Constitutional Court sit in Malabo. The Supreme Court has four chambers (Civil and Social, Penal, Administrative and Common) and consists of a President and 12 magistrates, from whom the President of each chamber is selected. There are Territorial High Courts in Malabo and Bata, which also sit as courts of appeal. Courts of first instance sit in Malabo and Bata, and may be convened in the other provincial capitals. Local courts may be convened when necessary.

President of the Supreme Court of Justice: MARTIN NDONG NSUE.

President of the Constitutional Court: SALVADOR ONDO NKUMU.

Attorney-General: CARLOS MANGUE.

Religion

More than 90% of the population are adherents of the Roman Catholic Church. Traditional forms of worship are also followed.

CHRISTIANITY

The Roman Catholic Church

Equatorial Guinea comprises one archdiocese and two dioceses.

Bishops' Conference

Arzobispado, Apdo 106, Malabo; tel. 333092909; fax 333092176; e-mail arzobispadomalabo@hotmail.com.

f. 1984; Pres. Most Rev. ILDEFONSO OBAMA OBONO (Archbishop of Malabo).

Archbishop of Malabo: Most Rev. ILDEFONSO OBAMA OBONO, Arzobispado, Apdo 106, Malabo; tel. 333092909; fax 333092176; e-mail arzobispadomalabo@hotmail.com.

Protestant Church

Iglesia Reformada Evangélica de Guinea Ecuatorial (Evangelical Reformed Church of Equatorial Guinea): Apdo 195, Malabo; f. 1960; c. 8,000 mems; Sec.-Gen. Pastor JUAN EBANG ELA.

The Press

Ebano: Malabo; f. 1940; weekly; govt-controlled.

El árbol del centro: Apdo 180, Malabo; tel. 333092186; fax 333093275; Spanish; cultural review; 6 a year; publ. by Centro Cultural Español de Malabo; Dir GLORIA NISTAL.

El Correo Deportivo: tel. 222259223 (mobile); e-mail lagacetademalabo@gmail.com; monthly; Dir ROBERTO MARTIN PRIETO.

La Gaceta: Malabo; tel. 222259223 (mobile); e-mail lagacetademalabo@gmail.com; f. 1996; monthly; Dir ROBERTO MARTÍN PRIETO; circ. 3,000.

El Lector: Malabo; f. 2011; fortnightly; Dir ANTONIO NSUE ADÁ.

La Verdad: Talleres Gráficos de Convergencia para la Democracia Social, Calle Tres de Agosto 72, Apdo 441, Malabo; publ. by the Convergencia para la Democracia Social; 5 annually; Editor PLÁCIDO MICÓ ABOGO.

Poto-poto: Bata; f. 1940; weekly; govt-controlled.

Voz del Pueblo: Malabo; publ. by the Partido Democrático de Guinea Ecuatorial.

PRESS ASSOCIATION

Asociación para la Libertad de Prensa y de Expresión en Guinea Ecuatorial (ASOLPEGE Libre): Calle Isla Cabrera 3, 5°, 46026 Valencia, Spain; tel. (660) 930629; e-mail asopge_ngo@hotmail.com; f. 2006 to replace ASOPGE (f. 1997); Pres. PEDRO NOLASCO NDONG OBAMA.

Asociación de Periodistas Profesionales de Guinea Ecuatorial: Malabo; f. 2007 by former Secretary of State for Information, Santiago Ngua.

Publisher

Centro Cultural Español de Malabo: Apdo 180, Malabo; tel. 333092186; fax 333092722; e-mail ccem@orange.gq.

Broadcasting and Communications

TELECOMMUNICATIONS

Dirección General de Correos y de Telecomunicaciones: Malabo; tel. 333092857; fax 333092515; Man. Dir M. DAUCHAT.

Guinea Ecuatorial de Telecomunicaciones, SA (GETESA): Calle Rey Boncoro 27, Apdo 494, Malabo; tel. 333092815; fax 333093313; e-mail info@getesa.gq; internet www.getesa.gq; f. 1987; 60% state-owned, 40% owned by France Telecom; Man. FRANCISCO NVE NSOGO.

RADIO

Radio Africa and Radio East Africa: Apdo 851, Malabo; e-mail pabcomain@aol.com; commercial station; owned by Pan American Broadcasting; music and religious programmes in English.

Radio Nacional de Guinea Ecuatorial: Apdo 749, Barrio Comandachina, Bata; Apdo 195, Avda 30 de Agosto 90, Malabo; tel. 333092260; fax 333092097; govt-controlled; commercial station; programmes in Spanish, French and vernacular languages; Dir (Bata) SEBASTIÁN ELÓ ASEKO; Dir (Malabo) JUAN EYENE OPKUA NGUEMA.

Radio Santa Isabel: Malabo; Spanish and French programmes.

Radio Televisión Asonga: Bata and Malabo; private; owned by Teodorín Ngumea Obiang.

TELEVISION

Televisión Nacional: Malabo; broadcasts in Spanish and French; Dir ERNESTO MFUMU MIKO.

Finance

(cap. = capital; res = reserves; dep. = deposits; m. = million; brs = branches; amounts in francs CFA)

BANKING

Central Bank

Banque des Etats de l'Afrique Centrale (BEAC): POB 501, Malabo; tel. 333092010; fax 333092006; e-mail beacmal@beac.int; internet www.beac.int; HQ in Yaoundé, Cameroon; agency also in Bata; f. 1973; bank of issue for mem. states of the Communauté économique et monétaire de l'Afrique centrale (CEMAC, fmrly Union douanière et économique de l'Afrique centrale), comprising Cameroon, the Central African Repub., Chad, the Repub. of the Congo, Equatorial Guinea and Gabon; cap. 88,000m., res 227,843m., dep. 4,110,966m. (Dec. 2009); Equatorial Guinea's deposits in 2010 totalled 776,000m; Gov. LUCAS ABAGA NCHAMA; Dir in Equatorial Guinea IVAN BACALE EBE MOLINA; 2 brs in Equatorial Guinea.

Commercial Banks

In 2008 there were four commercial banks in Equatorial Guinea.

Banco Nacional de Guinea Ecuatorial (BANGE): Bata; f. 2005; Dir-Gen. ROWELITO TANALIGA CAHILIG.

BGFIBANK Guinea Ecuatorial: Calle de Bata s/n, Apdo 749, Malabo; tel. 333096352; fax 333096373; e-mail agence_malabo@bgfi

.com; internet www.bgfi.com/site/sp/bgfibank-guinea-ecuatorial.461 .html; 55% owned by BGFIBANK, 35% owned by private shareholders, 10% state-owned; incorporated June 2001; cap. 5,000m., total assets 43,211m. (Dec. 2007); Chair. MELCHOR ESSONO EDJO; Dir-Gen. SERGE MICKOTO.

Caisse Commune d'Epargne et d'Investissement Guinea Ecuatorial (CCEI-GE): Calle del Presidente Nasser, Apdo 428, Malabo; tel. 333092203; fax 333093311; e-mail geccei@hotmail.com; 51% owned by Afriland First Bank (Cameroon); f. 1995; cap. and res 5,172m., total assets 81,191m. (Dec. 2003); Pres. BÁLTASAR ENGONGA EDJO'O; Dir-Gen. JOSEPH CÉLESTIN TINDJOU DJAMENI.

Commercial Bank Guinea Ecuatorial (CBGE): Carretera de Luba, Apdo 189, Malabo; e-mail cbgebank@cbc-bank.com; internet www.cbc-bank.com; f. 2003; cap. 1,500m. (Jan. 2003).

Société Générale des Banques en Guinée Equatoriale (SGBGE): Avda de la Independencia, Apdo 686, Malabo; tel. 333093337; fax 333093366; e-mail particuliers.sgbge@socgen.com; internet www.sgbge.gq; f. 1986; present name adopted 1998; 45.79% owned by Société Générale SA (France), 31.79% state-owned, 11.45% owned by Société Générale de Banques au Cameroun, 11.13% owned by local investors; cap. and res 2,780m., total assets 48,624m. (Dec. 2001); Chair. MARCELINO OWONO EDU; Man. Dir CHRISTIAN DELMAS; 5 brs in Bata, Ebebeyin, Luba and Malabo.

Development Banks

Banco de Fomento y Desarrollo (BFD): Malabo; f. 1998; 30% state-owned; cap. 50m.

Banque de Développement des Etats de l'Afrique Centrale: see Franc Zone

Financial Institution

Caja Autónoma de Amortización de la Deuda Pública: Ministry of the Economy, Trade and Business Devt, Apdo 404, Malabo; tel. 333093105; fax 333092043; management of state funds; Dir-Gen. RAFAEL TUN.

INSURANCE

Equatorial Guinean Insurance Company, SA (EGICO): Avda de la Libertad, Malabo; state-owned.

Trade and Industry

GOVERNMENT AGENCIES

Cámaras Oficiales Agrícolas de Guinea: Bioko and Bata; purchase of cocoa and coffee from indigenous planters, who are partially grouped in co-operatives.

Empresa General de Industria y Comercio (EGISCA): Malabo; f. 1986; parastatal body jtly operated with the French Société pour l'Organisation, l'Aménagement et le Développement des Industries Alimentaires et Agricoles (SOMDIA); import-export agency.

Oficina para la Cooperación con Guinea Ecuatorial (OCGE): Malabo; f. 1981; administers bilateral aid from Spain.

DEVELOPMENT ORGANIZATIONS

Agencia Española de Cooperación Internacional para el Desarrollo (AECID): Parque de las Avenidas de Africa, Malabo; tel. 333091621; fax 333092932; e-mail ucemalabo@guineanet.net; internet www.aecid.es.

Asociación Bienestar Familiar de Guinea Ecuatorial: Apdo 984, Malabo; tel. and fax (09) 33-13; e-mail abifage1@hotmail.com; family welfare org.

Asociación Hijos de Lommbe (A Vonna va Lommbe): Malabo; e-mail avvl@bisa.com; internet www.bisala.com/avvl.html; f. 2000; agricultural devt org.

Camasa: Finca Sampaka, Km 7 Camino a Luba, Malabo; tel. 333098692; e-mail casamallo@hotmail.com; internet www.camasa .net; f. 1906; agricultural devt on Bioko island; operates projects for the cultivation and export of cocoa, pineapple, coffee, vanilla, nutmeg, peppers and tropical flowers.

Centro de Estudios e Iniciativas para el Desarrollo de Guinea Ecuatorial (CEIDIGE): Malabo; e-mail ceidbata@intnet.gq; internet www.eurosur.org/CEIDGE/portada.html; umbrella group of devt NGOs; Pres. JOSÉ ANTONIO NSANG ANDEME.

Family Care Guinea Ecuatorial (FGCE): Malabo; f. 2000; health and education devt; Dir LAUREN TAYLOR STEVENSON.

Instituto Nacional de Promoción Agropecuaria (INPAGE): Malabo; govt agricultural devt agency; reorg. 2000.

Sociedad Anónima de Desarrollo del Comercio (SOADECO-Guinée): Malabo; f. 1986; parastatal body jtly operated with the French Société pour l'Organisation, l'Aménagement et le Développement des Industries Alimentaires et Agricoles (SOMDIA); devt of commerce.

CHAMBERS OF COMMERCE

Cámara de Comercio Agrícola y Forestal de Malabo: Avda de la Independencia, Apdo 51, Malabo; tel. 333092343; fax 333094462; Dir ENRIQUE MERCADER COASTA.

Cámara de Comercio de Bioko: Avda de la Independencia 43, Apdo 51, Malabo; tel. and fax 333094576; e-mail camara@orange.gq; Pres. GREGORIO BOHO CAMO.

INDUSTRIAL AND TRADE ASSOCIATIONS

INPROCAO: Malabo; production, marketing and distribution of cocoa.

Unión General de Empresas Privadas de la República de Guinea Ecuatorial (UGEPRIGE): Apdo 138, Malabo; tel. 222278326 (mobile); fax 333090559.

UTILITIES

Electricity

ENERGE: Malabo; state-owned electricity board.

Sociedad de Electricidad de Guinea Ecuatorial (SEGESA): Carretera de Luba, Apdo 139, Malabo; tel. 333093466; fax 333093329; e-mail segesa@internet.gq; state-owned electricity distributor; Man. Dir BENITO ONDO.

Major Companies

Abayak: Malabo; owned by President Obiang's family.

Efusilia: Malabo; owned by Armengol Ondo, President Obiang's brother.

ExxonMobil: Complejo Residencial Abajak, Malabo.

Guinea Ecuatorial de Petróleo (GEPetrol): Calle Acacio Mane 39, BP 965, Malabo; tel. 333096769; fax 333096692; e-mail bonifacio .monsuy@ge-petrol.com; internet www.equatorialoil.com/pages/ GEPetrol%20page.htm; f. 2001; state-owned petroleum company; National Dir CÁNDIDO NSUE OKOMO.

Shimmer International: Bata; controls 90% of wood production in Rio Muni.

Sociedad Equatoguineana de Bebidas: Bata; production and bottling of various brands of beer, water and soft drinks; Dir-Gen. CYRIL BRUNEL.

Sociedad Nacional de Gas de Guinea Ecuatorial (SONAGAS, G.E.): Malabo; e-mail j.ndong@sonagas-ge.com; internet www .sonagas-ge.com; f. 2005; oversees gas exploration and devt; Dir-Gen. JUAN ANTONIO NDONG.

Sociedad Nacional de Vigilancia (SONAVI): Malabo; owned by Armengol Ondo.

Total Ecuatoguineana de Gestión (GE—Total): Malabo; f. 1984; 50% state-owned, 50% owned by Total (France); petroleum marketing and distribution.

TRADE UNIONS

A law permitting the establishment of trade unions was introduced in 1992. However, trade unions have not been granted authorization to operate.

Transport

RAILWAYS

There are no railways in Equatorial Guinea.

ROADS

In 2000 there were an estimated 2,880 km of roads and tracks.

Bioko: a semi-circular tarred road serves the northern part of the island from Malabo down to Batete in the west and from Malabo to Basacato Grande in the east, with a feeder road from Luba to Moka and Bahía de la Concepción.

Río Muni: a tarred road links Bata with the town of Mbini (Río Benito) in the west; another road, partly tarred, links Bata with the frontier post of Ebebiyín in the east and then continues into Gabon; other earth roads join Acurenam, Mongomo and Anisok.

SHIPPING

The main ports are Bata (general cargo and most of the country's export timber), Malabo (general), Luba (bananas, timber and petroleum), Mbini and Cogo (timber).

CIVIL AVIATION

There are two international airports, at Malabo (Santa Isabel Airport) and Bata. Construction of a new runway at Bata began in 2011. All flights operated by carriers based in Equatorial Guinea are prohibited from flying in European Union airspace. SONAGESA, jointly operated by GEPetrol and SONAIR of Angola, offers direct connections between Malabo and Houston, TX, USA.

Air Consul: Apdo 77, Malabo; tel. and fax 333093291; e-mail airconsul@intnet.gq; Man. FERNANDEZ ARMESTO.

EGA—Ecuato Guineana de Aviación: Apdo 665, Malabo; tel. 333092325; fax 333093313; internet www.ecuatoguineana.com/ega/ega.htm; regional and domestic passenger and cargo services; Pres. MELCHOR ESONO EDJO.

Tourism

Tourism remains undeveloped. Future interest in this sector would be likely to focus on the unspoilt beaches of Río Muni and Bioko's scenic mountain terrain.

Defence

As assessed at November 2011, there were 1,100 men in the army, 120 in the navy and 100 in the air force. There was also a paramilitary force, referred to both as 'Antorchas' and 'Ninjas', which was trained by French military personnel. Military service is voluntary. Since 1979 Morocco has provided the bulk of the Presidential Guards, currently estimated at about 30 officers. It has also provided military advisers and training. Spain has also provided military advisers and training. Military aid has also been received from the USA. More recently, Israel has been providing military aid, advisers and training for special forces, including presidential security, and the aviation sector.

Defence Expenditure: Estimated at 3,800m. francs CFA in 2010.

Supreme Commander of the Armed Forces: Gen. (retd) OBIANG NGUEMA MBASOGO.

Inspector-Gen. of the Armed Forces and the Security Forces: Rear Adm. JOAQUÍN NDONG NVÉ.

Education

Education is officially compulsory and free for five years between the ages of six and 11 years. Primary education starts at six years of age and normally lasts for five years. Secondary education, beginning at the age of 12, spans a seven-year period, comprising a first cycle of four years and a second cycle of three years. In 2001/02 the total enrolment at primary and secondary schools was equivalent to 67% of the school-age population. According to UNESCO estimates, in 2002/03 total enrolment at primary schools included 66% of children in the relevant age-group (males 70%; females 63%), while secondary enrolment in 2000/01 included 24% of children in the relevant age-group (males 30%; females 18%). In 1999/2000 there were 1,003 pupils in higher education. Since 1979 assistance in the development of the educational system has been provided by Spain. Two higher education centres, at Bata and Malabo, are administered by the Spanish Universidad Nacional de Educación a Distancia. There is also a university, Universidad Nacional de Guinea Ecuatorial, founded in 1995, at Malabo and Bata, as well as the Escuela Nacional de Agricultura, a vocational college in Malabo. The French Government also provides considerable financial assistance. In September 2002 a new National Plan for Education was ratified. Its aims were to improve basic literacy and to introduce education on health-related topics. In 2003 spending on education represented 4.0% of total budgetary expenditure. According to UNESCO estimates, in 2010 the adult literacy rate was 93%, the highest in sub-Saharan Africa.

ERITREA

Introductory Survey

LOCATION, CLIMATE, LANGUAGE, RELIGION, FLAG, CAPITAL

The State of Eritrea, which has a coastline on the Red Sea extending for almost 1,000 km, is bounded to the north-west by Sudan, to the south and west by Ethiopia, and to the south-east by Djibouti. Its territory includes the Dahlak Islands, a low-lying coralline archipelago off shore from Massawa. Rainfall is less than 500 mm per year in lowland areas, increasing to 1,000 mm in the highlands. The temperature gradient is similarly steep: average annual temperatures range from 17°C (63°F) in the highlands to 30°C (86°F) in Massawa. The Danakil depression in the south-east, which is more than 130 m below sea-level in places, experiences some of the highest temperatures recorded, frequently exceeding 50°C (122°F). The major language groups in Eritrea are Afar, Bilien, Hedareb, Kunama, Nara, Rashaida, Saho, Tigre and Tigrinya. English is increasingly becoming the language of business and is the medium of instruction at secondary schools and at university. Arabic is also widely spoken. The population is fairly evenly divided between Tigrinya-speaking Christians (mainly Orthodox), the traditional inhabitants of the highlands, and the Muslim communities of the western lowlands, northern highlands and east coast; there are also systems of traditional belief adhered to by a small number of the population. The national flag (proportions 1 by 2) consists of a red triangle with its base corresponding to the hoist and its apex at the centre of the fly, in which is situated, towards the hoist, an upright gold olive branch with six clusters of three leaves each, framed by a wreath of two gold olive branches; the remainder of the field is green at the top and light blue at the base. The capital is Asmara.

CONTEMPORARY POLITICAL HISTORY

Historical Context

The Treaty of Ucciali, which was signed in 1889 between Italy and Ethiopia, gave the Italian Government control over what is today the State of Eritrea. Italian exploitation of the colony continued until the defeat of the Axis powers by the Allied forces in East Africa during the Second World War. The Eritrean national identity, which was established during the Italian colonial period, was further subjugated under British administration during 1941–52. As the Allied powers and the UN discussed the future of the former Italian colony, Ethiopian territorial claims helped to foment a more militant nationalism among the Eritrean population. In 1952 a federation was formed between Eritrea and Ethiopia; however, the absence of adequate provisions for the creation of federal structures allowed Ethiopia to reduce Eritrea's status to that of an Ethiopian province by 1962.

Resistance to the Ethiopian annexation was first organized in the late 1950s, and in 1961 the Eritrean Liberation Front (ELF) launched an armed struggle. In the mid-1970s a reformist group broke away from the ELF and formed the Popular Liberation Forces (renamed the Eritrean People's Liberation Front, EPLF, in 1977), and the military confrontation with the Ethiopian Government began in earnest. A major consequence of the split between the two Eritrean groups was the civil war of 1972–74. After two phases of desertion from the ELF to the EPLF, firstly in 1977–78 and secondly in 1985 (following a second civil war), the ELF was left without a coherent military apparatus.

Following the 1974 revolution in Ethiopia and the assumption of power by Mengistu Haile Mariam in 1977, thousands of new recruits joined the EPLF, and the armed struggle transformed into full-scale warfare. The numerically and materially superior Ethiopian forces achieved significant victories over the EPLF, which, following defeat in the highlands, was forced to retreat to its stronghold in the north of Eritrea. The EPLF launched counter-attacks throughout the late 1980s and slowly drove back the Ethiopian forces on all fronts. By 1989 the EPLF had gained control of the north and the west of the country, and in late 1989 the EPLF captured Massawa port, severing a major supply-route to the Ethiopian forces, who were by now besieged in Asmara. In May 1991 units of the EPLF entered Asmara, after the Ethiopian troops had fled, and immediately established an interim administration.

Following the liberation of Asmara by the EPLF, and of Addis Ababa, Ethiopia, by the Ethiopian People's Revolutionary Democratic Front (EPRDF), a conference was convened in London, United Kingdom, in August 1991. Both the USA and the Ethiopian delegation accepted the EPLF administration as the legitimate provisional Government of Eritrea, and the EPLF agreed to hold a referendum on independence in 1993. The provisional Government, which was to administer Eritrea during the two years prior to the referendum, drew most of its members from the EPLF. The Government struggled to rehabilitate and develop Eritrea's war-torn economy and infrastructure, and to feed a population largely dependent on food aid. The agricultural sector had been severely disrupted by the war, and urban economic activity was almost non-existent.

At the UN-supervised referendum held in April 1993, 99.8% of Eritreans who voted endorsed national independence. The anniversary of the liberation of Asmara, 24 May, was proclaimed Independence Day, and on 28 May Eritrea formally attained international recognition. In June Eritrea was admitted to the Organization of African Unity (OAU, now the African Union—AU, see p. 189). Following Eritrea's accession to independence, a four-year transitional period was declared, during which preparations were to proceed for establishing a constitutional and pluralist political system. At the apex of the transitional Government were three state institutions: the Consultative Council (the executive authority formed from the ministers, provincial administrators and heads of government authorities and commissions); the National Assembly (the legislative authority formed from the Central Committee of the EPLF, together with 30 members from the Provincial Assemblies and 30 individuals selected by the Central Committee); and the judiciary. One of the National Assembly's first acts was the election as Head of State of Issaias Afewerki, the Secretary-General of the EPLF, by a margin of 99 votes to five.

Domestic Political Affairs

In February 1994 the EPLF transformed itself into a political party, the People's Front for Democracy and Justice (PFDJ). An 18-member Executive Committee and a 75-member Central Committee were elected; President Afewerki was elected Chairman of the latter. In March the National Assembly adopted a series of resolutions whereby the former executive body, the Consultative Council, was formally superseded by a State Council. Other measures adopted included the creation of a 50-member Constitutional Commission and the establishment of a committee charged with the reorganization of the country's administrative divisions. It was decided that the National Assembly would henceforth comprise the 75 members of the PFDJ Central Committee and 75 directly elected members. However, no mechanism was announced for their election. All but eight of the 50 members of the Constitutional Commission were government appointees, and there was no provision for any opposition participation in the interim system.

A draft constitution was discussed at international conventions held by the Constitutional Commission in July 1994 and January 1995. In May the National Assembly approved proposals to create six administrative regions to replace the 10 regional divisions that had been in place since colonial rule. In November the Assembly approved new names for the regions and finalized details of their exact boundaries and sub-divisions; the new Constitution came into force in 1997.

It was initially announced that Eritrea's first post-independence elections, which were scheduled to have been held in 1998, but were postponed indefinitely following the outbreak of hostilities with Ethiopia (see below), would take place in December 2001. However, during 2001 the likelihood of elections taking place in that year diminished, as President Afewerki assumed an increasingly authoritarian position. In February he dismissed the Minister of Local Government, Mahmoud Ahmed Sherifo, and dissolved the electoral commission, which Sherifo had been appointed to head. In June Afewerki replaced the Ministers of

Trade and Industry and of Maritime Resources. They were among a group of 15 senior PFDJ officials, including 11 former government ministers, who, in May, had signed a letter publicly accusing Afewerki of working in an 'illegal and unconstitutional manner'. In August the Chief Justice of the Supreme Court was dismissed after he openly expressed his disapproval of Afewerki's continued interference in court operations. In mid-September six of the G15, as the signatories of the letter criticizing Afewerki had become known, were arrested, and the Government announced the 'temporary suspension' of the independent press. A few days later a further five members of the G15 were detained.

Although no formal postponement of the legislative elections was announced, the failure of the National Assembly to convene to ratify legislation on the electoral system and on political pluralism by December 2001 made further delay inevitable. In late January 2002 the National Assembly ratified the electoral law, but failed to set an election date. Meanwhile, dissident members of the ruling PFDJ, including several members of the G15, announced the formation, in exile, of a new political party, the Eritrean People's Liberation Front—Democratic Party (EPLF—DP).

During 2004 several parties took steps to form a viable opposition movement to the PFDJ. In February, following talks in Germany, the EPLF—DP announced that it would reform as the Eritrean Democratic Party (EDP), under the continued leadership of Mesfin Hagos. In May numerous former members of the ELF and the PFDJ combined to establish the Eritrean Popular Movement (EPM). In August two new coalitions were formed; the first united the EPM and four smaller parties under the umbrella of the Eritrean National Alliance (ENA), while the second brought the EDP, the ELF and the Eritrean Liberation Front—Revolutionary Council together. In late December representatives of these two alliances met in Khartoum, Sudan, for talks with the Ethiopian Prime Minister, Meles Zenawi, and the Sudanese President, Omar Hassan Ahmad al-Bashir, aimed at settling issues surrounding the border conflict with Ethiopia (see below). In 2004 the ENA was reorganized as the Eritrean Democratic Alliance (EDA) and in January 2005 Hiruy Tedla Bairu was elected leader of the coalition. In January 2008 the 11 opposition parties comprising the EDA met in Addis Ababa to consolidate the alliance after divisions had emerged in the previous year. Two additional parties were admitted to the coalition: the Eritrean Islamic Congress and the Eritrean People's Movement.

In August 2005 the Minister of Foreign Affairs, Ali Sayyid Abdullah, died and Muhammad Omar was appointed to succeed him on an interim basis. In April 2007 President Afewerki appointed Osman Salih Muhammad, hitherto Minister of Education, as Minister of Foreign Affairs. The education portfolio was assumed by the Administrator of Maakel Province, Semere Rusom.

Recent developments: party political changes

Despite a date for legislative elections remaining elusive in early 2010, political parties had begun preparing for an eventual poll with three main opposition blocs emerging. In May 2009 four opposition parties (the ELF, Islah, al-Khalas and the Eritrean Federal Democratic Movement) joined forces as the Eritrean Solidarity Front. Later that month the Eritrean People's Party announced it was to merge with the Democratic Movement of Gash-Setit and was continuing discussions with the EDP regarding a merger. In June the Red Sea Afar Democratic Organisation and the Democratic Movement for the Liberation of Eritrean Kunama signed an agreement establishing the Democratic Front of Eritrean Nationalities, while confirming their intention to continue to work under the umbrella of the EDA. However, Afewerki repeatedly stated his reluctance to implement a democratic framework and dismissed multi-party competition as a Western phenomenon alien to Eritrean culture. In August 2010 the EDA's 11 member organizations, together with other groups and civil society representatives, held a National Conference for Democratic Change in Addis Ababa, Ethiopia, during which plans were reportedly discussed to overthrow the Eritrean Government. The EDA claimed to have staged co-ordinated military attacks against government troops inside Eritrea in February, April and May, but the Eritrean Government maintained a stance of silence against such reports of attacks on its forces. Another National Conference for Democratic Change was convened in Hawassa, Ethiopia, in November 2011.

Internally Displaced Persons

According to estimates by the Internal Displacement Monitoring Centre (IDMC), in 2006 there remained some 40,000–45,000 internally displaced persons (IDPs) in Eritrea. In an effort to promote 'self-sufficiency', in September 2005 the Eritrean Government imposed severe restrictions on the distribution of food aid, and reduced from 1.3m. to 72,000 the number of people entitled to receive free food. The move was widely criticized, especially by the UN, and prompted fears of acute food shortages among the one-third of the population who were estimated to be dependent on humanitarian assistance. Government resettlement programmes reduced the number of IDPs to an estimated 32,000 by mid-2007. In October 2009 there were contradictory reports on the number of IDPs remaining in Eritrea; the Office for the Coordination of Humanitarian Affairs reported that all IDPs had been resettled or returned to their existing communities, while the Internal Displacement Monitoring Centre claimed an estimated 10,000 remained in Eritrea.

Foreign Affairs

Relations with Sudan

Relations between the transitional Government and Sudan, which had supported the EPLF during the war, deteriorated in December 1993, following an incursion by members of an Islamist group, the Eritrean Islamic Jihad (EIJ), into Eritrea from Sudan, during which all the members of the group, and an Eritrean army commander, were killed. In response, President Afewerki stressed the links between the EIJ and the Sudanese National Islamic Front, led by Dr Hassan at-Turabi, implying that the latter had prior knowledge of the incursion. However, following a swift denial by the Sudanese Government that it would interfere in the affairs of neighbouring states, Afewerki reaffirmed his support for the Sudanese authorities and his commitment to improving bilateral relations.

Relations between Eritrea and Sudan worsened in November 1994, when the Eritrean authorities accused Sudan of training 400 terrorists since August. In response, Sudan accused Eritrea of training some 3,000 Sudanese rebels in camps within Eritrea. In December Eritrea severed diplomatic relations with Sudan. Further destabilization was provoked in early 1995 by attacks and infiltration in Gash-Barka Province by the EIJ. The Eritrean authorities subsequently claimed to have identified six training camps on the Sudanese side of the border and also alleged that large numbers of Eritrean refugees in Sudan had been arrested by Sudanese security forces. Sudan responded by proposing Eritrea's suspension from the Intergovernmental Authority on Drought and Development (IGADD, now the Intergovernmental Authority on Development—IGAD, see p. 338), which had been attempting to mediate in Sudan's civil war. The Sudanese Government protested strongly against Eritrea's growing support for the Sudanese opposition grouping, the National Democratic Alliance (NDA), which held a number of conferences in Asmara in the mid-1990s.

In early 1999 Sudan took steps to resolve its differences with Ethiopia, thus increasing the tension between Eritrea and Sudan. In April, however, Sudan indicated its willingness also to improve relations with Eritrea, and in May a reconciliatory agreement was signed in Qatar, which, inter alia, restored diplomatic relations between the two countries. Following the renewed outbreak of hostilities between Eritrea and Ethiopia in May (see below), some 94,000 Eritreans crossed the border into Sudan. After the cessation of fighting in June, many Eritrean refugees were repatriated with the assistance of the UN High Commissioner for Refugees (UNHCR), and by January 2002 some 36,500 Eritreans had returned home. In January 2003 refugee status was withdrawn from more than 320,000 Eritreans in Sudan, although UNHCR maintained that its repatriation programme would continue until all those registered had been returned home. By the end of 2007 160,488 Eritrean refugees remained in Sudan, and in 2011 UNHCR estimated that some 100,000 persons were still living in camps along the border. In October UNHCR condemned the deportation of more than 300 Eritrean refugees from Sudan after they had been detained for several weeks and despite an agreement between the UN agency and the Sudanese Commissioner for Refugees to transfer Eritreans to Khartoum, where their asylum claims could be assessed.

In July 2001 Eritrea and Sudan signed an agreement on border security, which aimed to eradicate smuggling and illegal infiltration, as well as ensure the safe passage of people and goods across the common border. In December 2003 al-Bashir accused Eritrea of arming and training rebels in the Darfur region of Sudan and maintained that Eritrea was a destabilizing force in the region. Eritrea refuted the allegations. Relations improved in 2006, following two separate rounds of peace talks in Asmara between the Sudanese Government and the rebel coalition Eastern Front during June–July. Meanwhile, in mid-June President Afewerki met al-Bashir in Khartoum, and later that month the two countries agreed to restore diplomatic relations to ambassadorial level. However, in September al-Bashir accused Eritrea of interference in the Darfur region and urged Eritrea to expel the leaders of the National Redemption Front, which had launched attacks on Sudanese Government forces in Darfur, from Eritrean territory. Nevertheless, al-Bashir and the Eastern Front leadership returned to Asmara in mid-October to sign a peace agreement (see Sudan). In early November the common border between Eritrea and Sudan was officially re-opened. In June 2008 the Sudanese authorities banned all activity of Eritrean opposition groups that had been operating from Sudan, demonstrating a marked improvement in relations between the two countries. Al-Bashir visited Asmara in March 2009 and reiterated his commitment to the June 2008 agreement. In March 2010 talks were held in Tripoli, Libya, between Eritrea, Libya and Sudan. The respective presidential delegations met to discuss means of improving both regional and wider, African security. Bilateral agreements on trade and economic co-operation were signed in July and the Sudanese and Eritrean Governments continued to display commitment to their agreement to suspend their backing of opposition groups.

Conflict with Ethiopia

In September 1993 the first meeting of the Ethiopian-Eritrean joint ministerial commission was held in Asmara, during which agreement was reached on measures to allow the free movement of nationals between each country, and on co-operation regarding foreign affairs and economic policy. Meetings held between President Afewerki and the Ethiopian President, Meles Zenawi, in December underlined the good relations prevailing between the two Governments.

However, relations deteriorated in late 1997 following Eritrea's adoption of a new currency (the nakfa) to replace the Ethiopian birr and the subsequent disruption of cross-border trade. In May 1998 fighting erupted between Eritrean and Ethiopian troops in the border region after both countries accused the other of having invaded their territory. Hostilities escalated in June around Badme, Zalambessa and Assab, resulting in numerous casualties for both sides. A peace plan devised by the USA and Rwanda in early June proved unsuccessful, although later that month Eritrea and Ethiopia agreed to an aerial cease-fire, following US and Italian mediation. In November President Afewerki and Prime Minister Meles of Ethiopia were present at different sessions of a special meeting of the OAU mediation committee in Ouagadougou, which was also attended by the Heads of State of Burkina Faso, Zimbabwe and Djibouti. The committee's peace proposals were accepted by Ethiopia, but rejected by Eritrea, and in February 1999 the aerial cease-fire was broken and fighting resumed in the border region. In July both sides finally confirmed their commitment to the OAU's Framework Agreement. Afewerki announced that Eritrean troops would be withdrawn from all territory captured from Ethiopia since 6 May 1998. Under the agreement, Ethiopia was also required to withdraw from all Eritrean territory captured since 6 February 1999. After requesting clarification of technical arrangements to end the war, Ethiopia informed the OAU in September that it had rejected the peace agreement, owing to inconsistencies contained therein. Eritrea accused Ethiopia of deliberately stalling proceedings, while secretly preparing for a fresh offensive.

By late May 2000 Ethiopian forces had seized Zalambessa and Eritrean troops were withdrawn from the disputed areas, although Afewerki maintained that this was merely a 'gesture of goodwill' designed to revive the peace talks, which resumed in Algiers on 29 May. Two days later Meles stated that the war was over and that his troops had withdrawn from most of the territory it had captured from Eritrea. Following negotiations in early June both sides expressed their readiness, in principle, to accept the OAU's cease-fire agreement, and on 18 June the Ethiopian and Eritrean Ministers of Foreign Affairs signed an agreement, which provided for an immediate cease-fire and the deployment of a UN peace-keeping force in a 25-km temporary security zone (TSZ) inside Eritrea until the issue of the demarcation of the border had been settled. In September the UN Security Council approved the deployment of the UN Mission in Ethiopia and Eritrea (UNMEE), a 4,200-strong peace-keeping force, which was placed under the command of the Special Representative of the UN Secretary-General, Legwaila Joseph Legwaila. On 12 December Eritrea and Ethiopia signed an agreement in Algiers, which formally ended the conflict between the two countries. The agreement provided for a permanent cessation of all hostilities, the immediate return of all prisoners of war, the demarcation of the common border by an independent commission and the establishment of a Claims Commission to assess the issues of compensation and reparations. Furthermore, both countries pledged to co-operate with an independent investigation, which aimed to determine the origins of the conflict.

By late January 2001 the UNMEE force had been fully deployed and on 18 April, after all troops had been withdrawn from the border area, UNMEE declared the establishment of the TSZ, marking the formal separation of the Eritrean and Ethiopian forces. In late June UNMEE presented the final map of the TSZ to Eritrea and Ethiopia, although it emphasized that it would not influence the work of the neutral boundary commission charged with determining the border between the two countries. Despite this announcement, the Ethiopian Government expressed its dissatisfaction with the map. At the eighth meeting of the Military Co-ordination Commission (MCC) in August both countries reiterated their objections to the existing boundaries of the TSZ. In mid-September UNMEE's mandate was extended for a further six months, although Legwaila acknowledged that the mission faced an extremely difficult task in achieving lasting peace, as the two countries remained 'polarized', and also admitted that neither country had fully adhered to the terms of the cease-fire agreement. In mid-December Eritrea and Ethiopia began presenting their cases for border demarcation to the five-member Boundary Commission at the International Court of Justice (see p. 25) in The Hague, Netherlands. In mid-March 2002 UNMEE's mandate was extended until mid-September.

In March 2003 the Boundary Commission categorically ruled Badme to be Eritrean territory. Meles subsequently complained that the decision was 'wrong and unjust' and vowed to continue to contest the ruling. The demarcation of the border was delayed until October; both the MCC and the UN expressed their frustration at the slow progress being made. The UN Security Council stated that Ethiopia had committed itself under the 2000 Algiers agreement to accept the Boundary Commission's decision as 'final and binding' and urged it to accept and implement the ruling. Both Legwaila and the Chairman of the Boundary Commission, Elihu Lauterpacht, were critical of Ethiopia's lack of compliance with its obligations under the terms of the peace accord, and the ongoing impasse was further compounded by the Commission's announcement in late October that border demarcation had been delayed indefinitely. Ethiopia maintained that it had agreed to allow demarcation to take place in the eastern sector of the border region, but that it refused to accept the ruling in other areas and had expressed grave concerns about the competency of the Boundary Commission. Eritrea continued, however, to insist that the ruling be fully implemented.

UN concerns over the lack of progress on the part of both Eritrea and Ethiopia in implementing the border ruling continued during 2004. In March UNMEE's mandate was extended by a further six months. Following accusations by Eritrean officials in May of serious malpractice on the part of the UN forces, Legwaila issued an ultimatum to Eritrea that it should either co-operate with the UN peace-keeping forces or ask its troops to leave. In September UNMEE's mandate was extended until March 2005 and it was announced that the peace-keeping mission would be reduced with 550 Kenyan troops stationed on the eastern part of the border being replaced by helicopter patrols by the end of January. Meanwhile, in November 2004 Ethiopia stated that it had, in principle, accepted the Boundary Commission's ruling of April 2002 and was prepared to re-enter into talks with Eritrea regarding the demarcation of the border. However, Eritrea dismissed this announcement as little more than a further attempt by Ethiopia to stall the process.

Relations deteriorated further in early 2005 as the UN Security Council and the European Union (EU, see p. 276) expressed concern over troop redeployments on both sides of the border. UNMEE's mandate was extended by six months in March and the Security Council appealed to both countries to reduce troop numbers to December 2004 levels. In September 2005 UNMEE's mandate was again extended, until March 2006. In October 2005 Ethiopia reaffirmed its acceptance of the Boundary Commission's ruling, and signalled its willingness to recommence talks with Eritrea. Despite protests from Legwaila and the UN Secretary-General, Kofi Annan, later that month Eritrea imposed restrictions upon the movements of UN vehicles, including a ban upon all UNMEE helicopter flights on its side of the border. In late November the UN Security Council unanimously adopted Resolution 1640, which demanded an end to all restrictions on UNMEE activities and the full implementation of the Boundary Commission's ruling, while also evoking the possibility of sanctions against Eritrea and Ethiopia, should the two countries not comply. In December Eritrea requested that all UNMEE peacekeepers and staff from Canada, Russia, the USA and EU member states leave the country. Some 180 UN staff were subsequently moved into Ethiopia, along with peace-keeping troops, within the 10-day deadline set by Eritrean officials.

In early March 2006 representatives of Eritrea and Ethiopia attended a Boundary Commission meeting in London aimed at resolving the border dispute, during which an agreement was reached to hold further discussions in April. Those talks were, however, subsequently postponed until late May. Meanwhile, in late March Legwaila ended his term as Special Representative to the UN Secretary-General and expressed his disappointment at the continued impasse in the peace process. On 31 May the UN Security Council adopted Resolution 1681, which extended UNMEE's mandate for four months, while reducing the number of military personnel by 1,000 to 2,300. The Security Council called upon Eritrea to lift all restrictions placed upon UNMEE activities; however, the request was later rejected by the Eritrean authorities. In late September UNMEE's mandate was extended until 31 January 2007.

In mid-October 2006 UN officials urged Eritrea to withdraw 1,500 of its troops and 14 armoured vehicles from the TSZ; the Eritrean Government claimed that the soldiers were harvesting crops from state-run farms in the area. In mid-November both countries declined to attend a meeting of the Boundary Commission in The Hague to discuss border demarcation and subsequently rejected its recommendations. Following the meeting, the Boundary Commission issued a statement, which expressed frustration at both countries' refusal to co-operate with the Commission and insisted that, should no agreement be in place by November 2007, the Commission would unilaterally begin the physical demarcation of the border. Ethiopia later condemned the decision as 'illegal'. On 31 January 2007 the UN Security Council approved Resolution 1741, which extended UNMEE's mandate by six months, while further reducing the size of the mission, to 1,700 military personnel. UNMEE's mandate was subsequently further extended until the end of July 2008.

With Eritrea and Ethiopia continuing to dispute the demarcation of the common border, concerns that conflict could resume were heightened in September 2007 when both Governments deployed troops to the border region. In a letter to his Eritrean counterpart, the Ethiopian Minister of Foreign Affairs, Seyoum Mesfin, stated that the Ethiopian Government considered Eritrea to be in material breech of the Algiers agreement as its troops had occupied the TSZ and had restricted the movement of the UNMEE force. In November Eritrea accused Ethiopia of planning an invasion, although these allegations were strongly denied by the Ethiopian authorities. Both parties again insisted that they were committed to a peaceful resolution of the border dispute; however, neither side complied with the Boundary Commission's request of November 2006 physically to demarcate the border by the end of November 2007. In early December, prior to announcing its own dissolution, the Commission stated that the boundary that it had determined in November 2006 represented the official border between the two countries.

As a result of restrictions imposed by Eritrea, in early February 2008 UNMEE began preparations to withdraw its peacekeepers from that country and to relocate them across the border into Ethiopia. In previous months the UN had repeatedly urged the Eritrean Government to lift restrictions on the delivery of fuel supplies; however, these requests were not met and in mid-February UN personnel were forced to leave the area. It was subsequently reported that a number of peace-keepers had been prevented from leaving Eritrea and the UN Security Council expressed its concern at the 'impediments and logistical constraints' placed upon the force. Eritrea continued to restrict UNMEE operations and Ethiopia also placed constraints on UN peace-keeping units that had withdrawn from Eritrea; on 30 July the UN Security Council voted to adopt Resolution 1827, terminating the mandate of UNMEE. In September Meles issued a statement in which he dismissed the possibility of an attack by Eritrea, and went on to accuse Eritrea of supporting the Ogaden National Liberation Front, an ethnic Somali rebel group seeking the right to self-determination from the Ethiopian Government.

Arbitration efforts continued during 2008 and 2009, and an uneasy truce persisted, punctuated by occasional minor military clashes. (In August 2009 the Claims Commission awarded Ethiopia a total of US $174m. in compensation for war damages, while Eritrea received $164m., resulting in a net payment to Ethiopia of $10m.) The damages awarded to Eritrea included compensation for loss of property for people expelled from their land by Ethiopia, while the damages awarded to Ethiopia were to compensate for the human suffering and lost income of displaced persons. Eritrea, which was to pay Ethiopia $12.6m., stated that it would honour the ruling; however, Ethiopia rejected the ruling, declaring that the compensation awarded was insufficient.

In 2010 Ethiopia continued to accuse Eritrea of sponsoring its opposition movements, most notably the Oromo Liberation Front. Ethiopia also accused Eritrea of involvement in bomb attacks on a café and on a bus in northern Ethiopia near the Eritrean border in early 2010, and of attempting to disrupt the Ethiopian legislative elections in May. In March 2011, following a visit to New York, USA, during which, it was reported, he urged the international community to take action to prevent Eritrea from destabilizing the Horn of Africa region, Ethiopian Deputy Prime Minister and Minister of Foreign Affairs Hailemariam Desalegn announced a change of policy towards Eritrea from a defensive to a more belligerent stance. This new approach appeared to be confirmed the following month by Prime Minister Meles' offer of determined support to Eritrean opposition groups and his reiteration of claims that Eritrea was a conduit for foreign financing of terrorist groups in the region and had assisted in a foiled terrorist attack against the AU summit in Addis Ababa in January. The exiled Eritrean opposition in Ethiopia praised this active policy to bring about regime change. However, despite that fact that reports of the planned attack were also corroborated by the UN Monitoring Group on Somalia and Eritrea, the Eritrean ambassador to the AU denounced all the accusations as part of a campaign of disinformation by the Ethiopian authorities.

Relations with Djibouti

Relations with neighbouring Djibouti have also been problematic, mainly due to territorial disputes. In April 1996 tensions mounted when Eritrea was accused of attacking positions in the disputed region of Ras Doumeira, on the border between the two countries. Later that month Djibouti formally rejected a map submitted by Eritrean officials, claiming it included territory belonging to Djibouti. In 1998 diplomatic relations were suspended following Afewerki's accusation that Djibouti was lending support to Ethiopia in the Ethiopia–Eritrea border dispute, although relations were restored in March 2000. Tensions resurfaced, in April 2008, after it was reported that Eritrean forces had mobilized near Ras Doumeira and crossed into Djiboutian territory, although Afewerki strongly denied the allegations. Djibouti responded by increasing troop numbers in the region and recalled all police and soldiers demobilized in the previous five years. Despite diplomatic attempts to settle the dispute, including appeals for restraint from the AU, hostilities broke out in June and numerous casualties were reported on both sides. The fighting drew strong international condemnation: the UN launched an investigation but Eritrea refused to co-operate, denying any wrongdoing, and President Ismaïl Omar Guelleh of Djibouti demanded joint demilitarization in the border region, appealing to the UN Security Council for mediation. In January 2009 the UN Security Council adopted a resolution ordering Eritrea to withdraw its forces from the area; however, Eritrea refused to comply with the request and issued a strongly worded statement to the Security Council in May 2009 denying any involvement in the destabilization of either Djibouti or Somalia. In October the Djibouti Minister of Foreign Affairs and Co-operation accused Eritrea of arming and training militias to carry out acts of sabotage in Djibouti, and of fomenting chaos in the region. Following increasing pressure for the imposition of sanctions from numerous East African governments, in December the UN Security Council placed an arms embargo on Eritrea, imposed travel restrictions on political and military leaders and also froze the overseas funds and financial assets of those individuals. In March 2010 the EU imposed similar sanctions. (In May 2011 forces of the North Atlantic Treaty Organization (NATO) intercepted a cargo ship carrying a substantial quantity of arms from the Democratic People's Republic of Korea destined for Eritrea.) In June 2010 Afewerki and Guelleh signed an agreement to end the border dispute between Eritrea and Djibouti, entrusting responsibility for establishing a method of resolving the demarcation issue and normalizing relations to a commission of Qatari advisers.

Relations with Other Countries

In August 2011 Afewerki agreed to hold talks with Ugandan President Yoweri Kaguta Museveni, whose country provides the majority of troops to the AU peace-keeping mission in Somalia. The meeting was viewed by analysts as a conciliatory move on the part of Afewerki, who was becoming increasingly isolated in the region and had continued to be accused of supporting extremist groups in Somalia. However, Eritrea's application to rejoin IGAD (from which it had suspended itself in 2007) was postponed by IGAD's Council of Ministers later that month, who instead demanded the imposition of further UN sanctions against Eritrea. In November 2011 the Kenyan Minister of Foreign Affairs announced a review of diplomatic ties with Eritrea in the wake of a report that arms had been flown to the Somali town of Baidoa from Eritrea. Afewerki denied the allegations and appealed for an independent investigation to be carried out.

CONSTITUTION AND GOVERNMENT

Following independence a transitional Government was established, at the apex of which were three state institutions: the Consultative Council (the executive authority formed from the ministers, provincial administrators, and heads of government authorities and commissions); the National Assembly (the legislative authority comprising the Central Committee of the EPLF, 30 additional members from the Provincial Assemblies and 30 individuals selected by the Central Committee); and the judiciary. In March 1994 the Consultative Council was superseded by a State Council. At independence a four-year transitional period was declared, during which preparations were to proceed for the establishment of a constitutional and pluralist political system. Meanwhile, in March 1994 the National Assembly voted to alter its composition: it would thenceforth comprise the 75 members of the PFDJ Central Committee and 75 directly elected members.

In early 1997 the Government established a Constituent Assembly, comprising 527 members (150 from the National Assembly, with the remainder selected from representatives of Eritreans residing abroad or elected by regional assemblies), to discuss and ratify the draft constitution. On 23 May the Constituent Assembly adopted the Constitution, authorizing 'conditional' political pluralism and instituting a presidential regime, with a President elected for a maximum of two five-year terms. The President, as Head of State, would appoint a Prime Minister and judges of the Supreme Court; his or her mandate could be revoked should two-thirds of the members of the National Assembly so demand. The Constituent Assembly was disbanded, and a Transitional National Assembly (consisting of the 75 members of the PFDJ Central Committee, 60 members of the Constituent Assembly and 15 representatives of Eritreans residing abroad) was empowered to act as the legislature until the holding of elections to a new National Assembly. At May 2012 these had yet to take place.

REGIONAL AND INTERNATIONAL CO-OPERATION

Eritrea is a member of the African Union (AU, see p. 189), but did not participate actively in the AU for more than seven years following the recall of its AU ambassador in 2003. However, in January 2011 Eritrea reopened its AU mission in Addis Ababa and presented a new ambassador to the international organization. Eritrea is also a member of the Common Market for Eastern and Southern Africa (see p. 237) and of the Intergovernmental Authority on Development (IGAD, see p. 338), although the country unilaterally announced its suspension from IGAD in 2007. In July 2011 Eritrea requested that it be permitted formally to reactivate its membership of IGAD.

Eritrea became a member of the UN in 1993 and participates in the Group of 77 (G77, see p. 450) developing countries. Also in 1993 Eritrea was admitted to the group of African, Caribbean and Pacific (ACP) countries party to the Lomé Convention; in September 2001 Eritrea ratified the Cotonou Agreement (see p. 328), the successor of the Lomé Convention.

ECONOMIC AFFAIRS

In 2010, according to estimates by the World Bank, Eritrea's gross national income (GNI), measured at average 2008–10 prices, was US $1,792m., equivalent to $340 per head (or $540 per head on an international purchasing-power parity basis). During 2001–10, it was estimated, the population increased at an average annual rate of 3.6%. Gross domestic product (GDP) per head decreased, in real terms, by an average of 3.4% per year during 2001–10, while overall GDP remained constant in 2001–10; growth in 2010 was 2.2%.

By far the most important sector of the economy is agriculture, which sustains 90% of the population. In 2009, according to the African Development Bank (AfDB), agriculture (including forestry and fishing) accounted for an estimated 24.2% of GDP; the sector was forecast to engage an estimated 73.1% of the labour force in mid-2012, according to FAO. Most sedentary agriculture is practised in the highlands, where rainfall is sufficient to cultivate the main crops: sorghum, teff (an indigenous grain), sesame seed, potatoes, millet and barley. As a result of serious environmental degradation (caused directly and indirectly by the war of independence), water scarcity and unreliable rainfall, projects have been undertaken to build water reservoirs and small dams, while badly eroded hillsides have been terraced and new trees planted in order to prevent soil erosion. Fishing activity is on a very small scale—the total catch reached just 3,030 metric tons in 2009—although, according to the UN, sustainable yields of as much as 70,000 tons per year may be possible. In real terms, according to the World Bank, the GDP of the agricultural sector decreased at an average annual rate of 1.8% in 2001–09; according to the AfDB, agricultural GDP declined by 12.5% in 2008, but increased by 5.7% in 2009.

In 2009 industrial production (comprising mining, manufacturing, construction and utilities) accounted for an estimated 18.9% of GDP, according to the AfDB. Some 5.0% of the labour force were employed in the industrial sector in 1990. According to the World Bank, industrial GDP increased, in real terms, at an average annual rate of 1.5% in 2001–09; the GDP of the sector grew by 1.9% in 2008, but declined by 0.2% in 2009.

Eritrea's mineral resources are believed to be of significant potential value, although in 2009 mining and quarrying accounted for only 1.3% of GDP, according to the AfDB. Of particular importance, in view of Eritrea's acute energy shortage, is the possibility of large reserves of petroleum and natural gas beneath the Red Sea. An exploration agreement, with CMS Oil and Gas of the USA, was signed in 2001 following the end of the conflict with Ethiopia. Other mineral resources include potash, zinc, magnesium, copper, iron ore, marble and gold. New legislation on mining, adopted in 1995, declared all mineral resources to be state assets, but recognized an extensive role for private investors in their exploitation. In September 2004, following the discovery in August of high-grade gold and copper in Western Eritrea, the Eritrean authorities prohibited all mining exploration by foreign companies while it reassessed its mining legislation. The ban was lifted in January 2005, with the Government announcing the possibility of increasing its option to buy into projects from the current maximum of 20% to 30%.

The manufacturing sector provided an estimated 5.8% of GDP in 2009, according to the AfDB. Until mid-1997 imported petroleum was processed at the Assab refinery, the entire output of petroleum products of which was delivered to Ethiopia. In 1997 the Eritrean authorities announced that they would import refined petroleum for the immediate future. In late 2004 the Government suspended the sale of petrol to the public following fuel rationing precipitated by the rising cost of petroleum on world markets. According to the World Bank, the GDP of the manufacturing sector declined, in real terms, at an average annual rate of 4.3% in 2001–09; manufacturing GDP decreased by 0.7% in 2008 and by 0.2% in 2009, according to the AfDB.

According to the AfDB, the construction sector provided 11.7% of GDP in 2009.

Most electric energy is provided by four thermal power stations, which are largely dependent on imported fuel. Imports of fuel and energy comprised an estimated 8.9% of the total cost of imports in 2000. However, electricity is provided to only 10% of the population, the remainder relying on fuel wood and animal products. In mid-1999 the discovery of geothermal potential at the Alid volcanic centre raised hopes that Eritrea's energy problems could be alleviated. In 2004 the World Bank approved a grant of some US $50m. to support Eritrea's Power Distribution and Rural Electrification project, with a further $17.5m. approved in 2008.

According to the AfDB, the services sector contributed 56.9% of GDP in 2009. The dominant services are trade, public administration and transport. According to the World Bank, the GDP of the services sector increased, in real terms, at an average annual rate of 0.5% in 2001–09; the GDP of the sector expanded by 3.4% in 2009.

In 2010, according to the AfDB, Eritrea recorded a trade deficit of US $5,366m., while there was a surplus of $4,876m. on the current account of the balance of payments. In 2003 the principal sources of non-petroleum imports were the USA (accounting for an estimated 15.9% of the total), the United Arab Emirates and Italy. Exports in that year were mostly to Sudan (which took 19.7% of the total, compared with 83.8% in 2002) and Italy. Eritrea's principal exports in 2003 were food and live animals (36.4% of the total), crude materials and basic manufactures. The main non-petroleum imports in that year were food and live animals (40.5% of the total), machinery and transport equipment, and basic manufactures.

In 2009 it was estimated by the AfDB that Eritrea's budget deficit reached 4,585m. nakfa. Eritrea's general government gross debt was 38,872m. nakfa in 2009, equivalent to 135.0% of GDP. Eritrea's external debt at the end of 2008 totalled US $962m., of which $957.3m. was public and publicly guaranteed debt. The annual rate of inflation averaged 18.4% in 2001–10. Consumer prices increased by an estimated average of 33.0% in 2009 and by 12.7% in 2010. In 2003 unemployment and underemployment were estimated to affect as many as 50% of the labour force.

Since independence the Eritrean Government has experienced severe difficulties and many of its initial economic aims have not been realized. Vast expenditure (estimated to total at least US $1m. per day) on the war with Ethiopia, coupled with the failure of successive harvests, increased Eritrea's already considerable reliance on donations from aid organizations, and the need to feed, clothe and shelter the vast numbers of people displaced during the war placed a further strain on government finances. An IMF review in September 2009 noted the weakened economic performance of the country, largely as a consequence of the depressed global economic climate, while commenting on progress made in investment in irrigation projects to reduce the impact of irregular rainfall. The mining sector has expanded in recent years following the discovery of large mineral deposits around Bisha and Asmara and it was hoped that the development of this sector would, in the long term, reduce the dependence upon remittances from abroad, which are estimated to amount to some $400m. per year. The gold mine at Bisha poured its first gold at the end of 2010; it was estimated that proceeds from the export of gold could provide up to 40% of government revenue in the future. Higher metal price estimates in 2011 increased the value of reserves at the Bisha mine by 40% and its extraction lifetime was extended by three years to 13 years. A five-year National Development Plan presented by President Issaias Afewerki in June 2011 focused on supporting the agricultural sector in order to increase its contribution to the country's economy. The President outlined programmes to reinforce soil and water conservation in response to food shortages, and planned to implement measures to develop new and existing infrastructure facilities. Local agricultural projects were showing signs of success in late 2010 as new water pipelines were installed in the Gash-Barka region and in February 2011 the Ministry of Agriculture announced high yields in fruit and vegetables as a consequence of the installation of drip-irrigation systems. In addition, in the Dekemhare sub-zone the Ministry of Agriculture was supplying selected seeds and pesticides to local farmers and implementing livestock vaccination programmes in order to increase production. The five-year Plan also highlighted the growing importance of tourism and the need to promote this sector as a source of revenue; bay and port facilities were to be developed in 2011 and an airport was to be built on one of the Dahlak Islands. The Plan also incorporated a project to expand telecommunications and internet services throughout the country as soon as power-supply installations could be put in place.

PUBLIC HOLIDAYS

2013: 1 January (New Year's Day), 6 January (Epiphany), 24 May (Independence Day), 20 June (Martyrs' Day), 8 August* (Id al-Fitr, end of Ramadan), 1 September (anniversary of the start of the armed struggle), 15 October* (Id al-Adha/Arafat), 25 December (Christmas).

* These holidays are dependent on the Islamic lunar calendar and may vary by one or two days from the dates given.

Statistical Survey

Source (unless otherwise stated): Ministry of Trade and Industry, POB 1844, Asmara; tel. (1) 126155; fax (1) 120586.

Area and Population

AREA, POPULATION AND DENSITY*

Area (sq km)	121,144†
Population (census results)	
9 May 1984	
Males	1,374,452
Females	1,373,852
Total	2,748,304
Population (UN estimates at mid-year)‡	
2010	5,253,676
2011	5,415,280
2012	5,580,861
Density (per sq km) at mid-2012	46.1

* Including the Assab district.
† 46,774 sq miles.
‡ Source: UN, *World Population Prospects: The 2010 Revision*.

POPULATION BY AGE AND SEX
(UN estimates at mid-2012)

	Males	Females	Total
0–14	1,171,087	1,146,230	2,317,317
15–64	1,527,585	1,594,617	3,122,202
65 and over	53,576	87,766	141,342
Total	2,752,248	2,828,613	5,580,861

Source: UN, *World Population Prospects: The 2010 Revision*.

PRINCIPAL TOWNS
(estimated population at January 2012)

Asmara (capital)	1,376,318	Keren	82,198
Assab	101,284	Mitsiwa (Massawa)	53,090

Source: Stefan Helders, *World Gazetteer* (internet www.world-gazetteer.com).

BIRTHS AND DEATHS
(averages per year, UN estimates)

	1995–2000	2000–05	2005–10
Birth rate (per 1,000)	38.1	38.4	37.5
Death rate (per 1,000)	11.1	9.5	8.3

Source: UN, *World Population Prospects: The 2010 Revision*.

Life expectancy (years at birth, WHO estimates): 66 (males 64; females 68) in 2009 (Source: WHO, *World Health Statistics*).

ECONOMICALLY ACTIVE POPULATION
('000, FAO estimates at mid-year)

	2010	2011	2012
Agriculture, etc.	1,547	1,590	1,634
Total labour force (incl. others)	2,098	2,165	2,236

Source: FAO.

Health and Welfare

KEY INDICATORS

Total fertility rate (children per woman, 2009)	4.5
Under-5 mortality rate (per 1,000 live births, 2009)	55
HIV/AIDS (% of persons aged 15–49, 2009)	0.8
Hospital beds (per 1,000 head, 2006)	1.2
Physicians (per 1,000 head, 2004)	0.05
Health expenditure (2008): US $ per head (PPP)	18
Health expenditure (2008): % of GDP	3.1
Health expenditure (2008): public (% of total)	44.9
Access to water (% of persons, 2008)	61
Access to sanitation (% of persons, 2008)	14
Total carbon dioxide emissions ('000 metric tons, 2007)	578.9
Carbon dioxide emissions per head (metric tons, 2007)	0.1
Human Development Index (2011): ranking	177
Human Development Index (2011): value	0.349

For sources and definitions, see explanatory note on p. vi.

Agriculture

PRINCIPAL CROPS
('000 metric tons)

	2008	2009	2010*
Wheat	5.4	26.1	27.3
Barley	6.4	65.1	67.0
Maize	4.1	16.7	20.5
Millet	12.2	17.2	17.0
Sorghum	68.0	59.2	66.7
Potatoes	0.2	0.1	0.1
Broad beans, horse beans, dry	1.8	0.1	0.1
Peas, dry	—	2.0	2.0
Chick-peas	—	6.6	6.5
Lentils	—	0.6	0.6
Vetches	—	2.3	2.3
Groundnuts, with shell	0.6	1.3	1.3
Sesame seed	0.5	0.2	0.1

* FAO estimates.

Aggregate production ('000 metric tons, may include official, semi-official or estimated data): Total cereals 105.8 in 2008, 226.9 in 2009, 247.4 in 2010; Total roots and tubers 76.8 in 2008, 71.6 in 2009, 37.5 in 2010; Total vegetables (incl. melons) 40.1 in 2008, 47.5 in 2009, 43.3 in 2010.

Source: FAO.

LIVESTOCK
('000 head, year ending September, FAO estimates)

	2008	2009	2010*
Cattle	2,036	2,046	2,057
Sheep	2,249	2,260	2,272
Goats*	1,730	1,740	1,750
Camels	337	339	345
Chickens	1,198	1,204	1,250

* FAO estimates.

Source: FAO.

LIVESTOCK PRODUCTS
('000 metric tons)

	2008	2009	2010*
Cattle meat	17.2	23.0	22.0
Sheep meat	3.8†	4.0	4.1
Goat meat*	5.8	5.8	5.9
Chicken meat*	1.6	1.6	1.6
Camels' milk*	5.3	5.3	5.4
Cows' milk*	103.0	103.6	131.2
Goats' milk*	8.7	8.7	9.1
Sheep's milk*	5.3	5.4	5.5
Hen eggs*	1.9	1.7	1.9
Wool, greasy*	0.6	0.6	0.9

* FAO estimates.
† Unofficial figure.

Source: FAO.

Fishing

(metric tons, live weight of capture)

	2007	2008	2009
Requiem sharks	117	115	165
Sea catfishes	15	15	42
Threadfin breams	2	n.a.	62
Snappers and jobfishes	23	37	75
Narrow-barred Spanish mackerel	399	496	573
Tuna-like fishes	529	589	640
Barracudas	94	58	78
Carangids	67	46	79
Queenfishes	177	53	185
Penaeus shrimps	112	38	219
Total catch (incl. others)	1,932	1,665	3,030

Source: FAO.

Mining

('000 metric tons, unless otherwise indicated, estimates)

	2008	2009	2010
Gold (kilograms)	30.0	30.0	35.0
Marble ('000 sq m)	35.0	32.0	36.0
Limestone	3.0	3.0	3.0
Salt	7.5	7.5	7.8
Granite	25.0	25.0	25.0

Source: US Geological Survey.

Industry

SELECTED PRODUCTS
('000 metric tons, unless otherwise indicated, estimates)

	2008	2009	2010
Cement	45.0	45.0	45.0
Basalt	50.0	45.0	50.0
Gravel	80.0	78.0	80.0
Coral	65.0	60.0	58.0

Electric energy (million kWh): 287 in 2008.

Sources: US Geological Survey; UN Industrial Commodity Statistics Database.

Finance

CURRENCY AND EXCHANGE RATES

Monetary Units
100 cents = 1 nakfa.

Sterling, Dollar and Euro Equivalents (30 December 2011)
£1 sterling = 23.771 nakfa;
US $1 = 15.375 nakfa;
€1 = 19.894 nakfa;
1,000 nakfa = £42.07 = $65.04 = €50.27.

Note: Following its secession from Ethiopia in May 1993, Eritrea retained the Ethiopian currency, the birr. An exchange rate of US $1 = 5.000 birr was introduced in October 1992 and remained in force until April 1994, when it was adjusted to $1 = 5.130 birr. Further adjustments were made subsequently. In November 1997 the Government introduced a separate national currency, the nakfa, replacing (and initially at par with) the Ethiopian birr. The exchange rate in relation to the US dollar was initially set at the prevailing unified rate, but from 1 May 1998 a mechanism to provide a market-related exchange rate was established.

Average Exchange Rate (nakfa per US $)
2009 15.3750
2010 15.3750
2011 15.3750

BUDGET
(million nakfa)

Revenue*	2007	2008†	2009‡
Tax revenue	2,405	2,459	2,374
Direct taxes	1,512	1,719	1,580
Indirect domestic taxes	487	395	435
Import duties and taxes	406	345	360
Non-tax revenue	1,888	1,393	1,401
Total	4,293	3,853	3,775

Expenditure§	2007	2008†	2009‡
Current expenditure	5,900	6,905	6,824
Wages, salaries and allowances	2,234	2,275	2,430
Materials and services	2,316	2,531	2,398
Subsidies and transfers	706	1,311	931
Interest	644	788	1,065
Domestic	571	648	853
External	73	140	212
Capital expenditure	2,224	2,331	2,134
Central treasury	1,012	704	681
Externally financed	1,203	1,627	1,453
Total	8,124	9,236	8,958

* Excluding grants received (million nakfa): 628 in 2007; 604 in 2008 (estimate); 737 in 2009 (projected).
† Estimates.
‡ Projections.
§ Excluding net lending (million nakfa): –95 in 2007; 608 in 2008 (estimate); 139 in 2009 (projected).

Source: African Development Bank, *Interim Country Strategy Paper for Eritrea* (2009–11).

INTERNATIONAL RESERVES
(US $ million at 31 December)

	1999	2000	2001
Gold (national valuation)	19.7	10.4	10.5
Reserve position in IMF	0.0	0.0	0.0
Foreign exchange	34.2	25.5	39.7
Total	53.9	35.9	50.3

Foreign exchange: 25.3 in 2006; 34.3 in 2007; 57.9 in 2008.

IMF special drawing rights: 5.7 in 2009, 5.6 in 2010.

Source: IMF, *International Financial Statistics*.

MONEY SUPPLY
(million nakfa at 31 December)

	2008	2009	2010
Currency outside depository corporations	5,153	6,637	8,155
Transferable deposits	10,166	10,655	11,554
Other deposits	14,656	17,397	20,388
Broad money	29,976	34,689	40,097

Source: IMF, *International Financial Statistics*.

COST OF LIVING
(Consumer Price Index; base: 2000 = 100)

	2008	2009	2010
All items	349.0	464.1	523.0

Source: African Development Bank.

NATIONAL ACCOUNTS
(million nakfa at current prices)

Expenditure on the Gross Domestic Product

	2007	2008	2009
Private final consumption expenditure	17,165	17,534	25,023
Government final consumption expenditure	5,195	5,594	5,760
Gross capital formation	2,568	2,698	2,628
Total domestic expenditure	24,928	25,826	33,411
Exports of goods and services	1,170	940	1,293
Less Imports of goods and services	5,834	5,545	5,902
GDP in purchasers' values	20,264	21,220	28,801

Gross Domestic Product by Economic Activity

	2007	2008	2009
Agriculture, forestry and fishing	4,716	4,790	6,634
Mining and quarrying	269	267	360
Manufacturing	1,062	1,224	1,600
Construction	2,400	2,382	3,207
Wholesale and retail trade	3,553	3,705	5,041
Transport and communications	2,275	2,373	3,229
Other services	5,133	5,353	7,290
Sub-total	19,408	20,095	27,362
Indirect taxes (net)	856	1,126	1,439
GDP in purchasers' values	20,264	21,220	28,801

Source: African Development Bank.

BALANCE OF PAYMENTS
(US $ million)

	2000	2001*	2002†
Exports of goods f.o.b.	36.7	19.9	51.8
Imports of goods c.i.f.	–470.3	–536.7	–533.4
Trade balance	–433.5	–516.7	–481.7
Exports of services	60.7	127.5	132.6
Imports of services	–28.3	–33.4	–30.3
Balance on goods and services	–401.1	–422.6	–379.4
Other income (net)	–1.4	–4.6	–6.1
Balance on goods, services and income	–402.5	–427.2	–385.5
Private unrequited transfers (net)	195.7	175.0	205.6
Official unrequited transfers (net)	102.4	120.8	80.3
Current balance	–104.5	–131.4	–99.6
Capital account (net)	—	7.3	3.6
Financial account	98.7	94.8	64.6
Short-term capital (net)	–14.7	18.7	15.9
Net errors and omissions	–9.5	36.5	–7.6
Overall balance	–15.2	7.2	–39.0

* Preliminary figures.
† Estimates.

Source: IMF, *Eritrea: Selected Issues and Statistical Appendix* (June 2003).

2007 (Nakfa million): Trade balance –4,902; Services (net) 238; Income (net) –111; Current transfers (net) 3,537; *Current account* –1,238 (Source: African Development Bank).

2008 (Nakfa million): Trade balance –4,671; Services (net) 65; Income (net) –181; Current transfers (net) 3,626; *Current account* –1,160 (Source: African Development Bank).

2009 (Nakfa million): Trade balance –4,899; Services (net) 294; Income (net) –266; Current transfers (net) 3,423; *Current account* –1,449 (Source: African Development Bank).

2010 (Nakfa million): Trade balance –5,366; Services (net) 321; Income (net) –306; Current transfers (net) 4,876; *Current account* –474 (Source: African Development Bank).

External Trade

PRINCIPAL COMMODITIES
(distribution by SITC, US $ '000)

Imports c.i.f. (excl. petroleum)	2001	2002	2003
Food and live animals	110.9	153.0	175.2
Animal and vegetable oils, fats and waxes	13.6	7.4	19.3
Chemicals and related products	45.5	36.4	26.2
Basic manufactures	101.5	115.6	63.3
Machinery and transport equipment	107.4	155.9	97.2
Miscellaneous manufactured articles	34.0	46.9	40.7
Total (incl. others)	422.9	537.9	432.8

Exports f.o.b.	2001	2002	2003
Food and live animals	8.8	37.7	2.4
Crude materials (inedible) except fuels	3.0	6.0	2.1
Chemicals and related products	0.7	0.6	0.1
Basic manufactures	5.6	4.8	1.1
Miscellaneous manufactured articles	0.5	1.5	0.7
Total (incl. others)	19.0	51.8	6.6

Source: UN, *International Trade Statistics Yearbook*.

PRINCIPAL TRADING PARTNERS
(US $ million)

Imports c.i.f.	2001	2002	2003
Belgium	11.9	13.7	8.6
Germany	11.8	16.4	6.7
Italy	79.0	70.4	50.1
Netherlands	13.9	17.4	10.4
Saudi Arabia	70.0	70.0	45.4
United Arab Emirates	64.6	90.7	52.9
United Kingdom	9.6	10.0	11.7
USA	20.4	38.5	68.9
Total (incl. others)	422.9	537.9	432.8

Exports f.o.b.	2001	2002	2003
Djibouti	—	0.8	—
Germany	0.7	0.5	0.1
India	3.2	0.5	0.5
Italy	2.1	1.8	0.8
Netherlands	0.4	0.3	0.7
Saudi Arabia	0.3	0.1	—
Sudan	9.7	43.4	1.3
Total (incl. others)	19.0	51.8	6.6

Source: UN, *International Trade Statistics Yearbook*.

Transport

ROAD TRAFFIC
(motor vehicles in use)

	1996	1997	1998
Number of registered vehicles	27,013	31,276	35,942

2007 (vehicles registered at 31 December): Passenger cars 31,033; Buses and coaches 1,825; Vans and lorries 22,514; Motorcycles and mopeds 3,042 (Source: IRF, *World Road Statistics*).

SHIPPING

Merchant Fleet
(registered at 31 December)

	2007	2008	2009
Number of vessels	14	13	13
Displacement (grt)	14,478	13,075	13,075

Source: IHS Fairplay, *World Fleet Statistics*.

CIVIL AVIATION

	1996	1997	1998
Passengers ('000)	168.1	173.8	105.2

Tourism

ARRIVALS BY COUNTRY OF ORIGIN

	2007	2008	2009
Germany	825	742	775
India	2,973	395	718
Italy	2,023	2,108	1,944
Japan	743	773	151
Kenya	610	312	234
Sudan	2,413	3,570	5,866
United Kingdom	731	680	843
USA	506	499	511
Total (incl. others)	80,503	69,897	79,334

Tourism receipts (US $ million, incl. passenger transport): 61 in 2007; 46 in 2008; 26 in 2009.

Source: World Tourism Organization.

Communications Media

	2008	2009	2010
Telephones ('000 main lines in use)	40.4	48.5	54.2
Mobile cellular telephones ('000 subscribers)	108.6	141.1	185.3
Internet subscribers ('000)	6.5	7.0	7.1
Broadband subscribers	n.a.	100	100

Personal computers: 50,000 (10.1 per 1,000 persons) in 2008.

Television receivers ('000 in use): 100 in 2000.

Book production (1993): 106 titles (including 23 pamphlets) and 420,000 copies (including 60,000 pamphlets). Figures for books, excluding pamphlets, refer only to school textbooks (64 titles; 323,000 copies) and government publications (19 titles; 37,000 copies).

Sources: mainly UNESCO, *Statistical Yearbook*; International Telecommunication Union.

Education

(2009/10 unless otherwise indicated)

	Institutions*	Teachers	Pupils
Pre-primary	95	1,143	40,506
Primary	695	7,535	286,021
Secondary: General	44	6,152	246,778
Secondary: Teacher-training	2	47*	922*
Secondary: Vocational	n.a.	261	1,304
University and equivalent level	n.a.	634	10,198

* 2001/02 figure(s).

Sources: UNESCO Institute for Statistics; Ministry of Education, Asmara.

Pupil-teacher ratio (primary education, UNESCO estimate): 38.0 in 2009/10 (Source: UNESCO Institute for Statistics).

Adult literacy rate (UNESCO estimates): 66.6% (males 77.9%; females 56.0%) in 2009 (Source: UNESCO Institute for Statistics).

Directory

The Government

HEAD OF STATE

President: ISSAIAS AFEWERKI (assumed power May 1991; elected President by the National Assembly 8 June 1993).

CABINET
(May 2012)

The Government is formed by the People's Front for Democracy and Justice.

President: ISSAIAS AFEWERKI.

Minister of Defence: Gen. SEBHAT EPHREM.

Minister of Justice: FAWZIA HASHIM.

Minister of Foreign Affairs: OSMAN SALIH MUHAMMAD.

Minister of Information: ALI ABDU.

Minister of Finance: BERHANE ABREHE.

Minister of Trade and Industry: Dr GIORGIS TEKLEMIKAEL.

Minister of Agriculture: AREFAINE BERHE.

Minister of Labour and Human Welfare: ASKALU MENKERIOS.

Minister of Fisheries: AHMED HAJI ALI.

Minister of Construction: ABRAHA ASFAHA.

Minister of Energy and Mines: TESFAI GEBRESELASSIE.

Minister of Education: SEMERE RUSOM.

Minister of Health: Dr SALIH MEKKI.

Minister of Transport and Communications: WOLDEMIKAEL ABRAHA.

Minister of Tourism: AMNA NUR HUSSEIN.

Minister of Land, Water and the Environment: WOLDEMICHAEL GEBREMARIAM.

Minister of Local Government: NAIZGHI KIFLU.

MINISTRIES

Office of the President: POB 257, Asmara; tel. (1) 122132; fax (1) 125123.

Ministry of Agriculture: POB 1048, Asmara; tel. (1) 181499; fax (1) 181415.

Ministry of Construction: POB 841, Asmara; tel. (1) 114588; fax (1) 120661.

Ministry of Defence: POB 629, Asmara; tel. (1) 165952; fax (1) 124990.

Ministry of Education: POB 5610, Asmara; tel. (1) 113044; fax (1) 113866; internet www.erimoe.gov.er.

Ministry of Energy and Mines: POB 5285, Asmara; tel. (1) 116872; fax (1) 127652.

Ministry of Finance: POB 896, Asmara; tel. (1) 118131; fax (1) 127947.

Ministry of Fisheries: POB 923, Asmara; tel. (1) 120400; fax (1) 122185; e-mail mofisha@eol.com.er; f. 1994.

Ministry of Foreign Affairs: POB 190, Asmara; tel. (1) 127838; fax (1) 123788; e-mail tesfai@wg.eol.

Ministry of Health: POB 212, Asmara; tel. (1) 117549; fax (1) 112899.

Ministry of Information: POB 872, Asmara; tel. (1) 120478; fax (1) 126747; internet www.shabait.com.

Ministry of Justice: POB 241, Asmara; tel. (1) 127739; fax (1) 126422.

Ministry of Labour and Human Welfare: POB 5252, Asmara; tel. (1) 181846; fax (1) 181760; e-mail mlhw@eol.com.er.

Ministry of Land, Water and the Environment: POB 976, Asmara; tel. (1) 118021; fax (1) 123285.

Ministry of Local Government: POB 225, Asmara; tel. (1) 114254; fax (1) 120014.

Ministry of Tourism: POB 1010, Warsay Ave, Dembe Sembel (Green Building), Asmara; tel. (1) 154100; fax (1) 154081; e-mail eritreantourism@tse.com.er.

Ministry of Trade and Industry: POB 1844, Asmara; tel. (1) 126155; fax (1) 120586; e-mail berhanem69@yahoo.co.uk.

Ministry of Transport and Communications: POB 1840, Asmara; tel. (1) 114222; fax (1) 127048; e-mail motc.rez@eol.com.er.

Provincial Administrators

There are six administrative regions in Eritrea, each with regional, sub-regional and village administrations.

Anseba Province: SALMA HASSAN.

Debub Province: MUSTAFA NUR HUSSEIN.

Debubawi Keyih Bahri Province: OSMAN MOHAMED OMAR.

Gash-Barka Province: MUSA RAB'A.

Maakel Province: KAHSAI GEBREHIWET.

Semenawi Keyih Bahri Province: TSIGEREDA WOLDEGERGISH.

Legislature

NATIONAL ASSEMBLY

In accordance with transitional arrangements formulated in Decree No. 37 of May 1993, the National Assembly consists of the Central Committee of the People's Front for Democracy and Justice (PFDJ) and 60 other members: 30 from the Provincial Assemblies and an additional 30 members, including a minimum of 10 women, to be nominated by the PFDJ Central Committee. The legislative body 'outlines the internal and external policies of the government, regulates their implementation, approves the budget and elects a president for the country'. The National Assembly is to hold regular sessions every six months under the chairmanship of the President. In his role as Head of the Government and Commander-in-Chief of the Army, the President nominates individuals to head the various government departments. These nominations are ratified by the legislative body. In March 1994 the National Assembly voted to alter its composition: it would henceforth comprise the 75 members of the Central Committee of the PFDJ and 75 directly elected members. In May 1997, following the adoption of the Constitution, the Constituent Assembly empowered a Transitional National Assembly (comprising the 75 members of the PFDJ, 60 members of the former Constituent Assembly and 15 representatives of Eritreans residing abroad) to act as the legislature until elections were held for a new National Assembly.

Chairman of the Transitional National Assembly: ISSAIAS AFEWERKI.

Election Commission

Electoral Commission: Asmara; f. 2002; five mems appointed by the President; Commissioner RAMADAN MOHAMMED NUR.

Political Organizations

Afar Federal Alliance: e-mail afa_f@hotmail.com; f. 2003.

Democratic Movement for the Liberation of Eritrean Kunama: Postfach 620 124, 50694, Köln, Germany; e-mail kcs@baden-kunama.com; internet www.baden-kunama.com; based in Germany; represents the Kunama minority ethnic group.

Eritrean Democratic Alliance (EDA): internet www.erit-alliance.com; f. 1999 as the Alliance of Eritrean National Forces, became Eritrean National Alliance in 2002, adopted present name in 2004; broad alliance of 13 parties opposed to PFDJ regime; Chair. BERHANE YEMANE 'HANJEMA'; Sec.-Gen. HUSAYN KHALIFA.

Eritrean Democratic Party (EDP): e-mail info@selfi-democracy.com; internet www.selfi-democracy.com; f. 2001 as the Eritrean People's Liberation Front—Democratic Party (EPLF—DP); breakaway group from the PFDJ; name changed to above in 2004; Chair. MESFIN HAGOS.

Eritrean Islamic Jihad (EIJ): radical opposition group; in Aug. 1993 split into a military wing and a political wing.

Eritrean Islamic Party for Justice and Development (EIPJD) (Al-Hizb Al-Islami Al-Eritree Liladalah Wetenmiya): internet www.alkhalas.org; f. 1988 as Eritrean Islamic Jihad Movement; changed name to al-Khalas in 1998; political wing of EIJ; Leader KHALIL MUHAMMAD AMER.

Eritrean Liberation Front (ELF): f. 1958; commenced armed struggle against Ethiopia in 1961; subsequently split into numerous factions (see below); mainly Muslim support; opposes the PFDJ; principal factions:

Eritrean Liberation Front—Central Command (ELF—CC): f. 1982; Chair. ABDALLAH IDRISS.

Eritrean Liberation Front—National Council (ELF—NC): Leader Dr BEYENE KIDANE.

Eritrean Liberation Front—Revolutionary Council (ELF—RC): Chair. AHMED WOLDEYESUS AMMAR.

Eritrean People's Democratic Front (EPDF): e-mail main-office@sagem-eritra.org; internet www.democrasia.org; f. 2004 by merger of People's Democratic Front for the Liberation of Eritrea and a faction of ERDF; Leader TEWOLDE GEBRESELASSIE.

Eritrean Popular Movement (EPM): f. 2004; Leader ABDALLAH ADEM.

Eritrean Revolutionary Democratic Front (ERDF): e-mail webmaster@eritreana.com; internet www.eritreana.com; f. 1997 following merger of Democratic Movement for the Liberation of Eritrea and a faction of People's Democratic Front for the Liberation of Eritrea; Leader BERHANE YEMANE 'HANJEMA'.

Gash Setit Organization: Leader ISMAIL NADA.

People's Front for Democracy and Justice (PFDJ): POB 1081, Asmara; tel. (1) 121399; fax (1) 120848; e-mail webmaster@shaebia.org; internet www.shaebia.org; f. 1970 as the Eritrean Popular Liberation Forces, following a split in the Eritrean Liberation Front; renamed the Eritrean People's Liberation Front in 1977; adopted present name in Feb. 1994; Christian and Muslim support; in May 1991 took control of Eritrea and formed provisional Govt; formed transitional Govt in May 1993; Chair. ISSAIAS AFEWERKI; Sec.-Gen. ALAMIN MOHAMED SAID.

Red Sea Afar Democratic Organization: Afar opposition group; Sec.-Gen. IBRAHIM HAROUN.

Diplomatic Representation

EMBASSIES IN ERITREA

China, People's Republic: 16 Ogaden St, POB 204, Asmara; tel. and fax (1) 185271; fax (1) 185275; e-mail chemb@eol.com.er; Ambassador LI LIANSHENG.

Djibouti: POB 5589, Asmara; tel. (1) 354961; fax (1) 351831; Ambassador AHMAD ISSA (recalled in June 2008).

Egypt: 5 Dej Afworki St, POB 5570, Asmara; tel. and fax (1) 123294; Ambassador EIHAB EMAM HAMOUDA.

France: POB 209, Asmara; tel. (1) 125196; fax (1) 123288; e-mail cad.asmara@diplomatie.gouv.fr; internet ambafrance-er.org; Ambassador ROGER AUQUE.

Germany: SABA Building, 8th Floor, Warsay St, POB 4974, Asmara; tel. (1) 186670; fax (1) 186900; e-mail info@asmara.diplo.de; internet www.asmara.diplo.de; Ambassador KLAUS PETER SCHICK.

Iran: Asmara; Ambassador REZA AMERI.

Israel: 32 Abo St, POB 5600, Asmara; tel. (1) 188521; fax (1) 188550; e-mail info@asmara.mfa.gov.il; Ambassador ODED BEN-HAIM.

Italy: POB 220, 11 171–1 St, Asmara; tel. (1) 120160; fax (1) 121115; e-mail ambasciata.asmara@esteri.it; internet www.ambasmara.esteri.it; Ambassador GAETANO MARTINEZ TAGLIAVIA.

Libya: Asmara.

Norway: 11 173–1 St, POB 5801, Asmara; tel. (1) 122138; fax (1) 122180; e-mail emb.asmara@mfa.no; internet www.norway.gov.er; Ambassador KARI BJØRNSGAARD.

Russia: 21 Zobel St, POB 5667, Asmara; tel. (1) 127162; fax (1) 127164; e-mail rusemb@eol.com.er; Ambassador IGOR NIKOLAVIC.

Saudi Arabia: POB 5599, Asmara; tel. (1) 120171; fax (1) 121027; Ambassador NASSER ALI AL-HOTI.

South Africa: 51–53 Hitseito St 245, Tiravalo, POB 11447, Asmara; tel. (1) 152521; fax (1) 152538; e-mail saemb_asma@yahoo.com; Ambassador MAHOMED IQBAL DAWOOD.

Sudan: Asmara; tel. (1) 202072; fax (1) 200760; e-mail sudanemb@eol.com.er; Ambassador SALAH MOHAMED AL-HASSAN.

United Kingdom: 66–68 Mariam Ghimbi St, POB 5584, Asmara; tel. (1) 120145; fax (1) 120104; e-mail asmara.enquiries@fco.gov.uk; internet www.ukineritrea.fco.gov.uk; Ambassador AMANDA SUSANNAH TANFIELD.

USA: POB 211, 179 Ala St, Asmara; tel. (1) 120004; fax (1) 127584; e-mail usembassyasmara@state.gov; internet eritrea.usembassy.gov; Chargé d'affaires a.i. JOEL REIFMAN.

Yemen: POB 5566, Asmara; tel. (1) 114434; fax (1) 117921; Ambassador Dr ABDELKADIR MOHAMMED HADI.

Judicial System

The judicial system operates on the basis of transitional laws, which incorporate pre-independence laws of the Eritrean People's Liberation Front, revised Ethiopian laws, customary laws and post-independence enacted laws. The independence of the judiciary in the discharge of its functions is unequivocally stated in Decree No. 37, which defines the powers and duties of the Government. It is subject only to the law and to no other authority. The court structure is composed of first instance sub-zonal courts, appellate and first instance zonal courts, appellate and first instance high courts, a panel of high court judges, presided over by the President of the High Court, and a Supreme Court presided over by the Chief Justice, as a court of last resort. The judges of the Supreme Court are appointed by the President of the State, subject to confirmation by the National Assembly.

Supreme Court: Asmara.

High Court: POB 241, Asmara; tel. (1) 127739; fax (1) 201828; e-mail prshict@eol.com.er.

Religion

Eritrea is almost equally divided between Muslims and Christians. Most Christians are adherents of the Orthodox Church, although there are Protestant and Roman Catholic communities. A small number of the population follow traditional beliefs.

CHRISTIANITY

The Eritrean Orthodox Church

In September 1993 the separation of the Eritrean Orthodox Church from the Ethiopian Orthodox Church was agreed by the respective church leaderships. The Eritrean Orthodox Church announced that it was to create a diocese of each of the country's then 10 provinces. The first five bishops of the Eritrean Orthodox Church were consecrated in Cairo, Egypt, in September 1994. In May 1998 Eritrea's first Patriarch (Abune) was consecrated in Alexandria, Egypt. In January 2006 Eritrea's third Patriarch, Abune Antonios I (who had been under house arrest since August 2005), was deposed by the Holy Synod.

Patriarch (Abune): DIOSKOROS.

The Roman Catholic Church

An estimated 3% of the total population are Roman Catholics.

Bishop of Asmara: Rt Rev. ABBA MENGHISTEAB TESFAMARIAM, 19 Gonder St, POB 244, Asmara; tel. (1) 120206; fax (1) 126519; e-mail kimehret@gemel.com.er.

Bishop of Barentu: Rt Rev. THOMAS OSMAN, POB 9, Barentu; tel. and fax (1) 127283.

Bishop of Keren: Rt Rev. KIDANE YEBIO, POB 460, Keren; tel. (1) 401907; fax (1) 401604; e-mail cek@tse.com.er.

The Anglican Communion

Within the Episcopal Church in Jerusalem and the Middle East, Eritrea lies within the jurisdiction of the Bishop in Egypt.

Leader: ASFAHA MAHARY.

ISLAM

Eritrea's main Muslim communities are concentrated in the western lowlands, the northern highlands and the eastern coastal region.

Leader: Sheikh AL-AMIN OSMAN AL-AMIN.

The Press

There is no independent press in Eritrea.

Business Perspective: POB 856, Asmara; tel. (1) 121589; fax (1) 120138; monthly; Tigrinya, Arabic and English; publ. by Eritrean National Chamber of Commerce; Editor MOHAMMED-SFAF HAMMED.

Chamber News: POB 856, Asmara; tel. (1) 120045; fax (1) 120138; monthly; Tigrinya, Arabic and English; publ. by Asmara Chamber of Commerce.

Eritrea Profile: POB 247, Asmara; tel. (1) 114114; fax (1) 127749; e-mail eritreaprofile@yahoo.com; internet www.shabait.com; f. 1994; twice-weekly; English; publ. by the Ministry of Information; Man. Dir AZZAZI ZEREMARIAM; Editor-in-Chief YITSHAK YARED.

Hadas Eritra (New Eritrea): Asmara; f. 1991; six times a week; English, Tigrinya and Arabic; govt publ; Editor SAMSOM HAILE; circ. 49,200.

Newsletter: POB 856, Asmara; tel. (1) 121589; fax (1) 120138; e-mail encc@aol.com.er; monthly; Tigrinya, Arabic and English; publ. by

Eritrean National Chamber of Commerce; Editor MOHAMMED-SFAF HAMMED.

Broadcasting and Communications

Ministry of Transport and Communications (Communications Department): POB 4918, Asmara; tel. (1) 115847; fax (1) 126966; e-mail motc.rez@eol.com.er; Dir-Gen. MEKONNEN FISSEHAZION.

TELECOMMUNICATIONS

Eritrea Telecommunication Services Corpn (EriTel): 11 Semaetat St, POB 234, Asmara; tel. (1) 124655; fax (1) 120938; e-mail eritel@tse.com.er; internet www.tse.com.er; f. 1991; public enterprise; operates fixed-line and mobile cellular networks and internet services; Gen. Man. TESFASELASSIE BERHANE.

TFanus: 46 Daniel Comboni Street, POB 724, Asmara; tel. (1) 202590; fax (1) 126457; e-mail support@tfanus.com.er; internet www.tfanus.com.er; f. 1996; internet service provider.

BROADCASTING

Radio

Voice of the Broad Masses of Eritrea (Dimtsi Hafash): POB 242, Asmara; tel. (1) 120426; fax (1) 126747; govt-controlled; programmes in Arabic, Tigrinya, Tigre, Saho, Oromo, Amharic, Afar, Bilien, Nara, Hedareb and Kunama; Dir-Gen. GHIRMAY BERHE; Technical Dir BERHANE GEREZGIHER.

Voice of Liberty: Asmara; e-mail VoL@selfi-democracy.com; internet selfi-democracy.com; radio programme of the EDP; broadcasts for one hour twice a week.

Television

ERI-TV: Asmara; tel. (1) 116033; e-mail aslmelashe@yahoo.com; f. 1992; govt station providing educational, tech. and information service; broadcasting began in 1993; programming in Arabic, English, Tigre and Tigrinya; broadcasts for eight hours daily; Dir-Gen. ASMELASH ABRAHA.

Finance

(cap. = capital; res = reserves; dep. = deposits; m. = million; brs = branches; amounts in nakfa)

In November 1997 Eritrea adopted the nakfa as its unit of currency, replacing the Ethiopian birr, which had been Eritrea's monetary unit since independence.

BANKING

Central Bank

Bank of Eritrea: 21 Nakfa St 175, POB 849, Asmara; tel. (1) 123033; fax (1) 122091; e-mail kibreabw@boe.gov.er; f. 1993; bank of issue; Gov. KIBREAB W. MARIAM (acting).

Other Banks

Commercial Bank of Eritrea: 208 Liberty Ave, POB 219, Asmara; tel. (1) 121844; fax (1) 124887; e-mail gm.cber@gemel.com.er; f. 1991; cap. 400.0m., res 344.5m., dep. 13,791.6m. (Dec. 2004); Chair. BERHANE ABREHE; Gen. Man. YEMANE TESFAY; 15 brs.

Eritrean Development and Investment Bank: 29 Bedho St, POB 1266, Asmara; tel. (1) 126777; fax (1) 201976; e-mail edib@gemel.com .er; f. 1996; cap. 45m., total assets 194.2m. (Dec. 2003); provides medium- to long-term credit; Chair. HABTEAB TESFATSION; Gen. Man. Dr GOITOM W. MARIAM; 4 brs.

Housing and Commerce Bank of Eritrea: POB 235, Bahti Meskerem Sq., Asmara; tel. (1) 120350; fax (1) 202209; e-mail hcbgm@hcbe.com.er; internet erhcb.com; f. 1994; cap. 293m. (Dec. 2006); finances residential and commercial construction projects and commercial loans; Chair. HAGOS GHEBREHIWET; Gen. Man. BERHANE GHEBREHIWET; 10 brs.

INSURANCE

National Insurance Corporation of Eritrea Share Co (NICE): NICE Bldg, 171 Bidho Ave, POB 881, Asmara; tel. (1) 123000; fax (1) 123240; e-mail nice@nice-eritrea.com; internet www.nice-eritrea .com; f. 1992; partially privatized in 2004; 60% govt-owned; general and life; Gen. Man. ZERU WOLDEMICHAEL.

Trade and Industry

DEVELOPMENT ORGANIZATION

Eritrea Free Zones Authority: Asmara; f. 2001; CEO ARAIA TSEGGAI.

CHAMBER OF COMMERCE

Eritrean National Chamber of Commerce: POB 856, Asmara; tel. (1) 121589; fax (1) 120138; e-mail encc@gemel.com.er.

TRADE ASSOCIATION

Red Sea Trading Corporation: 29/31 Ras Alula St, POB 332, Asmara; tel. (1) 127846; fax (1) 124353; f. 1983; import and export services; operated by the PFDJ; Gen. Man. NEGASH AFWORKI.

UTILITIES

Electricity

Eritrean Electricity Corporation (EEC): POB 911, Asmara; fax (1) 121468; e-mail eeahrg@eol.com.er; Gen. Man. ABRAHAM WOLDEMICHAEL.

Water

Dept of Water Resources: POB 1488, Asmara; tel. (1) 119636; fax (1) 124625; e-mail wrdmlwe@eol.com.er; f. 1992; Dir-Gen. MEBRAHTU EYASSU.

Transport

Eritrea's transport infrastructure was severely damaged during the three decades of war prior to independence. International creditors have since provided loans for the repair and reconstruction of the road network and for the improvement of port facilities.

RAILWAYS

The 306-km railway connection between Agordat, Asmara and the port of Massawa was severely damaged during the war of independence and ceased operation in 1975. However, in 1999 an 81-km section of the Asmara–Massawa line (between Massawa and Embatkala) became operational, and in 2001 a further 18-km section, connecting Embatkala and Ghinda, was added. In February 2003 the reconstruction of the entire Asmara–Massawa line was completed. In 2007 work started on the reconstruction of the 124-km railway line west of Asmara to Akordat and Bisha, with the aim of eventually constructing a new international link from Bisha to Kassala, Sudan.

Eritrean Railway: POB 6081, Asmara; tel. (1) 123365; fax (1) 201785; Co-ordinator, Railways Rehabilitation Project AMANUEL GEBRESELLASIE.

ROADS

Eritrea has a long road network for its land base, totalling 18,540 km. Roads that are paved require considerable repair, as do many of the bridges across seasonal water courses destroyed in the war. The programme to rehabilitate the road between Asmara and the port of Massawa was completed in 2000.

SHIPPING

Eritrea has two major seaports: Massawa, which sustained heavy war damage in 1990, and Assab, which has principally served Addis Ababa, in Ethiopia. Under an accord signed between the Ethiopian and Eritrean Governments in 1993, the two countries agreed to share the facilities of both ports. Since independence, activity in Massawa has increased substantially; however, activity at Assab declined following the outbreak of hostilities with Ethiopia in May 1998. In 1998 a total of 463 vessels docked at Massawa, handling 1.2m. metric tons of goods; 322 vessels docked at Assab, which handled 1.0m. tons of goods. At 31 December 2009 Eritrea's registered merchant fleet numbered 13 vessels, with a total displacement of 13,075 grt.

Dept of Maritime Transport: POB 679, Asmara; tel. (1) 189156; fax (1) 186541; e-mail maritime@motc-gov.er; Dir-Gen. GHEBREMEDHIN HABTE KIDANE.

Port and Maritime Transport Authority: POB 851, Asmara; tel. (1) 111399; fax (1) 113647; Dir WELDE MIKAEL ABRAHAM.

BC Marine Services: 189 Warsay St, POB 5638, Asmara; tel. (1) 202672; fax (1) 12747; e-mail info@bc-marine.com; internet www .bc-marine.com; f. 2000; services include marine consultancy, marine survey and ship management; brs in Assab and Massawa; Dir Capt. NAOD GEBREAMLAK HAILE.

Cargo Inspection Survey Services: St No. 171-5-171, POB 906, Asmara; tel. (1) 120369; fax (1) 121767; e-mail gellatly@eol.com.er.

Eritrean Shipping Lines: 80 Semaetat Ave, POB 1110, Asmara; tel. (1) 120359; fax (1) 120331; e-mail ersl@eol.com.er; f. 1992; provides shipping services in Red Sea and Persian (Arabian) Gulf areas and owns and operates four cargo ships; Gen. Man. TOWELDE KELATI.

Maritime Shipping Services Corpn (MASSCO): POB 99, Massawa; tel. (1) 552729; fax (1) 552438; e-mail mascgm@eol.com.er; f. 1991 as Maritime Ship Services Enterprise; est. as a corpn 2006; shipping agents, stevedoring and shorehandling; Gen. Man. SIMON GHEBREGZIABHIER.

CIVIL AVIATION

There are three international airports: at Asmara, Assab and Massawa. There are also eight domestic airports.

Civil Aviation Department: POB 252, Asmara; tel. (1) 124335; fax (1) 124334; e-mail motc.rez@eol.com.er; handles freight and passenger traffic for eight scheduled carriers which use Asmara airport; Dir-Gen. PAULOS KAHSAY.

Eri-Air: Asmara; f. 2001; weekly charter flights to Italy; Man. Dirs TEWOLDE TESFAMARIAM, HAILEMARIAM GEBRECHRISTOS.

Eritrean Airlines: 89 Harnet Ave, POB 222, Asmara; tel. (1) 125500; fax (1) 125465; e-mail customer-rel@eritreanairlines.com.er; internet www.flyeritrea.com; CEO KUBROM DAFLA.

Nasair Eritrea: POB 11915, Asmara; tel. (1) 200700; fax (1) 117622; internet www.nasaireritrea.com; CEO NASR ELDIN IBRAHIM.

Tourism

The Ministry of Tourism is overseeing the development of this sector, although its advance since independence has been inhibited by the country's war-damaged transport infrastructure, and by subsequent conflicts with Ethiopia and other regional tensions. Eritrea possesses many areas of scenic and scientific interest, including the Dahlak Islands (a coralline archipelago rich in marine life), off shore from Massawa, and the massive escarpment rising up from the coastal plain and supporting a unique ecosystem. In 2009 79,334 tourists visited Eritrea. Tourist receipts in that year amounted to US $26m. Since May 2006 it has been necessary for foreign nationals to obtain a permit 10 days in advance in order to travel outside of the capital.

Eritrean Tourism Service Corpn: Asmara; operates govt-owned hotels.

Defence

As assessed at November 2011, Eritrea's active armed forces included an army of about 200,000, a navy of 1,400 and an air force of some 350; reserve forces numbered 120,000. National service is compulsory for all Eritreans between 18 and 40 years of age (with certain exceptions), for a 16-month period, including four months of military training. In September 2000 the UN Security Council approved the establishment of the UN Mission in Ethiopia and Eritrea (UNMEE, comprising 4,200 peace-keeping troops), which was subsequently deployed on the Eritrean side of the two countries' common border. UNMEE's mandate was periodically extended until the end of July 2008, when the UN Security Council adopted Resolution 1827, confirming the mission's termination.

Defence Expenditure: Budgeted at US $80m. in 2010.

Education

Education is provided free of charge in government schools and at the University of Asmara. There are also some fee-paying private schools. Education is officially compulsory for children between seven and 13 years of age. Primary education begins at the age of seven and lasts for five years. Secondary education, beginning at 12 years of age, lasts for as much as six years, comprising a first cycle of two years and a second of four years. According to UNESCO estimates, in 2009/10 primary enrolment included 34% of children in the relevant age-group (boys 36%; girls 31%), while the comparable ratio for secondary enrolment was only 29% (boys 32%; girls 25%). Total government expenditure on education and training in 2006 was estimated at the equivalent of 2.0% of GDP. In 2004/05 there were some 5,500 students enrolled on Bachelors degree courses at the University of Asmara; however, the University of Asmara was officially closed in September 2006. Higher education was henceforth to be provided by six newly established technical institutes, each associated with a relevant government ministry. The institutes provide education in the fields of science, technology, business and economics, social sciences, agriculture and marine training. In late 2010 two new schools were under construction in Gelalu sub-zone.

ESTONIA

Introductory Survey

LOCATION, CLIMATE, LANGUAGE, RELIGION, FLAG, CAPITAL

The Republic of Estonia is situated in north-eastern Europe. The country is bordered to the south by Latvia, and to the east by Russia. Estonia's northern coastline is on the Gulf of Finland, and its territory includes more than 1,520 islands, mainly off its western coastline in the Gulf of Rīga and the Baltic Sea. The largest of the islands are Saaremaa and Hiiumaa, in the Gulf of Rīga. The climate is influenced by Estonia's position between the Eurasian land mass and the Baltic Sea and the North Atlantic Ocean. The mean January temperature in Tallinn is −0.6°C (30.9°F); in July the mean temperature is 17.1°C (62.8°F). Average annual precipitation is 568 mm. The official language is Estonian, which is a member of the Baltic-Finnic group of the Finno-Ugric languages; it is closely related to Finnish. Many of the Russian residents, who comprise around one-quarter of the total population, do not speak Estonian. Most of the population profess Christianity. By tradition, Estonians belong to the Evangelical Lutheran Church. Smaller Protestant sects and the Eastern Orthodox Church are also represented. The national flag (proportions 7 by 11) consists of three equal horizontal stripes, of blue, black and white. The capital is Tallinn.

CONTEMPORARY POLITICAL HISTORY

Historical Context

The Russian annexation of Estonia, formerly under Swedish rule, was formalized in 1721. During the latter half of the 19th century, as the powers of the dominant Baltic German nobility declined, Estonians experienced a national cultural revival, which culminated in political demands for autonomy during the 1905 Russian Revolution, and for full independence after the beginning of the First World War. In March 1917 the Provisional Government in Petrograd (St Petersburg), which had taken power after the abdication of Tsar Nicholas II in February, approved autonomy for Estonia. A Maapäev (Provisional Council) was elected as the country's representative body. However, in October the Bolsheviks staged a coup in Tallinn. As German forces advanced towards Estonia in early 1918, the Bolshevik troops were forced to leave. The major Estonian political parties united to form the Estonian Salvation Committee, and on 24 February an independent Republic of Estonia was proclaimed. A Provisional Government, headed by Konstantin Päts, was formed, but Germany refused to recognize Estonia's independence, and the country was occupied by German troops. Following the capitulation of Germany in November, the Provisional Government assumed power. After a period of armed conflict between Soviet and Estonian troops, the Republic of Estonia and Soviet Russia signed the Treaty of Tartu on 2 February 1920, under the terms of which the Soviet Government recognized Estonia's independence and renounced any rights to its territory. Estonian independence was recognized by the major Western powers in January 1921, and Estonia was admitted to the League of Nations.

Independence lasted until 1940. During most of this time the country had a liberal-democratic political system, in which the Riigikogu (State Assembly) was the dominant political force. Significant social, cultural and economic advances were made in the 1920s, including radical land reform. However, the decline in trade with Russia and the economic depression of the 1930s, combined with the political problems of a divided parliament, caused public dissatisfaction. In March 1934 Prime Minister Päts seized power in a bloodless coup and introduced a period of authoritarian rule. The Riigikogu and political parties were disbanded, but in 1938 a new Constitution was adopted, which provided for a presidential system of government, with a bicameral legislature. In April 1938 Päts was elected President.

In August 1939 the USSR and Germany signed a non-aggression treaty (the Nazi-Soviet or Molotov-Ribbentrop Pact). The 'Secret Protocols' to the treaty provided for the occupation of Estonia (along with various other territories) by the USSR. In September Estonia was forced to sign an agreement that permitted the USSR to base Soviet troops there. In June 1940 the Government resigned, and the Soviet authorities appointed a new administration. In July elections were held, in which only candidates approved by the Soviet authorities were permitted to participate. On 21 July the Estonian Soviet Socialist Republic was proclaimed by the new legislature, and on 6 August the republic was formally incorporated into the USSR. Soviet rule in Estonia lasted less than one year. In that short period Soviet policy resulted in mass deportations of Estonians, the expropriation of property and severe restrictions on cultural life.

German forces entered Estonia in July 1941 and remained in occupation until September 1944. Thereafter, following a short-lived attempt to reinstate Estonian independence, Soviet troops occupied the whole of the country, and the process of 'sovietization' was resumed. By the end of 1949 most Estonian farmers had been forced to join collective farms. Heavy industry was expanded, with investment concentrated on electricity generation and the chemicals sector. Structural change in the economy was accompanied by increased political repression, with deportations of Estonians continuing until the death of Stalin (Iosif V. Dzhugashvili) in 1953. The most overt form of opposition to Soviet rule was provided by the 'forest brethren' (*metsavennad*), a guerrilla movement, which continued to conduct armed operations against Soviet personnel and institutions until the mid-1950s. In the late 1960s, as in other Soviet republics, more traditional forms of dissent appeared, concentrating on cultural issues, provoked by the increasing domination of the republic by immigrant Russians and other Slavs.

During the late 1970s and the 1980s the questions of 'russification' and environmental degradation became subjects of intense debate in Estonia. The policy of glasnost (openness), introduced by the Soviet leader, Mikhail Gorbachev, in 1986, allowed such discussion to spread beyond dissident groups. In August 1987 a demonstration attended by some 2,000 people commemorated the anniversary of the signing of the Nazi-Soviet Pact, and an Estonian Group for the Publication of the Molotov-Ribbentrop Pact (MRP-AEG) was subsequently formed. During 1988 the Nazi-Soviet Pact was duly published, and the MRP-AEG re-formed as the Estonian National Independence Party (ENIP), proclaiming the restoration of Estonian independence as its political objective. Another opposition group, the Estonian Popular Front (EPF), was formally constituted at its first congress in October, and included many members of the ruling Communist Party of Estonia (CPE). The EPF was more cautious than the ENIP, advocating the transformation of the USSR into a confederal system; the CPE was forced to adapt its policies to retain a measure of public support. On 16 November the Estonian Supreme Soviet (Supreme Council—legislature) adopted a declaration of sovereignty, which included the right to annul all-Union (USSR) legislation. The Presidium of the USSR Supreme Soviet declared the sovereignty legislation unconstitutional, but the Estonian Supreme Soviet affirmed its decision in December.

The adoption of Estonian as the state language was accepted by the Supreme Soviet in January 1989, and the tricolour of independent Estonia was reinstated as the official flag. Despite the successes of the opposition, differing political tactics were employed by the radical ENIP and the EPF. The ENIP refused to nominate candidates for elections to the all-Union Congress of People's Deputies in March. Instead, the ENIP leadership announced plans for the registration by citizens' committees of all citizens of the 1918–40 Republic of Estonia and their descendants. Voters on an electoral register, thus compiled, would elect an Eesti Kongress (Congress of Estonia) as the legal successor to the pre-1940 Estonian legislature. The EPF, however, participated in the elections to the Congress of People's Deputies and won 27 of the 36 contested seats. Five seats were won by the International Movement (Intermovement), a political group composed predominantly of ethnic Russians, which was established in July 1988 to oppose the growing influence of the Estonian opposition movements in the republic. In October 1989 delegates at the second congress of the EPF voted to adopt the restoration of Estonian independence as official policy. In November the Estonian Supreme Soviet voted to annul the 1940 decision of its predecessor to enter the USSR, declaring that the decision had been reached under coercion from Soviet armed forces.

On 2 February 1990 a mass rally was held to commemorate the anniversary of the 1920 Treaty of Tartu. Deputies attending the rally later met to approve a declaration urging the USSR Supreme Soviet to begin negotiations on restoring Estonia's independence. On 22 February 1990 the Estonian Supreme Soviet approved the declaration, and on the following day it voted to abolish the constitutional guarantee of power enjoyed by the CPE. This formal decision permitted largely free elections to take place to the Estonian Supreme Soviet in March. The EPF won 43 of the 105 seats, and 35 were won by the Association for a Free Estonia and other pro-independence groups. The remainder were won by members of the Intermovement. Candidates belonging to the CPE, which was represented in all these groups, won 55 seats. At the first session of the new legislature, Arnold Rüütel, previously Chairman of the Presidium of the Supreme Soviet, was elected to the new post of Chairman of the Supreme Soviet, in which was vested those state powers that had been the preserve of the First Secretary of the CPE. On 30 March the Supreme Soviet adopted a declaration that proclaimed the beginning of a transitional period towards independence and denied the validity of Soviet power in the republic.

In late February and early March 1990 some 580,000 people (excluding those who had migrated to Estonia after the Soviet occupation of 1940 and their descendants) took part in elections to the rival parliament to the Supreme Soviet, the Eesti Kongress. The Congress convened on 11–12 March 1990 and declared itself the constitutional representative of the Estonian people. The participants adopted resolutions demanding the restoration of Estonian independence and the withdrawal of Soviet troops from Estonia.

In April 1990 the Supreme Soviet elected Edgar Savisaar, a leader of the EPF, as Prime Minister, and on 8 May it voted to restore the first five articles of the 1938 Constitution, which described Estonia's independent status. The formal name of pre-1940 Estonia, the Republic of Estonia, was also restored, as were the state emblems, flag and anthem. Although formal economic sanctions were not imposed on Estonia (as was the case with Lithuania), relations with the Soviet authorities were severely strained. In mid-May President Gorbachev annulled the republic's declaration of independence, declaring that it violated the USSR Constitution. The Estonian leadership's request for negotiations on the status of the republic was refused by Gorbachev, who insisted that the independence declaration be rescinded before negotiations could begin. There was also opposition within the republic, mostly from ethnic Russians affiliated to the Intermovement.

When troops of the USSR's Ministry of the Interior attempted military intervention in the other Baltic republics (Latvia and Lithuania) in January 1991, the Estonian leadership anticipated similar confrontation. Barricades and makeshift defences were erected, but no military action was taken. However, events in Latvia and Lithuania intensified popular distrust of Estonian involvement in a new union, which was being negotiated by other Soviet republics. Consequently, Estonia refused to participate in a referendum on the future of the USSR, which took place in nine of the republics in March. The Estonian authorities had conducted a poll on the issue of independence earlier in the same month. According to the official results, 82.9% of the registered electorate took part, of whom 77.8% voted in favour of Estonian independence.

Domestic Political Affairs

When the conservative communist 'State Committee for the State of Emergency' announced that it had seized power in the USSR on 19 August 1991, Estonia, together with the other Baltic republics, expected military intervention to overthrow the pro-independence Governments. Gen. Fyodor Kuzmin, the Soviet commander of the Baltic military district, informed Rüütel that he was taking full control of Estonia. Military vehicles entered Tallinn on 20 August, and troops occupied the city's television station. However, the military command did not prevent a session of the Estonian Supreme Council from convening on the same day. Deputies adopted a resolution declaring the full and immediate independence of Estonia, thus ending the transitional period that had begun in March 1990. After it became evident, on 22 August 1991, that the Soviet coup had collapsed, the Government began to take measures against persons who had supported the coup. The anti-Government movements, including the Intermovement and the Communist Party of the Soviet Union, were banned in Estonia.

Consolidation of independent statehood

As the Estonian Government moved to assert its authority over former Soviet institutions, other countries quickly began to recognize its independence. On 6 September 1991 the recently formed USSR State Council finally recognized the re-establishment of Estonian independence. Later in the month Estonia, together with the other Baltic states, was admitted to the UN, as well as to the Conference on Security and Co-operation in Europe (CSCE), later the Organization for Security and Co-operation in Europe (OSCE, see p. 388). During the remainder of 1991 Estonia established diplomatic relations with most major states and was offered membership of leading international organizations. In internal politics, there was hope for a cessation of conflict between the Eesti Kongress and the Supreme Council, with the establishment of a Constitutional Assembly, composed of equal numbers of delegates from each body, which was to draft a new constitution. In January 1992, following a series of disputes with the Supreme Council, Savisaar resigned as Prime Minister and was replaced by the erstwhile Minister of Transport, Tiit Vähi. A new Council of Ministers was approved by the Supreme Council at the end of the month.

The draft Constitution was approved by some 91% of the electorate in a referendum held in June 1992. Under the recently adopted Citizenship Law, only citizens of pre-1940 Estonia and their descendants, or those who had successfully applied for citizenship, were entitled to vote. This ruling drew strong criticism from Russian leaders, who were concerned that the rights of Estonia's large Russian minority, most of whom had not been granted citizenship and were thus disenfranchised, were being violated. The new Constitution, which entered into force in July 1992, provided for a parliamentary system of government, with a strong presidency. Elections to the new legislature, the Riigikogu, were to be held in September, concurrently with a direct presidential election (although subsequent Presidents would be elected by the Riigikogu).

Legislative and presidential elections were duly held on 20 September 1992, with the participation of some 67% of the electorate. The country's Russian and other ethnic minorities, who represented 42% of the total population at that time, were again barred from voting (with the exception of those whose applications for citizenship had been granted). The elections to the 101-seat Riigikogu were contested by some 40 parties and movements, largely grouped into eight coalitions. The nationalist Pro Patria alliance emerged with the largest number of seats (29). The Secure Home alliance, which comprised some former communists, obtained 17 seats. The centrist Popular Front alliance (led by the EPF) won 15 seats. The Moderates electoral alliance obtained 12 seats, and the ENIP won 10 seats. None of the four candidates in the presidential election won an overall majority of the votes. The Riigikogu was thus required to choose from the two most successful candidates: Rüütel, now a leading member of the Secure Home alliance, and Lennart Meri, a former Minister of Foreign Affairs, who was supported by Pro Patria. In early October the Riigikogu elected Meri as Estonia's President.

A new coalition Government, comprising members of Pro Patria, the Moderates and the ENIP and headed by Mart Laar, the leader of Pro Patria, was announced in October 1992. Laar indicated that the principal objectives of his administration would be to negotiate the withdrawal of all Russian troops remaining in Estonia, as well as to accelerate the country's privatization programme. In November four of the five constituent parties of the Pro Patria alliance united to form the National Pro Patria Party (NPPP), with Laar as its Chairman.

In November 1993 Laar survived a vote of no confidence in the Riigikogu. Also in November, the EPF was disbanded. In January 1994 Laar reorganized four principal portfolios in the Council of Ministers, and in May–June four ministers resigned. Defections from the Pro Patria faction within the Riigikogu resulted in Laar's supporters retaining control of only 19 seats in the legislature by September. Following the revelation in that month that Laar had secretly contravened an agreement with the IMF, a vote of no confidence in the Prime Minister was endorsed by the Riigikogu. In October Andres Tarand, hitherto Minister of the Environment, was appointed to replace Laar. A new Council of Ministers, which included representatives of Pro Patria, the Moderates, the ENIP and liberal and right-wing parties, was announced in the following month.

The results of the legislative elections, held on 5 March 1993, reflected widespread popular dissatisfaction with the parties of the governing coalition. The largest number of seats in the Riigikogu (41 of the total of 101) was won by an alliance of the centrist Estonian Coalition Party (ECP, led by Vähi) and the Rural Union (in which Rüütel was a prominent figure). A coalition of the newly established Estonian Reform Party (ERP, led by Siim Kallas, the President of the Bank of Estonia) and liberal groups obtained 19 seats, followed by Savisaar's Estonian Centre Party (16). The NPPP (in coalition with the ENIP) won only eight seats, while the Moderates alliance obtained six seats. The Estonia is Our Home alliance (which represented the Russian-speaking minority) won six seats. The participation rate was almost 70%.

Vähi was confirmed as Prime Minister by the legislature in early April 1995, and the new Government—a coalition of the ECP/Rural Union and the Estonian Centre Party—was appointed later in the month. However, the Government survived only until early October, when it was revealed that Savisaar, the Minister of the Interior, had made clandestine recordings of conversations with other politicians concerning the formation of a new coalition government. The Estonian Centre Party subsequently refused to accept his dismissal by Vähi. As a result of the effective collapse of the coalition, Vähi and the remaining members of the Council of Ministers tendered their resignations. In mid-October President Meri reappointed Vähi as Prime Minister, and a coalition Government, comprising members of the ECP/Rural Union and the ERP, was formed in late October. In December the NPPP and the ENIP, which had campaigned jointly for the legislative elections in March, merged to form the Pro Patria Union (PPU).

A presidential election was held in the Riigikogu on 26 August 1996, contested by the incumbent, Meri, and Rüütel, now of the Estonian Country People's Party. Following two further inconclusive rounds of voting, a larger electoral college, comprising the 101 deputies of the legislature and 273 representatives of local government (as provided for by the Constitution), was convened on 20 September. As none of the five candidates contesting the election secured an overall majority, a further round of voting was held to choose between the leading candidates, Meri and Rüütel. The election was won by Meri, with 52% of the votes cast, and in October he was duly sworn in as President for a second term.

In October 1996 local government elections were held, in which the ERP gained control of the Tallinn city Government. In November the ECP concluded a co-operation agreement with the Estonian Centre Party, which had held no representation in the Government since October 1995. Disagreements among the coalition partners led to the collapse of the Tallinn city leadership, and Savisaar was appointed as the new Chairman of the city Government, replacing the newly elected ERP candidate. The ERP threatened to leave the Government unless the co-operation agreement with the Estonian Centre Party was cancelled, and in late November 1996 six ministers, including Kallas (hitherto the Minister for Foreign Affairs), resigned, causing the collapse of the ruling coalition. A minority Government, comprising the ECP, the Rural Union and independent members, was appointed in December. In early 1997 a series of allegations of abuse of office was made against Vähi. Although a legislative motion of no confidence, presented by the leaders of four opposition parties, was defeated by a narrow margin, Vähi tendered his resignation in February. Mart Siimann, the leader of the ECP parliamentary faction, was appointed Prime Minister, and was asked to form a new government. In March a new minority Government, again comprising the ECP, the Rural Union and independent members, was appointed. In September Vähi announced his resignation from the ECP and his retirement from political life. His position as Chairman of the ECP was assumed by Siimann.

The 1999 legislative elections

At legislative elections held on 7 March 1999, the Estonian Centre Party won 28 of the 101 seats available; the ERP and the PPU each secured 18 seats, the Moderates (in alliance with the People's Party) 17, the Estonian Country People's Party seven and the United People's Party of Estonia six. Just 57.4% of the electorate participated in the polls. Although the Estonian Centre Party obtained the largest number of seats, it was unable to form a majority coalition. A centre-right coalition Government was thus formed by the ERP, the PPU and the Moderates; Laar, by that time leader of the PPU, was appointed Prime Minister (the post he had held in 1992–94).

In May 1999 it was announced that some 300,000 non-citizens permanently resident in Estonia (principally comprising ethnic Russians) were to be allowed to participate in local elections to be held in October. At the elections, the governing ERP-PPU-Moderates alliance obtained control of 13 of Estonia's 15 county governments, and, in alliance with representatives of the Russian population, of Tallinn City Council, where Jüri Mõis was appointed Mayor of Tallinn, after resigning as Minister of the Interior. In November the Moderates' Party and the People's Party merged to form the People's Party Moderates. In June 2000 a new party, the Estonian People's Union (EPU), was formed by the merger of the Estonian Rural People's Party, the Rural Union and the Pensioners' and Families' Party. Mõis resigned in May 2001, after being threatened with a fifth confidence vote. A member of the PPU, Tõnis Palts, was elected as his successor.

Inconclusive rounds of voting in the presidential election took place in the Riigikogu on 27–28 August 2001. The first round of the election was contested by Tarand of the People's Party Moderates and Peeter Kreitzberg of the opposition Estonian Centre Party. Tarand was replaced as the candidate of the ruling coalition by Peeter Tulviste of the PPU in the second and third rounds of voting, but neither candidate emerged as the victor. An electoral college, composed of the 101 parliamentary deputies and 266 representatives of local government, was therefore convened on 21 September. Toomas Savi of the governing ERP (members of which had, hitherto, abstained from voting), and Rüütel, now the Honorary Chairman of the opposition EPU, participated at this stage, progressing to a second round, as the candidates with the greatest number of votes. Rüütel eventually emerged as the victor in the 'run-off' election, in which he secured 186 votes. He was sworn in as President on 8 October. The protracted electoral process had led to renewed demands for electoral reform, and some Estonians expressed concern at the election of a former communist official as President.

In September 2001 Mikhel Pärnoja tendered his resignation as Minister of Economic Affairs. In December the ERP announced that it was to leave the Tallinn city Government. It subsequently signed a coalition agreement with the Estonian Centre Party, in what was widely regarded as an attempt to distance itself from the increasingly unpopular national Government, of which it remained a part. Palts was forced to resign as Mayor, when a censure motion, brought by members of the Estonian Centre Party, was approved by a significant majority. His PPU left the city Government, and Savisaar was elected as Mayor of Tallinn in mid-December. These developments prompted Prime Minister Laar's Government to resign on 8 January 2002.

In mid-January 2002 the Estonian Centre Party and the ERP signed an agreement on the formation of an interim, coalition government, despite their contrasting political ideals; eight ministers were to be appointed from the Estonian Centre Party and six from the ERP. The parties of the coalition held fewer than one-half of the seats in the Riigikogu and, therefore, required the support of the EPU. On 22 January Kallas of the ERP was approved as Prime Minister, despite failing to obtain the support of his former government allies, the PPU and the People's Party Moderates.

Following a ruling by the Supreme Court prohibiting the formation of electoral blocs, in July 2002 the Riigikogu voted to permit their existence until 2005, in order to avoid a delay in holding the forthcoming local elections. The elections duly took place in October 2002. Parties represented in the national Government won the majority of the votes cast. In November Savisaar was re-elected as Mayor of Tallinn. Meanwhile, in response to their parties' poor performance, in late October Toomas Hendrik Ilves resigned as Chairman of the People's Party Moderates, and Laar resigned the chairmanship of the PPU. In February 2003 the Riigikogu approved an extension of the terms of local councils, from three years to four, in the first amendment to be made to the Constitution since its adoption. In early February the Minister of the Interior, Ain Seppik of the Estonian Centre Party, resigned, following severe criticism of his actions as a Supreme Court judge during the Soviet era.

Eleven parties participated in the parliamentary elections held on 2 March 2003, in which the Estonian Centre Party received 25.4% of the votes cast and 28 seats in the 101-member Riigikogu. The right-wing Union for the Republic Res Publica (founded in 2001) obtained 24.6% and 28 seats, and the ERP took 17.7% and 19 seats; the EPU, the PPU and the People's Party Moderates also secured representation in the Riigikogu. The level of participation by the electorate was 58.2%. Although the Estonian Centre Party secured the largest number of votes cast, in late March the Union for the Republic Res Publica, the ERP and the EPU reached agreement on the formation of a three-party government. After Savisaar declined the President's offer to form a government, on 2 April Juhan Parts, the leader of Union for the Republic Res Publica, was nominated as Prime Minister, and the new coalition Government was approved on 9 April. In September the Minister of Finance, Palts, resigned, after an investigation was initiated into allegations of tax evasion dating from before his appointment to the Council of Ministers; Taavi Veskimagi was appointed in his place. In February 2004 a congress of the People's Party Moderates voted formally to change the party's name to the Estonian Social Democratic Party (ESDP).

Accession to the European Union

Following Estonia's accession to the European Union (EU, see p. 276) in May 2004 (see Regional relations), in the following month the country took part in its first elections to the European Parliament. In October Savisaar resigned as Mayor of Tallinn, as the result of a vote of no confidence by the City Council. He was replaced by Palts. In November Margus Hanson resigned as Minister of Defence, following the theft from his home of classified documents. (His immunity from prosecution was removed in March 2005, and in November, after a criminal investigation, Hanson was given a fine for negligence.) Also in November 2004 Andrus Ansip, the new Minister of the Economy and Communications was elected Chairman of the ERP, replacing Kallas, who had been appointed as the country's representative to the European Commission. In December the Estonian Centre Party apparently sought to increase its support among the ethnic Russian population of Estonia, controversially signing a co-operation agreement with the de facto ruling party of Russia, United Russia. As a consequence, a number of Estonian Centre Party members who supported closer co-operation and integration with the EU left the party; by the end of January 2005 the party's faction in the Riigikogu had diminished from 28 to 19 members.

The Minister of Foreign Affairs, Kristiina Ojuland, was dismissed from office in February 2005, after a security audit revealed the disappearance of 91 classified documents. Ojuland and the ERP contested her dismissal, although the party ultimately accepted the appointment of Rein Lang as her successor. Nevertheless, on 21 March the Riigikogu adopted a motion of no confidence in Minister of Justice Ken-Marti Vaher, and three days later Parts announced the resignation of his Government. On 31 March the Estonian Centre Party, the ERP and the Estonian People's Party agreed to form a coalition, and Ansip was nominated to lead a new Government, which was sworn into office on 13 April. Municipal elections took place on 16 October (in which, for the first time, voting was permitted by way of the internet). The Estonian Centre Party won 25.5% of the votes cast nation-wide, followed by the ERP, the EPU and the PPU; the Union for the Republic Res Publica won just 8.5% of the ballot, compared with 15.2% in 2002. In Tallinn, the Estonian Centre Party won some 41% of the votes cast, but the party's Chairman, Savisaar, ultimately opted to retain his post as Minister of Economic Affairs and Communications, rather than be reappointed Mayor; in November another member of the party, Juri Ratas, was elected Mayor.

In mid-August 2006 the Estonian Centre Party and the EPU signed an agreement pledging their support for the candidacy of Rüütel in the forthcoming presidential election, scheduled to take place in the Riigikogu later that month. However, in the following week the two parties announced that they were to boycott the ballot after Rüütel announced that he would seek re-election only if the vote was decided by the electoral college system. In the initial ballot, held on 28 August, former Speaker of the legislature Ene Ergma, the sole candidate, attracted 65 votes, narrowly failing to secure the required two-thirds' majority (68 votes). Two further rounds of voting proved similarly inconclusive, with the former Minister of Foreign Affairs, Ilves (on both occasions the lone contender), securing 64 votes in each round. Responsibility for electing the President thus passed to the electoral college, which duly convened on 23 September and voted for Ilves over Rüütel by a margin of 174 to 162; Ilves was inaugurated on 9 October. Later that month Minister of the Environment Villu Reiljan tendered his resignation, amid widespread allegations that he had been involved in corrupt property deals. Also in October the PPU and the Union for the Republic Res Publica formally merged to form the Union of Pro Patria and Res Publica. (Following a lengthy dispute over its leadership, it had been agreed that Tõnis Lukas, hitherto Chairman of the PPU, and Taavi Veskimägi, hitherto Chairman of the Union for the Republic Res Publica, would co-chair the new party.)

Legislative elections were held on 4 March 2007, with the participation of 61.9% of the electorate. Following the successful trial of electronic voting in the municipal elections of 2005, all registered voters were entitled to cast their votes by way of the internet, although only a relatively small number did so. (Estonia became the first country to introduce internet voting at a national legislative election.) According to official results, the ERP was the most successful party at the elections, winning 31 seats and 27.8% of the votes cast, narrowly followed by the Estonian Centre Party, with 29 seats and 26.1% of the votes. The Union of Pro Patria and Res Publica secured 19 seats and 17.9% of the votes, the ESDP 10 seats and 10.6% of the votes, and the Estonian Greens and the EPU each obtained six seats and 7.1% of the votes. As in 2003, the Estonian Centre Party, despite its strong performance in the polls, was excluded from the new Government. In late March 2007 the ERP, the Union of Pro Patria and Res Publica, and the ESDP announced that they had agreed to form a centre-right coalition, which would command 60 of the 101 seats in the Riigikogu. A new Government, again under the premiership of Ansip, was installed on 4 April. Urmas Paet of the ERP was retained as Minister of Foreign Affairs; Jüri Pihl of the ESDP was awarded the interior portfolio, while Jaak Aaviksoo of the Union of Pro Patria and Res Publica assumed responsibility for defence. On the following day Savisaar was elected as Mayor of Tallinn, replacing Ratas, who had been elected as a Vice-President of the Riigikogu.

Divisions within the Government were evident in September 2008, as the coalition parties disagreed over measures to increase revenue and reduce expenditure in the 2009 budget, although a compromise was finally reached. An opinion poll published in the following month suggested that public support for the opposition Estonian Centre Party was exceeding that for the ERP for the first time since the March 2007 elections. In January 2009 the Minister of Social Affairs, Maret Maripuu of the ERP, announced her resignation from the Council of Ministers with effect from late February, despite having survived a vote of no confidence in the Riigikogu, which had been proposed by the three opposition parties in response to a severe delay in the disbursement of disability benefits; she was replaced by Hanno Pevkur, also of the ERP. In February the Government secured the approval of the Riigikogu for a supplementary budget further curtailing expenditure for 2009; the adoption of the austerity measures, which included a 10% reduction in public sector salaries, was linked to a vote of confidence in Ansip's administration.

Ansip dismissed the three ESDP ministers from the Government in May 2009, after disagreements with the party's Minister of Finance, Ivari Padar, over unemployment benefits and further proposals aimed at improving the country's fiscal position. Following the failure of talks to bring the EPU into the ruling coalition, the ERP and the Union of Pro Patria and Res Publica continued in office as a minority administration. In early June Jürgen Ligi of the ERP and Marko Pomerants of the Union of Pro Patria and Res Publica were appointed to the vacant positions of Minister of Finance and Minister of the Interior, respectively; the third ESDP minister, who had been responsible for population and ethnic affairs, was not replaced.

At elections to the European Parliament held on 7 June 2009, the Estonian Centre Party obtained two of the country's six seats, winning 26.1% of the votes cast. An independent candidate, Indrek Tarand, secured a seat, having received 25.8% of the votes cast, while the ERP, the Union of Pro Patria and Res Publica and the ESDP also each took one seat. In addition to the large share of the ballot garnered by Tarand, the elections were notable for the poor performance of the ESDP, which had been the most successful party in the 2004 European polls, winning three seats. The voter turn-out, at 43.9%, was also markedly higher than that recorded in 2004 (26.8%). The Estonian Centre Party was also victorious in municipal elections conducted on 18 October 2009, securing 31.2% of the votes cast nation-wide. The ERP won 16.8% of the votes and the Union of Pro Patria and Res Publica obtained 14.1%. In Tallinn, the Estonian Centre Party won 53.3% of the votes cast and 44 of the 79 seats on the City Council, with Savisaar re-elected as Mayor.

In early 2011 the campaign for the parliamentary elections, due to be held in March, was largely dominated by economic issues; the ruling coalition pledged to reduce taxes and to guarantee Estonia's continued economic growth if re-elected. However, from mid-December 2010 Savisaar, as both Mayor of Tallinn and Chairman of the Estonian Centre Party, became the focus of a political scandal, after he was accused of receiving illegal donations for his party. Savisaar denied all the allegations, which included claims that he had accepted €1.5m. from the President of Russian Railways, Vladimir Yakunin, on behalf of his party to grant Russia greater influence over Estonian affairs. Savisaar insisted that the funds were to be used for the construction of a Russian Orthodox church in Tallinn and that the allegations were intended to damage the Estonian Centre Party's reputation in advance of the forthcoming polls. Nevertheless, President Ilves was reported to have responded to the reports by declaring that he would veto any coalition government that was to include Savisaar's movement as a constituent party.

Recent developments: Ansip returned to power

On 23 March 2011 the ERP and the Union of Pro Patria and Res Publica reached a preliminary agreement to continue their governing coalition. Ansip subsequently appointed a new Government, in which several of the senior positions remained unchanged, including Ligi as Minister of Finance, Paet as Minister of Foreign Affairs and Pomerants as Minister of the Interior. Laar was appointed Minister of Defence, succeeding Aaviksoo, who became Minister of Education and Research.

In August 2011 a member of the Estonian United Left Party—which seeks to represent the rights of the Russian minority—attempted to take hostage staff members in the offices of the Ministry of Defence in Tallinn. The gunman opened fire inside the building before he was shot and killed by police. No one else was injured during the incident. The Minister of Defence was not present in the building at the time and it remained unclear whether the actions of the gunman were politically or personally motivated. In early December it emerged that two elected officials of Union of Pro Patria and Res Publica—a parliamentary deputy and a member of Tallinn City Council—had engaged in the sale of Estonian residence permits, in defiance of usual legal procedures, to entrepreneurs from Russia and other countries of the Commonwealth of Independent States. A parliamentary anti-corruption committee was convened to investigate the case, while in an attempt to protect the party's reputation, the two officials were expelled from the Union of Pro Patria and Res Publica, while two ministers belonging to the party—Minister of the Interior Vaher and Minister of Economic Affairs and Communications Parts, who were also allegedly implicated in the case, were to be subject to a vote of confidence from the party's ruling council. (The retention of both Vaher and Parts was endorsed later in the month).

At the end of January 2012 Urmas Reinsalu was elected as the leader of Union of Pro Patria and Res Publica, replacing Laar (who, having announced his intention to resign several months earlier, was given the title of Honorary Chairman). In mid-February Laar was hospitalized, having suffered a stroke. Consequently Aaviksoo assumed Laar's ministerial responsibilities in addition to his own, although it was anticipated that Laar would return to his post following his recovery. In early March 2012 some 16,000 teachers participated in three days of strike action in support of an increase in salaries of some 20% for 2012 and of 15% for each of 2013 and 2014. Members of other professions demonstrated their support for the striking teachers, including medical workers and railway staff. The Government proposed an increase in teaching salaries of 15% with effect from 2013, but this was deemed unacceptable by the principal education union. In March 2012 the EPU renamed itself the Estonian Conservative People's Party.

Foreign Affairs

Regional relations

Estonia pursues close relations with its Baltic neighbours, Latvia and Lithuania. In late 1991 the three states established a consultative interparliamentary body, the Baltic Assembly, with the aim of developing political and economic co-operation. The Baltic Assembly has maintained close links with the Nordic Council, and Estonia is also a member of the Council of the Baltic Sea States (see p. 254), established in March 1992. In January 2007 the Baltic states agreed to establish a joint Baltic Battalion (under Lithuanian command), which would participate in the NATO Response Force from January 2010. Meeting in Vilnius, Lithuania, in April 2009, the three Baltic Prime Ministers signed a declaration on the implementation of joint energy infrastructure projects and on the creation, by 2013, of a common Nordic-Baltic energy market. In June, furthermore, the three Prime Ministers, together with the heads of government of Denmark, Finland, Germany, Poland and Sweden and the President of the European Commission, signed a memorandum of understanding on a plan aimed at integrating Estonia, Latvia and Lithuania into the European energy market by establishing and strengthening network interconnections with neighbouring EU countries. It was announced in March 2012 that Estonia and Latvia would install a third electrical cable connecting the two countries. The cable, most of which would be situated in the Latvian side, was scheduled to be completed in 2020 and would increase capacity in the two countries by between 500 MW and 600 MW. Meanwhile, in 2011 it was confirmed that Estonia was to participate jointly with Lithuania, Latvia and Poland in the construction of a 1,300-MW nuclear power plant in Lithuania.

Since the restoration of Estonian independence in 1991, the republic's relations with its eastern neighbour, Russia, have been strained by a number of issues, most notably the presence of former Soviet troops and the rights of the large Russian minority in Estonia (equivalent to 25.5% of the population in January 2011, according to official figures, with a significantly higher proportion being recorded in Tallinn). Under the Citizenship Law of 1992 (a modified version of that adopted in 1938), non-ethnic Estonians who settled in the republic after its annexation by the USSR in 1940, and their descendants, were obliged to apply for naturalization. Many of the requirements for naturalization—including an examination in the Estonian language—were criticized by the Russian Government as being excessively stringent, and discriminatory against the Russian-speaking minority. A new citizenship law, adopted in January 1995, gave non-citizens until 12 July to apply for residence and work permits, by which time almost 330,000 people (more than 80% of the total) had submitted applications. The deadline was extended until 30 November 1996, and by October of that year some 110,000 people had taken Russian citizenship, while continuing to reside in Estonia. In May 1997 the Ministry of the Interior announced that Soviet passports were no longer valid in Estonia. In December 1998 the Riigikogu approved legislation requiring elected officials to demonstrate sufficient command of Estonian to participate in the basic bureaucratic procedures of office. The legislation became effective in May 1999, and on 1 July a further amendment to the Language Law, pertaining to those employed in the services sector, came into force. In April 2000, following a statement by the OSCE High Commissioner on National Minorities that the language legislation contradicted international standards on freedom of expression, the law was amended, to make knowledge of Estonian compulsory only where it was deemed necessary for the sake of public interest (for example, in areas such as public health and security). In November 2001 the requirement that electoral candidates be able to speak Estonian was abolished, although legislation adopted in the same month made Estonian the official language of parliament.

With the dissolution of the USSR in 1991, several thousand former Soviet troops remained stationed (under Russian command) on Estonian territory. Their withdrawal commenced in 1992, but the Russian leadership increasingly linked the progress of the troop withdrawals with the question of the citizenship, and other rights, of the Russian-speaking minority in Estonia. In July 1994 a bilateral agreement was reached, awarding civil and social guarantees to all Russian military pensioners in Estonia. The withdrawal of former Soviet troops was completed on 29 August.

A further cause of tension in Estonian–Russian relations concerned Estonia's demand for the return of some 2,000 sq km (770 sq miles) of territory that had been ceded to Russia in 1944. In June 1994 Russian President Boris Yeltsin ordered the unilateral demarcation of Russia's border with Estonia according to the post-1944 boundary, although no agreement with Estonia had been concluded. During 1995 Estonia abandoned its demand for the return of the disputed territories. Instead, the Estonian Government appealed only for minor amendments to be made to the existing line of demarcation, in order to improve border security; more importantly, it insisted that Russia recognize the 1920 Treaty of Tartu (in which Russia recognized Estonia's independence) as the basis of future relations between the two countries. However, the Russian Government maintained that the Treaty had lost its legal force, having been superseded by the declaration on bilateral relations signed by Russia and Estonia in 1991. In November 1996 the Estonian authorities announced that they were prepared to omit references to the Treaty of Tartu from the border agreement, and declared that it would be signed by Estonia and Russia at a summit of the OSCE in December. However, the Russian Government continued to refuse to sign the agreement.

Despite Russian misgivings, in September 2000 Estonia decreed that from 2001 a full visa regime would come into effect between the two countries (as part of Estonia's preparations for EU membership). Further tensions arose in December 2003, when the Riigikogu approved amendments to legislation on foreign nationals, which prevented Russian military pensioners from obtaining permanent residency in Estonia. The Russian Government warned that any abrogation of the bilateral agreement of July 1994 would be likely severely to damage Estonian–Russian relations. President Rüütel refused an invitation from Russian President Vladimir Putin to attend celebrations in Moscow, the Russian and former Soviet capital, on 9 May 2005, commemorating the 60th anniversary of the end of the Second World War in Europe, on the grounds that, for Estonia, it marked the beginning of almost 50 years of Soviet occupation. On 18 May the Ministers of Foreign Affairs of Estonia and Russia signed a border agreement. The treaty was ratified by the Riigikogu two days later, but the addition of a preamble making reference to the Soviet occupation of Estonia prompted Russia to revoke the agreement and demand renewed negotiations.

Hopes that bilateral relations might improve increased in June 2006 when the Russian ambassador to Estonia offered his country's condolences to Estonians on the anniversary of the Soviet mass deportations in 1941. However, in February 2007 the approval of legislation by the Riigikogu providing for the relocation of a Soviet war monument in Tallinn, together with draft legislation proposing a ban on politically motivated public displays of Soviet and Nazi symbols in Estonia, provoked intense indignation from the Russian Government. Russian Minister of Foreign Affairs Sergei Lavrov described the anticipated relocation of the monument as 'blasphemous', on the grounds that Soviet soldiers were buried beneath the monument, while Estonian President Ilves denounced the Riigikogu's approval of the legislation and assured the Russian authorities that he would veto the new law. When the monument was dismantled, in April, pending its relocation, several days of rioting ensued in Tallinn, as a result of which at least one person was killed and several hundred injured; at least 800 people were arrested. The Russian authorities submitted a formal protest to the Estonian ambassador in Moscow, while the Russian state-sponsored youth organization Nashi (Our Own) blockaded the Estonian embassy. In May Russia's state railway monopoly announced the suspension of deliveries of petroleum products to Estonia, purportedly on the grounds that it planned to carry out maintenance of the rail link to Estonia. The Estonian Minister of Foreign Affairs also claimed that elements in the Russian administration were responsible for a series of 'cyber-attacks' against the internet sites of Estonian government ministries, agencies and companies. (In March 2009 an activist with Nashi claimed that he and other members of the organization had organized these attacks.)

In June 2007 President Ilves made an official visit to the USA, during which US President George W. Bush endorsed the Estonian Government's proposal for the establishment of a North Atlantic Treaty Organization (NATO, see p. 370) 'cyber-defence' research centre in Tallinn, with US participation. In July the remains of eight Soviet soldiers previously under the war monument were reburied in Tallinn in an official ceremony (which the Russian ambassador to Estonia refused to attend). In January 2008 an ethnic Russian student resident in Estonia received a fine of 17,500 kroons for a cyber-attack against the ERP internet site. Also in that month the trial of four protesters accused of instigating unrest in April 2007 commenced in Tallinn; all four were acquitted of the charges against them in January 2009. Meanwhile, in May 2008 the defence force commanders of Estonia, Latvia, Lithuania, Italy, Germany, Spain and Slovakia signed a memorandum of understanding on the establishment of the NATO Cooperative Cyber Defence Centre of Excellence in Tallinn; the Centre received full NATO accreditation in October. In June 2008 the Estonian delegation, headed by President Ilves, withdrew from the fifth World Congress of Finno-Ugric Peoples, which was being held in the Russian town of Khanty-Mansiisk, in protest at a speech by the chairman of the foreign affairs committee of the Russian State Duma criticizing Estonia's treatment of its ethnic Russian minority. Prior to the opening of the Congress, Ilves had held brief talks with his recently elected Russian counterpart, Dmitrii Medvedev. In February 2009 the head of the security department at the Estonian Ministry of Defence during 2000–06, Herman Simm, pleaded guilty to treason and was sentenced to 12-and-a-half years' imprisonment for having reportedly passed classified Estonian, and later NATO, military documents to the Russian Foreign Intelligence Service over a period of more than 10 years. Although Estonian–Russian relations continued to be tense, it was considered significant that in early May 2010 Ilves became the first Estonian President to travel to Moscow to attend the annual Russian Victory Day parade (to commemorate the anniversary of the end of the Second World War).

An important focus of Estonia's foreign policy was the attainment of full membership of the EU. In July 1995 Estonia became an associate member, and in December it officially applied for full membership; formal accession negotiations began on 31 March 1998. In October 2002 the European Commission approved a report, which identified 10 countries, including Estonia, as ready to join the EU on 1 May 2004. A national referendum was held on 14 September 2003, in which voters were asked whether they supported Estonia's proposed accession to the EU in 2004 and the adoption of legislation amending the country's Constitution; 66.8% of the votes cast by 64.1% of the electorate were in favour of Estonia's accession, which duly took effect on 1 May 2004. In June Estonia was one of three new EU member states (alongside Lithuania and Slovenia) to be admitted to the exchange rate mechanism (ERM II) as a precursor to adopting the common European currency, the euro; the Estonian Government subsequently announced that it intended to adopt the euro by 1 January 2007. However, in April 2006 the Government acknowledged that it would not be in a position to meet this deadline, predominantly owing to high inflation. In March 2009 the Government approved a new deadline of 1 January 2011 for adopting the euro. As a result of the Government's successful fiscal programme, the European Commission announced on 12 May 2010 that Estonia had met the necessary economic criteria to proceed with this deadline; on 13 July EU ministers of finance endorsed Estonia's membership of the euro zone. Estonia thus formally adopted the common European currency on 1 January 2011, becoming the first Baltic state to join the euro zone.

Estonia ratified the draft European constitutional treaty in May 2006, but this was subsequently abandoned, after being rejected at referendums in France and the Netherlands. In December 2007 EU leaders signed a replacement treaty aimed at institutional reform, the Treaty of Lisbon, which was duly ratified by Estonia in June 2008, having been approved by 91 members of the Riigikogu, and entered into force in December 2009, following its ratification by all EU member states. Meanwhile, in December 2007 Estonia, together with eight other nations, implemented the EU's Schengen Agreement, enabling its citizens to travel to and from other signatory states without border controls.

Other external relations

In November 2006 US President George W. Bush made the inaugural visit to Estonia by a US Head of State, accompanied by US Secretary of State Condoleezza Rice. In a joint press conference given by Ilves and Bush, the US President thanked Ilves for the Estonian Government's support in the US-led 'war on terror' and expressed his appreciation for Estonian co-operation 'in the name of common aims and values'. In November 2008 Estonia joined the USA's programme for visa-free travel. At a meeting held in Washington, DC, USA, in late January 2011 between Estonia's Minister of Foreign Affairs, Urmas Paet, and US Secretary of State Hillary Clinton, the latter commended the Estonian authorities for the progress made since the restoration of independence in 1991, citing among other successes their 'commitment to good governance, the rule of law, and fiscal responsibility'.

Estonia joined NATO's 'Partnership for Peace' programme of military co-operation in March 1994. In November 2002, at a NATO summit meeting held in Prague, Czech Republic, Estonia was one of seven countries to be invited formally to accede to the Alliance, becoming a full member of NATO on 29 March 2004. Paet hosted an informal meeting of NATO foreign ministers in Tallinn in late April 2010.

CONSTITUTION AND GOVERNMENT

A new Constitution, based on that of 1938, was adopted by a referendum held on 28 June 1992 and took effect on 3 July. Legislative authority resides with the Riigikogu (State Assembly), which has 101 members, elected by universal adult suffrage for a four-year term. The Riigikogu elects the President (Head of State) for a term of five years. The President is also Supreme Commander of Estonia's armed forces. Executive power is held by the Council of Ministers, which is headed by the Prime Minister, who is nominated by the President. Judicial power is exercised by the Supreme Court, district courts and rural and city, as well as administrative, courts. For administrative purposes, Estonia is divided into 15 counties (*maakonds*), which in turn are subdivided into cities, rural municipalities and towns.

REGIONAL AND INTERNATIONAL CO-OPERATION

Estonia is a member of the Council of the Baltic Sea States (see p. 254), of the Baltic Council (see p. 462), of the Council of Europe (see p. 256), and of the Organization for Security and Co-operation in Europe (see p. 388). In 2004 it acceded to the European Union (see p. 276).

Estonia joined the UN in 1991, and was admitted to the World Trade Organization (see p. 433) in 1999 and to the Organisation for Economic Co-operation and Development (see p. 379) in 2010. The country is a member of the North Atlantic Treaty Organization (NATO, see p. 370) and hosts the NATO Cooperative Cyber Defence Centre of Excellence, which was established in 2008.

ECONOMIC AFFAIRS

In 2010, according to World Bank estimates, Estonia's gross national income (GNI), measured at average 2008–10 prices, was US $19,247m., equivalent to $14,370 per head (or $19,510 per head on an international purchasing-power parity basis). During 2001–10, according to World Bank estimates, the population declined at an average annual rate of 0.2%, while gross domestic product (GDP) per head increased, in real terms, by an average of 3.5% per year. According to World Bank estimates, overall GDP increased, in real terms, at an average annual rate of 3.3% during 20010–10; real GDP decreased by 13.9% in 2009, but increased by 1.8% in 2010.

Agriculture (including hunting, forestry and fishing) contributed 3.3% of GDP in 2010, when the sector provided 4.2% of employment. Animal husbandry is the main activity in the agricultural sector. Some 27.4% of Estonia's land is cultivable. The principal crops are grains, potatoes, and fruit and vegetables. Forestry products are also important. During 2001–08, according to World Bank estimates, agricultural GDP declined, in real terms, at an average annual rate of 1.9%; the GDP of the sector declined by 10.4% in 2007 but increased by 5.7% in 2008.

Industry (including mining and quarrying, manufacturing, construction, and power) contributed 28.5% of GDP in 2010, when the sector provided 30.5% of employment. The sector is dominated by machine-building, electronics and electrical engineering. During 2001–08, according to World Bank estimates, industrial GDP increased, in real terms, at an average annual rate of 7.3%; industrial GDP increased by 8.1% in 2007, but decreased by 4.8% in 2008.

Mining and quarrying contributed 1.4% of GDP in 2010, when the sector provided 1.2% of employment. Estonia's principal mineral resource is oil shale, and there are also deposits of peat, phosphorite ore, limestone and granite. There are total estimated reserves of oil shale of some 4,000m. metric tons. However, annual extraction of oil shale had declined to 17.9m. tons by 2010 (according to preliminary figures), compared with some 31m. tons in 1980. Phosphorite ore is processed to produce phosphates for use in agriculture, but development of the industry has been accompanied by increasing environmental problems. In 2000–07 the GDP of the mining and quarrying sector increased, in real terms, at an average annual rate of 6.3%. According to official figures, the GDP of the mining and quarrying sector increased by 11.9% in 2007.

In 2010 the manufacturing sector accounted for 16.4% of GDP and engaged 19.0% of the employed labour force. The sector is based on products of food- and beverage-processing (especially dairy products), textiles and clothing, fertilizers and other chemical products, and wood and timber products (particularly furniture). According to World Bank estimates, in 2001–08 the GDP of the manufacturing sector increased, in real terms, at an average annual rate of 7.4%; real manufacturing GDP increased by 6.2% in 2007, but declined by 4.2% in 2008.

The construction sector contributed 5.7% of GDP and engaged 8.4% of the employed labour force in 2010.

The country relies on oil shale for over 90% of its energy requirements. Estlink, an under-sea electrical cable connecting the electricity networks of Estonia and Finland, became operational in January 2007. In 2011 the Government announced that Estonia would participate jointly (taking a 20% share) with the Governments of Lithuania, Latvia and Poland in the construction of a 1,300-MW nuclear power plant at Visaginas, Lithuania; it was anticipated that construction of the plant would commence in 2012. In 2010 imports of mineral fuels accounted for 17.1% of total imports.

The services sector accounted for 68.2% of GDP and engaged 65.3% of the employed population in 2010. According to World Bank estimates, during 2001–08 the GDP of the services sector increased, in real terms, by an annual average rate of 6.2%; the GDP of the sector increased by 5.2% in 2007 but declined by 0.4% in 2008.

In 2010 Estonia recorded a visible trade deficit of US $330.7m., while there was a surplus of $673.2m. on the current account of the balance of payments. After 1991 trade with the West, particularly the Nordic countries, increased considerably. In 2010 Finland was Estonia's principal trading partner, accounting for 14.9% of imports and 17.0% of exports. Other important sources of imports were Germany, Latvia, Sweden, Russia, Lithuania and Poland. Sweden, Russia, Latvia, Germany and Lithuania were other important purchasers of exports. In 2010 the principal exports were machinery and mechanical appliances (22.6% of total export revenue), mineral fuels and oils, base metals, wood and charcoal, furniture, bedding, lamps and lighting fittings and prefabricated buildings, and vehicles. The principal imports in that year were machinery and mechanical appliances (23.6% of the total), mineral fuels and oils, base metals, chemical products and vehicles.

According to IMF estimates, in 2009 a budgetary surplus of 2,132m. kroons was recorded. Estonia's general government gross debt was 991m. euros in 2009, equivalent to 7.2% of GDP. Estonia's external debt totalled US $11,255m. at the end of 2005, of which $435m. was long-term public debt. In the same year the cost of debt-servicing was equivalent to 13.7% of the value of exports of goods and services. During 2000–10 the annual rate of inflation averaged 4.3%. Consumer prices increased by 2.9% in 2010. In 2010 some 16.9% of the labour force were officially registered as unemployed.

Although Estonia qualified for membership of the EU exchange rate mechanism (ERM II) in June 2004, only one month after it acceded to membership of the Union, subsequent economic developments, including an upturn in inflation, meant that it did not enter the euro zone as promptly as had been initially anticipated. In 2007 the rate of growth slowed, and in 2008 the economy entered recession, and the unemployment rate increased to 18%. The Government's economic priority was to maintain a fiscal deficit below the level of 3% of GDP required for euro adoption, and a number or reforms, including the liberalization of labour laws and an increase in the retirement age, were implemented to that end. In 2009 a supplementary budget reduced planned expenditure, and in that year some excise duties and the rate of value-added tax were increased. By the end of that year the inflation criterion for euro adoption had been met. The Government's macroeconomic and fiscal policies appeared to be vindicated when the country was admitted to the Organisation for Economic Co-operation and Development in December 2010, and when the euro was adopted as the national currency on 1 January 2011. Foreign investment increased during that year, while the adoption of the European common currency also made trade with other EU countries (which between them typically purchase around three-quarters of Estonian exports) more attractive. According to official sources, Estonia's real GDP grew by 7.6% in 2011. The economy's strong performance was attributed to the manufacturing, construction, and information and communications sectors. It was reported in late 2011 that Estonia had, at 6.7% of GDP in 2010, the lowest rate of national debt in the EU at that time. Moreover, in August 2011 Eurostat recorded that the rate of unemployment in Estonia had fallen during the previous 12 months from 18.8% to 13.8%. In the same month global credit ratings agency Standard & Poor's upgraded Estonia's rating, reflecting international confidence in the Government's economic policies. The IMF forecast real GDP growth to decline to 3.1% in 2012 as Estonia's export markets weakened as a result of the continuing euro debt crisis.

PUBLIC HOLIDAYS

2013: 1 January (New Year's Day), 24 February (Independence Day), 29 March (Good Friday), 1 May (Spring Day), 23 June (Victory Day, anniversary of the Battle of Võnnu in 1919), 24 June (Midsummer Day, Jaanipäev), 20 August (Restoration of Independence Day), 25–26 December (Christmas—Gregorian Calendar).

Statistical Survey

Source (unless otherwise stated): Statistical Office of Estonia (Statiskaamet), Endla 15, Tallinn 0100; tel. 625-9202; fax 625-9370; e-mail stat@stat.ee; internet www.stat.ee.

Area and Population

AREA, POPULATION AND DENSITY

Area (sq km)	45,227*
Population (census results)†	
12 January 1989	1,565,662
31 March 2000	
Males	631,851
Females	738,201
Total	1,370,052
Population (official estimates at 1 January)†	
2009	1,340,415
2010	1,340,127
2011	1,340,194
Density (per sq km) at 1 January 2011	29.6

* 17,462 sq miles.

† Figures refer to permanent inhabitants. The de facto total was 1,572,916 at the 1989 census and 1,356,931 at the 2000 census.

POPULATION BY AGE AND SEX
(official estimates at 1 January 2011)

	Males	Females	Total
0–14	105,869	99,831	205,700
15–64	436,919	469,453	906,372
65 and over	74,917	153,090	228,007
Total*	617,757	722,437	1,340,194

* Including 115 people (52 males and 63 females) whose age was unknown.

POPULATION BY ETHNIC GROUP
(1 January 2011)

	Number	% of total population
Estonian	924,100	68.9
Russian	341,450	25.5
Ukrainian	27,530	2.1
Belarusian	15,315	1.2
Others	31,799	2.4
Total	1,340,194	100.0

POPULATION BY COUNTY
(official estimates at 1 January 2011)

County	Area (sq km)*	Population	Density (per sq km)	County town (with population)
Harju	4,333	528,468	122.0	Tallinn (400,292)
Hiiu	1,023	10,000	9.8	Kärdla (3,635)
Ida-Viru	3,364	167,542	49.8	Jõhvi (12,723)†
Järva	2,460	35,963	14.6	Paide (9,764)
Jõgeva	2,604	36,550	14.0	Jõgeva (6,334)
Lääne	2,383	27,283	11.4	Haapsalu (11,604)
Lääne-Viru	3,628	66,861	18.4	Rakvere (16,578)
Pärnu	4,807	88,327	18.4	Pärnu (43,966)
Põlva	2,165	30,778	14.2	Põlva (6,584)
Rapla	2,980	36,652	12.3	Rapla (5,742)‡
Saare	2,922	34,577	11.8	Kuressaare (14,989)
Tartu	2,993	150,535	50.3	Tartu (103,740)
Valga	2,044	33,889	16.6	Valga (13,629)
Viljandi	3,423	55,275	16.1	Viljandi (19,880)
Võru	2,305	37,494	16.3	Võru (14,311)
Total	43,434	1,340,194	30.9	

* Excluding that part of Lake Peipsi that belongs to Estonia, and the area of Lake Võrtsjärv.

† Rural municipality.

‡ Estimated population at 1 January 2002.

PRINCIPAL TOWNS
(estimated population, excluding suburbs, at 1 January 2011)

Tallinn (capital)	400,292	Kohtla-Järve	44,107
Tartu	103,740	Pärnu	43,966
Narva	65,536		

BIRTHS, MARRIAGES AND DEATHS*

	Registered live births		Registered marriages		Registered deaths	
	Number	Rate (per 1,000)	Number	Rate (per 1,000)	Number	Rate (per 1,000)
2003	13,036	9.6	5,699	4.2	18,152	13.4
2004	13,992	10.4	6,009	4.5	17,685	13.1
2005	14,350	10.7	6,121	4.6	17,316	12.9
2006	14,877	11.1	6,954	5.2	17,316	12.9
2007	15,775	11.8	7,022	5.2	17,409	13.0
2008	16,028	12.0	6,127	4.6	16,675	12.4
2009	15,763	11.8	5,362	4.0	16,081	12.0
2010	15,825	11.8	5,066	3.8	15,790	11.8

* Revised figures, based on the results of the 1989 and 2000 population censuses.

Life expectancy (years at birth, official estimates): 75 (males 70; females 80) in 2009.

ECONOMICALLY ACTIVE POPULATION
(annual averages, '000 persons aged 15–74 years)

	2008	2009	2010
Agriculture, hunting and forestry	24.2	22.7	23.1
Fishing	1.1	1.3	1.0
Mining and quarrying	6.0	6.4	6.9
Manufacturing	135.0	113.8	108.4
Electricity, gas and water supply	10.5	10.1	11.0
Construction	81.0	58.3	47.9
Wholesale and retail trade	92.5	83.2	80.0
Hotels and restaurants	23.6	20.1	19.4
Transport, storage and communications	65.2	64.0	56.0
Financial intermediation	10.4	11.4	9.4
Real estate, renting and business activities	48.0	46.5	50.2
Public administration and defence; compulsory social security	38.4	36.7	40.4
Education	59.9	62.5	56.1
Health and social work	31.1	33.0	34.6
Other services	29.6	25.7	26.6
Total employed	656.5	595.8	570.9
Unemployed	38.4	95.1	115.9
Total labour force	694.9	690.9	686.8

Health and Welfare

KEY INDICATORS

Total fertility rate (children per woman, 2009)	1.7
Under-5 mortality rate (per 1,000 live births, 2009)	4
HIV/AIDS (% of persons aged 15–49, 2009)	1.2
Physicians (per 1,000 head, 2006)	3.3
Hospital beds (per 1,000 head, 2006)	5.6
Health expenditure (2008): US $ per head (PPP)	1,325
Health expenditure (2008): % of GDP	6.1
Health expenditure (2008): public (% of total)	77.8
Access to water (% of persons, 2008)	98
Access to sanitation (% of persons, 2008)	95
Total carbon dioxide emissions ('000 metric tons, 2007)	20,456.1
Carbon dioxide emissions per head (metric tons, 2007)	15.2
Human Development Index (2011): ranking	34
Human Development Index (2011): value	0.835

For sources and definitions, see explanatory note on p. vi.

Agriculture

PRINCIPAL CROPS

('000 metric tons)

	2008	2009	2010
Wheat	342.5	342.5	324.4
Barley	349.1	376.9	252.5
Rye	65.6	39.1	25.1
Oats	77.5	86.5	52.6
Triticale (wheat-rye hybrid)	21.8	22.6	8.8
Potatoes	125.2	139.1	163.4
Peas, dry	3.2	7.5	12.1
Rapeseed	111.1	136.0	131.0
Cabbages and other brassicas	19.8	18.6	16.3
Cucumbers and gherkins	8.6	9.4	12.1
Tomatoes	5.4	4.7	5.2
Carrots and turnips	15.6	20.9	22.8
Apples	2.2	5.4	2.0

Aggregate production ('000 metric tons, may include official, semi-official or estimated data): Total cereals 864.2 in 2008, 873.5 in 2009, 670.0 in 2010; Total roots and tubers 125.6 in 2008, 139.8 in 2009, 163.7 in 2010; Total vegetables (incl. melons) 64.6 in 2008, 70.7 in 2009, 74.0 in 2010; Total fruits (excl. melons) 5.5 in 2008, 9.2 in 2009, 5.1 in 2010.

Source: FAO.

LIVESTOCK

('000 head, year ending September)

	2008	2009	2010
Cattle	241	238	235
Pigs	379	365	365
Sheep	72	78	77
Chickens	1,478	1,757	1,792

Source: FAO.

LIVESTOCK PRODUCTS

('000 metric tons unless otherwise indicated)

	2008	2009	2010
Cattle meat	14.1	13.9	12.3
Pig meat	39.4	33.1	34.0
Chicken meat	13.2	14.9	16.0
Cows' milk	693.6	670.6	675.3
Hen eggs	9.2	10.8	11.4
Honey (metric tons)	501	575	681
Butter*	6.7	8.0	4.9
Cheese*	19.8	21.7	16.8

* FAO estimates.

Source: FAO.

Forestry

ROUNDWOOD REMOVALS

('000 cubic metres, excl. bark)

	2008	2009*	2010*
Sawlogs, veneer logs and logs for sleepers	2,232	2,457	3,330
Pulpwood	1,431	1,584	2,475
Other industrial wood	45	63	54
Fuel wood	1,152	1,296	1,701
Total	4,860	4,860	7,560

* Unofficial figures.

Source: FAO.

SAWNWOOD PRODUCTION

('000 cubic metres, incl. railway sleepers)

	2008	2009	2010*
Coniferous (softwood)	991	1,018	1,150
Broadleaved (hardwood)	129	110	210
Total	1,120	1,128	1,360

* Unofficial figures.

Source: FAO.

Fishing

('000 metric tons, live weight)

	2007	2008	2009
Capture	97.8	101.0	97.4
Atlantic herring	26.1	31.8	33.2
European sprat	51.0	48.6	47.3
Northern prawn	12.1	12.7	8.6
Aquaculture	0.8	0.8	0.7
Total catch	98.6	101.9	98.1

Source: FAO.

Mining

('000 metric tons)

	2008	2009	2010*
Oil shale	16,100	14,900	17,900
Peat	733	860	964

* Preliminary figures.

Industry

SELECTED PRODUCTS

('000 metric tons unless otherwise indicated)

	2008	2009	2010*
Distilled spirits ('000 hectolitres)	202.8	186.6	150.7
Wine ('000 hectolitres)	38.8	40.2	62.0
Beer ('000 hectolitres)	1,281.8	1,223.0	1,291.7
Soft drinks ('000 hectolitres)	1,094.5	903.6	535.7
Woven cotton fabric ('000 sq metres)	32,638	16,174	10,427
Carpets ('000 sq metres)	2,296	1,813	2,411
Footwear ('000 pairs)	1,167	1,016	1,167
Plywood ('000 cubic metres)	n.a.	21.8	36.0
Particle board ('000 cubic metres)	251.0	133.5	285.6
Fibreboard (million sq metres)	5.5	2.7	3.6
Chemical wood pulp	61.6	60.5	70.0
Paper	60.5	57.9	69.5
Nitrogenous fertilizers†	91.5	9.4	0.3
Building bricks (million)	42.4	14.6	21.2
Cement	808.0	326.2	375.0
Electric energy (million kWh)	10,581	8,780	12,964

* Preliminary figures.

† In terms of nitrogen (N).

Finance

CURRENCY AND EXCHANGE RATES

Monetary Units
100 cents = 1 euro (€).

Sterling, Dollar and Euro Equivalents (30 December 2011)
£1 sterling = 1.195 euros;
US $1 = 0.773 euros;
€10 = £8.37 = $12.94.

Average Exchange Rate (euros per US $)
2009 0.7198
2010 0.7550
2011 0.7194

Note: In June 1992 the kroon replaced the rouble of the former USSR in Estonia, initially at a rate of one kroon per 10 roubles. The kroon was included in the second European exchange rate mechanism (ERM II) from June 2004, with a central parity of 1 euro = 15.6466 kroons. On 1 January 2011 the euro was introduced to circulate alongside the kroon until 14 January, after which period the euro was formally adopted as the sole official currency of Estonia.

GOVERNMENT FINANCE

(general government transactions, non-cash basis, million kroons)*

Summary of Balances

	2007	2008	2009
Revenue	91,471	93,290	94,142
Less Expense	76,687	91,322	92,010
Net operating balance	14,784	1,968	2,132
Less Net acquisition of non-financial assets	8,483	9,249	5,942
Net lending/borrowing	6,301	−7,281	−3,811

Revenue

	2007	2008	2009
Tax revenue	51,754	50,449	48,622
Taxes on goods and services	32,478	29,712	31,518
Taxes on income, profits and capital gains	18,724	19,982	16,349
Taxes on property	552	755	755
Social contributions	26,588	29,914	28,828
Social security contribution	11,609	13,141	13,033
Total (incl. others)	91,471	93,290	94,142

Expense/Outlays

Expense by economic type†	2007	2008	2009
Compensation of employees	23,887	28,633	27,740
Use of goods and services	15,565	17,829	16,632
Consumption of fixed capital	3,674	4,152	4,496
Interest	418	588	699
Subsidies	2,152	2,526	2,151
Social benefits	24,781	30,805	34,559
Total (incl. others)	76,687	91,322	92,010

Outlays by function of government	2006	2007	2008
General public services	5,947	7,728	7,297
Defence	2,669	3,209	4,434
Public order and safety	4,376	5,422	6,892
Economic affairs	9,434	11,252	12,225
Environment protection	1,565	2,128	2,753
Housing and community amenities	76	1,533	1,569
Health	8,801	10,788	13,028
Recreation, culture and religion	4,861	4,905	5,776
Education	12,664	14,610	16,805
Social protection	19,722	23,462	29,492
Statistical discrepancy	268	133	301
Total	70,383	85,170	100,571

* Figures represent a consolidation of the operations of the Government, comprising all central and local government accounts.

† Including net acquisition of non-financial assets.

Source: IMF, *Government Finance Statistics Yearbook*.

INTERNATIONAL RESERVES

(US $ million at 31 December)

	2008	2009	2010
Gold (national valuation)	7.16	9.12	11.63
IMF special drawing rights	0.09	97.24	95.52
Reserve position in IMF	0.01	0.01	0.01
Foreign exchange	3,964.77	3,874.69	2,460.36
Total	3,972.03	3,981.06	2,567.52

Source: IMF, *International Financial Statistics*.

MONEY SUPPLY

(million kroons at 31 December)

	2008	2009	2010
Currency outside depository corporations	10,091	8,070	4,099
Transferable deposits	57,839	56,511	72,689
Other deposits	61,102	65,556	56,714
Securities other than shares	15,756	1,392	596
Broad money	144,788	131,529	134,098

Source: IMF, *International Financial Statistics*.

COST OF LIVING

(Consumer Price Index; base: 2000 = 100)

	2006	2007	2008
Food (incl. beverages)	124.2	135.8	155.1
Fuel and light	163.4	185.5	231.4
Clothing (incl. footwear)	114.0	118.0	122.5
Rent	154.1	195.3	187.4
All items (incl. others)	124.4	132.5	146.3

2009: Food 148.9; All items (incl. others) 146.3.

2010: Food 153.4; All items (incl. others) 150.6.

Source: ILO.

NATIONAL ACCOUNTS
(million euros at current prices)

Expenditure on the Gross Domestic Product

	2008	2009	2010
Final consumption expenditure	11,996.0	10,459.6	10,440.2
Households	8,656.9	7,200.8	7,235.1
Non-profit institutions serving households	207.7	212.6	214.3
General government	3,131.4	3,046.2	2,990.8
Gross capital formation	4,953.9	2,600.8	2,793.6
Gross fixed capital formation	4,848.6	2,969.3	2,694.3
Changes in inventories; Acquisitions, less disposals, of valuables	105.3	–368.5	99.3
Total domestic expenditure	16,949.8	13,060.4	13,233.8
Exports of goods and services	11,547.2	8,960.8	11,360.7
Less Imports of goods and services	12,244.5	8,153.6	10,378.0
Statistical discrepancy	51.6	–28.0	88.8
GDP in market prices	16,304.2	13,839.6	14,305.3

Gross Domestic Product by Economic Activity

	2008	2009	2010
Agriculture, forestry and fishing	438.1	332.3	411.1
Mining and quarrying	150.4	137.9	171.2
Manufacturing	2,228.8	1,704.9	2,047.5
Electricity, gas and water supply	496.0	523.2	633.2
Construction	1,438.0	830.1	712.8
Wholesale and retail trade; repair of motor vehicles, motorcycles and personal and household goods	1,944.3	1,440.2	1,486.8
Hotels and restaurants	211.0	147.3	137.6
Transport, storage and communications	1,139.6	937.2	1,104.9
Financial intermediation	617.8	467.1	449.4
Real estate, renting and business activities	1,482.6	1,368.2	1,358.5
Public administration and defence; compulsory social security	924.5	935.3	915.0
Education	684.5	654.2	635.0
Health and social work	517.7	487.6	470.3
Other community, social and personal service activities	2,239.3	1,981.7	1,962.9
Gross value added in basic prices	14,512.7	11,947.2	12,496.1
Taxes on products; *Less* Subsidies on products	1,791.5	1,892.3	1,809.1
GDP in market prices	16,304.2	13,839.6	14,305.3

BALANCE OF PAYMENTS
(US $ million)

	2008	2009	2010
Exports of goods f.o.b.	12,572.4	9,145.8	11,641.3
Imports of goods f.o.b.	–15,696.2	–9,921.1	–11,972.0
Trade balance	–3,123.8	–775.2	–330.7
Exports of services	5,192.1	4,434.7	4,527.9
Imports of services	–3,362.8	–2,535.2	–2,798.5
Balance on goods and services	–1,294.5	1,124.3	1,398.7
Other income received	1,700.0	917.0	907.3
Other income paid	–3,013.0	–1,614.1	–1,973.8
Balance on goods, services and income	–2,607.6	427.2	332.2
Current transfers received	726.1	709.4	788.7
Current transfers paid	–474.8	–395.7	–447.6
Current balance	–2,356.3	740.8	673.2

—continued	2008	2009	2010
Capital account (net)	285.1	690.2	693.8
Direct investment abroad	–1,130.6	–1,575.2	–127.2
Direct investment from abroad	1,748.5	1,908.2	1,539.1
Portfolio investment assets	943.9	–678.6	–364.6
Portfolio investment liabilities	–244.6	–1,408.3	–193.0
Financial derivatives assets	62.5	22.5	–3.5
Financial derivatives liabilities	9.3	–6.6	44.3
Other investment assets	–488.0	1,237.4	–1,736.2
Other investment liabilities	1,650.6	–815.1	–1,350.2
Net errors and omissions	239.4	–83.0	–287.7
Overall balance	719.9	32.2	–1,112.1

Source: IMF, *International Financial Statistics*.

External Trade

PRINCIPAL COMMODITIES
(distribution by HS, € million)

Imports c.i.f.	2008	2009	2010
Prepared foodstuffs; beverages, spirits and vinegar; tobacco and manufactured substitutes	639.5	531.9	581.7
Mineral products	1,735.0	1,420.5	1,614.2
Mineral fuels, mineral oils and products of their distillation; bituminous substances, etc.	1,707.4	1,392.0	1,580.4
Products of chemical or allied industries	873.0	693.6	734.8
Plastics, rubber and articles thereof	534.2	391.9	521.5
Plastics and articles thereof	434.5	324.2	423.5
Pulp of wood or of other fibrous cellulosic material; waste and scrap of paper or paperboard	240.1	202.0	223.2
Paper-making material; paper and paperboard and articles thereof	210.2	173.0	206.2
Textiles and textile articles	550.6	394.0	457.6
Base metals and articles of base metal	1,164.6	560.3	825.4
Iron and steel	531.9	183.0	322.1
Articles of iron and steel	314.8	203.5	253.4
Machinery and mechanical appliances; electrical equipment; sound and television apparatus	2,353.0	1,399.8	2,184.9
Nuclear reactors, boilers, machinery and mechanical appliances; parts thereof	1,035.7	583.4	714.0
Electrical machinery equipment and parts; sound and television apparatus parts and accessories	1,317.3	816.4	1,470.9
Vehicles, aircraft, vessels and associated transport equipment	1,194.3	451.7	656.2
Railway or tramway locomotives, rolling-stock and parts thereof	28.2	14.8	28.5
Vehicles other than railway or tramway rolling-stock, and parts and accessories	1,101.6	393.8	549.1
Total (incl. others)	10,896.4	7,269.9	9,250.4

Exports f.o.b.	2008	2009	2010
Live animals and animal products	255.6	233.3	319.2
Prepared foodstuffs; beverages, spirits and vinegar; tobacco and manufactured substitutes	350.2	301.7	349.9
Cocoa and cocoa preparations	7.4	11.9	15.2
Mineral products	1,026.8	1,083.5	1,376.4
Mineral fuels, mineral oils and products of their distillation	968.1	1,056.0	1,350.6
Products of chemical or allied industries	456.8	359.4	395.5
Plastics, rubber and articles thereof	266.7	203.2	279.6
Wood and articles thereof; wood charcoal	718.5	561.4	793.0
Pulp of wood or of other fibrous cellulosic material; waste and scrap of paper or paperboard	250.4	216.1	277.8
Paper-making material; paper and paperboard and articles thereof	122.3	97.8	122.0
Textiles and textile articles	354.3	261.4	300.2
Non-knitted clothing and accessories	156.1	121.3	140.8
Base metals and articles of base metal	1,012.4	559.2	793.9
Iron and steel	466.1	169.9	315.3
Articles of iron or steel	321.2	256.7	260.1
Machinery and mechanical appliances; electrical equipment; sound and television apparatus	1,847.1	1,268.6	1,978.5
Nuclear reactors, boilers, machinery and mechanical appliances; parts thereof	591.5	431.5	528.9
Electrical machinery equipment and parts; sound and television apparatus parts and accessories	1,255.6	837.1	1,449.6
Vehicles, aircraft, vessels and associated transport equipment	664.5	422.9	572.7
Miscellaneous manufactured articles	614.5	537.6	667.4
Furniture; bedding, mattresses, cushions, etc.; lamps and lighting fittings; prefabricated buildings	544.0	476.1	591.7
Total (incl. others)	8,470.1	6,486.9	8,747.8

PRINCIPAL TRADING PARTNERS
(€ million)

Imports c.i.f.	2008	2009	2010
Belarus	318.3	118.1	118.4
Belgium	218.9	153.0	155.1
China, People's Republic	232.3	145.4	281.6
Denmark	233.1	172.0	175.1
Finland	1,540.1	1,047.2	1,374.1
France	220.6	186.8	164.2
Germany	1,455.7	774.3	1,042.7
Hong Kong	68.4	42.7	64.8
Hungary	70.8	38.2	54.9
Italy	282.9	163.9	220.6
Japan	51.0	17.4	27.1
Latvia	987.6	764.7	1,014.3
Lithuania	966.1	792.9	724.2
Netherlands	362.2	257.4	308.3
Norway	74.0	94.4	128.5
Poland	497.5	410.5	586.2
Russia	832.4	597.4	762.8
Sweden	1,091.1	610.7	1,009.0
Ukraine	116.5	45.5	71.7
United Kingdom	315.9	162.4	187.6
USA	128.6	100.7	92.8
Total (incl. others)	10,896.4	7,269.9	9,250.4

Exports f.o.b.	2008	2009	2010
Belgium	101.2	123.0	112.3
China, People's Republic	53.7	54.8	112.2
Denmark	275.3	225.4	217.7
Finland	1,557.9	1,201.4	1,487.6
France	115.0	149.5	214.8
Germany	429.1	395.4	454.7
Hungary	17.3	16.3	17.3
Italy	104.9	73.5	80.7
Latvia	843.9	613.3	779.6
Lithuania	479.9	308.4	437.4
Netherlands	194.1	160.5	203.3
Norway	279.9	205.8	299.8
Poland	159.9	113.4	142.7
Russia	880.4	601.1	844.4
Sweden	1,169.5	816.5	1,364.5
Ukraine	141.0	72.3	88.4
United Kingdom	226.6	131.2	171.9
USA	407.4	274.0	330.9
Total (incl. others)	8,470.1	6,486.9	8,747.8

Transport

RAILWAYS
(traffic)

	2008	2009	2010
Passengers carried ('000)	5,284	4,886	4,803
Passenger-kilometres (million)	274.4	249.4	247.9
Freight carried ('000 metric tons)	53,561	38,400	46,726
Freight ton-kilometres (million)	5,960.9	5,934.1	6,642.3

ROAD TRAFFIC
('000 motor vehicles in use at 31 December)

	2008	2009	2010
Passenger cars	551.8	545.7	552.7
Buses and coaches	4.3	4.1	4.2
Lorries and vans	83.3	81.1	81.2
Motorcycles	17.6	18.6	19.7
Trailers	60.1	62.0	65.5

SHIPPING

Merchant Fleet
(registered at 31 December)

	2007	2008	2009
Number of vessels	122	116	115
Total displacement ('000 grt)	389.8	363.5	374.9

Source: IHS Fairplay, *World Fleet Statistics*.

International Sea-borne Freight Traffic
('000 metric tons)

	2008	2009	2010
Goods loaded	28,102	29,619	34,540
Goods unloaded	8,057	8,864	11,305

CIVIL AVIATION
(traffic on scheduled services)

	2008	2009	2010
Passengers carried ('000)	805.6	660.5	663.5
Passenger-km (million)	979.7	854.9	874.1

2007: Freight carried ('000 metric tons) 3.7; Total ton-km (million) 2.4.

Tourism

FOREIGN TOURIST ARRIVALS BY COUNTRY OF ORIGIN*

	2008	2009	2010
Finland	728,181	750,984	832,874
Germany	91,915	75,966	84,454
Latvia	79,527	68,320	72,684
Russia	82,280	93,947	141,964
Sweden	86,308	77,470	81,196
United Kingdom and Ireland	46,575	33,395	35,692
Total (incl. others)	1,433,346	1,380,540	1,563,952

* Figures refer to arrivals at registered accommodation establishments.

Tourism receipts (US $ million, incl. passenger transport): 1,361 in 2006; 1,416 in 2007; 1,662 in 2008 (Source: World Tourism Organization).

Communications Media

	2008	2009	2010
Telephones ('000 main lines in use)	498.1	492.8	482.2
Mobile cellular telephones ('000 subscribers)	1,624.5	1,570.5	1,652.8
Internet subscribers ('000)	324.5	342.9	n.a.
Broadband subscribers ('000)	281.5	301.1	326.5
Book production: titles	4,685	4,551	3,760
Book production: copies (million)	7.3	6.9	5.5
Daily newspapers: number	17	15	13
Non-daily newspapers: number	138	136	118
Other periodicals: number	1,254	1,166	1,153
Other periodicals: average annual circulation ('000 copies)	31,702.3	26,889.3	25,800.0

Radio receivers in use: 221,000 in 1996.

Television receivers in use: 900,000 in 2001.

Personal computers: 342,000 (255.1 per 1,000 persons) in 2008.

Sources: partly UN, *Statistical Yearbook*, and International Telecommunication Union.

Education

(2009/10 unless otherwise indicated)

	Institutions	Teachers	Students
Pre-primary	638	6,754*	64,300
Primary	323†	6,141*	76,026‡
General secondary	226	12,259§	94,935‡
Special	43	n.a.	3,779
Vocational and professional	51	870	28,012
Universities, etc.	33	6,842‖	69,113¶

* 2007/08.
† 2004/05.
‡ 2006/07.
§ 2001/02.
‖ 2005/06.
¶ Including students enrolled in evening and correspondence courses.

Pupil-teacher ratio (primary education, UNESCO estimate): 11.9 in 2008/09 (Source: UNESCO Institute for Statistics).

Adult literacy rate (UNESCO estimates): 99.8% (males 99.8%; females 99.8%) in 2009 (Source: UNESCO Institute for Statistics).

Directory

The Government

HEAD OF STATE

President: TOOMAS HENDRIK ILVES (elected by vote of the Riigikogu 23 September 2006; inaugurated 9 October 2006; re-elected 29 August 2011; inaugurated 10 October 2011).

COUNCIL OF MINISTERS
(May 2012)

A coalition of the Estonian Reform Party (ERP) and the Union of Pro Patria and Res Publica.

Prime Minister: ANDRUS ANSIP (ERP).

Minister of the Interior: KEN-MARTI VAHER (Union of Pro Patria and Res Publica).

Minister of Foreign Affairs: URMAS PAET (ERP).

Minister of Justice: KRISTEN MICHAL (ERP).

Minister of Economic Affairs and Communications: JUHAN PARTS (Union of Pro Patria and Res Publica).

Minister of Finance: JÜRGEN LIGI (ERP).

Minister of the Environment: KEIT PENTUS (ERP).

Minister of Culture: REIN LANG (ERP).

Minister of Education and Research: JAAK AAVIKSOO (Union of Pro Patria and Res Publica).

Minister of Agriculture: HELIR-VALDOR SEEDER (Union of Pro Patria and Res Publica).

Minister of Social Affairs: HANNO PEVKUR (ERP).

Minister of Defence: JAAK AAVIKSOO (acting) (Union of Pro Patria and Res Publica).

Minister of Regional Affairs: SIIM VALMAR KIISLER (Union of Pro Patria and Res Publica).

MINISTRIES

Office of the President: A. Weizenbergi 39, Tallinn 15050; tel. 631-6202; fax 631-6250; e-mail vpinfo@vpk.ee; internet www.president.ee.

Office of the Prime Minister: Stenbocki maja, Rahukohtu 3, Tallinn 15161; tel. 693-5701; fax 693-5554; e-mail riigikantselei@riigikantselei.ee; internet www.valitsus.ee.

Ministry of Agriculture: Lai 39/41, Tallinn 15056; tel. 625-6101; fax 625-6200; e-mail pm@agri.ee; internet www.agri.ee.

Ministry of Culture: Suur Karja 23, Tallinn 15076; tel. 628-2250; fax 628-2200; e-mail min@kul.ee; internet www.kul.ee.

Ministry of Defence: Sakala 1, Tallinn 15094; tel. 717-0022; fax 717-0001; e-mail info@kmin.ee; internet www.mod.gov.ee.

Ministry of Economic Affairs and Communications: Harju 11, Tallinn 15072; tel. 625-6342; fax 631-3660; e-mail info@mkm.ee; internet www.mkm.ee.

Ministry of Education and Research: Munga 18, Tartu 50088; tel. 735-0222; fax 730-1080; e-mail hm@hm.ee; internet www.hm.ee.

Ministry of the Environment: Narva mnt. 7A, Tallinn 15172; tel. 626-2802; fax 626-2801; e-mail keskkonnaministeerium@envir.ee; internet www.envir.ee.

Ministry of Finance: Suur-Ameerika 1, Tallinn 15006; tel. 611-3558; fax 611-3664; e-mail info@fin.ee; internet www.fin.ee.

Ministry of Foreign Affairs: Islandi Väljak 1, Tallinn 15049; tel. 637-7000; fax 637-7099; e-mail vminfo@vm.ee; internet www.vm.ee.

Ministry of the Interior: Pikk 61, Tallinn 15065; tel. 612-5008; e-mail info@siseministeerium.ee; internet www.siseministeerium.ee; Note: The Office of the Minister of Regional Affairs forms part of the Ministry of the Interior.

Ministry of Justice: Tõnismägi 5A, Tallinn 15191; tel. 620-8100; fax 620-8109; e-mail info@just.ee; internet www.just.ee.

Ministry of Social Affairs: Gonsiori 29, Tallinn 15027; tel. 626-9301; fax 699-2209; e-mail info@sm.ee; internet www.sm.ee.

President

On 29 August 2011 a presidential election was conducted in the 101-member Riigikogu (State Assembly). TOOMAS HENDRIK ILVES, the incumbent, was elected to a second term of office in the first round of voting, securing 73 votes, more than the requisite two-thirds' majority (68 votes). The only other candidate, INDREK TARAND, received 25 votes. ILVES assumed office on 10 October.

Legislature

Riigikogu
(State Assembly)

Lossi plats 1A, Tallinn 15165; tel. 631-6331; fax 631-6334; e-mail riigikogu@riigikogu.ee; internet www.riigikogu.ee.

Speaker: ENE ERGMA.

General Election, 6 March 2011

Parties	Votes	%	Seats
Estonian Reform Party	164,255	28.56	33
Estonian Centre Party	134,124	23.32	26
Union of Pro Patria and Res Publica	118,023	20.52	23
Estonian Social Democratic Party	98,307	17.09	19
Other parties	44,542	7.74	—
Individual candidates	15,882	2.76	—
Total	575,133	100.00	101

Election Commission

Estonian National Electoral Committee (Vabariigi Valimiskomisjon): Lossi plats 1A, Tallinn 15165; tel. 631-6540; fax 631-6541; e-mail info@vvk.ee; internet www.vvk.ee; Chair. HEIKI SIBUL.

Political Organizations

Estonian Centre Party (Eesti Keskerakond): Toom-Rüütli 3/5, Tallinn 10130; tel. 627-3460; fax 627-3461; e-mail keskerakond@keskerakond.ee; internet www.keskerakond.ee; f. 1991; absorbed the Estonian Green Party in 1998 and the Estonian Pensioners' Party in 2005; Chair. EDGAR SAVISAAR; Sec.-Gen. PRIIT TOOBAL; 9,000 mems.

Estonian Christian Democrats (Eesti Kristlikud Demokraadid): Jaama 2, 3rd Floor, Tallinn 11621; tel. 659-2357; fax 626-1431; e-mail ekd@erakond.eu; internet www.ekd.ee; f. 1998; fmrly Estonian Christian People's Party; present name adopted 2006; Chair. PEETER VÕSU.

Estonian Conservative People's Party (Eesti Konservatiivseks Rahvaerakonnaks): Pärnu mnt. 30–5, Tallinn 10141; tel. 616-1790; fax 616-1791; e-mail erl@erl.ee; f. 2000 as Estonian People's Union; present name adopted March 2012; right-wing; Chair. MARGO MILJAND; 10,000 mems (2009).

Estonian Greens (Erakond Eestimaa Rohelised): Haabersti kandekeskus, POB 4740, Tallinn 13503; tel. 502-6816; e-mail info@erakond.ee; internet roheline.erakond.ee; f. 2006; Chair. ALEKSANDER LAANE.

Estonian Reform Party (ERP) (Eesti Reformierakond): Tõnismagi 9, Tallinn 10119; tel. 680-8080; fax 680-8081; e-mail info@reform.ee; internet www.reform.ee; f. 1994; liberal; Chair. ANDRUS ANSIP; 11,151 mems (2012).

Estonian Social Democratic Party (ESDP) (Sotsiaaldemokraatlik Erakond): Ahtri 10A, Tallinn 10151; tel. 611-6040; fax 611-6050; e-mail kantselei@sotsdem.ee; internet www.sotsdem.ee; f. 1999 as the People's Party Moderates, by merger of the People's Party and the Moderates' Party; name changed in 2004; Chair. SVEN MIKSER; Sec.-Gen. RANDEL LÄNTS; 4,500 mems (2011).

Estonian United Left Party (Eestimaa Ühendatud Vasakpartei): Estonia pst. 7, Tallinn 10143; tel. 645-5335; fax 645-5336; e-mail info@vasak.ee; f. 2008 by merger of the Constitution Party (representing the Russian-speaking minority in Estonia) and the Estonian Left Party; Co-Chair. SERGEI JÜRGENS, HEINO RÜÜTEL; 2,500 mems (2008).

Union of Pro Patria and Res Publica (Isamaa ja Res Publica Liit—IRL): Paldiski mnt. 13, Tallinn 10137; tel. 624-0400; fax 669-1071; e-mail info@irl.ee; internet www.irl.ee; f. 2006 by merger of the Pro Patria Union (f. 1995) and the Union for the Republic Res Publica (f. 2001); centre-right; Chair. URMAS REINSALU; 9,000 mems (2008).

Diplomatic Representation

EMBASSIES IN ESTONIA

Austria: Vambola 6, Tallinn 10114; tel. 627-8740; fax 631-4365; e-mail tallinn-ob@bmeia.gv.at; Ambassador RENATE KOBLER.

Azerbaijan: Pirita tee 20T, Tallinn 10127; tel. 640-5050; fax 640-5051; e-mail tallinn@mission.mfa.gov.az; Ambassador TOFIG ZULFUGAROV.

Belarus: Magdaleena 3B, Tallinn 11312; tel. 651-5500; fax 655-8001; e-mail estonia@belembassy.org; internet www.estonia.belembassy.org; Chargé d'affaires a.i. VADIM LAZERKO.

Belgium: Rataskaevu 2–9, Tallinn 10123; tel. 627-4100; fax 627-4101; e-mail tallinn@diplobel.fed.be; internet www.diplomatie.be/tallinn; Ambassador NICOLAAS BUYCK.

Brazil: Hotell Kolm Õde, Pikk 71, Tallinn 10133; tel. 633-7070; fax 633-7871; e-mail brasemb.talin@itamaraty.gov.br; Ambassador VERGNIAUD ELYSEU FILHO.

Bulgaria: Lauteri 5, Tallinn 10114; tel. 648-0388; fax 648-1110; e-mail heiki@kranich.ee; Chargé d'affaires a.i. RALITSA DYUBRAILOVA.

China, People's Republic: Narva mnt. 98, Tallinn 15009; tel. 601-5830; fax 601-5833; e-mail chinaemb@online.ee; internet www.chinaembassy.ee; Ambassador QU ZHE.

Czech Republic: Lahe 4, Tallinn 10150; tel. 627-4400; fax 631-4716; e-mail tallinn@embassy.mzv.cz; internet www.mfa.cz/tallinn; Ambassador ALEXANDR LANGER.

Denmark: Wismari 5, Tallinn 15047; tel. 630-6400; fax 630-6421; e-mail tllamb@um.dk; internet estland.um.dk; Ambassador UFFE BALSLEV.

Finland: Kohtu 4, Tallinn 15180; tel. 610-3200; fax 610-3281; e-mail sanomat.tal@formin.fi; internet www.finland.ee; Ambassador ALEKSI HÄRKÖNEN.

France: Toom-Kuninga 20, Tallinn 15185; tel. 616-1600; fax 616-1608; e-mail info@ambafrance-ee.org; internet www.ambafrance-ee.org; Ambassador FRÉDÉRIC BILLET.

Georgia: Viru väljak 2, Tallinn 10111; tel. 698-8590; fax 641-3000; e-mail tallinn.emb@mfa.gov.ge; internet www.estonia.mfa.gov.ge; Ambassador RUSLAN ABASHIDZE.

Germany: Toom-Kuninga 11, Tallinn 15048; tel. 627-5300; fax 627-5304; e-mail info@tallinn.diplo.de; internet www.tallinn.diplo.de; Ambassador CHRISTIAN MATTHIAS SCHLAGA.

Greece: Pärnu mnt. 12, 2nd Floor, Tallinn 10148; tel. 640-3560; fax 640-3561; e-mail gremb.tal@mfa.gr; internet www.mfa.gr/tallinn; Ambassador POLYDORE KOKONAS.

Hungary: Narva mnt. 122, Tallinn 15025; tel. 605-1880; fax 605-4088; e-mail mission.tal@mfa.gov.hu; internet www.mfa.gov.hu/kulkepviselet/ee/ee; Ambassador ERIK HAUPT.

Ireland: Vene 2, 2nd Floor, Tallinn 10123; tel. 681-1888; fax 681-1889; e-mail tallinnembassy@dfa.ie; internet www.embassyofireland.ee; Ambassador PETER MCIVOR.

Italy: Vene 2, 3rd Floor, Tallinn 15075; tel. 627-6160; fax 631-1370; e-mail ambasciata.tallinn@esteri.it; internet www.ambtallinn.esteri.it; Ambassador ROSA MARIA CHICCO FERRARO.

Japan: Harju 6, Tallinn 15069; tel. 631-0531; fax 631-0533; e-mail info@ti.mofa.go.jp; internet www.ee.emb-japan.go.jp; Ambassador HIDEAKI HOSHI (resident in Helsinki, Finland).

Latvia: Tõnismägi 10, Tallinn 10119; tel. 627-7850; fax 627-7855; e-mail embassy.estonia@mfa.gov.lv; Ambassador KĀRLIS EIHENBAUMS.

Lithuania: Uus 15, Tallinn 15070; tel. 616-4991; fax 641-2013; e-mail amb.ee@urm.lt; internet ee.mfa.lt; Ambassador JUOZAS BERNATONIS.

Macedonia, former Yugoslav republic: Suurtüki 4 A/13, Tallinn 10133; tel. and fax 644-0494; e-mail nenad.kolev@mfa.gov.mk; Chargé d'affaires a.i. NENAD KOLEV.

Moldova: Tatari 20/9–10, Tallinn 10116; tel. 642-0203; fax 642-0204; e-mail tallinn@mfa.md; internet www.estonia.mfa.md; Ambassador VICTOR GUZUN.

Netherlands: Rahukohtu 4-I, Tallinn 10130; tel. 680-5500; fax 680-5501; e-mail info@netherlandsembassy.ee; internet www.netherlandsembassy.ee; Ambassador MAURITS R. JOCHEMS.

Norway: Harju 6, Tallinn 15054; tel. 627-1000; fax 627-1001; e-mail emb.tallinn@mfa.no; internet www.norra.ee; Ambassador LISE KLEVEN GREVSTAD.

Poland: Suur-Karja 1/Vana-Turg 2, Tallinn 10140; tel. 627-8201; fax 644-5221; e-mail eetalamb@msz.gov.pl; internet www.tallinn.polemb.net; Ambassador GRZEGORZ M. POZNAŃSKI.

Russia: Pikk 19, Tallinn 10133; tel. 646-4175; fax 646-4178; e-mail vensaat@online.ee; internet www.rusemb.ee; Ambassador YURII N. MERZLYAKOV.

Spain: Liivalaia 13–15, 6th Floor, Tallinn 10118; tel. 667-6651; fax 631-3767; e-mail emb.tallinn@mae.es; internet www.mae.es/embajadas/tallin; Ambassador ÁLVARO DE LA RIVA GUZMÁN DE FRUTOS.

Sweden: Pikk 28, Tallinn 15055; tel. 640-5600; fax 640-5695; e-mail swedemb@neti.ee; internet www.sweden.ee; Ambassador JAN PALMSTIERNA.

Turkey: Narva mnt. 30, Tallinn 10152; tel. 627-2880; fax 627-2885; e-mail embassy.tallinn@mfa.gov.tr; internet tallinn.emb.mfa.gov.tr; Ambassador AYŞENUR ALPASLAN.

Ukraine: Lahe 6, Tallinn 15170; tel. 601-5815; fax 601-5816; e-mail embassyofukraine@gmail.com; internet www.mfa.gov.ua/estonia; Ambassador VIKTOR V. KRYSHANIVSKY.

United Kingdom: Wismari 6, Tallinn 10136; tel. 667-4700; fax 667-4755; e-mail information@britishembassy.ee; internet www.ukinestonia.fco.gov.uk; Ambassador CHRISTOPHER B. HOLTBY.

USA: Kentmanni 20, Tallinn 15099; tel. 668-8100; fax 668-8265; e-mail usasaatkond@state.gov; internet estonia.usembassy.gov; Ambassador MICHAEL C. POLT.

Judicial System

Supreme Court (Riigikohus)

Lossi 17, Tartu 50093; tel. 730-9002; fax 730-9003; e-mail info@riigikohus.ee; internet www.nc.ee.

Chief Justice and Chairman of the Constitutional Review Chamber: MÄRT RASK.

Chairman of the Civil Chamber: ANTS KULL.

Chairman of the Criminal Chamber: PRIIT PIKAMÄE.

Chairman of the Administrative Law Chamber: TÕNU ANTON.

Office of the Chancellor of Justice (Õiguskantsleri Kantselei): Kohtu 8, Tallinn 15193; tel. 693-8404; fax 693-8401; e-mail info@oiguskantsler.ee; internet www.oiguskantsler.ee; f. 1993; reviews general application of legislative and executive powers and of local governments for conformity with the Constitution, supervises activities of state agencies in guaranteeing constitutional rights and freedoms; Chancellor of Justice INDREK TEDER.

Public Prosecutor's Office (Riigiprokuratuur): Wismari 7, Tallinn 15188; tel. 613-9400; fax 613-9402; e-mail info@prokuratuur.ee; internet www.prokuratuur.ee; State Prosecutor-Gen. NORMAN AAS.

Religion

CHRISTIANITY

Protestant Churches

Estonian Conference of Seventh-day Adventists (Seitsmenda Päeva Adventistide Kogudus Eesti Liit): Lille 18, Tartu 51010; tel. and fax 734-3211; e-mail info@advent.ee; internet www.advent.ee; f. 1917; Pres. DAVID NÕMMIK.

Estonian Evangelical Lutheran Church (Eesti Evangeelne Luterlik Kirik): Kiriku plats 3, Tallinn 10130; tel. 627-7350; fax 627-7352; e-mail konsistoorium@eelk.ee; internet www.eelk.ee; 172,000 mems; Archbishop Most Rev. ANDRES PÕDER.

Union of Free Evangelical Christian and Baptist Churches of Estonia (Eesti Evangeeliumi Kristlaste ja Baptistide Koguduste Liit): Koskla 18, Tallinn 10615; tel. 670-0698; fax 650-6008; e-mail liit@ekklesia.ee; internet www.ekklesia.ee; f. 1884; Pres. MEEGO REMMEL.

United Methodist Church in Estonia (Eesti Metodisti Kirik): EMK Kirikuvalitsus, Narva mnt. 51, Tallinn 10152; tel. 668-8497; fax 668-8498; e-mail keskus@metodistikirik.ee; internet www.metodistikirik.ee; f. 1907; forms part of the Northern European Area of the United Methodist Church; Superintendent TAAVI HOLLMAN.

The Eastern Orthodox Church

Since February 1996 the Estonian Apostolic Orthodox Church has been under the jurisdiction of the Ecumenical Patriarchate of Constantinople (based in İstanbul, Turkey), as it had been between 1923 and 1940. The Estonian Orthodox Church of the Moscow Patriarchate was officially registered in April 2002.

Estonian Apostolic Orthodox Church (Eesti Apostlik Õigeusu Kirik): Wismari 32, Tallinn 10136; tel. and fax 660-0780; e-mail eoc@eoc.ee; internet www.eoc.ee; Metropolitan of Tallinn and All Estonia STEPHANOS; 60 congregations.

Estonian Orthodox Church (Moscow Patriarchate) (Moskva Patriarhaadi Eesti Õigeusu Kirik/Estonskaya Pravoslavnaya Tserkov Moskovskogo Patriarkhata): Pikk 64/4, Tallinn 10133; tel. 641-1301; fax 641-1302; e-mail mpeok@orthodox.ee; internet www.orthodox.ee; Metropolitan of Tallinn and All Estonia KORNELIUS; 32 congregations.

The Roman Catholic Church

At 31 December 2009 there were an estimated 5,745 Roman Catholic adherents (of both the Latin and Byzantine rites) in Estonia.

Office of the Apostolic Administrator: Jaan Poska 47A, Tallinn 10150; tel. 601-3079; fax 601-3190; e-mail admapost@online.ee; internet katoliku.ee; Apostolic Administrator Most Rev. PHILIPPE JEAN-CHARLES JOURDAN (Titular Bishop of Pertusa).

ISLAM

Estonian Islamic Congregation: Sütiste 52–76, Tallinn 13420; tel. 652-2403; f. 1928; Chair. of Bd TIMUR SEIFULLEN.

JUDAISM

In the early 2000s there were an estimated 3,000 Jews resident in Estonia, principally in Tallinn.

Jewish Community of Estonia (Eesti Juudi Kogukond/Yevreiskaya Obshchina Estonii): Karu 16, Tallinn; POB 3576, Tallinn 10120; tel. and fax 643-8566; e-mail community@jewish.ee; internet www.jewish.ee; Chair. CILJA LAUD.

The Press

In 2010 there were 13 officially registered daily newspapers and 118 non-daily newspapers published in Estonia. In that year 1,153 periodicals were published.

PRINCIPAL NEWSPAPERS

In Estonian except where otherwise stated.

Äripäev (Business Daily): Pärnu mnt. 105, Tallinn 19094; tel. 667-0111; fax 667-0165; e-mail aripaev@aripaev.ee; internet www.aripaev.ee; f. 1989; five days a week; business and finance; Editor-in-Chief MEELIS MANDEL; circ. 14,200 (Jan. 2011).

Baltic Business News (BBN): Tallinn; tel. 667-0319; e-mail bbn@aripaev.ee; internet www.balticbusinessnews.com; daily; English; online; business and politics; affiliated with *Äripäev*; Editor TOOMAS HÕBEMÄGI.

Eesti Päevaleht (Estonian Daily): Narva mnt. 13, POB 433, Tallinn 10151; tel. 680-4400; fax 680-4401; e-mail mail@epl.ee; internet www.epl.ee; f. 1905; 6 a week; 50% owned by Ekspress Grupp; Editor-in-Chief LEA LARIN; circ. 30,000 (Jan. 2011).

Postimees (Postman): Maakri 23A, Tallinn 10145; tel. 666-2204; fax 666-2301; e-mail online@postimees.ee; internet www.postimees.ee; f. 1857; 6 a week; Editor-in-Chief MERIT KOPLI; circ. 60,300 (Jan. 2011).

SL Õhtuleht (Evening Gazette): Narva mnt. 13, POB 106, Tallinn 10151; tel. 614-4000; fax 614-4001; e-mail leht@ohtuleht.ee; internet www.ohtuleht.ee; f. 2000; 6 a week; 50% owned by Ekspress Grupp; popular; Editor-in-Chief VÄINO KOORBERG; circ. 53,300 (Jan. 2011).

Vesti dnya (News of the Day): Peterburi tee 53, Tallinn 11415; tel. 602-6865; fax 602-6867; e-mail vesti@vesti.ee; internet www.vesti.ee; five days a week; in Russian; also *Vesti nedeli* (News of the Week), Fridays; Chief Editor ALEKSANDR CHAPLYGIN; circ. 8,300 (2008).

PRINCIPAL PERIODICALS

Akadeemia: Ülikooli 21, Tartu 51007; tel. 742-3050; fax 744-1975; e-mail akadeemia@akad.ee; internet www.akad.ee; f. 1989; monthly; journal of the Union of Writers; Editor-in-Chief TOOMAS KIHO; circ. 2,090.

Eesti Arst (Estonian Physician): Pepleri 32, Tartu 51010; tel. 742-7825; fax 742-7825; e-mail eestiarst@eestiarst.ee; internet www

.eestiarst.ee; f. 1922; monthly; Editor-in-Chief ANDRES SOOSAAR; circ. 4,000.

Delovoye Vedomosti (Business Gazette): Pärnu mnt. 105, Tallinn 19094; tel. 667-0080; fax 667-0465; e-mail delo@mbp.ee; internet www.dv.ee; weekly; Russian; affiliated with business daily *Äripäev* (q.v.); Editor-in-Chief OKSANA KABRITS; circ. 4,800 (Jan. 2011).

Den za Dnem (Day to Day): Maakri 23A, Tallinn 10145; tel. 666-2511; fax 666-2395; e-mail tellimus@dzd.ee; internet www.dzd.ee; f. 1993; owned by Eesti Meedia (Schibsted Group); weekly; Russian; Editor-in-Chief YEVGENIYA GARANZHA; circ. 13,200 (Jan. 2011).

Eesti Ekspress (Estonian Express): Narva mnt. 11E, Tallinn 10151; tel. 669-8080; fax 669-8154; e-mail ekspress@ekspress.ee; internet www.ekspress.ee; f. 1923; published regularly till 1940; resumed publication in 1990; weekly; owned by Ekspress Grupp; Publr HANS H. LUIK; Editor-in-Chief PRIIT HÕBEMÄGI; circ. 33,400 (Jan. 2011).

Eesti Kirik (Estonian Church): Ülikooli 1, Tartu 51003; tel. 733-7790; fax 733-7792; e-mail ek@eelk.ee; internet www.eestikirik.ee; f. 1923; weekly; organ of the Estonian Evangelical Lutheran Church; Editor-in-Chief SIRJE SEMM; circ. 2,100.

Eesti Loodus (Estonian Nature): Veski 4, POB 110, Tartu 50002; tel. and fax 742-1143; e-mail toimetus@el.loodus.ee; internet www.loodusajakiri.ee/eesti_loodus; f. 1933; monthly; popular science; illustrated; Editor-in-Chief TOOMAS KUKK; circ. 5,200.

Eesti Naine (Estonian Woman): Maakri 23A, Tallinn 10145; tel. 666-2600; fax 666-2557; e-mail aita.kivi@kirjastus.ee; internet www.naistemaailm.ee; f. 1924; monthly; Editor AITA KIVI; circ. 24,000.

Hea Laps (Good Kid): Harju 1, Tallinn 10146; tel. 631-4428; e-mail tellimine@healaps.ee; internet www.healaps.ee; f. 1994; monthly; for children; Editor-in-Chief LEELO TUNGAL.

Horisont (Horizon): Endla 3, Tallinn 10122; tel. 610-4105; fax 610-4109; e-mail horisont@horisont.ee; internet www.horisont.ee; f. 1967; 6 a year; popular science; Editor-in-Chief KÄRT JÄNES-KAPP; circ. 3,000.

Keel ja Kirjandus (Language and Literature): Roosikrantsi 6, Tallinn 10119; tel. 644-9228; fax 644-1800; e-mail kk@eki.ee; internet www.eki.ee/keeljakirjandus; f. 1958; monthly; publ. by Academy of Sciences and Union of Writers; Editor-in-Chief JOEL SANG; circ. 900.

Kodukiri (Your Home): Maakri 23A, Tallinn 10145; tel. 666-2633; fax 666-2557; e-mail malle.pajula@kirjastus.ee; internet www.naistemaailm.ee; f. 1992; monthly; Editor-in-Chief MALLE PAJULA; circ. 50,000.

Komsomolskaya Pravda—Baltiya (Young Communist League Truth—Baltics): Lembitu tn. 8-2, Tallinn 10114; tel. 6688900; fax 6688902; e-mail info@kompravda.eu; internet www.kompravda.eu; f. 2007; weekly; in Russian; 'Northern European' edition of Komsomolskaya Pravda (Russia); Editor-in-Chief IGOR TETERIN; circ. 15,000 (Jan. 2011).

Maaleht (Country News): Narva mnt. 11E, Tallinn 10151; tel. 661-3300; fax 661-3344; e-mail ml@maaleht.ee; internet www.maaleht.ee; f. 1987; weekly; politics, culture, agriculture and country life; Editor-in-Chief AIVAR VIIDIK; circ. 42,800 (2008).

Oil Shale: Ehitajate tee 5, Tallinn 19086; tel. 501-1827; fax 620-3011; e-mail anto.raukas@gi.ee; internet www.kirj.ee/oilshale; f. 1984; quarterly; geology, chemistry, mining, oil shale industry; Editor-in-Chief ANTO RAUKAS; circ. 200.

Sirp: Voorimehe 9, Tallinn 10146; tel. 682-9076; fax 682-9071; e-mail sirp@sirp.ee; internet www.sirp.ee; f. 1940; weekly; the arts; Editor-in-Chief KAAREL TARAND; circ. 4,900 (2008).

Teater, Muusika, Kino (Theatre, Music, Cinema): Voorimehe 9, Tallinn 10146; tel. 683-3132; e-mail pille@temuki.ee; internet www.temuki.ee; f. 1982; monthly; Editor-in-Chief MADIS KOLK; circ. 1,500.

Vikerkaar (Rainbow): Voorimehe 9, Tallinn 10146; tel. 683-3140; fax 683-3101; e-mail vikerkaar@vikerkaar.ee; internet www.vikerkaar.ee; f. 1986; monthly; fiction, poetry, critical works; Editor-in-Chief MÄRT VÄLJATAGA; circ. 1,500.

NEWS AGENCY

BNS (Baltic News Service): Toompuiestee 35, Tallinn 15043; tel. 610-8800; fax 610-8811; e-mail bns@bns.ee; internet www.bns.ee; f. 1990; daily news bulletins in English, Estonian, Latvian, Lithuanian and Russian; Chief Exec. GEORGE SHABAD.

PRESS ORGANIZATIONS

Estonian Journalists' Union (Eesti Ajakirjanike Liit): Gonsiori 21/409, Tallinn 10147; tel. and fax 646-3699; e-mail eal@eal.ee; internet www.eal.ee; f. 1919; Dir PEETER ERNITS.

Estonian Newspaper Association (Eesti Ajalehtede Liit): Pärnu mnt. 67A, Tallinn 10134; tel. 646-1005; fax 631-1210; e-mail eall@eall.ee; internet www.eall.ee; f. 1990; 39 mem. newspapers; Man. Dir MART RAUDSAAR.

Estonian Press Council (Avaliku Sõna Nõukogu): Gonsiori 21, Tallinn 10147; tel. and fax 5300-5847; e-mail asn@asn.org.ee; internet www.asn.org.ee; f. 1997; non-governmental org.; Chair. Prof. EPP LAUK.

Publishers

Eesti Raamat (Estonian Book): Laki 26, Tallinn 12915; tel. and fax 658-7889; e-mail rein.poder.001@mail.ee; internet www.eestiraamat.ee; f. 1940; fiction for children and adults; Dir ANNE-ASTRI KASK.

Estonian Academy Publishers (EAP): Kohtu 6, Tallinn 10130; tel. 645-4504; fax 646-6026; e-mail niine@kirj.ee; internet www.kirj.ee; f. 1994; publishes nine academic journals incl. *Proceedings of the Estonian Academy of Sciences*, *Linguistica Uralica*, etc.; Dir ÜLO NIINE.

Ilmamaa: Vanemuise 19, Tartu 51014; tel. 742-7290; fax 742-7320; e-mail ilmamaa@ilmamaa.ee; internet www.ilmamaa.ee; f. 1993; general fiction, philosophy, cultural history; Chair. HANDO RUNNEL.

Ilo Publishing House: Tammsaare tee 47, Tallinn 11316; tel. 667-7855; fax 680-2230; e-mail ilo@ilo.ee; f. 1990; dictionaries, reference books, textbooks, history, management, psychology, law and children's books; Dir SIRJE-MAI PIHLAK.

Koolibri: POB 1793, Tallinn 11615; tel. 651-5300; fax 651-5301; e-mail koolibri@koolibri.ee; internet www.koolibri.ee; f. 1991; textbooks, dictionaries, children's books; Man. Dir KALLE KALJURAND.

Kunst (Fine Art): Lai 34, Tallinn 10133; POB 105, Tallinn 10502; tel. 641-1766; fax 641-1762; e-mail kunst.myyk@mail.ee; f. 1957; fine arts, fiction, tourism, history, biographies; Dir SIRJE HELME.

Logos: Narma mnt. 51, Tallinn 10152; tel. 66-88499; e-mail logos@logos.ee; internet www.logos.ee; f. 1991; Christian; Chair. TIINA NÕLVAK.

Monokkel: POB 311, Tallinn 10503; tel. 501-6307; fax 656-9176; e-mail monokkel@hot.ee; internet www.hot.ee/monokkel; f. 1988; history, fiction; Dir ANTS ÕÕBIK.

Olion: Laki 26, Tallinn 12915; tel. 655-0175; fax 655-0173; e-mail kirjastus@olion.ee; internet www.olion.ee; f. 1989; politics, reference, history, biographies, children's books; Dir HÜLLE UNT.

Tartu University Press: Tiigi 78, Tartu 50410; tel. 737-5961; fax 737-5944; e-mail tyk@ut.ee; internet www.tyk.ee; f. 1958; science, textbooks, etc.; Dir VAIKO TIGANE.

Tiritamm: Endla 3, Tallinn 10122; tel. and fax 656-3570; e-mail tiritamm@tiritamm.ee; internet www.eestikirjastused.com/tiritamm; f. 1991; children's books; Dir SIRJE SAIMRE.

Valgus: Tõnismägi 3A, Tallinn 10119; tel. 617-7010; fax 617-7016; e-mail info@kirjastusvalgus.ee; internet www.kirjastusvalgus.ee; f. 1965; scientific literature, resource materials and textbooks; Editor-in-Chief EVA KOLLI.

Varrak: Pärnu mnt. 67A, Tallinn 10134; tel. 616-1038; fax 616-1030; e-mail varrak@varrak.ee; internet www.varrak.ee; f. 1991; history, philosophy and sociology, literary fiction, science fiction, popular fiction and children's literature; Man. Dir PRIIT MAIDE.

PUBLISHERS' ASSOCIATION

Estonian Publishers' Association (Eesti Kirjastuste Liit): Roosikrantsi 6/207, Tallinn 10119; tel. 644-9866; fax 617-7550; e-mail kirjastusteliit@eki.ee; internet www.estbook.com; f. 1991; Chair. KADRI HALJAMAA.

Broadcasting and Communications

TELECOMMUNICATIONS

Service Providers

Eesti Telekom AS (Estonian Telecom Ltd): Valge 16, Tallinn 19095; tel. 611-1470; fax 631-1224; e-mail mailbox@telekom.ee; internet www.telekom.ee; f. 1992; privatized in 1999; subsidiaries include Eesti Mobiltelefon AS (EMT) and Elion Enterprises; CEO VALDO KALM.

Elisa Eesti: Sõpruse pst. 145, Tallinn 13417; tel. 681-1963; fax 681-1961; e-mail info@elisa.ee; internet www.elisa.ee; mobile cellular telecommunications; Exec. Dir SAMI SEPPÄNEN.

EMT: Valge 16, Tallinn 19095; tel. 639-7130; fax 639-7132; e-mail info@emt.ee; internet www.emt.ee; f. 1991; wholly-owned subsidiary of Eesti Telekom; CEO VALDO KALM.

Tele2 Eesti: Jõe 2A, Tallinn 10151; tel. 686-6866; fax 686-6877; e-mail info@tele2.ee; internet www.tele2.ee; mobile cellular telecommunications.

BROADCASTING

Supervisory Authority

Broadcasting Council: Gonsiori 21, Tallinn 15020; tel. 611-4305; fax 611-4457; e-mail rhn@er.ee; internet www.rhn.ee; mems appointed by Riigikogu (State Assembly); Chair. of Television AINAR RUUSSAAR; Chair. of Radio MARGUS ALLIKMAA.

Radio

The public broadcaster, Eesti Rahvusringhääling, was formed in 2007 by the merger of the public television and radio broadcasters. In 2005 there were additionally 28 private radio broadcasters operating in Estonia.

Eesti Rahvusringhääling (ERR) (Estonian Public Broadcasting): Gonsiori 27, Tallinn 15029; tel. 628-4100; fax 628-4155; e-mail err@err.ee; internet www.err.ee; f. 2007; radio broadcasts comprise five domestic channels (three in Estonian, one in Russian and one in English, French and German) and an external service in English; television broadcasts comprise one channel with programmes in Estonian and Russian; Chair. and Dir-Gen. MARGUS ALLIKMAA.

Raadio Elmar: Õpetaja 9A, Tartu 51003; tel. 742-7520; fax 774-2044; e-mail elmar@elmar.ee; internet www.elmar.ee; one of six radio stations owned by Trio Grupp; Dir JAAN HABICHT.

Raadio Kuku: Veerenni 58A, Tallinn 11314; tel. 630-7031; fax 630-7004; e-mail kuku@kuku.ee; internet www.kuku.ee; Chair. of Bd REIN LANG.

Raadio Sky Plus: Pärnu mnt. 139F, Tallinn 11317; tel. 678-8777; fax 678-8701; e-mail info@skyplus.fm; internet www.skyplus.fm; owned by Sky Media; Chief Exec. ILMAR KOMPUS.

Raadio Uuno: Veerenni 58A, Tallinn 11314; tel. 630-7080; fax 630-7085; e-mail uuno@uuno.ee; internet www.uuno.ee; f. 1994; Chair. REIN LANG.

Tartu Pereraadio (Tartu Family Radio): Annemõisa 8, Tartu 50708; tel. and fax 748-8458; e-mail pereraadio@pereraadio.ee; internet www.pereraadio.ee; f. 1994; Christian; Chief Exec. PAAVO PIHLAK.

Television

There are three national commercial television stations and one public broadcaster in Estonia. In addition, five cable television licences have been issued.

Eesti Rahvusringhääling (ERR) (Estonian Public Broadcasting): Gonsiori 27, Tallinn 15029; tel. 628-4100; fax 628-4155; e-mail err@err.ee; internet www.err.ee; f. 2007; radio broadcasts comprise five domestic channels (three in Estonian, one in Russian and one in English, French and German) and an external service in English; television broadcasts comprise one channel with programmes in Estonian and Russian; Chair. and Dir-Gen. MARGUS ALLIKMAA.

Kanal 2 (Channel 2): Maakri 23A, Tallinn 10145; tel. 666-2450; fax 666-2451; e-mail info@kanal2.ee; internet www.kanal2.ee; f. 1993; commercial; Chief Exec. URMAS ORU.

TV3: Peterburgi tee 81, Tallinn 11415; tel. 622-0200; fax 622-0201; e-mail tv3@tv3.ee; internet www.tv3.ee; f. 1996; owned by Modern Times Group (Sweden); Exec. Dir TOOMAS VARA.

Broadcasting Association

Association of Estonian Broadcasters (AEB) (Eesti Ringhäälingute Liit): Ülemiste tee 3A, Tallinn 11415; tel. and fax 633-3235; e-mail erl@online.ee; internet www.ringhliit.ee; f. 1992; 19 mems; Man. Dir URMAS LOIT.

Finance

(cap. = capital; res = reserves; dep. = deposits; m. = million; brs = branches; amounts in kroons, unless otherwise specified)

BANKING

Central Bank

Bank of Estonia (Eesti Pank): Estonia pst. 13, Tallinn 15095; tel. 668-0719; fax 668-0836; e-mail info@eestipank.ee; internet www.eestipank.info; f. 1919; closed 1940; re-established 1990; bank of issue; cap. 600.0m., res 4,253.5m., dep. 27,027.5m. (Dec. 2009); Gov. ANDRES LIPSTOK.

Commercial Banks

Estonian Credit Bank (Eesti Krediidipank): Narva mnt. 4, Tallinn 15014; tel. 669-0900; fax 661-6037; e-mail info@krediidipank.ee; internet www.krediidipank.ee; f. 1992; cap. €25.0.m., dep. €315.6m. (Dec. 2010); Pres. PAVEL GORBATSEVICH; Chair. of Bd ANDRUS KLUGE; 12 brs.

Sampo Pank (Sampo Bank): Narva mnt. 11, Tallinn 15015; tel. 680-0800; fax 675-2800; e-mail info@sampopank.ee; internet www.sampopank.ee; f. 1992; present name adopted 2000; wholly owned by Sampo Bank (Finland) (q.v.); cap. 898.0m., res 40.0m., dep. 20,345.0m. (Dec. 2006); Chair. of Management Bd AIVAR REHE; 13 brs.

SEB Pank (SEB Bank): Tornimäe 2, Tallinn 15010; tel. 665-5100; fax 665-5103; e-mail info@seb.ee; internet www.seb.ee; f. 1992 by the merger of 10 small banks; 100% owned by Scandinaviska Enskilda Banken (SEB—Sweden); cap. 665.6m., res 1,678.6m., dep. 62,157.2m. (Dec. 2009); fmrly SEB Eesti Ühispank; Chair. of Bd RIHO UNT; 90 brs.

Swedbank AS: Liivalaia 8, Tallinn 15040; tel. 631-0310; fax 631-0410; e-mail info@swedbank.ee; internet www.swedbank.ee; f. 1991; 100% owned by Swedbank (Sweden) (q.v.); fmrly AS Hansapank; present name adopted March 2009; cap. €202.8m., res €59.3m., dep. €21,193.2m. (Dec. 2008); Chair. of Council MICHAEL WOLF; Chair. of Bd HÅKAN BERG; 96 brs.

Tallinn Business Bank (Tallinna Äripank): Vana-Viru 7, Tallinn 15097; tel. 668-8000; fax 668-8001; e-mail info@tbb.ee; internet www.tbb.ee; f. 1991; cap. 229.8m., res 8.7m., dep. 1,322.2m. (Dec. 2009); Chair. of Bd VALERI HARITONOV.

Banking Association

Estonian Banking Association (Eesti Pangaliit): Ahtri 12, Tallinn 10151; tel. 611-6567; fax 611-6568; e-mail pangaliit@pangaliit.ee; internet www.pangaliit.ee; f. 1992; Chair. of Bd RIHO UNT.

STOCK EXCHANGE

Tallinn Stock Exchange (Tallinna Börs): Tartu mnt. 2, Tallinn 10145; tel. 640-8800; fax 640-8801; e-mail tallinn@nasdaqomx.com; f. 1995; 62% owned by the NASDAQ OMX Group (USA); Chair. of Man. Bd ANDRUS ALBER.

INSURANCE

In 2010 there were five insurance organizations providing life insurance and nine providing non-life insurance in Estonia.

Estonian Insurance Association (Eesti Kindlustusseltside Liit): Mustamäe tee 44, Tallinn 10621; tel. 667-1800; fax 667-1801; e-mail info@eksl.ee; internet www.eksl.ee; f. 1993; Chair. of Bd MART JESSE; 17 mem. cos.

Insurance Companies

ERGO: Tammsaare 47, Tallinn 11316; tel. 610-6500; fax 610-6501; e-mail info@ergo.ee; internet www3.ergo.ee; f. 1990; provides non-life insurance (as ERGO Kindlustuse) and life insurance (ERGO Elukindlustus); Chair. of Supervisory Bd THOMAS HANS SCHIRMER.

If P&C Insurance: Pronksi 19, Tallinn 10124; tel. 669-6684; fax 667-1101; internet www.if.ee; f. 1991 as Eesti Kindlustus; renamed AS Eesti Kindlustus 1996, AS Sampo Eesti Varakindlustus 1999, AS If Kindlustus 2002, and as above 2009; non-life; Chief Exec. TIMO VUORINEN.

QBE Kindlustuse Eesti: Sõpruse pst. 145, Tallinn 13417; tel. 667-1400; fax 667-1401; e-mail info@ee.qbe.com; internet www.qbeeurope.com/estonia; owned by QBE International (Australia); fmrly Nordea Kindlustus Eesti; present name adopted 2004; non-life.

SEB Elu- ja Pensionikindlustus (SEB Life Insurance & Pensions Estonia): Tornimäe 2, Tallinn 15010; tel. 665-5100; fax 665-5103; e-mail info@seb.ee; internet www.seb.ee; f. 1998; fmrly Ühispanga Elukindlustuse; wholly owned by SEB Eesti; life insurance, pensions; Chair. of Management Bd RIHO UNT.

Seesam Insurance AS: Vambola 6, Tallinn 10114; tel. 628-1800; fax 631-2109; e-mail seesam@seesam.ee; internet www.seesam.ee; f. 1991; owned by the OP-Pohjola Group; non-life; Chair. of Management Bd IVO KULDMÄE.

Swedbank Elukindlustus (Swedbank Life Insurance): Liivalaia 12, Tallinn 15036; tel. 613-1606; fax 613-1130; e-mail elukindlustus@swedbank.ee; internet www.swedbank.ee; wholly owned by Swedbank AS (Sweden); fmrly Hansa Elukindlustuse; present name adopted 2010; life insurance; Chief Exec. MINDAUGAS JUSIUS.

Trade and Industry

GOVERNMENT AGENCIES

Enterprise Estonia (Ettevõtluse Arendamise Sihtasutus): Lasnamäe 2, Tallinn 11412; tel. 627-9700; fax 627-9701; e-mail eas@eas.ee; internet www.eas.ee; f. 2000; Chair. ÜLARI ALAMETS.

Estonian Competition Authority (Kohkurentsiamet): Auna 6, Tallinn 10317; tel. 667-2400; fax 667-2401; e-mail info@konkurentsiamet.ee; internet www.konkurentsiamet.ee; f. 2008;

supervises competition, with specific powers in the sectors of fuel and energy, and electronic and postal communications; Dir-Gen. MÄRT OTS.

Estonian Investment and Trade Agency (EITA): Lasnamäe 2, Tallinn 11412; tel. 627-9700; fax 627-9701; e-mail invest@eas.ee; internet www.investinestonia.com; Dir URMAS SILMAN.

Estonian Regional and Local Development Agency (Eesti Regionaalse ja Kohaliku Arengu Sihtasutus—ERKAS): Ahtri 8, 3rd Floor, Tallinn 10151; tel. 694-3431; fax 694-3425; e-mail erkas@erkas.ee; internet www.erkas.ee; f. 2002; Chair. JÜRI ROOS.

Estonian Technical Surveillance Authority (Tehnilise Järelevalve Amet): Sõle 23A, 10614 Tallinn; tel. 667-2011; fax 667-2001; e-mail info@tja.ee; internet www.tja.ee; f. 2008; co-ordinates management of the use of radio frequencies (incl. broadcasting), manages numbering plan for telecommunications services, various responsibilities in the field of communications, incl. railways; Dir-Gen. RAIGO UUKKIVI.

CHAMBERS OF COMMERCE

Estonian Chamber of Agriculture and Commerce (Eesti Põllumajandus-Kaubanduskoda—EPKK): Vilmsi 53G, Tallinn 10147; tel. 600-9349; fax 600-9350; e-mail info@epkk.ee; internet www.epkk.ee; f. 1996; Chair. of Bd AAVO MÖLDER.

Estonian Chamber of Commerce and Industry (ECCI) (Eesti Kaubandus-Tööstuskoda): Toom-Kooli 17, Tallinn 10130; tel. 604-0060; fax 604-0061; e-mail koda@koda.ee; internet www.koda.ee; f. 1925; brs in Tartu, Jõhvi, Pärnu and Kuressaare; Pres. TOOMAS LUMAN.

INDUSTRIAL AND TRADE ASSOCIATIONS

Asscn of Construction Material Producers of Estonia (Eesti Ehitusmaterjalide Tootjate Liit—EETL): Pärnu mnt. 141, Tallinn 11314; tel. 648-1918; fax 648-9062; e-mail eetl@hot.ee; internet www.hot.ee/eetl; Man. Dir ENNO RABANE.

Asscn of Estonian Food Industry (Eesti Toiduainetööstuse Liit): Saku 15/105, Tallinn 11314; tel. 648-4978; fax 631-2718; e-mail info@toiduliit.ee; internet www.toiduliit.ee; f. 1993; Dir SIRJE POTISEPP.

Central Union of Estonian Farmers (Eestimaa Põllumeeste Keskliit): J. Vilmsi 53G, Tallinn 10147; tel. and fax 600-8616; e-mail info@eptk.ee; internet www.eptk.ee; f. 1990; Chair. of Bd ÜLLAS HUNT.

Estonian Asscn of Fisheries (Eesti Kalaliit): Peterburi tee 2F, Tallinn 11415; tel. 622-1300; fax 622-1302; e-mail kalaliit@online.ee; internet www.kalaliit.ee; f. 1995; 28 mems; Chair. TOOMAS KÕUHKNA; Man. Dir VALDUR NOORMÄGI.

Estonian Asscn of Information Technology and Telecommunication Companies (Eesti Infotehnoloogia ja Telekommunikatsiooni Liit): Lõõtsa 6, Tallinn 11415; tel. 617-7145; fax 617-7146; e-mail info@itl.ee; internet www.itl.ee; f. 2000; 36 mems; Pres. TAAVI KOTKA; Chair. URMAS KÕLLI.

Estonian Asscn of Small and Medium-sized Enterprises (EVEA) (Eesti Väike-Ja Keskmiste Ettevõtjate Assotsiatsioon): Liivalaia 9, Tallinn 10118; tel. 641-0920; fax 641-0916; e-mail evea@evea.ee; internet www.evea.ee; f. 1988; Pres. MARINA KAAS; CEO KERSTI KRAAS.

Estonian Forest Industries Asscn (Eesti Metsatööstuse Liit—EMTL): Viljandi mnt. 18A, Tallinn 11216; tel. 656-7643; fax 656-7644; e-mail info@emtl.ee; internet www.emtl.ee; f. 1996; Man. Dir OTT OTSMANN.

Estonian Meat Asscn (Eesti Lihaliit): Lai 39/41, Tallinn 10133; tel. 641-1179; fax 641-1035; e-mail lihaliit@hot.ee; f. 1989; Chair. of Bd AIGAR PINDMAA; Man. Dir PEETER GRIGORJEV.

Estonian Oil Asscn (Eesti Õliühing): Kiriku 6, Tallinn 10130; tel. 664-1247; fax 641-8471; e-mail toomas@oilunion.ee; internet www.oilunion.ee; f. 1993; Chair. RAIVO VARE; 12 mem. orgs.

Estonian Trade Council (Eesti Väliskaubanduse Liit): Tammsaare tee 47, Tallinn 11316; tel. 684-1252; fax 659-7017; e-mail icc@icc-estonia.ee; internet www.icc-estonia.ee; f. 1991; 110 mems; non-profit org.; promotes export trade; Chair. of Bd TIIT TAMMEMÄGI.

Federation of the Estonian Chemical Industry (Eesti Keemiatööstuse Liit): Peterburi tee 46, Tallinn 11415; tel. and fax 613-9775; e-mail info@keemia.ee; internet www.keemia.ee; f. 1991; Man. Dir HALLAR MEYBAUM.

Federation of the Estonian Engineering Industry (Eesti Masinatööstuse Liit—EML): Mustamäe tee 4, Tallinn 10621; tel. 611-5893; fax 656-6640; e-mail emliit@emliit.ee; internet www.emliit.ee; f. 1991; represents over 100 metalworking, machine-building, electrotechnics and electronics enterprises; Chair. of Bd JÜRI RIIVES.

Union of Estonian Automobile Enterprises (Eesti Autoettevõtete Liit): Akadeemia tee 20, Tallinn 12611; tel. 641-2511; fax 641-2523; e-mail al@autoettevoteliit.ee; internet www.autoettevoteteliit.ee; f. 1990; Chair. REIN SIIM; 77 mem. cos.

EMPLOYERS' ORGANIZATION

Estonian Employers' Confederation (Eesti Tööandjate Keskliit): Kiriku 6, Tallinn 10130; tel. 699-9301; fax 699-9310; e-mail ettk@ettk.ee; internet ettk.tooandjad.ee; f. 1991 as Confederation of Estonian Industry; Chair. of Bd MEELIS VIRKEBAU; Pres. ENN VESKIMÄGI; 24 brs.

UTILITIES

Electricity

Under terms agreed with the European Union, Estonia was permitted to postpone the liberalization of its electricity market until 2013, in order to allow the requisite investment to be made in the oil shale power plants that generate most of the country's electricity supply.

Operations of the Estlink submarine cable, connecting the electricity networks of Estonia and Finland, commenced in January 2007.

Eesti Energia (Estonian Energy Co): Laki 24, Tallinn 12915; tel. 715-2222; fax 715-2200; e-mail info@energia.ee; internet www.energia.ee; f. 1939; producer, transmitter and distributor of thermal and electric energy; manufacture of electric motors; electrical engineering; Chair. SANDOR LIIVE; 7,600 employees.

Gas

Eesti Gaas (Estonian Gas Co): Liivalaia 9, Tallinn 10118; tel. 630-3003; fax 631-3884; e-mail info@gaas.ee; internet www.gaas.ee; f. 1993; purchases and distributes natural gas; constructs pipelines; calibrates gas meters; Chair. TIIT KULLERKUPP; 255 employees.

Water

Tallinna Vesi (Tallinn Water Co): Ädala 10, Tallinn 10614; tel. 626-2200; fax 626-2300; e-mail tvesi@tvesi.ee; internet www.tallinnavesi.ee; f. 1997; supply and treatment of water; collection and treatment of waste water; 35.30% owned by United Utilities Tallinna (a subsidiary of United Utilities International, United Kingdom), 34.70% by Tallinn City Government (q.v.); CEO IAN PLENDERLEITH; 302 employees (April 2011).

TRADE UNIONS

Asscn of Estonian Energy Workers' Trade Unions (Eesti Energeetikatöötajate Ametiühingute Liit—EEAÜL): Gonsiori 3A, Tallinn 10117; tel. 715-5527; fax 715-5528; e-mail sander.vaikma@energia.ee; internet www.energeetik.ee; Chair. SANDER VAIKMA.

Confederation of Estonian Employee Unions (Teenistujate Ametiliitude Keskorganisatsioon—TALO): Gonsiori 21, Tallinn 10147; tel. 641-9800; e-mail talo@talo.ee; internet www.talo.ee; f. 1992; comprises nine mem. unions from the broadcasting, cultural, customs, education, engineering, journalism, radiology and scientific sectors; Chair. AGO TUULING.

Estonian Communication Workers and Service Workers' Trade Union (Eesti Side-ja Teenindustöötajate Ametiühingute Liit—ESTAL): Masti 2/5, Tallinn 11911; tel. 601-1606; fax 601-1124; e-mail estal@estal.ee; internet www.estal.ee; f. 1940 as Estonian Communication Workers' Trade Union; renamed as above in 2005; Chair. ÕIE VÄLJAS.

Estonian Light Industry Workers' Trade Union (Eesti Kergetööstustöötajate Ametiühingute Liit): Reimani 5/4, Tallinn 10124; tel. 661-2465; fax 661-2468; e-mail laivi@uninet.ee; mem. of Confederation of Estonian Trade Unions; Chair. LAIVI RÕÕMUS.

Estonian Trade Union Confederation (Eesti Ametiühingute Keskliit—EAKL): Pärnu mnt. 41A, Tallinn 10119; tel. 641-2800; fax 641-2801; e-mail eakl@eakl.ee; internet www.eakl.ee; f. 1990; 19 professional mem. orgs; Chair. HARRI TALIGA; estimated 40,000 individual mems (2008).

Estonian Transportation and Roadworkers' Union (Eesti Transpordi-ja Teetöötajate Ametiühing—ETTA): Kalju 7/1, Tallinn 10414; tel. 641-3129; fax 641-3131; e-mail etta@etta.ee; internet www.etta.ee; mem. of the Estonian Trade Union Confederation (q.v.); Chair. PEEP PETERSON.

Transport

RAILWAYS

In 2009 there were 929 km of railway track in use.

Edelaraudtee: Kaare 25, Türi 72213; tel. 385-7123; fax 385-7121; e-mail info@edel.ee; internet www.edel.ee; f. 1997; owned by GB Railways (United Kingdom); operates intercity passenger services on the routes: Tallinn–Tartu; Tallinn–Narva; Tartu–Varga; Tallinn–Vijandi–Pärnu; and Tartu–Orava; Dir KALVI PUKKA.

Eesti Raudtee (Estonian Railways): Toompuiestee 35, Tallinn 15073; tel. 615-8610; fax 615-8710; e-mail raudtee@evr.ee;

internet www.evr.ee; f. 1918; privatized in 2001; renationalization completed in 2007; rail infrastructure operator and freight carrier; Chair. of Management Bd KAIDO SIMMERMANN; Chair of Supervisory Bd TÕNIS HAAVEL; 1,821 employees (2009).

Elektriraudtee (Electric Railways): Vabaduse pst. 176, Tallinn 10917; tel. 673-7400; fax 673-7440; e-mail info@elektriraudtee.ee; internet www.elektriraudtee.ee; f. 1998; suburban passenger services in Tallinn region; Chair. KAIDA KAULER.

ROADS

In 2008 Estonia had a total road network of 58,034 km, of which 103 km were motorways and 3,940 km were main roads.

Estonian Road Administration (Maanteeamet): Pärnu mnt. 463A, Tallinn 10916; tel. 611-9300; fax 611-9360; e-mail info@mnt .ee; internet www.mnt.ee; f. 1990; govt org.; four regional road administrations; Dir-Gen. TAMUR TSAKKO.

INLAND WATERWAYS

In 2006 there were 320 km of navigable inland waterways.

SHIPPING

Tallinn is the main port for freight transportation. There are regular passenger services between Tallinn and Helsinki, Finland. At December 2009 the merchant fleet comprised 115 vessels, totalling 374,900 grt.

Estonian Maritime Administration (EMA) (Veeteede Amet): Valge 4, Tallinn 11413; tel. 620-5500; fax 620-5506; e-mail eva@ vta.ee; internet www.vta.ee; f. 1990; govt org.; administers and implements state maritime safety policies, ship-control, pilot, lighthouse and hydrography services; Gen. Dir ANDRUS MAIDE; 375 employees.

Principal Shipping Companies

Eesti Merelaevandus (ESCO) (Estonian Shipping Co): Sadama 4, Tallinn 15096; tel. 640-9500; fax 640-9595; e-mail online@eml.ee; internet www.eml.ee; f. 1940; owned by Tschudi Shipping Co (Norway); liner services, ship-chartering and cargo-shipping; Man. Dir TOM STAGE PETERSEN; 500 employees.

Saaremaa Laevakompanii (Saaremaa Shipping Co): Kohtu 1, Kuressaare 93812; tel. 452-4350; fax 452-4350; e-mail slk@ laevakompanii.ee; internet www.laevakompanii.ee; f. 1992; passenger and cargo services between mainland Estonia and Saaremaa, Hiiumaa and Vormsi islands; Dir-Gen. TÕNIS RIHVK.

Tallink Grupp: Tartu mnt. 13, Tallinn 10145; tel. 640-9800; fax 640-9810; e-mail info@tallink.ee; internet www.tallink.ee; f. 1989 as a joint-venture Estonian-Finnish co; in 1996–2002 known as Hansatee Grupp, reverted to previous name in 2002; passenger and cargo transport; operates high-speed ferries between Tallinn and Helsinki, Finland; also operates routes to St Petersburg, Russia, and Stockholm, Sweden; Chair. of Management Bd ENN PANT.

Shipowners' Association

Estonian Shipowners' Association (Eesti Laevaomanike Liit): Kopli 101, Tallinn 11712; tel. and fax 613-5528; e-mail reederid@hot .ee; Pres. Capt. TOIVO NINNAS.

Port Authorities

Port of Sillamäe (Sillamäe Sadam—Silport): Suur-Karja 5, Tallinn 10140; tel. 640-5271; fax 640-5279; e-mail silport@silport.ee; internet www.silport.ee; operations commenced Oct. 2005; deep sea port; navigable year-round; railway facilities; free trade zone; four terminals; privately owned; Chair. VITALY IVANOV.

Port of Tallinn (Tallinna Sadam): Sadama 25, Tallinn 15051; tel. 631-8555; fax 631-8166; e-mail ts@ts.ee; internet www.ts.ee; f. 1991; the Port of Tallinn consists of five constituent harbours: Old City, Muuga, Paljassaare, Paldiski South and Saaremaa; Chair. of Bd AIN KALJURAND; Harbour Master E. HUNT; 550 employees (2007).

CIVIL AVIATION

There is an international airport at Tallinn.

Civil Aviation Administration (Lennuamat): Rävala pst. 8, Tallinn 10143; tel. 610-3500; fax 610-3501; e-mail ecaa@ecaa.ee; internet www.ecaa.ee; f. 1990; Dir-Gen. KOIT KASKEL.

Avies: Lennujaama 2, Tallinn 11101; tel. 605-8022; fax 621-2951; e-mail info@avies.ee; internet www.avies.ee; f. 1991; domestic passenger services between Tallinn and Saaremaa and Hiiumaa islands, international scheduled and charter passenger and cargo services; Man. Dir VLADIMIR PISARKOV.

Estonian Air: Lennujaama 13, Tallinn 11101; tel. 640-1160; fax 640-1161; e-mail info@estonian-air.ee; internet www.estonian-air .com; f. 1991; 49% owned by Scandinavian Airlines (Denmark/ Norway/Sweden), 34% state-owned; passenger and cargo flights to destinations across Europe; Pres. TERO TASKILA.

Tourism

Estonia has a wide range of attractions for tourists, including the historic towns of Tallinn and Tartu, extensive nature reserves and coastal resorts. In 2006 the first deep-sea port for cruise ships was opened on Estonia's biggest island, Saaremaa. In 2010 there were 1,563,952 foreign visitors to Estonia (measured by arrivals at registered accommodation establishments). In 2008 receipts from tourism totalled US $1,662m.

Estonian Tourist Board (Turismiarenduskeskus): Liivalaia 13/ 15, Tallinn 10118; tel. 627-9770; fax 627-9777; e-mail tourism@eas .ee; internet www.visitestonia.com; f. 1990; Dir TARMO MUTSO.

Defence

As assessed at November 2011, Estonia's total armed forces numbered 5,750, comprising an army of 5,300 (including conscripts), a navy of 200, and an air force of 250. There was also a reserve militia of 30,000. The duration of military service is eight months, or eleven months for officers and some specialists. In February 1994 Estonia joined the North Atlantic Treaty Organization's (NATO) 'Partnership for Peace' programme of military co-operation, and became a full member of the Organization in March 2004.

Defence Expenditure: Budgeted at €336,000m. in 2012.

Commander of the Defence Forces: Brig.-Gen. RIHO TERRAS.

Chief of the General Staff: Col PEETER HOPPE.

Commander of the Army: Col INDREK SIREL.

Commander of the Navy: Capt. IGOR SCHVEDE.

Commander of the Air Force: Brig.-Gen. VALERI SAAR.

Education

Compulsory education begins at the age of seven and lasts for nine years. Students may then attend either general secondary school or vocational school. In 2009/10 there were 33 higher education institutions, at which 69,113 students were enrolled (including those undertaking evening and correspondence courses). In 2007/08 some 20% of students at primary and secondary schools received tuition in a language other than Estonian (mainly Russian). In 2007/08 enrolment at pre-primary schools included 90% of children in the corresponding age-group. In the same year enrolment in primary education included 94% of children in the relevant age-group, while secondary education enrolment included 89% of children in the relevant age-group. In 2006 enrolment in tertiary education was equivalent to 65% of those in the relevant age-group (males 49%; females 82%). Government outlays on education amounted to 16,805m. kroons in 2008 (16.7% of total expenditure in that year).

ETHIOPIA

Introductory Survey

LOCATION, CLIMATE, LANGUAGE, RELIGION, FLAG, CAPITAL

The Federal Democratic Republic of Ethiopia is a land-locked country in eastern Africa; it has a long frontier with Somalia near the Horn of Africa. South Sudan and Sudan lie to the west, Eritrea to the north, Djibouti to the north-east and Kenya to the south. The climate is mainly temperate because of the high plateau terrain, with an average annual temperature of 13°C (55°F), abundant rainfall in some years and low humidity. The lower country and valley gorges are very hot and subject to recurrent drought. The official language is Amharic, but many other local languages are also spoken. English is widely used in official and commercial circles. The Ethiopian Orthodox (Tewahido) Church, an ancient Christian sect, has a wide following in the north and on the southern plateau. In much of the south and east the inhabitants include Muslims and followers of animist beliefs. The national flag (proportions 1 by 2) has three equal horizontal stripes, of green, yellow and red, superimposed in the centre of which is a blue disk bearing a yellow pentagram, resembling a star, with single yellow rays extending outwards from the inner angles of the star. The capital is Addis Ababa.

CONTEMPORARY POLITICAL HISTORY

Historical Context

In September 1974 Emperor Haile Selassie was deposed by the armed forces and his imperial regime was replaced by the Provisional Military Administrative Council (PMAC), known popularly as the Dergue (Committee), led by Brig.-Gen. Teferi Benti. In December Ethiopia was declared a socialist state; however, a radical programme of social and economic reforms led to widespread unrest, and in February 1977 Lt-Col Mengistu Haile Mariam executed Teferi and his closest associates, and replaced him as Chairman of the PMAC and as Head of State.

During 1977–78, in an attempt to end opposition to the regime, the Government imprisoned or killed thousands of its opponents. Political power was consolidated in a Commission for Organizing the Party of the Working People of Ethiopia (COPWE), largely dominated by military personnel. In September 1984, at the COPWE's third congress, the Workers' Party of Ethiopia (WPE) was formally inaugurated. Mengistu was unanimously elected Secretary-General of the party, which modelled itself on the Communist Party of the Soviet Union. In February 1987, at a referendum, some 81% of the electorate endorsed a new Constitution and in June national elections were held to an 835-seat legislature, the National Shengo (Assembly). In September, at the inaugural meeting of the new legislature, the PMAC was abolished, and the People's Democratic Republic of Ethiopia was declared. The National Shengo unanimously elected Mengistu as President of the Republic, and a 24-member Council of State was also elected, to act as the Shengo's permanent organ.

Numerous groups, encouraged by the confusion resulting from the 1974 revolution, launched armed insurgencies against the Government. Of these, the most effective were based in the Ogaden, Eritrea and Tigrai regions. Somalia laid claim to the Ogaden, which is populated mainly by ethnic Somalis. Somali troops supported incursions by forces of the Western Somali Liberation Front, and in 1977 the Somalis made major advances in the Ogaden. In 1978, however, they were forced to retreat, and by the end of 1980 Ethiopian forces had gained control of virtually the whole of the Ogaden region.

The former Italian colony of Eritrea was merged with Ethiopia, in a federal arrangement, in September 1952, and annexed to Ethiopia as a province in November 1962. A secessionist movement, the Eritrean Liberation Front (ELF), was founded in Egypt in 1958. The ELF eventually split into several rival factions, the largest of which was the Eritrean People's Liberation Front (EPLF). In 1978 government troops re-established control in much of Eritrea, and the EPLF retreated to the northern town of Nakfa. In 1982 an offensive by government troops failed to capture Nakfa, and in 1984 the EPLF made several successful counter-attacks. In mid-1986 government forces abandoned the north-east coast to the rebels.

An insurgent movement also emerged in Tigrai province in the late 1970s. The Tigrai People's Liberation Front (TPLF) was armed and trained by the EPLF, but relations between the two groups deteriorated sharply in the mid-1980s. The TPLF was weakened by conflict with other anti-Government groups, and in 1985 and 1986 government forces had considerable success against the TPLF.

In September 1987 the newly elected National Shengo announced that five areas, including Eritrea and Tigrai, were to become 'autonomous regions' under the new Constitution. Eritrea was granted a considerable degree of self-government, but both the EPLF and the TPLF rejected the proposals. In March 1988 EPLF forces captured the town of Afabet; the TPLF took advantage of the movement of government forces to Eritrea and overran all the garrisons in north-western and north-eastern Tigrai. In early 1989, following major defeats in north-west Tigrai, government forces abandoned virtually the whole region to the TPLF.

Following the capture of Massawa port by the EPLF in February 1990 (presenting a direct threat to the continued survival of the Ethiopian army in Eritrea), President Mengistu was obliged to make a number of concessions. In March Ethiopian socialism was virtually abandoned, when the WPE was renamed the Ethiopian Democratic Unity Party, and membership was opened to non-Marxists. Mengistu began introducing elements of a market economy and dismantling many of the economic structures that had been established after the 1974 revolution.

By late April 1991, troops of the Ethiopian People's Revolutionary Democratic Front (EPRDF)—an alliance of the TPLF and the Ethiopian People's Democratic Movement (EPDM)—had captured Ambo, a town 130 km west of Addis Ababa, while EPLF forces were 50 km north of Assab, Ethiopia's principal port. On 21 May, faced with the prospect of the imminent defeat of his army, Mengistu fled the country. On 28 May, following the failure of negotiations in the United Kingdom, and with the public support of the USA, units of the EPRDF entered Addis Ababa. They encountered little resistance, and the EPRDF established an interim Government, pending the convening of a multi-party conference in July, which was to elect a transitional government. Meanwhile, the EPLF had gained control of the Eritrean capital, Asmara, and announced the establishment of a provisional Government to administer Eritrea until the holding of a referendum on the issue of independence.

In July 1991 a national conference adopted amendments to a national charter, presented by the EPRDF, and elected an 87-member Council of Representatives, which was to govern for a transitional period of two years, after which free national elections were to be held. The national charter provided guarantees for freedom of association and expression, and for self-determination for Ethiopia's various ethnic groups. The EPLF was not officially represented at the conference, but came to an agreement with the EPRDF, whereby the EPRDF accepted the formation of the EPLF's provisional Government of Eritrea and the determination by referendum of the future of the region. In late July the Council of Representatives established a commission to draft a new constitution and elected Meles Zenawi, the leader of the EPRDF (and of the TPLF), as Chairman of the Council, a position that made him President of the transitional Government and Head of State; in August it appointed a Council of Ministers. Following a referendum in April 1993 Eritrean independence was proclaimed on 24 May.

Domestic Political Affairs

Elections to a Constituent Assembly were conducted in Ethiopia in June 1994, in which the EPRDF won 484 of the 547 seats. The Constituent Assembly ratified a new Constitution in December, which provided for the establishment of a federal government and the division of the country (renamed the Federal Democratic Republic of Ethiopia) into nine states and two chartered cities. A new legislature, the Federal Parliamentary Assembly, was to be established, comprising two chambers: the House of People's Representatives (consisting of no more than 550 directly elected members) and the House of the Federation (composed of 117 deputies, elected by the new state assemblies). The EPRDF and its allies won an overwhelming victory in elections to the House of People's Representatives and state assemblies in May 1995. Most opposition parties boycotted the poll, although international observers accepted that the elections were conducted in a largely free and fair manner.

On 22 August 1995 the country's new Constitution and designation as the Federal Democratic Republic of Ethiopia were formally instituted. Later that day Dr Negasso Gidada, the EPRDF nominee, and a member of the Oromo People's Democratic Organization (OPDO, which was in alliance with the EPRDF), was elected President of the Federal Republic. A new Prime Minister, Meles Zenawi, was elected from among the members of the House of People's Representatives.

The trial of 69 former government officials, including ex-President Mengistu, opened in Addis Ababa in December 1994. The defendants, 23 of whom were being tried *in absentia* (including Mengistu, who was in exile in Zimbabwe), were accused of crimes against humanity and of genocide, perpetrated during 1974–91. In February 1997 the office of the Special Prosecutor announced that an additional 5,198 people would be indicted for war crimes and genocide, of whom nearly 3,000 would be tried *in absentia*. In April the Ethiopian High Court found 37 people (13 *in absentia*) guilty of crimes against humanity and genocide; they were sentenced to up to 20 years' 'rigorous' imprisonment. In December 2006 Mengistu, along with 71 others, was found guilty of genocide, and in January 2007 he was sentenced *in absentia* to life imprisonment. In May 2008 the life sentence was overturned by the Federal Supreme Court and Mengistu was sentenced to death, along with a number of his former political associates. The Zimbabwean authorities refused to extradite Mengistu, owing to his support for President Robert Mugabe's Zimbabwe African National Union during the liberation of Zimbabwe in the 1970s. However, in February 2009 a unity government that included the former opposition Movement for Democratic Change (MDC) was established in Zimbabwe. The MDC subsequently confirmed that the extradition of Mengistu would be 'high on the agenda' of the new administration.

Meanwhile, legislative elections were held on 14 May 2000: the OPDO won the largest number of seats in the House of People's Representatives, taking 178 of the 546 available. The OPDO's major partners in the EPRDF, the Amhara National Democratic Movement (ANDM—as the EPDM had been renamed in 1994) and the TPLF, gained 134 and 38 seats, respectively, securing the coalition a majority in the lower chamber. In October the new legislature was sworn in, and Meles was re-elected as Prime Minister.

In late June 2001 President Gidada was dismissed from the executive committee of the OPDO, after it was alleged that he had refused to accept the party's programme of reform and was providing support to dissidents opposed to Meles. Gidada, in turn, accused the Government of embarking on a campaign of propaganda against him. Gidada was also expelled from the EPRDF; however, he remained insistent that he would complete his presidential term, which was scheduled to end in October. By September Meles had succeeded in re-establishing control over the TPLF, and therefore the EPRDF, following his re-election as Chairman of the party. On 8 October 2001 Lt Girma Wolde Giorgis was elected by the legislature to replace Gidada as President. Later that month Prime Minister Meles effected a major reorganization of the Council of Ministers. In 2003 a number of new political parties and coalition organizations were formed, the most significant of which were the United Ethiopian Democratic Party, which was created by the merger of the Ethiopian Democratic Unity Party and the Ethiopian Democratic Party, and the United Ethiopian Democratic Forces (UEDF), under the leadership of Dr Beyene Petros.

From December 2003 clashes between the Anuak and Nuer communities over disputed land in the Gambela region of the country escalated. The increase in violence was precipitated by the killing of eight officials from the office of the UN High Commissioner for Refugees (UNHCR) and the Federal Agency for Refugee and Returnee Affairs, reportedly committed by the Anuak, who had been angered by the proposed construction on their land of a camp to house Nuer refugees. The Anuak community was the target of a number of revenge attacks, which resulted in the death of some 100 people (although opposition sources indicated that the actual casualty figures were much higher), and it was alleged that the Government had actively encouraged reprisals against the Anuak community. As the violence escalated some 15,000 Anuak, including the President of the region Okelo Akuai, sought refuge in Sudan. In late January 2004 some 200 people were killed after Anuak militants attacked a gold mine where many new settlers to the region were working. By mid-2004 the situation had calmed significantly and about 8,000 of those who had fled in January had returned to Gambela. In December UNHCR resumed operations in the region. An attack on a bus en route from Addis Ababa to Gambela in June 2006, in which at least 14 people died, was blamed on Anuak rebels.

The 2005 legislative elections

Legislative elections were held on 15 May 2005, although voting in the Somali regional state was postponed until 21 August. Provisional results for the House of People's Representatives, published by the National Electoral Board of Ethiopia (NEBE) in late May, awarded the EPRDF 302 seats, the Coalition for Unity and Democracy (CUD) 122 and the UEDF 57; the rate of voter participation was recorded at more than 90%. The results in some 300 constituencies were, however, disputed by both the EPRDF and opposition parties amid allegations of electoral fraud, while concerns over voting irregularities were also raised by observers from the European Union (EU, see p. 276). The NEBE agreed to undertake investigations in 143 of the contested constituencies and in June the EU brokered an agreement between the EPRDF and the CUD and the UEDF, according to which both sides pledged to accept the findings of the NEBE's investigations. The NEBE announced the official results of the legislative elections in early September, including results from the Somali regional state and from 31 constituencies where voting had been reheld, according to which the EPRDF took 327 seats, the CUD 109 seats and the UEDF 52 seats. A number of smaller parties secured the remaining seats. Despite agreeing to accept the NEBE's decision, the CUD renewed its allegations of electoral fraud and in early October some 100 CUD deputies boycotted the opening of the House of People's Representatives.

In November 2005 there were further violent clashes in Addis Ababa between police and demonstrators protesting against alleged voting irregularities in the legislative elections. It was reported that some 46 people were killed and around 150 people were injured during the confrontations. A number of senior members of the CUD were among some 130 people arrested later in November and who were subsequently charged with treason and attempted genocide. Proceedings against those accused, 25 of whom were being tried *in absentia*, commenced in the Federal High Court in February 2006. In March charges against 18 defendants were dropped. In June 2007 38 of the defendants were found guilty of violating the Constitution and 30 of those convicted were sentenced to life imprisonment, with the remainder handed lesser terms; however, in July all 38 were pardoned and freed from prison.

Meanwhile, in January 2006 the British Government announced that it was to suspend indefinitely its direct budgetary support to Ethiopia, owing to concerns over the political situation in the country. In May a new opposition coalition, the Alliance for Freedom and Democracy (AFD), was formed by the CUD and four rebel factions: the Ethiopian People's Patriotic Front; the Ogaden National Liberation Front (ONLF); the Oromo Liberation Front (OLF) and the Sidama Liberation Front. In August Meles announced that thousands of troops had been deployed against ONLF rebels, who were allegedly receiving support from Eritrea and Somali Islamists, in the Ogaden region. In the same month it was reported that around 150 members of the Ethiopian army had defected to Eritrea, including a senior commander who intended to join the OLF; two other key military figures allegedly followed in mid-September. In October it emerged that an official inquiry into the violent dispersal of demonstrations after the May 2005 elections had been suppressed by the Government; 193 protesters were reported to have been killed by Ethiopian security forces. Renewed violence in mid-November 2009 resulted in the deaths of a number of Ethiopian troops as ONLF rebels launched an offensive in the Ogaden region, seizing or destroying the military's weapons and equipment. In January 2010 the Ethiopian Government announced that it had detained some 100 OLF rebels following clashes near Moyale in which the OLF claimed to have killed at least three Ethiopian soldiers.

Meles reorganized the Council of Ministers in October 2008, appointing six new members; Shiferaw TekeleMariam was named Minister of Federal Affairs, replacing Siraj Fergesa, who was appointed Minister of Defence. Berhan Hailu, hitherto Minister of Information, was assigned the justice portfolio.

In April 2009 the Ethiopian Government arrested 40 individuals, mostly Amhara with military backgrounds, who they claimed were secretly members of a new opposition party, the Movement for Justice, Freedom and Democracy (Ginbot 7), which had adopted a platform sanctioning any means to effect political change. After being found guilty of plotting to overthrow the Government, in December five of the defendants were sentenced to death, while terms of life imprisonment were handed down to 33 others.

The 2010 general election

In October 2009 eight opposition organizations formed the Ethiopia Federal Democratic Unity Forum (FORUM) chaired by Dr Merara Gudina, leader of the Oromo People's Congress. It was reported in November that some 450 members of opposition parties had been arrested in an apparent attempt by the authorities to disrupt the opposition prior to the May 2010 legislative elections. Tensions increased further in the months leading up to the elections, with the FORUM and US-based Human Rights Watch (HRW) accusing the Government of orchestrating a campaign to suppress opposition activity. The FORUM alleged that its supporters had been subjected to harassment, intimidation and beatings. The situation deteriorated in March 2010, when a FORUM candidate was stabbed to death, which was followed by the murders of two FORUM activists in April and May, respectively. The Government denied any involvement in the killings and countered by blaming the opposition for the murder of one of its candidates in May. According to official sources, in the same month two people were also killed in a grenade attack at a meeting organized by the pro-Government OPDO. Meanwhile, in March Meles admitted that radio programming transmitted by the Voice of America (VOA), a worldwide broadcasting operation funded by the US Government, was being blocked within Ethiopia. Meles accused VOA of transmitting 'destabilizing propaganda' and likened its content to 1990s Rwandan broadcasts encouraging genocide, prompting condemnation by the US Administration.

The general election was held peacefully on 23 May 2010 and resulted in an emphatic victory for the EPRDF, which won 499 of the 547 seats contested. Pro-Government parties secured an additional 46 seats, while the FORUM (which had been weakened by internal divisions) only managed to gain control of a single seat; an independent candidate won the remaining seat. The rate of participation by the electorate was recorded at 93.4%. EU monitors announced that the election had not met international standards and criticized the Government's monopolization of state resources during campaigning, a stance reiterated by US officials, although African Union (see p. 189) observers defended the results. The EPRDF claimed that the outcome reflected voter satisfaction with the Government's economic policies. Opposition leaders denounced the results, citing electoral irregularities and accusing the authorities of fraud, allegations that the Government dismissed. Merara demanded a re-run of the election, but this was rejected by the NEBE and the Supreme Court in June.

Meles was unanimously re-elected as Prime Minister by the House of People's Representatives on 4 October 2010, and he appointed 10 new members to the Council of Ministers on the following day, although most of the major portfolios were unaltered. Most notable among the changes was the appointment of Hailemariam Desalegn as Deputy Prime Minister and Minister of Foreign Affairs. Birtukan Mideksa, a prominent opposition leader who had been sentenced to life imprisonment for treason after the post-election unrest in 2005, was pardoned and released from gaol shortly afterwards. (Birtukan had been freed in 2007 but was rearrested the following year.) Her release was viewed by some commentators as an attempt by the Government to appease its international partners in the wake of the election controversy. However, the EPRDF's victory came under further scrutiny later that month, when a HRW report claimed that the Government had systematically refused to allocate food aid to supporters of the opposition; the authorities denied this accusation.

Following their overwhelming defeat in the legislative elections, a number of opposition parties underwent a process of restructuring. The remaining members of the FORUM announced in July 2010 that they had disbanded their loose coalition and formed a six-party front, committing themselves to a permanent alliance and a common policy platform. A new opposition grouping, the Alliance for Liberty, Equality and Justice in Ethiopia, was founded in August by Ginbot 7, the Afar People's Party and the Ethiopian Movement for Unity and Justice, while local press reports in September noted the formation by seven opposition parties of the Ethiopian People's Democratic Front.

ONLF rebels attacked a military base in Malqaqa in May 2010 and claimed that they had gained control of the town, although the Government denied this and stated that the attack had been repelled and all rebels killed. In September the authorities announced that they had killed 123 ONLF fighters, who had reportedly crossed into Ethiopia from the 'Republic of Somaliland', but the rebels rejected this claim. Meanwhile, the leader of the United Western Somali Liberation Front, an Ogaden-based Islamist group, signed a peace deal with the Government in July, agreeing to disarm in exchange for an amnesty for its members. A similar peace agreement was signed by a faction of the ONLF, led by Salahdin Abdurahman Maow, in October. Both groups announced that they intended to regroup as political parties.

Recent developments: opposition arrests

In March 2011 it was announced that nearly 250 members of the FORUM, principally of the Oromo Federalist Democratic Movement (OFDM), had been arrested in an apparent attempt to pre-empt anti-Government protests such as those of the 'Arab Spring' in Middle East and North Africa. In the same month it was reported that Meles had replaced some 150 officials belonging to OPDO, after ordering their arrest on charges of corruption. In June Moga Firisa of the OFDM was elected as the new Chairman of the FORUM. In August human rights organization Amnesty International expressed concern at the detention by the authorities of 31 people, including two principal opposition leaders, on suspicion of participating in terrorist activities. In September five people, including opposition leader Andualem Arage and journalist Eskinder Nega, were arrested on the grounds that they were supporters of Ginbot 7 and involved in organizing acts of terrorism in the country; the detention earlier that month on similar charges of political activist Debebe Eshetu was also denounced by opposition groups.

Foreign Affairs

Regional relations

Relations with Somalia have been problematic since the Ogaden War of 1977–78. However, in April 1988 Ethiopia and Somalia agreed to re-establish diplomatic relations, to withdraw troops from their common border and to exchange prisoners of war. In November 2000 the President of Somalia, Abdulkassim Salad Hasan, visited Ethiopia and held talks with senior Ethiopian officials; however, the Ethiopian authorities continued to refuse to recognize officially the Hasan administration and urged it to reach agreements with its opponents. In January 2001 relations between the countries deteriorated, after the Somali Prime Minister accused Ethiopia of continuing to assist the Somali-based Rahawin Resistance Army, which had taken control of a number of towns in south-west Somalia, and of involvement in an assassination attempt on the Speaker of Somalia's transitional legislature. Later in the year Ethiopia agreed to mediate between the Somali Transitional National Government (TNG) and the Somali Reconciliation and Restoration Council, which had been established in Ethiopia in March to rival the TNG. Relations between Somalia and Ethiopia were further strained by Meles' claim that a number of members of al-Ittihad al-Islam (Islamic Union Party—which sought independence for Ethiopia's Ogaden province) were represented in the Somali TNG; the accusation was, however, forcefully denied by Hasan. Relations between Ethiopia and Somalia improved in early 2005 and Ethiopia signalled its support for the new Somali President, Col Abdullahi Yussuf Ahmed, following his election in January. In 2006, however, repeated accusations of incursions by Ethiopian troops in support of the TNG in Baidoa (where it had been relocated) caused relations to deteriorate once more. In October Meles admitted the presence of military trainers in Baidoa and described his country as being 'technically at war' with its neighbour and prepared for conflict. In late November it was reported that an Ethiopian military convoy had been ambushed by Islamist fighters near Baidoa; the following month supporters of the Somali Supreme Islamic Courts Council (SSICC, as the Union of Islamic Courts had been restyled) headed for Tiyeglow, a town near the Ethiopian border, with the intention of isolating the TNG in Baidoa. In mid-December the SSICC issued a deadline for Ethiopian troops to leave Somalia within one week or face a major attack; the following week, amid reports of heavy fighting between Ethiopian troops and Islamist militias near Baidoa, the SSICC urged all Somalis to join the 'war' against Ethiopia. At the end of the month Meles admitted for the first time to active military involvement by his country in Somalia, claiming that his troops were defending Ethiopia's sovereignty against what he termed terrorists and anti-Ethiopian elements. Ethiopia was supported in its actions by the African Union (AU, see p. 189), which conceded that the presence of Islamist militias so close to its borders might be perceived as a threat. The UN estimated that at the end of 2006 at least 8,000 Ethiopian troops were deployed in Somalia. In late June 2007 Meles pledged to withdraw Ethiopian forces from Somalia upon the arrival of an AU peace-keeping force, the AU Mission in Somalia (AMISOM); however, the pervading instability in Somalia meant that only a small number of the proposed 8,000 troops were deployed by mid-2007; in August the UN Security Council extended AMISOM's mandate by six months. Ethiopian forces were still present in February 2008—when the AMISOM mandate was extended by a further six months—as the number of peace-keepers deployed was still limited. In August the AMISOM mandate was extended again, and in November it was announced that all Ethiopian troops would leave Somalia by the end of the year; in January 2009 the last remaining soldiers withdrew. However, reports emerged during 2009 and 2010 of Ethiopian troops crossing into Somalia to engage insurgents belonging to the Somali Islamist group al-Shabaab. In November 2011 the Ethiopian Government denied reports that its forces were supporting the Somalian authorities and AMISOM in a large-scale military operation against al-Shabaab.

Following the military coup in Sudan in April 1985, full diplomatic relations were restored between Ethiopia and Sudan. Relations between the two countries were strained in the late 1980s, however, by the influx into Ethiopia of thousands of Sudanese refugees, fleeing from famine and civil war in southern Sudan. The vast majority of an estimated 380,000 refugees were reported to have returned to Sudan by early 1991, as a result of the civil war in Ethiopia. The change of government in Ethiopia in May 1991 led to a considerable improvement in relations, and in October President Meles and Sudan's leader, Lt-Gen. al-Bashir, signed an agreement on friendship and co-operation. In November 1999 Prime Minister Meles received al-Bashir in Addis Ababa, where they announced their intent to form closer economic ties between the two countries. In November 2004 the two countries finalized the demarcation of their common border on paper and requested financial assistance from international organizations in order to demarcate the border on the ground. In May 2008 it was announced that an agreement would soon be concluded. Despite Meles' insistence that no citizens would be displaced, in the following month there were reports that Ethiopians living in the border regions had been forced from their homes by Sudanese troops; there were also concerns that the demarcation would transfer holy and historic areas of Ethiopia to Sudan. In July Sudan accused Ethiopian troops of launching a cross-border raid on a police camp in which one officer was killed and several people wounded, although a spokesman for Prime Minister Meles denied the Ethiopian military's involvement. By November 2009 preparations had been finalized in Ethiopia for the deployment of a 200-strong air force unit to Darfur, in addition to the 1,600 ground troops already stationed in the region.

Ethiopia and the newly independent Eritrea signed a treaty of co-operation during a visit by the Eritrean President, Issaias Afewerki, to Addis Ababa in July 1993. The agreement included provisions on the joint utilization of resources and co-operation in the energy, transport, defence and education sectors. A further agreement, signed in late 1994, provided for the free movement of goods between the two countries without payment of customs dues.

In late 1997 relations with Eritrea deteriorated, following that country's adoption of a new currency (to replace the Ethiopian birr) and the subsequent disruption of cross-border trade. Fighting between Ethiopian and Eritrean troops erupted in early May 1998, with both countries accusing the other of having invaded their territory. Proposals by the UN Security Council and the Organization of African Unity (OAU), now the AU, to resolve the conflict were rejected by Eritrea, necessitating the convening of a special meeting of an OAU mediation committee in Ouagadougou, Burkina Faso, in November. Ethiopia welcomed the committee's proposals, which stressed the need to demilitarize and demarcate the disputed region, but Eritrea rejected the plans. Further mediation attempts to impose a cease-fire also failed.

In mid-May 2000 Ethiopian troops launched a major offensive near the disputed towns of Badme and Zalambessa, repelling the Eritrean forces. Despite demands from the UN, hostilities continued, and on 18 May the UN Security Council unanimously approved the imposition of a 12-month arms embargo on Ethiopia and Eritrea. Shortly afterwards Zalambessa fell to the Ethiopian forces, and on 25 May the Eritrean Government announced the withdrawal of its troops from all disputed areas. On 31 May Prime Minister Meles stated that Ethiopia had no territorial claims over Eritrea and that the war between the two countries was over; nevertheless, sporadic fighting continued to take place. In early June both sides expressed their willingness, in principle, to accept the OAU's peace proposals and on 18 June the Ethiopian and Eritrean Ministers of Foreign Affairs signed an agreement, which provided for an immediate cease-fire and the establishment of a 25-km temporary security zone (TSZ) on the Eritrean side of the common border until the issue of the final demarcation of the border had been settled. In mid-September the UN Security Council approved the deployment of a 4,200-strong UN Mission in Ethiopia and Eritrea (UNMEE).

In December 2000 Ethiopia and Eritrea signed an agreement in Algiers, which formally brought an end to the conflict. The agreement provided for a permanent cessation of all hostilities, the return of all prisoners of war, the demarcation of the common border by an independent commission, and the establishment of a Claims Commission to assess the issues of compensation and reparations. By late January 2001 the UNMEE force had arrived in the region and Ethiopian troops commenced their withdrawal from the territory they had captured from Eritrea. In March UNMEE's mandate was extended until September and on 16 April it was announced that the withdrawal of its forces was complete. In mid-May the arms embargo imposed on the two countries by the UN in May 2000 was lifted. In late June 2001 UNMEE presented the final map of the TSZ to Ethiopia and Eritrea, although it emphasized that it would not influence the work of the neutral Boundary Commission charged with determining the border between the two countries. Despite this announcement, the Ethiopian Government expressed its dissatisfaction with the map, and at the eighth Military Co-ordination Committee (MCC) meeting in August both countries again stated their objections to the current boundaries of the TSZ. In mid-September UNMEE's mandate was extended for a further six months.

In mid-December 2001 Ethiopia and Eritrea began presenting their cases for border demarcation to the five-member Boundary Commission at the International Court of Justice (see p. 25) in The Hague, Netherlands. In mid-March 2002 UNMEE's mandate was extended until mid-September. The Boundary Commission delivered its findings in April. Both Ethiopia and Eritrea had committed themselves in advance to the acceptance of the report, which was carefully balanced, thus allowing both sides to claim success. However, the Commission did not identify on which side of the boundary line Badme lay, stating that delineation had been delayed, as extensive de-mining was required prior to placing boundary markers. In the absence of any decision, both countries immediately claimed to have been awarded Badme. Ethiopia formally requested 'interpretation, correction and consultation' of the Boundary Commission's report in May; this was rejected in late June.

In early March 2003 the Boundary Commission reported to the UN Security Council that Ethiopia's requests for changes to the border ruling, in order to 'take better account of human and physical geography', threatened to undermine the peace process as a whole. Despite Ethiopia's claims that it had been promised that demarcations could be refined, later in March the Boundary Commission categorically ruled Badme to be Eritrean territory, thus rejecting Ethiopia's territorial claim over the town. Meles subsequently complained that the decision was 'wrong and unjust' and vowed to continue to contest the ruling.

The demarcation of the border, which had originally been scheduled to take place in May 2003, was postponed until July, and then further delayed until October. In a letter to the UN Security Council in October, Prime Minister Meles requested the establishment of a new body to resolve the crisis and again denounced the Boundary Commission's ruling as 'unacceptable'. However, the Security Council stated that Ethiopia had, under the 2000 Algiers accord, committed itself to accept the Boundary Commission's decision as 'final and binding' and urged it to accept and implement the border ruling. With no resolution to the ongoing impasse in sight, in late October the Boundary Commission announced that the demarcation of the border had been delayed indefinitely.

In 2004 UNMEE's mandate was extended by a further six months in March and again in September. In November Ethiopia indicated that it would co-operate with UNMEE when Meles announced a five-point plan aimed at resolving the disputed border issue and declared that Ethiopia had, in principle, accepted the Boundary Commission's ruling. Meles' statement was dismissed by the Eritrean authorities as an attempt by Ethiopia to further stall the process. In mid-December the UN withdrew some 550 Kenyan troops from the TSZ in an attempt to reduce the costs of its military presence in the area.

Ethiopia and Eritrea continued to increase troop numbers in the border area in 2005, raising fears of a return to conflict. However, Ethiopia sought to reassure the international community that troop movements and the construction of trenches on its side of the TSZ were for defensive purposes only. UNMEE's mandate was extended for six months in March and again in September. In November the UN Security Council adopted Resolution 1640, which demanded full acceptance by Ethiopia of the Boundary Commission's ruling regarding border demarcation, that Eritrea lift restrictions on UNMEE operations, and that troop numbers on both sides of the border be reduced with immediate effect.

In early March 2006 a Boundary Commission meeting took place in London, United Kingdom. Agreement was reached between Ethiopia and Eritrea to hold further talks the following month, although these were subsequently postponed. On 31 May UNMEE's mandate was extended for a further four months but reduced the number of military personnel in the region by 1,000 to 2,300; in September UNMEE's mandate was further extended until 31 January 2007. In mid-November 2006 both countries failed to attend a meeting of the Boundary Commission in The Hague and rejected its proposals; the Commission, in response, issued a statement informing them that in the event of no agreement having been reached by November 2007 it would begin the physical demarcation of the border. Ethiopia's relations with Eritrea came under further strain in December 2006, owing to the former's military support of pro-Government forces in Somalia, who were struggling to reclaim territory from Islamist militias. Reports that Eritreans were fighting alongside the Islamist forces were strongly denied by the Eritrean Government. On 31 January 2007 the UN Security Council's Resolution 1741 extended UNMEE'S mandate by six months and further reduced its personnel, to 1,700. UNMEE's mandate was again extended by six months in July, and on 30 January 2008 it was prolonged until the end of July 2008. By late 2007 neither side had complied with the Boundary Commission's request of November 2006 physically to demarcate the border. In early December, prior to announcing its own dissolution, the Commission stated that the boundary that it had determined in November 2006 represented the official border between the two countries.

Eritrean-imposed restrictions on the movements of UN peace-keeping personnel and the delivery of fuel led the UN to announce in early February 2008 that it was preparing to relocate its peace-keepers in Eritrea to Ethiopia. In previous months the UN had repeatedly urged the Eritrean Government to lift restrictions on the delivery of fuel supplies; however, these requests were not met and in mid-February UN personnel were forced to leave the area. It was subsequently reported that a number of peace-keepers had been prevented from leaving Eritrea and the UN Security Council expressed its concern at the 'impediments and logistical constraints' placed upon the force. UN Secretary-General Ban Ki-Moon warned of a possible return to hostilities if the peace-keeping force was withdrawn, but Eritrea continued to impede UN operations, eventually forcing UNMEE to abandon its mission in the region. On 30 July the UN Security Council adopted Resolution 1827, terminating the mandate of UNMEE; the last troops were withdrawn in October. In August 2009 the Claims Commission awarded Ethiopia a total of US $174m. in compensation for war damages, while Eritrea received $164m., resulting in a net payment to Ethiopia of $10m.

Arbitration efforts continued during 2008 and 2009, and an uneasy truce persisted, punctuated by occasional minor military clashes. However, in early January 2010 the Eritrean Government claimed that its troops had killed 10 Ethiopian soldiers after they attacked Eritrean positions near Zalambessa. The Ethiopian authorities denied that the incident had occurred and maintained that the Eritrean authorities were attempting to cover up an attack by a rebel Eritrean movement in which 25 Eritrean government soldiers were killed. Successive bomb attacks in Tigrai Region, bordering Eritrea, in April and May 2010 resulted in the deaths of five people. The Ethiopian Government blamed Eritrea for the explosions, claiming that they were an attempt by its neighbour to disrupt the legislative elections. In March 2011 Ethiopia warned that it would take all measures necessary against Eritrea, accusing it of planning attacks during the February AU Summit in Addis Ababa; furthermore, the Ethiopian Government openly declared its support for Eritrea's opposition groups and appealed for regime change. Ethiopia also maintained that al-Shabaab continued to receive weapons and assistance from Eritrea.

Other external relations

In 1984 some 13,000 Falashas, a Jewish group in Ethiopia, reached Sudan, from where they were flown to Israel in a secret airlift. In May 1991 Israel evacuated a further 14,000 Falashas from Addis Ababa; some 10,000 Falashmura (Ethiopian Christians whose forefathers had converted from Judaism) were subsequently granted Israeli citizenship on humanitarian grounds. In March 1999 Israel pledged to examine the possibility of bringing the estimated 19,000 Jews remaining in Ethiopia to Israel, and in April 2000 the Israeli Minister of the Interior visited Ethiopia to investigate the claims of some 26,000 Ethiopians who maintained that they belonged to the Falashmura community and were thus eligible to settle in Israel under Israeli law. In February 2003 the Israeli Government ruled that the Falashmura had been forced to convert to Christianity to avoid religious persecution and that they had the right to settle in Israel. In January 2004 Ethiopia and Israel agreed to allow the Falashmura to be flown to Israel; some 17,000 Falashmura and a further 3,000 Falashas arrived in Israel by May 2008. Israel resumed the transportation of Falashmura in January 2010, following a suspension of the airlift process in August 2008. The Israeli Government announced in November 2010 that the remaining Falashmura in Ethiopia, some 8,000 people, would be granted the right to immigrate to Israel. The process was expected to take place incrementally over the following four years.

In recent years the People's Republic of China has developed closer ties with Ethiopia and has made significant economic investment in the country. However, in late April 2007 members of the ONLF killed more than 70 people, including nine Chinese oil workers, in an attack on a petroleum installation in the Somali region; seven Chinese citizens were kidnapped, although they were released unharmed five days later.

In November 2010 Meles unexpectedly accused the Egyptian Government of supporting rebel groups within Ethiopia, an allegation that Egyptian President Muhammad Hosni Mubarak promptly denied. During 2010 Ethiopia (and other nations of the upper Nile) had exerted pressure on Egypt to accept revisions to a colonial-era agreement on sharing the River Nile's water resources, which was perceived as being unfairly weighted in Egypt's favour.

CONSTITUTION AND GOVERNMENT

Under the provisions of the Constitution, adopted in December 1994, the country became a federation, consisting of nine states and two chartered cities, the capital, Addis Ababa, and Dire Dawa. The states have their own parliamentary assemblies, which also elect representatives to the House of the Federation, the upper chamber of the Federal Parliamentary Assembly. The lower chamber, the House of People's Representatives, consists of no more than 550 directly elected deputies, who each serve terms of five years. The Federal Parliamentary Assembly elects a President as Head of State with a six-year term of office. However, the President fulfils mainly ceremonial functions, executive power being the preserve of the Prime Minister. The Prime Minister, who is elected by the House of People's Representatives, appoints the Council of Ministers (subject to approval by the legislature), and acts as Commander-in-Chief of the armed forces. Unless otherwise provided in the Constitution, the term of office of the Prime Minister is the duration of the mandate of the House of People's Representatives.

REGIONAL AND INTERNATIONAL CO-OPERATION

Ethiopia is a member of the African Union (see p. 189), and the headquarters of that organization are based in Addis Ababa. It is also a member of the Common Market for Eastern and Southern Africa (see p. 237) and of the Intergovernmental Authority on Development (see p. 338). In July 2001 Ethiopia ratified the

Cotonou Agreement (see p. 328), the successor of the Lomé Convention of the EU.

Ethiopia was one of the 51 founding member states of the UN, established in 1945, and participates in the Group of 77 (G77, see p. 450) developing countries. Ethiopia submitted a request for accession to the World Trade Organization (see p. 433) in January 2003.

ECONOMIC AFFAIRS

In 2010, according to estimates by the World Bank, Ethiopia's gross national income (GNI), measured at average 2008–10 prices, was US $32,409m., equivalent to $390 per head (or $1,030 per head on an international purchasing-power parity basis). During 2001–10, it was estimated, the population increased at an average annual rate of 2.3%, while gross domestic product (GDP) per head increased, in real terms, by an average of 5.9% per year. Overall GDP increased, in real terms, at an average annual rate of 8.4% during 2001–10; it increased by 10.1% in 2010.

Agriculture (including forestry and fishing) contributed 46.3% of GDP in 2010, according to the African Development Bank (AfDB), while the sector employed 80.2% of the labour force in March 2005. According to FAO estimates, the sector employed 76.2% of the labour force in mid-2012. The principal cash crop is coffee (which accounted for 30.0% of export earnings in 2010). The principal subsistence crops are cereals (teff, maize, sorghum, wheat and barley) and sugar cane. According to the World Bank, during 2001–10 agricultural GDP increased at an average annual rate of 6.2%; it increased by 5.8% in 2010.

Industry (including mining, manufacturing, construction and power) employed 6.6% of the labour force in March 2005, and provided 10.4% of GDP in 2010, according to the AfDB. During 2001–10, according to the World Bank, industrial GDP increased by an average of 9.4% per year. It rose by 8.8% in 2010.

According to the AfDB, mining contributed only 0.7% of GDP in 2010, and employed less than 0.3% of the labour force in March 2005. Ethiopia has reserves of petroleum, although these have not been exploited, and there are also deposits of copper and potash. Gold, tantalite, soda ash, kaolin, dimension stones, precious metals and gemstones, salt, and industrial and construction materials are mined. In April 2000 a US company discovered large petroleum deposits in the west of the country, and in June 2003 the Ethiopian Government granted a one-year exploration licence to Petronas of Malaysia. The licence was renewed in early 2004 to allow exploration over a larger area. During 2002/03–2006/07 mining GDP increased by an estimated average of 3.9% per year; growth in 2006/07 was an estimated 6.0%. According to the AfDB, the sector's GDP increased by 44.2% in 2010.

Manufacturing employed only 4.9% of the labour force in March 2005, and contributed 4.0% of GDP in 2010, according to the AfDB. During 2001–10, according to the World Bank, manufacturing GDP increased at an average annual rate of 7.7%. It increased by 9.8% in 2010.

Construction employed only 1.4% of the labour force in March 2005, and contributed 4.4% of GDP in 2010, according to the AfDB. The GDP of the sector increased by 10.9% in 2010.

In years of normal rainfall, energy is derived principally from Ethiopia's massive hydroelectric power resources. In 2007 96.2% of Ethiopia's electricity was produced by hydroelectric power schemes. Imports of mineral fuels accounted for 19.1% of the cost of total imports in 2010. In late 1995 the Government announced plans to develop geothermal energy sources at 15 sites in various regions of the country. Ethiopia's electricity generating capacity had reached 790 MW by 2006.

Services, which consisted mainly of wholesale and retail trade, public administration and defence, and transport and communications, employed 13.1% of the labour force in March 2005, and contributed 43.3% of GDP in 2010, according to the AfDB. The combined GDP of the service sectors increased, in real terms, at an average rate of 11.2% per year during 2001–10, according to the World Bank. It rose by 15.2% in 2010.

In 2010 Ethiopia recorded a visible trade deficit of US $4,964.6m., and there was a deficit of $425.4m. on the current account of the balance of payments. In 2010 the principal source of imports (24.0% of the total) was the People's Republic of China; other major suppliers were Saudi Arabia, India, the United Arab Emirates, the USA and Japan. The principal market for exports in that year were Germany (11.4% of the total), China, Somalia, the Netherlands, Sudan, Saudi Arabia and Switzerland. The principal exports in 2010 were oil seeds, coffee, and edible vegetables and roots and tubers, gold and cut flowers. The principal imports in that year were refined petroleum, electrical and electronic equipment, nuclear reactors, boilers, machinery, etc., and motor vehicles.

In the fiscal year 2010/11 Ethiopia's budgetary deficit was projected to reach 11,928m. birr. Ethiopia's general government gross debt was 140,716m. birr. in 2010, equivalent to 36.7% of GDP. Ethiopia is the principal African recipient of concessionary funding, and one of the largest recipients of European Union (EU) aid. In 2009 Ethiopia's total external debt was US $5,025m., of which $4,812m. was public and publicly guaranteed debt. In that year, the cost of servicing long-term public and publicly guaranteed debt and repayments to the IMF was equivalent to 1.6% of the value of exports of goods, services and income (excluding workers' remittances). The annual rate of inflation averaged 17.4% in 2005–10, according to the IMF. Consumer prices increased by 8.1% in 2010. In March 2005 1,653,700 people were registered as unemployed, representing 5.0% of the total labour force.

Ethiopia remains one of the poorest countries in the world, and the country's economy continues to suffer from the effects of recurrent, catastrophic drought, which severely disrupts agricultural production. The scarcity of land and the lack of agricultural development have resulted in massive environmental degradation and, in turn, widespread poverty and famine. The Ethiopian economy is also heavily dependent on assistance and grants from abroad, while political uncertainty, in particular with regard to ongoing instability in Ethiopia's relations with Eritrea and Somalia, poses further problems for the economy. Investment in the country's infrastructure was required to facilitate the distribution of aid supplies, and in June 2009 the AfDB approved a loan of some US $326m. for the completion of the second phase of the Mombasa-Nairobi-Addis Ababa Road Corridor Project. Furthermore, in September 2010 construction began of a 5,000-km railway system, to be used primarily for transporting goods, with financing provided by the Export-Import Bank of China. In 2008 the IMF approved a loan of $50m. under the Exogenous Shocks Facility to mitigate the impact of large increases in international prices for fuel, fertilizer and cereals; a further $240.6m. was approved in August 2009, and tranches of $58.7m. and $62.7m. were released in June and November 2010, respectively. In response to shortages in foreign exchange in 2009, the authorities devalued the currency by 9.9% in July, followed by a further devaluation of 16.7% in September 2010. A Growth and Transformation Plan (GTP) for 2010/11–2014/15 was finalized by the authorities in November 2010 and presented to the IMF, which considered the programme's high growth objectives to be over-ambitious, and advocated greater structural reform, with a focus on private sector development. The IMF estimated strong growth of 7.5% for Ethiopia in 2010/11, with a lower rate of about 6% projected for 2011/12, owing to continuing high inflation, restrictions on private bank lending, and a less favourable business environment.

PUBLIC HOLIDAYS

2013: 7 January* (Christmas), 19 January* (Epiphany), 24 January† (Mouloud, Birth of the Prophet), 2 March (Battle of Adowa), 1 May (May Day), 3 May* (Good Friday), 5 May (Patriots' Victory Day), 6 May* (Easter Monday), 28 May (Downfall of the Dergue), 7 August† (Id al-Fitr, end of Ramadan), 11 September (New Year's Day), 27 September* (Feast of the True Cross), 15 October† (Id al-Adha/Arafat).

* Coptic holidays.

† These holidays are dependent on the Islamic lunar calendar and may vary by one or two days from the dates given.

Note: Ethiopia uses its own solar calendar; the Ethiopian year 2004 began on 12 September 2011.

Statistical Survey

Source (unless otherwise stated): Central Statistical Authority, POB 1143, Addis Ababa; tel. (1) 553010; fax (1) 550334; internet www.csa.gov.et.

Area and Population

AREA, POPULATION AND DENSITY

Area (sq km)	1,133,380*
Population (census results)	
11 October 1994	53,477,265
28 May 2007	
Males	37,296,657
Females	36,621,848
Total	73,918,505
Population (UN estimates at mid-year)†	
2010	82,949,541
2011	84,734,260
2012	86,538,535
Density (per sq km) at mid-2012	76.4

* 437,600 sq miles.

† Source: UN, *World Population Prospects: The 2010 Revision*.

POPULATION BY AGE AND SEX

(UN estimates at mid-2012)

	Males	Females	Total
0–14	17,468,438	17,253,747	34,722,185
15–64	24,234,436	24,602,767	48,837,203
65 and over	1,369,037	1,610,110	2,979,147
Total	43,071,911	43,466,624	86,538,535

Source: UN, *World Population Prospects: The 2010 Revision*.

ADMINISTRATIVE DIVISIONS

(population at 2007 census)

	Population ('000)		
	Males	Females	Total
Regional States			
1 Tigrai	2,125	2,190	4,314
2 Afar	786	625	1,411
3 Amhara	8,637	8,577	17,214
4 Oromia	13,676	13,482	27,158
5 Somali	2,469	1,970	4,439
6 Benishangul/Gumuz	340	330	671
7 Southern Nations, Nationalities and Peoples	7,482	7,560	15,042
8 Gambela	160	147	307
9 Harari	92	91	183
Chartered Cities			
1 Dire Dawa	172	171	343
2 Addis Ababa	1,305	1,434	2,738
Total*	37,297	36,622	73,919

* Including 96,570 persons, detailed as 'special enumeration', not allocated to administrative divisions.

Note: Totals may not be equal to the sum of components, owing to rounding.

PRINCIPAL TOWNS

(population at 2007 census)

Addis Ababa (capital)	2,738,248	Bahir Dar	180,094
Dire Dawa	342,827	Awasa	159,013
Nazret	222,035	Jimma	120,600
Mekele	215,546	Dessie	120,029
Gondar	206,987	Debre Zeit	100,114

Mid-2010 (incl. suburbs, UN estimate): Addis Ababa (capital) 2,929,626 (Source: UN, *World Urbanization Prospects: The 2009 Revision*).

BIRTHS AND DEATHS

(annual averages, UN estimates)

	1995–2000	2000–05	2005–10
Birth rate (per 1,000)	43.9	38.8	33.3
Death rate (per 1,000)	15.2	13.0	10.5

Source: UN, *World Population Prospects: The 2010 Revision*.

Life expectancy (years at birth, WHO estimates): 54 (males 53; females 56) in 2009 (Source: WHO, *World Health Statistics*).

ECONOMICALLY ACTIVE POPULATION

('000 persons aged 10 years and over, March 2005)*

	Males	Females	Total
Agriculture, hunting, forestry and fishing	14,209.4	10,998.8	25,208.2
Mining and quarrying	51.4	30.6	82.1
Manufacturing	444.0	1,085.3	1,529.4
Electricity, gas and water	25.2	7.7	32.9
Construction	349.9	95.7	445.6
Wholesale and retail trade; repair of motor vehicles, motorcycles and personal and household goods	652.2	984.9	1,637.1
Hotels and restaurants	96.8	672.3	769.1
Transport, storage and communications	132.0	14.5	146.4
Financial intermediation	21.6	16.3	37.9
Real estate, renting and business services	36.1	16.2	52.3
Public administration and defence; compulsory social security	242.0	125.9	367.9
Education	178.2	104.5	282.7
Social work	45.6	32.5	78.1
Community, social and personal services	303.5	135.2	438.7
Households with employed persons	23.1	225.5	248.6
Extra-territorial organizations and bodies	42.7	25.1	67.9
Sub-total	16,853.7	14,571.0	31,424.9
Not classifiable by economic activity	6.5	3.8	10.3
Total employed	16,860.3	14,574.8	31,435.1
Unemployed	427.9	1,225.8	1,653.7
Total labour force	17,288.2	15,800.6	33,088.8

* Excluding armed forces.

Source: ILO.

Mid-2012 (FAO estimates in '000): Agriculture, etc. 33,142; Total labour force 43,466 (Source: FAO).

Health and Welfare

KEY INDICATORS

Total fertility rate (children per woman, 2009)	5.2
Under-5 mortality rate (per 1,000 live births, 2009)	104
HIV/AIDS (% of persons aged 15–49, 2007)	2.1
Physicians (per 1,000 head, 2003)	0.03
Hospital beds (per 1,000 head, 2006)	0.20
Health expenditure (2008): US $ per head (PPP)	37
Health expenditure (2008): % of GDP	4.3
Health expenditure (2008): public (% of total)	51.9
Access to water (% of persons, 2008)	38
Access to sanitation (% of persons, 2008)	12
Total carbon dioxide emissions ('000 metric tons, 2007)	6,503.6
Carbon dioxide emissions per head (metric tons, 2007)	0.1
Human Development Index (2011): ranking	174
Human Development Index (2011): value	0.363

For sources and definitions, see explanatory note on p. vi.

Agriculture

PRINCIPAL CROPS
('000 metric tons)

	2008	2009	2010
Wheat	2,463	3,076*	3,000*
Barley	1,352	1,750*	1,400*
Maize	3,776	3,897*	4,400*
Oats	31	43	43†
Millet (Dagusa)	484	560	565†
Sorghum	2,316	2,971*	2,997†
Potatoes	403	572*	786†
Sweet potatoes	526	451*	402†
Yams	228*	406*	407†
Sugar cane†	2,300	2,200	2,400
Beans, dry	241	285*	263†
Broad beans, horse beans, dry	689	611*	607†
Peas, dry	232	236*	232†
Chick peas	287	312*	310†
Lentils	94	124*	123†
Vetches	185	204*	203†
Groundnuts, with shell	45	46*	56†
Castor beans	7*	7*	8†
Rapeseed	48	23*	40†
Safflower seed	8	6*	4†
Sesame seed	187	261*	314*
Linseed	170	151*	150†
Cabbages and other brassicas	250	277*	257†
Tomatoes	42*	40*	41†
Onions and shallots, green†	22	26	26
Onions, dry	175	169*	205†
Garlic	104	180*	180†
Bananas	261	209*	172†
Oranges	29	44	39†
Mangoes, mangosteens and guavas	80†	66*	77†
Avocados	43	38*	34†
Papayas	250	260†	232†
Coffee, green	273	265*	270*

* Unofficial figure(s).
† FAO estimate(s).

Aggregate production ('000 metric tons, may include official, semi-official or estimated data): Total cereals 13,012 in 2008, 15,502 in 2009, 15,638 in 2010; Total roots and tubers 5,920 in 2008, 7,311 in 2009, 7,097 in 2010; Total vegetables (incl. melons) 1,391 in 2008, 1,640 in 2009, 1,679 in 2010; Total fruits (excl. melons) 866 in 2008, 792 in 2009, 684 in 2010.

Source: FAO.

LIVESTOCK
('000 head, year ending September)

	2008	2009	2010
Cattle	49,298	50,884*	50,884†
Sheep	26,117	25,017	25,980
Goats	21,799	21,961*	21,961†
Asses	5,422	5,715*	5,715†
Mules	374*	366*	366†
Horses	1,786	1,995*	1,995†
Camels	1009	760	808
Pigs†	29	29	29
Poultry	38,049	38,000†	38,000†

* Unofficial figure.
† FAO estimate(s).

Source: FAO.

LIVESTOCK PRODUCTS
('000 metric tons, FAO estimates)

	2008	2009	2010
Cattle meat	380.0	390.0	373.2
Sheep meat	81.5	85.0	86.5
Goat meat	67.9	65.5	66.3
Pig meat	1.7	2.0	1.6
Chicken meat	48.6	50.9	53.0
Game meat	83.0	89.6	84.7
Cows' milk	1,350	1,400	1774
Goats' milk	50.3	50.5	52.5
Sheep's milk	44.0	46.0	48.0
Hen eggs	34.0	30.9	35.1
Honey	42.0	40.7	45.3
Wool, greasy	7.3	7.6	14.4

Source: FAO.

Forestry

ROUNDWOOD REMOVALS
('000 cubic metres, excl. bark, FAO estimates)

	2007	2008	2009
Sawlogs, veneer logs and logs for sleepers	4	4	4
Pulpwood	7	7	7
Other industrial wood	2,917	2,917	2,917
Fuel wood	97,131	98,489	99,870
Total	100,059	101,417	102,798

2010: Figures assumed to be unchanged from 2009 (FAO estimates).

Source: FAO.

SAWNWOOD PRODUCTION
('000 cubic metres, incl. railway sleepers)

	2001	2002	2003
Coniferous (softwood)	25*	1	1
Broadleaved (hardwood)	35*	13	17
Total	60	14	18

* FAO estimate.

2004–10: Figures assumed to be unchanged from 2003 (FAO estimates).

Source: FAO.

Fishing

(metric tons, live weight of capture)

	2007	2008	2009
Common carp	284	313	293
Other cyprinids	1,651	1,672	1,936
Tilapias	5,425	7,180	7,554
North African catfish	2,823	3,384	3,143
Nile perch	2,597	3,243	2,740
Total catch (incl. others)	13,253	16,770	17,047

Source: FAO.

Mining

('000 metric tons, unless otherwise indicated, year ending 7 July)

	2006/07	2007/08	2008/09
Gold (kilograms)	4,368	3,465	4,872
Limestone	1,900*	1,900	2,000*
Gypsum and anhydrite	30	33	36*
Pumice	22	35	37*
Sandstone*	1,400	1,400	1,500

* Estimate(s).

Source: US Geological Survey.

Industry

SELECTED PRODUCTS

('000 metric tons, year ending 7 July, unless otherwise indicated)

	2000/01	2001/02	2002/03
Wheat flour	165	143	137
Macaroni and pasta	26	23	30*
Raw sugar	251	248*	295*
Wine ('000 hectolitres)	25	27*	32*
Beer ('000 hectolitres)	1,605	1,812*	2,123*
Mineral waters ('000 hectolitres)	395	395*	433*
Soft drinks ('000 hectolitres)	677	995	845*
Cigarettes (million)	1,904	1,511*	1,511*
Cotton yarn	5.7	7.7*	5.5*
Woven cotton fabrics ('000 sq m)	45,000	45,000*	41,000*
Nylon fabrics ('000 sq m)	1,300	1,000*	1,400*
Footwear (including rubber, '000 pairs)	n.a.	6,677	7,138
Soap	14.8	19.2*	11.6*
Tyres ('000)*	209	198	191
Clay building bricks ('000)*	20	22	21
Quicklime*	11	8	11
Cement*	819	919	890

* Year ending 31 December of later year.

Source: UN, *Industrial Commodity Statistics Yearbook*.

Raw sugar ('000 metric tons): 325.0 in 2004; 345.0 in 2005; 360.0 in 2006; 340.0 in 2007; 340 in 2008 (Source: UN Industrial Commodity Statistics Database).

Cement (hydraulic, '000 metric tons, year ending 7 July): 1,130.1 in 2003; 1,315.9 in 2004; 1,568.6 in 2005; 1,731 in 2006; 1,626 in 2007; 1,834 in 2008; 2,300 in 2009 (estimate) (Source: US Geological Survey).

Beer of millet ('000 metric tons): 220.7 in 2001; 208.0 in 2002; 244.1 in 2003 (Source: FAO).

Beer of barley ('000 metric tons, estimates): 502.6 in 2004; 545.1 in 2005; 618.9 in 2006; 634.5 in 2007; 630.6 in 2008; 776.9 in 2009 (Source: FAO).

Finance

CURRENCY AND EXCHANGE RATES

Monetary Units

100 cents = 1 birr.

Sterling, Dollar and Euro Equivalents (30 December 2010)

£1 sterling = 20.306 birr;
US $1 = 17.208 birr;
€1 = 18.066 birr;
100 birr = £4.92 = $5.81 = €5.54.

Average Exchange Rate (birr per US $)

2009 11.778
2010 14.410
2011 16.899

GENERAL BUDGET

(rounded figures, million birr, year ending 7 July)

Revenue	2004/05	2005/06	2006/07
Taxation	12,398	14,159	17,354
Taxes on income and profits	3,569	3,819	4,868
Personal income	1,132	1,414	1,828
Business profits	1,714	1,741	2,305
Domestic indirect taxes	2,721	3,111	3,997
Import duties	5,746	6,587	8,189
Other revenue	3,184	5,371	4,443
Reimbursements and property sales	193	310	168
Sales of goods and services	856	433	250
Total*	15,582	19,529	21,797

Expenditure	2004/05	2005/06	2006/07
Current expenditure	13,229	15,234	17,166
General services	5,816	6,522	7,073
Economic services	1,516	2,009	2,201
Social services	3,839	4,996	6,198
Interest and charges	1,011	1,054	1,207
External assistance (grants)†	721	586	411
Capital expenditure	11,343	14,041	18,398
Economic development	7,655	9,728	11,367
Social development	3,290	3,796	5,998
General services and compensation	397	517	1,033
External assistance (grants)†	1,513	2,196	3,081
Total	24,572	29,275	35,564

* Excluding grants received from abroad (million birr): 4,565 in 2004/05; 4,721 in 2005/06; 8,477 in 2006/07.

† Imputed value of goods and services provided, mainly aid in kind.

Source: IMF, *The Federal Democratic Republic of Ethiopia: Statistical Appendix* (July 2008).

2007/08 (million birr, year ending 7 July): *Revenue:* Taxation 23,801 (Direct taxes 6,628, Domestic indirect taxes 5,480, Import duties 11,693); Other revenue 5,993; Total 29,794 (excl. grants 9,911). *Expenditure:* Current expenditure 22,794 (Defence spending 3,453; Poverty-reducing expenditure 10,627; Interest and charges 1,133); Capital expenditure 24,121; Total 46,915 (Source: IMF, *Ethiopia: 2010 Article IV Consultation and First Review of the Arrangement under the Exogenous Shocks Facility—Staff Report; Staff Supplements; and Press Release on the Executive Board Discussion*—June 2010).

2008/09 (million birr, year ending 7 July): *Revenue:* Taxation 28,998 (Direct taxes 9,858, Domestic indirect taxes 7,325, Import duties 11,814); Other revenue 11,176; Total 40,174 (excl. grants 14,454). *Expenditure:* Current expenditure 27,176 (Defence spending 4,000; Poverty-reducing expenditure 12,629; Interest and charges 1,286); Capital expenditure 30,599; Total 57,774 (Source: IMF, *Ethiopia: 2010 Article IV Consultation and First Review of the Arrangement under the Exogenous Shocks Facility—Staff Report; Staff Supplements; and Press Release on the Executive Board Discussion*—June 2010).

2009/10 (million birr, year ending 7 July, estimates): *Revenue:* Taxation 42,831 (Direct taxes 14,507, Domestic indirect taxes 10,640, Import duties 17,685); Other revenue 10,461; Total 53,292 (excl. grants 12,730). *Expenditure:* Current expenditure 32,994 (Defence spending 4,000; Poverty-reducing expenditure 16,361; Interest and charges 1,587); Capital expenditure 39,062; Total 72,056 (Source: IMF, *The Federal Democratic Republic of Ethiopia: Second Review of the Arrangement under the Exogenous Shocks Facility—Staff Report; Press Release on the Executive Board Discussion; and Statement by the Executive Director for the Federal Democratic Republic of Ethiopia*—November 2010).

2010/11 (million birr, year ending 7 July, budget forecasts): *Revenue:* Taxation 53,735 (Direct taxes 17,969, Domestic indirect taxes 12,707, Import duties 23,059); Other revenue 9,575; Total 63,310 (excl. grants 18,744). *Expenditure:* Current expenditure 43,008 (Defence spending 4,581; Poverty-reducing expenditure 22,350; Interest and charges 3,013); Capital expenditure 50,974; Total 93,982 (Source: IMF, *The Federal Democratic Republic of Ethiopia: Second Review of the Arrangement under the Exogenous Shocks Facility—Staff Report; Press Release on the Executive Board Discussion; and Statement by the Executive Director for the Federal Democratic Republic of Ethiopia*—November 2010).

INTERNATIONAL RESERVES

(US $ million at 31 December, excluding gold)

	2007	2008	2009
IMF special drawing rights	0.1	—	27.4
Reserve position in IMF	11.6	11.5	11.8
Foreign exchange	1,278.1	859.0	1,741.7
Total	1,289.8	870.5	1,780.9

2010: IMF special drawing rights 150.0; Reserve position in IMF 11.6.

Source: IMF, *International Financial Statistics*.

MONEY SUPPLY
(million birr at 31 December)

	2006	2007	2008
Currency outside banks	11,606.4	14,445.8	17,432.9
Demand deposits at commercial banks	20,207.0	24,175.9	31,391.6
Total money (incl. others)	32,056.2	38,903.5	49,105.8

Source: IMF, *International Financial Statistics*.

COST OF LIVING
(Consumer Price Index; base: 2005 = 100)

	2008	2009	2010
All items	190.1	206.2	223.0

Source: IMF, *International Financial Statistics*.

NATIONAL ACCOUNTS
(million birr at current prices)

Expenditure on the Gross Domestic Product

	2008	2009	2010
Government final consumption expenditure	24,364	27,592	27,592
Private final consumption expenditure	216,432	293,463	341,447
Gross fixed capital formation	56,055	75,377	75,377
Total domestic expenditure	296,851	397,158	444,416
Exports of goods and services	28,317	35,233	35,233
Less Imports of goods and services	76,564	96,285	96,285
GDP in purchasers' values	248,605	335,380	383,364

Gross Domestic Product by Economic Activity

	2008	2009	2010
Agriculture, hunting, forestry and fishing	117,108	160,627	165,668
Mining and quarrying	944	1,270	2,475
Manufacturing	9,251	11,813	14,467
Electricity and water	3,481	3,717	4,457
Construction	12,000	16,074	15,882
Trade, hotels and restaurants	36,913	56,629	66,432
Finance, insurance and real estate	23,596	30,068	42,947
Transport and communications	9,350	12,766	15,967
Public administration and defence	8,370	10,320	11,577
Other services	12,463	15,501	17,922
Sub-total	233,476	318,785	357,794
Indirect taxes	16,785	19,139	28,412
Less imputed bank service charge	1,657	2,544	2,843
GDP in purchasers' values	248,605	335,380	383,364

Source: African Development Bank.

BALANCE OF PAYMENTS
(US $ million)

	2008	2009	2010
Exports of goods f.o.b.	1,554.7	1,538.1	2,400.0
Imports of goods f.o.b.	–7,206.3	–6,819.0	–7,364.5
Trade balance	–5,651.6	–5,280.9	–4,964.6
Exports of services	1,959.3	1,894.9	2,244.5
Imports of services	–2,410.3	–2,226.9	–2,546.5
Balance on goods and services	–6,102.6	–5,612.9	–5,266.6
Other income received	37.5	6.5	8.1
Other income paid	–35.9	–43.3	–71.7
Balance on goods, services and income	–6,101.0	–5,649.7	–5,330.1
Current transfers received	4,343.8	3,499.7	4,987.9
Current transfers paid	–48.5	–40.7	–83.2
Current balance	–1,805.7	–2,190.7	–425.4
Direct investment from abroad	108.5	221.5	288.3
Other investment assets	113.0	420.3	1,084.6
Investment liabilities	515.2	1,012.6	995.6
Net errors and omissions	1,450.7	–793.1	–2,929.9
Overall balance	381.6	–1,329.5	–986.8

Source: IMF, *International Financial Statistics*.

External Trade

PRINCIPAL COMMODITIES
(distribution by HS, US $ million)

Imports c.i.f.	2008	2009	2010
Cereals	576.9	368.2	421.8
Wheat and meslin	465.2	321.6	342.9
Animal, vegetable fats and oils, cleavage products, etc.	247.9	240.4	293.2
Palm oil and its fraction	201.6	204.8	251.0
Mineral fuels, oils, distillation products, etc.	2,053.8	1,305.7	1,850.2
Refined petroleum oils	1,971.3	1,222.5	1,740.2
Pharmaceutical products	213.4	323.2	282.1
Medicament mixtures (put in dosage)	144.2	256.5	230.0
Fertilizers	283.3	337.8	277.1
Mixtures of nitrogen, phosphorous and potassium fertilizers	209.9	250.3	190.3
Iron and steel	443.7	380.7	359.4
Bars and rods of iron	149.5	138.3	77.0
Articles of iron and steel	235.3	350.7	383.8
Structures (rods, angle, plates) of iron and steel	102.5	159.4	168.3
Tubes, pipes and hollow profiles of iron or steel	38.7	48.8	46.0
Nuclear reactors, boilers, machinery, etc.	920.3	1,025.8	1,257.1
Self-propelled bulldozer, angledozer, grader, excavator, etc.	230.4	183.4	165.5
Electrical and electronic equipment	1,016.4	1,175.1	1,272.4
Electric appliances for line telephony	448.7	414.0	596.4
Vehicles other than railway, tramway	525.7	520.4	942.3
Trucks, motor vehicles for the transport of goods	202.6	206.0	430.7
Total (incl. others)	8,680.3	7,973.9	9,692.2

Exports f.o.b.	2008	2009	2010
Live animals	46.4	62.0	146.6
Live bovine animals	26.6	36.7	86.0
Live trees, plants, bulbs, roots, cut flowers etc.	124.2	150.6	182.8
Cut flowers and flower buds for bouquets, fresh or dried	104.7	131.5	159.3
Edible vegetables and roots and tubers	223.7	294.0	452.7
Vegetables, fresh or chilled	83.5	168.5	271.4
Dried vegetables, shelled	117.0	104.1	151.2
Coffee, tea, mate and spices	574.4	382.9	805.7
Coffee	562.3	369.8	774.2
Oil seed, oleagic fruits, grain, seed, fruit, etc.	258.6	383.9	382.5
Oil seeds	250.3	380.3	375.2

Exports f.o.b.—*continued*	2008	2009	2010
Vegetable planting materials and vegetable products	30.6	0.1	—
Raw hides, skins (except furskins) and leather	91.0	42.8	74.4
Pearls, precious stones, metals, coins, etc.	80.2	93.0	203.7
Gold	79.9	92.5	201.9
Total (incl. others)	1,601.8	1,618.2	2,580.1

Source: Trade Map-Trade Competitiveness Map, International Trade Centre, www.intracen.org/marketanalysis.

PRINCIPAL TRADING PARTNERS
(US $ million)

Imports c.i.f.	2008	2009	2010
Belgium	83.2	56.5	100.3
Brazil	55.2	88.0	140.2
Bulgaria	93.5	45.7	62.7
China, People's Republic	1,750.4	1,920.4	2,323.5
Egypt	95.6	70.6	112.1
France (incl. Monaco)	134.0	108.2	119.9
Germany	285.0	193.5	232.9
India	635.6	638.9	698.2
Indonesia	98.0	86.8	98.3
Italy	501.1	412.8	440.6
Japan	382.0	358.5	533.5
Korea, Republic	146.0	136.9	106.5
Malaysia	203.9	215.4	258.1
Netherlands	72.7	98.8	91.6
Pakistan	177.4	253.0	60.7
Romania	84.8	55.0	19.6
Russia	105.1	166.0	103.0
Saudi Arabia	1,233.0	933.8	1,153.0
South Africa	61.5	63.4	66.1
Sudan	153.4	71.5	123.2
Thailand	75.3	77.7	142.6
Turkey	167.4	260.9	269.0
Ukraine	139.2	96.7	95.7
United Arab Emirates	725.8	310.1	547.3
United Kingdom	94.2	102.9	100.4
USA	401.5	476.3	544.9
Total (incl. others)	8,680.3	7,973.9	9,692.2

Exports f.o.b.	2008	2009	2010
Belgium	55.0	35.6	62.7
China, People's Republic	85.1	243.1	267.7
Djibouti	57.3	51.6	74.3
Egypt	13.1	15.7	51.3
France (incl. Monaco)	24.1	18.0	41.9
Germany	168.6	128.9	293.8
Greece	20.6	7.1	8.1
India	15.4	19.4	33.1
Israel	50.4	46.5	57.4
Italy	83.0	67.6	76.6
Japan	61.9	9.9	42.9
Jordan	19.7	19.0	18.7
Netherlands	119.2	143.3	192.0
Pakistan	14.4	9.8	27.0
Portugal	14.1	1.3	1.1
Saudi Arabia	123.2	114.1	162.2
Somalia	76.9	134.7	248.2
Sudan	74.1	76.9	167.6
Sweden	5.6	10.8	26.2
Switzerland-Liechtenstein	98.9	105.3	140.5
Turkey	39.2	30.1	36.9
United Arab Emirates	69.5	72.7	123.3
United Kingdom	47.7	58.2	64.0
USA	114.7	73.5	113.3
Yemen	28.8	20.7	20.6
Total (incl. others)	1,601.8	1,618.2	2,580.1

Source: Trade Map-Trade Competitiveness Map, International Trade Centre, www.intracen.org/marketanalysis.

Transport

RAILWAYS
(traffic, year ending 7 July)*

	2002/03	2003/04	2004/05
Addis Ababa–Djibouti:			
Passenger-km (million)	253	40	34
Freight (million net ton-km)	—	81	56

* Including traffic on the section of the Djibouti–Addis Ababa line that runs through the Republic of Djibouti. Data pertaining to freight include service traffic.

ROAD TRAFFIC
(motor vehicles in use, year ending 7 July)

	2000	2001	2002
Passenger cars	59,048	59,737	67,614
Buses and coaches	9,334	11,387	18,067
Lorries and vans	34,355	43,375	34,102
Motorcycles and mopeds	n.a.	2,198	2,575
Road tractors	6,809	1,275	1,396
Total	109,546	117,972	123,754

2007: Passenger cars 70,893; Buses and coaches 17,098; Lorries and vans 148,997; Motorcycles and mopeds 7,328.

Source: IRF, *World Road Statistics*.

SHIPPING

Merchant Fleet
(registered at 31 December)

	2007	2008	2009
Number of vessels	10	9	10
Displacement (grt)	122,729	117,747	117,957

Source: IHS Fairplay, *World Fleet Statistics*.

International Sea-borne Shipping
(freight traffic, '000 metric tons, year ending 7 July)

	1996/97	1997/98	1998/99
Goods loaded	242	201	313
Goods unloaded	777	1,155	947

Source: former Ministry of Transport and Communications, Addis Ababa.

CIVIL AVIATION
(traffic on scheduled services)

	2007	2008	2009
Kilometres flown (million)	69	75	75
Passengers carried ('000)	2,290	2,715	2,914
Passenger-km (million)	7,947	9,303	9,746
Total ton-km (million)	1,041	1,399	1,478

Source: UN, *Statistical Yearbook*.

Tourism

TOURIST ARRIVALS BY COUNTRY OF ORIGIN

	2006	2007	2008
Canada	7,349	8,391	8,574
Djibouti	4,650	4,562	5,038
France	6,649	7,338	8,965
Germany	7,428	11,691	12,643
India	7,975	8,895	10,560
Italy	8,386	9,882	11,235
Japan	2,402	1,905	2,012
Kenya	8,690	10,172	10,417
Netherlands	4,659	4,769	6,372
Saudi Arabia	8,463	8,330	7,160
Sudan	6,233	8,430	9,792
United Kingdom	16,076	17,094	18,283
USA	43,610	44,717	49,678
Yemen	4,724	4,269	5,641
Total (incl. others)*	290,458	311,947	330,157

* Including Ethiopian nationals residing abroad.

Receipts from tourism (US $ million, incl. passenger transport): 639 in 2006; 790 in 2007; 1,184 in 2008; 1,119 in 2009.

Source: World Tourism Organization.

Communications Media

	2008	2009	2010
Telephones ('000 main lines in use)	897.3	915.1	908.9
Mobile cellular telephones ('000 subscribers)	1,954.5	4,051.7	6,854.0
Internet subscribers ('000)	35.6	74.6	72.4
Broadband subscribers ('000)	1.5	3.5	4.1

Book production: 444 titles in 1999.

Non-daily newspapers: 135 in 2004.

Daily newspapers: 3 in 2004 (average circulation 358,000 copies).

Radio receivers ('000 in use): 11,340 in 2000.

Television receivers ('000 in use): 1,260 in 2000.

Personal computers: 532,000 (6.8 per 1,000 persons) in 2007.

Sources: UNESCO, *Statistical Yearbook*; UN, *Statistical Yearbook*; International Telecommunication Union.

Education

(1999/2000, unless otherwise indicated)

	Institutions	Teachers	Students
Pre-primary	834	13,763*	292,641*
Primary	11,490	234,215*	13,570,558*
Secondary: general	410	72,835*	3,618,719*
Secondary: teacher training	12	294	4,813
Secondary: skill development centres	25	367	2,474
Secondary: technical and vocational	25	9,052*	307,674*
University level	6	8,355†	264,822†
Other higher:			
Government	11	578	18,412
Non-government	4	140	8,376

* 2008/09 figure.

† 2007/08 figure.

Sources: Ministry of Education, Addis Ababa; UNESCO Institute for Statistics.

Pupil-teacher ratio (primary education, UNESCO estimate): 57.9 in 2008/09 (Source: UNESCO Institute for Statistics).

Adult literacy rate (UNESCO estimates): 35.9% (males 50.0%; females 22.8%) in 2008 (Source: UNESCO Institute for Statistics).

Directory

The Government

HEAD OF STATE

President: Lt Girma Wolde Giorgis (took office 8 October 2001; re-elected by vote of the House of People's Representatives 9 October 2007).

COUNCIL OF MINISTERS

(May 2012)

The Government is formed by members of the Amhara National Democratic Movement (ANDM), the South Ethiopian People's Democratic Movement (SEPDM), the Oromo People's Democratic Organization (OPDO), the Tigrai People's Liberation Front (TPLF), the Somali People's Democratic Party (SPDP) and one independent.

Prime Minister: Meles Zenawi.

Deputy Prime Minister and Minister of Foreign Affairs: Hailemariam Desalegn (SEPDM).

Minister of Defence: Siraj Fergesa (SEPDM).

Minister of Federal Affairs: Dr Shiferaw Tekelemariam (SEPDM).

Minister of Justice: Berhan Hailu (ANDM).

Minister of the Civil Service: Juniedy Sado (OPDO).

Minister of Finance and Economic Development: Sufyan Ahmed (OPDO).

Minister of Agriculture: Tefera Deribew (ANDM).

Minister of Industry: Mekonnen Manyazewal (Ind.).

Minister of Trade: Kebede Chane (ANDM).

Minister of Science and Technology: Desse Dalke (SEPDM).

Minister of Transport: Diriba Kuma (OPDO).

Minister of Cabinet Affairs and Head of the Office of the Prime Minister: Muktar Kedir (OPDO).

Minister of Communication and Information Technology: Debretsion Gebremikael (TPLF).

Minister of Urban Development and Construction: Mekuria Haile (SEPDM).

Minister of Water and Energy: Alemayehu Tegenu (OPDO).

Minister of Mines: Sinknesh Ejigu (OPDO).

Minister of Education: Demeke Mekonnen (ANDM).

Minister of Health: Dr Tewedros Adhanom (TPLF).

Minister of Labour and Social Affairs: Abdulfetah Abdulahi Hassen (SPDP).

Minister of Culture and Tourism: Amin Abdulkadir (ANDM).

Minister of Women, Youth and Children's Affairs: Zenebu Tadesse (ANDM).

Minister, Public Mobilization and Participation Adviser to the Prime Minister: Redwan Hussein (SEPDM).

Minister, Head of the Government Communication Office: BEREKET SIMON (ANDM).

Minister, Government Chief Whip: ASTER MAMO (OPDO).

Minister, Director-General of the Ethiopian Revenues and Customs Authority: MELAKU FANTA (ANDM).

MINISTRIES

Office of the President: POB 1031, Addis Ababa; tel. (11) 1551000; fax (11) 1552030.

Office of the Prime Minister: POB 1013, Addis Ababa; tel. (11) 1552044; fax (11) 1552020.

Office for Government Communication Affairs: Addis Ababa; tel. (11) 5540486; fax (11) 5540473; e-mail shekemal@yahoo.com.

Ministry of Agriculture: POB 62347, Addis Ababa; tel. (11) 5538134; fax (11) 5530776.

Ministry of the Civil Service: Addis Ababa.

Ministry of Communication and Information Technology: Addis Ababa.

Ministry of Culture and Tourism: POB 2183, Addis Ababa; tel. (11) 5512310; fax (11) 5512889; e-mail info@tourismethiopia.org; internet www.tourismethiopia.org.

Ministry of Defence: POB 1373, Addis Ababa; tel. (11) 5511777; fax (11) 5516053.

Ministry of Education: POB 1367, Addis Ababa; tel. (11) 1553133; fax (11) 1550877.

Ministry of Federal Affairs: POB 1031, Addis Ababa; tel. (11) 5512766; fax (11) 1552030.

Ministry of Finance and Economic Development: POB 1037, Addis Ababa; tel. (11) 1552800; fax (11) 1550118; internet www.mofaed.org.

Ministry of Foreign Affairs: POB 393, Addis Ababa; tel. (11) 5517345; fax (11) 5514300; e-mail mfa.addis@telecom.net.et; internet www.mfa.gov.et.

Ministry of Health: POB 1234, Addis Ababa; tel. (11) 5517011; fax (11) 5519366.

Ministry of Industry: Addis Ababa.

Ministry of Justice: POB 1370, Addis Ababa; tel. (11) 512288; fax (11) 517775; internet www.mojet.gov.et.

Ministry of Labour and Social Affairs: POB 2056, Addis Ababa; tel. (11) 5517080; fax (11) 5518396.

Ministry of Mines: POB 486, Addis Ababa; tel. (11) 5153689; fax (11) 5517874.

Ministry of Science and Technology: Addis Ababa.

Ministry of Trade: POB 704, Addis Ababa; tel. (11) 5518025; fax (11) 5514288; e-mail henok_fekadu@yahoo.com.

Ministry of Transport: Addis Ababa; tel. (11) 5516166; fax (11) 5515665; e-mail nigusmen@yahoo.com; internet www.motr.gov.et.

Ministry of Urban Development and Construction: POB 1238, Addis Ababa; tel. (11) 5518292; fax (11) 527969.

Ministry of Water and Energy: POB 486, Addis Ababa; tel. (11) 5153689; fax (11) 5517874.

Ministry of Women, Youth and Children's Affairs: POB 1364, Addis Ababa; tel. (11) 5517020.

Regional Governments

Ethiopia comprises nine regional governments, one chartered city (Addis Ababa) and one Administrative Council (Dire Dawa), which are vested with authority for self-administration. The executive bodies are respectively headed by Presidents (regional states) and Chairmen (Addis Ababa and Dire Dawa).

PRESIDENTS
(May 2012)

Tigrai: TSEGAYE BERHE.

Afar: ESMAEL ALISERO.

Amhara: AYALEW GOBEZE.

Oromia: Gen. ABADULA GEMEDA.

Somali: ABDULAHI HASAN MOHAMMED.

Benishangul/Gumuz: (vacant).

Southern Nations, Nationalities and Peoples: SHIFERAW SHIGUTTE.

Gambela: UMED UBONG.

Harari: MURAD ABDULHADIN.

CHAIRMEN
(May 2012)

Dire Dawa: ABDULAZIZ MOHAMMED.

Addis Ababa: KUMA DEMEKSA.

Legislature

FEDERAL PARLIAMENTARY ASSEMBLY

The legislature comprises an upper house, the House of the Federation (Yefedereshn Mekir Bet), with 108 seats (members are selected by state assemblies and are drawn one each from 22 minority nationalities and one from each professional sector of the remaining nationalities, and serve for a period of five years), and a lower house of no more than 550 directly elected members, the House of People's Representatives (Yehizbtewekayoch Mekir Bet), who are also elected for a five-year term.

Speaker of the House of the Federation: KASSA TEKLEBERHAN.

Deputy Speaker of the House of the Federation: MOHAMMED SIREE.

Yehizbtewekayoch Mekir Bet
(House of People's Representatives)

Speaker: ABADULA GEMEDA.

Deputy Speaker: SHITAYE MINALE.

General Election, 23 May 2010

Party	Seats
Ethiopian People's Revolutionary Democratic Front (EPRDF)	499
Somali People's Democratic Party (SPDP)	24
Benishangul Gumuz People's Democratic Party (BGPDP)	9
Afar National Democratic Party (ANDP)	8
Gambela People's Unity Democratic Movement (GPUDM)	3
Amhara National Democratic Movement (ANDM)	1
Ethiopia Federal Democratic Unity Forum (FORUM)	1
Harari National League (HNL)	1
Independent	1
Total	547

Election Commission

National Electoral Board of Ethiopia (NEB): POB 40812, Addis Ababa; tel. (11) 5153416; e-mail info@electionethiopia.org; internet www.electionethiopia.org; f. 1993; independent board of seven politically non-affiliated mems appointed, on the Prime Minister's recommendation, by the House of People's Representatives; Chair. KEMAL BEDRI KELO.

Political Organizations

A total of 79 political parties contested the 2010 legislative elections.

Afar National Democratic Party (ANDP): f. 1999; Chair. MOHAMED KEDIR.

Afar People's Democratic Organization (APDO): fmrly Afar Liberation Front (ALF); based in fmr Hararghe and Wollo Admin. Regions; Leader ISMAIL ALI SIRRO.

Benishangul Gumuz People's Democratic Party (BGPDP): f. 2009; Chair. HABTAMU HIKA.

Ethiopia Federal Democratic Unity Forum (FORUM): f. 2009; the Ethiopia Democratic Union Movement (EDUM) and the Somali Democratic Alliance Forces (SDAF) withdrew from the coalition in March 2010; Chair. MOGA FIRISA.

Ethiopian Social Democratic Party (ESDP): f. 1993 as the Council of Alternative Forces for Peace and Democracy in Ethiopia; opposes the EPRDF; Chair. Dr BEYENE PETROS.

Oromo Federalist Democratic Movement (OFDM): formed part of the Oromo Federalist Congress (OFC) for the 2010 elections; Chair. BULCHA DEMEKSA; Sec.-Gen. BEKELE JIRATA.

Oromo People's Congress (OPC): Addis Ababa; e-mail oromopeoplescongress@yahoo.com; internet www.oromopeoplescongress.org; f. 2007 by fmr mems of the ONC; formed part of the Oromo Federalist Congress (OFC) for the 2010 elections; Chair. Dr MERARA GUDINA.

Southern Ethiopia People's Democratic Union (SEPDU): f. 1994; Chair. TILAHUN EADESHAW.

Union of Tigrians For Democracy and Sovereignty (ARENA): f. 2007; Chair. GEBRU ASTRAT.

Unity For Democracy and Justice Party (ANDENET): f. 2008; Chair. Eng. GIZACHEW SHIFERAW.

Ethiopian Justice and Democratic Forces Front (EJDFF): f. 2008; Chair. GIRMAY HADERA.

Ethiopian Democratic Union (EDU): f. 2004; Chair. Dr KEBEDE HAILEMARIAM.

Ethiopian National Unity Party (ENUP): f. 2005; Chair. ZERIHUN GEBREGZIABER.

Oromia Liberation National Party (OLNP): Chair. Dr FARIS ISAYAS.

Unity of Southern Ethiopian Democratic Forces (USEDF): f. 2005; comprises Wolaita People's Democratic Front (WPDF), Gamo Democratic Union (GDU) and Gomogofa People's Democratic Union (GPDU); Chair. TEKLE BORENA.

Ethiopian National Democratic Party (ENDP): f. 1994 by merger of five pro-Govt orgs with mems in the Council of Representatives; comprises: the Ethiopian Democratic Organization, the Ethiopian Democratic Organization Coalition (EDC), the Gurage People's Democratic Front (GPDF), the Kembata People's Congress (KPC), and the Wolaita People's Democratic Front (WPDF); Chair. FEKADU GEDAMU.

Ethiopian People's Revolutionary Democratic Front (EPRDF): Addis Ababa; internet www.eprdf.org.et; f. 1989 by the TPLF as an alliance of insurgent groups seeking regional autonomy and engaged in armed struggle against the EDUP Govt; Chair. MELES ZENAWI; Vice-Chair. HAILEMARIAM DESALEGN; in May 1991, with other orgs, formed transitional Govt.

Amhara National Democratic Movement (ANDM): based in Tigrai; represents interests of the Amhara people; fmrly the Ethiopian People's Democratic Movement (EPDM); adopted present name in 1994; Chair. ADDISO LEGGESE.

Oromo People's Democratic Organization (OPDO): f. 1990 by the TPLF to promote its cause in Oromo areas; based among the Oromo people in the Shoa region; Leader Gen. ABADULA GEMEDA.

South Ethiopian People's Democratic Movement (SEPDM): f. 1992; Chair. HAILEMARIAM DESALEGN.

Tigrai People's Liberation Front (TPLF): f. 1975; the dominant org. within the EPRDF; Chair. MELES ZENAWI; Vice-Chair. SEYOUM MESFIN.

Gambela People's Unity Democratic Movement (GPUDM): f. 2008; Chair. UMOD OBONG ALUM.

Harari National League (HNL): f. 1994; Chair. YASIN HUSEIN.

Movement for Justice, Freedom and Democracy (Ginbot 7): 8647 Richmond Highway, Alexandria, VA 22309, USA; e-mail org@ginbot7.org; internet www.ginbot7.org; f. 2008; Leader BERHANU NEGA.

Ogaden National Liberation Front (ONLF): e-mail foreign@onlf.org; internet www.onlf.org; f. 1984; seeks self-determination for the Ogaden region; Chair. MOHAMED OMAR OSMAN.

Oromo Liberation Front (OLF): POB 73247, Washington, DC 20056, USA; tel. (202) 462-5477; fax (202) 332-7011; e-mail info@oromoliberationfront.org; internet www.oromoliberationfront.org; f. 1973; seeks self-determination for the Oromo people; participated in the Ethiopian transitional Govt until June 1992; Chair. DAWUD IBSA AYANA; Vice-Chair. ABDULFATTAH A. MOUSSA BIYYO.

Sidama Liberation Front (SLF): e-mail info@sidamaliberation-front.org; internet www.sidamaliberation-front.org; campaigns for self-determination for Sidama people.

Somali Abo Liberation Front (SALF): operates in fmr Bale Admin. Region; has received Somali military assistance; Sec.-Gen. MASURAD SHU'ABI IBRAHIM.

Somali People's Democratic Party (SPDP): St Jijiga Somali Regional 365; internet www.spdp.org.et; f. 1998 by merger of Ogaden National Liberation Front (ONLF) and the Ethiopian Somali Democratic League (ESDL—an alliance comprising the Somali Democratic Union Party, the Issa and Gurgura Liberation Front, the Gurgura Independence Front, the Eastern Gabooye Democratic Organization, the Eastern Ethiopian Somali League, the Horyal Democratic Front, the Social Alliance Democratic Organization, the Somali Abo Democratic Union, the Shekhash People's Democratic Movement, the Ethiopian Somalis' Democratic Movement and the Per Barreh Party); Chair. ABDIFETAH SHECK ABDULAHI; Sec.-Gen. AHMED ARAB ADEN.

United Ethiopian Democratic Forces (UEDF): POB 73246, Washington, DC 20056-3246, USA; e-mail UEDFHIBRET@yahoo.com; internet www.hebret.org; f. 2003; USA-based org.; Chair. Dr BEYENE PETROS; alliance comprises ESDP (q.v.) and the following parties:

Afar Revolutionary Democratic Unity Front (ARDUF): f. 1993.

All Amhara People's Organization (AAPO).

All Ethiopian Socialist Movement (MEISON): f. 1968.

Ethiopian Democratic Hibrehizb Unity Movement (EDHUM).

Ethiopian Medhin Democratic Party (MEDHIN): internet www.medhin.org; USA-based org.; Chair. Prof. SEYOUM GELAYE.

Ethiopian National United Front (ENUF): POB 21387, Washington, DC 20009-21387, USA; tel. (202) 785-1618; e-mail admin@enufforethiopia.net; internet www.enufforethiopia.net; f. 2001; USA-based org.; Chair. BEKELE MOLLA.

Ethiopian People's Federal Democratic Unity Party (HibreHizb): Vice-Sec. Lt AYALSEW DESSIE.

Ethiopian People's Revolutionary Party (EPRP): POB 73337, Washington, DC 20056, USA; tel. (202) 2914217; fax (202) 2917645; e-mail espic@aol.com; internet www.eprp.com; f. 1972; Leader MERSHA YOSEPH.

Gambella People's United Democratic Front.

Oromo National Council (ONC).

Oromo People's Liberation Organization (OPLO).

Southern Ethiopian People's Democratic Coalition (SEPDC): opposition alliance; Chair. Dr BEYENE PETROS.

Tigraian Alliance for National Democracy (TAND): Leader MEKONNEN ZELLELEW.

United Ethiopian Democratic Party (UEDP): POB 101458, Addis Ababa; tel. (11) 5508727; fax (11) 5508730; e-mail uedpmedhinpr@gmail.com; internet www.uedpmedhin.org; f. 2003 by the merger of Ethiopian Democratic Unity Party and the Ethiopian Democratic Party; Sec.-Gen. Dr ADMASSU GEBREYEHU.

United Oromo Liberation Forces (UOLF): f. 2000 in Asmara, Eritrea, as a common Oromo Front seeking to overthrow the Ethiopian Govt; Sec.-Gen. GALASA DILBO; alliance comprises:

Islamic Front for the Liberation of Oromia: Leader ABDELKARIM IBRAHIM HAMID.

Oromo Liberation Council (OLC).

Oromo Liberation Front (OLF): see above.

United Oromo People's Liberation Front (UOPLF).

Unity of Ethiopians for Democratic Change (UEDC): f. 2007 as replacement for the Alliance for Freedom and Democracy; coalition of political parties and rebel groups opposed to the Govt.

Benishangul People's Movement (BPM): rebel group operating in western Ethiopia.

Ethiopian People Patriotic Front: CP 182, 1211 Geneva 13, Switzerland; tel. 223406025; e-mail info@eppf.net; internet www.eppf.net; armed anti-Govt group operating mainly in north-western Ethiopia; Leader Prof. ALEBACHEW TEGEGNE.

Southern Ethiopia People's Front for Justice and Equality (SEPFJE): armed anti-Govt group operating in southern Ethiopia.

Tigrai People's Democratic Movement (TPDM): f. 1979; rebel group operating in northern Tigrai region of Ethiopia.

Western Somali Liberation Front (WSLF): POB 978, Mogadishu, Somalia; f. 1975; aims to unite the Ogaden region with Somalia; maintains guerrilla forces of c. 3,000 men; has received support from regular Somali forces; Sec.-Gen. ISSA SHAYKH ABDI NASIR ADAN.

Diplomatic Representation

EMBASSIES IN ETHIOPIA

Algeria: Woreda 23, Kebele 13, House No. 1819, POB 5740, Addis Ababa; tel. (11) 3719666; fax (11) 3719669; Ambassador NOUREDDINE AOUAM.

Angola: Woreda 18, Kebele 26, House No. 6, POB 2962, Addis Ababa; tel. (11) 5510085; fax (11) 5514922; Ambassador ARCANJO MARIA DO NASCIMENTO.

Australia: Addis Ababa; Ambassador LISA FILIPETTO.

Austria: POB 1219, Addis Ababa; tel. (11) 3712144; fax (11) 3712140; e-mail addis-abeba-ob@bmeia.gv.at; internet www.bmeia.gv.at/botschaft/addis-abeba.html; Ambassador Prof. Dr RUDOLF AGSTNER.

Belgium: Comoros St, Kebele 8, POB 1239, Addis Ababa; tel. (11) 6611813; fax (11) 6613646; e-mail addisababa@diplobel.fed.be; internet www.diplomatie.be/addisababa; Ambassador GUNTHER SLEEUWAGEN.

Benin: Addis Ababa; Ambassador EDOUARD AHO-GELLE.

Botswana: POB 22282, Addis Ababa; tel. (11) 715422; fax (11) 714099; Ambassador MANYEPEDZA PATRICK LESETEDI.

Brazil: Bole Sub-City, Kebele 2, House No. 2830, POB 2458, Addis Ababa; tel. (11) 6620401; fax (11) 6620412; e-mail embradisadm@ethionet.et; Ambassador IZABEL CRISTINA DE AZEVEDO.

Bulgaria: Bole Kifle Ketema, Kebele 06, Haile Gabreselassie Rd, POB 987, Addis Ababa; tel. (11) 6610032; fax (11) 6613373; e-mail bulemba@ethionet.et; internet www.mfa.bg/addis-ababa/; Chargé d'affaires a.i. EMIL TRIFONOV.

Burkina Faso: Kebele 19, House No. 281, POB 19685, Addis Ababa; tel. (11) 6615863; fax (11) 6625857; e-mail ambfet@telecom.net.et; Ambassador BRUNO ZIDOUEMBA.

Burundi: POB 3641, Addis Ababa; tel. (11) 4651300; e-mail burundi.emb@telecom.net.et; Ambassador EPIPHANIE KABUSHEMEYE.

Cameroon: Bole Rd, Woreda 18, Kebele 26, House No. 168, POB 1026, Addis Ababa; tel. (11) 5504488; fax (11) 5518434; Ambassador MARTIN AYAFAR CHINGGONG.

Canada: Nefas Silk Lafto Kifle Ketema 3, Kebele 4, House No. 122, POB 1130, Addis Ababa; tel. (11) 3713022; fax (11) 3713033; e-mail addis@international.gc.ca; internet www.canadainternational.gc.ca/ethiopia-ethiopie/index.aspx; Ambassador MICHÈLE LÉVESQUE.

Cape Verde: Kebele 3, House No. 107, POB 200093, Addis Ababa; tel. (11) 6635466; Chargé d'affaires a.i. CUSTODIA LIMA.

Chad: Bole Rd, Woreda 17, Kebele 20, House No. 2583, POB 5119, Addis Ababa; tel. (11) 6613819; fax (11) 6612050; Ambassador CHERIF MAHAMAT ZENE.

China, People's Republic: Jimma Rd, Woreda 24, Kebele 13, House No. 792, POB 5643, Addis Ababa; tel. (11) 3711960; fax (11) 3712457; e-mail chinaemb_et@mfa.gov.cn; internet et.china-embassy.org; Ambassador XIE XIAOYAN.

Congo, Democratic Republic: Makanisa Rd, Woreda 23, Kebele 13, House No. 1779, POB 2723, Addis Ababa; tel. (11) 3710111; fax (11) 3713485; Ambassador GÉRARD MAPANGO KEMISHANGA.

Congo, Republic: Woreda 3, Kebele 51, House No. 378, POB 5639, Addis Ababa; tel. (11) 5514188; fax (11) 5514331; Ambassador RAYMOND SERGE BALE.

Côte d'Ivoire: Woreda 23, Kebele 13, House No. 1308, POB 3668, Addis Ababa; tel. (11) 3711213; fax (11) 3712178; Ambassador GEORGES ABOA.

Cuba: Woreda 17, Kebele 19, House No. 197, POB 5623, Addis Ababa; tel. (11) 620459; fax (11) 620460; e-mail embacuba@ethiopia.cubaminrex.cu; Ambassador CLARA MARGARITA PULIDO.

Czech Republic: Kebele 15, House No. 289, POB 3108, Addis Ababa; tel. (11) 5516132; fax (11) 5513471; e-mail addisabeba@embassy.mzv.cz; internet www.mzv.cz/addisababa; Ambassador ZDENĚK DOBIÁŠ.

Denmark: Bole Kifle Ketema, Kebele 3, House No. 'New', POB 12955, Addis Ababa; tel. (11) 6187075; fax (11) 6187057; e-mail addamb@um.dk; internet www.etiopien.um.dk; Ambassador PERNILLE DAHLER KARDEL.

Djibouti: POB 1022, Addis Ababa; tel. (11) 6613200; fax (11) 6612786; Ambassador ISMAÏL GOULAL BOUDINE.

Egypt: POB 1611, Addis Ababa; tel. (11) 1226422; fax (11) 1226432; Ambassador TAREK GHONEIM.

Equatorial Guinea: Bole Rd, Woreda 17, Kebele 23, House No. 162, POB 246, Addis Ababa; tel. (11) 6626278; Ambassador (vacant).

Eritrea: POB 2571, Addis Ababa; tel. (11) 5512844; fax (11) 5514911; Chargé d'affaires a.i. SAHIH OMER.

Finland: Mauritania St, Kebele 12, House No. 1431, POB 1017, Addis Ababa; tel. (11) 3205920; fax (11) 3205923; e-mail sanomat.add@formin.fi; Ambassador KIRSTI AARNIO.

France: Kabana, POB 1464, Addis Ababa; tel. (11) 1236022; fax (11) 1236029; e-mail scacamb@ethionet.et; internet www.ambafrance-ethiopie.org; Ambassador JEAN-CHRISTOPHE BELLIARD.

Gabon: Woreda 17, Kebele 18, House No. 1026, POB 1256, Addis Ababa; tel. (11) 6611075; fax (11) 6613700; Ambassador (vacant).

The Gambia: Kebele 3, House No. 79, POB 60083, Addis Ababa; tel. (11) 6624647; fax (11) 6627895; e-mail gambia@ethionet.et; Ambassador Dr OMAR A. TOURAY.

Germany: Yeka Kifle Ketema (Khebena), Woreda 03, POB 660, Addis Ababa; tel. (11) 1235139; fax (11) 1235152; e-mail info@addis-abeba.diplo.de; internet www.addis-abeba.diplo.de; Ambassador LIESELORE CYRUS.

Ghana: Jimma Rd, Woreda 24, Kebele 13, House No. 108, POB 3173, Addis Ababa; tel. (11) 3711402; fax (11) 3712511; Ambassador JOHN EVONLAH AGGREY.

Greece: off Debre Zeit Rd, POB 1168, Addis Ababa; tel. (11) 4654911; fax (11) 4654883; internet www.telecom.net.et/~greekemb; Ambassador DIONISIOS KOUNTOUREAS.

Guinea: Debre Zeit Rd, Woreda 18, Kebele 14, House No. 58, POB 1190, Addis Ababa; tel. (11) 4651308; fax (11) 4651250; Ambassador SEKOU CAMARA.

Holy See: POB 588, Addis Ababa (Apostolic Nunciature); tel. (11) 3712100; fax (11) 3711499; Apostolic Nuncio Most Rev. GEORGE PANIKULAM (Titular Archbishop of Caudium).

India: Kabena, POB 528, Addis Ababa; tel. (11) 1552100; fax (11) 1552521; Ambassador GURJIT SINGH.

Indonesia: Mekanisa Rd, Higher 23, Kebele 13, House No. 1816, POB 1004, Addis Ababa; tel. (11) 3712104; fax (11) 3710873; e-mail kbriadis@ethionet.et; internet www.indonesia-addis.org.et; Ambassador RAMLI SA'UD.

Iran: 317–318 Jimma Rd, POB 1144, Addis Ababa; tel. (11) 3710037; fax (11) 3712299; internet www.iranembassy-addis.net; Ambassador MOHAMMED JAVAD ZAMANIAN KOOPAIE.

Ireland: Debre Zeit Rd, Woreda 20, Kebele 40, House No. 21, POB 9585, Addis Ababa; tel. (11) 4665050; fax (11) 4665020; e-mail addisababaembassy@dfa.ie; Ambassador SÍLE MAGUIRE.

Israel: Woreda 16, Kebele 22, House No. 283, POB 1266, Addis Ababa; tel. (11) 6460999; fax (11) 64619619; e-mail embassy@addisababa.mfa.gov.il; internet addisababa.mfa.gov.il; Ambassador BELAYNESH ZEVADIA.

Italy: Villa Italia, POB 1105, Addis Ababa; tel. (11) 1235717; fax (11) 1235689; e-mail ambasciata.addisabeba@esteri.it; internet www.ambaddisabeba.esteri.it; Ambassador RAFFAELE DE LUTIO.

Japan: Woreda 18, Kebele 7, House No. 653, POB 5650, Addis Ababa; tel. (11) 5511088; fax (11) 5511350; e-mail japan-embassy@telecom.net.et; internet www.et.emb-japan.go.jp; Ambassador HIROYUKI KISHINO.

Kenya: Woreda 16, Kebele 1, POB 3301, Addis Ababa; tel. (11) 610033; fax (11) 611433; Ambassador (vacant).

Korea, Democratic People's Republic: Woreda 20, Kebele 40, House No. 892, POB 2378, Addis Ababa; tel. (11) 6182828; Ambassador KIM HYOK CHOL.

Korea, Republic: Jimma Rd, Old Airport Area, POB 2047, Addis Ababa; tel. (11) 4655230; e-mail skorea.emb@telecom.net.et; Ambassador CHUNG SOONSUK.

Kuwait: Woreda 17, Kebele 20, House No. 128, POB 19898, Addis Ababa; tel. (11) 6615411; fax (11) 6612621; Ambassador FAEZ MOUBEL AL-MOUTEIRI.

Lesotho: Bole Sub-City, Kebele 03, House No. 2118, Addis Ababa; tel. (11) 6614368; fax (11) 6612837; e-mail lesotho-addis@foreign.gov.ls; Ambassador FINE MAEMA.

Liberia: Roosevelt St, Woreda 21, Kebele 4, House No. 237, POB 3116, Addis Ababa; tel. (11) 5513655; Ambassador Dr EDWARD GBOLOCO HOWARD CLINTON.

Libya: Ras Tessema Sefer, Woreda 3, Kebele 53, House No. 585, POB 5728, Addis Ababa; tel. (11) 5511077; fax (11) 5511383; Ambassador ALI ABDALLA AWIDAN.

Madagascar: Woreda 17, Kebele 19, House No. 629, POB 60004, Addis Ababa; tel. (11) 612555; fax (11) 610127; Ambassador JEAN PIERRE RAKOTOARIVONY.

Malawi: Bole Rd, Woreda 23, Kebele 13, House No. 1021, POB 2316, Addis Ababa; tel. (11) 3711280; fax (11) 3719742; e-mail malemb@telecom.net.et; Ambassador Dr ISAAC MUNLO.

Mali: Kebele 03, House No. 418, Addis Ababa; tel. (11) 168990; fax (11) 162838; e-mail keitamoone@maliembassy-addis.org; internet www.maliembassy-addis.org; Ambassador AMADOU NDIAYE.

Mauritania: Lidete Kifle Ketema, Kebele 2, House No. 431A, POB 200015, Addis Ababa; tel. (11) 3729165; fax (11) 3729166; Ambassador MOHAMED ABDELLAHI OULD BABANA.

Mauritius: Kebele 03, House No. 750, POB 200222, Kifle Ketema, Addis Ababa; tel. (1) 6615997; fax (1) 6614704; e-mail mmaddis@ethionet.et; Ambassador PREMDUT DOONGOOR.

Morocco: 210 Bole Rd, POB 60033, Addis Ababa; tel. (11) 5508440; fax (11) 5511828; e-mail morocco.emb@ethionet.et; Ambassador ABDELJEBBAR BRAHIME.

Mozambique: Woreda 17, Kebele 23, House No. 2116, POB 5671, Addis Ababa; tel. (11) 3729199; fax (11) 3729197; e-mail embamoc.etiopia@minec.gov.mz; Ambassador MANUEL TOMÁS LUBISSE.

Namibia: Bole Sub-City, Kebele 19, House No. 575, POB 1443, Addis Ababa; tel. (11) 6611966; fax (11) 6612677; e-mail nam.emb@ethionet.et; Ambassador KAKENA S. K. NANGULA.

Netherlands: Old Airport Zone, Kifle Ketema, Lideta, Kebele 02/03, POB 1241, Addis Ababa; tel. (11) 3711100; fax (11) 3711577; e-mail add@minbuza.nl; internet ethiopia.nlembassy.org; Ambassador HANS BLANKENBERG.

Niger: Woreda 9, Kebele 23, POB 5791, Addis Ababa; tel. (11) 4651305; fax (11) 4651296; Ambassador MAÏMOUNA DIAMBALLA.

Nigeria: POB 1019, Addis Ababa; tel. (11) 1550644; Chargé d'affaires a.i. CHIGOZIE OBI-NNADOZIE.

Norway: POB 8383, Addis Ababa; tel. (11) 3710799; fax (11) 3711255; e-mail emb.addisabeba@mfa.no; internet www.norway.org.et; Ambassador JENS-PETTER KJEMPRUD.

Poland: House No. 583, Dej Belay Zeleke Rd, Guelele Sub-City, Kebele 08, POB 27207/1000, Addis Ababa; tel. (11) 1574189; fax (11) 1574222; e-mail polemb@ethionet.et; internet www.addisabeba.polemb.net; Ambassador JAROSŁAW ROMAN SZCZEPANKIEWICZ.

Portugal: Sheraton Addis, Taitu St, POB 6002, Addis Ababa; tel. (11) 171717; fax (11) 173403; e-mail embportadis@hotmail.com; Ambassador Dr VERA MARIA FERNANDES.

Romania: Houses No. 9–10, Bole Kifle Ketema, Kebele 03, POB 2478, Addis Ababa; tel. (11) 6610156; fax (11) 6611191; e-mail roembaddis@ethionet.et; Chargé d'affaires a.i. GABRIEL BRANZARU.

Russia: POB 1500, Addis Ababa; tel. (11) 6612060; fax (11) 6613795; e-mail russemb@ethionet.et; Ambassador MIKHAIL Y. AFANASIEV.

Rwanda: POB 5618, Addis Ababa; tel. (11) 6610300; fax (11) 6610411; e-mail ambaddis@minaffet.gov.rw; internet www.ethiopia.embassy.gov.rw; High Commissioner JOSEPH NSENGIMANA.

Senegal: Africa Ave, POB 2581, Addis Ababa; tel. (11) 6611376; fax (11) 6610020; e-mail ambassene-addis@ethionet.et; Ambassador BASSIROU SÉNÉ.

Serbia: POB 1341, Addis Ababa; tel. (11) 5517804; fax (11) 5514192; e-mail serbembaddis@ethionet.et; Ambassador DRAGAN MOMCILOVIĆ.

Sierra Leone: Kefle Ketema-Nefas Silk Lafto, Kebele 05, House No. 2629, POB 5619, Addis Ababa; tel. (11) 3710033; fax (11) 3711911; e-mail salonembadd@yahoo.co.uk; Ambassador ANDREW GBEBAY BANGALI.

Slovakia: Bole Sub-City, Erer Ber Shola Residential Houses, Woreda 17, Kebele 14/15, House No. 123, POB 6627, Addis Ababa; tel. (11) 6450849; fax (11) 6474656; e-mail emb.addisababa@mzv.sk; internet www.mzv.sk/addisabeba.

Somalia: Bole Kifle Ketema, Kebele 20, House No. 588, POB 1643, Addis Ababa; tel. (11) 6180673; fax (11) 6180680; internet www.ethiopia.somaligov.net; Ambassador SAID AHMED NOOR.

South Africa: Alexander Pushkin St, Higher 23, Kebele 10, House No. 1885, Old Airport Area, POB 1091, Addis Ababa; tel. (11) 3713034; fax (11) 3711330; e-mail sa.embassy.addis@telecom.net.et; Ambassador CHRIS PEPANI.

Spain: Botswana St, POB 2312, Addis Ababa; tel. (11) 1222544; fax (11) 1222542; e-mail emb.addisabeba@maec.es; internet www.mae.es/embajadas/addisabeba/es/home; Ambassador MIGUEL FERNÁNDEZ-PALACIOS.

Sudan: Kirkos, Kebele, POB 1110, Addis Ababa; tel. (11) 5516477; fax (11) 5519989; e-mail sudan.embassy@telecom.net.et; Ambassador ABU ZAID AL-HASSAN.

Sweden: Ras Tessema Sefer, Woreda 3, Kebele 53, House No. 891, POB 1142, Addis Ababa; tel. (11) 5511255; fax (11) 5514558; e-mail ambassaden.addis-abeba@foreign.ministry.se; internet www.swedenabroad.com/addisabeba; Ambassador JENS ODLANDER.

Switzerland: Jimma Rd, Old Airport Area, POB 1106, Addis Ababa; tel. (11) 3711107; fax (11) 3712177; e-mail add.vertretung@eda.admin.ch; Ambassador DOMINIK LANGENBACHER.

Tanzania: POB 1077, Addis Ababa; tel. (11) 5511063; fax (11) 5517358; Ambassador (vacant).

Togo: Addis Ababa; Ambassador TILIOUFEI KOFFI ESAW.

Tunisia: Wereda 17, Kebele 19, Bole Rd, POB 100069, Addis Ababa; tel. (11) 6612063; fax (11) 6614568; Ambassador MOKHTAR CHAOUACHI.

Turkey: POB 1506, Addis Ababa; tel. (11) 6612321; fax (11) 6611688; e-mail turk.emb@ethionet.et; Ambassador ALI RIZA COLAK.

Uganda: Kirkos Kifle Ketema, Kebele 35, House No. 31, POB 5644, Addis Ababa; tel. (11) 5513088; fax (11) 5514355; e-mail uganda.emb@ethionet.et; Ambassador MULL KATENDE.

Ukraine: Woreda 17, Kebele 3, House No. 2116, POB 2358, Addis Ababa; tel. (11) 6611698; fax (11) 6621288; e-mail emb_et@mfa.gov.ua; Ambassador VLADYSLAV DEMYANENKO.

United Kingdom: POB 858, Addis Ababa; tel. (11) 6612354; fax (11) 6610588; e-mail britishembassy.addisababa@fco.gov.uk; internet www.ukinethiopia.gov.uk; Ambassador GREGORY DOREY.

USA: Entoto St, POB 1014, Addis Ababa; tel. (11) 5174000; fax (11) 5174001; e-mail pasaddis@state.gov; internet addisababa.usembassy.gov; Ambassador DONALD E. BOOTH.

Venezuela: Bole Kifle Ketema, Kebele 21, House No. 314–16, POB 1909, Addis Ababa; tel. (11) 6460601; fax (11) 5154162; Ambassador LUIS MARIANO JOUBERTT MATA.

Yemen: POB 664, Addis Ababa; Ambassador DARHAM NOMAN.

Zambia: Nifas Silk Kifle Ketema, Kebele 04, POB 1909, Addis Ababa; tel. (11) 3711302; fax (11) 3711566; e-mail zam.emb@ethionet.et; Ambassador (vacant).

Zimbabwe: POB 5624, Addis Ababa; tel. (11) 6613877; fax (11) 6613476; e-mail zimbabwe.embassy@telecom.net.et; Ambassador Dr ANDREW HAMA MTETWA.

Judicial System

The 1994 Constitution stipulates the establishment of an independent judiciary in Ethiopia. Judicial powers are vested in the courts, both at federal and state level. The supreme federal judicial authority is the Federal Supreme Court. This court has the highest and final power of jurisdiction over federal matters. The federal states of the Federal Democratic Republic of Ethiopia can establish Supreme, High and First-Instance Courts. The Supreme Courts of the federal states have the highest and the final power of jurisdiction over state matters. They also exercise the jurisdiction of the Federal High Court. According to the Constitution, courts of any level are free from any interference or influence from government bodies, government officials or any other source. In addition, judges exercise their duties independently and are directed solely by the law.

Federal Supreme Court: POB 6166, Addis Ababa; tel. (11) 1553400; fax (11) 1550278; e-mail webadmin@federalsupremecourt.gov.et; f. 1995; comprises civil, criminal and military sections; its jurisdiction extends to the supervision of all judicial proceedings throughout the country; the Supreme Court is also empowered to review cases upon which final rulings have been made by the courts (including the Supreme Court) where judicial errors have occurred; Pres. TEGNE GETANEH.

Federal High Court: POB 3483, Addis Ababa; tel. (11) 2751911; fax (11) 2755399; e-mail fedhc@telecom.net.et; hears appeals from the state courts; has original jurisdiction; Pres. WUBESHET SHIFERAW.

Awraja Courts: regional courts composed of three judges, criminal and civil.

Warada Courts: sub-regional; one judge sits alone with very limited jurisdiction, criminal only.

Religion

About 45% of the population are Muslims and about 40% belong to the Ethiopian Orthodox (Tewahido) Church. There are also significant Evangelical Protestant and Roman Catholic communities. The Pentecostal Church and the Society of International Missionaries carry out mission work in Ethiopia. There are also Hindu and Sikh religious institutions. It has been estimated that 5%–15% of the population follow animist rites and beliefs.

CHRISTIANITY

Ethiopian Orthodox (Tewahido) Church

The Ethiopian Orthodox (Tewahido) Church is one of the five oriental orthodox churches. It was founded in AD 328, and in 1989 had more than 22m. members, 20,000 parishes and 290,000 clergy. The Supreme Body is the Holy Synod and the National Council, under the chairmanship of the Patriarch (Abune). The Church comprises 25 archdioceses and dioceses (including those in Jerusalem, Sudan, Djibouti and the Western Hemisphere). There are 32 Archbishops and Bishops. The Church administers 1,139 schools and 12 relief and rehabilitation centres throughout Ethiopia.

Patriarchate Head Office: POB 1283, Addis Ababa; tel. (11) 1116507; internet webmaster@ethiopianorthodox.org; internet www.ethiopianorthodox.org; Patriarch (Abune) Archbishop PAULOS; Gen. Sec. L. M. DEMTSE GEBRE MEDHIN.

The Roman Catholic Church

At 31 December 2006 Ethiopia contained an estimated 68,138 adherents of the Alexandrian-Ethiopian Rite and 513,286 adherents of the Latin Rite.

Bishops' Conference: Ethiopian and Eritrean Episcopal Conference, POB 2454, Addis Ababa; tel. (11) 1550300; fax (11) 1553113; e-mail ecs@ethionet.et; internet www.ecs.org.et; f. 1966; Pres. Most Rev. BERHANEYESUS DEMEREW SOURAPHIEL (Metropolitan Archbishop of Addis Ababa).

Alexandrian-Ethiopian Rite

Adherents are served by one archdiocese (Addis Ababa) and two dioceses (Adigrat and Emdeber).

Archbishop of Addis Ababa: Most Rev. BERHANEYESUS DEMEREW SOURAPHIEL, Catholic Archbishop's House, POB 21903, Addis Ababa; tel. (11) 1111667; fax (11) 1551348; e-mail ecs@telecom.net.et.

Latin Rite

Adherents are served by the eight Apostolic Vicariates of Awasa, Gambela, Harar, Hosanna, Jimma-Bonga, Meki, Nekemte and Soddo.

Other Christian Churches

The Anglican Communion: Within the Episcopal Church in Jerusalem and the Middle East, the Bishop in Egypt has jurisdiction over seven African countries, including Ethiopia.

Armenian Orthodox Church: St George's Armenian Church, POB 116, Addis Ababa; f. 1923; Deacon VARTKES NALBANDIAN.

Ethiopian Evangelical Church (Mekane Yesus): POB 2087, Jomo Kenyatta Rd, Addis Ababa; tel. (11) 5533293; fax (11) 5534148; e-mail eecmyco@eecmy.org; internet www.eecmy.org; Pres. Rev. Dr WAKSEYOUM IDOSA; f. 1959; affiliated to Lutheran World Fed., All Africa Confed. of Churches and World Council of Churches; c. 5.57m. mems (2010).

Greek Orthodox Church: POB 571, Addis Ababa; tel. and fax (11) 1226459; Metropolitan of Axum Most Rev. PETROS YIAKOUMELOS.

Seventh-day Adventist Church: POB 145, Addis Ababa; tel. (11) 5511319; e-mail info@ecd.adventist.org; internet www.ecd.adventist.org; f. 1907; Pres. ALEMU HAILE; 130,000 mems.

ISLAM

Leader: Haji MOHAMMED AHMAD.

JUDAISM

A phased emigration to Israel of about 27,000 Falashas (Ethiopian Jews) took place during 1984–91. In February 2003 the Israeli Government ruled that the Falashmura (Ethiopian Christians whose forefathers had converted from Judaism) had been forced to convert to Christianity to avoid religious persecution and that they had the right to settle in Israel. In January 2004 Ethiopia and Israel agreed to allow the Falashmura to be flown to Israel; some 17,000 Falashmura and a further 3,000 Falashas arrived in Israel by May 2008. However, a further 8,700 Falashmura remained in a transit camp in Gondar in mid-2008 and the Israeli Government halted the transfer process in June. Israel resumed the transportation of Falashmura in January 2010, and in November 2010 the Israeli Government announced that the remaining Falashmura in Ethiopia—some 8,000 people—would be granted the right to immigrate to Israel. The process was expected to take place incrementally over the following four years.

The Press

DAILIES

Addis Zemen: POB 30145, Addis Ababa; internet www.addiszemen.com; f. 1941; Amharic; circ. 40,000.

The Daily Monitor: POB 22588, Addis Ababa; tel. (11) 1560788; e-mail themonitor@telecom.net.et; f. 1993; English; Editor-in-Chief NAMRUD BERHANE TSAHAY; circ. 6,000.

Ethiopian Herald: POB 30701, Addis Ababa; tel. (11) 5156690; f. 1943; English; Editor-in-Chief TSEGIE GEBRE-AMLAK; circ. 37,000.

PERIODICALS

Abyotawit Ethiopia: POB 2549, Addis Ababa; fortnightly; Amharic.

Addis Fortune: Tegene Bldg, 7th Floor, House No. 542, Ginbot Haya Ave, Kebele 03, POB 259, Addis Ababa; tel. (11) 4163020; fax (11) 4163039; internet www.addisfortune.com; weekly; English; Man. Editor TAMRAT G. GIORGIS.

Addis Tribune: Tambek International, POB 2395, Addis Ababa; tel. (11) 6615228; fax (11) 6615227; e-mail tambek@telecom.net.et; internet www.addistribune.com; f. 1992; weekly; English; Editor-in-Chief YOHANNES RUPHAEL; circ. 6,000.

Al-Alem: POB 30232, Addis Ababa; tel. (11) 6625936; fax (11) 6625777; f. 1941; publ. by the Ethiopian Press Agency; weekly; Arabic; Editor-in-Chief EYOB GIDEY; circ. 2,500.

Birritu: National Bank of Ethiopia, POB 5550, Addis Ababa; tel. (11) 5530040; fax (11) 5514588; e-mail mulget17@yahoo.com; internet www.nbe.gov.et; f. 1982; quarterly; Amharic and English; banking, insurance and macroeconomic news; owned by National Bank of Ethiopia; circ. 2,500; Editor-in-Chief (vacant); Dep. Editors-in-Chief MULUGETA AYALEW, BEKALU AYALEW.

Capital: POB 95, Addis Ababa; tel. (11) 5531759; fax (11) 5533323; e-mail syscom@telecom.net.et; internet www.capitalethiopia.com; f. 1998; weekly; Sunday; business and economics; Editor-in-Chief BEHAILU DESALEGN.

Ethiopian Reporter: Woreda 19, Kebele 56, House No. 221, POB 7023, Addis Ababa; tel. and fax (11) 4421517; e-mail mcc@telecom.net.et; internet www.ethiopianreporter.com; weekly; English and Amharic.

Maebel: Addis Ababa; weekly; Amharic; Editor-in-Chief ABERA WOGI.

Menilik: Editor-in-Chief ZELALEM GEBRE.

Meskerem: Addis Ababa; quarterly; theoretical politics; circ. 100,000.

Negarit Gazeta: POB 1031, Addis Ababa; irreg.; Amharic and English; official gazette.

Nigdina Limat: POB 2458, Addis Ababa; tel. (11) 5513882; fax (11) 5511479; e-mail aachamber1@telecom.net.et; monthly; Amharic; publ. by the Addis Ababa (Ethiopia) Chamber of Commerce; circ. 6,000.

Press Digest: POB 12719, Addis Ababa; tel. (11) 5504200; fax (11) 5513523; e-mail phoenix.universal@telecom.net.et; f. 1993; weekly.

Satenaw: Editor-in-Chief TAMRAT SERBESA.

Tequami: Addis Ababa; weekly; Editor-in-Chief SAMSON SEYUM.

Tobia Magazine: POB 22373, Addis Ababa; tel. (11) 1556177; fax (11) 1552654; monthly; Amharic; Man. GOSHU MOGES; circ. 30,000.

Tobia Newspaper: POB 22373, Addis Ababa; tel. (11) 1556177; fax (11) 1552654; e-mail akpac@telecom.net.et; weekly; Amharic; Man. GOSHU MOGES; circ. 25,000.

Tomar: Benishangul; weekly; Amharic; Editor-in-Chief BEFEKADU MOREDA.

Yezareitu Ethiopia (Ethiopia Today): POB 30232, Addis Ababa; weekly; Amharic and English; Editor-in-Chief IMIRU WORKU; circ. 30,000.

NEWS AGENCY

Ethiopian News Agency (ENA): Patriot St, POB 530, Addis Ababa; tel. (11) 1550011; fax (11) 1551609; e-mail feedback@ena.gov.et; internet www.ena.gov.et; f. 1942; Chair. NETSANET ASFAW.

PRESS ASSOCIATIONS

Ethiopian Free Press Journalists' Association (EFJA): POB 31317, Addis Ababa; tel. and fax (11) 1555021; e-mail efja@telecom.net.et; f. 1993; granted legal recognition in 2000; activities suspended in late 2003; Pres. KIFLE MULAT.

Ethiopian Journalists' Association: POB 30288, Addis Ababa; tel. (11) 1117852; fax (11) 5513365; Pres. KEFALE MAMMO.

Publishers

Addis Ababa University Press: POB 1176, Addis Ababa; tel. (11) 1119148; fax (11) 1550655; f. 1968; educational and reference works in English, general books in English and Amharic; Editor MESSELECH HABTE.

Berhanena Selam Printing Enterprise: POB 980, Addis Ababa; tel. (11) 1553233; fax (11) 1553939; f. 1921; fmrly Govt Printing Press; publishes and prints newspapers, periodicals, books, security prints and other miscellaneous commercial prints; Gen. Man. MULUWORK G. HIWOT.

Educational Materials Production and Distribution Enterprise (EMPDE): POB 5549, Addis Ababa; tel. (11) 6463555; fax (11) 6461295; f. 1999; textbook publishers.

Ethiopia Book Centre: POB 1024, Addis Ababa; tel. (11) 1123336; f. 1977; privately owned; publr, importer, wholesaler and retailer of educational books.

Kuraz Publishing Agency: POB 30933, Addis Ababa; tel. (11) 1551688; state-owned.

Mega Publishing: POB 423, Addis Ababa; tel. (11) 1571714; fax (11) 1571715; general publishers.

Broadcasting and Communications

TELECOMMUNICATIONS

Ethiopian Telecommunication Agency (ETA): Bekelobet, Tegene Bldg, Kirkos District, Kebele 02/03, House No. 542, POB 9991, Addis Ababa; tel. (11) 4668282; fax (11) 4655763; e-mail tele.agency@ethionet.et; internet www.eta.gov.et; aims to promote the devt of high quality, efficient, reliable and affordable telecommunication services in Ethiopia; Dir-Gen. ESHETU ALEMU.

Ethio Telecom (ETC): POB 1047, Addis Ababa; tel. (11) 6632597; fax (11) 6632674; e-mail etcweb@ethionet.et; internet www.ethionet.et; f. 1894; under the management of France Telecom since

December 2010; Chair. DEBRE TSION GEBRE MICHAEL; CEO JEAN-MICHEL LATUTE.

BROADCASTING

Radio

Radio Ethiopia: POB 654, Addis Ababa; tel. (11) 1551011; internet www.angelfire.com/biz/radioethiopia; f. 1941; Amharic, English, French, Arabic, Afar, Oromifa, Tigre, Tigrinya and Somali; Gen. Man. KASA MILOKO.

Radio Fana: POB 30702, Addis Ababa; internet www.radiofana.com; f. 1994; Amharic; operated by the EPRDF; Gen. Man. WOLDU YEMESSEL.

Radio Voice of One Free Ethiopia: broadcasts twice a week; Amharic; opposes current Govts of Ethiopia and Eritrea.

Voice of the Revolution of Tigrai: POB 450, Mekele; tel. (34) 4410545; fax (34) 4405485; e-mail vort@telecom.net.et; f. 1985; Tigrinya and Afargna; broadcasts 57 hours per week; supports Tigrai People's Liberation Front.

Television

Ethiopian Radio and Television Agency (ERTA): POB 5544, Addis Ababa; tel. (11) 5155326; fax (11) 5512685; e-mail gd1@erat.gov.et; internet www.erta.gov.et; f. 1964; semi-autonomous station; accepts commercial advertising; programmes transmitted from Addis Ababa to 26 regional stations; Chair. BEREKET SIMON.

Finance

(cap. = capital; res = reserves; dep. = deposits; m. = million; br(s). = branch(es); amounts in birr)

BANKING

Central Bank

In 2010 there were 16 banks and 22 microfinance institutions in Ethiopia.

National Bank of Ethiopia: Sudan Ave, POB 5558, Addis Ababa; tel. (11) 5517438; fax (11) 5514588; e-mail nbe.gov@ethionet.et; internet www.nbe.gov.et; f. 1964; bank of issue; cap. 500.0m., res 1,814.8m., dep. 35,781.3m. (June 2009); Chair. NEWAYE-KIRSTOS GEBREAB; Gov. TEKLEWOLD ATNAFU; Vice-Gov. ALEMSEGED ASSEFA; 1 br.

Other Banks

Awash International Bank SC: Africa Ave, Bole Rd, POB 12638, Addis Ababa; tel. (11) 6614482; fax (11) 6639159; e-mail awash.bank@ethionet.et; internet www.awash-international-bank.com; f. 1994; cap. 540.0m., res 750.0m., dep. 5,700m. (Dec. 2009); Chair. ATO BEKELE NEDI; Pres. LEIKUN BERHANU; 64 brs.

Bank of Abyssinia SC: Red Cross Bldg, Ras Desta Damtew Ave, POB 12947, Addis Ababa; tel. (11) 5530663; fax (11) 5514130; e-mail info@bankofabyssinia.com; internet www.bankofabyssinia.com; f. 1905; closed 1935 and reopened 1996; commercial banking services; cap. 313.1m., res 132.6m., dep. 4,583.5m., total assets 5,476.6m. (June 2009); Chair. DAGNACHEW MEHARI; Pres. ADDISU HABBA; 61 brs.

Commercial Bank of Ethiopia: Gambia St, POB 255, Addis Ababa; tel. (11) 5511271; fax (11) 5514522; e-mail cbe_cc@combanketh.com; internet www.combanketh.com; f. 1943; reorg. 1996; state-owned; cap. 4,000.0m., res 1,037.5m., dep. 43,480.3m. (June 2009); Chair. BEREKET SEMON; Pres. BEKALU ZELEKE; 331 brs.

Construction and Business Bank: Higher 21, Kebele 04, POB 3480, Addis Ababa; tel. (11) 5512300; fax (11) 5515103; e-mail cbbsics@ethionet.et; internet www.cbb.com.et; f. 1975 as Housing and Savings Bank; provides credit for construction projects and a range of commercial banking services; state-owned; cap. and res 80.8m., total assets 1,019.1m. (June 2003); Chair. TADESSE HAILE; Gen. Man. ADDISU HABBA; 20 brs.

Dashen Bank: Beklobet, Garad Bldg, Debre Zeit Rd, POB 12752, Addis Ababa; tel. (11) 4671803; fax (11) 4653037; e-mail dashen.bank@ethionet.et; internet www.dashenbanksc.com; f. 1995; share company; cap. 591.8m., res 340.2m., dep. 10,375.9m. (June 2010); Pres. LULSEGED TEFERI; Chair. TEKLU HAILE; 58 brs.

Development Bank of Ethiopia: Zosip Broz Tito St, POB 1900, Addis Ababa; tel. (11) 5511188; fax (11) 5511606; e-mail dbe@ethionet.et; internet www.dbe.com.et; f. 1909; provides devt finance for industry and agriculture, technical advice and assistance in project evaluation; state-owned; cap. and res 418.8m., total assets 3,163.2m. (June 2002); Chair. MELAKU FANTA; Pres. ESAYAS BAHRE; 32 brs.

Lion International Bank SC (LIB): Addis Ababa; tel. (11) 6626000; fax (11) 6625999; e-mail lionbank@ethionet.et; internet www.anbesabank.com; f. 2006; Chair. BERHANU G. MEDHIN; Pres. MERESSA GEBREMARIAM; 24 brs.

NIB International Bank SC: Africa Avenue, Dembel City Centre, 6th Floor, POB 2439, Addis Ababa; tel. (11) 5503304; fax (11) 5527213; e-mail nibbank@ethionet.et; internet www.nibbank-et.com; f. 1999; cap. 487.1m., res 132.0m., dep. 3,497.0m. (June 2009); Chair. DEMBEL BALCHA; Pres. AMERGA KASSA; 45 brs.

Oromia International Bank SC: POB 27530, Addis Ababa; tel. 1579760; fax 578673; internet www.orointbank.com; f. 2008; cap. 197.2m., res 13.8m., dep. 820.9m. (June 2010); Pres. ABIE SANO; 30 brs.

United Bank SC: Beklobet, Mekwor Plaza Bldg, Debe Zeit Rd, Kirkos District, Kebele 06, POB 19963, Addis Ababa; tel. (11) 4655222; fax (11) 4655243; e-mail hibretbank@ethionet.et; internet www.unitedbank.com.et; f. 1998; commercial banking services; cap. 355.2m., res 93.9m., dep. 3,615.7m. (June 2009); Chair. GETACHEW AYELE; Pres. BERHANU GETANEH; 50 brs.

Wegagen Bank: Dembel Bldg, 6th–7th Floor, Africa Ave, POB 1018, Addis Ababa; tel. (11) 5523800; fax (11) 5523521; e-mail wegagen@ethionet.et; internet www.wegagenbank.com.et; f. 1997; commercial banking services; cap. 517.6m., res 183.3m., dep. 3,942.7m. (June 2009); Chair. WONDWOSSON KEBEDE; Pres. and CEO ARAYA GEBRE EGIZHABER; 49 brs.

Zemen Bank: Josef Tito St, POB 1212, Addis Ababa; tel. (11) 5501111; fax (11) 5539042; e-mail customerservice@zemenbank.com; internet www.zemenbank.com; f. 2008; Chair. ERMYAS TEKIL AMELGA; Pres. and CEO BRUTAWIT DAWIT ABDI.

Bankers' Association

Ethiopian Bankers' Association: POB 23850, Addis Ababa; tel. and fax (11) 5533874; e-mail ethbankers@ethionet.et; f. 2001; Sec.-Gen. DEREJE DEGEFU.

INSURANCE

In 2010 there were 12 insurance companies operating in Ethiopia.

Africa Insurance Co: Woreda 17, Kebele 19, House 093, POB 12941, Addis Ababa; tel. (11) 6637716; fax (11) 6638253; e-mail africains@ethionet.et; internet www.africainsurance.com.et; f. 1994; Man. Dir and CEO KIROS JIRANIE.

Awash Insurance Co: Tebaber Berta Bldg, 4th Floor, Wolo Sefer, Ethio-China Rd, POB 12637, Addis Ababa; tel. (11) 5526050; fax (11) 5526091; e-mail aic@ethionet.et; internet www.awashinsurance.com; f. 1994; cap. 32.7m.; Chair. KANAA DABA; Gen. Man. TSEGAYE KEMSI; 21 brs.

Ethiopian Insurance Corpn: POB 2545, Addis Ababa; tel. (11) 5512400; fax (11) 5517499; e-mail eic.md@ethionet.et; internet www.eic.com.et; f. 1976; life, property and legal liabilities insurance cover; Man. Dir YEWONDWOSEN ETEFA.

Global Insurance Co SC: Gobena Aba Tigu St, Somale Tera, POB 180112, Addis Ababa; tel. (11) 1567400; fax (11) 1566200; e-mail globalinsu@ethionet.et; internet www.globalinsurancesc.com; f. 1997; cap. 24.8m.; Chair. AHMED ABUBAKER SHERIF; Man. Dir YAHYA MOHAMMED AFFAN (acting); 12 brs; 100 employees.

National Insurance Co of Ethiopia: POB 12645, Addis Ababa; tel. (11) 4661129; fax (11) 4650660; e-mail nice@telecom.net.et; Man. Dir and CEO HABTEMATIAM SHUMGIZAW.

Nile Insurance Co: POB 12836, Addis Ababa; tel. (11) 5537709; fax (11) 5514592; e-mail nileinsu@mail.telecom.net.et; f. 1995; Gen. Man. DAWIT G. AMANUEL.

Nyala Insurance SC: Mickey Leland St, POB 12753, Addis Ababa; tel. (11) 6626667; fax (11) 6626706; e-mail nisco@telecom.net.et; internet www.nyalainsurance.com; Chair. GETACHEW KIBRE SELASSIE; Man. Dir and CEO NAHU-SENAYE ARAYA.

Oromia Insurance Co SC (OIC): Biftu Bldg, 6th Floor, Ras Desta St, POB 10090, Addis Ababa; tel. (11) 5503138; fax (11) 5503192; e-mail oromiainsurance@ethionet.et; internet www.oromiainsurancecompany.com.et; f. 2009; Chair. ELIAS GENETI; CEO TESFAYE DESTA.

United Insurance Co SC: POB 1156, Addis Ababa; tel. (11) 5515656; fax (11) 5513258; e-mail united.insurance@telecom.net.et; Chair. GETAMESSAY DEGEFU; Man. Dir MESERET BEZABEH.

Trade and Industry

GOVERNMENT AGENCIES

Ethiopian Investment Agency: POB 2313, Addis Ababa; tel. (11) 5510033; fax (11) 5514396; e-mail ethiopian.invest@ethionet.et; internet www.ethioinvest.org; f. 1992; Dir-Gen. ABI WOLDEMESKEL.

Privatization and Public Enterprises Supervising Agency: POB 11835, Addis Ababa; tel. (11) 5530343; fax (11) 5513955; e-mail epa.etio@ethionet.et; internet www.ppesa.gov.et; Dir-Gen. BEYENE GEBREMESKEL.

DEVELOPMENT ORGANIZATION

Ethiopian Institute of Agricultural Research (EIAR): POB 2003, Addis Ababa; tel. (11) 6462633; fax (11) 6461294; internet www.eiar.gov.et; f. 1966; Dir-Gen. Dr SOLOMON ASSEFA.

CHAMBERS OF COMMERCE

Ethiopian Chamber of Commerce and Sectorial Associations: Mexico Sq., POB 517, Addis Ababa; tel. (11) 5514005; fax (11) 5517699; e-mail ethchamb@ethionet.et; internet www.ethiopianchamber.com; f. 1947; regional chambers in 11 localities; Pres. EYESSUSWORK ZAFU; Sec.-Gen. GASHAW DEBEBE.

Addis Ababa Chamber of Commerce: POB 2458, Addis Ababa; tel. (11) 5513882; fax (11) 5511479; e-mail AAchamber1@telecom.net.et; internet www.addischamber.com; Chair. MULU SOLOMON; Sec.-Gen. TESHOME BEYENE.

INDUSTRIAL AND TRADE ASSOCIATIONS

Ethiopian Association of Basic Metal and Engineering Industries: Bole Sub-City, House Number 0377, Addis Ababa; tel. and fax (11) 6293429; e-mail eabmei@ethionet.et; internet www.eabmei.org; Pres. SISAY TESFAYE; Gen. Man. SOLOMON MULUGETA.

Ethiopian Cement Corpn: POB 5782, Addis Ababa; tel. (11) 1552222; fax (11) 1551572; Gen. Man. REDI GEMAL.

Ethiopian Chemical Corpn: POB 5747, Addis Ababa; tel. (11) 6184305; Gen. Man. ASNAKE SAHLU.

Ethiopian Coffee Export Enterprise: POB 2591, Addis Ababa; tel. (11) 5515330; fax (11) 5510762; f. 1977; Chair. SUFIAN AHMED; Gen. Man. DERGA GURMESSA.

Ethiopian Food Corpn: POB 2345, Addis Ababa; tel. (11) 5518522; fax (11) 5513173; f. 1975; produces and distributes food items, incl. edible oil, ghee substitute, pasta, bread, maize, wheat flour, etc.; Gen. Man. BEKELE HAILE.

Ethiopian Fruit and Vegetable Marketing Enterprise: POB 2374, Addis Ababa; tel. (11) 5519192; fax (11) 5516483; f. 1980; sole wholesale domestic distributor and exporter of fresh and processed fruit and vegetables, and floricultural products; Gen. Man. KAKNU PEWONDE.

Ethiopian Grain Trade Enterprise: POB 3321, Addis Ababa; tel. (11) 4652436; fax (11) 4652792; e-mail egte@ethionet.et; internet www.egtemis.com; Gen. Man. BERHANE HAILU.

Ethiopian Horticulture Producers and Exporters Association (EHPEA): Haile Selassie Ave, opp. WARYT Bldg, Gelila Bldg, 2nd Floor; POB 22241, Addis Ababa; tel. (11) 6636750; fax (11) 6636753; e-mail ehpea@ethionet.et; internet www.ehpea.org; f. 2002; 87 mems; Pres. TSEGAYE ABEBE.

Ethiopian Import and Export Corpn (ETIMEX): Addis Ababa; tel. (11) 5511112; fax (11) 5515411; f. 1975; state trading corpn; import of building materials, foodstuffs, stationery and office equipment, textiles, clothing, chemicals, general merchandise, capital goods; Gen. Man. ASCHENAKI G. HIWOT.

Ethiopian Metal and Engineering Corpn: Addis Ababa; Man. Dir Brig.-Gen. KINFE DAGNEW.

Ethiopia Peasants' Association (EPA): f. 1978 to promote improved agricultural techniques, home industries, education, public health and self-reliance; comprises 30,000 peasant asscns with c. 7m. mems; Chair. (vacant).

Ethiopian Petroleum Enterprise: POB 3375, Addis Ababa; tel. and fax (11) 5512938; f. 1976; Gen. Man. YIGZAW MEKONNEN.

Ethiopian Pulses, Oilseeds and Spice Processors Exporters' Association: POB 5719, Addis Ababa; tel. (11) 1550597; fax (11) 1553299; f. 1975; Gen. Man. ABDOURUHMAN MOHAMMED.

Ethiopian Sugar Corpn: POB 133, Addis Ababa; tel. (11) 5519700; fax (11) 5513488; Dir-Gen. ABAY TSEHAYE.

Green Star Food Co LLC: POB 5579, Addis Ababa; tel. (11) 5526588; fax (11) 5526599; e-mail greenstar@telecom.net.et; f. 1984; fmrly the Ethiopian Livestock and Meat Corpn; production and marketing of canned and frozen foods; Gen. Man. DAWIT BEKELE.

National Leather and Shoe Corpn: POB 2516, Addis Ababa; tel. (11) 5514075; fax (11) 5513525; f. 1975; produces and sells semi-processed hides and skins, finished leather, leather goods and footwear; Gen. Man. GIRMA W. AREGAI.

Natural Gum Processing and Marketing Enterprise: POB 62322, Addis Ababa; tel. (11) 5527082; fax (11) 5518110; e-mail natgum@ethionet.et; internet www.naturalgum.ebigchina.com; f. 1976; state-owned; Gen. Man. TEKLEHAIMANOT NIGATU BEYENE.

Pharmaceuticals Fund and Supply Agency (PFSA): POB 976, Addis Ababa; tel. (11) 2763266; fax (11) 2751770; e-mail pfsa@ethionet.et; Dir-Gen. HAILESELASSIE BIHON.

UTILITIES

Electricity

Ethiopian Electric Power Corpn (EEPCo): De Gaulle Sq., POB 1233, Addis Ababa; tel. (11) 1560042; fax (11) 1550822; e-mail eelpa@telecom.net.et; internet www.eepco.gov.et; Chair. GIRMA BIRRU; Gen. Man. ATO MIHRET DEBEBE.

Water

Addis Ababa Water and Sewerage Authority: POB 1505; Addis Ababa; tel. (11) 6623902; fax (11) 6623924; e-mail aawsa.ha@ethionet.et; f. 1971; Gen. Man. ASEGID GETACHEW.

Water Resources Development Authority: POB 1045, Addis Ababa; tel. (11) 6612999; fax (11) 6611245; Gen. Man. GETACHEW GIZAW.

TRADE UNION

Confederation of Ethiopian Trade Unions (CETU): POB 3653, Addis Ababa; tel. (11) 5155473; fax (11) 5514532; e-mail cetu@telecom.net.et; f. 1975; comprises nine industrial unions and 22 regional unions with a total membership of 320,000 (1987); Pres. KASSAHUN FOLLO.

Transport

RAILWAYS

In 2010 construction of a 5,000-km railway network to link Addis Ababa with various parts of the country was started. Phase one of the five-year project included the construction of a new 2,000-km line to the border with Djibouti. Under phase two, there were plans to set up a 30-km light railway network in Addis Ababa. In 2011 the Indian government announced its intention to provide US $300m. towards a new railway line connecting Ethiopia and Djibouti.

Chemin de Fer Djibouti-Ethiopien (CDE): POB 1051, Addis Ababa; tel. (11) 5517250; fax (11) 5513997; f. 1909; adopted present name in 1981; jtly owned by Govts of Ethiopia and Djibouti; 781 km of track (660 km in Ethiopia), linking Addis Ababa with Djibouti; Pres. ISMAIL IBRAHIM HOUMED.

ROADS

In 2007 the total road network comprised an estimated 44,359 km of primary, secondary and feeder roads, of which 13.67% were paved, the remainder being gravel roads. In addition, there are some 30,000 km of unclassified tracks and trails. A highway links Addis Ababa with Nairobi in Kenya, forming part of the Trans-East Africa Highway. In mid-2003 work commenced on the second phase of the Road Sector Development Programme, which upgraded 80% and 63% of paved and gravel roads, respectively, to an acceptable condition by 2007.

Comet Transport SC: POB 2402, Addis Ababa; tel. (11) 4423962; fax (11) 4426024; e-mail cometrans@telecom.net.et; f. 1994; Gen. Man. ALEMU ASHENGO.

Ethiopian Freight Transport Corpn: POB 2538, Addis Ababa; tel. (11) 5515211; fax (11) 5519740; restructured into five autonomous enterprises in 1994.

Ethiopian Road Transport Authority: POB 2504, Addis Ababa; tel. (11) 5510244; fax (11) 5510715; e-mail kasahun_khmariam@yahoo.com; internet www.rta.gov.et; enforces road transport regulations, promotes road safety, registers vehicles and issues driving licences; Gen. Man. KASAHUN H. MARIAM.

Ethiopian Roads Authority: POB 1770, Addis Ababa; tel. (11) 5517170; fax (11) 5514866; e-mail era2@ethionet.et; internet www.era.gov.et; f. 1951; construction and maintenance of roads, bridges and airports; Dir-Gen. ZAID WOLDE GEBREAL.

Public Transport Corpn: POB 5780, Addis Ababa; tel. (11) 5153117; fax (11) 5510720; f. 1977; urban bus services in Addis Ababa and Jimma, and services between towns; restructured into three autonomous enterprises in 1994 and scheduled for privatization; Man. Dir AHMED NURU.

SHIPPING

The formerly Ethiopian-controlled ports of Massawa and Assab now lie within the boundaries of the State of Eritrea (q.v.). Although an agreement exists between the two Governments allowing Ethiopian access to the two ports, which can handle more than 1m. metric tons of merchandise annually, in mid-1998 Ethiopia ceased using the ports, owing to the outbreak of hostilities. Ethiopia's maritime trade currently passes through Djibouti (in the Republic of Djibouti), and also through the Kenyan port of Mombasa. An agreement was also signed in July 2003 to allow Ethiopia to use Port Sudan (in Sudan). At

31 December 2009 Ethiopia's registered merchant fleet numbered 10 vessels, with a total displacement of 117,957 grt.

Ethiopian Shipping Lines Corpn: POB 2572, Addis Ababa; tel. (11) 5518280; fax (11) 5519525; e-mail esl@ethionet.et; internet www.ethiopianshippinglines.com.et; f. 1964; serves Red Sea, Europe, Mediterranean, Gulf and Far East with its own fleet and chartered vessels; Chair. GETACHEW BELAY; Gen. Man. AMBACHEW ABRAHA.

Marine Transport Authority: POB 1238, Addis Ababa; tel. (11) 5158227; fax (11) 5515665; f. 1993; regulates maritime transport services; Dept Head ASKAL W. GEORGIS.

Maritime and Transit Services Enterprise: POB 1186, Addis Ababa; tel. (11) 5517564; fax (11) 5518197; e-mail mtse@telecom.net.et; internet www.telecom.net.et/~mtse; f. 1979; services include stevedoring, storehandling, bagging, forwarding and trucking; Chair. HAILEMARIAM DESSALEGN; Gen. Man. AHMED YASSIN.

CIVIL AVIATION

Ethiopia has two international airports (at Addis Ababa and Dire Dawa) and around 40 airfields. Bole International Airport in the capital handles 95% of international air traffic and 85% of domestic flights. A programme to modernize the airport, at an estimated cost of 819m. birr (US $130m.), was undertaken during 1997–2001. Construction of airports at Axum, Lalibela and Gondar was completed in April 2000.

Ethiopian Airlines: Bole International Airport, POB 1755, Addis Ababa; tel. (11) 6652222; fax (11) 6611474; e-mail publicrelations@ethiopianairlines.com; internet www.flyethiopian.com; f. 1945; operates regular domestic services and flights to 63 international destinations in Africa, Europe, Middle East, Asia and the USA; CEO TEWOLDE GEBREMARIAM.

Ethiopian Civil Aviation Authority (ECAA): POB 978, Addis Ababa; tel. (11) 6650200; fax (11) 6650281; e-mail civilaviation@ethionet.et; internet www.ecaa.gov.et; regulatory authority; provides air navigational facilities; Dir-Gen. Col WOSENYELEH HUNEGNAW.

Tourism

Ethiopia's tourist attractions include the early Christian monuments and churches, the ancient capitals of Gondar and Axum, the Blue Nile (or Tississat) Falls and the National Parks of the Simien and Bale Mountains. Tourist arrivals in 2008 totalled 330,157. In 2009 receipts from tourism (including passenger transport) amounted to US $1,119m.

Ministry of Culture and Tourism: POB 2183, Addis Ababa; tel. (11) 5512310; fax (11) 5512889; e-mail info@tourismethiopia.org; internet www.tourismethiopia.org.

Defence

Owing to hostilities with Eritrea in 1998–2000, there was a large increase in the size of the armed forces and in defence expenditure during this period. As assessed at November 2011, Ethiopia's active armed forces numbered an estimated 138,000, including an air force of some 3,000. In July 2000 the UN Security Council adopted a resolution (No. 1312) establishing the UN Mission in Ethiopia and Eritrea (UNMEE), which was to supervise the cease-fire and the implementation of a peace agreement between the two countries. UNMEE's mandate was periodically extended until the end of July 2008, when the UN Security Council confirmed its termination and all peace-keeping personnel were withdrawn. A total of 4,194 soldiers were stationed abroad, of which 159 were observers.

Defence Expenditure: Budgeted at 6,500m. birr in 2012.

Chief of Staff of the Armed Forces: Gen. SAMORA YUNIS.

Education

Education in Ethiopia is available free of charge, and, after a rapid growth in numbers of schools, it became compulsory between the ages of seven and 13 years. Since 1976 most primary and secondary schools have been controlled by local peasant associations and urban dwellers' associations. Primary education begins at seven years of age and lasts for eight years. Secondary education, beginning at 15 years of age, lasts for a further four years, comprising two cycles of two years, the second of which provides preparatory education for entry to the tertiary level. According to UNESCO estimates, in 2009/10 total enrolment at primary schools included 81% of children in the appropriate age-group (84% of boys; 79% of girls), while secondary enrolment was equivalent to 36% of children in the appropriate age-group (39% of boys; 32% of girls). There are 21 institutions of higher education in Ethiopia, including six universities (in Addis Ababa, Bahir Dar, Alemanya, Jimma, Awassa and Makele). A total of 291,610 students were enrolled in higher education in 2007/08, according to government statistics. In 2007 spending on education represented 23.3% of total government expenditure.

FIJI

Introductory Survey

LOCATION, CLIMATE, LANGUAGE, RELIGION, FLAG, CAPITAL

The Republic of Fiji comprises more than 300 islands, of which 100 are inhabited, situated about 1,930 km (1,200 miles) south of the equator in the Pacific Ocean. The four main islands are Viti Levu (on which almost 70% of the country's population lives), Vanua Levu, Taveuni and Kadavu. The climate is tropical, with temperatures ranging from 16°C to 32°C (60°F–90°F). Rainfall is heavy on the windward side. Fijian and Hindi are the principal languages but English is also widely spoken. In 2007 about 64% of the population were Christians (mainly Methodists), 28% Hindus and 6% Muslims. The national flag (proportions 1 by 2) is light blue, with the United Kingdom flag as a canton in the upper hoist. In the fly is the main part of Fiji's national coat of arms: a white field quartered by a red upright cross, the quarters containing sugar canes, a coconut palm, a stem of bananas and a dove bearing an olive branch; in chief is a red panel with a yellow crowned lion holding a white cocoa pod. The capital is Suva, on Viti Levu.

CONTEMPORARY POLITICAL HISTORY

Historical Context

The first Europeans to settle on the islands were sandalwood traders, missionaries and shipwrecked sailors, and in October 1874 Fiji was proclaimed a British possession. In September 1966 the British Government introduced a new Constitution for Fiji. It provided for a ministerial form of government, an almost wholly elected Legislative Council and the introduction of universal adult suffrage. Rather than using a common roll of voters, the Constitution introduced an electoral system that combined communal (Fijian and Indian) rolls with cross-voting. In September 1967 the Executive Council became the Council of Ministers, with Ratu Kamisese Mara, leader of the multiracial (but predominantly Fijian) Alliance Party (AP), as Fiji's first Chief Minister. Following a constitutional conference in April–May 1970, Fiji achieved independence, within the Commonwealth, on 10 October 1970. The Legislative Council was renamed the House of Representatives, and a second parliamentary chamber, the nominated Senate, was established. The British-appointed Governor became the first Governor-General of Fiji, while Ratu Sir Kamisese Mara (as he had become in 1969) took office as Prime Minister.

However, Fiji was troubled by racial tensions. Although the descendants of indentured Indian workers who were brought to Fiji in the late 19th century had grown to outnumber the native inhabitants, they were discriminated against in political representation and land ownership rights (see Land Ownership Issues for subsequent developments). A new electoral system was adopted in 1970 to ensure a racial balance in the legislature.

Domestic Political Affairs

At the legislative election held in March 1972 the Alliance Party secured 33 of the 52 seats in the House of Representatives, while the National Federation Party (NFP), traditionally supported by the Indian population, took 19 seats. At elections in March–April 1977 the NFP won 26 seats, but was unable to form a government, subsequently splitting into two factions. The AP governed in an interim capacity until the holding of a further election in September, when it was returned with its largest-ever majority. While the two main parties professed multiracial ideas, the Fijian Nationalist Party campaigned in support of its 'Fiji for the Fijians' programme in order to foster nationalist sentiment.

In 1980 Ratu Sir Kamisese Mara's suggestion that a government of national unity be formed was overshadowed by renewed political disagreement between the AP and the NFP over land ownership. Fijians owned 83% of the land and were strongly defending their traditional rights, while the Indian population was pressing for greater security of land tenure. The AP retained power at the legislative election held in July 1982, but its majority was reduced from 20 seats to four.

A new party, the Fiji Labour Party (FLP), was inaugurated in July 1985. Sponsored by the Fiji Trades Union Congress (FTUC), and under the presidency of Dr Timoci Bavadra, the FLP advocated the provision of free education and a national medical scheme, and hoped to work through farmers' organizations to win votes among rural electorates, which traditionally supported the NFP. During 1985–86 disagreements between the Government and the FTUC over economic policies led to an outbreak of labour unrest and the withdrawal, in June 1986, of government recognition of the FTUC as the unions' representative organization.

At a legislative election in April 1987 a coalition of the FLP and NFP won 28 seats (19 of which were secured by ethnic Indian candidates) in the House of Representatives, thus defeating the ruling AP, which took only 24 seats. The new Government, led by Bavadra, was therefore the first in Fijian history to contain a majority of ministers of Indian, rather than Melanesian, origin, although Bavadra himself was of Melanesian descent.

The coups of 1987 and subsequent events

On 14 May 1987 the Government was overthrown by a military coup, led by Lt-Col (later Maj.-Gen.) Sitiveni Rabuka. The Governor-General, Ratu Sir Penaia Ganilau, declared a state of emergency and appointed a 19-member advisory council, including Bavadra and Rabuka. Bavadra refused to participate in the council, denouncing it as unconstitutional and biased in its composition.

Widespread racial violence ensued, and there were several public demands for Bavadra's reinstatement as Prime Minister. In July 1987 the Great Council of Fijian Chiefs, comprising the country's 70 hereditary Melanesian leaders, approved plans for constitutional reform. In September negotiations began, on the initiative of Ganilau, between delegations led by the two former Prime Ministers, Bavadra and Mara, and it was subsequently announced that the two factions had agreed to form an interim bipartisan Government.

On 25 September 1987, however, Rabuka staged a second coup and announced his intention to declare Fiji a republic. Despite Ganilau's refusal to recognize the seizure of power, Rabuka revoked the Constitution on 1 October and proclaimed himself head of state, thus deposing Queen Elizabeth II. Ganilau conceded defeat and resigned as Governor-General. At a meeting in Canada, Commonwealth Heads of Government formally declared that Fiji's membership of the Commonwealth had lapsed. Rabuka installed an interim Cabinet comprising mainly ethnic Fijians. Several cases of violations of human rights by the Fijian army were reported, as the regime assumed powers of detention without trial and suspended all political activity. In December Rabuka resigned as head of state. Although he had previously refused to accept the post, Ganilau became the first President of the Fijian Republic. Mara was reappointed Prime Minister, and Rabuka became Minister of Home Affairs. The new interim Cabinet included 11 members of Rabuka's administration, but no former minister of Bavadra's deposed Government.

In February 1988 Rotuma (the only Polynesian island in the country), which lies to the north-west of Vanua Levu, declared itself politically independent of Fiji, the newly acquired republican status of which it refused to recognize. Fijian troops were dispatched to the island and swiftly quelled the dissent.

A new draft Constitution, approved by the interim Government in September 1988, was rejected by a multiracial constitutional committee, which considered unnecessary the specific reservation of the principal offices of state for ethnic Fijians. In September 1989 the committee published a revised draft, which was again condemned by Bavadra and the FLP-NFP coalition. In November Bavadra died and was replaced as leader of the FLP-NFP coalition by his widow, Adi Kuini Bavadra.

In January 1990 Rabuka resigned from the Cabinet and returned to his military duties. Mara agreed to remain as Prime Minister until the restoration of constitutional government. In June the Great Council of Chiefs approved the draft Constitution, while also stating its intention to form a new party, the Soqosoqo ni Vakavulewa ni Taukei (SVT) or Fijian Political Party, to advocate the cause of ethnic Fijians. The new Constitution was finally promulgated on 25 July by President Ganilau.

This was immediately condemned by the FLP-NFP coalition. Angered by the fact that a legislative majority was guaranteed to ethnic Fijians (who were allocated 37 of the 70 elective seats, compared with 27 Indian seats), and that the Great Council of Chiefs was to nominate ethnic Fijians to 24 of the 34 seats in the Senate and to appoint the President of the Republic, the opposition organized anti-Constitution demonstrations. The new Constitution was similarly condemned for its racial bias by India, New Zealand and Australia at the UN General Assembly meeting in October. In May 1991 the Commonwealth stated that Fiji would not be readmitted to the organization until it changed its Constitution. In July Rabuka resigned as Commander of the Armed Forces in order to rejoin the Cabinet as Deputy Prime Minister and Minister of Home Affairs, although towards the end of 1991 he relinquished the post and assumed the leadership of the SVT.

Disagreements between the Government and the FTUC re-emerged in 1991. In May the Government announced a series of reforms to the labour laws, including the abolition of the minimum wage, restrictions on strike action and derecognition of unions that did not represent at least two-thirds of the workforce. However, in late 1992 was the Government officially recognized the FTUC as the sole representative of workers in Fiji.

At the legislative election of May 1992 the SVT secured 30 of the 37 seats reserved for ethnic Fijians, while the NFP won 14 and the FLP 13 of the seats reserved for Indian representatives. The FLP agreed to participate in Parliament and to support Rabuka in his campaign for the premiership, in return for a guarantee from the SVT of a full review of the Constitution and of trade union and land laws. Rabuka was, therefore, appointed Prime Minister and formed a coalition Government (consisting of 14 members of the SVT and five others).

In December 1992 Rabuka formally invited the opposition leaders, Jai Ram Reddy of the NFP and Mahendra Chaudhry of the FLP (formerly the National Secretary of the FTUC), to form a government of national unity. The initiative was largely welcomed, but Indian politicians expressed reluctance to participate in a government in which political control remained fundamentally vested with ethnic Fijians, while nationalist extremists of the Taukei Solidarity Movement accused Rabuka of conceding too much political power to Fijian Indians. Following the appointment of a new Cabinet in June 1993, all 13 of the FLP legislative members began an indefinite boycott of Parliament, in protest against Rabuka's failure to implement the reforms that he had agreed to carry out in return for their support for his election to the premiership in June 1992.

In December 1993 President Ganilau died. He was replaced by Ratu Sir Kamisese Mara, who took office on 18 January 1994 (and was re-elected on 18 January 1999).

At the legislative election held in February 1994 the SVT won 31 of the 37 seats reserved for ethnic Fijians, while the Fijian Association Party (FAP, established in January by former members of the SVT) secured five. Of the 27 seats reserved for ethnic Indian representatives, 20 were secured by the NFP. The SVT subsequently formed a governing coalition with the General Voters' Party (GVP, which represented the interests of the General Electors—i.e. the minority Chinese and European communities and people from elsewhere in the Pacific region resident in Fiji) and an independent member, under the premiership of Rabuka, who announced the formation of a new Cabinet composed entirely of ethnic Fijians. In response to international concern regarding the continued existence of Fiji's racially biased Constitution, Rabuka announced in June that a Constitutional Review Commission had been established.

The issue of independence for the island of Rotuma was revived in September 1995 with the return of the King of Rotuma from exile in New Zealand. King Gagaj Sa Lagfatmaro, who had fled to New Zealand after receiving death threats during the military coups of 1987, appeared before the Constitutional Review Commission to petition for the island's independence within the Commonwealth, reiterating his view that Rotuma remained a British colony rather than a part of Fiji.

Racial tension intensified in October 1995, following the publication of the SVT's submission to the Constitutional Review Commission. In its report, the party detailed plans to abandon the present multiracial form of government, recommending instead the adoption of an electoral system based on racial representation, in which each ethnic group would select its own representatives. The expression of numerous extreme anti-Indian sentiments in the document was widely condemned (by both ethnic Fijians and ethnic Indians) as offensive.

Two of the four GVP members of the House of Representatives withdrew their support for the Government in early 1996, prompting an (unsuccessful) attempt by Rabuka to seek alternative coalition partners from among the opposition. The SVT was defeated in virtually every municipality at local elections in September.

Existing divisions within the Government were further exacerbated by the presentation to the House of Representatives, in September 1996, of the Constitutional Review Commission's report. The report included recommendations to enlarge the House of Representatives to 75 seats, with 25 seats reserved on a racial basis (12 for ethnic Fijians, 10 for Fijian Indians, two for General Electors and one for Rotuma Islanders), and also proposed that the size of the Senate should be reduced from 34 to 32 members (and the number of nominated ethnic Fijian senators be reduced from 24 to 15). It was also proposed that the Prime Minister should be a Fijian of any race, while the President should continue to be an indigenous Fijian. Rabuka and Mara both endorsed the findings of the report, while several nationalist parties and a number of SVT members of the House of Representatives expressed strong opposition to the proposals and formed a parliamentary coalition. The parliamentary committee reviewing the report agreed on a majority of the 700 recommendations, but proposed that the House of Representatives be enlarged to only 71 seats, with 46 seats reserved on a racial basis (23 for ethnic Fijians, 19 for Indians, three for General Electors and one for Rotuma Islanders) and 25 seats open to all races. A modified Constitution Amendment Bill was subsequently approved by both the House of Representatives and the Senate. Rabuka was anxious to reassure extremist nationalist Fijians that their interests would be protected under the amended Constitution and that indigenous Fijians would continue to play a pre-eminent role in government.

Despite opposition from both the FLP and the nationalist parties, Fiji was readmitted to the Commonwealth at a meeting of member states in October 1997. Rabuka was granted an audience with Queen Elizabeth II in London, at which he formally apologized for the military coups of 1987. The new Constitution took effect on 27 July 1998.

Following the death of the leader of the FAP, Josefata Kamikamica, Adi Kuini Vuikaba Speed (widow of former Prime Minister Bavadra) was elected leader of the party. Meanwhile, the GVP and the General Electors' Party merged to form the United General Party (UGP) under the leadership of the Minister for Tourism, Transport and Civil Aviation, David Pickering, and Rabuka was re-elected leader of the SVT. A new party, the Veitokani ni Lewenivanua Vakarisito (VLV, Christian Democratic Alliance), formed by several senior church and military leaders and former members of the nationalist Taukei Solidarity Movement, was widely criticized for its extremist stance.

At the legislative election held on 8–15 May 1999 Rabuka's coalition Government was defeated by Mahendra Chaudhry, leader of the FLP, who became Fiji's first ethnic Indian Prime Minister. Chaudhry's broadly based Government (a coalition of the FLP, FAP, VLV and the Party of National Unity—PANU) initially seemed threatened by the reluctance of FAP members to serve under an Indian Prime Minister. The leaders were persuaded to remain in the coalition in the interests of national unity, after the intervention of President Mara. Political stability was further marred by demands for Chaudhry's resignation by the Fijian Nationalist Vanua Takolavo Party (NVTLP), and by a number of arson attacks, allegedly linked to the former ruling SVT. Following the SVT's decisive election defeat, Rabuka resigned as party leader; he was replaced by Ratu Inoke Kubuabola, the former Minister for Communications, Works and Energy. Rabuka was later appointed the first independent Chairman of the newly autonomous Great Council of Chiefs. The NVTLP was widely suspected to have been responsible for three bomb explosions in Suva in August. In the same month a parliamentary vote of no confidence against Prime Minister Chaudhry was overwhelmingly defeated. In the latter half of 1999 there were persistent demands by various nationalist groups (including the SVT) that Chaudhry be replaced by a leader of indigenous Fijian descent, and a number of demonstrations were organized, expressing disillusionment with the Government.

The Government's decision to disband the Fiji Intelligence Service from December 1999 was criticized by the opposition as 'foolish' and racially motivated. Plans to amend a number of laws that did not comply with the terms of the new Constitution and proposals to alter the distribution of power between the President and the Prime Minister, along with reports that the Government was planning to withdraw state funds previously provided to assist indigenous Fijian business interests, prompted further criticism from the opposition, and in February 2000 a faction of the FAP announced its withdrawal from the governing coalition. Furthermore, it was announced in April that the extremist nationalist Taukei Movement (which had been inactive for several years) had been revived with the sole intention of removing the Prime Minister from office. The movement's campaign attracted considerable public support, which culminated in a march through Suva by some 5,000 people in early May, despite the army's reiteration of its support for Chaudhry.

The coup of 2000 and its repercussions

On 19 May 2000 a group of armed men, led by businessman George Speight, invaded the parliament building and ousted the Government, taking hostage Chaudhry and 30 other members of the governing coalition. President Mara condemned the coup and declared a state of emergency as Speight's supporters rampaged through the streets of Suva, looting and setting fire to Indian businesses. Speight declared that he had reclaimed Fiji for indigenous Fijians and had dissolved the Constitution. Moreover, he threatened to kill the hostages if the military intervened. Convening at Mara's invitation, the Great Council of Chiefs proposed the replacement of Chaudhry's Government with an interim administration, an amnesty for Speight and the rebels, and the amendment of the Constitution. Speight rejected the proposals, demanding that Mara also be removed from office. At the end of May Mara resigned and the Commander of the Armed Forces, Frank (Voreqe) Bainimarama, announced the imposition of martial law and a curfew to restore calm and stability to the country.

Negotiations between the newly installed Military Executive Council and the Great Council of Chiefs continued throughout June 2000. Following the release of the four female captives from the parliament building, the Military Executive Council demanded the release of all hostages. The Military Executive Council appointed an interim administration of 19 indigenous Fijians led by Laisenia Qarase (the former managing director of the Merchant Bank of Fiji), which was sworn in on 4 July. Speight announced that he would not recognize the interim authority, and most of Fiji's mainstream political parties similarly denounced it. By mid-July Chaudhry and the remaining hostages had been released by the rebels. In accordance with Speight's wishes, Ratu Josefa Iloilovatu Uluivuda (or Josefa Iloilo), hitherto the First Vice-President, was then installed as President.

Incidents of civil unrest continued, as Speight sought to manipulate existing grievances, particularly disputes over land ownership, in order to mobilize additional support. At the end of July 2000, however, Speight was finally arrested, along with dozens of his supporters, for breaking the terms of his amnesty by refusing to relinquish weapons. In early August more than 300 rebels appeared in court, charged with a variety of firearms and public order offences. Speight was similarly charged with several minor offences. On 11 August Speight and 14 of his supporters were formally charged with treason. Meanwhile, a police investigation into a commercial deal involving the Fijian mahogany trade began; Speight had been chairman of both Fiji Pine Corporation and Fiji Hardwood Corporation before being dismissed in 1999. Chaudhry subsequently stated his belief that the coup had been motivated by commercial vested interests.

In early November 2000 about 40 soldiers staged an unsuccessful mutiny at army headquarters in Suva. Troops loyal to Bainimarama, who narrowly escaped capture, retook the barracks following an eight-hour assault in which five rebels and four loyal soldiers were killed. It was later revealed that a number of the rebel soldiers had been involved in the coup in May. The Chairman of the Great Council of Chiefs, Rabuka, denied New Zealand's allegations that he had been involved in the mutiny. In November 2002 Capt. Shane Stevens was sentenced to life imprisonment after he was found guilty of leading the mutiny two years earlier; 14 other soldiers received lesser sentences for their part in the uprising. Bainimarama criticized the leniency of many of the sentences.

Later in November 2000 the High Court ruled that the existing Constitution remained valid and that the elected Parliament, ousted in the coup, remained Fiji's legitimate governing authority. Laisenia Qarase responded by lodging an appeal against the ruling and by declaring that the interim authority, of which he was leader, would continue as the country's national government until new elections could be organized and a new constitution drafted within 18 months.

In February 2001 an international panel of judges at the Court of Appeal began the hearing against the November 2000 ruling, which found the abrogation of the 1997 Constitution to be illegal. In its final judgment the court ruled that the 1997 Constitution remained the supreme law of Fiji, that the interim civilian government could not prove that it had the support of a majority of Fijian people and was therefore illegal, and that, following Mara's resignation, the office of President remained vacant. The ruling was welcomed by many countries in the region, including Australia and New Zealand, and appeared to be accepted by the interim authority, which announced that it would organize elections as soon as possible. However, in March 2001 Iloilo informed Chaudhry by letter that he had been dismissed as Prime Minister, claiming that by advising Iloilo to dissolve the authority in preparation for elections he had accepted that he no longer had the mandate of Parliament. Chaudhry rejected the decision as unconstitutional and unlawful. Ratu Tevita Momoedonu was appointed Prime Minister. However, Iloilo dismissed Momoedonu, on the advice of the Great Council of Chiefs, and reinstated Laisenia Qarase as head of the interim authority. It was announced that a legislative election would be held in August–September 2001, and would be conducted under the preferential voting system, similar to that of Australia, as used in Fiji's 1999 election.

There followed a period of factionalism and fragmentation among Fiji's political parties. George Speight had already been appointed President of the new Matanitu Vanua (MV—Conservative Alliance Party), despite having been charged with treason for his part in the 2000 coup. In May 2001 Qarase formed the Soqosoqo Duavata ni Lewenivanua (SDL—Fiji United Party), a new contender for the indigenous Melanesian vote, thus rivalling the established SVT. Another indigenous party, the Bai Kei Viti, was launched in June. Tupeni Baba, former Deputy Prime Minister in Chaudhry's Government, left the FLP and formed the New Labour United Party (NLUP). The election took place between 25 August and 1 September. Qarase's SDL was victorious, but failed to obtain an overall majority, securing 31 seats in the House of Representatives (increasing to 32 of the 71 seats after a by-election on 25 September). The FLP won 27 seats, the MV six seats and the NLUP two seats. International monitors were satisfied that the election had been contested in a fair manner.

Refusing to allow the FLP any representation in his new Cabinet, Qarase was accused of contravening a provision of the Constitution whereby a party winning more than 10% of the seats in the House of Representatives was entitled to a ministerial post. Two members of the MV were included in the Cabinet. Qarase claimed that Chaudhry had not accepted that the Government should be based fundamentally on nationalist Fijian principles. In October 2001, when members of the House of Representatives were sworn in, Chaudhry refused to accept the position of Leader of the Opposition, a role that consequently fell to Prem Singh, leader of the NFP. In December Parliament approved the Social Justice Bill, a programme of affirmative action favouring Fijians and Rotumans in education, land rights and business-funding policies.

The Prime Minister defended himself against demands for his resignation in January 2002 following allegations that he had contravened the Electoral Act by pledging some $F25m. of funds from the Ministry of Agriculture to pro-indigenous Fijian businesses during the 2001 election campaign. In February 2002, furthermore, an appeal court ruled that the Prime Minister had violated the Constitution by failing to incorporate any member of the opposition FLP in his Cabinet. Qarase had previously declared that he would resign if the legal challenge against him were to be successful. (The newly appointed Chief Justice, Daniel Fatiaki, was himself under scrutiny in mid-2002—the Chief Justice being appointed on the advice of the Prime Minister and the Leader of the Opposition, and being responsible for assembling the Supreme Court.) In September the High Court ruled that Prem Singh, the NFP leader, was not entitled to retain his parliamentary seat (the validity of certain votes cast at the 2001 election having been questioned). The disputed seat was therefore allocated to a member of the FLP. Also in September, in advance of a ruling by the Supreme Court on the issue of the inclusion of the FLP in the Cabinet, the Prime Minister effected a ministerial reorganization, assuming personal responsibility for a number of additional portfolios. In April 2003 the Commander of the Armed Forces, Cdre Frank Bainimarama, intervened in the ongoing dispute, stating that if the judicial ruling went against Qarase then he should resign. The Supreme Court finally delivered its ruling in mid-July, finding in favour of Chaudhry and declaring that, in order to uphold the Constitution, Qarase should form a new cabinet that included eight members of the FLP. Qarase responded by proposing to retain his current 22-member Cabinet and to add 14 FLP members. Both the opposition and the SVT leader, Sitiveni Rabuka, criticized the proposal, which would result in more than one-half of all members of the House of Representatives serving as government ministers. Chaudhry claimed that the positions offered to his party were too junior. However, Qarase remained intransigent, and at the end of August he formally nominated a Cabinet that included 14 FLP members (although Chaudhry was not among those named). The opposition reiterated its right to be consulted over the composition of the Cabinet.

Although in June 2002 the Prime Minister and the FLP leader had co-operated briefly in addressing the issue of the expiry of land leases, in August the FLP abandoned a second round of discussions on this issue and announced that it would boycott most of the proceedings in the current session of Parliament. Chaudhry accused the Government of attempting to accelerate the passage of six bills through Parliament without regard for the mandatory 30 days' notice of a bill being tabled. Tensions between the ruling SDL and the FLP and, moreover, between indigenous Fijians and Indian Fijians had been further exacerbated by anti-Indian comments made by the Minister for Women, Social Welfare and Land Resettlement, Asenaca Caucau, which the Prime Minister had not denounced. In September Qarase effected a reorganization of cabinet portfolios in which he assumed direct responsibility for the reform of the sugar industry and restated his commitment to resolve the long-standing issue of land leases.

The trial of George Speight and his accomplices on charges of treason opened in May 2001. (Speight was refused bail to enable him to occupy the seat that he won in the legislative election later in the year.) All the accused pleaded guilty to their involvement in the coup of May 2000, and at the conclusion of the trial in February 2002 Speight received the death sentence. However, within hours of the verdict President Iloilo signed a decree commuting the sentence to life imprisonment. Prison sentences of between 18 months and three years were imposed on 10 of Speight's accomplices, the charges of treason having been replaced by lesser charges of abduction. Between July 2002 and July 2004 a total of 86 people were arrested on charges relating to the coup, with the majority being found guilty of mutiny for their roles. In May 2004 Vice-President Ratu Jope Seniloli was charged with having attempted to oust President Mara during the coup, in addition to the existing charges against him. Also in May Speight made a further court appearance on charges of hostage-taking during the 2000 coup. Chaudhry and a member of Parliament, Ganesh Chand, were claiming US $3.6m. in compensation for the 56 days that they were held hostage in the government buildings by Speight and his accomplices. In August 2004 Seniloli was found guilty of treason and sentenced to four years' imprisonment. His appeal against the conviction was rejected in November; however, he was unexpectedly released from prison later that month on medical grounds, which were widely disputed. Upon his release, Seniloli resigned as Vice-President at the insistence of the military. In December the Great Council of Chiefs approved President Iloilo's proposal of Ratu Joni Madraiwiwi as the country's next Vice-President; Madraiwiwi took up the post in January 2005. In November 2004 paramount chief Ratu Inoke Takiveikata was sentenced to life imprisonment after being found guilty on several charges relating to the mutiny. (In June 2007, following claims about the impartiality of the presiding judge, a retrial of Takiveikata was ordered; however, in November 2007 he was again arrested, on separate charges of conspiracy to assassinate Bainimarama—see The coup of 2006 and abrogation of the Constitution.)

In June 2003, during a public reconciliation ceremony, the High Chief of a district of Vanua Levu publicly apologized for his involvement in the coup and announced a ban, in his locality, on words that differentiated ethnic Fijians from their Indian Fijian neighbours. Almost one year later the Great Council of Chiefs issued a historic public apology to all Indian Fijians for injustices committed against them during the coups of 1987 and 2000.

In May 2005 the Government announced plans for a Reconciliation, Tolerance and Unity Bill, which would allow the review of convictions relating to involvement in the 2000 coup and the pardoning of prisoners. However, the proposals provoked considerable opposition, particularly from the FLP and from Hindu organizations. In the same month the Minister for Transport, Simione Kaitani, and four other individuals appeared in court on coup-related charges. In June nine soldiers convicted for their role in the army mutiny in Labasa during the coup were released from prison.

The reappointment in March 2006, by the Great Council of Chiefs, of Iloilo as President and Madraiwiwi as Vice-President was welcomed by opposition leader Mahendra Chaudhry and by the military as contributing to national stability. A legislative election took place on 6–13 May. Although 25 political parties contested the election, only three of these won seats in the House of Representatives. The ruling SDL, which had joined forces with a number of smaller, conservative-leaning parties, secured 36 seats, while the FLP won 31 and the United People's Party (UPP—formerly the UGP—representing General Electors) two. The two successful independent candidates agreed to support the SDL. Various concerns over the conduct of the election were subsequently raised. The FLP and UPP both claimed that many potential voters had been omitted from electoral rolls, while in other constituencies thousands of excess voting forms had been printed. It was also reported that election officials had rejected 120 ballot boxes for being incorrectly labelled. Nevertheless, the Commonwealth observer group was broadly satisfied with the electoral process.

On 18 May 2006 Laisenia Qarase was sworn in for a second term of office. Following his reappointment, the Prime Minister offered seven of the 17 cabinet positions to the FLP, as required by the Constitution, although he restated his opposition to multi-party coalition government and hoped that Chaudhry would not accept the proposal. Chaudhry argued that his party was entitled to more seats and questioned the portfolios offered. The FLP was subsequently assigned nine positions in a 24-member Cabinet. Chaudhry himself declined to accept a cabinet role, choosing to remain as opposition leader, despite his party now forming part of the coalition Government.

The coup of 2006 and abrogation of the Constitution

Tensions between the Government and the military were exacerbated by Bainimarama's repeated accusations of racism and corruption within Qarase's administration throughout 2006. In February Bainimarama issued a statement declaring that he would prevent the Reconciliation, Tolerance and Unity Bill from becoming law, and in October he demanded the resignation of the Government if it failed to reject the Bill within three weeks. Australian officials intervened to refuse the military access to a consignment of ammunition landed at the port of Suva. While Bainimarama was absent from Fiji, visiting peace-keeping troops in the Middle East, an attempt was made to replace him. However, the Government's chosen replacement declined to accept the role and expressed support for Bainimarama. On 30 November Bainimarama issued a further ultimatum, giving Qarase 24 hours to comply with a list of demands. These demands included the removal of all members of the Government who had supported or benefited from the armed coup of 2000 and the suspension of three controversial pieces of legislation: the Reconciliation, Tolerance and Unity Bill, providing amnesties for those convicted of involvement in the 2000 coup; the Qoliqoli Bill, giving ethnic Fijians control of fishing rights and development of the coast; and the Indigenous Claims Tribunal Bill. In a public address on Fijian television, Qarase agreed to suspend the legislation condemned by Bainimarama as furthering the racist agenda of the Government. During November 2006 Australia stationed three warships off the Fijian coast in order to facilitate the evacuation of its nationals should this become necessary.

On 5 December 2006 soldiers took up positions outside the Prime Minister's official residence, seized strategic installations and erected road blocks around Suva. Bainimarama met President Iloilo, who authorized the dissolution of Parliament and the establishment of an interim administration. Bainimarama declared that he had assumed executive control of the country, appointing Dr Jona Senilagakali as interim Prime Minister and urging all cabinet ministers to resign within a month. The coup was condemned by New Zealand, the United Kingdom and Australia; Qarase's request for military intervention was refused by Australia, but various sanctions against the country were announced. A state of emergency was subsequently declared. The suspension of Fiji's participation in meetings of the Commonwealth was announced on 9 December. Despite widespread international condemnation, there was considerable support for the coup within Fiji. Organizations representing Indian Fijians expressed support for Bainimarama, as did the Fiji Human Rights Commission, which had questioned the legitimacy of Qarase's Government.

On 4 January 2007 Bainimarama returned executive power to President Iloilo, and on the following day, upon the resignation of Senilagakali, Bainimarama was sworn in as interim Prime Minister. Bainimarama's appointment was swiftly approved by the Great Council of Chiefs. An interim Government was subsequently sworn in; appointments included that of Mahendra Chaudhry as Minister for Finance, National Planning, Public Enterprise and the Sugar Industry, Ratu Epeli Nailatikau as Minister for Foreign Affairs and External Trade, and Aiyaz Sayed-Khaiyum as Attorney-General and Minister for Justice, Electoral Reform and Anti-Corruption. Also notable was the selection of Jone Navakamocea, a member of the previous Qarase administration, as Minister for Local Government, Urban Development and Public Utilities. Meanwhile, the Chief Justice of the Supreme Court, Daniel Fatiaki, was suspended pending an evaluation of the judiciary. In mid-January, amid reports of intimidation on the part of the military in the aftermath of the coup, President Iloilo issued a decree granting immunity to Bainimarama, Senilagakali and members of the military and police force in the event of disciplinary action or prosecution. In February Bainimarama announced plans to hold elections in 2010, following an assessment of electoral procedures and the completion of a census. This proposal appeared to have been revised in April 2007, when it was reported that the Fijian Government had agreed to the holding of legislative elections within two years, during discussions in Belgium with officials of the European Union (EU) on the issue of the release of development aid, suspended as a result of the coup.

In April 2007 the Great Council of Chiefs rejected Ratu Epeli Nailatikau, Minister for Foreign Affairs and External Trade, as a nominee for the post of Vice-President. The Council was suspended, and the Minister for Fijian Affairs, Heritage, Provincial Development and Multi-Ethnic Affairs, Ratu Epeli Ganilau, announced a review of its procedures. In July Ganilau clarified that the Council itself was not to be terminated, but that matters relating to membership were being assessed. Although the interim Government apparently rescinded the suspension in August, it was later reported that the composition of the Council had been altered. At the end of May Bainimarama declared an end to the state of emergency. In September a state of emergency was temporarily reimposed in response to the arrival in Suva of Laisenia Qarase, whose presence was regarded by the Government as a potential threat to stability; the order was rescinded in the following month. In early November some 16 arrests were made after plans for an apparent counter-coup, allegedly to include the assassination of Bainimarama, were reported to have been discovered. Several alleged conspirators, including a former senator, an intelligence official and paramount chief Ratu Inoke Takiveikata, who had been previously charged with mutiny (see The coup of 2000 and its repercussions), were subsequently indicted on charges such as treason and inciting mutiny.

A reorganization of the interim Cabinet was announced in January 2008, in which Bainimarama relinquished the home affairs and immigration portfolios, but assumed responsibility for others, including provincial development and indigenous and multi-ethnic affairs. Minor changes were made to the portfolios of leading cabinet members such as Aiyaz Sayed-Khaiyum and Chaudhry, while Ratu Epeli Nailatikau remained Minister for Foreign Affairs, with additional responsibility for international co-operation and civil aviation. Ratu Epeli Ganilau became Minister for Defence, National Security and Immigration. Bainimarama took charge of the 'People's Charter for Change, Peace and Progress', a directive proposed earlier in the year that established new regulations for government procedures. Bainimarama expected the Charter to result in amendments to the Constitution. The Charter, which was released in August and was undergoing a consultation process, advocated the forging of a 'common national identity', the introduction of an Anti-Discrimination Act, and a programme of reform in areas including governance and reconciliation. In anticipation of the forthcoming election, the Minister of Finance, National Planning, Sugar Industry and Public Utilities, Mahendra Chaudhry, resigned from the Interim Cabinet, along with two other members of the FLP, in mid-August. However, soon after, Bainimarama announced that the election schedule was dependent upon the implementation of electoral reform and would therefore be subject to further delays. Bainimarama assumed personal responsibility for finance and national planning, while other portfolios were distributed among existing ministers. In a further reorganization announced in September, Bainimarama took control of the foreign affairs portfolio, appointing Ratu Epeli Nailatikau as Minister for Provincial Development and Indigenous and Multi-Ethnic Affairs.

Meanwhile, in February 2008 it emerged that Bainimarama had assumed the role of Chairman of the Great Council of Chiefs; certain chiefs were to be barred from the new, smaller body. In late February it was announced that the National Security Council, which had been dissolved in 1999, and the Fiji Intelligence Services were to be reconstituted. Also in February 2008, Laisenia Qarase was charged with corruption and abuse of office by the Fiji Independent Commission Against Corruption; the allegations against the former premier pertained to his tenure as director of Fijian Holdings Ltd in 1999–2000. In March 2008 Qarase himself challenged the legality of the December 2006 coup and installation of an interim Government, but his case was dismissed by the High Court in October 2008. In March Chaudhry was cleared of tax evasion by a three-member panel; however, Qarase rejected the verdict.

In April 2009 the Court of Appeal overruled the High Court's decision, declaring that the Government installed by Bainimarama following the 2006 coup was illegal. However, the court rejected Qarase's appeal to be reinstated as Prime Minister, instead ordering President Iloilo to dissolve Parliament and to appoint an interim prime minister. Bainimarama resigned in response to the ruling. President Iloilo annulled the 1997 Constitution, reappointed himself as head of state and dismissed the entire judiciary; he then reappointed Bainimarama as Prime Minister and reinstated the Government, with modifications to some ministerial portfolios. The position of Vice-President was restored, Ratu Epeli Nailatikau being appointed to the post. President Iloilo also announced that elections would be held no later than 2014. Meanwhile, the building of the Reserve Bank of Fiji was occupied by the military, and the central bank's Governor was removed from office and reportedly detained. His replacement immediately announced that the Fijian currency had been devalued by 20%.

Once returned to power, Bainimarama enacted a Public Emergency Decree, outlawing gatherings of more than 100 people and imposing strict censorship laws whereby an authorized government official was to examine all news copy prior to publication. A number of international journalists were expelled from the country, and the Australian Broadcasting Corporation's radio transmitters were shut down. During subsequent weeks Bainimarama reinstated the Chief Magistrate and reopened the Magistrates' Court, reappointing the Chief Justice and judges of the High Court. Widespread international condemnation of the actions of President Iloilo and Prime Minister Bainimarama followed, with the UN, Australia and New Zealand offering to mediate in political dialogue to restore democracy. Bainimarama's refusal to set a date for democratic elections before 2014 resulted in Fiji's suspension from the Pacific Islands Forum (see p. 416) in May and the country's full suspension from the Commonwealth in September 2009.

In July 2009 Bainimarama announced plans for a new Constitution, to be enacted in 2013; the proposed Constitution, it was reported, would amend current land tenure arrangements under which indigenous Fijians owned 90% of land, and would lower the minimum voting age from 21 to 18 years. In late July 2009 interim President Iloilo, who was 88 years old and reportedly in ill health, announced his retirement, with effect from the beginning of August. (Iloilo died in February 2011.) Vice-President Nailatikau assumed the role in an acting capacity until October, when his position as President, for a term of three years, was confirmed. It was announced by Bainimarama that the newly recreated post of Vice-President would not be filled. Meanwhile, in July Bainimarama transferred responsibility for the foreign affairs portfolio to Ratu Inoke Kubuabola, hitherto Fiji's ambassador to Japan.

The Public Emergency Decree, first enacted by Bainimarama in April 2009, was subsequently extended. A senior minister of the Fiji Methodist Church, Rev. Manasa Lasaro, was briefly detained in May 2009 for breaching the decree in a sermon that criticized the Government. The Church's annual conference, due to be held in August, was banned on the premise that it planned to discuss political issues. In July a number of senior Church members were arrested on charges of organizing a meeting in contravention of the emergency decree. An additional decree, enacted in December, further reinforced the Government's control over public meetings and over the media.

Increasing suppression of dissent

In February 2010 Bainimarama was reported to have stated that he would relinquish his role as Prime Minister in advance of the proposed 2014 election; however, he planned to continue as Commander of the Armed Forces. In March 2010 the interim Prime Minister announced that all politicians who had served since 1987 were to be banned from contesting the 2014 election. Although the objective was apparently to change the political culture of Fiji, the decision was criticized by observers, who viewed the action as an attempt to influence the composition of the next Government.

In late February 2010 the High Court returned a verdict of guilty in the trial of eight men, including high chief Ratu Inoke Takiveikata, charged with conspiring to assassinate Bainimarama in 2007; the men were sentenced to terms of imprisonment ranging from three to seven years. In September 2010 the retrial of Takiveikata on charges of inciting the 2000 mutiny began (his original conviction having been declared invalid by the Court of Appeal in 2007—see The coup of 2000 and its repercussions); he was convicted in March 2011 and sentenced to life imprisonment.

Meanwhile, Amnesty International reiterated its concerns with regard to the situation in Fiji in early 2010; the human rights organization drew attention to the continued use of intimidation and discrimination in the suppression of freedom of expression and to the constraints placed on the independence of the judiciary. In April, furthermore, proposals for the imposition of stringent restrictions on the media provoked widespread criticism. The Media Industry Development Decree, which was to replace the emergency regulations implemented 12 months previously, would permit the authorities to enter news premises and seize any documentation, materials or equipment. The draft decree provided for fines of up to $F500,000 on media outlets found to have breached the regulations, while individual journalists, editors and publishers risked prison sentences in addition to substantial fines. Furthermore, restrictions were imposed on foreign ownership of the media. The International Federation of Journalists expressed concern that the draft decree would give all control of the media to officers appointed by the Bainimarama regime. The decree was enacted in June, whereupon it was announced that within three months all media organizations should have at least 90% Fijian ownership or risk closure. It was feared that the country's principal daily newspaper, the Australian-owned *Fiji Times*, would therefore be forced to close. In September, however, ownership of the newspaper was sold to a Suva-based company, the Motibhai Group. In October former Prime Minister Mahendra Chaudhry was charged with holding an illegal public gathering, in breach of the Public Emergency Decree, after he had attended a meeting with a group of sugar farmers; in February 2011 the charges were withdrawn on grounds of insufficient evidence, and Chaudhry urged that the emergency regulations be repealed.

The interim Deputy Prime Minister and Minister for Defence, National Security and Immigration, Ratu Epeli Ganilau, resigned from his post in November 2010, after disagreeing with a decision to deport an executive of the US-owned company Fiji Water (see Foreign Affairs). Ganilau's ministerial responsibilities were assumed by Joketani Cokanasiga, the Minister for Primary Industries. In March 2011 the Minister for Lands, Mineral Sources and Environment, Netani Sukanaivalu, resigned; responsibility for his portfolio was assumed by Bainimarama.

In early March 2011, despite a renewed appeal by Amnesty International that the Government respect the right to protest, plans for an anti-Government demonstration were cancelled owing to the presence of large numbers of security personnel at the proposed venue for the rally. Amnesty International noted that in the previous fortnight at least 10 politicians, trade unionists, critics of the Government and others had been arbitrarily arrested and subjected to severe physical assaults and other mistreatment by the Fiji military. The International Trade Union Confederation (ITUC) also expressed concern with regard to recent events in the country.

In May 2011 former army Chief of Staff Lt-Col Ratu Tevita Mara, son of the late former Prime Minister Ratu Sir Kamisese Mara, and former Commander of the Land Force Brig.-Gen. Pita Driti were charged with sedition and inciting mutiny after allegedly plotting to overthrow Bainimarama. Both men adamantly refuted the claims against them, insisting that the charges had been fabricated by the regime, which Lt-Col Mara denounced as 'a hateful dictatorship'. Lt-Col Mara fled to Tonga by sea a few days later, precipitating a diplomatic dispute between the Fijian and Tongan Governments (see Foreign Affairs). In February 2012 Brig.-Gen. Driti pleaded not guilty to two counts of uttering seditious comments and one count of inciting mutiny at the High Court in Suva.

In June 2011 it was announced that a dedicated Ministry of Sugar was to be established in Lautoka, on the west coast of Viti Levu, as part of government efforts to reform and revitalize the industry. Bainimarama was to retain responsibility for the portfolio, while Manasa Vaniqi was appointed to the newly created role of Permanent Secretary for Sugar.

In a report submitted to the Pacific Islands Forum in September 2011, the International Labour Organization noted with particular concern the use of the Public Emergency Decree introduced in 2009 to silence dissent. In late October 2011 Daniel Urai Manufolau, the President of the FTUC, was arrested on his return to Fiji from Australia, where he had met with a number of officials, including Prime Minister Julia Gillard, to discuss his concerns about the Bainimarama regime; he was subsequently charged with inciting political violence, having allegedly plotted to overthrow the interim Government. Urai, who staunchly denied the charges against him as a politically motivated fabrication, was released on bail in mid-November, pending his trial, which was expected to commence in mid-2012. The FTUC's General Secretary, Felix Anthony, was also arrested in early November 2011, following criticism of the interim Government's apparent campaign to curb the activities of trade unions, prompting vociferous protests by trade unionists and the international community; he was released six days later. In the same month the interim Government implemented the Essential National Industries Employment Decree, which prohibited trade unions from operating in selected industries, including the national airline, four major banks, broadcasting and telecommunications, and utilities. Also in November, three men were imprisoned for four years, having been convicted of disseminating anti-Government material.

In September 2011 Bainimarama offered assurances that a new constitution would be drafted for Fiji between September 2012 and September 2013, and pledged that the charter would establish a fully representative government based on an electoral system guaranteeing equal suffrage. (However, critics cited the Bainimarama regime's numerous alleged human rights violations as evidence of its lack of commitment to a truly democratic system of government.) The interim Prime Minister also announced that preparatory work was to commence in January 2012 on compiling an electronic register of voters for legislative elections scheduled to take place in 2014; $F5.9m. was allocated to the creation of the register in the 2012 national budget. Meanwhile, in late September Attorney-General Aiyaz Sayed-Khaiyum was awarded additional responsibility for the international trade portfolio, while retaining his existing ministerial posts.

At a preliminary hearing in October 2011, former Prime Minister Qarase pleaded not guilty to six counts of abuse of office and three counts of discharge of duty, charges first brought against him in 2008 (see The coup of 2006 and abrogation of the Constitution). Qarase's trial was due to commence in July 2012, having been postponed from November 2011, following a request by Qarase's lawyers for further disclosures from the prosecution to assist in the preparation of their defence.

Recent developments: introduction of the Public Order Act

The Public Emergency Decree in place since 2009 was rescinded in January 2012, in a development that was widely welcomed both within Fiji and further afield. However, hopes that the announcement might constitute an important development towards the restoration of democracy and augur an improvement in basic freedoms and human rights within Fiji were dashed shortly afterwards, when the details of a new Public Order Act that had been introduced in place of the emergency regulations were revealed. The highly controversial new legislation stipulated, *inter alia*, that actions taken by the Prime Minister or senior police officers could not be legally challenged under the Act; afforded the police new, wide-ranging powers, including the right to use force to disperse gatherings deemed to constitute a threat to public safety (while prohibiting both criminal and civil proceedings for any harm or loss caused by the use of such force); and imposed tighter controls on individuals suspected of breaking the law, as well as on the staging of meetings and other public gatherings. Widely regarded as being more repressive than the emergency regulations that it replaced, the Public Order Act provoked expressions of concern and disappointment from prominent figures within Fiji and the international community (see Foreign Affairs). Felix Anthony denounced the new legislation as a severe backwards step for the country's hopes of a democratic future, while former Prime Minister Chaudhry urged the Government to revoke the Act, arguing that it could not possibly enable the open and free environment necessary for proper political dialogue to take place concerning the drafting of a new constitution and the holding of legislative elections in 2014.

Two new ministers were appointed to the Cabinet in February 2012: Viliame Naupoto as Minister for Youth and Sports and Jone Usumate as Minister for Labour, Industrial Relations and Employment. Both portfolios had hitherto been held by Filipe Bole, who remained Minister for Education, National Heritage, Culture and Arts.

In early March 2012 Bainimarama outlined plans for the preparation of the new constitution: following a civic education programme and public consultations, in January 2013 a five-member Constitutional Commission would submit a draft constitution for the consideration of a Constituent Assembly, consisting of representatives of civil society groups, faith-based organizations, national institutions, political parties and the Government. It was anticipated that a new constitution would be approved by the end of February 2013. Bainimarama announced in mid-March 2012 that President Nailatikau had approved decrees formally abolishing the Great Council of Chiefs on the grounds that it had become highly politicized and 'perpetuated elitism'. However, the FLP criticized the move, asserting that the dissolution of the Council was a matter for indigenous Fijians to decide, while others accused the interim Government of seeking to curb potential dissent prior to negotiations on the new constitution.

Land Ownership Issues

In September 1995 the Government decided to transfer all state land (comprising some 10% of Fiji's total land area), hitherto administered by the Government Lands Department, to the Native Land Trust Board in order to allow the allocation of land to indigenous Fijians on the basis of native custom. However, concern among Fijian Indians increased following reports in early 1996 that many would not be able to renew their land leases (most of which were due to expire between 1997 and 2024) under the Agricultural Landlords and Tenants Act (ALTA). The reports were strongly denied by the Government, despite statements by several Fijian land-owning clans that Indians' leases would not be renewed. Moreover, a recently formed sugar-cane growers' association solely for ethnic Fijians, the Taukei Cane Growers' Association, announced its intention to campaign for ethnic Fijian control of the sugar industry, largely by refusing to renew land leases to ethnic Indians (who held some 85% of sugar farm leases). By the end of 2000 almost 2,000 land leases had expired, leaving many tenant farmers and their families homeless. Some 70 farmers, who had expressed a wish not to be resettled, received rehabilitation grants of $F28,000 in December 2000, although the authorities were criticized for their apparent slowness in processing the applications. In January 2001 the administration of native land leases was transferred from the ALTA to the Native Lands Trust Act (NLTA), prompting fears of increased bias in favour of ethnic Fijian landowners and further instability in the sugar industry. A further 1,500 leases expired during 2001.

A dispute between tribal landowners and the Government over compensation payments for land flooded by the Monosavu hydroelectric power station led to violence in July 1998. Landowners, who had been demanding compensation since the plant's construction in 1983, seized control of the station and carried out a series of arson attacks. In October 1998 the Government agreed to pay the landowners compensation totalling $A12m., but many rejected the offer. In October 2005 the dispute finally ended when landowners were paid a total of $A40m. in compensation for the use of their land by the Fiji Electricity Authority.

Meanwhile, the issue of the expiry of land leases continued to threaten Fiji's sugar industry. A committee, comprising members of both the SDL and FLP, was established to try to negotiate land leases that would satisfy both Indian Fijian tenants and their predominantly ethnic Fijian landowners. Most of the 30-year leases drawn up under the ALTA were expiring, and both tenants and the FLP were opposed to its replacement by the NLTA, which they saw as disproportionately favouring landowners. Two parliamentary bills had been approved by the Senate in April 2002, reducing the land under state control to around 1% of the total and increasing the amount under the Native Land Trust Board to over 90%. In August, however, the FLP withdrew from a second session of discussions on the issue of land leases. During 2003 more than 1,100 tenants on Vanua Levu were evicted following the expiry of their land leases. By late 2005 more than 3,500 farmers had received a total of $F26m. in assistance under the ALTA. In May 2009 the Fiji Independent Commission Against Corruption began an investigation into the Native Land Trust Board's lease renewal procedures.

Foreign Affairs

In November 1989 the Fijian Government expelled the Indian ambassador for allegedly interfering in Fiji's internal affairs, and the status of the Indian embassy was downgraded to that of a consulate. Relations between Fiji and India deteriorated as a result of the coup of May 1987, following which many ethnic Indians emigrated. In January 1989 statistical information, released by the interim Government, indicated that the islands' ethnic Fijians were in a majority for the first time since 1946. Following the adoption of significant constitutional reforms in 1997, diplomatic relations improved considerably, and in October the Indian Government invited Fiji to open a High Commission in New Delhi. In February 1999 India removed its trade embargo against Fiji (which had been in force for 10 years), and in May India reopened its High Commission in Suva. However, Fiji's relations with the international community suffered a major reversal following the coup of May 2000, which was condemned by the UN, the Commonwealth, the United Kingdom, Australia, New Zealand and several other nations in the region. In June Fiji was partially suspended from the Commonwealth (having been readmitted in October 1997 following its expulsion as a result of the coups of 1987) and a delegation of ministers of foreign affairs from the organization visited the islands to demand the reinstatement of the 1997 Constitution. Australia, New Zealand and the Commonwealth withheld formal recognition of Qarase's Government when Parliament opened in October 2001, but in December the Commonwealth Ministerial Action Group recommended that Fiji be readmitted to meetings of the Commonwealth. In November 2002 Qarase's Government confirmed its intention to reopen the Fijian High Commission in India, claiming that it was needed to cater for the new business and diplomatic links being fostered by the administration. (The mission was reopened in April 2004.) Sanctions imposed by the EU remained in place until early 2002. In late 2003 the EU announced the resumption of development aid to Fiji (suspended since 2000). The EU suspended non-humanitarian aid after the coup of December 2006. In December 2010, nevertheless, the EU concluded an Interim Economic Partnership Agreement with Fiji.

In May 2005 Fiji unexpectedly received President Chen Shui-bian of Taiwan. This unscheduled visit provoked considerable surprise, as Fiji had never recognized Taiwan and continued to maintain diplomatic relations with the People's Republic of China. However, during a five-day official visit to mainland China in the following month, Fiji's Prime Minister stressed his Government's continued support for a 'one China' policy. In April 2006 Premier Wen Jiabao of China made an official visit to Fiji in order to promote greater co-operation between the two countries. China's financial support to Fiji, in the form of aid and infrastructure development, was reported to have increased substantially between 2006 and 2009, and China was one of the few nations to continue such support following the abrogation of Fiji's Constitution in April 2009. In July–August 2010 Bainimarama visited China, declaring his preference for close relations with that country, rather than with Australia and New Zealand. In September President Nailatikau paid an official visit to China, and in November Bainimarama returned there, leading a trade mission. In January 2011 an aid agreement was concluded, whereby China was to provide US $4.5m. for development projects in Fiji. During a visit to Shenzhen, Guangdong, in August, President Nailatikau reiterated Fiji's adherence to the 'one China' policy, while both heads of state pledged further to bolster bilateral dialogue and co-operation in a wide range of fields, including political and economic engagement. Under a bilateral agreement signed in December, China was to provide the Fijian Government with US $3.3m. in grants intended to increase technical and economic co-operation.

In June 2007 New Zealand's high commissioner to Fiji was expelled because of alleged interference in the country's internal affairs. The decision prompted the New Zealand Prime Minister, Helen Clark, to announce plans for an expansion of existing sanctions against Fiji. In December 2008 Fiji expelled the acting high commissioner of New Zealand; the New Zealand Government responded by expelling her Fijian counterpart. Nevertheless, in January 2009, and again in January 2012, after heavy rains resulted in widespread flooding and a number of deaths in Fiji, New Zealand was one of several nations to offer immediate aid to the emergency relief effort, via non-governmental agencies.

The interim Government was also subject to international pressure with regard to the schedule for forthcoming elections, with several countries advising against significant delays. In March 2007 the Pacific Islands Forum Foreign Ministers convened to consider the conclusions of an 'eminent persons' group', which had travelled to Fiji to assess the situation. In addition to its criticism of alleged breaches of human rights after the coup, the group had decided that a swift return to democracy was desirable; as a consequence, the Pacific Islands Forum stressed the need for a revised timetable for elections. A joint working group subsequently outlined the necessary phases of the pre-election process. In August 2008 the interim Prime Minister asserted that the existing schedule for elections in March 2009 was not attainable in view of the need for electoral reforms; Cdre Bainimarama subsequently failed to attend a summit meeting of Pacific Islands Forum leaders. Following President Iloilo's abrogation of the Constitution in April 2009 (see Domestic Political Affairs), the Pacific Islands Forum set Bainimarama a deadline of 1 May to announce a 2009 date for democratic elections; failure to comply led to Fiji's suspension from the Forum. Australia and New Zealand considered the imposition of further sanctions against Fiji, but ultimately decided that such action would serve only to the detriment of the Fijian people. After Bainimarama refused to meet demands that an election date be set by 1 September, Fiji was fully suspended from the Commonwealth, a decision that entailed the severance of all Commonwealth aid. An envoy of the Commonwealth arrived in Fiji later in September to hold discussions with Bainimarama on Fiji's return to democracy; in October Fiji was barred from participating in the Commonwealth Games, to be held in New Delhi in 2010.

Relations between Fiji and Australia and New Zealand were severely damaged by the abrogation of the Constitution in April 2009. Both nations criticized the UN for continuing to employ Fijian peace-keepers, and Australia urged the international community to attempt to persuade Fiji to hold democratic elections. In November Bainimarama reportedly accused Australia and New Zealand of 'interfering' in Fiji's internal affairs, and ordered both nations' high commissioners to leave the country within 24 hours. In response, their Fijian counterparts were also expelled. However, in January 2010 relations between Fiji and New Zealand were reported to be improving: the two countries' ministers of foreign affairs agreed to increase the staff at their respective diplomatic missions, although this did not include the return of the high commissioners. In February 2011 a Pacific Islands Forum 'contact group' of ministers of foreign affairs met in Vanuatu, to discuss the situation in Fiji: the Fijian Minister for Foreign Affairs, Ratu Inoke Kubuabola, attended the meeting, which concluded that there had not been enough progress towards the restoration of democracy in Fiji for the contact group to recommend that the Forum change its policy on Fiji's membership; however, the group welcomed an invitation to visit Fiji within the next two months, although, in the event, this did not come to pass.

In July 2010 a regional organization, the Melanesian Spearhead Group, cancelled a planned meeting at which Bainimarama had been due to assume the rotating chairmanship of the Group: the previous chairman, Edward Natapei, the Prime Minister of Vanuatu, stated that allowing Bainimarama to take the chair would not be in accordance with the organization's democratic ideals. The Fijian Government immediately expelled the acting Australian high commissioner, accusing the Australian Government of having influenced the decision to cancel the meeting. In the same month Bainimarama convened an alternative meeting, entitled 'Engaging the Pacific', at which 10 Pacific island states were represented. In December, after Natapei had been replaced as Prime Minister of Vanuatu, Bainimarama was permitted to assume the chair of the Melanesian Spearhead Group. In January 2011 bilateral discussions with Kiribati took place, to improve the two countries' economic co-operation, in accordance with an agreement signed in September 2010. A similar agreement had been signed with Tuvalu earlier in 2010.

In February 2011 a dispute with Tonga concerning sovereignty over the uninhabited Teleki (Minerva) Reefs (claimed by Tonga in 1972) was submitted to UN officials for mediation. Bilateral tensions were further exacerbated by claims made by Bainimarama in May that the Tongan navy had assisted former army Chief of Staff Lt-Col Tevita Mara to flee from Fiji, where he had been charged with sedition and mutiny (see Domestic Political Affairs). In a statement published on the Fijian Government's website, Bainimarama stated that the Government 'takes strong exception to such breaches of Fiji's sovereignty'. The Tongan Government initially responded only to confirm that it had acted on a distress call from an island off the Fijian coast and that its navy had rescued one person. Later in May the Tongan Government rejected a Fijian request for Lt-Col Mara's extradition. It was reported in June that Lt-Col Mara had initiated in Australia a campaign to oust the Bainimarama regime. An extradition request subsequently submitted to the Australian Government by Fiji was rejected in July. In November the Australian Minister for Foreign Affairs condemned the arrest in Suva of two prominent FTUC leaders (see Domestic Political Affairs) as evidence of 'a concerted campaign by the Fiji authorities to target and intimidate trade unionists and other political opponents'.

The imposition of repressive new legislation in place of the Public Emergency Decree that was rescinded in January 2012 (see Domestic Political Affairs) elicited widespread censure from the international community. The ITUC condemned the continued limitations on freedom of association and assembly, arguing that the new Public Order Act constituted a severe reverse for hopes of a restoration of democracy in Fiji and further cemented the dictatorship of Bainimarama. New Zealand's Minister of Foreign Affairs, Murray McCully, expressed his disappointment concerning the new legislation but cautioned that it remained to be seen precisely how the new measures would be applied; rather more outspoken criticism of the Act by news publications within New Zealand prompted the Fijian Attorney-General, Aiyaz Sayed-Khaiyum, to describe that country's media as 'obtuse', arguing that the newly introduced measures were necessary to safeguard Fiji's national security.

Meanwhile, in March 2009 the US ambassador urged the interim Government to return to democratic rule, and Bainimarama accused him of interfering in Fiji's domestic affairs. In November 2010 the Fiji Government welcomed a decision by the USA to choose Fiji to host the office of the expanded US aid programme in the Pacific. However, in December Bainimarama threatened to expel the US ambassador, apparently in retaliation after the Fijian Chief Justice and two senior government officials had been refused admission to the USA in the previous month. In June 2011 the US Assistant Secretary of State for East Asia and Pacific Affairs, Kurt Campbell, expressed mounting unease about alleged human rights violations committed by the Bainimarama regime, stating that the US Administration was 'concerned' by the ongoing situation in Fiji. In a more positive development, in its *2011 Trafficking in Persons Report*, published that month, the US Department of State removed Fiji from its Tier 3 list of countries of particular concern with regard to human-trafficking, upgrading it to Tier 2 to reflect the Fijian Government's 'increased efforts' to address the issue in the previous 12 months. The report commended the establishment of a dedicated anti-trafficking police unit and the approval by the Government of a national action plan to combat human-trafficking. However, the report also noted that the Fijian authorities had failed to develop any formal procedures proactively to identify victims of trafficking.

During 2011 Bainimarama presided over the formal opening of three new diplomatic missions, in Indonesia (in April), South Africa (in July) and Brazil (in September). In December the Fijian Government announced that it was further to expand its diplomatic representation abroad by opening two more diplomatic missions, in the Republic of Korea (South Korea) and the United Arab Emirates, in mid-2012, thereby bringing the total number of such missions to 17. Meanwhile, Fiji established formal diplomatic relations with Ethiopia (in January 2011), Brunei (in April), Togo (in May), Malawi (in July), Bhutan, Cuba and Jordan (all in November) and Suriname (in December). Fiji was admitted as a member of the Non-aligned Movement (see p. 464) in May 2011, its membership bid having been accepted in January.

CONSTITUTION AND GOVERNMENT

Prior to the coup of December 2006, Fiji had a parliamentary form of government with a bicameral legislature, comprising the elected 71-seat House of Representatives and the appointed

Senate, with 32 members. The Constitution, which remained in place following the coup of 2006 but was revoked in April 2009, stated that 46 seats in the House were reserved on a racial basis (23 for ethnic Fijians, 19 for Indians, three for other races—General Electors—and one for Rotuma Islanders) and 25 seats were open to all races. The Senate was appointed by the President of the Republic, 14 members on the advice of the Great Council of Chiefs (a 52-member traditional body comprising every hereditary chief (Ratu) of a Fijian clan), nine on the advice of the Prime Minister, eight on the advice of the Leader of the Opposition and one on the advice of the Rotuma Island Council. In March 2012 the Great Council of Chiefs was abolished.

REGIONAL AND INTERNATIONAL CO-OPERATION

Fiji is a member of the Asian Development Bank (ADB, see p. 210), of the Pacific Community (see p. 413) and of the Colombo Plan (see p. 449). The country was suspended from the Pacific Islands Forum (see p. 416) in 2009. Fiji is a signatory of the South Pacific Regional Trade and Economic Co-operation Agreement (SPARTECA, see p. 418) and of the Lomé Conventions and successor Cotonou Agreement (see p. 328) with the European Union (EU). Fiji participates in the Melanesian Spearhead Group, which among other benefits provides for free trade among member countries (the others being Papua New Guinea, Solomon Islands and Vanuatu). The country is also a member of the UN's Economic and Social Commission for Asia and the Pacific (ESCAP, see p. 40)

Fiji became a member of the UN in 1970. It joined the World Trade Organization (WTO, see p. 433) in 1996. Fiji also participates in the Group of 77 (G77, see p. 450) developing countries. It is a member of the International Sugar Organization (see p. 446). Fiji was admitted to the Non-aligned Movement (see p. 464) in May 2011.

ECONOMIC AFFAIRS

In 2010, according to estimates by the World Bank, Fiji's gross national income (GNI), measured at average 2008–10 prices, was US $3,085m., equivalent to $3,580 per head (or $4,450 on an international purchasing-power parity basis). During 2001–10, it was estimated, the population increased at an average annual rate of 0.6%, while gross domestic product (GDP) per head increased, in real terms, by an annual average of 0.3%. Overall GDP rose at an average annual rate of 0.9% over the same period. According to revised figures from the Asian Development Bank (ADB), GDP decreased by 0.2% in 2010, rising by 2.1% in 2011.

In 2010 agriculture (including forestry and fishing) contributed an estimated 11.6% of GDP. According to figures from the ADB, in 2009 the sector engaged 1.3% of those in paid employment (excluding subsistence workers). The principal cash crop is sugar cane. However, production of sugar cane decreased by 10.0% in 2009 and by 16.2% in 2010, according to figures from FAO. In 2010 sugar and molasses together accounted for a provisional 6.0% of total export earnings, compared with 17.8% in 2008. Other significant export crops are coconuts and ginger, while the most important subsistence crop is paddy rice, production of which was estimated at 7,700 metric tons in 2010. Honey production was becoming an increasingly significant activity in the mid-2000s. The most important livestock products are beef and poultry meat. Fiji has significant timber reserves. Wood and wood products accounted for 5.2% of exports in 2010, when they were worth $F81.3m. Fishing is an important activity, and in 2010 fish products earned a provisional $F205.9m. in export revenue (13.3% of total export receipts). The entire agricultural sector was disrupted by unusually severe flooding in January 2009, which resulted in major losses of crops and livestock; further severe flooding was experienced in northern and western Fiji in early 2012. Meanwhile, losses also resulted from the impact of cyclones in December 2009 and in March 2010. According to the World Bank, during 2001–09 agricultural GDP decreased at an estimated average annual rate of 0.2%. The GDP of the agricultural sector contracted by 5.0% in 2010, but increased by 8.3% in 2011, according to the ADB.

Industry (including mining, manufacturing, construction and utilities) engaged 30.7% of the employed population in mid-2009. In 2010 the sector provided an estimated 21.7% of GDP. According to the World Bank, the GDP of the industrial sector was estimated to have decreased at an average rate of 0.3% per year during 2001–09. Industrial GDP increased by 8.1% in 2010 and by 0.3% in 2011, according to the ADB.

Mining contributed an estimated 1.4% of GDP in 2010. The sector engaged only 1.0% of the employed population in 2004. Following the resumption of gold-mining operations in October 2007, the sector recorded a good recovery in 2008 and 2009, and gold production rose substantially to reach 1,856 kg in 2010. Silver and copper are also mined. Operations at the country's first bauxite mine, in Nawailevu, commenced in November 2011. According to the ADB, during 2001–09 the mining sector's GDP declined at an average rate of 14.1% per year. Mining GDP declined by 13.8% in 2009.

Manufacturing contributed an estimated 15.8% of GDP in 2010, and engaged 13.6% of paid employees in 2004. The most important branch of the sector is food-processing, in particular sugar, molasses and coconut oil. The bottling of mineral water for export became increasingly important from the early 2000s, with production more than doubling between 2001 and 2005, and by 2010 exports of bottled water contributed a provisional 7.7% of total export earnings. The loss of preferential access to the US market for Fijian garments at the beginning of 2005 substantially reduced export receipts from this source. The contribution of garments to export earnings decreased from 18.8% of total revenue in 2004 to a provisional 6.2% in 2010. According to figures from the World Bank, the sector's GDP decreased at an estimated average annual rate of 1.0% during 2001–09. Manufacturing GDP decreased by an estimated 2.0% in 2009.

Construction contributed an estimated 2.9% of GDP in 2010, and engaged 5.4% of paid employees in 2004. According to figures from the ADB, the sector's GDP increased at an estimated average annual rate of 0.6% during 2001–09. Construction GDP increased by 4.7% in 2008, but decreased by 3.3% in 2009.

Energy is derived principally from hydroelectric power, which provided some 90% of Fiji's electricity in the late 1990s. Imports of mineral fuels represented a provisional 31.9% of the total cost of imports in 2010. A new wind farm was opened in 2007, as part of a plan for the country to become completely reliant on renewable energy sources.

The services sector engaged 68.0% of the employed population in mid-2009, and contributed an estimated 66.7% of GDP in 20010. Although intermittently affected by political unrest, tourism is a major source of foreign exchange. Revenue reached $F979.8m. in 2010. Visitor arrivals increased from 631,868 in 2010 to an estimated 674,913 in 2011. Australia and New Zealand are the most important sources of visitors. According to figures from the World Bank, during 2001–09 the sector's GDP rose at an average annual rate of 1.8%. The GDP of the services sector contracted by 1.4% in 2010, but expanded by 1.5% in 2011, according to the ADB.

Fiji consistently records a trade deficit, which was US $782.0m. in 2010, when the country also recorded a deficit of US $416.0m. on the current account of the balance of payments. The principal source of imports in 2010 was Singapore (33.2%). Other important suppliers were Australia, New Zealand and the People's Republic of China. The principal market for exports was Australia (17.8%). Other important markets included the USA, Japan, New Zealand and the United Kingdom. The principal imports in 2010 were mineral products (32.7% of total costs in that year), followed by machinery, mechanical appliances and electrical equipment, vegetable products, and chemical products, animals and animal products. Fiji's principal domestic exports were mineral products, prepared foodstuffs, and animals and animal products. Fiji also re-exports mineral fuels (including bunkers for ships and aircraft).

The overall budget deficit was estimated at $F211.8m. in 2010, equivalent to 3.6% of GDP. In 2011/12 aid from Australia was projected at $A37.5m. Aid from New Zealand in 2011/12 was budgeted at $NZ5.0m. Fiji's general government gross debt was $F3,327m. in 2010, equivalent to 55.8% of GDP. Fiji's outstanding external debt totalled an estimated US $422m. at the end of 2011. In that year the cost of debt-servicing was equivalent to 9.2% of the revenue from exports of goods and services. The average annual rate of inflation was 3.8% in 2001–10. Consumer prices rose by 8.7% in 2011. According to the ADB, an estimated 8.6% of the total labour force were unemployed in 2009. From the late 1980s remittances from Fijians working overseas assumed increasing importance, although in 2007–08 a substantial reduction in this source of income was recorded, partly owing to the decrease in the number of Fijian security personnel employed in the Middle East. Remittances from Fijian personnel serving in the British Army have become a significant source of income. The total value of remittances from overseas workers was reported to have risen by 56.5% in 2009, to reach US $294m., although this substantial increase was mainly due to the devaluation of the Fiji dollar in that year; a slight decline, to US $287m. was recorded in 2010.

The impact on Fiji's economy of the removal of the elected Government in the military coup of December 2006 was subsequently compounded by the sharp deterioration in global economic conditions in 2008/09 and by the political instability of 2009. The Fiji dollar was devalued by 20% in April 2009. Consumer spending remained weak in 2010, largely owing to high inflation. The European Union suspended financial aid to the sugar cane industry following the events of April 2009, and in August interim Prime Minister Bainimarama dissolved the Sugar Cane Growers' Council, reportedly claiming that it was attempting to influence national politics. As the country's sugar industry continued to contract in 2010–11, there were substantial job losses in the sector. However, tourism recorded a strong recovery in 2010 and 2011, when visitor numbers increased by 16.5% and 6.8%, respectively. In December 2010 the Tourist VAT Refund Scheme, to permit visitors to claim back value-added tax paid on goods purchased in Fiji, was enacted; meanwhile, the rate of VAT was raised from 12.5% to 15.0%. In March 2010 Cyclone Tomas caused serious damage in northern areas of Fiji, with the cost of repairs estimated at $F85m., while severe flooding was experienced in northern and western Fiji in early 2012. The 2012 budget, announced in November 2011, contained a number of austerity measures, including levies on credit card payments and luxury cars, an expansion of the existing tax on tourism services, and an increase in employers' pensions contributions. However, the budget also provided for an increase in public sector salaries, as well as reductions in income and corporate tax rates in a bid to increase consumer spending. Expenditure on infrastructural development, which was identified as being key to facilitating an increase in foreign trade levels, was increased by $F63m.; priority was to be given to several road, airport and water projects, including a scheme to improve the supply of safe, potable water, while a rural electrification project was also allocated increased funding. GDP growth of 2.1% was recorded in 2011, driven by robust post-cyclone recoveries in the agriculture and tourism sectors; the ADB forecast more moderate growth, of 1.0%, for 2012.

PUBLIC HOLIDAYS

2013 (provisional): 1 January (New Year's Day), 23 January* (Birth of the Prophet Muhammad), 29 March (Good Friday), 1 April (Easter Monday), 10 June (for Queen's Official Birthday), 11 October (Fiji Day), 4 November (for Deepavali), 25–26 December (Christmas).

* This Islamic holiday is dependent on the lunar calendar and may vary by one or two days from the date given.

Statistical Survey

Sources (unless otherwise stated): Bureau of Statistics, POB 2221, Government Bldgs, Suva; tel. 3315144; fax 3303656; internet www.statsfiji.gov.fj; Reserve Bank of Fiji, POB 1220, Suva; tel. 3313611; fax 3301688; e-mail info@rbf.gov.fj; internet www.reservebank.gov.fj.

AREA AND POPULATION

Area (incl. the Rotuma group): 18,376 sq km (7,095 sq miles). Land area of 18,333 sq km (7,078 sq miles) consists mainly of the islands of Viti Levu (10,429 sq km—4,027 sq miles) and Vanua Levu (5,556 sq km—2,145 sq miles).

Population: 775,077 at census of 25 August 1996; 837,271 (males 427,176, females 410,095) at census of 16 September 2007; *Mid-2012* (Secretariat of the Pacific Community estimate): 855,750 (Source: Pacific Regional Information System).

Density (at mid-2012): 46.6 per sq km.

Population by Age and Sex (Secretariat of the Pacific Community estimates at mid-2012): *0–14:* 242,691 (males 125,511, females 117,180); *15–64:* 570,294 (males 291,552, females 278,743); *65 and over:* 42,765 (males 19,330, females 23,435); *Total* 855,750 (males 436,392, females 419,358).

Principal Towns (population at 2007 census): Suva (capital) 74,481; Lautoka 43,473; Nadi 11,685; Lami 10,752; Labasa 7,706; Ba 6,826.

Ethnic Groups (2007 census): Fijians 475,739; Indians 313,798; Rotuman 10,771; Chinese 4,704; European 2,953; Others 29,306; Total 837,271.

Births, Marriages and Deaths (registrations, 2009 unless otherwise indicated): Live births 18,854 (birth rate 21.4 per 1,000); Marriages 7,076 in 2004 (marriage rate 8.6 per 1,000); Deaths 3,921 (death rate 4.8 per 1,000). Source: partly UN, *Population and Vital Statistics Report*.

Life Expectancy (years at birth, WHO estimates): 69 (males 66; females 73) in 2009. Source: WHO, *World Health Statistics*.

Economically Active Population (paid employment, persons aged 15 years and over, 2004): Agriculture, hunting, forestry and fishing 89,523; Mining and quarrying 3,222; Manufacturing 43,088; Electricity, gas and water 2,508; Construction 16,950; Trade, restaurants and hotels 66,043; Transport, storage and communications 22,551; Financing, insurance, real estate and business services 10,220; Community, social and personal services 61,936; *Total employed* 316,041. *Mid-2009* (paid employment, '000 persons, unless otherwise indicated): Agriculture 1.7; Industry 39.5; Services 87.6; Total employed 128.8; Unemployed 28.0; Total labour force (incl. subsistence workers) 327.0. Source: partly Asian Development Bank.

HEALTH AND WELFARE

Key Indicators

Total Fertility Rate (children per woman, 2009): 2.7.

Under-5 Mortality Rate (per 1,000 live births, 2009): 18.

HIV/AIDS (% of persons aged 15–49, 2009): 0.1.

Physicians (per 1,000 head, 2003): 0.5.

Health Expenditure (2008): US $ per head (PPP): 168.

Health Expenditure (2008): % of GDP: 3.5.

Health Expenditure (2008): public (% of total): 75.3.

Access to Water (% of persons, 2006): 47.

Access to Sanitation (% of persons, 2006): 71.

Total Carbon Dioxide Emissions ('000 metric tons, 2006): 1,608.5.

Carbon Dioxide Emissions Per Head (metric tons, 2006): 1.9.

Human Development Index (2011): ranking: 100.

Human Development Index (2011): value: 0.688.

For sources and definitions, see explanatory note on p. vi.

AGRICULTURE, ETC.

Principal Crops ('000 metric tons, 2010): Sugar cane 1,751; Coconuts 170.1 (FAO estimate); Rice, paddy 7.7 Cassava 51.7; Sweet potatoes 7.5; Yams 1.7; Taro 60.3; Aubergines (Eggplants) 3.7; Bananas 3.1 (FAO estimate); Pineapples 3.4; Ginger 2.3.

Livestock ('000 head, year ending 2010, FAO estimates): Cattle 312; Pigs 145; Sheep 6; Goats 255; Horses 46; Chickens 3,500; Ducks 85; Turkeys 70.

Livestock Products (metric tons, 2010): Poultry meat 14,726; Cattle meat 8,360 (FAO estimate); Goat meat 227; Pig meat 3,983 (FAO estimate); Hen eggs 5,707; Cows' milk 61,300 (FAO estimate); Honey 330 (FAO estimate).

Forestry ('000 cubic metres, 2010, FAO estimates): *Roundwood Removals* (excl. bark): Sawlogs and veneer logs 233; Pulpwood 206; Other industrial wood 6; Fuel wood 37; Total 482. *Sawnwood Production* (incl. sleepers): 90.

Fishing ('000 metric tons, live weight, 2009): Capture 39.6 (FAO estimate) (Albacore 7.2; Yellowfin tuna 2.6; Emperors—scavengers 0.8; Other marine fishes 21.0 (FAO estimate); Crustaceans 0.4 (FAO estimate); Molluscs 1.5); Aquaculture 0.2 (FAO estimate); *Total catch* 39.9 (FAO estimate) (excluding corals 1.0).

Source: FAO.

MINING

Production (kg, 2010, estimates): Gold 1,856; Silver 500 (Source: US Geological Survey).

INDUSTRY

Production (metric tons, 2009): Sugar 168,000; Molasses 131,000; Coconut oil 4,977; Flour 89,113; Soap 5,319; Cement 116,000; Paint ('000 litres) 3,217; Beer ('000 litres) 20,000; Soft drinks ('000 litres) 154,111; Cigarettes 367; Matches ('000 gross boxes) 114; Electric energy (million kWh) 809; Ice cream ('000 litres) 2,367; Toilet paper ('000 rolls) 17,179.

FINANCE

Currency and Exchange Rates: 100 cents = 1 Fiji dollar ($F). *Sterling, US Dollar and Euro Equivalents* (30 November 2011): £1 sterling = $F2.85; US $1 = $F1.828; €1 = $F2.453; $F100 = £35.05 = US $54.70 = €40.77. *Average Exchange Rate* ($F per US $): 1.5937 in 2008; 1.9557 in 2009; 1.9183 in 2010.

General Budget ($F million, 2010, provisional): *Revenue:* Current revenue 1,484.7 (Taxes 1,281.0, Non-taxes 203.7); Capital revenue 10.4; Grants 8.6; Total 1,503.7; *Expenditure:* General public services 205.5; Defence 97.0; Education 209.5; Health 113.9; Social security and welfare 3.9; Housing and community amenities 10.5; Economic services 115.5 (Agriculture 19.3; Industry 42.7; Transport, communications and other services 55.4); Total (incl. others) 1,715.5 (Current 1,332.6, Capital 382.9). Source: Asian Development Bank.

International Reserves (US $ million at 31 December 2010): Gold (valued at market-related prices) 1.17; IMF special drawing rights 78.69; Reserve position in IMF 25.02; Foreign exchange 615.63; *Total* 720.51. Source: IMF, *International Financial Statistics*.

Money Supply ($F million at 31 December 2010): Currency outside depository corporations 383.9; Transferable deposits 1,064.0; Other deposits 2,373.9; Securities other than shares 17.4; *Broad money* 3,839.2. Source: IMF, *International Financial Statistics*.

Cost of Living (Consumer Price Index; base: 2005 = 100): All items 115.8 in 2008; 120.0 in 2009; 126.7 in 2010.

Expenditure on the Gross Domestic Product ($F million at current prices, 2009): Government final consumption expenditure 983.5; Private final consumption expenditure 4,087.1; Increase in stocks 140.0; Gross fixed capital formation 1,064.1; *Total domestic expenditure* 6,274.7; Exports of goods and services 2,671.2; *Less* Imports of goods and services 3,414.6; *GDP in purchasers' values* 5,531.3. Source: Asian Development Bank.

Gross Domestic Product by Economic Activity ($F million at current prices, 2010, provisional): Agriculture, forestry and fishing 603.8; Mining and quarrying 73.4; Manufacturing 822.3; Electricity, gas and water 85.7; Construction 151.4; Wholesale and retail trade 979.9; Transport and communications 800.3; Finance, real estate, etc. 941.8; Public administration and defence 759.5; *Sub-total* 5,218.7; Indirect taxes, less subsidies 868.6; *GDP in purchasers' values* 6,087.4.

Balance of Payments (US $ million, 2010): Exports of goods f.o.b. 819.5; Imports of goods f.o.b. –1,601.4; *Trade balance* –782.0; Exports of services 861.2; Imports of services –509.5; *Balance on goods and services* –430.3; Other income received 78.3; Other income paid –179.9; *Balance on goods, services and income* –531.9; Current transfers received 168.7; Current transfers paid –52.7; *Current balance* –416.0; Capital account (net) 27.1; Direct investment abroad –5.8; Direct investment from abroad 196.2; Portfolio investment liabilities –0.1; Other investment assets 38.7; Other investment liabilities 36.5; Net errors and omissions 257.1; *Overall balance* 133.8 (Source: IMF, *International Financial Statistics*).

EXTERNAL TRADE

Principal Commodities ($F million, 2010, provisional): *Imports c.i.f.* (distribution by HS): Animals and animal products 205.4; Vegetable products 220.4; Prepared foodstuffs 164.5; Mineral products 1,129.5; Chemical products 209.5; Plastics and rubber 162.4; Textiles and textile articles 171.0; Base metals and articles thereof 174.7; Machinery, mechanical appliances and electrical equipment 447.3; Transportation equipment 182.2; Total (incl. others) 3,450.3. *Exports f.o.b.:* Animals and animal products 256.7; Vegetable products 75.1; Prepared foodstuffs 310.7; Mineral products 413.6; Wood and wood products 81.3; Textiles and textile articles 112.6; Pearls, precious or semi-precious stones and metals 94.1; Total (incl. others) 1,549.5.

Principal Trading Partners ($F million, 2010, provisional): *Imports c.i.f.:* Australia 700.2; China, People's Republic 210.3; France 29.1; Germany 4.5; Hong Kong 56.8; India 66.8; Indonesia 31.3; Japan 85.7; Malaysia 66.9; New Zealand 548.7; Singapore 1,146.8; Thailand 85.1; USA 124.1; Total (incl. others) 3,450.3. *Exports:* Australia 276.5; Japan 115.0; New Zealand 93.0; Samoa 31.4; Tonga 35.3; United Kingdom 80.6; USA 178.8; Total (incl. others) 1,549.5.

TRANSPORT

Road Traffic (motor vehicles registered at 31 December 2010): Private cars 89,422; Goods vehicles 43,722; Buses 2,279; Taxis 5,440; Rental vehicles 6,991; Motorcycles 5,127; Tractors 6,161; Total (incl. others) 167,085.

Shipping: *Merchant Fleet* (registered at 31 December 2009): Vessels 58; Total displacement ('000 grt) 35.2 (Source: IHS Fairplay, *World Fleet Statistics*). *International Freight Traffic* ('000 metric tons, 1990): Goods loaded 568; Goods unloaded 625 (Source: UN, *Monthly Bulletin of Statistics*).

Civil Aviation (traffic on scheduled services, 2010, unless otherwise indicated): Kilometres flown 25 million (2006); Passengers carried 908,651; Passenger-kilometres 2,312 million; Total ton-kilometres 356.6 million. Source: partly UN, *Statistical Yearbook*.

TOURISM

Foreign Visitors by Country of Residence (excluding cruise-ship passengers, 2010): Australia 318,185; Canada 12,970; Japan 12,011; New Zealand 97,857; Pacific Islands 39,198; United Kingdom 23,813; USA 53,122; Total (incl. others) 631,868.

Tourism Receipts ($F million): 853.8 in 2008; 816.9 in 2009; 979.8 in 2010.

COMMUNICATIONS MEDIA

Radio Receivers (1999): 545,000 in use*.

Television Receivers (2000): 92,000 in use†.

Telephones (2010): 129,800 main lines in use†‡.

Mobile Cellular Telephones (2010): 697,900 subscribers†‡.

Personal Computers: 50,000 (60.4 per 1,000 persons) in 2005†.

Internet Subscribers (2010): 39,000†.

Broadband Subscribers (2010): 23,200†.

Book Production (1980): 110 titles (84 books, 26 pamphlets); 273,000 copies (229,000 books, 44,000 pamphlets).

Daily Newspapers (2004): 3 (estimated combined circulation 44,000)*.

Non-daily Newspapers (2004): 3 (combined circulation 99,000 in 1988)*.

* Source: UNESCO Institute for Statistics.

† Source: International Telecommunication Union.

‡ 30 June 2011.

EDUCATION

Pre-Primary (2002, unless otherwise indicated): 451 schools (2003); 264 teachers; 7,076 pupils.

Primary (at 31 May 2009): 721 schools; 5,173 teachers; 129,444 pupils.

General Secondary (at 31 May 2009): 172 schools; 4,273 teachers; 67,072 pupils.

Vocational and Technical (at 31 May 2009): 69 institutions; 391 teachers; 2,387 students.

Teacher Training (at 31 May 2009): 4 institutions; 88 teachers; 633 students.

Medical (1989): 2 institutions; 493 students.

University (2004): 1 institution; 289 teachers; 16,444 students.

Pupil-teacher Ratio (primary education, UNESCO estimate): 26.0 in 2007/08 (Source: UNESCO Institute for Statistics).

Adult Literacy Rate (UN estimates, 1995–99): 92.9% (males 94.5%; females 91.4%). Source: UN Development Programme, *Human Development Report*.

Directory

The Government

HEAD OF STATE

President: Ratu EPELI NAILATIKAU (appointed Acting President 30 July 2009; inaugurated as President 5 November 2009).

Vice-President: (vacant).

CABINET

(May 2012)

Prime Minister, Minister for Finance, Strategic Planning and National Development and Statistics, Public Service, People's Charter for Change and Progress, Information, Provincial Development, iTaukei, Multi-Ethnic Affairs, Sugar, and Lands and Mineral Resources: Cdre FRANK (VOREQE) BAINIMARAMA.

Attorney-General and Minister for Justice, Anti-Corruption, Public Enterprises, Communications, Civil Aviation, Tourism and Industry and International and Internal Trade: AIYAZ SAYED-KHAIYUM.

Minister for Foreign Affairs and International Co-operation: Ratu INOKE KUBUABOLA.

Minister for Health: Dr NEIL SHARMA.

Minister for Women, Social Welfare and Poverty Alleviation: Dr JIKO LUVENI.

Minister for Education, National Heritage, Culture and Arts: FILIPE BOLE.

Minister for Labour, Industrial Relations and Employment: JONE USUMATE.

Minister for Local Government, Urban Development, Housing and Environment and Acting Minister for Defence, National Security and Immigration: Col SAMUELA SAUMATUA.

Minister for Public Utilities (Water and Energy), Works and Transport: TIMOCI LESI NATUVA.

Minister for Primary Industries: JOKETANI COKANASIGA.

Minister for Youth and Sports: Commdr VILIAME NAUPOTO.

MINISTRIES

Office of the President: Government House, Berkley Cres., Government Bldgs, POB 2513, Suva; tel. 3314244; fax 3301645.

Office of the Prime Minister: Government Bldgs, POB 2353, Suva; tel. 3211201; fax 3306034; e-mail pmsoffice@connect.com.fj; internet old.fiji.gov.fj/publish/pm_office.shtml.

Office of the Attorney-General: Government Bldgs, Victoria Parade, POB 2213, Suva; tel. 3309866; fax 3305421; internet www.ag.gov.fj.

Ministry of Communication: Suva.

Ministry of Defence, National Security and Immigration: Government Bldgs, POB 2349, Suva; tel. 3211401; fax 3300346; e-mail infohomaff@govnet.gov.fj.

Ministry of Education: Marela House, Thurston St, PMB, Suva; tel. 3314477; fax 3303511; internet www.education.gov.fj.

Ministry of Finance, Strategic Planning and National Development and Statistics: Government Bldgs, POB 2212, Suva; tel. 3307011; fax 3300834; e-mail psfinance@govnet.gov.fj.

Ministry of Foreign Affairs and International Co-operation: Government Bldgs, POB 2220, Suva; tel. 3309631; fax 3301741; e-mail info@foreignaffairs.gov.fj; internet www.foreignaffairs.gov.fj.

Ministry of Health: Government Bldgs, POB 2223, Suva; tel. 3306177; fax 3306163; e-mail info@health.gov.fj; internet www.health.gov.fj.

Ministry of Industry and Trade: Government Bldgs, POB 2118, Suva; tel. 3305411; fax 3302617; internet www.commerce.gov.fj.

Ministry of Information: Government Bldgs, POB 2225, Suva; tel. 3302102; fax 3305139; e-mail info@fiji.gov.fj; internet www.info.gov.fj.

Ministry of Justice: Government Bldgs, Victoria Parade, POB 2213, Suva; tel. 3309866; fax 3302404.

Ministry of Labour, Industrial Relations and Employment: Government Bldgs, POB 2216, Suva; tel. 3303500; fax 3304701; e-mail callcentre@labour.gov.fj; internet www.labour.gov.fj.

Ministry of Lands and Mineral Resources: Government Bldgs, POB 2222, Suva; tel. 3314399; fax 3305029; e-mail lis@lands.gov.fj; internet www.lands.gov.fj.

Ministry of Local Government, Urban Development, Housing and Environment: Government Bldgs, POB 2131, Suva; tel. 3304364; fax 3303515; e-mail msovaki@govnet.gov.fj.

Ministry of Primary Industries: Government Bldgs, POB 2218, Suva; tel. 3301611; fax 3301595.

Ministry of Provincial Development, iTaukei Affairs and Multi-Ethnic Affairs: Government Bldgs, POB 2100, Suva; tel. 3100909; fax 3312530; e-mail tvolau@govnet.gov.fj.

Ministry of Public Enterprises: Government Bldgs, POB 2278, Suva; tel. 3315577; fax 3315035; e-mail epowell.fj@gmail.com; internet www.fiji.gov.fj.

Ministry of Public Utilities (Water and Energy), Works and Transport: Government Bldgs, POB 2493, Suva; tel. 3384111; fax 3383198.

Ministry of Sugar: Sugar House, Marine Dr., Walu St, Lautoka.

Ministry of Tourism: Suva.

Ministry of Women, Social Welfare and Poverty Alleviation: POB 14068, Suva; tel. 3312681; fax 3312357.

Ministry of Youth and Sports: Government Bldgs, POB 2448, Suva; tel. 3315960; fax 3305348; e-mail vikash.nand@govnet.gov.fj; internet www.youth.gov.fj.

Legislature

Note: Parliament was dissolved on 6 December 2006, following the military coup of the previous day.

PARLIAMENT

Senate

The Senate was also known as the House of Review. The upper chamber comprised 32 appointed members.

House of Representatives

The lower chamber comprised 71 elected members: 23 representing ethnic Fijians, 19 representing ethnic Indians, three representing other races (General Electors), one for Rotuma Islanders and 25 seats open to all races.

General Election, 6–13 May 2006

	Communal Seats				
	Fijian	Indian	Other*	Open Seats	Total Seats
Fiji United Party (SDL)	23	—	—	13	36
Fiji Labour Party (FLP)	—	19	—	12	31
United People's Party	—	—	2	—	2
Independents	—	—	2	—	2
Total	23	19	4	25	71

* One Rotuman and three General Electors' seats.

Election Commission

Fiji Electoral Commission: Government Bldgs, POB 2528, Suva; tel. 3316225; fax 3302436; e-mail info@elections.gov.fj; internet www.elections.gov.fj; Senior Electoral Officer VILIAME VUIYANUCA; Acting Supervisor of Elections SORO TOUTOU.

Political Organizations

Fiji Indian Liberal Party: Rakiraki; f. 1991; represents the interests of the Indian community, particularly sugar-cane farmers and students; Sec. SWANI KUMAR.

Fiji Labour Party (FLP): Government Bldgs, POB 2162, Suva; tel. 3373317; fax 3373173; e-mail flp@connect.com.fj; internet www.flp.org.fj; f. 1985; Pres. SACHIDA NAND SHARMA (acting); Sec.-Gen. MAHENDRA PAL CHAUDHRY.

Fijian Association Party (FAP): Suva; f. 1995; est. by merger of Fijian Assen (breakaway faction of SVT) and the multiracial All Nationals Congress; Leader Adi KUINI SPEED; Pres. Ratu INOKE SERU.

Janata Party: Suva; f. 1995; est. by fmr mems of NFP and FLP.

National Alliance Party of Fiji: POB 2315, Suva; internet www.alliancefiji.com; f. 2005; Pres. Ratu EPELI GAVIDI GANILAU.

National Federation Party (NFP): POB 13534, Suva; tel. 3305811; fax 3305317; f. 1960; est. by merger of the multiracial (but mainly Indian) Fed. Party and Nat. Democratic Party; Leader ATTAR SINGH; Pres. RAMAN SINGH.

Nationalist Vanua Takolavo Party (NVTLP): Suva; Leader ILIESA DUVULOCO; Pres. VILIAME SAVU.

Party of National Unity (PANU): Ba; f. 1998; est. to lobby for increased representation for the province of Ba; merged with Bai Kei Viti and People's Nat. Party (Leader MELI BOGILEKA) in 2006; Leader Tui Ba Ratu SAIRUSI NAGAGAVOKA.

Soqosoqo Duavata ni Lewenivanua (SDL) (Fiji United Party): c/o House of Representatives, Suva; f. 2001; Leader LAISENIA QARASE; Pres. Ratu KALOKALO LOKI.

Soqosoqo ni Vakavulewa ni Taukei (SVT) (Fijian Political Party): Suva; f. 1990; est. by Great Council of Chiefs; supports constitutional dominance of ethnic Fijians but accepts multiracialism; Pres. Ratu SITIVENI RABUKA; Gen. Sec. EMA DRUAVESI.

United People's Party (UPP): Suva; f. 1998; est. by merger of General Electors' Party and General Voters' Party (fmrly General Electors' Asscn, one of the three wings of the Alliance Party—AP, the ruling party 1970–87); fmrly United General Party; present name adopted in 2004 to be more multiracial in scope; represents the interests of the minority Chinese and European communities and people from other Pacific Islands resident in Fiji; Pres. MICK BEDDOES; Vice-Pres. MARGARET ROUNDS.

Vanua Independent Party: Leader ILIESA TUVALOVO; Sec. URAIA TUISOVISOVI.

The Fiji Democracy and Freedom Movement (Pres. USAIA WAQATAIREWA) was established in Australia in 2009. Based in New Zealand, the Coalition for Democracy in Fiji was formed in 1987. Supporters of secession are concentrated in Rotuma.

Diplomatic Representation

EMBASSIES AND HIGH COMMISSIONS IN FIJI

Australia: 37 Princes Rd, POB 214, Suva; tel. 3382211; fax 3382065; e-mail public-affairs-suva@dfat.gov.au; internet www.fiji.embassy.gov.au; High Commissioner GLENN MILES (acting).

China, People's Republic: 183 Queen Elizabeth Dr., PMB, Nasese, Suva; tel. 3300215; fax 3300950; e-mail chinaemb_fj@mfa.gov.cn; internet fj.china-embassy.org/chn; Ambassador HUANG YONG.

France: Dominion House, 7th Floor, Thomson St, Suva; tel. 3310526; fax 3323901; e-mail presse@ambafrance-fj.org; internet www.ambafrance-fj.org; Ambassador GILLES MONTAGNIER.

India: POB 471, Suva; tel. 3301125; fax 3301032; e-mail hicomindsuva@is.com.fj; High Commissioner VINOD KUMAR.

Indonesia: Ra Marama Bldg, 6th Floor, 91 Gordon St, POB 878, Suva; tel. 3316697; fax 3316796; e-mail kbrisuva@connect.com; internet www.suva.deplu.go.id; Ambassador AIDIL CHANDRA SALIM.

Japan: Dominion House, 2nd Floor, POB 13045, Suva; tel. 3304633; fax 3302984; e-mail eojfiji@connect.com.fj; internet www.fj.emb-japan.go.jp; Ambassador EIICHI OSHIMA.

Kiribati: POB 17937, 36 MacGregor Rd, Suva; tel. 3302512; fax 3315335; High Commissioner RETETA RIMON.

Korea, Republic: Vanua House, 8th Floor, PMB, Suva; tel. 3300977; fax 3308059; e-mail korembfj@mofat.go.kr; internet fji.mofat.go.kr; Ambassador CHEONG HAE-WOOK.

Malaysia: Pacific House, 5th Floor, POB 356, Suva; tel. 3312166; fax 3303350; e-mail mwsuva@connect.com.fj; High Commissioner (vacant).

Marshall Islands: Government Bldgs, 41 Borron Rd, POB 2038, Suva; tel. 3387899; fax 3387115; e-mail amb.rmisuva@gmail.com; Ambassador FREDERICK H. MULLER.

Micronesia, Federated States: 37 Loftus St, POB 15493, Suva; tel. 3304566; fax 3304081; e-mail fsmsuva@sopacsun.sopac.org.fj; Ambassador GERSON JACKSON.

Nauru: Ratu Sukuna House, 7th Floor, Government Bldgs, 229–249 Victoria Parade, Suva; tel. 3313566; fax 3318311; e-mail naurulands@connect.com.fj; High Commissioner JARDEN KEPHAS.

New Zealand: Reserve Bank of Fiji Bldg, 10th Floor, Pratt St, POB 1378, Suva; tel. 3311422; fax 3300842; e-mail nzhc@connect.com.fj; internet www.nzembassy.com/fiji; Acting Head of Mission PHILLIP TAULA.

Papua New Guinea: 18 Rakua St, off Nailuva Rd, Government Bldgs, POB 2447, Suva; tel. 3304244; fax 3300178; e-mail kundufj@is.com.fj; High Commissioner PETER EAFEARE.

Solomon Islands: 34 Reki St, Government Bldgs, POB 2647, Suva; tel. 3100355; fax 3100356; e-mail solohicom@gmail.com; High Commissioner JOHN PATTESON OTI.

South Africa: Kimberly St, Suva; tel. 3311087; fax 3311086; e-mail freestate@connect.com.fj; internet www.sahcfiji.com; Chargé d'affaires ABBEY MATOTO PINDELO.

Tuvalu: 16 Gorrie St, POB 14449, Suva; tel. 3301355; fax 3308479; e-mail s.laloniu@yahoo.com; High Commissioner AUNESE MAKOI SIMATI.

United Kingdom: Victoria House, 47 Gladstone Rd, POB 1355, Suva; tel. 3229100; fax 3229132; e-mail publicdiplomacysuva@fco.gov.uk; internet ukinfiji.fco.gov.uk; Chargé d'affaires a.i. TIMOTHY SMART.

USA: 158 Princess Rd, Tamavua, Suva; tel. 3314466; fax 3308685; e-mail usembsuva@gmail.com; internet suva.usembassy.gov; Ambassador FRANKIE A. REED.

Vanuatu: Town House Apt Hotel, 3 Forster St, Suva; Chargé d'affaires KANAM WILSON NAPLAUI.

Judicial System

Justice is administered by the Supreme Court, the Fiji Court of Appeal, the High Court and the Magistrates' Courts. The Supreme Court of Fiji is the superior court of record, presided over by the Chief Justice. The 1990 Constitution provided for the establishment of Fijian customary courts and declared as final decisions of the Native Lands Commission in cases involving Fijian custom, etc. In April 2009, following the Court of Appeal's finding that the interim Government in place since the 2006 coup was illegal, the President of Fiji dismissed the entire judiciary.

Supreme Court: Suva; tel. 3211335; fax 3305242; e-mail enquiries@judicial.gov.fj; internet www.judiciary.gov.fj; Chief Justice ANTHONY GATES.

Court of Appeal: Victoria Parade, Suva; tel. 3211307; fax 3316284; President of the Court of Appeal (vacant).

High Court: Suva; Chief Registrar GANGA WAKISHTA ARACHCHI (acting).

Magistrates' Courts: there are 15 Magistrates' Courts, which allow for 22 sitting resident magistrates; Chief Magistrate USAIA RATUVILI.

Director of Public Prosecutions: 25 Gladstone Rd, Suva; tel. 3211793; Director CHRISTOPHER PRYDE.

Attorney-General: Government Bldgs, POB 2213, Suva; tel. 3309866; fax 3305421; internet www.ag.gov.fj; Attorney-General AIYAZ SAYED-KHAIYUM (Minister for Justice); Solicitor-General SHARVADA SHARAMA (acting).

Religion

CHRISTIANITY

Most ethnic Fijians are Christians. Methodists are the largest Christian group, followed by Roman Catholics. At the census of 2007 about 64.4% of the population were Christian (mainly Methodists, who comprised 34.6% of the total population).

Fiji Council of Churches: Government Bldgs, POB 2300, Suva; tel. and fax (1) 3313798; e-mail fijichurches@connect.com.fj; f. 1964; nine mem. churches; Pres. Rev. APIMELEKI QILIHO; Gen. Sec. Rev. ISIRELI LEDUA KACIMAIWAI.

The Anglican Communion

In April 1990 Polynesia, formerly a missionary diocese of the Church of the Province of New Zealand, became a full and integral diocese. The diocese of Polynesia is based in Fiji but also includes Wallis and Futuna, Tuvalu, Kiribati, French Polynesia, Cook Islands, Tonga, Samoa and Tokelau. There were an estimated 6,319 adherents in 2007.

Bishop of Polynesia: Archbishop Dr WINSTON HALAPUA, Bishop's Office, 8 Desvoeux Rd, POB 35, Suva; tel. 3304716; fax 3302687; e-mail episcopus@connect.com.fj.

The Roman Catholic Church

Fiji comprises a single archdiocese. At 31 December 2007 there were an estimated 97,692 adherents in the country.

Bishops' Conference: Episcopal Conference of the Pacific Secretariat (CEPAC), 14 Williamson Rd, POB 289, Suva; tel. 3300340; fax 3303143; e-mail cepac@connect.com.fj; f. 1968; 17 mems; Pres. Most Rev. ANTHONY SABLAN APURON (Archbishop of Agaña, Guam); Sec.-Gen. Fr ROGER MCCARRICK.

Archbishop of Suva: Mgr PETERO MATACA, Archdiocesan Office, Nicolas House, 35 Pratt St, POB 109, Suva; tel. 3301955; fax 3301565.

Other Christian Churches

Methodist Church in Fiji & Rotuma (Lotu Wesele e Viti): Epworth Arcade, Nina St, POB 357, Suva; tel. 3311477; fax 3303771; e-mail methodistchhq@connect.com.fj; f. 1835; autonomous since 1964; 212,831 mems (2007); Gen. Sec. Rev. TUIKILAKILA WAQAIRATU; Pres. Rev. AME TUGAUE.

Other denominations active in the country include the Assembly of God (with c. 7,000 mems), the Baptist Mission, the Congregational Christian Church and the Presbyterian Church.

HINDUISM

Most of the Indian community are Hindus. According to the census of 2007, 27.9% of the population were Hindus.

ISLAM

In 2007 some 6.3% of the population were Muslim. There are several Islamic organizations.

Fiji Muslim League: Samabula, POB 3990, Suva; tel. 3384566; fax 3370204; e-mail fijimuslim@connect.com.fj; f. 1926; Nat. Pres. HAFIZUD DEAN KHAN; Gen. Sec. MOHAMMAD TAABISH AKBAR; 26 brs and 3 subsidiary orgs.

SIKHISM

There were an estimated 2,540 Sikhs in Fiji in 2007.

Sikh Association of Fiji: Suva; Pres. MEJA SINGH.

BAHÁ'Í FAITH

National Spiritual Assembly: National Office, POB 639, Suva; tel. 3387574; fax 3387772; e-mail nsafiji@connect.com.fj; mems resident in 490 localities; national headquarters for consultancy and co-ordination.

The Press

NEWSPAPERS AND PERIODICALS

Coconut Telegraph: POB 249, Savusavu, Vanua Levu; f. 1975; monthly; serves rural communities; Editor LEMA LOW.

Fiji Calling: POB 12095, Suva; tel. 3305916; fax 3301930; publ. by Associated Media Ltd; every 6 months; English; Publr YASHWANT GAUNDER.

Fiji Cane Grower: POB 12095, Suva; tel. 3305916; fax 3305256.

Fiji Daily Post: 19 Ackland St, Viria East Industrial Subdivision, Vatuwaqa, Suva; tel. 3275176; fax 3275179; e-mail info@fijidailypost.com; internet www.fijidailypost.com; f. 1987 as *Fiji Post*, daily from 1989; English; 100% govt-owned since Sept. 2003; Chair. MALAKAI NAIYAGA; Editor-in-Chief ROBERT WOLFGRAMM.

Fiji Magic: POB 12095, Suva; tel. 3305916; fax 3302852; e-mail fijimagic@fijilive.com; internet www.fijilive.com/fijimagic; publ. by Associated Media Ltd; monthly; English; Publr YASHWANT GAUNDER; circ. 15,000.

Fiji Republic Gazette: Printing Dept, POB 98, Suva; tel. 3385999; fax 3370203; f. 1874; weekly; English.

Fiji Sun: 12 Amra St, Walubay, Suva; tel. 3307555; fax 3311455; e-mail leonec@fijisun.com.fj; internet www.fijisun.com.fj; re-est. 1999; daily; Editor LEONE CABENATABUA; CEO PETER LOMAS.

Fiji Times: 177 Victoria Parade, Suva; tel. 3304209; fax 3301521; e-mail timesnews@fijitimes.com.fj; internet www.fijitimes.com; f. 1869; fmrly owned by News Ltd (Australia); acquired by Motibhai Group in Sept. 2010 following introduction of legislation limiting foreign ownership of media organizations; daily; English; Publr HANK ARTS; Editor FRED WESLEY; circ. 34,000.

Fiji Trade Review: The Rubine Group, POB 12511, Suva; tel. 3313944; monthly; English; Publr GEORGE RUBINE; Editor MABEL HOWARD.

Islands Business: 46 Gordon St, POB 12718, Suva; tel. 3303108; fax 3301423; e-mail editor@ibi.com.fj; internet www.islandsbusiness.com; regional monthly news and business magazine featuring the Fiji Islands Business supplement; English; Editor-in-Chief LAISA TAGA; circ. 8,500.

Na Tui: 422 Fletcher Rd, Government Bldgs, POB 2071, Suva; f. 1988; weekly; Fijian; Publr TANIELA BOLEA; Editor SAMISONI BOLATAGICI; circ. 7,000.

Nai Lalakai: 20 Gordon St, POB 1167, Suva; tel. 3304111; fax 3301521; e-mail fijitimes@is.com.fj; f. 1962; publ. by Fiji Times Ltd; weekly; Fijian; Editor SAMISONI KAKAIVALU; circ. 18,000.

Pacific Business: POB 12095, Suva; tel. 3305916; fax 3301930; publ. by Associated Media Ltd; monthly; English; Publr YASHWANT GAUNDER.

Pacific Telecom: POB 12095, Suva; tel. 3300591; fax 3302852; e-mail review@is.com.fj; publ. by Associated Media Ltd; monthly; English; Publr YASHWANT GAUNDER.

PACNEWS: Level 2, Damodar Centre, Gordon St, Suva; tel. 3315732; fax 3317055; e-mail pacnews1@connect.com.fj; internet www.pina.com.fj; daily news service for the Pacific region; Editor MAKERETA KOMAI.

Pactrainer: PMB, Suva; tel. 3303623; fax 3303943; e-mail pina@is.com.fj; monthly; newsletter of Pacific Journalism Development Centre; Editor PETER LOMAS.

The Review: POB 12095, Suva; tel. 3305916; fax 3301930; e-mail review@is.com.fj; publ. by Associated Media Ltd; monthly; English; Publr YASHWANT GAUNDER.

Sartaj: John Beater Enterprises Ltd, Raiwaqa, POB 5141, Suva; f. 1988; weekly; Hindi; Editor S. DASO; circ. 15,000.

Shanti Dut: 20 Gordon St, POB 1167, Suva; f. 1935; publ. by Fiji Times Ltd; weekly; Hindi; Editor NILAM KUMAR; circ. 12,000.

Top Shot: Suva; f. 1995; golf magazine; monthly.

The Weekender: 2 Denison Rd, POB 15652, Suva; tel. 3315477; fax 3305346; publ. by Media Resources Ltd; weekly; English; Publr JOSEFATA NATA.

PRESS ASSOCIATIONS

Fiji Islands Media Association: c/o Vasiti Ivaqa, POB 12718, Suva; tel. 3303108; fax 3301423; national press assen; operates Fiji Press Club and Fiji Journalism Training Institute; Sec. NINA RATULELE.

Publishers

Fiji Times Ltd: POB 1167, Suva; tel. 3304111; fax 3301521; e-mail timesnews@fijitimes.com.fj; f. 1869; Propr News Corpn Ltd; largest newspaper publr; also publrs of books and magazines; Man. Dir ANNE FESSELL.

University of the South Pacific: Laucala Campus, Suva; tel. 3231000; fax 3301305; e-mail orga@usp.ac.fj; internet www.usp.ac.fj; f. 1986; education, natural history, regional interests; Pres. RAJESH CHANDRA.

GOVERNMENT PUBLISHING HOUSE

Printing and Stationery Department: POB 98, Suva; tel. 3385999; fax 3370203.

Broadcasting and Communications

TELECOMMUNICATIONS

Digicel Fiji: Kadavu House, Ground Floor, Victoria Parade, POB 13811, Suva; tel. 3310200; fax 3310201; e-mail customercarefiji@digicelgroup.com; internet www.digicelfiji.com; f. 2008; CEO DAVID BUTLER.

Fiji International Telecommunications Ltd (FINTEL): 158 Victoria Parade, POB 59, Suva; tel. 3312933; fax 3305606; e-mail inquiries@fintelfiji.com; internet www.fintel.com.fj; f. 1976; 51% govt-owned; 49% owned by Cable & Wireless Communications Plc (United Kingdom); Group CEO SAKARAIA TUILAKEPA; CEO IOANE KOROIVUKI.

Telecom Fiji Ltd (TFL): Ganilau House, Edward St, PMB, Suva; tel. 3304019; fax 3305595; e-mail contact@tfl.com.fj; internet www.tfl.com.fj; owned by Amalgamated Telecom Holdings; Chair. TOM RICKETTS; CEO ROHAN MAIL.

Vodafone Fiji Ltd: 168 Princes Rd, Tamavua, Suva; tel. 3312000; fax 3312007; e-mail aslam.khan@vodafone.com; internet www.vodafone.com.fj; 51% owned by Amalgamated Telecom Holdings Ltd, 49% by Vodafone International Holdings BV; GSM operator; CEO ASLAM KHAN.

In mid-2007 some 15 companies applied for mobile phone operators' licences.

BROADCASTING

All broadcasting licences were revoked by the interim Government in November 2009. Radio and television stations were issued with temporary licences.

Radio

Fiji Broadcasting Corporation Ltd—FBCL (Radio Fiji): 69 Gladstone Rd, POB 334, Suva; tel. 3314333; fax 3301643; internet www.fbc.com.fj; f. 1954; statutory body; jointly funded by govt grant and advertising revenue; Radio Fiji 1 broadcasts nationally on AM in

English and Fijian; Radio Fiji 2 broadcasts nationally on AM in English and Hindi; Gold FM broadcasts nationally on AM and FM in English; Mirchi FM and 2Day FM broadcast, mainly musical programmes, in Hindi and English, respectively; Bula FM broadcasts musical programmes in Fijian; CEO RIYAZ SAYED KHAIYUM.

Communications Fiji Ltd: 231 Waimanu Rd, PMB, Suva; tel. 3314766; fax 3303748; e-mail info@fm96.com.fj; internet www.cfl.com.fj; f. 1985; operates five commercial stations; FM 96, f. 1985, broadcasts 24 hours per day, on FM, in English; Navtarang, f. 1989, broadcasts 24 hours per day, on FM, in Hindi; Viti FM, f. 1996, broadcasts 24 hours per day, on FM, in Fijian; Legend FM, f. 2002, and Radio Sargam, f. 2004, broadcast musical programmes; Man. Dir WILLIAM PARKINSON; Gen. Man. IAN JACKSON.

Radio Light/Radio Naya Jiwan/Nai Talai: 15 Tower St, Government Bldgs, POB 2525, Suva; tel. and fax 3319536; e-mail radiolight@connect.com.fj; internet www.radiolight.org; f. 1990; non-profit religious organization; broadcasts in English (Radio Light FM 106, FM 93.6), Hindi (Radio Naya Jiwan FM 94.8) and Fijian (Nai Talai FM 103.4); Gen. Man. DOUGLAS ROSE.

Radio Pasifik: The University of the South Pacific, Suva; tel. 3232131; fax 3312591; e-mail blumel_d@usp.ac.fj; f. 1996; educational, operated by CFDL Multimedia Unit; broadcasts in English, Fijian, French, Bislama, Tongan, Hindi and other Pacific island languages.

Television

Fiji Television Ltd: 20 Gorrie St, Government Bldgs, POB 2442, Suva; tel. 3305100; fax 3304630; e-mail info@fijitv.com.fj; internet www.fijitv.info; f. 1994; operates two services, Fiji 1, a free channel, and Sky Fiji, a three-channel subscription service; Chair. ISOA KALOUMAIRA; Group CEO TARUN PATEL.

Film and Television Unit (FTU): c/o Department of Information, Government Bldgs, Suva; video library; production unit established by Govt and Hanns Seidel Foundation (Germany); a weekly news magazine and local documentary programmes.

Finance

BANKING

(cap. = capital; res = reserves; dep. = deposits; m. = million; brs = branches; amounts in Fiji dollars)

Central Bank

Reserve Bank of Fiji: Pratt St, PMB, Suva; tel. 3313611; fax 3302094; e-mail info@rbf.gov.fj; internet www.rbf.gov.fj; f. 1984; replaced Central Monetary Authority of Fiji (f. 1973); bank of issue; administers Insurance Act, Banking Act and Exchange Control Act; cap. 2.0m., res 39.1m. (Dec. 2009); Gov. BARRY WHITESIDE.

Commercial Bank

Bank South Pacific: cnr of Renwick Rd and Pratt St, PMB, Suva; tel. 3314400; fax 3318393; internet www.colonial.com.fj; f. 1974; est. as National Bank of Fiji; 51% acquired from Fiji Govt by Colonial Ltd in 1999 and renamed Colonial National Bank; above name adopted after acquisition of the Colonial Group by BSP in 2009; cap. 15.0m., res 0.3m. (June 2003), dep. 317.2m. (June 2004); Country Man. KEVIN MCCARTHY; 15 brs; 45 agencies.

Development Bank

Fiji Development Bank: 360 Victoria Parade, POB 104, Suva; tel. 3314866; fax 3314886; e-mail info@fdb.com.fj; internet www.fdb.com.fj; f. 1967; finances devt of natural resources, agriculture, transport, and other industries and enterprises; statutory body; applied for a commercial banking licence in Nov. 2004; cap. 56.1m., res 8.9m. (2005); Chair. ROBERT GORDON LYON; CEO DEVE TOGANIVALU; 9 brs.

Merchant Bank

Merchant Finance and Investment Company Ltd: 91 Gordon St, POB 14213, Suva; tel. 3314955; fax 3300026; e-mail info@mfl.com.fj; internet www.mfl.com.fj; f. 1986; fmrly Merchant Bank of Fiji Ltd; owned by Fijian Holdings Ltd (80%), South Pacific Trustees (20%); CEO UDAY RAJ SEN; 3 brs.

STOCK EXCHANGE

South Pacific Stock Exchange: Level 2, Plaza One, Provident Plaza, 33 Ellery St, POB 11689, Suva; tel. 3304130; fax 3304145; e-mail info@spse.com.fj; internet www.spse.com.fj; fmrly Suva Stock Exchange; name changed as above in 2000; Chair. MESAKE NAWARI; CEO JINITA PRASAD.

INSURANCE

Colonial Fiji Life Ltd: cnr of Renwick Rd and Pratt St, PMB, Suva; tel. 3314400; fax 3318393; internet www.colonial.com.fj; life and health; fmrly Blue Shield (Pacific) Ltd; owned by BSP Group, Australia; Man. Dir Ratu MALAKAI NAIYAG.

Dominion Insurance Ltd: 231 Waimanu Rd, POB 14468, Suva; tel. 3311055; fax 3303475; e-mail enquiries@dominioninsurance.com.fj; internet www.dominioninsurance.com.fj; general insurance; Chair. HARI PUNJA; Exec. Dir GARY S. CALLAGHAN.

FijiCare Insurance Ltd: 9/F, 343–359 FNPF Place, Victoria Parade, Suva; tel. 3302717; fax 3302119; e-mail inquiries@fijicare.com.fj; internet www.fijicare.com.fj; life and health; Chair. ROSS PORTER; Man. Dir PETER MCPHERSON.

New India Assurance Co Ltd: Harifam Centre, GPOB 71, Suva; tel. 3313488; fax 3302679; e-mail newindiasuva@connect.com.fj; internet www.niafiji.com; Chief Man. K. VENUKUMAR.

QBE Insurance (Fiji) Ltd: Queensland Insurance Center, 18 Victoria Parade, GPOB 101, Suva; tel. 3315455; fax 3300285; e-mail info.fiji@qbe.com; internet www.qbepacific.com/Insurance.html; owned by Australian interests; fmrly known as Queensland Insurance (Fiji) Ltd, name changed as above 2004; Gen. Man. MATTHEW KEARNS.

SUN Insurance: Kaunikuila House, Ground Floor, Laucala Bay Rd, Suva; tel. 3313822; fax 3313882; e-mail info@suninsurance.com.fj; internet www.suninsurance.com.fj; f. 1999; general; Chair. PADAM RAJ LALA; CEO ARCHIE SEETO.

Tower Insurance Fiji Ltd: Tower House, Thomson St, GPOB 950, Suva; tel. 3315955; fax 3301376; internet www.towerinsurance.com.fj; owned by New Zealand interests; Gen. Man. PAUL ABSELL.

Trade and Industry

GOVERNMENT AGENCIES

Fiji Islands Trade and Investment Bureau: Civic House, 6th Floor, Victoria Parade, POB 2303, Suva; tel. 3315988; fax 3301783; e-mail info@ftib.org.fj; internet www.ftib.org.fj; f. 1980; restyled 1988, to promote and stimulate foreign and local economic devt investment; Chair. ADRIAN SOFIELD; CEO JITOKO TIKOLEVU.

Training and Productivity Authority of Fiji (TPAF): Beaumont Rd, POB 6890, Nasinu; tel. 3392000; fax 3340184; e-mail info@tpaf.ac.fj; internet www.tpaf.ac.fj; fmrly Fiji National Training Council; present name assumed in 2002; Dir-Gen. JONE USAMATE.

DEVELOPMENT ORGANIZATIONS

Fiji Development Company Ltd: FNPF Place, 350 Victoria Parade, POB 161, Suva; tel. 3304611; fax 3304171; e-mail hfc@is.com.fj; f. 1960; subsidiary of the Commonwealth Development Corpn; Man. F. KHAN.

Fijian Development Fund Board: POB 122, Suva; tel. 3312601; fax 3302585; f. 1951; funds derived from payments from sales of copra by indigenous Fijians; funds used only for Fijian devt schemes; CEO VINCENT TOVATA.

Land Development Authority: POB 5442, Raiwaqa; tel. 3383155; fax 3387157; e-mail rsingh010@govnet.gov.fj; internet www.agriculture.org.fj; f. 1961; co-ordinates devt plans for land and marine resources; Chair. RITESHNI LATA SINGH.

CHAMBERS OF COMMERCE

Ba Chamber of Commerce: POB 99, Ba; tel. 6670134; fax 6670132; Pres. DINESH PATEL.

Fiji Chamber of Commerce and Industry: POB 14803, Suva; tel. 314040; fax 302641; Pres. PETER MASEY.

Labasa Chamber of Commerce: POB 992, Labasa; tel. 8811467; fax 8813009; Pres. ASHOK KARAN.

Lautoka Chamber of Commerce and Industry: POB 366, Lautoka; tel. 6661834; fax 6662379; e-mail vaghco@connect.com.fj; Pres. NATWARLAL VAGH.

Levuka Chamber of Commerce: POB 85, Levuka; tel. 3440248; fax 3440252; Pres. ISHRAR ALI.

Nadi Chamber of Commerce: POB 2735, Nadi; tel. 6701375; fax 6702406; e-mail rraju@connect.com.fj; Pres. RAM RAJU.

Nausori Chamber of Commerce: POB 228, Nausori; tel. 3478235; fax 3400134; Pres. MOTI LAL.

Sigatoka Chamber of Commerce: POB 882, Sigatoka; tel. 6500064; fax 6520006; Pres. TOM WAQA.

Suva Chamber of Commerce and Industry: 8 Dominion House, POB 337, Suva; tel. 3314044; fax 3302188; e-mail secretariat@suvachamber.org; internet www.suvachamber.org; f. 1902; Pres. Dr NUR BANO ALI; 150 mems.

Tavua-Vatukoula Chamber of Commerce: POB 698, Tavua; tel. 6680390; fax 6680390; Pres. SOHAN SINGH.

INDUSTRIAL AND TRADE ASSOCIATIONS

Fiji Kava Council: POB 17724, Suva; tel. 3386576; fax 3371844; Chair. Ratu JOSATEKI NAWALOWALO.

Fiji Sawmillers' Association: Yalalevu; e-mail jayd@islandchill.com; Pres. JAY DAYAL.

Fiji Sugar Corporation Ltd: Western House, 3rd Floor, cnr of Bila and Vidilo St, PMB, Lautoka; tel. 6662655; fax 6664685; nationalized 1974; buyer of sugar cane and raw sugar mfrs; Exec. Chair. ABDUL KHAN.

Mining and Quarrying Council: 42 Gorrie St, Suva; tel. 33313188; fax 3302183; e-mail employer@is.com.fj; Chief Exec. K. A. J. ROBERTS.

National Trading Corporation Ltd: POB 13673, Suva; tel. 3315211; fax 3315584; f. 1992; govt-owned body; develops markets for agricultural and marine produce locally and overseas; processes and markets fresh fruit, vegetables and ginger products; CEO APIAMA CEGUMALINA.

Native Lands Trust Board: GPOB 116, Suva; tel. 3312733; fax 3312014; e-mail info@nltb.com.fj; internet www.nltb.com.fj; manages holdings of ethnic Fijian landowners; Gen. Man. ALIPATE QETAKI.

Sustainable Forest Industries LTD (SFI): POB 1119, Nabua, Suva; tel. 3384999; fax 3370029; e-mail info@fijimahogany.com; internet www.fijimahogany.com; Man. Dir CHRISTOPHER DONLON.

EMPLOYERS' ORGANIZATIONS

Fiji Commerce and Employers Federation (FCEF): 42 Gorrie St, GPOB 575, Suva; tel. 3313188; fax 3302183; e-mail employer@fcef.com.fj; internet www.fcef.com.fj; f. 1960; represents 525 major employers with approx. 80,000 employees; fmrly Fiji Employers' Federation; Pres. DIGBY BOSSLEY; CEO NESBITT HAZELMAN.

Fiji Manufacturers' Association: POB 1308, Suva; tel. and fax 3318811; e-mail fma@connect.com.fj; internet fijimanufacturers.org; f. 1971; CEO DESMOND WHITESIDE; 68 mems.

Local Inter-Island Shipowners' Association: POB 152, Suva; fax 3303389; e-mail consortship@connect.com.fj; Pres. DURGA PRASAD; Sec. LEO B. SMITH.

Textile, Clothing and Footwear Council: POB 10015, Nabua; tel. 3384777; fax 3370446; Pres. KALPESH SOLANKI.

UTILITIES

Electricity

Fiji Electricity Authority (FEA): PMB, Suva; tel. 3311133; fax 3311882; e-mail ceo@fea.com.fj; internet www.fea.com.fj; f. 1966; govt-owned; responsible for the generation, transmission and distribution of electricity throughout Fiji; CEO HASMUKH PATEL.

Water

Water Authority of Fiji: Kings Road, Nasinu, Suva; tel. 3346777; CEO TONY FULLMAN.

TRADE UNIONS

Fiji Trades Union Congress (FTUC): 32 Des Voeux Rd, POB 1418, Suva; tel. 3315377; fax 3300306; e-mail ftucl@connect.com.fj; f. 1952; affiliated to ITUC; 35 affiliated unions; 33,000 mems; Pres. DANIEL URAI MANUFOLAU; Gen. Sec. FELIX ANTHONY.

Principal affiliated unions:

Association of USP Staff (AUSPS): POB U49, Suva; tel. 3232754; fax 3301305; e-mail ausps@usp.ac.fj; internet www.usp.ac.fj; f. 1977; Pres. Dr ROHIT KISHORE; Sec. KRISHNA RAGHUWAIYA.

Communication, Mining and General Workers' Union (CMGWU): 17 Knollys St, Suva; tel. 3300168; f. 1990; fmrly Fiji Post and Telecommunications Employees' Association; Gen. Sec. ATTAR SINGH.

Federated Airline Staff Association: Nadi Airport, POB 9259, Nadi; tel. 6722877; fax 6720068; e-mail fasa@ats.com.fj; Gen. Sec. VILIKESA NAULUMATUA.

Fiji Aviation Workers' Association: FTUC Complex, 32 Des Voeux Rd, POB 5351, Raiwaqa; tel. 3303184; fax 3311805; Pres. VALENTINE SIMPSON; Gen. Sec. ATTAR SINGH.

Fiji Bank and Finance Sector Employees' Union: 101 Gordon St, POB 853, Suva; tel. 3301827; fax 3301956; e-mail fbeu@connect.com.fj; internet www.fbfseu.org.fj; over 1,500 mems; Nat. Sec. PRAMOD K. RAE.

Fiji Electricity and Allied Workers' Union: POB 1390, Lautoka; tel. 6666353; e-mail feawu@connect.com.fj; Pres. LEONE SAKETA; Sec. J. A. PAUL.

Fiji Garment, Textile and Allied Workers' Union: c/o FTUC, Raiwaqa; f. 1992.

Fiji Nursing Association: 26 McGregor Rd, Suva; tel. 3305855; fax 3304881; e-mail fna@connect.com.fj; internet www.fijinursingassociation.com; f. 1957; Pres. S. MATIAVI; Gen. Sec. KUINI LUTUA.

Fiji Public Service Association: 298 Waimanu Rd, POB 1405, Suva; tel. 3311922; fax 3301099; e-mail fpsags@connect.com.fj; f. 1943; 4,000 mems; Pres. REIJIELI NARUMA; Gen. Sec. RAJESHWAR SINGH.

Fiji Sugar and General Workers' Union: 84 Naviti St, POB 330, Lautoka; tel. 6660746; fax 664888; 25,000 mems; Pres. SHIU LINGAM; Gen. Sec. FELIX ANTHONY.

Fiji Teachers' Union: 1–3 Berry Rd, Government Bldgs, POB 2203, Suva; tel. 3314099; fax 3305962; e-mail ftu@connect.com.fj; f. 1930; 4,300 mems; Pres. SHANDIL SATYA NAND; Gen. Sec. AGNI DEO SINGH.

Fijian Teachers' Association: POB 14464, Suva; tel. 3315099; fax 3304978; e-mail fta@connect.com.fj; internet fta.org.fj/fta; Pres. TEVITA KOROI; Gen. Sec. MAIKA NAMUDU.

Insurance Officers' Association: POB 71, Suva; tel. 3313488; Pres. JAGDISH KHATRI; Sec. DAVID LEE.

Mineworkers' Union of Fiji: POB 876, Tavua; f. 1986; Pres. JOSEPHA SADREU; Sec. KAVEKINI NAVUSO.

National Farmers' Union: POB 522, Labasa; tel. 8811838; 10,000 mems (sugar-cane farmers); Pres. SURENDRA LAL; Gen. Sec. MAHENDRA P. CHAUDHRY; CEO MOHAMMED LATIF SUBEDAR.

National Union of Factory and Commercial Workers: POB 989, Suva; tel. 3311155; fax 3303021; e-mail nufcw@connect.com.fj; 3,800 mems; Pres. CAMA TUILEVEUKA; Gen. Sec. JOHN V. MUDALIAR.

National Union of Hospitality, Catering and Tourism Industries Employees: Nadi Airport, POB 9426, Nadi; tel. 6700906; fax 6700181; e-mail nuhctie@connect.com.fj; Pres. PENI FINAU; Gen. Sec. DANIEL URAI.

Public Employees' Union: POB 781, Suva; tel. 3304501; 6,752 mems; Pres. SEMI TIKOICINA; Gen. Sec. VILIAME KAUTIA.

Transport and Oil Workers' Union: POB 903, Suva; tel. 3302534; f. 1988; est. by merger of Oil and Allied Workers' Union and Transport Workers' Union; Pres. J. BOLA; Sec. MICHAEL COLUMBUS.

There are several independent trade unions, including Fiji Registered Ports Workers' Union (f. 1947; Pres. JIOJI TAHOLOSALE).

Transport

RAILWAYS

Fiji Sugar Corporation Railway: Rarawai Mill, POB 155, Ba; tel. 6674044; fax 670505; for use in cane-harvesting season, May–Dec.; 595 km of permanent track and 225 km of temporary track (gauge of 600 mm), serving cane-growing areas at Ba, Lautoka and Penang on Viti Levu and Labasa on Vanua Levu; Gen. Man. ADURU KUVA.

ROADS

At the end of 2000 there were some 3,440 km of roads in Fiji, of which 49.2% were paved. A 500-km highway circles the main island of Viti Levu.

Land Transport Authority of Fiji: Lot 1, Daniva Rd, Valelevu, Nasinu; tel. 3392166; fax 3390026; e-mail infor@lta.com.fj; internet www.ltafiji.com; f. 1998; responsible for public transport services, vehicle registration, traffic management and road safety; Chair. GREG LAWLOR; CEO NAISA TUINACEVA.

SHIPPING

The principal ports of call are Suva, Lautoka, Levuka, Malau and Wairiki.

Fiji Islands Maritime Safety Administration (FIMSA): FIMSA House, Amra St, Walubay, POB 326, Suva; tel. 3315266; fax 3303251; e-mail mbuli@govnet.gov.fj; internet www.fimsa.gov.fj; regulatory body for maritime sector; Dir JOSATEKI TAGI.

Fiji Ports Corporation Ltd: POB 780, Suva; tel. 3312700; fax 3300064; e-mail fpcl@connect.com.fj; internet www.fijiports.com.fj; f. 2005; management and devt of Fiji's ports; CEO WAQA BAULEKA (acting); Chair. BEN NAIDU.

Ports Terminals Ltd: POB 780, Suva; f. 1998; subsidiary of Fiji Ports Corporation Ltd; stevedoring, pilotage and cargo handling at Suva and Lautoka ports; Gen. Man. EMINONI KURUSIGA.

Consort Shipping Line Ltd: Lot 4, Matua St, Suva; tel. 3313344; fax 3303389; e-mail consortshipping@connect.com.fj; internet www

.consortshipping.com.fj; f. 1986; est. following merger of Interport Shipping and Wong's Shipping Co; CEO HECTOR SMITH; Man. Dir JUSTIN SMIT.

Fiji Maritime Services Ltd: c/o Fiji Ports Workers and Seafarers Union, 36 Edinburgh Drive, Suva; f. 1989 by PAF and the Ports Workers' Union; services between Lautoka and Vanua Levu ports.

Pacific Agencies (Fiji) Ltd: Level 2, Gohil Complex, Toorak Rd, Suva; tel. 3315444; fax 3301127; e-mail info@pacshipfiji.com.fj; internet www.pacificagenciesfiji.com; f. 2000 after merger of Burns Philp and Forum Shipping; shipping agents, customs agents and international forwarding agents, crew handling; Gen. Man. GAVIN MCINTYRE.

Transcargo Express Fiji Ltd: POB 936, Suva; tel. 3313266; fax 3303389; e-mail consortship@connect.com.fj; f. 1974; Man. Dir LEO B. SMITH.

CIVIL AVIATION

There is an international airport at Nadi (about 210 km from Suva), a smaller international airport at Nausori (Suva) and numerous other airfields. Nadi is an important transit airport in the Pacific.

Airports Fiji Ltd: Nadi International Airport, Nadi; tel. 6725777; fax 6725161; e-mail info@afl.com.fj; internet www.airportsfiji.com; f. 1999; owns and operates 15 public airports in Fiji, incl. two international airports, Nadi International Airport and Nausori Airport; Chair. RICK RICKMAN; CEO TIMOCI TULSAWAU.

Air Pacific Ltd: Air Pacific Centre, Nadi International Airport, POB 9266, Nadi; tel. 6720777; fax 6720512; e-mail service@airpacific.com.fj; internet www.airpacific.com; f. 1951; est. as Fiji Airways, name changed in 1971; domestic and international services from Nausori Airport (serving Suva) to Nadi, and international services to Tonga, Solomon Islands, Cook Islands, Vanuatu, Samoa, Kiribati, Tuvalu, Hawaii, Japan, Hong Kong, Australia, New Zealand and the USA; 51% govt-owned, 46.05% owned by Qantas (Australia); Chair. NALIN PATEL; CEO and Man. Dir DAVE PFLIEGER.

Pacific Sun: Nadi International Airport, POB 9270, Nadi; tel. 6723555; fax 6723611; e-mail enquiries@pacificsun.com.fj; internet www.pacificsun.com.fj; f. 1980; wholly owned subsidiary of Air Pacific Ltd; acquired Sun Air 2007; scheduled flights to domestic and regional destinations; Gen. Man. SHAENAZ VOSS.

Vanua Air Charters: Labasa; f. 1993; provides domestic charter and freight services; Propr CHARAN SINGH.

Tourism

Scenery, climate, fishing and diving attract visitors to Fiji, where tourism is an important industry. However, the sector has been intermittently affected by political unrest. The number of visitor arrivals increased by 16.5% in 2010 to reach 631,868, of whom 75% were holiday-makers, rising further in 2011, to an estimated 674,913. Most visitors are from Australia, New Zealand, the USA, the United Kingdom and Japan. A total of 9,070 hotel rooms were available in 2006. Receipts from tourism totalled $F979.8m. in 2010.

Fiji Islands Hotels and Tourism Association (FIHTA): 42 Gorrie St, GPOB 13560, Suva; tel. 3302980; fax 3300331; e-mail info@fihta.com.fj; internet www.fihta.com.fj; fmrly Fiji Hotel Association; name changed as above in 2005; 90 active mems, over 300 assoc. mems; Pres. DIXON SEETO; Exec. Officer MICHAEL WONG.

Tourism Fiji: Nadi International Airport, POB 9217, Nadi; tel. 6722433; fax 6720141; e-mail marketing@tourismfiji.com.fj; internet www.fijime.com; Chair. DAVID PFLIEGER; CEO MICHAEL MEADE (acting).

Defence

As assessed at November 2011, Fiji's total armed forces numbered 3,500 (3,200 in the army and 300 in the navy). Reserves numbered approximately 6,000. The country's membership of the Commonwealth has entitled Fijians to work in the British armed forces; in mid-2006 about 2,000 Fijian soldiers were serving in Iraq with the British army. In addition, in November 2011 a total of 278 Fijian soldiers were serving in Iraq under the auspices of the UN Assistance Mission for Iraq (UNAMI). The country's defence budget for 2012 was an estimated $F116m.

Commander-in-Chief: President of the Republic.

Commander of the Armed Forces: Cdre FRANK (VOREQE) BAINIMARAMA.

Commander of the Land Force: Lt-Col MOSESE TIKOITOGA.

Commander of the Navy: FRANCIS KEAN.

Chief of Staff, Strategic Headquarters: Brig.-Gen. MOHAMMED AZIZ.

Education

Education in Fiji is compulsory and free at primary level. Primary education begins at six years of age and lasts for eight years. Secondary education, beginning at the age of 14, lasts for a further three years. State subsidies are available for secondary and tertiary education in cases of hardship. In May 2009 there were 721 state primary schools (with a total enrolment of 129,444 pupils) and 172 state secondary schools (with an enrolment of 67,072 pupils). There were 69 vocational and technical institutions (with 2,387 enrolled students). In the same year Fiji had four teacher-training colleges (with 633 students). The University of the South Pacific is based in Fiji. In 2004 university students (both on campus and at extension centres) totalled 16,444. The University of Fiji, a privately owned institution, was established in 2004. In January 2010 six government colleges merged to form the Fiji National University. Budgetary expenditure for 2010 allocated $F209.5m. for education, equivalent to 12.2% of total budgetary expenditure.

FINLAND

Introductory Survey

LOCATION, CLIMATE, LANGUAGE, RELIGION, FLAG, CAPITAL

The Republic of Finland lies in northern Europe, bordered to the far north by Norway and to the north-west by Sweden. Russia adjoins the whole of the eastern frontier. Finland's western and southern shores are washed by the Baltic Sea. The climate varies sharply, with warm summers and cold winters. The mean annual temperature is 5°C (41°F) in Helsinki and −0.4°C (31°F) in the far north. There are two official languages: more than 93% of the population speak Finnish and 6% speak Swedish. There is a small Sámi (Lapp) population in the north. The majority of the inhabitants profess Christianity; about 80% belong to the Evangelical Lutheran Church. The national flag (proportions 11 by 18) displays an azure blue cross (the upright to the left of centre) on a white background. The state flag has, at the centre of the cross, the national coat of arms (a yellow-edged red shield containing a golden lion and nine white roses). The capital is Helsinki.

CONTEMPORARY POLITICAL HISTORY

Historical Context

Finland formed part of the Kingdom of Sweden until 1809, when it became an autonomous Grand Duchy under the Russian Empire. During the Russian Revolution of 1917 the territory proclaimed its independence. Following a brief civil war, a democratic Constitution was adopted in 1919. The Soviet regime that came to power in Russia attempted to regain control of Finland, but acknowledged the country's independence in 1920.

Demands by the USSR for military bases in Finland and for the cession of part of the Karelian isthmus, in south-eastern Finland, were rejected by the Finnish Government in November 1939. As a result, the USSR attacked Finland, and the two countries fought the Winter War, a fiercely contested conflict lasting 15 weeks, before Finnish forces were defeated. Following its surrender, Finland ceded an area of 41,880 sq km (16,170 sq miles) to the USSR in March 1940. In the hope of recovering the lost territory, Finland joined Nazi Germany in attacking the USSR in 1941. However, a separate armistice between Finland and the USSR was concluded in 1944.

In accordance with a peace treaty signed in February 1947, Finland agreed to the transfer of about 12% of its pre-war territory (including the Karelian isthmus and the Petsamo area on the Arctic coast) to the USSR, and to the payment of reparations, which totalled about US $570m. when completed in 1952. Meanwhile, in April 1948 Finland and the USSR signed the Finno-Soviet Treaty of Friendship, Co-operation and Mutual Assistance (the YYA Treaty), which was extended for periods of 20 years in 1955, 1970 and again in 1983. A major requirement of the treaty was that Finland repel any attack made on the USSR by Germany, or its allies, through Finnish territory. (The treaty was replaced by a non-military agreement in 1992, see below.)

Domestic Political Affairs

Since independence in 1917, the politics of Finland have been characterized by coalition governments (including numerous minority coalitions) and the development of consensus between parties. The Social Democratic Party (SDP) and the Centre Party have usually been the dominant participants in government. The conservative opposition gained significant support at a general election in March 1979, following several years of economic crises. A new centre-left coalition Government was formed in May, however, by a former Prime Minister, Dr Mauno Koivisto, a Social Democrat. This four-party Government, comprising the Centre Party, the SDP, the Swedish People's Party and the Finnish People's Democratic League (an electoral alliance that included the communists), continued to pursue deflationary economic policies.

Dr Urho Kekkonen, who had been President since 1956, resigned in October 1981. Koivisto was elected President in January 1982. He was succeeded as head of the coalition by a former Prime Minister, Kalevi Sorsa, a Social Democrat. The coalition was re-formed in December 1982, without the Finnish People's Democratic League, which had refused to support austerity measures or an increase in defence spending.

At the general election of March 1983, the SDP won 57 of the 200 seats in the Parliament (Eduskunta), compared with 52 in the 1979 election, while the conservative opposition National Coalition Party (NCP) lost three seats. In May Sorsa formed another centre-left coalition, comprising the SDP, the Swedish People's Party, the Centre Party and the Finnish Rural Party.

The rise of conservative politics: 1987–1994

At a general election held in March 1987, the combined non-socialist parties gained a majority in the Eduskunta for the first time since the election of 1945. Although the SDP remained the largest single party, with 56 seats, the system of modified proportional representation enabled the NCP to gain an additional nine seats, winning a total of 53, while increasing its share of the votes cast by only 1%. President Koivisto eventually invited Harri Holkeri, a former Chairman of the NCP, to form a coalition Government comprising the NCP, the SDP, the Swedish People's Party and the Finnish Rural Party, thus avoiding a polarization of the political parties within the Eduskunta. Holkeri became the first conservative Prime Minister since 1946.

In February 1988 Koivisto retained office after the first presidential election by direct popular vote (in accordance with constitutional changes adopted in the previous year), following his campaign for a reduction in presidential power. He did not win the required absolute majority, however, and an electoral college was convened. Koivisto was re-elected after an endorsement by Holkeri, who had also contested the presidency and who had received the third highest number of direct votes (behind Paavo Väyrynen, the leader of the Centre Party).

At a general election held in March 1991, the Centre Party won 55 seats, the SDP 48 seats and the NCP 40. In April a coalition Government, comprising the Centre Party, the NCP, the Swedish People's Party and the Finnish Christian Union, took office. The new coalition constituted the country's first wholly non-socialist Government for 25 years. The Chairman of the Centre Party, Esko Aho, was appointed Prime Minister. In the first stage of a presidential election, which took place in January 1994, the two most successful candidates were Martti Ahtisaari (the SDP candidate and a senior UN official), with 25.9% of the votes cast, and Elisabeth Rehn (the Swedish People's Party candidate and Minister of Defence), with 22.0%, both of whom were supporters of Finland's application for membership of the European Union (EU, see p. 276), as the European Community had been restyled in late 1993. In accordance with constitutional changes adopted since the previous election (stipulating that, if no candidate gained more than 50% of the votes cast, the electorate should choose between the two candidates with the most votes), a second stage of the election took place in February 1994. Ahtisaari secured victory, with 53.9% of the votes cast, and took office in March.

The return of the SDP

At a general election held in March 1995, the SDP won 63 seats in the Eduskunta, the Centre Party secured 44 seats, the NCP 39 and the Left Alliance (formed in 1990 by a merger of the communist parties and the Finnish People's Democratic League) 22. A new coalition Government was formed in April, comprising the SDP, the NCP, the Swedish People's Party, the Left Alliance and the Green League. Paavo Lipponen, the leader of the SDP, replaced Aho as Prime Minister, and Sauli Niinistö, the Chairman of the NCP, became Deputy Prime Minister.

Following a general election held in March 1999, the SDP remained the largest party in the Eduskunta, with 51 seats. The Centre Party won 48 seats and the NCP 46. In April the five parties of the outgoing Government agreed to form a new coalition. Lipponen remained Prime Minister, while Niinistö was reappointed as Minister of Finance.

A presidential election was held in January and February 2000, at which Ahtisaari did not seek re-election, following his failure to secure the nomination of the SDP. The first round of the ballot was won by Tarja Halonen (the SDP candidate and Minister of Foreign Affairs), who received 40% of the votes cast; the second largest share of the vote (34.4%) was obtained by Aho. Having won a second round of voting on 6 February (with 51.6% of the votes cast), Halonen took office as the first female President of Finland on 1 March.

A new Constitution entered into force on 1 March 2000, under the provisions of which the executive power of the President was significantly reduced while the real authority of the Eduskunta was increased, with the power of decision-making being divided more equally between the Eduskunta, the Cabinet (Valtioneuvosto) and the President. In addition, the President was to co-operate more closely with the Cabinet on issues of foreign policy.

Following his defeat in the presidential election, Aho took leave from domestic politics for one year from August 2000; Anneli Jäätteenmäki, a former Minister of Justice, was elected to replace Aho as Chairman of the Centre Party during his sabbatical. Popular support for Jäätteenmäki's leadership of the Centre Party prompted Aho's resignation in mid-2002 and the election of Jäätteenmäki as Chairperson.

In November 2000 the stability of the coalition Government was threatened by a controversial proposal by an electricity company to build a fifth nuclear reactor in Finland, the first such proposal in Western Europe since the mid-1980s. The construction of the new reactor was approved by the Cabinet in January 2002 and by the Eduskunta in May, prompting the resignation of the Green League from the coalition Government. It was originally envisaged that the reactor would become operational in early 2009. However, following numerous delays this date was revised to 2013.

The 2003 and 2007 general elections

A general election was held on 16 March 2003; 69.7% of the electorate participated in the poll. The Centre Party gained the largest representation in the Eduskunta, winning 55 seats, while the SDP won 53. Although the SDP gained two seats, the three other members of the former governing coalition lost seats, with the NCP suffering the worst reverse, with the loss of six seats (winning 40 seats). In April the Centre Party formed a coalition Government with the SDP and the Swedish People's Party, with Jäätteenmäki as Finland's first woman Prime Minister.

Jäätteenmäki's premiership was, however, extremely short-lived. On 18 June 2003 she resigned following allegations that she had improperly used classified foreign ministry information to discredit the outgoing Prime Minister, Lipponen, and secure victory for the Centre Party in the general election. One of the documents, which were leaked by a presidential aide, Martti Manninen, recorded exchanges between Lipponen and the US President, George W. Bush, in December 2002, and was reportedly used by Jäätteenmäki to portray Lipponen as being overly supportive of US policy regarding Iraq; the majority of Finns were opposed to the US-led military action launched in Iraq in March 2003 to remove the regime of Saddam Hussain. The Deputy Chairman of the Centre Party, Matti Vanhanen, who had been assigned the post of Minister of Defence in the new Government, replaced Jäätteenmäki as Prime Minister. Jäätteenmäki, while rejecting allegations of wrongdoing, also stood down as Chairperson of the Centre Party; Vanhanen was elected to replace her in October. Jäätteenmäki and Manninen stood trial in March 2004; Jäätteenmäki was acquitted of inciting or assisting Manninen to divulge official secrets, but Manninen was found guilty of violating official secrecy and fined 80 days' salary.

Lipponen resigned as leader of the SDP in June 2005; Eero Heinäluoma, hitherto General Secretary of the party, was elected to succeed him. In September, as part of a government reorganization, Heinäluoma entered the Cabinet as Deputy Prime Minister and Minister of Finance, replacing Antii Kalliomäki, who was appointed Minister of Education.

A presidential election was held on 15 and 29 January 2006. Nine candidates contested the first round of voting, at which the incumbent, Halonen, received the largest share of the votes cast, with 46.3%, followed by Niinistö, representing the NCP, who secured 24.1%, and the Prime Minister, Vanhanen, the Centre Party candidate, with 18.6%. Halonen narrowly defeated Niinistö in a second round of voting, in which 77.2% of the electorate participated, with 51.8% of the votes cast.

At the general election held on 18 March 2007, the Centre Party narrowly retained its position as the largest party in the Eduskunta, securing 51 seats. The largest gains were made by the NCP, which won 50 seats. By contrast, the SDP suffered a significant loss, taking only 45 seats. The election was characterized by the lowest rate of voter participation since 1939, at just 67.9%. In April 2007 the Centre Party, the NCP, the Swedish People's Party and the Green League formed a new, centre-right coalition, with Vanhanen remaining as Prime Minister. For the NCP, the most notable appointments were Jyrki Katainen as Deputy Prime Minister and Minister of Finance and Ilkka Kanerva as Minister for Foreign Affairs. The new administration, which identified reducing taxes and increasing the employment rate as priorities, was the largest ever Finnish Cabinet and also the first in which female members outnumbered their male counterparts (accounting for 12 of the 20 ministers). In April 2008 Kanerva was forced to resign as Minister of Foreign Affairs, following revelations in the media that he had sent more than 200 text messages to an erotic dancer on his state-financed mobile telephone. He was succeeded by Alexander Stubb, also of the NCP, who had hitherto served as a member of the European Parliament.

Jutta Urpilainen was elected SDP Chairperson at the party's conference in June 2008, succeeding Heinäluoma, who had previously announced that he would not contest the election, following the SDP's poor performance in the March 2007 elections. At the close of the conference Urpilainen stressed the need for the party to return to its popular working-class values and strengthen its ties with civic organizations. None the less, at regional elections held in October 2008 the NCP overtook the SDP to become the largest party, winning 23.5% of the votes cast, compared with 21.2% for the SDP and 20.1% for the Centre Party. The nationalist True Finns increased its share of the vote to 5.4%.

Election campaign funding controversies

The admission on national television in May 2008 by the Chairman of the Centre Party's parliamentary group, Timo Kalli, that he had failed to disclose election campaign donations, owing to a lack of penalties in place for such a violation, prompted a series of similar revelations by other members of the Eduskunta, including several ministers. At the same time, it emerged that a significant proportion of parliamentary candidates in the 2007 elections, principally from the Centre Party, had received contributions from an association called Kehittyvien Maakuntien Suomi (KMS—Finland's Developing Regions) and, indeed, that the Prime Minister, Vanhanen, had received a €10,000 donation from the organization. The head of development of the Centre Party, Lasse Kontiola, subsequently admitted in an open letter to the party leadership that he had helped to establish the organization, which was funded by business executives, without the knowledge of senior members of the party. It also emerged that KMS, which accounted for 5% of all election spending by candidates at the 2007 elections, had been founded in the office of the Secretary of the Centre Party, Jarmo Korhonen. Combined with a report published in December 2007 by the Group of States against Corruption (GRECO), which criticized a lack of transparency in the political process, these revelations contributed to a growing public disaffection with Finnish politics. New rules covering party financing were swiftly agreed by all the principal parties prior to the local elections in October 2008.

The issue of irregularities in election campaign funding arose again in mid-2009, when the Prime Minister was accused by the opposition SPD of lying about a campaign funding meeting. The accusation referred to a session in the Eduskunta one year earlier, during which Vanhanen had claimed he did not remember a meeting with the donor Nova Group, a real estate provider, which transferred large sums of money to the Centre Party via KMS. In June Vanhanen contradicted his previous statement about the meeting, but dismissed accusations of mendacity, claiming he had previously suffered a lapse of memory. The issue continued to dominate the political discourse throughout the following months, with further revelations of funding irregularities, principally with regard to the Centre Party, but also involving other parties. At the end of September a current affairs programme on the public broadcasting company YLE alleged that Vanhanen had received a bribe in the 1990s in the form of free building materials from a construction company that had benefited from contracts from Nuorisosäätiö (the Youth Foundation), a housing organization with close links to the Centre Party, which had been chaired by Vanhanen from 1998–2003 and which had made a large donation to Vanhanen's presidential election campaign in 2006. Vanhanen vehemently denied the accusations and resisted calls for his resignation. A motion of no confidence in the Prime Minister, brought by the opposition in early October in protest against his role in the political funding scandals, was defeated by 128 votes to 57.

In December 2009 Vanhanen unexpectedly announced that he would not stand for re-election as Chairman of the Centre Party at the party conference in June 2010, owing to health reasons. He initially claimed that an impending operation would not allow him to fulfil the dual obligations of party Chairman and Prime Minister, although he later admitted that there were other reasons for his resignation that he would reveal at a future date; it was widely speculated that the recent campaign funding controversy had contributed to his decision. In June party members elected Mari Kiviniemi, the Minister of Public Administration and Local Government, to succeed Vanhanen as Chairwoman. One week later, as expected, Vanhanen submitted his resignation as Prime Minister along with those of his ministers, and on 22 June Kiviniemi was sworn in as Prime Minister at the head of a renewed Cabinet: this was unchanged from the outgoing administration save for the appointment of Tapani Tölli, also of the Centre Party, who filled Kiviniemi's place as Minister of Public Administration and Local Government.

The issue of Vanhanen's campaign funding caused renewed controversy in September 2010 when the Chancellor of Justice, Jaakko Jonkka, concluded an investigation into the former Prime Minister's connection with Nuorisosäätiö. Jonkka stated that he believed that Vanhanen had acted unlawfully when, as premier, he had authorized a grant from the state-administered Raha-automaattiyhdistys (RAY—Finland's Slot Machine Association) to the housing charity, despite the latter's contribution to his campaign fund. Jonkka referred the case to the Eduskunta's constitutional law committee, which in February 2011 decided that Vanhanen was guilty of dereliction of duty by not declaring his conflict of interest; however, it concluded that the charge was not serious enough to warrant Vanhanen's trial by the High Court of Impeachment. Later in February the committee's decision was ratified by a plenary session of the Eduskunta.

Recent developments: the 2011 general election

The general election held on 17 April 2011 was characterized by a massive increase in support for the True Finns, which took 19.0% of the votes cast and won 39 seats in the Eduskunta (34 more than at the 2007 election), thus becoming the third largest party. The NCP narrowly emerged as the largest grouping in the legislature for the first time in its history, with 20.4% of the vote and 44 seats (a loss of six), while the SDP came second with 42 seats. All of the parliamentary parties apart from the True Finns suffered losses, but the greatest decline in support was for the Centre Party, which took 35 seats (a loss of 16) and fell from first to fourth place. The participation rate, at 70.4%, was the highest since 1995. The True Finns, while maintaining its traditional anti-immigration stance, had focused its campaign on opposition to financial support for debt-stricken countries in the euro area (in particular Portugal, which had requested emergency funding from other euro area countries earlier in April 2011); the party had benefited from growing popular resentment that Finland, whose public finances were among the soundest in the EU, was being expected to rescue countries perceived as imprudent. Kiviniemi conceded defeat immediately after the results were known and announced that the Centre Party would not participate in the formation of a new administration. The Chairman of the NCP and outgoing Deputy Prime Minister and Minister of Finance, Jyrki Katainen, began negotiations to form a government in early May. In mid-May the True Finns withdrew from these talks, refusing to comply with Katainen's demand that prospective coalition partners support EU policy, notably regarding financial assistance for euro area countries at risk of default. As the coalition negotiations continued, in late May the Eduskunta approved an EU plan for the provision of loans worth €78,000m. to Portugal over a three-year period.

On 17 June 2011 Katainen announced the formation of a six-party coalition, comprising—in addition to the NCP—the SDP, the Left Alliance, the Green League, the Swedish People's Party and the Christian Democrats. The broad-based coalition held a comfortable majority of 126 of the 200 parliamentary seats, leaving just the True Finns and the Centre Party in opposition. Five days later the Eduskunta formally elected Katainen as Prime Minister and a new Cabinet was appointed. The NCP and the SDP were each allocated six of the 19 ministerial portfolios, the Left Alliance, the Green League and the Swedish People's Party two apiece and the Christian Democrats one. Jutta Urpilainen, the Chairperson of the SDP, became Deputy Prime Minister and Minister of Finance, while her party colleague, Erkki Tuomioja, returned to the post of Minister of Foreign Affairs (which he had previously held in 2000–07), succeeding Alexander Stubb of the NCP, who was named Minister of European Affairs and Foreign Trade. Prime Minister Katainen pledged to balance the budget by 2015 through a combination of reductions in public expenditure and tax rises. At the behest of the SDP, which had voted against bail-outs for Greece and Ireland while in opposition, the Government was also to insist that any future EU financial assistance for heavily indebted members of the euro area be subject to strict conditions (see Regional Relations). A motion of no confidence in the Government, tabled by The Finns (the new English name adopted by the True Finns in August) in protest against the response to the sovereign debt crisis in the euro area, was defeated in December by 116 votes to 73.

The Eduskunta adopted various revisions to the Constitution in October 2011. The changes included the stipulation that the Prime Minister would formally represent Finland within the EU, rather than the President, the explicit recognition of Finland's membership of the EU, and provision for citizens to propose new laws to parliament if they could collect the signatures of 50,000 supporters. The amendments were signed into law in November and took effect in March 2012.

A presidential election was held on 22 January and 5 February 2012. The incumbent Halonen was ineligible for re-election, having served the maximum two terms permitted by the Constitution. At the first round of voting, contested by eight candidates, Niinistö, who had been narrowly defeated in the 2006 poll and had served as Speaker of the Eduskunta during the 2007–11 legislative term, received the largest share of the votes cast, with 37.0%, followed by Pekka Haavisto, the Green candidate, who secured 18.8%, Paavo Väyrynen, representing the Centre Party, with 17.5%, and Timo Soini, the Chairman of The Finns, with 9.4%. Niinistö easily defeated Haavisto in the second round of voting, at which a turn-out of 66.0% was recorded, with 62.6% of the votes cast. He took office on 1 March 2012, becoming the first President from the NCP since 1956. The fact that both candidates in the second round were pro-European was notable, the economic difficulties in the euro area having been a major theme of the electoral campaign, although the Eurosceptic Väyrynen and Soini together garnered more than one-quarter of the vote.

Foreign Affairs

Regional relations

Finland has traditionally maintained a neutral stance in foreign affairs. It joined the UN and the Nordic Council in 1955, but became a full member of the European Free Trade Association (EFTA) only in 1986, although a free trade agreement between Finland and the European Community (EC) took effect in 1974. In 1989 Finland joined the Council of Europe. In 1991, following the collapse of the USSR, Finland unilaterally abrogated the 1948 Finno-Soviet Treaty of Friendship, Co-operation and Mutual Assistance, which had bound Finland to a military defence alliance with the USSR and prevented the country from joining any international organization (including the EC) whose members posed a military threat to the USSR. In March 1992 the Finnish Government formally applied to join the EC. Following a referendum in which 56.9% of votes cast were in favour of membership, Finland left EFTA and joined the European Union (EU, see p. 276), as the EC had been restyled, in 1995.

Finland has proved its commitment to European integration, joining the Economic and Monetary Union (EMU), which commenced on 1 January 1999. Its political parties and the general populace have demonstrated a broad consensus on Finland's participation in the EU and on the importance of strengthening and enlarging the EU. In particular, Finland regards its role in the EU as one of advocacy for the so-called 'Northern Dimension'—the Nordic and Baltic countries and Russia. In December 2006 the Eduskunta approved the ratification of the Treaty establishing a Constitution for Europe, which aimed to facilitate the smooth functioning of the EU, following its enlargement in May 2004. The constitutional treaty was subsequently replaced by the Treaty of Lisbon, following its rejection at referendums in France and the Netherlands. In 2008 the Eduskunta ratified the Treaty of Lisbon, which retained many of the provisions of the constitutional treaty, which entered into effect across the EU on 1 December 2009. More specifically, Finnish foreign policy in the late 2000s advocated that the EU develop a closer strategic relationship with Russia, preserve and improve its strategic relationship with the USA, and develop stronger economic and strategic ties with Asia, in particular the People's Republic of China.

Although the coalition Government that took office in Finland in June 2011 did not include the Eurosceptic True Finns, which had made large gains at the April general election, the new administration insisted that it would impose strict conditions on its support for future emergency financial assistance from the EU's European Financial Stability Facility (EFSF) to debt-stricken members of the euro area, including the involvement of the private sector and the provision of collateral to Finland by recipient countries. In August the Governments of Finland and Greece, which was seeking a second financial rescue package in addition to assistance agreed in May 2010, reached a provisional agreement under which Greece would place a sum of money equal to Finland's contribution to its emergency funding plan into a Finnish escrow account as collateral. However, this bilateral accord prompted several other euro area members to demand similar arrangements as a condition of their contributions to new funding for Greece, leading to a delay in the implementation of a second bail-out for that country. Following protracted negotiations, the dispute was resolved in October, when euro area ministers responsible for finance concluded a new, more complex, collateral agreement; notably, any country requesting collateral would itself have to fulfil certain conditions in exchange, including the payment of its share of the capital of the European Stability Mechanism (a permanent rescue fund that was due to come into force in July 2012), at the time of its establishment rather than over a five-year period. Although this new arrangement was available in principle to all countries contributing to the rescue plan for Greece, only Finland opted to pursue it. The Greek and Finnish Governments duly signed a new agreement on collateral in February 2012, following which the Eduskunta approved Finland's participation in a further EFSF funding plan for Greece. Meanwhile, at a meeting of EU ministers of internal affairs in September 2011, Finland, together with the Netherlands, vetoed the admission of Bulgaria and Romania to the EU's Schengen area (which would allow the removal of border controls between these states and existing members of the area), owing to concerns regarding corruption and organized crime.

The pursuance of friendly relations with the USSR, and latterly Russia, has generally been regarded as a priority in Finnish foreign affairs. In October 1989 Mikhail Gorbachev became the first Soviet head of state to visit Finland since 1975, and recognized Finland's neutral status. The Finno-Soviet Treaty of Friendship was replaced in January 1992 by a 10-year agreement, signed by Finland and Russia, which involved no military commitment. The agreement was to be automatically renewed for five-year periods unless annulled by either signatory. The new treaty also included undertakings by the two countries not to use force against each other and to respect the inviolability of their common border and each other's territorial integrity. Finnish foreign policy towards Russia in the late 2000s included advocacy for a closer strategic relationship between the EU and Russia. In February 2010 Finland gave its final approval for the construction of a Russian-owned gas pipeline, Nord Stream, under the Baltic Sea, amid concerns from countries bordering the sea over the pipeline's potential environmental impact. The pipeline, which would carry gas directly from Russia to Germany, thus bypassing Russia's neighbours, commenced operations in September 2011.

Other external relations

Although Finland did not become a member of the North Atlantic Treaty Organization (NATO, see p. 370), owing to its policy of military neutrality, it did join NATO's Partnership for Peace framework in 1994 and co-operates with NATO in certain NATO-led operations. Finland contributed troops to the International Security Assistance Force (ISAF) in Afghanistan from 2002 and the Kosovo Force (KFOR) operation responsible for establishing and maintaining security in Kosovo from 1999, and also participated in the peace-keeping force in Bosnia and Herzegovina, from which it withdrew its troops in 2009. The debate surrounding membership of NATO was reinvigorated following the Russian action in Georgia in 2008. Despite support for an application for full NATO membership from senior figures of the NCP, the President and a majority of the public remained averse to such a measure. In its January 2009 security and defence policy report, however, the Government stated that it would continue to uphold the possibility of seeking full membership of NATO in the future. Meanwhile, in January 1997 Finland began participation in two of the then 13 EU 'battlegroups', to be deployed in crisis areas in rotation. Finland also contributed troops to an EU Force (EUFOR) mission in Bosnia and Herzegovina and to the UN Mission in the Central African Republic and Chad (MINURCAT) until the end of its mandate in December 2010.

Relations between Finland and the USA are cordial. US policy before the dissolution of the USSR was to support Finnish neutrality and, thereafter, was to engage actively in trade and economic relations. Following the terrorist attacks of 11 September 2001 in the USA, Finland did not participate in the US-led retaliatory military action against the Taliban regime in Afghanistan. Finnish military personnel did, however, take part in the subsequent peace-keeping operation in Afghanistan. Finland was opposed to military action against the regime of Saddam Hussain in Iraq in early 2003 without a UN Security Council resolution, but indicated that it would be prepared to take part in military action under UN auspices and in possible humanitarian and peace-keeping operations. In the event, Finland pledged US $5.1m. for reconstruction in Iraq, but did not send any troops. Representatives of groups involved in the conflict in Iraq held discussions in Helsinki in September 2007. Facilitated by a conflict prevention organization founded by former President Ahtisaari, the talks resulted in an agreement on a set of principles for negotiations aimed at achieving national reconciliation. Ahtisaari also mediated in a series of peace negotiations between the Indonesian Government and separatist rebels from the Indonesian province of Aceh in 2005, which led to the signature of a peace agreement in August of that year.

CONSTITUTION AND GOVERNMENT

The Constitution of Finland entered into force on 1 March 2000, amending the Constitution of July 1919. Finland has a republican Constitution, under the provisions of which executive power is divided between the Eduskunta (Parliament), the Valtioneuvosto (Cabinet) and the President. The unicameral Eduskunta has 200 members, elected by universal adult suffrage for four years on the basis of proportional representation. The President is elected for six years by direct popular vote. Legislative power is exercised by the Eduskunta. The Eduskunta elects the Prime Minister, who is then appointed by the President. The other government ministers are appointed by the President on the basis of nominations by the Prime Minister. At April 2011, following many municipal mergers, Finland was divided into 336 municipalities, which are guaranteed self-government and are entitled to levy taxes. The Åland Islands are guaranteed self-government. In their native region the Sámi have linguistic and cultural autonomy.

REGIONAL AND INTERNATIONAL CO-OPERATION

Finland joined the European Union (EU, see p. 276) in 1995, and participated in the introduction of the single European currency, the euro, in January 1999. Finland is a member of the Nordic Council (see p. 464), the Arctic Council, the Council of Europe (see p. 256), the Council of the Baltic Sea States (see p. 254) and the Organization for Security and Co-operation in Europe (OSCE, see p. 388).

Finland joined the UN in 1955. As a contracting party to the General Agreement on Tariffs and Trade, Finland joined the World Trade Organization (WTO, see p. 433) on its establishment in 1995. Finland is a member of the Organisation for Economic Co-operation and Development (OECD, see p. 379) and participates in the Partnership for Peace framework of the North Atlantic Treaty Organization (NATO, see p. 370).

ECONOMIC AFFAIRS

In 2010, according to estimates by the World Bank, Finland's gross national income (GNI), measured at average 2008–10 prices, was US $252,958m., equivalent to $47,160 per head (or $37,180 per head on an international purchasing-power parity basis). During 2001–10, it was estimated, the population increased at an average annual rate of 0.4%, while gross domestic product (GDP) per head increased, in real terms, by an average of 1.4% per year. Overall GDP increased, in real terms, at an average annual rate of 1.8% in 2001–10; GDP contracted by 8.2% in 2009, but grew by 3.1% in 2010.

Agriculture (including hunting, forestry and fishing) contributed an estimated 3.0% of GDP in 2010 and employed 4.5% of the working population in 2008. Forestry is the most important branch of the sector. Animal husbandry is the predominant form of farming. The major crops are barley, oats, wheat and potatoes. During 2001–10 agricultural GDP increased, in real terms, by an average of 2.6% per year; agricultural GDP increased by 1.7% in 2010.

Industry (including mining, manufacturing, construction and power) provided 28.5% of GDP in 2010 and employed 25.4% of the working population in 2008. Industrial GDP increased, in real terms, by an average of 2.1% per year during 2001–10; industrial GDP declined significantly by 20.6% in 2009 largely due to an increase in production costs, but increased by 11.2% in 2010.

Mining and quarrying contributed 0.5% of GDP in 2010 and employed 0.2% of the working population in 2008. Gold is the major mineral export, and zinc ore, copper ore and lead ore are also mined in small quantities. The GDP of the mining sector increased, in real terms, at an average rate of 6.6% per year during 2001–10; mining GDP declined by 3.1% in 2009 but increased significantly by 25.5% in 2010.

Manufacturing provided 18.0% of GDP in 2010 and employed 17.2% of the working population in 2008. The most important branches of manufacturing measured by value of output in 2006 were electrical and optical equipment, including the electronics industry (particularly mobile telephones), pulp, paper and paper products, metal products, chemical products and non-electrical machinery and equipment. The GDP of the manufacturing sector increased, in real terms, at an average rate of 2.0% per year during 2001–10; the sector's GDP declined significantly by 24.8% in 2009, followed by an increase of 12.8% in 2010.

Construction provided 6.7% of GDP in 2010 and employed 7.2% of the working population in 2008. Construction GDP increased, in real terms, by an average of 2.8% per year during 2001–10; the sector's GDP declined by 6.5% in 2009 but increased by 9.4% in 2010.

Of total energy generated in 2008, 29.6% was derived from nuclear energy, 22.1% from hydroelectric power, 11.8% from coal and 14.5% from natural gas. In early 2011 there were four nuclear reactors in operation. Construction of a fifth nuclear plant, a 1,600-MW nuclear reactor in Olkiluoto in south-west Finland, following numerous delays, was scheduled for completion in 2013, four years later than originally planned and hugely over budget. Despite these difficulties, the construction of two further commercial reactors was being considered in 2010–11. Imports of mineral fuels comprised 18.4% of the total cost of imports in 2010.

Services provided 68.5% of GDP in 2010 and engaged 70.2% of the employed labour force in 2008. In real terms, the combined GDP of the services sector increased at an average rate of 1.5% per year during 2001–10; the sector's GDP declined by 4.6% in 2009, but it increased by 1.6% in 2010.

In 2010 Finland recorded a visible trade surplus of US $3,947m., and there was a surplus of $4,459m. on the current account of the balance of payments. In 2010 the principal source of imports was Russia (providing 17.8% of total imports); other major sources were Germany, Sweden and the People's Republic of China. Sweden was the principal market for exports in the same year (accounting for 11.4% of total exports); other major purchasers were Germany, Russia, the USA, the Netherlands and the People's Republic of China. The European Union (EU, see p. 276) accounted for 55.0% of exports and 54.0% of imports in 2010. The principal exports in 2010 were machinery and transport equipment (mainly electronic products, notably mobile telephones), basic manufactures (mainly paper and paperboard), chemicals and related products and mineral fuels and lubricants. The principal imports were machinery and transport equipment, mineral fuels and lubricants, basic manufactures, and chemicals and related products.

In 2010, according to official figures, there was a general government deficit of €4,564m., equivalent to 2.5% of GDP. Finland's general government gross debt was €87,216m. in 2010, equivalent to 48.4% of GDP. The average annual rate of inflation was 1.6% during 2001–11. Consumer prices increased by 1.2% in 2010 and by 3.5% in 2011. The average rate of unemployment was 8.4% in 2010.

Finland's economy depends chiefly on exports, notably paper and high-technology products. Finland was one of the strongest performing economies in the euro area in the late 1990s and 2000s. However, Finland's external trade was severely affected by the global economic downturn that began in late 2008, with exports decreasing by more than one-fifth and real GDP contracting by 8.2% in 2009. By mid-2010 strong growth in the world economy, particularly in Finland's principal trading partners (Russia, Germany and Sweden), had brought about a recovery in the country's exports and GDP, which increased by 8.6% and 3.1%, respectively, in 2010. After a solid performance in the first half of year, the economy slowed in late 2011, as external demand, in particular, weakened, amid uncertainty in the euro area resulting from the sovereign debt crisis affecting some members. In December 2011 the Ministry of Finance forecast growth of 2.6% for that year and of only 0.4% for 2012, partly owing to an anticipated contraction in both public and private investment and dwindling domestic demand. Fiscal stimulus measures introduced during the economic downturn had a detrimental effect on public finances, and the general government balance moved into deficit in 2009 for the first time in 10 years. However, the deficit of 2.5% of GDP recorded in 2010 was still the second smallest in the euro area, after Luxembourg (although the central government deficit was considerably higher, at 5.5%). None the less, the high costs associated with the demographic pressures of a rapidly ageing population, in conjunction with generous welfare benefits, were expected to put further pressure on public finances in the medium term. The new Government that took office in June 2011 aimed to balance the budget by 2015; to this end, the budget for 2012 contained a combination of reductions in expenditure and indirect tax rises, although corporate tax was lowered with the aim of stimulating growth and job creation. The general and central government deficits were forecast to narrow to 1.2% and 3.8% of GDP, respectively, in 2011. Meanwhile, government debt remained relatively low in euro area terms, and in early 2012 Finland was one of only four euro area countries to retain an AAA credit rating.

PUBLIC HOLIDAYS

2013: 1 January (New Year's Day), 6 January (Epiphany), 29 March (Good Friday), 1 April (Easter Monday), 1 May (May Day), 9 May (Ascension Day), 19 May (Whit Sunday), 21–22 June (Midsummer), 2 November (All Saints' Day), 6 December (Independence Day), 24–26 December (Christmas).

Statistical Survey

Source (unless otherwise stated): Statistics Finland, 00022 Helsinki; tel. (9) 17342220; fax (9) 17342279; e-mail library@stat.fi; internet www.stat.fi.

Note: Figures in this survey include data for the autonomous Åland Islands.

Area and Population

AREA, POPULATION AND DENSITY

Area (sq km)	
Land	303,892
Inland water	34,538
Total	338,430*
Population (census results)	
31 December 1995	5,116,826
31 December 2000	
Males	2,529,341
Females	2,651,774
Total	5,181,115
Population (official estimates at 31 December)	
2008	5,326,314
2009	5,351,427
2010	5,375,276
Density (per sq km) at 31 December 2010	17.7†

* 130,668 sq miles; including Åland Islands (1,553 sq km—600 sq miles).

† Land area only.

POPULATION BY AGE AND SEX

(official estimates at 31 December 2010)

	Males	Females	Total
0–14	453,645	434,032	887,677
15–64	1,793,061	1,753,497	3,546,558
65 and over	391,710	549,331	941,041
Total	2,638,416	2,736,860	5,375,276

REGIONS

(population at 31 December 2010)

	Land area (sq km)*	Population	Density (per sq km)*
Uusimaa (Nyland)†	9,097	1,532,309	168.5
Varsinais-Suomi (Egentliga Finland)	10,662	465,183	43.6
Satakunta	7,957	227,031	28.5
Kanta-Häme (Egentliga Tavastland)	5,200	174,555	33.6
Pirkanmaa (Birkaland)	12,446	487,923	39.2
Päijät-Häme (Päijänne-Tavastland)	5,125	201,772	39.4
Kymenlaakso (Kymmenedalen)	5,148	182,382	35.4
Etelä-Karjala (Södra Karelen)	5,613	133,703	23.8
Etelä-Savo (Södra Savolax)	13,980	154,668	11.1
Pohjois-Savo (Norra Savolax)	16,769	247,943	14.8
Pohjois-Karjala (Norra Karelen)	17,763	165,866	9.3
Keski-Suomi (Mellersta Finland)	16,704	273,637	16.4
Etelä-Pohjanmaa (Södra Österbotten)	13,444	193,504	14.4
Pohjanmaa (Österbotten)	7,749	177,946	23.0
Keski-Pohjanmaa (Mellersta Österbotten)	5,019	68,321	13.6
Pohjois-Pohjanmaa (Norra Österbotten)	35,504	394,965	11.1
Kainuu (Kajanaland)	21,501	82,073	3.8
Lappi (Lappland)	92,661	183,488	2.0
Ahvenanmaa (Åland)	1,552	28,007	18.0
Total	303,892	5,375,276	17.7

* According to regional divisions at 1 January 2011; excluding inland waters, totalling 34,538 sq km.

† Including the former Itä-Uusimaa (Östra Nyland) region, which was consolidated with Uusimaa from 1 January 2011.

PRINCIPAL TOWNS

(estimated population at 31 December 2010)*

Helsinki (Helsingfors) (capital)	588,549	Lahti	101,588
Espoo (Esbo)	247,970	Kuopio	96,793
Tampere (Tammerfors)	213,217	Kouvola	88,072
Vantaa (Vanda)	200,055	Pori (Björneborg)	83,032
Turku (Åbo)	177,326	Joensuu	73,305
Oulu (Uleåborg)	141,671	Lappeenranta (Villmanstrand)	71,982
Jyväskylä	130,816	Hämeenlinna	66,829

* According to regional divisions at 1 January 2011.

BIRTHS, MARRIAGES AND DEATHS

	Registered live births*		Registered marriages†		Registered deaths*	
	Number	Rate (per 1,000)	Number	Rate (per 1,000)	Number	Rate (per 1,000)
2003	56,630	10.9	25,815	5.0	48,996	9.4
2004	57,758	11.0	29,342	5.6	47,600	9.1
2005	57,745	11.0	29,283	5.6	47,928	9.1
2006	58,840	11.2	28,236	5.4	48,065	9.1
2007	58,729	11.1	29,497	5.6	49,077	9.3
2008	59,530	11.2	31,014	5.8	49,094	9.2
2009	60,430	11.3	29,836	5.6	49,883	9.3
2010	60,980	11.4	29,952	5.6	50,887	9.5

* Including Finnish nationals temporarily outside the country.

† Data relate only to marriages in which the bride was domiciled in Finland.

Life expectancy (years at birth, WHO estimates): 80 (males 77; females 83) in 2009 (Source: WHO, *World Health Statistics*).

ECONOMICALLY ACTIVE POPULATION

('000 persons aged 15 to 74 years)

	2006	2007	2008
Agriculture, forestry and fishing	114	113	114
Mining and quarrying	5	5	5
Manufacturing	443	445	438
Electricity, gas and water	17	16	17
Construction	162	174	184
Wholesale and retail trade; repair of motor vehicles, and household goods	303	311	314
Hotels and restaurants	78	84	89
Transport, storage and communications	181	175	174
Financial intermediation and insurance	47	50	52
Real estate and business activities	289	308	315
Public administration and defence; compulsory social security	137	137	139
Education	170	166	162
Health and social work	371	373	384
Other community, social and personal service activities	137	141	144
Household service activities	7	7	8

—continued	2006	2007	2008
Extra-territorial organizations and bodies	1	1	1
Sub-total	2,461	2,506	2,540
Not classifiable by economic activity	4	6	13
Total employed	2,465	2,512	2,553
Unemployed	204	183	172
Total labour force	2,669	2,695	2,726

Note: Unemployment data for 2008 are not strictly comparable with other years, owing to revised methodology.

Source: ILO.

2009 ('000 persons aged 15 to 74 years): Total employed 2,457; Unemployed 221; Total labour force 2,678.

2010 ('000 persons aged 15 to 74 years): Total employed 2,447; Unemployed 224; Total labour force 2,672.

Health and Welfare

KEY INDICATORS

Total fertility rate (children per woman, 2009)	1.8
Under-5 mortality rate (per 1,000 live births, 2009)	3
HIV/AIDS (% of persons aged 15–49, 2009)	0.1
Physicians (per 1,000 head, 2006)	3.3
Hospital beds (per 1,000 head, 2006)	7.0
Health expenditure (2008): US $ per head (PPP)	3,299
Health expenditure (2008): % of GDP	8.8
Health expenditure (2008): public (% of total)	70.7
Total carbon dioxide emissions ('000 metric tons, 2007)	64,123.7
Carbon dioxide emissions per head (metric tons, 2007)	12.1
Human Development Index (2011): ranking	22
Human Development Index (2011): value	0.882

For sources and definitions, see explanatory note on p. vi.

Agriculture

PRINCIPAL CROPS
('000 metric tons; farms with arable land of 1 ha or more)

	2008	2009	2010
Wheat	787.5	887.0	724.4
Barley	2,128.6	2,171.0	1,340.2
Rye	60.8	41.7	68.5
Oats	1,213.4	1,114.7	809.7
Mixed grain	37.2	45.3	46.5
Potatoes	684.4	755.3	659.1
Rapeseed	88.9	139.9	178.5
Sugar beet	468.0	559.0	542.1
Cucumbers and gherkins	40.0	39.4	42.6
Carrots and turnips	60.8	70.6	67.5

Aggregate production ('000 metric tons, may include official, semi-official or estimated data): Total cereals 4,229 in 2008, 4,261 in 2009, 2,992 in 2010; Total roots and tubers 684 in 2008, 755 in 2009, 659 in 2010; Total vegetables (incl. melons) 232 in 2008, 252 in 2009, 243 in 2010; Total fruits (excl. melons) 17 in 2008, 19 in 2009, 17 in 2010.

Source: FAO.

LIVESTOCK
('000 head at 1 May; farms with arable land of 1 ha or more)

	2008	2009	2010
Horses*	69	72	74
Cattle	915	918	926
Sheep	122	118	126
Pigs†	1,483	1,381	1,367
Poultry	6,090	5,224	4,896

* Including horses not on farms.

† Including piggeries of dairies.

Source: FAO.

LIVESTOCK PRODUCTS
('000 metric tons)

	2008	2009	2010
Cattle meat	81.9	82.1	83.0
Pig meat	217.1	205.8	203.2
Chicken meat	100.9	94.9	96.3
Cows' milk*	2,310.9	2,332.0	2,346.3
Hen eggs	58.3	53.9	61.5

* Millions of litres.

Source: FAO.

Forestry

ROUNDWOOD REMOVALS
('000 cubic metres, excl. bark)

	2008	2009	2010
Sawlogs, veneer logs and logs for sleepers	19,893.1	15,737.0	19,993.3
Pulpwood	26,072.1	20,963.8	25,983.4
Fuel wood	4,705.2	4,952.3	4,974.8
Total	50,670.5	41,653.1	50,951.5

Source: FAO.

SAWNWOOD PRODUCTION
('000 cu m, incl. railway sleepers)

	2008	2009	2010
Coniferous (softwood)	9,800.0	8,000.0	9,400.0
Broadleaved (hardwood)	81.0	72.5	73.0
Total	9,881.0	8,072.5	9,473.0

Source: FAO.

Fishing

('000 metric tons, live weight)

	2007	2008	2009
Capture	164.7	148.6	154.6
Roaches	5.9	3.6	3.6
Northern pike	10.8	8.8	8.8
European perch	14.6	10.8	10.6
Vendace	4.1	4.2	4.2
Atlantic herring	89.4	83.7	90.8
European sprat	24.6	24.3	23.2
Aquaculture	13.0	13.4	13.6
Rainbow trout	12.1	12.6	12.7
Total catch	177.7	162.1	168.2

Note: Figures exclude aquatic mammals, recorded by number rather than by weight. The catch of grey seals was: 218 in 2007; 360 in 2008; 390 in 2009.

Source: FAO.

Mining

('000 metric tons unless otherwise indicated)

	2007	2008	2009
Copper ore*	13.6	13.0†	13.0†
Nickel ore*	55.0	43.0	10.3
Zinc ore*	72.1	51.9	56.4
Chromium ore‡	556	614	247
Cobalt (metric tons)§	5,862	6,301	4,665
Mercury (metric tons)	45	33	6
Silver (metric tons)§	33.4	59.4	60.0

—*continued*	2007	2008	2009
Gold (kg)§	2,727	2,064	1,785
Platinum (kg)§	461	214	265
Phosphate rock (incl. apatite, metric tons)‖	860	780	660
Peat: for fuel	8,671	6,933	5,576
Peat: for horticulture	1,145	1,552	876

* Figures refer to the metal content of ores.

† Estimated production.

‡ Figures refer to the gross weight of chromite. The estimated chromic oxide content (in '000 metric tons) was: 210 in 2007; 218 in 2008; 210 in 2009 (estimate).

§ Figures refer to production of metal and (for cobalt) powder and salts.

‖ Figures refer to gross weight. The phosphorus oxide content (in metric tons) was: 325 in 2007; n.a. in 2008–09.

Source: US Geological Survey.

Industry

SELECTED PRODUCTS

('000 metric tons, unless otherwise indicated)

	2002	2003	2004*
Cellulose	7,503	7,446	7,852
Newsprint	1,190	1,238	1,217
Other paper, boards and cardboards	11,362	12,113	13,218
Plywoods and veneers ('000 cu m)	1,135	1,168	1,388
Cement	1,198	1,493	1,270
Pig iron and ferro-alloys	2,829	3,091	3,037
Electricity (net, million kWh)	71,618	80,377	82,171
Sugar	161	202	193
Rolled steel products (metric tons)	3,975	4,090	4,157
Cigarettes (million)	4,130	3,946	n.a.

* Preliminary data.

2005: Cement 1,537,000 metric tons (Source: US Geological Survey); Electricity (net) 67,657m. kWh.

2006: Cement 1,685,000 metric tons (Source: US Geological Survey); Electricity (net) 78,623m. kWh.

2007: Cement 1,743,000 metric tons (Source: US Geological Survey); Electricity (net) 77,817m. kWh.

2008: Cement 1,633,000 metric tons (Source: US Geological Survey); Electricity (net) 74,475m. kWh.

2009: Cement 1,052,000 metric tons (Source: US Geological Survey); Electricity (net) 69,207m. kWh.

2010: Electricity (net) 76,968m. kWh (preliminary).

Finance

CURRENCY AND EXCHANGE RATES

Monetary Units

100 cent = 1 euro (€).

Sterling and Dollar Equivalents (30 December 2011)

£1 sterling = 1.195 euros;
US $1 = 0.773 euros;
€10 = £8.37 = $12.94.

Average Exchange Rate (euros per US $)

2009 0.7198
2010 0.7550
2011 0.7194

Note: The national currency was formerly the markka (Finnmark). From the introduction of the euro, with Finnish participation, on 1 January 1999, a fixed exchange rate of €1 = 5.94573 markkaa was in operation. Euro notes and coins were introduced on 1 January 2002. The euro and local currency circulated alongside each other until 28 February, after which the euro became the sole legal tender.

BUDGET

(€ million)

Revenue	2010	2011*	2012†
Taxes and other levies	32,207	35,830	38,200
Taxes on income and property	10,061	11,844	12,119
Taxes on turnover	14,416	15,365	16,450
Excise duties	5,284	5,990	6,700
Other taxes	2,339	2,520	2,809
Other levies	107	111	123
Miscellaneous revenues	5,069	4,703	4,849
Sub-total	37,276	40,533	43,049
Interest on investments and profits received	1,486	1,752	2,009
Loans receivable	11,561	8,241	7,295
Total	50,323	50,527	52,353

Expenditure	2010	2011*	2012†
President of the Republic	15	22	19
Parliament	120	133	143
Council of State	78	79	82
Ministry of Foreign Affairs	1,174	1,268	1,283
Ministry of Justice	813	836	856
Ministry of the Interior	1,329	1,222	1,245
Ministry of Defence	2,732	2,856	2,853
Ministry of Finance	16,278	15,294	16,196
Ministry of Education	6,374	6,730	6,663
Ministry of Agriculture and Forestry	2,761	2,829	2,704
Ministry of Transport and Communications	2,252	2,059	2,375
Ministry of Employment and the Economy	2,592	3,423	3,367
Ministry of Social Affairs and Health	11,165	11,518	12,111
Ministry of the Environment	307	323	271
Public debt	1,890	1,933	2,185
Total	49,880	50,527	52,353

* Preliminary, excluding supplementary budget.

† Budget proposals.

INTERNATIONAL RESERVES

(US $ million at 31 December)

	2008	2009	2010
Gold (Eurosystem valuation)	1,366.7	1,744.3	2,228.2
IMF special drawing rights	239.0	1,883.9	1,841.0
Reserve position in IMF	248.1	423.4	565.9
Foreign exchange	6,492.3	7,403.2	4,919.9
Total	8,346.1	11,454.9	9,555.0

Source: IMF, *International Financial Statistics*.

MONEY SUPPLY

(incl. shares, depository corporations, national residency criteria, € million at 31 December)

	2008	2009	2010
Currency issued	12,992	13,817	14,392
Bank of Finland	8,844	9,907	10,978
Demand deposits	55,893	65,439	69,958
Other deposits	51,292	41,706	44,734
Securities other than shares	67,186	65,280	68,516
Money market fund shares	9,346	9,223	8,039
Shares and other equity	28,745	29,845	31,607
Other items (net)	–14,802	–2,893	7,398
Total	219,496	222,418	244,643

Source: IMF, *International Financial Statistics*.

COST OF LIVING
(Consumer Price Index; base: 2005 = 100)

	2009	2010	2011
Food and non-alcoholic beverages	114.6	110.5	116.8
Alcoholic beverages and tobacco	116.8	121.7	122.7
Clothing and footwear	99.6	101.0	102.7
Housing, water, electricity, gas and other fuels	113.1	115.5	122.8
Furniture, household equipment	105.7	107.8	109.9
Health	105.2	107.2	108.2
Transport	102.2	106.7	111.0
Communication	92.1	90.4	89.1
Recreation and culture	102.8	103.8	104.1
Education	113.1	118.4	121.8
Restaurants and hotels	115.0	116.1	119.0
Miscellaneous goods and services	109.7	109.6	113.8
All items	108.3	109.7	113.5

NATIONAL ACCOUNTS
(€ million at current prices)

National Income and Product

	2008	2009	2010
Compensation of employees	73,430	72,959	74,550
Employers' social contributions	18,077	17,338	17,826
Operating surplus	43,545	33,464	38,153
Domestic factor incomes	135,052	123,761	130,529
Consumption of fixed capital	29,558	29,291	28,858
Gross domestic product at factor cost	164,610	153,052	159,387
Indirect taxes	24,339	23,529	24,338
Less Subsidies	3,298	3,314	3,472
GDP in purchasers' values	185,651	173,267	180,253
Factor income received from abroad *Less* Factor income paid abroad	959	2,989	3,137
Gross national product	186,610	176,256	183,390
Less Consumption of fixed capital	29,558	29,291	28,858
National income in market prices	157,052	146,965	154,532
Other current transfers from abroad *Less* Other current transfers from abroad	−1,968	−2,140	−2,070
National disposable income	155,084	144,825	152,462

Expenditure on the Gross Domestic Product

	2008	2009	2010
Government final consumption expenditure	41,733	43,361	44,276
Private final consumption expenditure	95,479	94,060	98,480
Changes in inventories	1,730	−2,095	−451
Acquisitions, less disposals, of valuables	67	67	66
Gross fixed capital formation	39,759	33,982	33,888
Total domestic expenditure	178,768	169,375	176,259
Exports of goods and services	86,958	64,356	72,643
Less Imports of goods and services	79,991	61,525	70,298
Statistical discrepancy	−84	1,061	1,649
GDP in purchasers' values	185,651	173,267	180,253
GDP at constant 2000 prices	166,908	153,214	157,998

Gross Domestic Product by Economic Activity

	2008	2009	2010
Agriculture, hunting, forestry and fishing	4,588	4,231	4,769
Mining and quarrying	638	548	746
Manufacturing	34,959	25,386	28,218
Electricity, gas and water	4,462	4,846	5,216
Construction	11,874	10,960	10,545
Wholesale and retail trade; repair of motor vehicles, motorcycles, and personal and household goods	16,497	15,145	15,578
Hotels and restaurants	2,667	2,540	2,609
Transport, storage and communication	16,539	15,874	16,164
Financial intermediation and insurance	4,577	4,352	4,324
Real estate and business activities	24,494	24,738	25,490
Administrative and support service activities	5,237	5,000	5,300
Public administration and defence; compulsory social security	9,449	9,619	9,730
Education	7,715	7,965	8,260
Health and social work	14,121	14,801	15,251
Other community, social and personal services	4,566	4,677	4,742
Household service activities	123	162	153
Sub-total	162,506	150,844	157,095
Taxes, less subsidies, on products	23,145	22,423	23,158
GDP in purchasers' values	185,651	173,267	180,253

BALANCE OF PAYMENTS
(US $ million)

	2008	2009	2010
Exports of goods f.o.b.	96,918	62,910	70,132
Imports of goods f.o.b.	−87,215	−58,648	−66,186
Trade balance	9,703	4,262	3,947
Exports of services	31,879	28,045	27,847
Imports of services	−30,671	−27,101	−27,650
Balance on goods and services	10,911	5,207	4,144
Other income received	23,174	15,279	18,327
Other income paid	−25,011	−13,166	−15,805
Balance on goods, services and income	9,074	7,320	6,666
Current transfers received	2,386	2,262	2,243
Current transfers paid	−4,761	−4,606	−4,450
Current balance	6,699	4,976	4,459
Capital account (net)	246	202	212
Direct investment abroad	−8,442	−4,944	−10,647
Direct investment from abroad	−2,286	456	7,072
Portfolio investment assets	−1,299	−39,382	−29,520
Portfolio investment liabilities	7,157	29,106	20,967
Financial derivatives liabilities	1,670	3,020	−430
Other investment assets	−13,544	−6,282	−25,284
Other investment liabilities	28,346	25,441	33,845
Net errors and omissions	−18,308	−10,076	−2,847
Overall balance	238	2,516	−2,173

Source: IMF, *International Financial Statistics*.

External Trade

PRINCIPAL COMMODITIES
(€ million)

Imports c.i.f.	2008	2009	2010
Food and live animals	2,586.9	2,610	2,849
Beverages and tobacco	543.2	458	493
Crude materials (inedible) except fuels	5,393.5	2,659	4,582
Mineral fuels, lubricants, etc.	10,913.3	7,250	9,488
Animal and vegetable oils and fats	109.8	140	299
Chemicals and related products	6,468.4	5,066	5,922

Imports c.i.f.—*continued*	2008	2009	2010
Basic manufactures	7,634.8	5,205	6,352
Machinery and transport equipment	21,574.7	13,863	14,755
Miscellaneous manufactured articles	5,216.1	4,626	5,071
Total (incl. others)	62,084.1	43,250	51,500

Exports f.o.b.	2008	2009	2010
Food and live animals	1,177.1	996	1,105
Beverages and tobacco	144.4	137	135
Crude materials (inedible) except fuels	3,241.5	2,171	3,559
Mineral fuels, lubricants, etc.	4,489.0	2,877	4,211
Animal and vegetable oils and fats	61.7	39	50
Chemicals and related products	5,401.4	4,577	5,870
Basic manufactures	18,293.4	12,632	16,566
Machinery and transport equipment	28,639.1	18,129	16,914
Miscellaneous manufactured articles	3,324.7	2,708	2,979
Total (incl. others)	65,513.0	44,897	52,372

PRINCIPAL TRADING PARTNERS
(€ million)*

Imports c.i.f.	2008	2009	2010
Belgium	1,410.6	962	1,223
China, People's Republic	4,364.9	3,434	3,776
Denmark	1,454.7	1,168	1,238
Estonia	1,376.8	978	1,248
France	2,108.7	1,945	2,012
Germany	8,707.4	6,313	6,836
Italy	1,865.9	1,220	1,429
Japan	1,253.0	848	905
Netherlands	2,604.2	1,977	2,798
Norway	1,676.7	1,004	1,195
Russia	10,140.4	7,026	9,163
Sweden	6,167.7	4,306	5,220
United Kingdom	2,570.1	1,449	1,603
USA	1,853.4	1,486	1,767
Total (incl. others)	62,084.1	43,250	51,500

Exports f.o.b.	2008	2009	2010
Belgium	1,636.0	1,223	1,518
China, People's Republic	2,058.7	1,854	2,687
Denmark	1,380.6	873	1,008
Estonia	1,438.0	905	1,099
France	2,287.8	1,653	1,775
Germany	6,557.1	4,625	5,264
Italy	2,161.1	1,340	1,365
Netherlands	3,368.4	2,625	3,545
Norway	1,969.1	1,345	1,406
Russia	7,611.6	4,044	4,689
Spain	1,887.6	1,021	1,067
Sweden	6,578.1	4,405	5,987
United Kingdom	3,595.2	2,349	2,504
USA	4,146.0	3,482	3,672
Total (incl. others)	65,513.0	44,897	52,372

* Imports by country of production; exports by country of consumption.

Transport

RAILWAYS
(traffic)

	2008	2009	2010
Passengers ('000 journeys)	69,937	67,555	68,950
Passenger-km (million)	4,100	3,900	4,000
Freight carried ('000 metric tons)	41,937	32,860	35,795
Freight ton-km (million)	10,800	8,900	9,800

ROAD TRAFFIC
(registered motor vehicles at 31 December)

	2008	2009	2010
Passenger cars	2,700,492	2,776,664	2,877,484
Lorries and vans	424,498	443,912	464,408
Motorcycles	204,859	216,443	226,877
Tractors	364,334	370,565	376,807
Snowmobiles*	112,923	117,051	121,976

* Excluding Åland Islands.

Buses and coaches: 10,716 in 2004.

SHIPPING

Merchant Fleet
(registered at 31 December)

	2007	2008	2009
Number of vessels	289	287	284
Total displacement ('000 grt)	1,570.1	1,564.9	1,459.3

Source: IHS Fairplay, *World Fleet Statistics*.

International Sea-borne Freight Traffic

	2008	2009	2010
Number of vessels entered	30,126	24,810	25,373
Goods ('000 metric tons):			
loaded	44,293	37,518	41,786
unloaded	58,113	45,052	51,488

CANAL TRAFFIC

	2008	2009	2010
Vessels in transit	34,255	42,199	47,778
Goods carried ('000 metric tons)	2,116	1,083	1,660

CIVIL AVIATION
(traffic on scheduled services)

	2007	2008	2009
Kilometres flown (million)	140	148	139
Passengers carried ('000)	8,289	7,917	7,423
Passenger-km (million)	16,416	17,859	16,389
Total ton-km (million)	1,981	2,162	1,969

Source: UN, *Statistical Yearbook*.

Tourism

FOREIGN TOURIST ARRIVALS
(overnight stays at accommodation establishments)

Country of residence	2008	2009	2010
Estonia	205,627	167,816	205,429
France	230,448	212,887	213,414
Germany	579,970	525,880	510,280
Italy	167,416	151,658	142,389
Netherlands	182,077	169,213	165,779
Norway	182,531	149,279	159,377
Russia	1,030,333	979,526	1,056,24
Sweden	571,904	494,002	517,849
United Kingdom	547,719	464,292	406,272
USA	204,387	166,893	178,482
Total (incl. others)	5,502,542	4,890,006	5,005,068

Tourism receipts (US $ million, incl. passenger transport, unless otherwise indicated): 4,861 in 2008; 4,141 in 2009; 2,809 in 2010 (excl. passenger transport, provisional) (Source: World Tourism Organization).

Communications Media

	2008	2009	2010
Newspapers:			
number	201	201	179
total circulation ('000 copies)	3,066	2,960	2,886
Other periodicals: number	3,313	3,156	3,056
Book production: titles	13,419	12,714	12,017
Telephones ('000 main lines in use)*	1,650	1,430	1,250
Mobile cellular telephones ('000 subscribers)*	6,830	7,700	8,390
Internet users ('000 aged 15 years and over)*	4,438.2	4,393.1	n.a.
Broadband subscribers ('000)*	1,591.9	1,533.8	1,532.7

* Source: International Telecommunication Union.

Personal computers: 2,625,000 (500.4 per 1,000 persons) in 2005 (Source: International Telecommunication Union).

Radio receivers ('000 in use): 7,700 in 1997 (Source: UNESCO, *Statistical Yearbook*).

Television receivers ('000 in use): 3,580 in 2000 (Source: International Telecommunication Union).

Education

(2004)

	Institutions	Teachers†	Students
Comprehensive schools*	3,720	44,313	602,300
Senior secondary schools	436	7,295	127,200
Vocational and professional institutions	302	14,058	199,500
Polytechnics	31	6,034	143,200
Universities	20	7,755	174,000

* Comprising six-year primary stage and three-year lower secondary stage.
† 2003 figures.

2005: *Students:* Comprehensive schools 586,381; Senior secondary schools 118,111; Vocational and professional institutions 243,398; Polytechnics 132,783; Universities 176,061.

2006: *Students:* Comprehensive schools 578,918; Senior secondary schools 117,260; Vocational and professional institutions 256,872; Polytechnics 132,560; Universities 176,555.

2007: *Students:* Comprehensive schools 570,689; Senior secondary schools 115,253; Vocational and professional institutions 266,479; Polytechnics 133,284; Universities 176,304.

2008: *Students:* Comprehensive schools 561,061; Senior secondary schools 114,240; Vocational and professional institutions 275,498; Polytechnics 132,501; Universities 164,068.

2009: *Students:* Comprehensive schools 553,329; Senior secondary schools 112,088; Vocational and professional institutions 281,572; Polytechnics 135,033; Universities 168,475.

2010: *Students:* Comprehensive schools 546,423; Senior secondary schools 111,778; Polytechnics 138,852; Universities 169,404.

Pupil-teacher ratio (primary education, UNESCO estimate): 13.6 in 2008/09 (Source: UNESCO Institute for Statistics).

Directory

The Government

HEAD OF STATE

President: SAULI NIINISTÖ (took office 1 March 2012).

CABINET

(Valtioneuvosto)
(May 2012)

A coalition comprising the National Coalition Party (NCP), the Social Democratic Party (SDP), the Left Alliance (Vas), the Swedish People's Party (SPP), the Green League (Green), and the Christian Democrats (CD).

Prime Minister: JYRKI KATAINEN (NCP).

Minister of Finance: JUTTA URPILAINEN (SDP).

Minister of Foreign Affairs: ERKKI TUOMIOJA (SDP).

Minister of European Affairs and Foreign Trade: ALEXANDER STUBB (NCP).

Minister of International Development: HEIDI HAUTALA (Green).

Minister of Justice: ANNA-MAJA HENRIKSSON (SPP).

Minister of the Interior: PÄIVI RÄSÄNEN (CD).

Minister of Defence: STEFAN WALLIN (SPP).

Minister of Public Administration and Local Government: HENNA VIRKKUNEN (NCP).

Minister of Education and Science: JUKKA GUSTAFSSON (SDP).

Minister of Culture and Sport: PAAVO ARHINMÄKI (Vas).

Minister of Agriculture and Forestry: JARI KOSKINEN (NCP).

Minister of Transport: MERJA KYLLÖNEN (Vas).

Minister of Economic Affairs: JYRI HÄKÄMIES (NCP).

Minister of Labour: LAURI IHALAINEN (SDP).

Minister of Social Affairs and Health: PAULA RISIKKO (NCP).

Minister of Health and Social Services: MARIA GUZENINA-RICHARDSON (SDP).

Minister of the Environment: VILLE NIINISTÖ (Green).

Minister of Housing and Communications: KRISTA KIURU (SDP).

MINISTRIES

Office of the President: Mariankatu 2, 00170 Helsinki; tel. (9) 661133; fax (9) 638247; e-mail presidentti@tpk.fi; internet www.presidentti.fi.

Prime Minister's Office: Snellmaninkatu 1A, Helsinki; POB 23, 00023 Government; tel. (9) 16001; fax (9) 16022165; e-mail info@vnk.fi; internet www.vnk.fi.

Ministry of Agriculture and Forestry: Hallituskatu 3A, Helsinki; POB 30, 00023 Government; tel. (9) 16001; fax (9) 16054202; e-mail kirjaamo.mmm@mmm.fi; internet www.mmm.fi.

Ministry of Defence: Eteläinen Makasiinikatu 8, POB 31, 00131 Helsinki; tel. (9) 16001; fax (9) 653254; e-mail tiedotus@defmin.fi; internet www.defmin.fi.

Ministry of Education and Culture: Meritullinkatu 10, Helsinki; POB 29, 00023 Government; tel. (9) 16004; fax (9) 1359335; e-mail kirjaamo@minedu.fi; internet www.minedu.fi.

Ministry of Employment and the Economy: Aleksanterinkatu 4, 00170 Helsinki; POB 32, 00023 Government; tel. (10) 606000; fax (9) 16062166; e-mail kirjaamo@tem.fi; internet www.tem.fi.

Ministry of the Environment: Kasarmikatu 25, Helsinki; POB 35, 00023 Government; tel. (20) 610100; fax (20) 690160; e-mail kirjaamo.ym@ymparisto.fi; internet www.ymparisto.fi.

Ministry of Finance: Snellmaninkatu 1A, Helsinki; POB 28, 00023 Government; tel. (9) 16001; fax (9) 16033123; e-mail valtiovarainministerio@vm.fi; internet www.vm.fi.

Ministry of Foreign Affairs: Merikasarmi, Laivastokatu 22, POB 176, 00023 Helsinki; tel. (9) 16005; fax (9) 629840; e-mail kirjaamo.um@formin.fi; internet formin.finland.fi.

Ministry of the Interior: Kirkkokatu 12, Helsinki; POB 26, 00023 Government; tel. (71) 8780171; fax (71) 8788555; e-mail kirjaamo@intermin.fi; internet www.intermin.fi.

Ministry of Justice: Eteläesplanadi 10, Helsinki; POB 25, 00023 Government; tel. (9) 16003; fax (9) 16067730; e-mail oikeusministerio@om.fi; internet www.om.fi.

Ministry of Social Affairs and Health: Meritullinkatu 8, 00170 Helsinki; POB 33, 00023 Government; tel. (9) 16001; fax (9) 16074126; e-mail kirjaamo.stm@stm.fi; internet www.stm.fi.

Ministry of Transport and Communications: Yliopistonkatu 5, Helsinki; POB 31, 00023 Government; tel. (9) 16002; fax (9) 16028596; e-mail info@lvm.fi; internet www.lvm.fi.

President and Legislature

PRESIDENT

Presidential Election, 22 January and 5 February 2012

	First round votes (%)	Second round votes (%)
Sauli Niinistö (NCP)	37.0	62.6
Pekka Haavisto (Green)	18.8	37.4
Paavo Väyrynen (Centre)	17.5	—
Timo Soini (The Finns)	9.4	—
Paavo Lipponen (SDP)	6.7	—
Paavo Arhinmäki (Left Alliance)	5.5	—
Eva Biaudet (SPP)	2.7	—
Sari Essayah (CD)	2.5	—
Total	100.0	100.0

PARLIAMENT

Suomen Eduskunta

Mannerheimintie 30, 00102 Helsinki; tel. (9) 4321; fax (9) 4322274; e-mail parliament@parliament.fi; internet www.eduskunta.fi.

Speaker: EERO HEINÄLUOMA (SDP).

Secretary-General: SEPPO TIITINEN.

General Election, 17 April 2011

Party	Votes	% of votes	Seats
Kansallinen Kokoomus (National Coalition Party)	599,138	20.38	44
Suomen Sosialidemokraattinen Puolue (Finnish Social Democratic Party)	561,558	19.10	42
Perussuomalaiset/ Sannfinländarna (True Finns)	560,075	19.05	39
Suomen Keskusta (Finnish Centre Party)	463,266	15.76	35
Vasemmistoliitto (Left Alliance)	239,039	8.13	14
Vihreä Liitto (Green League)	213,172	7.25	10
Svenska Folkpartiet (Swedish People's Party)	125,785	4.28	9
Suomen Kristillisdemokraatit (Finnish Christian Democrats)	118,453	4.03	6
Others	59,085	2.01	1*
Total	2,939,571	100.00	200

* Including a representative of the Åland Islands.

Election Commission

Democracy and Language Affairs Unit: POB 25, 00023 Government; Eteläesplanadi 10, 00130 Helsinki; tel. (9) 16067572; fax (9) 16067792; e-mail vaalit@om.fi; internet www.vaalit.fi; dept of the Ministry of Justice; Dir JOHANNA SUURPÄÄ.

Political Organizations

In December 2012 there were 15 registered political parties in Finland.

Itsenäisyyspuolue (IP) (Independence Party): Nikinsaarentie 31, 62900 Alajärvi; tel. (40) 565366; fax (06) 5574728; e-mail info@ipu.fi; internet www.itsenaisyyspuolue.fi; promotes national independence and social equality; Chair. ANTTI PESONEN.

Kansallinen Kokoomus (National Coalition Party—NCP): Kansakoulukuja 3A, 2nd Floor, 00100 Helsinki; tel. (20) 7488488; fax (20) 7488505; e-mail info@kokoomus.fi; internet www.kokoomus.fi; f. 1918; moderate conservative political ideology; Chair. JYRKI KATAINEN; Party Sec. TARU TUJUNEN; Chair. Parliamentary Group JAN VAPAAVUORI; 41,000 mems.

Köyhien Asialla (For The Poor): Elsankuja 2B 9, 02230 Espoo; tel. (50) 5291171; e-mail info@koyhienasialla.fi; internet www.koyhienasialla.fi; f. 2002; Chair. TERTTU SAVOLA.

Muutos 2011 (M11) (Change 2011): POB 34, 24101 Salo; tel. (40) 7333467; e-mail jiri.keronen@muutos2011.fi; internet www.muutos2011.fi; f. 2010; Chair. MARJUKKA KAAKKOLA; Sec. TAPIO ÄYRÄVÄINEN; 403 mems.

Perussuomalaiset (The Finns): Mannerheimintie 40B 56, 00100 Helsinki; tel. (9) 0207430800; fax (9) 0207430801; e-mail peruss@perussuomalaiset.fi; internet www.perussuomalaiset.fi; f. 1995 by mems of defunct Suomen Maaseudun Puolue (Finnish Rural Party); changed its official English name from True Finns in 2011; Swedish name, Sannfinländarna; Chair. TIMO SOINI; Sec.-Gen. OSSI SANDVIK.

Piraattipuolue (Pirate Party of Finland): Pähkinätie 13, 16710 Hollola kk; tel. (45) 1327960; e-mail info@piraattipuole.fi; internet www.piraattipuole.fi; f. 2009; campaigns for freedom of speech and reform of copyright and intellectual property laws; Chair. HARRI KIVISTÖ.

Suomen Keskusta (Finnish Centre Party): Apollonkatu 11A, 00100 Helsinki; tel. (10) 2897000; fax (10) 2897240; e-mail puoluetoimisto@keskusta.fi; internet www.keskusta.fi; f. 1906; radical centre party founded to promote the interests of the rural population, now reformist movement favouring individual enterprise, equality and decentralization; Chair. MARI KIVINIEMI; Party Sec. TIMO LAANINEN; Chair., Parliamentary Group TIMO KALLI; over 200,000 mems.

Suomen Kommunistinen Puolue (SKP) (Communist Party of Finland): Haapaniemenkatu 7–9B, 9th Floor, 00530 Helsinki; tel. (9) 77438150; fax (9) 77438160; e-mail skp@skp.fi; internet www.skp.fi; f. 1918; incorporated into Vasemmistoliitto (Left Alliance) in 1990; refounded 1997 following disputes in the latter party; Chair. YRJÖ HAKANEN; Sec.-Gen. JUHA-PEKKA VÄISÄNEN; 3,000 mems.

Suomen Kristillisdemokraatit (Finnish Christian Democrats—CD): Karjalankatu 2C, 7th Floor, 00520 Helsinki; tel. (9) 34882200; fax (9) 34882228; e-mail kd@kd.fi; internet www.kd.fi; f. 1958 as Suomen Kristillinen Liitto (Finnish Christian Union); present name adopted 2001; Chair. PÄIVI RÄSÄNEN; Sec.-Gen. ASMO MAANSELKÄ; Chair. Parliamentary Group BJARNE KALLIS; 12,000 mems.

Suomen Sosialidemokraattinen Puolue (Finnish Social Democratic Party—SDP): Saariniemenkatu 6, 00530 Helsinki; tel. (9) 478988; fax (9) 712752; e-mail palaute@sdp.fi; internet www.sdp.fi; f. 1899; constitutional socialist programme; mainly supported by the urban working and middle classes; Chair. JUTTA URPILAINEN; Gen. Sec. MIKAEL JUNGNER; Chair. Parliamentary Group EERO HEINÄLUOMA; 50,000 mems.

Suomen Työväenpuolue (Finnish Workers' Party): POB 780, 00101 Helsinki; tel. (40) 7641163; e-mail tyovaenpuolue@suomi24.fi; internet www.tyovaenpuolue.org; f. 1999; Chair. JUHANI TANSKI; Sec.-Gen. HEIKKI MÄNNIKKÖ.

Svenska Folkpartiet (Swedish People's Party—SPP): POB 430, Simonkatu 8A, 00101 Helsinki; tel. (9) 693070; fax (9) 6931968; e-mail info@sfp.fi; internet www.sfp.fi; f. 1906; liberal party representing the interests of the Swedish-speaking minority; Chair. STEFAN WALLIN; Sec.-Gen. ULLA ACHRÉN; Chair. Parliamentary Group ULLA-MAJ WIDEROOS; 37,000 mems.

Vapauspuolue-Suomen tulevaisuus (Liberty Party-Future of Finland): POB 51, 33201 Tampere; tel. (44) 2028447; e-mail info@vapauspuolue.fi; internet www.vapauspuolue.fi; f. 2010; Chair. KALEVI HELO; Sec. SAKARI SALMI.

Vasemmistoliitto (Vas) (Left Alliance): Viherniemenkatu 5, 2nd Floor, 00530 Helsinki; tel. (9) 7737700; fax (9) 77474200; e-mail vas@vasemmistoliitto.fi; internet www.vasemmisto.fi; f. 1990 by merger of the Finnish People's Democratic League (f. 1944), the Communist Party of Finland (f. 1918), the Democratic League of Finnish Women, and left-wing groups; Chair. PAAVO ARHINMÄKI; Sec.-Gen. SIRPA PUHAKKA; Chair. Parliamentary Group ANNIKA LAPINTIE; 10,000 mems.

Vihreä Liitto (Green League): Fredrikinkatu 33A, 3rd Floor, 00120 Helsinki; tel. (9) 58604160; fax (9) 58604161; e-mail vihreat@vihreat.fi; internet www.vihreat.fi; f. 1987; Chair. and Leader VILLE NIINISTÖ; Sec.-Gen. PANU LATURI; c. 4,400 mems.

Diplomatic Representation

EMBASSIES IN FINLAND

Argentina: Bulevardi 5A 11, 00120 Helsinki; tel. (9) 42428700; fax (9) 42428701; e-mail embassy@embargentina.fi; internet www.embargentina.fi; Ambassador ROBERTO DANIEL PIERINI.

Austria: Unioninkatu 22, 00130 Helsinki; tel. (9) 6818600; fax (9) 665084; e-mail helsinki-ob@bmeia.gv.at; internet www.bmeia.gv.at/botschaft/helsinki.html; Ambassador MARGIT WÄSTFELT.

Belarus: Unioninkatu 18, 00130 Helsinki; e-mail finland@mfa.gov.by; Ambassador VLADIMIR N. DRAZHIN.

Belgium: Kalliolinnantie 5, 00140 Helsinki; tel. (9) 170412; fax (9) 628842; e-mail helsinki@diplobel.fed.be; internet www.diplomatie.be/helsinki; Ambassador Ivo Goemans.

Brazil: Itäinen puistotie 4B 1, 00140 Helsinki; tel. (9) 6841500; fax (9) 650084; e-mail brasemb@brazil.fi; internet www.brazil.fi; Ambassador Norton de Andrade Mello Rapesta.

Bulgaria: Kuusisaarentie 2B, 00340 Helsinki; tel. (9) 4584055; fax (9) 4584550; e-mail bulembfi@yahoo.com; internet www.mfa.government.bg/bg/71/; Chargé d'affaires a.i. Ralitza Djubrailova-Tchorbadjiyska.

Canada: Pohjoisesplanadi 25B, 00100 Helsinki; POB 779, 00101 Helsinki; tel. (9) 228530; fax (9) 601060; e-mail hsnki@international.gc.ca; internet www.canadainternational.gc.ca/finland-finlande; Ambassador Chris Shapardanov.

Chile: Erottajankatu 11, 2nd Floor, 00130 Helsinki; tel. (9) 6126780; fax (9) 61267825; e-mail info@embachile.fi; internet www.embachile.fi; Ambassador Eduardo Pablo Tapia Riepel.

China, People's Republic: Vanha Kelkkamäki 11, 00570 Helsinki; tel. (9) 22890110; fax (9) 22890168; e-mail chinaemb_fi@mfa.gov.cn; internet www.chinaembassy-fi.org; Ambassador Huang Xing.

Croatia: Kruunuvuorenkatu 5, 4th Floor, 00160 Helsinki; tel. (9) 6850170; fax (9) 6222221; e-mail croemb.helsinki@mvpei.hr; Ambassador Dr Damir Kušen.

Cuba: Frederikinkatu 61, 3rd Floor, 00100 Helsinki; tel. (9) 6802022; fax (9) 643163; e-mail cuba@cuba.fi; internet emba.cubaminrex.cu/finlandia; Ambassador Sergio González González.

Cyprus: Bulevardi 5A 19, 00120 Helsinki; tel. (9) 6962820; fax (9) 677428; e-mail mail@cyprusembassy.fi; internet www.cyprusembassy.fi; Ambassador Filippos Kritiotis.

Czech Republic: Armfeltintie 14, 00150 Helsinki; tel. (9) 6120880; fax (9) 630655; e-mail helsinki@embassy.mzv.cz; internet www.mfa.cz/helsinki; Ambassador Martin Tomčo.

Denmark: Mannerheimintie 8, 6th Floor, POB 1042, 00100 Helsinki; tel. (9) 6841050; fax (9) 6985156; e-mail helamb@um.dk; internet www.ambhelsingfors.um.dk; Ambassador Jens-Otto Horslund.

Egypt: Itäinen puistotie 2, 00140 Helsinki; tel. (9) 4777470; fax (9) 47774721; e-mail secretaryofembassy@hotmail.com; Ambassador Muhammad Abd al-Hamid Muhammad Kassem.

Estonia: Itäinen puistotie 10, 00140 Helsinki; tel. (9) 6220260; fax (9) 62202610; e-mail embassy.helsinki@mfa.ee; internet www.estemb.fi; Ambassador Mart Tarmak.

France: Itäinen puistotie 13, 00140 Helsinki; tel. (9) 618780; fax (9) 61878342; e-mail ambassade.france@pp.htv.fi; internet www.ambafrance-fi.org/france_finlande; Ambassador Eric Lebédel.

Germany: Krogiuksentie 4B, 00340 Helsinki; POB 5, 00331 Helsinki; tel. (9) 458580; fax (9) 45858258; e-mail info@helsinki.diplo.de; internet www.helsinki.diplo.de; Ambassador Dr Thomas Götz.

Greece: Maneesikatu 2A 4, 00170 Helsinki; tel. (9) 6229790; fax (9) 2781200; e-mail greek.embassy@kolumbus.fi; internet www.greekembassy.fi; Ambassador Christos Kontovounisios.

Hungary: Kuusisaarenkuja 6, 00340 Helsinki; tel. (9) 484144; fax (9) 480497; e-mail mission.hel@kum.hu; internet www.mfa.gov.hu/emb/helsinki; Ambassador Kristóf Forrai.

Iceland: Pohjoisesplanadi 27C, 00100 Helsinki; tel. (9) 6122460; fax (9) 61224620; e-mail icemb.helsinki@utn.stjr.is; internet www.iceland.org/fi; Ambassador Elin Flygenring.

India: Satamakatu 2A 8, 00160 Helsinki; tel. (9) 2289910; fax (9) 6221208; e-mail indianembassy@indianembassy.fi; internet www.indianembassy.fi; Ambassador Aladiyan Manickam.

Indonesia: Kuusisaarentie 3, 00340 Helsinki; tel. (9) 4470370; fax (9) 4582882; e-mail info@indonesian-embassy.fi; internet www.indonesian-embassy.fi; Ambassador Elias Ginting.

Iran: Kulosaarentie 9, 00570 Helsinki; tel. (9) 6869240; fax (9) 68692410; e-mail embassy@iran.fi; internet www.iran.fi; Ambassador Saeed Rasoul Moussavi.

Iraq: Lars Sonckintie 2, 00570 Helsinki; tel. (9) 6818870; fax (9) 6848977; e-mail hlsemb@iraqmofamail.net; Ambassador Abdul Karim Mehdi.

Ireland: Erottajankatu 7A, 00130 Helsinki; POB 33, 00131 Helsinki; tel. (9) 6824240; fax (9) 646022; e-mail helsinkiembassy@dfa.ie; internet www.embassyofireland.fi; Ambassador Dermot Brangan.

Israel: Yrjönkatu 36A, 00100 Helsinki; tel. (9) 6812020; fax (9) 1356959; e-mail info@helsinki.mfa.gov.il; internet helsinki.mfa.gov.il; Ambassador Dan Ashbel.

Italy: Itäinen puistotie 4A, 00140 Helsinki; tel. (9) 6811280; fax (9) 6987829; e-mail ambasciata.helsinki@esteri.it; internet www.ambhelsinki.esteri.it; Ambassador Giorgio Visetti.

Japan: Unioninkatu 20–22, 00130 Helsinki; tel. (9) 6860200; fax (9) 633012; e-mail inquiry@hk.mofa.go.jp; internet www.fi.emb-japan.go.jp; Ambassador Hiroshi Maruyama.

Korea, Republic: Erottajankatu 7A, 00130 Helsinki; tel. (9) 2515000; fax (9) 25150055; e-mail korembfi@mofat.go.kr; internet fin.mofat.go.kr; Ambassador Park Dong-Sun.

Latvia: Armfeltintie 10, 00150 Helsinki; tel. (9) 47647244; fax (9) 47647288; e-mail embassy.finland@mfa.gov.lv; internet www.mfa.gov.lv/fi/helsinki; Ambassador Juris Bone.

Lithuania: Rauhankatu 13A, 00170 Helsinki; tel. (9) 6844880; fax (9) 68448820; e-mail info@lithuania.fi; internet fi.mfa.lt; Ambassador Arunas Jievaltas.

Malaysia: Aleksanterinkatu 17, 00100 Helsinki; tel. (9) 69697142; fax (9) 69697144; e-mail malhsinki@kln.gov.my; internet www.kln.gov.my/perwakilan/helsinki; Ambassador Choong Kit Cheah.

Mexico: Simonkatu 12A, 7th Floor, 00100 Helsinki; tel. (9) 5860430; fax (9) 6949411; e-mail mexican.embassy@welho.com; Ambassador Agustín Gutiérrez Canet.

Morocco: Unioninkatu 15A, 00300 Helsinki; tel. (9) 6122480; fax (9) 635160; e-mail embassy.of.morocco@co.inet.fi; Ambassador Dr Mina Tounsi.

Netherlands: POB 886, 00101 Helsinki; Erottajankatu 19B, 00130 Helsinki; tel. (9) 228920; fax (9) 22892228; e-mail hel@minbuza.nl; internet www.netherlands.fi; Ambassador Nicolaas Beets.

Norway: Rehbinderintie 17, 00150 Helsinki; tel. (9) 6860180; fax (9) 657807; e-mail emb.helsinki@mfa.no; internet www.norja.fi; Ambassador Leidulv Namtvedt.

Peru: Annankatu 31–33C 44, 00100 Helsinki; tel. (9) 7599400; fax (9) 75994040; e-mail embassy.peru@peruemb.inet.fi; internet www.peruembassy.fi; Ambassador Dr Pablo Portugal.

Philippines: Regus Luna House, Rooms 624–625, 6th Floor, Mannerheimintie 12B, 00100 Helsinki; tel. (9) 25166322; fax (9) 25166100; e-mail admin@helsinkipe.org; Chargé d'affaires a.i. Blesila C. Cabrera.

Poland: Armas Lindgrenintie 21, 00570 Helsinki; tel. (9) 618280; fax (9) 6847477; e-mail helsinki.amb.info@msz.gov.pl; internet www.helsinki.polemb.net; Ambassador Janusz Niesyto.

Portugal: Unioninkatu 22, 00130 Helsinki; tel. (9) 6824370; fax (9) 663550; e-mail emb.port@portugal.fi; Chargé d'affaires a.i. Jorge de Aranda.

Romania: Stenbäckinkatu 24, 00250 Helsinki; tel. (9) 2414414; fax (9) 2413272; e-mail romania@romania.fi; internet helsinki.mae.ro; Ambassador Marian Cătălin Avramescu.

Russia: Tehtaankatu 1B, 00140 Helsinki; tel. (9) 661876; fax (9) 661006; e-mail rusembassy@co.inet.fi; internet www.rusembassy.fi; Ambassador Aleksandr Yu. Rumyantsev.

Saudi Arabia: Stenbäckinkatu 26, 00250 Helsinki; tel. (9) 4778870; fax (9) 4543060; e-mail secretary@saudiembassy.fi; Chargé d'affaires a.i. Jamal I. M. Nasef.

Serbia: Kulosaarentie 36, 00570 Helsinki; tel. (9) 6848522; fax (9) 6848783; e-mail info.ambascghki@kolumbus.fi; internet www.helsinki.mfa.rs; Ambassador Vera Mavrić.

Slovakia: Annankatu 25, 00100 Helsinki; tel. (9) 68117810; fax (9) 68117820; e-mail emb.helsinki@mzv.sk; internet www.mzv.sk/helsinki; Ambassador Juraj Podhorský.

Slovenia: Eteläesplanadi 24A, 00130 Helsinki; POB 9, 00101 Helsinki; tel. (9) 2289940; fax (9) 6944775; e-mail vhe@gov.si; internet www.helsinki.embassy.si; Ambassador Tone Kajzer.

South Africa: Rahapajankatu 1A 5, 3rd Floor, 00160 Helsinki; tel. (9) 68603100; fax (9) 68603160; e-mail saembfin@dirco.gov.za; internet www.southafricanembassy.fi; Ambassador Cleopus Phaswana Moloto.

Spain: Kalliolinnantie 6, 00140 Helsinki; tel. (9) 6877080; fax (9) 170923; e-mail emb.helsinki@maec.es; internet www.maec.es/embajadas/helsinki/es/home; Ambassador Marcos Vega Gómez.

Sweden: POB 329, 00171 Helsinki; Pohjoisesplanadi 7B, 00170 Helsinki; tel. (9) 6877660; fax (9) 655285; e-mail ambassaden.helsingfors@foreign.ministry.se; internet www.sverige.fi; Chargé d'affaires a.i. Örjan Berner.

Switzerland: Uudenmaankatu 16A, 00120 Helsinki; tel. (9) 6229500; fax (9) 62295050; e-mail hel.vertretung@eda.admin.ch; internet www.eda.admin.ch/helsinki; Ambassador Maurice Darier.

Thailand: Eteläesplanadi 22C, 3rd Floor, 00130 Helsinki; tel. (9) 6122640; fax (9) 61226466; e-mail info@thaiembassy.fi; internet www.thaiembassy.fi; Chargé d'affaires a.i. Worawoot Pongprapapant.

Tunisia: Liisankatu 14B 31, 00170 Helsinki; tel. (9) 68039614; fax (9) 68039610; e-mail at.helsinki@kolumbus.fi; Chargé d'affaires Ali Ben Malek.

Turkey: Puistokatu 1B A 3, 00140 Helsinki; tel. (9) 6811030; fax (9) 655011; e-mail turkish.embassy@welho.com; internet www.helsinki.be.fscnet.net; Ambassador Hüseyin Selah Korutürk.

Ukraine: Vähäniityntie 9, 00570 Helsinki; tel. (9) 2289000; fax (9) 2289001; e-mail embassy@ukraine.fi; internet www.ukraine.fi; Ambassador Andrii Deshchytsia.

United Kingdom: Itäinen puistotie 17, 00140 Helsinki; tel. (9) 22865100; fax (9) 22865262; e-mail info.helsinki@fco.gov.uk; internet www.ukinfinland.fco.gov.uk; Ambassador Matthew Lodge.

USA: Itäinen puistotie 14 B, 00140 Helsinki; tel. (9) 616250; fax (9) 61625800; e-mail arc@usembassy.fi; internet finland.usembassy.gov; Ambassador Bruce J. Oreck.

Venezuela: Bulevardi 1A 62, 00100 Helsinki; tel. (9) 6860440; fax (9) 640971; e-mail embavenefin@embavene.fi; internet www.embavene.fi; Chargé d'affaires a.i. Ernesto Navazio Mossucca.

Viet Nam: Kulosaarentie 12, 00570 Helsinki; tel. (9) 6229900; fax (9) 62299022; e-mail vietnamfinland@gmail.com; internet www.vietnamembassy-finland.org; Ambassador Doan Ngoc Boi.

Judicial System

The administration of justice is independent of the Government and judges can be removed only by judicial sentence. The compulsory retirement age for judges is 67.

SUPREME COURT

Korkein oikeus/Högsta domstolen
Pohjoisesplanadi 3, POB 301, 00171 Helsinki; tel. (10) 3640000; fax (10) 3640154; e-mail korkein.oikeus@oikeus.fi; internet www.kko.fi.

Consists of a President and at least 15 Justices appointed by the President of the Republic. Final court of appeal in civil and criminal cases, supervises judges and executive authorities.

President: Pauliine Koskelo.

Justices: Kari Raulos, Mikko Tulokas, Kati Hidén, Kari Kitunen, Gustav Bygglin, Liisa Mansikkamäki, Pertti Välimäki, Pasi Aarnio, Juha Häyhä, Hannu Rajalahti, Ilkka Rautio, Timo Esko, Soile Poutianen, Marjut Jokela, Jukka Sippo, Jorma Rudanko, Pekka Koponen, Ari Kantor.

SUPREME ADMINISTRATIVE COURT

Korkein hallinto-oikeus/Högsta förvaltningsdomstolen
Unioninkatu 16, POB 180, 00131 Helsinki; tel. (10) 3640200; fax (10) 3640382; e-mail korkein.hallinto-oikeus@oikeus.fi; internet www.kho.fi.

Consists of a President and 20 Justices appointed by the President of the Republic. Highest tribunal for appeals in administrative cases.

President: Pekka Hallberg.

Justices: Olof Olsson, Esa Aalto, Pirkko Ignatius, Pekka Vihervuori, Heikki Kanninen, Kari Kuusiniemi, Niilo Jääskinen, Ahti Vapaavuori, Irma Telivuo, Matti Pellonpää, Tuula Pynnä, Anne E. Niemi, Matti Halén, Sakari Vanhala, Eila Rother, Riitta Mutikainen, Hannele Ranta-Lassila, Hannu Ranta, Timo Viherkenttä, Eija Siitari-Vanne.

COURTS OF APPEAL

There are Courts of Appeal at Turku, Vaasa, Kuopio, Helsinki, Kouvola, and Rovaniemi, consisting of a President and an appropriate number of members.

ADMINISTRATIVE COURTS

There are eight Administrative Courts, which hear the appeals of private individuals and corporate bodies against the authorities in tax cases, municipal cases, construction cases, social welfare and health care cases and other administrative cases. In certain of these, the appeal must be preceded by a complaint to a separate lower appellate body. The state and municipal authorities also have a right of appeal in certain cases.

DISTRICT COURTS

Courts of first instance for almost all suits. Appeals lie to the Court of Appeal, and then to the Supreme Court. The composition of the District Court is determined by the type of case to be heard. Civil cases and 'ordinary' criminal cases can be considered by one judge. Other criminal cases and family law cases are heard by a judge and a panel of three lay judges (jurors). Other civil cases are heard by three legally qualified judges. There are 66 District Courts.

SPECIAL COURTS

In addition there are a number of special courts with more restricted jurisdictions. These are the High Court of Impeachment; the Insurance Court; the Labour Court; and the Market Court. There is no constitutional court in Finland, but the Constitutional Committee of Parliament has been entrusted with the process of verifying the compatibility of new legislation with the Constitution.

CHANCELLOR OF JUSTICE

The Oikeuskansleri (Chancellor of Justice) is responsible for ensuring that authorities and officials comply with the law. He is the chief public prosecutor, and acts as counsel for the Government.

Chancellor of Justice: Jaakko Jonkka.

Chancellor of Justice's Office: POB 20, 00023 Government; Snellmaninkatu 1A, Helsinki; tel. (9) 16001; fax (9) 16023975; e-mail kirjaamo@okv.fi; internet www.okv.fi.

PARLIAMENTARY OMBUDSMAN

The Eduskunnan Oikeusasiamies is the Finnish Ombudsman appointed by the Eduskunta to supervise the observance of the law.

Parliamentary Ombudsman: Petri Jääskeläinen.

Office of the Parliamentary Ombudsman: Arkadiankatu 3, 00102 Helsinki; tel. (9) 4321; fax (9) 4322268; e-mail ombudsman@parliament.fi; internet www.ombudsman.fi; f. 1919; Parl. Ombudsman Petri Jääskeläinen.

In addition to the Chancellor of Justice and the Parliamentary Ombudsman, there are also specialized authorities that have similar duties in more limited fields. These include the Consumer Ombudsman, the Ombudsman for Equality, the Data Protection Ombudsman, the Ombudsman for Aliens and the Bankruptcy Ombudsman.

Religion

In 2009 79.9% of the population were members of the Evangelical Lutheran Church and around 1.1% belonged to the Orthodox Church. Some 17.7% of the population professed no religious affiliation.

CHRISTIANITY

Suomen ekumeeninen neuvosto/Ekumeniska rådet i Finland (Finnish Ecumenical Council): Katajanokankatu 7A, POB 185, 00161 Helsinki; tel. (9) 1802369; fax (9) 174313; e-mail heikki.huttunen@ekumenia.fi; internet www.ekumenia.fi; f. 1917; 11 mem. churches; Pres. Rt Rev. Teemu Sippo; Gen. Sec. Rev. Heikki Huttunen.

National Churches

Suomen evankelis-luterilainen kirkko (Evangelical Lutheran Church of Finland): Council for International Relations, Satamakatu 11, POB 185, 00161 Helsinki; tel. (9) 18021; fax (9) 1802350; e-mail kirkkohallitus@evl.fi; internet www.evl.fi; 4.3m. mems (2010); Leader Archbishop Dr Kari Mäkinen.

Suomen Ortodoksinen Kirkko (Orthodox Church of Finland): Karjalankatu 1, 70110 Kuopio; tel. (206) 100210; fax (206) 100211; e-mail kirkollishallitus@ort.fi; internet www.ort.fi; 60,000 mems; Leader Archbishop Leo of Karelia and All Finland.

The Roman Catholic Church

Finland comprises the single diocese of Helsinki, directly responsible to the Holy See. At 31 December 2006 there were 9,429 adherents in the country (around 0.2% of the population). The Bishop participates in the Scandinavian Episcopal Conference (based in Sweden).

Bishop of Helsinki: Rt Rev. Teemu Sippo, Rehbinderintie 21, 00150 Helsinki; tel. (9) 6877460; fax (9) 639820; e-mail curia@catholic.fi; internet www.catholic.fi.

Other Churches

Finlands svenska baptistsamfund (Finland Swedish Baptist Union): POB 54, 65101 Vasa; Rådhusgatan 44, 5th Floor, 65100 Vasa; tel. (6) 3464500; fax (6) 3464510; e-mail fsb@baptist.fi; internet www.baptist.fi; f. 1856; publishes *Missionsstandaret* (12 a year); 1,300 mems; Gen. Sec. Peter Sjöblom.

Finlands svenska metodistkyrka (United Methodist Church in Finland—Swedish-speaking): Apollogatan 5, 00100 Helsinki; e-mail kyrkostyrelsen@metodistkyrkan.fi; internet www.metodistkyrkan.fi; f. 1881; 1,000 mems; District Superintendent Rev. Tom Hellsten.

Jehovan Todistajat (Jehovah's Witnesses): POB 68, 01301 Vantaa; Puutarhatie 60, 01300 Vantaa; tel. (9) 825885; fax (9) 82588285; internet www.watchtower.org; 19,366 mems.

Myöhempien Aikojen Pyhien Jeesuksen Kristuksen Kirkko (The Church of Jesus Christ of Latter-day Saints—Mormon): Neitsytpolku 3A, 00140 Helsinki; tel. (9) 6962750; fax (9) 69627510; e-mail 2015803@ldschurch.org; internet www.mormonit.fi; 4,604 mems; Mission Pres. D.M. RAWLINGS.

Suomen Adventtikirkko (Seventh-day Adventist Church in Finland): POB 94, 33101 Tampere; Ketarantie 4E, 33680 Tampere; tel. (3) 3611111; fax (3) 3600454; e-mail mervi.tukiainen@adventtikirkko.fi; internet www.adventtikirkko.fi; f. 1894; 5,469 mems; Pres. ATTE HELMINEN; Sec. ANNE VRCELJ.

Suomen Baptistikirkko (Baptists—Finnish-speaking): Kissanmaankatu 19, 33530 Tampere; tel. (30) 3138100; e-mail porttis@hotmail.com; internet www.baptisti.fi; 692 mems; Pres. JARI PORTAANKORVA.

Suomen Metodistikirkko (United Methodist Church—Finnish-speaking): Punavuorenkatu 2B 17, 00120 Helsinki; tel. (9) 628135; fax (9) 6224558; e-mail suomen@metodistikirkko.fi; internet www.metodistikirkko.fi; 782 mems; District Superintendent Rev. TIMO VIRTANEN.

Suomen Vapaakirkko (Evangelical Free Church of Finland): POB 198, 13101 Hämeenlinna; tel. (3) 6445150; fax (3) 6122153; e-mail svk@svk.fi; internet www.svk.fi; f. 1923; 15,150 mems; Pres. Rev. HANNU VUORINEN.

The Anglican Church and the Salvation Army are also active in the country.

BAHÁ'Í FAITH

Suomen Bahá'í-yhteisö (Bahá'í Community of Finland): POB 423, 00101 Helsinki; tel. (9) 790875; fax (9) 790058; e-mail info@bahai.fi; internet www.bahai.fi; f. 1953; 700 mems.

JUDAISM

Helsingin Juutalainen Seurakunta (Jewish Community of Helsinki): Synagogue and Community Centre, Malminkatu 26, 00100 Helsinki; tel. (9) 6854584; fax (9) 6948916; e-mail srk@jchelsinki.fi; internet www.jchelsinki.fi; 1,200 mems; Pres. RONY SMOLAR; Exec. Dir DAN KANTOR.

ISLAM

Between 1990 and 2000 the number of Muslims increased from 1,000 to approximately 20,000. There are around 20 registered mosques or religious communities.

Suomen Islamilainen Yhdyskunta (Islamic Society of Finland): Lonnrotinkatu 22A 3, POB 87, 00101 Helsinki; tel. (9) 2782551; fax (9) 6121156; e-mail yhdyskunta@rabita.fi; internet www.rabita.fi; Imam ANAS HAJJAR.

The Press

In 2009 there were 201 newspapers in Finland; the total circulation for all types of newspaper was some 3.2m. A number of dailies are printed in Swedish. The most popular daily papers are *Helsingin Sanomat*, *Ilta-Sanomat*, *Aamulehti* and *Iltalehti*.

PRINCIPAL DAILIES

(average net circulation figures, for the year 2010, unless otherwise indicated)

Helsinki

Helsingin Sanomat: Töölönlahdenkatu 2, POB 18, 00089 Sanomat; tel. (9) 1221; fax (9) 1222366; e-mail janne.virkkunen@sanomat.fi; internet www.hs.fi; f. 1889; independent; Publr and Senior Editor-in-Chief MIKAEL PENTIKÄINEN; circ. 374,503 (weekdays), 447,682 (weekend).

Hufvudstadsbladet: Mannerheimvägen 18, POB 217, 00101 Helsinki; tel. (9) 12531; fax (9) 642930; e-mail nyheter@hbl.fi; internet www.hbl.fi; f. 1864; Swedish-language; independent; Editor-in-Chief JENS BERG; circ. 47,702 (weekdays), 50,030 (weekend).

Iltalehti: Aleksanterinkatu 9, POB 372, 00100 Helsinki; tel. (10) 665100; fax (9) 177313; e-mail il.toimitus@iltalehti.fi; internet www.iltalehti.fi; f. 1981; afternoon; independent; Man. Dir KARI KIVELÄ; Editor-in-Chief PANU POKKINEN; circ. 107,052 (weekdays), 136,245 (weekend).

Ilta-Sanomat: Töölönlahdenkatu 2, POB 45, 00089 Sanomat; tel. (9) 1221; fax (9) 1223419; e-mail uutiset@sanoma.fi; internet www.iltasanomat.fi; f. 1932; afternoon; 6 a week; independent; Publr and Editor-in-Chief TAPIO SADEOJA; circ. 150,351 (weekdays), 189,524 (weekend).

Kauppalehti (Finnish Business Daily): Eteläesplanadi 20, POB 189, 00101 Helsinki; tel. (10) 665101; fax (10) 6652423; internet www.kauppalehti.fi; f. 1898; weekdays; Man. Dir JUHA-PETRI LOIMOVUORI; Editor-in-Chief HANNU LEINONEN; circ. 70,118.

Uutispäivä Demari: Haapaniemenkatu 7–9B, 17th and 18th Floors, 00530 Helsinki; POB 338, 00531 Helsinki; tel. (9) 701041; fax (9) 7010567; e-mail toimitus@demari.fi; internet www.demari.fi; f. 1895; chief organ of the Social Democratic Party; Man. Dir HEIKKI NYKANEN; Editor-in-Chief JUHA PELTONEN; circ. 14,119.

Hämeenlinna

Hämeen Sanomat: Vanajantie 7, POB 530, 13111 Hämeenlinna; tel. (3) 61511; fax (3) 6151492; e-mail toimitus@hameensanomat.fi; internet www.hameensanomat.fi; f. 1879; independent; Man. Dir PAULI UUSI-KILPONEN; Editor-in-Chief PAULI UUSI-KILPONEN; circ. 28,296.

Joensuu

Karjalainen: Kosti Aaltosentie 9, 80140, Joensuu; POB 99, 80141 Joensuu; tel. (13) 2551; fax (13) 2552363; e-mail toimitus@karjalainen.fi; internet www.karjalainen.fi; f. 1874; independent; Man. Dir RAIMO PUUSTINEN; Editor PASI KOIVUMAA; circ. 45,584.

Jyväskylä

Sanomalehti Keskisuomalainen Oy: Aholaidantie 3, POB 159, 40101 Jyväskylä; tel. (14) 622000; fax (14) 622272; internet www.ksml.fi; f. 1871; Editor-in-Chief PEKKA MERVOLA; circ. 73,559.

Kemi

Pohjolan Sanomat: Sairaalakatu 2, 94100 Kemi; tel. (10) 6656555; fax (10) 6656322; e-mail ps.toimitus@pohjolansanomat.fi; internet www.pohjolansanomat.fi; f. 1915; Man. Dir MARTTI NIKKANEN; Editor-in-Chief HEIKKI LÄÄKKÖLÄ; circ. 20,070 (weekdays), 20,221 (Sat.).

Kokkola

Keskipohjanmaa: Eteläväylä, POB 45, 67101 Kokkola; tel. (20) 7504400; fax (20) 7504488; e-mail toimitus@kpk.fi; internet www.keskipohjanmaa.net; f. 1917; independent; Man. Dir EINO LAUKKA; Editor-in-Chief LASSI JAAKKOLA; circ. 25,479.

Kotka

Kymen Sanomat: Tornatorintie 3, 48100 Kotka; POB 27, 48101 Kotka; tel. (5) 210015; fax (5) 21005206; e-mail uutiset@kymensanomat.fi; internet www.kymensanomat.fi; f. 1902; independent; Man. Dir JARMO KOSKINEN; Editor PEKKA LAKKA; circ. 23,208.

Kouvola

Kouvolan Sanomat: Lehtikaari 1, POB 40, 45101 Kouvola; tel. (5) 280014; fax (5) 28004706; e-mail toimitus@kouvolansanomat.fi; internet www.kouvolansanomat.fi; f. 1909; independent; Man. Dir JUHA OKSANEN; Editor-in-Chief PEKKA LAKKA; circ. 27,273 (weekdays), 27,610 (Sat.).

Kuopio

Savon Sanomat: Vuorikatu 21, POB 68, 70101 Kuopio; tel. (17) 303111; fax (17) 303375; e-mail lukijansanomat@iwn.fi; internet www.savonsanomat.fi; f. 1907; independent; Man. Dir HEIKKI AURASMAA; Editor-in-Chief JARI TOURUNEN; circ. 61,546.

Lahti

Etelä-Suomen Sanomat: Ilmarisentie 7, POB 80, 15101 Lahti; tel. (3) 75751; fax (3) 7575466; e-mail heikki.hakala@ess.fi; internet www.ess.fi; f. 1914; independent; Man. Dir JUKKA OTTELA; Editor-in-Chief HEIKKI HAKALA; circ. 58,400.

Lappeenranta

Etelä-Saimaa: Lauritsalantie 1, POB 3, 53501 Lappeenranta; tel. (5) 538813; fax (5) 53883206; e-mail lukijat@esaimaa.fi; internet www.esaimaa.fi; f. 1885; independent; Editor PEKKA LAKKA; circ. 30,288 (weekdays), 30,816 (Sat.).

Mikkeli

Länsi-Savo: Teollisuuskatu 2–6, 50130 Mikkeli; POB 6, 50101 Mikkeli; tel. (15) 3501; fax (15) 3503337; e-mail asiakaspalvelu@lansi-savo.fi; internet www.lansi-savo.fi; independent; Man. Dir JUKKA TIKKA; Editor-in-Chief TAPIO HONKAMAA; circ. 25,018.

Oulu

Kaleva: Lekatie 1, 90140 Oulu; POB 170, 90401 Oulu; tel. (8) 5377111; fax (8) 5377206; e-mail kaleva@kaleva.fi; internet www.kaleva.fi; f. 1899; independent; Man. Dir TAISTO RISKI; Editor-in-Chief MARKKU MANTILA; circ. 78,216 (weekdays), 80,324 (weekend).

Pori

Satakunnan Kansa: Pohjoisranta 11E, POB 58, 28100 Pori; tel. (10) 665132; fax (10) 6658330; e-mail sk.toimitus@satakunnankansa.fi; internet www.satakunnankansa.fi; f. 1873; independent; Editor-in-Chief PETRI HAKALA; circ. 49,989.

Rovaniemi

Lapin Kansa: Veitikantie 2–8, 96100 Rovaniemi; tel. (10) 665022; fax (10) 6657720; e-mail lktoimitus@lapinkansa.fi; internet www.lapinkansa.fi; f. 1928; independent; Man. Dir JUHA RUOTSALAINEN; Editor-in-Chief ANTTI KOKKONEN; circ. 32,691 (weekdays), 32,887 (Sat.).

Salo

Salon Seudun Sanomat: Örninkatu 14, POB 117, 24101 Salo; tel. (2) 77021; fax (2) 7702200; e-mail jarmo.vahasilta@sss.fi; internet www.sss.fi; independent; Man. Dir KIRSTI KIRJONEN; Editor-in-Chief JUKKA HOLMBERG; circ. 21,828.

Savonlinna

Itä-Savo: Olavinkatu 60, POB 101, 57101 Savonlinna; tel. (15) 3503400; fax (15) 3503444; e-mail asiakaspalvelu@ita-savo.fi; internet www.ita-savo.fi; Man. Dir JUHA PELKONEN; Editor-in-Chief TUOMO YLI-HUTTALA; circ. 16,674.

Seinäjoki

Ilkka: Koulukatu 10, 60100 Seinäjoki; POB 60, 60101 Seinäjoki; tel. (6) 2477830; fax (6) 4186500; e-mail ilkka.toimitus@ilkka.fi; internet www.ilkka.fi; f. 1906; independent; Man. Dir MATTI KORKIATUPA; Editor-in-Chief MATTI KALLIOKOSKI; circ. 53,768.

Tampere

Aamulehti: Itäinenkatu 11, 33210 Tampere; tel. (10) 665111; fax (10) 6653140; e-mail matti.apunen@aamulehti.fi; internet www.aamulehti.fi; f. 1881; Editor JOUKO JOKINEN; circ. 131,539.

Turku

Turun Sanomat: Länsikaari 15, POB 95, 20101 Turku; tel. (2) 2693297; fax (2) 2693274; e-mail ts.toimitus@ts-group.fi; internet www.turunsanomat.fi; f. 1904; independent; Man. Dir MIKKO KETONEN; Editors-in-Chief KARI VAINIO, RIITTA MONTO; circ. 107,119.

Tuusula

Keski-Uusimaa: Klaavolantie 5, POB 52, 04301 Tuusula; tel. (9) 273000; fax (9) 27300205; e-mail toimitus@keskiuusimaa.fi; internet www.keskiuusimaa.fi; independent; Man. Dir JORMA HÄMÄLÄINEN; Editor-in-Chief PENTTI KIISKI; circ. 20,444.

Vaasa

Pohjalainen: Hietasaarenkatu 19, 65100 Vaasa; POB 37, 65101 Vaasa; tel. (6) 3249111; fax (6) 3249355; e-mail toimitus@pohjalainen.fi; internet www.pohjalainen.fi; f. 1903; independent; Man. Dir MATTI KORKIATUPA; Editor KALLE HEISKANEN; circ. 25,517.

Vasabladet: Hietasaarenkatu 20, POB 52, 65101 Vaasa; tel. (6) 3260211; fax (6) 3129003; e-mail nyheter@vasabladet.fi; internet www.vasabladet.fi; f. 1856; Swedish-language; liberal independent; Man. Dir JENS LILLSUNDE; Editor-in-Chief CAMILLA BERGGREN; circ. 21,529.

PRINCIPAL PERIODICALS

7 päivää: Pursimiehenkatu 29–31A, 00150 Helsinki; POB 124, 00151 Helsinki; tel. (9) 177777; fax (9) 177477; e-mail toimitus@seiska.fi; internet www.seiska.fi; f. 1992; weekly; television and radio; Editor-in-Chief EEVA-HELENA JOKITAIPALE; circ. 224,047.

Ahjo: Hakaniemenranta 1, POB 107, 00531 Helsinki; tel. (20) 774001; fax (20) 7741240; e-mail metalli.posti@metalliliitto.fi; internet www.metalliliitto.fi; 16 a year; for metal industry employees; Editor-in-Chief HEIKKI PISKONEN; circ. 173,000.

Aku Ankka (Donald Duck): Lapinmäentie 1, 00350 Helsinki; POB 100, 00040 Helsinki; tel. (9) 1201; fax (9) 1205569; e-mail asiakaspalvelu@sanomamagazines.fi; internet www.akuankka.fi; f. 1951; weekly; children's; Editor-in-Chief JUKKA HEISKANEN; circ. 317,529.

Apu: Hitsaajankatu 10, 00081 Helsinki; tel. (9) 75961; fax (9) 75983101; e-mail matti.saari@apu.fi; internet www.apu.fi; f. 1933; weekly; family journal; Editor-in-Chief MATTI SAARI; circ. 184,212.

Avotakka: Risto Rytintie 33, 00081 A-lehdet, Helsinki; tel. (9) 75961; fax (9) 75983110; e-mail soili.ukkola@a-lehdet.fi; internet www.avotakka.fi; f. 1967; monthly; interior decoration; Editor-in-Chief SOILI UKKOLA; circ. 81,271.

Diabetes: Kirjoniementie 15, 33680 Tampere; tel. (3) 2860111; fax (3) 3600462; e-mail diabetesliitto@diabetes.fi; internet www.diabetes.fi; f. 1949; 10 a year; health; publ. by Finnish Diabetes Asscn; Editor-in-Chief HEIKKI HAKALA; circ. 61,292.

Eeva: Risto Rytintie 33, 00081 A-lehdet, Helsinki; tel. (9) 75961; fax (9) 786858; e-mail eeva@a-lehdet.fi; internet www.eeva.fi; f. 1933; monthly; women's; Editor-in-Chief LIISA JÄPPINEN; circ.96,326.

Erä: Maistraatinportti 1, 00015 Kuvalehdet, Helsinki; tel. (9) 156665; fax (9) 1566511; e-mail sepp.suuronen@kuvalehdet.fi; internet www.eralehti.fi; monthly; fishing and outdoor leisure; Editor SEPPO SUURONEN; circ. 46,352.

ET-lehti: Lapinmäentie 1, 00350 Helsinki; POB 100, 00040 Sanoma Magazines; tel. (9) 1201; fax (9) 1205428; e-mail kaisa.larmela@helsinkimedia.fi; internet www.et-lehti.fi; monthly; over-50s magazine; Editor-in-Chief MAIJA TOPPILA; circ. 235,914.

Gloria: Lapinmäentie 1, 00350 Helsinki; POB 100, 00040 Sanoma Magazines; tel. (9) 1201; fax (9) 1205427; e-mail gloria@sanomamagazines.fi; internet www.gloria.fi; monthly; women's; Editor-in-Chief SAMI SYKKÖ; circ. 54,144.

Hevosurheilu: Tulkinkuja 3, 02650 Espoo; tel. (20) 7605300; fax (20) 7605390; e-mail hevosurheilu@hevosurheilulehti.fi; internet www.hippos.fi/hippos/hevosurheilu_lehti; independent; horse racing; Editor-in-Chief JORMA KEMILÄINEN; circ. 25,494.

Hymy: Maistraatinportti 1, 00015 Kuvalehdet, Helsinki; tel. (9) 156665; fax (9) 1566511; e-mail esko.tulusto@kuvalehdet.fi; internet www.hymy.fi; monthly; family journal; Editor SAMI LOTILA; circ. 91,111.

Hyvä Terveys: Lapinmäentie 1, 00350 Helsinki; POB 100, 00040 Sanoma Magazines; tel. (9) 1201; fax (9) 1205456; e-mail hyva.terveys@sanomamagazines.fi; internet www.hyvaterveys.fi; 15 a year; health; Editor-in-Chief SATU VASANTOLA; circ. 132,478.

IT-Invalidityö: Mannerheimintie 107, 00280 Helsinki; tel. (9) 613191; fax (9) 1461443; e-mail fmd@invalidiliitto.fi; internet www.invalidiliitto.fi/portal/fi; 12 a year; for handicapped people; Editor-in-Chief SINIKKA RANTALA; circ. 32,141.

Kaksplus: Maistraatinportti 1, 00015 Kuvalehdet; tel. (9) 1566591; fax (9) 1566550; e-mail kaksplus@kuvalehdet.fi; internet kaksplus.fi; f. 1969; monthly; for families with young children; Editor-in-Chief JAANA SARKKI; circ. 32,153.

Kansan Uutiset: Vilhonvuorenkatu 11C 7, 00500 Helsinki; POB 64, 00501 Helsinki; tel. (9) 759601; fax (9) 75960319; e-mail ku@kansanuutiset.fi; internet www.kansanuutiset.fi; f. 1957; organ of the Left Alliance; Editor-in-Chief JANNE MÄKINEN; circ. 13,616.

Katso: Pursimiehenkatu 29–31A, 00150 Helsinki; POB 124, 00151 Helsinki; tel. (9) 86217000; fax (9) 86217177; e-mail asiakaspalvelu@katso.fi; internet www.katso.fi; f. 1960; weekly; TV, radio, film and video; Editor-in-Chief EEVA-HELENA JOKITAIPALE; circ. 34,187.

Kauneus ja terveys: Risto Rytintie 33, 00081 A-lehdet, Helsinki; tel. (9) 75961; fax (9) 75983106; e-mail asiakaspalvelu@a-lehdet.fi; internet www.kauneusjaterveys.fi; monthly; health and beauty; Editor TITTA KIURU; circ. 73,290.

Kirkko ja kaupunki: POB 279, Hietalahdenranta 13, 00181 Helsinki; tel. (9) 0207542255; fax (9) 0207542343; e-mail kirkkojakaupunki@kotimaa.fi; internet www.kirkkojakaupunki.fi; weekly; church and community; Editor-in-Chief SEPPO SIMOLA; circ. 203,279.

Kodin Kuvalehti: Lapinmäentie 1, 00350 Helsinki; POB 100, 00040 Helsinki; tel. (9) 1201; fax (9) 1205468; e-mail kodin.kuvalehti@sanomamagazines.fi; internet www.kodinkuvalehti.fi; fortnightly; family magazine; Editor LEENA KARO; circ. 177,714.

Kotilääkäri: Maistraatinportti 1, 00015 Kuvalehdet, Helsinki; tel. (9) 15661; fax (9) 145650; e-mail kotilaakari@kuvalehdet.fi; internet www.kotilaakari.fi; f. 1889; monthly; health and beauty; Editor-in-Chief MARJATTA LEINO; circ. 46,205.

Kotiliesi: Maistraatinportti 1, 00015 Kuvalehdet, Helsinki; tel. (9) 156665; fax (9) 1566511; internet www.kotiliesi.fi; f. 1922; fortnightly; women's; Editor-in-Chief LEENI PELTONEN; circ. 140,297.

Kotivinkki: Ruoholahdenkatu 21, 00180 Helsinki; tel. (9) 773951; fax (9) 77395399; internet www.kotivinkki.fi; monthly; women's; Editor-in-Chief OUTI GYLDÉN; circ. 101,512.

Maaseudun Tulevaisuus (The Rural Future): Simonkatu 6, POB 440, 00100 Helsinki; tel. (9) 204132100; fax (9) 204132370; e-mail toimitus@maaseuduntulevaisuus.fi; internet www.maaseuduntulevaisuus.fi; f. 1916; independent; Man. Dir HEIKKI LAURINEN; Editor-in-Chief LAURI KONTRO; circ. 83,158 (2010).

Me Naiset: POB 100, 00040 Helsinki; Lapinmäentie 1, 00350 Helsinki; tel. (9) 1201; fax (9) 1205414; e-mail menaiset@sanomamagazines.fi; internet www.menaiset.fi; f. 1952; weekly; women's; Editor MARJO VUORINEN; circ. 142,931.

Metsälehti: Soidinkuja 4, 00700 Helsinki; tel. (20) 7729121; fax (20) 7729139; e-mail outi.karemaa@metsakustannus.fi; internet www.metsakustannus.fi; f. 1933; fortnightly; forestry; owned by the

Forestry Development Centre Tapio; Editor-in-Chief Eliisa Kallioniemi; circ. 37,854.

MikroBitti: Lapinmäentie 1, 00350 Helsinki; POB 100, 00040 Sanoma Magazine; tel. (9) 1201; fax (9) 1205456; e-mail otto@mikrobitti.fi; internet www.mbnet.fi; f. 1984; Editor-in-Chief Otto Aalto; circ. 88,308.

MikroPC: Annankatu 34–36B, 00100 Helsinki; POB 920, 00101 Helsinki; tel. (20) 44240; e-mail asiakaspalvelu@talentum.com; internet mikropc.net; 12 a year; computers; Editor-in-Chief Kauko Ollila; circ. 30,122.

Partio: Töölönkatu 55, 00250 Helsinki; tel. (9) 88651100; fax (9) 88651199; e-mail info@partio.fi; internet www.partio.fi; 6 a year; the Scout movement; Editor Minna Helle; circ. 44,866.

Pellervo: POB 77, Simonkatu 6, 00101 Helsinki; tel. (9) 4767501; fax (9) 6948845; e-mail toimisto@pellervo.fi; internet www.pellervo.fi; f. 1899; monthly; agricultural and co-operative, home and country life journal; organ of the Confederation of Finnish Co-operatives; Editor-in-Chief Teemu Pakarinen; circ. 31,961.

PerusSuomalainen: Mannerheimintie 40B 56, 00100 Helsinki; tel. (20) 7430800; fax (20) 7430801; e-mail peruss@perussuomalaiset.fi; internet www.perussuomalaiset.fi; f. 1996; 12 a year; organ of the Perussuomalaiset/Sannfinländarna (PS—True Finns); Editor Harry Lindell; circ. 100,000.

Pirkka: POB 410, 00811 Helsinki; tel. (9) 42427330; internet www.pirkka.fi; 10 a year; Swedish; Editor-in-Chief Minna Järvenpää; circ. 1,720,139.

Reserviläinen: Döbelninkatu 2, 00260 Helsinki; tel. (9) 40562016; fax (9) 40562096; e-mail toimitus@reservilainen.fi; internet www.reservilainen.fi; 8 a year; military; Editor Mirva Brola; circ. 69,000.

Sähköviesti/Elbladet: Fredrikinkatu 51–53B, POB 100, 00101 Helsinki; tel. (9) 530520; fax (9) 53052900; e-mail ari.vesa@energia.fi; internet www.energiaviesti.fi; f. 1939; quarterly; publ. by Finnish Energy Industries; Editor-in-Chief Ari J. Vesa; circ. 601,387.

Seura: Maistraatinportti 1, 00015 Kuvalehdet; tel. (9) 15661; fax (9) 145650; e-mail seura@kuvalehdet.fi; internet www.seura.fi; f. 1934; weekly; family journal; Editor-in-Chief Saija Hakoniemi; circ. 180,779.

STTK—lehti: POB 421, 00101 Helsinki; tel. (9) 131521; fax (9) 652367; e-mail marja-liisa.rajakangas@sttk.fi; internet www.sttk.fi; 8 a year; organ of STTK (Finnish Confed. of Professionals); Editor-in-Chief Marja-Liisa Rajakangas; circ. 30,000.

Suomen Kuvalehti: Maistraatinportti 1, 00240 Helsinki; tel. (9) 15661; fax (9) 1566212; e-mail suomen.kuvalehti@kuvalehdet.fi; internet www.suomenkuvalehti.fi; f. 1916; weekly; illustrated news; Editor-in-Chief Tapani Ruokanen; circ. 96,791.

Suosikki: Maistraatinportti 1, 00240 Helsinki; tel. (9) 15661; fax (9) 145650; e-mail suosikki@kuvalehdet.fi; internet www.suosikki.fi; f. 1961; owned by Yhtyneet Kuvalehdet Oy; monthly; youth magazine, music, films, fashion; Editor-in-Chief Ville Kormilainen; circ. 31,760.

Suuri Käsityölehti: Lapinmäentie 1, 00350 Helsinki; POB 100, 00040 Helsinki; tel. (9) 1201; fax (9) 1205352; e-mail suuri.kasityolehti@sanomamagazines.fi; internet www.suurikasityo.fi; f. 1974; monthly; needlework, knitting and dressmaking magazine; Editor-in-Chief Heidi Laaksonen; circ. 67,238.

Talouselämä: Annankatu 34–36B, 00100 Helsinki; POB 920, 00101 Helsinki; tel. (9) 204424390; fax (9) 204424108; e-mail te@talentum.fi; internet www.talouselama.fi; f. 1938; 43 a year; economy, business; Man. Dir Juha Blomster; Editor-in-Chief Reijo Ruokanen; circ. 80,101.

Taloustaito: Kalevankatu 4, 00100 Helsinki; tel. (9) 618871; fax (9) 604435; e-mail antti.marttinen@veronmaksajat.fi; internet www.taloustaito.fi; economics and taxation; Editor-in-Chief Anti Marttinen; circ. 236,362.

Tieteen Kuvalehti: Siltasaarenkatu 18–20A, 00530 Helsinki; tel. (20) 5637608; internet tieku.fi; f. 1986; every 3 weeks; science, nature, technology; publ. by Bonnier Publications Int; Editor Jens Henneberg; circ. 47,216.

Tekniikan Maailma: Maistraatinportti 1, 00240 Helsinki; tel. (9) 15661; fax (9) 1566511; e-mail tekniikan.maailma@kuvalehdet.fi; internet www.tekniikanmaailma.fi; f. 1953; 22 a year; motoring, technology, aviation, photography; Editor-in-Chief Velimatti Honkanen; circ. 148,216.

Tekniikka & Talous: Annankatu 34–36B, 00100 Helsinki; POB 920, 00101 Helsinki; tel. (20) 4424100; fax (20) 4424101; e-mail tilpal@talentum.fi; internet www.tekniikkatalous.fi; Editor-in-Chief Timo Tolsa; circ. 95,853.

Tiede: Lapinmäentie 1, 00350 Helsinki; POB 100, 00040 Sanoma Magazines; tel. (9) 1201; e-mail tiede@sanomamagazines.fi; internet www.tiede.fi; f. 1980; popular science; Editor-in-Chief Jukka Ruukki; circ. 60,635.

Trendi: Ruoholahdenkatu 21, 00180 Helsinki; tel. (9) 773951; fax (9) 77395399; e-mail trendi.toimitus@forma.fi; internet www.trendi.fi; 12 a year; women's lifestyle; Editor-in-Chief Elina Tanskanen; circ. 44,899.

Tuulilasi: Risto Rytintie 33, 00081 A-lehdet, Helsinki; tel. (9) 75961; fax (9) 75983103; e-mail tuulilasi@a-lehdet.fi; internet www.tuulilasi.fi; f. 1963; 16 a year; motoring; Editor-in-Chief Lauri Larmela; circ. 80,071.

Työ Terveys Turvallisuus: Topeliuksenkatu 41A, 00250 Helsinki; tel. (30) 4741; fax (30) 4742478; e-mail info-ttt@ttl.fi; internet www.ttl.fi; f. 1971; 6 a year; occupational safety and health; Editor-in-Chief Harri Vainio; circ. 60,008.

Valitut Palat: Pitäjänmäentie 14, 00380 Helsinki; POB 106, 00381 Helsinki; tel. (9) 503441; fax (9) 5034499; e-mail asiakaspalvelu@valitutpalat.fi; internet www.valitutpalat.fi; monthly; Finnish Reader's Digest; Editor-in-Chief Ilkka Virtanen; circ. 197,287.

Veikkaaja: Töölönlahdenkatu 2, POB 45, 00089 Helsinki; tel. (9) 1221; fax (9) 1223419; e-mail veikkaaja@iltasanomat.fi; internet www.veikkaaja.fi; Editor-in-Chief Tapio Sadeoja; circ. 49,891.

Voi hyvin: Risto Rytintie 33, 00081 A-lehdet, Helsinki; tel. (9) 75961; fax (9) 75983109; e-mail voihyvin@a-lehdet.fi; internet www.voihyvin.fi; f. 1986; 8 a year; health, well-being; Editor-in-Chief Krista Launonen; circ. 43,773.

Yhteishyvä: Fleminginkatu 34, 00510 Helsinki; tel. (9) 1882621; fax (9) 1882626; e-mail kirsi.ervola@sok.fi; internet www.yhteishyva.fi; f. 1905; monthly; free to members of co-operative group; Editor-in-Chief Kirsi Ervola; circ. 1,677,754.

NEWS AGENCY

Oy Suomen Tietotoimisto (STT): Albertinkatu 33, 00180 Helsinki; POB 550, 00101 Helsinki; tel. (9) 695811; fax (9) 69581335; e-mail toimitus@stt.fi; internet www.stt.fi; f. 1887; 8 regional bureaux; independent national agency distributing domestic and international news in Finnish and Swedish; CEO and Editor-in-Chief Mika Pettersson.

PRESS ASSOCIATIONS

Aikakauslehtien Liitto (Finnish Periodical Publishers' Association): Lönnrotinkatu 11A, POB 267, 00121 Helsinki; tel. (9) 22877280; fax (9) 603478; e-mail toimisto@aikakauslehdet.fi; internet www.aikakauslehdet.fi; f. 1946; aims to further the interests of publishers of magazines and periodicals, to encourage co-operation between publishers, and to improve standards; Chair. Raili Mäkinen.

Sanomalehtien Liitto—Tidningarnas Förbund (Finnish Newspapers Association): Lönnrotinkatu 11, POB 415, 2nd Floor, 00120 Helsinki; tel. (9) 22877300; fax (9) 607989; e-mail info@sanomalehdet.fi; internet www.sanomalehdet.fi; f. 1908; represents newspapers' interests; 188 mem. newspapers; Exec. Dir Jukka Holmberg.

Suomen Journalistiliitto—Finlands Journalistförbund r.y. (Union of Journalists): Hietalahdenkatu 2B 22, POB 252, 00180 Helsinki; tel. (9) 6122330; fax (9) 605396; e-mail info@journalistiliitto.fi; internet www.journalistiliitto.fi; f. 1921; 15,000 mems; Pres. Arto Nieminen; Sec.-Gen. Eila Hyppönen.

Publishers

Alfamer Oy: Hämeentie 109–111, 00550 Helsinki; tel. (9) 7742810; fax (9) 77428111; e-mail alfamer@alfamer.fi; internet www.alfamer.fi; motor sports, militaria; Man. Dir Esko Vartiainen.

Amino-Kustannus: Hämeenkatu 25B, POB 55, 33201 Tampere; tel. (50) 3389865; e-mail books@aminokustannus.fi; internet www.aminokustannus.fi; non-fiction, children's; Man. Tuula Laamanen.

Art House Oy: Bulevardi 19C, 00120 Helsinki; tel. (9) 6940752; fax (9) 6933762; e-mail myynti@arthouse.fi; internet www.arthouse.fi; f. 1975; Finnish and foreign fiction, non-fiction, popular science, horror, fantasy, science fiction, detective fiction; Publr Paavo Haavikko.

Basam Books Oy: Hämeentie 155A 6, POB 42, 00561 Helsinki; tel. and fax (9) 75793839; e-mail info@basambooks.fi; internet www.basambooks.fi; f. 1993; independent; literary fiction, poetry, non-fiction; Publr Batu Samaletdin.

Gummerus Kustannus Oy: Arkadiankatu 23B, POB 749, 00101 Helsinki; tel. (10) 6836200; fax (9) 58430200; e-mail info@gummerus.fi; internet www.gummerus.fi; f. 1872; fiction, non-fiction, reference, dictionaries, languages; independent; Man. Dir Ilkka Kylmälä.

Karisto Oy: Paroistentie 2, POB 102, 13101 Hämeenlinna; tel. (3) 63151; fax (3) 6161565; e-mail kustannusliike@karisto.fi; internet www.karisto.fi; f. 1900; non-fiction and fiction, printing; Man. Dir Mika Kotilainen.

Kirjapaja: Hietalahdenranta 13, POB 279, 00181 Helsinki; tel. (20) 7542000; fax (20) 7542341; e-mail mira.pitkanen@kirjapaja.fi; internet www.kirjapaja.fi; f. 1942; Christian literature, general fiction, non-fiction, reference, juvenile; Vice-Pres ANNE-MARIA LANTTA.

Kustannus-Mäkelä Oy: POB 14, 03601 Karkkila; tel. (9) 2257995; fax (9) 2257660; e-mail makela@kustannusmakela.fi; internet www.kustannusmakela.fi; f. 1971; juvenile, fiction; Man. Dir ORVO MÄKELÄ.

Oy Like Kustannus Ltd: Uudenmaankatu 10, 00120 Helsinki; tel. (9) 6229970; fax (9) 1351372; e-mail like@like.fi; internet www.like.fi; f. 1987; film literature, fiction, non-fiction, comics; Man. Dir PÄIVI ISOSAARI.

Maahenki Oy: Eerikinkatu 28, 00180 Helsinki; tel. (9) 7512020; fax (9) 75120211; e-mail maahenki@msl.fi; internet www.maahenki.fi; art, nature; Man. Dir ULLA SARVIALA.

Otava Publishing Co Ltd: Uudenmaankatu 10, 00120 Helsinki; tel. (9) 19961; fax (9) 1996560; e-mail otava@otava.fi; internet www.otava.fi; f. 1890; part of Otava-United Magazines Group Ltd; non-fiction, fiction, children's and textbooks; Man. Dir PASI VAINIO.

Schildts Förlags Ab: Georgsgatan 18, 00120 Helsinki; tel. (9) 8870400; fax (9) 8043257; e-mail schildts@schildts.fi; internet www.schildts.fi; f. 1913; subjects mainly in Swedish; Man. Dir JOHAN JOHNSON.

Söderströms Förlag: Georgsgatan 29A, POB 870, 00101 Helsinki; tel. (9) 68418620; fax (9) 68418610; e-mail soderstrom@soderstrom.fi; internet www.soderstrom.fi; f. 1891; all subjects in Swedish only; Man. Dir BARBRO TEIR.

Suomalaisen Kirjallisuuden Seura, SKS (Finnish Literature Society): Mariankatu 3, 00170 Helsinki; tel. (20) 1131231; fax (9) 13123220; e-mail sks@finlit.fi; internet www.finlit.fi/books; f. 1831; Finnish language and literature, linguistics, folklore, cultural studies and history; Publishing Dir PÄIVI VALLISAARI.

Tammi Publishers: Korkeavuorenkatu 37, 00130 Helsinki; tel. (9) 6937621; fax (9) 69376270; e-mail tammi@tammi.fi; internet www.tammi.fi; f. 1943; fiction, general, non-fiction, children's, juvenile, textbooks, educational materials, audio books; owned by Bonnier AB; Pres. MARIA CURMAN.

Weilin & Göös Oy: Bulevardi 12, 00120 Helsinki; tel. (9) 43771; fax (9) 4377270; e-mail asiakaspalvelu@wg.fi; internet www.wg.fi; f. 1872; non-fiction, encyclopaedias; Dir JAANA KORPI.

Werner Söderström Corpn (WSOY): POB 222, 00121 Helsinki; Bulevardi 12, 00120 Helsinki; tel. (9) 61681; fax (9) 61683560; internet www.wsoy.fi; f. 1878; fiction and non-fiction, science, juvenile, textbooks, reference, comics, the printing industry; Pres. ANNA BAIJARS.

PUBLISHERS' ASSOCIATION

Suomen Kustannusyhdistys (Finnish Book Publishers' Association): Lönnrotinkatu 11A, POB 177, 00121 Helsinki; tel. (9) 22877250; fax (9) 6121226; e-mail sirkku.palomaki@kustantajat.fi; internet www.kustantajat.fi; f. 1858; Pres. VELI-PEKKA ELONEN; Dir SAKARI LAIHO; 100 mems.

Broadcasting and Communications

REGULATORY AUTHORITY

Finnish Communications Regulatory Authority (FICORA): Itämerenkatu 3A, POB 313, 00181 Helsinki; tel. (9) 69661; fax (9) 6966410; e-mail info@ficora.fi; internet www.ficora.fi; f. 1988; affiliated to Ministry of Transport and Communications; CEO ASTA SIHVONEN-PUNKKA.

TELECOMMUNICATIONS

DNA Ltd: Ansatie 6A B, POB 41, 01741 Vantaa; tel. (44) 0440; internet www.dna.fi; f. 2007; offers mobile communications services through DNA Finland Ltd and fixed-network broadband and television services through DNA Services Ltd; Chair. LEINO JARMO; CEO RIITTA TIURANIEMI.

Elisa Corpn: Ratavartijankatu 5, Helsinki; POB 1, 00061 Elisa; tel. (10) 26000; fax (10) 26060; internet www.elisa.com; Chair. RISTO SIILASMAA; CEO VELI-MATTI MATTILA.

Finnet International Ltd: Sinebrychoffinkatu 11, POB 949, 00101 Helsinki; tel. (9) 315315; fax (9) 605531; e-mail fl@finnet.fi; internet www.finnet.fi; Chair. RISTO LINTURI.

Telecon Ltd: POB 55, 02231 Espoo; tel. (40) 9526900; e-mail info@telecon.fi; internet www.telecon.fi; f. 1980; Man. Dir JOUKO JOKINEN.

TeliaSonera Finland Oyj: Teollisuuskatu 15, Helsinki; POB 220, 00051 Sonera; tel. (20) 401; fax (20) 4069100; e-mail yritysasiakaspalvelu@sonera.com; internet www.teliasonera.fi; f. 2002 by merger of Telia AB (Sweden) and Sonera Ltd; Chair. ANDERS NARVINGER; Pres. and CEO LARS NYBERG.

BROADCASTING

Radio

The first commercial radio stations were introduced in 1985 and stations proliferated rapidly to reach 59 by 1990. The economic recession of the early 1990s led to the collapse of many commercial stations. However, the industry began to recover in the late 1990s, notably with the launch of the first national commercial radio station, Radio Nova, in May 1997. In 1999 RAB Finland was established to promote and develop the Finnish private radio industry by providing extensive information services free of charge to media planners, buyers and advertisers. By 2008 the number of commercial radio stations had risen again to reach 57.

In May 1999 the first part of the national Digital Audio Broadcast (DAB) network was launched by Yleisradio (YLE—Finnish Broadcasting Company) with 10 transmitters (rising to 11 in 2001), covering 2m. people (approximately 40% of the population). The Finnish DAB transmitter network was closed down in 2005; YLE continued its digital transmissions through the Digital Video Broadcasting (DVB) television network.

Yleisradio Oy (YLE) (Finnish Broadcasting Company): YLE Centre, Radiokatu 5, 00024 Helsinki; tel. (9) 14801; fax (9) 14803216; e-mail fbc@yle.fi; internet www.yle.fi; f. 1926; 99.9% state-owned, with management appointed by the Administrative Council; Chair. KARI NEILIMO; Dir-Gen. LAURI KIVINEN.

YLE Radio 1 (Radio Ylen Ykkönen): POB 6, 00024 Helsinki; 24-hour arts and culture in Finnish; Dir HEIKKI PELTONEN.

YLE R2 (YleX): POB 17, 00024 Helsinki; tel. (9) 14801; fax (9) 1482650; e-mail satu.keto-kantele@yle.fi; internet ylex.fi; f. 2003; 24-hour popular culture for young people in Finnish; Dir SATU KETO-KANTELE.

YLE R3 (Radio Suomi): 24-hour news, current affairs, sport, regional programmes in Finnish; Dir MARJA KESKITALO.

YLE R4 (Radio Extrem): Swedish-language channel for young people; Dir (vacant).

YLE R5 (Radio Vega): POB 62, 00024 Rundradion; tel. (9) 14801; e-mail mika.kosunen@yle.fi; internet www.yle.fi/vega; news, current affairs, art, culture and regional programmes in Swedish; Dir MIKA KOSUNEN.

YLE Radio Finland: POB 78, 00024 Yleisradio; tel. (9) 14804320; fax (9) 14801169; e-mail rfinland@yle.fi; internet www.yle.fi/rfinland; broadcasts in Finnish, Swedish, English, German, French, Russian and Classical Latin.

YLE Sámi Radio: POB 38, 99871 Inari; tel. (16) 6757500; fax (16) 6757501; e-mail sami.radio@yle.fi; internet www.yle.fi/samiradio; Sámi-language network covering northern Lapland.

Digita Oy: Jämsänkatu 2, 00520 Helsinki; POB 135, 00521 Helsinki; tel. (20) 411711; fax (20) 4117234; e-mail info@digita.fi; internet www.digita.fi; f. 1999; operates the radio and television broadcasting network covering the whole of Finland; 36 main broadcasting stations and 151 substations; Man. Dir SIRPA OJALA.

Groove FM: Pursimiehenkatu 29–31C, 00150 Helsinki; tel. (20) 7768360; e-mail juha.kakkuri@groovefm.fi; internet www.groovefm.fi; Station Dir JUHA KAKKURI.

Iskelmä: Tallberginkatu 1C, 00180 Helsinki; tel. (20) 7474000; e-mail erkka.jaakkola@sbs.fi; internet www.iskelma.fi; Media Dir JUHA OURILA.

NRJ: Kiviaidankatu 2I, 00210 Helsinki; tel. (9) 681900; fax (9) 68190102; e-mail marko.lintussari@nrj.fi; internet www.nrj.fi; Man. Dir ANTTI PAKKALA.

RadioMedia: Lönnrotinkatu 11A, POB 312, 00121 Helsinki; tel. (9) 22877340; fax (9) 648221; e-mail info@radiomedia.fi; internet www.radiomedia.fi; f. 1999; promotes Finnish private radio industry by providing extensive information services free of charge; Man. Dir STEFAN MÖLLER.

Radio Nova: Ilmalankatu 2C, POB 123, 00241 Helsinki; tel. (9) 88488700; fax (9) 88488720; e-mail toimitus@radionova.fi; internet www.radionova.fi; largest commercial radio station; 74% owned by Alma Media; Marketing Dir PÄIVI NURMESNIEMI.

Radio SuomiPOP: Pursimiehenkatu 29–31C, 00150 Helsinki; tel. (20) 7768360; e-mail studio@radiosuomipop.fi; internet www.radiosuomipop.fi; Station Dir JUHA KAKKURI.

The Voice: Tallberginkatu 1C, 00180 Helsinki; tel. (20) 7474000; e-mail toimitus@voice.fi; internet www.voice.fi; Sales Man. MIKA SALLINEN.

Television

Digital Video Broadcasting (DVB) began in Finland in 2001. Analogue transmission networks were closed down from 1 September 2007.

Yleisradio (YLE): (see above) operates 5 national channels: TV 1, TV 2, YLE FST (in Swedish), TV Finland (digital satellite channel broadcast in Nordic countries and elsewhere in Europe) and YLE Teema (a specialized channel for culture, education and science)

YLE/TV 1: POB 97, 00024 Yleisradio; tel. (9) 14801; fax (9) 14803424; e-mail riitta.pihlajamaki@yle.fi; internet www.yle.fi/tv1; f. 1957; programmes in Finnish; Channel Controller RIITTA PIHLAJAMÄKI.

YLE TV2: POB 196, 33101 Tampere; tel. (3) 3456111; fax (3) 3456892; e-mail ilkka.saari@yle.fi; internet www.yle.fi/tv2; f. 1964; programmes in Finnish and Swedish; Channel Controller ILKKA SAARI.

Canal Digital Finland Oy: POB 866, 33101 Tampere; tel. (20) 7699000; fax (20) 7699006; e-mail asiakaspalvelu@canaldigital.fi; internet www.canaldigital.fi; f. 1998; subsidiary of Telenor ASA (Norway).

MTV Finland: Ilmalantori 2, Helsinki; tel. (9) 6224176; e-mail palaute@mtv3.fi; internet www.mtv3.fi; f. 1957; independent nationwide commercial television company comprising 9 channels: MTV3 and Subtv, as well as 7 subscription channels (MTV3 MAX, MTV3 Fakta, MTV Ava, MTV3 Sarja, MTV3 Scifi, Sub Juniori and Sub Leffa); became part of Alma Media Corpn in 1998; acquired by Bonnier (Sweden) in 2005; Pres. and CEO PEKKA KARHUVAARA.

Nelonen Media (Sanoma Entertainment Finland Oy): POB 350, 00151 Helsinki; Tehtaankatu 27–29D, 00150 Helsinki; tel. (9) 45451; fax (9) 4545400; e-mail hans.edin@nelonen.fi; internet www.nelonenmedia.fi; f. 1997; fmrly Oy Ruutunelonen Ab; independent commercial television co; part of Sanoma Group; Pres. HANS EDIN.

Finance

The Bank of Finland is the country's central bank and the centre of Finland's monetary and banking system. It functions 'under guarantee and supervision of the Eduskunta (Parliament) and the Bank supervisors delegated by the Eduskunta'.

At the end of 2008 there were a total of 336 banks operating in Finland.

BANKING

(cap. = capital; res = reserves; dep. = deposits; m. = million; brs = branches; amounts in euros)

Supervisory Authority

Financial Supervisory Authority (FIN-FSA): Snellmaninkatu 6, POB 103, 00101 Helsinki; tel. (10) 8315339; fax (10) 8315328; e-mail finanssivalvonta@finanssivalvonta.fi; internet www.finanssivalvonta.fi; f. 2009 to replace the Financial Supervision Authority and the Insurance Supervisory Authority; maintains confidence in the financial markets by supervising the markets and the bodies working within them; Chair. PENTTI HAKKARAINEN; Dir-Gen. ANNELI TUOMINEN.

Central Bank

Suomen Pankki/Finlands Bank (Bank of Finland): Snellmaninaukio, POB 160, 00101 Helsinki; tel. (10) 8311; fax (9) 174872; e-mail info@bof.fi; internet www.bof.fi; f. 1811; Bank of Issue under the guarantee and supervision of the Eduskunta; cap. 841m., res 1,334m., dep. 14,402m. (Dec. 2010); Gov. ERKKI LIIKANEN; 4 brs.

Commercial Banks

Nordea Bank Finland PLC (Nordea Pankki Suomi Oyj): Aleksanterinkatu 36B, 00100 Helsinki; tel. (9) 1651; fax (9) 16554500; internet www.nordea.fi; f. 1995; cap. 2,319m., res 3,448m., dep. 141,223m. (Dec. 2010); CEO CHRISTIAN CLAUSEN; 416 brs.

Sampo Bank PLC: Hiililaiturinkuja 2, Helsinki; POB 1568, 00075 Sampo; tel. (10) 5460000; fax (10) 5462533; e-mail hannu.vuola@sampopankki.fi; internet www.sampopankki.fi; f. 1886 as Postisäästöpankki; name changed as above 2001; owned by Danske Bank (Denmark) (q.v.); cap. 106m., res 271.1m., dep. 18,043.2m. (Dec. 2010); CEO ILKKA HALLAVO; 63 brs.

Co-operative Banks

Association of Finnish Local Co-operative Banks: Yliopistonkatu 7, 00101 Helsinki; tel. (9) 6811700; fax (9) 68117070; internet www.paikallisosuuspankit.fi; f. 1997; central organization of local co-operative banking group, which comprises 42 local co-operatives; cap. 200m., dep. 1,600m., total assets 2,062m. (Dec. 2000); 140 brs.

Pohjola Bank PLC: Teollisuuskatu 1B, 00510 Helsinki; POB 308, 00013 Helsinki; tel. (10) 252011; fax (10) 2522002; internet www.pohjola.com; f. 1902 as Osuuspankkien Keskuspankki Oyj; current name adopted 2008; cap. 428m., res 1,081m., dep. 18,753m. (Dec. 2010); part of OP–Pohjola Group Central Co-operative; Chair. REIJO KARHINEN; Pres. and CEO ERKKI MIKAEL SILVENNOINEN; 677 brs.

Savings Bank

Aktia Bank Plc (Aktia Savings Bank PLC): Mannerheimintie 14, POB 207, 00100 Helsinki; tel. (10) 2475000; fax (10) 2476356; e-mail aktia@aktia.fi; internet www.aktia.fi; f. 1852 as Helsingfors Sparbank; current name adopted 2008; cap. 163m., res 53.7m., dep. 4,811.4m. (Dec. 2010); Chair. DAG WALLGREN; Man. Dir JUSSI LAITINEN; approx. 90 brs.

Mortgage Banks

OP-Asuntoluottopankki (OP Mortgage Bank): POB 308, 00101 Helsinki; tel. (9) 4041; fax (9) 4042620; e-mail iloniemi@pohjola.com; f. 2000; part of OP–Pohjola Group Central Co-operative; Man. Dir LAURI ILONIEMI.

Sampo Asuntoluottopankki (Sampo Housing Loan PLC): Fabianinkatu 27, 00100 Helsinki; tel. (10) 5160100; fax (10) 5160016; internet www.sampo.fi; f. 2000; fmrly Suomen Asuntoluottopankki, renamed as above 2005; part of Sampo Group; Chair. BJÖRN WAHLROOS; Man. Dir and CEO KARI STADIGH; cap. 6m., total assets 25m. (Dec. 2000).

Investment Bank

Nordiska Investeringsbanken (Nordic Investment Bank): Fabianinkatu 34, POB 249, 00171 Helsinki; tel. (10) 618001; fax (10) 6180725; e-mail info@nib.int; internet www.nib.int; f. 1975; owned by Govts of Denmark, Estonia, Finland, Iceland, Latvia, Lithuania, Norway and Sweden; all member countries are represented on the Bd of Dirs by their ministers responsible for finance and the economy; cap. 418.6m., res 1,632.2m., dep. 6,822.2m. (Dec. 2010); Pres. and CEO JOHNNY ÅKERHOLM.

Banking Associations

Finanssialan Keskusliitto r.y. (Federation of Finnish Financial Services): Bulevardi 28, 00120 Helsinki; tel. (20) 7934200; fax (20) 7934202; e-mail fk@fkl.fi; internet www.fkl.fi; f. 2007 by merger of the Finnish Bankers' Association, the Federation of Finnish Insurance Companies, the Employers' Association of Finnish Financial Institutions and the Finnish Finance Houses' Association; Chair. KARI STADIGH; Man. Dir PIIA-NOORA KAUPPI.

Säästöpankkiliitto (Finnish Savings Banks Association): Linnoitustie 9, POB 68, 02601 Espoo; tel. (9) 548051; fax (20) 6029108; e-mail pasi.kamari@saastopankki.fi; internet www.saastopankki.fi; f. 1906; 33 mems; Chair. JUSSI HAKALA; Man. Dir PASI KÄMÄRI; 256 brs.

Suomen Hypoteekkiyhdistys (Mortgage Society of Finland): Yrjönkatu 9A, 2nd Floor, 00120 Helsinki; POB 509, 00101 Helsinki; tel. (9) 228361; fax (9) 647443; e-mail hypo@hypo.fi; internet www.hypo.fi; f. 1860; cap. 36m., total assets 336m. (Dec. 2000); Pres. MATTI INHA.

STOCK EXCHANGE

NASDAQ OMX Helsinki: Fabianinkatu 14, POB 361, 00131 Helsinki; tel. (9) 616671; fax (9) 61667368; e-mail nordicexchange.helsinki@nasdaqomx.com; internet www.nasdaqomx.com; f. 1912 as Helsingin Pörssi; merged with OMX AB (Sweden) in 2003; became part of OMX Nordic Exchange with Copenhagen (Denmark), Reykjavík (Iceland) and Stockholm (Sweden) exchanges in 2006; acquired by NASDAQ Stock Market, Inc (USA) in 2008; Group CEO ROBERT GREIFELD.

INSURANCE

In January 2011 there were 63 insurance companies operating in Finland, 24 of which were branches of foreign insurance companies.

A-Vakuutus Oy (A-Vakuutus Mutual Insurance Co): Lapinmäentie 1, 00350 Helsinki; tel. (10) 253000; fax (10) 2532908; e-mail a-vakuutus@a-vakuutus.fi; internet www.a-vakuutus.fi; non-life; Man. Dir JOUKO PÖLÖNEN.

Eurooppalainen Insurance Co Ltd: Lapinmäentie 1, 00013 Pohjola; tel. (10) 253000; fax (10) 5592205; internet www.eurooppalainen.fi; f. 1922; non-life; part of Pohjola Bank plc; Man. Dir JOUNI AALTONEN.

Garantia Insurance Co Ltd: Salomonkatu 17A, 9th Floor, POB 600, 00101 Helsinki; tel. (20) 7479800; fax (20) 7479801; internet www.garantia.fi; non-life; Man. Dir MIKAEL ENGLUND.

If Vahinkovakuutusyhtiö Oy (If P & C Insurance Ltd): Niittyportti 4, 02200 Espoo; tel. 10191515; fax 105144028; internet www.if.fi; f. 1999; subsidiary of Sampo plc; property and casualty; Chair. KARI STADIGH.

Keskinäinen Eläkevakuutusyhtiö Ilmarinen (Ilmarinen Mutual Pension Insurance Co): Porkkalankatu 1, 00018 Ilmarinen;

tel. (10) 28411; fax (10) 2843445; e-mail info@ilmarinen.fi; internet www.ilmarinen.fi; f. 1961; statutory employment pensions; Man. Dir HARRI SAILAS.

Keskinäinen Eläkevakuutusyhtiö Tapiola (Tapiola Mutual Pension Insurance Co): Revontulentie 7, POB 9, 02010 Tapiola; tel. (9) 4531; internet www.tapiola.fi; Pres. ASMO KALPALA; Man. Dir JUHA-PEKKA HALMEENMÄKI.

Keskinäinen Henkivakuutusosakeyhtiö Suomi (Suomi Mutual Life Assurance Co): Aleksanterinkatu 15B, 00100 Helsinki; POB 1068, 00101 Helsinki; tel. (10) 2530066; fax (10) 2527806; e-mail hvpalvelukeskus@suomi-yhtio.fi; internet www.suomi-yhtio.fi; f. 1890; life insurance; Pres. and CEO JARI SOKKA.

Keskinäinen Henkivakuutusyhtiö Tapiola (Tapiola Mutual Life Assurance Co): 02010 Tapiola; tel. (9) 4531; fax (9) 4532146; internet www.tapiola.fi; Pres. ASMO KALPALA; Man. Dir MINNA KOHMO.

Keskinäinen työeläkevakuutusyhtiö Varma (Varma Mutual Pension Insurance Co): Salmisaarenranta 11, POB 1, 00098 Varma; tel. (10) 2440; fax (10) 2444752; e-mail info@varma.fi; internet www.varma.fi; f. 1998; fmrly Varma-Sampo; Man. Dir MATTI VUORIA.

Keskinäinen Vakuutusyhtiö Fennia (Fennia Mutual Insurance Co): Kansakoulukuja 1, 00100 Helsinki; tel. (10) 5031; fax (10) 5037680; e-mail efasiakas@fennia.fi; internet www.fennia.fi; f. 1882; non-life; Man. Dir ANTII KULJUKKA.

Keskinäinen Vakuutusyhtiö Kaleva (Kaleva Mutual Insurance Co): Bulevardi 56, 00100 Helsinki; POB 347, 00101 Helsinki; tel. (10) 515225; fax (10) 5167501; internet www.kalevavakuutus.fi; f. 1874; Man. Dir MATTI RANTANEN.

Keskinäinen Vakuutusyhtiö Tapiola (Tapiola General Mutual Insurance Co): 02010 Tapiola; tel. (9) 4531; fax (9) 4532146; internet www.tapiola.fi; non-life; Pres. ASMO KALPALA; Man. Dir JUHA-PEKKA HALMEENMÄKI.

Lähivakuutus Keskinäinen Yhtiö (Local Insurance Mutual Co): Lintuvaarantie 2, POB 50, 02601 Espoo; tel. (20) 5222111; fax (20) 5222332; e-mail myynti@lahivakuutus.fi; internet www.lahivakuutus.fi; f. 1917; non-life; Man. Dir PAULIINA HAIJANEN.

Mandatum Life Insurance Co ltd: Bulevardi 56, 00101 Helsinki; tel. (10) 515225; internet www.mandatumlife.fi; f. 1997; subsidiary of Sampo plc; CEO PETRI NIEMISVIRTA.

Nordea Life Assurance Finland: Aleksis Kiven Katu 9, 00020 Helsinki; tel. (9) 16527601; fax (9) 8594622; internet www.nordea.fi/selekta; Man. Dir PEKKA LUUKKANEN.

Palonvara Mutual Insurance Co: Saimaankatu 20, 15140 Lahti; tel. (20) 5226960; fax (20) 5226961; e-mail palvelu@palonvara.fi; internet www.palonvara.fi; f. 1912; non-life; Man. Dir JUKKA HERTTI.

Pohjantähti Keskinäinen Vakuutusyhtiö (Pohjantähti Mutual Insurance Co): Keinusaarentie 2, POB 164, 13101 Hämeenlinna; tel. (20) 7634000; fax (3) 5899890; internet www.pohjantahti.fi; f. 1895; non-life; Pres. and CEO EERO YLÄ-SOININMÄKI.

Spruce Insurance Ltd: POB 330, 00101 Helsinki; tel. 108611; fax 108621197; e-mail jaana.dromberg@kemira.com; f. 1948; non-life; owned by Kemira Oyj; Man. Dir JAANA DROMBERG.

Vahinkovakuutusosakeyhtiö Pohjola (Pohjola Non-Life Insurance Co Ltd): Lapinmäentie 1, 00013 Pohjola; tel. (10) 253000; fax (10) 5592205; internet www.pohjola.fi; f. 1891; non-life; Chair. REIJO KARHINEN; Pres. MIKAEL SILVENNOINEN.

Veritas Eläkevakuutus (Veritas Pension Insurance Co Ltd): Olavintie 2, POB 133, 20101 Turku; tel. (10) 55010; fax (10) 5501690; e-mail veritas@veritas.fi; internet www.veritas.fi; Pres. PETER BOSTRÖM; Man. Dir JAN-ERIK STENMAN.

Insurance Associations

Federation of Accident Insurance Institutions: Bulevardi 28, POB 275, 00121 Helsinki; tel. (9) 680401; fax (9) 68040514; internet www.tvl.fi; f. 1920; publishes *Tapaturmavakuutuslehti* quarterly (circ. 3,300); Man. Dir JUSSI KAUMA.

Finnish Motor Insurers' Centre: Bulevardi 28, 00120 Helsinki; tel. (40) 4504750; fax (40) 4504696; internet www.liikennevakuutuskeskus.fi; f. 1938; Man. Dir ULLA NIKU-KOSKINEN.

Finnish Pension Alliance TELA: Lastenkodinkuja 1, 00180 Helsinki; tel. (10) 6806700; fax (10) 6806706; e-mail tela@tela.fi; internet www.tela.fi; f. 1964; Man. Dir SUVI-ANNE SIIMES.

Nordic Nuclear Insurers: Kalevankatu 18A, 00100 Helsinki; tel. (9) 6803410; fax (9) 68034115; internet www.atompool.com; Man. Dir EERO HOLMA.

Trade and Industry

GOVERNMENT AGENCIES

Finpro: Porkkalankatu 1, POB 358, 00181 Helsinki; tel. (20) 46951; fax (20) 4695200; e-mail info@finpro.fi; internet www.finpro.fi; f. 1919 as Finnish Export Association; Chair. MIKAEL MÄKINEN; Pres. and CEO KARI HÄYRINEN.

Invest in Finland Bureau: Kaivokatu 8, 6th Floor, 00100 Helsinki; tel. (10) 7730300; fax (10) 7730301; e-mail info@investinfinland.fi; internet www.investinfinland.fi; promoting foreign investments to Finland; Chair., Bd of Dirs PAUL PAUKKU; CEO TUOMO AIRAKSINEN.

CHAMBERS OF COMMERCE

Helsingin Seudun Kauppakamari (Helsinki Region Chamber of Commerce): Kalevankatu 12, 00100 Helsinki; tel. (9) 228601; fax (9) 22860228; e-mail kauppakamari@helsinki.chamber.fi; internet www.helsinki.chamber.fi; f. 1917; Man. Dir HEIKKI J. PERÄLÄ; 6,500 mems.

Keskuskauppakamari (Central Chamber of Commerce of Finland): Aleksanterinkatu 17, POB 1000, 00101 Helsinki; tel. (9) 42426200; fax (9) 650303; e-mail keskuskauppakamari@chamber.fi; internet www.keskuskauppakamari.fi; f. 1918; CEO RISTO E. J. PENTTILÄ; 17,911 mems; represents 19 regional chambers of commerce.

INDUSTRIAL AND TRADE ASSOCIATIONS

Betoniteollisuus r.y. (Finnish Concrete Industry Asscn): Unioninkatu 14, POB 11, 00131 Helsinki; tel. (9) 12991; fax (9) 1299291; e-mail jussi.mattila@betoni.com; internet www.betoni.com; f. 1929; Chair. LAURI KIVEKÄS; Man. Dir JUSSI MATTILA; 48 mems.

Kalatalouden Keskusliitto (Federation of Finnish Fisheries Associations): Malmin kauppatie 26, 00700 Helsinki; tel. (9) 6844590; fax (9) 68445959; e-mail kalastus@ahven.net; internet www.ahven.net; f. 1891; Sec. MARKKU MYLLYLÄ; 616,000 mems.

Kesko Oyj (Finnish Retail Specialist): Satamakatu 3, 00016 Helsinki; tel. (10) 5311; fax (9) 174398; internet www.kesko.fi; f. 1941; retailer-owned wholesale corporation, trading in foodstuffs, textiles, shoes, consumer goods, hardware, agricultural and builders' supplies, and machinery; Chair. HEIKKI TAKAMÄKI.

Maa- ja metsataloustuottajain Keskusliitto MTK r.y. (Central Union of Agricultural Producers and Forest Owners): Simonkatu 6, POB 510, 00100 Helsinki; tel. (20) 4131; fax (20) 4132409; e-mail michael.hornborg@mtk.fi; internet www.mtk.fi; f. 1917; Pres. JUHA MARTTILA; Sec.-Gen. ANTTI SAHI; 154,000 mems.

Metsäteollisuus r.y. (Finnish Forest Industries' Federation): POB 336, 00171 Helsinki; Snellmaninkatu 13, 00170 Helsinki; tel. (9) 13261; fax (9) 1324445; e-mail forest@forestindustries.fi; internet www.forestindustries.fi; f. 1918; Chair. JUHA VANHAINEN; mems: 120 cos in the forestry industry and sales or trade asscns.

Sähköenergialiitto r.y. (Finnish Electricity Association): c/o Oy Turku Energia, POB 105, 20101 Turku; tel. 505573257 (mobile); e-mail sener.energia@gmail.com; internet www.sener.fi; f. 1926; 76 mems; research on electricity networks and electrical applications; Man. JARKKO LEHTONEN.

Suomalaisen Työn Liitto (Association for Finnish Work): Mikonkatu 17A, 00100 Helsinki; POB 429, 00101 Helsinki; tel. (9) 6962430; fax (9) 69624333; e-mail stl@avainlippu.fi; internet www.avainlippu.fi; f. 1978; public relations for Finnish products and for Finnish work; Chair. of Council MAURI PEKKARINEN; Chair., Bd of Dirs PEKKA SAIRANEN; Man. Dir LARS COLLIN; c. 1,200 mems.

Suomen Kaupan Liitto (Federation of Finnish Commerce): Eteläranta 10, 00130 Helsinki; POB 340, 00131 Helsinki; tel. (9) 172850; fax (9) 17285120; e-mail tiedotus@suomenkauppa.fi; internet www.suomenkauppa.fi; f. 2005 by merger of the Federation of Finnish Commerce and Trade and the Commercial Employers' Association; Man. Dir JUHANI PEKKALA; 36 mem. asscns with more than 10,000 firms.

Svenska lantbruksproducenternas centralförbund (Central Union of Swedish-speaking Agricultural Producers): Fredriksgatan 61A 34, 00100 Helsinki; tel. (9) 5860460; fax (9) 6941358; e-mail holger.falck@slc.fi; internet www.slc.fi; f. 1945; Chair. HOLGER FALCK; 14,000 mems.

Teknisen Kaupan Liitto (Association of Finnish Technical Traders): Sarkiniementie 3, 4th Floor, 00210 Helsinki; tel. (9) 6824130; fax (9) 68241310; e-mail tekninen.kauppa@tkl.fi; internet www.tkl.fi; f. 1918; organization of the main importers dealing in steel and metals, machines and equipment, heavy chemicals and raw materials; Chair. HEIMO AHO; Man. Dir KLAUS KATARA; 400 mems.

EMPLOYERS' ORGANIZATIONS

Elinkeinoelämän Keskusliitto (EK) (Confederation of Finnish Industries): Eteläranta 10, 00130 Helsinki; POB 30, 00131 Helsinki;

tel. (9) 42020; fax (9) 42022299; e-mail netti@ek.fi; internet www.ek.fi; f. 1907; aims to promote co-operation between cos and mem. organizations and to protect the interests of mems in employment issues; 35 asscns consisting of about 16,000 enterprises with 950,000 employees; Chair. SAKARI TAMMINEN; Dir-Gen. LEIF FAGERNÄS.

Autoliikenteen Työnantajaliitto r.y. (Employers' Federation of Road Transport): Nuijamiestentie 7, 00400 Helsinki; tel. (9) 47899480; fax (9) 5883995; e-mail mari.vasarainen@alt.fi; internet www.alt.fi; f. 1945; Chair. ANTTI NORRLIN; Man. Dir HANNU PARVELA; c. 1,000 mems.

Elintarviketeollisuusliitto r.y. (Finnish Food and Drink Industries' Federation): Pasilankatu 2, POB 115, 00240 Helsinki; tel. (9) 148871; fax (9) 14887201; e-mail info@etl.fi; internet www.etl.fi; Chair. MATTI KARPPINEN; Dir-Gen. HEIKKI JUUTINEN.

Kemianteollisuus (KT) r.y. (Chemical Industry Federation): Eteläranta 10, POB 4, 00131 Helsinki; tel. (9) 172841; fax (9) 630225; internet www.chemind.fi; Chair. HARRI KERMINEN; Dir-Gen. TIMO LEPPÄ.

Kenkä- ja Nahkateollisuus r.y. (Association of Finnish Shoe and Leather Industries): Eteläranta 10, 00130 Helsinki; tel. (9) 172841; fax (9) 179588; e-mail olavi.viljanmaa@jalas.com; Chair. OLAVI VILJANMAA.

Kumiteollisuus r.y. (Rubber Manufacturers' Association of Finland): Eteläranta 10, 7th Floor, 00130 Helsinki; POB 4, 00131 Helsinki; tel. (9) 172841; fax (9) 630225; e-mail tuula.rantalaiho@kumiteollisuus.fi; internet www.kumiteollisuus.fi; f. 1961; Chair. KIM GRAN; Man. Dir TUULA RANTALAIHO; 17 mems.

Lääketeollisuus r.y. (Pharma Industry Finland—PIF): Porkkalankatu 1, 00180 Helsinki; POB 206, 00181 Helsinki; tel. (9) 61504900; fax (9) 61504940; e-mail pif@pif.fi; internet www.pif.fi; Chair. OVE ULJAS; Gen. Man. SUVI-ANNE SIIMES.

Muoviteollisuus r.y. (Finnish Plastics Industries Federation): Eteläranta 10, 00131 Helsinki; tel. (9) 172841; fax (9) 171164; e-mail vesa.karha@plastics.fi; internet www.plastics.fi; Chair. PETRI ROLIG; Man. Dir VESA KÄRHÄ.

Palvelualojen Toimialaliitto r.y. (Association of Support Service Industries): Eteläranta 10, POB 11, 00131 Helsinki; tel. (9) 172841; fax (9) 176877; e-mail webmaster@palvelualojentoimialaliitto.com; internet www.palvelualojentoimialaliitto.com; f. 1992; Chair. and Man. Dir MIKAEL JUNGNER.

Puusepänteollisuuden Liitto r.y. (Association of the Finnish Furniture and Joinery Industries): Snellmaninkatu 13, 00170 Helsinki; POB 336, 00171 Helsinki; tel. (9) 13261; fax (9) 1324445; e-mail jukka.nevala@forestindustries.fi; internet www.puusepanteollisuus.fi; f. 1917; Chair. PEKKA SAIRANEN; Dir-Gen. TIMO JAATINEN; 80 mem. cos.

Rakennusteollisuus (RT) r.y. (Confederation of Finnish Construction Industries): Unioninkatu 14, POB 381, 00130 Helsinki; tel. (9) 12991; fax (9) 628264; e-mail rt@rakennusteollisuus.fi; internet www.rakennusteollisuus.fi; f. 2001; Dir-Gen. TIMO U. KORHONEN; Man. Dir TARMO PIPATTI; 2,700 mem. cos.

Rannikko- ja Sisävesiliikenteen Työnantajaliitto (RASILA) r.y. (Coastal and Inland Waterway Employers' Association): Satamakatu 4A, POB 155, 00160 Helsinki; tel. (9) 62267312; fax (9) 669251; Chair. STEFAN HÅKANS; Man. Dir HENRIK LÖNNQVIST.

Satamaoperaattorit r.y. (Finnish Port Operators' Asscn): Köydenpunojankatu 8, POB 268, 00181 Helsinki; tel. (9) 6859530; fax (9) 68595353; e-mail juha.mutru@satamaoperaattorit.fi; internet www.satamaoperaattorit.fi; f. 1906; fmrly Suomen Lastauttajain Liitto (SLL) r.y; Chair. KARI SAVOLAINEN; Man. Dir JUHU MUTRU.

Suomen Varustamot r.y. (Finnish Shipowners' Association): see under Shipping.

Suunnittelu- ja konsulttitoimistojen liitto (SKOL) r.y. (Finnish Association of Consulting Firms—SKOL): Eteläranta 10, POB 10, 00131 Helsinki; tel. (9) 19231; fax (9) 624462; e-mail skolry@teknologiateollisuus.fi; internet www.skolry.fi; f. 1951; Chair. KIMMO FISCHER; Man. Dir TIMO MYLLYS; 215 mems.

Teknokemian Yhdistys r.y. (Finnish Cosmetic, Toiletry and Detergent Association): Eteläranta 10, 00130 Helsinki; POB 311, 00131 Helsinki; tel. (9) 172841; fax (9) 666561; e-mail info@teknokem.fi; internet www.teknokem.fi; Dir KIRSI-MARJA KOSKELO; CEO SARI KARJOMAA; 66 mems.

Teknologiateollisuus r.y. (Technology Industries of Finland): Eteläranta 10, POB 10, 00131 Helsinki; tel. (9) 19231; fax (9) 624462; e-mail martti.maenpaa@teknologiateollisuus.fi; internet www.teknologiateollisuus.fi; f. 1903 as Metalliteollisuuden Keskusliitto r.y.; Chair. JORMA ELORANTA; Man. Dir MARTTI MÄENPÄÄ.

Tieto- ja tekniikka-alojen työnantajaliitto (TIKLI) r.y. (Employers' Asscn TIKLI): Yrjönkatu 13A, 5th Floor, POB 264, 00121 Helsinki; tel. (20) 5955000; fax (20) 5955001; e-mail info@tikli.fi; internet www.tikli.fi; fmrly Sähkö- ja telealan työnantajaliitto r.y; Chair. JUKKA ALHO; Dir-Gen. HARRI HIETALA; 180 mems.

Työnantajain Yleinen Ryhmä r.y. (Finnish Employers' General Group): Eteläranta 10, 00130 Helsinki; tel. (9) 1724264; fax (9) 179588; e-mail sari.vannela@ryhma.ttliitot.fi; Chair. MARKKU JOKINEN; Exec. Dir SARI VANNELA.

Viestinnän Keskusliitto (Fed. of the Finnish Media Industry): Lönnrotinkatu 11A, POB 291, 00121 Helsinki; tel. (9) 22877200; fax (9) 603527; e-mail hakan.gabrielsson@vkl.fi; internet www.vkl.fi; Man. Dir VALTTERI NIIRANEN.

Yleinen Teollisuusliitto r.y. (General Industry Association): Eteläranta 10, 7th Floor, POB 325, 00130 Helsinki; tel. (9) 6220410; fax (9) 176135; internet www.ytl.fi; Chair. MARKKU TALONEN; Man. Dir MARKKU KÄPPI.

Kultaseppien Työnantajaliitto r.y. (Employers' Association of Goldsmiths): Eteläranta 10, 00130 Helsinki; tel. (9) 172841; fax (9) 630225; e-mail sari.vannela@ryhma.ttliitot.fi; Chair. ILKKA RUOHOLA.

Suomen Kiinteistöliitto r.y. (Finnish Real Estate Federation): Annankatu 24, 3rd Floor, 00100 Helsinki; tel. (9) 16676761; fax (9) 16676400; e-mail info@kiinteistoliitto.fi; internet www.kiinteistoliitto.fi; f. 1907; Pres. MATTI INHA; Man. Dir HARRI HILTUNEN; 26 mem asscns.

Tupakkateollisuusliitto r.y. (Finnish Tobacco Industries' Federation): Eteläranta 10, POB 325, 00131 Helsinki; tel. (9) 62204155; fax (9) 176135; e-mail paavo.heiskanen@ytl.fi; Chair. KARI HEIKKILÄ.

UTILITIES

Electricity

Fortum Oyj: Keilaniementie 1, 02150 Espoo; POB 1, 00048 Fortum; tel. (10) 4511; fax (10) 4524777; e-mail asiakapavelu@fortum.com; internet www.fortum.fi; f. 1998 following merger of the Imatran Voima Group and the Neste Group; 51.5% state-owned; generation, distribution and sale of electricity and heat, as well as the operation and maintenance of power plants; listed on the Helsinki exchange in Dec. 1998; Chair. MATTI LEHTI; Pres. and CEO TAPIO KUULA.

Kemijoki Oy: Valtakatu 11, POB 8131, 96101 Rovaniemi; tel. (16) 7401; fax (16) 7402325; e-mail info@kemijoki.fi; internet www.kemijoki.fi; f. 1954; electric power; 66.99% state-owned; Chair. of Supervisory Bd JUSSI JÄRVENTAUS; Pres. and CEO AIMO TAKALA; 266 employees.

Pohjolan Voima Oy (PVO): Töölönkatu 4, POB 40, 00101 Helsinki; tel. (9) 693061; fax (9) 69306335; e-mail info@pvo.fi; internet www.pohjolanvoima.fi; Pres. and CEO LAURI VIRKKUNEN.

Regional electricity providers operate, of which the largest is Helsingin Energia.

Helsingin Energia (Helsinki Energy): Kampinkuja 2, 00090 Helen; tel. (9) 6171; fax (9) 6172360; e-mail helsingin.energia@helen.fi; internet www.helen.fi; f. 1909; municipal undertaking; generates and distributes electrical power and district heating; distributes natural gas; Man. Dir SEPPO RUOHONEN.

Gas

Gasum Oy: Miestentie 1, POB 21, 02151 Espoo; tel. (20) 4471; fax (20) 4478619; e-mail minna.ojala@gasum.fi; internet www.gasum.fi; f. 1994; 31% owned by Fortum, 25% owned by OAO Gazprom (Russia), 24% state-owned and 20% owned by E.ON Ruhrgas International AG (Germany); imports and sells natural gas, owns and operates natural gas transmission system; operates 3 subsidiaries, Gasum Energiapalvelut Oy, Gasum Paikallisjakelu Oy and Kaasupörssi Oy; Pres. and CEO ANTERO JÄNNES.

Water

Helsingin Vesi (Helsinki Water): Iimalankuja 2A, 00240 Helsinki; POB 301, 00066 Helsinki; tel. (9) 15613010; fax (9) 15613011; e-mail vesiliitos.helsinki@hsy.fi; internet www.hsy.fi; responsible for water supply and sewerage of the greater Helsinki area; Man. Dir RAIMO INKINEN.

CO-OPERATIVES

Pellervo (Confederation of Finnish Co-operatives): Simonkatu 6, POB 77, 00101 Helsinki; tel. (9) 4767501; fax (9) 6948845; e-mail toimisto@pellervo.fi; internet www.pellervo.fi; f. 1899; central organization of co-operatives; Man. Dir VEIKKO HÄMÄLÄINEN; 400 mem. societies (incl. 11 central co-operative societies).

Munakunta (Co-operative Egg Producers' Association): Piispanristintie 8, POB 6, 20761 Piispanristi; tel. (2) 214420; fax (2) 2144222; e-mail jan.lahde@munakunta.fi; internet www.kultamuna.fi; f. 1922; Man. Dir JAN LÄHDE; 500 mems.

Suomen Osuuskauppojen Keskusliitto (SOKL) r.y. (Finnish Co-operative Union): Fleminginkatu 34, POB 1, 00088 Helsinki; tel. (10) 768011; f. 1908; Chair. Jukka Huiskonen; Man. Dir Taavi Heikkilä; 44 mems.

Valio Ltd (Finnish Co-operative Dairies' Association): Meijeritie 6, 00370 Helsinki; POB 10, 00039 Valio; tel. (10) 381121; fax (9) 5625068; e-mail pekka.laaksonen@valio.fi; internet www.valio.fi; f. 1905; production and marketing of dairy products; Pres. and CEO Pekka Laaksonen.

TRADE UNIONS

Akava (Confederation of Unions for Professional and Managerial Staff): Rautatieläisenkatu 6, 00520 Helsinki; tel. (20) 7489400; fax (9) 1502603; e-mail arja.joivio@akava.fi; internet www.akava.fi; f. 1950; 34 affiliates, incl. asscns of doctors, engineers, social workers and teachers; Pres. Matti Viljanen; total membership 552,800.

Suomen Ammattiliittojen Keskusjärjestö (SAK) r.y. (Central Organization of Finnish Trade Unions): Siltasaarenkatu 3A, POB 157, 00531 Helsinki; tel. (20) 774000; fax (20) 7740225; e-mail sak@sak.fi; internet www.sak.fi; f. 1907; 22 affiliated unions comprising over 1m. mems; Pres. Lauri Lyly.

Principal affiliated unions:

Auto- ja Kuljetusalan Työntekijäliitto (AKT) r.y. (Finnish Transport Workers' Union AKT): John Stenbergin ranta 6, POB 313, 00531 Helsinki; tel. (9) 613110; fax (9) 739287; e-mail nesrin.can@akt.fi; internet www.akt.fi; f. 1948; Pres. Timo Räty; Sec. Arto Sorvali; 50,505 mems.

Julkisten ja Hyvinvointialojen Liitto r.y. (JHL) (Public and Welfare Sectors): POB 101 Sörnäisten rantatie 23, 00500 Helsinki; POB 101, 00531 Helsinki; tel. (10) 770331; fax (10) 7703477; e-mail merja.launis@jhl.fi; internet www.jhl.fi; f. 2006 by merger of 6 unions; Pres. Tuire Santamäki-Vuori; 220,000 mems.

Metallityöväen Liitto r.y. (Metalworkers): Hakaniemenranta 1, POB 107, 00531 Helsinki; tel. (20) 774001; fax (20) 7741050; e-mail metalli.posti@metalliliitto.fi; internet www.metalliliitto.fi; f. 1899; Pres. Riku Aalto; Sec. Matti Mäkelä; 165,500 mems.

Palvelualojen ammattiliitto PAM r.y. (Service Union United): Paasivuorenkatu 4–6A, POB 54, 00530 Helsinki; tel. (20) 774002; fax (20) 7742039; e-mail pam@pam.fi; internet www.pam.fi; f. 1987 as Liikealan ammattiliitto r.y.; present name adopted 2000; Pres. Ann Selin; Vice-Pres Anssi Vuorio, Kaarlo Julkunen; 210,000 mems.

Paperiliitto r.y. (Paperworkers): Paasivuorenkatu 4–6A, POB 326, 00531 Helsinki; tel. (9) 70891; fax (9) 7012279; e-mail info@paperiliitto.fi; internet www.paperiliitto.fi; f. 1906; Pres. Jouko Ahonen; Gen. Sec. Petri Vanhala; 47,040 mems.

Posti- ja logistiikka-alan unioni (PAU) r.y. (Post and Logistics): John Stenbergin ranta 6, 00530 Helsinki; tel. (9) 613116; fax (9) 61311750; e-mail pau@pau.fi; internet www.pau.fi; Pres. Esa Vilkuna; Gen. Sec. Arto Sieranta; 32,000 mems.

Puu- ja erityisalojen Liitto r.y. (Wood and Allied Workers): Haapaniemenkatu 7–9B, POB 318, 00531 Helsinki; tel. (9) 615161; fax (9) 7532506; e-mail puuliitto@puuliitto.fi; internet www.puuliitto.fi; f. 1993 by merger of 2 unions; Pres. Kalevi Vanhala; 45,586 mems.

Rakennusliitto r.y. (Construction Workers): Siltasaarenkatu 4, POB 307, 00531 Helsinki; tel. (20) 774003; fax (20) 7743062; e-mail info@rakennusliitto.fi; internet www.rakennusliitto.fi; f. 1924; Pres. Matti Niemi Harjuniemi; 84,000 mems.

Rautatieläisten Liitto r.y. (RAUTL) (Railwaymen): Hakaniemenranta 1, 00530 Helsinki; POB 205, 00531 Helsinki; tel. (9) 774941; fax (9) 7015941; e-mail mauri.lunden@rautl.fi; internet www.rautl.fi; f. 1906; Pres. Vesa Mauriala; 14,458 mems.

Sähköalojen ammattiliitto r.y. (Electrical Workers): Aleksanterinkatu 15, 33100 Tampere; POB 747, 33101 Tampere; tel. (3) 2520111; fax (3) 2520210; e-mail lauri.lyly@sahkoliitto.fi; internet www.sahkoliitto.fi; f. 1955; Pres. Martti Alakoski; Gen. Sec. Timo Punkki; 32,000 mems.

Suomen Elintarviketyöläisten Liitto (SEL) r.y. (Food Workers): Siltasaarenkatu 6, POB 213, 00531 Helsinki; tel. (20) 774004; fax (20) 7740604; internet www.selry.fi; f. 1905; Pres. Veli-Matti Kuntonen; 36,000 mems.

Suomen Merimies-Unioni SM-U r.y. (Seamen): John Stenbergin ranta 6, 00530 Helsinki; tel. (9) 6152020; fax (9) 61520227; e-mail pekka.teravainen@smu.fi; internet www.smu.fi; f. 1916; Pres. Simo Zitting; Sec. Kenneth Bondas; 11,000 mems.

TEAM (Teollisuusalojen ammattiliitto r.y.): Siltasaarenkatu 2, 00530 Helsinki; POB 324, 00531 Helsinki; tel. (9) 773971; fax (9) 739995; internet www.teamliitto.fi; f. 2010 by merger of Kemianliitto-Kemifacket r.y. and Viestintäalan ammattiliitto r.y.; Pres. Timo Vallittu; 67,000 mems.

STTK (Finnish Confederation of Professionals): Mikonkatu 8A, 6th Floor, 00100 Helsinki; POB 421, 00101 Helsinki; tel. (9) 131521; fax (9) 652367; e-mail mikko.maenpaa@sttk.fi; internet www.sttk.fi; f. 1946; Pres. Mikko Mäenpää.

There are 20 affiliated trade unions, including the following:

Erityisalojen Toimihenkilöliitto ERTO r.y. (Special Service and Clerical Employees): Asemamiehenkatu 4, 00520 Helsinki; tel. (9) 613231; fax (9) 61323202; e-mail jasenpalvelu@erto.fi; internet www.erto.fi; f. 1968; Pres. Tapio Huttula; 30,000 mems.

Julkis- ja yksityisalojen toimihenkilöliitto r.y. (Jyty) (Federation of Public and Private Sector Employees): Asemamiehenkatu 4, 00520 Helsinki; tel. (20) 7893799; fax (20) 7893790; e-mail merja.ailus@jytyliitto.fi; internet www.jytyliitto.fi; f. 1918 as Kunnallisvirkamiesliitto KVL r.y.; present name adopted 2005; Pres. Merja Ailus; 70,000 mems and 270 mem. asscns.

Palkansaajajärjestö Pardia r.y. (Confederation of State Employees' Unions): Ratamestarinkatu 11, 00520 Helsinki; tel. (75) 3247500; fax (75) 3247575; e-mail toimisto@pardia.fi; internet www.pardia.fi; 22 mem. unions comprising 60,000 mems; Pres. Antti Palola.

Suomen lähi- ja perushoitajaliitto SuPer r.y. (Practical Nurses): Ratamestarinkatu 12, 00520 Helsinki; tel. (9) 2727910; fax (9) 27279120; e-mail juhani.palomaki@superliitto.fi; internet www.superliitto.fi; f. 1948; Pres. Juhani Palomäki; 74,000 mems.

Tehy (Union of Health and Social-Care Professionals): Asemamiehenkatu 4, 00520 Helsinki; POB 10, 00060 Tehy; tel. (9) 54227000; fax (9) 61500278; e-mail tehy.international@tehy.fi; internet www.tehy.fi; f. 1982; Pres. Jaana Laitinen-Pesola; 131,000 mems.

Toimihenkilöunioni (TU) (Union of Salaried Employees): Selkämerenkuja 1A, POB 183, 00181 Helsinki; tel. (9) 172731; fax (9) 17273330; e-mail petteri.ojanen@toimihenkilounioni.fi; internet www.toimihenkilounioni.fi; Pres. Antti Rinne; 120,000 mems.

Vakuutusväen Liitto VvL ry (Insurance Employees' Union): Asemamiehenkatu 2, 00520 Helsinki; tel. (9) 85672400; fax (9) 85672401; e-mail kirsi.kovanen@vvl.fi; internet www.vvl.fi; f. 1945; Pres. Sirpa Komonen; Gen. Sec. Kirsi Kovanen; 10,000 mems.

Transport

ADMINISTRATIVE BODIES

Liikennevirasto (Finnish Transport Agency): Opastinsilta 12A, POB 33, 00521 Helsinki; tel. (20) 637373; fax (20) 6373700; e-mail viestinta@liikennevirasto.fi; internet www.fta.fi; f. 2010 by merger of waterways section of Finnish Maritime Administration, Finnish Rail Administration and Finnish Road Administration; attached to the Ministry of Transport and Communications; responsible for maintenance and development of transport infrastructure; Dir-Gen. Tervala Juhani.

TraFi (Transport Safety Agency): Kumpulantie 9, POB 320, 00101 Helsinki; tel. (20) 618500; fax (20) 6185095; e-mail riitta-liisa.linnakko@trafi.fi; internet www.trafi.fi; f. 2010 by merger of 4 sectoral bodies; attached to Ministry of Transport and Communications; responsible for safety and supervision of maritime, rail and road traffic and civil aviation; Dir-Gen. Kari Wihlman.

RAILWAYS

Finland had 5,919 km of wide-gauge (1,524 mm of Russian gauge) railways in 2009, of which 3,067 km were electrified, providing internal services and connections with Sweden and Russia. The state rail network is owned by the Finnish Transport Agency which oversees the maintenance and development of the country's rail network, (see Administrative Bodies), while VR Group operates train services on the network. A high-speed rail link between Helsinki and St Petersburg, Russia became operational in December 2010. An underground railway service has been provided by Helsinki City Transport since 1982. In 2010 it was proposed to build a 312-km cross-border railway line linking Finland's main railway hub of Kolari to Skibotn in Norway. An 18-km railway route connecting the Helsinki-Vantaa airport and the adjacent Aviapolis business and commercial district to the Helsinki commuter rail network was under construction in 2012. The line, known as the Ring Rail Line Kehärata, was expected to open in 2015.

Karhula-Sunila Railway: Ratakatu 8, 48600 Karhula; tel. (5) 298221; fax (5) 298225; f. 1937; goods transport; privately owned; operates 10 km of railway (1,524 mm gauge); Man. Pertti Honkala.

VR Group: Vilhonkatu 13, POB 488, 00101 Helsinki; tel. (307) 10; fax (307) 21500; e-mail contactcenter@vr.fi; internet www.vr.fi; began operating 1862; joint-stock co since 1995; operates 5,784 km of railways; Pres. and CEO MIKAEL ARO; Chief Financial Officer HELI OLLILA.

ROADS

Finland had 78,161 km of highways at 1 January 2009, of which 13,328 km were main roads (including 765 km of motorway). Some 65% of the road network was paved in that year. In 2007 €780m. was spent on road infrastructure, including private roads.

Destia: Heidehofintie 2, POB 206, 01301 Helsinki; tel. (20) 44411; fax (20) 4442297; e-mail destia@destia.fi; internet www.destia.fi; f. 2008 to assume activities of fmr Tieliikelaitos (Finnish Road Enterprise); state-owned enterprise; provides transport infrastructure and transport environment services; Pres. and CEO HANNU LEINONEN.

INLAND WATERWAYS

Finland has a total of 19,500 km (approx.) of public, charted fairways. Lakes cover 33,672 sq km. The inland waterway system comprises 7,842 km of buoyed-out channels, 40 open canals and 37 lock canals. Merchant shipping routes include about 4,000 km. The total length of canals is 116 km. The most economically significant canal is the Saimaa Canal, which is 43 km long and connects Lake Saima to the Gulf of Finland. In 2006 cargo vessel traffic on inland waterways (including on the Saimaa Canal) amounted to 2.4m. metric tons, timber floating amounted to 0.9m. tons and passenger traffic to 479,709 passengers. The Finnish Transport Agency (see Administrative Bodies) is responsible for maintaining the inland waterways.

SHIPPING

The chief port of export is Kotka. Reclamation of land was carried out to build a second container port in Kotka. It opened in 2001 and has the capacity to handle 500,000 20-ft equivalent units (TEUs) of cargo per year. The main port of import is Helsinki, which has three specialized harbours. The West Harbour handles most of the container traffic, the North Harbour cargo ferry traffic and the South Harbour passenger traffic. Other important international ports are Turku (Åbo), Rauma and Hamina. The Transport Safety Agency (see Administrative Bodies) is responsible for maritime administration. At December 31 2009 the merchant fleet numbered 284 registered vessels, with a combined displacement of 1.46m. grt.

Port Authority Association

Suomen Satamaliitto (Finnish Port Association): Toinen Linja 14, 00530 Helsinki; tel. (9) 7711; fax (9) 7530474; e-mail info@finnports.com; internet www.finnports.com; f. 1923; 30 mems; Man. Dir MARKKU MYLLY.

Port Authorities

HaminaKotka: Merituulentie 424, POB 196, 48310 Kotka; tel. (20) 7908800; fax (20) 7908891; e-mail office@haminakotka.fi; internet www.portofkotka.fi; merged with the Port of Hamina in May 2011; Man. Dir KIMMO NASKI.

Helsinki: Port of Helsinki, Olympiaranta 3, POB 800, 00099 Helsinki; tel. (9) 3101621; fax (9) 31033802; e-mail port.helsinki@hel.fi; internet www.portofhelsinki.fi; Man. Dir KIMMO MÄKI.

Rauma: Port of Rauma, Hakunintie 19, 26100 Rauma; tel. (2) 8344712; fax (2) 8226369; e-mail harbour.office@portofrauma.com; internet www.portofrauma.com; Port Dir HANNU ASUMALAHTI; Harbour Master and Port Security Officer TANJA ROBERTS.

Turku: Turku Port Authority, Linnankatu 90, 20100 Turku; tel. (2) 2674111; fax (2) 2674125; e-mail turkport@port.turku.fi; internet www.port.turku.fi; Man. Dir CHRISTIAN RAMBERG; Harbour Master KARI RIUTTA.

Shipowners' Association

Suomen Varustamot r.y. (Finnish Shipowners' Association): Hämeentie 19, 00500 Helsinki; tel. (10) 8410500; fax (10) 8410599; e-mail info@shipowners.fi; internet www.shipowners.fi; f. 1932 as Suomen Varustamoyhdistys r.y; adopted current name in June 2008 following a merger with the Cargo Ship Association and the Åland Shipowners' Association; 24 mems; Chair. THOMAS FRANCK, OLOF WIDEN.

Principal Companies

ESL Shipping Oy: Lintulahdenkuja 10, POB 91, 00501 Helsinki; tel. (9) 5211; fax (9) 5219999; e-mail operations@eslshipping.fi; internet www.eslshipping.fi; world-wide tramp services; subsidiary of Aspo Oyj; Pres. MARKUS KARJALAINEN.

Finnlines PLC: Porkkalainkatu 20A, POB 197, 00180 Helsinki; tel. (10) 34350; fax (10) 3435200; e-mail info.fi@finnlines.com; internet www.finnlines.fi; f. 1949; liner and contract services between Finland and other European countries; overland and inland services combined with direct sea links; Pres. and CEO UWE BAKOSCH; 85 cargo ferries.

Alfons Håkans Oy Ab: Linnankatu 36C, 20100 Turku; tel. (2) 515500; fax (2) 2515873; e-mail office.turku@alfonshakans.fi; internet www.alfonshakans.fi; Man. Dir and Chair. STEFAN HÅKANS; 32 tugs and 4 barges.

Rettig Oy Ab Bore: Bulevardi 46, POB 115, 00121 Helsinki; tel. (9) 61883300; fax (9) 61883398; e-mail info@bore.eu; internet www.bore.eu; f. 1897; acquired Bror Husell Chartering Ab in 2005 and Rederi Ab Engship in 2006; Man. Dir THOMAS FRANCK; 17 cargo ships, 3 car carriers and 1 bulk vessel.

RG Line Oy Ab: Satamaterminaali, 65170 Vaasa; tel. (20) 7716810; fax (20) 7716820; e-mail info@rgline.com; internet www.rgline.com; operates ferry services across the Gulf of Bothnia from Vaasa to Umeå.

Tallink Silja Oy: Keilaranta 9, POB 43, 02151 Espoo; tel. (9) 18041; fax (9) 1804402; internet www.tallinksilja.com; f. 2006 by merger of Tallink Finland Oy and Silja Oy; part of the AS Tallink Group; passenger and cargo services in the Baltic; CEO ENN PANT; 19 vessels.

CIVIL AVIATION

An international airport is situated at Helsinki-Vantaa, 19 km from Helsinki. International and domestic services also operate to and from airports at Ivalo, Joensuu, Jyväskylä, Kajaani, Kemi-Tornio, Kruunupyy, Kuopio, Lappeenranta, Mariehamn, Oulu, Pori, Rovaniemi, Savonlinna, Tampere-Pirkkala, Turku, Vaasa and Varkaus. Domestic services are available at airports at Enontekiö, Kittilä, Kuusamo and Mikkeli. The Transport Safety Agency (see Administrative Bodies) is the regulatory authority for civil aviation.

Finavia Corporation: Lentäjäntie 3, POB 50, 01531 Vantaa; tel. (20) 708000; fax (20) 7082090; e-mail info@finavia.fi; internet www.finavia.fi; state-owned commercial enterprise; provides air navigation services and maintains state-owned airports; Pres. and CEO SAMULI HAAPASALO.

Principal Airlines

Blue1: POB 168, 01531 Vantaa; tel. (20) 5856000; fax (20) 5856001; e-mail blue1@blue1.com; internet www.blue1.com; f. 1988 as Air Botnia; name changed in 2004; domestic and international services; member of SAS Group since 1998 and of Star Alliance since 2004; Pres. and CEO STEFAN WENTJÄRVI.

Finnair Oyj: Tietotie 11A, POB 15, 01053 Vantaa; tel. (9) 81881; fax (9) 8184979; e-mail maria.mroue@finnair.fi; internet www.finnair.com; f. 1923; 55.8% state-owned; 12 domestic services, 39 European services and 12 international services (to Asia and North America); Pres. and CEO MIKA VEHVILÄINEN.

Tourism

Europe's largest inland water system, vast forests, magnificent scenery and the possibility of holiday seclusion are Finland's main attractions. Most visitors come from Sweden, Germany, Russia, the United Kingdom, the Netherlands and Norway. Overnight stays by foreign tourists at registered accommodation establishments totalled 5,005,068 in 2010, compared with 4,890,006 in 2009. Receipts from tourism (including passenger traffic) amounted to an estimated US $2,809m. in 2010.

Matkailun edistämiskeskus (Finnish Tourist Board): Töölönkatu 11, POB 625, 00101 Helsinki; tel. (10) 6058000; fax (10) 6058333; e-mail mek@mek.fi; internet www.mek.fi; f. 1973; Dir-Gen. JAAKKO LEHTONEN.

Defence

As assessed at November 2011, the armed forces of Finland numbered 22,100 comprising an army of 16,000 (including 11,000 conscripts), a navy of 3,500 (including 1,900 conscripts) and an air force of 2,600 (including 750 conscripts). There were also some 340,000 reserves and a 2,875-strong border guard (under the Ministry of the Interior). Finland was committed to two European Union (EU) 'battlegroups' as its contribution to the EU's rapid reaction force. The Nordic battlegroup, which was led by Sweden and also contained troops from Norway, Estonia and Ireland, was ready for deployment to crisis areas from the beginning of 2008. The second battlegroup was with Germany and the Netherlands.

Defence Expenditure: Budget estimated at €2,520m. in 2012.

Chief of Defence: Gen. ARI PUHELOINEN.

Education

The Ministry of Education and Culture is the central body responsible for providing education. Tuition is free and the core curriculum is the same for all students. All children are entitled to receive one year of voluntary pre-primary education, usually at the age of six years. Compulsory schooling is provided in comprehensive schools and lasts for nine years, divided into a six-year lower stage, beginning at the age of seven, and a three-year upper stage (or lower secondary stage), beginning at the age of 13. Some comprehensive schools offer a voluntary 10th year in which additional basic education is provided. After comprehensive school, pupils may continue their studies, either at a general upper secondary school or a vocational upper secondary school. The upper secondary school curriculum is designed for three years but may be completed in two or four years. Courses leading to basic vocational qualifications take three years to complete. The matriculation examination taken at the end of three years of general upper secondary school gives eligibility for higher education, as do a Finnish polytechnic degree, a post-secondary level vocational qualification or a three-year vocational diploma. In 2008/09 enrolment at pre-primary level included 66% of children in the relevant age-group. Enrolment at primary schools in that year included 96% of those in the relevant age-group, while the comparable rate for secondary enrolment was also 96%. Higher education is provided by 20 universities and 28 polytechnics. In 2005 enrolment at tertiary level was equivalent to 92% of those in the relevant age-group. Of total proposed budgetary expenditure by the central Government in 2010, €6,186m. (equivalent to 12.3% of total proposed expenditure) was allocated to the Ministry of Education and Culture.

FINNISH EXTERNAL TERRITORY
THE ÅLAND ISLANDS

Introductory Survey

LOCATION, LANGUAGE, RELIGION, FLAG, CAPITAL

The Åland Islands are a group of more than 6,000 islands (of which some 60 are inhabited) in the Gulf of Bothnia, between Finland and Sweden. About 91% of the inhabitants are Swedish-speaking, and Swedish is the official language; of the remaining population, about 5% are Finnish-speaking. The majority profess Christianity and 88.5% belong to the Evangelical Lutheran Church of Finland. The flag displays a red cross, bordered with yellow, on a blue background, the upright of the cross being to the left of centre. The capital is Mariehamn, which is situated on Åland, the largest island in the group.

CONTEMPORARY POLITICAL HISTORY

For geographical and economic reasons, the Åland Islands were traditionally associated closely with Sweden. In 1809, when Sweden was forced to cede Finland to Russia, the islands were incorporated into the Finnish Grand Duchy. However, following Finland's declaration of independence from the Russian Empire in 1917, the Ålanders demanded the right to self-determination and sought to be reunited with Sweden, with support from the Swedish Government. In 1920 Finland granted the islands autonomy but refused to acknowledge their secession, and in 1921 the Åland question was referred to the League of Nations. In June the League granted Finland sovereignty over the islands, while directing that certain conditions pertaining to national identity be included in the autonomy legislation offered by Finland and that the islands should be a neutral and non-fortified region. Elections were held in accordance with the new legislation, and the new provincial parliament (Landsting) held its first plenary session on 9 June 1922. The revised Autonomy Act of 1951 provided for independent rights of legislation in internal affairs and for autonomous control over the islands' economy. This Act could not be amended or repealed by the Finnish legislature without the consent of the Landsting.

In 1988 constitutional reform introduced the principle of a majority parliamentary government, to be formed by the Lantrådskandidat, the member of the Landsting nominated to conduct negotiations between the parties. These negotiations may yield two alternative outcomes: either the nominee will submit a proposal to create a new government or the nominee will fail to reach agreement on a new government (in which case renewed negotiations will ensue). The first formal parliamentary government and opposition were duly established. The governing coalition consisted of the three largest parties that had been elected to the Landsting in October 1987 (the Centre Party, the Liberals and the Moderates), which together held 22 seats in the 30-member legislature.

At a general election held in October 1991 the Centre Party increased its representation in the Landsting to 10, while the Liberal Party won seven seats, and the Moderates and Social Democrats won six and four seats, respectively. The Centre and Moderate Parties formed a new coalition Government, in which the Liberal Party was replaced by the Social Democratic Party.

A revised Autonomy Act, providing Åland with a greater degree of autonomous control, took effect on 1 January 1993. The rules regarding legislative authority were modernized, and the right of the Åland legislature (henceforth known as the Lagting) to enact laws was extended. Åland was given greater discretion with respect to its budget, and the revised Act also introduced changes in matters such as right of domicile, land-ownership regulations and administrative authority. The Autonomy Act contains a provision that, in any treaty which Finland may conclude with a foreign state and to which Åland is a party, the Lagting must consent to the statute implementing the treaty in order for the provision to enter into force in Åland. A referendum on the issue of Åland's proposed accession to membership of the European Union (EU, see p. 276) in 1995 was held in November 1994, immediately after similar referendums in Finland and Sweden had shown a majority in favour of membership. (A small majority of Åland citizens had supported Finland's membership.) Despite low participation in the referendum, 73.7% of the votes cast supported membership and Åland duly joined the EU, together with Finland and Sweden, on 1 January 1995. Under the terms of the treaty of accession, Åland was accorded special exemption from tax union with the EU in order to stimulate the ferry and tourism industries. (In 1998 two of Europe's largest ferry operators, Silja and Viking—both Finnish, re-routed their major services via Åland in order to continue to conduct duty-free sales, which were later abolished within the rest of the EU.)

A general election was held in October 1995. The Centre Party secured nine seats and the Liberal Party won eight, while the Moderates and Social Democrats maintained the representation that they had achieved in the previous parliament. The new coalition Government was composed of members of the Centre and Moderate Parties and one independent.

At a general election held in October 1999 the Centre Party and the Liberal Party each won nine seats. The Moderate Party secured only four seats, while the Social Democrats maintained their level of representation. The Obunden Samling (Non-aligned Coalition) won four seats. A coalition Government was formed comprising the Centre Party, the Moderate Party and the Independents. In March 2001, following a motion of no confidence in the Lagting, the Chairman (Lantråd) of the Government, Roger Nordlund of the Centre Party, dissolved the coalition and formed a new administration comprising members of the Centre Party and the Liberal Party.

A general election was held on 19 October 2003, at which the Centre Party and the Liberal Party each won seven seats. The two parties formed a new Government in coalition with the Social Democrats (who had won six seats) and the Moderate Party (with four seats), under Nordlund.

In August 2004 the Finnish Government agreed new, more stringent regulations securing the islands' demilitarized status, following reports that this had been violated by troop movements over the past two decades.

In January 2005, following a motion of no confidence in the Lagting, the governing coalition was dissolved and Nordlund formed a new administration comprising members of the Centre Party, the Social Democrats and the Moderate Party.

In May 2006 the European Court of Justice (ECJ) ruled that Finland was in breach of EU regulations on tobacco products by allowing the continued sale of *snus* (Swedish oral tobacco) in the Åland Islands. (The sale of oral tobacco was prohibited in the EU in 1992, but Sweden was granted an exemption from the ban when it joined the Union in 1995.) Trade in *snus*, particularly on ferries registered in the Islands, had been worth several million euros annually. As Finland had no powers to legislate in health matters in the Islands, the matter was referred to the Lagting, which in January 2007 adopted legislation with the aim of complying with the Court's judgment; however, this was deemed insufficient by the European Commission, as it only prohibited *snus* (rather than oral tobacco in general) from entering the market, and did not apply to the sale of *snus* on vessels registered in the Åland Islands once they had left Finnish territorial waters. In October the European Commission referred the case to the Court of Justice for a second time. Consequently, the Lagting adopted further legislation, which was enacted in January 2008, introducing an outright ban on *snus* sales on Åland-registered ships, including in Swedish territorial waters; as a result, the European Commission withdrew its case against Finland later in 2008.

The opposition Liberal Party became the largest party in the Lagting following a general election held on 21 October 2007, at which it won 10 seats. The Centre Party won eight seats, while the Independents took four. The representation of the Moderate Party and the Social Democrats declined to three seats each. A turn-out of 67.8% was recorded. The Liberal Party and the Centre Party subsequently formed a coalition Government, under Viveka Eriksson, the Liberal leader.

In September 2008 Finland ratified the Lisbon Treaty, which aimed to improve decision-making in the enlarged EU. However, the Åland Islands, which under the amended Act of Autonomy was also required to ratify the treaty, demanded concessions from the Finnish Government prior to ratification. The Åland Government's demands included a seat in the European Parliament, the right to appear before the European Court of Justice (where Åland had been represented by Finland in the case regarding *snus* sales), participation in the meetings of the Council and shared control over the principle of subsidiarity (that the EU should only act when an objective can be better achieved at the supranational level). By November 2009 no formal concessions appeared to have been granted by the Finnish Government; none the less, on 25 November the Lagting voted to ratify the treaty, six days before it was scheduled to enter into effect across the EU. Earlier in November the Lagting's legal affairs committee had recommended that the legislature approve the treaty, but urged the Åland Government to continue to seek greater participation for the islands in EU affairs.

At a general election held on 16 October 2011, the ruling coalition partners, the Liberal Party and the Centre Party, lost their majority, their respective representation declining to six and seven seats. The

Social Democrats increased its number of seats, to six, while the Moderates and the Independents each secured four seats and the separatist Åland's Future three. A turn-out of 66.6% was recorded. Later that month a new coalition Government, comprising the Social Democrats, the Centre Party, the Independents and the Moderates, was formed under Camilla Gunell of the Social Democrats.

GOVERNMENT

The Åland Islands are governed according to the Autonomy Act, which was introduced in 1920, revised in 1951 and further revised with effect from January 1993. The Islands' demilitarized status and autonomy are guaranteed by international treaties. The legislative body is the Lagting, comprising 30 members, elected every four years on a basis of proportional representation. All Ålanders over the age of 18 years, possessing Åland regional citizenship, have the right to vote and to seek election. An Executive Council (Landskapsregeringen), consisting of five to seven members, is elected by the Lagting, and its Chairman (Lantråd) is the highest-ranking politician in Åland after the Speaker (Talman) of the Lagting. The President has the right to veto Lagting decisions only when the Lagting exceeds its legislative competence, or when there is a threat to the security of the country. The Governor of Åland represents the Government of Finland and is appointed by the Finnish President (with the agreement of the Speaker of the Åland legislature). The Åland Islands elects one representative to the Finnish Parliament, the Eduskunta. There are 16 municipalities in the Åland Islands.

REGIONAL CO-OPERATION

The Åland Islands joined the European Union (EU, see p. 276) in 1995, together with Finland, following a referendum in November 1994.

ECONOMIC AFFAIRS

In 2008 the gross domestic product (GDP) of the Åland Islands, measured at current prices, was €1,044.6m. In 2009 4.3% of the working population were employed in agriculture (including hunting, forestry and fishing), which contributed 2.8% of GDP in 2008. Forests covered 60% of the islands in 2010, and only 9.0% of the total land area was arable. The principal crops are cereals, sugar beet, potatoes and fruit. Dairy farming and sheep rearing are also important.

Industry (including mining, manufacturing, construction and power) provided 12.5% of GDP in 2008, and employed 14.7% of the working population in 2009. Manufacturing contributed 5.0% of GDP in 2008 and engaged 6.6% of the working population in 2009.

Since 1960 the economy of the islands has expanded and diversified. Fishing has declined as a source of income, and shipping (particularly the operation of ferry services between Finland and Sweden), trade and tourism have become the dominant economic sectors. In 2008 services accounted for 84.7% of GDP and engaged 78.5% of the employed labour force in 2009. The transport sector, including shipping, employed 13.7% in 2009, and, together with storage and communications, contributed 33.9% of GDP in 2008. The political autonomy of the islands and their strategic location between Sweden and Finland have contributed to expanding banking and trade sectors; financial services engaged 3.3% of the employed labour force in 2009, while trade and hotels employed 13.5%. Tourist arrivals totalled 442,527 in 2009 with a slight decrease in 2010 when the number of total arrivals was 423,893.

The Finnish state collects taxes, duties and fees from the Åland Islands, which receives 0.45% of total Finnish government income in return. If the taxes raised in the Åland Islands exceed 0.5% of corresponding Finnish tax revenues, the islands receive the excess amount in the form of a tax redemption. Consumer prices increased at an average annual rate of 1.5% in 2001–10; prices rose by 1.8% in 2010. The unemployment rate stood at 3.1% in 2011. Finland participated in Economic and Monetary Union (EMU), introducing the single European currency, the euro, in January 1999. The Finnish currency, the markka, was used by the islands until the end of 2001. Euro notes and coins were introduced on 1 January 2002, and, as in Finland as a whole, the common European currency, the euro, became the sole legal tender from 1 March 2002.

Statistical Survey

Source: Statistics Åland, POB 1187, 22111 Mariehamn; tel. (18) 25490; fax (18) 19495; e-mail info@asub.ax; internet www.asub.ax.

AREA AND POPULATION

Area: 13,324 sq km (5,144 sq miles), of which 1,553 sq km (600 sq miles) is land and 11,772 sq km (4,545 sq miles) is water.

Population (official figures at 31 December 2010): 28,007 (males 13,953, females 14,054).

Density (land area only, 31 December 2010): 18.0 per sq km.

Population by Age and Sex (official figures at 31 December 2010): *0–14:* 4,582 (males 2,399, females 2,183); *15–64:* 18,280 (males 9,196, females 9,084); *65 and over:* 5,145 (males 2,358, females 2,787); *Total* 28,007 (males 13,953, females 14,054).

Principal Towns (official figures at 31 December 2010): Mariehamn (capital) 11,190; Godby 879; Storby 503; Prästgården 419; Ödkarby 357; Söderby 342.

Births, Marriages and Deaths (2010 unless otherwise indicated): Registered live births 286 (birth rate 10.2 per 1,000); Marriages (2009) 120 (marriage rate 4.3 per 1,000); Deaths 233 (death rate 8.3 per 1,000).

Life Expectancy (years at birth, 2005–09): 81.5 (males 79.7; females 83.1).

Immigration and Emigration (2010): Immigrants 873 (Finland 292; Sweden 391); Emigrants 649 (Finland 251; Sweden 348).

Employment (2009): Agriculture, fishing and aquaculture 587; Mining and quarrying 12; Manufacturing 900; Electricity, gas, steam and air conditioning supply 80; Water supply, sewerage, waste management and remediation activities 100; Construction 924; Wholesale and retail trade, and repair of motor vehicles 1,318; Transportation and storage 1,878; Accommodation and food services 534; Information and communication 505; Finance and insurance activities 446; Real estate 77; Professional, scientific and technical activities 441; Administrative and support services 328; Public administration and defence 1,065; Education 797; Health and social work 2,541; Arts, entertainment and recreation 346; Other service activities 464; *Sub-total* 13,343; Activities not classified 344; *Total employed* 13,687; Unemployed 416; *Total labour force* 14,103.

HEALTH AND WELFARE

Physicians (2003): 59.

Hospital Beds (2010): 199.

AGRICULTURE, ETC.

Agricultural Production (metric tons, 2010, unless otherwise indicated): Milk ('000 litres) 14,459; Beef 548; Pork 25 (2008); Mutton 95; Poultry 1,497 (2002); Eggs 236 (2009); Wheat 3,492; Rye 871 (2008); Triticale (wheat-rye hybrid) 81 (2003); Barley and oats 1,972; Peas 1 (2006); Turnip rape 40 (2006); Sugar beet 4,010; Potatoes 14,705; Onions 7,205; Cucumbers 111 (2008); Leeks 78 (2008); Chinese cabbage and lettuce 911; Apples 3,192; Strawberries ('000 litres) 22 (2008); Tomatoes 153 (2008); Parsley ('000 bunches) 94 (2008); Dill ('000 bunches) 155 (2008); Celery 23 (2008); Carrots 39 (2008).

Livestock (2009): Cattle 7,694; Pigs 294; Hens 12,780; Sheep 13,124; Horses 257.

Forestry Production (cu m, roundwood, 2010): Logs 60,897; Pulp 143,025.

Fishing (metric tons, live weight, 2010): Capture 3,415 (Baltic herring and sprat 2,686; Cod 521; Whitefish 43; Perch 69; Pike-perch 11; Pike 11); Aquaculture 4,118; *Total catch* 7,533.

INDUSTRY

Selected Indicators (2010): Electric energy 72m. kWh (incl. 53m. kWh from wind power); Dwellings completed 241 (preliminary).

FINANCE

Currency: Finnish currency was used until the end of 2001. Euro notes and coins were introduced on 1 January 2002, and the euro became the sole legal tender from 1 March. For details of exchange rates, see the chapter on Finland.

Budget (€ '000, 2009): Revenue 287,684; Expenditure 304,982.

Cost of Living (Consumer Price Index; base: 2000 = 100): All items 114.4 in 2008; 114.7 in 2009; 116.8 in 2010.

Expenditure on the Gross Domestic Product (€ million at current prices, 2004): Wages and salaries 383; Employers' contribution to social security 103; Operating surplus 257; Fixed capital depreciation 140; *Total domestic expenditure* 883; Indirect taxes 117; *Less* Subsidies 38; *GDP in market prices* 963.

Gross Domestic Product by Economic Activity (€ million at current prices, 2008): Agriculture, hunting, forestry and fishing 27.0; Manufacturing 48.4; Construction 51.2; Energy supply and water 6.5; Trade, restaurants and hotels 87.3; Transport, storage and communications 298.2; Financing, insurance, real estate and business services 202.0; Government services 215.8; Unallocated banking services –30.0; Other community, social and personal services 58.4; Non-profit institutions 15.1; *GDP at factor cost* 979.9; Indirect taxes 127.9; *Less* Subsidies 63.2; *GDP in purchasers' values* 1,044.7.

EXTERNAL TRADE

2010 (€ '000): *Imports:* Total 179,406 (Live animals and products thereof 24,417; Articles of plastics and rubber 13,573; Pulp and paper 20,324; Machinery, equipment and appliances 35,021); *Exports:* Total 49,815 (Articles of plastics and rubber 14,794; Wood and cork and products thereof 6,792). Note: Figures exclude trade with mainland Finland.

TRANSPORT

Road Traffic (registered motor vehicles, 31 December 2010): Private motor cars 19,240; Vans 3,915; Lorries 674; Buses 43; Motorcycles 1,373; Tractors 3,637.

Shipping (2008): *Merchant Fleet:* 64 vessels; total displacement 1,141,971 grt. Note: Figures include 19 vessels registered under flags other than Åland or Finland, total displacement 594,281 grt. *Traffic:* 8,135 vessels entered; 2,224,692 passenger arrivals (incl. ferry services).

Civil Aviation (traffic, Mariehamn airport, 2009): Passengers 56,193; Freight 11 metric tons; Post 307 metric tons.

TOURISM

Tourist Arrivals (2010): 423,893 (177,697 from Finland).

EDUCATION

Primary and Secondary Schools (2010): Institutions 23 (Comprehensive schools 22, of which 9 also offer upper-stage education, Upper-stage only 1); Pupils 2,841 (Comprehensive schools 1,840, Upper-stage schools 1,001).

Pupils Enrolled in Post-Comprehensive Education (2010): Preparatory study programme 483 (males 187, females 296); Vocational 803 (males 445, females 358); Other 57 (males 22, females 35); Åland Polytechnic 506 (males 322, females 184).

Directory

Government and Legislature

The legislative body is the Lagting, comprising 30 members, elected every four years on a basis of proportional representation. All Ålanders over the age of 18 years, possessing Åland regional citizenship, have the right to vote and to seek election. An Executive Council (Landskapsregeringen), consisting of five to seven members, is elected by the Lagting, and its Chairman (Lantråd) is the highest-ranking politician in Åland after the Speaker (Talman) of the Lagting. The President has the right to veto Lagting decisions only when the Lagting exceeds its legislative competence, or when there is a threat to the security of the country. The Governor of Åland represents the Government of Finland and is appointed by the Finnish President (with the agreement of the Speaker of the Åland legislature).

Governor: PETER LINDBÄCK.

LANDSKAPSREGERINGEN
(Executive Council)

Självstyrelsegården, POB 1060, 22111 Mariehamn; tel. (18) 25000; fax (18) 19155; e-mail marina.sundstrom@regeringen.ax; internet www.regeringen.ax.

The governing coalition comprises members of the Social Democrats, the Centre Party, the Independents and the Moderates. Its composition in May 2012 was as follows:

Chairman (Lantråd): CAMILLA GUNELL (Social Democrats).

Deputy Chairman (Vicelantråd) and Minister of Finance: ROGER NORDLUND (Centre Party).

Minister for Administrative Affairs: GUN-MARI LINDHOLM (Independents).

Minister for Infrastructure: VERONICA THÖRNROOS (Centre Party).

Minister for Social and Environmental Affairs: CARINA AALTONEN (Social Democrats).

Minister for Enterprise: FREDRIK KARLSTRÖM (Independents).

Minister for Education and Culture: JOHAN EHN (Moderates).

LAGTING
(Parliament)

Självstyrelsegården, POB 69, 22101 Mariehamn; tel. (18) 25000; fax (18) 13302; e-mail susanne.eriksson@regeringen.ax; internet www.lagtinget.ax.

Speaker (Talman): ROGER NORDLUND (Centre Party).

Election, 16 October 2011

	Votes	% of votes	Seats
Åländsk Center (Centre Party)	3,068	23.65	7
Liberalerna på Åland (Liberal Party)	2,630	20.27	6
Ålands Socialdemokrater (Social Democrats)	2,404	18.53	6
Moderaterna på Åland (Moderates of Åland)	1,810	13.95	4
Obunden Samling (Independents)	1,639	12.63	4
Ålands Framtid (Åland's Future)	1,286	9.91	3
Valmansf. för Henrik Appelqvist	138	1.06	—
Total	12,975	100.00	30

Political Organizations

Unless otherwise indicated, the address of each of the following organizations is: Ålands Lagting, POB 69, 22101 Mariehamn; tel. (18) 25000; fax (18) 13302.

Åländsk Center (Centre Party): tel. (18) 25360; fax (18) 16630; e-mail centern@lagtinget.ax; internet www.centern.ax; f. 1976; Chair. HARRY JANSSON.

Ålands Framtid (Åland's Future): tel. (18) 25366; e-mail info@alandsframtid.ax; internet www.alandsframtid.ax; f. 2003; separatist; Leader ANDERS ERIKSSON; Sec. BIRGITTA BERGMAN-JANSSON.

Ålands Socialdemokrater (Social Democrats): Ekonomiegatan 1, POB 69, Mariehamn; tel. (18) 25461; e-mail anders.hallback@lagtinget.ax; internet www.socialdemokraterna.ax; Chair. CAMILLA GUNELL; Sec. ANDERS HALLBÄCK.

Liberalerna på Åland (Liberal Party): tel. (18) 25362; fax (18) 16075; e-mail liberalerna@lagtinget.ax; internet www.liberalerna.ax; Chair. VIVEKA ERIKSSON; Gen. Sec. CHRISTINA JOHANSSON-GAMMALS.

Moderaterna Åland (Moderates of Åland): tel. (18) 25357; e-mail moderat@lagtinget.ax; internet www.moderaterna.ax; Chair. JOHAN EHN.

Obunden Samling (Independents): tel. (18) 25368; e-mail danne.sundman@lagtinget.ax; internet www.obs.ax; f. 1987; Chair. GUN-MARI LINDHOLM.

Religion

The majority of the islands' population is Christian. At 31 December 2006 there were 23,820 adherents of the Evangelical Lutheran Church of Finland, accounting for 88.5% of the population. There were also small numbers of Jehovah's Witnesses (49), Roman Catholics (39), Greek Orthodox Christians (24) and Adventists (12); 58 people practised other religions.

The Press

Ålandstidningen: Strandgatan 16, POB 50, 22101 Mariehamn; tel. (18) 26026; fax (18) 15755; e-mail niklas.lampi@alandstidningen.ax; internet www.tidningen.ax; 6 a week; f. 1891; Man. Dir DAN-JOHAN DAHLBLOM; Editor-in-Chief NIKLAS LAMPI; circ. 10,355 (2007).

Nya Åland: Uppgårdsvägen 6, POB 21, 22100 Mariehamn; tel. (18) 23444; fax (18) 23450; e-mail redaktion@nyan.ax; internet www.nyan.ax; f. 1981; 5 a week; Man. Dir STEFAN NORRGRANN; Editor-in-Chief JONAS BLADH; circ. 7,256 (2005).

Broadcasting and Communications

TELECOMMUNICATIONS

Ålands Mobiltelefon Ab: POB 1230, 22101 Mariehamn; tel. (18) 291464; e-mail info@amt.ax; internet www.gsm.aland.fi; f. 1989; licensed to operate both GSM- and UMTS-networks on the islands.

Ålands Telefonandelslag: Hantverkargränd 1, 22150 Jomala; tel. (18) 41053; fax (18) 41299; e-mail jomala@altel.ax; internet www.altel.ax; f. 1910.

Mariehamns Telefon Ab: Ålandsvägen 52, POB 1228, 22111 Mariehamn; tel. (18) 27044; fax (18) 15900; e-mail anders@mtel.ax; internet www.mtel.ax; f. 1892; Dir ANDERS JOHNSSON.

RADIO AND TELEVISION

Ålands Radio och TV Ab: Ålandsvägen 24, POB 140, 22101 Mariehamn; tel. (18) 26060; fax (18) 26520; e-mail info@radiotv.ax; internet www.radiotv.ax; f. 1996; broadcasts radio programmes in Swedish, 115.5 hours a week; operates 3 analogue and 5 digital television channels; Man. Dir PIA ROTHBERG-OLOFSSON; Editor-in-Chief ASTRID OLHAGEN.

Steel FM: Strandgränd 2, 22100 Mariehamn; tel. (18) 16200; fax (18) 22079; e-mail mail@steelfm.net; internet www.steelfm.net; commercial radio broadcaster; Dir FREDRIK KARLSTRÖM.

TV Åland: Elverksgatan 1, 22100 Mariehamn; tel. (18) 14035; fax (18) 14037; e-mail redaktion@tv.ax; internet www.tv.ax; f. 1984; television producer and broadcaster; broadcasts by cable to 75% of islands; Dir KAJ GRUNDSTRÖM.

Finance

BANKS

(cap. = capital; res = reserves; dep. = deposits; m. = million; amounts in euros; brs = branches)

Ålandsbanken Abp (Bank of Åland): Nygatan 2, POB 3, 22100 Mariehamn; tel. (204) 29011; fax (204) 29228; e-mail aland@alandsbanken.fi; internet www.alandsbanken.fi; f. 1919 as Ålands Aktiebank; name changed to Bank of Åland Ltd 1980, changed as above in 1998; merged with Ålands Hypoteksbank Ab in November 1995; cap. 23.3m., res 67.7m., dep. 2,568.4m. (Dec. 2010); Man. Dir PETER WIKLÖF; 24 brs.

Andelsbanken för Åland: Köpmansgatan 2, POB 34, 22101 Mariehamn; tel. (18) 26000; e-mail info@andelsbanken.ax; co-operative; mem. of OP–Pohjola Group; Dirs HÅKAN CLEMES, ROLAND KARLSSON.

Nordea Bank Finland PLC and Pohjola Bank PLC are also represented.

INSURANCE

Alandia Group: Ålandsvägen 31, POB 121, 22101 Mariehamn; tel. (18) 29000; fax (18) 12290; e-mail mhamn@alandia.com; internet www.alandia.com; f. 1938; life, non-life and marine; comprises 3 subsidiaries; Man. Dir LEIF NORDLUND.

Ålands Ömsesidiga Försäkringsbolag (Åland Mutual Insurance Co): Köpmansgatan 6, POB 64, 22101 Mariehamn; tel. (18) 27600; fax (18) 27610; e-mail info@omsen.ax; internet www.omsen.ax; f. 1866; life and non-life; Chair. STURE CARLSSON; Man. Dir GÖRAN LINDHOLM.

Trade and Industry

CHAMBER OF COMMERCE

Ålands Handelskammare: Nygatan 6, 22100 Mariehamn; tel. (18) 29029; fax (18) 21129; e-mail info@chamber.ax; internet www.chamber.ax; f. 1945; Chair. EDGAR VIKSTRÖM; Man. Dir DANIEL DAHLÉN.

TRADE ASSOCIATION

Ålands Företagareförening (Åland Business Asscn): Skarpansvägen 17, 22100 Mariehamn; tel. (18) 23277; fax (18) 23288; e-mail ombudsman@foretagare.ax; internet www.foretagare.ax; f. 1957; c. 250 mem. cos; Chair. DICK JANSSON; Sec. JONNY MATTSSON.

EMPLOYERS' ORGANIZATIONS

Ålands Arbetsgivareförening (Åland Employers' Asscn): Nygatan 6, 22100 Mariehamn; tel. (18) 29474; fax (18) 21129; f. 1969; Chair. KJELL CLEMES.

Ålands Fiskodlarförening (Åland Fish Farmers' Asscn): Tingsvägen 3, 22710 Föglö; tel. (18) 17834; fax (18) 17833; e-mail info@fiskodlarna.aland.fi; internet www.fiskodlarna.aland.fi; Chair. MARCUS ERIKSSON; Sec. ANDREAS ENQUIST.

Ålands Köpmannaförening (Åland Businessmen's Asscn): Nygatan 6, 22100 Mariehamn; tel. (18) 13650; fax (18) 16519; e-mail kopmannaforeningen@aland.net; internet www.akf.ax; f. 1927; Chair. TOM FORSBOM; Sec. STEFAN BLOMQVIST.

Ålands Producentförbund (Åland Agricultural Producers' Asscn): Ålands Landsbygdscentrum, Jomalagårdsväg 17, 22150 Jomala; tel. (18) 329840; fax (18) 329801; e-mail birgitta.eriksson@landsbygd.aland.fi; f. 1946; Chair. ANDERS ENGLUND; Man. Dir BIRGITTA ERIKSSON.

UTILITIES

Electricity

Ålands Elandelslag: Godbyvägen 193, 22100 Mariehamn; tel. (18) 39250; fax (18) 31562; e-mail info@el.ax; internet www.el.ax; distribution; Man. Dir JAN WENNSTRÖM.

Ålands Vindenergi Andelslag: Hamngatan 8, 22100 Mariehamn; tel. (18) 526300; fax (18) 12090; e-mail info@alandsvindenergi.ax; internet www.alandsvindenergi.ax; operates the 16 wind power farms on the Åland islands, 9 of which it owns; produces roughly 7% of energy consumed on the islands; Chair. ANNETTE LARSON; Man. Dir HENRIK LINDQVIST.

Kraftnät Åland: Elverksgatan 10, POB 71, 22101 Mariehamn; tel. (18) 5395; fax (18) 539250; e-mail info@kraftnat.ax; internet www.kraftnat.ax; production; Man. Dir JAN KAHLROTH.

Water

Ålands Vatten Ab: Vattenverksvägen 34, 22150 Jomala; tel. (18) 32860; fax (18) 31471; e-mail alandsvatten@vatten.ax; internet www.vatten.ax; f. 1970; supplies water to 70% of population; Man. Dir CHRISTIAN NORDAS.

VA-verket: Torggatan 17, POB 5, 22101 Mariehamn; tel. (18) 5310; fax (18) 531206; e-mail info@mariehamn.ax; internet www.mariehamn.ax; Dir JOUNI HUHTALA.

TRADE UNIONS

FFC-facken på Åland: POB 108, 22101 Mariehamn; tel. (18) 16207; fax (18) 17207; internet www.facket.ax; Chair. STURLE FJÄDER; Gen. Sec. CHRISTINA HENRIKSSON.

Tjänstemannaorganisationerna på Åland, TCÅ r.f. (Union of Salaried Employees in Åland): Norragatan 1B5, 22100 Mariehamn; tel. (18) 16210; e-mail facket@tca.ax; Chair. YVONNE ASPHOLM; Dir MARIE-SUSANNE STENWALL.

Transport

The islands are linked to the Swedish and Finnish mainlands by ferry services and by air services from Mariehamn airport. There are no railways, but local bus services are available, along with inter-island ferries.

Ålandstrafiken: Strandgatan 25, 22100 Mariehamn; tel. (18) 525100; fax (18) 17815; e-mail info@alandstrafiken.ax; internet www.alandstrafiken.ax; operates buses on the islands and ferry services between the islands.

ROADS

In 2006 there was a road network of 914.4 km, of which 738.9 km were paved. There is also a bicycle route network, covering some 356.5 km in 2006.

SHIPPING

Ferry services operate from the Åland Islands to Sweden, the Finnish mainland and Estonia.

Principal Companies

Birka Line Abp: Torggatan 2, POB 158, 22101 Mariehamn; tel. (18) 28050; fax (18) 15118; e-mail brage.jansson@birkaline.com; internet www.birkaline.com; f. 1971; shipping service; Man. Dir BRAGE JANSSON.

Birka Cargo Ab Ltd: Torggatan 2B, POB 175, 22101 Mariehamn; tel. (18) 28050; fax (18) 23223; e-mail info@birkacargo.com; internet www.birkacargo.com; f. 1990 as United Shipping Ltd Ab; 7 ro-ro vessels; Man. Dir STEFAN AXBERG.

Lundqvist Rederierna: Norra Esplanadgatan 9B, 22100 Mariehamn; tel. (18) 26050; fax (18) 26428; e-mail info@lundqvist.aland.fi; internet www.lundqvist.aland.fi; f. 1927; tanker and ro-ro services; Man. Dir BEN LUNDQVIST; total tonnage c. 820,000 dwt.

Rederiaktiebolaget Eckerö (Eckerö Linjen): Torggatan 2, POB 158, 22101 Mariehamn; tel. (18) 28030; fax (18) 28380; e-mail info@eckerolinjen.fi; internet www.eckerolinjen.fi; f. 1960; operates ferry routes between the Åland Islands and Sweden, and between Finland and Estonia; Man. Dir BJÖRN BLOMQVIST.

Rederiaktiebolaget Gustaf Erikson: Norra Esplanadgatan 4B, POB 49, 22101 Mariehamn; tel. (18) 27070; fax (18) 12670; e-mail info@geson.aland.fi; internet www.geson.ax; f. 1913; manages dry cargo and refrigerated vessels; Man. Dir GUN ERIKSON-HJERLING.

Rederi Ab Lillgaard: Köpmansgatan 9, POB 136, 22101 Mariehamn; tel. (18) 13120; fax (18) 17220; e-mail info@lillgaard.aland.fi; internet www.lillgaard.aland.fi; f. 1966; operates services from the Åland Islands to the Finnish mainland and Sweden; Man. Dir ANDERS NORDLUND.

Viking Line Abp: Norragatan 4, POB 166, 22101 Mariehamn; tel. (18) 27000; fax (18) 16944; e-mail nn@vikingline.fi; internet www.vikingline.fi; f. 1963; operates cruise and ferry services between Finland and Sweden and throughout the Baltic Sea; 7 car/passenger vessels; total tonnage 212,474 grt; Chair. BEN LUNDQVIST; Man. Dir and Chief Exec. MIKAEL BACKMAN.

CIVIL AVIATION

The islands' airport is at Mariehamn. In 2008 the airport handled 62,110 passengers, 135 metric tons of freight and 223 tons of post. It is served by Finnair and AirÅland Ab.

AirÅland Ab: Mariehamns Airport, Flygfältsvägen 67, 22120 Mariehamn; tel. (18) 17110; fax (18) 23730; e-mail info@airaland.com; internet www.airaland.com; f. 2005; routes from Mariehamn to Helsinki and Stockholm; the Swedish company NextJet operates all AirÅland Ab flights; CEO CARIN HOLMQVIST.

Tourism

The Åland archipelago has numerous bays, inlets, islands and open stretches of water, and is an area of great natural beauty. Cycling, canoeing, kayaking and hiking attract tourists to the islands. Major tourist attractions include the Maritime Museum, the museum ship Pommern and the Maritime Quarter. Most visitors are from the Nordic countries, particularly from mainland Finland and Sweden. In 2010 tourist arrivals totalled 423,893 (including 177,697 from Finland).

Ålands Turist Förbund (Åland Tourism Board): Storagatan 8, 22100 Mariehamn; tel. (18) 24000; fax (18) 24265; e-mail info@visitaland.com; internet www.visitaland.com; f. 1989; Man. Dir ANNICA JANSSON.

Ålands Turist och Konferens Ab: Hotell Arkipelag, Strandgatan 31, 22100 Mariehamn; tel. (18) 15349; fax (18) 21077; e-mail info@turist-konferens.aland.fi; internet www.turist-konferens.aland.fi; Man. Dir HENRIK NORDSTRÖM.

Defence

By law, the archipelago is demilitarized. For general details, see the chapter on Finland.

Education

The education system is similar to that of Finland, except that Swedish is the language of instruction and Finnish an optional subject.

FRANCE

Introductory Survey

LOCATION, CLIMATE, LANGUAGE, RELIGION, FLAG, CAPITAL

The French Republic is situated in Western Europe. It is bounded to the north by the English Channel (la Manche), to the east by Belgium, Luxembourg, Germany, Switzerland and Italy, to the south by the Mediterranean Sea, Andorra, Monaco, and Spain, and to the west by the Atlantic Ocean. The Mediterranean island of Corsica is part of metropolitan France, while 12 overseas possessions (French Guiana, Guadeloupe, Martinique, Réunion, French Polynesia, Mayotte, Saint-Barthélemy, Saint-Martin, Saint Pierre and Miquelon, the Wallis and Futuna Islands, the French Southern and Antarctic Territories and New Caledonia) also form an integral part of the Republic. The climate is temperate throughout most of the country, but in the south it is of the Mediterranean type, with warm summers and mild winters. The principal language is French; additionally, small minorities speak Alsatian, Basque, Breton, Corsican and Provençal, among other regional languages and dialects. A majority of French citizens profess Christianity, and about 74% of the population are adherents of the Roman Catholic Church. Other Christian denominations are represented, and there are also Muslim and Jewish communities. The national flag (proportions 2 by 3) has three equal vertical stripes, of blue, white and red. The capital is Paris.

CONTEMPORARY POLITICAL HISTORY

Historical Context

In September 1939, following Nazi Germany's invasion of Poland, France and the United Kingdom declared war on Germany, thus entering the Second World War. In June 1940 France was forced to sign an armistice, following a swift invasion and occupation of French territory by German forces. After the liberation of France from German occupation in 1944, a provisional Government took office under Gen. Charles de Gaulle, leader of the Free French forces during the wartime resistance. The war in Europe ended in May 1945, when German forces surrendered at Reims. In 1946, following a referendum, the Fourth Republic was established and de Gaulle announced his intention to retire from public life.

France had 26 different Governments from 1946 until the Fourth Republic came to an end in 1958 with an insurrection in Algeria (then an overseas department) and the threat of civil war. In May 1958 the President, René Coty, invited Gen. de Gaulle to form a government. In June the National Assembly (Assemblée nationale) invested de Gaulle as Prime Minister, with the power to rule by decree for six months. A new Constitution, approved by referendum in September, was promulgated in October; thus the Fifth Republic came into being, with de Gaulle taking office as President in January 1959. The new system provided for a strong presidency, the authority of which would be strengthened by national referendums and a stable executive.

The early years of the Fifth Republic were overshadowed by the Algerian crisis. De Gaulle granted Algeria independence in 1962, withdrew troops and repatriated French settlers. In May 1968 students and workers joined in a revolt against the Government's authoritarian education and information policies, low wage rates and lack of social reform. For a time the Republic appeared threatened, but the student movement collapsed and the general strike was settled by large wage rises. In April 1969 President de Gaulle resigned following his defeat in a referendum on regional reform.

Domestic Political Affairs

Georges Pompidou, who had been Prime Minister from 1962–68, was elected President in June 1969. The Gaullist government coalition was returned at a general election in March 1973. Pompidou died in April 1974. In the presidential election held in May, Valéry Giscard d'Estaing, formerly leader of the centre-right Républicains Indépendants (RI), narrowly defeated François Mitterrand, the First Secretary of the Parti Socialiste (PS). A coalition Government was formed from members of the RI, the Gaullist Union des Démocrates pour la République (UDR) and the centrist parties. In August 1976 Jacques Chirac resigned as Prime Minister and subsequently undertook to transform the UDR into a new party, the Rassemblement pour la République (RPR). In February 1978 the governing non-Gaullist parties formed the Union pour la Démocratie Française (UDF) to compete against RPR candidates in the National Assembly elections held in March, when the governing coalition retained a working majority.

In the April/May 1981 presidential election Mitterrand defeated Giscard d'Estaing. At elections for a new National Assembly, held in June, the PS and associated groups, principally the Mouvement des Radicaux de Gauche (MRG), won an overall majority of seats, following which four members of the Parti Communiste Français (PCF) were appointed to the Council of Ministers. The new Government introduced a programme of social and labour reforms, including the nationalization of several major industrial enterprises and financial institutions.

Legislative elections took place in March 1986, using a party-list based system of proportional representation for the first time. Although the PS remained the largest single party in the new National Assembly, the centre-right parties, led by an RPR-UDF alliance, commanded a majority of seats. The PCF suffered a severe decline in support, while the far-right Front National (FN) won legislative representation for the first time. A period of political 'cohabitation' ensued as Mitterrand invited the RPR leader, Chirac, to form a new Council of Ministers.

In April 1986 Chirac introduced legislation that allowed his Government to legislate by decree on economic and social issues and on the proposed reversion to a voting system comprising single-member constituencies for legislative elections. However, Mitterrand insisted on exercising the presidential right to withhold approval of decrees that reversed the previous Government's social reforms. In July Chirac thus resorted to the 'guillotine' procedure (setting a time-limit for consideration of legislative proposals) to gain parliamentary consent for legislation providing for the privatization of 65 state-owned companies, which, since it had been approved by the predominantly right-wing Senate (Sénat) and the Constitutional Council (Conseil Constitutionnel), the President was legally bound to approve.

Mitterrand was re-elected as President in May 1988, defeating Chirac. A general election took place in June, with a reintroduced single-seat majority voting system, at which an alliance of the PS and the MRG secured the largest number of seats. Michel Rocard of the PS, who had been appointed as Prime Minister following the presidential election, regained that role. Rocard resigned in May 1991 and was succeeded by Edith Cresson, France's first female Prime Minister. However, following the poor performance of the PS in regional elections in March 1992, in April Mitterrand appointed Pierre Bérégovoy to replace Cresson. In June the National Assembly approved constitutional changes allowing the ratification of the Treaty on European Union (the Maastricht Treaty), subject to approval by referendum. In the referendum, held in September, 51.1% of voters supported the treaty's ratification.

At elections to the National Assembly, held in March 1993, the RPR won 247 of the 577 seats, the UDF 213 and the PS 54. Chirac had made it known that he was not available for the post of Prime Minister as he intended to concentrate on his candidacy in the 1995 presidential election. Another RPR member, Edouard Balladur, was therefore appointed premier.

In the first round of voting in the presidential election, on 23 April 1995, Lionel Jospin, the PS candidate, obtained 23% of the votes, while Chirac and Balladur, both representing the RPR, took 21% and 19%, respectively. Jean-Marie Le Pen, the leader of the FN, won 15%. In the second round, on 7 May, Chirac (with 53% of the votes) defeated Jospin. Chirac appointed Alain Juppé (Minister of Foreign Affairs in the previous Government) as Prime Minister. Juppé formed an administration in which the principal portfolios were evenly distributed between the RPR and the UDF.

At legislative elections held in May–June 1997, the PS secured 241 seats, the RPR 134 and the UDF 108. The unexpected victory of the PS, which began a further period of 'cohabitation', was widely attributed to dissatisfaction with Juppé's administration and the imposition of economic austerity measures necessitated under the terms of Economic and Monetary Union (EMU, see p. 312) within the European Union (EU, see p. 276). Jospin became Prime Minister, and formed a 'plural left' coalition.

In March 1999 a Paris public prosecutor upheld a ruling of the Constitutional Council that the President of the Republic enjoyed immunity from prosecution for all crimes, other than high treason, for the duration of his presidential term. This decision, which was confirmed by an appeal court ruling in January 2000, followed the disclosure of documentation purporting to show that Chirac had been aware of the existence of at least 300 fictitious employees, reputedly including RPR members or supporters, on the payroll of the Paris city council during his tenure as Mayor in 1977–95. In September 2000 a transcript of a videotape made by Jean-Claude Méry, a former RPR official who had been imprisoned on charges of embezzlement in the mid-1990s, was published posthumously in *Le Monde*. In the recording Méry stated that Chirac had personally ordered him to arrange for municipal funds to be diverted to political parties. In December Michel Roussin, who had been Chirac's principal private secretary from 1989–93, was arrested, while the former unofficial treasurer for the RPR was questioned. Their testimony, which was leaked to the press, included details of the systematic levying of an illegal commission on public works contracts awarded by the council.

In April 2001 the investigating judge in the case, Eric Halphen, announced the existence of consistent evidence implicating Chirac in the alleged illegal use of funds in the Paris city council, but stated that the doctrine of presidential immunity prevented Chirac from being brought to trial. New revelations concerning Chirac's alleged involvement in financial malpractice emerged in June: the President was alleged to have spent up to 2.4m. francs (a figure subsequently increased to 3.1m. francs) of state 'secret funds'—issued annually by the Office of the Prime Minister for the security services, to pay bonuses to staff, and as a contingency fund—on airline tickets and luxury hotel bills for himself and his family in 1992–95, although suspicions were voiced that the finance for these holidays might have originated from the alleged illicit commission payments made by building firms to the Paris city council. Chirac declared himself innocent of all charges made against him, and confirmed that he would not participate in any court case. In September 2001 the Appeal Court dismissed Halphen as the leading investigator into the case regarding the use of illicit funds in the Paris city council; Halphen was ruled to have exceeded his powers by calling the President as a witness, and by introducing certain items of evidence, including Méry's videotape. Although the case could be tried again, this decision effectively ruled out any development in the case so long as Chirac remained President. In October the Court of Cassation confirmed the Constitutional Council's ruling that an incumbent President could not be prosecuted, additionally ruling that a head of state could not undergo formal investigation while in power, even for offences allegedly committed prior to taking office.

Meanwhile, the tensions caused by the prolonged period of 'cohabitation' from 1997 prompted moves towards constitutional change. In June 2000 the National Assembly approved a reduction in the presidential term from seven to five years, in order to bring it into line with the life of a parliament. Amid concerns that the Senate might not support the bill by the two-thirds' majority required, Chirac called a referendum. Held on 24 September, the referendum attracted only a 30.6% participation rate. Of those who voted, 73.2% were in favour of the change, which would take effect from the 2002 presidential election. In May 2001 the Constitutional Council approved a proposal, aimed at preventing a further period of 'cohabitation', to hold the presidential election in advance of the parliamentary elections due in May 2002.

The 2002 presidential election

The first round of the presidential election was held on 21 April 2002. Prior to the first round, Chirac and Jospin had been widely expected to progress to a second round. However, partly as a result of the wide choice of candidates (16), a relatively low rate of participation (only 69.2% of the electorate cast valid votes), and a campaign focus on issues related to 'insecurity' and law and order, Jospin polled only 16.2% of the valid votes cast, while Chirac won 19.9% and Le Pen 16.9%. The splintering of the governmental 'plural left' coalition proved detrimental for Jospin and the PS, as four of the coalition partners presented individual candidates for the presidency, together securing 16.3% of votes cast. The qualification of Le Pen for the second-round poll precipitated widespread demonstrations, and the majority of the defeated candidates rallied around Chirac as a candidate who represented 'republican values'. In the second round, on 5 May, the turn-out increased slightly, to 75.4%. Chirac's victory, with 82.2% of the valid votes cast, was widely interpreted as a resounding defeat for the far right. On 6 May Chirac appointed Jean-Pierre Raffarin, of Démocratie Libérale (DL), as Prime Minister. Raffarin appointed an interim Government; among the principal appointments were Nicolas Sarkozy as Minister of the Interior, Interior Security and Local Freedoms, Michèle Alliot-Marie as Minister of Defence and Dominique de Villepin as Minister of Foreign Affairs. Chirac was subsequently instrumental in the organization of a new centre-right electoral alliance, which was initially titled the Union pour la Majorité Présidentielle (UMP).

At the legislative elections in June 2002 the UMP, which incorporated the greater part of the RPR and DL, and significant elements of the UDF, succeeded in becoming the largest grouping in the National Assembly, with 355 of the 577 seats, while a further 43 representatives of other parties of the centre-right and right were elected, thus ensuring a clear working majority for the pro-presidential grouping. Of the 176 seats awarded to parties of the broad left, the PS was the most successful, with 140 deputies. The new Government was largely unchanged from the interim administration and cited law and order, a programme of decentralization, and further privatizations among its priorities. In the aftermath of the legislative elections, the UMP consolidated its position, formally constituting itself as the Union pour un Mouvement Populaire in November 2002, absorbing the RPR and DL, in addition to factions of the UDF and the Rassemblement pour la France; Juppé was elected as President of the party.

Further concerns at the extent of corrupt practices in public life were raised during the trial in late 2003 of Juppé and 26 other defendants on charges that the Paris city council and private companies had illegally paid staff of the RPR during Juppé's tenure as Secretary-General of the party (in 1988–95) and as Deputy Mayor of Paris (1983–95). In January 2004 Juppé was found guilty and given an 18 months' suspended prison sentence; 13 other business executives also received suspended prison sentences in the case. Juppé was also banned from holding public office for a period of 10 years, but was permitted to remain in office as Mayor of Bordeaux, and as a parliamentary deputy, pending an appeal. Although the constitutional immunity from prosecution and investigation of the President of the Republic prevented any inquiry into Chirac's behaviour, the judges ruled that Juppé had been directly subordinate to Chirac in his capacity as President of the RPR. (Moreover, Chirac was the Mayor of Paris for the entire duration of Juppé's service as the Deputy Mayor.) Following Juppé's conviction, Chirac and other leading figures in the UMP rallied to his support. (In December 2004 the appeal court upheld the conviction, but reduced the length of the ban on holding public office from 10 years to one; Juppé subsequently resigned as Mayor of Bordeaux, having relinquished the UMP presidency in July.)

In March 2003 the two houses of Parliament (Parlement), meeting in congress, approved several constitutional changes relating to the proposed decentralization programme, which provided for the eventual possibility of territorial units receiving varying degrees of autonomy and powers, for the institution of deliberative assemblies and for the holding of local referendums in such territories. Moreover, the amendments permitted the introduction of legislation pertaining to decentralization on a temporary, or experimental, basis. Notably, the first article of the Constitution was amended to assert that the organization of the Republic was decentralized. However, attempts to implement policies that utilized the new constitutional provisions initially proved unsuccessful—in a local referendum in Corsica in July voters rejected proposals to reorganize the administration of the island, and in December voters in the Overseas Departments of Guadeloupe and Martinique rejected proposals to restructure and simplify their territorial administration.

A major topic of political debate in 2003 and early 2004 concerned the wearing of the *hijab* (headscarf) by female Muslim schoolchildren and students during classes at state educational establishments. Although a 1989 ruling of the Council of State (Conseil d'État) declared that the wearing of religious symbols in state schools did not violate the principle of the secularity of the state, formalized in 1905, so long as they were deemed to be of a 'non-ostentatious' nature, the ruling had subsequently been used to exclude a number of Muslim students from educational establishments. Legislation explicitly forbidding the wearing of the veil and other conspicuous religious symbols, including Jewish skullcaps and large Christian crosses, in state-run schools and colleges came into effect in September 2004.

Widespread public discontent with the Government was reflected in the results of regional and cantonal elections held in March 2004, following which the parties of the centre-right lost control of 13 regions to parties of the left and centre-left, which thereby controlled all of the regions of metropolitan France excluding Alsace and Corsica. Raffarin tendered his resignation as Prime Minister on 30 March, but was immediately reappointed to that position by President Chirac. Sarkozy was appointed as Minister of State, Minister of the Economy, Finance and Industry in a new Government formed the following day, and was replaced as Minister of the Interior, Internal Security and Local Freedoms by de Villepin. However, in November Sarkozy was elected President of the UMP, following the resignation of Juppé in July. There was widespread speculation that Sarkozy intended to use the leadership of the ruling party as a platform from which to launch his candidature in the presidential election due in 2007. Following the insistence of President Chirac that the head of the UMP would not be permitted simultaneously to hold ministerial office, Sarkozy resigned from the Government.

Despite opposition from left-wing parties and nation-wide demonstrations organized by trade unions, in March 2005 the National Assembly approved proposals intended further to relax the regulations controlling the 35-hour working week, which had been introduced by Jospin in 2000.

De Villepin appointed Prime Minister

In May 2005 a national referendum took place on the ratification of the Treaty establishing a Constitution for Europe. Following an intense campaign, in which Chirac and leading members of the UMP and the PS had demonstrated their support for the EU constitutional treaty, 54.9% of those voting rejected its ratification. Raffarin subsequently resigned as Prime Minister. He was succeeded by de Villepin, while Sarkozy returned to the Government as Minister of State, Minister of the Interior and Land Management.

In October 2005 violence broke out in Clichy-sous-Bois, a suburb of Paris largely populated by immigrant communities and suffering from high unemployment and poor social housing, following the death of two youths who had allegedly been fleeing a police identity check. Rioting erupted in the area, subsequently spreading to several neighbouring suburbs in the department of Seine-Saint-Denis, to the north-east of Paris. Sarkozy promised the families of the two youths (both of whom were of African extraction) a full investigation into the circumstances surrounding their deaths, but his uncompromising stance towards the rioters, notably his language, which some condemned as inflammatory in tone, provoked sharp criticism from some commentators and politicians, even within the Government. By early November some 300 towns and cities across France were experiencing unrest, mainly led by young males of African origin, while some 9,500 riot police had been deployed in an attempt to curb the violence. As the violence claimed a fatality, de Villepin announced a series of enhanced security measures and a programme aimed at improving education, employment and housing in deprived suburban areas. None the less, rioting continued, and on 8 November de Villepin announced a state of emergency, which granted préfets additional powers to issue house-arrest warrants and restrict public gatherings. Sarkozy announced that all convicted rioters who were not of French nationality would be deported, including those holding residence permits (at the time amounting to around 120 of the 1,800 arrested since the start of the riots). In mid-November, as the violence subsided, Chirac announced a scheme to train 50,000 young people in impoverished suburban areas by 2007. By this time nearly 300 schools and public buildings had been burned and 4,770 people had been arrested. In late November 2005 de Villepin proposed amendments to immigration legislation intended to make it more difficult for foreigners to gain entry to France by marrying French nationals and for immigrants to bring in family members. In December the Prime Minister launched a national campaign against discrimination, with measures including the imposition of fines on businesses found to have practised discrimination and incentives for companies to locate in deprived areas and to employ young people. The state of emergency was lifted in January 2006.

In April 2006, following a series of mass demonstrations and strike action in Paris and other cities, the Government abandoned plans for a new employment contract that would have allowed employers in small companies to dismiss workers aged under 26 more easily during their first two years of employment. De Villepin's popularity suffered a further reverse in May, following allegations of his involvement in a scandal that had originated in July 2004, when a French magistrate received documents that purported to show that a number of senior politicians, including Sarkozy, held secret offshore accounts with a Luxembourg bank, Clearstream, in which illegal payments allegedly relating to the 1991 sale of eight French naval vessels to Taiwan had been deposited. A subsequent investigation proved that the documents had been falsified. However, in late April 2006 a former senior intelligence officer testified that de Villepin had asked him to conduct an investigation into the allegations before they were known publicly. Sarkozy's supporters alleged that de Villepin had ordered the investigation in an attempt to discredit his principal rival for the UMP nomination in the forthcoming presidential election. De Villepin admitted that he had been made aware of the allegations in January 2004 and had ordered the intelligence services to investigate, but denied any wrongdoing. In May 2006 the Prime Minister comfortably survived a vote of confidence in the National Assembly. Nevertheless, the investigation into Clearstream continued.

In January 2007 the UMP elected Sarkozy unopposed as the party's candidate for the presidency, in accordance with a change to the party's statutes allowing members to select the presidential candidate. De Villepin and Chirac initially declined publicly to declare their support for Sarkozy, whose programme promised a break with Chirac's policies and combined an agenda of liberal economic reforms and protectionism with authoritarian policies on immigration and law and order. In March 2007 Sarkozy resigned from the Government, along with the Minister of Health and Social Protection, Xavier Bertrand, who was to manage Sarkozy's electoral campaign. At a PS congress in November, Ségolène Royal, the President of the Poitou Charentes Regional Council, was elected as the party's presidential candidate.

The first round of the presidential election, held on 22 April 2007, was contested by 12 candidates. Sarkozy and Royal progressed to the second round of voting, winning 31.2% and 25.9% of the valid votes cast, respectively. The UDF candidate, François Bayrou, won 18.6% of the vote, while Le Pen's support declined to only 10.4%. The rate of participation in the election was high, at 83.8% of eligible voters. At the second round of the election, held on 6 May, Sarkozy was elected as President, securing 53.1% of the valid votes cast.

The Sarkozy presidency

Sarkozy formally acceded to the presidency on 16 May 2007. François Fillon, a close adviser of the President, who had been Minister of National Education, Higher Education and Research in 2004–05, was appointed Prime Minister, while Juppé returned to government office as Minister of State, Minister of Ecology and Sustainable Development. The new Council of Ministers included prominent figures from across the political divide, in an attempt to accord the Government greater political legitimacy in its implementation of radical reforms. Bernard Kouchner, a member of Royal's presidential campaign team and former minister under Jospin, was appointed Minister of Foreign and European Affairs, while Hervé Morin, a member of the UDF, was allocated the defence portfolio. Among other notable appointments were those of Jean-Louis Borloo as Minister of the Economy, Finance and Employment, Michèle Alliot-Marie as Minister of the Interior, the Overseas Possessions and Territorial Collectivities, and Rachida Dati as Minister of Justice.

At elections to the National Assembly, held on 10 and 17 June 2007, the UMP remained the largest party in the legislature, but with a reduced majority, winning 313 of 577 seats. The PS, which was in disarray following the loss of the presidential election and the defection of Kouchner, confounded many observers by improving upon a poor performance in the first round of voting, taking a total of 186 seats. Prior to the elections the UDF was restyled the Mouvement Démocrate (MoDem) by its leader, Bayrou, while former members of the UDF allied to the President formed a new party, the Nouveau Centre. In the event the Nouveau Centre won 22 seats, while MoDem won just three. Following the elections Sarkozy reappointed Fillon as Prime Minister and effected a government reorganization. Borloo assumed the role vacated by Juppé, who failed to win re-election to the National Assembly, and Borloo was, in turn, replaced as Minister of the Economy, Finance and Employment by Christine Lagarde (hitherto Minister of Agriculture and Fisheries). Michel

Barnier, a former Minister of Foreign Affairs, replaced Lagarde in her previous role.

Investigations into allegations of wrongdoing on the part of members of the previous administration continued. In July 2007 Chirac (having lost his right to immunity from prosecution following the end of his presidency) was questioned by magistrates over his alleged involvement in the payment of wages to RPR supporters under false pretences during his tenure as Mayor of Paris. In November Chirac was placed under formal investigation with regard to a separate inquiry into misuse of public funds in relation to the alleged existence of fictitious city council employees during his mayoralty; he denied any wrongdoing. In October 2009 an investigating judge ordered Chirac and nine aides to stand trial on charges of embezzlement and breach of trust in relation to this affair. Furthermore, Chirac was placed under formal investigation in relation to the illicit payment of RPR supporters in December and ordered to stand trial in this case in November 2010. Chirac's trial in both cases commenced in March 2011. (The Paris city council had withdrawn a civil claim against Chirac in September 2010, after accepting an offer by the former President and the UMP to pay a total of €2.2m. in reparation.) In December 2011 Chirac was convicted of the charges against him and received a two-year suspended prison sentence; although he continued to plead his innocence, he announced that he lacked the strength to appeal against the verdict. Two of Chirac's co-defendants were acquitted, while six of the other seven were also sentenced to suspended prison terms. Meanwhile, De Villepin was placed under formal investigation by magistrates leading inquiries into the Clearstream affair in July 2007. Towards the end of 2008 it was announced that de Villepin was to stand trial for complicity in false accusation and using forgeries, among other charges, in relation to the Clearstream affair. De Villepin claimed that the charges were politically motivated, owing to his rivalry with Sarkozy. The trial of de Villepin and four other defendants commenced in September 2009. In January 2010 de Villepin was cleared of the four charges against him, but three of the remaining defendants were convicted for their roles in the affair. De Villepin was again cleared of the charges against him in September 2011, following a second trial resulting from an appeal by the prosecution against his acquittal. Meanwhile, De Villepin established a new political movement, République Solidaire, in June 2010, and relinquished his membership of the UMP in February 2011. In December he announced his candidacy for the 2012 presidential election; however, he was unable to secure the required number of endorsements from mayors or elected officials in order to stand.

In October 2007 new legislation increasing restrictions on immigration was approved by Parliament. The legislation included provisions for the evaluation of individual immigrants' knowledge of French language and culture and the compilation of population statistics based on ethnicity. Opposition to the legislation, however, focused on the provision for voluntary DNA testing of immigrants from non-EU countries who were suspected of falsely claiming to have a relative resident in France. The measure provoked an angry response from the Minister-Delegate for Urban Policy, Fadela Amara, and prompted the PS to refer the proposed legislation to the Constitutional Council. In November the Constitutional Council approved the provision on DNA testing, but declared the compilation of population statistics by ethnicity to be unconstitutional.

In February 2008 the FN leader, Le Pen, was convicted of conspiring to justify war crimes and denying crimes against humanity, following comments he had made regarding the occupation of France by German forces in 1940–44 in an interview in a far-right periodical in 2005. He received a three-month suspended prison sentence and a fine of €10,000.

In July 2008 significant constitutional changes were narrowly approved by the National Assembly and the Senate. Parliament was awarded new powers to oversee certain presidential appointments and to set its own agenda for one-half of its sessions (where formerly the entire agenda was decided by the Prime Minister and the Council of Ministers). The use of motions of confidence to force legislation through the National Assembly was restricted and Parliament had to be notified of any deployment of troops within three days, while parliamentary approval was required for military action extending beyond four months. The President was limited to two terms of office and curbs were imposed on the President's emergency powers, but the President was permitted to address Parliament in a joint session, a right that had been denied to the holder of that office since 1875.

In January 2009 Sarkozy effected a minor reorganization of the Council of Ministers. Brice Hortefeux, hitherto Minister of Immigration, Integration, National Identity and Shared Development, replaced Xavier Bertrand as Minister of Labour, Social Relations, the Family, Solidarity and Urban Affairs. Bertrand had succeeded Patrick Devedjian as Secretary-General of the UMP a month earlier, when Devedjian joined the Council of Ministers with responsibility for implementing a recovery plan for the economy. Hortefeux was succeeded by Eric Besson, a former PS deputy who had joined Sarkozy's Government in 2007. Later in January large numbers of public and private sector workers took part in a one-day nation-wide strike organized by trade unions in protest at an economic stimulus plan, which the unions criticized for its perceived failure to offer adequate protection for workers and wages. The strike, which represented the most serious challenge to Sarkozy's authority since his election to the presidency, resulted in widespread disruption. Rejecting concessions, including new welfare measures and tax reductions for the low-paid, as inadequate, union and opposition leaders called a further one-day nation-wide strike in March, which attracted greater support than the previous day of action.

Sarkozy carried out a further ministerial reorganization in June 2009, precipitated by the election of Rachida Dati and Michel Barnier to the European Parliament. Alliot-Marie replaced Dati as Minister of State, Keeper of the Seals and Minister of Justice and Freedoms, and was in turn succeeded by Hortefeux as Minister of the Interior, the Overseas Possessions and Territorial Collectivities.

Debate on national identity

In June 2009 Sarkozy exercised his new-found right under the recent constitutional amendments to outline the Government's policy for the forthcoming year before a joint session of Parliament at the Palace of Versailles, an event viewed by many commentators as a manifestation of the President's increasing assumption of political and executive control at the expense of the Prime Minister. Sarkozy provoked controversy during his speech by expressing support for a proposed parliamentary inquiry on the wearing of all-enveloping female Islamic dress. His declaration that the burka was 'not welcome' in France helped to revive political debate on Islamic clothing, some five years after the wearing of conspicuous religious symbols had been outlawed in public buildings. In January 2010 a parliamentary committee on the issue published its conclusions, recommending a ban on wearing the veil in 'public services' (including hospitals and public transport facilities, which would be able to refuse their services to women thus attired). Meanwhile, in November 2009 Eric Besson, Minister of Immigration, Integration, National Identity and Shared Development, announced the start of a debate on French national identity, which would include public consultations organized by local authorities, with the aim of addressing tensions in community relations exemplified by the controversy over the burka. In February 2010 Fillon announced a series of government proposals arising from the debate: these included measures to strengthen the teaching of 'republican values' in schools and a requirement that candidates for French citizenship sign a charter of rights and responsibilities. Moreover, in March the Prime Minister revealed that the Government would introduce a bill to outlaw the full Islamic veil. The proposed legislation, which outlawed the covering of the face in public and prescribed penalties of one year's imprisonment and a fine of €30,000 for anyone forcing a woman to wear a full-face veil, was approved by the National Assembly in July and by the Senate in September. Following confirmation of its legality by the Constitutional Council, the law was promulgated in October and entered into force in April 2011. Also in April, a week before the ban on the Islamic veil took effect, the UMP hosted a debate on the compatibility of religious practices with France's secular laws. Islamic leaders declined to participate in the debate, as did the Prime Minister, who warned that it risked stigmatizing Muslims. In the event, issues discussed included the Muslim practice of holding prayer meetings in the street when mosques were too crowded, the refusal of Muslim women to be treated by male doctors, and the withdrawal of Muslim schoolchildren from lessons in mandatory subjects such as physical education and biology. In September the Government announced a ban with immediate effect on praying outdoors in Paris, prompting criticism from some Muslim groups, which accused the Government of bowing to pressure from the FN. Later that month the first two women to be convicted of wearing the full Islamic veil in public were fined €120 and €80, respectively. In January 2012 it emerged that, in a non-binding decision in response to a complaint by a French Sikh man, the UN Human Rights Committee had concluded that France's insistence that Sikhs remove their turbans when being photographed for official documents constituted a violation of religious freedom under the International Covenant on Civil and Political Rights.

The Government suffered a heavy defeat at regional elections held on 14 and 21 March 2010. The PS, led by Martine Aubry, who had narrowly defeated the former presidential candidate Ségolène Royal in a controversial leadership contest in November 2008, achieved its best result for 30 years. In the second round of voting, the PS in alliance with Europe Ecologie (an electoral coalition led by Les Verts) and other parties of the left, won 54.1% of the votes cast, emerging with control of all but one of metropolitan France's 22 regions (having added the Territorial Collectivity of Corsica to the 20 regions hitherto controlled by the left). The UMP and its right-wing allies won 35.4% of the votes cast, while the FN performed strongly, winning 9.4% of the vote; many commentators believed that the recent debate on national identity and Islamic dress had contributed to the FN's resurgence by encouraging anti-immigrant sentiment. Sarkozy's standing had been adversely affected by his attempts at unpopular reforms, notably a planned increase in the retirement age. Following the regional elections, Sarkozy effected a minor government reorganization, dismissing the minister responsible for labour, Xavier Darcos, and appointing Eric Woerth, hitherto Minister of the Budget, Public Finances, the Civil Service and State Reform, in his stead.

Pension reforms and the deportation of Roma

In mid-June 2010 Eric Woerth, the Minister of Labour, Solidarity and the Civil Service, announced details of the Government's plans for reform of the state pension system, which formed part of wider efforts to reduce the burgeoning budget deficit. Notably, the proposals envisaged raising the minimum retirement age from 60 to 62 by 2018 and the qualifying age for a full pension from 65 to 67. Trade unions organized a one-day strike and rallies later that month in protest against the pension reforms, having already staged nation-wide demonstrations in May in anticipation of Woerth's announcement. In July both the President and Woerth were damaged by accusations that they had received allegedly illegal donations to the UMP and to Sarkozy's 2007 presidential election campaign from Liliane Bettencourt, the principal shareholder of the L'Oréal cosmetics business, whose financial affairs were subject to a police investigation. Woerth's position was complicated by his role as treasurer of the UMP and by the fact that his wife had worked for a company managing Bettencourt's finances. Sarkozy and Woerth strongly rejected the allegations, made by a former accountant of Bettencourt, and Woerth resigned as treasurer of the UMP on the President's advice. In February 2012 Woerth, who had left the Government in a reorganization in November 2010, was placed under formal investigation on suspicion of influence-peddling in connection with allegations that he had secured France's highest award, the National Order of the Legion of Honour, for Bettencourt's financial manager, Patrice de Maistre, after his wife had begun working for Maistre. Meanwhile, two secretaries of state, Alain Joyandet and Christian Blanc, resigned from the Government in July 2010 over claims that they had been profligate with public funds. As Parliament began to consider the pension legislation in early September, trade unions renewed their protests against the planned reforms. Several days of action, involving strikes and demonstrations across the country, were organized in September and October, attended by up to 1.2m. people according to official figures (or 3.5m. according to the unions) and causing severe disruption to public transport, schools and other services. None the less, the legislation secured parliamentary approval in October, following some minor concessions by the Government, and was promulgated in November. (In November 2011 the Government decided to bring forward the increase in the minimum retirement age from 2018 to 2017.)

A government decision taken in July 2010 to expel Roma migrants provoked condemnation from opposition parties, human rights groups and members of the European Commission and European Parliament. The policy was introduced in response to an attack on a police station by a group of Roma, following an incident in which a young traveller who had driven through a checkpoint without stopping had been shot dead by a gendarme. President Sarkozy ordered the dismantlement of 300 unauthorized Roma camps within three months and the immediate return of Roma who had committed public order offences or were living in France illegally to their countries of origin, mainly Romania and Bulgaria (citizens of which required work or residency permits if they wished to remain in France longer than three months). The President also pledged to withdraw French citizenship from foreign-born persons convicted of serious offences such as threatening the life of a police officer. With opinion polls indicating significant public support for such strict measures, critics claimed that Sarkozy's principal motivation was to improve his personal popularity and to attract voters away from the FN. As the deportation of Roma continued, in late September the European Commission threatened to initiate legal proceedings against France unless the French Government could demonstrate that it would incorporate a directive on the free movement of EU citizens within the Union into French law. The Government subsequently provided the assurances demanded by the Commission, promising to include the necessary measures in a new immigration bill recently presented to Parliament. In accordance with earlier pledges, this proposed legislation required candidates for French citizenship to sign a charter of rights and responsibilities and, most controversially, provided for the removal of citizenship from anyone who had acquired it within the previous 10 years if they were sentenced to at least five years' imprisonment by a French or foreign court. The immigration bill was approved by the National Assembly in October, despite opposition from some UMP deputies, but rejected by the Senate in February 2011. A revised version of the bill, which did not include the provision related to the removal of citizenship, was adopted by Parliament in May. Meanwhile, in February it was announced that more than 3,700 Roma had been returned to their countries of origin since July 2010, and that 70% of unauthorized Roma camps had been dismantled.

Recent developments: towards the 2012 elections

Sarkozy effected a government reorganization in November 2010, retaining Fillon as Prime Minister and appointing Alain Juppé as Minister of State, Minister of Defence and Veterans. Notable departures included those of Woerth and of former socialist Bernard Kouchner, who had publicly expressed reservations about the expulsion of Roma. Xavier Bertrand returned to the Council of Ministers as Minister of Labour, Employment and Health, while Minister of State Michèle Alliot-Marie replaced Kouchner as Minister of Foreign and European Affairs, being succeeded herself as Keeper of the Seals and Minister of Justice and Freedoms by Michel Mercier, hitherto Minister of Rural Affairs and Planning. Jean-François Copé, the UMP's leader in the National Assembly, additionally became Secretary-General of the organization, charged with preparing the party for the presidential and legislative elections due in 2012. A further reorganization in February 2011 was occasioned by the resignation of Alliot-Marie, who had sustained harsh criticism for her close links to the regime of the recently deposed Tunisian President, Zine al-Abidine Ben Ali (see Foreign Affairs). She was replaced as Minister of Foreign and European Affairs by Juppé, whose defence portfolio was assumed by Gérard Longuet. Sarkozy also dismissed Brice Hortefeux as Minister of the Interior, the Overseas Possessions, the Territorial Collectivities and Immigration, replacing him with Claude Guéant.

Jean-Marie Le Pen retired as President of the FN at a party conference in January 2011; his daughter, Marine Le Pen, was elected as his successor, subsequently declaring her intention to contest the presidency in 2012. Also in January, the PS confirmed that it would hold a primary election in October, in which any registered French voter who supported left-wing values could take part, in order to select its presidential candidate. Royal had surprised other members of the party in November 2010 with her early announcement that she intended to seek the PS presidential nomination; François Hollande, Aubry's predecessor as First Secretary of the party, declared his candidacy in March 2011, followed by Aubry herself in June. Dominique Strauss-Kahn, a former finance minister and Managing Director of the IMF since September 2007, had also been considered a likely contender. However, his arrest in New York, USA, in May, on charges of sexually assaulting a hotel chambermaid, led to his resignation from the IMF and effectively ended his presidential ambitions, at least for 2012, despite the charges against him being withdrawn in August. An investigation into an allegation against Strauss-Kahn of attempted rape by a French journalist was also discontinued in October. Strauss-Kahn was subsequently implicated in a further scandal, being placed under formal investigation by magistrates in March 2012 over his alleged involvement in a prostitution ring.

Meanwhile, the PS and the FN both performed strongly in elections to departmental councils in March 2011, taking 24.9% and 15.1% of votes cast, respectively, in the first round held on 20 March, with the UMP barely surpassing the FN in terms of its share of the vote, taking less than 17.0%; in the second round, on 27 March, the PS secured 35.4% of votes cast, the UMP 20.0% and the FN 11.6%. At indirect partial elections to the Senate held on 25 September, the centre-right parties, dominated by the UMP, lost their majority in the upper chamber for the first time since the establishment of the Fifth Republic in 1958. Jean-Pierre Bel of the PS was duly elected President of the Senate on 1 October, defeating the incumbent, Gérard Larcher of the UMP.

The appointment of Christine Lagarde as Strauss-Kahn's replacement at the IMF necessitated a ministerial reorganization in June 2011. Among the changes, François Baroin, hitherto Minister of the Budget, Public Finances, the Civil Service and State Reform, and Government Spokesman, succeeded Lagarde as Minister of the Economy, Finance and Industry, while Valérie Pécresse assumed responsibility for all of Baroin's former portfolios, with the exception of that of the civil service, which was allocated to François Sauvadet. Laurent Wauquiez replaced Pécresse as Minister of Higher Education and Research. Also in June, Georges Tron, who had been forced to resign as Secretary of State for the Civil Service in late May, was placed under formal investigation over claims, which he denied, that he had raped and sexually assaulted two former colleagues at the town hall of Draveil, where he was Mayor.

Hollande was selected as the presidential candidate of the PS at the party's primary election, defeating Aubry with 56.6% of the votes cast in a second round held on 16 October 2011, in which almost 2.9m. people voted. Six candidates had contested the first round, on 9 October, at which Hollande had won 39.2% of the vote and Aubry 30.4%; Arnaud Montebourg, who advocated far-ranging political and constitutional reforms, was notably placed third, with 17.2% of the vote, while Royal secured only 6.9%. With a solid lead in opinion polls, Hollande presented his election manifesto in January 2012, pledging to create 60,000 jobs in the education sector and 150,000 jobs for young people, and to introduce a 15% increase in tax on bank profits and a new, higher rate of income tax of 45% for those earning more than €150,000 per year; he later additionally proposed a 75% rate of tax on annual incomes exceeding €1m. and stated that the EU's 'fiscal compact' would not be ratified by France without some renegotiation. The decision by the credit rating agency Standard & Poor's to downgrade France's long-term sovereign debt rating to AA+ that month represented a significant reverse for Sarkozy and his Government, which had emphasized the importance of retaining the country's AAA rating when announcing austerity measures in November 2011. Sarkozy did not confirm his intention to seek re-election until February 2012, when he defended his economic policies, including raising the retirement age and lowering the number of state employees, insisting that France's economic position would have deteriorated further without such action. In March, in an apparent attempt to court right-wing voters, the President proposed reducing the number of immigrants to France from 180,000 to 100,000 per year, citing the difficulty of integrating 'too many foreigners'.

The first round of the presidential election was held on 22 April 2012. Hollande narrowly defeated Sarkozy, with 28.63% of votes against the latter's 27.18%. Marine Le Pen came third with 17.9% of votes, her pledge to give French citizens priority over foreigners for jobs, housing and social welfare proving popular amid rising unemployment, although she only narrowly succeeded in securing the 500 pledges of support from mayors or local officials required to stand. (Her attempt to persuade the Constitutional Council that the names of elected officials who endorse a presidential candidate should not be made public had failed in February.) Other presidential candidates included Jean-Luc Mélenchon, representing the Front de Gauche (a left-wing alliance comprising primarily the PCF, the Parti de Gauche and the Gauche Unitaire), who secured 11.1% of votes, Bayrou, the President of MoDem (9.13% of votes), and Eva Joly, for Europe Ecologie Les Verts (2.31%). At the second round of elections held on 6 May Hollande defeated Sarkozy, winning 51.62% of the votes, compared with Sarkozy's 48.38%.

The Situation in Corsica

Demands for the independence of Corsica increased markedly during the 1960s and 1970s, with particular discontent being expressed at the resettlement there of French citizens displaced from Algeria following its independence in 1962. In 1972 the status of Corsica was upgraded to that of a region, administered by a centrally appointed préfet. (It had hitherto formed an administrative department within the region of Provence-Alpes-Côte d'Azur.) The assassination of two gendarmes at Aléria, in eastern Corsica, in August 1975, marked a significant escalation in the campaign for Corsican independence; from 1976 the clandestine Fronte di Liberazione Naziunale di a Corsica (FLNC) was regarded as the leading pro-independence organization. Also in 1976 Corsica was subdivided into two departments, Corse-du-Sud and Haute-Corse. However, demands for greater autonomy or independence persisted, with intermittent bombing campaigns conducted by separatists both in Corsica and in continental France. As a result of decentralization legislation of 1982, the status of Corsica was elevated to that of a Territorial Collectivity (Collectivité territoriale), with its own directly elected 61-seat assembly, and an administration with augmented executive powers. In April 1991 the National Assembly adopted legislation that granted greater autonomy to Corsica; a seven-member executive council was to be formed, chosen from a 51-member Corsican Assembly (Assemblée de Corse), which would be elected in 1992.

In February 1998, in the most serious act of violence committed by separatist militants to date, the Préfet of Corsica, Claude Erignac, was assassinated. The killing was condemned by the FLNC and the primary suspect in the case, Yvan Colonna, was convicted of murder in December 2007 and sentenced to life imprisonment. In March 2009 an appeal court upheld his conviction and added the stipulation that he serve a minimum of 22 years in prison. In June 2010 the Court of Cassation annulled the appeal court's verdict on the grounds of procedural irregularities. However, following a retrial, Colonna's life sentence was upheld in June 2011. Meanwhile, peace negotiations involving the Government and representatives of Corsica commenced in Paris in December 1999. Four Corsican militant groups called an unconditional cease-fire, and pledged to disarm should their aims, including the recognition of the Corsican people as a nation, and the granting of official status to the Corsican language on the island, be achieved. The peace process resulted in agreement on a number of proposals known as the Matignon Accords, which were approved in the Corsican Assembly in July 2000. Under the proposals, subject to the maintenance of peace on Corsica, and the approval of the National Assembly, a referendum would be held on eventual revisions to the Constitution in 2004, prior to the introduction of a single political and administrative body for the island with formal, but limited, legislative powers, replacing the two existing administrative departments. The proposals also provided for instruction in the Corsican language to take place in all primary schools. Although most militant groups maintained a cease-fire following the signature of the accords, increasing concern was expressed at the prevalence of organized crime in Corsica, while sporadic, low-level attacks by militants continued. In May 2001 the National Assembly approved a more moderate version of the bill to amend the status of Corsica, with a view to presenting a text that would be acceptable to the Constitutional Council; consequently, Corsican language instruction at primary schools was to be optional, rather than compulsory, and the French Parliament would be required to pass enabling legislation before local legislation approved by the Corsican Assembly could take effect. By September the process envisaged by the accords appeared to be stalling; the moderate nationalist leader, Jean-Guy Talamoni, who had been involved in negotiating the accords, announced that the moderate separatist Corsica Nazione had decided to withdraw from the provisions of the accords. The final bill on greater autonomy, which had been subject to further amendments received the approval of both legislative houses by December. In January 2002 the Constitutional Council ruled that the section of the bill that permitted the Corsican Assembly to amend national legislation on the island was illegitimate, although the section of the law that permitted the optional use of Corsican language in primary schools was approved.

In April 2002, following the defeat of Jospin in the first round of the presidential election and a statement by Chirac to the effect that Corsican aspirations for greater autonomy were insignificant, nationalists on the island announced their withdrawal from the Matignon process. In May the FLNC-Union des Combatants (FLNC-UDC—as the main faction of the organization was now known) announced that it was to resume its dissident campaign, while stating its preference for a negotiated settlement. In June the new centre-right Government unexpectedly announced that it was to seek several amendments to the Constitution that would permit the eventual decentralization of a number of powers, and that Corsica could be expected to be affected by these measures. In July Nicolas Sarkozy, the Minister of the Interior, visited Corsica, where he announced efforts to relaunch a dialogue with nationalists. The Prime Minister, Jean-Pierre Raffarin, also travelled to the island. However, amid scepticism regarding the Government's intentions, the number of small-scale bomb attacks on the island increased sharply in 2002, to reach the highest annual total recorded (in excess of 220) since 1997. In February 2003 the Corsican Assembly voted in favour of a proposal, supported by Sarkozy, whereby the two administrative departments in Corsica were to be replaced by a single collectivity, subject to the approval of these measures by a referendum in Corsica. Following the approval in March by the National Assembly of constitutional changes that permitted local referendums, it was announced that such a plebiscite was to be held in July. Although several separatist groups, including the FLNC-UDC, Corsica Nazione, and the political wing of the FLNC-UDC, Indipendenza, announced their support for the proposals, other more radical groups expressed concern that plans to devolve limited legislative and additional tax-raising powers to the new collectivity, which had been included in the Matignon Accords, had not been revived. At the referendum, held on 6 July, the proposal was defeated, with 51.0% of the votes against the restructuring. A relatively high turn-out of 60.5% was recorded.

Following the defeat of the Government's proposals in the referendum, there was an escalation of violence by Corsican separatist groups, both in Corsica and in mainland France. The FLNC-UDC, which announced in July 2003 that it was to end its cease-fire, claimed responsibility for two bomb attacks in Nice and a series of bombings in Corsica later in July. In October Sarkozy announced that measures to combat widespread violence, terrorism and organized crime on Corsica would now be a priority of the Government. However, the incidence of bombings and other attacks accelerated in 2004, despite the FLNC-UDC's reiteration in May of its commitment to the unconditional cease-fire. Many of these attacks were on North African Muslims, most of which were claimed by the Clandestini Corsi group. In March 2005 the FLNC-UDC ended its cease-fire to coincide with the start of the trial in Paris of its suspected leader, Charles Pieri, who was accused of extortion, misappropriation of funds, financing terrorism and associating with criminals for a terrorist enterprise. Pieri, who had been imprisoned since December 2003, was convicted and sentenced to a 10-year custodial sentence and was released in December 2009.

Militant activity in Corsica continued throughout 2006, with the FLNC-UDC claiming responsibility for a series of attacks. In May 2007 13 members of a militant separatist organization, FLNC des anonymes, were convicted by a court in Paris of perpetrating a series of bombings in Corsica during 2001–02 and received sentences of between one and 11 years' imprisonment, while the apparent leader of FLNC des anonymes, Antoine Marchini, was sentenced to 12 years' imprisonment for his role in the attacks. In December militants carried out a series of bombings on the island, following the conviction of Colonna and the arrest of 13 members of Corsica Nazione suspected of involvement in bomb attacks carried out in 2006–07.

The political situation in Corsica remained tense in 2008. In January around 500 protesters occupied the Corsican Assembly in Ajaccio after a demonstration led by nationalist groups and trade unions. During the occupation offices within the Assembly building were set on fire. Five people were arrested in connection with the arson attack and placed under judicial investigation. The initial judicial hearing at a court in Ajaccio was marked by violent clashes between separatist protesters and police in the regional capital and in Bastia. Three of the defendants were acquitted by a court in Ajaccio in May, while a fourth was acquitted in October; all four were members of U Rinnovu, a nationalist movement founded in 1998. Meanwhile, in May 2008 a hitherto unrecognized organization, FLNC 1976, claimed responsibility for 26 recent attacks in Corsica, including the destruction of public buildings, police stations and holiday homes. The newly formed movement sought to reunite the various factions of the FLNC, namely, the FLNC-UDC and the FLNC du 22 Octobre (founded in October 2002). In February 2009 Corsa Nazione, U Rinnovu and two other nationalist movements merged to form a new pro-independence political party, Corsica Libera, led by Talamoni.

In January 2010 the FLNC-UDC claimed responsibility for 14 bomb attacks, which had taken place over the previous months, and renewed its threats against the authorities, in protest at a controversial 20-year development plan supported by the mainland French Government and the Corsican executive. The Construction and Sustainable Development Plan of Corsica (Plan d'aménagement et de développement durable de la Corse—Padduc), which envisaged sanctioning development on previously protected land, also attracted criticism from environmental groups and moderate pro-independence parties. At the regional elections in March a left-wing grouping led by Paul Giacobbi of the Parti Radical de Gauche won 24 of the 51 seats in the Corsican Assembly, following 26 years of political dominance by the right; Giacobbi was elected President of the Executive Council.

Developments in the Overseas Territories

In November 1998, following a lengthy campaign for the independence of the Pacific overseas territory of New Caledonia by indigenous Melanesian (Kanak) separatists, a referendum on self-determination was held in the territory. At the referendum a gradual transfer of powers to local institutions was approved, and the Republican Constitution was amended accordingly. Further enabling legislation was approved by Parliament in February 1999, and certain powers were transferred to local institutions in subsequent years. Notably, the constitutional amendments approved in March 2003 that sought to permit other communities eventually to gain increased autonomy were not to apply to New Caledonia.

Proposals to restructure the administration of France's Caribbean overseas territories, Guadeloupe and Martinique, were rejected in referendums held in July 2003. However, in concurrent referendums held in Saint-Barthélemy and Saint-Martin, the electorate voted in favour of seceding from Guadeloupe to assume the status of Overseas Collectivities (Collectivités d'outre-mer). The administrative process was completed in February 2007, when it was approved by the Constitutional Council.

In January 2004 the National Assembly approved an organic law and an ordinary law, the combined effect of which was to grant autonomous status to French Polynesia; this legislation was finally approved, with minor amendments, in February, by the Constitutional Council. At a referendum held in the Overseas Collectivity of Mayotte in March 2009, the electorate voted overwhelmingly in favour of becoming an Overseas Department with the same political status as metropolitan departments. The result was welcomed by the French Government, but the African Union and the Government of the Comoros, which claims sovereignty over Mayotte, rejected the referendum. The change took effect at the end of March 2011.

Foreign Affairs

Regional relations

France was a founder member of the European Community, which became the European Union (EU, see p. 276) in 1992 under the Treaty on European Union (the Maastricht Treaty). The French Government was an enthusiastic proponent of efforts to strengthen integration within the EU, most notably the Treaty establishing a Constitution for Europe. Following the rejection of the constitutional treaty at referendums in France and the Netherlands in 2005, in December 2007 a new treaty was signed in Lisbon, Portugal, by the heads of state or of government of the 27 EU member countries. The so-called Lisbon Treaty was ratified by Parliament in February 2008, and entered into force across the EU in December 2009.

In May 1992 France and Germany announced that they would establish a joint defence force of 50,000 troops, the Eurocorps, which was intended to provide a basis for a European army under the aegis of Western European Union, and which became operational in November 1995. Belgium, Spain and Luxembourg also agreed to participate in the force. In January 1993 an agreement was signed between NATO and the French and German Governments, establishing formal links between the Eurocorps and NATO's military structure. In late 2000 it was announced that France would contribute 12,000 troops, of a total of more than 60,000 that would form a European rapid reaction force, to participate in peace-keeping missions from 2003. Proposals for a new autonomous European military command headquarters near Brussels, Belgium, with the capacity to plan and execute European operations autonomously, were put forward by Belgium, France, Germany and Luxembourg, following a meeting in Brussels in April 2003. The proposal was opposed by several EU states, notably the United Kingdom, which feared that NATO would be undermined. A compromise was reached in December, under which a small cell of planning staff would be created, situated in NATO's military headquarters in Brussels, which would only be used if NATO declined involvement and national European headquarters needed support. Under a new European plan devised to compensate for the inadequacies of the rapid reaction force, which, although theoretically declared ready for action in May 2003, in practice was adversely affected by shortfalls in equipment, a series of EU 'battlegroups' were established for deployment to crisis areas by 2007. France was the sole contributor to one battlegroup and also participated in two others, one with Belgium and one with Germany, Belgium and Luxembourg. Measures to increase European military integration, including once again proposals for the establishment in Brussels of the first permanent headquarters for planning EU military missions, were outlined by France in June 2008. In March 2009 Sarkozy won a vote of confidence in the National Assembly over his decision to bring France back into NATO's integrated military command structure, despite criticism from opponents that it would weaken French independence from the USA. Sarkozy insisted that the country would benefit from being able to take part in strategic decision-making and emphasized the fact that France would retain its independent nuclear capability and autonomy in defence decisions. In May 2011 the foreign ministers of the so-called 'Weimar Triangle' grouping, comprising France, Germany and Poland, agreed to pursue a trilateral initiative for the establishment of an EU civil and military planning headquarters independent of NATO. Furthermore, in July senior military officers from the three countries signed a technical agreement on the creation of a Weimar Triangle EU battlegroup, which would comprise 1,700 troops and become operational in 2013.

Following the election of Sarkozy as President in May 2007, relations between France and Germany deteriorated. The German Government expressed its opposition to several of Sarkozy's initiatives on foreign affairs, notably the negotiation of accords on nuclear energy with Libya and French plans to form a so-called Mediterranean Union, comprising the seven EU member states in the Mediterranean region (Cyprus, France, Greece, Italy, Malta, Portugal and Spain) and certain littoral Middle Eastern and North African states. Germany feared that the organization would undermine the ongoing Euro-Mediterranean Partnership (the Barcelona Process—a framework launched in 1995 for co-operation between all EU member states and 10 other Mediterranean states). However, in March 2008 Sarkozy and the German Chancellor, Angela Merkel, announced that an agreement had been reached, under which all EU member states would be involved in the formation of the new union, which was restyled the Union for the Mediterranean and inaugurated in July. The Union also included the 10 Mediterranean partners in the Barcelona Process, including Turkey, which agreed in March to participate, following reassurances from France that the Union would not, as originally envisaged, function as an alternative to Turkey's membership of the EU. (Sarkozy's election campaign platform had included a pledge to oppose Turkey's accession to the EU.)

Tensions arose between Sarkozy and Merkel in May 2010, at an emergency summit of leaders of euro area member states in Brussels, over the proposed establishment of the European Financial Stability Facility (EFSF), a temporary fund to support member countries suffering severe financial difficulties with the aim of preserving the stability of the currency. Sarkozy reportedly threatened to withdraw France from economic and monetary union if Germany did not support the €440,000m. fund before agreement on its creation was finally reached. Relations between the two leaders subsequently improved, however, and they jointly advocated the establishment of a permanent crisis mechanism, the European Stability Mechanism (ESM), on which EU heads of government reached agreement in October. At bilateral talks in December, Sarkozy and Merkel affirmed their commitment to the single currency and also welcomed the stationing of a battalion of German troops in the French town of Illkirch-Graffenstaden, near Strasbourg, the first time German troops had been based in France since the Second World War. In February 2011 Sarkozy and Merkel jointly proposed a European 'competitiveness pact' aimed at eliminating economic policy differences and ensuring more rigorous supervision of fiscal commitments. However, they encountered significant opposition from other leaders. In early December, prior to a summit meeting of EU heads of state and of government, Sarkozy and Merkel again united to propose a series of measures aimed at strengthening economic and fiscal policy co-ordination and surveillance within the euro area, including a commitment to balanced budgets and automatically triggered sanctions for any country recording a fiscal deficit exceeding 3% of gross domestic product. Amid mounting concern regarding the sovereign debt crisis in the euro area, the majority of EU member states agreed, in principle, to the proposals at the summit meeting, with the exception of the United Kingdom, which vetoed their incorporation into an existing treaty owing to its opposition to a tax on financial transactions. In March 2012 the heads of state and of government of 25 of the 27 EU member states signed the so-called 'fiscal compact' (the Treaty on Stability, Co-ordination and Governance), with the Czech Republic joining the United Kingdom in withholding its assent. The compact required ratification by 12 euro area countries to take effect. Meanwhile, the strength of the relationship between Sarkozy and Merkel was reflected in February by the German Chancellor's pledge of support for Sarkozy's re-election in the French presidential contest scheduled for April.

A dispute with Italy emerged in April 2011 after the Italian Government granted temporary residence permits to some 20,000 recent immigrants (mostly Tunisians fleeing the civil unrest in their home country), thereby allowing them to travel freely within the EU. Large numbers of Tunisian migrants had attempted to cross the border into France in the preceding weeks, many of whom had been returned by the French authorities. Tensions eased after France and Italy agreed to undertake joint patrols of the Tunisian coast in an attempt to prevent migrants from reaching the Italian island of Lampedusa by boat. However, the dispute escalated later in the month after France denied entry to a train carrying Tunisian migrants from Italy, prompting a protest by the latter country, which claimed France was in breach of the EU's Schengen agreement on internal borders. (The European Commission later stated that France had acted within its rights in turning back the migrants.) Sarkozy subsequently met the Italian Prime Minister, Silvio Berlusconi, and both leaders declared their intention to seek reform of the Schengen agreement so as to allow the establishment of temporary border controls in a greater range of circumstances. In June the heads of government of the EU member states agreed, in principle, to introduce a safeguard mechanism to Schengen area procedures, which would allow extraordinary national border controls to be imposed for a limited time in response to exceptional circumstances. However, the French, German and Spanish ministers responsible for internal affairs rejected the European Commission's proposals for this mechanism as inadequate in September, objecting to a five-day limit on the restoration of border controls, after which time the authorization of the Commission would be required. Sarkozy continued to advocate a reform of the Schengen agreement in the following months, and in March 2012, at a presidential election campaign rally held in Paris, he threatened to suspend France's membership of the Schengen area in the absence of progress within the next 12 months on revisions that would curb illegal immigration.

Other external relations

France has been active in promoting the establishment of regional peace-keeping forces in Africa. In the early 1990s French troops were dispatched to Rwanda to train government forces and to supply military equipment, following the outbreak of armed conflict between the Government and the opposition Front patriotique rwandais. In April 1994 French troops re-entered Rwanda to establish a 'safe humanitarian zone' for refugees fleeing the civil war. Evidence emerged in early 1998 that appeared to support allegations that France had sold arms to Rwanda during the massacres in 1994 (after the imposition of a UN embargo on the delivery of military equipment to any party in the conflict). The Rwandan Government rejected the findings of a commission of inquiry, subsequently established to investigate the affair, which effectively exonerated France. Bilateral relations further deteriorated following the decision in November 2006 by a French magistrate to issue arrest warrants for nine senior Rwandan military and government officials on suspicion of involvement in the killing in 1994 of the former Rwandan President, Juvénal Habyarimana. The magistrate also alleged that the incumbent Rwandan President, Paul Kagame, had ordered the missile attack in which Habyarimana was killed; however, under French law, as a head of state, Kagame was immune from prosecution. The Rwandan Government denied the allegations, and accused France of attempting to undermine and, ultimately, overthrow it. Rwanda subsequently severed relations with France. In January 2008 the French Minister of Foreign and European Affairs, Bernard Kouchner, visited Rwanda in an attempt to improve relations between the two countries. Despite a further deterioration in relations occasioned by the publication by the Rwandan Government in August of a report alleging the involvement of several senior French military and political figures (among them, Mitterrand and de Villepin) in the 1994 massacres, full diplomatic relations were restored in November 2009. In February 2010 Sarkozy became the first French President to visit Rwanda since 1984; during his visit he admitted that France and the international community had made 'mistakes' in their failure to prevent the massacres. In March 2010, just one week after Sarkozy's visit, Agathe Habyarimana, the widow of the former President, who was the subject of an extradition request by Rwandan prosecutors for her alleged role in the genocide, was arrested at her home near Paris; however, in September 2011 a French court in Paris rejected the Rwandan request for her extradition. A French judge, Marc Trévidic, placed six senior Rwandan military officials—including the Minister of Defence, Gen. James Kabarebe, and the Chief of Defence Staff, Lt-Gen. Charles Kayonga—under judicial investigation in December 2010 in connection with the killing of former Rwandan President Habyarimana after questioning them in Burundi for several days (with the agreement of the Rwandan authorities); the warrants for their arrest that were issued in 2006 were revoked. In January 2012, however, Trévidic announced that a team of technical experts that had been charged with re-examining the attack in which Habyarimana was killed had concluded that the evidence indicated that the missiles involved could not have been fired from a base occupied by forces loyal to Kagame. Meanwhile, Kagame visited France in September 2011 in an attempt to strengthen bilateral relations, holding talks with Sarkozy.

From late 2002 more than 3,000 French troops were dispatched to Côte d'Ivoire to assist the 550 French troops already based there, initially to protect French citizens resident in the country from civil unrest and subsequently to monitor a ceasefire between Ivorian government troops and rebel forces in the north of the country. Following the recommencement of military operations by Ivorian government forces against the rebel-controlled north in November 2004, nine French troops were killed during an air strike on 6 November. The French military, acting on the direct orders of President Chirac, responded by disabling the Ivorian air force on the ground. France's perceived intervention in the conflict provoked riots in the principal city, Abidjan, and elsewhere, and numerous attacks occurred against French civilians and targets. French troops entered Abidjan to secure the international airport and protect French and other foreign citizens, airlifting an estimated 9,000 people out of the city. (The French Government subsequently admitted that its forces had killed some 20 Ivorian civilians during clashes with rioters; the Ivorian authorities claimed the number was significantly higher.) Some 600 troops were subsequently flown in to reinforce the French military presence in Côte d'Ivoire, while diplomatic relations between the two countries remained tense. France reduced its military presence in Côte d'Ivoire from 2,400 troops at early 2008 to 1,800 by late 2008 and to 900 by mid-2009. In December 2010 the French Government advised the 15,000 French nationals in Côte d'Ivoire to leave the country temporarily, amid security concerns following a disputed presidential election in the previous month. In April 2011 French troops stationed in the country assisted forces loyal to Alassane Ouattara, who was recognized internationally as the winner of the presidential election, to oust outgoing President Laurent Gbagbo, who had refused to cede office. President Sarkozy attended Ouattara's formal inauguration as Ivorian President in May. Sarkozy and Ouattara signed a joint security agreement in January 2012, during a state visit by the Ivorian President to France. By this time the number of French troops in Côte d'Ivoire, which had been increased to some 1,600 during the first half of 2011, had again been reduced, to 450, with a further reduction, to 300, envisaged; according to the security agreement, their main role was to train local forces.

Relations between France and Angola were adversely affected in 2008 by the opening of a trial of 42 people charged with involvement in illegal arms transactions with Angola in 1993–98. The Angolan President, José Eduardo dos Santos, was implicated in allegations of corruption in connection with the arms deals, while senior French political figures, including Jean-Christophe Mitterrand, the son of the former President, who had acted as adviser to his father on African affairs, and Charles Pasqua, who had been the Minister of the Interior in 1986–88, were among the defendants. The trial, which centred on the sale of weapons and equipment worth US $790m to Angola by an Israeli business executive and his French associate, ended in March 2009. In October all but six of the defendants were convicted; Pasqua was sentenced to one year's imprisonment, while Mitterrand received a two-year suspended sentence and a substantial fine. However, Pasqua's conviction was overturned by an appeals court in April 2011.

France's relations with the USA have frequently been characterized by a desire to establish French independence of action, particularly with regard to military concerns and international relations. In the aftermath of the attacks in New York and Washington, DC, attributed to the militant Islamist al-Qa'ida organization, on 11 September 2001, France offered full military and logistical support to the USA, including the dispatch to Afghanistan of marines, engineers and members of the Special Forces, in its campaign against al-Qa'ida. However, France criticized several aspects of the foreign policy of the Administration of US President George W. Bush. Although France supported UN Security Council Resolution 1441 (presented by the USA and the United Kingdom) in November 2002, which demanded the expedited admittance of UN weapons inspectors to Iraq, it opposed any UN Security Council resolution that would authorize any automatic resort to force against Iraq, and was a prominent opponent of the US-led military action that commenced later in March 2003. However, following the conclusion of large-scale hostilities in Iraq, France gave full support to UN Security Council Resolution 1483, approved in May, which recognized the Coalition Provisional Authority as the legal occupying power in Iraq.

The election of Sarkozy as President in May 2007 precipitated a significant improvement in relations between France and the USA. Following US pleas for members of NATO to increase the deployment of forces in Afghanistan, Sarkozy announced in April 2008 that he would send an additional 700 troops to the country. The deployment of a further 250 French troops in Afghanistan was announced in July 2010. A phased withdrawal of French troops from Afghanistan commenced in October 2011, as part of NATO's plan to end its combat mission in that country by the end of 2014. Following the killing of four French soldiers by a member of the Afghan National Army in January 2012, President Sarkozy held talks with Afghan President Hamid Karzai and announced that France would complete its withdrawal of combat troops from Afghanistan by the end of 2013, a year ahead of the deadline envisaged by NATO. François Hollande, Sarkozy's main rival in the French presidential election due to be held in April and May 2012, had notably pledged to end France's mission in Afghanistan by the end of that year if elected. At February 2012 France was contributing some 3,600 troops towards NATO's International Security Assistance Force (ISAF) in Afghanistan—the fifth largest contingent after the USA, the United Kingdom, Germany and Italy.

One of the priorities of French foreign policy under the presidency of Sarkozy was to secure an increased role for France in the Middle East. In August 2007 Sarkozy used his first major speech on foreign policy to reiterate his opposition to Iran's nuclear enrichment programme, which many governments in developed countries feared was intended to facilitate the development of an Iranian nuclear force. France was a strong proponent of imposing stricter sanctions against Iran in early 2012, amid ongoing concerns regarding its nuclear enrichment programme, and in January EU ministers responsible for foreign affairs reached agreement on an embargo on Iranian petroleum exports from July and a freeze on the assets of the Iranian central bank in the EU. Iran halted oil sales to British and French companies in February.

In December 2007 Sarkozy announced that France was to suspend diplomatic relations with Syria, accusing the Syrian Government of obstructing international efforts to achieve a consensus regarding the appointment of a new President in Lebanon, while also demanding Syria's co-operation regarding the formation of an international tribunal to investigate the assassination, in 2005, of the former Lebanese Prime Minister, Rafik Hariri. Syria reacted unfavourably to Sarkozy's intervention and suspended all co-operation with France over Lebanon. In an effort to improve relations between the two countries and assuage Syria's international isolation, Sarkozy undertook a visit to Syria in September 2008, where he met with his counterpart, Bashar al-Assad, along with officials from Turkey and Qatar, for talks on Lebanon. In late April 2011 Sarkozy was one of several foreign leaders to urge the Syrian authorities to halt the violent suppression of anti-Government protests that had commenced in mid-March. In August, by which time it was estimated that more than 2,000 people had been killed since the uprising began, Sarkozy called for President Assad to relinquish office. France was also a strong advocate of exerting greater international pressure on Assad's administration to end the violence in Syria, supporting two draft UN Security Council resolutions condemning government repression in that country in October 2011 and February 2012, but these were vetoed by both the People's Republic of China and Russia. Meanwhile, during a visit to the Persian (Arabian) Gulf area in January 2008, Sarkozy announced that France was to establish a permanent military base in Abu Dhabi, the United Arab Emirates (UAE). The President also signed an agreement with the UAE, under which France was to assist the development of a programme to produce nuclear energy in that country. The French base in Abu Dhabi was officially inaugurated by Sarkozy during a further visit to the UAE in May 2009. A visit to Iraq by Sarkozy in February 2009—the first by a French head of state since 2003—signalled the President's willingness to renew bilateral ties with the country.

Initiatives by President Sarkozy to establish closer diplomatic and economic relations with Libya provoked widespread criticism. In July 2007 Sarkozy travelled to Libya for an official state visit, during which he signed an agreement on defence co-operation and a memorandum of understanding on the development of civil nuclear technology in Libya. A state visit to France in December by Qaddafi provoked criticism both from opposition figures and from some politicians aligned with the Government. Qaddafi and Sarkozy signed several agreements during the visit, including, most controversially, contracts for the sale of military equipment to Libya and a further agreement on nuclear energy.

The French Government was criticized for its slow response to large-scale pro-democracy demonstrations in Tunisia that eventually led to the flight from that country of its President, Zine al-Abidine Ben Ali, in January 2011. Criticism was particularly focused on the Minister of State, Minister of Foreign and European Affairs, Michèle Alliot-Marie, who had been on holiday in Tunisia when the protests began in the previous month, after she suggested that the French authorities might assist Ben Ali's administration to 'restore calm' and later admitted having accepted two free flights on an aircraft owned by a Tunisian businessman with close links to Ben Ali. Alliot-Marie resigned in February (see Domestic Political Affairs). In contrast to its initial response to the situation in Tunisia, France was swift to show its support for the popular movement against Qaddafi's regime in Libya that emerged in mid-February. As the situation in Libya descended into civil war, on 10 March France became the first country to recognize the National Transitional Council, based in the rebel-held city of Benghazi, as the legitimate representative of the Libyan people. Later in March France led international efforts to secure a UN Security Council resolution authorizing an air exclusion zone over Libya. Following the adoption on 17 March of Resolution 1973, which permitted UN member states to take 'all necessary measures' (short of military occupation) to protect civilians in Libya, French and British air and naval forces played a particularly prominent role in the international coalition against Qaddafi's forces, which came under NATO command at the end of March. France also supplied arms to rebel forces, despite concerns that this could be regarded as a breach of Resolution 1973. After Qaddafi and his forces had been ejected from the Libyan capital, Tripoli, in August, Sarkozy, together with British Prime Minister David Cameron, visited the city in September. The NATO operation in Libya ended in October, following the capture by opposition forces of the last remaining government-controlled city and the death of Qaddafi.

France's relations with Turkey were severely strained from late 2011 by the adoption by the French Parliament of legislation outlawing the denial of killings deemed by French law to constitute genocide, including the massacre of Armenians under the Ottoman Empire during the First World War, which Parliament had voted to recognize as genocide in 2001. The penalty for those convicted of denying genocide was one year's imprisonment and a fine of €45,000. Following the bill's approval by the National Assembly in December 2011, the Turkish Prime Minister, Recep Tayyip Erdoğan, recalled the Turkish ambassador to France and suspended bilateral political and military co-operation. The legislation was approved by the Senate in January 2012, but a group of legislators subsequently referred it to the Constitutional Council, which ruled in late February that the law infringed on freedom of expression. President Sarkozy, who had supported the legislation, insisting that it applied to all acts of genocide and was not aimed at any state in particular, requested that the Government draft new legislation criminalizing the denial of genocide, taking into account the Council's decision.

CONSTITUTION AND GOVERNMENT

The Constitution of the Fifth Republic was promulgated in 1958 following its approval at a referendum. Under its terms, legislative power is held by the bicameral Parliament (Parlement), comprising a Senate (Sénat) and a National Assembly (Assemblée nationale). The Senate currently has 343 members, who are elected by an electoral college (311 for metropolitan France, 19 for the overseas possessions, and 12 for French nationals abroad). A law approved by Parliament in July 2003 introduced a number of reforms to senatorial elections; henceforth, senators were to be elected for a term of six years, with one-half of the seats renewable every three years (compared with a term of nine years and one-third of the seats renewable every three years previously). With effect from 2011, the number of senators was to be increased to 348, and the minimum age for eligible candidates to the Senate was to be reduced from 35 to 30 years. (The first stage of reform, whereby the number of senators increased from 321 to 331, took place at the partial senatorial elections held in September 2004; this number was subsequently increased to 343 at the partial senatorial elections held in September 2008.) The National Assembly has 577 members, with 555 for metropolitan France and 22 for the overseas possessions. Members of the National Assembly are elected by universal adult suffrage, under a single-member constituency system of direct election, using a second ballot if the first ballot failed to produce an absolute majority for any one candidate. The term of the National Assembly is five years, subject to dissolution. Executive power is held by the President. Since 1962 the President has been directly elected by popular vote (using two ballots if necessary). A constitutional amendment passed in October 2000 shortened the term of office from seven to five years, and a further amendment enacted in July 2008 limited the President to a maximum of two consecutive terms in office. The President appoints a Council of Ministers, headed by the Prime Minister, which administers the country and is responsible to Parliament.

Metropolitan France comprises 22 administrative regions containing 96 departments. Under the decentralization law of March 1982, administrative and financial power in metropolitan France was transferred from the préfets, who became Commissaires de la République, to locally elected departmental assemblies (Conseils généraux) and regional assemblies (Conseils régionaux). Corsica has its own directly elected legislative assembly (the Assemblée de Corse). The 12 overseas possessions comprise five Overseas Regions and Departments (Régions et départements d'outre mer—French Guiana, Guadeloupe, Martinique, Mayotte and Réunion); five Overseas Collectivities (Collectivités d'outre mer—French Polynesia, Saint-Barthélemy, Saint-Martin, Saint Pierre and Miquelon and the Wallis and Futuna Islands); and two other territories (the French Southern and Antarctic Territories, and New Caledonia—which has a unique status as a *sui generis* Collectivity); all of which are integral parts of the French Republic. At a referendum held in the Overseas Collectivity of Mayotte in March 2009, the electorate voted overwhelmingly in favour of becoming an Overseas Department of France; the change took effect at the end of March 2011.

REGIONAL AND INTERNATIONAL CO-OPERATION

France was a founder member of the European Community, now the European Union (EU, see p. 276), and uses the single currency, the euro. France is also a member of the Council of Europe (see p. 256), which is based in Strasbourg, and the Organization for Security and Co-operation in Europe (OSCE, see p. 388). France is the host nation for the European Space Agency (see p. 273).

France was a founder member of the UN in 1945, and is a permanent member of the Security Council. As a contracting party to the General Agreement on Tariffs and Trade, France joined the World Trade Organization (WTO, see p. 433) on its establishment in 1995. France participates in the Group of Eight major industrialized nations (G8, see p. 463) and the Group of 20 major industrialized and systemically important emerging market nations (G20, see p. 454). France is also a member of the North Atlantic Treaty Organization (NATO, see p. 370) and the Organisation for Economic Co-operation and Development (OECD, see p. 379), which has its headquarters in Paris. It presides over the Franc Zone (see p. 332).

ECONOMIC AFFAIRS

In 2010, according to estimates by the World Bank, France's gross national income (GNI), measured at average 2008–10 prices, was US $2,749,821m., equivalent to $42,390 per head (or $34,440 on an international purchasing-power parity basis). During 2001–10, it was estimated, the population increased by an average of 0.7% per year, while gross domestic product (GDP) per head increased, in real terms, by an average of 0.4% per year. Overall GDP increased, in real terms, at an average rate of 1.1% per year in 2001–10; real GDP declined by 2.7% in 2009, but increased by 1.5% in 2010.

Agriculture (including forestry and fishing) contributed 1.7% of GDP in 2009 and engaged 3.1% of the economically active population in 2008. The principal crops are wheat, sugar beet, maize and barley. Livestock, dairy products and wine are also important. According to World Bank figures, agricultural GDP increased, in real terms, by an average of 0.8% per year in 2001–09; it grew by 3.4% in 2009.

Industry (including mining, manufacturing, construction and power) provided 18.8% of GDP in 2009 and employed 23.2% of the working population in 2008. Industrial GDP decreased, in real terms, by an average of 0.5% per year during 2001–09; according to World Bank figures, it declined by 1.5% in 2008 and by 9.0% in 2009.

Mining and quarrying contributed 0.2% of GDP in 2001, and employed 0.1% of the working population in 2008. Petroleum and natural gas are extracted and metallic minerals, including iron ore, copper and zinc, are mined. The production of coal, an industry which used to dominate the sector, finished in 2004 with the closure of France's last operating coal mine.

Manufacturing provided 10.6% of GDP in 2009 and employed 15.1% of the working population in 2008. Manufacturing GDP decreased, in real terms, at an average annual rate of 1.0% in 2001–09, according to World Bank figures; the sector declined by 2.5% in 2008 and by 11.0% in 2009.

The construction sector provided 6.4% of GDP in 2009 and employed 7.2% of the working population in 2008.

France has only limited fossil fuel resources and in the early 2000s was the world's largest producer of nuclear power per head of population. In 2008 nuclear power provided 77.1% of total electricity production and hydroelectric power 11.2%. In 2010 France had 58 nuclear power stations, many of which would need to be replaced in around 2020. Construction on a new nuclear reactor, the European Pressurized Reactor, began at Flamanville in Normandy in 2007 and the reactor was scheduled to be operational in 2016. Construction of a second new reactor was due to begin in 2012. Imports of energy products comprised 13.5% of the value of total merchandise imports in 2010; in the early 2000s the major sources of petroleum imported to France were Saudi Arabia and Norway.

Services accounted for 79.4% of GDP in 2009 and employed 73.7% of the working population in 2008. France is consistently the country with the largest number of tourist visitors in the world; there were an estimated 76,827,000 tourist arrivals in 2009, and tourism receipts in that year totalled US $59,391m., according to the World Tourism Organization. The GDP of the services sector increased, in real terms, at an average rate of 1.5% per year in 2001–09, according to World Bank figures; it rose by 0.6% in 2008, but declined by 1.0% in 2009.

In 2010 France recorded a trade deficit of US $71,210m., and there was a deficit of $44,500m. on the current account of the balance of payments. In 2010 the principal source of imports (providing 17.3% of the total) was Germany; other major sources were the People's Republic of China, Belgium, Italy, Spain and the USA. Germany was also the principal market for exports in that year (accounting for 16.2% of the total); other major trading partners were Italy, Belgium, Spain, the United Kingdom and the USA. The European Union (EU) as a whole provided 59.9% of imports in 2010 and took 61.1% of exports. The principal exports in 2010 were nuclear reactors and machinery, motor vehicles, aircraft and spacecraft, and electrical and electronic equipment. The principal imports in that year were mineral fuels and lubricants, nuclear reactors and machinery, electrical and electronic equipment, and motor vehicles.

The general government deficit for 2010 was €136,900m., equivalent to 7.1% of GDP. France's general government gross debt was €1,591,200m. in 2010, equivalent to 82.3% of GDP. The average annual rate of inflation in 2001–11 was 1.8%. Consumer prices increased by 2.12% in 2011, according to official figures. The rate of unemployment was 9.1% in 2010.

The French economy was the second largest in Europe in 2010, after Germany. France was less severely affected than most advanced economies by the global financial crisis and downturn that began in late 2008, partly owing to the country's high levels of government spending and generous social security provisions, which helped to maintain consumer demand. The economy emerged from recession in mid-2009 after four quarters of negative growth, and GDP declined by just 2.7% in 2009 (compared with 4.3% in the euro area as a whole), before rising by 1.5% in 2010 and an estimated 1.7% in 2011. However, the unemployment rate remained high in 2011, at 9.4% in metropolitan France in the final quarter of the year. Particularly affected were young workers, of whom 22.4% were unemployed, largely owing to the division of the labour market into a two-tiered system of well-remunerated, highly protected, permanent jobs and poorly paid, fixed-term and temporary jobs. Moreover, stimulus measures introduced to counter the economic crisis had exacerbated the fiscal deficit, which amounted to 7.1% of GDP in 2010. The Government aimed to reduce the deficit to 5.7% of GDP in 2011, to 4.5% in 2012 and to below the EU-mandated limit of 3% by 2013. To this end, the Government of Nicolas Sarkozy announced two austerity plans in August and November 2011, together aimed at achieving savings of €18,000m. in 2012, with an emphasis more on tax rises than expenditure reductions. Specific measures included a temporary increase in the income tax rate, from 41% to 44%, for those earning more than €500,000 a year, bringing forward an increase in the retirement age from 60 to 62 from 2018 to 2017, and the introduction of an additional 5% levy on companies with turnovers in excess of €250m. None the less, the credit rating agency Standard & Poor's lowered France's long-term sovereign debt rating from AAA to AA+ in January 2012; France's largest banks had already suffered downgradings in their ratings by the Moody's agency in September and December 2011, mainly owing to borrowing difficulties and exposure to Greek sovereign debt. In January 2012 the Government revised its growth forecast for that year downwards, from 1.0% to 0.5%, amid a deteriorating economic outlook and the ongoing debt crisis in the euro area.

PUBLIC HOLIDAYS

2013: 1 January (New Year's Day), 1 April (Easter Monday), 1 May (Labour Day), 8 May (Liberation Day), 9 May (Ascension Day), 20 May (Whit Monday), 14 July (National Day, Fall of the Bastille), 15 August (Assumption), 1 November (All Saints' Day), 11 November (Armistice Day), 25 December (Christmas Day).

Statistical Survey

Source (unless otherwise stated): Institut national de la statistique et des études économiques, 18 blvd Adolphe Pinard, 75675 Paris Cedex 14; tel. 1-45-17-50-50; internet www.insee.fr.

Note: Unless otherwise indicated, figures in this survey refer to metropolitan France, excluding the Overseas Possessions.

Area and Population

AREA, POPULATION AND DENSITY

Area (sq km)	543,965*
Population (census results, *de jure*)†	
8 March 1999‡	
Males	28,419,419
Females	30,101,269
Total	58,520,688
1 January 2009§	62,465,709
Population (official estimates at 1 January)‖	
2010	62,791,013
2011	63,127,768
2012	63,460,768
Density (per sq km) at 1 January 2012	116.7

* 210,026 sq miles.

† Excluding professional soldiers and military personnel outside the country with no personal residence in France.

‡ Data are provisional. The revised total is 58,518,395. Figures include double counting.

§ New census methodology. Data refer to median figures based on the collection of raw data over a five-year period (2005–10).

‖ Provisional figures.

POPULATION BY AGE AND SEX

(official estimates at 1 January 2012, provisional)

	Males	Females	Total
0–14	5,956,587	5,686,557	11,643,144
15–64	20,209,965	20,617,221	40,827,186
65 and over	4,578,868	6,411,570	10,990,438
Total	30,745,420	32,715,348	63,460,768

NATIONALITY OF THE POPULATION

(numbers resident in France at 1999 census, revised figures)

Country of citizenship	Population	%
France	55,257,502	94.42
Portugal	553,663	0.95
Morocco	504,096	0.86
Algeria	477,482	0.82
Turkey	208,049	0.36
Italy	201,670	0.34
Spain	161,762	0.28
Tunisia	154,356	0.26
Germany	78,381	0.31
Belgium	66,666	0.11
Yugoslavia*	50,543	0.09
Poland	33,758	0.06
Others	772,760	1.32
Total	58,520,688	100.00

* The successor states of the former Socialist Federal Republic of Yugoslavia, comprising Bosnia and Herzegovina, Croatia, the former Yugoslav republic of Macedonia, Slovenia and the Federal Republic of Yugoslavia (now Montenegro and Serbia).

REGIONS

(population at 1 January 2011, official estimates)

	Area (sq km)	Population	Density (per sq km)	Principal city
Alsace	8,280.2	1,860,243	224.7	Strasbourg
Aquitaine	41,308.4	3,258,176	78.9	Bordeaux
Auvergne	26,012.9	1,347,794	51.8	Clermont-Ferrand
Basse-Normandie	17,589.3	1,476,937	84.0	Caen
Bourgogne (Burgundy)	31,582.0	1,647,708	52.2	Dijon
Bretagne (Brittany)	27,207.9	3,221,451	118.4	Rennes
Centre	39,150.9	2,551,372	65.2	Orléans
Champagne–Ardenne	25,605.8	1,334,998	52.1	Châlons-en-Champagne
Corse (Corsica)	8,679.8	312,936	36.1	Ajaccio
Franche-Comté	16,202.3	1,177,295	72.7	Besançon
Haute-Normandie	12,317.4	1,843,118	149.6	Rouen
Ile-de-France	12,012.3	11,866,900	987.9	Paris
Languedoc-Roussillon	27,375.8	2,661,449	97.2	Montpellier
Limousin	16,942.3	746,691	44.1	Limoges
Lorraine	23,547.4	2,354,876	100.0	Nancy
Midi-Pyrénées	45,347.9	2,916,076	64.3	Toulouse
Nord-Pas-de-Calais	12,414.1	4,038,280	325.3	Lille
Pays de la Loire	32,081.8	3,594,865	112.1	Nantes
Picardie (Picardy)	19,399.5	1,919,367	98.9	Amiens
Poitou-Charentes	25,809.5	1,780,379	69.0	Poitiers
Provence-Alpes-Côte d'Azur	31,399.6	4,944,390	157.5	Marseille
Rhône-Alpes	43,698.2	6,272,467	143.5	Lyon
Total	543,965.4	63,127,768	116.1	—

PRINCIPAL TOWNS*

(incl. suburbs, estimated population at 1 January 2007)

Paris (capital)	10,197,678	Metz	322,459
Marseille–Aix-en-Provence	1,433,462	Montpellier	320,760
Lyon	1,422,331	Tours	307,146
Lille	1,014,586	Saint-Etienne	283,996
Nice	946,630	Rennes	281,734
Toulouse	858,233	Avignon	275,613
Bordeaux	809,224	Orléans	268,470
Nantes	569,961	Clermont-Ferrand	261,239
Toulon	546,801	Béthune	258,967
Douai-Lens	512,029	Mulhouse	239,859
Strasbourg	440,704	Dijon	237,925
Grenoble	427,739	Le Havre	235,818
Rouen	389,876	Angers	226,809
Valenciennes	355,709	Reims	211,966
Nancy	330,232	Brest	205,195

* Data refer to contiguous urban agglomerations (*unités urbaines*).

Mid-2010 ('000, incl. suburbs, UN estimates): Paris 10,485; Lyon 1,468; Marseille–Aix-en-Provence 1,469; Lille 1,033; Nice 977; Toulouse 912; Bordeaux 838 (Source: UN, *World Urbanization Prospects: The 2007 Revision*).

BIRTHS, MARRIAGES AND DEATHS*

	Registered live births		Registered marriages		Registered deaths	
	Number	Rate (per 1,000)	Number	Rate (per 1,000)	Number	Rate (per 1,000)
2004	767,816	12.7	271,598	4.5	509,429	8.4
2005	774,355	12.7	276,303	4.5	527,533	8.7
2006	796,896	13.0	267,260	4.4	516,416	8.4
2007	785,985	12.7	267,194	4.3	521,016	8.4
2008	796,044	12.8	258,739	4.2	532,131	8.6
2009	793,420	12.7	245,151	3.9	538,116	8.6
2010	802,224	12.8	n.a.	n.a.	540,469	8.6
2011	797,000	12.6	n.a.	n.a.	544,000	8.6

* Including data for national armed forces outside the country.

Life expectancy (years at birth, WHO estimates): 81 (males 78; females 85) in 2009 (Source: WHO, *World Health Statistics*).

ECONOMICALLY ACTIVE POPULATION
(annual averages, '000 persons aged 15 years and over)

	2006	2007	2008
Agriculture, forestry and fishing	931.5	875.9	789.1
Mining and quarrying	29.0	24.3	25.5
Manufacturing	3,984.8	3,949.8	3,877.2
Electricity, gas and water supply	245.8	200.4	201.2
Construction	1,705.4	1,755.1	1,860.0
Wholesale and retail trade; repair of motor vehicles, motorcycles and personal and household goods	3,352.8	3,538.8	3,421.3
Hotels and restaurants	911.1	878.8	870.5
Transport, storage and communications	1,518.9	1,602.9	1,640.7
Financial intermediation	807.4	826.0	793.3
Real estate, renting and business activities	2,662.6	2,666.0	2,784.8
Public administration and defence; compulsory social security	2,407.2	2,563.3	2,652.5
Education	1,776.7	1,735.9	1,791.6
Health and social work	3,066.4	3,143.4	3,215.0
Other community, social and personal service activities	1,102.9	1,156.9	1,161.8
Households with employed persons	580.7	592.4	607.9
Extra-territorial organizations and bodies	18.4	18.9	19.0
Sub-total	25,101.7	25,528.8	25,711.4
Not classifiable by economic activity	31.8	36.4	201.8
Total employed	25,133.5	25,565.2	25,913.2
Unemployed	2,435.0	2,222.0	2,071.0
Total labour force	27,568.5	27,787.2	27,984.2
Males	14,556.5	14,613.9	14,688.9
Females	13,012.0	13,173.3	13,296.0

Source: ILO.

Health and Welfare

KEY INDICATORS

Total fertility rate (children per woman, 2009)	1.9
Under-5 mortality rate (per 1,000 live births, 2009)	4
HIV/AIDS (% of persons aged 15–49, 2007)	0.4
Physicians (per 1,000 head, 2006)	3.4
Hospital beds (per 1,000 head, 2005)	7.3
Health expenditure (2008): US $ per head (PPP)	3,851
Health expenditure (2008): % of GDP	11.2
Health expenditure (2008): public (% of total)	75.9
Total carbon dioxide emissions ('000 metric tons, 2007)	371,452.7
Carbon dioxide emissions per head (metric tons, 2007)	6.0
Human Development Index (2011): ranking	20
Human Development Index (2011): value	0.884

For sources and definitions, see explanatory note on p. vi.

Agriculture

PRINCIPAL CROPS
('000 metric tons)

	2008	2009	2010
Wheat	39,006.4	38,332.2	38,207.0
Rice, paddy	111.5	138.0	118.5
Barley	12,171.6	12,875.8	10,102.0
Maize	15,818.5	15,288.2	13,975.0
Rye	123.5	129.8	121.7
Oats	472.0	573.0	447.8
Sorghum (excl. sorghum for forage and silage)	231.0	312.8	287.0
Buckwheat	98.0	114.5	125.9
Triticale (wheat-rye hybrid)	1,821.8	2,015.6	2,057.2
Potatoes	6,872.0	7,174.6	6,582.2
Sugar beet	30,321.2	35,160.3	31,910.4
Broad beans, horse beans, dry	314.7	438.3	480.9
Peas, dry	450.6	547.0	1,098.1
Soybeans (soya beans)	63.1	109.3	140.0
Sunflower seed	1,598.3	1,720.2	1,633.1
Rapeseed	4,721.3	5,588.5	4,815.5
Linseed	14.6	20.6	35.0*
Cabbages and other brassicas	225.5	206.8	197.4
Artichokes	44.9	46.6	42.2
Lettuce and chicory	426.7	421.3	398.2
Spinach	123.5	130.6	104.8
Tomatoes	617.6	602.9	587.6
Cauliflowers and broccoli	355.3	369.4	371.0
Pumpkins, squash and gourds	195.3	193.2	190.9*
Cucumbers and gherkins	138.9	138.5	138.7
Onions and shallots, green	43.3	40.1	45.4
Onions, dry	151.3	164.3	145.3*
Beans, green	45.1	43.6	41.0†
Peas, green	349.8	664.4	406.1
String beans	343.5	338.2	318.2†
Carrots and turnips	301.5	320.0	328.7
Maize, green	479.7	362.5	341.1†
Mushrooms and truffles	29.9	28.2	23.1
Chicory roots	125.5	164.0	107.6
Cantaloupes and other melons	278.9	301.2	295.2
Apples	1,701.8	1,729.6	1,711.2
Pears	159.9	187.6	173.7
Apricots	94.5	190.4	139.6
Sweet cherries	40.4	53.6	45.9
Peaches and nectarines	301.1	347.5	324.4
Plums and sloes	161.0	238.5	280.4
Strawberries	44.1	46.7	46.6
Grapes	6,019.2	6,104.3	5,849.0
Kiwi fruit	65.7	75.1	70.4
Tobacco, unmanufactured	16.3	17.8	18.4

* Unofficial figure.
† FAO estimate.

Aggregate production ('000 metric tons, may include official, semi-official or estimated data): Total cereals 70,108.2 in 2008, 70,034.2 in 2009, 65,675.7 in 2010; Total roots and tubers 6,872.0 in 2008, 7,174.6 in 2009, 6,582.2 in 2010; Total vegetables (incl. melons) 5,205.1 in 2008, 5,331.5 in 2009, 5,020.8 in 2010; Total fruits (excl. melons) 8,640.5 in 2008, 9,033.5 in 2009, 8,691.8 in 2010.

Source: FAO.

LIVESTOCK
('000 head, year ending 30 September)

	2008	2009	2010
Cattle	20,046.9	19,805.4	19,620.9
Pigs	14,947.4	14,718.9	14,531.9
Sheep	8,189	8,093	7,977
Goats	1,283	1,329	1,349
Horses	452	453	453
Asses*	15	15	15
Mules*	15	15	15
Chickens	118,687	122,364	124,249
Ducks	22,844	21,913	22,531
Turkeys	24,855	24,197	23,596

* FAO estimate(s).

Source: FAO.

LIVESTOCK PRODUCTS
('000 metric tons)

	2008	2009	2010
Cattle meat	1,502.9	1,515.8	1,550.2
Sheep meat	129.9	125.6	121.9
Pig meat	2,274.1	2,261.6	2,259.7
Chicken meat	1,081.8	1,069.2	1,103.0
Duck meat	272.1	264.5	276.0
Turkey meat	448.7	419.4	406.8
Cows' milk	23,564.9	22,653.1	23,301.2
Sheep's milk	244.2	145.1	259.2
Goats' milk	567.3	645.2	645.2
Honey	14.9	15.5	16.0
Hen eggs	946.8	918.3	946.6
Wool, greasy*	10	9	5

* FAO estimates.

Source: FAO.

Forestry

ROUNDWOOD REMOVALS
('000 cubic metres, excluding bark)

	2008	2009	2010
Sawlogs, veneer logs and logs for sleepers	18,268	19,040	17,829
Pulpwood	9,115	9,708	11,154
Other industrial wood	342	332	321
Fuel wood	25,032	25,366	26,174
Total	52,757	54,447	55,477

Source: FAO.

SAWNWOOD PRODUCTION
('000 cubic metres, including railway sleepers)

	2008	2009	2010
Coniferous (softwood)	7,608	6,462	6,916
Broadleaved (hardwood)	1,735	1,423	1,420
Total	9,343	7,885	8,336

Source: FAO.

Fishing

('000 metric tons, live weight)

	2007	2008	2009
Capture*	513.4	460.4	411.2
Saithe (Pollock)	20.8	21.4	8.2
Atlantic herring	22.1	22.1	3.7
European pilchard (Sardine)	38.7	29.7	39.3
Skipjack tuna	34.6	34.1	37.0
Yellowfin tuna	44.1	53.6	39.9
Atlantic mackerel	17.4	14.2	12.3
Blue whiting (Poutassou)	20.0	19.9	7.0
Monkfishes (Angler)	22.4	18.7	18.2
Aquaculture	237.6	238.5*	233.9
Rainbow trout	32.3	34.2	32.8
Pacific cupped oyster	110.8	103.8	103.5
Blue mussel	56.7	64.5	61.6
Total catch*	751.0	698.8	645.1

* FAO estimate(s).

Note: Figures exclude aquatic plants ('000 metric tons, all capture): 39.8 in 2007; 39.8 in 2008 (FAO estimate); 18.6 in 2009. Figures also exclude coral (metric tons): 8.2 in 2007; 8.4 in 2008; 9.0 in 2009; and sponges (metric tons, FAO estimates): 0.5 in 2007; 0.4 in 2008; 0.3 in 2009. Also excluded are aquatic mammals, recorded by number rather than by weight. The number of common dolphins caught was: 16 in 2007; 22 in 2008; 145 in 2009.

Source: FAO.

Mining

('000 metric tons unless otherwise indicated)

	2007	2008	2009
Crude petroleum ('000 barrels)	7,242	7,117	6,624
Natural gas (marketed production, million cu m)	1,642	1,472	1,444
Silver (kg)*†	700	—	—
Gold (kg)†*	1,500	1,500	1,500
Kaolin and kaolinitic clay‡	307	624	519
Salt*	6,140	6,240	6,200
Gypsum and anhydrite (crude)*	3,500	3,500	3,351
Mica*	20	20	20
Talc (crude)*	420	420	420

* Estimates.

† Figures refer to the metal content of ores and concentrates.

‡ Figures refer to marketable production.

Source: US Geological Survey.

Industry

SELECTED PRODUCTS
('000 metric tons unless otherwise indicated)

	2007	2008	2009
Wheat flour	4,513	4,537	n.a.
Wine ('000 hl)*	4,712	4,269	4,679
Chemical wood pulp*	1,423	1,413	1,025
Newsprint*	1,088	1,064	873
Liquefied petroleum gas ('000 barrels)†	30,358	33,860	33,000‡
Motor gasoline (petrol—'000 barrels)†	142,069	141,195	140,000‡
Jet fuels and kerosene ('000 barrels)†	44,293	44,462	44,000‡
Distillate fuel oil ('000 barrels)†	259,550	275,148	275,000‡
Residual fuel oil ('000 barrels)†	73,803	73,342	73,000‡
Coke-oven coke	4,591	4,594	n.a.
Pig iron	12,426	11,372	n.a.
Crude steel	19,250	17,879	n.a.
Aluminium (unwrought—primary)†	428	389	345‡
Lead (unwrought)†‡	88.0	82.0	86.6
Zinc (incl. slab and secondary)†	129.0	118.9	118.0‡
Electric energy (incl. Monaco, million kWh)	569,755	574,868	n.a.

* Source: FAO.

† Source: US Geological Survey.

‡ Estimates.

2010: Wine ('000 hl) 4,542, Chemical wood pulp 1,073, Newsprint 984 (Source: FAO).

Source (unless otherwise indicated): UN Industrial Commodities Statistics Database.

Finance

CURRENCY AND EXCHANGE RATES

Monetary Units
100 cent = 1 euro (€).

Sterling and Dollar Equivalents (30 December 2011)
£1 sterling = 1.195 euros;
US $1 = 0.773 euros;
€10 = £8.37 = $12.94.

Average Exchange Rate (euros per US $)

2009	0.7198
2010	0.7550
2011	0.7194

Note: The national currency was formerly the French franc. From the introduction of the euro, with French participation, on 1 January 1999, a fixed exchange rate of €1 = 6.5596 French francs was in operation. Euro notes and coins were introduced on 1 January 2002. The euro and local currency circulated alongside each other until 17 February, after which the euro became the sole legal tender.

GOVERNMENT FINANCE

(general government transactions, € '000 million)

Revenue	2008	2009	2010
Taxes	515.4	473.7	495.0
Taxes on income and inheritance	223.6	186.8	204.1
Taxes on capital	7.9	7.5	7.7
Taxes on production and imports	288.6	284.9	287.4
Social contributions	350.0	353.5	360.5
Other revenue	100.0	101.7	102.1
Total	965.4	928.8	957.6

Expenditure	2008	2009	2010
Compensation of employees	247.0	254.3	259.4
Use of goods and services	97.7	104.8	110.6
Interest	56.6	46.1	47.2
Subsidies	27.0	31.7	33.4
Grants	344.8	365.4	378.1
Other social benefits	109.8	114.1	117.9
Other expenses	81.5	87.7	86.9
Net acquisition of non-financial assets	65.6	67.8	61.0
Total	1,030.0	1,071.9	1,094.5

INTERNATIONAL RESERVES

(US $ million at 31 December)

	2008	2009	2010
Gold*	69,308	86,444	110,424
IMF special drawing rights	966	15,234	15,000
Reserve position in IMF	2,270	3,671	4,589
Foreign exchange	30,382	27,729	36,211
Total	102,926	133,078	166,224

* Valued at market-related prices.

Source: IMF, *International Financial Statistics*.

MONEY SUPPLY

(incl. shares, depository corporations, national residency criteria, € million at 31 December)

	2008	2009	2010
Currency issued	147,301	153,733	160,096
Banque de France	72,341	79,107	83,780
Demand deposits	434,852	464,723	502,493
Other deposits	980,643	1,036,281	1,081,448
Securities other than shares	1,147,892	1,096,611	1,164,674
Money market fund shares	476,301	474,001	391,301
Shares and other equity	474,755	525,244	574,225
Other items (net)	–592,587	–501,333	–441,119
Total	3,069,157	3,249,260	3,433,118

Source: IMF, *International Financial Statistics*.

COST OF LIVING

(Consumer Price Index, December of each year; base: January 1998 = 100)

	2009	2010	2011
Food (incl. non-alcoholic beverages)	123.7	125.2	129.5
Alcoholic beverages and tobacco	159.9	165.0	171.8
Clothing and footwear	107.4	107.7	110.9
Housing, water, gas, electricity, etc.	132.8	138.0	143.3
Furniture and household items	113.9	114.2	117.0
Health care and pharmaceuticals	103.3	102.6	102.6
Transport	129.9	135.3	140.9
Post and telecommunications	83.6	82.1	79.8
Leisure and culture (goods and services)	91.7	90.9	90.4
Education	132.8	136.7	139.2
Hotels, cafés and restaurants	130.1	131.8	135.1
All items (incl. others)	120.0	122.1	125.1

NATIONAL ACCOUNTS

(€ '000 million at current prices)

National Income and Product

(preliminary)

	2007	2008	2009
Compensation of employees	974.3	1,004.7	1,005.4
Gross operating surplus and mixed income	667.5	686.7	653.9
Gross domestic product (GDP) at factor cost	1,641.8	1,691.4	1,659.3
Taxes on production and imports	290.4	293.8	288.5
Less Subsidies	36.9	36.6	40.6
GDP in market prices	1,895.3	1,948.5	1,907.1
Primary income from abroad	191.3	186.9	148.7
Primary income paid abroad	–169.2	–167.5	–133.0
Gross national income (GNI)	1,917.3	1,968.0	1,922.8
Less Consumption of fixed capital	–252.3	269.2	272.7
Net national income	1,665.1	1,698.8	1,650.2
Current transfers from abroad	14.6	15.6	14.6
Less Current transfers paid abroad	–42.4	–44.8	–47.7
Net national disposable income	1,637.3	1,669.6	1,617.1

Expenditure on the Gross Domestic Product

(revised figures)

	2008	2009	2010
Final consumption expenditure	1,549.6	1,562.6	1,604.1
Households	1,063.7	1,057.8	1,084.8
Non-profit institutions serving households	36.0	37.8	39.4
General government	449.9	467.0	479.9
Gross capital formation	424.3	360.8	374.1
Gross fixed capital formation	411.9	373.0	373.3
Changes in inventories	11.5	–12.7	0.2
Acquisitions, less disposals, of valuables	0.9	0.5	0.6
Total domestic expenditure	1,973.9	1,923.4	1,978.2
Exports of goods and services	521.0	440.9	492.2
Less Imports of goods and services	561.7	475.2	537.5
GDP in market prices	1,933.2	1,889.2	1,932.8

Gross Domestic Product by Economic Activity

(preliminary)

	2007	2008	2009
Agriculture, forestry and fishing	37.5	35.7	30.0
Industry (incl. energy)	241.8	238.6	213.4
Food products, beverages and tobacco	29.9	31.7	25.7
Consumer goods industries	35.6	33.5	33.5
Automobile industry	12.8	11.6	11.2
Equipment goods industries	48.9	49.9	44.6
Intermediate goods industries	81.1	79.8	67.2
Energy	33.4	32.1	31.2
Construction	106.6	116.5	111.0
Mainly market services	948.2	982.1	976.1
Trade	169.5	177.5	172.3
Transportation	74.4	77.4	78.5
Financial activities	79.3	80.9	87.3
Real estate and renting activities	242.7	250.8	251.9
Business services	287.1	297.7	286.2
Domestic and personal services	95.1	97.8	99.8
Mainly non-market services	364.4	377.6	391.3
Education, health, social work	233.4	242.6	251.4
General government and non-profit institutions serving households	130.9	135.0	139.9
Gross value added at basic prices	1,698.4	1,750.5	1,721.7
Taxes on products	209.5	210.6	201.1
Less Subsidies	12.6	12.7	15.7
GDP in market prices	1,895.3	1,948.5	1,907.1

BALANCE OF PAYMENTS
(US $ '000 million)*

	2008	2009	2010
Exports of goods f.o.b.	605.33	475.87	517.15
Imports of goods f.o.b.	–692.60	–535.82	–588.36
Trade balance	–87.28	–59.94	–71.21
Exports of services	166.33	144.64	144.97
Imports of services	–141.87	–130.33	–132.21
Balance on goods and services	–62.82	–45.63	–58.45
Other income received	269.07	210.54	208.46
Other income paid	–221.06	–166.70	–159.57
Balance on goods, services and income	–14.80	–1.78	–9.56
Current transfers received	29.13	26.07	24.06
Current transfers paid	–64.21	–64.15	–59.01
Current balance	–49.88	–39.87	–44.50
Capital account (net)	1.04	0.46	0.07
Direct investment abroad	–159.94	–103.08	–84.39
Direct investment from abroad	66.54	35.12	33.67
Portfolio investment assets	–158.60	–106.29	28.60
Portfolio investment liabilities	184.78	452.95	128.93
Financial derivatives liabilities	–16.64	–22.88	45.17
Other investment assets	70.04	73.70	–159.72
Other investment liabilities	27.62	–261.95	39.50
Net errors and omissions	23.02	–18.82	20.45
Overall balance	–12.02	9.35	7.79

* Figures refer to transactions of metropolitan France, French Guiana, Guadeloupe, Martinique, Réunion and Monaco with the rest of the world.

Source: IMF, *International Financial Statistics*.

External Trade

(Note: Figures refer to the trade of metropolitan France, French Guiana, Guadeloupe, Martinique, Réunion and Monaco with the rest of the world.)

PRINCIPAL COMMODITIES
(distribution by HS, US $ million)

Imports*	2008	2009	2010
Mineral fuels, oils, distillation products, etc.	117,496.8	71,975.4	82,758.9
Crude petroleum oils	59,821.0	31,789.7	35,319.2
Petroleum oils, not crude	26,030.7	17,664.3	23,518.0
Petroleum gases	24,791.8	17,690.2	18,163.8
Organic chemicals	18,442.4	15,360.4	16,952.9
Pharmaceutical products	22,172.2	24,538.9	25,010.5
Plastics and articles thereof	25,260.9	20,022.0	23,082.3
Iron and steel	22,228.8	11,406.9	14,462.1
Nuclear reactors, boilers, machinery, etc.	85,215.5	64,491.3	67,218.7
Electrical, electronic equipment	56,442.3	47,247.0	56,123.6
Vehicles other than railway, tramway	70,983.9	53,143.4	55,954.1
Cars (incl. station wagons)	36,803.6	30,481.1	31,166.6
Total (incl. others)	695,004.3	540,502.3	599,171.5

Exports	2008	2009	2010
Mineral fuels, oils, distillation products, etc.	30,141.7	16,391.9	18,719.1
Petroleum oils, not crude	18,808.3	10,459.2	12,439.6
Pharmaceutical products	32,275.5	33,340.8	33,536.7
Plastics and articles thereof	23,053.3	17,300.6	19,403.7
Iron and steel	22,185.2	13,079.8	16,615.8
Nuclear reactors, boilers, machinery, etc.	75,974.1	56,251.7	58,802.0
Turbo-jets, turbo-propellers and other gas turbines	9,951.8	9,303.5	9,819.3
Electrical, electronic equipment	47,957.6	38,722.3	43,487.9
Electronic integrated circuits and microassemblies	6,245.6	4,569.5	7,086.0
Vehicles other than railway, tramway	61,853.1	42,737.5	47,147.8
Cars (incl. station wagons)	27,747.4	19,901.6	21,089.0
Parts and accessories of motor vehicles	19,603.9	14,912.8	16,978.6
Aircraft, spacecraft, and parts thereof	38,141.2	34,546.6	46,404.1
Aircraft (helicopter, aeroplanes) and spacecraft (satellites)	31,637.1	29,184.4	40,818.5
Total (incl. others)	594,505.0	464,112.8	511,651.0

* Including re-imports.

Source: Trade Map-Trade Competitiveness Map, International Trade Centre, www.intracen.org/marketanalysis.

PRINCIPAL TRADING PARTNERS
(US $ million)

Imports*	2008	2009	2010
Algeria	7,082.5	3,817.9	3,073.6
Belgium	59,139.9	44,696.2	46,993.3
China, People's Republic	45,461.9	41,252.6	48,872.7
Czech Republic	6,891.6	5,876.0	6,640.4
Germany	113,901.6	88,206.8	103,433.8
Ireland	8,983.4	8,389.5	7,745.4
Italy	56,530.1	42,981.6	44,971.0
Japan	13,998.7	10,767.9	11,719.3
Libya	5,052.5	3,135.8	6,263.2
Netherlands	28,179.7	22,853.7	25,188.4
Norway	12,381.5	6,629.9	6,490.6
Poland	9,549.7	7,788.1	9,124.2
Russia	20,159.6	12,938.9	16,136.1
Spain	45,316.8	34,255.2	37,184.8
Sweden	9,297.6	6,497.8	7,474.2
Switzerland	15,700.0	13,725.1	14,600.1
Turkey	7,828.7	7,019.1	7,159.7
United Kingdom	33,670.7	25,172.3	25,974.0
USA	38,295.7	34,722.7	35,234.6
Total (incl. others)	695,004.3	540,502.3	599,171.5

Exports	2008	2009	2010
Algeria	8,108.2	6,959.6	6,933.3
Belgium	45,318.0	35,348.7	38,471.5
China, People's Republic	13,285.3	10,943.3	14,551.3
Germany	86,841.5	68,985.0	82,988.7
Hong Kong	3,745.1	3,294.9	5,578.6
Italy	52,423.5	39,242.6	41,337.6
Japan	8,254.7	6,648.8	7,793.3
Morocco	6,260.1	4,823.0	5,281.2
Netherlands	25,132.6	19,107.8	21,333.8
Poland	9,906.6	7,179.0	7,849.8
Portugal	7,565.4	6,022.6	5,547.5
Russia	10,364.3	7,069.4	8,319.0
Saudi Arabia	3,329.8	3,511.4	5,190.5
Singapore	6,798.9	5,939.6	6,663.0
Spain	49,916.9	37,242.6	37,979.6
Sweden	8,056.4	5,717.6	6,694.3
Switzerland	17,686.1	14,028.5	15,054.3
Turkey	8,402.7	6,731.6	8,303.3
United Arab Emirates	5,188.5	4,836.4	4,522.0
United Kingdom	46,710.2	33,747.3	34,343.8
USA	35,110.1	27,346.8	29,230.6
Total (incl. others)	594,505.0	464,112.8	511,651.0

* Including re-imports.

Source: Trade Map-Trade Competitiveness Map, International Trade Centre, www.intracen.org/marketanalysis.

Transport

RAILWAYS
(traffic)

	2006	2007	2008
Paying passengers ('000 journeys)	1,013,000	1,042,860	1,085,540
Passenger-km (million)	n.a.	80,370	85,030
Freight carried ('000 metric tons)	107,710	105,710	97,440
Freight ton-km (million)	n.a.	40,630	37,270

Source: Société Nationale des Chemins de fer Français, Paris.

ROAD TRAFFIC
('000 motor vehicles in use at 31 December)

	2006	2007	2008
Passenger cars	30,400	30,700	30,850
Lorries and vans	6,179	6,270	6,280
Buses and coaches	83	83	84
Motorcycles and mopeds	2,482	1,300	2,710

Source: International Road Federation, *World Road Statistics*.

INLAND WATERWAYS

	2003	2004	2005
Freight carried ('000 metric tons)	54,661	57,994	59,510
Freight ton-km (million)	6,890	7,316	7,856

Source: Voies navigables de France.

SHIPPING

Merchant Fleet
(registered at 31 December)

	2007	2008	2009
Number of vessels	746	775	785
Total displacement ('000 grt)	1,168.6	1,286.7	1,225.3

Source: IHS Fairplay, *World Fleet Statistics*.

Sea-borne Freight Traffic
('000 metric tons)

	2003	2004	2005
Goods loaded	93,010	96,100	100,660
Goods unloaded	220,610	223,580	227,100

2010: Goods loaded 99,864; Goods unloaded 199,308.

Source: UN, *Monthly Bulletin of Statistics*.

CIVIL AVIATION
(revenue traffic on scheduled services)*

	2008	2009	2010
Passengers carried ('000)	63,729	61,086	60,759
Passenger-km (million)	172,446	166,181	167,959
Total ton-km (million)	5,852	4,809	4,955

* Including data for airlines based in French overseas possessions.

Source: Direction Générale de l'Aviation Civile.

Tourism

FOREIGN TOURIST ARRIVALS BY COUNTRY OF ORIGIN
('000, estimates)

	2007	2008	2009
Belgium and Luxembourg	9,355	9,409	10,906
Germany	13,041	11,645	10,698
Italy	8,141	8,233	7,253
Netherlands	6,824	6,244	7,231
Scandinavian states	1,512	1,668	1,484
Spain	5,599	5,640	4,880
Switzerland	5,303	5,065	5,442
United Kingdom and Ireland	15,009	14,374	12,915
USA	3,399	3,328	3,064
Total (incl. others)	80,851	79,220	76,827

Receipts from tourism (US $ million, excl. passenger transport): 56,573 in 2008; 49,398 in 2009; 46,319 in 2010 (provisional).

Source: World Tourism Organization.

Communications Media

	2008	2009	2010
Telephones ('000 main lines in use)	35,100	35,400	35,300
Mobile cellular telephones ('000 subscribers)	57,972	59,600	63,200
Internet subscribers ('000)	18,810	20,500	21,800
Broadband subscribers ('000)	17,830	19,900	21,345

Personal computers: 40,000 (652.0 per 1,000 persons) in 2006.

Television receivers ('000 in use): 37,500 in 2001.

Radio receivers ('000 in use): 55,300 in 1997.

Book production: 51,837 titles in 2000.

Daily newspapers (2005): 103 titles (total average circulation 9,973m.).

Non-daily newspapers (1999, excl. newspapers published on Sundays only): 245 titles (total average circulation 2,236,000 copies).

Other periodicals (1993): 2,683 titles (circulation 120,018,000 copies in 1991).

Sources: UN, *Statistical Yearbook*; UNESCO Institute for Statistics, International Telecommunication Union.

Education

(2004/05, public and private, metropolitan France, French Guiana, Guadeloupe, Martinique and Réunion)

	Students ('000)		
	Males	Females	Total
Pre-primary	1,335.7	1,273.8	2,609.5
Primary	2,011.2	1,913.4	3,924.6
Integration and adaptation schooling	30.9	20.5	51.4
Secondary:			
Lower	1,626.2	1,568.1	3,194.3
Upper—Professional	389.0	324.8	713.8
Upper—General/Technical	681.0	834.6	1,515.5
Higher	n.a.	n.a.	2,268.4

Source: Ministry of National Education, Higher Education and Research, Paris.

Students ('000, 2010/11, public and private, metropolitan France, French Guiana, Guadeloupe, Martinique and Réunion): Pre-primary 2,539.1; Primary 4,080.8; Integration and adaptation schooling 44.3; Secondary (Lower) 3,126.4; Secondary (Upper—Professional) 705.5; Secondary (Upper—General/Technical) 1,425.7; Higher 2,318.7.

Institutions (2010/11, public and private, metropolitan France, French Guiana, Guadeloupe, Martinique and Réunion): Pre-primary 16,189, Primary and Integration and adaptation schooling 37,609, Secondary (Lower) 7,018, Secondary (Upper—Professional) 1,637, Secondary (Upper—General/Technical) 2,640, Higher (Universities) 79, Higher (Other) 4,363.

Teachers (2004/05, public and private, metropolitan France, French Guiana, Guadeloupe, Martinique and Réunion, excl. trainee teachers): Pre-primary, Primary and Integration and adaptation schooling 364,315, Secondary (Lower) 237,277, Secondary (Upper) 250,367, Higher 87,724.

Directory

The Government

HEAD OF STATE

President: NICOLAS SARKOZY (took office 16 May 2007).

Note: François Hollande was elected President on 6 May 2012 and was expected to take office on 15 May.

COUNCIL OF MINISTERS
(May 2012)

The Government is composed mainly of members of the Union pour un Mouvement Populaire.

Prime Minister and Minister of Ecology, Sustainable Development, Transport and Housing: FRANÇOIS FILLON.

Minister of State, Minister of Defence and Veterans: GÉRARD LONGUET.

Minister of State, Minister of Foreign and European Affairs: ALAIN JUPPÉ.

Keeper of the Seals, Minister of Justice and Freedoms: MICHEL MERCIER.

Minister of the Interior, the Overseas Possessions, the Territorial Collectivities and Immigration: CLAUDE GUÉANT.

Minister of the Economy, Finance and Industry: FRANÇOIS BAROIN.

Minister of Public Service: FRANÇOIS SAUVADET.

Minister of Labour, Employment and Health: XAVIER BERTRAND.

Minister of National Education, Youth and Community Life: LUC CHATEL.

Minister of the Budget, Public Finances and State Reform, and Government Spokesman: VALÉRIE PÉCRESSE.

Minister of Higher Education and Research: LAURENT WAUQUIEZ.

Minister of Agriculture, Food, Fisheries, Rural Affairs and Planning: BRUNO LE MAIRE.

Minister of Culture and Communication: FRÉDÉRIC MITTERRAND.

Minister of Solidarity and Social Cohesion: ROSELYNE BACHELOT-NARQUIN.

Minister of Urban Planning: MAURICE LEROY.

Minister of Sport: DAVID DOUILLET.

Minister in the Office of the Prime Minister, in charge of Relations with Parliament: PATRICK OLLIER.

Minister in the Ministry of the Economy, Finance and Industry, in charge of Industry, Energy and the Digital Economy: ERIC BESSON.

Minister in the Ministry of Foreign and European Affairs, in charge of Co-operation: HENRI DE RAINCOURT.

Minister in the Ministry of the Interior, the Overseas Possessions, the Territorial Collectivities and Immigration, in charge of the Territorial Collectivities: PHILIPPE RICHERT.

Minister in the Ministry of Foreign and European Affairs, in charge of European Affairs: JEAN LEONETTI.

Minister in the Ministry of Labour, Employment and Health, in charge of Apprenticeship and Vocational Training: NADINE MORANO.

Minister in the Ministry of the Interior, the Overseas Possessions, the Territorial Collectivities and Immigration, in charge of the Overseas Possessions: MARIE-LUCE PENCHARD.

Minister in the Ministry of Ecology, Sustainable Development, Transport and Housing, in charge of Transport: THIERRY MARIANI.

Secretary of State in the Ministry of the Economy, Finance and Industry, in charge of Foreign Trade: PIERRE LELLOUCHE.

Secretary of State in the Ministry of Labour, Employment and Health, in charge of Health: NORA BERRA.

Secretary of State in the Ministry of Ecology, Sustainable Development, Transport and Housing, in charge of Housing: BENOIST APPARU.

Secretary of State in the Ministry of Defence and Veterans: MARC LAFFINEUR.

State Secretary in the Ministry of Solidarity and Social Cohesion: MARIE-ANNE MONTCHAMP.

Secretary of State in the Ministry of Solidarity and Social Cohesion, in charge of Family: CLAUDE GREFF.

Secretary of State in the Ministry of the Economy, Finance and Industry, in charge of Trade, Crafts, Small and Medium-Sized Enterprises, Tourism, Services, Professions and Consumption: FRÉDÉRIC LEFÈBVRE.

Secretary of State in the Ministry of National Education, Youth and Community Life, in charge of Youth and Community Life: JEANNETTE BOUGRAB.

MINISTRIES

Office of the President: Palais de l'Elysée, 55–57 rue du Faubourg Saint Honoré, 75008 Paris; tel. 1-42-92-81-00; fax 1-47-42-24-65; internet www.elysee.fr.

Office of the Prime Minister: Hôtel de Matignon, 57 rue de Varenne, 75007 Paris; tel. 1-42-75-80-00; fax 1-42-75-78-31; e-mail premier-ministre@premier-ministre.gouv.fr; internet www.premier-ministre.gouv.fr.

Ministry of Agriculture, Food, Fisheries, Rural Affairs and Planning: 78 rue de Varenne, 75349 Paris Cedex 07; tel. 1-49-55-49-55; fax 1-49-55-40-39; e-mail infodoc@agriculture.gouv.fr; internet www.agriculture.gouv.fr.

Ministry of the Budget, Public Finances and State Reform: 139 rue de Bercy, 75572 Paris Cedex 12; tel. 1-40-04-04-04; fax 1-43-43-75-97; e-mail dircom-cnt@dircom.finances.gouv.fr; internet www.budget.gouv.fr.

Ministry of Culture and Communication: 3 rue de Valois, 75001 Paris; tel. 1-40-15-80-00; fax 1-40-15-81-72; e-mail point.culture@culture.fr; internet www.culture.gouv.fr.

Ministry of Defence and Veterans: 14 rue Saint Dominique, 75007 Paris; tel. 1-42-19-30-11; fax 1-47-05-40-91; e-mail courrier-ministre@sdbc.defense.gouv.fr; internet www.defense.gouv.fr.

Ministry of Ecology, Sustainable Development, Transport and Housing: 92055 La Défense Cedex; tel. 1-40-81-21-22; internet www.developpement-durable.gouv.fr.

Ministry of the Economy, Finance and Industry: 139 rue de Bercy, 75572 Paris Cedex 12; tel. 1-40-04-04-04; fax 1-43-43-75-97; e-mail mediateur@finances.gouv.fr; internet www.minefe.gouv.fr.

Ministry of Foreign and European Affairs: 37 quai d'Orsay, 75351 Paris Cedex 07; tel. 1-43-17-53-53; fax 1-43-17-52-03; internet www.diplomatie.gouv.fr.

Ministry of Higher Education and Research: 1 rue Descartes, 75231 Paris Cedex 05; tel. 1-55-55-90-90; e-mail sup-info@education.gouv.fr; internet www.enseignementsup-recherche.gouv.fr.

Ministry of the Interior, the Overseas Possessions, the Territorial Collectivities and Immigration: place Beauvau, 75008 Paris; tel. 1-49-27-49-27; fax 1-43-59-89-50; e-mail sirp@interieur.gouv.fr; internet www.interieur.gouv.fr.

Ministry of Justice and Freedoms: 13 place Vendôme, 75042 Paris Cedex 01; tel. 1-44-77-60-60; fax 1-44-77-60-00; e-mail cyberjustice@justice.gouv.fr; internet www.justice.gouv.fr.

Ministry of Labour, Employment and Health: 127 rue de Grenelle, 75007 Paris; tel. 1-44-38-38-38; fax 1-44-38-20-20; internet www.travail-solidarite.gouv.fr.

Ministry of National Education, Youth and Community Life: 110 rue de Grenelle, 75357 Paris Cedex 07; tel. 1-55-55-10-10; fax 1-45-51-53-63; e-mail info-desco@education.gouv.fr; internet www.education.gouv.fr.

Ministry of Public Service: 101 rue de Grenelle, 75007 Paris Cedex 07; tel. 1-77-72-61-00; internet www.fonction-publique.gouv.fr.

Ministry of Solidarity and Social Cohesion: 127 rue de Grenelle, 75007 Paris; tel. 1-44-38-38-38; fax 1-44-38-20-20; internet www.travail-solidarite.gouv.fr.

Ministry of Sport: 14 ave Duquesne, 75700 Paris; tel. 1-40-56-60-00; internet www.sante-sports.gouv.fr.

Ministry of Urban Planning: 14 rue Saint Dominique, 75007 Paris; tel. 1-42-75-80-00; internet www.ville.gouv.fr.

President and Legislature

PRESIDENT

Presidential Election, First Ballot, 22 April 2012

Candidates	Votes	% of votes
François Hollande (Parti Socialiste)	10,273,480	28.63
Nicolas Sarkozy (Union pour un Mouvement Populaire)	9,754,316	27.18
Marine Le Pen (Front National)	6,421,802	17.90
Jean-Luc Mélenchon (Front de Gauche)*	3,985,089	11.10
François Bayrou (Mouvement Démocrate)	3,275,395	9.13
Eva Joly (Europe Ecologie Les Verts)	828,381	2.31
Nicolas Dupont-Aignan (Debout la République)	644,043	1.79
Philippe Poutou (Nouveau Parti Anticapitaliste)	411,182	1.15
Nathalie Arthaud (Lutte Ouvrière)	202,561	0.56
Jacques Cheminade (Solidarité et Progrès)	89,552	0.25
Total	35,885,801	100.00

* A coalition of left-wing parties, including the Parti de Gauche and the Parti Communiste.

Presidential Election, Second Ballot, 6 May 2012

Candidate	Votes	% of votes
François Hollande (Parti Socialiste)	18,000,668	51.64
Nicolas Sarkozy (Union pour un Mouvement Populaire)	16,860,685	48.36
Total	34,861,353	100.00

PARLEMENT
(Parliament)

Assemblée nationale
(National Assembly)

126 rue de l'Université, 75355 Paris Cedex 07; tel. 1-40-63-60-00; fax 1-45-55-75-23; e-mail infos@assemblee-nationale.fr; internet www.assemblee-nationale.fr.

President: BERNARD ACCOYER (UMP).

General Election, 10 June and 17 June 2007

Party	% of votes cast in first ballot	% of votes cast in second ballot*	Seats
Union pour un Mouvement Populaire (UMP)	33.30	47.26	313
Parti Socialiste (PS)	24.11	35.26	186
Le Nouveau Centre	4.85	3.92	22†
Parti Communiste Français (PCF)	4.82	3.26	15
Parti Radical de Gauche (PRG)	1.54	2.15	7
Les Verts	4.51	3.19	4
Mouvement Démocrate (MoDem)	0.41	—	3†
Rassemblement pour la France (RPF)	0.37	0.29	3
Mouvement pour la France (MPF)	0.80	—	1
Front National (FN)	11.34	1.85	—
Pôle Républicain (PR)	1.19	0.06	—
Chasse Pêche Nature Traditions (CPNT)	1.67	—	—
Ligue Communiste Révolutionnaire (LCR)	1.27	—	—
Lutte Ouvrière (LO)	1.20	—	—
Mouvement National Républicain (MNR)	1.09	—	—
Various right-wing candidates‡	3.65	1.29	9
Various left-wing candidates	1.09	1.27	15
Regionalist candidates	0.26	0.14	1
Various ecologist candidates§	1.17	—	—
Various far-left candidates‖	0.32	—	—
Various far-right candidates¶	0.24	—	—
Others[1]	0.77	0.06	1
Total	100.00	100.00	577

* Held where no candidate had won the requisite overall majority in the first ballot, between candidates who had received at least 12.5% of the votes in that round. The total number of valid votes cast was 25,246,045 in the first round, and 21,221,026 in the second round.

† In May 2007 the Union pour la Démocratie Française (UDF) was restyled as the Mouvement Démocrate (MoDem) by the party leader, François Bayrou, to oppose the UMP party of the President, Nicolas Sarkozy. The UDF was formally reconstituted as the MoDem in November. The Nouveau Centre was formed in May 2007 by elements of the UDF allied to the President.

‡ Including, notably, candidates of the Droite Libérale Chrétienne and the Centre National des Indépendants et Paysans.

§ Including, notably, candidates of Génération Ecologie-Les Bleus and the Mouvement Ecologiste Indépendant.

‖ Including, notably, candidates of the Parti des Travailleurs, Les Motivé-e-s and Les Alternatifs.

¶ Including, notably, candidates of the Parti National Républicain, La France aux Français and the Parti Nationaliste Français.

[1] Including, notably, candidates of the Rassemblement des Contribuables Français, the Parti de la Loi Naturelle and the Union pour la Semaine de Quatre Jours.

Sénat
(Senate)

15 rue de Vaugirard, 75291 Paris Cedex 06; tel. 1-42-34-20-00; fax 1-42-34-26-77; e-mail communication@senat.fr; internet www.senat.fr.

President: JEAN-PIERRE BEL (PS).

Senators are elected for a term of six years, with one-half of the seats renewable every three years; seats are allocated through a combination of majority voting and proportional representation. The minimum age for eligible candidates to the Sénat is 30 years.

A partial election to the Sénat took place on 25 September 2011, when the number of senators was increased to 348. The strength of the parties at 11 October 2011 was as follows:

Grouping	Seats
Groupe Socialiste, Apparentés et Groupe Europe Écologie Les Verts Rattaché	140
Groupe Union pour un Mouvement Populaire	132
Groupe de l'Union Centriste et Républicaine	31
Groupe Communiste Républicain et Citoyen	21
Groupe du Rassemblement Démocratique et Social Européen	16
Non-attached	8
Total	348

Territorial Collectivity of Corsica

In 1992 Corsica officially assumed the status of a Territorial Collectivity (Collectivité territoriale), in accordance with legislation approved by Parliament in the previous year, gaining a degree of political and administrative autonomy. The island of Corsica is generally considered as one of the 22 *régions* of metropolitan France.

The 51-member Corsican Assembly (Assemblée de Corse) was constituted following elections held in March 1992. Members of the Assembly are elected by universal suffrage for a term of six years, according to a system of proportional representation. Three additional seats are allocated to the list receiving the largest number of votes. The nine-member Executive Council (Conseil Exécutif) is elected by the Assembly from among the members of the largest parliamentary group.

President of the Executive Council (Conseil Exécutif): PAUL GIACOBBI (PRG—L'Alternance).

Members: PAUL MARIE BARTOLI, EMMANUELLE DE GENTILI, PIERRE GHIONGA, MARIA GUIDICELLI, JEAN-LOUIS LUCIANI, MARIE-THÉRÈSE OLIVESI, VANINA PIERI, JEAN ZUCCARELLI.

President of the Corsican Assembly: DOMINIQUE BUCCHINI (PCF—L'Alternance).

Corsican Assembly (Assemblée de Corse): 22 cours Grandval, 20187 Ajaccio Cedex 1; tel. 4-95-51-64-64; fax 4-95-51-67-75; e-mail contact@corse.fr; internet www.corse.fr; f. 1982.

Election, 14 and 21 March 2010

	Seats
L'Alternance*	24
Rassembler pour la Corse†	12
Femu a Corsica‡	11
Corsica Libera	4
Total	51

* Electoral list comprising the Parti Radical de Gauche (PRG), the Parti Communiste Français (PCF), the Parti de Gauche (PG), the Parti Socialiste (PS) and allies.

† Electoral list comprising the Union pour un Mouvement Populaire (UMP) and allies.

‡ Moderate nationalist electoral list.

Political Organizations

Les Alternatifs: 40 rue de Malte, 75011 Paris; tel. 1-43-57-44-80; fax 1-43-57-64-50; e-mail contact@alternatifs.org; internet www.alternatifs.org; f. 1997; socialist, ecologist, feminist; Spokesperson JEAN-JACQUES BOISLAROUSSIE.

Chasse Pêche Nature Traditions (CPNT): BP 87546, 64075 Pau Cedex; tel. 5-59-14-71-71; fax 5-59-14-71-72; e-mail cpnt@cpnt.asso.fr; internet www.cpnt.asso.fr; f. 1989 as Chasse-Pêche-Traditions; emphasizes defence of rural traditions and the sovereignty of the state within Europe; Pres. FRÉDÉRIC NIHOUS; Sec.-Gen. EDDIE PUYJALON.

Corsica Libera: 1 rue Miot, BP 304, 20297 Bastia Cedex; tel. 4-95-31-66-96; fax 4-95-31-78-91; e-mail corsicalibera@corsicalibera.com; internet www.corsicalibera.com; f. 2009 by merger of 4 Corsican separatist parties, incl. Corsica Nazione (f. 1992); Pres. ERIC SIMONI; Leader JEAN-GUY TALAMONI.

Debout la République (DLR): 17 rue des Rossignols, BP 18, 91330 Yerres; tel. 1-69-49-17-37; e-mail courrier@debout-la-republique.fr; internet www.debout-la-republique.fr; f. 2008; Gaullist, republican; Pres. NICOLAS DUPONT-AIGNAN; Sec.-Gen. JEAN-PIERRE ANTONI.

Europe Ecologie Les Verts: 247 rue du Faubourg Saint-Martin, 75010 Paris; tel. 1-53-19-53-19; fax 1-53-19-03-93; e-mail verts@lesverts.fr; internet www.lesverts.fr; f. 1984; ecologist; fmrly called Les Verts; name changed to above following merger with Europe Ecologie in Nov. 2010; Nat. Sec. CÉCILE DUFLOT.

Front National (FN): 76–78 rue des Suisses, 92000 Nanterre; tel. 1-41-20-20-00; fax 1-41-12-10-86; e-mail contact@frontnational.com; internet www.frontnational.com; f. 1972; extreme right-wing nationalist; Pres. MARINE LE PEN; Sec.-Gen. STEEVE BRIOIS.

Génération Ecologie: 35 ave du Pont Juvenal, 34000 Montepellier; tel. and fax 9-52-47-48-40; e-mail webge@hotmail.fr; internet www.generation-ecologie.fr; f. 1991; ecologist; Pres. YVES PIETRASANTA; Sec.-Gen. MONIQUE BACCELLI.

Lutte Ouvrière (LO): BP 233, 75865 Paris Cedex 18; tel. 1-48-10-86-20; fax 1-48-10-86-26; e-mail contact@lutte-ouvriere.org; internet www.lutte-ouvriere.org; f. 1968; Trotskyist; Spokesperson NATHALIE ARTHAUD.

Mouvement Démocrate (MoDem): 133 bis rue de l'Université, 75007 Paris; tel. 1-53-59-20-00; fax 1-53-59-20-59; internet www.mouvementdemocrate.fr; f. 1978 as the Union pour la Démocratie Française (UDF) to unite for electoral purposes non-Gaullist 'majority' candidates; reconstituted as a unified party in 1998; reconstituted in November 2007 to oppose the UMP; elements of the UDF allied to the President, Nicolas Sarkozy, left the party and formed the Nouveau Centre in May 2007; Pres. FRANÇOIS BAYROU.

Mouvement Ecologiste Indépendant (MEI): 26 ter rue Nicolaï, 75012 Paris; tel. 3-84-47-48-80; e-mail jacques.lancon@orange.fr; f. 1994; ecologist; 1,000 mems; Pres. ANTOINE WAECHTER; Nat. Sec. JACQUES LANÇON.

Mouvement National Républicain (MNR): BP 10008, 93161 Noisy-le-Grand Cedex; tel. 9-51-45-84-93; fax 9-51-45-84-93; e-mail presse@m-n-r.fr; internet www.m-n-r.fr; f. 1999 by breakaway faction of FN; extreme right-wing nationalist; Pres. BRUNO MÉGRET; Sec.-Gen. HUBERT SAVON.

Mouvement pour la France (MPF): 16 bis ave de la Motte Picquet, 75007 Paris; tel. 1-53-63-53-00; fax 1-73-00-10-51; e-mail communication@pourlafrance.fr; internet www.pourlafrance.fr; f. 1994; far-right, nationalist; Pres. PHILIPPE DE VILLIERS; Sec.-Gen. PATRICK LOUIS.

Mouvement Républicain et Citoyen (MRC): 3 ave de Corbéra, 75012 Paris; tel. 1-55-78-05-40; fax 1-44-83-83-10; e-mail contact@mrc-france.org; internet www.mrc-france.org; f. 2002 as Pôle Républicain on the basis of the Mouvement des Citoyens; present name adopted 2003; socialist; sceptical of increased European integration or devolution of powers from the nation state; Pres. JEAN-LUC LAURENT.

Le Nouveau Centre: 84 rue de Grenelle, 75007 Paris; tel. 1-44-39-28-00; fax 1-44-39-28-09; e-mail contact@le-nouveaucentre.org; internet www.le-nouveaucentre.org; f. 2007 by members of the UDF allied to the President, Nicolas Sarkozy, and his UMP party; Pres. HERVÉ MORIN; Sec.-Gen. PHILIPPE VIGIER; Parliamentary Leader FRANÇOIS SAUVADET.

Nouveau Parti Anticapitaliste (NPA): 2 rue Richard Lenoir, 93100 Montreuil; tel. 1-48-70-42-30; fax 1-48-59-39-59; internet www.npa2009.org; f. Feb. 2009 to replace the dissolved Ligue Communiste Révolutionnaire (LCR); socialist, democratic, ecologist; seeks to break with traditional hierarchical party structures; 9,123 mems; Principal Speakers MYRIAM MARTIN, CHRISTINE POUPIN.

Parti Communiste Français (PCF): 2 place du Colonel Fabien, 75019 Paris; tel. 1-40-40-12-12; fax 1-40-40-13-56; e-mail pcf@pcf.fr; internet www.pcf.fr; advocates independent foreign policy; formed the Front de Gauche with the Parti de Gauche in 2008; Nat. Sec PIERRE LAURENT.

Parti de Gauche (PG): BP 30007, 91301 Massy Cedex; e-mail contact@lepartidegauche.fr; internet www.lepartidegauche.fr; f. 2008 by former members of PS and MARS-Gauche Républicaine; left-wing, republican; formed the Front de Gauche with the Parti Communiste Français in 2008; Leader JEAN-LUC MÉLENCHON.

Parti Radical: 1 place de Valois, 75001 Paris; tel. 1-42-61-02-02; fax 1-42-61-02-04; e-mail contact@partiradical.net; internet www.partiradical.net; f. 1901; democratic socialist; fmrly affiliated to UMP; Pres. JEAN-LOUIS BORLOO; Sec.-Gen. LAURENT HÉNART.

Parti Radical de Gauche (PRG): 13 rue Duroc, 75007 Paris; tel. 1-45-66-67-68; fax 1-45-66-47-93; e-mail pascalcedan@prg.com.fr; internet www.planeteradicale.org; f. 1972 as the Mouvement des Radicaux de Gauche; left-wing; Pres. JEAN-MICHEL BAYLET.

Parti Socialiste (PS): 10 rue de Solférino, 75333 Paris Cedex 07; tel. 1-45-56-77-00; fax 1-47-05-15-78; e-mail infops@parti-socialiste.fr; internet www.parti-socialiste.fr; f. 1971; First Sec. HARLEM DÉSIR.

Rassemblement pour l'Indépendance et la Souveraineté de la France (RIF): BP 10014, 75362 Paris Cedex 08; tel. and fax 1-46-44-94-16; e-mail secretariat.rif@tele2.fr; internet www.r-i-f.org; f. 2003; nationalist, opposed to the transfer of powers from nation states to the European Union; Pres. PAUL MARIE COÛTEAUX; Sec.-Gen. ALAIN BOURNAZEL.

République Solidaire: 14 pl. Henri Bergson, 75008 Paris; tel. 1-71-26-72-91; internet www.republiquesolidaire.fr; f. 2010; republican; Pres. JEAN-PIERRE GRAND; Sec.-Gen. MARC BERNIER.

Solidarité et Progrès (S&P): BP 27, 92114 Clichy Cedex; tel. 1-76-69-14-50; fax 1-47-39-05-80; internet www.solidariteetprogres.org; f. 1996; associated with LaRouche movement; Pres. JACQUES CHEMINADE.

Union pour un Mouvement Populaire (UMP): 55 rue La Boétie, 75384 Paris Cedex 08; tel. 1-40-76-60-00; e-mail webmaster@u-m-p.org; internet www.u-m-p.org; f. 2002; founded as Union pour la Majorité Présidentielle by members of the former Rassemblement pour la République and Démocratie Liberale parties, in conjunction with elements of the UDF, now MoDem (q.v.); centre-right grouping formed to ensure that President Jacques Chirac had a majority grouping in the Assemblée nationale; 317,771 mems. (Jan. 2007); Sec.-Gen. JEAN-FRANÇOIS COPÉ; First Vice-Pres. JEAN-PIERRE RAFFARIN.

Associated organizations include:

Centre National des Indépendants et Paysans (CNI): 6 rue Quentin Bauchart, 75008 Paris; tel. 1-47-23-47-00; fax 1-47-23-47-03; e-mail contact@cni.asso.fr; internet www.cni.asso.fr; f. 1949; right-wing; Pres. GILLES BOURDOULEIX; Sec.-Gen. BRUNO NORTH.

La Gauche Moderne: 89 blvd Magenta, 75010 Paris; e-mail webmaster@lagauchemoderne.org; internet www.lagauchemoderne.org; moderate, left-wing; f. 2007 to support President Nicolas Sarkozy and his UMP party; Pres. JEAN-MARIE BOCKEL.

Diplomatic Representation

EMBASSIES IN FRANCE

Afghanistan: 32 ave Raphaël, 75016 Paris; tel. 1-45-25-05-29; fax 1-42-24-47-14; e-mail contact@ambafghanistan-fr.com; internet www.ambafghane-paris.com; Ambassador Dr OMAR SAMAD.

Albania: 57 ave Marceau, 75116 Paris; tel. 1-47-23-31-00; fax 1-47-23-59-85; e-mail contact@amb-albanie.fr; internet www.amb-albanie.fr; Ambassador YLLJET ALIÇKA.

Algeria: 50 rue de Lisbonne, 75008 Paris; tel. 1-53-93-20-20; fax 1-53-93-20-69; e-mail chancellerie@amb-algerie.fr; internet www.amb-algerie.fr; Ambassador MISSOUM SBIH.

Andorra: 51 bis rue de Boulainvilliers, 75016 Paris; tel. 1-40-06-03-30; fax 1-40-06-03-64; e-mail ambaixada@andorra.ad; internet www.amb-andorre.fr; Ambassador MARIA UBACH FONT.

Angola: 19 ave Foch, 75116 Paris; tel. 1-45-01-58-20; fax 1-45-00-33-71; e-mail sg@emb-ang.fr; internet www.emb-ang.fr; Ambassador MIGUEL DA COSTA.

Antigua and Barbuda: 43 ave de Friedland, 75008 Paris; tel. 1-53-96-93-96; fax 1-53-75-15-69; e-mail carl.roberts@antigua-barbuda.com; Ambassador Dr CARL ROBERTS (resident in London, United Kingdom).

Argentina: 6 rue Cimarosa, 75116 Paris; tel. 1-44-05-27-00; fax 1-44-05-27-18; e-mail efranpriv@noos.fr; internet www.ambassadeargentine.net; Ambassador ALDO FERRER.

Armenia: 9 rue Viète, 75017 Paris; tel. 1-42-12-98-00; fax 1-42-12-98-03; e-mail ambarmen@wanadoo.fr; Ambassador VIGUEN TCHITETCHIAN.

Australia: 4 rue Jean Rey, 75724 Paris Cedex 15; tel. 1-40-59-33-00; fax 1-40-59-33-10; e-mail info.paris@dfat.gov.au; internet www.france.embassy.gov.au; Ambassador RIC WELLS.

Austria: 6 rue Fabert, 75007 Paris; tel. 1-40-63-30-63; fax 1-45-55-63-65; e-mail paris-ob@bmeia.gv.at; internet www.amb-autriche.fr; Ambassador Dr URSULA PLASSNIK.

Azerbaijan: 78 ave d'Iéna, 75016 Paris; tel. 1-44-18-60-20; fax 1-44-18-60-25; e-mail ambazer@wanadoo.fr; Ambassador ELCHIN AMIRBAYOV.

Bahrain: 3 bis place des Etats-Unis, 75116 Paris; tel. 1-47-23-48-68; fax 1-47-20-55-75; e-mail ambassade@ambahrein-france.com; internet www.ambahrein-france.com; Ambassador Dr NASSER AL-BELOOSHI.

Bangladesh: 39 rue Erlanger, 75016 Paris; tel. 1-46-51-90-33; fax 1-46-51-90-35; e-mail bangembpar@yahoo.com; Ambassador MOHAMMED ENAMUL KABIR.

Belarus: 38 blvd Suchet, 75016 Paris; tel. 1-44-14-69-79; fax 1-44-14-69-70; e-mail france@mfa.gov.by; internet france.mfa.gov.by; Ambassador ALEKSANDR A. PAVLOVSKY.

Belgium: 9 rue de Tilsitt, 75840 Paris Cedex 17; tel. 1-44-09-39-39; fax 1-47-54-07-64; e-mail paris@diplobel.fed.be; internet www.diplomatie.be/paris; Ambassador PATRICK VERCAUTEREN DRUBBEL.

Benin: 87 ave Victor Hugo, 75116 Paris; tel. 1-45-00-98-82; fax 1-45-01-82-02; e-mail contact@ambassade-benin.fr; internet www.ambassade-benin.fr; Ambassador ALBERT AGOSSOU.

Bolivia: 12 ave Président Kennedy, 75016 Paris; tel. 1-42-24-93-44; fax 1-45-25-86-23; e-mail embolivia.paris@wanadoo.fr; Ambassador LUZMILA CARPIO SANGÜEZA.

Bosnia and Herzegovina: 174 rue de Courcelles, 75017 Paris; tel. 1-42-67-34-22; fax 1-40-53-85-22; e-mail amb.pariz@mvp.gov.ba; Ambassador NINA SAJIĆ.

Brazil: 34 cours Albert 1er, 75008 Paris; tel. 1-45-61-63-00; fax 1-42-89-03-45; e-mail ambassade@bresil.org; internet www.bresil.org; Ambassador JOSÉ MAURICIO BUSTANI.

Brunei: 7 rue de Presbourg, 75116 Paris; tel. 1-53-64-67-60; fax 1-53-64-67-83; e-mail ambassade.brunei@wanadoo.fr; Ambassador Dato' Paduka ZAINIDI Haji SIDUP.

Bulgaria: 1 ave Rapp, 75007 Paris; tel. 1-45-51-85-90; fax 1-45-51-18-68; e-mail bulgamb@wanadoo.fr; internet www.amb-bulgarie.fr; Ambassador MARIN RAYKOV.

Burkina Faso: 159 blvd Haussmann, 75008 Paris; tel. 1-43-59-90-63; fax 1-42-56-50-07; e-mail contact@ambaburkina-fr.org; internet ambaburkina-fr.org; Ambassador JOSEPH PARÉ.

Burundi: 10–12 rue de l'Orme, 75019 Paris; tel. 1-45-20-60-61; fax 1-45-20-02-54; e-mail ambabu.paris@wanadoo.fr; Ambassador GASPARD MUSAVYARABONA.

Cambodia: 4 rue Adolphe Yvon, 75116 Paris; tel. 1-45-03-47-20; fax 1-45-03-47-40; e-mail arc@ambcambodgeparis.info; internet www.ambcambodgeparis.info; Ambassador UCH KIMAN.

Cameroon: 73 rue d'Auteuil, 75016 Paris; tel. 1-47-43-98-33; fax 1-46-51-24-52; Ambassador LEJEUNE MBELLA MBELLA.

Canada: 35 ave Montaigne, 75008 Paris; tel. 1-44-43-29-00; fax 1-44-43-29-99; e-mail paris_webmaster@international.gc.ca; internet www.canadainternational.gc.ca/france; Ambassador MARC LORTIE.

Cape Verde: 3 rue de Rigny, 75008 Paris; tel. 1-42-12-73-50; fax 1-40-53-04-36; e-mail ambassade-cap-vert2@wanadoo.fr; internet www.ambassadecapvert.fr; Ambassador JOSÉ ARMADO DUARTE.

Central African Republic: 30 rue des Perchamps, 75116 Paris; tel. 1-45-25-39-74; fax 1-45-27-48-11; e-mail accueil@amb-rcaparis.org; internet www.amb-rcaparis.org; Ambassador JEAN WILLYBIRO SAKO.

Chad: 65 rue des Belles Feuilles, 75116 Paris; tel. 1-45-53-36-75; fax 1-45-53-16-09; e-mail ambassadedutchadparis@wanadoo.fr; Ambassador HISSÈNE BRAHIM TAHA.

Chile: 2 ave de la Motte-Picquet, 75007 Paris; tel. 1-44-18-59-60; fax 1-44-18-59-61; e-mail echile@amb-chili.fr; internet chileabroad.gov.cl/francia; Ambassador JORGE EDWARDS VALDÉS.

China, People's Republic: 11 ave George V, 75008 Paris; tel. 1-49-52-19-50; fax 1-47-20-24-22; e-mail chinaemb_fr@mfa.gov.cn; internet www.amb-chine.fr; Ambassador KONG QUAN.

Colombia: 22 rue de l'Elysée, 75008 Paris; tel. 1-42-65-46-08; fax 1-42-66-18-60; e-mail eparis@cancilleria.gov.co; internet www.embcolfrancia.com; Ambassador GUSTAVO ADOLFO CARVAJAL SINISTERRA.

Comoros: 20 rue Marbeau, 75116 Paris; tel. 1-40-67-90-54; fax 1-40-67-72-96; Ambassador ABDALLAH MIRGHANE.

Congo, Democratic Republic: 32 cours Albert 1er, 75008 Paris; tel. 1-42-25-57-50; fax 1-45-62-16-52; e-mail contact@ambardcparis.com; internet www.ambardcparis.com; Ambassador CHRISTIAN ILEKA ATOKI.

Congo, Republic: 37 bis rue Paul Valéry, 75116 Paris; tel. 1-45-00-60-57; fax 1-40-67-17-33; e-mail ambacongo_france@yahoo.fr; Ambassador HENRI LOPES.

Costa Rica: 4, Square Rapp, 4ème étage, 75007 Paris; tel. 1-45-78-96-96; fax 1-45-78-99-66; e-mail embcr@wanadoo.fr; internet www.ambassade-costarica.org; Ambassador CARLOS BONILLA SANDOVAL.

Côte d'Ivoire: 102 ave Raymond Poincaré, 75116 Paris; tel. 1-53-64-62-62; fax 1-45-00-47-97; e-mail rciparis@ambassadecotedivoire.fr; internet www.ambassadecotedivoire.fr; Ambassador ALLY COULIBALY.

Croatia: 7 sq. Thiers, 75116 Paris; tel. 1-53-70-02-80; fax 1-53-70-02-90; e-mail vrh.pariz@mvep.hr; internet www.amb-croatie.fr; Ambassador MIRKO GALIČ.

Cuba: 16 rue de Presles, 75015 Paris; tel. 1-45-67-55-35; fax 1-45-66-80-92; e-mail embacu@ambacuba.fr; internet embacuba.cubaminrex.cu; Ambassador ORLANDO REQUEIJO GUAL.

Cyprus: 23 rue Galilée, 75116 Paris; tel. 1-47-20-86-28; fax 1-40-70-13-44; e-mail paris@mfa.gov.cy; Ambassador MARIOS LYSSIOTIS.

Czech Republic: 15 ave Charles Floquet, 75007 Paris; tel. 1-40-65-13-00; fax 1-40-65-13-13; e-mail paris@embassy.mzv.cz; internet www.mzv.cz/paris; Ambassador MARIE CHATARDOVA.

Denmark: 77 ave Marceau, 75116 Paris; tel. 1-44-31-21-21; fax 1-44-31-21-88; e-mail paramb@um.dk; internet www.ambparis.um.dk; Ambassador ANNA DORTE RIGGELSEN.

Djibouti: 26 rue Emile Ménier, 75116 Paris; tel. 1-47-27-49-22; fax 1-45-53-50-53; e-mail ambassadeur@ambdjibouti.org; Ambassador RACHAD FARAH.

Dominican Republic: 45 rue de Courcelles, 75008 Paris; tel. 1-53-63-95-95; fax 1-45-63-35-63; e-mail embajadom@wanadoo.fr; internet www.amba-dominicaine-paris.com; Ambassador LAURA FAXAS.

Ecuador: 34 ave de Messine, 75008 Paris; tel. 1-45-61-10-21; fax 1-42-56-06-64; e-mail embajadaenfrancia@ambassade-equateur.fr; internet www.ambassade-equateur.fr; Ambassador CARLOS JÁTIVA NARANJO.

Egypt: 56 ave d'Iéna, 75116 Paris; tel. 1-53-67-88-30; fax 1-47-23-06-43; e-mail ambassadedegypteaparis@hotmail.com; internet www.ambassade-egypte.com; Ambassador NASSER KAMEL.

El Salvador: 12 rue Galilée, 75116 Paris; tel. 1-47-20-42-02; fax 1-40-70-01-95; e-mail embparis@wanadoo.fr; Ambassador FRANCISCO GALINDO-VELEZ.

Equatorial Guinea: 29 blvd de Courcelles, 75008 Paris; tel. 1-45-61-98-20; fax 1-45-61-98-25; e-mail embarege_paris@hotmail.com; Ambassador EDUARDO NDONG ELO NZANG.

Eritrea: 1 rue de Staël, 75015 Paris; tel. 1-43-06-15-56; fax 1-43-06-07-51; Ambassador FASSIL GEBRESELASSIE TEKLE.

Estonia: 17 rue de la Baume, 75008 Paris; tel. 1-56-62-22-00; fax 1-49-52-05-65; e-mail estonie@mfa.ee; internet www.est-emb.fr; Ambassador SVEN JÜRGENSON.

Ethiopia: 35 ave Charles Floquet, 75007 Paris; tel. 1-47-83-83-95; fax 1-43-06-52-14; e-mail embeth@free.fr; Ambassador TESHOME TOGA.

Finland: 1 place de Finlande, 75007 Paris; tel. 1-44-18-19-20; fax 1-45-55-51-57; e-mail sanomat.par@formin.fi; internet www.amb-finlande.fr; Ambassador PILVI-SISKO VIERROS-VILLENEUVE.

Gabon: 41 rue de la Bienfaisance, 75008 Paris; tel. 1-72-70-01-50; fax 1-72-81-05-89; e-mail cab.ambassadegabonfrance@yahoo.fr; internet www.affaires-etrangeres.gouv.ga/ambassade/france; Ambassador GERMAIN NGOYO MOUSSAVOU.

The Gambia: 117 rue St Lazare, 75008 Paris; tel. 1-72-74-82-61; fax 1-53-04-05-99; e-mail ambgambia_france117@hotmail.com; Ambassador MOSES BENJAMIN JALLOW.

Georgia: 104 ave Raymond Poincaré, 75116 Paris; tel. 1-45-02-16-16; fax 1-45-02-16-01; e-mail ambassade.georgie@mfa.gov.ge; internet www.france.mfa.gov.ge; Ambassador MAMUKA KUDAVA.

Germany: 13–15 ave Franklin D. Roosevelt, 75008 Paris; tel. 1-53-83-45-00; fax 1-43-59-74-18; e-mail ambassade@amb-allemagne.fr; internet www.paris.diplo.de; Ambassador REINHARD SCHÄFERS.

Ghana: 8 Villa Saïd, 75116 Paris; tel. 1-45-00-09-50; fax 1-45-00-81-95; e-mail ambghanaparis@yahoo.fr; Ambassador GENEVIÈVE DELALI TSEGAH.

Greece: 17 rue Auguste Vacquerie, 75116 Paris; tel. 1-47-23-72-28; fax 1-47-23-73-85; e-mail mfapar@wanadoo.fr; internet www.amb-grece.fr; Ambassador CONSTANTIN CHALASTANIS.

Guatemala: 2 rue Villebois-Marueil, 75017 Paris; tel. 1-42-27-78-63; fax 1-47-54-02-06; internet www.ambassadeduguatemala.com; Ambassador ANAISABEL PRERA FLORES.

Guinea: 51 rue de la Faisanderie, 75116 Paris; tel. 1-47-04-81-48; fax 1-47-04-57-65; e-mail accueil@ambaguinee-paris.org; Ambassador AMARA CAMARA.

Guinea-Bissau: 94 rue Saint Lazare, 75009 Paris; tel. 1-48-74-36-39; fax 1-48-78-36-39; e-mail ambaguineebxo@wanadoo.fr; Ambassador JOÃO SOARES DA GAMA.

Haiti: 10 rue Théodule Ribot, BP 275, 75017 Paris; tel. 1-47-63-47-78; fax 1-42-27-02-05; e-mail ambhaitiparis@orange.fr; Chargé d'affaires a.i. FRITZNER GASPARD.

Holy See: 10 ave du Président Wilson, 75116 Paris (Apostolic Nunciature); tel. 1-53-23-01-50; fax 1-47-23-65-44; e-mail noncapfr@wanadoo.fr; Apostolic Nuncio Most Rev. LUIGI VENTURA.

Honduras: 8 rue Crevaux, 75116 Paris; tel. 1-47-55-86-45; fax 1-47-55-86-48; e-mail ambassade.honduras@yahoo.com; Ambassador CARMEN ORTEZ ELEONORA WILLIAMS.

Hungary: 5 bis sq. de l'ave Foch, 75116 Paris; tel. 1-45-00-94-97; fax 1-56-36-02-68; e-mail mission.par@kum.hu; internet www.mfa.gov.hu/emb/paris; Ambassador LASZLO TROCSANYI.

Iceland: 52 ave Victor Hugo, 75116 Paris; tel. 1-44-17-32-85; fax 1-40-67-99-96; e-mail icemb.paris@utn.stjr.is; internet www.iceland.org/fr; Ambassador BERGLIND ÁSGEIRSDÓTTIR.

India: 15 rue Alfred Dehodencq, 75016 Paris; tel. 1-40-50-70-70; fax 1-40-50-09-96; e-mail pic.2@wanadoo.fr; internet www.amb-inde.fr; Ambassador RAKESH SOOD.

Indonesia: 47–49 rue Cortambert, 75016 Paris; tel. 1-45-03-07-60; fax 1-45-04-50-32; e-mail komparis@online.fr; internet www.amb-indonesie.fr; Ambassador REZLAN ISHAR JENIE.

Iran: 4 ave d'Iéna, 75116 Paris; tel. 1-40-69-79-03; fax 1-40-70-01-57; e-mail contact@amb-iran.fr; internet www.amb-iran.fr; Ambassador ALI AHANI.

Iraq: 64 ave Foch, 75016 Paris; tel. 1-45-53-33-70; fax 1-45-53-33-80; e-mail paremb@iraqmfamail.com; internet www.amb-iraq.fr; Ambassador FARID MUSTAFA KAMIL YASSEIN.

Ireland: 12 ave Foch, 75116 Paris; tel. 1-44-17-67-00; fax 1-44-17-67-50; e-mail paris@dfa.ie; internet www.embassyofireland.fr; Ambassador PAUL KAVANAGH.

Israel: 3 rue Rabelais, 75008 Paris; tel. 1-40-76-55-00; fax 1-40-76-55-55; e-mail information@paris.mfa.gov.il; internet paris1.mfa.gov.il; Ambassador YOSSI GAL.

Italy: 51 rue de Varenne, 75343 Paris Cedex 07; tel. 1-49-54-03-00; fax 1-45-54-04-10; e-mail ambasciata.parigi@esteri.it; internet www.ambparigi.esteri.it; Ambassador GIOVANNI CARACCIOLO DI VIETRI.

Japan: 7 ave Hoche, 75008 Paris; tel. 1-48-88-62-00; fax 1-42-27-50-81; e-mail info-fr@ps.mofa.go.jp; internet www.fr.emb-japan.go.jp; Ambassador ICHIRO KOMATSU.

Jordan: 80 blvd Maurice Barrès, 92200 Neuilly-sur-Seine; tel. 1-55-62-00-00; fax 1-55-62-00-06; e-mail amjo.paris@wanadoo.fr; Ambassador DINA KAWAR.

Kazakhstan: 59 rue Pierre Charron, 75008 Paris; tel. 1-45-61-52-00; fax 1-45-61-52-01; e-mail info@amb-kazakhstan.fr; internet www.amb-kazakhstan.fr; Ambassador NURLAN DANENOV.

Kenya: 3 rue Freycinet, 75116 Paris; tel. 1-56-62-25-25; fax 1-47-20-44-41; e-mail info@ambassade-kenya.fr; internet www.kenyaembassyparis.org; Ambassador SALMA AHMED.

Korea, Republic: 125 rue de Grenelle, 75007 Paris; tel. 1-47-53-01-01; fax 1-47-53-00-41; e-mail koremb-fr@mofat.go.kr; internet fra.mofat.go.kr; Ambassador HEUNG-SHIN PARK.

Kuwait: 2 rue de Lübeck, 75116 Paris; tel. 1-47-23-54-25; fax 1-47-20-33-59; Ambassador ALI SULAIMAN AL-SAEID.

Laos: 74 ave Raymond Poincaré, 75116 Paris; tel. 1-45-53-02-98; fax 1-47-57-27-89; e-mail ambalaoparis@wanadoo.fr; internet www.laoparis.com; Ambassador KHOUANTA PHALIVONG.

Latvia: 6 villa Saïd, 75116 Paris; tel. 1-53-64-58-10; fax 1-53-64-58-19; e-mail embassy.france@mfa.gov.lv; internet www.am.gov.lv/paris; Ambassador SANITA PAVLUTA-DESLANDES.

Lebanon: 3 villa Copernic, 75116 Paris; tel. 1-40-67-75-75; fax 1-40-67-16-42; e-mail na@ambliban.fr; internet www.ambassadeliban.fr; Ambassador BOUTROS ASSAKER.

Liberia: 12 place du Général Catroux, 75017 Paris; tel. 1-47-63-58-55; fax 1-42-12-76-14; e-mail libem.paris@wanadoo.fr; Ambassador DUDLEY MCKINLEY THOMAS.

Libya: 2 rue Charles Lamoureux, 75116 Paris; tel. 1-47-04-71-60; fax 1-47-55-96-25; Sec. of the People's Bureau AL-SHIABANI MANSOUR ABUHAMOUD.

Lithuania: 22 blvd de Courcelles, 75017 Paris; tel. 1-40-54-50-50; fax 1-40-54-50-75; e-mail chancellerie@amb-lituanie.fr; internet fr.mfa.lt; Ambassador JOLANTA BALČIŪNIENĖ.

Luxembourg: 33 ave Rapp, 75007 Paris; tel. 1-45-55-13-37; fax 1-45-51-72-29; e-mail paris.amb@mae.etat.lu; internet paris.mae.lu; Ambassador GEORGES SANTER.

Macedonia, former Yugoslav republic: 5 rue de la Faisanderie, 75116 Paris; tel. 1-45-77-10-50; fax 1-45-77-14-84; e-mail paris@mfa.gov.mk; Ambassador AGRON BUDJAKU.

Madagascar: 4 ave Raphaël, 75016 Paris; tel. 1-45-04-62-11; fax 1-45-03-58-70; e-mail accueil@ambassade-madagascar.fr; internet www.ambassade-madagascar.fr; Ambassador NARISOA RAJAONARIVONY.

Malaysia: 2 bis rue Bénouville, 75116 Paris; tel. 1-45-53-11-85; fax 1-47-27-34-60; e-mail malparis@kln.gov.my; internet www.kln.gov.my/web/fra_paris; Ambassador Dato' ABD AL-AZIZ BIN Haji ZAINAL.

Mali: 89 rue du Cherche-Midi, 75263 Paris Cedex 06; tel. 1-45-48-58-43; fax 1-45-48-55-34; e-mail ambamali.paris@wanadoo.fr; Ambassador BOUBACAR SIDIKI TOURE.

Malta: 23 rue d'Artois, 75008 Paris; tel. 1-56-59-75-90; fax 1-45-62-00-36; e-mail maltaembassy.paris@gov.mt; Ambassador Dr MARK MIGGIANI.

Mauritania: 5 rue de Montévidéo, 75116 Paris; tel. 1-45-04-88-54; fax 1-40-72-82-96; e-mail ambassade.mauritanie@wanadoo.fr; Ambassador CHEYAKH OULD ELY.

Mauritius: 127 rue de Tocqueville, 75017 Paris; tel. 1-42-27-30-19; fax 1-40-53-02-91; e-mail ambassade.maurice@online.fr; Ambassador MARIE JOSEPH JACQUES CHASTEAU DE BALYON.

Mexico: 9 rue de Longchamp, 75116 Paris; tel. 1-53-70-27-70; fax 1-47-55-65-29; e-mail embfrancia@sre.gob.mx; internet www.sre.gob.mx/francia; Ambassador CARLOS DE ICAZA GONZÁLEZ.

Moldova: 1 rue de Sfax, 75116 Paris; tel. 1-40-67-11-20; fax 1-40-67-11-23; e-mail ambassade.moldavie@wanadoo.fr; Ambassador OLEG SEREBRIAN.

Monaco: 22 blvd Suchet, 75116 Paris; tel. 1-45-04-74-54; fax 1-45-04-45-16; e-mail ambassade.en.france@gouv.mc; Ambassador SOPHIE THÉVENOUX.

Mongolia: 5 ave Robert Schuman, 92100 Boulogne-Billancourt; tel. 1-46-05-28-12; fax 1-46-05-30-16; e-mail info@ambassadedemongolie.fr; internet www.ambassademongolie.fr; Ambassador SHÜKHERIIN ALTANGEREL.

Montenegro: 216 blvd Saint-Germain, 75007 Paris; tel. 1-53-63-80-30; fax 1-42-22-83-90; e-mail ambasadacg@orange.fr; Ambassador IRENA RADOVIC.

Morocco: 5 rue Le Tasse, 75016 Paris; tel. 1-45-20-69-35; fax 1-45-20-22-58; e-mail info@amb-maroc.fr; internet www.amb-maroc.fr; Ambassador MOSTAPHA SAHEL.

Mozambique: 82 rue Laugier, 75017 Paris; tel. 1-47-64-91-32; fax 1-44-15-90-13; e-mail embamoc.franca@minec.gov.mz; Ambassador ALEXANDRE DA CONCEIÇÃO ZANDAMELA.

Myanmar: 60 rue de Courcelles, 75008 Paris; tel. 1-56-88-15-90; fax 1-45-62-13-30; e-mail me-paris@wanadoo.fr; Ambassador U KYAW ZWAR MINN.

Namibia: 80 ave Foch, 75016 Paris; tel. 1-44-17-32-65; fax 1-44-17-32-73; e-mail info@embassyofnamibia.fr; internet www.embassyofnamibia.fr; Ambassador FRIEDA NANGULA ITHETE.

Nepal: 45 bis rue des Acacias, 75017 Paris; tel. 1-46-22-48-67; fax 1-42-27-08-65; e-mail nepalinparis@noos.fr; internet www.nepalembassy.org; Ambassador MOHAN KRISHNA SHRESTHA.

Netherlands: 7–9 rue Eblé, 75007 Paris; tel. 1-40-62-33-00; fax 1-40-62-34-56; e-mail ambassade@amb-pays-bas.fr; internet www.amb-pays-bas.fr; Ambassador HUGO HANS SIBLESZ.

New Zealand: 7 rue Léonard de Vinci, 75116 Paris; tel. 1-45-01-43-43; fax 1-45-01-43-44; e-mail nzembassy.paris@fr.oleane.com; internet www.nzembassy.com/france; Ambassador ROSEMARY BANKS.

Niger: 154 rue de Longchamp, 75116 Paris; tel. 1-45-04-80-60; fax 1-45-04-79-73; e-mail ambassadeniger@wanadoo.fr; Ambassador ABDERAHAMANE MAYAKI ASSANE.

Nigeria: 173 ave Victor Hugo, 75116 Paris; tel. 1-47-04-68-65; fax 1-47-04-47-54; e-mail ambassador@nigeriafrance.com; internet www.nigeriafrance.com; Ambassador GORDON H. BRISTOL.

Norway: 28 rue Bayard, 4e étage, 75008 Paris; tel. 1-53-67-04-00; fax 1-53-67-04-40; e-mail emb.paris@mfa.no; internet www.norvege.no; Ambassador TARALD O. BRAUTASET.

Oman: 50 ave d'Iéna, 75116 Paris; tel. 1-47-23-01-63; fax 1-47-23-77-10; Ambassador AHMED BIN NASSER BIN HAMAD AL-MAHERZI.

Pakistan: 18 rue Lord Byron, 75008 Paris; tel. 1-45-62-23-32; fax 1-45-62-89-15; e-mail pakemb_paris@yahoo.com; Ambassador SHAFKAT SAEED.

Panama: 145 ave de Suffren, 75015 Paris; tel. 1-45-66-42-44; fax 1-45-67-99-43; e-mail panaemba.francia@wanadoo.fr; Ambassador HENRY J. FAARUP.

Paraguay: 1 rue St Dominique, 75007 Paris; tel. 1-42-22-85-05; fax 1-42-22-83-57; e-mail paraguay.ambassade@wanadoo.fr; internet www.mre.gov.py/embaparfrancia; Chargé d'affaires a.i. JULIO CÉSAR DUARTE VAN HUMBECK.

Peru: 50 ave Kléber, 75116 Paris; tel. 1-53-70-42-03; fax 1-47-04-32-55; e-mail perou.ambassade@amb-perou.fr; internet www.amb-perou.fr; Ambassador CRISTINA VELITA DE LABOUREIX.

Philippines: 4 Hameau de Boulainvilliers, 75016 Paris; tel. 1-44-14-57-00; fax 1-46-47-56-00; e-mail ambaphilparis@wanadoo.fr; internet www.philembassyparis.com; Ambassador CRISTINA ORTEGA.

Poland: 1 rue de Talleyrand, 75343 Paris Cedex 07; tel. 1-43-17-34-05; fax 1-43-17-35-07; e-mail info@ambassade.pologne.net; internet www.paris.polemb.net; Ambassador TOMASZ ORŁOWSKI.

Portugal: 3 rue de Noisiel, 75116 Paris; tel. 1-47-27-35-29; fax 1-44-05-94-02; e-mail mailto@embaixada-portugal-fr.org; internet www.embaixada-portugal-fr.org; Ambassador FRANCISCO MANUEL SEIXAS DA COSTA.

Qatar: 1 rue de Tilsitt, 75008 Paris; tel. 1-45-51-90-71; fax 1-45-51-77-07; e-mail paris@mofa.gov.qa; internet www.qatarambassade.com; Ambassador MUHAMMAD JAHAM ABD AL-AZIZ AL-KUWARI.

Romania: 5 rue de l'Exposition, 75007 Paris; tel. 1-47-05-10-46; fax 1-45-56-97-47; e-mail secretariat@amb-roumanie.fr; internet paris.mae.ro; Ambassador BOGDAN MAZURU.

Russia: 40–50 blvd Lannes, 75116 Paris; tel. 1-45-04-05-50; fax 1-45-04-17-65; e-mail ambrus@wanadoo.fr; internet www.france.mid.ru; Ambassador ALEKSANDRE ORLOV.

Rwanda: 12 rue Jadin, 75017 Paris; tel. 1-71-19-91-91; fax 1-71-19-99-95; e-mail ambarwanda.paris@gmail.com; Ambassador JACQUES KABALE NYANGEZI.

San Marino: 22 rue d'Artois, 75008 Paris; tel. and fax 1-47-23-04-75; e-mail saint-marin@wanadoo.fr; Ambassador GIANPIERO SAMORI.

Saudi Arabia: 5 ave Hoche, 75008 Paris; tel. 1-56-79-40-00; fax 1-56-79-40-01; e-mail amb.arabiesaoudite@gmail.com; Ambassador Dr MUHAMMAD BIN ISMAIL AL-ASHEKH.

Senegal: 14 ave Robert Schuman, 75007 Paris; tel. 1-47-05-39-45; fax 1-45-56-04-30; e-mail repsen@wanadoo.fr; internet www.ambasseneparis.com; Ambassador MAÏMOUNA SOURANG NDIR.

Serbia: 5 rue Léonard de Vinci, 75116 Paris; tel. 1-40-72-24-24; fax 1-40-72-24-11; e-mail ambasadapariz@wanadoo.fr; internet www.amb-serbie.fr; Ambassador DUŠAN T. BATAKOVIĆ.

Seychelles: 51 ave Mozart, 75016 Paris; tel. 1-42-30-57-47; fax 1-42-30-57-40; e-mail ambsey@aol.com; Ambassador CLAUDE MOREL.

Singapore: 12 sq. de l'ave Foch, 75116 Paris; tel. 1-45-00-33-61; fax 1-45-00-61-79; e-mail singemb_par@sgmfa.gov.sg; internet www.mfa.gov.sg/paris; Ambassador TAN YORK CHOR.

Slovakia: 125 rue de Ranelagh, 75016 Paris; tel. 1-77-93-73-330; fax 1-42-88-76-53; e-mail emb.paris@mzv.sk; internet www.mzv.sk/paris; Ambassador MAREK EŠTOK.

Slovenia: 28 rue Bois-le-Vent, 75016 Paris; tel. 1-44-96-50-71; fax 1-45-24-67-05; e-mail vpa@gov.si; Ambassador VERONIKA STABEJ.

Somalia: 26 rue Dumont d'Urville, 75116 Paris; tel. 1-45-00-88-98; Ambassador (vacant).

South Africa: 59 quai d'Orsay, 75343 Paris Cedex 07; tel. 1-53-59-23-23; fax 1-45-50-31-98; e-mail info@afriquesud.net; internet www.afriquesud.net; Ambassador DOLANA MSIMANG.

Spain: 22 ave Marceau, 75008 Paris Cedex 08; tel. 1-44-43-18-00; fax 1-47-23-59-55; e-mail emb.paris@mae.es; internet www.maec.es/subwebs/embajadas/paris; Ambassador CARLOS BASTARRECHE SAGÜES.

Sri Lanka: 16 rue Spontini, 75016 Paris; tel. 1-55-73-31-31; fax 1-55-73-18-49; e-mail sl.france@wanadoo.fr; internet www.srilankaembassy.fr; Ambassador DAYAN JAYATHILLEKA.

Sudan: 11 rue Alfred Dehodencq, 75016 Paris; tel. 1-42-25-55-71; fax 1-54-63-66-73; e-mail ambassade-du-soudan@wanadoo.fr; Ambassador MUHAMMAD FARAH ELFAHAL.

Sweden: 17 rue Barbet-de-Jouy, 75007 Paris; tel. 1-44-18-88-00; fax 1-44-18-88-40; e-mail info@amb-suede.fr; internet www.swedenabroad.com/paris; Ambassador GUNNAR LUND.

Switzerland: 142 rue de Grenelle, 75007 Paris; tel. 1-49-55-67-00; fax 1-49-55-67-67; e-mail par.vertretung@eda.admin.ch; internet www.eda.admin.ch/paris; Ambassador JEAN-JACQUES DE DARDEL.

Syria: 20 rue Vaneau, 75007 Paris; tel. 1-40-62-61-00; fax 1-47-05-92-73; e-mail ambassade-syrie@wanadoo.fr; Ambassador LAMIA SHAKKUR.

Tanzania: 13 ave Raymond Poincaré, 75116 Paris; tel. 1-53-70-63-66; fax 1-47-55-05-46; e-mail ambtanzanie@wanadoo.fr; Ambassador BEGUM KARIM-TAJ.

Thailand: 8 rue Greuze, 75116 Paris; tel. 1-56-26-50-50; fax 1-56-26-04-45; e-mail thaipar@wanadoo.fr; Ambassador VIRAPHAND VACHARATHIT.

Togo: 8 rue Alfred Roll, 75017 Paris; tel. 1-43-80-12-13; fax 1-43-80-06-05; e-mail france@ambassadetogo.org; Ambassador CALIXTE BATOSSIE MADJOULBA.

Tunisia: 25 rue Barbet-de-Jouy, 75007 Paris; tel. 1-45-55-95-98; fax 1-45-56-02-64; e-mail atn.paris@wanadoo.fr; Ambassador MUHAMMAD RAOUF NAJAR.

Turkey: 16 ave de Lamballe, 75016 Paris; tel. 1-53-92-71-12; fax 1-45-20-41-91; e-mail paris.be@mfa.gov.tr; internet paris.emb.mfa.gov.tr; Ambassador TAHSIN BURCUOĞLU.

Turkmenistan: 13 rue Picot, 75116 Paris; tel. 1-47-55-05-36; fax 1-47-55-05-68; e-mail turkmenamb@free.fr; Ambassador TCHARY G. NIYAZOV.

Uganda: 13 ave Raymond Poincaré, 75116 Paris; tel. 1-56-90-12-20; fax 1-45-05-21-22; e-mail uganda.embassy@club-internet.fr; Ambassador ELIZABETH PAULA NAPEYOK.

Ukraine: 21 ave de Saxe, 75007 Paris; tel. 1-43-06-07-37; fax 1-43-06-02-94; e-mail ambassade-ukraine@wanadoo.fr; internet www.mfa.gov.ua/france; Ambassador OLEXANDR KUPCHYSHYN.

United Arab Emirates: 2 blvd de la Tour Maubourg, 75007 Paris; tel. 1-44-34-02-00; fax 1-47-55-61-04; e-mail ambassade.emirats@wanadoo.fr; internet www.amb-emirats.fr; Ambassador MOHAMED ABDULLAH AL-MEER RAEES.

United Kingdom: 35 rue du Faubourg St Honoré, 75383 Paris Cedex 08; tel. 1-44-51-31-00; fax 1-44-51-32-34; e-mail public.paris@fco.gov.uk; internet ukinfrance.fco.gov.uk; Ambassador Sir PETER RICKETTS.

USA: 2 ave Gabriel, 75382 Paris Cedex 08; tel. 1-43-12-22-22; fax 1-42-66-97-83; internet france.usembassy.gov; Ambassador CHARLES H. RIVKIN.

Uruguay: 15 rue Le Sueur, 75116 Paris; tel. 1-45-00-81-37; fax 1-45-01-25-17; e-mail amburuguay.urugalia@fr.oleane.com; Ambassador Dr OMAR GONZÁLEZ MESA.

Uzbekistan: 22 rue d'Aguesseau, 75008 Paris; tel. 1-53-30-03-53; fax 1-53-30-03-54; e-mail contact@ouzbekistan.fr; internet www.ouzbekistan.fr; Ambassador BAKHROM ALOEV.

Venezuela: 11 rue Copernic, 75116 Paris; tel. 1-45-53-29-98; fax 1-47-55-64-56; e-mail info@amb-venezuela.fr; internet www.embavenez-paris.com; Ambassador JESÚS ARNALDO PÉREZ.

Viet Nam: 62–66 rue Boileau, 75016 Paris; tel. 1-44-14-64-00; fax 1-45-24-39-48; e-mail vnparis@club-internet.fr; Ambassador DUONG CHI DUNG.

Yemen: 25 rue Georges Bizet, 75116 Paris; tel. 1-53-23-87-87; fax 1-47-23-69-41; e-mail ambyemenparis@easynet.fr; Ambassador KHALED ISMAIL AL-AKWA'A.

Zambia: 18 ave de Tourville, 75007 Paris; tel. 1-56-88-12-70; fax 1-56-88-03-50; e-mail zambiansparis@wanadoo.fr; Ambassador ANDREW MULENGA.

Zimbabwe: 10 rue Jacques Bingen, 75017 Paris; tel. 1-56-88-16-00; fax 1-56-88-16-09; e-mail zimparisweb@wanadoo.fr; internet www.ambassade-zimbabwe.com; Ambassador DAVID HAMADZIRIPI.

Judicial System

The judiciary is independent of the Government. Judges of the Court of Cassation (Cour de cassation) and the First President of the Court of Appeal (Cour d'appel) are appointed by the executive from nominations of the High Council of the Judiciary.

Subordinate cases are heard by Tribunaux d'instance and more serious cases by Tribunaux de grande instance. Parallel to these Tribunals are the Tribunaux de commerce, for commercial cases, composed of judges elected by traders and manufacturers among themselves. These do not exist in every district. Where there is no Tribunal de commerce, commercial disputes are judged by Tribunaux de grande instance.

The Boards of Arbitration (Conseils des prud'hommes) consist of an equal number of workers or employees and employers ruling on the differences that arise over Contracts of Work.

The Correctional Courts (Tribunaux correctionnels) for criminal cases correspond to the Tribunaux de grande instance for civil cases. They pronounce on all graver offences (*délits*), including those involving imprisonment. Offences committed by juveniles of under 18 years go before specialized tribunals.

From all these Tribunals appeal lies to the Court of Appeal (Cours d'appel).

The Courts of Assize (Cours d'assises) have no regular sittings, but are called when necessary to try every important case, such as murder. They are presided over by judges who are members of the Courts of Appeal, and are composed of elected judges (jury). Their decision is final, except where shown to be wrong in law, and then recourse is to the Court of Cassation. The Court of Cassation is not a supreme court of appeal but a higher authority for the proper application of the law. Its duty is to see that judgments are not contrary either to the letter or the spirit of the law; any judgment annulled by the Court involves the trying of the case anew by a court of the same category as that which made the original decision.

A programme of extensive reforms in the judicial system, which aimed to reduce political control of the judiciary and to increase citizens' rights, was introduced in stages between 1997 and 2001. A notable innovation introduced by these reforms was the introduction of the convention that a person accused of a crime is presumed innocent unless otherwise proven.

In 2011 reforms to reduce the number of judicial districts, from 1,190 to 862 were completed.

Court of Cassation
(Cour de cassation)

5 quai de l'Horloge, 75055 Paris RP; tel. 1-44-32-95-95; fax 1-44-32-78-29; e-mail webmstre@courdecassation.fr; internet www.courdecassation.fr.

First President: Vincent Lamanda.

Presidents of Chambers: Christian Charruault (1ère Chambre civile), Dominique Loriferne (2ème Chambre civile), Alain Lacabarats (3ème Chambre civile), Claire Favre (Chambre commerciale, financière et économique), Evelyne Collomp (Chambre sociale), Bertrand Louvel (Chambre criminelle).

There are 88 Counsellors and 65 Junior Counsellors.

Solicitor-General: Jean-Claude Marin.

There are seven First Attorneys-General and 29 Attorneys-General.

Chief Clerk of the Court: Claire Collet.

President of the Council of Advocates at the Court of Cassation: Didier Le Prado.

Paris Court of Appeal
(Cour d'appel de Paris)

34 quai des Orfèvres, 75055 Paris Cedex 01; tel. 1-44-32-52-52; internet www.ca-paris.justice.fr.

First President: Jacques Degrandi.

There are also 61 Presidents of Chambers.

Solicitor-General: François Falletti.

There are also 124 Counsellors, 22 Attorneys-General and 36 Deputies.

Tribunal de grande instance de Paris

4 blvd du Palais, 75055 Paris RP; tel. 1-44-32-51-51; fax 1-43-29-12-55; internet www.tgi-paris.justice.fr.

President: Jacques Degrandi.

Solicitor of the Republic of Paris: Jean-Claude Marin.

Tribunal de commerce de Paris

1 quai de Corse, 75181 Paris Cedex 04; tel. 1-44-32-83-83; fax 1-40-46-07-28; e-mail sandrine.carret@greffe-tc-paris.fr; internet www.greffe-tc-paris.fr.

President: Perrette Rey.

Administrative Tribunals
(Tribunaux administratifs)

Certain cases arising between civil servants (when on duty) and the Government, or between any citizen and the Government are judged by special administrative courts.

The Administrative Tribunals (Tribunaux administratifs), of which there are 29 in metropolitan France and nine in the overseas possessions, are situated in the capital of each area; the Council of State (Conseil d'Etat) has its seat in Paris.

Tribunal des conflits

Decides whether cases shall be submitted to the ordinary or administrative courts.

President: The Keeper of the Seals, Minister of Justice.

Vice-President: Marie-France Mazars.

There are also three Counsellors of the Court of Cassation (Cour de cassation) and four Counsellors of State.

Audit Court
(Cour des comptes)

13 rue Cambon, 75001 Paris Cedex 01; tel. 1-42-98-95-00; fax 1-42-60-01-59; e-mail contact@ccomptes.fr; internet www.ccomptes.fr.

An administrative tribunal competent to judge the correctness of public accounts. It is the arbiter of common law of all public accounts laid before it. The judgments of the Court may be annulled by the Council of State (Conseil d'Etat).

First President: Didier Migaud.

Presidents of Chambers: Christian Babusiaux, Alain Hespel, Jean Picq, Alain Pichon, Jean-Pierre Bayle, Rolande Ruellan, Christian Descheemaeker, Claire Bazy-Malaurie.

Solicitor-General: Jean-François Bénard.

Chambres régionales et territoriales des comptes

In 1983 jurisdiction over the accounts of local administrations (*régions, départements* and *communes*) and public institutions (hospitals, council housing, etc.) was transferred from the Audit Court (Cour des comptes) to local *Chambres régionales*. *Chambres territoriales* were subsequently created in New Caledonia (in 1988), French Polynesia (in 1990), and Mayotte, Saint-Barthélémy, Saint-Martin and Saint Pierre and Miquelon (in 2007). The 32 courts (26 *Chambres régionales* and six *Chambres territoriales*) are autonomous but under the jurisdiction of the state. Appeals may be brought before the Audit Court.

Council of State
(Conseil d'Etat)

1 Place du Palais-Royal, 75100 Paris 01 SP; tel. 1-40-20-80-00; fax 1-40-20-80-08; e-mail chantal.leveque@conseil-etat.fr; internet www.conseil-etat.fr.

The Council of State (Conseil d'Etat) is the consultative organ of the Government and the supreme administrative court. It gives opinions to the Government in the legislative and administrative domain (interior, finance, public works and social sections) and has three functions in administrative jurisdiction: to judge in the first and last resort such cases as appeals against excess of power laid against official decrees or individuals; to judge appeals against judgments made by Tribunaux administratifs, Cours administratives d'appel and resolutions of courts of litigation; and to annul decisions made by various specialized administrative authorities that adjudicate without appeal, such as the Audit Court (Cour des comptes).

President: The Prime Minister.

Vice-President: Jean-Marc Sauvé.

Presidents of Sections: Marie-Dominique Hagelsteen, Olivier Schrameck, Yannick Moreau, Pierre-François Racine, Bernard Stirn, Yves Robineau, Michel Pinault.

General Secretary: Christophe Devys.

Constitutional Council
(Conseil constitutionnel)

2 rue de Montpensier, 75001 Paris; tel. 1-40-15-30-00; fax 1-40-20-93-27; e-mail informatique@conseil-constitutionnel.fr; internet www.conseil-constitutionnel.fr.

President: Jean-Louis Debré.

Members: Valéry Giscard d'Estaing (ex officio), Jacques Chirac (ex officio), Pierre Steinmetz, Jacqueline de Guillenchmidt, Jean-Louis Pezant, Renaud Denoix de Saint-Marc, Guy Canivet, Michel Charasse, Hubert Haenel, Jacques Barrot.

Religion

CHRISTIANITY

Conseil d'Eglises Chrétiennes en France: 58 ave de Breteuil, 75007 Paris; tel. 1-72-36-69-60; fax 1-73-72-96-67; e-mail conseil.eglises.chretienne@cef.fr; f. 1987; ecumenical organization comprising representatives from all Christian denominations to express opinions on social issues; 21 mems; Pres. Pastor Claude Baty, Cardinal André Vingt-Trois, Most Rev. Emmanuel (Adamakis); Secs Pastor Gill Daudé, Fr Michel Mallèvre, Archbishop Arsenios Kardamakis.

The Roman Catholic Church

For ecclesiastical purposes, France comprises nine Apostolic Regions, together forming 22 archdioceses (of which one, Strasbourg, is directly responsible to the Holy See), 70 dioceses (including one, Metz, directly responsible to the Holy See) and one Territorial Prelature. The Archbishop of Paris is also the Ordinary for Catholics of Oriental Rites. At 31 December 2006 an estimated 74.4% of the population were adherents of the Roman Catholic Church.

Bishops' Conference

Conférence des Evêques de France, 58 ave de Breteuil, 75007 Paris; tel. 1-72-36-68-00; fax 1-73-72-97-22; e-mail cef@cef.fr; internet www.cef.fr; Pres. Cardinal André Vingt-Trois (Archbishop of Paris); Sec.-Gen. Fr Antoine Hérouard.

Archbishop of Lyon and Primate of Gaul: Cardinal Philippe Barbarin, Archevêché, 1 place de Fourvière, 69321 Lyon Cedex 05; tel. 4-72-38-80-98; fax 4-78-36-06-00; e-mail petre@@lyon.catholique.fr; internet lyon.catholique.fr.

Archbishop of Aix et Arles: Most Rev. Christophe Dufour.

Archbishop of Albi: Most Rev. Jean Marie Henri Legrez.

Archbishop of Auch: Most Rev. Maurice Gardès.

Archbishop of Avignon: Most Rev. Jean-Pierre Marie Cattenoz.

Archbishop of Besançon: Most Rev. André Jean René Lacrampe.

Archbishop of Bordeaux: Cardinal JEAN-PIERRE RICARD.

Archbishop of Bourges: Most Rev. ARMAND MAILLARD.

Archbishop of Cambrai: Most Rev. FRANÇOIS GARNIER.

Archbishop of Chambéry: Most Rev. PHILIPPE BALLOT.

Archbishop of Clermont: Most Rev. HIPPOLYTE SIMON.

Archbishop of Dijon: Most Rev. ROLAND MINNERATH.

Archbishop of Marseille: Most Rev. GEORGES PAUL PONTIER.

Archbishop of Montpellier: Most Rev. PIERRE-MARIE CARRÉ.

Archbishop of Paris: Cardinal ANDRÉ VINGT-TROIS.

Archbishop of Poitiers: PASCAL JEAN MARCEL WINTZER.

Archbishop of Reims: Most Rev. THIERRY JORDAN.

Archbishop of Rennes: Most Rev. PIERRE D'ORNELLAS.

Archbishop of Rouen: Most Rev. JEAN-CHARLES DESCUBES.

Archbishop of Sens-Auxerre: Most Rev. YVES PATENÔTRE.

Archbishop of Strasbourg: Most Rev. JEAN-PIERRE GRALLET.

Archbishop of Toulouse: Most Rev. ROBERT JEAN-LOUIS LE GALL.

Archbishop of Tours: Most Rev. BERNARD-NICOLAS JEAN-MARIE AUBERTIN.

Protestant Churches

There are some 950,000 Protestants in France.

Eglise méthodiste: 3 rue Paul Verlaine, 30100 Alès; tel. 4-66-86-20-72; the total Methodist community was estimated at 1,000 mems in 2001.

Fédération protestante de France: 47 rue de Clichy, 75311 Paris Cedex 09; tel. 1-44-53-47-12; fax 1-42-81-40-01; e-mail courrier@protestants.org; internet www.protestants.org; f. 1905; Pres. Pastor CLAUDE BATY; Gen. Sec. Pastor YVES PARREND.

The Federation includes:

Armée du Salut (Foundation and Congregation): 60 rue des Frères Flavien, 75976 Paris Cedex 20; tel. 1-43-62-25-00; fax 1-43-62-25-57; e-mail info@armeedusalut.fr; internet www.armeedusalut.fr; f. 1881; Pres. Lt-Col ALAIN DUCHÊNE.

Communauté protestante évangélique de Vannes: 18 blvd Edouard Herriot, 56000 Vannes; tel. and fax 2-97-47-16-75; e-mail communauteprotestante.vannes@wanadoo.fr; Pres. of the Council of the Church MARK PLUNIER.

Eglise évangélique luthérienne de France: 24 ave Wilson, 25200 Montbéliard; tel. 3-81-95-28-67; fax 3-81-94-20-70; e-mail eelf.montbeliard@wanadoo.fr; internet www.eelf.org; 10,400 mems (2010); f. 1872; Pres. Pastor JOËL DAUTHEVILLE; Sec. JEANNIE FAVRE.

Eglise protestante de la Confession d'Augsbourg d'Alsace et de Lorraine: 1 quai St Thomas, BP 80022, 67081 Strasbourg Cedex; tel. 3-8825-90-00; fax 3-88-25-90-99; e-mail contact@uepal.fr; internet www.uepal.fr; 210,000 mems; member of Union des Eglises Protestantes d'Alsace et de Lorraine; Pres. Prof. JEAN-FRANÇOIS COLLANGE.

Eglise protestante évangélique de Rochefort: 42 Quéreux de la Laiterie, 17300 Rochefort; tel. 5-46-87-10-82.

Eglise protestante réformée d'Alsace et de Lorraine: 1 quai St Thomas, BP 80022, 67081 Strasbourg Cedex; tel. 3-88-25-90-00; fax 3-88-25-90-99; e-mail contact@uepal.fr; member of Union des Eglises Protestantes d'Alsace et de Lorraine; 33,000 mems; Pres. Pastor GEOFFROY GOETZ.

Eglise réformée de France: 47 rue de Clichy, 75311 Paris Cedex 09; tel. 1-48-74-90-92; fax 1-42-81-52-40; e-mail contact@unacerf.org; internet www.eglise-reformee-fr.org; 350,000 mems; Pres. Nat. Council Pastor LAURENT SCHLUMBERGER; Gen. Sec. Pastor ESTHER WIELAND-MARET.

Fédération des Eglises évangéliques baptistes de France: 47 rue de Clichy, 75311 Paris Cedex 09; tel. 1-53-20-15-40; fax 1-53-20-15-41; e-mail secretariat@feebf.com; internet www.feebf.com; 6,000 mems; f. 1910; Pres. JEAN DUPUPET.

Mission évangélique tzigane de France: 'Les Petites Brosses', 45500 Neuvoy; tel. 2-38-67-03-18; 100,000 mems; f. 1946; Pres. Pastor GEORGES MEYER; Sec. MARIO HOLDENBAUM.

Mission populaire évangélique de France: 47 rue de Clichy, 75009 Paris Cedex 09; tel. 1-48-74-98-58; fax 1-48-78-52-37; e-mail mpef@free.fr; internet www.missionpopulaire.org; 4,000 mems; f. 1871; Pres. Pastor BERTRAND VERGNIOL.

Union des Eglises évangéliques libres de France: 12 rue Claude-Perrault, 31500 Toulouse; tel. 5-61-26-06-18; fax 5-61-99-92-82; e-mail pierre.lacoste@protstants.org; internet www.ueel.org; 2,500 mems; Pres. Pastor PIERRE LACOSTE; Sec. RAYMOND CHAMARD.

Union Nationale des Eglises réformées évangéliques indépendantes de France: 74 rue Henri Revoil, 30900 Nîmes; tel. 4-66-23-51-66; fax 4-66-23-59-98; e-mail unerei@wanadoo.fr; internet erei.free.fr; f. 1938; 13,000 mems; Pres. PHILIPPE GIARDET; Sec.-Gen. GÉRARD FINES.

Scots Kirk Paris (Church of Scotland): 17 rue Bayard, 75008 Paris; tel. and fax 1-48-78-47-94; e-mail scotskirk@wanadoo.fr; internet www.scotskirkparis.com; Minister Rev. JIM COWIE.

The Orthodox Church

There are about 200,000 Orthodox believers in France, of whom 100,000 are Russian Orthodox and 50,000 Greek Orthodox. There are 85 parishes and eight monasteries.

Administration of Russian Orthodox Churches in Western Europe (Jurisdiction of the Ecumenical Patriarchate): Cathédrale St Alexandre-Nevski, 12 rue Daru, 75008 Paris; tel. and fax 1-46-22-38-91; e-mail administration.diocesaine@exarchat.eu; internet www.exarchat.eu; Pres. Most Rev. GABRIEL (Archbishop of Russian Orthodox Churches in Western Europe and Exarch of the Ecumenical Patriarch).

Assembly of the Orthodox Churches of France (Greek Orthodox Church): Cathédrale St Stéphane, 7 rue Georges Bizet, 75116 Paris; tel. 1-47-20-82-35; fax 1-47-20-83-15; e-mail eglise.orthodoxe.grecque@wanadoo.fr; f. 1997; Metropolitan of France Most Rev. EMMANUEL (ADAMAKIS).

Russian Orthodox Church (Moscow Patriarchate): 26 rue Péclet, 75015 Paris; tel. 1-48-28-99-90; fax 1-48-28-74-54; e-mail presse@egliserusse.eu; internet www.egliserusse.eu; the diocese of Chersonesus covers France, Portugal, Spain and Switzerland; Archbishop of Chersonesus INNOCENT (VASILIYEV).

The Anglican Communion

Within the Church of England, France forms part of the diocese of Gibraltar in Europe. The Bishop is resident in London (United Kingdom).

Archdeacon of France: Ven. KENNETH LETTS, Presbytère Anglican, 11 rue de la Buffa, 06000 Nice; tel. 4-93-87-19-83; fax 4-93-82-25-09; e-mail anglican@free.fr.

Other Christian Denominations

Société Religieuse des Amis (Quakers, Assemblée de France)/ Centre Quaker International: 11 ave des Quakers, 30111 Congénies; tel. 1-45-48-74-23; e-mail quaker.paris@aliceadsl.fr; internet quaker.chez-alice.fr; f. 1920; 10 meetings nation-wide; Clerk ROGER ANDRIANALY.

ISLAM

In numerical terms, Islam is the second most important religion in France; in 2006 there were about 5m. adherents, of whom some 35% resided in the Ile-de-France region.

Conseil français du culte musulman (CFCM): 270 rue Lecourbe, 75015 Paris; tel. 1-45-58-05-73; fax 1-45-58-24-06; internet www.lecfcm.fr; f. 2003 to represent Islamic interests to the public authorities; Pres. Dr DALIL BOUBAKEUR; Vice-Pres FOUAD ALAOUI; Sec.-Gen. HAYDAR DEMIRYUREK.

Fédération Nationale des Musulmans de France (FNMF): 33 rue Polonceau, 75018 Paris; e-mail fnmf1@aol.com; f. 1985; 20 asscns; Pres. MOHAMED BECHARI.

Institut Musulman de la Grande Mosquée de Paris: 2 bis place du Puits de l'Ermite, 75005 Paris; tel. 1-45-35-97-33; fax 1-45-35-16-23; e-mail rectorat@mosquee-de-paris.net; internet www.mosquee-de-paris.net; f. 1926; cultural, diplomatic, social, judicial and religious sections; research and information and commercial annexes; Rector Dr DALIL BOUBAKEUR.

Ligue nationale des Musulmans de France: 83 rue Romain Rolland, 93260 Les Lilas; tel. 8-92-68-18-30; e-mail lnmf@wanadoo.fr; internet www.lnmf.net.

JUDAISM

There are about 650,000 Jews in France.

Conseil représentatif des institutions juives de France (CRIF): 39 rue Broca, 75005 Paris; tel. 1-42-17-11-11; fax 1-42-17-11-50; e-mail infocrif@crif.org; internet www.crif.org; 63 asscns; Pres. ROGER CUKIERMAN.

Consistoire Central—Union des Communautés Juives de France: 19 rue Saint Georges, 75009 Paris; tel. 1-49-70-88-00; fax 1-42-81-03-66; e-mail administration@consistoirecentral.fr; internet www.consistoiredefrance.fr; f. 1808; 230 asscns; Chief Rabbi of France GILLES BERNHEIM; Pres. JOËL MERGUI; Dir-Gen. FRÉDÉRIC ATTALI.

Consistoire Israélite de Paris: 17 rue Saint Georges, 75009 Paris; tel. 1-40-82-26-26; internet www.consistoire.org; f. 1808; 40,000 mems; Pres. MOÏSE COHEN; Chief Rabbi of Paris DAVID MESSAS; Chief Rabbi of the Consistoire Israélite de Paris ALAIN GOLDMANN.

Fonds social juif unifié (FSJU): Espace Rachi, 39 rue Broca, 75005 Paris; tel. 1-42-17-10-00; fax 1-42-17-10-82; e-mail info@fsju.org; internet www.fsju.org; f. 1950; unites the principal organizations supporting Jewish cultural, educational and social activity in France, and seeks to establish closer links between French Jewry and Israel; Pres. PIERRE BESNAINOU; Dir DAVID SAADA.

BAHÁ'Í FAITH

Centre National Bahá'í: 45 rue Pergolèse, 75116 Paris; tel. 1-45-00-90-26; e-mail info@bahai.fr; internet www.bahai-fr.org.

The Press

Most major daily newspapers are owned by individual publishers or by the powerful groups that have developed round either a company or a single personality. The major groups are as follows:

Amaury Group: 25 ave Michelet, 93408 Saint Ouen Cedex; tel. 1-40-10-30-30; fax 1-40-11-15-26; owns *Le Parisien*, *Aujourd'hui en France*, the sports daily *L'Equipe*, the bi-weekly magazine *France Football*, the weekly *L'Equipe Magazine*, and the monthly *Vélo Magazine*; Man. Dir MARIE-ODILE AMAURY.

Bayard Presse: 3–5 rue Bayard, 75393 Paris Cedex 08; tel. 1-44-35-60-60; fax 1-44-35-61-61; e-mail communication@bayard-presse.com; internet www.bayardpresse.fr; f. 1873; Roman Catholic press group; owns 143 publs world-wide, incl. the national daily *La Croix*, the magazines *Pèlerin*, *Panorama*, *Notre Temps* and several specialized religious publications; Pres. GEORGES SANEROT.

Lagardère Active: 121 ave de Malakoff, 75216 Paris Cedex 16; tel. 1-40-69-16-00; fax 1-40-69-18-54; e-mail contactpresse@hfp.fr; internet www.lagardere.com; f. 2006 by merger of Hachette Filipacchi Médias (f. 1999) and Lagardère Active; controls magazines in France incl. *Paris-Match*, *Pariscope*, *Jeune et Jolie*, *Photo*, *France-Dimanche*, *Elle*, *Télé 7 Jours*; owns 220 magazines world-wide; CEO DENIS OLIVENNES; Editorial Dir BRUNO LESOUËF.

Mondadori France: 43 rue du Colonel Pierre-Avia, 75015 Paris; tel. 1-46-48-48-48; e-mail contact@mondadori.fr; internet www.mondadori.fr; fmrly Editions Mondiales, and subsequently Emap France; present name adopted 2006; owned by Arnoldo Mondadori Editore, SpA (Italy); controls more than 40 magazines in France, incl. *Nous Deux*, *FHM*, *Science et Vie*, *Télé-Star*, *Top Santé*, *Télépoche*, *Auto Plus* and also specialized magazines; Man. Dir ERNESTO MAURI.

DAILY NEWSPAPERS (PARIS)

La Croix: 18 rue Barbès, 92128 Montrouge Cedex; tel. 1-74-31-60-60; fax 1-74-31-60-69; e-mail lecteurs.lacroix@bayard-presse.com; internet www.la-croix.com; f. 1883; Roman Catholic; Editor JEAN-BAPTISTE DE FOMBELLE; Dir DOMINIQUE QUINIO; circ. in France 98,918 (2012).

Les Echos: 16 rue du Quatre Septembre, 75112 Paris Cedex 02; tel. 1-49-53-65-65; fax 1-45-61-48-92; e-mail redassist@lesechos.fr; internet www.lesechos.fr; f. 1908; acquired by Groupe LVMH in 2007; economic and financial; Editor-in-Chief HENRI GIBIER; circ. in France 119,613 (2012).

L'Equipe: 4 rue Rouget-de-l'Isle, 92130 Issy-les-Moulineaux Cedex; tel. 1-40-93-20-20; fax 1-40-93-20-08; e-mail courrierdeslecteurs@lequipe.presse.fr; internet www.lequipe.fr; f. 1946; sport; owned by Groupe Amaury; Chair. LOUIS GILLET; Editorial Dir FABRICE JOUHAUD; circ. in France 279,615 (2011).

Le Figaro: 14 blvd Haussmann, 75009 Paris; tel. 1-42-21-62-00; fax 1-42-21-64-05; internet www.lefigaro.fr; f. 1828; owned by Groupe Dassault; morning; news and literary; magazine on Saturdays; 3 weekly supplements; Pres. SERGE DASSAULT; Dir-Gen. OLIVIER COSTA DE BEAUREGARD; Editorial Dir FRANZ-OLIVIER GIESBERT; circ. in France 329,367 (2011).

France-Soir: 13 rue Camille Desmoulins, 92130 Issy-les-Moulineaux; tel. 1-56-21-00-00; internet www.francesoir.fr; f. 1941 as *Défense de la France*; present title adopted 1944; Editor RÉMY DESSARTS; circ. in France 23,934 (2008).

L'Humanité: 32 rue Jean Jaurès, 93528 Saint-Denis Cedex; tel. 1-49-22-72-72; fax 1-49-22-74-00; internet www.humanite.presse.fr; f. 1904; communist; morning; Pres. PATRICK LE HYARIC; Editorial Dir PATRICK APEL-MULLER; circ. 49,061 (2008).

International Herald Tribune: 6 bis rue des Graviers, 92521 Neuilly-sur-Seine Cedex; tel. 1-41-43-93-00; fax 1-41-43-93-38; e-mail iht@iht.com; internet www.iht.com; f. 1887; present name adopted 1966; owned by The New York Times Co (USA); English language; Publr STEPHEN DUNBAR-JOHNSON; Man. Editor ALISON SMALE; world-wide circ. 240,322 (2008).

Le Journal Officiel de la République Française: 26 rue Desaix, 75727 Paris Cedex 15; tel. 1-40-58-75-00; fax 1-45-79-17-84; e-mail info@journal-officiel.gouv.fr; internet www.legifrance.gouv.fr; f. 1870; official journal of the Government; publishes laws, decrees, parliamentary proceedings, and economic bulletins; Dir XAVIER PATIER.

Libération: 11 rue Béranger, 75154 Paris Cedex 03; tel. 1-42-76-17-89; fax 1-42-72-94-93; internet www.liberation.com; f. 1973; 37.8% owned by Edouard de Rothschild; Pres. and Editorial Dir NICOLAS DEMORAND; circ. in France119,165 (2011).

Metro: 35 rue Greneta, 75002 Paris; tel. 1-55-34-45-00; fax 1-55-34-45-03; e-mail courrier@publications-metro.fr; internet www.metrofrance.com; f. 2002; distributed free of charge in Paris, Marseille, Lyon, Toulouse, Lille, Bordeaux, Nice, Nantes, Rennes, Strasbourg and Cannes; Propr Metro International (Sweden); Dir-Gen. SOPHIE SACHNINE; Editor CHRISTOPHE JOLY; circ. 490,382 (2011).

Le Monde: 80 blvd Auguste Blanqui, 75707 Paris Cedex 13; tel. 1-42-17-20-00; fax 1-42-17-21-21; e-mail lemonde@lemonde.fr; internet www.lemonde.fr; f. 1944; independent; Chair., Supervisory Bd PIERRE BERGÉ; Dir of Publication ERIK IZRAELEWICZ; Editorial Dir SYLVIE KAUFFMANN; circ. in France 292,062 (2011).

Paris-Turf: Société des Editions France Libre, Bâtiment 270, 45 ave Victor Hugo, BP 60279 Aubervilliers, 93534 La Plaine Saint-Denis Cedex; e-mail info@paris-turf.com; internet www.paris-turf.com; horse racing; Editorial Dir FRANÇOIS HALLOPÉ; circ. 55,894 (2011).

Le Parisien: 25 ave Michelet, 93405 Saint-Ouen Cedex; tel. 1-40-10-30-30; fax 1-40-10-35-16; e-mail courriers@leparisien.com; internet www.leparisien.fr; f. 1944; morning; sold in Paris and surrounding areas; Dir-Gen. JEAN HORNAIN; Editorial Dir THIERRY BORSA; circ. in France (incl. *Aujourd'hui en France*) 454,298 (2011).

Le Quotidien du Médecin: 21 rue Camille Desmoulins, 92789 Issy-les-Moulineaux Cedex; tel. 1-73-28-13-11; fax 1-73-28-13-10; e-mail redaction@quotimed.com; internet www.quotimed.com; medical journal; Pres. and Dir-Gen. Dr GÉRARD KOUCHNER; Editorial Dir RICHARD LISCIA; circ. 179,949 (Dec. 2011).

La Tribune: 26 rue d'Oradour-sur-Glane, 75725 Paris Cedex 15; tel. 1-44-82-16-16; fax 1-44-82-17-92; e-mail directiondelaredaction@latribune.fr; internet www.latribune.fr; economic and financial; Pres., Dir of Publication VALÉRIE DECAMP; Editorial Dir JACQUES ROSSELIN; circ. in France 77,122 (2008).

20 Minutes: 50–52 blvd Hausmann, 75427 Paris Cedex 09; tel. 1-53-26-65-65; fax 1-53-26-65-68; e-mail redac-chef@20minutes.fr; internet www.20minutes.fr; f. 2002; distributed free of charge; Propr Schibsted (Norway); Pres. PIERRE-JEAN BOZO; circ. (2008) 475,287 (Paris), 782,091 (total France).

SUNDAY NEWSPAPERS (PARIS)

Le Journal du Dimanche: 121 ave de Malakoff, 75216 Paris Cedex 16; tel. 1-40-69-16-00; fax 1-40-69-18-54; internet www.lejdd.fr; owned by Groupe Lagardère; Editorial Dir DENIS OLIVENNES; circ. 257,257 (2011).

Le Parisien Dimanche: 25 ave Michelet, 93405 Saint Ouen Cedex; tel. 1-40-10-30-30; fax 1-40-10-35-16; e-mail infoat@leparisien.fr; internet www.leparisien.fr; circ. 199,204 (2011).

PRINCIPAL PROVINCIAL DAILY NEWSPAPERS

Amiens

Le Courrier Picard: 29 rue de la République, BP 1021, 80010 Amiens Cedex 01; tel. 3-22-82-60-00; fax 3-22-82-60-11; e-mail courrier@courrier-picard.fr; internet www.courrier-picard.fr; f. 1944; Chair./Man. MICHEL COLLET; Editor-in-Chief DIDIER LOUIS; circ. 58,239 (2011).

Angers

Le Courrier de l'Ouest: 4 blvd Albert Blanchoin, BP 10728, 49007 Angers Cedex 01; tel. 2-41-68-86-88; fax 2-41-44-31-43; e-mail redac.angers@courrier-ouest.com; internet www.courrierdelouest.fr; f. 1944; acquired in 2005 by Ouest-France group; Pres. and Man. Dir MATTHIEU FUCHS; Editor-in-Chief PATRICE GULLIER; circ. 99,253 (2008).

Angoulême

La Charente Libre: 16903 Angoulême Cedex 09; tel. 5-45-94-16-00; fax 5-45-94-16-19; e-mail charente@charentelibre.fr; internet www.charentelibre.com; Publishing Dir JEAN-PIERRE BARJOU; Editorial Dir JACQUES GUYON; Editor-in-Chief JEAN-LOUIS HERVOIS; circ. 34,929 (2011).

Auxerre

L'Yonne Républicaine: 8–12 ave Jean Moulin, 89000 Auxerre; tel. 3-86-49-52-00; fax 3-86-46-52-35; e-mail direction@lyonne-republicaine.fr; internet www.lyonne-republicaine.fr; f. 1944; Pres. and Dir-Gen. JEAN-PIERRE CAILLARD; Editor-in-Chief DIDIER LAGEDAMON; circ. 36,134 (2008).

Bordeaux

Sud-Ouest: 23 quai de Queyries, 33094 Bordeaux Cedex; tel. 5-35-31-31-31; fax 5-56-00-32-17; e-mail contact@sudouest.com; internet www.sudouest.com; f. 1944; independent; Pres. and Dir of Publication BRUNO FRANCESCHI; Editor-in-Chief PATRICK VENRIES; circ. 288,524 (2011).

Bourges

Le Berry Républicain: 1–3 place Berry, 18023 Bourges Cedex; tel. 2-48-27-63-63; fax 2-48-48-17-19; e-mail redaction.berry@centrefrance.com; internet www.leberry.fr; Editor-in-Chief BERNARD STEPHAN; circ. 34,915 (weekdays), 11,350 (Sun.) (2011).

Chalon-sur-Saône

Le Journal de Saône-et-Loire: 9 rue des Tonneliers, BP 134, 71100 Chalon-sur-Saône; tel. 3-85-44-68-68; fax 3-85-93-02-96; e-mail infos@lejsl.com; internet www.lejsl.com; f. 1826; Editor-in-Chief MICHEL MEKKI; circ. 58,831 (2008).

Chartres

L'Echo Républicain: 21 rue Vincent Chevard, 28000 Chartres; tel. 2-37-88-88-88; fax 2-37-91-17-42; internet www.lechorepublicain.fr; f. 1929; Pres. and Dir-Gen. RICHARD METZGER; Editor-in-Chief HUGUES DE LESTAPIS; circ. 31,575 (2011).

Clermont-Ferrand

La Montagne: 245 rue du Clos Four, 63056 Clermont-Ferrand Cedex 2; tel. 4-73-17-17-17; fax 4-73-17-18-19; e-mail lamontagne@centrefrance.com; internet www.lamontagne.fr; f. 1919; independent; Pres. and Dir-Gen. JEAN-PIERRE CAILLARD; Editors-in-Chief PHILIPPE ROUSSEAU, PHILIPPE VAZEILLE; circ. 183,982 (2011).

Dijon

Le Bien Public-Les Dépêches: 7 blvd du Chanoîne Kir, BP 550, 21015 Dijon Cedex; tel. 3-80-42-42-42; fax 3-80-42-44-35; e-mail bienpublic@lebienpublic.fr; internet www.bienpublic.com; f. 1850 as Le Bien Public; merged with *Les Dépêches* in 2001; Pres. JEAN VIANSSON PONTÉ; Editor-in-Chief JEAN-LOUIS PIERRE; circ. 43,378 (2011).

Epinal

Vosges Matin: 40 quai des Bons Enfants, 88000 Epinal Cedex; tel. 3-29-82-98-00; fax 3-29-82-99-29; e-mail vomredacweb@vosgesmatin.fr; internet www.vosgesmatin.fr; f. 1945; Editor-in-Chief GÉRARD NOËL; circ. 26,232 (2008).

Grenoble

Le Dauphiné Libéré: Isles des Cordées, 38913 Veurey-Voroize Cedex; tel. 4-76-88-71-00; fax 4-76-88-70-96; e-mail redaction@ledauphine.com; internet www.ledauphine.com; f. 1945; Pres., Dir-Gen. and Editor-in-Chief HENRI-PIERRE GUILBERT; circ. 227,187 (2011).

Lille

La Voix du Nord: 8 place du Général de Gaulle, BP 549, 59023 Lille Cedex; tel. 3-20-78-40-40; fax 3-20-78-42-44; e-mail contact@lavoixdunord.fr; internet www.lavoixdunord.fr; f. 1944; Dir-Gen. JACQUES HARDOIN; Editor-in-Chief JEAN-MICHEL BRETONNIER; circ. 259,912 (2011).

Limoges

L'Echo du Centre: 29 rue Claude-Henri Gorceix, 87022 Limoges Cedex 09; tel. 5-55-04-49-99; fax 5-55-04-49-78; internet www.l-echo.info; f. 1943; five edns; communist; Dir of Publication GUY DUMIGNARD; Editor-in-Chief BERNARD CUNY.

Le Populaire du Centre: 15 rue du Général-Catroux, BP 541, 87011 Limoges Cedex 1; tel. 5-55-58-59-00; fax 5-55-58-59-77; e-mail lepopulaire@centrefrance.com; internet www.lepopulaire.fr; f. 1905; Chair. and Dir of Publication ALAIN VÉDRINE; Editor-in-Chief OLIVIER BONNICHON; circ. 40,884 (2011).

Lyon

Le Progrès: 4 rue Montrochet, 69002 Lyon; tel. 4-72-22-23-23; fax 4-78-90-52-40; internet www.leprogres.fr; f. 1859; Dir of Publication PIERRE FANNEAU; circ. 202,794 (2011).

Tribune de Lyon: 9 rue de l'Arbre sec, 69001 Lyon; tel. 4-72-69-15-15; fax 4-72-44-92-04; e-mail fsapy@tribunedelyon.fr; internet www.tribunedelyonhebdo.fr; f. 2005; daily; Dir of Publication FRANÇOIS SAPY; circ. 2,543 (2010).

Le Mans

Le Maine Libre: 28–30 place de l'Eperon, BP 299, 72013 Le Mans Cedex 2; tel. 2-43-83-72-50; fax 2-43-28-28-19; e-mail redaction@maine-libre.com; internet www.lemainelibre.fr; acquired in 2005 by the Ouest-France group; Pres. and Dir-Gen. MATTHIEU FUCHS; Editor-in-Chief JÉRÔME GLAIZE; circ. 44,973 (2011).

Marseille

La Marseillaise: 19 cours d'Estienne d'Orves, BP 1862, 13001 Marseille Cedex 01; tel. 4-91-57-75-00; fax 4-91-57-75-25; internet www.journal-lamarseillaise.com; f. 1944; communist; Man. Dir PAUL BIAGGINI; Editor-in-Chief ROLLAND MARTINEZ.

MarseillePlus: 248 ave Roger-Salengro, 13015 Marseille; tel. 4-91-84-00-00; fax 4-91-84-80-07; e-mail redaction@marseilleplus.com; internet www.marseilleplus.com; f. 2002; Mon.–Fri. mornings; distributed free of charge; Editorial Dir GUILHEM RICAVY; circ. 60,718 (2011).

La Provence: 248 ave Roger-Salengro, 13015 Marseille; tel. 4-91-84-45-45; fax 4-91-84-49-95; e-mail contact@laprovence.com; internet www.laprovence.com; f. 1996 by merger of *Le Provençal* with *Le Méridional*; Dir of Publication STÉPHANE DUHAMEL; Editorial Dir HEDI DAHMANI; circ. 130,388 (2011).

Metz

Le Républicain Lorrain: 3 ave des Deux Fontaines, 57140 Woippy; tel. 3-87-34-17-89; fax 3-87-34-17-90; e-mail pm.pernet@republicain-lorrain.fr; internet www.republicain-lorrain.fr; f. 1919; independent; Dir-Gen. and Dir of Publication PIERRE WICKER; Editor-in-Chief JACQUES VIRON; circ. 123,592 (2011).

Montpellier

Midi Libre: Mas de Grille, 34923 Montpellier Cedex 09; tel. 4-67-07-67-07; fax 4-67-07-68-13; internet www.midilibre.com; f. 1944; Pres. and Dir of Publication ALAIN PLOMBAT; Editorial Dir PHILIPPE PALAT; circ. 140,375 (2011).

Montpellier Plus: Mas de Grille, 34923 Montpellier Cedex 09; tel. 4-67-07-69-45; internet www.montpellierplus.com; f. 2005 by *Midi Libre*; daily; distributed free of charge; circ. 30,080 (2011).

Morlaix

Le Télégramme: 7 voie d'accès au Port, BP 243, 29672 Morlaix; tel. 2-98-62-11-33; fax 2-98-63-45-45; e-mail telegramme@bretagne-online.com; internet www.letelegramme.com; f. 1944; fmrly *Le Télégramme de Brest et de l'Ouest*; Pres. and Man. Dir EDOUARD COUDURIER; Editor-in-Chief MARCEL QUIVIGER; circ. 204,785 (2011).

Mulhouse

L'Alsace: 18 rue de Thann, 68945 Mulhouse Cedex 09; tel. 3-89-32-70-00; fax 3-89-32-11-26; e-mail redaction@alsapresse.com; internet www.alsapresse.com; f. 1944; Chair. JACQUES ROMANN; Editor-in-Chief FRANCIS LAFFON; circ. 97,244 (2008).

Nancy

L'Est Républicain: rue Théophraste-Renaudot, Nancy Houdemont, 54185 Heillecourt Cedex; tel. 3-83-59-80-26; fax 3-83-59-80-13; e-mail secretariat.general@estrepublicain.fr; internet www.estrepublicain.fr; f. 1889; Dir of Publication PIERRE WICKER; Editor-in-Chief RÉMI GODEAU; circ. 149,172 (2011).

Nantes

Presse Océan: 15 rue Deshoulières, BP 22418, 44024 Nantes Cedex 01; tel. 2-40-44-24-00; fax 2-40-44-24-40; e-mail redac.locale.nantes@presse-ocean.com; internet www.presseocean.fr; f. 1944; acquired in 2005 by the Ouest-France group; Dir of Publication MATTHIEU FUCHS; Editor-in-Chief DOMINIQUE LUNEAU; circ. 32,684 (2011).

Nevers

Le Journal du Centre: 3 rue du Chemin de Fer, BP 106, 58001 Nevers; tel. 3-86-71-45-27; fax 3-86-71-45-20; e-mail redaction.jdc@centrefrance.com; internet www.lejdc.fr; f. 1943; Dir of Publication JEAN-PIERRE CAILLARD; Editor-in-Chief JEAN-YVES VIF; circ.27,940 (2011).

Nice

Nice-Matin: 214 route de Grenoble, BP 4, 06290 Nice Cedex 03; tel. 4-93-18-28-38; fax 4-93-83-93-97; internet www.nicematin.fr; f. 1945; Dir of Publication DOMINIQUE BERNARD; Editor-in-Chief OLIVIER BISCAYE; circ. 101,882 (2011).

Orléans

La République du Centre: rue de la Halte, 45770 Saran; tel. 2-38-78-79-80; fax 2-38-78-79-79; e-mail dleger@larep.com; internet www.larep.com; f. 1944; Dir of Publication JEAN-PIERRE CAILLARD; Editor-in-Chief CHRISTINE BROUDIC; circ. 39,905 (2011).

Perpignan

L'Indépendant: 'Le Mas de la Garrigue', 2 ave Alfred Sauvy, 66605 Rivesaltes Cedex; tel. 4-68-64-88-88; fax 4-68-64-88-38; internet www.lindependant.com; f. 1846; daily; also *Indépendant-Dimanche* (Sun.); Pres. OLIVIER GEROLAMI; Editorial Dir JOSÉ LOZANO; circ. 60,119 (2011).

Reims

L'Union: 5 rue de Talleyrand, 51083 Reims Cedex; tel. 3-26-50-50-50; fax 3-26-50-51-69; e-mail dirgen@journal-lunion.fr; internet www.lunion.presse.fr; f. 1944; Chair. JACQUES TILLIER; Editor-in-Chief SÉBASTIEN LACROIX; circ. 106,381 (2008).

Rennes

Ouest-France: 10 rue du Breil, 35051 Rennes Cedex 09; tel. 2-99-32-60-00; fax 2-99-32-60-25; internet www.ouest-france.fr; f. 1944; publ. by non-profit-making Association pour le soutien des principes de la démocratie humaniste; 40 local editions (weekdays), 9 editions (Sun.); the largest circulation of any daily newspaper in France; Chair. and Man. Dir FRANÇOIS RÉGIS HUTIN; Editor-in-Chief JEAN-LUC ÉVIN; circ. Mon.–Fri. 748,223; Sun. 359,174 (2011).

Roubaix

Nord-Eclair: 42 rue du Général Sarrail, 59100 Roubaix Cedex 1; tel. 3-20-25-02-50; fax 3-20-25-62-98; e-mail contact@nordeclair.fr; internet www.nordeclair.fr; f. 1944; Pres. JACQUES HARDOIN; Dir-Gen. and Editorial Dir JEAN-RENÉ LORE; circ. 24,267 (2011).

Rouen

Paris-Normandie: 33 rue des Grosses Pierres, BP 40047, 76250 Deville-lès-Rouen; tel. 2-35-14-56-56; fax 2-35-14-56-15; e-mail redaction.web@paris-normandie.fr; internet www.paris-normandie.com; f. 1944; Pres. and Dir-Gen. PHILIPPE HERSANT; Editor-in-Chief SOPHIE BLOCH; circ. 52,606 (2011).

Strasbourg

Les Dernières Nouvelles d'Alsace: 17–21 rue de la Nuée Bleue, BP 406/R1, 67077 Strasbourg Cedex; tel. 3-88-21-55-00; fax 3-88-21-56-41; e-mail dnasug@sdv.fr; internet www.dna.fr; f. 1877; non-party; Dir-Gen. FRANCIS HIRN; Editor-in-Chief DOMINIQUE JUNG; circ. 168,238 (2011).

Toulon

Var Matin: 214 route de Grenoble, BP 4, 06290 Nice Cedex 3; tel. 4-93-18-28-38; fax 4-94-63-49-98; internet www.varmatin.com; f. 1975; Dir of Publication Dominique BERNARD; Editor-in-Chief OLIVIER BISCAYE; circ. 70,209 (2011).

Toulouse

La Dépêche du Midi: ave Jean Baylet, 31095 Toulouse Cedex; tel. 5-62-11-33-00; fax 5-61-44-74-74; internet www.ladepeche.com; f. 1870; Dir of Publication BRUNO PACHENT; Editor-in-Chief JEAN-CLAUDE SOULERY; circ. 177,863 (2011).

Tours

La Nouvelle République du Centre-Ouest: 232 ave de Grammont, 37048 Tours Cedex 1; tel. 2-47-31-70-00; fax 2-47-31-70-70; e-mail nr.redactionenchef@nrco.fr; internet www.lanouvellerepublique.fr; f. 1944; non-party; Pres. OLIVIER SAINT-CRICQ; Editor-in-Chief BRUNO BÉCARD; circ. 183,482 (2011).

Troyes

L'Est-Eclair: 71 ave du Maréchal Leclerc, 10120 St André les Vergers; tel. 3-25-71-75-75; fax 3-25-79-58-54; e-mail redaction@lest-eclair.fr; internet www.lest-eclair.fr; f. 1945; Pres. and Dir of Publication JACQUES TILLIER; Editor-in-Chief PATRICK PLANCHENAULT; circ. 25,852 (2011).

SELECTED PERIODICALS

(average net circulation figures for 2010, unless otherwise stated)

Current Affairs and Politics

Annales—Histoire, Sciences sociales: 54 blvd Raspail, 75006 Paris; tel. 1-49-54-24-75; fax 1-49-54-26-88; e-mail antoine.lilti@ehess.fr; internet www.editions.ehess.fr/revues/annales-histoire-sciences-sociales; f. 1929; 6 a year; Dir ANTOINE LILTI.

Armées d'Aujourd'hui: Délégation à l'Information et à la Communication de la Défense,14 rue Saint-Dominique, 75700 Paris; tel. 1-56-77-23-03; fax 1-56-77-23-04; e-mail journalistes@dicod.defense.gouv.fr; 10 a year; military and technical; produced by the Délégation à l'Information et à la Communication de la Défense; Editor-in-Chief Commdt DESTEFANIS OLIVIER; circ. 100,000 (2008).

Le Canard Enchaîné: 173 rue Saint Honoré, 75051 Paris Cedex 01; tel. 1-42-60-31-36; fax 1-42-27-97-87; e-mail redaction@lecanardenchaine.fr; internet www.canardenchaine.com; f. 1915; weekly; satirical; Dir MICHEL GAILLARD; Editors-in-Chief CLAUDE ANGELI, ERIK EMPTAZ; circ. 340,090 (2005).

Charlie Hebdo: 44 rue de Turbigo, 75003 Paris; tel. 1-44-61-96-10; fax 1-44-61-96-11; e-mail redaction@charliehebdo.fr; internet www.charliehebdo.fr; f. 1992 (as revival of 1969–81 publication); left-wing, satirical; Editor and Dir of Publication PHILIPPE VAL; Editor-in-Chief GÉRARD BIARD.

Commentaire: 116 rue du Bac, 75007 Paris; tel. 1-45-49-37-82; fax 1-45-44-32-18; e-mail infos@commentaire.fr; internet www.commentaire.fr; f. 1978; quarterly; Dir JEAN-CLAUDE CASANOVA.

Courrier International: 8 rue Jean-Antoine de Baïf, 75212 Paris Cedex 13; tel. 1-46-46-16-00; fax 1-46-46-16-01; e-mail communication@courrierinternational.com; internet www.courrierinternational.com; f. 1990; weekly; current affairs and political; Pres. and Editorial Dir PHILIPPE THUREAU-DANGIN; circ. 206,006.

Défense Nationale: Ecole Militaire, BP 8607, 75325 Paris Cedex 07; tel. 1-44-42-38-23; fax 1-44-42-31-89; e-mail contact@defnat.com; internet www.defnat.com; f. 1939; 11 a year; publ. by Cttee for Study of National Defence; military, economic, political and scientific problems; Dir Gen. BERNARD NORLAIN; Editor-in-Chief JEAN DUFOURCQ.

L'Express: 29 rue de Châteaudun, 75308 Paris Cedex 09; tel. 1-75-55-10-00; fax 1-75-55-12-05; e-mail courrier@lexpress.fr; internet www.lexpress.fr; f. 1953; weekly, Thur.; Editorial Dir CHRISTOPHE BARBIER; circ. 438,187.

L'Humanité Dimanche (HD): 32 rue Jean Jaurès, 93528 Saint-Denis Cedex; tel. 1-49-22-72-72; fax 1-49-22-74-00; internet www.humanite.presse.fr; f. 2006 to replace *L'Humanité Hebdo*; current affairs; weekly (Sun.); Editor PATRICK APEL-MULLER.

Marianne: 32 rue René Boulanger, 75484 Paris Cedex 10; tel. 1-53-72-29-00; fax 1-53-72-29-72; e-mail p.cohen3@gmail.com; internet www.marianne2.fr; f. 1997; weekly, Sat.; current affairs; Dir MAURICE SZAFRAN; Editorial Dir LAURENT NEUMANN; circ. 266,285.

Le Monde Diplomatique: 1 ave Stephen Pichon, 75013 Paris Cedex; tel. 1-53-94-96-01; fax 1-53-94-96-26; e-mail secretariat@monde-diplomatique.fr; internet www.monde-diplomatique.fr; f. 1954; monthly; international affairs; Pres. and Editorial Dir SERGE HALIMI; circ. 160,179.

Le Nouvel Observateur: 12 place de la Bourse, 75002 Paris; tel. 1-44-88-34-34; e-mail direction@nouvelobs.com; internet hebdo.nouvelobs.com; f. 1964; weekly, Thur.; left-wing political and literary; Pres. and Editor-in-Chief LAURENT JOFFRIN; circ. 500,337.

Paris-Match: 151 rue Anatole-France, 93200 Levallois-Perret Cedex; tel. 1-41-34-72-46; fax 1-41-34-79-59; e-mail parismatch@hfp.fr; internet www.parismatch.com; f. 1949; weekly, Thur.; magazine of French and world affairs; Editorial Dir OLIVIER ROYANT; Editor-in-Chief GILLES MARTIN-CHAUFFIER; circ. 678,096.

Passages: 10 rue Clément, 75006 Paris; tel. 1-43-25-23-57; fax 1-43-25-63-65; e-mail passages4@wanadoo.fr; internet www.passages-forum.fr; f. 1987; quarterly; multidisciplinary discussions of geostrategic issues, seeking to present major contemporary events in an ethical and historical perspective; Dir EMILE H. MALET.

Le Peuple: 263 rue de Paris, Case 432, 93514 Montreuil Cedex; tel. 1-48-18-83-05; fax 1-48-59-28-31; e-mail lepeuplecgt@free.fr; internet www.lepeuple-cgt.com; f. 1921; fortnightly; official organ of the Confédération Générale du Travail (trade union confederation); Dir DANIEL PRADA; Editor-in-Chief FRANÇOISE DUCHESNE.

Le Point: 74 ave du Maine, 75014 Paris; tel. 1-44-10-10-10; fax 1-44-10-12-19; e-mail support@lepoint.fr; internet www.lepoint.fr; f. 1972; weekly, Thur.; politics and current affairs; Pres. and Dir-Gen. FRANZ-OLIVIER GIESBERT; Editor-in-Chief MICHEL COLOMÈS; circ.407,388.

Politique Internationale: 11 rue du Bois de Boulogne, 75116 Paris; tel. 1-45-00-15-26; fax 1-45-00-16-87; internet www.politiqueinternationale.com; f. 1978; quarterly; Dir-Gen. PATRICK WAJSMAN; Editor-in-Chief ANNE LE FUR.

Regards: 5 villa des Pyrénées, 75020 Paris; e-mail remi.douat@regards.fr; internet www.regards.fr; monthly; communist; politics, current affairs, culture; Dir of Publication CATHERINE TRICOT; Editor-in-Chief RÉMI DOUAT.

Revue des Deux Mondes: 97 rue de Lille, 75007 Paris; tel. 1-47-53-61-94; fax 1-47-53-61-99; e-mail contact@revuedesdeuxmondes.fr; internet www.revuedesdeuxmondes.fr; f. 1829; 10 a year; current affairs; Pres. MARC LADREIT DE LACHARRIÈRE; Editor-in-Chief MICHEL CRÉPU.

Rivarol: 1 rue d'Hauteville, 75010 Paris; tel. 1-53-34-97-97; fax 1-53-34-97-98; e-mail contact@rivarol.com; internet www.rivarol.com; f. 1951; weekly; conservative; political, literary and satirical; Dir and Editor-in-Chief CAMILLE-MARIE GALIC.

Technikart: Passage du Cheval-Blanc, 2 rue de la Roquette, 75011 Paris; tel. 1-43-14-33-44; fax 1-43-14-33-40; e-mail rturcat@technikart.com; internet www.technikart.com; monthly; cultural review; Editor-in-Chief RAPHAËL TURCAT; circ. 38,500 (2008).

La Vie: 8 rue Jean-Antoine-de-Baïf, 75212 Paris Cedex 13; tel. 1-48-88-46-00; fax 1-48-88-46-01; e-mail vie.forum@mp.com.fr; internet www.lavie.fr; f. 1945; acquired by Le Monde SA in 2000; weekly; general, Christian; Dir of Publication JEAN-MARIE MONTEL; circ. 139,220.

VSD: 15 rue Galvani, 75809 Paris Cedex 17; tel. 1-56-99-47-00; fax 1-56-99-51-28; e-mail lecteurs@vsd.fr; internet www.vsd.fr; f. 1977; weekly, Wed.; current affairs, leisure; Dir of Publication PHILIPPE LABI; Editor-in-Chief PHILIPPE BOURBEILLON; circ. 175,132.

The Arts

L'Architecture d'Aujourd'hui: 43 ave Hoche, 75005 Paris; e-mail redaction@larchitecturedaujourdhui.fr; internet www.larchitecturedaujourdhui.fr; f. 1930; relaunched in 2009; 6 a year.

Art & Décoration: 16–18 rue de l'Amiral Mouchez, 75686 Paris Cedex 14; tel. 1-45-65-48-48; e-mail redaction@art-decoration.fr; internet www.art-decoration.fr; f. 1897; 8 a year; Dir JEAN MASSIN; Editor-in-Chief GUILLAUME EXCOFFIER; circ. 316,823.

Beaux Arts Magazine: 3 carrefour de Weiden, 92130 Issy-les-Moulineaux; tel. 1-41-08-38-00; e-mail courrier@beauxartsmagazine.com; internet www.beauxartsmagazine.com; monthly; review of art, architecture, cinema, design; Dir of Publication THIERRY TAITTINGER; Editor-in-Chief FABRICE BOUSTEAU; circ. 61,710.

Critique: 7 rue Bernard Palissy, 75006 Paris; tel. 1-44-39-39-20; fax 1-44-39-39-23; e-mail critique@wanadoo.fr; f. 1946; 9 a year; publ. by Les Éditions de Minuit; general review of French and foreign literature, philosophy, art, social sciences and history; Dir PHILIPPE ROGER.

Diapason: 33 rue du Colonel Pierre Avia, 75754 Paris Cedex 15; tel. 1-41-33-50-00; fax 1-41-33-57-18; e-mail diapason.redac@mondadori.fr; internet www.diapasonmag.fr; f. 1956; monthly; classical music; Editor-in-Chief EMMANUEL DUPUY; circ. 36,479.

Esprit: 212 rue Saint Martin, 75003 Paris; tel. 1-48-04-92-90; fax 1-48-04-50-53; e-mail redaction@esprit.presse.fr; internet www.esprit.presse.fr; f. 1932; 10 a year; philosophy, history, sociology; Dir OLIVIER MONGIN; Editor-in-Chief MARC-OLIVIER PADIS.

Les Inrockuptibles: 24 rue Saint Sabin, 75011 Paris; tel. 1-42-44-16-16; fax 1-42-44-16-00; e-mail christian.fevret@inrocks.com; internet www.lesinrocks.com; f. 1986; weekly, Tue.; music, cinema, literature and television; Editorial Dir BERNARD ZEKRI; circ. 54,583.

Lire: 29 rue de Châteaudun, 75308 Paris Cedex 09; tel. 1-75-55-10-00; fax 1-75-55-17-04; e-mail redaction@lire.fr; internet www.lire.fr; f. 1975; monthly; literary review; Editorial Dir FRANÇOIS BUSNEL; circ. 71,088.

Livres de France: 35 rue Grégoire-de-Tours, 75006 Paris; tel. 1-44-41-28-00; fax 1-43-29-77-85; f. 1979; 11 a year; Dir JEAN-MARIE DOUBLET.

Livres-Hebdo: 35 rue Grégoire-de-Tours, 75006 Paris; tel. 1-44-41-28-00; fax 1-43-29-77-85; internet www.livreshebdo.fr; f. 1979; weekly; book publishing; Editor-in-Chief CHRISTINE FERRAND.

Le Magazine Littéraire: 74 ave du Maine, 75014 Paris; tel. 1-44-10-10-10; fax 1-44-10-13-94; e-mail courrier@magazine-litteraire.com; internet www.magazine-litteraire.com; f. 1966; monthly; literature; Editorial Dir JOSEPH MACÉ-SCARON; circ. 38,420.

Le Matricule des Anges: BP 20225, 34004 Montpellier Cedex 1; tel. and fax 4-67-92-29-33; e-mail lmda@lmda.net; internet www.lmda.net; f. 1992; monthly; literary criticism; Dir of Publication THIERRY GUICHARD.

La Quinzaine Littéraire: 135 rue Saint-Martin, 75194 Paris Cedex 04; tel. 1-48-87-48-58; fax 1-48-87-13-01; e-mail selis@wanadoo.fr; internet www.quinzaine-litteraire.net; f. 1966; fortnightly; Dir MAURICE NADEAU; Editor-in-Chief ERIC PHALIPPOU.

Rock & Folk: 12 rue Mozart, 92587 Clichy Cedex; tel. 1-41-40-32-32; internet www.rocknfolk.com; f. 1966; monthly; music; publ. by Éditions Larivière; Editor-in-Chief PHILIPPE MANŒUVRE; circ. 41,932.

Les Temps Modernes: 26 rue de Condé, 75006 Paris; tel. 1-43-29-08-47; fax 1-40-51-83-38; e-mail les.temps.modernes@free.fr; f. 1945 by J.-P. Sartre; 6 a year; literary review; publ. by Gallimard; Dir CLAUDE LANZMANN.

Economic and Financial

Capital: 15 rue Galvani, 75809 Paris Cedex 17; tel. 1-44-15-30-00; e-mail contact@capital.fr; internet www.capital.fr; f. 1991; monthly; business, finance; Editor-in-Chief FRANÇOIS GENTHIAL; circ. 351,771.

Challenges: 33 rue Vivienne, 75002 Paris; tel. 1-58-65-03-03; e-mail pf@challenges.fr; internet www.challenges.fr; weekly; economics and politics; Editor-in-Chief VINCENT BEAUFILS; circ. 241,872.

L'Expansion: 29 rue de Châteaudun, 75308 Paris Cedex 09; tel. 1-75-55-10-00; internet www.lexpansion.com; f. 1967; monthly; economics and business; Editorial Dir CHRISTINE KERDELLANT; circ. 150,853.

Marchés Tropicaux et Méditerannéens: 1 rue du Dahomey, 75011 Paris; tel. 1-55-25-87-30; fax 1-43-70-12-31; e-mail info@marches-tropicaux.com; internet www.mtm-news.com; f. 1945; weekly; analysis and information on Africa and the Mediterranean region; Dir of Publication MYRTILLE DELAMARCHE; Editor-in-Chief ANAÏS DUBOIS.

Mieux Vivre Votre Argent: 29 rue de Châteaudun, 75308 Paris Cedex 09; tel. 1-75-55-10-00; fax 1-75-55-11-40; e-mail jpviallon@mieuxvivre.fr; internet www.votreargent.fr; monthly; f. 1918; investment, economics; Editorial Dir JEAN-ANTOINE BOUCHEZ; Editor-in-Chief JEAN-FRANÇOIS FILLIATRE; circ. 233,428.

Le Monde-Initiatives: 1–3 ave Stephen Pichon, 75013 Paris; tel. 1-53-94-96-60; fax 1-53-94-96-80; e-mail initiatives@lemonde.fr; f. 2002; monthly; circ. 50,000 (2002).

Le Nouvel Economiste: 5 passage Piver, 75011 Paris; tel. 1-75-44-41-00; e-mail patrick.arnoux@nouveleconomiste.fr; internet www.nouveleconomiste.fr; f. 1976; weekly, Thur.; Pres. and Editorial Dir HENRI J. NIJDAM; circ. 15,652.

L'Usine Nouvelle: Antony Parc II–10, place du Général de Gaulle, 92160 Antony Cedex; tel. 1-77-92-92-92; fax 1-56-79-42-34; internet www.usinenouvelle.com; f. 1945; weekly (Thur.); technical and industrial journal; Editorial Dir LAURENT GUEZ; Editor-in-Chief THIBAUT DE JAEGHER; circ. 54,924.

Valeurs Actuelles: 3–5 rue Saint Georges, 75009 Paris; tel. 1-40-54-11-31; fax 1-40-54-12-85; internet www.valeursactuelles.com; f. 1966; weekly; politics, economics, international affairs; Dir-Gen. GUILLAUME ROQUETTE; circ. 83,211.

La Vie Financière: 14 rue Chapon, 75003 Paris; tel. 1-53-01-70-70; fax 1-53-01-71-13; e-mail jlchampetier@laviefinanciere.com; internet www.laviefinanciere.com; f. 1945; weekly; economics and finance; Editorial Dir GÉRARD BLANDIN; circ. 84,956 (2008).

History and Geography

Annales de Géographie: 21 rue de Montparnasse, 75006 Paris; fax 1-40-46-49-93; e-mail infos@armand-colin.com; f. 1891; every 2 months.

Cahiers de Civilisation Médiévale: 24 rue de la Chaine, 86022 Poitiers; tel. 5-49-45-45-63; fax 5-49-45-45-73; e-mail blaise.royer@univ-poitiers.fr; internet www.mshs.univ-poitiers.fr/cescm; f. 1958; Centre d'études Supérieures de Civilisation Médiévale; quarterly; pluri-disciplinary medieval studies, concentrating on the 10th–12th centuries; Dir MARTIN AURELL; circ. 1,000 (2011).

GEO: 43–45 ave de Clichy, 75850 Paris Cedex 17; tel. 1-56-99-60-83; e-mail kmontemont@prisma-presse.com; internet www.geomagazine.fr; f. 1979; monthly; architecture, culture, people, photo-journalism, travel; Editor-in-Chief ERIC MEYER; circ. 300,123.

La Géographie: 184 blvd Saint Germain, 75006 Paris; tel. 1-45-48-54-62; fax 1-42-22-40-93; e-mail socgeo@socgeo.org; internet www.socgeo.org; f. 1821; quarterly of the Société de Géographie; Chair. Prof. JEAN-ROBERT PITTE.

L'Histoire: 74 ave du Maine, 75014 Paris; tel. 1-44-10-10-10; fax 1-44-10-54-47; e-mail courrier@histoire.presse.fr; internet www.histoire.presse.fr; f. 1978; monthly; Dir-Gen. PHILIPPE CLERGET; Editor-in-Chief VALÉRIE HANNIN; circ. 64,054.

Historia: 74 ave du Maine, 75014 Paris; tel. 1-44-10-10-10; fax 1-44-10-12-94; e-mail pczete@tallandier.fr; internet www.historia.fr; f. 1909; monthly; Editor-in-Chief PIERRE BARON; circ. 84,377.

National Geographic France: 13 rue Henri Barbusse, 92230 Gennevilliers; tel. 1-73-05-60-96; e-mail nationalgeographic@ngm-f.com; internet www.nationalgeographic.fr; f. 1999; monthly; geography, people, science, travel; Dir MARTIN TRAUTMANN; Editor-in-Chief FRANÇOIS MAROT; circ. 117,270.

Revue d'Histoire Diplomatique: 13 rue Soufflot, 75005 Paris; tel. 1-43-54-05-97; fax 1-46-34-07-60; e-mail librairie@pedone.info; internet www.pedone.info; f. 1887; quarterly; Dirs MAURICE VAISSE, GEORGES-HENRI SOUTOU.

Revue Historique: 56 rue Jacob, 75006 Paris; tel. 1-58-71-71-35; e-mail revuehistorique@puf.com; f. 1876; quarterly; Dirs CLAUDE GAUVARD, JEAN-FRANÇOIS SIRINELLI.

Revue de Synthèse: Centre International de Synthèse, 45 rue d'Ulm, 75005 Paris; tel. 1-44-32-26-55; fax 1-44-32-22-56; e-mail revuedesynthese@ens.fr; internet www.revue-de-synthese.eu; f. 1900; 4 a year; history, philosophy, social sciences; Dir and Editor-in-Chief ERIC BRIAN.

Home, Fashion and General

Be: 149 rue Anatole France, 92534 Levallois-Perret Cedex; tel. 1-41-34-60-00; e-mail contact@be.com; internet www.be.com; f. 2000; weekly; women's magazine; publ. by Lagardère Active; Dir VALÉRIE BROUCHOUD; circ. 176,365.

Closer: 43 rue du Colonel Pierre Avia, 75015 Paris; tel. 1-46-48-48-14; internet www.closermag.fr; f. 2005; weekly; publ. by Mondadori France; celebrity news, TV, radio, films; Editor-in-Chief JEROME PATALANO; circ. 507,173.

Cosmopolitan: 10 blvd des Frères Voisin, 92792 Issy-les-Moulineaux Cedex 9; tel. 1-41-46-88-88; fax 1-41-48-84-93; internet www.cosmopolitan.fr; f. 1973; monthly; Editor-in-Chief SYLVIE OVERNOY; circ. 419,193.

Elle: 149 rue Anatole France, 92300 Levallois-Perret; tel. 1-41-34-60-00; fax 1-41-34-67-97; e-mail ellemagazine@hfp.fr; internet www.elle.fr; f. 1945; monthly; Dir-Gen. ANNE-MARIE COUDERC; Editor-in-Chief VALÉRIE TORANIAN; circ. 408,798.

Femme Actuelle: 13 rue Henri Barbusse, 92624 Gennevilliers; tel. 1-73-05-46-46; e-mail lectrices@femmeactuelle.fr; internet www.femmeactuelle.fr; f. 1984; weekly, Mon.; Editorial Dir MARYSE BONNET; circ. 944,231.

Ici-Paris: 10 rue Thierry Le Luron Immeuble Omega, 82592 Levallois-Perret; tel. 1-41-34-60-00; fax 1-41-34-89-34; f. 1945; weekly; celebrity gossip, news; publ. by Lagadère Active; Editors-in-Chief GIANNI LORENZON, JOËL LAFFAY; circ. 370,010.

Le Journal de la Maison: 124 rue Danton, 92598 Levallois-Perret; tel. 1-41-34-60-00; fax 1-41-10-13-01; e-mail ccorvaisier@hfp.fr; internet journal-de-la-maison.dekio.fr; monthly; home; Editor-in-Chief ANNE GASTINEAU; circ. 175,977.

Marie-Claire: 10 blvd des Frères Voisin, 92792 Issy-les-Moulineaux Cedex 9; tel. 1-41-46-88-88; fax 1-41-46-86-86; e-mail mcredac@gmc.tm.fr; internet www.marieclaire.fr; f. 1954; monthly; Editor-in-Chief CHRISTINE LEIRITZ; circ. 485,507.

Marie-France: 10 blvd des Frères Voisin, 92792 Issy-Les-Moulineaux; tel. 1-41-46-88-88; e-mail mfredac@gmc.tm.fr; f. 1944; monthly; circ. 190,301.

Maxi: 30–32 rue de Chabrol, 75010 Paris; tel. 1-40-22-75-00; fax 1-48-24-08-40; e-mail courrier@maxi.presse.fr; internet www.maxi-mag.fr; f. 1986; weekly; 100% subsidiary of Bauer Group; Editor-in-Chief KATHARINA HORBATSCH; circ. 471,712.

Modes et Travaux: 8 rue François Ory, 92543 Montrouge Cedex; tel. 1-46-48-48-48; fax 1-46-48-19-00; f. 1919; monthly; publ. by Mondadori France; Editor PATRICIA WAGNER; circ. 435,810.

Notre Temps: 18 rue Barbès, 92128 Montrouge; tel. 1-74-31-60-60; fax 1-74-31-60-90; e-mail redaction@notretemps.com; internet www.notretemps.com; f. 1968; monthly; for retired people; Editor-in-Chief CÉCILE CASCIANO; circ. 872,002.

Nous Deux: 1 rue du Colonel Pierre Avia, 75015 Paris; tel. 1-46-48-48-90; fax 1-46-48-43-20; e-mail contact@mondadori.fr; f. 1947; weekly; Editor MARION MINUIT; circ. 323,137.

Parents: 10 rue Thierry-le-Luron, 92592 Levallois-Perret Cedex; tel. 1-41-34-60-00; fax 1-41-34-70-79; internet www.parents.fr; monthly; magazine for parents; Editorial Dir CATHERINE LELIÈVRE; circ. 296,469.

Pleine Vie: 48 rue Guynemer, 92865 Issy-Les-Moulineaux Cedex 9; tel. 1-41-33-50-00; e-mail jeanne.thiriet@mondadori.fr; internet www.pleinevie.fr; f. 1997; monthly; intended for women aged 50 and over; Editor JEANNE THIRIET; circ. 875,813.

Point de Vue: 23 rue du Châteaudun, 75308 Paris Cedex 09; tel. 1-75-55-10-00; e-mail info@pointdevue.fr; internet www.pointdevue.fr; f. 1945; weekly, Wed.; general illustrated; publ. by Roularta Media; Editorial Dir COLOMBE PRINGLE; circ. 252,524.

Prima: 73–75 rue La Condamine, 75854 Paris Cedex 17; tel. 1-44-90-67-50; internet www.prima.fr; f. 1982; monthly; intended for women of 40 years and over; also **Prima Maison** and **Prima Cuisine Gourmande**; Editor-in-Chief ARMELLE OGER; circ. 478,179.

Psychologies Magazine: 149–151 rue Anatole France, 92534 Levallois Perret Cedex; tel. 1-41-34-60-00; internet www.psychologies.com; monthly; Dir-Gen. ARNAUD DE SAINT SIMON; Editor-in-Chief LAURENCE RAVIER; circ. 380,447.

Public: 149 rue Anatole France, 92534 Levallois-Perret Cedex; tel. 1-41-34-92-37; fax 1-41-34-90-98; internet www.public.fr; f. 2003; weekly, Mon.; celebrity news, TV, radio, films; Editorial Dir NICOLAS PIGASSE; circ. 480,936.

Questions de Femmes: 117 rue de la Tour, 75116 Paris; tel. 1-45-03-80-00; fax 1-45-03-80-23; e-mail fazire@groupe-ayache.com; internet www.questionsdefemmes.com; f. 1996; monthly; Editor-in-Chief FABIENNE AZIRE; circ. 79,468.

Santé Magazine: 22 rue Letellier, 75015 Paris; tel. 1-43-23-16-60; e-mail direction@santemagazine.fr; internet www.santemagazine.fr; f. 1976; monthly; health; Editor-in-Chief ALINE PERRAUDIN; circ. 303,575.

Top Santé: 1 rue du Colonel Pierre Avia, 75015 Paris; tel. 1-46-48-43-84; e-mail cathy.vichery@mondadori.fr; internet www.topsante.com; f. 1990; monthly; health; Editor SOPHIE DELAUGÈRE; circ. 373,476.

Vivre Plus: 3–5 rue Bayard, 75393 Paris Cedex 08; tel. 1-44-35-60-60; fax 1-44-35-60-37; internet www.vivreplus.fr; f. 2004 as *Côté Femme* ; restyled as above 2006; monthly; aimed at women aged 40 years and above; Editors-in-Chief ODILE AMBLARD, MARIE-MADELEINE LAMY.

Vogue Paris: 56A rue du Faubourg Saint Honoré, 75008 Paris; tel. 1-53-43-60-00; fax 1-53-43-61-61; e-mail magazine@vogueparis.com; internet www.vogue.fr; monthly; Editor-in-Chief EMMANUELLE ALT; Publr XAVIER ROMATET; circ. 153,248.

Voici: 15 rue Galvani, 75809 Paris Cedex 17; tel. 1-56-99-47-00; e-mail voici@prisma-presse.com; internet www.voici.fr; f. 1987; weekly, Mon.; celebrity news, TV, radio, films; Editor-in-Chief LOÏC SELLIN; circ. 426,238.

Leisure Interests and Sport

Cahiers du Cinéma: 65 rue Montmartre, 75002 Paris; tel. 1-53-44-75-75; fax 1-43-43-95-04; e-mail teraha.cducinema@lemonde.fr; internet www.cahiersducinema.com; f. 1951; monthly; film reviews; Dir of Publication ANDREW PRICE; Editor-in-Chief STÉPHANE DELORME; circ. 21,385.

Le Chasseur Français: 48 rue Guynemer, 92865 Issy-les-Moulineaux Cedex 9; tel. 1-41-33-22-01; fax 1-41-33-22-90; internet www.lechasseurfrancais.com; f. 1885; monthly; hunting, shooting, fishing; Dir of Publication ERNESTO MAURI; Editor-in-Chief JEAN-PHILIPPE LOUIS; circ. 366,506.

France-Football: 4 cours de l'Ile Seguin, BP 10302, 92102 Boulogne-Billancourt Cedex; tel. 1-40-93-20-20; fax 1-40-93-20-17; internet www.francefootball.fr; f. 1947; twice weekly; owned by Amaury Group; Editorial Dir DENIS CHAUMIER; circ. 149,832 (Tues.), 100,225 (Fri.).

Le Journal de Mickey: 10 rue Thierry Le Luron, 92592 Levallois-Perret; tel. 1-41-34-88-73; fax 1-41-34-93-90; internet www.journaldemickey.com; f. 1934; weekly; cartoon magazine; publ. by Disney Hachette Presse; circ. 133,448.

Pariscope: 151 rue Anatole France, 92534 Levallois-Perret Cedex; tel. 1-41-34-60-60; fax 1-41-34-78-30; f. 1965; listings and reviews of events in Paris and Ile-de-France; weekly; Dir-Gen. BRUNO LESOUEF; Editorial Dir NATHALIE PESICIC; circ. 61,771.

Photo: 151 rue Anatole France, 92300 Levallois-Perret Cedex; tel. 1-41-34-73-27; fax 1-41-34-71-52; e-mail photo@photo.fr; internet www.photo.fr; f. 1967; monthly; specialist photography magazine; Editorial Dir ERIC COLMET-DAÂGE; circ.35,544.

Positif: 38 rue Milton, 75009 Paris; tel. 1-43-26-17-80; fax 1-43-26-29-77; e-mail posed@wanadoo.fr; internet www.revue-positif.net; f. 1952; monthly; film reviews; publ. by Editions Scope.

Première: 149 rue Anatole France, 92534 Levallois-Perret Cedex; tel. 1-41-34-60-00; fax 1-41-34-89-92; internet www.premiere.fr; monthly; film reviews; Dir of Publication BRUNO LESOUËF; circ. 152,078.

Télé 7 Jours: 149 rue Anatole France, 92534 Levallois-Perret Cedex; tel. 1-41-34-60-00; fax 1-41-34-79-70; e-mail courriert7j@hfp.fr; internet www.tele7.fr; weekly; television; Editorial Dir THIERRY MOREAU; circ. 1,481,865.

Télé Poche: 43 rue du Colonel Pierre Avia, 75015 Paris; tel. 1-41-33-53-50; fax 1-41-33-57-48; e-mail pierreyves.simon@emapfrance.com; internet www.telepoche.fr; f. 1966; weekly; publ. by Mondadori France; television; Pres. and Dir-Gen. ARNAUD ROY DE PUYFONTAINE; Editor-in-Chief ERIC PAVON; circ. 576,605.

Télérama: 8 rue Jean-Antoine de Baïf, Paris 75212 Cedex 13; tel. 1-55-30-55-30; fax 1-47-64-02-04; internet www.telerama.fr; f. 1972; weekly, Wed.; radio, TV, film, literature and music; Dir PHILIPPE THUREAU-DANGIN; circ. 640,946.

Télé Star: 43 rue du Colonel Pierre Avia, 75015 Paris; tel. 1-41-33-53-50; e-mail lecteurs.telestar@mondadori.fr; internet www.telestar.fr; f. 1976; weekly; television; Editorial Dir CATHERINE RAMBERT; circ. 1,034,683.

Télé Z: 10 ave de Messine, 75008 Paris; tel. 1-53-83-93-40; fax 1-53-89-97-71; internet www.telez.fr; weekly; television; Dir LAURENT D'EPENOUX; circ. 1,614,772.

Vélo Magazine: 4 rue Rouget de Lisle, 92793 Issy-les-Moulineaux; tel. 1-40-93-20-20; fax 1-40-93-20-09; e-mail redac@velomagazine.fr; internet www.velomagazine.fr; monthly; cycling; Editor-in-Chief GILLES COMTE; circ. 55,763.

Voiles et Voiliers: 21 rue du Faubourg Saint-Antoine, 75550 Paris Cedex 11; tel. 1-44-87-87-87; fax 1-44-87-87-79; internet www.voilesetvoiliers.com; monthly; sailing and nautical sports; Dir CHARLES DE FRÉMINVILLE; circ. 57,974.

Religion and Philosophy

Actualité Juive: 14 rue Raymonde Salez, 93260 Les Lilas; tel. 1-43-60-20-20; fax 1-43-60-20-21; e-mail a-j-presse@actuj.com; internet www.actuj.com; weekly; Dir LYDIA BENATTAR; circ. 17,000 (2004).

Etudes: 14 rue d'Assas, 75006 Paris; tel. 1-44-39-48-48; fax 1-44-39-48-17; e-mail etudes@free.fr; internet www.revue-etudes.com; f. 1856; monthly; general interest; Editor-in-Chief PIERRE DE CHARENTENAY.

France Catholique: 60 rue de Fontenay, 92350 Le Plessis-Robinson; tel. 1-46-30-79-06; fax 1-46-30-04-64; e-mail france-catholique@wanadoo.fr; internet www.france-catholique.fr; weekly; Dir FRÉDÉRIC AIMARD; Editor-in-Chief GÉRARD LECLERC; circ. 16,000 (2004).

Le Monde des Religions: 80 blvd Auguste-Blanqui, 75707 Paris Cedex 13; tel. 1-48-88-46-00; fax 1-42-27-04-19; e-mail contact@lemondedesreligions.fr; internet www.le-monde-des-religions.fr; f. 2003 to replace *Actualité des Religions*; 6 a year; Editorial Dir FRÉDÉRIC LENOIR; circ. 55,747.

Pèlerin: 18 rue Barbès, 92128 Montrouge; tel. 1-74-31-60-60; fax 1-74-31-60-21; e-mail pelerin@bayard-presse.com; internet www.pelerin.info; f. 1873; weekly; Dir GEORGES SANEROT; Editor-in-Chief ANTOINE D'ABBUNDO; circ. 238,633.

Philosophie Magazine: 10 rue Ballu, 75009 Paris; tel. 1-43-80-46-10; internet www.philomag.com; f. 2006; monthly; Dir FABRICE GERSCHEL; Editor-in-Chief ALEXANDRE LACROIX; circ. 51,105.

Prier: 8 rue Jean-Antoine de Baïf, 75212 Paris Cedex 13; tel. 1-48-88-46-00; fax 1-42-27-29-03; e-mail contacts-prier@mp.com.fr; internet www.prier.presse.fr; f. 1978; monthly; review of modern prayer and contemplation; Editor ERIC VINSON.

Réforme: 53–55 ave du Maine, 75014 Paris; tel. 1-43-20-32-67; fax 1-43-21-42-86; e-mail reforme@reforme.net; internet www.reforme.net; f. 1945; weekly; considers current affairs from a Protestant Christian perspective; Dir JEAN-LUC MOUTON; Editor-in-Chief NATHALIE DE SENNVILLE-LEENHARDT; circ. 6,000 (2003).

Revue des Sciences Philosophiques et Théologiques: Le Saulchoir, 43 bis rue de la Glacière, 75013 Paris; tel. 1-44-08-71-99; internet www.rspt.org; f. 1907; quarterly; Dir GILLES BERCEVILLE.

Silence: Ecologie, Alternatives, Non-violence: 9 rue Dumenge, 69317 Lyon Cedex 04; tel. 4-78-39-55-33; fax 4-78-28-85-12; internet www.revuesilence.net; f. 1982; monthly.

Témoignage Chrétien: 3–5 rue de Metz, 75010 Paris; tel. 1-44-83-82-82; fax 1-44-83-82-88; e-mail initialeduprenom.nom@temoignagechretien.fr; internet www.temoignagechretien.fr; f. 1941; weekly; Christianity and politics; Pres. and Dir of Publication HUBERT DEBBASCH; Editor-in-Chief LUC CHATEL.

La Voix Protestante: 14 rue de Trévise, 75009 Paris; tel. 1-47-70-23-53; fax 1-48-01-09-13; e-mail direction@lavoixprotestante.org; internet www.erf-rp.org; monthly review of Protestant churches in Paris and Eastern regions; Dir DANIEL CASSOU.

Science and Technology

Air et Cosmos: 1 bis ave de la République, 75011 Paris; tel. 1-49-29-30-00; fax 1-49-29-32-01; e-mail air-cosmos@air-cosmos.com; internet www.aerospacemedia.com; f. 1963; weekly; aerospace; Dir-Gen. and Editorial Dir ROBERT MONTEUX; Editor-in-Chief JEAN-PIERRE CASAMAYOU; circ. 21,393.

Annales de Chimie—Science des Matériaux: Lavoisier SAS, 14 rue de Provigny, 94236 Cachan Cedex; tel. 1-47-40-67-00; fax 1-47-40-67-02; e-mail acsm@lavoisier.fr; internet acsm.revuesonline.com; f. 1789; 6 a year; chemistry and material science.

L'Argus de l'Automobile: 52 rue de la Victoire, 75009 Paris; tel. 1-53-29-11-18; fax 1-49-27-09-50; internet www.argusauto.com; f. 1927; motoring weekly; Dir ALEXANDRINE BRETON DES LOŸS; circ. 23,814.

Astérisque: Société Mathématique de France, Institut Henri Poincaré, 11 rue Pierre et Marie Curie, 75231 Paris Cedex 05; tel. 1-44-27-67-99; fax 1-40-46-90-96; e-mail nathalie.christiaen@ens.fr; internet smf.emath.fr/Publications/Asterisque; f. 1973; 6–8 a year; mathematics; Editor-in-Chief YVES ANDRÉ; Sec. NATHALIE CHRISTIAËN.

L'Astronomie: 3 rue Beethoven, 75016 Paris; tel. 1-42-24-13-74; fax 1-42-30-75-47; e-mail redac.saf@wanadoo.fr; internet www.saf-lastronomie.com; f. 1887; monthly; publ. by Société Astronomique de France; Editor-in-Chief MARIE-CLAUDE PASKOFF.

Auto-Moto: 151 rue Anatole France, 92534 Levallois-Perret Cedex; tel. 1-41-34-95-25; fax 1-41-34-95-26; e-mail redaction@autonews.fr; internet www.autonews.fr; monthly; cars; Dir BRUNO LESOUËF; Editor-in-Chief CHRISTOPHE BOULAIN; circ. 275,322 (2008).

Auto Plus: 8 rue François Ory, 92543 Montrouge Cedex; tel. 1-41-33-51-16; fax 1-41-33-57-06; e-mail olivier.bernis@mondadori.fr; internet www.autoplus.fr; fortnightly; cars; Editor-in-Chief OLIVIER BERNIS; circ. 296,478.

Biochimie: Centre universitaire des Saints Pères, 45 rue des Saints Pères, 75270 Paris Cedex 06; tel. 1-42-86-33-77; fax 1-42-86-33-73; e-mail redaction.biochemie@ibpc.fr; internet www.elsevier.com/locate/biochi; f. 1914; monthly; biochemistry; Editor-in-Chief RICHARD BUCKINGHAM.

Electronique Pratique: 3 blvd Ney, 75018 Paris; tel. 1-44-65-80-80; fax 1-44-65-80-90; e-mail contact@electroniquepratique.com; internet www.electroniquepratique.com; monthly; electronics; Dir PATRICK VERCHER; Editor-in-Chief BERNARD DUVAL.

Industries et Technologies: 10 place du Général de Gaulle, 92160 Antony Cedex; tel. 1-77-92-92-92; fax 1-77-92-98-51; e-mail p.wagner@industries-technologies.com; internet www.industries-technologies.com; f. 1958 as Industries et Techniques; present name adopted 2002; monthly; Editor-in-Chief RIDHA LOUKIL.

Ingénieurs de l'Automobile: Editions VB,7 rue Jean Mermoz, 78000 Versailles; tel. 1-39-20-88-05; fax 1-39-20-88-06; e-mail vblcda@lcda.fr; internet www.lcda.fr/ingenieurs/ing-ensavoirplus; f. 1927; 6 a year; technical automobile review, in French and English; Editor-in-Chief ERIC BIGOURDAN; circ. 9,000 (2007).

Matériaux et Techniques: EDP Sciences, 17 ave du Hoggar, Parc d'Activités de Courtaboeuf, BP 112, 91944 Les Ulis Cedex A; tel. 1-69-18-75-75; fax 1-69-28-84-91; e-mail edps@edpsciences.org; internet www.mattech-journal.org; f. 1913; 6 a year; review of engineering research and progress on industrial materials; publ. by EDP Sciences; Editor-in-Chief RENÉ GRAS.

Le Monde Informatique: IDG Communications France, 5 rue Chantecoq, 92808 Puteaux Cedex; tel. 1-41-97-61-61; fax 1-49-04-79-04; e-mail redac_weblmi@it-news-info.com; internet www.lemondeinformatique.fr; f. 1981; weekly; information science; Editor-in-Chief SERGE LEBLAL; circ. 29,236 (2006).

Le Moniteur des Travaux Publics et du Bâtiment: 17 rue d'Uzès, 75108 Paris Cedex 02; tel. 1-40-13-30-30; fax 1-40-13-50-21; e-mail contact.groupemoniteur@groupemoniteur.fr; internet www.lemoniteur-expert.com; f. 1903; weekly; construction; Chair. JACQUES GUY; Dir of Publication GUILLAUME PROT; circ. 52,754.

Psychologie Française: c/o Nicole Dubois, Département de Psychologie, Université Nancy II, BP 3397, 54015 Nancy Cedex; e-mail nicole.dubois@univ-nancy2.fr; f. 1956; quarterly; review of the Société Française de Psychologie, publ. by Elsevier France; Editor DENIS BROUILLET.

La Recherche: 74 ave du Maine, 75014 Paris; tel. 1-40-10-10-10; fax 1-40-10-54-30; e-mail courrier@larecherche.fr; internet www.larecherche.fr; monthly; review of the Société d'éditions scientifiques; Dir of Publication PHILIPPE CLERGET; Editor-in-Chief ALINE RICHARD; circ. 47,794.

Science et Vie: 1 rue du Colonel Pierre Avia, 75015 Paris; tel. 1-46-48-48-48; fax 1-46-48-48-67; e-mail svmens@mondadori.fr; internet www.science-et-vie.com; f. 1913; monthly; Dir of Publication JEAN-LUC BREYSSE; Editorial Dir MATTHIEU VILLIERS; circ. 274,612 (2008).

Sciences et Avenir: 12 pl. de la Bourse, 75002 Paris; tel. 1-44-88-34-34; e-mail redaction@sciences-et-avenir.com; internet sciencesetavenirmensuel.nouvelobs.com; monthly; Dir of Publication DENIS OLIVENNES; circ. 263,859.

NEWS AGENCIES

Agence France-Presse (AFP): 13 place de la Bourse, 75002 Paris; tel. 1-40-41-46-46; fax 1-40-41-46-32; e-mail contact@afp.com; internet www.afp.fr; f. 1944; 24-hour service of world political, financial, entertainment, science and technology, sporting news, and photographs; 86 bureaux, 34 sub-bureaux and 2,900 correspondents world-wide; Pres. and Dir-Gen. EMMANUEL HOOG; Editor-in-Chief ERIC WISHART.

Agence Parisienne de Presse: 18 rue Saint Fiacre, 75002 Paris; tel. 1-42-36-95-59; fax 1-42-33-83-24; f. 1949; Man. Dir MICHEL BURTON.

Infomedia M.C.: 8 rue de la Michodière, 75002 Paris; tel. 1-47-42-14-33; fax 1-47-42-14-39; f. 1988; economic and financial news; Dir FRANÇOIS COUDURIER.

PRESS ASSOCIATIONS

Comité de Liaison de la Presse: 13 rue Lafayette, 75009 Paris; tel. 1-53-20-90-56; e-mail comite-liaison-presse@orange.fr; liaison organization for press, radio and cinema.

Fédération Française des Agences de Presse (FFAP): Paris; tel. 1-42-93-42-57; fax 1-42-93-15-32; e-mail info@agencesdepresse .fr; internet www.ffap.fr; comprises 5 syndicates (news, photographs, television, general information and multimedia) with a total membership of 109 agencies; Pres. ARNAUD HAMELIN; Dir JACQUES MORANDAT.

Fédération Nationale de la Presse Française (FNPF): 13 rue La Fayette, 75009 Paris; tel. 1-53-20-90-50; f. 1944; mems: Syndicat de la Presse Quotidienne Nationale, Syndicat Professionnel de la Presse Magazine et d'Opinion, Syndicat de la Presse Quotidienne Départementale, Fédération de la Presse Périodique Régionale, Fédération Nationale de la Presse d'Information Spécialisée; Pres. ALAIN DETTERNICH.

Fédération Nationale de la Presse d'Information Spécialisée: 37 rue de Rome, 75008 Paris; tel. 1-44-90-43-60; fax 1-44-90-43-72; e-mail contact@fnps.fr; internet www.fnps.fr; comprises Syndicat National de la Presse Agricole et Rurale (SNPAR), Syndicat National de la Presse Médicale et des Professions de Santé (SNPM), Syndicat de la Presse Culturelle et Scientifique (SPCS), Syndicat de la Presse Economique, Juridique et Politique (SPEJP), Syndicat de la Presse Professionnelle (SP—PRO), Syndicat de la Presse Magazine et Spécialisée (SPMS) and Syndicat de la Presse Sociale (SPS), representing some 1,350 specialized or professional publications; CEO JEAN-MICHEL HUAN.

Fédération de la Presse Périodique Régionale: 72 rue d'Hauteville, 75010 Paris; tel. 1-45-23-98-00; fax 1-45-23-98-01; e-mail sphr@sphr.fr; internet www.sphr.fr; f. 1970; present name adopted 1992; mems: Syndicat de la Presse Hebdomadaire Régionale, Syndicat National des Publications Régionales, Syndicat de la Presse Judiciaire de Province, Syndicat National de la Presse Judiciaire; represents 250 regional periodical publications; Pres. ERIC LEJEUNE; Sec.-Gen. WILLIAMS CAPTIER.

Syndicat de la Presse Quotidienne Régionale: 17 place des Etats-Unis, 75116 Paris; tel. 1-40-73-80-20; fax 1-47-20-48-94; internet www.spqr.fr; f. 1986; regional dailies; Pres. MICHEL COMBOUL; Dir-Gen. BRUNO HOCQUART DE TURTOT.

PRESS INSTITUTE

Institut Français de Presse: 4 rue Blaise Desgoffe, 75006 Paris; tel. 1-44-41-57-93; fax 1-53-63-53-28; e-mail ifp@u-paris2.fr; f. 1951; university training programme in mass communication and journalism; maintains research and documentation centre; open to research workers, students, journalists; Dir JOSIANE JOUËT.

Publishers

Actes Sud: Le Méjan, place Nina-Berberova, BP 90038, 13633 Arles; tel. 4-90-49-86-91; fax 4-90-96-95-25; e-mail contact@actes-sud.fr; internet www.actes-sud.fr; f. 1978; French and translated literature, music, theatre, studies of Arabic and Islamic civilizations; Pres. FRANÇOISE NYSSEN; Editorial Dir BERTRAND PY.

Editions Albin Michel: 22 rue Huyghens, 75014 Paris Cedex 14; tel. 1-42-79-10-00; fax 1-43-27-21-58; e-mail virginie.caminade@albin-michel.fr; internet www.albin-michel.fr; f. 1901; general, fiction, history, classics; Pres. FRANCIS ESMÉNARD; Man. Dir RICHARD DUCOUSSET.

Armand Colin Editeur: 21 rue du Montparnasse, 75006 Paris Cedex 06; tel. 1-44-39-54-47; fax 1-40-46-49-93; e-mail infos@armand-colin.com; internet www.armand-colin.com; f. 1870; imprint of Hachette Livre; literature, history, human and social sciences, university textbooks; Dir-Gen. JEAN-CHRISTOPHE TAMISIER.

Assouline: 26 pl. Vendome, 75001 Paris; tel. 1-42-60-33-84; fax 1-42-60-33-85; e-mail production@assouline.com; internet www.assouline .com; f. 1994; art, fashion, design, lifestyle; Dir PROSPER ASSOULINE.

Editions de l'Atelier/Editions Ouvrières: 51-55 rue Hoche, 94200 Ivry-sur-Seine; tel. 1-45-15-20-20; fax 1-45-15-20-22; e-mail contact@editionsatelier.com; internet www.editionsatelier.com; f. 1929; religious, educational, political and social, including labour movement; Dir-Gen. BERNARD STÉPHAN.

Groupe Bayard: 18 rue Barbès, 92128 Montrouge Cedex; tel. 1-74-31-60-60; fax 1-74-31-60-69; e-mail communication@bayardpresse .com; internet www.groupebayard.com; f. 1870; children's books, religion, human sciences; Pres. GEORGES SANEROT; Man. Dir HUBERT CHICOU.

Beauchesne Editeur: 7 Cité du Cardinal Lemoine, 75005 Paris; tel. 1-53-10-08-18; fax 1-53-10-85-19; e-mail contact@editions-beauchesne.com; internet www.editions-beauchesne.com; f. 1850; scripture, religion and theology, philosophy, religious history, politics, encyclopaedias; Man. Dir JEAN-ETIENNE MITTELMANN.

Editions Belfond: 12 ave d'Italie, 75627 Paris Cedex 13; tel. 1-44-16-05-00; fax 1-44-16-05-06; e-mail belfond@placedesediteurs.com; internet www.belfond.fr; f. 1963; fiction, poetry, documents, history, arts; Chair. JÉRÔME TALAMON; Man. Dir FABIENNE DELMOTE.

Berger-Levrault: 3 rue Ferrus, 75014 Paris; tel. 1-40-64-42-32; fax 1-40-64-42-30; e-mail ble@berger-levrault.fr; internet www .berger-levrault.fr; f. 1676; fine arts, health, social and economic sciences, law; Pres. and Dir-Gen. ALAIN SOURISSEAU; Man. Dirs PIERRE-MARIE LEHUCHER, FRANÇOIS POTIER.

Bordas: 89 blvd Blanqui, 75013 Paris; tel. 1-72-36-40-00; fax 1-72-36-40-10; e-mail cjacqueson@bordas.tm.fr; internet www .editions-bordas.com; f. 1946; imprint of Editis; encyclopaedias, dictionaries, history, geography, arts, children's and educational; Pres. OLIVIER QUERENET DE BREVILLE; Dir of Publication CATHERINE LUCET.

Buchet-Chastel: 7 rue des Canettes, 75006 Paris; tel. 1-44-32-05-60; fax 1-44-32-05-61; e-mail buchet.chastel@buchet-chastel.fr; internet www.libella.fr/buchet-chastel; f. 1929; literature, music, crafts, religion, practical guides; part of the Libella publishing group; Chair. VERA MICHALSKI; Gen. Man. FRANÇOISE DILLEMANN.

Editions Calmann-Lévy: 31 rue de Fleurus, 75006 Paris; tel. 1-49-54-36-02; e-mail editions@calmann-levy.com; internet www .editions-calmann-levy.com; f. 1836; French and foreign literature, history, social sciences, economics, sport, leisure; Chair. JEAN-ETIENNE COHEN-SEAT.

Editions Casterman: 36 rue du Chemin Vert, 75011 Paris; tel. 1-55-28-12-00; fax 1-55-28-12-60; e-mail info@casterman.com; internet www.casterman.com; f. 1780; juvenile, comics, fiction, education, leisure, art; since 1999 subsidiary of Flammarion; Chair. and Man. Dir SIMON CASTERMAN.

Editions du Cerf: 29 blvd de La Tour Maubourg, 75340 Paris Cedex 07; tel. 1-44-18-12-12; fax 1-45-56-04-27; internet www .editionsducerf.fr; f. 1929; religion, history, philosophy; Chair. MICHEL BON; Editorial Dir NICOLAS-JEAN SED; Man. Dir ERIC DE CLERMONT-TONNERRE.

Editions Champ Vallon: rue Gérin, 01420 Seyssel; tel. and fax 4-50-56-15-51; e-mail info@champ-vallon.com; internet www .champ-vallon.com; f. 1980; social sciences, literary history, literary criticism; Dirs MYRIAM MONTEIRO-BRAZ, PATRICK BEAUNE.

Editions Chiron: 1 rue Guynemer, 78114 Magny-les-Hameaux; tel. 1-30-48-74-50; fax 1-34-98-02-44; e-mail info@editionschiron.com; internet www.editionschiron.com; f. 1907; sport, education, fitness, health, dance, games; Dir THIERRY HEUNINCK.

Editions Dalloz: 31–35 rue Froidevaux, 75685 Paris Cedex 14; tel. 1-40-64-54-54; fax 1-40-64-54-97; e-mail ventes@dalloz.fr; internet www.dalloz.fr; f. 1824; law, philosophy, political science, business and economics; imprint of Hachette Livre; Pres. and Dir-Gen. RENAUD LEFEBVRE.

Dargaud: 15–27 rue Moussorgski, 75895 Paris Cedex 18; tel. 1-53-26-32-32; fax 1-53-26-32-00; e-mail contact@dargaud.fr; internet www.dargaud.fr; f. 1943; juvenile, cartoons, comics, video, graphic novels; Dir-Gen. JEAN-CHRISTOPHE DELPIERRE.

De Boccard, Edition-Diffusion: 11 rue de Médicis, 75006 Paris; tel. 1-43-26-00-37; fax 1-43-54-85-83; e-mail deboccard@deboccard .com; internet www.deboccard.com; f. 1866; history, archaeology, religion, orientalism, medievalism; Man. Dir DOMINIQUE CHAULET.

La Découverte: 9 bis rue Abel Hovelacque, 75013 Paris; tel. 1-44-08-84-01; fax 1-44-08-84-39; e-mail ladecouverte@editionsladecouverte.com; internet www.editionsladecouverte.fr; f. 1959; imprint of Editis; economic, social and political science, literature, history; Man. Dir FRANÇOIS GÈZE.

Editions Denoël: 9 rue du Cherche-Midi, 75278 Paris Cedex 06; tel. 1-44-39-73-73; fax 1-44-39-73-90; internet www.gallimard.fr/catalog/html/grp/denoel.htm; f. 1930; imprint of Editions Gallimard; general literature, science fiction, crime, history; Dir-Gen. OLIVIER RUBINSTEIN.

La Documentation Française: 29 quai Voltaire, 75344 Paris Cedex 07; tel. 1-40-15-70-00; fax 1-40-15-72-30; e-mail depcom@ladocumentationfrancaise.fr; internet www .ladocumentationfrancaise.fr; f. 1945; government publs; politics, law, economics, culture, science; Man. Dir OLIVIER CAZENAVE; Dir of Publication XAVIER PATIER.

Dunod: 5 rue Laromiguière, 75005 Paris Cedex; tel. 1-40-46-35-00; fax 1-40-46-49-95; e-mail infos@dunod.com; internet www.dunod .com; f. 1800; science, computer science, electronics, economics, accountancy, management, psychology and humanities; imprint of Hachette Livre; Dir-Gen. NATHALIE DE BAUDRY D'ASSON.

Edilarge Editions Ouest-France: 13 rue du Breil, 35063 Rennes Cedex; tel. 2-99-32-58-27; fax 2-99-32-58-30; e-mail commercial@

edilarge.fr; internet www.edilarge.fr; history, guides; subsidiary of Ouest-France group; fmrly Editions Ouest-France; Chair. FRANCOIS-XAVIER HUTIN; Dir-Gen. SERVANE BIGUAIS.

Edisud: 30 ave des Ecoles Militaires, 13100 Aix-en-Provence; tel. 4-42-21-61-44; fax 4-42-21-56-20; e-mail info@edisud.com; internet www.edisud.com; f. 1971; Dir CHARLY-YVES CHAUDOREILLE.

Editis: 30 pl. d'Italie, 75702 Paris Cedex 13; tel. 1-53-53-30-00; fax 1-72-36-47-10; e-mail benoit.liva@vupublishing.net; internet www.editis.com; f. 1835 as Havas; renamed Vivendi Universal Publishing 2001, then VUP-Investima 10 in 2003; present name adopted Oct. 2003; wholly owned subsidiary of Grupo Planeta since May 2008; education, literature, reference; imprints include Bordas, La Découverte, Editions First, Fleuve Noir, Editions Nathan, Editions Robert Laffont, Le Robert; Dir of Publishing ALAIN KOUCK.

Editions Eyrolles: 61 blvd Saint Germain, 75240 Paris Cedex 05; tel. 1-44-41-11-11; fax 1-44-41-11-44; e-mail editeurs@editions-eyrolles.com; internet www.editions-eyrolles.com; f. 1918; science, computing, technology, electronics, management, law; Man. Dir JEAN-PIERRE TISSIER.

Fayard: 13 rue du Montparnasse, 75006 Paris; tel. 1-45-49-82-00; fax 1-45-49-82-54; e-mail rights@editions-fayard.fr; internet www.editions-fayard.fr; f. 1857; literature, biography, history, religion, essays, music; CEO OLIVIER NORA.

Editions des Femmes Antoinette Fouque: 35 rue Jacob, 75006 Paris; tel. 1-42-22-60-74; fax 1-42-22-62-73; e-mail contact@desfemmes.fr; internet www.desfemmes.fr; f. 1973; mainly women authors; fiction, essays, art, history, politics, psychoanalysis, talking books; Dir ANTOINETTE FOUQUE.

Editions First: 60 rue Mazarine, 75006 Paris; tel. 1-45-49-60-00; fax 1-45-49-60-01; e-mail firstinfo@efirst.com; internet www.efirst.com; f. 1992; imprint of Editis; general non-fiction; Pres. VINCENT BARBARE.

Editions Flammarion: 87 quai Panhard et Levassor, 75647 Paris Cedex 13; tel. 1-40-51-31-00; fax 1-43-29-21-48; internet editions.flammarion.com; f. 1876; general literature, art, human sciences, sport, children's books, medicine; subsidiary of Flammarion Group; Chair. TERESA CREMISI.

Editions Fleurus: 15–27 rue Moussorgski, 75018 Paris; tel. 1-53-26-33-35; fax 1-53-26-33-36; e-mail editionsfleurus@fleurus-mame.fr; internet www.editionsfleurus.com; f. 1944; arts, education, leisure; Chair. VINCENT MONTAGNE; Man. Dir PIERRE-MARIE DUMONT; also Fleurus Idées, Fleurus Enfants, Fleurus Jeunesse, Mame, Tardy, Critérion, Desclée, Droguet et Ardant.

Fleuve Noir: 12 ave d'Italie, 75627 Paris Cedex 13; tel. 1-44-16-05-00; fax 1-44-16-05-07; e-mail deborah.druba@universpoche.com; internet www.fleuvenoir.fr; f. 1949; imprint of Editis; crime, thrillers, fantasy and science fiction; Chair. JEAN-CLAUDE DUBOST; Editorial Dir DEBORAH DRUBA.

Editions Foucher: 58 rue Jean Bleuzen, 92170 Vanves Cedex; tel. 1-41-23-65-65; e-mail cfages@editions-foucher.fr; internet www.editions-foucher.fr; f. 1936; science, economics, law, medicine textbooks; Dir of Publication OLIVIER JAOUI.

Editions Gallimard: 5 rue Sébastien-Bottin, 75328 Paris Cedex 7; tel. 1-49-54-42-00; fax 1-45-44-94-03; e-mail pub@gallimard.fr; internet www.gallimard.fr; f. 1911; general fiction, literature, history, poetry, children's, philosophy; Dir ANTOINE GALLIMARD; Editorial Dir TERESA CREMISI.

Editions Grasset et Fasquelle: 61 rue des Saints Pères, 75006 Paris; tel. 1-44-39-22-00; fax 1-42-22-64-18; e-mail dfanelli@grasset.fr; internet www.grasset.fr; f. 1907; contemporary literature, criticism, general fiction and children's books; Pres. OLIVIER NORA.

Librairie Gründ: 60 rue Mazarine, 75006 Paris; tel. 1-45-49-60-00; fax 1-45-49-60-01; e-mail grund@grund.fr; internet www.grund.fr; f. 1880; art, natural history, children's books, guides; Chair. ALAIN GRÜND; Dir VINCENT BARBARE.

Hachette Livre: 43 quai de Grenelle, 75905 Paris Cedex 15; tel. 1-43-92-30-00; fax 1-43-92-30-30; internet www.hachette.com; f. 1826; fifth largest publisher in profit terms world-wide in 2004; group comprises over 40 publishing houses in France and abroad, particularly in the UK and Spain; Pres. and Dir-Gen. ARNAUD NOURRY.

L'Harmattan Edition: 7 rue de l'Ecole Polytechnique, 75005 Paris; tel. 1-40-46-79-20; fax 1-43-25-82-03; e-mail harmat@worldnet.fr; internet www.editions-harmattan.fr; f. 1975; politics, human sciences, developing countries; Dir DENIS PRYEN.

Editions Hatier: 8 rue d'Assas, 75278 Paris Cedex 06; tel. 1-49-54-49-54; fax 1-40-49-00-45; e-mail informationspedagogiques@editions-hatier.fr; internet www.editions-hatier.fr; f. 1880; children's books, fiction, history, science, nature guides; Chair. BERNARD FOULON; Dir-Gen. CÉLIA ROSENTRAUB.

Hermann: 6 rue de la Sorbonne, 75005 Paris; tel. 1-45-57-45-40; fax 1-40-60-12-93; e-mail hermann.sa@wanadoo.fr; internet www.editions-hermann.fr; f. 1876; sciences and art, humanities; Editorial Dir ARTHUR COHEN.

Editions Ibolya Virag: 21 rue du Grand Prieuré, 75001 Paris; tel. and fax 1-43-38-56-05; fax 1-43-38-43-14; e-mail iboya_virag@hotmail.com; f. 1996; fiction, history, Central and Eastern Europe, Russia and Central Asia; Dir IBOLYA VIRAG.

J'ai Lu: 87 quai Panhard et Levassor, 75647 Paris Cedex 13; tel. 1-40-51-31-00; fax 1-43-29-21-48; e-mail ajasmin@jailu.com; internet www.jailu.com; f. 1958; fiction, paperbacks; subsidiary of Flammarion Group; Chair. CHARLES-HENRI FLAMMARION; Man. Dir BERTRAND LOBRY.

Editions Julliard: 24 ave Marceau, 75008 Paris; tel. 1-53-67-14-00; fax 1-53-67-14-14; internet www.laffont.fr/julliard/index.htm; f. 1942; general literature, biography, essays; imprint of Editions Robert Laffont/Editis; Dirs BETTY MIALET, BERNARD BARRAULT.

Editions du JurisClasseur: 141 rue de Javel, 75747 Paris Cedex 15; tel. 1-45-58-93-76; fax 1-45-58-94-00; e-mail editorial@juris-classeur.com; internet www.juris-classeur.com; member of Groupe Lexis-Nexis (ReedElsevier); imprints include Litec and Légisoft; law, economics, taxation; Dirs ANJER HOLL, MARIELLE BERNARD.

Karthala Editions: 22–24 blvd Arago, 75013 Paris; tel. 1-43-31-15-59; fax 1-45-35-27-05; e-mail karthala@wanadoo.fr; internet www.karthala.com; f. 1980; politics, history, geography, anthropology, religious studies, Christianity, Islam, the Arabic-speaking world; CEO ROBERT AGENEAU.

Editions Koutoubia: 266 ave Daumesnil, 75012 Paris; tel. 1-43-25-02-80; fax 1-80-82-55-21; e-mail infocontact@editions-koutoubia.eu; internet www.editions-koutoubia.eu; f. 2009; subsidiary of Editions Alphée (Monaco); Mediterranean culture, history and society; Dir HENRY BONNIER.

Jeanne Laffitte: 25 Cours d'Estienne d'Orves, BP 1903, 13225 Marseille Cedex 01; tel. 4-91-59-80-43; fax 4-91-54-25-64; e-mail librairie@jeanne-laffitte.com; internet www.jeanne-laffitte.com; f. 1972; art, geography, culture, medicine, history; Chair. and Man. Dir JEANNE LAFFITTE.

Editions Robert Laffont: 24 ave Marceau, 75381 Paris Cedex 08; tel. 1-53-67-14-00; fax 1-53-67-14-14; e-mail gmessina@robert-laffont.fr; internet www.laffont.fr; f. 1941; imprint of Editis; Pres. and Dir-Gen. LEONELLO BRANDOLINI.

Larousse: 21 rue du Montparnasse, 75283 Paris Cedex 06; tel. 1-44-39-44-00; fax 1-44-39-43-43; e-mail livres-larousse@larousse.fr; internet www.larousse.com; f. 1852; general, specializing in dictionaries, illustrated books on scientific subjects, encyclopaedias, classics; imprint of Hachette Livre; Pres. and Dir-Gen. PHILIPPE MERLET.

Editions J.-C. Lattès: 17 rue Jacob, 75006 Paris; tel. 1-44-41-74-00; fax 1-43-25-30-47; e-mail mpageix@editions-jclattes.fr; internet www.editions-jclattes.fr; f. 1968; imprint of Hachette Livre; general fiction and non-fiction, biography; Man. Dir ISABELLE LAFFONT.

Letouzey et Ané: 87 blvd Raspail, 75006 Paris; tel. 1-45-48-80-14; fax 1-45-49-03-43; e-mail letouzey@free.fr; internet www.letouzey.com; f. 1885; theology, religion, archaeology, history, ecclesiastical encyclopaedias and dictionaries, biography; Man. Dir FLORENCE LETOUZEY.

LGDJ—Montchrestien: 31 rue Falguière, 75741 Paris Cedex 15; tel. 1-56-54-16-00; fax 1-56-54-16-49; e-mail info@eja.fr; internet www.lgdj.fr; f. 1836; law and economy; Chair. LIONEL GUÉRIN; Dir EMMANUELLE FILIBERTI.

Le Livre de Poche: 31 rue de Fleurus, 75006 Paris Cedex 06; tel. 1-49-54-37-00; fax 1-49-54-37-01; internet www.livredepoche.com; f. 1953; general literature, dictionaries, encyclopaedias; Gen. Man. CÉCILE BOYER-RUNGE.

Editions Magnard: 5 allée de la 2ème Division Blindée, 75015 Paris; fax 1-42-79-46-80; e-mail contact@magnard.fr; internet www.magnard.fr; f. 1933; children's and educational books; subsidiary of Editions Albin Michel; Man. Dir JEAN-MANUEL BOURGOIS.

Elsevier Masson: 62 rue Camille Desmoulins, 92442 Issy les Moulineaux Cedex; tel. 1-71-16-55-99; e-mail infos@elsevier-masson.fr; internet www.elsevier-masson.fr; f. 2005; medicine and science, books and periodicals; publrs for various academies and societies; subsidiary of Elsevier; Pres. STÉPHANIE VAN DUIN.

Mercure de France: 26 rue de Condé, 75006 Paris; tel. 1-55-42-61-90; e-mail mercure@mercure.fr; internet www.mercuredefrance.fr; f. 1893; general fiction, history, biography, sociology; Pres. and Man. Dir ISABELLE GALLIMARD; Editor NICOLAS BREHAL.

Editions de Minuit: 7 rue Bernard Palissy, 75006 Paris; tel. 1-44-39-39-20; fax 1-44-39-39-23; e-mail contact@leseditionsdeminuit.fr; internet www.leseditionsdeminuit.fr; f. 1945; general literature; Man. Dir IRÈNE LINDON.

Editions Nathan: 25 ave Pierre de Coubertin, 75211 Paris Cedex 13; tel. 1-45-87-50-00; fax 1-47-07-57-57; e-mail frubert@nathan.fr;

internet www.nathan.fr; f. 1881; educational books for all levels; Man. Dir CATHERINE LUCET.

Editions Payot-Rivages: 106 blvd Saint Germain, 75006 Paris; tel. 1-44-41-39-90; fax 1-44-41-39-69; e-mail editions@payotrivages.com; internet www.payot-rivages.fr; f. 1917; literature, human sciences, philosophy; Chair. and Dir JEAN-FRANÇOIS LAMUNIÈRE.

A. et J. Picard: 82 rue Bonaparte, 75006 Paris; tel. 1-43-26-96-73; fax 1-43-26-42-64; e-mail livres@librairie-picard.com; internet www.abebooks.com/home/libpicard; f. 1869; archaeology, architecture, history of art, history, pre-history, auxiliary sciences, linguistics, musicological works, antiquarian books; Chair. and Man. Dir CHANTAL PASINI-PICARD.

Editions Plon: 76 rue Bonaparte, 75284 Paris Cedex 06; tel. 1-44-41-35-00; fax 1-44-41-30-53; e-mail stephane.billerey@editions-plon.com; internet www.plon.fr; f. 1884; imprint of Editis; fiction, history, anthropology, human sciences, biography; Chair. OLIVIER ORBAN.

Editions P.O.L.: 33 rue Saint André des Arts, 75006 Paris; tel. 1-43-54-21-20; fax 1-43-54-11-31; e-mail pol@pol-editeur.fr; internet www.pol-editeur.fr; literature; arts; Dir-Gen. PAUL OTCHAKOVSKI-LAURENS.

Presses de la Cité: 12 ave d'Italie, 75625 Paris Cedex 13; tel. 1-44-16-05-00; e-mail pressesdelacite@placedesediteurs.com; internet www.pressesdelacite.com; f. 1944; subsidiary of Editis; fiction and factual literature for general audience; Dir JEAN ARCACHE.

Presses de Sciences Po: 117 blvd Saint-Germain, 75006 Paris; tel. 1-45-49-83-64; fax 1-45-49-83-34; e-mail info.presses@sciences-po.fr; internet www.pressesdesciencespo.fr; f. 1975; history, politics, linguistics, economics, sociology, health, sustainable development; Dir MARIE-GENEVIÈVE VANDESANDE.

Presses Universitaires de France: 6 ave Reille, 75014 Paris Cedex 14; tel. 1-58-10-31-00; fax 1-58-10-31-82; e-mail info-ventes@puf.com; internet www.puf.com; f. 1921; philosophy, psychology, psychoanalysis, psychiatry, education, sociology, theology, history, geography, economics, law, linguistics, literature, science; Chair. (vacant).

Presses Universitaires de Grenoble: Saint Martin-d'Héres, 38040 Grenoble Cedex 09; tel. 4-76-82-56-52; fax 4-76-82-78-35; e-mail pug@pug.fr; internet www.pug.fr; f. 1972; psychology, law, economics, management, history, statistics, literature, medicine, science, politics; Man. Dir SYLVIE BIGOT.

Presses Universitaires de Nancy: 42–44 ave de la Libération, BP 3347, 54014 Nancy Cedex; tel. 3-54-50-46-90; fax 3-54-50-46-94; e-mail pun@univ-nancy2.fr; internet www.univ-nancy2.fr/pun; f. 1976; literature, history, law, social sciences, politics; Dir-Gen. FERRI BRIQUET.

Editions Privat: 10 rue des Arts, BP 38028, 31080 Toulouse Cedex 06; tel. 5-61-33-77-00; fax 5-34-31-64-44; e-mail info@editions-privat.com; internet www.editions-privat.com; f. 1839; regional, national and international history, heritage, health; Pres. PIERRE-YVES REVOL.

Editions du Seuil: 25 blvd Romain Rolland, 75993 Paris Cedex 14; tel. 1-40-46-50-50; fax 1-40-46-43-00; e-mail contact@seuil.com; internet www.seuil.com; f. 1936; acquired by La Martinière in 2003; modern literature, fiction, illustrated books, non-fiction; Pres. and Dir-Gen. OLIVIER BÉTOURNÉ.

Editions du Signe: 1 rue Alfred Kastler, BP 94, Eckbolsheim, 67038 Strasbourg Cedex 02; tel. 3-88-78-91-91; fax 3-88-78-91-99; e-mail info@editionsdusigne.fr; internet www.editionsdusigne.fr; f. 1987; Christianity; Chair. and Man. Dir CHRISTIAN RIEHL.

Editions Stock: 31 rue de Fleurus, 75006 Paris Cedex 06; tel. 1-49-54-36-55; fax 1-49-54-36-62; e-mail hamalric@editions-stock.fr; internet www.editions-stock.fr; f. 1710; literature, translations, biography, human sciences, guides; Chair. and Editorial. Dir JEAN-MARC ROBERTS; Sec.-Gen. MARIE-CHARLOTTE D'ESPOUY.

Succès du Livre: 60 rue St André des Arts, 75006 Paris; tel. 1-44-41-65-00; fax 1-44-41-65-36; internet www.succesdulivre.com; f. 1987; fiction, biography; Pres. ALEXANDRE FALCO.

Editions de la Table Ronde: 33 rue Saint-André-des-Arts, 75006 Paris; tel. 1-40-46-70-70; fax 1-40-46-71-01; e-mail editionslatableronde@editionslatableronde.fr; internet www.editionslatableronde.fr; f. 1944; fiction, essays, religion, travel, theatre, youth; Dir-Gen. ALICE DÉON.

Editions Tallandier: 2 rue Rotrou, 75006 Paris; tel. 1-40-46-43-88; fax 1-40-46-43-98; e-mail contact@tallandier.com; internet www.tallandier.com; f. 1865; history, reference; Dir BERNARD WOUTS.

Editions Tawhid: 8 rue Notre Dame, 69006 Lyon; tel. 4-72-74-19-39; fax 4-78-24-01-56; e-mail tawhid@islam-france.com; internet www.islam-france.com; Islamic interest; Dir TARIQ RAMADAN.

Editions Vigot: 23–27, rue de l'Ecole de Médecine, 75006 Paris; tel. 1-43-29-54-50; fax 1-46-34-56-12; e-mail ventelibraires@vigot.fr; internet www.vigot.fr; f. 1890; medicine, pharmacology, nature, veterinary science, sport, fitness, tourism, cookery; Chair. CHRISTIAN VIGOT; Man. Dir DANIEL VIGOT.

Librairie Philosophique J. Vrin: 6 place de la Sorbonne, 75005 Paris; tel. 1-43-54-03-47; fax 1-43-54-48-18; e-mail contact@vrin.fr; internet www.vrin.fr; f. 1911; university textbooks, philosophy, education, science, law, religion; Dir of Publication DENIS ARNAUD.

Librairie Vuibert: 5 allée de la 2ème Division Blindée, 75015 Paris; tel. 1-42-79-44-00; fax 1-42-79-46-80; e-mail valerie.devillers@vuibert.fr; internet www.vuibert.com; f. 1877; school and university textbooks, psychology, law; subsidiary of Editions Albin Michel.

XO Editions: 33 ave du Maine, BP 142, 75755 Paris Cedex 15; tel. 1-56-80-26-80; fax 1-56-80-26-72; e-mail edito@xoeditions.com; internet www.xoeditions.com; f. 2000; general fiction, biography, current affairs, politics; Dir BERNARD FIXOT.

PUBLISHERS' AND BOOKSELLERS' ASSOCIATIONS

Cercle de la Librairie (Syndicat des Industries et Commerces du Livre): 35 rue Grégoire de Tours, 75006 Paris Cedex; tel. 1-44-41-28-05; fax 1-44-41-28-19; internet www.editionsducercledelalibrairie.com; f. 1847; a syndicate of the book trade, grouping the principal asscns of publishers, booksellers and printers; Chair. DENIS MOLLAT; Man. Dir PHILIPPE BEAUVILLARD.

Chambre Syndicale de l'Edition Musicale: 74 rue de la Fédération, 75015 Paris; tel. 1-48-74-09-29; e-mail csdem@csdem.org; internet www.csdem.org; f. 1925; music publishers' asscn; Pres. NELLY QUEROL.

Fédération Française Syndicale de la Librairie: 24 place de la République, 14100 Lisieux; tel. 2-31-62-16-87; fax 2-31-63-97-37; f. 1892; booksellers' asscn; Chair. COLETTE HEDOUX.

Syndicat National de l'Edition: 115 blvd Saint-Germain, 75006 Paris; tel. 1-44-41-40-50; fax 1-44-41-40-77; internet www.sne.fr; f. 1892; publishers' asscn; 575 mems; Chair. SERGE EYROLLES.

Syndicat National de la Librairie Ancienne et Moderne: 4 rue Gît-le-Cœur, 75006 Paris; tel. 1-43-29-46-38; fax 1-43-25-41-63; e-mail slam-livre@wanadoo.fr; internet www.slam-livre.fr; f. 1914; booksellers' asscn; 250 mems; Pres. ALAIN MARCHISET.

Broadcasting and Communications

TELECOMMUNICATIONS

Regulatory Authorities

Agence Nationale des Fréquences (ANFR): 78 ave du Général de Gaulle, BP 400, 94704 Maisons-Alfort Cedex; tel. 1-45-18-72-73; fax 1-45-18-72-00; e-mail rtte@anfr.fr; internet www.anfr.fr; Pres. ARNAUD MIQUEL; Dir-Gen. GILLES BRÉGANT.

Autorité de Régulation des Communications Electroniques et des Postes (ARCEP): 7 sq. Max Hymans, 75730 Paris Cedex 15; tel. 1-40-47-70-00; fax 1-40-47-71-98; e-mail courrier@arcep.fr; internet www.arcep.fr; f. 2005; fmrly Autorité de Régulation des Télécommunications; Chair. JEAN-LUDOVIC SILICANI; Dir-Gen. PHILIPPE DISTLER.

Major Service Providers

Alcatel-Lucent: 3 ave Octave Gréard, 75007 Paris; tel. 1-40-76-10-10; fax 1-40-76-14-00; e-mail execoffice@alcatel-lucent.com; internet www.alcatel-lucent.com; f. 2006 by merger of Alcatel (f. 1898) and Lucent (USA, f. 1996); telecommunications and business systems, broadband access, terrestrial and submarine optical networks; Chair. PHILIPPE CAMUS; CEO BEN VERWAAYEN.

Bouygues Télécom: 32 ave Hoche, 75008 Paris; tel. 1-44-20-10-00; internet www.bouygtel.com; f. 1994; mobile cellular telecommunications; Pres. and Dir-Gen. PHILIPPE MARIEN.

France Télécom: 6 place d'Alleray, 75505 Paris Cedex 15; tel. 1-44-44-22-22; fax 1-44-44-80-34; e-mail infos.groupe@orange-ftgroup.com; internet www.francetelecom.com; 33.1% state-owned, following privatization in 2004; acquired Orange (UK) in 2000; Chair. and CEO STÉPHANE RICHARD.

Orange: 6 place d'Alleray, 75505 Paris Cedex 15; tel. 1-55-22-22-22; fax 1-55-22-25-50; internet www.orange.fr; f. 2006; mobile cellular telecommunications and internet access; CEO STÉPHANE RICHARD.

Groupe Iliad (Free): 8 rue de la Ville l'Evêque, 75008 Paris; tel. (1) 73-50-20-00; fax (1) 73-50-20-01; e-mail presse@iliad.fr; internet www.iliad.fr; f. 1991; provides fixed-line telecommunications, broadband internet and television through subsidiaries Free, One.Tel and Iliad Télécom; subsidiary Free Mobile awarded licence to operate mobile cellular telecommunications in 2009; Pres. CYRIL POIDATZ; Dir-Gen. MAXIME LOMBARDINI.

Numericable: 10 rue Albert Einstein, 77420 Champs-sur-Marne; tel. 1-55-92-46-00; fax 1-55-92-46-90; e-mail communication@

ncnumericable.com; internet www.numericable.fr; f. 2006 by merger of NC Numéricâble (f. 1997) and Noos (f. 1986); fixed-line operator, consumer internet access, cable television; Dir-Gen. PIERRE DANON.

SFR: 1 place Carpeaux, Tour Séquoia, 92915 Paris La Défense Cedex; tel. 8-05-77-66-66; internet www.sfr.fr; f. 1993; mobile cellular telecommunications; 100% owned by Vivendi SA; merged with Neuf Cegetel in 2008; 15m. subscribers (March 2010); Pres. and Dir-Gen. JEAN-BERNARD LÉVY; Dir-Gen. PIERRE TROTOT.

BROADCASTING

Conseil Supérieur de l'Audiovisuel (CSA): Tour Mirabeau, 39–43 quai André Citroën, 75739 Paris Cedex 15; tel. 1-40-58-38-00; fax 1-45-79-00-06; internet www.csa.fr; f. 1989 as replacement for the Commission Nationale de la Communication et des Libertés (CNCL); supervises all French broadcasting; awards licences to private radio (including digital radio) and television stations, allocates frequencies, has a co-decisional power to appoint chairs of public broadcasting companies, monitors programme standards; consists of 9 members, appointed for 6 years: 3 nominated by the Pres. of the Republic; 3 by the Pres. of the Assemblée nationale; and 3 by the Pres. of the Sénat; Pres. MICHEL BOYON; Gen. Man. OLIVIER JAPIOT.

Institut National de l'Audiovisuel: 4 ave de l'Europe, 94360 Bry-sur-Marne Cedex; tel. 1-49-83-26-74; fax 1-49-83-23-89; e-mail assistance@ina.fr; internet www.ina.fr; f. 1975; research and professional training in the field of broadcasting; radio and TV archives, TV production; Publ. *Les Nouveaux Dossiers de l'Audiovisuel*; (6 a year); Pres. and Dir-Gen. MATHIEU GALLET.

Télédiffusion de France (TDF): 106 ave Marx Dormoy, 92120 Montrouge; tel. 1-55-95-10-00; e-mail e-tdf@tdf.fr; internet www.tdf.fr; f. 1975; partly privatized 1987; restructured in 2007; comprises 3 sections: TDF France, TDF Multimedia and TDF International; responsible for broadcasting programmes produced by the production companies, for the organization and maintenance of the networks, for study and research into radio and television equipment; broadcasts digital terrestial television; Dir-Gen. OLIVIER HUART.

Radio

State-controlled Radio

Public radio services are provided by three entities: Radio France for the domestic audience; Réseau France Outre-Mer for the French overseas departments and territories; and Radio France Internationale for foreign countries (and those of foreign origin in France).

Société Nationale de Radiodiffusion (Radio France): 116 ave du Président Kennedy, 75786 Paris Cedex 16; tel. 1-56-40-22-22; fax 1-56-40-35-87; internet www.radio-france.fr; f. 1975; planning and production of radio programmes; provides 7 national services, 43 local stations and 2 European services; Pres. and Dir-Gen. JEAN-LUC HAAS.

France Bleu: Maison de Radio France, 75220 Paris Cedex 16; tel. 1-56-40-37-86; e-mail brigitte.tauzin@radiofrance.com; internet www.francebleu.com; f. 1980, restructured 2000; network of domestic services; Dir ANNE BRUCY.

France Culture: tel. 1-56-40-27-91; e-mail caroline.cesbron@radiofrance.com; internet franceculture.com; domestic, nation-wide service; Dir OLIVIER POIVRE D'ARVOR.

France-Info: tel. 1-56-40-20-43; e-mail romain.beignon@radiofrance.com; internet www.france-info.com; domestic, nation-wide service; continuous news and information; f. 1987; Dir PHILIPPE CHAFFANJON.

France Inter: tel. 1-56-40-37-57; e-mail emmanuel.perreau@radiofrance.com; internet www.franceinter.com; domestic, nation-wide service; general programmes, for entertainment and information; Dir PHILIPPE VAL.

France Musique: tel. 1-56-40-36-12; e-mail christophe.sillieres@radiofrance.com; internet www.francemusique.com; domestic, nation-wide service; Dir OLIVIER MOREL-MAROGER.

Le Mouv': tel. 5-62-30-70-16; internet www.lemouv.com; domestic, nation-wide service; music and general interest for people aged 18–35; f. 1997; Dir PATRICE BLANC FRANCARD.

Réseau FIP: tel. 1-56-40-16-15; internet www.fipradio.fr; f. 1971; comprises 10 local stations; continuous music; Dir JULIEN DELLI FIORI.

Radio France Internationale (RFI): 116 ave du Président Kennedy, BP 9516, 75786 Paris Cedex 16; tel. 1-56-40-12-12; fax 1-56-40-47-59; internet www.rfi.fr; f. 1975; broadcasts on MW and FM transmitters, mainly to Africa, Eastern Europe, North America, the Caribbean, South-East Asia and the Middle East, in French; also broadcasts in 19 other languages: Albanian, Arabic, Bulgarian, Cambodian, Créole, Croatian, English, Farsi, German, Laotian, Mandarin, Polish, Portuguese, Romanian, Russian, Serbian, Spanish, Turkish, Vietnamese; Pres. and Dir-Gen. ALAIN DE POUZILHAC.

Réseau France Outre-mer (RFO): 35–37 rue Danton, 92240 Malakoff; tel. 1-55-22-71-00; fax 1-55-22-74-76; e-mail rfo@rfo.fr; internet www.rfo.fr; f. 1983; frmly FR3 DOM-TOM; controls broadcasting in the French overseas territories; 10 local stations providing 2 radio networks, 2 television channels, the latter broadcasting material from various state and private channels as well as local programmes, and 1 satellite television channel; Dir CLAUDE ESCLATINE.

Independent Radio

BFM: 12 rue d'Oradour sur Glane, 75015 Paris; tel. 1-71-19-11-81; fax 1-71-19-11-80; e-mail stemplet@radiobfm.com; internet www.radiobfm.com; f. 1992; broadcasts on cable and 14 FM frequencies; politics, economics; Pres. ALAIN WEILL; Dir-Gen. NICOLAS LESPAULE.

Chérie FM: 22 rue Boileau, 75203 Paris Cedex 16; tel. 1-40-71-40-00; e-mail vgrandclaude@nrj.fr; internet www.cheriefm.fr; broadcasts popular music and entertainment programming on FM nationwide; mem. of Groupe NRJ.

Europe 1: 26 bis rue François, 75008 Paris; tel. 1-53-35-72-60; fax 1-47-23-19-00; e-mail courrier@europe1.fr; internet www.europe1.fr; owned by Groupe Lagardère, which also owns Europe 2 (for younger listeners) and RFM; broadcasting on long wave and 99 FM frequencies; Pres. DENIS OLIVENNES.

Nostalgie: 22 rue Boileau, 75203 Paris Cedex 16; tel. 1-40-71-40-00; e-mail sbosc@nrj.fr; internet www.nostalgie.fr; mem. of Groupe NRJ; broadcasts popular music and entertainment programming on FM nation-wide; Dir STÉPHANE BOSC.

NRJ: 22 rue Boileau, 75203 Paris Cedex 16; tel. 1-40-71-40-00; e-mail vgrandclaude@nrj.fr; internet www.nrj.fr; broadcasts contemporary popular music and entertainment programming on FM nation-wide; Pres. and Dir-Gen. JEAN-PAUL BAUDECROUX.

Radio Classique: 12 bis place Henri Bergson, 75382 Paris Cedex 08; tel. 1-40-08-50-00; fax 1-40-08-50-80; internet www.radioclassique.fr; f. 1983; classical music; Pres. FRANCIS MOREL.

Radio Monte-Carlo (RMC): 12 rue d'Oradour sur Glane, 75740 Paris Cedex 15; tel. 1-71-19-11-91; fax 1-71-19-11-90; internet www.rmcinfo.fr; broadcasting on long wave and 148 FM frequencies; information, talk and sports programmes.

RTL: 22 rue Bayard, 75008 Paris; tel. 1-41-86-21-49; fax 1-40-70-42-72; e-mail contact@rtl.fr; internet www.rtl.fr; broadcasting on long wave and 150 FM frequencies; CEO CHRISTOPHER BALDELLI.

Skyrock: 37 bis rue Grenéta, 75002 Paris; tel. 1-44-88-82-00; fax 1-44-88-89-57; internet www.skyrock.com; f. 1986; contemporary rap and hip-hop music; Pres. PIERRE BELLANGER; Dir-Gen. FRANK CHENEAU.

Television

In November 2011 France completed the transfer from analogue to digital television.

State-controlled Television

France Télévisions: 7 esplanade Henri-de-France, 75907 Paris; tel. 1-56-22-60-00; fax 1-56-22-60-21; internet www.francetelevisions.fr; f. 1992; supervisory authority for the national public television networks (France 2, France 3 and France 5: see below); Pres. RÉMY PFLIMLIN; Sec.-Gen. YVES ROLLAND.

France 2: 7 esplanade Henri-de-France, 75907 Paris Cedex 15; tel. 1-56-22-42-42; fax 1-56-22-55-87; e-mail contact@france2.fr; internet www.france2.fr; f. 1975; general programmes for a nation-wide audience; Dir-Gen. BERTRAND MOSCA.

France 3 (F3): 7 esplanade Henri-de-France, 75907 Paris Cedex 15; tel. 1-56-22-30-30; internet www.france3.fr; f. 1975 as France Régions 3 (FR3); general programmes for a nation-wide audience (with a larger proportion of cultural and educational programmes than France 2), and regional programmes transmitted from 13 regional stations; Dir-Gen. FRANÇOIS GUILBEAU.

France 4: 7 esplanade Henri-de-France, 75907 Paris Cedex 15; tel. 1-56-22-68-68; fax 1-56-22-68-69; e-mail yann.renoard@francetv.fr; internet www.france4.fr; f. 2005; 100% owned by France Télévisions; digital TV station; creative and cultural programming; Dir-Gen. EMMANUELLE GUILBART.

France 5: 2–4 rue Horace Vernet, 92785 Issy-les-Moulineaux Cedex 09; tel. 1-56-22-91-91; e-mail telespectateurs@france5.fr; internet www.france5.fr; f. 1994 as La Cinquième; present name adopted 2002; educational programmes and documentaries; Dir-Gen. BRUNO PATINO.

France 24: 5 rue des Nations Unies, 92445 Issy-les-Moulineaux; tel. 1-73-01-24-24; fax 1-73-01-24-56; e-mail webdesk@france24.com; internet www.france24.com; f. 2006; jointly owned by TF1 and France Télévisions; cable, satellite and internet broadcasts; 24-hour news broadcasts in Arabic, English and French; aims to present international news from a French perspective; CEO ALAIN DE POUZILHAC.

ARTE France: 8 rue Marceau, 92785 Issy-les-Moulineaux Cedex 09; tel. 1-55-00-77-77; fax 1-55-00-77-00; internet www.arte.tv; f. 1992 to replace La Sept; arts, cultural programmes, in French and German; Pres. VÉRONIQUE CAYLA; Dir-Gen. ANNE DURUPTY.

TV5 Monde: 131 ave de Wagram, 75017 Paris; tel. 1-44-18-55-55; internet www.tv5.org; f. 1984; broadcasts French-language programmes via satellite and cable to 203 countries world-wide; 49% owned by Audiovisuel Extérieur de la France, 12.58% by France Télévisions and 3.29% by ARTE France; Pres. and Dir-Gen. ALAIN DE POUZILHAC; Dir of Programmes FREDERICK-LOUIS BOULAY.

Television programmes for France's overseas departments and territories are provided by Réseau France Outre-mer (see under Radio).

Independent Television

Canal Plus: 1 place du Spectacle, 92863 Issy-Les-Moulineaux Cedex 9; tel. 1-71-35-35-35; fax 1-44-25-12-34; internet www.canalplus.fr; f. 1984; 80% owned by Vivendi, 20% by Groupe Lagadère; coded programmes financed by audience subscription; uncoded programmes financed by advertising sold by Canal Plus; specializes in drama (including films) and sport; launched a 'pay-per-view' service for sports events in 1996; produces 21 theme channels in 6 countries; Pres. and Dir-Gen. BERTRAND MÉHEUT.

demain.tv: 1 rue Patry, 92220 Bagneux; tel. 1-45-36-89-00; fax 1-45-36-89-01; e-mail contact@demain.fr; internet www.demain.fr; f. 1997; information about employment for job-seekers; Dir-Gen. EMMANUEL DES MOUTIS.

Direct8: Tour Bolloré, 31-32 quai de Dion-Bouton, 92811 Puteaux; tel. 1-46-96-48-88; fax 1-46-96-40-28; e-mail emissions@direct8.net; internet www.direct8.fr; f. 2005; free-to-air digital television channel; 60% owned by Groupe Canal Plus and 40% owned by Bolloré Média; Pres. VINCENT BOLLORÉ; Dir of Programmes GUY LAGACHE.

Gulli: 12 rue d'Oradour-sur-Glane, 75015 Paris; tel. 1-56-36-55-55; fax 1-56-36-55-59; e-mail tachaine@gullitv.fr; internet www.gullitv.fr; f. 2005; free-to-air digital television channel for children; Dir-Gen. ANTOINE VILLENEUVE.

i>TELE: 6 allée de la 2ème DB, 75015 Paris; tel. 1-53-91-50-00; fax 1-53-91-51-45; e-mail communication.itele@canal-plus.com; internet www.itele.fr; f. 1999; free-to-air digital television channel; 24-hr news broadcasts; part of Groupe Canal Plus; Dir-Gen. CÉCILIA RAGUENEAU.

LCI (La Chaîne Info): 1 Quai du Point du Jour, 92656 Boulogne-Billancourt Cedex; tel. 1-41-41-12-34; e-mail ccomfi@tf1.fr; internet lci.tf1.fr; f. 1994; news, information; part of Groupe TF1; Pres. NONCE PAOLINI; Dir-Gen. ERIC REVEL.

M6: 89 ave Charles de Gaulle, 92575 Neuilly-sur-Seine Cedex; tel. 1-41-92-61-61; fax 1-41-92-66-10; e-mail pholl@m6.fr; internet www.m6.fr; f. 1986 as TV6; re-formed as M6 1987; 48.43% owned by RTL Group; subsidiaries include W9 (a free-to-air digital television channel); specializes in drama, music and magazines; Chair., Man. Bd NICOLAS DE TAVERNOST.

NT1: 132 ave du Président Wilson, 93213 La Plaine-Saint-Denis; tel. 1-49-22-20-01; fax 1-49-22-20-71; e-mail contact@nt1.fr; internet www.nt1.tv; free-to-air digital television channel; owned by AB Groupe; Pres. CLAUDE BERDA.

Télévision Française 1 (TF1): 1 quai du Point du Jour, 92656 Boulogne-Billancourt Cedex; tel. 1-41-41-12-34; fax 1-41-41-28-40; internet www.tf1.fr; f. 1975 as a state-owned channel, privatized 1987; 43.1% owned by Bouygues SA; general programmes; Pres. and Dir-Gen. NONCE PAOLINI.

Finance

(cap. = capital; res = reserves; dep. = deposits; m. = million; brs = branches; amounts in euros)

BANKING

Central Bank

Banque de France: 31 rue Croix des Petits Champs, 75001 Paris; tel. 1-42-92-42-92; fax 1-42-92-45-00; e-mail infos@banque-france.fr; internet www.banque-france.fr; f. 1800; nationalized 1946; became independent 1994; acts as banker to the Treasury, issues bank notes, controls credit and money supply and administers France's gold and currency assets; in 1993 the Assemblée nationale approved legislation to make the Banque de France an independent central bank, with a General Council to supervise activities and appoint the principal officials, and a 9-member monetary policy committee, independent of government control, to be in charge of French monetary policy; a member of the European System of Central Banks since June 1998; cap. and res 25,870m., dep. 118,397m., total assets 506,050m. (Dec. 2009); Gov. CHRISTIAN NOYER; 130 brs.

Financing Institution

Société de financement de l'économie française (SFEF): Paris; f. Oct. 2008 to assist the banking sector in the financial crisis; 66% owned by a group of 7 banks, 34% owned by the state; provider of government-guaranteed loans to banks; Chair. FRANÇOISE MALRIEU; Dir-Gen. HENRY RAYMOND.

State Savings Bank

Caisse des dépôts et consignations: 56 rue de Lille, 75356 Paris Cedex 07; tel. 1-58-50-00-00; fax 1-58-50-02-46; internet www.caissedesdepots.fr; f. 1816; manages state savings system, holds widespread investments in industrial cos; res 3,434m., dep. 85,634m., total assets 269,520m. (Dec. 2010); Dir-Gen. AUGUSTIN DE ROMANET; 1 br.

Commercial Banks

Allianz Banque: Tour Neptune, 20 place de Seine, La Défense, 92400 Courbevoie; tel. 1-53-24-48-48; fax 1-53-24-48-41; e-mail serviceclient@banqueagf.fr; internet www.allianzbanque.fr; f. 2000; affiliated to Group Allianz; Pres. PASCAL THÉBÉ; Dir-Gen. FABIEN WATHLÉ.

Arkea Banque Enterprises et Institutionnels: allée Louis Lichou, 29480 Le Relecq-Kerhuon Cedex; tel. 2-99-29-92-00; fax 2-98-43-83-03; e-mail banque-ei@arkea.com; internet www.arkea-banque-ei.com; f. 1985; present name adopted 2000; subsidiary of Crédit Mutuel Arkéa; cap. 152.6m., res 77.6m., dep. 3,700.8m. (Dec. 2009); Chair. MARCEL GARNIER; Pres., Executive Bd GILBERT RICHARD.

Banca Intesa (France): 23 rue Linois, 75725 Paris Cedex 15; tel. 1-45-23-72-22; fax 1-45-23-70-90; e-mail hoff@bcif.fr; internet www.bcif.fr; f. 1918 as Banca Commerciale Italiana (France); present name adopted 2003; 99.99% owned by Intesa Sanpaolo SpA (Italy); cap. 160.3m., res 34.9m., dep. 788.5m. (Dec. 2006); Chair. ALBERTO VALDEMBRI; Dir-Gen. EUGENIO GUICCIARDI.

Banque BIA: 67 ave Franklin D. Roosevelt, 75008 Paris; tel. 1-53-76-62-62; fax 1-42-89-09-59; e-mail contact@bia-paris.fr; internet www.bia-paris.fr; f. 1975 as Banque Intercontinentale Arabe; present name adopted 2006; 50% owned by Banque Extérieure d'Algérie, 50% by Libyan Arab Foreign Bank; cap. 158.1m., res 1.6m., dep. 966.5m. (Dec. 2010); Chair. MUHAMMAD LOUKAL.

Banque de Bretagne: 18 quai Duguay-Trouin, 35084 Rennes Cedex; tel. 2-99-01-75-75; fax 2-99-01-75-00; internet www.bdbretagne.com; f. 1909; 100% owned by BNP Paribas; cap. 52.9m., res 13.4m., dep. 2,464.4m. (Dec. 2010); Pres. JEAN-CLAUDE LALLEMENT; 70 brs.

Banque CIC Est: 31 rue Jean Wenger-Valentin, 67958 Strasbourg Cedex 9; tel. 3-88-37-61-23; fax 3-88-37-61-81; internet www.cic.fr; f. 2008 from merger of CIC Banque SNVB and CIC Banque CIAL; 100% owned by Crédit Industriel et Commercial; cap. 225.0m., res 905.8m., dep. 46.7m. (Dec. 2008); Chair. PHILIPPE VIDAL; Gen. Mans LUC DYMARSKI, PIERRE JACHEZ.

Banque CIC Sud Ouest: 42 cours du Chapeau Rouge, 33000 Bordeaux; tel. 5-56-00-59-50; fax 5-57-85-55-74; internet www.cic.fr/sb; f. 1880 as Société Bordelaise de Crédit Industriel et Commercial et de Dépôts; present name adopted in 2010; 100% owned by Crédit Industriel et Commercial; cap. 155m., res 49m., dep. 7,430m. (Dec. 2009); Chair. and Dir-Gen. JEAN-JACQUES TAMBURINI; 209 brs.

Banque CIO-BRO: BP 84001, 2 ave Jean-Claude Bonduelle, 44040 Nantes Cedex 1; tel. 0-83-97-89-37; fax 2-40-12-93-80; e-mail cio-international@cio.cic.fr; internet www.cic.fr/cio-bro; f. 2006 by merger of Crédit Industriel de l'Ouest (f. 1957) and Banque Régionale de l'Ouest (f. 1913); 100% owned by Crédit Industriel et Commercial; Chair. MICHEL MICHENKO; Man. Dir JEAN-PIERRE BICHON.

Banque de l'Economie du Commerce et de la Monétique: 34 rue du Wacken, 67913 Strasbourg Cedex 9; tel. 3-88-14-74-74; fax 3-88-14-75-10; e-mail becm@becm.creditmutuel.fr; internet www.becm.fr; f. 1992 as Banque de l'Economie—Crédit Mutuel; cap. 378.3m., dep. 1,546.7m., total assets 8,320.4m. (Dec. 2006); Chief Exec. RENÉ DANGEL; 37 brs.

Banque Espírito Santo et de la Vénétie: 45 ave Georges Mandel, 75116 Paris; tel. 1-44-34-48-00; fax 1-44-34-48-48; e-mail besv@besv.fr; internet www.besv.fr; f. 1945; present name adopted 1998; absorbed Via Banque in 2002; 42% owned by Espirito Santo Financial Group SA (Luxembourg); cap. 75.1m., res 65.8m., dep. 301m. (Dec. 2010); Pres. PHILLIPE GUIRAL.

Banque Fédérative du Crédit Mutuel: 34 rue du Wacken, 67000 Strasbourg; tel. 3-88-14-88-14; fax 3-88-14-67-00; internet www.bfcm.creditmutuel.fr; f. 1895; cap. 1,302m., res 7,726m., dep. 133,199m. (Dec. 2010); Pres. and Chair. ETIENNE PFLIMLIN; Dir-Gen. MICHEL LUCAS; 16 brs.

Banque Nationale de Paris Intercontinentale: 12 rue Chauchat, 75009 Paris; tel. 1-40-14-22-11; fax 1-40-14-69-34; internet www.bnpgroup.com; f. 1940; present name adopted 1972; 100% owned by BNP Paribas; cap. 30.5m., res 5.0m., dep. 8.9m. (Dec. 2008); Chair. and Dir-Gen. BAUDOUIN PROT.

Banque Neuflize OBC: 3 ave Hoche, 75008 Paris; tel. 1-56-21-70-00; fax 1-56-21-84-60; internet www.neuflizeobc.fr; f. 1966 as De Neuflize, Schlumberger, Mallet & Cie; acquired clients of fmr Banque OBC—Odier Bungener Courvoisier and adopted present name 2006; 100% owned by ABN AMRO France; private banking; cap. 383.5m., res 168.3m., dep. 4,981.9m. (Dec. 2010); Chair., Supervisory Bd CHRIS VOGELZANG; Pres. and Chair., Management Bd PHILLIPE VAYSSETTES; 12 brs.

Banque Palatine: 42 rue d'Anjou, 75382 Paris Cedex 08; tel. 1-55-27-94-94; e-mail contact@palatine.fr; internet www.palatine.fr; f. 1971; fmrly Banque Sanpaolo; present name adopted 2005; 100% owned by Caisse Nationale des Caisses d'Epargne; cap. 538.8m., res 172.7m., dep. 7,615.9m. (Dec. 2010); Chair. NICOLAS MERINDOL; Pres. DANIEL KARYOTIS; 60 brs.

BNP Paribas: 16 blvd des Italiens, 75009 Paris; tel. 1-40-14-45-46; fax 1-40-14-69-40; internet www.bnpparibas.com; f. 2000 by merger of Banque Nationale de Paris and Paribas; cap. 25,711m., res 169m., dep. 772,986m. (Dec. 2010); Pres. BAUDOUIN PROT; CEO JEAN-LAURENT BONNAFÉ.

Cetelem: 14 bis blvd de l'Hôpital, 75221 Paris Cedex 05; tel. 1-55-43-55-43; fax 1-55-43-55-30; e-mail frederic.tardy@cetelem.fr; internet www.cetelem.fr; f. 1953; owned by BNP Paribas; cap. 848.8m., res 1,423.3m., dep. 32,906.8m. (Dec. 2006); Chair. and CEO FRANÇOIS VILLEROY DE GALHAU.

CIC Nord Ouest: 33 ave le Corbusier, BP 567, 59800 Lille; tel. 3-20-12-64-64; fax 3-20-12-64-05; e-mail brouchbr@cmcic.fr; internet www.cic.fr; f. 2006 by merger of Banque Scalbert-Dupont (f. 1977) and Crédit Industriel de Normandie (f. 1932); 100% owned by Crédit Industriel et Commercial; cap. 591m., res 7,221m., dep. 214,842m. (Dec. 2009); Chair. STELLI PRÉMAOR; Gen. Man. COTTE ERIC.

Compagnie Financière Edmond de Rothschild Banque: 47 rue du Faubourg St Honoré, 75401 Paris Cedex 08; tel. 1-40-17-25-25; fax 1-40-17-24-02; e-mail info@lcfr.fr; internet www.lcf-rothschild.fr; f. 1971; present name adopted 1986; cap. 83.1m., res 187m., dep. 1,255.2m. (Dec. 2010); Chair., Exec. Bd MICHEL CICUREL; Gen. Man. GUY GRYMBERG.

Crédit Agricole Corporate and Investment Bank (Calyon): 9 quai Paul Doumer, 92920 Paris La Défense Cedex; tel. 1-41-89-00-00; fax 1-41-89-36-33; internet www.ca-cib.com; f. 1975 as Banque Indosuez, subsequently Crédit Agricole Indosuez and Calyon Corporate and Investment Bank; present name adopted 2010; 100% owned by Crédit Agricole; merchant and offshore banking; cap. 6,056m., res 7,545m., dep. 220,914m. (Dec. 2010); Pres. JEAN PAUL CHIFFLET; Chief Exec. JEAN YVES HOCHER; 15 brs in France, 44 outside France.

Crédit Foncier de France: 19 rue des Capucines, 75001 Paris Cedex 01; tel. 1-42-44-80-00; fax 1-42-44-86-99; e-mail cbuying-france@creditfoncier.fr; internet www.creditfoncier.fr; f. 1852; 100% owned by Caisses d'Epargne et de Prévoyance; mortgage banking; cap. 1,198m., res 1,157m., dep. 128,224m. (Dec. 2009); Chair., Bd of Dirs FRANÇOIS DROUIN; Chief Exec. FRANÇOIS BLANCARD; 200 brs.

Crédit Industriel et Commercial (CIC): 6 ave de Provence, 75452 Paris Cedex 09; tel. 1-45-96-96-96; fax 1-45-96-96-66; internet www.cic.fr; f. 1990 by merger; present name adopted 1999; 70.81% owned by Banque Fédérative du Crédit Mutuel; cap. 591m., res 7,221m., dep. 214,131m. (Dec. 2009); Chair., Supervisory Bd ETIENNE PFIMLIN; Chair., Management Bd MICHEL LUCAS.

Crédit du Nord: 59 blvd Haussmann, 75008 Paris; tel. 1-40-22-40-22; fax 3-20-57-74-05; internet www.credit-du-nord.fr; f. 1974 by merger; name changed as above in 1976; 80% owned by Société Générale; cap. 740.3m., res 1,019.1m., dep. 30,260.9m. (Dec. 2009); Pres. ALAIN PY; 675 brs.

Fortis Banque France: 29–30 quai de Dion Bouton, 92800 Puteaux; tel. 1-55-67-89-00; e-mail courrier@fortis.com; internet www.fortisbanque.fr; f. 1920 as Banque Parisienne de Crédit au Commerce et à l'Industrie; present name adopted 2000; 99.94% owned by Fortis Bank (Belgium); cap. 157.5m., res 201.2m., dep. 6,388.3m. (Dec. 2007); Pres. and Chair. of Bd MICHEL PÉBEREAU; 99 brs.

HSBC France: 103 ave des Champs-Elysées, 75419 Paris Cedex 08; tel. 1-40-70-70-40; fax 1-40-70-70-09; e-mail contact@hsbc.fr; internet www.hsbc.fr; 100% owned by HSBC Bank PLC (United Kingdom); f. 2005 by merger of CCF (fmrly Crédit Commercial de France) with 3 other banks; cap. 337.0m., res 154m., dep. 59,922m. (Dec. 2010); CEO CHRISTOPHE DE BACKER; 223 brs in France.

HSBC Hervet: 184 ave Frédéric et Irène Joliot Curie, 92729 Nanterre Cedex; tel. 1-57-66-52-56; fax 1-57-66-54-16; e-mail marketing@banque-hervet.fr; internet www.hsbc-hervet.fr; f. 1830; 97.9% owned by HSBC France; present name adopted 2005; Chair. of Bd and Pres. FRANÇOIS MORLAT; CEO JACQUES-EMMANUEL BLANCHET; 86 brs.

HSBC Private Bank France: 117 ave des Champs-Elysées, 75386 Paris Cedex 08; tel. 1-49-52-20-00; fax 1-49-52-20-99; internet www.hsbcprivatebankfrance.com; f. 2003 by merger; 100% owned by HSBC Holdings plc; cap. 43m., res 138.5m., dep. 869m. (Dec. 2009); Chief Exec. ANTOINE CAHUZAC.

LCL—Le Crédit Lyonnais: 19 blvd des Italiens, 75002 Paris; tel. 1-42-95-70-00; fax 1-42-68-37-19; internet www.lcl.com; f. 1863 as Crédit Lyonnais; present name adopted 2005; privatized 1999; acquired by Crédit Agricole in June 2003; cap. 1,848m., res 2,310m., dep. 77,802m. (Dec. 2010); Chair. of Bd GEORGES PAUGET; Chief Exec. CHRISTIAN DUVILLET; 1,950 brs.

Lyonnaise de Banque: 8 rue de la République, 69001 Lyon; tel. 4-78-92-02-12; fax 4-78-92-03-00; e-mail ddi@lb.cicomore.fr; internet www.cic.fr/lb; f. 1865 as Société Lyonnaise de Dépôts et de Crédit Industriel; name changed as above in 1988; 100% owned by Crédit Industriel et Commercial; cap. 260.8m., res 577.2m., dep. 27,653m. (Dec. 2009); Chair. and Chief Exec. RÉMY WEBER; 368 brs.

Natixis: 45 rue Saint Dominique, 75007 Paris Cedex 02; tel. 1-58-32-30-00; internet www.natixis.com; f. 1999 as Natexis Banques Populaires; present name adopted 2006; 71.54% owned by BPCE (France); cap. 4,653m., res 4,353m., dep. 189,359m. (Dec. 2010); Chair. FRANÇOIS PEROL; CEO LAURENT MIGNON.

Société Générale: Tour Société Générale, 17 cours Valmy, 92972 Paris La Défense; tel. 1-42-14-20-00; fax 1-53-43-87-69; internet www.socgen.com; f. 1864; name changed as above in 1983; cap. 933m., res 23,465m., dep. 536,147m. (Dec. 2010); Chair. FRÉDÉRIC OUDÉA; 2,000 brs in France.

Société Marseillaise de Crédit (SMC): 75 rue Paradis, 13006 Marseille; tel. 4-91-13-33-33; fax 4-91-13-33-16; e-mail infos@smc.fr; internet www.smc.fr; f. 1865; owned by Crédit du Nord (France); cap. 16.0m., res 244.2m., dep. 3,072.2m. (Dec. 2009); Chair. and Chief Exec. EMMANUEL BARTHÉLÉMY; Gen. Man. and Pres. OLIVIER DELAPORTE; 154 brs.

Union de Banques Arabes et Françaises (UBAF): 190 ave Charles de Gaulle, 92523 Neuilly-sur-Seine; tel. 1-46-40-61-01; fax 1-47-38-13-88; e-mail ubaf.paris@ubaf.fr; internet www.ubaf.fr; f. 1970; 47.01% owned by Crédit Agricole CIB, 52.68% by Arab interests; commercial, Islamic and merchant banking; cap. 250.7m., res 11.9m., dep. 1,147.6m. (Dec. 2010); Chair., Supervisory Bd FAROUK EL-OKDAH; Chair., Management Bd SERGE DE BEAUFORT.

VTB Bank (France) SA (BCEN—Eurobank): 79–81 blvd Haussmann, 75382 Paris Cedex 08; tel. 1-40-06-43-21; fax 1-40-06-48-48; internet www.vtb.fr; f. 1921 as Comptoir Parisien de Banque et de Change; changed name to Banque Commerciale pour l'Europe du Nord in 1972; present name adopted 2006; 87.04% owned by VTB Bank (Austria); cap. 185.3m., res –62m., dep. 286.3m. (Dec. 2009); Chair., Supervisory Council OGLA DERGUNOVA; Chair., Executive Bd RICHARD VORNBERG.

Co-operative and Savings Banks

BPCE: 50 ave Pierre Mendès, Paris Cedex 13; tel. 1-58-40-41-42; internet www.bpce.fr; f. 2009 by merger of Banque Fédérale des Banques Populaires (BFBP) with Caisse Nationale des Caisses d'Epargne (CNCE); controls and co-ordinates 20 co-operative Banques Populaires (including those listed below) and 17 Caisses d'Epargne; Chair. FRANÇOIS PÉROL.

Banque Populaire d'Alsace: 4 quai Kléber, 67000 Strasbourg; tel. 3-88-62-77-11; fax 3-88-62-70-35; e-mail contact@alsace.banquepopulaire.fr; internet www.alsace.banquepopulaire.fr; f. 2003 by merger of Banque Populaire de la Région Economique de Strasbourg and Banque Populaire du Haut Rhin; cap. 331m., res 155.4m., dep. 6,739.6m. (Dec. 2010); Pres. THIERRY CAHN; Dir-Gen. DOMINIQUE DIDON; 96 brs.

Banque Populaire Aquitaine Centre Atlantique: 10 quai des Queyries, 33072 Bordeaux Cedex; tel. 5-49-08-65-20; e-mail contact@bpaca.banquepopulaire.fr; internet www.bpaca.banquepopulaire.fr; formed by merger of Banque Populaire du Sud-Ouest and Banque Populaire Centre-Atlantique; Chair. JACQUES RAYNAUD; Gen. Man. DOMINIQUE GARNIER.

Banque Populaire Bourgogne Franche-Comté: 14 blvd de la Trémouille, BP 310, 21008 Dijon Cedex; tel. 8-20-33-75-00; fax 8-20-20-36-20; internet www.bpbfc.banquepopulaire.fr; f. 2002 by merger of Banque Populaire de Bourgogne and Banque Populaire de Franche-Comté, du Mâconnais et de l'Ain; cap. 437.7m., res 290.6m., dep. 9,874.4m. (Dec. 2010); Pres. MICHAEL GRASS; Dir-Gen. BERNARD JEANNIN; 151 brs.

Banque Populaire Côte d'Azur (BPCA): BP 241, 457 promenade des Anglais, 06024 Nice; tel. 4-93-21-52-00; fax 4-93-21-54-45; e-mail contact@cotedazur.banquepopulaire.fr; internet www.cotedazur.banquepopulaire.fr; f. 1986; present name adopted

2002; cap. 158.2m., res 302.2m., dep. 4,008.8m. (Dec. 2010); Pres. BERNARD FLEURY; Gen. Man. JEAN-FRANÇOIS COMAS; 90 brs.

Banque Populaire Loire et Lyonnais: 141 rue Garibaldi, BP 3152, 69003 Lyon; tel. 4-89-95-55-55; fax 4-78-71-03-99; e-mail contact@bp2l.banquepopulaire.fr; internet www.loirelyonnais.banquepopulaire.fr; f. 2000 by merger of Banque Populaire de Lyon and Banque Populaire de la Loire; cap. 202.5m., res 318.1m., dep. 5,777.9m. (Dec. 2009); Chair. JEAN BRUNET-LECOMTE; Gen. Man. OLIVIER DE MARIGNAN.

Banque Populaire du Massif Central: BP 53, 18 blvd Jean Moulin, 63002 Clermont-Ferrand; tel. 4-73-23-46-23; fax 4-73-23-47-99; internet www.massifcentral.banquepopulaire.fr; f. 1920; cap. 158m., res 73.7m., dep. 4,422m. (Dec. 2010); Gen. Man. CATHERINE HALBERSTADT.

Banque Populaire Rives de Paris: 76–78 ave de France, 75024 Paris Cedex 13; tel. 1-40-92-61-00; fax 1-46-57-61-53; internet www.rivesparis.banquepopulaire.fr; f. 2004 by merger of BICS-Banque Populaire and Banque Populaire Nord de Paris; cap. 579.9m., res 346.9m., dep. 13,955.7m. (Dec. 2010); Chair. MARC JARDIN; Gen. Man. JEAN CRITON.

BRED Banque Populaire: 18 quai de la Rapée, 75604 Paris Cedex 12; tel. 1-48-98-60-00; fax 1-40-04-71-57; e-mail webmaster@bred.fr; internet www.bred.fr; f. 1919; present name adopted 1994; cap. 1,759.3m., res -59.2m., dep. 17,412.4m. (Dec. 2010); Chair. STEVE GENTILI; Gen. Man. and Chief Exec. JEAN MICHEL LATY; 339 brs (including 70 in the French Overseas Departments).

Crédit Coopératif: BP 211, Parc de la Défense, 33 rue des Trois Fontanot, 92002 Nanterre; tel. 1-47-24-85-00; fax 1-47-24-89-25; e-mail din@coopanet.com; internet www.credit-cooperatif.coop; f. 1893; present name adopted 2001; joined the Banque Fédérale des Banques Populaires group in 2002; merged with Caisse Centrale de Crédit Coopératif in 2003; cap. 535.6m., res 315.3m., dep. 8,998.7m. (Dec. 2009); Chair., Pres. and Gen. Man. JEAN-LOUIS BANCEL.

Caisse Centrale du Crédit Mutuel: 88–90 rue Cardinet, 75847 Paris Cedex 17; tel. 1-44-01-10-10; fax 1-44-01-12-30; internet www.creditmutuel.com; f. 1963; central organization of 10 autonomous banks (Caisses Fédérales); cap. 125m., res 267.8m., dep. 5,978.2m. (Dec. 2011); Chair. BERNARD FLOURIOT; Gen. Man. ALAIN FRADIN.

Crédit Agricole: 91–93 blvd Pasteur, 75015 Paris; tel. 1-43-23-52-02; fax 1-43-23-20-28; internet www.credit-agricole.fr; f. 1920; central institution for co-operative banking group comprising 39 Caisses Regionales and a central bank (CNCA); emphasis on agribusiness; cap. 7,205m., res 37,199m., dep. 710,446m. (Dec. 2010); Pres. RENÉ CARRON; Chief Exec. JEAN LAURENT; 9,130 brs.

Crédit Mutuel Arkéa: 1 rue Louis Lichou, 29480 Le Relecq-Kerhoun; tel. 2-98-00-22-22; fax 2-98-00-27-24; internet www.arkea.com; f. 2002; co-operative and mutual savings bank; cap. 1,283m., res 2,040m., dep. 31,409.9m. (Dec. 2010); Chair. JEAN-PIERRE DENIS; Gen. Man. RONAN LE MOAL.

Supervisory Body

Association Française des Etablissements de Crédit et des Entreprises d'Investissement (AFECEI): 36 rue Taitbout, 75009 Paris; tel. 1-48-01-88-88; fax 1-48-24-13-31; e-mail atassi@afecei.asso.fr; internet www.afecei.asso.fr; f. 1984; advises Govt on monetary and credit policy and supervises the banking system; 14 mems; Pres. FRANÇOIS PEROL; Dir-Gen. ARIANE OBOLENSKY.

Banking Association

Fédération Bancaire Française: 18 rue La Fayette, 75440 Paris Cedex 09; tel. 1-48-00-52-52; fax 1-42-46-76-40; e-mail fbf@fbf.fr; internet www.fbf.fr; f. 1941; 450 mems; Pres. BAUDOUIN PROT; Dir-Gen. ARIANE OBOLENSKY.

STOCK EXCHANGE

Euronext Paris: 39 rue Cambon, 75001 Paris; tel. 1-49-27-10-00; fax 1-49-27-11-71; e-mail info@euronext.com; internet www.euronext.fr; formed in 2000 by merger of Amsterdam, Paris and Brussels exchanges, and joined in 2002 by the Lisbon stock exchange and the London futures exchange LIFFE; merged with New York Stock Exchange in 2007 to form NYSE Euronext; Chair. JAN-MICHIEL HESSELS.

Stock Exchange Associations

Autorité des Marchés Financiers (AMF): 17 place de la Bourse, 75082 Paris Cedex 2; tel. 1-53-45-60-00; fax 1-53-45-61-00; e-mail centrededoc@amf-france.org; internet www.amf-france.org; f. 2003 by merger of Commission des Opérations de Bourse and Conseil des Marchés Financiers; 350 mems (2007); Pres. JEAN-PIERRE JOUYET; Sec.-Gen. GÉRARD RAMEIX.

Fédération Française des Clubs d'Investissement (FFCI): 39 rue Cambon, 75001 Paris; tel. 1-42-60-12-47; fax 1-42-60-10-14; e-mail info@clubinvestissement.com; internet www.ffci.fr; f. 1968; fmrly Fédération Nationale des Associations de Clubs d'Investissement (FNACI); represents investment clubs in matters concerning public and political institutions; Pres. DOMINIQUE LEBLANC; Sec.-Gen. ALDO SICURANI.

INSURANCE

AG2R La Mondiale: 32 ave Emile Zola, Mons en Baroeul, 59370 Lille Cedex 9; tel. 3-20-67-37-00; internet www.ag2rlamondiale.fr; f. 1905; renamed as above in 2010 following merger of La Mondiale and AG2R; life insurance; Dir-Gen. ANDRÉ RENAUDIN.

Allianz (AGF): 87 rue de Richelieu, 75002 Paris Cedex 02; tel. 1-44-86-20-00; fax 1-44-86-42-42; e-mail ecrire@allianz.fr; internet www.allianz.fr; f. 1968 by merger; affiliated to Allianz (Germany); name changed as above 2009; insurance and reinsurance; Pres. JEAN-PHILIPPE THIERRY; Dirs-Gen. LAURENT MIGNON, FRANÇOIS THOMAZEAU, LOUIS DE MONTFERRAND, JEAN-FRANÇOIS LEQUOY.

Assurances du Crédit Mutuel IARD, SA: BP 373 R 10, 34 rue du Wacken, 67010 Strasbourg Cedex; tel. 3-88-14-90-90; fax 3-88-14-90-00; internet www.creditmutuel.fr; Pres. MICHEL LUCAS; Dir ALAIN FRADIN.

Aviva: 52 rue de la Victoire, 75009 Paris; e-mail veronique_eriaud@aviva.fr; internet www.aviva.fr; f. 1998 as CGU France by merger to incorporate fmr Abeille Assurances; present name adopted 2002; affiliated to CGNU Group (United Kingdom); CEO PHILIPPE MASO Y GUELL RIVET.

AXA Assurances IARD: 313 Terrasses de l'Arche, 92727 Nanterre Cedex; tel. 1-47-74-10-01; fax 1-47-74-10-01; internet www.axa.fr; CEO NICOLAS MOREAU; Chair., Management Bd HENRI DE CASTRIES.

Caisse Centrale des Assurances Mutuelles Agricoles: 8–10 rue d'Astorg, 75008 Paris; tel. 1-44-56-77-77; fax 1-44-56-79-46; e-mail relations.exterieures@groupama.com; internet www.groupama.com; affiliated to Groupama; CEO THIERRY MARTEL.

Caisse Nationale de Prévoyance-Assurances (CNP): 4 place Raoul Dautry, 75716 Paris Cedex 15; tel. 1-42-18-88-88; fax 1-42-34-70-14; internet www.cnp.fr; general insurance; Pres EDMOND ALPHANDÉRY; CEO GILLES BENOIST.

Cardif: 8 rue du Port, 92728 Nanterre Cedex; tel. 1-41-42-83-00; internet www.cardif.fr; general insurance; Dir-Gen. ERIC LOMBARD.

GAN Assurances: 8–10 rue d'Astorg, Paris 75008; tel. 1-70-94-20-00; fax 1-42-47-67-66; e-mail gan.rimbault.philippe@wanadoo.fr; internet www.ganassurances.fr; f. 1820, fire; f. 1830, life; f. 1865, accident; affiliated to Groupama; Pres. JEAN-FRANÇOIS LEMOUX; Dir ERIC GELPE.

Garantie Mutuelle des Fonctionnaires: 76 rue de Prony, 75857 Paris Cedex 17; tel. 1-47-54-10-10; fax 1-47-54-18-97; e-mail webgmf@gmf.fr; internet www.gmf.fr; f. 1934; Pres. and CEO THIERRY DEREZ.

Generali France: 11 blvd Haussmann, 75311 Paris Cedex 09; tel. 1-58-38-74-00; fax 1-58–38–74–01; e-mail dep-agence-web-interne@generali.fr; internet www.generali-patrimoine.fr; subsidiary of Groupe Generali (Italy); Pres. and CEO CLAUDE TENDIL.

Groupama Vie: 8–10 rue d'Astorg, 75008 Paris; tel. 1-49-31-31-31; fax 1-49-31-31-98; e-mail webmaster@groupama.fr; internet www.groupama.com; life insurance; Dir PIERRE BEAUMIN.

Mutuelles du Mans Assurances (MMA): 14 blvd Alexandre Oyon, 72030 Le Mans Cedex 09; tel. 2-43-41-72-72; fax 2-43-41-72-26; internet www.mma.fr; f. 1828; life and general insurance; comprises 3 companies: MMA-IARD, DAS and MMA-VIE; Pres. and Dir-Gen. JEAN-CLAUDE SEYS; Dir-Gen. JACQUES LENORMAND.

Predica: 50 rue de la Procession, 75724 Paris Cedex 15; tel. 1-43-23-58-00; fax 1-43-23-03-47; e-mail communication-pole-assurances@ca-predica.fr; internet www.ca-predica.fr; affiliated to Crédit Agricole; general insurance; Pres. GUY CHATEAU; Chair. GÉRARD OUVRIER BUFFET.

Previposte: BP 7162, 4 place Raoul Dautry, 75716 Paris Cedex 15; tel. 1-42-18-81-37; fax 1-42-18-94-94; life insurance; Pres. GÉRARD MÉNÉROUD; Dir MARTINE FRIANT.

Suravenir: BP 103, 232 rue Général Paulet, 29802 Brest Cedex 09; tel. 2-98-34-65-00; fax 2-98-34-65-11; e-mail relations-client@suravenir.fr; internet www.suravenir.fr; f. 1984; general insurance; Pres., Bd JEAN-PIERRE CORLAY; Pres., Management Bd HUMBERT DE FRESNOYE.

UAF Patrimoine: 50-56 rue de la Procession, 75015 Paris; internet www.uafpatrimoine.fr; life insurance; part of Predica; Dir ERIC MORVAN.

Insurance Associations

Chambre Syndicale des Courtiers d'Assurances (CSCA): 91 rue Saint Lazare, 75009 Paris; tel. 1-48-74-19-12; fax 1-42-82-91-10;

e-mail csca@csca.fr; internet www.csca.fr; f. 2006; c. 1,000 mems; Chair. DOMINIQUE SIZES.

Fédération Française des Courtiers d'Assurances et de Réassurances (FCA): 91 rue Saint Lazare, 75009 Paris; tel. 1-48-74-19-12; fax 1-42-82-91-10; e-mail csca@csca.fr; internet www.csca.fr; f. 1991; Chair. ROBERT LEBLANC; c. 700 mems.

Syndicat Français des Assureurs-Conseils: 14 rue de la Grange Batelière, 75009 Paris; tel. 1-55-33-51-51; fax 1-48-00-93-01; e-mail sfac@sfac-assurance.fr; internet www.sfac-assurance.fr; Pres. ALAIN MORICHON.

Fédération des Agents Généraux d'Assurances (AGEA): 104 rue Jouffroy d'Abbans, 75847 Paris Cedex 17; tel. 1-44-01-18-00; fax 1-43-18-72-60; e-mail regis.devaux@agea.fr; internet www.agea.fr; Pres. PHILIPPE DE ROBERT.

Fédération Française des Sociétés d'Assurances (FFSA): 26 blvd Haussmann, 75311 Paris; tel. 1-42-47-90-00; fax 1-42-47-93-11; internet www.ffsa.fr; f. 1937; Pres. BERNARD SPITZ; Sec.-Gen. GILLES WOLKOWITSCH.

Trade and Industry

GOVERNMENT AGENCIES

Agence Française pour les Investissements Internationaux (AFII) (Invest In France Agency—IFA): 77 blvd Saint-Jacques, 75680 Paris Cedex 14; tel. 1-44-87-17-17; fax 1-40-74-73-29; e-mail info@afii.fr; internet www.invest-in-france.org; f. 2001; promotes and assists foreign investment in France; Pres. DAVID APPIA; Man. Dir SERGE BOSCHER.

Conseil du Commerce de France: 40 blvd Malesherbes, 75008 Paris; tel. 1-40-15-03-03; fax 1-40-15-97-22; e-mail conseilducommerce@cdcf.com; internet www.cdcf.com; Pres. GÉRARD ATLAN; Sec.-Gen. FANNY FAVOREL-PIGE.

UBIFRANCE—l'Agence Française pour le développement international des entreprises: 77 blvd Saint-Jacques, 75998 Paris Cedex 14; tel. 1-40-73-30-00; fax 1-40-73-39-79; e-mail Claire.rocheteau@ubifrance.fr; internet www.ubifrance.fr; f. 2004 by merger of the Centre Français du Commerce Extérieur and the association UBIFrance; Minister-delegate for External Trade ANNE MARIE IDRAC; Dir-Gen. CHRISTOPHE LECOURTIER.

DEVELOPMENT ORGANIZATIONS

Agence pour la Création d'Entreprises (APCE): 14 rue Delambre, 75682 Paris Cedex 14; tel. 1-42-18-58-58; fax 1-42-18-58-00; e-mail info@apce.com; internet www.apce.com; Pres. JEAN-CLAUDE VOLOT; Dir-Gen. PHILIPPE MATHOT.

Groupe IDI: 18 ave Matignon, 75008 Paris; tel. 1-55-27-80-00; fax 1-40-17-04-44; e-mail idi@idi.fr; internet www.idi.fr; f. 1970 as Institut de Développement Industriel; provides venture capital, takes equity shares in small and medium-sized businesses; Chair. CHRISTIAN LANGLOIS MEURINNE; CEO F. MARMISSOLLE.

CHAMBERS OF COMMERCE

There are Chambers of Commerce in all the larger towns for all the more important commodities produced or manufactured.

Assemblée des Chambres Françaises de Commerce et d'Industrie: 45 ave de la Grande Armée, 75858 Paris Cedex 17; tel. 1-40-69-37-00; fax 1-47-20-61-28; e-mail contactsweb@acfci.cci.fr; internet www.acfci.cci.fr; f. 1964; unites 154 local and 21 regional Chambers of Commerce and Industry; Pres. JEAN-FRANÇOIS BERNARDIN.

Chambre de Commerce et d'Industrie de Paris: 27 ave de Friedland, 75382 Paris Cedex 08; tel. 1-55-65-55-65; fax 1-55-65-78-68; e-mail cpdp@ccip.fr; internet www.ccip.fr; f. 1803; 307,000 mems in Paris and surrounding regions (Hauts de Seine, Seine-Saint-Denis and Val de Marne); Pres. PIERRE SIMON; Dir-Gen. PIERRE TROUILLET.

INDUSTRIAL AND TRADE ASSOCIATIONS

Armateurs de France: 47 rue de Monceau, 75008 Paris; tel. 1-53-89-52-52; fax 1-53-89-52-53; e-mail info@armateursdefrance.org; internet www.armateursdefrance.org; f. 1903; fmrly Comité Central des Armateurs de France; shipping; Pres. CHRISTIAN GARIN; Delegate-Gen. ANNE-SOPHIE AVE; 110 mems.

Assemblée Permanente des Chambres d'Agriculture (APCA): 9 ave George V, 75008 Paris; tel. 1-53-57-10-10; fax 1-53-57-10-05; e-mail accueil@apca.chambagri.fr; internet paris.apca.chambagri.fr; f. 1929; agriculture; Pres. GREY VASSEUR; Dir-Gen. ROLAND BAUD.

Association Nationale des Industries Alimentaires (ANIA): 21 rue Leblanc, 75015 Paris; tel. 1-53-83-86-00; fax 1-53-83-92-37; e-mail infos@ania.net; internet www.ania.net; f. 1971; food produce; Pres. JEAN-RENÉ BUISSON.

Chambre Syndicale de l'Ameublement, Négoce de Paris et de l'Ile de France: 15 rue de la Cerisaie, 75004 Paris; tel. 1-42-72-13-79; fax 1-42-72-02-36; e-mail info@meubleparis.net; internet www.franceameublement.fr; f. 1860; furnishing; Chair. NICOLE PHILIBERT; 350 mems.

Chambre Syndicale des Céramistes et Ateliers d'Art de France: 8 rue Jadin, 75017 Paris; tel. 1-44-01-08-30; fax 1-44-01-08-35; e-mail info@ateliersdart.com; internet www.ateliersdart.com; f. 1886; craft and design trades; Chair. SERGE NICOLE; Sec.-Gen. NICOLE CRESTOU; 2,800 mems.

Comité des Constructeurs Français d'Automobiles: 2 rue de Presbourg, 75008 Paris; tel. 1-49-52-51-00; fax 1-47-23-74-73; e-mail ccfa@ccfa.fr; internet www.ccfa.fr; f. 1909; motor manufacturing; Chair. XAVIER FELS; 6 mems.

Comité National des Pêches Maritimes et des Elevages Marins (CNPMEM): 134 ave de Malakoff, 75116 Paris; tel. 1-72-71-18-00; fax 1-72-71-18-50; e-mail cnpmem@comite-peches.fr; internet www.comite-peches.fr; marine fisheries; Pres. PIERRE-GEORGES DACHICOURT.

Comité Professionnel du Pétrole: 212 ave Paul Doumer, 92508 Rueil-Malmaison Cedex; tel. 1-47-16-94-60; fax 1-47-08-10-57; e-mail contact@cpdp.org; internet www.cpdp.org; f. 1950; petroleum industry; 80 mems; Pres. OLIVIER GANTOIS.

Commissariat à l'Energie Atomique (CEA) (Atomic Energy Commission): Bâtement le ponant D, 25 rue Leblanc, 75015 Paris; tel. 1-64-50-20-59; fax 1-64-560-12-15; e-mail dcom@aramis.cea.fr; internet www.cea.fr; f. 1945; promotes the uses of nuclear energy in science, industry and national defence; involved in research on nuclear materials; reactor development; fundamental research; innovation and transfer of technologies; military applications; biotechnologies; robotics; electronics; new materials; radiological protection and nuclear safety; Gen. Administrator and High Commissioner BERNARD BIGOT.

Confédération des Industries Céramiques de France: 114 rue La Boétie, 75008 Paris; tel. 1-58-18-30-40; fax 1-42-66-09-00; e-mail cicf@ceramique.org; f. 1937; ceramic industry; Chair. PHILIPPE MAURISSET; Sec.-Gen. DELPHINE PALOUX-HUSSON; 85 mems, 5 affiliates.

Confédération du Négoce Bois-Matériaux (FFNB): 215 bis blvd St Germain, 75007 Paris; tel. 1-45-48-28-44; fax 1-45-48-42-89; e-mail contact@cnbm.fr; internet www.cnbm.fr; timber trade; Pres. GÉRAUD SPIRE; Dir-Gen. LAURENT MARTIN-SAINT-LÉON.

Les Entreprises du Medicament (LEEM): 88 rue de la Faisanderie, 75782 Paris Cedex 16; tel. 1-45-03-88-70; fax 1-45-03-39-25; e-mail dcre@leem.org; internet www.leem.org; fmrly Syndicat National de l'Industrie Pharmaceutique; pharmaceuticals; Chair. CHRISTIAN LAJOUX; 326 mem. cos.

FEBEA (France) (Fédération des Enterprises de la Beauté): 137 rue de l'Université, 75007 Paris; tel. 1-56-69-67-89; fax 1-56-69-67-90; e-mail febea@febea.fr; internet www.febea.fr; makers of perfume, cosmetics and toiletries; Pres. ALAIN GRANGÉ CABANE; 300 mems.

Fédération des Chambres Syndicales de l'Industrie du Verre: 114 rue la Boétie, 75008 Paris; tel. 1-42-65-60-02; fax 1-42-66-23-88; e-mail contact@fedeverre.fr; internet www.fedeverre.fr; f. 1874; glass industry; Pres. MICHEL GARDES.

Fédération des Chambres Syndicales des Minerais, Minéraux Industriels et Métaux non-Ferreux (FEDEM): 17 rue de l'Amiral Hamelin, 75016 Paris; tel. 1-40-76-44-0; e-mail contact@fedem.fr; internet www.fedem.fr; f. 1945; minerals and non-ferrous metals; Chair. CATHERINE TISSOT-COLLE; Delegate-Gen. CLAIRE DE LANGERON; 16 affiliated syndicates.

Fédération des Exportateurs de Vins et Spiritueux de France: 7 rue de Madrid, 75008 Paris; tel. 1-45-22-75-73; fax 1-45-22-94-16; e-mail contact@fevs.com; internet www.fevs.com; f. 1922 as Commission d'Exportation des Vins de France; exporters of wines and spirits; Pres. CLAUDE DE JOUVENCEL; 450 mems.

Fédération Française de l'Acier: 5 rue Luigi Cherubini, 93212 La Plaine Saint-Denis Cedex; tel. 1-71-92-20-18; fax 1-71-92-25-00; e-mail svp.clients@ffa.fr; internet www.ffa.fr; f. 1945; steel-making; Pres. PHILIPPE DARMAYAN.

Fédération Française du Bâtiment: 33 ave Kléber, 75784 Paris Cedex 16; tel. 1-40-69-51-00; fax 1-45-53-58-77; e-mail ffbbox@ffb.fr; internet www.ffbatiment.fr; f. 1906; building trade; Pres. DIDIER RIDORET; 57,000 mems.

Fédération Française des Industries Lainière et Cotonnière (FFILC): BP 121, 37–39 rue de Neuilly, 92582 Clichy Cedex; tel. 1-47-56-31-48; fax 1-47-37-06-20; e-mail uitcotonlaine@textile.fr; internet www.textile.fr; f. 1902; manufacturing of wool, cotton and associated textiles; Pres. CAMILLE AMALRIC; 400 mems.

Fédération Française de la Tannerie-Mégisserie (FFTM): 122 rue de Provence, 78087 Paris; tel. 1-45-22-96-45; fax 1-42-93-37-44; e-mail fftm@leatherfrance.com; internet www.leatherfrance.com; f. 1885; leather industry; 100 mems.

Fédération des Industries Electriques, Electroniques et de Communication (FIEEC): 11–17 rue Hameline, 75783 Paris Cedex 16; tel. 1-45-05-70-70; fax 1-45-53-03-93; e-mail comm@fieec.fr; internet www.fieec.fr; f. 1925; electrical and electronics industries; Chair. HENRI STARCK; Delegate-Gen. ERIC JOURDE; c. 1,000 mems.

Fédération des Industries Mécaniques: 39–41 rue Louis Blanc, 92400 Courbevoie; tel. 1-47-17-60-00; fax 1-47-17-64-37; e-mail webmaster@mail.fimeca.com; internet www.fim.net; f. 1840; mechanical and metal-working; Pres. JÉRÔME FRANTZ; Dir-Gen. CLAUDE CHARRIER.

Fédération des Industries Nautiques: 200 Port de Javel Haut, 75015 Paris; tel. 1-44-37-04-00; fax 1-45-77-21-88; e-mail info@fin.fr; internet www.fin.fr; f. 1964; pleasure-boating; Pres. JEAN-FRANÇOIS FOUNTAINE; Gen. Man. PHILLIPPE FOURRIER; 750 mems.

Fédération Nationale du Bois: 6 rue François 1er, 75008 Paris; tel. 1-56-69-52-00; fax 1-56-69-52-09; e-mail infos@fnbois.com; internet www.fnbois.com; f. 1884; timber and wood products; Chair. LAURENT DENORMANDIE; 1,850 mems.

Fédération Nationale des Chambres Syndicales des Horlogers, Bijoutiers, Joailliers et Orfèvres (HBJO): 249 rue Saint Martin, 75003 Paris; tel. 1-44-54-34-00; fax 1-44-54-34-07; e-mail fedhbjo@wanadoo.fr; internet www.fedehbjo.com; jewellery, watch- and clock-making; Pres. GÉRARD ATLAN; Delegate-Gen. CAROLE GROUESY; 1,300 mems.

Fédération Nationale de l'Industrie Laitière: 42 rue de Châteaudun, 75314 Paris Cedex 09; tel. 1-49-70-72-85; fax 1-42-80-63-94; e-mail fnil@atla.asso.fr; internet www.maison-du-lait.com; f. 1946; dairy products; Pres. OLIVIER PICOT.

Fédération Nationale des Industries Electrométallurgiques, Eléctrochimiques et Connexes (FNIEEC): 30 ave de Messine, 75008 Paris; tel. 1-40-76-44-53; fax 1-45-63-61-54; Chair. JACQUES GANI.

Fédération Nationale de la Musique: 62 rue Blanche, 75009 Paris; tel. 1-48-74-09-29; fax 1-42-81-19-87; f. 1964; includes Chambre Syndicale de la Facture Instrumentale, Syndicat National de l'Edition Phonographique and other groups; musical instruments, publications and recordings; Chair. PIERRE HENRY; Sec.-Gen. FRANÇOIS WELLEBROUCK.

Les Fondeurs de France: 45 rue Louis Blanc, 92038 Paris La Défense Cedex; tel. 1-43-34-76-67; fax 1-43-34-76-37; e-mail contact@fondeursdefrance.org; internet www.fondeursdefrance.org; f. 1897; metal casting; Dir-Gen. JEAN-LUC BRILLANCEAU; 300 mems.

Groupe Intersyndical de l'Industrie Nucléaire (GIIN): 39–41 rue Louis Blanc, 92400 Courbevoie; tel. 1-47-17-62-78; fax 1-47-17-68-91; e-mail contact@giin.fr; internet www.giin.fr; f. 1959; aims to promote the interests of the French nuclear industry; 200 member firms.

Groupement des Industries de Construction et d'Activités Navales: 47 rue de Monceau, 75008 Paris; tel. 1-53-89-52-00; fax 1-53-89-52-15; e-mail contact@gican.asso.fr; internet www.gican.asso.fr; f. 2009; owned by the French marine industry; Chair. JEAN-MARIE POIMBOEUF; Delegate-Gen. JEAN-MARIE CARNET.

Groupement des Industries Françaises Aéronautiques et Spatiales (GIFAS): 8 rue Galilée, 75116 Paris; tel. 1-44-43-17-00; fax 1-40-70-91-41; e-mail infogifas@gifas.asso.fr; internet www.gifas.asso.fr; f. 1910; aerospace industry; Pres. JEAN-PAUL HERTEMAN; 273 mems.

Syndicat Général des Cuirs et Peaux: 18 blvd Montmartre, 75009 Paris; tel. 1-45-08-08-54; fax 1-40-39-97-31; e-mail cuirsetpeaux@wanadoo.fr; internet www.sgcp.net; f. 1977; present name adopted 1996; untreated leather and hides; Chair. DANIEL BELLIARD; 22 mems.

Syndicat Général des Fabricants d'Huile et de Tourteaux de France: 118 ave Achille Peretti, 92200 Neuilly-sur-Seine; tel. 1-46-37-22-06; fax 1-46-37-15-60; f. 1928; edible oils; Pres. HENRI RIEUX; Sec.-Gen. JEAN-CLAUDE BARSACQ.

Union des Armateurs à la Pêche de France: 59 rue des Mathurins, 75008 Paris; tel. 1-42-66-32-60; fax 1-47-42-91-12; e-mail uapf75@wanadoo.fr; f. 1945; fishing vessels; Chair. PATRICK SOISSON; Delegate-Gen. MARC GHIGLIA.

Union des Fabricants de Porcelaine de Limoges: 7 bis rue du Général Cérez, 87000 Limoges; tel. 5-55-77-29-18; fax 5-55-77-36-81; e-mail ufpl@porcelainelimoges.org; porcelain manufacturing; Chair. BERTRAND RAYNAUD; Sec.-Gen. MARIE-THÉRÈSE PASQUET.

Union des Industries Chimiques (UIC): Le Diamant A, 14 rue de la République, 92800 Paris La Défense Cedex 10; tel. 1-46-53-11-00; fax 1-46-96-00-59; e-mail uicgeneral@uic.fr; internet www.uic.fr; f. 1860; chemical industry; Pres. OLIVIER HOMOLLE; 25 affiliated unions.

Union des Industries Métallurgiques et Minières (UIMM): 56 ave de Wagram, 75017 Paris; tel. 1-40-54-20-20; fax 1-47-66-22-74; e-mail uimm@uimm.fr; internet www.uimm.fr; metallurgy and mining; Chair. FRÉDÉRIC SAINT-GEOURS; 223 mems.

Union des Industries Papetières pour les Affaires Sociales (UNIPAS): 154 blvd Haussmann, 75008 Paris; tel. 1-53-89-25-25; fax 1-53-89-25-26; e-mail contact@unipas.org; internet www.unipas.org; f. 1864; paper, cardboard and cellulose; Chair. JEAN-PIERRE QUÉRÉ; Sec.-Gen. ARNAUD COUVREUR.

Union des Industries Textiles: BP 121, 37–39 rue de Neuilly, 92113 Clichy Cedex; tel. 1-47-56-31-00; fax 1-47-30-25-28; e-mail uit@textile.fr; internet www.textile.fr; f. 1900; textiles; Chair. LUCIEN DEVEAUX; 649 mems. cos (2010).

Union des Métiers et des Industries de l'Hôtellerie (UMIH): 22 rue d'Anjou, 75008 Paris; tel. 1-44-94-19-94; fax 1-47-42-15-20; e-mail fnih@imagenet.fr; internet www.umih.fr; hospitality; Chair. ROLAND HÉGUY.

Union Nationale de l'Imprimerie et de la Communication (UNIC): 68 blvd Saint Marcel, 75005 Paris; tel. 1-44-08-64-46; fax 1-43-36-09-51; e-mail unic@com-unic.fr; internet www.com-unic.fr; f. 2008 by merger of Fédération de l'Imprimerie et de la Communication Graphique (FICG) and Syndicat National des Industries de la Communication Graphique et de l'Imprimerie Françaises (SICOGIF); printing, communication and design; Pres. JACQUES CHIRAT; 1,300 mems.

Union professionnelle artisanale (UPA): 53 rue Ampère, 75017 Paris; tel. 1-47-63-31-31; fax 1-47-63-31-10; e-mail upa@upa.fr; internet www.upa.fr; f. 1975; unites crafts and other manual workers in 3 trade bodies and more than 100 regional organizations; Chair. JEAN LARDIN.

EMPLOYERS' ORGANIZATIONS

Association Française des Entreprises Privées (AGREF): Paris; represents the interests of 81 of the largest enterprises in France; Chair. JEAN-MARTIN FOLZ.

Centre des Jeunes Dirigeants d'Entreprise (CJD): 19 ave Georges V, 75008 Paris; tel. 1-53-23-92-50; fax 1-40-70-15-66; e-mail cjd@cjd.net; internet www.cjd.net; f. 1938; asscn for young entrepreneurs (under 45 years of age); Pres. GONTRAN LEJEUNE; 3,000 mems.

Confédération Générale des Petites et Moyennes Entreprises (CGPME): 10 terrasse Bellini, 92806 Puteaux Cedex; tel. 1-47-62-73-73; fax 1-47-73-08-86; e-mail contact@cgpme.org; internet www.cgpme.org; small and medium-sized cos; Chair. JEAN-FRANÇOIS ROUBAUD.

Les Entrepreneurs et Dirigeants Chrétiens (Les EDC): 24 rue Hamelin, 75116 Paris; tel. 1-45-53-09-01; fax 1-47-27-43-32; e-mail lesedc@lesedc.org; internet www.lesedc.org; fmrly Centre Français du Patronat Chrétien; asscn of Christian employers; Nat. Pres. PIERRE DESCHAMPS.

Entreprise et Progrès: 41 blvd Malesherbes, 75008 Paris; tel. 1-45-74-52-62; fax 1-45-74-52-63; e-mail enterprise.et.progres@wanadoo.fr; internet www.entreprise-progres.net; f. 1970; represents 110 enterprises; Pres. PHILIPPE CHARRIER; Sec.-Gen. BEATRICE BOURGES.

Entreprises de Taille Humaine Indépendantes et de Croissance (ETHIC): 260 blvd Saint Germain, 75007 Paris; tel. 1-71-18-33-68; fax 1-71-18-33-76; e-mail asdevillers@ethic.fr; internet www.ethic.fr; f. 1976; represents small enterprises and promotes ethical values in business; Pres. SOPHIE DE MENTHON.

Mouvement des Entreprises de France (MEDEF): 55 ave Bosquet, 75330 Paris Cedex 07; tel. 1-53-59-19-19; fax 1-45-51-20-44; internet www.medef.fr; f. 1998 to replace Conseil National du Patronat Français; employers' asscn grouping 700,000 cos from all sectors of activity in 85 professional feds and 152 regional orgs; Pres. LAURENCE PARISOT; Dir-Gen. PIERRE-HENRI RICAUD.

UTILITIES

Electricity

EDF: 22–30 ave de Wagram, 75382 Paris Cedex 8; tel. 1-40-42-79-40; fax 1-40-42-22-22; e-mail masteredf@edfgdf.fr; internet www.edf.fr; established under the Electricity and Gas Industry Nationalization Act of 1946 as Electricité de France; responsible for generating and supplying electricity for distribution to consumers in metropolitan France; 15% of the company was sold to the private sector in November 2005; Chair. and CEO HENRI PROGLIO.

Gas

GDF SUEZ: 23 rue Philibert Delorme, 75840 Paris Cedex 17; tel. 1-47-54-24-35; fax 1-47-54-74-42; internet www.gdfsuez.com; established as Gaz de France under the Electricity and Gas Industry

Nationalization Act of 1946; responsible for distribution of gas in metropolitan France; partially privatized in 2005; present name adopted in July 2008 following merger with Suez; merged with International Power (United Kingdom) in 2011; Chair. and CEO GÉRARD MESTRALLET.

Water

Lyonnaise des Eaux: 1 rue d'Astorg, 75008 Paris; e-mail sophie.le.scaon@lyonnaise-des-eaux.fr; internet www.lyonnaise-des-eaux.fr; f. 1858; fmrly Suez-Lyonnaise des Eaux; present name adopted 2001; Pres. and CEO JEAN-LOUIS CHAUSSADE.

Veolia Eau (Veolia Water): 52 rue d'Anjou, 75384 Paris Cedex 8; tel. 1-49-24-49-24; fax 1-49-24-69-59; e-mail webmaster@veoliawater.com; internet www.veoliawater.com; f. 1853 as the Compagnie Générale des Eaux; subsidiary of Veolia Environnement; provides drinking water and manages waste water; Chair. HENRI PROGLIO; CEO JEAN-MICHEL HERREWYN.

TRADE UNIONS

There are three major trade union organizations:

Confédération Française Démocratique du Travail (CFDT): 4 blvd de la Villette, 75955 Paris Cedex 19; tel. 1-42-03-80-00; fax 1-53-72-85-67; e-mail international@cfdt.fr; internet www.cfdt.fr; f. 1919 as Confédération Française des Travailleurs Chrétiens—CFTC; present title and constitution adopted 1964; moderate; co-ordinates 1,500 trade unions, 95 departmental and overseas unions, 3 confederal unions and 14 affiliated professional federations, all of which are autonomous. There are also 22 regional orgs; 833,108 mems; affiliated to European Trade Union Confederation and to ITUC; Sec.-Gen. FRANÇOIS CHÉRÈQUE.

Affiliated federations:

CFDT-Agroalimentaire (FGA-CFDT) (Agribusiness): 47–49 ave Simon Bolivar, 75950 Paris Cedex 19; tel. 1-56-41-50-50; fax 1-56-41-50-30; e-mail fga@cfdt.fr; internet www.fga-cfdt.fr; f. 1980; Sec.-Gen. HERVÉ GARNIER; 60,000 mems.

CFDT-Banques et Sociétés Financières (Financial Institutions): 47–49 ave Simon Bolivar, 75950 Paris Cedex 19; tel. 1-56-41-54-50; fax 1-56-41-54-51; e-mail federation@banques.cfdt.fr; internet www.banques.cfdt.fr; Sec.-Gen. LUC MATHIEU.

CFDT-Cadres (Managers and Professionals): 47–49 ave Simon Bolivar, 75950 Paris Cedex 19; tel. 1-56-41-55-00; fax 1-56-41-55-01; e-mail contact@cadres.cfdt.fr; internet www.cadres-plus.net; Sec.-Gen. JEAN-PAUL BOUCHET.

CFDT-Chimie-Energie (FCE-CFDT) (Chemical Energy): 47–49 ave Simon Bolivar, 75950 Paris Cedex 19; tel. 1-56-41-53-00; fax 1-56-41-53-01; e-mail fce@fce.cfdt.fr; internet www.fce.cfdt.fr; f. 1946; Sec.-Gen. PATRICK PIERRON; 62,000 mems.

CFDT-Communication, Conseil, Culture (F3C) (Communications, Advisory and Cultural Federation): 47–49 ave Simon Bolivar, 75950 Paris Cedex 19; tel. 1-56-41-54-00; fax 1-56-41-54-01; e-mail f3c@cfdt.fr; internet www.f3c-cfdt.fr; f. 2005; Sec.-Gen. HERVÉ MORLAND.

CFDT-Construction-Bois (FNCB-CFDT) (Builders, Woodworkers, Architects, Town Planners): 47–49 ave Simon Bolivar, 75950 Paris Cedex 19; tel. 1-56-41-55-60; fax 1-56-41-55-61; e-mail fncb@cfdt.fr; internet www.cfdt-construction-bois.fr; f. 1934; Sec.-Gen. GILLES DANTOT.

CFDT-Education Nationale (SGEN-CFDT) (National Education): 47–49 ave Simon Bolivar, 75950 Paris Cedex 19; tel. 1-56-41-51-00; fax 1-56-41-51-11; e-mail fede@sgen-cfdt.org; internet www.sgen-cfdt.org; f. 1937; Sec.-Gen. THIERRY CADART.

CFDT-Etablissements et Arsenaux de l'Etat: 2–8 rue Gaston Rébuffat, 75940 Paris Cedex 19; tel. 1-56-41-56-80; fax 1-56-41-56-89; e-mail feae@cfdt.fr; internet www.cfdt-feae.com; Sec.-Gen. JACQUES LEPINARD.

CFDT-Finances et Affaires Economiques (Finance): 2–8 rue Gaston Rébuffat, 75940 Paris Cedex 19; tel. 1-56-41-55-55; fax 1-56-41-55-59; e-mail finances@cfdt.fr; f. 1936; civil servants and workers within government financial departments; Sec.-Gen. PHILIPPE LECLEZIO.

CFDT-Fonctionnaires et Assimilés (UFFA) (Civil Servants): 47–49 ave Simon Bolivar, 75950 Paris Cedex 19; tel. 1-56-41-54-40; fax 1-56-41-54-44; e-mail uffa@cfdt.fr; f. 1932; Sec.-Gen. BRIGITTE JUMEL.

CFDT-Formation et Enseignement Privés (Independent education): 47–49 ave Simon Bolivar, 75950 Paris Cedex 19; tel. 1-56-41-54-70; fax 1-56-41-54-71; e-mail contact@fep.cfdt.fr; internet www.fep.cfdt.fr; Sec.-Gen. XAVIER NAU.

CFDT-Interco (Local Government Workers): 47–49 ave Simon Bolivar, 75950 Paris Cedex 19; tel. 1-56-41-52-52; fax 1-56-41-52-51; e-mail interco@cfdt.fr; internet www.interco.cfdt.fr; Sec.-Gen. MARIE-ODILE ESCH.

CFDT-Métallurgie et Mines (Miners, Machinery and Metal Workers): 47–49 ave Simon Bolivar, 75950 Paris Cedex 19; tel. 1-56-41-50-70; fax 1-56-41-50-96; e-mail mines-metallurgie@fgmm.cfdt.fr; internet www.fgmm.cfdt.fr; Sec.-Gen. DOMINIQUE GILLIER.

CFDT-Protection Sociale, Travail, Emploi (Social Security): 2–8 rue Gaston Rébuffat, 75940 Paris Cedex 19; tel. 1-56-41-51-50; fax 1-56-41-51-51; e-mail federation@pste.cfdt.fr; internet www.pste-cfdt.org; Sec.-Gen. MARTIAL GARCIA.

CFDT-Retraités (UCR) (Retired People): 49 ave Simon Bolivar, 75950 Paris Cedex 19; tel. 1-56-41-55-20; fax 1-56-41-55-21; e-mail contact@retraites.cfdt.fr; internet www.cfdt-retraites.fr; Sec.-Gen. MICHEL DEVACHT.

CFDT-Services (Trade, Insurance, Legal, Property and other Service Sector Professions): Tour Essor, 14 rue Scandicci, 93508 Pantin Cedex; tel. 1-48-10-65-90; fax 1-48-10-65-95; e-mail services@cfdt.fr; internet www.cfdt-services.fr; Sec.-Gen. GILLES DESBORDES.

CFDT-Services de Santé et Services Sociaux (Health and Social Workers): 47–49 ave Simon Bolivar, 75950 Paris Cedex 19; tel. 1-56-41-52-00; fax 1-42-02-48-08; e-mail webmaster-sante@sante-sociaux.cfdt.fr; internet www.fed-cfdt-sante-sociaux.org; Sec.-Gen. YOLANDE BRIAND.

CFDT-Transports-Equipement (Transport, Public Works and Housing—FGTE): 47–49 ave Simon Bolivar, 75950 Paris Cedex 19; tel. 1-56-41-56-03; fax 1-42-02-49-96; e-mail federation@fgte-cfdt.org; internet www.fgte.org; f. 1977; Sec.-Gen. JOËL LECOQ.

Confédération Générale du Travail (CGT) (Labour): 263 rue de Paris, 93516 Montreuil Cedex; tel. 1-48-18-80-00; fax 1-49-88-18-57; e-mail info@cgt.fr; internet www.cgt.fr; f. 1895; National Congress is held every 3 years; Sec.-Gen. BERNARD THIBAULT; 700,000 mems.

Affiliated federations:

CGT-Agro-Alimentaire et Forestière (FNAF) (Food Producers): 263 rue de Paris, Case 428, 93514 Montreuil Cedex; tel. 1-48-18-83-27; fax 1-48-51-57-49; e-mail fnaf@fnaf-cgt.com; Sec.-Gen. FREDDY HUCK.

CGT-Banques et Assurance (Banking and Insurance): 263 rue de Paris, Case 537, 93515 Montreuil Cedex; tel. 1-48-18-83-40; fax 1-49-88-16-36; e-mail fspba@cgt.fr; internet www.cgt-banque-assurance.fr; Sec.-Gen. PATRICK LICHAU.

CGT-Bois Ameublement Connexes (Woodworkers): 263 rue de Paris, Case 414, 93514 Montreuil Cedex; tel. 1-48-18-81-61; fax 1-48-51-59-91; e-mail cgt.bois1@wanadoo.fr; Sec.-Gen. HENRI SANCHEZ.

CGT-Cheminots (Railway Workers): 263 rue de Paris, Case 546, 93515 Montreuil Cedex; tel. 1-49-88-61-00; fax 1-48-57-95-65; e-mail coord@cheminotcgt.fr; internet www.cheminotcgt.fr; Sec.-Gen. DIDIER LE RESTE.

CGT-Commerce (Business): 263 rue de Paris, Case 425, 93514 Montreuil Cedex; tel. 1-48-18-83-11; fax 1-48-18-83-19; e-mail fd.commerce.services@cgt.fr; internet www.commerce.cgt.fr; Sec.-Gen. MICHÈLE CHAY.

CGT-Construction (Building): 263 rue de Paris, Case 413, 93514 Montreuil Cedex; tel. 1-48-18-81-60; fax 1-48-59-10-37; e-mail construction@cgt.fr; internet www.construction.cgt.fr; Sec.-Gen. ERIC AUBIN.

CGT-Equipement et Environnement (Capital Works and Environment): 263 rue de Paris, Case 543, 93515 Montreuil Cedex; tel. 1-48-18-82-81; fax 1-48-51-62-50; e-mail equipement@cgt.fr; internet www.equipement.cgt.fr; Sec.-Gen. JEAN-MARIE RECH.

CGT-Education Recherche Culture (CGT-FERC) (Education, Research and Culture): 263 rue de Paris, Case 544, 93515 Montreuil Cedex; tel. 1-48-18-82-44; fax 1-49-88-07-43; e-mail ferc@cgt.fr; internet www.ferc.cgt.fr; Sec.-Gen. RICHARD BERAUD.

CGT-Finances (Finance): 263 rue de Paris, Case 540, 93515 Montreuil Cedex; tel. 1-48-18-82-21; fax 1-48-18-82-52; e-mail finances@cgt.fr; internet www.finances.cgt.fr; Sec.-Gen. CHRISTOPHE DELECOURT.

CGT-Fonctionnaires (CGT-UGFF) (Civil Servants): 263 rue de Paris, Case 542, 93514 Montreuil Cedex; tel. 1-48-18-82-31; e-mail ugff@cgt.fr; internet www.ugff.cgt.fr; f. 1946; groups National Education, Finance, Technical and Administrative, Civil Servants, Police, etc.; comprises some 70 national unions and 6 professional federations; Sec.-Gen. JEAN-MARC CANON.

CGT-Industries Chimiques (Chemical Industries): 263 rue de Paris, Case 429, 93514 Montreuil Cedex; tel. 1-48-18-80-36; fax 1-48-18-80-35; e-mail fnic@cgt.fr; internet www.fnic.cgt.fr; Sec.-Gen. JEAN-MICHEL PETIT.

CGT-Industries du Livre, du Papier et de la Communication (FILPAC) (Printing, Paper Products and Media): 263 rue de Paris, Case 426, 93514 Montreuil Cedex; tel. 1-48-18-80-24; fax 1-48-51-99-07; e-mail filpac@filpac-cgt.fr; internet www.filpac-cgt.fr; Sec.-Gen. MICHEL MULLER.

CGT-Ingénieurs, Cadres et Techniciens (CGT-UGICT) (Engineers, Managerial Staff and Technicians): 263 rue de Paris, Case 408,

93516 Montreuil Cedex; tel. 1-48-18-81-25; fax 1-48-51-64-57; e-mail ugict@cgt.fr; internet www.ugict.cgt.fr; f. 1963; Sec.-Gen. MARIE-JO KOTLICKI.

CGT-Intérimaires (Temporary Workers): 263 rue de Paris, Case 460, 93514 Montreuil Cedex; tel. 1-48-18-84-16; fax 1-48-18-82-59; e-mail contact@interim.cgt.fr; internet www.interim.cgt.fr; Pres. YANNIC POULAIN.

CGT-Journalistes: 263 rue de Paris, Case 570, 93514 Montreuil Cedex; tel. 1-48-18-81-78; fax 1-48-51-58-08; e-mail snj@cgt.fr; internet www.snj.cgt.fr; Sec.-Gen. MICHEL DIARD.

CGT-Marine Marchande (Merchant Marine): Cercle Franklin, 119 cours de la République, 76000 Le Havre; tel. 2-35-25-04-81; fax 2-35-24-23-77; e-mail off-march@cgt.fr; Sec.-Gen. CHARLES NARELLI.

CGT-Maritimes (Seamen): 263 rue de Paris, Case 420, 93514 Montreuil Cedex; tel. 1-48-18-84-21; fax 1-48-51-59-21; e-mail fnsm@cgt.fn; Sec.-Gen. ALAIN MERLET.

CGT-Métallurgie (FTM-CGT) (Metalworkers): 263 rue de Paris, Case 433, 93514 Montreuil Cedex; tel. 1-48-18-21-21; fax 1-48-59-80-66; e-mail accueil@cgt.fr; internet www.ftm-cgt.fr; f. 1891; Sec.-Gen. PHILIPPE MARTINEZ.

CGT-Mines-Energie (FNME-CGT): 263 rue de Paris, 93516 Montreuil Cedex; tel. 1-56-93-26-50; fax 1-56-93-27-20; e-mail fnme@fnme-cgt.fr; internet www.fnme-cgt.fr; Sec.-Gen. FRÉDÉRIC IMBRECHT.

CGT-Organismes Sociaux (Social Services): 263 rue de Paris, Case 536, 93515 Montreuil Cedex; tel. 1-48-18-83-56; fax 1-48-59-24-75; e-mail fede@orgasociaux.cgt.fr; internet www.orgasociaux.cgt.fr; Sec.-Gen. CATHERINE LEMOINE.

CGT-Pénitentiaires (Prison Workers): 263 rue de Paris, Case 542, 93514 Montreuil Cedex; tel. 1-48-18-82-42; fax 1-48-18-82-50; e-mail ugsp@cgt.fr; internet www.ugsp-cgt.org; Sec.-Gen. CÉLINE VERZELETTI.

CGT-Police: 263 rue de Paris, Case 550, 93514 Montreuil Cedex; tel. 1-48-51-51-83; fax 1-48-51-14-43; e-mail cgtpolice@cgt.fr; internet www.police.cgt.fr; f. 1906; Sec.-Gen. MICHEL GASTALDI.

CGT-Ports et Docks: 263 rue de Paris, Case 424, 93514 Montreuil Cedex; tel. 1-48-18-82-96; fax 1-48-18-82-94; e-mail portsetdocks-cgt@wanadoo.fr; Sec.-Gen. TONY HAUTBOIS.

CGT-Postes et Télécommunications (CGT-FAPT): 263 rue de Paris, Case 545, 93515 Montreuil Cedex; tel. 1-48-18-54-00; fax 1-48-59-25-22; e-mail fede@cgt-ptt.fr; internet cgtptt.free.fr; Sec.-Gen. ALAIN GAUTHERON.

CGT-Professionnels de la Vente (Sales Workers): Bourse du Travail, 3 rue du Château d'eau, 75010 Paris; tel. 1-42-39-02-99; fax 1-42-39-09-11; e-mail cgt.commerciaux@wanadoo.fr; internet www.cgt-provente.com; Sec.-Gen. ALAIN SERRE.

CGT-Santé, Action Sociale (Health and Social Services): 263 rue de Montreuil, Case 538, 93514 Montreuil Cedex; tel. 1-48-18-20-99; fax 1-48-18-29-80; e-mail santeas@cgt.fr; internet www.cgt.fr/santeas; f. 1907; Sec.-Gen. NADINE PRIGENT.

CGT-Services Publics (Community Services): 263 rue de Paris, Case 547, 93514 Montreuil Cedex; tel. 1-48-18-83-74; fax 1-48-51-98-20; e-mail fdsp@cgt.fr; internet www.spterritoriaux.cgt.fr; Sec.-Gen. BAPTISTE TALBOT.

CGT-Sociétés d'études (Research, Service Sector Workers, Translators, Accountants, Notaries): 263 rue de Paris, Case 421, 93514 Montreuil Cedex; tel. 1-48-18-84-34; fax 1-48-18-84-86; e-mail fsetud@cgt.fr; internet www.soc-etudes.cgt.fr; f. 1980; Pres. NOËL LECHAT.

CGT-Spectacle, Audiovisuel et Action Culturelle (Theatre, Media and Culture): 14–16 rue des Lilas, 75019 Paris; tel. 1-48-03-87-60; fax 1-42-40-90-20; e-mail cgtspectacle@fnsac-cgt.com; internet www.fnsac-cgt.com; Sec.-Gen. JEAN VOIRIN.

CGT-Tabac et Allumettes (Tobacco and Matches): 263 rue de Paris, Case 422, 93514 Montreuil Cedex; tel. 1-48-18-84-19; fax 1-48-51-54-53; e-mail tabacs.allumettes@cgt.fr; Sec.-Gen. FRÉDÉRIQUE BARTLETT.

CGT-Textiles, Habillement, Cuir (Textiles): 263 rue de Paris, Case 415, 93514 Montreuil Cedex; tel. 1-48-18-82-98; fax 1-48-18-83-01; e-mail thc@cgt.fr; internet www.thc-cgt-textile.fr; Sec.-Gen. MAURAD RABHI.

CGT-Transports: 263 rue de Paris, Case 423, 93514 Montreuil Cedex; tel. 1-48-18-80-82; fax 1-48-18-82-54; e-mail transports@cgt.fr; internet www.transports.cgt.fr; Sec.-Gen. PAUL FOURIER.

CGT-Travailleurs de l'Etat (State Employees): 263 rue de Paris, Case 541, 93515 Montreuil Cedex; tel. 1-48-18-86-86; fax 1-48-18-86-87; e-mail trav-etat@cgt.fr; internet www.fnte.cgt.fr; Sec.-Gen. JEAN-LOUIS NAUDET.

CGT-Verre-Céramique (Glassworkers, Ceramics): 263 rue de Paris, Case 417, 93514 Montreuil Cedex; tel. 1-48-18-80-13; fax 1-48-18-80-11; e-mail ver-ceram@cgt.fr; internet www.verreceram-cgt.fr; Sec.-Gen. MOHAMMED OUSSEDIK.

Force Ouvrière (FO): 141 ave du Maine, 75680 Paris Cedex 14; tel. 1-40-52-82-00; fax 1-40-52-82-02; internet www.force-ouvriere.fr; f. 1948 by breakaway from the more left-wing CGT; mem. of ITUC and of the European Trade Union Confederation; Sec.-Gen. JEAN-CLAUDE MAILLY; c. 1m. mems.

Affiliated federations:

Fédération Générale Force Ouvrière (FGFO) (Building, Public Works, Wood, Ceramics, Paper, Cardboard and Building Materials): 170 ave Parmentier, 75010 Paris; tel. 1-42-01-30-00; fax 1-42-39-50-44; e-mail fgfoconstruction@orange.fr; internet www.federationgeneralefo.com; Sec.-Gen. FRANCK SERRA.

FO-Action Sociale: 7 passage Tenaille, 75680 Paris Cedex 14; tel. 1-40-52-85-80; fax 1-40-52-85-79; e-mail lafnas@fnasfo.fr; internet fnasfo.fr; Sec.-Gen. PASCAL CORBEX.

FO-Administration Générale de l'Etat: 46 rue des Petites Ecuries, 75010 Paris; tel. 1-42-46-40-19; fax 1-42-46-19-57; e-mail fagefo@wanadoo.fr; internet www.fage-fo.com; f. 1948; Sec.-Gen. JEAN-CLAUDE LE BOURSICAUD.

FO-Agriculture, Alimentation et Tabacs (Agriculture, Food and Tobacco): 7 passage Tenaille, 75680 Paris Cedex 14; tel. 1-40-52-85-10; fax 1-40-52-85-12; e-mail fgtafo@fgta-fo.org; internet www.fgtafo.fr; Sec.-Gen. RAFAËL NEDZYNSKI.

FO-Cadres et Ingénieurs (UCI) (Managers, Engineers): 2 rue de la Michodière, 75002 Paris; tel. 1-47-42-39-69; fax 1-47-42-03-53; e-mail contact@fo-cadres.fr; internet www.fo-cadres.fr; Sec.-Gen. ERIC PERES.

FO-Cheminots (Railway Workers): 61 rue de la Chapelle, 75018 Paris; tel. 1-55-26-94-00; fax 1-55-26-94-01; e-mail federation@fo-cheminots.com; internet www.fo-cheminots.com; f. 1948; Sec.-Gen. ERIC FALEMPIN.

FO-Coiffure, Esthétique, Parfumerie (Hairdressers, Beauticians and Perfumery): 131 rue Damrémont, 75018 Paris; tel. 1-53-01-61-13; fax 1-53-01-61-45; e-mail fcoiffure@force-ouvriere.fr; Sec.-Gen. GUY MARIN.

FO-Communications (Post and Telecommunications): 60 rue Vergniaud, 75640 Paris Cedex 13; tel. 1-40-78-31-50; fax 1-40-78-30-58; e-mail federation@fo-com.com; internet www.fo-com.com; f. 1947; Sec.-Gen. JACQUES LEMERCIER.

FO-Cuirs, Textiles, Habillement (Leather, Textiles and Clothing): 7 passage Tenaille, 75680 Paris Cedex 14; tel. 1-40-52-83-00; fax 1-40-52-82-99; e-mail fvanderosieren@force-ouvriere.fr; Sec.-Gen. DOMINIQUE MAGIN.

FO-Défense, Industries de l'Armement et Secteurs Assimilés (Defence and Arms Manufacture): 46 rue des Petites Ecuries, 75010 Paris; tel. 1-42-46-00-05; fax 1-45-23-12-89; e-mail fediasa@force-ouvriere.fr; internet www.fodefense.com; Sec.-Gen. GILLES GOULM.

FO-Employés et Cadres (Office Workers and Private Sector Managerial Staff): 28 rue des Petits Hôtels, 75010 Paris; tel. 1-48-01-91-91; fax 1-48-01-91-92; e-mail fecfo@force-ouvriere.fr; internet www.fecfo.fr; Sec.-Gen. SERGE LEGAGNOA.

FO-Energie et Mines (Energy and Mines): 60 rue Vergniaud, 75640 Paris Cedex 13; tel. 1-44-16-86-20; fax 1-44-16-86-32; e-mail federation@fnem-fo.fr; internet www.fnem-fo.fr; Sec.-Gen. MAX ROYER.

FO-Enseignement, Culture et Formation Professionnelle (Teaching): 6–8 rue Gaston-Lauriau, 93513 Montreuil Cedex; tel. 1-56-93-22-22; fax 1-56-93-22-20; e-mail fnecfpfo@fr.oleane.com; internet fo-fnecfp.fr; Sec.-Gen. HUBERT RAGUIN.

FO-Equipements, Environnement, Transports et Services (Transport and Public Works): 46 rue des Petites Ecuries, 75010 Paris; tel. 1-44-83-86-20; fax 1-48-24-38-32; internet www.fets-fo.fr; f. 1932; Sec.-Gen. JEAN HEDOU.

FO-Fédéchimie (Chemical Industries): 60 rue Vergniaud, 75640 Paris Cedex 13; tel. 1-45-80-14-90; fax 1-45-80-08-03; e-mail fedechimie_cgtfo@wanadoo.fr; internet www.fedechimie-cgtfo.com; f. 1948; Sec.-Gen. HERVÉ QUILLET.

FO-Finances: 46 rue des Petites Ecuries, 75010 Paris; tel. 1-42-46-75-20; fax 1-47-70-23-92; e-mail fo.finances@wanadoo.fr; internet www.financesfo.fr; Sec.-Gen. LAURENT AUBURSIN.

FO-Fonctionnaires (Civil Servants): 46 rue des Petites Ecuries, 75010 Paris; tel. 1-44-83-65-55; fax 1-42-46-97-80; e-mail contact@fo-fonctionnaires.fr; internet www.fo-fonctionnaires.fr; Sec.-Gen. ANNE BALTAZAR.

FO-Livre (Printing Trades): 7 passage Tenaille, 75680 Paris Cedex 14; tel. 1-40-52-85-00; fax 1-40-52-85-01; e-mail psacquepee@force-ouvriere.fr; Sec.-Gen. PATRICE SACQUÉPÉE.

FO-Métaux (Metals): 9 rue Baudouin, 75013 Paris; tel. 1-53-94-54-00; fax 1-45-83-78-87; e-mail contact@fo-metaux.fr; internet www.fo-metaux.com; Sec.-Gen. FRÉDÉRIC HOMEZ.

FO-Mineurs, Miniers et Similaires (Mine Workers): 7 passage Tenaille, 75014 Paris; tel. 1-40-52-85-50; fax 1-40-52-85-48; e-mail fo.mineurs@orange.fr; Sec.-Gen. JEAN-PIERRE DAMM.

FO-Pharmacie, Officine-Industrie VM, Droguerie-Répartition, Laboratoire d'Analyse (Pharmacists, Druggists and Analytical Laboratories): 7 passage Tenaille, 75680 Paris Cedex 14; tel. 1-40-52-85-60; fax 1-40-52-85-61; e-mail fopharma@wanadoo.fr; internet www.fo-pharmacie.com; Sec.-Gen. JACQUES TECHER.

FO-Police: 146–148 rue Picpus, 75012 Paris; tel. 1-53-46-11-00; fax 1-44-68-07-41; e-mail xbeugnet@force-ouvriere.fr; f. 1948; Sec.-Gen. NICOLAS COMTE.

FO-Services des Départements et Régions (Local and Regional Government): 46 rue des Petits Ecuries, 75010 Paris; tel. 1-42-46-50-52; fax 1-47-70-26-06; e-mail msimonnin@force-ouvriere.fr; f. 1984; Sec.-Gen. MICHÈLE SIMONNIN.

FO-Services Publics et de Santé (Health and Public Services): 153–155 rue de Rome, 75017 Paris; tel. 1-44-01-06-00; fax 1-42-27-21-40; e-mail fosps@force-ouvriere.fr; internet www.fo-publics-sante.org; f. 1947; Sec.-Gen. DIDIER BERNUS.

FO-Spectacles, Audiovisuel, Presse, Multimedia (FASAPFO) (Theatre, Broadcasting, Press, Multimedia): 2 rue de la Michodière, 75002 Paris; tel. 1-47-42-35-86; fax 1-47-42-39-45; e-mail fasap-fo@wanadoo.fr; Sec.-Gen. FRANÇOISE CHAZAUD.

FO-Transports et Logistique: 7 passage Tenaille, 75680 Paris Cedex 14; tel. 1-40-52-85-45; fax 1-40-52-85-09; e-mail secretariat@fo-transports.com; internet www.fo-transports.com; Sec.-Gen. GÉRARD MARTINEZ.

Other federations:

Confédération Française de l'Encadrement (CFE—CGC): 59–63 rue du Rocher, 75008 Paris; tel. 1-55-30-12-12; fax 1-55-30-13-13; e-mail presse@cfecgc.fr; internet www.cfecgc.fr; f. 1944; organizes managerial staff, professional staff and technicians; co-ordinates unions in every industry and sector; Nat. Pres. BERNARD VAN CRAEYNEST; Sec.-Gen. CAROLE COUVERT; 160,000 mems (2006).

Confédération Française des Travailleurs Chrétiens (CFTC): 13 rue des Ecluses Saint Martin, 75483 Paris Cedex 10; tel. 1-44-52-49-00; fax 1-44-52-49-18; e-mail eurint@cftc.fr; internet www.cftc.fr; f. 1919; present form in 1964 after majority CFTC became CFDT (see above); mem. European Trade Union Confederation, World Confederation of Labour; Chair. JACQUES VOISIN; Gen. Sec. PHILLIPE LOUIS; 132,000 mems.

Fédération Nationale des Syndicats Autonomes de l'Enseignement Supérieur et de la Recherche: 48 rue Vitruve, 75020 Paris; tel. 1-46-59-01-01; fax 1-46-59-01-23; e-mail autonomesup@free.fr; internet autonomesup.com; f. 1948; higher education and research; Pres. JEAN-LOUIS CHARLET; Sec.-Gen. MICHEL GAY.

Fédération Nationale des Syndicats d'Exploitants Agricoles (FNSEA) (National Federation of Farmers' Unions): 11 rue de la Baume, 75008 Paris; tel. 1-53-83-47-47; fax 1-53-83-48-48; e-mail fnsea@fnsea.fr; internet www.fnsea.fr; f. 1946; comprises 92 departmental federations and 32,000 local unions; Pres. JEAN-MICHEL LEMÉTAYER; Dir-Gen. PATRICK FERRÈRE; 600,000 mems.

Fédération Syndicale Unitaire (FSU): 104 rue Romain Rolland, 93260 Les lilas; tel. 1-41-63-27-30; fax 1-41-63-15-48; e-mail fsu.nationale@fsu.fr; internet www.fsu.fr; f. 1993; federation of civil service and education workers' unions; Sec.-Gen. BERNADETTE GROISON; 163,000 mems.

Syndicat National Unitaire des Instituteurs Professeurs d'écoles et PEGC (SNUipp): 128 blvd Blanqui, 75013 Paris; tel. 1-44-08-69-30; fax 1-44-08-69-40; internet www.snuipp.fr; f. 1993; primary school teachers; Sec.-Gen. GILLES MOINDROT.

UNSA Education: 87 bis ave Georges Gosnat, 94853 Ivry-sur-Seine Cedex; tel. 1-56-20-29-50; fax 1-56-20-29-89; e-mail national@unsa-education.org; internet www.unsa-education.org; f. 1948; federation of teachers' unions; comprises 24 mem. unions; fmrly Fédération de l'Education Nationale; Sec.-Gen. PATRICK GONTHIER.

Transport

RAILWAYS

Most of the French railways are controlled by the Société Nationale des Chemins de fer Français (SNCF), established in 1937, while the Réseau Ferré de France (RFF, f. 1997) manages track and infrastructure. The SNCF is divided into 22 *régions* (areas). In 2009 the RFF operated 29,273 km of track, of which 15,687 km were electrified. A high-speed service (*train à grande vitesse*—TGV) operates between Paris and various other destinations: Lyon (TGV Sud-Est), extending to Marseille or Nîmes (TGV Méditerranée), Bordeaux or Nantes (TGV Atlantique), Lille (TGV Nord Europe) and Strasbourg and destinations in Germany, Luxembourg and Switzerland (TGV Est Européen). The Rhine-Rhône high-speed line opened in 2011 linking central and eastern France with Germany and Switzerland. Further high-speed lines, between Nîmes and Montpellier and Brittany and the Loire Valley, were expected to be completed by 2016. The Parisian transport system is controlled by a separate authority, the Régie Autonome des Transports Parisiens (RATP). A number of small railways in the provinces are run by independent organizations.

Réseau Ferré de France (RFF): 92 ave de France, 75648 Paris Cedex 13; tel. 1-53-94-30-00; fax 1-53-94-38-00; internet www.rff.fr; f. 1997 to assume ownership and financial control of national rail infrastructure; state-owned; Pres. HUBERT DE MESNIL; Asst Gen. Dir ALAIN QUINET.

Société Nationale des Chemins de fer Français (SNCF): 34 rue du Commandant Mouchotte, 75699 Paris Cedex 14; tel. 1-53-25-60-00; fax 1-53-25-61-08; e-mail webcom@sncf.fr; internet www.sncf.fr; f. 1937; Pres. GUILLAUME PÉPY.

Channel Tunnel (Le Tunnel sous la Manche)

Groupe Eurotunnel: BP 69, Coquelles Cedex; tel. 3-21-00-65-43; internet www.eurotunnel.fr; Anglo-French consortium contracted to design, finance and construct the Channel Tunnel under a concession granted for a period up to 2052 (later extended to 2086); receives finance exclusively from the private sector, including international commercial banks; the Channel Tunnel was formally opened in May 1994; operates a series of road vehicle 'shuttle' trains and passenger and freight trains through the Channel Tunnel; Chair. and Chief Exec. JACQUES GOUNON; Man. Dir JEAN-PIERRE TROTIGNON.

ROADS

At 31 December 2008 there were 11,100 km of motorways (*autoroutes*), 9,100 km of highways, 381,000 km of secondary roads and 550,000 km of other roads.

Fédération Nationale des Transports Routiers (FNTR): 6 rue Ampère, 75017 Paris; tel. 1-44-29-04-29; fax 1-44-29-04-01; e-mail contact@fntr.fr; internet www.fntr.fr; f. 1933; road transport; Chair. JEAN-CHRISTOPHE PIC; 12,500 mem. cos.

METROPOLITAN TRANSPORT

Régie Autonome des Transports Parisiens (RATP): 54 quai de la Rapée, 75599 Paris Cedex 12; tel. 1-58-78-20-20; fax 1-58-78-31-70; internet www.ratp.fr; f. 1949; state-owned; operates the Paris underground (comprising 16 lines totalling 200 km, and 381 stations), Réseau Express Régional (RER) suburban railways (totalling 115 km in 2007), 3 suburban tramlines, and 345 bus routes; Chair. and CEO PIERRE MONGIN.

Five provincial cities also have underground railway systems: Marseille, Lyon, Lille, Rennes and Toulouse. Tram networks have been constructed in several provincial cities since the 1980s.

INLAND WATERWAYS

At 20 February 2007 there were 8,501 km of navigable waterways, of which 1,621 km were accessible to craft of 3,000 metric tons.

Voies navigables de France: 175 rue Ludovic Boutleux, BP 30820, 62408 Béthune Cedex; tel. 3-21-63-24-24; fax 3-21-63-24-42; e-mail direction-generale@vnf.fr; internet www.vnf.fr; f. 1991; management and development of France's inland waterways; responsible for 3,800 km of navigable canals and 2,900 km of navigable rivers; Pres. ALAIN GEST; Dir-Gen. MARC PAPINUTTI.

SHIPPING

Seven of the major ports, Marseille, Le Havre, Dunkerque, Nantes Saint-Nazaire, Rouen, Bordeaux and La Rochelle, are operated by autonomous authorities (Grands Ports Maritimes), although the state retains supervisory powers.

Conseil supérieur de la marine marchande (CSMM): 3 pl. de Fontenoy, 75007 Paris; tel. 1-44-49-81-84; e-mail jean-marie.berthet@developpement-durable.gouv.fr; internet www.csmm.equipement.gouv.fr; f. 1896; merged with the Conseil National des Communautés Portuaires (f. 1987) in 2002; govt consultative and co-ordinating body for maritime transport, ports and port authorities; 39 mems, including 12 trade union mems; Pres. MICHEL QUIMBERT; Sec.-Gen. JEAN-MARIE BERTHET.

Direction du Transport Maritime, des Ports et du Littoral (DTMPL): 22 rue Monge, 75005 Paris; tel. 1-40-81-72-11; fax 1-40-81-72-15; e-mail dtmpl@equipement.gouv.fr; f. 1997; govt body responsible for the economic development of port and civil maritime activities and the protection of the coast; Dir DIDIER SIMMONET.

Grand Port Maritime de Bordeaux: 3 pl. Gabriel, 33075 Bordeaux; tel. 5-56-90-58-00; fax 5-56-90-58-80; e-mail postoffice@

bordeaux-port.fr; internet www.bordeaux-port.fr; Dir-Gen. CHRISTOPHE MASSON.

Grand Port Maritime de Dunkerque: 2505 route de l'Ecluse Trystram, BP 46534, 59386 Dunkerque Cedex 01; tel. 3-28-28-78-78; fax 3-28-28-78-77; e-mail info@portdedunkerque.fr; internet www.portdedunkerque.fr; Dir-Gen. MARTINE BONNY.

Grand Port Maritime du Havre: Terre-Plein de la Barre, BP 1413, 76067 Le Havre Cedex; tel. 2-32-74-74-00; fax 2-32-74-74-29; e-mail internetpah@havre-port.fr; internet www.havre-port.fr.

Grand Port Maritime de La Rochelle: BP 70394, 170001 La Rochelle Cedex 1; tel. (5) 46-00-53-60; fax (5) 46-43-12-54; internet www.larochelle.port.fr; Dir-Gen. NICOLAS GAUTHIER.

Grand Port Maritime de Marseille: 23 pl. de la Joliette, BP 1965, 13226 Marseille Cedex 02; tel. 4-91-39-40-00; fax 4-91-39-57-00; e-mail gpmm@marseille-port.fr; internet www.marseille-port.fr; Dir-Gen. JEAN-CLAUDE TERRIER.

Grand Port Maritime de Nantes Saint Nazaire: 18 quai Ernest Renaud, BP 18609, 44186 Nantes Cedex 4; tel. 2-40-44-20-20; fax 2-40-44-21-81; e-mail ser.com@nantes.port.fr; internet www.nantes.port.fr; f. 1966; Dir-Gen. JEAN-PIERRE CHALUS.

Grand Port Maritime de Rouen: 34 blvd de Boisguilbert, BP 4075, 76022 Rouen Cedex 03; tel. 2-35-52-54-56; fax 2-35-52-54-13; e-mail dg@rouen.port.fr; internet www.rouen.port.fr; Dir-Gen. PHILIPPE DEISS.

Port de Calais: 24 blvd des Alliés, BP 199, 62104 Calais Cedex; tel. 3-21-96-31-20; fax 3-21-34-08-92; e-mail ccic@calais.cci.fr; internet www.calais-port.com; Pres. HENRI RAVISSE.

Principal Shipping Companies

Note: Not all the vessels belonging to the companies listed below are registered under the French flag.

Brittany Ferries: Port du Bloscon, BP 72, 29688 Roscoff Cedex; tel. 2-98-29-28-13; fax 2-98-29-27-00; e-mail service.client@brittany-ferries.fr; internet www.brittany-ferries.fr; f. 1972 as Bretagne-Angleterre-Irlande (BAI); transport between France, Ireland, Spain and the United Kingdom; Chair. JEAN MARC ROUÉ; Man. Dir MARTINE JOURDREN.

Compagnie Maritime Marfret: 13 quai de la Joliette, 13002 Marseille; tel. 4-91-56-91-00; fax 4-91-56-91-01; e-mail bvidil@marfret.fr; internet www.marfret.fr; f. 1951 as Marseille-Fret; name changed to present in 1987; freight services to the Mediterranean, South America, the Caribbean, Canada and northern Europe; Chair RAYMOND VIDIL; Dir-Gen. BERNARD VIDIL.

Consortium Européen de Transports Maritimes (CETRAMAR): 87 ave de la Grande Armée, 75782 Paris Cedex 16; tel. 1-40-66-11-11; fax 1-45-00-77-35; f. 1964; Chair. PHILIPPE POIRIER D'ANGÉ D'ORSAY; Man. Dir ANDRÉ MAIRE; displacement 564,291 grt.

Corsica Ferries: 5 bis rue Chanoîne Leschi, BP 275, 20296 Bastia; tel. 4-95-32-95-95; fax 4-95-32-14-71; e-mail resa1@corsicaferries.com; internet www.corsica-ferries.fr; affiliated to Groupe Lota Maritime; passenger and freight ferry services between Corsica, Sardinia, mainland France, and mainland Italy; Pres. PASCAL LOTA.

Esso France: 2 rue des Martinets, 92569 Rueil-Malmaison Cedex; tel. 1-47-10-60-00; fax 1-47-10-60-03; internet www.esso.com/europe-french/fr_homepage.asp; f. 1952; merged with Mobil Oil Française in 2003; Chair. and Man. Dir PATRICK HEINZLE.

Groupe CMA—CGM: 4 quai d'Arenc, 13235 Marseille Cedex 02; tel. 4-88-91-90-00; fax 4-88-91-90-95; e-mail webmaster@cma-cgm.com; internet www.cma-cgm.com; f. 1996 by merger of Compagnie Générale Maritime and Compagnie Maritime d'Affrètement; freight services to USA, Canada, the Caribbean, Central and South America, the Mediterranean, the Middle East, the Far East, India, Australia, New Zealand, Indonesia, East Africa and other Pacific and Indian Ocean areas; 25 ships owned; Chair. JACQUES R. SAADÉ; CEO FARID T. SALEM; displacement 1,900,000 grt (2001).

Louis Dreyfus Armateurs (LDA): 28 quai Gallieni, 92158 Suresnes Cedex; tel. 1-70-38-60-00; fax 1-70-79-15-02; e-mail gehannep@lda.fr; internet www.lda.fr; gas and bulk carriers; Pres. PHILIPPE LOUIS-DREYFUS; CEO PIERRE GEHANNE.

Maersk Tankers France SAS: 35 ter ave André Morizet, 92100 Boulogne Billancourt; tel. 1-46-99-60-15; fax 1-72-70-34-90; e-mail partankmng@maersk.com; internet www.maersktankers.com; subsidiary of A.P. Møller-Mærsk AS (Denmark); fmrly Broström Tankers, SAS; name changed to present in June 2010; oil product and chemical coastal tankers and tramping.

Navale Française SA: 8 blvd Victor Hugo, 34000 Montpellier; tel. 4-67-58-82-12; fax 4-67-92-98-34; Chair. MARC CHEVALLIER.

Société d'Armement et de Transport (Socatra): 9 allées de Tourny, 33000 Bordeaux; tel. 5-56-00-00-56; fax 5-56-40-16-77; e-mail management@socatra.com; internet www.socatra.com; f. 1977; Chair. F. BOZZONI; Man. Dir M. DUBOURG.

Société Européenne de Transport Maritime: 9 allées de Tourny, 33000 Bordeaux; tel. 5-56-00-00-56; fax 5-56-48-51-23; Man. Dirs GILLES BOUTHILLIER, FERNAND BOZZONI; displacement 53,261 grt.

Société Nationale Maritime Corse-Méditerranée (SNCM): 61 blvd des Dames, BP 1963, 13226 Marseille Cedex 02; tel. 4-91-56-32-00; fax 4-91-56-36-36; e-mail info@sncm.fr; internet www.sncm.fr; passenger and roll-on/roll-off ferry services between France and Corsica, Sardinia, North Africa; 25% state-owned, managed by Veolia Transport (owners of a 28% share) from 2006; Chair. PIERRE VIEU; displacement 141,454 grt.

Société Services et Transports: route du Hoc Gonfreville-L'Orcher, 76700 Harfleur; tel. 2-35-24-72-00; fax 2-35-53-36-25; petroleum and gas transport, passenger transport; Chair. YVES ROUSIER; Man. Dir JACQUES CHARVET; displacement 118,274 grt.

CIVIL AVIATION

The principal international airports are at Orly and Roissy-Charles de Gaulle (Paris), Bordeaux, Lille, Lyon, Marseille, Nice, Strasbourg and Toulouse.

Aéroports de Paris: 291 blvd de Raspail, 75675 Paris Cedex 14; tel. 1-43-35-70-00; fax 1-43-35-72-00; e-mail webmaster@adp.fr; internet www.adp.fr; f. 1945; majority state-controlled authority in charge of Paris airports at Orly and Roissy-Charles de Gaulle, 11 other airports for light aircraft, including Le Bourget, and a heliport at Issy-les-Moulineaux; Chair. and CEO. PIERRE GRAFF; Man. Dir FRANÇOIS RUBICHON.

Airlines

Air France: 45 rue de Paris, 95747 Roissy Cedex; tel. 1-41-56-78-00; fax 1-41-56-70-29; internet www.airfrance.fr; f. 1933; 18.6% state-owned; merged with KLM (Netherlands) in 2004; internal, international, European and intercontinental services; 240 destinations in 105 countries world-wide; Chair. and CEO ALEXANDRE DE JUNAIC.

Brit Air: Aéroport, CS 27925-29679 Morlaix; tel. 2-98-63-63-63; fax 2-98-62-77-66; internet www.britair.com; f. 1973; domestic and European flights; wholly owned by Air France; Pres. and Dir-Gen. MARC LAMIDEY.

Corsairfly: 2 ave Charles Lindbergh, 94636 Rungis Cedex; tel. 1-49-79-49-59; tel. www.corsairfly.com; f. 1981; scheduled flights between metropolitan France and Italy, Madagascar, Morocco, Kenya, and the French overseas possessions, and chartered flights to other medium- and long-range destinations; owned by TUI AG Group (Germany); Pres. PIERRE CHESNEAU; Man. Dir HERVÉ PIERRET.

Hex'Air: Aéroport Le Puy, 43320 Loudes; tel. 4-71-08-62-28; fax 4-71-08-04-10; e-mail contact@hexair.com; internet www.hexair.com; f. 1991; domestic services; Pres. and Dir-Gen. ALEXANDRE ROUCHON.

Régional—Compagnie Aérienne Européenne: Aéroport Nantes Atlantique, 44345 Bouguenais Cedex; tel. 2-40-13-53-00; fax 2-40-13-53-08; e-mail contact@regional.com; internet www.regional.com; f. 2001 by merger of Flandre Air, Proteus and Regional Airlines; operates European and domestic flights; subsidiary of Air France; Pres. and Dir-Gen. JEAN-YVES GROSSE.

XL Airways France: Bâtiment Mars, Continental Sq. II, 3 place de Berlin, 95727 Roissy Cedex; tel. 1-70-03-15-86; internet www.xlairways.fr; f. 1995 as Star Airlines; acquired by XL Leisure Group (United Kingdom) in 2006; charter and scheduled flights between France and Corsica, Cuba, the Dominican Republic, Egypt, Italy, the Maldives, Mexico, Morocco, Senegal and Tunisia; Dir-Gen. LAURENT MAGNIN.

Airline Associations

Fédération Nationale de l'Aviation Marchande (FNAM): 28 rue de Châteaudun, 75009 Paris; tel. 1-45-26-23-24; fax 1-45-26-23-95; e-mail info@fnam.fr; internet www.fnam.fr; f. 1991; Pres. LIONEL GUÉRIN; Delegate-Gen. JEAN-PIERRE LE GOFF.

Chambre Syndicale du Transport Aérien (CSTA): 28 rue de Châteaudun, 75009 Paris; tel. 1-45-26-23-24; fax 1-45-26-23-95; e-mail info@fnam.fr; f. 1947; represents French airlines at national level; Pres. LIONEL GUÉRIN.

Tourism

France is the world's most popular tourist destination. Paris is famous for its boulevards, historic buildings, theatres, art treasures, fashion houses, restaurants and night clubs. The Mediterranean and Atlantic coasts and the French Alps are the most popular tourist resorts. Among other attractions are the many ancient towns, the châteaux of the Loire, the fishing villages of Brittany and Normandy, and spas and places of pilgrimage, such as Vichy and Lourdes. The theme park, Disneyland Resort Paris, also attracts large numbers of tourists. There were 76.8m. tourist arrivals in 2009; tourism receipts totalled US $46,319m. in 2010, according to provisional figures. Most visitors are from the United Kingdom, Germany, the Netherlands, Belgium and Italy.

Atout France: 79–81 rue de Clichy, 75009 Paris; tel. 1-42-96-70-00; fax 1-42-96-70-11; internet fr.franceguide.com; f. 2009 following merger of Maison de la France and ODIT France; Pres. RENAUD DONNEDIEU DE VABRES; Dir-Gen. CHRISTIAN MANTEI.

Direction du Tourisme: 23 place de Catalogne, 75014 Paris; tel. 1-70-39-93-00; internet www.tourisme.gouv.fr; Dir MICHEL CHAMPON.

There are Regional Tourism Committees in the 22 metropolitan regions. There are more than 3,600 Offices de Tourisme and Syndicats d'Initiative (tourist offices operated by the local authorities) throughout France.

Defence

French military policy is decided by the Supreme Defence Council. Military service was compulsory until November 2001, when legislation to create fully professional armed forces took effect. As assessed at November 2011, the total active armed forces numbered 238,591, comprising an army of 130,600, a navy of 40,353, an air force of 52,669, and other staff numbering 14,969. In addition, there was a paramilitary gendarmerie of 103,376. Civilian forces stood at 70,976 (army 20,600; navy 7,091; air force 7,517; paramilitary gendarmerie 1,925; other staff 35,768), while reserves stood at 33,686 (army 18,500; navy 6,012; air force 5,186; other staff 3,988); there were also 40,000 paramilitary reserves. France is a member of the North Atlantic Treaty Organization (NATO) and possesses its own nuclear weapons. France withdrew from the integrated military command of NATO in 1966 but re-entered it in April 2009. In November 2004 the European Union (EU) ministers responsible for defence agreed to create a number of 'battlegroups' (each comprising about 1,500 troops), which could be deployed at short notice to crisis areas around the world. The EU battlegroups, two of which were to be ready for deployment at any one time, following a rotational schedule, reached full operational capacity from 1 January 2007. France was the sole contributor to one battlegroup and also participated in two others, one with Belgium and one with Germany, Belgium and Luxembourg.

Defence Expenditure: Budgeted at €40,200m. in 2012.

Chief of Staff of the Armed Forces: Adm. EDOUARD GUILLAUD.

Chief of Staff of the Ground Forces: Gen. BERTRAND RACT-MADOUX.

Chief of Staff of the Navy: Adm. BERNARD ROGEL.

Chief of Staff of the Air Forces: Gen. JEAN-PAUL PALOMÉROS.

Director-General of the National Gendarmerie: JACQUES MIGNAUX.

Education

Responsibility for education in France rests with the Ministry of National Education, Youth and Community Life, which defines the curriculum to be followed in schools. Administrative control of the education system, from primary to higher levels, is delegated to 30 educational districts (*académies*). Education is compulsory and free for children aged six to 16 years. In 2008/09 enrolment at primary level included 98% of children in the relevant age-group, while enrolment at secondary level also included 99% of children in the relevant age-group. Primary education begins at six years of age and lasts for five years. At the age of 11 all pupils enter the first cycle of the *enseignement secondaire*, with a four-year general course at a *collège*. At the age of 15 pupils may enter the second cycle at a *lycée générale et technologique*, choosing a course leading to the general or technological *baccalauréat* examination after three years. Alongside the *lycées générales et technologiques*, vocational education is provided in the *lycées professionnels*, where pupils prepare for the professional *baccalauréat* over three years or a vocational qualification (*certificat d'aptitude professionnelle*—CAP) over two years. In 2009/10 16.9% of pupils attended France's 8,780 private schools (including *écoles élémentaires*, *collèges* and *lycées*), most of which are administered by the Roman Catholic Church.

The minimum qualification for entry to university is the *baccalauréat* and anyone possessing that qualification is entitled to receive a university education. There are three levels of university education. The first degree, the *licence*, is obtained after three years of study. The *master recherche* and *master professionnel* are obtained after five years of study; the *master recherche* is required for progress to the *doctorat*, while the *master professionnel* provides vocational education. The *doctorat* requires eight years' study and the submission of a thesis. Universities are complemented by the prestigious *grandes écoles*, entry to which is by competitive examination; these institutions have traditionally supplied France's administrative élite. Enrolment at tertiary level in 2005/06 was equivalent to 56% of students in the relevant age-group (males 49%; females 64%).

Expenditure on education and research in France (including the overseas departments) by the central Government was budgeted at €78,200m. for 2009 (equivalent to 25.3% of total central Government expenditure).

FRENCH OVERSEAS POSSESSIONS

Ministry of the Interior, the Overseas Possessions, the Territorial Collectivities and Immigration: 27 rue Oudinot, 75007 Paris, France; tel. 1-53-69-20-00; internet www.outre-mer.gouv.fr.

Minister of the Interior, the Overseas Possessions, the Territorial Collectivities and Immigration: CLAUDE GUÉANT.

The national flag of France, proportions two by three, with three equal vertical stripes, of blue, white and red, is used in the Overseas Possessions.

French Overseas Regions and Departments

As amended in March 2003, the Constitution defines French Guiana, Guadeloupe, Martinique and Réunion as being simultaneously Overseas Regions (Régions d'outre-mer) and Overseas Departments (Départements d'outre-mer) within the French Republic. National legislation is fully applicable, although, other than in the areas of justice, the police, the armed forces and public freedoms, some provision is made for local adaptation within the framework of the law. At a referendum held in the Overseas Collectivity (Collectivité d'outre-mer) of Mayotte in March 2009, the electorate voted in favour of becoming an Overseas Department of France. The change took effect at the end of March 2011.

FRENCH GUIANA

Introductory Survey

LOCATION, CLIMATE, LANGUAGE, RELIGION, CAPITAL

French Guiana (Guyane) lies on the north coast of South America, with Suriname to the west and Brazil to the south and east. The climate is humid, with a season of heavy rains from April to July and another short rainy season in December and January. Average temperature at sealevel is 27°C (85°F), with little seasonal variation. French is the official language, but a Creole patois is also spoken. The majority of the population belongs to the Roman Catholic Church, although other Christian churches are represented. The capital is Cayenne.

CONTEMPORARY POLITICAL HISTORY

Historical Context

French occupation commenced in the early 17th century. After brief periods of Dutch, English and Portuguese rule, the territory was finally confirmed as French in 1817. The colony steadily declined, after a short period of prosperity in the 1850s as a result of the discovery of gold in the basin of the Approuague river. French Guiana, including the notorious Devil's Island, was used as a penal colony and as a place of exile for convicts and political prisoners before the practice was halted in 1937. The colony became a Department of France in 1946.

Domestic Political Affairs

French Guiana's reputation as an area of political and economic stagnation was dispelled by the growth of pro-independence sentiments, and the use of violence by a small minority, compounded by tensions between the Guyanais and large numbers of immigrant workers. In 1974 French Guiana was granted regional status, as part of France's governmental reorganization, thus acquiring greater economic autonomy. In that year, none the less, demonstrations against unemployment, the worsening economic situation and French government policy with regard to the Department led to the detention of leading trade unionists and pro-independence politicians. Further industrial and political unrest in the late 1970s prompted the Parti Socialiste Guyanais (PSG), then the strongest political organization, to demand greater autonomy for the Department. In 1980 there were several bomb attacks against 'colonialist' targets by an extremist group, Fo nou Libéré la Guyane. Reforms introduced by the French Socialist Government in 1982–83 devolved some power over local affairs to the new Conseil régional (Regional Council). In the 1983 election to the Conseil régional the left-wing parties gained a majority of votes, but not of seats, and the balance of power was held by the separatist Union des Travailleurs Guyanais (UTG), the political wing of which became the Parti National Populaire Guyanais (PNPG) in 1985. At the election to the Conseil général (General Council) held in 1985, the PSG and left-wing independents secured a majority of seats.

For the general election to the Assemblée nationale (National Assembly) in 1986, French Guiana's representation was increased from one to two deputies. The PSG increased its strength on the Conseil régional following a simultaneous election to that body, and Georges Othily of the PSG was re-elected President of the Conseil. Left-wing parties again won a majority of seats at the election to the Conseil général in 1988. In September 1989 Othily was elected to take French Guiana's seat in the French Sénat (Senate). Othily had been expelled from the PSG for having worked too closely with the opposition parties. However, he attracted support from those who regarded the party's domination of French Guiana as corrupt. In December Othily formed his own party, the Forces Démocratiques Guyanaises (FDG), which included other dissident members of the PSG.

The PSG dominated in elections to both the Conseil général and the Conseil régional in 1992: party leader Elie Castor retained the presidency of the Conseil général while PSG Secretary-General Antoine Karam was elected as President of the Conseil régional. In a referendum in September, 67% of voters in French Guiana approved ratification of the Treaty on European Union (see p. 276), although a high abstention rate was recorded.

At the 1993 elections to the Assemblée nationale Léon Bertrand of the Gaullist Rassemblement pour la République (RPR) was re-elected, along with Christiane Taubira-Delannon, the founder of the independent left-wing Walwari movement and an outspoken critic of existing policies for the management of French Guiana's natural resources. The PSG's representation in the Conseil général fell following the 1994 cantonal elections; none the less, one of its members, Stéphan Phinéra-Horth, was subsequently elected President of the Conseil.

A boycott of classes by secondary school pupils, who were demanding improved conditions of study, escalated in late 1996 into a crisis that was regarded as exemplifying wider social tensions between the Department and metropolitan France. The refusal of the Prefect, Pierre Dartout, to receive schools' representatives prompted protests in Cayenne, which swiftly degenerated into rioting and looting. The central Government dispatched anti-riot police to assist the local security forces, and it was announced that the Secretary of State for Overseas Departments and Territories, Jean-Jacques de Peretti, and the Minister of National Education, François Bayrou, would visit French Guiana. However, the conviction, shortly afterwards, of several people implicated in the rioting provoked further protests and clashes with security forces, and a one-day general strike in Cayenne, organized by the UTG, was widely observed. The extent of the security forces' actions in suppressing the demonstrations was criticized, as was the approach of the Department's administrators. An agreement on the students' material demands was reached, but, to considerable local acclaim, the ministers announced the establishment of separate Academies for French Guiana, Guadeloupe and Martinique, as well as additional primary educational facilities, and a programme was declared to improve academic standards in secondary schools. In all, the measures were to cost the French Government more than 500m. francs.

In April 1997 violent incidents followed the arrest of five pro-independence activists suspected of setting fire to the home of the public prosecutor during the disturbances of November 1996. Five others, including leading members of the UTG and the PNPG, were subsequently detained in connection with the arson incident. The transfer of all 10 detainees to Martinique prompted further violent protests in Cayenne: police reinforcements were dispatched by the central Government to help suppress the violence.

In 1997 Léon Bertrand and Christiane Taubira-Delannon were both re-elected to the Assemblée nationale in elections that were marked by a high rate of abstention. Elections to the Conseils régional and général were held in 1998. The PSG lost seats on both bodies. Karam was re-elected to the presidency of the Conseil régional. André Lecante, an independent left-wing councillor, was elected as President of the Conseil général, defeating the incumbent, Phinéra-Horth. In September Georges Othily was re-elected to the Sénat.

Demands for further autonomy

In January 1999 representatives of 10 separatist organizations from French Guiana, Guadeloupe and Martinique, including the Mouvement de la Décolonisation et d'Emancipation Sociale (MDES) and the PNPG, signed a joint declaration denouncing 'French colonialism', in which they stated their intention to campaign for the reinstatement of the three Caribbean Overseas Departments on a UN list of territories to be decolonized. Following a series of meetings, in December the Presidents of the regional councils of French Guiana, Guadeloupe and Martinique signed a joint declaration in Basse-Terre, Guadeloupe, affirming their intention to propose, to the President and the Government, a legislative amendment aimed at creating a new status of overseas region. However, the Secretary of State for Overseas Departments and Territories, Jean-Jack Queyranne, in early 2000 dismissed the declaration as unconstitutional and exceeding the mandate of politicians responsible. In March, during a visit to the Department by Queyranne, rioting broke out following his refusal to meet a delegation of separatist organizations. Later that month the Conseil régional overwhelmingly rejected reforms proposed by Queyranne, which included the creation of a Congrès (Congress) in French Guiana, as well as the extension of the Departments' powers in areas such as regional co-operation. Nevertheless, the proposals were approved by the Assemblée nationale in November, and ratified by the Constitutional Council in the following month.

In November 2000 several people were injured following riots in Cayenne. The riots followed a pro-autonomy march, organized by the UTG. Protesters claimed they had been excluded from talks on French Guiana's status. Nevertheless, discussions were held in December in Paris attended by Queyranne's successor, Christian Paul, various senior politicians from French Guiana and representatives from the PSG, the RPR, Walwari, and the FDG. In 2001, following further consultations, it was agreed that a document detailing proposals for increased autonomy for French Guiana was to be drawn up by local officials and was to be presented to the French Government for approval. These proposals included: the division of the territory into four districts; the creation of a Territorial Collectivity (Collectivité territoriale), governed by a 41-member Assembly elected for a five-year term; and the establishment of an independent executive council. There was also a request that the territory be given control over legislative and administrative affairs, as well as legislative authority on matters concerning French Guiana alone. In November the French Government announced itself to be in favour of the suggested constitutional developments; in March 2003 a constitutional amendment conferred the status of Overseas Region (Région d'outre-mer) on French Guiana.

At elections to the presidency of the Conseil général in 2001, the left-wing independent candidate Joseph Ho-Ten-You defeated André Lecante. At the legislative elections held in 2002, Taubira-Delannon was re-elected to the Assemblée nationale.

In September 2001 Christian Paul announced the establishment of a number of measures designed to improve security in the Department. Plans included a 20% increase in the police force, the creation of a small 'peace corps' and a continuous police presence in the town of Maripasoula and its surrounding region, following concerns over the security of gold prospectors in the area. In 2002 the gendarmerie, in co-operation with the national police, began a series of operations in the south of the Department aimed at stopping the illegal gold trade. As well as causing extensive environmental damage, unlicensed gold-mining operations were a chief cause of illegal immigration, and a focus for other criminal activities, such as drugs-smuggling and gun-running.

In elections to the Conseil régional in March 2004 the PSG won a majority of seats. Antoine Karam was duly re-elected as President of the Conseil. In May 2005 a national referendum was held on ratification of the European Union constitutional treaty: in the Department 60.1% of participating voters were in favour of adopting the treaty; however, voter turn-out was low, at just 23.1%. The treaty was ultimately rejected by a majority of voters in metropolitan France.

At the first round of the national presidential election in April 2007, the Union pour un Mouvement Populaire (UMP) candidate, Nicolas Sarkozy, won 41% of the votes cast in the Department, ahead of Ségolène Royal of the PS, who attracted 33% of ballot. At the second round, held on 6 May, Sarkozy secured the presidency, winning 53% of the votes cast in the Department. Meanwhile, at elections to the Assemblée nationale, held on 10 and 17 June, Taubira-Delannon, representing Walwari, and Chantal Berthelot of the PSG secured the Department's two seats. Following municipal elections held on 10 March 2008, Alain Tien-Long replaced Pierre Désert as President of the Conseil général. At an election held on 21 September Georges Patient and Jean-Etienne Antoinette were elected as the Department's senate representatives.

Efforts to halt illegal gold-mining were intensified in 2008. In February, during a visit to French Guiana, President Sarkozy announced a four-month deployment of gendarmes and military personnel in Operation Harpie, which aimed to disrupt unlicensed mining activities and combat illegal immigration, especially from Brazil. As part of his visit, Sarkozy met Brazilian President Lula da Silva and agreed to increase border co-operation between the two countries. Operation Harpie was expanded and renewed for a further six months in April 2009. However, with the problem of illegal gold-mining persisting, Operation Harpie became a permanent mission from March 2010.

Recent developments: referendum on autonomy

President Sarkozy, during a visit to the region in June 2009, proposed a series of referendums on the issue of increased autonomy for the French Overseas Regions in the Caribbean. French Guiana's plebiscite was duly held on 10 January 2010. The electorate, fearful of losing economic support from mainland France and unwilling to confer greater power upon the local political élite, voted overwhelmingly to reject any increase in autonomy, with 69.8% voting against the proposal. The rate of participation by the electorate was 48.2%. A further referendum on institutional reform was held on 24 January, and 57.5% of participants voted in favour of changing the status of French Guiana to a collectivité unique (single collectivity), replacing the existing two-tier departmental and regional administrative structure. Only 27.4% of the electorate took part in the plebiscite. The authorities hoped that the merger of the departmental and regional levels of government (expected to take place in 2014) would increase efficiency and reduce operating costs. In mid-2011 the Assemblée nationale approved legislation to facilitate this transition to a collectivité unique. Polls were scheduled for March 2014 to elect the 51 members of a new, consolidated legislative body, which would replace the Conseil régional and the Conseil général.

At elections to the Conseil régional held on 14 and 21 March 2010, the UMP list secured 21 of the 31 council seats, with 56.1% of the ballot. The left-wing list, led by Walwari and the MDES, obtained the remaining 10 seats and won 43.9% of the votes cast. Rodolphe Alexandre was elected as President of the Conseil régional. The rate of participation by the electorate was 50.5%. Municipal elections were conducted on 20 and 27 March 2011, following which Alain Tien-Long was re-elected as President of the Conseil général. In April Denis Labbé was appointed as Prefect, replacing Daniel Férey.

CONSTITUTION AND GOVERNMENT

France is represented in French Guiana by an appointed Prefect. There are two councils with local powers: the Conseil général, with 19 members, and the Conseil régional, with 31 members. Both are elected by universal adult suffrage for a period of six years. French Guiana elects two representatives to the Assemblée nationale in Paris, and sends two elected representatives to the Sénat. French Guiana is also represented at the European Parliament.

ECONOMIC AFFAIRS

In 2003 French Guiana's gross domestic product (GDP), measured at current prices, was US $1,551m., equivalent to $8,300 per head. Between 1990 and 2001, according to UN estimates, GDP increased, in real terms, at an average rate of 3.1% per year; growth in 2001 was 1.6%. Between the censuses of 1999 and 2006, according to provisional figures, the population increased at an average annual rate of 3.9%. According to official figures, in 2009 French Guiana's GDP was €3,212.1m., equivalent to €14,028 per head.

Agriculture (including fishing) engaged an estimated 1.6% of the economically active population in 2007. In 2003 the sector contributed 4.6% of GDP. In 2008 agricultural products accounted for some 16.5% of total export earnings, at €15.9m. The dominant activities are fisheries and forestry, although the contribution of the latter to export earnings has declined in recent years. In 2009 shrimp production (excluding farmed shrimp) was recorded at 1,326 metric tons. The aquaculture industry faced competition from shrimp producers in Latin America and Asia and rising fuel prices and in 2005 the Compagnie Française de Pêche Nouvelle went into liquidation. The principal crops for local consumption are cassava, vegetables and rice, and sugar cane is grown for making rum; rum production in 2010 was 2,019 hl. Livestock rearing was also largely for subsistence. In 2009 Guianese abattoirs produced an estimated 1,276 tons of meat, mostly pork, poultry and beef. Rice, pineapples and citrus fruit are cultivated for export. According to UN estimates, agricultural GDP decreased at an average annual rate of 0.8% in 1990–98; in 1998 agricultural GDP increased by an estimated 0.3%.

Industry, including construction and agrarian and food industries, contributed an estimated 20.3% to GDP in 2003, while in 2007 it engaged 16.1% of the employed labour force. The mining sector is dominated by the extraction of gold, which involves small-scale alluvial operations as well as larger local and multinational mining concerns. The first new concession in 70 years was awarded to Cambior in 2004 for a 25-year period. The US Geological Survey estimated gold production in 2010 at a provisional 2,000 kg. Gold exports in 2008 were put at €35.7m., a 28.8% decrease on the previous year and indicative of the general decline in the economic contribution of the precious metal. Crushed rock for the construction industry is the only other mineral extracted in significant quantities, although exploratory drilling of known diamond deposits began in 1995. Deposits of bauxite, columbo-tantalite and kaolin are also present. There is little manufacturing activity, except for the processing of fisheries products (mainly shrimp-freezing) and the distillation of rum. In 1990–98 industrial GDP (excluding construction) increased at an average annual rate of 7.8%. The construction sector engaged 7.6% of the employed labour force in 2007. It expanded at an average of 2.0% per year in 1990–98.

French Guiana's Petit-Saut 116-MW hydroelectric dam, on the Sinnamary river, provided most of the territory's electrical energy requirements, and was expected to do so for about 30 years. Imports of fuels and combustibles accounted for 12.0% of total imports in 2008.

The services sector engaged an estimated 82.3% of the employed labour force in 2007 and, according to official sources, contributed 75.2% of GDP in 2003. The European Space Agency's satellite-launching centre at Kourou has provided a considerable stimulus to the economy, most notably the construction sector (which engaged an estimated 6.8% of the employed labour force in 2006). The space centre was estimated to contribute approximately one-quarter of French Guiana's GDP and approximately one-half of its tax revenues. In 2011 there were seven rocket launches. The tourism sector expanded in the last two decades of the 20th century, although its potential is limited by the lack of infrastructure away from the coast. In 2007 some 108,801 visitor arrivals were recorded, while receipts from tourism totalled US $49m. in the same year. In 2003 it was estimated that tourism contributed 3% of GDP.

French Guiana recorded a trade deficit of some €923.5m in 2010. In 2008 the principal source of imports was metropolitan France (which supplied 45.6% of total imports); the Department's other major suppliers were Trinidad and Tobago, Martinique and Germany. Metropolitan France was also the principal market for exports in that year (38.7%); other important purchasers were Switzerland (15.6%), Germany and Italy. The principal imports in 2008 were products of agriculture and food industries, car industry products and fuels and combustibles; the principal exports were metals and metal products, car industry products, and products of agriculture and food industries.

According to the 2008 regional budget, expenditure totalled €106.7m., while revenue was €110.7m. The departmental budget for that year put revenue at €274.0m., while expenditure was €218.4m. The annual rate of inflation averaged 1.8% in 2001–10; the average rate of inflation in 2010 was 0.2%. Unemployment in 2007 was estimated at 19.4% of the total labour force. However, there is a shortage of skilled labour, offset partly by immigration. In 2008 the number of unemployed grew to 12,834, compared with 11,697 in the previous year.

Economic development in French Guiana has been hindered by the Department's location, poor infrastructure away from the coast and lack of a skilled indigenous labour force, although there is considerable potential for further growth in the fishing, forestry, mining and tourism (notably eco-tourism) sectors. A particular concern was the high rate of unemployment (21.0% at mid-2011). French Guiana's geographical characteristics—large parts of the territory are accessible only by river—have resulted in difficulties in regulating key areas of the economy, such as gold-mining and forestry. Despite registering GDP growth of 3.6% in 2009, according to official data, French Guiana did not escape the negative effects of the global financial crisis in that year, with the country experiencing declining levels of investment, a reduction in gold output, and lower tax revenues. The economy remained sluggish in 2010, and high unemployment persisted. However, a recovery in exports (particularly gold exports, which had benefited from rising prices) was a positive development, and strong internal demand resulted in GDP expanding by 2.5% in that year. The value of gold shipments rose again in 2011, but production levels were in long-term decline. A significant offshore petroleum discovery was announced in September, potentially containing up to 700m. barrels of oil. Further exploratory drilling was scheduled to be conducted during 2012, although, if the deposit proved to be commercially viable, production was not expected to commence until at least 2020.

PUBLIC HOLIDAYS

2013: 1 January (New Year's Day), 11–12 February (Lenten Carnival), 13 February (Ash Wednesday), 1 April (Easter Monday), 1 May (Labour Day), 8 May (Liberation Day), 9 May (Ascension Day), 20 May (Whit Monday), 10 June (Abolition of Slavery), 14 July (National Day, Fall of the Bastille), 15 August (Assumption), 1 November (All Saints' Day), 11 November (Armistice Day), 25 December (Christmas Day).

Statistical Survey

Sources (unless otherwise indicated): Institut National de la Statistique et des Etudes Economiques (INSEE), Service Régional de Guyane, ave Pasteur, BP 6017, 97306 Cayenne Cédex; tel. 5-94-29-73-00; fax 5-94-29-73-01; internet www.insee.fr/fr/insee_regions/guyane; Chambre de Commerce et d'Industrie de la Guyane (CCIG), Hôtel Consulaire, pl. de l'Esplanade, BP 49, 97321 Cayenne Cédex; tel. 5-94-29-96-00; fax 5-94-29-96-34; internet www.guyane.cci.fr.

AREA AND POPULATION

Area: 83,534 sq km (32,253 sq miles).

Population: 157,213 at census of 8 March 1999; 224,469 at census of 1 January 2009. Note: According to new census methodology, data in 2009 refer to median figures based on the collection of raw data over a five-year period (2006–11). *1 January 2010* (estimate): 232,223. *Mid-2012* (UN estimate): 243,171 (Source: UN, *World Population Prospects: The 2010 Revision*.

Density (at mid-2012): 2.9 per sq km.

Population by Age and Sex (UN estimates at mid-2012): *0–14:* 79,414 (males 40,409, females 39,005); *15–64:* 152,570 (males 75,929, females 76,641); *65 and over:* 11,187 (males 5,355, females 5,832); *Total* 243,171 (males 121,693, females 121,478) (Source: UN, *World Population Prospects: The 2010 Revision*).

Principal Towns (population at 1999 census): Cayenne (capital) 50,594; Saint-Laurent-du-Maroni 19,211; Kourou 19,107; Matoury 18,032; Rémire-Montjoly 15,555; Mana 5,445; Macouria 5,050; Maripasoula 3,710. *Mid-2009* (UN estimate, incl. suburbs): Cayenne 62,437 (Source: UN, *World Urbanization Prospects: The 2009 Revision*).

Births, Marriages and Deaths (2009): Registered live births 6,171 (birth rate 26.9 per 1,000); Registered marriages 611 (marriage rate 2.7 per 1,000); Registered deaths 699 (death rate 3.1 per 1,000).

Life Expectancy (years at birth): 76.3 (males 73.0; females 80.2) in 2010. Source: Pan American Health Organization.

Economically Active Population (persons aged 15 years and over, 1999): Agriculture, forestry and fishing 2,888; Construction 3,256; Industry 3,524; Trade 4,573; Transport 1,616; Education, health and social services 8,990; Public administration 10,337; Other services 8,259; Total employed 43,443 (males 25,703, females 17,740). *2007* (provisional estimates at 31 December): Agriculture 803; Industry 4,111; Construction 3,712; Trade 4,426; Services 35,677; Total employed 48,729; Unemployed 11,697; Total labour force 60,426. Note: Figures for employment exclude unsalaried workers. *31 December 2008:* Unemployed 12,834.

HEALTH AND WELFARE

Key Indicators

Total Fertility Rate (children per woman, 2010): 3.1.

Under-5 Mortality Rate (per 1,000 live births, 2010): 14.2.

Physicians (per 1,000 head, c. 2001): 1.4.

Hospital Beds (per 1,000 head, 2005): 3.0.

Access to Water (% of persons, 2004): 84.

Access to Sanitation (% of persons, 2004): 78.

Source: mostly Pan American Health Organization.

For other sources and definitions, see explanatory note on p. vi.

AGRICULTURE, ETC.

Principal Crops ('000 metric tons, 2010, FAO estimates): Rice, paddy 8.5; Cassava 28.7; Sugar cane 4.0; Cabbages and other brassicas 4.9; Tomatoes 4.0; Cucumbers and gherkins 1.6; Beans, green 1.3; Bananas 3.8; Plantains 3.3. *Aggregate Production* ('000 metric tons, may include official, semi-official or estimated data): Total vegetables (incl. melons) 17.4; Total fruits (excl. melons) 17.6.

Livestock ('000 head, 2010, FAO estimates): Cattle 14.0; Pigs 20.0; Sheep 1.0.

Livestock Products (metric tons, 2010, FAO estimates): Cattle meat 290; Pig meat 410; Chicken meat 550; Cows' milk 350; Hen eggs 640.

Forestry ('000 cubic metres, 2010, FAO estimates): *Roundwood Removals* (excl. bark): Sawlogs, veneer logs and logs for sleepers 84.3; Other industrial wood 9.0; Fuel wood 122.0; Total 215.3. *Sawnwood Production* (incl. railway sleepers): Total 15.

Fishing (metric tons, live weight, 2009): Capture 4,134 (Marine fishes 2,808; Shrimps 1,326); Aquaculture 35 (FAO estimate); *Total catch* 4,169 (FAO estimate).

Source: FAO.

MINING

Production ('000 metric tons unless otherwise indicated, 2010, estimates): Cement 62,000; Gold (metal content of ore, kilograms, reported figure) 2,000; Sand 1,500. Source: US Geological Survey.

INDUSTRY

Production: Rum 2,019 hl in 2010; Electric energy 716 million kWh in 2009 (Source: l'Institut d'Emission des Départements d'Outre-mer, *Rapport Annuel 2010*).

FINANCE

Currency and Exchange Rates: 100 cent = 1 euro (€). *Sterling and Dollar Equivalents* (30 December 2011): £1 sterling = €1.195; US $1 = €0.773; €10 = £8.37 = $12.94. *Average Exchange Rate* (euros per US dollar): 0.720 in 2009; 0.755 in 2010; 0.719 in 2011. Note: The national currency was formerly the French franc. From the introduction of the euro, with French participation, on 1 January 1999, a fixed exchange rate of €1 = 6.55957 French francs was in operation. Euro notes and coins were introduced on 1 January 2002. The euro and French currency circulated alongside each other until 17 February, after which the euro became the sole legal tender. Some of the figures in this Survey are still in terms of francs.

Budgets (excl. debt rescheduling, € million, 2008, unless otherwise indicated): *Regional Government:* Current revenue 65.9 (Taxes 50.5); Capital revenue 44.9; Total 110.7. Current expenditure 50.1; Capital expenditure 56.6; Total 106.7. *Departmental Government* (2008): Revenue 274.0; Expenditure 218.4. Source: Département des Etudes et des Statistiques Locales.

Money Supply (million French francs at 31 December 1996): Currency outside banks 3,000; Demand deposits at banks 1,621; *Total money* 4,621.

Cost of Living (Consumer Price Index; base: 2000 = 100): All items 118.2 in 2008; 119.0 in 2009; 119.2 in 2010. Source: ILO.

Gross Domestic Product (US $ million at constant 1990 prices): 1,668 in 2001; 1,695 in 2002; 1,722 in 2003. Source: UN, *Statistical Yearbook*.

Expenditure on the Gross Domestic Product (€ million at current prices, 2009, estimates): Total final consumption expenditure 3,170 (General government and non-profit institutions serving households 1,599, Households 1,571); Gross capital formation 927; *Total domestic expenditure* 4,097; Exports of goods and services 1,033; *Less* Imports of goods and services 1,553; Statistical discrepancy –365; *GDP in purchasers' values* 3,212. Source: Institut d'Emission des Départements d'Outre-mer, *Guyane: Rapport Annuel 2010*.

Gross Domestic Product by Economic Activity (€ million at current prices, 2003): Agriculture, hunting, forestry and fishing 95; Food industries 39; Manufacturing 180; Energy 40; Construction 163; Services 1,564 (Restaurants and hotels 42, Transport –85, Commerce 223, Other market services 560; Non-market services 824); *Sub-total* 2,081; Financial intermediation services indirectly measured –42; Import duties, less subsidies 169; *GDP in purchasers' values* 2,207.

EXTERNAL TRADE

Principal Commodities (€ million, 2008): *Imports c.i.f.:* Products of agriculture and food industries 161.9; Pharmaceutical products 59.3; Home equipment 56.1; Car industry products 161.5; Mechanical equipment 122.0; Electronic equipment 56.6; Fuels and combustibles 127.6; Total (incl. others) 1,065.0. *Exports f.o.b.:* Products of agriculture and food industries 15.9; Car industry products 23.5; Mechanical equipment 3.2; Electronic equipment 7.8; Metals and products thereof 36.7; Total (incl. others) 96.3. *2010* (€ million): Total imports 1,081.8; Total exports 158.3 (Source: Institut d'Emission des Départements d'Outre-mer, *Guyane: Rapport Annuel 2010*).

Principal Trading Partners (€ million, 2008): *Imports c.i.f.:* France (metropolitan) 485.4; Germany 31.9; Italy 17.6; Martinique 38.4; Netherlands 21.2; Spain 17.0; Trinidad and Tobago 51.4; Total (incl. others) 1,065.0. *Exports f.o.b.:* France (metropolitan) 37.3; Germany 11.4; Guadeloupe 7.7; Italy 9.5; Martinique 8.3; Spain 2.5; Switzerland 15.0; Total (incl. others) 96.3. *2010* (€ million): Total imports 1,081.8; Total exports 158.3 (Source: Institut d'Emission des Départements d'Outre-mer, *Guyane: Rapport Annuel 2010*).

TRANSPORT

Road Traffic ('000 motor vehicles in use, 2001): Passenger cars 32.9; Commercial vehicles 11.9 (Source: UN, *Statistical Yearbook*). *2002:* 50,000 motor vehicles in use.

International Sea-borne Shipping (traffic, 2005 unless otherwise indicated): International vessels entered 115; Goods loaded 25,103 metric tons; Goods unloaded 472,567 metric tons (Source: CCIG); Passengers carried 275,300 (1998).

Civil Aviation (2009): Freight carried (incl. post) 5,475 metric tons; Passengers carried 425,000.

TOURISM

Tourist Arrivals by Country (2007): France 62,016; Guadeloupe 14,362; Martinique 22,739; Total (incl. others) 108,801.

Receipts from Tourism (US $ million, incl. passenger transport): 49 in 2007.

Source: World Tourism Organization.

COMMUNICATIONS MEDIA

Radio Receivers ('000 in use): 104 in 1997.

Television Receivers ('000 in use): 37 in 1998.

Telephones ('000 main lines in use): 45.5 in 2010.

Mobile Cellular Telephones ('000 subscribers): 217.7 in 2009.

Personal Computers ('000 in use): 33 in 2004.

Internet Users ('000): 58.0 in 2009.

Broadband Subscribers ('000): 30.2 in 2009.

Daily Newspaper: 1 in 1996 (average circulation 2,000 copies).

Sources: UNESCO, *Statistical Yearbook*; UN, *Statistical Yearbook*; International Telecommunication Union.

EDUCATION

Pre-primary (2008/09): 40 institutions; 14,003 students (13,187 state, 816 private).

Primary (2008/09): 114 institutions (106 state, 8 private); 26,454 students (24,792 state, 1,662 private).

Specialized Pre-primary and Primary (2008/09): 433 students (428 state, 5 private).

Secondary (2008/09): 42 institutions (37 state, 5 private); 30,814 students (29,102 state, 1,712 private). Source: Rectorat de la Guyane *Enquête 19 (1st degré)* and *Enquête 19 (2nd degré)*.

Higher (2007/08): 2,653 students.

Teachers (2008/09 unless otherwise indicated): *Primary:* 2,243 teachers (2,121 state, 122 private); *Secondary:* 2,433 teachers (2,285 state, 148 private); *Higher* (2004/05): 63 teachers. Source: Ministère de l'Education Nationale, *Repères et références statistiques*.

Adult Literacy Rate: 83.0% (males 83.6%, females 82.3%) in 1998. Source: Pan American Health Organization.

Directory

The Government

(May 2012)

HEAD OF STATE

President: NICOLAS SARKOZY.

Prefect: DENIS LABBÉ, Préfecture, 1 rue Fiedmont, BP 7008, 97307 Cayenne Cédex; tel. 5-94-39-45-00; fax 5-94-30-02-77; e-mail courrier@guyane.pref.gouv.fr; internet www.guyane.pref.gouv.fr.

DEPARTMENTAL ADMINISTRATION

President of the General Council: ALAIN TIEN-LIONG, Hôtel du Département, pl. Léopold Héder, BP 5021, 97397 Cayenne Cédex; tel. 5-94-29-55-00; fax 5-94-29-55-25; e-mail atienliong@cg973.fr; internet www.cg973.fr.

President of the Economic and Social Committee: ROGER-MICHEL LOUPEC, 66 ave du Général de Gaulle, 97300 Cayenne; tel. 5-94-28-96-01; fax 5-94-30-73-65; e-mail cesr@cr-guyane.fr.

President of the Culture, Education and Environment Committee: JEAN-PIERRE BACOT, 66 ave du Général de Gaulle, 97300 Cayenne; tel. 5-94-25-66-84; fax 5-94-37-94-24; e-mail ccee@cr-guyane.fr; internet www.cr-guyane.fr.

President of the Regional Council: RODOLPHE ALEXANDRE (UMP), Cité Administrative Régionale, 4179 route de Montabo, Carrefour de Suzini, BP 7025, 97307 Cayenne Cédex; tel. 5-94-29-20-20; fax 5-94-31-95-22; e-mail cabcrg@cr-guyane.fr; internet www.cr-guyane.fr.

Elections, 14 and 21 March 2010

	Seats
Guyane 73*	21
Deux Ans: Un Marathon pour Bâtir†	10
Total	31

* Electoral list comprising the Union pour un Mouvement Populaire (UMP) and allies.

† Electoral list comprising various left-wing parties led by Walwari and the Mouvement de Décolinisation et d'Emancipation Sociale (MDES).

REPRESENTATIVES TO THE FRENCH PARLIAMENT

Deputies to the French National Assembly: CHRISTIANE TAUBIRA-DELANNON (Walwari), CHANTAL BERTHELOT (PSG).

Representatives to the French Senate: GEORGES PATIENT (Groupe Socialiste), JEAN-ETIENNE ANTOINETTE (Groupe Socialiste).

Political Organizations

Forces Démocratiques de Guyane (FDG): 41 rue du 14 Juillet, BP 403, 97300 Cayenne; tel. 5-94-28-96-79; fax 5-94-30-80-66; e-mail g.othily@senat.fr; f. 1989 by a split in the PSG; Pres. ALICK EGOUY; Sec.-Gen. GIL HORTH.

Mouvement de Décolonisation et d'Emancipation Sociale (MDES): 21 rue Maissin, 97300 Cayenne; tel. 5-94-30-55-97; fax 5-94-30-97-73; e-mail mdes.parti@wanadoo.org; internet www.mdes.org; f. 1991; pro-independence; Sec.-Gen. MAURICE PINDARD.

Parti Socialiste (PS): 7 rue de l'Adjudant Pindard, 97300 Cayenne Cédex; tel. 5-94-37-81-33; fax 5-94-37-81-56; e-mail fede973.partisocialiste@wanadoo.fr; internet guyane.parti-socialiste.fr; departmental br. of the metropolitan party; Leader LÉON JEAN BAPTISTE EDOUARD; Sec. PAUL DEBRIETTE.

Parti Socialiste Guyanais (PSG): 1 Cité Césaire, BP 46, 97300 Cayenne; tel. 5-94-28-11-44; fax 5-94-28-46-92; e-mail partisocialisteguyanais@orange.fr; internet www.psg-guyane.com; f. 1956; left-wing; Sec.-Gen. MARIE JOSÉ LALSIE.

Union pour un Mouvement Populaire (UMP): 42 rue du Docteur Barrat, 97300 Cayenne; tel. 5-94-28-80-74; fax 5-94-28-80-75; internet www.u-m-p.org; f. 2002 as Union pour la Majorité Presidentielle by mems of the fmr Rassemblement pour la République and Union pour la Démocratie Française; centre-right; departmental br. of the metropolitan party; Pres., Departmental Cttee RÉMY-LOUIS BUDOC.

Les Verts Guyane: 64 rue Madame Payé, 97300 Cayenne; tel. 5-94-40-97-27; e-mail tamanoir.guyane@wanadoo.fr; internet guyane.lesverts.fr; ecologist; departmental br. of the metropolitan party; Regional Sec. JOSÉ GAILLOU.

Walwari: 35 rue Schoelcher, BP 803, 97300 Cayenne Cédex; tel. 5-94-30-31-00; fax 5-94-31-84-95; e-mail info@walwari.org; internet www.walwari.org; f. 1993; left-wing; Leader CHRISTIANE TAUBIRA-DELANNON; Sec.-Gen. JOËL PIED.

Judicial System

Courts of Appeal: see Judicial System, Martinique.

Tribunal de Grande Instance: Palais de Justice, 9 ave du Général de Gaulle, 97300 Cayenne; Pres. PIERRE GOUZENNE.

Religion

CHRISTIANITY

The Roman Catholic Church

French Guiana comprises the single diocese of Cayenne, suffragan to the archdiocese of Fort-de-France, Martinique. Some 80% of the population are Roman Catholics. French Guiana participates in the Antilles Episcopal Conference, currently based in Port of Spain, Trinidad and Tobago.

Bishop of Cayenne: Rt Rev. EMMANUEL M. P. L. LAFONT, Evêché, 24 rue Madame Payé, BP 378, 97328 Cayenne Cédex; tel. 5-94-28-98-48; fax 5-94-30-20-33; e-mail emmanuel.lafont@wanadoo.fr; internet www.guyane.catholique.fr.

The Anglican Communion

Within the Church in the Province of the West Indies, French Guiana forms part of the diocese of Guyana. The Bishop is resident in Georgetown, Guyana. There were fewer than 100 adherents in 2000.

Other Churches

In 2000 there were an estimated 7,000 Protestants and 7,200 adherents professing other forms of Christianity.

Assembly of God: 1051 route de Raban, 97300 Cayenne; tel. 5-94-35-23-04; fax 5-94-35-23-05; e-mail jacques.rhino@wanadoo.fr; internet www.addguyane.fr; Pres. JACQUES RHINO; c. 500 mems.

Church of Jesus Christ of Latter-day Saints (Mormons): Route de la Rocade, 97305 Cayenne; c. 368 mems.

Seventh-day Adventist Church: Mission Adventiste de la Guyane, 39 rue Schoëlcher, BP 169, 97324 Cayenne Cédex; tel. 5-94-25-64-26; fax 5-94-37-93-02; e-mail adventiste.mission@orange.fr; f. 1949; Pres. and Chair. ALAIN LIBER; 2,164 mems.

The Jehovah's Witnesses are also represented.

The Press

France-Guyane: 17 rue Lallouette, BP 428, 97329 Cayenne; tel. 5-94-29-70-00; fax 5-94-29-70-02; e-mail france.guyane@media-antilles.fr; internet www.franceguyane.fr; daily; Publishing Dir FRÉDÉRIC AURAND; Local Dir MARC AUBURTIN; Editor-in-Chief JÉRÔME RIGOLAGE; circ. 9,000.

L'Hebdo de Guyane: pl. Léopold Héder, 97300 Cayenne; tel. 5-94-29-55-55; fax 5-94-29-55-54; e-mail communication@cg973.fr; publ. by the Conseil général; 5 a week; Editor-in-Chief TCHISSÉKA LOBELT.

La Semaine Guyanaise: 6 ave Louis Pasteur, 97300 Cayenne; tel. 5-94-31-09-83; fax 5-94-31-95-20; e-mail semaine.guyanaise@nplus.gf; internet www.semaineguyanaise.com; weekly (Thurs.); Dir ALAIN CHAUMET; Editor-in-Chief JÉRÔME VALLETTE.

Oka.Mag': 11 rue Abel Azor, 18 Cité Manil, 97310 Kourou; tel. 5-94-22-01-44; fax 5-94-32-17-66; e-mail oka.mag@wanadoo.fr; internet www.okamag.fr; f. 2001; 6 a year; Amerindian interest; Pres. and Editor-in-Chief DANIEL FRANÇOIS; circ. 15,000.

Ròt Kozé: 21 rue Maissin, 97300 Cayenne; tel. 5-94-30-55-97; fax 5-94-30-97-73; e-mail webmaster@mdes.org; internet www.mdes.org; f. 1990; left-wing organ of the MDES party; monthly; Dir MAURICE PINDARD.

Publishers

Editions Anne C.: 8 Lot Mapaou, route de Baduel, BP 212, 97325 Cayenne; tel. and fax 5-94-35-20-10; e-mail canne@nplus.gf; f. 1998; French-Creole children's and youth literature; Dir NICOLE PARFAIT-CHAUMET.

Ibis Rouge Editions: chemin de la Levée, BP 267, 97357 Matoury; tel. 5-94-35-95-66; fax 5-94-35-95-68; e-mail jlm@ibisrouge.fr; internet www.ibisrouge.fr; f. 1995; general literature, French-Creole, and academic; Gen. Man. JEAN-LOUIS MALHERBE; agencies in Guadeloupe and Martinique.

PUBLISHERS' ASSOCIATION

Promolivres Guyane: BP 96, 97394 Rémire-Montjoly Cédex; tel. 5-94-29-55-56; fax 5-94-38-52-82; e-mail promolivreguyane@wanadoo.fr; f. 1996; asscn mems incl. editors, booksellers, journalists and librarians; promotes French Guianese literature; Pres. TCHISSÉKA LOBELT.

Broadcasting and Communications

TELECOMMUNICATIONS

Digicel Antilles Françaises Guyane: see Martinique—Telecommunications.

France Telecom: 76 ave Voltaire, BP 8080, 97300 Cayenne; tel. 5-94-39-91-15; fax 5-94-39-91-00; e-mail eline.miranda@francetelecom.com.

Orange Caraïbe: see Guadeloupe—Telecommunications.

Outremer Telecom: 112 ave du Général de Gaulle, 97300 Cayenne; tel. 5-94-28-71-15; fax 5-94-23-93-59; e-mail communication@outremer-telecom.fr; internet www.outremer-telecom.fr; f. 1998; mobile telecommunications provider; Group CEO JEAN-MICHEL HEGESIPPE.

ONLY: 112 ave du Général de Gaulle, 97300 Cayenne; tel. 5-94-28-71-15; fax 5-94-23-93-59; e-mail contact@outremer-telecom.fr; internet www.only.fr; f. 2004 as Outremer Telecom Guyane; subsidiary of Outremer Telecom, France; present name adopted following merger of Volubis, ONLY and OOL in 2006; mobile and fixed telecommunications provider.

BROADCASTING

Guyane 1ère (Outre-mer Première): ave le Grand Boulevard, Z.A.D. Moulin à Vent, 97354 Rémire-Montjoly; tel. 5-94-25-67-00; fax 5-94-25-67-64; internet guyane.la1ere.fr; acquired by Groupe France Télévisions in 2004; fmrly Société Nationale de Radio-Télévision Française d'Outre-mer; name changed to Réseau France Outre-mer (RFO) in 1998; present name adopted in 2010; Radio-Guyane Inter accounts for 46.6% of listeners (2003); Télé Guyane/RFO1 and RFO (Tempo) account for 52.3% and 7.5% of viewers, respectively (2003); Dir.-Gen. GENEVIÈVE GIARD; Regional Dir FRED AYANGMA.

Radio

KFM Guyane: 6 rue François Arago, 97300 Cayenne; tel. 5-94-31-30-38; fax 5-94-37-84-20; internet www.kfmguyane.skyrock.com; f. 1993 as Radio Kikiwi; present name adopted 2003.

Métis FM: Cayenne; internet www.metis.fm; popular music station.

Mig FM Guyane: 100 ave du Général de Gaulle, 97300 Cayenne; tel. 5-94-30-77-67; fax 5-94-31-86-81; f. 1995; Creole.

NRJ Guyane: 2 blvd de la République, 97300 Cayenne; tel. 5-94-39-54-88; fax 5-94-39-54-79; e-mail wladimir@nrjguyane.com; internet www.nrjguyane.com; f. 2006; commercial radio station; Man MARC HO-A-CHUCK.

Ouest FM Guyane: Cayenne; tel. 5-94-38-29-19; e-mail contact@ouestfm.net; internet www.ouestfm.net; commercial music station.

Radio Joie de Vivre: 39 rue Schoëlcher, 97324 Cayenne Cédex; BP 169, 97300 Cayenne; tel. 5-94-31-29-00; fax 5-94-29-47-26; f. 1993; operated by the Seventh-day Adventist church; Gen. Man. ESAÏE AUGUSTE.

Radio Littoméga (RLM): 24 blvd Malouet, BP 108, 97320 Saint-Laurent-du-Maroni; tel. 5-94-34-22-09; e-mail centre.cl@wanadoo.fr; internet www.rlm100.com; f. 1994; Dir ARIELLE BERTRAND.

Radio Mosaïque: 11 rue Sainte-Catherine, cité Brutus, 97300 Cayenne; tel. 5-94-30-94-76; e-mail guyanes@free.fr; commercial radio station; Man. BÉRIL BELVU.

Radio Ouassailles: rue Maurice Mongeot, 97360 Mana; tel. 5-94-34-80-96; fax 5-94-34-13-89; e-mail radio.ouassailles@wanadoo.fr; f. 1994; French and Creole; Man. RÉMY AUBERT.

Radio Saint-Gabriel: Salle Paul VI, Cité Mirza, 97300 Cayenne; tel. 5-94-31-17-11; fax 5-94-28-17-51; e-mail radiosaintgabriel@wanadoo.fr; f. 2001; Roman Catholic; Man. HENRI-CLAUDE ASSÉLOS.

Radio Toucan Fréquence International (TFI): 1 pl. du Vidé, BP 68, 97300 Kourou; tel. 5-94-32-96-11; fax 5-94-39-71-61; e-mail direction@tfifm.com; internet www.tfifm.com; f. 1983; part of Groupe I-Medias Antilles-Guyane; commercial radio station.

Radio UDL (Union Défense des Libertés): 7 rue Félix Eboué, BP 5, 97393 Saint-Laurent-du-Maroni; tel. 5-94-34-10-61; fax 5-94-34-04-78; e-mail radio.udl@wanadoo.fr; internet www.udlguyane.com; f. 1982; Man. JEAN GONTRAND.

Radio Voix dans le Désert: 5 chemin du Château, 97300 Cayenne; tel. 5-94-31-73-95; fax 01-73-76-88-00; e-mail president@rvld.fr; internet www.rvld.fr; f. 1993; operated by the Assembly of God church; Pres. EDDY LAUTRIC.

Television

Antenne Créole Guyane: 31 ave Louis Pasteur, 97300 Cayenne; tel. 5-94-28-82-88; fax 5-94-29-13-08; e-mail acg@acg.gf; internet www.acg.gf; f. 1994; sole local private TV station; gen. interest with focus on music and sports; produces 30% of own programmes; received by 95% of the population, accounting for 25% of viewers (2003); Pres. MARC HO-A-CHUCK; Gen. Man. WLADIMIR MANGACHOFF.

Canal+ Guyane: 14 Lotissement Marengo, Z. I. de Collery, 97300 Cayenne; tel. 8-10-50-15-02; fax 5-94-30-53-35; internet www.canalplus-caraibes.com/guyane; f. 1996; subsidiary of Groupe Canal+, France; satellite TV station; Dir OLEG BACCOVICH.

Finance

(cap. = capital; res = reserves; dep. = deposits; m. = million; brs = branches; amounts in French francs)

BANKING

Central Bank

Institut d'Emission des Départements d'Outre-mer (IEDOM): 8 rue Christophe Colomb, BP 6016, 97306 Cayenne Cédex; tel. 5-94-29-36-50; fax 5-94-30-02-76; e-mail direction@iedom-guyane.fr; internet www.iedom.fr; f. 1959; Dir-Gen. NICOLAS DE SÈZE; Dir JEAN-PIERRE DERANCOURT.

Commercial Banks

Banque Française Commerciale Antilles-Guyane (BFC Antilles-Guyane): 8 pl. des Palmistes, BP 111, 97345 Cayenne; tel. 5-94-29-11-11; fax 5-94-30-13-12; e-mail service-client@bfc-ag.com; internet www.bfc-ag.com; f. 1985; Regional Dir JOCELYN MATHIAS.

BNP Paribas Guyane SA: 2 pl. Victor Schoëlcher, BP 35, 97300 Cayenne; tel. 5-94-39-63-00; fax 5-94-30-23-08; e-mail bnpg@bnpparibas.com; internet www.bnpparibas.com; f. 1964 following purchase of BNP Guyane (f. 1855); name changed July 2000; 94% owned by BNP Paribas SA, 3% by BNP Paribas Martinique and 3% by BNP Paribas Guadeloupe; cap. 71.7m., res 100.0m., dep. 2,007m. (Dec. 1994); Dir and CEO ANTOINE GARCIA; Gen. Sec. JACQUES SALGE; 2 brs.

Crédit Agricole: see Martinique—Finance.

Development Bank

Société Financière pour le Développement Economique de la Guyane (SOFIDEG): PK 3, 700 route de Baduel, BP 860, 97339 Cayenne Cédex; tel. 5-94-29-94-29; fax 5-94-30-60-44; e-mail sofideg@nplus.gf; f. 1982; bought from the Agence Française de Développement (AFD—q.v.) by BRED-BP in 2003; Dir FRANÇOIS CHEVILLOTTE.

Insurance

Allianz IARD: 34 rue Léopold Heder, BP 462, 97300, Cayenne Cédex; tel. 5-94-30-27-66; fax 5-94-30-69-09; e-mail agfguyana@wanadoo.fr; internet www.allianz.fr; life and short-term insurance; Dir (Latin America) Dr HELGA JUNG.

Groupama Antilles Guyane: see Martinique—Insurance.

Trade and Industry

GOVERNMENT AGENCIES

Direction de l'Agriculture et de la Forêt (DAF): Parc Rebard, BP 5002, 97305 Cayenne Cédex; tel. 5-94-29-63-74; fax 5-94-29-63-63; e-mail daf.guyane@agriculture.gouv.fr; internet daf.guyane.agriculture.gouv.fr; Dir FRANÇOIS CAZOTTES.

Direction Régionale et Départementale des Affaires Maritimes (DRAM): 2 bis, rue Mentel, BP 6008, 97306 Cayenne Cédex; tel. 5-94-29-36-15; fax 5-94-29-36-16; e-mail Dram-Guyane@developpement-durable.gouv.fr; responsible for shipping, fishing and other maritime issues at a nat. and community level; Dir STÉPHANE GATTO.

Direction Régionale de l'Industrie, de la Recherche et de l'Environnement (DRIRE): Pointe Buzaré, BP 7001, 97307 Cayenne Cédex; tel. 5-94-29-75-30; fax 5-94-29-07-34; e-mail drire-antilles-guyane@industrie.gouv.fr; internet www.ggm.drire.gouv.fr; active in industry, business services, transport, public works, tourism and distribution; Regional Dir JOEL DURANTON.

DEVELOPMENT ORGANIZATIONS

Agence de l'Environnement et de la Maîtrise de l'Energie (ADEME): 28 ave Léopold Heder, 97300 Cayenne Cédex; tel. 5-94-31-73-60; fax 5-94-30-76-69; e-mail ademe.guyane@ademe.fr; internet www.ademe-guyane.fr; Dir SUZANNE PONS.

Agence Française de Développement (AFD): Lotissement les Héliconias, route de Baduel, BP 1122, 97345 Cayenne Cédex; tel. 5-94-29-90-90; fax 5-94-30-63-32; e-mail afdcayenne@afd.fr; internet www.afd-guyane.org; fmrly Caisse Française de Développement; Dir ROBERT SATGE.

Agence Régionale de Développement économique de la Guyane (ARD): 1 pl. Schoëlcher, BP 325, 97325 Cayenne Cédex; tel. 5-94-25-66-66; fax 5-94-25-43-19; f. 2009 to replace Agence pour la Création et le Développement des Entreprises en Guyane; Dir PASCAL VELINORE.

Fédération des Organisations Amérindiennes de Guyane (FOAG): Centre des Cultures, rue Capt. Charles Claude, 97319 Awala Yalirnapo; tel. 6-94-42-27-76; fax 5-94-33-50-06; e-mail foag@

nplus.gf; f. 1993; civil liberties org. representing the rights of the indigenous peoples of French Guiana; Pres. FÉLIX TIOUKA; Sec.-Gen. Chief JEAN AUBÉRIC CHARLES.

CHAMBERS OF COMMERCE

Chambre d'Agriculture: 8 ave du Général de Gaulle, BP 544, 97333 Cayenne Cédex; tel. 5-94-29-61-95; fax 5-94-31-00-01; e-mail chambre.agriculture.973@orange.fr; Pres. CHRISTIAN EPAILLY; Dir (vacant).

Chambre de Commerce et d'Industrie de la Guyane (CCIG): Hôtel Consulaire, pl. de l'Esplanade, BP 49, 97321 Cayenne Cédex; tel. 5-94-29-96-00; fax 5-94-29-96-34; e-mail contact@guyane.cci.fr; internet www.guyane.cci.fr; Pres. JEAN-PAUL LE PELLETIER.

Chambre de Métiers: 41 Lotissement, Artisanal Zone Galmot, 97300 Cayenne Cédex; tel. 5-94-25-24-70; fax 5-94-30-54-22; e-mail m.toulemonde@cm-guyane.fr; internet www.cm-guyane.fr; Pres. HARRY CONTOUT; Sec.-Gen. CLÉMENTINE JOHANES.

Jeune Chambre Economique de Cayenne: 1 Cité A. Horth, route de Montabo, BP 1094, Cayenne; tel. 5-94-31-62-99; fax 5-94-31-76-13; internet www.jcicayenne.com; f. 1960; Pres. RENÉE-LINE SABAS; Gen. Sec. CÉLINE GENTILI.

EMPLOYERS' ORGANIZATIONS

Groupement Régional des Agriculteurs de Guyane (GRAGE): PK 15 route nationale 1, Domaine de Soula, 97355 Macouria; tel. 5-94-38-71-26; e-mail 973@confederationpaysanne.fr; internet www.grage.gf; affiliated to the Confédération Paysanne; Pres. SYLVIE HORTH.

MEDEF Guyane: 27A Résidence Gustave Stanislas, Source de Baduel, BP 820, 97338 Cayenne Cédex; tel. 5-94-31-17-71; fax 5-94-30-32-13; e-mail updg@nplus.gf; f. 2005; fmrly Union des Entreprises de Guyane; Pres. ADRIEN AUBIN.

Ordre des Pharmaciens du Département Guyane: 7 ave du Général de Gaulle, 97300 Cayenne; tel. 5-94-32-17-62; fax 5-94-32-17-66; e-mail delegation_guyane@ordre.pharmacien.fr; internet www.ordre.pharmacien.fr; Pres LILIANE POGNON, EJULIBERTE PAULLAC MAM LAM FOUCK.

Syndicat des Transformateurs du Bois de Guyane (STBG): Menuisserie Cabassou, PK 4.5, route de Cabassou, 97354 Remire-Montjoly; tel. 5-94-31-34-49; fax 5-94-35-10-51; f. 2002; represents artisans using wood; Pres. YVES ELISE; Sec. FRANÇOIS AUGER.

UTILITIES

Electricity

EDF Guyane: blvd Jubelin, BP 6002, 97306 Cayenne; tel. 5-94-39-64-00; fax 5-94-30-10-81; internet guyane.edf.com; electricity producer; Gen. Man. DENIS GIRARD.

Water

Société Guyanaise des Eaux: 2738 route de Montabo, BP 5027, 97306 Cayenne Cédex; tel. 5-94-25-59-26; fax 5-94-30-59-60; internet www.suez-environnement.fr; f. 1978; CEO JEAN-LOUIS CHAUSSADE; Gen. Man. RODOLPHE LELIEVRE.

TRADE UNIONS

Centrale Démocratique des Travailleurs Guyanais (CDTG): 99–100 Cité Césaire, BP 383, 97328 Cayenne Cédex; tel. 5-94-31-02-32; fax 5-94-31-81-05; e-mail sg.cdtg@wanadoo.fr; internet cdtg-guyane.com; affiliated to the Confédération Française Démocratique du Travail; Sec.-Gen. GÉRARD FAUBERT.

Affiliated unions incl.:

SGEN-CFDT: 99–100 Cité Césaire, BP 383, 97328 Cayenne Cédex; tel. 5-94-31-02-32; fax 5-94-35-71-17; e-mail guyane@sgen.cfdt.fr; affiliated to the Fédération des Syndicats Généraux de l'Education Nationale et de la Recherche; represents teaching staff; Sec.-Gen. MARTINE NIVOIX.

Fédération Syndicale Unitaire Guyane (FSU): Mont Lucas, Bâtiment G, No C37, 97300 Cayenne; tel. 5-94-30-05-69; fax 5-94-38-36-58; e-mail fsu973@fsu.fr; f. 1993; departmental br. of the Fédération Syndicale Unitaire; represents public sector employees in teaching, research and training, and also agriculture, justice, youth and sports, and culture; Sec. ALAIN BRAVO.

Union Départementale Confédération Française des Travailleurs Chrétiens Guyane (UD CFTC): 19 lot Gibelin 1, BP 763, 97351 Matoury Cédex; tel. 5-94-35-63-14; fax 5-94-90-59-05; e-mail lydie.leneveu@wanadoo.fr; Sec. LYDIE LENEVEU.

Union Départementale Force Ouvrière de Guyane (FO): 4 ave Pasteur, 97300 Cayenne; tel. and fax 5-94-31-79-66; e-mail force-ouvriere-guyane@orange.fr; internet guyane.force-ouvriere.org; Sec.-Gen. DOMINIQUE BONADEI.

Union des Travailleurs Guyanais (UTG): 40 ave Digue Ronjon, BP 265, 97326 Cayenne Cédex; tel. 5-94-31-26-42; fax 5-94-30-82-46; e-mail utg1@wanadoo.fr; Sec.-Gen. ALBERT DARNAL.

UNSA Education Guyane: 46 rue Vermont Polycarpe, BP 807, 97300 Cayenne Cédex; tel. 5-94-31-02-10; fax 5-94-31-30-08; e-mail 973@se-unsa.org; internet sections.se-unsa.org/973; Sec.-Gen. LAURENT LECANTE.

Transport

RAILWAYS

There are no railways in French Guiana.

ROADS

In 2004 there were 1,300 km (808 miles) of roads in French Guiana, of which 397 km were main roads. Much of the network is concentrated along the coast, although proposals for a major new road into the interior of the Department were under consideration.

SHIPPING

Dégrad-des-Cannes, on the estuary of the river Mahury, is the principal port, handling the majority of maritime traffic. There are other ports at Le Larivot, Saint-Laurent-du-Maroni and Kourou. Saint-Laurent is used primarily for the export of timber, and Le Larivot for fishing vessels. There are river ports on the Oiapoque and on the Approuague. There is a ferry service across the Maroni river between Saint-Laurent and Albina, Suriname. The rivers provide the best means of access to the interior, although numerous rapids prevent navigation by large vessels. A bridge across the Oyapock river, funded by the Governments of France and Brazil, was expected to be inaugurated in 2012.

Compagnie Maritime Marfret: Immeuble Face Scierie Patoz, Z. I. Degrad des Cannes, 97354 Rémire-Montjoly; tel. 5-94-31-04-04; fax 5-94-35-18-44; e-mail jccelse@marfret.fr; internet www.marfret.fr; Gen. Man. JEAN-CHRISTIAN CELSE-L'HOSTE.

SOMARIG (Société Maritime et Industrielle de la Guyane): Z. I. de Dégrad-des-Cannes, Rémire-Montjoly, BP 81, 97354 Cayenne Cédex; tel. 5-94-35-42-00; fax 5-94-35-53-44; e-mail cay.genmbox@cma-cgm.com; internet www.cma-cgm.com; f. 1960; owned by Groupe CMA—GGM (France); Man. Dir HERVÉ ROUCHON.

CIVIL AVIATION

Rochambeau International Airport, situated 17.5 km (11 miles) from Cayenne, is equipped to handle the largest jet aircraft. There are also airports at Maripasoula, Saul and Saint Georges. Access to remote inland areas is frequently by helicopter.

Air Guyane: Aéroport de Rochambeau, 97300 Matoury; tel. 5-94-29-36-30; fax 5-94-30-54-37; e-mail reservations@airguyane.com; internet www.airguyane.com; f. 1980; 46% owned by Guyane Aéro Invest, 20% owned by Sodetraguy; operates domestic services; Pres. CHRISTIAN MARCHAND.

Tourism

The main attractions are the natural beauty of the tropical scenery and the Amerindian villages of the interior. In 2005 there were 27 hotels with some 1,184 rooms. Receipts from tourism in 2007 were US $49m. while in 2009 tourist arrivals totalled 109,000.

Comité du Tourisme de la Guyane: 12 rue Lallouette, BP 801, 97338 Cayenne Cédex; tel. 5-94-29-65-00; fax 5-94-29-65-01; e-mail ctginfo@tourisme-guyane.com; internet www.tourisme-guyane.com; Pres. SYLVIE DESERT; Dir-Gen. ERIC MADELEINE.

Délégation Régionale au Tourisme, au Commerce et à l'Artisanat pour la Guyane: 9 rue Louis Blanc, BP 7008, 97300 Cayenne Cédex; tel. 5-94-28-92-90; fax 5-94-31-01-04; e-mail 973.pole3e@dieccte.gouv.fr; Delegate DIDIER BIRONNEAU (acting).

L'Ensemble Culturel Régional (ENCRE): 82 ave du Général de Gaulle, BP 6007, 97306 Cayenne Cédex; tel. 5-94-28-94-00; fax 5-94-28-94-04; e-mail encre.crg@wanadoo.fr; f. 2004 by merger of Ecole Nationale de Musique et de Danse and Office Culturel de la Région Guyane; fmrly Asscn Régionale de Développement Culturel; Pres. ANTOINE KARAM.

Fédération des Offices du Tourisme et Syndicat d'Initiative de la Guyane (FOTSIG): 12 rue Lallouette, BP 702, 97301 Cayenne; tel. 5-94-30-96-29; fax 5-94-31-23-41; e-mail frguyane@fnotsi.net; Pres. JULIETTE GOUSSET.

Defence

As assessed at November 2011, France maintained a military force of 1,769 in French Guiana. The headquarters is in Cayenne. There was also a gendarmerie of about 700 personnel.

Education

Education is modelled on the French system and is compulsory for children between six and 16 years of age. Primary education begins at six years of age and lasts for five years. Secondary education, beginning at 11 years of age, lasts for up to seven years, comprising a first cycle of four years and a second of three years. Education at state schools is provided free of charge. In 2009/10 there were 40 pre-primary schools, 116 primary schools and 45 secondary schools. In the same period there were 41,849 students in pre-primary and primary education, while in secondary education there were 29,750 students, of whom some 94% were educated in the state sector. Higher education in law, administration and French language and literature is provided by a branch of the Université des Antilles et de la Guyane in Cayenne; there is also a teacher-training college (IUFM), a technical institute at Kourou and an agricultural college. In 2009/10 some 2,689 students were enrolled in higher education in French Guiana. The French Government increased expenditure in the education sector in 2000–06, including €71m. on the construction of new school buildings.

GUADELOUPE

Introductory Survey

LOCATION, CLIMATE, LANGUAGE, RELIGION, CAPITAL

Guadeloupe is the most northerly of the Windward Islands group in the West Indies. Dominica lies to the south, and Antigua and Montserrat to the north-west. Guadeloupe is formed by two large islands, Grande-Terre and Basse-Terre, separated by a narrow sea channel (but linked by a bridge), with a smaller island, Marie-Galante, to the south-east, and another, La Désirade, to the east. The climate is tropical, with an average temperature of 26°C (79°F), and a more humid and wet season between June and November. French is the official language, but a Creole patois is widely spoken. The majority of the population profess Christianity, and belong to the Roman Catholic Church. The capital is the town of Basse-Terre; the other main town and the principal commercial centre is Pointe-à-Pitre, on Grande-Terre.

CONTEMPORARY POLITICAL HISTORY

Historical Context

Guadeloupe was first occupied by the French in 1635, and has remained French territory, apart from a number of brief occupations by the British in the 18th and early 19th centuries. It gained departmental status in 1946.

Domestic Political Affairs

The deterioration of the economy and an increase in unemployment provoked industrial and political unrest during the 1960s and 1970s, including outbreaks of serious rioting in 1967. Pro-independence parties (which had rarely won more than 5% of the total vote at elections in Guadeloupe) resorted, in some cases, to violence as a means of expressing their opposition to the economic and political dominance of white, pro-French landowners and government officials. In 1980 and 1981 there was a series of bomb attacks on hotels, government offices and other targets by a group called the Groupe de Libération Armée, and in 1983 and 1984 there were further bombings by a group styling itself the Alliance Révolutionnaire Caraïbe (ARC). Further sporadic acts of violence continued in 1985–88.

In 1974 Guadeloupe was granted the status of a Region, and an indirectly elected Conseil régional (Regional Council) was formed. In direct elections to a new Conseil régional in 1983 the centre-right coalition succeeded in gaining a majority of the seats and control of the administration. In 1984 Lucette Michaux-Chevry, the President of the Conseil général (General Council), formed a new conservative centre party, Le Parti de la Guadeloupe, which remained in alliance with the right-wing Rassemblement pour la République (RPR). However, at the election for the Conseil général held in 1985, the left-wing combination of the Parti Socialiste (PS) and the Parti Communiste Guadeloupéen (PCG) gained a majority of seats on the enlarged Conseil, and the PS leader, Dominique Larifla, was elected its President. In July demonstrations and a general strike, organized by pro-separatist activists in order to obtain the release of a leading member of the Mouvement Populaire pour une Guadeloupe Indépendante, quickly intensified into civil disorder and rioting in the main commercial centre, Pointe-à-Pitre.

For the 1986 general election to the Assemblée nationale (National Assembly), Guadeloupe's representation was increased from three to four deputies. In the concurrent elections for the Conseil régional, the two left-wing parties together won a majority of seats. As a result, José Moustache of the RPR was replaced as President of the Conseil by Félix Proto of the PS. The left-wing parties also won a majority of seats at the election to the Conseil général in the same year, and Larifla was re-elected President of the Conseil.

In April 1989 the separatist Union Populaire pour la Libération de la Guadeloupe (UPLG) organized protests in Port Louis to demand the release of 'political prisoners', which led to violent clashes with the police. A number of activists of the now disbanded ARC (including its leader, Luc Reinette) staged a hunger strike while awaiting trial in Paris, accused in connection with politically motivated offences. Anti-Government demonstrations took place in the following month. Demands included the release of the prisoners held in France, a rejection of the Single European Act and the granting of a series of social measures. In June the Assemblée nationale approved legislation granting an amnesty for crimes that had taken place before July 1988, and that were intended to undermine the authority of the French Republic in the Overseas Departments. The agreement of those seeking greater independence in Guadeloupe to work within the democratic framework had gained parliamentary support for the amnesty. In March 1990 the UPLG declared that it would henceforth participate in elections, and would seek associated status (rather than full independence) for Guadeloupe.

In March 1992 concurrent elections were held to the Conseil général and the Conseil régional. Larifla was re-elected as President of the former, despite his refusal to contest as part of the local official PS list of candidates and his leadership of a group of 'dissident' PS members. In the election to the Conseil régional the official PS list (headed by Frédéric Jalton) secured nine seats and the dissident PS members seven. Former members of the PCG, who had formed a new organization, the Parti Progressiste Démocratique Guadeloupéen (PPDG), won five seats. The RPR, the centre-right Union pour la Démocratie Française (UDF) and other right-wing candidates formed an electoral alliance, Objectif Guadeloupe, to contest the elections, together securing 15 of the 41 seats in the Conseil régional. Jalton's refusal to reach an agreement with the 'dissident' PS members prompted Larifla's list to support the presidential candidacy of Michaux-Chevry. Thus, despite an overall left-wing majority in the Conseil régional, the right-wing Michaux-Chevry was elected as President. In December, however, the French Conseil d'état declared the election to the Conseil régional invalid, owing to the failure of Larifla's list to pay a registration deposit. Other heads of lists were subsequently found to have submitted incomplete documents to the election commission, and (although malpractice was discounted) the electoral code necessitated that they be declared ineligible for election to the Conseil régional for one year. Fresh elections took place in January 1994, at which Objectif Guadeloupe took 22 seats, while the PS and 'dissident' PS retained a total of only 10 seats.

In a referendum on 20 September 1992 68% of voters in Guadeloupe endorsed ratification of the Treaty on European Union (see p. 276), although a high abstention rate was recorded.

The persistence of divisions between the socialists was evident at the 1993 election to the Assemblée nationale. Michaux-Chevry was re-elected, as were Eric Moutoussamy (for the PPDG) and Jalton. Larifla, meanwhile, was defeated by Edouard Chammougon, a candidate of the independent right. The left retained control of the Conseil général following cantonal elections in 1994. Larifla was subsequently re-elected President of the Conseil.

At municipal elections in June 1995, Michaux-Chevry became mayor of Basse-Terre. Michaux-Chevry and Larifla were elected to the French Sénat (Senate) in September; Philippe Chaulet of the RPR was subsequently elected to take Michaux-Chevry's seat in the Assemblée nationale.

The RPR performed strongly in the election to the Conseil régional in March 1998; Michaux-Chevry was re-elected President of the Conseil. The composition of the Conseil général remained largely unchanged following concurrent cantonal elections, although the RPR doubled its representation; Marcellin Lubeth, of the PPDG, was elected to the presidency, defeating Larifla.

Social and industrial unrest intensified in Guadeloupe in October 1999, prior to a two-day visit by Prime Minister Lionel Jospin. Demonstrations escalated into rioting in Pointe-à-Pitre, following the sentencing of Armand Toto—a leading member of the Union Générale des Travailleurs de la Guadeloupe (UGTG)—to four months' imprisonment for assaulting two policemen and threatening to kill another while occupying the premises of a motor vehicle company in support of a dismissed worker. Moreover, banana producers demonstrated around the port of Basse-Terre, demanding aid for the restructuring of their businesses as compensation for a significant decline in banana prices on the European market. Jospin announced an emergency plan for the banana sector.

Demands for further autonomy

Following a series of meetings, in December 1999 the Presidents of the Conseils régionaux of French Guiana, Guadeloupe and Martinique signed a joint declaration in Basse-Terre, affirming their intention to propose a legislative amendment aimed at creating a new status of overseas region. The declaration, however, was dismissed by the Secretary of State for Overseas Departments and Territories, Jean-Jack Queyranne, in February 2000 as unconstitutional. Amended proposals regarding the institutional evolution of Guadeloupe were approved by the Assemblée nationale in November, and in December they were ratified by the Constitutional Council.

In municipal elections held in March 2001 Michaux-Chevry was re-elected mayor of Basse-Terre, despite corruption charges against her; however, she relinquished the post to Pierre Martin, in order to comply with regulations that no official may hold more than two elected posts simultaneously (she already held the positions of Senator and President of the Conseil régional). Henri Bangou of the PPDG was also re-elected to the mayoralty of Pointe-à-Pitre. In the concurrently held election to the presidency of the Conseil général, Jacques Gillot of Guadeloupe Unie, Socialisme et Réalité (GUSR) defeated Marcellin Lubeth of the PPDG.

Following a meeting of members of the Conseil régional and the Conseil général in June 2001, a series of administrative restructuring proposals was agreed upon. These included: the division of the territory into four districts; the creation of a Territorial Collectivity (Collectivité territoriale), governed by a 41-member Assembly elected for a five-year term; and the establishment of an independent executive council. Furthermore, the proposals included a request that the territory be given control over legislative and administrative affairs, as well as legislative authority on matters concerning Guadeloupe alone. In March 2003 the French parliament approved constitutional changes that, *inter alia*, allowed for local referendums to be held on proposals for greater decentralization in overseas possessions. Under the changes, the Department of Guadeloupe was also designated an Overseas Region (Région d'outre-mer). In the referendum, held on 7 December, some 73% of participating voters rejected legislative reforms that envisaged the replacement of the Conseil général and the Conseil régional with a single assembly, owing to fears that restructuring would lead to autonomy for the Department and the consequent loss of central government funding. However, at the referendums concurrently held in the dependencies of Saint-Barthélemy and Saint-Martin, a clear majority of voters in each commune (95.5% and 76.2%, respectively) were in favour of seceding from Guadeloupe to form separate Overseas Collectivities (Collectivités d'outre-mer—q.v.). The reorganization was subsequently approved by the French Sénat on 6 February 2007 and by the Assemblée nationale the following day. On 21 February Saint-Barthélemy and the French part of Saint-Martin were formally designated Overseas Collectivities. Following elections to their respective Conseils territoriaux (Territorial Councils), held in early July 2007, the two Overseas Collectivities acceded to administrative independence. Each Overseas Collectivity was to elect one representative to the Sénat (in 2008) and one deputy to the Assemblée nationale (in 2012); in the interim, they were to continue to be represented by Guadeloupean parliamentarians.

In June 2002 all four incumbent deputies were defeated in an election to the Assemblée nationale; they were replaced by Gabrielle Louis-Carabin and Joël Beaugendre, both representing the Union pour la Majorité Présidentielle (UMP), a right-wing alliance that included the Objectif Guadeloupe, Eric Jalton, also of a right-wing coalition, and Victorin Lurel of the PS. The RPR subsequently merged into the successor party to the UMP, Union pour un Mouvement Populaire (also known as the UMP).

At an election to the Conseil régional in March 2004 the UMP alliance, led by Michaux-Chevry, was resoundingly defeated by the Guadeloupe pour Tous list, a coalition comprising the PS, the PPDG, the GUSR and other left-wing candidates. Victorin Lurel of the PS subsequently became President of the Conseil régional.

The arrest of the trade union leader Michel Madassamy in October 2004 led to a deterioration in the social situation. Madassamy was accused of vandalizing two petrol tankers during the blockade of a service station in Point-à-Pitre in November 2003. In March 2004 he had been found guilty and sentenced to 10 months' imprisonment. Following a failed appeal process, Madassamy was taken into custody in October. The UGTG challenged the legality of the arrest, and Madassamy began a hunger strike. Several hundred protesters took to the streets in Point-à-Pitre in late October, leading to a number of arrests. Madassamy was granted conditional release in November pending a further hearing in January 2005 when the judge ruled that he should serve a further eight months in prison.

In late May 2005 a national referendum was held on ratification of the European Union constitutional treaty: some 58.6% of participating voters in the Department were in favour of adopting the treaty; however, only 22% of the electorate exercised their right to vote. The treaty was ultimately rejected by a majority of voters in metropolitan France.

At the first round of the national presidential election, held on 22 April 2007, Nicolas Sarkozy of the UMP won 42.6% of the votes cast in Guadeloupe, ahead of PS candidate Ségolène Royal, who attracted 38.3% of the vote. At the second round, held on 6 May, Sarkozy emerged victorious, winning 49.2% of the vote in the Department. At elections to the Assemblée nationale, held on 10 and 17 June, Gabrielle Louis-Carabin of the UMP, Victorin Lurel of the PS and Eric Jalton of the PCG were re-elected, while Jeanny Marc-Matthiasin of the GUSR was also successful. At municipal elections held in March 2008 Michaux-Chevry was again elected mayor of Basse-Terre. The PS and GUSR retained control of the Conseil général, and Gillot was subsequently re-elected as its President.

Recent developments: referendum on autonomy

From January 2009 the island suffered overwhelming disruption as a result of a general strike organized by Lyannaj Kont Pwofitasyon (LKP—League against Profiteering), an alliance of 47 trade unions, political parties and other associations, over the rising cost of living. Violent protests continued throughout February, resulting in the death of a union official, and military police from metropolitan France were deployed in order to restore order. On 5 March the 44-day strike ended and businesses began to reopen after a deal was agreed between the unions, the local authorities and employers' representatives, involving widespread measures to improve living standards. Notably, the wages of the lowest-paid workers were to be supplemented by a monthly payment of €200. However, a further LKP-led demonstration, attended by over 1,000 protesters, was organized to coincide with the visit of President Sarkozy to the archipelago in June. During his visit Sarkozy proposed a referendum on the issue of increased autonomy for Guadeloupe, but this option was subsequently rejected by the Guadeloupean authorities. Nevertheless, in accordance with legislation approved by the Assemblée nationale in late 2010, the territory's institutions were to be restructured by 2014. The exact nature of this reform was under debate in early 2012, although the number of elected representatives was expected to be reduced from 81 to 45.

In an election to the Conseil régional held in March 2010, the PS-led list, Tous pour la Guadeloupe, secured an overwhelming victory in the first round of voting, with 56.5% of the ballot, gaining 31 of the 41 council seats. The UMP alliance, Ensemble pour la Guadeloupe, and the left-wing Région Autrement obtained four seats each, with 14.0% and 12.4% of the votes cast, respectively, while the Pou Gwadloup an nou ay list took the remaining two seats with 7.0% of the ballot. Victorin Lurel was re-elected as President of the Conseil régional. The rate of participation by the electorate was 49.8%. Left-wing candidates performed strongly in the municipal polls conducted on 20 and 27 March 2011, and Gillot was subsequently re-elected as President of the Conseil général. Gillot was also re-elected to the Sénat on 25 September, while Felix Desplan of the PS and Jacques Cornano, a left-wing independent, secured the territory's other two Sénat seats. Meanwhile, in August Amaury de Saint-Quentin was appointed as Prefect, replacing Jean-Luc Michel Fabre.

CONSTITUTION AND GOVERNMENT

France is represented in Guadeloupe by an appointed prefect. There are two councils with local powers: the 42-member Conseil général (General Council) and the 41-member Conseil régional (Regional Council). Both are elected by universal adult suffrage for a period of up to six years. Guadeloupe elects four deputies to the Assemblée nationale in Paris, and sends three indirectly elected representatives to the Sénat. The Department is also represented at the European Parliament.

ECONOMIC AFFAIRS

In 2001, according to UN estimates, Guadeloupe's gross domestic product (GDP), measured at current prices, was US $4,460m., equivalent to $10,323 per head. During 1990–2001 GDP increased, in real terms, at an average annual rate of 2.2%; growth in 2001 was 4.6%. Between the censuses of 1999 and 2006, according to provisional figures, the population decreased at an average annual rate of 0.8%. In 2009, according to official estimates, Guadeloupe's GDP, measured at current prices, was €8,160m., equivalent to €18,170 per head.

Agriculture, hunting, forestry and fishing contributed an estimated 2.7% of GDP in 2006 and engaged an estimated 1.7% of the employed population in 2008. In 2009 agricultural produce (including that related to agrarian production and food industries) accounted for 55.2% of exports. The principal cash crops are bananas and sugar cane. Yams, sweet potatoes and plantains are the chief subsistence crops. Fishing, mostly at an artisanal level, fulfils about two-thirds of domestic requirements, and there is some shrimp-farming. According to UN estimates, agricultural GDP decreased at an average annual rate of 0.3% in 1990–98; the sector increased by 4.1% in 1998.

The industrial sector (including mining, manufacturing, construction, power and food industries) contributed an estimated 14.9% of GDP in 2006 and engaged an estimated 12.3% of the employed population in 2008. Construction contributed 9.6% of GDP in 2006 and engaged an estimated 4.8% of the working population in 2008. The main manufacturing activity is food processing, particularly sugar production, rum distillation, and flour-milling. The sugar industry declined in the 1990s, owing to deteriorating equipment and a reduction in the area planted with sugar cane (from 20,000 ha in 1980 to 9,960 ha in 2009). Industrial GDP (excluding construction) increased at an average annual rate of 5.2% in 1990–98. Construction expanded at an average rate of 2.2% per year in the same period.

Of some 700,000 tons of petroleum imported annually, about one-third is used for the production of electricity. Efforts are currently being concentrated on the use of renewable energy resources—notably solar, geothermal and wind power—for energy production; there is also thought to be considerable potential for the use of bagasse (a by-product of sugar cane) as a means of generating energy in Guadeloupe. The 64 MW power plant at Le Moule produces some 400m. kWh of electricity annually—almost one-third of Guadeloupe's requirements—using a mixture of coal (75%) and bagasse (25%). Imports of fuels and combustibles accounted for 11.9% of total expenditure on imports in 2009. In 2010 Guadeloupe's total electricity consumption was 1,788m. kWh.

The services sector engaged an estimated 85.9% of the employed population in 2008 and provided an estimated 82.4% of GDP in 2006. Tourism is the Department's principal source of income, and there is significant potential for the further development of the sector, particularly eco-tourism. In 2008 tourist arrivals totalled some 433,358, and receipts from tourism amounted to US $384m. In the same year 93.9% of arrivals came from metropolitan France or dependent territories.

In 2010 Guadeloupe recorded a trade deficit of some €655.5m. In 2009 the value of exports was €149.2m., less than one-10th of the total value of imports, which were worth €1,799.5m. In 2008 the principal source of imports was metropolitan France (52.1%), which was also the principal market for exports (38.5%). The USA, Germany, and Trinidad and Tobago are also important trading partners. The principal exports in 2009 were sugar, bananas, boats and rum. The principal imports were machinery and transport equipment (mainly road vehicles), food and live animals, miscellaneous manufactured articles, basic manufactures and chemicals.

Guadeloupe's budget surplus was estimated by the metropolitan authorities to amount to some €92m. in 2005. The departmental budget for 2006 was balanced, with expenditure and revenue of €562.8m. The regional budget was balanced in 2008. The annual rate of inflation averaged 1.9% in 2001–10. In 2010 the annual inflation rate was 2.8%. Some 27.1% of the labour force was unemployed in 2007.

Economic growth in Guadeloupe has been restricted by certain inherent problems: its location; the fact that the domestic market is too narrow to stimulate the expansion of the manufacturing base; the lack of primary materials; and the inflated labour and service costs compared with those of neighbouring countries. Guadeloupe's banana sector was adversely affected by the end of the EU's quota system from 2006 and the gradual elimination of tariffs on non-European bananas from 2010 led to a further contraction in the sector. The sugar industry was also adversely affected by modernization. The global financial crisis had a severe impact upon the territory, and GDP contracted by 4.8% in 2009, according to official data. Tourist numbers decreased, owing to the combined effects of the economic downturn and the violent demonstrations of early 2009, which tarnished the island's reputation. Nevertheless, the economy recovered in 2010, with higher levels of investment and domestic consumption supporting GDP growth of 2.7%. There was also a revival in the tourism sector, owing in part to the holding of the 'Route du Rhum' yacht race, which attracted some 10,000 additional visitors to the islands in late 2010. Agricultural performance was undermined by adverse weather conditions, while ash from a volcanic eruption on the neighbouring island of Montserrat in February also caused significant damage to crops. Economic activity appeared subdued in 2011. The unemployment rate declined but was still very high (22.6% at mid-2011). Rising inflation, precipitated by increases in fuel prices during 2010–11, was a further concern.

PUBLIC HOLIDAYS

2013: 1 January (New Year's Day), 11–12 February (Lenten Carnival), 13 February (Ash Wednesday), 29 March–1 April (Easter), 1 May (Labour Day), 8 May (Victory Day), 9 May (Ascension Day), 20 May (Whit Monday), 10 June (Abolition of Slavery), 14 July (National Day), 15 August (Assumption), 1 November (All Saints' Day), 11 November (Armistice Day), 25 December (Christmas Day).

Statistical Survey

Sources (unless otherwise indicated): Institut National de la Statistique et des Etudes Economiques (INSEE), Service Régional de la Guadeloupe, ave Paul Lacavé, BP 96, 97102 Basse-Terre; tel. 5-90-99-02-50; internet www.insee.fr/fr/regions/guadeloupe; Service de Presse et d'Information, Ministère des Départements et Territoires d'Outre-mer, 27 rue Oudinot, 75700 Paris 07 SP, France; tel. 1-53-69-20-00; fax 1-43-06-60-30; internet www.outre-mer.gouv.fr.

AREA AND POPULATION

(Note: In July 2007 Saint-Barthélemy and Saint-Martin seceded from Guadeloupe to become Overseas Collectivities.)

Area: 1,630 sq km (629.3 sq miles), comprising continental Guadeloupe 1,438 sq km (Basse-Terre à l'Ouest 848 sq km, Grande-Terre à l'Est 590 sq km) and dependencies 194 sq km (La Désirade 22 sq km, Iles des Saintes 14 sq km, Marie-Galante 158 sq km).

Population: 422,496 at census of 8 March 1999; 401,554 at census of 1 January 2009. Note: According to new census methodology, data in 2009 refer to median figures based on the collection of raw data over a five-year period (2006–11). *1 January 2010* (estimate): 404,394. *Mid-2012* (UN estimate): 465,283 (Source: UN, *World Population Prospects: The 2010 Revision*).

Density (at mid-2012): 285.4 per sq km.

Population by Age and Sex (UN estimates at mid-2012): *0–14:* 101,498 (males 51,724, females 49,774); *15–64:* 303,354 (males 141,906, females 161,448); *65 and over:* 60,431 (males 25,623, females 34,808); *Total* 465,283 (males 219,253, females 246,030). Source: UN, *World Population Prospects: The 2010 Revision*.

Principal Towns (population at 1999 census): Les Abymes 63,054; Saint-Martin 29,078; Le Gosier 25,360; Baie-Mahault 23,389; Pointe-à-Pitre 20,948; Le Moule 20,827; Petit Bourg 20,528; Sainte Anne 20,410; Basse-Terre (capital) 12,410.

Births, Marriages and Deaths (2009): Registered live births 5,487 (birth rate 13.6 per 1,000); Registered marriages 1,440 (marriage rate 3.6 per 1,000); Registered deaths 2,850 (death rate 7.1 per 1,000). *2010* (provisional): Registered live births 5,283 (birth rate 13.1 per 1,000); Registered deaths 2,860 (death rate 7.1 per 1,000).

Life Expectancy (years at birth): 79.4 (males 76.4, females 82.5) in 2010. Source: Pan American Health Organization.

Economically Active Population (persons aged 15 years and over, 1990 census): Agriculture, hunting, forestry and fishing 8,391; Industry and energy 9,630; Construction and public works 13,967; Trade 15,020; Transport and telecommunications 6,950; Financial services 2,802; Other marketable services 26,533; Non-marketable services 34,223; *Total employed* 117,516 (males 68,258, females 49,258); Unemployed 54,926 (males 25,691, females 29,235); *Total labour force* 172,442 (males 93,949, females 78,493). *2008* (provisional estimates at 31 December): Agriculture 1,741; Mining and quarrying 171; Manufacturing 5,896; Electricity, water and sanitation 1,635; Construction 4,826; Trade 11,482; Hotels and restaurants 3,521; Transportation and storage 4,909; Communication 1,823; Finance and insurance 2,720; Real estate activities 576; Professional services 9,236; Public administration 21,526; Education 10,783; Health and other social services 14,186; Other services 6,443; Total 101,474. Note: Figures for employment exclude 7,727 non-salaried workers. *2009* (estimate at 31 December): Unemployed 47,870.

HEALTH AND WELFARE

Key Indicators

Total Fertility Rate (children per woman, 2010): 2.1.

Under-5 Mortality Rate (per 1,000 live births, 2010): 8.5.

Physicians (per 1,000 head, c. 2001): 1.4.

Hospital Beds (per 1,000 head, 2004): 6.1.

Access to Water (% of persons, 2004): 98.

Access to Sanitation (% of persons, 2004): 64.

Source: mainly Pan American Health Organization.

For other sources and definitions, see explanatory note on p. vi.

AGRICULTURE, ETC.

Principal Crops ('000 metric tons, 2010, FAO estimates): Sweet potatoes 1.9; Sugar cane 870.0; Cabbages and other brassicas 1.9; Lettuce and chicory 3.4; Tomatoes 3.9; Cucumbers and gherkins 5.2; Bananas 68.0 Plantains 6.4. *Aggregate Production* ('000 metric tons, may include official, semi-official or estimated data): Total roots and tubers 14.8; Total vegetables (incl. melons) 45.3; Total fruits (excl. melons) 87.4.

Livestock ('000 head, year ending September 2010, FAO estimates): Cattle 75.0; Chickens 300.

Livestock Products ('000 metric tons, 2010, FAO estimates): Cattle meat 2.9; Pig meat 1.5; Chicken meat 1.4; Hen eggs 2.0.

Forestry ('000 cu m, 2010, FAO estimates): *Roundwood Removals* (excl. bark): Sawlogs, veneer logs and logs for sleepers 0.3; Fuel wood 15.0; Total 15.3. *Sawnwood Production* (incl. railway sleepers): Total 1.0.

Fishing (metric tons, live weight, 2009, FAO estimates): Capture 10,000 (Common dolphinfish 700; Other mackerel-like fishes 1,600; Marine fishes 7,000; Stromboid conchs 550); Aquaculture 12; *Total catch* 10,012.

Source: FAO.

MINING

Production ('000 metric tons, 2009, estimates): Cement 230; Pumice 210; Salt 49. Source: US Geological Survey.

INDUSTRY

Production (2010): Sugar 60,000 metric tons; Rum 64,832 hl; Electric energy 1,788 million kWh. Source: Institut d'Emission des Départements d'Outre-mer, *Guadeloupe: Rapport Annuel 2010*.

FINANCE

Currency and Exchange Rates: The French franc was used until the end of February 2002. Euro notes and coins were introduced on 1 January 2002, and the euro became the sole legal tender from 18 February. Some of the figures in this Survey are still in terms of francs. For details of exchange rates, see French Guiana.

Budget: *French Government* (€ million, 2005): Revenue 1,132; Expenditure 1,040. *Regional Budget* (€ million, 2008): Current revenue 261.0 (Taxes 182.3, Other current revenue 78.7); Capital revenues 44.7; Total 305.7. Current expenditure 148.9; Capital expenditure 156.8; Total 305.7 (Source: Département des Etudes et des Statistiques Locales). *Departmental Budget* (excl. debt rescheduling, € million, 2006): Revenue 562.8; Expenditure 562.8 (Source: Département des Etudes et des Statistiques Locales).

Money Supply (million French francs at 31 December 1996): Currency outside banks 1,148; Demand deposits at banks 6,187; Total money 7,335.

Cost of Living (Consumer Price Index; base: 2000 = 100): All items 118.4 in 2008; 118.7 in 2009; 122.0 in 2010. Source: ILO.

Gross Domestic Product (US $ million at constant 1990 prices): 3,543 in 2001; 3,707 in 2002; 3,844 in 2003. Source: UN, *Statistical Yearbook*.

Expenditure on the Gross Domestic Product (€ million at current prices, 2009, estimates): Total final consumption expenditure 8,571; Changes in inventories –420; Gross fixed capital formation 1,653; *Total domestic expenditure* 9,804; Exports of goods and services 522; *Less* Imports of goods and services 2,192; Statistical discrepancy 26; *GDP in purchasers' values* 8,160. Source: Institut d'Emission des Départements d'Outre-mer, *Guadeloupe: Rapport Annuel 2010*.

Gross Domestic Product by Economic Activity (€ million at current prices, 2006): Agriculture, hunting, forestry and fishing 197; Food industries 87; Other manufacturing 265; Energy 37; Construction 713; Services 6,094 (Restaurants and hotels 253, Transport 249, Commerce 948, Other market services 2,269, Non-market services 2,375); *Sub-total* 7,393; Financial intermediation services indirectly measured (FISIM) –325; Import duties, less subsidies 690; *GDP in purchasers' values* 7,758.

EXTERNAL TRADE

Principal Commodities (€ million, 2009): *Imports c.i.f.:* Products of agriculture and food industries 350.3; Pharmaceutical products 179.4; Home equipment 102.3; Car industry products 211.6; Mechanical equipment 121.2; Electronic equipment 73.8; Fuels and combustibles 214.0; Total (incl. others) 1,799.5. *Exports f.o.b.:* Products of agriculture and food industries 82.3; Boats, planes, trains, and motorcycles 5.5; Mechanical equipment 7.6; Electronic equipment 5.0; Metals and metallic products 6.3; Total (incl. others) 149.2. *2010* (€ million): Total imports 2,213.5; Total exports 155.8 (Source: Institut d'Emission des Départements d'Outre-mer, *Guadeloupe: Rapport Annuel 2010*).

Principal Trading Partners (€ million, 2008): *Imports c.i.f.:* Aruba 98; China, People's Repub. 87; France (metropolitan) 1,355; Germany 110; Italy 65; Martinique 210; Spain 40; USA 146; Total (incl. others) 2,601. *Exports f.o.b.:* France (metropolitan) 79; French Guiana 40; Germany 3; Martinique 44; Poland 5; Portugal 4; USA 4; Total (incl. others) 205. *2010* (€ million): Total imports 2,213.5; Total exports 155.8 (Source: Institut d'Emission des Départements d'Outre-mer, *Guadeloupe: Rapport Annuel 2010*).

TRANSPORT

Road Traffic ('000 motor vehicles in use, 2002): Passenger cars 117.7; Commercial vehicles 31.4. Source: UN, *Statistical Yearbook*.

Shipping: *Merchant Fleet* (vessels registered, '000 grt at 31 December 1992): Total displacement 6 (Source: Lloyd's Register-Fairplay, *World Fleet Statistics*). *International Sea-borne Traffic* (1995, unless otherwise indicated): Freight vessels entered 1,257; Freight vessels departed 1,253; Gross freight handled 2,973,169 metric tons; Containers handled 154,263 TEUs; Passengers carried 924,446 (2004).

Civil Aviation (2009): Freight carried 12,419 metric tons; Passengers carried 1,726,000.

TOURISM

Tourist Arrivals by Country (2000): Canada 10,431; France 440,779; Italy 15,670; Switzerland 9,766; USA 92,474; Total (incl. others) 623,134. *2004:* France 391,910; Total (incl. others) 423,172. *2005:* France 406,871; Total (incl. others) 433,358. *2006:* France 352,140; Total (incl. others) 383,518. *2007:* France 391,910; Total (incl. others) 423,172. *2008:* France 406,871; Total (incl. others) 433,358.

Receipts from Tourism (US $ million, incl. passenger transport): 306 in 2005; 299 in 2006; 344 in 2007; 384 in 2008.

Source: partly World Tourism Organization.

COMMUNICATIONS MEDIA

Radio Receivers ('000 in use): 113 in 1997.

Television Receivers ('000 in use): 118 in 1997.

Telephones ('000 main lines in use): 255.7 in 2010.

Mobile Cellular Telephones ('000 subscribers): 314.7 in 2004.

Personal Computers: 90,000 in 2004.

Internet Users ('000): 109.0 in 2009.

Daily Newspaper: 1 (estimate) in 1996 (estimated average circulation 35,000 copies).

Sources: UNESCO, *Statistical Yearbook*; UN, *Statistical Yearbook*; International Telecommunication Union.

EDUCATION

Pre-primary (2008/09): 22,411 students (20,362 state, 2,049 private).

Primary (2008/09): 37,650 students (33,797 state, 3,853 private).

Specialized Pre-primary and Primary (2005/06): 1,253 students (1,041 state, 212 private).

Secondary (2008/09): 52,547 students (47,134 state, 5,413 private).

Higher (2007/08): 8,718 students. Source: Ministère de l'Education Nationale, de la Recherche et de la Technologie.

Teachers (2007/08 unless otherwise indicated): *Primary:* 3,382 (3,139 state, 243 private); *Secondary:* 4,675 (4,223 state, 452 private); *Higher* (2004/05): 203. Source: Ministère de l'Education Nationale, *Repères et références statistiques*.

Institutions (2002/03): 136 pre-primary; 220 primary. Source: Ministère de l'Education Nationale, de l'Enseignement Supérieur et de la Recherche, *Repères et références statistiques sur les enseignements, la formation et la recherche 2003*.

Adult Literacy Rate: 90.1 (males 89.7; females 90.5) in 1998. Source: Pan American Health Organization.

Directory

The Government

(May 2012)

HEAD OF STATE

President: NICOLAS SARKOZY.

Prefect: AMAURY DE SAINT-QUENTIN, Préfecture, Palais d'Orléans, rue Lardenoy, 97109 Basse-Terre Cédex; tel. 5-90-99-39-00; fax 5-90-81-58-32; e-mail webmestre@guadeloupe.pref.gouv.fr; internet www.guadeloupe.pref.gouv.fr.

DEPARTMENTAL ADMINISTRATION

President of the General Council: Dr JACQUES GILLOT (GUSR), Hôtel du Département, blvd Félix Eboué, 97109 Basse-Terre; tel. 5-

90-99-77-77; fax 5-90-99-76-00; e-mail info@cg971.fr; internet www.cg971.fr.

President of the Economic and Social Committee: JOCELYN JALTON, 16 rue Peynier, 97100 Basse-Terre; tel. 5-90-41-05-25; fax 5-90-41-05-23; e-mail cr-cesr-guadeloupe@wanadoo.fr; internet www.cr-guadeloupe.fr.

President of the Culture, Education and Environment Committee: JEAN-JACQUES JEREMIE, 16 rue Peynier, 97100 Basse-Terre; tel. 5-90-41-05-15; fax 5-90-41-05-23; e-mail cr-cesr-guadeloupe@wanadoo.fr; internet www.cr-guadeloupe.fr.

President of the Regional Council: VICTORIN LUREL (PS), 1 rue Paul Lacavé, Petit-Paris, 97109 Basse-Terre; tel. 5-90-80-40-40; fax 5-90-81-34-19; internet www.cr-guadeloupe.fr.

Elections, 14 and 21 March 2010

	Seats
Tous pour la Guadeloupe*	31
Ensemble pour la Guadeloupe†	4
Région Autrement‡	4
Pou Gwadloup an nou ay	2
Total	41

* Comprising the Parti Socialiste (PS) and other left-wing candidates.

† Comprising the Union pour un Mouvement Populaire (UMP) and other right-wing candidates.

‡ Comprising smaller left-wing parties and dissident socialists.

REPRESENTATIVES TO THE FRENCH PARLIAMENT

Deputies to the French National Assembly: ERIC JALTON (PCG), GABRIELLE LOUIS-CARABIN (UMP), JEANNY MARC-MATTHIASIN (GUSR), VICTORIN LUREL (PS).

Representatives to the French Senate: JACQUES GILLOT (Groupe Socialiste), FÉLIX DES PLAN (Groupe Socialiste), JACQUES CORNANO (Groupe Socialiste).

Political Organizations

Combat Ouvrier: BP 213, 97156 Pointe-à-Pitre Cédex; tel. 5-90-26-23-58; e-mail redaction@combat-ouvrier.net; internet www.combat-ouvrier.net; Trotskyist; associated with national party Lutte Ouvrière; mem. of the Internationalist Communist Union; Leader JEAN-MARIE NOMERTIN.

Guadeloupe Unie, Socialisme et Réalité (GUSR): Pointe-à-Pitre; e-mail gusr@ais.gp; internet perso.mediaserv.net/gusr; 'dissident' faction of the Parti Socialiste; Pres. GUY LOSBAR.

Konvwa pou Liberasyon Nasyon Gwadloup (KLNG): Pointe-à-Pitre; f. 1997; pro-independence; Leader LUC REINETTE.

Parti Communiste Guadeloupéen (PCG): 119 rue Vatable, 97110 Pointe-à-Pitre; tel. 5-90-88-23-07; f. 1944; Sec.-Gen. FÉLIX FLÉMIN.

Parti Socialiste (PS): 8 Résidence Légitimus, blvd Légitimus, 97110 Pointe-à-Pitre; tel. and fax 5-90-21-65-72; fax 5-90-83-20-51; e-mail fede971@parti-socialiste.fr; internet www.parti-socialiste.fr; divided into 2 factions to contest the March 1992 and March 1993 elections; Regional Sec. MAX MATHIASIN.

Pou Gwadloup an nou ay: Pointe-à-Pitre; youth party; Leader CÉDRIC CORNET.

Union pour un Mouvement Populaire (UMP): Les Portes de Saint Martin Bellevue, 97150 Saint Martin; tel. and fax 5-90-87-50-01; fax 5-90-87-75-72; e-mail ump-sxm@laposte.net; internet www.u-m-p.org; f. 2002; centre-right; local br. of the metropolitan party; Pres., Departmental Cttee LAURENT BERNIER.

Les Verts Guadeloupe: 5 rue François Arago, 97110 Pointe-à-Pitre; tel. 5-90-35-41-90; fax 5-90-25-02-62; internet guadeloupe.lesverts.fr; ecologist; departmental br. of the metropolitan party; Regional spokespersons HARRY DURIMEL, JOCELYNE HATCHI.

Other political organizations included Mouvement pour la Démocratie et le Développement (MDDP), Union Populaire pour la Libération de la Guadeloupe (UPLG), Mouvman Gwadloupéyen (MG), Parti Progressiste Démocratique Guadeloupéen (PPDG), Renouveau Socialiste; and the coalitions Priorité à l'Education et à l'Environnement and Union pour une Guadeloupe Responsable.

Judicial System

Cour d'Appel: Palais de Justice, 4 blvd Félix Eboué, 97100 Basse-Terre; tel. 5-90-80-63-36; fax 5-90-80-63-39; First Pres. HENRY ROBERT; Procurator-Gen. CHRISTINE PENICHON.

There are two Tribunaux de Grande Instance and four Tribunaux d'Instance.

Religion

The majority of the population belong to the Roman Catholic Church.

CHRISTIANITY

The Roman Catholic Church

Guadeloupe comprises the single diocese of Basse-Terre, suffragan to the archdiocese of Fort-de-France, Martinique. Some 76% of the population are Roman Catholics. The Bishop participates in the Antilles Episcopal Conference, based in Port of Spain, Trinidad and Tobago.

Bishop of Basse-Terre: (vacant), Evêché, pl. Saint-Françoise, BP 369, 97100 Basse-Terre Cédex; tel. 5-90-81-36-69; fax 5-90-81-98-23; e-mail eveche@catholique-guadeloupe.info.

OTHER CHURCHES

Seventh-day Adventist Church: Eglise Adventiste de la Guadeloupe, BP 19, 97151 Pointe-à-Pitre Cédex; tel. 5-90-82-79-76; fax 5-90-83-44-24; e-mail adventiste.federation@wanadoo.fr; internet www.adventiste-gpe.org; f. 1931; Pres. ALAIN ANGERVILLE; Sec. DANIEL LOUSSALA; 11,957 members (2007).

Other denominations active in Guadeloupe include the Baptist Church and Jehovah's Witnesses.

The Press

France Antilles: ZAC Moudong Sud, 97122 Baie-Mahault; tel. 5-90-90-25-25; fax 5-90-91-78-31; e-mail f.breland@media-antilles.fr; internet www.guadeloupe.franceantilles.fr; f. 1964; subsidiary of Groupe France Antilles; daily; Chair. PHILIPPE HERSANT; Man. Dir FRÉDÉRIC AURAND; circ. 50,000.

Match: 33 rue Peynier, 97110 Pointe-à-Pitre; tel. 5-90-82-18-68; fax 5-90-82-01-87; fortnightly; Dir MARIE ANTONIA JABBOUR; circ. 6,000.

Nouvelles Etincelles: 119 rue Vatable, 97110 Pointe-à-Pitre; tel. 5-90-91-12-77; fax 5-90-83-69-90; f. 1944 as l'Etincelle, organ of the Parti Communiste Guadeloupéen (q.v.); present name adopted 2005; weekly; Editor-in-Chief DANIK ZANDRONIS; circ. 5,000.

Sept Mag Communication: Immeuble Curaçao, voie Verte, 97122 Baie-Mahault; weekly; Dir JACQUES CANNEVAL; circ. 30,000.

Terre de Guadeloupe: Immeuble Pluriel, 3 rue Ferdinand Forest, 97122 Baie-Mahault; tel. 5-90-25-20-20; fax 5-90-38-29-61; f. 2003; publ. by Groupe Maximini; monthly; local and environmental issues; CEO JEAN-YVES FRIXON; Publ. Dir THIERRY ELFGANG; circ. 60,000; also publ. *Maximini News* (f. 2005, daily, circ. 3,500).

TV Magazine Guadeloupe: 1 rue Paul Lacavé, BP 658, 97169 Pointe-à-Pitre; tel. 5-90-90-25-25; weekly.

Publishers

Editions Caret (Centre Antillais de Recherche et d'Edition de Textes): BP 165, 97190 Le Gosier; tel. and fax 5-90-84-82-29; e-mail caret@wanadoo.fr; French-Creole language, culture and fiction; Dir JACQUELINE PICARD.

Editions Exbrayat: 12 Allée des Marguerites, Les Jardins d'Arnouville, 97170 Petit-Bourg; tel. 5-90-26-32-33; fax 5-90-26-32-66; internet commerce.ciel.com/exbrayat; Dir PAQUITA EXBRAYAT-SANCHEZ.

Editions Jasor: 46 rue Schoëlcher, 97110 Pointe-à-Pitre; tel. 5-90-91-18-48; fax 5-90-21-07-01; e-mail editionsjasor@wanadoo.fr; French-Creole culture, biography and language, and youth fiction; Dir RÉGINE JASOR.

PLB Editions: route de Mathurin, 97190 Gosier; tel. 5-90-89-91-17; fax 5-90-89-91-05; e-mail plbeditions@wanadoo.fr; internet www.plbeditions.com; f. 1997; regional natural history and French-Creole youth fiction; Dirs CHANTAL MATTET, THIERRY PETIT LE BRUN.

Broadcasting and Communications

TELECOMMUNICATIONS

Digicel Antilles Françaises Guyane: see Martinique—Telecommunications.

Orange Caraïbe: BP 2203, 97196 Jarry Cédex; tel. 5-90-38-45-55; fax 8-10-50-05-59; e-mail webmaster@orange.gp; internet www.orangecaraibe.com; f. 1996; subsidiary of Orange France; mobile cellular telephone operator; network coverage incl. Martinique and French Guiana; Dir-Gen. JEAN-PHILIPPE GAY.

Outremer Telecom: SCI, Brand, voie Verte, Z. I. de Jarry, 97122 Baie-Mahault; e-mail communication@outremer-telecom.fr; internet www.outremer-telecom.fr; f. 1998; mobile telecommunications provider; Group CEO JEAN-MICHEL HEGESIPPE.

ONLY: SCI, Brand, voie Verte, Z. I. de Jarry, 97122 Baie-Mahault; e-mail communication@outremer-telecom.fr; internet www.outremer-telecom.fr; f. 1998 as Outremer Telecom Guadeloupe; present name adopted following merger of Volubis, ONLY and OOL in 2006; subsidiary of Outremer Telecom, France; fixed and mobile telecommunications provider.

BROADCASTING

Guadeloupe 1ère (Outre-mer Première): Morne Bernard Destrellan, BP 180, 97122 Baie-Mahault Cédex; tel. 5-90-60-96-96; fax 5-90-60-96-82; e-mail rfo@rfo.fr; internet guadeloupe.la1ere.fr; f. 1964; acquired by Groupe France Télévisions in 2004; fmrly Société Nationale de Radio-Télévision Française d'Outre-mer; name changed as Réseau France Outre-mer (RFO) in 1998; present name adopted in 2010; radio and TV; Dir-Gen. Geneviève Giard; Regional Dir Liliane Francil.

Radio

Kilti FM: Impasse Augustin Fresnel, Immeuble 590, Z. I. de Jarry, 97122 Baie-Mahault; tel. 5-90-32-52-61; fax 5-90-25-66-03; e-mail kiltifm@wanadoo.fr; f. 2006; French and Creole.

NRJ Guadeloupe: 2 blvd de la Marne, 97200 Fort-de-France; tel. 5-96-63-63-63; fax 5-96-73-73-15; e-mail webmaster@nrjantilles.com; internet www.nrjantilles.com; Dir Franck Férandier-Sicard; Dir Jean-Christophe Martinez.

Ouest FM: Immeuble Vivies, rue Thomas Edyson, Z. I. Jarry, 97122 Baie-Mahault; tel. 5-90-32-01-32; fax 5-90-26-02-97; e-mail contact@ouestfm.com; internet www.ouestfm.net; f. 2008; commercial radio station; French.

Radio Caraïbes International (RCI Guadeloupe): Carrefour Grand Camp, BP 40, 97151 Pointe-à-Pitre Cédex; tel. 5-90-83-96-96; fax 5-90-83-96-97; internet gp.rci.fm; f. 1962; Dir Frank Ferandier-Sicard; Man. Thierry Fundéré.

Radio Contact: 40 bis, rue Lamartine, 97110 Pointe-à-Pitre; tel. 5-90-82-25-41; fax 5-96-91-56-77; internet www.radio-contact.net; operated by l'Asscn Citoyenne de Sauvegarde et de Défense des Intérêts des Guadeloupéens; Dir Octavie Losio; Man. Henri Yoyotte.

Radio Gayak Media Delkaribe: BP 535, 97135 Pointe-à-Pitre Cédex; tel. 6-90-55-85-15; fax 5-90-83-12-30; e-mail gaston971@yahoo.fr; internet www.radiogayak.com; operated by the l'Asscn Guadeloupéenne de Défense et de Valorisation du Patrimoine Historique, Culturel et de l'Environnement; French and Creole; Dir Jean Adélaïde; Man. Danik Ibrahim Zandwonis.

Radio Haute Tension: route de Petit Marquisat, Routhiers, 97130 Capesterre Belle Eau; tel. 5-90-99-08-12; e-mail hautetension2@wanadoo.fr; internet www.radiohautetension.fr; f. 1986; Dir Huguette Hubert; Man. Ruddy Cornelie.

Radio Inter S'Cool (RIS): Lycée Ducharmoy, 97120 Saint-Claude; tel. and fax 5-90-80-38-40; e-mail contact@gupilvision.com; internet www.radiointerscool.net; educational and school-focused programmes; French and Creole; Pres. Jaques Remus.

Radio Tanbou: 153 résidence Espace, 97110 Pointe-à-Pitre; tel. 5-90-21-66-45; fax 5-90-21-66-48; e-mail kontak@radyotanbou.com; internet www.radyotanbou.com; French and Creole; operated by the l'Asscn pour le Développement de l'Information et de la Culture Guadeloupéenne.

Virgin Radio: Pointe-à-Pitre; internet www.virginradio.fr; f. 1987 as Europe 2 Fréquence Alizée; adopted current name 2008; commercial music station; Dir-Gen. Jean-Christophe Lestra.

Zouk Radio: Immeuble Général Bricolage, Petit Pérou, 97139 Les Abymes; tel. 5-90-89-25-80; fax 5-90-89-26-22; internet www.zoukradio.fr; commercial music station; French and Creole.

Other radio stations include: Média Tropical Guadeloupe; Radio Actif; Radio Arago; Radio Basses Internationale; Radio Bélo; Radio Climax; Radio Cosmique One; Radio Côte sous le Vent; Radio Éclair; Radio Horizon; Radio Karata; Radio Madras; Radio Massabielle; Radio Saint-Martin; Radio Saphir; Radio Sofaïa Altitude; Radio Souffle de Vie; Radio Tonic; and Radio Vie Meilleure.

Television

Antilles Télévision (ATV): see Martinique—Television.

Archipel 4: Immeuble Debs-Montauban, 97190 Gosier; tel. 5-93-21-05-20; f. 2002; Chair. Jean-Claude Thomaseau.

Canal Plus Antilles: Immeuble Canal Media, Moudong Centre Jarry, 97122 Baie-Mahault; tel. 5-90-38-09-00; fax 5-90-38-09-04; e-mail mrichol@canalantilles.gp; internet www.canalantilles.com; f. 1993; subsidiary of Groupe Canal Plus, France; satellite TV station; Pres. Jean-Noël Tronc.

Canal 10: Immeuble CCL, blvd de Houelbourg, ZI de Jarry, BP 2271, 97122 Baie-Mahault; tel. 5-90-26-73-03; fax 5-90-26-61-25; e-mail contact@canal10-tv.com; internet www.canal10-tv.com; f. 1990; focus on social, economic and cultural issues in Guadeloupe; produces 100% of its programmes; Man. Michel Rodriguez.

Eclair TV (ETV): Basse-Terre Télévision, Pintade, 97100 Basse-Terre; tel. 5-90-60-15-30; fax 5-90-60-15-33; e-mail eclairfm.com@orange.fr; f. 1998; community station local to Basse-Terre; Pres. (vacant).

La Une Guadeloupe (L'A1): 20 rue Henri Becquerel, Z. I. de Jarry, 97122 Baie-Mahault; tel. 5-90-38-06-06; fax 5-90-38-06-07; f. 1998; fmrly TCI; gen. interest; purchases 65% of programmes from TF1, France (2003); Pres. José Gaddarkhan.

Finance

(cap. = capital; res = reserves; dep. = deposits; m. = million; brs = branches; amounts in euros unless otherwise indicated)

BANKING

Central Bank

Institut d'Emission des Départments d'Outre-mer (IEDOM): Parc d'activité la Providence, ZAC de Dothémare, BP 196, 97139 Les Abymes; tel. 5-90-93-74-00; fax 5-90-93-74-25; e-mail iedom-pap-etudes@iedom-guadeloupe.fr; internet www.iedom.fr; Dir Charles Apanon.

Commercial Banks

Banque des Antilles Françaises: Parc d'Activités de la Jaille, BP 46, Bâtiments 5 et 6, 97122 Baie-Mahault; tel. 5-90-38-50-38; fax 5-90-38-62-92; internet www.bdaf.fr; f. 1967 by merger of Banque de la Martinique and Banque de la Guadeloupe; subsidiary of Financière Océor, France; cap. 55.9m., res –7.7m., dep. 1,095.9m. (Dec. 2009); Pres. and Chair. Christian Camus; Gen. Man. Didier Loing; 19 brs.

Banque Française Commerciale Antilles-Guyane (BFC Antilles-Guyane): Z. I. de Jarry, ZAC de Moudong Sud, 97122 Baie-Mahault; tel. 5-90-25-19-50; fax 5-90-25-19-49; e-mail f.aujoulat@bfc-ag.com; internet www.bfc-ag.com; f. 1976 as br. of Banque Française Commerciale, SA, separated 1984; cap. 51.1m., res 3.7m., dep. 656.9m. (Dec. 2009); Group Dir Anicette Lubin; Gen. Man. Jean Marguier.

BNP Paribas Guadeloupe: pl. de la Rénovation, BP 161, 97155 Pointe-à-Pitre; tel. 5-90-90-58-58; fax 5-90-90-04-07; internet guadeloupe.bnpparibas.net; f. 1941; subsidiary of BNP Paribas, France; CEO Thomas Courtois; Gen. Sec. Jean-Luc Riviere; 12 brs.

BRED Banque Populaire (BRED-BP): Immeuble Simcar, blvd Marquisat de Houelbourg, Z. I. Jarry, 97122 Baie-Mahault; tel. 5-90-82-65-46; internet www.bred.banquepopulaire.fr; cap. 242m. (Oct. 2005); Regional Man. Thierry Moreau.

Crédit Agricole de la Guadeloupe: Petit Pérou, 97176 Abymes Cédex; tel. 5-90-90-65-65; fax 5-90-90-65-89; e-mail catelnet@ca-guadeloupe.fr; internet www.ca-guadeloupe.fr; total assets 1,228.1m. (Dec. 2003); Pres. Christian Fléreau; Gen. Man. Roger Wunschel; 30 brs.

Crédit Maritime de la Guadeloupe: 36 rue Achille René-Boisneuf, BP 292, 97175 Pointe-à-Pitre; tel. 5-90-21-08-40; fax 5-90-89-52-42; e-mail pointe-a-pitre-agence-cmm@creditmaritime.com; internet www.creditmaritime-outremer.com; Dir Gérard Cadic; 4 agencies.

Société Générale de Banque aux Antilles (SGBA): 30 rue Frébault, BP 55, 97152 Pointe-à-Pitre; tel. 5-90-25-49-77; fax 5-90-25-49-78; e-mail sgba@wanadoo.fr; internet www.sgba.fr; f. 1979; cap. 32.6m., res –15.3m., dep. 360.5m. (Dec. 2009); Pres. Jean-Louis Mattei; Gen. Man. Michel Pecheur; 5 brs in Guadeloupe, 3 brs in Martinique.

Development Bank

Société de Crédit pour le Développement de Guadeloupe (SODEGA): Carrefour Raizet Baimbridge, BP 54, 97152 Pointe-à-Pitre; tel. 5-90-82-65-00; fax 5-90-90-17-91; e-mail credit@sodega.fr; internet www.sodega.fr; f. 1970; bought from the Agence Française de Développement (q.v.) by BRED Banque Populaire (q.v.) in 2003.

INSURANCE

Allianz Vie France: Le Patio de Grand Camp, BP 212, 97156 Pointe-à-Pitre Cédex; tel. 5-90-21-38-88; fax 5-90-82-78-25; e-mail agf.guavie@wanadoo.fr; internet www.allianz.fr; life insurance.

GAN Guadeloupe: 59–61 rue Achille René Boisneuf, BP 152, 97171 Pointe-à-Pitre Cédex; tel. 5-90-89-32-00; fax 5-90-04-43; internet www.groupama.es; subsidiary of Groupama, France; Dir-Gen. Alexandre Pascal; Man. Gilles Cano.

Mutuelle d'Assurance de Guadeloupe (MAG): Immeuble Capma & Capmi, blvd Légitimus, (face à Air France), 97110 Pointe-à-Pitre Cédex; tel. 5-90-82-22-71; fax 5-90-91-19-40; internet www.monceauassurances.com; fmrly Capma & Capmi.

Optimum Assurances: 3 bis rue Henri Bequerel, Jarry, 97122 Baie-Mahault; tel. 5-90-26-96-47; fax 5-90-26-81-27; internet www.assurances-guadeloupe.info; Dir-Gen. URBALD REINE.

WAB Assurances: Immeuble Stratégie, Moudong Sud, 97122 Baie-Mahault Cédex; tel. 5-90-32-66-66; fax 5-90-32-66-74; e-mail philippe.bech@wab-assu.com; internet www.wabassu.fr; f. 2005; Dir-Gen. PHILIPPE BECH.

Trade and Industry

GOVERNMENT AGENCIES

Direction de l'Alimentation, de l'Agriculture et de la Forêt (DAAF): Jardin Botanique, 97100 Basse-Terre; tel. 5-90-99-09-09; fax 5-90-99-09-10; e-mail daaf971@agriculture.gouv.fr; internet daaf971@agriculture.gouv.fr; Dir VINCENT FAUCHER.

Direction Régionale des Affaires Maritimes (DRAM): 20 rue Henri Becquerel, BP 2466, 97085 Jarry; tel. 5-90-41-95-50; fax 5-90-90-07-33; e-mail Dram-Guadeloupe@developpement-durable.gouv.fr; responsible for shipping, fishing and other maritime issues at a national and community level; Dir FRÉDÉRIC BLUA.

Direction Régionale du Commerce Extérieur Antilles-Guyane (DRCE): see Martinique—Trade and Industry.

Direction Régionale de l'Industrie, de la Recherche et de l'Environnement (DRIRE): 552 rue de la Chapelle, Z. I. Jarry, 97122 Baie-Mahault; tel. 5-90-38-03-47; fax 5-90-38-03-50; e-mail pierre.juan@industrie.gouv.fr; internet www.ggm.drire.gouv.fr; active in industry, business services, transport, public works, tourism and distribution; Departmental Co-ordinator MICHEL MASSON.

DEVELOPMENT ORGANIZATIONS

Agence de l'Environnement et de la Maîtrise de l'Energie (ADEME): Immeuble Café Center, rue Ferdinand Forest, Z. I. Jarry, 97122 Baie-Mahault; tel. 5-90-26-78-05; fax 5-90-26-87-15; e-mail ademe.guadeloupe@ademe.fr; internet www.ademe.fr; developing energy and waste management; Man. CLAUDE COROSINE.

Agence Française de Développement (AFD): Parc d'activités de la Jaille, Bâtiment 7, BP 110, 97122 Baie-Mahault; tel. 5-90-89-65-65; fax 5-90-83-03-73; e-mail afdpointeaPitre@afd.fr; internet www.afd-guadeloupe.org; fmrly Caisse Française de Développement; Man. PHILIPPE BAUDUIN.

CHAMBERS OF COMMERCE

Chambre d'Agriculture de la Guadeloupe: Espace régional Agricole, Convenance BP 35, 97122 Baie-Mahault; tel. 5-90-25-17-17; fax 5-90-26-07-22; e-mail cda_direction@guadeloupe.chambagri.fr; Pres. ERIC NELSON; Dir JOËL PEDURAND.

Chambre de Commerce et d'Industrie de Région des Iles de Guadeloupe: Hôtel Consulaire, rue Félix Eboué, 97110 Pointe-à-Pitre Cédex; tel. 5-90-93-76-00; fax 5-90-90-21-87; e-mail contact@pointe-a-pitre.cci.fr; internet www.pointe-a-pitre.cci.fr; f. 1832; Pres. COLETTE KOURY; Sec. HENRI NAGAPIN; 34 full mems and 17 assoc. mems.

Chambre de Métiers et de l'Artisanat de la Guadeloupe (CMA): route Choisy, BP 61, 97120 Saint-Claude; tel. 5-90-80-23-33; fax 5-90-80-08-93; e-mail sgstc@cmguadeloupe.org; internet www.cmguadeloupe.org; Pres. JOËL LOBEAU; 11,630 mems (2005).

EMPLOYERS' ORGANIZATIONS

Association des Moyennes et Petites Industries (AMPI): rue Pierre et Marie Curie, Z.I. Jarry, BP 2325, 97187 Jarry Cédex; tel. 5-90-26-38-27; fax 5-90-95-52-57; e-mail mpi.guadeloupe@wanadoo.fr; internet www.industrieguadeloupe.com; f. 1974; Pres. FRANK DOQUIN; Gen. Sec CHRISTOPHE WACHTER; 116 mem. cos.

Interprofession Guadeloupéenne pour la Canne à Sucre (IGUACANNE): Espace Régional Agricole de Convenance, 97122 Baie-Mahault; f. 2005; represents sugar cane growers, sugar producers and professional bodies; Pres. ATHANASE COQUIN.

Ordre des pharmaciens du département Guadeloupe: Immeuble Capital 16, 1°, ZAC de Houelbourg, SUD 2, 97122 Baie-Mahault; tel. 5-90-21-66-05; fax 5-90-21-66-07; e-mail delegation_guadeloupe@ordre.pharmacien.fr; Pres. MAGGY CHEVRY-NOL.

Syndicat des Producteurs-Exportateurs de Sucre et de Rhum de la Guadeloupe et Dépendances: Z. I. Jarry, 97122 Baie-Mahault; BP 2015, 97191 Pointe-à-Pitre; tel. 5-90-23-53-15; fax 5-90-23-52-34; f. 1937; Pres. M. VIGNERON; 4 mems.

Union des Entreprises-Mouvement des Entreprises de France (UDE-MEDEF): Immeuble SCI BTB, voie Principale de Jarry, Baie-Mahault; tel. 5-90-26-83-58; fax 5-90-26-83-67; e-mail ude.medef@medef-guadeloupe.com; Pres. WILLY ANGÈLE.

UTILITIES

Electricity

EDF Guadeloupe: BP 85, 97153 Pointe-à-Pitre; tel. 5-90-82-40-34; fax 5-90-83-30-02; e-mail marie-therese.fournier@edfgdf.fr; internet guadeloupe.edf.fr; electricity producer; Man. MAX BORDELAIS.

Water

Veolia Water—Compagnie Générale des Eaux Guadeloupe: Centre de la Guadeloupe, 7 Morne Vergain, BP 17, 97139 Abymes, Pointe-à-Pitre; tel. 5-90-89-76-76; fax 5-90-91-39-10; e-mail mail-elise@gde-guadeloupe.com; internet www.generaledeseaux.gp; fmrly SOGEA; Dir (Americas) AUGUSTE LAURENT.

TRADE UNIONS

Centrale des Travailleurs Unis de la Guadeloupe (CTU): Logement Test 14, Bergevin, 97110 Pointe-à-Pitre; BP 120, 97153 Pointe-à-Pitre Cédex; tel. 5-90-28-96-36; fax 5-90-28-81-16; e-mail ctu.gpe@wanadoo.fr; internet ctuguadeloupe.fr; f. 1999 by merger of the FASU-G and Centrale Syndicale des Travailleurs de la Guadeloupe; represents public and private sector workers; collegial directorate of 11 Secs-Gen; Sec.-Gen. ALEX LOLLIA; 3,500 mems.

Confédération Générale du Travail de la Guadeloupe (CGTG): 4 Cité Artisanale de Bergevin, BP 779, 97110 Pointe-à-Pitre Cédex; tel. 5-90-82-34-61; fax 5-90-91-04-00; f. 1961; Sec.-Gen. JEAN-MARIE NOMERTIN; 5,000 mems.

Fédération Départementale des Syndicats d'Exploitants de la Guadeloupe (FDSEA): Chambre d'Agriculture, Rond-Point de Destrellan, BP 150, 97122 Baie-Mahault; tel. 5-90-26-06-47; fax 5-90-26-48-82; e-mail fdsea971@yahoo.fr; affiliated to the Fédération Nationale des Syndicats d'Exploitants; Pres. ERIC NELSON.

Fédération Syndicale Unitaire Guadeloupe (FSU): BP 82, 97005 Pointe-à-Pitre Cedéx; tel. 5-90-23-13-66; fax 5-90-23-19-83; e-mail fsu971@fsu.fr; internet sd971.fsu.fr; f. 1993; departmental br. of the Fédération Syndicale Unitaire; represents public sector employees in teaching, research and training, and also agriculture, justice, youth and sports, and culture; Sec. GUY-LUC BELROSE.

SE-UNSA Guadeloupe (Le Syndicat des Enseignants UNSA): Immeuble Jabol, 5ème étage, 1 rue de la Clinique, 97139 Les Abymes; tel. 5-90-82-22-04; fax 5-90-83-08-64; e-mail 971@se-unsa.org; internet www.syndicat-enseignant-unsa-guadeloupe.fr; Sec.-Gen. GIRARD PELAGE.

Union Départementale de la Confédération Française des Travailleurs Chrétiens (UD/UR CFTC): BP 154, 97122 Baie-Mahault Cédex; tel. 5-90-26-20-62; e-mail udurcftc.gpe@orange.fr; f. 1937; Pres. SÉVERINE NOYER; 3,500 mems.

Union Départementale des Syndicats Force Ouvrière: 59 rue Lamartine, BP 687, 97110 Pointe-à-Pitre; tel. 5-90-82-86-83; fax 5-90-82-16-12; e-mail udfoguadeloupe@force-ouvriere.fr; internet www.force-ouvriere.fr; Gen. Sec. MAX EVARISTE; 1,500 mems.

Union Générale des Travailleurs de la Guadeloupe (UGTG): rue Paul Lacavé, 97110 Pointe-à-Pitre; tel. 5-90-83-10-07; fax 5-90-89-08-70; e-mail ugtg@ugtg.org; internet www.ugtg.org; f. 1973; confederation of pro-independence trade unions incl. Union des Agents de la Sécurité Sociale (UNASS), l'Union des Employés du Commerce (UEC), Union des Travailleurs de l'Etat et du Département (UTED), l'Union des Travailleurs des Collectivités (UTC), l'Union des Travailleurs de l'Hôtellerie, du Tourisme et de la Restauration (UTHTR), l'Union des Travailleurs des Produits Pétroliers (UTPP), l'Union des Travailleurs de la Santé (UTS), and l'Union des Travailleurs des Télécommunications (UTT); Gen. Sec. ELIE DOMOTA; 4,000 mems.

Union Interprofessionnelle Régionale CFDT de la Guadeloupe (UIR CFDT): 104 Immeuble Les Chicanes, 97139 Grand-Camp Abymes; tel. 5-90-83-16-50; fax 5-90-20-42-61; e-mail cfdt.gpe@wanadoo.fr; affiliated to the Fédération des Syndicats Généraux de l'Education Nationale et de la Recherche; represents teaching staff.

Union des Moyennes et Petites Entreprises de Guadeloupe (UMPEG): 17 Immeuble Coupole, Grand Camp, 97139 Abymes, Pointe-à-Pitre; tel. 5-90-91-79-31; fax 5-90-93-09-18; Pres. EDOUARD VAINQUEUR.

Transport

RAILWAYS

There are no railways in Guadeloupe.

ROADS

In 1990 there were 2,069 km (1,286 miles) of roads in Guadeloupe, of which 323 km were Routes Nationales.

SHIPPING

The Port Autonome de la Guadeloupe comprises five sites. The two principal seaports are at Pointe-à-Pitre, which offers both cargo-handling and passenger facilities, and the container terminal at Jarry (Baie-Mahault); the smaller port of Basse-Terre caters to freight and inter-island passenger traffic. There is also a sugar terminal at Folle-Anse (Saint-Louis); and a marina at Bas-du-Fort with 1,000 berths for pleasure craft.

Agence Petrelluzzi Transit et Maritime: 17 rue de la Chapelle, 97122 Baie Mahault; tel. 5-90-38-12-12; fax 5-90-26-69-26; e-mail info@transitpetrelluzzi.com; internet transitpetrelluzzi.com; f. 1896; Dir PATRICK PETRELLUZZI.

Compagnie Générale Maritime Antilles-Guyane: Route du WTC, Zone Portuaire, BP 92, 97122 Baie-Mahault; tel. 5-90-25-57-00; fax 5-90-25-57-81; e-mail ptp.mbellemare@cma-cgm.com; internet www.cma-cgm.com; subsidiary of CMA-CGM, France; shipping agents, stevedoring; Gen. Man. MARLÈNE BELLEMERE.

Port Autonome de la Guadeloupe: Quai Ferdinand de Lesseps, BP 485, 97165 Pointe-à-Pitre Cédex; tel. 5-90-68-61-70; fax 5-90-68-61-71; e-mail v-sene@port-guadeloupe.com; internet www.port-guadeloupe.com; port authority; Pres. GIL THÉMINE; Dir-Gen. LAURENT MARTENS.

Compagnie Générale Portuaire: Marina Bas-du-Fort, 97110 Pointe-à-Pitre; tel. 5-90-93-66-20; fax 5-90-90-81-53; e-mail marina@marina-pap.com; internet www.marina-pap.com; port authority; Man. PHILIPPE CHEVALLIER; Harbour Master TONY BRESLAU; 1,000 berths for non-commercial traffic.

Société Guadeloupéenne de Consignation et Manutention (SGCM): 8 rue de la Chapelle, BP 2360, 97001 Jarry Cédex; tel. 5-90-38-05-55; fax 5-90-26-95-39; e-mail gerard.petrelluzzi@sgcm.fr; f. 1994; shipping agents, stevedoring; also operates Navimar Cruises inter-island tour co; Gen. Man. GERARD PETRELLUZZI; 17 berths.

Transcaraïbes S.A.: BP 2453, 97085 Pointe-à-Pitre; tel. 5-90-26-63-27; fax 5-90-26-67-49; e-mail transcaraibes.gpe@wanadoo.fr; f. 1976; shipping agents, stevedoring; office in Martinique; Gen. Man. ERIK URGIN.

CIVIL AVIATION

Raizet International Airport is situated 3 km (2 miles) from Pointe-à-Pitre and is equipped to handle jet-engined aircraft. There are smaller airports on the islands of Marie-Galante, La Désirade and Saint-Barthélémy. The island is served by a number of regional airlines, including LIAT (see Antigua and Barbuda).

Air Antilles Express: Aeroport Pôle Caraibes, Point-à-Pitre; tel. 5-90-21-14-47; e-mail ar@media-caraibes.com; internet www.airantilles.com; f. 2002; subsidiary of Compagnie Aerienne Inter Regionale Express, France; serves Guadeloupe, Martinique, St-Barthélemy, St-Martin and the Dominican Republic; seasonal flights to San Juan, La Romana, Antigua and St Lucia; Dir CHRISTIAN MARCHAND.

Air Caraïbes (CAT): Aéroport International Guadeloupe, Pôle Caraïbes, 97139 Abymes; tel. 5-90-82-47-41; fax 5-90-82-47-49; e-mail drh@aircaraibes.com; internet www.aircaraibes.com; f. 2000 following merger of Air St Martin, Air St Barts, Air Guadeloupe and Air Martinique; owned by Groupe Dubreuil; operates daily inter-island, regional and international services within the Caribbean, and flights to Brazil, French Guiana and Paris; CEO SERGE TSYGALNITZKY; 16 aircraft; 800,000 passengers (2006).

Air Caraïbes Atlantique: Aéroport, 97232 Le Lamentin; f. 2003; subsidiary of Air Caraïbes; services between Pointe-à-Pitre, Fort-de-France (Martinique) and Paris; Pres. FRANÇOIS HERSEN.

Tourism

Guadeloupe is a popular tourist destination, especially for visitors from metropolitan France (who account for some 89% of tourists) and the USA. The main attractions are the beaches, the mountainous scenery and the unspoilt beauty of the island dependencies. In 2009 some 408,000 tourists visited Guadeloupe. Receipts from tourism totalled US $384m. in 2008. In 2005 there were 93 hotels, with some 6,632 rooms.

Comité du Tourisme: 5 sq. de la Banque, BP 555, 97166 Pointe-à-Pitre Cédex; tel. 5-90-82-09-30; fax 5-90-83-89-22; e-mail info@lesilesdeguadeloupe.com; internet www.lesilesdeguadeloupe.com; Pres. JOSETTE BOREL-LINCERTIN; Dir THIERRY GARGAR.

Délégation Régionale au Tourisme, au Commerce et l'Artisanat: 5 rue Victor Hugues, 97100 Basse-Terre; tel. 5-90-81-10-44; fax 5-90-81-94-82; e-mail drtourisme.guadeloupe@wanadoo.fr; Dir CHRISTIAN FOURCRIER.

Syndicat d'Initiative de Pointe-à-Pitre: Centre Commercial de la Marina, 97110 Pointe-à-Pitre; tel. 5-90-90-70-02; fax 5-90-90-74-70; e-mail syndicatinitiativedepap@wanadoo.fr; internet www.sivap.gp; Pres. DENYS FORTUNE; Man. NADIA DEGLAS.

Defence

As assessed at November 2011, France maintained a military force of about 1,057 in Fort-de-France (Martinique).

Education

The education system is similar to that of metropolitan France (see chapter on French Guiana). In 2009/10 there were 134 pre-primary and 209 primary schools. In 2009/10 secondary education was provided at 92 institutions. In 2009/10 there were 22,198 students in pre-primary and 37,185 in primary education, while in secondary education there were 51,580 students, of whom some 90% attended state schools. There were also two teacher-training institutes, and colleges of agriculture, fisheries, hotel management, nursing, midwifery and child care. A branch of the Université des Antilles et de la Guyane, at Pointe-à-Pitre, has faculties of law and economics, sciences, medicine, sports science and humanities. In 2009/10 there was a total of 9,078 students in higher education.

MARTINIQUE

Introductory Survey

LOCATION, CLIMATE, LANGUAGE, RELIGION, CAPITAL

Martinique is one of the Windward Islands in the West Indies, with Dominica to the north and Saint Lucia to the south. The island is dominated by the volcanic peak of Mont Pelée. The climate is tropical, but tempered by easterly and north-easterly breezes. The more humid and wet season runs from July to November, and the average temperature is 26°C (79°F). French is the official language, but a Creole patois is widely spoken. The majority of the population professes Christianity and belongs to the Roman Catholic Church. The capital is Fort-de-France.

CONTEMPORARY POLITICAL HISTORY

Historical Context

Martinique has been a French possession since 1635. The prosperity of the island was based on the sugar industry, which was devastated by the volcanic eruption of Mont Pelée in 1902. Martinique became a Department of France in 1946, when the Governor was replaced by a Prefect, and an elected Conseil général (General Council) was created.

During the 1950s there was a growth of nationalist feeling, as expressed by Aimé Césaire's Parti Progressiste Martiniquais (PPM) and the Parti Communiste Martiniquais (PCM). However, economic power remained concentrated in the hands of the *békés* (descendants of white colonial settlers), who owned most of the agricultural land and controlled the lucrative import-export market. This provided little incentive for innovation or self-sufficiency, and fostered resentment against lingering colonial attitudes.

Domestic Political Affairs

In 1974 Martinique, together with Guadeloupe and French Guiana, was given regional status as part of France's governmental reorganization. An indirectly elected Conseil régional (Regional Council) was created, with some control over the local economy. In 1982 and 1983 the socialist Government of President François Mitterrand made further concessions towards autonomy by giving the local councils greater control over taxation, local police and the economy. At the first direct elections to the new Conseil régional, held in February 1983, left-wing parties (the PPM, the PCM and the Fédération Socialiste de la Martinique—FSM) won a majority of seats. This success, and the election of Césaire as President of the Conseil régional, strengthened his influence against the pro-independence elements in his own party. (Full independence for Martinique attracted support from only a small minority of the population; the majority sought reforms that would bring greater autonomy, while retaining French control.) The Mouvement Indépendantiste Martiniquais (MIM), the most vocal of the separatist parties, fared badly in the elections, obtaining less than 3% of the total vote. At an election to the enlarged Conseil général in 1985, the left-wing parties increased their representation, but the centre-right coalition of the Union pour la Démocratie Française (UDF) and the Rassemblement pour la République (RPR) maintained their control of the administration.

At the general election to the Assemblée nationale (National Assembly) in 1986, Martinique's representation was increased from three to four deputies. Césaire and a member of the FSM were elected from a unified list of left-wing candidates, while the RPR and the UDF (which had also presented a joint list) each won one seat. In the concurrent election to the Conseil régional the left-wing parties (including the PPM, the FSM and the PCM) won a narrow majority of seats. Césaire retained the presidency of the Council until 1988, when he relinquished the post to Camille Darsières (the Secretary-General of the PPM). Indirect elections were held also held in 1986 for Martinique's two seats in the Sénat. The left-wing parties again united, and Martinique acquired a left-wing senator for the first time since 1958, a PPM member, while the other successful candidate belonged to the UDF.

Left-wing candidates secured all four seats at elections to the Assemblée nationale in 1988 and the parties of the left also achieved a majority at elections to the Conseil général. Emile Maurice of the RPR was, none the less, elected President of the Conseil général for a seventh term.

In 1990 the results of the 1986 election to the Conseil régional were annulled because of a technicality, and another election was held. Pro-independence candidates secured nine seats (of which seven were won by the MIM). The PPM-FSM-PCM coalition lost its absolute majority on the Conseil régional; Camille Darsières was, however, re-elected to the presidency of the Conseil régional. At an election to the Conseil général in 1992, left-wing parties secured a narrow majority. Claude Lise, a PPM deputy to the Assemblée nationale, was elected President of the Conseil. In concurrent elections to the Conseil régional the RPR and the UDF, contesting the election as the Union pour la France (UPF), won the most seats. Emile Capgras of the PCM was elected President of the Conseil régional.

In September 1992 72% of voters in Martinique approved ratification of the Treaty on European Union (see p. 276), although the abstention rate was high.

There was a marked swing in favour of the parties of the right at the 1993 elections to the Assemblée nationale: André Lesueur and Pierre Petit of the RPR were elected, as was a third right-wing candidate, Anicet Turinay of the UPF. In September 1995 Lise was elected to the Sénat, while the incumbent PPM representative, Rodolphe Désiré, was returned to office.

At elections to the Assemblée nationale in 1997, Turinay and Petit, representing the RPR, were re-elected, together with Camille Darsières of the PPM. Alfred Marie-Jeanne, the First Secretary and a founding member of the MIM, was elected in a constituency hitherto held by the RPR. At elections to the Conseil régional in the following year, the left retained its majority. Marie-Jeanne was elected President of the Conseil régional. In a concurrent election to the Conseil général the left again increased its majority; Lise was re-elected to the presidency of the Conseil général.

A two-month strike by workers in the banana sector, which had severely disrupted economic activity around the port of Fort-de-France, was ended in January 1999, when a pay agreement was reached. However, the social climate deteriorated further in May, as the Toyota motor company and the Roger Albert distribution group were affected by strike action. In early October tension escalated as trade unions blocked access to the main industrial and commercial zones around the capital for two days. Subsequent negotiations between the local authorities and a trade union delegation resulted in a conclusion to the dispute at Roger Albert, but, despite mediation efforts, industrial action at Toyota continued. Trade unions organized a week-long blockade of the port of Fort-de-France in protest against proposed redundancies at the car plant. Later that month, prior to a two-day visit to Martinique by Prime Minister Lionel Jospin, banana producers occupied the headquarters of the French naval forces for several days, demanding the disbursement of exceptional aid to compensate for a dramatic decline in prices on the European market. The Prime Minister announced an emergency plan for the banana sector and agreed, in principle, to a proposal for greater autonomy for the local authorities in conducting relations with neighbouring countries and territories. In November, following two weeks of negotiations, the Toyota dispute was resolved; a pay increase was awarded and dismissal proceedings against 12 employees were annulled.

Following a series of meetings, in December 1999 the Presidents of the Conseils régionaux of French Guiana, Guadeloupe and Martinique signed a joint declaration in Basse-Terre, Guadeloupe, affirming their intention to propose, to the Government, a legislative amendment aimed at creating a new status of overseas region, despite an earlier statement to the contrary by Jospin. Modified proposals regarding the institutional future and socio-economic development of the Departments were approved by the Assemblée nationale and in December were ratified by the Constitutional Council. Following a meeting of members of the Conseil régional and the Conseil général in late June 2001, a series of proposals on greater autonomy was agreed upon. These included: the division of the territory into four districts; the creation of a Territorial Collectivity (Collectivité territoriale), governed by a 41-member Assembly elected for a five-year term; and the establishment of an independent executive council. Furthermore, the proposals included a request that the territory be given control over legislative and administrative affairs, as well as legislative authority on matters concerning Martinique alone. In March 2003 the two houses of the French parliament approved constitutional changes that, *inter alia*, allowed for local referendums to be held on proposals for greater decentralization in overseas possessions. The status of Overseas Region (Région d'outre-mer) was also conferred on Martinique. In the referendum, held on 7 December, some 51% of participating voters rejected legislative reforms that envisaged the replacement of the Conseil général and the Conseil régional with a single assembly.

In municipal elections held in March 2001 the PPM retained control of the majority of municipalities. In the concurrently held election to the Conseil général, Lise was re-elected President. At elections to the Assemblée nationale in June 2002, Marie-Jeanne was re-elected, while Turinay lost his seat to Louis-Joseph Manscour of the PS, and Darsières lost his to Pierre-Jean Samot of the left-wing Bâtir le Pays Martinique (BPM); Alfred Almont, representing the right-wing alliance of the Union pour la Majorité Présidentielle (UMP) and the RPR, secured the remaining seat. The RPR subsequently merged into the successor party to the UMP, the Union pour un Mouvement Populaire (also known as the UMP). In March 2003 the French Conseil constitutionnel ordered Samot to resign for having broken campaign funding rules. A by-election was held in May 2003, which was won by Philippe Edmond-Mariette, also of BPM.

At an election to the Conseil régional in March 2004 the Patriotes Martiniquais, a pro-independence alliance, comprising the MIM, the Conseil National des Comités Populaires and the Alliance pour le Pays Martinique (which was absorbed by the two larger groupings after the first round of voting), won an overwhelming majority, obtaining 28 of the 41 council seats. A joint list comprising the PPM and other left-wing candidates obtained nine seats, while the right-wing Forces Martiniquaises de Progrès secured the remaining four seats.

In May 2005 a national referendum was held on ratification of the European Union constitutional treaty: 69% of voters in the Department were in favour of adopting the treaty, although the turn-out of the electorate was only 28%. The treaty was ultimately rejected by a majority of voters in metropolitan France. In December more than 1,000 protesters took part in demonstrations in Fort-de-France against a law, approved in the previous February, that proposed changing the school syllabus to reflect the 'positive' role of French colonialism. In January 2006 the relevant article of law was removed in accordance with a ruling by the Conseil constitutionnel that it lay outside the competence of the legislature.

In the first round of the national presidential election, held on 22 April 2007, Ségolène Royal of the PS won 48.5% of the votes cast on the island, ahead of Nicolas Sarkozy, the UMP candidate, who attracted 33.8% of the ballot. At the second round, held on 6 May, Royal won 60.5% of the vote in the Department. However, nationally, Sarkozy emerged victorious, securing 53.1% of the votes overall. At elections to the Assemblée nationale, held on 10 and 17 June, Marie-Jeanne, Manscour and Almont were all re-elected, while Serge Letchimy of the PPM was also successful. Following elections to the Conseil général in March 2008 Lise was again re-elected as the Conseil's President.

A general strike began in early February 2009 in protest against the increasingly high cost of living, following similar unrest in Guadeloupe. Riot police were sent from metropolitan France in an effort to control the demonstrations, and violent confrontations between police and protesters ensued. The strike, which caused significant economic disruption, ended on 11 March, although a further, small-scale, demonstration was organized in the following month by union leaders protesting against rising unemployment.

Recent developments: referendum on autonomy

A referendum on the issue of increased autonomy for the island was held on 10 January 2010. The electorate, fearful of losing economic support from mainland France and unwilling to confer greater power upon the local political élite, voted overwhelmingly to reject any increase in autonomy, with 78.9% voting against the proposal. The rate of participation by the electorate was 55.4%. A further referendum on institutional reform was held on 24 January, and 68.3% of participants voted in favour of changing the status of Martinique to a collectivité unique (single collectivity), replacing the existing two-tier departmental and regional administrative structure. Only 35.8%

of the electorate took part in the plebiscite. The authorities hoped that the merger of the departmental and regional levels of government (expected to take place in 2014) would increase efficiency and reduce operating costs. A joint committee to examine the institutional transition, comprising members of the Conseil régional and the Conseil général, agreed in mid-2010 that the collectivité unique would be officially designated the Collectivité de la Martinique. In mid-2011 the Assemblée nationale approved legislation to facilitate this transition. Polls were scheduled for March 2014 to elect the 51 members of a new, consolidated legislative body, which would replace the Conseil régional and the Conseil général. In turn, the new assembly would then elect a nine-member executive council.

Meanwhile, in elections to the Conseil régional on 14 and 21 March 2010, the PPM won a decisive victory, with 48.4% of the ballot, gaining 26 of the Council's 41 seats. The MIM secured 12 seats and the UMP-led list obtained the remaining three, with 41.0% and 10.6% of the votes cast, respectively. Letchimy was duly elected as President of the Conseil régional. The rate of participation by the electorate was 55.1%. Following the UMP's poor electoral performance, in May a group of disaffected members formed a new right-wing party, the Parti Régionaliste Martiniquais. Left-wing candidates performed strongly in the municipal polls conducted on 20 and 27 March 2011, following which the BPM's Josette Manin (representing a PPM-led coalition) was elected as Martinique's first female President of the Conseil général. Also in that month, Laurent Prévost was appointed as Prefect. In September Serge Larcher of the PPM was re-elected to the Sénat, while another left-wing candidate, Maurice Antiste, won control of the island's second Sénat seat.

CONSTITUTION AND GOVERNMENT

France is represented in Martinique by an appointed prefect. There are two councils with local powers: the 45-member Conseil général (General Council) and the 41-member Conseil régional (Regional Council). Both are elected by universal adult suffrage for a period of up to six years. Martinique elects four deputies to the Assemblée nationale in Paris, and sends two indirectly elected representatives to the Sénat. The Department is also represented at the European Parliament.

ECONOMIC AFFAIRS

In 2009, according to official estimates, Martinique's gross domestic product (GDP), measured at current prices, was estimated at €7,716m., equivalent to US $19,160 per head. During 1990–2001, according to UN estimates, GDP increased, in real terms, at an average rate of 1.5% per year; growth in 2001 was 2.1%. Between the censuses of 1999 and 2006, according to provisional figures, the population increased at an average annual rate of 0.5%.

Agriculture, hunting, forestry and fishing contributed 2.2% of GDP in 2006, and according to provisional figures engaged an estimated 3.3% of the active labour force in 2008. The principal cash crops are bananas, sugar cane (primarily for the production of rum), limes, melons and pineapples. The cultivation of cut flowers is also of some significance. Roots and tubers and vegetables are grown for local consumption. Agricultural production increased at an average rate of 1.3% per year during 1990–98; the sector declined by 0.2% in 1999.

According to provisional figures, the industrial sector (including construction and public works) engaged 13.6% of the employed population in 2008 and contributed 14.0% of GDP in 2006. The most important manufacturing activities are petroleum refining (exports of fuels and combustibles accounted for 58.1% of the value of total exports in 2008) and the production of agricultural products (11.8% of exports in 2008), the production of rum being of particular significance. Other areas of activity include metals, cement, chemicals, plastics, wood, printing and textiles.

In 2008 construction engaged a preliminary 6.3% of the employed labour force and in 2006 the sector contributed 6.2% to GDP.

Energy is derived principally from mineral fuels. In 2008 imports of fuels and combustibles (including crude petroleum destined for the island's refinery) accounted for 21.6% of the value of total imports.

The services sector engaged a provisional 83.1% of the employed population in 2008 and provided 83.8% of GDP in 2006. Tourism is a major activity on the island and one of the most important sources of foreign exchange: in 2009 441,648 visitor arrivals were recorded while earnings from the tourism industry totalled an estimated €302m.; some 80.3% of visitors were from metropolitan France in the same year. In 2010 some 475,886 visitor arrivals were recorded.

In 2010 Martinique's trade deficit totalled €2,205.1m., compared with f€1,757m. in the previous year. In 2009 Martinique's export earnings were worth only approximately 13.2% of the total value of imports. Metropolitan France was the principal source of imports (54.9% in 2008); Guadeloupe was the principal market for exports (57.2%) in that year. French Guiana, member countries of the European Union (EU, see p. 276) and the USA were also significant trading partners. The principal exports were fuels and combustibles, agricultural products and food industries. The principal imports included fuels and combustibles, food industry products and car industry products.

In 2008 the regional budget showed a deficit of €14.2m. In that year, the departmental budget showed a surplus of €170.8m. The annual rate of inflation averaged 1.9% in 2001–10; consumer prices decreased by 0.3% in 2009, but increased by 1.6% in 2010. Some 21.4% of the labour force was unemployed in 2008.

Martinique's economic development has created a society that combines a relatively high standard of living with a weak economic base in agricultural and industrial production, as well as a chronic trade deficit, with high levels of unemployment and emigration. The linking of wage levels to those of metropolitan France, despite the island's lower level of productivity, has increased labour costs and restricted development. Martinique's economy was badly affected by the global financial crisis from 2008, and GDP contracted by 6.5% in 2009, according to official data, mainly owing to a dramatic fall in investment. Tourist numbers decreased in 2009, owing to the combined effects of the economic downturn and the violent demonstrations of that year, which damaged the island's reputation and deterred visitors. Nevertheless, the economy recovered in 2010, with increasing internal demand and a resurgent tourism industry driving GDP growth of 4.6%. Exports also rose sharply during the year, although activity in the construction and agricultural sectors was subdued. Tourism indicators remained positive in the first half of 2011, but the rest of the economy appeared to be struggling. Moreover, the unemployment rate (20.8% at mid-2011) was still very high and inflation, which had been rising since 2010 owing to higher fuel prices, was continuing its upward trend.

PUBLIC HOLIDAYS

2013: 1 January (New Year's Day), 11–12 February (Lenten Carnival), 13 February (Ash Wednesday), 29 March–1 April (Easter), 1 May (Labour Day), 8 May (Victory Day), 9 May (Ascension Day), 20 May (Whit Monday), 10 June (Abolition of Slavery), 14 July (National Day), 15 August (Assumption), 1 November (All Saints' Day), 11 November (Armistice Day), 25 December (Christmas Day).

Statistical Survey

Sources (unless otherwise indicated): Institut National de la Statistique et des Etudes Economiques (INSEE), Service Régional de Martinique, Centre Administratif Delgrès, blvd de la Pointe des Sables, Hauts de Dillon, BP 641, 97262 Fort-de-France Cédex; tel. 5-96-60-73-73; fax 5-96-60-73-50; e-mail antilles-guyane@insee.fr; internet www.insee.fr/fr/regions/martinique; Ministère des Départements et Territoires d'Outre-mer, 27 rue Oudinot, 75700 Paris 07 SP; tel. 1-53-69-20-00; fax 1-43-06-60-30; internet www.outre-mer.gouv.fr.

AREA AND POPULATION

Area: 1,100 sq km (424.7 sq miles).

Population: 381,427 at census of 8 March 1999; 396,404 at census of 1 January 2009. Note: According to new census methodology, data in 2009 refer to median figures based on the collection of raw data over a five-year period (2006–11). *1 January 2010* (estimate): 399,637. *Mid-2012* (UN estimate): 408,301 (Source: UN, *World Population Prospects: The 2010 Revision*).

Density (at mid-2012): 371.2 per sq km.

Population by Age and Sex (UN estimates at mid-2012): *0–14:* 76,755 (38,912 males, 37,843 females); *15–64:* 269,162 (125,862 males, 143,300 females); *65 and over:* 62,384 (26,181 males, 36,203 females); *Total:* 408,301 (190,955 males, 217,346 females).

Principal Towns (at 2006 census): Fort-de-France (capital) 90,347; Le Lamentin 39,847; Le Robert 23,856; Schoelcher 21,419; Sainte-Marie 19,528; Le François 19,201; Saint-Joseph 17,107; Ducos 15,977. *2007* (official estimates): Fort-de-France (capital) 89,794; Le Lamentin 39,442; Le Robert 24,068; Schoelcher 21,510.

Births, Marriages and Deaths (2009 unless otherwise indicated): Registered births 5,174 (birth rate 13.0 per 1,000); Registered marriages 1,357 (marriage rate 3.4 per 1,000); Registered deaths 2,770 (death rate 6.9 per 1,000). *2010:* Birth rate 12.1 per 1,000; Death rate 8.0 per 1,000. Source: partly Pan American Health Organization.

Life Expectancy (years at birth): 79.9 (males 76.9; females 82.6) in 2010. Source: Pan American Health Organization.

Economically Active Population (persons aged 15 years and over, 1998): Agriculture and fishing 7,650; Industry 7,103; Construction and public works 10,405; Trade 16,196; Transport 4,383; Financial services and real estate 3,354; Business services 8,376; Public services 14,179; Education 14,991; Health and social security 10,676;

Administrative services 18,742; *Total employed* 116,055 (males 62,198, females 53,857); Unemployed 48,537 (males 22,628, females 25,909); *Total labour force* 164,592 (males 84,826, females 79,766). *2008* (provisional figures at 31 December): Agriculture 4,113; Mining and quarrying 157; Manufacturing 7,158; Electricity, water and sanitation 1,957; Construction 7,962; Trade 15,349; Hotels and restaurants 4,398; Transportation and storage 5,676; Communication 2,432; Finance and insurance 3,139; Real estate activities 837; Professional services 12,139; Public administration 21,925; Education 11,367; Health and other social services 16,905; Extra-territorial activities 14; Other services 10,980; Total 126,508. Note: Figures for employment exclude 8,633 non-salaried workers. *2009* (estimate at 31 December): Unemployed 39,531.

HEALTH AND WELFARE

Key Indicators

Total Fertility Rate (children per woman, 2010): 1.9.

Under-5 Mortality Rate (per 1,000 live births, 2010): 8.1.

Physicians (per 1,000 head, c. 2001): 19.7.

Hospital Beds (per 1,000 head, 2008): 4.1.

Source: mainly Pan American Health Organization.

For definitions and other sources, see explanatory note on p. vi.

AGRICULTURE, ETC.

Principal Crops ('000 metric tons, 2010, FAO estimates): Yams 1.5; Sugar cane 223.4; Lettuce and chicory 6.9; Tomatoes 5.4; Cucumbers and gherkins 5.7; Bananas 192.0; Plantains 13.7; Pineapples 1.7. *Aggregate Production* ('000 metric tons, may include official, semi-official or estimated data): Total vegetables (incl. melons) 37.7; Total fruits (excl. melons) 208.9.

Livestock ('000 head, year ending September 2010, FAO estimates): Cattle 21; Sheep 15; Pigs 15; Goats 8.

Livestock Products ('000 metric tons, 2010, FAO estimates): Cattle meat 1.2; Pig meat 1.0; Chicken meat 1.2; Cows' milk 2.7; Hen eggs 2.7.

Forestry ('000 cubic metres, 2010, FAO estimates): *Roundwood Removals* (excl. bark): Sawlogs, veneer logs and logs for sleepers 2.4; Fuel wood 10.0; Total 12.4. *Sawnwood Production* (incl. railway sleepers): 1.0.

Fishing (metric tons, live weight, 2009): Capture 6,200—FAO estimate (Clupeoids 4,000; Common dolphinfish 210—FAO estimate; Other marine fishes 1,050—FAO estimate; Caribbean spiny lobster 190; Clams, etc. 700); Aquaculture 110—FAO estimate *Total catch* 6,310—FAO estimate.

Source: FAO.

MINING

Production ('000 metric tons, 2009, estimates): Cement 221; Pumice 130; Salt 200. Source: US Geological Survey.

INDUSTRY

Production ('000 metric tons, 2008, unless otherwise indicated): Motor spirit (petrol) 167; Kerosene 146; Gas-diesel (distillate fuel) oils 185; Residual fuel oils 323; Liquefied petroleum gas 29; Electric energy (million kWh) 1,237 (Source: UN Industrial Commodity Statistics Database). *2009:* Raw sugar 5,600 metric tons; Rum (hl) 70.6. *2010:* Raw sugar 4,000 metric tons; Rum (hl) 68.0. (Source: Institut d'Emission des Départements d'Outre-mer, *Rapport Annuel 2010*).

FINANCE

Currency and Exchange Rates: The French franc was used until the end of 2001. Euro notes and coins were introduced on 1 January 2002, and the euro became the sole legal tender from 18 February. Some of the figures in this Survey are still in terms of francs. For details of exchange rates, see French Guiana.

Budget: *French Government* (million French francs, 1998): Revenue 4,757; Expenditure 8,309. *Regional Budget* (€ million, 2008): Current revenue 232.2 (Taxes 174.1, Other current revenue 58.1); Capital revenue 61.9; Total 294.1. Current expenditure 165.1; Capital expenditure 143.2; Total 308.3. *Departmental Budget* (forecasts, million French francs, 2001): Tax revenue 836.9 (Departmental taxes 332.0, Fuel tax 295.0, Transfer taxes, etc. 58.0, Motor vehicle tax 68.0, Fiscal subsidy 53.0); Other current revenue 886.6 (Refunds of social assistance 65.0, Operational allowance 315.0, Decentralization allowance 477.0); Capital revenue 499.5 (EU development funds 71.0, Capital allowances 59.0, Other receipts 101.4, Borrowing 270.0); Total 2,223.0. Current expenditure 1,482.2 (Finance service 57.1, Permanent staff 394.7, General administration 65.1, Other indirect services 69.0, Administrative services 108.4, Public health 49.9, Social assistance 503.6, Support costs of minimum wage 99.8, Economic services 114.7); Capital expenditure 740.8 (Road system 139.5, Networks 47.9, Education and culture 111.5, Other departmental programmes 101.6, Other public bodies 83.7, Other programmes 96.3, Non-programme expenditure 162.3); Total 2,223.0. *2008* (€ million, excl. debt rescheduling): Total revenue 667.7; Total expenditure 496.9. Source: partly Département des Etudes et des Statistiques Locales.

Money Supply (million French francs at 31 December 1998): Currency outside banks 924; Demand deposits at banks 6,330; Total money 7,254.

Cost of Living (Consumer Price Index at January; base: 1998 = 100): All items (excluding tobacco) 120.0 in 2008; 121.3 in 2009; 121.7 in 2010.

Gross Domestic Product (€ million at current prices): 7,893 in 2007; 8,043 in 2008 (estimate); 7,716 in 2009 (estimate). Source: Institut d'Emission des Départements d'Outre-mer, *Rapport Annuel 2010*.

Expenditure on the Gross Domestic Product (€ million at current prices, 2009, estimates): Total final consumption expenditure 8,079.6 (General government and non-profit institutions serving households 3,315.7, Households 4,763.9); Changes in stocks –252.9; Gross fixed capital formation 1,474.1; *Total domestic expenditure* 9,300.8; Exports of goods and services 592.1; *Less* Imports of goods and services 2,179.8; Statistical discrepancy 2.9; *GDP in purchasers' values* 7,716.0. Source: Institut d'Emission des Départements d'Outre-mer, *Martinique: Rapport Annuel 2010*.

Gross Domestic Product by Economic Activity (€ million at current prices, 2006): Agriculture 160; Food industries 122; Other manufacturing 282; Energy 164; Construction 453; Services 6,088 (Restaurants and hotels 232, Transport 222, Commerce 852, Other market services 2,387, Non-market services 2,395); *Sub-total* 7,269; *Less* Financial intermediation services indirectly measured 298; Taxes, less subsidies 667; *GDP in purchasers' values* 7,638.

EXTERNAL TRADE

Principal Commodities (€ million, 2008): *Imports c.i.f.:* Products of food industries 391.5; Leather and clothing 90.5; Pharmaceutical products 185.3; Home equipment 151.3; Car industry products 320.2; Mechanical equipment 184.3; Electronics and electrical equipment 147.5; Chemicals, rubber and plastics 195.7; Metals and metal products 123.3; Fuels and combustibles 598.3; Total (incl. others) 2,766.0. *Exports f.o.b.:* Products of agriculture, forestry and fishing 43.3; Products of food industries 51.9; Metals and metal products 11.6; Fuels and combustibles 213.4; Total (incl. others) 367.1. *2010* (€ million): Total imports 2,539.6; Total exports 334.5 (Source: Institut d'Emission des Départements d'Outre-mer, *Martinique: Rapport Annuel 2010*).

Principal Trading Partners (€ million, 2008): *Imports c.i.f.:* Aruba 78; France (metropolitan) 1,519; Germany 72; Guadeloupe 44; Italy 45; Japan 36; Netherlands 54; Spain 26; United Kingdom 326; USA 199; Total (incl. others) 2,766. *Exports f.o.b.:* Antigua 4; France (metropolitan) 90; French Guiana 38; Guadeloupe 210; Netherlands Antilles 3; USA 9; Total (incl. others) 367. *2010* (€ million): Total imports 2,539.6; Total exports 334.5 (Source: Institut d'Emission des Départements d'Outre-mer, *Martinique: Rapport Annuel 2010*).

TRANSPORT

Road Traffic ('000 motor vehicles in use, 1995): Passenger cars 95.0; Commercial vehicles 21.5. Source: UN, *Statistical Yearbook*.

Shipping: *Merchant Fleet* (vessels registered '000 grt at 31 December, 1992): 1 (Source: Lloyd's Register of Shipping). *International Sea-borne Traffic* (2006, provisional figures): Goods loaded 950,000 metric tons (petroleum products 359,000 metric tons); Goods unloaded 2,302,000 metric tons (petroleum products 1,109,000 metric tons).

Civil Aviation (2009): Freight (incl. post) carried 11,247 metric tons; Passengers carried 1,495,000.

TOURISM

Tourist Arrivals by Country (excl. same-day visitors and cruise ship arrivals, 2003): France (metropolitan) 357,726; Guadeloupe 40,668; French Guiana 10,619; Total (incl. others) 453,159. *2009* (excl. same-day visitors and cruise ship arrivals): Total 441,648 (France 354,846; French Guiana 7,141; Guadeloupe 38,094; USA 6,290). *2010* (excl. same-day visitors and cruise ship arrivals): Total 475,886. (Source: partly Institut d'Emission des Départements d'Outre-mer, *Martinique: Rapport Annuel 2010*).

Receipts from Tourism (€ million, incl. passenger transport): 299 in 2007; 316 in 2008; 302 in 2009. (Source: World Tourism Organization).

COMMUNICATIONS MEDIA

Radio Receivers ('000 in use): 82 in 1997.

Television Receivers ('000 in use): 62 in 1999.

Telephones ('000 main lines in use): 172.0 in 2010.

Mobile Cellular Telephones ('000 subscribers): 295.4 in 2004.

Personal Computers: 82,000 in 2004.

Internet Users ('000): 170.0 in 2009.

Broadband Subscribers: 6,000 in 2010.

Daily Newspaper: 1 (estimate) in 1996 (estimated average circulation 30,000 copies).

Sources: UNESCO, *Statistical Yearbook*; UN, *Statistical Yearbook*; International Telecommunication Union.

EDUCATION

Pre-primary (2008/09): 17,079 students (16,048 state, 1,031 private).

Primary (2008/09): 29,611 students (27,306 state, 2,305 private).

Specialized Pre-primary and Primary (2008/09): 318 students.

Secondary (2008/09): 44,277 students (40,264 state, 4,013 private).

Higher (2007/08, unless otherwise indicated): 8,985 students. Source: Ministère de l'Education Nationale, de la Recherche et de la Technologie. *Université Antilles-Guyane (Campus de Schoelcher):* 5,344 students in 2003/04. Source: Préfecture de Martinique, *Livret d'accueil des services de l'Etat en Martinique*.

Teachers (2004/05): *Primary:* 3,031 (2,787 state, 244 private); *Secondary:* 4,553 (4,177 state, 376 private); *Higher:* 186. Source: Ministère de l'Education Nationale, *Repères et références statistiques—édition 2005*.

Institutions (2003/04): 258 primary schools; 41 lower secondary schools; 22 state upper secondary schools; 24 private institutions. Source: Préfecture de Martinique, *Livret d'accueil des services de l'Etat en Martinique*.

Adult Literacy Rate: 98.0% (males 97.6%, females 98.3%) in 2005. Source: Pan American Health Organization.

Directory

The Government

(May 2012)

HEAD OF STATE

President: NICOLAS SARKOZY.

Prefect: LAURENT PRÉVOST, Préfecture, 82 rue Victor Sévère, BP 647–648, 97262 Fort-de-France Cédex; tel. 5-96-39-36-00; fax 5-96-71-40-29; e-mail contact.prefecture@martinique.pref.gouv.fr; internet www.martinique.pref.gouv.fr.

DEPARTMENTAL ADMINISTRATION

President of the General Council: JOSETTE MANIN (PPM), Conseil général de la Martinique, blvd Chevalier Sainte-Marthe, 97200 Fort-de-France Cédex; tel. 5-96-55-26-00; fax 5-96-73-59-32; internet www.cg972.fr.

President of the Economic and Social Committee: MICHEL CRISPIN, Hôtel de la Région, ave Gaston Deferre, Plateau Roy Cluny, BP 601, 97200 Fort-de-France; tel. 5-96-59-63-00; fax 5-96-59-64-31; e-mail cesr-s@region-martinique.com; internet www.cr-martinique.fr.

President of the Culture, Education and Environment Committee: CLAUDE PETIT, Hôtel de la Région, ave Gaston Deferre, Plateau Roy Cluny, BP 601, 97200 Fort-de-France; e-mail ccee@cr-martinique.fr; fax www.cr-martinique.fr.

President of the Regional Council: SERGE LETCHIMY (PPM), Hôtel de la Région, ave Gaston Deferre, BP 601, 97200 Fort-de-France Cédex; tel. 5-96-59-63-00; fax 5-96-72-68-10; e-mail service.communication@cr-martinique.fr; internet www.cr-martinique.fr.

Elections, 14 and 21 March 2010

	Seats
Parti Progressiste Martiniquais	26
Mouvement Indépendantiste Martiniquais	12
Rassembler la Martinique*	3
Total	41

* Electoral list comprising the Union pour un Mouvement Populaire (UMP) and allies.

REPRESENTATIVES TO THE FRENCH PARLIAMENT

Deputies to the French National Assembly: LOUIS-JOSEPH MANSCOUR (FSM), ALFRED ALMONT (UMP), SERGE LETCHIMY (PPM), ALFRED MARIE-JEANNE (MIM).

Representatives to the French Senate: SERGE LARCHER (PPM), MAURICE ANTISTE (Groupe Socialiste).

Political Organizations

Bâtir le Pays Martinique: Fort-de-France; f. 1998; left-wing; split from the Parti Communiste Martiniquais; Leader PIERRE-JEAN SAMOT; Nat. Sec. DAVID ZOBDA.

Combat Ouvrier: BP 821, 97258 Fort-de-France Cédex; e-mail redaction@combat-ouvrier.net; internet www.combat-ouvrier.net; Trostskyist; mem. of the Communist Internationalist Union; Leader GHISLAINE JOACHIM-ARNAUD.

Conseil National des Comités Populaires (CNCP): 8 rue Pierre et Marie Curie, Terres Sainville, 97200 Fort-de-France; tel. 5-96-63-75-23; e-mail cncp@netcaraibes.com; internet www.m-apal.com; f. 1983; pro-independence party affiliated to the Union Général des Travailleurs de Martinique; contested the 2004 regional elections in alliance with the MIM; Pres. JOSETTE MASSOLIN; Spokesperson ROBERT SAÉ.

Fédération Socialiste de la Martinique (FSM): 52 rue du Capitaine Pierre-Rose, 97200 Fort-de-France; tel. 5-96-60-14-88; fax 5-96-63-81-06; e-mail federation.socialiste-martinique@wanadoo.fr; internet martinique.parti-socialiste.fr; local br. of the Parti Socialiste (PS); Fed. Sec. LOUIS JOSEPH MANSCOUR; Spokesperson FRÉDÉRIC BUVAL.

Forces Martiniquaises de Progrès (FMP): 12 rue Ernest Deproge, 97200 Fort-de-France; tel. 5-96-57-74-10; fax 5-96-63-36-19; e-mail miguel.laventure@fmp-regionales.org; internet www.jrdmedias.com/laventure/index.html; f. 1998 to replace the local br. of the Union pour la Démocratie Française; Pres. MIGUEL LAVENTURE.

Mouvement des Démocrates et Écologistes pour une Martinique Souveraine (MODEMAS): Fort-de-France; f. 1992; left-wing, pro-independence; Pres. GARCIN MALSA.

Mouvement Indépendantiste Martiniquais (MIM): Fort-de-France; internet www.mim-matinik.org; f. 1978; pro-independence party; First Sec. ALFRED MARIE-JEANNE.

Mouvement Populaire Franciscain: angle des rues Couturier et Holo, 97240 Le François; tel. 5-96-54-20-40; e-mail direction@pont-abel.fr; left-wing; Leader MAURICE ANTISTE.

Osons Oser: Fort-de-France; f. 1998; right-wing; affiliated with the metropolitan Union pour un Mouvement Populaire (UMP); Pres. PIERRE PETIT; Vice-Pres. JENNY DULYS-PETIT.

Parti Communiste Martiniquais (PCM): angle des rues A. Aliker et E. Zola, Terres-Sainville, 97200 Fort-de-France; tel. 5-96-71-86-83; fax 5-96-63-13-20; e-mail ed.justice@wanadoo.fr; internet journal-justice-martinique.com; f. 1957; Sec.-Gen. GEORGES ERICHOT.

Parti Progressiste Martiniquais (PPM): Ancien Réservoir de Trénelle, 97200 Fort-de-France; tel. 5-96-71-88-01; fax 5-96-72-68-56; e-mail contact@ppm-martinique.fr; internet www.ppm-martinique.fr; f. 1958; left-wing; Leader SERGE LETCHIMY; Sec.-Gen. DIDIER LAGUERRE.

Parti Régionaliste Martiniquais: Fort-de-France; f. 2010 by fmr mems of UMP (q.v.); right-wing; Pres. CHANTAL MAIGNAN; Sec.-Gen. CHRISTIAN RAPHA.

Rassemblement Démocratique pour la Martinique (RDM): Résidence Pichevin 2, Bâtiment Hildevert, Les Hauts du Port, 97200 Fort-de-France; tel. 5-96-71-89-97; internet rfdm.e-monsite.com; f. 2006; Sec.-Gen. CLAUDE LISE.

Union pour un Mouvement Populaire (UMP): angle des rues de la République et Vincent Allègre, 97212 Saint Joseph; tel. 5-96-57-96-68; fax 5-96-57-32-68; internet www.u-m-p.org; centre-right; local br. of the metropolitan party; Pres., Departmental Cttee MARC SEFIL.

Les Verts Martinique: Lotissement Donatien, 54 rue Madinina, Cluny, 97200 Fort-de-France; tel. and fax 5-96-71-58-21; e-mail louisleonce@wanadoo.fr; ecologist; departmental br. of the metropolitan party; Leader LOUIS-LÉONCE LECURIEUX-LAFFERONNAY.

Judicial System

Cour d'Appel de Fort-de-France: ave St John Perse, Morne Tartenson, BP 634, 97262 Fort-de-France Cédex; tel. 5-96-70-62-62; fax 5-96-63-52-13; e-mail ca-fort-de-france@justice.fr; highest court of appeal for Martinique and French Guiana; First Pres. HERVÉ EXPERT; Procurator-Gen. JEAN JACQUES BOSC.

There are two Tribunaux de Grande Instance, at Fort-de-France and Cayenne (French Guiana), and three Tribunaux d'Instance (two in Fort-de-France and one in Cayenne).

Religion

The majority of the population belong to the Roman Catholic Church.

CHRISTIANITY

The Roman Catholic Church

Some 80% of the population are Roman Catholics. Martinique comprises the single archdiocese of Fort-de-France. The Archbishop participates in the Antilles Episcopal Conference, based in Port of Spain, Trinidad and Tobago.

Archbishop of Fort-de-France and Saint-Pierre: Most Rev. GILBERT MARIE MICHEL MÉRANVILLE, Archevêché, 5–7 rue du Révérend Père Pinchon, BP 586, 97207 Fort-de-France Cédex; tel. 5-96-63-70-70; fax 5-96-63-75-21; e-mail archeveche-martinique@wanadoo.fr.

Other Churches

Among the denominations active in Martinique are the Assembly of God, the Evangelical Church of the Nazarene and the Seventh-day Adventist Church.

The Press

Antilla: Le Lamentin, BP 46, 97281 Fort-de-France, Cédex 1; tel. 5-96-75-48-68; fax 5-96-75-58-46; e-mail antilla@orange.fr; f. 1981; weekly; politics and economics; Publ. Dir ALFRED FORTUNE; Editor-in-Chief TONY DELSHAM.

France Antilles: pl. François Mitterrand, 97207 Fort-de-France; tel. 5-96-59-08-83; fax 5-96-60-29-96; e-mail redaction.fa@media-antilles.fr; internet www.martinique.franceantilles.fr; f. 1964; subsidiary of Groupe France Antilles; daily; Editor PAUL-HENRI COSTE; circ. 30,000 (Martinique edn).

Journal Asé Pléré Annou Lité (Journal APAL): 8 rue Pierre et Marie Curie, Terres Sainville, 97200 Fort-de-France; tel. 5-96-63-75-23; fax 5-96-70-30-82; e-mail journ.apal@orange.fr; internet www.m-apal.com; f. 1983; monthly; organ of the Conseil Nat. des Comités Populaires (q.v.) and the Union Général des Travailleurs de Martinique (q.v.); Dir ROBERT SAÉ.

Justice: rue André Aliker, 97200 Fort-de-France; tel. 5-96-71-86-83; fax 5-96-63-13-20; e-mail ed.justice@wanadoo.fr; internet journal-justice-martinique.com; f. 1920; weekly; organ of the Parti Communiste Martinique (q.v.); Dir FERNAND PAPAYA; circ. 8,000.

Lutte Ouvrière: 1111 Rés Matéliane, l'aiguille, 97128 Goyave; e-mail contact@lutte-ouvriere.org; internet www.lutte-ouvriere.org; f. 1970; fortnightly; communist; Publ. Dir MICHEL RODINSON; circ. 14,000.

Le NAIF-Magazine: Résidence K, Pointe des Nègres, route Phare, 97200 Fort-de-France; tel. 5-96-61-62-55; fax 5-96-61-85-76; e-mail docedouard@yahoo.fr; internet www.wmaker.net/lenaif; weekly; publ. by CIC; Owner CAMILLE CHAUVET.

Le Progressiste: c/o Parti Progressiste Martiniquais, Ancien Réservoir de Trénelle, 97200 Fort-de-France; tel. 5-96-71-88-01; e-mail d.compere@ool.fr; internet www.ppm-martinique.fr; weekly; organ of the PPM; Publ. Dir DANIEL COMPERE; circ. 13,000.

TV Magazine: pl. François Mitterand, 97232 Lamentin; tel. 5-96-42-60-77; fax 5-96-42-98-70; e-mail tv.mag@media-antilles.fr; f. 1989; weekly; Editor-in-Chief RUDY RABATHALY.

Publishers

Editions Desormeaux: Z. I. la Jambette, 97232 Fort-de-France; tel. 5-96-50-30-30; fax 5-96-50-30-70; e-mail info.desormeaux@gmail.com; internet www.editions-desormeaux.com; French-Creole history, language, culture, culinaria, natural history, academic and fiction.

Editions Exbrayat: 5 rue des Oisillons, route de Balata, 97234 Fort-de-France; tel. 5-96-64-60-58; fax 5-96-64-70-42; e-mail andre.exbrayat@exbrayat.com; internet commerce.ciel.com/exbrayat; regional art, history, natural history, culinaria, maps and general fiction; 2 brs in Guadeloupe; Commercial Dir PAQUITA EXBRAYAT-SANCHEZ; Sec. HERMINIE MARIE-CLAIRE.

Editions Lafontaine: Bâtiment 12, Maniba, 97222 Case Pilote; tel. and fax 5-96-78-87-98; e-mail info@editions-lafontaine.com; internet www.editions-lafontaine.com; f. 1994; Creole, French and English literature, general fiction, culture, history, youth and educational; Dir JEANNINE 'JALA' LAFONTAINE.

Broadcasting and Communications

TELECOMMUNICATIONS

Digicel Antilles Françaises Guyane: Oasis, Quartier Bois Rouge, 97224 Ducos; tel. 8-10-63-56-35; fax 5-96-42-09-01; e-mail contact@digicelgroup.fr; internet www.digicel.fr; f. 2000 as Bouygues Telecom Caraïbe; acquired from Bouygues Telecom, France, in 2006; mobile cellular telephone operator; network coverage incl. Guadeloupe and French Guiana; CEO (French Caribbean) YANN KEREBEL; Dir.-Gen. (Martinique) SÉBASTIEN AUBÉ.

Orange Caraïbe: see Guadeloupe—Telecommunications.

Outremer Telecom: Z. I. la Jambette, BP 280, 97285 Lamentin Cédex 2; e-mail communication@outremer-telecom.fr; internet www.outremer-telecom.fr; f. 1998; mobile telecommunications provider; CEO JEAN-MICHEL HEGESIPPE.

ONLY: Z. I. la Jambette, BP 280, 97285 Lamentin Cédex 2; e-mail communication@outremer-telecom.fr; internet www.outremer-telecom.fr; f. 1998 as Outremer Telecom Martinique; present name adopted following merger of Volubis, ONLY and OOL in 2006; telecommunications provider; subsidiary of Outremer Telecom, France; Head of Operations (French West Indies and French Guiana) FRÉDÉRIC HAYOT.

BROADCASTING

Martinique 1ère (Outre-mer Première): La Clairière, BP 662, 97263 Fort-de-France; tel. 5-96-59-52-00; fax 5-96-59-52-26; internet martinique.la1ere.fr; acquired by Groupe France Télévisions in 2004; fmrly Société Nationale de Radio-Télévision Française d'Outre-mer; name changed to Réseau France Outre-mer (RFO) in 1998; present name adopted in 2010; Dir-Gen. GENEVIÈVE GIARD; Regional Dir JEAN-PHILIPPE PASCAL.

Radio

Radio Asé Pléré Annou Lité (Radio APAL) (Radio Pèp-la): 8 rue Pierre et Marie Curie, Terres Sainville, 97200 Fort-de-France; tel. 5-96-63-75-23; fax 5-96-70-30-82; e-mail radio.apal@orange.fr; internet www.m-apal.com; f. 1989; affiliated to the Conseil Nat. des Comités Populaires (q.v.) and the Union Général des Travailleurs de Martinique (q.v.); French and Creole; Dir MICHEL NE'DAN; Station Man. JEAN-CLAUDE LOUIS-SYDNEY.

Radio Banlieue Relax (RBR): 107 ave Léona Gabriel, Cité Dillon, 97200 Fort-de-France; tel. 5-96-60-00-90; fax 5-96-73-06-53; e-mail radio.br@orange.fr; internet www.rbrfm.com; f. 1981; regional social and cultural programmes; Pres. FRANTZ CLÉORON; Dir JEAN-ÉTIENNE JEANNOT.

Radio Canal Antilles (RCA): plateau Fofo, 97233 Schoelcher; tel. 5-96-61-74-19; fax 5-96-61-23-58; internet membres.multimania.fr/canalantilles; f. 1980; fmrly Radio 105; regional social and cultural programmes; Radio France Internationale relay; Pres. SERGE POGNON.

Radio Caraïbes International (RCI Martinique): 2 blvd de la Marne, 97200 Fort-de-France Cédex; tel. 5-96-63-98-70; fax 5-96-63-26-59; internet www.rcimartinique.fm; commercial radio station; Dir JOSÉ ANELKA; Station Man. VINCENT CHRÉTIEN; Editor-in-Chief JEAN-PHILIPPE LUDON.

Radio Evangile Martinique (REM): 54 Route des Religieuses, 97200 Fort-de-France; tel. 5-96-70-68-48; fax 5-96-70-17-51; e-mail rem@evgi.net; internet rem.evgi.net; f. 1993; Pres. RAYMOND SORMAIN; Dir LUCIEN COIQUE.

Radio Fréquence Atlantique (RFA): 10 rue du Docteur Laveran, 97232 Le Lamentin; tel. 5-96-42-35-51; fax 5-96-51-04-26; e-mail r.f.a@wanadoo.fr; internet www.radiorfa.fr; operated by Société Martiniquaise de Communication; Dir JOSEPH LEVI.

Other radio stations include: Chérie FM (formerly Campêche FM); Difé Radio; Fun Radio (formerly Maxxi FM); Radio 22; Radio Actif Martinique; Radio Alizés; Radio Archipel; Radio Espérance; Radio Espoir; Radio Inter Tropicale; Radio Solidarité Rurale—La Voix des Mornes; and West Indies Radio.

Television

Antilles Télévision (ATV): 28 ave des Arawacks, Chateauboeuf, 97200 Fort-de-France; tel. 5-96-75-44-44; fax 5-96-75-55-65; e-mail contact@atvweb.fr; internet www.antillestelevision.com; f. 1993; general interest; accounts for 22% of viewers; also broadcasts to French Guiana and Guadeloupe; Chair. FABRICE JEAN-JEAN; Dir-Gen. DANIEL ROBIN; Editor-in-Chief KARL SIVATTE.

Canal Plus Antilles: see Guadeloupe—Television.

Kanal Martinique Télévision (KMT) (Kanal Matinik Télévision): voie 7, Renéville, 97200 Fort-de-France; tel. 5-96-63-64-85; e-mail webmaster@kmttelevision.com; internet kmttelevision.com; f. 2004; operated by l'Asscn pour le Développement des Techniques Modernes de Communication; Pres. ROLAND LAOUCHEZ.

Finance

(cap. = capital; res = reserves; dep. = deposits; m. = million; brs = branches; amounts in euros)

BANKING

Central Bank

Institut d'Emission des Départements d'Outre-mer (IEDOM): 1 blvd du Général de Gaulle, BP 512, 97206 Fort-de-France Cédex; tel. 5-96-59-44-00; fax 5-96-59-44-04; e-mail agence@iedom-martinique.fr; internet www.iedom.fr; Dir PHILIPPE LA COGNATA.

Commercial Banks

Banque des Antilles Françaises: see Guadeloupe—Finance.

BNP Paribas Martinique: 72 ave des Caraïbes, BP 588, 97200 Fort-de-France; tel. 5-96-59-46-02; fax 5-96-63-71-42; e-mail michel.lafont@bnpparibas.com; internet martinique.bnpparibas.net; f. 1941; subsidiary of BNP Paribas, France; 12 brs; Gen. Man. ALAIN THOLLIEZ.

BRED Banque Populaire: Z. I. la Jambette, 97232 Le Lamentin; tel. 5-96-63-77-63; e-mail courrier-direct@bred.fr; internet www.bred.banquepopulaire.fr; cap. 242m. (Oct. 2005); Regional Man. BRUNO DUVAL; brs in Martinique and French Guiana.

Crédit Agricole: rue Case Nègre, pl. d'Armes, BP 370, 97232 Le Lamentin Cédex 2; tel. 8-20-39-93-10; fax 5-96-51-37-12; internet www.ca-martinique.fr; f. 1950; total assets 1,263m. (Dec. 2004); Pres. GUY RANLIN; Gen. Man. JEAN-MARIE CARLI; 30 brs in Martinique and French Guiana.

Société Générale de Banque aux Antilles (SGBA): see Guadeloupe—Finance.

INSURANCE

AGF Allianz Vie France: ZAC de l'Etang Z'Abricots, Bâtiment C, 97200 Fort-de-France; tel. 5-96-50-55-61; fax 5-96-50-55-71; e-mail marvie1@agfmar.com; internet www.allianz.fr; life insurance; subsidiary of Allianz Group.

Assurance Outre-mer: Hauts Dillon Delgres, Fort-de-France; tel. 5-96-73-09-70; fax 5-96-70-09-25; e-mail accueil@assurance-outremer.fr; internet www.assurance-outremer.com; Dir-Gen THIERRY COAT.

DPA Assurance: 126 route des Religieuses 97200 Fort de France; tel. 5-96-63-84-49; fax 5-96-63-09-52; e-mail dp.a@wanadoo.fr; internet www.dpa-assurances.com.

Groupama Antilles Guyane: 10 Lotissement Bardinet Dillon, BP 559, 97242 Fort-de-France Cédex; tel. 5-96-75-33-33; fax 5-96-75-06-78; internet www.groupama.fr; f. 1978; Dir-Gen. DIDIER COURIER; 6 brs in Martinique, 7 brs in Guadeloupe, 3 brs in French Guiana.

Groupement Français d'Assurances Caraïbes (GFA Caraïbes): 46–48 rue Ernest Desproges, 97205 Fort-de-France; tel. 5-96-59-04-04; fax 5-96-73-19-72; e-mail contact@gfa-caraibes.fr; internet www.gfacaraibes.fr; subsidiary of Gruppo Generali, Italy; Chair. JEAN-CLAUDE WULLENS; Man. Dir STÉPHANE COUDOUR.

Trade and Industry

GOVERNMENT AGENCIES

Direction Régionale du Commerce Extérieur Antilles-Guyane (DRCE): Bureaux 406 et 408, BP 647, 97262 Fort-de-France Cédex; tel. 5-96-39-49-90; fax 5-96-60-08-14; e-mail drceantilles@missioneco.org; internet www.tresor.economie.gouv.fr/region/antilles-guyane; Regional Dir MICHEL ROUSSELLIER; Regional Asst. (Martinique) XAVIER BUCHOUX.

Direction Régionale de l'Industrie, de la Recherche et de l'Environnement (DRIRE): see French Guiana—Trade and Industry.

Direction de la Santé et du Développement Social (DSDS): Centre d'Affaires AGORA, l'Etang Z'abricots, Pointe des Grives, BP 658, 97263 Fort-de-France Cédex; tel. 5-96-39-42-43; fax 5-96-60-60-12; e-mail josiane.pinville@sante.gouv.fr; internet www.martinique.sante.gouv.fr; Dir CHRISTIAN URSULET.

DEVELOPMENT ORGANIZATIONS

Agence Française de Développement (AFD): 1 blvd du Général de Gaulle, BP 804, 97244 Fort-de-France Cédex; tel. 5-96-59-44-73; fax 5-96-59-44-88; e-mail afdfortdefrance@groupe-afd.org; internet www.afd.fr; fmrly Caisse Française de Développement; Man. ERIC BORDES.

Secrétariat Général pour les Affaires Régionales (SGAR)—Bureau de la Coopération Régionale: Préfecture, 97262 Fort-de-France; tel. 5-96-39-49-78; fax 5-96-39-49-59; e-mail jean-charles.barrus@martinique.pref.gouv.fr; successor to the Direction de l'Action Economique Régionale (DAER); research, documentation, and technical and administrative advice on investment in industry and commerce; Chief JEAN-CHARLES BARRUS.

CHAMBERS OF COMMERCE

Chambre d'Agriculture: pl. d'Armes, BP 312, 97286 Le Lamentin Cédex 2; tel. 5-96-51-75-75; fax 5-96-51-93-42; e-mail ca972@martinique.chambagri.fr; internet www.martinique.chambagri.fr; Pres. LOUIS-DANIEL BERTOME; Dir NICAISE MONROSE.

Chambre de Commerce et d'Industrie de la Martinique: 50 rue Ernest Desproge, BP 478, 97200 Fort-de-France Cédex; tel. 5-96-55-28-00; fax 5-96-60-66-68; e-mail dic@martinique.cci.fr; internet www.martinique.cci.fr; f. 1907; Pres. MANUEL BAUDOUIN; Dir-Gen. FRANTZ SABIN.

Chambre des Métiers et de l'Artesanat de la Martinique: 2 rue du Temple, Morne Tartenson, BP 1194, 97200 Fort-de-France; tel. 5-96-71-32-22; fax 5-96-70-47-30; e-mail cmm972@wanadoo.fr; internet www.cma-martinique.com; f. 1970; Pres. HERVÉ LAUREOTE; Sec.-Gen. HERVÉ ETILÉ; 8,000 mems.

INDUSTRIAL ORGANIZATION

Association Martiniquaise pour la Promotion de l'Industrie (AMPI): Centre d'Affaires de la Martinique, Bâtiment Pierre, 1er étage, Californie, BP 1042, 97232 Le Lamentin; tel. 5-96-50-74-00; fax 5-96-50-74-37; e-mail industrie@ampi.mq; internet www.industriemartinique.com; f. 1972 as Asscn des Moyennes et Petites Industries; 119 mem. cos; Pres. PIERRE MARIE-JOSEPH; Sec.-Gen. RICHARD CRESTOR.

EMPLOYERS' ORGANIZATIONS

Banalliance: Centre d'Affaires le Baobab, rue Léon Gontran Damas, 97232 Le Lamentin; tel. 5-96-57-42-42; fax 5-96-57-35-18; f. 1996; banana growers' alliance; Pres. DANIEL DISER; Dir-Gen. SANDRA ALEXIA; 220 mems.

Banamart: Quartier Bois Rouge, 97224 Ducos; tel. 5-96-42-43-44; fax 5-96-51-47-70; internet www.banamart.com; f. 2005 by merger of SICABAM and GIPAM; represents banana producers; Pres. NICOLAS MARRAUD DES GROTTES; Dir-Gen. PIERRE MONTEUX.

Ordre des Médecins de la Martinique: 80 rue de la République, 97200 Fort-de-France; tel. 5-96-63-27-01; fax 5-96-60-58-00; e-mail martinique@972.medecin.fr; Pres. HELENON RAYMOND; Sec.-Gen. ELANA EMILE.

Ordre des Pharmaciens de la Martinique: Apt G-01, Immeuble Gaëlle, Résidence Studiotel-Grand Village, BP 587, 97233 Schoelcher; tel. 5-96-52-23-67; fax 5-96-52-20-92; e-mail delegation_martinique@ordre.pharmacien.fr; internet www.ordre.pharmacien.fr; Pres. JEAN BIGON.

UTILITIES

Electricity

EDF Martinique (Electricité de France Martinique): Pointe des Carrières, BP 573, 97242 Fort-de-France Cédex 01; tel. 5-96-59-20-00; fax 5-96-60-29-76; e-mail edf-services-martinique@edfgdf.fr; internet www.edf.fr/martinique; f. 1975; electricity supplier; successor to Société de Production et de Distribution d'Electricité de la Martinique (SPDEM); Chair. and CEO HENRI PROGLIO; 174,753 customers (2006).

Water

Veolia Water-Société Martiniquaise des Eaux (SME): pl. d'Armes, BP 213, 97284 Le Lamentin Cédex 02; tel. 5-96-51-80-51; fax 5-96-51-80-55; internet www.martiniquaisedeseaux.com; f. 1977 as Société Martiniquaise des Eaux.

TRADE UNIONS

Centrale Démocratique Martiniquaise du Travail (CDMT): Maison des Syndicats, Jardin Desclieux, 97200 Fort-de-France; tel. 5-96-70-19-86; fax 5-96-71-32-25; Sec.-Gen. PHILIPPE PIERRE-CHARLES.

Confédération Générale du Travail de la Martinique (CGTM): Maison des Syndicats, blvd Général de Gaulle, 97200 Fort-de-France; tel. 5-96-70-25-89; fax 5-96-63-80-10; e-mail contact@cgt-martinique.fr; internet www.cgt-martinique.fr; f. 1961; affiliated to World Fed. of Trade Unions; Sec.-Gen. GHISLAINE JOACHIM-ARNAUD.

Fédération Départementale des Syndicats d'Exploitants Agricoles de la Martinique (FDSEA): Immeuble Chambre d'Agriculture, pl. d'Armes, 97232 Le Lamentin; tel. 5-96-51-61-46; fax 5-96-57-05-43; e-mail fdsea.martinique@wanadoo.fr; affiliated to the Fédération Nationale des Syndicats d'Exploitants Agricoles; Pres. BÉRARD CAPGRAS.

Fédération Syndicale Unitaire Martinique (FSU): route des Réligieuses, Bâtiment B, Cité Bon Air, 97200 Fort-de-France; tel. 5-96-63-63-27; fax 5-96-71-89-43; e-mail fsu@fsu-martinique.fr; internet www.fsu-martinique.fr; f. 1993; departmental br. of the Fédération Syndicale Unitaire; represents public sector employees in teaching, research and training, and also agriculture, justice, youth and sports, and culture; Sec. YVON JOSEPH-HENRI.

Union Départementale Confédération Française des Travailleurs Chrétiens Martinique (UD CFTC): Maison des Syndicats, Jardin Desclieux, 97200 Fort-de-France; tel. 5-96-71-95-10; fax 5-96-60-39-10; e-mail cftc972@wanadoo.fr; internet www.cftc.fr.

Union Départementale Force Ouvrière Martinique (UD-FO): rue Bouillé, BP 1114, 97248 Fort-de-France Cédex; tel. 5-96-70-07-04; fax 5-96-70-18-20; e-mail udfomartinique@wanadoo.fr; internet www.force-ouvriere.fr; affiliated to the Int. Trade Union Confederation; Sec.-Gen. ERIC BELLEMARE.

Union Générale des Travailleurs de Martinique (UGTM): 8 rue Pierre et Marie Curie, Terres Sainville, 97200 Fort-de-France; tel. 5-96-63-75-23; fax 5-96-70-30-82; e-mail ugtm.centrale@wanadoo.fr; f. 1999; Pres. LÉON BERTIDE; Sec.-Gen. PATRICK DORÉ.

Union Régionale Martinique: Maison des Syndicats, rue de la Sécurité Jardin Desclieux, Salles 5–7, 97200 Fort-de-France; tel. 5-96-72-64-74; fax 5-96-70-16-80; e-mail ur-martinique@unsa.org; internet www.unsa.org.

UNSA Education Martinique (UE): Maison des Syndicats, Salles 4–5, Jardin Desclieux, 97200 Fort-de-France; tel. 5-96-72-64-74; fax 5-96-70-16-80; e-mail unsa-education972@orange.fr; Sec.-Gen. MIREILLE JACQUES.

Transport

RAILWAYS

There are no railways in Martinique.

ROADS

There were 2,077 km (1,291 miles) of roads in 1998, of which 261 km were motorways and first-class roads.

SHIPPING

CMA-CGM CGM Antilles-Guyane: ZIP de la Pointe des Grives, BP 574, 97242 Fort-de-France Cédex; tel. 5-96-55-32-00; fax 5-96-63-08-87; e-mail fdf.jgourdin@cma-cgm.com; internet www.cma-cgm.com; subsidiary of CMA-CGM, France; also represents other passenger and freight lines; Pres. RODOLPHE SAADÉ; Man. Dir JACQUES GOURDIN.

Direction des Concessions Services Portuaires: quai de l'Hydro Base, BP 782, 97244 Fort-de-France Cédex; tel. 5-96-59-00-00; fax 5-96-71-35-73; e-mail port@martinique.port.fr; internet www.martinique.port.fr; port services management; Dir ZÉBINA CHRISTINE.

Direction Régionale des Affaires Maritimes (DRAM): blvd Chevalier de Sainte-Marthe, BP 620, 97261 Fort-de-France Cédex; tel. 5-96-60-80-30; fax 5-96-60-79-80; e-mail dram-martinique@equipement.gouv.fr; Dir OLIVIER MORNET.

CIVIL AVIATION

Fort-de-France–Le Lamentin international airport is located at Le Lamentin, 12 km from Fort-de-France and is equipped to handle jet-engined aircraft. The regional airline LIAT (based in Antigua and Barbuda) provides scheduled services to the island connecting it with all the islands of the Eastern Caribbean.

Direction des Services Aéroportuaires: BP 279, 97285 Le Lamentin; tel. 5-96-42-16-00; fax 5-96-42-18-77; e-mail aeroport@martinique.cci.fr; internet www.martinique.aeroport.fr; Dir FRANTZ THODIARD.

Air Caraïbes: see Guadeloupe—Transport.

Tourism

Martinique's tourist attractions are its beaches and coastal scenery, its mountainous interior, and the historic towns of Fort-de-France and Saint-Pierre. In 2005 there were 97 hotels, with some 4,676 rooms. In 2010 the number of tourists who stayed on the island totalled 475,886. Receipts from tourism were €245.9m. in 2009.

Comité Martiniquais du Tourisme: Immeuble Beaupré, Pointe de Jaham, 97233 Schoelcher; tel. 5-96-61-61-77; fax 5-96-61-22-72; e-mail infos.cmt@martiniquetourisme.com; internet www.martiniquetourisme.com; Pres. KARINE ROY-CAMILLE.

Délégation Régionale au Tourisme: 41 rue Gabriel Périé, 97200 Fort-de-France; tel. 5-96-71-42-68; fax 5-96-73-00-96; e-mail drtmartinique.ndl@wanadoo.fr; Delegate VALÉRIE LEOTURE.

Fédération Martiniquaise des Offices de Tourisme et Syndicats d'Initiative (FMOTSI): Maison du Tourisme Vert, 9 blvd du Général de Gaulle, BP 491, 97207 Fort-de-France Cédex; tel. 5-96-63-18-54; fax 5-96-70-17-61; e-mail contact@fmotsi.net; internet www.fmotsi.net; f. 1984; Pres. JOSÉ REINETTE; Sec.-Gen. JEAN-MARC LUSBEC.

Defence

As assessed at November 2011, France maintained a military force of about 1,057 and a gendarmerie, headquartered in Fort-de-France.

Education

The educational system is similar to that of metropolitan France (see chapter on French Guiana). In 2009/10 there were 80 pre-primary schools, 182 primary schools and 80 secondary schools. In 2009/10 there were 46,124 pupils in pre-primary and primary education, while in secondary education there were 42,740 students, of whom some 91% attended state schools. Higher education in law, French language and literature, human sciences, economics, medicine and Creole studies is provided in Martinique by a branch of the Université des Antilles et de la Guyane. During 2007/08 some 5,249 students were enrolled at the university in Martinique; in 2009/10 there were 8,942 students enrolled in higher education on the island. There are also two teacher-training institutes, and colleges of agriculture, fisheries, hotel management, nursing, midwifery and childcare. Departmental expenditure on education and culture was estimated at €44.1m. in 2006.

MAYOTTE

Introductory Survey

LOCATION, CLIMATE, LANGUAGE, RELIGION, CAPITAL

Mayotte forms part of the Comoros archipelago, which lies between the island of Madagascar and the east coast of the African mainland. The territory comprises a main island, Mayotte (Mahoré), and a number of smaller islands. The climate is tropical, with temperatures averaging between 24°C and 27°C (75°F to 81°F) throughout the year. The official language is French, but Shimaore (Maorese) and Shibushi are also spoken. Islam is the main religion. The capital is Dzaoudzi, which is connected to the island of Pamandzi by a causeway.

CONTEMPORARY POLITICAL HISTORY

Historical Context

Since the Comoros unilaterally declared independence in July 1975, Mayotte has been administered separately by France. The independent Comoran state claims sovereignty of Mayotte, and officially represents it in international organizations, including the UN. In December 1976 France introduced the special status of Territorial

Collectivity (Collectivité territoriale) for the island. Following a coup in the Comoros in May 1978, Mayotte rejected the new Government's proposal that it should rejoin the other islands under a federal system, and reaffirmed its intention of remaining linked to France. In December 1979 the Assemblée nationale approved legislation that extended Mayotte's special status for another five years, during which the islanders were to be consulted. In October 1984, however, the Assemblée nationale further prolonged Mayotte's status, and the referendum on the island's future was postponed indefinitely.

Domestic Political Affairs

Relations between the main political party on Mayotte, the Mouvement populaire mahorais (MPM) and the French Government rapidly deteriorated after the Franco-African summit in November 1987, when the French Prime Minister, Jacques Chirac, expressed reservations concerning the elevation of Mayotte to the status of a Overseas Department (Département d'outre-mer), despite his announcement, in early 1986, that he shared the MPM's aim to upgrade Mayotte's status. In the second round of the French presidential election, which took place in May 1988, François Mitterrand, the incumbent President and the candidate of the Parti socialiste (PS), received 50.3% of the votes cast on Mayotte, defeating Chirac, the candidate of the Rassemblement pour la république (RPR). At elections to the French Assemblée nationale, which took place in June, Henry Jean-Baptiste was re-elected as Mayotte's representative to that body. (Later that month, he joined the newly formed centrist group in the Assemblée nationale, the Union du centre—UDC.) In elections to the Conseil général in September and October, the MPM retained the majority of seats.

In 1989–90 concern about the number of Comoran immigrants seeking employment on the island resulted in an increase in racial tension. A paramilitary organization, known as Caiman, was subsequently formed in support of the expulsion of illegal immigrants, but was refused legal recognition by the authorities. In June 1992 growing resentment resulted in further attacks against Comoran immigrants resident in Mayotte. In early September representatives of the MPM met the French Prime Minister, Pierre Bérégovoy, to request the reintroduction of entry visas to restrict immigration from the Comoros. Later that month the MPM organized a boycott of Mayotte's participation in the French referendum on the Treaty on European Union (see p. 276), in support of the provision of entry visas.

At elections to the Assemblée nationale, which took place in March 1993, Jean-Baptiste was returned, securing 53.4% of the votes cast, while the Secretary-General of the RPR, Mansour Kamardine, received 44.3% of the votes.

Elections to the Conseil général (which was enlarged from 17 to 19 members) took place in March 1994: the MPM retained 12 seats, while the RPR secured four seats, and independent candidates three seats. During an official visit to Mayotte in November, the French Prime Minister, Edouard Balladur, announced the reintroduction of entry visas as a requirement for Comoran nationals, and the adoption of a number of security measures, in an effort to reduce illegal immigration to the island. In January 1995 the Comoran Government suspended transport links between Mayotte and the Comoros in response to the measure. In the first round of the French presidential election in April, Balladur received the highest number of votes on Mayotte (although Chirac subsequently won the election).

In elections to the French Sénat (Senate) in September 1995, the incumbent MPM representative, Marcel Henry, was returned by a large majority. During a visit to Mayotte in October, the French Secretary of State for Overseas Departments and Territories pledged that a referendum on the future status of the island would be conducted by 1999. In October 1996 he confirmed that two commissions, one based in Paris and the other in Mayotte, were preparing a consultation document, which would be presented in late 1997, and announced that the resulting referendum would take place before the end of the decade.

Partial elections to fill nine seats in the Conseil général were held in March 1997; the MPM secured three seats (losing two that it had previously held), the RPR won three seats, the local PS one seat, and independent right-wing candidates two seats. In elections to the Assemblée nationale Jean-Baptiste, representing the alliance of the Union pour la démocratie française (UDF) and the Force démocrate, defeated Kamardine, securing 51.7% of the votes cast in the second round of voting, which took place in June.

In July 1997 the relative prosperity of Mayotte was believed to have prompted separatist movements on the Comoran islands of Nzwani and Mwali to demand the restoration of French rule, and subsequently to declare their independence in August. Illegal immigration from the Comoros continued to prove a major concern for the authorities on Mayotte; during January–February 1997 some 6,000 Comorans were expelled from the island, with many more agreeing to leave voluntarily.

Meanwhile, uncertainty remained over the future status of Mayotte. In April 1998 one of the commissions charged with examining the issue submitted its report, which concluded that the present status of Territorial Collectivity was no longer appropriate, but did not advocate an alternative. In May the MPM declared its support for an adapted form of departmental administration, and urged the French authorities to decide on a date for a referendum. In July Pierre Bayle succeeded Philippe Boisadam as Prefect. In May 1999 Younoussa Bamana, the leader of the MPM, made an appeal that the inhabitants of Mayotte be allowed to organize their own vote on their future, and later that month Jean-Baptiste introduced draft legislation to the Assemblée nationale, which proposed the holding of a referendum regarding the island's future before the end of 1999. In August, following negotiations between the French Secretary of State for Overseas Departments and Territories, Jean-Jack Queyranne, and island representatives, Mayotte members of the RPR and the PS and Bamana signed a draft document providing for the transformation of Mayotte into a Departmental Collectivity (Collectivité départementale), if approved at a referendum. However, both Henry and Jean-Baptiste rejected the document. The two politicians subsequently announced their departure from the MPM and formed a new political party entitled the Mouvement départementaliste mahorais (MDM), while reiterating their demands that Mayotte be granted full overseas departmental status.

Mayotte becomes a Departmental Collectivity

Following the approval of Mayotte's proposed new status by the Conseil général (by 14 votes to five) and the municipal councils, an accord to this effect was signed by Queyranne and political representatives of Mayotte on 27 January 2000. On 2 July a referendum was held, in which the population of Mayotte voted overwhelmingly in favour of the January accord, granting Mayotte the status of Departmental Collectivity for a period of 10 years. In November the commission established to define the terms of Mayotte's new status published a report, which envisaged the transfer of executive power from the Prefect to the Conseil général by 2004, the dissolution of the position of Prefect by 2007 and the concession of greater powers to the local Government, notably in the area of regional co-operation.

At elections to the Conseil général, held in March 2001, no party established a majority. The MPM experienced significant losses, with only four of its candidates being elected, while the RPR won five seats, the Mouvement des citoyens (MDC) two, the MDM one, the PS one, and various right-wing independent candidates six seats. Bamana was re-elected as President of the Conseil général. The French parliament approved Mayotte's status as a Departmental Collectivity in July 2001. In September Philippe de Mester succeeded Bayle as Prefect.

In the first round of the French presidential election, which was held on 21 April 2002, Chirac received the highest number of votes on Mayotte, winning 43.0% of the valid votes cast; the second round, held on 5 May, was also won resoundingly by Chirac, who secured 88.3% of votes cast on the island, defeating the candidate of the extreme right-wing Front National, Jean-Marie Le Pen. At elections to the Assemblée nationale, held in June, Kamardine, representing the recently formed Union pour la majorité présidentielle (UMP, which incorporated the RPR, the Démocratie libérale and significant elements of the UDF), defeated the MDM-UDF candidate, Siadi Vita. Jean-Jacques Brot replaced de Mester as Prefect in July. In November the UMP was renamed the Union pour un mouvement populaire.

At elections to the Conseil général in March 2004, the UMP won eight seats in alliance with the MPM, which secured one seat, while the MDM and the MDC, also in alliance, obtained five and two seats, respectively; independent candidates were elected to the remaining three seats. With the election of Saïd Omar Oili, an independent, as President of the Conseil général on 2 April, executive power was transferred from the Prefect to the Conseil. In January 2005 Jean-Paul Kihl replaced Brot as Prefect. In late May a national referendum on ratification of the European Union (EU) constitutional treaty was held: 86.5% of Mayotte's electorate voted in favour of adopting the treaty; however, it was ultimately rejected by a majority of French voters. In late November more than 500 trade union members protested in Mamoudzou as part of a general strike for greater social equality with metropolitan France. There was a further two-day strike in mid-December involving some 200 union members.

In early November 2005 a French parliamentary commission—which included Kamardine—was convened to report on the state of illegal immigration in Mayotte. The commission's first report, which was published in mid-February 2006, found that there were between 45,000 and 60,000 illegal immigrants living in Mayotte, of whom 90% were Comoran. (According to the census of 2002 the official French population numbered 160,265.) The number of births on the island had risen by more than 50% over a 10-year period, reaching 7,676 in 2004, of which some two-thirds were to women lacking official documentation. The report also detailed that between 10,000 and 15,000 immigrants were employed in the unofficial economy with the complicity of the Mahoris populace. The report proposed closer co-operation with the Comoran authorities. Recommendations to stem the flow of immigrants included, inter alia, the introduction of biometric identity cards in Mayotte and the Comoros; the construction of a maternity clinic on the Comoran island of Nzwani; and an increase in the number of border police. The French Ministry of the Interior targeted the expulsion of 12,000 illegal immigrants from Mayotte in 2006; the total number expelled in 2005 exceeded 4,500.

Nicolas Sarkozy of the UMP secured 30.5% of the votes cast on Mayotte in the first round of the French presidential election, held on 22 April 2007. However, in the second round, which took place on 6 May, Ségolène Royal of the PS won 60.0% of the votes cast, although Sarkozy was elected to the presidency. At elections to the Assemblée nationale, held on 10 and 17 June, Kamardine was defeated by Abdoulatifou Aly, who was affiliated to the Mouvement démocrate (MoDem), which had been formed following the presidential election by François Bayrou, the leader of the UDF, to oppose Sarkozy's UMP.

Meanwhile, in February 2007 Vincent Bouvier replaced Kihl as Prefect and, although that position was scheduled to be abolished in 2007, Bouvier remained in the post until July 2008, when Denis Robin assumed the position. Also in February 2007 new legislation approved by the French Assemblée nationale introduced statutory and institutional measures granting Mayotte many of the powers afforded to territories with full overseas departmental status, with the exception of certain fiscal, financial and social welfare powers. This followed a constitutional amendment in 2003 whereby Mayotte acquired the status of Overseas Collectivity (Collectivité d'outre-mer) and expedited the process towards becoming an Overseas Department. The 2007 legislation provided a framework for measures to be implemented to facilitate the transfer of full fiscal control to Mayotte by January 2014.

Elections for 10 of the 19 seats in the Conseil général took place over two rounds held on 9 and 16 March 2008. The UMP, the MDM and the Nouvel élan pour Mayotte (founded in 2007 by Omar Oili) all secured two seats, the PS won one seat and three seats were taken by independent candidates. On 20 March Ahamed AttoumaniI Douchina was elected to replace Omar Oili as President of the Conseil.

Recent developments: Mayotte becomes an Overseas Department

The question of Mayotte's status once again became prevalent in April 2008 when the Conseil général adopted a resolution providing for the transfer of Mayotte's status from that of Overseas Collectivity to an Overseas Department. The resolution required that a public consultation on the matter be held within 12 months. In January 2009 the text of the question to be put to the Mayotte electorate was approved and Sarkozy declared that the consultation would take place on 29 March. At the referendum, which was held as scheduled, 95.2% of voters approved of Mayotte attaining the status of an Overseas Department within the French Republic (in contradiction to the recognition of the island by the African Union and the Comoran Government as an inseparable part of the Comoran state). Some 61% of those eligible to vote participated in the ballot. In October 2010 the French Sénat adopted the departmentalization of Mayotte and the following month the Assemblée nationale approved the appropriate legislation; the change in status was scheduled to take place in March 2011.

Meanwhile, in August 2009 Hubert Derache replaced Robin as Prefect. In early December protests on Pamandzi against the rise in the cost of living, and in particular in response to the increased cost of transport in the territory, resulted in some 15 people being injured during clashes with the security forces. In January 2010 President Sarkozy made a brief visit to Mayotte during which he discussed the issue of immigration with local officials. It was estimated that as many as one-third of the residents of Mayotte had entered the territory illegally from the Comoros. In 2009 about 16,000 Comorans had been deported from Mayotte.

In November 2010 trade unions on Mayotte organized a day of strike action to demand better working conditions and pay. Indexation had been used in Réunion to ensure salaries increased in line with living costs; however, Mayotte workers had not received the same benefit.

On 31 March 2011 Mayotte officially became the 101st Department of France and the fifth Overseas Department. On 3 April Daniel Zaïdani was elected President of the Conseil général and in July Thomas Degos replaced Derache as Prefect. In October the authorities of Mayotte made an official request to the EU (transferred in December to the European Commission) to recognize Mayotte as a Région ultrapériphérique (RUP) of France; a final decision on this petition was expected in mid-2012. Recognition as an RUP would allow Mayotte to draw upon EU funds to aid its economic development. In the short term, €2m. was to be released from January 2012 over two years.

Persistent unrest on the island caused by the continued high cost of living led to a 44-day-long general strike in October and early November, followed by a further two days' shutdown in December. The French Prime Minister, François Fillon, dispatched Denis Robin, a former Prefect of the island, to attempt to mediate an agreement between trade unions, employers and the Government to end the strike action. In late December an agreement was signed, imposing until March 2012 a reduction in the price of 11 staple goods, including nine food products, domestic gas and sand; in addition, families with modest incomes were to receive food tokens.

(For further details of the recent history of the island, see the Comoros.)

CONSTITUTION AND GOVERNMENT

The Constitution of the Fifth Republic of France, adopted by referendum on 28 September 1958 and promulgated on 6 October 1958 applies on Mayotte. The French Government is represented in Mayotte by an appointed Prefect. There is a Conseil général, with 19 members, elected by universal adult suffrage. Mayotte elects one deputy to the Assemblée nationale, and one representative to the Sénat. Mayotte is also represented at the European Parliament. Mayotte acquired the status of Overseas Department in March 2011.

ECONOMIC AFFAIRS

Mayotte's gross domestic product (GDP) per head in 2009 was €6,575, according to official figures. Total GDP in that year amounted to €1,396m. Between the censuses of 2002 and 2007 the population of Mayotte increased at an average annual rate of 3.1%.

The economy is based mainly on agriculture. In 2007 8.5% of the employed labour force were engaged in this sector. The principal export crops are ylang ylang (an ingredient of perfume) and vanilla. Mayotte imports large quantities of foodstuffs, which comprised 22.7% of the value of total imports in 2010. In 2003 it was estimated that some 44% of the population was dependent on *gratte* (subsistence) farming. Cassava, maize and pigeon peas are cultivated for domestic consumption; while rice is widely eaten there is little domestic production. More than 90% of farms grow bananas, often mixed with coconuts (grown for their milk and oil, both of which are used in cooking); together banana and coconut plantations occupy some 45% of agricultural land (approximately 20,000 ha in total, some 55% of the surface area of Mayotte). Mangoes are also widespread, and around one-third of mango trees grow wild. Livestock-rearing (of cattle, goats—for meat—and chickens) and fishing are also important activities. Aquaculture was first introduced in 1998 and in 2005 there were five producers catering mainly to the export market.

Industry (which is dominated by the construction sector) engaged 12.7% of the employed population in 2007. There are no mineral resources on the island. Imports of mineral products comprised 3.0% of the value of total imports in 2010 and base metals and metal products comprised 6.2%. Mayotte also imports considerable quantities of machinery (20.5% of the value of total imports) and transport equipment (8.8%).

Services engaged 78.8% of the employed population in 2007. The annual number of tourist arrivals (excluding cruise-ship passengers) totalled 52,800 in 2010; receipts from tourism in 2006 amounted to €16.3m.

In 2010 Mayotte recorded a trade deficit of €372.7m. The principal export in 2010 was fish; exports of ylang ylang were also significant. The principal imports in that year were foodstuffs, machinery and appliances, transport equipment, chemical products, and base metals and metal products. The principal source of imports in 2009 was France (50.8%); the People's Republic of China was also a major supplier. France was also the principal market for exports (taking 40.0% of exports in that year); the other significant purchasers were the Comoros and Réunion.

In 2010 Mayotte's total budgetary revenue was €330m., while total expenditure was €307m. Mayotte recorded inflation of 0.9% in the year to December 2009. Some 17.6% of the labour force was unemployed in 2009.

Mayotte suffers from a persistently high trade deficit, owing to its reliance on imports, and is largely dependent on French aid. As Mayotte's labour force has continued to increase (mostly owing to a high birth rate and the continued arrival of immigrants, many of them entering the territory illegally—see Recent History, above), youth unemployment has caused particular concern. However, local farmers have expressed fears that 'unofficial' labourers whom they rely upon to carry out manual work that local Mahoris refuse to accept will be removed from the country, thus potentially reducing agricultural output. The French Government agreed a new, six-year development contract with Mayotte for 2008–14 valued at €551m., and also made provision for significant expenditure to increase access to clean drinking water and to improve sanitation, as well as the development of renewable energy sources. The long-term aim of the contract was to ensure Mayotte's economic and social autonomy. It was envisaged that the transfer of Mayotte's status from that of Overseas Collectivity to an Overseas Department would provide a number of economic benefits to the territory, and during a visit to Mayotte in January 2010 the French President, Nicolas Sarkozy, pledged additional state funding towards the construction of schools and of social housing for some 40,000 inhabitants by 2016. However, by April 2011 the construction industry was in serious decline and the Conseil général was obliged to freeze spending owing to high levels of public debt. With its new status as a French Department, measures were adopted in 2011 to align, by increments, Mayotte's minimum wage with that of France. Although there were plans to extend Dzaoudzi Pamandzi International Airport and the French Minister in charge of Oversees Territories announced a €50m. recovery plan for Mayotte based almost entirely on public sector construction, the trade unions remained sceptical about the island's imminent economic recovery. These concerns appeared to be justified by the fact that at the end of 2011 it was reported that some 89 companies had requested permission to place their staff on short-time employment contracts.

PUBLIC HOLIDAYS

The principal holidays of metropolitan France are observed.

Statistical Survey

Source (unless otherwise indicated): Institut National de la Statistique et des Études Économiques (INSEE) de Mayotte; Z.I. Kawéni, BP 1362, 97600 Mamoudzou; tel. 269-61-36-35; fax 269-61-39-56; e-mail antenne-mayotte@insee.fr; internet www.insee.fr/fr/regions/mayotte/default.asp.

AREA AND POPULATION

Area: 374 sq km (144 sq miles).

Population: 160,265 at census of 30 July 2002; 186,452 at census of 31 July 2007. *Mid-2010* (official estimate): 186,452.

Density (at mid-2010): 498.5 per sq km.

Population by Age and Sex (UN estimates at mid-2012): *0–14:* 100,505 (males 51,465, females 49,040); *15–64:* 112,526 (males 54,554, females 57,972); *65 and over:* 4,140 (males 2,146, females 1,994); *Total* 217,171 (males 108,165, females 109,006) (Source: UN, *World Population Prospects: The 2010 Revision*).

Population by Country of Origin (2002, before adjustment for double counting): Mayotte 103,705; France 6,323; Comoros 45,057; Madagascar-Mauritius-Seychelles 4,601; Total (incl. others) 160,301.

Principal Towns (population of communes at 2007 census): Mamoudzou 53,022; Koungou 19,831; Dzaoudzi (capital) 15,339; Dembeni 10,141.

Births and Deaths (2007): Registered live births 7,658 (birth rate 41.1 per 1,000); Registered deaths 587 (death rate 3.1 per 1,000). *2009:* Birth rate 39.0 per 1,000; Death rate 3.0 per 1,000.

Life Expectancy (years at birth): 74.5 (males 72.0; females 76.0) in 2004.

Economically Active Population (persons aged 14 years and over, census of 31 July 2007): Agriculture and fishing 3,204; Construction 3,024; Other industry 1,805; Wholesale and retail trade 3,154; Hotels and restaurants 609; Transport, telecommunications and real estate 5,043; Public administration 6,535; Education, health and social care 7,247; Other services 7,289; *Total employed* 37,910 (males 24,157, females 13,753); Unemployed 13,614 (males 5,922, females 7,692); *Total labour force* 51,524 (males 30,079, females 21,445). *2009* (labour force survey March–June, persons aged 15 years and over): Total employed 35,600; Unemployed 7,600; Total labour force 43,200.

HEALTH AND WELFARE

Key Indicators

Total Fertility Rate (children per woman, 2004): 4.5.

Physicians (per 1,000 head, 1997): 0.4.

Hospital Beds (per 1,000 head, 1997): 1.4.

For definitions see explanatory note on p. vi.

AGRICULTURE, ETC.

Livestock (2003): Cattle 17,235; Goats 22,811; Chickens 80,565.

Fishing (metric tons, live weight, 2009): Capture 15,130 (Skipjack tuna 6,709; Yellowfin tuna 5,496); Aquaculture 126 (FAO estimate); *Total catch* 15,256 (FAO estimate). Source: FAO.

INDUSTRY

Electric Energy (million kWh, consumption): 171 in 2010.

FINANCE

Currency and Exchange Rates: 100 cent = 1 euro. *Sterling and Dollar Equivalents* (30 December 2012): £1 sterling = €1.195; US $1 = €0.773; €10 = £8.37 = US $12.94. *Average Exchange Rate* (euros per US dollar): 0.7198 in 2009; 0.7550 in 2010; 0.7194 in 2011. The French franc was used until the end of February 2002. Euro notes and coins were introduced on 1 January 2002, and the euro became the sole legal tender from 18 February. Some of the figures in this Survey are still in terms of French francs.

Budget of the Collectivity (€ million, 2010): Total revenue 330; Total expenditure 307.

French State Expenditure (€ million, 2010): Direct expenditure 394.7; Indirect expenditure 94.8; *Total expenditure* 489.6.

Money Supply (million French francs at 31 December 1997): Currency outside banks 789; Demand deposits 266; Total money 1,055.

Cost of Living (Consumer Price Index for December; base: December 2006 = 100): 108.5 in 2008; 109.5 in 2009; 112.4 in 2010.

Expenditure on the Gross Domestic Product (€ million, 2009, INSEE estimates): Government final consumption expenditure 726; Private final consumption expenditure 799; Gross fixed capital formation 372; *Total domestic expenditure* 1,897; Exports of goods and services 31; *Less* Imports of goods and services 532; *GDP in purchasers' values* 1,396.

EXTERNAL TRADE

Principal Commodities (€ million, 2010): *Imports c.i.f.* (excl. hydrocarbons): Foodstuffs 85.7; Mineral products 11.4; Chemical products 31.9; Plastic materials and rubber 12.0; Base metals and metal products 23.6; Machinery and appliances 77.5; Transport equipment 33.2; Total (incl. others) 377.7. *Exports f.o.b.:* Farmed fish 0.4; Ylang ylang 0.2; Re-exports 0.1; Total (incl. others) 5.0 (Source: Institut d'Emission des Départements d'Outre-mer, *Rapport Annuel 2010*).

Principal Trading Partners (€ million, 2009): *Imports:* Brazil 7.5; China, People's Republic 28.8; France (Metropolitan) 185.0; Mauritius 4.5; South Africa 5.8; United Arab Emirates 8.2; Total (incl. others) 364.3. *Exports* (incl. re-exports): Total 5.1. Note: The principal markets for exports are France (Metropolitan—some 40% of exports in 2009), Comoros (15% in 2009) and Réunion.

TRANSPORT

Road Traffic (2008): Motor vehicles in use 7,781.

Shipping (2006, unless otherwise indicated): *Maritime Traffic:* Vessel movements 530 (2005); Goods unloaded 390,954 metric tons; Goods loaded 66,278 metric tons; Passengers 23,437 (arrivals 7,697, departures 15,740). *Barges* (2002): Passengers 11,845; Light vehicles 532. *Cruise Ships* (2005): Vessel movements 36; Passengers 6,857.

Civil Aviation (2010): *Passengers Carried:* 304,775. *Freight Carried:* 1,597 metric tons. *Post Carried:* 534 metric tons.

TOURISM

Foreign Tourist Arrivals (excl. cruise-ship passengers): 37,957 in 2008; 49,500 in 2009; 52,800 in 2010.

Foreign Tourist Arrivals by Country of Residence (2010): France (metropolitan) 25,200; Réunion 23,300; Total (incl. others) 52 800.

Tourism Receipts (€ million): 13.7 in 2004; 14.5 in 2005; 16.3 in 2006.

COMMUNICATIONS MEDIA

Telephones ('000 main lines in use, 2010): 10.0.

Mobile Cellular Telephones ('000 subscribers, 2008): 48.1.

Internet Users ('000, 2000): 1.8.

Source: International Telecommunication Union.

EDUCATION

Pre-primary: 71 schools (2007); 15,868 pupils (2010).

Primary: 118 schools (2007); 33,857 pupils (2010).

General Secondary: 19 schools (2009); 18,710 pupils (2010).

Vocational and Technical: 9 institutions (2009); 6,784 students (2010).

Students Studying in France or Réunion (2009): Secondary 1,452; Higher 2,253; *Total* 3,705.

Teaching Staff (2008): Primary 2,354; Secondary 1,769.

Directory

The Government

(May 2012)

HEAD OF STATE

President: NICOLAS SARKOZY.

Prefect: THOMAS DEGOS.

DEPARTMENTAL ADMINISTRATION

President of the General Council: DANIEL ZAÏDANI (AUT), 108 rue de l'Hôpital, BP 101, 97600 Mamoudzou; tel. 269-61-12-33; fax 269-61-10-18; internet www.cg976.fr.

REPRESENTATIVES TO THE FRENCH PARLIAMENT

Deputy to the French National Assembly: ABDOULATIFOU ALY (Mouvement Démocrate).

Representatives to the French Senate: ADRIEN GIRAUD (Divers Droite), SOIBAHADINE IBRAHIM RAMADANI (UMP).

GOVERNMENT DEPARTMENTS

Office of the Prefect: BP 676, Kawéni, 97600 Mamoudzou; tel. 269-63-50-00; fax 269-60-18-89; e-mail communication@mayotte.pref.gouv.fr; internet www.mayotte.pref.gouv.fr.

Department of Agriculture and Forestry: 15 rue Mariazé, BP 103, 97600 Mamoudzou; tel. 269-61-12-13; fax 269-61-10-31; e-mail daf976@agriculture.gouv.fr; internet www.hydro-mayotte.agriculture.gouv.fr.

Department of Education: rue Sarahangué, BP 76, 97600 Mamoudzou; tel. 269-61-10-24; fax 269-61-09-87; e-mail vice-rectorat@ac-mayotte.fr; internet www.ac-mayotte.fr.

Department of Health and Social Security: rue de l'Hôpital, BP 104, 97600 Mamoudzou; tel. 269-61-12-25; fax 269-61-19-56.

Department of Public Works: rue Mariazé, BP 109, 97600 Mamoudzou; tel. 269-61-12-54; fax 269-61-07-11; e-mail de-mayotte@equipement.gouv.fr.

Department of Work, Employment and Training: 3 bis, rue Mahabou, BP 174, 97600 Mamoudzou; tel. 269-61-16-57; fax 269-61-03-37; internet www.dtefp-mayotte.travail.gouv.fr.

Department of Youth and Sports: 14 rue Mariazé, BP 94, 97600 Mamoudzou; tel. 269-61-60-50; fax 269-61-82-10; e-mail dd976@jeunesse-sports.gouv.fr.

Political Organizations

Fédération du front national (FN): route nationale 1, M'tsahara, 97630 M'tzamboro; BP 1331, 97600 Mamoudzou Cédex; tel. and fax 269-60-50-24; Regional Sec. HAMADA OUSSENI.

Fédération de Mayotte de l'union pour un mouvement populaire (UMP): route nationale, Immeuble 'Jardin Créole', 97600 Mamoudzou; tel. 269-61-64-64; fax 269-60-87-89; e-mail alisouf@ump976.org; centre-right; local branch of the metropolitan party; Departmental Pres. ASSANI HAMISSI; Departmental Sec. ALI SOUF.

Fédération du mouvement national républicain (MNR) de Mayotte: 15 rue des Réfugiers, 97615 Pamandzi; tel. and fax 269-60-33-21; Departmental Sec. ABDOU MIHIDJAY.

Mouvement des citoyens (MDC): Chirongui; Leader ALI HALIFA.

Mouvement départementaliste mahorais (MDM): 97610 Dzaoudzi; f. 2001 by fmr mems of the MPM; Pres. ZOUBERT ADINANI; Sec.-Gen. MOHAMED ALI BEN ALI.

Mouvement de la gauche ecologiste de Mayotte: 6 avenue Mamanne, Quartier Artisanal, Localité de Pamandzi, 97600 Pamandzi; tel. and fax 269-61-09-70; internet mayotte.lesverts.fr; fmrly Les Verts Mayotte; affiliated to Mouvement de la Gauche Réunionnaise; Gen. Sec. AHAMADA SALIME.

Mouvement populaire mahorais (MPM): route de Vahibé, Passamainti, 97600 Mamoudzou; Leader YOUNOUSSA BAMANA.

Parti socialiste (PS): Dzaoudzi; local branch of the metropolitan party; Fed. Sec. IBRAHIM ABUBACAR.

Judicial System

Palais de Justice: Immeuble Espace, BP 106 (Kawéni), 97600 Mamoudzou; tel. 269-61-11-15; fax 269-61-19-63.

Tribunal de Grande Instance

16 rue de l'hôpital, BP 106, 97600 Mamoudzou; tel. 269-61-11-15; fax 269-61-19-63; Pres. JEAN-BAPTISTE FLORI; Prosecutor JEAN-LOUIS BEC.

Procureur de la République: JEAN-LOUIS BEC.

Tribunal d'Instance: Pres. ALAIN CHATEAUNEUF.

Religion

Muslims comprise about 98% of the population. Most of the remainder are Christians, mainly Roman Catholics.

CHRISTIANITY

The Roman Catholic Church

Mayotte is within the jurisdiction of the Apostolic Administrator of the Comoros.

Office of the Apostolic Administrator: 7 rue de l'hôpital, BP 1012, 97600 Mamoudzou; tel. and fax 269-61-11-53; fax 269-61-48-25; e-mail mcatholique@wanadoo.fr.

The Press

Albalad: Mamoudzou; internet www.albaladmayotte.com; f. 2010; owned by Al Waseet International; daily; French; Editor-in-Chief RICHARD VINCENT; circ. 5,000.

Flash Infos Mayotte: Société Mahoraise de Presse, 7 rue Salamani Cavani/M'Tsapéré, BP 60, 97600 Mamoudzou; tel. 269-61-20-04; fax 269-60-35-90; e-mail flash-infos@wanadoo.fr; internet www.mayottehebdo.com; f. 1999; owned by Somapresse; daily e-mail bulletin; Dir LAURENT CANAVATE.

Le Mahorais: 11 centre commercial, Lukida, 97600 Mamoudzou; tel. 269-61-66-75; fax 269-61-66-72; e-mail lemahorais@wanadoo.fr; internet www.lemahorais.com; weekly; French; Publ. Dir SAMUEL BOSCHER; Editor-in-Chief LUCIE TOUZÉ.

Le Mawana: BP 252, Z.I. Kawéni, 97600 Mamoudzou; tel. 269-61-73-84; f. 2005; weekly; French; Publ. Dir MADI ABDOU N'TRO.

Mayotte Hebdo: Société Mahoraise de Presse, 7 rue Salamani Cavani/M'Tsapéré, BP 60, 97600 Mamoudzou; tel. 269-61-20-04; fax 269-60-35-90; e-mail contact@mayottehebdo.com; internet www.mayottehebdo.com; f. 2000; weekly; French; incl. the economic supplement *Mayotte Eco* and cultural supplement *Tounda* (weekly); owned by Somapresse; Dir LAURENT CANAVATE; circ. 2,300.

Zan'Goma: Impasse du Jardin Fleuri, Cavani, 97600 Mamoudzou; f. 2005; monthly; French; Publ. Dir MONCEF MOUHOUDHOIRE.

Broadcasting and Communications

TELECOMMUNICATIONS

Mayotte Télécom Mobile: 27, pl. Mariaźe, 97600 Mamoudzou; mobile cellular telephone operator; local operation of Société Réunionnaise du Radiotéléphone based in Réunion.

RADIO AND TELEVISION

Mayotte 1ère: BP 103, 97610 Dzaoudzi; tel. 269-60-10-17; fax 269-60-18-52; e-mail annick.henry@rfo.fr; internet mayotte.la1ere.fr; f. 1977; acquired by Groupe France Télévisions in 2004; fmrly Réseau France Outre-mer, name changed as above in 2010; radio broadcasts in French and more than 70% in Mahorian; television transmissions began in 1986; a satellite service was launched in 2000; Dir-Gen. GENEVIÈVE GIARD; Regional Dir GERALD PRUFER.

Finance

(br(s). = branch(es))

BANKS

In 2010 there were three commercial banks, two mutual banks and two other financial institutions in Mayotte.

Issuing Authority

Institut d'Émission des Départements d'Outre-mer: ave de la Préfecture, BP 500, 97600 Mamoudzou; tel. 269-61-05-05; fax 269-61-05-02; internet agence@iedom-mayotte.fr; internet www.iedom.fr; Dir VICTOR-ROBERT NUGENT.

Commercial Banks

Banque Française Commerciale Océan Indien: route de l'Agriculture, BP 222, 97600 Mamoudzou; tel. 269-61-10-91; fax 269-61-17-40; e-mail pleclerc@bfcoi.com; internet www.bfcoi.com; f. 1976; jtly owned by Société Générale and Mauritius Commercial Bank Ltd; Pres. Gérald Lacaze; brs at Dzaoudzi and Sada.

Banque de la Réunion: 30 pl. Mariage, 97600 Mamoudzou; tel. 269-61-20-30; fax 269-61-20-28; internet www.banquedelareunion.fr; owned by Groupe Banque Populaire et Caisse d'Epargne (France); 2 brs.

BRED Banque Populaire: Centre d'Affaires Mayotte, pl. Mariage, Z.I. 3, 97600 Mamoudzou; tel. 269-64-80-86; fax 269-60-51-10; internet www.bred.fr; owned by Groupe Banque Populaire et Caisse d'Epargne (France).

INSURANCE

AGF: pl. Mariage, BP 184, 97600 Mamoudzou; tel. 269-61-44-33; fax 269-61-14-89; e-mail jl.henry@wanadoo.fr; Gen. Man. Jean-Luc Henry.

Groupama: BP 665, Z.I. Nel, Lot 7, 97600 Mamoudzou; tel. 269-62-59-92; fax 269-60-76-08.

Prudence Créole: Centre Commercial et Médical de l'Ylang, BP 480, 97600 Mamoudzou; tel. 269-61-11-10; fax 269-61-11-21; e-mail prudencecreolemayotte@wanadoo.fr; 87% owned by Groupe Générali; 2 brs.

Vectra Paic Océan Indien: BP 65, 55 champs des Ylangs, 97680 Combani; tel. 269-62-44-54; fax 269-62-46-97; e-mail cfonteneau@wanadoo.fr.

Trade and Industry

DEVELOPMENT ORGANIZATION

Agence Française de Développement (AFD): ave de la Préfecture, BP 500, 97600 Mamoudzou; tel. 269-61-05-05; fax 269-61-05-02; e-mail afdmamoudzou@groupe-afd.org; internet www.afd.fr; Dir Patrick Peaucellier.

EMPLOYERS' ORGANIZATIONS

Mouvement des Entreprises de France Mayotte (MEDEF): Z.I. Kawéni, Immeuble GMOI, BP 570, 97600 Mamoudzou; tel. 269-61-44-22; fax 269-61-46-10; e-mail contact@medef-mayotte.com; internet www.medef-mayotte.com; Pres. Michel Taillefer.

Ordre National des Médecins: BP 675 Kawéni, 97600 Mamoudzou; tel. 269-61-02-47; fax 269-61-36-61.

UTILITIES

Electricity

Electricité de Mayotte (EDM): BP 333, Z.I. Kawéni, 97600 Kawéni; tel. 269-61-44-44; fax 269-60-10-92; e-mail edm.mayotte@wanadoo.fr; internet www.electricitedemayotte.com; f. 1997; subsidiary of SAUR; Dir-Gen. Augusto Soares dos Reis.

Water

Syndicat intercommunal de l'eau et de l'assainissement de Mayotte (SIEAM): BP 289, 97600 Mamoudzou; tel. 269-62-11-11; fax 269-62-10-31; Pres. Maoulida Soula.

TRADE UNIONS

Confédération Inter-Syndicale de Mayotte (CISMA-CFDT): 18 rue Mahabou, BP 1038, 97600 Mamoudzou; tel. 269-61-12-38; fax 269-61-36-16; f. 1993; affiliated to the Confédération Française Démocratique du Travail; Gen. Sec. Saïd Boinali.

Affiliated unions incl.:

ScDEN-CGT: BP 793 Kawéni, 97600 Mamoudzou; tel. and fax 269-62-53-35; e-mail scdencgt.mayotte@free.fr; internet www.cgt-mayotte.info; affiliated to the Confédération Générale du Travail; represents teaching staff; Sec.-Gen. Khémaïs Saidani.

SGEN-CFDT: c/o CISMA, 18 rue Mahabou, BP 1038, 97600 Mamoudzou; tel. 269-61-12-38; fax 269-61-18-09; e-mail mayotte@sgen.cfdt.fr; internet etranger.sgencfdt.free.fr/Mayotte/index.htm; affiliated to the Fédération des Syndicats Généraux de l'Education Nationale et de la Recherche; represents teaching staff; Sec.-Gen. Françoise Holzapfel.

Fédération Départementale des Syndicats d'Exploitants Agricoles de Mayotte (FDSEAM): 150 rue Mbalamanga-Mtsapéré, 97600 Mamoudzou; tel. and fax 269-61-34-83; e-mail fdsea.mayotte@wanadoo.fr; f. 1982; affiliated to the Fédération Nationale des Syndicats d'Exploitants; Pres. Ambody Ali; Dir Ali Bacar.

SNES Mayotte (SNES-FSU): 12 Résidence Bellecombe, 110 Lotissement Les Trois Vallées, Majicavo, 97600 Mamoudzou; tel. 269-62-50-58; fax 269-62-53-39; e-mail mayotte@snes.edu; internet www.mayotte.snes.edu; affiliated to the Syndicat National des Enseignements de Second Degré; represents teaching staff in secondary education; Sec. Frédéric Louvier.

Union Départementale Force Ouvrière de Mayotte (FO): Z. I. de Kaweni, Rond Point El-Farouk, BP 1109, 97600 Mamoudzou; tel. 269-61-18-39; fax 269-61-22-45; e-mail utfo.mayotte@wanadoo.fr; Sec.-Gen. Hamidou Madi MColo.

Transport

ROADS

In 2011 the road network totalled approximately 230 km, of which 90 km were main roads.

SHIPPING

Coastal shipping is provided by locally owned small craft. There is a deep-water port at Longoni. Construction of a second quay at Longoni was proposed under the 2006 budget; in December 2008 the Agence Française de Développement approved the allocation of a €10m. loan towards the extension of Longoni port.

Service des Affaires Maritimes: BP 37, 97615 Pamandzi; tel. 269-60-31-38; fax 269-60-31-39; e-mail c.mait.sam-mayotte@developpment-durable.gouv.fr; Head of Service Olivier Bisson.

Service des Transports Maritimes (STM): BP 186, 97600 Dzaoudzi; tel. 269-64-39-72; fax 269-60-80-25; e-mail denys.cormy@cg976.fr; internet www.mayotte-stm.com; Dir Denys Cormy; 8 vessels.

CIVIL AVIATION

There is an airport at Dzaoudzi, serving daily commercial flights to the Comoros; four-times weekly flights to Réunion; twice-weekly services to Madagascar; and weekly services to Kenya and Mozambique. In January 2004 plans were approved for the construction of a new runway to allow the commencement of direct flights to Paris, France. The proposed establishment of Air Mayotte International was abandoned in September of that year. Plans for a new terminal at the airport in Dzaoudzi were announced in late 2010 as a result of which the number of visitors passing through the airport each year was to increase to 615,000 by 2025. Air Austral announced plans to commence a direct air service to Paris by late 2011; the scheduled launch date was subsequently delayed until March 2012.

Air Austral: pl. Mariage, BP 1429, 97600 Mamoudzou; tel. 269-60-90-90; fax 269-61-61-94; e-mail mayotte@air-austral.com; internet www.air-austral.com; Pres. Gérard Ethève.

Tourism

Tropical scenery provides the main tourist attraction. Excluding cruise-ship passengers, Mayotte received 52,800 visitors in 2010; tourism receipts totalled €16.3m. in 2006. In 2007 there were nine hotels, with a total of some 366 rooms.

Comité Départemental du Tourisme de Mayotte (CDTM): rue Amiral Lacaze 5, 97400 Saint-Denis, Réunion; tel. 269-61-09-09; fax 269-61-03-46; e-mail mayottetourisme.lareunion@orange.fr; internet www.mayotte-tourisme.com; Dir George Mecs.

RÉUNION

Introductory Survey

LOCATION, CLIMATE, LANGUAGE, RELIGION, CAPITAL

Réunion is an island in the Indian Ocean, lying about 800 km (500 miles) east of Madagascar. The climate varies greatly according to altitude: at sea level it is tropical, with average temperatures between 20°C (68°F) and 28°C (82°F), but in the uplands it is much cooler, with average temperatures between 8°C (46°F) and 19°C (66°F). Rainfall is abundant, averaging 4,714 mm annually in the uplands, and 686 mm at sea level. The population is of mixed origin, including people of European, African, Indian and Chinese descent. The official language is French. A large majority of the population are Christians belonging to the Roman Catholic Church. The capital is Saint-Denis.

CONTEMPORARY POLITICAL HISTORY

Historical Context

Réunion was first occupied by France in 1642, and was ruled as a colony until 1946, when it received full departmental status. In 1974 it became an Overseas Department (Département d'outre-mer) with the status of a region.

In 1978 the Organization of African Unity (OAU, now the African Union, see p. 189) adopted a report recommending measures to hasten the independence of the island, and condemned its occupation by a 'colonial power'. However, this view seemed to have little popular support in Réunion. Although the left-wing political parties on the island advocated increased autonomy (amounting to virtual self-government), few people were in favour of complete independence.

Domestic Political Affairs

In June 1992 a delegation from the Conseil régional (Regional Council) met French President François Mitterrand to submit proposals for economic reforms, in accordance with the aim of establishing parity between Réunion and metropolitan France. In early July, however, the French Government announced increases in social security benefits that were substantially less than had been expected, resulting in widespread discontent on the island. In September the Parti communiste réunionnais (PCR), which in alliance with the Free-DOM list of independent candidates controlled 26 of the 45 seats in the Conseil régional, demanded that the electorate refuse to participate in the forthcoming French referendum on ratification of the Treaty on European Union (see p. 276), in protest at the alleged failure of the French Government to recognize the requirements of the Overseas Departments. At the referendum, which took place later that month, the ratification of the treaty was approved by the voters of Réunion, although only 26.3% of the registered electorate voted.

In March 1993 Dr Camille Sudre, the President of the Conseil régional, announced that he was to contest a seat on behalf of the Free-DOM–PCR alliance in the forthcoming elections to the French Assemblée nationale. However, at the elections, which took place later that month, Sudre was defeated by Jean-Paul Virapoullé in the second round of voting, while another incumbent right-wing deputy, André Thien Ah Koon (who contested the elections on behalf of the Union pour la France—UPF), also retained his seat. The PCR, the Parti socialiste (PS) and the Rassemblement pour la république (RPR) each secured one of the remaining seats.

At elections to the 47-seat Conseil général, which took place in March 1994, the PCR retained 12 seats, while the number of PS deputies increased to 12. The number of seats held by the RPR and the Union pour la démocratie française (UDF) declined to five and 11, respectively. The RPR and UDF subsequently attempted to negotiate an alliance with the PCR; however, the PCR and PS established a coalition (despite the long-standing differences between the two parties), thereby securing the support of 24 of the 47 seats in the Conseil général. In April a member of the PS, Christophe Payet, was elected President of the Conseil général; the right-wing parties (which had held the presidency of the Conseil général for more than 40 years) boycotted the poll. The PS and PCR signed an agreement whereby the two parties were to control the administration of the Conseil général jointly, and indicated that centrist deputies might be allowed to join the alliance.

In the second round of the French presidential election, which took place in May 1995, the socialist candidate, Lionel Jospin, secured 56% of the votes cast on Réunion, while Jacques Chirac, the official candidate of the RPR, won 44% of the votes (although Chirac obtained the highest number of votes overall).

Equality with metropolitan France

With effect from the beginning of 1996 the social security systems of the Overseas Departments were aligned with those of metropolitan France. In February Alain Juppé, the French Prime Minister, invited representatives from the Overseas Departments to Paris to participate in discussions on social equality and development. The main issue uniting the political representatives from Réunion was the need to align the salaries of civil servants on the island with those in metropolitan France. Several trade unionists declared themselves willing to enter into negotiations, on condition that only new recruits would be affected. Paul Vergès, joint candidate of the PCR and the PS, was elected to the Sénat in April, securing 51.9% of the votes cast. In the by-election to replace Paul Vergès, which took place in September, Claude Hoarau, the PCR candidate, was elected as a deputy to the Assemblée nationale with 56.0% of the votes cast. A new majority alliance between Free-DOM, the RPR and the UDF was subsequently formed in the Conseil régional, with the re-election of its 19-member permanent commission in October.

In October 1996 the trial of a number of politicians and business executives, who had been arrested in 1993–94 on charges of corruption, took place, after three years of investigations. Jacques de Châteauvieux, the Chairman of Groupe Sucreries de Bourbon, was found guilty of bribery, and was imprisoned, while two senior executives from the French enterprise Compagnie Générale des Eaux were given suspended sentences. Some 20 others were also found guilty of corruption. Pierre Vergès surrendered to the authorities in December and appeared before a magistrate in Saint-Pierre, where he was subsequently detained; in February 1997 he was released by the Court of Appeal.

Four left-wing candidates were successful in elections to the Assemblée nationale held in May and June 1997. Claude Hoarau (PCR) retained his seat and was joined by Huguette Bello and Elie Hoarau, also both from the PCR, and Michel Tamaya (PS), while Thien Ah Koon, representing the RPR-UDF coalition, was re-elected.

In February 1998 the PCR (led by Paul Vergès), the PS and several right-wing mayors presented a joint list of candidates, known as the Rassemblement, to contest forthcoming elections. In the elections to the Conseil régional, which took place on 15 March, the Rassemblement secured 19 seats, while the UDF obtained nine seats and the RPR eight, with various left-wing candidates representing Free-DOM winning five. Vergès was elected President of the Conseil régional on 23 March, with the support of the deputies belonging to the Rassemblement and Free-DOM groups. In concurrent elections to an expanded 49-member Conseil général, right-wing candidates (including those on the Rassemblement's list) secured 27 seats, while left-wing candidates obtained 22 seats, with the PCR and the PS each winning 10 seats. At the end of the month Jean-Luc Poudroux, of the UDF, was elected President of the Conseil général, owing to the support of two left-wing deputies.

At municipal elections, held in March 2001, the left-wing parties experienced significant losses. Notably, the PS mayor of Saint-Denis, Michel Tamaya, was defeated by the RPR candidate, René-Paul Victoria. The losses were widely interpreted as a general rejection of Jospin's proposals to create a second department on the island. At elections to the Conseil général, held concurrently, the right-wing parties also made substantial gains, obtaining 38 of the 49 seats; the UDF retained its majority, and Poudroux was re-elected as President. In July Elie Hoarau was obliged to resign from the Assemblée nationale, following his conviction on charges of electoral fraud, as a result of which he received a one-year prison sentence and was barred from holding public office for a period of three years.

In the first round of the presidential election, which was held on 21 April 2002, Jospin secured 39.0% of the valid votes cast in the Department (although he was eliminated nationally), followed by Chirac, who received 37.1%. In the second round, on 5 May, Chirac overwhelmingly defeated the candidate of the extreme right-wing Front National, Jean-Marie Le Pen, with 91.9% of the vote. At elections to the Assemblée nationale in June, Thien Ah Koon, allied to the new Union pour la majorité présidentielle (UMP, which had recently been formed by the merger of the RPR, the Démocratie libérale and elements of the UDF), and Bello were re-elected. Tamaya lost his seat to Victoria of the UMP, Claude Hourau lost to Bertho Audifax of the UMP, while Elie Hourau, who was declared ineligible to stand for re-election, was replaced by Christophe Payet of the PS. (In November the UMP was renamed the Union pour un mouvement populaire.)

In elections to the Conseil régional, which took place on 21 and 28 March 2004, the Alliance, a joint list of candidates led by the PCR, secured 27 seats. The UMP won 11 seats, and an alliance of the PS and Les Verts Réunion obtained seven seats. Following concurrent elections to the Conseil général, to renew 25 of the 49 seats, right-wing candidates held 30 seats, while left-wing candidates held 19. On 1 April Nassimah Dindar of the UMP was elected to succeed Poudroux as President of the Conseil général. Paul Vergès was re-elected as President of the Conseil régional on the following day. In February 2005 Gélite Hoarau replaced Paul Vergès as the PCR's representative to the Sénat.

In late May 2005 a national referendum on ratification of the proposed constitutional treaty of the European Union was held: 59.9% of Réunion's electorate joined with a majority of French voters in rejecting the treaty; voter turn-out on the island was around 53%.

Recent developments: presidential and local elections

In the first round of the French presidential election, held on 22 April 2007, Ségolène Royal of the PS secured 46.2% of the votes cast in Réunion, while Nicolas Sarkozy of the UMP received 25.1%. Both, therefore, proceeded to the second round of voting on 6 May in which Sarkozy claimed victory at national level; however, voting on Réunion again went in favour of Royal, who received 63.6% of the island vote. At legislative elections in June Victoria and Bello both retained their seats in the Assemblée nationale, but Audifax lost his seat to Jean-Claude Fruteau of the PS. Didier Robert of the UMP defeated Paul Vergès, while Patrick Lebreton of the PS was also elected. In March 2008 Dindar was re-elected to the presidency of the Conseil général.

In January 2009 workers in Guadeloupe, a French overseas territory in the Caribbean, commenced industrial action in protest against rising fuel and food prices and the deterioration of living conditions on the island. The unrest soon spread to other departments, including Réunion, where unemployment had reached 25.2% in February and living costs had increased significantly. In early March thousands of workers took to the streets of Saint-Denis, demanding a 20% reduction in the price of basic goods, and a wage increase of €200 per month for low-paid workers. The protests turned violent as demonstrators began throwing stones and police responded by firing tear gas to disperse the crowds.

In January 2010 President Sarkozy visited Réunion for the first time since his election to the presidency. Also in that month Michel Lalande replaced Pierre-Henry Maccioni as Prefect. Elections to the Conseil régional took place on 14 and 21 March 2010 at which the La Réunion en confiance alliance led by Robert won 27 seats. The Liste de l'alliance, headed by Vergès' PCR, took 12 seats, while the PS-led Pour une Réunion plus juste avec l'union des socialistes alliance secured six seats. On 26 March Robert was elected to succeed Vergès as President of the Conseil régional.

In October 2011 a fire broke out in Maïdo forest in the National Park, threatening areas of endemic plants, rare wildlife species and key micro-habitats for biodiversity. (The site was inscribed on the World Heritage List in July 2010). The French authorities were heavily criticized by local and metropolitan officials for taking six days to react and their delay in sending fire-fighting planes; some 2,824 ha of land were destroyed before the fire could be brought under control. In early 2012 several nights of social unrest were reported; initially the protests were directed at the high cost of fuel prices with transporters blocking fuel outlets, but subsequently protests at the generally high cost of living spread across the island and security forces were brought in from France to quell the violence. Some 233 arrests were made and nine police officers were injured, according to the Prefecture. Negotiations between local politicians, civil society representatives, transporters and petrol companies were held by Lalande and an agreement was reached to lower prices of fuel and electricity for households on modest income and to freeze prices for 60 staple products from 1 March onwards.

CONSTITUTION AND GOVERNMENT

The Constitution of the Fifth Republic of France, adopted by referendum on 28 September 1958 and promulgated on 6 October 1958 applies on Réunion. France is represented in Réunion by an appointed Prefect. There are two councils with local powers: the 49-member Conseil général and the 45-member Conseil régional. Both are elected for up to six years by direct universal suffrage. Réunion sends five directly elected deputies to the Assemblée nationale in Paris and three indirectly elected representatives to the Sénat. The Department is also represented at the European Parliament.

REGIONAL AND INTERNATIONAL CO-OPERATION

Réunion is represented by France in the Indian Ocean Commission (IOC, see p. 450) which it joined in 1986. Réunion was given the right to host ministerial meetings of the IOC, but would not be allowed to occupy the presidency, owing to its status as a non-sovereign state. As an integral part of France, Réunion belongs to the European Union (see p. 276).

ECONOMIC AFFAIRS

Réunion's gross national income (GNI) in 1995 was estimated at 29,200m. French francs, equivalent to about 44,300 francs per head. Between the censuses of 1999 and 2006, Réunion's population increased at an average annual rate of 1.5%. In 2009, according to official figures, Réunion's gross domestic product (GDP), measured at current prices, was €14,400m.; in 2009 GDP per head totalled €17,520. GDP increased, in real terms, at an average annual rate of 5.9% in 2000–09; it declined in 2009 by 2.7%.

Agriculture (including hunting, forestry and fishing) contributed 1.3% of GDP in 2007, and engaged 1.6% of the salaried working population in 2008. The principal cash crops are sugar cane (sugar accounted for 37.9% of export earnings in 2007), maize, tobacco, vanilla, and geraniums and vetiver root, which are cultivated for the production of essential oils. Fishing and livestock production are also important to the economy. According to the UN, agricultural GDP increased at an average annual rate of 3.9% during 1990–2000; growth in 2001 was 3.1%.

Industry (including mining, manufacturing, construction and power) contributed 16.6% of GDP in 2007, and employed 16.0% of the working salaried population in 2008. The principal branch of manufacturing is food-processing, particularly the production of sugar and rum. Other significant sectors include the fabrication of construction materials, mechanics, printing, metalwork, textiles and garments, and electronics. According to the UN, industrial GDP (excluding construction) increased at an average annual rate of 4.3% during 1990–99; growth in 2001 was 3.7%.

There are no mineral resources on the island. Energy is derived principally from thermal and hydroelectric power. Power plants at Bois-Rouge and Le Gol produce around 45% of the island's total energy requirements; almost one-third of the electricity generated is produced using bagasse, a by-product of sugar cane. Imports of fuel comprised 10.8% of the value of total imports in 2010.

Services (including transport, communications, trade and finance) contributed 82.0% of GDP in 2007, and employed 82.4% of the salaried working population in 2008. The public sector accounts for more than two-thirds of employment in the services sector. Tourism is also significant; in 2010, 420,300 tourists visited Réunion, and tourism revenue totalled €292.9m. in 2007.

Réunion's economy is overwhelmingly dependent on imports and as a result the island recorded a trade deficit of €3,983.7m. in 2010. The principal sources of imports in 2010 were France (54.2%), Singapore and the People's Republic of China. The principal market for exports in 2010, were France (31.6%), Mayotte, Madagascar and Spain. The principal exports in 2010 were prepared foodstuffs, transport equipment, electrical and electronic equipment and industrial and household waste. The principal imports in 2010 were electrical and electronic equipment and components, prepared foodstuffs, transport equipment, refined petroleum products, pharmaceutical products, metal products, textiles and footwear, miscellaneous manufactured products, plastic products and chemicals and perfumes.

In 2008 the budget balanced at €835m. The departmental budget for 2009 amounted to €1,415.0m.; some 62.5% of revenue was to be provided by the state. The annual rate of inflation averaged 1.8% in 2001–10; consumer prices increased by 1.5% in 2010. An estimated 23.6% of the labour force were unemployed in December 2008.

Réunion has a relatively developed economy, but is dependent on financial aid from France. The economy has traditionally been based on agriculture, and is, therefore, vulnerable to poor climatic conditions. From the 1990s the production of sugar cane (which dominates that sector) was adversely affected by increasing urbanization, which resulted in a decline in agricultural land; however, sugar still accounted for 38% of export earnings in 2007, and although export quantities fell in 2009 they grew by 4.4% in 2010. Favourable economic progress has been largely sustained by tourism and economists have identified Réunion's need to expand external trade, particularly with fellow IOC members, if the island's economy is to continue to prosper. It was hoped that a decision to allow Réunion to negotiate co-operation agreements with regional states from 2004 would enhance its trading position. The tourism sector experienced a reverse in 2006, however, with visitor numbers and revenue vastly reduced, and consequent job losses in the sector. Réunion experienced a small recovery in 2007 before the global economic crisis in 2008 and 2009 adversely affected tourism revenue. In 2010 the French Institut national de la statistique et des études économiques (INSEE) estimated that the island had received some 420,300 visitors, a decline of 0.4% compared with the previous year. Réunion's rate of unemployment was 23.6% in 2007, among the highest of all the French Departments; however, this did represent a reduction from 31.9% in 2005. Unemployment among Réunion's youth (aged 15–24) has remained high—from 49.1% in 2005 it continued to increase to 49.6% in 2009 and to 55.3% in mid-2010. During a visit to Réunion in January 2010 the French President, Nicolas Sarkozy, announced plans to create a 'green laboratory' on Réunion with the intention of making the island energy self-sufficient by 2030. A consequent injection of public subsidies into solar projects led to a 21.7% rise in the creation of enterprises on the island; INSEE, however, noted that 96.2% of these enterprises had no salaried workers. In August 2011 a study was presented by the French Commissioner for Indian Ocean Development to the island authorities that highlighted a lack of international opening on an economic level, the small size of undercapitalized local companies and an absence of 'risk culture'. The report recommended the rationalizing of aid for international companies to create an export platform for a shared strategy for 2012 and 2013.

PUBLIC HOLIDAYS

2013: 1 January (New Year's Day), 1 April (Easter Monday), 1 May (Labour Day), 8 May (Liberation Day), 9 May (Ascension Day), 20 May (Whit Monday), 14 July (National Day, Fall of the Bastille), 15 August (Assumption), 1 November (All Saints' Day), 11 November (Armistice Day), 20 December (Abolition of Slavery Day), 25 December (Christmas Day).

Statistical Survey

Source (unless otherwise indicated): Institut National de la Statistique et des Études Économiques, Service Régional de la Réunion, 15 rue de l'Ecole, 97490 Sainte-Clotilde; tel. 262-48-81-00; fax 262-41-09-81; internet www.insee.fr/fr/insee_regions/reunion.

AREA AND POPULATION

Area: 2,507 sq km (968 sq miles).

Population: 706,180 (males 347,076, females 359,104) at census of 8 March 1999; 816,364 at census of 1 January 2009. Note: According to new census methodology, data in 2009 refer to median figures based on the collection of raw data over a five-year period (2006–11). *1 January 2010:* 833,000. *Mid-2012* (UN estimate): 865,480 (Source: UN, *World Population Prospects: The 2010 Revision*).

Density (at mid-2012): 345.2 per sq km.

Population by Age and Sex (UN estimates at mid-2012): *0–14:* 219,343 (males 111,204, females 108,139); *15–64:* 572,107 (males 280,076, females 292,031); *65 and over:* 74,030 (males 32,465, females 41,565); *Total* 865,480 (males 423,745, females 441,735) (Source: UN, *World Population Prospects: The 2010 Revision*.

Principal Towns (population at census of January 2006): Saint-Denis (capital) 138,314; Saint-Paul 99,291; Saint-Pierre 74,480; Le Tampon 69,849; Saint-André 51,817; Saint-Louis 49,455. *Mid-2009* (incl. suburbs, UN estimate): Saint-Denis 140,906 (Source: UN, *World Urbanization Prospects: The 2009 Revision*).

Births, Marriages and Deaths (2010 unless otherwise indicated): Registered live births 14,146 (birth rate 17.4 per 1,000); Registered marriages (2009) 2,919 (marriage rate 3.6 per 1,000); Registered deaths (2009) 4,109 (death rate 5.1 per 1,000).

Life Expectancy (years at birth, 2008): Males 74.6; females 82.1.

Economically Active Population (persons aged 15 years and over, 1999 census): Agriculture, hunting, forestry and fishing 9,562; Mining, manufacturing, electricity, gas and water 13,424; Construction 11,003; Wholesale and retail trade 24,658; Transport, storage and communications 5,494; Financing, insurance and real estate 4,851; Business services 11,225; Public administration 39,052; Education 23,325; Health and social work 17,376; Other services 13,707; *Total employed* 173,677 (males 100,634, females 73,043); Unemployed 124,203 (males 63,519, females 60,684); *Total labour force* 297,880 (males 164,153, females 133,727). Figures exclude 967 persons on compulsory military service (males 945, females 22). *2008* (salaried workers at 1 January, preliminary): Agriculture 3,262; Industry (incl. energy) 14,431; Construction 18,658; Trade 27,112; Transport 7,718; Financial activities and real estate 6,102; Private services 19,484; Business services 19,819; Health and welfare 18,340; Education 23,474; Public administration 48,174; Total employed 206,574. Note: Total excludes 26,626 non-salaried workers. *Unemployed* (at 1 January 2008): 72,133.

HEALTH AND WELFARE

Key Indicators

Total Fertility Rate (children per woman, 2004): 2.5.

Physicians (per 1,000 head, 2011): 2.1.

Hospital Beds (per 1,000 head, 2000): 3.7.

For definitions, see explanatory note on p. vi.

AGRICULTURE, ETC.

Principal Crops ('000 metric tons, 2010, FAO estimates): Maize 13.8; Potatoes 7.4; Sugar cane 1,930.0; Cabbages and other brassicas 2.7; Lettuce and chicory 4.5; Tomatoes 11.8; Cauliflowers and broccoli 5.2; Pumpkins, squash and gourds 0.8; Eggplants (Aubergines) 0.8; Onions and shallots, green 4.7; Beans, green 3.8; Carrots and turnips 2.0; Bananas 7.2; Tangerines, mandarins, clementines and satsumas 3.4; Mangoes, mangosteens and guavas 2.5; Pineapples 17.6. *Aggregate Production* ('000 metric tons, may include official, semi-official or estimated data): Total vegetables (incl. melons) 46.3; Total fruits (excl. melons) 59.4.

Livestock ('000 head, 2010, FAO estimates): Cattle 33.2; Pigs 80.7; Sheep 1.0; Goats 40.0; Chickens 15,000.

Livestock Products ('000 metric tons, 2010, FAO estimates): Cattle meat 1.7; Pig meat 12.0; Chicken meat 16.8; Rabbit meat 2.1; Cow's milk 29.8; Hen eggs 6.7.

Forestry ('000 cu m, 1991): *Roundwood Removals:* Sawlogs, veneer logs and logs for sleepers 4.2; Other industrial wood 0.9 (FAO estimate); Fuel wood 31.0 (FAO estimate); Total 36.1. *Sawnwood Production:* 2.2. *1992–2010:* Annual production assumed to be unchanged from 1991 (FAO estimates).

Fishing (metric tons, live weight, 2009, all capture, FAO estimates): Albacore 560; Yellowfin tuna 472; Bigeye tuna 503; Swordfish 942; Common dolphinfish 60; *Total catch* (incl. others) 3,000.

Source: FAO.

INDUSTRY

Selected Products (metric tons, 2010, unless otherwise indicated): Sugar 207,000; Oil of geranium 2 (2007); Oil of vetiver root 0.4 (2002); Rum (hl) 93,704; Electric energy (million kWh) 2,699 (Source: partly Institut d'Emission des Départements d'Outre-mer, *Rapport Annuel 2010*).

FINANCE

Currency and Exchange Rates: The French franc was used until the end of February 2002. Euro notes and coins were introduced on 1 January 2002, and the euro became the sole legal tender from 18 February. Some of the figures in this Survey are still in terms of francs. For details of exchange rates, see Mayotte.

Budget (€ million): *Regional Budget* (2008): Revenue 835 (Taxes 279, Transfers received 291, Loans 265); Expenditure 835 (Current expenditure 265, Capital 571). *Departmental Budget* (2009): Revenue 1,415.0 (State endowments 884.5, Direct and indirect taxes 392.3, Loans 60.0, Other subsidies—Europe and other bodies) 39.4, Other revenues and receipts 38.8); Expenditure 1,415.0 (Social welfare 843.2, General services 278.8, Development 56.2, Teaching 62.0, Networks and infrastructure 43.9, Security 53.2, Planning and environment 10.6, Culture, societies, youth and sports 10.7, Traffic 56.3). Source: Conseil général, *Le Budget du Département*.

Money Supply (million francs at 31 December 1996): Currency outside banks 4,050; Demand deposits at banks 7,469; Total money 11,519.

Cost of Living (Consumer Price Index; base: 2000 = 100): All items 118.2 in 2008; 118.8 in 2009; 120.6 in 2010. Source: ILO.

Expenditure on the Gross Domestic Product (€ million at current prices, 2010): Private final consumption expenditure 9,590; Government final consumption expenditure 5,720; Gross capital formation 3,150; *Total domestic expenditure* 18,460; Exports of goods 280; *Less* Imports of goods 4,260; Tourist expenditure 300; Statistical discrepancy 120; *GDP in market prices* 14,900.

Gross Domestic Product by Economic Activity (€ million at current prices, 2007): Agriculture, forestry and fishing 177; Mining, manufacturing, electricity, gas and water 917; Construction 1,274; Wholesale and retail trade 1,182; Transport and communications 820; Finance and insurance 704; Public administration 1,521; Education, health and social work 3,128; Other services (incl. hotels and restaurants) 3,472; *Sub-total* 13,196; *Less* Financial intermediation services indirectly measured 462; *Gross value-added at basic prices* 12,734; Taxes on products, *less* subsidies on products 1,235; *GDP in market prices* 13,969.

EXTERNAL TRADE

Principal Commodities (€ million, 2010): *Imports:* Agriculture, forestry and fishing 91.6; Mining and quarrying 63.5 (Natural hydrocarbons 63.0); Prepared foodstuffs 652.8; Refined petroleum products 458.8; Electrical and electronic equipment and components 834.3 (Information products and electronics 346.1, Electronic equipment and household electrical goods 259.8, Industrial and agricultural machinery 228.4); Transport equipment 529.6; Other industrial products 1,570.9 (Textiles and footwear 235.6, Paper and paperboard 142.8, Chemicals and perfumes 214.2, Pharmaceutical products 265.5, Plastic products 229.6, Metal products 247.8, Miscellaneous manufactured products 235.6); Printed books 63.0; Total 4,265.2. *Exports:* Agriculture, forestry and fishing 4.6; Industrial and household waste 15.0; Prepared foodstuffs 171.5; Refined petroleum products 8.1; Electrical and electronic equipment and components 29.8 (Information products and electronics 16.6, Electronic equipment and household electrical goods 3.0, Industrial and agricultural machinery 10.2); Transport equipment 30.1; Other industrial products 24.0 (Textiles and footwear 2.6, Paper and paperboard 1.8, Chemicals and perfumes 6.4, Pharmaceutical products 0.9, Plastic products 1.7, Metal products 5.9, Miscellaneous manufactured products 4.8); Total 281.5. Note: Totals may not be equal to the sum of components, owing to rounding (Source: Source: Institut d'Emission des Départements d'Outre-mer, *Rapport Annuel 2010*).

Principal Trading Partners (€ million, 2010): *Imports:* Belgium 52.1; China, People's Republic 287.5; France 2,312.8; Germany 200.6; Italy 89.8; Singapore 389.8; South Africa 100.0; Spain 62.0; Total (incl. others) 4,265.2. *Exports f.o.b.:* France 88.9; Hong Kong 13.4; Italy 6.7; Japan 10.5; Madagascar 15.1; Mauritius 7.4; Mayotte 26.5; Spain 18.0; USA 8.4; Total (incl. others) 281.5.

TRANSPORT

Road Traffic (1 January 2005): Motor vehicles in use 338,500.

Shipping: *Merchant Fleet* (total displacement at 31 December 1992): 21,000 grt (Source: UN, *Statistical Yearbook*); *Traffic* (2007): Passenger arrivals 14,667; Passenger departures 16,225; Vessels entered 709; Freight unloaded 3,652,600 metric tons; Freight loaded 559,500 metric tons; Containers unloaded 111,952 TEUs; Containers loaded 112,921 TEUs.

Civil Aviation (2010): Passenger arrivals 1,014,874; Passenger departures 1,015,540; Freight unloaded 21,265 metric tons; Freight loaded 8,048 metric tons (Source: Institut d'Emission des Départements d'Outre-mer, *Rapport Annuel 2010*).

TOURISM

Tourist Arrivals: 396,400 in 2008; 421,900 in 2009; 420,300 in 2010 (Source: Institut d'Emission des Départements d'Outre-mer, *Rapport Annuel 2010*).

Arrivals by Country of Residence (2010): France (metropolitan) 346,200; Other EU 17,200; Mauritius 18,400; Total (incl. others) 420,300 (Source: Institut d'Emission des Départements d'Outre-mer, *La Réunion: Rapport Annuel 2010*).

Tourism Receipts (€ million): 308.8 in 2005; 224.8 in 2006; 292.9 in 2007.

COMMUNICATIONS MEDIA

Television Receivers ('000 in use, 1998): 130 in use. Source: UNESCO, *Statistical Yearbook*.

Telephones ('000 main lines in use, 2010): 480.9. Source: International Telecommunication Union.

Mobile Cellular Telephones ('000 subscribers, 2008): 579.2. Source: International Telecommunication Union.

Personal Computers ('000 in use, 2004): 279. Source: International Telecommunication Union.

Internet Users ('000, 2009): 300. Source: International Telecommunication Union.

Broadband Subscribers ('000, 2009): 185. Source: International Telecommunication Union.

Book Production (1992): 69 titles (50 books; 19 pamphlets). Source: UNESCO, *Statistical Yearbook*.

Daily Newspapers (1996): 3 (estimated average circulation 55,000 copies). Source: UNESCO, *Statistical Yearbook*.

Non-daily Newspapers (1988, estimate): 4 (average circulation 20,000 copies). Source: UNESCO, *Statistical Yearbook*.

EDUCATION

Pre-primary and Primary (2009/10, unless otherwise indicated): Schools 532 (pre-primary 174, primary 358 in 2003/04); public sector pupils 112,603 (pre-primary 41,019, primary 70,241, special education and disabled 1,343); private pupils 9,134 (pre-primary 3,282, primary 5,852).

Secondary (2008/09, unless otherwise indicated): Schools 121 (112 public sector, 9 private) (2005/06); pupils 101,262 (public sector 94,977, private 6,285).

University (2008/09): Institution 1; students 11,310.

Other Higher (2006/07): Students 4,988.

Teaching Staff (31 December 2007): Pre-primary and primary 6,866; Secondary 9,178; University 498; Other higher 476.

Directory

The Government

(May 2012)

HEAD OF STATE

President: Nicolas Sarkozy.

Prefect: Michel Lalande, Préfecture, pl. du Barachois, 97405 Saint-Denis Cédex; tel. 262-40-77-77; fax 262-41-73-74; e-mail courrier@reunion.pref.gouv.fr; internet www.reunion.pref.gouv.fr.

DEPARTMENTAL ADMINISTRATION

President of the Conseil général: Nassimah Dindar (UMP), Hôtel du Département, 2 rue de la Source, 97488 Saint-Denis Cédex; tel. 262-90-30-30; fax 262-90-39-99; internet www.cg974.fr.

President of the Conseil régional: Didier Robert (UMP), Hôtel de Région Pierre Lagourgue, ave René Cassin, Moufia, BP 7190, 97719 Saint-Denis Cédex 9; tel. 262-48-70-00; fax 262-48-70-71; e-mail region.reunion@cr-reunion.fr; internet www.regionreunion.com.

Election, Conseil Régional, 14 and 21 March 2010

Party	Seats
La Réunion en confiance*	27
Liste de l'alliance†	12
Pour une Réunion plus juste avec l'union des socialistes‡	6
Total	45

* An alliance led by the UMP.
† An alliance led by the PCR.
‡ An alliance led by the PS.

REPRESENTATIVES TO THE FRENCH PARLIAMENT

Deputies to the French National Assembly: Huguette Bello (NI), Jean-Claude Fruteau (PS), Patrick Lebreton (PS), Didier Robert (UMP), René-Paul Victoria (UMP).

Representatives to the French Senate: Gélita Hoarau (CRC), Anne-Marie Payet (Union Centriste), Jean-Paul Virapoullé (UMP).

GOVERNMENT OFFICES

Direction des Actions de Solidarité et d'Intégration (DASI): 26 ave de la Victoire, 97488 Saint-Denis Cédex; tel. 262-90-35-44; fax 262-90-39-94.

Direction de l'Aménagement et du Développement Territorial: ave de la Victoire, 97488 Saint-Denis Cédex; tel. 262-90-86-86; fax 262-90-86-70.

Direction des Déplacements et de la Voirie (DDV): 6 allée Moreau, Le Chaudron, 97490 Sainte-Clotilde; tel. 262-20-38-08; fax 262-94-17-90; e-mail dtransports@cg974.fr.

Direction du Développement Rural, de l'Agriculture et de la Forêt (DDRAF): ave de la Victoire, 97488 Saint-Denis Cédex; tel. 262-90-35-24; fax 262-90-39-89.

Direction de l'Eau: 14 allée de la forêt, 97400 Saint-Denis Cédex; tel. 262-30-84-84; fax 262-30-84-85; e-mail office@eaureunion.fr; internet www.eaureunion.fr.

Direction de l'Environnement et de l'Energie (DEE): 16 rue Jean Chatel, 97400 Saint-Denis Cédex; tel. 262-90-24-00; fax 262-90-24-19.

Direction des Finances: ave de la Victoire, 97488 Saint-Denis Cédex; tel. 262-90-39-39; fax 262-90-39-92; e-mail d.finances@cg974.fr; internet www.cg974.fr.

Direction Générale des Services (DGS): 2 rue de la Source, 97488 Saint-Denis Cédex; tel. 262-90-30-92; fax 262-90-39-99.

Direction de l'Informatique (DI): 19 route de la Digue, 97488 Saint-Denis Cédex; tel. 262-90-32-90; fax 262-90-32-99.

Direction de la Logistique (DL): 2 rue de la Source, 97488 Saint-Denis Cédex; tel. 262-90-31-38; fax 262-90-39-91.

Direction du Patrimoine (DP): 6 bis rue Rontaunay, 97488 Saint-Denis Cédex; tel. 262-90-86-81; fax 262-90-86-90.

Direction de la Promotion Culturelle et Sportive (DPCS): 18 rue de Paris, 97488 Saint-Denis Cédex; tel. 262-94-87-00; fax 262-94-87-26.

Direction des Ressources Humaines (DRH): 2 rue de la Source, 97488 Saint-Denis Cédex; tel. 262-90-34-65; fax 262-90-34-91.

Direction de la Vie Educative: ave de la Victoire, 97488 Saint-Denis Cédex; tel. 262-90-36-96; fax 262-90-37-21.

Political Organizations

Front national (FN)—Fédération de la Réunion (FN): Saint-Denis; tel. 262-51-38-97; e-mail fatna@frontnational.com; internet www.frontnational.com; f. 1972; extreme right-wing; Sec. (vacant).

Mouvement démocrate (MoDem): Saint-Denis; internet www.mouvementdemocrate.fr; f. 2007; fmrly Union pour la Démocratie Française (UDF); centrist.

Mouvement pour l'indépendance de la Réunion (MIR): f. 1981 to succeed the fmr Mouvement pour la Libération de la Réunion; grouping of parties favouring autonomy; Leader Anselme Payet.

Mouvement national républicain (MNR)—Fédération de la Réunion: tel. 262-22-34-69; Sec. RÉMI BERTIN.

Parti communiste réunionnais (PCR): Saint-Denis; f. 1959; Pres. PAUL VERGÈS; Sec.-Gen. ELIE HOARAU.

Mouvement pour l'egalité, la démocratie, le développement et la nature: affiliated to the PCR; advocates political unity; Leader RENÉ PAYET.

Parti radical de gauche (PRG)—Fédération de la Réunion: 18 rue des Demoiselles, Hermitage les Bains, 97434 Saint-Gilles-les-Bains; tel. 262-33-94-73; internet www.prg93.org; f. 1977; fmrly Mouvement des Radicaux de Gauche; advocates full independence and an economy separate from, but assisted by, France; Pres. RÉMY MASSAIN.

Parti socialiste (PS)—Fédération de la Réunion (PS): 190 route des Deux Canons Immeuble, Futura, 97490 Saint-Clotilde; tel. 262-29-32-06; fax 262-28-53-03; e-mail psreunion@wanadoo.fr; internet www.parti-socialiste.fr; left-wing; Sec. ANNETTE GILBERT.

Union pour un mouvement populaire (UMP)—Fédération de la Réunion: 6 bis blvd Vauban, BP 11, 97461 Saint-Denis Cédex; tel. 262-20-21-18; fax 262-41-73-55; f. 2002; centre-right; local branch of the metropolitan party; Departmental Sec. DIDIER ROBERT.

Les verts Réunion: Apt 30, Res ARIAL, 132 rue Général de Gaulle, 97400 Saint-Denis; tel. 262-55-73-52; fax 262-25-03-03; e-mail sr-verts-reunion@laposte.net; internet lesverts.fr; ecologist; Regional Sec. VINCENT DEFAUD.

Judicial System

Cour d'appel: Palais de Justice, 166 rue Juliette Dodu, 97488 Saint-Denis; tel. 262-40-58-58; fax 262-20-16-37; Pres. JEAN-FRANÇOIS GABIN.

There are two Tribunaux de Grande Instance, one Tribunal d'Instance, two Tribunaux pour Enfants and two Conseils de Prud'hommes.

Religion

A substantial majority of the population are adherents of the Roman Catholic Church. There is a small Muslim community.

CHRISTIANITY

The Roman Catholic Church

Réunion comprises a single diocese, directly responsible to the Holy See. The number of adherents was equivalent to 80% of the population.

Bishop of Saint-Denis de la Réunion: Mgr GILBERT GUILLAUME MARIE-JEAN AUBRY, Evêché, 36 rue de Paris, BP 55, 97461 Saint-Denis Cédex; tel. 262-94-85-70; fax 262-94-85-73; e-mail eveche .lareunion@wanadoo.fr; internet www.diocese-reunion.org.

The Press

DAILIES

Journal de l'Ile de la Réunion: Centre d'affaires Cadjee, 62 blvd du Chaudron, BP 40019, 97491 Sainte-Clotilde Cédex; tel. 262-48-66-00; fax 262-48-66-50; internet www.clicanoo.re; f. 1951; CEO and Dir of Publication JEAN-BAPTISTE MARIOTTI; Editor-in-Chief YVES MONT-ROUGE; circ. 35,000.

Quotidien de la Réunion et de l'Océan Indien: BP 303, 97712 Saint-Denis Cédex 9; tel. 262-92-15-10; fax 262-28-25-28; e-mail laredaction@lequotidien.re; internet www.lequotidien.re; f. 1976; Dir MAXIMIN CHANE KI CHUNE; circ. 38,900.

Témoignages: 6 rue du Général Emile Rolland, BP 1016, 97828 Le Port Cédex; tel. 262-55-21-21; e-mail temoignages@wanadoo.fr; internet www.temoignages.re; f. 1944; affiliated to the Parti communiste réunionnais (q.v.); daily; Dir JEAN-MAX HOARAU; Editor-in-Chief ALAIN ILAN CHOJNOW; circ. 6,000.

PERIODICALS

Al-Islam: Centre Islamique de la Réunion, BP 437, 97459 Saint-Pierre Cédex; tel. 262-25-45-43; fax 262-35-58-23; e-mail centre-islamique-reunion@wanadoo.fr; internet www .islam-reunion.com; f. 1975; 4 a year; Dir ISSAC GANGAT.

L'Eco Austral: Technopole de la Réunion 2, rue Emile Hugot, BP 10003, 97801 Saint-Denis Cédex 9; tel. 262-41-51-41; fax 262-41-31-14; internet www.ecoaustral.com; f. 1993; monthly; regional economic issues; Editor ALAIN FOULON; circ. 50,000.

L'Economie de la Réunion: c/o INSEE, Parc Technologique, 10 rue Demarne, BP 13, 97408 Saint-Denis Messag Cédex 9; tel. 262-48-89-35; fax 262-48-89-89; e-mail insee-contact@insee.fr; internet www .insee.fr/reunion; 4 a year; Dir PASCAL CHEVALIER; Editor-in-Chief COLETTE BERTHIER.

Lutte Ouvrière—Ile de la Réunion: BP 184, 97470 Saint-Benoît; fax 262-48-00-98; e-mail contact@lutte-ouvriere-ile-de-la-reunion .org; internet www.lutte-ouvriere.org/en-regions/la-reunion; monthly; Communist; digital.

Le Mémento Industriel et Commercial Réunionnais: 80 rue Pasteur, BP 397, 97468 Saint-Denis; tel. 262-21-94-12; fax 262-41-10-85; e-mail memento@memento.fr; internet www.memento.fr; f. 1970; monthly; Editor-in-Chief GEORGES-GUILLAUME LOUAPRE-POTTIER; circ. 20,000.

La Réunion Agricole: Chambre d'Agriculture, 24 rue de la Source, BP 134, 97463 Saint-Denis Cédex; tel. 262-94-25-94; fax 262-21-06-17; e-mail herve.cailleaux@reunion.chambagri.fr; f. 2007; monthly; Dir JEAN YVES MINATCHY; Chief Editor HERVÉ CAILLEAUX; circ. 8,000.

Leader Réunion: 14 rue de la Guadeloupe, ZA Foucherolles, 97490 Sainte-Clotilde; tel. 262-92-10-60; Dir of Publication CAROLE MANOTE.

Visu: 97712 Saint-Denis Cédex 9; tel. 262-90-20-60; fax 262-90-20-61; weekly; Editor-in-Chief PHILIPPE PEYRE; circ. 53,000.

NEWS AGENCY

Imaz Press Réunion: 12 rue Victor MacAuliffe, 97400 Saint-Denis; tel. 262-20-05-65; fax 262-20-05-49; e-mail ipr@ipreunion.com; internet www.ipreunion.com; f. 2000; photojournalism and news agency; Dir RICHARD BOUHET.

Broadcasting and Communications

TELECOMMUNICATIONS

Orange Réunion: 35 blvd du Chaudron, BP 7431, 97743 Saint-Denis Cédex 9; tel. 262-20-02-00; fax 262-20-67-79; internet reunion .orange.fr; f. 2000; subsidiary of Orange France; mobile cellular telephone operator.

Outremer Telecom Réunion: 12 et 14 rue Henri Cornu, Technopole de la Réunion, BP 150, 97801 Saint-Denis, Cedex 9; tel. 262-20-023-00; fax 262-97-53-99; internet www.outremer-telecom.fr; telecommunications provider.

Société Réunionnaise du Radiotéléphone (SRR): 21 rue Pierre Aubert, 97490 Sainte-Clotide; BP 17, 97408 Saint-Denis, Messag Cédex 9; tel. 262-48-19-70; fax 262-48-19-80; internet www.srr.fr; f. 1995; subsidiary of SFR Cegetel, France; mobile cellular telephone operator; CEO JEAN-PIERRE HAGGAÏ; 431,719 subscribers in Réunion, 46,341 in Mayotte (as Mayotte Télécom Mobile) in 2003.

BROADCASTING

Réunion 1ère: 1 rue Jean Chatel, 97716 Saint-Denis Cédex; tel. 262-40-67-67; fax 262-21-64-84; internet reunion.la1ere.fr; acquired by Groupe France Télévisions in 2004; fmrly Réseau France Outre-mer, present name adopted in 2010; radio and television relay services in French; broadcasts two television channels (Télé-Réunion and Tempo) and three radio channels (Radio-Réunion, France-Inter and France-Culture); Dir-Gen. GENEVIÈVE GIARD; Regional Dir ROBERT .

Radio

In 2005 there were 46 licensed private radio stations. These included:

Antenne Réunion Radio: Saint-Denis; e-mail direction@ antennereunion.fr; internet www.antennereunion.fr; f. 2011.

Cherie FM Réunion: 3 rue de Kerveguen, 97400 Sainte-Clotilde; tel. 262-97-32-00; fax 262-97-32-32; Editor-in-Chief LEA BERTHAULT.

NRJ Réunion: 3 rue de Kerveguen, 97490 Sainte-Clotilde; tel. 262-97-32-00; fax 262-97-51-10; e-mail c.duboc@h2r.re; commercial radio station; Station Man. SYLVAIN PEGUILLAN.

Radio Festival: 3 rue de Kerveguen, 97490 Sainte-Clotilde; tel. 262-97-32-00; fax 262-97-32-32; e-mail redaction@radiofestival.fr; internet www.radiofestival.re; f. 1995; commercial radio station; Pres. MARIO LECHAT; Editor-in-Chief JEAN-PIERRE GERMAIN.

Radio Free-DOM: 131 rue Jules Auber, BP 666, 97400 Saint-Denis Cédex; tel. 262-41-51-51; fax 262-21-68-64; e-mail freedom@freedom .fr; internet www.freedom.fr; f. 1981; commercial radio station; Dir Dr CAMILLE SUDRE.

Television

Antenne Réunion: rue Emile Hugot, BP 80001, 97801 Saint-Denis Cédex 9; tel. 262-48-28-28; fax 262-48-28-26; e-mail direction@ antennereunion.fr; internet www.antennereunion.fr; f. 1991; broadcasts 10 hours daily; Pres. CHRISTOPHE DUCASSE; Dir-Gen. PHILIPPE ROUSSEL.

Canal Réunion: 6 rue René Demarne, Technopole de la Réunion, 97490 Sainte-Clotilde; tel. 262-97-98-99; fax 262-97-98-90; e-mail contact@canalreunion.net; internet www.canalreunion.com; subscription television channel; broadcasts a minimum of 19 hours daily; Chair. JEAN-NOEL TRONC; Dir JEAN-BERNARD MOURIER.

TV-4: 8 chemin Fontbrune, 97400 Saint-Denis; tel. 262-52-73-73; broadcasts 19 hours daily.

Other privately owned television services include TVB, TVE, RTV, Télé-Réunion and TV-Run.

Finance

(cap. = capital; res = reserves; dep. = deposits; m. = million; brs = branches)

BANKING

Central Bank

Institut d'Émission des Départements d'Outre-mer: 4 rue de la Compagnie des Indes, 97487 Saint-Denis Cédex; tel. 262-90-71-00; fax 262-21-41-32; e-mail agence@iedom-reunion.fr; internet www.iedom.fr/reunion; Dir ARNAUD BELLAMY-BROWN.

Commercial Banks

Banque Française Commerciale Océan Indien (BFCOI): 60 rue Alexis de Villeneuve, BP 323, 97466 Saint-Denis Cédex; tel. 262-40-55-55; fax 262-25-21-47; e-mail webmaster@bfcoi.com; internet www.bfcoi.com; f. 1976; cap. €16.7m., res €65.9m., dep. €1,302.4m. (Dec. 2008); Pres. PIERRE GUY-NOEL; Gen. Man. ROGER MUNOZ; 8 brs.

Banque Nationale de Paris Intercontinentale: 67 rue Juliette Dodu, BP 113, 97463 Saint-Denis; tel. 262-40-30-02; fax 262-41-39-09; e-mail contactreunion@bnpparibas.com; internet www.bnpgroup.com; f. 1927; 100% owned by BNP Paribas; Chair. MICHEL PEBEREAU; Man. Dir DANIEL DEGUIN; 16 brs.

Banque de la Réunion (BR), SA: 27 rue Jean Chatel, 97711 Saint-Denis Cédex; tel. 262-40-01-23; fax 262-40-00-61; internet www.banquedelareunion.fr; f. 1853; owned by Groupe Banque Populaire et Caisse d'Epargne (France); cap. €65.4m., res €112.0m., dep. €2,010.8m. (Dec. 2008); Pres. BRUNO DELETRE; Gen. Man. BENOÎT CATEL; 20 brs.

BRED-Banque Populaire: 33 rue Victor MacAuliffe, 97461 Saint-Denis; tel. 262-90-15-60; fax 262-90-15-99.

Crédit Agricole de la Réunion: Parc Jean de Cambiaire, Cité des Lauriers, BP 84, 97462 Saint-Denis Cédex; tel. 262-40-81-81; fax 262-40-81-40; internet www.ca-reunion.fr; f. 1949; total assets €2,564m. (Dec. 2004); Chair. CHRISTIAN DE LA GIRODAY; Gen. Man. PIERRE MARTIN.

Development Bank

Société Financière pour le Développement Economique de la Réunion (SOFIDER): 3 rue Labourdonnais, BP 867, 97477 Saint-Denis Cédex; tel. 262-40-32-32; fax 262-40-32-00; internet www.sofider.re; part of the Agence Française de Développement; Dir-Gen. CLAUDE PÉRIOU.

INSURANCE

More than 20 major European insurance companies are represented in Saint-Denis.

AGF Vie La Réunion: 185 ave du Général de Gaulle, BP 797, 97476 Saint-Denis Cédex; tel. 262-94-72-23; fax 262-94-72-26; e-mail agfoi-vie@agfoi.com.

Capma & Capmi: 18 rue de la Cie des Indes, 97499 Saint-Denis; tel. 262-21-10-56; fax 262-20-32-67.

Groupama Océan Indien et Pacifique: 13 rue Fénelon, BP 626, 97473 Saint-Denis Cédex; tel. 262-26-12-61; fax 262-41-50-79; Chair. DIDIER FOUCQUE; Gen. Man. MAURICE FAURE (acting).

Trade and Industry

GOVERNMENT AGENCIES

Agence de Gestion des Initiatives Locales en Matière Européenne (AGILE)—Cellule Europe Réunion: 3 rue Felix Guyon, 97400 Saint-Denis; tel. 262-90-10-80; fax 262-21-90-72; e-mail celleurope@agile-reunion.org; internet www.agile-reunion.org; responsible for local application of EU structural funds; Dir SERGE JOSEPH.

Agence Régionale de Santé Océan Indien (ARS-OI): 2 bis ave Georges Brassens, CS 60050, 97408 Saint-Denis Messag Cédex 9; tel. 262-97-90-00; e-mail ars-oi-delegation-reunion@ars.sante.fr; internet www.ars.ocean-indien.sante.fr; f. 2010; responsible for implementation of health policies in Réunion and Mayotte; Dir-Gen. CHANTAL DE SINGLY.

Conseil Economique et Social de la Réunion (CESR): 10 rue du Béarn, BP 7191, 97719 Saint-Denis Messag Cédex; tel. 262-97-96-30; fax 262-97-96-31; e-mail cesr-reunion@cesr-reunion.fr; internet www.cesr-reunion.fr; f. 1984; Pres. JEAN-RAYMOND MONDON; Dir DIDIER LAMOTTE.

Direction Départementale de la Jeunesse, des Sports et de la Vie Associative de la Réunion (DDJS): 14 allée des Saphirs, 97487 Saint-Denis Cédex; tel. 262-20-96-40; fax 262-20-96-41; e-mail dd974@jeunesse-sports.gouv.fr; internet www.ddjs-reunion.jeunesse-sports.gouv.fr; Departmental Dir RÉGIS BERTOGLI.

Direction Régionale des Affaires Culturelles de la Réunion (DRAC): 23 rue Labourdonnais, BP 224, 97464 Saint-Denis Cédex; tel. 262-21-91-71; fax 262-41-61-93; e-mail drac-la.reunion@culture.gouv.fr; internet www.reunion.pref.gouv.fr/drac; f. 1992; responsible to the French Ministry of Culture; Regional Dir JEAN-MARC BOYER.

Direction Régionale du Commerce Extérieur (DRCE): 3 rue Serge Ycard, 97490 Sainte-Clotilde; tel. 262-92-24-70; fax 262-92-24-76; e-mail reunion@missioneco.org; internet www.missioneco.org/reunion; Dir PHILIPPE GENIER.

Direction Régionale de l'Environnement (DIREN): 12 allée de la Forêt, Parc de la Providence, 97400 Saint-Denis; tel. 262-94-78-11; fax 262-94-72-55; e-mail estelle.loiseau@reunion.ecologie.gouv.fr; internet www.reunion.ecologie.gouv.fr; Regional Dir BERTRAND GALTIER.

Direction Régionale de l'Industrie, de la Recherche et de l'Environnement: 130 rue Léopold Rambaud, 97495 Sainte-Clotilde Cédex; tel. 262-92-41-10; fax 262-29-37-31; internet www.reunion.drire.gouv.fr; Reg. Dir JEAN-CHARLES ARDIN; Sec.-Gen. JACQUELINE LECHEVIN.

DEVELOPMENT ORGANIZATIONS

Agence de Développement de la Réunion (AD): rue Serge Ycart, BP 33, 97490 Sainte-Clotilde Cedex; tel. 262-92-24-92; fax 262-92-24-88; e-mail info@adreunion.com; internet www.adreunion.com; JISMY SOUPRAYENMESTRY.

Agence Française de Développement (AFD): 44 rue Jean Cocteau, BP 2013, 97488 Saint-Denis Cédex; tel. 262-90-00-90; fax 262-21-74-58; e-mail afdstdenis@re.groupe-afd.org; Dir LAURENT FONTAINE.

Association pour le Développement Industriel de la Réunion: 8 rue Philibert, BP 327, 97466 Saint-Denis Cédex; tel. 262-94-43-00; fax 262-94-43-09; e-mail adir@adir.info; internet www.adir.info; f. 1975; Pres. MAURICE CERISOLA; Sec.-Gen. FRANÇOISE DELMONT DE PALMAS; 190 mems.

Chambre d'Agriculture de la Réunion: 24 rue de la Source, BP 134, 97463 Saint-Denis Cédex; tel. 262-94-25-94; fax 262-21-06-17; e-mail president@reunion.chambagri.fr; internet www.reunion.chambagri.fr; Pres. JEAN-YVES MINATCHY; Gen. Man. JEAN-FRANÇOIS APAYA.

Jeune Chambre Economique de Saint-Denis de la Réunion: 25 rue de Paris, BP 1151, 97483 Saint-Denis; f. 1963; Chair. STÉPHANE CAZANOVE; 30 mems.

Société de Développement Economique de la Réunion (SODERE): 26 rue Labourdonnais, 97469 Saint-Denis; tel. 262-20-01-68; fax 262-20-05-07; f. 1964; Chair. RAYMOND VIVET; Man. Dir ALBERT TRIMAILLE.

CHAMBERS OF COMMERCE

Chambre de Commerce et d'Industrie de la Réunion (CCIR): 5 bis rue de Paris, BP 120, 97463 Saint-Denis Cédex; tel. 262-94-20-00; fax 262-94-22-90; e-mail sg.dir@reunion.cci.fr; internet www.reunion.cci.fr; f. 1830; Pres. ERIC MAGAMOOTOO; Dir MOHAMED AHMED.

Chambre de Métiers et de l'Artisanat: 42 rue Jean Cocteau, BP 261, 97465 Saint-Denis Cédex; tel. 262-21-04-35; fax 262-21-68-33; e-mail cdm@cm-reunion.fr; internet www.cm-reunion.fr; f. 1968; Pres. BERNARD PICARDO; Sec. BENJAMINE DE OLIVEIRA; 14 mem. orgs.

EMPLOYERS' ASSOCIATIONS

Conseil de l'Ordre des Pharmaciens: 1 bis rue Sainte Anne, Immeuble le Concorde, Appt. 26, 1er étage, 97400 Saint-Denis; tel. 262-41-85-51; fax 262-21-94-86; e-mail delegation_reunion@ordre.pharmacien.fr; Pres. CHRISTIANE VAN DE WALLE.

Fédération Régionale des Coopératives Agricoles de la Réunion (FRCA): 8 bis, route de la Z. I. No. 2 97410, Saint-Pierre; tel. 262-96-24-40; fax 262-96-24-41; internet www.frca-reunion.coop; f. 1979; Pres. JEAN-FLORE BARRET; Sec.-Gen. RITO FERRERE; 27 mem. orgs.

Coopérative Agricole des Huiles Essentielles de Bourbon (CAHEB): 83 rue de Kerveguen, 97430 Le Tampon; BP 43, 97831 Le Tampon; tel. 262-27-02-27; fax 262-27-35-54; e-mail caheb@geranium-bourbon.com; f. 1963; represents producers of essential oils; Pres. MARIE ROSE SEVERIN; Sec.-Gen. LAURENT JANCI.

Société Coopérative Agricole Fruits de la Réunion: 18 Bellevue Pâturage, 97450 Saint-Louis; fax 262-91-41-04; f. 2002; Pres. CHRISTIAN BARRET.

Union Réunionnaise des Coopératives Agricoles (URCOOPA): Z. I. Cambaie, BP 90, 97862 Saint-Paul Cedex; tel. 262-45-37-10; fax 262-45-37-05; e-mail urcoopa@urcoopa.fr; internet www.urcoopa.fr; f. 1982; represents farmers; comprises Coop Avirons (f. 1967), Société Coopérative Agricole Nord-Est (CANE), SICA Lait (f. 1961), and CPPR; Pres. ARY MONDON; Dir-Gen. OLIVIER RONIN.

Mouvement des Entreprises de France Réunion (MEDEF): 14 rampes Ozoux, BP 354, 97467 Saint-Denis; tel. 262-20-01-30; fax 262-41-68-56; e-mail medef.reunion@wanadoo.fr; Pres. FRANÇOIS CAILLÉ.

Ordre National de Médecins: 3 résidence Laura, 4 rue Milius, 97400 Saint-Denis; tel. 262-20-11-58; fax 262-21-08-02; e-mail reunion@974.medecin.fr; internet www.odmreunion.net; Pres. Dr YVAN TCHENG.

Syndicat des Fabricants de Sucre de la Réunion: 23 rue Raymond Vergès, Quartier Français, 97441 Sainte-Suzanne; tel. 262-72-18-00; fax 261-72-18-01; e-mail ft@sfsnuu.com; Chair. JEAN-FRANÇOIS MOSER; Dir FLORENT THIBAULT.

Syndicat des Pharmaciens de la Réunion: 1 ave Marcel Hoarau, 97490 Sainte-Clotilde; tel. 262-28-53-60; fax 262-28-79-67; e-mail synd974@resopharma.fr; Pres. FRÉDE SAUTRON.

Syndicat des Producteurs de Rhum de la Réunion: chemin Frédéline, BP 354, 97453 Saint-Pierre Cédex; tel. 262-25-84-27; fax 262-35-60-92; Chair. OLIVIER THIEBLIN.

TRADE UNIONS

CFE-CGC de la Réunion: 1 Rampes Ozoux, Résidence de la Rivière, Appt 2A, BP 873, 97477 Saint-Denis Cédex; tel. 262-90-11-95; fax 262-90-11-99; e-mail union@cfecgcreunion.com; internet www.cfecgcreunion.com; departmental br. of the Confédération Française de l'Encadrement-Confédération Générale des Cadres; represents engineers, teaching, managerial and professional staff and technicians; Pres. ALAIN IGLICKI; Sec.-Gen. DANIEL THIAW-WING-KAI.

Confédération Générale du Travail de la Réunion (CGTR): 144 rue du Général de Gaulle, BP 1132, 97482 Saint-Denis Cédex; Sec.-Gen. GEORGES MARIE LEPINAY.

Fédération Départementale des Syndicats d'Exploitants Agricoles de la Réunion (FDSEA): 105 rue Amiral Lacaze, Terre Sainte, 97410 Saint-Pierre; tel. 262-96-33-53; fax 262-96-33-90; e-mail fdsea-reunion@wanadoo.fr; affiliated to the Fédération Nationale des Syndicats d'Exploitants; Sec.-Gen. JEAN-BERNARD HOARAU.

Fédération Réunionnaise du Bâtiment et des Travaux Publics: BP 108, 97462 Saint-Denis Cédex; tel. 262-41-70-87; fax 262-21-55-07; Pres. J. M. LE BOURVELLEC.

Fédération Syndicale Unitaire Réunion (FSU): 4 rue de la Cure, BP 279, 97494 Sainte-Clotilde Cédex; tel. 262-86-29-46; fax 262-22-35-28; e-mail fsu974@fsu.fr; internet sd974.fsu.fr; f. 1993; departmental br. of the Fédération Syndicale Unitaire; represents public sector employees in sectors incl. teaching, research, and training, and also agriculture, justice, youth and sports, and culture; Sec. CHRISTIAN PICARD.

Union Départementale Confédération Française des Travailleurs Chrétiens (UD CFTC): Résidence Pointe des Jardins, 1 rue de l'Atillerie, 97400 Saint-Denis; tel. 262-41-22-85; fax 262-41-26-85; e-mail usctr@wanadoo.fr.

Union Départementale Force Ouvrière de la Réunion (FO): 81 rue Labourdonnais, BP 853, 97477 Saint-Denis Cédex; tel. 262-21-31-35; fax 262-41-33-23; e-mail eric.marguerite@laposte.net; Sec.-Gen. ERIC MARGUERITE.

Union Interprofessionnelle de la Réunion (UIR-CFDT): 58 rue Fénelon, 97400 Saint-Denis; tel. 262-90-27-67; fax 262-21-03-22; e-mail uir.cfdt@wanadoo.fr; affiliated to the Confédération Française Démocratique du Travail; Sec.-Gen. JEAN-PIERRE RIVIERE.

Affiliated unions incl.:

FEP-CFDT Réunion: 58 rue Fénélon, 97400 Saint-Denis; tel. 262-90-27-67; fax 262-21-03-22; e-mail jpmarchau@uir-cfdt.org; affiliated to the Fédération Formation et Enseignement Privés; represents private sector teaching staff.

SGEN-CFDT: 58 rue Fénélon, 97400 Saint-Denis; tel. 262-90-27-72; fax 262-21-03-22; e-mail reunion@sgen.cfdt.fr; internet www.sgen-cfdt-reunion.org; mem. of Union Interprofessionnelle de la Réunion; represents teaching staff; Sec.-Gen. JEAN-LOUIS BELHÔTE.

Union Régionale UNSA-Education: BP 169, 97464 Saint-Denis Cédex; tel. 262-20-02-25; fax 262-21-58-65; e-mail urreunio@unsa.org; represents teaching staff; Sec.-Gen. ERIC CHAVRIACOUTY.

Transport

ROADS

A route nationale circles the island, generally following the coast and linking the main towns. Another route nationale crosses the island from south-west to north-east linking Saint-Pierre and Saint-Benoît. In 1994 there were 370 km of routes nationales, 754 km of departmental roads and 1,630 km of other roads; 1,300 km of the roads were bituminized. Discussions began in the mid-2000s regarding a proposed 'tram-train' network that would link Saint-Benoît to Saint-Joseph via Saint-Denis. However, by mid-2012 no progress had been made with this project.

Société d'Economie Mixte des Transports, Tourisme, Equipements et Loisirs (SEMITTEL): 24 chemin Benoite-Boulard, 97410 Saint-Pierre; tel. 262-55-40-60; fax 262-55-49-56; e-mail semittel@semittel.fr; f. 1984; bus service operator; Pres. MARRIE PERIANAYAGOM.

Société des Transports Départementaux de la Réunion (SOTRADER): 2 allée Bonnier, 97400 Saint-Denis; tel. 262-94-89-40; fax 262-94-89-50; f. 1995; bus service operator; Dir-Gen. FRÉDÉRIC DELOUYE.

SHIPPING

In 1986 work was completed on the expansion of the Port de la Pointe des Galets, which was divided into the former port in the west and a new port in the east (the port Ouest and the port Est), known together as Port Réunion. In 2009 some 3.3m. metric tons of freight were unloaded and 594,700 tons loaded at the two ports. The Chambre de Commerce et d'Industrie de la Réunion also manages three yachting marinas.

Port Authority (Concession Portuaire): rue Evariste de Parny, BP 18, 97821 Le Port Cédex; tel. 262-42-90-00; fax 262-42-47-90; internet www.reunion.port.fr; Dir BRUNO DAVIDSEN.

CMA CGM Réunion: 85 rue Jules Verne, Z.I. No. 2, BP 2007, 97822 Le Port Cédex; tel. 262-55-10-10; fax 262-43-23-04; e-mail lar.genmbox@cma-cgm.com; internet www.cmacgm.com; f. 1996 by merger of Cie Générale Maritime and Cie Maritime d'Affrètement; shipping agents; Man. Dir VALÉRIE SEVENO.

Mediterranean Shipping Co France (Réunion), S.A. (MSC): 1 bis, Gustave Eiffel, Z.A.C. 2000, BP 221, 97825 Le Port Cédex; tel. 262-42-78-00; fax 262-42-78-10; e-mail msclareunion@mscfr.mscgva.ch; internet www.mscreunion.com.

Réunion Ships Agency (RSA): 17 rue R. Hoareau, BP 10186, 97825 Le Port Cédex; tel. 262-43-33-33; fax 262-42-03-10; e-mail rsa@indoceanic.com; internet www.indoceanic.com; f. 1975; subsidiary of Indoceanic Services; Man. Dir HAROLD JOSÉ THOMSON.

Société d'Acconage et de Manutention de la Réunionnaise (SAMR): 3 ave Théodore Drouhet, Z.A.C. 2000, BP 40, 97821 Le Port Cédex; tel. 262-55-17-55; fax 262-55-17-62; stevedoring; Pres. DOMINIQUE LAFONT; Man. MICHEL ANTONELLI.

Société de Manutention et de Consignation Maritime (SOMACOM): 3 rue Gustave Eiffel, Zac 2000, BP 97420, Le Port; tel. 262-42-60-00; fax 262-42-60-10; stevedoring and shipping agents; Gen. Man. DANIEL RIGAT.

Société Réunionnaise de Services Maritimes (SRSM): 3 ave Théodore Drouhet, Z.A.C. 2000, BP 2006, 97822 Le Port Cédex; tel. 262-55-17-55; fax 262-55-17-62; e-mail n.hoarau@dri-reunion.com; freight only; Man. MICHEL ANTONELLI.

CIVIL AVIATION

Réunion's international airport, Roland Garros-Gillot, is situated 8 km from Saint-Denis. A programme to develop the airport was completed in 1994. In 1997 work commenced on the extension of its terminal, at a cost of some 175m. French francs, and the project was completed in 2002. The Pierrefonds airfield, 5 km from Saint-Pierre, commenced operating as an international airport in December 1998 following its development at an estimated cost of nearly 50m. French francs. Air France, Corsair and Air Austral operate international services. In 2009 Roland Garros-Gillot handled some 1.75m. passengers, while Pierrefonds airport handled 126,651 passengers.

Air Austral: 4 rue de Nice, 97400 Saint-Denis; tel. 262-90-90-91; fax 262-29-28-95; e-mail reservation@air-austral.com; internet www.airaustral.com; f. 1975; subsidiary of Air France; Dir-Gen. GÉRARD ETHEVE.

Tourism

Réunion's attractions include spectacular scenery and a pleasant climate. In January 2010 the island had some 2,090 hotel rooms. In 2010 some 420,300 tourists visited Réunion. Receipts from tourism in 2009 were €305.8m.

Délégation Régionale au Commerce, à l'Artisanat et au Tourisme: Préfecture de la Réunion, 97400 Saint-Denis; tel. 262-40-77-58; fax 262-50-77-15; Dir PHILIPPE JEAN LEGLISE.

L'île de la Réunion Tourisme (IRT): pl. du 20 décembre 1848, BP 615, 97472 Saint-Denis Cédex; tel. 262-21-00-41; fax 262-21-00-21; e-mail ctr@la-reunion-tourisme.com; internet www.reunion.fr; fmrly Comité du Tourisme de la Réunion; name changed as above in 2009; Pres. JACQUELINE FARREYROL.

Office du Tourisme Intercommunal du Nord: 2 pl. Etienne Regnault, 97400 Saint-Denis; tel. 262-41-83-00; fax 262-21-37-76; e-mail info@ot-nordreunion.com; Pres. FRÉDÉRIC FOUCQUE; Dir CATHERINE GLAVNIK.

Defence

Réunion is the headquarters of French military forces in the Indian Ocean and French Southern and Antarctic Territories. As assessed at November 2009, there were 1,000 French troops stationed on Réunion and Mayotte, including a gendarmerie.

Education

Education is modelled on the French system, and is compulsory for 10 years between the ages of six and 16 years. Primary education begins at six years of age and lasts for five years. Secondary education, which begins at 11 years of age, lasts for up to seven years, comprising a first cycle of four years and a second of three years. In the academic year 2009/10 there were 41,019 pupils enrolled at pre-primary schools and 70,241 at primary schools. In the academic year 2008/09 there were 101,262 pupils enrolled at secondary schools. There is a university, with several faculties, providing higher education in law, economics, politics, and French language and literature, and a teacher-training college. In 2008/09 11,310 students were enrolled at the university.

French Overseas Collectivities

As amended in March 2003, the Constitution defines French Polynesia, Saint Pierre and Miquelon, and the Wallis and Futuna Islands as having the status of Overseas Collectivities (Collectivités d'outre-mer) within the French Republic. Under an organic law of February 2007, Saint-Barthélemy and Saint-Martin were, additionally, each accorded the status of Overseas Collectivity. The territories within this category have a greater degree of independence than do the Overseas Departments and Territories, with the particular status of each being defined by an individual organic law. Local assemblies may establish internal legislation. An organic law of February 2004 accords to French Polynesia the unique designation of Overseas Country (Pays d'outre-mer), while it retains the legal status of an Overseas Collectivity. Mayotte, which was previously an Overseas Collectivity became an Overseas Department of France at the end of March 2011.

FRENCH POLYNESIA

Introductory Survey

LOCATION, CLIMATE, LANGUAGE, RELIGION, FLAG, CAPITAL

French Polynesia comprises several scattered groups of islands in the South Pacific Ocean, lying about two-thirds of the way between the Panama Canal and New Zealand. Its nearest neighbours are the Cook Islands, to the west, and the Line Islands (part of Kiribati), to the north-west. French Polynesia consists of the following island groups: the Windward Islands (Iles du Vent—including the islands of Tahiti and Moorea) and the Leeward Islands (Iles Sous le Vent—located about 160 km north-west of Tahiti) which, together, constitute the Society Archipelago; the Tuamotu Archipelago, which comprises some 80 atolls scattered east of the Society Archipelago in a line stretching north-west to south-east for about 1,500 km; the Gambier Islands, located 1,600 km south-east of Tahiti; the Austral Islands, lying 640 km south of Tahiti; and the Marquesas Archipelago, which lies 1,450 km north-east of Tahiti. There are 35 islands and 83 atolls in all, of which 76 are populated. The average monthly temperature throughout the year varies between 20°C (68°F) and 29°C (84°F), and most rainfall occurs between November and April, the average annual precipitation being 1,625 mm (64 ins). The official languages are French and Tahitian. Seven Polynesian languages and their dialects are spoken by the indigenous population. The principal religion is Christianity; about 54% of the population is Protestant and some 38% Roman Catholic. The official flag is the French tricolour. Subordinate to this, the French Polynesian flag (proportions 2 by 3), comprises three horizontal stripes, of red, white (half the depth) and red, with, in the centre, the arms of French Polynesia, consisting of a representation in red of a native canoe, bearing a platform supporting five stylized persons, on a circular background (five wavy horizontal dark blue bands, surmounted by 10 golden sunrays). The capital is Papeete, on the island of Tahiti.

CONTEMPORARY POLITICAL HISTORY

Historical Context

Tahiti, the largest of the Society Islands, and the other island groups were annexed by France in the late 19th century. The islands were governed from France under a decree of 1885 until 1946, when French Polynesia became an Overseas Territory, administered by a Governor in Papeete. A Territorial Assembly and a Council of Government were established to advise the Governor.

Between May 1975 and May 1982 a majority in the Territorial Assembly sought independence for French Polynesia. Following pressure by Francis Sanford, leader of the largest autonomist party in the Assembly, a new Constitution for the Territory was negotiated with the French Government and approved by a newly elected Assembly in 1977. Under the provisions of the new statute, France retained responsibility for foreign affairs, defence, monetary matters and justice, but the powers of the territorial Council of Government were increased, especially in the field of commerce. The French Governor was replaced by a High Commissioner, who was to preside over the Council of Government and was head of the administration, but had no vote. The Council's elected Vice-President, responsible for domestic affairs, was granted greater powers. An Economic, Social and Cultural Council, responsible for all development matters, was also created, and French Polynesia's economic zone was extended to 200 nautical miles (370 km) from the islands' coastline.

Domestic Political Affairs

Following elections to the Territorial Assembly in May 1982, the Gaullist Tahoera'a Huiraatira (People's Rally), led by Gaston Flosse, which secured 13 of the 30 seats, formed successive ruling coalitions, first with the Ai'a Api (New Land) party and in September with the Pupu Here Ai'a Te Nunaa Ia Ora party. Seeking self-government, especially in economic matters, elected representatives of the Assembly held discussions with the French Government in Paris in 1983, and in September 1984 a new statute was approved by the French Assemblée nationale (National Assembly). This allowed the territorial Government greater powers, mainly in the sphere of commerce and development; the Council of Government was replaced by a Council of Ministers, whose President was to be elected from among the members of the Territorial Assembly. Flosse became the first President of the Council of Ministers.

At elections held in March 1986 the Tahoera'a Huiraatira gained the first outright majority to be achieved in the Territory, winning 24 of the 41 seats in the Territorial Assembly. Leaders of opposition parties subsequently expressed dissatisfaction with the election result, claiming that the Tahoera'a Huiraatira victory had been secured only as a result of the allocation of a disproportionately large number of seats in the Territorial Assembly to one of the five constituencies. The constituency at the centre of the dispute comprised the Mangareva and Tuamotu islands, where the two French army bases at Hao and Mururoa constituted a powerful body of support for Flosse and the Tahoera'a Huiraatira, which, in spite of winning a majority of seats, had obtained a minority of individual votes in the election. At concurrent elections for French Polynesia's two seats in the Assemblée nationale in Paris, Flosse and Alexandre Léontieff, the candidates of the Rassemblement pour la République (RPR—to which the Tahoera'a Huiraatira was affiliated, latterly the Union pour un Mouvement Populaire), were elected, Flosse subsequently ceding his seat to Edouard Fritch. Later in March the French Prime Minister, Jacques Chirac, appointed Flosse to a post in the French Council of Ministers, assigning him the portfolio of Secretary of State for South Pacific Affairs.

In April 1986 Flosse was re-elected President of the Council of Ministers. However, he was severely criticized by leaders of the opposition for his allegedly inefficient and extravagant use of public funds, and was accused, in particular, of corrupt electoral practice. Flosse resigned as President in February 1987, and was replaced by Jacques Teuira.

In December 1987, amid growing discontent over his policies, Teuira and the entire Council of Ministers resigned and were replaced by a coalition of opposition parties and the Te Tiaraama party (a breakaway faction of the Tahoera'a Huiraatira) under the presidency of Alexandre Léontieff. The Léontieff Government survived several challenges in the Territorial Assembly to its continuation in office during 1988–89. Amendments to the Polynesian Constitution, which were approved by the French legislature and enacted by July 1990, augmented the powers of the President of the Council of Ministers and increased the competence of the Territorial Assembly.

At territorial elections in March 1991 the Tahoera'a Huiraatira won 18 of the 41 seats. Flosse then formed a coalition with the Ai'a Api, thereby securing a majority of 23 seats in the Territorial Assembly. Emile Vernaudon, leader of the Ai'a Api, was elected President of the Assembly and Flosse was elected President of the Council of Ministers. In September Flosse announced the end of the coalition between his party and the Ai'a Api, accusing Vernaudon of disloyalty, and signed a new alliance with the Pupu Here Ai'a Te Nunaa Ia Ora, led by Jean Juventin.

In April 1992 Flosse was found guilty of fraud (relating to an illegal sale of government land to a member of his family) and there were widespread demands for his resignation. In November Juventin and Léontieff were charged with 'passive' corruption, relating to the construction of a golf course by a Japanese company. In the following month the French Court of Appeal upheld the judgment against Flosse, who received a six-month, suspended prison sentence. The case provoked a demonstration by more than 3,000 people in January 1993, demanding the resignation of Flosse and Juventin. In September 1994 Flosse succeeded in having the conviction rescinded, on a procedural issue, in a second court of appeal. In October 1997, however, Léontieff was found guilty of accepting substantial bribes in order to facilitate a business venture and was sentenced to three years' imprisonment (one-half of which was to be suspended). In May 1998 Léontieff was sentenced to a further three years' imprisonment (two of which were to be suspended) for corruption.

When the French authorities resumed nuclear testing in September 1995 (see Nuclear Testing and Relations with Metropolitan France), peaceful protests in Tahiti rapidly developed into full-scale riots, as several thousand demonstrators rampaged through Papeete, demanding an end to French rule. Violent clashes with police, and the burning of dozens of buildings in Papeete during the riots, left much of the capital in ruins.

In November 1995 the Territorial Assembly adopted a draft statute of autonomy, which proposed the extension of the Territory's powers to areas such as fishing, mining and shipping rights, international transport and communications, broadcasting and the offshore economic zone. However, France would retain full responsibility for defence, justice and security in the islands. Advocates of independence for French Polynesia criticized the statute for promising only relatively superficial changes, while failing to increase the democratic rights of the islanders. The statute was approved by the French Assemblée nationale in December and entered into force in April 1996.

At territorial elections held in May 1996 the Tahoera'a Huiraatira achieved an outright majority, although the principal pro-independence party, Tavini Huiraatira/Front de Libération de la Polynésie (FLP), made considerable gains throughout the Territory (largely owing to increased popular hostility towards France since the resumption of nuclear-weapons tests at Mururoa Atoll—see Nuclear Testing and Relations with Metropolitan France). The Tahoera'a Huiraatira secured 22 of the 41 seats in the Territorial Assembly, while Tavini Huiraatira won 10 seats. Other anti-independence parties won a total of eight seats and an additional pro-independence grouping secured one seat. Flosse defeated the pro-independence leader, Oscar Temaru, by 28 votes to 11 to remain as President of the Council of Ministers later in the month, and Justin Arapari was elected President of the Territorial Assembly. Allegations of voting irregularities led to legal challenges, which annulled the results in 11 constituencies. Following by-elections in May 1998 for the 11 seats, the Tahoera'a Huiraatira increased its representation by one seat. Tavini Huiraatira again claimed that the elections had not been fairly conducted.

At elections for French Polynesia's two seats in the French Assemblée nationale in May 1997 Michel Buillard and Emile Vernaudon, both supporters of the RPR, were elected with 52% and 59% of total votes cast, respectively. However, Oscar Temaru was a strong contender for the western constituency seat, securing 42% of the votes. Flosse was re-elected as the Territory's representative to the French Sénat (Senate) in September 1998.

In March 1999 proposals to increase French Polynesia's autonomy, as part of constitutional reforms, were announced in Paris. These proposals followed an initial agreement between the Territory and the French Government in late 1998 on the future of French Polynesia. In October 1999 the French Sénat adopted a constitutional amendment, approved by the Assemblée nationale in June, designating French Polynesia as an Overseas Country (Pays d'outre-mer) and creating a new Polynesian citizenship. Although France was to retain control over areas such as foreign affairs, defence, justice and electoral laws, French Polynesia would have the power to negotiate with other Pacific countries and sign its own international treaties. The constitutional amendment was presented to a joint session of the French Sénat and Assemblée nationale for final ratification in January 2000, although no decision on the matter was taken.

In November 1999 Flosse was found guilty of corruption, on charges of accepting more than 2.7m. French francs in bribes from the owner of an illegal casino, allegedly to help fund his party. Flosse was sentenced to a two-year suspended prison term, a large fine and a one-year ban on seeking office. Demonstrations, organized by the pro-independence FLP, took place in Tahiti, in protest at Flosse's refusal to resign from his post as President of the Council of Ministers. In October 2000 Flosse lodged an appeal with the High Court, which reversed the ruling in May 2001. In November 2002 the Court of Appeal in Paris announced that Flosse should be pardoned.

In December 2000 provision was made for the number of seats in the Territorial Assembly to be increased from 41 to 49, in an attempt to reflect demographic changes more accurately. At elections in May 2001, the Tahoera'a Huiraatira won 28 seats, securing a fifth successive term in office. The pro-independence Tavini Huiraatira took 13 seats. Flosse was subsequently re-elected President of the Council of Ministers.

In January 2002 representatives of state and local government met to review the first five years of the Restructuring Fund, an agreement implemented in 1996 to further the economic autonomy of Polynesia and to regulate financial subsidies to the Territory following the cessation of nuclear testing (Nuclear Testing and Relations with Metropolitan France). The President and Prime Minister of France took part in similar meetings in mid-2002, when it was agreed that funding would be extended for 10 years after 2006. In June 2002 elections for the Territory's two seats in the Assemblée nationale were won by Tahoera'a Huiraatira candidates Michel Buillard and Béatrice Vernaudon.

In December 2002 the French Sénat approved legislation providing for a constitutional amendment that would allow French Polynesia (along with Wallis and Futuna) to be designated as an Overseas Country; both chambers of the French legislature ratified the amendments to the Constitution in March 2003. In July the Territorial Assembly and the Government ratified the amendments. Meanwhile, in May 2003 it was announced that French Polynesia (together with New Caledonia) was to be allocated one additional seat in the French Sénat. About 2,000 islanders, led by Oscar Temaru, demonstrated in favour of self-determination during an official visit to French Polynesia by President Jacques Chirac in July 2003.

The final text of the autonomy statute was approved by the Assemblée nationale in January 2004, and a decree formally designating French Polynesia as an Overseas Country of France was signed by President Chirac in March. French Polynesia was thus granted greater authority over matters such as labour law, civil aviation and regional relations, with France retaining control of law and order, defence and money supply. In April 2004 the local legislature was dissolved, in preparation for the holding of an election to a new 57-member Assembly in May.

At elections for the newly expanded French Polynesia Assembly held on 23 May 2004, the Tahoera'a Huiraatira, led by Gaston Flosse, won 28 of the 57 seats. An opposition coalition, the Union pour la démocratie (UPD), comprising the pro-independence Tavini Huiraatira and various minor parties, secured 27 seats and the remaining two seats were taken by opposition parties favouring autonomy. The Tahoera'a Huiraatira thus lost its overall majority in the Assembly for the first time in 20 years. Flosse disputed the results, claiming that there had been irregularities in the electoral process. In June the new legislature elected Antony Géros of Tavini Huiraatira as President of the Assembly. Oscar Temaru, leader of Tavini Huiraatira, was elected President of the Council of Ministers and announced the composition of a streamlined 10-member cabinet two days later.

In early September divisions over the 2004 appropriation bill brought the legislative process to a halt. Three members of the Assembly resigned from the UPD coalition, two of them to sit as independents, with the third joining the opposition Tahoera'a Huiraatira. In early October separate motions of no confidence were filed against the Government by the Tahoera'a Huiraatira and the newly formed Te' Avei'a (Te Ara) party, comprising six former members of the ruling UPD coalition and the Tahoera'a Huiraatira. In early October Oscar Temaru twice appealed to the French Government to dissolve the Assembly and to hold new elections. In mid-October 22,000 people took part in the largest demonstration ever witnessed in French Polynesia, demanding the dissolution of the Assembly. The French Minister for Overseas Territories, Brigitte Girardin, refused to accept that such demands were justified. The motions of no confidence were endorsed by 29 of the 57 legislators (the members of the UPD refusing to vote), thus requiring the Assembly to choose a new President of the Council of Ministers. The 23 Tahoera'a Huiraatira and six Te' Avei'a members elected Gaston Flosse as President. However, the UPD members boycotted the vote and refused to recognize Flosse's authority. Temaru and his ministers refused to vacate the presidential building. Flosse's newly appointed 17-member Council of Ministers, which was largely drawn from his previous administration and included former Vice-President Edouard Fritch, was forced to operate at adjacent buildings.

The validity of Oscar Temaru's removal and the subsequent vote to elect Gaston Flosse as President of the Council of Ministers were both upheld by the French Conseil d'Etat (State Council). Under the new autonomy statute, the Assembly could vote to dissolve itself if it received a petition from 10% of the electorate, roughly equivalent to 15,000 people; by 19 November 2004 the UPD claimed to have collected 42,890 signatures, representing some 28% of the electorate. Both Temaru and Flosse sent delegations to Paris, to make representations to the French Government, led respectively by Nicole Bouteau (leader of the No Oe e Te Nunaa party) and Edouard Fritch. Temaru claimed that an audit of the accounts of the previous Flosse administration (1999–2004), begun in September, had been stopped. The French Conseil d'Etat began investigations into the conduct of the May legislative election and in mid-November declared the results in the Windward Islands null and void, thus requiring the holding of by-elections within three months. The decision also meant that the 37 legislators affected automatically lost their seats, among them Flosse, Temaru and the President of the Assembly, Antony Géros, who was replaced by Hiro Tefaarere. At the end of November leading representatives from all parties were summoned to Paris for discussions, which included Flosse, Temaru, Nicole Bouteau, Philip Schyle (of the Fe'tia Api party) and Jacky Briant (of the Heiura-Greens party). Despite an initial agreement in principle to hold a fresh legislative election, the talks broke down in early December. In mid-December the French Conseil d'Etat validated Gaston Flosse's appointment as President.

By-elections were held in the Windward Islands constituency on 13 February 2005. The parties of Nicole Bouteau and Philip Schyle stood on a joint platform (the Alliance pour une Démocratie Nouvelle—ADN) offering a 'third way'. Gaston Flosse's Tahoera'a Huiraatira won 10 of the 37 seats, having secured 40.0% of the votes. The seven-party UPD coalition, led by Oscar Temaru, won 25 seats, receiving 46.9% of the votes. The newly formed ADN took the constituency's remaining two seats. Overall, therefore, the Tahoera'a Huiraatira and the UPD now held 27 seats each in the Assembly. The ADN held three seats but refused to co-operate with either the Tahoera'a Huiraatira or the UPD, as a result of which neither of the two groupings was able to form a majority. Temaru brought a motion of no confidence against President Flosse, which was endorsed by 30 of the 57 members. The Assembly had 14 days within which to elect a new President of the Council of Ministers, while Flosse and his Government remained in office in an interim capacity. Temaru announced that he would be standing again for the presidency, while the Tahoera'a Huiraatira put forward Gaston Tong Sang, the serving Minister for Small and Medium-sized Enterprises, Industry, Trade and Energy. Temaru was elected as President by 29 votes to 26 on 4 March, following an initial boycott by members of the Tahoera'a Huiraatira. There were two blank ballots cast, believed to have been those of Nicole Bouteau and Philip Schyle. Temaru promptly announced the composition of his new 17-member Council of Ministers, which included Louis Frébault as Minister for Outer Islands Development, the portfolio he had held under the recent Flosse administration. Jacqui Drollet was reappointed as Vice-President. In April Antony Géros was returned as President of the Assembly, having received 28 of the 57 votes.

During March and April 2005 fuel supplies were interrupted by a blockade of the port by members of the Groupement d'Interventions de la Polynésie (GIP) protesting at a government review of the 1,300-member organization. The GIP had been established by President Gaston Flosse in 1998 to provide relief assistance to areas throughout the region affected by natural disasters; latterly, the organization had diversified into other areas including security, cleaning services and logistics. However, owing to its close links with Flosse, the GIP had developed the reputation of a 'private militia'. Temaru reportedly accused Flosse of trying to destabilize the Government through the GIP, and a police investigation into reports of an 'intelligence unit' within the GIP was conducted. The organization was subsequently divided into two separate bodies, for land and sea operations, with a renewed focus on disaster relief, and renamed To'a Arai ('vigilante force'); the GIP was officially dissolved in January 2006.

In July 2005 the former Secretary-General of the Tahoera'a Huiraatira and minister under Flosse, Jean-Christophe Bouissou, left the party to form the Rautahi party. He was joined in September by two more former ministers, Temauri Foster and Emma Algan: as a result, the Tahoera'a Huiraatira held 23 seats in the Assembly and the UPD 29 seats. Meanwhile, Anne Boquet replaced Michel Mathieu as French High Commissioner, and Emmanuel Porlier was appointed as French Polynesia's permanent representative to the European Union (EU, see p. 276) in Brussels. In early November the Government presented an economic reform programme that included a proposed increase in the minimum wage; however, the programme envisaged raising the necessary revenue through a 'solidarity' tax on personal income. Public protest culminated in a four-day general strike and demonstrations in Papeete at the end of that month. The Temaru Government was forced to seek alternative sources of revenue, principally by increasing the duty on alcohol and tobacco. In early December two more members of the Tahoera'a Huiraatira left the party, to sit as independent members of the Assembly, reducing the party's standing to 21 seats, compared with the 29 seats held by the UPD.

In February 2006 Temaru signed a new agreement with Anne Boquet, on behalf of the French Government, regarding the proportion of the economic development grant (dotation générale de développement économique—DGDE—see Economic Affairs) that could be used towards the Government's operating costs: the proportion would be reduced from 50% in 2005 to 35% in 2006, to 30% in 2007 and to 20% from 2008. The Tahoera'a Huiraatira lodged eight complaints with the French Conseil d'Etat against the introduction of new taxes, which included the levies on alcohol and tobacco. It was also reported that the budget approved for 2006 had been calculated on the basis that up to 45% of the DGDE would be allocated to operating costs. The Audit Office ruled that the budget was 'imbalanced' by some 2,000m. francs CFP and gave the Temaru Government 30 days in which to present a revised budget or face the possibility of state intervention. A revised budget was approved by the court in mid-March. Meanwhile, in January the Minister for Post and Telecommunications and Sports, Emile Vernaudon, was convicted of having used public property for personal benefit while serving as Mayor of Mahina (a district of Papeete) between 1992 and 1999; he received a one-year suspended prison sentence and was fined US $30,000. In April 2006 Antony Géros was replaced as President of the Assembly by Philip Schyle, of the Fe'tia Api party, who had secured 29 of the 57 members' votes.

In June 2006 a criminal court in Tahiti found former President Gaston Flosse guilty of corruption in relation to his son's purchase of a hotel. Flosse was given a three-month suspended prison sentence, but was not disqualified from his positions as member of the French Polynesian Assembly and representative to the Sénat in Paris. In October members of the O Oe To Oe Rima trade union protesting at rises in the cost of living, along with former employees of the recently dissolved GIP who were demanding compensation, erected road blockades in Papeete. After two weeks of disruption, hundreds of protesters gained access to the presidential palace and other government buildings, demanding that Oscar Temaru, who was attending a meeting of the Pacific Islands Forum (see p. 416) in Fiji, return to Papeete for negotiations. Security forces were deployed to eject the protesters and restore stability. In November reports emerged of dissent within the ruling coalition; in December the French Polynesian Assembly approved a motion of no confidence submitted by the opposition against the Government, resulting in President Temaru's removal from office. In late December 31 of the 57 members of the legislature voted in favour of installing Gaston Tong Sang, member of the Tahoera'a Huiraatira party and Mayor of Bora Bora, as President.

At the beginning of January 2007 Tong Sang appointed his cabinet, providing several positions for former ministers of the Temaru Government. In mid-January a vote on a no-confidence motion submitted to the legislature by the opposition failed to garner enough support to oust the new Government. Meanwhile, President Tong Sang paid an official visit to France in what was widely regarded as an attempt to improve relations with the French Government following the relatively tense period of Temaru's presidency. In February hundreds of supporters of the opposition took to the streets of Papeete to demand the holding of new elections. In March the former Minister for Post and Telecommunications and Sports, Emile Vernaudon, was convicted of corruption and therefore barred from public office. He was given a suspended 18-month prison sentence (in December he was arrested on further charges). In April Edouard Fritch, the former Vice-President of French Polynesia, was elected President of the Assembly, receiving only one vote more than his rival, Antony Géros. In the same month the formation of the Te Niu Hau Manahune (Principle of Democracy) party was announced. At its inaugural convention the party elected Teina Maraera, the Mayor of Rangiroa, as President, stated its aim of establishing a federal system for French Polynesian archipelagos and declared its support for the candidate of the Union pour un Mouvement Populaire (UMP), Nicolas Sarkozy, in the forthcoming French presidential election. At the second round of this election in May approximately 52% of French Polynesian voters chose Sarkozy, while 48% voted for the candidate of the Parti Socialiste, Ségolène Royal (a slightly narrower margin than in metropolitan France). In June, at French legislative elections, the two Tahoera'a Huiraatira candidates were elected as deputies to the Assemblée nationale: Buillard, an incumbent deputy, defeated Temaru to regain one of the seats, while Bruno Sandras was newly elected to the second seat. Temaru was convicted of 'racial discrimination' in July, having used a derogatory term to describe non-Tahitians.

Political instability within French Polynesia continued to pose a threat during 2007. Gaston Tong Sang's Government survived a second unsuccessful motion of no confidence submitted by the opposition in June, but in July it suffered a serious set-back with the withdrawal of the Tahoera'a Huiraatira, Tong Sang's own party, from the majority grouping in the Assembly. The decision signalled a major shift in local politics, which had perhaps been foreshadowed by the intensification of criticism of Tong Sang by the Tahoera'a Huiraatira leader, Gaston Flosse. Five members of the Tahoera'a Huiraatira resigned from the Council of Ministers. Flosse later admitted that negotiations were taking place between the Tahoera'a Huiraatira and Temaru's Tavini Huiraatira, an unexpected revelation given the traditional rivalry and lack of consensus between the parties. However, it appeared that the two parties had a common goal: the removal of the Tong Sang Government. The precarious situation had already prompted the French Government to announce plans for political reform, and Christian Estrosi, the French Minister-Delegate for the Overseas Possessions, urged politicians to 'act responsibly', holding talks with Tong Sang, Flosse, Temaru and other politicians in an attempt to resolve the continuing instability. However, Tong Sang was finally removed from office at the end of August, when a third no-confidence motion in his leadership was approved by 35 Assembly members. The French Conseil d'Etat subsequently ruled that, should the Assembly's selection of a new President require a second round of voting, a relative majority, rather than an absolute majority, would be sufficient. In mid-September Oscar Temaru was elected President, having received 26 votes to defeat the two other candidates, Edouard Fritch and Gaston Tong Sang, in the first round, and 27 votes to secure the presidency in the second round, in which Fritch garnered 17 votes. A new Council of Ministers was duly announced, in which Temaru assumed responsibility for international relations and other portfolios, while Antony Géros was appointed Vice-President and Minister of Finance, Housing and Land Issues.

At a parliamentary session later in September 2007, Temaru stated that a 'pact' had been negotiated between the two major political parties (taken to mean Tavini Huiraatira and the Tahoera'a Huiraatira), thus ensuring a clear majority in the Assembly, which, it was hoped, would lead to greater political stability. In October Temaru attended discussions in France with the newly elected French President, Nicolas Sarkozy, while reform legislation was being prepared for submission to the French Assemblée nationale. Temaru, who was reportedly not entirely satisfied with the schedule, nevertheless 'respected' Sarkozy's decision to call early elections. In November proposals for reform, which included the introduction of two election rounds and the setting of a maximum of 15 appointees to the Council of Ministers, were approved by the French Sénat. Meanwhile, following his defeat, Tong Sang announced the creation of the O Porinetia To Tatou Ai'a (Polynesia, Our Homeland) party, which elected him as its President in December. Flosse was re-elected President of the Tahoera'a Huiraatira, while Fritch was named 'President-Delegate', a new position that was expected to ensure his eventual succession to the most senior position in the party.

At the first round of elections, held on 27 January 2008, the To Tatou Ai'a coalition, of which Tong Sang's O Porinetia To Tatou Ai'a was a leading member, secured more votes in important constituencies than Temaru's political alliance, the Union for Democracy (UPLD) and the Tahoera'a Huiraatira. At the second round of elections on 10 February, To Tatou Ai'a was confirmed as the coalition with the largest representation in the legislature, winning a total of 27 seats, while the UPLD secured 20 and the Tahoera'a Huiraatira only 10. Owing to the lack of an overall majority, discussions on the establishment of a coalition ensued, and the election of Edouard Fritch of the Tahoera'a Huiraatira as President of the Assembly suggested that the two pro-autonomy parties had reached an agreement. The Assembly then conducted a vote to select the next President of French Polynesia. Gaston Flosse unexpectedly declared his candidacy and was able to defeat Tong Sang after Temaru, the third candidate, withdrew, and Flosse gained the support of members of the UPLD. A new parliamentary alliance, between the Tahoera'a Huiraatira and the UPLD, had been established: the Union pour le Développement, la Stabilité et la Paix (Union for Development, Stability and Peace—UDSP). A new cabinet, incorporating several ministers of the previous Temaru Government, was appointed in late February; it included Fritch in the position of Vice-President and Minister for Vocational Training, Labour, Social Dialogue and Municipalities Development. Temaru was elected Assembly President, after Fritch's resignation left a vacancy.

Increasing political instability

The installation of a new Government did not bring the expected political stability. In April 2008 the establishment of Te Mana o Te May Motu, a new parliamentary grouping said to be allied with To Tatou Ai'a, was announced. Later in that month a no-confidence motion submitted by Tong Sang against the Flosse Government garnered 29 out of 57 votes in the Assembly, resulting in Flosse's removal from office; two members of Flosse's coalition group had reportedly defected to Te Mana o Te May Motu. Tong Sang was elected President, and he subsequently appointed a Council of Ministers comprising coalition partners and one member of the Tahoera'a Huiraatira. In July Adolphe Colrat replaced Anne Boquet as the French High Commissioner. In the following month a former Minister for Industry and Small and Medium Businesses and President of the Assembly, Hiro Tefaarere, formed a new political party, naming it A rohi (Let's Act). Tefaarere expressed frustration with the prevailing political situation, which was perceived to be dominated by the pro- and anti-independence movements. In September Gaston Flosse was re-elected as a representative to the French Sénat, while Richard Tuheiava, a member of the UPLD, secured the newly created second seat for French Polynesia. As a sign of the rift between Flosse and the UMP, the latter had supported the senatorial campaign of Gaston Tong Sang and Béatrice Vernaudon of To Tatou Ai'a. Flosse resigned from the UMP, and he was subsequently charged with misuse of public funds relating to his time in office (see below). In late December 2008 the Government lost its majority in the Assembly when one member of the coalition withdrew, resulting in an impasse over budget legislation, amid claims that Tong Sang's position had become untenable.

In February 2009 Tong Sang resigned as President, prompted by an impending motion of no confidence filed by a new opposition alliance comprising the UPLD, the Tahoera'a Huiraatira and the Rautahi party, the latter having defected from the To Tatou Ai'a coalition. Within days Oscar Temaru was elected as President, garnering 37 votes in comparison with Tong Sang's 20 in the second round. Edouard Fritch was subsequently elected to replace Temaru as President of the Assembly. The newly appointed Council of Ministers included Antony Géros as Vice-President and Minister for Development of the Municipalities and for Lands, and Georges Puchon as Minister for Economy, Finance, Budget, Public Accounts, Fiscal Reform and Small and Medium Enterprises.

Also in February 2009, Gaston Flosse was convicted of theft, having been found guilty of misappropriating some 2.4m. francs CFP of public funds in order to pay catering expenses incurred during celebrations for his expected election victory in 2004. He received a suspended one-year prison sentence and a fine of 2m. francs CFP, in addition to being barred from holding public office for a year. The former chief accountant of Flosse and a Tahoera'a Huiraatira treasurer also received suspended prison sentences and were fined. Flosse appealed against the conviction, and in November 2011 the element of the sentence suspending his occupation of public office for one year was overturned. Flosse was thus able to retain his French parliamentary seat. In a further prosecution in May 2010 Flosse was fined after being convicted of obstructing an investigation into a former intelligence unit that had operated during his presidency, by destroying the records of its activities, and in October the French Polynesian Court of Appeal upheld his conviction. The Court of Cassation in France similarly upheld the conviction in September 2011.

In April 2009, meanwhile, Philip Schyle, of Gaston Tong Sang's To Tatou Ai'a coalition, returned to the position of President of the Assembly, following a parliamentary vote in which Edouard Fritch of the Tahoera'a Huiraatira, who had been appointed to the position only two months previously, was overwhelmingly defeated. Shortly after Schyle's election by the legislature, President Temaru presented a new Council of Ministers, incorporating several supporters of Gaston Tong Sang in the coalition Government.

In October 2009 six legislators representing the outer islands, who claimed that their views had been disregarded, withdrew from the coalition Government, and consequently Oscar Temaru's support in the Assembly was seriously reduced. In November, amid mounting public concern at the ongoing political instability, a demonstration to protest against a forthcoming parliamentary motion of no confidence took place in Papeete. Nevertheless, 29 members of the Assembly supported the motion, and the Government was thus removed from office. Gaston Tong Sang was appointed to replace Temaru, thus becoming President for the third time since 2006, and Edouard Fritch returned to the vice-presidency.

In January 2010 President Sarkozy referred to the political situation in French Polynesia as a 'comedy', and announced that he would initiate further reforms of the electoral system and institutions there, in order to provide greater political stability. While Tong Sang was visiting France for discussions (which encompassed the nuclear compensation issue—Nuclear Testing and Relations with Metropolitan France) in that month, he submitted a proposal that the French Polynesian President be directly chosen by the local electorate, rather than elected by the members of the French Polynesian Assembly, with the objective of increasing political stability. While not opposed to Tong Sang's suggestion, the Minister for Overseas Possessions, Marie-Luce Penchard, attributed the instability of recent years to the conduct of French Polynesian politicians and their frequent shifts of allegiance.

Also in January 2010 it was reported that a group of residents on the island of Moorea, wishing to register their protest against the high cost of living, claimed to have seceded from French Polynesia. The rebels claimed to have established a new republic, Hau Pakumotu. In the same month a French administrator, Ghyslain Chatel, was abruptly removed from his post, following the intervention of the High Commissioner, who had been investigating allegations of nepotism in relation to the award of a contract for public works on Moorea. Local media suggested that the situation had been exacerbated by frequent disagreements between Colrat and Chatel since the latter's arrival in French Polynesia two years previously.

In February 2010 thousands of islanders were forced to evacuate their homes when the most severe cyclone for decades struck French Polynesia; the Tuamotu Archipelago was the worst affected area. Hundreds of houses were seriously damaged or completely destroyed by Cyclone Oli. The cost of repairs to housing and infrastructure was unofficially estimated to be in the region of 2,000m. francs CFP.

In April 2010, following Philip Schyle's unexpected resignation as President of the French Polynesian Assembly, Oscar Temaru defeated Gaston Flosse and Jean-Christophe Bouissou in the election for the vacant post; the result indicated that the coalition between Flosse's party, the Tahoera'a Huiraatira, and Tong Sang's To Tatou Ai'a had been seriously undermined. Tong Sang immediately asked President Sarkozy to dissolve the French Polynesian Assembly, urging that an early legislative election be scheduled. Sarkozy replied that electoral reform was necessary before any election could take place. In June a general strike, lasting for more than a week, disrupted transport and other services; the group of 11 unions that organized the strike stated that its principal aim was to draw attention to increasing unemployment and poverty. In September and October further discussions on electoral reform took place: the French Government suggested that any motion of no confidence (the instrument that had frequently been used to defeat recent administrations) should require the support of at least 60% of members of the Assembly. It also suggested that the Society Archipelago adopt an electoral system separate from that of the other islands, and that the number of seats in the Assembly be reduced. Members of all the principal political groupings criticized the proposals. In January 2011 Richard Didier replaced Colrat as the French High Commissioner in French Polynesia.

Also in January 2011, Emile Vernaudon, the former Minister for Post and Telecommunications and the former long-serving mayor of Mahina, was found guilty of misusing funds amounting to 114m. francs CFP belonging to the Office des Postes et Télécommunications (OPT—the state-owned post and telecommunications company) in 2005 and 2006. Vernaudon was sentenced to five years in prison and barred from holding public office for five years. Furthermore, 11 other officials, including former ministers Georges Puchon, Patrick Bordet and Natacha Taurua, were convicted of similar offences in connection with the OPT. The sentence against Vernaudon was upheld at appeal in May 2011.

In December 2010 the proposed budget for the following year, which included reductions in expenditure, was rejected by the legislature. The Assembly approved the budget in February 2011, but President Tong Sang refused to accept the vote, publishing his own version of the budget in official journals. The matter of which budget was valid was referred to the French Supreme Court. Tong Sang dismissed Vice-President Edouard Fritch and five cabinet ministers in March for failing to support his proposed budget. A week later, however, a motion to annul Tong Sang's budget was approved by 44 of the 57 members of the French Polynesian Assembly, and at the beginning of April he was removed from office following his defeat in a parliamentary motion of no confidence, which was supported by 29 of the Assembly's members. Oscar Temaru, leader of the pro-independence Tavini Huiraatira, thus returned to the position of President.

The composition of the new Government was announced in early April 2011. President Temaru assumed personal charge of the portfolios of international and regional relations, tourism and international air transport. The incoming Vice-President, Antony Géros, was allocated responsibility for budget and community development, while Pierre Frébault was appointed Minister for Economy, Finance, Labour and Employment. The ministers dismissed by Tong Sang in the previous month for opposing his budget were all reinstated. In mid-April Jacqui Drollet defeated three other candidates to secure election to the post of President of the French Polynesian Assembly.

In the largest trial in French Polynesian history, a total of 87 people appeared in court in April 2011 in connection with payments made to individuals during the presidency of Gaston Flosse in 1990s. In what became known as the 'phantom jobs case', it was alleged that Flosse had secured the support of numerous politicians, journalists, trade unionists and clergymen by paying them a salary for jobs that did not exist. In October Flosse was found guilty of making corrupt payments and was sentenced to four years' imprisonment. A total of 56 people were convicted in the case.

Meanwhile, the deteriorating economic situation in French Polynesia continued to cause concern, and in April 2011 more than 3,000 people joined a demonstration outside the parliament buildings to protest against a perceived lack of action by politicians to address issues such as rising unemployment. In May the French Government agreed to provide a loan of €41.9m. from the Agence Française de Développement to ease the economic crisis. In the following month the French Polynesian Assembly approved an economic reform plan, thought to have been a requirement of the French loan. The plan envisaged a number of controversial measures, including salary reductions of up to 50% for public sector workers and the closure of GIE Tahiti Tourisme's 11 overseas offices and of the news agency Agence Tahitienne de Presse. In November the Government presented its budget for 2012, which forecast income of US $1,500m. and revenue some 9% lower than the previous year. New taxes on imports from Europe were included in the proposals, although the introduction of income tax was expected to be delayed until 2014. The budget was approved by 29 votes in the Assembly in December.

Recent developments: further electoral reforms

In April 2011 the French Government approved draft legislation amending the islands' electoral system, which was adopted by the Sénat in May and by the Assemblée nationale in June, and was promulgated by President Sarkozy in August. The reforms, which were all aimed at increasing political stability in the islands, included a new system of proportional representation (whereby the winning list in the second round of polling would receive one-third of the 57 seats in the Assembly, with the remainder distributed according to the lists' relative strength); a reduction in the number of members of the Council of Ministers from up to 15 to between seven and 10; and a requirement of 60% of votes, rather than a simple majority, for a motion of no confidence to succeed. In addition, the President of the Council of Ministers of French Polynesia would be limited to serving a maximum of two consecutive terms. Contrary to earlier proposals, the number of seats in the Assembly was maintained at 57. However, having hitherto comprised six electoral constituencies, the islands would henceforth constitute one, albeit composed of eight sections: three for the Windward Islands (Iles du Vent—Society Islands) and one each for the Leeward Islands (Iles Sous le Vent—Society Islands), the Gambier Islands-East Tuamotu Archipelago, the West Tuamotu Archipelago, the Austral Islands and the Marquesas Islands.

In September 2011 Oscar Temaru caused controversy and risked jeopardizing relations with France when he lobbied leaders at a Pacific Islands Forum meeting to support French Polynesia's bid to be reinscribed on the UN's List of Non-Self-Governing Territories. (Former French President Charles de Gaulle had removed French Polynesia from the list in 1946.) The Pacific Islands Forum declined to endorse the decolonization campaign, although the leaders of Vanuatu and Solomon Islands spoke in favour of French Polynesia's reinscription on the list at the UN General Assembly in New York, USA, in that month. Temaru provoked further controversy among French loyalists by referring to the islands at the international gathering by their indigenous name of Maohi Nui.

Nuclear Testing and Relations with Metropolitan France

France's use of French Polynesia for the purposes of nuclear testing was a highly controversial issue. In July 1962 the French Government transferred its nuclear-testing facilities to Mururoa and Fangataufa atolls, in the Tuamotu Archipelago, establishing the Centre d'Expérimentation du Pacifique (CEP). The first nuclear device was tested at Fangataufa four years later in July 1966. In July 1985 the *Rainbow Warrior*, the flagship of the anti-nuclear environmentalist group Greenpeace, which was to have led a protest flotilla to Mururoa, was sunk in Auckland Harbour, New Zealand, in an explosion that killed one crew member. Two agents of the French secret service, the Direction Générale de Sécurité Extérieure (DGSE), were subsequently convicted of manslaughter and imprisoned in New Zealand (see the chapter on New Zealand for further details). According to official reports, between 1966 and 1974 France conducted 46 atmospheric tests in the Territory; 147 underground tests were carried out between 1975 and 1991. In April 1992 the French Government announced that nuclear tests would be suspended until the end of the year. In January 1993 French Polynesia accepted assistance worth 7,000m. francs CFP in compensation for lost revenue and in aid for development projects.

Shortly after his election in May 1995, President Jacques Chirac announced that France would resume nuclear testing, with a programme of eight tests between September 1995 and May 1996. The decision provoked almost universal outrage in the international community, and was condemned for its apparent disregard for regional opinion, as well as for undermining the considerable progress made towards a worldwide ban on nuclear testing. Scientists also expressed concern at the announcement; some believed that further explosions at Mururoa might lead to the collapse of the atoll, which had already been weakened considerably. Large-scale demonstrations and protest marches throughout the region were accompanied by boycotts of French products and the suspension of several trade and defence co-operation agreements. Opposition to the French Government intensified in July 1995, when French commandos violently seized *Rainbow Warrior II*, the flagship of Greenpeace, and its crew, which had been protesting peacefully near the test site. Chirac continued to defy mounting pressure from within the EU, from Japan and Russia, as well as from Australia, New Zealand and the South Pacific region, to reverse the decision to carry out the tests.

French Polynesia became the focus of world attention when the first test of this series took place in September 1995. The action prompted further statements of condemnation from Governments around the world, and provoked major demonstrations in many countries, as well as in Tahiti (see Domestic Political Affairs). In defiance of international opinion, a further five tests were carried out, the sixth and final one being conducted in January 1996. In early 1996 the French Government confirmed reports by a team of independent scientists that radioactive isotopes had leaked into the waters surrounding the atoll, but denied that they represented a threat to the environment. However, following the election of a new socialist administration in France in mid-1997, the French Minister of the Environment demanded in August 1998 that the matter be investigated further, stating that she had not been reassured by the initial reports. Work to dismantle facilities at the test site began in 1997 and was completed in July 1998. Some 1,800 French military personnel were present at the CEP site in 1998.

In early 1999 a study by the French Independent Research and Information Commission reported that there was serious radioactive leakage into underground water, lagoons and the ocean at Mururoa and Fangataufa atolls. In May, furthermore, a French government official admitted that fractures had been found in the coral cone at the Mururoa and Fangataufa nuclear testing sites. During President Chirac's visit to Papeete in July 2003 some 200 members of an association of those formerly employed at Mururoa and Fangataufa—Moruroa e Tatou—staged a demonstration to demand that France recognize the existence of a connection between nuclear testing and the subsequent health problems of those involved. The Nuclear Veterans' Association continued to seek compensation from the French Government: according to the group around 30% of some 15,000 former nuclear workers were either suffering—or had died—from cancers or related diseases.

In May 2005 a French research centre published declassified secret reports from 1966 on nuclear testing in the Gambier Islands, which suggested that the French military had deliberately suppressed information about the extent of contamination from radioactive fall-out. In October a French Polynesian commission of inquiry visited Mangareva, Tureia and Hao with officials from the French Commission for Independent Research and Information on Radioactivity. The commission reported that, contrary to the information given to the public, each of the 46 atmospheric tests between 1966 and 1974 had caused radioactive fall-out on the islands around the test sites; and, furthermore, that the military had failed to predict how weather conditions would affect dispersion of the fall-out.

In March 2006 a new nuclear veterans' association, Tamarii Moruroa, was established, urging that an independent inquiry be conducted by the International Atomic Energy Agency. The association sought to distinguish itself from Moruroa e Tatou by acknowledging the positive role that the tests had played in advancing medical science in particular. In August it emerged that a study conducted by an eminent French scientist had linked a 'small but clear' rise in cases of thyroid cancer in the French Polynesian region to the nuclear tests. A French government representative later admitted that some of the tests might have affected the health of inhabitants of a number of islands. Medical examinations were to be offered to those thought most likely to be at risk.

In January 2009 France agreed to finance the rehabilitation of its former military base on the atoll of Hao. The 'clean-up' operation, which was expected to take seven years, was projected to cost the equivalent of US $80m. In March it was announced that the French Government was to establish an independent commission to examine individual compensation claims from civilian and military workers affected by the nuclear tests, and in December the French legislature voted in favour of compensation payments; 18 illnesses, including leukaemia and thyroid cancer, were to be formally recognized by the French Government. Prior to the adoption of the legislation, an estimated 2,000 demonstrators attended a peaceful march in Papeete, claiming that the scope of the new law was inadequate. In July 2011 the French authorities announced that seven of the eight compensation claims made under the new law had been rejected. In the same month, during commemorations of the 45th anniversary of the beginning of the nuclear test programme in French Polynesia, Jaques Chirac Square was renamed 2 July 1966 Square after the date of the first nuclear test at Mururoa.

In February 2010 French Polynesia concluded a new agreement with France, under which the DGDE, which had been introduced to offset the loss of revenue resulting from the closure of the nuclear testing facilities, would be replaced at the end of the year by three new financial instruments, as part of an arrangement that would continue to take into consideration the economic legacy of the nuclear testing programme. However, the annual sum provided would remain unchanged, at some 18,000m. francs CFP (nearly €151m.). About 60% of this funding was to be disbursed by the French Polynesian Government, while more than 30% was to be allocated to approved infrastructure projects. In March 2011, amid increasing fears for the stability of Mururoa Atoll, the local Government urged the French President to dispatch experts to the area to assess the risks to the population if the atoll were to collapse and release radiation.

CONSTITUTION AND GOVERNMENT

French Polynesia was designated as an Overseas Country (Pays d'outre-mer) within the French Republic in 2004. Its status is that of an Overseas Collectivity (Collectivité d'outre-mer). The French Government is represented in French Polynesia by its High Commissioner, and controls various important spheres of government, including defence, foreign diplomacy and justice. A local Assembly, with 57 members (increased from 49 at the May 2004 election), is elected for a five-year term by universal adult suffrage. The Assembly may elect a President of an executive body, the Council of Ministers, who in turn submits a list of between seven and 10 members of the Assembly to serve as ministers (decreased from 15 in legislation promulgated by the French President in August 2011), for approval by the Assembly.

In addition, French Polynesia elects two deputies to the French Assemblée nationale (National Assembly) in Paris and two representatives to the French Sénat (Senate), all chosen on the basis of universal adult suffrage. French Polynesia is also represented at the European Parliament.

REGIONAL AND INTERNATIONAL CO-OPERATION

French Polynesia forms part of the Franc Zone (see p. 332), and is an associate member of the UN's Economic and Social Commission for Asia and the Pacific (ESCAP, see p. 40). Although France is also a member of the organization, French Polynesia has membership in its own right of the Pacific Community (see p. 413), which is based in New Caledonia and provides technical advice, training and assistance in economic, cultural and social development to the region. In October 2006 French Polynesia became an associate member of the Pacific Islands Forum (see p. 416). For the first time in August 2008, representatives of French Polynesia, in the islands' capacity of associate member of the organization, attended a summit meeting of the Pacific Islands Forum, held in Niue. In November 2011 leaders from French Polynesia, American Samoa, the Cook Islands, Niue, Samoa, Tokelau, Tonga and Tuvalu formed the Polynesian Leaders' Group. The group was expected to hold annual meetings with the aim of sharing knowledge in the areas of the economy, education and the environment and of promoting culture, tradition and languages.

ECONOMIC AFFAIRS

In 2000, according to World Bank estimates, French Polynesia's gross national income (GNI), measured at average 1998–2000 prices, was US $3,795m., equivalent to $16,150 per head (or $24,680 per head on an international purchasing-power parity basis). During 2001–10, it was estimated, the population rose at an average annual rate of 1.3%. Gross domestic product (GDP) per head increased, in real terms, by an average of 1.4% per year during 1995–2000. According to the UN's Economic and Social Commission for Asia and the Pacific (ESCAP), GDP per head increased at an average annual rate of 1.7% in 2000–05. Overall GDP increased at an average annual rate of 3.3% in 1995–2000 and of 1.9% in 2000–05. According to UN estimated figures, real GDP increased by 2.1% in 2009, when GDP at constant 2005 prices reached 384,320.4m. francs CFP.

According to UN estimates, agriculture, forestry and fishing contributed only 2.5% of GDP in 2009. The sector engaged 9.2% of the employed labour force at the 2007 census. Coconuts are the principal cash crop, and in 2010, according to FAO, the estimated harvest was 134,100 metric tons. The quantity of copra exported increased from 5,365.6 tons in 2004 to 5,703.1 tons in 2005; however, the value of copra exports decreased from 297.6m. francs CFP to 291.9m. Monoï oil is produced by macerating tiaré flowers in coconut oil, and in 2007 355 tons of the commodity (representing an increase of 36% over the previous year) were exported. Vegetables, fruit (including pineapples, citrus fruit and noni fruit), vanilla and coffee are also cultivated. In 2007 vanilla exports reached 10.9 tons, and export revenue totalled 230m. francs CFP. Most commercial fishing, principally for tuna, is conducted, under licence, by Japanese and Korean fleets. The total fish catch in 2009 was 12,434 tons. In addition, production by the aquaculture sector, mainly shrimps, reached 39 tons. Another important activity is the production of cultured black pearls. The quantity of cultured pearls totalled 9,131 kg in 2008, when export earnings reached 8,316m. francs CFP (compared with 20,173.2m. in 2000). According to UN figures, the GDP of the agricultural sector contracted at an average annual rate of 2.9% in 2000–09. Compared with the previous year, agricultural GDP was estimated to have increased by 0.9% in 2009.

According to UN estimates, industry (comprising mining, manufacturing, construction and utilities) provided 12.9% of GDP in 2009. In 2007 17.3% of the employed labour force were engaged in the industrial sector. According to the UN, industrial GDP increased at an average annual rate of 0.8% in 2000–09. Compared with the previous year, the GDP of the industrial sector was estimated to have expanded by 1.6% in 2009. There is a small manufacturing sector, which is heavily dependent on agriculture. Coconut oil and copra are produced, as are beer, dairy products and vanilla essence. Deposits of phosphates and cobalt were discovered during the 1980s.

According to UN estimates, mining, manufacturing and utilities provided 7.3% of GDP in 2009 (with manufacturing alone accounting for 5.6%). Mining and manufacturing engaged 6.4% of the employed labour force in 2007, and utilities a further 0.6%. The sectoral GDP decreased at an average annual rate of 0.3% in 2000–09, according to figures from the UN. Compared with the previous year, the GDP of the sector was estimated to have expanded by 1.6% in 2009.

Construction is an important industrial activity, contributing 5.6% of GDP in 2009, and engaging 10.3% of the employed labour force in 2007. According to the UN, the sectoral GDP decreased at an average annual rate of 1.5% in 2000–09. Compared with the previous year, the GDP of the sector was estimated to have expanded by 1.5% in 2009.

Hydrocarbon fuels are the main source of energy in French Polynesia, with the Papeete thermal power station providing about three-quarters of the electricity produced. Mineral fuels accounted for 13.0% of the total value of merchandise imports in 2010. Hydroelectric power dams, with the capacity to generate more than one-third of the electricity requirements of Tahiti's population, have been constructed. Solar energy is also increasingly important, especially on the less-populated islands. Electricity production on Tahiti reached 649.3m. kWh in 2009.

The services sector provided 84.6% of GDP in 2009, and engaged 73.4% of the employed labour force in 2007. The GDP of the services sector expanded at an average annual rate of 2.5% in 2000–09, according to UN estimates. Compared with the previous year, the sector's GDP was estimated to have increased by 2.2% in 2009. Tourism is a major source of revenue. In 2011 162,776 tourists visited French Polynesia, compared with 153,919 in the previous year. In 2010 26.5% of visitor arrivals were from the USA, 23.7% from France and 8.9% from Japan. Receipts from tourism in 2009 totalled an estimated US $736m.

In 2010, according to the Institut d'Émission d'Outre-Mer (IEOM—the French overseas reserve bank), French Polynesia recorded a visible trade deficit of 147,941m. francs CFP. On the current account of the balance of payments there was a surplus of 98m. francs CFP. In 2010, according to provisional official figures, the total cost of imports (excluding military transactions) reached 155,333.1m. francs CFP, while the value of exports totalled 13,868.3m. francs CFP. In 2010 the principal sources of imports were France (which provided 28.1% of total imports), Singapore, the USA, the People's Republic of China and New Zealand. The principal markets for exports in that year were Hong Kong (accounting for 29.8% of the total), Japan, France and the USA. The principal imports included prepared foodstuffs, beverages, spirits and vinegar, and tobacco and manufactured substitutes (which together accounted for 18.8% of the value of imports), and machinery and mechanical appliances, electrical equipment, and sound and television apparatus; the principal exports were cultured pearls, precious and semi-precious stones and related items (providing some 58.4% of total export revenue).

The 2009 budget was expected to be balanced, with revenue equalling expenditure at 140,567m. francs CFP. In the 2010 budget, spending amounted to 142,950m. francs CFP, of which operational expenditure accounted for 106,649m. and investments 36,301m. In 2003 an economic development grant (DGDE) from metropolitan France, amounting to some 18,000m. francs CFP (almost €151m.) annually and to be paid in perpetuity, was introduced to offset the loss of revenue resulting from the closure of the nuclear testing facilities. The DGDE was replaced by three new financial instruments at the end of 2010, but the annual sum provided remained unchanged. About 60% of the funding was to be disbursed by the French Polynesian Government, while about 30% was to be allocated to approved infrastructure projects. In 2010 state expenditure by France in French Polynesia totalled 178,943m. francs CFP, nearly 11.5% of which was on the military budget.

The annual rate of inflation averaged 1.5% during 2000–10. Consumer prices rose by 1.3% in 2010. A high unemployment rate (11.7% of the labour force in 2007) has been exacerbated by the predominance of young people in the population.

In June 2011 the Government of Oscar Temaru, which had taken office in April of that year, approved a dramatic economic reform plan. The plan proposed controversial measures, such as a reduction in public sector salaries of up to 50% and the closure of GIE Tahiti Tourisme's 11 overseas offices and of news agency Agence Tahitienne de Presse, which were believed to be conditions attached to the provision of a loan of €41.9m. from France. The financial assistance was intended to ease the acute financial crisis in the islands, which had resulted in rising unemployment and led to a demonstration in April by some 3,000 people demanding that politicians address the situation more effectively. The budget approved in December 2011 forecast a decline in revenue of some 9% and noted that GDP per head had decreased by some 10% over the previous seven years. In an attempt to increase revenue, the budget included new taxes on imports from Europe. Vice-President Antony Géros (also in charge of the budget, among other portfolios) stated that all sectors of the economy were in crisis, apart from tourism. After four years of decline, owing partly to the contraction of the economy of the USA, the leading source of visitors to French Polynesia, tourist arrivals increased by 5.8% in 2011, to 162,776. Visitors from the USA, Australia and New Zealand rose by 20.4%, 18.6% and 7.9%, respectively, while arrivals from other countries continued to decrease. During 2010 and 2011 investor confidence remained weak, and international credit monitoring agencies continued to cite political instability as a major factor in the successive downgrading of their ratings for French Polynesia. Analysts maintained that, in view of the fact that the public sector accounted for 70% of GDP and that the system of taxation was based largely on import duties and other indirect taxes, a reduction in government involvement in the economy had become essential.

PUBLIC HOLIDAYS

2013: 1 January (New Year's Day), 5 March (Arrival of the Gospel), 29 March (Good Friday), 1 April (Easter Monday), 1 May (Labour Day), 8 May (Liberation Day), 9 May (Ascension Day), 20 May (Whit Monday), 29 June (Internal Autonomy Day), 14 July (Fall of the Bastille), 15 August (Assumption), 1 November (All Saints' Day), 11 November (Armistice Day), 25 December (Christmas Day).

Statistical Survey

Source (unless otherwise indicated): Institut Statistique de la Polynésie Française, Immeuble Uupa, 1er étage, rue Edouard Ahne, BP 395, 98713 Papeete; tel. 473434; fax 427252; e-mail ispf@ispf.pf; internet www.ispf.pf.

AREA AND POPULATION

Area: Total 4,167 sq km (1,609 sq miles); Land area 3,521 sq km (1,359 sq miles).

Population: 245,516 at census of 7 November 2002; 259,706 (males 133,109, females 126,597) at census of 20 August 2007. *By Island Group* (2007 census): Society Archipelago 227,848 (Windward Islands 194,683, Leeward Islands 33,165); Marquesas Archipelago 8,658; Austral Islands 6,304; Tuamotu-Gambier Islands 16,896; Total 259,706. *2011* (official estimate at 1 January): 269,972.

Density (land area only, at 1 January 2011): 76.7 per sq km.

Population by Age and Sex (UN estimates at mid-2012): *0–14:* 67,254 (males 34,239, females 33,015); *15–64:* 190,943 (males 98,325, females 92,618); *65 and over:* 18,532 (males 8,991, females 9,541); *Total* 276,729 (males 141,555, females 135,174) (Source: UN, *World Population Prospects: The 2010 Revision*.

Ethnic Groups (census of 15 October 1983): Polynesian 114,280; 'Demis' 23,625 (Polynesian-European 15,851, Polynesian-Chinese 6,356, Polynesian-Other races 1,418); European 19,320; Chinese 7,424; European-Chinese 494; Others 1,610; Total 166,753. *1988 Census* ('000 persons): Polynesians and 'Demis' 156.3; Others 32.5.

Principal Towns (population at 2007 census): Faa'a 29,781; Papeete (capital) 26,050; Punaauía 25,399; Moorea-Maiao 16,507; Pirae 14,551; Mahina 14,356; Paea 12,084; Taiarapu-Est 11,538; Papara 10,634.

Births, Marriages and Deaths (2010): Registered live births 4,579 (birth rate 17.0 per 1,000); Marriages 1,330 (marriage rate 5.0 per 1,000); Registered deaths 1,261 (death rate 4.7 per 1,000).

Life Expectancy (official estimates, years at birth, 2010): 75.6 (males 73.2; females 78.3).

Economically Active Population (persons aged 14 years and over, 2007 census, excluding persons in military service): Agriculture, hunting, forestry and fishing 8,809; Mining and manufacturing 6,081; Electricity, gas and water 585; Construction 9,825; Trade, restaurants and hotels 21,064; Transport, storage and communications 7,049; Financial services 1,666; Real estate, housing and services to business 4,391; Other private services 5,326; Education, health and social welfare 15,115; Public administration 15,347; *Total employed* 95,258 (males 56,674, females 38,584); Unemployed 12,668 (males 7,006, females 5,662); *Total labour force* 107,926 (males 63,680, females 44,246). *2009* (salaried workers at 31 December): Agriculture, hunting, forestry and fishing 1,958; Mining and quarrying 170; Manufacturing 4,469; Electricity, gas and water 677; Construction 5,433; Trade, restaurants and hotels 16,861; Transport, storage and communications 6,471; Financial services 1,638; Real estate, housing and services to business 4,915; Public administration 14,885; Education 632; Health and social welfare 3,559; Other community, social and personal services 3,057; Persons employed in private households 1,375; Total 66,100. Note: Figures for 2009 exclude 10,600 non-salaried workers and 11,285 civil servants and armed forces personnel.

HEALTH AND WELFARE

Key Indicators

Total Fertility Rate (children per woman, 2010): 2.1.

Physicians (per 1,000 head, 2009): 1.8.

Total Carbon Dioxide Emissions ('000 metric tons, 2007): 806.1.

Carbon Dioxide Emissions Per Head (metric tons, 2007): 3.1.

For definitions, see explanatory note on p. vi.

AGRICULTURE, ETC.

Principal Crops (metric tons, 2010, FAO estimates): Cassava 4,400; Other roots and tubers 5,500; Sugar cane 3,000; Vegetables and melons 6,924; Pineapples 3,500; Coconuts 134,100; Vanilla 60; Coffee, green 20.

Livestock (year ending September 2010, FAO estimates): Cattle 7,300; Horses 2,200; Pigs 31,000; Goats 16,500; Sheep 440; Chickens 270,000; Ducks 32,000.

Livestock Products (metric tons, 2010, FAO estimates): Cattle meat 170; Pig meat 1,220; Goat meat 75; Chicken meat 630; Cows' milk 1,200; Hen eggs 3,000; Other poultry eggs 88; Honey 50.

Fishing (metric tons, live weight, 2009): Capture 12,434 (Skipjack tuna 1,282; Albacore 3,170; Yellowfin tuna 1,067; Bigeye tuna 484; Blue marlin 369; Wahoo 214; Common dolphinfish 417; Other marine fishes 5,101); Aquaculture 39; Total catch 12,473. Note: Figures exclude pearl oyster shells: 1,866.

Source: FAO.

INDUSTRY

Selected Products (metric tons, 2010, unless otherwise indicated): Copra 7,879; Coconut oil 6,879; Oilcake 4,461; Electric energy (2009, Tahiti only) 649.3m. kWh. Source: partly Institut d'Emission d'Outre-Mer.

FINANCE

Currency and Exchange Rates: 100 centimes = 1 franc de la Communauté française du Pacifique (franc CFP or Pacific franc). *Sterling, Dollar and Euro Equivalents* (30 December 2011): £1 sterling = 142.591 francs CFP; US $1 = 92.226 francs CFP; €1 = 119.332 francs CFP; 1,000 francs CFP = £7.01 = $10.84 = €8.38. *Average Exchange Rate* (francs CFP per US $): 85.89 in 2009; 90.10 in 2010; 94.44 in 2011. Note: Until 31 December 1998 the value of the franc CFP was fixed at 5.5 French centimes (1 French franc = 18.1818 francs CFP). Since the introduction of the euro, on 1 January 1999, an official exchange rate of 1,000 francs CFP = €8.38 (€1 = 119.332 francs CFP) has been in operation. Accordingly, the value of the franc CFP has been adjusted to 5.4969 French centimes (1 French franc = 18.1920 francs CFP), representing a 'devaluation' of 0.056%.

Territorial Budget (million francs CFP, 2009, budget): *Revenue:* 140,567 (Taxes 107,003, Other revenues 4,087, State grants 18,123, Loans 11,354). *Expenditure:* 140,567 (Current 106,016, Capital 23,900, Debt-servicing 10,651). Source: Institut d'Emission d'Outre-Mer.

French State Expenditure (million francs CFP): 148,618 (incl. military budget 22,315) in 2005; 159,100 (incl. military budget 24,000) in 2006; 169,563 (incl. military budget 21,668) in 2007; 167,809 (incl. military budget 21,662) in 2008; 175,572 (incl. military budget 21,005) in 2009.

Money Supply (million francs CFP at 31 December 2010): Currency in circulation 14,781; Demand deposits 157,218; *Total money* 171,998. Source: Institut d'Emission d'Outre-Mer.

Cost of Living (Consumer Price Index, annual averages; base: 2000 = 100): All items 114.4 in 2008; 114.6 in 2009; 116.1 in 2010. Source: UN, *Monthly Bulletin of Statistics*.

Gross Domestic Product (million francs CFP at constant 2005 prices): 367,556.1 in 2007; 376,575.8 in 2008; 384,320.4 in 2009. Source: UN Statistics Division, National Accounts Main Aggregates Database.

Expenditure on the Gross Domestic Product (million francs CFP at current prices, 2009): Government final consumption expenditure 41,878.4; Private final consumption expenditure 398,672.3; Increase in stocks 852.2; Gross fixed capital formation 98,433.9; *Total domestic expenditure* 539,836.8; Exports of goods and services 70,012.2; *Less* Imports of goods and services 220,176.9; *GDP in purchasers' values* 389,672.1. Source: UN National Accounts Main Aggregates Database.

Gross Domestic Product by Economic Activity (million francs CFP at current prices, 2009): Agriculture, hunting, forestry and fishing 9,967.4; Mining, electricity, gas and water 6,451.8; Manufacturing 22,364.2; Construction 22,377.9; Trade, restaurants and hotels 96,303.7; Transport, storage and communications 29,627.9; Other activities 209,691.5; *Sub-total* 396,784.4; Net of indirect taxes –7,112.3 (obtained as a residual); *GDP in purchasers' values* 389,672.1. Source: UN National Accounts Main Aggregates Database.

Balance of Payments (million francs CFP, 2010): Exports of goods 14,425; Imports of goods –162,366; *Trade balance* –147,941; Exports of services 86,041; Imports of services –57,349; *Balance on goods and services* –119,249; Other income (net) 54,592; *Balance on goods, services and income* –64,657; Current transfers (net) 64,820; Capital account (net) –65; *Current balance* 98; Direct investment (net) 503; Portfolio investment (net) –175; Other investment (net) 9,783; *Overall balance* 10,207. Source: Institut d'Emission d'Outre-Mer.

EXTERNAL TRADE

Principal Commodities (million francs CFP, 2010, excl. military transactions, provisional): *Imports c.i.f.:* Live animals and animal products 7,669.3 (Meat and edible meat offal 7,598.0); Prepared foodstuffs; beverages, spirits and vinegar; tobacco and manufactured substitutes 29,242.5; Mineral products 20,273.5 (Mineral fuels, mineral oils and products of their distillation; bituminous substances; mineral waxes 20,270.5); Products of chemical or allied industries 13,597.7 (Pharmaceutical products 7,254.8); Plastics, rubber and articles thereof 5,710.8; Paper-making materials; paper and paperboard and articles thereof 4,270.6; Textiles and textile articles 4,328.1; Base metals and articles thereof 9,745.5; Machinery and mechanical appliances; electrical equipment; sound and television apparatus 27,627.4 (Nuclear reactors, boilers, machinery, mechanical appliances and parts 13,453.8; Electrical machinery, equipment, etc. 14,173.6); Vehicles, aircraft, vessels and associated transport equipment 16,448.5 (Aircraft and aeronautical craft 695.0; Sea or river vessels 3,833.7; Road vehicles, parts and accessories 11,758.8); Miscellaneous manufactured articles 5,507.3; Total (incl. others) 155,333.1. *Exports f.o.b.:* Fish and crustaceans, molluscs and other aquatic invertebrates 674.3; Prepared foodstuffs; beverages, spirits and vinegar; tobacco and manufactured substitutes 2,463.8 (Preparations of vegetables, fruit, nuts or other parts of plants 754.4); Natural or cultured pearls, precious or semi-precious stones, precious metals and articles thereof; imitation jewellery; coin 8,098.2; Vehicles, aircraft, vessels and associated transport equipment 1,999.7 (Aircraft, spacecraft and parts 244.4); Total (incl. others) 13,868.3.

Principal Trading Partners (million francs CFP, 2010, excl. military transactions, provisional): *Imports:* Australia 4,972.9; Belgium 2,341.2; China, People's Republic 14,670.8; France 43,573.4; Germany 5,234.4; Indonesia 1,464.0; Italy 3,984.3; Japan 4,191.5; Korea, Republic of 2,424.5; Netherlands 1,638.0; New Zealand 12,577.5; Singapore 19,791.4; Spain 1,854.0; Thailand 4,701.1; United Kingdom 1,978.0; USA 15,635.1; Total (incl. others) 155,333.1. *Exports:* Australia 290.1; Belgium 12.3; Canada 45.4; China, People's Republic 309.2; France 1,784.5; Germany 124.4; Hong Kong 4,129.8; Japan 2,777.1; New Caledonia 358.0; New Zealand 219.4; USA 1,597.2; Total (incl. others) 13,868.3.

TRANSPORT

Road Traffic (1987): Total vehicles registered 54,979. *2007 Census:* Private cars 4,602; Vans 3,108; Trucks 80; Special vehicles 19; Two wheelers 3,463; Trailers 20; Total 11,292. *2009:* Four-wheelers 15,909; Two-wheelers 2,432; Total 18,341.

Shipping (2010, unless otherwise indicated): *International Traffic:* Passengers carried 27,852 (2003); Freight handled 961,526 (loaded 41,648, unloaded 919,878) metric tons. *Domestic Traffic* (2009): Passengers carried 1,715,455; Total freight handled 397,493 metric tons.

Civil Aviation (2010): *International Traffic:* Passengers carried 512,169; Freight handled 9,393 metric tons. *Domestic Traffic:* Passengers carried 662,629; Freight handled 2,638 metric tons.

TOURISM

Visitors: 196,496 in 2008; 160,447 in 2009; 153,919 in 2010.

Tourist Arrivals by Country of Residence (2010): Australia 6,945; Canada 5,468; France 36,544; Germany 4,256; Italy 11,208; Japan 13,761; New Caledonia 3,940; New Zealand 5,128; Spain 4,104; Switzerland 519; United Kingdom 2,840; USA 40,735; Total (incl. others) 153,919. Source: Institut d'Emission d'Outre-Mer.

Tourism Receipts (US $ million, incl. passenger transport): 807 in 2007; 745 in 2008; 736 in 2009. Source: World Tourism Organization.

COMMUNICATIONS MEDIA

Radio Receivers (1997): 128,000 in use*.

Television Receivers (2000): 44,000 in use†.

Telephones (2010): 54,900 main lines in use†.

Mobile Cellular Telephones (subscribers, 2010): 215,900†.

Personal Computers (number in use, 2005): 28,000†.

Internet Subscribers (2009): 30,500†.

Broadband Subscribers (2010): 32,200†.

Daily Newspapers (2000): 2.

* Source: UNESCO, *Statistical Yearbook*.

† Source: International Telecommunication Union.

EDUCATION

Pre-primary (2008/09, unless otherwise indicated): 40 schools (2006/07); 408 teachers (1996/97); 14,306 pupils.

Primary (incl. special schools and young adolescents' centres, 2010/11, unless otherwise indicated): 231 schools (incl. pre-primary); 2,811 teachers (1996/97); 39,991 pupils.

Secondary (2010/11, unless otherwise indicated): 51 schools (first and second cycles, 2008/09); 2,035 teachers (general secondary only, 1998/99); 32,418 pupils.

Tertiary (2006/07, unless otherwise indicated): 50 teachers (1999); 681 students.

Source: partly Institut d'Emission d'Outre-Mer.

Directory

The Government

High Commissioner: Richard Didier (took office 24 January 2011).

Secretary-General: Alexandre Rochatte.

COUNCIL OF MINISTERS

(May 2012)

The Government is led by Tavini Huiraatira No Te Ao Ma'ohi.

President, also in charge of International and Regional Relations, Tourism and International Air Transport: Oscar Manutahi Temaru.

Vice-President, also in charge of Budget, Community Development, Digital Economy, Communication, Relations with French Polynesia's Institutions, Government Spokesman: Antony Géros.

Minister for Economy, Finance, Labour and Employment, in charge of Fiscal Reforms, Vocational Training, Administrative Reforms and Public Service: Pierre Frébault.

Minister for Public Utilities, Land Transport, in charge of Ports and Airports: James Salmon.

Minister for Marine Resources, in charge of Pearl Farming Industries, Fisheries, Aquaculture and Green Technologies: Temauri Foster.

Minister for Education, Youth and Sports, in charge of Higher Education, Research and Associations: Tauhiti Nena.

Minister for Planning and Housing, in charge of Land Affairs and Urban Matters: Louis Frébault.

Minister for Environment, Energy and Mining: Jacky Bryant.

Minister for Health and Solidarity, in charge of Social Welfare Protection: Charles Tetaria.

Minister for Culture, Crafts and Family, in charge of Women's Affairs: Chantal Tahiata.

Minister for Agriculture, Livestock, in charge of Biotechnologies: Kalani Teixeira.

Minister for Outer Islands Development and Transport, in charge of Coconut Plantations Revival: Daniel Herlemme.

GOVERNMENT OFFICES

Office of the High Commissioner of the Republic: BP 115, 98713 Papeete; tel. 468686; fax 468689; e-mail courrier@polynesie-francaise.pref.gouv.fr; internet www.polynesie-francaise.pref.gouv.fr.

Office of the President of the Government: ave Pouvana'a A Opa, BP 2551, 98713 Papeete; tel. 472000; fax 472210; internet www.presidence.pf.

Government of French Polynesia: BP 2551, Papeete; tel. 472000; fax 419781.

Economic, Social and Cultural Council (CESC): Immeuble Te Raumaire, ave Bruat, BP 1657, 98713 Papeete; tel. 416500; fax 419242; e-mail cesc@cesc.pf; internet www.cesc.pf; f. 1977; est. as Economic and Social Council; present name adopted in 1990; Pres. Jean Tama; Sec.-Gen. Alexa Bonnette.

Ministry of Culture and Handicrafts: BP 2551, 98713 Papeete; tel. 508620; fax 508622; e-mail ambroise.colombani@artisanat.min.gov.pf; internet www.artisanat.gov.pf.

Ministry of Economic Reform, External Trade, Industry and Enterprise: Bâtiment de la Culture, rue des Poilus Tahitiens, Quartier Buillard, Papeete; tel. 484000; fax 484014.

Ministry of Education, Higher Education and Research: rue Tuterai Tane, BP 2551, 98713 Papeete; tel. 544900; fax 544901; e-mail secretariat@education.min.gov.pf; internet www.education.gov.pf.

Ministry of Finance, Budget, Public Expenditure and Fiscal Reform: BP 2551, 98713 Papeete; tel. 484000; fax 484014; e-mail secretariat@finances.gov.pf; internet www.postes.gov.pf.

Ministry of Health and Ecology: Bâtiment de la Direction de la Santé, 1er étage, Papeete; tel. 460099; fax 433942; internet www.sante.gov.pf.

Ministry of Labour and Employment: Bâtiment du Gouvernement, 1er étage, ave Pouvana'a A Opa, Papeete; tel. 472440; fax 855777.

Ministry of Land Affairs, Planning, Housing and Public Works: Bâtiment Administratif A2, 5ème étage, rue du Commandant Destremeau, BP 2551, 98713 Papeete; tel. 468019; fax 483792; e-mail secretariat@equipement.min.gov.pf; internet www.equipement.gov.pf.

Ministry of Maritime Resources: Immeuble Te Fenua, rue Dumont d'Urville, 98713 Papeete; tel. 549575; fax 454343; e-mail secretariat@maritime.min.gov.pf; internet www.mer.gov.pf.

Ministry of Outer Islands Development and Domestic Transport: Immeuble Papineau, 5ème étage, rue Tepano Jaussen, BP 2551, 98713 Papeete; tel. 478350; fax 478357; internet www.transports-interinsulaires.gov.pf.

Ministry of Rural Economy: Bâtiment du Gouvernement, ave Pouvana'a A Opa, Papeete; tel. 504455; fax 504460.

Ministry of Solidarity and Family Affairs: Immeuble Papineau, 6ème étage, rue Tepano Jaussen, BP 2551, Papeete; tel. 478383; fax 478302; e-mail secretariat.mfc@famille.min.gov.pf; internet www.famille.gov.pf.

Ministry of Tourism and International Air Transport: Fare Manihini, rond-point de la Base Marine, blvd Pomare, BP 2551, 98713 Papeete; tel. 803000; e-mail contact@tourisme.min.gov.pf.

Ministry of Youth and Sports: Immeuble ICA, 4ème étage, Colline Putiaoro, Quartier de la Mission, 98713 Papeete; tel. 501075; fax 501077; internet www.jeunesse.gov.pf.

Legislature

ASSEMBLÉE

President: Jacqui Drollet.

Assembly: Assemblée de la Polynésie Française, rue du Docteur Cassiau, BP 28, 98713 Papeete; tel. 416300; fax 416372; e-mail communication@assemblee.pf; internet www.assemblee.pf.

Election (second round), 10 February 2008*

Party	Seats
To Tatou Ai'a†	27
Union pour la Démocratie (UPLD)‡	20
Tahoera'a Huiraatira	10
Total	57

* Unofficial results. Three of the 57 seats were determined at the first round of voting, held on 27 January 2008, when the requisite absolute majority was secured.

† Coalition led by O Porinetia To Tatou Ai'a.

‡ Coalition led by Tavini Huiraatira.

PARLEMENT

Deputies to the French Assemblée Nationale: Michel Buillard (Tahoera'a Huiraatira/Union pour un Mouvement Populaire—UMP), Bruno Sandras (Tahoera'a Huiraatira/UMP).

Representatives to the French Sénat: Gaston Flosse (Tahoera'a Huiraatira), Richard Tuheiava (Union pour la Démocratie—UPLD).

Political Organizations

Ai'a Api (New Land): BP 11185, 98709 Mahina, Tahiti; tel. 504596; fax 504598; e-mail courrier@aiaapi.pf; internet www.aiaapi.pf; f. 1982 after split in Te E'a Api; Pres. Emile Vernaudon.

Fe'tia Api (New Star): c/o Assemblée de la Polynésie Française, BP 140 512, Arue; tel. 416131; fax 416136; f. 1996; part of Alliance pour une Démocratie Nouvelle coalition; Leader Philip Schyle.

Heiura-Les Verts Polynésiens: BP 44, Bora Bora; tel. and fax 677174; e-mail heiura@heiura-lesverts.pf; internet www.heiura-lesverts.pf; ecologist; Sec.-Gen. Jacky Bryant.

Ia Mana Te Nunaa (Power to the People): rue du Commandant Destrémau, BP 1223, Papeete; tel. 426699; f. 1976; advocates 'socialist independence'; Sec.-Gen. Jacqui Drollet.

No Oe E Te Nunaa (This Country is Yours): Immeuble Fara, rue Nansouty, BP 40205, Fare Tony, 98713 Papeete; tel. 423718; e-mail contact@noetn.com; internet www.noetn.com; favours autonomy; part of Alliance pour une Démocratie Nouvelle coalition; Leader NICOLE MOEA BOUTEAU; Sec.-Gen. ROSALIE TIRIANA ZAVAN.

O Porinetia To Tatou Ai'a (Polynesia, Our Homeland): BP 4061, 98713 Papeete; tel. 584848; fax 504888; e-mail contact@oporinetia.pf; internet www.oporinetia.pf; f. 2007; est. by fmr members of Tahoera'a Huiraatira; leading mem. of To Tatou Ai'a coalition; Pres. GASTON TONG SANG.

Pupu Here Ai'a Te Nunaa Ia Ora: BP 3195, Papeete; tel. 420766; f. 1965; advocates autonomy.

Rautahi (Rally for French Polynesia): BP 60 013, Faa'a Centre; tel. 762000; e-mail rautahi-rpf@mail.pf; internet www.rautahi-be.org; f. 2005; est. by fmr mems of Tahoera'a Huiraatira; Pres. JEAN-CHRISTOPHE BOUISSOU.

Taatiraa No Te Hau: BP 2916, Papeete; tel. 437494; fax 422546; f. 1977; Pres. ROBERT TANSEAU.

Tahoera'a Huiraatira (People's Rally): rue du Commandant Destremeau, BP 471, Papeete; tel. 429898; fax 450004; e-mail courrier@tahoeraahuiraatira.pf; internet tahoeraahuiraatira.pf; f. 1977; fmrly l'Union Tahitienne; supports links with France, with internal autonomy; affiliated to the metropolitan Union pour un Mouvement Populaire (UMP); Pres. GASTON FLOSSE; Pres.-Delegate EDOUARD FRITCH; Sec.-Gen. BRUNO SANDRAS.

Tapura Amui No Te Faatereraa Manahune-Tuhaa Pae: c/o Assemblée de la Polynésie Française, BP 140 512, Arue; represents the Austral Islands; Leader CHANTAL FLORES.

Tavini Huiraatira No Te Ao Ma'ohi/Front de Libération de la Polynésie (Polynesian People's Servant): c/o Assemblée de la Polynésie Française, BP 140 512, Arue; tel. 733865; f. 1977; leading mem. of Union pour la Démocratie (Union for Democracy—UPLD) coalition; independence movement; anti-nuclear; Leader OSCAR TEMARU.

Te' Avei'a (Te Ara): BP 11 362, 98709 Mahina, Tahiti; tel. and fax 851385; e-mail mail@teaveia.pf; internet www.teaveia.pf; f. 2004; est. by fmr mems of Fe'tia Api and Tavini Huiraatira; Pres. ANTONIO PEREZ.

Te Henua Enana Kotoa: Papeete; Leader LOUIS TAATA.

Te Niu Hau Manahune (Principle of Democracy): Rangiroa; f. 2007; Leader TEINA MARAEURA; Sec.-Gen. HINANO TEANOTOGA.

Judicial System

Audit Office: Chambre Territoriale des Comptes, rue Edouard Ahnne, BP 331, 98713 Papeete; tel. 509710; fax 509719; e-mail ctcpf@pf.ccomptes.fr; Pres. JACQUES BASSET; Clerk of the Court MARIE-HÉLÈNE ANDRIOT.

Court of Administrative Law: rue Pouvana'a A Opa, BP 4522, 98713 Papeete; tel. 509025; fax 451724; e-mail tadelapolynesiefrancaise@mail.pf; internet polynesie-francaise.tribunal-administratif.fr; Pres. BERNARD LEPLAT; Cllrs CHANSEREY MUM, MARIE-CHRISTINE LUBRANO, DANIÈLE GONNOT; Clerk of the Court DONA GERMAIN.

Court of Appeal: Cour d'Appel de Papeete, 42 ave Pouvana'a A Opa, BP 101, 98713 Papeete; tel. 415500; fax 424416; e-mail sec.pp.ca-papeete@justice.fr; internet www.ca-papeete.justice.fr; Pres. OLIVIER AIMOT; Attorney-Gen. SERGE SAMUEL; Clerk of the Court RENE ARLANDA.

Court of the First Instance: Tribunal de Première Instance de Papeete, ave Bruat, BP 4633, 78718 Papeete; tel. 415500; fax 454012; e-mail sec.pr.tpi-papeete@justice.fr; internet www.ca-papeete.justice.fr; Pres. GUY RIPOLL; Procurator JOSÉ THOREL; Clerk of the Court KARL LEQUEUX.

Religion

About 54% of the population are Protestants and 38% are Roman Catholics.

CHRISTIANITY

Protestant Church

At mid-2000 there were an estimated 110,000 Protestants.

Maohi Protestant Church: BP 113, Papeete; tel. 460600; fax 419357; e-mail eepf@mail.pf; f. 1884; autonomous since 1963; fmrly l'Eglise Evangélique en Polynésie Française (Etaretia Evaneria I Porinetia Farani); Pres. of Council Rev. TAAROANUI MARAEA; c. 95,000 mems.

The Roman Catholic Church

French Polynesia comprises the archdiocese of Papeete and the suffragan diocese of Taiohae o Tefenuaenata (based in Nuku Hiva, Marquesas Is). At 31 December 2007 there were an estimated 101,090 adherents in French Polynesia. The Archbishop and the Bishop participate in the Episcopal Conference of the Pacific, based in Fiji.

Archbishop of Papeete: (vacant), Archevêché, BP 94, Vallée de la Mission, 98713 Papeete; tel. 420251; fax 424032; e-mail catholic@mail.pf.

Other Churches

Other denominations active in French Polynesia include the Assemblies of God, Church of Jesus Christ of Latter-day Saints (Mormon), Sanito and Seventh-day Adventist missions. At mid-2000 there were an estimated 30,000 adherents to other forms of Christianity.

The Press

La Dépêche de Tahiti: Ave George Clémenceau, BP 50, 98713 Papeete; tel. 464343; fax 464393; e-mail journalistes@ladepeche.pf; internet www.ladepeche.pf; f. 1964; acquired by Groupe France Antilles in 1988; daily; French; Man. Dir and Editor RICHARD BROZAT; circ. 20,500.

Fenua'Orama: BP 629, 98713 Papeete; tel. 475293; fax 475297; e-mail fenuaorama@hersantmedia.pf; publ. by Groupe France Antilles; monthly; women's lifestyle; Editor-in-Chief DANIEL PARDON; circ. 13,700.

L'Hebdo Maohi: Papeete; tel. and fax 4581827; e-mail journal@hebdo.pf; internet www.hebdo.pf; weekly; Man. and Publ. Dir TERII PAQUIER; circ. 3,000.

Journal Officiel de la Polynésie Française: c/o Imprimerie Officielle, 43 rue des Poilus Tahitiens, BP 117, 98713 Papeete; tel. 500580; fax 425261; e-mail imprimerie.officielle@imprimerie.gov.pf; f. 2004 as *Compte Rendu Intégral des Débats de l'Assemblée de la Polynésie Française*; bi-weekly; publ. by the Imprimerie Officielle; Dir CLAUDINO LAURENT; circ. 100.

Les Nouvelles de Tahiti: Immeuble Sarateva, Carrefour de la Fautaua, BP 629, Papeete; tel. 475200; fax 475209; e-mail redac@lesnouvelles.pf; internet www.lesnouvelles.pf; f. 1957; daily; French; Gen. Man. EDMUND TRAN; Editor-in-Chief MURIEL PONTAROLLO; circ. 6,500.

Le Semeur Tahitien: BP 94, 98713 Papeete; tel. 502350; e-mail catholic@mail.pf; f. 1909; 22 a year; French; publ. by the Roman Catholic Church.

Tahiti Beach Press: BP 887, 98713 Papeete; tel. 426850; fax 423356; e-mail tahitibeachpres@mail.pf; internet www.tahitibeachpress.com; f. 1980; monthly; English; Publr G. WARTI; circ. 10,000.

Tahiti Pacifique Magazine: BP 368, Maharepa, Moorea; tel. 562894; fax 563007; e-mail tahitipm@mail.pf; internet tahiti-pacifique.com; monthly; French; Dir and Editor ALEX W. DU PREL; circ. 6,500.

Ve'a Katorika: BP 94, 98713 Papeete; e-mail catholic@mail.pf; f. 1909; monthly; publ. by the Roman Catholic Church.

Ve'a Porotetani: BP 113, Papeete; tel. 460623; fax 419357; e-mail eepf@mail.pf; f. 1921; monthly; French and Tahitian; publ. by the Maohi Protestant Church; Dir TAARII MARAEA; Editor-in-Chief EVA RAAPOTO; circ. 5,000.

Other publications include *Le To'ere*, weekly; *Conso + Info Plus*, *Tahiti Business*, and *Ve'a Ora Magazine*, monthly; and *Dixit* and *Fenua Economie*, annually.

NEWS AGENCY

Agence France-Presse (AFP): BP 629, Papeete; tel. 508100; fax 508109.

Publishers

Editions Haere Pō: BP 1958, Papeete 98713; tel. and fax 480401; e-mail haerepotahiti@mail.pf; internet www.haerepo.org; f. 1981; travel, history, linguistics, literature, culture, anthropology, religion, land tenure and local interest.

Au Vent des Iles: BP 5670, 98716 Pirae; tel. 509595; fax 509597; e-mail mail@auventdesiles.pf; internet www.auventdesiles.pf; f. 1992; South Pacific interest, fiction and trade; Gen. Man. CHRISTIAN ROBERT.

GOVERNMENT PRINTER

Imprimerie Officielle: 43 rue des Poilus Tahitiens, BP 117, 98713 Papeete; tel. 500580; fax 425261; e-mail imprimerie.officielle@imprimerie.gov.pf; f. 1843; printers, publrs; Dir CLAUDINO LAURENT.

Broadcasting and Communications

TELECOMMUNICATIONS

Office des Postes et Télécommunications (OPT): Hôtel des Postes, 8 rue de la Reine Pomare IV, 98714 Papeete; tel. 414242; fax 436767; e-mail contact@opt.pf; internet www.opt.pf; state-owned telecommunications co; subsidiaries incl. Tahiti Nui Telecom (international voice services), Tikiphone (mobile network), Mana (internet service), Tahiti Nui Satellite (satellite broadcaster), ISS (software and network solutions); Chair. FRANÇOIS VOIRIN; Dir-Gen. BENJAMIN TEIHOTU (acting).

Tahiti Nui Telecommunications (TNT): BP 11843, 98709 Mahina; tel. 415400; fax 437553; e-mail admin.tnt@tahitinui-telecom.com; internet www.tahitinui-telecom.com; f. 2001; owned by OPT; provides international telephone services; Chair. JEAN-CLAUDE TERIIEROOITERAI.

Tikiphone SAS (Vini): POB 440, 98713 Papeete; tel. 481313; fax 487248; internet www.tikiphone.pf; f. 1994; subsidiary of OPT; operates Vini, French Polynesia's first mobile telephone network; more than 208,000 subscribers; Gen. Man. YANNICK TERIIEROOITERAI.

Regulatory Authority

Agence de Réglementation du Numérique: Immeuble Toriki, rue Dumont d'Urville, Quartier Orovini, BP 5019, 98716 Pirae; tel. 544535; fax 532801; e-mail direction@arn.gov.pf; internet www.arn.pf; fmrly Services des Postes et Télécommunications; name changed as above 2011; Dir TAMATOA POMMIER.

BROADCASTING

Radio

RFO Polynésie: Centre Pamatai, Faa'a, BP 60125, 98702 Papeete; tel. 861616; fax 861611; e-mail rfopfr@mail.pf; internet polynesie.la1ere.fr; f. 1934; public service radio and television station operated by Réseau France Outre-Mer (RFO), Paris; daily programmes in French and Tahitian; Dir-Gen. GENEVIÈVE GIARD; Regional Dir MICHEL KOPS.

Private Stations

Since 2004 some 17 stations have been licensed. There are currently around 25 commercial radio stations in French Polynesia.

NRJ Tahiti: BP 50, 98718 Papeete; tel. and fax 421042; fax 464346; internet www.nrj.pf; affiliated to NRJ France; French; entertainment; broadcasts 14 hrs daily; Station Man. NADINE RICHARDSON.

Radio Maohi: Maison des Jeunes, Pirae; tel. 819797; fax 825493; e-mail tereo@mail.pf; French and Tahitian; owned by the political party Tahoera'a Huiraatira; ceased broadcasting between March 2008 and May 2009.

Radio One: Fare Ute, BP 3601, 98713 Papeete; tel. 434100; fax 422421; e-mail contact@radio1.pf; internet www.radio1.pf; French; relays Europe 1 news bulletins from Paris; CEO SONIA ALINE.

Radio (Te Reo O) Tefana (La Voix de Tefana): BP 6295, 98702 Faa'a; tel. 819797; fax 825493; e-mail tereo@mail.pf; f. 1987; French and Tahitian; affiliated to the Tavini Huiraatira party; Pres. VITO MAAMAATUAIAHUTAPU; Dir and Station Man. TERIIMATEATA MANA; Editor-in-Chief MICAËL TAPUTU.

Radio Te Vevo O Te Tiaturiraa: 51 rue Dumont d'Urville, BP 1817, 98713 Papeete; tel. 412341; fax 412322; e-mail contacts@mail.pf; religious; affiliated with the Assemblies of God church; Treas. THIERRY ALBERT.

Other radio stations include Pacific FM, Radio Fara, Radio la Voix de l'Espérance (LVDL), Radio Ma'ohi-RTL, Radio Maria No Te Hau, Radio Paofai, Radio Te Vevo No Papara, Star FM and Tiare FM.

Television

RFO Polynésie: see Radio

TNS (Tahiti Nui Satellite): 8 rue de la Reine Pomare IV, 98714 Papeete; tel. 414370; fax 432707; e-mail tns@opt.pf; internet www.tns.pf; f. 2000; 100% owned by the Office des Postes et Télécommunications; news and entertainment; relays 25 television channels and 6 radio channels, in French, Tahitian and English, incl. TNTV; also relays ABC Asia Pacific Television, Australia, and Canal Plus, France; Man. VETEA TROUCHE-BONNO; over 10,000 subscribers.

TNTV (Tahiti Nui Television): Quartier Mission, BP 348, 98713 Papeete; tel. 473636; fax 532721; e-mail redaction@tntv.pf; internet www.tntv.pf; f. 2000; broadcasts in French and Tahitian 19 hours daily; Chair. JOËL ALLAIN; Dir-Gen. YVES HAUPERT.

Finance

(cap. = capital; res = reserves; dep. = deposits; m. = million; brs = branches; amounts in francs CFP)

BANKING

Commercial Banks

Banque de Polynésie SA: 355 blvd Pomare, BP 530, 98713 Papeete; tel. 466666; fax 466664; e-mail bdp@sg-bdp.pf; internet www.sg-bdp.pf; f. 1973; 80% owned by Société Générale, France; cap. 1,380.0m., res 5,214.3m., dep. 133,725.2m. (Dec. 2009); Chair. JEAN-LOUIS MATTEI; Gen. Man. FRÉDÉRIC COIN; 14 brs.

Banque de Tahiti SA: 38 rue François Cardella, BP 1602, 98713 Papeete; tel. 417000; fax 423376; e-mail contact@bt.pf; internet www.banque-tahiti.pf; f. 1969; owned by Financière Océor (95.4%); merged with Banque Paribas de Polynésie in 1998; cap. 1,814.8m., res 5,271.2m., dep. 180,703.7m. (Dec. 2008); Chair. CHRISTIAN CAMUS; Dir-Gen. PATRICE TEPELIAN; 18 brs.

Banque SOCREDO—Société de Crédit et de Développement de l'Océanie: 115 rue Dumont d'Urville, BP 130, 98713 Papeete; tel. 415123; fax 415283; e-mail socres@bank-socredo.pf; internet www.socredo.pf; f. 1959; public body; in partnership with French cos BNP Paribas, Cardif Assurance and Crédit Agricole, which provide technical assistance; cap. 22,000.0m., res 6,774.9m., dep. 205,874.1m. (Dec. 2009); Pres. MICHEL JACQUIER; Gen. Man. JAMES ESTALL; 26 brs.

Insurance

AGF Vie & AGF IART Polynésie Française: Immeuble Sienne, rue Dumont d'Urville, BP 4452, 98713 Papeete; tel. 549100; fax 549101; e-mail gestion-vie@agf.pf; internet www.allianz.fr; life and general non-life insurance.

GAN Pacifique: 9 ave Bruat, BP 339, 98713 Papeete; tel. 503150; fax 431918; subsidiary of Groupama, France; general non-life insurance; Chair. JEAN-FRANÇOIS LEMOUX; CEO PASCAL ALEXANDRE.

Poe-ma Insurances: Marina Fare Ute, BP 4652, 98713 Papeete; tel. 502650; fax 450097; e-mail info@poema.pf; internet www.poema.pf; f. 1991; general non-life insurance; Man. Dir VINCENT GEORGE.

Trade and Industry

GOVERNMENT AGENCIES

Direction Générale des Affaires Economiques (DGAE): Fare Ute, Bâtiment des Affaires Economiques, BP 504, 98713 Papeete; tel. 509797; fax 434477; e-mail dgae@economie.gov.pf; internet www.affaires-economiques.gov.pf; Dir PATRICE PERRIN.

Etablissement Public des Grands Travaux (EGT): 51 rue du Commandant Destremeau, BP 9030, Motu Uta, 98715 Papeete; tel. 508100; fax 508102; e-mail contact@egt.pf; internet www.egt.pf; responsible for public works; Pres. JONAS TAHUAITU; Dir ERIC NOBLE-DEMAY.

Service de l'Artisanat Traditionnel (ART): Immeuble Lejeune, 1er étage, 82 rue du Général de Gaulle, BP 4451, 98713 Papeete; tel. 545400; fax 532321; e-mail secretariat@artisanat.gov.pf; f. 1984; Dir LAETITIA GALENON.

Service de l'Emploi, de la Formation et de la Insertion Professionnelles (SEFI): Immeuble Papineau, rue Tepano Jaussen, 2ème étage, BP 540, 98713 Papeete; tel. 461212; fax 450280; internet www.sefi.pf; Dir PAUL NATIER.

Service du Commerce Extérieur: 53 rue Nansouty, Immeuble Teissier au 1er étage, BP 20727, 98713 Papeete; tel. 506464; fax 436420; e-mail commerceexterieur@economie.gov.pf; internet www.tahiti-export.pf; Dir WILLIAM VANIZETTE.

Service du Développement de l'Industrie et des Métiers (SDIM): BP 9055, Motu Uta, 98715 Papeete; tel. 502880; fax 412645; e-mail infos@sdim.pf; internet www.sdim.pf; f. 1988; industry and small-business devt administration; Dir DENIS GRELLIER.

Société de Financement du Développement de la Polynésie Française (SOFIDEP): Centre Paofai, Bâtiment BC, 1er étage, blvd Pomare, BP 345, 98713 Papeete; tel. 509330; fax 509333; e-mail sem.sofidep@mail.pf; Dir PIERRE FONTAINE.

DEVELOPMENT ORGANIZATIONS

Agence Française de Développement (AFD): Immeuble Hokule'a, 2 rue Cook Paofai, BP 578, 98713 Papeete; tel. 544600; fax 544601; e-mail afdpapeete@pf.groupe-afd.org; internet www.afd.fr; public body; devt finance institute; Dir FRANÇOIS GIOVALUCCHI.

Moruroa e Tatou (Moruroa et Nous): 403 blvd Pomare, BP 5456, 98716 Pirae, Papeete; tel. 460666; e-mail moruroaetatou@mail.pf; internet www.moruroaetatou.com; f. 2001; represents fmr employees of the Centre d'Expérimentation du Pacifique (CEP) and their families; Pres. Roland Pouira Oldham; c. 4,500 mems.

SODEP (Société pour le Développement et l'Expansion du Pacifique): BP 4441, Papeete; tel. 429449; f. 1961; est. by a consortium of banks and private interests; regional devt and finance co.

CHAMBERS OF COMMERCE

Chambre de Commerce, d'Industrie, des Services et des Métiers de Polynésie Française (CCISM): 41 rue du Docteur Cassiau, BP 118, 98713 Papeete; tel. 472700; fax 540701; e-mail info@cci.pf; internet www.ccism.pf; f. 1880; Pres. Gilles Yau; Gen. Man. Abner Gilloux; 34 mems.

Chambre d'Agriculture et de la Pêche Lagonaire: route de l'Hippodrome, BP 5383, Pirae; tel. 425393; fax 438754; e-mail courrier@vanille.pf; f. 1886; Pres. Henri Tauraa; Sec.-Gen. Jacques Roomataaroa; 10 mems.

Jeune Chambre Economique de Tahiti: BP 20669, Papeete; tel. 810114; fax 702703; e-mail contact@jcitahiti.com; internet www.jcitahiti.com; Pres. Sandira Derock.

EMPLOYERS' ORGANIZATIONS

Confédération Générale des Petites et Moyennes Entreprises de Polynésie Française Te Rima Rohi (CGPME): BP 1733, 98713 Papeete; tel. 426333; fax 835608; e-mail courrier@cgpme.pf; internet www.cgpme.pf; Pres. Christophe Plée; c. 1,000 mems.

Affiliated organizations include:

Chambre Syndicale des Fleuristes de Polynésie Française: tel. 800505; fax 573649; e-mail tahitifleurs@mail.pf; f. 2007; Pres. Alain Menard.

Syndicat des Gérants de Stations Services (SGSS): tel. 455479; fax 427314; Pres. Christian Bastien.

Syndicat des Restaurants, Bars et Snacks Bars de Polynésie Française (SRBSBPF): Le Mandarin, BP 302, 98713 Papeete; tel. 503350; fax 421632; e-mail charl.beaumont@mail.pf; Pres. Charles Beaumont.

Syndicat Polynésien des Entreprises et Prestataires de Service (SPEPS): tel. 584629; fax 545641; e-mail rdp@mail.pf; Pres. Sébastien Bouzard (acting).

Union Polynésienne de l'Hôtellerie (UPHO): 76 rue Wallis, BP 1733 Motu Uta, Papeete; tel. 426333; fax 429553; e-mail chris.beaumont@mail.pf; Pres. Christophe Beaumont.

Union Polynésienne des Professions Libérales (UPPL): BP 4554, Papeete; e-mail gibeaux.tahiti@mail.pf; Pres. Charlie Gibeaux.

Conseil des Entreprises de Polynésie Française (CEPF): Immeuble Farnham, rue Clappier, BP 972, 98713 Papeete; tel. 541040; fax 423237; e-mail cepf@cepf.pf; internet www.cepf.pf; f. 1983; fmrly Conseil des Employeurs; affiliated to Mouvement des Entreprises de France (MEDEF); comprises 15 professional and interprofessional orgs, representing 500 cos; Pres. Luc Tapeta-Servonnat; Sec.-Gen. Jean-Claude Lecuelle.

Affiliated organizations include:

Association des Transporteurs Aériens Locaux de Polynésie Française (ATAL): BP 314, 98713 Papeete; tel. 864004; fax 864009; Pres. Marcel Galenon.

Association Tahitienne des Professionnels de l'Audiovisuelle: Papeete.

Chambre Syndicale des Commissionnaires en Douane, Agents de Fret et Déménageurs de Polynésie Française: BP 972, 98713 Papeete; tel. 541040; fax 423237; e-mail cscdafd@cepf.pf; Pres. Titaina Bourne.

Comité de Polynésie de l'Association Française des Banques: Papeete; tel. 426603; fax 26605; Pres. Eric Pommier.

Fédération Générale du Commerce: BP 1607, 98713 Papeete; tel. 541042; fax 422359; e-mail fgc@mail.pf; internet www.fgc.pf; Pres. Jacques Billon-Tyrard; Sec. Patricia Lo Monaco.

Organisation Professionnelle du Conseil de l'Intérim et de la Formation: Papeete.

Syndicat des Agences Maritimes au Long Cours: BP 274, 98713 Papeete; tel. 428972; fax 432184; e-mail amitahiti@amitahiti.pf; Pres. Maeva Siu.

Syndicat des Employeurs du Secteur de l'Assurance (SESA): BP 358, 98713 Papeete; tel. 506262; fax 506263; Pres. Alain Lebris.

Syndicat des Industriels de Polynésie Française (SIPOF): Immeuble Farnham, BP 3521, 98713 Papeete; tel. 541040; fax 423237; e-mail sipof@cepf.pf; internet www.sipof.pf; f. 1974; represents workers in industry, engineering, manufacturing and printing; Pres. Francis Guebel; Sec. Sébastien Mollard; 2,240 mems in 62 cos.

Syndicat Professionnel des Concessionnaires Automobiles: BP 916, 98713 Papeete; tel. 454545; fax 431260; Pres. Paul Yeo Chichong.

Union des Industriels de la Manutention Portuaire (UNIM): BP 570, 98713 Papeete; tel. 545700; fax 426262; Pres. Jules Changues.

Groupement Interprofessionnel du Monoï de Tahiti (GIMT): BP 14 165, Arue, Tahiti; tel. 414851; fax 431849; internet www.monoidetahiti.pf; f. 1992; asscn of monoï manufacturers.

UTILITIES

Electricity

Electricité de Tahiti (EDT): route de Puurai, BP 8021, Faa'a-Puurai; tel. 867704; fax 834439; e-mail edt@edt.pf; internet www.edt.pf; subsidiary of Groupe Suez, France; Pres. Hervé Dubost-Martin; Gen. Man. Christian Lekieffre; c. 60,000 customers (2005).

Water

Société Polynésienne des Eaux et Assainissements: BP 20795, 98713 Papeete; fax 421548; e-mail spea@spea.pf.

TRADE UNIONS

Under French Polynesian legislation, to be officially recognized, trade unions must receive the vote of at least 5% of the work-force at professional elections.

Chambre Syndicale des Métiers du Génie Civil et des Travaux Publics (CSMGCTP): BP 51120, 98716 Pirae; tel. 502100; fax 436922; Pres. Daniel Palacz.

Confédération des Syndicats des Travailleurs de Polynésie/Force Ouvrière (CSTP/FO): Immeuble Farnham, 1er étage, BP 1201, 98713 Papeete; tel. 426049; fax 450635; e-mail pfrebault@cstp-fo.pf; Pres. Coco Teraiefa Chang; Sec.-Gen. Patrick Galenon.

Confédération des Syndicats Indépendants de la Polynésie Française (CSIP): Immeuble Allegret, 1er étage, ave du Prince Hinoï, BP 468, 98713 Papeete; tel. 532274; fax 532275; Sec.-Gen. Cyril Le Gayic.

Confédération Syndicale A Tia I Mua (CFDT): Fare Ia Ora, Mamao, BP 4523, Papeete; tel. 544010; fax 450245; e-mail atiaimua@ifrance.com; affiliated to the Confédération Française Démocratique du Travail; Gen. Sec. Jean-Marie Yan Tu.

Conseil Fédéral des Syndicats Libres de Polynésie O Oe To Oe Rima: Immeuble Brown, 1er étage, BP 52866, 98716 Pirae; tel. 483445; fax 483445; Gen. Sec. Ronald Terorotua.

Union Fédérale des Syndicats Autonomes/Confédération OTAHI (OTAHI UFSA): ancien Immeuble SETIL, 1er étage, ave du Prince Hinoi, BP 148, 98713 Papeete; tel. 450654; fax 451327; Sec.-Gen. Lucie Tiffenat.

Transport

ROADS

French Polynesia has 792 km of roads, of which about one-third are bitumen-surfaced and two-thirds stone-surfaced.

Direction des Transports Terrestres: 93 avenue Pomare V, Fariipiti, BP 4586, 98713 Papeete; tel. 502060; fax 436021; e-mail dtt@transport.gov.pf; internet www.transports-terrestres.pf; f. 1988; Dir Roland Tsu.

SHIPPING

The principal port is at Papeete, on Tahiti.

Port Authority: Port Autonome de Papeete, BP 9164, Motu Uta, 98715 Papeete; tel. 474800; fax 421950; e-mail portppt@portppt.pf; internet www.portdepapeete.pf; Harbour Master Marcel Pelletier; Port Dir Patrick Bordet.

Agence Maritime Internationale de Tahiti: BP 274, 98713 Papeete; tel. 428972; fax 432184; e-mail amitahiti@amitahiti.pf; internet www.amitahiti.com; f. 1978; services from Asia, the USA, Australia, New Zealand and Europe; Gen. Mans Jean Siu, Maeva Siu.

CMA CGM Papeete: 2 rue Wallis, BP 96, Papeete; tel. 545252; fax 436806; e-mail ppt.genmbox@cma-cgm.com; fmrly CGM Tour du Monde SA; shipowners and agents; international freight services; Gen. Man. Stephane Mercadal.

Compagnie Polynésienne de Transport Maritime: BP 220, 98713 Papeete; tel. 426242; fax 434889; e-mail aranui@mail.pf; internet www.aranui.com; shipping co; CEO Jean Wong; Gen. Man. Philippe Wong.

EURL Transport Maritime des Tuamotu Ouest: BP 1816, 98713 Papeete; tel. 422553; fax 422557; inter-island passenger service; Dir Siméon Richmond.

SA Compagnie Française Maritime de Tahiti: Immeuble Importex, No. 45, Fare Ute, POB 368, 98713 Papeete; tel. 426393; fax 420617; e-mail taporo@mail.pf; Pres. and Man. MORTON GARBUTT.

SARL Société de Transport Insulaire Maritime (STIM): BP 635, 98713 Papeete; tel. 549954; fax 452444; Dir ROLAND PAQUIER.

Société de Navigation des Australes: BP 1890, Papeete; tel. 509609; fax 420609; e-mail snathp@mail.pf; inter-island passenger service; Dir HERVÉ DANTON.

CIVIL AVIATION

There is one international airport, Faa'a airport, 6 km from Papeete, on Tahiti, and there are numerous smaller airports and aerodromes throughout French Polynesia. Since October 2004 the Government has commissioned studies into the possible siting of a new international airport on Tubai in the Austral Islands, or in the Marquesas at either Nuku Hiva or Hiva Oa. International services are operated by Air France, Air Tahiti Nui, Air New Zealand, LAN-Chile, Hawaiian Airlines (USA) and Air Calédonie International.

Service d'Etat de l'Aviation Civile: BP 6404, 98702, Faa'a, Papeete; tel. 861000; fax 861009; e-mail webmaster@seac.pf; internet www.seac.pf; Dir THIERRY RÉVIRON.

Aéroport de Tahiti (ADT): BP 60161, 98702, Faa'a Centre; tel. 866060; fax 837391; e-mail secretariat@tahiti-aeroport.pf; internet www.tahiti-aeroport.pf; f. 2010; 50% govt-owned; management and devt of airports at Faa'a, Bora Bora, Raiatea and Rangiroa; Dir-Gen. ALAIN BERQUEZ.

Air Moorea: BP 6019, 98702 Faa'a; tel. 864262; fax 864269; e-mail direction@airmoorea.pf; internet www.airmoorea.pf; f. 1968; operates internal services between Tahiti and Moorea Island and domestic charter flights; Pres. MARCEL GALENON; CEO FREDDY CHANSEAU.

Air Tahiti: BP 314, 98713 Papeete; tel. 864012; fax 864069; e-mail direction.generale@airtahiti.pf; internet www.airtahiti.aero; f. 1953; Air Polynésie 1970–87; operates domestic services to 46 islands; Chair. CHRISTIAN VERNAUDON; Gen. Man. MARCEL GALENON.

Air Tahiti Nui: Immeuble Dexter, Pont de l'Est, BP 1673, 98713 Papeete; tel. 460303; fax 460290; e-mail fly@airtahitinui.pf; internet www.airtahitinui.com; f. 1996; commenced operations 1998; scheduled services to the USA, France, Japan, New Zealand and Australia; CEO ETIENNE HOWAN.

Tourism

Tourism is an important and developed industry in French Polynesia, particularly on Tahiti. Tourist arrivals decreased from 218,241 in 2007 to 153,919 in 2010, but increased to 162,776 in 2011. Most visitors were from the USA, France and Japan. The number of hotels increased from 44 in 2001 to 49 in 2005, while the number of available rooms decreased from 4,418 to 3,326 during the same period. In 2009 earnings from tourism were an estimated US $736m.

GIE Tahiti Tourisme: Fare Manihini, blvd Pomare, BP 65, 98713 Papeete; tel. 504030; fax 436619; e-mail hvaxelaire@tahiti-tourisme.pf; internet www.tahiti-tourisme.pf; f. 1966 as autonomous public body; transformed into private corpn in 1993; relaunched Dec. 2005 following merger between GIE Tahiti Tourisme and Tahiti Manava Visitors' Bureau; Chair. HEREMOANA MAAMAATUAIAHUTAPU; CEO ANNE-SOPHIE LESUR.

Service du Tourisme (SDT): Paofai Bldg (Entry D), blvd Pomare, Papeete; tel. 476200; fax 476202; e-mail sdt@tourisme.gov.pf; govt dept; manages Special Fund for Tourist Development; Dir GÉRARD VANIZETTE.

Defence

As assessed at November 2011, France maintained a force of 607 army and 450 navy personnel in French Polynesia. France began testing nuclear weapons at Mururoa and Fangataufa atolls, in the Tuamotu Archipelago, in 1966. The military presence has been largely connected with the Centre d'Expérimentation du Pacifique (CEP) and the Commission d'Energie Atomique (CEA). An indefinite suspension of tests was announced in mid-1993. In June 1995, however, the French Government announced its decision to resume nuclear testing at Mururoa Atoll. The final test was conducted in January 1996. The defence budget for 2006 was 24,000m. francs CFP.

Commander of the French Armed Forces in French Polynesia, of the Pacific Maritime Area and of the Centre d'Expérimentation du Pacifique: Rear-Adm. JÉRÔME RÉGNIER.

Education

Education is compulsory for eight years between six and 14 years of age. It is free of charge for day pupils in government schools. Primary education, lasting six years, is financed by the territorial budget, while secondary and technical education are supported by state funds. A total of 14,306 children were enrolled in kindergarten in 2008/09. In 2010/11 39,991 pupils attended primary school. Secondary education was provided by public lycées, public high schools and private or church schools. A total of 32,418 pupils attended secondary school in 2010/11. The French Polynesian Government assumed responsibility for secondary education in 1988. Technical and professional education includes eight technical institutions, a tourism training programme, preparation for entrance to the metropolitan Grandes Ecoles, a National Conservatory for Arts and Crafts and training centres for those in the construction industry, health services, traditional handicrafts, primary school teaching and social work. The French University of the Pacific was established in French Polynesia in 1987. In 1999 it was divided into two separate branches, of which the University of French Polynesia is now based in Papeete. In 2009/10 a total of 2,922 students were enrolled at the Papeete branch. In 2004 French state spending on education, higher education and research amounted to 50,500m. francs CFP.

SAINT-BARTHÉLEMY

Saint-Barthélemy is one of the Leeward Islands in the Lesser Antilles. The volcanic island lies in the Caribbean Sea, 230 km north-west of Guadeloupe and 20 km south-east of Saint-Martin. St-Barthélemy occupies only 21 sq km, but has green-clad volcanic hillsides, as well as white beaches and surrounding reefs and islets. The climate is tropical, moderated by the sea, with an annual average temperature of 27.5°C (81°F) and a more humid and wet season between May and November. The island normally receives about 1,100 mm (43 ins) of rain annually. According to official estimates, at 1 January 2009 Saint-Barthélemy had a permanent population of 9,057 predominantly white inhabitants of Breton, Norman and Poitevin descent. There are fewer descendants of the Swedish, who ruled Saint-Barthélemy for almost one century (until a referendum in 1878). French is the official language, but English and two Creole patois are widely spoken. A Norman dialect of French is also still sometimes in use. The majority of the population professes Christianity and belongs to the Roman Catholic Church. The principal town is Gustavia, its main port, in the south-west.

On 7 December 2003 the Guadeloupean dependency of Saint-Barthélemy participated in a Department-wide referendum on Guadeloupe's future constitutional relationship with France. Although the proposal to streamline administrative and political processes was defeated, an overwhelming majority of those participating in Saint-Barthélemy, 95.5%, voted in favour of secession from Guadeloupe to form a separate Overseas Collectivity (Collectivité d'outre-mer). The reorganization was subsequently approved by the French Sénat on 6 February 2007 and by the Assemblée nationale the following day. On 21 February the island was formally designated an Overseas Collectivity.

Legislative elections to form a 19-member legislative assembly, the Conseil territorial (Territorial Council), were held in July 2007. At the first round of elections, held on 1 July, the Saint-Barth d'abord/Union pour un Mouvement Populaire (UMP) list, headed by Bruno Magras, won a clear majority of 72.2% of the total votes cast, thereby obviating the need for a second round. The election was also contested by three other groupings: the Tous unis pour St-Barthélemy list, lead by Karine Miot-Richard, the Action Equilibre et Transparence list headed by Maxime Desouches—each of which secured 9.9% of the ballot—and Benoît Chauvin's Ensemble pour St-Barthélemy, which attracted the remaining 7.9% of the votes cast. Some 70.6% of the electorate participated in the election. The Saint-Barth d'abord/UMP list obtained 16 of the 19 legislative seats, while the three other contenders were allocated one seat each. On 15 July Magras assumed the presidency of the Conseil territorial and Saint-Barthélemy was officially installed as an Overseas Collectivity.

At an election held on 21 September 2008 Michel Magras of the UMP was elected as the territory's representative to the French Sénat. Pending the election of one deputy to the Assemblée nationale (in 2012), the territory was to continue to be represented by Victorin Lurel of the Parti Socialiste, one of the deputies for Guadeloupe. In

December 2011 Philippe Chopin replaced Jacques Simonnet as Prefect. In elections to the Conseil territorial on 18 March 2012, Magras's party, Saint-Barth d'abord, increased its share of the votes cast (to 73.8% from 72.2% in 2007) and retained its 16 seats. The list led by Tous pour Saint Barth increased its representation to two seats while the remaining seat was secured by Saint Barth en Mouvement

Prefect-Delegate: PHILIPPE CHOPIN.

Conseil Territorial

Hôtel de la Collectivité, BP 133, Gustavia; e-mail contact@comstbarth.fr; internet www.comstbarth.fr.

President: BRUNO MAGRAS (Saint-Barth d'abord/UMP).

Election, 18 March 2012

	Seats
Saint-Barth d'abord	16
Tous pour Saint Barth	2
Saint Barth en Mouvement	1
Total	19

Representative to the French Senate: MICHEL MAGRAS (UMP).

SAINT-MARTIN

The French Overseas Collectivity (Collectivité d'outre-mer) of Saint-Martin forms the northern half of the island of Saint Martin (the remainder, Sint Maarten, being part of the Kingdom of the Netherlands). The small volcanic island lies among the Leeward group of the Lesser Antilles in the Caribbean Sea, 8 km south of the British Overseas Territory of Anguilla and 265 km north-west of the French Overseas Department of Guadeloupe, of which Saint-Martin was formerly a dependency. The 10.2-km border between the French and the Dutch territories of the island is the only land frontier in the Lesser Antilles. Saint-Martin occupies about 60% of the island (51 sq km or 20 sq miles). The climate is tropical and moderated by the sea. Saint-Martin normally receives about 1,000 mm (43 ins) of rain annually. According to official estimates, at 1 January 2009 Saint-Martin had a population of 37,461. French is the official language, but a Creole patois is widely spoken, as well as English, Dutch and Spanish. The majority of the population professes Christianity and belongs to the Roman Catholic Church. The principal town is Marigot, in the south-west of the territory, on the north coast of the island, between the sea and the Simpson Bay Lagoon.

On 7 December 2003 the Guadeloupean dependency of Saint-Martin participated in a Department-wide referendum on Guadeloupe's future constitutional relationship with France. Although the proposal to streamline administrative and political processes was defeated, a majority of those participating in Saint-Martin, 76.2%, elected to secede from Guadeloupe to form a separate Overseas Collectivity. The reorganization was subsequently approved by the French Sénat on 6 February 2007 and by the Assemblée nationale the following day. On 21 February the territory of Saint-Martin was formally designated an Overseas Collectivity.

Legislative elections to form a 23-member legislative assembly to be known as the Conseil territorial (Territorial Council) were held in July 2007. At the first round ballot, held on 1 July, the Union pour le Progrès/Union pour un Mouvement Populaire (UPP/UMP) list, headed by Louis-Constant Fleming, won 40.4% of the total votes cast, while the Rassemblement, responsabilité et réussite (RRR) list, led by Alain Richardson, secured 31.9%, and Jean-Luc Hamlet's Réussir Saint-Martin obtained 10.9% of the vote. As no list emerged with an absolute majority, a further round of voting was contested by the three parties that had secured more than 10% of the vote. At this second round, held on 8 July, the UPP/UMP list won 49.0% of the vote and obtained 16 of the 23 legislative seats, the RRR received 42.2% of the vote (six seats), and Réussir Saint-Martin 8.9% (one seat). Voter participation was slightly higher, at 50.8%. Fleming assumed the presidency of the Conseil territorial on 15 July, and Saint-Martin was officially installed as an Overseas Collectivity. However, in July 2008 Fleming was forced to resign the presidency after the French Conseil d'Etat disqualified him from his seat on the Conseil territorial for one year, owing to irregularities in his financial accounts for the 2007 election campaign. In August the Conseil territorial elected Frantz Gumbs as its new President; however, in April 2009 the Conseil d'Etat annulled the election of Gumbs due to voting irregularities. First Vice-President Daniel Gibbs was installed as interim President pending a re-run of the election, which was to be held within 30 days. On 5 May Gumbs was re-elected as President with 16 votes, defeating Alain Richardson, who received six votes, and Marthe Ogoundélé, who gained one vote.

Meanwhile, at an election held on 21 September 2008 Fleming, representing the UMP, was elected as Saint-Martin's representative to the French Sénat. Pending the election of a deputy to the Assemblée nationale (scheduled for 2012), the territory was to continue to be represented therein by Victorin Lurel of the Parti Socialiste, one of the deputies for Guadeloupe. In December 2011 Philippe Chopin replaced Jacques Simonnet as Prefect. First-round elections to the Conseil territorial took place on 18 March 2012. The RRR won the largest percentage of valid votes (34.1%, or 3,077 votes), just ahead of the list headed by Daniel Gibbs (Team Daniel Gibbs 2012), which secured 32.0% (2,889 votes). The UPP attracted 13.3% of the ballot. The RRR consolidated its success at a second round of voting, held on 25 March; the party secured 56.9% of the ballot (5,451 votes), compared to Team Daniel Gibbs 2012, which attracted 43.1% (4,134 votes). Alain Richardson was sworn in as President of the Conseil Territorial on 1 April.

Prefect-Delegate: PHILIPPE CHOPIN.

Conseil Territorial

Hôtel de la Collectivité, rue de Hôtel de Ville, BP 374, Marigot; tel. 5-90-87-50-04; fax 5-90-87-88-53; internet www.com-saint-martin.fr.

President: ALAIN RICHARDSON.

Election, 18 and 25 March 2012

	% of first round votes	% of second round votes
Rassemblement, responsabilité et réussite (RRR)	34.1	56.9
Team Daniel Gibbs 2012	32.0	43.1
Union pour le Progrès (UPP)	13.3	—
Saint Martin pour Tous	9.4	—
Movement for the Advancement of the People (MAP)	7.4	—
Génération Solidaire	3.7	—
Total	100.0	100.0

Representative to the French Senate: LOUIS-CONSTANT FLEMING (UMP).

SAINT PIERRE AND MIQUELON

Introductory Survey

LOCATION, CLIMATE, LANGUAGE, RELIGION, CAPITAL

The territory of Saint Pierre and Miquelon (Iles Saint-Pierre-et-Miquelon) consists of a number of small islands which lie about 25 km (16 miles) from the southern coast of Newfoundland and Labrador, Canada, in the North Atlantic Ocean. The principal islands are Saint Pierre, Miquelon (Grande Miquelon) and Langlade (Petite Miquelon)—the last two being linked by an isthmus of sand. Winters are cold, with temperatures falling to –20°C (–4°F), and summers are mild, with temperatures averaging between 10° and 20°C (50° and 68°F). The islands are particularly affected by fog in June and July. The language is French, and the majority of the population profess Christianity and belong to the Roman Catholic Church. The capital is Saint-Pierre, on the island of Saint Pierre.

CONTEMPORARY POLITICAL HISTORY

Historical Context

The islands of Saint Pierre and Miquelon are the remnants of the once extensive French possessions in North America. They were confirmed as French territory in 1815.

Domestic Political Affairs

Saint Pierre and Miquelon gained departmental status in July 1976. The departmentalization proved unpopular with many of the islanders, since it incorporated the territory's economy into that of the European Community (EC, now European Union, see p. 276—EU), and was regarded as failing to take into account the islands' isolation and dependence on Canada for supplies and transport links. In 1982 socialist and other left-wing candidates, campaigning for a change in the islands' status, were elected unopposed to all seats in the Conseil général (General Council). Saint Pierre and Miquelon was excluded from the Mitterrand administration's decentralization reforms, undertaken in 1982.

In 1976 Canada imposed an economic interest zone extending to 200 nautical miles (370 km) around its shores. Fearing the loss of traditional fishing areas and thus the loss of the livelihood of the fishermen of Saint Pierre, the French Government claimed a similar zone around the islands. Hopes of discovering valuable reserves of petroleum and natural gas in the area heightened the tension between France and Canada.

In December 1984 legislation was approved giving the islands the status of a Territorial Collectivity (Collectivité territoriale) with effect from 11 June 1985. This was intended to allow Saint Pierre and Miquelon to receive the investment and development aid suitable for its position, while allaying Canada's fears of EC exploitation of its offshore waters. Local representatives, however, remained apprehensive about the outcome of negotiations between the French and Canadian Governments to settle the dispute over coastal limits. (France continued to claim a 200-mile fishing and economic zone around Saint Pierre and Miquelon, while Canada wanted the islands to have only a 12-mile zone.) The dispute was submitted to international arbitration. Discussions began in March 1987, and negotiations to determine quotas for France's catch of Atlantic cod over the period 1988–91 were to take place simultaneously. In the meantime, Canada and France agreed on an interim fishing accord, which would allow France to increase its cod quota. The discussions collapsed in October, however, and French trawlers were prohibited from fishing in Canadian waters. In February 1988 Albert Pen and Gérard Grignon, Saint Pierre's elected representatives to the French legislature, together with two members of the Saint Pierre administration and 17 sailors, were arrested for fishing in Canadian waters. This episode, and the arrest of a Canadian trawler captain in May for fishing in Saint Pierre's waters, led to an unsuccessful resumption of negotiations in September. An agreement was reached on fishing rights in March 1989, whereby France's annual quotas for Atlantic cod and other species were determined for the period until the end of 1991. At the same time the Governments agreed upon the composition of an international arbitration tribunal which would delineate the disputed maritime boundaries and exclusive economic zones.

In July 1991 the international arbitration tribunal began its deliberations in New York. The tribunal's ruling, issued in June 1992, was generally deemed to be favourable to Canada. France was allocated an exclusive economic zone around the territory totalling 2,537 square nautical miles (8,700 sq km), compared with its demand for more than 13,000 square nautical miles. The French authorities claimed that the sea area granted would be insufficient to sustain the islands' fishing community. Talks on new fishing quotas for the area off Newfoundland (known as Newfoundland and Labrador from 2001) failed, and, in the absence of a new agreement, industrial fishing in the area was effectively halted until November 1994, when the Governments of the two countries signed an accord specifying new quotas for a period of at least 10 years. In the following month deputies in the Assemblée nationale (National Assembly) expressed concern that the terms of the agreement would be detrimental to Saint Pierre and Miquelon's interests, although the Government asserted that the accord recognized the islanders' historic fishing rights in Canadian waters.

In September 1992 some 64% of voters approved ratification of the Treaty on European Union (see p. 276), although only a small percentage of the electorate participated in the referendum. At elections to the Sénat in 1993, Albert Pen, representing the Parti Socialiste (PS), was narrowly defeated at a second round of voting by Victor Reux of the right-wing Rassemblement pour la République (RPR), since 1994 the Secretary of the islands' Economic and Social Council. Gérard Grignon, of the centre-right Union pour la Démocratie Française (UDF), was re-elected to the Assemblée nationale at a second round of voting in June 1997.

A number of government proposals regarding the socio-economic and institutional development of the Overseas Departments, certain provisions of which were also to be applied to Saint Pierre and Miquelon, were provisionally accepted by the Assemblée nationale in May 2000, and subsequently adopted by the Sénat (following a number of modifications). The proposals were definitively approved by the Assemblée nationale in November and were ratified by the Constitutional Council in December. Measures included provisions for improving and supporting the economic development of the islands, as well as the introduction of proportional representation in elections to the Conseil général. In the June 2002 general election Grignon, representing an alliance of the Union pour la Majorité Présidentielle and the UDF, was re-elected to the Assemblée nationale, with 69% of the second round votes.

In March 2003, as part of a wider constitutional reform, the islands were given the status of an Overseas Collectivity (Collectivité d'outre-mer). At elections to the Sénat in September 2004 the mayor of Miquelon, Denis Detcheverry, narrowly defeated the mayor of Saint Pierre, Karine Claireaux. In May 2005 a national referendum was held on ratification of the European Union constitutional treaty: 62.7% of the local electorate voted in favour of adopting the treaty; however, voter turn-out was only 37.1%. The treaty was ultimately rejected by a majority of voters in metropolitan France. At elections to the Conseil général in March 2006 Archipel Demain won 13 of Saint Pierre's 15 seats; the left-wing Cap sur l'Avenir (CSA) took the remaining two seats. Archipel Demain also won three of the four available seats allocated to Miquelon; SPM Ensemble took the remaining seat. Stéphane Artano of Archipel Demain was elected President of the Conseil général.

Further provisions of the 2003 constitutional reform were effected in February 2007, following the approval by the French Sénat and the Assemblée nationale of an organic law that amended the statutes and institutions of French Overseas Possessions. The legislation redesignated the Conseil général as a Conseil territorial (Territorial Council) and granted local government wider fiscal powers and greater control over the operation of the exclusive economic zone. In the first round of the presidential election, held on 22 April, Ségolène Royal of the PS obtained 26.6% of the votes cast on the islands, ahead of Nicolas Sarkozy of the Union pour un Mouvement Populaire (UMP), who received 24.9%. Royal subsequently won 60.9% of the islands' votes in the second round, on 6 May; however, Sarkozy was elected President nationally. In the second round of the elections to the Assemblé nationale on 17 June, Grignon was narrowly defeated by Annick Girardin, representing the Parti Radical de Gauche in association with CSA. In October 2009 Jean-Régis Borius succeeded Jean-Pierre Berçot as Prefect of the territory. In 2011 Artano remained as President of the Conseil despite having been convicted, in November 2009, of misappropriation of public funds and fined €7,500 by the territory's Higher Court of Appeal. Artano had approved expense claims deemed excessive from his predecessor, Marc Plantegenest. Plantegenest was fined €60,000 and given a four-month suspended prison sentence. Both men appealed the convictions, but in November 2010 the original decision was upheld.

In September 2011 the mayor of Saint Pierre, Karine Claireaux, representing the PS, was elected to the Sénat. Claireaux secured a majority in the first round of voting, defeating Grignon, who was representing the UMP, and Detcheverry, the outgoing senator. In November Patrice Latron succeeded Jean-Régis Borius as Prefect of the territory. The elections to the Conseil territorial in March 2012 were contested by Archipel Demain and the left-wing, CSA-led Ensemble pour l'Avenir electoral list: Archipel Demain secured 15 seats; CSA candidates won the remaining four seats. At the end of March Artano was re-elected as President of the Conseil.

CONSTITUTION AND GOVERNMENT

The French Government is represented in Saint Pierre by an appointed Prefect. There is a Conseil territorial (Territorial Council, known as the Conseil général—General Council—until February 2007), with 19 members (15 for Saint Pierre and four for Miquelon), elected by adult universal suffrage for a period of six years. Saint Pierre and Miquelon elects one deputy to the Assemblée nationale and one representative to the Sénat in Paris.

ECONOMIC AFFAIRS

The soil and climatic conditions of Saint Pierre and Miquelon do not favour agricultural production, which is mainly confined to smallholdings, except for market-gardening and the production of eggs and chickens.

The principal economic activity of the islands is traditionally fishing and related industries. However, the sector has been severely affected by disputes with Canada regarding territorial waters and fishing quotas, and employed just 2.7% of the working population in 1999. By 2005 the fishing fleet had been reduced to some 26 vessels, of which only 15 were considered to be active. New arrangements have been to the detriment of Saint Pierre and Miquelon, although there is some optimism regarding the potential for the exploitation of shellfish, notably mussels and scallops; since 2000 Export Development Canada has been developing commercial scallop farms in the islands' waters. The total fish catch increased from 747 metric tons in 1996 to 6,485 tons in 2000, before falling to 3,802 tons in 2001. By 2008 the total catch had recovered to 4,621 tons, before declining to 1,761 tons in 2009.

Fish-processing—producing frozen and salted fish, and fish meal for fodder—provided the basis for industrial activity, employing around 100 people in 2006. Much of the fish processed was imported. Electricity is generated by two thermal power stations, with a combined capacity of 26.2 MW, and a wind power station (on Miquelon) with a capacity of 0.6 MW. The resolution of a boundary dispute between the Canadian provinces of Nova Scotia and Newfoundland and Labrador in 2002 accorded the islands about 500 sq miles of waters over the Gulf of Saint Lawrence basin, believed to contain substantial reserves of petroleum and gas. In May 2005, following four years of negotiations, the Governments of France and Canada signed an agreement on the exploration and exploitation of 'transboundary' hydrocarbon fields. Two Canadian oil companies were given exclusive licences to explore the area until April 2006. In 2009 ConocoPhillips Canada and Bardoil Energy SPM, a locally registered company, filed applications for two exploration licences within the French exclusive economic zone. However, in mid-2010 it was reported that ConocoPhillips had withdrawn its application.

The replenishment of ships' (mainly trawlers') supplies was formerly an important economic activity, but has now also been adversely affected by the downturn in the industrial fishing sector. Efforts were made to promote tourism, and the opening of the Saint Pierre–Montréal air route in 1987 led to an increase in air traffic in the 1990s. In 1999 the completion of a new airport capable of accommodating larger aircraft further improved transport links. Tourist arrivals in 2010 were estimated at 12,322.

In 2010 Saint Pierre and Miquelon recorded a trade deficit of €67.1m. Most trade is with Canada and France and other countries of the EU (see p. 276). The only significant exports are fresh and frozen fish, which provided 38% of the total value of non-entrepôt exports in 2010. The principal imports are food and beverages and mineral fuels. Items such as clothing and other consumer goods are generally imported from France.

The annual rate of inflation averaged 6.0% in 1997–2005; consumer prices increased by 4.1% in 2008, but declined by 0.8% in 2009. Some 12.8% of the labour force were unemployed at the 1999 census. The rate of unemployment in 2011 was estimated at 7.4%.

Given the decline of the fishing sector, the development of the ports of Saint Pierre and Miquelon and the expansion of tourism (particularly from Canada and the USA) are regarded locally as the principal means of maintaining economic progress. In December 2005 a report commissioned by the Sénat recommended expanding trade links with Canada. The report also identified hydrocarbon exploration as a future source of revenue, if not from direct exploitation of resources within Saint Pierre and Miquelon's own territory, then by providing services to companies operating in Canadian waters, where oil deposits were already being worked. In March 2009 the French authorities announced that the country intended to submit a claim before the UN Commission on the Limits of the Continental Shelf to thousands of square miles of sea bed around Saint Pierre and Miquelon, thought to be rich with petroleum deposits. The announcement was in anticipation of Canada's completion of a five-year project to map the Atlantic sea bed off its eastern coast. It was expected that Canada would take all measures to contest the claim. The islands remain highly dependent on budgetary assistance from the French central Government, and face potential problems in the future due to their ageing population, with increasing numbers of young people leaving the islands to study and work in mainland France and Canada. Youth unemployment is also high, with 27.8% of people aged 20–24 seeking work in 2006. In mid-2011 the islands' largest fish-processing company and a major local employer, SPM Seafoods International, was placed in receivership. The development was expected to have severe consequences for the fishing sector.

PUBLIC HOLIDAYS

2013: 1 January (New Year's Day), 1 April (Easter Monday), 1 May (Labour Day), 8 May (Liberation Day), 9 May (Ascension Day), 20 May (Whit Monday), 14 July (National Day, Fall of the Bastille), 15 August (Assumption), 1 November (All Saints' Day), 11 November (Armistice Day), 25 December (Christmas Day).

Statistical Survey

Source: Préfecture, pl. du Lieutenant-Colonel Pigeaud, BP 4200, 97500 Saint-Pierre; tel. 41-10-10; fax 41-47-38.

AREA AND POPULATION

Area: 242 sq km (93.4 sq miles): Saint Pierre 26 sq km, Miquelon-Langlade 216 sq km.

Population: 6,125 at census of March 2006; 6,314 (Saint Pierre 5,699, Miquelon Langlade 615) at census of 1 January 2009. Note: According to new census methodology, data in 2009 refer to median figures based on the collection of raw data over a five-year period (2006–11).

Density (at 1 January 2009): 26.1 per sq km.

Births, Marriages and Deaths (1997): Live births 92; Marriages 36; Deaths 51. *2009:* Live births 64; Deaths 45.

Economically Active Population (1999): Fish and fish-processing 76; Other manufacturing 194; Construction 261; Transport 150; Trade 418; Financial services 79; Real estate services 7; Business services 383; Education 490; Government employees 732; *Total employed* 2,790; Unemployed 408; *Total labour force* 3,198. *2006 census* (preliminary): Total employed 2,876; Registered unemployed 318; Total labour force 3,194 (males 1,751, females 1,443).

AGRICULTURE

Principal Crops (metric tons, 2010, unless otherwise indicated): Lettuce ('000 heads, 2007) 67.9; Tomatoes 6 (FAO estimate); Strawberries 1 (FAO estimate) (Source: partly FAO).

Livestock ('000 head, 2010, FAO estimates): Sheep 0.2; Chickens 40; Ducks 1 (Source: FAO).

FISHING

Total Catch (all capture, metric tons, live weight, 2009): Atlantic cod 542; Yellowtail flounder 87; Rays 6; Queen crab 169; Total (incl. others) 1,761.

Source: FAO.

FINANCE

Currency and Exchange Rates: French currency was used until the end of 2001. Euro notes and coins were introduced on 1 January 2002, and the euro became the sole legal tender from 18 February. Some of the figures in this Survey are still in terms of French francs. For details of exchange rates, see French Guiana.

Expenditure by Metropolitan France (million francs, 1997): 280.

Budget (€ 'million, 2009): *Revenue:* Current 28.8 (Direct taxes 11.3; Indirect taxes 10.5; Capital 17.5; Total 46.3. *Expenditure:* Current 23.2; Capital 15.8; Total 38.9.

Money Supply (million francs at 31 December 1997): Currency outside banks 281; Demand deposits at banks 897; Total money 1,178.

Cost of Living (Consumer Price Index at December; base: December 1998 = 100): 142.7 in 2008; 141.7 in 2009.

Expenditure on the Gross Domestic Product (€ million at current prices, 2007): Government final consumption expenditure 82.7; Private final consumption expenditure 110.4; Gross fixed capital formation 40.2; Change in stocks –1.2; *Total domestic expenditure* 232.1; Exports of goods and services 8.3; *Less* Imports of goods and services 79.2; *GDP in purchasers' values* 161.1 (Source: Institut d'Emission des Départements d'Outre-mer).

Gross Domestic Product by Economic Activity (€ million, 2004): Agriculture 1.0; Fishing 2.9; Construction 16.6; Other industry 4.8; Trade 21.3; Hotels and restaurants 3.9; Real estate and renting 15.1; Transport and communications 8.4; Financial services 7.4; Public administration and other non-market services 67.2; *Total* 148.7.

EXTERNAL TRADE

Total (€ million, 2010): *Imports:* 71.4 (Food and beverages 14.5, Mineral fuels 11.3, Other—largely raw materials 45.6); *Exports:* 5.0 (Fresh or frozen fish 1.9; Crustaceans (fresh), refrigerated 0.6). Note: Totals for imports and exports exclude entrepôt movements (€0.5m. of imports–mostly fish for food manufacturing, and €1.5m. of exports) (Source: Institut d'Emission des Départements d'Outre-mer).

Note: Most trade is with Canada, France (imports), other countries of the European Union (exports) and the USA.

TRANSPORT

Road Traffic (2010): 6,026 motor vehicles in use.

Shipping (2007): Ships entered 867 (Source: Service des Douanes).

Civil Aviation (2010): Passengers carried 45,558; Freight carried 95.4 metric tons (Source: Service de l'Aviation Civile de Saint Pierre et Miquelon).

TOURISM

Tourist Arrivals: 15,098 in 2008; 11,767 in 2009; 12,323 in 2010.

Tourist Arrivals by Country of Residence (2010): France 1,725; Other (mostly Canada and USA) 10,598; Total 12,323.

Source: Institut d'Emission des Départements d'Outre-mer.

COMMUNICATIONS MEDIA

Radio Receivers (estimate, '000 in use): 5.0 in 1997.

Television Receivers (estimate, '000 in use): 3.5 in 1997.

EDUCATION

Primary (2002): 8 institutions; 73 teachers; 736 students.

Secondary (2002): 2 institutions; 56 teachers; 329 students.

Technical (2002): 1 institution; 25 teachers; 134 students.

Source: Service de l'Education Nationale de Saint Pierre et Miquelon.

Note: At the time of the 2006 census, 211 students of higher education were studying outside of Saint Pierre and Miquelon.

Directory

The Government

(May 2012)

HEAD OF STATE

President: NICOLAS SARKOZY.

Prefect: PATRICE LATRON, pl. du Lieutenant-Colonel Pigeaud, BP 4200, 97500 Saint-Pierre; tel. 41-10-10; fax 41-47-38; e-mail courrier@saint-pierre-et-miquelon.pref.gouv.fr; internet www.saint-pierre-et-miquelon.pref.gouv.fr.

DEPARTMENTAL ADMINISTRATION

President of the Economic and Social Committee: MAX OLAISOLA, 4 rue Bordas, 97500 Saint-Pierre; tel. 41-45-50; fax 41-42-45; e-mail comite.ec.soc.spm@cheznoo.net.

REPRESENTATIVES TO THE FRENCH PARLIAMENT

Deputy to the French National Assembly: ANNICK GIRARDIN (PRG-SPM).

Representative to the French Senate: KARINE CLAIREAUX (PS).

Conseil Territorial

2 pl. de Monseigneur François Maurer, BP 4208, 97500 Saint-Pierre; tel. 41-01-02; fax 41-22-97; e-mail cgspm@wanadoo.fr.

The Conseil territorial (fmrly the Conseil général) has 19 mems: Saint Pierre 15, Miquelon four. The last election to the Conseil territorial was held in March 2012; as a result of those elections, the composition of the Conseil by party was as follows: Archipel Demain 15, Cap sur l'Avenir four.

President: STÉPHANE ARTANO.

Political Organizations

Archipel Demain: 1 rue des Français Libres, BP 1179, 97500 Saint-Pierre; tel. 41-42-19; fax 41-48-06; e-mail contact@archipeldemain.fr; internet www.archipeldemain.fr; f. 1985; Pres. GÉRARD GRIGNON; Sec.-Gen. BERNARD BRIAND; incl. Archipel Demain Miquelon (Leader CÉLINE GASPARD).

Cap sur l'Avenir (CSA): 7 rue René Autin, BP 4477, 97500 Saint-Pierre; tel. 41-99-08; fax 41-99-97; e-mail agirardin@assemblee-nationale.fr; internet www.capsurlavenir-expression.net; f. 2000; left-wing and green coalition; associated with the PRG-SPM; Pres. ANNICK GIRARDIN.

Ensemble pour Construire: BP 305, 97500 Saint-Pierre; e-mail ensemblepourconstruire@cheznoo.net; internet www.ensemblepourconstruire.com; affiliated with the metropolitan Parti Socialiste; supported the Ensemble pour l'Avenir electoral list during the 2012 elections to the Conseil territorial; Pres. KARINE CLAIREAUX.

Parti Radical de Gauche SPM (PRG-SPM): 7 rue René Autin, BP 4477, 97500 Saint-Pierre; tel. 41-99-08; fax 41-99-97; internet www.planeteradicale.org/-St-Pierre-et-Miquelon; local br. of the metropolitan party; associated with CSA; Pres. YANNICK CAMBRAY; Sec. TATIANA VIGNEAU.

SPM Ensemble: c/o Mairie de Miquelon, 2 rue du Baron de l'espérance, Miquelon, 97500 Saint-Pierre; internet spmensemble.oldiblog.com; f. 2006; left-wing, independent; advocates parity between the islands of Saint-Pierre and Miquelon; STÉPHANE COSTE.

Union pour un Mouvement Populaire (UMP): 15 rue Ange Gautier, BP 113, 97500 Saint-Pierre; tel. 41-35-73; fax 41-29-97; e-mail contact@ump975.net; internet www.ump975.net; centre-right; local br. of the metropolitan party; Pres., Departmental Cttee FRANÇOIS ZIMMERMANN.

Judicial System

Tribunal Supérieur d'Appel: 14 rue Emile Sasco, BP 4215, 97500 Saint-Pierre; tel. 41-03-20; fax 41-03-23; e-mail francois.billon@justice.fr; Presiding Magistrate JEAN-YVES GOUEFFON; Procurator HERVÉ LEROY.

Tribunal de Première Instance: 4 rue Borda, BP 4215, 97500 Saint-Pierre; tel. 41-03-20; fax 41-41-03-23; Presiding Magistrate VÉRONIQUE VEILLARD.

Religion

Almost all of the inhabitants are adherents of the Roman Catholic Church.

CHRISTIANITY

The Roman Catholic Church

The islands form the Apostolic Vicariate of the Iles Saint-Pierre et Miquelon. At 31 December 2006 there were an estimated 6,076 adherents.

Vicar Apostolic: MARIE PIERRE FRANÇOIS AUGUSTE GASCHY (Titular Bishop of Usinaza), Vicariat Apostolique, BP 4245, 97500 Saint-Pierre; tel. 41-02-40; fax 41-47-09; e-mail mission-catho.spm@wanadoo.fr.

Other Churches

Eglise Evangélique de Saint-Pierre et Miquelon: 5 bis rue Paul Lebailly, BP 4325, 97500 Saint-Pierre; tel. 41-92-39; fax 41-59-75; e-mail pasteurspm@cheznoo.net; internet www.cheznoo.net/eglise_evangelique.spm; f. 1995; affiliated to the Fédération Nationale des Assemblées de Dieu de France and Commission des Eglises Evangéliques d'Expression Française à l'Extérieure; Pastor FRANCIS NOVERT.

The Press

L'Echo des Caps Hebdo: rue Georges Daguerre, BP 4213, 97500 Saint-Pierre; tel. 41-10-90; fax 41-49-33; e-mail echohebd@cheznoo.net; f. 1982; weekly; Dir KARINE CLAIREAUX; Editor-in-Chief DIDIER GIL; circ. 3,000.

Recueil des Actes Administratifs: 4 rue du Général Leclerc, BP 4233, 97500 Saint-Pierre; tel. 41-24-50; fax 41-20-85; e-mail imprimeriepref@cheznoo.net; f. 1866; monthly; Dir DANIEL KOELSCH.

Le Vent de la Liberté: 1 rue Amiral Muselier, BP 1179, 97500 Saint-Pierre; tel. 41-42-19; fax 41-48-06; e-mail archipel@cheznoo.net; f. 1986; monthly; Dir GÉRARD GRIGNON; circ. 550.

Broadcasting and Communications

TELECOMMUNICATIONS

SPM Telecom: 6 pl. du Général de Gaulle, BP 4253, 97500 Saint Pierre; tel. 41-00-15; fax 41-00-19; e-mail accueil@spmtelecom.com; internet www.spmtelecom.com; Dir XAVIER BOWRING.

RADIO AND TELEVISION

Réseau Outre-mer 1ère: BP 4227, 97500 Saint-Pierre; tel. 41-11-11; fax 41-22-19; internet saintpierremiquelon.la1ere.fr; acquired by Groupe France Télévisions in 2004; fmrly Société Nationale de Radio-Télévision Française d'Outre-mer, became Réseau France Outre-mer (RFO) in 1998, present name adopted in 2010; broadcasts 24 hours of radio programmes daily on three stations and 195 hours of television programmes weekly on two channels, Télé St Pierre et Miquelon and Tempo; Gen. Man. YVES GARNIER; Regional Dir MOZARIO GABBANI.

Radio Atlantique: 1er étage du Centre Culturel et Sportif, BP 1282, 97500 Saint-Pierre; tel. 41-24-93; fax 41-56-33; e-mail radioatlantique@cheznoo.net; internet www.cheznoo.net/radioatlantique; f. 1982; private; broadcasts 24 hours of radio programmes daily; Pres. PASCAL DAIREAUX; Sec. ANDRÉ URTIZBÉRÉA.

Finance

(cap. = capital, res = reserves, dep. = deposits; m. = million; amounts in euros)

BANKING

Central Bank

Institut d'Emission des Départements d'Outre-mer (IEDOM): 4 rue de la Roncière, BP 4202, 97500 Saint-Pierre; tel. 41-43-57; fax 41-58-55; e-mail agence@iedom-spm.fr; internet www.iedom.fr; Dir FABRICE DUFRESNE.

Commercial Bank

Banque de Saint-Pierre et Miquelon (BDSPM): 2 rue Jacques Cartier, BP 4223, 97500 Saint-Pierre; tel. 41-07-00; fax 41-07-42; internet www.bdspm.fr; f. 1889; name changed as above in 2009, following merger with Crédit Saint Pierrais; subsidiary of Groupe BPCE, France; cap. 15.4m., res 0.2m., dep. 147.5m. (Dec. 2009); Pres. PHILIPPE GARSUAULT; Gen. Man. PIERRE BALSAN; 2 brs.

INSURANCE

Cabinet Paturel Assurances, Allianz: 29 bis rue Boursaint, BP 4288, 97500 Saint-Pierre; tel. 41-04-40; fax 41-51-65; e-mail npaturel@allianz-spm.fr; internet www.allianz-spm.fr; Man. NATHALIE PATUREL.

Mutuelle des Iles: 52 rue Maréchal Foch, BP 1112, 97500 Saint-Pierre; tel. 41-28-69; fax 41-51-13.

Trade and Industry

DEVELOPMENT AGENCIES

Agence Française de Développement (AFD): 22 place du Général de Gaulle, BP 4202, 97500 Saint-Pierre; tel. 41-06-00; fax 41-25-98; e-mail ledom-spm@iedom-spm.fr; internet saintpierreetmiquelon.afd.fr; fmrly Caisse Française de Développement; Man. FABRICE DUFRESNE.

Société de Développement et de Promotion de l'Archipel (SODEPAR): Palais Royal, rue Borda, BP 4365, 97500 Saint-Pierre; tel. 41-15-15; fax 41-15-16; e-mail sodepar.spm@sodepar.com; internet www.sodepar.com; f. 1989; economic devt agency; Chair. STÉPHANE ARTANO; Dir FRANÇOISE LETOURNEL.

CHAMBER OF COMMERCE

Chambre d'Agriculture, de Commerce, d'Industrie, de Métiers et de l'Artisanat (CACIMA): 4 rue Constant-Colmay, BP 4207, 97500 Saint-Pierre; tel. 41-45-12; fax 41-32-09; e-mail cacim@ccimspm.org; internet www.cacimaspm.fr; Pres. XAVIER BOWRING; Sec. ROMUALD DERRIBLE.

TRADE UNIONS

Syndicat des Armateurs à la Pêche Côtière: BP 937, 97500 Saint-Pierre; tel. 41-30-13; fax 41-73-89; e-mail kenavo@cheznoo.net; Pres. JEAN BEAUPERTUIS.

Syndicat CFDT (Union Interprofessionnelle SPM): 15 rue du Docteur Dunan, BP 4352, 97500 Saint-Pierre; tel. 41-23-20; fax 41-27-99; e-mail cfdt.spm@cheznoo.net; internet www.cfdtspm.com; affiliated to the Confédération Française Démocratique du Travail; Sec.-Gen. VÉRONIQUE PERRIN.

Union Départementale Force Ouvrière: 15 rue du Docteur Dunan, BP 4241, 97500 Saint-Pierre; tel. 41-25-22; fax 41-46-55; e-mail udfospm975@cheznoo.net; affiliated to the Confédération Générale du Travail-Force Ouvrière; Sec.-Gen. ALAIN TANGUY.

Union Intersyndicale CGT de Saint-Pierre et Miquelon: rue du 11 Novembre, 97500 Saint-Pierre; tel. 41-41-86; fax 41-30-21; e-mail cgtsp@cheznoo.net; affiliated to the Confédération Générale du Travail; Sec.-Gen. RONALD MANET.

UNSA-Education: rue du Docteur Dunan, 97500 Saint-Pierre; tel. 41-38-05; fax 41-34-08; e-mail 975@se-unsa.org; represents teaching staff; Sec.-Gen. ANDRÉ URTIZBEREA.

Transport

SHIPPING

Packet boats and container services operate between Saint-Pierre and Halifax, Nova Scotia (Canada), Boston, MA (USA), and France. There is a ferry service between Saint-Pierre, Miquelon and Newfoundland and Labrador. The seaport at Saint-Pierre has three jetties and 1,200 metres of quays.

Alliance Europe Le Havre: 1 rue Abbé Pierre Gervain, 97500 Saint-Pierre; tel. 20-53-53; fax 20-53-86; e-mail mc.spm@alliance-europe.fr; internet alliance-europe.fr; f. 2004 as successor to Compagnie Maritime des Transports Frigorifiques (f. 1980); operates weekly container and ro-ro shipping services between Saint Pierre and Miquelon and ports in northern Europe; also operates air freight service; Gen. Man. MARIANNICK SPENS.

Régie de Transports Maritimes: pl. du Général de Gaulle, BP 4468, 97500 Saint-Pierre; tel. 41-08-75; fax 41-98-95; e-mail rtm@cg975.fr; internet www.cg975.fr; govt-operated; operates inter-island passenger ferry services and services between Saint-Pierre and Newfoundland, Canada; Dir CAROLINE CECCHETTI.

CIVIL AVIATION

There is an airport on Saint Pierre, served by airlines linking the territory with five destinations in Canada. Construction of a new airport, able to accommodate larger aircraft and thus improve air links, was completed in 1999.

Service de l'Aviation Civile de Saint-Pierre et Miquelon: Aérodrome Saint-Pierre Pointe Blanche, BP 4265, 97500 Saint-Pierre; tel. 41-18-00; fax 41-18-18; e-mail sacspm@aviation-civile.gouv.fr; internet www.cheznoo.net/sacspm; Dir LUC COLLET.

Air Saint-Pierre: 18 rue Albert Briand, Saint-Pierre, BP 4225, 97500 Saint-Pierre; tel. 41-00-00; fax 41-00-02; e-mail contact@airsaintpierre.com; internet www.airsaintpierre.com; f. 1964; connects the territory directly with Newfoundland and Labrador, Nova Scotia and Québec, Canada; Pres. RÉMY L. BRIAND; Man. THIERRY BRIAND.

Tourism

There were an estimated 11,450 tourist arrivals in 2011. In 2010 there were 18 establishments offering tourist accommodation.

Comité Régional du Tourisme: pl. du Général de Gaulle, BP 4274, 97500 Saint-Pierre; tel. 41-02-00; fax 41-33-55; e-mail info@st-pierre-et-miquelon.info; internet www.st-pierre-et-miquelon.info; f. 1989; fmrly Service Loisirs Accueil; Pres. FRANÇOIS RIVOLLET; Dir PIERRE-YVES CASTAING.

Defence

France is responsible for the islands' defence.

Education

The education system is modelled on the French system, and education is compulsory for children aged between six and 16 years. In 2002 there were eight primary schools, two secondary schools (one of which is private and has a technical school annex) and one technical school. At the time of the 2006 census, 211 students of higher education were studying outside Saint Pierre and Miquelon. Agreements with universities in New Brunswick, Newfoundland and Labrador and Nova Scotia allow students from Saint Pierre and Miquelon to enjoy the same rights as Canadian students.

THE WALLIS AND FUTUNA ISLANDS

Introductory Survey

LOCATION, CLIMATE, LANGUAGE, RELIGION, CAPITAL

Wallis and Futuna comprises two groups of islands: the Wallis Islands, including Wallis Island (also known as Uvea) and 10 islets *(motu)* on the surrounding reef, and Futuna (or Hooru) to the south-west, comprising the two small islands of Futuna and Alofi. The islands are located north-east of Fiji and west of Samoa. Temperatures are generally between about 23°C (73°F) and 30°C (86°F), and there is a cyclone season between December and March. French and the indigenous Polynesian languages Wallisian (Uvean) and Futunian are spoken throughout the islands. Nearly all of the population is nominally Roman Catholic. The capital is Mata'Utu, on Wallis Island.

CONTEMPORARY POLITICAL HISTORY

Historical Context

French protectorate status was formalized for Wallis and for the two kingdoms of Futuna in the 19th century. The islands were subsequently treated as a dependency of New Caledonia. During the Second World War (1939–45), Wallis was used as an air force base by the USA. In 1959 the traditional Kings and chiefs requested integration into the French Republic. The islands formally became an Overseas Territory in July 1961, following a referendum in December 1959, in which 94.4% of the electorate requested this status (almost all the opposition was in Futuna, which itself recorded dissent from only 22.2% of the voters; Wallis was unanimous in its acceptance).

Although there was no movement in Wallis and Futuna seeking secession of the Territory from France (in contrast with the situation in the other French Pacific Territories, French Polynesia and New Caledonia), the two Kings whose kingdoms share the island of Futuna requested in November 1983, through the Territorial Assembly, that the island groups of Wallis and Futuna become separate Overseas Territories of France, arguing that the administration and affairs of the Territory had become excessively concentrated on the island of Wallis.

Domestic Political Affairs

At elections to the 20-member Territorial Assembly in March 1982, the Rassemblement pour la République (RPR) and its allies won 11 seats, while the remaining nine were secured by candidates belonging to, or associated with, the Union pour la Démocratie Française (UDF). Later that year one member of the Lua Kae Tahi, a group affiliated to the metropolitan UDF, defected to the RPR group. In November 1983, however, three of the 12 RPR members joined the Lua Kae Tahi, forming a new majority. In the subsequent election for President of the Territorial Assembly, this 11-strong bloc of UDF-associated members supported the ultimately successful candidate, Falakiko Gata, even though he had been elected to the Territorial Assembly in 1982 as a member of the RPR.

In April 1985 Falakiko Gata formed a new political party, the Union Populaire Locale (UPL), which was committed to giving priority to local, rather than metropolitan, issues.

In 1987 a dispute broke out between two families both laying claim to the throne of Sigave, the northern kingdom on the island of Futuna. The conflict arose following the deposition of the former King, Sagato Keletaona, and his succession by Sosefo Vanaï. The intervention of the island's administrative authorities, who attempted to ratify Vanaï's accession to the throne, was condemned by the Keletaona family as an interference in the normal course of local custom, according to which such disputes are traditionally settled by a fight between the protagonists.

At elections to the Territorial Assembly held in March 1987, the UDF (together with affiliated parties) and the RPR each won seven seats. However, by forming an alliance with the UPL, the RPR maintained its majority, and Falakiko Gata was subsequently re-elected President. At elections to the French Assemblée nationale (National Assembly) in June 1988, Benjamin Brial was re-elected deputy. However, when the result was challenged by an unsuccessful candidate, Kamilo Gata, the election was investigated by the French Constitutional Council and the result declared invalid, owing to electoral irregularities. When the election was held again in January 1989, Kamilo Gata was elected deputy, obtaining 57.4% of the total votes.

Statistical information, gathered in 1990, showed that the emigration rate of Wallis and Futuna islanders had risen to over 50%. In October of that year 13,705 people (of whom 97% were Wallisians and Futunians) lived in the Territory, while 14,186 were resident in New Caledonia. At the 1996 census the number of Wallisians and Futunians resident in New Caledonia had increased to 17,563. According to the results, a proportion of the islanders had chosen to emigrate to other French Overseas Possessions or to metropolitan France, mainly owing to the lack of employment opportunities in the islands.

At elections to the Territorial Assembly in March 1992 the newly founded Taumu'a Lelei secured 11 seats, while the RPR won nine. The new Assembly was remarkable for being the first since 1964 in which the RPR did not hold a majority. At elections to the French Assemblée nationale in March 1993, Kamilo Gata was re-elected deputy, obtaining 52.4% of the total votes cast to defeat Clovis Logologofolau. In June 1994 the Union Locale Force Ouvrière organized a general strike in protest at the increasing cost of living in the Territory and the allegedly inadequate education system. It was reported that demonstrations continued for several days, during which the Territorial Assembly building was damaged in an arson attack.

In October 1994 it was reported that the King of Sigave (or Keletaona), Lafaele Malau, had been deposed by a unanimous decision of the kingdom's chiefs. The action followed the appointment of two customary leaders to represent the Futunian community in New Caledonia, which had led to unrest among the inhabitants of Sigave.

At elections to the Territorial Assembly in December 1994 the RPR secured 10 seats, while a coalition group, Union Populaire pour Wallis et Futuna (UPWF), won seven, and independent candidates three. Mikaele Tauhavili was subsequently elected President of the Assembly.

The refusal by 10 of the 20 members of the Territorial Assembly to adopt budgetary proposals in January 1996 led to appeals for the dissolution of the Government by France and the organization of new elections. The budget (which, at US $20m., was some $4.5m. smaller than in the previous year) aroused opposition for its apparent lack of provision for development funds, particularly for the islands' nascent tourist industry.

Elections to the Territorial Assembly took place in March 1997. A participation rate of 87.2% was recorded at the poll, in which RPR candidates secured 14 seats and left-wing candidates (including independents and members of various political groupings) won six seats. Victor Brial, a representative of the RPR, was elected President of the Territorial Assembly. At the second round of elections to the French Assemblée nationale, on 1 June, Brial defeated Kamilo Gata, obtaining 3,241 votes (51.3% of the total).

Allegations that irregularities had occurred in the elections of March 1997 were investigated and upheld for 11 of the seats. As a result, new elections were organized for the 11 seats in September 1998, following which the RPR's representation in the Assembly was reduced to from 14 to 11 seats, while left-wing and independent members increased their share of seats from six to nine. Also in September 1998, in a second round of voting, Fr Robert Laufoaulu was elected to the French Sénat (Senate), defeating Kamilo Gata in a vote by the Territorial Assembly. Laufoaulu, a priest and director of Catholic education in the islands, stood as a left-wing candidate, nominated by RPR candidates, but was elected with the support of right-wing politicians.

In March 1999 festivities were held to commemorate the 40th anniversary of the accession of the King of Wallis Island (or Lavelua) Tomasi Kulimoetoke.

In January 2001 two candidates of the RPR contested the presidency of the Territorial Assembly. Patalione Kanimoa was elected by the majority of the RPR (eight votes) and of the UPWF (four votes). Soane Muni Uhila, the previous President of the Territorial Assembly, then formed a new party, La Voix des Peuples Wallisiens et Futuniens, along with five other RPR dissidents. The new majority RPR-UPWF grouping elected Albert Likuvalu (of the UPWF) president of the permanent commission.

In June 2001 senior officials from Wallis and Futuna and from New Caledonia agreed on a project to redefine their bilateral relationship under the Nouméa Accord (see the chapter on New Caledonia) on greater autonomy, signed in 1998. The Accord gave the New Caledonian authorities the power to control immigration from Wallis and Futuna; following decades of migration, the population of Wallis and Futuna was 15,000, while the number of migrants and descendants from the islands in New Caledonia had risen to 20,000. In exchange for controlling immigration, New Caledonia stated that it would make a financial contribution to economic development in Wallis and Futuna. The Nouméa Accord also envisaged a separate arrangement allowing for open access to New Caledonia for residents of Wallis and Futuna.

In January 2002 a delegation from Wallis and Futuna met President Jacques Chirac in Paris to discuss the situation of members of their community living in New Caledonia. Under the Nouméa Accord, New Caledonia was to have signed a separate agreement with Wallis and Futuna better to define the islanders' status, with particular regard to the job market.

An election was held in March 2002 for the 20 seats of the Territorial Assembly. The RPR won 12 of the seats, while socialist candidates, or affiliated independents, won eight. Some 82.7% of some 9,500 registered voters cast their vote. The election campaign was the first to give parties coverage on television and radio, provided by the national broadcasting company. The Territory's only newspaper, *Te-Fenua Fo'ou*, ceased publication in April, following a dispute over the King of Wallis's alleged support for an electoral candidate, Make Pilioko. The newspaper contested that Pilioko, a former member of the Territorial Assembly, was unfit for office, having been convicted in 1999 of misuse of public funds. The publisher and editor of *Te-Fenua Fo'ou*, respectively Michel Boudineau and Laurent Gourlez (both of whom were French), were summoned before the King and ordered not to publish any further articles on the matter. However, the newspaper asserted its right to freedom of expression and, in defiance of the King, printed and distributed its next edition from New Caledonia. The police subsequently removed computers and other equipment from the newspaper's office in Mata'Utu. Boudineau filed a complaint with the French authorities for theft and obstruction of press freedom but, none the less, was forced to close the publication.

At elections to the Assemblée nationale in June 2002, Victor Brial, representing a coalition of the Union pour la Majorité Présidentielle (subsequently Union pour un Mouvement Populaire—UMP) and the RPR, was re-elected as the Wallis and Futuna deputy to the French legislature, winning 50.4% of the votes cast in the first round. (The RPR was fully absorbed into the UMP structure that year.) However, in December the Constitutional Council ruled that the result was invalid as certain ballot papers had been improperly marked; Brial (now representing the UMP) subsequently won the by-election in March 2003. Meanwhile, Christian Job replaced Alain Waquet as Chief Administrator of the islands in August 2002. In November Soane Patita Maituka was enthroned as King of Alo (known as the Tu'i Agaifo) following the deposition of Sagato Alofi in the previous month. In the following month the French Sénat approved a bill providing for a constitutional amendment that would allow Wallis and Futuna (along with French Polynesia) to be designated as an Overseas Country (Pays d'outre-mer); both houses of the French legislature in Paris ratified the amendments to the Constitution in March 2003. Wallis and Futuna was given the status of an Overseas Collectivity (Collectivité d'outre-mer). In July, during an official visit to New Caledonia, President Chirac received a delegation from Wallis and Futuna.

In October 2003 Pasilio Keletaona was deposed as King of Sigave by members of his own clan. He was succeeded in March 2004 by Visesio Moeliku. In December 2003 the President of New Caledonia signed an accord governing relations between France, New Caledonia and Wallis and Futuna. The conclusion of the agreement, which had been negotiated two years previously in an attempt to address the situation of the 20,000 Wallis and Futuna islanders permanently resident in New Caledonia, had been delayed by the continuing ethnic tensions there. Under the agreement, Wallis and Futuna and New Caledonia were henceforth to deliver separate public services. Concerns had been raised by the former's increasing debt (estimated to total 2,500m. francs CFP) to the Government of New Caledonia, a major creditor being the New Caledonian hospital. It was therefore hoped that Wallis and Futuna would become more self-sufficient in the areas of health and secondary education and that the islanders would be encouraged to remain on Wallis and Futuna, while those already settled in New Caledonia would become more integrated.

Between February and April 2003 the postal service was affected by strike action, which was resolved in favour of the striking workers. During May–June 2004 a strike prevented television and radio transmissions from the Territory's main broadcasting company, and again the dispute was resolved in favour of the striking employees, whose demands included the resignation of the station manager.

In January 2005 Xavier de Fürst replaced Christian Job as Chief Administrator of the islands. In the following month Albert Likuvalu, representing the newly formed Alliance grouping, a coalition of UDF members and left-wing independents, was elected President of the Territorial Assembly by 11 votes to nine, replacing Patalione Kanimoa of the UMP grouping. The Alliance comprised three members of the UDF and two left-wing ministers, including Likuvalu himself; they were supported by the UPWF grouping.

In January 2005 the local court found the Lavelua's grandson, Tomasi Tuugahala, guilty of unintentional homicide while driving under the influence of alcohol. Tuugahala took refuge in the Lavelua's palace and refused to surrender himself to the police. The King of Wallis and his chiefs claimed that the matter had been settled in accordance with traditional custom, but the incident brought them into confrontation with the French authorities and with pro-reform groups in Wallis and Futuna who wished to depose the Lavelua. In May the King's Prime Minister, Kapeliele Faupala, criticized de Fürst for interfering in traditional affairs and urged him to leave the island. Later in the month Tuugahala gave himself up to the authorities and was flown to New Caledonia to begin an 18-month prison sentence. However, in June de Fürst suspended allowances and salaries to the Lavelua and his Council of Ministers, while officially recognizing an alternative council composed of members of rival royal families from Futuna, headed by Clovis Logologofolau, whose previous posts had included that of President of the Territorial Assembly.

In August 2005 the King of Wallis reiterated a pledge of allegiance to France but maintained that the crisis was the result of de Fürst's interference. In September the alternative council of ministers announced its intention to install Chief Sosefo Mautamakia as King of Wallis. Supporters of the incumbent Lavelua took to the streets in protest, mounting blockades and occupying the international airport; meanwhile, in the New Caledonian capital of Nouméa, a group of some 500 supporters marched to the French High Commission to present a petition demanding the intervention of France. The Secretary-General of the French High Commission in New Caledonia, Louis Lefranc, was dispatched to undertake negotiations; he reaffirmed France's recognition of Tomasi Kulimoetoke as Lavelua and overruled de Fürst's earlier decisions. As a result of negotiations among the royal clans themselves, no attempt was made to install a new King. In November Emeni Simete of the UMP replaced Albert Likuvalu as President of the Territorial Assembly.

In March 2006 the two Kings of Futuna, accompanied by ministers of the kingdoms and members of the local assembly, travelled to France to meet President Jacques Chirac, Prime Minister Dominique de Villepin and other senior government officials. The delegation emphasized the need for improved transport links between Futuna and Wallis, citing disruption caused on Futuna by severe weather conditions in early 2006 and the temporary halt to flights between the two islands because of a faulty aircraft. The Futuna delegation reportedly claimed that President Chirac had assured them that their island would be designated as a sub-prefecture. In August Xavier de Fürst was replaced by Richard Didier as Chief Administrator.

Recent developments

In January 2007 a delegation from Wallis visited Futuna, amid reported tensions between the islands, to present a memorandum of understanding encompassing the three kingdoms, the details of which were not immediately publicized. At the legislative election conducted on 1 April, the level of participation reached an estimated 74% of registered voters. Three new members were elected to the Territorial Assembly, with many votes reportedly cast according to clan loyalties. Pesamino Taputai was subsequently selected to succeed Emeni Simete as the Assembly's President, receiving the support of 12 of the 20 members. In his inaugural speech Taputai urged the islands' leaders to address the various issues that continued to impede good relations between Wallis and Futuna.

The results of Wallis and Futuna's participation in the second round of the French presidential election in May 2007 showed similar levels of support for the two candidates: Nicolas Sarkozy of the UMP, who secured a majority overall, received 50.2% of the votes cast locally, while the Parti Socialiste (PS) candidate, Ségolène Royal, received 49.8%. Elections to the French Assemblée nationale were held in June, with the incumbent UMP deputy, Victor Brial, winning the first round with 33.7% of the votes cast. However, in the second round Brial was defeated by the PS-affiliated candidate, Albert Likuvalu, who received 51.8% of the votes. In September it was announced that the 2013 South Pacific Mini Games were to be held in Wallis and Futuna; it was envisaged that the event would require significant development of the islands' infrastructure. In early October 2007 the King of Tonga, George Tupou V, paid a personal visit to Wallis and Futuna. Later in the month the French Minister-Delegate for the Overseas Possessions, Christian Estrosi, also visited the islands; the hosting of the South Pacific Mini Games was discussed during his three-day visit. In December the islands' former deputy to the Assemblée nationale, Victor Brial, was elected President of the Territorial Assembly. Brial received 13 out of 20 votes, including those of members affiliated with the UMP and the Mouvement Démocrate (MoDem—formerly known as the UDF), while his only opponent, Siliako Lauhéa, received six.

From mid-2006 the health of the King of Wallis, Lavelua Tomasi Kulimoetoke, had deteriorated to the extent that he was unable to attend official events. He died in May 2007, after 48 years in office. Following his death, the subject of his successor was declared taboo for six months. The Council of Ministers of Wallis temporarily exercised royal duties and was charged with choosing a new king. In July 2008 the Council announced its decision to nominate Kapiliele Faupala, who had presided over the local Council of Ministers since 2004. Despite some vocal opposition to Faupala's nomination by certain other royal clans on the island of Wallis, his coronation took place later in July 2008 at a ceremony in Mata'Utu. Meanwhile, it had emerged in August 2007 that Soane Patita Maituka, the King of Alo, was in hospital in New Caledonia with a serious illness. In February 2008, following criticism of the style of leadership of the Tu'i Agaifo and the reaching of a unanimous decision by the four chiefly clans of Alo, the King was removed from office. Petelo Vikena, a former public servant, was subsequently chosen to replace him, and his coronation took place in November 2008. However, the choice of Vikena was not supported by some chiefly clans, which criticized the unilateral appointment by the chiefly council and the lack of consensus.

In July 2008, the French Government appointed Philippe Paolantoni as the new Chief Administrator of Wallis and Futuna, to succeed Richard Didier. In the French senatorial elections of September Fr Robert Laufoaulu, the senator representing Wallis and Futuna, was re-elected for a second six-year term at the first round of voting, securing a majority sufficient to preclude the need for the contest to proceed to a second round.

In January 2010, amid reports of acts of vandalism against royal property, Petelo Vikena abdicated as King of Alo. Meanwhile, the monarch of Sigave, Visesio Moeliku, was reported to have relinquished his position several months previously. The kingdom of Futuna was thus placed in an unusual situation, being required to function without either of its two Kings. In July Polikalepo Kolivai was crowned King of Sigave, although two rival clans refused to recognize his accession.

In March 2010 a cyclone was reported to have destroyed 90% of traditional houses on Futuna. Most of the island's crops and many public amenities were also destroyed. French military aircraft based in New Caledonia, followed by a warship, brought emergency supplies of food and other necessities, and in June the French Minister in charge of the Overseas Possessions, Marie-Luce Penchard, undertook to provide financial and technical assistance for rebuilding Futuna's infrastructure. In the same month Penchard, while visiting New Caledonia, signed an agreement on the status of migrants from Wallis and Futuna in New Caledonia, who were more numerous than those remaining in Wallis and Futuna itself (see above).

From April 2010 the supply of electricity and water on Wallis was intermittently disrupted when employees of the utility company Electricité et Eau de Wallis et Futuna (EEWF, a subsidiary of the French Groupe Suez) staged a strike, reportedly in support of an executive who had been dismissed for misconduct. In July the King of Wallis announced that the contract with EEWF had been terminated (although such an action was not legally within his powers), and the company's offices were taken over by a small group of employees, who stated that they were establishing a new company and claimed to be acting with the support of the King. Hundreds of people participated in protests, urging the restoration of power and water supplies. Later in July the new Chief Administrator, Michel Jeanjean, who had taken office earlier in that month, authorized the police to intervene to allow access to the power plant, after which normal supplies were apparently resumed.

In December 2010 Victor Brial was replaced as President of the Territorial Assembly by Siliaki Lauhéa, the leader of the UPWF. Lauhéa was himself succeeded in October by Pesamino Taputai (who had held the post from April to December 2007).

In July 2011 the Australian Parliamentary Secretary for Pacific Island Affairs, Richard Marles, became the first Australian member of Parliament to visit Wallis and Futuna. Along with France's Minister in charge of the Overseas Possessions, Marie-Luce Penchard, he had travelled to Wallis and Futuna to join celebrations marking the 50th anniversary of the islands' status as a French Overseas Territory. During their visits the two ministers discussed regional co-operation in the Pacific, and Marles stated his country's commitment to continue to provide support in times of humanitarian crisis and to assist in the protection of the islands' vital fisheries resources.

Ongoing concern about the rising cost of living culminated in demonstrations throughout the islands attended by some 1,500 people in November 2011. Protesters demanding lower fuel prices and air fares marched to the government buildings in Mata'Utu, where they were met by local politicians and Chief Administrator Jeanjean. The demonstrations coincided with widespread strike action by public sector employees demanding the same system of pay indexation as their French state counterparts.

An election for the 20 seats of the Territorial Assembly was conducted on 25 March 2012. The turn-out was high, at 86.0% of the 8,897 registered voters. Notably, the incumbent President of the Territorial Assembly, Pesamino Taputai, and his two predecessors, Siliaki Lauhéa and Victor Brial, all failed to secure re-election to the legislature. Vetelino Nau of the UPWF was elected as President of the Territorial Assembly on 4 April, receiving 11 out of 20 votes, including those of six unaffiliated members.

CONSTITUTION AND GOVERNMENT

The Overseas Collectivity (Collectivité d'outre-mer) of Wallis and Futuna is administered by a representative of the French Government, the Chief Administrator, who is assisted by the Territorial Assembly. The Assembly has 20 members and is elected for a five-year term. The three traditional kingdoms, one on Wallis and two sharing Futuna, have equal rights, although the Kings' powers are limited. In addition, Wallis and Futuna elects one deputy to the French Assemblée nationale (National Assembly) in Paris and one representative to the French Sénat (Senate). The islands may also be represented at the European Parliament.

REGIONAL AND INTERNATIONAL CO-OPERATION

Wallis and Futuna forms part of the Franc Zone (see p. 332). Although France is also a member of the organization, Wallis and Futuna has membership in its own right of the Pacific Community (see p. 413), which is based in New Caledonia and provides technical advice, training and assistance in economic, cultural and social development to the region. Wallis and Futuna was granted observer status at the Pacific Islands Forum (see p. 416) in 2006 and submitted an application for associate membership in 2008.

ECONOMIC AFFAIRS

In 1995 it was estimated that Wallis and Futuna's gross domestic product (GDP) was US $28.7m., equivalent to some $2,000 per head. Most monetary income in the islands is derived from government employment and from remittances sent home by islanders employed in New Caledonia and metropolitan France.

Agricultural activity is of a subsistence nature. Yams, taro, bananas, cassava and other food crops are also cultivated. Tobacco is grown for local consumption. Pigs, goats and chickens are reared on the islands. Apiculture was revived in 1996, and in 2000 honey production was sufficient to meet the demands of the local market. Fishing activity in the exclusive economic zone of Wallis and Futuna increased during the 1990s; the total catch was estimated at 750 metric tons in 2009, compared with 70 tons in 1991.

Mineral fuels are the main source of electrical energy, although it is hoped that hydroelectric power can be developed, especially on Futuna. There is a 4,000-kW thermal power station on Wallis, and a 2,600-kW thermal power station was completed on Futuna in 2000. The hydroelectric power station on the Vainifao river, on Futuna, provided 10% of the production needed. Total electricity output in 2010 reached 19.8m. kWh.

There were 291 businesses operating in Wallis and Futuna in 2000, of which 24 were in the industrial and artisanal sector, 68 in construction and 199 in the service and commercial sectors; 47 of those businesses were located on Futuna. A new commercial centre opened in Wallis in 2002. The tourism sector is very limited. In 2008 Wallis had four hotels and Futuna two establishments. In November 2005 the French Government agreed to provide some €8m. towards expanding the domestic airport at Vele, on Futuna, to receive international traffic. Foreign visitor arrivals, mainly from New Caledonia and France, totalled 2,456 in 2006.

In 2010 the cost of the islands' imports reached 5,772.0m. francs CFP. In 2010 the major imports were prepared foodstuffs (30.4% of the total value of imports), followed by fuels (16.0%), transport equipment (7.6%), mechanical equipment (6.2%), and chemicals, rubber and plastic products (5.1%). Exports of Trochus shells produced revenue of 11.6m. francs CFP in 2006. However, total exports declined to 1.0m. francs CFP in 2009. Traditional food products, mother of pearl (from the Trochus shell) and handicrafts are the only significant export commodities. Exports of copra from Wallis ceased in 1950, and from Futuna in the early 1970s. The principal sources of imports in 2007 were France, which supplied 28% of the total, Singapore (14%) and Australia (13%). In 2004 most of the islands' exports were purchased by Italy. In August 2001 the frequency of supplies to Wallis and Futuna was significantly improved when the Sofrana shipping company, based in Auckland, began operating a new route linking New Zealand, Tonga and the Samoas to Wallis and Futuna.

There was a deficit of 239m. francs CFP on the territorial budget in 2006. French aid to Wallis and Futuna increased from a total of 7,048m. francs CFP in 1999 to 12,064.2m. francs CFP in 2008. In December 2002 France proposed a broad 15-year sustainable development strategy for Wallis and Futuna.

The annual rate of inflation in 1989–2007 averaged 1.7%. The annual rate of inflation at June 2009 was recorded as 0.3%. The high level of unemployment has remained a major economic and social issue; 12.8% of the total labour force was classified as unemployed and seeking work at the time of the 2008 census. More than 50% of those in formal employment are engaged in the public sector.

In 2003 the Assemblée nationale in Paris approved the Overseas Territories Development Bill, providing support for economic and social development in Wallis and Futuna (together with French Polynesia and New Caledonia) by attracting foreign investment. In early 2007 France concluded an agreement with Wallis and Futuna to provide US $50m. over the period 2007–11 for the purposes of infrastructural development. Priority was also to be given to the areas of health, education and vocational training. In March 2008 it was announced that the European Union (EU, see p. 276) had allocated the sum of €16.49m. to development projects in Wallis and Futuna, under the 10th European Development Fund (EDF) encompassing the period 2008–13. Areas of focus were expected to include sources of renewable energy, improved management of the islands' natural resources and sustainable development, in addition to the priority sectors of education and health. In November 2008 it was announced that France was to allocate an additional €50,000 to aid the reforestation programme on the islands. A new programme of training, to be carried out by French military personnel, which aimed to address youth unemployment by improving the skills of those aged between 18 and 25 years, was announced in October 2009. About 80% of Futuna's crops were reported to have been destroyed in the cyclone of March 2010, leading to serious food shortages. By May, according to the French Government, a total of $700,000 had been allocated to the relief effort. The island's infrastructure was badly damaged, necessitating the implementation of a major repair programme. Furthermore, supplies of electricity and water on Wallis were disrupted during 2010 by a dispute at the local utility company. The rising cost of living, particularly the prices of food, fuel and transport, dominated the economic affairs of the islands in 2011 and led to large demonstrations in November of that year (see Contemporary Political History).

PUBLIC HOLIDAYS

2013: 1 January (New Year's Day), 5 March (Missionary Day), 1 April (Easter Monday), 1 May (Labour Day), 8 May (Liberation Day), 9 May (Ascension Day), 20 May (Whit Monday), 14 July (Fall of the Bastille), 8 September (Internal Autonomy Day), 24 September (anniversary of possession by France), 1 November (All Saints' Day), 11 November (Armistice Day), 25 December (Christmas Day).

Statistical Survey

Source (unless otherwise indicated): Service Territorial de la Statistique et des Etudes Economiques, Immeuble Pukavila, RT1, BP 638, Mata'Utu, Falaleu, 98600 Wallis; tel. 722403; fax 722487; e-mail stats@wallis.co.nc; internet www.spc.int/prism/Country/WF/WF index.html.

AREA AND POPULATION

Area (sq km): 142. *By Island:* Uvea (Wallis Island) 78; Futuna Island 46; Alofi Island 18. The Collectivity also includes a group of uninhabited volcanic and coralline islets (18 sq km).

Population: Total population 14,944 at census of 22 July 2003. Total population 13,445 (males 6,669, females 6,776) at census of 21 July 2008: Wallis Island—Uvea 9,207; Futuna Island 4,238 (Alo 2,655, Sigave 1,583).

Density (2008 census): 94.7 per sq km.

Population by Age and Sex (2008 census): *0–14:* 4,081 (2,181 males, 1,900 females); *15–64:* 8,387 (4,047 males, 4,340 females); *65 and over:* 977 (441 males, 536 females); *Total:* 13,445 (6,669 males, 6,776 females).

Principal Villages (population at 2008 census): Mata'Utu (capital) 1,120; Taoa 623; Utufua 622.

Births, Marriages and Deaths (2008): Registered live births 185 (birth rate 13.6 per 1,000); Registered marriages 53 (marriage rate 3.9 per 1,000); Registered deaths 90 (death rate 6.7 per 1,000).

Life Expectancy (years at birth): 74.3 (males 73.1; females 75.5) in 2003.

Economically Active Population (2008 census): Total employed 3,373 (males 1,867, females 1,506); Unemployed persons seeking work 496 (males 296, females 200); Total labour force 3,869 (males 2,163, females 1,706).

HEALTH AND WELFARE

Key Indicators

Total Fertility Rate (children per woman, census of 2008): 2.0.

Under-5 Mortality Rate (per 1,000 live births, average of 2005–2008): 5.2.

Physicians (per 1,000 head, 2003): 0.7.

Access to Sanitation (% of persons, census of July 2003): 80.9.

Access to Water (% of persons, census of July 2003): 68.5.

For definitions, see explanatory note on p. vi.

AGRICULTURE, ETC.

Principal Crops ('000 metric tons, 2010, FAO estimates): Cassava 2.1; Taro (coco yam) 1.6; Yams 0.6; Other roots and tubers 1.1; Coconuts 3.7; Vegetables and melons 0.6; Bananas 6.1. *Aggregate Production* ('000 metric tons, may include official, semi-official or estimated data): Total fruits (excl. melons) 11.6; Total roots and tubers 5.4.

Livestock ('000 head, year ending September 2010, FAO estimates): Pigs 25; Goats 7; Chickens 65.

Livestock Products (metric tons, 2010, FAO estimates): Pig meat 315; Goat meat 15; Chicken meat 48; Cows' milk 48; Hen eggs 50; Honey 10.

Fishing (metric tons, live weight, 2009, FAO estimates): Total catch 750 (Marine fishes 743). Figures exclude Trochus shells (metric tons) 29.

Source: FAO.

INDUSTRY

Selected Products (metric tons, 2010, unless otherwise indicated): Coconut oil 164 (FAO estimate); Copra 252.5 (2006, FAO estimate); Electric energy 19.8m. kWh (Wallis Island 16.7; Futuna Island 3.1). Sources: FAO; Institut d'Emission d'Outre-Mer.

FINANCE

Currency and Exchange Rates: see French Polynesia.

Territorial Budget (million francs CFP, 2006): *Revenue:* Current 2,683; Capital 189; Fiscal adjustment –14; Total 2,858. *Expenditure:* Current 2,850; Capital 247; Total 3,097.

Aid from France ('000 million francs CFP, 2008): Total expenditure 12.1 (Education 5.7, Health 3.1, Other expenditure by Ministère de l'Outre-Mer 3.3). Source: Institut d'Emission d'Outre-Mer.

Money Supply (million francs CFP at 31 December 2010): Currency in circulation 2,137; Demand deposits 3,581; *Total money* 5,718. Source: Institut d'Emission d'Outre-Mer.

Cost of Living (Consumer Price Index at June; base: June 2008 = 100): All items 100.3 in 2009.

EXTERNAL TRADE

Principal Commodities (million francs CFP): *Imports c.i.f.* (2009): Prepared foodstuff 1,756; Pharmaceutical and cosmetic products 273; Household equipment 284; Transport equipment 436; Mechanical equipment 355; Electrical and electronic equipment 274; Chemicals, rubber and plastic products 297; Fuels 923; Total (incl. others) 5,772. *Exports f.o.b.* (2001): Preparations of molluscs and other aquatic invertebrates 0.3; Coral and shells 5.5; Braids and mats of vegetable material 0.9; Total 5.6. *2009:* Total exports 1.0. Source: mainly Institut d'Emission d'Outre-Mer.

Principal Trading Partners: *Imports c.i.f.* ('000 million francs CFP, 2007): Australia 0.7; Fiji 0.3; France (incl. Monaco) 1.5; New Caledonia 0.3; New Zealand 0.5; Singapore 0.8; Total (incl. others) 5.4. *Exports f.o.b.* (million francs CFP, 2004): Italy 4.6; Total 4.6. Source: mainly Institut d'Emission d'Outre-Mer.

TRANSPORT

Road Traffic (vehicles in use, 2001): Scooters 1,093; Cars 1,293. Source: Ministère de l'Agriculture, de l'Alimentation, de la Pêche et des Affaires Rurales, *Recensement agricole du territoire 2001*.

Shipping: *Merchant Fleet* (31 December 2008): Vessels registered 8; Displacement ('000 grt): 92.3. Source: Lloyd's Register-Fairplay, *World Fleet Statistics*.

Civil Aviation (2010): *Domestic Traffic:* Aircraft movements 1,413; Passenger movements 13,191; Freight handled 27.7 metric tons; Mail handled 11.1 metric tons. *International Traffic:* Aircraft movements 332; Passenger movements 28,654; Freight handled 176.2 metric tons; Mail handled 77.3 metric tons. Source: Institut d'Emission d'Outre-Mer.

TOURISM

Foreign Visitors (2006): *Total Arrivals:* 2,456. *Overnight Stays in Hotel Establishments:* 607.

Foreign Visitor Arrivals by Nationality (2006): Australia 37; Fiji 45; France 674; French Polynesia 62; New Caledonia 1,310; Total (incl. others) 2,456.

COMMUNICATIONS MEDIA

Telephones (2010): 3,100 main lines installed.

Internet Users (2009): 1,300.

Broadband Subscribers (2010): 1,100.

Source: International Telecommunication Union.

EDUCATION

Pre-primary (2005): 3 institutions; 260 pupils.

Primary (2010, unless otherwise indicated): 18 institutions (2008); 2,156 pupils (incl. pre-primary). Source: Institut d'Emission d'Outre-Mer.

Secondary (2010, unless otherwise indicated): 7 institutions (2 vocational) (2006); 1,901 students. Source: Institut d'Emission d'Outre-Mer.

Higher (students, 2005/06): 14 in New Caledonia; 60 in metropolitan France; 6 in French Polynesia. Source: Institut d'Emission d'Outre-Mer.

Teachers (2003): Pre-primary and primary 168; Secondary 209.

Adult Literacy Rate (census of July 2003): 78.8% (males 78.2%; females 79.3%).

Directory

The Government

(May 2012)

Chief Administrator (Administrateur Supérieur): MICHEL JEANJEAN.

CONSEIL DU TERRITOIRE

The council is chaired by the Chief Administrator and comprises the members by right (the Kings of Wallis, Sigave and Alo) and three appointed members.

GOVERNMENT OFFICES

Government Headquarters: Bureau de l'Administrateur Supérieur, BP 16, Mata'Utu, Havelu, Hahake, 98600 Uvea, Wallis Islands; tel. 722727; fax 722300; e-mail adsupwf@wallis.co.nc; internet www.adsupwf.org.

Department of Catholic Schools: Direction Diocésaine de l'Enseignement Catholique, BP 80, Mata'Utu, 98600 Uvea, Wallis Islands; tel. 722766; e-mail decwf.wallis@wallis.co.nc; responsible for pre-primary and primary education since 1969.

Department of Cultural Action: BP 131, Mata'Utu, Aka'aka, 98600 Uvea, Wallis Islands; tel. 722667; fax 722563; e-mail culture.wf@mail.wf.

Department of the Environment: BP 294, Mata'Utu, Havelu, Hahake, 98600 Uvea, Wallis Islands; tel. 720351; fax 720597; e-mail senv@mail.wf.

Department of Justice: BP 12, Mata'Utu, Havelu, Hahake, 98600 Uvea, Wallis Islands; tel. 722715; fax 722531; e-mail tpi@wallis.co.nc.

Department of Labour and Social Affairs Inspection (SITAS): BP 385, Mata'Utu, Hahake, 98600 Uvea; tel. 722288; fax 722384; e-mail sitas.wf@mail.wf.

Department of Public Works and Rural Engineering: BP 13, Mata'Utu, Kafika, Hahake, 98600 Uvea, Wallis Islands; tel. 722626; fax 722115; e-mail tpwallis@mail.wf.

Department of Rural Affairs and Fisheries: BP 19, Mata'Utu, Aka'aka, 98600 Uvea, Wallis Islands; tel. 722606; fax 722544; e-mail ecoru.futuna@wallis.co.nc.

Department of Youth and Sports: BP 51, Mata'Utu, Kafika, Hahake, 98600 Uvea; tel. 722188; fax 722322; e-mail jeusport@mail.wf.

Health Agency: Agence de Santé, BP 4G, 98600 Uvea, Wallis Islands; tel. 720700; fax 723399; e-mail sante@adswf.org; operates two hospitals at Sia on Uvea and Kaleveleve on Futuna, respectively.

Legislature

ASSEMBLÉE TERRITORIALE

The Territorial Assembly has 20 members and is elected for a five-year term. Within the Assembly, ministers may form political groupings of five members or more. These groupings are not necessarily formed along party lines, and alliances may be made in support of a common cause. The most recent general election took place on 25 March 2012.

President: VETELINO NAU (UPWF).

Territorial Assembly: Assemblée Territoriale, BP 31, Mata'Utu, Havelu, Hahake, 98600 Uvea, Wallis Islands; tel. 722004; fax 721807; e-mail cab-pres.at@wallis.co.nc.

PARLEMENT

Deputy to the French National Assembly: ALBERT LIKUVALU (PS).

Representative to the French Senate: Fr ROBERT LAUFOAULU (UMP).

The Kingdoms

WALLIS

(Capital: Mata'Utu on Uvea)

Lavelua, King of Wallis: KAPILIELE FAUPALA.

Council of Ministers (Aliki Fau): The Council is composed of six ministers who assist the King:

Kivalu: the Prime Minister and King's spokesman at official meetings.

Mahe: the second Prime Minister and King's counsel.

Kulitea: responsible for cultural and customary matters.

Uluimonoa: responsible for the sea.

Fotuatamai: responsible for health and hygiene.

Mukoifenua: responsible for land and agriculture.

In addition, the Puliuvea is responsible for the King's security and the maintenance of public order.

The Kingdom of Wallis is divided into three administrative districts (Hihifo, Hahake, Mua), and its traditional hierarchy includes three district chiefs (Faipule), 20 village chiefs (Pule) and numerous hamlet chiefs (Lagiaki).

SIGAVE

(Capital: Leava on Futuna)

Keletaona, King of Sigave: POLIKALEPO KOLIVAI.

Council of Ministers: six ministers, chaired by the King.

The Kingdom of Sigave is located in the north of the island of Futuna; there are five village chiefs.

ALO

(Capital: Ono on Futuna)

Tu'i Agaifo, King of Alo: (vacant).

Council of Ministers: five ministers, chaired by the King.

The Kingdom of Alo comprises the southern part of the island of Futuna and the entire island of Alofi. There are nine village chiefs.

Political Organizations

Alliance: c/o Assemblée Territoriale; f. 2005; coalition of UDF mems and left-wing independents; Pres. APITONE MUNIKIHAAFATA.

Mouvement Démocrate (MoDem): c/o Assemblée Territoriale; fmrly known as Union pour la Démocratie Française; name changed as above in 2007; centrist; based on Uvean (Wallisian) support.

Union pour un Mouvement Populaire (UMP): c/o Assemblée Territoriale; f. 2002; est. as Union pour la Majorité Présidentielle; includes fmr mems of Rassemblement pour la République; centre-right; local br. of the metropolitan party; Territorial Leader ROBERT LAUFOAULU.

Union pour Wallis et Futuna (UPWF): c/o Assemblée Territoriale; f. 1994; est. as Union Populaire pour Wallis et Futuna; affiliated to Parti Socialiste of France since 1998; Leader SILIAKO LAUHÉA.

Judicial System

The Statute provided for two parallel judicial systems: customary law, which applied to the indigenous population; and French State law. The competencies of the respective systems are not always clearly defined, which has been a cause of tensions between the indigenous monarchy and the French authorities. On Uvea, under customary law there are separate courts for civil matters (Fono Puleaga) and village matters (Fono Fenua). Disputes over land are dealt with by the Council of the Territory, presided over by the King. A similar system exists on Futuna. Judgments may be referred to a Chambre d'Annulation at the Court of Appeal at Nouméa, New Caledonia.

Court of the First Instance: Tribunal de Première Instance, BP 12, Havelu, Mata'Utu, Hahake, 98600 Uvea, Wallis Islands; tel. 722715; fax 722531; e-mail pr.tpi@wallis.co.nc; f. 1983; Pres. FRANCIS ALARY.

Religion

Almost all of the inhabitants profess Christianity and are adherents of the Roman Catholic Church.

CHRISTIANITY

The Roman Catholic Church

The Territory comprises a single diocese, suffragan to the archdiocese of Nouméa (New Caledonia). The diocese estimated that there were 14,400 adherents at 31 December 2007. The Bishop participates in the Catholic Bishops' Conference of the Pacific, currently based in Fiji.

Bishop of Wallis and Futuna: GHISLAIN MARIE RAOUL SUZANNE DE RASILLY, Evêché Lano, BP G6, Mata'Utu, 98600 Uvea, Wallis Islands; tel. 722932; fax 722783; e-mail eveche.wallis@wallis.co.nc.

The Press

'Uvea Mo Futuna: Tuku'atu Ha'afuasia, Uvea, Wallis Islands; e-mail filihau@uvea-mo-futuna.com; f. 2002; daily; electronic; Editor FILIHAU ASI TALATINI.

The Territory's only newspaper, *Te-Fenua Fo'ou*, was forced to close in April 2002, following a dispute with the King of Wallis. *Fenua Magazine* was launched by a group of local business people in September 2002 but closed in September 2003 owing to a lack of advertising revenue. There is currently no printed press in Wallis and Futuna.

Broadcasting and Communications

TELECOMMUNICATIONS

France Câbles et Radio Wallis et Futuna (FCR WF): Télécommunications Extérieures de Wallis et Futuna, BP 54, Mata'Utu, 98600 Uvea, Wallis Islands; tel. 722436; fax 722255; e-mail fcr@mail.wf; owned by France Telecom; Man. JACQUES PAMBRUN.

Service des Postes et Télécommunications: BP 00, Mata'Utu, 98600 Uvea, Hahake, Wallis Islands; tel. 720809; fax 722662; e-mail pio.tui@wallis.co.nc; internet www.spt.wf; Dir MANUELE TAOFIFENUA; Head of Postage Stamp Section PIO TUI.

BROADCASTING

Radio and Television

France Télévisions Pôle Wallis et Futuna: BP 102, Pointe Matala, Mata'Utu, 98600 Uvea, Wallis Islands; tel. 721300; fax 722446; e-mail rfo.wallis@wallis.co.nc; internet wallisfutuna.rfo.fr; f. 1979; acquired by Groupe France Télévisions in 2004; fmrly Radiodiffusion Française d'Outre-mer, present name adopted in 1998; transmitters at Mata'Utu (Uvea) and Alo (Futuna); programmes broadcast 24 hours daily in Uvean (Wallisian), Futunian and French; a television service on Uvea, transmitting for 12 hours daily in French, began operation in 1986; a television service on Futuna was inaugurated in 1994; satellite television began operation in 2000; Regional Dir JEAN-JACQUES AGOSTINI; Station Man. LOUIS AUGUSTE; Editor-in-Chief NORBERT TAOFIFENUA.

Finance

BANKING

Bank of Issue

Institut d'Emission d'Outre-Mer: BP G5, Mata'Utu, Havelu, Hahake, 98600 Uvea, Wallis Islands; tel. 722505; fax 722003; e-mail direction@ieomwf.fr; internet www.ieom.fr/wallis-et-futuna; f. 1998; Dir RAYMOND COFFRE.

Other Banks

Agence Française de Développement: BP G5, Mata'Utu, 98600 Uvea, Wallis Islands; tel. 722505; fax 722003; e-mail afdmatautu@groupe-afd.org; fmrly Caisse Française de Développement; devt bank; Man. RAYMOND COFFRE.

Banque de Wallis et Futuna: BP 59, Mata'Utu, 98600 Uvea, Wallis Islands; tel. 722124; fax 722156; e-mail maurice.j.lasante@bnpparibas.com; internet nc.bnpparibas.net; f. 1991; 51% owned by BNP Paribas (New Caledonia); CEO MAURICE LASANTE.

Paierie de Wallis et Futuna: BP 29, Mata'Utu, 98600 Uvea, Wallis Islands; tel. 722929; fax 722120; Man. MARCEL BUSH.

Insurance

GAN Assurances: BP 52, Mata'Utu, Hahake, 98600 Uvea, Wallis Islands; subsidiary of GAN Assurances, France; general non-life insurance.

Poe-ma Insurances: Matala'a, Utufua, Mua, BP 728, Vaitupu, 98600 Uvea, Wallis Islands; tel. 450096; fax 450097; e-mail poema@mail.pf.

Trade and Industry

UTILITIES

Electricité et Eau de Wallis et Futuna (EEWF): BP 28, Mata'Utu, 98600 Uvea, Wallis Islands; tel. 721500; fax 721196; e-mail eewf@wallis.co.nc; 32.4% owned by the territory and 66.6% owned by Electricité et Eau de Calédonie (Groupe Suez, France); production and distribution of electricity on Wallis and Futuna; production and distribution of potable water on Wallis since 1986; Dir JEAN-MARC PETIT.

TRADE UNIONS

Union Interprofessionnelle CFDT Wallis et Futuna (UI CFDT): BP 178, Mata'Utu, 98600 Uvea, Wallis Islands; tel. 721880; Sec.-Gen. KALOLO HANISI.

Union Territoriale Force Ouvrière: BP 325, Mata'Utu, 98600 Uvea, Wallis Islands; tel. 721732; fax 721732; Sec.-Gen. CHRISTIAN VAAMEI.

Transport

ROADS

Uvea has a few kilometres of road, one route circling the island, and there is also a partially surfaced road circling the island of Futuna; the only fully surfaced roads are in Mata'Utu.

SHIPPING

There are two wharves on Uvea for bulk goods, at Mata'Utu, and liquid fuels, at Halalo, respectively. There is one wharf at Leava on Futuna. Wallis and Futuna is served by two container ships: the *Southern Moana*, operated jointly by Moana Services of New Caledonia and Pacific Direct Line of New Zealand between Auckland (New Zealand), Nouméa (New Caledonia) and the islands; and the *Sofrana Bligh*, operated by SOFRANA between Auckland and the islands. Plans to expand the harbour facilities at Mata'Utu and to make improvements to the fishing port of Halalo have been subject to delay.

Société Française Navigation (SOFRANA): BP 24, Mata'Utu, 98600 Uvea, Wallis Islands; tel. 720511; fax 720568; f. 1986; subsidiary of Sofrana Unilines, New Zealand; 1 vessel.

CIVIL AVIATION

There is an international airport in Hihifo district on Uvea, about 5 km from Mata'Utu. Air Calédonie International (Aircalin—New Caledonia) is the only airline to serve Wallis and Futuna. The company operates five flights a week from Wallis to Futuna, one flight a week from Wallis to Tahiti (French Polynesia) and two flights a week from Wallis to Nouméa (New Caledonia). The airport on Futuna is at Pointe Vele, in the south-east, in the Kingdom of Alo; work began in 2005 to upgrade Vele airport to receive international traffic, originally scheduled to be completed by the end of 2008. The Compagnie Aérienne de Wallis et Futuna (Air Wallis) was established in 2004, as a joint venture between the Government and local business interests; however, the project was delayed in 2005.

Service d'Etat de l'Aviation Civile de Wallis et Futuna: BP 01, Mata'Utu, Malae, Hihifo, 98600 Uvea, Wallis Islands; tel. 721201; fax 722954; e-mail seac-wf.encadrement@mail.wf; Dir PATRICK PEZZETTA.

Tourism

Tourism remains undeveloped. There are four small hotels on Uvea, Wallis Islands. In 2006 foreign visitors to the islands totalled 2,456. In 2008 Wallis had four hotels and Futuna two establishments. The 2013 Pacific Mini Games were to be held on Wallis and Futuna.

Defence

Defence is the responsibility of France. The French naval command for the Pacific area is based in French Polynesia.

Education

In 2008 there were 18 primary schools and seven secondary schools (including two vocational schools) in Wallis and Futuna. Primary and pre-primary pupils totalled 2,156 and secondary students 1,901 in 2010. In 2005/06 a total of 80 students were attending various universities overseas.

Other French Overseas Territories

The other French territories are the French Southern and Antarctic Territories, and New Caledonia. The latter has a unique status as a Collectivité *sui generis* within the framework of the French Republic. Powers are devolved to New Caledonia under the terms of the 1998 Nouméa Accord.

THE FRENCH SOUTHERN AND ANTARCTIC TERRITORIES

Introduction

The French Southern and Antarctic Territories (Terres australes et antarctiques françaises) are administered under a special statute. The territory comprises Adélie Land, a narrow segment of the mainland of Antarctica together with a number of offshore islets, three groups of sub-Antarctic islands (the Kerguelen and Crozet Archipelagos, and Saint-Paul and Amsterdam Islands) in the southern Indian Ocean, and the Iles Eparses, in the Indian Ocean, comprising Bassas da India, Juan da Nova, Europa and Les Glorieuses, which are also claimed by Madagascar, and Tromelin, also claimed by Madagascar and Mauritius.

Under the terms of legislation approved by the French Government in 1955, the French Southern and Antarctic Territories were placed under the authority of a chief administrator, responsible to the government member for the overseas possessions. The Prefect and Chief Administrator is assisted by a Consultative Council, which meets at least twice annually. The Council is composed of seven members who are appointed for five years by the government member for the overseas possessions (from among members of the Office of Scientific Research and from those who have participated in scientific missions in the sub-Antarctic islands and Adélie Land). Under the terms of a decree promulgated in 1997, administration of the French Southern and Antarctic Territories was formally transferred from Paris to Saint-Pierre, Réunion, in April 2000. The Iles Eparses, administrative control of which was transferred from the Prefect of Réunion to the Prefect and Chief Administrator of the French Southern and Antarctic Territories in January 2005, became an integral part of the French Southern and Antarctic Territories under an organic law promulgated in February 2007.

From 1987 certain categories of vessels were allowed to register under the flag of the Kerguelen Archipelago, provided that 25% of their crew (including the captain and at least two officers) were French. These specifications were amended to 35% of the crew and at least four officers in April 1990. Under new legislation enacted in May 2005 this 'Kerguelen Register' was replaced with a new French International Register, whereby, *inter alia*, the captain and one officer would be required to be a French national, and 35% of the crew would be required to be from member countries of the European Union.

A permanent French base was established in 1950 at Martin de Viviès, on Amsterdam Island, followed by a second at Port-aux-Français, in the Kerguelen Archipelago, in 1951. The first permanent French base on the mainland was built in 1952 at Port Martin. Having been destroyed by fire, it was replaced in 1956 by a new permanent base at Dumont d'Urville. A fourth base was opened in 1964 at Alfred Faure on Ile de la Possession, in the Crozet Archipelago. In 1992 the French Government created a Public Interest Group, the Institut Français pour la Recherche et la Technologie Polaires (IFRTP—renamed the Institut Polaire Français Paul Emile Victor—IPEV—in 2002), to assume responsibility for the organization of scientific and research programmes in the French Southern and Antarctic Territories. Under an agreement between the IFRTP and Italy's Programma Nazionale di Ricerche in Antartide in 1993, work began on a joint project, Concordia, with a permanent base to be established at Dome C. Concordia was officially opened for winter operation in 2005. France is a signatory to the Antarctic Treaty (see p. 615).

Fishing for crayfish and Patagonian toothfish in the territories' Exclusive Economic Zone is strictly regulated by quotas (see Statistical Survey). During 2005/06 six companies were licensed to fish in the zone. Following the implementation of a new satellite surveillance system in February 2004, illegal fishing incursions were believed to have been reduced by some 90% by November 2005. An agreement to increase co-operation between France and Australia in combating illegal fishing in the southern Antarctic was signed in 2007 and was ratified by Australia in 2011 (it had previously been ratified by the French Government).

Limited numbers of tourists have since 1994 been permitted to visit Crozet, Kerguelen and Amsterdam: about 60 tourists travel to the territories each year aboard the supply and oceanographic vessel *Marion Dufresne II*. In 2006 Crozet, Kerguelen, Amsterdam and Saint Paul were designated as nature and marine reserves.

Statistical Survey

Area (sq km): Kerguelen Archipelago 7,215, Crozet Archipelago 340, Amsterdam Island 58, Saint-Paul Island 8, Adélie Land (Antarctica) 432,000, Iles Eparses 39 (Bassas da India 1, Europa 28, Juan de Nova 4, Les Glorieuses 5, Tromelin 1).

Population (the population, comprising members of scientific missions, fluctuates according to season, being higher in the summer, but the average is around 200; the figures given are approximate): Kerguelen Archipelago, Port-aux-Français 80; Amsterdam Island at Martin de Viviès 30; Adélie Land at Base Dumont d'Urville 27; the Crozet Archipelago at Alfred Faure (on Ile de la Possession) 35; Saint-Paul Island is uninhabited; Total population (April 2000): 172. *2003/04:* Adélie Land at Base Concordia 41 (joint French-Italian team).

Fishing (catch quotas in metric tons): *2002/03–2006/07:* Crayfish (spiny lobsters) in Amsterdam and Saint-Paul: 390. *2007/08:* Patagonian toothfish (caught by French and foreign fleets) in the Kerguelen and Crozet Archipelagos: 6,000.

Currency: French currency was used until the end of 2001. Euro notes and coins were introduced on 1 January 2002, and the euro became the sole legal tender from 18 February. For details of exchange rates, see French Guiana.

Budget: €33.4m. in 2005, of which official subventions comprised €281,800.

External Trade: Exports consist mainly of crayfish and other fish to France and Réunion. The Territories also derive revenue from the sale of postage stamps and other philatelic items.

Directory

Government: rue Gabriel Dejean, 97410 Saint Pierre, Réunion; tel. 262-96-78-78; fax 262-96-78-06; e-mail didier.hespel@taaf.fr; internet www.taaf.fr; Prefect, Chief Administrator PASCAL BOLOT.

Consultative Council: Pres. JEAN-PIERRE CHARPENTIER-VULLIEZ.

Publications: The central administration in Réunion produces two quarterly publications relating to the French Southern and Antarctic Territories: the legal bulletin *Journal officiel des Terres australes et antarctiques françaises* and a newsletter, *Terres Extrêmes*.

Institut Polaire Français Paul Emile Victor (IPEV): Technopôle de Brest-Iroise, BP 75, 29280 Plouzané, France; tel. 2-98-05-65-00; fax 2-98-05-65-55; e-mail infoipev@ipev.fr; internet www.institut-polaire.fr; f. 1992 as Institut Français pour la Recherche et la Technologie Polaires, name changed 2002; Dir GÉRARD JUGIE; 5 permanent bases.

Research Stations: There are meteorological stations and geophysical research stations on Kerguelen, Amsterdam, Adélie Land and Crozet. Research in marine microbiology is conducted from the Crozet and Kerguelen Archipelagos, and studies of atmospheric pollution are carried out on Amsterdam Island. Additionally, a joint French-Italian research station, Concordia, operates at Dome C. The French atomic energy authority, the Commissariat à l'énergie atomique, also maintains a presence on Crozet, Kerguelen and Adélie Land.

Transport: An oceanographic and supply vessel, the *Marion Dufresne II*, operated by the French Government, provides regular links between Réunion and the sub-Antarctic islands. A polar research vessel, *Astrolabe*, owned by the Groupe Bourbon and operating from Hobart, Tasmania, calls five times a year at the Antarctic mainland.

NEW CALEDONIA

Introductory Survey

LOCATION, CLIMATE, LANGUAGE, RELIGION, CAPITAL

New Caledonia comprises one large island and several smaller ones, lying in the South Pacific Ocean, about 1,500 km (930 miles) east of Queensland, Australia. The main island, New Caledonia (Grande Terre), is long and narrow, and has a total area of 16,372 sq km. Rugged mountains divide the west of the island from the east, and there is little flat land. The nearby Loyalty Islands, which are administratively part of New Caledonia, are 1,981 sq km in area, and a third group of islands, the uninhabited Chesterfield Islands, lies about 400 km north-west of the main island. The islands are surrounded by the world's largest continuous coral barrier reef, encompassing some 40,000 sq km. The climate is generally mild, with an average temperature of about 24°C (75°F) and a rainy season between December and March. The average rainfall in the east of the main island is about 2,000 mm (80 ins) per year, and in the west about 1,000 mm (40 ins). French is the official language and the mother tongue of the Caldoches (French settlers). The indigenous Kanaks (Melanesians) also speak Melanesian languages: 29 languages were taken into account at the census of 1996, when it was recorded that 38% of the total indigenous Kanak population spoke a Melanesian language. Other immigrants speak Polynesian and Asian languages. New Caledonians almost all profess Christianity, the majority of whom are Roman Catholics. There is a substantial Protestant minority. The capital is Nouméa, on the main island.

CONTEMPORARY POLITICAL HISTORY

Historical Context

New Caledonia became a French possession in the 19th century, when the island was annexed as a dependency of Tahiti. A separate administration was subsequently established, and a conseil général was elected to defend local interests. France took possession of Melanesian land and began mining nickel and copper. This displacement of the indigenous Kanak population provoked a number of rebellions. New Caledonia became an Overseas Territory of the French Republic in 1946. In 1956 the first Territorial Assembly, with 30 members, was elected by universal adult suffrage, although the French Governor effectively retained control of the functions of government. New Caledonian demands for a measure of self-government were answered in 1976 by a new statute, which gave the Council of Government, elected from the Territorial Assembly, responsibility for certain internal affairs. The post of Governor was replaced by that of French High Commissioner to the Territory. In 1978 the Kanak-supported, pro-independence parties obtained a majority of the posts in the Council of Government. In early 1979, however, the French Government dismissed the Council, following its failure to support a proposal for a 10-year 'contract' between France and New Caledonia, because the plan did not acknowledge the possibility of New Caledonian independence. The Territory was then placed under the direct authority of the High Commissioner.

Domestic Political Affairs

A general election was held in July 1979, but a new electoral law, which affected mainly the pro-independence parties, ensured that minor parties were not represented in the Assembly. Two parties loyal to France (Rassemblement pour la Calédonie dans la République—RPCR—and Fédération pour une Nouvelle Société Calédonienne—FNSC) together won 22 of the 36 seats.

Following the election of François Mitterrand as President of France, tension increased in September 1981 after the assassination of Pierre Declercq, the Secretary-General of the pro-independence party, Union Calédonienne (UC). In December of that year the French Government made proposals for change that included equal access for all New Caledonians to positions of authority, land reforms and the fostering of Kanak cultural institutions. To assist in effecting these reforms, the French Government simultaneously announced that it would rule by decree for a period of at least one year. In 1982 the FNSC joined with the opposition grouping, Front Indépendantiste (FI), to form a government that was more favourable to the proposed reforms.

In November 1983 the French Government proposed a five-year period of increased autonomy from July 1984 and a referendum in 1989 to determine New Caledonia's future. The statute was opposed in New Caledonia, both by parties in favour of earlier independence and by those against, and it was rejected by the Territorial Assembly in April 1984. However, the proposals were approved by the French Assemblée nationale (National Assembly) in September 1984. Under the provisions of the statute, the Territorial Council of Ministers was given responsibility for many internal matters of government, its President henceforth being an elected member instead of the French High Commissioner; a second legislative chamber, with the right to be consulted on development planning and budgetary issues, was created at the same time. All of the main parties seeking independence (except the Libération Kanak Socialiste—LKS—party, which left the FI) boycotted elections for the new Territorial Assembly in November 1984 and, following the dissolution of the FI, formed a new movement, the Front de Libération Nationale Kanak Socialiste (FLNKS). On 1 December the FLNKS Congress established a 'provisional' Government, headed by Jean-Marie Tjibaou. The elections to the Territorial Assembly attracted only 50.1% of the electorate, and the anti-independence party RPCR won 34 of the 42 seats. An escalation of violence began in November, and in the following month three settlers were murdered by pro-independence activists and 10 Kanaks were killed by *métis* (mixed race) settlers.

In January 1985 Edgard Pisani, the new High Commissioner, announced a plan by which the Territory might become independent 'in association with' France on 1 January 1986, subject to the result of a referendum in July 1985. Kanak groups opposed the plan, insisting that the indigenous population be allowed to determine its own fate. At the same time, the majority of the population, which supported the RPCR, demonstrated against the plan and in favour of remaining within the French Republic. A resurgence of violence followed the announcement of Pisani's plan, and a state of emergency was declared after two incidents in which a leading member of the FLNKS was killed by security forces and the son of a French settler was killed by Kanak activists.

In April 1985 the French Prime Minister, Laurent Fabius, put forward new proposals for the future of New Caledonia, whereby the referendum on independence was deferred until an unspecified date not later than the end of 1987. Meanwhile, the Territory was to be divided into four regions, each to be governed by its own elected autonomous council, which would have extensive powers in the spheres of planning and development, education, health and social services, land rights, transport and housing. The elected members of all four councils together would serve as regional representatives in a Territorial Congress (to replace the Territorial Assembly).

The 'Fabius plan' was well received by the FLNKS, although the organization reaffirmed the ultimate goal of independence. It was also decided to maintain the 'provisional Government' under Jean-Marie Tjibaou at least until the end of 1985. The RPCR condemned the plan, and the proposals were rejected by the predominantly anti-independence Territorial Assembly in May. Nevertheless, the necessary legislation was approved by the French Assemblée nationale in July, and the Fabius plan entered into force. Elections were held in September, and as expected only in the region around Nouméa, where the bulk of the population was non-Kanak, was an anti-independence majority recorded. However, the pro-independence Melanesians, in spite of their majorities in the three non-urban regions, would be in a minority in the Territorial Congress.

The FLNKS boycotted the general election to the French Assemblée nationale in March 1986, in which only about 50% of the eligible voters in New Caledonia participated. In May the French Council of Ministers approved a draft law providing for a referendum to be held in New Caledonia within 12 months, whereby voters would choose between independence and a further extension of regional autonomy. In December, in spite of strong French diplomatic opposition, the UN General Assembly voted to reinscribe New Caledonia on the UN list of non-self-governing territories, thereby affirming the population's right to self-determination.

The FLNKS decided to boycott the referendum on 13 September 1987, at which 98.3% of the votes cast were in favour of New Caledonia's continuation as part of the French Republic and only 1.7% of those cast favoured independence. Of the registered electorate, almost 59% voted, a higher level of participation than expected, although 90% of the electorate abstained in constituencies inhabited by a majority of Kanaks.

In October 1987 seven pro-French loyalists were acquitted on a charge of murdering 10 Kanak separatists in 1984. Jean-Marie Tjibaou, who reacted to the ruling by declaring that his supporters would have to abandon their stance of pacifism, and his deputy, Yeiwéné Yeiwéné, were indicted for 'incitement to violence'. In April 1988 four gendarmes were killed, and 27 held hostage in a cave on the island of Uvéa (the neighbouring Wallis Island), by supporters of the FLNKS. Two days later, Kanak separatists prevented about one-quarter of the Territory's polling stations from opening when local elections were held. The FLNKS boycotted the elections. Although 12 of the gendarmes taken hostage were subsequently released, six members of a French anti-terrorist squad were captured. French security forces immediately laid siege to the cave, and in the following month made an assault upon it, leaving 19 Kanaks and two gendarmes dead. Following the siege, allegations that three Kanaks had been executed or left to die, after being arrested, led to an announcement by the new French Socialist Government that a judicial inquiry into the incident was to be opened.

At the elections to the French Assemblée nationale in June 1988, both New Caledonian seats were retained by the RPCR. Michel Rocard, the new French Prime Minister, chaired negotiations in Paris, between Jacques Lafleur (leader of the RPCR) and Jean-Marie Tjibaou, who agreed to transfer the administration of the Territory to Paris for 12 months. Under the provisions of the agreement (known as the Matignon Accord), the Territory was to be divided into three administrative Provinces prior to a territorial plebiscite on independence to be held in 1998. Only people resident in the Territory in 1988, and their direct descendants, would be allowed to vote in the plebiscite. The agreement also provided for a programme of economic development, training in public administration for Kanaks, and institutional reforms. The Matignon Accord was presented to the French electorate in a referendum, held on 6 November 1988, and approved by 80% of those voting (although an abstention rate of 63% of the electorate was recorded). The programme was approved by a 57% majority in New Caledonia, where the rate of abstention was 37%. In November, under the terms of the agreement, 51 separatists were released from prison, including 26 Kanaks implicated in the incident on Uvéa.

In May 1989 the leaders of the FLNKS, Jean-Marie Tjibaou and Yeiwéné Yeiwéné, were murdered by separatist extremists, alleged to be associated with the Front Uni de Libération Kanak (FULK). This grouping had hitherto formed part of the FLNKS, but it opposed the Matignon Accord. Elections to the three Provincial Assemblies were nevertheless held, as scheduled, in June: the FLNKS won a majority of seats in the North Province and the Loyalty Islands Province. The RPCR obtained a majority in the South Province, and it also emerged as the dominant party in the Territorial Congress, with 27 of the 54 seats; the FLNKS secured 19 seats.

The year of direct rule by France ended, as agreed, on 14 July 1989, when the Territorial Congress and Provincial Assemblies assumed the administrative functions allocated to them in the Matignon Accord. In November the French Assemblée nationale approved an amnesty (as stipulated in the Matignon Accord) for all who had been involved in politically motivated violence in New Caledonia before August 1988, despite strong opposition from the right-wing French parties. In April 1991 the LKS announced its intention to withdraw from the Matignon Accord, accusing the French Government, as well as several Kanak political leaders, of seeking to undermine Kanak culture and tradition. At elections for the New Caledonian representative to the French Sénat (Senate) in September 1992, the RPCR's candidate, Simon Loueckhote, narrowly defeated Roch Wamytan, the Vice-President of the FLNKS.

In October 1994 Lafleur proposed that New Caledonia abandon the planned 1998 referendum on self-determination, in favour of a 30-year agreement with France, similar to the Matignon Accord, but with provision for greater autonomy in judicial matters. However, the UC rejected the proposal and reiterated its demand for a gradual transfer of power from France to New Caledonia, culminating in a return to sovereignty in 1998.

At provincial elections in July 1995 the RPCR remained the most successful party, although its dominance was reduced considerably. The RPCR retained an overall majority in the Territorial Congress, while the FLNKS remained the second largest party. Considerable gains were made by a newly formed party led by Nouméa businessman Didier Leroux, Une Nouvelle-Calédonie pour Tous (UNCT). However, a political crisis subsequently arose as a result of the UNCT's decision to align itself with the FLNKS, leaving the RPCR with a minority of official positions in the congressional committees. Lafleur would not accept a situation in which the UNCT appeared to be the dominant party in the chamber, and Pierre Frogier, the RPCR President of the Congress, refused to convene a congressional sitting under such circumstances. The deadlock was broken only when the FLNKS proposed the allocation of congressional positions on a proportional basis.

Elections to the French Assemblée nationale in May–June 1997 were boycotted by the pro-independence FLNKS and LKS, resulting in a relatively low participation rate among the electorate. Lafleur and Frogier, both RPCR candidates, were elected to represent New Caledonia. Intensive negotiations involving the RPCR, the FLNKS and the French Government took place in late 1995 and early 1996. France's refusal to grant final approval for a large-scale nickel smelter project in the North Province (see Economic Affairs) until the achievement of consensus in the discussions on autonomy prompted accusations of blackmail from several sources within the Territory and increased suspicions that metropolitan France would seek to retain control of the islands' valuable mineral resources in any settlement on New Caledonia's future status. The issue proved to be a serious obstacle and resulted in the virtual cessation of negotiations between the two sides during the remainder of 1996. The FLNKS argued that the smelter project should be administered by local interests, consistent with the process of reallocating responsibility for the economy from metropolitan France to the Territory as advocated in the Matignon Accord. Their demands were supported by widespread industrial action in the mining sector during late 1996.

In February 1997 the French Minister for Overseas Territories, Jean-Jacques de Peretti, travelled to New Caledonia in an attempt to achieve an exchange agreement on nickel between the Société Minière du Sud Pacifique (SMSP), controlled by the North Province, and a subsidiary of the French mining conglomerate Eramet, Société Le Nickel (SLN). The minister failed to resolve the dispute during his visit; however, at the end of the month, in a complete reversal of its previous position, the French Government announced its decision not to compensate SLN for any losses incurred. The decision provoked strong criticism from SLN and Eramet, and attracted protests from shareholders and employees of the company. During March large-scale demonstrations were held by the UC and the pro-independence trade union, the Union Syndicale des Travailleurs Kanak et des Exploités (USTKE), in support of SMSP's acquisition of the smelter. Meanwhile, another trade union, USOENC (which represented a high proportion of SLN employees), organized a protest rally against the unequal exchange of mining sites. Frustrated at SLN's seemingly intransigent position during the negotiations, the FLNKS organized protests and blockades at all the company's major mining installations and restricted shipments of ore around New Caledonia. Consequently, four mines were forced to close, while a 25% reduction in working hours was imposed on 1,500 mine workers. In January 1998 Roch Wamytan urged the French Prime Minister, Lionel Jospin, to settle the dispute by the end of the month in order that official negotiations on the political future of New Caledonia, in preparation for the referendum, might begin. The position of the FLNKS had been somewhat undermined by the decision, in the previous month, of a breakaway group of pro-independence politicians—including prominent members of the UC, the Parti de Libération Kanak (PALIKA), and the LKS—to begin negotiations with the RPCR concerning the dispute. These moderate supporters of independence formed the Fédération des Comités de Coordination des Indépendantistes (FCCI) in 1998.

In February 1998, in response to the demands of Kanak political leaders, the French Government, Eramet, SMSP and others signed the Bercy Accord, whereby Eramet was to relinquish control of its site at Koniambo, located in the North Province, in exchange for the Poum mine, operated by SMSP, in the South Province. (The Bercy Accord was the foundation for the 'rebalancing' of New Caledonia's economy under the Nouméa Accord—see below—by creating wealth beyond the South Province.) In April SMSP formed a joint venture with the Canadian mining company Falconbridge to develop the Koniambo nickel deposits. If construction of a nickel smelter had not begun by the end of 2005, control of the nickel deposits was to revert from SMSP to SLN. Meanwhile, the French Government agreed to pay compensation of some 1,000m. French francs to Eramet for the reduction in the company's reserves. An agreement was concluded in February 1999 to enable the transfer of 30% of SLN's share capital (and 8% of Eramet's capital) to a newly created company representing local interests, the Société Territoriale Calédonienne de Participation Industrielle (STCPI), to be owned by the development companies of the three New Caledonian provinces. In July 2000, following two years of negotiations, New Caledonia's political leaders signed an agreement on the formation of the STCPI, the new company to be owned equally by PROMOSUD (representing the South Province) and NORDIL (combining the interests of the North Province and the Loyalty Islands). In September shares in SLN and Eramet were transferred to the STCPI, reducing Eramet's interest in SLN from 90% to 60%.

The Nouméa Accord

Tripartite negotiations on the constitutional future of New Caledonia resumed in Paris in late February 1998 between representatives of the French Government, the FLNKS and the RPCR. In April, following a final round of talks in Nouméa, an agreement was concluded by the three sides. The agreement, which became known as the Nouméa Accord, postponed the referendum on independence for a period of between 15 and 20 years but provided for a gradual transfer of powers to local institutions, with the exception of defence, foreign policy, law and order, justice and monetary affairs, which were to remain the responsibility of the French Government until after the referendum. The document also acknowledged the negative impact of many aspects of French colonization on New Caledonia and emphasized the need for greater recognition of the importance of the Kanak cultural identity in the political development of the islands. The Nouméa Accord was signed on 5 May.

In July 1998 both chambers of the French legislature voted in favour of adopting the proposed changes regarding the administration of New Caledonia, which were to be incorporated in an annex to the French Constitution. In the following month the French Minister for Overseas Territories, Jean-Jack Queyranne, returned to New Caledonia for discussion on draft legislation for the devolution process. In September a new political group, the Comité Provisoire pour la Défense des Principes Républicains de la Nouvelle-Calédonie Française, was formed in opposition to the Nouméa Accord, with support from members of the Front National and other right-wing parties. The UNCT, which was dissatisfied with several aspects of the accord, also urged its supporters to vote against the agreement.

The Nouméa Accord, which designated New Caledonia as an Overseas Country (Pays d'outre-mer) of France, was presented to the electorate in a referendum on 8 November 1998, when it was decisively approved, with 71.9% of votes cast in favour of the agreement. The North Province registered the strongest vote in favour of the agreement (95.5%), while the South Province recorded the most moderate level of approval (62.9%). In late December the French Assemblée nationale unanimously approved draft legislation regarding the definitive adoption of the accord. The Sénat similarly approved the legislation in February 1999. However, in March of that year the French Constitutional Council declared its intention to allow any French person who had resided in New Caledonia for 10 years or more to vote in provincial elections. This decision was criticized by Roch Wamytan, leader of the FLNKS, as well as by politicians in the French Assemblée nationale and Sénat, who claimed that this was in breach of the Nouméa Accord, whereby only those residing in New Caledonia in 1998 would be permitted to vote in provincial elections. Pro-independence groups threatened to boycott the elections (to be held in May). In response to this, the French Government announced that the Accord would be honoured, claiming that the Constitutional Council had breached the Nouméa Accord, and stating that this contravention would be rectified. In June the French Council of Ministers announced that it had drafted legislation restricting eligibility for voting in provincial elections and in any future referendums on sovereignty, to those who had been eligible to vote in the November 1998 referendum on the Nouméa Accord, and to their children upon reaching the age of majority. This decision was condemned by the right-wing Front National, and by Lafleur, leader of the RPCR.

At the general election held on 9 May 1999, no party gained an absolute majority. However, Lafleur's anti-independence RPCR won 24 of the 54 seats in the Congress and formed a coalition with the recently established FCCI and, on an informal level, with the Front National, thus creating an anti-independence block of 31 seats in the chamber. The pro-independence FLNKS won 18 seats. Simon Loueckhote was re-elected as President of the Congress in late May. Results of the elections in the Loyalty Islands were officially challenged by the moderate independence parties, LKS and FCCI, as well as by the RPCR, following the issue by the electoral commissioner for the Province of a report claiming that a large number of irregularities had occurred. A new election was held in June 2000, at which a coalition of the RPCR, FCCI, LKS and FULK obtained 44.8% of votes and six seats. The FLNKS obtained 37.3% of votes and six seats, and PALIKA 17.8% of votes and two seats. The composition of the Congress therefore remained unchanged.

On 28 May 1999 the Congress elected Jean Lèques as the first President of the Government of New Caledonia, under the increased autonomy terms of the Nouméa Accord. The new Government was elected on the basis of proportional representation and replaced the French High Commissioner as New Caledonia's executive authority. The election of Léopold Jorédié, leader of the FCCI, as Vice-President was denounced by the FLNKS, which argued that, as it was the second largest party in the Congress and had been a joint negotiator in the Nouméa Accord, the post should have gone to its leader, Roch Wamytan. In December Vice-President Jorédié received a one-year suspended prison sentence following accusations of misuse of public funds. Jorédié was charged with illegally obtaining grants totalling an estimated 5.5m. francs CFP, for the benefit of his son.

At the FLNKS's annual conference, held in November 2000, Roch Wamytan was re-elected President of the party (Wamytan was also narrowly re-elected leader of the UC); at the same time a new pro-independence party, the Groupe UC du Congrès, formed by a breakaway faction of the UC, was officially recognized by both the UC and the FLNKS.

Municipal elections confirmed the predominance of the RPCR in the south in March 2001, when it won 39 of the 49 seats in Nouméa. However, overall the RPCR controlled only 14 of the 33 municipalities in New Caledonia, while pro-independence parties, principally the UC, PALIKA, LKS and FLNKS, held 19. The FLNKS won a majority in the north and took all three communes in the Loyalty Islands. Jean Lèques resigned as President and was replaced by fellow RPCR politician, Frogier, in April. Déwé Gorodey of the FLNKS was elected Vice-President. The election to the two most senior posts took place after the Congress had elected an 11-member Government consisting of seven RPCR-FCCI coalition members, three from the FLNKS and one from the UC.

In October 2001 the French Conseil d'Etat (State Council) ruled that the 11th seat in the New Caledonian Government had been incorrectly allocated to the FLNKS following the local elections of April 2001. As a result, FCCI leader Raphaël Mapou replaced Aukusitino Manuohalalo of the FLNKS as Minister for Social Security and Health. Roch Wamytan was replaced as President of the UC by his deputy, Pascal Naouna. In November Wamytan lost the presidency of the FLNKS, following a leadership struggle between its two main factions, the UC and PALIKA. The political bureau of the FLNKS was to lead the party until its internal disputes were settled.

Prior to the French legislative elections of June 2002, RPCR became affiliated to the metropolitan Union pour la Majorité Presidentielle—latterly Union pour un Mouvement Populaire—to form Le Rassemblement-UMP. The UC and PALIKA could not agree upon their choice of President for the FLNKS. The UC therefore refused to take part in the elections and urged its supporters to abstain from the poll, thereby depriving the President of PALIKA, Paul Néaoutyine, of any chance of re-election to the Assemblée nationale in Paris. Lafleur, now representing Le Rassemblement-UMP, was thus re-elected as a deputy, as was Frogier also for Le Rassemblement-UMP.

In November 2002 the sole UC member of the Government, Gerald Cortot, resigned, prompting the immediate dissolution of the Government, as stipulated in the Nouméa Accord. The Council of Ministers was reduced to 10 members, and the Congress appointed a new administration, with Frogier reappointed as President; the incoming Government contained seven members of the Rassemblement-UMP-FCCI coalition, two from the FLNKS and one from the UC.

In May 2003 it was announced that New Caledonia (together with French Polynesia) would be granted one additional seat in the French Sénat. (This change finally took effect at the senatorial elections of September 2011.) Also in May 2003, at a congress of the FLNKS, officials of the party reportedly claimed that the terms of the Nouméa Accord were not being fully observed by the French Government. In July USTKE called a general strike to coincide with a visit to New Caledonia by President Jacques Chirac and organized a rally attended by 2,000 protesters. Chirac's four-day visit also provoked demonstrations by several hundred members of the UC. Kanak representatives, meanwhile, expressed dismay at their exclusion from meetings with the French President.

Legislative elections took place on 9 May 2004. Le Rassemblement-UMP lost its majority in the South Province, where it won only 16 of the 40 seats, and thus in the Congress of New Caledonia, occupying only 16 of the 54 seats. The results demonstrated an increase in support for the pro-independence movements, notably the recently formed Avenir Ensemble, which secured 19 seats in the South Province and proceeded to take 16 seats in the Congress. Each Provincial Assembly in turn elected its President: Philippe Gomès of Avenir Ensemble became President of the South Province, replacing Lafleur; Néaoutyine of the Union Nationale pour l'Indépendance (UNI) was re-elected in the North Province; and Néko Hnépeune, also of the UNI-FLNKS alliance, was elected President in the Loyalty Islands. At its inaugural meeting in late May the incoming Congress elected Harold Martin of Avenir Ensemble as its President and began the process of appointing a new Government. In early June Marie-Noëlle Thémereau of Avenir Ensemble and Gorodey of the UNI-FLNKS were respectively nominated President and Vice-President. However, the Government disintegrated within hours, following the resignation of three Rassemblement-UMP cabinet ministers, who claimed that they were entitled to four seats under power-sharing terms set out in the Nouméa Accord. The Congress granted Le Rassemblement-UMP the seats, but with the result that the decision of the Council of Ministers on its leadership reached a stalemate. In late June, following negotiations that also involved the French High Commissioner in New Caledonia and discussions in Paris between Martin and the French Government, a new vote returned Thémereau and Gorodey to their elected posts. The incoming Government endorsed a code of conduct that emphasized the importance of consensus-building among the parties. In January 2005 representatives of Avenir Ensemble for the first time took part in discussions with the French Government in Paris.

In October 2004 an operating licence was granted to Canadian mining company Inco for the development of a proposed nickel-cobalt plant at Goro in the South Province (see Economic Affairs). Concerns about the disposal of industrial waste into the sea had been raised in a public inquiry in the previous August and in February 2005 protesters from a Kanak environmental organization, Rééb̀hu Nùù, blockaded the Goro site. In December Goro was again blockaded, this time by protesters from another Kanak organization, the Conseil Autochtone pour la Gestion des Ressources Naturelles en Kanaky Nouvelle-Calédonie (CAUGERN), which had been formed in July. CAUGERN received the support of USTKE and the local Customary Senate in raising concerns relating to the socio-economic and political impact of nickel-mining activities, as well as with regard to the environmental repercussions.

In early December 2005 Eramet instigated a legal challenge at the Tribunal de grande instance, in Paris, over the transfer of control of the Koniambo mine to the Canadian mining company Falconbridge and SMSP. Under the terms of the Bercy Accord (see above), the transfer was to be completed by the end of the year. However, Eramet claimed that Falconbridge had not fulfilled certain conditions, as a result of which control of the mine would remain with Eramet's subsidiary, SLN. In mid-December some 2,000 protesters were reported to have demonstrated in Nouméa in support of the transfer, which was seen as empowering the indigenous Kanak population of the North Province. Initially the French Government had promised financial and tax concessions to Falconbridge, but in late November announced that it would be unable to make a commitment until the drafting of the following year's budget. In early December, with the support of SMSP, Falconbridge undertook to finance the entire cost of the project. Later that month the French court rejected Eramet's challenge and the transfer was completed.

In 2006 plans for a merger between Inco and Falconbridge were cancelled; Falconbridge was subsequently acquired by a Swiss-based company, Xstrata PLC. (Under the terms of a 2007 agreement, Xstrata Nickel has a 49% stake and the SMSP Group a 51% stake in the Koniambo joint venture.) Inco became a wholly owned subsidiary of the Brazilian enterprise, Companhia Vale do Rio Doce (CVRD). In April the development of the Goro Nickel mine again became a major issue when members of the Kanak environmental organization Réébhù Nùù, opposed to the project because of its environmental impact, blockaded access routes to the mining site and caused damage to equipment estimated at US $10m. Construction work at the nickel plant was halted, and Frogier, who continued as New Caledonia's deputy to the Assemblée nationale in Paris, submitted a request to the French Government for the deployment of additional police officers to New Caledonia. The FLNKS assumed the role of mediator on behalf of Réébhù Nùù, Goro Nickel, the New Caledonian Government and community leaders, while USTKE announced its support for the Réébhù Nùù campaign. Following reassurances about the security of the site, Goro Nickel announced that it would restart construction work. However, opposition to the project remained, and demonstrations continued. In June a New Caledonian court ruled that the possible environmental consequences of the scheme had not been comprehensively investigated, and cancelled its licence to operate; however, the company's construction licence remained intact. In July Réébhù Nùù, joined by CAUGERN, warned of further action if Goro Nickel failed to halt construction by a deadline of 24 September. On 25 September the CSTNC began a general strike to demand the expulsion of several hundred Filipino employees of Goro Nickel and the resignations of local government officials. In November Réébhù Nùù succeeded in gaining an injunction from a French court on Goro Nickel's construction of a waste facility. This ruling was rescinded in February 2007. Mounting costs and continuing local opposition further delayed the project, which was not expected to reach full production until 2013.

In April 2006 Lafleur founded a new political party with Simon Loueckhote, the Rassemblement pour la Calédonie (Rally for Caledonia—RPC). In early 2007, the French legislature approved a constitutional amendment that limited voting rights to those who had been resident in New Caledonia prior to 1998. Due to enter into force in 2009, the legislation did not cover the French legislative and presidential elections of 2007. Nicolas Sarkozy of the UMP defeated Ségolène Royal of the Parti Socialiste in the second round, garnering 62.9% of the votes in New Caledonia (Royal received 37.1%). The discrepancy between their respective proportions of the vote was significantly smaller within France. Elections to the Assemblée nationale were held in June. Although the Rassemblement-UMP candidates, incumbent deputy Frogier and Gaël Yanno, received the largest number of votes in their respective constituencies, their failure to secure an absolute majority resulted in the scheduling of a second round. Avenir Ensemble candidates, along with former Rassemblement-UMP member Lafleur, did not receive enough votes to proceed to the next stage. In the second round, Yanno secured a decisive victory over FLNKS candidate Charles Washetine, the Minister for Education and Research, while Frogier was re-elected, defeating Charles Pidjot of the FLNKS by a smaller margin.

As had been widely anticipated, Thémereau of Avenir Ensemble, resigned from the position of President in July 2007, although the Council of Ministers was to remain in place until the appointment of a new Government. Frogier was elected President of the Congress of New Caledonia in late July, following reports that Avenir Ensemble and Le Rassemblement-UMP had signed an agreement, a so-called 'majority accord', which the President of the RPC, Loueckhote, had also entered into. An initial attempt to form a multi-party Council of Ministers in early August failed after the FLNKS, dissatisfied with the number of ministerial posts it had been allocated, withdrew its support. The Congress elected a new Council of Ministers in August, meeting the FLNKS's demand for four cabinet positions out of a total of 11. Martin was subsequently elected President and Gorodey returned to the position of Vice-President.

In October 2007 the French High Commissioner in New Caledonia, Michel Mathieu, resigned amid reports of a disagreement with the French Minister-Delegate for the Overseas Possessions, Christian Estrosi, who had signalled a new approach to the issue of strike action in New Caledonia. The appointment of Yves Dassonville as Mathieu's replacement was approved in the same month, and Dassonville took office in November. In January 2008 a USTKE strike in Nouméa escalated into violence following police intervention; several people were injured, and in April a total of 23 members of USTKE, including the union's leader, were given prison sentences for their involvement in the clashes. In November Louis Kotra Uregei was elected President of the Parti Travailliste, which had been formed in the previous year in conjunction with USTKE. Meanwhile, municipal elections were held in March. In July when Frogier was re-elected as President of the Congress, he received significantly fewer votes than in the previous year, owing to the division into factions of Avenir Ensemble led by Martin and Gomès, the latter of which had nominated Thémereau for the position.

Recent developments: the elections of 2009 and beyond

In March 2009, as required by the Nouméa Accord, the New Caledonian Congress unanimously approved new legislation governing the operations of the nickel industry (see Economic Affairs). Legislative elections were held in the Territory's three provinces on 10 May, whereupon each Provincial Assembly elected its President. Pierre Frogier of Le Rassemblement-UMP replaced Philippe Gomès as President of the South Province. Paul Néaoutyine, leader of the UNI, was re-elected in the North Province. In the Loyalty Islands Néko Hnépeune, also of the UNI-FLNKS, was re-elected as President. Members of anti-independence parties occupied 31 of the 54 seats in the New Caledonian Congress, (of which Le Rassemblement-UMP took 13). Calédonie Ensemble, established in 2008 by former members of Avenir Ensemble and led by Gomès, was allocated 10 seats. The pro-independence groups made some gains and took 23 seats, eight of which were occupied by the UC and eight by the UNI.

At its inaugural session, the Congress chose Gomès as the Territory's President; Gomès also assumed responsibility for the mining portfolio. Disagreements delayed the election of the Vice-President until mid-June 2009, when Pierre Ngaihoni of the UC was appointed to the position. Other appointments to the Council of Ministers included that of Philippe Germain, whose responsibilities included economic affairs. Martin replaced Frogier as President of the New Caledonian Congress. However, the Parti Travailliste lodged a formal complaint with regard to the conduct of the elections and in October 2009, following the confirmation of irregularities relating mainly to the extensive use of proxy votes, the results of the Loyalty Islands were declared invalid by the Conseil d'Etat in France. The province thus returned to the polls on 6 December: the UC-FLNKS alliance was reported to have retained six seats in the Provincial Assembly; the Parti Travailliste increased its representation from two to four seats, the LKS won two seats and two seats were taken by another pro-independence grouping.

Industrial unrest continued intermittently. A dispute at the local airline, arising from the dismissal of an employee, developed into rioting in May 2009, when the police used tear gas and grenades to quell the disturbance. In June the union called a general strike following the refusal by Air Calédonie to pay striking workers during several weeks of industrial action and the sentencing of USTKE leader Gérard Jodar to one year's imprisonment. A further confrontation between USTKE demonstrators and the police occurred in July, during a visit from France of the new Minister for Overseas Possessions, Marie-Luce Penchard. Businesses in Nouméa were similarly disrupted by USTKE action. An estimated 20,000 demonstrators, including business leaders and politicians, joined a march in Nouméa to protest against the disruption. In October three USTKE members were found guilty of involvement in the violence during the protests and each defendant was sentenced to one year's imprisonment, eight months of which were suspended.

Meanwhile, the gradual process of transferring powers from metropolitan France continued, as stipulated in the Nouméa Accord (with the exception of certain areas such as defence and foreign policy, which were to remain the responsibility of the French Government until after the referendum on independence that was to take place between 2014 and 2018). With responsibility for primary education, post and telecommunications, training in public administration, labour, external trade and mining having already been granted to the New Caledonian authorities, in November 2009 the local Congress unanimously approved the transfer of responsibility for various other areas from the French authorities; these included secondary education, private primary education, and the policing and security of domestic maritime transport and of internal air transport. New Caledonia was expected to assume control of most of these responsibilities during 2011–13. Secondary education became the responsibility of New Caledonia in January 2012, although the French Government was to continue to pay the salaries of teaching staff with an annual contribution of US $500m.

In June 2010 President Gomès was indicted for allegedly abusing his position in 2005–06, as the then President of the South Province, when a company owned by him had sold equipment to a mining company to which he had awarded an operating licence: Gomès denied the charge, claiming that it was politically motivated.

In June 2010 Marie-Luce Penchard again visited New Caledonia and held discussions with the various party leaders in order to establish the agenda for a meeting on the further implementation of the Nouméa Accord, which took place in Paris later that month. It was resolved at a subsequent meeting that a committee of experts would be established to study the options for the future political status of New Caledonia. At the same time the French Government undertook to provide 45,000m. francs CFP in development assistance for New Caledonia during the period 2011–15. In July 2010 the French Prime Minister, François Fillon, paid a visit to New Caledonia, during which the 'Kanak' flag (which had formed a symbol of the pro-independence movement over the past 20 years) was, with the approval of the Congress, officially raised for the first time, concurrently with the French national flag. However, the display of two flags was regarded by some as symbolizing disunity, and President Gomès, among others, argued that a new single flag should be designed to represent New Caledonia following decolonization.

In September 2010 Dassonville and Gomès signed a formal agreement on the transfer of powers from the metropolitan Government. Gomès emphasized that France should honour its undertaking to meet the costs of the transfer of powers. A new French High Commissioner, Albert Dupuy, replaced Dassonville in October 2010.

In February 2011 members of the pro-independence UC withdrew from the Council of Ministers, on the grounds that Gomès was opposed to the use of two flags. Under the terms of the Nouméa Accord, such a resignation automatically results in the removal from office of the entire Government and fresh elections to the government within two weeks. Gomès, who was in favour of designing a new flag, protested that the dispute regarding the flag was a ploy to remove him from office. He accused Le Rassemblement-UMP of allying itself with the UC to this end and pledged to disrupt future governments until a fresh general election was called. In early March the Congress elected a new 11-member collegial Government, in proportion to the parties' representation in the legislature. However, the new administration collapsed within minutes after one of the incoming ministers of Calédonie Ensemble duly submitted his resignation. Martin of Avenir Ensemble, who had replaced Gomès of Calédonie Ensemble as President, continued in office in an interim capacity, with Guy Tuyienon of the UC as his Vice-President. The crisis intensified a fortnight later when another Government, comprising six anti-independence and five pro-independence ministers was again appointed, only to disintegrate immediately when Calédonie Ensemble withdrew. In April, following a further unsuccessful attempt to establish a government, Marie-Luce Penchard travelled to New Caledonia in an attempt to resolve the crisis.

In May 2011, following three days of negotiations in Paris between political leaders from New Caledonia and members of the French Government, the French Prime Minister François Fillon announced that the Congress would elect a new collegial government on 10 June, rather than proceed with an early general election as initially requested by Gomès. Fillon was simultaneously planning amendments to New Caledonia's electoral law that would provide for greater political stability by allowing a new administration a period of 18 months free from the upheaval caused by ministerial resignations. At the election to the Government in June, Martin was re-elected as President and Tuyienon as Vice-President. Despite initial threats to withdraw once again, Calédonie Ensemble agreed to remain in the collegial Government following the election. The French Prime Minister hosted further talks in Paris between the signatories to the Nouméa Accord in July to review the agreement in advance of its entering its final phase (2014–18) when, under the terms of the Accord, a referendum on independence could be held in the Territory.

In August 2011 Nicolas Sarkozy made his first presidential visit to the Pacific islands. During his visit he endorsed the Government's recent decision to use the indigenous Kanak flag alongside the French tricolour in all official settings. He also appealed for restraint between different political groups and condemned the violence on Maré Island earlier that month when, during a blockade of the island's airport in a dispute over high local air fares and land ownership, four people had been killed and more than 20 injured in clashes between armed groups.

At elections to the French Sénat in September 2011, New Caledonia was allocated an additional seat, thus two seats were contested. Pierre Frogier and Hilarion Vendégou, both representing the UMP group, were successful, ending Frogier's mandate as a deputy of the French Assemblée nationale.

Regional Affairs

During a visit to Nouméa in September 2008, the French Minister of Defence, Hervé Morin, stated that the number of French military personnel stationed in New Caledonia was to be reduced by between 10% and 15%, partly owing to the islands' proximity to the regional power of Australia. New Caledonia was to be designated as a regional hub for marine defence. Closer co-operation with the armed forces of both Australia and New Zealand was envisaged following visits to Nouméa by senior delegations from these two countries in April 2009. A new defence co-operation agreement between France and Australia entered into force in July 2009, and in March 2010 a senior delegation, which included the French High Commissioner in New Caledonia, the President of the local Government and the Presidents of the three provinces, was invited to visit Australia, where the leadership hoped to enlist support for New Caledonia's objective of becoming a full (rather than an associate) member of the Pacific Islands Forum (see p. 416). Other matters under discussion included bilateral trade relations. In November the first annual bilateral consultation between New Caledonia and Australia took place. New Caledonia's application for full membership of the Pacific Islands Forum was rejected at a meeting of the organization in September 2011.

In early 2010 a bilateral co-operation agreement with Vanuatu, first signed in June 2006, was renewed for a period of five years. The accord provided for greater collaboration in the areas of education, health, culture, trade, law and order, and good governance. In June 2010 a mission of the Melanesian Spearhead Group, led by the Prime Minister of Vanuatu, Edward Natapei, and including senior ministers from Fiji, Papua New Guinea and Solomon Islands, visited New Caledonia and expressed concern at the slow progress being made in implementing the Nouméa Accord, and in particular at the persistent economic and social imbalance between the provinces of New Caledonia.

CONSTITUTION AND GOVERNMENT

New Caledonia was designated as an Overseas Country (Pays d'outre-mer) in 1999. Its status of Collectivité *sui generis*, conferred following a constitutional revision of 2003, is unique within the French Republic in that the local assembly is permitted to pass its own laws and a local citizenship may be bestowed upon permanent residents. The French Government is represented in New Caledonia by its High Commissioner, and controls a number of important spheres, including external relations and defence. In July 1989 administrative reforms were introduced, as stipulated in the Matignon Accord (which had been approved by national referendum in November 1988). New Caledonia was divided into three Provinces (North, South and Loyalty Islands), each governed by an assembly, which is elected on a proportional basis. The members of the three Provincial Assemblies together form the Congress. Members are subject to re-election every five years. The responsibilities of the Congress include New Caledonia's budget and fiscal affairs, infrastructure and primary education, while the responsibilities of the Provincial Assemblies include local economic development, land reform and cultural affairs. The Government of New Caledonia is elected by the Congress, and comprises between seven and 11 members. Under the terms of the Nouméa Accord (which was approved by a referendum in November 1998), the Government replaces the French High Commissioner as New Caledonia's executive authority. A gradual transfer of power from metropolitan France to local institutions was to be effected over a period of between 15 and 20 years under the terms of the Nouméa Accord.

In addition, New Caledonia elects two deputies to the French Assemblée nationale in Paris and two representatives to the French Sénat (Senate) on the basis of universal adult suffrage; one Economic and Social Councillor is also nominated. New Caledonia may also be represented at the European Parliament.

REGIONAL AND INTERNATIONAL CO-OPERATION

New Caledonia forms part of the Franc Zone (see p. 332). It is an associate member of the UN's Economic and Social Commission for Asia and the Pacific (ESCAP, see p. 40) and a member, in its own right, of the Pacific Community (see p. 413). New Caledonia became an associate member of the Pacific Islands Forum (see p. 416) in 2006. New Caledonia's application for full membership of the Pacific Islands Forum was rejected at a meeting of the organization in September 2011. The Front de Libération Nationale Kanak Socialiste (FLNKS) was admitted to the Melanesian Spearhead Group in 1990.

ECONOMIC AFFAIRS

In 2000, according to World Bank estimates, New Caledonia's gross national income (GNI) at average 1998–2000 prices totalled US $2,989.6m., equivalent to $14,060 per head (or $22,210 per head on an international purchasing-power parity basis). During 2001–10, it was estimated, the population rose at an average annual rate of 1.7%. According to the UN Economic and Social Commission for Asia and the Pacific (ESCAP), gross domestic product (GDP) per head decreased, in real terms, by an annual average of 0.6% during 1990–2000 and by 1.2% in 2000–05. However, overall GDP increased at an average annual rate of 1.6% in 1990–2000, rising by 0.5% annually in 2000–05. According to UN estimates, in comparison with the previous year, GDP was estimated to have expanded by 0.6% in 2008 and 2009, in the latter year reaching $6,379.7m. at constant 2005 prices.

Agriculture, forestry and fishing contributed only an estimated 3.7% of GDP in 2009. In 2009 2.7% of the employed labour force were engaged in the sector. Maize, yams, sweet potatoes and coconuts have traditionally been the principal crops, and pumpkins (squash) became an important export crop for the Japanese market from the 1990s. Livestock consists mainly of cattle, pigs and poultry. The main fisheries products are albacore, tuna and prawns (most of which are exported to Japan). The aquaculture industry has expanded steadily, with production of blue shrimp reaching 1,860 metric tons in 2009, in comparison with 691 tons in 1994. In 2009 exports of marine products were worth 1,832m. francs CFP, thus accounting for 1.2% of total exports. The GDP of the agricultural sector was estimated to have increased at an average annual rate of 6.0% in 1995–2000 and by an annual average of 1.1% in 2000–05. Compared with the previous year, agricultural GDP rose by 1.5% in 2006.

Industry (comprising mining, manufacturing, construction and utilities) provided an estimated 23.6% of GDP in 2009. The industrial sector employed 22.7% of the working population in 2009. The GDP of the industrial sector was estimated to have expanded at an average annual rate of 3.9% in 1995–2000, before contracting by an annual average of 1.4% in 2000–05. In comparison with the previous year, industrial GDP increased by 1.0% in 2006.

Although mining employed only 1.5% of New Caledonia's working population in 2009, it constitutes the most important industrial activity. In 2009 the mining and processing of nickel contributed an estimated 4.9% of GDP. New Caledonia is a major producer of ferro-nickel and is believed to possess about one-quarter of the world's nickel reserves. Output of nickel ore was 8.7m wet tons in 2010. In 2011 the export revenue from nickel ore, ferro-nickel and nickel matte was 126,674m. francs CFP, accounting for 86.1% of total export revenue. Following various delays, the Goro Nickel plant, one of the largest such construction projects in the world, was not expected to reach full production capacity before 2013, when it was anticipated that 60,000 metric tons of nickel and at least 4,300 tons of cobalt would be produced annually. The similarly controversial Koniambo facility, with an annual production capacity of 60,000 tons was expected to enter into production in 2012, reaching full production levels in 2014. In 1999 a joint French and Australian research mission made an offshore discovery of what was believed to be the world's largest gas deposit, measuring an estimated 18,000 sq km. It was hoped that this might indicate the presence of considerable petroleum reserves.

The manufacturing sector, which engaged 10.3% of the employed labour force in 2009, consists mainly of small and medium-sized enterprises, most of which are situated around the capital, Nouméa, producing building materials, furniture, salted fish, fruit juices and perishable foods. Food-processing and other manufacturing activities accounted for an estimated 6.4% of GDP in 2009.

The construction sector provided 12.5% of GDP in 2009 and engaged 9.9% of the employed labour force in 2009.

Electrical energy is provided mainly by thermal power stations (some 80% in 2004), by hydroelectric plants, and more recently by wind power. Mineral products accounted for 19.2% of total imports in 2011. As part of the Government's plans to reduce expensive imports of diesel fuel, a target was set to provide 60,000 kWh of wind-generated electricity by 2010, equivalent to some 15% of New Caledonia's energy requirements. Plans for the nickel plant at Koniambo envisaged the construction of a 390-MW power station. In 2009 production of electric energy reached an estimated 1,944m. kWh.

Service industries contributed an estimated 72.7% of GDP in 2009 and engaged 74.5% of the employed labour force in 2009. The GDP of the services sector was estimated to have declined at an average annual rate of 0.8% in 1995–2000, rising by an annual average of 1.0% in 2000–05. The GDP of the services sector increased by 1.2% in 2006, compared with the previous year. However, the tourism sector in New Caledonia has failed to witness an expansion similar to that experienced in many other Pacific islands, and tourist arrivals have been intermittently affected by political unrest. The majority of tourists come from France, Japan, Australia and New Zealand. The number of visitor arrivals by air decreased from 103,672 in 2008 to 99,379 in 2009, with a continuing decline reported to 98,562 in 2010. The number of visiting cruise-ship passengers also declined, from 152,250 in 2008 to 131,231 in 2009, but was reported to have risen substantially in 2010. Receipts from tourism were estimated to have decreased from €153.0 in 2008 to €146.0 in 2009.

In 2009 New Caledonia's trade deficit was 121,071m. francs CFP, and there was a deficit of 77,956m. francs CFP on the current account of the balance of payments in that year. The principal imports in 2011 were mineral products, machinery and electrical equipment, transport equipment, foodstuffs, chemical products and base metals and articles. In 2011 the principal exports remained nickel products, prawns and fish. France was the main supplier of imports in 2011, accounting for 22.1% of the total. Other important suppliers of imports were Singapore (14.6%) and Australia. The principal markets for New Caledonia's exports in 2011 were France, representing 24.6% of the total, Japan (19.4%), France (17.2%), Australia, Taiwan, Korea and the People's Republic of China.

The 2010 budget projected expenditure of 161,500m. francs CFP. A sum of €26.4m. was allocated by France towards protection of natural heritage and as financial assistance in preparation for the 2011 Pacific Games, which were hosted by New Caledonia. Over the period 2011–15 France was to provide development assistance of 45,000m. francs CFP for New Caledonia.

The annual rate of inflation in Nouméa averaged 1.7% in 2001–10. Consumer prices rose by 2.6% in 2010. An unemployment rate of 16.3% was recorded at the 2004 census. In 2009 the total of those registered as unemployed averaged 6,981, equivalent to 7.8% of the total labour force.

The economy of New Caledonia has been dominated by the nickel industry. The Koniambo mining project was expected to become operational in mid-2012 and to produce 60,000 tons of nickel metal annually by 2014 (equivalent to 5% of global production). The Goro plant was to generate a similar output by 2013. Both operations were to continue to receive substantial tax concessions from the French Government. A nickel stabilization fund was also established: with an initial allocation of 1,500m. francs CFP, the fund was intended to counter substantial fluctuations in international nickel prices, which were reported to have decreased by two-thirds during 2009. However, nickel prices reportedly rose by nearly 40% in 2010 (largely owing to Chinese demand for stainless steel). The tourist industry confronted major challenges; in addition to the relatively high cost of living in New Caledonia, substantial increases in air fares became necessary. In 2009 the number of tourist arrivals declined to its lowest level for 15 years, and in 2010 and 2011 Air Calédonie was reported to be in serious financial difficulty. Nevertheless, the continuing decline in arrivals by air was believed to have been offset by a substantial increase in cruise-ship visitors in 2010. The holding of the Pacific Games in New Caledonia, however, in August–September 2011 went some way towards improving the performance of the tourism sector in that year. The increasing cost of living, particularly of food and transport, resulted in popular demonstrations and industrial action throughout 2011. In October a committee of politicians and trades unionists produced a report on the apparent growing economic inequalities in New Caledonian society. The report cited high energy and transport costs, inadequate taxation, high import levies and a lack of competition among wholesale distributors as the principal factors contributing to this situation. It recommended a series of measures including greater transparency in the pricing of goods, the removal of tax 'loopholes', increased taxation on higher salaries and a levy on the purchase of expensive property.

PUBLIC HOLIDAYS

2013 (provisional): 1 January (New Year's Day), 5 March (Missionary Day), 1 April (Easter Monday), 1 May (Labour Day), 8 May (Liberation Day), 9 May (Ascension Day), 20 May (Whit Monday), 26 June (Commemoration of Matignon and Nouméa Accords), 14 July (Fall of the Bastille), 8 September (Internal Autonomy Day), 24 September (Anniversary of possession by France), 1 November (All Saints' Day), 11 November (for Armistice Day), 25 December (Christmas Day).

Statistical Survey

Source (unless otherwise stated): Institut de la Statistique et des Etudes Economiques, BP 823, 98845 Nouméa; tel. 275481; fax 288148; internet www.isee.nc.

AREA AND POPULATION

Area (sq km): New Caledonia island (Grande Terre) 16,372; Loyalty Islands 1,981 (Lifou 1,207, Maré 642, Ouvéa 132); Isle of Pines 152; Belep Archipelago 70; Total 18,575 (7,172 sq miles).

Population: 230,789 at census of 31 August 2004; 245,580 at census of 27 July 2009. *Population by Province* (2009 census): Loyalty Islands 17,436; North Province 45,137; South Province 183,007. *2012* (UN estimate at mid-year): 258,734 (Source: UN, *World Population Prospects: The 2010 Revision*).

Density (mid-2012): 13.9 per sq km.

Population by Age and Sex (UN estimates at mid-2012): *0–14:* 63,436 (males 32,447, females 30,989); *15–64:* 173,218 (males 86,478, females 86,740); *65 and over:* 22,080 (males 10,260, females 11,820); *Total* 258,734 (males 129,185, females 129,549) (Source: UN, *World Population Prospects: The 2010 Revision*.

Ethnic Groups (census of 1996): Indigenous Kanaks (Melanesians) 86,788; French and other Europeans 67,151; Wallisians and Futunians (Polynesian) 17,763; Tahitians (Polynesian) 5,171; Indonesians 5,003; Others 14,960.

Principal Towns (population of communes at census of 2009): Nouméa (capital) 97,579; Mont-Doré 25,683; Dumbéa 24,103; Païta 16,358.

Births, Marriages and Deaths (2009, unless otherwise indicated, preliminary): Registered live births 4,112 (birth rate 16.7 per 1,000); Registered marriages 932 (marriage rate 3.8 per 1,000); Registered deaths 1,235 (death rate 5.0 per 1,000).

Life Expectancy (years at birth, 2007): 75.9 (males 71.8; females 80.3).

Economically Active Population (salaried workers, annual averages, 2009): Agriculture, hunting, forestry and fishing 2,198; Mining and quarrying 1,238; Manufacturing 8,473; Electricity, gas and water 842; Construction 8,136; Trade (vehicle repairs and domestic goods) 9,348; Hotels and restaurants 4,171; Transport and communications 5,275; Financing activities 1,899; Real estate and business services 6,564; Education 188; Health and welfare 1,938; Domestic services for households 3,492; Community, social and personal services 2,845; Other services 60; Non-market services 25,565; *Total employed* 82,232; Unemployed 6,981; *Total labour force* 89,213.

HEALTH AND WELFARE

Key Indicators

Total Fertility Rate (children per woman, 2007): 2.2.

Physicians (per 1,000 head, 2008): 2.2.

Hospital Beds (per 1,000 head, 2003): 3.7.

Total Carbon Dioxide Emissions ('000 metric tons, 2007): 2,846.9.

Carbon Dioxide Emissions Per Head (metric tons, 2007): 11.7.

For definitions, see explanatory note on p. vi.

AGRICULTURE, ETC.

Principal Crops ('000 metric tons, 2010): Maize 3.3; Potatoes 0.9; Sweet potatoes 1.9 (FAO estimate); Cassava 1.7 (FAO estimate); Yams 7.3 (FAO estimate); Coconuts 17.0 (FAO estimate); Vegetables (incl. melons) 5.6; Bananas 1.1.

Livestock ('000 head, year ending September 2010, FAO estimates): Horses 12.0; Cattle 90.0; Pigs 37.0; Sheep 2.3; Goats 8.2; Poultry 600.

Livestock Products (metric tons, 2010): Cattle meat 3,419; Pig meat 2,255; Chicken meat 876; Cows' milk 316; Hen eggs 2,992.

Forestry ('000 cubic metres, 2010, unless otherwise indicated): *Roundwood Removals:* Sawlogs and veneer logs 12.7; Fuel wood 11.8; Other industrial wood 2.0 (FAO estimate); Total 26.5. *Sawnwood Production:* 3.3 (all broadleaved) in 1994. *1995–2010:* Sawnwood production assumed to be unchanged from 1995 (FAO estimates).

Fishing (metric tons, live weight, 2009): Capture 3,545 (Albacore 1,649; Yellowfin tuna 487; Other marine fishes 284; Sea cucumbers 364); Aquaculture 1,920 (Blue shrimp 1,860); Total catch 5,465 (excl. trochus shells 277).

Source: FAO.

MINING

Production: Nickel ore (metal content, '000 metric tons) 102.6 in 2008; Nickel ore ('000 wet tons) 8,709 in 2010. Source: Institut d'Emission d'Outre-Mer.

INDUSTRY

Production (2010, provisional): Ferro-nickel 39,802 metric tons (nickel content); Nickel matte 13,917 metric tons (nickel content); Electric energy 1,944 million kWh (2009); Cement 138,114 metric tons (Source: mainly US Geological Survey).

FINANCE

Currency and Exchange Rates: see French Polynesia.

French Government Budget Expenditure ('000 million francs CFP, incl. military expenditure): 132.3 in 2007; 137.8 in 2008 (preliminary); 137.0 in 2009 (preliminary).

Territorial Budget (million francs CFP, 2010): *Revenue:* Current 165,753 (Direct taxes 61,082; Indirect taxes 50,159); Capital 6,722; Total 172,475. *Expenditure:* Current 155,569 (Transfers to provinces 61,946); Capital 11,730; Total 167,299.

Money Supply (million francs CFP at 31 December 2010): Currency in circulation 14,666; Demand deposits 245,223; *Total money* 259,889. Source: Institut d'Emission d'Outre-Mer.

Cost of Living (Consumer Price Index for Nouméa, December each year; base: December 1992 = 100): All items 132.1 in 2008; 132.3 in 2009; 135.9 in 2010.

Gross Domestic Product (US $ million at constant 2005 prices): 6,964.6 in 2008; 7,131.8 in 2009; 7,378.5 in 2010. Source: UN Statistics Division, National Accounts Main Aggregates Database.

Expenditure on the Gross Domestic Product (million francs CFP at current prices, 2009, estimates): Government final consumption expenditure 186,486; Private final consumption expenditure 477,588; Gross capital formation 288,599; Change in inventories –6,847; *Total domestic expenditure* 945,824; Exports of goods and services 116,726; *Less* Imports of goods and services 310,434; *GDP in purchasers' values* 752,116.

Gross Domestic Product by Economic Activity (€ million at current prices, 2009, estimates): Agriculture, hunting, forestry and fishing 11,406; Nickel mining and processing 33,840; Food processing 14,190; Miscellaneous manufacturing 30,194; Electricity, gas and water 12,775; Construction 86,191; Trade 89,444; Transport and telecommunications 50,148; Banks and insurance 25,881; Business services 56,865; Services to households 150,596; Public administration 128,810; *Sub-total* 690,341; *Less* Financial intermediation services indirectly measured 18,097; *Gross value added in basic prices* 672,244; Taxes and subsidies on products (net) 79,872; *GDP in market prices* 752,116.

Balance of Payments (million francs CFP, 2009): Exports of goods 80,544; Imports of goods –201,615; *Trade balance* –121,071; Exports of services 43,634; Imports of services –95,504; *Balance on goods and services* –172,941; Other income received 53,761; Other income paid –16,107; *Balance on goods, services and income* –135,287; Current transfers received 87,877; Current transfers paid –30,546; *Current balance* –77,956; Capital account (net) 500; Direct investment (net) 93,420; Portfolio investment assets 65,735; Portfolio investment liabilities –51,197; Other investment assets 325,160; Other investment liabilities –362,541; *Overall balance* –6,878. Source: Institut d'Emission d'Outre-Mer.

EXTERNAL TRADE

Principal Commodities (million francs CFP, 2011): *Imports:* Food products, beverages and tobacco 37,638; Mineral products 60,822; Chemical products 19,550; Plastic and rubber articles 11,249; Paper and paper articles 4,749; Textiles and textile articles 6,902; Base metals and articles thereof 16,132; Machinery and mechanical appliances, and electrical equipment 45,635; Transport equipment 35,139; Total (incl. others) 316,761. *Exports:* Nickel ore 27,325; Ferro-nickel 76,167; Nickel matte 23,182; Marine products 1,832 (Prawns 1,013); Total (incl. others) 147,114.

Principal Trading Partners (million francs CFP, 2011): *Imports:* Australia 30,228; France 69,930; Japan 6,230; New Zealand 13,220; Singapore 46,270; USA 14,369; Total (incl. others) 316,761. *Exports:* Australia 18,702; China, People's Republic 8,822; France 25,308; Japan 28,475; Korea, Republic 13,703; South Africa 2,675; Taiwan 15,986; USA 6,263; Total (incl. others) 147,114.

TRANSPORT

Road Traffic (motor vehicles in use, 2001): Total 85,499.

Shipping (2009): *Domestic Traffic* ('000 metric tons): Freight unloaded 2,906; Freight loaded 90. *International Traffic:* Freight unloaded 1,399 metric tons; Freight loaded 3,735 metric tons. *Merchant Fleet* (vessels registered, '000 grt, at 31 December 1992): 14.

Civil Aviation (La Tontouta international airport, Nouméa, 2009): *Passenger Traffic:* Passengers arriving 231,327; Passengers departing 231,922. *Freight Traffic:* Freight unloaded 5,055 metric tons; Freight loaded 1,395 metric tons (Source: Department of Civil Aviation).

TOURISM

Foreign Arrivals: *Arrivals by Air:* 103,672 in 2008; 99,379 in 2009; 98,562 in 2010. *Cruise-ship Passenger Arrivals:* 124,467 in 2007; 152,250 in 2008; 131,231 in 2009.

Tourist Arrivals by Country of Residence (2010): Australia 17,551; France 24,960; Japan 18,534; New Zealand 6,406; Total (incl. others) 98,562 (Source: Institut d'Emission d'Outre-Mer).

Tourism Receipts (€ million): 152.5 in 2007; 153.0 in 2008 (estimate); 146.0 in 2009 (estimate).

COMMUNICATIONS MEDIA

Radio Receivers (1997): 107,000 in use*.

Television Receivers (2000): 106,000 in use†.

Telephones (2010): 72,200 main lines in use†.

Mobile Cellular Telephones (2010): 220,800 subscribers†.

Internet Subscribers (2009): 33,100†.

Broadband Subscribers (2010): 38,200†.

Personal Computers: 40,000 (170.7 per 1,000 persons) in 2006†.

Daily Newspapers (1999): 1.

* Source: UNESCO, *Statistical Yearbook*.
† Source: International Telecommunication Union.

EDUCATION

Pre-primary (2010, unless otherwise indicated): 83 schools (2004); 12,946 pupils.

Primary (2010, unless otherwise indicated): 286 schools (incl. pre-primary); 1,966 teachers (2009, incl. pre-primary); 23,654 pupils (incl. special education).

Secondary (2009, unless otherwise indicated): 76 schools; 2,763 teachers (2009, incl. higher); 32,490 pupils.

Higher (2005): 4 institutions; 111 teaching staff.

Adult Literacy Rate (1989): Males 94.0%; Females 92.1%.

Directory

The Government

(May 2012)

STATE GOVERNMENT

High Commissioner: ALBERT DUPUY (took office November 2010).

Secretary-General: THIERRY SUQUET.

LOCAL GOVERNMENT

Secretary-General: JACQUES WADRAWANE.

COUNCIL OF MINISTERS

The coalition Government is led by Avenir Ensemble.

President, responsible for Regional Co-operation, External Relations, Customs, Agriculture and Fisheries and International Air Transport: HAROLD MARTIN.

Vice-President and Minister for Mines, Equipment and Infrastructure, Development Plan NC 2025, Domestic Air Travel and Transport (Surface and Marine): GILBERT TYUIENON.

Minister for Defence: PHILIPPE GOMÈS.

Minister for Energy, Budget and Financial Affairs, Digital Economy, Communication and Broadcasting, Higher Education and Research: SONIA BACKES.

Minister for Economy: ANTHONY LECREN.

Minister for Culture and Citizenship, Women Affairs and Relations with the Communes: DÉWÉ GORODEY.

Minister for Youth and Sports, Primary and Secondary Education and Social Dialogue: JEAN-CLAUDE BRIAULT.

Minister for Civil Services: PHILIPPE DUNOYER.

Minister for Human Resources and Labour and Employment: GEORGES MANDAQUE.

Minister for Health and Society and Vocational Training: SYLVIE ROBINEAU.

Minister for Ecology and Sustainable Development: HELEN IEKAWE.

GOVERNMENT OFFICES

Office of the High Commissioner: Haut-commissariat de la République en Nouvelle-Calédonie, 1 ave du Maréchal Foch, BP C5, 98844 Nouméa Cedex; tel. 266300; fax 272828; e-mail haussariat@nouvelle-caledonie.gouv.fr; internet www.nouvelle-caledonie.gouv.fr.

Secretariat-General of the High Commissioner: 9 bis rue de la République, BP C5, 98844 Nouméa Cedex; tel. 246711; fax 246740; internet www.nouvelle-caledonie.gouv.fr.

New Caledonian Government: Présidence du Gouvernement, 8 route des Artifices, Artillerie, BP M2, 98849 Nouméa Cedex; tel. 246565; fax 246580; e-mail presidence@gouv.nc; internet www.gouv.nc.

Office of the Secretary-General of the Government of New Caledonia: 8 route des Artifices, BP M2, 98849 Nouméa Cedex; tel. 246532; fax 246620; e-mail alain.swetschkin@gouv.nc; internet www.gouv.nc.

GOVERNMENT DEPARTMENTS

Department of the Budget and Financial Affairs (DBAF): 18 ave Paul Doumer, BP M2, 98849 Nouméa Cedex; tel. 256083; fax 283133; e-mail dbaf@gouv.nc.

Department of Civil Aviation: 179 rue Gervolino, BP H01, 98849 Nouméa Cedex; tel. 265200; fax 265202; e-mail dac-nc@aviation-civile.gouv.fr; internet www.dac.nc.

Department of Computer Technology (DTSI): 127 rue Arnold Daly, Magenta Ouemo, BP 15101, 98804 Nouméa Cedex; tel. 275888; fax 281919; e-mail dtsi@gouv.nc.

Department of Cultural and Customary Affairs (DACC): 8 rue de Sébastopol, BP T5, 98852 Nouméa Cedex; tel. 269766; fax 269767; e-mail secretariat.dacc@gouv.nc.

Department of Economic Affairs (DAE): 7 rue du Général Galliéni, BP 2672, 98846 Nouméa Cedex; tel. 232250; fax 232251; e-mail dae@gouv.nc; internet www.dae.gov.nc.

Department of Education (DENC): Immeuble Foch, 19 ave du Maréchal Foch, BP 8244, 98807 Nouméa Cedex; tel. 239600; fax 272921; e-mail denc@gouv.nc; internet www.denc.gouv.nc.

Department of Fiscal Affairs (DSF): Hôtel des Impôts, 13 rue de la Somme, BP D2, 98848 Nouméa Cedex; tel. 257500; fax 251166; e-mail dsf@gouv.nc; internet www.dsf.gouv.nc.

Department of Health and Social Services (DASS): 5 rue Général Galliéni, BP N4, 98851 Nouméa Cedex; tel. 243700; fax 243702; e-mail dass@gouv.nc; internet www.dass.gouv.nc.

Department of Human Resources and Civil Service (DRHFPT): 18 ave Paul Doumer, BP M2, 98849 Nouméa Cedex; tel. 256000; fax 274700; e-mail drhfpt@gouv.nc; internet www.drhfpt.gouv.nc.

Department of Industry, Mines and Energy (DIMENC): 1 ter rue Edouard Unger, 1ère, Vallée du Tir, BP 465, 98845 Nouméa Cedex; tel. 270230; fax 272345; e-mail dimenc@gouv.nc; internet www.dimenc.gouv.nc.

Department of Infrastructure, Topography and Land Transport (DITTT): 1 bis rue Edouard Unger, 1ère, Vallée du Tir, BP A2, 98848 Nouméa Cedex; tel. 280300; fax 281760; e-mail dittt@gouv.nc; internet www.dittt.gouv.nc.

Department of Labour and Employment (DTE): 12 rue de Verdun, BP 141, 98845 Nouméa Cedex; tel. 275572; fax 270494; e-mail dte@gouv.nc; internet www.dtnc.gouv.nc.

Department of Veterinary, Food and Rural Affairs (DAVAR): 209 rue Auguste Bénébig, Haut Magenta, BP 256, 98845 Nouméa Cedex; tel. 255100; fax 255129; e-mail davar@gouv.nc; internet www.davar.gouv.nc.

Department of Vocational Training (DFPC): 19 ave du Maréchal Foch, BP 110, 98845 Nouméa Cedex; tel. 246622; fax 281661; e-mail dfpc@gouv.nc; internet www.dfpc.gouv.nc.

Department of Youth and Sports (DJS): 23 rue Jean Jaurès, BP 810, 98845 Nouméa Cedex; tel. 252384; fax 254585; e-mail djsnc@gouv.nc; internet www.djs.gouv.nc.

Legislature

ASSEMBLÉES PROVINCIALES

Members of the Provincial Assemblies are elected on a proportional basis for a five-year term. Each Provincial Assembly elects its President. A number of the members of the Provincial Assemblies sit together to make up the Congress of New Caledonia. The Assembly of the North Province has 22 members (including 15 sitting for the Congress), the Loyalty Islands 14 members (including seven for the Congress) and the South Province has 40 members (including 32 for the Congress).

North Province: BP 41, 98860 Koné; tel. 417100; fax 472475; e-mail presidence@province-nord.nc; internet www.province-nord.nc; Pres. PAUL NÉAOUTYINE (UNI-FLNKS).

South Province: Hôtel de la Province Sud, route des Artifices, Port Moselle, BP L1, 98849 Nouméa Cedex; tel. 258000; fax 274900; e-mail cabinet@province-sud.nc; internet www.province-sud.nc; Pres. PIERRE FROGIER (Le Rassemblement-UMP).

Loyalty Islands Province: BP 50, Wé, 98820 Lifou; tel. 455100; fax 451440; e-mail presidence@loyalty.nc; internet www.province-iles.nc; Pres. NÉKO HNÉPEUNE (UNI-FLNKS).

Election, 10 May 2009 (provisional results by province)

Party	North	South	Loyalty Islands
Le Rassemblement-UMP	1	15	—
Union Calédonienne-Front de Libération Nationale Kanak Socialiste (UC-FLNKS)	8	—	6
Calédonie Ensemble	—	11	—
Union Nationale pour l'Indépendance (UNI)	9	—	—
L'Avenir Ensemble	—	8	—
Front de Libération Nationale Kanak Socialiste (FLNKS)	—	4	—
Union Nationale pour l'Indépendance-Front de Libération Nationale Kanak Socialiste (UNI-FLNKS)	—	—	4
Parti Travailliste	3	—	2
Dynamique Autochtone (Le Mouvement de la Diversité)	—	—	2
Rassemblement pour la Calédonie	—	2	—
Une Province Pour Tous	1	—	—
Total	22	40	14

Note: in October 2009, following the confirmation of irregularities in the conduct of the election, notably with regard to the use of proxy votes, the results of the Loyalty Islands were declared invalid by the Conseil d'Etat in France. The province thus returned to the polls on 6 December: the UC-FLNKS alliance was reported to have retained six seats, the Parti Travailliste increased its representation to four seats, the Libération Kanak Socialiste (LKS) won two seats and two seats were taken by another pro-independence grouping

CONGRÈS

A proportion of the members of the three Provincial Assemblies sit together, in Nouméa, as the Congress of New Caledonia. There are 54 members (32 from the South Province, 15 from the North Province and seven from the Loyalty Islands Province) of a total of 76 sitting in the Provincial Assemblies.

President: ROCH WAMYTAN, Congrès de la Nouvelle-Calédonie, 1 blvd Vauban, BP P3, 98851 Nouméa Cedex; tel. 273129; fax 270219; e-mail courrier@congres.nc; internet www.congres.nc.

Election, 10 May 2009 (provisional results for New Caledonia as a whole)

Party	Votes	%	Seats
Le Rassemblement-UMP	19,888	20.60	13
Calédonie Ensemble	16,253	16.83	10
Union Calédonienne	11,247	11.65	8
Union Nationale pour l'Indépendance	10,162	10.52	8
L'Avenir Ensemble-Le Mouvement de la Diversité	11,308	11.71	6
Parti Travailliste	7,692	7.97	3
Front de Libération Nationale Kanak Socialiste	5,342	5.53	3
Rassemblement pour la Calédonie	4,304	4.46	2
Libération Kanak Socialiste	1,852	1.92	1
Others	8,510	8.81	—
Total	96,558	100.00	54

PARLEMENT

Deputies to the French National Assembly: GAËL YANNO (UMP); Pierre Frogier was also a deputy until his election to the Senate in September 2011.

Representatives to the French Senate: (elected in September 2011) PIERRE FROGIER (UMP), HILARION VENDÉGOU (UMP).

Political Organizations

L'Avenir Ensemble (AE): 2 bis blvd Vauban, 98800 Nouméa; tel. 281179; fax 281011; e-mail avenirensemble@lagoon.nc; internet www.avenirensemble.nc; f. 2004; combined list incl. fmr mems of Rassemblement pour la Calédonie dans la République and Alliance pour la Calédonie; anti-independence party; supports unification of all ethnic groups; Leader HAROLD MARTIN.

Calédonie Ensemble (CE): 13 route de Vélodrome, 98800 Nouméa; tel. 288905; fax 288906; internet www.caledonieensemble.nc; f. 2008; anti-independence party est. by fmr mems of L'Avenir Ensemble; Leader PHILIPPE GOMÈS.

Fédération des Comités de Coordination des Indépendantistes (FCCI): 42 ter rue de Verdun, Nouméa; internet www.fcci-nc.org; f. 1998; est. by breakaway group of FLNKS; includes Front du Développement des Iles Loyauté and Front Uni de Libération Kanak; Leaders LÉOPOLD JORÉDIÉ, RAPHAËL MAPOU, FRANÇOIS BURCK.

Front Calédonien (FC): extreme right-wing; Leader M. SARRAN.

Front de Libération Nationale Kanak Socialiste (FLNKS): 9 rue Austerlitz, Immeuble SAM3, 98800 Nouméa Cedex; tel. 265880; fax 265887; f. 1984; est. following dissolution of Front Indépendantiste; pro-independence; Pres. PAUL NÉAOUTYINE; a grouping of the following parties:

Parti de Libération Kanak (PALÉIKA): f. 1975; Leader PAUL NÉAOUTYINE.

Rassemblement Démocratique Océanien (RDO): Nouméa; f. 1994; est. by breakaway faction of Union Océanienne (f. 1989); supports Kanak sovereignty; Pres. ALOISIO SAKO.

Union Calédonienne (UC): 4 rue de la Gazelle, Aérodrome de Magenta, Nouméa; tel. 272599; fax 276257; e-mail info@union-caledonienne.org; internet www.union-caledonienne.org; f. 1952; pro-independence; left FLNKS coalition prior to elections of 2004 but subsequently returned; 11,000 mems; Pres. CHARLES PIDJOT; Sec.-Gen. DANIEL YEIWÉNÉ.

Union Progressiste Mélanésienne (UPM): f. 1974; est. as Union Progressiste Multiraciale; Pres. VICTOR TUTUGORO; Sec.-Gen. RENÉ POROU.

Front National (FN): 12 bis rue du Général Mangin, 98800 Nouméa; tel. 258068; fax 258064; e-mail george@province-sud.nc; internet www.frontnational.com; right-wing; Leader GUY GEORGE.

Génération Calédonienne: f. 1995; youth-based; aims to combat corruption in public life; Pres. JEAN-RAYMOND POSTIC.

Le Groupe MUR: BP 1211, 98845 Nouméa Cedex; tel. and fax 419385; coalition of Mouvement des Citoyens Calédoniens, Union Océanienne (f. 1989) and Rassemblement des Océaniens dans la Calédonie; Jt Pres TINO MANUOHALALO (MCC), MICHEL HEMA (UO), MIKAELE TUIFUA (ROC).

Libération Kanak Socialiste (LKS): Maré, Loyalty Islands; moderate, pro-independence; contested the 2009 elections in the Loyalty Islands as Dynamique Autochtone; Leader NIDOÏSH NAISSELINE.

Le Mouvement de la Diversité (LMD): 98802 Nouméa; tel. 997700; fax 240620; internet www.lmd.nc; f. 2009; allied to L'Avenir Ensemble; Pres. SIMON LOUECKHOTE.

Parti Travailliste: Nouméa; f. 2007; Pres. LOUIS KOTRA UREGEI.

Le Rassemblement-UMP: 13 rue de Sébastopol, BP 306, 98845 Nouméa; tel. 282620; fax 284033; e-mail contact@rassemblement.nc; internet www.rassemblement.nc; f. 1976; est. as Rassemblement pour la Calédonie dans la République; affiliated to the metropolitan Union pour un Mouvement Populaire; in favour of retaining the status quo in New Caledonia; Leader PIERRE FROGIER; Sec.-Gen. ERIC GAY.

A coalition of the following parties:

Centre des Démocrates Sociaux (CDS): f. 1971; Leader JEAN LÈQUES.

Parti Républicain (PR): Leader PIERRE MARESCA.

Rassemblement pour la Calédonie (RPC): Nouméa; f. 2006; Leader (vacant).

Union Calédonienne Renouveau (UC Renouveau): Hôtel de la province des îles Loyauté, BP 50, Wé Lifou; tel. 455100; fax 451440; Leader JACQUES LALIE.

Union Nationale pour l'Indépendance (UNI): c/o Le Congrès de la Nouvelle Calédonie, Nouméa ; Leader PAUL NÉAOUTYINE.

Minor political organizations that participated in the elections of May 2009 included: Avance, Calédonie Mon Pays, Génération Destin Commun, Ouverture Citoyenne, and Patrimoine et Environnement avec les Verts.

Judicial System

Court of Administrative Law: 85 ave du Général de Gaulle, Immeuble Carcopino 3000, 4ème étage, BP 63, 98851 Nouméa Cedex; tel. 250630; fax 250631; e-mail greffe.ta-noumea@juradm.fr; internet www.ta-noumea.juradm.fr; f. 1984; Pres. GUY LAPORTE; Cllrs MICHEL M. BICHET, ARSÈNE IBO, MARIE-THÉRÈSE LACAU.

Court of Appeal: Palais de Justice, BP F4, 98848 Nouméa; tel. 279357; fax 269185; e-mail pp.ca-noumea@justice.fr; internet www.ca-noumea.justice.fr; First Pres. THIERRY DRACK; Procurator-Gen. ANNIE BRUNET-FURSTER.

Court of the First Instance: 2 blvd Extérieur, BP F4, 98848 Nouméa; tel. 279372; fax 276531; e-mail p.tpi-noumea@justice.fr;

Pres. JEAN PRADAL; Procurator of the Republic CLAIRE LANET; there are two subsidiary courts, with resident magistrates, at Koné (North Province) and Wé (Loyalty Islands Province).

Customary Senate of New Caledonia: Conseil Consultatif Coutumier, 68 ave J. Cook, BP 1059, Nouville; tel. 242000; fax 249320; e-mail senat-coutumier@gouv.nc; f. 1990; consulted by Local Assembly and French Govt on matters affecting land, Kanak tradition and identity; composed of 16 elected mems (two from the regional council of each of the eight custom areas) for a six-year period; Pres. JULIEN BOANEMOI.

Religion

The majority of the population is Christian, with Roman Catholics comprising about 55% of the total in 2002. About 3% of the inhabitants, mainly Indonesians, are Muslims.

CHRISTIANITY

The Roman Catholic Church

The Territory comprises a single archdiocese, with an estimated 131,000 adherents in December 2007. The Archbishop participates in the Catholic Bishops' Conference of the Pacific, based in Fiji.

Archbishop of Nouméa: Most Rev. MICHEL-MARIE-BERNARD CALVET, Archevêché, 4 rue Mgr-Fraysse, BP 3, 98845 Nouméa; tel. 265353; fax 265352; e-mail archeveche@ddec.nc; internet www.ddec.nc/diocese.

The Anglican Communion

Within the Church of the Province of Melanesia, New Caledonia forms part of the diocese of Vanuatu. The Archbishop of the Province is the Bishop of Central Melanesia (resident in Honiara, Solomon Islands). At mid-2000 there were an estimated 160 adherents.

Protestant Churches

At mid-2000 there were an estimated 30,000 adherents.

Eglise évangélique en Nouvelle-Calédonie et aux Iles Loyauté: BP 277, Nouméa; f. 1960; Pres. Rev. SAILALI PASSA; Gen. Sec. Rev. TELL KASARHEROU.

Other churches active in the Territory include the Assembly of God, the Free Evangelical Church, the New Apostolic Church, the Pentecostal Evangelical Church, the Presbyterian Church and the Tahitian Evangelical Church. At mid-2000 there were an estimated 15,500 adherents professing other forms of Christianity.

The Press

L'Avenir Calédonien: 10 rue Gambetta, Nouméa; organ of the Union Calédonienne; Dir GABRIEL PAÏTA.

La Calédonie Agricole: BP 111, 98845 Nouméa Cedex; tel. 243160; fax 284587; internet www.formagri.nc; quarterly; official publ. of the Chambre d'Agriculture; Pres. GÉRARD PASCO; Man. YANNICK COLLETTE; Chief Editors PIERRE ARDORINO, SOPHIE GOLFIER; circ. 4,000.

Le Chien Bleu: BP 16018, Nouméa; tel. 288505; fax 261819; e-mail courrier@lechienbleu.nc; internet www.lechienbleu.nc; monthly; satirical; Man. Editor ETIENNE DUTAILLY.

Eglise de Nouvelle-Calédonie: BP 3, 98845 Nouméa; fax 265352; f. 1976; monthly; official publ. of the Roman Catholic Church; circ. 450.

Les Infos: 42 route de l'Anse-Vata, BP 8134, 98807 Nouméa; tel. 251808; fax 251882; e-mail lesinfos@lagoon.nc; weekly; Editor-in-Chief THIERRY SQUILLARIO.

Journal Officiel de la Nouvelle-Calédonie: Imprimerie Administrative, BP M2, 98849, Nouméa Cedex; tel. 256001; fax 256021; e-mail webmestre.juridoc@gouv.nc; internet www.juridoc.gouv.nc; f. 1853; est. as *Bulletin Officiel de la Nouvelle-Calédonie*; present name adopted in 1988; only the paper version is official; twice a week; publ. by Govt of New Caledonia; record of state legislative devts in New Caledonia.

Mwà Véé: Centre Tjibaou, BP 378, 98845 Nouméa; tel. 414555; fax 414556; e-mail adck@adck.nc; f. 1993; quarterly; French; publ. by l'Agence de Développement de la Culture Kanak; Kanak history, culture and heritage; Publr EMMANUEL KASARHE'ROU; Editor GÉRARD DEL RIO.

Les Nouvelles Calédoniennes: 41–43 rue de Sébastopol, BP G5, 98848 Nouméa; tel. 272584; fax 281627; e-mail xserre@canl.nc; internet www.lnc.nc; f. 1971; daily; Publr FRÉDÉRIC AURAND; Gen. Man. FRANÇOIS LEVASSOR; Editor-in-Chief XAVIER SERRE; circ. 18,500.

Tazar: Immeuble Gallieni II, 12 rue de Verdun, 98800 Nouméa; tel. 282277; fax 283443; monthly; publ. by Mission d'Insertion des Jeunes de la Province Sud; youth.

Télé 7 Jours: Route de Vélodrome, BP 2080, 98846 Nouméa Cedex; tel. 284598; weekly.

NEWS AGENCY

Agence France-Presse (AFP): 15 rue Docteur Guégan, 98800 Nouméa; tel. 263033; fax 278699; Correspondent FRANCK MADOEUF.

Publishers

Editions d'Art Calédoniennes: 3 rue Guynemer, BP 1626, Nouméa; tel. 277633; fax 281526; art, reprints, travel.

Editions du Santal: 5 bis rue Emile-Trianon, 98846 Nouméa; tel. and fax 262533; history, art, travel, birth and wedding cards; Dir PAUL-JEAN STAHL.

Grain de Sable: BP 577, 98845 Nouméa; tel. and fax 273057; e-mail graindesable@canl.nc; internet www.pacific-bookin.com; literature, travel; Publr LAURENCE VIALLARD.

Ile de Lumière: BP 8401, Nouméa Sud; tel. 289858; history, politics.

Savannah Editeur SNP: Yacht Marianne, BP 3086, 98846 Nouméa; tel. 784711; e-mail savannahmarc@hotmail.com; f. 1994; est. as Savannah Edns; present name adopted in 2006; sports, travel, leisure; Publr JOËL MARC.

Société d'Etudes Historiques de la Nouvelle-Calédonie: BP 63, 98845 Nouméa; tel. 767155; e-mail seh-nc@lagoon.nc; f. 1969; Pres. VALET GABRIEL.

Broadcasting and Communications

TELECOMMUNICATIONS

Citius: Immeuble Administratif, 1 rue du Contre Amiral Joseph Bouzet, Route de Nouville, 98800 Nouméa; tel. 266604; fax 266642; e-mail visio@citius.nc; internet www.citius.nc; f. 2008.

Offices des Postes et Télécommunications (OPT): Le Waruna, 2 rue Monchovet, Port Plaisance, 98841 Nouméa Cedex; tel. 268217; fax 262927; e-mail direction@opt.nc; internet www.opt.nc; provides postal and fixed-line tel. services, and operates Mobilis mobile cellular tel. network (f. 2003); Dir-Gen. JEAN-YVES OLLIVAUD.

BROADCASTING

Radio

Nouvelle-Calédonie 1ère: Réseau France Outre-mer (RFO), 1 rue Maréchal Leclerc, Mont Coffyn, BP G3, 98848 Nouméa Cedex; tel. 239999; fax 239975; e-mail comrfonc@francetv.fr; internet nouvellecaledonie.la1ere.fr; f. 1942; fmrly Radiodiffusion Française d'Outre-mer (RFO); French; relays Radio Australia's French service; Dir-Gen. CLAUDE ESCLATINE; Regional Dir WALLES KOTRA.

NRJ Nouvelle-Calédonie: 41–43 rue Sébastopol, BP G5, 98848 Nouméa; tel. 263434; fax 279447; e-mail nrj@nrj.nc; internet www.nrj.nc; f. 1984; Dir RICARDO GREMY.

Radio Djiido (Kanal K): Résidence La Caravelle, 3 rue Sainte Cécile, Vallée du Tir, BP 10459, 98805 Nouméa Cedex; tel. 778768; fax 272187; e-mail radiodjiido@radiodjiido.nc; internet www.radiodjiido.nc; f. 1985; pro-independence community station; broadcasts in French; socio-cultural programmes; 60% local news, 30% regional, 10% international; Station Man. THIERRY KAMÉRÉMOIN; Editor-in-Chief CÉDRICK WAKAHUGNEME.

Radio Océane: 1 ave d'Auteuil, Lotissement FSH, Koutio, 98835 Dumbéa; tel. 410095; fax 410099; e-mail oceane.fm@lagoon.nc; Dir YANN DUVAL.

Radio Rythme Bleu: 8 ave Foch, BP 578, 98845 Nouméa Cedex; tel. 254646; fax 284928; e-mail rrb@lagoon.nc; f. 1984; music and local, nat. and int. news; Pres. CHRISTIAN PROST; Dir ELIZABETH NOUAR.

Television

RFO-Télé Nouvelle-Calédonie: Réseau France Outre-mer (RFO), 1 rue Maréchal Leclerc, Mont Coffyn, BP G3, 98848 Nouméa Cedex; tel. 239999; fax 239975; internet www.rfo.fr; f. 1965; part of the France Télévisions group, France; three channels; Gen. Man. BERNARD JOYEUX; Editor-in-Chief GONZAGUE DE LA BOURDONNAYE.

Canal+ Calédonie: 30 rue de la Somme, BP 1797, 98845 Nouméa; tel. 265343; fax 265338; e-mail abonnement@canal-caledonie.com; internet www.canalcaledonie.com; subsidiary of Canal Plus, France; subscription service; broadcasts 24 hours daily; CEO SERGE LAMAGNÈRE.

Canal Outre-mer (Canal+): Nouméa; f. 1995; cable service.

Finance

(cap. = capital; res = reserves; dep. = deposits; m. = million; brs = branches; amounts in francs CFP unless otherwise stated)

BANKING

Agence Française de Développement: 1 rue Barleux, BP JI, 98849 Nouméa Cedex; tel. 242600; fax 282413; e-mail afdnoumea@afd.fr; Man. Jean-Yves Clavel.

Banque Calédonienne d'Investissement (BCI): 54 ave de la Victoire, BP K5, 98849 Nouméa; tel. 256565; fax 274035; e-mail bci@bci.nc; internet www.bci.nc; f. 1988; cap. 7,500m. (Dec. 2003); Chair. Didier Leroux; Dir-Gen. Jean-Pierre Gianotti.

Banque de Nouvelle-Calédonie: 10 ave Foch, BP L3, 98849 Nouméa Cedex; tel. 257402; fax 275619; e-mail contact@bnc.nc; internet www.bnc.nc; f. 1974; adopted present name in 2002; 95.8% owned by Financière Océor, France; cap. 3,858.3m., res 1,294.2m., dep. 66,873.0m. (Dec. 2004); Pres. Christian Camus; Gen. Man. Sylvain Faure; 7 brs.

BNP Paribas Nouvelle-Calédonie (France): 37 ave Henri Lafleur, BP K3, 98849 Nouméa Cedex; tel. 258400; fax 258459; e-mail bnp.nc@bnpparibas.com; internet nc.bnpparibas.net/fr; f. 1969; est. as Banque Nationale de Paris; present name adopted in 2001; cap. €28.0m., res €315.6m. (Dec. 2001); Pres. Jean-Pascal Dumans; Gen. Man. Jean-Francois Aracil; 10 brs.

Société Générale Calédonienne de Banque: 44 rue de l'Alma, Siège et Agence Principale, BP G2, 98848 Nouméa Cedex; tel. 256300; fax 256322; e-mail svp.sgcb@canl.nc; internet www.sgcb.com; f. 1981; total assets 1,086m. (Dec. 2007); Gen. Man. Jean-Pierre Dufour; Chair. Jean-Louis Mattei; 21 brs.

INSURANCE

AGF Vie & AGF IART Nouvelle-Calédonie: 99 ave du Générale de Gaulle, BP 152, 98845 Nouméa; tel. 283838; fax 281628; e-mail agfvienc@agfvie.nc; life and general non-life insurance.

GAN Pacifique: 30 route de la Baie des Dames, Immeuble Le Centre-Ducos, BP 7953, 98800 Nouméa Cedex; tel. 243070; fax 278884; e-mail ganoumea@canl.nc; subsidiary of GAN Assurances, France; general non-life insurance; Chair. Jean-François Lemoux; Dir-Gen. Patrick Reynaud.

Poe-ma Insurances: 3 rue Sébastopol, BP 8069, 98807 Nouméa; tel. 274263; fax 274267; e-mail info@poema.nc; Bureau Man. Frederic Ducos.

Trade and Industry

DEVELOPMENT ORGANIZATIONS

Agence de Développement de la Culture Kanak (ADCK): Centre Culturel Tjibaou, rue des Accords de Matignon, BP 378, 98845 Nouméa Cedex; tel. 414555; fax 414546; e-mail adck@adck.nc; internet www.adck.nc; Pres. Marie-Claude Tjibaou; Dir Emmanuel Kasarherou.

Agence de Développement Economique de la Nouvelle-Calédonie (ADECAL): 15 rue Guynemer, BP 2384, 98846 Nouméa Cedex; tel. 249077; fax 249087; e-mail adecal@offratel.nc; internet www.adecal.nc; f. 1995; promotes investment within New Caledonia; Gen. Man. Jean-Michel Arlie.

Agence de Développement Rural et d'Aménagement Foncier (ADRAF): 1 rue de la Somme, BP 4228, 98847 Nouméa Cedex; tel. 258600; fax 258604; e-mail adraf@adraf.nc; internet www.adraf.nc; f. 1986, reorg. 1989; acquisition and redistribution of land; Chair. Michel Mathieu; Dir-Gen. Jules Hmaloko.

Conseil Economique et Social: 30 route Baie des Dames, Immeuble Le Centre, Ducos, BP 4766, 98847 Nouméa Cedex; tel. 278517; fax 278509; e-mail ces@gouv.nc; internet www.ces.gouv.nc; represents trade unions and other orgs involved in economic, social and cultural life; Pres. Robert Lamarque; Sec.-Gen. François-Paul Bufnoir.

Institut Calédonien de Participation (ICAP): 1 rue Barleux, BP J1, 98849 Nouméa; tel. 276218; fax 282280; e-mail icap@icap.nc; internet www.icap.nc; f. 1989; est. to finance devt projects and encourage the Kanak population to participate in the market economy; Pres. Paul Néaoutyine; Man. Yves Goyetche.

Institut pour le Développement des Compétences en Nouvelle-Calédonie: 1 rue de la Somme, BP 497, 98845 Nouméa Cedex; tel. 281082; fax 272079; e-mail idc.nc@idcnc.nc; internet www.idcnc.nc; f. 2006; Dir Philippe Martin.

Société de Développement et d'Investissement des Iles Loyauté (SODIL SA): 12 rue du Général Mangin, Immeuble Richelieu, BP 2217, 98846 Nouméa Cedex; tel. 276663; fax 276709; e-mail sodil@lagoon.nc; f. 1991; financing, promotion and sustainable devt of industry, tourism and artisanal cos; priority areas are transport, food-processing, aquaculture, and regional and int. tourism; Pres. Hnaejë Hamu; Man. Samuel Hnepeune.

Société d'Equipement de Nouvelle-Calédonie (SECAL): 28 rue du Général Mangin, BP 2517, 98846 Nouméa Cedex; tel. 232666; fax 232676; e-mail contact@secal.nc; internet www.secal.nc; f. 1971; urban management and devt, public sector construction and civil engineering; Pres. Simone Mignard.

Société de Financement et de Développement de la Province Sud (PROMOSUD): BP 295, 98845 Nouméa Cedex; tel. 241972; fax 271326; e-mail info@promosud.nc; internet www.promosud.nc; f. 1991; financing, promotion and economic devt of cos in priority sectors, incl. tourism, fishing and aquaculture, and processing industries; Pres. Pierre Bretegnier; Man. Thierry Payen.

Société de Financement et d'Investissement de la Province Nord (SOFINOR): 85 ave du Général de Gaulle, BP 66, 98800 Nouméa; tel. 281353; fax 281567; e-mail dirgen@smsp.nc; internet www.sofinor.nc; f. 1990; economic devt, management and financing; priority areas include mining and metal production, aquaculture and fishing, tourism, transport, real estate and engineering; Pres. Guigui Dounehote; Man. Louis Mapou.

CHAMBERS OF COMMERCE

Chambre d'Agriculture: 3 rue A. Desmazures, BP 111, 98845 Nouméa Cedex; tel. 243160; fax 284587; e-mail direction@canc.nc; f. 1909; Pres. Gérard Pasco; Dir Yannick Couette; 33 mems.

Chambre de Commerce et d'Industrie: 15 rue de Verdun, BP M3, 98849 Nouméa Cedex; tel. 243100; fax 243131; e-mail cci@cci.nc; internet www.cci.nc; f. 1879; Pres. André Desplat; Gen. Man. Michel Merzeau; 12,000 mems.

Chambre de Métiers et de l'Artisanat: 10 ave James Cook, BP 4186, 98846 Nouméa Cedex; tel. 282337; fax 282729; e-mail cma@cma.nc; internet www.cma.nc; Pres. Jean-Claude Merlet; Sec.-Gen. Paul Sanchez.

EMPLOYERS' ORGANIZATION

MEDEF de Nouvelle-Calédonie (Fédération Patronale des Chefs d'Entreprise en Nouvelle-Calédonie): 6 rue Jean Jaurès, 98800 Nouméa Cedex; tel. 273525; fax 274037; e-mail medefnc@medef.nc; internet www.medef.nc; f. 1936; represents leading cos of New Caledonia in defence of professional interests, co-ordination, documentation and research in socio-economic fields; affiliated to Mouvement des Entreprises de France; Pres. Jean-François Bouillaguet.

UTILITIES

Electricity

Electricité et Eau de Nouvelle-Calédonie (EEC): 15 rue Jean Chalier, PK 4, 98800 Nouméa Cedex; tel. 463636; fax 463510; e-mail clientele@eec.nc; internet www.eec.nc; f. 1929; est. as UNLECO; present name adopted in 1984; subsidiary of GDF SUEZ, France; producers and distributors of electricity; Chair. François Guichard; Gen. Man. Yves Morault.

Société Néo-Calédonienne d'Energie (ENERCAL): 87 ave du Général de Gaulle, BP C1, 98848 Nouméa Cedex; tel. 250250; fax 250253; e-mail jbegaud@canl.nc; f. 1955; 16% owned by EDEV, France; production and distribution of electricity; Chair. Jean-Pierre Aifa; Gen. Man. Jean Bégaud.

Water

Société Calédonienne des Eaux (CDE): 13 rue Edmond Harbulot, PK 6, BP 812, 98845 Nouméa Cedex; tel. 413720; fax 438128; e-mail patrick.chantre@cde.nc; water distribution; Gen. Man. Alain Carbonel.

TRADE UNIONS

Confédération Générale des Travailleurs de Nouvelle-Calédonie (COGETRA): incorporates:

Syndicat de la Fonction Publique Territoriale (SFPT): 3 rue Edouard Unger, Maison des Syndicats, Vallée du Tir, BP 10453, 98805 Nouméa Cedex; tel. and fax 271820; e-mail cogetra_nc@yahoo.fr; f. 1998; Pres. Françoise Armand.

Union des Secteurs Généraux du Commerce et de l'Industrie de Nouvelle-Calédonie: 3 rue Edouard Unger, Maison des Syndicats, Vallée du Tir, BP 1612, 98845 Nouméa Cedex; tel. 276450; fax 245270; e-mail usgcinc@cogetra.nc; f. 1966; Pres. Jean-Pierre Kabar.

Confédération Générale du Travail-Force Ouvrière de Nouvelle-Calédonie (CGT-FO NC): 13 rue Jules Ferry, BP R2, 98851 Nouméa Cedex; tel. 274950; fax 278202; e-mail cgtfonc@lagoon.nc; f. 1984; Sec.-Gen. Jacques Bernaleau.

Confédération Syndicale des Travailleurs de Nouvelle-Calédonie (CSTNC): 49 rue Auer Ducos, 98800 Nouméa; tel. and fax 269648; e-mail cst-nc@laposte.net; Sec.-Gen. SYLVAIN NÉA.

Fédération des Fonctionnaires, Agents et Ouvriers de la Fonction Publique (FSFAOFP): 3 rue Edouard Unger, Maison des Syndicats, Vallée du Tir, BP 820, 98845 Nouméa Cedex; tel. and fax 273532; fax 273917; e-mail lafede@lagoon.nc; f. 1946; represents civil servants and public sector employees; Sec.-Gen. JOÃO D'ALMEIDA.

Union des Syndicats des Ouvriers et Employés de Nouvelle-Calédonie (USOENC): 3 rue Edouard Unger, Maison des Syndicats, Vallée du Tir, BP 2534, 98846 Nouméa Cedex; tel. 259640; fax 250164; e-mail usoenc@canl.nc; f. 1968; affiliated to the Int. Metalworkers' Fed; Sec.-Gen. DIDIER GUÉNANT-JEANSON; 4,011 mems (2005).

Union Syndicale des Travailleurs Kanak et des Exploités (USTKE): 2 rue Ali Raleb, Vallée du Tir, BP 4372, Nouméa; tel. 277210; fax 277687; e-mail contact@ustke.org; internet www.ustke.org; f. 1981; Pres. MARIE-PIERRE GOYETCHE.

Union Territoriale de la Confédération Française de l'Encadrement-Confédération Générale des Cadres (UT-CFE-CGC): Centre Commercial La Belle Vie, 224 rue Jacques Ikékawé, PK 6, BP 30536, 98895 Nouméa Cedex; tel. and fax 410300; fax 410310; e-mail utcfecgc@utcfecgc.nc; internet www.utcfecgc.nc; f. 1996; territorial br. of the Confédération Française de l'Encadrement-Confédération Générale des Cadres; Pres. CHRISTOPHE COULSON; Sec.-Gen. JEAN MARIE ARMAND.

Other unions include the Fédération des Cadres et Collaborateurs en Nouvelle-Calédonie (f. 1968), Syndicat Libre Unité Action (f. 1995), Syndicat National du Personnel Navigant Commercial (f. 1984) and Syndicat des Ouvriers de Travaux Publics et Municipaux (f. 1962).

Transport

ROADS

In 2005 there was a total of 4,926 km of roads in New Caledonia; of these, some 2,559 km were unsealed. There were some 410,680 km of urban roads and 890,450 km of rural tracks. There was a further estimated 350 km of unrecorded urban roads within Nouméa.

Société Anonyme des Voies Express à Péage (SAVEXPRESS): 15 rue de Verdun, BP M3, 98849 Nouméa Cedex; tel. 411930; fax 412899; e-mail savexpress@savexpress.nc; f. 1979; highway management and devt; Pres. GUY GEORGE; Man. MAXIME CHASSOT.

SHIPPING

Most traffic is through the port of Nouméa. Passenger and cargo services, linking Nouméa to other towns and islands, are regular and frequent. There is also a harbour for yachts and pleasure craft at Nouméa.

Port Autonome de la Nouvelle-Calédonie: 34 ave James Cook, BP 14, 98845 Nouméa Cedex; tel. 255000; fax 275490; e-mail noumeaportnc@canl.nc; Port Man. PHILIPPE LAFLEUR; Harbour Master EDMUND MARTIN.

Moana Services: 2 bis rue Berthelot, BP 2099, 98846 Nouméa; tel. 273898; fax 259315; e-mail moana@canl.nc; internet www.moana.nc; f. 2000; shipping and logistics agency; representatives for Moana Shipping (Wallis), Maersk Line (Denmark) and Canadian Steamship Lines (Canada); Gen. Man. LUCIEN BOURGADE.

SEM de la Baie de la Moselle (SODEMO): rue de la Frégate-Nivôse, BP 2960, 98846 Nouméa; tel. 277197; fax 277129; e-mail contact@sodemo.nc; internet www.sodemo.nc; f. 1987; operates Port Moselle for pleasure craft and boatyard; Pres. JEAN WASMAN; Man. FRANÇOIS LE BRUN.

Sofrana NC: 14 ave James Cook, BP 1602, 98845 Nouméa; tel. 275191; fax 272611; e-mail info@sofrana.nc; internet www.sofrana.nc; f. 1968; subsidiary of Sofrana Holding; shipping agents and stevedores; barge operators; Chair. JEAN-BAPTISTE LEROUX; Gen. Man. FRANÇOIS BURNOUF.

CIVIL AVIATION

There is an international airport, La Tontouta, 47 km from Nouméa, and an internal network, centred on Magenta airport, which provides air services linking Nouméa to other towns and islands. In a major expansion of the airport, a new terminal opened in April 2011, while final developments were scheduled for completion in 2012. Air Calédonie International (Aircalin) operates flights to various Asia-Pacific destinations. Other airlines providing services to the island include Air New Zealand, Air Vanuatu and Qantas.

Air Calédonie: Aérodrome de Magenta, BP 212, 98845 Nouméa Cedex; tel. 250302; fax 254869; e-mail direction@air-caledonie.nc; internet www.air-caledonie.nc; f. 1954; services throughout mainland New Caledonia and its islands; operates four aircraft; Pres. NIDOÏSH NAISSELINE; CEO WILLIAM IHAGE.

Air Calédonie International (Aircalin): 47 rue de Sébastopol, BP 3736, 98846 Nouméa Cedex; tel. 265546; fax 272772; internet www.aircalin.com; f. 1983; 27% owned by Agence pour la Desserte Aérienne de la Nouvelle-Calédonie (NC Air Transport Agency), 72% by Caisse Nationale des Caisses d'Epargne et de Prévoyance, 1% by others; services to Sydney and Brisbane (Australia), Auckland (New Zealand), Nadi (Fiji), Papeete (French Polynesia), Wallis and Futuna Islands, Port Vila (Vanuatu), Osaka and Tokyo (Japan) and Seoul (Republic of Korea); Chair. CHARLES LAVOIX; Pres. and CEO JEAN-MICHEL MASSON.

Cofely Airport Pacific: La Tontouta International Airport, BP 5, 98840 La Tontouta; tel. 352600; fax 352601; e-mail secretariat@cofely-airport-pacific.nc; f. 1995; fmrly Tontouta Air Service; renamed as above 2011; owned by Endel Group; operates Tontouta airport and freight management services; Gen. Man. ELVIR PEROCEVIC.

Tourism

The number of visitors arriving by air in New Caledonia declined from 99,379 in 2009 to 98,562 in 2010; in the latter year 25.3% came from France, 18.8% from Japan and 17.8% from Australia. The number of visiting cruise-ship passengers declined from 152,250 in 2008 to 131,231 in 2009. A total of 2,643 hotel rooms were available in 2004. In 2009 receipts from tourism were estimated at €146.0m. New Caledonia hosted the Pacific Games in August–September 2011.

GIE Nouvelle-Calédonie Tourisme Point Sud: Galerie Nouméa Centre, 20 rue Anatole France, BP 688, 98845 Nouméa Cedex; tel. 242080; fax 242070; e-mail info@nctps.com; internet www.nouvellecaledonietourisme-sud.com; f. 2001; Dir-Gen. PATRICK MOISAN.

GIE Nouvelle-Calédonie Tourisme Province Nord: Centre Commercial Le Village, 35 ave du Maréchal Foch, BP 115, 98845 Nouméa Cedex; tel. 277805; fax 274887; e-mail info@tourismeprovincenord.nc; internet www.tourismeprovincenord.nc; f. 2003; Dir JACQUELINE RIAHI.

Defence

As assessed at November 2011, France maintained a force of 757 army and 510 navy personnel, as well as a gendarmerie, in New Caledonia. The French naval command for the Pacific area is based in French Polynesia.

Commander of the French Armed Forces in New Caledonia: Brig.-Gen. JEAN-FRANÇOIS PARLANTI.

Education

Education is compulsory for 10 years between six and 16 years of age. Schools are operated by both the State and churches, under the supervision of three Departments of Education: the Provincial department responsible for primary level education, the New Caledonian department responsible for primary level inspection, and the State department responsible for secondary level education. Primary education begins at six years of age, and lasts for five years; secondary education, beginning at 11 years of age, comprises a first cycle of four years and a second, three-year cycle. Overall, in 2006 73.7% of pre-primary and primary pupils, and 67.6% of secondary pupils, were enrolled at public institutions. In 2010 there were 12,946 pupils enrolled in pre-primary education, 23,654 in primary education (including special education) and in 2009 there were 32,463 in secondary education (including vocational training). Four institutions provide higher education. Students may also attend universities in France. In 1987 the French University of the Pacific (based in French Polynesia) was established, with a centre in Nouméa, and divided into two universities in 1999. Several other vocational tertiary education centres exist in New Caledonia, including a teacher-training college and two agricultural colleges. In 2003 total public expenditure on education was 66,914m. francs CFP, of which some 42,362m. francs CFP was provided by the French State.

GABON

Introductory Survey

LOCATION, CLIMATE, LANGUAGE, RELIGION, FLAG, CAPITAL

The Gabonese Republic is an equatorial country on the west coast of Africa, with Equatorial Guinea and Cameroon to the north and the Republic of the Congo to the south and east. The climate is tropical, with an average annual temperature of 26°C (79°F) and an average annual rainfall of 2,490 mm (98 ins). The official language is French, but Fang (in the north) and Bantu dialects (in the south) are also widely spoken. About 60% of the population are Christians, mainly Roman Catholics. Most of the remainder follow animist beliefs. The national flag (proportions 3 by 4) has three equal horizontal stripes, of green, yellow and blue. The capital is Libreville.

CONTEMPORARY POLITICAL HISTORY

Historical Context

Formerly a province of French Equatorial Africa, Gabon was granted internal autonomy in November 1958, and proceeded to full independence on 17 August 1960. Léon M'Ba, the new Republic's President, established Gabon as a one-party state. Following his death in November 1967, M'Ba was succeeded by the Vice-President, Albert-Bernard (later Omar) Bongo, who organized a new ruling party, the Parti démocratique gabonais (PDG). Gabon enjoyed political stability and rapid economic growth in the 1970s, underpinned by substantial foreign investment in the development and exploitation of its petroleum reserves. However, the social and economic problems that accompanied the subsequent decline in world petroleum prices led to the emergence in 1981 of a moderate opposition group, the Mouvement de redressement national (MORENA), which demanded the restoration of a multi-party system and formed a government-in-exile in Paris, France, from where it unsuccessfully sought to put forward a candidate to challenge Bongo in the presidential election held in November 1986.

Domestic Political Affairs

In May 1989 the Chairman of MORENA, Fr Paul M'Ba Abessole, visited Gabon and, after a meeting with Bongo, announced that he and many of his supporters would return to Gabon. In January 1990 representatives of MORENA announced that M'Ba Abessole had been dismissed from the leadership of the movement, following his declaration of support for the Government. M'Ba Abessole subsequently formed a breakaway faction, known as MORENA des bûcherons (renamed Rassemblement national des bûcherons—RNB—in 1991 to avoid confusion with the rival MORENA—originels).

A number of arrests took place in October 1989, following an alleged conspiracy to overthrow the Government. It was claimed that the plot had been initiated by Pierre Mamboundou, the leader of the Union du peuple gabonais (UPG, an opposition movement based in Paris). In early 1990 Bongo announced that extensive political reforms were to be introduced and that the ruling party was to be replaced by a new organization, the Rassemblement social-démocrate gabonais (RSDG).

In March 1990 the PDG announced that a multi-party system was to be introduced at the end of a five-year transitional period of political reform under the aegis of the RSDG. Later that month a national conference, attended by representatives of more than 70 political organizations, rejected these proposals and demanded the immediate establishment of a multi-party system and the formation of a new government, which would hold office only until legislative elections could take place. Bongo acceded to the decisions of the conference, and in late April Casimir Oyé Mba, the Governor of the Banque des états de l'Afrique centrale, was appointed Prime Minister of a transitional administration, which included several opposition members. In May constitutional changes were approved that would facilitate the transition to a multi-party political system. Future elections to the presidency would be contested by more than one candidate, and the tenure of office would be reduced to five years, renewable only once.

Legislative elections were scheduled for 16 and 23 September 1990. The first round of the elections was disrupted by violent protests by voters who claimed that the PDG was engaging in electoral fraud. Following further allegations of widespread electoral malpractices, results in 32 constituencies were declared invalid, although the election of 58 candidates (of whom 36 were members of the PDG) was confirmed. The interim Government subsequently conceded that electoral irregularities had taken place, and further voting was postponed until 21 and 28 October. At the elections the PDG won an overall majority in the 120-member Assemblée nationale, with 62 seats, while opposition candidates secured 55 seats.

In November 1990 a Government of National Unity, under Oyé Mba, was formed. Sixteen posts were allocated to members of the PDG, while the remaining eight portfolios were distributed among members of five opposition parties. A new draft Constitution, which was promulgated on 22 December, endorsed reforms that had been included in the transitional Constitution, introduced in May. Further measures included the proposed establishment of an upper house, the Sénat, which was to control the balance and regulation of power. A Constitutional Council was to replace the administrative chamber of the Supreme Court, and a National Communications Council was to be formed to ensure the impartial treatment of information by the state media.

The final composition of the Assemblée nationale was determined in March 1991, when elections took place in five constituencies, where the results had been annulled, owing to alleged malpractice. Following the completion of the elections, the PDG held a total of 66 seats in the Assemblée nationale, while various opposition groups held 54 seats. The two most prominent opposition movements, the Parti gabonais du progrès (PGP) and the RNB, held 19 and 17 seats, respectively.

In May 1991 six opposition parties formed an alliance, the Co-ordination de l'opposition démocratique (COD), in protest against the delay in the implementation of the new Constitution. The COD also demanded the appointment of a new Prime Minister, the abolition of certain institutions under the terms of the Constitution, and the liberalization of the state-controlled media. Following a general strike, organized by the COD, Bongo announced the resignation of the Council of Ministers, and declared that he was prepared to implement fully the new Constitution. He also claimed that, in accordance with the Constitution, several institutions, including the High Court of Justice, had been dissolved, and that a Constitutional Court and a National Communications Council had been established. However, opposition parties within the COD refused to be represented in a new Government of National Unity, of which Oyé Mba was appointed as Prime Minister. In June Oyé Mba appointed a new coalition Government, in which 14 members of the previous Council of Ministers retained their portfolios. Members of MORENA—originels, the Union socialiste gabonaise (USG) and the Association pour le socialisme au Gabon were also represented in the Government.

Bongo re-elected

Bongo was re-elected to the presidency on 5 December 1993, winning 51.2% of the votes cast, while M'Ba Abessole secured 26.5% of the votes. The official announcement of the results prompted rioting by opposition supporters. Five deaths were reported after security forces suppressed the unrest, and a national curfew and state of alert were subsequently imposed. M'Ba Abessole, however, claimed victory and formed a Haut conseil de la République, later redesignated as the Haut conseil de la résistance (HCR), which included the majority of opposition presidential candidates, and a parallel government. Despite reports by international observers that the elections had been conducted fairly, the opposition appealed to the Constitutional Court to annul the results, on the grounds that the Government had perpetrated electoral malpractice.

The Constitutional Court ruled against the appeal by the opposition and endorsed the election results, and on 22 January 1994 Bongo was officially inaugurated as President. In mid-

February the national curfew and the state of alert, which had been in force since December 1993, were repealed, but later that month were reimposed, after a general strike, in support of demands for an increase in salaries to compensate for a devaluation of the CFA franc in January, degenerated into violence. Strike action was suspended after four days, following negotiations between the Government and trade unions; nine people had been killed during that period, according to official figures (although the opposition claimed that a total of 38 had died).

In March 1994 the Assemblée nationale approved a constitutional amendment that provided for the establishment of a Sénat (which the opposition had resisted) and repealed legislation prohibiting unsuccessful presidential candidates from participating in the Government within a period of 18 months. In August the opposition parties announced that they were prepared to participate in a coalition government, on condition that it was installed as a transitional organ pending legislative elections. In September negotiations between the Government and opposition took place in Paris, under the auspices of the Organization of African Unity (OAU, now the African Union—AU, see p. 189), in order to resolve remaining differences concerning the results of the presidential election and the proposed formation of a government of national unity.

At the end of September 1994 an agreement was reached whereby a transitional coalition government was to be installed, with local government elections scheduled to take place after a period of one year, followed by legislative elections six months later; the electoral code was to be revised and an independent electoral commission established, in an effort to ensure that the elections be conducted fairly. In early October Oyé Mba resigned from office and dissolved the Council of Ministers. Shortly afterwards Bongo appointed Dr Paulin Obame-Nguema of the PDG as Prime Minister. Obame-Nguema subsequently formed a 27-member Council of Ministers, which included six opposition members. The composition of the new Government was, however, immediately criticized by the opposition, on the grounds that it was entitled to one-third of ministerial portfolios in proportion to the number of opposition deputies in the Assemblée nationale; the HCR announced that the opposition would boycott the new administration, which, it claimed, was in violation of the Paris accord. Four opposition members consequently refused to accept the portfolios allocated to them, although two of these finally agreed to join the Government. (The portfolios that remained vacant were later assigned to a further two opposition members.)

At a national referendum held on 24 July 1995 the constitutional provisions adopted under the terms of the Paris accord were approved by 96.5% of votes cast, with 63% of the electorate participating. At the beginning of May 1996, following a meeting attended by all the officially recognized political parties, Bongo agreed to establish a Commission nationale électorale (National Election Commission—CNE) to formulate an electoral timetable, in consultation with all the official parties. It was also decided that access to state-controlled media and election funding should be equitably divided. On 20 May the Assemblée nationale's mandate expired, and Obame-Nguema's Government resigned at the beginning of June, in accordance with the Paris accord. Bongo, however, rejected the resignation on the grounds that the Government should, before leaving office, organize the elections and finalize pending agreements with the IMF and the World Bank.

Legislative elections were rescheduled on several occasions, owing to the delay in the release of the local election results and the failure to revise electoral registers in time. The PDG obtained 47 of the 55 seats that were decided in the first round of voting on 15 December 1996. The opposition disputed the results and urged a boycott of the second round of voting. The PDG secured a substantial majority of the seats decided in the second round, which was held on 29 December, winning 84 seats, while the RNB obtained seven, the PGP six and independent candidates four, with a further 14 seats shared by the Cercle des libéraux réformateurs (CLR), the UPG, the USG and others. Polling was unable to proceed for the five remaining seats, and results in a number of other constituencies were later annulled, owing to irregularities. (Following by-elections held in August 1997, during which five people were reportedly killed in violent incidents in north-east Gabon, the PDG held 88 seats, the PGP nine and the RNB five.) Guy Ndzouba Ndama was elected President of the new Assemblée nationale. Obame-Nguema was reappointed Prime Minister on 27 January, and a new Council of Ministers, dominated by members of the PDG, was announced on the following day. The PGP, the main opposition party represented in the Assemblée nationale, had refused to participate in the new Government.

Elections to the new Sénat took place on 26 January and 9 February 1997, with senators to be elected by members of municipal councils and departmental assemblies. The PDG won 53 of the Sénat's 91 seats, while the RNB secured 20 seats, the PGP four, the Alliance démocratique et républicaine (ADERE) three, the CLR one, and the Rassemblement pour la démocratie et le progrès (RDP) one, with independent candidates obtaining nine seats. The results for a number of seats were annulled, however, and in subsequent by-elections, held later that year, the PDG increased its representation to 58 seats, while the RNB held 20 seats and the PGP four.

Constitutional amendments

In April 1997 a congress of deputies and senators adopted constitutional amendments which extended the presidential term to seven years, provided for the creation of the post of Vice-President and formally designated the Sénat as an upper chamber of a bicameral legislature. Opposition demands that a referendum be held were ignored. The Vice-President was to deputize for the President as required, but was not to have any power of succession. In late May Didjob Divungui-di-N'Dingue, a senior member of the ADERE and a candidate in the 1993 presidential election, was appointed to the new post.

In September 1998 opposition parties withdrew their members from the CNE in protest against alleged irregularities in the voter registration process for the forthcoming presidential poll. At the election, which was held on 6 December, Bongo was re-elected with 66.6% of votes cast, while Mamboundou of the HCR received 16.5% of the votes and M'Ba Abessole of the RNB secured 13.4%. The reported rate of participation was 53.8%. Opposition parties rejected the results, again alleging electoral malpractice, and called for fresh elections to be held. None the less, Bongo was inaugurated as President on 21 January 1999, and a new 42-member Council of Ministers, headed by Jean-François Ntoutoume Emane, was subsequently appointed.

Elections to the Assemblée nationale took place on 9 and 23 December 2001. Three opposition parties accused the Government of falsely inflating voter registration lists and boycotted the elections, while others called for the first round to be annulled, as a result of reputed irregularities and high abstention rates, reported to have reached some 80% in urban areas. In the event, the elections were postponed in three districts until 6 January 2002, owing to violent incidents, and voting was repeated on 20 January in a further two constituencies where candidates had received the same number of votes and in a third district where violence had marred the initial ballot. An outbreak of the Ebola virus resulted in the indefinite postponement of voting in the north-eastern district of Zadie. The PDG won 86 seats in the Assemblée, which were supplemented by 19 seats secured by independents with links to the PDG and other parties affiliated to the ruling party. Opposition parties obtained a total of 14 seats (the Rassemblement pour le Gabon—RPG—as the RNB had been restyled, eight, the Parti social-démocrate—PSD—two and the UPG one). A new, enlarged 39-member Council of Ministers, which included four opposition representatives, was appointed in late January. Ntoutoume Emane was reappointed as Prime Minister, while M'Ba Abessole was named Minister of State for Human Rights and Missions.

During March and April 2002 the Constitutional Court annulled the results of voting in the December 2001 elections to the Assemblée nationale in 12 constituencies owing to irregularities. On 26 May and 9 June by-elections took place in these 12 constituencies and in Zadie; the PDG won 10 of the 13 seats contested, increasing its representation to 88 seats. Elections to the Sénat took place on 9 February 2003; the PDG won more than 60 of the upper chamber's 91 seats, followed by the RPG, which secured eight seats.

In July 2003 the Assemblée nationale voted to revoke the Constitution's limit on the number of terms of office for which the President was eligible to seek re-election. Opposition politicians claimed that Bongo thus intended to become 'President-for-Life' by means of continuous fraud in future presidential elections. In September, in response to a series of strikes and protests, the Government and representatives of labour groups announced the signing of a so-called 'social truce', which included commitments to lower the prices of essential items and reduce the extent of political patronage over the following three years. However, renewed protests over reductions in state expenditure in early 2004 appeared to threaten the viability of the agreement.

In early September 2004 President Bongo Ondimba (who had added his father's name to his own in November 2003) carried out a minor cabinet reorganization, in which several leading opposition figures were awarded ministerial portfolios in the newly enlarged 44-member Council of Ministers. It was widely believed that the inclusion of opposition leaders in the Government was intended to reduce the number of candidates opposing Bongo and the PDG in the presidential and legislative elections scheduled for 2005 and 2006, respectively. In October 2005 disquiet arose among opposition groups, following the decision of the CNE to exclude nine presidential candidates, two of whom subsequently appealed successfully against their exclusion, from contesting the election.

At the presidential election held on 27 November 2005 Bongo Ondimba was re-elected, receiving 79.2% of votes cast. Mamboundou, the candidate of the UPG, received 13.6%, while Zacharie Myboto, a former government minister representing the newly formed Union gabonaise pour la démocratie et le développement (UGDD), received 6.6%. The rate of voter participation was recorded at 63.5%. Mamboundou and Myboto disputed the validity of the results, alleging electoral malpractice, and each claimed victory for himself. However, a delegation of international election observers, including a representative from the French Sénat, declared the elections to have been largely free and transparent. The ensuing unrest caused by supporters of the defeated candidates was broadly quelled following the deployment of security forces throughout the country in January 2006. On 20 January President Bongo Ondimba appointed Jean Eyéghé Ndong of the PDG as Prime Minister and later that month Ndong unveiled a new, expanded Council of Ministers composed overwhelmingly of PDG members.

The PDG consolidates power

Legislative elections took place on 17 December 2006, although voting in seven constituencies was postponed until 24 December for logistical reasons. The PDG retained control of the Assemblée nationale, winning 82 of the 120 seats, while parties allied to the PDG secured a further 17 seats; the opposition won 17 seats (the UPG secured the largest number of opposition seats with eight) and independents won four. Electoral observers endorsed the results, but the opposition complained that it had not been given adequate access to state media during the election campaign. In late January 2007 Ndong, who had been reappointed to the premiership, announced a largely unchanged 50-member Council of Ministers, which was again dominated by members of the PDG. Results in 20 constituencies were subsequently annulled owing to allegations of procedural irregularities and fraud. By-elections were held on 10 June 2007 at which the PDG won 11 of the 20 seats available. Parties allied to the PDG won six seats, while the opposition took two; the remaining seat was secured by an independent candidate.

In July 2007 Louis-Gaston Mayila was dismissed from the post of Vice-Prime Minister, Minister of National Solidarity, Social Affairs, Welfare and the Fight against Poverty. Jean-François Ndongou subsequently assumed responsibility for those portfolios. Shortly before Mayila was dismissed he had announced the formation of a new political party, the Union pour la nouvelle République (UPNR), and had therefore positioned himself as a potential challenger to Bongo Ondimba's presidency.

In December 2007 President Bongo Ondimba appointed a new Government, retaining Ndong as Prime Minister but dismissing Emmanuel Ondo Methogo, hitherto Vice-Prime Minister, Minister of Relations with Parliament and Constitutional Institutions. The new Government comprised just three Vice-Prime Ministers and 10 Ministers-delegate, reduced from 15 in the previous cabinet, in an attempt to increase efficiency within the administration. A further governmental reorganization was effected in February 2008, following the appointment of Jean Ping, hitherto Vice-Prime Minister, Minister of Foreign Affairs, Co-operation, Francophone Affairs and Regional Integration, to the position of Chairperson of the Commission of the AU. Laure Olga Gondjout replaced Ping.

In October 2008 Paul Toungui was appointed Minister of State, Minister of Foreign Affairs, Co-operation, Francophone Affairs and Regional Integration, while Blaise Louembé replaced him as Minister of the Economy, Finance, the Budget and Privatization. A governmental reorganization was carried out in mid-January 2009, when eight new ministers were sworn in. At elections to the Sénat held on 18 January the ruling PDG retained its majority, winning 75 of the 102 seats in the upper house.

The death of President Bongo Ondimba

On 8 June 2009 the death was announced of President Bongo Ondimba. It was reported that he had died of a heart attack while receiving medical treatment in Spain; he had 'temporarily' withdrawn from public duties the previous month following the death of his wife in March. Under the terms of the Constitution, interim power was transferred to Rose Francine Rogombé, the President of the Sénat, who was charged with responsibility for organizing a presidential election within 45 days. Despite requests by the political opposition for a delay to the timetable to allow for a thorough revision of the electoral register, the Constitutional Court declared that the ballot would take place on 30 August. The PDG's selection of Ali Bongo Ondimba, the son of the former President and Minister of National Defence, as its presidential candidate resulted in serious divisions within the party and in mid-June Prime Minister Ndong announced the resignation of his Government and his intention to contest the election as an independent candidate. Interim President Rogombé named Paul Biyoghé Mba as Ndong's successor and the outgoing Government was reappointed virtually unchanged.

Recent developments: the presidency of Ali Bongo Ondimba

At the presidential election, which was held as scheduled on 30 August 2009, Bongo Ondimba secured 41.7% of the valid votes cast, and independent candidate André Mba Obame (the Minister of the Interior) was placed second with 25.9%, while Mamboundou, again representing the UPG, secured 25.2% of the votes. Violent protests ensued, most notably in Libreville and Port-Gentil, resulting in the deaths of at least three people and French business interests and diplomatic offices in Gabon were attacked. It was subsequently announced that a recount of the votes would take place; finally on 12 October the Constitutional Court announced that Bongo had secured 141,665 valid votes, equating to 41.8%, while the number of votes attributed to Mamboundou and Mba Obame were amended to 86,875 (25.6%) and 85,814 (25.3%), respectively, thus reversing their placings in the election.

Ali Bongo Ondimba was sworn in as President on 16 October 2009 and a new Government, reduced in size from 44 to 30 members, was appointed the following day. Biyoghé Mba retained the premiership and Angélique Ngoma was named Minister of National Defence, while Anicette Nang Ovika became Minister of Justice, Keeper of the Seals. No opposition party members were accorded ministerial positions. The new President pledged to implement wide-ranging reforms, including the imposition of salary caps for the heads of parastatals and an audit of the civil service.

In February 2010 three political movements representing the Fang ethnic group (the UGDD, the Mouvement africain de développement and the Rassemblement national des républicains) united under the leadership of Mba Obame to form the Union nationale. However, in January 2011 the Ministry of the Interior announced the dissolution of the Union nationale and accused Mba Obame of treason after he declared himself the victor of the 2009 presidential election and appointed a 19-member parallel government. Rallies held in support of Mba Obame degenerated into violent clashes between demonstrators and the security forces. Mba Obame and his associates fled to the Libreville premises of the UN Development Programme, refusing to leave until late February 2011 due to safety concerns. Numerous media outlets that had provided coverage of Mba Obame and other opposition figures had their operations suspended by the government-controlled Conseil national de la communication throughout 2011 and early 2012. Although Mba Obame's right, as a parliamentarian, to immunity from prosecution had been revoked in May 2011, no formal charges had been brought against the opposition leader by early 2012.

Meanwhile, in January 2011 President Bongo Ondimba effected a reorganization of the Council of Ministers, appointing 10 new ministers. Most notable among the changes announced were the respective appointments of Emmanuel Issozet as Minister of the Budget, Public Accounts and the Civil Service, responsible for State Reform, and of Pacôme Rufin Ondzounga as Minister of National Defence. In March three military officials were sentenced to gaol terms of up to seven years after being found guilty of planning to stage a coup against President Bongo Ondimba in 2009.

Legislative elections were conducted on 17 December 2011. According to the official results, the ruling PDG secured an overwhelming victory, winning 114 seats in the Assemblée nationale. Of the remaining six seats, the RPG secured three, while the CLR, the PSD and the UPNR each obtained a single seat. The rate of participation by the electorate was only 34.3%. Numerous opposition parties had urged a boycott, arguing that the elections would lack transparency since biometric voting cards had not been issued. None the less, AU observers endorsed the results, although they reported some 'shortcomings'. In early January 2012 the Constitutional Court announced that it had received a total of 45 appeals against the election results.

Foreign Affairs

Regional relations

In March 2003 relations with Equatorial Guinea became tense, following Gabon's occupation of the uninhabited island of Mbagne (Mbañé, Mbanie), which lies in potentially oil-rich waters in Corisco Bay, north of Libreville. Both countries claimed sovereignty over the island. Equatorial Guinea rejected Bongo's proposal for joint exploitation of any petroleum reserves found in the vicinity of the island, despite an official visit to Libreville in early May by the Equato-Guinean President, Gen. (Theodoro) Obiang Nguema Mbasogo. Attempts to reach a negotiated settlement failed in December, although the two countries agreed to the appointment of a UN mediator in the dispute in January 2004 and in July a provisional agreement was reached to explore jointly for petroleum in the disputed territories. In February 2006 Bongo Ondimba and Obiang Nguema agreed, under the auspices of UN Secretary-General Kofi Annan in Geneva, Switzerland, to work on an accord to resolve the dispute. However, in late 2006 negotiations were suspended indefinitely. In February 2011 Obiang Nguema and Ali Bongo Ondimba attended a meeting hosted by Annan's successor, Ban Ki-Moon, in New York, USA, and confirmed that they would seek the intervention of the International Court of Justice in settling the dispute.

The Gabonese and Cameroonian ministers responsible for foreign affairs met in Yaoundé, the capital of Cameroon, in March 2011. It was agreed that a bilateral border security commission would be established, and numerous accords relating to, *inter alia*, agriculture, fishing, tourism and education were concluded. With the security situation improving in the Republic of the Congo, in July the Gabonese Government terminated the refugee status that had been granted to Congolese fleeing recurrent outbreaks of factional violence. In response, the office of the UN High Commissioner for Refugees increased its efforts to repatriate the 9,500 Congolese still sheltering in Gabon, although the Gabonese Government also permitted the former refugees to apply for residency.

Other external relations

President Omar Bongo Ondimba pursued a policy of close co-operation with France in the fields of economic and foreign affairs. Relations became strained in March 1997, however, when allegations that Bongo had been a beneficiary in an international fraud emerged during a French judicial investigation into the affairs of the petroleum company Elf Aquitaine (now part of Total). In October 1999 a further judicial investigation into the affairs of Elf Aquitaine, carried out by Swiss authorities, revealed that André Tarallo (a senior Elf Aquitaine executive) had used bank accounts in that country secretly to transfer large sums of money to several African heads of state, among them Bongo. Bongo denied personally receiving direct payments from Elf and maintained that such 'bonus' payments were made only to the Gabonese Government. However, a report released in November, following a separate investigation by the US Congress into money-laundering and corruption among political figures, alleged further improper financial dealing between Bongo and Elf. In March 2003 the trial commenced in Paris of 37 defendants accused of permitting the embezzlement of the equivalent of some €300m. of funds from Elf Aquitaine. In November Tarallo was sentenced to four years' imprisonment and fined €2m., while 29 others also received terms of imprisonment. Tarallo was released from prison on the grounds of ill-health in January 2004; however, his sentence was increased to seven years' imprisonment, following appeals by the prosecution in March 2005. Following the election of Nicolas Sarkozy to the French presidency in May 2007, relations between France and Gabon became increasingly strained. National identity had formed the basis of Sarkozy's election campaign and he pledged to implement stricter immigration policies. In early 2008 two Gabonese students were deported and several weeks of tension ensued when the French Minister-Delegate for Co-operation and the Francophonie announced plans to terminate the 'Francafrique' policy preserving France's influence in Africa; however, that minister was later removed in a governmental reorganization in Paris in March. A visit to Gabon by a delegation of French officials in April signalled an improvement in relations. Nevertheless, in February 2009 the French authorities announced that they had frozen a number of Bongo Ondimba's bank accounts, following a ruling by a court in Bordeaux, France, in October 2008 that he return a payment of some €450,000 made to him in order to secure the release of a French businessman who had been imprisoned in Libreville in 1996.

In November 2009, on his first visit abroad since acceding to the presidency, Ali Bongo Ondimba met with President Sarkozy in Paris and in February 2010 Sarkozy made a reciprocal visit to Gabon. Relations between the two leaders appeared cordial and their discussions centred on future co-operation between their respective countries. A visit to Gabon by French Prime Minister François Fillon in July 2011 was censured by opposition groups critical of France's support of President Bongo Ondimba. Nevertheless, Fillon announced that the French garrison in Gabon would be upgraded to the status of France's main military base in the region. Reports emerged in September alleging that former French President Jacques Chirac, former French Prime Minister Dominique de Villepin and other prominent French politicians had received clandestine payments totalling US $20m. from the leaders of several ex-French colonies in Africa, including Omar Bongo Ondimba. In exchange, the African leaders allegedly secured French support for their respective regimes. Chirac and de Villepin rejected these accusations, while Gabon downplayed any involvement. However, in November a former government official in Omar Bongo Ondimba's administration corroborated these allegations and further claimed that the former Gabonese President had transferred similar payments to Sarkozy.

Following a visit to Gabon in February 2004 by the Chinese President, Hu Jintao, agreements were signed providing for greater economic co-operation between the two countries; most notably, the French oil corporation Total concluded an agreement to export Gabonese oil to the People's Republic of China. Relations were further strengthened following Bongo's visit to China in September, during which he secured some US $5m. in aid from the Jintao administration.

CONSTITUTION AND GOVERNMENT

The Constitution of March 1991 provides for a multi-party system, and vests executive power in the President, who is directly elected by universal suffrage for a period of seven years. The President appoints the Prime Minister, who is Head of Government and who (in consultation with the President) appoints the Council of Ministers. Legislative power is vested in the Assemblée nationale, comprising 120 members, who are elected by direct universal suffrage for a term of five years, and the 102-member Sénat, which is elected by members of municipal councils and departmental assemblies for a term of six years. The independence of the judiciary is guaranteed by the Constitution. Gabon is divided into nine provinces, each under an appointed governor, and 37 prefectures.

REGIONAL AND INTERNATIONAL CO-OPERATION

Gabon is a member of the African Union (see p. 189), of the Central African organs of the Franc Zone (see p. 333) and of the Communauté économique des états de l'Afrique centrale (CEEAC, see p. 449).

Gabon became a member of the UN in 1960. As a contracting party to the General Agreement on Tariffs and Trade, Gabon joined the World Trade Organization (see p. 433) on its establishment in 1995. Gabon participates in the Group of 15 (G15, see p. 450) and the Group of 77 (G77, see p. 450) developing countries. Gabon served as a non-permanent member of the UN Security Council in 2010 and 2011.

ECONOMIC AFFAIRS

In 2010, according to estimates by the World Bank, Gabon's gross national income (GNI), measured at average 2008–10 prices, was US $11,655m., equivalent to $7,740 per head (or $13,150 per head on an international purchasing-power parity basis). During 2001–10, it was estimated, the population increased at an average annual rate of 2.0%, while gross domestic product (GDP) per head increased, in real terms, by an average of 0.2% per year. Overall GDP increased, in real terms, at an average annual rate of 2.2% in 2001–10. GDP declined by 1.4% in 2009, but increased by 5.7% in 2010.

Agriculture (including forestry and fishing) contributed an estimated 5.8% of GDP in 2009, according to the African Development Bank (AfDB). About 24.7% of the labour force was estimated to be employed in the agricultural sector in mid-2012, according to FAO estimates. Cocoa, coffee, oil palm and rubber are cultivated for export. Gabon has yet to achieve self-sufficiency in staple crops: imports of food and live animals accounted for 13.0% of the value of total imports in 2006. The principal subsistence crops are plantains, cassava and yams. The exploitation of Gabon's forests (which cover about 75% of the land area) is a principal economic activity. In 2006 cork and wood accounted for an estimated 6.3% of total exports. Although Gabon's territorial waters contain important fishing resources, their commercial exploitation is minimal. According to World Bank estimates, agricultural GDP increased at an average annual rate of 1.2% in 2001–10; a decline of 1.1% was recorded in 2009, but agricultural GDP increased by 3.8% in 2010.

Industry (including mining, manufacturing, construction and power) contributed an estimated 56.5% of GDP in 2009, according to AfDB figures. About 14.1% of the working population were employed in the sector in 1991. According to World Bank estimates, industrial GDP increased at an average annual rate of 1.0% in 2001–10; industrial GDP contracted by 2.5% in 2009, but it expanded by 2.9% in 2010.

Mining accounted for an estimated 47.6% of GDP in 2009 (with the majority of that contributed by the petroleum sector alone). In 2006 sales of petroleum and petroleum products provided an estimated 85.6% of export revenue. Production of crude petroleum was estimated at 245,000 barrels per day (b/d) in 2010, down from some 371,000 b/d in 1997. However, recent explorations have doubled oil reserves compared with 1996 levels. At the end of 2010 Gabon had proven petroleum reserves of 3,684m. barrels. Proven natural gas reserves totalled 1,000,000m. cu ft at the end of 2010. Gabon is among the world's foremost producers and exporters of manganese (which contributed an estimated 3.1% of export earnings in 2006). In 2010 3,200 metric tons of manganese was mined. Major reserves of iron ore remain undeveloped, although in September 2004 a Chinese company signed an agreement to exploit some 1,000m. tons of Gabonese iron ore, and there are also substantial niobium (columbium) reserves at Mabounie. Small amounts of gold are extracted, and the existence of many mineral deposits, including talc, barytes, phosphates, rare earths, titanium and cadmium, has also been confirmed. In 1996–2002, according to the IMF, mining GDP declined at an estimated average annual rate of 6.5%. The IMF estimated a decline of 2.1% in mining GDP in 2002.

According to AfDB figures, the manufacturing sector contributed an estimated 4.8% of GDP in 2009. The principal activities are the refining of petroleum and the processing of other minerals, the preparation of timber and other agro-industrial processes. The chemicals industry is also significant. According to World Bank estimates, manufacturing GDP increased at an average annual rate of 2.4% in 2001–10. It increased by 3.0% in 2010.

The construction sector contributed 2.3% of GDP in 2009, according to AfDB figures. The sector grew by 3.5% in 2008 but contracted by 3.3% in 2009.

In 2008 43.8% of electrical energy was provided by hydroelectric power, with the remainder provided by petroleum (31.2%) and natural gas (24.7%). Imports of mineral fuels and lubricants comprised an estimated 4.0% of the total value of merchandise imports in 2006. Construction began of a new hydroelectric dam in Mitzic in December 2010 by French company Bouygues SA; the project was expected to cost US $108m. with a projected capacity of 40 MW.

Services engaged 18.8% of the economically active population in 1991 and, according to AfDB figures, provided 37.7% of GDP in 2009. According to World Bank estimates, the GDP of the services sector increased at an average annual rate of 3.3% in 2001–10; services GDP declined by 0.6% in 2009, but increased by 7.9% in 2010.

According to preliminary figures, in 2008 Gabon recorded a trade surplus of 2,248,200m. francs CFA, and there was a surplus of 1,091,400m. francs CFA on the current account of the balance of payments. In 2006 the principal source of imports (39.9%) was France (including Monaco); other major sources were Belgium and the USA. The principal market for exports in that year was the USA (58.4%); the People's Republic of China, France (including Monaco) and Singapore were also important purchasers. The principal exports in 2006 were mineral fuels and lubricants and cork and wood. The principal imports in that year were food and live animals, road vehicles, chemicals and related products, industrial machinery and equipment and iron and steel.

In 2009 there was a projected budgetary surplus of 110,200m. francs CFA. Gabon's general government gross debt was 1,635,410m. francs CFA in 2010, equivalent to 25.1% of GDP. Gabon's external debt totalled US $2,130m. at the end of 2009, of which $2,022m. was public and publicly guaranteed debt. In 2005 the cost of servicing long-term public and publicly guaranteed debt and repayments to the IMF was equivalent to 3.4% of the value of exports of goods, services and income (excluding workers' remittances). In 2001–10 the average annual rate of inflation was 2.1%. Consumer prices increased by 1.5% in 2010. The Government estimated about 20% of the labour force to be unemployed in 1996.

Gabon's potential for economic growth is based on its considerable mineral and forestry resources. Petroleum provides the country's principal source of income, and at the end of 2010 the country had proven oil reserves of 3,684m. barrels. However, these reserves were in decline, and the Government's efforts to increase revenue from non-oil sectors (predominantly mining, agriculture, forestry and tourism) had been only moderately successful. Following his accession to the presidency, in October 2009 Ali Bongo Ondimba pledged that by 2012 the Government would be spending at least €500m. per year on infrastructure projects, and that the country would aim to become a centre for specialist medical research and training in tourism, forestry and architecture. The promotion of eco-tourism, capturing profits from the carbon-trading market and promoting sustainable forestry projects were prioritized, and the export of unprocessed timber was banned in January 2010 to encourage the creation of a domestic processing industry. The Government intended to use around 40% of budgetary revenue in 2010–17 to create 100,000 jobs per year. Real GDP growth was estimated by the IMF at 5.7% in 2010 and 5.6% in 2011, driven mainly by high levels of government spending, increased economic activity in the mining sector and a recovery in exports. Nevertheless, these figures remained well below the ambitious targets set by the Gabonese authorities, which aimed to sustain GDP growth of 10% over at least one-half of the period 2010–17. In an attempt to boost growth and economic diversification, a Special Economic Zone was established near the capital in September 2011; the Government hoped to attract investment into the Zone by offering generous tax incentives. In a complementary move, loans totalling US $439m. were secured from the AfDB in late 2011 to fund a variety of infrastructural development projects. Despite these measures, the IMF forecast average annual GDP growth of only 2.5% during 2012–15.

PUBLIC HOLIDAYS

2013: 1 January (New Year's Day), 23 January* (Mouloud, Birth of Muhammad), 12 March (Anniversary of Renovation, foundation of the Parti démocratique gabonais), 1 April (Easter Monday), 1 May (Labour Day), 20 May (Whit Monday), 7 August* (Id al-Fitr, end of Ramadan), 17 August (Anniversary of Independence), 14 October* (Id al-Adha, Feast of the Sacrifice), 1 November (All Saints' Day), 25 December (Christmas).

* These holidays are dependent on the Islamic lunar calendar and may vary by one or two days from the dates given.

Statistical Survey

Source (unless otherwise stated): Direction Générale de la Statistique et des Etudes Economiques, Ministère de la Planification et de la Programmation du Développement, BP 2119, Libreville; tel. 01-72-13-69; fax 01-72-04-57; e-mail plan@dgsee.yahoo.fr; internet www.stat-gabon.org.

Area and Population

AREA, POPULATION AND DENSITY

Area (sq km)	267,667*
Population (census results)	
31 July 1993	
Males	501,784
Females	513,192
Total	1,014,976
1 December 2003	1,269,000†
Population (UN estimates at mid-year)‡	
2010	1,505,463
2011	1,534,258
2012	1,563,873
Density (per sq km) at mid-2012	5.8

* 103,347 sq miles.
† Provisional (Source: UN, *Population and Vital Statistics Report*).
‡ Source: UN, *World Population Prospects: The 2010 Revision*.

POPULATION BY AGE AND SEX

(UN estimates at mid-2012)

	Males	Females	Total
0–14	273,325	268,206	541,531
15–64	479,641	474,637	954,278
65 and over	31,915	36,149	68,064
Total	784,881	778,992	1,563,873

Source: UN, *World Population Prospects: The 2010 Revision*.

REGIONS

(1993 census)

Region	Area (sq km)	Population	Density (per sq km)	Chief town
Estuaire	20,740	463,187	22.3	Libreville
Haut-Ogooué	36,547	104,301	2.9	Franceville
Moyen-Ogooué	18,535	42,316	2.3	Lambaréné
N'Gounié	37,750	77,781	2.1	Mouila
Nyanga	21,285	39,430	1.9	Tchibanga
Ogooué-Ivindo	46,075	48,862	1.1	Makokou
Ogooué-Lolo	25,380	43,915	1.7	Koulamoutou
Ogooué-Maritime	22,890	97,913	4.3	Port-Gentil
Woleu-N'Tem	38,465	97,271	2.5	Oyem
Total	267,667	1,014,976	3.8	

PRINCIPAL TOWNS

(population at 1993 census)

Libreville (capital)	419,596	Mouila	16,307
Port-Gentil	79,225	Lambaréné	15,033
Franceville	31,183	Tchibanga	14,054
Oyem	22,404	Koulamoutou	11,773
Moanda	21,882	Makokou	9,849

Mid-2009 (incl. suburbs, UN estimate): Libreville (capital) 619,000 (Source: UN, *World Urbanization Prospects: The 2009 Revision*).

BIRTHS AND DEATHS

(annual averages, UN estimates)

	1995–2000	2000–05	2005–10
Birth rate (per 1,000)	33.2	29.7	27.4
Death rate (per 1,000)	10.2	10.4	9.4

Source: UN, *World Population Prospects: The 2010 Revision*.

Life expectancy (years at birth, WHO estimates): 62 (males 60; females 64) in 2009 (Source: WHO, *World Health Statistics*).

ECONOMICALLY ACTIVE POPULATION

('000 persons, 1991, estimates)

	Males	Females	Total
Agriculture, etc.	187	151	338
Industry	62	9	71
Services	69	26	95
Total labour force	318	186	504

Source: UN Economic Commission for Africa, *African Statistical Yearbook*.

2005 (persons aged 15 years and over): Total employed 639,180; Unemployed 115,499; Total labour force 664,117.

Mid-2012 (estimates in '000): Agriculture, etc. 185; Total 749 (Source: FAO).

Health and Welfare

KEY INDICATORS

Total fertility rate (children per woman, 2009)	3.2
Under-5 mortality rate (per 1,000 live births, 2009)	69
HIV/AIDS (% of persons aged 15–49, 2009)	5.2
Physicians (per 1,000 head, 2004)	0.3
Hospital beds (per 1,000 head, 2006)	2.0
Health expenditure (2008): US $ per head (PPP)	384
Health expenditure (2008): % of GDP	2.6
Health expenditure (2008): public (% of total)	43.7
Access to water (% of persons, 2008)	87
Access to sanitation (% of persons, 2008)	33
Total carbon dioxide emissions ('000 metric tons, 2007)	2,033.5
Carbon dioxide emissions per head (metric tons, 2007)	1.4
Human Development Index (2011): ranking	106
Human Development Index (2011): value	0.674

For sources and definitions, see explanatory note on p. vi.

Agriculture

PRINCIPAL CROPS

('000 metric tons, FAO estimates)

	2008	2009	2010
Maize	35	46	40
Cassava (Manioc)	243	307	270
Taro (Cocoyam)	55	70	55
Yams	164	210	168
Sugar cane	220	240	240
Groundnuts, with shell	20	18	18
Oil palm fruit	34	20	20
Bananas	14	12	14
Plantains	275	288	297
Natural rubber	14	13	14

Aggregate production ('000 metric tons, may include official, semi-official or estimated data): Total cereals 36 in 2008, 47 in 2009, 41 in 2010; Total roots and tubers 465 in 2008, 591 in 2009, 496 in 2010; Total vegetables (incl. melons) 38 in 2008, 39 in 2009, 36 in 2010; Total fruits (excl. melons) 302 in 2008, 311 in 2009, 325 in 2010.

Source: FAO.

LIVESTOCK
('000 head, year ending September, FAO estimates)

	2006	2007	2008
Cattle	35	36	37
Pigs	212	213	215
Sheep	195	196	196
Goats	90	91	92
Chickens	3,100	3,100	3,200

2009–10: Figures assumed to be unchanged from 2008 (FAO estimates).

Source: FAO.

LIVESTOCK PRODUCTS
('000 metric tons, FAO estimates)

	2008	2009	2010
Cattle meat	1.1	1.1	1.1
Pig meat	3.2	3.2	3.2
Chicken meat	3.8	3.8	3.8
Rabbit meat	1.9	1.9	1.9
Game meat	20.7	22.0	25.1
Cows' milk	1.8	1.8	1.9
Hen eggs	2.2	1.9	2.1

Source: FAO.

Forestry

ROUNDWOOD REMOVALS
('000 cubic metres)

	2005	2006	2007
Sawlogs, veneer logs and logs for sleepers	3,200	3,500	3,400
Fuel wood*	1,070	1,070	1,070
Total*	4,270	4,570	4,470

* FAO estimates.

2008–10: Production assumed to be unchanged from 2007 (FAO estimates).

Source: FAO.

SAWNWOOD PRODUCTION
('000 cubic metres, incl. railway sleepers)

	2008	2009	2010
Total	197	199	230

Source: FAO.

Fishing

('000 metric tons, live weight)

	2006	2007	2008
Capture	41.5	38.5*	30.0*
Tilapias	3.8	4.3	4.5*
Other freshwater fishes	4.8	4.8*	4.8*
Barracudas	0.6	0.5	0.4
Bobo croakers	1.5	1.5*	1.4
West African croakers	3.4	2.3*	1.1
Lesser African threadfin	1.5	1.2	0.8
Bonga shad	10.6	11.3	8.3
Sardinellas	1.9	1.1	—
Penaeus shrimp	1.4	0.4*	0.1*
Aquaculture	0.1	0.1	0.1
Total catch	41.6	38.6*	30.1*

* FAO estimate.

2009: Figures assumed to be unchanged from 2008 (FAO estimates).

Source: FAO.

Mining

	2008	2009	2010
Crude petroleum ('000 barrels)	85,775	83,950	89,425
Natural gas (million cu m)	80	n.a.	n.a.
Diamonds (carats)	500	500	500
Manganese ore ('000 metric tons): gross weight*	3,150	1,950	3,200
Manganese ore ('000 metric tons): metal content†	100	50	100
Gold (kg)*‡	300	300	300

* Figures refer to the metal content of ore.

† Figures refer to the weight of chemical-grade pellets.

‡ Excluding production smuggled out of the country (estimated at more than 400 kg annually).

Source: US Geological Survey.

Industry

PETROLEUM PRODUCTS
('000 metric tons)

	2006	2007	2008
Motor spirit (petrol)	44	56	70
Kerosene	23	25	31
Distillate fuel oils	213	260	326
Residual fuel oils and asphalt	324	356	446
Butane	6.7	14.0	13.5

Source: mostly UN Industrial Commodity Statistics Database.

SELECTED OTHER PRODUCTS

	2003	2004	2005
Plywood ('000 cu mm)	37.8	52.8	68.1
Veneer sheets ('000 cu mm)	198.2	120.7	175.2
Alcoholic beverages ('000 hl)	755.9	750.1	852.1
Soft drinks ('000 hl)	568.4	537.9	587.0

Hydraulic cement ('000 metric tons, estimates): 230 in 2008; 250 in 2009; 200 in 2010 (Source: US Geological Survey).

Electric energy (million kWh): 1,610 in 2005; 1,723 in 2006; 1,844 in 2007; 2,040 in 2008 (Source: UN Industrial Commodity Statistics Database).

Finance

CURRENCY AND EXCHANGE RATES

Monetary Units

100 centimes = 1 franc de la Coopération financière en Afrique centrale (CFA).

Sterling, Dollar and Euro Equivalents (30 December 2011)

£1 sterling = 783.813 francs CFA;
US $1 = 506.961 francs CFA;
€1 = 655.957 francs CFA;
10,000 francs CFA = £12.76 = $19.73 = €15.24.

Average Exchange Rate (francs CFA per US $)

2009	472.19
2010	495.28
2011	471.87

Note: An exchange rate of 1 French franc = 50 francs CFA, established in 1948, remained in force until January 1994, when the CFA franc was devalued by 50%, with the exchange rate adjusted to 1 French franc = 100 francs CFA. This relationship to French currency remained in effect with the introduction of the euro on 1 January 1999. From that date, accordingly, a fixed exchange rate of €1 = 655.957 francs CFA has been in operation.

BUDGET

('000 million francs CFA)

Revenue*	2007	2008†	2009†
Petroleum revenue	958.5	1,296.7	632.4
Non-petroleum revenue	677.8	714.3	750.3
Direct taxes	193.5	232.7	256.0
Indirect taxes	130.3	133.4	145.7
Value-added tax	92.4	86.0	87.0
Taxes on international trade and transactions	281.9	275.5	271.2
Other revenue	72.1	72.7	77.4
Total	1,636.3	2,011.0	1,382.6

Expenditure‡	2007	2008†	2009†
Current expenditure	837.8	917.0	843.5
Wages and salaries	301.8	320.8	370.0
Goods and services	190.4	205.3	191.5
Transfers and subsidies	226.8	268.1	183.2
Interest payments	118.8	122.8	98.8
Domestic	26.6	22.8	12.3
External	92.2	100.0	86.6
Capital expenditure	246.8	295.0	306.1
Domestically financed investment	198.6	244.1	235.5
Externally financed investment	48.2	50.9	70.6
Capital grants	—	0.0	8.7
Capital transfers	—	38.7	55.7
Total	1,084.6	1,250.7	1,214.0

* Excluding grants received ('000 million francs CFA): 0.2 in 2007; 6.0 in 2008 (projection); 4.0 in 2009 (projection).

† Projections.

‡ Excluding net lending and road maintenance and other special funds ('000 million francs CFA): 39.3 in 2004 (funds only); 58.4 in 2005; 55.8 in 2006; 81.0 in 2007; 101.8 in 2008 (funds only, projection); 62.4 in 2009 (projection).

Source: IMF, *Gabon: Second and Third Reviews Under the Stand-By Arrangement and Requests for Waiver of Nonobservance of Performance Criteria and Modification of Performance Criterion—Staff Report; Press Release on the Executive Board Discussion; and Statement by the Executive Director for Gabon* (March 2009).

INTERNATIONAL RESERVES

(US $ million at 31 December)

	2008	2009	2010
Gold*	1.86	—	9.64
IMF special drawing rights	0.47	208.20	204.53
Reserve position in IMF	0.70	0.80	0.83
Foreign exchange	1,922.33	1,784.24	1,530.53
Total	1,925.36	1,993.24	1,745.53

* Valued at market-related prices.

Source: IMF, *International Financial Statistics*.

MONEY SUPPLY

('000 million francs CFA at 31 December)

	2008	2009	2010
Currency outside banks	230.01	249.40	221.53
Demand deposits at commercial and development banks	531.60	505.90	688.83
Total money (incl. others)	774.36	766.23	918.11

Source: IMF, *International Financial Statistics*.

COST OF LIVING

(Consumer Price Index; base: 2000 = 100)

	2007	2008	2009
Clothing	109.8	109.5	107.2
Rent, water, electricity, gas and other fuels	113.1	123.4	128.5
All items (incl. others)	112.7	118.5	120.8

2010: All items (incl. others) 122.6.

Food (Consumer Price Index; base: 2007 = 100): 107.8 in 2008; 111.8 in 2009; 116.7 in 2010.

Source: ILO.

NATIONAL ACCOUNTS

('000 million francs CFA at current prices)

Expenditure on the Gross Domestic Product

	2007	2008	2009
Government final consumption expenditure	670	709	791
Private final consumption expenditure	1,758	1,932	2,038
Gross fixed capital formation	1,291	1,331	1,250
Changes in inventories	4	32	27
Total domestic expenditure	3,723	4,004	4,106
Exports of goods and services	3,558	4,401	2,893
Less Imports of goods and services	1,802	1,951	1,868
GDP at purchasers' values	5,478	6,454	5,131

Gross Domestic Product by Economic Activity

	2007	2008	2009
Agriculture, livestock, hunting, forestry and fishing	269	264	277
Mining and quarrying	2,853	3,684	2,282
Manufacturing	250	251	230
Electricity, gas and water	70	81	88
Construction	102	113	112
Trade, restaurants and hotels	303	333	350
Finance, insurance and real estate	611	668	687
Transport and communications	281	295	267
Public administration and defence	402	432	506
GDP at factor cost	5,140	6,121	4,799
Indirect taxes	338	333	332
GDP at purchasers' values	5,478	6,454	5,131

Note: Deduction for imputed bank service charge assumed to be distributed at origin.

Source: African Development Bank.

BALANCE OF PAYMENTS

('000 million francs CFA)

	2007*	2008†
Exports of goods f.o.b.	3,459.2	4,283.0
Petroleum	2,781.6	3,341.5
Imports of goods f.o.b.	−1,731.0	−2,034.8
Trade balance	1,728.2	2,248.2
Services and other income (net)	−730.7	−1,001.5
Balance on goods, services and income	997.5	1,246.7
Current transfers (net)	−137.5	−155.3
Current balance	860.0	1,091.4
Capital transfers (net)	0.0	132.3
Direct investment (net)	214.1	358.0
Portfolio investments (net)	445.2	48.3
Other investment assets and liabilities (net)	−1,512.3	−1,308.5
Overall balance	7.0	321.5

* Estimates.

† Projections.

Source: IMF, *Gabon: Second and Third Reviews Under the Stand-By Arrangement and Requests for Waiver of Nonobservance of Performance Criteria and Modification of Performance Criterion—Staff Report; Press Release on the Executive Board Discussion; and Statement by the Executive Director for Gabon* (March 2009).

External Trade

PRINCIPAL COMMODITIES
('000 million francs CFA)

Imports	2004	2005	2006
Food and live animals	186.0	216.3	223.9
Meat and meat preparations	52.5	65.5	66.0
Cereal and cereal preparations	55.7	60.6	58.5
Beverages and tobacco	33.8	41.9	45.7
Mineral fuels, lubricants, etc.	30.6	53.0	67.0
Petroleum, petroleum products and related materials	25.1	46.7	61.3
Chemicals and related products	102.2	141.3	158.4
Medicinal and pharmaceutical products	39.8	50.1	53.1
Basic manufactures	162.5	258.9	319.7
Iron and steel	44.1	98.0	127.5
Machinery and transport equipment	340.6	591.1	737.9
General industrial machinery and equipment	75.2	143.4	151.1
Electrical machinery, apparatus and appliances	42.8	86.4	81.0
Road vehicles	91.8	130.8	171.6
Miscellaneous manufactured articles	78.5	126.4	131.1
Total (incl. others)	964.9	1,471.9	1,724.9

Exports	2004	2005	2006
Crude materials (inedible), except fuels	426.3	563.9	593.1
Cork and wood	271.3	371.4	381.9
Metalliferous ore and metal scrap	153.1	181.9	189.3
Manganese ores and concentrates	151.1	178.8	186.7
Mineral fuels, lubricants, etc.	2,117.9	4,259.7	5,149.8
Basic manufactures	124.8	113.4	125.1
Cork and wood manufactures	101.0	103.8	119.9
Veneers, plywood, particle board and other wood	100.6	103.6	119.8
Total (incl. others)	2,780.0	5,068.5	6,015.2

Source: UN, *International Trade Statistics Yearbook*.

PRINCIPAL TRADING PARTNERS
(US $ million)

Imports c.i.f.	2004	2005	2006
Argentina	7.4	10.2	12.4
Belgium	106.1	179.1	244.5
Brazil	16.4	32.2	32.0
Cameroon	30.1	53.4	60.0
China, People's Republic	14.5	27.0	45.2
Côte d'Ivoire	19.1	10.2	14.1
France (incl. Monaco)	393.8	578.6	688.8
Germany	14.1	20.6	34.8
India	10.3	11.8	14.5
Italy	26.5	37.4	32.5
Japan	29.1	48.9	52.2
Netherlands	40.0	39.5	48.3
Norway	1.1	10.4	1.7
Singapore	4.6	30.7	10.5
South Africa	20.3	21.7	31.0
Spain	21.9	29.2	41.5
Sweden	7.4	9.8	16.8
Thailand	27.2	25.9	28.0
United Arab Emirates	9.8	14.9	18.9
United Kingdom	40.0	34.6	32.8
USA	44.2	95.3	126.6
Total (incl. others)	964.9	1,471.9	1,724.9

Exports f.o.b.	2004	2005	2006
Australia	0.1	65.3	0.0
China, People's Republic	175.2	203.0	635.8
Congo, Democratic Republic	14.7	8.4	16.2
France (incl. Monaco)	246.2	233.7	425.3
Iceland	117.0	0.0	0.3
India	45.4	94.9	128.4
Italy	54.8	63.3	67.7
Korea, Democratic People's Republic	1.4	63.7	0.9
Netherlands	7.0	29.1	22.1
Norway	31.1	41.2	20.2
Senegal	1.5	8.6	43.3
Singapore	3.4	42.7	318.4
South Africa	38.4	93.5	117.8
Spain	33.6	107.4	82.4
Switzerland-Liechtenstein	53.4	273.3	156.4
Thailand	31.1	56.2	127.0
United Kingdom	4.8	1.6	74.3
Ukraine	29.1	34.8	17.9
USA	1,363.6	3,367.8	3,514.6
Total (incl. others)	2,780.0	5,068.5	6,015.2

Source: UN, *International Trade Statistics Yearbook*.

Transport

RAILWAYS
(traffic)

	2003	2004	2005
Passengers carried ('000)	206.8	214.4	218.5
Freight carried ('000 metric tons)	2,967.7	3,455.8	3,923.8

ROAD TRAFFIC
(estimates, motor vehicles in use)

	1994	1995	1996
Passenger cars	22,310	24,000	24,750
Lorries and vans	14,850	15,840	16,490

Source: IRF, *World Road Statistics*.

SHIPPING

Merchant Fleet
(registered at 31 December)

	2007	2008	2009
Number of vessels	49	49	50
Total displacement ('000 grt)	13.8	14.0	14.4

Source: IHS Fairplay, *World Fleet Statistics*.

International Sea-borne Freight Traffic
('000 metric tons, Port-Gentil and Owendo)

	2002	2003	2004
Goods loaded	15,429	16,005	17,144
Goods unloaded	763	739	776

Source: IMF, *Gabon: Statistical Appendix* (May 2005).

CIVIL AVIATION
(traffic on scheduled services)

	2003	2004	2005
Kilometres flown (million)	8	9	9
Passengers carried ('000)	386	431	465
Passenger-kilometres (million)	655	750	829
Total ton-kilometres (million)	112	128	140

Source: UN, *Statistical Yearbook*.

Passengers carried ('000): 535.3 in 2007; 545.6 in 2008; 524.9 in 2009 (Source: World Bank, World Development Indicators database).

Tourism

	2001	2002	2003
Tourist arrivals	169,191	208,348	222,257
Tourism receipts (US $ million, incl. passenger transport)	46	77	84

Receipts from tourism (US $ million, incl. passenger transport): 74 in 2004; 13 in 2005.

Source: World Tourism Organization.

Communications Media

	2008	2009	2010
Telephones ('000 main lines in use)	33.2	36.5	30.4
Mobile cellular telephones ('000 subscribers)	1,300.0	1,373.0	1,610.0
Internet subscribers ('000)	13.8	20.2	22.2
Broadband subscribers ('000)	2.2	3.7	4.1

Radio receivers ('000 in use): 600 in 1999.

Television receivers ('000 in use): 400 in 2001.

Daily newspapers: 2 (estimated average circulation 34,800 copies) in 1998; 1 in 2004.

Personal computers: 47,000 (33.7 per 1,000 persons) in 2006.

Sources: UNESCO Institute for Statistics; UN, *Statistical Yearbook*; International Telecommunication Union.

Education

(2003/04, unless otherwise indicated, estimates)

	Institutions	Teachers	Pupils: Males	Pupils: Females	Pupils: Total
Pre-primary	9*	517†	7,784†	7,784†	15,568†
Primary	1,175*	7,807	142,268	139,103	281,371
Secondary:					
General	88‡	3,102†	43,892§	39,303§	83,195§
Technical and vocational	11‡	394†	5,025‖	2,562‖	7,587‖
Tertiary	2*	585¶	4,806¶	2,667¶	7,473¶

* 1991/92 figure.
† 2000/01 figure.
‡ 1996 figure.
§ 1999/2000 figure.
‖ 2001/02 figure.
¶ 1998/99 figure.

Source: UNESCO Institute for Statistics.

Pupil-teacher ratio (primary education, UNESCO estimate): 36.0 in 2003/04 (Source: UNESCO Institute for Statistics).

Adult literacy rate (UNESCO estimates): 87.7% (males 91.4%; females 84.1%) in 2009 (Source: UNESCO Institute for Statistics).

Directory

The Government

HEAD OF STATE

President: ALI BONGO ONDIMBA (inaugurated 16 October 2009).

Vice-President: DIDJOB DIVUNGUI-DI-N'DINGUE.

COUNCIL OF MINISTERS
(May 2012)

The Government is formed by members of the Parti démocratique gabonais.

Prime Minister and Head of Government: RAYMOND NDONG SIMA.

Minister of Justice, Keeper of the Seals, Government Spokesperson: IDA RETENO ASSONOUET.

Minister of Foreign Affairs, International Co-operation and Francophone Affairs, responsible for the NEPAD and Regional Integration: EMMANUEL ISSOZET NGONDET.

Minister of Health: LÉON NZOUBA.

Minister of Agriculture, Stockbreeding, Fisheries and Rural Development: JULIEN NKOGHÉ BÉKALÉ.

Minister of the Promotion of Investment, Public Works, Transport, Housing and Tourism, responsible for Territorial Management: MAGLOIRE NGAMBIA.

Minister of the Digital Economy, Communication and Posts: BLAISE LOUEMBÉ.

Minister of National Education, Higher and Technical Education and Professional Training, responsible for Culture, Youth and Sports: SÉRAPHIN MOUNDOUNGA.

Minister of Water and Forests: GABRIEL NTCHANGO.

Minister of Small and Medium-sized Enterprises, Handicrafts and Trade: FIDÈLE MENGUE M'ENGOUANG.

Minister of the Interior, Public Security, Immigration and Decentralization: JEAN-FRANÇOIS NDONGOU.

Minister of National Defence: PACÔME RUFIN ONDZOUNGA.

Minister of the Family and Social Affairs: HONORINE NZET BITÉGUÉ.

Minister of Industry and Mines: RÉGIS IMMONGAULT TATAGANI.

Minister of the Economy, Employment and Sustainable Development: LUC OYOUBI.

Minister of the Budget, Public Accounts and the Civil Service: CHRISTIANE ROSE OSSOUKA RAPONDA.

Minister of Petroleum, Energy and Hydraulic Resources: ETIENNE NGOUBOU.

Minister-delegate to the Prime Minister, responsible for State Reform: CALIXTE ISIDORE NSIE EDANG.

Minister-delegate to the Minister of Foreign Affairs, responsible for the NEPAD and Regional Integration: DOMINIQUE NGUIENO.

Ministers-delegate to the Minister of Agriculture, Stockbreeding, Fisheries and Rural Development: CÉLESTINE OGUEWA BA.

Minister-delegate to the Minister of Health: ALICE BIKISA NEMBE.

Minister-delegate to the Minister of the Interior, responsible for Security: AIMÉ-POPA NTZOUTSI MOUYAMA.

Minister-delegate to the Minister of the Digital Economy, Communication and Posts: FRANÇOISE ASSENGONE OBAME.

Minister-delegate to the Minister of National Education, Higher and Technical Education and Professional Training, responsible for Culture, Youth and Sports: ERNEST WALKER ONINWIN.

Minister-delegate to the Minister of the Budget, Public Accounts and the Civil Service, responsible for the Civil Service: RAPHAËL NGAZOUZET.

Ministers-delegate to the Minister of Promotion of Investment, Public Works, Transport, Housing and Tourism: JEAN EMMANUEL BIE (Transport), CHRISTIANE LECKAT (Housing).

Minister-delegate to the Minister of National Education, Higher and Technical Education and Professional Training, responsible for Technical Education and Professional Training: PAULETTE MOUNGUENGUI.

Minister-delegate to the Minister of the Economy, Employment and Sustainable Development: DÉSIRÉ GUEDON.

MINISTRIES

Office of the Prime Minister: BP 546, Libreville; tel. 77-89-81.

Ministry of Agriculture, Stockbreeding, Fisheries and Rural Development: BP 3974 & 199, Libreville; tel. 76-13-78; fax 77-37-44.

Ministry of the Budget, Public Accounts and the Civil Service: BP 165, Libreville; tel. 79-50-00; fax 79-57-37; internet www.finances.gouv.ga.

Ministry of the Digital Economy, Communication and Posts: Libreville.

Ministry of the Economy, Employment and Sustainable Development: Libreville.

Ministry of the Family and Social Affairs: Libreville.

Ministry of Foreign Affairs, International Co-operation and Francophone Affairs: BP 2245, Libreville; tel. 72-95-21; fax 72-91-73.

Ministry of Health: BP 50, Libreville; tel. 76-36-11.

Ministry of Industry and Mines: Libreville.

Ministry of the Interior, Public Security, Immigration and Decentralization: BP 2110, Libreville; tel. 74-35-06; fax 72-13-89.

Ministry of Justice: BP 547, Libreville; tel. 74-66-28; fax 72-33-84.

Ministry of National Defence: BP 13493, Libreville; tel. and fax 77-86-96.

Ministry of National Education, Higher and Technical Education, Professional Training, Culture, Youth and Sports: BP 6, Libreville; tel. 72-44-61; fax 72-19-74.

Ministry of Petrol, Energy and Hydraulic Resources: Libreville.

Ministry of the Promotion of Investment, Public Works, Transport, Housing and Tourism: Libreville.

Ministry of Small and Medium-sized Enterprises, Handicrafts and Trade: BP 3096, Libreville; tel. 74-59-21.

Ministry of Transport: BP 803, Libreville; tel. 74-71-96; fax 77-33-31.

Ministry of Water and Forests: Libreville.

President and Legislature

PRESIDENT

Presidential Election, 30 August 2009

Candidate	Valid votes	% of valid votes
Ali Bongo Ondimba (PDG)	141,952	41.73
André Mba Obame (Ind.)	88,028	25.88
Pierre Mamboundou (UPG)	85,797	25.22
Zacharie Myboto (UGDD)	13,418	3.94
Casimir Oyé Mba (Ind.)	3,118	0.92
Pierre-Claver Maganga Moussavou (PSD)	2,576	0.76
Bruno Ben Moubamba (Ind.)	963	0.28
Georges Bruno Ngoussi (Ind.)	915	0.27
Jules Artides Bourdès Ogouliguende (CDJ)	695	0.20
Albert Ondo Ossa (Ind.)	674	0.20
Others	2,028	0.60
Total	340,178*	100.00

* The total number of votes officially attributed to candidates by the Constitutional Court amounted to 340,164. However, that body declared the total number of valid votes cast to be 340,178. Additionally, there were 17,443 spoiled ballots. Several of the defeated candidates formally protested against the results and a recount of the votes was subsequently held. On 12 October the Constitutional Court announced that Bongo had secured 141,665 valid votes, equating to 41.79%, while the number of votes attributed to Mamboundou and Mba Obame was amended to 86,875 (25.64%) and 85,814 (25.33%), respectively, thus reversing their placings in the election. No figures for the remaining candidates or the total number of votes cast were made available.

ASSEMBLÉE NATIONALE

President: GUY NDZOUBA NDAMA.

Secretary-General: JEAN-BAPTISTE YAMA-LEGNONGO.

General Election, 17 December 2011

Party	Seats
Parti démocratique gabonais (PDG)	114*
Rassemblement pour le Gabon (RPG)	3
Cercle des libéraux réformateurs (CLR)	1
Parti social-démocrate (PSD)	1
Union pour la nouvelle République (UPNR)	1
Total	120

* One seat was won in alliance with the Parti gabonais du centre indépendant (PGCI).

SÉNAT

President: ROSE FRANCINE ROGOMBÉ.

Secretary-General: FÉLIX OWANSANGO DEACKEU.

Election, 18 January 2009

Party	Seats
Parti démocratique gabonais (PDG)	75
Rassemblement pour le Gabon (RPG)	6
Parti gabonais du centre indépendent (PGCI)	3
Union du peuple gabonais (UPG)	3
Cercle des libéraux réformateurs (CLR)	2
Parti social-démocrate (PSD)	2
Union gabonaise pour la démocratie et le développement (UGDD)	2
Alliance démocratique et républicaine (ADERE)	1
Independents	8
Total	102

Election Commission

Commission électorale nationale autonome et permanente (CENAP): Libreville; f. 2006 to replace the Commission nationale électorale; Pres. appointed by the Constitutional Court; Pres. RENÉ ABOGHÉ ELLA.

Political Organizations

Alliance démocratique et républicaine (ADERE): Pres. MBOUMBOU NGOMA; Sec.-Gen. DIDJOB DIVUNGUI-DI-N'DINGUE.

Cercle des libéraux réformateurs (CLR): f. 1993 by breakaway faction of the PDG; Leader JEAN-BONIFACE ASSELE.

Congrès pour la démocratie et la justice (CDJ): tel. 70-00-00; e-mail contact@bourdes-gabon.com; internet www.bourdes-gabon.com; Pres. JULES BOURDÈS OGOULIGUENDE.

Front national (FN): f. 1991; Leader MARTIN EFAYONG.

Mouvement d'emancipation socialiste du peuple: Leader MOUANGA MBADINGA.

Parti démocratique gabonais (PDG): Immeuble PETROGAB, BP 75384, Libreville; tel. 70-31-21; fax 70-31-46; internet www.pdg-gabon.org; f. 1968; sole legal party 1968–90; Leader ALI BONGO ONDIMBA; Sec.-Gen. FAUSTIN BOUKOUBI.

Parti gabonais du centre indépendant (PGCI): allied to the PDG; Leader JÉRÔME OKINDA.

Parti gabonais du progrès (PGP): f. 1990; Pres. (vacant); Vice-Pres. JOSEPH-BENOÎT MOUITY.

Parti social-démocrate (PSD): f. 1991; Leader PIERRE-CLAVER MAGANGA MOUSSAVOU.

Rassemblement des démocrates républicains (RDR): Leader MAX MEBALE M'OBAME.

Rassemblement pour la démocratie et le progrès (RDP): Pres. ALAIN CLAUDE BILIE BI NZE.

Rassemblement pour le Gabon (RPG): f. 1990 as MORENA des bûcherons; renamed Rassemblement national des bûcherons in 1991, name changed as above in 2000; allied to the PDG; Leader Fr PAUL M'BA ABESSOLE; Vice-Pres. Prof. VINCENT MOULENGUI BOUKOSSO.

Rassemblement national des bûcherons—Démocratique (RNB): Libreville; f. 1991; Leader PIERRE ANDRÉ KOMBILA.

Union démocratique et sociale (UDS): f. 1996; Leader HERVÉ ASSAMANET.

Union nationale (UN): f. 2010 through the merger of the Union gabonaise pour la démocratie et le développement (UGDD), the Mouvement africain de développement (MAD) and the Rassemblement national des républicains (RNR); forcibly dissolved by the Government in January 2011; Leader ZACHARIE MYBOTO.

Union pour la nouvelle République: Immeuble Score, 657 ave du Col Parant, BP 4049, Libreville; tel. 77-40-13; fax 77-40-17; e-mail info@louisgastonmayila.com; internet www.louisgastonmayila.com; f. 2007 following the merger of the Front pour l'unité nationale (FUNDU) and the Rassemblement des républicains indépendants (RRI); Leader LOUIS-GASTON MAYILA.

Union du peuple gabonais (UPG): BP 6048, Awendjé, Libreville; tel. 07-14-61-61 (mobile); internet www.upg-gabon.org; f. 1989 in Paris, France; Leader (vacant); Sec.-Gen. DAVID BADINGA.

Union pour le progrès national (UPN): Leader DANIEL TENGUE NZOUNDO.

Diplomatic Representation

EMBASSIES IN GABON

Algeria: Bord de mer, BP 4008, Libreville; tel. 44-34-80; fax 44-34-81; e-mail algerie@ambassade-lbv-algerie.com; internet www.ambassade-lbv-algerie.com; Ambassador DJIHED-EDDINE BELKAS.

Angola: BP 4884, Libreville; tel. 73-04-26; fax 73-76-24; Chargé d'affaires EMÍLIO JOSÉ DE CARVAHLO GUERRA.

Benin: BP 3851, Akebe, Libreville; tel. 73-76-82; fax 73-77-75; e-mail ambassade.benin@inet.ga; internet www.maebenin.bj/Libreville.htm; Ambassador SYMPHORIEN CODJO ACHODÉ.

Brazil: blvd de l'Indépendance, BP 3899, Libreville; tel. 76-05-35; fax 74-03-43; e-mail emblibreville@inet.ga; internet libreville.itamaraty.gov.br; Ambassador BRUNO LUIZ DOS SANTOS COBUCCIO.

Cameroon: blvd Léon Mba, BP 14001, Libreville; tel. 73-28-00; Ambassador SAMUEL MVONDO AYOLO.

Central African Republic: Libreville; tel. 72-12-28; Ambassador (vacant).

China, People's Republic: blvd Triomphale Omar Bongo, BP 3914, Libreville; tel. 74-32-07; fax 74-75-96; e-mail gzy@internetgabon.com; Ambassador LI FUSHUN.

Congo, Democratic Republic: BP 2257, Libreville; tel. 74-32-53; Ambassador KABANGI KAUMBU BULA.

Congo, Republic: BP 269, Libreville; tel. 73-29-06; e-mail ambacobrazzalibreville@yahoo.fr; Ambassador EDOUARD ROGER OKOULA.

Côte d'Ivoire: Charbonnages, BP 3861, Libreville; tel. 73-82-70; fax 73-82-87; e-mail ambacigabon@yahoo.fr; Ambassador ROGER DJELLÉ GNOHITÉ.

Egypt: Immeuble Floria, 1 blvd de la Mer, Quartier Batterie IV, BP 4240, Libreville; tel. 73-25-38; fax 73-25-19; Ambassador AHMED MUHAMMAD TAHA AWAD.

Equatorial Guinea: BP 1462, Libreville; tel. 75-10-56; Ambassador JOSÉ ESONO BACALE.

France: 1 rue du pont Pirah, BP 2125, Libreville; tel. 79-70-00; fax 79-70-09; e-mail scac@ambafrance-ga.org; internet www.ambafrance-ga.org; Ambassador JEAN-DIDIER ROISIN.

Germany: blvd de l'Indépendance, Immeuble les Frangipaniers, BP 299, Libreville; tel. 76-01-88; fax 72-40-12; e-mail amb-allegmagne@inet.ga; internet www.libreville.diplo.de; Ambassador CHRISTIAN RUMPLECKER.

Guinea: BP 4046, Libreville; tel. 73-85-09; fax 73-85-11; Ambassador MOHAMED SAMPIL.

Italy: Immeuble Personnaz et Gardin, 321 rue de la Mairie, BP 2251, Libreville; tel. 74-28-92; fax 74-80-35; e-mail ambasciata.libreville@esteri.it; internet www.amblibreville.esteri.it; Ambassador RAFFAELE DE BENEDICTIS.

Japan: blvd du Bord de Mer, BP 2259, Libreville; tel. 73-22-97; fax 73-60-60; Ambassador MOTOI KATO.

Korea, Republic: BP 2620, Libreville; tel. 73-40-00; fax 73-99-05; e-mail gabon-ambcoree@mofat.go.kr; internet gab.mofat.go.kr; Ambassador KIM SEONG-JIN.

Lebanon: BP 3341, Libreville; tel. and fax 73-68-77; e-mail amb.lib.gab@inet.ga; Ambassador MICHELIN BAZ.

Mali: BP 4007, Quartier Batterie IV, Libreville; tel. 73-82-73; fax 73-82-80; e-mail ambamaga@yahoo.fr; Ambassador TRAORÉ ROKIATOU GUIKINE.

Mauritania: BP 3917, Libreville; tel. 74-31-65; fax 74-01-62; Ambassador El Hadj THIAM.

Morocco: blvd de l'Indépendance, Immeuble CK 2, BP 3983, Libreville; tel. 77-41-51; fax 77-41-50; e-mail sifamalbv@inet.ga; Ambassador ALI BOJI.

Nigeria: ave du Président Léon-M'Ba, Quartier blvd Léon-M'Ba, BP 1191, Libreville; tel. 73-22-03; fax 73-29-14; e-mail nigeriamission@internetgabon.com; Ambassador JOSEPH CHIBUZO EZEMA.

Russia: BP 3963, Libreville; tel. 72-48-69; fax 72-48-70; e-mail ambrusga@inet.ga; internet www.gabon.mid.ru; Ambassador VLADIMIR E. TARABRIN.

São Tomé and Príncipe: BP 489, Libreville; tel. 72-09-94; Ambassador URBINO JOSÉ GONHALVES BOTELÇO.

Senegal: Quartier Sobraga, BP 3856, Libreville; tel. 77-42-67; fax 77-42-68; e-mail ambasengab@yahoo.fr; Ambassador ABDOU MALAL DIOP.

South Africa: Immeuble les Arcades, 142 rue des Chavannes, BP 4063, Libreville; tel. 77-45-30; fax 77-45-36; e-mail libreville.consular@foreign.gov.za; Ambassador T. SHOPE-LINNEY.

Spain: Immeuble Diamant, 2ème étage, blvd de l'Indépendance, BP 1157, Libreville; tel. 72-12-64; fax 74-88-73; e-mail ambespga@mail.mae.es; Ambassador D. CÉSAR ALBA Y FÚSTER.

Togo: BP 14160, Libreville; tel. 73-29-04; fax 73-32-61; Ambassador ESSOHOHANAM ADEWI.

Tunisia: BP 3844, Libreville; tel. 73-28-41; Ambassador EZZEDINE KERKENI.

Ukraine: BP 23746, Libreville; tel. 44-51-03; e-mail emb_ga@mfa.gov.ua; Ambassador SERGIY MISHUSTIN.

USA: blvd du Bord de Mer, BP 4000, Libreville; tel. 76-20-03; fax 74-55-07; e-mail clolibreville@state.gov; internet libreville.usembassy.gov; Ambassador ERIC D. BENJAMINSON.

Judicial System

Justice is dispensed on behalf of the Gabonese people by the three autonomous chambers of the Supreme Court (judicial, administrative and accounting), the Constitutional Court, the Council of State, the Court of Accounts, the Courts of Appeal, the Provincial Courts, the High Court and the other special courts of law.

Supreme Court: BP 1043, Libreville; tel. 72-17-00; three chambers: judicial, administrative and accounting; Pres. BENJAMIN PAMBOU-KOMBILA.

Constitutional Court: BP 547, Libreville; tel. 76-62-88; fax 76-10-17; has jurisdiction on: the control of the constitutionality of laws before promulgation; all electoral litigations; all matters concerning individual fundamental rights and public liberties; the interpretation of the Constitution; and arbitration of conflicts of jurisdiction arising among the state's institutions; Pres. MARIE MADELEINE MBORANTSUO.

Council of State: BP 547, Libreville; tel. 72-17-00.

Courts of Appeal: Libreville and Franceville.

Court of State Security: Libreville; 13 mems; Pres. FLORENTIN ANGO.

Conseil Supérieur de la Magistrature: Libreville; Pres. (vacant); Vice-Pres. BENJAMIN PAMBOU-KOMBILA (ex officio).

Religion

About 60% of Gabon's population are Christians, mainly adherents of the Roman Catholic Church. About 40% are animists and fewer than 1% are Muslims.

CHRISTIANITY

The Roman Catholic Church

Gabon comprises one archdiocese, four dioceses and one apostolic prefecture. Some 50% of the population are Roman Catholics.

Bishops' Conference

Conférence Episcopale du Gabon, BP 2146, Libreville; tel. 72-20-73.

f. 1989; Pres. Most Rev. TIMOTHÉE MODIBO-NZOCKENA (Bishop of Franceville).

Archbishop of Libreville: Most Rev. BASILE MVÉ ENGONE, Archevêché, Sainte-Marie, BP 2146, Libreville; tel. and fax 72-20-73; e-mail basilemve@yahoo.fr.

Protestant Churches

Christian and Missionary Alliance: BP 13021, Libreville; tel. 73-24-39; e-mail fdgabon@gmail.com; active in the south of the country; Dir Dr DAVID THOMPSON; 115 org. mem. churches, 11,226 baptized mems.

Eglise Evangélique du Gabon: BP 10080, Libreville; tel. 72-41-92; f. 1842; independent since 1961; 205,000 mems; Pres. Pastor GLIÇANT ASSOUMOU EDZANG ONDO; Sec. Rev. CLÉMENT AUBAME MEZUI.

The Evangelical Church of South Gabon and the Evangelical Pentecostal Church are also active in Gabon.

The Press

Le Bûcheron: BP 6424, Libreville; tel. 72-50-20; f. 1990; weekly; official publ. of the Rassemblement pour le Gabon; Editor Désiré Ename.

Bulletin Evangélique d'Information et de Presse: BP 80, Libreville; monthly; religious.

Bulletin Mensuel de Statistique de la République Gabonaise: BP 179, Libreville; monthly; publ. by Direction Générale de l'Economie.

La Concorde: Libreville; f. 2005; owned by TV+ group; daily; Dir François Ondo Edou; circ. 10,000.

L'Economiste Gabonais: BP 3906, Libreville; quarterly; publ. by the Centre gabonais du commerce extérieur.

Gabon Libre: BP 6439, Libreville; tel. 72-42-22; weekly; Dir Dzime Ekang; Editor René Nzovi.

Gabon-Matin: BP 168, Libreville; daily; publ. by Agence Gabonaise de Presse; Man. Hilarion Vendany; circ. 18,000.

Gabon Show: Libreville; f. 2004; independent; satirical; printed in Cameroon; Man. Editor Fulbert Wora; weekly; circ. 3,000.

Gris-Gris International: Paris; f. 1990; weekly; independent; satirical; distribution forbidden in 2001; Editor-in-Chief Raphael Ntoutoume Nkoghe; Editor Michel Ongoundou.

Journal Officiel de la République Gabonaise: BP 563, Libreville; f. 1959; fortnightly; Man. Emmanuel Obamé.

Ngondo: BP 168, Libreville; monthly; publ. by Agence Gabonaise de Presse.

Le Peuple: BP 2170, Libreville; tel. 06-03-09-94 (mobile); e-mail lepeuple@lepeuple.info; internet www.lepeuple.info; f. 2002; weekly; Dir of Publication and Editor-in-Chief Augustin Mveme Obiang.

Le Progressiste: blvd Léon-M'Ba, BP 7000, Libreville; tel. 74-54-01; f. 1990; Dir Benoît Mouity Nzamba; Editor Jacques Mourende-Tsioba.

La Relance: BP 268, Libreville; tel. 72-93-08; weekly; publ. of the Parti démocratique gabonais; Pres. Jacques Adiahénot; Dir René Ndemezo'o Obiang.

Le Réveil: BP 20386, Libreville; tel. and fax 73-17-21; weekly; Man. Albert Yangari; Editor René Nzovi; circ. 8,000.

Sept Jours: BP 213, Libreville; weekly.

La Tribune des Affaires: BP 2234, Libreville; tel. 72-20-64; fax 74-12-20; monthly; publ. of the Chambre de Commerce, d'Agriculture, d'Industrie et des Mines du Gabon.

L'Union: Sonapresse, BP 3849, Libreville; tel. 73-58-61; fax 73-58-62; e-mail mpg@inet.ga; f. 1974; 75% state-owned; daily; official govt publ; Dir-Gen. Albert Yanagri; circ. 20,000.

Zoom Hebdo: Carrefour London, BP 352, Libreville; tel. 76-44-54; fax 74-67-50; e-mail zoomhebdo@assala.net; internet www.zoomhebdo.com; Friday; f. 1991; Dir-Gen. Hans Raymond Kwaaitaal; circ. 12,000–20,000.

NEWS AGENCIES

Agence Gabonaise de Presse (AGP): BP 168, Libreville; tel. 44-35-07; fax 44-35-09; internet www.agpgabon.ga; f. 1960; Dir Lin Joël Ndembet.

Association Professionnelle de la Presse Ecrite Gabonaise (APPEG): BP 3849, Libreville; internet www.gabon-presse.org.

BERP International: BP 8483, Libreville; tel. 06-06-62-91 (mobile); fax 01-77-58-81; e-mail berp8483@hotmail.com; internet www.infosplusgabon.com/berp.php3; f. 1995; Dir Antoine Lawson.

Publishers

Gabonaise d'Imprimerie (GABIMP): BP 154, Libreville; tel. 70-20-88; fax 70-31-85; e-mail gabimp@inet.ga; f. 1973; Dir Claire Vial.

Multipress Gabon: blvd Léon-M'Ba, BP 3875, Libreville; tel. 73-22-33; fax 73-63-72; e-mail mpg@inet.ga; internet multipress-gabon.com; monopoly distributors of magazines and newspapers; f. 1973; Chair. Paul Bory; Jean-Luc Phalempin.

Société Imprimerie de Gabon: BP 9626, Libreville; f. 1977; Man. Dir Akwang Rex.

Société nationale de Presse et d'Edition (SONAPRESSE): BP 3849, Libreville; tel. and fax 73-58-60; e-mail unionplus@intergabon.com; internet union.sonapresse.com; f. 1975; Man. Dir Albert Yangari.

Broadcasting and Communications

TELECOMMUNICATIONS

At the end of 2011 there were four providers of mobile cellular telephone services in Gabon, while Gabon Télécom was the sole provider of fixed-line services.

Regulatory Authority

Agence de Régulation des Télécommunications (ARTEL): Quartier Haut de Gué-Gué, face Bureau de la Francophonie, BP 50000, Libreville; tel. 44-68-11; fax 44-68-06; e-mail artel@inet.ga; internet www.artel.ga; f. 2001; regulatory authority; Pres. Lin Mombo; Dir-Gen. Serge Essongué Ewampongo.

Infrastructure and Development

Agence Nationale des Infrastructures Numériques et des Fréquences: Cours Pasteur, Immeuble de la Solde, BP 798, Libreville; tel. 79-52-77; internet www.aninf.ga; f. 2011; Dir-Gen. Alex Bernard Bongo Ondimba.

Service Providers

Airtel Gabon SA: 124 ave Bouët, Montagne Sainte, BP 9259, Libreville; tel. 07-28-01-11 (mobile); e-mail info.africa@airtel.com; internet africa.airtel.com/gabon; f. 2000; fmrly Zain Gabon, present name adopted 2010; Dir-Gen. Louis Lubala.

Gabon Télécom: Immeuble du Delta Postal, BP 20000, Libreville; tel. 78-70-00; fax 78-67-70; e-mail gabontelecom@gabontelecom.ga; f. 2001; provider of telecommunications, incl. satellite, internet and cellular systems; 51% owned by Maroc Telecom; Dir-Gen. Oussalah Lhoussaine.

Libertis: Immeuble du Delta Postal, BP 20000, Libreville; tel. 06-22-22-22 (mobile); e-mail contact@libertis.ga; internet www.libertis.ga; f. 1999; mobile cellular telephone operator; Dir-Gen. Mostapha Laarabi; 250,000 subscribers in 2006.

Moov Gabon: Immeuble Rénovation, bvld du Bord de Mer, BP 12470, Libreville; tel. 76-83-83; fax 76-83-88; internet www.moov.ga; f. 2000; Dir-Gen. Frédéric Feraille.

USAN Gabon: Libreville; e-mail info@azur-gabon.com; internet www.azur-gabon.com; f. 2009; provides mobile cellular services under Azur network; Dir-Gen. Bruno Valat.

BROADCASTING

Conseil National de la Communication: BP 6437, Libreville; tel. 72-82-60; fax 72-82-71; e-mail infos@cnc.ga; f. 1991; Pres. Jean Ovono Essono.

Radio

The national network, 'La Voix de la Rénovation', and a provincial network broadcast for 24 hours each day in French and local languages.

Africa No. 1: BP 1, Libreville; tel. 74-07-34; fax 74-21-33; e-mail africaradio1@yahoo.fr; internet www.africa1.com; f. 1981; 35% state-controlled; int. commercial radio station; daily programmes in French and English; Pres. Elmahjour Ammar Gomaa; Sec.-Gen. Louis Barthélemy Mapangou.

Radiodiffusion-Télévision Gabonaise (RTG): BP 150, Libreville; tel. 73-20-25; fax 73-21-53; internet www.rtg1.ga; f. 1959; state-controlled; broadcasts two channels RTG1 and RTG2; Dir-Gen. (RTG1) David Ella Mintsa; Dir-Gen. (RTG2) Florence Mbani; Dir of Radio Gilles Terence Nzoghe.

Radio Fréquence 3: f. 1996.

Radio Génération Nouvelle: f. 1996; Dir Jean-Boniface Assele.

Radio Mandarine: f. 1995.

Radio Soleil: f. 1995; affiliated to Rassemblement pour le Gabon.

Radio Unité: f. 1996.

Television

Radiodiffusion-Télévision Gabonaise (RTG): see Radio.

Radio Télévision Nazareth (RTN): BP 9563, Libreville; tel. 76-82-58; fax 72-20-44; e-mail rtntv@yahoo.fr; Pres. and Dir-Gen. Georges Bruno Ngoussi.

Télé-Africa: BP 4269, Libreville; tel. 72-49-22; fax 76-16-83; f. 1985; private channel; daily broadcasts in French.

Télédiffusion du Gabon: f. 1995.

TV Sat (Société de Télécommunications Audio-Visuelles): Immeuble TV SAT BP 184, Libreville; tel. 72-49-22; fax 76-16-83; f. 1994.

TV+: Immeuble Dumez, Bord de mer, BP 8344, Libreville; operation suspended in Jan. 2012; Owner André Mba Obame.

Finance

(cap. = capital; res = reserves; dep. = deposits; m. = million; brs = branches; amounts in francs CFA)

BANKING

In 2008 there were five commercial banks and four other financial institutions in Gabon.

Central Bank

Banque des Etats de l'Afrique Centrale (BEAC): BP 112, Libreville; tel. 76-13-52; fax 74-45-63; e-mail beaclbv@beac.int; internet www.beac.int; HQ in Yaoundé, Cameroon; f. 1973; bank of issue for mem. states of the Communauté économique et monétaire de l'Afrique centrale (CEMAC, fmrly Union douanière et économique de l'Afrique centrale), comprising Cameroon, the Central African Repub., Chad, the Repub. of the Congo, Equatorial Guinea and Gabon; cap. 88,000m., res 227,843m., dep. 4,110,966m. (Dec. 2007); Gov. LUCAS ABAGA NCHAMA; Dir in Gabon DENIS MEPOREWA; 4 brs in Gabon.

Commercial Banks

Banque Internationale pour le Commerce et l'Industrie du Gabon, SA (BICIG): ave du Colonel Parant, BP 2241, Libreville; tel. 76-26-13; fax 74-40-34; e-mail bicigdoi@inet.ga; internet bicig-gabon.com; f. 1973; 26.30% state-owned, 46.67% owned by BNP Paribas SA; cap. 18,000m., res 8,495m., dep. 310,220m., (Dec. 2009); Pres. ETIENNE GUY MOUVAGHA TCHIOBA; Dir-Gen. CLAUDE AYO-IGUENDHA; 9 brs.

Banque Internationale pour le Gabon: Immeuble Concorde, blvd de l'Indépendance, BP 106, Libreville; tel. 76-26-26; fax 76-20-53.

BGFI Bank: blvd de l'Indépendence, BP 2253, Libreville; tel. 76-40-35; fax 74-08-94; e-mail agence_libreville@bgfi.com; internet www.bgfi.com; f. 1972 as Banque Gabonaise et Française Internationale (BGFI); name changed as above in March 2000; 8% state-owned; cap. 25,065.4m., res 32,117.8m., dep. 349,064.6m. (Dec. 2006); Chair. PATRICE OTHA; Gen. Man. HENRI-CLAUDE OYIMA; 3 brs.

Citibank: 810 blvd Quaben, rue Kringer, BP 3940, Libreville; tel. 73-19-16; fax 73-37-86; total assets 1,000m. (Dec. 2004); Dir-Gen. FUNMI ADE AJAYI; Dep. Dir-Gen. JULIETTE WEISTFLOG.

Financial Bank Gabon: Immeuble des Frangipaniers, blvd de l'Indépendance, BP 20333, Libreville; tel. 77-50-78; fax 72-41-97; e-mail financial.gabon@financial-bank.com; internet www.orabank.net; f. 2002; cap. 1,250m., res –394.3m., dep. 21,594.9m. (Dec. 2006); 85.47% owned by Oragroup SA (Togo); Pres. RENÉ-HILAIRE ADIAHENO; Dir-Gen. MAMOUDOU KANE.

Union Gabonaise de Banque, SA (UGB): ave du Colonel Parant, BP 315, Libreville; tel. 77-70-00; fax 76-46-16; e-mail ugbdio@internetgabon.com; internet ugb-interactif.com; f. 1962; 25% state-owned, 56.25% owned by Crédit Lyonnais (France); cap. 7,400.0m., res 10,281.5m., dep. 215,799.1m. (Dec. 2009); Chair. MARCEL DOUPAMBY-MATOKA; Man. Dir REDOUNE BENNIS; 4 brs.

Development Banks

Banque Gabonaise de Développement (BGD): rue Alfred Marche, BP 5, Libreville; tel. 76-24-29; fax 74-26-99; e-mail infos@bgd-gabon.com; internet www.bgd-gabon.com; f. 1960; 69.01% state-owned; cap. 25,200m., res 7,677m. (Dec. 2006); Dir-Gen. ROGER MBA.

Banque Nationale de Crédit Rural (BNCR): ave Bouet, BP 1120, Libreville; tel. 72-47-42; fax 74-05-07; f. 1986; 74% state-owned; under enforced administration since March 2002; total assets 5,601m. (Dec. 2000); Pres. GÉRARD MEYO M'EMANE; Man. JOSEPH KOYAGBELE.

Banque Populaire du Gabon: 413 blvd de l'Indépendance, BP 6663, Libreville; tel. 72-86-89; fax 72-86-91.

BICI-Bail Gabon: Immeuble BICIG, 5ème étage, ave du Colonel Parant, BP 2241, Libreville; tel. 77-75-52; fax 77-48-15; internet www.bicig.ga/bicibail.htm; BNP Paribas-owned.

Société Financière Transafricaine (FINATRA): blvd de l'Indépendance, BP 8645, Libreville; tel. and fax 77-40-87; e-mail finatra@bgfi.com; internet www.bgfi.com; f. 1997; 50% owned by BGFI Bank; cap. 2,000m., total assets 14,613m. (Dec. 2003); Dir-Gen. MARIE CÉLINE NTSAME-MEZUI.

Société Gabonaise de Crédit Automobile (SOGACA): Immeuble SOGACA, BP 63, Libreville; tel. 76-08-46; fax 76-01-03; car finance; 43% owned by CFAO Gabon, 10% state-owned; cap. and res 2,828.0m., total assets 18,583.0m. (Dec. 2003); Pres. M. LAPLAGNOLLE; Dir-Gen. THIERRY PAPILLION.

Société Gabonaise de Crédit-Bail (SOGABAIL): Immeuble SOGACA, BP 63, Libreville; tel. 77-25-73; fax 76-01-03; e-mail sogaca@assala.net; 25% owned by CFAO Gabon, 14% state-owned; cap. and res 2,980.4m., total assets 4,123.2m.; Pres. M. LAPLAGNOLLE; Dir-Gen. THIERRY PAPILLON.

Société Nationale d'Investissement du Gabon (SONADIG): BP 479, Libreville; tel. 72-09-22; fax 74-81-70; f. 1968; state-owned; cap. 500m.; Pres. ANTOINE OYIEYE; Dir-Gen. NARCISSE MASSALA TSAMBA.

Financial Institution

Caisse Autonome d'Amortissement du Gabon: BP 912, Libreville; tel. 74-41-43; management of state funds; Dir-Gen. MAURICE EYAMBA TSIMAT.

INSURANCE

Agence Gabonaise d'Assurance et de Réassurance (AGAR): BP 1699, Libreville; tel. 74-02-22; fax 76-59-25; f. 1987; Dir-Gen. ANGE GOULOUMES.

Assinco: BP 7812, Libreville; tel. 72-19-25; fax 72-19-29; e-mail assinco@assinco-sa.com; internet assinco-sa.com; Dir EUGÉNIE DENDÉ.

Assureurs Conseils Franco-Africains du Gabon (ACFRA-GABON): BP 1116, Libreville; tel. 72-32-83; Chair. FRÉDÉRIC MARRON; Dir M. GARNIER.

Assureurs Conseils Gabonais (ACG): Immeuble Shell-Gabon, rue de la Mairie, BP 2138, Libreville; tel. 74-32-90; fax 76-04-39; e-mail acg@ascoma.com; represents foreign insurance cos; Dir MICHELLE VALETTE.

Axa Assurances Gabon: BP 4047, Libreville; tel. 79-80-80; fax 74-14-46; e-mail axa-assurances@axa-gabon.ga; internet www.axa.com; Dir JOËL MULLER.

Commercial Union: Libreville; tel. 76-43-00; Exec. Dir M. MILAN.

Fédération gabonaise des assureurs (FEGASA): BP 4005, Libreville; tel. 74-45-29; fax 77-58-23; Pres. JACQUES AMVAMÉ.

Gras Savoye Gabon: ave du Colonel Parant, BP 2148, Libreville; tel. 74-31-53; fax 74-68-38; e-mail contact@ga.grassavoye.com; internet www.ga.grassavoye.com; Dir CHRISTOPHE ROUDAUT.

Groupement Gabonais d'Assurances et de Réassurances (GGAR): Libreville; tel. 74-28-72; f. 1985; Chair. RASSAGUIZA AKEREY; Dir-Gen. DENISE OMBAGHO.

NSIA Gabon: Résidence les Frangipaniers, Blvd de l'Indépendance, BP 2221–2225, Libreville; tel. 72-13-90; fax 74-17-02; e-mail nsiagabon@groupensia.com; internet www.nsiagabon.com; f. 2000 by acquisition of Assurances Mutuelles du Gabon; name changed as above in 2006; owned by NSIA Participations S.A. Holding (Côte d'Ivoire); Dir-Gen. CÉSAR EKOMIE-AFENE.

Société Nationale Gabonaise d'Assurances et de Réassurances (SONAGAR): ave du Colonel Parant, BP 3082, Libreville; tel. 72-28-97; f. 1974; owned by l'Union des Assurances de Paris (France); Dir-Gen. JEAN-LOUIS MESSAN.

SOGERCO-Gabon: BP 2102, Libreville; tel. 76-09-34; f. 1975; general; Dir M. RABEAU.

Union des Assurances du Gabon-Vie (UAG-Vie): ave du Colonel Parant, BP 2137, Libreville; tel. 74-34-34; fax 72-48-57; e-mail uagvie@uagvie.com; internet www.sunu-group.com; life insurance; 80.65% owned by Groupe SUNU; Pres. ALBERT ALEWINA CHAVIHOT; Dir-Gen. APOLLINAIRE EVA ESSANGONE.

Trade and Industry

GOVERNMENT AGENCIES

Conseil Economique et Social du Gabon: BP 1075, Libreville; tel. 73-19-46; fax 73-19-44; comprises representatives from salaried workers, employers and Govt; commissions on economic, financial and social affairs, and forestry and agriculture; Pres. ANTOINE DE PADOUE MBOUMBOU MIYAKOU.

Agence de Promotion des Investissements Privés (APIP): BP 13740, Front de Mer, Libreville; tel. 76-87-65; fax 76-87-64; e-mail apip@netcourrier.com; internet www.invest-gabon.com; f. 2002; promotes private investment; Dir-Gen. LÉON PAUL NGOULAKIA.

Fonds Gabonais d'Investissement Stratégique: Libreville; f. 2010; Pres. CLAUDE AYO INGUENDA; SERGE THIERRY MICKOTO CHAVAGNE.

DEVELOPMENT ORGANIZATIONS

Agence Française de Développement (AFD): blvd de l'Indépendance, BP 64, Libreville; tel. 74-33-74; fax 74-51-25; e-mail afdlibreville@groupe-afd.org; internet www.afd.fr; fmrly Caisse Française de Développement; Dir FRANÇOIS PARMANTIER.

Agence Nationale des Grands Travaux (ANGT): Immeuble du bord de mer, 1er étage, à côté de l'ancien gouvernorat, BP 23765,

Libreville; tel. 07-04-62-77 (mobile); e-mail info@angtmedia.com; f. 2010; Dir-Gen. HENRI OHAYON.

Agence Nationale de Promotion de la Petite et Moyenne Entreprise (PromoGabon): BP 2111, Libreville; tel. 06-26-79-19 (mobile); fax 74-89-59; f. 1964; state-controlled; promotes and assists small and medium-sized industries; Pres. SIMON BOULAMATARI; Man. Dir GEORGETTE ONGALA.

Agence de Régulation du Marché des Produits Forestiers: Libreville; Dir-Gen. PIERRE NGAVOURA.

Centre Gabonais de Commerce Extérieur (CGCE): Immeuble Rénovation, 3ème étage, BP 3906, Libreville; tel. 72-11-67; fax 74-71-53; promotes foreign trade and investment in Gabon; Gen. Dir PIERRE SOCKAT.

Commerce et Développement (CODEV): BP 2142, Libreville; tel. 76-06-73; f. 1976; 95% state-owned; import and distribution of capital goods and food products; Chair. and Man. Dir JÉRÔME NGOUA-BEKALE.

Conservation et Utilisation Rationelle des Ecosystèmes Forestiers en Afrique Centrale (ECOFAC): BP 15115, Libreville; tel. 73-23-43; fax 73-23-45; e-mail coordination@ecofac.org; internet www.ecofac.org.

Fonds de Garantie pour le Logement (FGL): Libreville; f. 2011.

Groupes d'Etudes et de Recherches sur la Démocratie et le Développement Economique et Social au Gabon (GERDDES-Gabon): BP 13114, Libreville; tel. 06-25-14-38 (mobile); fax 07-38-04-20 (mobile); e-mail gerddesgabon@yahoo.fr; internet gerddes-gabon.asso-web.com; f. 1991; Pres. MARYVONNE C. NTSAME NDONG.

Institut Gabonais d'Appui au Développement (IGAD): BP 20423, Libreville; tel. and fax 74-52-47; e-mail igad@inet.ga; f. 1992; Dir-Gen. CHRISTIAN RENARDET.

Office Gabonais d'Amélioration et de Production de Viande (OGAPROV): BP 245, Moanda; tel. 66-12-67; f. 1971; devt of private cattle farming; manages ranch at Lekedi-Sud; Pres. PAUL KOUNDA KIKI; Dir-Gen. VEYRANT OMBÉ EPIGAT.

Palmiers et Hévéas du Gabon (PALMEVEAS): BP 75, Libreville; f. 1956; state-owned; palm-oil devt.

Programme Régionale de Gestion de l'Information Environnementale en Afrique Centrale (PRGIE): BP 4080, Libreville; tel. 76-30-19; fax 77-42-61; e-mail urge@adie-prgie.org; internet www.adie-prgie.org.

Société de Développement de l'Agriculture au Gabon (AGROGABON): BP 2248, Libreville; tel. 76-40-82; fax 76-44-72; f. 1976; 93% state-owned; acquired by the Société Industrielle Agricole du Tabac Tropical in April 2004; Man. Dir ANDRÉ PAUL-APANDINA.

Société de Développement de l'Hévéaculture (HEVEGAB): BP 316, Libreville; tel. 72-08-29; fax 72-08-30; f. 1981; acquired by the Société Industrielle Agricole du Tabac Tropical in April 2004; devt of rubber plantations in the Mitzic, Bitam and Kango regions; Chair. FRANÇOIS OWONO-NGUEMA; Man. Dir JANVIER ESSONO-ASSOUMOU.

Société Gabonaise de Recherches et d'Exploitations Minières (SOGAREM): Libreville; state-owned; research and devt of gold mining; Chair. ARSÈNE BOUNGUENZA; Man. Dir SERGE GASSITA.

Société Gabonaise de Recherches Pétrolières (GABOREP): BP 564, Libreville; tel. 75-06-40; fax 75-06-47; exploration and exploitation of hydrocarbons; Chair. HUBERT PERRODO; Man. Dir P. F. LECA.

Société Nationale de Développement des Cultures Industrielles (SONADECI): Libreville; tel. 76-33-97; f. 1978; state-owned; agricultural devt; Chair. PAUL KOUNDA KIKI; Man. Dir GEORGES BEKALÉ.

CHAMBER OF COMMERCE

Chambre de Commerce, d'Agriculture, d'Industrie et des Mines du Gabon: BP 2234, Libreville; tel. 72-20-64; fax 74-12-20; f. 1935; regional offices at Port-Gentil and Franceville; Pres. JEAN BAPTISTE BIKALOU; Sec.-Gen. LIN-FRANÇOIS MADJOUPAL.

EMPLOYERS' ORGANIZATIONS

Confédération Patronale Gabonaise: Immeuble les Frangipaniers, blvd de l'Indépendence, BP 410, Libreville; tel. 76-02-43; fax 74-86-52; e-mail infocpg@patronatgabonais.ga; internet www.confederation-patronale-gabonaise.org; f. 1959; represents industrial, mining, petroleum, public works, forestry, banking, insurance, commercial and shipping interests; Pres. HENRI-CLAUDE OYIMA; Sec.-Gen. CHRISTIANE QUINIO.

Syndicat des Entreprises Minières du Gabon (SYNDIMINES): BP 260, Libreville; Pres. ANDRÉ BERRE; Sec.-Gen. SERGE GREGOIRE.

Syndicat des Importateurs Exportateurs du Gabon (SIMPEX): Libreville; Pres. ALBERT JEAN; Sec.-Gen. R. TYBERGHEIN.

Syndicat des Industries du Gabon: BP 2175, Libreville; tel. 72-02-29; fax 74-52-13; e-mail sociga@ga.imptob.com; Pres. JACQUES-YVES LAUGE.

Syndicat des Producteurs et Industriels du Bois du Gabon: BP 84, Libreville; tel. 72-26-11; fax 77-44-43.

Syndicat Professionnel des Usines de Sciages et Placages du Gabon: Port-Gentil; f. 1956; Pres. PIERRE BERRY.

Union des Représentations Automobiles et Industrielles (URAI): BP 1743, Libreville; Pres. M. MARTINENT; Sec. R. TYBERGHEIN.

Union Nationale du Patronat Syndical des Transports Urbains, Routiers et Fluviaux du Gabon (UNAPASY-TRUFGA): BP 1025, Libreville; f. 1977; represents manufacturers of vehicle and construction parts; Pres. LAURENT BELLAL BIBANG-BI-EDZO; Sec.-Gen. AUGUSTIN KASSA-NZIGOU.

UTILITIES

Société d'Energie et d'Eau du Gabon (SEEG): BP 2187, Libreville; tel. 76-78-07; fax 76-11-34; e-mail laroche.lbv@inet.ga; internet www.seeg-gabon.com; f. 1950; 51% owned by Vivendi (France); controls 35 electricity generation and distribution centres and 32 water production and distribution centres; Pres. and Dir-Gen. FRANÇOIS OMBANDA.

TRADE UNIONS

Confédération Gabonaise des Syndicats Libres (CGSL): BP 8067, Libreville; tel. 77-37-82; fax 74-45-25; e-mail c.libres@voila.fr; f. 1991; Sec.-Gen. FRANCIS ETIENNE MAYOMBO; 19,000 mems (2007).

Confédération Syndicale Gabonaise (COSYGA): BP 14017, Libreville; tel. 06-68-07-26 (mobile); fax 74-21-70; e-mail mintsacosyga@yahoo.fr; f. 1969 by the Govt, as a specialized organ of the PDG, to organize and educate workers, to contribute to social peace and economic devt, and to protect the rights of trade unions; Gen. Sec. MARTIN ALLINI; 14,610 mems (2007).

Organisation Nationale des Employés du Pétrole (ONEP): Libreville; Sec.-Gen. GUY ROGER AURAT RETENO.

Transport

RAILWAYS

The construction of the Transgabonais railway, which comprises a section running from Owendo (the port of Libreville) to Booué (340 km) and a second section from Booué to Franceville (357 km), was completed in 1986. By 1989 regular services were operating between Libreville and Franceville. Some 2.9m. metric tons of freight and 215,000 passengers were carried on the network in 1999, which in that year totalled 814 km. In 1998 the railways were transferred to private management.

Société d'Exploration du Chemin de Fer Transgabonais (SETRAG): BP 578, Libreville; tel. 70-24-78; fax 70-20-38; operates Transgabonais railway; 84% owned by COMILOG; Chair. MARCEL ABEKE.

ROADS

In 2004 there were an estimated 9,170 km of roads, including 2,793 km of main roads and 6,377 km of secondary roads; about 10.2% of the road network was paved.

AGS Frasers: BP 9161, Libreville; tel. 70-23-16; fax 70-41-56; e-mail direction-gabon@ags-demenagement.com; internet www.agsfrasers.com; Man. BERNARD DURET.

APRETRAC: BP 4542, Libreville; tel. 72-84-93; fax 74-40-45; e-mail apretrac@assala.net; Dir CHRISTOPHE DISSOU.

A.R.T.: BP 9391, Libreville; tel. 70-57-26; fax 70-57-28; freight; Dir-Gen. PHILIPPE BERGON.

Compagnie Internationale de Déménagement Transit (CIDT): BP 986, Libreville; tel. 76-44-44; fax 76-44-55; e-mail cidg@internetgabon.com; Dir THIERRY CARBONIE.

Fonds d'Entretien Routier–Deuxième Génération (FER 2): Galerie des Jardins d'Ambre, BP 16201, Libreville; tel. 76-93-90; fax 76-93-96; e-mail info@fer-gabon.org; internet www.fer-gabon.org; f. 1993; Pres. RAPHAËL MAMIAKA; Dir-Gen. LANDRY PATRICK OYAYA.

GETMA Gabon: BP 7510, Libreville; tel. 70-28-14; fax 70-40-20; e-mail claude.barone@assala.net; Dir CLAUDE BARONE.

Trans form: BP 7538, Libreville; tel. 70-43-95; fax 70-21-91; e-mail transformgab@yahoo.fr; f. 1995; Dir JEAN-PIERRE POULAIN.

Transitex: BP 20323, Libreville; tel. 77-84-26; fax 77-84-35; e-mail helenepedemonte@transitex.ga; freight; Man. FRÉDÉRIC GONZALEZ.

INLAND WATERWAYS

The principal river is the Ogooué, navigable from Port-Gentil to Ndjolé (310 km) and serving the towns of Lambaréné, Ndjolé and Sindara.

Compagnie de Navigation Intérieure (CNI): BP 3982, Libreville; tel. 72-39-28; fax 74-04-11; f. 1978; scheduled for privatization; responsible for inland waterway transport; agencies at Port-Gentil, Mayumba and Lambaréné; Chair. JEAN-PIERRE MENGWANG ME NGYEMA; Dir-Gen. FRANÇOIS OYABI.

SHIPPING

The principal deep-water ports are Port-Gentil, which handles mainly petroleum exports, Owendo, 15 km from Libreville, which services mainly barge traffic, and Mayumba. The main ports for timber are at Owendo, Mayumba and Nyanga, and there is a fishing port at Libreville. A new terminal for the export of minerals, at Owendo, was opened in 1988. In 2009 the merchant shipping fleet numbered 50 and had a total displacement of 14,400 grt.

Compagnie de Manutention et de Chalandage d'Owendo (COMACO): BP 2131, Libreville; tel. 70-26-35; f. 1974; Pres. GEORGES RAWIRI; Dir in Libreville M. RAYMOND.

Office des Ports et Rades du Gabon (OPRAG): Owendo, BP 1051, Libreville; tel. 70-00-48; fax 70-37-35; e-mail info@ports-gabon.com; internet ports-gabon.com; f. 1974; 25-year management concession acquired in April 2004 by the Spanish PIP group; national port authority; Pres. ALI BONGO; Dir-Gen. RIGOBERT IKAMBOUAYAT NDÉKA.

SAGA Gabon: Zone OPRAG, BP 518, Port-Gentil; tel. 55-58-19; fax 55-21-71; e-mail sagalbv@internetgabon.com; internet www.saga.fr; Chair. G. COGNON; Man. Dir DANIEL FERNÁNDEZ.

SDV Gabon: Zone Portuaire d'Owendo, BP 77, Libreville; tel. 70-26-36; fax 70-23-34; e-mail shipping.lbv@ga.dti.bollore.com; internet www.sdv.com; freight by land, sea and air.

Société Nationale d'Acconage et de Transit (SNAT): BP 3897, Libreville; tel. 70-04-04; fax 70-13-11; e-mail snat.direction@ga.dti.bollore.com; freight transport and stevedoring; Dir-Gen. MARC GÉRARD.

Société Nationale de Transports Maritimes (SONATRAM): BP 3841, Libreville; tel. 74-44-04; fax 74-59-87; f. 1976; relaunched 1995; 51% state-owned; river and ocean cargo transport; Man. Dir RAPHAEL MOARA WALLA.

SOCOPAO–Gabon: Immeuble Socapao, Zone Portuaire d'Owendo, BP 4, Libreville; tel. 02-56-09-13; fax 02-55-45-43; e-mail socopaolibreville@vpila.fr; f. 1983; freight transport and storage; Dir DANIEL BECQUERELLE.

CIVIL AVIATION

There are international airports at Libreville, Port-Gentil and Franceville, and 65 other public and 50 private airfields, linked mostly with the forestry and petroleum industries.

Agence Nationale de l'Aviation Civile (ANAC): BP 2212, Libreville; e-mail anac@anac-gabon.com; internet www.anac.ga; f. 2008; Pres. EMMANUEL NZÉ-BÉKALÉ; Dir-Gen. DOMINIQUE OYINAMONO.

Air Service Gabon (ASG): BP 2232, Libreville; tel. 73-24-08; fax 73-60-69; e-mail reservation@airservice.aero; internet www.airservice.aero; f. 1965; charter flights; Chair. JEAN-LUC CHEVRIER; Gen. Man. FRANÇOIS LASCOMBES.

Gabon Airlines SA: Aéroport International Léon M'ba, BP 12913, Libreville; tel. 72-02-02; internet www.gabonairlines.com; f. 2006; internal and international cargo and passenger services; Pres. and Dir-Gen. ANDRÉ GIACOMINI.

Gabon Fret: BP 20384, Libreville; tel. 73-20-69; fax 73-44-44; e-mail gabonfret.gf@gabonfret.com; internet www.gabonfret.com; f. 1995; air freight handlers; Dir DOMINIQUE OYINAMONO.

Nouvelle Air Affaires Gabon: BP 3962, Libreville; tel. 73-25-13; fax 73-49-98; e-mail online@sn2ag.com; internet www.sn2ag.com; f. 1975; domestic passenger chartered and scheduled flights, and medical evacuation; Chair. HERMINE BONGO ONDIMBA.

Société de Gestion de l'Aéroport de Libreville (ADL): BP 363, Libreville; tel. 73-62-44; fax 73-61-28; e-mail dg@adlgabon.com; internet www.adlgabon.com; f. 1988; 26.5% state-owned; management of airport at Libreville; Pres. CHANTAL LIDJI BADINGA; Dir-Gen. JEAN-MARC SANSOVINI.

Tourism

Tourist arrivals were estimated at 222,257 in 2003, and receipts from tourism totalled US $13m. in 2005. The tourism sector is being extensively developed, with new hotels and associated projects and the promotion of national parks.

Centre Gabonais de Promotion Touristique (GABONTOUR): 622 ave du Colonel Parant, BP 2085, Libreville; tel. 72-85-04; fax 72-85-03; e-mail accueil@gabontour.ga; internet www.gabontour.ga; f. 1988; Dir-Gen. ALBERT ENGONGA BIKORO.

Office National Gabonais du Tourisme: BP 161, Libreville; tel. 72-21-82.

Defence

As assessed at November 2011, the army consisted of 3,200 men, the air force of 1,000 men and the navy of an estimated 500 men. Paramilitary forces (gendarmerie) numbered 2,000. Military service is voluntary. France maintains a detachment of 762 troops in Gabon.

Defence Expenditure: Budgeted at an estimated 125,000m. francs CFA for 2011.

Commander-in-Chief of the Armed Forces: Gen. JEAN-CLAUDE ELLA EKOGHA.

Education

Education is officially compulsory and free of charge for 10 years between six and 16 years of age. According to UNESCO estimates, in 2000/01 80% of children in the relevant age-group (81% of boys; 80% of girls) attended primary schools, while in 2001/02 enrolment at secondary schools was equivalent to 53% of children in the relevant age-group. Primary and secondary education is provided by the State and mission schools. Primary education begins at the age of six and lasts for five years. Secondary education, beginning at 12 years of age, lasts for up to seven years, comprising a first cycle of four years and a second of three years. The Université Omar Bongo is based at Libreville and the Université des Sciences et des Techniques de Masuku at Franceville. In 1998 7,473 students were enrolled at institutions providing tertiary education. Many students go to France for university and technical training. In 2000 spending on education represented 3.8% of total budgetary expenditure.

THE GAMBIA

Introductory Survey

LOCATION, CLIMATE, LANGUAGE, RELIGION, FLAG, CAPITAL

The Republic of The Gambia is a narrow territory around the River Gambia on the west coast of Africa. Apart from a short coastline on the Atlantic Ocean, the country is a semi-enclave in Senegal. The climate is tropical, with a rainy season from July to September. Away from the river swamps most of the terrain is covered by savannah bush. Average temperatures in Banjul range from 23°C (73°F) in January to 27°C (81°F) in July, while temperatures inland can exceed 40°C (104°F). English is the official language, while the principal vernacular languages are Mandinka, Fula and Wolof. About 85% of the inhabitants are Muslims; most of the remainder are Christians, and there are a small number of animists. The national flag (proportions 2 by 3) has red, blue and green horizontal stripes, with two narrow white stripes bordering the central blue band. The capital is Banjul.

CONTEMPORARY POLITICAL HISTORY

Historical Context

Formerly administered with Sierra Leone, The Gambia became a separate British colony in 1888. Party politics rapidly gained momentum following the establishment of a universal adult franchise in 1960. Following legislative elections in May 1962, the leader of the People's Progressive Party (PPP), Dr (later Sir) Dawda Kairaba Jawara, became Premier. Full internal self-government followed in October 1963. On 18 February 1965 The Gambia became an independent country within the Commonwealth, with Jawara as Prime Minister. The country became a republic on 24 April 1970, whereupon Jawara took office as President. He was re-elected in 1972 and again in 1977.

The first presidential election by direct popular vote was held in May 1982. Jawara, who was opposed by the leader of the National Convention Party (NCP), Sheriff Mustapha Dibba, was re-elected, with 72% of the votes cast. In the concurrent legislative elections the PPP won 27 of the 35 elective seats in the House of Representatives. At legislative elections in March 1987 the PPP took 31 of the 36 directly elected seats in the House of Representatives. In the presidential election Jawara was re-elected with 59% of the votes cast; Dibba received 27% of the votes, and Assan Musa Camara, a former Vice-President who had recently formed the Gambian People's Party (GPP), won 14%. Rumours of financial impropriety, corruption and the abuse of power at ministerial level persisted throughout the decade.

Plans were announced in August 1981 for a confederation of The Gambia and Senegal, to be called Senegambia. The confederal agreement came into effect in February 1982; a Confederal Council of Ministers, headed by President Abdou Diouf of Senegal (with President Jawara as his deputy), held its inaugural meeting in January 1983, as did a 60-member Confederal Assembly. However, the confederation was dissolved in September, and a period of tension between the two countries followed: The Gambia alleged that the Senegalese authorities had introduced trade and travel restrictions, while Senegal accused The Gambia of harbouring rebels of the Mouvement des forces démocratiques de la Casamance (MFDC), an organization seeking independence for the Casamance region—which is virtually separated from the northern segment of Senegal by the enclave of The Gambia. In January 1991 the two countries signed an agreement of friendship and co-operation.

Jawara was elected for a sixth time in April 1992, receiving 58% of the votes cast, while Dibba took 22%. In elections to the House of Representatives the PPP retained a clear majority, with 25 elected members. The NCP secured six seats, the GPP two and independent candidates the remaining three.

Domestic Political Affairs

On 22 July 1994 Jawara was deposed by a self-styled Armed Forces Provisional Ruling Council (AFPRC), a group of five young army officers led by Lt (later Col) Yahya Jammeh, in a bloodless coup. The AFPRC suspended the Constitution and banned all political activity. Jammeh pronounced himself Head of State and appointed a mixed civilian and military Government. Purges of the armed forces and public institutions were implemented, and in November it was announced that 10 of Jawara's former ministers would be tried on charges of corruption.

The AFPRC's timetable for a transition to civilian rule, published in October 1994, envisaged a programme of reform culminating in the inauguration of new elected institutions in December 1998. The length of the transition period prompted criticism both internationally and domestically. In November 1994 Jammeh commissioned a National Consultative Committee (NCC) to make recommendations regarding a possible shortening of the period of transition to civilian rule; the NCC proposed a return to civilian government in 1996.

The draft of a report by a Constitutional Review Commission (established in April 1995) was published in March 1996. Opponents of the AFPRC criticized provisions of the Constitution that, they alleged, had been formulated with the specific intention of facilitating Jammeh's election to the presidency (although the Head of State had frequently asserted that he would not seek election).

The constitutional referendum took place on 8 August 1996. The rate of participation was high (85.9%), and 70.4% of voters endorsed the new document. A presidential decree was issued in the following week reauthorizing party political activity. Shortly afterwards, however, a further decree (Decree 89) was promulgated, according to which all holders of executive office in the 30 years prior to July 1994 were to be prohibited from seeking public office, with the PPP, the NCP and the GPP barred from contesting the forthcoming presidential and parliamentary elections. Thus, the only parties from the Jawara era authorized to contest the elections were the People's Democratic Organization for Independence and Socialism (PDOIS) and the People's Democratic Party. The effective ban on the participation of all those associated with political life prior to the military take-over in the restoration of elected institutions was strongly criticized by the Commonwealth Ministerial Action Group on the Harare Declaration (CMAG, see p. 240), which had hitherto made a significant contribution to the transition process.

In August 1996 the establishment of a political party supporting Jammeh, the Alliance for Patriotic Reorientation and Construction (APRC), was reported. In early September Jammeh resigned from the army, in order to contest the presidency as a civilian, as required by the Constitution. According to official results of the presidential election held on 26 September, Jammeh secured the presidency with 55.8% of the votes cast, ahead of Ousainou Darboe, the leader of the United Democratic Party (UDP), who received 35.8%. The rate of participation by voters was again high, especially in rural areas, although observers, including CMAG, expressed doubts as to the credibility of the election results. The dissolution of the AFPRC was announced the same day. Jammeh was inaugurated as President on 18 October.

Legislative elections took place on 2 January 1997 and the Gambian authorities, opposition groups and most international observers expressed broad satisfaction at the conduct of the poll. The APRC won an overwhelming majority of seats, securing 33 elective seats (including five in which the party was unopposed). The UDP obtained seven elective seats, the National Reconciliation Party (NRP) two, the PDOIS one and independent candidates two. The overall rate of participation by voters was 73.2%. As Head of State, Jammeh was empowered by the Constitution to nominate four additional members of parliament, from whom the Speaker and Deputy Speaker would be chosen. The opening session of the National Assembly, on 16 January, denoted the full entry into force of the Constitution and thus the inauguration of the Second Republic. Under the new Constitution, ministers of cabinet rank were designated Secretaries of State, and the Government was reorganized to this effect in March.

In May 2001 the National Assembly and the President approved a number of constitutional amendments, which were to be submitted to a referendum. The opposition protested that the proposed changes, including the extension of the presidential term from five to seven years, the introduction of a presidential prerogative to appoint local chiefs, and the replacement of the permanent Independent Election Commission (IEC) with an ad hoc body, would further increase the powers of the President and precipitate acts of electoral fraud at the forthcoming parliamentary and presidential elections.

The 2001 presidential election

In July 2001 Jammeh announced the abrogation of Decree 89, although several prominent individuals who had participated in pre-1994 administrations, including Jawara and Sabally, remained prohibited from seeking public office. None the less, the PPP, the NCP and the GPP were subsequently re-established. In August the UDP, the PPP and the GPP formed a coalition and announced that Darboe would be its presidential candidate in the election scheduled for October.

A number of violent incidents were reported during the week before the presidential election. Nevertheless, the presidential election was held, as scheduled, on 18 October 2001. Jammeh was re-elected to the presidency, with 52.8% of the votes cast, according to official results, ahead of Darboe, who won 32.6% of the votes. Although Darboe conceded defeat, members of the opposition subsequently disputed the legitimacy of the results, reiterating claims of incorrect practice in the distribution of voting credentials and in the counting of ballots. None the less, international observers described the poll as being largely free and fair. In late December, at his inauguration, President Jammeh granted an unconditional amnesty to Jawara, guaranteeing the former President's security should he decide to return to The Gambia.

In December 2001 the UDP-PPP-GPP coalition announced that it would boycott legislative elections scheduled for January 2002, as a result of the alleged addition of some 50,000 foreign citizens to electoral lists and the reputed transfer of voters between the electoral lists of different constituencies. Having denied these accusations, the IEC announced that the APRC had secured 33 of the 48 elective seats in the enlarged National Assembly, in constituencies where the party was unopposed owing to the boycott. At the elections, which took place on 17 January, the APRC won 12 of the 15 contested seats, giving the party an overall total of 45 elective seats; the PDOIS obtained two seats, and the NRP one. Electoral turn-out was reportedly low. An additional five members of parliament were appointed by President Jammeh, in accordance with the Constitution. Dibba, whose NCP had formed an alliance with the APRC prior to the elections, was appointed Speaker of the new National Assembly.

In May 2002 the National Assembly approved legislation that imposed stricter regulations over the print media, in accordance with which all journalists not working for the state-controlled media would be required to register with a National Media Commission (NMC). The law was condemned by the Gambia Press Union, which announced that it would not co-operate with the Commission. In early June Jawara returned to The Gambia from exile; at the end of the month he was officially received by Jammeh and later tendered his resignation as leader of the PPP. In July legislation was adopted that allowed Jammeh to appoint up to 20 secretaries of state to his Cabinet, instead of 15.

In June 2003 the NMC was created, despite continuing opposition from journalists, and was given far-reaching powers, including the authority to imprison journalists for terms of up to six months. Reports continued throughout 2003 and 2004 of journalists being arrested or subjected to harassment. In September 2003 the editor-in-chief of *The Independent*, Abdoulaye Sey, was reportedly detained for four days, shortly after the newspaper published an article criticizing Jammeh. In October the newspaper's offices in Banjul were set on fire and in April 2004 the printing press was destroyed. In early December legislation providing for terms of imprisonment of up to three years for journalists found guilty of libel or sedition, and obliging members of the media to re-register with the state, was approved by the National Assembly, despite protests by members of the Gambian and international media. In mid-December Deyda Hydara, the editor of the independent newspaper *The Point*, who had been severely critical of the new legislation, was murdered in Banjul. The incident precipitated a demonstration in the capital, reportedly attended by several hundred journalists, and later that month a one-week media strike was observed. In January 2005 Reporters sans frontières appealed for an independent commission to be established to investigate the murder of Hydara and maintained that it had been carried out by a contract killer.

The National Alliance for Democracy and Development (NADD), a coalition of five opposition parties, including the NRP, the PDOIS and the UDP, was formed in January 2005 with the aim of presenting a single candidate to contest the presidential election scheduled to take place in late 2006. In June 2005 four deputies, among them three opposition leaders—Hamat Bah of the NRP and Sidia Jatta and Halifa Sallah of the PDOIS—were expelled from the National Assembly following their registration as members of the NADD. According to Gambian law, deputies were not permitted to switch allegiance between political parties during the term of a parliament. By-elections to the vacant seats were held in September at which the NADD retained three of the contested constituencies, while the APRC took the remaining seat. In November Bah and Sallah, along with another senior member of the NADD, Omar Jallow, were arrested and charged with sedition. They were released on bail in mid-December and in February 2006 all charges against them were dropped. However, in the same month a rift in the NADD became apparent, with the NRP and the UDP withdrawing and forming a new coalition.

In mid-July 2006 the Chairman of the IEC was unexpectedly dismissed from office. It was subsequently announced that a presidential election was to be held on 22 September, at which Jammeh won 67.3% of the votes cast. His nearest rival was Darboe (candidate for the UDP, the NRP and the Gambia Party for Democracy and Progress) with 26.7%, while Halifa Sallah of the NADD was placed third with some 6.0%. Some 59% of the eligible electorate participated in the ballot.

Jammeh's third elective term

The ruling APRC won 42 seats at legislative elections held on 25 January 2007, while the UDP took four seats, the NADD one seat and an independent candidate one seat. Sallah and Bah failed to be re-elected to the National Assembly. The rate of voter participation was officially recorded at 41.7%.

A Cabinet reorganization was effected in September 2007 in which Crispin Grey-Johnson was appointed Secretary of State for Foreign Affairs and National Assembly Matters, while Ousman Jammeh assumed the newly created petroleum, energy and mineral resources portfolio. Further governmental changes were implemented in November when Secretary of State for Health and Social Welfare Dr Tamsir Mbowe was dismissed. Although no official reason was given, Mbowe was earlier reported to have made controversial claims that President Jammeh had succeeded in finding a cure for HIV/AIDS. The following month Maj. Dr Malick Njie was named as Mbowe's successor.

In March 2008 the Cabinet came under further scrutiny when allegations of fraud and inefficiency were reported; two ministers were subsequently dismissed. Dr Omar Touray assumed responsibility for the foreign affairs portfolio in a further cabinet change later that month, while two minor governmental reorganizations, effected in February 2009, saw the communication, information and technology and higher education, research, science and technology portfolios placed under the remit of the Office of the President.

The National Assembly adopted amendments to the Constitution in April 2009, providing for a change in the title of members of the Government from Secretary of State to Minister, in line with general international practice. The restriction on the number of cabinet ministers that may be appointed was also removed.

Halifa Sallah was arrested and detained in June 2009 along with a number of other journalists and editors, reportedly accused of being disrespectful to President Jammeh with regard to the murder of Hydara in 2004 in articles published in Sallah's newspaper *Foroyaa*. Sallah proclaimed the arrests unlawful and unconstitutional and alleged that the detainees had been held for an extended period of time without being informed of the charges against them. In July 2009 six journalists were imprisoned on charges of sedition; they were pardoned and released from gaol in September, although President Jammeh reiterated that those who were disrespectful towards him would be subjected to punishment.

The army Chief of Defence Staff, Gen. Lang Tombong Tamba, was dismissed in October 2009 and replaced by his hitherto deputy Brig.-Gen. Massaneh Kinteh. A further four senior military officials, including the Commander of the National Guards, were also dismissed. In early February 2010 President Jammeh implemented a major reorganization of the Government, appointing four new ministers and creating a new Ministry of Economic Planning and Industrial Development. Jammeh carried out a further two reorganizations in March.

In early March 2010 six senior members of the security forces, including the Commander of the Navy, Sarjo Fofona, were removed from their posts and placed under arrest. The Executive Director of the National Drug Enforcement Agency, Ebrima Bun Sanneh, and his deputy, Bakary Bojang, were also dismissed and placed in detention. Later that month Cham, Tamba and Fofona, *inter alios*, were accused of planning a coup against the Jammeh regime during the previous year and were charged with treason. Eight of the accused, including Tamba and other high-ranking military officers, were found guilty in July and received death sentences, a decision that was condemned by the European Union (EU). (In June prosecutors also accused Tamba and Fofona of taking part in a plot to overthrow the President in 2006. Both received jail sentences of 20 years on this charge in May 2011.) Critics of the regime claimed that the coup plot was a fabrication devised by Jammeh to remove potential political rivals, while the human rights organization Amnesty International alleged that some of the sentenced men had been subjected to torture. Further arrests were made in November in relation to the alleged 2009 coup conspiracy; the detainees included high-ranking intelligence personnel.

Senior UDP official Femi Peters was fined and imprisoned for one year in April 2010 after being convicted of orchestrating an illegal public meeting, prompting expressions of concern from the EU, the United Kingdom and the USA. An appeal against his sentence was rejected in August, although Peters was released from gaol in December. Meanwhile, in June the UDP designated Darboe as its candidate in the 2011 presidential election. At a UDP rally in September, Darboe proposed the formation of an opposition coalition to compete more effectively against Jammeh in the election.

The President carried out another cabinet reorganization in June 2010, most notably replacing Ousman Jammeh with Dr Mamadou Tangara as Minister of Foreign Affairs, International Co-operation and Gambians Abroad. The Office of the President assumed responsibility for the energy and higher education portfolios in the same month. Abdou Kolley, after being replaced as Minister of Finance and Economic Affairs in March, was restored to his former position in a further government reorganization in July. Abdoulie Bojang became Speaker of the National Assembly in November. Additional changes were made to the Government in early 2011, following the death of the Minister of Health and Social Welfare, Dr Abu Bakarr Gaye. Fatim Badjje, who had been dismissed as Minister of Information and Communication Infrastructure in 2009, returned to the Cabinet as Gaye's replacement in February 2011, while in January Mambury Njie, hitherto the Minister of Economic Planning and Industrial Development, had assumed responsibility for the finance and economic affairs portfolio. Also in January Mikailu Abdulahi was appointed Director of Public Prosecution (he had previously deputized this position) after the incumbent, Richard Chenge, a Nigerian national, had been ordered to leave The Gambia.

Meanwhile, following indications that criminals were increasingly utilizing The Gambia as a drugs transshipment base, including the seizure by Gambian police of 2.3 metric tons of cocaine in June 2010, new anti-narcotics legislation was approved in October. The measures included the potential imposition of the death penalty on those convicted of heroin or cocaine possession. Subsequently, in October 2011 eight foreign nationals received jail sentences of 50 years each for attempting to traffic 2.1 tons of cocaine through The Gambia to Europe in June 2009. One of the accused reportedly died in prison.

Recent developments: Jammeh retains the presidency

In March 2011 the head of the IEC announced that a presidential election would take place on 24 November, to be followed by legislative elections in early 2012 and local government elections in 2013. In a registration period for the upcoming elections, held from 5 May to 17 June, 837,029 voters were registered, according to the IEC. President Jammeh stated that his party, the APRC, would not campaign, as he was confident of being re-elected. In a statement made in July, on the 17th anniversary of his accession to power, Jammeh proclaimed that no coup or election could unseat him, suggesting that he ruled the country by divine mandate. Several opposition politicians publicly stated that the shortening of the election campaign period to 11 days placed them at a significant electoral disadvantage, given the President's permanent access to national media. A report published in July by the Observatory for the Protection of Human Rights Defenders expressed concern at the repression of journalists and civil society in the Gambia, and voiced fears that such instances could increase as the election approached, while Amnesty International also declared that it harboured serious concerns about the observance of human rights during the election.

Meanwhile, in June 2011 the former Minister of Communications and Information Technology, Amadou Scatred Janneh, was one of four people arrested on suspicion of conspiracy to commit treason and sedition. The four were allegedly members of a civil society organization named Coalition for Change—The Gambia (CCG), which claimed to challenge dictatorship and promote basic freedoms through non-violent action.

In October 2011 the IEC announced that parliamentary elections would be held on 29 March 2012, following a nomination period from 8–10 March and an official campaign period from 14–27 March. Also in October 2011 the various opposition parties announced that they had failed to agree on a single joint candidate to oppose Jammeh in the upcoming presidential election.

Subsequently, in the presidential election held on 24 November 2011, Jammeh was re-elected to the office of the President for a fourth term, receiving 71.5% of votes cast. His nearest opponent, Darboe of the UDP, won 17.4% of the votes, while Hamat Bah, representing a United Front of four opposition parties—the Gambia People's Democratic Party (GPDP), the NADD, the NRP, and the PDOIS—took 11.1%. The rate of voter participation was 83%. Two days prior to the polling date, the Economic Community of West African States (see p. 264) had announced that it would not be observing the elections, stating that conditions within the country—including domination of mass media by the ruling party, a lack of neutrality in state institutions, and widespread intimidation of the opposition and electorate—were not conducive to the holding of free and fair elections. Nevertheless, the elections were observed by missions from the African Union, the Commonwealth, and the Organization of Islamic Co-operation (OIC). These bodies broadly agreed that the elections had been conducted in a fair and transparent manner, though the African Union mission observed in its report that the APRC had benefited from superior media access and financial resources, while the Commonwealth report drew attention to the shortened campaign period as possibly disadvantageous to the opposition parties.

Meanwhile, in December 2011 former justice minister and maritime law expert Fatou Bensouda was appointed Chief Prosecutor to the International Criminal Court in the Hague, the Netherlands. Bensouda thus became the first African to be appointed to the post, and there was speculation that her appointment reflected a desire on the part of the court to deflect accusations that it excessively targets the African continent in its prosecutions.

In February 2012 Jammeh effected a major reorganization of his Cabinet; only eight members of the outgoing Government were retained, although Tangara and Njie were again respectively appointed to head the foreign affairs and finance ministries.

The legislative elections, which were held as scheduled on 29 March 2012, were boycotted by all opposition parties with the exception of the NRP, which took one seat. The APRC was unopposed in 25 constituencies and won 43 of the 48 elective seats available. The remaining four seats were secured by independent candidates. The rate of voter participation was put at 50% by the IEC. The following month Jammeh annnounced that Njie had replaced Tangara as Minister of Foreign Affairs, International Co-operation and Gambians Abroad. Tangara became Minister of Fisheries, Water Resources and National Assembly Matters, while Kolley was again appointed to head the finance ministry. Later in April, in a further reorganization of the Government, Tangara was moved to head the higher education ministry, with President Jammeh assuming responsibility for Tangara's former portfolio.

Foreign Affairs

Regional relations

After the 1994 coup The Gambia's traditional aid donors and trading partners suspended much co-operation, although vital aid projects generally continued. The Jammeh administration therefore sought new links: diplomatic relations with Libya, severed in 1980, were restored in November 1994, and numerous co-operation agreements ensued. Links with the Republic of China (Taiwan), ended in 1974, were re-established in July 1995, whereupon Taiwan became one of The Gambia's major sources of funding.

Despite the presence in Senegal of prominent opponents of his Government, Jammeh also sought to improve relations with that country, and in January 1996 the two countries signed an agreement aimed at increasing bilateral trade and at minimizing cross-border smuggling; a further trade agreement was concluded in April 1997. In June the two countries agreed to take joint measures to combat insecurity, illegal immigration, arms-trafficking and drugs-smuggling. In January 1998 the Government of Senegal welcomed an offer by Jammeh to mediate in the conflict in the southern province of Casamance: the separatist Mouvement des forces démocratiques de la Casamance (MFDC) is chiefly composed of the Diola ethnic group, of which Jammeh is a member. In December 2000 the Gambian Government sent a delegation to participate in talks between the MFDC and the Senegalese Government. At the end of 2002 there were some 4,230 refugees from Casamance resident in The Gambia, although by late 2004 only 500 were registered with the Office of the UN High Commissioner for Refugees. A dispute between the two countries arose in August 2005 when Gambian authorities increased the price of the ferry across the Gambia river at Banjul and in retaliation Senegalese lorry drivers commenced a blockade of the common border. The conflict was resolved in October, under the mediation of the Nigerian President, Olusegun Obasanjo, and an agreement was reached to build a bridge over the Gambia river. However, renewed fighting in Senegal's Casamance province from March 2006 resulted in the movement of some 10,000 refugees into The Gambia, including a number of rebel leaders sought by the Senegalese authorities.

The Government severed diplomatic relations with Iran in November 2010. No formal explanation for this action was provided; however, during the previous month the Nigerian authorities had intercepted a consignment of illegal weapons from Iran that was allegedly en route to The Gambia, and Gambian officials intimated that the two events were connected. The final destination of the arms shipment was reportedly a property in The Gambia belonging to President Jammeh (although the Gambian Government dismissed this claim), and there was speculation in Senegal that the weapons would have been smuggled across the border to the MFDC to aid the separatist insurgency, raising tensions between the two West African nations. Nevertheless, during an official visit to Senegal in January 2011, the Gambian Minister of Foreign Affairs, International Co-operation and Gambians Abroad, Mamadou Tangara, held discussions with high-ranking Senegalese officials (including President Abdoulaye Wade), which precipitated an improvement in bilateral relations. In February Senegal and The Gambia agreed to establish a Boundary Management Commission to address matters relating to their common border. In August, in an official state visit to The Gambia, Wade reiterated the hope that President Jammeh would assist in enabling a peaceful resolution to the situation in The Gambia.

Other external relations

Relations with the United Kingdom were strained in 2001, following the expulsion of the British Deputy High Commissioner, Bharat Joshi, from The Gambia in late August. The Gambian authorities alleged that the diplomat had interfered in the country's internal affairs, following his attendance at an opposition meeting, but emphasized that the action had been taken against Joshi, and not the United Kingdom. However, in late September the Gambian Deputy High Commissioner in London was expelled from the United Kingdom, and further retaliatory measures were implemented against The Gambia. Relations were restored during 2002, although in January of that year the EU (see p. 276) representative, George Marc-André, was declared *persona non grata* by the Gambian authorities and requested to leave the country. In September 2011 the President of Guinea, Alpha Condé, accused the Government of The Gambia, alongside that of Senegal, of complicity in an assassination attempt made against him that July.

CONSTITUTION AND GOVERNMENT

The Constitution of the Second Republic of The Gambia, which was approved in a national referendum on 8 August 1996, entered into full effect on 16 January 1997. The Constitution provides for the separation of the powers of the executive, legislative and judicial organs of state. Under its terms, the Head of State is the President of the Republic, who is directly elected by universal adult suffrage. No restriction is placed on the number of times a President may seek re-election. Legislative authority is vested in the National Assembly, elected for a five-year term and comprising 48 members elected by direct suffrage and five members nominated by the President of the Republic. The President appoints government members, who are responsible both to the Head of State and to the National Assembly. Tribalism and other forms of sectarianism in politics are forbidden. The Gambia is divided into eight local government areas.

REGIONAL AND INTERNATIONAL CO-OPERATION

The Gambia is a member of the African Union (see p. 189), of the Economic Community of West African States (ECOWAS, see p. 264), of the Community of Sahel-Saharan States—CEN-SAD (see p. 449) and of the Gambia River Basin Development Organization (OMVG, see p. 450).

The Gambia became a member of the UN in 1965, was admitted to the World Trade Organization (WTO, see p. 433) in 1996 and also participates in the Group of 77 (G77, see p. 450) developing countries.

ECONOMIC AFFAIRS

In 2010, according to estimates by the World Bank, The Gambia's gross national income (GNI), measured at average 2008–10 prices, was US $770m., equivalent to $450 per head (or $1,290 on an international purchasing-power parity basis). During 2001–10, it was estimated, the population increased at an average annual rate of 2.9%, while gross domestic product (GDP) per head increased by 0.7%. Overall GDP increased, in real terms, at an average annual rate of 3.6% in 2001–10; GDP increased by 5.0% in 2010.

Agriculture (including forestry and fishing) contributed 27.7% of GDP in 2009, according to the African Development Bank (AfDB). According to FAO, 75.4% of the labour force were estimated to be employed in the sector in mid-2012. The dominant agricultural activity has traditionally been the cultivation of groundnuts, and exports of that commodity accounted for an estimated 68.2% of domestic export earnings in 1999. However, in 2009 groundnuts accounted for just 4.7% of total exports. The significant decline was attributed to poor production (owing to transport problems) and a change in licensing requirements that left just one company in operation in the sector. A significant proportion of the groundnut crop is frequently smuggled for sale in Senegal. Cotton, citrus fruits, mangoes, avocados and sesame seed are also cultivated for export. The principal staple crops are millet, maize, rice and sorghum, although The Gambia remains heavily dependent on imports of rice and other basic foodstuffs. Fishing makes an important contribution to the domestic food supply. In 2001 the Government announced the construction of a major new fishing port in Banjul, at a cost of US $10m. According to the World Bank, agricultural GDP increased at an average annual rate of 1.9% in 2001–10; growth of 4.0% was recorded in 2010.

Industry (including manufacturing, construction, mining and power) contributed 12.4% of GDP in 2009, according to the AfDB. About 10.3% of the labour force were employed in the sector at the time of the 1993 census. According to the World Bank, industrial GDP increased at an average annual rate of 7.3% in 2001–10; growth in 2010 was 6.4%.

The Gambia has few viable mineral resources, although seismic surveys have indicated the existence of petroleum deposits off shore. Deposits of kaolin and salt are currently unexploited. In early 2008 the discovery of commercially exploitable quantities of uranium was announced. Mining contributed 1.8% of GDP in 2009, according to the AfDB, and the GDP of the sector grew by 8.8% in that year.

Manufacturing contributed 5.5% of GDP in 2009, according to the AfDB, and employed 6.6% of the labour force in 1993. The sector is dominated by agro-industrial activities, most importantly the processing of groundnuts and fish. Beverages and construction materials are also produced for the domestic market. According to the AfDB, manufacturing GDP increased at an average annual rate of 3.5% in 2000–07; growth in 2009 was 0.4%.

According to the AfDB, construction contributed 3.6% of GDP in 2009, while the construction sector alone employed 3.0% of the total labour force in 1993. The sector grew by 3.0% in 2009.

The Gambia is highly reliant on imported energy. According to the UN, imports of mineral fuels and lubricants comprised an estimated 15.6% of the value of total merchandise imports in 2009.

The services sector contributed 59.9% of GDP in 2009, according to the AfDB, and employed about 34.3% of the labour force in 1993. The tourism industry is of particular significance as a generator of foreign exchange. Tourism contributed about 16% of annual GDP in the late 2000s, and employed some 10,000 workers at that time. The Jammeh administration has expressed its intention further to exploit the country's potential as a transit point for regional trade and also as a centre for regional finance and telecommunications. The GDP of the services sector increased at an average annual rate of 6.2% in 2001–10; growth in 2010 was 6.3%.

In 2010 The Gambia recorded an estimated visible trade deficit of US $68.9m., while there was a surplus of $17.2m. on the current account of the balance of payments. In 2009 the principal source of imports was Côte d'Ivoire, which supplied an estimated 14.3% of total imports; other major sources were the People's Republic of China, the United Kingdom, Brazil, Germany and the Netherlands. The largest market for exports in that year was Senegal (an estimated 26.8% of total exports). Other major purchasers were France and the United Kingdom. The Gambia's principal exports in 2009 were food and live animals (which contributed 37.0% of total exports and chiefly comprised vegetables and fruits), groundnut oil, machinery and transport equipment, and groundnuts. The principal imports in 2009 were food and live animals (contributing 25.4% of imports), machinery and transport equipment, minerals fuels and lubricants, petroleum and petroleum products, chemicals and related products, and animal and vegetable oils.

In 2009, according to the IMF, there was an overall budget deficit of D773m. (equivalent to 3.1% of GDP). The Gambia's general government gross debt was D14,926m. in 2010, equivalent to 57.0% of GDP. The Gambia's total external debt was US $520m. at the end of 2009, of which $449m. was public and publicly guaranteed debt. In that year, the cost of servicing long-term public and publicly guaranteed debt and repayments to the IMF was equivalent to 8.9% of the value of exports of goods, services and income (excluding workers' remittances). According to ILO the average annual rate of inflation was 7.1% in 2001–10; consumer prices increased by an average of 5.0% in 2010. The rate of unemployment was estimated at some 26% of the labour force in mid-1994.

Relations between The Gambia and the international financial community have often been strained, particularly owing to concerns over alleged inaccuracies in economic data provided by the Gambian authorities. However, in 2007 the Government elicited praise from the IMF for stabilizing the economy and the Fund agreed to resume assistance through a three-year Poverty Reduction and Growth Facility. The IMF approved increased assistance of US $9.2m. in February 2009 to reduce the detrimental impact of the global financial crisis on the country's key sectors. Subsequently, under the redesignated Extended Credit Facility, the IMF disbursed $3.0m. to the Government in February 2010 and a further $3.6m. in January 2011. The Gambian authorities also received loans from the Islamic Development Bank totalling $44.9m. in October 2010; the funds were to be used to finance education and infrastructure projects. Despite the impact of the global economic crisis, which produced a significant decline in tourist arrivals and remittances from abroad, overall GDP grew by around 6.5% per year in 2008–10, according to the IMF, driven in particular by increased agricultural production and a related revival in the manufacturing and trade services sector. The Gambian central bank, meanwhile, evaluated GDP growth for 2010 at 6.1%, but predicted a decline to 5.5% in 2011, as a consequence of the slowdown in the agricultural sector. Moreover, external debt remained high despite debt relief initiatives, with interest payments placing a significant strain on government finances. In November, the IMF estimated that 22.5% of government revenue was being used to pay the interest on domestic and international debts. The IMF also noted that tax revenues had fallen steadily as a proportion of GDP since 2007, to less than 12.5% in 2011. There were also concerns regarding rising food prices and the vulnerability of the agricultural sector to fluctuating weather conditions, while poverty remained pervasive among the Gambian population. The Government was expected to take steps to reduce poverty with the implementation of a Programme for Accelerated Growth and Employment (PAGE) in 2012–15. Negotiations with the IMF for a new three-year Extended Credit Facility agreement to support the PAGE began in May 2011.

PUBLIC HOLIDAYS

2013: 1 January (New Year's Day), 23 January* (Eid al-Moulid, Birth of the Prophet), 18 February (Independence Day), 29 March (Good Friday), 1 April (Easter Monday), 1 May (Workers' Day), 22 July (Anniversary of the Second Republic), 7* (Eid al-Fitr, end of Ramadan), 15 August (Assumption/St Mary's Day), 14 October* (Eid al-Kebir, Feast of the Sacrifice), 13 November (Ashoura), 25 December (Christmas).

* These holidays are dependent on the Islamic lunar calendar and may vary by one or two days from the dates given.

Statistical Survey

Sources (unless otherwise stated): Department of Information Services, 14 Daniel Goddard St, Banjul; tel. 4225060; fax 4227230; Central Statistics Department, Central Bank Building, 1/2 Ecowas Ave, Banjul; tel. 4228364; fax 4228903; e-mail director@csd.gm; internet www.gambia.gm/Statistics/statistics.html.

Area and Population

AREA, POPULATION AND DENSITY

Area (sq km)	11,295*
Population (census results)	
15 April 1993	1,038,145
15 April 2003†	
Males	687,781
Females	676,726
Total	1,364,507
Population (UN estimates at mid-year)‡	
2010	1,728,394
2011	1,776,103
2012	1,824,775
Density (per sq km) at mid-2012	161.6

* 4,361 sq miles.
† Provisional.
‡ Source: UN, *World Population Prospects: The 2010 Revision*.

ETHNIC GROUPS

1993 census (percentages): Mandinka 39.60; Fula 18.83; Wolof 14.61; Jola 10.66; Serahule 8.92; Serere 2.77; Manjago 1.85; Bambara 0.84; Creole/Aku 0.69; Others 1.23.

POPULATION BY AGE AND SEX

(UN estimates at mid-2012)

	Males	Females	Total
0–14	398,746	392,881	791,627
15–64	481,596	512,417	994,013
65 and over	20,372	18,763	39,135
Total	900,714	924,061	1,824,775

Source: UN, *World Population Prospects: The 2010 Revision*.

ADMINISTRATIVE DIVISIONS

(population at 2003 census, provisional results)

Banjul	34,828	Kanifing	322,410
Basse	183,033	Kerewan	172,806
Brikama	392,987	Kuntaur	79,098
Georgetown	106,799	Mansakonko	72,546

PRINCIPAL TOWNS
(population at 1993 census)

Serrekunda	151,450	Lamin	10,668
Brikama	42,480	Gunjur	9,983
Banjul (capital)	42,407	Basse	9,265
Bakau	38,062	Soma	7,925
Farafenni	21,142	Bansang	5,405
Sukuta	16,667		

Mid-2009 (incl. suburbs, UN estimate): Banjul 436,447 (Source: UN, *World Urbanization Prospects: The 2009 Revision*).

BIRTHS AND DEATHS
(annual averages, UN estimates)

	1995–2000	2000–05	2005–10
Birth rate (per 1,000)	44.7	42.4	39.3
Death rate (per 1,000)	12.2	10.9	9.8

Source: UN, *World Population Prospects: The 2010 Revision*.

Life expectancy (years at birth, WHO estimates): 60 (males 58; females 61) in 2009 (Source: WHO, *World Health Statistics*).

ECONOMICALLY ACTIVE POPULATION*
(persons aged 10 years and over, 1993 census)

	Males	Females	Total
Agriculture, hunting and forestry	82,886	92,806	175,692
Fishing	5,610	450	6,060
Mining and quarrying	354	44	398
Manufacturing	18,729	2,953	21,682
Electricity, gas and water supply	1,774	84	1,858
Construction	9,530	149	9,679
Wholesale and retail trade; repair of motor vehicles, motorcycles and personal and household goods	33,281	15,460	48,741
Hotels and restaurants	3,814	2,173	5,987
Transport, storage and communications	13,421	782	14,203
Financial intermediation	1,843	572	2,415
Other community, social and personal service activities	25,647	15,607	41,254
Sub-total	196,889	131,080	327,969
Activities not adequately defined	10,421	6,991	17,412
Total labour force	207,310	138,071	345,381

* Figures exclude persons seeking work for the first time, but include other unemployed persons.

Mid-2012 (estimates in '000): Agriculture, etc. 640; Total labour force 849 (Source: FAO).

Health and Welfare

KEY INDICATORS

Total fertility rate (children per woman, 2009)	5.0
Under-5 mortality rate (per 1,000 live births, 2009)	103
HIV/AIDS (% of persons aged 15–49, 2009)	2.0
Physicians (per 1,000 head, 2003)	0.1
Hospital beds (per 1,000 head, 2005)	0.8
Health expenditure (2008): US $ per head (PPP)	75
Health expenditure (2008): % of GDP	5.5
Health expenditure (2008): public (% of total)	48.1
Access to water (% of persons, 2008)	92
Access to sanitation (% of persons, 2008)	67
Total carbon dioxide emissions ('000 metric tons, 2007)	395.7
Carbon dioxide emissions per head (metric tons, 2007)	0.2
Human Development Index (2011): ranking	168
Human Development Index (2011): value	0.420

For sources and definitions, see explanatory note on p. vi.

Agriculture

PRINCIPAL CROPS
('000 metric tons)

	2008	2009	2010
Rice, paddy	38.3	79.0	99.9
Maize	44.9	54.6	66.0
Millet	125.6	144.9	158.0
Sorghum	25.6	31.9	39.0
Cassava (Manioc)*	8.4	7.4	7.6
Groundnuts, with shell	109.6	122.0	137.6
Oil palm fruit*	35.0	35.0	35.0
Guavas, mangoes and mangosteens*	1.2	1.3	1.2

* FAO estimates.

Aggregate production ('000 metric tons, may include official, semi-official or estimated data): Total cereals 235.2 in 2008, 311.0 in 2009, 363.5 in 2010; Total pulses 3.3 in 2008, 2.7 in 2009, 2.9 in 2010; Total vegetables (incl. melons) 11.7 in 2008, 9.3 in 2009, 12.2 in 2010; Total fruits (excl. melons) 8.1 in 2008, 8.9 in 2009, 8.6 in 2010.

Source: FAO.

LIVESTOCK
('000 head, year ending September)

	2008	2009	2010
Cattle	420	432	425
Goats	374	380	352
Sheep	200	215	251
Pigs	25	27	29
Asses	42	43	42
Horses	41	37	38
Chickens	720	800	850

Source: FAO.

LIVESTOCK PRODUCTS
('000 metric tons, FAO estimates)

	2008	2009	2010
Cattle meat	4.0	4.1	4.1
Goat meat	1.0	1.0	1.0
Sheep meat	0.6	0.6	0.6
Chicken meat	1.1	1.2	1.2
Game meat	1.2	1.2	1.2
Cows' milk	8.8	9.1	9.3
Hen eggs	0.9	0.9	0.9

Source: FAO.

Forestry

ROUNDWOOD REMOVALS
('000 cubic metres, excluding bark, FAO estimates)

	2007	2008	2009
Sawlogs, veneer logs and logs for sleepers*	106	106	106
Other industrial wood†	7	7	7
Fuel wood	666	675	684
Total	779	788	797

* Assumed to be unchanged since 1994.
† Assumed to be unchanged since 1993.

2010: Production assumed to be unchanged since 2009 (FAO estimates).

Source: FAO.

Fishing

('000 metric tons, live weight of capture)

	2007	2008	2009
Tilapias	0.7	1.1	1.2
Sea catfishes	4.0	3.5	3.8
Bonga shad	13.9	11.7	12.6
Sardinellas	4.4	7.1	7.6
Sharks, rays, skates	0.4	0.5	0.5
Total catch (incl. others)	43.6	42.6	45.9

Source: FAO.

Mining

	2007	2008	2009*
Clay (metric tons)	6,713	n.a.	n.a.
Laterites (metric tons)	187	115	100
Silica sand ('000 metric tons)	712	1,065	1,000
Zircon (metric tons)	355	n.a.	n.a.

* Estimated figures.

Source: US Geological Survey.

Industry

SELECTED PRODUCTS

('000 metric tons, unless otherwise stated)

	2007	2008	2009
Beer of barley*	1.7	2.6	3.5
Palm oil—unrefined*	2.6	2.5	2.1
Groundnut oil	13.5*	16.0†	13.6†
Electric energy (million kWh)‡	229	242.0	n.a.

* FAO estimate(s).

† Unofficial figure.

‡ Source: UN Industrial Commodity Statistics Database.

Beer of millet ('000 metric tons, FAO estimates): 50.4 in 2003, 55.4 in 2004–05.

Source: mainly FAO.

Finance

CURRENCY AND EXCHANGE RATES

Monetary Units

100 butut = 1 dalasi (D).

Sterling, Dollar and Euro Equivalents (31 October 2011)

£1 sterling = 48.2651 dalasi;
US $1 = 30.1205 dalasi;
€1 = 42.1717 dalasi;
1,000 dalasi = £20.72 = $33.20 = €23.71.

Average Exchange Rate (dalasi per US $)

2008	22.192
2009	26.644
2010	28.012

BUDGET

(million dalasi)

Revenue*	2009	2010†	2011†
Tax revenue	3,518	3,991	4,069
Direct taxes	974	1,185	1,288
Domestic taxes on goods and services	1,395	1,572	1,713
Taxes on international trade	1,148	1,234	1,068
Non-tax revenue	371	421	522
Total	3,889	4,413	4,590

Expenditure*	2009	2010†	2011†
Current expenditure	3,622	4,014	4,850
Wages and salaries	1,192	1,499	1,672
Other goods and services	1,689	1,752	2,259
Interest payments	741	762	919
Internal	588	586	739
External	153	176	180
Capital expenditure	1,924	1,692	1,244
Gambia Local Fund	586	365	358
Foreign financed	1,338	1,327	886
Total	5,545	5,706	6,094

* Excluding grants received (million dalasi): 1,021 in 2009; 1,061 in 2010 (budget projection); 1,062 in 2011 (budget projection).

† Budget projections.

‡ Excluding lending minus repayments (million dalasi): 138 in 2009; –31 in 2010 (budget projection); 23 in 2011 (budget projection).

Source: IMF, *The Gambia: Seventh Review of the Arrangement Under the Extended Credit Facility, Request for Rephasing of the Eighth Review and Extension of the Arrangement, and Request for Waivers of Nonobservance of Performance Criteria—Staff Report; Informational Annex; Public Information Notice; Press Release on the Executive Board Discussion; and Statement by the Alternate Executive Director for The Gambia* (January 2011).

INTERNATIONAL RESERVES

(US $ million at 31 December)

	2008	2009	2010
IMF special drawing rights	0.10	38.58	37.88
Reserve position in IMF	2.29	2.33	2.37
Foreign exchange	114.13	183.26	161.37
Total	116.52	224.18	201.63

Source: IMF, *International Financial Statistics*.

MONEY SUPPLY

(million dalasi at 31 December)

	2008	2009	2010
Currency outside banks	1,832.91	2,004.81	2,064.62
Demand deposits at commercial banks	3,286.69	3,594.96	3,957.34
Total money	5,119.60	5,599.77	6,021.96

Source: IMF, *International Financial Statistics*.

COST OF LIVING

(Consumer Price Index for Banjul and Kombo St Mary's; base: 1974 = 100)

	1997	1998	1999
Food	1,511.8	1,565.8	1,628.8
Fuel and light	2,145.8	1,854.9	2,076.0
Clothing*	937.5	981.8	999.9
Rent	1,409.6	1,431.3	1,428.6
All items (incl. others)	1,441.5	1,457.3	1,512.8

* Including household linen.

All items (Consumer Price Index for Banjul and Kombo St Mary's; base: 2005 = 100): 112.3 in 2008; 117.4 in 2009; 123.4 in 2010 (Source: IMF, International Financial Statistics).

NATIONAL ACCOUNTS

(million dalasi at current prices)

Expenditure on the Gross Domestic Product

	2007	2008	2009
Government final consumption expenditure	984	1,747	1,885
Private final consumption expenditure	18,252	19,279	20,813
Gross fixed capital formation	5,797	5,957	6,430
Increase in stocks	699	626	676
Total domestic expenditure	25,732	27,609	29,804
Exports of goods and services	1,634	1,465	1,581
Less Imports of goods and services	6,809	6,095	6,579
GDP in purchasers' values	20,556	22,978	24,806

Gross Domestic Product by Economic Activity

	2007	2008	2009
Agriculture, hunting, forestry and fishing	4,044	5,590	6,417
Mining and quarrying	343	374	406
Manufacturing	1,327	1,241	1,278
Electricity, gas and water	317	334	355
Construction	712	820	829
Wholesale and retail trade; restaurants and hotels	6,587	6,824	6,693
Finance, insurance and real estate	2,049	2,543	2,841
Transport and communications	2,385	2,231	2,467
Public administration and defence	561	832	894
Other services	749	953	969
Sub-total	19,074	21,742	23,149
Less Imputed bank service charge	672	743	868
GDP at factor cost	18,402	20,999	22,279
Indirect taxes, *less* subsidies	2,154	1,980	2,527
GDP in market prices	20,556	22,978	24,806

Source: African Development Bank.

BALANCE OF PAYMENTS

(US $ million, year ending 30 June)

	2008	2009	2010
Exports of goods f.o.b.	205.50	174.17	167.38
Imports of goods f.o.b.	-274.55	-259.96	-236.31
Trade balance	-69.05	-85.79	-68.93
Exports of services	117.58	104.19	88.26
Imports of services	-85.65	-82.57	-71.60
Balance on goods and services	-37.12	-64.16	-52.27
Other income received	12.72	11.68	14.35
Other income paid	-47.15	-19.78	-22.40
Balance on goods, services and income	-71.56	-72.26	-60.31
Current transfers received	96.48	160.21	212.75
Current transfers paid	-21.99	-58.79	-135.28
Current balance	2.93	29.16	17.16
Direct investment from abroad	70.79	39.45	37.14
Other investment assets	1.30	20.06	20.30
Investment liabilities	-67.99	-40.58	-73.40
Net errors and omissions	-29.71	-27.82	-94.48
Overall balance	-22.68	20.26	-93.28

Source: IMF, *International Financial Statistics*.

External Trade

PRINCIPAL COMMODITIES

(US $ million)

Imports c.i.f.	2007	2008	2009
Food and live animals	74.5	73.4	77.1
Cereal and cereal preparations	31.6	34.5	39.4
Beverages and tobacco	6.6	5.9	5.1
Crude materials, inedible (excluding fuels)	7.6	7.4	4.2
Mineral fuels, lubricants, etc.	54.1	64.1	47.3
Petroleum, petroleum products and related materials	53.5	63.3	47.2
Animal and vegetable oils	18.5	16.9	21.9
Chemicals and related products	16.1	23.1	22.8
Medicinal and pharmaceutical products	8.9	8.6	13.3
Basic manufactures	39.4	43.2	42.9
Textile yarn, fabrics, made-up articles and related products	15.0	14.0	11.7
Non-metallic mineral manufactures	10.6	13.7	18.3
Machinery and transport equipment	80.2	65.7	61.6
Machinery specialized for particular industries	9.5	4.1	8.3
Telecommunications, sound recording and reproducing equipment	9.3	6.0	5.9
Road vehicles	41.9	38.3	30.8
Miscellaneous manufactured articles	23.9	22.6	20.9
Total (incl. others)	320.9	322.2	303.9

Exports f.o.b.	2007	2008	2009
Food and live animals	6.1	6.7	24.4
Fish, crustaceans, molluscs and preparations thereof	3.2	3.4	5.2
Vegetables and fruit	1.5	2.9	9.1
Beverages and tobacco	—	0.4	0.1
Crude materials, inedible (excluding fuels)	1.9	3.5	8.2
Animal and vegetable oils, fats and waxes	3.0	0.1	7.4
Machinery and transport equipment	0.8	0.9	5.2
Road vehicles	0.6	0.4	2.0
Total (incl. others)	12.5	13.7	66.0

Source: UN, *International Trade Statistics Yearbook*.

PRINCIPAL TRADING PARTNERS

(US $ million)

Imports c.i.f.	2007	2008	2009
Belgium	12.4	9.8	11.4
Brazil	11.4	13.8	17.3
China, People's Repub.	34.0	34.7	34.9
Côte d'Ivoire	21.5	28.8	43.5
Denmark	46.2	23.7	4.9
France (incl. Monaco)	9.5	8.8	10.2
Germany	26.3	35.1	17.2
Hong Kong	6.5	6.2	3.9
India	6.5	5.6	10.7
Japan	8.8	6.1	4.5

Imports c.i.f.—*continued*	2007	2008	2009
Netherlands	18.0	22.7	17.2
Senegal	8.8	9.7	5.6
Singapore	4.7	4.5	5.6
Spain	7.4	3.7	6.5
Thailand	0.5	4.3	10.8
Turkey	1.7	4.3	8.5
United Arab Emirates	6.7	11.7	8.6
United Kingdom	24.7	26.1	23.7
USA	41.8	35.2	7.1
Total (incl. others)	320.9	322.2	303.9

Exports f.o.b.	2007	2008	2009
France (incl. Monaco)	1.7	0.3	4.9
Netherlands	0.8	1.6	0.9
Senegal	3.2	2.4	17.7
United Kingdom	2.5	1.4	4.9
Total (incl. others)	12.5	13.7	66.0

Source: UN, *International Trade Statistics Yearbook*.

Transport

ROAD TRAFFIC
(motor vehicles in use, estimates)

	2002	2003	2004
Passenger cars	7,919	8,168	8,109
Buses	2,261	1,300	1,200
Lorries and vans	1,531	1,862	1,761

2007: Passenger cars 8,815; Buses and coaches 1,012; Vans and lorries 2,601.

Source: IRF, *World Road Statistics*.

SHIPPING

Merchant Fleet
(registered at 31 December)

	2007	2008	2009
Number of vessels	15	15	15
Total displacement (grt)	34,635	34,635	34,635

Source: IHS Fairplay, *World Fleet Statistics*.

International Sea-borne Freight Traffic
('000 metric tons)

	1996	1997	1998
Goods loaded	55.9	38.1	47.0
Goods unloaded	482.7	503.7	493.2

CIVIL AVIATION
(traffic on scheduled services)

	1992	1993	1994
Kilometres flown (million)	1	1	1
Passengers carried ('000)	19	19	19
Passenger-km (million)	50	50	50
Total ton-km (million)	5	5	5

Source: UN, *Statistical Yearbook*.

Tourism

FOREIGN VISITORS BY COUNTRY OF ORIGIN*

	2007	2008	2009
Belgium	2,746	3,192	3,118
Denmark	4,372	4,540	4,547
Germany	6,418	5,289	3,539
Netherlands	15,921	18,920	14,246
Norway	3,212	5,324	4,123
Sweden	7,458	8,370	8,302
United Kingdom	66,042	62,108	63,937
USA	1,297	1,394	1,930
Total (incl. others)	142,626	146,759	141,569

* Air charter tourist arrivals.

Receipts from tourism (US $ million, incl. passenger transport): 100 in 2007; 81 in 2008; 64 in 2009.

Source: World Tourism Organization.

Communications Media

	2008	2009	2010
Telephones ('000 main lines in use)	48.9	48.5	48.8
Mobile cellular telephones ('000 subscribers)	1,166.1	1,312.9	1,478.3
Internet users ('000)	114.2	130.1	n.a.
Broadband subscribers	300	300	400

Personal computers (number in use): 57,000 (35.3 per 1,000 persons) in 2005.

Television receivers (number in use): 4,000 in 2000.

Radio receivers ('000 in use): 196 in 1997.

Daily newspapers: 2 in 2004 (average circulation 2,100 copies in 1998).

Non-daily newspapers: 4 in 1996 (estimated average circulation 6,000 copies).

Book production: 10 titles in 1998 (10,000 copies).

Sources: UNESCO Institute for Statistics; UNESCO, *Statistical Yearbook*; UN, *Statistical Yearbook*; International Telecommunication Union.

Education

(2006/07)

	Institutions	Teachers	Students		
			Males	Females	Total
Primary	491	4,428	108,540	111,883	220,423
Junior Secondary	186	2,385	34,432	32,047	66,479
Senior Secondary	66	845	19,024	14,697	33,721

Source: Department of State for Education, Banjul.

Pupil-teacher ratio (primary education, UNESCO estimate): 36.6 in 2008/09 (Source: UNESCO Institute for Statistics).

Adult literacy rate (UNESCO estimates): 46.5% (males 57.6%; females 35.8%) in 2009 (Source: UNESCO Institute for Statistics).

Directory

The Government

HEAD OF STATE

President: Col (retd) Alhaji YAHYA A. J. J. JAMMEH (proclaimed Head of State 26 July 1994; elected President 26 September 1996, re-elected 18 October 2001, 22 September 2006 and 24 November 2011).

Vice-President: ISATOU NJIE-SAIDY.

THE CABINET
(May 2012)

President and Minister of Defence, Fisheries, Water Resources and National Assembly Matters: Col (retd) Alhaji YAHYA A. J. J. JAMMEH.

Vice-President and Minister of Women's Affairs: Dr ISATOU NJIE-SAIDY.

Minister of Finance and Economic Affairs: ABDOU KOLLEY.

Minister of Tourism and Culture: FATOU MASS JOBE-NJIE.

Minister of Foreign Affairs, International Co-operation and Gambians Abroad: MAMBURY NJIE.

Minister of Higher Education, Research, Science and Technology: Dr MAMADOU TANGARA.

Minister of Health and Social Welfare: FATIM BADJI.

Minister of Trade, Regional Integration and Employment: KEBBA S. TOURAY.

Minister of Basic and Secondary Education: FATOU LAMIN FAYE.

Minister of Forestry and the Environment: FATOU GAYE.

Minister of Petroleum: TENENG MBA JAITEH.

Minister of Local Government and Lands: LAMIN WAA JUWARA.

Minister of Justice and Attorney-General: LAMIN JOBARTEH.

Minister of the Interior: OUSMAN SONKO.

Minister of Youth and Sports: ALIEU K. JANNEH.

Minister of Agriculture: SOLOMON OWENS.

Minister of Works, Construction and Infrastructure: FRANCIS LITI MBOGE.

MINISTRIES

Office of the President: PMB, State House, Banjul; tel. 4223811; e-mail info@statehouse.gm; internet www.statehouse.gm.

Office of the Vice-President: State House, Banjul; tel. 4227605; fax 4224401; e-mail info@ovp.gov.gm; internet www.ovp.gov.gm.

Ministry of Agriculture: The Quadrangle, Banjul; tel. 4228270; fax 4229325; e-mail info@moa.gov.gm; internet www.moa.gov.gm.

Ministry of Basic and Secondary Education: Willy Thorpe Bldg, Banjul; tel. 4228232; fax 4224180; e-mail info@mobse.gov.gm; internet www.mobse.gov.gm.

Ministry of Finance and Economic Affairs: The Quadrangle, POB 9686, Banjul; tel. 4227221; fax 4227954; e-mail info@mof.gov.gm; internet www.mof.gov.gm.

Ministry of Fisheries, Water Resources and National Assembly Matters: Marina Parade, Banjul; tel. 4227773; fax 4225009; e-mail info@mofwrnam.gov.gm; internet www.mofwrnam.gov.gm.

Ministry of Foreign Affairs, International Co-operation and Gambians Abroad: 4 Marina Parade, Banjul; tel. 4223577; fax 4227917; e-mail info@mofa.gov.gm; internet www.mofa.gov.gm.

Ministry of Forestry and the Environment: Kairaba Ave, Serekunda; tel. 4399447; fax 4399518; e-mail info@mofen.gov.gm; internet www.mofen.gov.gm.

Ministry of Health and Social Welfare: The Quadrangle, Banjul; tel. 4228624; fax 4229325; e-mail info@moh.gov.gm; internet www.moh.gov.gm.

Ministry of Higher Education, Research, Science and Technology: Bertil Harding Highway, Kotu, Banjul; tel. 4466752; fax 4465408; e-mail info@moherst.gov.gm; internet www.moherst.gov.gm.

Ministry of Information and Communication Infrastructure: GRTS Bldg, MDI Rd, Kanifing, Banjul; tel. 4378028; fax 4378029; e-mail info@moici.gov.gm; internet www.moici.gov.gm.

Ministry of the Interior: 5 J. R. Forster St, Banjul; tel. 4223277; fax 4201320; e-mail info@moi.gov.gm; internet www.moi.gov.gm.

Ministry of Justice and Attorney-General's Chambers: Marina Parade, Banjul; tel. 4225352; fax 4229908; e-mail info@moj.gov.gm; internet www.moj.gov.gm.

Ministry of Local Government and Lands: The Quadrangle, Banjul; tel. 4222022; fax 4225261; e-mail info@molgl.gov.gm; internet www.molgl.gov.gm.

Ministry of Petroleum: Bertil Harding Highway, Kotu, Banjul; tel. 8806317; fax 8200896; e-mail info@mop.gov.gm; internet www.mop.gov.gm.

Ministry of Tourism and Culture: New Administrative Bldg, The Quadrangle, Banjul; tel. 4229844; fax 4227753; e-mail info@motc.gov.gm; internet www.motc.gov.gm.

Ministry of Trade, Regional Integration and Employment: Central Bank Bldg, Independence Dr., Banjul; tel. 4228868; fax 4227756; e-mail info@motie.gov.gm; internet www.motie.gov.gm.

Ministry of Works, Construction and Infrastructure: MDI Rd, Kanifing, Banjul; tel. 4375761; fax 4375765; e-mail info@mowci.gov.gm; internet www.mowci.gov.gm.

Ministry of Youth and Sports: The Quadrangle, Banjul; tel. 4225264; fax 4225267; e-mail info@moys.gov.gm; internet www.moys.gov.gm.

President and Legislature

PRESIDENT

Presidential Election, 24 November 2011

Candidate	Valid votes	% of valid votes
Yahya A. J. J. Jammeh (APRC)	470,550	71.54
Ousainou N. Darboe (UDP)	114,177	17.36
Hamat Bah (Independent)	73,060	11.11
Total*	657,787	100.00

* In addition, there were 264 invalid votes.

NATIONAL ASSEMBLY

Speaker: ABDOULIE BOJANG.

National Assembly: Parliament Buildings, Independence Dr., Banjul; tel. 4227241; fax 4225123; e-mail assemblyclerk@yahoo.com; internet www.nationalassembly.gm.

General Election, 29 March 2012*

Party	Votes	% of votes	Seats
Alliance for Patriotic Reorientation and Construction (APRC)	80,289	51.82	43
National Reconciliation Party (NRP)	14,606	9.43	1
Independents	60,055	38.76	4
Total	154,950	100.00	48†

* The election was boycotted by six of the seven main opposition parties, including the United Democratic Party and the National Alliance for Democracy and Development.

† The President of the Republic is empowered by the Constitution to nominate five additional members of parliament. The total number of members of parliament is thus 53.

Election Commission

Independent Electoral Commission (IEC): Election House, Bertil Harding Highway, Kanifing East Layout, POB 793 Banjul; tel. 4373804; fax 4373803; e-mail info@iec.gm; internet www.iec.gm; f. 1997; Chair. Alhaji MUSTAPHA CARAYOL.

Political Organizations

Alliance for Patriotic Reorientation and Construction (APRC): Sankung Sillah Bldg, Kairaba Ave, Banjul; tel. 9745687; f. 1996; governing party; Chair. President YAHYA A. J. J. JAMMEH.

Gambia Moral Congress (GMC): 78 Bertil Harding Highway, Kotu, Banjul; e-mail info@Gambia-Congress.org; internet www.gambia-congress.org; f. 2008; Exec. Chair. MAI N. K. FATTY.

The Gambia Party for Democracy and Progress (GPDP): POB 4014, Kombo St Mary, Serrekunda; tel. 9955226; f. 2004; Sec.-Gen. HENRY GOMEZ.

National Alliance for Democracy and Development (NADD): 30 Papa Sarr St, Churchill, Serrekunda; f. Jan. 2005 to contest 2006 elections; Co-ordinator HALIFA SALLAH; comprises parties listed below.

People's Democratic Organization for Independence and Socialism (PDOIS): POB 2306, 1 Sambou St, Churchill, Serrekunda; tel. and fax 4393177; e-mail foroyaa@qanet.gm; f. 1986; socialist; Leaders HALIFA SALLAH, SAM SARR, SIDIA JATTA.

People's Progressive Party (PPP): c/o Omar Jallow, Ninth St East, Fajara M Section, Banjul; tel. and fax 4392674; f. 1959; fmr ruling party in 1962–94; centrist; Chair. OMAR JALLOW.

National Convention Party (NCP): 38 Sayerr Jobe Ave, Banjul; tel. 6408128 (mobile); f. 1977; left-wing; Leader EBRIMA JANKO SANYANG.

National Democratic Action Movement (NDAM): 1 Box Bar Rd, Nema, Brikama Town, Western Division, Banjul; tel. 7788882; e-mail ndam_gambia@hotmail.com; f. 2002; reformist; Leader and Sec.-Gen. LAMIN WAA JUWARA.

National Reconciliation Party (NRP): 69 Daniel Goddard St, Banjul; tel. 4201371; fax 4201732; f. 1996; formed an alliance with the UDP in 2006; Leader HAMAT N. K. BAH.

United Democratic Party (UDP): 1 Rene Blain St, Banjul; tel. 4221730; fax 4224601; e-mail info@udpgambia.com; internet www.udpgambia.com; f. 1996; formed an alliance with the NRP in 2006 and with the GMC in 2011; reformist; Sec.-Gen. and Leader OUSAINU N. DARBOE; Nat. Pres. DEMBO BOJANG.

Diplomatic Representation

EMBASSIES AND HIGH COMMISSIONS IN THE GAMBIA

Cuba: C/801, POB 4627, Banjul; tel. and fax 4495382; e-mail embacuba@ganet.gm; Ambassador MARIA INES FERNANDEZ.

Guinea-Bissau: 78 Atlantic Rd, Fajara (Bakau), Banjul; tel. 4226862; Ambassador FRANCISCA MARIA MONTEIRA SILVA VAZ TURPIN.

Libya: Independence Dr., Banjul; tel. 4223213; fax 4223214; Ambassador Dr ALI MUHAMMAD DUKALY.

Nigeria: 52 Garba Jalumpa Ave, Bakau, POB 630, Banjul; tel. 4495803; fax 4496456; e-mail nighcgambia@yahoo.com; High Commissioner ESTHER JOHN AUDU.

Senegal: 159 Kairaba Ave, POB 385, Banjul; tel. 4373752; fax 4373750; Ambassador DIAMÉ SIGNATÉ.

Sierra Leone: 67 Daniel Goddard St, Banjul; tel. 4228206; fax 4229819; e-mail mfodayyumkella@yahoo.co.uk; High Commissioner Alhaji KEMOH FADIKA.

Taiwan (Republic of China): 26 Radio Gambia Rd, Kanifing South, POB 916, Banjul; tel. 4374046; fax 4374055; e-mail rocemb@gamtel.gm; Ambassador SAMUEL CHEN.

United Kingdom: 48 Atlantic Rd, Fajara, POB 507, Banjul; tel. 4495133; fax 4496134; e-mail bhcbanjul@fco.gov.uk; internet ukingambia.fco.gov.uk/en; High Commissioner DAVID MORELY.

USA: The White House, Kairaba Ave, Fajara, PMB 19, Banjul; tel. 4392856; fax 4392475; e-mail consularbanjul@state.gov; internet banjul.usembassy.gov; Ambassador PAMELA ANN WHITE.

Judicial System

The judicial system of The Gambia is based on English Common Law and legislative enactments of the Republic's parliament, which include an Islamic Law Recognition Ordinance whereby an Islamic Court exercises jurisdiction in certain cases between, or exclusively affecting, Muslims.

The Constitution of the Second Republic guarantees the independence of the judiciary. The Supreme Court is defined as the final court of appeal. Provision is made for a special criminal court to hear and determine all cases relating to theft and misappropriation of public funds.

Supreme Court of The Gambia

Law Courts, Independence Dr., Banjul; tel. 4227383; fax 4228380.

Consists of the Chief Justice and up to six other judges.

Chief Justice: EMMANUEL A. AGIM.

The **Banjul Magistrates Court**, the **Kanifing Magistrates Court** and the **Divisional Courts** are courts of summary jurisdiction presided over by a magistrate or in his absence by two or more lay justices of the peace. There are resident magistrates in all divisions. The magistrates have limited civil and criminal jurisdiction, and appeal from these courts lies with the Supreme Court. **Islamic Courts** have jurisdiction in matters between, or exclusively affecting, Muslim Gambians and relating to civil status, marriage, succession, donations, testaments and guardianship. The Courts administer Islamic *Shari'a* law. A cadi, or a cadi and two assessors, preside over and constitute an Islamic Court. Assessors of the Islamic Courts are Justices of the Peace of Islamic faith. **District Tribunals** have appellate jurisdiction in cases involving customs and traditions. Each court consists of three district tribunal members, one of whom is selected as president, and other court members from the area over which it has jurisdiction.

Attorney-General: LAMIN JOBARTEH.

Solicitor-General: PA HARRY JAMMEH.

Religion

About 85% of the population are Muslims. The remainder are mainly Christians, and there are small numbers of animists, mostly of the Diola and Karoninka ethnic groups.

ISLAM

Banjul Central Mosque: King Fahd Bin Abdul Aziz Mosque, Box Bar Rd, POB 562, Banjul; tel. 4228094; Imam Ratib Alhaji TAFSIR GAYE.

Supreme Islamic Council: Banjul; Chair. Alhaji BANDING DRAMMEH; Vice-Chair. Alhaji OUSMAN JAH.

CHRISTIANITY

Christian Council of The Gambia: MDI Rd, Kanifing, POB 27, Banjul; tel. 4392092; f. 1966; seven mems (churches and other Christian bodies); Chair. Rt Rev. ROBERT P. ELLISON (Roman Catholic Bishop of Banjul); Sec.-Gen. Rev. EDU GOMEZ.

The Anglican Communion

The diocese of The Gambia, which includes Senegal and Cape Verde, forms part of the Church of the Province of West Africa. The Archbishop of the Province is the Bishop of Koforidua, Ghana. There are about 1,500 adherents in The Gambia.

Bishop of The Gambia: Rt Rev. Dr SOLOMON TILEWA JOHNSON, Bishopscourt, POB 51, Banjul; tel. 4228405; fax 4229495; e-mail anglican@qanet.gm.

The Roman Catholic Church

The Gambia comprises a single diocese (Banjul), directly responsible to the Holy See. Some 3% of the population are Roman Catholics. The diocese administers a development organization (Caritas, The Gambia), and runs 63 schools and training centres. The Gambia participates in the Inter-territorial Catholic Bishops' Conference of The Gambia and Sierra Leone (based in Freetown, Sierra Leone).

Bishop of Banjul: Rt Rev. ROBERT PATRICK ELLISON, Bishop's House, POB 165, Banjul; tel. 4391957; fax 4390998; e-mail rpel202@yahoo.co.uk.

Protestant Churches

Abiding Word Ministries (AWM): 156 Mosque Rd, PMB 207, Serrekunda Post Office, Serrekunda; tel. 7640126; fax 4374069; e-mail info@awmgambia.com; internet www.awmgambia.com; f. 1988; Senior Pastor Rev. FRANCIS FORBES.

Evangelical Lutheran Church in The Gambia: POB 5275, Brikama West Coast Region; tel. 9083755; fax 7043336; e-mail leadership@elctg.org; internet www.elctg.org.

Methodist Church: 1 Macoumba Jallow St, POB 288, Banjul; tel. 4227506; fax 4228510; f. 1821; Chair. and Gen. Supt Rev. NORMAN A. GRIGG.

BAHÁ'Í FAITH

National Spiritual Assembly: POB 2532, Serrekunda; tel. 4229015; e-mail nsagambia@gamtel.gm; internet bci.org/bahaigambia.

The Press

All independent publications are required to register annually with the Government and to pay a registration fee.

The Daily Express: Banjul; f. 2006; independent; Man. Dir SAM OBI.

The Daily News: 65 Kombo Sillah Dr., Churchill's Town, POB 2849, Serrekunda; tel. 8905629; e-mail dailynews34@yahoo.com; internet dailynews.gm; f. 2009; 3 a week; Dir MADI M. K. CEESAY; Editor-in-Chief SAIKOU JAMMEH.

The Daily Observer: Gacem Rd, Kanifing Industrial Area, Bakau, POB 131, Banjul; tel. 414425; fax 4496878; e-mail webmaster@

observer.gm; internet www.observer.gm; f. 1992; daily; pro-Govt; Man. Dir (vacant).

Foroyaa (Freedom): 1 Sambou St, Churchill's Town, POB 2306, Serrekunda; tel. and fax 4393177; e-mail online@foroyaa.gm; internet www.foroyaa.gm; f. 1987; daily; publ. by the PDOIS; Editors HALIFA SALLAH, SAM SARR, SIDIA JATTA.

The Gambia Daily: Dept of Information, 14 Daniel Goddard St, Banjul; tel. 4225060; fax 4227230; e-mail gamna@gamtel.gm; f. 1994; govt organ; Dir of Information EBRUMA COLE; circ. 500.

The Independent: next to A–Z Supermarket, Kairaba Ave, Banjul; f. 1999; 2 a week; independent; Gen. Man. MADI CEESAY; Editor-in-Chief MUSA SAIDYKHAN.

The Point: 2 Garba Jahumpa Rd, Fajara, POB 66, Banjul; tel. 4497441; fax 4497442; e-mail thepoint13@yahoo.com; internet www.thepoint.gm; f. 1991; 3 a week; Editor-in-Chief PAP SAINE; circ. 3,000.

NEWS AGENCY

The Gambia News Agency (GAMNA): Dept of Information, 14 Daniel Goddard St, Banjul; tel. 4225060; fax 4227230; e-mail gamna@gamtel.gm; Dir EBRIMA COLE.

PRESS ASSOCIATION

The Gambia Press Union (GPU): 78 Mosque Rd, Serrekunda, POB 1440, Banjul; tel. and fax 4377020; e-mail gpu@qanet.gm; internet www.gambiapressunion.org; f. 1978; affiliated to West African Journalists' Association; Pres. NDEY TAPHA SOSSEH; Sec.-Gen. EMIL TOURAY.

Publishers

National Printing and Stationery Corpn: Sankung Sillah St, Kanifing; tel. 4374403; fax 4395759; f. 1998; state-owned.

Baroueli: 73 Mosque Rd, Serrekunda, POB 976, Banjul; tel. 4392480; e-mail baroueli@qanet.gm; f. 1986; educational.

Observer Company: Bakau New Town Rd, Kanifing, PMB 131, Banjul; tel. 4496087; fax 4496878; e-mail webmaster@observer.gm; internet www.observer.gm; f. 1995; indigenous languages and non-fiction.

Sunrise Publishers: POB 955, Banjul; tel. 4393538; e-mail sunrise@qanet.gm; internet www.sunrisepublishers.net; f. 1985; regional history, politics and culture; Man. PATIENCE SONKO-GODWIN.

Broadcasting and Communications

TELECOMMUNICATIONS

In 2011 the Gambia telecommunications sector comprised three mobile cellular telephone operators and one fixed-line operator. A fifth licence was issued to Nigeria-owned Globacom in 2010

Africell (Gambia): 43 Kairaba Ave, POB 2140, Banjul; tel. 4376022; fax 4376066; e-mail mmakkaoui@africell.gm; internet www.africell.gm; f. 2001; provider of mobile cellular telecommunications; CEO ALIEU BADARA MBYE.

Comium Gambia: 27 Kairaba Ave, Pipeline, KSMD, Banjul; tel. 6601601; fax 6601602; e-mail info@comium.gm; internet www.comium.gm; f. 2007; operates mobile cellular telephone network under the Nakam brand; Man. Dir AMER ATWI.

The Gambia Telecommunications Co Ltd (GAMTEL): Gamtel House, 3 Nelson Mandela St, POB 387, Banjul; tel. 4229999; fax 4228004; e-mail gen-info@gamtel.gm; internet www.gamtel.gm; f. 1984; state-owned; Man. Dir BABOUCAR SANYANG (acting).

Gamcel: 59 Mamadi Maniyang Highway, Kanifing; tel. 4398169; fax 4372932; internet www.gamcel.gm; f. 2000; wholly owned subsidiary of GAMTEL providing mobile cellular telephone services.

QCell Gambia: QCell House, Kairaba Ave, Serrekunda; tel. 3333111 (mobile); fax 4376311; internet www.qcell.gm; f. 2008; mobile cellular services; CEO MUHAMMED JAH.

BROADCASTING

Radio

The Gambia Radio and Television Services (GRTS): GRTV Headquarters, MDI Rd, Kanifing, POB 158, Banjul; tel. 4373913; fax 4374242; e-mail bora@gamtel.gm; internet www.grts.gm; f. 1962; state-funded, non-commercial broadcaster; radio broadcasts in English, Mandinka, Wolof, Fula, Diola, Serer and Serahuli; Dir-Gen. Alhaji MODOU SANYANG.

Citizen FM: Banjul; independent commercial broadcaster; broadcasts news and information in English, Wolof and Mandinka; rebroadcasts selected programmes from the British Broadcasting Corpn; operations suspended in Oct. 2001; Propr BABOUCAR GAYE; News Editor EBRIMA SILLAH.

Farafenni Community Radio: Farafenni; tel. 9931964; Gen. Man. SAINEY DIBBA.

FM B Community Radio Station: Brikama; tel. 4483000; fax 4484100; e-mail brikamacommunityradio@yahoo.co.uk; f. 1998; FM broadcaster; Admin. Man. BAKARY K. TOURAY.

Radio 1 FM: 44 Kairaba Ave, POB 2700, Serrekunda; tel. 4396076; fax 4394911; e-mail george.radio1@qanet.gm; f. 1990; private station broadcasting FM music programmes to the Greater Banjul area; Dir GEORGE CHRISTENSEN.

Radio Gambia: Mile 7, Banjul; tel. 4495101; fax 4495923; e-mail semafye@hotmail.com.

Sud FM: Buckle St, POB 64, Banjul; tel. 4222359; fax 4222394; e-mail sudfm@gamtel.gm; licence revoked in 2005; Man. MAMADOU HOUSSABA BA.

Teranga FM: Sinchu Alhagie Village, Kombo North, West Coast Region; f. 2009; Man. ISMAILA SISAY.

West Coast Radio: Manjai Kunda, POB 2687, Serrekunda; tel. 4460911; fax 4461193; e-mail info@westcoast.gm; internet www.westcoast.gm; FM broadcaster; Man. Dir PETER GOMEZ.

Unique FM: Garba Jahumpa Rd, Bakau; tel. 7555777; internet www.uniquefm.gm; f. 2007; Man. LAMIN MANGA.

The Gambia also receives broadcasts from Radio Democracy for Africa (f. 1998), a division of the Voice of America, and the British Broadcasting Corpn.

Television

The Gambia Radio and Television Services (GRTS): see Radio; television broadcasts commenced 1995.

There is also a private satellite channel, Premium TV.

Finance

(cap. = capital; res = reserves; dep. = deposits; m. = million; br(s). = branch(es); amounts in dalasi)

BANKING

At the end of 2010 there were 14 banks operating in the country, of which one was an Islamic bank and 13 were conventional commercial banks.

Central Bank

Central Bank of The Gambia: 1–2 ECOWAS Ave, Banjul; tel. 4228103; fax 4226969; e-mail info@cbg.gm; internet www.cbg.gm; f. 1971; bank of issue; monetary authority; cap. 81.0m., res 4.3m., dep. 1,702.7m. (Dec. 2009); Gov. MODOU BAMBA SAHO.

Other Banks

Access Bank (Gambia) Ltd: 47 Kairaba Ave, Fajara, KSMD; tel. 4396679; fax 4396640; e-mail jammehm@accessbankgambia.com; internet www.accessbankplc.com/gm; f. 2007; Man. Dir LEAK OJIOGO.

Arab-Gambian Islamic Bank: 7 ECOWAS Ave, POB 1415, Banjul; tel. 4222222; fax 4223770; e-mail info@agib.gm; internet www.agib.gm; f. 1996; 21.1% owned by The Gambia National Insurance Co Ltd, 20.0% owned by Islamic Development Bank (Saudi Arabia); cap. and res 9.0m., total assets 116.9m. (Dec. 2001); Chair. SUZANNE IROCHE; Man. Dir SALISU SIRAJO; 1 br.

Bank PHB: 11A Liberation Ave, POB 211, Banjul; tel. 4227944; fax 4229312; e-mail mgcisse@ibc.gm; internet gambia.bankphb.com; f. 1968; fmrly International Bank for Commerce (Gambia) Ltd, name changed as above August 2008 following acquisition by Bank PHB Nigeria; cap. 60m., res 59.9m., dep. 434.6m. (Dec. 2006); Man. Dir CHUKS CHIBUNDU; 2 brs.

Banque Sahelo-Saherienne pour l'Investissement et Commerce Gambie Ltd: 52 Kairaba Ave, PMB 204, KMC; tel. 4498078; fax 4498080; e-mail bsic@bsicgambia.gm; f. 2008; Gen. Man. YOUSEF SGHAYER AHMED TURKMAN.

Ecobank Gambia Ltd: 42 Kairaba Ave, POB 3466, Serrekunda; tel. 4399030; fax 4399034; e-mail egacustomercare@ecobank.com; cap. 79.5m., dep. 629m. (Dec. 2009); Man. Dir FITZGERALD ODONKOR.

First International Bank Ltd: 2 Kairaba Ave, Serrekunda; tel. and fax 4396580; e-mail info@fibgm.com; internet www.fibankgm.com; f. 1999; 61.9% owned by Slok Ltd (Nigeria); cap. 150.7m., res 6.8m., dep. 570.3m. (Dec. 2010); Chair. EDRISSA JOBE; Man. Dir YASSIN BAYO; 8 brs.

Guaranty Trust Bank (Gambia): 56 Kairaba Ave, Fajara, POB 1958, Banjul; tel. 4376371; fax 4376398; e-mail webmaster@gambia

.gtbplc.com; internet www.gambia.gtbplc.com; f. 2002; subsidiary of Guaranty Trust Bank PLC (Nigeria); Chair. AMADOU SAMBA; Man. Dir LEKAN SANUSI.

International Commercial Bank (Gambia) Ltd: GIPFZA House, Ground Floor, 48 Kairaba Ave, Serrekunda, KMC, POB 1600, Banjul; tel. 4377878; fax 4377880; e-mail icbank@icbank-gambia.com; internet www.icbank-gambia.com; f. 2005; CEO LALIT MOHAN TEWARI; 3 brs.

Oceanic Bank Gambia: Adam's Shopping Center, Bertil Hardling Highway, Kololi, POB 1884, Banjul; tel. 4466711; fax 4466710; e-mail Info@oceanicbankgambia.com; internet www.oceanicbankgambia.com; a subsidiary of Oceanic Bank International PLC (Nigeria); Man. Dir KINGSLEY KEINDE ADEBISI.

Prime Bank Gambia Ltd: 42 Kairaba Ave, KSMD, Banjul; tel. 4399283; fax 4399044; e-mail info@primebankgambia.com; internet www.primebankgambia.gm; f. 2009; Chair. G. W. HAIKAL; Exec. Dir FADI A. MENDY.

Skye Bank Gambia: 70 Kairaba Ave, Fajara, KSM; tel. 4414370; e-mail info@skyebankgm.com; subsidiary of Skye Bank PLC (Nigeria); Man. Dir AKIM YUSUF.

Standard Chartered Bank (Gambia) Ltd: 8/10 ECOWAS Ave, POB 259, Banjul; tel. 4202929; fax 4202692; e-mail Humphrey.Mukwereza@gm.standardchartered.com; internet www.standardchartered.com/gm; f. 1894; 75% owned by Standard Chartered Holdings BV, The Netherlands; cap. 60m., res 157.6m., dep. 2,183.7m. (Dec. 2009); Chair. MOMODOU B. A. SENGHORE; CEO HUMPHREY MUKWEREZA; 5 brs.

Trust Bank Ltd (TBL): 3–4 ECOWAS Ave, POB 1018, Banjul; tel. 4225777; fax 4225781; e-mail info@trustbank.gm; internet www.trustbank.gm; f. 1997; fmrly Meridien BIAO Bank Gambia Ltd; 22.54% owned by Data Bank, 36.97% by Social Security and Housing Finance Corpn; cap. 60.0m., res 183.7m., dep. 2,477.1m. (Dec. 2009); Chair. KEN OFORI ATTA; Man. Dir PA MACOUMBA NJIE; 8 brs.

Zenith Bank (Gambia) Ltd: 49 Kairaba Ave, Fajara, POB 2823, Serrekunda; tel. 4399471; f. 2008; subsidiary of Zenith Bank PLC; Man. Dir EMEKA ANYAEGBUNA.

INSURANCE

In 2010 there were 11 insurance companies operating in the country.

Capital Express Assurance (Gambia) Ltd: 22 Anglesea St, POB 268, Banjul; tel. 4227480; fax 4229219; e-mail capinsur@gamtel.gm; f. 1985; subsidiary of Capital Express Assurance Limited (Nigeria); CEO KUNLE ADEGBOYE.

The Gambia National Insurance Co Ltd (GNIC): 19 Kairaba Ave, Fajara, KSMD, POB 750, Banjul; tel. 4395725; fax 4395716; e-mail info@gnic.gm; internet www.gnic.gm; f. 1974; privately owned; Chair. MATARR O. DRAMMEH; Man. Dir FYE K. CEESAY; 3 brs.

Global Security Insurance Co Ltd: 73A Independence Dr., POB 1400, Banjul; tel. 4223716; fax 4223715; e-mail global@gamtel.gm; f. 1996; Man. Dir KWASU DARBOE.

Great Alliance Insurance Co: 10 Nelson Mandela St, POB 1160, Banjul; tel. 4227839; fax 4229444; f. 1989; Pres. BAI MATARR DRAMMEH; Man. Dir DEBORAH H. FORSTER.

IGI Gamstar Insurance Co Ltd: 79 Daniel Goddard St, POB 1276, Banjul; tel. 4228610; fax 4229755; e-mail gamstarinsurance@hotmail.com; f. 1991; Man. Dir FRANK UCHE.

International Insurance Co. Ltd: Duwa Jabbi Bldg, 5 OAU Blvd, POB 1254, Banjul; tel. 4202761; fax 4202763; e-mail iic@gamtel.gm; Man. Dir SENOR THOMAS.

Londongate (Gambia) Insurance Co: 1–3 Liberation Ave, POB 602, Banjul; tel. 4201740; fax 4201742; e-mail izadi@londongate.gm; internet www.londongate.co.uk/gambia_profile.htm; f. 1999; owned by Boule & Co Ltd; Man. Dir SHAHROKH IZADI.

New Vision Insurance Co Ltd: 3–4 ECOWAS Ave, POB 239, Banjul; tel. 4223045; fax 4223040; Dir BIRAN BAH.

Prime Insurance Co Ltd: 10C Nelson Mandela St, POB 277, Banjul; tel. 4222476; e-mail prime@qanet.gm; f. 1997; Gen. Man. JARREH F. M. TOURAY.

Sunshine Insurance Company Ltd: 7/8 Nelson Mandela St, Banjul; tel. 4202645; fax 4202648; e-mail sunshine.insurance@qanet.gm; Man. Dir ALMAMY B. JOBARTEH.

Takaful Gambia Ltd: 22 Serign Modou Sillah St, Banjul; tel. 4227480; fax 4229219; e-mail info@takaful.gm; Man. Dir MAMODOU M. JOOF.

Insurance Association

Insurance Association of The Gambia (IAG): Banjul; tel. 4229952; fax 4201637; e-mail info@iag.gm; internet www.iag.gm; f. 1987; Pres. DAWDA SARGE; Sec.-Gen. HENRY M. JAWO.

Trade and Industry

GOVERNMENT AGENCIES

The Gambia Investment and Export Promotion Agency (GIEPA): GIEPA House, 48A Kairaba Ave, Serrekunda, KMC, POB 757, Banjul; tel. 4377377; fax 4377379; e-mail info.gipfza@qanet.gm; internet www.gipfza.gm; f. 2001; fmrly The Gambia Investment Promotion and Free Zones Agency (f. 2001), the implementing agency of the Gateway Project, funded by the World Bank and the Gambian Government, responsible for fostering local and foreign direct investment; name changed as above in 2010; Chair. FATOU SINYAN MERGAN; CEO FATOU M. JALLOW.

Indigenous Business Advisory Services (IBAS): POB 2502, Bakau; tel. 4496098; e-mail payibas@gamtel.gm; Man. Dir MANGA SANYANG.

DEVELOPMENT AGENCY

The Gambia Rural Development Agency (GARDA): Soma Village, Jarra West, PMB 452, Serrekunda; tel. 4496676; fax 4390095; f. 1990; Exec. Dir KEBBA BAH.

CHAMBER OF COMMERCE

The Gambia Chamber of Commerce and Industry (GCCI): 55 Kairaba Ave, KSMD, POB 3382, Serrekunda; tel. 4378929; fax 4378936; e-mail gcci@gambiachamber.com; internet www.gambiachamber.com; f. 1967; Pres. BAI MATARR DRAMMEH; CEO EDRISSA MASS JOBE.

INDUSTRIAL AND TRADE ASSOCIATIONS

Association of Gambian Entrepreneurs (AGE): POB 200, Banjul; tel. 4393494.

The Gambia Cotton Growers Association: Banjul; Pres. ALPHA BAH; Sec.-Gen. OMAR SUMPO CEESAY.

UTILITIES

Public Utilities Regulatory Authority (PURA): 94 Kairaba Ave, Bakau; tel. 4399601; fax 4399905; e-mail info@pura.gm; internet www.pura.gm; f. 2001; monitors and enforces standards of performance by public utilities; Chair. ABDOULIE TOURAY; Dir-Gen. ALAGI B. GAYE.

National Water and Electricity Co Ltd (NAWEC): 53 Mamady Manjang Highway, Kanifing, POB 609, Banjul; tel. 4376607; fax 4375990; e-mail nawecmd@qanet.gm; internet www.nawec.gm; f. 1996; in 1999 control was transferred to the Bassau Development Corpn, Côte d'Ivoire, under a 15-year contract; electricity and water supply, sewerage services; Chair. MUSTAPHA COLLEY; Man. Dir MOMODOU JALLOW.

TRADE UNIONS

Agricultural Workers' Association (AWA): Banjul; Pres. Sheikh TIJAN SOSSEH; 247 mems.

Association of Gambian Sailors (AGS): c/o 31 OAU Blvd, POB 698, Banjul; tel. 4223080; fax 4227214; Sec.-Gen. ABDOU SANYANG.

The Gambia Dock and Maritime Workers' Union: Albert Market, POB 852, Banjul; tel. 4229448; fax 4225049; Sec.-Gen. LANDING SANYANG.

The Gambia Labour Union: 6 Albion Pl., POB 508, Banjul; f. 1935; Pres. B. B. KEBBEH; Gen. Sec. MOHAMED M. CEESAY; 25,000 mems.

The Gambia National Trades Union Congress (GNTUC): Trade Union House, 31 OAU Blvd, POB 698, Banjul; Pres. MUSTAPHA WADA; Sec.-Gen. EBRIMA GARBA CHAM.

Gambia Teachers' Union (GTU): POB 133, Banjul; tel. and fax 4392075; e-mail gtu@gamtel.gm; f. 1937; Pres. LAMIN DARBOE (acting); Sec.-Gen. ANTOINETTE CORR-JACK.

The Gambia Workers' Confederation: Trade Union House, 72 OAU Blvd, POB 698, Banjul; tel. and fax 4222754; e-mail gambiawc@hotmail.com; f. 1958 as The Gambia Workers' Union; present name adopted in 1985; Sec.-Gen. PA MOMODOU FAAL; 52,000 mems (2007).

Transport

The Gambia Public Transport Corpn: Factory St, Kanifing Housing Estate, POB 801, Kanifing; tel. 4392230; fax 4392454; f. 1975; operates road transport and ferry services; Man. Dir BAKARY HUMA.

RAILWAYS

There are no railways in The Gambia.

ROADS

In 2004 there were an estimated 3,742 km of roads in The Gambia, of which 1,652 km were main roads, and 1,300 km were secondary roads. In that year only 19.3% of the road network was paved. Some roads are impassable in the rainy season. The expansion and upgrading of the road network is planned, as part of the Jammeh administration's programme to improve The Gambia's transport infrastructure. Among intended schemes is the construction of a motorway along the coast, with the aid of a loan of US $8.5m. from Kuwait. In early 1999 Taiwan agreed to provide $6m. for road construction programmes, and in early 2000 work began on the construction of a dual carriageway between Serrekunda, Mandina and Ba, supported by funds from the Islamic Development Fund and the Organization of the Petroleum Exporting Counties. In 2006 the European Union provided a grant of €44m. to rehabilitate five roads.

SHIPPING

The River Gambia is well suited to navigation. A weekly river service is maintained between Banjul and Basse, 390 km above Banjul, and a ferry connects Banjul with Barra. Small ocean-going vessels can reach Kaur, 190 km above Banjul, throughout the year. Facilities at the port of Banjul were modernized and expanded during the mid-1990s, with the aim of enhancing The Gambia's potential as a transit point for regional trade. In 1999 three advanced storage warehouses were commissioned with total storage space of 8,550 sq m. The Gambia's merchant fleet consisted of 15 vessels, totalling 34,635 grt, at 31 December 2009.

The Gambia Ports Authority: 34 Liberation Ave, POB 617, Banjul; tel. 4227269; fax 4227268; e-mail info@gamport.gm; internet www.gambiaports.com; f. 1972; Man. Dir MOHAMMED LAMIN GIBBA.

Gambia River Transport Co Ltd: 61 Wellington St, POB 215, Banjul; tel. 4227664; river transport of groundnuts and general cargo; Man. Dir LAMIN JUWARA; 200 employees.

The Gambia Shipping Agency Ltd: 1A Cotton St, POB 257, Banjul; tel. 4227518; fax 4227929; e-mail Thomas.nielsen@bollore.com; f. 1984; shipping agents and forwarders; Gen. Man. THOMAS NIELSEN; 30 employees.

Interstate Shipping Co (Gambia) Ltd: 43 Buckle St, POB 220, Banjul; tel. 4229388; fax 4229347; e-mail interstate@gamtel.gm; transport and storage; Man. Dir B. F. SAGNIA.

Maersk Gambia Ltd: 80 OAU Blvd, POB 1399, Banjul; tel. 4224450; fax 4224025; e-mail gamsalimp@maersk.com; f. 1993; owned by Maersk Line.

CIVIL AVIATION

Banjul International Airport is situated at Yundum, 27 km from the capital. Construction of a new terminal, at a cost of some US $10m., was completed in late 1996. Facilities at Yundum have been upgraded by the US National Aeronautics and Space Administration, to enable the airport to serve as an emergency landing site for space shuttle vehicles.

The Gambia Civil Aviation Authority (GCAA): Banjul International Airport, Yundum; tel. 4472831; fax 4472190; e-mail dggcaa@qanet.gm; internet www.gambia.gm/gcaa; f. 1991; Man. Dir MALICK CHAM (acting).

The Gambia International Airlines: PMB 353, Banjul; tel. 4472770; fax 4223700; internet www.gia.gm; f. 1996; state-owned; sole handling agent at Banjul, sales agent; Chair. ISATOU HYDARA; Man. Dir BAKARY NYASSI (acting).

Slok Air International (Gambia) Ltd: 55 Kairaba Ave, POB 2697, Banjul; e-mail info@slok-air.com; internet www.slok-air.com; commenced operations in The Gambia in 2004; CEO ABDULKAREEM IDRIS.

Tourism

Tourists are attracted by The Gambia's beaches and also by its abundant birdlife. A major expansion of tourism facilities was carried out in the early 1990s. Although there was a dramatic decline in tourist arrivals in the mid-1990s (owing to the political instability), the tourism sector recovered well. In 2009 some 141,569 tourists visited The Gambia and in that year estimated earnings from tourism were US $64m. While visitor numbers remained constant in the late 2000s, the global financial crisis was reported to have impacted negatively on The Gambia's tourism industry, with earning falling by some 35% between 2007 and 2009. An annual 'Roots Festival' was inaugurated in 1996, with the aim of attracting African-American visitors to The Gambia.

The Gambia Hotel Association: c/o Golden Beach Hotel, Coastal Rd, POB 2345, Bijilo; tel. 4465111; fax 4463722; e-mail gambiahotels@gamtel.gm; internet www.gambiahotels.gm; Chair. ALIEU SECKA.

The Gambia Tourist Authority: Kololi, POB 4085, Bakau; tel. 4462491; fax 4462487; e-mail info@gta.gm; internet www.visitthegambia.gm; f. 2001; Chair. and Dir-Gen. ALIEU MBOGE.

Defence

As assessed at November 2011, the Gambian National Army comprised 800 men (including a marine unit of about 70 and the National Guards) in active service. The Armed Forces comprise the Army, the Navy and the National Guards. Military service has been mainly voluntary; however, the Constitution of the Second Republic, which entered into full effect in January 1997, makes provision for conscription.

Defence Expenditure: Estimated at D189m. in 2010.

Chief of Defence Staff: Brig.-Gen. MASSANEH KINTEH.

Commander of the Gambian National Army: Brig.-Gen. SERIGN MODOU NJIE.

Commander of the Navy: Commodore SILLAH KUJABBIE (acting).

Education

Primary education, beginning at seven years of age, is free but not compulsory and lasts for nine years. It is divided into two cycles of six and three years. Secondary education, from 16 years of age, lasts for a further three years. According to UNESCO estimates, in 2009/10 total enrolment at primary schools included 66% of children in the relevant age-group (boys 64%; girls 67%), while secondary enrolment was equivalent to 54% of the appropriate age-group (boys 56%; girls 53%). The Jammeh administration has, since 1994, embarked on an ambitious project to improve educational facilities and levels of attendance and attainment. A particular aim has been to improve access to schools for pupils in rural areas. Post-secondary education is available in teacher training, agriculture, health and technical subjects. Some 1,591 students were enrolled at tertiary establishments in 1994/95. In 1977 The Gambia introduced Koranic studies at all stages of education, and many children attend Koranic schools (*daara*). The University of The Gambia, at Banjul, was officially opened in 2000. Some 2,842 students were enrolled at the university in 2009/10. In 2004 current expenditure by the central Government on education was an estimated D224.3m., equivalent to 17.5% of non-interest current expenditure.

GEORGIA

Introductory Survey

LOCATION, CLIMATE, LANGUAGE, RELIGION, FLAG, CAPITAL

Georgia is situated in the west and central South Caucasus, on the southern foothills of the Greater Caucasus mountain range. There is a frontier with Turkey to the south-west and a western coastline on the Black Sea. The northern frontier with Russia follows the axis of the Greater Caucasus. To the south lies Armenia, and to the south-east is Azerbaijan. Two territories within Georgia were outside the control of the central Government in mid-2012: Abkhazia (which has the formal status of an autonomous republic), in the north-west, and the former Autonomous Oblast of South Ossetia, in the north. Another autonomous republic within Georgia, Adjara, is located in the south-west. The Black Sea coast and the Rion plains have a warm, humid, subtropical climate, with annual rainfall of more than 2,000 mm and average temperatures of 6°C (42°F) in January and 23°C (73° F) in July. Eastern Georgia has a more continental climate, with cold winters and hot, dry summers. The official language is Georgian, a member of the South Caucasian (Kartavelian) language group, which is written in the Georgian script. Most of the population are adherents of Christianity; the principal denomination is the Georgian Orthodox Church. Islam is professed by Ajarians, Azeris, Kurds and some others. The national flag (proportions 100 by 147) consists of a white field, with a centred red cross and a smaller red cross in each quarter. The capital is Tbilisi.

CONTEMPORARY POLITICAL HISTORY

Historical Context

A powerful kingdom in medieval times, Georgia subsequently came under periods of foreign domination, and was annexed by the Russian Empire from the 19th century. An independent Georgian state was established on 26 May 1918, ruled by a Menshevik Socialist Government. Although it received recognition from the Bolshevik Government of Soviet Russia in May 1920, Bolshevik troops invaded Georgia and proclaimed a Georgian Soviet Socialist Republic (SSR) on 25 February 1921. In December 1922 it was absorbed into the Transcaucasian Soviet Federative Socialist Republic (TSFSR), which, on 22 December, became a founder member of the USSR. In 1936 the TSFSR was disbanded and Georgia reverted to the status of an SSR.

During the 1930s Georgians suffered persecution under the Soviet leader, Stalin (Iosif V. Dzhugashvili), himself a Georgian. Most members of the Georgian leadership were dismissed after Stalin's death in 1953, and demonstrations in support of Stalin in the Georgian capital, Tbilisi, in 1956 were violently dispersed. In 1972 the First Secretary of the Communist Party of Georgia (CPG), Eduard Shevardnadze, attempted to remove officials who had been accused of corruption. Shevardnadze remained leader of the CPG until 1985, when he became Minister of Foreign Affairs of the USSR.

The increased freedom of expression that followed the election of Mikhail Gorbachev as Soviet leader in 1985 allowed the formation of 'unofficial groups', which were prominent in organizing demonstrations in November 1988 against russification in Georgia. In February 1989 Abkhazians renewed a campaign, begun in the 1970s, for secession from Georgia (see Abkhazia). Counter-demonstrations were staged in Tbilisi, to demand that Georgia's territorial integrity be preserved. On the night of 8–9 April 1989 Soviet security forces attacked demonstrators in Tbilisi, who were advocating Georgian independence, killing 16 people and injuring many more. Despite the subsequent resignation of state and party officials (including the First Secretary of the CPG, Jumber Patiashvili), anti-Soviet sentiment increased sharply. In November the Georgian Supreme Soviet (Supreme Council—legislature), which was dominated by CPG members, declared the supremacy of Georgian laws over all-Union (USSR) laws. In February 1990 the same body declared Georgia 'an annexed and occupied country', and in the following month abolished the CPG's monopoly on power. Legislation permitting full multi-party elections was adopted in August.

In early 1990 principal political parties formed the pro-independence Round Table–Free Georgia coalition. Meanwhile, more radical parties, united in the National Forum, announced their intention to boycott the elections to the Georgian Supreme Soviet and, instead, elect a rival parliament, the 'National Congress'. Some 51% of the electorate participated in these unofficial elections, held on 30 September.

In the elections to the Supreme Soviet, held on 28 October and 11 November 1990, the Round Table–Free Georgia coalition, led by Zviad Gamsakhurdia, a former dissident, won 155 seats in the 250-seat chamber, and 64% of the votes cast. The CPG won 64 seats, while the remainder were won by the Georgian Popular Front (GPF), smaller coalitions and independents. All 14 political parties and coalitions involved in the election campaign, including the CPG, declared support for Georgia's independence. The elections were boycotted by many non-ethnic Georgians, since parties limited to one area of the country were prevented from participating.

The new Supreme Soviet convened on 14 November 1990 and elected Gamsakhurdia as its Chairman. It also agreed to rename the territory the Republic of Georgia and to adopt the white, black and cornelian red-coloured flag of the 1918–21 Georgian state (and of the Menshevik Party of that period). Tengiz Sigua was appointed Chairman of the Council of Ministers. The new Supreme Soviet declared illegal the conscription of Georgians into the Soviet armed forces. Many young men were reported to have joined nationalist paramilitary groups or the National Guard (a de facto republican army), which the Supreme Soviet established in January 1991.

The Georgian authorities boycotted the all-Union referendum on the future of the USSR, held in March 1991, but polling stations were opened in Abkhazia, in military barracks, and in the territories of the former autonomous oblast of South Ossetia (which had been abolished in December 1990). It was reported that in Abkhazia almost the entire non-Georgian population voted to preserve the Union, and that in South Ossetia only nine people voted against the preservation of the USSR. On 31 March 1991 the Government conducted a referendum on the restoration of Georgian independence. Of those eligible to vote, 95% participated in the referendum, 93% of whom voted for independence, according to official figures. On 9 April the Georgian Supreme Council approved a decree formally restoring Georgia's independence. Georgia thus became the first republic to secede from the USSR. Direct elections to the newly established post of executive President, held in May, were won by Gamsakhurdia, who received 86.5% of the votes cast. Voting did not take place in Abkhazia or South Ossetia.

Domestic Political Affairs

Gamsakhurdia's actions during the failed Soviet coup by conservative communists in Moscow, the Russian and Soviet capital, in August 1991 were strongly criticized, as he initially refrained from publicly condemning the coup leaders (although the CPG was subsequently disbanded). After the coup collapsed, Gamsakhurdia's position became tenuous. Tengiz Kitovani, the former leader of the National Guard (who had been dismissed by Gamsakhurdia in August), announced that 15,000 of his men were no longer subordinate to the President. Kitovani was joined in opposition to Gamsakhurdia by Sigua, who resigned as Chairman of the Council of Ministers in mid-August. In September 30 opposition parties united and organized a series of demonstrations to demand Gamsakhurdia's resignation. Several people were killed in clashes between Kitovani's troops and those forces loyal to Gamsakhurdia. Gamsakhurdia ordered the arrest of prominent opposition leaders and imposed a state of emergency in Tbilisi.

In December 1991 armed conflict broke out in Tbilisi, as the opposition, led by Kitovani and by Jaba Ioseliani, the leader of the paramilitary *Mkhedrioni* (Horsemen), resorted to force to oust the President. More than 100 people were believed to have been killed. On 2 January 1992 the opposition declared Gamsakhurdia deposed and formed a Military Council, which appointed Sigua as acting Chairman of the Council of Ministers.

Gamsakhurdia and some of his supporters ('Zviadists') fled Georgia four days later. The office of President was abolished, and the functions of Head of State were, instead, to be exercised by the Chairman of the Supreme Council. Sigua subsequently formed a new Government.

The return of Eduard Shevardnadze

In March 1992 Shevardnadze returned to Georgia, and a State Council was created to replace the Military Council in legislative and executive matters. The State Council, of which Shevardnadze was designated Chairman, comprised 50 members, drawn from all the major political organizations, and included Sigua, Ioseliani and Kitovani. By April government troops had re-established control in the rebellious areas. In July, however, a deputy premier was taken hostage by Zviadists in western Georgia. This was followed by the kidnapping of the Minister of Internal Affairs, and several other officials. In response, the State Council dispatched more than 3,000 National Guardsmen to Abkhazia, where the hostages were believed to be held, prompting armed resistance by Abkhazian militia. By August several of the hostages had been released.

An estimated 75% of the electorate participated in elections to the Supreme Council held on 11 October 1992, contested by more than 30 parties and alliances. Voting did not take place in South Ossetia, Mingrelia (south-east of Abkhazia) and parts of Abkhazia. The largest number of seats in the 235-seat legislature (29) was won by the centrist Peace bloc. Shevardnadze was the sole candidate at the concurrent direct election of the legislature's Chairman (Head of State), winning more than 95% of the total votes cast. The new Supreme Council convened in November.

Shevardnadze was rapidly confronted by opposition from within his own administration, prompting the dismissal, in May 1993, of Kitovani as Minister of Defence. In August the Council of Ministers tendered its resignation. In September Shevardnadze appointed a new Council of Ministers, headed by Otar Patsatsia, a former CPG official, and offered his own resignation, which was, however, rejected by the Supreme Council. By late September, already confronted by the growing political and economic crisis and military defeat in Abkhazia, Shevardnadze's position was made more precarious by a Zviadist resurgence in western Georgia, with Gamsakhurdia's forces capturing the Black Sea port of Poti, preventing all rail traffic from reaching Tbilisi. As the rebel forces advanced eastwards, Shevardnadze persuaded the Supreme Council to agree to Georgia's membership of the Commonwealth of Independent States (CIS, see p. 246), established in December 1991 by 11 former Soviet republics. In October 1993 Russian troops were dispatched to Georgia, and by November the Zviadists had been entirely routed from the country. In January 1994 it was reported that Gamsakhurdia had committed suicide, although the exact circumstances of his death remained obscure.

Meanwhile, following the restoration of a degree of stability in Georgia (excluding Abkhazia), although assassinations and other acts of political violence remained common, Shevardnadze created his own party, the Citizens' Union of Georgia (CUG). Sigua and Kitovani established a National Liberation Front (NLF) with the declared aim of regaining control of Abkhazia, although the organization was banned after Kitovani led an armed convoy of some 350 NLF supporters towards Abkhazia in January 1995.

In August 1995 the Supreme Council adopted a new Constitution, which provided for a strong executive presidency and a 235-member unicameral Sakartvelos Parlamenti (Parlamenti—Georgian Parliament). The Government was to be directly subordinate to the President, and the post of Prime Minister was to be abolished; the most senior position in the Government was henceforth to be that of the Minister of State. The country (the official title of which was, henceforth, to be, simply Georgia) was described as 'united and undivided'; however, the territorial status of Abkhazia and Adjara was not defined, while the incorporation of the former South Ossetian territories into various other regions was confirmed. The official signing of the Constitution, which had been scheduled for 29 August, was postponed until 17 October following an assassination attempt against Shevardnadze. Igor Giorgadze, the Minister of State Security, was subsequently named by state prosecutors as the chief instigator of the plot. Giorgadze, along with two other alleged plotters, fled abroad.

A presidential election was held on 5 November 1995, in which Shevardnadze won almost 75% of the votes cast. The election of Parlamenti was held concurrently with the presidential election. A mixed system of voting was employed: 150 seats were to be filled by proportional representation, while 85 deputies were to be elected by majority vote in single-member constituencies. Only three parties contesting the proportional seats succeeded in obtaining the 5% of the votes required to obtain representation on this basis. Of these, Shevardnadze's CUG won the largest number of seats (90), followed by the National Democratic Party of Georgia (31) and the All-Georgian Union of Revival (25 seats), chaired by Aslan Abashidze, the leader of the Autonomous Republic of Adjara. A further two rounds of voting were required before all 85 posts allocated to deputies elected on the basis of single-mandate seats were filled. The CUG held a total of 107 seats. Approximately 64% of the registered electorate was reported to have participated in the legislative elections. Parlamenti convened in late November, electing as its Chairman Zurab Zhvania, the General Secretary of the CUG. In December Shevardnadze formed a new Government, with Nikoloz Lekishvili as Minister of State.

Meanwhile, in late 1995 criminal proceedings commenced in Tbilisi against Kitovani, in connection with the NLF's attempted raid on Abkhazia earlier in the year. In September 1996 Kitovani was convicted on charges of establishing an illegal armed formation and was sentenced to eight years' imprisonment. (He was released in May 1999.) Meanwhile, in May 1996 Ioseliani was convicted of complicity in the assassination attempt against Shevardnadze in August 1995 and imprisoned. (He was released in April 2000 and died in March 2003.) In June 1996 supporters of Gamsakhurdia received lengthy prison sentences for their roles in the civil conflict of 1993.

In February 1998 Shevardnadze survived a further attempt on his life. In March Guram Absandze, a former Minister of Finance, was arrested in Moscow and returned to Georgia to stand trial on charges of organizing the attempted assassination. Absandze was sentenced to 17 years' imprisonment in August 2001 (although he was later pardoned). Further arrests were made in May 1999, in connection with a new plot to overthrow Shevardnadze. All of those arrested were reported to have links with Giorgadze; one of the accused died in detention, and 10 others were sentenced to terms of imprisonment in November 2001. In July 1998 Shevardnadze conducted a major ministerial reorganization. In August the hitherto ambassador to Russia, Vazha Lortkipanidze, was appointed Minister of State. In October an abortive two-day armed Zviadist insurrection took place in western Georgia. Following the escape of the captured rebel leaders, the Minister of State Security, Jemal Gakhokidze, resigned in late October.

In July 1999 Parlamenti approved a constitutional amendment, increasing the quota to achieve parliamentary representation in those seats elected on the basis of proportional representation from 5% to 7%. Legislative elections, held in two rounds, on 31 October and 14 November, were contested by 32 parties and blocs, with the participation of 68% of the electorate. The CUG obtained 130 seats. The Union for the Revival of Georgia bloc, led by Abashidze, and the Industry Will Save Georgia (IWSG) bloc secured 58 seats and 15 seats, respectively. Despite opposition allegations of irregularities, observers from the Organization for Security and Co-operation in Europe (OSCE, see p. 388) declared the elections lawful. The new Parlamenti re-elected Zhvania as Chairman.

In the presidential election of 9 April 2000, Shevardnadze secured 79.8% of the votes cast. Electoral violations were noted by the OSCE, but the Parliamentary Assembly of the Council of Europe (PACE, see p. 256) and the Central Electoral Commission (CEC) reported no major infringements of voting procedure. On 11 May Parlamenti endorsed the appointment of Giorgi Arsenishvili as Minister of State, prior to the formation of a new Council of Ministers.

In September 2001 the Minister of Justice, Mikheil Saakashvili, resigned, apparently in response to a perceived lack of support for his anti-corruption campaign. Shortly afterwards, he founded a new political party, the National Movement (NM). Also in September Shevardnadze resigned as Chairman of the CUG. In October public discontent culminated in large-scale protests in Tbilisi, after security officials raided Rustavi 2, an independent television station that had been critical of the Government. (In July a journalist for the station, who had been carrying out an investigation into official corruption, had been murdered.) Zhvania urged both the Minister of State Security and the Minister of Internal Affairs to resign in order to avert further protests. However, the latter refused to comply with this request, and popular protests intensified. On 1 November Shevardnadze dismissed the Government. The Prosecutor-

General subsequently resigned, as did Zhvania; he was replaced as parliamentary Chairman by Nino Burjanadze. Later in the month, a new Government was formed, with Avtandil Jorbenadze as Minister of State. Zhvania founded a new 'reformist' political party, the United Democrats (UD), in June 2002. At municipal elections, held in that month, the CUG suffered a serious reverse, and the New Conservative Party (NCP), formed, like the UD, in a split from the CUG, won the largest number of seats nation-wide. Jorbenadze was subsequently elected as Chairman of the CUG.

The 'rose revolution' and the Saakashvili presidency

On 2 November 2003 elections were held to Parlamenti. Preliminary results indicated that the pro-presidential For a New Georgia bloc had obtained the majority of the votes cast. However, international monitors from the Council of Europe and the OSCE noted electoral irregularities, and there were widespread allegations of electoral malpractice and the falsification of results. On 4 November thousands of people assembled in Tbilisi to protest against the conduct of the elections, and Saakashvili (who claimed that his NM had attracted the most support) led demands for Shevardnadze's resignation. Further large-scale protest demonstrations subsequently took place in Tbilisi and elsewhere.

On 20 November 2003 the CEC announced the final results of the elections (although five members of the Commission refused to endorse the results). The For a New Georgia bloc received a total of 57 seats in Parlamenti (including 38 of the 150 seats allocated by proportional representation), followed by Abashidze's renamed Democratic Union of Revival (DUR), with 39 seats (33 on a proportional basis), and the NM, with 36 seats (32 on a proportional basis). The Georgian Labour Party (GLP) obtained 21 seats, the Burjanadze-Democrats (B-D) bloc, formed by Zhvania and Burjanadze, 16, the New Right bloc 15 and the IWSG bloc two; 16 seats were won by independents, and elections were scheduled to be repeated in other constituencies. The leaders of the NM and the B-D bloc reiterated their claims that the results were invalid, while international critics of the conduct of the election notably included the USA. A referendum, held concurrently with the parliamentary elections, approved an eventual reduction in the number of parliamentary deputies to a maximum of 150. Saakashvili announced his intention to organize a protest march on 22 November, with the intent of preventing the new legislature from convening. On 21 November the Secretary of the National Security Council, Tedo Japaridze, proposed that new polls be scheduled once Parlamenti had convened. However, the next day some 30,000 demonstrators proceeded to the parliament building, precipitating what became known as the 'rose revolution'. Troops attached to the Ministry of Internal Affairs failed to prevent protesters from besieging the main parliamentary chamber, and Shevardnadze was evacuated from the building. He subsequently declared a nation-wide state of emergency. The Russian Minister of Foreign Affairs, Igor Ivanov, was dispatched to Tbilisi, and on 23 November Shevardnadze and Saakashvili attended a meeting, mediated by Ivanov, at which Shevardnadze agreed to tender his resignation, in return for guarantees of immunity from prosecution. Burjanadze immediately assumed the presidency in an interim capacity, pending a presidential election, and the state of emergency was lifted the following day. Jorbenadze and several other senior ministers resigned on 25 November 2003, and on the same day the Supreme Court annulled the results of the legislative elections for the 150 mandates allocated by proportional representation. (The single-member constituency mandates were to remain valid.) On 27 November Zhvania was approved as Minister of State, and new appointments were made to the posts of Minister of Internal Affairs, Minister of Foreign Affairs, Minister of Finance and Chairman of the CEC.

In the presidential election, held on 4 January 2004, Mikheil Saakashvili obtained 96.3% of the votes cast, and the electoral turn-out was 88.0%. On 14 January the legislature adopted a new national flag, hitherto the party flag of the NM, and a new Prosecutor-General was appointed. On 25 January Saakashvili was inaugurated as President. In early February Parlamenti adopted several constitutional amendments, proposed by Saakashvili, providing for the reintroduction of the post of prime minister and the removal of the government by means of two consecutive legislative votes of no confidence. On 17 February Parlamenti approved the composition of a new Government, headed by Zhvania as Prime Minister. The members of the Government, none of whom had served in the Shevardnadze administration, were predominantly young and Western-educated. In March Saakashvili announced the appointment of Salomé Zurabishvili, hitherto the French ambassador to Georgia, as Minister of Foreign Affairs, after she had been granted Georgian citizenship.

Elections to fill the 150 proportional seats in Parlamenti were held on 28 March 2004. A coalition of the NM and the UD won 67.3% of the votes cast and 135 seats (giving them a total of 152 seats of the 235 in Parlamenti, including their single-member constituency mandates). Although international observers commended the overall conduct of the elections, some violations were reported. The Rightist Opposition—an alliance of IWSG and the NCP—was the only other grouping to secure seats in the legislature on a party-list basis (with 7.5% of the votes and 15 seats—giving them 23 seats overall). Abashidze, whose DUR obtained 6.0% of the proportional votes, claimed that the results had been falsified. On 22 April Parlamenti re-elected Burjanadze as Chairman. In June Parlamenti approved Zhvania's proposals for a ministerial reorganization. Irakli Okruashvili became Minister of Internal Affairs, replacing Giorgi Baramidze, who was appointed Minister of Defence, while Kakha Bendukidze, a prominent Georgian industrialist with major business interests in Russia, was appointed Minister of the Economy. In the same month the Republican Party of Georgia (RPG) announced that it would no longer co-operate with the NM-UD bloc, becoming an opposition party; however, this depleted the pro-presidential parliamentary faction by only four, with two of the party's deputies continuing to support the Government. In November the NM and the UD merged to form the United National Movement (UNM), headed by Saakashvili. In December Okruashvili was appointed as Minister of Defence, while Baramidze became Deputy Prime Minister with responsibility for European Integration; the Ministry of State Security was merged with the Ministry of Internal Affairs, and Bendukidze was promoted to become State Minister, responsible for Economic Reform.

On 3 February 2005 Prime Minister Zhvania was discovered dead, apparently from poisoning attributed to a domestic gas leak. On 17 February Parlamenti approved a reorganized Government, headed by the hitherto Minister of Finance, Zurab Noghaideli; Valeri Chechelashvili, hitherto Ambassador to Russia, succeeded him in his former role, while Konstantine Kemularia, hitherto Chairman of the Supreme Court, became Deputy Prime Minister and Minister of Justice. On 23 February Parlamenti endorsed the constitutional amendments providing for a reduction in the number of parliamentary deputies that had been approved by referendum in November 2003; the new measures were to take effect from the legislative elections scheduled for 2008. Meanwhile, in June 2005 Aleksi Aleksishvili was appointed as Minister of Finance, following the dismissal of Chechelashvili, who was accused of bribery. On 1 July legislation was approved by Parlamenti, providing for the election of the mayor of Tbilisi by the Tbilisi City Council, rather than directly by the electorate, thereby contravening the policy of direct election for which the NM had campaigned while in opposition.

On 13 October 2005 Parlamenti ratified the Framework Convention for the Protection of National Minorities (with a number of modifications), honouring one of Georgia's commitments on joining the Council of Europe in 1999. However, delays in the preparation of the document prompted a number of deputies to demand the dismissal of Minister of Foreign Affairs Zurabishvili; her removal on 19 October prompted protest rallies by up to 5,000 of her supporters. She was replaced by Gela Bezhuashvili. In March 2006 Zurabishvili announced the formation of new political movement, Georgia's Way.

In late March 2006 three opposition factions—the Democratic Front (comprising the Conservative Party of Georgia—CPG—and the RPG), the NCP and IWSG—launched a boycott of parliamentary proceedings, in protest at Parlamenti's decision to remove the mandate of an RPG deputy suspected of improper business activities. Also in March a protest against the reportedly routine use of violence by police officers was staged outside the parliament building in Tbilisi. Four officers belonging to the interior ministry's special police force were arrested on suspicion of the killing of a bank employee, Sandro Girgvliani, and in July they were convicted and sentenced to between seven and eight years' detention. On 21 July Giorgi Khaindrava was dismissed as State Minister, responsible for Conflict Resolution, following his outspoken criticism of what he regarded as Minister of Internal Affairs Vano Merabishvili's inadequate response to the killing of Girgvliani. As one-third (six members) of the Government had now been dismissed since its formation, the administration was constitutionally compelled to resign. A new, substantially unchanged, Government was approved in Parlamenti in late July.

On 28 August 2006 President Saakashvili issued a decree rescheduling municipal elections, which had been expected to take place in December, for 5 October; the deadline for candidates to submit their applications was, moreover, to be later that same day, a public holiday, prompting complaints from the opposition. In September 29 people associated with the Justice Party were arrested on suspicion of plotting a coup; 13 of those arrested were subsequently charged. At the municipal elections on 5 October, the UNM secured a resounding victory, attracting 66.5% of the total votes cast. There were numerous allegations of electoral irregularities and malpractice. On 10 November Okruashvili was dismissed as Minister of Defence, after he made controversial comments regarding South Ossetia; he was replaced by Davit Kezerashvili. Okruashvili was appointed as Minister of Economic Development, although he resigned from that position several days later.

In January 2007 President Saakashvili signed into force a series of constitutional amendments, as a result of which the President would no longer be authorized to dismiss or appoint judges, nor be involved in the activities of the High Council of Justice. The amendments also stipulated that presidential and legislative elections were henceforth to be conducted simultaneously, thereby bringing forward the next presidential election by several months to late 2008.

In September 2007 Parlamenti approved a government reorganization. Later in the month Okruashvili, who had established a new opposition party, the Movement for a United Georgia (MUG), publicly accused Saakashvili of corruption and of conspiring to kill a prominent Georgian businessman resident in the United Kingdom, Arkadi (Badri) Patarkatsishvili, who owned several media organizations in Georgia. Two days later Okruashvili was arrested on charges of financial malpractice relating to his work as Minister of Defence, prompting a large rally staged outside the parliamentary building to demand his release and early legislative elections. Early in October Okruashvili withdrew the accusations of criminal behaviour he had made against Saakashvili, and also confessed to criminal charges against him; he was released on bail. In November he stated that he had been forced to retract the accusations while in detention, and left Georgia. Later that month he was arrested and detained in Germany in response to a request of the Georgian authorities, but was subsequently transferred to France, where he was released on bail in January 2008. In March a Georgian court found Okruashvili guilty of embezzlement, and sentenced him *in absentia* to 11 years' imprisonment. In April it was announced that France had granted Okruashvili political asylum.

Meanwhile, in October 2007 a 10-party opposition alliance presented a joint manifesto to the authorities, demanding that elections to Parlamenti be conducted in early 2008, the electoral system be reformed, new election bodies be established, and political prisoners be released. In November Patarkatsishvili declared that he would provide funding to the opposition for organized protests. In early November the opposition led a campaign of rallies outside the parliamentary building, and issued a demand for Saakashvili's resignation. On 7 November special forces violently dispersed opposition supporters; later that day the Government declared a national state of emergency, under which broadcasts of the Imedi television channel (partially owned by Patarkatsishvili) were suspended by the police. On the following day Saakashvili announced that a presidential election would be held on 5 January 2008, to be followed by a referendum on the scheduling of early legislative elections. The authorities announced that two opposition leaders, including Shalva Natelashvili, the Chairman of the GLP, had been charged with espionage and conspiring to overthrow the Government with Russian support, and that Patarkatsishvili was suspected of complicity. On 16 November the state of emergency was ended by parliamentary decree; on the same day Saakashvili dismissed Noghaideli and nominated Vladimer (Lado) Gurgenidze, hitherto the Chairman of the Bank of Georgia, to the premiership. A reorganized Government was subsequently approved by Parlamenti. On 25 November Saakashvili resigned the presidency, as required by the Constitution, in order to campaign for the forthcoming election; Burjanadze replaced him in an interim capacity. In early December Imedi resumed broadcasts.

President Saakashvili re-elected

The alliance of nine opposition parties agreed to nominate Levan Gachechiladze, a non-partisan parliamentary deputy, to contest the presidential election. In December 2007 Patarkatsishvili announced his withdrawal from the poll (although his name remained on the ballot) and returned to the United Kingdom, claiming that the Georgian authorities planned his assassination. At the presidential election, which was contested by seven candidates on 5 January 2008, Saakashvili was re-elected with 53.5% of votes cast; Gachechiladze secured 25.7% of the votes. At the concurrent referendum on the scheduling of early legislative elections, some 79.9% of votes cast were in favour of the proposal. The CEC officially recognized the election results on 13 January and Saakashvili was inaugurated on 20 January. Parlamenti approved a reorganized administration in late January (with opposition deputies boycotting the session). In February the death of Patarkatsishvili at his British residence prompted speculation that he had been assassinated, but medical investigations concluded that he had died from natural causes. On 26 February Parlamenti adopted constitutional amendments providing for legislative elections to be brought forward to May; however, voting on other significant reforms (including the reduction of the quota required for parliamentary representation from 7% to 5%) was postponed, owing to the continued opposition legislative boycott. On 12 March Parlamenti adopted further constitutional amendments, reducing the number of legislative deputies from 235 to 150, of whom 75 were to be elected by proportional representation and 75 in single-member constituencies. On 21 March Saakashvili issued a decree scheduling the parliamentary elections for 21 May.

In early May 2008 Saakashvili appointed Ekaterine (Eka) Tkeshelashvili (Prosecutor-General since January) as Minister of Foreign Affairs, replacing Davit Bakradze, who had resigned in April in order to head the UNM list of candidates in the forthcoming elections. In the parliamentary elections, held on 21 May, the UNM secured 59.2% of votes cast on a party-list basis and 119 seats overall in the legislative elections, while the Joint Opposition (National Council, New Rights) alliance—comprising eight parties, among them MUG, Georgia's Way, the CPG and the New Rights, as well as four individual deputies—won 17.7% of votes and 17 seats. Although an international observer mission issued a generally positive assessment of the election results, the Joint Opposition accused the authorities of extensive electoral malpractice, and announced a boycott of the new Parlamenti. Bakradze was elected parliamentary Chairman in June.

On 9 August, two days after military conflict with Russia broke out in South Ossetia (see Regional relations, below, and the section on South Ossetia elsewhere in this chapter), which subsequently spread to other regions of Georgia, Parlamenti approved a presidential decree declaring a state of war with Russia, and martial law within Georgia. In October 2008, in the aftermath of the conflict, as a result of which Georgia lost control of those territories within Abkhazia and South Ossetia in which it had hitherto maintained a presence, Saakashvili dismissed Gurgenidze as Prime Minister. Grigol Mgaloblishvili, hitherto Ambassador to Turkey, was nominated to replace him. Parlamenti approved the appointment of Mgaloblishvili and four new ministers on 1 November. An opposition demonstration was staged in early November to demand Saakashvili's resignation, after political leaders accused him of responsibility for Georgia's effective defeat in the military conflict with Russia. Meanwhile, a number of formerly prominent supporters of Saakashvili expressed increasing dissatisfaction with his leadership. In November Burjanadze established a new opposition party, the Democratic Movement—United Georgia (DM—UG), and in early December Noghaideli also announced the creation of a political association, the Movement for Fair Georgia (MFG). In November, a group of opposition deputies that did not support the parliamentary boycott formed a new party, the Democratic Party of Georgia, headed by Gia Tortladze. In December Saakashvili reorganized the Government; Vasil (Davit) Sikharulidze, hitherto Ambassador to the USA, became Minister of Defence, and Grigol Vashadze was appointed Minister of Foreign Affairs. Shortly beforehand, it was announced that Irakli Alasania, the Permanent Representative of Georgia to the UN, had submitted his resignation; after returning to Georgia, he criticized the Government and demanded that Saakashvili step down. Burjanadze (who also criticized Saakashvili) demanded that an early presidential election be conducted. Later in December Saakashvili announced that he would propose a constitutional amendment providing for a significant reduction in presidential powers. On 30 January 2009 Mgaloblishvili tendered his resignation as Prime Minister on grounds of ill health, although media reports referred to a dispute between him and Saakashvili. On the same day Saakashvili nominated First Deputy Prime Minister and Minister of Finance Nika Gilauri to succeed him.

Approval of new Constitution

Meanwhile, divisions emerged within the main opposition groups over a strategy to bring about a change of government; in late February 2009 Alasania demanded that Saakashvili schedule a referendum on an early presidential election, while four opposition parties, including the DM—UG, instead threatened to resume continuous protests outside the parliamentary building unless Saakashvili resign. Meanwhile, Alasania established a new informal opposition alliance, the Alliance for Georgia, comprising the RPG and the New Rights. In late March the Ministry of Internal Affairs announced that its forces had arrested 10 suspects, of whom nine were members of the DM—UG, on charges of the illegal purchase of armaments; Burjanadze dismissed broadcast video evidence as part of a campaign by the authorities against her party. Shortly afterwards, two opposition members were arrested for allegedly planning an uprising against the Government. In April large demonstrations demanding the resignation of Saakashvili and his administration commenced in Tbilisi and other major cities; these protests, which were attended by as many as 50,000 people on occasion, continued daily until late July, notably outside the parliamentary building in Tbilisi, while demonstrators also blocked numerous principal highways in the city.

Meanwhile, on 5 May 2009, the authorities announced that they had acted to forestall an army mutiny at a military base east of Tbilisi. The authorities retracted initial claims that the rebels were acting on behalf of Russia in an attempt to destabilize Georgia and disrupt forthcoming North Atlantic Treaty Organization (NATO, see p. 370) military exercises. In early July a commission empowered to draft a new Georgian Constitution, headed by a former President of the Constitutional Court, Avtandil Demetrashvili, was convened, although representatives of the main opposition declined invitations to participate. In mid-July Alasania established a new opposition party, Our Georgia—Free Democrats.

In August 2009 Gilauri dismissed Lasha Zhvania as Minister of Economic Development; he was replaced by the hitherto Ambassador to Spain, Zurab Pololikashvili. One day after Pololikashvili's appointment, President Saakashvili transferred Sikharulidze to the position of foreign affairs adviser to the President; he was succeeded as Minister of Defence by Bachana Akhalaia. Akhalaia's appointment was criticized by numerous human rights groups and opposition figures, including Burjanadze, who held Akhalaia responsible for overseeing the maltreatment of prisoners during the period that he had headed Georgia's penitential department.

In December 2009 a woman and her child were killed during the controversial destruction of a memorial to Georgian soldiers who had died fighting in the Soviet Army in the Second World War in Kutaisi. President Saakashvili dismissed the regional governor of Imereti Mkhare, based in Kutaisi, in response to the deaths, while in February 2010 three directors of the company that had undertaken the demolition were imprisoned on charges of flouting safety regulations. Also in February Noghaideli, in his capacity as leader of the MFG, signed a co-operation agreement with Boris Gryzlov, the Chairman of the Supreme Council of the de facto ruling party of Russia, United Russia. This development was strongly criticized by senior members of the ruling UNM, but obtained the support of some opposition parties, including the New Rights. In early March Burjanadze also made a visit to Russia, where she met Russian premier Vladimir Putin and Minister of Foreign Affairs Sergei Lavrov. Considerable controversy was provoked in mid-March when the Imedi TV channel (the Director-General of which was a close ally of President Saakashvili) broadcast a fabricated news bulletin, which purported to show an ongoing invasion of Georgia by Russia, and announced that Saakashvili had been assassinated and that several prominent opposition figures, among them Burjanadze and Noghaideli, had expressed support for the invasion. The Georgian National Communications Commission ordered Imedi TV to apologize to the public for the broadcast, which had provoked mass panic domestically and also attracted international criticism.

Despite the widespread criticism of Saakashvili following the 2008 military conflict with Russia, the UNM secured a decisive victory in nation-wide local elections on 30 May 2010, receiving more than 65% of votes cast nation-wide. In the first direct mayoral election in Tbilisi, the incumbent, Giorgi Ugulava of the UNM, retained the office with about 55% of the votes, defeating Alasania. OSCE and Council of Europe observers issued a report stating that the conduct of the elections had demonstrated progress towards meeting democratic commitments but noted continuing shortcomings, including incidences of malpractice. In June a statue of Stalin was removed from its prominent position in the main square of his hometown, Gori; the authorities announced that a memorial to the victims of the 2008 conflict was to take its place, and that the statue was to be relocated to the grounds of the museum dedicated to Stalin in the town. In July Saakashvili reorganized the Government, notably appointing Ramaz Nikolaishvili as Minister of Regional Development and Infrastructure, replacing Davit Tkeshelashvili (who had additionally served as First Deputy Prime Minister, and who was transferred to a senior position in the presidential office).

On 19 July 2010 the state commission submitted proposed constitutional amendments to Parlamenti; the main opposition parties (which had refused to participate in drafting the amendments) and prominent civil society organizations urged further discussion, and complained of a lack of media coverage and public debate. On 15 October Parlamenti approved by 112 votes a new Constitution, providing for the transfer of many powers from the President to the Prime Minister and the Government, including regarding the appointment and dismissal of ministers and other officials, in foreign policy and in law initiation. The new text was to take effect upon the inauguration of the President after the next presidential election, scheduled for October 2013. Many domestic and international observers suggested that the changes were designed to allow Saakashvili, who was constitutionally prohibited from seeking re-election, to retain substantial powers as a future premier. In addition, the authorities attracted criticism for failing to consider the final opinion of the Council of Europe's Venice Commission (which at the invitation of the Government had been involved in the drafting of the new Constitution), which had welcomed significant improvements to the constitutional system but recommended the further strengthening of the powers of the legislature. Meanwhile, in October 2010 a number of prominent opposition leaders, including Gachechiladze and Okruashvili established a new political movement, the Georgian Party. In November Ekaterine Tkeshelashvili was appointed Deputy Prime Minister, State Minister, responsible for Reintegration, replacing Temur Iakobashvili, who was nominated as Georgia's ambassador to the USA. Later that month one person was killed in a bomb attack near GLP offices in central Tbilisi (following similar explosions near the US embassy in September and near the principal railway station in the city in October). In November Zurabishvili resigned as leader of Georgia's Way; she was succeeded by Kakha Seturidze. In January 2011 members of the MFG voted to remove Noghaideli from the chairmanship of the party, replacing him with Sergo Javkhidzre; Noghaideli subsequently established a new party, Fair Georgia. On 28 June a court in Tbilisi convicted 15 people (three *in absentia*) of acts of terrorism in connection with the bomb attacks in Tbilisi in late 2010 (see Regional relations).

Recent developments: anti-Government protests

On 21 May 2011 several days of anti-Government protests, led by Burjanadze, began in Tbilisi and Batumi. On 26 May (Independence Day) police forces violently dispersed the crowd, resulting in the death of at least four people. More than 100 protesters were arrested, including opposition leader Badri Bitsadze. (A number of policemen were subsequently dismissed and others reprimanded for the excessive use of force.) At the end of May Parlamenti approved controversial new legislation prohibiting the public display of Nazi and Soviet symbols, and placing restrictions on former Soviet officials from holding office. On 4 June Gachechiladze and other senior members of the Georgian Party announced their resignation from the party, effectively leaving it without leadership in the country. On 17 June Dmitri Gvindadze was appointed Minister of Finance, replacing Kakha Baindurashvili, who was appointed as the Chairman of the Supervisory board of the state-owned postal service, which was in the process of being privatized. Later in June eight opposition activists were charged by a Tbilisi court with possession of armaments, in connection with an alleged conspiracy by Okruashvili (who remained in France) and the Georgian Party to organize a Russian-supported insurrection in Georgia; Okruashvili was charged *in absentia* with forming an armed group. In June the UNM submitted proposed changes to the electoral law, and subsequently signed an agreement with several other parties, including the Christian Democratic Movement and the New Rights (previously members of the eight-party coalition); however, the agreement was rejected by the remaining six parties of the coalition. On 1 July a constitutional amendment was approved, providing for the relocation of Parlamenti from Tbilisi to the country's second largest city, Kutaisi, after the 2012 elections. In early July 2011 large demonstrations, orchestrated by elements within the Georgian Orthodox Church and led by priests, were staged in Tbilisi in protest at the introduction of legislation extending new rights to minority religious groups. In mid-October Gilauri appointed the hitherto governor of the Samegrelo-Zemo Svaneti Mkhare, Zaza Gorozia, as Minister of Agriculture, in place of Bakur Kvezereli.

In October 2011 a billionaire businessman, Bidzina Ivanishvili, announced that he intended to oppose Saakashvili in the next presidential election; in December he formed a movement known as Georgian Dream, with the stated aim of also contesting the 2012 parliamentary elections. Later in December Parlamenti adopted legislation that imposed restrictions on financing political parties. Meanwhile, Ivanishvili's Georgian citizenship was abrogated by a presidential order, on the grounds that he had contravened regulations by obtaining French, as well as Georgian and Russian citizenship, and in January 2012 he appointed his wife, Ekaterina Khvedelidze, to head Georgian Dream. In February Ivanishvili formally established Georgian Dream as a coalition incorporating Our Georgia—Free Democrats, the RPG, the National Forum and other opposition leaders. Ivanishvili subsequently announced his willingness to rescind his French citizenship, although his request that his Georgian citizenship be reinstated was rejected by the authorities in early April. The founding congress of Georgian Dream as a political party was held later in the month.

Adjara

The Autonomous Republic of Adjara, in south-west Georgia, proved to be the least troubled of the country's three autonomous territories (for information on the other two territories, which claim secession from Georgia, see the separate sections within this chapter on Abkhazia and South Ossetia). Despite being of ethnic Georgian origin, the Ajars retained a sense of separate identity, owing to their adherence to Islam. In April 1991 there were prolonged demonstrations in protest against proposals to abolish Adjaran autonomy. Elections to the Supreme Council (legislature) of Adjara were held in September 1996, and Aslan Abashidze was re-elected Chairman of the Adjaran Supreme Council (regional leader), a position he had held since 1991. (Abashidze had concurrently been a Deputy Chairman of the Georgian Supreme Council in 1991–95.)

In November 2001 Abashidze contested unopposed a direct election to the new post of Head of the Republic, which replaced that of Chairman of the Adjaran Supreme Council. In the same month he was appointed as President Shevardnadze's personal representative for conflict resolution in Abkhazia. In early December Adjara's new bicameral legislature (composed of the Council of the Republic and the Senate) held its inaugural session, following the implementation of amendments to the region's Constitution, which had been agreed in July.

Following the disputed Georgian legislative elections of November 2003 (see above), Abashidze announced the dispatch of hundreds of supporters to Tbilisi, in an attempt to prevent the overthrow of Shevardnadze's regime. (According to the official results of the elections, Abashidze's Democratic Union of Revival had been the second-placed party across Georgia.) In response to Shevardnadze's resignation on 23 November, Abashidze declared a state of emergency in Adjara. He subsequently pledged to boycott the national presidential election due to be held in January 2004, condemning it as unconstitutional. However, following international pressure, the poll was conducted in the region. Meanwhile, a number of opposition movements had become active in the region, amid reports of their repression by the local authorities. In March, after the newly elected Georgian President, Mikheil Saakashvili, was prevented from entering Adjara, he issued an ultimatum, demanding that Abashidze recognize the authority of the central Government and ensure that forthcoming national parliamentary elections were conducted freely and fairly in the region. Economic sanctions were subsequently imposed on Adjara, while Abashidze declared a renewed state of emergency and a curfew. Following Russian mediation, Abashidze agreed to allow the organization of elections in Adjara, in exchange for the removal of the economic blockade and the withdrawal of Georgian troops from neighbouring areas. The state of emergency was suspended, and legislative elections proceeded as part of the nation-wide ballot on 28 March.

Tensions escalated further on 2 May 2004, when Abashidze ordered the destruction of bridges linking Adjara with neighbouring regions of Georgia, following military manoeuvres by government troops close to the border, despite assurances by Saakashvili that the Government did not intend to take military action against the region. Saakashvili immediately threatened to dismiss Abashidze, unless the Adjaran leader agreed to comply with the 'framework of the Georgian Constitution' within a period of 10 days. Large public demonstrations against Abashidze ensued. Following discussions with the Chairman of the Security Council of the Russian Federation (and former Minister of Foreign Affairs), Igor Ivanov, on 5 May Abashidze resigned and departed for Russia. Saakashvili immediately imposed presidential rule on the region, and on 6 May Parlamenti voted to approve the President's authority to dismiss the legislature and the Government of the Autonomous Republic of Adjara and to schedule new elections. The Adjaran Supreme Council also voted to abolish the post of Head of the Republic, scheduled new parliamentary elections and dissolved itself. Immunity from prosecution was extended to armed groups that surrendered their weapons within seven days. Levan Varshalomidze was appointed as the head of an interim council to rule the region. On 20 June elections to the new unicameral legislature of Adjara, the Supreme Council, took place. The Saakashvili—Victorious Adjara party received 75% of the votes cast and 28 of the 30 seats in the Council; the Republican Party won the remaining two seats. On 1 July Parlamenti approved legislation, whereby the President of Georgia was granted the authority to dismiss the Adjaran Government, dissolve the parliament and annul legislation. Mikheil Makharadze was elected Chairman of the newly elected Supreme Council; Varshalomidze was the sole candidate for Chairman of the Government. Abashidze's personal fortune and estate were confiscated by the authorities on the grounds that they had been acquired illegally. In December a warrant was issued for Abashidze's arrest on charges of abuse of office, terrorist offences and embezzlement. The relocation of the Constitutional Court of Georgia from Tbilisi to Abashidze's former residence in Batumi took effect from September 2006. In January 2007 Saakashvili signed into effect a number of constitutional amendments, under which, *inter alia*, the mandate of the Supreme Council was to be extended until late 2008, so that the next legislative regional elections would be conducted concurrently with those to Parlamenti.

On 30 July 2008 the Supreme Council adopted amendments to the region's electoral code, prior to forthcoming legislative elections, scheduled to take place on 4 October: the Council was to be reduced from 30 to 18 deputies; the minimum proportion of votes required for parties to obtain representation on this basis was reduced from 7% to 5%; and the composition of the local Central Election Commission (CEC) was reformed to include opposition representatives. In September, following the conflict in South Ossetia and other parts of Georgia (see below), the CEC rescheduled the elections to the Supreme Council for 3 November. A number of opposition parties subsequently declared a boycott of the poll; the rate of participation by the electorate on 3 November was registered at some 44.9%. Saakashvili's UNM secured about 78.8% of votes cast, while the Christian Democratic Movement (which had been established by a former associate of Abashidze, Giorgi Targamadze, in February) became the only other party to gain representation in the Supreme Council, with 14.7% of votes.

In late March 2009 the head of the republican branch of the opposition DM—UG party, Zurab Avaliani, was detained, along with nine other men, pending trial on charges of illegal arms-smuggling and plotting politically motivated violence. (Avaliani was subsequently sentenced to one year and six months' imprisonment on charges of illegal possession of firearms.) In April 2010, despite his membership of the ruling UNM, Varshalomidze openly criticized the centralization of powers in Georgia and demanded the restoration of a greater degree of autonomy to Adjara. In May the head of the Georgian Ministry of Internal Affairs emergency situations service in Adjara was killed in an explosion near Batumi; in early 2011, following the arrest of two suspects, the Georgian authorities claimed that the killing had been ordered by Russian military intelligence agents based in Abkhazia.

Foreign Affairs

Regional relations

Georgia was one of only four republics of those that had constituted the USSR not to join the CIS at its formation in December 1991. However, as civil and separatist conflicts threatened to destroy the country, Shevardnadze was forced to reverse policy on the CIS, and in late 1993 the republic was admitted to that body. Georgia's relations with Russia were strained by developments in Abkhazia from 1992. However, in February 1994 Georgia and Russia signed a 10-year treaty of friendship and co-operation, which provided, *inter alia*, for the establishment of Russian military bases in Georgia. In 1996 President Shevardnadze and the Georgian legislature threatened to close the military bases, unless Russia adopted a firmer stance against the separatists in South Ossetia and Abkhazia. In May 1999 Georgia failed to renew its adherence to the CIS Collective Security Treaty.

The lifting of customs and travel restrictions on the Russian–Abkhazian border in September 1999 angered Georgia, and further tension occurred later in the year, owing to the renewed conflict in Russia's Chechen Republic (Chechnya). Georgia denied allegations that it was harbouring Chechen soldiers and selling arms to Chechen separatists. During 2000 there were violent disturbances and kidnappings in the Pankisi Gorge, close to the Chechen border, which was inhabited by both ethnic Chechens and refugees from Chechnya. In December Shevardnadze reiterated Georgia's refusal to carry out joint operations in the area with Russian troops. Russia's decision to implement a full visa regime for Georgian citizens entering its territory from January 2001 caused further antagonism, particularly since citizens of Abkhazia and South Ossetia were to be exempt from the requirement. In January 2002 Georgian security forces launched a campaign to restore order to the Pankisi region. Later that month the Georgian Deputy Minister of State Security was shot dead in the Pankisi Gorge. In February four police officers were held hostage for three days in the Gorge. In the same month the US chargé d'affaires in Georgia announced that international Islamist militants were believed to have established bases in the Pankisi Gorge, a claim that the Georgian authorities appeared unable to refute. In May a US-led military-training programme commenced in Georgia, to equip the armed forces for operations in Pankisi. In August Georgia accused Russia of perpetrating an act of aggression, and announced its preparedness to repel subsequent attacks, when the aerial bombardment of the Pankisi Gorge by unmarked aircraft led to at least one death; Russia denied responsibility for the attack. In September Russian President Vladimir Putin wrote to the UN Secretary-General, warning that unless the Georgian Government was prepared to suppress the Chechen rebels alleged to be operating from within its territory, Russia would take unilateral action to counteract the threat. In early October Georgia extradited five suspected Chechen militants to Russia. Later that month Presidents Shevardnadze and Putin reached an agreement, according to which the two countries were to resume joint patrols of their common border, and seek to resolve border issues by diplomatic means.

Relations with Russia deteriorated after the accession to power in Georgia of President Mikheil Saakashvili, largely as a result of the pro-Western orientation of the new administration, as well as concern in Russia that the means by which Saakashvili had come to prominence (involving civil disorder following disputed elections) might be emulated by opponents of the Russian regime. In January 2006 two natural gas pipelines and a power line supplying power to Georgia from Russia were damaged by a series of explosions that remained unexplained. The decision of the Georgian Parlamenti, in mid-February, to request the replacement of Russian peace-keepers in South Ossetia with international forces threatened to aggravate tensions in relations. In February Russia suspended its visa arrangements with Georgia, in protest at Georgia's perceived obstruction of the provision of visas for military personnel, and a visit to Russia by Georgian Prime Minister Zurab Noghaideli was postponed by the Russian authorities. In March Russia banned the import of wine from Georgia, ostensibly owing to suspected contamination with pesticides (having hitherto been the main market of Georgian wine exports). In September Georgian security forces detained four Russian military officers on suspicion of espionage. In October President Saakashvili announced that the officers had been transferred to the authority of the OSCE, which arranged for their return to Russia. In response to the detention of the officers, Russia withdrew its ambassador from Georgia, cut all transport and postal links between the two countries, and expelled several hundred ethnic Georgians (who the Russian authorities stated were illegal immigrants) from Russia. (Russia's ambassador returned to Tbilisi in January 2007, although economic sanctions imposed by Russia against Georgia remained in place.) In March 2006, following repeated postponements by the Russian Government, Georgia and Russia signed an agreement providing for a Russian withdrawal from the military base that it maintained at Akhalkalaki and headquarters at Tbilisi by the end of 2007, and from the second base at Batumi in 2008. In the event, the withdrawal of Russian forces from the military bases was completed in November 2007, earlier than scheduled, although the continued deployment of Russian peace-keeping forces in Abkhazia and South Ossetia remained a source of tension.

In August 2007 the Georgian authorities issued an announcement urging the international community to condemn the alleged violation of Georgian airspace by two military aircraft originating from Russia, and the apparent launch of a missile near South Ossetia. The Russian Government strongly denied the allegations; however, international experts subsequently confirmed that at least one aircraft had entered Georgian airspace from Russia. Following the imposition of a national state of emergency in early November, Georgia expelled three Russian embassy staff, on the grounds that they were engaged in subversive activities against the Government, prompting Russia to expel three Georgian diplomats in retaliation.

In July 2008 the Russian authorities acknowledged that four Russian aircraft had entered airspace over South Ossetia, claiming that the purpose of the mission was to deter Georgia from flying unmanned military reconnaissance drones over the region.

After Georgian troops attacked Tskhinvali and other regions of South Ossetia on 7–8 August 2008, Russian troops entered the territory through the Roki tunnel, purportedly to protect the security of Russian citizens, rapidly obtaining control over the region. In a statement subsequently shown to be greatly exaggerated, Russian President Dmitrii Medvedev accused Georgia of perpetrating 'genocide', claiming that up to 2,000 people had been killed as a result of the Georgian attack. Russian aircraft commenced bombardment of Georgian targets, including the town of Gori, the port of Poti and the military base at Senaki. On 9 August Parlamenti approved a presidential decree declaring a state of war with Russia, and martial law within Georgia. On 12 August President Medvedev ordered an end to Russia's military operations. Georgia and Russia agreed to a peace plan, mediated by French President Nicolas Sarkozy on behalf of the EU, providing for an immediate cease-fire and the withdrawal of Russian troops to pre-conflict positions. However, Russia failed to implement fully the withdrawal of troops as stipulated. On 14 August Parlamenti voted unanimously in favour of Georgia's withdrawal from the CIS. On 26 August 2008 Medvedev endorsed a resolution, which had been approved in both chambers of the Russian legislature, officially recognizing South Ossetia and Abkhazia as independent, sovereign states. Georgia, the USA and EU condemned the decision, and by 2012 only a small number of states had similarly extended recognition. On 29 August Georgia formally suspended diplomatic relations with Russia.

Following an EU-mediated peace agreement, reached on 8 September 2008; Russia announced that 3,800 of its troops were to remain in each of South Ossetia and Abkhazia, although all remaining forces would be withdrawn from all other Georgian territories within 10 days of the deployment of EU monitors. On 17 September Russia signed friendship, economic and military co-operation treaties with South Ossetia and Abkhazia. Following the deployment of the European Union Monitoring Mission in Georgia (EUMM) on 1 October, the withdrawal of the remaining Russian troops from areas adjacent to the two secessionist territories was verified by the deadline of 10 October. However, Georgia claimed that Russia was in violation of the cease-fire agreement, on the grounds that it retained troops in areas previously held by Georgian forces, and that the number of troops in South Ossetia and Abkhazia exceeded the pre-conflict levels. Meanwhile, on 9 October the Council of CIS Foreign Ministers officially suspended Georgia's membership. (Georgia's full withdrawal from the organization was consequently to take place in August 2009.) In mid-October negotiations between Russia and Georgia were abandoned, after the Georgian delegation rejected Russian demands that the representatives of South Ossetia and Abkhazia be invited to participate. The appointment, on 22 October, of a Prime Minister of South Ossetia who had previously worked for the Russian Federal Security Service (FSB) was a source of controversy in Georgia. In November discussions between Russian, US and Georgian representatives, which were also attended by South Ossetian and Abkhazian officials, were reconvened in Geneva, Switzerland, under the aegis of the UN, EU and OSCE (and subsequently continued to be held at intervals). At the end of December the mandate of the OSCE mission in Georgia (deployed in South Ossetia since 1992) expired, owing to Russia's refusal to approve a further extension after its demand that OSCE monitors in Georgia and South Ossetia be allocated separate mandates was rejected by most other member states. In February 2009 OSCE states agreed to extend until the end of June the mandate of 20 military monitoring officers deployed in areas of Georgia adjacent to South Ossetia after the 2008 conflict, although discussions on the mandate of the pre-existing OSCE mission remained at an impasse. Meanwhile, a report by Human Rights Watch, issued in January 2009, concluded that both Russia and Georgia had committed numerous violations of the laws of war, citing 'indiscriminate and disproportionate attacks' by both sides; following investigations by both Governments, Russia (despite its earlier claims) had only been able to attribute 162 fatalities to Georgian forces.

In March 2009 it was reported that the separatist authorities of South Ossetia and Abkhazia were to implement agreements with Russia for the joint patrol of their borders with the remainder of Georgia. Later that month Russia confirmed that military bases were to be established in Abkhazia and South Ossetia, and envisaged the organization of joint military exercises between Russian troops and members of the territories' defence forces. On 30 April Russian President Dmitrii Medvedev signed border treaties with Abkhazia and South Ossetia, which provided for Russia to guard the state borders of Abkhazia prior to the establishment of Abkhazian border forces. The EU expressed 'deep concern' at both agreements, which it stated violated the terms of the peace agreement. The mandate of UNOMIG expired on 15 June; Russia had used its veto to prevent the approval of a UN Security Council resolution providing for its extension.

The publication of an independent fact-finding report, supported by the EU, into the 2008 conflict in September 2009 was a cause of some controversy in both Georgia and Russia. The report concluded that Georgia had instigated the conflict, and that its initial attack upon Tshkhinvali was not warranted by international law, while Russia's military response was condemned as being disproportionate, and its recognition of South Ossetia and Abkhazia as independent states was also deemed to be in violation of international law.

Contacts between Russia and Georgia remained effectively 'frozen' during 2009, although the only road crossing between Russia and those territories controlled by the Georgian authorities, at Verkhnyi Lars–Kazbegi, closed since 2006, re-opened in March 2010. Both Medvedev and the Russian Minister of Foreign Affairs Sergei Lavrov reiterated that they would not enter into negotiations with Saakashvili, but increasingly made contacts with prominent members of the Georgian opposition. In October 2010 the Russian Ministry of Foreign Affairs denounced as an attempt to destabilize the region a decision by the Georgian authorities to abolish visa requirements for the residents of Russia's seven North Caucasus republics.

Meanwhile, accusations by the Georgian Government of Russian subversive activity hampered any progress towards reconciliation at the internationally mediated negotiations. In November Georgia announced the arrest of 13 people suspected of being members of a Russian espionage network, including four Russian citizens. In early December six people were arrested in connection with a series of explosions in Tbilisi. On 25 June 2011 a Russian military officer who had been based in Abkhazia, Yevgenii Borisov, was sentenced to 30 years' imprisonment *in absentia* for organizing the bomb attacks; Borisov's deputy received a life sentence *in absentia* and a further four defendants were sentenced to terms of 30 years (one *in absentia*), while lesser sentences were imposed on the remaining eight. The Russian Government strongly denied Borisov's involvement, after Georgia issued an international arrest warrant against him.

Following an appeal brought by Georgia against Russia, which accused Russian forces of ethnically motivated abuses in both South Ossetia and Abkhazia during the 2008 conflict, in April 2011 the International Court of Justice dismissed the case, on the grounds that Georgia had made no attempt to resolve the dispute with Russia beforehand. Also in April it was reported that a Russian military officer and two ethnic Georgians had been killed in a clash in the Gali district of Abkhazia. On 20 May Parlamenti issued a resolution that the massacre of ethnic Circassians in the northern Caucasus by Tsarist Russia in the mid-19th century constituted genocide. In November, following ongoing discussions between Georgian and Russian representatives in Bern, Switzerland, since March, it was announced that the negotiators had finally reached an agreement that would allow Russia to join the World Trade Organization (WTO, see p. 433); under a compromise arrangement, trade between Russia and Abkhazia and South Ossetia was to be controlled by Swiss monitors. A presidential decree, announced by Saakashvili in late February 2012 as a gesture of reconciliation, ended visa restrictions on Russian citizens, who were henceforth permitted to remain in Georgia for 90 days without a visa. In early March the Russian Ministry of Foreign Affairs announced that it was prepared to consider the introduction of reciprocal arrangements for Georgian citizens who wished to visit Russia, along with a restoration of diplomatic relations between the two countries.

Other external relations

Relations with the USA became increasingly cordial in the mid-2000s. US Secretary of State Colin Powell attended Saakashvili's inauguration as President in January 2004, and in February Saakashvili visited Washington, DC, USA, where he attended talks with US President George W. Bush. In May 2005 President Bush made a brief state visit to Georgia, during which he praised the 'rose revolution' and endorsed the Government's efforts to bring about reform. In September 2005 Saakashvili and the US Secretary of State, Condoleezza Rice, signed an agreement, under which the USA was to disburse some US $300m. in aid to Georgia over a period of five years. In February 2006 Georgian and US representatives signed a further agreement, pledging to increase co-operation in combating the smuggling of nuclear and radioactive materials, which had been a persistent source of concern in Georgia and the wider Caucasus region. In July Saakashvili visited Washington, DC, where he again met Bush and Rice on which occasion President Bush affirmed his support for Georgian aspirations to NATO membership. In September the USA pledged to grant Georgia $40m. as part of a programme of US military assistance. In 2007 Georgia's presence in Iraq was increased from 850 personnel to 2,000. In September 2008, following the military conflict with Russia (see Regional relations), US Vice-President Dick Cheney announced that the USA would pledge US $1,000m. in reconstruction aid to Georgia. In January 2009 Georgia and the USA signed a bilateral charter on strategic partnership, which was to increase co-operation in defence, trade, energy and other areas. Although the new Administration of President Barack Obama, which took office later that month, sought to achieve a rapprochement with Russia, in July Vice-President Joe Biden visited Tbilisi and reaffirmed US support for the Saakashvili administration. In July 2010 US Secretary of State Hillary Clinton visited Tbilisi, where, meeting Saakashvili, she expressed support for Georgia's efforts to restore its territorial integrity. In August 2011 the US Senate adopted a resolution (which prompted protests from the Russian Government) condemning the continuing presence of Russian troops in Abkhazia and South Ossetia. Following discussions with Obama in Washington, DC, in January 2012, Saakashvili announced plans for significantly increased defence co-operation between Georgia and the USA.

In April 1996 Georgia (together with Armenia and Azerbaijan) signed an agreement on partnership and co-operation with the EU, and in January 1999 it joined the Council of Europe. In March 2005 the European Commission recommended strengthening relations with Georgia under its European Neighbourhood Policy, in which Georgia had been included in June 2004. In November 2002 Georgia formally applied for membership of NATO. In October 2004 NATO approved a two-year Individual Partnership Action Plan with Georgia. At a NATO summit meeting, conducted in Bucharest, Romania, on 2–4 April 2008, the Alliance expressed support for the membership aspirations of Georgia (and Ukraine), but failed to extend offers of a Membership Action Plan (MAP). With the aim of strengthening relations with Eastern European countries and addressing integration aspirations, in December the European Commission presented an Eastern Partnership proposal for Georgia, Armenia, Azerbaijan, Ukraine, Moldova and Belarus; the new programme, offering further economic integration and envisaging enhanced trade and visa arrangements, was officially inaugurated in May. Following a summit meeting in Lisbon, Portugal, in November 2010, NATO issued a final declaration reiterating support for Georgia's eventual full membership of the Alliance. In December 2011 the Georgian Government welcomed a statement by NATO that officially named Georgia (*inter alia*) as an 'aspirant' state.

what, to around 8%, by the end of 2011. A further priority was the promotion of Georgia as a regional trade and logistic centre, following the establishment of free industrial zones at the port of Poti (in association with the United Arab Emirates state agency, RAKIA) and in Kutaisi. In April 2011 the Government announced that it was to issue a new, 10-year Eurobond for $500m. Meanwhile, there was increasing speculation that Russia's sanctions on Georgian agricultural exports (notably of wine) would be ended; in late 2011 it was announced that the Georgian and Russian Governments had reached a compromise agreement (involving the monitoring of trade between Russian and the regions of Abkhazia and South Ossetia) that would allow Russia to join the World Trade Organization (WTO, see p. 433). In December the EU declared that Georgia had made satisfactory progress in implementing reforms preparatory to EU integration, and that negotiations would begin on the establishment of a free trade area under the Eastern Partnership framework (see Other external relations). In early 2012 the Georgian and USA also announced that they had agreed to enter into dialogue on increased economic co-operation, including a possible free trade agreement.

PUBLIC HOLIDAYS

2013: 1–2 January (New Year), 7 January (Christmas), 19 January (Theophany), 3 March (Mothers' Day), 8 March (International Women's Day), 21 March (Nowruz, Spring Holiday), 9 April (Restoration of Independence Day), 3–6 May (Easter and Commemoration of the Deceased), 9 May (Victory Day), 12 May (St Andrew's Day), 26 May (Independence Day), 28 August (Assumption), 14 October (Mtskhetoba), 23 November (St George's Day).

Statistical Survey

Source (unless otherwise indicated): National Statistics Office of Georgia, 0181 Tbilisi, Guramishvili 39, Tskneti; tel. (32) 36-72-10; fax (32) 36-72-13; e-mail info@geostat.ge; internet www.geostat.ge.

Area and Population

AREA, POPULATION AND DENSITY

Area (sq km)	69,700*
Population (census results)†	
12 January 1989	5,400,841
17 January 2002‡	
Males	2,061,753
Females	2,309,782
Total	4,371,535
Population (official estimates at 1 January)§	
2009	4,385,400
2010	4,436,400
2011	4,469,200
Density (per sq km) at 1 January 2011	64.1

* 26,911 sq miles.

† Population is *de jure*. The de facto total at the 2002 census was 4,355,700.

‡ Those territories of the former autonomous oblast (district) of South Ossetia that remained outside Georgian government control, as well as those of the separatist 'Republic of Abkhazia', were not included in the census of 2002. It was estimated that around 230,000 people lived in these territories.

§ Excluding the territories not under the control of the central Government.

POPULATION BY AGE AND SEX

('000, official estimates at 1 January 2011)

	Males	Females	Total
0–14	400.3	359.1	759.4
15–64	1,494.2	1,599.0	3,093.2
65 and over	232.8	383.8	616.6
Total	2,127.3	2,341.9	4,469.2

POPULATION BY ETHNIC GROUP

(2002 census result, excl. areas outside Georgian government control)

	Number ('000)	% of total population
Georgian	3,661.2	83.8
Azeri	284.8	6.5
Armenian	248.9	5.7
Russian	67.7	1.5
Ossetian	38.0	0.9
Kurdish	20.8	0.5
Others	50.1	1.1
Total (incl. others)	4,371.5	100.0

ADMINISTRATIVE DIVISIONS

('000, official population estimates at 1 January 2011*)

Territory	Population	Principal city
Autonomous Republic		
Adjara	390.6	Batumi (124.3)
Mkharebi (Regions)		
Guria	140.3	Ozurgeti (78.4)
Imereti	704.5	Kutaisi (194.7)
Kakheti	406.2	Telavi (71.0)
Kvemo Kartli	505.7	Rustavi (120.8)
Mtskheta-Mtianeti	109.3	Mtskheta (57.3)
Racha-Lechkumi and Kvemo-Svaneti	47.3	Ambrolauri (14.3)
Samegrelo-Zemo Svaneti†	477.1	Zugdidi (176.6)
Samstkhe-Javakheti	212.8	Akhaltsikhe (48.2)
Shida Kartli‡	313.0	Gori (145.3)
Capital City		
Tbilisi	1,162.4	—
Total	4,469.2	—

* These figures exclude the population of the 'Republic of Abkhazia'.

† Including population of Kodori Gorge (Upper Abkhazia).

‡ Most of the territories of South Ossetia are included in Shida Kartli Mkhare.

PRINCIPAL TOWNS

(estimates at 1 January 2011)

Tbilisi (capital)	1,162,400	Marneuli*	128,100
Kutaisi	194,700	Batumi	124,300
Zugdidi*	176,600	Rustavi	120,800
Gori*	145,300	Gardabani*	98,700

* Figure refers to the population of the municipality.

BIRTHS, MARRIAGES AND DEATHS

	Registered live births		Registered marriages		Registered deaths	
	Number	Rate (per 1,000)	Number	Rate (per 1,000)	Number	Rate (per 1,000)
2003	46,194	10.7	12,696	2.9	46,055	10.6
2004	49,572	11.5	14,866	3.4	48,793	11.3
2005	46,512	10.7	18,012	4.1	42,984	9.9
2006	47,795	10.9	21,845	5.0	42,255	9.6
2007	49,287	11.2	24,891	5.7	41,178	9.4
2008	56,565	12.9	31,414	7.2	43,011	9.8
2009	63,377	14.4	31,752	7.2	46,625	10.6
2010	62,585	14.1	34,675	7.8	47,864	10.7

Life expectancy (years at birth, WHO estimates): 71 (males 67; females 75) in 2009 (Source: WHO, *World Health Statistics*).

CONSTITUTION AND GOVERNMENT

Under the Constitution of August 1995, as subsequently revised, the President of Georgia is Head of State and the head of the executive, and also Commander-in-Chief of the Armed Forces. The President is directly elected for a five-year term (and may not hold office for more than two consecutive terms). The Government is accountable to the President, to whom it acts as an advisory body. The Government is headed by the Prime Minister. The supreme legislative body is the unicameral Sakartvelos Parlamenti (Georgian Parliament), which is directly elected for four years. Of the 150 parliamentary deputies, 75 are elected on the basis of proportional representation and 75 in single-member constituencies. A new Constitution, approved by Parlamenti in October 2010, and which was to take effect after the presidential election scheduled for 2013, transfers many powers from the President to the Prime Minister and the Government. Judicial power is exercised by the Supreme Court, the members of which are elected by the Sakartvelos Parlamenti, on the recommendation of the President, and by general courts. Georgia contains two nominally autonomous territories: the Autonomous Republic of Adjara; and Abkhazia. The status of Abkhazia and South Ossetia were both disputed; following conflict in August 2008, both territories became entirely under the control of their respective separatist authorities, with Russian military support. Those parts of the country under central government control are divided into nine mkharebi (regions—singular mkhare) headed by trustees (governors) appointed by the President, and the city of Tbilisi, headed by a mayor. A second tier of local government comprises seven cities of special status and 60 districts (raions), and a third tier comprises a total of 966 villages and settlements.

REGIONAL AND INTERNATIONAL CO-OPERATION

Georgia is a member of the Organization of the Black Sea Economic Co-operation (see p. 402), the Council of Europe (see p. 256) and the Organization for Democracy and Economic Development (GUAM, see p. 465).

Georgia joined the UN in 1992 and became a full member of the World Trade Organization (WTO, see p. 433) in 2000.

ECONOMIC AFFAIRS

In 2010, according to estimates by the World Bank, Georgia's gross national income (GNI), measured at average 2008–10 prices, was US $11,976m., equivalent to $2,690 per head (or $4,960 per head on an international purchasing-power parity basis). During 2001–10, it was estimated, the population decreased by an average of 0.2% per year, while gross domestic product (GDP) per head increased, in real terms, at an average annual rate of 6.2%. According to the World Bank, overall GDP increased, in real terms, by an average of 6.4% annually during 2001–10. Real GDP decreased by 3.8% in 2009, but increased by 6.3% in 2010, according to official estimates.

Agriculture contributed 8.3% of GDP in 2010, and the sector engaged 53.4% of the total employed labour force in 2007. Georgia's favourable climate allows the cultivation of subtropical crops, such as tea and oranges. Other fruits (including wine grapes), flowers, tobacco and grain are also cultivated, and hazelnuts have increased in importance in recent years. The mountain pastures are used for sheep- and goat-farming. In 2002 private farms accounted for 94% of the agricultural crop harvest. During 2001–10, according to the World Bank, agricultural GDP declined, in real terms, by an average of 0.2% per year. Real agricultural GDP decreased by 4.8% in 2010, according to official figures.

Industry contributed 22.0% of GDP in 2010, and the sector engaged 10.4% of the total employed labour force in 2007. The most significant parts of the sector are the agro-processing and energy industries. According to the World Bank, industrial GDP increased, in real terms, at an average annual rate of 7.4% in 2001–10. According to official figures, real GDP in the industrial sector decreased by 3.5% in 2009, but increased by 9.1% in 2010, with manufacturing contributing substantially to this growth.

Mining and quarrying accounted for just 1.0% of GDP in 2010, and the sector engaged 0.3% of the total employed labour force in 2007. The principal minerals extracted are manganese ore, petroleum and coal. There are also deposits of copper, gold, silver and natural gas. During 2003–10, according to the official figures, mining GDP increased, in real terms, by an average of 5.8% per year; real GDP of the sector increased by 4.6% in 2010.

The manufacturing sector (including household processing) contributed 9.1% of GDP in 2010, and the sector engaged 4.9% of the total employed labour force in 2007. Manufacturing GDP increased, in real terms, by an annual average rate of 8.1% in 2001–10, according to World Bank estimates. Real manufacturing GDP decreased by 8.5% in 2009, but increased by 20.2% in 2010.

The construction sector contributed 6.0% of GDP in 2010, and the sector engaged 4.2% of the employed labour force in 2007. According to official figures during 2003–10 construction GDP increased, in real terms, by an average of 10.0% per year; the sector's GDP declined, in real terms, by 3.1% in 2009, but increased by 6.5% in 2010.

Hydroelectric power provided 84.8% of the country's electricity in 2008. However, Georgia's largest hydroelectric power station was located in the secessionist region of Abkhazia, and the IMF estimated that more than one-third of the power it produced was consumed without payment. Imports of mineral fuels and lubricants comprised 17.6% of total imports in 2009. After 1999 Georgia was involved in a number of regional development projects to deliver both petroleum and gas through international pipelines. However, Georgia also hoped to develop its own energy resources. New gas-turbine electricity generators commenced operations in 2006, and the country proposed to reconstruct several hydroelectric power plants, as part of measures intended to make the country self-sufficient in electricity.

The services sector contributed 69.8% of GDP in 2010, and the sector engaged 36.2% of the employed labour force in 2007. Trade and transport and communications are the sector's most significant areas of activity, with telecommunications and hotels and restaurants demonstrating the greatest growth in the early 2000s. According to the World Bank, the GDP of the services sector increased, in real terms, at an average annual rate of 8.1% in 2001–10. According to the official figures, real sectoral GDP decreased by 4.8% in 2009, but increased by 10.1% in 2010.

In 2010 Georgia recorded a visible trade deficit of US $2,586.3m., and there was a deficit of $1,464.8m. on the current account of the balance of payments. In 2010 Turkey was the principal source of imports (accounting for 16.9% of the total); other major sources were Ukraine, Azerbaijan, the People's Republic of China, Germany and Russia. The principal market for exports in that year was Azerbaijan (accounting for 15.5% of the total); other important purchasers were Turkey, the USA, Armenia, Ukraine and Canada. The principal imports in 2009 were machinery and transport equipment (23.7% of total imports), mineral fuels and lubricants, food and live animals, chemicals, miscellaneous manufactured articles and manufactured goods classified chiefly by material. The principal exports in that year were crude materials (inedible) except fuels (17.6% of total exports), manufactured goods, food and live animals, machinery and transport equipment, beverages and tobacco and chemicals.

In 2010 there was a budgetary deficit of 869.2m. lari (equivalent to 4.2% of GDP). Georgia's general government gross debt was 8,124m. lari in 2010, equivalent to 39.1% of GDP. At the end of 2009 Georgia's total external debt was US $4,231m., of which $2,596m. was public and publicly guaranteed debt. In that year, the cost of servicing long-term public and publicly guaranteed debt and repayments to the IMF was equivalent to 4.7% of the value of exports of goods, services and income (excluding workers' remittances). According to IMF estimates, the annual rate of inflation averaged 6.8% during 2001–10; consumer prices in five major cities increased by 3.0% in 2009 and by 11.2% in 2010. In 2010 the average rate of unemployment was 16.3%.

In 1992 Georgia became a member of the IMF and the World Bank, and also joined the European Bank for Reconstruction and Development (EBRD, see p. 271).

The administration of President Mikheil Saakashvili, which came to power in 2004, introduced wide-ranging reforms, and implemented anti-corruption measures, and foreign direct investment increased substantially. A Russian embargo on the import of various Georgian foodstuffs and beverages, implemented in 2005 forced the country to seek new markets. Heightened tensions with Russia were also marked by steep increases in the prices charged to Georgia for imports of natural gas. While Georgia was able to diversify its sources of energy imports, the country was affected adversely by the international financial crisis from late 2008. In August 2009 an IMF stand-by arrangement was extended in duration until June 2011, and the funding available under the programme increased to US $1,200m. Following a contraction in GDP in 2009, a recovery ensued in 2010–11. The annual rate of inflation increased sharply in the second half of 2010, partly owing to increases in the international prices of food and energy), but was estimated to have reduced some-

ECONOMICALLY ACTIVE POPULATION
(annual averages, '000 persons)*

	2005	2006	2007
Agriculture, hunting and forestry	947.8	966.4	910.5
Mining and quarrying	5.8	3.4	4.7
Manufacturing	89.8	81.5	82.7
Electricity, gas and water supply	23.4	18.4	18.2
Construction	43.1	54.8	71.2
Wholesale and retail trade; repair of motor vehicles and personal and household goods	188.2	168.1	168.8
Hotels and restaurants	16.3	16.9	18.0
Transport, storage and communications	69.3	77.8	71.7
Financial intermediation	13.3	14.3	17.3
Real estate, renting and business activities	25.9	26.9	34.7
Public administration and defence; compulsory social security	81.8	78.5	64.3
Education	130.9	132.2	124.2
Health and social work	58.0	52.2	59.9
Other community, social and personal service activities	38.2	41.9	43.9
Private households with employed persons	9.2	11.7	11.1
Extra-territorial organizations and bodies	3.3	2.3	2.9
Sub-total	1,744.3	1,747.3	1,704.3
Activities not adequately defined	0.3	—	—
Total employed	1,744.6	1,747.3	1,704.3
Unemployed	279.3	274.5	261.0
Total labour force	2,023.9	2,021.8	1,965.3
Males	1,074.4	1,085.9	1,031.8
Females	949.5	935.9	933.5

* Figures exclude employment in the informal sector, estimated to total about 750,000 persons at the end of 1997, and those employed in the armed forces.

2008: Total employed 1,601.9; Unemployed 315.8; Total labour force 1,917.8.

2009: Total employed 1,656.1; Unemployed 335.6; Total labour force 1,991.8.

2010: Total employed 1,628.1; Unemployed 316.9; Total labour force 1,944.9.

Source: mainly ILO.

Health and Welfare

KEY INDICATORS

Total fertility rate (children per woman, 2009)	1.6
Under-5 mortality rate (per 1,000 live births, 2009)	29
HIV/AIDS (% of persons aged 15–49, 2009)	0.1
Physicians (per 1,000 head, 2006)	4.7
Hospital beds (per 1,000 head, 2006)	3.7
Health expenditure (2008): US $ per head (PPP)	433
Health expenditure (2008): % of GDP	8.7
Health expenditure (2008): public (% of total)	30.9
Access to water (% of persons, 2008)	98
Access to sanitation (% of persons, 2008)	95
Total carbon dioxide emissions ('000 metric tons, 2007)	6,027.3
Carbon dioxide emissions per head (metric tons, 2007)	1.4
Human Development Index (2011): ranking	75
Human Development Index (2011): value	0.733

For sources and definitions, see explanatory note on p. vi.

Agriculture

PRINCIPAL CROPS
('000 metric tons)

	2008	2009	2010
Wheat	80.3	53.9	48.4
Barley	49.3	20.0	23.3
Maize	328.2	291.0	141.1
Potatoes	193.4	216.8	228.8
Sunflower seed	15.1	2.3	2.6
Cabbages and other brassicas	41.9	39.6	27.1
Tomatoes	62.6	51.4	56.0
Cucumbers and gherkins	18.6	30.9	28.6
Onions, dry	11.1	10.2	19.0
Watermelons	52.8	43.7	40.9
Oranges	1.9	1.5	1.4
Apples	41.5	80.7	21.1
Pears	16.4	11.1	13.7
Sour (Morello) cherries	4.0	4.0	3.0
Peaches and nectarines	13.7	17.6	6.9
Plums and sloes	12.6	6.3	6.7
Grapes	175.8	150.1	120.7
Hazelnuts (with shell)	18.7	21.8	28.8
Tea	5.4	5.8	3.5
Tobacco, unmanufactured	0.1	0.1	0.1*

* FAO estimate.

Aggregate production ('000 metric tons, may include official, semi-official or estimated data): Total cereals 467.6 in 2008, 374.5 in 2009, 220.2 in 2010; Total treenuts 26.1 in 2008, 31.1 in 2009, 36.1 in 2010; Total roots and tubers 193.4 in 2008, 216.8 in 2009, 228.8 in 2010; Total vegetables (incl. melons) 217.8 in 2008, 214.0 in 2009, 216.6 in 2010; Total fruits (excl. melons) 364.6 in 2008, 394.9 in 2009, 260.0 in 2010.

Source: FAO.

LIVESTOCK
('000 head at 1 January)

	2008	2009	2010
Horses*	42.0	40.0	40.0
Cattle	1,031.3	1,045.5	1,014.7
Buffaloes	17.2	18.0†	17.5†
Pigs	109.9	86.4	135.2
Sheep	711.0	690.0	602.3
Goats	86.1	79.4	71.5
Chickens†	5,700	6,200	6,190
Turkeys†	400	482	485

* FAO estimates.
† Unofficial figure(s).

Source: FAO.

LIVESTOCK PRODUCTS
('000 metric tons)

	2008	2009	2010
Cattle meat	25.1	29.2	26.7
Sheep meat*	7.5	4.1	4.9
Pig meat	11.4	8.2	12.8
Chicken meat	12.9	12.4	11.6
Cows' milk*	632.8	539.4	520.0
Hen eggs*	24.3	23.9	24.6

* Unofficial figures.

Source: FAO.

Forestry

ROUNDWOOD REMOVALS
('000 cu m, excl. bark, unofficial figures)

	2005	2006	2007
Sawlogs, veneer logs and logs for sleepers	81.0	168.2	105.0
Other industrial wood	81.0	—	—
Fuel wood	453.9	473.0	733.0
Total	615.9	641.2	838.0

2008–10: Production assumed to be unchanged from 2007 (FAO estimates).

Source: FAO.

SAWNWOOD PRODUCTION
('000 cu m, incl. railway sleepers)

	2005	2006	2007
Coniferous (softwood)	6.9*	55.0	30.0
Broadleaved (hardwood)	215.0†	45.0	40.0
Total	221.9*	100.0	70.0

* FAO estimate.
† Unofficial figure.

2008–10: Production assumed to be unchanged from 2007 (FAO estimates).

Source: FAO.

Fishing

(metric tons, live weight)

	2007	2008	2009
Capture*	18,197	26,512	25,050
Mullets	0	1	1
Surmullets	4	0	n.a.
European anchovy	17,447	25,938	24,500
Sea snails	600	500*	476*
Aquaculture	180	180*	210*
Total catch*	18,377	26,692	25,260

* FAO estimate(s).

Source: FAO.

Mining

('000 metric tons unless otherwise indicated)

	2005	2006	2007
Coal	5.1	8.3	8.3*
Crude petroleum	66.7	63.5	63.5*
Natural gas (million cu m)	14.8	21.4	21.4*
Manganese ore	251.8	328.6	350.0
Cement*	450.0	450.0	450.0

* Estimated production.

2008 (estimates): Manganese ore 400.0; Cement 450.0.

2009 (estimates): Manganese ore 350.0; Cement 400.0.

Source: US Geological Survey.

Industry*

SELECTED PRODUCTS
('000 metric tons, unless otherwise indicated)

	2006	2007	2008
Refined sugar	122.4	133.9	n.a.
Wine ('000 hectolitres)	225.5	160.0	182.9
Beer ('000 hectolitres)	734	709	625
Vodka and liqueurs ('000 hectolitres)	93	75	98
Soft drinks ('000 hectolitres)	1,644	1,828	1,462
Mineral water ('000 hectolitres)	782	n.a.	1,132
Cigarettes (million)	3,791	4,874	5,156
Residual fuel oils	4	13	17
Building bricks (million)	12.8	12.4	10.2
Electric energy (million kWh)	7,362	8,329	8,441

Source: mainly UN, *Industrial Commodity Statistics Yearbook* and Database.

Wine ('000 metric tons): 53 in 2004 (unofficial figure); 87 in 2005 (unofficial figure); 85 in 2006; 135 in 2007; 97 in 2008 (FAO estimate); 90 in 2009 (FAO estimate); 97 in 2010 (FAO estimate).

* Data for those areas of South Ossetia outside central government control and for the separatist 'Republic of Abkhazia' are not included.

Finance

CURRENCY AND EXCHANGE RATES

Monetary Units
100 tetri = 1 lari.

Sterling, Dollar and Euro Equivalents (30 November 2011)
£1 sterling = 2.588 lari;
US $1 = 1.658 lari;
€1 = 2.225 lari;
100 lari = £38.64 = $60.30 = €44.94.

Average Exchange Rate (lari per US $)
2008 1.4908
2009 1.6705
2010 1.7823

Note: On 25 September 1995 Georgia introduced the lari, replacing interim currency coupons at the rate of 1 lari = 1,000,000 coupons. From April 1993 the National Bank of Georgia had issued coupons in various denominations, to circulate alongside (and initially at par with) the Russian (formerly Soviet) rouble. From August 1993 coupons became Georgia's sole legal tender, but their value rapidly depreciated. The transfer from coupons to the lari lasted one week, and from 2 October 1995 the lari became the only permitted currency in Georgia.

BUDGET
(million lari)*

Revenue†	2006	2007	2008
Tax revenue	3,149.4	4,391.1	4,752.7
Taxes on income	385.9	526.7	1,296.3
Taxes on profits	341.1	554.8	592.1
Value-added tax	1,332.4	1,973.7	2,069.0
Excise	335.6	428.6	518.5
Customs duties	132.4	52.0	51.9
Other taxes	118.9	133.2	224.9
Social taxes	502.8	722.0	—
Other current revenue	521.7	880.7	484.2
Capital revenue	564.5	643.8	724.0
Total	4,235.5	5,915.6	5,960.9

Expenditure‡	2006	2007	2008
General state services	515.2	775.0	1,510.1
Defence	722.2	1,502.9	1,552.1
Public order and safety	382.9	725.3	1,010.6
Education	414.2	458.3	553.8
Health	225.9	256.2	313.1
Social protection	690.1	640.1	323.0
Recreation, culture and religion	139.6	177.1	202.1
Other expenditure§	1,374.1	1,548.2	1,470.5
Total	4,464.1	6,083.1	6,935.2

* Figures represent a consolidation of the State Budget (covering the central Government and local administrations) and extrabudgetary funds.
† Excluding grants received (million lari): 194.3 in 2006; 116.9 in 2007; 617.3 in 2008.
‡ Including net lending.
§ Includes expenditure on fuel energy services, agriculture, forestry, fisheries and hunting, and transport and communications in 2007, and includes expenditure on economic affairs, housing and community amenities, and environmental protection in 2008.

2009 (million lari): *Revenue:* Tax revenue 4,388.9; Other current revenue 487.1; Capital revenue 456.3; Total revenue 5,332.3 (excl. grants 388.6). *Expenditure:* Wages and salaries 1,048.3; Use of goods and services 1,105.2; Interest 171.2; Subsidies 613.5; Social benefits 1,505.9; Grants 8.8; Other expenditure 944.3; Capital expenditure 1,252.7; Total expenditure 6,649.8.

2010 (million lari): *Revenue:* Tax revenue 4,867.5; Other current revenue 526.2; Capital revenue 286.1; Total revenue 5,679.8 (excl. grants 472.1). *Expenditure:* Wages and salaries 1,120.2; Use of goods and services 1,138.6; Interest 206.1; Subsidies 380.0; Social benefits 1,623.6; Grants 10.5; Other expenditure 1,001.3; Capital expenditure 1,540.8; Total expenditure 7,021.1.

INTERNATIONAL RESERVES
(excl. gold, US $ million at 31 December)

	2008	2009	2010
IMF special drawing rights	12.31	218.73	222.41
Reserve position in the IMF	0.02	0.02	0.02
Foreign exchange	1,467.84	1,891.58	2,041.36
Total	1,480.16	2,110.32	2,263.79

Source: IMF, *International Financial Statistics*.

MONEY SUPPLY
(million lari at 31 December)

	2008	2009	2010
Currency outside depository corporations	1,082.55	1,229.44	1,372.99
Transferable deposits	1,348.20	1,274.87	2,037.60
Other deposits	1,874.37	2,152.47	2,865.14
Broad money	4,305.13	4,656.77	6,275.73

Source: IMF, *International Financial Statistics*.

COST OF LIVING
(Consumer Price Index for five cities*; base: December 2003 = 100)

	2008	2009	2010
Food and non-alcoholic beverages	157.7	163.7	201.0
Alcoholic beverages and tobacco	150.3	151.8	170.7
Clothing and footwear	97.7	88.2	88.8
Housing, utilities and other fuels	174.0	165.7	169.7
Household furnishings and maintenance	128.2	123.2	128.0
Health	152.7	156.2	162.9
Transport	134.7	143.3	153.6
Education	101.6	150.2	151.5
Recreation and culture	111.3	112.0	111.5
All items (incl. others)	145.4	149.8	166.6

* Tbilisi, Kutaisi, Batumi, Gori and Telavi.

NATIONAL ACCOUNTS
(million lari at current prices)

National Income and Product

	2008	2009	2010
Compensation of employees	4,422.7	5,227.3	6,010.3
Net operating surplus	7,194.7	4,870.6	5,974.2
Net mixed income	2,921.5	3,475.7	3,647.9
Domestic primary incomes	14,538.9	13,573.6	15,632.4
Consumption of fixed capital	1,758.0	1,751.4	2,126.8
Gross domestic product (GDP) at factor cost	16,296.9	15,325.0	17,759.2
Taxes on production and imports	2,864.2	2,752.3	3,089.5
Less Subsidies	86.3	91.3	105.3
GDP in market prices	19,074.9	17,986.0	20,743.4
Primary incomes received from abroad	760.1	706.1	742.8
Less Primary incomes paid abroad	1,016.9	902.5	1,383.4
Gross national income (GNI)	18,818.0	17,789.5	20,102.8
Less Consumption of fixed capital	1,758.0	1,751.4	2,126.8
Net national income	17,060.0	16,038.1	17,976.0
Current transfers from abroad	1,718.3	1,735.3	2,108.3
Less Current transfers paid abroad	121.7	118.6	151.7
Net disposable income	18,656.6	17,654.8	19,932.6

Expenditure on the Gross Domestic Product

	2008	2009	2010
Government final consumption expenditure	4,936.3	4,399.5	4,371.0
Private final consumption expenditure	14,659.5	14,675.8	15,527.2
Increase in stocks	853.1	–412.5	468.7
Gross fixed capital formation	4,098.5	2,755.4	4,009.0
Total domestic expenditure	24,547.4	21,418.1	24,375.9
Exports of goods and services	5,459.2	5,348.9	7,250.0
Less Imports of goods and services	11,140.4	8,801.3	10,945.1
Statistical discrepancy	208.6	20.2	62.6
GDP in market prices	19,074.9	17,986.0	20,743.4
GDP at constant 2003 prices	12,491.4	12,019.7	12,771.3

Gross Domestic Product by Economic Activity

	2008	2009	2010
Agriculture, forestry and fishing	1,551.1	1,457.1	1,509.9
Mining and quarrying	128.9	123.3	181.0
Manufacturing	1,509.4	1,263.9	1,654.8
Electricity, gas and water supply	434.3	490.8	534.2
Processing of products by households	482.6	521.8	536.9
Construction	1,058.3	1,004.3	1,100.0
Wholesale and retail trade; repair of motor vehicles, motorcycles and personal and household goods	2,680.9	2,344.1	3,024.9
Hotels and restaurants	395.7	346.4	411.7
Transport, storage and communications	1,813.0	1,746.3	2,076.9
Financial intermediation	442.0	452.7	476.7
Real estate, renting and business activities*	1,130.0	1,161.9	1,478.1
Public administration and defence; compulsory social security	2,850.1	2,457.6	2,343.1
Education	671.2	757.5	874.0
Health and social services	835.2	1,021.4	1,202.0
Other community, social and personal services	748.4	604.6	825.5
Private households with employed persons	14.3	17.0	20.1
Sub-total	16,745.4	15,770.8	18,249.9
Less Financial intermediation services indirectly measured	223.5	224.4	235.5
Gross value added in basic prices	16,521.8	15,546.3	18,014.4
Taxes on products	2,639.3	2,530.9	2,834.3
Less Subsidies on products	86.3	91.3	105.3
GDP in market prices	19,074.9	17,986.0	20,743.4

* Including imputed rent of owner-occupied dwellings.

BALANCE OF PAYMENTS
(US $ million)

	2008	2009	2010
Exports of goods f.o.b.	2,428.0	1,893.6	2,462.2
Imports of goods f.o.b.	–6,264.2	–4,292.6	–5,048.5
Trade balance	–3,836.2	–2,399.0	–2,586.3
Exports of services	1,260.5	1,313.6	1,599.3
Imports of services	–1,239.4	–973.9	–1,084.5
Balance on goods and services	–3,815.1	–2,059.3	–2,071.5
Other income received	494.2	422.7	416.3
Other income paid	–655.1	–540.7	–776.3
Balance on goods, services and income	–3,976.2	–2,177.3	–2,431.5
Current transfers received	819.8	929.4	1,051.7
Current transfers paid	–81.7	–71.0	–85.0
Current balance	–3,238.9	–1,318.9	–1,464.8

—continued	2008	2009	2010
Capital account (net)	112.3	182.5	206.1
Direct investment abroad	–70.0	1.1	–5.9
Direct investment from abroad	1,564.0	658.4	814.5
Portfolio investment assets	0.7	–1.1	–0.6
Portfolio investment liabilities	125.9	13.2	252.7
Financial derivatives assets	11.1	1.1	1.7
Financial derivatives liabilities	–3.3	–0.5	–1.0
Other investment assets	–264.1	191.5	–408.0
Other investment liabilities	922.4	564.3	459.3
Net errors and omissions	–30.6	54.7	–15.8
Overall balance	–869.6	346.1	–161.8

Source: IMF, *International Financial Statistics*.

External Trade

PRINCIPAL COMMODITIES
(distribution by SITC, US $ million)

Imports	2007	2008	2009
Food and live animals	687.7	738.6	584.7
Beverages and tobacco	86.5	126.1	110.6
Crude materials (inedible) except fuels	75.2	128.8	88.0
Mineral fuels and lubricants, etc.	913.3	1,088.2	768.9
Chemicals and related products	444.1	553.1	465.2
Manufactured goods classified chiefly by material	1,019.9	985.4	585.9
Machinery and transport equipment	1,449.1	2,015.2	1,035.4
Miscellaneous manufactured articles	497.9	603.6	690.6
Total (incl. others)	5,212.2	6,301.5	4,366.1

Exports	2007	2008	2009
Food and live animals	149.8	103.8	168.5
Beverages and tobacco	143.2	138.3	123.8
Crude materials (inedible) except fuels	263.3	329.3	199.7
Chemicals and related products	118.4	157.8	105.3
Manufactured goods classified chiefly by material	261.8	393.8	181.1
Machinery and transport equipment	152.8	191.0	151.5
Total (incl. others)	1,232.1	1,495.3	1,133.6

2010: Total imports 5,248.5; Total exports 1,574.1.

PRINCIPAL TRADING PARTNERS
(US $ million)

Imports c.i.f.	2008	2009	2010
Armenia	72.1	41.9	46.2
Austria	70.3	51.9	51.5
Azerbaijan	607.4	410.2	483.5
Belgium	61.3	39.9	50.8
Brazil	104.2	76.0	80.6
Bulgaria	124.1	152.8	131.7
China, People's Republic	298.3	174.7	335.1
Czech Republic	59.9	46.3	57.8
France	98.5	66.0	74.7
Germany	497.3	302.1	331.8
Greece	57.5	62.0	72.7
Iran	52.1	29.9	55.1
Italy	183.8	130.1	136.6
Japan	119.8	108.4	170.4
Kazakhstan	54.8	23.3	94.5
Netherlands	134.1	105.3	105.3
Poland	51.5	46.1	55.7
Romania	92.4	115.1	140.8
Russia	423.3	291.6	290.4
Switzerland	50.2	38.0	34.5
Turkey	940.5	787.9	887.0
Turkmenistan	135.0	74.3	59.2

Imports c.i.f.*—continued*	2008	2009	2010
Ukraine	657.7	421.2	560.1
United Arab Emirates	276.9	110.4	159.2
United Kingdom	91.2	59.5	65.6
USA	358.1	231.6	177.8
Total (incl. others)	6,301.5	4,500.2	5,248.5

Exports f.o.b.	2008	2009	2010
Armenia	123.4	88.9	159.7
Azerbaijan	203.9	165.6	243.5
Belgium	7.2	13.5	21.8
Bulgaria	108.2	82.3	62.1
Canada	131.8	117.2	86.7
France	39.9	5.8	9.8
Germany	33.1	23.0	31.8
Israel	2.4	1.6	4.1
Italy	17.1	23.3	23.4
Kazakhstan	22.0	20.5	48.0
Mexico	53.0	—	4.1
Russia	29.8	21.1	34.3
Spain	19.7	15.3	32.6
Turkey	262.9	225.8	214.1
Turkmenistan	6.3	10.7	12.2
Ukraine	134.2	84.0	103.3
United Arab Emirates	11.2	16.7	27.8
United Kingdom	43.6	8.2	17.1
USA	102.2	36.9	180.5
Total (incl. others)	1,495.3	1,133.6	1,574.1

Transport

RAILWAYS
(traffic)

	2007	2008	2009
Passengers carried (million)	3.9	3.4	3.1
Passenger-km (million)	773.9	674.5	626.0
Freight ('000 tons)	22,230.0	21,181.2	17,104.0
Freight net ton-km (million)	6,927.5	6,515.7	5,417.0

ROAD TRAFFIC
('000 motor vehicles in use)

	2008	2009	2010
Passenger cars	466.9	500.9	536.1
Buses	47.4	42.9	45.9
Lorries and vans	57.7	54.4	59.7
Total (incl. others)	573.6	606.9	652.0

SHIPPING

Merchant Fleet
(registered at 31 December)

	2007	2008	2009
Number of vessels	398	289	295
Total displacement ('000 grt)	1,048.4	678.4	707.9

Source: IHS Fairplay, *World Fleet Statistics*.

CIVIL AVIATION
(traffic on scheduled services)

	2007	2008	2009
Passengers carried ('000)*	200	200	200
Passenger-km (million)	474.8	485.7	378.5
Freight ('000 metric tons)	1.1	0.7	0.4
Total ton-km (million)	3.6	1.9	1.1

* Figures are rounded.

Tourism

FOREIGN TOURIST ARRIVALS

Country of residence	2007	2008	2009
Armenia	243,133	281,463	351,049
Azerbaijan	281,629	344,936	418,992
Germany	14,081	13,267	15,351
Greece	12,380	12,914	14,300
Israel	16,450	17,413	16,757
Russia	91,361	114,459	127,937
Turkey	248,028	351,410	384,482
Ukraine	28,932	32,988	39,339
United Kingdom	9,775	8,951	10,633
USA	14,818	15,652	16,934
Total (incl. others)	1,051,769	1,290,107	1,500,049

Tourism receipts (US $ million, incl. passenger transport): 440 in 2007; 505 in 2008; 531 in 2009.

Source: World Tourism Organization.

Communications Media

	2008	2009	2010
Telephones ('000 main lines in use)	618	620	1,105.9
Mobile cellular telephones ('000 subscribers)	2,755.1	2,837.0	3,980.0
Internet subscribers ('000)	99.6	176.5	254.1
Broadband subscribers ('000)	112.1	150.0	253.9
Newspapers: titles	221	199	225
Newspapers: circulation ('000)	700	500	800

Personal computers: 1,170,000 (271.7 per 1,000 persons) in 2008.

Radio receivers ('000 in use): 3,020 in 1997.

Television receivers ('000 in use): 2,590 in 2000.

Book production (incl. pamphlets): 581 titles in 1996 (834,000 copies); 697 titles in 1999.

Sources: partly UN, *Statistical Yearbook*; UNESCO, *Statistical Yearbook*; and International Telecommunication Union.

Education

(2008/09 unless otherwise indicated)

	Institutions	Students*
Pre-primary schools†	1,197	77,922
General education: schools (primary)‡§ General education: schools (secondary)§	2,430	595,400
General education: evening schools†	14	n.a.
State secondary professional schools	30	2,177
Private secondary professional schools	4	434
State higher schools (incl. universities)‖	21	74,056
Private higher schools (incl. universities)‖	108	28,654

* Some figures are rounded.

† Data for 2005/06.

‡ Including primary schools covering part of the secondary syllabus.

§ Data for 2010/11.

‖ Data for 2009/10.

Teachers (2007/08, unless otherwise indicated): Pre-primary 7,783 (2004/05); Total in general day schools 79,891 (2009/10); Total in secondary professional schools 873 (803 public, 70 private—2008/09); Total full- and part-time professors in institutes of higher education 11,424 in 2008 (7,142 in public institutions, 4,282 in non-state institutions).

Pupil-teacher ratio (primary education, UNESCO estimate): 8.2 in 2009/10 (Source: UNESCO Institute for Statistics).

Adult literacy rate (UNESCO estimates): 99.7% (males 99.8%; females 99.7%) in 2009 (Source: UNESCO Institute for Statistics).

Directory

The Government

HEAD OF STATE

President: MIKHEIL SAAKASHVILI (elected 4 January 2004; re-elected 5 January 2008; inaugurated 20 January 2008).

GOVERNMENT

(May 2012)

Prime Minister: NIKOLOZ (NIKA) GILAURI.

Deputy Prime Minister, State Minister, responsible for European and Euro-Atlantic Integration: GIORGI BARAMIDZE.

Deputy Prime Minister, State Minister, responsible for Re-integration: EKATERINE (EKA) TKESHELASHVILI.

Minister of Regional Development and Infrastructure: RAMAZ NIKOLAISHVILI.

Minister of Finance: DMITRI GVINDADZE.

State Minister, responsible for Diaspora Affairs: MIRZA DAVITAIA.

Minister of Foreign Affairs: GRIGOL VASHADZE.

Minister of Education and Science: DIMITRI SHASHKIN.

Minister of Economic and Sustainable Development: VERA KOBALIA.

Minister of Defence: BACHANA AKHALAIA.

Minister of Internal Affairs: IVANE MERABISHVILI.

Minister of Justice: ZURAB ADEISHVILI.

Minister of Agriculture: ZAZA GOROZIA.

Minister of Environmental Protection: GIORGI KHACHIDZE.

Minister of Energy and Natural Resources: ALEKSANDRE KHETAGURI.

Minister of Culture and the Protection of Monuments: NIKOLOZ RURUA.

Minister of Internally Displaced Persons from the Occupied Territories, Accommodation, and Refugees of Georgia: KOBA SUBELIANI.

Minister of Health, Labour and Social Protection: ZURAB CHIABERASHVILI.

Minister of Prisons and Probation: KHATUNA KALMAKHELIDZE.

Minister of Sports and Youth Affairs: VLADIMER VARDZELASHVILI.

MINISTRIES

Office of the President: 0103 Tbilisi, M. Abdushelishvili 1; tel. (32) 228-27-36; fax (32) 228-27-14; e-mail secretariat@admin.gov.ge; internet www.president.gov.ge.

Chancellery of the Government: 0105 Tbilisi, P. Ingorovka 7; tel. (32) 292-22-43; fax (32) 292-10-69; e-mail primeminister@geo.gov.ge; internet www.government.gov.ge.

Office of the Deputy Prime Minister, State Minister, responsible for European and Euro-Atlantic Integration: 0134 Tbilisi, P. Ingorovka 7; tel. and fax (32) 293-28-67; e-mail info@eu-nato.gov.ge; internet www.eu-nato.gov.ge.

Office of the State Minister, responsible for Diaspora Affairs: 0177 Tbilisi, Tamarashvili 15A; tel. and fax (32) 239 71 24; e-mail info@diaspora.gov.ge; internet www.diaspora.gov.ge.

Office of the State Minister, responsible for Reintegration: 0134 Tbilisi, P. Ingorovka 7; tel. (32) 298-92-56; fax (32) 292-16-50; e-mail press@smr.gov.ge; internet www.smr.gov.ge.

Ministry of Agriculture: 0179 Tbilisi, Gelovani 6; tel. (32) 237-80-09; fax (32) 237-80-13; e-mail ministry@maf.ge; internet moa.gov.ge.

Ministry of Culture and the Protection of Monuments: 0105 Tbilisi, Sanapiro 4; tel. (32) 293-22-55; fax (32) 299-99-66; e-mail culturegovge@gmail.com; internet www.mcs.gov.ge.

Ministry of Defence: 0112 Tbilisi, Gen. Kvinitadze 20; tel. (32) 291-04-21; fax (32) 291-06-45; e-mail pr@mod.gov.ge; internet www.mod.gov.ge.

Ministry of Economic and Sustainable Development: 0108 Tbilisi, Chanturia 12; tel. (32) 299-10-11; fax (32) 293-28-46; e-mail ministry@economy.ge; internet www.economy.ge.

Ministry of Education and Science: 0102 Tbilisi, D. Uznadze 52; tel. (32) 220-02-20; fax (32) 243-88-12; e-mail pr@mes.gov.ge; internet www.mes.gov.ge.

Ministry of Energy and Natural Resources: 0105 Tbilisi, Gulua 6; tel. (32) 235-78-00; fax (32) 235-78-28; e-mail mail@menr.gov.ge; internet www.minenergy.gov.ge.

Ministry of Environmental Protection: 0114 Tbilisi, G. Gulua 6; tel. and fax (32) 272-72-34; e-mail press@moe.gov.ge; internet www.moe.gov.ge.

Ministry of Finance: 0114 Tbilisi, V. Gorgasali 16; tel. (32) 226-14-44; fax (32) 245-74-55; e-mail minister@mof.ge; internet www.mof.ge.

Ministry of Foreign Affairs: 0108 Tbilisi, Sh. Chitadze 4; tel. (32) 294-50-00; fax (32) 294-50-01; e-mail inform@mfa.gov.ge; internet www.mfa.gov.ge.

Ministry of Health, Labour and Social Protection: 0119 Tbilisi, A. Cereteli 144; tel. (32) 251-00-33; fax (32) 251-00-19; e-mail press@moh.gov.ge; internet www.moh.gov.ge.

Ministry of Internal Affairs: 0114 Tbilisi, Gulua 10; tel. (32) 274-62-50; fax (32) 241-10-17; e-mail monitoringi@mia.gov.ge; internet www.police.ge.

Ministry of Internally Displaced Persons from the Occupied Territories, Accommodation, and Refugees of Georgia: 0177 Tbilisi, Tamarashvili 15A; tel. (32) 231-15-98; fax (32) 231-15-96; e-mail presscentre@mra.gov.ge; internet www.mra.gov.ge.

Ministry of Justice: 0146 Tbilisi, Gorgasali 24A; tel. (32) 240-52-02; fax (32) 275-82-37; e-mail press-center@justice.gov.ge; internet www.justice.gov.ge.

Ministry of Prisons and Probation: 0177 Tbilisi, Al. Qazbegi 42; tel. (32) 231-27-34; fax (32) 231-19-01; e-mail info@mcla.gov.ge; internet www.mcla.gov.ge.

Ministry of Regional Development and Infrastructure: 0177 Tbilisi, Al. Qazbegi 12; tel. (32) 251-05-91; e-mail press@mrdi.gov.ge; internet www.mrdi.gov.ge.

Ministry of Sports and Youth Affairs: 0162 Tbilisi, Cholokashvili 9; tel. (32) 223-54-33; fax (32) 229-20-49; e-mail office@msy.gov.ge; internet msy.gov.ge.

President

Presidential Election, 5 January 2008

Candidates	Votes	%
Mikheil Saakashvili	1,060,042	53.47
Levan Gachechiladze	509,234	25.69
Arkadi (Badri) Patarkatsishvili	140,826	7.10
Others	226,827	11.44
Total*	1,982,318	100.00

* Including 45,389 invalid votes (2.29% of the total).

Legislature

Sakartvelos Parlamenti
(Georgian Parliament)

0118 Tbilisi, Rustaveli 8; tel. (32) 293-61-70; fax (32) 299-93-86; e-mail hdstaff@parliament.ge; internet www.parliament.ge.

Chairman: DAVIT BAKRADZE.

General Election, 21 May 2008

Parties and blocs	%*	Seats A†	Seats B†	Seats Total
United National Movement—Victorious Georgia	59.18	48	71	119
Joint Opposition (National Council, New Rights) bloc‡	17.73	15	2	17
Giorgi Targamadze—Christian Democrats	8.66	6	—	6
Shalva Natelashvili—Labour Party	7.44	6	—	6
Republican Party of Georgia	3.78	—	2	2
Others	3.21	—	—	—
Total	100.00	75	75	150

* Percentage refers to the share of the vote cast for seats awarded on the basis of party lists.

† Of the 150 seats in the Sakartvelos Parlamenti, 75 (A) are awarded according to proportional representation on the basis of party lists, and 75 (B) are elected in single-mandate constituencies.

‡ An electoral alliance of the Conservative Party of Georgia; Freedom; the Georgian People's Party; the Georgian Troupe; Georgia's Way; the Movement for a United Georgia; the National Forum; the New Rights; and four individual candidates.

Election Commission

Central Electoral Commission of Georgia (CEC): 0108 Tbilisi, Aghmashenebeli 13-km; tel. (32) 251-00-51; e-mail correspondence@cec.gov.ge; internet www.cec.gov.ge; Chair. ZURAB KHARATISHVILI.

Political Organizations

In early 2008 some 190 political parties and alliances were registered with the Central Electoral Commission. The following were among the most prominent parties in early 2012:

Christian Democratic Movement (CDM) (Kristian-demokratebi): 0162 Tbilisi, Tsagareli 59; tel. (32) 214-10-33; fax (32) 214-10-38; e-mail info@cdm.ge; internet www.cdm.ge; f. 2008; contested 2008 legislative elections as Giorgi Targamadze—Christian Democrats; Chair. GIORGI TARGAMADZE.

Conservative Party of Georgia: 0179 Tbilisi, Arakishvili 15; tel. and fax (32) 222-61-23; e-mail office@conservatives.ge; f. 2001; contested 2008 legislative elections as mem. of the Joint Opposition (National Council, New Rights) bloc; Chair. ZVIAD DZIDZIGURI.

Democratic Movement—United Georgia (Demokratiuli modzraoba—ertiani sakartvelo): 0160 Tbilisi, Abuladze 8; tel. (32) 255-03-77; e-mail mail@democrats.ge; internet www.democrats.ge; f. 2008; opposed to regime of Pres. Saakashvili; Chair. NINO BURJANADZE.

Democratic Party of Georgia: c/o Sakartvelos Parlamenti, 0118 Tbilisi, Rustaveli 8, Room N709; f. 2008; right-of-centre; Chair. GIA TORTLADZE.

Freedom (Tavisupleba): Tbilisi; f. 2004 by a son of former President Zviad Gamsakhurdia; nationalist; contested 2008 legislative elections as mem. of the Joint Opposition (National Council, New Rights) bloc; Leader KONSTANTINE GAMSAKHURDIA.

Georgian Dream (Qartuli Ocneba): 0105 Tbilisi, Erekle II Moedani 3; tel. (32) 2260-47-67; e-mail info@georgiandream.ge; internet www.georgiandream.ge; f. 2011 as social organization, became a political party in 2012; opposed to administration of Pres. Saakashvili; founded by prominent businessman Bidzina Ivanishvili; Leader EKATERINA KHVEDELIDZE.

Georgian Labour Party (Sakartvelos leiboristuli partia): 0112 Tbilisi, Javakhishvili 88; tel. (32) 294-39-22; fax (32) 294-29-22; e-mail labour_info@caucasus.net; internet www.labour.ge; f. 1997; contested 2008 legislative elections as Shalva Natelashvili—Labour Party; Chair. SHALVA NATELASHVILI.

Georgian Party: Tbilisi; f. 2010; opposed to administration of Pres. Saakashvili; Co-Chair. IRAKLI OKRUASHVILI (in exile), EROSI KITSMARISHVILI.

Georgian People's Party: Tbilisi; f. 2006; contested 2008 legislative elections as mem. of the Joint Opposition (National Council, New Rights) bloc; Chair. KOBA DAVITASHVILI.

Georgian Social Democratic Party (Sakartvelos sotsial-demokratiuli partia): 0108 Tbilisi, Tskhra Aprilis 2; tel. (32) 299-95-50; fax (32) 298-42-57; f. 1990; contested (subsequently annulled) 2003 legislative elections as mem. of the Jumber Patiashvili-Unity bloc; Chair. Prof. JEMAL KAKHNIASHVILI.

Georgia's Way (Sakartvelos gza): 0108 Tbilisi, Barnovi 60; tel. and fax (32) 291-45-46; f. 2006; contested 2008 legislative elections (as Salomé Zurabishvili—Georgia's Way) as mem. of the Joint Opposition (National Council, New Rights) bloc; Leader KAKHA SETURIDZE.

Movement for a Fair Georgia (Modzraoba samartliani sakartvelostvis): 0160 Tbilisi, Lvovi 56; tel. (32) 291-92-22; f. 2008; opposes regime of Pres. Saakashvili; signed co-operation agreement with de facto ruling party of Russia, United Russia, in Feb. 2010; Chair. SERGO JAVKHIDZE.

Movement for a United Georgia (Modzraoba ertiani sakartvelostvis): Tbilisi; f. 2007; contested 2008 legislative elections as mem. of the Joint Opposition (National Council, New Rights) bloc; Honorary Chair. IRAKLI OKRUASHVILI (in exile); Chair. GIA TORTLADZE; Gen. Sec. (vacant).

National Forum: Tbilisi; f. 2006; contested 2008 legislative elections as mem. of the Joint Opposition (National Council, New Rights) bloc; Leader KAKHA SHARTAVA.

New Rights (Axali Memarjveneebi—Axlebi): 0114 Tbilisi, J. Kalandadze 3; tel. (32) 272-07-75; fax (32) 272-38-58; e-mail nrp@nrp.ge; internet www.nrp.ge; f. 2001 as New Conservative Party; contested 2008 legislative elections as mem. of the Joint Opposition (National Council, New Rights) bloc; mem. of the Alliance for Georgia opposition grouping formed in 2009; Chair. Dr DAVID GAMKRELIDZE; Gen. Sec. DAVID SAGANELIDZE.

Our Georgia—Free Democrats (Chveni Sakartvelo—Davisuphali demokratebi): 0194 Tbilisi, E. Cherkezishvili 4; tel. (32) 210-48-83; e-mail contact@ag.ge; f. 2009; right-of-centre; opposed to administration of Pres. Saakashvili; mem. of the Alliance for Georgia opposition grouping formed in 2009; Leader IRAKLI ALASANIA.

Republican Party of Georgia (Sakartvelos respublikuri partia): 0108 Tbilisi, Phanaskerteli 20/81; tel. (32) 292-00-58; fax (32) 298-34-76; e-mail usupashvili@republicans.ge; internet www.republicans.ge; f. 1995; absorbed Georgian Popular Front (f. 1989); politically, economically and socially liberal; mem. of the Alliance for Georgia opposition grouping formed in 2009; Chair. DAVID USUPASHVILI.

Tophadze-Industrials (Tophadze-Mretsvelebi): 0105 Tbilisi, Marjvena Sanapiro 7; tel. (32) 294-09-81; f. 1999; fmrly Industry Will Save Georgia; contested 2008 legislative elections as mem. of New Right Alliance-Tophadze Industrial bloc; Leader GIORGI TOPHADZE.

Union of Georgian Traditionalists (Kartvel Traditsirnalistta kazshiri): 0108 Tbilisi, Virsaladze 10; tel. (32) 298-39-55; fax (32) 298-79-59; f. 1990; founded the People's Forum for Welfare and Democracy in 2005, to campaign for the direct election of city mayors and regional governors; monarchist; Chair. AKAKI ASATIANI.

United National Movement (UNM) (Ertiani natsionaluri modzraoba): 0118 Tbilisi, Lesya Ukrainka 1; tel. (32) 292-30-84; fax (32) 292-30-91; e-mail info@unm.ge; internet www.unm.ge; f. Nov. 2004 by merger of National Movement and United Democrats; nationalist; participated in 2008 legislative elections as United National Movement—Victorious Georgia; Chair. MIKHEIL SAAKASHVILI; Sec.-Gen. ZURAB MELIKISHVILI.

Unity (Ertoba): 0105 Tbilisi, Tavisuplebis Moedani; tel. (32) 292-30-65; fax (32) 293-46-94; e-mail ertoba@post.com; f. 2001; contested (subsequently annulled) 2003 legislative elections as mem. of the Jumber Patiashvili-Unity bloc; Co-Chair. JUMBER PATIASHVILI, ALEKSANDER CHACHIA.

Diplomatic Representation

EMBASSIES IN GEORGIA

Armenia: 0102 Tbilisi, Tetelashvili 4; tel. (32) 295-17-23; fax (32) 296-42-87; e-mail armemb@caucasus.net; internet www.armenianembassy.ge; Ambassador HOVHANNES MANUKIAN.

Azerbaijan: Tbilisi, Kipshidzse 2/1; tel. (32) 225-35-26; fax (32) 225-00-13; e-mail tbilisi@mission.mfa.gov.az; internet www.azembassy.ge; Ambassador AZER TOFIG HUSEYN.

Brazil: 0105 Tbilisi, Tavisuplebis Moedani 4; tel. (32) 277-91-96; fax (32) 277-91-65; e-mail brasemb.tbilisi@itamaraty.gov.br; Ambassador CARLOS ALBERTO LOPES ASFORA.

Bulgaria: 0102 Tbilisi, D. Agmashenebeli 61; tel. (32) 291-01-94; fax (32) 291-02-70; e-mail bgembassy.georgia@gol.ge; internet www.mfa.bg/bg/25/; Ambassador BRANIMIR RADEV.

China, People's Republic: 0179 Tbilisi, Barnov 52, POB 224; tel. (32) 225-26-70; fax (32) 225-09-96; e-mail chinaemb_ge@mfa.gov.cn; internet ge.china-embassy.org; Ambassador CHEN JIANFU.

Czech Republic: 0162 Tbilisi, Chavchavadze 37/6; tel. (32) 291-69-40; fax (32) 291-67-44; e-mail tbilisi@embassy.mzv.cz; internet www.mzv.cz/tbilisi; Ambassador IVAN JESTŘÁB.

Estonia: 0171 Tbilisi, Saburtalo, Likhauri 4; tel. (32) 236-51-22; fax (32) 236-51-38; e-mail tbilisisaatkond@mfa.ee; internet www.tbilisi.vm.ee; Ambassador TOOMAS LUKK.

France: 0108 Tbilisi, Gogebashvili 15; tel. (32) 299-99-76; fax (32) 295-33-75; e-mail ambafrance@access.sanet.ge; internet www.ambafrance-ge.org; Ambassador ERIC FOURNIER.

Germany: 0103 Tbilisi, Telavi 20, Sheraton Metekhi Palace Hotel; tel. (32) 244-73-00; fax (32) 244-73-64; e-mail info@tiflis.diplo.de; internet www.tiflis.diplo.de; Ambassador Dr ORTWIN HENNIG.

Greece: 0179 Tbilisi, T. Tabldze 37D; tel. (32) 291-49-70; fax (32) 291-49-80; e-mail gremb.tbi@mfa.gr; internet www.greekembassy.ge; Ambassador ELEFTHERIOS PROIOS.

Holy See: 0108 Tbilisi, Jgenti 40, Nutsubidze Plateau; tel. (32) 253-76-01; fax (32) 253-67-04; e-mail nuntius@vatican.ge; Apostolic Nuncio MAREK SOLCZYŃSKI (Titular Archbishop of Caesarea in Mauretania).

Hungary: 0160 Tbilisi, Lvovi 83; tel. (32) 239-90-08; fax (32) 239-90-04; e-mail hunembtbs@gmail.com; internet www.mfa.gov.hu/kulkepviselet/GE/hu; Ambassador SÁNDOR SZABÓ.

Iran: 0160 Tbilisi, Chavchavadze 80; tel. (32) 291-36-56; fax (32) 291-36-28; e-mail iranemb@geo.net.ge; Ambassador MAJID SAMAR-ZADEH SABER.

Iraq: 0179 Tbilisi, Kobuleti 16; tel. (32) 291-35-96; fax (32) 229-45-03; e-mail iraqiageoemb@yahoo.com; Ambassador TAYEB MOHAMMED TAYEB.

Israel: 0102 Tbilisi, D. Agmashenebeli 61; tel. (32) 296-44-57; fax (32) 295-52-09; e-mail press@tbilisi.mfa.gov.il; internet tbilisi.mfa.gov.il; Ambassador YUVAL FUCHS.

Italy: 0108 Tbilisi, Chitadze 3A; tel. (32) 299-64-18; fax (32) 299-64-15; e-mail embassy.tbilisi@esteri.it; internet www.ambtbilisi.esteri.it; Ambassador FEDERICA FAVI.

Japan: Tbilisi, Krtsanisi 7D; tel. (32) 275-21-11; fax (32) 275-21-20; e-mail protocol@embjapan.ge; Ambassador MASAYOSHI KAMOHARA.

Kazakhstan: 0179 Tbilisi, Shatberashvili 23; tel. (32) 299-76-84; fax (32) 229-24-24; e-mail dmkazaida@inbox.ru; Chargé d'affaires ADIL TURSUNOV.

Latvia: 0160 Tbilisi, Odessa 4; tel. (32) 224-48-58; fax (32) 238-14-06; e-mail embassy.georgia@mfa.gov.lv; Ambassador ELITA GAVELE.

Lithuania: 0162 Tbilisi, T. Abuladze 25; tel. (32) 291-29-33; fax (32) 222-17-93; e-mail amb.ge@urm.lt; internet ge.mfa.lt; Ambassador JONAS PASLAUSKAS.

Netherlands: 0103 Tbilisi, Telavi 20, Sheraton Metekhi Palace Hotel; tel. (32) 227-62-00; fax (32) 227-62-32; e-mail tbi@minbuza.nl; internet www.dutchembassy.ge; Ambassador PIETER JAN LANGENBERG.

Poland: 0108 Tbilisi, Zubalashvili 19; tel. (32) 292-03-98; fax (32) 292-03-97; e-mail tbilisi.amb.sekretariat@msz.gov.pl; internet www.tbilisi.polemb.net; Ambassador URSULA DOROSZEWSKA.

Romania: Tbilisi, Kushitashvili 7; tel. (32) 238-53-10; fax (32) 238-52-10; e-mail ambasada@caucasus.net; Ambassador (vacant).

Spain: Tbilisi, Rustaveli 24, 1st Floor; tel. (32) 230-54-64; fax (32) 299-60-06; e-mail emb.tiflis@maec.es; Chargé d'affaires JOSÉ ANTONIO ZORILLA ÁLVAREZ.

Sweden: Tbilisi, Tabidze 12; tel. (32) 255-03-20; fax (32) 225-12-26; e-mail ambassaden.tbilisi@sida.se; Ambassador DIANA JANSE.

Switzerland: 0114 Tbilisi, Krtsanisi 11; tel. (32) 275-30-01; fax (32) 275-30-06; e-mail tif.vertretung@eda.admin.ch; internet www.eda.admin.ch/tbilisi; Ambassador Dr GUENTHER BAECHLER.

Turkey: 0162 Tbilisi, Chavchavadze 35; tel. (32) 225-20-72; fax (32) 222-06-66; e-mail tiblisbe@dsl.ge; internet tbilisi.emb.mfa.gov.tr; Ambassador LEVENT MURAT BURHAN.

Ukraine: 0160 Tbilisi, Oniashvili 75; tel. (32) 231-11-61; fax (32) 231-11-81; e-mail emb_ge@mfa.gov.ua; internet www.mfa.gov.ua/georgia; Ambassador VASYL H. TSYBENKO.

United Kingdom: 0114 Tbilisi, Krtsanisi 51; tel. (32) 227-47-47; fax (32) 227-47-92; e-mail british.embassy.tbilisi@fco.gov.uk; internet ukingeorgia.fco.gov.uk; Ambassador JUDITH GOUGH.

USA: 0131 Tbilisi, Balanchivadze 11; tel. (32) 227-70-00; fax (32) 227-77-01; e-mail consulate-tbilisi@state.gov; internet georgia.usembassy.gov; Ambassador JOHN R. BASS.

Judicial System

Constitutional Court: 6010 Adjara, Batumi, M. Abashidze 16-18; tel. (422) 27-00-99; fax (422) 27-01-44; e-mail const@constcourt.ge; internet www.constcourt.ge; f. 1996; consists of 9 members; Pres. GIORGI PAPUASHVILI.

Supreme Court

0110 Tbilisi, Zubalashvili 32; tel. (32) 299-01-64; fax (32) 299-70-01; e-mail info@supremecourt.ge; internet www.supremecourt.ge; Chair. KONSTANTIN KUBLASHVILI.

Procurator-General: MURTAZ ZODELAVA, 0133 Tbilisi; tel. (32) 240-54-05; internet www.justice.gov.ge/index.php?lang_id=ENG &sec_id=106.

High Council of Justice: 0144 Tbilisi, Bochorma 12; tel. (32) 227-31-00; fax (32) 227-31-01; e-mail council@hcoj.gov.ge; internet www .hcoj.gov.ge; f. 1997; 15-member council that co-ordinates the appointment of judges and their activities; Chair. KONSTANTIN KUBLASHVILI (Chair. of the Supreme Court); Exec. Sec. VALERIAN TSERTSVADZE.

Religion

CHRISTIANITY

The Orthodox Church

The Georgian Orthodox Church is divided into 27 dioceses.

Georgian Patriarchate: 0105 Tbilisi, Erekle II Moedani 1; tel. (32) 299-03-78; fax (32) 298-71-14; e-mail info@patriachate.ge; internet www.patriarchate.ge; Catholicos-Patriarch of All Georgia ILIA II.

The Roman Catholic Church

The Apostolic Administrator of Latin Rite Catholics of the Caucasus is resident in Tbilisi. At 31 December 2007 there were an estimated 50,000 adherents within the territory covered by the Administration (which includes Armenia in addition to Georgia).

Apostolic Administrator of Latin Rite Catholics of the Caucasus: Most Rev. GIUSEPPE PASOTTO (Titular Bishop of Musti), 0105 Tbilisi, G. Abesadze 6; tel. and fax (32) 99-60-50; e-mail ammapost@ geo.net.ge.

The Armenian Apostolic Church

Primate of the Armenian Apostolic Church in Georgia: Rt Rev. Bishop VAZGEN MIRZAKHANIAN, 0105 Tbilisi, Krasilnaya 5, St Gevork Church; tel. (32) 272-17-50.

ISLAM

The principal Islamic communities in Georgia are those among the Ajars and Abkhaz (who are Sunni Muslims) and Azeris (who are Shi'ite). There is only one mosque in Tbilisi, which is shared by Sunni and Shi'ite communities. A new Muslim Affairs Department was established in 2011, to assume the jurisdiction over Georgia hitherto held by the Spiritual Board of Muslims of the Caucasus, based in Azerbaijan.

Muslim Affairs Department of Georgia: 0105 Tbilisi, Botankuri 32; f. 2011; non-governmental organization; Chair Mufti JAMAL BAGSHADZE.

JUDAISM

A large part of the country's long-established Jewish population emigrated, particularly to Israel, after the collapse of the USSR. In 2009 there were an estimated 30,000 Jews in Georgia, with the largest communities in Tbilisi and Kutaisi.

The Press

PRINCIPAL NEWSPAPERS

In 2005 88 newspaper titles were printed. Those listed below appear in Georgian, except where otherwise stated.

Droni (The Times): 0108 Tbilisi, Kostava 14; tel. (32) 299-56-54; e-mail newspdroni@usa.net; internet www.droni.ge; 2 a week; Editor-in-Chief GIORGI CHOCHISHVILI.

Georgia Today: 0105 Tbilisi, Nato Vachnadze 9; tel. (32) 292-08-30; fax (32) 292-08-82; e-mail info@georgiatoday.ge; internet www .georgiatoday.ge; f. 2000; weekly; in English; Gen. Man. GEORGE SHARASHIDZE.

Georgian Times: 0107 Tbilisi, Kikodze 12; tel. (32) 293-44-05; fax (32) 293-49-63; e-mail editor@geotimes.ge; internet www.geotimes .ge; f. 1993; weekly, Mondays; in English, Georgian and Russian; Editors DALI BZHALAVA, NANA GAGUA.

Iberia Spektri (Iberian Spectrum): 0105 Tbilisi, Machabeli 11; tel. (32) 298-73-87; fax (32) 298-73-88; Editor IRAKLI GOTSIRIDZE.

The Messenger: 0108 Tbilisi, Belinski 43; tel. (32) 293-91-69; fax (32) 293-62-32; e-mail messenger@messenger.com.ge; internet www .messenger.com.ge; f. 1919, revived 1990 and 1993; daily; in English; Editor-in-Chief ZAZA GACHECHILADZE.

Respublika (Republic): 0196 Tbilisi, Kostava 14; tel. and fax (32) 293-43-91; f. 1990; weekly; independent; Editor J. NINUA; circ. 40,000.

Rezonansi (Resonance): 0102 Tbilisi, D. Agmashenebeli 89/24; tel. (32) 237-79-69; fax (32) 238-79-69; e-mail resonancenewspaper@ yahoo.com; internet www.resonancedaily.com; f. 1990; daily; Editor-in-Chief LASHA TUGUSHI; circ. 7,000.

Sakartvelo (Georgia): 0196 Tbilisi, Kostava 14; tel. (32) 299-92-26; 5 a week; organ of the Georgian Parliament; Editor SERGO JANASHIA.

Svobodnaya Gruziya (Free Georgia): 0108 Tbilisi, D. Agmashenebeli 61; tel. (32) 255-01-31; fax (32) 255-01-61; e-mail new@ caucasus.net; internet www.svobodnaya-gruzia.com; f. 1922 as *Zarya Vostoka* (Dawn of the East); present name adopted 1991; in Russian; Editor-in-Chief TATO LASKHISHVILI; circ. 5,000.

PRINCIPAL PERIODICALS

Dila (The Morning): 0196 Tbilisi, Kostava 14; tel. (32) 293-41-30; e-mail dila1904@yahoo.com; internet www.dila.ge; f. 1904; present name adopted 1947; bimonthly; illustrated; for 5- to 12-year-olds; Editor-in-Chief DODO TSIVTSIVADZE; circ. 4,500.

Liberali: Tbilisi; internet www.liberali.ge; f. 2009; weekly; current affairs, politics; Editor-in-Chief SHORENA SHAVERDASHVILI; circ. 5,000 (2010).

Literaturnaya Gruziya (Literary Georgia): 0108 Tbilisi, Kostava 5; tel. (32) 222-47-37; e-mail abzianidze@hotmail.com; f. 1957; quarterly journal; politics, art and fiction; in Russian; Editor Prof. ZAZA ABZIANIDZE.

Metsniereba da Tekhnologiebi (Science and Technologies): 0108 Tbilisi, Rustaveli 52, Georgian Academy of Sciences; e-mail tech@gw .acnet.ge; f. 1949; monthly; journal of the Georgian Academy of Sciences; English, Georgian and Russian; Editor VLADIMER CHAVCHANIDZE.

Nakaduli (Stream): 0108 Tbilisi, Kostava 14; tel. (32) 293-31-81; f. 1926; fmrly *Pioneri*; monthly journal of the Ministry of Education and Science; illustrated; for 10- to 15-year-olds; Editor MANANA GELASHVILI; circ. 5,000.

Sakartvelos Metsnierebata Erovnuli Akademiis Moambe/ Bulletin of Georgian National Academy of Sciences: 0108 Tbilisi, Rustaveli 52; tel. (32) 299-75-93; fax (32) 299-88-91; e-mail bulletin@science.org.ge; internet www.science.org.ge/bulletin; f. 1940; 3 a year; in Georgian and English; Editor-in-Chief THOMAS V. GAMKRELIDZE.

Saunje (Treasure): 0107 Tbilisi, Dadiani 2; tel. (32) 272-47-31; f. 1974; 6 a year; organ of the Union of Writers of Georgia; foreign literature in translation; Editor S. NISHNIANIDZE.

Tabula: Tbilisi; tel. (32) 242-03-00; fax (32) 291-61-21; e-mail info@ tabula.ge; internet www.tabula.ge; f. 2010; politics and current affairs; supports administration of Pres. Saakashvili and free-market economics; Chief Editor TAMAR CHERGOLEISHVILI.

NEWS AGENCIES

Inter-Press: 0160 Tbilisi, Iosebidze 49; tel. (32) 238-78-00; fax (32) 245-07-80; e-mail interpress@ipn.ge; internet www.interpressnews .ge; f. 2000; in Georgian, Russian and English.

Kavkasia-Press (Caucasus Press): 0108 Tbilisi, Kiacheli 13; tel. (32) 292-29-19; fax (32) 293-35-99; e-mail en-edit@caucasus.net.

Prime News Agency (PNA): 0105 Tbilisi, Leselidze 28; tel. (32) 292-32-63; fax (32) 292-32-65; e-mail info@primenewsonline.com; f. 1997; news on Armenia, Azerbaijan and Georgia; Gen. Man. DEMNA CHAGELISHVILI.

Sarke Information Agency: 0102 Tbilisi, D. Agmashenebeli 54; tel. (32) 295-06-59; fax (32) 295-08-37; e-mail info@sarke.com; internet www.sarke.com; f. 1992; professional agency for economic and business news in Georgia; privately owned; Dir VALERIAN KHUKHUNASHVILI; Editor-in-Chief VICTORIA GUJELASHVILI.

JOURNALISTS' ASSOCIATIONS

Independent Association of Georgian Journalists: 0105 Tbilisi, Lermontov 10; tel. (599) 296-52-52; fax (32) 293-44-05; e-mail pochkhua@geotimes.ge; f. 2000; Pres. ZVIAD POCHKHUA.

Journalists' Federation of Georgia: 0105 Tbilisi, Erekle II Moedani 6; tel. (32) 298-24-46; e-mail foraf@geotvr.ge.

Publishers

Bakur Sulakauri Publishing (Bakur Sulakauris Gamomtsemlobs): 0112 Tbilisi, D. Agmashenebeli 150; tel. (32) 291-09-54; fax (32) 291-11-65; e-mail info@sulakauri.ge; internet www.sulakauri.ge; f. 1999; reference, school textbooks, fiction and children's literature; Dir BAKUR SULAKAURI.

Ganatleba (Education): 0164 Tbilisi, Chubinashvili 50; tel. (32) 295-50-97; f. 1957; educational, literature; Dir L. KHUNDADZE.

Georgian National Universal Encyclopedia: 0108 Tbilisi, Rustaveli 52; e-mail zurab_abashidze@hotmail.com; unit of the Georgian National Academy of Sciences; Editor-in-Chief ZURAB ABASHIDZE.

Meridian Publishing Co (Sh. P. Kh. Gamomtsemloba 'Meridiani'): Tbilisi, A. Kazbegi 45; tel. (32) 239-15-22; fax (32) 295-56-35; e-mail info@meridianpub.com; f. 1994; academic and schools; Editor-in-Chief GIORGI GIGINEISHVILI.

Metsniereba (Sciences): 0160 Tbilisi, Gamrekeli 19; tel. and fax (32) 237-22-97; e-mail publicat@gw.acnet.ge; f. 1941; owned by Georgian Academy of Sciences; Dir DAVID KOLOTAURI; Editor CISANA KARTOZIA.

Nakaduli (Stream): 0194 Tbilisi, Pekini 28; tel. (32) 238-46-52; e-mail ngvineria@yahoo.com; f. 1938; books for children and youth.

Sakartvelo (Georgia): 0102 Tbilisi, Marjanishvili 5; tel. (32) 295-42-01; f. 1921; fmrly *Sabchota Sakartvelo* (Soviet Georgia); political, scientific and fiction; Dir JANSUL GVINJILIA.

Tbilisi State University Publishing House: 0128 Tbilisi, Chavchavadze 14; tel. (32) 225-14-32; e-mail publishing@tsu.ge; f. 1933; scientific and educational literature; Dir TAMAR EBRALIDZE.

Broadcasting and Communications

TELECOMMUNICATIONS

In 2010 there were 1.1m. fixed telephone lines and 4.0m. subscriptions to mobile telephone services in the country.

Georgian National Communications Commission (Sakartvelos Komunikatsiebis Erovnuli Komisia): 0144 Tbilisi, Ketevan Tsamebuli Ave/Bochorma 50/18; tel. (32) 292-16-67; fax (32) 292-16-25; e-mail post@gncc.ge; internet www.gncc.ge; f. 2000; Chair. IRAKLI CHIKOVANI.

Geocell (Geoseli): 0160 Tbilisi, Gotua 3, POB 48; tel. (32) 277-01-77; fax (32) 277-01-01; e-mail contact@geocell.com.ge; internet www.geocell.com.ge; f. 1996; mobile cellular communications.

Magti: 0186 Tbilisi, Politkovskaya 5; tel. (32) 217-17-17; fax (32) 217-11-71; e-mail office@magtigsm.ge; internet www.magticom.ge; f. 1997; mobile cellular communications; launched 3G mobile services July 2006; Dir DAVID LEE.

Silknet: 0112 Tbilisi, Tsinamdzgvrishvili 95; tel. (32) 210-00-00; fax (32) 210-00-01; internet www.silknet.com; fmrly United Telecommunications Co of Georgia, operating under the brand names Vaneks and Elektrosvyaz Ajarii, present name adopted March 2010; owned by Bank TuranAlem (Kazakhstan); CEO GIORGI GUGUNISHVILI.

Telecom Georgia (Sakartvelos Telekomi): 0108 Tbilisi, Rustaveli 31; tel. (32) 244-18-00; fax (32) 244-18-29; e-mail sandro@telecom.ge; f. 1994; provides international telecommunications services; 100% owned by Metromedia International Group Inc (USA); Gen. Dir OTAR ZUMBURIDZE.

BROADCASTING

Television

Georgian Public Broadcasting (SSM) (Sakartvelos Sazogadoebrivi Mautsqebeli): 0171 Tbilisi, Kostava 68; tel. (32) 240-93-77; e-mail info@gpb.ge; internet www.gpb.ge; f. 2005; comprises two television channels: Public TV (f. 1956) and Second Channel (f. 1971), and two radio stations: Public Radio (f. 1925) and Radio Two (f. 1995); Gen. Dir GIORGI CHANTURIA.

Adjara TV: 6000 Adjara, Batumi, M. Abashidze 41; tel. (422) 27-43-70; fax (422) 27-43-84; e-mail info@adjaratv.ge; internet www.adjaratv.ge; Chief Exec. TEA TSETSKHLADZE.

Imedi TV: 0159 Tbilisi, Lubliana 5; tel. (32) 246-33-10; fax (32) 246-30-41; e-mail contact@imedi.ge; internet www.imedi.ge; f. 2001; Dir-Gen. GIORGI ARVELADZE.

Mze TV (Sun TV): 0171 Tbilisi, Kostava 75B; tel. (32) 233-55-98; e-mail reklama@mze.ge; internet www.mze.ge; f. 2003; 78% owned by Rustavi 2; Dir ZAZA TANANASHVILI (acting).

PIK-TV (First Information Caucasian TV): Tbilisi; tel. (57) 729-39-79; e-mail i.nikagosian@pik.tv; internet www.pik.tv; f. 2011; broadcasts in Russian; Gen. Dir YEKATERINA KOTRIKADZE.

Rustavi 2: 0177 Tbilisi, Vazha-Pshavela 45; tel. (32) 220-11-11; fax (32) 253-69-11; e-mail tv@rustavi2.com; internet www.rustavi2.com; f. 1994; independent; Gen. Dir IRAKLI CHIKOVANI.

Radio

Georgian Public Broadcasting: see Television.

Radio Imedi: 0159 Tbilisi, Lubliana 5; tel. (32) 233-10-59; e-mail info@radio-imedi.ge; internet www.radio-imedi.ge; f. 2001; national broadcasting, 24 hours; news; Dir IRAKLI KHETERELI.

Radio Sakartvelo (Radio Georgia): 0159 Tbilisi, Marshal Gelovani 2; tel. (32) 238-30-30; fax (32) 233-60-60; e-mail tamara@fortuna.ge; internet www.fortuna.ge; f. 1999; owns and operates 4 stations, incl. Radio Fortuna and Radio Fortuna Plus; popular and classical music; Gen. Dir GURAM CHIGOGIDZE.

Finance

(cap. = capital; res = reserves; dep. = deposits; m. = million; brs = branches; amounts in lari, unless otherwise indicated)

BANKING

Central Bank

National Bank of Georgia: 0105 Tbilisi, Leonidze 3–5; tel. (32) 244-25-44; fax (32) 244-25-77; e-mail info@nbg.gov.ge; internet www.nbg.gov.ge; f. 1991; cap. 15.0m., res 108.8m., dep. 2,750.9m. (Dec. 2009); Pres. and Chair. of Bd GIORGI KADAGIDZE.

Other Banks

In 2007 some 19 commercial banks were in operation in Georgia.

Bank of Georgia (Sakartvelos Banki): 0105 Tbilisi, Pushkin 3; tel. (32) 244-44-44; fax (32) 244-42-47; e-mail ir@bog.ge; internet www.bankofgeorgia.ge; f. 1991; present name adopted 1994; cap. 31.3m., res 502.6m., dep. 2,161.3m. (Dec. 2010); 77.5% owned by BNY (Nominees) Ltd (United Kingdom); CEO IRAKLI GILAURI; 25 brs.

Bank Republic: 0179 Tbilisi, Gr. Abashidze 2; tel. (32) 290-90-90; fax (32) 292-55-44; e-mail info@republic.ge; internet www.republic.ge; f. 1991; 60% owned by Société Générale (France); cap. 48.3m., res 43.6m., dep. 486.7m. (Dec. 2010); Chair. of Bd LASHA PAPASHVILI; CEO CHRISTIAN CARMAGNOLLE.

Basisbank: 0103 Tbilisi, K. Tsamebuli 1; tel. (32) 292-29-22; fax (32) 298-65-48; e-mail info@basisbank.ge; internet www.basisbank.ge; f. 1993; cap. 5.9m., res 8.0m., dep.96.3m. (Dec. 2010); Gen. Dir ZURAB TSIKHISTAVI.

Cartu Bank: 0162 Tbilisi, Chavchavadze 39A; tel. (32) 292-55-92; fax (32) 291-22-79; e-mail cartubank@cartubank.ge; internet www.cartubank.ge; f. 1996; cap. 54.7m., res 3.8m., dep. 122.0m. (Dec. 2010); Chair. of Bd GIORGI CHRDILELI; Dir-Gen. GIORGI KVIRIKASHVILI; 5 brs.

Kor Standard Bank (Standartbank): 0162 Tbilisi, Chavchavadze 43; tel. (32) 250-77-00; fax (32) 250-77-07; e-mail mail@standardbank.ge; internet www.standardbank.ge; f. 2000; name changed from Agro-Business Bank (ABG) in 2005; development bank; cap. 75.0m., dep. 178.2m., total assets 239.4m. (Dec. 2010); Gen. Dir GEORGE GLONTI; 61 brs.

Liberty Bank: 0162 Tbilisi, Chavchavadze 74; tel. and fax (32) 255-55-00; e-mail info@libertybank.ge; internet www.libertybank.ge; f. 2002; frmly People's Bank of Georgia; name changed as above after 91.2% stake acquired by Liberty Investments Holding in 2009; cap. 28.9m., res 38.4m., dep. 462.8m. (Dec. 2010); CEO LADO GURGENIDZE.

ProCredit Bank, Georgia: 0112 Tbilisi, D. Agmashenebeli 154; tel. (32) 220-22-22; fax (32) 224-37-53; e-mail info@procreditbank.ge; internet www.procreditbank.ge; f. 1999; present name adopted 2003; cap. 68.5m., res 18.6m., dep. 480.5m. (Dec. 2010); Gen. Dir MAYA MEREDOVA; 58 brs.

TaoPrivatBank: 0119 Tbilisi, Tsereteli 114; tel. (32) 255-55-55; fax (32) 235-50-80; e-mail hotlinetpb@privatbank.ge; internet www.tpbank.ge; f. 1992; name changed as above 2007; cap. 58.0m., res 16.4m., dep. 113.5m. (Dec. 2009); Gen. Dir VLADIMER UGULAVA.

TBC Bank: 0102 Tbilisi, Marjanishvili 7; tel. (32) 227-27-27; fax (32) 277-27-74; e-mail info@tbcbank.com.ge; internet www.tbcbank.com.ge; f. 1992; 55% owned by international financial institutions; cap. 15.1m., res 233.5m., dep. 1,412.4m. (Dec. 2010); Pres. of Bd of Dirs VAKHTANG BUTSKHRIKIDZE; 13 brs.

VTB Georgia (VneshTorgBank Georgia): 0102 Tbilisi, Uznadze 37; tel. (32) 250-55-05; fax (32) 299-91-39; e-mail info@vtb.com.ge; internet www.vtb.com.ge; f. 1995 as United Georgian Bank; name changed as above 2006; 84.7% owned by VTB OJSC (Russia); 9.0% owned by European Bank for Reconstruction and Development; cap. 148.0m., res 1.6m., dep. 180.9m. (Dec. 2010); Dir-Gen. ARCHIL KONTSELIDZE; 19 brs.

STOCK EXCHANGE

Georgian Stock Exchange (Sakartvelos Saphondo Birsha): 0162 Tbilisi, Chavchavadze 74A; tel. (32) 222-07-18; fax (32) 225-18-76;

e-mail info@gse.ge; internet www.gse.ge; f. 1999; Chair. of Supervisory Bd GEORGE LOLADZE; Gen. Dir VAKHTANG SVANADZE.

INSURANCE

Insurance State Supervision Service of Georgia (Sakartvelos Dazghvevis Sakhelmtsipho Zedamkhedvelobis Samsakhuri): 0164 Tbilisi, G. Chitaia 21; tel. (32) 295-64-89; fax (32) 295-71-42; e-mail isssg@inbox.ge; internet www.insurance.caucasus.net; f. 1997; provides state regulation of insurance activity; Dir ARCHIL TSERTSVADZE.

Aldagi BCI Insurance Co (Aldagi Bisiai Sadazghvevo kompania): 0179 Tbilisi, Qazgegis 3-5, Melikishvili 10; tel. (32) 244-48-08; fax (32) 229-49-05; e-mail aldagi@aldagi.com.ge; internet www.bci.ge; formed by merger of Aldagi Insurance Co and British-Caucasian Insurance Co.

Alpha Insurance Co: 0100 Tbilisi, Vazha Phshavelas 27 B; tel. (32) 239-15-01; fax (32) 239-93-70; e-mail info@aversi.ge; f. 2009; subsidiary of Aversi Pharma; Dir PAATA KURTANIDZE.

GPI (Georgian Pension and Insurance) Holding Co (Jipiai Holdingi): 0171 Tbilisi, Kostava 67; tel. (32) 250-51-11; fax (32) 236-52-22; e-mail info@gpih.ge; internet www.gpih.ge; f. 2001; majority share owned by Vienna Insurance Group—VIG (Austria); merged with VIG-owned IRAO Insurance Co in 2011, retaining separate brands; Gen. Dir GIORGI KVIRIKADZE.

IC Group Insurance Co: 0162 Tbilisi, Mosashvili 24; tel. (32) 220-88-88; fax (32) 291-24-27; e-mail icgroup@icgroup.ge; internet www.icgroup.ge; f. 2005; acquired People's Insurance Co in 2009.

Imedi L International Co: 0162 Tbilisi, Chavchavadze Ave 20; tel. (32) 225-00-88; fax (32) 229-30-75; e-mail imedi-l@imedi-l.com; internet www.imedi-l.com.ge; f. 1995; Dir ALEXANDER LORTKIPANIDZE.

Unison Insurance Co: 0160 Tbilisi, Budapeshti 15; tel. (32) 299-19-91; fax (32) 295-22-40; e-mail unison@unison.ge; internet www.unison.ge; f. 2011; Gen. Dir EDUARD VAKHTANGISHVILI.

Trade and Industry

GOVERNMENT AGENCY

National Investment Agency: Invest In Georgia: 0108 Tbilisi, Chanturia 12; tel. (32) 243-34-33; fax (32) 298-27-55; e-mail enquiry@investingeorgia.org; internet www.investingeorgia.org; f. 2002 to promote foreign direct investment; Dir KETI BOCHORISHVILI.

CHAMBERS OF COMMERCE

Georgian Chamber of Commerce and Industry (Sakartvelos Savachro-Samoetsvelo Palata): 0100 Tbilisi, Berdznis 29; tel. (32) 272-07-10; fax (32) 272-31-90; e-mail info@gcci.ge; internet www.gcci.ge; f. 1960; brs in Sukhumi and Batumi; Chair. JEMAL INAISHVILI.

Chamber of Commerce and Industry of Adjara (Acharas Savachro-Samoetsvelo Palata): 6000 Adjara, Batumi, Melashvili 26; tel. (422) 27-28-41; fax (422) 27-28-43; e-mail acci@acci.ge; internet www.acci.ge; f. 2004; Pres. TAMAZ SHAVADZE; Exec. Dir IRAKLI SAMNIDZE.

TRADE ASSOCIATIONS

Agricultural Development Association of Georgia (ADA): 0102 Tbilisi, Doki 2; tel. (995) 958-86-28; e-mail ada@access.sanet.ge; Chair. ALEXANDER LAZASHVILI.

Association of Georgian Exporters: 0177 Tbilisi, Jikia 5; tel. (32) 224-43-02; fax (32) 224-43-03; e-mail gea@gepa.org.ge; Gen. Dir TAMAZ AGLADZE.

Georgian Employers' Association (GEA): 0177 Tbilisi, Gazapkhuli 14; tel. (32) 221-02-54; fax (32) 223-21-71; e-mail employer@employer.ge; internet www.employer.ge; f. 2000; Dir ELGUJA MELADZE.

UTILITIES

Regulatory Authorities

Georgian National Energy Regulation Committee (SEMEK) (Sakartvelos Energetikis Maregulirebeli Erovnuli Komisia): 4600 Kutaisi, Chechelashvili 26; tel. (431) 225-61-20; fax (431) 225-61-21; e-mail mail@gnerc.org; internet www.gnerc.org; f. 1997; Chair. GURAM CHALAGASHVILI.

State Agency for the Regulation of Oil and Gas Resources (SAROGR): 0177 Tbilisi, Al. Qazbegi 45; tel. and fax (32) 225-33-11; e-mail sarogr@access.sanet.ge; f. 1999; Pres. ANDRIA KOTETISHVILI.

Electricity

In February 2007 Energo-Pro (Czech Republic) completed its purchase of 62.5% of Georgia's electricity distribution market, including six hydroelectric power plants and two distribution companies.

Electricity System Commercial Operator (ESCO) (Elektroenergetikuli Sistamis Komertsiuli Operatori): 0105 Tbilisi, Tskneti, Baratashvili 2; tel. and fax (32) 260-19-15; e-mail office@esco.ge; internet www.esco.ge; f. 2006; trades electricity and reserve capacity in order to maintain the balance of supply and demand; Gen. Dir IRINA MILORAVA.

Georgian State Electrosystem (GSE) (Sakartvelos Sakhelmtsipho Elektrosistema—SSE): 0105 Tbilisi, Baratashvilis 2; tel. (32) 251-02-02; fax (32) 298-37-04; e-mail info@gse.com.ge; internet www.gse.com.ge; f. 2002 by merger; operator of electricity transmission grid; Chair. of Managing Bd SULKHAN ZUMBURIDZE.

Gas

Georgian Oil and Gas Corpn (GOGC) (Sakartvelos Navtobisa da Gazis Korporatsia) (SNGK): 0190 Tbilisi, Kakhetis Gzatketsili 21; tel. (32) 224-40-40; fax (32) 224-40-41; e-mail public@gogc.ge; internet www.gogc.ge; f. 1997; state-owned; exclusive operator, owner, user, disposer and manager of natural and liquid gas imports and transit in Georgia; Gen. Dir ZURAB JANJGHAVA.

KazTransGaz Tbilisi: 0194 Tbilisi, Mitskevich 18A; tel. (32) 238-76-25; fax (32) 237-56-51; e-mail info@ktg-tbilisi.ge; internet www.tbilgazi.ge; fmrly Tbilgazi; gas distribution co for the Tbilisi region; privatized in 2006; 100% owned by KazTransGaz (Kazakhstan); Dir-Gen. GIORGI KOIAVA.

Water

Tbilisi Water Utility (Tbilisis Tskali): 0179 Tbilisi, M. Kostava 1st Alley 33; tel. (32) 248-71-10; scheduled for privatization; fmrly Tbiltskalkanali; water supply and sewerage system; Dir GIORGI GELBAKIANI.

TRADE UNION CONFEDERATION

Georgian Trade Union Confederation (GTUC) (Sakartvelos Prophesiuli Kavshirebis Gaertianeba): 0100 Tbilisi, Vazha Phshavelas 43; tel. and fax (32) 238-29-95; e-mail gtua@geo.net.ge; internet www.gtuc.ge; f. 1995; total membership approx. 259,172; in Feb. 2005 the association ceded 90% of its property to the state; Chair. IRAKLI PETRIASHVILI; 25 mem. unions.

Transport

RAILWAYS

In 2010 Georgia's rail network (including the sections within the secessionist republic of Abkhazia) totalled approximately 1, 566 km., of which 1,486 km. were electrified. In December 2004 an agreement was signed on the construction of a rail link between Kars, in Turkey, and Akhalkalaki, in Georgia, continuing to Azerbaijan; this was scheduled to open in 2012.

In 2011 the Tbilisi Metro comprised two lines with 22 stations, totalling 26.4 km in length.

Georgian Railways (Sakartvelos Rkinigza): 0112 Tbilisi, Tamar Mepis 15; tel. (32) 219-95-73; fax (32) 219-95-72; e-mail sag@railway.ge; internet www.railway.ge; f. 1872; Chair. and Dir-Gen. IRAKLI EZUGBAIA.

Tbilisi Metro: 0112 Tbilisi, Vagzlis Moedani 2; tel. (32) 235-77-77; fax (32) 293-41-41; e-mail info@metro.ge; f. 1966; Gen. Dir ZURAB KIKALISHVILI.

ROADS

In 2007 the total length of roads in use was an estimated 20,329 km (including 1,495 km of main roads and 3,354 km of secondary roads). Some 94% of the total network was hard-surfaced.

SHIPPING

There are international shipping services to and from Black Sea and Mediterranean ports. The main ports are at Batumi and Poti. At 31 December 2009 the Georgian merchant fleet comprised 295 vessels, with a combined displacement of 707,900 grt.

Batumi Sea Port (Batumis Sazghvao Navsadguri): 6003 Adjara, Batumi, Gorgbashvilis 3; tel. and fax (422) 27-62-61; e-mail info@batumiport.com; internet www.batumiport.com; operates five terminals: petroleum terminal, container terminal, railway ferry, dry cargo terminal and passenger terminal; owned by KazTransOil (Kazakhstan) (q.v.); Chair. ABAI TURIKENBAEVI; Gen. Dir VYACHESLAV KHARTYAN.

Poti Sea Port (Photis Sazghvao Navsadguri): 4401 Samegrelo-Zemo Svaneti Mkhare, Poti, D. Agmashenebeli 52; tel. (393) 22-06-60; fax (393) 22-06-88; e-mail contact@potiseaport.com; f. 1858; commercial port; Gen. Dir RONI SAABI.

CIVIL AVIATION

Georgia's primary airport is Tbilisi International Airport, Lochini. There are three other airports in operation in Batumi, Kutaisi and Senaki.

Civil Aviation Authority: 0160 Tbilisi, Al. Qazbegi 12; tel. (32) 236-30-29; fax (32) 294-75-09; e-mail g.mzhavanadze@gcaa.org.ge; f. 2002; Dir GIORGI MZHAVANADZE.

Georgian Airways (Jorjian Airveisi): 0108 Tbilisi, Rustaveli 12; tel. (32) 299-97-30; fax (32) 299-96-60; e-mail info@georgian-airways.com; internet www.georgian-airways.com; f. 2004; privately owned; flights to destinations in Europe and the Middle East; Chair. of Bd of Dirs TAMAZ GAIASHVILI.

Tourism

Georgia's numerous sites of interest to tourists include the historic buildings of Tbilisi and the ancient Georgian capital of Mtskheta, the cave cities at Uplistsikhe and Vardzia, the mountain landscapes of Kazbegi and Svaneti. According to the World Tourism Organization, there were 1,500,049 tourist arrivals in 2009, when receipts from tourism (including passenger transport) totalled US $531m.

Department of Tourism and Resorts: 0162 Tbilisi, Chavchavadze 80; tel. (32) 222-61-25; fax (32) 229-40-52; forms part of the Ministry of Economic and Sustainable Development; Chair. (vacant).

Defence

Following the dissolution of the USSR in December 1991, Georgia began to create a unified army from the various existing paramilitary and other groups. Compulsory military service lasts for 18 months. As assessed at November 2011, total armed forces numbered some 20,655: an army of 17,767, an air force of 1,310 and a National Guard of 1,578. There were also paramilitary forces of 11,700, comprising a border guard of 5,400 and 6,300 troops controlled by the Ministry of Internal Affairs. The navy was merged with the coast guard in 2009, also under the auspices of the Ministry of Internal Affairs.

In March 1994 Georgia joined the 'Partnership for Peace' programme of military co-operation of the North Atlantic Treaty Organization (NATO). In November 2004 Georgia became the first country to present an Individual Partnership Action Plan to NATO.

An Organization for Security and Co-operation in Europe (OSCE) Mission to Georgia was deployed from 1992 until 2008 to support the peace process in South Ossetia and Abkhazia. Following conflict in Georgia in early August 2008 and subsequent peace agreements (see History), the European Union Monitoring Mission in Georgia (EUMM) commenced deployment on 1 October; the EUMM comprised some 340 personnel, including 200 monitors contributed by 22 countries. Russia had announced its intention to maintain 3,800 troops each in South Ossetia and Abkhazia and to establish military bases there. At the end of August 2009, however, the Chief of the General Staff of the Russian armed forces stated that the number of Russian troops in Abkhazia and South Ossetia had been reduced to 1,700 in each. (As assessed at November 2011, there were 6,900 Russian troops within the internationally recognized boundaries of Georgia.)

Defence Expenditure: Budgeted at 647m. lari in 2011.

Chief of the General Staff: Maj.-Gen. DEVI CHANKOTADZE.

Commander of the Land Forces: Col IVERI SUBELIANI (acting).

Commander of the Air Forces: Col GOCHA SHINGAZRDILOV.

Education

Education is compulsory for nine years, between the ages of six and 14. Primary education begins at six years of age. Secondary education, beginning at the age of 10, lasts for a maximum of seven years, comprising a compulsory cycle of five years and an optional second cycle of two years. In 2006/07 pre-primary enrolment included 40.9% of children in the relevant age-group. In 2006/07 primary enrolment included 93.7% of the relevant age-group, when the ratio for secondary enrolment was 81.9%.

In addition to state institutions, many private institutions of higher education were opened after 1991; there were 108 in 2009/10. In 2009/10 there were 102,710 students enrolled at institutions of higher education (including universities). In 2008 state expenditure on education amounted to 553.8m. lari (8.0% of total consolidated state budgetary expenditure.

GEORGIAN SECESSIONIST TERRITORIES

Two regions within the constitutional boundaries of Georgia, Abkhazia (Apsny) and South Ossetia, have declared independence from the Georgian state, and in practice exist separately from Georgia. In neither case has the independence of the proclaimed republics been widely recognized, with Russia being the principal supporter of the ensuing secessionist polities.

ABKHAZIA

Introductory Survey

LOCATION, CLIMATE, LANGUAGE, RELIGION, FLAG, CAPITAL

Abkhazia is situated in the north-west of Georgia, and covers an area of 8,665 sq km. Russia lies to the north, across the River Psou, while the remainder of Georgia lies to the east, across the River Ingur (Enguri). The south-western boundary is with the Black Sea. The climate is mild and mostly subtropical. Average temperatures in the principal city, Sukhumi, range from 7°C (44°F) in January to 23°C (73°F) in July, although the climate in the mountainous regions is substantially cooler Precipitation averages around 1,390 mm per year in the lowlands, but in the highlands may exceed 3,000 mm. The population principally speak Abkhaz, a language of the North-western Caucasian family that is usually written in a form of the Cyrillic script, although Russian is also in general use. Although most Abkhaz outside Abkhazia are Muslims, a survey undertaken in the territory in 2003 found that a small majority of the population of the territory were adherents of Orthodox Christianity, with around one-sixth of the population adhering to Islam. The separatist authorities use a flag (proportions 1 by 2) with seven horizontal stripes, alternately green and white. A red canton contains a white hand surmounted by an arch of seven white stars. The principal city and capital of the self-proclaimed 'Republic' is Sukhumi (Sukhum, known as Aqwa in Abkhaz).

CONTEMPORARY POLITICAL HISTORY

Historical Context

Formerly a colony of the Eastern Roman or 'Byzantine' Empire, Abkhazia was an important power in the ninth and 10th centuries, but it was later dominated by Georgian, Turkish and Russian rulers. For much of the Soviet period it formed a nominally Autonomous Republic (ASSR) within the Georgian Soviet Socialist Republic (SSR). However, following the Bolshevik occupation of 1921, it was initially granted the status of an SSR, before the Soviet leader, Stalin (Iosif V. Dzhugashvili), absorbed it into Georgia in 1931 (which, itself, constituted part of the Transcaucasian Soviet Federative Socialist Republic until 1936). Tens of thousands of ethnic Georgians were subsequently resettled in Abkhazia, particularly in the western regions. A movement for secession from Georgia was revived in 1989, by which time the predominately Muslim Abkhaz comprised only 17.8% of the area's population, and Georgians constituted the largest ethnic group (45.7%). The Georgian Government repeatedly rejected Abkhazian secessionist demands, which were also fiercely resisted by the local Georgian population. In July 1989 violent clashes erupted between ethnic Georgians and Abkhaz in Sukhumi (Sukhum or Sokhumi), the republic's capital, resulting in 14 deaths. A state of emergency was imposed throughout Abkhazia, but further inter-ethnic violence ensued. In 1989 the total population was 537,000, of which 17.8% were Abkhazians, and 45.7% ethnic Georgians.

In August 1990 the Abkhazian Supreme Soviet voted to declare independence from Georgia. This declaration was pronounced invalid by the Georgian Supreme Soviet. Later in the month Georgian deputies in the Abkhazian legislature succeeded in reversing the declaration of independence, and inter-ethnic unrest continued. Following the overthrow of Zviad Gamsakhurdia as President of Georgia in January 1992, there was renewed unrest in Abkhazia, as large numbers of ethnic Georgians demonstrated in support of Gamsakhurdia. In July the Abkhazian legislature declared Abkhazia's sovereignty as the 'Republic of Abkhazia'.

Domestic Political Affairs

A period of armed conflict began in August 1992, when the Georgian Government dispatched some 3,000 members of the National Guard to the republic, in order to release senior officials who had been taken hostage by supporters of Gamsakhurdia and who were being held in Abkhazia (see above). The Chairman of the Abkhazian legislature and leader of the independence campaign, Vladislav Ardzinba, retreated north with his forces. The situation was complicated by the dispatch of Russian paratroopers to the region to protect Russian (former Soviet) military bases, amid reports that Russia was supplying military assistance to the separatists. In October separatist forces regained control of northern Abkhazia; hostilities intensified further in the first half of 1993. A provisional peace agreement was signed in July by Georgian and Abkhazian leaders. The cease-fire held until September, when Abkhazian forces recaptured Sukhumi after 11 days of intense fighting. Almost all Georgian forces were expelled from Abkhazia, and the Georgian Head of State, Eduard Shevardnadze, was forced to flee Sukhumi by air, under heavy bombardment, after the leader of the pro-Shevardnadze administration in Abkhazia, Zhiuli Shartava, was assassinated. Several hundred people were believed to have been killed during the fighting, and more than 200,000 people (mostly ethnic Georgians) fled Abkhazia. Many thousands of the refugees were subsequently stranded, in freezing conditions, near the mountainous south-eastern border region of Abkhazia, where large numbers perished. In December Georgian and Abkhazian officials signed an eight-point 'memorandum of understanding' at UN-sponsored talks in Geneva, Switzerland. A small number of UN military personnel, part of the UN Observer Mission in Georgia (UNOMIG), were subsequently dispatched to Sukhumi in a peace-keeping capacity.

Outbreaks of violence continued throughout 1994, although peace talks were held at regular intervals. The fundamental disagreement between the Georgian and Abkhazian delegations concerned the future status of Abkhazia: Ardzinba demanded full independence, while the Georgian Government insisted on the preservation of Georgia's territorial integrity. However, a full cease-fire was declared in May, in accordance with which 2,500 CIS (mainly Russian) peace-keepers were deployed in June, joining an augmented UN observer force. Nevertheless, hostilities continued.

In November 1994 the Abkhazian legislature adopted a new Constitution, declaring the 'Republic of Abkhazia' to be a sovereign state. Ardzinba was elected as President. The Georgian Government condemned this declaration of sovereignty, and the peace negotiations were suspended. Protests were also expressed by the USA, Russia and the UN Security Council, all of which reaffirmed their recognition of Georgia's territorial integrity. Peace talks were resumed in 1995, despite periodic outbreaks of violence. In January 1996, at a summit meeting of CIS leaders in Moscow, it was agreed to implement Shevardnadze's request for economic sanctions to be imposed against Abkhazia until it consented to rejoin Georgia.

On 23 November 1996 elections to the secessionist Abkhazian 'legislature', the People's Assembly, were held. In March 1997 the Abkhazian faction in Parlamenti staged a hunger strike, demanding the withdrawal of the CIS peace-keeping forces from Abkhazia. However, the peace-keepers' mandate was repeatedly extended. The mandate of UNOMIG, which expired on 31 July, was subsequently granted successive six-monthly extensions. Russian proposals for a settlement of the conflict, which provided for substantial autonomy for Abkhazia within Georgia, were welcomed by Shevardnadze, but rejected by Ardzinba. In August, for the first time since 1992, Ardzinba visited Tbilisi, together with the Russian Minister of Foreign Affairs, Yevgenii Primakov, where they met Shevardnadze. In November 1997 it was agreed to establish a joint Co-ordinating Council, in which representatives of the parties to the conflict, as well as Russian, UN and European Union (EU, see p. 276) delegates, were to participate.

In May 1998 Abkhazian troops attempted to enter the neutral zone between Abkhazia and the remainder of Georgia, resulting in tens of thousands of ethnic Georgian refugees fleeing the region. Negotiations resumed in June; Georgia's principal demand was the prompt and unconditional repatriation to Gali of some 35,000 ethnic Georgians who had been forced to flee. In January 1999 Ardzinba agreed to permit the refugees to return to Gali from 1 March, although their return and the convening of proposed peace talks in Gali were hindered by a one-month blockade of the road bridge permitting access to Abkhazia. On 3 October Ardzinba, the sole candidate, was re-elected President. The election was declared illegal by international observers. In a referendum held concurrently, 97% of the votes cast were reported to have upheld Abkhazian independence. In July 2000 a UN-sponsored protocol on stabilization measures was signed by Abkhazia and Georgia, although violent incidents continued.

In March 2001, at a summit meeting held in Yalta, Crimea, Ukraine, under UN auspices, Abkhazia and Georgia signed an accord renouncing the use of force. Hostilities resumed in October, when a UN helicopter was shot down over the Kodori Gorge, killing all nine passengers. The operations of UNOMIG were suspended, and violence in the region intensified; Abkhazian officials blamed the attack on Georgian guerrillas and on dissidents from the Chechen Republic within Russia. The Abkhazian authorities blamed Georgia for subsequent aerial attacks on villages in the Kodori Gorge; Georgia, in turn, attributed responsibility for the attacks to Russia, and made repeated allegations of violations of Georgian airspace by Russian aircraft in October–November. The Georgian Government dispatched troops to the region in October, ostensibly to protect the ethnic Georgian population, in what the UN deemed a violation of the 1994 cease-fire agreement.

In October 2001 Parlamenti voted to request the immediate withdrawal of the CIS peace-keeping forces from Abkhazia; however, Shevardnadze argued against their removal, as no substitute force was forthcoming. In January 2002 the Georgian and Abkhazian authorities signed a protocol, providing for the withdrawal of Georgian troops from the Kodori Gorge; a further protocol was signed in April, precipitating the withdrawal of the troops. In the same month the Abkhazian authorities suspended their participation in the UN-sponsored Co-ordinating Council. Meanwhile, UNOMIG resumed its activities in February, following the extension of its mandate. At a CIS summit meeting held in March Shevardnadze and the Russian President, Vladimir Putin, agreed to amend the mandate of the CIS peace-keeping forces, to satisfy Georgian demands, among them the inclusion of forces from countries other than Russia. Abkhazian Legislative elections, held on 2 March, were deemed to be illegal by the Georgian Government. In July the UN Security Council adopted Resolution 1427, which urged the resumption of negotiations on Abkhazia's status within Georgia.

In January 2003 the Georgian National Security Council ruled that the country would not approve a renewal of the CIS peace-keepers' mandate (which had recently expired) unless a number of conditions were met. In February the National Security Council finally agreed to remove all objections to the renewal of the peace-keepers' mandate, and in early March, following talks in Sochi, Presidents Shevardnadze and Putin issued a joint statement, according to which they agreed to expedite the repatriation of displaced persons to Abkhazia. In addition, they agreed to extend indefinitely the mandate of the CIS peace-keeping forces, until either Georgia or Abkhazia demanded their withdrawal.

The Presidency of Sergei Bagapsh, 2004–11

An internationally unrecognized presidential election took place on 3 October 2004, in which former Prime Minister of Abkhazia Raul Khajimba, the candidate endorsed by Ardzinba and supported by Russia, was initially declared the winner. However, Khajimba's rival Sergei Bagapsh was ultimately judged to have received the most votes, by a narrow margin. Khajimba disputed this result, demanding the annulment of the ballot. An agreement was reached on 6 December, under the mediation of Russian officials, according to which the two candidates were to participate jointly in a new election. Bagapsh was to contest the presidency, with Khajimba as his Vice-President, and with the powers of the latter role to be augmented by an amendment to the separatist territory's 'constitution'. In the repeated election on 12 January 2005, Sergei Bagapsh was elected as President with some 90% of the votes cast; following his inauguration in February, Bagapsh nominated Aleksandr Ankvab, a close ally, as Prime Minister. Despite Russia's apparent preference for Khajimba's presidential candidacy, Bagapsh also sought a strategic union with Russia.

In October 2005 Parlamenti adopted a resolution establishing a deadline of 15 June 2006 for the Russian peace-keeping forces in the region to demonstrate compliance with their mandate. In February 2006 negotiations took place, under the aegis of the UN, in Geneva between representatives of the Georgian and Abkhazian authorities. In May the UN-sponsored Co-ordinating Council convened in Tbilisi to oversee talks between the two sides. In July Georgian forces launched an operation to disarm an armed militia group, *Monadire* (Hunter), in the upper Kodori Gorge, capture its leader, Emzar Kvitsiani, and 'restore constitutional order' to the region. On 27 July President Saakashvili announced that Georgian forces had, for the first time in 13 years, regained full control of the Kodori Gorge and surrounding regions; on the following day Saakashvili ordered the Abkhazian parliament-in-exile to relocate to Chkhalta, in the newly captured region, which was officially designated Upper Abkhazia, as part of efforts to ensure that eventual Georgian control over all of Abkhazia be restored. In an address at a session of the UN General Assembly in September, Saakashvili stated that Georgia would acquiesce to an agreement on the non-resumption of hostilities and the safe return of refugees only if Russian peace-keeping troops in Abkhazia were replaced by a multinational police force. In October the UN Security Council adopted a resolution that urged Georgia to refrain from 'provocative' actions in Abkhazia and underlined the significance of Russian peace-keeping forces there.

On 4 and 18 March 2007 some 108 candidates contested the elections for Abkhazia's 35-member legislature, which were denounced by the Georgian Government. In mid-March three military helicopters made a series of aerial bombings in the Georgian-controlled Kodori Gorge. Both the Russian and separatist Abkhazian authorities denied any involvement in the attacks, although reports stated that the helicopters had entered the territory from Russian airspace. Following the announcement in July that Russia was to host the 2014 Winter Olympic Games in Sochi, near the border with Abkhazia, reports that Russian enterprises intended to import materials for the construction of sports facilities from Abkhazia (with considerable potential benefit to the local economy) prompted strong protests from Georgia. The widespread granting of Russian passports to residents of Abkhazia (and of South Ossetia) was a significant source of tension between Georgia and Russia from the mid-2000s. This tension intensified in early 2008; in March Russia announced its unilateral withdrawal from the CIS sanctions against the separatist Abkhazian regime imposed in 1996. Also in March 2008 the separatist Abkhazian authorities rejected a new proposal for a resolution of the status of the territory (granting it extensive autonomous powers within Georgia) presented by President Saakashvili.

In May 2008 Russia (which in April had announced that it was to establish closer relations with the separatist territories) dispatched 400 troops to Abkhazia, with the stated intention of repairing a railway line; Georgia formally protested at the measure. In June a bomb exploded in Sukhumi, prompting the Abkhazian authorities, which claimed that Georgian special forces had perpetrated that and other attacks with the aim of destabilizing the region, to close the border between Abkhazia and the remainder of Georgia. On 9 August, following the onset of hostilities in and around South Ossetia, the Abkhazian separatists declared that their forces had commenced military action to expel Georgian troops from the Kodori Gorge. Two days later Russia announced that some 9,000 Russian troops had been dispatched to Abkhazia; on 12 August Abkhazian forces, with Russian support, were reported to have regained control of the Kodori Gorge. Later in August a mass demonstration was staged in Abkhazia to urge Russia to recognize the region's independence. An EU-mediated peace agreement was reached on 8 September; Russia announced its intention of maintaining 3,800 troops in each of Abkhazia and South Ossetia. Following Russia's official recognition, on 26 August, of Abkhazia and South Ossetia as independent states, on 24 September the Abkhazian People's Assembly ratified a friendship and co-operation treaty committing Russia to military support; the treaty had been signed by the leaders of the two separatist Republics and the Russian President on 17 September. Bagapsh confirmed that two Russian military bases would be established in Abkhazia, and announced that the security of the border between Abkhazia and the remainder of Georgia would be strengthened. Meanwhile, on 6 September the President of Nicaragua, Daniel Ortega, announced that his country was to formally recognize the independence of both Abkhazia and South Ossetia, becoming the second state to do so. On 9 October the Council of CIS Foreign Ministers, officially confirming the suspension of Georgia's membership of the organization, also announced the suspension of the activities of the CIS peace-keeping forces in Abkhazia. Despite opposition from the Abkhazian authorities, EU monitors were deployed in Abkhazia for the first time in early November. In late January 2009 the United Abkhazia movement, founded in 2004, and which was closely associated with Bagapsh and with the de facto ruling party of Russia, United Russia, was formally reconstituted as a political party. In March 2009 concerns increased that the stated intention of the Abkhazian (and South Ossetian) authorities to enforce conscription into their armed forces of all local inhabitants regardless of ethnicity would be regarded as provocation by the Georgian Government, after an ethnic Georgian, accompanied by some 70 women and children from his village, fled Abkhazia in order to evade this conscription. Later in March the Russian Government signed an agreement providing for the extension of some 2,360m. roubles in financial aid to Abkhazia. The Belarusian President Alyaksandr Lukashenka, after meeting Bagapsh, also offered financial assistance to Abkhazia, while declining to recognize the territory as an independent state. In the same month a military agreement allowing a Russian military base to remain in the territory for 49 years was signed. On 30 April Russian President Dmitrii Medvedev signed border treaties with Abkhazia and South Ossetia, which provided for Russia to guard the state borders of Abkhazia prior to the establishment of Abkhazian border forces. The EU expressed 'deep concern' at both agreements, which it stated violated the terms of the peace agreement of late August 2008. Meanwhile, in March 2009 separatist officials set residents a deadline of 20 March, by which time they would be required to renounce their Georgian citizenship and receive Abkhazian (or Russian) passports. In the same month it was reported that schools in Gali were being subject to pressure to abandon Georgian-language teaching and to use textbooks written in Russian.

Georgia protested on 11 April 2009 against the 'provocative military manoeuvres' of the Russian navy in the Black Sea off the coast of Abkhazia, and on 13 April the Georgian Ministry of Defence accused Russia of having increased its military presence in the Gali district of Abkhazia, as well as within South Ossetia. The Russian military responded that it had undertaken 'preventive measures' in response to growing political disorder in Georgia.

A joint statement, issued in May 2009, by the opposition Forum of National Unity of Abkhazia (FNEA) and a war veterans' union strongly criticized Bagapsh after he granted various economic concessions, including the transfer of control, for a period of 10 years, over Abkhazia's airport and railways, to Russia. In late May the authorities signed a five-year agreement giving Rosneft, the Russian state-owned oil company, the right to prospect for petroleum and natural gas off Abkhazia's Black Sea coast. At the end of the month Khajimba resigned as Vice-President, following a number of disagreements with Bagapsh (the position remained vacant until February 2010). On 27 July the EU extended the mandate of its monitoring mission until 14 September 2010 (when it was again extended), and urged that the mission be granted the unhindered access to Abkhazia and South Ossetia that had hitherto been denied it.

On 12 August 2009 Putin, as Russian premier, visited Abkhazia to reaffirm Russian support for the separatist regime, announcing that Russia would finance the reinforcement of Abkhazia's borders and further Russian military operations within the territory, in addition to providing budgetary aid. On the same day two explosions in Sukhumi and Gagra killed two people and injured three. The Abkhazian authorities blamed Georgian security services for the blasts. At the end of the month the Russian Army's Chief of the General Staff, Gen. Nikolai Makarov, stated that troop levels had been reduced to 1,700 in both Abkhazia and South Ossetia. In September Venezuela became the third state to recognize the independence of both Abkhazia and South Ossetia. (An Abkhazian embassy opened in the Venezuelan capital, Caracas in July 2010, and Bagapsh subsequently made an official visit to the country.) An independent fact-finding report published in September 2009, with support from the EU, described Russia's recognition of South Ossetia and Abkhazia as independent states as constituting a violation of international law.

In the (internationally unrecognized) presidential election held on 12 December 2009, contested by five candidates, Bagapsh was overwhelmingly elected to a further term of office, receiving, according to official figures, 61.2% of the votes cast; his nearest rival was Khajimba, with 15.3%. The official rate of participation was enumerated at 73.5%. On 12 February 2010 Bagapsh was inaugurated to a new presidential term, and Ankvab was appointed to the still vacant post of Vice-President; one day later he was replaced as Prime Minister by Sergei Shamba, hitherto Minister of Foreign Affairs. On 17 February Abkhazia signed an agreement with Russia allowing the construction of a land base at Gudauta which would accommodate up to 3,000 Russian land troops for at least 49 years.

In April 2010, following a visit to Sukhumi by a UN ambassador and the EU Special Representative for the South Caucasus, Bagapsh announced that UN and EU observer missions would no longer be admitted into Abkhazia. In August, shortly after a visit to Abkhazia by Russian President Dmitrii Medvedev, Russia announced that it had deployed anti-aircraft missiles in the territory; the EU expressed concern, stating that the deployment would be in contravention of the cease-fire agreement. In early September Shamba stated that unless Georgia officially recognized Abkhazia's independence it would be impossible for ethnic Georgian refugees to return to the region. On 7 September the UN General Assembly adopted a non-binding resolution (following similar resolutions in 2008 and 2009) reiterating the right of return of all displaced persons and refugees to breakaway Abkhazia and South Ossetia. On 13 September the International Court of Justice opened hearings on a case brought by Georgia against Russia, which it accused of violating the International Convention on the Elimination of All Forms of Racial Discrimination in South Ossetia and Abkhazia. (In April 2011 the Court dismissed the case without any right of appeal, on the grounds that Georgia had made no attempt to settle the dispute with Russia before bringing the case to the Court.) In a concession to demands by the Abkhaz and South Ossetian delegations in the ongoing negotiations in Geneva, President Saakashvili, addressing the European Parliament in November 2010, declared that Georgia would 'never use military force to restore its territorial integrity'; although the Presidents of Abkhazia and South Ossetia issued similar pledges, Russia welcomed the announcement without making a reciprocal affirmation. In February 2011 a voter turnout of only 38.8% was reported in (internationally unrecognized) local elections in Abkhazia.

Recent developments: the search for international recognition

On 29 May 2011 Bagapsh died, as a result of complications from a lung operation; an election to the Abkhazian presidency was subsequently scheduled for 26 August. On 26 August Ankvab, who had been acting President since Bagapsh's death, was elected President of Abkhazia, obtaining 54.9% of the votes cast in a poll contested by three candidates (including Shamba) and in which 71.9% of the electorate participated. On 26 September Ankvab was inaugurated as President. One day later he appointed Leonid Lakerbaya as Prime Minister, and a new Government was appointed during October.

Abkhazia made only limited progress during 2011 towards obtaining international recognition for the secessionist administration. In late May the Pacific island state of Vanuatu announced that it had become the fifth state to recognize Abkhazian statehood (it was the first of these five states not to extend such recognition to South Ossetia). However, despite claims that agreement had been signed by the Prime Ministers of Abkhazia and Vanuatu, the declaration of recognition was subsequently disputed by various factions of the Vanuatu Government. Following the inauguration of a new Prime Minister in Vanuatu in June, recognition was rescinded, but it was reinstated in the following month. Tuvulu recognized the statehood of Abkhazia in September, and the hosting of the World Domino Championship in Sukhumi in October, in which representatives of 25 countries and territories participated, was intended to constitute a further attempt to raise the profile of the territory internationally. (At that time the only countries to recognize the statehood of the 'Republic of Abkhazia' were Nauru, Nicaragua, Russia, Tuvalu, Vanuatu and Venezuela.)

On 22 February 2012 an assassination attempt against Ankvab was staged by unidentified assailants, who attacked the presidential convoy near Sukhumi, killing two of his bodyguards. The first round of elections to the Abkhazian secessionist legislature were held on 10 March, with a second round in 20 of the single-mandate constituencies on 24 March. It was announced by the regions's electoral commission that independent candidates nominated by civic 'initiative groups' had secured 26 of the 35 seats, while the opposition FNEA had received four seats and United Abkhazia, which supported Ankvab, three seats. (Polls were to be repeated in two constituencies at a later date, owing, respectively, to insufficient voter turnout and electoral irregularities in the first round.) The opening session of the new National Assembly took place on 3 April, when a deputy of long standing, Valerii Bganba, was elected Speaker. Meanwhile, on 16 March, Medvedev announced the creation of a new post, of Representative of the Russian President to Abkhazia (similar posts were also created later that month for South Ossetia and the Moldovan secessionist territory of Transnistria). Taimuraz Mamsurov, the Head of the Republic of North Osetiya—Alaniya was appointed additionally to that role. By mid-April six suspects (of whom two were subsequently released) had been detained in the investigation into the assassination attempt against Ankvab. However, two of the suspects, including former Minister of the Interior, Almasbei Kchach, were found dead during April, with both deaths being officially attributed to suicide.

PUBLIC HOLIDAYS

2013: 1–2 January (New Year), 7 January (Christmas), 14 January (Azhurnyhua, Creation of the World and Renewal), 8 March (International Women's Day), 9 May (Victory Day), 30 September (Liberation Day), 14 October* (Kurbannykhua, Feast of the Sacrifice), 26 November (Constitution Day).

* This holiday is dependent on the Islamic lunar calendar and may vary by one or two days from the date given.

Directory

The Government of the 'Republic of Abkhazia'

President: ALEKSANDR ANKVAB.

Vice-President: MIKHAIL LOGUA.

CABINET OF MINISTERS

(May 2012)

Prime Minister: LEONID I. LAKERBAYA.

First Deputy Premier: INDIRA VARDANIYA.

Deputy Premier: VLADIMIR DELBA.

Deputy Premier: ALEKSANDR STRANICHKIN.

Chief of the Apparatus of the Cabinet of Ministers: MARINA LADARIYA.

Minister of Finance: DAVID IRADYAN.

Minister of Defence: Gen.-Col MIRAB KISHMARIYA.

Minister of Internal Affairs: Gen.-Maj. OTAR KHETSIYA.

Minister of Foreign Affairs: VYACHESLAV CHIRIKBA.

Minister of Justice: YEKATERINA ONISHCHENKO.

Minister of the Economy: KRISTINA OZGAN.

Minister of Taxes and Duties: RAUF A. TSIMTSBA .

Minister of Agriculture: BESLAN JOPUA.

Minister of Education: DAUR NACHKEBIYA.

Minister of Culture: NUGZAR LOGUA.

Minister of Health: ZURAB G. MARSHAN.

Minister of Labour and Social Development: OLGA KOLTUKOVA.

Note: The Chairmen of the State Customs Committee, and of the State Committees for The Management of Property and Privatization, of Resorts and Tourism, of Youth Affairs and Sport, of Repatriation, and of Ecology and Nature are also members of the Cabinet of Ministers.

MINISTRIES

Office of the President: 384900 Abkhazia, Sukhumi, nab. Makhajirov 32; tel. (8402) 22-46-22; fax (8402) 22-71-17; e-mail sukhum-krma@yandex.ru.

Office of the Prime Minister: 384900 Sukhumi, ul. nab. Makhajirov 72; tel. (8402) 26-12-22; e-mail info@govabk.org; internet www.govabk.org.

Office of the Cabinet of Ministers: 384900 Sukhumi, ul. nab. Makhajirov 32; tel. (8402) 26-46-21; e-mail info@govabk.org; internet www.govabk.org.

Ministry of Agriculture: 384900 Sukhumi, ul. Lakoba 21; tel. (8402) 26-19-05.

Ministry of Culture: 384900 Sukhumi, ul. Lakoba 21; tel. (8402) 26-14-41; e-mail mc_ra@mail.ru; internet mkra.org.

Ministry of Defence: 384900 Sukhumi, Abjuiskoye shosse 57; tel. (8402) 26-57-86.

Ministry of the Economy: 384900 Sukhumi, ul. Lakoba 21; tel. (8402) 26-45-81.

Ministry of Education: 384900 Sukhumi, ul. Zvanba 9; tel. (8402) 26-46-51; e-mail minobr-ra@yandex.ru.

Ministry of Finance: 384900 Sukhumi, ul. Lakoba 21; tel. (8402) 26-30-05; e-mail minfinra@yandex.ru.

Ministry of Foreign Affairs: 384900 Sukhumi, ul. Lakoba 21; tel. (8402) 26-57-92; fax (8402) 26-34-45; e-mail mid@abhazia.net; internet mfaabkhazia.net.

Ministry of Health: 384900 Sukhumi, ul. Zvanba 20; tel. and fax (8402) 26-10-77; e-mail mz_apsny@rambler.ru.

Ministry of Internal Affairs: 384900 Sukhumi, ul. Akademika Marra 35; tel. (8402) 26-86-82; e-mail minfinra@yandex.ru; internet mvdra.org.

Ministry of Justice: 384900 Sukhumi, ul. Lakoba 21; tel. (8402) 26-67-66.

Ministry of Labour and Social Development: 384900 Sukhumi, ul. Zvanba 9; tel. and fax (8402) 26-97-13; e-mail mintruda@mail.ru.

Ministry of Taxes and Duties: 384900 Sukhumi, ul. Lakoba 109; tel. (8402) 26-97-03; fax (8402) 26-97-58; e-mail mns_ra@mail.ru.

The Autonomous Republic of Abkhazia

Note: the following representatives of the officially recognized Abkhazian Government were formerly based in Chkhalta, and their remit only extended, de facto, over those regions of Upper (Eastern) Abkhazia under the control of the Georgian authorities. However, following the conflict of August 2008, these regions reverted to the control of the internationally unrecognized 'Republic of Abkhazia'. A nominal Government of the territory, listed below, continued to be based in Tbilisi, with additional representative offices in Kutaisi and Zugdidi.

Chairman of the Government: GIORGI BARAMIA.

Minister of Education and Culture: DALI KHOMERIKI.

Minister of Finance: TAMAZ KVARTSKHELIA.

Minister of the Economy: NODAR CHKHARTISHVILI.

Minister of Regional Management: Brig.-Gen. KORNELI SALIA.

Minister of Health, Labour and Social Welfare: LEKSO LAGVILAVA.

Minister of Special Assignments: ZAUR JALAGONIA.

Minister of Upper Abkhazia Affairs: MEVLUD JACHVLIANI.

Note: the Chairmen of the Departments for: Refugee Affairs; Justice; and Agriculture, Environmental Protection and Natural Resources are also members of the Government of the Autonomous Republic of Abkhazia.

Representative Office of the Government of the Autonomous Republic of Abkhazia: 0177 Tbilisi, Kosta Khetagurovi 2; tel. (32) 296-64-53; fax (32) 295-32-89; e-mail dkekelia@abkhazia.gov.ge; internet www.abkhazia.gov.ge.

Chairman of the Supreme Council of the Autonomous Republic of Abkhazia: ELGUJA (GIA) GVAZAVA.

President

Presidential Election, 26 August 2011

Candidates	Votes	%
Aleksandr Ankvab	58,657	54.90
Sergei Shamba	22,456	21.02
Raul Khajimba	21,177	19.82
Against all candidates	2,023	1.89
Total*	106,845	100.00

* Including 2,532 invalid votes (2.37% of the total).

Legislature

The National Assembly of the Republic of Abkhazia

384900 Abkhazia, Sukhumi; tel. (8402) 22-76-84; internet www.parlamentra.info.

Speaker: VALERII BGANBA.

General Election, 10 March and 24 March 2012

Parties and blocs	Seats
Independent	26
Forum of National Unity of Abkhazia	4
United Abkhazia	3
Vacant*	2
Total	33

* No candidates were elected in two constituencies, where elections were to be re-run on 6 May and 20 May, respectively.

Political Organizations

The following are among the principal political parties to operate in Abkhazia.

Communist Party of Abkhazia: 384900 Sukhumi; f. 1921; reconstructed as an independent political org. after the fall of the USSR in 1991; First Sec. LEV SHAMBA.

Forum of National Unity of Abkhazia: 384900 Sukhumi; f. 2005 as social organization, constituted as political party in 2008; Chair. RAUL KHAJIMBA.

Party of the Economic Development of Abkhazia: 384900 Sukhumi, ul. Lakoba 34; tel. (840) 226-04-44; e-mail info@era-abkhazia.org; internet www.era-abkhazia.org; f. 2007; economically reformist, supportive of business interests; signed co-operation agreement with People's Party of Abkhazia (q.v.) in 2008; Chair. BESLAN BUTBA.

People's Party of Abkhazia (Kiaraz): 384900 Sukhumi, ul. Guliya 6; tel. 226-19-57; fax 226-17-77; internet www.kiaraz.org; f. 1992; democratic centralist party; signed co-operation agreement with Party of the Economic Devt of Abkhazia (q.v.) in 2008; Chair. YAKUB LAKOBA.

Social Democratic Party of Abkhazia: Sukhumi; f. 2004; Chair. GENNADII ALAMIYA.

United Abkhazia: Sukhumi; f. 2004 as a socio-political movement, constituted as a political party 2009; Chair. DAUR TARBA.

SOUTH OSSETIA

Introductory Survey

LOCATION, CLIMATE, LANGUAGE, RELIGION, FLAG, CAPITAL

South Ossetia is situated in the north of Georgia, and covers an area of 3,900 sq km. It borders Russia (principally the Republic of North Osetiya—Alaniya) to the north, the boundary comprising part of the Great Caucasus Range, while the remainder of Georgia lies to the west, south, and east. The climate of South Ossetia is milder than that of the North Caucasus, although snowfall can occur in the highlands at any time of year. Average temperatures in Tshkhinvali range from 5°C (41°F) in January to 20°C (68°F) in July. Precipitation in southern lowland regions averages 350mm–600mm per year, but amounts to 1,000mm–1,800mm in the highlands. The population speak Ossetian, an Indo-European language of the Persian group commonly written in the Cyrillic script, while Russian and Georgian are also in use. Most Ossetians are adherents of Orthodox Christianity. The separatist authorities use a flag (proportions 1 by 2) with three equal horizontal stripes, of white, red and yellow. The principal city and capital of the self-proclaimed 'Republic' is Tshkhinvali.

CONTEMPORARY POLITICAL HISTORY

Historical Context

Ossetia (Osetiya), the original inhabitants of which are an Orthodox Christian East Iranian people, was divided into two territories under Stalin, with North Osetiya (later North Osetiya—Alaniya) falling under Russian jurisdiction as a nominally autonomous republic and South Ossetia assuming the lesser status of an autonomous oblast (region) within Georgia. At the census of 1979 ethnic Ossetians comprised 66% of the oblast's population. The long-standing Georgian animosity towards the Ossetians was exacerbated by the Ossetians' traditional pro-Russian stance. Tensions intensified in 1989, when Ossetian demands for greater autonomy and eventual reunification with North Osetiya (and thus integration into Russia) led to violent clashes between local Georgians and Ossetians. Troops of the Soviet Ministry of Internal Affairs were dispatched to South Ossetia in January 1990, but in September the South Ossetian Supreme Soviet (legislature) proclaimed South Ossetia's independence from Georgia (as the 'South Ossetian Soviet Democratic Republic') and its state sovereignty within the USSR. This decision was declared unconstitutional by the Georgian Supreme Soviet, which in December revoked the region's nominally autonomous status. Following renewed violence, the Georgian legislature declared a state of emergency in Tskhinvali, the principal city in South Ossetia.

Domestic Political Affairs

In January 1991 Soviet President Gorbachev annulled both South Ossetia's declaration of independence and the Georgian Supreme Soviet's decision of December 1990. Violence continued throughout 1991, with the resulting displacement of many thousands of refugees, despite a series of short-lived cease-fires. In December the South Ossetian Supreme Soviet declared a state of emergency and a general mobilization, in response to the Georgian Government's dispatch of troops to the region. In the same month the South Ossetian legislature adopted a second declaration of the region's independence, as well as a resolution in favour of its integration into Russia. The resolutions were endorsed at a referendum held in the region in January 1992. Hostilities continued, compounded by the intervention of Georgian government troops. The situation was further complicated by the arrival of volunteer fighters from North Osetiya.

In June 1992 negotiations between Shevardnadze and President Boris Yeltsin of Russia led to an agreement to secure a lasting cease-fire and a peaceful solution to the conflict (in which more than 400 Georgians and 1,000 Ossetians had been killed since 1989). The Joint Peace-keeping Forces (JPKF), comprising Georgian, Ossetian and Russian troops, was deployed in July 1992, and the return of refugees began. An OSCE Mission to Georgia was established in December. However, some parts of South Ossetia remained effectively a seceded territory; on 23 December 1993 the separatist authorities introduced a new 'Constitution', which referred to the territory as the 'Republic of South Ossetia'. (The region was characterized by the existence of discrete areas controlled either by supporters of the central Government in Tbilisi, or of the separatist 'Republic', a state of affairs that continued until 2008.) In July 1995 representatives from Georgia, Russia, North Osetiya and South Ossetia reopened talks on a political settlement, under the aegis of the OSCE. In April 1996 a memorandum 'on strengthening mutual trust and security measures' was initialled in Tskhinvali; it was signed in Moscow in the following month. Meetings were subsequently held between President Shevardnadze and Ludvig Chibirov, the Chairman of the South Ossetian legislature, to negotiate South Ossetia's political status. In September the separatist legislature approved an amendment to its Constitution to allow the introduction of a presidential system of government; Chibirov was elected to the post of 'President' on 10 November.

Quadripartite negotiations were held throughout 1997. Talks held in Moscow in March confirmed the principle of Georgia's territorial integrity, while allowing a measure of self-determination for South Ossetia. In September Shevardnadze and Chibirov signed an agreement on the return of refugees to South Ossetia. Legislative elections took place in the regions of South Ossetia controlled by separatists in May 1999; the local Communist Party (CP) secured about 39% of the votes cast. In April 2001 a referendum was held in South Ossetia, at which 69% of those who participated voted in favour of adopting amendments to the 1993 Constitution, which included the designation of both Georgian and Russian as official languages, in addition to Ossetian.

Eduard Kokoyev (Kokoiti) elected President

In a presidential election held in November–December 2001 a Russian-based businessman, Eduard Kokoyev (Kokoiti), emerged as the victor, after a second round of voting, securing 55% of the votes cast. Although Kokoyev declared himself to be willing to resume talks with Georgia, he also expressed an interest in developing closer ties with Russia and North Osetiya. Kokoyev was inaugurated on 18 December; in subsequent months he oversaw a policy of granting Russian citizenship to many local residents. Kokoyev's Unity Party won a majority of seats in legislative elections held on 23 May 2004.

Proposals for the granting to South Ossetia of broad autonomy, presented by the Georgian authorities in 2004–05, were consistently rejected by the separatist leadership. In late 2005 Kokoyev submitted his own proposals, which endorsed President Saakashvili's proposed format for resolving the conflict (focusing on demilitarization, confidence-building, and social and economic reconstruction, prior to a decision on South Ossetia's political status), but without imposing a timetable. In early 2006 Parlamenti adopted a resolution, urging the Government to replace Russian peace-keepers deployed in South Ossetia as part of the JPKF with an international force, following concern that Russian troops had been providing armaments to separatists. Amid rising tensions, Georgia announced proposals for the demilitarization of the conflict zone, and a willingness to participate in talks with the aim of resolving the conflict. In July Oleg Alborov, secretary of South Ossetia's 'National Security Council', was killed when a bomb exploded outside his residence in Tskhinvali. South Ossetian officials alleged that the attack had been staged at the orders of Georgia. In August South Ossetian officials began issuing Russian passports to residents of the territory, provoking outrage from the Georgian Government; it was reported by the following year that most of the citizens in those regions under separatist control had been issued with Russian passports.

On 12 November 2006 a presidential election was held in those areas of South Ossetia controlled by the separatist authorities. Kokoyev was overwhelmingly elected to a second term in office, reportedly attracting 98.1% of the votes cast. The poll coincided with a referendum, in which voters were asked whether or not South Ossetia should preserve its de facto independent status. Results released by the 'South Ossetian Central Election Commission' indicated that 99% of those who voted had cast their ballots in favour of independence; voter turn-out was reported to be 95.2% of the registered electorate. Concurrently, what was termed an 'alternative election' for a regional President was held in those South Ossetian territories controlled by Georgia; this poll was won by Dmitry Sanakoyev, a former rebel leader. A referendum held in these territories also overwhelmingly expressed approval for the commencement of negotiations with the central authorities in Tbilisi on the establishment of a federal Georgian state, of which South Ossetia would form a unit. Although these polls were not officially recognized, nationally or internationally, Sanakoyev adopted the title 'President of South Ossetia' and announced the formation of an alternative 'Government', based in the village of Kurta, in December. Also in December Parlamenti approved draft legislation concerning restitution for victims of the South Ossetian conflict. In March 2007 President Saakashvili visited Kurta, and extended an offer to rebuild infrastructure damaged by the fighting in the early 1990s. However, the President's visit was not welcomed by the South Ossetian authorities led by Kokoyev, who accused Saakashvili of attempting to fuel tensions in the region. On 10 May Sanakoyev became head of the new Provisional Administration of South Ossetia, officially established under a resolution by Parlamenti on 8 May.

Renewed military conflict

From early 2008 peace-keeping officials reported an increasing number of minor cease-fire violations in South Ossetia. In July the Russian authorities acknowledged that four Russian aircraft had entered airspace over South Ossetia, claiming that the purpose of the mission was to deter Georgia from flying unmanned military reconnaissance drones over the region. According to the South Ossetian separatist authorities, six people were killed in a Georgian bombardment of Tskhinvali on 1 August, following attacks on South Ossetian villages, while Georgia claimed that South Ossetian forces had initiated the hostilities. Continuing exchanges of fire and shelling were reported to have resulted in a number of deaths. On 3 August the separatist South Ossetian authorities began to evacuate children to Russia.

On 7–8 August 2008 Georgian troops commenced a concerted offensive, including an aerial bombardment, against Tskhinvali; the Georgian Government announced that its troops had entered the city and had secured control of most of South Ossetia, and stated that its purpose had been to 'restore constitutional order'. In response, Russia sent a substantial deployment of troops into South Ossetia, purportedly to protect the security of Russian citizens resident there. After an intensive counter-offensive, the Russian military (supported by volunteer militias, particularly from Chechnya) rapidly claimed to have gained control of Tskhinvali and repulsed the Georgian troops; the separatists also gained control of neighbouring regions hitherto under Georgian control. Looting, retaliatory attacks against ethnic Georgians, and burning of Georgian villages were subsequently reported by human rights organizations. In a statement subsequently shown to be greatly exaggerated, the recently elected Russian President, Dmitrii Medvedev, accused Georgia of perpetrating 'genocide' against the ethnic Ossetian population, and alleged that up to 2,000 people had been killed as a result of the Georgian attack on Tskhinvali. Russian aircraft commenced bombardment of Georgian targets, including the port of Poti and the military base at Senaki. On 26 August Russia recognized South Ossetia and Abkhazia as independent, sovereign states. Georgia, the USA and EU condemned the decision. (In September Nicaragua became the second state to recognize the independence of the two regions, and Venezuela and Nauru were the only countries to do so during 2009.)

Following an EU-mediated peace agreement, reached on 8 September 2008, the deployment of EU monitors commenced in Georgia on 1 October; the Russian Government had announced that 3,800 Russian troops were to remain in each of South Ossetia and Abkhazia. On 17 September Russia signed friendship, economic and military co-operation treaties with the leaders of South Ossetia and Abkhazia. On 3 October, prior to the scheduled deployment of Russian troops, a car bomb at a Russian military base near Tskhinvali killed some nine Russian troops; Kokoyev attributed the attack to Georgian special forces. The appointment of Aslanbek Bulantsev, previously the head of the Russian Federal Security Service (FSB) directorate's financial department in Vladikavkaz, North Osetiya—Alaniya, as Prime Minister on 22 October, replacing Yurii Morozov, prompted renewed Georgian accusations that the province was effectively being annexed. A report by US-based Human Rights Watch, issued in January 2009, concluded that South Ossetian forces had perpetrated numerous abuses against ethnic Georgians in the territory, including abductions and killings. It was reported that the cease-fire was tenuous, with UN, OSCE and EU monitors unable to separate opposing forces deployed in the border region. In March 2009 the Russian Government signed an agreement providing for the extension of some 2,800m. roubles in financial aid to South Ossetia; the territory was also to receive 8,500m. roubles in post-conflict reconstruction aid. On 29 March a Georgian policeman died and six others were injured in an explosion while patrolling the borders of South Ossetia; 11 other police officers had been killed in the region since the imposition of the official cease-fire. In the same month it was reported that the separatist authorities of South Ossetia and Abkhazia were to implement agreements with Russia for the joint patrol of their borders with the remainder of Georgia, while Russia confirmed that military bases were to be established in Abkhazia and South Ossetia, and envisaged the organization of joint military exercises between Russian troops and members of the territories' defence forces.

In April 2009 the electoral commission refused to register the opposition People's Party led by Roland Kelekhsayev for the legislative elections to be held in the following month; a few days previously it had permitted a newly established group, which the opposition claimed comprised allies of Kokoyev, to register under the same name. It also rejected the candidacy of Vyacheslav Gobozov, the Chairman of the Fatherland Party, which described itself as providing constructive and moderate opposition. In the elections, held on 31 May, three parties, all of which were perceived as broadly supportive of Kokoyev, won seats in the legislature. Kokoyev's Unity Party received 46.3% of the votes cast and secured 17 seats; the People's Party won 22.6% of the votes and nine seats, while the CP obtained 22.2% of the votes and eight seats. On 27 July the EU extended the mandate of its monitoring mission until 14 September 2010 (when it was again extended), and urged that the mission be granted the unhindered access to Abkhazia and South Ossetia that had hitherto been denied it.

Following a series of reported disputes over the control of reconstruction funding, Kokoyev dismissed Bulantsev as Prime Minister on 3 August 2009. Vadim Brovtsev, the head of a firm producing construction materials in Chelyabinsk, in the Russian Urals, was appointed to the post the following day. The anniversary of the declaration of independence—which was formally recognized only at that time by Russia and Nicaragua (although Venezuela and Nauru extended recognition later in the year)—was marked by the renewed affirmation of support from the Russian leadership (despite the announcement of a reduction in the quantity of Russian troops to be based in the territory). In Tskhinvali, the authorities staged several official ceremonies on 26 August, including one to mark the official inauguration of a Gazprom-financed gas pipeline linking South Ossetia with North Osetiya—Alaniya, enabling the region to receive gas directly from Russia. In September Russia and South Ossetia signed a defence agreement (similar to a treaty agreed between Russia and Abkhazia), which permitted Russia to maintain military bases in the territory for a period of at least 49 years.

The publication of an independent fact-finding report in September 2009, supported by the EU, was a cause of some controversy in both Georgia and Russia. The report concluded that Georgia had instigated the conflict, and that its initial attack upon Tshkhinvali was not warranted by international law, while Russia's military response was condemned as being disproportionate, and its recognition of South Ossetia and Abkhazia as independent states was also deemed to be in violation of international law.

In April 2010 Brovtsev attracted increasing government and media pressure, owing to allegations of official involvement by the separatist authorities in the embezzlement of Russian funds allocated for the post-conflict reconstruction. In a concession to demands by the Abkhaz and South Ossetian delegations in the ongoing negotiations in Geneva, President Saakashvili, addressing the European Parliament in November 2010, declared that Georgia would 'never use military force to restore its territorial integrity'; although the Presidents of Abkhazia and South Ossetia issued similar pledges, Russia welcomed the announcement without making a reciprocal affirmation. In January 2011 Russian and South Ossetian troops conducted joint military exercises in the territory. In the same month the European Court of Human Rights dismissed 1,549 legal appeals submitted by a group of Russian and South Ossetian peace-keepers over human rights violations during the hostilities in South Ossetia in August 2008.

Recent Developments: the 2011 and 2012 presidential elections

On 15 June 2011 the Supreme Court of South Ossetia ruled against proposals to hold a referendum on the amendment of the 'Republic's' Constitution, providing for the abolition of restrictions on the number of terms a president was permitted to serve, but decided that its legislature was permitted to authorize such a measure. On 5 October the South Ossetian legislature voted to remove Stanislav Kochiyev as its Chairman, in protest at his persistent opposition to the proposed constitutional changes. The presidential election, which was conducted on 13 and 27 November, appeared to have been won in the second round by former Minister of Education, Alla Jioyeva, who defeated Russian-supported candidate Anatolii Bibilov, with around 59% of votes cast. On 29 November, however, the Supreme Court upheld a challenge to the result by Bibilov and ordered that a new election be conducted. However, Jioyeva was to be barred from participation in the new election, owing to apparent irregularities in her campaign. Popular protests ensued and the arrest of a number of local activists was reported. Jioyeva denounced the planned repeated poll as illegitimate and announced her intention to stage her own 'inauguration' ceremony on 10 February 2012. On 9 February, however, she was hospitalized, during a raid on her offices by security forces. In the first round of the repeated election, held on 25 February, contested by four candidates, the head of the region's security service, Leonid Tibilov was placed first, with 42.5% of the votes cast, according to preliminary figures, and his nearest challenger was a special envoy for human rights issues, David Sanakoyev, with 24.6%. (Bibilov did not contest the election.) At the 'run-off' poll, held on 8 April, Tibilov was elected to the presidency, with 54.1% of the votes cast. Sanakoyev officially recognized the legitimacy of the election results, while urging that alleged incidents of irregularities be investigated. Tibilov was inaugurated as President on 19 April. On 25 April Tibilov signed a decree dismissing Brovtsev as acting premier, and appointed Rostik Khutayev, a businessman from Samara, Russia, as his successor (in an acting capacity, pending parliamentary approval), with instructions to form a new Government. Tibilov announced that an investigation was to be opened into alleged wide-spread corruption, and the apparent embezzlement of funding supplied by Russia by the outgoing administration. At that time the statehood of the 'Republic of South Ossetia' was recognized by the following five countries: Nauru, Nicaragua, Russia, Tuvalu, Venezuela. Meanwhile, on 26 March, Medvedev announced the creation of a new post, of Representative of the Russian President to South Ossetia (similar posts were also created in the same month for Abkhazia and the Moldovan secessionist territory of Transnistria). Aleksandr Tkachev, who had been recently appointed to a fourth term as the Governor of the neighbouring Krasnodar Krai (province) of Russia, was appointed additionally to that role.

PUBLIC HOLIDAYS

2013: 1–2 January (New Year), 7 January (Christmas), 8 March (International Women's Day), 1 May (Labour Day), 9 May (Victory Day), 13–16 May (Easter), 26 August (Independence Day).

Directory

The Government of the 'Republic of South Ossetia'

President: LEONID TIBILOV (elected 8 April 2012, inaugurated 19 April).

CABINET OF MINISTERS
(May 2012)

Note: the formation of a new Cabinet of Ministers was expected to take place following the inauguration of LEONID TIBILOV as President in April 2012. Tbilov nominated RUSTIK KHUGAYEV as acting Chairman on 25 April, replacing VADIM BROVTSEV. With the exception of the chairmanship, the following list details the outgoing administration, which resigned from office on 19 April.

Chairman: RUSTIK KHUGAYEV (acting).

Head of the Presidential Administration: ARSEN GAGLOYEV.

First Deputy Chairman: ALEKSANDR ZELIG.

Deputy Chairman: DOMENTII KULUMBEGOV.

Minister of Foreign Affairs: MURAT JIOYEV.

Minister of Defence: VALERII YAKHNOVETS.

Minister of Internal Affairs: VALERII VALIYEV.

Minister of Civil Defence, Emergency Situations and Clean-up Operations: ANATOLII BIBILOV.

Minister of Justice: TAMAZI DOGUZOV.

Minister of Finance: IRINA SYTNIK.

Minister of Economic Development: KONSTANTIN KOLIYEV.

Minister of Education, Science and Youth Policy: ARYANA JIOYEVA.

Minister of Health and Social Development: OTAR GASSIYEV.

Minister of Culture: MAKHARBEG KOKOYEV.

Minister of Capital and Road Construction and Architecture: CHERMAN KHUGAYEV.

MINISTRIES

Office of the Presidency and Government: 100001 Tskhinvali, ul. Khetgurova 1; tel. (9974) 45-00-01; fax (44) 45-47-63; e-mail ospress@yandex.ru; internet presidentrso.ru.

Ministry of Capital and Road Construction and Architecture: 100001 Tskhinvali, ul. Khetgurova 1; tel. (9974) 45-00-01; fax (44) 45-47-63.

Ministry of Civil Defence, Emergency Situations and Clean-up Operations: 100001 Tskhinvali, ul. Khetgurova 1; tel. (9974) 45-00-01; fax (44) 45-47-63.

Ministry of Culture: 100001 Tskhinvali, ul. Stalina 12; tel. (9974) 45-34-81.

Ministry of Defence: 100001 Tskhinvali, ul. Khetgurova 1; tel. (9974) 45-00-01; fax (44) 45-47-63.

Ministry of Economic Development: 100001 Tskhinvali, ul. Khetgurova 1; tel. (9974) 45-00-01; fax (44) 45-47-63.

Ministry of Education, Science and Youth Policy: 100001 Tskhinvali, ul. Khetgurova 1; tel. (9974) 45-00-01; fax (44) 45-47-63.

Ministry of Finance: 100001 Tskhinvali, ul. Stalina 18, 4th Floor; tel. (9974) 45-26-52; e-mail ospress@yandex.ru; internet www.minfinrso.com.

Ministry of Foreign Affairs: 100001 Tskhinvali, ul. Stalina 18, 4th Floor; tel. and fax (9974) 45-22-43; e-mail mfa-rso@mail.ru; internet mfa-rso.su.

Ministry of Health and Social Development: 100001 Tskhinvali, ul. Khetgurova 1; tel. (9974) 45-00-01; fax (44) 45-47-63.

Ministry of Internal Affairs: 100001 Tskhinvali, ul. Khetgurova 1; tel. (9974) 45-00-01; fax (44) 45-47-63.

Ministry of Justice: 100001 Tskhinvali, ul. Khetgurova 1; tel. (9974) 45-00-01; fax (44) 45-47-63.

President

Presidential Election, First Round, 25 March 2012, preliminary results

Candidates	%
Leonid Tibilov	42.48
David Sanakoyev	24.58
Dmitrii Medoyev	23.79
Stanislav Kochiyev	5.26
Against all candidates	0.80
Total*	100.00

* Including invalid votes (3.09% of the total).

Second Round, 8 April 2012, final results

Candidates	Votes	%
Leonid Tibilov	15,786	54.12
David Sanakoyev	12,439	42.65
Against all candidates	279	0.96
Total*	29,166	100.00

* Including 662 invalid votes (2.27% of the total).

Legislature

Elections to the 34-member Parliament of the Republic of South Ossetia were held on 31 May 2009.

The Parliament of the Republic of South Ossetia
100001 Tskhinvali.

Speaker: ZURAB KOKOYEV (acting).

General Election, 31 May 2009, preliminary results

Parties and blocs	Votes	%	Seats
Unity South Ossetian Republican Political Party	21,246	46.38	17
People's Party of the Republic of South Ossetia	10,345	22.58	9
Communist Party of the Republic of South Ossetia	10,194	22.25	8
Fatherland Republican Socialist Party of South Ossetia	2,918	6.37	—
Total*	45,813	100.00	34

* Including 1,110 invalid votes (equivalent to 2.42% of the total).

Political Organizations

In early 2012 the following political parties were registered in South Ossetia.

Communist Party of the Republic of South Ossetia (CP): c/o 100001 Tskhinvali. Parliamentary Bldg; internet kpruo.ru; f. 1993; supports the unification of South Ossetia and North Osetiya—Alaniya; Chair. STANISLAV KOCHIYEV.

Fatherland Republican Socialist Party of South Ossetia (Fydybasta): Tshkinvali; supports the devt of an inclusive democratic state, opposed to regime of Pres. Kokoyev; Leader STANISLAV GOBOZOV.

A Just Ossetia (Raestag Ir/Spravedlivaya Osetiya): 100001 Tskhinvali; f. 2009; Chair. KOSTA KOSHTE.

People's Party of the Republic of South Ossetia: 100001 Tskhinvali, ul. Geroev 3; e-mail npruo@km.ru; internet www.npruo.ru; supports an independent, democratic and socially liberal South Ossetia; Chair. KAZEMIR PLIYEV.

Unity South Ossetian Republican Political Party: c/o 100001 Tskhinvali, Parliamentary Bldg; f. 2003; supports a strong state with an executive presidency, and the integration of South Ossetia with North Osetiya—Alaniya and a strengthening of links with the Russian Federation; Chair. ZURAB KOKOYEV.

GERMANY

Introductory Survey

LOCATION, CLIMATE, LANGUAGE, RELIGION, FLAG, CAPITAL

The Federal Republic of Germany, which was formally established in October 1990 upon the unification of the Federal Republic of Germany (FRG, West Germany) and the German Democratic Republic (GDR, East Germany), lies in the heart of Europe. It is bordered by nine countries: Denmark to the north, the Netherlands, Belgium, Luxembourg and France to the west, Switzerland and Austria to the south, and the Czech Republic and Poland to the east. The climate is temperate, with an annual average temperature of 9°C (48°F), although there are considerable variations between the North German lowlands and the Bavarian Alps. The language is German. There is a small Sorbian-speaking minority (numbering about 100,000 people). About 31% of the population are Roman Catholics and a further 31% are members of the Evangelical Lutheran (Protestant) church. The national flag (proportions 3 by 5) consists of three equal horizontal stripes, of black, red and gold. The capital is Berlin.

CONTEMPORARY POLITICAL HISTORY

Historical Context

Following the defeat of the Nazi regime and the ending of the Second World War in 1945, Germany was divided, according to the Berlin Agreement, into US, Soviet, British and French occupation zones. Berlin was similarly divided. The former German territories east of the Oder and Neisse rivers, with the city of Danzig (now Gdańsk), became part of Poland, while the northern part of East Prussia, around Königsberg (now Kaliningrad), was transferred to the USSR. After the failure of negotiations to establish a unified German administration, the US, French and British zones were integrated economically in 1948. In May 1949 a provisional Constitution, the Basic Law (Grundgesetz), came into effect in the three zones (except in Saarland), and federal elections were held in August. On 21 September 1949 a new German state, the Federal Republic of Germany (FRG), was established in the three western zones. The FRG was governed from Bonn in North Rhine-Westphalia (Nordrhein-Westfalen). (Saarland was not incorporated into the FRG until 1957.) In October 1949 Soviet-occupied Eastern Germany declared itself the German Democratic Republic (GDR), with the Soviet zone of Berlin as its capital. This left the remainder of Berlin (West Berlin) as an effective enclave of the FRG within the territory of the GDR, although it remained formally under British, French and US occupation.

The FRG and the GDR developed sharply divergent political and economic systems. The leaders of the GDR created a socialist state, based on the Soviet model. As early as 1945 large agricultural estates in eastern Germany were nationalized, followed in 1946 by major industrial concerns. Exclusive political control was exercised by the Sozialistische Einheitspartei Deutschlands (SED, Socialist Unity Party of Germany), which had been formed in April 1946 by the merger of the Communist Party of Germany and the branch of the Sozialdemokratische Partei Deutschlands (SPD, Social Democratic Party of Germany) in the Soviet zone. Other political parties in eastern Germany were under the strict control of the SED, and no independent political activity was permitted.

The transfer, as war reparations, of foodstuffs, livestock and industrial equipment to the USSR from eastern Germany had a devastating effect on the area's economy in the immediate post-war period. In June 1953 increasing political repression and severe food shortages led to uprisings and strikes, which were suppressed by Soviet troops. The continued failure of the GDR to match the remarkable economic recovery of the FRG prompted a growing number of refugees to cross from the GDR to the FRG (between 1949 and 1961 an estimated 2.5m. GDR citizens moved permanently to the FRG). Emigration was accelerated by the enforced collectivization of many farms in 1960, and in August 1961 the GDR authorities hastily constructed a guarded wall between East and West Berlin (the Berlin Wall).

Domestic Political Affairs

In May 1971 Walter Ulbricht was succeeded as First Secretary (later restyled General Secretary) of the SED by Erich Honecker. Ulbricht remained Chairman of the Council of State (Head of State), a post that he had held since 1960, until his death in August 1973. He was initially succeeded in this office by Willi Stoph, but in October 1976 Stoph returned to his previous post as Chairman of the Council of Ministers, and Honecker became Chairman of the Council of State. Under Honecker, despite some liberalization of relations with the FRG, there was little relaxation of repressive domestic policies. Honecker strongly opposed the political and economic reforms that began in the USSR and some other Eastern European countries in the mid-1980s.

The 1949 elections in the FRG resulted in victory for the conservative Christlich-Demokratische Union Deutschlands (CDU, Christian Democratic Union of Germany), together with its sister party in Bavaria, the Christlich-Soziale Union (CSU, Christian Social Union). The SPD was the largest opposition party. Dr Konrad Adenauer, the leader of the CDU, was elected Federal Chancellor by the Bundestag (Federal Assembly); Theodor Heuss became the first President of the Republic, the constitutional head of state (a largely ceremonial position). Under Adenauer's chancellorship (which lasted until 1963) and the direction of Dr Ludwig Erhard, his Minister of Economics (and successor as Chancellor), the FRG rebuilt itself rapidly to become one of the most affluent and economically dynamic states in Europe, as well as an important strategic ally of other Western European states and the USA. The Paris Agreement of 1954 gave full sovereign status to the FRG from 5 May 1955, and also granted it membership of the North Atlantic Treaty Organization (NATO, see p. 370).

The CDU/CSU held power in coalition with the SPD from 1966 to 1969, under the chancellorship of Dr Kurt Kiesinger, but lost support at the 1969 general election, allowing the SPD to form a coalition Government with the Freie Demokratische Partei (FDP, Free Democratic Party), under the chancellorship of Willy Brandt, the SPD leader. Following elections in November 1972, the SPD became, for the first time, the largest party in the Bundestag. In May 1974, however, Brandt resigned as Chancellor after the discovery that his personal assistant had been a clandestine agent of the GDR. He was succeeded by Helmut Schmidt, also of the SPD. The SPD-FDP coalition retained a majority in the Bundestag at the elections of 1976 and 1980. In September 1982 the coalition collapsed when the two parties failed to agree on budgetary measures. In October the FDP formed a Government with the CDU/CSU, under the chancellorship of the CDU leader, Dr Helmut Kohl. This new partnership was consolidated by the results of the general election of March 1983, when the CDU/CSU substantially increased its share of the vote. The CDU/CSU-FDP coalition retained office after the general election of January 1987.

During 1949–69 the FRG, under the CDU/CSU, remained largely isolated from Eastern Europe, owing to the FRG Government's refusal to recognize the GDR as an independent state or to maintain diplomatic relations with any other states that recognized the GDR. When Brandt became Chancellor in 1969, he adopted a more conciliatory approach to relations with Eastern Europe and, in particular, towards the GDR, a policy which came to be known as Ostpolitik. In 1970 formal discussions were conducted between representatives of the GDR and the FRG for the first time, and there was a significant increase in diplomatic contacts between the FRG and the other countries of Eastern Europe. In 1970 treaties were signed with the USSR and Poland, in which the FRG formally renounced claims to the eastern territories of the Third Reich and recognized the 'Oder–Neisse line' as the border between Germany (actually the GDR) and Poland. Further negotiations between the GDR and the FRG, following a quadripartite agreement on West Berlin in September 1971, clarified access rights to West Berlin and also allowed West Berliners to visit the GDR. In December 1972 the two German states signed a Basic Treaty, agreeing to develop normal, neighbourly relations with each other, to settle all differences without resort to force, and to respect each other's independence. The treaty permitted both the FRG and the GDR to join the UN in September 1973, and allowed many western countries to establish diplomatic relations with the GDR, although both German states continued to deny each other formal diplomatic recognition.

In December 1981 the first official meeting for 11 years took place between the two countries' leaders, when Chancellor Schmidt travelled to the GDR for discussions with Honecker. Inter-German relations deteriorated following the deployment, in late 1983, of US nuclear missiles in the FRG, and the subsequent siting of additional Soviet missiles in the GDR. Nevertheless, official contacts were maintained, and Honecker made his first visit to the FRG in September 1987.

The fall of the Berlin Wall

Relations between the two German states were dramatically affected by political upheavals that occurred in the GDR in late 1989 and 1990. In the latter half of 1989 many thousands of disaffected GDR citizens emigrated illegally to the FRG, via Czechoslovakia, Poland and Hungary. The exodus was accelerated by the Hungarian Government's decision, in September 1989, to permit citizens of the GDR to leave Hungary without exit visas. Meanwhile, there was a growth in popular dissent within the GDR, led by Neues Forum (New Forum), an independent citizens' action group which had been established to encourage discussion of democratic reforms, justice and environmental issues.

In early October 1989, following official celebrations to commemorate the 40th anniversary of the foundation of the GDR, anti-Government demonstrations erupted in East Berlin and other large towns. Eventually, as the demonstrations attracted increasing popular support, intervention by the police ceased. In mid-October, as the political situation became more unsettled, Honecker resigned as General Secretary of the SED, Chairman of the Council of State and Chairman of the National Defence Council, citing reasons of ill health. He was replaced in all these posts by Egon Krenz, a senior member of the SED Politburo. Krenz immediately initiated a dialogue with Neues Forum (which was legalized in November) and with church leaders. There was also a noticeable liberalization of the media, and an amnesty was announced for all persons who had been detained during the recent demonstrations and for those imprisoned for attempting to leave the country illegally. However, large demonstrations, to demand further reforms, continued in many towns throughout the GDR.

On 7 November 1989, in a further attempt to placate the demonstrators, the entire membership of the GDR Council of Ministers resigned. On the following day the SED Politburo also resigned and was replaced. On 9 November restrictions on foreign travel for GDR citizens were ended, and all border crossings to the FRG were opened. During the weekend of 10–11 November an estimated 2m. GDR citizens crossed into West Berlin, and the GDR authorities began to dismantle sections of the Berlin Wall. Dr Hans Modrow, a leading member of the SED who was regarded as an advocate of greater reforms, was appointed Chairman of a new Council of Ministers. The new Government pledged to introduce comprehensive political and economic reforms and to hold free elections in 1990.

In early December 1989 the Volkskammer (the GDR's legislature) voted to remove provisions in the Constitution that protected the SED's status as the single ruling party. However, the mass demonstrations continued, prompted by revelations of corruption and personal enrichment by the former leadership and of abuses of power by the State Security Service (Staatssicherheitsdienst, known colloquially as the Stasi, which was subsequently disbanded). A special commission was established to investigate such charges, and former senior officials, including Honecker and Stoph, were expelled from the SED and placed under house arrest, pending legal proceedings. As the political situation became increasingly unstable, the SED Politburo and Central Committee, including Krenz, resigned, and both bodies, together with the post of General Secretary, were abolished. Shortly afterwards, Krenz also resigned as Chairman of the Council of State; he was replaced by Dr Manfred Gerlach, the Chairman of the Liberal-Demokratische Partei Deutschlands (LDPD, Liberal Democratic Party of Germany). Dr Gregor Gysi, a prominent defence lawyer who was sympathetic to the opposition, was elected to the new post of Chairman of the SED (restyled the Partei des Demokratischen Sozialismus—PDS, Party of Democratic Socialism, in February 1990).

In December 1989 and January 1990 all-party talks took place in the GDR, resulting in the formation, in early February, of a new administration, designated the Government of National Responsibility (still led by Modrow), to remain in office until elections were held. The GDR's first free legislative elections took place on 18 March 1990, with the participation of 93% of those eligible to vote. The East German CDU obtained 40.8% of the total votes cast, while the newly re-established East German SPD and the PDS secured 21.8% and 16.4%, respectively. In April a coalition Government was formed, headed by Lothar de Maizière, leader of the Eastern CDU. Five parties were represented in the new Government: the CDU, the SPD, the Liga der Freien Demokraten (League of Free Democrats) and two smaller parties. The PDS was not invited to join the coalition.

The reunification of Germany

As a result of the changes within the GDR and the subsequent free contact between Germans of east and west, the reunification of the two German states became a realistic possibility. In November 1989 Chancellor Kohl proposed a plan for the eventual unification of the two countries by means of an interim confederal arrangement. In December Kohl made his first visit to the GDR, where he held discussions with the East German leadership. The two sides agreed to develop contacts at all levels and to establish joint economic, cultural and environmental commissions. The GDR Government initially insisted that the GDR remain a sovereign, independent state. However, in February 1990, in response to growing popular support among GDR citizens for unification, Modrow publicly advocated the establishment of a united Germany. Shortly afterwards, Kohl and Modrow met in Bonn, where they agreed to establish a joint commission to achieve full economic and monetary union between the GDR and the FRG. The new coalition Government of the GDR, formed in April, pledged its determination to achieve German unification in the near future. In mid-May the legislatures of the GDR and the FRG approved the Treaty Between the FRG and the GDR Establishing a Monetary, Economic and Social Union, which came into effect on 1 July. Later in July the Volkskammer approved the re-establishment on GDR territory of the five *Länder* (states)—Brandenburg, Mecklenburg--Western Pomerania (Mecklenburg-Vorpommern), Saxony (Sachsen), Saxony-Anhalt (Sachsen-Anhalt) and Thuringia (Thüringen)—which had been abolished by the GDR Government in 1952. On 31 August 1990 the Treaty Between the FRG and the GDR on the Establishment of German Unity was signed in East Berlin by representatives of the two Governments. The treaty stipulated, *inter alia*, that the newly restored *Länder* would accede to the FRG on 3 October 1990, and that the 23 boroughs of East and West Berlin would jointly form the *Land* (state) of Berlin.

Owing to the complex international status of the FRG and the GDR and the two countries' membership of opposing military alliances (respectively, NATO and the Warsaw Pact), the process of German unification also included negotiations with other countries. In February 1990 representatives of 23 NATO and Warsaw Pact countries agreed to establish the so-called 'two-plus-four' talks (the FRG and the GDR, plus the four countries that had occupied Germany after the Second World War—France, the USSR, the United Kingdom and the USA) to discuss the external aspects of German unification. In June both German legislatures approved a resolution recognizing the inviolability of Poland's post-1945 borders, stressing that the eastern border of a future united Germany would remain along the Oder–Neisse line. In July, at bilateral talks in the USSR with Chancellor Kohl, the Soviet leader, Mikhail Gorbachev, agreed that a united Germany would be free to join whichever military alliance it wished, thus permitting Germany to remain a full member of NATO. The USSR also pledged to withdraw its armed forces (estimated at 370,000 in 1990) from GDR territory within four years, and it was agreed that a united Germany would reduce the strength of its armed forces to 370,000 within the same period. This agreement ensured a successful result to the 'two-plus-four' talks, which were concluded in September in the Soviet capital, Moscow, where the Treaty on the Final Settlement with Respect to Germany was signed. In late September the GDR withdrew from the Warsaw Pact.

On 1 October 1990 representatives of the four countries that had occupied Germany after the Second World War met in New York, USA, to sign a document in which Germany's full sovereignty was recognized. Finally, on 3 October, the two German states were formally unified. On the following day, at a session of the Bundestag (which had been expanded to permit the representation of former deputies of the GDR Volkskammer), five prominent politicians from the former GDR were sworn in as

Ministers without Portfolio in the Federal Government. The Federal President, Richard von Weizsäcker, became the first President of the reunified nation.

Prior to unification, the CDU, the SPD and the FDP of the GDR had merged with their respective counterparts in the FRG to form three single parties. At state elections in the newly acceded *Länder*, held in mid-October 1990, the CDU won control of four *Land* legislatures, while the SPD gained a majority only in Brandenburg. This surge of support for Chancellor Kohl and the CDU was confirmed by the results of elections to the Bundestag in early December (the first all-German elections since 1933), at which the CDU and CSU secured a total of 319 seats in the 662-member Bundestag. Kohl was formally re-elected to the post of Federal Chancellor in January 1991, immediately after the formation of the new Federal Government. This comprised 20 members, but included only three politicians from the former GDR. The FDP's representation was increased from four to five ministers, reflecting the party's increased representation in the legislature. In June 1991 the Bundestag voted in favour of Berlin as the future seat of the legislature and of government; the transfer of most organs of government from Bonn to Berlin took place in 1999.

Events following reunification: 1991–98

One of the most serious problems confronting the Government following unification was that of escalating unemployment in eastern Germany, as a result of the introduction of market-orientated reforms intended to integrate the economic system of the former GDR with that of the rest of the country. A substantial increase in the crime rate in eastern Germany was also recorded. A further disturbing social issue, particularly in the eastern *Länder*, was the resurgence of extreme right-wing and neo-Nazi groups. Moreover, there were also fears of a resurgence of political violence, following a series of terrorist acts culminating in the assassination, in April 1991, of Detlev Rohwedder, the executive head of the Treuhandanstalt (the trustee agency that had been established in March 1990 to supervise the privatization of state-owned enterprises in the former GDR). Responsibility for this and other attacks was claimed by the Rote Armee Fraktion (Red Army Faction), an extreme left-wing terrorist organization that had been active in the FRG during the 1970s. (The Red Army Faction eventually disbanded in 1998.)

Investigations into the abuse of power by the former GDR administration, conducted during the early 1990s, prompted the dismissal or resignation from government posts of several former SED politicians. In January 1991 the authorities temporarily suspended efforts to arrest Honecker on charges of manslaughter (for complicity in the deaths of people who had been killed while attempting to escape from the GDR), owing to the severe ill health of the former GDR leader. In March it was announced that Honecker had been transferred, without the permission of the German authorities, to the USSR, and in December he took refuge in the Chilean embassy in Moscow. In January 1992 some 2m. Stasi files were opened to public scrutiny. In February Erich Mielke, the former head of the Stasi, was brought to trial on charges of murder, and in September Markus Wolf, the former head of East Germany's intelligence service, was charged with espionage, treason and corruption; both were subsequently found guilty and each was sentenced to six years' imprisonment. Meanwhile, Honecker returned to Germany from Russia in July 1992. He was brought to trial in November, together with five other defendants (among them Mielke and Stoph), on charges of manslaughter and embezzlement. In April 1993, however, the charges against Honecker were suspended. (The former East German leader, who was terminally ill, had been allowed to leave for Chile in January of that year; he died in May 1994.) Stoph was also released on grounds of ill health.

In May 1994 Roman Herzog, the candidate of the CDU (previously the President of the Federal Constitutional Court) was elected Federal President by the Bundesversammlung (Federal Convention, a body comprising the members of the Bundestag and delegates chosen by the regional legislatures); he took office in July.

The CDU/CSU-FDP coalition was re-elected at a general election held in October 1994; its majority in the Bundestag was, however, sharply reduced, from 134 to 10 seats. In November the ruling coalition negotiated a new political programme, which prioritized the creation of jobs. Shortly afterwards Kohl was formally re-elected as the Federal Chancellor.

In May 1995 the Federal Constitutional Court ruled that alleged former East German spies should not be prosecuted by federal courts regarding crimes that were committed against the Federal Republic on behalf of the former GDR prior to unification; consequently, in October the 1992 conviction of Markus Wolf was overturned. In November 1996 the Constitutional Court ruled that the legal principles of the FRG regarding human rights could be retroactively applied to actions carried out within the former GDR. Thus, in May 1997 Wolf was convicted on charges of abduction, coercion and assault, receiving a suspended sentence of two years' imprisonment. In August Egon Krenz and two other former senior SED members, Günther Schabowski and Günther Kleiber, were found guilty of the manslaughter and attempted manslaughter of people who had sought to flee the former GDR; all three were sentenced to terms of imprisonment. Krenz's conviction was upheld in 2001, following an unsuccessful appeal to the European Court of Human Rights. Schabowski and Kleiber were pardoned in September 2000.

The activities of extreme right-wing organizations increased significantly in 1997, and during the latter half of the year a series of incidents was reported that suggested the infiltration of some sections of the armed forces by neo-Nazi interests. In April 1998 the extreme right-wing and openly xenophobic Deutsche Volksunion (DVU, German People's Union) won unprecedented support at an election to the *Land* parliament for the economically depressed region of Saxony-Anhalt in eastern Germany, securing 12.9% of the votes cast.

Tensions within the CDU/CSU-FDP coalition became apparent in 1997, mainly concerning the desirability and means of meeting the 'convergence criteria' for participation in European Economic and Monetary Union (EMU) by 1999. Record levels of unemployment continued to cause concern, as well as an unexpectedly large deficit on the 1997 budget. In April 1998, despite evidence of widespread opposition to the new single European currency, the Bundestag voted strongly in favour of Germany's participation in EMU.

The SPD-led coalition: 1998–2005

At the general election held in September 1998 the CDU/CSU-FDP coalition was decisively defeated by the SPD, which won 298 of the 669 seats in the Bundestag. Following the election, Kohl resigned as Chairman of the CDU; he was replaced by the party's parliamentary leader, Dr Wolfgang Schäuble. Meanwhile, the SPD and Bündnis 90/Die Grünen (Alliance 90/The Greens, which held 47 seats) swiftly negotiated a coalition pact. In October Gerhard Schröder of the SPD, formerly the Minister-President of Lower Saxony (Niedersachsen), was elected Federal Chancellor by a large majority of Bundestag members. The new Federal Government included three ministers representing Bündnis 90/Die Grünen, the most prominent of whom was the new Federal Vice-Chancellor and Minister of Foreign Affairs, Joschka Fischer. Oskar Lafontaine, the Chairman of the SPD, was appointed Minister of Finance.

Lafontaine resigned in March 1999, apparently in protest at an evident lack of support for his economic policies and management from within both the business community and the Government; he also vacated his seat in the Bundestag and the chairmanship of the SPD. Hans Eichel of the SPD was appointed as the new Minister of Finance. In the following month Schröder was elected to the post of Chairman of the SPD. In May Johannes Rau, the candidate of the SPD (hitherto Minister-President of North Rhine-Westphalia) was elected Federal President, taking office in July.

During November 1999 the opposition CDU became embroiled in a scandal concerning the discovery of a system of secret bank accounts, which had been used to deposit undisclosed donations to the party throughout the 1990s. (In accordance with the Basic Law, all substantial funding of political parties must be declared.) Allegations subsequently emerged that the CDU leadership had covertly accepted a large bribe from the then state-owned French oil company Elf Aquitaine, in connection with its purchase in 1992 of an eastern German oil refinery. It was also alleged that, in 1998, the CDU had granted an export licence to an arms exporting interest in return for an undeclared party donation. The former Chancellor, Kohl, admitted knowledge of some secret party funding, but repeatedly refused to name any sources; in January 2000 Kohl was forced to resign from his honorary chairmanship of the CDU after he became the subject of a criminal investigation. In that month Schäuble established an independent inquiry into the funding scandal, which subsequently revealed that irregularities had persisted for decades in German politics. In February Schäuble resigned as Chairman of the CDU, accepting responsibility for mishandling the funding scandal.

The CDU's Secretary-General, Angela Merkel, was elected Chairman at the party congress in April 2000. Merkel, who had secured significant support as a result of her determination to expose the CDU's financial irregularities, was considered more liberal than her predecessors. In May the state prosecutor concluded that there were sufficient grounds for the criminal prosecution of Kohl on charges of fraud and bribery (although, as an incumbent member of the legislature, Kohl was immune from prosecution). In his testimony in June to the parliamentary committee Kohl again admitted accepting illegal secret contributions to party funds, but denied allegations that such donations had influenced government policy decisions. In February 2001 Kohl accepted the proposal of the state prosecutor that he should pay a fine of DM 300,000 in exchange for the abandonment of the criminal investigation into his acceptance of illegal contributions; this arrangement subsequently gained judicial approval. The parliamentary inquiry continued, however, as did Kohl's refusal to name the illegal contributors to his party.

In December 1999 the Government agreed to pay a substantial sum in compensation to people who had worked as forced labourers for German companies or been deprived of their assets under the Nazi regime; it was hoped that this would forestall a growing number of lawsuits taken out against German industrial interests and banks by survivors of the Holocaust. Chancellor Schröder announced that the Government would provide one-half of the proposed DM 10,000m. fund; the remainder was to be raised by Germany's largest banks and companies. The compensation agreement was signed in July 2000, and, following the resolution of legal difficulties, payments began in May 2001.

In June 2000, following months of negotiations between the Government and the nuclear industry, Schröder announced that an agreement had been concluded to decommission the country's 19 nuclear power plants (which accounted for almost one-third of power requirements) without compensation by 2021. Although a significant number of members of Bündnis 90/Die Grünen had favoured an immediate cessation of nuclear power generation, in September 2001 the Federal Government adopted a bill regulating the phasing out of nuclear power, which was subsequently approved by the Bundestag.

In August 2000, in response to growing fears concerning the escalation of neo-Nazi violence against immigrants, the Government announced a series of measures to combat racist attacks. An application to the Constitutional Court to ban the extremist right-wing Nationaldemokratische Partei Deutschlands (NPD, National Democratic Party of Germany) on the grounds that it was anti-Semitic, racist and supported violence was approved by the Bundesrat (Federal Council, the upper chamber of the legislature) in November and by the Bundestag in December. In January 2002, however, the Court postponed hearing the case when it emerged that one of the senior NPD activists whose statements were to be used in evidence against the party was an informant for the Bundesamt für Verfassungsschutz (BfV—Office for the Protection of the Constitution); the Court dismissed the case in March 2003.

In late September 2001, following attacks on New York and Washington, DC, USA by suspected Islamist extremists, the Government abolished the so-called 'religious privilege', thus removing legal protection for, and allowing the banning of, any religious organization suspected of promoting terrorism. In December police raided the premises of 20 militant Islamist groups throughout Germany, some of which were suspected of having links with the al-Qa'ida organization of the Saudi-born militant Islamist Osama bin Laden (which was widely believed to have organized the attacks in the USA in September). Evidence subsequently emerged that at least three of the presumed perpetrators of the US atrocities had recently lived in Hamburg and other German cities. Plans to introduce more liberal immigration laws were abandoned, and further new legislation was introduced to increase national security, including the extension of existing anti-terrorism legislation, which had hitherto only covered terrorist acts in Germany, to apply, in addition, to such acts committed in other countries. Measures to block funding channels for militant activists allowed the police access to bank account details of alleged terrorists. Further steps to control money-laundering were introduced, including the foundation of a centralized Financial Intelligence Unit.

At the general election held on 22 September 2002 the SPD-Bündnis 90/Die Grünen coalition was re-elected with a reduced majority of nine seats. The SPD's position was, however, severely weakened and the Government's popularity suffered as a result of financial austerity measures adopted in an attempt to ward off economic recession. At two *Land* elections in February 2003 the SPD suffered emphatic defeats by the CDU, which thus strengthened the CDU's majority in the Bundesrat to such an extent that it was able to block government legislation.

In August 2003 the Federal Government approved the 12 bills that comprised Schröder's Agenda 2010 package of economic reforms, the main aims of which were to reduce the rate of unemployment and to revive Germany's stagnant economy. The proposals were, however, deeply unpopular among the general public, trade unions (which had long been traditional allies of the SPD) and many members of the SPD. Bills to reform health provision and labour regulations were adopted by the Bundestag in September, as were welfare and tax reforms in October. Most notably, the welfare legislation proposed the merging of unemployment benefit and social welfare payments (in effect reducing the level of benefits paid). Tax reductions were proposed to stimulate consumption and thereby reduce public indebtedness (which was at its highest level in Germany's post-war history). For the majority, however, most of the benefits accrued from these reductions were likely to be swiftly cancelled out by a lowering of tax concessions and subsidies. In November the CDU used its majority in the Bundesrat to block the legislation on debt-financed tax reductions, fearing that the debt burden would overwhelm the economy rather than revive it. The tax legislation was eventually approved in December; under the amended bill, the tax reductions were to be reduced from the originally proposed €22,000m. to approximately €15,000m.

At the SPD conference held in November 2003, Schröder was re-elected Chairman of the party; however, many SPD members felt that the Agenda 2010 reforms were a betrayal of the party's core values, and during 2003 the party lost some 5% of its membership. In December the various bills comprising Agenda 2010, including the amended tax reductions, were finally adopted by both legislative bodies. Bitterness and divisions remained within the SPD, however, with the party leadership increasingly being seen as isolated from the rest of the membership. Consequently, in February 2004 Schröder announced his resignation as Chairman of the SPD; he was, however, to remain in his post as Chancellor. The SPD elected Franz Müntefering as its new leader at a special party conference in March.

In May 2004 the Bundesversammlung elected Dr Horst Köhler (hitherto the Managing Director of the International Monetary Fund—IMF), the joint candidate of the CDU and the FDP, as the new Federal President; he was inaugurated on 1 July. (Köhler was elected Federal President for a second term in May 2009.)

In July 2004 the Bundesrat adopted legislation on the reform (and ultimately a reduction) of unemployment and social welfare benefits. Opposition was strong throughout Germany, but particularly so in the *Länder* of the former GDR, where long-term unemployment was endemic. For six weeks many thousands took to the streets in weekly protests, held in Berlin and several other cities throughout Germany. Lafontaine, the former Minister of Finance, demanded Schröder's resignation, openly incited revolt within the SPD and threatened to support a left-wing political movement composed of disaffected SPD members and trade unionists. None the less, the legislation on welfare reform took effect in January 2005. Declining support for the SPD was demonstrated in *Land* elections in 2004-05, reflecting not only the widespread anger at the reforms, but also the long-standing frustration of many east Germans at the failure to achieve economic integration of the east since reunification.

Following the SPD's defeat in North Rhine-Westphalia in May 2005, Schröder announced his intention to call an early general election, ostensibly because the CDU's increased majority in the Bundesrat rendered his Government unviable. As the Basic Law does not technically allow early elections, Schröder called and deliberately lost a vote of confidence in his administration in July, thereby enabling President Köhler to dissolve the Bundestag. Two legal challenges against this process were dismissed by the Federal Constitutional Court in August, and the election was confirmed for 18 September.

As the rift between Schröder and the left wing of the SPD deepened, Lafontaine left the party and, in July 2005, established a new party with the PDS and other defectors from the SPD, known as Linkspartei.PDS (Die Linke—Left Party.PDS). Die Linke formed an electoral alliance with another left-wing grouping, Wahlalternative Arbeit und soziale Gerechtigkeit (WASG—Electoral Alternative Jobs and Social Justice). Its manifesto included the repeal of social reforms, an increase in the minimum wage and the imposition of higher taxes on the rich. The party swiftly gained considerable support, particularly in the east. (In June 2007, at a special conference in Berlin, the two parties completed a formal merger, as Die Linke, under the joint leadership of Lafontaine and Prof. Lothar Bisky.)

The 'grand coalition': 2005–09

At the election to the Bundestag, held on 18 September 2005, the CDU/CSU won a total of 225 of the 614 seats (later increased to 226 following a delayed ballot in one constituency), while the SPD secured 222. Despite neither party winning a majority, both Merkel and Schröder asserted their claims to the chancellorship. Owing to the strong performance of Die Linke, which won 54 seats, neither the CDU/CSU nor the SPD could form a majority government with their preferred coalition partners (respectively the FDP, with 61 seats, and Bündnis 90/Die Grünen, with 51 seats). Moreover, neither party was willing to form a coalition with Die Linke. Following three weeks of negotiations, during which coalitions involving the FDP and Bündnis 90/Die Grünen with either the CDU/CSU or the SPD were mooted and rejected, Merkel was designated Chancellor on 10 October at the head of a 'grand coalition' of the CDU/CSU and SPD. The coalition agreement focused on a programme of job creation, economic reform and reform of the federal system. Many of the more radical reforms proposed by the CDU in its election campaign, including plans for a reduction in income tax for those earning high salaries and the liberalization of employment legislation, were abandoned. Müntefering was designated Vice-Chancellor and Minister of Labour and Social Affairs, and the SPD retained control of a total of eight of the 14 ministries. Merkel was formally elected as Federal Chancellor by the Bundestag on 22 November, becoming both the first woman and the first former citizen of the GDR to lead the country.

Amendments to 25 articles of the Basic Law were approved by the Bundestag on 30 June 2006 and by the Bundesrat on 7 July. The amendments were intended to simplify relations between the two legislative houses, as well as between the Federal and *Land* Governments, and to define their respective responsibilities more clearly. The reforms were intended to expedite the legislative process, since the amendments substantially reduced the number of bills needing approval from the Bundesrat. Conversely, the *Land* Governments represented in the Bundesrat gained increased authority over services, including schools and prisons. In early July the coalition partners reached an agreement on the reform of health care provision, which was intended to reduce rising costs and to limit reliance on employers' contributions to finance health insurance schemes. Despite initial opposition among members of both the CDU and the SPD, the proposals were formally approved by the Bundestag in February 2007. Implementation of the reforms was completed on 1 January 2009.

In mid-July 2006 anti-terrorism legislation adopted following the 11 September 2001 attacks in the USA was renewed for a five-year period by the Government. Under the renewed legislation, the Bundesnachrichtendienst (BND—the federal intelligence service) was given greater powers, including access to information regarding passengers on international flights. In August 2006 explosive devices were discovered on trains in Dortmund and Koblenz, but they failed to detonate: two men of Lebanese origin were subsequently convicted of attempted murder. In September 2007 three men, believed to have been trained by a militant Islamist group, were charged with planning to perpetrate attacks using car bombs in Germany; a fourth suspect was arrested in connection with the plot in November 2008. In March 2010 all four were convicted and sentenced to terms of imprisonment.

At an SPD conference in October 2007, party members voted to approve a policy programme that appeared to move the party toward the left. Prior to the conference, some senior members of the party, including Müntefering, had criticized proposals to relax some of the measures included in the Schröder Government's Agenda 2010 programme. In November 2007 Müntefering announced his resignation from the Government, citing personal reasons. Olaf Scholz was appointed to replace him as Minister of Labour and Social Affairs, while the Minister of Foreign Affairs, Frank-Walter Steinmeier, assumed the additional role of Vice-Chancellor. In September 2008 continuing internal disagreements within the SPD culminated in the resignation of Kurt Beck as party Chairman. At a special meeting of the party leadership held in that month, Müntefering was nominated as his successor. Steinmeier was appointed as interim Chairman, pending a special party conference in October at which Müntefering was elected to the role on a permanent basis; Steinmeier had earlier been selected as the party's candidate for the chancellorship at the next federal election.

In June 2008 the Government approved a draft bill to provide extensive new powers for the Bundeskriminalamt (Federal Criminal Police Office—BKA) to combat terrorism, allowing the BKA to search computers via the internet, monitor telephone conversations and put an individual's home under surveillance, even if he or she was not suspected of a crime. Despite strong criticism from the opposition and from human rights groups, the legislation was passed by the Bundestag in November, and was approved by the Bundesrat in December, following the inclusion of several amendments, notably that prior permission by the judiciary would always be required for remote searches of computers.

During 2008 and 2009 the Government sought to mitigate the effects of world-wide recession on the German economy. In October 2008 it announced that it would guarantee private bank deposits, in order to maintain confidence in the banking system, and over the following three months it announced new spending totalling some €80,000m., to stimulate the economy (see under Economic Affairs). The CSU Federal Minister of Economics and Technology, Michael Glos, resigned from that post in early February 2009, expressing dissatisfaction with his role in the Government and a lack of support from Merkel; he was replaced by Karl-Theodor zu Guttenberg, hitherto Secretary-General of the CSU. Disagreements between the SPD and the CDU intensified in early 2009, leading to the postponement of policy initiatives, including environmental measures and labour market reforms. In March Steinmeier and Müntefering criticized Merkel for her response to the economic downturn, citing her refusal to support proposals from SPD ministers, most notably including legislation designed to increase the Government's powers to act against tax havens.

Return to power of Merkel at 2009 election

At the general election on 27 September 2009 the CDU/CSU together won 239 of the 622 seats in the Bundestag, while the SPD sustained a severe loss of support, securing 146 seats (compared with 222 in 2005). The FDP significantly increased its representation, winning 93 seats, while Die Linke and Bündnis 90/Die Grünen also increased the number of seats that they won (to 76 and 68, respectively). Prior to the election Angela Merkel had strongly indicated that the FDP was the preferred coalition partner of the CDU/CSU. As the parties together held a clear majority of seats in the Bundestag, negotiations on forming a coalition proceeded swiftly. Following the conclusion of an agreement on policy, which included a commitment to the tax reductions demanded by the FDP, the new Government was sworn in on 28 October: it included the FDP Chairman, Guido Westerwelle, as Vice-Chancellor and Minister of Foreign Affairs, while another FDP member, Rainer Brüderle, became Minister of Economics and Technology. FDP members were also allocated the ministries in charge of justice, health and development. Wolfgang Schäuble, previously the Minister of the Interior, became Minister of Finance, and the defence portfolio was given to Karl-Theodor zu Guttenberg of the CSU, previously the Minister of Economics and Technology. After the election Franz Müntefering resigned from the chairmanship of the SPD and was replaced by Sigmar Gabriel, a former Minister of the Environment.

In November 2009 the Chief of Staff of the Bundeswehr (armed forces), Gen. Wolfgang Schneiderhan, together with an official in the Federal Ministry of Defence, resigned in response to a controversy over an air attack by US forces in Afghanistan in September, which had been requested by a German commander in the area (see Foreign Affairs). It was alleged by a national newspaper, *Bild*, that the Ministry of Defence had withheld information on the number of civilians killed in the attack. On the day after their resignations the Minister of Labour and Social Affairs, Franz Josef Jung, who had been Minister of Defence at the time of the attack and who had previously defended the Government's handling of the affair, also resigned. (He was replaced by Ursula von der Leyen, who had hitherto held responsibility for family affairs.) A parliamentary inquiry into the events began in December, and the affair reinforced widespread public disquiet over Germany's military involvement in Afghanistan, which had been presented by the Government as a mission to assist reconstruction rather than as participation in the conflict there. In December the Government gained parliamentary approval for measures intended to accelerate economic recovery, which included tax reductions (for individuals and businesses) that had been favoured by the FDP. Critics of the plan expected it to add to an already unprecedented level of public debt.

In January 2010 Lafontaine announced his retirement as joint Chairman of Die Linke and as a member of the Bundestag, owing to ill health. At a party conference in May Klaus Ernst and Gesine Lötzsch were elected to succeed him and Lothar Bisky, who had also retired as joint Chairman of the party. In February 2010 the Federal Constitutional Court ruled that the controversial reform of unemployment and social welfare benefits introduced by the Schröder Government in 2004 was unconstitutional, on the grounds that it failed to guarantee a 'dignified minimum' income for the recipients of benefits. The Court ordered the Government to implement a new system of welfare benefits by January 2011; however, the changes demanded by the Court were expected to require a significant increase in government expenditure, adding to the already high public deficit.

Recent developments: a decline in support for the CDU and FDP

In early May 2010 the legislature approved loans to Greece amounting to €22,400m. over a three-year period, as part of the emergency assistance approved earlier in that month by the ministers responsible for finance of countries participating in the single European currency, the euro (see Regional Relations). The unpopularity of this measure within Germany at a time of domestic economic austerity was believed to have led to a decline in support for the CDU at a regional election in North Rhine-Westphalia on 9 May: the CDU, which had previously formed a coalition administration there with the FDP, secured 34.6% of the votes cast, compared with 44.8% at the previous election in 2005, while the SPD also lost support, and Bündnis 90/Die Grünen and Die Linke made considerable gains. (Negotiations on the formation of a new administration in North Rhine-Westphalia continued until July, when the SPD and Bündnis 90/Die Grünen formed a minority government, reliant on the support of Die Linke.) As a result of the CDU's defeat in North Rhine-Westphalia, the Federal Government lost its majority in the Bundesrat. Later in May the Minister-President of Hesse, Roland Koch, a senior conservative member of the CDU, resigned from his post in what was perceived as a withdrawal of support for Merkel's leadership.

On 31 May 2010 President Köhler unexpectedly announced his resignation, following criticism of comments he had made about Germany's military involvement in Afghanistan, which were interpreted by some as implying that Germany's commercial interests justified military deployment abroad. The President of the Bundesrat, Jens Böhrnsen, assumed the position of interim head of state until the election of a new Federal President on 30 June. Christian Wulff of the CDU (hitherto Minister-President of Lower Saxony) was the successful candidate in the presidential election, defeating Joachim Gauck, a pastor and respected former East German dissident: however, since as many as three rounds of voting in the Bundesversammlung had been necessary to ensure a sufficient majority in his support, the election was regarded as a humiliating rebuke for the Government. Meanwhile, earlier in June there were widespread protests following the Government's announcement of a four-year programme of economic austerity measures, with the aim of reducing the budgetary deficit.

In September 2010 the Government announced a delay in the planned closure of Germany's 17 remaining nuclear power stations: the operations of the most recently built nuclear plants were to continue for a further 14 years beyond 2021 (the deadline originally decided by the SPD-led Government in 2000), while older plants were to continue in use for eight years after 2021. It was stipulated that the companies operating the nuclear power stations should make substantial contributions to the development of renewable energy sources. Despite large anti-nuclear demonstrations, the plan was approved by the Bundestag in late October 2010. In November the Minister of Defence, zu Guttenberg, announced that, controversially, conscription to the armed forces was to be suspended with effect from July 2011, and was to be replaced by voluntary military or community service.

During 2010 there were indications that Germany was making a rapid recovery from recession, and that unemployment was decreasing. In November Angela Merkel was re-elected unopposed to the leadership of the CDU. In February 2011 zu Guttenberg was accused of using unattributed material in the doctoral thesis that he had submitted in 2006: he denied the allegations of plagiarism, but the University of Bayreuth revoked his doctorate, and on 1 March 2011, despite Merkel's support, he resigned from his ministerial post. He was replaced as Minister of Defence by Thomas de Maizière, hitherto Minister of the Interior, a position now allocated to Hans-Peter Friedrich (chairman of the CSU group in the Bundestag).

At an election in Hamburg in February 2011 the CDU (which had hitherto governed the city in coalition with Bündnis 90/Die Grünen) obtained only 21.9% of the votes (compared with 42.6% at the previous election in 2008); the SPD won 48.3% (increasing from 34.1% previously), thus securing an absolute majority in the city legislature. Following a severe earthquake in Japan in March 2011, which seriously damaged the Fukushima nuclear power station, large demonstrations opposing nuclear power took place in four German cities. The Government ordered safety reviews to be undertaken at all the country's nuclear power stations, and the temporary closure of the seven oldest nuclear reactors, together with a three-month suspension of the decision taken in September 2010 to prolong the production of nuclear power. In May 2011 the Government announced the permanent closure of the seven oldest reactors, and the closure of the remainder by 2022. Critics of the revised policy expressed the fear that despite a proposed acceleration in the development of renewable sources of energy, there would be an increase in emissions of carbon dioxide from coal- and gas-fired power stations, while the transmission of wind-derived energy was expected to require unpopular lines of high pylons in environmentally sensitive areas.

At regional elections held in March 2011 Bündnis 90/Die Grünen, which opposed nuclear power, attracted greatly increased support. In Saxony-Anhalt the CDU won 32.5% of the votes (compared with 36.2% at the previous election in 2006), and formed a coalition with the SPD (21.5%), as before; Bündnis 90/Die Grünen almost doubled their share of the votes, to 7.1%, but the FDP's share declined from 6.6% to 3.8%, and the party thus lost its representation in the *Land* legislature, since parties winning less than 5% of the votes were not allocated seats. In Baden-Württemberg, controlled by the CDU since the 1950s, the share of the votes won by Bündnis 90/Die Grünen increased to 24.2% (from 11.7% at the previous election in 2006), reflecting not only concern about nuclear power but also the unpopularity of a proposed urban transport development project in Stuttgart; although the CDU won 39.0% of the votes (compared with 44.2% in 2006), its former coalition partner, the FDP, won only 5.3%, and Bündnis 90/Die Grünen formed a coalition with the SPD (which had won 23.1%), led by Winfried Kretschmann, the first member of Bündnis 90/Die Grünen to become a *Land* premier. On the same day, at an election in Rhineland-Palatinate (previously controlled by the SPD), the share of the votes won by Bündnis 90/Die Grünen more than tripled, to 15.4% (from 4.6% at the previous election in 2006), and here too the party formed a coalition with the SPD (which had won 35.7%, compared with 46.6% previously); although the CDU had slightly increased its share of the votes, to 35.3%, the FDP won only 4.2%, thus once again losing its representation in the *Land* legislature. In response Rainer Brüderle, the Federal Minister of Economics and Technology, resigned from the leadership of the FDP in Rhineland-Palatinate. In early April 2011 Guido Westerwelle resigned as national Chairman of the FDP and as Federal Vice-Chancellor, but retained his post as Minister of Foreign Affairs. In May Philipp Rösler, hitherto the Minister of Health, replaced Westerwelle as Chairman of the FDP and Vice-Chancellor, also assuming Brüderle's post as Minister of Economics and Technology.

Further *Land* elections in 2011 continued to reveal a decline in the popularity of Angela Merkel's party, the CDU, and of its federal coalition partner, the FDP (particularly the latter, whose advocacy of tax reductions and relatively sceptical attitude towards the European Union (EU) had failed to attract support); the share of the votes won by Bündnis 90/Die Grünen, on the other hand, consistently increased. In Bremen, in May, the governing coalition of the SPD and Bündnis 90/Die Grünen was returned to power: the SPD won 38.6% of the votes, while support for Bündnis 90/Die Grünen increased to 22.5% (from 16.4% at the previous election in 2007), thus overtaking the CDU (with 20.4%) for the first time in a regional election. The FDP won only 2.4% of votes, thus yet again losing all its seats. In September 2011, in Mecklenburg-Western Pomerania, the ruling 'grand coalition' of the SPD and the CDU was re-elected, winning 35.7% and 23.1% of the votes respectively, while the FDP, with 2.7%, again lost its representation, and Bündnis 90/Die Grünen, with 8.4%, entered the legislature and was thus represented in all 16 *Land* legislatures for the first time. Also in September, at an election in Berlin, the SPD won 28.3% of the votes (slightly less than the 30.8% it obtained at the previous election in 2006), while the CDU increased its support to 23.4% (from 21.3%), but the FDP only obtained 1.8% and therefore lost its seats in the city's legislature. Bündnis 90/Die Grünen increased its support to 17.6% (from 13.1%), and the Piratenpartei Deutschland (Pirate Party Germany, originally formed in 2006 to campaign for, among other things, freedom of information) unexpectedly entered the city legislature, winning 8.9% of the votes. Although the SPD had been expected to form a coalition with Bündnis 90/ Die Grünen, this was prevented by the latter's refusal to support a motorway extension, and in November 2011 the SPD formed a 'grand coalition' in Berlin with the CDU. At an early election in Saarland held in March 2012 following the collapse of the ruling coalition, the FDP failed to keep seats in the legislature, with preliminary figures showing its share of the vote reduced from 9.2% in 2009 to 1.2%; the CDU kept its 19 seats with 35.2% of the vote; the SPD's share increased from 24.5% in 2009 to 30.6%, while support for Die Linke and Bündnis 90/Die Grünen was slightly reduced, at 16.1% and 5% of the vote respectively (down from 21.3% and 5.9% in 2009). The Piratenpartei secured four seats in the legislature for the first time, with 7.4% of votes. An election was expected to be held in North Rhine-Westphalia in May 2012 following the dissolution of the minority Government, which lost a vote on its proposed budget in the legislature.

In late September 2011 a vote took place in the federal legislature on the proposed enhancement of the European Financial Stability Facility (EFSF) so as to assist Greece and other members of the euro area that were experiencing severe economic difficulties. Despite dissent within the ruling coalition parties, and public resentment at the high cost of supporting other EU members, the Government won the vote, which had been regarded as a test of confidence in the Chancellor's European policy (see Regional relations).

In November 2011 the existence of a violent neo-Nazi group, based in Zwickau, was revealed only after the suicide of two of its members: the group was believed to have been responsible for 10 murders, mostly of people of Turkish origin, since 2000, and for two bomb attacks and a number of bank robberies. There was widespread concern that the police and security services had not identified the group earlier, owing to an apparent lack of co-ordination. Suspected accomplices who were subsequently arrested included a former official of the extreme right-wing NPD. In December 2011 federal and state ministers responsible for internal affairs agreed to make a new attempt to ban the NPD, which, although unsuccessful in federal elections, currently had representation in two *Land* legislatures (Mecklenburg-Western Pomerania and Saxony); a previous attempt to ban the party had been rejected by the Constitutional Court in 2003 (see above). In January 2012 ministers approved the establishment of a national register of right-wing extremists.

In February 2012 President Wulff resigned, after prosecutors had asked the Bundestag to remove his presidential immunity from prosecution, in order to allow possible legal proceedings against him for improper conduct: Wulff had received a low-interest home loan from the wife of a businessman in 2008, and subsequently denied (in the legislature of Lower Saxony, where he was then Minister-President) having financial dealings with the businessman, and in December 2011 he had allegedly attempted to prevent a prominent newspaper, *Bild*, from reporting the story. On resigning Wulff denied that he had done anything illegal, but acknowledged that he had lost public trust. Horst Seehofer, the President of the Bundesrat, assumed Wulff's responsibilities in an interim capacity. Joachim Gauck, the unsuccessful candidate in the 2010 presidential election, was nominated for the post of Federal President by the SPD and Bündnis 90/Die Grünen, with the support of Merkel: Gauck was elected in March 2012, securing 991 votes out of 1,228 valid votes, by the Federal Convention (Bundesversammlung) specially convened for the purpose. Beate Klarsfeld, the candidate put forward by Die Linke, secured 126 votes.

Foreign Affairs

Regional relations

The orientation of Germany's foreign policy after unification broadly followed that of the FRG. The united Germany remained committed to a leading role in the European Community (EC—now EU), of which the FRG was a founding member, and NATO, while placing greater emphasis on defence co-operation with France. The country was also strongly committed to close relations with Eastern Europe, in particular with the USSR and, subsequently, its successor states.

In December 1992 the Bundestag ratified the Treaty on European Union (the Maastricht Treaty). At the same time the lower house approved an amendment to the Basic Law (negotiated in May 1992 with the *Länder*), whereby the state assemblies would be accorded greater involvement in the determination of German policy within the EC. The Bundesrat ratified the Maastricht Treaty later in December 1992. In April 1998 the Bundestag approved Germany's participation in EMU, which took effect in January 1999. Following the eventual approval of the draft EU constitutional treaty on 18 June 2004 by the Heads of State and of Government of the member countries of the EU, the German Government expressed its desire that Germany ratify the document as soon as possible. Legislative ratification, which required a two-thirds' majority in both houses, was secured in May 2005. However, following the subsequent rejection of the proposed constitution at public referendums in France and the Netherlands, the process of ratification in other member countries halted. In June 2007 Merkel, who held the presidency of the Council of the EU for the first half of the year, hosted an EU summit meeting in Brussels, Belgium, at which a preliminary agreement was reached for a reform treaty to replace the defunct constitutional treaty. The reform treaty was signed by EU leaders in Lisbon, Portugal, in December 2007, and was ratified by the Bundestag in May 2008. In June 2009 the Federal Constitutional Court responded to a legal challenge by members of the federal legislature (mostly belonging to Die Linke) who claimed that the so-called Treaty of Lisbon was incompatible with German law: the Court ruled that the treaty was compatible with the law, but that new domestic legislation must be adopted to ensure greater participation by the Bundestag in EU decisions affecting Germany. The Treaty of Lisbon entered into effect across the EU in December 2009. In May 2010 the German Government, with other countries participating in the common European currency, the euro, undertook to provide assistance for the severely indebted Greek economy, and to establish a temporary emergency fund, the EFSF, in order to ensure financial stability within the euro area. Merkel argued that the Treaty of Lisbon should be amended to provide a permanent mechanism for helping member states to avoid insolvency, and the establishment of the European Stability Mechanism (ESM, originally intended to enter into effect in mid-2013, following the expiry of the EFSF, and later brought forward to July 2012) was agreed by EU heads of state and government in December 2010.

During 2011 the German Government undertook a leading role in maintaining the stability of the euro area, by providing assistance for heavily indebted member states (although this was widely unpopular among German tax-payers), and by urging the adoption of more rigorous rules and closer EU integration to prevent future sovereign debt crises. In May the Bundestag approved Germany's contribution to an assistance programme for Portugal, but proposals for a second 'bail-out' for Greece, to prevent that country being obliged to default on its debts, proved more controversial, particularly among members of Angela Merkel's own party, the CDU, and the FDP. In June the Minister of Finance, Wolfgang Schäuble, declared that German support for a new assistance programme for Greece was conditional upon a 'quantified and substantial contribution' by holders of Greek government bonds, i.e. private-sector creditors, such as banks, who would be obliged to reschedule the debts owed and suffer losses as a result. This suggestion was opposed by the European Central Bank as being equivalent to Greece defaulting on its debt, which might lead to a disastrous decline in the credit ratings of other heavily indebted EU members. In September the Bundestag voted in favour of enhancing the EFSF by increasing Germany's guarantee commitments to €211,000m. Merkel repeatedly urged the adoption of measures for closer fiscal and economic integration and enforceable budgetary discipline in the EU, but at a meeting of EU heads of state and government in December proposals for a 'fiscal compact' to be incorporated in amendments to the Treaty of Lisbon were defeated when the United Kingdom imposed its veto, after safeguards for British financial services were not forthcoming. The 'fiscal compact' was expected to be adopted, instead, by a separate intergovernmental treaty, according to which members would agree to adopt binding legislation on balancing their budgets; failure to adhere to this would incur penalties imposed by the European Court of Justice. At a further summit meeting in January 2012 it was announced that all EU members except the Czech Republic and the United

Kingdom had agreed to support the compact (which was formally concluded in March). In February EU ministers of finance finally agreed upon a second assistance programme for Greece, with the aim of reducing Greece's debt to 120% of gross domestic product by 2020. The programme, involving loans of more than €130,000m. and (as demanded by Germany) reductions in the value of bonds held by private creditors, was conditional upon extremely stringent reductions in public spending, under external supervision, and many Greeks expressed considerable resentment of Germany, which they regarded as primarily responsible for what were perceived as the harsh and humiliating conditions of the agreement. The assistance was approved by the Bundestag in late February 2012. However, the German Government resisted a proposal by the IMF and the Netherlands Government that the ESM should be expanded (from the originally envisaged size of €500,000m.) by adding to it the remaining funds of the EFSF in order to create a larger 'firewall' against future debt crises.

From late 2002 Germany and France began a phase of markedly cordial bilateral relations, partly owing to both countries' opposition to the US-led military action in Iraq (see below). The two countries were also united in their attitude towards the proposed EU constitution, and in the defence of their budgetary deficits, which were in excess of the limits set by the EU's Stability and Growth Pact. While close relations with France remained a priority following Merkel's election as Chancellor in November 2005, Merkel believed that Germany had worked too exclusively with France in the past and announced her intention to strengthen relations with smaller EU states and the USA. Following the election in May 2007 of Nicolas Sarkozy as French President, the attitudes of the two leaders appeared to diverge, especially with regard to a series of agreements signed by Sarkozy during late 2007 for the sale of nuclear technology to countries in the Middle East and French proposals regarding the formation of a so-called Mediterranean Union, membership of which was to be limited to the seven EU member states in the Mediterranean region and Middle Eastern and African littoral countries. The German Government, which was thus excluded from the grouping, opposed the project on the grounds that it could undermine the influence of the ongoing Euro-Mediterranean Partnership (the Barcelona Process—a framework launched in 1995 for co-operation between all EU member states and 10 other Mediterranean states). However, in March 2008, following negotiations between French and German representatives, Merkel and Sarkozy announced an agreement on the formation of the new union, which was launched in July and restyled the Union for the Mediterranean, and which incorporated all EU member states. In February 2011 the German and French Governments initiated what later became known as the Euro-Plus Pact, an agreement among EU members to work towards raising the age at which workers qualified for pensions, abolishing wage indexation, harmonizing corporate taxes, and creating legally binding limits on budget deficits. During 2011, as the two governments co-operated in seeking a solution to the euro area debt crisis, the French Government disagreed with Germany's insistence on the involvement of private investors in reducing Greece's debt (since several French banks held large amounts of Greek debt), but supported the 'fiscal compact' on budgetary discipline (see above).

Germany's relations with Poland were for a long time influenced by the Second World War. In the course of the negotiations on EU enlargement during the 1990s, Germany strongly supported Poland's accession (which took place in May 2004), citing the need for reconciliation with its eastern neighbour. In August 2004 Chancellor Schröder attended a ceremony in Warsaw to mark the 60th anniversary of the failed uprising there, during which he acknowledged the 'immeasurable suffering' inflicted by Nazi troops on Poland. The Polish Government, as well those of Estonia, Latvia, Lithuania and Ukraine, opposed the construction of a pipeline to transport natural gas to Germany from Russia (see below), fearing that it could be used to divert energy away from those countries for political reasons. Further disagreement occurred in June 2007 after the Polish Government objected to proposals supported by Germany for the reform of voting procedures within the EU institutions. However, the appointment in November of a new, largely pro-EU Government in Poland improved relations between the two countries: the new Polish Prime Minister, Donald Tusk, visited Berlin in mid-December for a meeting with Merkel, following which the two leaders affirmed the friendly nature of relations between Germany and Poland, and promised close co-operation over the planned gas pipeline.

In October 2005 preliminary negotiations for the possible accession of Turkey to the EU began. Germany has a substantial Turkish population, and Schröder was supportive of its bid for EU membership, but with the election of Merkel, who was opposed to Turkey's accession, as Chancellor in November 2005, Germany's continued support became more doubtful. In February 2008, during a visit to Germany, the Turkish Prime Minister, Reçep Tayyip Erdoğan, urged the sizable Turkish population within Germany to retain their ethnic identity, and provoked an angry reaction from several German politicians, who expressed fears that such remarks by their Turkish counterparts could undermine efforts to integrate people of Turkish origin into German society. In January 2010 the Minister of Foreign Affairs, Guido Westerwelle, visited Turkey and declared his support for Turkey's entry to the EU, provided that domestic reforms were undertaken.

In the early 21st century Russia was the source of around one-third of Germany's natural gas requirements, and the security of this supply (about 80% of which arrived via Ukraine) was of major concern to the German Government. During a visit to Germany in September 2005 the Russian President, Vladimir Putin, finalized an agreement with Chancellor Schröder on the construction of a pipeline directly linking Russia and Germany under the Baltic Sea. The 'Nord Stream' pipeline (actually twin pipelines) was intended to transport up to 27,500m. cu m of Russian natural gas per year to Western Europe. It was approved by neighbouring countries, despite environmental concerns; construction began in April 2010 and transport of gas through the first of the pipelines began in November 2011, with completion of the two lines scheduled for late 2012. In March 2008 Merkel became the first EU leader to visit Russia after the election of Dmitrii Medvedev as Russian President earlier in that month. In January 2009 she held emergency talks with Putin, who had assumed the position of Russian Prime Minister, following the temporary severance of gas supplies to several EU member states, including Germany, during the latest of a series of disputes between Russia and Ukraine over energy prices. In November 2010, during a visit by Putin, Merkel expressed support for Russia's application to join the World Trade Organization (see p. 433) and for the eventual establishment of a free trade area between Russia and the EU.

Other external relations

Following the Iraqi invasion and annexation of Kuwait in August 1990, the German Government expressed support for the deployment of US-led allied forces in the region of the Persian (Arabian) Gulf, and contributed substantial amounts of financial and technical aid to the effort to liberate Kuwait, although there were mass demonstrations against the allied action in many parts of Germany. Despite criticism from certain countries participating in the alliance, Germany did not contribute troops to the allied force, in accordance with a provision in the Basic Law that was widely interpreted as prohibiting intervention outside the area of NATO operations. In July 1992, however, the Government announced that it was to send a naval destroyer and reconnaissance aircraft to the Adriatic Sea to participate in the UN force monitoring the observance of UN sanctions on the Federal Republic of Yugoslavia (FRY). This deployment was subsequently approved by the Bundestag. In April 1993 the Constitutional Court ruled that German forces could join the UN operation to enforce an air exclusion zone over Bosnia and Herzegovina. Germany dispatched troops to assist the UN relief effort in Somalia in mid-1993. In May 1994 the Constitutional Court declared the participation of German military units in collective international defence and security operations, with the approval of the Bundestag in each instance, to be compatible with the Basic Law. From March to early June 1999 Germany participated in the NATO military offensive against the FRY, despite misgivings from left-wing elements within the ruling SPD-Bündnis 90/Die Grünen coalition. From 2004 onwards Germany participated in the EU peace-keeping operation in Bosnia and Herzegovina, where about 120 German soldiers were deployed at the end of 2010.

In the aftermath of the terrorist attacks in the USA on 11 September 2001, Schröder pledged 'unlimited solidarity' with the US Administration, and announced plans to send 3,900 troops to take part in the US-led military action in Afghanistan, although these plans were strongly opposed by the majority of members of the junior partner in the governing coalition, Bündnis 90/Die Grünen. In November Schröder narrowly won a parliamentary vote on the troop deployment, which was linked to a vote of confidence in his Government. In November 2002 the Bundestag voted to extend the deployment of troops in Afghanistan by a further year, and the mandate was thereafter renewed annually, with the size of the German contingent participating in the International Security Assistance Force (ISAF) increasing to almost 5,000 by 2011. In February 2008 the German Government rejected a US request to send further troops to southern Afghanistan, where NATO forces were increasingly engaged in direct combat with supporters of the former fundamentalist Islamist regime, the Taliban. In September 2009 a number of Afghan civilians were killed in an air attack by US forces on two petrol tankers that had been seized by Taliban members near the northern city of Kunduz: the air attack had been requested by a local German commander. The incident led to the resignation in November of the Chief of Staff of the Bundeswehr, and of an official in the Federal Ministry of Defence. Although the mandate for maintaining German forces in Afghanistan was again renewed by the Bundestag in December, the events reinforced domestic opposition to their deployment in that country. From mid-2010 the German Government increased to 200 the number of German police officers involved in training and developing the Afghan police force. In December 2011 it was announced that the number of German troops participating in ISAF would be reduced in 2012, in accordance with the planned phasing-out of the ISAF mission by 2014.

Germany opposed US plans for the reconstruction of Iraq following the removal of Saddam Hussain in March–April 2003 and advocated instead greater UN involvement and the swifter transfer of governing powers to Iraqis. In September, however, Chancellor Schröder offered to provide resources for the training of Iraqi police, security staff and military personnel (while continuing to refuse to send German peace-keeping troops to Iraq). The continuing 'war on terror' precipitated further tensions in late 2005, following reports that the USA's Central Intelligence Agency (CIA) had routed over 400 flights through German airports, allegedly with the knowledge of the Minister of the Interior, as part of its programme of 'extraordinary rendition'. Under this programme, it was alleged, suspected Islamist militants were secretly transferred to third countries, some of which were suspected of practising torture, for interrogation. When the US Secretary of State, Condoleezza Rice, visited Germany in December she admitted that suspects were flown abroad for interrogation but denied that they were tortured. Germany's relations with the USA improved after Merkel took office, and the importance of bilateral co-operation was emphasized during her first official visit to the USA in January 2006, which was returned by the US President, George W. Bush, in July. In November 2009 Merkel visited the USA for discussions with President Barack Obama, during which she requested that US nuclear weapons should no longer be stationed in Germany. In April 2010 Merkel attended a meeting of heads of state and government in Washington, DC, to discuss the security of nuclear materials, both military and civilian, and the possible threat of their being used by terrorists. During 2010 and 2011 the US Government voiced concern over Germany's consistently large export surplus, urging that Germany should stimulate domestic demand for the benefit of other exporters.

In February 2011 a popular movement began against Col Muammar al-Qaddafi's regime in Libya, which by March had descended into civil war. Chancellor Merkel was criticized for abstaining from a vote on a UN Security Council resolution, proposed by the United Kingdom, France and Lebanon, authorizing an air exclusion zone over Libya. Germany was the only Western nation to abstain from the vote, which none the less resulted in the adoption of a resolution that permitted UN member states to take 'all necessary measures' (short of military occupation) to protect civilians in Libya.

The People's Republic of China is one of Germany's principal trading partners. From 2002 China became Germany's second largest export market outside Europe (after the USA), and by 2010 China had become Germany's principal supplier of imports. Angela Merkel made an official visit to China in July 2010, when the two Governments announced that intergovernmental consultations would take place annually, and in June 2011 the Chinese Premier, Wen Jiabao, visited Germany; during his visit, a number of agreements on economic and other co-operation were concluded.

CONSTITUTION AND GOVERNMENT

The Basic Law (*Grundgesetz*), which came into force in the British, French and US Zones of Occupation in Germany (excluding Saarland) on 23 May 1949, became the Constitution of the entire German nation with the accession of the five newly re-established eastern *Länder* (states) and East Berlin to the Federal Republic on 3 October 1990.

Germany is a federal republic with a bicameral legislature. The country's main legislative organ, is the Bundestag (Federal Assembly), with 622 deputies, who are elected for four years by universal adult suffrage (using a mixed system of proportional representation and direct voting). The upper chamber is the Bundesrat (Federal Council), which consists of 69 members representing the 16 *Länder*. Each *Land* has between three and six seats, depending on the size of its population. The term of office of Bundesrat members varies in accordance with *Land* election dates.

Executive authority rests with the Federal Government (Bundesregierung), led by the Federal Chancellor (Bundeskanzler), who is elected by an absolute majority of the Bundestag and appoints the other Ministers. The Federal President (Bundespräsident) is elected by a Federal Convention (Bundesversammlung), which meets only for this purpose and consists of the Bundestag and an equal number of members elected by *Land* parliaments. The President is a constitutional head of state with little influence on government.

Germany is composed of 16 *Länder* (states). Each *Land* has its own constitution, legislature and government, with the right to enact laws except on matters that are the exclusive right of the Federal Government, such as defence, foreign affairs and finance. Education, police, culture and environmental protection are in the control of the *Länder*. Local responsibility for the execution of Federal and *Land* laws is undertaken by the *Gemeinden* (communities).

REGIONAL AND INTERNATIONAL CO-OPERATION

Germany was a founding member of the European Community, now European Union (EU, see p. 276) and participated in the introduction of the single European currency, the euro, in January 1999. It is also a member of the Council of Europe (see p. 256), of the Organization for Security and Co-operation in Europe (OSCE, see p. 388), and of the Council of the Baltic Sea States.

Germany joined the UN in 1973; it was elected as a non-permanent member of the Security Council for the period 2011–12. As a contracting party to the General Agreement on Tariffs and Trade, Germany joined the World Trade Organization (WTO, see p. 433) on its establishment in 1995. Germany is a member of the Organisation for Economic Co-operation and Development (OECD, see p. 379) and the North Atlantic Treaty Organization (NATO, see p. 370). It participates in the Group of Eight major industrialized nations (G8, see p. 463) and the Group of 20 major industrialized and systemically important emerging market nations (G20, see p. 454).

ECONOMIC AFFAIRS

In 2010, according to estimates by the World Bank, Germany's gross national income (GNI), measured at average 2008–10 prices, was US \$3,537,180m., equivalent to \$43,290 per head (or \$38,140 per head on an international purchasing-power parity basis). During 2001–10 Germany's population registered a decrease of 0.1%, while gross domestic product (GDP) per head grew, in real terms, by an average of 0.9% annually. According to the UN, overall GDP expanded, in real terms, at an average annual rate of 0.9% in 2001–10; GDP increased by 3.6% in 2010.

Agriculture (including hunting, forestry and fishing) engaged 2.3% of the employed labour force in 2008, and provided 0.9% of Germany's GDP in 2010. The principal crops are wheat, sugar beet, barley and potatoes. Wine production is also important in western Germany. According to the UN, agricultural GDP decreased, in real terms, at an average annual rate of 0.4% in 2001–10; it declined by 0.4% in 2010.

Industry (including mining, power, manufacturing and construction) engaged 29.7% of the employed labour force in 2008 and contributed 27.9% of GDP in 2010. According to UN figures, industrial GDP increased at an average annual rate of 0.3% in 2001–10; it decreased by 16.3% in 2009 but increased by 10.1% in 2010.

The mining sector engaged 0.3% of the employed labour force in 2008 and, with energy, gas and water supply, contributed 3.0% of GDP in 2010. The principal mining activities are the extraction of lignite (low-grade brown coal), hard coal and salts. According to the UN, GDP of mining along with utilities increased, in real terms, at an average annual rate of 0.3% in 2001–10; it decreased by 10.3% in 2010.

The manufacturing sector employed 19.3% of the employed labour force in 2008, and provided 20.7% of GDP in 2010. Measured by value of output, the principal branches of manufacturing in 2004 were motor vehicles and parts (accounting for 20.1% of the total), non-electric machinery (11.4%), chemical products (9.7%) and food products (9.0%). According to UN figures, real manufacturing GDP increased at an average annual rate of 0.2% in 2001–10; it contracted by 18.1% in 2009 but expanded by 11.5% in 2010.

The construction sector employed 6.0% of the employed labour force in 2008, and provided 4.1% of GDP in 2010. According to the UN, the GDP of the sector declined by an average annual rate of 2.1% during 2001–10; construction GDP decreased by 1.8% in 2009 but increased by 1.5% in 2010.

Of the total energy produced in 2008, coal accounted for 46.0%, nuclear power for 23.5%, natural gas for 13.9% and hydroelectric power for 3.3%. In September 2010, in a reversal of a decision in 2000 to end the use of nuclear power by 2021, the Government announced plans to delay the closure of its 17 nuclear power plants, some by a further 14 years. In March 2011, following radiation leaks from a nuclear plant in Japan that had been damaged in an earthquake, this decision was suspended and seven nuclear reactors were temporarily closed for safety checks. In 2010 imports of mineral fuels accounted for an estimated 11.4% of Germany's total imports.

Services engaged 68.1% of the employed labour force in 2008, and contributed 71.2% of GDP in 2010. According to the UN, the GDP of the services sector increased, in real terms, at an average annual rate of 1.4% in 2001–10. Financial services, real estate, renting and business activities accounted for 30.5% of GDP in 2010. Trade, transport and communications accounted for 17.2% of GDP in 2010. The real GDP of this sector grew at an average annual rate of 1.3% in 2001–10. Overall services GDP fell by 2.4% in 2009, but grew by 2.4% in 2010.

In 2010 Germany recorded a visible trade surplus of US $204.72m., and there was a surplus of $187.94m. on the current account of the balance of payments. Germany was the world's largest exporter of goods in the years 2004–08, although exports from the People's Republic of China exceeded those from Germany in 2009 by over $20,000m in that year. Germany conducted more than one-half of its total trade with other countries of the European Union (EU, see p. 276) in 2008. France is the most significant individual trading partner, supplying 7.7% of imports and purchasing 9.5% of exports, according to provisional figures, in 2010. Other principal sources of imports in that year were China (9.5% of imports), the Netherlands (8.5%), the USA and Italy; the other major purchasers of exports were the USA (6.8% of exports), the Netherlands, the United Kingdom, Italy, Austria and China. The principal imports in 2010 were machinery and transport equipment (accounting for 34.5% of the total, with road vehicles and parts comprising 7.4%), chemicals and related products, basic manufactures, mineral fuels and lubricants and food and live animals. The principal exports were machinery and transport equipment (accounting for 47.0% of the total, with road vehicles and parts comprising 15.9%), chemicals and related products, basic manufactures, and miscellaneous manufactured articles.

The general government deficit for 2009 was €72,910.0m., equivalent to 3.0% of GDP. In 2010 general government gross debt was €2,079,630m., equivalent to 84.0% of GDP. Annual inflation averaged 1.6% during 2001–10. Consumer prices rose by an annual average of 2.3% in 2011. Unemployment averaged 7.5% of the labour force in 2009. The unemployment rate was 7.6% in March 2011.

Germany is the largest economy in Europe, although the area comprising the former German Democratic Republic (East Germany) remains less prosperous than the former Federal Republic of Germany (West Germany). The country experienced a resurgence of growth from 2004–07, owing to the rapid growth of exports, partly due to high demand for German machinery from emerging market economies. However, following the rapid deterioration in global financial conditions from the end of 2007, GDP growth slowed significantly to 1.3% in 2008 as the German economy officially entered a recession, contracting in the last three quarters of that year. As a major exporter (particularly of machinery and vehicles), Germany was vulnerable to the global decline in demand, which was exacerbated by the rise in the value of the euro, and caused a sharp decline in industrial output. German banks demonstrated some resilience during the global financial crisis, owing to their comparatively low ratios of debt to capital, although the Government was forced to intervene to support several banks. The general government deficit of 3.3% in 2005, which breached the 3.0% higher limit permitted under the EU's Stability and Growth Pact, had been eliminated to achieve a balanced budget by 2008, largely as a result of a rise in tax revenues, owing to rapid economic growth and the expansion of employment. In November 2008 and January 2009 measures were adopted to stimulate the economy, requiring a supplementary budget, with a substantial rise in borrowing: as a result, in 2009 the budgetary deficit amounted to 3.2% of GDP, thus once again exceeding the EU limit. During 2009 unemployment remained at a level similar to that of the previous year, largely because of a system of short-time working, initiated at the beginning of 2009, whereby the Government subsidized companies that retained their employees while reducing working hours. Germany's GDP declined by 4.7% in 2009, the largest contraction in the country's post-war history. In 2010, however, there was a substantial economic recovery: GDP increased by 3.6%, reflecting an unexpectedly rapid growth in exports and investment, although there was only a small increase in domestic consumer demand. The budgetary deficit was estimated at 3.5% of GDP in 2010, and in June the Government announced a controversial programme of austerity measures, with the aim of reducing the deficit to below 3.0% of GDP by 2013 and achieving a balanced budget by 2016. The budgetary deficit decreased more quickly than anticipated, to 1% of GDP in 2011, reflecting an increase in tax revenues. GDP growth was maintained in 2011, at 3.0%, although there was a slight contraction in the final quarter of the year. Unemployment fell to its lowest level for 20 years in December 2011, at 6.8%. The Government predicted weaker GDP growth of 0.7% in 2012, owing to a reduction in exports caused by the economic difficulties of the euro area and an anticipated decline in demand in Asia.

PUBLIC HOLIDAYS

2013: 1 January (New Year's Day), 6 January (Epiphany)*, 29 March (Good Friday), 1 April (Easter Monday), 1 May (Labour Day), 9 May (Ascension Day), 20 May (Whit Monday), 30 May (Corpus Christi)*, 15 August (Assumption)*, 3 October (Day of Unity), 31 October (Reformation Day)*, 1 November (All Saints' Day)*, 20 November (Day of Prayer and Repentance)*, 25–26 December (Christmas), 31 December (New Year's Eve).

* Religious holidays observed in certain *Länder* only.

Statistical Survey

Source (unless otherwise indicated): Statistisches Bundesamt, 65180 Wiesbaden; tel. (611) 752405; fax (611) 753330; e-mail info@destatis.de; internet www.destatis.de.

Area and Population

AREA, POPULATION AND DENSITY

Area (sq km)*	357,124
Population (official estimates at 31 December)	
2008	82,002,356
2009	81,802,257
2010	81,751,602
Males	40,112,425
Females	41,639,177
Density (per sq km) at 31 December 2010	228.9

* 137,886 sq miles.

2011 (official population estimate at 31 December, preliminary): 81,800,000.

POPULATION BY AGE AND SEX

(UN estimates at mid–2012)

	Males	Females	Total
0–14	5,562,358	5,298,720	10,861,078
15–64	27,316,580	26,757,096	54,073,676
65 and over	7,352,606	9,703,478	17,056,084
Total	40,231,544	41,759,294	81,990,838

Source: UN, *World Population Prospects: The 2010 Revision*.

LÄNDER

(official population estimates at 31 December 2010)

	Area (sq km)	Population ('000)	Density (per sq km)	Capital
Baden-Württemberg	35,751	10,754	301	Stuttgart
Bayern (Bavaria)	70,550	12,539	177	München
Berlin	892	3,461	3,861	Berlin
Brandenburg	29,482	2,503	85	Potsdam
Bremen	404	661	1,637	Bremen
Hamburg	755	1,786	2,349	Hamburg
Hessen (Hesse)	21,115	6,067	287	Wiesbaden
Mecklenburg-Vorpommern (Mecklenburg-Western Pomerania)	23,189	1,642	71	Schwerin
Niedersachsen (Lower Saxony)	47,635	7,918	166	Hannover
Nordrhein-Westfalen (North Rhine-Westphalia)	34,088	17,845	524	Düsseldorf
Rheinland-Pfalz (Rhineland-Palatinate)	19,854	4,004	202	Mainz
Saarland	2,569	1,018	398	Saarbrücken
Sachsen (Saxony)	18,420	4,149	226	Dresden
Sachsen-Anhalt (Saxony-Anhalt)	20,449	2,335	115	Magdeburg
Schleswig-Holstein	15,799	2,834	179	Kiel
Thüringen (Thuringia)	16,172	2,235	139	Erfurt
Total	357,124	81,752	229	—

Note: Totals may not be equal to the sum of components, owing to rounding.

PRINCIPAL TOWNS

('000 population at 31 December 2009, estimates)

Berlin (capital)	3,442.7	Mannheim	312.0
Hamburg	1,774.2	Karlsruhe	292.0
München (Munich)	1,330.4	Wiesbaden	277.5
Köln (Cologne)	998.1	Münster	275.5
Frankfurt am Main	671.9	Augsburg	263.6
Stuttgart	601.6	Gelsenkirchen	259.7
Düsseldorf	586.2	Aachen (Aix-la-Chapelle)	258.4
Dortmund	581.3	Mönchengladbach	258.3
Essen	576.3	Braunschweig (Brunswick)	247.4
Bremen	547.7	Chemnitz	243.1
Hannover (Hanover)	521.0	Kiel	238.3
Leipzig	518.9	Krefeld	235.4
Dresden	517.1	Halle an der Saale*	232.3
Nürnberg (Nuremberg)	503.7	Magdeburg	230.5
Duisburg	491.9	Freiburg im Breisgau	221.9
Bochum	376.3	Oberhausen	214.0
Wuppertal	351.1	Lübeck	209.8
Bielefeld	323.1	Erfurt	203.8
Bonn	319.8		

* Including Halle-Neustadt.

BIRTHS, MARRIAGES AND DEATHS

	Registered live births		Registered marriages		Registered deaths	
	Number	Rate (per 1,000)	Number	Rate (per 1,000)	Number	Rate (per 1,000)
2003	706,721	8.6	382,911	4.6	853,946	10.3
2004	705,622	8.5	395,992	4.8	818,271	9.9
2005	685,795	8.3	388,451	4.7	830,270	10.1
2006	672,724	8.2	373,681	4.5	821,627	10.0
2007	684,862	8.3	368,922	4.5	827,155	10.1
2008	682,514	8.3	377,055	4.6	844,439	10.3
2009	665,126	8.1	378,439	4.6	854,544	10.4
2010*	677,947	8.3	382,047	4.7	858,768	10.5

* Preliminary results.

Life expectancy (years at birth, WHO estimates): 80 (males 78; females 83) in 2009 (Source: WHO, *World Health Statistics*).

IMMIGRATION AND EMIGRATION

('000 persons)

	2006	2007	2008
Immigrant arrivals	661.9	675.6	682.1
Emigrant departures	639.1	632.4	737.9

2009 ('000 persons, preliminary): Immigrant arrivals 721; Emigrant departures 734.

ECONOMICALLY ACTIVE POPULATION

(sample surveys, '000 persons aged 15 years and over, at March unless otherwise indicated)

	2006	2007	2008
Agriculture, hunting and forestry	837	854	866
Fishing	6	5	6
Mining and quarrying	116	107	109
Manufacturing	8,157	8,395	8,516
Electricity, gas and water	316	334	346
Construction	2,446	2,527	2,521
Wholesale and retail trade; repair of motor vehicles, motorcycles and personal and household goods	5,281	5,308	5,290

—continued	2006	2007	2008
Hotels and restaurants	1,381	1,428	1,459
Transport, storage and communications	2,060	2,148	2,146
Financial intermediation	1,306	1,303	1,301
Real estate, renting and business activities	3,735	3,909	4,171
Public administration and defence; compulsory social security	2,901	2,916	2,836
Education	2,174	2,237	2,290
Health and social work	4,264	4,398	4,515
Other community, social and personal service activities	2,125	2,058	2,112
Private households with employed persons	187	206	216
Extra-territorial organizations and bodies	29	29	33
Total employed	37,322	38,163	38,734
Unemployed	4,279	3,608	3,141
Total labour force	41,601	41,771	41,875
Males	22,820	22,834	22,878
Females	18,781	18,936	18,997

Source: ILO.

Health and Welfare

KEY INDICATORS

Total fertility rate (children per woman, 2009)	1.3
Under-five mortality rate (per 1,000 live births, 2009)	4
HIV/AIDS (% of persons aged 15–49, 2009)	0.1
Physicians (per 1,000 head, 2006)	3.4
Hospital beds (per 1,000 head, 2006)	8.3
Health expenditure (2008): US $ per head (PPP)	3,922
Health expenditure (2008): % of GDP	10.5
Health expenditure (2008): public (% of total)	74.6
Total carbon dioxide emissions ('000 metric tons, 2007)	787,291.0
Carbon dioxide emissions per head (metric tons, 2007)	9.6
Human Development Index (2011): ranking	9
Human Development Index (2011): value	0.905

For sources and definitions, see explanatory note on p. vi.

Agriculture

PRINCIPAL CROPS
('000 metric tons)

	2008	2009	2010
Wheat	25,989	25,192	24,107
Barley	11,967	12,288	10,412
Maize	5,106	4,527	4,073
Rye	3,744	4,329	2,903
Oats	793	826	600
Triticale (wheat-rye hybrid)	2,381	2,514	2,199
Potatoes	11,369	11,618	10,202
Sugar beet	23,003	25,919	23,858
Broad beans, dry	38	47	56
Sunflower seed	49	57	47
Rapeseed	5,155	6,307	5,698
Cabbages and other brassicas	806	841	787
Cauliflowers and broccoli	156	168	152
Cucumbers and gherkins	237	263	243
Onions, dry	408	433	387
Beans, green	49	45	41
Carrots and turnips	547	570	554
Grapes	1,429	1,306	1,008
Apples	1,047	1,071	835
Pears	38	52	39
Cherries	25	39	31
Plums and sloes	31	73	49
Strawberries	151	159	157
Currants	11	12	12

Aggregate production ('000 metric tons, may include official, semi-official or estimated data): Total cereals 50,105 in 2008, 49,809 in 2009, 44,413 in 2010; Total roots and tubers 11,369 in 2008, 11,618 in 2009, 10,202 in 2010; Total vegetables (incl. melons) 3,470 in 2008, 3,662 in 2009, 3,338 in 2010; Total fruits (excl. melons) 2,802 in 2008, 2,810 in 2009, 2,201 in 2010.

Source: FAO.

LIVESTOCK
('000 head at December)

	2008	2009	2010
Horses	543.0*	545.0*	461.8
Cattle	12,969.7	12,944.9	12,809.5
Pigs	26,686.8	26,948.3	26,509.0
Sheep	2,437.0	2,350.4	2,088.5
Goats	190	220	150
Chickens	115,000*	118,000*	114,113
Geese and guinea fowls	300*	290*	278
Ducks	2,700*	2,750*	3,164
Turkeys	11,500*	12,000*	11,344

* FAO estimate.

Source: FAO.

LIVESTOCK PRODUCTS
('000 metric tons)

	2008	2009	2010
Cattle meat	1,199.4	1,189.6	1,205.0
Sheep meat	38.5	38.3	38.3
Pig meat	5,121.6	5,264.5	5,488.4
Chicken meat	746.9	785.9	837.1
Cows' milk	28,656.3	29,198.7	29,628.9
Goats' milk*	35.3	34.4	36.4
Hen eggs	789.6	698.1	664.3
Honey	15.7	16.5	23.1
Wool, greasy*	12.0	12.5	12.8

* FAO estimates.

Source: FAO.

Forestry

ROUNDWOOD REMOVALS
('000 cubic metres, excluding bark)

	2008	2009	2010
Sawlogs, veneer logs and logs for sleepers	31,241	25,481	29,749
Pulpwood	12,655	10,860	12,659
Other industrial wood	2,910	2,645	2,980
Fuel wood	8,561	9,087	9,031
Total	55,367	48,073	54,418

Source: FAO.

SAWNWOOD PRODUCTION
('000 cubic metres, including railway sleepers)

	2008	2009	2010
Coniferous (softwood)	18,093	19,657	21,161
Broadleaved (hardwood)	1,094	1,116	1,190
Total	19,187	20,773	22,351

Source: FAO.

Fishing

('000 metric tons, live weight)

	2007	2008	2009
Capture	295.8	280.1	250.3
Freshwater fishes	18.8	18.8	18.8
Atlantic cod	16.8	17.4	18.6
Saithe (Pollock)	16.4	16.6	15.7
Blue whiting (Poutassou)	34.7	25.3	5.0
Atlantic herring	50.0	46.7	37.5
European sprat	31.0	31.0	29.2
Sardinellas	12.1	—	—
Atlantic horse mackerel	5.8	13.0	16.5
Atlantic mackerel	18.6	15.4	22.4
Common shrimp	15.9	17.9	17.3
Aquaculture	45.0	44.0	40.0
Common carp	9.2	10.9	9.9
Rainbow trout	23.2	22.0	21.1
Blue mussel	10.5	6.9	3.6
Total catch	340.8	324.1	290.3

Note: Figures exclude aquatic mammals, recorded by number rather than by weight. The number of harbour porpoises caught was: 27 in 2007; 8 in 2008; 8 in 2009.

Source: FAO.

Mining

('000 metric tons, unless otherwise indicated)

	2004	2005	2006
Hard coal	25,859	24,907	20,882
Brown coal	181,903	177,875	176,290
Crude petroleum	3,516	3,573	4,929
Salt (unrefined)	8,242	n.a.	n.a.

Crude petroleum ('000 metric tons): 4,640 in 2007; 2,586 in 2008.

Natural gas (petajoules): 654 in 2006; 609 in 2007; 526 in 2008 (Source: UN Industrial Commodity Statistics Database).

2008 ('000 metric tons unless otherwise indicated): Coal, lignite 175,313; Coal, anthracite and bituminous 17,077; Crude petroleum ('000 42-gallon barrels) 22,400; Natural gas, marketable (million cu m) 15,377 (Source: US Geological Survey).

2009 ('000 metric tons unless otherwise indicated): Coal, lignite 169,857; Coal, anthracite and bituminous 13,766; Crude petroleum ('000 42-gallon barrels) 20,500; Natural gas, marketable (million cu m) 14,380 (Source: US Geological Survey).

Industry

SELECTED PRODUCTS

('000 metric tons, unless otherwise indicated)

	2007	2008	2009
Margarine	430	403	405
Flour	4,942	5,044	4,986
Refined sugar	3,644	3,375	4,012
Beer ('000 hl)	94,781	91,123	88,005
Cigarettes (million)	214,458	223,633	212,834
Cotton yarn (pure and mixed)	36	30	19
Woven cotton fabrics ('000 sq m)	245,508	205,643	136,624
Newsprint	2,623	2,734	2,487
Motor spirit (petrol)	24,408	23,448	23,624
Diesel oil*	35,188	33,569	32,939
Cement	33,804	33,983	30,664
Sulphuric acid	2,052	2,125	1,796
Nitrogenous fertilizers	1,319	1,329	1,341
Artificial resins and plastics	17,776	17,274	15,454
Synthetic rubber	1,033	1,027	958
Soap	222	260	290
—continued	2007	2008	2009
Aluminium (unwrought):			
primary	314	320	213
secondary	1,034	1,064	710
Refined lead (unwrought)	292	325	315
Refined zinc (unwrought)	265	262	n.a.
Passenger cars and minibuses ('000)	6,360	6,100	5,386
Bicycles ('000)	1,731	n.a.	1,322
Lenses, incl. contact ('000)	434,520	433,567	n.a.
Footwear ('000 pairs)†	11,662	10,961	n.a.
Electricity (million kWh)	576,017	572,175	n.a.

* Including light heating oil.

† Excluding rubber and plastic footwear.

Finance

CURRENCY AND EXCHANGE RATES

Monetary Units

100 cent = 1 euro (€).

Sterling and Dollar Equivalents (30 December 2011)

£1 sterling = 1.195 euros;
US $1 = 0.773 euros;
€10 = £8.37 = $12.94.

Average Exchange Rate (euros per US $)

2009 0.7198
2010 0.7550
2011 0.7194

Note: The national currency was formerly the Deutsche Mark (DM). From the introduction of the euro, with German participation, on 1 January 1999, a fixed exchange rate of €1 = DM 1.95583 was in operation. Euro notes and coins were introduced on 1 January 2002. The euro and local currency circulated alongside each other until 28 February, after which the euro became the sole legal tender.

GOVERNMENT FINANCE

(general government transactions, non-cash basis, € '000 million)

Summary of Balances

	2007	2008	2009
Revenue	1,065.8	1,088.5	1,066.0
Less Expense	1,064.9	1,089.6	1,140.6
Net operating balance	0.9	−1.1	−74.5
Less Net acquisition of non-financial assets	−5.4	−4.0	−1.8
Net lending/borrowing	6.3	2.8	−72.7

Revenue

	2007	2008	2009
Taxes	580.6	594.9	569.0
Taxes on income, profits and capital gains	303.4	313.2	285.3
Taxes on goods and services	256.6	261.7	264.6
Social contributions	400.2	407.8	409.9
Grants	4.5	4.2	3.3
Other revenue	80.5	81.6	83.9
Total	1,065.8	1,088.5	1,066.1

Expense/Outlays

Expense by economic type	2007	2008	2009
Compensation of employees	168.3	170.7	177.6
Use of goods and services	100.0	104.9	111.4
Consumption of fixed capital	38.3	39.4	39.8
Interest	67.3	66.7	62.2
Subsidies	27.2	27.8	31.5
Grants	19.7	21.4	21.0
Social benefits	597.3	606.8	640.1
Other expense	46.6	52.0	56.9
Total	1,064.7	1,089.7	1,140.5

Outlays by functions of government*	2007	2008	2009
General public services	144.6	148.4	146.6
Defence	25.4	26.6	27.8
Public order and safety	37.2	38.4	40.2
Economic affairs	76.2	84.3	86.8
Environmental protection	11.5	11.9	15.6
Housing and community amenities	20.3	19.5	17.8
Health	149.1	155.3	164.8
Recreation, culture and religion	14.6	15.2	15.8
Education	96.7	99.5	104.7
Social protection	485.0	491.4	518.7
Total	1,060.6	1,090.5	1,138.8

* Including net acquisition of non-financial assets.

Source: IMF, *Government Finance Statistics Yearbook*.

INTERNATIONAL RESERVES

(US $ million at 31 December)

	2008	2009	2010
Gold (Eurosystem valuation)	94,906	120,922	154,202
IMF special drawing rights	2,198	19,101	18,769
Reserve position in IMF	2,382	3,896	6,169
Foreign exchange	38,557	36,928	37,356
Total	138,043	180,847	216,496

Source: IMF, *International Financial Statistics*.

MONEY SUPPLY

(incl. shares, depository corporations, national residency criteria, € '000 million at 31 December)

	2008	2009	2010
Currency issued	213.3	208.4	217.2
Deutsche Bundesbank	335.1	355.2	374.3
Demand deposits	831.8	1,015.5	1,105.8
Other deposits	1,990.8	1,860.2	1,867.0
Securities other than shares	1,692.7	1,576.0	1,479.4
Money market fund shares	16.4	11.4	9.8
Shares and other equity	378.2	378.8	380.6
Other items (net)	–505.2	–458.5	–496.6
Total	4,618.0	4,591.8	4,563.2

Source: IMF, *International Financial Statistics*.

COST OF LIVING

(Consumer Price Index for all private households; base: 2005 = 100)

	2008	2009	2010
Food	112.3	110.9	112.5
Alcohol and tobacco	108.4	111.3	113.0
Clothes and shoes	101.4	102.8	103.7
Housing, energy and fuel	108.5	108.9	110.1
Furniture and household goods	102.5	104.2	104.6
Health	103.0	104.0	104.7
Transport	110.5	108.3	112.1
Communications	91.8	89.8	88.0
Recreation and culture	99.8	101.4	101.3
Education	137.9	132.3	131.8
Restaurants and hotels	106.3	108.7	109.9
Miscellaneous goods and services	105.9	107.5	108.4
All items	106.6	107.0	108.2

NATIONAL ACCOUNTS

(€ million at current prices, rounded to nearest €10m.)

National Income and Product

	2008	2009	2010
Compensation of employees	1,223,280	1,225,860	1257,820
Net operating surplus/mixed income	647,740	565,970	645,710
Domestic primary incomes	1,871,020	1,791,830	1,903,530
Consumption of fixed capital	367,160	366,090	353,160
Gross domestic product (GDP) at factor cost	2,238,180	2,157,920	2,256,690
Net taxes on production and imports*	243,020	239,180	242,110
GDP in market prices	2,481,200	2,397,100	2,498,800
Balance of primary income from abroad	39,650	33,840	36,480
Gross national income (GNI)	2,520,850	2,430,940	2,535,280
Less Consumption of fixed capital	367,160	366,090	353,160
Net national income	2,153,690	2,064,850	2,182,120
Current transfers from abroad	12,860	10,820	11,320
Less Current transfers paid abroad	44,990	43,190	48,950
Net national disposable income	2,121,560	2,032,480	2,144,490

* Data obtained as residuals.

Expenditure on the Gross Domestic Product

	2008	2009	2010
Government final consumption expenditure	449,600	472,140	484,690
Private final consumption expenditure	1,413,220	1,411,060	1,445,010
Increase in stocks	–12,430	–27,270	–10,780
Gross fixed capital formation	471,360	422,690	448,150
Total domestic expenditure	2,321,750	2,278,620	2,367,070
Exports of goods and services	1,177,870	978,790	1,152,280
Less Imports of goods and services	1,018,420	860,310	1,020,550
GDP in purchasers' values	2,481,200	2,397,100	2,498,800

Gross Domestic Product by Economic Activity

	2008	2009	2010
Agriculture, hunting, forestry and fishing	19,960	17,310	19,480
Mining and quarrying* Electricity, gas and water supply*	65,460	65,580	68,080
Manufacturing	504,220	408,800	463,800
Construction	89,830	92,140	92,490
Wholesale and retail trade; repair of motor vehicles, motorcycles and personal and household goods; and transport and communications	396,660	373,650	385,550
Financial intermediation Real estate, renting and business activities†	655,810	666,690	682,130
Public administration and defence; compulsory social security Education Health and social work Other community, social and personal service activities, incl. hotels and restaurants Private households with employed persons	492,860	516,440	528,020
Gross value added in basic prices	2,224,800	2,140,610	2,239,550
Taxes, less subsidies, on products*	256,400	256,490	259,250
GDP in market prices	2,481,200	2,397,100	2,498,800

* Data obtained as residuals.

† Including deduction for financial intermediation services indirectly measured.

BALANCE OF PAYMENTS
(US $ '000 million)

	2008	2009	2010
Exports of goods f.o.b.	1,501.80	1,160.99	1,303.33
Imports of goods f.o.b.	–1,238.77	–972.49	–1,098.61
Trade balance	263.03	188.50	204.72
Exports of services	254.68	232.59	237.81
Imports of services	–291.53	–257.12	–263.44
Balance on goods and services	226.18	163.97	179.09
Other income received	288.35	248.68	230.54
Other income paid	–237.28	–178.37	–170.89
Balance on goods, services and income	277.26	234.28	238.73
Current transfers received	27.20	24.25	22.73
Current transfers paid	–76.34	–69.90	–73.52
Current balance	228.11	188.63	187.94
Capital account (net)	–0.19	0.07	–0.82
Direct investment abroad	–81.23	–77.97	–108.36
Direct investment from abroad	4.79	38.92	46.13
Portfolio investment assets	23.42	–96.13	–231.13
Portfolio investment liabilities	50.01	–19.99	61.37
Financial derivatives liabilities	–47.72	15.16	–22.92
Other investment assets	–221.77	136.14	–163.59
Other investment liabilities	40.00	–191.10	233.76
Net errors and omissions	7.33	18.62	–0.24
Overall balance	2.74	12.36	2.13

Source: IMF, *International Financial Statistics*.

OVERSEAS DEVELOPMENT AID
(€ million)

	2007	2008	2009
Bilateral	5,807	6,283	5,096
Multilateral	3,171	3,410	3,578
Total	8,978	9,693	8,674

External Trade

PRINCIPAL COMMODITIES
(distribution by SITC, € million)

Imports c.i.f.	2008	2009	2010*
Food and live animals	46,072	44,285	45,720
Crude materials (inedible) except fuels	29,600	21,284	30,719
Mineral fuels, lubricants, etc.	112,988	76,315	92,154
Petroleum, petroleum products, etc.	74,603	44,865	60,720
Chemicals and related products	100,299	89,670	101,965
Organic chemicals	21,405	17,408	20,381
Medicinal and pharmaceutical products	32,524	34,303	35,832
Basic manufactures	116,142	80,837	101,514
Machinery and transport equipment	276,206	234,724	278,357
Power-generating machinery and equipment	24,559	21,089	24,070
General industrial machinery, equipment and parts	31,570	24,254	27,441
Office machines and automatic data-processing equipment	28,801	24,190	29,503
Telecommunications and sound equipment	24,940	22,555	25,445

Imports c.i.f.—*continued*	2008	2009	2010*
Other electrical machinery, apparatus and appliances	53,767	46,341	63,192
Road vehicles (incl. air-cushion vehicles) and parts	66,447	57,143	59,648
Other transport equipment	25,618	25,183	33,700
Miscellaneous manufactured articles	85,669	81,402	88,417
Articles of apparel and clothing accessories (excl. footwear)	22,745	22,602	24,623
Total (incl. others)	805,842	664,615	806,164

Exports f.o.b.	2008	2009	2010*
Food and live animals	40,100	38,227	40,009
Chemicals and related products	148,017	130,702	150,276
Medical and pharmaceutical products	46,724	47,550	50,492
Basic manufactures	140,886	108,309	126,584
Machinery and transport equipment	481,091	378,133	451,151
Power-generating machinery and equipment	35,377	29,889	35,526
Machinery specialized for particular industries	48,615	34,826	39,961
General industrial machinery and equipment	74,298	59,461	65,708
Office machines and automatic data-processing equipment	21,692	18,870	20,262
Telecommunications and sound equipment	17,568	14,021	16,407
Electrical machinery, apparatus and appliances	74,807	60,263	75,132
Road vehicles (incl. air-cushion vehicles) and parts	162,545	118,537	152,751
Other transport equipment	30,150	29,429	33,069
Miscellaneous manufactured articles	98,017	87,670	97,579
Total (incl. others)	984,140	803,312	959,497

* Provisional.

PRINCIPAL TRADING PARTNERS
(€ million)

Imports c.i.f.	2008	2009	2010*
Austria	33,180.1	27,565.1	34,315.1
Belgium	36,622.7	28,040.9	33,699.5
China, People's Republic	60,825.1	56,706.2	76,528.4
Czech Republic	27,548.0	24,005.9	29,623.2
Denmark	11,907.4	10,587.0	11,096.5
Finland	7,756.8	5,302.7	6,023.3
France	63,368.6	53,338.5	61,751.2
Hungary	16,815.1	13,765.6	16,700.5
Ireland	16,131.7	13,815.0	14,032.4
Italy	46,841.8	37,196.8	43,666.7
Japan	23,129.8	18,946.1	22,064.8
Korea, Republic	9,180.0	7,801.8	11,102.5
Netherlands	67,970.6	55,583.5	68,767.2
Norway	22,323.3	17,160.7	17,109.7
Poland	25,874.8	22,161.0	28,416.4
Russia	37,086.8	25,187.8	31,780.2
Spain	20,700.7	18,958.7	22,258.5
Sweden	13,672.3	10,166.4	13,229.7
Switzerland-Liechtenstein	31,666.3	28,480.7	32,886.1
Turkey	9,735.3	8,338.5	9,907.9
United Kingdom	41,646.0	32,457.4	38,593.5
USA	46,463.5	39,282.5	45,063.0
Total (incl. others)	805,842.5	664,614.9	806,164.1

Exports f.o.b.	2008	2009	2010*
Austria	54,688.6	46,093.5	53,721.1
Belgium	49,933.6	41,839.5	46,406.7
China, People's Republic	34,065.3	37,272.5	53,636.4
Czech Republic	27,600.6	22,032.0	26,967.6
Denmark	16,006.9	12,808.7	14,166.6
Finland	9,643.4	7,085.2	7,812.5
France	93,717.9	81,304.1	90,694.4
Hungary	17,360.0	11,675.1	14,265.3
Italy	62,014.8	50,619.5	58,476.8
Japan	12,731.7	10,875.1	13,113.8
Netherlands	65,798.8	53,195.1	63,235.2
Poland	40,750.3	31,121.8	38,053.3
Russia	32,312.4	20,620.9	26,360.9
Spain	42,676.1	31,280.5	34,380.8
Sweden	20,091.4	15,546.5	19,634.1
Switzerland-Liechtenstein	39,579.3	35,994.5	42,207.6
Turkey	15,129.4	11,624.9	16,192.0
United Kingdom	64,175.4	53,239.9	59,487.4
USA	71,428.2	54,356.4	65,570.3
Total (incl. others)	984,139.8	803,311.8	959,497.4

* Provisional.

Transport

FEDERAL RAILWAYS
(traffic)

	2008	2009	2010
Passengers (million)	2,337	2,323	2,370
Passenger-km (million)	81,765	n.a.	n.a.
Freight net ton-km (million)	115,652	95,834	107,317

ROAD TRAFFIC
('000 licensed vehicles at 1 January)

	2008	2009	2010
Passenger cars	41,183.6	41,321.2	41,737.6
Lorries	2,323.1	2,346.7	2,385.1
Buses	75.1	75.3	76.4
Motorcycles	3,566.1	3,658.6	3,762.6
Trailers	5,642.3	5,774.8	5,910.7

SHIPPING

Inland Waterways

	2008	2009	2010
Freight ton-km (million)	64,057	55,497	62,278

Merchant Fleet
(registered at 31 December)

	2007	2008	2009
Number of vessels	885	961	948
Displacement ('000 grt)	12,934.2	15,282.8	15,157.1

Source: IHS Fairplay, *World Fleet Statistics*.

Sea-borne Traffic

	1997	1998	1999
Vessels entered ('000 net registered tons):*			
domestic (coastwise)	19,785	43,667	21,213
international	260,553	263,470	269,637
Vessels cleared ('000 net registered tons):*			
domestic	19,664	67,036	20,529
international	235,110	237,071	246,887
Freight unloaded ('000 metric tons):†			
international	136,249	140,846	137,759
Freight loaded ('000 metric tons):†			
international	69,058	69,098	73,858
Total domestic freight ('000 metric tons)	8,011	7,444	10,005

* Loaded vessels only.

† Including transshipments.

CIVIL AVIATION
(traffic on scheduled services)

	2007	2008	2009
Kilometres flown (million)	1,484	1,548	1,425
Passengers carried ('000)	105,911	107,942	103,397
Passenger-km (million)	214,655	220,759	205,371
Total ton-km (million)	29,670	30,074	27,097

Source: UN, *Statistical Yearbook*.

Tourism

FOREIGN TOURIST ARRIVALS
('000)*

Country of residence	2008	2009	2010
Austria	1,204.8	1,252.4	1,387.7
Belgium and Luxembourg	1,213.3	1,271.0	1,347.3
Denmark	1,110.4	1,138.9	1,214.3
France	1,220.1	1,249.5	1,366.2
Italy	1,421.5	1,444.1	1,524.1
Japan	597.7	538.0	605.2
Netherlands	3,584.9	3,692.1	3,917.6
Poland	575.2	514.6	604.3
Spain	809.4	761.1	842.8
Sweden	853.8	762.7	859.3
Switzerland	1,773.8	1,856.9	2,028.4
United Kingdom	1,968.5	1,749.7	1,986.9
USA	1,973.7	1,938.8	2,206.3
Total (incl. others)	24,884.0	24,219.6	26,875.3

* Figures refer to arrivals at all accommodation types.

Tourism receipts (€ million, excl. passenger transport): 39,912 in 2008; 34,650 in 2009; 34,675 in 2010 (provisional) (Source: World Tourism Organization).

Communications Media

	2008	2009	2010
Telephones ('000 main lines in use)	50,300	47,500	45,600
Mobile cellular telephones ('000 subscribers)	105,523	105,000	104,560
Internet users ('000)	64,092	65,125	n.a.
Broadband subscribers ('000)	22,644	24,892	26,090

Personal computers: 54,000,000 (655.5 per 1,000 persons) in 2006.

Source: International Telecommunication Union.

Television receivers ('000 in use, 2000): 48,170.

Radio receivers ('000 in use, 1997): 77,800.

Book production (titles, including pamphlets, 1996): 71,515.

Daily newspapers (2004): 347, average circulation ('000 copies) 22,100.

Non-daily newspapers (2004): 34, average circulation ('000 copies) 6,100.

Sources: UNESCO, *Statistical Yearbook*; UN, *Statistical Yearbook*.

Education

(2007/08 unless otherwise indicated)

	Teachers	Students
Pre-primary*	215,920	2,385,856
Primary*	242,329	3,150,822
Secondary:		
lower secondary	410,096*	4,985,838
upper secondary:		
general	105,133	1,242,102
vocational	83,007	1,679,166
Post-secondary non-tertiary:		
general	7,450	516,359
vocational	18,766	
Higher:		
non-university institutions	287,744†	671,686‡
universities and equivalent institutions		1,415,503‡

* 2008/09.

† 2005/06.

‡ 2009/10, preliminary.

Source: mainly UNESCO Institute for Statistics.

Pupil-teacher ratio (primary education, UNESCO estimate): 13.0 in 2008/09 (Source: UNESCO Institute for Statistics).

Directory

The Government

HEAD OF STATE

Federal President: JOACHIM GAUCK (assumed office 18 March 2012).

THE FEDERAL GOVERNMENT
(May 2012)

A coalition of the Christlich-Demokratische Union Deutschlands (CDU—Christian Democratic Union), with its sister party in Bavaria, the Christlich-Soziale Union (CSU—Christian Social Union), and the Freie Demokratische Partei (FDP—Free Democratic Party).

Federal Chancellor: ANGELA MERKEL (CDU).

Federal Vice-Chancellor and Federal Minister of Economics and Technology: PHILIPP RÖSLER (FDP).

Federal Minister of Foreign Affairs: GUIDO WESTERWELLE (FDP).

Federal Minister of the Interior: HANS-PETER FRIEDRICH (CSU).

Federal Minister of Justice: SABINE LEUTHEUSSER-SCHNARRENBERGER (FDP).

Federal Minister of Finance: WOLFGANG SCHÄUBLE (CDU).

Federal Minister of Labour and Social Affairs: URSULA VON DER LEYEN (CDU).

Federal Minister of Food, Agriculture and Consumer Protection: ILSE AIGNER (CSU).

Federal Minister of Defence: THOMAS DE MAIZIÈRE (CDU).

Federal Minister of Family Affairs, Senior Citizens, Women and Youth: KRISTINA SCHRÖDER (CDU).

Federal Minister of Health: DANIEL BAHR (FDP).

Federal Minister of Transport, Building and Urban Affairs: PETER RAMSAUER (CSU).

Federal Minister of the Environment, Nature Conservation and Nuclear Safety: NORBERT RÖTTGEN (CDU).

Federal Minister of Education and Research: ANNETTE SCHAVAN (CDU).

Federal Minister of Economic Co-operation and Development: DIRK NIEBEL (FDP).

Head of the Federal Chancellery and Minister for Special Tasks: RONALD POFALLA (CDU).

MINISTRIES

Office of the Federal President: 11010 Berlin; Bundespräsidialamt, Spreeweg 1, 10557 Berlin; tel. (30) 20000; fax (30) 20001999; e-mail poststelle@bpra.bund.de; internet www.bundespraesident.de.

Federal Chancellery: Bundeskanzler-Amt, Willy-Brandt Str. 1, 10557 Berlin; tel. (30) 40000; fax (30) 40002357; e-mail internetpost@bpa.bund.de; internet www.bundeskanzlerin.de.

Press and Information Office of the Federal Government: 11044 Berlin; Dorotheenstr. 84, 10117 Berlin; tel. (30) 182720; fax (30) 18102720; e-mail posteingang@bpa.bund.de; internet www.bundesregierung.de.

Federal Ministry of Defence: Stauffenbergstr. 18, 10785 Berlin; tel. (30) 18242424; fax (30) 18248240; e-mail poststelle@bmvg.bund.de; internet www.bmvg.de.

Federal Ministry of Economic Co-operation and Development: Dahlmannstr. 4, 53113 Bonn; tel. (228) 995350; fax (228) 995353500; e-mail info@bmz.bund.de; internet www.bmz.de.

Federal Ministry of Economics and Technology: 11019 Berlin; Scharnhorststr. 34–37, 10115 Berlin; tel. (30) 201419; fax (30) 20147010; e-mail info@bmwi.bund.de; internet www.bmwi.de.

Federal Ministry of Education and Research: Heinemannstr. 2, 53175 Bonn; tel. (228) 99570; fax (228) 995783601; e-mail information@bmbf.bund.de; internet www.bmbf.de.

Federal Ministry of the Environment, Nature Conservation and Nuclear Safety: Alexanderstr. 3, 10178 Berlin; tel. (30) 183050; fax (30) 183052044; e-mail service@bmu.bund.de; internet www.bmu.de.

Federal Ministry of Family Affairs, Senior Citizens, Women and Youth: Glinkastr. 24, 10117 Berlin; tel. (30) 185550; fax (30) 185554400; e-mail poststelle@bmfsfj.bund.de; internet www.bmfsfj.de.

Federal Ministry of Finance: 11016 Berlin; Wilhelmstr. 97, 10117 Berlin; tel. (30) 186820; fax (30) 186823260; e-mail poststelle@bmf.bund.de; internet www.bundesfinanzministerium.de.

Federal Ministry of Food, Agriculture and Consumer Protection: 11055 Berlin; Wilhelmstr. 54, 10117 Berlin; tel. (30) 185290; fax (30) 185293179; e-mail poststelle@bmelv.bund.de; internet www.bmelv.de.

Federal Ministry of Foreign Affairs: 11013 Berlin; Werderscher Markt 1, 10117 Berlin; tel. (30) 18170; fax (30) 18173402; e-mail poststelle@auswaertiges-amt.de; internet www.auswaertiges-amt.de.

Federal Ministry of Health: 11055 Berlin; Friedrichstr. 108, 10117 Berlin; tel. (30) 184414900; fax (30) 184411921; e-mail poststelle@bmg.bund.de; internet www.bmg.bund.de.

Federal Ministry of the Interior: Alt-Moabit 101D, 10559 Berlin; tel. (30) 186810; fax (30) 186812926; e-mail poststelle@bmi.bund.de; internet www.bmi.bund.de.

Federal Ministry of Justice: Mohrenstr. 37, 10117 Berlin; tel. (30) 185800; fax (30) 185809525; e-mail poststelle@bmj.bund.de; internet www.bmj.bund.de.

Federal Ministry of Labour and Social Affairs: Wilhelmstr. 49, 10117 Berlin; tel. (30) 185270; fax (30) 185271830; e-mail info@bmas.bund.de; internet www.bmas.de.

Federal Ministry of Transport, Building and Urban Affairs: Invalidenstr. 44, 10115 Berlin; tel. (30) 183003060; fax (30) 183001942; e-mail buergerinfo@bmvbs.bund.de; internet www.bmvbs.de.

Legislature

Bundestag (Federal Assembly)

Pl. der Republik 1, 11011 Berlin; tel. (30) 2270; fax (30) 22736878; e-mail mail@bundestag.de; internet www.bundestag.de.

President: Prof. Dr NORBERT LAMMERT (CDU).

Vice-Presidents: EDUARD OSWALD (CDU), Dr WOLFGANG THIERSE (SPD), Dr HERMANN OTTO SOLMS (FDP), KATRIN GÖRING-ECKARDT (Bündnis 90/Die Grünen), PETRA PAU (Die Linke).

General Election, 27 September 2009

Parties and Groups	Votes*	% of votes*	Seats
Christlich-Demokratische Union Deutschlands/Christlich-Soziale Union (CDU/CSU)†	14,658,515	33.80	239
Sozialdemokratische Partei Deutschlands (SPD)	9,990,488	23.03	146
Freie Demokratische Partei (FDP)	6,316,080	14.56	93
Die Linke	5,155,933	11.89	76
Bündnis 90/Die Grünen	4,643,272	10.71	68
Others	2,606,902	6.01	—
Total	43,371,190	100.00	622

* Figures refer to valid second votes (i.e. for state party lists). The total number of valid first votes (for individual candidates) was 43,248,000. In addition, there were 757,575 invalid first votes and 634,385 invalid second votes.

† Of which the CDU received 11,828,277 votes (27.27%—194 seats) and the CSU received 2,830,238 votes (6.53%—45 seats).

Bundesrat (Federal Council)

Niederkirchnerstr. 1-4, 10117 Berlin; tel. (18) 9100; fax (30) 189100400; e-mail bundesrat@bundesrat.de; internet www.bundesrat.de.

The Bundesrat has 69 members. Each *Land* (state) has three, four, five or six votes, depending on the size of its population, and may send as many members to the sessions as it has votes. The head of government of each *Land* is automatically a member of the Bundesrat. Members of the Federal Government attend the sessions, which are held every two to three weeks.

President: HORST SEEHOFER (CSU) (1 Nov. 2011–31 Oct. 2012).

Länder	Seats
Nordrhein-Westfalen (North Rhine-Westphalia)	6
Bayern (Bavaria)	6
Baden-Württemberg	6
Niedersachsen (Lower Saxony)	6
Hessen (Hesse)	5
Sachsen (Saxony)	4
Rheinland-Pfalz (Rhineland-Palatinate)	4
Berlin	4
Schleswig-Holstein	4
Brandenburg	4
Sachsen-Anhalt (Saxony-Anhalt)	4
Thüringen (Thuringia)	4
Hamburg	3
Mecklenburg-Vorpommern (Mecklenburg-Western Pomerania)	3
Saarland	3
Bremen	3
Total	69

The Land Governments

The 16 *Länder* of Germany are autonomous but not sovereign states, enjoying a high degree of self-government and extensive legislative powers. Thirteen of the *Länder* have a Landesregierung (Government) and a Landtag (Assembly). The equivalent of the Landesregierung in Berlin, Bremen and Hamburg is the Senat (Senate). The equivalent of the Landtag is the Abgeordnetenhaus (House of Representatives) in Berlin and the Bürgerschaft (City Council) in Bremen and Hamburg.

BADEN-WÜRTTEMBERG

The Constitution was adopted by the Assembly in Stuttgart on 11 November 1953 and came into force on 19 November. The Minister-President, who is elected by the Assembly, appoints and dismisses Ministers. The Government is currently formed by a coalition Bündnis 90/Die Grünen and the SPD.

Minister-President: WINFRIED KRETSCHMANN (Bündnis 90/Die Grünen).

Landtag von Baden-Württemberg

Haus des Landtags, Konrad-Adenauer-Str. 3, 70173 Stuttgart; tel. (711) 20630; fax (711) 2063299; e-mail post@landtag-bw.de; internet www.landtag-bw.de.

President of Assembly: WILLI STÄCHELE (CDU).

Election, 27 March 2011

Party	Seats
Christlich-Demokratische Union Deutschlands (CDU)	60
Bündnis 90/Die Grünen	36
Sozialdemokratische Partei Deutschlands (SPD)	35
Freie Demokratische Partei (FDP)	7
Total	138

The *Land* is divided into four administrative districts: Stuttgart, Karlsruhe, Tübingen and Freiburg.

BAYERN (BAVARIA)

The Constitution of Bavaria provides for a unicameral Assembly and a Constitutional Court. Provision is also made for referendums. The Minister-President, who is elected by the Assembly for five years, appoints the Ministers and Secretaries of State with the consent of the Assembly. The Government is currently formed by a coalition of the CSU and the FDP.

Minister-President: HORST SEEHOFER (CSU).

Bayerischer Landtag

Landtagsamt, Maximilaneum, 81627 München; tel. (89) 41260; fax (89) 41261392; e-mail landtag@bayern.landtag.de; internet www.bayern.landtag.de.

President of Assembly: BARBARA STAMM (CSU).

Election, 28 September 2008

Party	Seats
Christlich-Soziale Union (CSU)	92
Sozialdemokratische Partei Deutschlands (SPD)	39
Freie Wähler	21
Bündnis 90/Die Grünen	19
Freie Demokratische Partei (FDP)	16
Total	187

Bayern is divided into seven districts: Mittelfranken, Oberfranken, Unterfranken, Schwaben, Niederbayern, Oberpfalz and Oberbayern.

BERLIN

The House of Representatives (Abgeordnetenhaus) is the legislative body. The executive agency is the Senate, which is composed of the Governing Mayor (Regierender Bürgermeister) and up to 10 Senators, from among whom the deputy mayor is elected. The Governing Mayor and the senators are elected by a majority of the House of Representatives. The Senate is responsible to the House of Representatives and dependent on its confidence.

Regierender Bürgermeister: KLAUS WOWEREIT (SPD).

Abgeordnetenhaus von Berlin (House of Representatives)

Niederkirchnerstr. 5, 10117 Berlin; tel. (30) 23250; e-mail verwaltung@parlament-berlin.de; internet www.parlament-berlin.de.

President of House of Representatives: WALTER MOMPER (SPD).

Election, 18 September 2011

Party	Seats
Sozialdemokratische Partei Deutschlands (SPD)	48
Christlich-Demokratische Union Deutschlands (CDU)	39
Bündnis 90/Die Grünen	30
Die Linke	20
Piratenpartei Deutschland	15
Total	152

BRANDENBURG

The Constitution of Brandenburg was adopted on 14 June 1992 and came into force on 20 August. It was amended on 7 April 1999. The Assembly elects the Minister-President, who appoints Ministers. The Government is currently formed from a coalition of the SPD and Die Linke.

Minister-President: MATTHIAS PLATZECK (SPD).

Landtag Brandenburg

Postfach 601064, 14410 Potsdam; Am Havelblick 8, 14473 Potsdam; tel. (331) 9660; fax (331) 9661210; e-mail poststelle@landtag.brandenburg.de; internet www.landtag.brandenburg.de.

President of Assembly: GUNTER FRITSCH (SPD).

Election, 27 September 2009

Party	Seats
Sozialdemokratische Partei Deutschlands (SPD)	31
Die Linke	26
Christlich-Demokratische Union Deutschlands (CDU)	19
Freie Demokratische Partei (FDP)	7
Bündnis 90/Die Grünen	5
Total	88

BREMEN

The Constitution of the Free Hanseatic City of Bremen was approved by referendum on 12 October 1947. The main constitutional organs are the City Council (Bürgerschaft), the Senate and the Constitutional Court. The Senate is the executive organ elected by the Council for the duration of its own tenure of office. The Senate elects from its own ranks two Mayors (Bürgermeister), one of whom becomes President of the Senate. Decisions of the Council are subject to the delaying veto of the Senate. The Government is currently formed from a coalition of the SPD and Bündnis 90/Die Grünen.

First Bürgermeister and President of the Senate: JENS BÖHRNSEN (SPD).

Bremische Bürgerschaft (Bremen City Council)

Am Markt 20, 28195 Bremen; tel. (421) 3614555; fax (421) 36112492; e-mail geschaeftsstelle@buergerschaft.bremen.de; internet www.bremische-buergerschaft.de.

President of the City Council: CHRISTIAN WEBER (SPD).

Election, 22 May 2011

Party	Seats
Sozialdemokratische Partei Deutschlands (SPD)	36
Bündnis 90/Die Grünen	21
Christlich-Demokratische Union Deutschlands (CDU)	20
Die Linke	5
Bürger in Wut (BIW)	1
Total	83

HAMBURG

The Constitution of the Free and Hanseatic City of Hamburg was adopted in June 1952. The City Council (Bürgerschaft) elects the President of the Senate (government), who appoints and dismisses members of the Senate. The Senate is currently composed of members of the SPD.

President of Senate and First Bürgermeister: OLAF SCHOLZ (SPD).

Bürgerschaft der Freien und Hansestadt Hamburg (Hamburg City Council)

Rathaus, Rathausmarkt 1, 20095 Hamburg; tel. (40) 428312408; fax (40) 428312558; e-mail oeffentlichkeitsservice@bk.hamburg.de; internet www.hamburgische-buergerschaft.de.

President: LUTZ MOHAUPT (CDU).

Election, 20 February 2011

Party	Seats
Sozialdemokratische Partei Deutschlands (SPD)	62
Christlich-Demokratische Union Deutschlands (CDU)	28
Bündnis 90/Die Grünen—Grüne Alternative Liste (GAL)	14
Freie Demokratische Partei (FDP)	9
Die Linke	8
Total	121

HESSEN (HESSE)

The Constitution of this *Land* dates from 1 December 1946. The Minister-President is elected by the Assembly, and appoints and dismisses Ministers with its consent. The Assembly can force the resignation of the Government by a vote of no confidence. The Government is currently formed by a coalition of the CDU and the FDP.

Minister-President: VOLKER BOUFFIER (CDU).

Hessischer Landtag

Schlosspl. 1–3, 65183 Wiesbaden; tel. (611) 3500; fax (611) 350434; e-mail oeffentlichkeit@ltg.hessen.de; internet www.hessischer-landtag.de.

President of Assembly: NORBERT KARTMANN (CDU).

Election, 18 January 2009

Party	Seats
Christlich-Demokratische Union Deutschlands (CDU)	46
Sozialdemokratische Partei Deutschlands (SPD)	29
Freie Demokratische Partei (FDP)	20
Bündnis 90/Die Grünen	17
Die Linke	6
Total	118

Hessen is divided into three governmental districts: Kassel, Giessen and Darmstadt.

MECKLENBURG-VORPOMMERN (MECKLENBURG-WESTERN POMERANIA)

The Constitution was adopted by the Assembly on 14 May 1993. The Assembly elects the Minister-President, who appoints and dismisses Ministers. The Government is currently formed by a coalition of the SPD and the CDU.

Minister-President: Dr ERWIN SELLERING (SPD).

Landtag Mecklenburg-Vorpommern

Schloss, Lennéstr. 1, 19053 Schwerin; tel. (385) 5250; fax (385) 5252141; e-mail poststelle@landtag-mv.de; internet www.landtag-mv.de.

President of Assembly: SYLVIA BRETSCHNEIDER (SPD).

Election, 4 September 2011

Party	Seats
Sozialdemokratische Partei Deutschlands (SPD)	27
Christlich-Demokratische Union Deutschlands (CDU)	18
Die Linke	14
Bündnis 90/Die Grünen	7
Nationaldemokratische Partei Deutschlands (NPD)	5
Total	71

NIEDERSACHSEN (LOWER SAXONY)

The Constitution was adopted by the Assembly on 19 May 1993 and came into force on 1 June. The Minister-President is elected by the Assembly, with whose consent he/she appoints and dismisses Ministers. The Government is currently formed from a coalition of the CDU and the FDP.

Minister-President: DAVID MCALLISTER (CDU).

Landtag Niedersachsen

Hinrich-Wilhelm-Kopf-Pl. 1, 30159 Hannover; tel. (511) 30300; fax (511) 30302806; e-mail poststelle@lt.niedersachsen.de; internet www.landtag-niedersachsen.de.

President of Assembly: HERMANN DINKLA (CDU).

Election, 27 January 2008

Party	Seats
Christlich-Demokratische Union Deutschlands (CDU)	68
Sozialdemokratische Partei Deutschlands (SPD)	48
Freie Demokratische Partei (FDP)	13
Bündnis 90/Die Grünen	12
Die Linke	11
Total	152

NORDRHEIN-WESTFALEN (NORTH RHINE-WESTPHALIA)

The present Constitution was adopted by the Assembly on 6 June 1950, and was endorsed by the electorate in the elections held on 18 June. The Government is presided over by the Minister-President, who appoints Ministers. In March 2012 the minority Government comprising the SPD and Bündnis 90/Die Grünen was dissolved. An early election was to be held on 13 May 2012.

Minister-President: HANNELORE KRAFT (SPD).

Landtag von Nordrhein-Westfalen

Postfach 101143, 40002 Düsseldorf; Pl. des Landtags 1, 40221 Düsseldorf; tel. (211) 8840; fax (211) 8842258; e-mail email@landtag.nrw.de; internet www.landtag.nrw.de.

President of Assembly: ECKHARD UHLENBERG (CDU).

Election, 9 May 2010

Party	Seats
Christlich-Demokratische Union Deutschlands (CDU)	67
Sozialdemokratische Partei Deutschlands (SPD)	67
Bündnis 90/Die Grünen	23
Freie Demokratische Partei (FDP)	13
Die Linke	11
Total	181

The *Land* is divided into five governmental districts: Düsseldorf, Münster, Arnsberg, Detmold and Köln.

RHEINLAND-PFALZ (RHINELAND-PALATINATE)

The three chief agencies of the Constitution of this *Land* are the Assembly, the Government and the Constitutional Court. The Minister-President is elected by the Assembly, with whose consent he or she appoints and dismisses Ministers. Following the election of 27 March 2011, the SPD formed a coalition with Die Grünen.

Minister-President: KURT BECK (SPD).

Landtag Rheinland-Pfalz

Postfach 3040, 55020 Mainz; Deutschhauspl. 12, 55116 Mainz; tel. (6131) 2080; fax (6131) 2082447; e-mail poststelle@landtag.rlp.de; internet www.landtag.rlp.de.

President of Assembly: JOACHIM MERTES (SPD).

Election, 27 March 2011

Party	Seats
Sozialdemokratische Partei Deutschlands (SPD)	42
Christlich-Demokratische Union Deutschlands (CDU)	41
Bündnis 90/Die Grünen	18
Total	101

SAARLAND

Under the Constitution, which came into force on 1 January 1957, Saarland was politically integrated into the FRG as a *Land.* It was economically integrated into the FRG in July 1959. The Minister-President is elected by the Assembly. Following an early election on 25 March 2012, the CDU formed a coalition with the SPD.

Minister-President: ANNEGRET KRAMP-KARRENBAUER (CDU).

Landtag des Saarlandes

Postfach 101833, 66018 Saarbrücken; Franz-Josef-Röder Str. 7, 66119 Saarbrücken; tel. (681) 50020; fax (681) 5002546; e-mail r.riemann@landtag-saar.de; internet www.landtag-saar.de.

President of the Assembly: HANS LEY (CDU).

Election, 25 March 2012 (preliminary results)

Party	Seats
Christlich-Demokratische Union Deutschlands (CDU)	19
Sozialdemokratische Partei Deutschlands (SPD)	17
Die Linke	9
Piratenpartei Deutschland	4
Bündnis 90/Die Grünen	2
Total	51

SACHSEN (SAXONY)

The Constitution of Sachsen was adopted on 26 May 1992 and came into force on 6 June. The Assembly elects the Minister-President and can force the resignation of the Government by a vote of no confidence, if a majority of parliamentarians can agree on a replacement candidate. The Government is currently formed from a coalition of the CDU and FDP.

Minister-President: STANISLAW TILLICH (CDU).

Sächsischer Landtag

Postfach 120705, 01008 Dresden; Bernhard-von-Lindenau Pl. 1, 01067 Dresden; tel. (351) 49350; fax (351) 4935900; e-mail info@slt.sachsen.de; internet www.landtag.sachsen.de.

President of Assembly: Dr MATTHIAS RÖSSLER (CDU).

Election, 30 August 2009

Party	Seats
Christlich-Demokratische Union Deutschlands (CDU)	58
Die Linke	29
Sozialdemokratische Partei Deutschlands (SPD)	14
Freie Demokratische Partei (FDP)	14
Bündnis 90/Die Grünen	9
Nationaldemokratische Partei Deutschlands (NPD)	8
Total	132

Sachsen is divided into three districts: Chemnitz, Dresden and Leipzig.

SACHSEN-ANHALT (SAXONY-ANHALT)

The Constitution of Sachsen-Anhalt was adopted on 16 July 1992. The Assembly elects the Minister-President, who appoints and dismisses Ministers. The Government is formed by a coalition of the CDU and SPD.

Minister-President: Dr REINER HASELOFF (CDU).

Landtag von Sachsen-Anhalt

Dompl. 6–9, 39104 Magdeburg; tel. (391) 5600; fax (391) 5601123; e-mail kontakt@lt.sachsen-anhalt.de; internet www.landtag.sachsen-anhalt.de.

President of Assembly: DETLEF GÜRTH (CDU).

Election, 20 March 2011

Party	Seats
Christlich-Demokratische Union Deutschlands (CDU)	41
Die Linke	29
Sozialdemokratische Partei Deutschlands (SPD)	26
Bündnis 90/Die Grünen	9
Total	105

SCHLESWIG-HOLSTEIN

The Provisional Constitution was adopted by the Assembly on 13 December 1949. The Assembly elects the Minister-President, who appoints and dismisses Ministers. The Government is currently formed by a coalition of the CDU and the FDP.

Minister-President: PETER HARRY CARSTENSEN (CDU).

Landtag Schleswig-Holstein

Düsternbrooker Weg 70, 24105 Kiel; tel. (431) 9880; fax (431) 9881119; e-mail annette.wiese-krukowska@landtag.ltsh.de; internet www.landtag.ltsh.de.

President of Assembly: TORSTEN GEERDTS (CDU).

Election, 27 September 2009

Party	Seats
Christlich-Demokratische Union Deutschlands (CDU)	34
Sozialdemokratische Partei Deutschlands (SPD)	25
Freie Demokratische Partei (FDP)	15
Bündnis 90/Die Grünen	12
Die Linke	5
Südschleswigscher Wählerverband (SSW)	4
Total	95

THÜRINGEN (THURINGIA)

The Constitution of Thüringen was adopted on 25 October 1993. The Assembly elects the Minister-President and can force the resignation of the Government by a vote of no confidence, if a majority of parliamentarians agree on a replacement candidate. The Government is currently formed by a coalition of the CDU and the SPD.

Minister-President: CHRISTINE LIEBERKNECHT (CDU).

Thüringer Landtag

Jürgen-Fuchs Str. 1, 99096 Erfurt; tel. (361) 3772006; fax (361) 3772004; e-mail pressestelle@landtag.thueringen.de; internet www.thueringen.de/tlt.

President of Assembly: BIRGIT DIEZEL (CDU).

Election, 30 August 2009

Party	Seats
Christlich-Demokratische Union Deutschlands (CDU)	30
Die Linke	27
Sozialdemokratische Partei Deutschlands (SPD)	18
Freie Demokratische Partei (FDP)	7
Bündnis 90/Die Grünen	6
Total	88

Election Commission

Bundeswahlleiter (Federal Returning Officer): Statistisches Bundesamt, 65180 Wiesbaden; tel. (611) 754863; fax (611) 724000; e-mail bundeswahlleiter@destatis.de; internet www.bundeswahlleiter.de; Federal Returning Officer RODERICH EGELER (Pres., Federal Office of Statistics); Deputy Federal Returning Officer PETER WEIGL.

Political Organizations

Bündnis 90/Die Grünen (Alliance 90/Greens): Pl. vor dem Neuen Tor 1, 10115 Berlin; tel. (30) 284420; fax (30) 28442210; e-mail info@gruene.de; internet www.gruene.de; f. 1993; merger of Bündnis 90 (f. 1990, as an electoral political asscn of citizens' movements of the former GDR) and Die Grünen (f. 1980, largely composed of the membership of the Grüne Aktion Zukunft, the Grüne Liste, Umweltschutz and the Aktionsgemeinschaft Unabhängiger Deutscher, also including groups of widely varying political views); essentially left-wing party programme includes ecological issues, democratization of society at all levels, social justice, comprehensive disarmament; Chair. CLAUDIA ROTH, CEM ÖZDEMIR; Parliamentary Leaders RENATE KÜNAST, JÜRGEN TRITTIN; Sec.-Gen. STEFFI LEMKE.

Bürger in Wut (BIW) (Citizens in Rage): Torstr. 195, 10115 Berlin; tel. (30) 208664660; fax (30) 208664661; e-mail info@buerger-in-wut.de; internet www.buerger-in-wut.de; f. 2004; supports free democracy; Chair. JAN TIMKE.

Christlich-Demokratische Union Deutschlands/Christlich-Soziale Union (CDU/CSU) (Christian Democratic and Christian Social Union): alliance of the CDU and its sister party in Bavaria, the CSU; forms a single group in the Bundestag; Parliamentary Leader VOLKER KAUDER.

CDU: Konrad-Adenauer-Haus, Klingelhöferstr. 8, 10785 Berlin; tel. (30) 220700; fax (30) 22070111; e-mail info@cdu.de; internet www.cdu.de; f. 1945; became a federal party in 1950; advocates united action between Catholics and Protestants for rebuilding German life on a Christian-Democratic basis, while guaranteeing private property and the freedom of the individual, and for a 'free and equal Germany in a free, politically united and socially just Europe'; other objectives are to guarantee close ties with allies within NATO and the EU; c. 520,000 mems; Chair. Dr ANGELA MERKEL; Sec.-Gen. HERMANN GRÖHE.

CSU: Franz Josef Strauss-Haus, Nymphenburger Str. 64, 80335 München; tel. (89) 12430; fax (89) 1243299; e-mail info@csu-bayern.de; internet www.csu.de; f. 1945; Christian Social party, aiming for a free market economy 'in the service of man's economic and intellectual freedom'; also combines national consciousness with support for a united Europe; 181,000 mems; Chair. HORST SEEHOFER; Sec.-Gen. ALEXANDER DOBRINDT.

Deutsche Kommunistische Partei (DKP) (German Communist Party): Hoffnungstr. 18, 45127 Essen; tel. (201) 1778890; fax (201) 17788929; e-mail pv@dkp-online.de; internet www.dkp.de; Chair. BETTINA JÜRGENSEN.

Deutsche Volksunion (DVU) (German People's Union): Postfach 540626, 22506 Hamburg; tel. (01805) 007432; fax (9181) 290720; e-mail info@dvu.de; internet www.dvu.de; f. 1987; extreme right-wing nationalist; Chair. MATTHIAS FAUST.

Freie Demokratische Partei (FDP) (Free Democratic Party): Thomas-Dehler-Haus, Reinhardtstr. 14, 10117 Berlin; tel. (30) 28495820; fax (30) 28495822; e-mail fdp-point@fdp.de; internet www.fdp-bundespartei.de; f. 1948; represents democratic liberalism and makes the individual the focal point of the state and its laws and economy; in Aug. 1990 incorporated the 3 liberal parties of the former GDR—the Association of Free Democrats, the German Forum Party and the FDP; publishes *Elde*; c. 70,000 mems; Chair PHILIPP RÖSLER; Parliamentary Leader RAINER BRÜDERLE; Sec.-Gen. PATRICK DÖRING.

Freie Wähler (FW) (Independent Voters): Freystadter Str. 28, 92361 Berngau; tel. and fax (9181) 254590; e-mail cordula.breitenfellner@freie-waehler-deutschland.de; internet www.freie-waehler-deutschland.de; f. 1946; non-ideological, centrist; regional orgs in Baden-Württemberg, Bavaria, Hesse, North Rhine-Westphalia, Rhineland-Palatinate and Saxony; Chair. HUBERT AIWANGER; c. 280,000 mems.

Die Linke (Left Party): Karl-Liebknecht-Haus, Kleine Alexanderstr. 28, 10178 Berlin; tel. (30) 240090; fax (30) 2411046; e-mail bundesgeschaeftsstelle@die-linke.de; internet www.die-linke.de; successor to the Sozialistische Einheitspartei Deutschlands (SED—Socialist Unity Party, f. 1946 as a result of the unification of the Social Democratic Party and the Communist Party in Eastern Germany), which had been the dominant political force in the GDR until late 1989; renamed Partei des Demokratischen Sozialismus 1990; restyled Linkspartei.PDS 2005; adopted present name 2007 following merger with Wahlalternative Arbeit und soziale Gerechtigkeit (WASG—Electoral Alternative Jobs and Social Justice); has renounced Stalinism, opposes fascism, right-wing extremism and xenophobia, advocates a socially and ecologically sustainable market economy with public, collective and private ownership of the means of production, opposes terrorism, supports international disarmament and peaceful solutions to international conflicts; Chair. KLAUS ERNST; Parliamentary Leader GREGOR GYSI; Secs-Gen. CAREN LAY, WERNER DREIBUS.

Nationaldemokratische Partei Deutschlands (NPD) (National Democratic Party of Germany): Postfach 840157, 12531 Berlin; Seelenbinderstr. 42, 12555 Berlin; tel. (30) 650110; fax (30) 65011140; e-mail parteizentrale@npd.de; internet www.npd.de; f. 1964; right-wing; 7,000 mems; youth organization Junge Nationaldemokraten (JN), 6,000 mems; Chair. HOLGER APFEL; Sec.-Gen. PETER MARX.

Neues Forum (New Forum): Winsstr. 60, 10405 Berlin; tel. (30) 2479404; fax (30) 24725605; e-mail info@neuesforum.de; internet www.neuesforum.de; f. 1989 as a citizens' action group; played prominent role in democratic movement in former GDR; campaigns for peace, social justice and protection of the environment; Leaders SABINE SCHAAF, REINHARD SCHULT, KLAUS TONNDORF.

Piratenpartei Deutschland (Pirate Party Germany): Pflugstr. 9A, 10115 Berlin; tel. (30) 27572040; fax (30) 609897517; e-mail fragen@piratenpartei.de; internet www.piratenpartei.de; f. 2006; advocates freedom of information, environmental protection, transparency of government; Chair. BERND SCHLÖMER.

Die Republikaner (REP) (Republican Party): Berliner Str. 9, 13187 Berlin; tel. (1805) 737000; fax (1805) 737111; e-mail info@rep.de; internet www.rep.de; f. 1983; conservative right-wing; publishes *Neue Republik*; c. 15,000 mems; Chair. Dr ROLF SCHLIERER.

Sozialdemokratische Partei Deutschlands (SPD) (Social Democratic Party of Germany): Willy-Brandt-Haus, Wilhelmstr. 141, 10963 Berlin; tel. (30) 259910; fax (30) 25991410; e-mail parteivorstand@spd.de; internet www.spd.de; f. 1863; maintains that a vital democracy can be built only on the basis of social justice; advocates for the economy as much competition as possible, as much planning as necessary to protect the individual from uncontrolled economic interests; favours a positive attitude to national defence, while supporting controlled disarmament; rejects any political ties with communism; 548,491 mems (July 2007); Chair. SIGMAR GABRIEL; Parliamentary Leader FRANK-WALTER STEINMEIER; Sec.-Gen. ANDREA NAHLES.

Südschleswigscher Wählerverband (SSW) (South Schleswig Voters' Committee): Schiffbrücke 42, 24939 Flensburg; tel. (461) 14408310; fax (461) 14408313; e-mail info@ssw.de; internet www

.ssw.de; f. 1948; represents the Danish minority in Schleswig-Holstein and Friesian community in northern Germany; Chair. FLEMMING MEYER; Gen. Sec. MARTIN LORENZEN.

There are also numerous other small parties, none of which is represented in the Bundestag, covering all shades of the political spectrum and various regional interests.

Diplomatic Representation

EMBASSIES IN GERMANY

Afghanistan: Taunusstr. 3, Ecke Kronbergerstr. 5, 14193 Berlin; tel. (30) 20673510; fax (30) 20673525; e-mail info@botschaft-afghanistan.de; internet www.botschaft-afghanistan.de; Ambassador Prof. Dr ABDUL RAHMAN ASHRAF.

Albania: Friedrichstr. 231, 10969 Berlin; tel. (30) 2593040; fax (30) 25931890; e-mail kanzlei@botschaft-albanien.de; internet www.botschaft-albanien.de; Ambassador VALTER IBRAHIMI.

Algeria: Görschstr. 45–46, 13187 Berlin; tel. (30) 437370; fax (30) 48098716; e-mail info@algerische-botschaft.de; internet www.algerische-botschaft.de; Ambassador MADJID BOUGUERRA.

Angola: Wallstr. 58, 10179 Berlin; tel. (30) 2408970; fax (30) 24089712; e-mail botschaft@botschaftangola.de; internet www.botschaftangola.de; Ambassador ALBERT CORREIA NETO.

Argentina: Kleiststr. 23–26, 10787 Berlin; tel. (30) 2266890; fax (30) 2291400; e-mail info@embargent.de; internet www.embargent.de; Ambassador VICTORIO MARIA JOSE TACCETTI.

Armenia: Nussbaumallee 4, 14050 Berlin; tel. (30) 4050910; fax (30) 40509125; e-mail armgermanyembassy@mfa.am; internet www.botschaft-armenien.de; Ambassador ARMEN MARTIROSYAN.

Australia: Wallstr. 76–79, 10179 Berlin; tel. (30) 8800880; fax (30) 880088210; e-mail info.berlin@dfat.gov.au; internet www.germany.embassy.gov.au; Ambassador PETER MARTIN TESCH.

Austria: Stauffenbergstr. 1, 10785 Berlin; tel. (30) 202870; fax (30) 2290569; e-mail berlin-ob@bmeia.gv.at; internet www.oesterreichische-botschaft.de; Ambassador Dr RALPH SCHEIDE.

Azerbaijan: Hubertusallee 43, 14193 Berlin; tel. (30) 2191613; fax (30) 21916152; e-mail berlin@mission.mfa.gov.az; internet www.azembassy.de; Ambassador PARVIZ SHAHBAZOV.

Bahrain: Klingelhöfer Str. 7, 10785 Berlin; tel. (30) 86877777; fax (30) 86877788; Ambassador IBRAHIM MAHMOUD AHMED ABDULLAH.

Bangladesh: Dovestr. 1, 5th Floor, 10587 Berlin; tel. (30) 3989750; fax (30) 39897510; e-mail info@bangladeshembassy.de; internet www.bangladeshembassy.de; Ambassador MOSUD MANNAN.

Belarus: Am Treptower Park 32, 12435 Berlin; tel. (30) 5363590; fax (30) 53635923; e-mail germany@mfa.gov.by; internet www.germany.mfa.gov.by; Ambassador ANDREI GIRO.

Belgium: Jägerstr. 52–53, 10117 Berlin; tel. (30) 206420; fax (30) 20642200; e-mail berlin@diplobel.fed.be; internet www.diplomatie.be/berlin; Ambassador RENIER WILLEM JOSEPH NIJSKENS.

Benin: Englerallee 23, 14195 Berlin; tel. (30) 23631470; fax (30) 236314740; Ambassador ISIDORE BIO.

Bolivia: Wichmannstr. 6, 10787 Berlin; tel. (30) 2639150; fax (30) 26391515; e-mail embajada.bolivia@berlin.de; internet www.bolivia.de; Ambassador WALTER PRUDENCIO MAGNE VÉLIZ.

Bosnia and Herzegovina: Ibsenstr. 14, 10439 Berlin; tel. (30) 81471210; fax (30) 81471211; e-mail mail@botschaftbh.de; internet www.botschaftbh.de; Chargé d'affaires a.i. JASMINKA AJANOVIĆ.

Brazil: Wallstr. 57, 10179 Berlin; tel. (30) 726280; fax (30) 72628320; e-mail brasil@brasemberlim.de; internet www.brasilianische-botschaft.de; Ambassador EVERTON VIEIRA VARGAS.

Brunei: Kronenstr. 55–58, 10117 Berlin; tel. (30) 20607600; fax (30) 20607666; e-mail berlin@brunei-embassy.de; Ambassador MOHAMMAD YUSOF ABU BAKAR.

Bulgaria: Mauer Str. 11, 10117 Berlin; tel. (30) 2010922; fax (30) 2086838; e-mail embassy.berlin@mfa.bg; internet www.mfa.bg/de/24; Ambassador RADI DRAGNEV NAIDENOV.

Burkina Faso: Karolingerpl. 10–11, 14052 Berlin; tel. (30) 30105990; fax (30) 301059920; e-mail embassy_burkina_faso@t-online.de; internet www.embassy-bf.org; Ambassador MARIE ODILE BONKOUNGOU BALIMA.

Burundi: Berliner Str. 36, 10715 Berlin; tel. (30) 2345670; fax (30) 23456720; e-mail info@burundi-embassy-berlin.com; internet www.burundi-embassy-berlin.com; Ambassador ANATOLE BACANAMWO.

Cambodia: Benjamin-Vogelsdorff-Str., 13187 Berlin; tel. (30) 48637901; fax (30) 48637973; e-mail rec-berlin@t-online.de; internet www.kambodscha-botschaft.de; Ambassador WIDHYA CHEM.

Cameroon: Kurfürstendamm 136, 10711 Berlin; tel. (30) 89068090; fax (30) 890680929; e-mail berlin@ambacam.de; internet www.ambacam.de; Ambassador JEAN-MARC MPAY.

Canada: Leipziger Pl. 17, 10117 Berlin; tel. (30) 203120; fax (30) 20312590; e-mail berlin@international.gc.ca; internet www.canadainternational.gc.ca/germany-allemagne; Ambassador PETER M. BOEHM.

Cape Verde: Stavanger Str. 16, 10439 Berlin; tel. (30) 20450955; fax (30) 20450966; e-mail info@embassy-capeverde.de; internet www.embassy-capeverde.de; Ambassador JORGE HOMERO TOLENTINO ARAÚJO.

Chad: Lepsiusstr. 114, 12165 Berlin; tel. (30) 31991620; fax (30) 319916220; e-mail contact@ambatchadberlin.com; internet www.ambatchadberlin.com; Ambassador Dr HASSAN TCHONAI ELIMI.

Chile: Mohrenstr. 42, 10117 Berlin; tel. (30) 7262035; fax (30) 726203603; e-mail comunicaciones@echilealemania.de; internet www.embajadaconsuladoschile.de; Ambassador JORGE EDUARDO O'RYAN SCHÜTZ.

China, People's Republic: Märkisches Ufer 54, 10179 Berlin; tel. (30) 275880; fax (30) 27588221; internet www.china-botschaft.de; Ambassador WU HONGBO.

Colombia: Kurfürstenstr. 84, 5th Floor, 10787 Berlin; tel. (30) 2639610; fax (30) 26396125; e-mail info@botschaft-kolumbien.de; internet www.botschaft-kolumbien.de; Ambassador JUAN MAYR MALDONADO.

Congo, Democratic Republic: Im Meisengarten 133, 53179 Bonn; tel. and fax (228) 9349237; e-mail ambardc-rfa@t-online.de; Ambassador KAMANGA CLEMENTINE SHAKEMBO.

Congo, Republic: Grabbeallee 47, 13156 Berlin; tel. (30) 49400753; fax (30) 48479897; e-mail botschaftkongobzv@hotmail.de; Chargé d'affaires a.i. HENRI DIMI.

Costa Rica: Dessauer Str. 28–29, 10963 Berlin; tel. (30) 26398990; fax (30) 26557210; e-mail emb@botschaft-costarica.de; internet www.botschaft-costarica.de; Ambassador JOSÉ JOAQUÍN CHAVERRI SIEVERT.

Côte d'Ivoire: Schinkelstr. 10, 14193 Berlin; tel. (30) 8906960; fax (30) 890696206; e-mail contact@ambaci.de; internet www.ambaci.de; Ambassador HOUADJA LÉON ADOM KACOU.

Croatia: Ahornstr. 4, 10787 Berlin; tel. (30) 21915514; fax (30) 23628965; e-mail info@kroatische-botschaft.de; internet de.mfa.hr; Ambassador Dr MIRO KOVAČ.

Cuba: Stavangerstr. 20, 10439 Berlin; tel. (30) 44717319; fax (30) 9164553; e-mail embacuba-berlin@t-online.de; internet emba.cubaminrex.cu/alemania; Ambassador RAÚL BECERRA EGAÑA.

Cyprus: Wallstr. 27, 10179 Berlin; tel. (30) 3086830; fax (30) 27591454; e-mail info@botschaft-zypern.de; internet www.botschaft-zypern.de; Chargé d'affaires a.i. ELENA RAFTI.

Czech Republic: Wilhelmstr. 44, 10117 Berlin; tel. (30) 226380; fax (30) 2294033; e-mail berlin@embassy.mzv.cz; internet www.mzv.cz/berlin; Ambassador RUDOLF JINDRÁK.

Denmark: Rauchstr. 1, 10787 Berlin; tel. (30) 50502000; fax (30) 50502050; e-mail beramb@um.dk; internet www.tyskland.um.dk; Ambassador PER POULSEN-HANSEN.

Dominican Republic: Dessauer Str. 28–29, 10963 Berlin; tel. (30) 25757760; fax (30) 25757761; e-mail info@embajadadominicana.de; Ambassador GABRIEL RAFAEL CALVENTI.

Ecuador: Joachimstaler Str. 10–12, 10719 Berlin; tel. (30) 8009695; fax (30) 800969699; e-mail alemania@embassy-ecuador.org; Ambassador JORGE ENRIQUE JURADO MOSQUERA.

Egypt: Stauffenbergstr. 6–7, 10785 Berlin; tel. (30) 4775470; fax (30) 4771049; e-mail embassy@egyptian-embassy.de; internet www.egyptian-embassy.de; Ambassador RAMZY EZZ EL-DIN RAMZY.

El Salvador: Joachim-Karnatz-Allee 47, 10557 Berlin; tel. (30) 2064660; fax (30) 22488244; e-mail embasalvarfa@googlemail.com; internet www.botschaft-elsalvador.de; Ambassador ANITA CRISTINA ESCHER ECHEVERRÍA.

Equatorial Guinea: Rohlfsstr. 17–19, 14195 Berlin; tel. (30) 88663877; fax (30) 88663879; e-mail botschaft@guinea-ecuatorial.de; internet www.botschaft-aequatorialguinea.de; Ambassador CÁNDIDO MUATETEMA RIVAS.

Eritrea: Stavangerstr. 18, 10439 Berlin; tel. (30) 4467460; fax (30) 44674621; e-mail embassyeritrea@t-online.de; internet www.botschaft-eritrea.de; Ambassador PETROS TSEGGAI ASGHEDOM.

Estonia: Hildebrandstr. 5, 10785 Berlin; tel. (30) 25460602; fax (30) 25460601; e-mail embassy.berlin@mfa.ee; internet www.estemb.de; Ambassador WILLIAM MART LAANEMÄE.

Ethiopia: Boothstr. 20A, 12207 Berlin; tel. (30) 772060; fax (30) 7720626; e-mail emb.ethiopia@t-online.de; internet www.aethiopien-botschaft.de; Ambassador FESSEHA ASGHEDOM TESSEMA.

Finland: Rauchstr. 1, 10787 Berlin; tel. (30) 505030; fax (30) 50503333; e-mail sanomat.ber@formin.fi; internet www.finnland.de; Ambassador PÄIVI LUOSTARINEN.

France: Pariser Pl. 5, 10117 Berlin; tel. (30) 590039000; fax (30) 590039110; e-mail kanzlei@botschaft-frankreich.de; internet www.ambafrance-de.org; Ambassador MAURICE GOURDAULT-MONTAGNE.

Gabon: Hohensteinerstr. 16, 14197 Berlin; tel. (30) 89733440; fax (30) 89733444; e-mail botschaft@botschaft-gabun.de; internet www.botschaft-gabun.de; Ambassador JEAN-CLAUDE BOUYOBART.

Georgia: Heinrich-Mann-Str. 32, 13156 Berlin; tel. (30) 4849070; fax (30) 48490720; e-mail info@botschaftvongeorgien.de; Ambassador GABRIELA VON HABSBURG.

Ghana: Stavanger Str. 17 und 19, 10439 Berlin; tel. (30) 5471490; fax (30) 44674063; e-mail chancery@ghanaemberlin.de; internet www.ghanaemberlin.de; Ambassador PAUL KING ARYENE.

Greece: Jägerstr. 54–55, 10117 Berlin; tel. (30) 20612900; fax (30) 20450908; e-mail pressinfo@griechische-botschaft.de; internet www.griechenland-botschaft.de; Ambassador DIMITRIS RALLIS.

Guatemala: Joachim-Karnatz-Allee 45–47, 10557 Berlin; tel. (30) 2064363; fax (30) 20643659; e-mail embaguate.alemania@t-online.de; internet www.botschaft-guatemala.de; Ambassador CARLOS HUMBERTO JIMÉNEZ LICONA.

Guinea: Jägerstr. 67–69, 10117 Berlin; tel. (30) 20074330; fax (30) 200743333; e-mail berlin@ambaguinee.de; Ambassador Dr IBRAHIMA SORY SOW.

Haiti: Uhlandstr. 14, 10623 Berlin; tel. (30) 88555134; fax (30) 88554135; e-mail haibot@aol.com; Chargé d'Affaires a.i. EMMANUEL CHARLES.

Holy See: Lilienthalstr. 3A, 10965 Berlin; tel. (30) 616240; fax (30) 61624300; e-mail apostolische@nuntiatur.de; internet www2.nuntiatur.de; Apostolic Nuncio Most Rev. JEAN-CLAUDE PÉRISSET (Titular Archbishop of Iustiniana Prima).

Honduras: Cuxhavenerstr. 14, 10555 Berlin; tel. (30) 39749709; fax (30) 39749712; e-mail informacion@embahonduras.de; Ambassador EFRAÍN ANIBAL DÍAZ ARRIVILLAGA.

Hungary: Unter den Linden 76, 10117 Berlin; tel. (30) 203100; fax (30) 2291314; e-mail infober@kum.hu; internet www.mfa.gov.hu/kulkepviselet/de; Ambassador Dr JÓZSEF CZUKOR.

Iceland: Rauchstr. 1, 10787 Berlin; tel. (30) 50504000; fax (30) 50504300; e-mail infoberlin@mfa.is; internet www.botschaft-island.de; Ambassador GUNNAR SNORRI GUNNARSSON.

India: Tiergartenstr. 17, 10785 Berlin; tel. (30) 257950; fax (30) 25795102; e-mail infowing@indianembassy.de; internet www.indianembassy.de; Ambassador SUJATHA SINGH.

Indonesia: Lehrter Str. 16–17, 10557 Berlin; tel. (30) 478070; fax (30) 44737142; internet www.botschaft-indonesien.de; Ambassador EDDY PRATOMO.

Iran: Podbielskiallee 65–67, 14195 Berlin; tel. (30) 843530; fax (30) 54353535; e-mail iran.botschaft@t-online.de; internet berlin.mfa.gov.ir; Ambassador ALI REZA SHEIKH ATTAR.

Iraq: Riemeisterstr. 20, 14169 Berlin; tel. (30) 814880; fax (30) 81488222; e-mail info@iraqiembassy-berlin.de; internet www.iraqiembassy-berlin.de; Ambassador HUSSAIN MAHMOUD FADHLALLA.

Ireland: Jägerstr. 51, 10117 Berlin; tel. (30) 220720; fax (30) 22072299; e-mail berlin@dfa.ie; internet www.embassyofireland.de; Ambassador DANIEL GERARD MULHALL.

Israel: Auguste-Viktoria-Str. 74–76, 14193 Berlin; tel. (30) 89045500; fax (30) 89045309; e-mail botschaft@israel.de; internet www.israel.de; Ambassador YAKOV HADAS-HANDELSMAN.

Italy: Hiroshimastr. 1–7, 10785 Berlin; tel. (30) 254400; fax (30) 25440120; e-mail segreteria.berlino@esteri.it; internet www.ambberlino.esteri.it; Ambassador MICHELE VALENSISE.

Jamaica: Schmargendorfer Str. 32, 12159 Berlin; tel. (30) 85994511; fax (30) 85994540; e-mail info@jamador.de; internet www.jamador.de; Ambassador JOY ELFREDA WHEELER.

Japan: Hiroshimastr. 6, 10785 Berlin; tel. (30) 210940; fax (30) 21094228; e-mail info@botschaft-japan.de; internet www.de.emb-japan.go.jp; Ambassador TAKESHI NAKANE.

Jordan: Heerstr. 201, 13595 Berlin; tel. (30) 36996051; fax (30) 36996011; e-mail jordan@jordanembassy.de; internet www.jordanembassy.de; Ambassador MAZEN IZZEDDIN AL-TAL.

Kazakhstan: Nordendstr. 14–17, 13156 Berlin; tel. (30) 47007111; fax (30) 47007125; e-mail info@botschaft-kaz.de; internet www.botschaft-kasachstan.de; Ambassador NURLAN ONZHANOV.

Kenya: Markgrafenstr. 63, 10969 Berlin; tel. (30) 2592660; fax (30) 25926650; e-mail office@embassy-of-kenya.de; internet www.kenyaembassyberlin.de; Ambassador KENNEDY NYAUNCHO OSINDE.

Korea, Democratic People's Republic: Glinkastr. 5–7, 10117 Berlin; tel. (30) 20625990; fax (30) 22651929; e-mail info@dprkorea-emb.de; Ambassador RI SI-HONG.

Korea, Republic: Stülerstr. 8–10, 10787 Berlin; tel. (30) 260650; fax (30) 2606551; e-mail koremb-ge@mofat.go.kr; internet www.koreaemb.de; Ambassador MOON TAE-YOUNG.

Kosovo: Wallstr. 65, 10179 Berlin; tel. (30) 24047690; fax (30) 240476929; e-mail embassy.germany@ks-gov.net; Ambassador VILSON MIRDITA.

Kuwait: Griegstr. 5–7, 14193 Berlin; tel. (30) 8973000; fax (30) 89730010; e-mail info@kuwait-botschaft.de; internet www.kuwait-botschaft.de; Ambassador MUSAED RASHED AL-HAROUN.

Kyrgyzstan: Otto-Suhr-Allee 146, 10585 Berlin; tel. (30) 34781338; fax (30) 34781362; e-mail info@botschaft-kirgisien.de; internet www.botschaft-kirgisien.de; Ambassador BOLOT OTUNBAEV.

Laos: Bismarckallee 2A, 14193 Berlin; tel. (30) 89060647; fax (30) 89060648; Ambassador KHAMVONE PHANOUVONG.

Latvia: Reinerzstr. 40–41, 14193 Berlin; tel. (30) 82600222; fax (30) 82600233; e-mail embassy.germany@mfa.gov.lv; internet www.mfa.gov.lv/berlin; Ambassador ILGVARS KLAVA.

Lebanon: Berliner Str. 127, 13187 Berlin; tel. (30) 4749860; fax (30) 47487858; e-mail lubnan@t-online.de; internet www.libanesische-botschaft.info; Ambassador RAMEZ DIMECHKIÉ.

Lesotho: Kurfürstenstr. 84, 10787 Berlin; tel. (30) 2575720; fax (30) 25757222; e-mail embleso@yahoo.com; Ambassador Dr MAKASE NYAPHISI.

Liberia: Kurfürstenstr. 84, 10787 Berlin; tel. (30) 26391194; fax (30) 26394893; e-mail info@liberiaembassygermany.de; internet www.liberiaembassygermany.de; Ambassador ETHEL DAVIES.

Libya: Podbielskiallee 42, 14195 Berlin; tel. (30) 2005960; fax (30) 20059699; e-mail info@libysche-botschaft.de; internet www.libysche-botschaft.de; Chargé d'Affaires a.i. ALI MASEDNAH AL-KHOTANY.

Liechtenstein: Mohrenstr. 42, 10117 Berlin; tel. (30) 52000630; fax (30) 52000631; e-mail vertretung@ber.llv.li; Ambassador Prince STEFAN OF LIECHTENSTEIN.

Lithuania: Charitéstr. 9, 10117 Berlin; tel. (30) 8906810; fax (30) 89068115; e-mail info@botschaft-litauen.de; internet de.mfa.lt; Ambassador MINDAUGAS BUTKUS.

Luxembourg: Klingelhöfer Str. 7, 10785 Berlin; tel. (30) 2639570; fax (30) 26395727; e-mail berlin.amb@mae.etat.lu; Ambassador MARTINE SCHOMMER.

Macedonia, former Yugoslav republic: Koenigsallee 2–4, 14193 Berlin; tel. (30) 89069522; fax (30) 89541194; e-mail berlin@mfa.gov.mk; Ambassador KORNELIJA UTEVSKA-GLIGOROVSKA.

Madagascar: Seepromenade 92, 14612 Falkensee (Brandenburg); tel. (3322) 23140; fax (3322) 231429; e-mail info@botschaft-madagaskar.de; internet www.botschaft-madagaskar.de; Ambassador ALPHONSE SEM RALISON.

Malawi: Westfälische Str. 86, 10709 Berlin; tel. (30) 8431540; fax (30) 84315430; e-mail malawiberlin@aol.com; internet www.malawi-berlin.com; Ambassador ISSAC CHIKWEKWERE LAMBA.

Malaysia: Klingelhöferstr. 6, 10785 Berlin; tel. (30) 8857490; fax (30) 88574950; e-mail mwberlin@malemb.de; internet www.malemb.de; Ambassador IBRAHIM BIN ABDULLAH.

Mali: Kurfürstendamm 72, 10709 Berlin; tel. (30) 3199883; fax (30) 31998848; e-mail ambmali@1019freenet.de; internet www.ambassade-mali-berlin.de; Ambassador FATOUMATA SIRE DIAKITE.

Malta: Klingelhöfer Str. 7, 10785 Berlin; tel. (30) 2639110; fax (30) 26391123; e-mail maltaembassy.berlin@gov.mt; Ambassador CARL (CHARLES) XUEREB.

Mauritania: Kommandantenstr. 80, 10117 Berlin; tel. (30) 2065883; fax (30) 20674750; e-mail ambarim.berlin@gmx.de; Ambassador OULD MOHAMED M'BARECK BEBBE.

Mauritius: Kurfürstenstr. 84, 10787 Berlin; tel. (30) 2639360; fax (30) 26558323; e-mail berlin@mauritius-embassy.de; internet www.mauritius-embassy.de; Ambassador SAROJINI SEENEEVASSEN.

Mexico: Klingelhöferstr. 3, 10785 Berlin; tel. (30) 2693230; fax (30) 269323700; e-mail mail@mexale.de; internet embamex.sre.gob.mx/alemania; Ambassador FRANCISCO GONZÁLEZ DÍAZ.

Moldova: Gotlandstr. 16, 10439 Berlin; tel. (30) 44652970; fax (30) 44652972; e-mail office@botschaft-moldau.de; internet www.botschaft-moldau.de; Ambassador AURELIU CIOCOI.

Monaco: Klingelhöferstr. 7, 10785 Berlin; tel. (30) 2639033; fax (30) 2690344; e-mail ambassademonaco@aol.com; Ambassador CLAUDE JOËL GIORDAN.

Mongolia: Dietzgenstr. 31, 13156 Berlin; tel. (30) 4748060; fax (30) 47480616; e-mail mongolbot@aol.com; internet www.botschaft-mongolei.de; Ambassador BALDORJ DAVAADORJ.

Montenegro: Dessauer Str. 28–29, 2nd Floor, 10963 Berlin; tel. (30) 51651070; fax (30) 516510712; e-mail germany@mfa.gov.me; Ambassador VLADIMIR RADULOVIĆ.

Morocco: Niederwallstr. 39, 10117 Berlin; tel. (30) 2061240; fax (30) 20612420; e-mail kontakt@botschaft-marokko.de; internet www.maec.gov.ma/berlin; Ambassador Dr OMAR ZNIBER.

Mozambique: Stromstr. 47, 10551 Berlin; tel. (30) 39876500; fax (30) 39876503; e-mail info@embassy-of-mozambique.de; Ambassador AMADEU PAULO SAMUEL DA CONCEIÇÃO.

Myanmar: Thielallee 19, 14195 Berlin; tel. (30) 2061570; fax (30) 20615720; e-mail info@botschaft-myanmar.de; internet www.botschaft-myanmar.de; Ambassador U TIN WIN.

Namibia: Reichsstr. 17, 14052 Berlin; tel. (30) 2540950; fax (30) 25409555; e-mail namibiaberlin@aol.com; internet www.namibia-botschaft.de; Ambassador NEVILLE MELVIN GERTZE.

Nepal: Guerickestr. 27, 2nd Floor, 10587 Berlin; tel. (30) 34359920; fax (30) 34359906; e-mail neberlin@t-online.de; internet www.nepalembassy-germany.com; Ambassador SURESH PRASAD PRADHAN.

Netherlands: Klosterstr. 50, 10179 Berlin; tel. (30) 209560; fax (30) 20956441; e-mail nlgovbln@bln.nlamb.de; internet www.niederlandeweb.de; Ambassador MARNIX KROP.

New Zealand: Atrium, Friedrichstr. 60, 10117 Berlin; tel. (30) 206210; fax (30) 20621114; e-mail nzembber@infoem.org; internet www.nzembassy.com/germany; Ambassador PETER HOWARD RIDER.

Nicaragua: Joachim-Karnatz-Allee 45, 10557 Berlin; tel. (30) 2064380; fax (30) 22487891; e-mail embajada.berlin@embanic.de; Chargé d'affaires a.i. KARLA LUZETTE BETETA BRENES.

Niger: Machnower Str. 24, 14165 Berlin; tel. (30) 80589660; fax (30) 80589662; e-mail ambaniger@t-online.de; Ambassador AMINATOU GAOH.

Nigeria: Neue Jakobstr. 4, 10179 Berlin; tel. (30) 212300; fax (30) 21230212; e-mail info@nigeriaembassygermany.org; internet www.nigeriaembassygermany.org; Ambassador ABDU USMAN ABUBAKAR.

Norway: Rauchstr. 1, 10787 Berlin; tel. (30) 505050; fax (30) 505055; e-mail emb.berlin@mfa.no; internet www.norwegen.no; Ambassador SVEN ERIK SVEDMAN.

Oman: Clayallee 82, 14195 Berlin; tel. (30) 8100510; fax (30) 81005199; Ambassador Dr ZAINAB BINT ALI BIN SAID AL-QASIMIYAH.

Pakistan: Schaperstr. 29, 10719 Berlin; tel. (30) 21244299; fax (30) 21244499; e-mail mail@pakemb.de; internet www.pakemb.de; Chargé d'affaires a.i. MAZHAR JAVED.

Panama: Wichmannstr 6, 10787 Berlin; tel. (30) 22605811; fax (30) 22605812; e-mail info@botschaft-panama.de; internet www.botschaft-panama.de; Ambassador JAVIER HELMUT CALVO QUIROS.

Paraguay: Hardenbergstr. 12, 10623 Berlin; tel. (30) 3199860; fax (30) 31998617; e-mail consulado@embapar.de; Ambassador RAUL ALBERTO FLORENTIN ANTOLA.

Peru: Mohrenstr. 42, 10117 Berlin; tel. (30) 2064103; fax (30) 20641077; e-mail info@embaperu.de; internet www.botschaft-peru.de; Ambassador JOSÉ ANTONIO MEIER ESPINOSA.

Philippines: Uhlandstr. 97, 10715 Berlin; tel. (30) 8649500; fax (30) 8732551; e-mail info@philippine-embassy.de; internet www.philippine-embassy.de; Ambassador MARIA CLEOFE NATIVIDAD.

Poland: Lassenstr. 19–21, 14193 Berlin; tel. (30) 223130; fax (30) 2213155; e-mail info@botschaft-polen.de; internet www.berlin.polemb.net; Ambassador Dr MAREK WŁADYSŁAW PRAWDA.

Portugal: Zimmerstr. 56, 10117 Berlin; tel. (30) 590063500; fax (30) 590063600; e-mail mail@botschaftportugal.de; internet www.botschaftportugal.de; Ambassador LUÍS DE ALMEIDA SAMPAIO.

Qatar: Hagenstr. 56, 14193 Berlin; tel. (30) 862060; fax (30) 86206150; e-mail berlin@mofa.gov.qa; Ambassador ABD AL-RAHMAN MUHAMMAD AL-KHULAIFI.

Romania: Dorotheenstr. 62–66, 10117 Berlin; tel. (30) 21239202; fax (30) 21239399; e-mail office@rumaenische-botschaft.de; internet berlin.mae.ro; Ambassador Dr LAZĂR COMĂNESCU.

Russia: Unter den Linden 63–65, 10117 Berlin; tel. (30) 2291110; fax (30) 2299397; e-mail info@russische-botschaft.de; internet www.russische-botschaft.de; Ambassador VLADIMIR M. GRININ.

Rwanda: Jägerstr. 67–69, 10117 Berlin; tel. (30) 20916590; fax (30) 209165959; e-mail info@rwanda-botschaft.de; internet www.rwanda-botschaft.de; Ambassador CHRISTINE NKULIKIYINKA.

Saudi Arabia: Tiergartenstr. 33–34, 10785 Berlin; tel. (30) 8892500; fax (30) 88925179; Ambassador Prof. Dr OSSAMA ABD AL-MAJID ALI SHOBOKSHI.

Senegal: Dessauerstr. 28–29, 10963 Berlin; tel. (30) 8562190; fax (30) 85621921; internet www.botschaft-senegal.de; Ambassador HENRI ANTOINE TURPIN.

Serbia: Taubertstr. 18, 14193 Berlin; tel. (30) 8957700; fax (30) 8252206; e-mail info@botschaft-smg.de; internet berlin.mfa.rs; Ambassador Prof. Dr IVO VISKOVIĆ.

Sierra Leone: Herwarthstr. 4, 12207 Berlin; tel. (30) 77205850; fax (30) 772058529; e-mail slembassybonn@hotmail.com; internet www.slembassy-germany.org; Ambassador JONGOPIE SIAKA STEVENS.

Singapore: Friedrichstr. 200, 10117 Berlin; tel. (30) 2263430; fax (30) 22634355; e-mail singemb_ber@sgmfa.gov.sg; internet www.singapore-embassy.de; Ambassador JACKY FOO KONG SENG.

Slovakia: Hildebrandstr. 25, 10785 Berlin; tel. (30) 88926200; fax (30) 88926222; e-mail emb.berlin@mzv.sk; internet www.mzv.sk/berlin; Ambassador IGOR SLOBODNÍK.

Slovenia: Hausvogteipl. 3–4, 10117 Berlin; tel. (30) 2061450; fax (30) 20614570; e-mail vbn@gov.si; internet berlin.veleposlanistvo.si; Ambassador MITJA DROBNIČ.

Somalia: Heilmanring 10, 13627 Berlin; tel. (30) 80201438; Ambassador MOHAMUD MOHAMED TIFOW.

South Africa: Tiergartenstr. 18, 10785 Berlin; tel. (30) 220730; fax (30) 22073190; e-mail berlin.info@foreign.gov.za; internet www.suedafrika.org; Ambassador MAKHENKESI ARNOLD STOFILE.

Spain: Lichtensteinallee 1, 10787 Berlin; tel. (30) 2540070; fax (30) 25799557; e-mail emb.berlin.inf@maec.es; internet www.maec.es/subwebs/embajadas/berlin; Ambassador RAFAEL DEZCALLAR DE MAZARREDO.

Sri Lanka: Niklasstr. 19, 14163 Berlin; tel. (30) 80909749; fax (30) 80909757; e-mail info@srilanka-botschaft.de; internet www.srilanka-botschaft.de; Ambassador UPALI SARRATH KONGAHAGE.

Sudan: Kurfürstendamm 151, 10709 Berlin; tel. (30) 8906980; fax (30) 89409693; e-mail poststelle@sudan-embassy.de; internet www.sudan-embassy.de; Ambassador Dr BAHA AD-DIN HANAFI MANSOUR WAHEESH.

Sweden: Rauchstr. 1, 10787 Berlin; tel. (30) 505060; fax (30) 50506789; e-mail ambassaden.berlin@foreign.ministry.se; internet www.swedenabroad.com/berlin; Ambassador STAFFAN CARLSSON.

Switzerland: Otto-von-Bismarck-Allee 4A, 10557 Berlin; tel. (30) 3904000; fax (30) 3911030; e-mail ber.vertretung@eda.admin.ch; internet www.eda.admin.ch/berlin; Ambassador Dr URS CHRISTIAN TIMOTHEUS GULDIMANN.

Syria: Rauchstr. 25, 10787 Berlin; tel. (30) 501770; fax (30) 50177311; e-mail info@syrianembassy.de; internet www.syrianembassy.de; Ambassador RADWAN LOUTFI.

Tajikistan: Perleberger Str. 43, 10559 Berlin; tel. (30) 3479300; fax (30) 34793029; e-mail info@botschaft-tadschikistan.de; Ambassador IMOMUDIN M. SATTOROV.

Tanzania: Eschenallee 11, 14050 Berlin; tel. (30) 3030800; fax (30) 30308020; e-mail info@tanzania-gov.de; internet www.tanzania-gov.de; Ambassador AHMADA RWEYEMAMU NGEMERA.

Thailand: Lepsiusstr. 64–66, 12163 Berlin; tel. (30) 794810; fax (30) 79481511; e-mail general@thaiembassy.de; internet www.thaiembassy.de; Ambassador CHARIVAT SANTAPUTRA.

Togo: Grabbeallee 43, 13156 Berlin; tel. (30) 49908968; fax (30) 49908967; e-mail info@botschaft-togo.de; internet www.botschaft-togo.de; Ambassador ESSOHANAM COMLA PAKA.

Tunisia: Lindenallee 16, 14050 Berlin; tel. (30) 3641070; fax (30) 30820683; Ambassador ELYES GHARIANI.

Turkey: Rungestr. 9, 10179 Berlin; tel. (30) 275850; fax (30) 27590915; e-mail info@tuerkischebotschaft.de; internet www.tuerkischebotschaft.de; Ambassador HÜSEYIN AVNI KARSLIOĞLU.

Turkmenistan: Langobardenallee 14, 14052 Berlin; tel. (30) 30102452; fax (30) 30102453; Ambassador BERDYMURAT REDJEPOV.

Uganda: Axel-Springer-Str. 54A, 10117 Berlin; tel. (30) 24047556; fax (30) 24047557; e-mail ugembassy@yahoo.de; Ambassador FRANCIS KAMUJANDUZI BUTAGIRA.

Ukraine: Albrechtstr. 26, 10117 Berlin; tel. (30) 288870; fax (30) 28887163; e-mail ukremb@ukrainishe-botschaft.de; internet www.mfa.gov.ua/germany; Ambassador NATALIA ZARUDNA.

United Arab Emirates: Hiroshimastr. 18–20, 10787 Berlin; tel. (30) 516516; fax (30) 51651900; e-mail uae@uaeembassy.de; internet www.uae-embassy.de; Ambassador MUHAMMAD AHMAD AL-MAHMUD.

United Kingdom: Wilhelmstr. 70–71, 10117 Berlin; tel. (30) 204570; e-mail ukingermany@fco.gov.uk; internet ukingermany.fco.gov.uk; Ambassador SIMON MCDONALD.

USA: Clayallee 170, Pariser Pl. 2, 14191 Berlin; tel. (30) 2385174; fax (30) 83051215; internet germany.usembassy.gov; Ambassador PHILLIP D. MURPHY.

Uruguay: Budapester Str. 39, 10787 Berlin; tel. (30) 2639016; fax (30) 26390170; e-mail urubrande@t-online.de; Chargé d'Affaires a.i. CONRADO SILVEIRA RODRIGUEZ.

Uzbekistan: Perleberger Str. 62, 10559 Berlin; tel. (30) 3940980; fax (30) 39409862; e-mail botschaft@uzbekistan.de; internet www.uzbekistan.de; Ambassador DILSHOD AKHATOV.

Venezuela: Schillstr. 9–10, 10785 Berlin; tel. (30) 8322400; fax (30) 83224020; e-mail embavenez.berlin@botschaft-venezuela.de; internet www.botschaft-venezuela.de; Chargé d'affaires a.i. CARLOS ALBERTO QUERALES RIVERO.

Viet Nam: Elsenstr. 3, 12435 Berlin; tel. (30) 53630108; fax (30) 53630200; e-mail info@vietnambotschaft.org; internet www.vietnambotschaft.org; Ambassador DO HOA BINH.

Yemen: Budapester Str. 37, 10787 Berlin; tel. (30) 8973050; fax (30) 89730562; e-mail info@botschaft-jemen.de; internet www.botschaft-jemen.de; Chargé d'Affaires a.i. Dr GAMAL OMAR HASSAN AL-AKBARI.

Zambia: Axel-Springer-Str. 54A, 10117 Berlin; tel. (30) 2062940; fax (30) 20629419; e-mail info@zambiaembassy.de; internet www.zambiaembassy.de; Chargé d'Affaires a.i. EVANS KIWA CHENGETA.

Zimbabwe: Kommandantenstr. 80, 10117 Berlin; tel. (30) 2062263; fax (30) 20455062; e-mail zimberlin@t-online.de; Ambassador HEBSON MAKUVISE.

Judicial System

Justice is administered in accordance with the federal structure through the courts of the Federation and the *Länder*, as well as the Federal Constitutional Court and the Constitutional Courts of the *Länder*. Judges are independent and responsible to the law. They are not removable except by the decision of a court. One-half of the judges of the Federal Constitutional Court are elected by the Bundestag and the other half by the Bundesrat. A committee for the selection of judges participates in the appointment of judges of the Superior Federal Courts.

FEDERAL CONSTITUTIONAL COURT

Bundesverfassungsgericht

Postfach 1771, 76006 Karlsruhe; Schlossbezirk 3, 76131 Karlsruhe; tel. (721) 91010; fax (721) 9101382; e-mail bverfg@bundesverfassungsgericht.de; internet www.bundesverfassungsgericht.de.

President: Prof. Dr ANDREAS VOSSKUHLE.

Vice-President: Prof. Dr FERDINAND KIRCHHOF.

Judges of the First Senate: Prof. Dr FERDINAND KIRCHHOF, Prof. Dr REINHARD GAIER, Prof. Dr MICHAEL EICHBERGER, WILHELM SCHLUCKEBIER, Prof. Dr JOHANNES MASING, Prof. Dr ANDREAS L. PAULUS, Prof. Dr SUSANNE BAER, Prof. Dr GABRIELE BRITZ.

Judges of the Second Senate: Prof. Dr ANDREAS VOSSKUHLE, Prof. Dr GERTRUDE LÜBBE-WOLFF, Dr MICHAEL GERHARDT, Prof. HERBERT LANDAU, Prof. Dr PETER HUBER, PETER MÜLLER, MONIKA HERMANNS, Dr SIBYLLE KESSAL-WULF.

SUPERIOR FEDERAL COURTS

Bundesarbeitsgericht (Federal Labour Court)

Hugo-Preuss-Pl. 1, 99084 Erfurt; tel. (361) 26360; fax (361) 26362000; internet www.bundesarbeitsgericht.de.

President: INGRID SCHMIDT.

Vice-President: Dr RUDI MÜLLER-GLÖGE.

Bundesgerichtshof (Federal Court of Justice)

Herrenstr. 45A, 76133 Karlsruhe; tel. (721) 1590; fax (721) 1592512; e-mail poststelle@bgh.bund.de; internet www.bundesgerichtshof.de.

President: Prof. Dr KLAUS TOLKSDORF.

Vice-President: WOLFGANG SCHLICK.

Presidents of the Senate: Prof. Dr JOACHIM BORNKAMM, Prof. Dr WULF GOETTE, WILFRIED TERNO, Prof. Dr WOLFGANG KRÜGER, Prof. Dr ROLF KNIFFKA, WOLFGANG BALL, Dr GERHARD GANTER, Dr FLOCK, ULRICH WIECHERS, Dr MEO-MICAELA HAHNE, ARMIN NACK, Dr ERNEMANN, Dr RUTH RISSING-VAN SAAN, CLEMENS BASDORF, JÖRG-PETER BECKER.

Federal Prosecutor-General: HARALD RANGE.

Bundessozialgericht (Federal Social Court)

Graf-Bernadotte-Pl. 5, 34119 Kassel; tel. (561) 31071; fax (561) 3107475; e-mail pressestelle@bsg.bund.de; internet www.bsg.bund.de.

President: PETER MASUCH.

Vice-President: Dr RUTH WETZEL-STEINWEDEL.

Bundesverwaltungsgericht (Federal Administrative Court)

Postfach 100854, 04008 Leipzig; Simsonpl. 1, 04107 Leipzig; tel. (341) 20070; fax (341) 20071000; e-mail pressestelle@bverwg.bund.de; internet www.bverwg.de.

President: Dr MARION ECKERTZ-HÖFER.

Vice-President: (vacant).

Presidents of the Senate: KLEY, Prof. Dr RUBEL, VORMEIER, NEUMANN, SAILER, Prof. Dr RENNERT, BIER, Prof. Dr BERLIT.

Bundesfinanzhof (Federal Financial Court)

Postfach 860240, 81629 München; Ismaninger Str. 109, 81675 München; tel. (89) 92310; fax (89) 9231201; e-mail bundesfinanzhof@bfh.bund.de; internet www.bundesfinanzhof.de.

President: Prof. Dr RUDOLF MELLINGHOFF.

Vice-President: HERMANN-ULRICH VISKORF.

Presidents of the Senate: HEIDE BOEKER, Prof. Dr FRANZ DÖTSCH, Prof. Dr DIETMAR GOSCH, MONIKA VÖLLMEKE, Dr KLAUS-PETER MÜLLER-EISELT, Prof. Dr HANS-JOACHIM KANZLER, Prof. Dr HEINRICH WEBER-GRELLET, Dr SUSE MARTIN, Prof. Dr PEZZER.

Religion

CHRISTIANITY

Arbeitsgemeinschaft Christlicher Kirchen in Deutschland (Council of Christian Churches in Germany): Postfach 900617, 60446 Frankfurt a.M.; Ludolfusstr. 2–4, 60487 Frankfurt a.M.; tel. (69) 2470270; fax (69) 24702730; e-mail info@ack-oec.de; internet www.oekumene-ack.de; 20 affiliated Churches, including the Roman Catholic Church and the Orthodox Church in Germany.

The Roman Catholic Church

Germany comprises seven archdioceses and 20 dioceses. At 31 December 2006 there were an estimated 25,660,563 adherents (about 31.2% of the population).

Bishops' Conference

Deutsche Bischofskonferenz, Postfach 2962, 53019 Bonn; Kaiserstr. 161, 53113 Bonn; tel. (228) 1030; fax (228) 103299; e-mail pressestelle@dbk.de; internet www.dbk.de; Pres. Dr ROBERT ZOLLITSCH (Archbishop of Freiburg im Breisgau); Sec. Dr HANS LANGENDÖRFER.

Archbishop of Bamberg: Prof. Dr LUDWIG SCHICK, Dompl. 3, 96049 Bamberg; tel. (951) 5020; fax (951) 502250.

Archbishop of Berlin: RAINER MARIA WOELKI, Postfach 040856, 10064 Berlin; Niederwallstr. 8–9, 10117 Berlin; tel. (30) 326840; fax (30) 32684276.

Archbishop of Freiburg im Breisgau: Dr ROBERT ZOLLITSCH, Schoferstr. 2, 79098 Freiburg i. Br.; tel. (761) 2188243; fax (761) 2188427; e-mail erzbischof@ordinariat-freiburg.de; internet www.erzbistum-freiburg.de.

Archbishop of Hamburg: Dr WERNER THISSEN, Postfach 101925, 20013 Hamburg; Danzigerstr. 52A, 20099 Hamburg; tel. (40) 24877100; fax (40) 24877233; e-mail pforte@egv-erzbistum-hh.de; internet www.erzbistum-hamburg.de.

Archbishop of Köln (Cologne): Cardinal Dr JOACHIM MEISNER, Marzellenstr. 32, 50668 Köln; tel. (221) 16420; fax (221) 16421700; e-mail info@erzbistum-koeln.de; internet www.erzbistum-koeln.de.

Archbishop of München (Munich) and Freising: Cardinal Dr REINHARD MARX, Postfach 100551, 80079 München; Rochsusstr. 5–7, 80333 München; tel. (89) 21370; fax (89) 21371585; e-mail pressestelle@erzbistum-muenchen.de; internet www.erzbistum-muenchen.de.

Archbishop of Paderborn: HANS-JOSEF BECKER, Erzbischöfliches Generalvikariat, Dompl. 3, 33098 Paderborn; tel. (5251) 1251287; fax (5251) 1251470; e-mail info@erzbistum-paderborn.de; internet www.erzbistum-paderborn.de.

Commissariat of German Bishops—Catholic Office: Postfach 040660, 10063 Berlin; Hannoversche Str. 5, 10115 Berlin; tel. (30) 288780; fax (30) 28878108; e-mail post@kath-buero.de; internet www.kath-buero.de; represents the German Conference of Bishops before the Federal Govt and international institutions on political issues; Leader Prelate Dr KARL JÜSTEN.

Central Committee of German Catholics (ZdK): Postfach 40141, 53175 Bonn; Hochkreuzallee 246, 53175 Bonn; tel. (228) 382970; fax (228) 3829744; e-mail info@zdk.de; internet www.zdk.de; f. 1868; represents Catholic laymen and lay-organizations in Germany; Pres. ALOIS GLÜCK; Gen. Sec. Dr STEFAN VESPER.

The Evangelical (Protestant) Church

In 2006 the Evangelische Kirche in Deutschland, which includes the Lutheran, Uniate and Reformed Protestant Churches, had some 25m. members, amounting to about 30.5% of the population.

Evangelische Kirche in Deutschland (EKD) (Evangelical Church in Germany): Herrenhäuser Str. 12, 30419 Hannover; tel. (511) 27960; fax (511) 2796707; e-mail presse@ekd.de; internet www.ekd.de; the governing bodies of the EKD are its Synod of 120 clergy and lay members, which meets at regular intervals, the Conference of member churches, and the Council, composed of 15 elected members; the EKD has an ecclesiastical secretariat of its own (the Evangelical Church Office), including a special office for foreign relations; Chair. of the Council NIKOLAUS SCHNEIDER.

Synod of the EKD: Herrenhäuser Str. 12, 30419 Hannover; tel. (511) 2796114; fax (511) 2796707; e-mail synode@ekd.de; Pres. KATRIN GÖRING-ECKARDT.

Deutscher Evangelischer Kirchentag (German Evangelical Church Convention): Postfach 1555, 36005 Fulda; Magdeburger Str. 59, 36037 Fulda; tel. (661) 969500; fax (661) 9695090; e-mail fulda@kirchentag.de; internet www.kirchentag.de; Pres. KATRIN GÖRING-ECKARDT; Gen. Sec. Dr ELLEN UEBERSCHÄR.

Churches and Federations within the EKD:

Reformierter Bund (Reformed Alliance): Knochenhauerstr. 33, 30159 Hannover; tel. (511) 1241808; fax (511) 1241811; e-mail info@reformierter-bund.de; internet www.reformierter-bund.de; f. 1884; unites the Reformed Territorial Churches and Congregations of Germany (with an estimated 2m. mems). The central body of the Reformed League is the 'Moderamen', the elected representation of the various Reformed Churches and Congregations; Moderator Rev. PETER BUKOWSKI; Gen. Sec. Rev. JÖRG SCHMIDT.

Union Evangelischer Kirchen in der EKD (UEK): Herrenhäuser Str. 12, 30419 Hannover; tel. (511) 2796529; fax (511) 2796717; e-mail postfach@uek-online.de; internet www.uek-online.de; f. 2003 by merger of Arnoldshainer Konferenz and Evangelische Kirche der Union; union of 13 regional churches (10 United, two Reformed and one Lutheran) with approx. 13.4m. mems; promotes unity among churches in the EKD; Chair. Bishop Dr ULRICH FISCHER (Evangelical Church of Baden); Vice-Chair. CHRISTIAN DRÄGERT (Evangelical Church in the Rhineland), BRIGITTE ANDRAE (Evangelical Church in Central Germany).

Bremen Evangelical Church: Franziuseck 2–4, 28199 Bremen; tel. (421) 55970; fax (421) 5597265; e-mail kirchenkanzlei@kirche-bremen.de; internet www.kirche-bremen.de; Pres. BRIGITTE BOEHME.

Church of Lippe: Postfach 2153, 32711 Detmold; Leopoldstr. 27, 32756 Detmold; tel. (5231) 97660; fax (5231) 976850; e-mail lka@lippische-landeskirche.de; internet www.lippische-landeskirche.de; Supt Dr MARTIN DUTZMANN.

Evangelical Church in Baden: Blumenstr. 1, 76133 Karlsruhe; tel. (721) 91750; fax (721) 9175553; e-mail info@ekiba.de; internet www.ekiba.de; Bishop Dr ULRICH FISCHER.

Evangelical Church in Berlin-Brandenburg-schlesiche Oberlausitz: Georgenkirchstr. 69, 10249 Berlin; tel. (30) 2434400; fax (30) 24344500; e-mail info@ekbo.de; internet www.ekbo.de; Bishop Dr MARKUS DRÖGE.

Evangelical Church in Hessen and Nassau: Pauluspl. 1, 64285 Darmstadt; tel. (6151) 4050; fax (6151) 405220; e-mail info@ekhn.de; internet www.ekhn.de; Pres. Dr VOLKER JUNG.

Evangelical Church in the Rhineland: Postfach 300339, 40403 Düsseldorf; Hans-Böckler-Str. 7, 40476 Düsseldorf; tel. (211) 45620; fax (211) 4562490; e-mail pressestelle@ekir.de; internet www.ekir.de; Pres. NIKOLAUS SCHNEIDER.

Evangelical Church of Kurhessen-Waldeck: Postfach 410260, 34114 Kassel-Wilhelmshöhe; Wilhelmshöher Allee 330, 34131 Kassel; tel. (561) 93780; fax (561) 9378400; e-mail landeskirchenamt@ekkw.de; internet www.ekkw.de; Bishop Prof. Dr MARTIN HEIN.

Evangelical Church of the Palatinate: Dompl. 5, 67346 Speyer; tel. (6232) 6670; fax (6232) 667480; e-mail landeskirchenrat@evkirchepfalz.de; internet www.evpfalz.de; Pres. CHRISTIAN SCHAD.

Evangelical Church of Westfalen: Altstädter Kirchpl. 5, 33602 Bielefeld; tel. (521) 5940; fax (521) 594129; e-mail landeskirchenamt@lka.ekvw.de; internet www.ekvw.de; Pres. ALFRED BUSS.

Evangelical-Lutheran Church in Central Germany: Am Dom 2, 39104 Magdeburg; tel. (391) 5346225; fax (391) 5346226; e-mail ilse.junkermann@ekmd.de; internet www.ekmd.de; 858,453 mems; Bishop ILSE JUNKERMANN.

Vereinigte Evangelisch-Lutherische Kirche Deutschlands (VELKD) (The United Evangelical-Lutheran Church of Germany): Postfach 210220, 30419 Hannover; Herrenhäuserstr. 12, 30419 Hannover; tel. (511) 2796526; fax (511) 2796182; e-mail zentrale@velkd.de; internet www.velkd.de; f. 1948; 10.4m. mems; unites all but 3 of the Lutheran territorial Churches within the Evangelical Church in Germany; Presiding Bishop Dr JOHANNES FRIEDRICH (Munich).

Evangelical-Lutheran Church in Bavaria: Katharina-von-Bora-Str. 11, 80333 München; tel. (89) 55950; fax (89) 5595666; e-mail landesbischof@elkb.de; internet www.bayern-evangelisch.de; 2.6m. mems; Bishop Dr JOHANNES FRIEDRICH.

Evangelical-Lutheran Church in Braunschweig: Dietrich-Bonhoeffer-Str. 1, 38300 Wolfenbüttel; tel. (5331) 8020; fax (5331) 802707; e-mail info@lk-bs.de; internet www.landeskirche-braunschweig.de; Bishop Dr FRIEDRICH WEBER.

Evangelical-Lutheran Church of Hannover: Haarstr. 6, 30169 Hannover; tel. (511) 5635830; fax (511) 56358311; e-mail landesbischoefin@evlka.de; internet www.evlka.de; 2.8m. mems; Bishop RALF MEISTER.

Evangelical-Lutheran Church of North Elbe: Postfach 3449, 24033 Kiel; Dänische Str. 21–35, 24103 Kiel; tel. (431) 97975; fax (431) 9797655; e-mail info.nka@nordelbien.de; internet www.nordelbien.de; Chair. Rt Rev. GERHARD ULRICH (Schleswig and Holstein).

Evangelical-Lutheran Church of Schaumburg-Lippe: Herderstr. 27, 31665 Bückeburg; tel. (5722) 96017; fax (5722) 96028; e-mail lka@landeskirche-schaumberg-lippe.de; internet www.landeskirche-schaumburg-lippe.de; Bishop Dr KARL-HINRICH MANZKE.

Also affiliated to the EKD:

Evangelical-Lutheran Church in Oldenburg: Philosophenweg 1, 26121 Oldenburg; tel. (441) 77010; fax (441) 77012199; e-mail info@kirche-oldenburg.de; internet www.kirche-oldenburg.de; 446,899 mems; Bishop JAN JANSSEN.

Evangelical-Lutheran Church in Württemberg: Postfach 101342, 70012 Stuttgart; Augustenstr. 124, 70197 Stuttgart; tel. (711) 2227658; fax (711) 2227681; e-mail kontakt@elk-wue.de; internet www.elk-wue.de; Bishop FRANK OTFRIED JULY.

Evangelical-Lutheran Church of Mecklenburg: Münzstr. 8-10, Postfach 111063, 19010 Schwerin; tel. (385) 51850; fax (385) 5185170; e-mail okr@ellm.de; internet www.kirche-mv.de; 196,272 mems; Bishop Dr ANDREAS VON MALTZAHN.

Evangelical-Lutheran Church of Saxony: Rampische Str. 29, 01067 Dresden; tel. (351) 3105724; fax (351) 3400281; e-mail bischof@evlks.de; internet www.evlks.de; 784,706 mems; Bishop JOCHEN BOHL.

Evangelical-Reformed Church: Saarstr. 6, 26789 Leer; tel. (491) 91980; fax (491) 9198251; e-mail info@reformiert.de; internet www.reformiert.de; Pres. Rev. JANN SCHMIDT.

Herrnhuter Brüdergemeine/Europäisch-Festländische Brüder-Unität (European Continental Province of the Moravian Church): Badwasen 6, 73087 Bad Boll; tel. (7164) 94210; fax (7164) 942199; f. 1457; there are 25 congregations in Germany, Denmark, Estonia, Latvia, the Netherlands, Sweden, Albania and Switzerland, with approx. 18,000 mems; Chair. FRIEDER VOLLPRECHT.

Other Protestant Churches

Arbeitsgemeinschaft Mennonitischer Gemeinden in Deutschland (Association of Mennonite Congregations in Germany): Stauferstr. 43, 85051 Ingolstadt; tel. (841) 9008216; e-mail amg.frieder.boller@mennoniten.de; internet www.mennoniten.de; f. 1886; re-organized 1990; Chair. Pastor FRIEDER BOLLER.

Bund Evangelisch-Freikirchlicher Gemeinden in Deutschland K.d.ö.R. (Union of Evangelical Free Churches (Baptists) in Germany): Johann-Gerhard-Oncken-Str. 7, 14641 Wustermark; tel. (33234) 74105; fax (33234) 74199; e-mail befg@baptisten.de; internet www.baptisten.de; f. 1942; Pres. HARTMUT RIEMENSCHNEIDER; Gen. Sec. REGINA CLAAS.

Bund Freier evangelischer Gemeinden (Covenant of Free Evangelical Churches in Germany): Postfach 4005, 58426 Witten; Goltenkamp 4, 58452 Witten; tel. (2302) 9370; fax (2302) 93799; e-mail bund@feg.de; internet www.feg.de; f. 1854; Pres. ANSGAR HÖRSTING; Administrator KLAUS KANWISCHER; 39,500 mems.

Evangelisch-altreformierte Kirche von Niedersachsen (Evangelical Reformed Church of Lower Saxony): Hauptstr. 33 49824 Laar; tel. (5947) 242; e-mail beukel@ewetel.net; f. 1838; Sec. Rev. Dr GERRIT JAN BEUKER.

Evangelisch-methodistische Kirche (United Methodist Church): Ludolfusstr. 2–4, 60487 Frankfurt a.M.; tel. (69) 2425210; fax (69) 242521129; e-mail bischoefin@emk.de; internet www.emk.de; f. 1968; Presiding Bishop ROSEMARIE WENNER.

Freikirche der Siebenten-Tags-Adventisten (Seventh-Day Adventist Church): Postfach 4260, 73745 Ostfildern; Senefelderstr.

15, 73760 Ostfildern; tel. (711) 4481914; fax (711) 4481960; e-mail info@adventisten.de; internet www.adventisten.de; f. 1863; Pres. Dr TED N. C. WILSON.

Die Heilsarmee in Deutschland (Salvation Army in Germany): Salierring 23–27, 50677 Köln; tel. (221) 208190; fax (221) 2081951; e-mail info@heilsarmee.de; internet www.heilsarmee.de; f. 1886; Leader Col HORST CHARLET.

Mülheimer Verband Freikirchlich-Evangelischer Gemeinden (Pentecostal Church): Habenhauser Dorfstr. 27, 28279 Bremen; tel. (421) 8399130; fax (421) 8399136; e-mail mv-bremen@t-online.de; f. 1913.

Selbständige Evangelisch-Lutherische Kirche (Independent Evangelical-Lutheran Church): Schopenhauerstr. 7, 30625 Hannover; tel. (511) 557826; fax (511) 551588; e-mail selk@selk.de; internet www.selk.de; f. 1972; Pres. Bishop HANS JOERG VOIGT; Exec. Sec. Rev. MICHAEL SCHAETZEL; 34,934 mems.

Other Christian Churches

Other Christian churches had 4.5m.–5m. members in 2005, of whom 1.5m.–2m. persons were members of Orthodox churches.

Alt-Katholische Kirche (Old Catholic Church): Gregor-Mendel-Str. 28, 53115 Bonn; tel. (228) 232285; fax (228) 238314; e-mail ordinariat@alt-katholisch.de; internet www.alt-katholisch.de; seceded from the Roman Catholic Church as a protest against the declaration of Papal infallibility in 1870; belongs to the Utrecht Union of Old Catholic Churches; in full communion with the Anglican Communion; Bishop Dr MATTHIAS RING; 25,000 mems.

Apostelamt Jesu Christi: Madlower Hauptstr. 39, 03050 Cottbus; tel. (355) 541227.

Armenisch-Apostolische Orthodoxe Kirche in Deutschland (Armenian Apostolic Orthodox Church in Germany): Allensteiner Str. 5, 50735 Köln; tel. (221) 7126223; fax (221) 7126267; e-mail armenische_dioezese@hotmail.com; Archbishop KAREKIN BEKDJIAN.

Griechisch-Orthodoxe Metropolie von Deutschland (Greek Orthodox Metropolitanate of Germany): Postfach 300555, 53185 Bonn; Dietrich-Bonhoeffer-Str. 2, 53227 Bonn; tel. (228) 9737840; fax (228) 97378424; e-mail sekretariat@orthodoxie.net; internet www.orthodoxie.net; f. 1963; Metropolitan of Germany and Exarch of Central Europe AUGOUSTINOS LABARDAKIS.

Religiöse Gesellschaft der Freunde (Quäker) (Religious Society of Friends—Quakers): Planckstr. 20, 10117 Berlin; tel. (30) 2082284; fax (30) 20458142; internet www.quaeker.org; f. 1925; 260 mems.

Russische Orthodoxe Kirche—Berliner Diözese (Russian Orthodox Church): Postfach 17, 10267 Berlin; Wildensteiner Str. 10, 10318 Berlin; tel. (30) 50379488; fax (30) 5098153; e-mail red.stimme@snafu.de; Archbishop of Berlin and Germany Archbishop FEOFAN.

ISLAM

An estimated 4.3m. Muslims were living in Germany in 2009.

Zentralrat der Muslime in Deutschland eV (ZMD) (Central Council of Muslims in Germany): Steinfelder Gasse 32, 50670 Köln; tel. (221) 1394450; fax (221) 1394681; e-mail sekretariat@zentralrat.de; internet www.zentralrat.de; f. 1994; 19 mem. asscns; Pres. Dr AYUUB AXEL KÖHLER.

JUDAISM

The membership of Jewish synagogues in Germany numbered some 108,000 in 2006.

Zentralrat der Juden in Deutschland (Central Council of Jews in Germany): Postfach 040207, 10061 Berlin; Tucholskystr. 9, Leo-Baeck-Haus, 10117 Berlin; tel. (30) 2844560; fax (30) 28445613; e-mail info@zentralratdjuden.de; internet www.zentralratdjuden.de; Pres. Dr DIETER GRAUMANN; Sec.-Gen. STEPHAN J. KRAMER.

Jüdische Gemeinde zu Berlin (Jewish Community in Berlin): Oranienburger Str 28–31, 10117 Berlin; tel. (30) 880280; fax (30) 880282679; e-mail service@jg-berlin.org; internet www.jg-berlin.org; Pres. LALA SÜSSKIND.

The Press

A significant feature of the German press is the large number of daily newspapers published in regional centres, of which the *Westdeutsche Allgemeine Zeitung* in Essen has the largest circulation. The most important national publications are *Bild* in Hamburg and *Süddeutsche Zeitung* in Munich, followed by the *Frankfurter Allgemeine Zeitung* in Frankfurt am Main and Berlin's *Die Welt*.

There are strict limits on press ownership. In 1968 a government commission stipulated various restrictions on the proportions of circulation that any one publishing group should be allowed to control: (1) 40% of the total circulation of newspapers or 40% of the total circulation of magazines; (2) 20% of the total circulation of newspapers and magazines together; (3) 15% of the circulation in one field if the proportion owned in the other field is 40%. However, many of the most important newspapers and magazines are controlled by large publishing groups.

Axel Springer Verlag AG: Axel-Springer-Str. 65, 10888 Berlin; and Axel-Springer-Pl. 1, 20355 Hamburg; tel. (30) 25910; fax (30) 251606; tel. (40) 34700; fax (40) 345811; internet www.asv.de; f. 1946; includes 5 major dailies *Berliner Morgenpost*, *Bild*, *BZ*, *Die Welt*, *Hamburger Abendblatt*, 3 Sunday papers *Bild am Sonntag*, *BZ am Sonntag*, *Welt am Sonntag*, and radio, television, women's and family magazines; Chair. Dr MATHIAS DÖPFNER.

Bauer Verlagsgruppe: Burchardstr. 11, 20077 Hamburg; and Charles-de-Gaulle-Str. 8, 81737 München; tel. (40) 30190; fax (40) 30191043; tel. (89) 67860; fax (89) 6374404; internet www.bauerverlag.de; f. 1875; publ. 42 magazines in Germany, incl. *Auf einen Blick*, *Bravo*, *Neue Post*, *Tina*, *tv14*, *tv Hören und Sehen*, *TV Movie*; Pres. HEINZ HEINRICH BAUER.

Gruner + Jahr AG & Co KG: Am Baumwall 11, 20459 Hamburg; tel. (40) 37030; fax (40) 37036000; e-mail unternehmenskommunikation@guj.de; internet www.guj.de; publ., among others, *Brigitte*, *Capital*, *Eltern*, *Financial Times Deutschland*, *GEO*, *Schöner Wohnen* and *Stern*; Chair. Dr BERND BUCHHOLZ.

Hubert Burda Media Holding GmbH & Co KG: Arabellastr. 23, 81925 München; tel. (89) 9250-0; e-mail info@hubert-burda-media.com; internet www.burda.de; f. 1908; publs 74 magazine titles in Germany, incl. *Bild + Funk*, *Bunte*, *Burda Modemagazin*, *Elle*, *Focus*, *Freizeit Revue*, *Freundin*, *Meine Familie & Ich*; Chair. Dr HUBERT BURDA.

WAZ Mediengruppe: Friedrichstr. 34-38, 45128 Essen; tel. (201) 804-0; fax (201) 8041644; e-mail kontakt@waz-mediengruppe.de; internet www.waz-mediengruppe.de; f. 1976; publ. regional dailies, incl. *Westdeutsche Allgemeine Zeitung*, and magazines incl. *Frau Aktuell* and *Gong*; Man. Dirs BODO HOMBACH, CHRISTIAN NIENHAUS.

PRINCIPAL DAILIES

Aachen

Aachener Zeitung: Dresdner Str. 3, 52068 Aachen; Postfach 500110, 52085 Aachen; tel. (241) 5101310; fax (241) 5101360; e-mail redaktion@zeitungsverlag-aachen.de; internet www.az-web.de; f. 1946; Editor-in-Chief BERND MATHIEU; circ. 128,711 (Dec. 2011, with *Aachener Nachrichten*).

Augsburg

Augsburger Allgemeine: Curt-Frenzel-Str. 2, 86167 Augsburg; tel. (821) 7770; fax (821) 7772039; e-mail redaktion@augsburger-allgemeiner.de; internet www.augsburger-allgemeine.de; Editor-in-Chief WALTER ROLLER; circ. 331,637 (March 2012, with *Allgäuer Zeitung*).

Bautzen

Serbske Nowiny: Tuchmacherstr. 27, 02625 Bautzen; tel. (3591) 577233; fax (3591) 577202; e-mail redaktion@serbske-nowiny.de; internet www.serbske-nowiny.de; evening; Sorbian; Editor BENEDIKT DYRLICH.

Berlin

Berliner Kurier: Karl-Liebknecht-Str. 29, 10178 Berlin; tel. (30) 23279; fax (30) 23275533; e-mail post@berliner-kurier.de; internet www.berliner-kurier.de; f. 1990; evening; publ. by Berliner Verlag GmbH; Editor-in-Chief HANS-PETER BUSCHHEUER; circ. 117,456 (Dec. 2011).

Berliner Morgenpost: Axel-Springer-Str. 65, 10888 Berlin; tel. (30) 25910; fax (30) 2516071; e-mail redaktion@morgenpost.de; internet www.morgenpost.de; f. 1898; publ. by Ullstein GmbH; Editor-in-Chief CARSTEN ERDMANN; circ. 126,411 (Dec. 2011).

Berliner Zeitung: Karl-Liebknecht-Str. 29, 10178 Berlin; tel. (2) 23279; fax (30) 23275533; e-mail berliner-zeitung@berliner-zeitung.de; internet www.berliner-zeitung.de; f. 1945; morning (except Sun.); publ. by Berliner Verlag GmbH; Editor UWE VORKÖTTER; circ. 144,229 (Dec. 2011).

B.Z.: B.Z. Ullstein GmbH, Kurfürstendamm 21–22, 10719 Berlin; tel. (30) 25910; fax (30) 259173006; e-mail redaktion@bz-berlin.de; internet www.bz-berlin.de; f. 1877; Mon.–Sat.; Editor-in-Chief PETER HUTH; circ. 161,726 (Dec. 2011, with *B.Z. am Sonntag*).

Der Tagesspiegel: Askanischer Pl. 3, 10963 Berlin; tel. (30) 290210; fax (30) 26009332; e-mail redaktion@tagesspiegel.de; internet www.tagesspiegel.de; f. 1945; Editors-in-Chief STEPHAN-ANDREAS CASDORFF, LORENZ MAROLDT; circ. 131,178 (Dec. 2011).

Die Welt: Axel-Springer-Str. 65, 10888 Berlin; tel. (30) 25910; fax (30) 259171606; internet www.welt.de; f. 1946; publ. by Axel

Springer Verlag AG; Editor-in-Chief JAN-ERIC PETERS; circ. 263,817 (Dec. 2011, Mon.–Fri. only).

Bielefeld

Neue Westfälische: Niedernstr. 21–27, 33602 Bielefeld; Postfach 100225, 33502 Bielefeld; tel. (521) 5550; fax (521) 555348; e-mail redaktion@neue-westfaelische.de; internet www.nw-news.de; f. 1967; publ. by Zeitungsgruppe Neue Westfälische; Editor-in-Chief THOMAS SEIM; circ. 253,082 (Dec. 2011).

Braunschweig
(Brunswick)

Braunschweiger Zeitung: Hamburger Str. 277, 38114 Braunschweig; Postfach 8052, 38130 Braunschweig; tel. (531) 39000; fax (531) 3900610; e-mail chefredaktion@bzv.de; internet www.braunschweiger-zeitung.de; Editor-in-Chief ARMIN MAUS; circ. 157,105 (Dec. 2011).

Bremen

Weser-Kurier: Martinistr. 43, 28195 Bremen; Postfach 107801, 28078 Bremen; tel. (421) 36710; fax (421) 36711000; e-mail chefredaktion@weser-kurier.de; internet www.weser-kurier.de; f. 1945; Editor-in-Chief SILKE HELLWIG; circ. 168,424 (Dec. 2011, with *Bremer Nachrichten*).

Chemnitz

Freie Presse: Brückenstr. 15, 09111 Chemnitz; Postfach 261, 09002 Chemnitz; tel. (371) 6560; fax (371) 65617070; e-mail die.tageszeitung@freiepresse.de; internet www.freiepresse.de; f. 1963; morning; Editor TORSTEN KLEDITZSCH; circ. 277,442 (Dec. 2011, incl. regional edns).

Cottbus

Lausitzer Rundschau: Str. der Jugend 54, 03050 Cottbus; Postfach 100279, 03002 Cottbus; tel. (355) 4810; fax (355) 481245; e-mail redaktion@lr-online.de; internet www.lr-online.de; independent; morning; Editor-in-Chief JOHANNES FISCHER; circ. 93,042 (Dec. 2011).

Darmstadt

Darmstädter Echo: Holzhofallee 25–31, 64295 Darmstadt; Postfach 100155, 64276 Darmstadt; tel. (6151) 387373; fax (6151) 387900; e-mail chefredaktion@darmstaedter-echo.de; internet www.echo-online.de; f. 1945; Editor-in-Chief JÖRG RIEBARTSCH; circ. 88,828 (Dec. 2011).

Dortmund

Westfälische Rundschau: Rundschau-Haus, Brüderweg 9, 44047 Dortmund; tel. (231) 95730; e-mail zentralredaktion@wr.de; internet www.wr.de; publ. by WAZ Mediengruppe; Editor-in-Chief MALTE HINZ; circ. 210,000 (2008).

Dresden

Sächsische Zeitung: Haus der Presse, Ostra-Allee 20, 01067 Dresden; tel. (351) 48640; fax (351) 48642354; e-mail redaktion@sz-online.de; internet www.sz-online.de; f. 1946; morning; publ. by Gruner + Jahr AG; Editor-in-Chief THOMAS SCHULTZ-HOMBERG; circ. 285,000 (Dec. 2011).

Düsseldorf

Handelsblatt: Kasernenstr. 67, 40213 Düsseldorf; Postfach 102741, 40018 Düsseldorf; tel. (211) 8870; fax (211) 8872980; e-mail handelsblatt@vhb.de; internet www.handelsblatt.de; Mon.–Fri.; business and finance; publ. by Verlagsgruppe Handelsblatt GmbH; Editor-in-Chief BERND ZIESEMER; circ. 147,208 (Dec. 2011).

Rheinische Post: Zülpicherstr. 10, 40549 Düsseldorf; tel. (211) 5050; fax (211) 5051929; internet www.rp-online.de; f. 1946; Editor-in-Chief SVEN GÖSMANN; circ. 373,810 (Dec. 2011, incl. regional edns).

Westdeutsche Zeitung: Königsallee 27, 40212 Düsseldorf; tel. (211) 83820; fax (211) 83822225; e-mail westdeutsche.zeitung@wz-newsline.de; internet www.wz-newsline.de; Editor-in-Chief MARTIN VOGLER; circ. 159,246 (Dec. 2011).

Erfurt

Thüringer Allgemeine: Gottstedter Landstr. 6, 99092 Erfurt; tel. (361) 2274; fax (361) 2275007; e-mail redaktion@thueringer-allgemeine.de; internet www.thueringer-allgemeine.de; f. 1946; morning; Editor-in-Chief PAUL-JOSEF RAUE; circ. 338,500 (Sept. 2011, with *Ostthüringer Zeitung* and *Thüringische Landeszeitung*).

Essen

Neue Ruhr Zeitung/Neue Rhein Zeitung: Friedrichstr. 34–38, 45128 Essen; tel. (201) 8040; fax (201) 8041070; e-mail redaktion@nrz.de; internet www.derwesten.de/nachrichten/nrz.html; f. 1946; Editor-in-Chief RÜDIGER OPPERS; circ. 180,000.

Westdeutsche Allgemeine Zeitung: Friedrichstr. 34–38, 45128 Essen; tel. (201) 8040; fax (201) 8042841; e-mail zentralredaktion@waz.de; internet www.derwesten.de/nachrichten/faz.html; f. 1948; Editor-in-Chief ULRICH REITZ; circ. 580,000.

Frankfurt am Main

Frankfurter Allgemeine Zeitung: Hellerhofstr. 2–4, 60327 Frankfurt a.M.; tel. (69) 75910; fax (69) 75912332; e-mail info@faz.net; internet www.faz.net; f. 1949; Editors WERNER D'INKA, BERTHOLD KOHLER, Dr GÜNTHER NONNENMACHER, Dr FRANK SCHIRRMACHER, HOLGER STELTZNER; circ. 380,427 (Dec. 2011).

Frankfurter Neue Presse: Frankenallee 71–81, 60327 Frankfurt a.M.; Postfach 100801, 60008 Frankfurt a.M.; tel. (69) 75010; fax (69) 75014846; e-mail fnp.redaktion@fsd.de; internet www.fnp.de; independent; Editor-in-Chief RAINER M. GEFELLER.

Frankfurter Rundschau: Karl-Gerold-Pl. 1, 60594 Frankfurt a.M.; tel. (69) 21991; fax (69) 21993720; e-mail politik@fr-online.de; internet www.fr-online.de; f. 1945; Editor-in-Chief Dr UWE VORKÖTTER; circ. 124,479 (Dec. 2011).

Freiburg im Breisgau

Badische Zeitung: Pressehaus, Basler Str. 88, 79115 Freiburg i. Br.; tel. (761) 4960; fax (761) 4965029; e-mail redaktion@badische-zeitung.de; internet www.badische-zeitung.de; f. 1946; Editor-in-Chief THOMAS HAUSER; circ. 148,061 (Dec. 2011).

Gera

Ostthüringer Zeitung: Alte Str. 3, 04626 Löbichau; tel. (3447) 524; fax (3447) 525914; e-mail redaktion@otz.de; internet www.otz.de; morning; Editor-in-Chief ULLRICH ERZIGKEIT.

Hagen

Westfalenpost: Schürmannstr. 4, 58097 Hagen; tel. (2331) 9170; fax (2331) 9174206; e-mail westfalenpost@westfalenpost.de; internet www.derwesten.de/nachrichten/wp.html; f. 1946; publ. by WAZ Mediengruppe; Editor-in-Chief STEFAN HANS KLÄSENER.

Halle an der Saale

Mitteldeutsche Zeitung: Delitzscher Str. 65, 06112 Halle (Saale); tel. (345) 5650; fax (345) 5654350; e-mail service@mz-web.de; internet www.mz-web.de; f. 1946 as *Freiheit* (organ of the ruling party in the GDR); refounded 1990 following unification; publ. by M. DuMont Schauberg Gruppe; Editors-in-Chief HANS-JÜRGEN GREYE, HARTMUT AUGUSTIN; circ. 221,404 (Dec. 2011).

Hamburg

Bild: Axel-Springer-Pl. 1, 10969 Hamburg; tel. (40) 34700; fax (40) 345811; internet www.bild.de; f. 1952; publ. by Axel Springer Verlag AG; Chief Editor KAI DIEKMANN; circ. 2,715,105 (Dec. 2011).

Financial Times Deutschland: Am Stubbenhuk 3, 20459 Hamburg; tel. (40) 319900; fax (40) 31990214; e-mail leserservice@ftd.de; internet www.ftd.de; f. 2000; publ. by Gruner + Jahr AG & Co KG in jt venture with *Financial Times* (UK); Editor-in-Chief STEFFEN KLUSMANN; circ. 102,782 (Dec. 2011).

Hamburger Abendblatt: Axel-Springer-Pl. 1, 20355 Hamburg; tel. (40) 34700; fax (40) 34726110; internet www.abendblatt.de; publ. by Axel Springer Verlag AG; Editor-in-Chief LARS HAIDER; circ. 212,263 (Dec. 2011).

Hamburger Morgenpost: Griegstr. 75, 22763 Hamburg; tel. (40) 8090570; fax (40) 9057640; e-mail verlag@mopo.de; internet www.mopo.de; publ. by Morgenpost Verlag; Editor-in-Chief FRANK NIGGEMEIER; circ. 107,584 (Dec. 2011).

Hannover
(Hanover)

Hannoversche Allgemeine Zeitung: August-Madsack-Str. 1, 30559 Hannover; tel. (511) 5180; fax (511) 5182899; e-mail redaktion@haz.de; internet www.haz.de; Editors-in-Chief HENDRIK BRANDT, MATTHIAS KOCH; circ. 540,570 (Dec. 2011).

Heidelberg

Rhein-Neckar-Zeitung: Neugasse 2, 69117 Heidelberg; tel. (6221) 5190; fax (6221) 519217; e-mail rnz-kontakt@rnz.de; internet www.rnz.de; f. 1945; morning; Publrs JOACHIM KNORR, WINFRIED KNORR, INGE HOELTZCKE, DANIEL SCHULZE; circ. 92,754 (Dec. 2011).

Ingolstadt

Donaukurier: Stauffenbergstr. 2A, 85051 Ingolstadt; tel. (841) 96660; fax (841) 9666255; e-mail ingolstadt.redaktion@donaukurier.de; internet www.donaukurier.de; f. 1872; Editor-in-Chief GERD SCHNEIDER; circ. 88,772 (Dec. 2011).

Kassel

Hessische/Niedersächsische Allgemeine: Frankfurter Str. 168, 34121 Kassel; Postfach 101009, 34010 Kassel; tel. (561) 20300; fax (561) 2032406; e-mail info@hna.de; internet www.hna.de; f. 1959; independent; Editor-in-Chief HORST SEIDENFADEN; circ. 224,507 (Dec. 2011).

Kempten

Allgäuer Zeitung: Heisinger Str. 14, 87437 Kempten; Postfach 3155, 87440 Kempten; tel. (831) 2060; fax (831) 206123; e-mail redaktion@azv.de; internet www.all-in.de; f. 1945; Publrs GEORG FÜRST VON WALDBURG-ZEIL, GÜNTER HOLLAND, ELLINOR HOLLAND; circ. 102,874 (Dec. 2011).

Kiel

Kieler Nachrichten: Fleethörn 1–7, 24103 Kiel; Postfach 1111, 24100 Kiel; tel. (431) 9030; fax (431) 9032935; internet www.kn-online.de; publ. by Axel Springer Verlag; Editor-in-Chief JÜRGEN HEINEMANN; circ. 103,053 (Dec. 2011).

Koblenz

Rhein-Zeitung: August-Horch-Str. 28, 56070 Koblenz; tel. (261) 89200; fax (261) 892770; e-mail redaktion@rhein-zeitung.net; internet www.rhein-zeitung.de; Editor-in-Chief CHRISTIAN LINDNER; circ. 198,688 (Mon.–Fri.), 216,837 (Sat.) (2011).

Köln
(Cologne)

Express: Postfach 100410, 50450 Köln; Amsterdamer Str. 192, 50735 Köln; tel. (221) 2240; fax (211) 2242700; e-mail info@express.de; internet www.express.de; f. 1964; publ. by DuMont Schauberg Gruppe; Editor-in-Chief RUDOLF KREITZ; circ. 182,498 (Dec. 2011).

Kölner Stadt-Anzeiger: Amsterdamer Str. 192, 50735 Köln; tel. (221) 2240; fax (221) 2242524; internet www.ksta.de; f. 1876; Editor-in-Chief PETER PAULS; circ. 328,092 (Dec. 2011, with *Kölnische Rundschau*).

Kölnische Rundschau: Stolkgasse 25–45, 50667 Köln; Postfach 102145, 50461 Köln; tel. (221) 1632551; fax (221) 1632491; e-mail koeln@kr-redaktion.de; internet www.rundschau-online.de; f. 1946; Publr HELMUT HEINEN.

Konstanz

Südkurier: Max-Stromeyer-Str. 178, 78467 Konstanz; Postfach 102001, Presse- und Druckzentrum, 78420 Konstanz; tel. (7531) 9990; fax (7531) 991485; e-mail chefredaktion@suedkurier.de; internet www.suedkurier.de; f. 1945; Editor-in-Chief STEFAN LUTZ; circ. 131,191 (Dec. 2011).

Leipzig

Leipziger Volkszeitung: Peterssteinweg 19, 04107 Leipzig; tel. (341) 21810; fax (341) 21811640; e-mail post@lvz-online.de; internet www.lvz-online.de; f. 1894; morning; publ. by Verlagsgesellschaft Madsach and Axel Springer Verlag AG; Editor-in-Chief JAN EMENDÖRFER; circ. 217,014 (Dec. 2011).

Leutkirch im Allgäu

Schwäbische Zeitung: Rudolf-Roth-Str. 18, 88299 Leutkirch im Allgäu; Postfach 1145, 88291 Leutkirch im Allgäu; tel. (7561) 80100; fax (7561) 80378; e-mail redaktion@schwaebische-zeitung.de; internet www.schwaebische-zeitung.de; f. 1945; Editor-in-Chief HENDRIK GROTH; circ. 175,051 (Dec. 2011).

Lübeck

Lübecker Nachrichten: Herrenholz 10–12, 23556 Lübeck; tel. (451) 1440; fax (451) 1441022; e-mail redaktion@ln-luebeck.de; internet www.ln-online.de; f. 1945; Tues.–Sun.; publ. by Axel Springer Verlag AG; Editor-in-Chief GERALD GOETSCH; circ. 104,033 (Dec. 2011).

Ludwigshafen

Die Rheinpfalz: Amtsstr. 5–11, 67059 Ludwigshafen; Postfach 211147, 67011 Ludwigshafen; tel. (621) 590201; fax (621) 5902272; e-mail rheinpfalz@rheinpfalz.de; internet www.rheinpfalz.de; Editor-in-Chief MICHAEL GARTHE; circ. 243,572 (Dec. 2011).

Magdeburg

Volksstimme: Bahnhofstr. 17, 39104 Magdeburg; tel. (391) 59990; fax (391) 388400; e-mail chefredaktion@volksstimme.de; internet www.volksstimme.de; f. 1890; morning; 18 regional edns; publ. by Magdeburger Verlags- und Druckhaus GmbH; Editor-in-Chief ALOIS KÖSTER; circ. 193,615 (Dec. 2011, incl. regional edns).

Mainz

Allgemeine Zeitung: Erich-Dombrowski-Str. 2, 55127 Mainz; tel. (6131) 4830; fax (6131) 485868; e-mail az-mainz@vrm.de; internet www.main-rheiner.de; f. 1850; publ. by Verlagsgruppe Rhein-Main; Editor-in-Chief FRIEDRICH ROEINGH; circ. 95,494 (March 2008, incl. regional edns).

Mannheim

Mannheimer Morgen: Dudenstr. 12–26, 68167 Mannheim; Postfach 102164, 68021 Mannheim; tel. (621) 39201; fax (621) 3921376; e-mail redaktion@mamo.de; internet www.morgenweb.de; f. 1946; Editor-in-Chief HORST ROTH; circ. 125,634 (Dec. 2011).

München
(Munich)

Abendzeitung: Rundfunkpl. 4, 80335 München; tel. (89) 23770; fax (89) 2377409; e-mail info@abendzeitung.de; internet www.abendzeitung.de; f. 1948; evening; Editor-in-Chief ARNO MAKOWSKY; circ. 131,399 (Dec. 2011).

Münchner Merkur: Paul-Heyse-Str. 2–4, 80336 München; tel. (89) 53060; fax (89) 5306408; internet www.merkur-online.de; Editor-in-Chief KARL SCHERMANN; circ. 268,762 (Dec. 2011).

Süddeutsche Zeitung: Hultschiner Str. 8, 81677 München; tel. (89) 21830; fax (89) 21839715; e-mail wir@sueddeutsche.de; internet www.sueddeutsche.de; f. 1945; publ. by Süddeutscher-Verlag GmbH; Editor-in-Chief KURT KISTER; circ. 427,748 (Dec. 2011).

TZ: Paul-Heyse-Str. 2–4, 80336 München; tel. (89) 53060; fax (89) 5306552; e-mail sekretariat@tz-online.de; internet www.tz-online.de; f. 1968; Editor-in-Chief RUDOLF BÖGEL; circ. 141,250 (Dec. 2011).

Münster

Westfälische Nachrichten: An der Hansalinie 1, 48163 Münster; tel. (251) 6900; fax (251) 6904570; internet www.wn.de; Editor-in-Chief Dr NORBERT TIEMANN; circ. 210,030 (June 2008, incl. regional edns).

Neubrandenburg

Nordkurier: Friedrich-Engels-Ring 29, 17033 Neubrandenburg; tel. (395) 45750; fax (395) 4575694; e-mail chefredaktion@nordkurier.de; internet www.nordkurier.de; Editor-in-Chief Dr ANDRÉ UZULIS; circ. 88,841 (Dec. 2011).

Nürnberg
(Nuremberg)

Nürnberger Nachrichten: Marienstr. 9–11, Postfach 90327, 90402 Nürnberg; tel. (911) 2160; fax (911) 2162432; e-mail info@nordbayern.de; internet www.nn-online.de; f. 1945; Editor-in-Chief HEINZ-JOACHIM HAUCK; circ. 282,469 (Dec. 2011).

Oldenburg

Nordwest-Zeitung: Peterstr. 28–34, 26121 Oldenburg; Postfach 2527, 26015 Oldenburg; tel. (441) 998801; fax (441) 99882029; internet www.nwz-online.de; publ. by Nordwest-Zeitung Verlagsgesellschaft mbH & Co KG; Editor-in-Chief ROLF SEELHEIM; circ. 123,706 (Dec. 2011).

Osnabrück

Neue Osnabrücker Zeitung: Breiter Gang 10–16 and Grosse Str. 17–19, 49074 Osnabrück; Postfach 4260, 49032 Osnabrück; tel. (541) 3100; fax (541) 310485; e-mail redaktion@neue-oz.de; internet www.neue-oz.de; f. 1967; Editor-in-Chief RALF GEISENHANSLÜKE; circ. 282,238 (Dec. 2011).

Passau

Passauer Neue Presse: Medienstr. 5, 94036 Passau; tel. (851) 8020; fax (851) 802256; e-mail info@pnp.de; internet www.pnp.de; f. 1946; Editor-in-Chief ERNST FUCHS; circ. 166,010 (Dec. 2011).

Potsdam

Märkische Allgemeine: Friedrich-Engels-Str. 24, 14473 Potsdam; Postfach 601153, 14411 Potsdam; tel. (331) 28400; fax (331) 2840310; e-mail chefredaktion@mazonline.de; internet www

.maerkischeallgemeine.de; f. 1990; morning; independent; Chief Editor Dr KLAUS ROST; circ. 138,092 (Dec. 2011).

Regensburg

Mittelbayerische Zeitung: Kumpfmühler Str. 9, 93047 Regensburg; tel. (941) 207270; fax (941) 207307; e-mail mittelbayerische@mittelbayerische.de; internet www.mittelbayerische.de; f. 1945; Editor-in-Chief MANFRED SAUERER; circ. 119,375 (Dec. 2011).

Rostock

Ostsee-Zeitung: Richard-Wagner-Str. 1A, 18055 Rostock; tel. (81) 3650; fax (81) 365244; e-mail redaktion@ostsee-zeitung.de; internet www.ostsee-zeitung.de; f. 1952; publ. by Axel Springer Verlag AG; Editor-in-Chief JAN EMENDÖRFER; circ. 149,553 (Dec. 2011, incl. regional edns).

Saarbrücken

Saarbrücker Zeitung: Gutenbergstr. 11–23, 66117 Saarbrücken; tel. (681) 5020; fax (681) 502501; internet www.saarbruecker-zeitung.de; f. 1761; Editor PETER STEFAN HERBST; circ. 149,308 (Dec. 2011).

Stuttgart

Stuttgarter Nachrichten: Plieninger Str. 150, 70567 Stuttgart; Postfach 104452, 70039 Stuttgart; tel. (711) 72050; fax (711) 72057138; e-mail cvd@stn.zgs.de; internet www.stuttgarter-nachrichten.de; f. 1946; Editor-in-Chief CHRISTOPH REISINGER; circ. 201,729 (Dec. 2011, with *Stuttgarter Zeitung).*

Stuttgarter Zeitung: Plieninger Str. 150, 70567 Stuttgart; Postfach 106032, 70049 Stuttgart; tel. (711) 72050; fax (711) 72051112; e-mail redaktion@stz.zgs.de; internet www.stuttgarter-zeitung.de; f. 1945; Editor-in-Chief JOACHIM DORFS.

Trier

Trierischer Volksfreund: Hanns-Martin-Schleyer-Str. 8, 54294 Trier; Postfach 3770, 54227 Trier; tel. (651) 71990; fax (651) 7199990; e-mail redaktion@volksfreund.de; internet www.volksfreund.de; Editor-in-Chief ISABELL FUNK; circ. 92,685 (Dec. 2011).

Würzburg

Main-Post: Berner Str. 2, 97084 Würzburg; tel. (931) 60010; fax (931) 6001242; e-mail redaktion@mainpost.de; internet www.mainpost.de; f. 1883; independent; Editor-in-Chief MICHAEL REINHARD; circ. 128,325 (Dec. 2011).

SUNDAY AND WEEKLY PAPERS

Bayernkurier: Nymphenburger Str. 64, 80636 München; tel. (89) 120040; fax (89) 12004133; e-mail redaktion@bayernkurier.de; internet www.bayernkurier.de; f. 1950; weekly; organ of the CSU; Editor-in-Chief PETER HAUSMANN; circ. 63,364 (Dec. 2011).

Bild am Sonntag: Axel-Springer-Pl. 1, 20350 Hamburg; tel. (40) 34700; fax (40) 34726110; internet www.bild-am-sonntag.de; f. 1956; Sunday; publ. by Axel Springer Verlag AG; Editor-in-Chief WALTER MAYER; circ. 1,394,173 (Dec. 2011).

B.Z. am Sonntag: Axel-Springer-Str. 65, 10888 Berlin; tel. (30) 25910; fax (30) 259173131; e-mail redaktion@bz-berlin.de; internet www.bz-berlin.de; f. 1992; publ. by Ullstein GmbH; Editor-in-Chief PETER HUTH; circ. 88,670 (Dec. 2011).

Frankfurter Allgemeine Sonntagszeitung: Hellerhofstr. 2–4, 60327 Frankfurt a.M.; tel. (69) 75910; fax (69) 75911773; e-mail sonntagszeitung@faz.de; internet www.faz.de; Sunday; Publrs WERNER D'INKA, BERTHOLD KOHLER, GÜNTHER NONNENMACHER, FRANK SCHIRRMACHER, HOLGER STELTZNER; circ. 401,337 (Dec. 2011).

Sonntag Aktuell: Plieninger Str. 150, 70567 Stuttgart; Postfach 104462, 70039 Stuttgart; tel. (711) 72050; fax (711) 72057138; e-mail redaktion@soak.zgs.de; internet www.sonntag-aktuell.de; Sunday; Editor-in-Chief ANDREAS BRAUN; circ. 643,139 (Dec. 2011).

Welt am Sonntag: Axel-Springer-Str. 65, 10888 Berlin; tel. (30) 25910; fax (30) 259171606; e-mail leserbriefe@wams.de; internet www.welt.de; f. 1948; Sunday; publ. by Axel Springer Verlag AG; Editor-in-Chief JAN-ERIC PETERS; circ. 402,287 (Dec. 2010).

Die Zeit: Buceriusstr., Eingang Speersort 1, Pressehaus, 20095 Hamburg; tel. (40) 32800; fax (40) 327111; e-mail diezeit@zeit.de; internet www.zeit.de; f. 1946; weekly; Editor-in-Chief GIOVANNI DI LORENZO; circ. 537,129 (Dec. 2011).

SELECTED PERIODICALS

Agriculture

Bauernzeitung: Postfach 310448, 10634 Berlin; Wilhelmsaue 37, 10713 Berlin; tel. (30) 464060; fax (30) 46406319; e-mail info@bauernverlag.de; internet www.bauernzeitung.de; f. 1960; weekly; covers agricultural news in Brandenburg, Mecklenburg-Western Pomerania, Saxony, Saxony-Anhalt and Thüringen; Editor-in-Chief Dr THOMAS TANNEBERGER; circ. 24,192 (Sept. 2008).

Bayerisches Landwirtschaftliches Wochenblatt: Postfach 200523, 80005 München; Bayerstr. 57, 80335 München; tel. (89) 53098901; fax (89) 5328537; e-mail ulrich.graf@dlv.de; internet www.wochenblatt-dlv.de; f. 1810; weekly; organ of the Bayerischer Bauernverband; Editor-in-Chief JOHANNES URBAN; circ. 102,515 (Sept. 2008).

dlz agrarmagazin: Postfach 400580, 80705 München; Lothstr. 29, 80797 München; tel. (89) 127051; fax (89) 12705546; e-mail dlv.muenchen@dlv.de; internet www.dlz-agrarmagazin.de; monthly; publ. by Deutscher Landwirtschaftsverlag GmbH; Editor-in-Chief DETLEF STEINERT; circ. 77,349 (Sept. 2008).

Eisenbahn-Landwirt: Postfach 2026, 76008 Karlsruhe; Ostring 6, 76131 Karlsruhe; tel. (721) 62830; fax (721) 628310; e-mail info@druck-verlag-sw.de; internet www.druck-verlag-sw.de; f. 1918; monthly; gardening; organ of the Hauptverband der Bahn-Landwirtschaft; publ. by Druckhaus Karlsruhe, Druck + Verlagsgesellschaft Südwest mbH; Dir ROLF HAASE; circ. 82,683 (Sept. 2008).

Landpost: Wollgrasweg 31, 70599 Stuttgart; tel. (711) 167790; fax (711) 4586093; e-mail info@vdaw.de; internet www.vdaw.de; f. 1945; weekly; agriculture and gardening; Editor ERICH REICH; circ. 15,409 (Oct. 2010).

Top Agrar: Postfach 7847, 48042 Münster; Hülsebrockstr. 2–8, 48165 Münster; tel. (2501) 801640; fax (2501) 801654; e-mail redaktion@topagrar.com; internet www.topagrar.com; monthly; focusing on key agricultural issues; Editors BERTHOLD ACHLER, HEINZ-GÜNTER TOPÜTH, Dr LUDGER SCHULZE PALS; circ. 115,225 (Oct. 2010).

The Arts and Literature

Art. Das Kunstmagazin: Am Baumwall 11, 20459 Hamburg; tel. (40) 37030; fax (40) 37035618; e-mail kunst@art-magazin.de; internet www.art-magazin.de; f. 1979; monthly; publ. by Gruner + Jahr AG & Co KG; Editor-in-Chief TIM SOMMER; circ. 53,336 (2010).

Cinema: Christoph-Probst-Weg 1, 20251 Hamburg; tel. (40) 41310; fax (40) 41312024; e-mail info@milchstrasse.de; internet www.cinema.de; monthly; film reviews, interviews; publ. by Cinema Verlag GmbH; Editor-in-Chief ARTUR JUNG; circ. 83,925 (Oct. 2010).

Literarische Welt: Axel-Springer-Str. 65, 10888 Berlin; tel. (30) 25910; fax (30) 259171606; e-mail literaturwelt@welt.de; internet www.welt.de/kultur/literarischewelt; f. 1971; weekly; literary supplement of *Die Welt*; Editor THOMAS SCHMID.

Musikexpress: Mehringdamm 33, 10960 Berlin; tel. (30) 881880; fax (30) 88188223; e-mail redaktion@musikexpress.de; internet www.musikexpress.de; f. 1983; monthly; popular music; publ. by Axel Springer Mediahouse Berlin GmbH; Editor-in-Chief RAINER SCHMIDT.

Neue Rundschau: S. Fischer Verlag GmbH, Hedderichstr. 114, 60596 Frankfurt a.M.; tel. (69) 60620; fax (69) 6062319; e-mail neuerundschau@fischerverlage.de; f. 1890; quarterly; literature and essays; Editors HANS-JÜRGEN BALMES, JÖRG BONG, ALEXANDER RÖSLER, OLIVER VOGEL; circ. 3,000.

Praxis Deutsch: Im Brande 17, 30926 Seelze/Velber; tel. (511) 400040; fax (511) 40004170; e-mail redaktion.pd@friedrich-verlag.de; internet www.friedrich-verlag.de; 6 a year; German language and literature; publ. by Erhard Friedrich Verlag GmbH; circ. 11,341 (Sept. 2008).

Schnitt—das Filmmagazin: Breite Str. 118-120, 50667 Köln; tel. (221) 2858703; fax (221) 2858704; e-mail info@schnitt.de; internet www.schnitt.de; f. 1996; quarterly; film reviews, essays; Editor-in-Chief CHRISTIAN LAILACH.

Theater der Zeit: Klosterstr. 68, 10179 Berlin; tel. (30) 24722414; fax (30) 24722415; e-mail redaktion@theaterderzeit.de; internet www.theaterderzeit.de; f. 1946; 10 a year; theatre, drama, opera, children's theatre, puppet theatre, dance; Editors HARALD MÜLLER, Dr FRANK RADDATZ, DORTE LENA EILERS, SEBASTIAN KIRSCH, LENA SCHNEIDER; circ. 5,000.

Theater heute: Knesebeckstr. 59–61, 10719 Berlin; tel. (30) 25449510; fax (30) 25449512; e-mail redaktion@theaterheute.de; internet www.theaterheute.de; f. 1960; monthly, with a yearbook in August; Editors BARBARA BURCKHARDT, EVA BEHRENDT, Dr FRANZ WILLE; circ. 15,000.

xia intelligente architektur: Fasanenweg 18, 70771 Leinfelden-Echterdingen; tel. (711) 7591286; fax (711) 7591410; e-mail ait-red@ait-online.de; internet www.xia-online.de; f. 1890; quarterly; Editor Dr DIETMAR DANNER; circ. 16,458 (Oct. 2010).

Economics, Finance and Industry

Absatzwirtschaft: Postfach 101102, 40002 Düsseldorf; Kasernenstr. 67, 40213 Düsseldorf; tel. (211) 8870; fax (211) 8871420; e-mail absatzwirtschaft@fachverlag.de; internet www.absatzwirtschaft.de; f. 1958; monthly; marketing; Editor-in-Chief CHRISTOPH BERDI; circ. 26,163 (Oct. 2010).

Börse Online: Postfach 800227, 81602 München; Weihenstephaner Str. 7, 81673 München; tel. (89) 4152200; fax (89) 4152383; e-mail kontakt@boerse-online.de; internet www.boerse-online.de; f. 1987; weekly; German and international stocks and stock-related investments; publ. by Gruner + Jahr AG & Co KG; Editor-in-Chief STEFANIE BURGMAIER; circ. 85,711 (Oct. 2010).

Capital: G+J Wirtschaftsmedien, Am Baumwall 11, 20459 Hamburg; tel. (40) 31990; fax (40) 31990310; e-mail capital@capital.de; internet www.capital.de; f. 1962; monthly; business magazine; publ. by Gruner + Jahr AG & Co KG; Editor-in-Chief Dr STEFFEN KLUSMANN; circ. 173,041 (Oct. 2010).

Creditreform: Postfach 101102, 40002 Düsseldorf; Kasernenstr. 67, 40213 Düsseldorf; tel. (211) 8870; fax (211) 8872980; e-mail creditreform-service@fachverlag.de; internet www.creditreform-magazin.de; f. 1879; Editor-in-Chief INGO SCHENK; circ. 126,000 (Oct. 2010).

H&V Journal Handelsvermittlung und Vertrieb: Siegel-Verlag Otto Müller GmbH, Mainzer-Land-Str. 238, 60326 Frankfurt a.M.; tel. (69) 75890950; fax (69) 75890960; e-mail hv-journal@svffm.de; internet www.svffm.de; f. 1949; monthly; Editor-in-Chief Dr ANDREAS PAFFHAUSEN; circ. 11,891 (Oct. 2010).

Impulse: Stubbenhuk 3, 20459 Hamburg; tel. (40) 31990584; fax (40) 31990595; e-mail chefredaktion@impulse.de; internet www.impulse.de; f. 1980; monthly; business and entrepreneurship; publ. by Gruner + Jahr AG & Co KG; Editor-in-Chief Dr NIKOLAUS FÖRSTER; circ. 110,387 (Oct. 2010).

Industrieanzeiger: Ernst–Mey–Str. 8, 70771 Leinfelden-Echterdingen; tel. (711) 7594451; fax (711) 7594398; e-mail werner.goetz@konradin.de; internet www.industrieanzeiger.de; f. 1879; 30 a year; Editor-in-Chief WERNER GÖTZ; circ. 40,037 (Oct. 2010).

Management International Review: Johannes Gutenburg-Universität, Jaco-Welder-Weg 9, 55128 Mainz; tel. (6131) 3923767; fax (6131) 3923004; e-mail mir-online@uni-mainz.de; internet www.mir-online.de; f. 1960; 6 a year; English; publ. by Gabler Verlag; Editors Prof. Dr MICHAEL-JÖRG OESTERLE (Mainz), Prof. Dr JOACHIM WOLF (Kiel).

VDI Nachrichten: VDI-Pl. 1, 40468 Düsseldorf; tel. (211) 61880; fax (211) 6188112; e-mail redaktion@vdi-nachrichten.com; internet www.vdi-nachrichten.com; f. 1923; weekly, Fri.; technology and economics; Editor-in-Chief RUDOLF SCHULZE; circ. 162,537 (Dec. 2010).

WirtschaftsWoche: Kasernenstr. 67, 40213 Düsseldorf; tel. (211) 8870; fax (211) 887972114; e-mail wiwo@wiwo.de; internet www.wiwo.de; weekly; business; Editor-in-Chief ROLAND TICHY; circ. 184,708 (Oct. 2010).

Home, Fashion and General

Bild der Frau: Axel-Springer-Pl. 1, 20350 Hamburg; tel. (40) 34700; e-mail service@bildderfrau.de; internet www.bildderfrau.de; f. 1983; weekly; publ. by Axel Springer Verlag AG; Editor-in-Chief SANDRA IMMOOR; circ. 991,744 (Oct. 2010).

Bravo: Charles-de-Gaulle-Str. 8, 81737 München; tel. (89) 67860; fax (89) 6702033; e-mail post@bravo.de; internet www.bravo.de; weekly; publ. by Bauer Verlagsgruppe; for young people; Editor-in-Chief PHILIPP JESSEN; circ. 484,221 (Oct. 2010).

Brigitte: Am Baumwall 11, 20459 Hamburg; tel. (40) 37034679; fax (40) 37035845; e-mail infoline@brigitte.de; internet www.brigitte.de; f. 1954; fortnightly; women's magazine; also publishes *Brigitte Balance* (2 a year; circ. 130,000) and *Brigitte Woman* (monthly; circ. 294,928); publ. by Gruner + Jahr AG & Co KG; Editor-in-Chief ANDREAS LEBERT; circ. 692,680 (Oct. 2010).

Bunte: Arabellastr. 23, 81925 München; tel. (89) 92500; fax (89) 92503427; e-mail bunte@burda.com; internet www.bunte.de; f. 1948; weekly; celebrity gossip; publ. by Bunte Entertainment Verlag GmbH; Editor-in-Chief PATRICIA RIEKEL; circ. 662,668 (Oct. 2010).

Burda Modemagazin: Am Destendamm 1, 77652 Offenburg; tel. (781) 840; fax (781) 843291; e-mail info@burdastyle.de; internet www.burdastyle.de; f. 1949; monthly; fashion, patterns; publ. by Hubert Burda Media Holding GmbH & Co KG; Editor-in-Chief DAGMAR BILY; circ. 135,095 (Oct. 2010).

Cosmopolitan: MVG Medien Verlagsgesellschaft mbH & Co, Arabellastr. 30, 81925 München; tel. (89) 92340; fax (89) 9234618; e-mail info@cosmopolitan.de; internet www.cosmopolitan.de; f. 1980; monthly; lifestyle; Editor-in-Chief PETRA WINTER; circ. 367,503 (Oct. 2010).

Elle: Arabellastr. 23, 81925 München; tel. (89) 92503355; fax (89) 92503040; e-mail elleonline@elle.burda.com; internet www.elle.de; monthly; fashion; also publishes *Elle Decoration* (6 a year; circ. 122,905); publ. by Hubert Burda Media Holding GmbH & Co KG; Editor-in-Chief SABINE NEDELCHEV; circ. 226,172 (Oct. 2010).

Eltern: Weihenstephanerstr. 7, 81673 München; tel. (89) 415200; fax (89) 4152651; e-mail redaktion@eltern.de; internet www.eltern.de; f. 1966; monthly; for parents of young children; also publishes *Eltern Family* (monthly; for parents of older children; circ. 142,971); publ. by Gruner + Jahr AG & Co KG; Editor-in-Chief MARIE-LUISE LEWICKI; circ. 317,221 (Oct. 2010).

Essen & Trinken: Am Baumwall 11, 20459 Hamburg; tel. (40) 37034214; fax (40) 37034212; e-mail service@essen-und-trinken.de; internet www.essen-und-trinken.de; f. 1972; monthly; food and drink; also publishes *Essen & Trinken Für Jeden Tag* (monthly; recipes; circ. 169,938); publ. by Gruner + Jahr AG & Co KG; Editor-in-Chief STEPHAN SCHAEFER; circ. 177,709 (Oct. 2010).

Familie & Co: Kaiser-Joseph-Str. 263, 79098 Freiburg i. Br.; tel. (761) 70578559; fax (761) 70578656; e-mail redaktion@familymedia.de; internet www.familie.de; f. 1996; monthly; publ. by Family Media GmbH & Co; also publishes *Baby & Co* (circ. 99,424; Editor-in-Chief HAUKE JOHANNSEN; circ. 178,321 (Oct. 2010).

Frau aktuell: Adlerstr. 22, Düsseldorf; tel. (211) 36660; fax (211) 3666200; e-mail frauaktuell@waso.de; f. 1965; weekly; publ. by Westdeutsche Zeitschriftenverlag GmbH & Co KG; circ. 204,716 (Oct. 2010).

Frau im Spiegel: Münchener Str. 101/09, 85737 Ismaning; tel. (89) 272700; fax (89) 272708990; e-mail fis@mzv-direkt.de; internet www.frau-im-spiegel.de; f. 1947; weekly; aimed at women over 35; also publishes *Frau im Spiegel Legenden* (quarterly; focusing on a particular celebrity; publ. by WZV Westdeutsche Zeitschriftenverlag GmbH; Editor-in-Chief INGO WIBBEKE; circ. 312,985 (Oct. 2010).

Frau im Trend: Burda Senator Verlag GmbH, Arabellastr. 23, 81925 Munich; tel. (89) 92500; e-mail info@hubert-burda-media.com; women's magazine; Editor-in-Chief THOMAS OTTO; circ. 359,626 (Oct. 2010).

Frau und Mutter: Prinz Georg Str. 44, 40477 Düsseldorf; tel. (211) 4499240; fax (211) 4499275; e-mail redaktion@kfdfum.de; internet www.frauundmutter.de; monthly; women's magazine published by the Catholic Women's Community; Editors BARBARA LECKEL, NIKOLA HOLLMAN; circ. 556,150 (Oct. 2010).

Freizeit Revue: Hubert-Burda-Pl. 1, 77652 Offenburg; tel. (781) 8401; internet www.freizeitfreunde.de; weekly; celebrities, food, health and beauty; publ. by Hubert Burda Media Holding GmbH & Co KG; Editor-in-Chief ROBERT PÖLZER; circ. 964,362 (Oct. 2010).

Freundin: Arabellastr. 23, 81925 München; tel. (89) 92500; fax (89) 92503991; e-mail freundin@burda.com; internet www.freundin.com; f. 1948; fortnightly; for young women; publ. by Hubert Burda Media Holding GmbH & Co KG; Editor-in-Chief ULRIKA ZEITLINGER; circ. 526,680 (Oct. 2010).

Für Sie: Jahreszeitenverlag GmbH, Possmoorweg 2, 22301 Hamburg; tel. (40) 27173574; fax (40) 27172059; e-mail redaktion@fuer-sie.de; internet www.fuer-sie.de; fortnightly; women's magazine; Editor-in-Chief UTE KRÖGER; circ. 470,237 (Oct. 2010).

Gala: Schaarsteinweg 14, 20459 Hamburg; tel. (40) 37030; fax (40) 37034364; e-mail redaktion@gala.de; internet www.gala.de; f. 1994; weekly; celebrity gossip; publ. by Norddeutsche Verlagsgesellschaft mbH; Editor-in-Chief PETER LEWANDOWSKI; circ. 341,284 (Oct. 2010).

GEO: Am Baumwall 11, 20459 Hamburg; tel. (40) 37030; fax (40) 37035648; e-mail briefe@geo.de; internet www.geo.de; f. 1976; monthly; reports on science, politics and religion; publ. by Gruner + Jahr AG & Co KG; also publishes *GEO Epoche* (quarterly; history; circ. 130,593), *GEO Saison* (monthly; travel; circ. 99,508), *GEO Special* (6 a year; travel; circ. 73,009), *Geolino* (monthly; general interest for children aged 8–14 years; circ. 223,988); Editor-in-Chief PETER-MATTHIAS GAEDE; circ. 337,237 (Oct. 2010).

Guter Rat: Superillu Verlag GmbH & Co KG, Zimmerstr. 28, 10969 Berlin; tel. (30) 23876600; fax (30) 23876395; e-mail kontakt@guter-rat.de; internet www.guter-rat.de; f. 1945; monthly; consumer magazine; Editor-in-Chief WERNER ZEDLER; circ. 254,035 (Oct. 2010).

Das Haus: Postfach 810164, 81901 München; Arabellastr. 23, 81925 München; tel. (89) 92500; fax (89) 92503055; e-mail userservice@haus.de; internet www.haus.de; 10 a year; home improvement; pub. by Hubert Burda Media Holding GmbH & Co KG; Editor-in-Chief GABY MIKETTA; circ. 1,808,307 (Sept. 2008).

How To Spend It: Stubbenhuk 3, 20459 Hamburg; tel. (40) 31990232; fax (40) 31990214; e-mail htsi@guj.de; internet www.howtospendit.de; f. 2001; 10 a year; luxury lifestyle; publ. by Financial Times Deutschland GmbH & Co KG; Editor STEFFEN KLUSMANN; circ. 100,000.

Living At Home: Am Baumwall 11, 20459 Hamburg; tel. (40) 37034267; fax (40) 37035838; internet www.livingathome.de; f. 2000; monthly; lifestyle magazine covering furnishing, decorating, cooking, entertaining and gardening; publ. by LaH Multimedia GmbH; Editor-in-Chief NADJA STAVENHAGEN; circ. 171,027 (Oct. 2010).

Meine Familie & Ich: Arabellastr. 23, 81925 München; tel. (89) 92500; fax (89) 92503030; e-mail redaktion@daskochrezept.de; internet www.daskochrezept.de; 13 a year; food and drink, health and beauty; publ. by MFI Verlag GmbH; Editor-in-Chief BIRGITT MICHA; circ. 365,180 (Oct. 2010).

Neue Post: Postfach 2427, Burchardstr. 11, 20077 Hamburg; tel. (40) 30194123; fax (40) 30194133; e-mail info@bauerdigital.de; internet neue-post.wunderweib.de; weekly; celebrity gossip, women's interest; publ. by Heinrich Bauer Verlagsgruppe; Editor-in-Chief HANSJÖRN MUDER; circ. 747,464 (Oct. 2010).

Petra: Jahreszeiten Verlag GmbH, Possmoorweg 2, 22301 Hamburg; tel. (40) 27173009; fax (40) 27173020; e-mail redaktion@petra.de; internet www.petra.de; monthly; health and beauty; Editor-in-Chief NINA MAURISCHAT; circ. 222,828 (Oct. 2010).

Readers Digest Deutschland: Postfach 106020, 70049 Stuttgart; Verlag Das Beste GmbH, Vordernbergstr. 6, 70191 Stuttgart; tel. (711) 66020; fax (711) 6602547; e-mail verlag@readersdigest.de; internet www.readersdigest.de; f. 1948; owned by Reader's Digest Assen Inc., Pleasantville, NY (USA); magazines, general, serialized and condensed books, music and video programmes; Man. Dir WERNER NEUNZIG; circ. 730,418 (Oct. 2010).

Schöner Wohnen: Am Baumwall 11, 20459 Hamburg; tel. (40) 37032226; fax (40) 37032258; e-mail info@schoener-wohnen.de; internet www.schoener-wohnen.de; f. 1960; monthly; homes and gardens; publ. by Gruner + Jahr AG & Co KG; Editor-in-Chief ULRICH WEIß; circ. 272,976 (Oct. 2010).

7 Tage: Postfach 2071, 76490 Baden-Baden; Rotweg 8, 76532 Baden-Baden; tel. (7221) 35010; fax (7221) 3501204; e-mail kontakt@klambt.de; internet www.klambt.de; f. 1843; weekly, Sat.; celebrities, women's interest; Editor-in-Chief PETER VIKTOR KULIG; circ. 105,863 (Sept. 2008).

Law

Der Betrieb: Postfach 101102, 40002 Düsseldorf; Grafenberger Allee 293 40237, Düsseldorf; tel. (211) 8871454; fax (211) 8871450; e-mail der-betrieb@fachverlag.de; internet www.der-betrieb.de; weekly; business administration, revenue law, corporate law, labour and social legislation; Editor MARKO WIECZOREK; circ. 21,508 (Oct. 2010).

Deutsche Richterzeitung: Geschäftsstelle des Deutschen Richterbundes, Kronenstr. 73/74, 10117 Berlin; tel. (30) 2061250; fax (30) 20612525; e-mail info@drb.de; internet www.driz.de; f. 1909; monthly; publ. by Carl Heymanns Verlag; Chair., Editorial Bd LOTHAR JÜNEMANN; circ. 11,000.

Juristenzeitung: Postfach 2040, 72010 Tübingen; Wilhelmstr. 18, 72074 Tübingen; tel. (7071) 9230; fax (7071) 51104; e-mail info@mohr.de; internet www.mohr.de; f. 1944; fortnightly; Editors MATTHIAS JESTAEDT, HERBERT ROTH, ROLF STÜRNER, JOACHIM VOGEL; circ. 4,500 (2008).

Juristische Rundschau: Postfach 303421, 10728 Berlin; Lützowstr. 33, 10785 Berlin; tel. (30) 26005322; fax (30) 26005329; e-mail jr@degruyter.com; internet www.degruyter.de; f. 1925; monthly; publ. by De Gruyter Rechtswissenschaften Verlags GmbH; Editors-in-Chief Prof. Dr DIRK OLZEN, Dr GERHARD SCHÄFER.

Neue Juristische Wochenschrift: Postfach 110241, 60037 Frankfurt a.M.; Beethovenstr. 7B, 60325 Frankfurt a.M.; tel. (69) 7560910; fax (69) 75609149; e-mail redaktion@njw.de; internet www.njw.de; f. 1947; weekly, Fri.; Editors-in-Chief Prof. Dr ACHIM SCHÜNDER, CHRISTOPH WENK-FISCHER; circ. 39,168 (Oct. 2010).

Rabels Zeitschrift für ausländisches und internationales Privatrecht: Mittelweg 187, 20148 Hamburg; tel. (40) 41900263; fax (40) 41900288; e-mail heinrich@mpipriv.de; internet www.mpipriv.de; f. 1927; quarterly; German, English and French contributions, English summaries; Editors JÜRGEN BASEDOW, HOLGER FLEISCHER, REINHARD ZIMMERMANN.

Versicherungsrecht: Klosestr. 20–24, 76137 Karlsruhe; tel. (721) 35090; fax (721) 3509206; e-mail info@vvw.de; internet www.vvw.de; f. 1950; insurance law; 3 a month; Editor Prof. Dr EGON LORENZ; circ. 7,500 (2008).

Zeitschrift für die gesamte Strafrechtswissenschaft: Postfach 303421, 10728 Berlin; Lützowstr. 33, 10785 Berlin; tel. (30) 26005261; fax (30) 26005329; e-mail recht@degruyter.com; internet www.degruyter.de; f. 1881; quarterly; publ. by De Gruyter Rechtswissenschaften Verlags GmbH; Editor-in-Chief Prof. Dr KRISTIAN KÜHL.

Leisure Interests and Sport

AUTO BILD: Axel-Springer-Pl. 1, 20350 Hamburg; tel. (40) 34700; fax (40) 345660; e-mail redaktion@autobild.de; internet www.autobild.de; f. 1986; weekly; publ. by Axel Springer Verlag AG; Editor-in-Chief BERND WIELAND; circ. 592,507 (Oct. 2010).

Auto Motor und Sport: Leuschnerstr. 1, 70174 Stuttgart; tel. (711) 1821416; fax (711) 1822220; e-mail redaktion_ams@motorpresse.de; internet www.auto-motor-und-sport.de; fortnightly; publ. by Motor Presse Stuttgart GmbH & Co KG; Editor-in-Chief BERND OSTMANN; circ. 408,679 (Oct. 2010).

Bild + Funk: Münchener Str. 101/09, 85737 Ismaning; tel. (89) 272700; fax (89) 2707290; weekly, Fri.; publ. by Gong Verlag GmbH & Co KG; radio and television; Editor-in-Chief CARSTEN PFEFFERKORN; circ. 175,424 (Oct. 2010).

Computer Bild Spiele: Axel-Springer-Pl. 1, 20350 Hamburg; tel. (40) 34729136; fax (40) 34726749; e-mail leserbriefe@computerbildspiele.de; internet www.computerbildspiele.de; f. 1999; monthly; computer gaming; publ. by Axel Springer Verlag AG; Editor-in-Chief CHRISTIAN BIGGE; circ. 227,570 (Oct. 2010).

FF Magazin: Meyer & Meyer Fachverlag & Buchhandel GmbH, Von-Coels-Str. 390, 52080 Aachen; tel. (241) 958100; fax (241) 9581010; e-mail verlag@m-m-sports.com; internet www.ff-magazin.com; f. 2004; 10 a year; women's football; Editor-in-Chief MARTINA VOSS; circ. 30,000.

Flora Garten: Stubbenhuk 10, 20459 Hamburg; tel. (40) 37033771; fax (40) 37035682; internet www.floragarten.de; f. 1985; monthly; gardening; publ. by Gruner + Jahr AG & Co KG; Editor-in-Chief HOLGER RADLOFF; circ. 101,001 (Oct. 2010).

Funk Uhr: Brieffach 4460, 20350 Hamburg; tel. (40) 34726315; fax (40) 34722601; e-mail funkuhrabo@axelspringer.de; f. 1952; weekly; television listings; publ. by Axel Springer Verlag AG; Editors-in-Chief Dr THOMAS GARMS, JAN VON FRENDELL; circ. 583,409 (Oct. 2010).

GameStar: Lyonel-Feininger-Str. 26, 80807 München; tel. (89) 36086660; fax (89) 36086652; e-mail brief@gamestar.de; internet www.gamestar.de; f. 1996; monthly; computer gaming; publ. by IDG Entertainment Media GmbH; Editor-in-Chief MICHAEL TRIER; circ. 118,549 (Oct. 2010).

Gong: Postfach 400748, 80707 München; Gong Verlag GmbH & Co KG, Münchner Str. 101/09, 85737 Ismaning; tel. (89) 272700; fax (89) 272707490; e-mail kontakt@gongverlag.de; internet www.gong.de; f. 1948; radio and TV weekly; Editor-in-Chief CARSTEN PFEFFERKORN; circ. 302,513 (Oct. 2010).

Hörzu: Postfach 4110, Axel-Springer-Pl. 1, 20355 Hamburg; tel. (40) 34700; fax (40) 34729629; e-mail leserbriefe@hoerzu.de; internet www.hoerzu.de; f. 1946; weekly; radio and television; publ. by Axel Springer Verlag AG; Editor-in-Chief CHRISTIAN HELLMANN; circ. 1,403,212 (Oct. 2010).

Kicker-Sportmagazin: Badstr. 4–6, 90402 Nürnberg; tel. (911) 2160; fax (911) 9922420; e-mail info@kicker.de; internet www.kicker.de; f. 1920; 2 a week; illustrated sports magazine; publ. by Olympia Verlag GmbH; Editor-in-Chief RAINER HOLZSCHUH; circ. (Oct. 2010) 249,549 (Mon.), 213,338 (Thurs.).

Mein schöner Garten: Am Kestendamm 1, 77652 Offenburg; tel. (781) 8401; fax (781) 842254; e-mail garten@burda.com; internet www.mein-schoener-garten.de; monthly; gardening; publ. by Hubert Burda Media GmbH & Co KG; Editor-in-Chief ANDREA KÖGEL; circ. 394,155 (Oct. 2010).

Sport Bild: Axel-Springer-Str. 65, 10888 Hamburg; tel. (40) 34723689; fax (40) 34722085; e-mail sportbild@sportbild.de; internet www.sportbild.de; f. 1988; weekly; publ. by Axel Springer Verlag AG; Editor-in-Chief MANFRED HART; circ. 454,630 (Oct. 2010).

TV Digital: Axel-Springer-Pl. 1, 20355 Hamburg; tel. (40) 34700; fax (40) 34729629; e-mail leserservice@tvdigital.de; internet www.tvdigital.de; f. 2004; fortnightly; publ. by Axel Springer Verlag AG; Editor-in-Chief CHRISTIAN HELLMANN; circ. 1,656,558 (Sept. 2008).

TV Hören und Sehen: Burchardstr. 11, 20077 Hamburg; tel. (40) 30190; fax (40) 30191991; e-mail briefe@tv-hoeren-und-sehen.de; internet www.tvhus.de; f. 1962; weekly; television listings; publ. by Heinrich Bauer Verlagsgruppe; Editor-in-Chief UWE BOKELMANN; circ. 838,163 (Oct. 2010).

Medicine, Science and Technology

Angewandte Chemie: Postfach 101161, 69451 Weinheim; Boschstr. 12, 69469 Weinheim; tel. (6201) 606315; fax (6201) 606328; e-mail angewandte@wiley-vch.de; internet www.angewandte.de; f. 1888; applied chemistry; weekly; also publishes international edn in English; publ. by Wiley-VCH Verlag GmbH & Co KGaA; Editor-in-Chief PETER GÖLITZ.

Ärztliche Praxis: Gabrielenstr. 9, 80636 München; tel. (89) 89817404; fax (89) 89817400; e-mail khp@rbi.de; internet www.aerztlichepraxis.de; weekly; publ. by Reed Business Information GmbH; Editor-in-Chief ANDREAS BORCHERT; circ. 56,243 (Sept. 2008).

Chemie Ingenieur Technik: Postfach 101161, 69451 Weinheim; Boschstr. 12, 69469 Weinheim; tel. (6201) 606520; fax (6201) 606203; e-mail cit@wiley.com; internet www.cit-journal.de; f. 1928; monthly;

publ. by Wiley-VCH Verlag GmbH & Co KG; Editor Dr BARBARA BÖCK.

Der Chirurg: Tiergartenstr. 17, 69121 Heidelberg; tel. (6221) 4870; fax (6221) 4878461; e-mail friederike.fellenberg@springer.com; internet www.derchirurg.de; f. 1928; surgery; monthly; publ. by Springer Science + Business Media Deutschland GmbH; Editors Prof. Dr JOACHIM JÄHNE, Prof. Dr VOLKER SCHUMPELICK.

Computer Bild: Axel-Springer-Pl. 1, 20350 Hamburg; tel. (40) 34724300; fax (40) 34724683; e-mail redaktion@computerbild.de; internet www.computerbild.de; f. 1996; fortnightly; publ. by Axel Springer Verlag AG; Editor-in-Chief CHRISTIAN BIGGE; circ. 588,394 (Oct. 2010).

Deutsche Apotheker Zeitung: Postfach 101061, 70009 Stuttgart; Birkenwaldstr. 44, 70191 Stuttgart; tel. (711) 25820; fax (711) 2582290; e-mail daz@deutscher-apotheker-verlag.de; internet www.deutscher-apotheker-verlag.de; f. 1861; weekly, Thurs.; Editor-in-Chief PETER DITZEL; circ. 29,280 (Oct. 2010).

Deutsche Medizinische Wochenschrift: Postfach 301120, 70469 Stuttgart; Rüdigerstr. 14, 70469 Stuttgart; tel. (711) 89310; fax (711) 8931298; e-mail martin.middeke@thieme.de; internet www.thieme.de/dmw; f. 1875; weekly; Editor-in-Chief Prof. Dr MARTIN MIDDEKE; circ. 7,397 (Oct. 2010).

Deutsche Zahnärztliche Zeitschrift: Deutscher Ärzte-Verlag, Dieselstr. 2, 50859 Köln; tel. (2234) 7011242; fax (2234) 70116242; e-mail dey@aerzteverlag.de; internet www.online-dzz.de; f. 1945; monthly; dental medicine; Editors Prof. Dr GEURTSEN, Prof. Dr G. HEYDECKE; circ. 17,000 (Jan. 2011).

Elektro Automation: Ernst-Mey-Str. 8, 70771 Leinfelden-Echterdingen; tel. (711) 75340; fax (711) 7594390; e-mail info@konradin.de; internet www.ea-online.de; f. 1948; monthly; publ. by Konradin Verlag Robert Kohlhammer GmbH; Editor-in-Chief STEFAN ZIEGLER; circ. 18,037 (Oct. 2010).

Erziehung und Wissenschaft: Stamm Verlag GmbH, Goldammerweg 16, 45134 Essen; tel. (201) 843000; fax (201) 472590; e-mail info@stamm.de; internet www.erziehungundwissenschaft.de; f. 1948; monthly; organ of the Gewerkschaft Erziehung und Wissenschaft; national edn, plus 5 regional edns; Editor-in-Chief ULF RÖDDE; circ. 252,453 (Oct. 2010).

Geographische Rundschau: Georg-Westermann-Allee 66, 38104 Braunschweig; tel. (531) 708385; fax (531) 708374; e-mail gr@westermann.de; internet www.geographischerundschau.de; f. 1949; 11 a year; Man. Editor REINER JUENGST; circ. 8,000.

Handchirurgie, Mikrochirurgie, Plastische Chirurgie: Postfach 300504, 70445 Stuttgart; Rüdigerstr. 14, 70469 Stuttgart; tel. (711) 89310; fax (711) 8931453; f. 1969; 6 a year; Editors K.-J. PROMMERSBERGER, R. E. GIUNTA; circ. 1,600.

International Journal of Earth Sciences (Geologische Rundschau): Geologische Vereinigung e.V., Vulkanstr. 23, 56743 Mendig; tel. (02652) 989360; fax (02652) 989361; e-mail info@g-v.de; internet www.g-v.de; f. 1910; 8 a year; English; general, geological; publ. by Springer Science + Business Media Deutschland GmbH; Editor-in-Chief Prof. Dr WOLF-CHRISTIAN DULLO.

International Journal of Materials Research (Zeitschrift für Metallkunde): Max-Planck-Institut für Metallforschung, Heisenbergstr. 3, 70569 Stuttgart; tel. (711) 6893520; fax (711) 6893522; e-mail ruehle@mf.mpg.de; monthly; publ. by Carl Hanser Verlag; Editors Dr M. RÜHLE, Prof. Dr G. PETZOW.

Journal of Neurology: Springer Verlag, Tiergartenstr. 17, 69121 Heidelberg; tel. (6221) 4878434; fax (6221) 48768434; e-mail christine.lodge@springer.com; internet www.jon.springer.de; f. 1891; official journal of the European Neurological Society; Editors-in-Chief Prof. Dr G. SAID, Dr R. BARKER.

Medizinische Klinik: Neumarkter Str. 43, 81673 München; tel. (89) 43721300; fax (89) 43721399; e-mail verlag@urban-vogel.de; internet www.urban-vogel.de; f. 1904; monthly; official organ of the Deutsche Gesellschaft für Innere Medizin; publ. by Verlag Urban & Vogel GmbH; Editor ANNA-MARIA WORSCH; circ. 20,118 (Oct. 2010).

Nachrichten aus der Chemie: Postfach 900440, 60444 Frankfurt a.M.; Varrentrappstr. 40-42, 60486 Frankfurt a.M.; tel. (69) 79170; fax (69) 7917463; e-mail gdch@gdch.de; internet www.gdch.de; f. 1953; monthly; journal of the German Chemical Society; Editor-in-Chief Dr ERNST GUGGOLZ; circ. 30,051 (Oct. 2010).

National Geographic Deutschland: Am Baumwall 11, 20459 Hamburg; tel. (40) 37030; fax (40) 37035598; internet www.nationalgeographic.de; f. 1999; monthly; culture, history, nature, the Earth, the universe, people, animals, archaeology, paleontology, travel, research, expeditions; also publishes *NG World* (German and English; monthly; for children aged 7–13 years; circ. 91,021); Editor-in-Chief THOMAS SCHMIDT; circ. 186,037 (Oct. 2010).

Natur + Kosmos: Konradin Medien GmbH, Bretonischer Ring 13, 85630 Grasbrunn; tel. (89) 45616220; fax (89) 45616300; e-mail redaktion-natur@konradin.de; internet www.natur.de; f. 1904; monthly; popular nature journal; Editor-in-Chief ILONA JERGER; circ. 58,882 (Oct. 2010).

Naturwissenschaftliche Rundschau: Postfach 101061, 70009 Stuttgart; Birkenwaldstr. 44, 70191 Stuttgart; tel. (711) 2582289; fax (711) 2582283; e-mail nr@wissenschaftliche-verlagsgesellschaft.de; internet www.naturwissenschaftliche-rundschau.de; f. 1948; publ. by Gesellschaft Deutscher Naturforscher und Ärzte; monthly; scientific; Editor Dr KLAUS REHFELD; circ. 2,500.

Planta Medica: Postfach 301120, 70451 Stuttgart; Georg Thieme Verlag, Rüdigerstr. 14, 70469 Stuttgart; tel. (711) 89310; fax (711) 8931298; e-mail kunden.service@thieme.com; internet www.thieme.de/fz/plantamedica; f. 1953; 18 a year; journal of the Society of Medicinal Plant Research; Editor-in-Chief Prof. Dr LUC PIETERS.

P.M.: Weihenstephaner Str. 7, 81673 München; tel. (89) 415200; fax (89) 4152565; e-mail kontakt@pm-magazin.de; internet www.pm-magazin.de; f. 1978; monthly; technology, natural sciences, medicine, psychology, nature and the environment, history, philosophy, anthropology, culture, multimedia, the internet; publ. by Gruner + Jahr AG & Co KG; Editor-in-Chief THOMAS VAŠEK; circ. 328,330 (Oct. 2010).

rfe-Electrohandler: Am Friedrichshain 22, 10407 Berlin; tel. (30) 42151313; fax (30) 42151251; e-mail rfe.redaktion@hussberlin.de; internet www.rfe-eh.de; f. 1952; monthly; technology and marketing of consumer goods, electronics, digital imaging, multimedia, audio, video, broadcasting, TV; Man. Editor MATTHIAS ZSCHUNKE; circ. 16,303 (Sept. 2008).

Zeitschrift für Allgemeinmedizin: Postfach 301120, 70451 Stuttgart; Rüdigerstr. 14, 70469 Stuttgart; tel. (711) 8931532; fax (711) 8931408; e-mail silke.karl@thieme.de; internet www.thieme.de/fz/zfa; f. 1924; monthly; general and family medicine; publ. by Georg Thieme Verlag; Editors Prof. Dr E. BAUM, Prof. Dr M. KOCHEN, Prof. Dr E. HUMMERS-PRADIER, Prof. Dr W. NIEBLING.

Zeitschrift für Zahnärztliche Implantologie: Deutscher Ärtze-Verlag, Dieselstr. 2, 50859 Köln; tel. (2234) 7011241; fax (2234) 70116241; e-mail schubert@aerzteverlag.de; internet www.online-zzi.de; f. 1984; quarterly; dental medicine, implantology; Editors Prof. Dr STEFAN SCHULTZE-MOSGAU, Dr SEBASTIAN SCHMIDINGER, Dr KARL-LUDWIG ACKERMANN, Prof. Dr MARTIN LORENZONI; circ. 9,100 (March 2012).

Zentralblatt für Neurochirurgie (Central European Neurosurgery): Friedrich-Wilhelms Universität, Sigmund-Freud-Str. 25, 53127 Bonn; tel. (228) 2876501; fax (228) 2876573; e-mail zblneurochir@thieme.de; f. 1936; quarterly; German and English; neuro-surgery, spinal surgery, traumatology; Editor Prof. Dr J. SCHRAMM; circ. 1,650 (2008/09).

Politics, History and Current Affairs

akzente: Dag-Hammarskjöld-Weg 1-5, 65760 Eschborn; tel. (6196) 790; fax (6196) 791115; e-mail akzente@giz.de; internet www.giz.de; quarterly; politics, essays, photo-journalism, int. and devt co-operation; publ. by the Deutsche Gesellschaft für Internationale Zusammenarbeit (GIZ) GmbH; Editor WOLFGANG BARINA; circ. 8,000.

Deutschland: Frankfurter Societäts-Druckerei GmbH, Frankenallee 71–81, 60327 Frankfurt a.M.; tel. (69) 75014352; fax (69) 75014361; e-mail redaktion.deutschland@fsd.de; internet www.magazine-deutschland.de; 2 in a month; edns in German, Arabic, Chinese, English, French, Hungarian, Japanese, Portuguese, Russian, Spanish, Turkish; Editor-in-Chief PETER HINTEREDER; circ. 378,123 (Sept. 2008).

Eulenspiegel: Gubener Str. 47, 10243 Berlin; tel. (30) 2934630; fax (30) 29346321; e-mail verlag@eulenspiegel-zeitschrift.de; internet www.eulenspiegel-zeitschrift.de; f. 1946; political, satirical and humorous monthly; Editor-in-Chief Dr MATHIAS WEDEL; circ. 100,000.

FOCUS: Arabellastr. 23, 81925 München; tel. (89) 92500; fax (89) 92502026; e-mail anzeigen@focus.de; internet www.focus.de; f. 1993; weekly; political, general; publ. by FOCUS Magazin Verlag GmbH; Editors-in-Chief WOLFRAM WEIMER, ULI BAUR; circ. 601,516 (Jan. 2011).

Gesellschaft-Wirtschaft-Politik (GWP): Sürderstr. 22A, 51375 Leverkusen; tel. (2171) 344594; fax (2171) 344693; e-mail redaktion@gwp-pb.de; internet www.budrich-journals.de; f. 1951; quarterly; economics, politics, education; publ. by Verlag Barbara Budrich; Editors Prof. Dr SIBYLLE REINHARDT, Prof. Dr STEFAN HRADIL, Prof. Dr ROLAND STURM, EDMUND BUDRICH.

Internationale Politik: Rauchstr. 17–18, 10787 Berlin; tel. (30) 25423146; fax (30) 25423167; e-mail ip@dgap.org; internet www.internationalepolitik.de; f. 1946; monthly, 11 a year; journal of the German Council on Foreign Relations; edns in English (*IP International Edition*, quarterly) and Russian (bimonthly); publ. by Frankfurter Societäts-Druckerei GmbH, Frankfurt a.M; Editor-in-Chief Dr SYLKE TEMPEL; circ. 7,000.

Merkur (Deutsche Zeitschrift für europäisches Denken): Mommsenstr. 27, 10629 Berlin; tel. (30) 32709414; fax (30) 32709415; e-mail merkur.zeitschrift@snafu.de; internet www.online-merkur.de; f. 1947; monthly, 11 a year; literary, political; Editors KARL HEINZ BOHRER, KURT SCHEEL; circ. 4,800.

Neue Gesellschaft/Frankfurter Hefte: c/o Friedrich-Ebert-Stiftung Berlin, Hiroshimastr. 17, 10785 Berlin; tel. (30) 269357151; fax (30) 269359238; e-mail ng-fh@fes.de; internet www.ng-fh.de; f. 1946; monthly; cultural, political; Editor-in-Chief THOMAS MEYER; circ. 6,000.

Der Spiegel: Brandstwiete 19, 20457 Hamburg; tel. (40) 380800; fax (40) 30072247; e-mail spiegel@spiegel.de; internet www.spiegel.de; f. 1947; weekly; political, general; Editor-in-Chief RÜDIGER DITZ; circ. 1,022,512 (Oct. 2010).

Stern: Am Baumwall 11, 20459 Hamburg; tel. (40) 37030; e-mail info@stern.de; internet www.stern.de; f. 1948; weekly; news, history, lifestyle; publ. by Gruner + Jahr AG & Co KG; also publishes *Stern Fotographie* (quarterly; circ. 10,000) and *Stern Gesund Leben* (6 a year; circ. 65,139); Editor-in-Chief FRANK THOMSEN; circ. 911,185 (Oct. 2010).

Universitas: Postfach 101061, 70009 Stuttgart; Birkenwaldstr. 44, 70191 Stuttgart; tel. (711) 2582240; fax (711) 2582290; e-mail universitas@hirzel.de; internet www.hirzel.de/universitas; f. 1946; monthly; scientific, literary and philosophical; Editors Dr CHRISTIAN ROTTA, DIRK KATZSCHMANN; circ. 3,200.

VdK-Zeitung: Wurzerstr. 4A, 53175 Bonn; tel. (228) 820930; fax (228) 8209343; e-mail kontakt@vdk.de; internet www.vdk.de; f. 1950; monthly; publ. by Sozialverband VdK Deutschland eV; also maintains office in Munich; Editors JOSEF MÜSSENICH, ALBRECHT ENGEL, MICHAEL PAUSDER; circ. 1,372,528 (Oct. 2010).

vorwärts: Postfach 610322, 10925 Berlin; Stresemannstr. 30, 10963 Berlin; tel. (30) 25594100; fax (30) 25594192; e-mail verlag@vorwaerts.de; internet www.vorwaerts.de; f. 1994; affiliated to the Social Democratic Party (SPD); publ. by Berliner vorwärts Verlagsgesellschaft mbH; Editor-in-Chief UWE KNÜPFER; circ. 454,903 (Oct. 2010).

Religion and Philosophy

chrismon plus rheinland: Postfach 302255, 40402 Düsseldorf; Kaiserswerther Str. 450, 40474 Düsseldorf; tel. (211) 43690150; fax (211) 43690100; e-mail redaktion@chrismon-rheinland.de; internet www.chrismon-rheinland.de; f. 2004; monthly; Protestant; Editor-in-Chief VOLKER GÖTTSCHE; circ. 19,612 (Oct. 2010).

Christ in der Gegenwart: Hermann-Herder-Str. 4, 79104 Freiburg i. Br.; tel. (761) 2717276; fax (761) 2717243; e-mail cig@herder.de; internet www.christ-in-der-gegenwart.de; f. 1948; weekly; Editor-in-Chief JOHANNES RÖSER; circ. 32,240 (Oct. 2010).

Christlicher Digest: Okenstr. 23, 77652 Offenburg; tel. (781) 289928420; fax (781) 289928500; e-mail info@christlicherdigest.de; internet www.christlicherdigest.de; f. 2002 by merger of Evangelischer Digest (f. 1958), Katholischer Digest (f. 1949) and Der Sonntagsbrief (f. 1974); monthly, 10 a year; publ. by Verlag Christlicher Digest GmbH & Co KG; Editor FRED HEINE; circ. 40,000.

Der Dom: Karl-Schurz-Str. 26, 33100 Paderborn; tel. (5251) 153241; fax (5251) 153133; e-mail redaktion@derdom.de; internet www.derdom.org; f. 1946; weekly, Sun.; Catholic; publ. by Bonifatius GmbH, Druck-Buch-Verlag; Editor-in-Chief MATTHIAS NÜCKEL; circ. 33,500 (Dec. 2012).

Katholische Sonntagszeitung für Deutschland: Verlag Christliche Familie GmbH, Komödienstr. 48, 50667 Köln; tel. (821) 502420; fax (821) 5024241; e-mail redaktion@suv.de; internet www.katholische-sonntagszeitung.de; f. 1885; weekly; Publr Dr JOHANNES MÜLLER; circ. 62,193 (Oct. 2010).

Katholisches Sonntagsblatt: Postfach 4280, 73745 Ostfildern; Senefelderstr. 12, 73760 Ostfildern; tel. (711) 4406121; fax (711) 4406170; e-mail redaktion@kathsonntagsblatt.de; internet www.kathsonntagsblatt.de; f. 1848; weekly; publ. by Schwabenverlag AG; Editor-in-Chief REINER SCHLOTTHAUER; circ. 49,222 (Oct. 2010).

Kirche+Leben: Cheruskerring 19, 48147 Münster; tel. (251) 48390; fax (251) 4839122; e-mail info@bmv-verlag.de; internet www.kirche-und-leben.de; f. 1945; weekly; Catholic; Editor-in-Chief Dr HANS-JOSEF JOEST; circ. 197,967 (Oct. 2010).

Kirchenzeitung für das Erzbistum Köln: Postfach 102041, 50460 Köln; Ursulapl. 1, 50668 Köln; tel. (221) 1619131; fax (221) 1619216; e-mail redaktion@kirchenzeitung-koeln.de; internet www.kirchenzeitung-koeln.de; weekly; Editor-in-Chief STEPHAN GEORG SCHMIDT; circ. 39,788 (Oct. 2010).

Philosophisches Jahrbuch: Philosophie Department Lehrstuhl III, Ludwig-Maximilians-Universität München, Geschwister-Scholl-Pl. 1, 80539 München; e-mail redaktion.phj@lrz.uni-muenchen.de; f. 1893; 2 a year; publ. by Verlag Karl Alber GmbH; Editor MARCELA GARCÍA.

PRESS ORGANIZATION

Deutscher Presserat (German Press Council): Gerhard-von-Are-Str. 8, 53111 Bonn; tel. (228) 985720; fax (228) 9857299; e-mail info@presserat.de; internet www.presserat.de; f. 1956; self-regulatory body, composed of publishers and journalists; formulates guidelines and investigates complaints against the press; Dir LUTZ TILLMANNS.

NEWS AGENCIES

ddp (Deutscher Depeschendienst GmbH): Panoramastr. 1A, 10178 Berlin; tel. (30) 231220; fax (30) 23122182; e-mail info@ddp.de; internet www.ddp.de; f. 1971; merged with fmr official news agency of the GDR (Allgemeiner Deutscher Nachrichtendienst) 1992; maintains 22 branch offices in Germany; provides a daily news service and features in German; Man. Dir Dr MATTHIAS SCHULZE; Editor-in-Chief JOACHIM WIDMANN.

dpa (Deutsche Presse-Agentur GmbH): Mittelweg 38, 20148 Hamburg; tel. (40) 411332310; fax (40) 411332319; e-mail info@dpa.com; internet www.dpa.de; f. 1949; supplies all the daily newspapers, broadcasting stations and more than 1,000 further subscribers throughout Germany with its international, national and regional text, photo, audio, graphics and online services; English, Spanish, Arabic and German language news is also transmitted via direct satellite and the internet to press agencies, newspapers, radio and television stations, online services and non-media clients in more than 100 countries; 1,200 employees worldwide; Dir-Gen. MALTE VON TROTHA; Editor-in-Chief WOLFGANG BÜCHNER.

PRESS AND JOURNALISTS' ASSOCIATIONS

Bundesverband Deutscher Zeitungsverleger eV (German Newspaper Publishers' Association): Markgrafenstr. 15, 10969 Berlin; tel. (30) 7262980; fax (30) 726298299; e-mail bdzv@bdzv.de; internet www.bdzv.de; 11 affiliated *Land* asscns; Pres. HELMUT HEINEN; Chief Sec. Dr VOLKER SCHULZE.

Deutscher Journalisten-Verband (German Journalists' Association): Charlottenstr. 17, 10117 Berlin; tel. (30) 72627920; fax (30) 726279213; e-mail djv@djv.de; internet www.djv.de; 17 *Land* asscns; Chair. MICHAEL KONKEN; Man. Dir KAJO DÖHRING.

Verband Deutscher Zeitschriftenverleger eV (VDZ) (Association of German Magazine Publishers): Haus der Presse, Markgrafenstr. 15, 10969 Berlin; tel. (30) 726298101; fax (30) 7262898103; e-mail info@vdz.de; internet www.vdz.de; 7 affiliated *Land* asscns; Pres. Dr HUBERT BURDA; Man. Dir WOLFGANG FÜRSTNER.

Verein der Ausländischen Presse in Deutschland eV (VAP) (Foreign Press Association): Pressehaus 1306, Schiffbauerdamm 40, 10117 Berlin; tel. (30) 22489547; fax (30) 22489549; e-mail info@vap-deutschland.org; internet www.vap-deutschland.org; f. 1906; c. 400 mems; Chair. ROZALIA ROMANIEC.

Publishers

The following is a selection of the most prominent German publishing firms:

ADAC Verlag GmbH: Am Westpark 8, 81373 München; tel. (89) 76760; fax (89) 76762500; e-mail adac@adac.de; internet www.adac.de; f. 1958; guidebooks, legal brochures, maps, magazines; Pres. Dr PETER MEYER.

Aufbau Verlagsgruppe GmbH: Lindenstr. 20–25, 10969 Berlin; tel. (30) 283940; fax (30) 28394100; e-mail info@aufbau-verlag.de; internet aufbau-verlag.de; f. 1945; fiction, non-fiction, classical literature; Dirs RENÉ STRIEN, TOM ERBEN.

J. P. Bachem Verlag GmbH: Ursulapl. 1, 50668 Köln; tel. (221) 1619900; fax (221) 1619909; e-mail verlag@bachem.de; internet www.bachem-verlag.de; f. 1818; history, dialect, art history, architecture, sociology and walking/cycling tours of the Cologne and Rhine area; church and society; Dir CLAUS BACHEM.

Bauverlag BV GmbH: Avenwedderstr. 55, 33311 Gütersloh; tel. (1805) 5522533; fax (1805) 5522535; e-mail leserservice@bauverlag.de; internet www.bauverlag.de; f. 2002 following the merger of Fachzeitschriften GmbH (Gütersloh) and Bauverlag GmbH (Walluf); civil engineering, architecture, environment, energy, etc.; Dir KARL-HEINZ MÜLLER.

Verlag C. H. Beck oHg: Postfach 400340, 80703 München; Wilhelmstr. 9, 80801 München; tel. (89) 381890; fax (89) 38189398; e-mail info@beck.de; internet www.beck.de; f. 1763; law, science, theology, archaeology, philosophy, philology, history, politics, art, literature; Dirs Dr HANS DIETER BECK, WOLFGANG BECK.

Bibliographisches Institut und F. A. Brockhaus GmbH: Postfach 100311, 68167 Mannheim; Dudenstr. 6, 68003 Mannheim; tel. (621) 390101; fax (621) 3901391; internet www.bifab.de; f. 1805;

encyclopaedias, dictionaries, atlases, textbooks, calendars; Chair. Dr ALEXANDER BOB; Dirs TIMO BLÜMER, KLAUS KÄMPFE-BURGHARDT.

BLV Buchverlag GmbH & Co KG: Lothstr. 19, 80797 München; tel. (89) 1202120; fax (89) 120212120; e-mail blv.verlag@blv.de; internet www.blv.de; f. 1946; gardening, nature, sports, fitness, hunting, fishing, food and drink, health; Man. Dir RAINER TRETTER.

Breitkopf & Härtel: Postfach 1707, Walkmühlstr. 52, 65195 Wiesbaden; tel. (611) 450080; fax (611) 4500859; e-mail info@breitkopf.com; internet www.breitkopf.com; f. 1719; music and music books; Dir LIESELOTTE SIEVERS.

Bruckmann Verlag GmbH: Infanteriestr. 11A, 80797 München; tel. (89) 1306990; fax (89) 130699100; e-mail info@bruckmann.de; internet www.bruckmann.de; f. 1858; travel guides, illustrated travel books, video cassettes; Man. Dir CLEMENS SCHÜSSLER.

Bund-Verlag GmbH: Postfach, 60424 Frankfurt a.M.; Heddernheimer Landstr. 144, 60439 Frankfurt a.M.; tel. (69) 7950100; fax (69) 79501010; e-mail kontakt@bund-verlag.de; internet www.bund-verlag.de; f. 1947; labour and social law; Man. Dir RAINER JÖDE.

Verlag Georg D. W. Callwey GmbH & Co: Streitfeldstr. 35, 81673 München; tel. (89) 4360050; fax (89) 436005113; e-mail buch@callwey.de; internet www.callwey.de; f. 1884; architecture, gardens, crafts; Man. Dir LUTZ BANDTE.

Carlsen Verlag GmbH: Postfach 500380, 22703 Hamburg; Völckersstr. 14–20, 22765 Hamburg; tel. (40) 398040; fax (40) 39804390; e-mail info@carlsen.de; internet www.carlsen.de; f. 1953; children's and comic books; Dirs KLAUS HUMANN, JOACHIM KAUFMANN.

Delius Klasing Verlag: Siekerwall 21, 33602 Bielefeld; tel. (521) 5590; fax (521) 55988114; e-mail info@delius-klasing.de; internet www.delius-klasing.de; f. 1911; yachting, motor boats, surfing, mountain biking, race biking, basketball, motor cars; Dir KONRAD DELIUS.

Deutsche Verlags-Anstalt (DVA): Neumarkter Str. 28, 81673 München; tel. (89) 41360; fax (89) 41363721; e-mail markus.desaga@dva.de; internet www.randomhouse.de/dva; f. 1831; general; owned by Random House Group Ltd (United Kingdom).

Deutscher Taschenbuch Verlag GmbH & Co KG (DTV): Postfach 400422, 80704 München; Friedrichstr. 1A, 80801 München; tel. (89) 381670; fax (89) 346428; e-mail verlag@dtv.de; internet www.dtv.de; f. 1961; general fiction, history, music, reference, children, natural and social sciences, medicine, textbooks; Man. Dirs WOLFGANG BALK, BERND BLÜM.

Egmont vgs Verlagsgesellschaft mbH: Postfach 101251, 50452 Köln; Gertrudenstr. 30–36, 50667 Köln; tel. (221) 208110; fax (221) 2081166; e-mail info@vgs.de; internet www.vgs.de; f. 1970; fiction, hobbies, natural sciences, culture, popular culture, cinema, television, history; Dir Dr MICHAEL SCHWEINS.

Eichborn Verlag: Kaiserstr. 66, 60329 Frankfurt a.M.; tel. (69) 2560030; fax (69) 25600330; internet www.eichborn.de; f. 1980; literature, non-fiction, guidebooks, humour, cartoons; Man. Dir Dr MATTHIAS KIERZEK.

Bildungsverlag EINS GmbH: Hansestr. 115, 51149 Köln; tel. (220) 38982100; fax (220) 38982190; e-mail info@bildungsverlag1.de; internet www.bildungsverlag1.de; f. 2001 by merger of Gehlen, Kieser, Stam Verlag, Wolf, Dürr+Kessler and Konkordia; educational; Dir WILMAR DIEPGROND.

Elsevier GmbH: Postfach 201930, 80019 München; Hackerbrücke 6, 80335 München; tel. (89) 53830; fax (89) 5383939; e-mail info@elsevier.de; internet www.elsevier.de/journals; f. 1878; biological science, medical science; Dirs OLAF LODBROK, MARTIN LUDWIG, MARTIN BECK.

S. Fischer Verlag GmbH: Postfach 700355, 60553 Frankfurt a.M.; Hedderichstr. 114, 60596 Frankfurt a.M.; tel. (69) 60620; fax (69) 6062319; e-mail info@fischerverlage.de; internet www.fischerverlage.de; f. 1886; general, paperbacks; Publr Dr JÖRG BONG; Man. Dirs MONIKA SCHOELLER, MICHAEL JUSTUS, Dr UWE ROSENFELD.

Franz Cornelsen Bildungsgruppe: Mecklenburgische Str. 53, 14197 Berlin; tel. (30) 897850; fax (30) 89786299; e-mail mail@franz-cornelsen-bildungsholding.de; internet www.franz-cornelsen-bildungsholding.de; f. 1946 as Cornelsen Verlag GmbH & Co; name changed to present in 2010; school textbooks, educational software; Man. Dirs HARMUTH BRILL, WOLF-RÜDGER FELDMANN, MARTIN HÜPPE, Dr TILMANN MICHALETZ.

Franzis Verlag GmbH: Gruber Str. 46A, 85586 Poing; tel. (8121) 950; fax (8121) 19951696; e-mail info@franzis.de; internet www.franzis.de; f. 1924; Gen. Mans THOMAS KÄSBOHRER, WERNER MÜTZEL.

GRÄFE UND UNZER Verlag GmbH: Grillparzerstr. 12, 81675 München; tel. (89) 41981150; fax (89) 41981406; e-mail sarah.kirchner@graefe-und.unzer.de; internet www.graefe-und-unzer.de; f. 1722; cookery and wine, fitness, health and well-being, self-help, gardening, nature, pets; Man. Dir ANNETTE BEETZ.

Walter de Gruyter GmbH & Co KG Verlag: Postfach 303421, 10728 Berlin; Genthiner Str. 13, 10785 Berlin; tel. (30) 260050; fax (30) 26005251; e-mail info@degruyter.com; internet www.degruyter.com; f. 1919; humanities and theology, literary studies, linguistics, law, natural sciences, medicine, mathematics; imprints: De Gruyter Rechtswissenschaften Verlags, Max Niemeyer Verlag, K. G. Saur Verlag and Dr Arthur L. Sellier & Co; Man. Dir Dr SVEN FUND.

Carl Hanser Verlag GmbH & Co KG: Postfach 860420, 81631 München; Kolbergerstr. 22, 81679 München; tel. (89) 998300; fax (89) 984809; e-mail info@hanser.de; internet www.hanser.de; f. 1928; modern literature, plastics, technology, chemistry, science, economics, computers, children's books; Man. Dirs WOLFGANG BEISLER, STEPHAN D. JOSS, MICHAEL KRÜGER.

Harenberg Kommunikation Verlags- und Mediengesellschaft mbH & Co KG: Postfach 101852, 44018 Dortmund; Königswall 21, 44137 Dortmund; tel. (231) 90560; fax (231) 9056110; e-mail post@harenberg.de; internet www.harenberg.de; f. 1973; almanacs, encyclopaedias, calendars, periodicals; Man. Dir CHRISTOPH HELLERUNG.

Haufe-Lexware GmbH & Co KG: Munzinger Str. 9, 79111 Freiburg i. Br.; tel. (761) 8980; fax (761) 898993184; e-mail presselexware@haufe-lexware.com; internet haufe-lexware.com; f. 1934; business, law, taxation, information management, finance, social science; Man. Dirs MARTIN LAQUA, MARKUS REITHWIESNER.

Verlag Herder GmbH: Hermann-Herder-Str. 4, 79104 Freiburg i. Br.; tel. (761) 27170; fax (761) 2717520; e-mail info@herder.de; internet www.herder.de; f. 1801; religion, philosophy, psychology, history, education, art, encyclopaedias, children's books, gift books, periodicals; Proprs Dr HERMANN HERDER, MANUEL GREGOR HERDER.

Wilhelm Heyne Verlag: Bayerstr. 71–73, 80335 München; tel. (01805) 990505; e-mail vertrieb.verlagsgruppe@randomhouse.de; internet www.heyne.de; f. 1934; fiction, biography, history, cinema, etc.; Publr ULRICH GENZLER.

Hoffmann und Campe Verlag: Harvestehuder Weg 42, 20149 Hamburg; tel. (40) 441880; fax (40) 44188202; e-mail email@hoca.de; internet www.hoffmann-und-campe.de; f. 1781; biography, fiction, history, economics, science; Man. Dirs GÜNTER BEG, MARKUS KLOSE.

Hüthig GmbH: Postfach 102869, 69018 Heidelberg; Im Weiher 10, 69121 Heidelberg; tel. (6221) 4890; fax (6221) 489481; e-mail fachmedien@huethig.de; internet www.huethig.de; f. 1925; chemistry, chemical engineering, metallurgy, dentistry, etc.; Dir FABIAN MÜLLER.

Axel Juncker Verlag GmbH: Postfach 401120, 80711 München; Mies-van-der-Rohe-Str. 1, 80807 München; tel. (89) 360960; fax (89) 36096222; e-mail redaktion@axel-juncker.de; internet www.langenscheidt.de; f. 1972; dictionaries, language courses, reference; Man. Dir ANDREAS LANGENSCHEIDT.

S. Karger GmbH: Wilhelmstr. 20A, 79098 Freiburg i. Br.; tel. (761) 452070; fax (761) 4520714; e-mail information@karger.de; internet content.karger.com; f. 1890; medicine, psychology, natural sciences; Dirs THOMAS KARGER, GABRIELLA KARGER TRAVELLA, SIBYLLE GROSS.

Verlag Kiepenheuer & Witsch GmbH & Co KG: Postfach 102062, 50460 Köln; Bahnhofsvorpl. 1, 50667 Köln; tel. (221) 376850; fax (221) 3768511; e-mail verlag@kiwi-verlag.de; internet www.kiwi-verlag.de; f. 1947; general fiction, biography, history, sociology, politics; Man. Dirs HELGE MANCHOW, PETER ROIK.

Ernst Klett Verlag GmbH: Postfach 106016, 70049 Stuttgart; Rotebühlstr. 77, 70178 Stuttgart; tel. (711) 66720; fax (711) 6672000; e-mail pr@klett.de; internet www.klett.de; f. 1897; primary school and secondary school textbooks, atlases, teaching aids; Publr MICHAEL KLETT.

Verlag W. Kohlhammer GmbH: Hessbrühlstr. 69, 70565 Stuttgart; tel. (711) 78630; fax (711) 78638430; e-mail kohlhammer@kohlhammer.de; internet www.kohlhammer.de; f. 1866; periodicals, general textbooks; Man. Dirs Dr JÜRGEN GUTBROD, LEOPOLD FREIHERR VON UND ZU WEILER.

Kösel-Verlag: Flüggenstr. 2, 80639 München; tel. (89) 178010; fax (89) 17801111; e-mail info@koesel.de; internet www.koesel.de; f. 1593; philosophy, religion, psychology, spirituality, family and education.

Kreuz Verlag GmbH: Hermann-Herder-Str. 4, 79104 Freiburg i. Br.; tel. (761) 27170; fax (761) 2717520; e-mail service@verlagkreuz.de; internet www.kreuzverlag.de; f. 1983; theology, psychology, pedagogics; Dirs OLAF CARSTENS, MANUEL HERDER, HANS DIETER VOGT.

Verlag der Kunst GmbH: Neckarstr. 13, 72622 Nürtingen; tel. (70) 2256343; fax (70) 2253286; e-mail info@verlag-kunst-kunsttherapie.de; internet www.verlag-kunst-kunsttherapie.de; f. 1952; art books and reproductions; Dir ROGER N. GREENE.

Peter Lang GmbH—Internationaler Verlag der Wissenschaften: Postfach 940225, 60460 Frankfurt a.M.; Eschborner Landstr. 42–50, 60489 Frankfurt a.M.; tel. (69) 7807050; fax (69) 78070550; e-mail zentrale.frankfurt@peterlang.com; internet www.peterlang

.de; sociology, politics, communications, linguistics, science of law, literature, theology, economics, education; Dir Dr JÖRG MEIDENBAUER.

Langenscheidt-Verlag: Postfach 401120, 80711 München; Mies-van-der-Rohe Str. 1, 80807 München; tel. (89) 360960; fax (89) 36096222; e-mail mail@langenscheidt.de; internet www.langenscheidt.de; f. 1856; foreign languages, German for foreigners, dictionaries, textbooks, language guides, CDs, CD-ROMs, software, electronic dictionaries; Man. Dir JAN HENNE DE DIJN.

Bastei Lübbe GmbH & Co KG: Schanzenstr. 6–20, 51063 Köln; tel. (221) 82000; internet www.luebbe.de; f. 1964; general fiction and non-fiction, biography, history, etc.; Publr STEFAN LÜBBE; Man. Dir THOMAS SCHIERACK.

Hermann Luchterhand Verlag GmbH: Postfach 2352, 56513 Neuwied; Heddesdorfer Str. 31, 56564 Neuwied; tel. (2631) 8012000; fax (2631) 8012204; e-mail info@wolterskluwer.de; internet www.luchterhand.de; f. 1924; insurance, law, taxation, labour; imprint of Wolters Kluwer Deutschland GmbH; Man. Dir Dr ULRICH HERMANN.

Mairdumont: Marco-Polo-Zentrum, 73760 Ostfildern; tel. (711) 45020; fax (711) 4502310; internet www.mairdumont.com; f. 1848; road maps, atlases, tourist guides; Man. Dirs Dr STEPHANIE MAIR-HUYDTS, Dr THOMAS BRINKMANN, UWE ZACHMANN.

J. B. Metzler Verlag: Postfach 103241, 70028 Stuttgart; Werastr. 21–23, 70182 Stuttgart; tel. (711) 21940; fax (711) 2194119; e-mail info@metzlerverlag.de; internet www.metzlerverlag.de; f. 1682; literature, music, linguistics, history, cultural studies, philosophy, textbooks; Dir VOLKER DABELSTEIN.

Verlag Moderne Industrie AG & Co KG: Justus-von-Liebig-Str. 1, 86899 Landsberg; tel. (8191) 1250; fax (8191) 125211; e-mail info@mi-verlag.de; internet www.mi-verlag.de; f. 1952; management, investment, technical; Man. Dir FABIAN MÜLLER.

Verlagsgesellschaft Rudolf Müller GmbH & Co KG: Postfach 410949, 50869 Köln; Stolberger Str. 84, 50933 Köln; tel. (221) 54970; fax (221) 5497326; e-mail rmh@rudolf-mueller.de; internet www.rudolf-mueller.de; f. 1840; architecture, construction, engineering, education; Publrs Dr CHRISTOPH MÜLLER, RUDOLF M. BLESER.

MVS Medizinverlage Stuttgart GmbH & Co KG: Oswald-Hesse-Str. 50, 70469 Stuttgart; tel. (711) 89310; fax (711) 8931706; e-mail kunden.service@thieme.de; internet www.medizinverlage.de; imprints are Karl F. Haug, Hippokrates, Sonntag, Enke, Parey and TRIAS und Haug Sachbuch; CEO Dr THOMAS SCHERB.

Verlag Friedrich Oetinger GmbH: Postfach 658230, 22374 Hamburg; Poppenbütteler Chaussee 53, 22397 Hamburg; tel. (40) 60790902; fax (40) 6072326; e-mail oetinger@verlagsgrupper-oetinger.de; internet www.oetinger.de; f. 1946; juvenile, illustrated books; Man. Dirs SILKE WEITENDORF, JAN WEITENDORF, TILL WEITENDORF, KLAUS-PETER STEGEN.

Pabel-Moewig Verlag KG: Karlsruher Str. 31, 76437 Rastatt; tel. (7222) 130; fax (7222) 13218; e-mail info@vpm.de; internet www.vpm-online.de; f. 1989; Gen. Man. WALTER A. FUCHS.

Piper Verlag GmbH: Georgenstr. 4, 80799 München; tel. (89) 3818010; fax (89) 338704; e-mail info@piper.de; internet www.piper.de; f. 1904; literature, philosophy, theology, psychology, natural sciences, political and social sciences, history, biographies, music; Dirs MARCEL HARTGES, HANS-JOACHIM HARTMANN.

Verlagsgruppe Random House GmbH: Neumarkter Str. 28, 81673 München; tel. (89) 41360; fax (89) 41363721; e-mail vertrieb.verlagsgruppe@randomhouse.de; internet www.randomhouse.de; f. 1994; general, reference; Chair. Dr JOERG PFUHL.

Ravensburger Buchverlag Otto Maier GmbH: Robert-Bosch-Str. 1, 88214 Ravensburg; tel. (751) 860; fax (751) 861311; e-mail buchverlag@ravensburger.de; internet www.ravensburger.de; f. 1883; subsidiary of Ravensburger AG; Man. Dirs ULRIKE METZGER, JOHANNES HAUENSTEIN.

Philipp Reclam jun. Verlag GmbH: Siemensstr. 32, 71254 Ditzingen bei Stuttgart; tel. (7156) 1630; fax (7156) 163197; e-mail info@reclam.de; internet www.reclam.de; f. 1828; literature, literary criticism, fiction, history of culture and literature, philosophy and religion, biography, fine arts, music; Dirs FRANK R. MAX, FRANZ SCHÄFER.

Rowohlt Verlag GmbH: Hamburgerstr. 17, 21465 Reinbek bei Hamburg; tel. (40) 72720; fax (40) 7272319; e-mail info@rowohlt.de; internet www.rowohlt.de; f. 1908/1953; politics, science, fiction, translations of international literature; Dirs PETER KRAUS VOM CLEFF, ALEXANDER FEST, LUTZ KETTMANN.

K. G. Saur Verlag GmbH: Postfach 401649, 80716 München; Mies-van-der-Rohe-Str. 1, 80707 München; tel. (89) 769020; fax (89) 76902150; e-mail info@degruyter.com; internet www.saur.de; f. 1949; library science, reference, dictionaries, encyclopaedias, books, journals, microfiches, CD-ROMs, DVDs, online databases; brs in Leipzig, Osnabrück and Zürich (Switzerland); an imprint of Walter de Gruyter GmbH & Co KG.

Schattauer GmbH: Postfach 104543, 70040 Stuttgart; Hoelderlinstr. 3, 70174 Stuttgart; tel. (711) 229870; fax (711) 2298750; e-mail info@schattauer.de; internet www.schattauer.de; f. 1949; medicine and related sciences; Man. Dirs DIETER BERGEMANN, Dr WULF BERTRAM.

Verlag Dr Otto Schmidt KG: Postfach 511026, 50946 Köln; Gustav-Heinemann-Ufer 58, 50968 Köln; tel. (221) 9373801; fax (221) 93738900; e-mail info@otto-schmidt.de; internet www.otto-schmidt.de; f. 1905; university textbooks, jurisprudence, tax law; Man. Dir Dr FELIX HEY.

Egmont Franz Schneider Verlag GmbH: Postfach 101251, 50452 Köln; Gertrudenstr. 30–36, 50667 Köln; tel. (221) 208110; fax (221) 2081166; e-mail info@schneiderbuch.de; internet www.schneiderbuch.de; f. 1913; children's books; Man. Dir FRANK KNAU.

Springer Science+Business Media Deutschland GmbH: Heidelberger Pl. 3, 14197 Berlin; tel. (30) 827870; fax (30) 8214091; internet www.springer.com; f. 1842; wholly owned subsidiary of Springer Science+Business Media Netherlands BV; CEO DERK HAANK.

Stollfuss Verlag Bonn GmbH & Co KG: Dechenstr. 3–11, 53115 Bonn; tel. (228) 7240; fax (228) 72491181; e-mail info@stollfuss.de; internet www.stollfuss.de; reference, fiscal law, economics, investment, etc.; Man. Dir WOLFGANG STOLLFUSS.

Suhrkamp Verlag GmbH & Co KG: Pappelallee 78–79, 10437 Berlin; tel. (30) 7407440; fax (30) 740744199; e-mail info@suhrkamp.de; internet www.suhrkamp.de; f. 1950; modern German and foreign literature, philosophy, poetry; Chair. ULLA UNSELD-BERKÉWICZ.

SYBEX Verlags- und Vertriebs-GmbH: Emil-Hoffmann-Str. 1, 50996 Köln; tel. (2236) 3999200; fax (2236) 3999229; e-mail sybex@sybex.de; internet www.sybex.de; f. 1981; computer books and software; Man. Dirs HOLGER SCHNEIDER, ANJA SCHRIEVER.

Georg Thieme Verlag: Postfach 301120, 70451 Stuttgart; Rüdigerstr. 14, 70469 Stuttgart; tel. (711) 89310; fax (711) 8931298; e-mail info@thieme.com; internet www.thieme.de; f. 1886; medicine and natural sciences; Man. Dirs Dr ALBRECHT HAUFF, Dr WOLFGANG KNÜPPE.

Thienemann Verlag GmbH: Blumenstr. 36, 70182 Stuttgart; tel. (711) 210550; fax (711) 2105539; e-mail info@thienemann.de; internet www.thienemann.de; f. 1849; picture books, children's books, juveniles; Dir KLAUS WILLBERG.

Verlag Eugen Ulmer GmbH & Co: Wollgrasweg 41, 70599 Stuttgart; tel. (711) 45070; fax (711) 4507120; e-mail info@ulmer.de; internet www.ulmer.de; f. 1868; agriculture, horticulture, science, periodicals; Dir MATTHIAS ULMER.

Verlag Ullstein GmbH: Charlottenstr. 13, 10969 Berlin; tel. (30) 25913570; fax (30) 25913523; f. 1894; literature, art, music, theatre, contemporary history, biography; Pres. Dr JÜRGEN RICHTER.

Ullstein Buchverlage GmbH: Friedrichstr. 126, 10117 Berlin; tel. (30) 23456300; fax (30) 23456303; e-mail info@ullstein-buchverlage.de; internet www.ullsteinbuchverlage.de; f. 1894; general fiction, history, art, philosophy, religion, psychology; Dir SIV BUBLITZ.

Verlag Ullstein GmbH: Charlottenstr. 13, 10969 Berlin; tel. (30) 25913570; fax (30) 25913523; f. 1894; literature, art, music, theatre, contemporary history, biography; Pres. Dr JÜRGEN RICHTER.

Wiley-VCH Verlag GmbH & Co KGaA: Boschstr. 12, 69469 Weinheim; tel. (6201) 6060; fax (6201) 606328; e-mail service@wiley-vch.de; internet www.wiley-vch.de; f. 1921; natural sciences, especially chemistry, chemical engineering, civil engineering, architecture, biotechnology, materials science, life sciences, information technology and physics, scientific software, business, management, computer science, finance and accounting; Man. Dirs CHRISTOPHER J. DICKS, BIJAN GHAWAMI, WILLIAM PESCE.

Verlag Klaus Wingefeld: Lachergt. 7, 86919 Holzhausen; e-mail info@kinderbuchverlag.de.

PRINCIPAL ASSOCIATION OF BOOK PUBLISHERS AND BOOKSELLERS

Börsenverein des Deutschen Buchhandels eV (German Publishers and Booksellers Association): Postfach 100442, 60004 Frankfurt a.M.; Grosser Hirschgraben 17–21, 60311 Frankfurt a.M.; tel. (69) 13060; fax (69) 1306201; e-mail info@boev.de; internet www.boersenverein.de; f. 1825; Chair. Dr GOTTFRIED HONNEFELDER; Man. Dir ALEXANDER SKIPIS.

Broadcasting and Communications

REGULATORY AUTHORITY

Bundesnetzagentur für Elektrizität, Gas, Telekommunikation, Post und Eisenbahnen (Bundesnetzagentur) (Federal Network Agency for Electricity, Gas, Telecommunications, Post and Railways): Tulpenfeld 4, 53113 Bonn; Postfach 8001, 53105 Bonn; tel. (228) 140; fax (228) 148872; e-mail poststelle@bnetza.de; internet www.bundesnetzagentur.de; f. 1997; fmrly Regulierungsbehörde für Telekommunikation und Post, renamed 2005; responsible for supervising the liberalization and deregulation of the post and telecommunications sector, as well as electricity, gas and railways; Pres. MATTHIAS KURTH.

TELECOMMUNICATIONS

Deutsche Telekom AG: Postfach 2000, 53105 Bonn; Friedrich-Ebert-Allee 140, 53113 Bonn; tel. (228) 1810; fax (228) 18171915; e-mail info@telekom.de; internet www.telekom.de; f. 1989; partially privatized 1995 with further privatization pending; 14.8% state-owned, 16.9% owned by Kreditanstalt für Wiederaufbau, 68.3% owned by private shareholders; fmr monopoly over national telecommunications network removed 1998; Chair., Supervisory Bd Prof. Dr ULRICH LEHNER; Chair., Management Bd and CEO RENÉ OBERMANN.

E-Plus Service GmbH & Co. KG: Edison-Allee 1, 14473 Potsdam; tel. (211) 4480; fax (211) 4482222; e-mail kundenservice@eplus.de; internet www.eplus.de; f. 1993; 13.6m. subscribers (June 2007); owned by KPN Mobile NV (Netherlands); Chair., Supervisory Bd EELCO BLOK; Chair., Management Bd and CEO THORSTEN DIRKS.

Mobilcom debitel AG: Hollerstr. 126, 24782 Büdelsdorf; tel. (180) 5022240; e-mail info@mobilcom.de; internet www.mobilcom-debitel.de; f. 2009 following merger with mobilCom Communicationstecknik AG; mobile cellular telecommunications and internet service provider; Mans STEPHAN BRAUER, JOACHIM PREISIG, CHRISTOPH VILANEK.

Telefónica O_2 Germany GmbH & Co OHG: Georg-Brauchle-Ring 23–25, 80992 München; tel. (89) 24421201; fax (89) 24421209; internet www.de.o2.com; f. 1995 as VIAG Interkom; name changed to O_2 Germany in 2002; mobile cellular telecommunications; acquired by Telefónica SA (Spain) 2006; 18.3m. subscribers (March 2010); CEO RENÉ SCHUSTER.

T-Mobile Deutschland GmbH: POB 300463, 53184 Bonn; Landgrabenweg 151, 53227 Bonn; tel. (228) 93631717; fax (228) 93631719; e-mail info@telekom.de; internet www.t-mobile.de; f. 1993; 34.3m. subscribers (June 2007); subsidiary of Deutsche Telekom AG; Chair., Management Bd GEORG PÖLZL.

Vodafone D2 GmbH: Am Seestern 1, 40547 Düsseldorf; tel. (211) 5330; fax (211) 5332200; e-mail kontakt@vodafone.com; internet www.vodafone.de; f. 1992 as Mannesmann Mobilfunk GmbH; present name adopted 2000; 38m. subscribers (March 2010); subsidiary of Vodafone Group PLC (UK); acquired fixed-line services provider Arcor AG in 2008; Chair., Management Bd and CEO FRIEDRICH JOUSSEN.

BROADCASTING

Radio

Regional public radio stations are co-ordinated by the ARD (see below). There are also numerous regional commercial radio stations.

In early 2009 Digital Audio Broadcasting (DAB) services were available to approximately 80% of the population.

Public Stations

Arbeitsgemeinschaft der öffentlich-rechtlichen Rundfunkanstalten der Bundesrepublik Deutschland (ARD) (Association of Public Law Broadcasting Organizations): Bertramstr. 8, 60320 Frankfurt a.M.; tel. (69) 15687211; fax (69) 15687100; e-mail info@ard.de; internet www.ard.de; f. 1950; Chair. PETER BOUDGOUST; the co-ordinating body of Germany's public service radio and television organizations; each of the following organizations broadcasts radio and television channels:

Bayerischer Rundfunk (BR): Rundfunkpl. 1, 80355 München; tel. (89) 590001; fax (89) 59002375; e-mail info@br.de; internet www.bronline.de; Dir-Gen. Prof. Dr ULRICH WILHELM.

Deutsche Welle: Kurt-Schumacher-Str. 3, 53113 Bonn; tel. (228) 4290; fax (228) 4293000; e-mail info@dw-world.de; internet www.dw-world.de; f. 1953; German short-wave radio (DW-Radio), satellite television service (DW-TV) and online service; broadcasts daily in 30 languages for Europe and overseas; Dir-Gen. ERIK BETTERMANN.

Hessischer Rundfunk (hr): Bertramstr. 8, 60320 Frankfurt a.M.; tel. (69) 1551; fax (69) 1552900; internet www.hr-online.de; Dir-Gen. Dr HELMUT REITZE.

Mitteldeutscher Rundfunk (mdr): Kanstr. 71–73, 04275 Leipzig; tel. (341) 3000; fax (341) 3006788; e-mail zuschauerservice@mdr.de; internet www.mdr.de; f. 1992; Dir-Gen. Prof. Dr KAROLA WILLE.

Norddeutscher Rundfunk (NDR): Rothenbaumchaussee 132–134, 20149 Hamburg; tel. (40) 41560; fax (40) 447602; e-mail info@ndr.de; internet www.ndr.de; f. 1956; Dir-Gen. LUTZ MARMOR.

Radio Bremen: Diepenau 10, 28195 Bremen; tel. (421) 2460; fax (421) 24641200; e-mail info@radiobremen.de; internet www.radiobremen.de; f. 1945; Dir-Gen. JAN METZGER.

Rundfunk Berlin-Brandenburg (rbb): Masurenallee 8–14, 14057 Berlin; tel. (30) 97993-0; fax (30) 97993-19; e-mail presse@rbb-online.de; internet www.rbb-online.de; f. 2003; Dir-Gen. DAGMAR REIM.

Saarländischer Rundfunk (SR): Funkhaus Halberg, 66100 Saarbrücken; tel. (681) 6020; fax (681) 6023874; e-mail info@sr-online.de; internet www.sr-online.de; f. 1952; Dir-Gen. THOMAS KLEIST.

Südwestrundfunk (SWR): Neckarstr. 230, 70150 Stuttgart; tel. (49) 9290; fax (49) 9292600; e-mail info@swr.de; internet www.swr.de; Dir-Gen. PETER BOUDGOUST.

Westdeutscher Rundfunk (WDR): Appellhofpl. 1, 50667 Köln; tel. (221) 2200; fax (221) 2204800; e-mail redaktion@wdr.de; internet www.wdr.de; Dir-Gen. MONIKA PIEL.

Deutschlandradio: Raderberggürtel 40, 50968 Köln; tel. (221) 3450; fax (221) 3454802; e-mail hoererservice@dradio.de; internet www.dradio.de; f. 1994 by merger of Deutschlandfunk, Deutschlandsender Kultur and RIAS Berlin; national public service radio broadcaster; 3 stations: Deutschlandfunk, Deutschlandradio Kultur and DRadio Wissen; jtly managed by ARD and ZDF; Dir-Gen. Dr WILLI STEUL.

Commercial Radio

Verband Privater Rundfunk und Telemedien eV (VPRT) (Asscn of Commercial Broadcasters and Audiovisual Cos): Stromstr. 1, 10555 Berlin; tel. (30) 398800; fax (30) 39880148; e-mail info@vprt.de; internet www.vprt.de; f. 1984; 140 mems (April 2011); Man. Dir CLAUS GREWENIG.

Television

There are three main public service television channels. The autonomous regional broadcasting organizations combine to provide material for the First Programme, which is produced by ARD. The Second Programme (Zweites Deutsches Fernsehen—ZDF) is completely separate and is controlled by a public corporation of all the *Länder*. It is partly financed by advertising. The Third Programme (ARTE Deutschland) provides a cultural and educational service in the evenings only, with contributions from both ARD and ZDF. There are also three other public service channels (KI.KA, Phoenix and 3Sat), which are jointly managed by ARD and ZDF. Commercial television channels also operate.

Analogue broadcasting was discontinued throughout Germany in early December 2008.

Public Stations

ARD: Programmdirektion Deutsches Fernsehen: Arnulfstr. 42, 80335 München; tel. (89) 59003344; fax (89) 59003249; e-mail info@daserste.de; internet www.daserste.de; co-ordinates the regional public service television organizations (see Radio, above); Chair. MONIKA PIEL; Dir of Programmes VOLKER HERRES.

ARTE Deutschland TV GmbH: Postfach 100213, 76483 Baden-Baden; tel. (7221) 9369-0; fax (7221) 9369-70; internet www.arte.tv; f. 1991; arts, cultural programmes, in French and German; Pres. Dr VÉRONIQUE CAYLA.

KI.KA—Der Kinderkanal ARD/ZDF: Gothaer Str. 36, 99094 Erfurt; tel. (361) 2181890; fax (361) 2181848; e-mail kika@kika.de; internet www.kika.de; f. 1997; children's programming; jtly managed by ARD and ZDF; Dir Prof. Dr KAROLA WILLE.

Phoenix: Langer Grabenweg 45-47, 53175 Bonn; tel. (1802) 8217; fax (1802) 8213; e-mail info@phoenix.de; internet www.phoenix.de; f. 1997; digital channel broadcasting news and current affairs programmes; jtly managed by ARD and ZDF; Dir of Programming CHRISTOPH MINHOFF.

Zweites Deutsches Fernsehen (ZDF): 55100 Mainz; tel. (6131) 700; fax (6131) 7012157; e-mail info@zdf.de; internet www.zdf.de; f. 1961 by the *Land* govts as a second television channel; Dir-Gen. MARKUS SCHÄCHTER; Dir of Programmes Dr THOMAS BELLUT.

3Sat: ZDF-Str. 1, 55127 Mainz; tel. (6131) 700; fax (6131) 702157; e-mail info@zdf.de; internet www.3sat.de; f. 1984; satellite channel broadcasting cultural programmes in Germany, Austria and German-speaking areas of Switzerland; 32.5% each owned by ARD and

ZDF, 25.0% owned by ÖRF (Austria) and 10.0% owned by SRG SSR idée suisse (Switzerland); Dir-Gen. Dr MARKUS SCHÄCHTER.

Commercial Television

ProSiebenSat.1 Media AG: Medienallee 7, 85774 Unterföhring; tel. (89) 950710; fax (89) 95071122; e-mail info@prosiebensat1.com; internet www.prosiebensat1.com; f. 2000 by merger of ProSieben Media AG (f. 1989) and Sat.1 (f. 1984); operates Sat.1, ProSieben, Kabel eins and sixx; Chair., Management Bd THOMAS EBELING; Chair., Supervisory Bd GÖTZ MÄUSER.

RTL Television GmbH: Picassopl. 1, 50679 Köln; tel. (49) 2214560; fax (49) 2214561690; e-mail pressezentrum@rtl.de; internet www.rtl-television.de; f. 1984; subsidiary of RTL Group (Luxembourg); CEO ANKE SCHÄFERKORDT.

Sky Deutschland AG: Medienallee 26, 85774 Unterföhring; tel. (89) 995802; fax (89) 99586239; e-mail info@sky.de; internet www.sky.de; f. 1988; fmrly called Premiere Fernsehen GmbH & Co KG; name changed to present in 2009; subscriber service offering 53 television channels; 49.9% stake owned by News Corporation (USA); CEO BRIAN SULLIVAN.

Verband Privater Rundfunk und Telemedien eV (VPRT): see under Radio; represents privately owned satellite, cable and digital television cos.

VOX Film- und Fernseh- GmbH: Picassopl. 1, 50679 Köln; tel. (221) 9534370; e-mail mail@vox.de; internet www.vox.de; f. 1991; cable, satellite and digital terrestrial channel broadcasting entertainment programmes; 99.7% owned by RTL Group (Luxembourg) and 0.3% owned by Development Company for Television Program; CEO FRANK HOFFMANN.

Association

Bundesverband Digitale Wirtschaft eV (BVDW): Berliner Allee 57, 40212 Düsseldorf; tel. (211) 6004560; fax (211) 60045633; e-mail info@bvdw.org; internet www.bvdw.org; 700 mems (July 2008); Pres. ARNDT GROTH; Man. Dir TANJA FELLER.

Finance

(cap. = capital; res = reserves; dep. = deposits; m. = million; brs = branches; amounts in euros)

The Deutsche Bundesbank, the central bank of Germany, consists of the central administration in Frankfurt am Main (considered to be the financial capital of the country), nine main regional offices (*Hauptverwaltungen*) and 47 smaller branches. In carrying out its functions as determined by law the Bundesbank is independent of the Federal Government, but is required to support the Government's general economic policy. As a member of the European System of Central Banks (ESCB), the Bundesbank implements the single monetary policy determined by the Governing Council of the European Central Bank (ECB).

All credit institutions other than the Bundesbank are subject to supervision through the Federal Financial Supervisory Authority (Bundesanstalt für Finanzdienstleistungsaufsicht) in Bonn. Banks outside the central banking system are divided into three groups: private commercial banks, credit institutions incorporated under public law and co-operative credit institutions. All these commercial banks are 'universal banks', conducting all kinds of customary banking business. There is no division of activities. As well as the commercial banks there are a number of specialist banks, such as private or public mortgage banks.

The group of private commercial banks includes all banks incorporated as a company limited by shares (Aktiengesellschaft—AG, Kommanditgesellschaft auf Aktien—KGaA) or as a private limited company (Gesellschaft mit beschränkter Haftung—GmbH) and those which are known as 'regional banks' because they do not usually function throughout Germany; and those banks which are established as sole proprietorships or partnerships and mostly have no branches outside their home town. The main business of all private commercial banks is short-term lending. The private bankers fulfil the most varied tasks within the banking system.

The public law credit institutions are the savings banks (*Sparkassen*) and the *Landesbank-Girozentralen*. The latter act as central banks and clearing houses on a national level for the savings banks. Laws governing the savings banks limit them to certain sectors—credits, investments and money transfers—and they concentrate on the areas of home financing, municipal investments and the trades. In early 2009 there were 446 *Sparkassen* and 10 *Landesbank-Girozentralen* in Germany.

The head institution of the co-operative system is the DZ BANK (Deutsche Zentral-Genossenschaftsbank AG). In early 2009 there were 1,210 credit co-operatives, including central institutions.

In April 2010 there were 1,963 banks in Germany.

SUPERVISORY BODY

Bundesanstalt für Finanzdienstleistungsaufsicht (BaFin) (Federal Financial Supervisory Authority): Postfach 1253, 53002 Bonn; Graurheindorfer Str. 108, 53117 Bonn; tel. (228) 41080; fax (228) 41081550; e-mail poststelle@bafin.de; internet www.bafin.de; f. 2002; independent body within federal administration; supervises banks, financial services providers, insurance cos and securities trading; Pres. JOCHEN SANIO.

BANKS

The Central Banking System

Germany participates in the ESCB, which consists of the ECB and the national central banks of all European Union (EU) member states.

Deutsche Bundesbank: Postfach 100602, 60006 Frankfurt a.M.; Wilhelm-Epstein-Str. 14, 60431 Frankfurt a.M.; tel. (69) 95660; fax (69) 95663077; e-mail presse-information@bundesbank.de; internet www.bundesbank.de; f. 1957; aims, in conjunction with the other members of the ESCB, to maintain price stability in the euro area. The Bundesbank, *inter alia*, holds and maintains foreign reserves of the Federal Republic of Germany, arranges for the execution of domestic and cross-border payments and contributes to the stability of payment and clearing systems. The Bundesbank (which has nine regional offices—*Hauptverwaltungen*—and 47 smaller branches) is the principal bank of the Federal *Land* Govts, carrying accounts for public authorities, executing payments and assisting with borrowing on the capital market. The Bundesbank has reserve positions in, and claims on, the IMF and the ECB. The Executive Board determines the Bundesbank's business policy; members of the Federal Govt may take part in the deliberations of the Board; cap. 2,500m., res 2,500m., dep. 131,673m. (Dec. 2009); Pres. Prof. Dr JENS WEIDMANN; Vice-Pres. SABINE LAUTENSCHLÄGER.

Hauptverwaltung Bayern: Ludwigstr. 13, 80539 München; tel. (89) 28895; fax (89) 28893598; e-mail pressestelle.hv-muenchen@bundesbank.de; internet www.bundesbank.de/hv/hv_muenchen.php; Pres. ALOIS MÜLLER.

Hauptverwaltung Berlin: Postfach 120163, 10591 Berlin; Leibnizstr. 10, 10625 Berlin; tel. (30) 34750; fax (30) 34751990; e-mail pressestelle.hv-berlin@bundesbank.de; internet www.bundesbank.de/hv/hv_berlin.php; Pres. CLAUS TIGGES.

Hauptverwaltung Düsseldorf: Postfach 101148, 40002 Düsseldorf; Berliner Allee 14, 40212 Düsseldorf; tel. (211) 8740; fax (211) 8742424; e-mail stab.hv-duesseldorf@bundesbank.de; internet www.bundesbank.de/hv/hv_duesseldorf.php; Pres. NORBERT MATYSIK.

Hauptverwaltung Frankfurt: Postfach 111232, 60047 Frankfurt a.M.; Taunusanlage 5, 60329 Frankfurt a.M.; tel. (69) 23880; fax (69) 23881044; e-mail pressestelle.hv-frankfurt@bundesbank.de; internet www.bundesbank.de/hv/hv_frankfurt.php; Pres. HANS-JOACHIM KOHSE.

Hauptverwaltung Hamburg: Postfach 570348, 22772 Hamburg; Willy-Brandt-Str. 73, 20459 Hamburg; tel. (40) 37070; fax (40) 37073342; e-mail pressestelle.hv-hamburg@bundesbank.de; internet www.bundesbank.de/hv/hv_hamburg.php; Pres. ADELHEID SAILER-SCHUSTER.

Hauptverwaltung Hannover: Postfach 245, 30002 Hannover; Georgspl. 5, 30159 Hannover; tel. (511) 30330; fax (511) 30332500; e-mail pressestelle.hv-hannover@bundesbank.de; internet www.bundesbank.de/hv/hv_hannover.php; Pres. STEPHAN FREIHERR VON STENGLIN.

Hauptverwaltung Leipzig: Postfach 901121, 04358 Leipzig; Str. des 18. Oktober 48, 04103 Leipzig; tel. (341) 8600; fax (341) 8602389; e-mail pressestelle.hv-leipzig@bundesbank.de; internet www.bundesbank.de/hv/hv_leipzig.php; Pres. HANS CHRISTOPH POPPE.

Hauptverwaltung Rheinland-Pfalz und Saarland: Postfach 3009, 55020 Mainz; Hegelstr. 65, 52122 Mainz; tel. (6131) 3770; e-mail pressestelle.hv-mainz@bundesbank.de; internet www.bundesbank.de/hv/hv_mainz.php; Pres. STEFAN HARDT.

Hauptverwaltung Stuttgart: Postfach 106021, 70049 Stuttgart; Marstallstr. 3, 70173 Stuttgart; tel. (711) 9440; fax (711) 9441903; e-mail hv-stuttgart@bundesbank.de; internet www.bundesbank.de/hv/hv_stuttgart.php; Pres. BERNHARD SIBOLD.

Private Commercial Banks

In 2007 204 private commercial banks were operating in Germany. The most prominent of these are listed below:

Bayerische Hypo- und Vereinsbank AG (HypoVereinsbank): Kardinal-Faulhaber-Str. 1, 80333 München; tel. (89) 3780; fax (89) 378113422; e-mail info@unicreditgroup.de; internet www.hypovereinsbank.de; f. 1998 by merger of Bayerische Hypotheken- und Wechsel Bank AG (f. 1835) and Bayerische Vereinsbank AG (f. 1869); 95.4% owned by UniCredito Italiano SpA; cap. 2,407m., res

16,927m., dep. 247,894m. (Dec. 2009); Chair., Supervisory Bd FEDERICO GHIZZONI; Chair., Bd of Management Dr THEODOR WEIMER.

Berliner Volksbank eG: 10892 Berlin; Budapester Str. 35, 10787 Berlin; tel. (30) 30630; fax (30) 30631550; e-mail service@berliner-volksbank.de; internet www.berliner-volksbank.de; f. 1880; cap. 248.8m., res 263.3m., dep. 9,153m. (Dec. 2009); Chair., Management Bd Dr HOLGER HATJE; 170 brs.

BHF-Bank Aktiengesellschaft: Bockenheimer Landstr. 10, 60323 Frankfurt a.M.; tel. (69) 7180; fax (69) 7182296; e-mail corp-comm@bhf-bank.com; internet www.bhf-bank.com; f. 1970 by merger of Frankfurter Bank (f. 1854) and Berliner Handels-Gesellschaft (f. 1856); current name adopted 2005; cap. 200m., res 423m., dep. 14,823m. (Dec. 2009); Man. Dir MATTHIAS GRAF VON KROCKOW; 11 brs.

Commerzbank AG: Kaiserpl., 60311 Frankfurt a.M.; tel. (69) 13620; fax (69) 285389; e-mail info@commerzbank.com; internet www.commerzbank.de; f. 1870; acquired Dresdner Bank in Jan. 2009; 25.0% stake owned by Federal Govt; cap. 20,225m., res –1,697m., dep. 415,477m. (Dec. 2010); Chair., Supervisory Bd KLAUS-PETER MÜLLER; Chair., Management Bd MARTIN BLESSING.

Deutsche Bank AG: Theodor-Heuss-Allee 70, 60486 Frankfurt a.M.; tel. (69) 9100; fax (69) 91034225; e-mail deutsche.bank@db.com; internet www.deutsche-bank.de; f. 1870; cap. 2,380m., res 20,464m., dep. 627,844m. (Dec. 2010); Chair., Supervisory Bd Dr CLEMENS BÖRSIG; Co-Chair., Management Bd Dr JOSEF ACKERMANN (until June 2012), ANSHU JAIN (from June 2012), JÜRGEN FITSCHEN (from June 2012); 983 brs.

HSBC Trinkaus & Burkhardt AG: Königsallee 21–23, 40212 Düsseldorf; tel. (211) 9100; fax (211) 910616; internet www.hsbctrinkhaus.de; f. 1785; current name adopted 2006; cap. 75.4m., res 447.7m., dep. 11,328.4m. (Dec. 2010); Chair., Management Bd ANDREAS SCHMITZ; 6 brs.

Sal. Oppenheim Jr & Cie KGaA: Postfach 102743, 50467 Köln; Unter Sachsenhausen 4, 50667 Köln; tel. (221) 14501; fax (221) 1451512; e-mail info@oppenheim.de; internet www.oppenheim.de; f. 1789; name changed as above in 2010; cap. 900m., res 1,042m., dep. 17,889m. (Dec. 2008); Chair. MATTHIAS GRAF VON KROCKOW; 10 brs.

SEB AG: 60283 Frankfurt a.M.; Ulmenstr. 30, 60283 Frankfurt a.M.; tel. (69) 2580; fax (69) 2587578; e-mail info@seb.de; internet www.seb.de; f. 1958 as BfG Bank AG; adopted current name 2001; owned by Skandinaviska Enskilda Banken AB (Sweden); cap. 775m., res 1,524m., dep. 53,797m. (Dec. 2008); Chair., Management Bd JAN SINCLAIR; 175 brs.

Targobank AG & Co KGaA: Postfach 101818, 40009 Düsseldorf; Kasernenstr. 10, 40213 Düsseldorf; tel. (211) 89840; fax (211) 8984222; internet www.targobank.de; f. 1926 as KKB Bank KGaA; acquired by Crédit Mutuel Group (France) in 2008; present name adopted in 2010; cap. 135m., res 601m., dep. 10,152m. (Dec. 2004); Chair., Management Bd FRANZ JOSEF NICK; 286 brs.

UBS Deutschland AG: Landstr. 2–4, 60313 Frankfurt a.M.; tel. (69) 21790; fax (69) 21796511; internet www.ubs.com/deutschland; f. 1998 as Warburg Dillon Read AG by merger of Schweizerischer Bankverein (Deutschland) and Union Bank of Switzerland (Deutschland) AG; present name adopted 2005; cap. 176m., res 266.8m., dep. 32,237.6m. (Dec. 2009); Chair. and CEO STEPHAN ZIMMERMANN; 13 brs.

Public-Law Credit Institutions

Together with the private banks, the banks incorporated under public law (savings banks—*Sparkassen*—and their central clearing houses—*Landesbank-Girozentralen*) play a major role within the German banking system. In early 2009 there were 446 savings banks and 10 central clearing houses.

BayernLB: Brienner Str. 18, 80333 München; tel. (89) 217101; fax (89) 217123578; e-mail kontakt@bayernlb.de; internet www.bayernlb.de; f. 1972 as Bayerische Landesbank Girozentrale; present name adopted 2002; cap. 6,241m., res 4,145m., dep. 194,003m. (Dec. 2010); Chair., Management Bd GERD HÄUSLER.

Bremer Landesbank Kreditanstalt Oldenburg-Girozentrale (Bremer Landesbank): Domshof 26, 28195 Bremen; tel. (421) 3320; fax (421) 3322322; e-mail kontakt@bremerlandesbank.de; internet www.bremerlandesbank.de; f. 1983; 92.5% owned by Norddeutsche Landesbank and 7.5% owned by Bremen city council; cap. 748m., res 244m., dep. 21,670m. (Dec. 2010); Chair. Dr STEPHAN ANDREAS KAULVERS.

DekaBank Deutsche Girozentrale: Mainzer Landstr. 16, 60325 Frankfurt am Main; tel. (69) 71470; fax (69) 71471376; e-mail konzerninfo@deka.de; internet www.dekabank.de; f. 1999 by merger of Deutsche Girozentrale-Deutsche Kommunalbank and Dekabank GmbH; present name adopted 2002; central institution of *Sparkassen* org.; issues bonds (*Pfandbriefe*); cap. 286m., res 252.5m., dep. 50,878.4m. (Dec. 2010); Chair., Management Bd FRANZ S. WAAS.

HSH Nordbank AG: Gerhart-Hauptmann-Pl. 50, 20095 Hamburg; tel. (40) 33330; fax (40) 333334001; e-mail info@hsh-nordbank.com; internet www.hsh-nordbank.com; f. 2003 by merger of Hamburgische Landesbank-Girozentrale and Landesbank Schleswig-Holstein Girozentrale; 12.37% owned by Hamburg city council, 10.97% by Schleswig-Holstein *Land* Govt; cap. 2,635m., res 741m., dep. 76,646m. (Dec. 2010); CEO Dr PAUL LERBINGER.

Landesbank Baden-Württemberg (LBBW): Postfach 106049, 70049 Stuttgart; Am Hauptbahnhof 2, 70173 Stuttgart; tel. (711) 1270; fax (711) 12743544; e-mail kontakt@lbbw.de; internet www.lbbw.de; f. 1999 by merger of Landesgirokasse, L-Bank Landeskreditbank Baden-Württemberg and Südwestdeutsche Landesbank Girozentrale; 19.57% owned by *Land* Govt of Baden-Württemberg; cap. 2,584m., res 6,320m., dep. 66,076m. (Dec. 2010); Chair., Management Bd HANS-JÖRG VETTER.

Landesbank Berlin AG: Alexanderpl. 2, 10178 Berlin; tel. (30) 869801; fax (30) 86983074; e-mail information@lbb.de; internet www.lbb.de; f. 1818; name changed as above in 2006; cap. 1,900m., res 920m., dep. 54,773m. (Dec. 2010); Chair., Management Bd Dr JOHANNES EVERS; 150 brs.

Landesbank Hessen-Thüringen Girozentrale (Helaba): Main Tower, Neue Mainzer Str. 52–58, 60297 Frankfurt a.M.; tel. (69) 913201; fax (69) 291517; e-mail presse@helaba.de; internet www.helaba.de; f. 1953; 10% owned by Hesse *Land* Govt, 5% by Thuringia *Land* Govt; cap. 477m., res 2,474m., dep. 42,861m. (Dec. 2010); Chair., Management Bd HANS-DIETER BRENNER.

Landesbank Saar (SaarLB): Ursulinenstr. 2, 66111 Saarbrücken; tel. (681) 38301; fax (681) 3831200; e-mail service@saarlb.de; internet www.saarlb.de; f. 1941; name changed as above in 2003; 49.9% owned by Bayerische Landesbank, 35.2% by Saarland *Land* Govt; cap. 284m., res 34.6m., dep. 13,454.1m. (Dec. 2010); Chair., Management Bd THOMAS-CHRISTIAN BUCHBINDER.

Norddeutsche Landesbank Girozentrale (NORD/LB): Friedrichswall 10, 30159 Hannover; tel. (511) 3610; fax (511) 3612502; e-mail info@nordlb.de; internet www.nordlb.de; f. 1970 by merger of several north German banks; cap. 1,085m., res 2,626m., dep. 88,833m. (Dec. 2010); Chair., Management Bd Dr GUNTER DUNKEL; 108 brs.

WestLB AG: Herzogstr. 15, 40217 Düsseldorf; tel. (211) 82601; fax (211) 8266119; e-mail presse@westlb.de; internet www.westlb.de; f. 2002; cap. 967m., res –196m., dep. 69,245m. (Dec. 2010); Chair., Management Bd DIETRICH VOIGTLÄNDER; 14 brs.

Central Bank of Co-operative Banking System

DZ BANK AG (Deutsche Zentral-Genossenschaftsbank): Pl. der Republik, 60265 Frankfurt a.M.; tel. (69) 744701; fax (69) 74471685; e-mail mail@dzbank.de; internet www.dzbank.de; f. 1949; cap. 3,160m., res 568m., dep. 204,833m. (Dec. 2010); Chair., Management Bd WOLFGANG KIRSCH; 46 brs.

DZ BANK is a specialist wholesale bank and is the central institution in the German co-operative banking sector, which comprises local co-operative banks, three regional central banks and a number of specialist financial institutions. In January 2009 there were 1,210 credit co-operatives, including central institutions.

Specialist Banks

Although Germany is considered the model country for universal banking, banks that specialize in certain types of business are also extremely important. A selection of the most prominent among these is given below:

Aareal Bank AG: Paulinenstr. 15, 65189 Wiesbaden; tel. (611) 3480; fax (611) 3482549; e-mail aareal@aareal-bank.com; internet www.aareal-bank.com; f. 1923; privatized 1989; fmrly DePfa Bank AG, present name adopted 2002; cap. 128m., res 926m., dep. 35,736m. (Dec. 2009); Chair. Dr WOLF SCHUMACHER.

Berlin-Hannoversche Hypothekenbank AG (Berlin Hyp): Budapester Str. 1, 10787 Berlin; tel. (30) 259990; fax (30) 25999131; e-mail kommunikation@berlinhyp.de; internet www.berlinhyp.de; f. 1996 by merger; cap. 658.3m., res 70.5m., dep. 39,642.6m. (Dec. 2009); Chair., Management Bd Dr JOHANNES EVERS; Chair., Supervisory Bd JAN BETTINK.

COREALCREDIT BANK AG: Postfach 170162, 60075 Frankfurt a.M.; Grüneburgweg 58-62, 60322 Frankfurt a.M.; tel. (69) 71790; fax (69) 7179100; e-mail info@corealcredit.de; internet www.corealcredit.com; f. 1962 as Allgemeine Hypotheken Bank AG; name changed to Allgemeine HypothekenBank Rheinboden in 2001; present name adopted 2007; specializes in commercial property market; cap. 100.3m., res 1,363.3m., dep. 4,758.8m. (Dec. 2010); Chair., Management Bd Dr CLAUS NOLTING; 6 brs.

Deutsche Hypothekenbank AG: Georgspl. 8, 30159 Hannover; tel. (511) 30450; fax (511) 3045459; e-mail mail@deutsche-hypo.de; internet www.deutsche-hypo.de; f. 1872; subsidiary of Norddeutsche Landesbank Girozentrale; cap. 725m., res 590m., dep. 15,214.9m. (Dec. 2010); Chair., Supervisory Bd Dr GUNTER DUNKEL; Chair., Management Bd JÜRGEN ALLERKAMP; 6 brs.

Deutsche Pfandbriefbank AG: Von-der-Tann-Str. 2, 80539 München; tel. (89) 28800; fax (89) 288010319; e-mail info@hyporealestate.de; internet www.hyporealestate.com; f. 2001 as HVB Real Estate Bank AG; adopted current name 2009 following merger with Depfa Deutsche Pfandbriefbank AF; part of Hypo Real Estate Group (under state control since 2009); cap. 1,379m., res 5,291m., dep. 79,971m. (Dec. 2010); Chair., Supervisory Bd Dr BERND THIEMANN; Chair., Management Bd MANUELA BETTER.

Deutsche Postbank AG: Friedrich-Ebert-Allee 114–126, 53113 Bonn; tel. (228) 9200; fax (228) 92035151; e-mail presse@postbank.de; internet www.postbank.de; f. 1990; 51.98% owned by Deutsche Bank AG; cap. 547m., res 1,595m., dep. 163,293m. (Dec. 2010); Chair., Management Bd STEFAN JÜTTE; 850 brs.

Eurohypo AG: Helfmann-Park 5, 65760 Eschborn; tel. (69) 25480; fax (69) 254871204; e-mail internetredaktion@eurohypo.com; internet www.eurohypo.com; f. 2002 by merger of Deutsche Hyp (f. 1862), Eurohypo (f. 1862) and Rheinhyp (f. 1871); wholly owned by Commerzbank AG; cap. 913.7m., res 4,740.3m., dep. 111,628.9m. (Dec. 2009); CEO and Chair., Management Bd Dr THOMAS KÖNTGEN; 16 brs.

IKB Deutsche Industriebank AG: Postfach 101118, 40002 Düsseldorf; Wilhelm-Bötzkes-Str. 1, 40474 Düsseldorf; tel. (211) 82210; fax (211) 82213959; e-mail info@ikb.de; internet www.ikb.de; f. 1949; Industriekreditbank AG; name changed as above in 1991; cap. 1,621.3m., res –400.2m., dep. 32,786.4m. (March 2010); Chair., Management Bd HANS JÖRG SCHÜTTLER; 7 brs.

KfW Bankengruppe (Kreditanstalt für Wiederaufbau): Postfach 111141, 60046 Frankfurt a.M.; Palmengartenstr. 5–9, 60325 Frankfurt a.M.; tel. (69) 74310; fax (69) 74312944; e-mail info@kfw.de; internet www.kfw.de; f. 1948; 80% owned by Federal Govt and 20% by *Land* Govts; cap. 3,300m., res 7,266m., dep. 384,008m. (Dec. 2010); Chair., Management Bd Dr ULRICH SCHRÖDER.

Münchener Hypothekenbank eG (MünchenerHyp): Karl-Scharnagl-Ring 10, 80539 München; tel. (89) 538780; fax (89) 5387900; e-mail serviceteam800@muenchenerhyp.de; internet www.muenchenerhyp.de; f. 1896; cap. 483.9m., res 279.3m., dep. 34,658.7m. (Dec. 2009); Chair., Supervisory Bd KONRAD IRTEL; Chair., Management Bd Dr LOUIS HAGEN; 11 brs.

Bankers' Organizations

Bankenverband—Bundesverband deutscher Banken (Association of German Banks): Postfach 040307, 10062 Berlin; Burgstr. 28, 10178 Berlin; tel. (30) 16630; fax (30) 16631399; e-mail bankenverband@bdb.de; internet www.bdb.de; f. 1951; Gen. Man. MICHAEL KEMMER.

Bundesverband der Deutschen Volksbanken und Raiffeisenbanken eV (BVR) (Federal Association of German Co-operative Banks): Schellingstr. 4, 10785 Berlin; tel. (30) 20210; fax (30) 20211900; e-mail info@bvr.de; internet www.bvr.de; f. 1972; Pres. UWE FRÖHLICH; 1,121 mems (2011).

Bundesverband Öffentlicher Banken Deutschlands eV (VÖB) (Association of German Public Sector Banks): Lennéstr. 11, 10785 Berlin; tel. (30) 81920; fax (30) 8192222; e-mail presse@voeb.de; internet www.voeb.de; 33 mems and 28 assoc. mems; Pres. CHRISTIAN BRAND; Chair. Dr HANS RECKERS.

Deutscher Sparkassen- und Giroverband eV (German Savings Banks Assen): Charlottenstr. 47, 10117 Berlin; tel. (30) 202250; fax (30) 20225250; e-mail info@dsgv.de; internet www.dsgv.de; Pres. HEINRICH HAASIS.

STOCK EXCHANGES

Bayerische Börse AG: Karolinenplatz 6, 80333 München; tel. (89) 5490450; fax (89) 54904531; e-mail info@boerse-muenchen.de; internet www.boerse-muenchen.de; f. 1830; 106 mems; Chair., Supervisory Bd Dr DIETER CHRISTINE BORTENLÄNGER; Chair., Management Bd ANDREAS SCHMIDT.

Berlin: Börse Berlin AG, Fasanenstr. 85, 10623 Berlin; tel. (30) 3110910; fax (30) 31109179; e-mail kundenbetreuung@boerse-berlin.de; internet www.boerse-berlin.de; f. 1685; 109 mems; Pres. Dr JÖRG WALTER.

Düsseldorf: Börse Düsseldorf AG, Ernst-Schneider-Pl. 1, 40212 Düsseldorf; tel. (211) 13890; fax (211) 133287; e-mail kontakt@boerse-duesseldorf.de; internet www.boerse-duesseldorf.de; f. 1935; 110 mem. firms; Chair. DIRK ELBERSKIRCH.

Frankfurt am Main: Deutsche Börse AG, Börsenpl. 4, 60313 Frankfurt a.M.; tel. (69) 2110; fax (69) 21111021; internet www.exchange.de; f. 1585 as Frankfurter Wertpapierbörse; 269 mems; CEO RETO FRANCIONI; Chair., Supervisory Bd KURT F. VIERMETZ.

North Germany (Hamburg): BÖAG Börsen AG, Kleine Johannisstr. 2–4, 20457 Hamburg; tel. (40) 3613020; fax (40) 36130223; internet www.boersenag.de; f. 1999 by merger of Hanseatische Wertpapierbörse Hamburg and Niedersächsische Börse zu Hannover; 109 mems; Pres. UDO BANDOW; Chair. Dr THOMAS LEDERMANN.

North Germany (Hannover): BÖAG Börsen AG, Rathenaustr. 2, 30159 Hannover; tel. (511) 327661; fax (511) 324915; e-mail s.lueth@boersenag.de; internet www.boersenag.de; f. 1999 by merger of Hanseatische Wertpapierbörse Hamburg and Niedersächsische Börse zu Hannover; 81 mems; Chair. Prof. Dr HANS HEINRICH PETERS.

Stuttgart: Boerse-Stuttgart AG, Börsenstr. 4, 70174 Stuttgart; tel. (711) 2229850; fax (711) 222985555; e-mail info@boerse-stuttgart.de; internet www.boerse-stuttgart.de; f. 1861; 121 mems; Pres. ROLF LIMBACH; Man. Dir Dr CHRISTOPH MURA.

INSURANCE

German law specifies that property and accident insurance may not be jointly underwritten with life, sickness, legal protection or credit insurance by the same company. Insurers are therefore obliged to establish separate companies to cover the different classes of insurance. In March 2010 there were 2,217 insurance companies operating in Germany.

Aachener und Münchener Lebensversicherung AG: Aachen-Münchener-Pl. 1, 52064 Aachen; tel. (241) 4560; fax (241) 4565678; e-mail service@amv.de; internet www.amv.de; f. 1868; subsidiary of Generali Deutschland Holding AG; Chair. MICHAEL WESTKAMP.

Allianz AG: Königinstr. 28, 80802 München; tel. (89) 38000; fax (89) 38003425; e-mail info@allianz.de; internet www.allianz.de; f. 1890; Chair., Supervisory Bd Dr WERNER ZEDELIUS; Chair., Management Bd MICHAEL DIEKMANN.

Allianz Lebensversicherungs-AG: Königinstr. 28, 80802 München; tel. (89) 38000; fax (89) 349941; e-mail lebensversicherung@allianz.de; internet www.allianzgroup.com; f. 1922; Chair., Supervisory Bd HENNING SCHULTE-NOELLE; Chair., Management Bd MICHAEL DIEKMANN.

Allianz Private Krankenversicherungs AG: Fritz-Schäffer-Str. 9, 81737 München; tel. (89) 67850; fax (89) 67856523; e-mail service.apkv@allianz.de; internet www.allianz.de; f. 1925; Chair, Supervisory Bd. Dr MAXIMILIAN ZIMMERER; Chair, Management Bd. Dr BIRGIT KÖNIG.

Allianz Versicherungs AG: Königinstr. 28, 80802 München; tel. (89) 38000; fax (89) 38003425; e-mail info@allianz.de; internet www.allianz.de; f. 1985; Chair. Dr WERNER ZEDELIUS.

AXA Krankenversicherung AG: Colonia-Allee 10–20, 50167 Köln; tel. (1803) 556622; fax (221) 14832602; f. 1962; 100% owned by AXA Konzern AG; Chair., Management Bd Dr FRANK KEUPER; Chair., Supervisory Bd Dr GERNOT SCHLOESSER.

AXA Lebensversicherung AG: Colonia-Allee 10–20, 51067 Köln; tel. (1803) 556622; fax (221) 14822750; e-mail service@axa.de; internet www.axa.de; f. 1853; Chair., Supervisory Bd CLAAS KLEYBOLDT; Chair., Management Bd Dr CLAUS-MICHAEL DILL.

AXA Versicherung AG: Colonia-Allee 10–20, 50670 Köln; tel. (221) 14819727; fax (221) 14822740; e-mail service@axa.de; internet www.axa.de; f. 1839 as Colonia Kölnischer Freuer Versicherung AG; present name adopted 2001; non-life insurance; Chair., Supervisory Bd CLAAS KLEYBOLDT; Chair., Management Bd Dr CLAUS-MICHAEL DILL.

Continentale Krankenversicherung AG: Ruhrallee 92, 44139 Dortmund; tel. (231) 9190; fax (231) 9193255; e-mail info@continentale.de; internet www.continentale.de; f. 1926; Chair. ROLF BAUER.

DBV-Winterthur Lebensversicherung AG: Frankfurter Str. 50, 65178 Wiesbaden; tel. (1803) 328100; fax (1803) 328400; e-mail info@dbv-winterthur.de; internet www.dbv.de; f. 1872; Chair. BERNHARD GERTZ.

Debeka Krankenversicherungsverein AG: Ferdinand-Sauerbruch-Str. 18, 56073 Koblenz; tel. (261) 4980; fax (261) 4985555; e-mail kundenservice@debeka.de; internet www.debeka.de; f. 1905; Chair. P. GREISLER; Gen. Man. UWE LAUE.

Deutsche Krankenversicherung AG: Postfach 100865, 50448 Köln; Aachener Str. 300, 50933 Köln; tel. (1801) 358222; fax (1801) 5786000; e-mail service@dkv.com; internet www.dkv.com; f. 1927; Chair. Dr CLEMENS MUTH.

ERGO Lebensversicherung AG: Überseering 45, 22297 Hamburg; tel. (40) 63760; fax (40) 63763302; e-mail prr@hamburg-mannheimer.de; internet www.ergo.de; subsidiary of ERGO Versicherungsgruppe AG; f. 1899; Chair. Dr DANIEL VON BORRIES.

Gothaer Versicherungsbank Versicherungsverein AG: Arnoldipl. 1, 50969 Köln; tel. (221) 30800; fax (221) 308103; e-mail info@gothaer.de; internet www.gothaer.de; f. 1820; Chair., Supervisory Bd Dr KLAUS MURMANN; Chair., Management Bd Dr WOLFGANG PEINER.

Haftpflicht-Unterstützungs-Kasse kraftfahrender Beamter Deutschlands AG in Coburg (HUK-COBURG): Bahnhofspl., 96448 Coburg; tel. (9561) 960; fax (9561) 963636; e-mail info@

huk-coburg.de; internet www.huk.de; f. 1933; CEO Dr WOLFGANG WEILER.

HDI Direkt Versicherung AG: Riethorst 2, 30659 Hannover; tel. (221) 14461988; fax (511) 6454545; e-mail vertragsservice@hdi-gerling.de; internet www.hdi-gerling.de; Chair. Dr CHRISTIAN HINSCH.

HDI-Gerling Industrie Versicherung AG: HDI-Pl. 1, 30659 Hannover; tel. (511) 6450; fax (511) 6454545; e-mail vertragsservice@hdi-gerling.de; internet www.hdi-gerling.de; f. 2001; Chair. H. K. HAAS; CEO Dr CHRISTIAN HINSCH.

HDI-Gerling Lebensversicherung AG: Charles de Gaulle Platz 1, 50679 Köln; tel. (221) 1445599; fax (221) 1443833; e-mail leben.service@hdi-gerling.de; internet www.hdi-gerling.com; f. 1918; Chair. HEINZ-PETER ROß.

IDUNA Vereinigte Lebensversicherung AG für Handwerk, Handel und Gewerbe: Neue Rabenstr. 15–19, 20354 Hamburg; tel. (40) 41244801; fax (40) 41242958; e-mail info@signal-iduna.de; internet www.signal-iduna.de; f. 1914; Chair., Supervisory Bd G. KÜTZ; Gen. Man. REINHOLD SCHULTE.

LVM Versicherungen: Kolde-Ring 21, 48126 Münster; tel. (251) 7020; fax (251) 7021099; e-mail info@lvm.de; internet www.lvm.de; f. 1896; Chair. JOCHEN BORCHERT; Gen. Man. ROBERT BARESEL.

SIGNAL Krankenversicherung AG: Joseph-Scherer-Str. 3, 44139 Dortmund; tel. (231) 1350; fax (231) 1354638; e-mail info@signal-iduna.de; internet www.signal-iduna.de; f. 1907; Chair., Supervisory Bd G. KUTZ; Gen. Man. REINHOLD SCHULTE.

Talanx AG: Riethorst 2, 30659 Hannover; tel. (511) 37470; fax (511) 37472525; e-mail info@talanx.com; internet www.talanx.com; f. 1996; owned by HDI Haftpflichtverband der Deutschen Industrie VaG; Chair., Supervisory Bd WOLF-DIETER BAUMGARTL; CEO HERBERT K. HAAS.

Volksfürsorge Deutsche Lebensversicherung AG: Postfach 106420, 20043 Hamburg; tel. (40) 28654477; fax (40) 28653369; e-mail service@volksfuersorge.de; internet www.volksfuersorge.de; f. 1913.

Württembergische AG Versicherungs-Beteiligungsgesellschaft: Gutenbergstr. 30, 70176 Stuttgart; tel. (711) 662723400; fax (711) 662722520; e-mail keu@wuerttembergische.de; internet www.wuerttembergische.de; f. 1828; Chair., Supervisory Bd ALEXANDER ERDLAND; Chair., Management Bd NORBERT HEINEN.

Reinsurance

DARAG Deutsche Versicherungs- und Rückversicherungs-AG: Hafenstr. 32A, 22880 Wedel; tel. (41) 370160; fax (41) 37016179; e-mail info@darag.de; internet www.darag.de; f. 1958; re-formed 1990; fire and non-life, technical, cargo transport, marine hull, liability, aviation insurance and reinsurance; Chair., Management Bd GARNDT GOSSMANN.

Deutsche Rückversicherung AG: Postfach 10, 290110 Düsseldorf; Hansaallee 177, 40549 Düsseldorf; tel. (211) 455401; fax (211) 4554199; e-mail info@deutscherueck.de; internet www.deutscherueck.de; f. 1951; Gen. Man. Dr ARNO JUNKE.

General Reinsurance AG: Postfach 102244, 50668 Köln; Theodor-Heuss-Ring 11, 50668 Köln; tel. (221) 97380; fax (221) 9738494; e-mail askgenre@genre.com; internet www.genre.com; f. 1846; acquired by General Re in 2009; name changed as above in 2010; Chair. FRANKLIN MONTROSS, IV.

Hamburger Internationale Rückversicherung AG: Postfach 1161, 25452 Rellingen; Halstenbeker Weg 96A, 25462 Rellingen; tel. (4101) 4710; fax (4101) 471298; f. 1965; Chair., Exec. Bd Dr WOLFGANG EILERS.

Hannover Rückversicherung AG: Postfach 610369, 30603 Hannover; Karl-Wiechert-Allee 50, 30625 Hannover; tel. (511) 56040; fax (511) 56041188; e-mail info@hannover-re.com; internet www.hannover-re.com; f. 1966; Chair., Supervisory Bd H. HAAS; Chair., Management Bd U. WALLIN.

Münchener Rückversicherungs-Gesellschaft AG (Munich RE): Königinstr. 107, 80802 München; tel. (89) 38910; fax (89) 399056; e-mail info@munichre.com; internet www.munichre.com; f. 1880; all classes of reinsurance; Chair. Dr NIKOLAUS VON BOMHARD.

R + V Versicherung-AG Reinsurance: Raiffeisenplatz 1, 65189 Wiesbaden; tel. (01802) 7858633; fax (611) 5334500; e-mail ruv@ruv.de; internet www.ruv.de; f. 1935; all classes of reinsurance; Chair. Dr FREDERICK CASPERS.

Swiss Re Germany AG: Dieselstr. 11, 85774 Unterföhring bei München; tel. (89) 38440; fax (89) 38442279; e-mail info.srmuc@swissre.com; internet www.swissre.com; Chair. Dr WALTER B. KIELHOLZ; Gen. Man. M. LIÈS.

Principal Insurance Association

Gesamtverband der Deutschen Versicherungswirtschaft eV (German Insurance Assen): Wilhelmstr. 43/43G, 10117 Berlin; tel. (30) 20205000; fax (30) 20206000; e-mail berlin@gdv.de; internet www.gdv.de; f. 1948; affiliating 3 mem. asscns and 464 mem. cos; Pres. ROLF-PETER HOENEN (Coburg); CEO Dr FRANK VON FÜRSTENWERTH.

Trade and Industry

GOVERNMENT AGENCIES

Bundesverband Grosshandel, Aussenhandel, Dienstleistungen eV (Federation of German Wholesale and Foreign Trade): Am Weidendamm 1A, 10117 Berlin; tel. (30) 59009950; fax (30) 590099519; e-mail info@bga.de; internet www.bga.de; f. 1949; wholesale, foreign trade and services sector; Man. Dir GERHARD HANDKE; 77 mem. asscns.

Finanzmarktstabilisierungsanstalt (Financial Market Stabilization Agency): Taunusanlage 6 60329 Frankfurt a.M.; tel. (69) 23883000; fax (69) 9566509090; e-mail info@soffin.de; internet www.soffin.de; f. Oct. 2008 by Federal Govt to manage a stabilization fund; provides emergency funding for financial institutions; may grant up to €400m. to guarantee debt securities and liabilities, and up to €10m. for recapitalization; Chair., Management Cttee Dr HANNES REHM.

Germany Trade & Invest: Friedrichstr. 60, 10117 Berlin; tel. (30) 2000990; fax (30) 200099111; e-mail info@gtai.de; internet www.gtai.com; f. 2009 following merger of Bundesagentur für Aussenwirtschaft with Invest in Germany GmbH; promoted by Federal Ministry of Economics and Technology and the Federal Government Commissioner for the New Federal States; Chief Exec. Dr JÜRGEN FRIEDRICH.

Hauptverband des Deutschen Einzelhandels eV: Am Weidendamm 1A, 10117 Berlin; tel. (30) 7262500; fax (30) 72625099; e-mail hde@einzelhandel.de; internet www.einzelhandel.de; f. 1947; Chair. JOSEF SANKTJOHANSER; Exec. Dir STEFAN GENTH.

Zentralverband Gewerblicher Verbundgruppen: Haus des Handels, Am Weidendamm 1A, 10117 Berlin; tel. (30) 590099663; fax (30) 59099617; e-mail info@zgv-online.de; internet www.zgv-online.de; f. 1992; Pres. WILFRIED HOLLMANN; c. 400 mems.

CHAMBERS OF COMMERCE

Deutscher Industrie- und Handelkammerstag eV (DIHK) (Association of German Chambers of Industry and Commerce): Breite Str. 29, 10178 Berlin; tel. (30) 203080; fax (30) 203081000; e-mail infocenter@dihk.de; internet www.dihk.de; Pres. HANS HEINRICH DRIFTMANN; Chief Exec. Dr MARTIN WANSLEBEN; affiliates 80 Chambers of Industry and Commerce.

There are Chambers of Industry and Commerce in all the principal towns and also 13 regional associations including:

Arbeitsgemeinschaft der Industrie- und Handelskammern in Mecklenburg-Vorpommern: Ludwig-Bölkow-Haus, Graf-Schack-Allee 12, 19053 Schwerin; tel. (385) 51030; fax (385) 5103999; e-mail info@schwerin.ihk.de; internet www.ihkzuschwerin.de; Pres. HANS THON; Man. Dir KLAUS-MICHAEL ROTHE.

Arbeitsgemeinschaft Hessischer Industrie- und Handelskammern: Börsenpl. 4, 60313 Frankfurt a.M.; tel. (69) 21971384; fax (69) 21971448; internet www.ihk-hessen.de; Chair. MATHIAS MÜLLER; Sec.-Gen. MATTHIAS GRÄSSLE; 10 mems.

Arbeitsgemeinschaft Norddeutscher Industrie- und Handelskammern (IHK Nord): Adolphspl. 1, 20457 Hamburg; tel. (40) 36138459; fax (40) 36138553; e-mail info@ihk-nord.de; internet www.ihk-nord.de; Chair. FRANK HORCH; Sec. Dr MAIKE BIELFELDT.

Baden-Württembergischer Industrie- und Handelskammertag: Jägerstr. 40, 70174 Stuttgart; tel. (711) 22550060; fax (711) 22550077; e-mail info@bw.ihk.de; internet www.bw.ihk.de; Pres. Dr PETER KULITZ; Man. Dir MICHAEL DEFFNER.

Bayerischer Industrie- und Handelskammertag eV (BIHK): Max-Joseph-Str. 2, 80333 München; tel. (89) 51160; fax (89) 5116290; e-mail info@bihk.de; internet www.bihk.de; Pres Prof. Dr ERICH GREIPL, PETER DRIESSEN; Sec.-Gen. Dr REINHARD DÖRFLER; 900,000 mems.

IHK-Arbeitsgemeinschaft Rheinland-Pfalz: Herzogenbuscher Str. 12, 54292 Trier; tel. (651) 97770; fax (651) 9777150; e-mail infocenter@trier.ihk.de; internet www.ihk-arbeitsgemeinschaft-rlp.de; Pres. PETER ADRIAN; four mems.

IHK Industrie- und Handelskammer Erfurt: Arnstädter Str. 34, 99096 Erfurt; tel. (361) 34840; fax (361) 3485950; e-mail info@erfurt.ihk.de; internet www.erfurt.ihk.de; f. 1991; Pres. NIELS LUND CHRESTENSEN.

IHK Schleswig-Holstein: Bergstr. 2, 24103 Kiel; tel. (431) 51940; fax (431) 5194234; e-mail ihk@kiel.ihk.de; internet www

.ihk-schleswig-holstein.de; Chair. Christoph Andreas Leicht; Man. Dir Peter Michael Stein.

Industrie- und Handelskammer Hannover: Schiffgraben 49, 30175 Hannover; tel. (511) 31070; fax (511) 3107333; e-mail info@hannover.ihk.de; internet www.hannover.ihk.de; f. 1899; Pres. Dr Hannes Rehm; Man. Dir Dr Wilfried Prewo.

Industrie- und Handelskammer in Südwestsachsen (Chemnitz, Plauen, Zwickau): Postfach 464, 09004 Chemnitz; Str. der Nationen 25, 09111 Chemnitz; tel. (371) 69001240; fax (371) 6900191240; e-mail hofmann@chemnitz.ihk.de; internet www.chemnitz.ihk24.de.

Industrie- und Handelskammer Magdeburg: Postfach 1840, Alter Markt 8, 39104 Magdeburg; tel. (391) 56930; fax (391) 5693193; e-mail kammer@magdeburg.ihk.de; internet www.magdeburg.ihk.de; f. 1825; Pres. Klaus Olbricht.

Industrie- und Handelskammer Potsdam: Breite Str. 2a–c, 14467 Potsdam; tel. (331) 2786251; fax (331) 2786190; e-mail ullmann@potsdam.ihk.de; internet www.potsdam.ihk24.de; f. 1990; public; 72,000 mem. cos; Pres. Dr Victor Stimming; CEO René Kohl.

Vereinigung der Industrie- und Handelskammern in Nordrhein-Westfalen: Marienstr. 8, 40212 Düsseldorf; tel. (211) 367020; fax (211) 3670221; e-mail info@ihk-nrw.de; internet www.ihk-nrw.de; Pres. Paul Bauwens-Adenauer; Chief Exec. Dr Ralf Mittelstädt; 16 mems.

INDUSTRIAL AND TRADE ASSOCIATIONS

Bundesverband der Deutschen Industrie eV (Federation of German Industry): Breite Str. 29, 10178 Berlin; tel. (30) 20281566; fax (30) 20282566; e-mail presse@bdi.eu; internet www.bdi.eu; Pres. Hans-Peter Keitel; Dir-Gen. Dr Markus Kerber.

Arbeitsgemeinschaft Keramische Industrie eV (Ceramics): Postfach 1624, 95090 Selb; Schillerstr. 17, 95100 Selb; tel. (9287) 8080; fax (9287) 70492; e-mail info@keramverband.de; internet www.keramverbaende.de; Pres. Franz Kook; Man. Peter Frischholz.

Bundesverband Baustoffe—Steine und Erden eV (Building Materials): Postfach 610486, 10928 Berlin; Kochstr. 6–7, 10969 Berlin; tel. (30) 72619990; fax (30) 726199912; e-mail info@bvbaustoffe.de; internet www.baustoffindustrie.de; f. 1948; Pres. Dr Gernot Schaefer; Chief Dir Dr Michael Weissenhorn.

Bundesverband der Deutschen Entsorgungswirtschaft (BDE) (Waste Disposal and Recycling): Behrenstr. 29, 10117 Berlin; tel. (30) 59003350; fax (30) 590033599; e-mail info@bde-berlin.de; internet www.bde-berlin.de; Pres. Peter Hoffmeyer; Dir-Gen. Anne Baum-Rudischhauser.

Bundesverband der Deutschen Gießerei-Industrie (BDG) (Foundries): Postfach 101961, 40010 Düsseldorf; Sohnstr. 70, 40237 Düsseldorf; tel. (211) 6871215; fax (211) 6871205; e-mail info@bdguss.de; internet www.bdguss.de; f. 1865; Pres. Hans-Dieter Honsel; Man. Dir Kay-Uwe Präfke.

Bundesverband der Deutschen Luft- und Raumfahrtindustrie eV (BDLI) (German Aerospace Industries Asscn): Friedrichstr. 60, 10117 Berlin; tel. (30) 2061400; fax (30) 20614090; e-mail info@bdli.de; internet www.bdli.de; f. 1955; Pres. Dr Thomas Enders; Man. Dir Dietmar Schrick.

Bundesverband Druck und Medien eV (Printing and Media): Postfach 1869, 65008 Wiesbaden; Biebricher Allee 79, 65187 Wiesbaden; tel. (611) 8030; fax (611) 803113; e-mail info@bvdm-online.de; f. 1947; Pres. Manfred Adrian; Man. Dir Thomas Mayer; 12 mem. asscns.

Bundesverband Glasindustrie eV (Glass): Postfach 101753, 40008 Düsseldorf; Am Bonneshof 5, 40474 Düsseldorf; tel. (211) 4796134; fax (211) 9513751; e-mail info@bvglas.de; internet www.bvglas.de; Chair. Paul Neeteson; 4 mem. asscns.

Bundesverband Schmuck, Uhren, Silberwaren und Verwandte Industrien eV (Jewellery, Clocks and Silverware): Poststr. 1, 75172 Pforzheim; tel. (7231) 1455510; fax (7231) 1455521; e-mail info@bv-schmuck-uhren.de; internet www.bv-schmuck-uhren.de; Pres. Dr Philipp Reisert; Man. Dir Dr Alfred Schneider.

Bundesvereinigung der Deutschen Ernährungsindustrie eV (BVE) (Food): Claire-Waldorf-Str. 7, 10117 Berlin; tel. (30) 2007860; fax (30) 200786299; e-mail bve@bve-online.de; internet www.bve-online.de; f. 1949; Chair. Jürgen Abraham; Chief Gen. Man. Prof. Dr Matthias Horst.

Bundesverband der Deutschen Gießerei-Industrie (BDG) (Foundries): Postfach 101961, 40010 Düsseldorf; Sohnstr. 70, 40237 Düsseldorf; tel. (211) 6871215; fax (211) 6871205; e-mail info@bdguss.de; internet www.bdguss.de; f. 1865; Pres. Hans-Dieter Honsel; Man. Dir Kay-Uwe Präfke.

Centralvereinigung Deutscher Wirtschaftsverbände für Handelsvermittlung und Vertrieb (Trade and Marketing): Am Weidendamm 1a, 10117 Berlin; tel. (30) 72625600; fax (30) 72625699; e-mail centralvereinigung@cdh.de; internet www.cdh.de; f. 1902; Pres. Heinrich Schmidt; Gen. Sec. Dr Andreas Paffhausen; 18,000 mems.

Deutscher Hotel- und Gaststättenverband eV (DEHOGA): Am Weidendamm 1a, 10117 Berlin; tel. (30) 7262520; fax (30) 72625242; f. 1949; Pres. Ernst Fischer; Gen. Sec. Ingrid Hartges; over 75,000 mems.

Gemeinschaftsausschuss der Deutschen gewerblichen Wirtschaft (Joint Committee for German Industry and Commerce): Köln; tel. (221) 370800; fax (221) 3708730; f. 1950; a discussion forum for the principal industrial and commercial orgs; Pres. Dr Tyll Necker; 16 mem. orgs.

GermanFashion Modeverband Deutschland eV: An Lyskirchen 14, 50676 Köln; tel. (221) 77440; fax (221) 7744137; e-mail info@germanfashion.net; internet www.germanfashion.net.

Gesamtverband der deutschen Textil und Modeindustrie eV (Textiles and Clothing): Postfach 5340, 65728 Eschborn; Frankfurter Str. 10–14, 65760 Eschborn; tel. (6196) 9660; fax (6196) 42170; e-mail info@textil-mode.de; internet www.textil-online.de; f. 1948; Dir-Gen. Dr Wolf R. Baumann.

Gesamtverband kunststoffverarbeitende Industrie eV (GKV) (Plastics): Am Hauptbahnhof 12, 60329 Frankfurt a.M.; tel. (69) 271050; fax (69) 232799; e-mail tenhagen-gkv@t-online.de; internet www.gkv.de; f. 1950; Chair. Günter Schwank; Sec.-Gen. Joachim den Hagen; 750 mems.

Hauptverband der Deutschen Bauindustrie eV (Building): Kurfürstenstr. 129, 10785 Berlin; tel. (30) 212860; fax (30) 21286240; e-mail info@bauindustrie.de; internet www.bauindustrie.de; f. 1948; Pres. Prof. Thomas Bauer; Dir-Gen. Michael Knipper; 23 mem. asscns.

Hauptverband der Deutschen Holz und Kunststoffe verarbeitenden Industrie und verwandter Industriezweige eV (HDH) (Woodwork and Plastic): Flutgraben 2, 53604 Bad-Honnef; tel. (2224) 93770; fax (2224) 937777; e-mail info@hdh-ev.de; internet www.hdh-ev.de; f. 1948; Pres. Helmut Lübke; Man. Dir Dirk-Uwe Klaas; 24 mem. asscns.

Hauptverband der Papier, Pappe und Kunststoffe verarbeitenden Industrie eV (HPV) (Paper, Board and Plastic): Strubbergstr. 70, 60489 Frankfurt a.M.; tel. (69) 9782810; fax (69) 97828130; e-mail info@hpv-ev.org; internet www.hpv-ev.org; f. 1948; 10 regional groups, 20 production groups; Pres. Lutz Boeder; Dir-Gen. Thomas Beck; 1,300 mems.

Mineralölwirtschaftsverband eV (German Petroleum Association): Georgenstr. 25, 10117 Berlin; tel. (30) 20220530; fax (30) 20220555; e-mail info@mwv.de; internet www.mwv.de; f. 1946; Chair. Dr Uwe Franke; Man. Dir Dr Klaus Picard.

SPECTARIS—Deutscher Industrieverband für optische, medizinische und mechatronische Technologien eV (German Industrial Asscn for Optical, Medical and Mechatronical Technologies): Saarbrücker Str. 38, 10405 Berlin; tel. (30) 4140210; fax (30) 41402133; e-mail info@spectaris.de; internet www.spectaris.de; f. 1949; Chair. Dr Michael Kaschke; Dir Sven Behrens.

Verband der Automobilindustrie eV (Motor Cars): Postfach 170563, 60079 Frankfurt a.M.; Westendstr. 61, 60325 Frankfurt a.M.; tel. (69) 975070; fax (69) 97507261; e-mail info@vda.de; internet www.vda.de; Pres. Prof. Dr Bernd Gottschalk.

Verband der Chemischen Industrie eV (Chemical Industry): mainzer Landstr. 55, 60329 Frankfurt a.M.; tel. (69) 25560; fax (69) 25561471; e-mail vci@vci.de; internet www.chemische-industrie.de; f. 1877; Pres. Dr Klaus Engel; Dir-Gen. Dr Utz Tillmann; 1,579 mems.

Verband Deutscher Maschinen- und Anlagenbau eV (VDMA) (German Engineering Federation): Postfach 710864, 60498 Frankfurt a.M.; Lyoner Str. 18, 60528 Frankfurt a.M.; tel. (69) 66030; fax (69) 66031511; e-mail kommunikation@vdma.org; internet www.vdma.org; f. 1892; Pres. Dieter Brucklacher; Gen. Man. Dr Hannes Hesse.

Verband Deutscher Papierfabriken eV (Paper): Adenauerallee 55, 53113 Bonn; tel. (228) 267050; fax (228) 2670562; Pres. Dr Wolfgang Palm; Dir-Gen. Klaus Windhagen.

Verband der Kali- und Salzindustrie eV (Potash and Salt): Reinhardtstr. 18a, 10117 Berlin; tel. (30) 84710690; fax (30) 847106921; e-mail info.berlin@vks-kalisalz.de; internet www.vks-kalisalz.de; f. 1905; Chair. Norbert Steiner; Man. Dir Hartmut Behnsen.

Verband für Schiffbau und Meerestechnik eV (German Shipbuilding and Ocean Industries Asscn): Steinhoeft 11, 20459 Hamburg; tel. (40) 2801520; fax (40) 28015230; e-mail info@vsm.de; internet www.vsm.de; f. 1884; Man. Dirs Werner Lundt, Dr Ralf Soeren Marquardt.

Verein der Zuckerindustrie (Sugar): Am Hofgarten 8, 53113 Bonn; tel. (228) 22850; fax (228) 2285100; e-mail wvz-vdz@

zuckerverbaende.de; internet www.zuckerverbaende.de; f. 1850; Chair. Horst W. Mewis; Dir-Gen. Dr Dieter Langendorf.

Vereinigung Rohstoffe und Bergbau eV (German Mining Association): Postfach 120736, 10597 Berlin; Am Schillertheater 4, 10625 Berlin; tel. (30) 31518242; fax (30) 31518235; e-mail info@v-r-b.de; internet www.v-rohstoffe-bergbau.de; f. 1953; Pres. Joachim Geisler; Gen. Man. Dr Heinz-Norbert Schächter; 13 mem. asscns.

Wirtschaftsverband der Deutschen Kautschukindustrie eV (WDK) (Rubber): Zeppelinallee 69, 60487 Frankfurt a.M.; tel. (69) 79360; fax (69) 7936165; e-mail info@wdk.de; internet www.wdk.de; f. 1894; Pres. Paul Eberhard-Krug; Gen. Man. Fritz Katzensteiner; 87 mems.

Wirtschaftsverband Erdöl- und Erdgasgewinnung eV (Association of German Oil and Gas Producers): Brühlstr. 9, 30169 Hannover; tel. (511) 121720; fax (511) 1217210; e-mail info@erdoel-erdgas.de; internet www.erdoel-erdgas.de; f. 1945; Pres. Dr Gernot Kalkoffen; Gen. Man. Josef Schmid.

Wirtschaftsverband Stahlbau und Energietechnik (SET) (Steel and Energy): Postfach 320420, 40419 Düsseldorf; Sternstr. 36, 40479 Düsseldorf; tel. (211) 4987092; fax (211) 4987036; e-mail info@set-online.de; internet www.set-online.de; Chair. Klaus Dieter Rennert; Dir-Gen. R. Maass.

WSM—Wirtschaftsverband Stahl- und Metallverarbeitung eV (Steel and Metal-processing Industry): Kaiserwerther Str. 135, 40474 Düsseldorf; tel. (211) 4564108; fax (211) 4564169; e-mail hwolff@wsm-net.de; internet www.wsm-net.de; Pres. Jürgen R. Thumann; Dir-Gen. Dr Andreas Moehlenkamp.

WirtschaftsVereinigung Metalle (Metal): Postfach 105463, 40045 Düsseldorf; Am Bonneshof 5, 40474 Düsseldorf; tel. (211) 47960; fax (211) 4796400; e-mail info@wvmetalle.de; internet www.wvmetalle.de; Pres. Dr Karl-Heinz Dörner; Dir-Gen. Martin Kneer.

Wirtschaftsvereinigung Stahl (Steel): Postfach 105464, 40045 Düsseldorf; Sohnstr. 65, 40237 Düsseldorf; tel. (211) 67070; fax (211) 6707310; e-mail wvstahl@wvstahl.de; internet www.stahl-online.de; Pres. Hans-Jürgen Kerkhoff.

Wirtschaftsvereinigung Ziehereien und Kaltwalzwerke eV (Metal): Drahthaus, Kaiserswerther Str. 137, 40474 Düsseldorf; tel. (211) 478060; fax (211) 4780622; Chair. and Gen. Man. Dr Friedrich Uenhaus.

Zentralverband des Deutschen Handwerks: Mohrenstr. 20/21, 10117 Berlin; tel. (30) 206190; fax (30) 20619460; e-mail info@zdh.de; internet www.zdh.de; f. 1949; Pres. Otto Kentzler; Gen. Sec. Holger Schwannecke; 54 mem. chambers, 37 asscns.

Zentralverband Elektrotechnik- und Elektronikindustrie eV (ZVEI) (Electrical and Electronic Equipment): Postfach 701261, 60591 Frankfurt a.M.; Stresemannallee 19, 60596 Frankfurt a.M.; tel. (69) 63020; fax (69) 6302317; e-mail zvei@zvei.org; internet www.zvei.org; f. 1918; Pres. Friedhelm Loh; Exec. Dir Dr Klaus Mittelbach; 1,400 mems.

EMPLOYERS' ORGANIZATIONS

Bundesvereinigung der Deutschen Arbeitgeberverbände (BDA) (Confederation of German Employers' Associations): Breite Str. 29, 10178 Berlin; tel. (30) 20330; fax (30) 20331055; e-mail bda@arbeitgeber.de; internet www.bda-online.de; f. 1904; represents the professional and regional interests of German employers in the social policy field, affiliates 14 regional asscns and 53 branch asscns, of which some are listed under industrial asscns; Pres. Prof. Dr Dieter Hundt; Man. Dir Dr Reinhard Göhner.

Affiliated associations:

Arbeitgeberverband der Cigarettenindustrie eV (Employers' Association of Cigarette Manufacturers): Kapstadtring 10, 22297 Hamburg; tel. (40) 63784841; fax (40) 63784841; e-mail md@adc-online.de; internet www.adc-online.de; f. 1949; Pres. Michael Wenzel; Dir Michael Dreier.

Arbeitgeberverband der Deutschen Binnenschiffahrt eV (Employers' Association of German Inland Waterway Transport): Dammstr. 15–17, 47119 Duisburg; tel. (203) 8000631; fax (203) 8000621; e-mail info@schulschiff-rhein.de; internet www.schulschiff-rhein.de; f. 1974; Pres. Volker Seefeldt; Dir Jörg Rusche.

Arbeitgeberverband der Deutschen Kautschukindustrie (ADK) eV (German Rubber Industry Employers' Association): Schiffgraben 36, 30175 Hannover; tel. (511) 85050; fax (511) 8505203; e-mail info@adk-verband.de; internet www.adk-ev.de; Pres. Dr Sven Vogt; Gen. Man. Dr Volker Schmidt.

Arbeitgeberverband Deutscher Eisenbahnen eV (German Railway Employers' Association): Volksgartenstr. 54a, 50677 Köln; tel. (221) 9318450; fax (221) 93184588; e-mail info@agvde.de; internet www.agvde.de; Pres. Rolf Bender; Dir Dr Hans-Peter Ackmann.

Arbeitgeberverband des Privaten Bankgewerbes eV (Private Banking Employers' Association): Burgstr. 28, 10178 Berlin; tel. (30) 590011270; fax (30) 590011279; e-mail service@agvbanken.de; internet www.agvbanken.de; f. 1954; 140 mems; Pres. Ulrich Sieber; Dir Dr Gerd Benrath.

Arbeitgeberverband der Versicherungsunternehmen in Deutschland (Employers' Association of Insurance Companies): Arabellastr. 29, 81925 München; tel. (89) 9220010; fax (89) 92200150; e-mail agvvers@agv-vers.de; internet www.agv-vers.de; f. 1950; Pres. and Dir-Gen. Dr Josef Beutelmann; Dir-Gen. Dr Michael Niebler.

Bundesarbeitgeberverband Chemie eV (Federation of Employers' Associations in the Chemical Industry): Postfach 1280, 65002 Wiesbaden; Abraham-Lincoln-Str. 24, 65189 Wiesbaden; tel. (611) 778810; fax (611) 7788123; e-mail info@bavc.de; internet www.bavc.de; f. 1949; Pres. Dr Eggert Voscherau; Dir Hans Paul Frey; 10 mem. asscns.

Bundesarbeitgeberverband Glas und Solar eV: Postfach 200219, 80002 München; Max-Joseph-Str. 5, 80333 München; tel. (89) 41119430; fax (89) 411194344; e-mail info@bavglassolar.de; internet www.bavglassolar.de; f. 2010; fmrly Arbeitgeberverband der Deutschen Glasindustrie eV; Pres. Thomas Kietschmann; Gen. Man. Harms Lefnaer.

Bundesarbeitgeberverband Glas und Solar eV: Postfach 200219, 80002 München; Max-Joseph-Str. 5, 80333 München; tel. (89) 41119430; fax (89) 411194344; e-mail info@bavglassolar.de; internet www.bavglassolar.de; f. 2010; fmrly Arbeitgeberverband der Deutschen Glasindustrie eV; Pres. Thomas Kietschmann; Gen. Man. Harms Lefnaer.

Gesamtmetall—Gesamtverband der Arbeitgeberverbände der Metall- und Elektro-Industrie eV (Federation of the Metal Trades Employers' Associations): Postfach 060249, 10052 Berlin; Vossstr. 16, 10117 Berlin; tel. (30) 551500; e-mail info@gesamtmetall.de; internet www.gesamtmetall.de; f. 1898; Pres. Martin Kannegiesser; 22 mem. asscns.

Gesamtverband der Deutschen Land- und Forstwirtschaftlichen Arbeitgeberverbände eV (Federation of Agricultural and Forestry Employers' Associations): Claire-Waldoff-Str. 7, 10117 Berlin; tel. (30) 31904407; fax (30) 31904431; e-mail presse@bauernverband.net; internet www.bauernverband.de; Pres. Gerd Sonnleitner; Sec. Dr Helmut Born.

Vereinigung der Arbeitgeberverbände der Deutschen Papierindustrie eV (Federation of Employers' Associations of the German Paper Industry): Postfach 1232, 76585 Gernsbach; Scheffelstr. 29, 76593 Gernsbach; tel. (228) 2672810; fax (228) 215270; e-mail vap@papierzentrum.org; internet www.vap-papier.de; Pres. Eberhard Potempa; Dir Stephan Meißner; 8 mem. asscns.

Vereinigung der Arbeitgeberverbände energie- und versorgungswirtschaftlicher Unternehmungen (Employers' Federation of Energy and Power Supply Enterprises): Theaterstr. 3, 30159 Hannover; tel. (511) 911090; fax (511) 9110940; e-mail agv.energie@t-online.de; internet www.vaeu.de; f. 1962; Pres. Hartmut Geldmacher; Dir Jobst Kleineberg; 7 mem. asscns.

Regional employers' associations:

Arbeitgeber- und Wirtschaftsverbände Sachsen-Anhalt eV (Employers' and business associations of Saxony-Anhalt): Postfach 4152, 39106 Magdeburg; Humboldtstr. 14, 39112 Magdeburg; tel. (391) 6288819; fax (391) 6288810; e-mail info@aw-sa.de; internet www.wir-setzen-akzente.de; Pres. Klemens Gutmann; Gen. Man. Matthias Menger; 31 mem. asscns.

Landesvereinigung Baden-Württembergischer Arbeitgeberverbände eV: Postfach 700501, 70574 Stuttgart; Löffelstr. 22–24, 70597 Stuttgart; tel. (711) 76820; fax (711) 7651675; e-mail info@agv-bw.de; internet www.agv-bw.de; f. 1951; Pres. Dr Dieter Hundt; Dir Peer-Michael Dick; 42 mem. asscns.

Landesvereinigung der Unternehmensverbände Nordrhein-Westfalen eV (North Rhine-Westphalia Federation of Employers' Associations): Postfach 300643, 40406 Düsseldorf; Uerdinger Str. 58–62, 40474 Düsseldorf; tel. (211) 45730; fax (211) 4573179; e-mail info@unternehmernrw.net; internet www.unternehmernrw.net; Pres. Horst-Werner Maier-Hunke; Dir Dr Luitwin Mallmann; 92 mem. asscns.

Landesvereinigung Unternehmerverbände Rheinland-Pfalz eV (LVU) (Federation of Employers' Associations in the Rhineland Palatinate): Postfach 2966, 55019 Mainz; Hindenburgstr. 32, 55118 Mainz; tel. (6131) 55750; fax (6131) 557539; e-mail contact@lvu.de; internet www.lvu.de; f. 1963; Pres. Dr Gerhard F. Braun.

Die Unternehmensverbände im Lande Bremen eV (Federation of Employers' Associations in the Land of Bremen): Postfach 100727, 28007 Bremen; Schiller Str. 10, 28195 Bremen; tel. (421) 368020; fax (421) 3680249; e-mail info@uvhb.de; internet www

.uvhb.de; Pres. INGO KRAMER; Dir CORNELIUS NEUMANN-REDLIN; 18 mem. asscns.

Unternehmerverbände Niedersachsen eV (UVN) (Federation of Employers' Associations in Lower Saxony): Schiffgraben 36, 30175 Hannover; tel. (511) 8505243; fax (511) 8505268; e-mail uvn@uvn-online.de; internet www.uvn-online.de; f. 1951; Pres. WERNER M. BAHLSEN; Dir Dr VOLKER MÜLLER; 65 mem. asscns.

UVNord—Vereinigung der Unternehmensverbände in Hamburg und Schleswig-Holstein eV (Federation of Employers' Associations in Hamburg and Schleswig-Holstein): Postfach 601969, 22219 Hamburg; Kapstadtring 10, 22297 Hamburg; tel. (40) 63785120; fax (40) 63785151; e-mail froehlich@uvnord.de; internet www.uvnord.de; Pres. Prof. Dr ULI WACHHOLTZ; Dir Dr MICHAEL THOMAS FRÖHLICH; 59 mem. asscns.

vbw—Vereinigung der Bayerischen Wirtschaft eV (Federation of Employers' Associations in Bavaria): Postfach 202026, 80020 München; Max-Joseph-Str. 5, 80333 München; tel. (89) 55178100; fax (89) 55178111; e-mail info@vbw-bayern.de; internet www.vbw-bayern.de; Pres. RANDOLF RODENSTOCK; Gen. Man. BERTRAM BROSSARDT; 83 mem. asscns.

Verband der Wirtschaft Thüringens eV (Association of Thuringian Management): Postfach 900353, 99007 Erfurt; Lossiusstr. 1, 99094 Erfurt; tel. (361) 67590; fax (361) 6759222; e-mail info@vwt.de; internet www.vwt.de; Pres. WOLGANG ZAHN; Dir STEPHAN FAUTH; 44 mem. asscns.

Vereinigung der Unternehmensverbände in Berlin und Brandenburg eV (Federation of Employers' Associations in Berlin and Brandenburg): Am Schillertheater 2, 10625 Berlin; tel. (30) 310050; fax (30) 31005160; e-mail uvb@uvb-online.de; internet www.uvb-online.de; Pres. BURKHARD ISCHLER; 60 mem. asscns.

Vereinigung der hessischen Unternehmerverbände eV (Hessian Federation of Enterprise Associations): Postfach 500561, 60394 Frankfurt a.M.; Emil-von-Behring-Str. 4, 60439 Frankfurt a.M.; tel. (69) 958080; fax (69) 95808126; e-mail info@vhu.de; internet www.vhu.de; f. 1947; Pres. Prof. DIETER WEIDEMANN; Dir and Sec. VOLKER FASBENDER; 60 mem. asscns.

Vereinigung der Saarländischen Unternehmensverbände eV (Federation of Employers' Associations in Saarland): Postfach 650433, 66143 Saarbrücken; Harthweg 15, 66119 Saarbrücken; tel. (681) 954340; fax (681) 9543474; e-mail kontakt@vsu.de; internet www.vsu.de; Pres. Dr OSWALD BUBEL; Dir Dr JOACHIM MALTER; 19 mem. asscns.

Vereinigung der Sächsischen Wirtschaft eV (VSW) (Federation of Employers' Associations in Saxony): Postfach 300200, 01131 Dresden; Washingtonstr. 16/16A, 01139 Dresden; tel. (351) 255930; fax (351) 2559378; e-mail vsw@hsw-mail.de; internet www.wirtschaftsverbaende-sachsen.de; Pres. BODO FINGER; Gen. Man. Dr ANDREAS WINKLER; 40 mem. asscns.

Vereinigung der Unternehmensverbände für Mecklenburg-Vorpommern eV (Federation of Employers' Associations of Mecklenburg-Western Pomerania): Graf-Schack-Allee 10, 19053 Schwerin; tel. (385) 6356100; fax (385) 6356151; e-mail info@vumv.de; internet www.vumv.de; Pres. HANS-DIETER BREMER; Dir Dr THOMAS KLISCHAN; 30 mem. asscns.

UTILITIES

Regulatory Authority

Bundesnetzagentur für Elektrizität, Gas, Telekommunikation, Post und Eisenbahnen: see Telecommunications.

Electricity and Gas

Supply of electricity and gas is dominated by four companies (RWE, E.ON, Vattenfall Europe and EnBW). A large number of regional utilities, many of which are part-owned by the four major companies, supply electricity and gas to towns and municipalities in one or more of the federal *Länder*.

Energie Baden-Württemberg AG (EnBW): Durlacher Allee 93, 76131 Karlsruhe; tel. (49) 7216300; e-mail kontakt@enbw.com; internet www.enbw.com; production, distribution and supply of electricity and gas; CEO HANS-PETER VILLIS.

E.ON AG: E.ON-Pl. 1, 40479 Düsseldorf; tel. (211) 45790; fax (211) 4579501; e-mail info@eon.com; internet www.eon.com; f. 2000 by merger of VEBA AG and VIAG AG; production, distribution and supply of electricity and gas; operates in 19 countries world-wide; Chair. and CEO Dr JOHANNES TEYSSEN.

E.ON Energie AG: Brienner Str. 40, 80333 München; tel. (89) 125401; fax (89) 12543906; e-mail info@eon-energie.com; internet www.eon-energie.com; f. 2000 by merger of Bayernwerk AG and Preussenelektra AG; production, transmission and supply of electricity; subsidiary of E.ON AG; Chair. Prof. Dr KLAUS-DIETER MAUBACH.

E.ON Ruhrgas AG: Huttropstr. 60, 45138 Essen; tel. (201) 18400; fax (201) 1843766; e-mail info@eon-ruhrgas.com; internet www.eon-ruhrgas.com; f. 1926; distribution and supply of natural gas; subsidiary of E.ON AG; Chair., Management Bd Dr BERNHARD REUTERSBERG.

EWE AG: Donnerschweer Str. 22–26, 26122 Oldenburg; tel. (441) 48050; fax (441) 48053999; e-mail info@ewe.de; internet www.ewe.de; f. 1943; supplier of electricity and natural gas; serves northern Germany; Chair., Management Bd Dr WERNER BRINKER.

GASAG Berliner Gaswerke AG: Voßstr. 20, 10117 Berlin; tel. (30) 78720; fax (30) 78724794; e-mail service@gasag.de; internet www.gasag.de; f. 1992; regional gas supplier for Berlin; Man. Dirs ANDREAS PROHL, OLAF CZERNOMORIEZ.

GasVersorgung Süddeutschland GmbH (GVS): Am Wallgraben 135, 70565 Stuttgart; tel. (711) 78120; fax (711) 78121411; e-mail sunc@gvs-erdgas.de; internet www.gvs-erdgas.de; f. 1961; supplies gas to 750 towns and municipalities in Baden-Württemberg; CEO PAOLO CONTI.

Mainova AG: Solmsstr. 38, 60623 Frankfurt a.M.; tel. (69) 21302; fax (69) 21381122; internet www.mainova.de; f. 1998 by merger of Stadtwerke Frankfurt and Maingas AG; supply of electricity, natural gas and water in Frankfurt am Main and surrounding area; 75.2% owned by Frankfurt a.M. city administration, 24.4% owned by Thüga AG; Chair. Dr PETRA ROTH.

MITGAS Mitteldeutsche Gasversorgung GmbH: Postfach 300552, 06025 Halle (Saale); tel. (34605) 60; fax (34605) 61610; e-mail service@mitgas.de; internet www.mitgas.de; f. 2000; regional gas supplier with customers in Saxony, Saxony-Anhalt and Thuringia; 24.60% owned by VNG-Beteiligungs-GmbH; Man. Dirs CARL-ERNST GIESTING, Dr ANDREAS AUERBACH.

RWE AG: Postfach 103061, 45030 Essen; Opernpl. 1, 45128 Essen; tel. (201) 1200; internet www.rwe.de; f. 1898; production, distribution and supply of electricity, gas and water; subsidiaries in 6 European countries (Czech Republic, Hungary, the Netherlands, Poland, Slovakia, the UK) and the USA; Pres. and CEO Dr JÜRGEN GROßMAN (until July 2012), JÜRGEN GROSSMAN (from July 2012).

swb AG: Theodor-Heuss-Allee 20, 28215 Bremen; tel. (421) 3590; fax (421) 3592499; e-mail info@swb-gruppe.de; internet www.swb-gruppe.de; f. 1854; supplies electricity, natural gas and water in Bremen and northern Germany; 100% owned by EWE AG; Chair., Management Bd Dr WILLEM SCHOEBER.

Vattenfall Europe AG: Chausseestr. 23, 10115 Berlin; tel. (30) 818222; fax (30) 81823950; e-mail info@vattenfall.de; internet www.vattenfall.de; f. 2002 by merger of Bewag, HEW, LAUBAG and VEAG; production, distribution and supply of electricity; Chair., Management Bd TUOMO J. HATAKKA.

WINGAS GmbH & Co KG: Friedrich-Ebert-Str. 160, 34119 Kassel; tel. (561) 3010; fax (561) 3011702; e-mail info@wingas.de; internet www.wingas.de; f. 1993; distribution of natural gas; also supplies gas to public utilities, regional gas suppliers, industrial facilities and power plants; jt venture of Wintershall Holding AG and Gazprom (Russia); Chair. Dr GERHARD KÖNIG; Man. Dir ARTOUR CHAKHDINAROV.

Water

Responsibility for water supply lies with the municipalities. As a result, there are over 6,000 water supply utilities in Germany. The ownership structures of those utilities are diverse. Many municipalities have formed limited or joint-stock companies with private sector partners to manage water supply, such as the supplier for the capital (Berliner Wasserbetriebe), while others have contracted private companies to provide water services.

Berliner Wasserbetriebe: Neue Jüdenstr. 1, 10179 Berlin; tel. (800) 2927587; fax (30) 86442810; internet www.bwb.de; f. 1856; supplier of water and sanitation services to Berlin; subsidiary of Berlinerwasser Gruppe (50.1% owned by Berlin regional Govt, 24.95% each by RWE AG and Veolia Environment (France); Chair., Management Bd JÖRG SIMON.

Gelsenwasser AG: Willy-Brandt-Allee 26, 45891 Gelsenkirchen; tel. (209) 7080; fax (209) 708650; e-mail info@gelsenwasser.de; internet www.gelsenwasser.de; privately owned enterprise, supplying water and sanitation services by agreement with several municipalities in North Rhine-Westphalia and across Germany; also supplies electricity and gas; Chair., Management Bd HENNING R. DETERS.

Association

Bundesverband der Energie- und Wasserwirtschaft eV (BDEW) (German Association of Energy and Water Companies): Reinhardtstr. 32, 10117 Berlin; tel. (30) 3001990; fax (30) 3001993900; e-mail info@bdew.de; internet www.bdew.de; f. 2007; c. 1,800 mems; Pres. EWALD WOSTE; Chair., Management Bd HILDEGARD MÜLLER.

TRADE UNIONS

The main German trade union federations are the Deutscher Gewerkschaftsbund (DGB), the Deutscher Beamtenbund und Tarifunion (dbb) and the Christlicher Gewerkschaftsbund Deutschlands (CGB). Following German unification in October 1990, the trade unions of the former GDR were absorbed into the member unions of the DGB.

National Federations

Christlicher Gewerkschaftsbund Deutschlands (Christian Workers' Union—CGB): Obentrautstr. 57, 10963 Berlin; tel. (30) 21021730; fax (30) 21021740; e-mail cgb.bund@cgb.info; internet www.cgb.info; f. 1899; 16 affiliated unions; Pres. MATTHÄUS STREBL; Gen. Sec. GUNTER SMITS; c. 280,000 mems.

dbb beamtenbund und tarifunion (Civil Servants' Federation): Friedrichstr. 169–170, 10117 Berlin; tel. (30) 408140; fax (30) 40814999; e-mail post@dbb.de; internet www.dbb.de; f. 1918; 40 affiliated unions; Pres. PETER HEESEN; 1.3m. mems (2007).

Deutscher Gewerkschaftsbund (DGB): Henriette-Herz-Pl. 2, 10178 Berlin; tel. (30) 240600; fax (30) 24060324; e-mail info.bvv@dgb.de; internet www.dgb.de; f. 1949; 8 affiliated unions; Pres. MICHAEL SOMMER; Vice-Pres. INGRID SEHRBROCK; 6,441,045 mems (2007).

Principal Unions

Christliche Gewerkschaft Metall (CGM): Jahnstr. 12, 70597 Stuttgart; tel. (711) 24847880; fax (711) 248478821; e-mail info@cgm.de; internet www.cgm.de; f. 1899; represents workers in the metals and electronics sectors; mem. union of CGB; Pres. REINHARDT SCHILLER.

DHV—Die Berufgewerkschaft (Commerce and Administration): César-Klein-Ring 40, 22309 Hamburg; tel. (40) 6328020; fax (40) 63280225; e-mail dhv@dhv-cgb.de; internet www.dhv-cgb.de; mem. union of CGB; Pres. JÖRG HEBSACKER; Gen. Sec. HENNING RÖDERS; c. 80,000 mems.

GDL—Gewerkschaft Deutscher Lokomotivführer (Train Drivers' Union): Baumweg 45, 60316 Frankfurt a.M.; tel. (69) 4057090; fax (69) 405709129; e-mail info@gdl.de; internet www.gdl.de; f. 1867; mem. of dbb; Pres. CLAUS WESELSKY; c. 34,000 mems.

Gewerkschaft Erziehung und Wissenschaft (GEW) (German Education Union): Reifenberger Str. 21, 60489 Frankfurt a.M.; tel. (69) 789730; fax (69) 78973201; e-mail info@gew.de; internet www.gew.de; mem. union of DGB; Pres. ULRICH THOENE; 258,119 mems (Dec. 2009).

Gewerkschaft Nahrung-Genuss-Gaststätten (Food, Beverages, Tobacco, Hotel and Catering and allied Workers): Haubachstr. 76, 22765 Hamburg; tel. (40) 380130; fax (40) 3892637; e-mail hauptverwaltung@ngg.net; internet www.ngg.net; f. 1949; mem. union of DGB; Pres. FRANZ-JOSEF MÖLLENBERG; 207,947 mems (Dec. 2007).

Gewerkschaft der Polizei (Police): Stromstr. 4, 10555 Berlin; tel. (30) 3999210; fax (30) 39921211; e-mail gdp-bund-berlin@gdp-online.de; internet www.gdp.de; f. 1950; mem. union of DGB; Chair. KONRAD FREIBERG; Sec. FRANK RICHTER; 168,433 mems (Dec. 2007).

IG Bau—Industriegewerkschaft Bauen-Agrar-Umwelt (Building and Construction Trade): Olof-Palme-Str. 19, 60439 Frankfurt a.M.; tel. (69) 957370; fax (69) 95737800; e-mail presse@igbau.de; internet www.igbau.de; mem. union of DGB; Pres. KLAUS WIESEHÜGEL; 351,723 mems (Dec. 2007).

IG BCE—Industriegewerkschaft Bergbau, Chemie, Energie (Mining, Chemical and Energy Industrial Union): Königsworther Pl. 6, 30167 Hannover; tel. (511) 76310; fax (511) 7000891; e-mail info@igbce.de; internet www.igbce.de; f. 1997 by merger of Chemical, Paper and Pulp and Ceramic Workers' Union, Mining and Energy Workers' Union and Leather Workers' Union; mem. union of DGB; Pres. HUBERTUS SCHMOLDT; 702,332 mems. (June 2008).

IG Metall—die Gewerkschaft in Produktion und Dienstleistung der Bereiche Metall-Elektro, Textil-Bekleidung, Holz-Kunststoff (Metal, Textiles, Clothing, Wood and Plastics Workers): Wilhelm-Leuschner-Str. 79, 60329 Frankfurt a.M.; tel. (69) 66930; fax (69) 66932843; e-mail presse.igm@igmetall.de; internet www.igmetall.de; f. 1891; mem. union of DGB; Chair. BERTHOLD HUBER; 2,306,283 mems (Dec. 2007).

Transnet (Transport Workers): Chausseestr. 84, 10115 Berlin; tel. (30) 42439075; fax (30) 42439071; e-mail presse@transnet.org; internet www.transnet.org; f. 1948 as Gewerkschaft der Eisenbahner Deutschlands; present name adopted 2000; mem. union of DGB; Pres. ALEXANDER KIRCHNER; 239,468 mems (Dec. 2007).

ver.di—Vereinte Dienstleistungsgewerkschaft (United Services Union): Paula-Thiede-Ufer 10, 10179 Berlin; tel. (30) 69560; fax (30) 69563141; e-mail info@verdi.de; internet www.verdi.de; f. 2001 by merger of Gewerkschaft Handel, Banken und Versicherungen, Industriegewerkschaft Medien, Gewerkschaft Öffentliche Dienste, Transport und Verkehr, Deutsche Postgewerkschaft and Deutsche Angestellten-Gewerkschaft; mem. union of DGB; Chair. FRANK BSIRSKE; 2,094,455 mems (Dec. 2010).

Verkehrsgewerkschaft GDBA: Westendstr. 52, 60325 Frankfurt a.M.; tel. (69) 7140010; fax (69) 71400141; e-mail verkehrsgewerkschaft@gdba.de; internet www.gdba.de; f. 1948; represents employees in the transportation, service and telecommunications sectors; mem. union of dbb; Pres. KLAUS-DIETER HOMMEL.

Transport

RAILWAYS

At 2010 the length of state-owned track in Germany was 33,708 km, of which 19,820 km were electrified. High-speed InterCity Express (ICE) trains operate between several German cities, and offer links to Austria (Vienna and Innsbruck), Belgium (Brussels and Liège), Denmark (Copenhagen and Arhus), France (Paris), the Netherlands (Arnhem, Utrecht and Amsterdam) and Switzerland (Zürich and Interlaken).

Regulatory Bodies

Eisenbahn-Bundesamt (EBA) (Federal Railway Authority): Heinemannstr. 6, 53119 Bonn; tel. (228) 98260; fax (228) 9826199; e-mail poststelle@eba.bund.de; internet www.eisenbahn-bundesamt.de; supervisory and authorizing body; ensures safety of railway passengers; supervises construction; inspects and approves rolling stock and monitors safe condition of railway infrastructure and signalling; Pres. GERALD HÖRSTER.

Bundeseisenbahnvermögen (BEV) (Federal Railroad Assets): Kurt-Georg-Kiesinger-Allee 2, 53175 Bonn; tel. (228) 30770; fax (228) 3077160; e-mail bonn@bev.bund.de; internet www.bev.bund.de; Pres. MARIE-THERES NONN.

Federal Railway

Deutsche Bahn AG (German Railways): Potsdamer Pl. 2, 10785 Berlin; tel. (30) 29761131; fax (30) 29761919; e-mail medienbetreuung@bku.db.de; internet www.db.de; f. 1994 by merger of Deutsche Bundesbahn and Deutsche Reichsbahn; state-owned; CEO and Chair., Management Bd RÜDIGER GRUBE; Chair., Supervisory Bd Dr UTZ-HELLMUTH FELCHT.

Metropolitan Railways

Berliner Verkehrsbetriebe (BVG) (Berlin Transport Authority): Anstalt des öffentlichen Rechts, Holzmarktstr. 15–17, 10783 Berlin; tel. (30) 19449; fax (30) 25649256; e-mail info@bvg.de; internet www.bvg.de; f. 1929; operates 144.9 km of underground railway; also runs tram and bus services; Chair., Management Bd Dr SIGRID EVELYN NIKUTTA.

Hamburger Hochbahn AG: Steinstr. 20, 20095 Hamburg; tel. (40) 32880; fax (40) 326406; e-mail info@hochbahn.de; internet www.hochbahn.de; f. 1911; operates 100.7 km of underground railway on 3 lines; fourth line under construction, scheduled for completion in 2011; also operates 120 bus routes; Chair., Management Bd GÜNTER ELSTE; Chair., Supervisory Bd Dr MICHAEL FREYTAG.

Münchner Verkehrsgesellschaft mbH (MVG): Emmy-Noether-Str. 2, 80287 München; tel. (89) 21910; fax (89) 21912405; e-mail info@swm.de; internet www.mvg-mobil.de; subsidiary of Stadtwerke München GmbH; operates underground railway (6 lines totalling 91 km), tramway (10 lines totalling 71 km), 67 bus lines (452 km); Chair., Management Bd HERBERT KÖNIG.

VAG Verkehrs-Aktiengesellschaft: 90338 Nürnberg; Südliche Fürther Str. 5, 90429 Nürnberg; tel. (911) 2830; fax (911) 2834800; e-mail vag@vag.de; internet www.vag.de; wholly owned subsidiary of Städtische Werke Nürnberg GmbH; operates underground railway (3 lines totalling 31 km), tramway (5 lines totalling 34 km) and bus services (53 routes); Chair., Management Bd JOSEF HASLER; Chair., Supervisory Bd Dr MICHAEL REINDL.

Association

Verband Deutscher Verkehrsunternehmen (VDV) (Association of German Transport Undertakings): Kamekestr. 37–39, 50672 Köln; tel. (221) 579790; fax (221) 514272; e-mail info@vdv.de; internet www.vdv.de; f. 1895; public transport, freight transport by rail; publishes *Der Nahverkehr* (10 a year), *Bus + Bahn* (monthly) and *Güterbahnen* (quarterly); Pres. JÜRGEN FENSKE; Exec. Dir Dr CLAUDIA LANGOWSKY.

ROADS

At 1 January 2008 there were 12,645 km of motorway, 40,203 km of highways and 413,289 km of secondary roads in a total road network of 644,288 km.

INLAND WATERWAYS

The inland waterways network in Germany centres around the Rhine, Danube and Elbe rivers. There are around 7,500 km of navigable inland waterways, including the Main–Danube Canal, linking the North Sea and the Black Sea, which was opened in 1992. Inland shipping accounts for about 12.1% of total freight traffic.

Associations

Bundesverband der Deutschen Binnenschiffahrt eV (BDB): Dammstr. 15–17, 47119 Duisburg; tel. (203) 8000650; fax (203) 8000621; e-mail infobdb@binnenschiff.de; internet www.binnenschiff.de; f. 1978; central Inland Waterway Association to further the interests of operating firms; Pres. Dr GUNTHER JAEGERS; Man. Dirs JENS SCHWANEN, JÖRG RUSCHE.

Bundesverband Öffentlicher Binnenhäfen eV: Ernst-Reuter-Haus, Str. des 17. Juni 114, 10623 Berlin; tel. (30) 39881981; fax (30) 340608553; e-mail info-boeb@binnenhafen.de; internet www.binnenhafen.de; Man. Dir BORIS KLUGE.

Bundesverband der Selbstständigen Abteilung Binnenschiffahrt eV (BDS): August-Bier-Str. 18, 53129 Bonn; tel. (228) 746337; fax (228) 746569; e-mail zentrale@bds-binnenschiffahrt.de; internet www.bds-binnenschiffahrt.de; Man. Dir ANDREA BECKSCHÄFER.

Deutsche Binnenreederei AG: Revaler Str. 100, 10245 Berlin; tel. (30) 29376101; fax (30) 29376201; e-mail dbr@binnenreederei.de; internet www.binnenreederei.de; f. 1949; Dir-Gen. PIOTR CHAJDEROWSKI.

Unternehmensverband Hafen Hamburg eV: Mattentwiete 2, 20457 Hamburg; tel. (40) 3789090; fax (40) 37890970; e-mail info@uvhh.de; internet www.uvhh.de; Pres. KLAUS-DIETER PETERS.

Verein für europäische Binnenschiffahrt und Wasserstrassen eV (VBW): Dammstr. 15–17, 47119 Duisburg; tel. (203) 8000627; fax (203) 8000628; e-mail info@vbw-ev.de; internet www.vbw-ev.de; f. 1877; represents all brs of the inland waterways; Pres. Dr PHILIPPE GRULOIS.

SHIPPING

The port of Hamburg is the largest in Germany and the fourth largest in Europe. Other principal ports are Bremerhaven, Rostock-Überseehafen and Wilhelmshaven. At 31 December 2009 the merchant fleet totalled 948 vessels, with a combined displacement of 15.2m. grt. Some important shipping companies are:

Argo Shipping GmbH: Postfach 107529, 28075 Bremen; Am Wall 187–189, 28195 Bremen; tel. (421) 2575184; fax (421) 2575432; e-mail argoshipping@argo-adler.de; internet www.argo-adler.de; f. 1896; shipowners; Propr MAX ADLER.

Aug. Bolten, Wm. Miller's Nachfolger GmbH & Co KG: Postfach 112269; Mattentwiete 8, 20457 Hamburg; tel. (40) 36010; fax (40) 3601423; e-mail info@aug-bolten.de; internet www.aug-bolten.de; shipowner, manager and broker, port agent; Man. Dirs OLE KRAFT, MICHAEL SAY.

Bugsier- Reederei- und Bergungs-Gesellschaft mbH & Co: Johannisbollwerk 10, 20459 Hamburg; tel. (40) 311110; fax (40) 313693; e-mail info@bugsier.de; internet www.bugsier.de; salvage, towage, tugs, ocean-going heavy lift cranes, submersible pontoons, harbour tugs; Man. Dirs J. W. SCHUCHMANN.

Christian F. Ahrenkiel GmbH & Co KG: An der Alster 45, 20099 Hamburg; tel. (40) 248380; fax (40) 24838375; e-mail info@ahrenkiel.net; internet www.ahrenkiel.net; f. 1950; shipowners, operators and managers; Man. Dir KLAUS G. WOLFF.

DAL Deutsche Afrika-Linien/John T. Essberger GmbH & Co KG: Palmaille 45, 22767 Hamburg; tel. (40) 380160; fax (40) 38016629; e-mail info@rantzau.de; internet www.dal.biz; Europe and South Africa; Man. Dirs Dr E. VON RANTZAU, H. VON RANTZAU.

Deutsche Seereederei GmbH: Lange Str. 1A, 18055 Rostock; tel. (381) 4584043; fax (381) 4584001; e-mail info@deutsche-seereederei.de; internet www.deutsche-seereederei.de; shipping, tourism, real estate, industry and finance; Man. Dir ARNO PÖKER.

Ernst Russ GmbH: Alsterufer 10, 20354 Hamburg; tel. (40) 414070; fax (40) 41407111; e-mail info@ernst-russ.de; internet www.ernst-russ.de; f. 1893; world-wide.

F. Laeisz Schiffahrtsgesellschaft mbH & Co KG: Postfach 111111, 20411 Hamburg; Trostbrücke 1, 20457 Hamburg; tel. (40) 368080; fax (40) 364876; e-mail info@laeisz.de; internet www.laeisz.de; f. 1983; CEO NIKOLAUS H. SCHÜES.

Hamburg Südamerikanische Dampfschiffahrts-Gesellschaft KG: Postfach 111533, 20415 Hamburg; Willy-Brandt-Str. 59–61, 20457 Hamburg; tel. (40) 37050; fax (40) 37052400; e-mail central@ham.hamburgsud.com; internet www.hamburgsud.com; f. 1871; world-wide services; Chair. Dr OTTMAR GAST.

Hapag-Lloyd AG: Ballindamm 25, 20095 Hamburg; tel. (40) 30010; fax (40) 336432; e-mail info.de@hlag.com; internet www.hapag-lloyd.com; f. 1970; 61.6% stake owned by Albert Ballin consortium (comprising city of Hamburg, Kühne Holding AG, Signal Iduna, HSH Nordbank, M.M.Warburg Bank and HanseMerkur); 38.4% stake owned by TUI AG; Chair. MICHAEL BEHRENDT.

John T. Essberger GmbH & Co KG: Postfach 500429, Palmaille 45, 22767 Hamburg; tel. (40) 380160; fax (40) 38016579; f. 1924; Man. Dirs Dr E. VON RANTZAU, H. VON RANTZAU.

KG Fisser & v. Doornum GmbH & Co: Bernhard-Nocht-Str. 113, 20359 Hamburg; tel. (40) 441860; fax (40) 4108050; e-mail management@fissership.com; internet www.fissership.com; f. 1879; tramping services; Man. Dirs CHRISTIAN FISSER, SVEN HEYMANN.

Oldenburg-Portugiesische Dampfschiffs-Rhederei GmbH & Co KG: Postfach 110869, 20408 Hamburg; Kajen 10, 20459 Hamburg; tel. (40) 361580; fax (40) 364131; e-mail info@opdr.de; internet www.opdr.de; f. 1882; Gibraltar, Spain, Portugal, Madeira, North Africa, Canary Islands; Man. Dirs TILL OLE BARRELET, MARK WILKINSON.

Oldendorff Carriers GmbH & Co KG: Postfach 2153, 23509 Lübeck; Willy-Brandt-Allee 6, 235544 Lübeck; tel. (451) 15000; fax (451) 73522; internet www.oldendorff.com; formerly Egon Oldendorff; Chair. HENNING OLDENDORFF; CEO PETER TWISS.

Peter Döhle Schiffahrts-KG: Elbchaussee 370, 22609 Hamburg; tel. (40) 381080; fax (40) 38108255; e-mail empfang@doehle.de; internet www.doehle.de; shipbrokers, chartering agent, shipowners; Pres. JOCHEN DÖHLE.

Rhein-, Maas und See-Schiffahrtskontor GmbH: Krausstr. 1A, 47119 Duisburg; tel. (203) 8040; fax (203) 804330; e-mail rms-team@rheinmaas.de; internet www.rheinmaas.de; f. 1948.

Sloman Neptun Schiffahrts-AG: Postfach 101469, 28014 Bremen; Langenstr. 44, 28195 Bremen; tel. (421) 17630; fax (421) 1763321; e-mail info@sloman-neptun.com; internet www.sloman-neptun.com; f. 1873; liner services from Northern Europe and Mediterranean to North Africa; gas carriers; agencies; Mans SVEN-MICHAEL EDYE, DIRK LOHMANN.

Walther Möller & Co: Postfach 501029, 22710 Hamburg; Gr. Elbstr. 14, 22767 Hamburg; tel. (40) 3803910; fax (40) 38039199; e-mail chartering@wmco.de; internet www.wmco.de.

Shipping Organizations

Verband Deutscher Reeder eV (German Shipowners' Association): Postfach 305580, 20317 Hamburg; Esplanade 6, 20354 Hamburg; tel. (40) 350970; fax (40) 35097211; e-mail vdr@reederverband.de; internet www.reederverband.de; Pres. MICHAEL BEHRENDT; Man. Dir UTA ORDEMANN.

Zentralverband der Deutschen Seehafenbetriebe eV (Federal Association of German Seaport Operators): Am Sandtorkai 2, 20457 Hamburg; tel. (40) 3662034; fax (40) 366377; e-mail info@zds-seehaefen.de; internet www.zds-seehaefen.de; f. 1934; Chair. DETTHOLD ADEN; 199 mems.

CIVIL AVIATION

There are two international airports in the Berlin region (a third, Tempelhof airport, closed in October 2008) and further international airports at Dresden, Düsseldorf, Frankfurt, Hamburg, Hannover, Köln-Bonn, Leipzig, München and Stuttgart. Construction of a major new international airport at Schönefeld, south-east of Berlin, commenced in 2007; the Berlin-Brandenburg International Airport was scheduled to be operational by June 2012.

Air Berlin GmbH & Co Luftverkehrs KG: Saatwinkler Damm 42-43, 13627 Berlin; tel. (1805) 737800; fax (30) 41021003; e-mail serviceteam@airberlin.com; internet www.airberlin.com; f. 1979; offers flights to 97 destinations in Germany and other European countries; CEO HARTMUT MEHDORN.

Condor Flugdienst GmbH: Condor Pl. 1, 60549 Frankfurt am Main; tel. (6107) 9390; fax (6107) 939440; internet www.condor.com; f. 1956; subsidiary of Thomas Cook AG; low-cost airline; Chair., Management Bd RALF TECKENTRUP; Chair., Supervisory Bd HEINER WILKENS.

Deutsche Lufthansa AG: Flughafen-Bereich West, 60546 Frankfurt a.M.; tel. (69) 6960; fax (69) 69633022; internet konzern.lufthansa.com; f. 1953; extensive world-wide network; Chair., Supervisory Bd Dr JÜRGEN WEBER; Chair., Exec. Bd CHRISTOPH FRANZ.

Germania Fluggesellschaft: Riedemannweg 58, 13627 Berlin; tel. (30) 254020; fax (30) 522808361; e-mail info@germania.aero; internet www.germania-flug.de; f. 1979; operates as Germania; charter and scheduled flights.

Germanwings GmbH: Germanwings-Str. 2, 51147 Köln; tel. (900) 1919100; fax (220) 31027300; e-mail kontakt@germanwings.com; internet www.germanwings.com; f. 2002; low-cost airline, offers flights to 60 destinations within Europe; owned by Deutsche Lufthansa AG; CEO THOMAS WINKELMANN.

LTU Lufttransport-Unternehmen GmbH: Flughafen, Halle 8, 40474 Düsseldorf; tel. (211) 9418888; fax (211) 9418881; e-mail internet@ltu.de; internet www.ltu.de; f. 1955; charter and scheduled services; owned by Air Berlin GmbH & Co Luftverkehrs KG; CEO HELMUT WEIXLER.

Lufthansa Cargo AG: Flughafen-Bereich West, Tor 25, Gebäude 451, 60546 Frankfurt a.M.; tel. (69) 6960; fax (69) 69691185; e-mail lhcargo@dlh.de; internet www.lufthansa-cargo.de; f. 1994; wholly owned subsidiary of Deutsche Lufthansa AG; freight-charter worldwide; Chair., Management Bd KARL ULRICH GARNADT; Chair., Supervisory Bd STEFAN GEMKOW.

Lufthansa CityLine GmbH: Flughafen Köln/Bonn, Waldstr. 247, 51147 Köln; tel. (2203) 5960; fax (2203) 596801; e-mail lh-cityline@dlh.de; internet www.lufthansacityline.com; scheduled services; subsidiary of Deutsche Lufthansa AG; Man. Dirs CHRISTIAN TILLMANS, Dr KLAUS FROESE.

TUIfly GmbH: Flughafenstr. 10, Postfach 420240, 30855 Langenhagen; tel. (511) 97270; fax (511) 9727739; internet www.tuifly.com; f. 2007 following merger of Hapag-Lloyd Flug and Hapag-Lloyd Express; charter and scheduled passenger services; Exec. Chair. MICHAEL FRENZEL.

Tourism

Germany's tourist attractions include spas, summer and winter resorts, mountains, medieval towns and castles, and above all a variety of fascinating cities. The North and Baltic Sea coasts, the Rhine Valley, the Black Forest, the mountains of Thuringia, the Erzgebirge and Bavaria are the most popular areas. The total number of foreign visitors was 26.9m. in 2010; preliminary estimates for receipts from tourism in 2010 totalled €34,675m.

Deutsche Zentrale für Tourismus eV (DZT) (German National Tourist Board): Beethovenstr. 69, 60325 Frankfurt a.M.; tel. (69) 97464287; fax (69) 97464233; e-mail info@d-z-t.com; internet www.germany-tourism.de; f. 1948; CEO PETRA HEDORFER.

Defence

Germany is a member of the North Atlantic Treaty Organization (NATO). Military service is compulsory for a period of nine months. In October 2006 the Government endorsed a review of German defence policy, which contained proposals to redefine the primary role of the Bundeswehr from border defence to intervention in international conflicts. Under the proposals, the Bundeswehr would be expanded to allow for the deployment of up to 14,000 troops in five international missions simultaneously. As assessed at November 2011, Germany's armed forces totalled some 251,465. This included an army of 105,291, a navy of 19,179, an air force of 44,565, a joint support service of 57,495 and a joint medical service of 24,935. There was also a reserve of 40,396 (army 15,351; navy 1,867; air force 4,914; joint support service 12,871; joint medical service 4,970; and MoD 423). In November 2010 the Minister of Defence announced that conscription to the armed forces was to be suspended with effect from July 2011, and was to be replaced by voluntary military or community service.

As assessed at November 2011, the USA had 54,198 troops stationed in Germany and the United Kingdom 17,870, while France maintained forces of 2,800 personnel. Canada had 287 troops stationed in Germany.

In November 2004 the European Union (EU) ministers responsible for defence agreed to create a number of 'battlegroups' (each comprising about 1,500 men), which could be deployed at short notice to crisis areas around the world. The EU battlegroups, two of which were to be ready for deployment at any one time, following a rotational schedule, reached full operational capacity from 1 January 2007. Germany was committed to participate in three battlegroups.

Defence Expenditure: Budget estimated at €30,900m. for 2012.

Chief of Staff of the Bundeswehr: Lt-Gen. VOLKER WIEKER.

Education

The Basic Law (*Grundgesetz*) assigns control of the education system to the governments of the *Länder* and to the *Schulamt* (lower-level school supervisory authorities). There is, however, quite close co-operation to ensure a large degree of conformity in the system. Enrolment at pre-primary level included 91.2% of children in the relevant age-group in 2009. Compulsory schooling, which is free, begins at six years of age and continues for nine years (or 10 years in some *Länder*). Until the age of 18 years, all young people who do not continue to attend a full-time school must attend the *Berufsschule* (a part-time vocational school). Primary education lasts four years (six years in Berlin and Brandenburg). In 2008/09 enrolment at primary level included 97% of children in the relevant age-group. Attendance at the *Grundschule* (elementary school) is obligatory for all children, after which their education continues at secondary school. Secondary education, which lasts for up to nine years, is divided into lower secondary, which is compulsory, between the ages of 10 and 15/16 years, and upper secondary, which lasts from 15/16 years of age to 18/19 years. At the end of the lower secondary cycle pupils who reach the required standard receive a leaving certificate, the *Hauptabschluss* or *Mittlerer Schulabschluss*. There are four principal types of secondary school: the *Gymnasium* (grammar school), the *Realschule* (intermediate school), the *Hauptschule* (high school) and the *Gesamtschule* (comprehensive school). At upper secondary, admission to the *Gymnasiale Oberstufe* (which has also been established in schools other than the *Gymnasium*) is dependent on high achievement in the lower secondary leaving certificate, and admission to vocational education at upper secondary level is also based on achievement at lower secondary level. The *Abitur* (grammar school leaving certificate) is a prerequisite for entry into university education. Post-secondary non-tertiary education takes place at *Berufsfachschule* (vocational schools), *Fachoberschule* (technical colleges), at evening classes or through a dual system of vocational school and training in a work placement. Tertiary education includes universities, *Technische Hochschule* (technical colleges), *Fachhochschule* (universities of applied sciences), teacher training colleges and colleges of art and music. According to preliminary official figures, 1,415,503 students were enrolled in universities and equivalent institutions in 2009/10, and a further 671,686 were enrolled in non-university higher education.

In 2009 government expenditure on education amounted to €104,700m. (4.4% of total expenditure).

GHANA

Introductory Survey

LOCATION, CLIMATE, LANGUAGE, RELIGION, FLAG, CAPITAL

The Republic of Ghana lies on the west coast of Africa, with Côte d'Ivoire to the west and Togo to the east. It is bordered by Burkina Faso to the north. The climate is tropical, with temperatures generally between 21°C and 32°C (70°–90°F) and average annual rainfall of 2,000 mm (80 ins) on the coast, decreasing inland. English is the official language, but there are 10 major national languages (each with more than 250,000 speakers), the most widely spoken being Akan, Ewe, Mole-Dagomba and Ga. Many of the inhabitants follow traditional beliefs and customs. Christians comprise an estimated 69% of the population. The national flag (proportions 2 by 3) has three equal horizontal stripes, of red, yellow and green, with a five-pointed black star in the centre of the yellow stripe. The capital is Accra.

CONTEMPORARY POLITICAL HISTORY

Historical Context

Ghana was formed as the result of a UN-supervised plebiscite in May 1956, when the British-administered section of Togoland, a UN Trust Territory, voted to join the Gold Coast, a British colony, in an independent state. Ghana was duly granted independence, within the Commonwealth, on 6 March 1957 and Dr Kwame Nkrumah, the Prime Minister of the former Gold Coast since 1952, became Prime Minister of the new state. Ghana became a republic on 1 July 1960, with Nkrumah as President. In 1964 the Convention People's Party, led by Nkrumah, was declared the sole authorized party.

In February 1966 Nkrumah was deposed in a military coup, the leaders of which established a governing National Liberation Council, led by Gen. Joseph Ankrah. In April 1969 Ankrah was replaced by Brig. (later Lt-Gen.) Akwasi Afrifa, and a new Constitution was introduced. Power was returned in October to an elected civilian Government, led by Dr Kofi Busia. However, in reaction to increasing economic and political difficulties, the army again seized power in January 1972, under the leadership of Lt-Col (later Gen.) Ignatius Acheampong. In July 1978 Acheampong was deposed by his deputy, Lt-Gen. Frederick Akuffo, who assumed power in a bloodless coup. Tensions within the army became evident in May 1979, when junior military officers staged an unsuccessful coup attempt. The alleged leader of the conspirators, Flight-Lt Jerry Rawlings, was imprisoned, but was subsequently released by other officers. On 4 June he and his associates successfully seized power, amid popular acclaim, established the Armed Forces Revolutionary Council, and introduced measures to eradicate corruption. Acheampong and Akuffo were among nine senior officers who were convicted on charges of corruption and executed.

Civilian rule was restored in September 1979; however, on 31 December 1981 Rawlings seized power for a second time, and established a governing Provisional National Defence Council (PNDC), with himself as Chairman. The PNDC's policies initially received strong support, but discontent with the regime and with the apparent ineffectiveness of its economic policies was reflected by a series of coup attempts.

Domestic Political Affairs

In July 1990, in response to pressure from Western aid donors to introduce further democratic reforms, the PNDC announced that a National Commission for Democracy (NCD) would organize a series of regional debates to consider Ghana's political and economic future. In December Rawlings announced proposals for the introduction of a constitution by the end of 1991; the PNDC was to consider recommendations presented by the NCD, and subsequently to convene a consultative body to determine constitutional reform.

In March 1991 the NCD presented a report on the democratic process, which recommended the election of an executive President for a fixed term, the establishment of a legislature and the creation of the post of Prime Minister. In May the PNDC endorsed the restoration of a multi-party system and approved the NCD's recommendations, although the formation of political associations remained prohibited. Later in May the Government announced the establishment of a 260-member Consultative Assembly, which was to present a draft constitution to the PNDC. The Government also appointed a nine-member committee of constitutional experts, who, in August, submitted a series of recommendations for constitutional reform, which included the establishment of a parliament and a council of state. It was proposed that the President, who would also be Commander-in-Chief of the Armed Forces, would be elected by universal suffrage for a four-year term of office, while the leader of the party that commanded a majority in the legislature would be appointed as Prime Minister. Later in August Rawlings announced that presidential and legislative elections were to take place in late 1992. In December 1991 the Government established an Interim National Electoral Commission (INEC), which was to be responsible for the demarcation of electoral regions and the supervision of elections and referendums. In March 1992 Rawlings announced a programme for transition to a multi-party system, which was to be completed on 7 January 1993.

At the end of March 1992 the Consultative Assembly approved the majority of the constitutional recommendations that had been submitted to the PNDC. However, the proposed creation of the post of Prime Minister was rejected by the Assembly; executive power was to be vested in the President, who would appoint a Vice-President. Opposition groups subsequently objected to a provision in the draft Constitution that members of the Government be exempt from prosecution for human rights violations allegedly committed during the PNDC's rule. At a national referendum on 28 April, however, the draft Constitution was approved by 92% of votes cast, with 43.7% of the electorate voting.

On 18 May 1992 the Government introduced legislation permitting the formation of political associations; political parties were henceforth required to apply to the INEC for legal recognition, although emergent parties were not permitted to use names or slogans associated with 21 former political organizations that remained proscribed. In June a number of political associations were established, many of which were identified with supporters of former President Nkrumah; six opposition movements, including the People's National Convention (PNC) were subsequently granted legal recognition. In the same month a coalition of pro-Government organizations, the National Democratic Congress (NDC), was formed to contest the forthcoming elections on behalf of the PNDC. However, an existing alliance of Rawlings' supporters, the Eagle Club, refused to join the NDC, and created its own political organization, the Eagle Party (later known as the EGLE—Every Ghanaian Living Everywhere—Party). In August the Government promulgated a new electoral code, which included a provision that in the event that no presidential candidate received more than 50% of votes cast the two candidates with the highest number of votes would contest a second round within 21 days. In September Rawlings officially retired from the air force (although he retained the post of Commander-in-Chief of the Armed Forces in his capacity as Head of State), in accordance with the new Constitution, and accepted a nomination to contest the presidential election as a candidate of the NDC. The NDC, the EGLE Party and the National Convention Party (NCP) subsequently formed a pro-Government electoral coalition, the Progressive Alliance.

Rawlings was elected President on 3 November 1992, securing 58.3% of the votes cast. The four opposition parties that had presented candidates, the PNC, the New Patriotic Party (NPP), the National Independence Party (NIP) and the People's Heritage Party (PHP), claimed that there had been widespread electoral malpractice, although international observers maintained that, despite isolated irregularities, the election had been conducted fairly. Later in November these four parties withdrew from the forthcoming legislative elections (scheduled for 8 December), in protest at the Government's refusal to comply with their demands for the compilation of a new electoral register and the investigation of alleged misconduct during the presidential election. As a result, the legislative elections were postponed until 22 December, and subsequently by a further week, and the nomination of new candidates permitted. In December the opposition claimed that many of its members had left Ghana, as a result of widespread intimidation by the Government. In the legislative elections, which took place on 29 December, the NDC secured 189 of the 200 seats in the Parliament, while the NCP obtained eight seats, the EGLE Party one seat and independent candidates the remaining two. According to official figures, however, only 29% of the electorate voted in the elections.

Establishment of the Fourth Republic

On 7 January 1993 Rawlings was sworn in as President of what was designated the Fourth Republic, the PNDC was dissolved and the new Parliament was inaugurated. In May a 17-member Council of Ministers, which included several ministers who had served in the former PNDC administration, was inaugurated. In December the PHP, the NIP and a faction of the PNC, all of which comprised supporters of ex-President Nkrumah, merged to form a new organization, the People's Convention Party (PCP).

Presidential and parliamentary elections were scheduled for December 1996 and a consolidation of the opposition parties took place prior to the deadline for the nomination of candidates in September. In May the Popular Party for Democracy and Development merged with the PCP and declared its support for unity with the NPP. In August the NPP and the PCP formed an electoral coalition, the Great Alliance; it was subsequently announced that John Kufuor, of the NPP, was to be the Great Alliance's presidential candidate. The NCP stated that it would support the NDC in the forthcoming elections, while the PNC announced its intention to contest the elections alone. In September the NDC nominated Rawlings as its presidential candidate. By 18 September, the official deadline for the nomination of candidates, only the Great Alliance, the Progressive Alliance (the NDC, the EGLE Party and the Democratic People's Party—DPP) and the PNC had succeeded in having their nomination papers accepted. In November a network of independent Domestic Election Observers was created to oversee the elections.

In the presidential election, which took place on 7 December 1996, Rawlings was re-elected, with 57.2% of the votes cast, while Kufuor secured 39.8%. In the parliamentary elections the NDC's representation was reduced to 133 seats, while the NPP won 60 seats, the PCP five and the PNC one seat. Voting was postponed in one constituency, owing to a legal dispute concerning the eligibility of candidates. (The seat was subsequently won by the NPP in a by-election in June 1997.) Despite opposition claims of malpractice, international observers declared that the elections had been conducted fairly, and an electoral turn-out of 76.8% was reported. At the end of December the PCP announced that the Great Alliance had broken down. On 7 January 1997 Rawlings was sworn in as President.

In August 1998 the NCP and the PCP merged to form the Convention Party. An earlier attempt by the party to register as the Convention People's Party (CPP) had been rejected on the grounds that the use of the name of a proscribed party was unconstitutional. (This decision was reversed in 2000, however, when the Convention Party was permitted to adopt the name and logo of Nkrumah's former party.) In October 1998 the NPP nominated Kufuor to stand as its presidential candidate, in elections due to be held in 2000. At an NDC congress in December 1998 the position of 'Life Chairman' of the party was created for Rawlings, who confirmed that he would comply with the terms of the Constitution and not stand for a third term as President, and subsequently announced that the incumbent Vice-President, Prof. John Evans Atta Mills, was to contest the election on behalf of the NDC. In June 1999, owing to dissatisfaction within the NDC at the changes carried out at the party congress and at Rawlings' pronouncement regarding his successor, a group of party members broke away to form a new political organization, the National Reform Party (NRP). At the end of April Mills had been elected unopposed as the NDC presidential candidate.

An estimated 62% of the electorate voted in the elections, which took place on 7 December 2000. Observers from the Organization of African Unity (now the African Union, see p. 189) declared the elections to have been held in an orderly and fair manner. In the elections to the 200-seat Parliament the NPP won 100 seats, while the NDC obtained 92 seats, the PNC three, the CPP one, and independent candidates four. The NPP thus became the largest parliamentary party for the first time, gaining an unprecedented degree of support in rural areas. In the presidential election Kufuor won 48.2% of the valid votes cast, and Mills 44.5%, thus necessitating a second round, which proceeded on 28 December; Kufuor was elected to the presidency, with 56.9% of the valid votes cast.

The Kufuor presidency

On 7 January 2001 Kufuor was inaugurated as President and subsequently appointed a new Government, which notably included one member from each of the CPP, the NRP and the PNC. In February it was announced that members of the military were to be forbidden from celebrating the anniversaries of the coups staged by Rawlings in 1979 and 1981, and that their participation in quasi-political organizations was also to be prohibited. In addition, Kufuor ordered the suspension of the heads of six public sector financial institutions, to facilitate an investigation into allegations of embezzlement. Also in February 2001 Kufuor announced that a National Reconciliation Commission (NRC) was to be established to investigate allegations of human rights abuses and other violations committed by state representatives. According to proposed legislation, the NRC would be charged with investigating three periods of military rule and unconstitutional government since independence (24 February 1966–21 August 1969, 13 January 1972–23 September 1979 and 31 December 1981–6 January 1983), although the NRC would also be permitted to investigate complaints relating to events outside these periods. The NRC was officially launched in May and commenced public hearings in January 2003, by which time some 2,800 complaints had been received, mostly relating to events that took place under military regimes.

In March 2002 the Minister of the Interior and the Minister for the Northern Region both resigned, following the deaths of some 40 people during clashes between the Mamprusi and Kusasi ethnic groups in the north of Ghana, which had been prompted by the abduction and murder of Ya-na Yakuba Andani, king of the Dagomba, in Yendi. A commission of inquiry was established, headed by traditional leaders, and a state of emergency was declared. The state of emergency ended in the majority of districts in October 2003, but remained in place in Tamale municipality and Yendi district until August 2004. Unrest, however, continued during 2005. Renewed violence broke out in mid-2009, in which three people were killed. A curfew was established in an attempt to curtail the fighting.

Meanwhile, in April 2002 the election of Dr Obed Asamoah as the new Chairman of the NDC created divisions within the party between supporters of Asamoah and Rawlings. In September a number of accusations of financial impropriety were made against Rawlings and his former associates. In November, following the arrest of three NDC deputies on charges of fraud and the reckless loss of state revenues, the NDC boycotted the Parliament in protest; this followed an earlier boycott over a controversial US $1,000m. development loan. In February 2004 Rawlings appeared before the NRC to answer questions about the murders of three high court judges and a retired military officer in 1982, and about extrajudicial military killings in 1984. In July 2004 the NRC ended its hearings, prior to the submission of its report in October, which recommended that victims of state brutality receive compensation and that state institutions, including the security services, be reformed.

In October 2004 four presidential candidates submitted their nominations to the Chairman of the Electoral Commission (EC). As expected, Kufuor represented the NPP, while Mills was selected as the candidate for the NDC. Also contesting the election were George Aggudey of the CPP and Edward Mahama of the PNC for the Grand Coalition, which comprised the PNC and the EGLE Party. The parliamentary and presidential elections were held as scheduled on 7 December 2004. Kufuor was declared the winner of the presidential election after securing 52.4% of the valid votes cast, while Mills won 44.6%. Mahama and Aggudey took 1.9% and 1.0%, respectively. In the parliamentary elections the NPP won 128 seats, with 55.6% of the vote, while the NDC won 94 seats, the PNC four and the CPP three. The new Parliament was inaugurated on 7 January 2005. On the same day Kufuor and Aliu Mahama were sworn in as President and Vice-President, respectively, following which Kufuor reorganized the Government.

In January 2006 the African Peer Review Mechanism, a programme of voluntary assessment organized by the New Partnership for Africa's Development (see p. 190), published its report on Ghana. The report, while commending overall development, criticized endemic corruption and the ongoing civil unrest in the north of the country. In late April President Kufuor effected an extensive government reshuffle. Notably, Joseph Ghartey was appointed Attorney-General and Minister of Justice, while Albert Kan Dapaah assumed responsibility for the interior portfolio, and portfolios for aviation and national security were created. In October Kufuor alleged that former President Rawlings had been seeking foreign support in order to overthrow the Government.

In May 2007 the EC convened a meeting to discuss a controversial proposal that would allow Ghanaians living abroad to vote in national elections, prompting public protests and a NDC boycott of Parliament. In July eight cabinet ministers tendered their resignation, having declared their intention to contest the presidential election. Among those to step down was Minister of Defence Dr Kwame Addo Kufuor, the brother of the President; a governmental reorganization was subsequently effected in which Akwasi Osei-Adjai was named Minister of Foreign Affairs, Regional Integration and NEPAD; Dapaah later received the defence portfolio.

The 2008 elections: Mills becomes President

With Kufuor ineligible for re-election, nominations for candidates to the presidency were announced in December 2007; Nana Addo Dankwa Akufo-Addo, who had held the foreign affairs portfolio until July, was to represent the NPP, while Mills was again selected as the candidate of the NDC. A governmental reorganization was effected in May 2008, following the dismissal earlier that year of the Minister of National Security and the Minister of Energy. Felix Owusu-Adjapong subsequently assumed the energy portfolio, but the national security post remained vacant. In September the Minister of Finance and Economic Planning, Kwadwo Baah-Wiredu, died suddenly in South Africa, leaving the post vacant pending the December elections.

As preparations for the presidential and legislative elections began in late August 2008 violence threatened to undermine the conduct of the ballot. Conflict at a political rally, believed to be a result of continued unrest over the murder of Andani in Dagomba in 2002, left at least three people dead and many more injured. The announcement by the EC that the electoral register could contain as many as 1m. false names further heightened tensions. Nevertheless, voting proceeded in a largely peaceful atmosphere. In the first round of the presidential election on 7 December 2008 Akufo-Addo won 49.1% of the votes cast while Mills secured 47.9%. (Of the six other candidates, none took more than 1.3% of the popular vote.) As no candidate had secured more than 50% of the valid votes cast, Mills and Akufo-Addo contested a second round of voting, held on 28 December, at which Mills emerged the winner with some 50.2% of votes cast. He was inaugurated as President on 7 January 2009. Following legislative elections, held concurrently with the first round of the presidential election, the NDC became the largest party in the Parliament, with 113 of the 230 seats, while the NPP's representation was reduced to 109 seats; the PNC took two seats and the CPP one seat.

The new Cabinet included Dr Kwabena Duffuor as Minister of Finance and Economic Planning, Cletus Avoka as Minister of the Interior and Lt-Gen. (retd) Joseph Henry Smith as Minister of Defence, while Betty Mould Iddrisu was named as the first female Attorney-General and Minister of Justice. The Minister of Health, Dr George Sepa Yankey, and the Minister of State at the Presidency, Seidu Amadu, resigned in October following allegations that they had accepted bribes from a British construction company, which had the previous month been ordered by a British court to pay fines of more than US $7m. for offering illegal payments to officials in Ghana in the 1990s; five other senior Ghanaian officials were also implicated in the alleged corruption. (However, following a police investigation, all seven officials were exonerated in June 2011.) Mills carried out a reorganization of the Government in January 2010; notably, Martin Amidu, a former Deputy Attorney-General, replaced Avoka as Minister of the Interior. In January 2011 Mills effected another government reorganization, which included the appointment of Amidu as Attorney-General and Minister of Justice, while Benjamin Kunbuor (hitherto Minister of Health) became the new Minister of the Interior.

Recent developments: constitutional reform

In January 2010 President Mills inaugurated a nine-member Constitution Review Commission (CRC), which was charged with recommending changes to the 1992 Constitution for approval at a referendum. Community and district constitutional review consultations, with the aim of soliciting public contributions to the work of the CRC, began in April. It was reported that public opinion strongly favoured restructuring of the principal state organs, and in particular a redistribution and separation of power between the presidential executive and the legislature. In December 2011 Mills received the CRC's final report, which recommended, *inter alia*, restricting the President's power of appointment, strengthening Parliament and the independence of the judiciary, and greater decentralization to local government. The report also advocated the creation of a National Development Planning Commission, the abrogation of the death penalty and, controversially, the preservation of the constitutional clauses granting former PNDC members immunity from prosecution.

Mills' authority had been undermined throughout his presidency by the relentless, public criticism of his administration by former President Rawlings. The divisions within the NDC culminated in July 2011, when Rawlings' wife, Nana Konadu Agyeman Rawlings, stood against Mills in a primary election to select the ruling party's 2012 presidential candidate. In the event, Mills secured the NDC presidential nomination after winning 97% of the votes cast, reinforcing his control over the party. (Akufo Addo had again been elected as the NPP's presidential candidate in August 2010.) There was media speculation that Nana Rawlings and her supporters would resign from the NDC and form a new party, but this failed to transpire.

The EC planned to introduce a new biometric system to register voters prior to the 2012 presidential and legislative elections. However, the NPP expressed concern that this new registration system would lack a concomitant biometric verification mechanism to prevent fraud, and in October 2011 the opposition party intimated that it would boycott the elections if this matter were not addressed. The Government argued that biometric verification would be too expensive to implement, preferring instead to direct funding towards strengthening security at polling stations. In accordance with a Supreme Court judgment, Mills declared in November that prisoners would be entitled to vote in the upcoming elections and that special measures to facilitate this would be effected. NPP officials claimed that this announcement was motivated by the NDC's desire to secure the votes of prison inmates. Paa Kwesi Nduom, the CPP's presidential candidate in 2008, resigned from the party in December 2011 and subsequently announced the establishment of the Progressive People's Party.

Foreign Affairs

Ghana was in 2011 the fifth largest African contributing nation to UN peace-keeping operations and the 10th largest of all peace-keeping contributing nations. At the end of that year Ghana contributed 2,989 personnel to UN peace-keeping missions world-wide. Ghana notably deployed large contingents in the Democratic Republic of the Congo (DRC), the Darfur region of Sudan, Liberia and Côte d'Ivoire, and outside Africa contributed 877 troops to the UN Interim Force in Lebanon. In late 2005 Ghana was elected as a non-permanent member of the UN Security Council.

In October 1992 Ghana denied claims that it was implicated in subversive activity by Togolese dissidents based in Ghana and in March 1993 the Rawlings administration further denied allegations, made by the Togolese Government, of Ghanaian complicity in an armed attack on the residence of Togo's President, Gen. Gnassingbé Eyadéma. In January 1994 relations with Togo deteriorated further, following an attempt to overthrow the Togolese Government, which the Togolese authorities claimed had been staged by armed dissidents based in Ghana. The Ghanaian chargé d'affaires in Togo was arrested, and Togolese forces killed 12 Ghanaians and attacked a customs post and several villages near the border. Ghana, however, denied any involvement in the coup attempt, and threatened to retaliate against further acts of aggression. Later that year, however, relations improved, and in November full diplomatic links were formally restored. In December Togo's border with Ghana (which had been closed in January 1994) was reopened. Following the death of Eyadéma in early 2005 and the subsequent unrest in Togo precipitated by the assumption of power by Eyadéma's son, Faure Gnassingbé, some 15,000 Togolese refugees were reported to have registered in Ghana. In August 2009 President Gnassingbé visited Ghana for meetings with President Mills and senior security officials to discuss improved border security and the control of cross-border crime and drugs- and people-trafficking. In May 2010 it was reported that some 3,500 refugees had fled from Ghana into northern Togo, as a result of renewed ethnic conflict and land disputes in the north of the country.

During the conflict in Liberia (q.v.), which commenced in December 1989, Ghana contributed troops to the Monitoring Group (ECOMOG) of the Economic Community of West African

States (ECOWAS, see p. 264). As Chairman of the ECOWAS Conference of Heads of State and Government, Rawlings mediated negotiations between the warring Liberian factions in the mid-1990s, and by mid-1997 some 17,000 Liberian refugees had arrived in Ghana. In 2003 Ghana also hosted peace negotiations concerning Liberia, and from September contributed troops to the ECOWAS Mission in Liberia (ECOMIL). In October the Ghanaian troops were transferred to a longer-term UN stabilization force, the UN Mission in Liberia (UNMIL, see p. 94), which replaced ECOMIL, with a mandate to support the implementation of a comprehensive peace agreement in that country. In late 2005 there were some 40,000 Liberian refugees registered in Ghana, a number of whom were in the process of repatriation, and by the end of 2010 the number of Liberian refugees remaining in Ghana was 11,585. Due to the improving security climate in Liberia, the Ghanaian Government planned to revoke in June 2012 the refugee status that had been granted to Liberians who had fled the conflict in their country. After this date, former refugees would be required to return to Liberia or apply for residency in Ghana. In February 2010 the Liberian President, Ellen Johnson-Sirleaf, made a two-day visit to Ghana following which it was agreed to reactivate the Ghana-Liberia Permanent Joint Commission for Co-operation. Ghana contributed 736 personnel to UNMIL at December 2011.

In June 1997 Ghana, Côte d'Ivoire, Guinea and Nigeria formed the 'committee of four', which was established by ECOWAS to monitor the situation in Sierra Leone, following the staging of a military coup; troops were dispatched to participate in a peace-keeping force. Following the reinstatement of the democratically elected Government in March, ECOMOG units remained in the country and continued to launch attacks against rebel forces, which still retained control of a number of areas. In December 2005 the Ghanaian troops participating in the UN Mission in Sierra Leone (UNAMSIL) returned to Ghana on the termination of the peace-keeping mission.

In November 2001 some 400 Ghanaian troops were dispatched to participate in peace-keeping duties in the DRC, under the auspices of the UN Mission in the Democratic Republic of the Congo (MONUC, see p. 97). In 2011 Ghana continued to participate in the UN peace-keeping contingent (which had been reconstituted as the UN Organization Stabilization Mission in the Democratic Republic of the Congo—MONUSCO), contributing 487 personnel at December.

After the outbreak of an armed rebellion in Côte d'Ivoire (q.v.) in September 2002, Ghana denied accusations by the Ivorian rebels that it had intervened in support of President Laurent Gbagbo. In October Ghana pledged to provide troops to an ECOWAS military mission in Côte d'Ivoire (ECOMICI), and the first contingent of the 266 Ghanaian soldiers to be contributed was deployed in February 2003. Further ECOWAS summit meetings on Côte d'Ivoire took place in Accra in March and November 2003. Ghanaian troops in Côte d'Ivoire were to be transferred to a UN Operation in Côte d'Ivoire (UNOCI, see p. 96), which was deployed from April 2004. A conference held in Accra in August 2004 led to the signing of a peace accord between rival Ivorian factions, Accra III. At December 2011 546 Ghanaian personnel were deployed in Côte d'Ivoire as part of UNOCI. Political instability and factional violence in Côte d'Ivoire following a disputed presidential election in late 2010 precipitated the inflow of large numbers of Ivorian refugees into Ghana (estimated to total 18,000 by October 2011). Alassane Ouattara, who had been sworn in as the new Ivorian President in May 2011 after months of fighting, visited Ghana in October and pressured Mills to extradite Ivorian refugees accused of committing human rights abuses during the post-election turmoil. A repatriation accord was also signed by Ghana, Côte d'Ivoire and the office of the UN High Commissioner for Refugees, to facilitate the voluntary return of Ivorian refugees, while former fighters were to be resettled in other countries.

Although in March 2011 the United Kingdom pledged to increase aid to Ghana to £100m. by 2014/15 (up from £85m. in 2010/11), British Prime Minister David Cameron caused controversy in Ghana in late 2011 by indicating that aid would be reduced to nations that failed to reform discriminatory laws against homosexuals. President Mills firmly rejected any liberalization of Ghana's conservative laws regarding homosexuality and criticized Cameron for encroaching on domestic Ghanaian affairs.

CONSTITUTION AND GOVERNMENT

Under the terms of the Constitution, which was approved by national referendum on 28 April 1992, Ghana has a multi-party political system. Executive power is vested in the President, who is the Head of State and Commander-in-Chief of the Armed Forces. The President is elected by direct universal suffrage for a maximum of two four-year terms of office. Legislative power is vested in a 230-member unicameral Parliament, which is elected by direct universal suffrage for a four-year term. The President appoints a Vice-President, and nominates a Council of Ministers, subject to approval by the Parliament. The Constitution also provides for a 25-member Council of State, principally comprising regional representatives and presidential nominees, and a 20-member National Security Council, chaired by the Vice-President, which act as advisory bodies to the President.

Ghana has 10 regions, each headed by a Regional Minister, who is assisted by a regional co-ordinating council. The regions constitute 110 administrative districts, each with a District Assembly, which is headed by a District Chief Executive. Regional colleges, which comprise representatives selected by the District Assemblies and by regional Houses of Chiefs, elect a number of representatives to the Council of State.

REGIONAL AND INTERNATIONAL CO-OPERATION

Ghana is a member of the African Union (see p. 189) and of the Economic Community of West African States (ECOWAS, see p. 264).

Ghana became a member of the UN in 1957 and was admitted to the World Trade Organization (WTO, see p. 433) in 1995. Ghana also participates in the Group of 77 (G77, see p. 450) developing countries. Ghana is also a member of the International Cocoa Organization (ICCO, see p. 445), and of the International Coffee Organization (ICO, see p. 445). In May 2004 Ghana became a full member of the Community of Sahel-Saharan States (see p. 449).

ECONOMIC AFFAIRS

In 2010, according to estimates by the World Bank, Ghana's gross national income (GNI), measured at average 2008–10 prices, was US $30,080m., equivalent to $1,230 per head (or $1,600 on an international purchasing-power parity basis). During 2001–10, it was estimated, the population increased at an average annual rate of 2.4%, while gross domestic product (GDP) per head increased, in real terms, by an average of 3.4% per year. Overall GDP increased at an average annual rate of 6.0% in 2001–10; growth in 2010 was 6.6%.

Agriculture (including forestry and fishing) contributed 29.9% of GDP in 2010, according to estimates by the Bank of Ghana. An estimated 54.0% of the economically active population was employed in the sector in mid-2012, according to FAO. The principal cash crop is cocoa beans, contributing 25.6% of total exports in 2008. Ghana is the world's second largest producer after Côte d'Ivoire, and some 700,000 metric tons of cocoa beans were harvested in 2007/08. Coffee, bananas, cassava, oil palm, coconuts, limes, kola nuts and shea-nuts (karité nuts) are also produced. The development of the palm oil and cassava sectors was underway. Timber production is also important, with the forestry sector accounting for 3.7% of GDP in 2010, and cork and wood, and manufactures thereof, contributing 3.9% of total export earnings in 2008. Fishing satisfies more than three-quarters of domestic requirements, and contributed 2.3% of GDP in 2010. During 2006–10, according to the Bank of Ghana, agricultural GDP increased at an average annual rate of 4.5%; growth in 2010 was 5.3%.

According to Bank of Ghana estimates, industry (including mining, manufacturing, construction and power) contributed 18.6% of GDP in 2010. According to the Bank of Ghana, industrial GDP increased at an average annual rate of 7.7% in 2006–10; growth in 2010 was 5.6%.

Mining contributed 1.8% of GDP in 2010, according to the Bank of Ghana. Gold and diamonds are the major minerals exported (in 2009 gold production was 79,883 kg), although Ghana also exploits large reserves of bauxite and manganese ore. The Government is attempting to increase exploitation of salt, bauxite and clay. According to Bank of Ghana estimates, the GDP of the mining sector increased by an average of 5.9% per year in 2006–10; mining GDP grew by 7.7% in 2010.

Manufacturing contributed 6.8% of GDP in 2010, according to Bank of Ghana estimates. The most important sectors are food processing, textiles, vehicles, cement, paper, chemicals and petroleum. Manufacturing GDP increased at an average annual rate of 2.1% in 2006–10; the GDP of the sector fell by 1.3% in 2009, but increased by 7.6% in 2010.

According to Bank of Ghana estimates, the construction sector contributed 8.6% of GDP in 2010. The GDP of the sector increased at an average annual rate of 17.7% in 2006–10; the sector's GDP increased by 2.5% in 2010.

According to figures published by the World Bank, some 74.1% of Ghana's production of electricity was from hydroelectric power in 2008, with the Akosombo and Kpong plants being the major sources, and 25.9% from petroleum (an increase from 8.5% in 2000). In mid-2004 it was announced that the World Bank was providing a loan of US $60m. to increase the production of the thermal power generator, Takoradi II. In November 2004 the World Bank agreed to finance the construction of the West African Gas Pipeline, which was to supply natural gas from Nigeria to Ghana, Benin and Togo; the first gas was delivered in 2010. Imports of petroleum comprised just 0.8% of the total value of merchandise imports in 2008. Electricity is exported to Benin and Togo.

The services sector contributed 51.4% of GDP in 2010, according to estimates by the Bank of Ghana. The GDP of the services sector increased at an average annual rate of 7.7% in 2006–10; growth in 2010 was 9.8%.

In 2010 Ghana recorded a visible trade deficit of US $2,962.0m, and there was a deficit of $2,700.5m. on the current account of the balance of payments. In 2008 the principal source of imports was the People's Republic of China (11.7%); other major sources were Nigeria, the USA and Belgium. South Africa was the principal market for exports (taking 44.0% of the total) in that year; other important purchasers were India, and the Netherlands. The principal exports in 2008 were food and live animals (which accounted for 33.3% of total export earnings), and cork and wood. The principal imports in 2008 were machinery and transport equipment (principally road vehicles and parts), basic manufacturers (iron and steel), crude petroleum, food and live animals, and chemicals and related products, road vehicles and parts and mineral fuels, lubricants, etc.

Ghana's overall budget deficit for 2009 was 1,282.4m. Ghana cedis. Ghana's general government gross debt was 13,256m. Ghana cedis in 2009, equivalent to 36.2% of GDP. Ghana's external debt totalled US $5,720m. at the end of 2009, of which $4,126m. was public and publicly guaranteed debt. In that year the cost of debt-servicing long-term public and publicly guaranteed debt and repayments to the IMF was equivalent to 0.8% of the value of exports of goods, services and income (excluding workers' remittances). In 20001–10 the average annual rate of inflation was 16.1%. Consumer prices increased by 10.7% in 2010. In 1995 some 41,000 people were registered as unemployed in Ghana.

Although Ghana's economy had made steady progress since the transfer to civilian rule in 1992, the new Government of President John Atta Mills, which came to power in early 2009, faced a number of challenges in order to maintain this positive momentum. The country remained vulnerable to unfavourable weather conditions, and continued reliance on three main export commodities, namely gold, cocoa and timber, had increased Ghana's exposure to the vagaries of the global market for those products. In mid-2009 the IMF approved a three-year credit arrangement (totalling about US $602.6m.) for Ghana, and in September the Government announced a series of structural reforms following the adverse effects of the international economic downturn. Economic growth recovered, to an estimated 5.7%, in 2010, partly owing to rises both in volumes and prices of gold and cocoa. According to IMF estimates, real GDP expanded by 13.7% in 2011. This dramatic increase in growth, one of the highest rates world-wide, was driven predominantly by petroleum production, which commenced in December 2010 and was forecast to reach 110,000 barrels per day by 2012. Under the terms of legislation adopted in March 2011, the Government was obliged to transfer 30% of oil revenue to various stabilization funds. GDP growth in 2011 was also supported by further increases in gold and cocoa output and by consistently high international prices for these commodities, while the construction and service sectors also registered renewed economic activity. A record cocoa harvest was reported at the end of the 2010/11 season, although cocoa-smuggling from Côte d'Ivoire had allegedly distorted the production figures. To fund new infrastructure projects, viewed as critical to Ghana's long-term economic development, in July 2011 Parliament approved increased government spending and in the following month endorsed a $3,000m. concessionary Chinese loan. The 2012 budget aimed to reduce the fiscal deficit, partly through the imposition of additional taxes on mining companies, although critics argued that this measure would deter investors. Nevertheless, strong global prices for petroleum and Ghana's other exports were projected to contribute to robust real GDP growth of 7.3% in 2012, and the economy was also expected to benefit from the start of natural gas production by 2013.

PUBLIC HOLIDAYS

2013: 1 January (New Year's Day), 6 March (Independence Day), 29 March–1 April (Easter), 1 May (Labour Day), 25 May (African Union Day), 1 July (Republic Day), 7 August* (Eid-al-Fitr, end of Ramadan), 21 September (Founder's Day), 14 October* (Eid-al-Adha, Feast of the Sacrifice), 3 December (National Farmers' Day), 25–26 December (Christmas).

* These holidays are dependent on the Islamic lunar calendar and may vary by one or two days from the dates given.

Statistical Survey

Source (except where otherwise stated): Ghana Statistical Service, POB GP1098, Accra; tel. (30) 2671732; fax (30) 2671731; internet www.statsghana.gov.gh.

Area and Population

AREA, POPULATION AND DENSITY

Area (sq km)	238,539*
Population (census results)	
26 March 2000	18,912,079
26 September 2010 (provisional)	
Males	11,801,661
Females	12,421,770
Total	24,223,431
Population (UN estimates at mid-year)	
2011	24,965,819
2012	25,545,937
Density (per sq km) at mid-2012	107.1

* 92,100 sq miles.

POPULATION BY AGE AND SEX

(UN estimates at mid-2012)

	Males	Females	Total
0–14	4,999,349	4,761,804	9,761,153
15–64	7,514,243	7,262,965	14,777,208
65 and over	483,288	524,288	1,007,576
Total	12,996,880	12,549,057	25,545,937

Source: UN, *World Population Prospects: The 2010 Revision*.

REGIONS
(population at 2000 census)

Region	Area ('000 sq km)	Population	Density (per sq km)	Capital
Ashanti	24.39	3,612,950	148.1	Kumasi
Brong Ahafo	39.56	1,815,408	45.9	Sunyani
Central	9.83	1,593,823	162.1	Cape Coast
Eastern	19.32	2,106,696	109.0	Koforidua
Greater Accra	3.24	2,905,726	896.8	Accra
Northern	70.38	1,820,806	25.9	Tamale
Upper East	8.84	576,583	65.2	Bolgatanga
Upper West	18.48	920,089	49.8	Wa
Volta	20.57	1,635,421	79.5	Ho
Western	23.92	1,924,577	80.5	Takoradi
Total	238.54	18,912,079	79.3	

PRINCIPAL TOWNS
(population at 1984 census)

Accra (capital)	867,459	Takoradi	61,484
Kumasi	376,249	Cape Coast	57,224
Tamale	135,952	Sekondi	31,916
Tema	131,528		

Mid-2010 (incl. suburbs, UN estimates): Accra 2,341,882; Kumasi 1,834,084 (Source: UN, *World Urbanization Prospects: The 2009 Revision*).

BIRTHS AND DEATHS
(annual averages, UN estimates)

	1995–2000	2000–05	2005–10
Birth rate (per 1,000)	35.0	33.8	32.6
Death rate (per 1,000)	10.4	9.6	8.3

Source: UN, *World Population Prospects: The 2010 Revision*.

Life expectancy (years at birth, WHO estimates): 60 (males 57; females 64) in 2009 (Source: WHO, *World Health Statistics*).

ECONOMICALLY ACTIVE POPULATION
(1984 census)

	Males	Females	Total
Agriculture, hunting, forestry and fishing	1,750,024	1,560,943	3,310,967
Mining and quarrying	24,906	1,922	26,828
Manufacturing	198,430	389,988	588,418
Electricity, gas and water	14,033	1,404	15,437
Construction	60,692	3,994	64,686
Trade, restaurants and hotels	111,540	680,607	792,147
Transport, storage and communications	117,806	5,000	122,806
Financing, insurance, real estate and business services	19,933	7,542	27,475
Community, social and personal services	339,665	134,051	473,716
Total employed	2,637,029	2,785,451	5,422,480
Unemployed	87,452	70,172	157,624
Total labour force	2,724,481	2,855,623	5,580,104

2000 census ('000 persons aged 7 years and over): Total economically active population 9,039.3.

Source: ILO.

Mid-2012 (estimates in '000): Agriculture, etc. 6,394; Total 11,838 (Source: FAO).

Health and Welfare

KEY INDICATORS

Total fertility rate (children per woman, 2009)	4.2
Under-5 mortality rate (per 1,000 live births, 2009)	69
HIV/AIDS (% of persons aged 15–49, 2009)	1.8
Physicians (per 1,000 head, 2004)	0.2
Hospital beds (per 1,000 head, 2005)	0.9
Health expenditure (2008): US $ per head (PPP)	114
Health expenditure (2008): % of GDP	7.8
Health expenditure (2008): public (% of total)	50.0
Access to water (% of persons, 2008)	82
Access to sanitation (% of persons, 2008)	13
Total carbon dioxide emissions ('000 metric tons, 2007)	9,801.2
Carbon dioxide emissions per head (metric tons, 2007)	0.4
Human Development Index (2011): ranking	135
Human Development Index (2011): value	0.541

For sources and definitions, see explanatory note on p. vi.

Agriculture

PRINCIPAL CROPS
('000 metric tons)

	2008	2009	2010
Rice, paddy	301.9	391.4	491.6
Maize	1,470.0	1,619.5	1,871.7
Millet	193.8	245.5	219.0
Sorghum	330.9	350.5	324.4
Sweet potatoes*	112.3	122.1	130.3
Cassava (Manioc)	11,351.1	12,230.6	13,504.1
Taro (Cocoyam)	1,688.3	1,504.0	1,354.8
Yams	4,894.8	5,777.9	5,960.5
Sugar cane*	145.0	145.0	145.0
Groundnuts, with shell	470.1	485.1	530.9
Coconuts	316.3†	273.8†	297.9*
Oil palm fruit	1,896.8	2,103.6	2,004.3
Tomatoes	284.0*	317.5	350.0*
Chillies and peppers, green*	282.2	176.2	294.1
Onions, dry*	44.4	49.1	50.0
Beans, green*	29.3	23.3	27.6
Okra*	89.7	71.4	82.5
Bananas	63.0	65.0	64.5*
Plantains	3,337.6	3,562.5	3,537.7
Oranges	550.0	560.0	556.1*
Lemons and limes*	43.7	46.7	46.0
Pineapples*	70.0	74.7	73.7
Cocoa beans	680.8	710.6	632.0
Natural rubber	16.6	19.1	15.0†

* FAO estimate(s).

† Unofficial figure.

Aggregate production ('000 metric tons, may include official, semi-official or estimated data): Total cereals 2,297 in 2008, 2,607 in 2009, 2,907 in 2010; Total roots and tubers 18,046 in 2008, 19,635 in 2009, 20,950 in 2010; Total vegetables (incl. melons) 744 in 2008, 649 in 2009, 819 in 2010; Total fruits (excl. melons) 4,146 in 2008, 4,396 in 2009, 4,364 in 2010.

Source: FAO.

LIVESTOCK
('000 head, year ending September)

	2008	2009	2010
Horses	2.6	2.6	2.7
Asses*	14.0	14.0	14.0
Cattle	1,422	1,438	1,454
Pigs	506	521	536
Sheep	3,529	3,642	3,759
Goats	4,405	4,625	4,855
Chickens	39,816	43,320	44,000*

* FAO estimate(s).

Source: FAO.

LIVESTOCK PRODUCTS
('000 metric tons, FAO estimates)

	2008	2009	2010
Cattle meat	25.4	25.5	25.5
Sheep meat	15.9	16.4	16.9
Goat meat	13.7	14.3	14.3
Pig meat	17.0	17.5	17.5
Chicken meat	44.5	48.0	48.7
Game meat	64.9	69.3	74.1
Cows' milk	37.2	37.7	38.7
Hen eggs	33.7	36.7	36.7

Source: FAO.

Forestry

ROUNDWOOD REMOVALS
('000 cubic metres, excl. bark)

	2008	2009	2010
Sawlogs, veneer logs and logs for sleepers	1,392	1,300	1,300*
Fuel wood*	35,363	36,564	36,564
Total	36,755	37,864	37,864

* FAO estimate(s).

Source: FAO.

SAWNWOOD PRODUCTION
('000 cubic metres, incl. railway sleepers)

	2008	2009	2010
Total (all broadleaved)	513	522	522*

* FAO estimate.

Source: FAO.

Fishing

('000 metric tons, live weight)

	2007	2008	2009
Capture	330.5	359.8	321.8
Freshwater fishes	84.8	85.0	88.7
Bigeye grunt	21.9	17.7	17.4
Red pandora	9.1	6.4	3.9
Round sardinella	40.8	24.9	19.5
Madeiran sardinella	10.2	15.8	6.3
European anchovy	10.1	40.6	54.4
Skipjack tuna	34.6	37.4	36.1
Yellowfin tuna	15.5	14.3	18.4
Atlantic bumper	9.9	9.9	2.6
Aquaculture	3.8	5.6	7.2
Total catch	334.3	365.4	328.9

Source: FAO.

Mining

('000 metric tons, unless otherwise indicated)

	2007	2008	2009
Bauxite	748	796	440
Manganese ore: gross weight	1,173	1,261	1,007
Manganese ore: metal content*	410	440	350
Silver (kg)†	3,300*	3,200*	3,928
Gold (kg)‡	72,209	72,980	79,883*
Salt (unrefined)*	124	239	200
Diamonds ('000 carats)	895	643	376

* Estimated figure(s).

† Silver content of exported doré.

‡ Gold content of ores and concentrates, excluding smuggled or undocumented output.

Crude petroleum: 400,000 barrels in 2004.

Source: US Geological Survey.

Industry

SELECTED PRODUCTS
('000 metric tons unless otherwise indicated)

	2002	2003	2004
Groundnut oil*	98.9	76.4	61.5
Coconut oil	6.5*	7.0†	7.0†
Palm oil†	108.0	108.4	114.0
Palm kernel oil*	15.0	17.5	20.7
Butter of karité nuts (shea butter)*	8.4	9.8	18.3
Beer of barley*	100.0	100.0	100.0
Beer of millet*	66.6	73.8	60.2
Beer of sorghum*	234.6	258.3	340.7
Gasoline (petrol)	5,850	5,580	5,580†
Jet fuel	625	625	625†
Kerosene	1,950	1,950	1,950†
Distillate fuel oil	4,450	4,450	4,450†
Residual fuel oil	1,250	1,250	1,250†
Cement†	1,900	1,900	1,900
Aluminium (unwrought)‡	117	16	—
Electric energy (million kWh)	7,273	5,882	6,039

* FAO estimate(s).

† Provisional or estimated figure(s).

‡ Primary metal only.

2005: Groundnut oil 63.8 (FAO estimate); Coconut oil 7.0 (unofficial figure); Palm oil 117.0 (unofficial figure); Palm kernel oil 17.0 (FAO estimate); Beer of barley 136.0 (FAO estimate); Cement 1,800 (estimated figure); Aluminium (unwrought) 13; Electric energy (million kWh) 6,788.

2006: Groundnut oil 90.3 (FAO estimate); Coconut oil 7.0 (unofficial figure); Palm oil 121.0 (unofficial figure); Palm kernel oil 21.0 (FAO estimate); Beer of barley 137.5 (FAO estimate); Cement 1,800 (estimated figure); Aluminium (unwrought) 80 (estimated figure); Electric energy (million kWh) 8,429.

2007: Groundnut oil 32.4 (FAO estimate); Coconut oil 7.0 (unofficial figure); Palm oil 122.0 (unofficial figure); Palm kernel oil 16.0 (unofficial figure); Beer of barley 129.5 (FAO estimate); Cement 1,800 (estimated figure); Electric energy (million kWh) 6,978.

2008: Groundnut oil 63.4 (FAO estimate); Coconut oil 7.0 (unofficial figure); Palm oil 128.0 (unofficial figure); Palm kernel oil 16.0 (unofficial figure); Beer of barley 138.5 (FAO estimate); Cement 1,800 (estimated figure); Electric energy (million kWh) 8,323.

2009: Groundnut oil 65.5 (FAO estimate); Coconut oil 7.0 (unofficial figure); Palm oil 130.0 (unofficial figure); Palm kernel oil 16.0 (unofficial figure); Beer of barley 142.0 (FAO estimate); Cement 1,800 (estimated figure); Electric energy (million kWh) 8,958.

2010: Groundnut oil 72.2 (FAO estimate); Coconut oil 7.0 (FAO estimate); Palm oil 120.0 (unofficial figure); Palm kernel oil 16.0 (unofficial figure); Beer of barley 155.2 (FAO estimate); Electric energy (million kWh) 10,166.

Sources: FAO; US Geological Survey; Energy Commission of Ghana.

Finance

CURRENCY AND EXCHANGE RATES

Monetary Units
100 Ghana pesewas = 1 Ghana cedi.

Sterling, Dollar and Euro Equivalents (30 September 2011)
£1 sterling = 2.3742 Ghana cedis;
US $1 = 1.5224 Ghana cedis;
€1 = 2.0557 Ghana cedis;
10 Ghana cedis = £4.21 = $6.57 = €4.86.

Average Exchange Rate (Ghana cedis per US $)

2008	1.0579
2009	1.4088
2010	1.4310

Note: A new currency, the Ghana cedi, equivalent to 10,000 new cedis (the former legal tender), was introduced over a six-month period beginning in July 2007. Some statistical data in this survey are still presented in terms of the former currency, the new cedi.

GENERAL BUDGET

(million Ghana cedis)

Revenue*	2007	2008	2009
Tax revenue	3,081.9	3,892.8	4,485.2
Income and property	940.4	1,253.2	1,716.9
Personal (PAYE)	401.5	526.5	773.5
Company tax	399.8	539.1	661.9
Domestic goods and services	473.1	444.9	330.2
Petroleum tax	403.3	386.2	278.7
International trade	576.6	719.4	762.7
Import duties	543.1	679.4	745.9
Value added tax	834.2	1,088.0	1,268.4
National health insurance levy	257.7	318.3	319.0
Other	—	69.0	88.0
Non-tax revenue	112.8	125.8	461.3
Total	3,194.7	4,018.6	4,946.5

Expenditure†	2007	2008	2009‡
Recurrent expenditure	3,228.0	4,468.5	4,904.3
Wages and salaries	1,418.8	1,987.6	2,478.7
Goods and services	565.0	648.5	621.2
Transfers	611.8	685.6	603.9
National Health Fund (NHF)	291.8	256.5	153.5
Reserve fund	192.5	467.6	168.3
Interest payments	440.0	679.2	1,032.3
Domestic (accrual)	322.2	481.9	773.5
External (accrual)	117.8	197.3	258.8
Capital expenditure	1,630.2	2,481.2	2,425.7
Domestic	903.8	1,564.8	799.1
External	726.4	916.4	1,626.6
Total	5,244.3	7,228.6	7,330.1

* Excluding grants received (million Ghana cedis): 857.2 in 2007; 820.8 in 2008; 1,101.2 in 2009.

† Including net lending (million Ghana cedis): 0.9 in 2007; 0.0 in 2008; 0.0 in 2009.

‡ Provisional.

INTERNATIONAL RESERVES

(US $ million at 31 December)

	2004	2005	2006
Gold (national valuation)	122.6	144.5	177.9
IMF special drawing rights	20.7	1.1	1.2
Foreign exchange	1,605.9	1,751.8	2,089.1
Total	1,749.2	1,897.4	2,268.2

IMF special drawing rights: 0.6 in 2007; 0.4 in 2008; 455.4 in 2009; 448.6 in 2010.

Source: IMF, *International Financial Statistics*.

MONEY SUPPLY

(million Ghana cedis at 31 December)

	2008	2009	2010
Currency outside depository corporations	1,663.8	2,082.4	2,929.2
Transferable deposits	3,867.2	4,638.9	5,709.8
Other deposits	2,756.4	3,872.7	4,998.3
Broad money	8,287.5	10,594.0	13,637.3

Source: IMF, *International Financial Statistics*.

COST OF LIVING

(Consumer Price Index; prices at December; base: 2000 = 100)

	2007	2008	2009
Food	300.6	346.2	400.6
Clothing	275.6	306.9	378.2
Rent, water, electricity and other fuels	543.9	640.8	653.5
All items (incl. others)	331.9	386.8	461.2

2010: Food 424.9; All items (incl. others) 510.6.

Source: ILO.

NATIONAL ACCOUNTS

(million Ghana cedis at current prices)

Expenditure on the Gross Domestic Product

	2008	2009	2010
Government final consumption expenditure	3,393	4,294	4,388
Private final consumption expenditure	25,729	28,349	35,860
Increase in stocks / Gross fixed capital formation	6,474	7,565	9,118
Total domestic expenditure	35,595	40,208	49,366
Exports of goods and services	7,554	10,720	13,539
Less Imports of goods and services	13,425	15,482	18,982
Statistical discrepancy	455	1,151	2,309
GDP in purchasers' values	30,179	36,598	46,232
GDP in constant 2006 prices	21,592	22,454	24,187

Gross Domestic Product by Economic Activity

	2008	2009	2010
Agriculture and livestock	7,041	9,154	10,295
Forestry and logging	1,072	1,314	1,614
Fishing	762	874	1,001
Mining and quarrying	693	740	757
Manufacturing	2,277	2,478	2,941
Electricity and water	384	413	634
Construction	2,500	3,144	3,706
Transport, storage and communications	3,884	4,415	5,409
Wholesale and retail trade, restaurants and hotels	3,426	4,305	5,294
Finance, insurance, real estate and business services	2,274	3,009	4,185
Public administration and defence	1,799	2,479	3,024
Education	1,132	1,506	1,877
Health and social work	381	513	674
Other community, social and personal services	1,039	1,318	1,722
Sub-total	28,664	35,662	43,132
Indirect taxes, less subsidies	1,514	936	3,100
GDP at market prices	30,179	36,598	46,232

BALANCE OF PAYMENTS

(US $ million)

	2008	2009	2010
Exports of goods f.o.b.	5,269.7	5,839.7	7,960.1
Imports of goods f.o.b.	–10,268.5	–8,046.3	–10,922.1
Trade balance	–4,998.8	–2,206.6	–2,962.0
Exports of services	1,800.9	1,769.7	1,477.3
Imports of services	–2,298.2	–2,943.1	–3,003.2
Balance on goods and services	–5,496.0	–3,380.0	–4,488.0
Other income received	85.6	101.1	52.9
Other income paid	–344.2	–397.6	–587.9
Balance on goods, services and income	–5,754.6	–3,676.5	–5,022.9
Current transfers (net)	2,211.5	2,078.0	2,322.4
Current balance	–3,543.1	–1,598.5	–2,700.5
Capital account (net)	463.3	563.9	337.5
Direct investment abroad	–8.8	–6.9	—
Direct investment from abroad	1,220.4	1,684.7	2,527.4
Portfolio investment assets		41.3	723.0
Portfolio investment liabilities	–49.0	–84.9	–102.5
Other investment liabilities	643.5	1,452.0	822.7
Net errors and omissions	515.3	–1,022.3	–163.0
Overall balance	–758.5	1,029.4	1,444.6

Source: IMF, *International Financial Statistics*.

External Trade

PRINCIPAL COMMODITIES
(distribution by SITC, US $ million)

Imports c.i.f.	2006	2007	2008
Food and live animals	648.6	931.7	1,097.7
Fish, crustaceans and molluscs, and preparations thereof	120.2	164.6	120.5
Fish, fresh, chilled or frozen	108.2	138.7	97.1
Cereals and cereal preparations	238.5	320.4	502.4
Rice	118.2	158.4	214.4
Sugar and honey	81.4	118.1	92.0
Crude materials (inedible), except fuels	88.0	95.4	126.3
Mineral fuels, lubricants, etc.	733.9	904.2	1,180.4
Crude petroleum and oils obtained from bituminous materials	684.9	790.6	1,084.0
Petroleum products, refined	25.4	83.7	69.0
Chemicals and related products	574.1	832.4	951.7
Basic manufactures	915.3	1,289.2	1,504.0
Non-metallic mineral manufactures	244.7	322.3	362.7
Iron and steel	131.5	275.4	343.6
Machinery and transport equipment	1,809.4	2,686.7	3,106.3
Power-generating machinery and equipment	90.2	236.2	212.4
Machinery specialized for particular industries	228.0	325.0	435.6
General industrial machinery and equipment, and parts thereof	198.9	293.7	361.5
Telecommunications, sound recording and reproducing equipment	213.9	250.0	405.0
Other electric machinery, apparatus and appliances, and parts thereof	210.2	348.7	367.0
Road vehicles and parts*	790.8	1,112.4	1,188.0
Passenger motor vehicles (excluding buses)	415.3	557.1	544.4
Motor vehicles for the transport of goods or materials	250.0	355.6	399.3
Miscellaneous manufactured articles	482.6	418.3	409.2
Total (incl. others)	5,328.8	7,278.3	8,536.1

* Data on parts exclude tyres, engines and electrical parts.

Exports f.o.b.	2006	2007	2008
Food and live animals	1,480.9	1,219.1	1,266.8
Fish, crustaceans and molluscs, and preparations thereof	51.5	61.0	43.9
Fish, prepared or preserved	35.2	31.4	19.7
Vegetables and fruit	163.0	76.7	143.5
Fruit and nuts, fresh, dried	141.9	37.6	122.3
Fruit, fresh or dried	13.7	10.8	7.0
Pineapples, fresh or dried	12.9	10.0	6.2
Coffee, tea, cocoa, spices and manufactures thereof	1,242.9	1,057.8	1,048.3
Cocoa	1,239.1	1,049.2	1,039.8
Cocoa beans, raw, roasted	1,096.3	896.4	974.1
Cocoa butter and paste	88.5	62.0	15.1
Cocoa butter (fat or oil)	53.3	85.7	44.9
Crude materials (inedible) except fuels	169.5	344.8	349.1
Cork and wood	80.2	163.4	147.3
Wood, non-coniferous species, sawn, planed, tongued, grooved, etc.	77.6	155.1	138.2
Wood, non-coniferous species, sawn lengthwise, sliced or peeled	67.6	138.5	123.8
Mineral fuels, lubricants, etc.	16.2	26.8	50.6
Basic manufactures	506.3	253.0	236.3
Cork and wood manufactures (excl. furniture)	200.5	135.5	138.3
Veneers, plywood, 'improved' wood and other wood, worked.	117.9	129.0	130.7
Wood sawn lengthwise, veneer sheets, etc., up to 6 mm in thickness	49.1	73.1	55.4
Aluminium and aluminium alloys, unwrought	34.8	22.8	23.9
Machinery and transport equipment	13.9	68.7	97.4
Gold, non-monetary, unwrought or semi-manufactured	1,130.7	1,458.7	1,713.9
Total (incl. others)	3,614.0	3,533.8	3,809.9

Source: UN, *International Trade Statistics Yearbook*.

2009 (million Ghana cedis): Total imports c.i.f. 6,698.3; total exports f.o.b. 2,962.7.

PRINCIPAL TRADING PARTNERS
(US $ million)

Imports c.i.f.	2006	2007	2008
Australia	70.2	105.6	127.7
Belgium	300.9	431.0	428.9
Brazil	114.2	194.7	182.1
Canada	110.4	143.3	234.9
China, People's Republic	504.0	806.1	999.6
Congo, Republic	118.4	192.8	253.8
France (incl. Monaco)	197.3	173.2	235.0
Germany	288.6	396.5	328.0
India	205.8	319.2	369.9
Indonesia	90.5	149.8	156.0
Italy (incl. San Marino)	170.8	262.5	171.5
Japan	121.2	163.8	188.8
Korea, Republic	119.5	199.0	243.7
Netherlands	193.4	270.5	285.6
Nigeria	510.0	502.6	745.0
South Africa	204.8	293.9	365.9
Spain	98.2	142.6	115.2
Sweden	103.7	158.9	264.9
Thailand	115.1	170.2	224.3
United Kingdom	474.0	411.1	370.7
USA	352.3	555.8	653.5
Total (incl. others)	5,328.8	7,278.3	8,536.1

Exports f.o.b.	2006	2007	2008
Belgium	144.9	61.9	43.3
Burkina Faso	456.0	163.1	81.7
China, People's Republic	38.8	32.7	71.6
Côte d'Ivoire	10.0	26.0	28.9
Denmark	7.2	21.6	18.7
Estonia	68.8	40.1	50.3
France (incl. Monaco)	164.7	119.5	91.2
Germany	96.4	77.1	56.6
India	58.9	78.4	203.0
Italy (incl. San Marino)	90.7	43.8	62.6
Japan	72.8	77.4	19.6
Malaysia	94.7	121.8	120.5
Netherlands	402.6	425.7	447.5
Nigeria	69.8	80.5	86.0
South Africa	932.8	1,312.0	1,676.2
Spain	50.9	64.3	59.8
Switzerland-Liechtenstein	245.4	210.2	100.7
Turkey	61.1	12.8	54.9
United Kingdom	144.8	209.8	140.5
USA	106.3	83.9	108.1
Total (incl. others)	3,614.0	3,533.8	3,809.9

Source: UN, *International Trade Statistics Yearbook*.

2009 (million Ghana cedis): Total imports c.i.f. 6,698.3; total exports f.o.b. 2,962.7.

Transport

RAILWAYS
(traffic)

	2002	2003	2004
Passenger-km (million)	61	86	80
Net ton-km (million)	244	242	216

Source: UN, *Statistical Yearbook*.

ROAD TRAFFIC
(motor vehicles in use at 31 December)

	2001	2002	2003
Passenger cars	90,800	91,200	91,000
Lorries and vans	121,100	123,500	124,300

Source: UN, *Statistical Yearbook*.

2007 (motor vehicles in use at 31 December): Passenger cars 493,770; Buses and coaches 121,113; Vans and lorries 158,379; Motorcycles and mopeds 149,063 (Source: IRF: *World Road Statistics*).

SHIPPING

Merchant Fleet
(registered at 31 December)

	2007	2008	2009
Number of vessels	235	239	236
Total displacement ('000 grt)	118.2	116.9	116.0

Source: IHS Fairplay, *World Fleet Statistics*.

International Sea-borne Freight Traffic
(estimates, '000 metric tons)

	1991	1992	1993
Goods loaded	2,083	2,279	2,424
Goods unloaded	2,866	2,876	2,904

Source: UN Economic Commission for Africa, *African Statistical Yearbook*.

CIVIL AVIATION
(traffic on scheduled services)

	2002	2003	2004
Kilometres flown (million)	12	12	5
Passengers carried ('000)	256	241	96
Passenger-km (million)	912	906	363
Total ton-km (million)	107	101	41

Source: UN, *Statistical Yearbook*.

Tourism

ARRIVALS BY NATIONALITY

	2004	2005	2006
Côte d'Ivoire	28,069	25,155	25,921
France	21,096	10,089	11,915
Germany	28,168	14,094	17,132
Liberia	15,310	14,472	16,938
Netherlands	14,133	13,663	14,673
Nigeria	80,131	47,983	56,278
Togo	17,472	11,888	13,859
United Kingdom	50,547	36,747	36,795
USA	38,508	50,475	62,795
Total (incl. others)*	583,819	428,533	497,129

* Includes Ghanaian nationals resident abroad: 158,917 in 2004; 159,821 in 2005; 155,826 in 2006.

Total tourist arrivals ('000): 587 in 2007; 698 in 2008; 803 in 2009 (provisional).

Receipts from tourism (US $ million, excl. passenger transport): 908 in 2007; 919 in 2008; 968 in 2009 (provisional).

Source: World Tourism Organization.

Communications Media

	2008	2009	2010
Telephones ('000 main lines in use)	143.9	267.4	277.9
Mobile cellular telephones ('000 subscribers)	11,570.4	15,108.9	17,436.9
Internet subscribers ('000)	28.9	92.7	53.1
Broadband subscribers ('000)	23.0	28.9	50.1

Personal computers: 250,000 (10.7 per 1,000 persons) in 2008.

Source: International Telecommunication Union.

Radio receivers ('000 in use): 4,400 in 1997.

Television receivers ('000 in use): 2,390 in 2000.

Daily newspapers: 4 titles in 1998 (average circulation 260,000).

Book production (titles, 1998): 7.

Sources: UNESCO Institute for Statistics; UNESCO, *Statistical Yearbook*; UN, *Statistical Yearbook*.

Education

(2008/09 unless otherwise indicated)

			Students ('000)		
	Institutions	Teachers	Males	Females	Total
Pre-primary	n.a.	37,789	671.9	666.6	1,338.5
Primary	13,115*	110,508	1,882.3	1,776.8	3,659.1
Junior secondary	6,394*	73,211	566.6	485.5	1,052.1
Senior secondary	512*	25,943	280.5	208.7	489.2
Tertiary	n.a.	7,698	127.6	75.8	203.4

* 1998/99 figure.

1998/99: *Teacher training* 38 institutions; *Technical institutes* 61 institutions; *Polytechnics* 8 institutions; *Universities* 7 institutions.

Source: UNESCO and former Ministry of Education, Accra.

Pupil-teacher ratio (primary education, UNESCO estimate): 33.1 in 2008/09 (Source: UNESCO Institute for Statistics).

Adult literacy rate (UNESCO estimates): 66.6% (males 72.8%; females 60.4%) in 2009 (Source: UNESCO Institute for Statistics).

Directory

The Government

HEAD OF STATE

President and Commander-in-Chief of the Armed Forces: Prof. JOHN EVANS ATTA MILLS (inaugurated 7 January 2009).

Vice-President: JOHN DRAMANI MAHAMA.

CABINET
(May 2012)

Minister of Finance and Economic Planning: Dr KWABENA DUFFUOR.

Minister of Defence: Lt-Gen. (retd) JOSEPH HENRY SMITH.

Minister of the Interior: WILLIAM KWASI ABOAH.

Minister of Foreign Affairs and Regional Integration: Alhaji MUHAMMED MUMUNI.

Attorney-General, Minister of Justice: Dr BENJAMIN KUNBUOR.

Minister of Roads and Highways: JOE GIDISU.

Minister of Local Government and Rural Development: SAMUEL OFUSO-AMPOFO.

Minister of Health: ALBAN BAGBIN.

Minister of Food and Agriculture: KWESI AWHOI.

Minister of Education: LEE OCRAN.

Minister of Trade and Industry: HANNAH TETTEH.

Minister of Communications: HARUNA IDDRISU.

Minister of Water Resources, Works and Housing: ENOCH TEYE MENSAH.

Minister of the Environment, Science and Technology: HANI SHERRY AYITEY.

Minister of Energy: Dr JOE OTENG ADJEI.

Minister of Lands and Natural Resources: MIKE ALLEN HAMMAH.

Minister of Transport: Alhaji COLLINS DAUDA.

Minister of Employment and Social Welfare: MOSES ASAGA.

Minister of Women's and Children's Affairs: JULIANA JOCELYN AZUMAH MENSAH.

Minister of Tourism: AKUA SENA DANSUA.

Minister of Information: FRITZ BAFFOUR.

Minister of Youth and Sports: CLEMENT KOFI HUMADO.

Minister of Culture and Chieftaincy: ALEXANDER ASUM-AHENSAH.

Ministers of State at the Presidency: RAFATU HALUTIE DUBIE, STEPHEN AMOANOR KWAO, JOHN GYETUAH, DOMINIC AZIMBE AZUMAH.

In addition there were 28 Deputy Ministers.

REGIONAL MINISTERS
(May 2012)

Ashanti: KWAKU AGYEMANG-MENSAH.

Brong Ahafo: KWADWO NYAMEKYE-MARFO.

Central: AMA BENYIWA-DOE.

Eastern: VICTOR EMMANUEL SMITH.

Greater Accra: NII ARMAH ASHITEY.

Northern: MOSES MAGBENBA.

Upper East: MARK WAYONGO.

Upper West: AMIN AMIDU SULEMANI.

Volta: HENRY KAMEL FORD.

Western: PAUL EVANS AIDOO.

MINISTRIES

Office of the President: POB 1627, Osu, Accra; tel. (30) 2666997; internet www.oop.gov.gh.

Ministry of Communications: POB M38, Accra; tel. (30) 2666465; fax (30) 2667114; e-mail info@moc.gov.gh; internet www.moc.gov.gh.

Ministry of Culture and Chieftaincy: POB 1627, State House, Accra; tel. (30) 2685012; fax (30) 2678361; e-mail chieftancycultur@yahoo.com.

Ministry of Defence: Burma Camp, Accra; tel. (30) 2775665; fax (30) 2772241; e-mail kaddok@internetghana.com.

Ministry of Education: POB M45, Accra; tel. (30) 2666070; fax (30) 2664067.

Ministry of Employment and Social Welfare: POB 1627, State House, Accra; tel. (30) 2684532; fax (30) 2663615.

Ministry of Energy: FREMA House, Spintex Rd, POB T40 (Stadium Post Office), Stadium, Accra; tel. (30) 2683961; fax (30) 2668262; e-mail moen@energymin.gov.gh; internet www.energymin.gov.gh.

Ministry of the Environment, Science and Technology: POB M232, Accra; tel. (30) 2660005.

Ministry of Finance and Economic Planning: POB M40, Accra; tel. (30) 2665587; fax (30) 2666079; e-mail minister2009@mofep.gov.gh; internet www.mofep.gov.gh.

Ministry of Food and Agriculture: POB M37, Accra; tel. (30) 2663036; fax (30) 2668245; e-mail info@mofa.gov.gh; internet www.mofa.gov.gh.

Ministry of Foreign Affairs and Regional Integration: Treasury Rd, POB M53, Accra; tel. (30) 2664952; fax (30) 2665363; e-mail ghmaf00@ghana.com.

Ministry of Health: POB M44, Accra; tel. (30) 2684208; fax (30) 2663810; e-mail info@moh-ghana.org; internet www.moh-ghana.org.

Ministry of Information: POB M41, Accra; tel. and fax (30) 2229870; e-mail webmaster@mino.gov.gh; internet www.ghana.gov.gh.

Ministry of the Interior: POB M42, Accra; tel. (30) 2684400; fax (30) 2684408; e-mail mint@mint.gov.gh; internet www.mint.gov.gh.

Ministry of Justice and Attorney-General's Department: POB M60, Accra; tel. (30) 2665051; fax (30) 2667609; e-mail info@mjag.gov.gh.

Ministry of Lands and Natural Resources: POB M212, Accra; tel. (30) 2687314; fax (30) 2666801; e-mail motgov@hotmail.com; internet www.ghana-mining.org/ghweb/en/ma.html.

Ministry of Local Government and Rural Development: POB M50, Accra; tel. (30) 2682018; fax (30) 2682003.

Ministry of Roads and Highways: Accra; tel. (30) 2618668; fax (30) 2672676; internet www.mrt.gov.gh.

Ministry of Tourism: POB 4386, Accra; tel. (30) 2666314; fax (30) 2666182; e-mail humphrey.kuma@tourism.gov.gh; internet www.touringghana.com.

Ministry of Trade and Industry: POB M47, Accra; tel. (30) 2663327; fax (30) 2662428; e-mail info@moti.gov.gh; internet www.moti.gov.gh.

Ministry of Transport: POB M57, Accra; tel. (30) 2681780; fax (30) 2681781; e-mail info@mot.gov.gh; internet mot.gov.gh.

Ministry of Water Resources, Works and Housing: POB M43, Accra; tel. (30) 2665940; fax (30) 2685503; e-mail mwh@ighmail.com.

Ministry of Women's and Children's Affairs: POB M186, Accra; tel. (30) 2255411; fax (30) 2688182; e-mail info@mowacgov.com; internet www.mowacghana.net.

Ministry of Youth and Sports: Accra.

President and Legislature

PRESIDENT

Presidential Election, First Round, 7 December 2008

Candidate	Valid votes	% of valid votes
Nana Akufo-Addo (NPP)	4,159,439	49.13
John Evans Atta Mills (NDC)	4,056,634	47.92
Paa Kwesi Nduom (CPP)	113,494	1.34
Edward Nasigre Mahama (PNC)	73,494	0.87
Emmanuel Ansah Antwi (DFP)	27,889	0.33
Kwesi Amoafo Yeboah (Ind.)	19,342	0.23
Thomas Ward-Brew (DPP)	8,653	0.10
Kwabena Adjei (RPD)	6,889	0.08
Total	8,465,834*	100.00

* Excluding 205,438 spoiled papers.

Presidential Election, Second Round, 28 December 2008

Candidate	Valid votes	% of valid votes
John Evans Atta Mills (NDC)	4,521,032	50.23
Nana Akufo-Addo (NPP)	4,480,446	49.77
Total	9,001,478*	100.00

* Excluding 92,886 spoiled papers.

PARLIAMENT

Parliament: Parliament House, Accra; tel. (30) 2664042; fax (30) 2665957; e-mail clerk@parliament.gh; internet www.parliament.gh.

Speaker: JOYCE BAMFORD-ADDO.

General Election, 7 December 2008

Party	Seats
National Democratic Congress (NDC)	113
New Patriotic Party (NPP)	109
People's National Convention (PNC)	2
Convention People's Party (CPP)	1
Independents	4
Total	229*

* The result in the remaining constituency was not immediately made available.

COUNCIL OF STATE

Chairman: Prof. DANIEL ADZEI BEKOE.

Election Commission

Electoral Commission (EC): POB M214, Accra; tel. (30) 2228421; internet www.ec.gov.gh; f. 1993; appointed by the President; Chair. Dr KWADWO AFARI-GYAN.

Political Organizations

Convention People's Party (CPP): 64 Mango Tree Ave, Asylum Down, POB 10939, Accra-North; tel. (30) 2227763; e-mail info@conventionpeoplesparty.org; internet conventionpeoplesparty.org; f. 1998 as Convention Party by merger of the National Convention Party (f. 1992) and the People's Convention Party (f. 1993); present name adopted in 2000; Nkrumahist; Chair. LADI NYLANDER; Gen. Sec. IVOR KOBBINA GREENSTREET.

Democratic Freedom Party (DFP): POB 1040, Accra; tel. (30) 2237590; internet votedfp.org; f. 2006; Leader Dr OBED YAO ASAMOAH.

Democratic People's Party (DPP): 698/4 Star Ave, Kokomlemle, Accra; tel. (30) 2221671; f. 1992; Chair. THOMAS WARD-BREW; Gen. Sec. G. M. TETTEY.

EGLE (Every Ghanaian Living Everywhere) Party: POB TN 16132, Teshie Nungua, Accra; tel. (30) 2713994; fax (30) 2776894; f. 1992 as the Eagle Party.

Great Consolidated People's Party (GCPP): Citadel House, POB 3077, Accra; tel. (30) 2311498; f. 1996; Nkrumahist; Chair. (vacant); Sec.-Gen. NICHOLAS MENSAH.

National Democratic Congress (NDC): 641/4 Ringway Close, POB 5825, Kokomlemle, Accra-North; tel. (30) 2223195; fax (30) 2220743; e-mail info@ndc.org.gh; internet www.ndc2008.com; f. 1992; party of fmr Pres. Jerry Rawlings; Chair. Dr KWABENA ADJEI; Gen. Sec. JOHNSON ASIEDU NKETIAH.

National Reform Party (NRP): 31 Mango Tree Ave, Asylum Down, POB 19403, Accra-North; tel. (30) 2228578; fax (30) 2227820; f. 1999 by a breakaway group from the NDC; Sec.-Gen. OPOKU KYERETWIE.

New Patriotic Party (NPP): C912/2 Duade St, Kokomlemle, POB 3456, Accra-North; tel. (30) 2227951; fax (30) 2224418; f. 1992; Gen. Sec. NANA OHENE NTOW.

People's National Convention (PNC): POB AC 120, Arts Centre, Accra; tel. (30) 2236389; f. 1992; Nkrumahist; Chair. Alhaji AHMED RAMADAN; Gen. Sec. BERNARD MORNAH.

Reformed Patriotic Democrats (RPD): POB 13274, Kumasi; tel. 243616660 (mobile); f. 2007 by former mems of the NPP; Sec.-Gen. FRANCIS KYEI (acting).

United Ghana Movement (UGM): 1 North Ridge Cres., POB C2611, Cantonments, Accra; tel. (30) 2225581; fax (30) 2223506; e-mail info@ugmghana.org; f. 1996 by a breakaway group from the NPP; Chair. WEREKO BROBBY.

United Renaissance Party (URP): Nima Hwy, POB 104, Accra-North; tel. (30) 28914411; f. 2006; Chair. KOFI WAYO.

Diplomatic Representation

EMBASSIES AND HIGH COMMISSIONS IN GHANA

Algeria: 22 Josif Broz Tito Ave, POB 2747, Cantonments, Accra; tel. (30) 2776719; fax (30) 2776828; Ambassador LARBI KATTI.

Angola: Accra; Ambassador ANA MARIA TELES CARREIRA.

Benin: 19 Volta St, Second Close, Airport Residential Area, POB 7871, Accra; tel. (30) 2774860; fax (30) 2774889; Ambassador PIERRE SADELER.

Brazil: Millennium Heights Bldg 2A, 14 Liberation Link, Airport Commercial Area, POB CT3859, Accra; tel. (30) 2774908; fax (30) 2778566; e-mail brasemb@africaonline.com.gh; internet www.embrazil.com.gh; Ambassador LUIS IRENE GALA.

Bulgaria: 3 Kakramadu Rd, POB 3193, East Cantonments, Accra; tel. (30) 2772404; fax (30) 2774231; e-mail bulemb2003@yahoo.com; internet www.mfa.bg/accra; Chargé d'affaires a.i. GEORGE MITEV.

Burkina Faso: 772 Asylum Down, off Farrar Ave, POB 65, Accra; tel. (30) 2221988; fax (30) 2221936; e-mail ambafaso@ghana.com; Ambassador PIERRE SEM SANOU.

Canada: 42 Independence Ave, Sankara Interchange, POB 1639, Accra; tel. (30) 2211521; fax (30) 2211523; e-mail accra@international.gc.ca; internet www.canadainternational.gc.ca/ghana; High Commissioner TRUDY KERNIGHAN.

China, People's Republic: 6 Agostino Neto Rd, Airport Residential Area, POB 3356, Accra; tel. (30) 2777073; fax (30) 2774527; e-mail chinaemb_gh@mfa.gov.cn; internet gh.chineseembassy.org; Ambassador GONG JIANZHONG.

Côte d'Ivoire: 9 18th Lane, off Cantonments Rd, POB 3445, Christiansborg, Accra; tel. (30) 2774611; fax (30) 2773516; e-mail acigh@ambaci-ghana.org; Ambassador BERNARD HUI KOUTOUA.

Cuba: 20 Amilcar Cabral Rd, Airport Residential Area, POB 9163 Airport, Accra; tel. (30) 2775868; fax (30) 2774998; e-mail embghana@africaonline.com.gh; Ambassador (vacant).

Czech Republic: C260/5, 2 Kanda High Rd, POB 5226, Accra-North; tel. (30) 2223540; fax (30) 2225337; e-mail accra@embassy.mzv.cz; internet www.mzv.cz/accra; Ambassador MILOSLAV MACHÁLEK.

Denmark: 67 Dr Isert Rd, North Ridge, POB CT596, Accra; tel. (30) 2253473; fax (30) 2228061; e-mail accamb@um.dk; internet www.ambaccra.um.dk; Ambassador CARSTEN NILAUS PEDERSEN.

Egypt: 38 Senchi St, Airport Residential Area, Accra; tel. (30) 2776795; fax (30) 2777579; e-mail boustaneaccra@hotmail.com; Ambassador IBRAHIM SAEED.

Ethiopia: 2 Milne Close, Airport Residential Area, POB 1646, Accra; tel. (30) 2775928; fax (30) 2776807; e-mail ethioemb@ghana.com; Ambassador GIFTY ABASIGA ABABULGU.

France: 12th Rd, off Liberation Ave, POB 187, Accra; tel. (30) 2214550; fax (30) 2214589; e-mail info@ambafrance-gh.org; internet www.ambafrance-gh.org; Ambassador FRANCIS HURTUT.

Germany: 6 Ridge St, North Ridge, POB 1757, Accra; tel. (30) 2211000; fax (30) 2221347; e-mail info@accra.diplo.de; internet www.accra.diplo.de; Ambassador Dr MARIUS HAAS.

Guinea: 11 Osu Badu St, Dzorwulu, POB 5497, Accra-North; tel. (30) 2777921; fax (30) 2760961; e-mail embagui@ghana.com; Ambassador MAMADOU FALILOU BAH.

Holy See: 8 Drake Ave, Airport Residential Area, POB 9675, Accra; tel. (30) 2777759; fax (30) 2774019; e-mail nuncio@ghana.com; Apostolic Nuncio Most Rev. LÉON KALENGA BADIKEBELE (Titular Archbishop of Magnetum).

India: 9 Ridge Rd, Roman Ridge, POB CT 5708, Cantonments, Accra; tel. (30) 2775601; fax (30) 2772176; e-mail indiahc@ncs.com.gh; internet www.indiahc-ghana.com; High Commissioner RUCHI GHANASHYAM.

Iran: 12 Arkusah St, Airport Residential Area, POB 12673, Accra-North; tel. (30) 2774474; fax (30) 2777043; Ambassador MOHAMMED SULEYMANI.

Israel: Accra; Ambassador SHARON BAR-LI.

Italy: Jawaharlal Nehru Rd, POB 140, Accra; tel. (30) 2775621; fax (30) 2777301; e-mail ambasciata.accra@esteri.it; internet www.ambaccra.esteri.it; Ambassador LUCA FRATINI.

Japan: Fifth Ave, POB 1637, West Cantonments, Accra; tel. (30) 2765060; fax (30) 2762553; Ambassador KEIICHI KATAKAMI.

Korea, Democratic People's Republic: 139 Nortei Ababio Loop, Ambassadorial Estate, Roman Ridge, POB 13874, Accra; tel. (30) 2777825; Ambassador KIM PYONG GI.

Korea, Republic: 3 Abokobi Rd, POB GP13700, East Cantonments, Accra-North; tel. (30) 2776157; fax (30) 2772313; e-mail ghana@mofat.go.kr; internet gha.mofat.go.kr; Ambassador LEE SANG-HAK.

Lebanon: F864/1, off Cantonments Rd, Osu, POB 562, Accra; tel. (30) 2776727; fax (30) 2764290; e-mail lebanon@its.com.gh; Ambassador JAWDAT EL-HAJJAR.

Liberia: 10 Odoi Kwao St, Airport Residential Area, POB 895, Accra; tel. (30) 2775641; fax (30) 2775987; Ambassador RUDOLPH P. VON BALLMOOS.

Libya: 14 Sixth St, Airport Residential Area, POB 9665, Accra; tel. (30) 2774819; fax (30) 2774953; Secretary of People's Bureau Dr ALI AHMED GHUDBAN.

Malaysia: 18 Templesi Lane, Airport Residential Area, POB 16033, Accra; tel. (30) 2763691; fax (30) 2764910; e-mail mwaccra@africaonline.com.gh; High Commissioner Dato' HAJJAH RAZINAH GHAZALI.

Mali: 1st Bungalow, Liberia Rd, Airport Residential Area, POB 1121, Accra; tel. and fax (30) 2666942; e-mail ambamali@ighmail.com; Ambassador Gen. TOUMANY SISSOKO.

Netherlands: 89 Liberation Rd, Ako Adjei Interchange, POB CT1647, Accra; tel. (30) 2214350; fax (30) 2773655; e-mail acc@minbuza.nl; internet www.ambaccra.nl; Ambassador (vacant).

Niger: E104/3 Independence Ave, POB 2685, Accra; tel. (30) 2224962; fax (30) 2229011; Ambassador ABDOULMOUMINE HADJIO.

Nigeria: 20/21 Onyasia Cres., Roman Ridge Residential Area, Accra; tel. (30) 2776158; fax (30) 2774395; e-mail nighicomgh@yahoo.com; High Commissioner MUHAMMED OBANIKORO.

Russia: Jawaharlal Nehru Rd, Switchback Lane, POB 1634, Accra; tel. (30) 2775611; fax (30) 2772699; e-mail russia@4u.com.gh; internet www.ghana.mid.ru; Ambassador VLADIMIR V. BARBIN.

Senegal: 8F Odoi Kwao St, Airport Residential Area, PMB CT 342, Cantonments, Accra; tel. (30) 2770285; fax (30) 2770286; e-mail senegalaccra@hotmail.fr; Ambassador CHÉRIF OUMAR DIAGNÉ.

Sierra Leone: 83A Senchi St, Airport Residential Area, POB 55, Cantonments, Accra; tel. (30) 2769190; fax (30) 2769189; e-mail slhc@ighmail.com; High Commissioner MOKOWA ADU- GYAMFI.

South Africa: Speed House 1, 3rd Soula St, Labone North POB 298, Accra; tel. (30) 2740450; fax (30) 2762381; e-mail sahcgh@africaonline.com.gh; High Commissioner (vacant).

Spain: Drake Ave Extension, Airport Residential Area, PMB KA44, Accra; tel. (30) 2774004; fax (30) 2776217; e-mail emb.accra@mae.es; Ambassador JULIA ALICIA OLMO Y ROMERO.

Switzerland: Kanda Highway, North Ridge, POB 359, Accra; tel. (30) 2228125; fax (30) 2223583; e-mail acc.vertretung@eda.admin.ch; internet www.eda.admin.ch/accra; Ambassador ANDREA SEMADENI.

Togo: Togo House, near Cantonments Circle, POB C120, Accra; tel. (30) 2777950; fax (30) 2765659; e-mail togamba@ighmail.com; Ambassador JEAN-PIERRE GBIKPI-BENISSAN.

United Kingdom: Osu Link, off Gamel Abdul Nasser Ave, POB 296, Accra; tel. and fax (30) 2221665; fax (30) 2213274; e-mail high.commission.accra@fco.gov.uk; internet ukinghana.fco.gov.uk; High Commissioner Dr PETER EDWARD JONES.

USA: 24 Fourth Circular Rd, POB 194, Cantonments, Accra; tel. (30) 2741150; fax (30) 2741692; e-mail pressaccra@state.gov; internet ghana.usembassy.gov; Ambassador DONALD GENE TEITELBAUM.

Judicial System

The civil law in force in Ghana is based on the Common Law, doctrines of equity and general statutes which were in force in England in 1874, as modified by subsequent Ordinances. Ghanaian customary law is, however, the basis of most personal, domestic and contractual relationships. Criminal Law is based on the Criminal Procedure Code, 1960, derived from English Criminal Law, and since amended. The Superior Court of Judicature comprises a Supreme Court, a Court of Appeal, a High Court and a Regional Tribunal; Inferior Courts include Circuit Courts, Circuit Tribunals, Community Tribunals and such other Courts as may be designated by law. In 2001 'fast-track' court procedures were established to accelerate the delivery of justice.

Supreme Court

Consists of the Chief Justice and not fewer than nine other Justices. It is the final court of appeal in Ghana and has jurisdiction in matters relating to the enforcement or interpretation of the Constitution.

Chief Justice: GEORGINA THEODORA WOOD.

Court of Appeal: Consists of the Chief Justice and not fewer than five Judges of the Court of Appeal. It has jurisdiction to hear and determine appeals from any judgment, decree or order of the High Court.

High Court: Comprises the Chief Justice and not fewer than 12 Justices of the High Court. It exercises original jurisdiction in all matters, civil and criminal, other than those for offences involving treason. Trial by jury is practised in criminal cases in Ghana and the Criminal Procedure Code, 1960, provides that all trials on indictment shall be by a jury or with the aid of Assessors.

Circuit Courts: Exercise original jurisdiction in civil matters where the amount involved does not exceed 100,000 new cedis. They also have jurisdiction with regard to the guardianship and custody of infants, and original jurisdiction in all criminal cases, except offences where the maximum punishment is death or the offence of treason. They have appellate jurisdiction from decisions of any District Court situated within their respective circuits.

District Courts: To each magisterial district is assigned at least one District Magistrate who has original jurisdiction to try civil suits in which the amount involved does not exceed 50,000 new cedis. District Magistrates also have jurisdiction to deal with all criminal cases, except first-degree felonies, and commit cases of a more serious nature to either the Circuit Court or the High Court. A Grade I District Court can impose a fine not exceeding 1,000 cedis and sentences of imprisonment of up to two years and a Grade II District Court may impose a fine not exceeding 500 new cedis and a sentence of imprisonment of up to 12 months. A District Court has no appellate jurisdiction, except in rent matters under the Rent Act.

Juvenile Courts: Jurisdiction in cases involving persons under 17 years of age, except where the juvenile is charged jointly with an adult. The Courts comprise a Chairman, who must be either the District Magistrate or a lawyer, and not fewer than two other members appointed by the Chief Justice in consultation with the Judicial Council. The Juvenile Courts can make orders as to the protection and supervision of a neglected child and can negotiate with parents to secure the good behaviour of a child.

National Public Tribunal: Considers appeals from the Regional Public Tribunals. Its decisions are final and are not subject to any further appeal. The Tribunal consists of at least three members and not more than five, one of whom acts as Chairman.

Regional Public Tribunals: Hears criminal cases relating to prices, rent or exchange control, theft, fraud, forgery, corruption or any offence which may be referred to them by the Provisional National Defence Council.

Special Military Tribunal: Hears criminal cases involving members of the armed forces. It consists of between five and seven members.

Attorney-General: Dr BENJAMIN KUNBUOR.

Religion

According to the 2000 census, 69% of the population were Christians and 16% Muslims, while 7% followed indigenous beliefs.

CHRISTIANITY

Christian Council of Ghana: POB GP919, Accra; tel. (30) 2776678; fax (30) 2776725; e-mail info@christiancouncilofghana.org; internet www.christiancouncilofghana.org; f. 1929; advisory body comprising 16 mem. churches and 2 affiliate Christian orgs (2005); Chair. Most Rev. Prof. EMMANUEL ASANTE; Gen. Sec. Rev. Dr FRED DEEGBE.

The Anglican Communion

Anglicans in Ghana are adherents of the Church of the Province of West Africa, comprising 14 dioceses and a missionary region, of which nine are in Ghana.

Archbishop of the Province of West Africa and Bishop of Accra: Most Rev. JUSTICE OFEI AKROFI, Bishopscourt, POB 8, Accra; tel. (30) 2662292; fax (30) 2668822; e-mail adaccra@ghana.com.

Bishop of Cape Coast: Rt Rev. DANIEL ALLOTEY, Bishopscourt, POB A233, Adisadel Estates, Cape Coast; tel. (33) 2132502; fax (33) 2132637; e-mail danallotey@priest.com.

Bishop of Ho: Rt Rev. MATTHIAS MEDADUES-BADOHU, Bishopslodge, POB MA 300, Ho; e-mail matthiaskwab@googlemail.com.

Bishop of Koforidua: Rt Rev. FRANCIS QUASHIE, POB 980, Koforidua; tel. (34) 2022329; fax (34) 2022060; e-mail cpwa_gh@yahoo.com; internet koforidua.org.

Bishop of Kumasi: Rt Rev. DANIEL YINKAH SAFO, Bishop's Office, St Cyprian's Ave, POB 144, Kumasi; tel. and fax (32) 2024117; e-mail anglicandioceseofkumasi@yahoo.com.

Bishop of Sekondi: Rt Rev. JOHN KWAMINA OTOO, POB 85, Sekondi; tel. (31) 20669125; e-mail angdiosek@yahoo.co.uk.

Bishop of Sunyani: Rt Rev. THOMAS AMPAH BRIENT, Bishop's House, POB 23, Sunyani, BA; tel. (35) 2027205; fax (35) 2027203; e-mail anglicandiocesesyi@yahoo.com.

Bishop of Tamale: Rt Rev. EMMANUEL ANYINDANA ARONGO, POB 110, Tamale NR; tel. (37) 2022639; fax (37) 2022906; e-mail bishopea2000@yahoo.com.

Bishop of Wiawso: Rt Rev. ABRAHAM KOBINA ACKAH, POB 4, Sefwi, Wiawso; e-mail bishopackah@yahoo.com.

The Roman Catholic Church

Ghana comprises four archdioceses, 15 dioceses and one apostolic vicariate. Some 13% of the total population are Roman Catholics.

Ghana Bishops' Conference

National Catholic Secretariat, POB 9712, Airport, Accra; tel. (30) 2500491; fax (30) 2500493; e-mail dscncs@africaonline.com.gh; internet www.ghanacbc.org.

f. 1960; Pres. Rt Rev. LUCAS ABADAMLOORA (Bishop of Navrongo-Bolgatanga).

Archbishop of Accra: Most Rev. GABRIEL CHARLES PALMER-BUCKLE, Chancery Office, POB 247, Accra; tel. (30) 2222728; fax (30) 2231619; e-mail cpalmerbuckle@yahoo.com; internet www.accracatholic.org.

Archbishop of Cape Coast: Most Rev. MATTHIAS KOBENA NKETSIAH, Archbishop's House, POB 112, Cape Coast; tel. (33) 2133471; fax (33) 2133473; e-mail archcape@ghanacbc.com.

Archbishop of Kumasi: Most Rev. THOMAS KWAKU MENSAH, POB 99, Kumasi; tel. (32) 2024012; fax (32) 2029395; e-mail cadiokum@ghana.com.

Archbishop of Tamale: Most Rev. PHILIP NAAMEH, Archbishop's House, Gumbehini Rd, POB 42, Tamale; tel. and fax (37) 2022425; e-mail tamdio2@yahoo.co.uk.

Other Christian Churches

African Methodist Episcopal Zion Church: POB MP522, Mamprobi, Accra; tel. (30) 2669200; f. 1898; Pres. Rt Rev. WARREN M. BROWN.

Christian Methodist Episcopal Church: POB AN 7639, Accra; tel. 244630267 (mobile); internet www.cmetenth.org/Ghana%20Regional%20Conference.htm; Pres. KENNETH W. CARTER; Mission Supervisor Rev. ADJEI K. LAWSON.

Church of Pentecost: POB 2194 Accra; tel. (30) 2777611; fax (30) 2774721; e-mail cophq@thechurchofpentecost.com; internet www.thecophq.org; Chair. Apostle Dr OPOKU ONYINAH; Gen. Sec. Apostle ALFRED KODUAH; 1,503,057 mems.

Evangelical-Lutheran Church of Ghana: POB KN197, Kaneshie, Accra; tel. (30) 2223487; fax (30) 2220947; e-mail elcga@africaonline.com.gh; Pres. Rt Rev. Dr PAUL KOFI FYNN; 27,521 mems (2010).

Evangelical-Presbyterian Church of Ghana: 19 Main St, Tesano, PMB, Accra-North; tel. (30) 2220381; fax (30) 2233173; e-mail epchurch@ghana.com; f. 1847; Moderator Rev. FRANCIS AMENU; 295,000 mems.

Ghana Baptist Convention: PMB, Kumasi; tel. (30) 225215; fax (30) 228592; e-mail mail@gbconvention.org; internet www.gbconvention.org; f. 1963; Pres. Rev. Dr KOJO OSEI-WUSUH; Sec. Rev. KOJO AMO; 65,000 mems.

Ghana Mennonite Church: POB 5485, Accra; fax (30) 2220589; f. 1957; Moderator Rev. THEOPHILUS TETTEH; Sec. JOHN ADETA; 5,000 mems.

Ghana Union Conference of Seventh-day Adventists: POB GP1016, Accra; tel. (30) 2223720; fax (30) 2227024; e-mail guc@adventistsghana.org; internet www.adventistgh.org; f. 1943; Pres. Pastor SAMUEL A. LARMIE; Sec. Pastor KWAME KWANIN-BOAKYE; 268,171 mems.

Methodist Church of Ghana: Wesley House, E252/2, Liberia Rd, POB 403, Accra; tel. (30) 2670355; fax (30) 2679223; e-mail mcghqs@ucomgh.com; internet www.methodistchurch-gh.org; Presiding Bishop Most Rev. Dr ROBERT ABOAGYE-MENSAH; 584,969 mems (2007).

Presbyterian Church of Ghana: POB 106, Accra; tel. (30) 2662511; fax (30) 2665594; e-mail pcghg@yahoo.com; internet www.pc-ghana.org; f. 1828; Moderator Rt Rev. YAW FRIMPONG-MANSON; Clerk Rev. Dr CHARLES GYANG DUAH; 422,500 mems.

The African Methodist Episcopal Church, the Christ Reformed Church, the F'Eden Church, the Gospel Revival Church of God and the Religious Society of Friends (Quakers) are also active in Ghana.

ISLAM

In 2000 some 16% of the population of Ghana were Muslims, with a particularly large concentration in the Northern Region. The majority are Malikees.

Coalition of Muslim Organizations (COMOG): Accra; Pres. Alhaji Maj. MOHAMMED EASAH.

Ghana Muslim Representative Council: Accra.

Chief Imam: Sheikh USMAN NUHU SHARABUTU.

BAHÁ'Í FAITH

National Spiritual Assembly: POB 7098, Accra-North; tel. (30) 2222127; e-mail bahaighana@yahoo.com; Sec. GLADYS QUARTEY-PAPAFIO.

The Press

DAILY NEWSPAPERS

The Daily Dispatch: 1 Dade Walk, North Labone, POB C1945, Cantonments, Accra; tel. (30) 2763339; e-mail ephson@usa.net; Editor BEN EPHSON.

Daily Graphic: Graphic Communications Group Ltd, 3 Graphic Rd, POB 742, Accra; tel. (30) 2684001; fax (30) 2234754; e-mail gpack@graphic.com.gh; internet www.graphic.com.gh; f. 1950; state-owned; Editor RANSFORD TETTEH; circ. 100,000.

Daily Guide: Accra; internet dailyguideghana.com; owned by Western Publications Ltd; Editor GINA BLAY.

Ghanaian Chronicle: 37 Bobo St, Tesano, PMB, Accra-North; tel. (30) 2232713; fax (30) 2232608; e-mail chronicl@africaonline.com.gh; internet www.ghanaian-chronicle.com; Editor EMMANUEL AKLI; circ. 60,000.

The Ghanaian Times: New Times Corpn, Ring Rd West, POB 2638, Accra; tel. (30) 228282; fax (30) 220733; e-mail info@newtimes.com.gh; internet www.newtimes.com.gh; f. 1958; state-owned; Editor ENIMIL ASHON; circ. 45,000.

The Mail: POB CT4910, Cantonments, Accra; e-mail mike@accra-mail.com; internet www.accra-mail.com; Editor Alhaji ABDUL RAHMAN HARUNA ATTAH.

The Statesman: DTD 10 Sapele Loop, Kokomlemle, Accra; tel. and fax (30) 2220057; fax (30) 2220043; e-mail statesman_gh@yahoo.com; internet www.thestatesmanonline.com; f. 1949; official publ. of the New Patriotic Party; Editor-in-Chief ASARE OTCHERE-DARKO; Editor FRANK AGYEI-TWUM.

The Telescope: Takoradi; f. 2005; Editor LOUIS HENRY DANSO.

PERIODICALS

Thrice Weekly

The Independent: Clear Type Press Bldg Complex, off Graphic Rd, POB 4031, Accra; tel. and fax (30) 2661091; f. 1989; Editor ANDREW ARTHUR.

Network Herald: 34 Crescent Rd, Labone, Accra; tel. (30) 2701184; fax (30) 2762173; e-mail support@ghana.com; internet www.networkherald.gh; f. 2001; Editor ELVIS QUARSHIE.

Bi-Weekly

Ghana Palaver: Palaver Publications, POB WJ317, Wejia, Accra; tel. (30) 2850495; e-mail editor@ghana-palaver.com; internet www.ghana-palaver.com; f. 1994; Editor JOJO BRUCE QUANSAH.

The Ghanaian Lens: Accra; Editor KOBBY FIAGBE.

The Ghanaian Voice: Newstop Publications, POB 514, Mamprobi, Accra; tel. (30) 2324644; fax (30) 2314939; Editor CHRISTIANA ANSAH; circ. 100,000.

Weekly

Business and Financial Times: POB CT16, Cantonments, Accra; tel. and fax (30) 2785366; fax (30) 2775449; e-mail info@thebftonline.com; internet www.thebftonline.com; f. 1989; 3 a week; Editor WILLIAM SELASSY ADJADOGO; circ. 40,000.

The Crusading Guide: POB 8523, Accra-North; tel. (30) 2763339; fax (30) 2761541; internet www.ghanaweb.com/CrusadingGuide; Editor KWEKU BAAKO, Jr.

Free Press: Tommy Thompson Books Ltd, POB 6492, Accra; tel. (30) 2225994; independent; Editor FRANK BOAHENE.

Ghana Life: Ghana Life Publications, POB 11337, Accra; tel. (30) 2229835; Editor NIKKI BOA-AMPONSEM.

Ghana Market Watch: Accra; internet www.ghanamarketwatch.com; f. 2006; financial; CEO AMOS DOTSE.

Graphic Showbiz: Graphic Communications Group Ltd, POB 742, Accra; tel. (30) 2684001; fax (30) 2684025; e-mail graphicshowbiz@gmail.com; internet www.graphicghana.info; f. 2000; state-owned; Editor NANABANYIN DADSON.

Graphic Sports: Graphic Communications Group Ltd, POB 742, Accra; tel. (30) 2228911; fax (30) 2234754; e-mail info@graphicghana.com; state-owned; Editor FELIX ABAYATEYE; circ. 60,000.

Gye Nyame Concord: Accra; e-mail gnconcord@yahoo.com; internet www.ghanaweb.com/concord.

The Heritage: POB AD676, Arts Center, Accra; tel. (30) 2236051; fax (30) 2237156; e-mail heritagenewspaper@yahoo.co.uk; internet www.theheritagenews.com; Chair. STEPHEN OWUSU; Editor A. C. OHENE.

The Mirror: Graphic Communications Group Ltd, POB 742, Accra; tel. (30) 2228911; fax (30) 2234754; e-mail info@graphicghana.com; internet www.graphicghana.info; f. 1953; state-owned; Sat.; Editor E. N. O. PROVENCAL; circ. 90,000.

The National Democrat: Democrat Publications, POB 13605, Accra; Editor ELLIOT FELIX OHENE.

Public Agenda: Box MP2989, Accra-North; tel. (21) 2238820; e-mail pagenda@4u.com.gh; f. 1994; Editor AMOS SAFO; circ. 12,000.

The Standard: Standard Newspapers & Magazines Ltd, POB KA 9712, Accra; tel. (30) 2513537; fax (30) 2500493; e-mail snam.ncs@ghanacbc.org; internet www.ghanacbc.org; Roman Catholic; Editor ISAAC FRITZ ANDOH; circ. 10,000.

The Vanguard: Accra; Editor OSBERT LARTEY.

The Weekend: Newstop Publications, POB 514, Mamprobi, Accra; tel. (30) 2324644; fax (30) 2314939; Editor EMMANUEL YARTEY; circ. 40,000.

Weekly Spectator: New Times Corpn, Ring Rd West, POB 2638, Accra; tel. (30) 2228282; fax (30) 2229398; internet spectator.newtimesonline.com/spectator; state-owned; f. 1963; Sun.; Editor ENIMIL ASHON; circ. 165,000.

Other

The African Woman Magazine: Ring Rd West, POB AN 15064, Accra; tel. and fax (30) 2241636; e-mail mail@theafricanwoman.com; internet www.theafricanwoman.com; f. 1957; monthly; Editor NII ADUMUAH ORGLE.

AGI Newsletter: c/o Asscn of Ghana Industries, POB 8624, Accra-North; tel. (30) 2779023; e-mail agi@agighana.org; internet www.agighana.org; f. 1974; monthly; Editor CARLO HEY; circ. 1,500.

AGOO: Newstop Publications, POB 514, Mamprobi, Accra; tel. (30) 2324644; fax (30) 2314939; monthly; lifestyle magazine; Publr KOJO BONSU.

Armed Forces News: General Headquarters, Directorate of Public Relations, Burma Camp, Accra; tel. (30) 2776111; f. 1966; quarterly; Editor ADOTEY ANKRAH-HOFFMAN; circ. 4,000.

Business Watch: Sulton Bridge Co Ltd, POB C3447, Cantonments, Accra; tel. (30) 2233293; monthly.

Christian Messenger: Presbyterian Book Depot Bldg, POB 3075, Accra; tel. and fax (30) 2663124; e-mail danbentil@yahoo.com; f. 1883; English-language; fortnightly; Editor GEORGE MARTINSON; circ. 40,000.

Ghana Journal of Science: National Science and Technology Press, Council for Scientific and Industrial Research, POB M32, Accra; tel. (30) 2500253; monthly; Editor Dr A. K. AHAFIA.

Ghana Review International (GRi): POB GP14307, Accra; tel. (30) 2677437; fax (30) 2677438; e-mail accra@ghanareview.com; internet www.ghanareview.com; publishes in Accra, London and New York; CEO NANA OTUO ACHEAMPONG; print circ. 100,000.

Ghana Today: Information Services Dept, POB 745, Accra; tel. (30) 2228011; fax (30) 2228089; e-mail isd@mino.gov.gh; English; political, economic, investment and cultural affairs; Dir ELVIS ADANYINA.

Ideal Woman (Obaa Sima): POB 5737, Accra; tel. (30) 2221399; f. 1971; monthly; Editor KATE ABBAM.

New Legon Observer: POB LG 490, Accra, Ghana; tel. (30) 2512503; fax (30) 2512504; e-mail newlegonobserver@ug.edu.gh; internet www.egnghana.org/publications/newLegonObserver.php; f. 2007; publ. by Ghana Society for Development Dialogue; fortnightly; Acting Editor ERNEST ARYEETEY.

The Post: Ghana Information Services, POB 745, Accra; tel. (30) 2228011; fax (30) 2228089; e-mail isd@mino.gov.gh; f. 1980; monthly; current affairs and analysis; Dir ALPHONSE KOBLAVIE (acting); circ. 25,000.

Radio and TV Times: Ghana Broadcasting Corpn, Broadcasting House, POB 18167, Accra; tel. (30) 2508927; fax (30) 2773612; f. 1960; quarterly; Editor SAM THOMPSON; circ. 5,000.

Students World: POB M18, Accra; tel. (30) 2774248; fax (30) 2778715; e-mail afram@wwwplus.co.za; f. 1974; monthly; educational; Man. Editor ERIC OFEI; circ. 10,000.

Uneek: POB 230, Achimota, Accra; tel. (30) 2543853; fax (30) 2231355; e-mail info@uneekmagazine.com; internet www.uneekmagazine.com; f. 1998; monthly; leisure, culture; CEO and Editor FRANCIS ADAMS.

The Watchman: Watchman Gospel Ministry, POB GP4521, Accra; tel. and fax (30) 2500631; e-mail watchmannewspaper@yahoo.com; f. 1986; Christian news; fortnightly; Pres. and CEO DIVINE P. KUMAH; Chair. Dr E. K. OPUNI; circ. 5,000.

Other newspapers include **The Catalyst**, **The Crystal Clear Lens**, **The Enquirer** and **Searchlight**. There are also internet-based news sites, including **Ghana Today**, at www.ghanatoday.com and **ThisWeekGhana**, at www.thisweekghana.com.

NEWS AGENCY

Ghana News Agency: POB 2118, Accra; tel. (30) 2662381; fax (30) 2669841; e-mail ghnews@ghana.com; internet www.ghananewsagency.org; f. 1957; Gen. Man. NANA APPAU DUAH; 10 regional offices and 110 district offices.

PRESS ASSOCIATION

Ghana Journalists' Association: POB 4636, Accra; tel. and fax (30) 2234694; e-mail info@gjaghana.org; internet gjaghana.org; Pres. RANSFORD TETTEH.

Publishers

Advent Press: Osu La Rd, POB 0102, Osu, Accra; tel. (30) 2777861; fax (30) 2775327; e-mail eaokpoti@ghana.com; f. 1937; publishing arm of the Ghana Union Conference of Seventh-day Adventists; Gen. Man. EMMANUEL C. TETTEH.

Adwinsa Publications (Ghana) Ltd: Advance Press Bldg, 3rd Floor, School Rd, POB 92, Legon, Accra; tel. and fax (30) 2501515; e-mail adwinsa@yahoo.com; internet www.adwinsa.8k.com; f. 1977; general, educational; Man. Dir KWABENA AMPONSAH.

Afram Publications: C 184/22 Midway Lane, Abofu-Achimota, POB M18, Accra; tel. (30) 2412561; e-mail aframpub@pubchgh.com; internet www.aframpublications.com.gh; f. 1973; textbooks and general; Man. Dir ERIC OFEI.

Africa Christian Press: POB 30, Achimota, Accra; tel. (30) 2244147; fax (30) 2220271; e-mail acpbooks@ghana.com; f. 1964; religious, fiction, theology, children's, leadership; Gen. Man. RICHARD A. B. CRABBE.

Allgoodbooks Ltd: POB AN10416, Accra-North; tel. (30) 2664294; fax (30) 2665629; e-mail allgoodbooks@hotmail.com; f. 1968; children's; Man. Dir MARY ASIRIFI.

Asempa Publishers: POB GP919, Accra; tel. (30) 2233084; fax (30) 2235140; e-mail asempa@ghana.com; f. 1970; religion, social issues, African music, fiction, children's; Gen. Man. SARAH O. APRONTI.

Catholic Book Centre: North Liberia Rd, POB 3285, Accra; tel. (30) 2226651; fax (30) 2237727.

Educational Press and Manufacturers Ltd: POB 9184, Airport-Accra; tel. (30) 2220395; f. 1975; textbooks, children's; Man. G. K. KODUA.

Encyclopaedia Africana Project: POB 2797, Accra; tel. (30) 2776939; fax (30) 2779228; e-mail eap@africaonline.com.gh; internet encyclopaediaafricana.org; f. 1962; reference; Dir GRACE BANSA.

Frank Publishing Ltd: POB MB414, Accra; tel. (30) 2240711; f. 1976; secondary school textbooks; Man. Dir FRANCIS K. DZOKOTO.

Ghana Publishing Co Ltd (Assembly Press): POB 124, Accra; tel. (30) 2664338; fax (30) 2664330; e-mail info@ghanapublishingcompany.com; internet www.ghanapublishingcompany.com; f. 1965; state-owned; textbooks and general fiction and non-fiction; Chair. Rev. HELENA OPOKU-SARKODIE; Man. Dir DAVID K. DZREKE (acting).

Ghana Universities Press: POB GP4219, Accra; tel. (30) 2513401; fax (30) 2513402; f. 1962; scholarly, academic and general and textbooks; CEO Dr K. M. GANU.

Sam-Woode Ltd: A.979/15 Dansoman High St, POB 12719, Accra-North; tel. (30) 2305287; fax (30) 2310482; e-mail samwoode@ghana.com; internet samwoode.com; f. 1984; educational and children's; Chair. KWESI SAM-WOODE.

Sedco Publishing Ltd: Sedco House, 5 Tabon St, North Ridge, POB 2051, Accra; tel. (30) 2221332; fax (30) 2220107; e-mail info@sedcopublishing.com; internet www.sedcopublishing.com; f. 1975; educational; Chair. COURAGE K. SEGBAWU; Man. Dir FRANK SEGBAWU.

Sub-Saharan Publishers: PO Box 358, Legon, Accra; tel. and fax (30) 2233371; e-mail sub-saharan@ighmail.com; Man. Dir AKOSS OFORI-MENSAH.

Unimax Macmillan Ltd: 42 Ring Rd South Industrial Area, POB 10722, Accra-North; tel. (30) 2227443; fax (30) 2225215; e-mail info@unimacmillan.com; internet www.unimacmillan.com; representative of Macmillan UK; atlases, educational and children's; Man. Dir EDWARD ADDO.

Waterville Publishing House: 101 Miamona Cl., South Industrial Area, POB 195, Accra; tel. (30) 2689973; fax (30) 2689974; e-mail e.amoh@a-riiscompany; internet a-riiscompany.com; f. 1963; general fiction and non-fiction, textbooks, paperbacks, Africana; Man. Dir EMMANUEL AMOH.

Woeli Publishing Services: POB NT601, Accra New Town; tel. and fax (30) 2229294; e-mail woelipublishing@yahoo.co.uk; f. 1984; children's, fiction, academic; Dir W. A. DEKUTSEY.

PUBLISHERS' ASSOCIATIONS

Ghana Book Development Council: POB M430, Accra; tel. (30) 2229178; f. 1975; govt-financed agency; promotes and co-ordinates writing, production and distribution of books; Exec. Dir D. A. NIMAKO.

Ghana Book Publishers' Association (GBPA): POB LT471, Laterbiokorshie, Accra; tel. (30) 2912764; fax (30) 2810641; e-mail ghanabookpubs@yahoo.co.uk; internet www.ghanabookpublishers.org; f. 1976; Pres. ASARE KONADU YAMOAH.

Private Newspaper Publishers' Association of Ghana (PRINPAG): POB 125, Darkuman, Accra; Exec. Sec. KENTEMAN NII LARYEA SOWAH.

Broadcasting and Communications

TELECOMMUNICATIONS

In 2011 there were five companies operating in the telecommunications sector in Ghana. Airtel Ghana and Vodafone Ghana provided both mobile cellular and fixed line telephone services, whereas the three other operators provided solely mobile cellular telephone services. In that year there were 284,721 subscribers to fixed line services and 21.2m. subscribers to mobile services.

Regulatory Authority

National Communication Authority (NCA): 1 Rangoon Close, POB 1568, Cantonments, Accra; tel. (30) 2776621; fax (30) 2763449; e-mail info@nca.org.gh; internet www.nca.org.gh; f. 1996; regulatory body; Chair. KOFI TOTOBI QUAKYI; Dir-Gen. PAAROCK ASSUMAN VANPERCY.

Major Telecommunications Companies

Airtel Ghana: PMB, Accra; e-mail customercare.gh@gh.airtel.com; internet www.gh.zain.com; f. 2008; name changed as above in 2010; provides both mobile cellular and fixed line telephone services; Man. PHILIP SOWAH; 2.63m. subscribers (Dec. 2011).

Expresso Telecoms Ghana: POB 10208, Accra; tel. 28282100 (mobile); fax 28210103 (mobile); internet www.expressotelecom.com; frmly Kasapa Telecom Ltd; present name adopted 2010; owned by Expresso Telecom Group (UAE); Man. Dir EL AMIR AHMED EL AMIR YOUSIF; 186,751 subscribers (Dec. 2011).

Millicom Ghana Ltd: Millicom Place, Barnes Rd, PMB 100, Accra; tel. 277551000 (mobile); fax 277503999 (mobile); e-mail info@tigo.com.gh; internet www.tigo.com.gh; f. 1990; mobile cellular telephone services through the network Tigo; Man. Dir CARLOS CACERES; 3.92m. subscribers (Dec. 2011).

MTN Ghana: Auto Parts Bldg, 41A Graphic Rd, South Industrial Area, POB 281, International Trade Fair Lane, Accra; tel. 244300000 (mobile); fax (30) 2231974; e-mail customercare@mtn.com.gh; internet www.mtn.com.gh; f. 1994; Ghana's largest mobile cellular telephone provider, through the network MTN (formerly Areeba); 100% owned by MTN (South Africa); CEO MICHAEL IKPOKI; 10.15m. subscribers (Dec. 2011).

Vodafone Ghana: Telecom House, nr Kwame Nkrumah Circle, PMB 221, Accra-North; tel. (30) 2200200; fax (30) 2221002; e-mail info.gh@vodafone.com; internet www.vodafone.com.gh; f. 1995; name changed as above in 2008, following acquisition of 70% shares in Ghana Telecommunications Company (GT) by Vodafone Group PLC (United Kingdom), 30% govt-owned; operates mobile cellular, fixed line networks and data services; Chair. KOBINA QUANSAH; CEO KYLE WHITEHALL; 4.55m. subscribers (Dec. 2011).

BROADCASTING

There are internal radio broadcasts in English, Akan, Dagbani, Ewe, Ga, Hausa and Nzema, and an external service in English and French. There are three transmitting stations, with a number of relay stations. The Ghana Broadcasting Corporation operates two national networks, Radio 1 and Radio 2, which broadcast from Accra, and four regional FM stations. In January 2010 the Minister for Communications announced that the Government intended to switch off the analogue television signal in all regional capitals by the end of 2012 and that digital broadcasting would commence earlier in that year.

Ghana Broadcasting Corpn (GBC): Broadcasting House, Ring Rd Central, Kanda, POB 1633, Accra; tel. and fax (30) 2227779; e-mail radioghana@yahoo.com; internet www.gbcghana.com; f. 1935; Dir-Gen. BERIFI AFARI APENTENG; Dir of TV CHARLES KOFI BUCKNOR; Dir of Radio YAW OWUSU ADDO.

CitiFM: 11 Tettey Loop, Adabraka, Accra; tel. (30) 2226171; fax (30) 2224043; e-mail info@citifmonline.com; internet www.citifmonline.com; f. 2004; Man. Dir SAMUEL ATTA MENSAH.

Joy FM: 355 Faanofa St, Kokomlemle, POB 17202, Accra; tel. (30) 2701199; fax (30) 2224405; e-mail info@myjoyonline.com; internet www.myjoyonline.com; f. 1995; news, information and music broadcasts; Dir KWESI TWUM.

Metro TV: POB C1609, Cantonments, Accra; tel. (30) 2765701; fax (30) 2765703; e-mail admin@metroworld.tv; internet www.metrotv.com.gh; Chair. KWADWO DABO FRIMPONG; CEO TALAL FATTAL.

Radio Ada: POB KA9482, Accra; tel. (30) 2500907; fax (30) 2516442; e-mail radioada@kalssinn.net; f. 1998; community broadcasts in Dangme; Dirs ALEX QUARMYNE, WILNA QUARMYNE.

Radio Gold FM: POB 17298, Accra; tel. (30) 3300281; fax (30) 3300284; e-mail radiogold@ucomgh.com; internet www.myradiogoldlive.com; Man. Dir BAFFOE BONNIE.

Sky Broadcasting Co Ltd: 45 Water Rd, Kanda Overpass, North Ridge, POB CT3850, Cantonments, Accra; tel. (30) 2225716; fax (30) 2221983; e-mail vayiku@yahoo.com; internet www.spirit.fm; f. 2000; Gen. Man. STEVE ESHUN.

TV3: 12th Rd, Kanda (opposite French embassy), Accra; tel. (30) 2763458; fax (30) 2763450; e-mail info@tv3.com.gh; internet www.tv3.com.gh; f. 1997; private television station; progamming in English and local languages; CEO SANTOKH SINGH.

Vibe FM: Pyramid House, 3rd Floor, Ring Rd Central, Accra; internet www.vibefm.com.gh; educational; CEO MIKE COOKE.

Finance

(cap. = capital; res = reserves; dep. = deposits; m. = million; br(s). = branch(es); amounts in new cedis, unless otherwise indicated)

BANKING

The commercial banking sector comprised 26 commercial banks, three development banks, five merchant banks and five foreign banks in 2008. There were also 134 rural and community banks and 44 non-banking financial institutions.

Central Bank

Bank of Ghana: 1 Thorpe Rd, POB 2674, Accra; tel. (30) 2666902; fax (30) 2662996; e-mail bogsecretary@bog.gov.gh; internet www.bog.gov.gh; f. 1957; bank of issue; cap. 10.0m., res 741.1m., dep. 3,685.9m. (Dec. 2009); Gov. KWESI BEKOE AMISSAH-ARTHUR.

Commercial Banks

Amalgamated Bank Ltd: 131–3 Farrar Ave, Cantonments, POB CT1541, Accra; tel. (30) 2249690; fax (30) 2249697; e-mail enquiries@amalbank.com.gh; internet www.amalbank.com.gh; f. 1997; cap. 7.2m., res 19.6m., dep. 300.9m. (Dec. 2009); Chair. STEPHAN ATA; Man. Dir MENSON TORKORNOO.

Fidelity Bank: Ridge Towers, PMB 43, Cantonments, Accra; tel. (30) 2214490; fax (30) 2678868; e-mail info@myfidelitybank.net; internet www.fidelitybank.com.gh; f. 2006; cap. 25.9m., res 4.9m., dep. 315.1m. (Dec. 2009); Chair. WILLIAM PANFORD BRAY; CEO and Man. Dir EDWARD EFFAH; 8 brs.

Ghana Commercial Bank Ltd: Thorpe Rd, POB 134, Accra; tel. (30) 2664914; fax (30) 2662168; e-mail gcbmail@gcb.com.gh; internet www.gcb.com.gh; f. 1953; 21.4% state-owned; cap. 72.0m., res 80.3m., dep. 1,259.4m. (Dec. 2009); Chair. PRYCE KOJO THOMPSON; Man. Dir SIMON DORNOO; 136 brs.

NTHC Ltd: Martco House, Okai Mensah Link, off Kwame Nkrumah Ave, POB 9563, Adabraka, Accra; tel. (30) 2238492; fax (30) 2229975; e-mail nthc@ghana.com; internet www.nthcghana.com; fmrly National Trust Holding Co Ltd; f. 1976 to provide stockbrokerage services, asset management and financial advisory services; cap. 9,000m. (2001); Chair. KWADWO OWUSU-TWENEBOA; Man. Dir Dr A. W. Q. BARNOR.

Prudential Bank Ltd: 8 Nima Ave, Ring Rd Central, PMB GPO, Accra; tel. (30) 2781201; fax (30) 2781210; e-mail headoffice@prudentialbank.com.gh; internet www.prudentialbank.com.gh; f. 1996; Exec. Chair. JOHN SACKAH ADDO; Man. Dir STEPHEN SEKYERE ABANKWA; 16 brs.

The Trust Bank Ltd: Re-insurance House, 68 Kwame Nkrumah Ave, POB 1862, Accra; tel. (30) 2240049; fax (30) 2240059; e-mail trust@ttbgh.com; internet www.thetrustbank.com.gh; f. 1996; 35% owned by Banque Belgolaise (Belgium), 33% owned by the Social Security and National Insurance Trust; cap. 25.0m., res 13.8m., dep.

223.1m. (Dec. 2009); Chair. ALBERT D. OSEI; Man. Dir LAWRENCE YIRENKYI-BOAFO; 6 brs.

uniBank (Ghana) Ltd: Royal Castle Rd, POB AN15367, Kokomlemle, Accra; tel. (30) 2233328; fax (30) 2253695; e-mail info@unibankghana.com; internet www.unibankghana.com; f. 2001; total assets 69.2m. (Dec. 2007); Chair. OPOKU-GYAMFI BOATENG; Man. Dir AMMISHADDAI ADU OWUSU-AMOAH.

Development Banks

Agricultural Development Bank (ADB): ADB House, 37 Independence Ave, POB 4191, Accra; tel. (30) 2770403; fax (30) 2784893; e-mail info@agricbank.com; internet www.agricbank.com; f. 1965; 51.8% state-owned, 48.2% owned by Bank of Ghana; credit facilities for farmers and commercial banking; cap. and res 390,064.5m., dep. 968,713.0m. (Dec. 2002); Chair. Alhaji IBRAHIM ADAM; Man. Dir STEPHEN KPORDZIH; 50 brs.

National Investment Bank Ltd (NIB): 37 Kwame Nkrumah Ave, POB 3726, Accra; tel. (30) 2661701; fax (30) 2661730; e-mail info@nib-ghana.com; internet www.nib-ghana.com; f. 1963; 86.4% state-owned; provides long-term investment capital, jt venture promotion, consortium finance man. and commercial banking services; cap. 70.0m., res –9.6m., dep. 336.7m. (Dec. 2009); Chair. EMMANUEL ABLO; Man. Dir Dr P. A. KURANCHIE; 27 brs.

Merchant Banks

CAL Bank Ltd: 23 Independence Ave, POB 14596, Accra; tel. (30) 2680068; fax (30) 2680081; e-mail info@calbank.net; internet www.calbank.net; f. 1990; cap. 25.0m., res 32.0m., dep. 276.9m. (Dec. 2009); Chair. PAAROCK VANPERCY; Man. Dir FRANK BRAKO ADU, Jr.

Databank: 61 Barnes Rd, Adabraka, PMB, Ministries Post Office, Accra; tel. (30) 2610610; fax (30) 2681443; e-mail info@databankgroup.com; internet www.databankgroup.com; f. 1990; Exec. Chair. KEN OFORI-ATTA; Exec. Dir R. YOFI GRANT; 3 brs.

Ecobank Ghana Ltd (EBG): 19 7th Ave, Ridge West, POB 16746, Accra; tel. (30) 2681166; fax (30) 2680428; e-mail ecobankgh@ecobank.com; internet www.ecobank.com; f. 1989; 92.2% owned by Ecobank Transnational Inc (Togo, operating under the auspices of the Economic Community of West African States); cap. 100.0m., res 106.9m., dep. 1,012.2m. (Dec. 2009); Chair. LIONEL VAN LARE DOSOO; Man. Dir SAMUEL ASHITEY ADJEI; 7 brs.

First Atlantic Merchant Bank Ltd: Atlantic Pl., 1 Seventh Ave, Ridge West, POB C1620, Cantonments, Accra; tel. (30) 2682203; fax (30) 2479245; e-mail info@firstatlanticbank.com.gh; internet www.firstatlanticbank.com.gh; f. 1994; cap. 7.0m., res 9.2m., dep. 261.2m. (Dec. 2009); Chair. PHILIP OWUSU; Man. Dir JUDE ARTHUR.

Merchant Bank (Ghana) Ltd: Merban House, 44 Kwame Nkrumah Ave, POB 401, Accra; tel. (30) 2666331; fax (30) 2667305; e-mail info@merchantbank.com.gh; internet www.merchantbank.com.gh; f. 1972; cap. 25.0m., res 23.3m., dep. 611.6m. (Dec. 2009); Chair. MARIAN ROSAMOND BARNOR; Man. Dir JOSEPH TETTEH (acting); 15 brs.

Foreign Banks

Barclays Bank of Ghana Ltd (UK): Barclays House, High St, POB 2949, Accra; tel. (30) 2664901; fax (30) 2669254; e-mail barclays.ghana@barclays.com; internet www.barclays.com/africa/ghana; f. 1971; 90% owned by Barclays Bank Plc; 10% owned by Govt of Ghana; total assets 1,196m. (Dec. 2007); Man. Dir BENJAMIN DABRAH; 62 brs.

Guaranty Trust Bank (Ghana) Ltd: 25A Castle Rd, Ambassadorial Area Ridge, PMB CT416, Accra; tel. (30) 2676474; fax (30) 2662727; e-mail gh.corporateaffairs@gtbank.com; internet www.gtbghana.com; f. 2004; 70% owned by Guaranty Trust Bank Plc, 15% owned by Netherlands Development Finance Co (FMO), 15% owned by Alhaji Yusif Ibrahim; Man. Dir. DOLAPO OGUNDIMU.

International Commercial Bank (Ghana) Ltd (Taiwan): Meridian House, Ring Rd Central, PMB 16, Accra; tel. (30) 2236136; fax (30) 2238228; e-mail icb@icbank-gh.com; internet www.icbank-gh.com; f. 1996; cap. and res 31,205m., total assets 218,318m. (Dec. 2003); CEO LALGUDI KRISHNAMURTHY GANAPATHIRAMAN; 11 brs.

SG-SSB Bank Ltd: Ring Rd Central, POB 13119, Accra; tel. (30) 2202001; fax (30) 2248920; internet www.sg-ssb.com.gh; f. 1976 as Social Security Bank; 51.0% owned by Société Générale, France; cap. 62.3m., res 28.4m., dep. 420.9m. (Dec. 2009); Chair. GÉRALD LACAZE; Man. Dir ALAIN BELLISSARD; 37 brs.

Stanbic Bank Ghana: Valco Trust House, Castle Rd Ridge, POB CT2344, Cantonments, Accra; tel. (30) 2687670; fax (30) 2687669; e-mail stanbicghana@stanbic.com.gh; internet www.stanbic.com.gh; f. 1999; subsidiary of the Standard Bank of South Africa Ltd; cap. and res 14,981m., total assets 97,253m. (Dec. 2001); Chair. DENNIS W. KENNEDY; Man. Dir ANDANI ALHASSAN; 2 brs.

Standard Chartered Bank Ghana Ltd (UK): High St, POB 768, Accra; tel. (30) 2664591; fax (30) 2667751; internet www.standardchartered.com/gh; f. 1896 as Bank of British West Africa; cap. 61.1m., res 41.1m., dep. 844.5m. (Dec. 2009); Chair. PETER SULLIVAN; Country CEO KWEKU BEDU ADDO; 19 brs.

Zenith Bank Ghana (Nigeria): Premier Towers, Liberia Rd, PMB CT393, Accra; tel. (30) 2660075; fax (30) 2660087; e-mail info@zenithbank.com.gh; internet www.zenithbank.com; Chair. MARY CHINERY-HESSE; CEO DANIEL ASIEDU.

Banking Association

Ghana Association of Bankers (GAB): Accra; tel. (30) 2670629; internet ghanaassociationofbankers.com; f. 1980; CEO DANIEL ATO KWAMINA MENSAH.

STOCK EXCHANGE

Ghana Stock Exchange (GSE): Cedi House, 5th Floor, Liberia Rd, POB 1849, Accra; tel. (30) 2669908; fax (30) 2669913; e-mail info@gse.com.gh; internet www.gse.com.gh; f. 1990; 35 listed cos in early 2009; Chair. NORBERT KUDJAWU; Man. Dir KOFI YAMOAH.

INSURANCE

In 2004 there were 19 insurance companies.

Donewell Insurance Co Ltd: Fihankra House, POB 2136, Osu, Accra; tel. (30) 2760483; fax (30) 2760484; e-mail info@donewellinsurance.com; internet www.donewellinsurance.com; f. 1992; Chair. JOHN S. ADDO; Man. Dir PERRY ATAWORA ADAMBA.

Enterprise Insurance Co Ltd: Enterprise House, 11 High St, POB GP50, Accra; tel. (30) 2666847; fax (30) 2666186; e-mail enquiries@eicghana.com; internet www.eicghana.net; f. 1972; Chair. TREVOR TREFGARNE; Man. Dir GEORGE OTOO.

Ghana Union Assurance Co Ltd: F828/1 Ring Rd East, POB 1322, Accra; tel. (30) 2780627; fax (30) 2780647; e-mail gua@ghanaunionassurancecompany.com; f. 1973; insurance underwriting; Man. Dir NANA AGYEI DUKU.

Metropolitan Insurance Co Ltd: Caledonian House, Kojo Thompson Rd, POB GP20084, Accra; tel. (30) 2220966; fax (30) 2237872; e-mail met@metinsurance.com; internet www.metinsurance.com; f. 1991; Chair. SAM E. JONAH; CEO KWAME-GAZO AGBENYADZIE.

SIC Insurance Co Ltd: 28/29 Ring Road East, Osu, POB 2363, Accra; tel. (30) 2780600; fax (30) 2662205; e-mail sicinfo@sic-gh.com; internet www.sic-gh.com; f. 1962; 60% state-owned; all classes of insurance; Chair. MAX COBBINA; Man. Dir BENJAMIN K. ACOLATSE.

Social Security and National Insurance Trust (SSNIT): Pension House, POB MB 149, Accra; tel. (30) 266773; fax (30) 2686373; e-mail public@ssnit.org.gh; internet www.ssnit.org.gh; f. 1972; covers over 974,666 contributors (Feb. 2012); Dir-Gen. FRANK ODOOM.

Starlife Assurance Co Ltd: C653/3 5th Cres., Asylum Down, Accra; tel. (30) 2258946; fax (30) 2258947; e-mail info@starlifegh.com; internet www.starlifegh.com; f. 2005; CEO Dr KWABENA DUFFUOR; Man. Dir FRANK OPPONG YEBOAH.

Vanguard Assurance Co Ltd: 21 Independence Ave, POB 1868, Accra; tel. (30) 2666485; fax (30) 2782921; e-mail vacmails@vanguardassurance.com; internet www.vanguardassurance.com; f. 1974; foreign travel, general accident, marine, motor and life insurance; Chair. KWADWO OBUAOBISA KETEKU; CEO GIDEON AMENYEDOR; 13 brs.

Trade and Industry

GOVERNMENT AGENCIES

Divestiture Implementation Committee: F35, 5 Ring Rd East, North Labone, POB CT102, Cantonments, Accra; tel. (30) 2772049; fax (30) 2773126; e-mail info@dic.com.gh; internet www.dic.com.gh; f. 1988; Exec. Sec. BENSON POKU-ADJEI.

Environmental Protection Agency (EPA): 91 Starlets Rd, POB M326, Accra; tel. (30) 2664697; fax (30) 2662690; e-mail epaed@africaonline.com.gh; internet www.epa.gov.gh; f. 1974; Chair. EMMANUEL F. SIISI-WILSON; Exec. Dir JONATHAN A. ALLOTEY.

Export Development and Investment Fund (EDIF): Ridge Tower, 13th Floor, Ridge, POB M493, Accra; tel. (30) 2671567; fax (30) 2671573; e-mail info@edifghana.org; f. 2000; Chief Exec. AGYABENG ANTWI-AGYEI (acting); Chair. Prof. FRANCIS DODOO (acting).

Forestry Commission of Ghana (FC): 4 3rd Ave Ridge, PMB 434, Accra; tel. (30) 2401210; fax (30) 2401197; e-mail info@hq.fcghana.com; internet www.fcghana.com; CEO SAMUEL AFARI-DARTEY.

Ghana Export Promotion Authority (GEPA): Republic House, Tudu Rd, POB M146, Accra; tel. (30) 2683153; fax (30) 2677256; internet www.gepaghana.com; f. 1974; Chair. KOBINA ADE COKER; CEO AGYEMAN KWADWO OWUSU.

Ghana Free Zones Board: POB M626, Accra; tel. (30) 2780535; fax (30) 2785036; e-mail info@gfzb.com; internet www.gfzb.com; f. 1995; approves establishment of cos in export-processing zones; Exec.-Sec. KWADWO TWUM BOAFO.

Ghana Heavy Equipment Ltd (GHEL): Old Warehouse under the Bridge, Airport West, POB 1524, Accra; tel. (30) 2680118; fax (30) 2660276; e-mail info@ghelghana.com; internet ghelghana.com; fmrly subsidiary of Ghana National Trading Corpn; organizes exports, imports and production of heavy equipment; CEO YIDANA MAHAMI.

Ghana Investment Promotion Centre (GIPC): Public Services Commission Bldg, Ministries, POB M193, Accra; tel. (30) 2665125; fax (30) 2663801; e-mail info@gipcghana.com; internet www.gipc.org.gh; f. 1994; negotiates new investments, approves projects, registers foreign capital and decides extent of govt participation; Chair. Dr ISHMAIL YAMSON; CEO GEORGE ABOAGYE.

Ghana Minerals Commission (MINCOM): 12 Switchback Rd Residential Area, POB M248, Cantonments, Accra; tel. (30) 2771318; fax (30) 2773324; e-mail mincom@mc.ghanamining.org; internet www.ghanamining.org; f. 1986 to regulate and promote Ghana's mineral industry; CEO BENJAMIN NII AYI ARYEE.

Ghana National Petroleum Authority (NPA): Centurion Bldg No. 11, 5 Circular Rd, PMB CT, Accra; tel. (30) 2766196; fax (30) 2766193; e-mail info@npa.gov.gh; internet www.npa.gov.gh; f. 2005; oversees petroleum sector; Chair. KOJO FYNN; Chief Exec. ALEX MOULD.

Ghana Standards Board: POB MB245, Accra; tel. (30) 2500065; fax (30) 2500092; e-mail info@gsb.gov.gh; internet www.gsb.gov.gh; f. 1967; establishes and promulgates standards; promotes standardization, industrial efficiency and devt and industrial welfare, health and safety; operates certification mark scheme; 402 mems; Chair. WILLIAM ABOAH; Exec. Dir GEORGE BEN CRENTSIL (acting).

Ghana Trade Fair Co Ltd: Trade Fair Centre, POB 111, Accra; tel. (30) 2776611; fax (30) 2772012; e-mail gftc@ghana.com; internet www.gitf-europe.de; f. 1989; CEO EBENEZER ERASMUS OKPOTI KONEY (acting).

Ghana Trade and Investment Gateway Project (GHATIG): POB M47, Accra; tel. (30) 2663439; fax (30) 2773134; e-mail gateway1@ghana.com; promotes private investment and trade, infrastructural devt of free-trade zones and export-processing zones.

GNPA Ltd: POB 15331, Accra; tel. (30) 2228321; fax (30) 2221049; e-mail info@gnpa-ghana.com; internet www.gnpa-ghana.com; f. 1976 as Ghana National Procurement Agency; state-owned; part of Ministry of Trade and Industry; procures and markets a wide range of goods and services locally and abroad.

National Board for Small-scale Industries (NBSSI): POB M85, Accra; tel. (30) 2668641; fax (30) 2661394; e-mail nbssided@ghana.com; f. 1985; part of Ministry of Trade and Industry; promotes small and medium-scale industrial and commercial enterprises by providing credit, advisory services and training; Exec. Dir LUKMAN ABDUL-RAHIM.

DEVELOPMENT ORGANIZATIONS

Agence Française de Développement (AFD): 8th Rangoon Close, Ring Rd Central, POB 9592, Airport, Accra; tel. (30) 2778755; fax (30) 2778757; e-mail afdaccra@afd.fr; internet www.afd.fr; f. 1985; fmrly Caisse Française de Développement; Resident Man. BRUNO LECLERC.

Private Enterprise Foundation (PEF): POB CT1671, Cantonments, Accra; tel. (30) 2515603; fax (30) 2515600; e-mail info@pefghana.org; internet www.pefghana.org; f. 1994; promotes development of private sector; Pres. ASARE AKUFFO.

Social Investment Fund: Accra; tel. (21)778921; fax (21) 778404; internet sifinghana.org; f. 1998; Chair. JACOB BENJAMIN QUARTEY-PAPAFIO; Exec. Dir JOSEPH ACHEAMPONG (acting).

CHAMBER OF COMMERCE

Ghana National Chamber of Commerce and Industry (GNCCI): Adabla Plaza, 2nd Floor, 3 Oroko St, Kokomlemle, POB 2325, Accra; tel. (30) 27012780; fax (30) 2255202; e-mail info@ghanachamber.org; internet www.ghanachamber.org; f. 1961; promotes and protects industry and commerce, organizes trade fairs; 2,500 individual mems and 10 mem. chambers; Pres. SETH ADJEI BAAH; CEO EMMANUEL DONI-KWAME.

INDUSTRIAL AND TRADE ORGANIZATIONS

Federation of Associations of Ghanaian Exporters (FAGE): POB M124, Accra; tel. (30) 2766176; fax (30) 2766253; e-mail fage-ghana@gmx.net; internet www.fageplus.com; non-governmental, not-for-profit org. for exporters of non-traditional exports; over 2,500 mems.

Forestry Commission of Ghana, Timber Industry Development Division (TIDD): 4 Third Ave, Ridge, POB MB434, Accra; tel. (30) 2221315; fax (30) 2220818; e-mail info@hq.fcghana.com; internet www.ghanatimber.org; f. 1985; promotes the development of the timber industry and the sale and export of timber.

Ghana Cocoa Board (COCOBOD): Cocoa House, 41 Kwame Nkrumah Ave, POB 933, Accra; tel. (30) 2661872; fax (30) 2665893; e-mail cocobod@cocobod.gh; internet www.cocobod.gh; f. 1947; monopoly purchaser of cocoa until 1993; responsible for purchase, grading and export of cocoa, coffee and shea nuts; also encourages production and scientific research aimed at improving quality and yield of these crops; controls all exports of cocoa; subsidiaries include the Cocoa Marketing Co (Ghana) Ltd and the Cocoa Research Institute of Ghana; Chair. Dr PERCIVAL YAW KURANCHIE; CEO ANTHONY FOFEI.

Grains and Legumes Development Board: POB 4000, Kumasi; tel. (32) 2024231; fax (32) 2024778; e-mail gldb@africaonline.com.gh; f. 1970; subsidiary of Ministry of Food and Agriculture; produces, processes and stores seeds and seedlings, and manages national seed security stocks; Chair. Dr GODFRIED ADJEI DIXON; Exec. Dir Dr ROBERT AGYEIBI ASUBOAH.

EMPLOYERS' ORGANIZATION

Ghana Employers' Association (GEA): State Enterprises Commission Bldg, POB GP2616, Accra; tel. (30) 2678455; fax (30) 2678405; e-mail gea@ghanaemployers.com; internet www.ghanaemployers.com; f. 1959; 600 mems (2006); Pres. TERENCE RONALD DARKO; Vice-Pres. SAMER CHEDID.

Affiliated Bodies

Association of Ghana Industries (AGI): Addison House, 2nd Floor, Trade Fair Centre, POB AN8624, Accra-North; tel. (30) 2779023; fax (30) 2763383; e-mail agi@agighana.org; internet www.agighana.org; f. 1957; Pres. NANA OWUSU AFARI; Exec. Dir ANDREW LAWSON; c. 500 mems.

Ghana Booksellers' Association: POB 10367, Accra-North; tel. (30) 2773002; fax (30) 2773242; e-mail minerva@ghana.com; Pres. FRED J. REIMMER; Gen. Sec. ADAMS AHIMAH.

Ghana Chamber of Mines: 22 Sir Arku Korsah Rd, Airport Residential Area, POB 991, Accra; tel. (30) 2760652; fax (30) 2760653; e-mail chamber@ghanachamberofmines.org; internet www.ghanachamberofmines.org; f. 1928; Pres. DANIEL OWIREDU; CEO Dr TONI AUBYNN.

Ghana Timber Association (GTA): POB 1020, Kumasi; tel. and fax (32) 2025153; f. 1952; promotes, protects and develops timber industry; Pres. BOATENG OPOKU.

UTILITIES

Regulatory Bodies

Energy Commission (EC): FREMA House, Plot 40, Spintex Rd, PMB Ministries, Accra; tel. (30) 2813756; fax (30) 2813764; e-mail info@energycom.gov.gh; internet www.energycom.gov.gh; f. 2001; Chair. Prof. ABEEKU BREW-HAMMOND; Exec. Sec. Dr ALFRED OFOSU AHENKORAH.

Public Utilities Regulatory Commission (PURC): 51 Liberation Rd, African Liberation Circle, POB CT3095, Cantonments, Accra; tel. (30) 2244181; fax (30) 2244188; e-mail purcsec@purc.com.gh; internet www.purc.com.gh; f. 1997; Chair. EMMANUEL ANNAN.

Electricity

Electricity Co of Ghana (ECG): Electro-Volta House, POB 521, Accra; tel. (30) 2676727; fax (30) 2666262; e-mail ecgho@ghana.com; internet www.ecgonline.info; Chair. Dr KWEKU OSAFO; Man. Dir CEPHAS GAKPO.

Ghana Grid Company Ltd (GRIDCo): POB CS 7979, Tema; tel. (30) 27011185; fax (30) 2676180; e-mail gridco@gridcogh.com; internet www.gridcogh.com; f. 2006; CEO CHARLES A. DARKU.

Volta River Authority (VRA): Electro-Volta House, 28th February Rd, POB MB77, Accra; tel. (30) 2664941; fax (30) 2662610; e-mail prunit@vra.com; internet www.vra.com; f. 1961; govt owned; controls the generation and distribution of electricity; Northern Electricity Department of VRA f. 1987 to distribute electricity in northern Ghana; CEO KWEKU ANDOH AWORTWI.

Water

In mid-2006 the Volta Basin Authority (VBA) was created by Ghana, Benin, Burkina Faso, Côte d'Ivoire, Mali and Togo to manage the resources of the Volta River basin.

Ghana Water Co Ltd (GWCL): POB MB194, Accra; tel. (30) 2666781; fax (30) 2663552; e-mail info@gwcl.com.gh; internet www.gwcl.com.gh; f. 1965 to provide, distribute and conserve water supplies for public, domestic and industrial use, and to establish, operate and control sewerage systems; jointly managed by Aqua Vitens (the Netherlands) and Rand Water (South Africa); Chair. ARNOLD H. K. SESHIE; Man. Dir KWEKU BOTWE.

CO-OPERATIVES

Department of Co-operatives: POB M150, Accra; tel. (30) 2666212; fax (30) 2772789; f. 1944; govt-supervised body, responsible for registration, auditing and supervision of co-operative socs; Registrar R. BUACHIE-APHRAM.

Ghana Co-operatives Council Ltd (GACOCO): POB 4034, Accra; tel. 244267014 (mobile); fax (30) 2672014; e-mail gacopco@yahoo.com; f. 1951; co-ordinates activities of all co-operative socs and plays advocacy role for co-operative movement; comprises 11 active nat. asscns and 2 central orgs; Sec.-Gen. ALBERT AGYEMAN PREMPEH.

The national associations and central organizations include the Ghana Co-operative Marketing Asscn Ltd, the Ghana Co-operative Credit Unions Asscn Ltd, the Ghana Co-operative Distillers and Retailers Asscn Ltd, and the Ghana Co-operative Poultry Farmers Asscn Ltd.

TRADE UNIONS

Ghana Federation of Labour: POB Trade Fair 509, Accra; tel. (30) 2252105; fax (30) 2307394; e-mail gflgh@hotmail.com; Sec.-Gen. ABRAHAM KOOMSON; 10,540 mems.

Ghana National Association of Teachers (GNAT): POB 209, Accra; tel. (30) 2221576; fax (30) 2226286; e-mail info@ghanateachers.org; internet www.ghanateachers.org; f. 1931; Pres. SAMUEL ALOBUIA (acting); Gen. Sec. IRENE DUNCAN ADANUSA; 178,000 mems (2003).

Ghana Trades Union Congress (TUC): Hall of Trade Unions, Liberia Rd, POB 701, Accra; tel. (30) 2662568; fax (30) 2667161; e-mail info@ghanatuc.org; internet www.ghanatuc.org; f. 1945; 17 affiliated unions; Chair. ALEX K. BONNEY; Sec.-Gen. KOFI ASAMOAH.

General Agricultural Workers' Union (GAWU): Hall of Trade Unions, 5th Floor, Liberia Rd, POB 701, Accra; tel. (30) 2665514; fax (30) 2672468; e-mail gawughanatuc@yahoo.com; f. 1959; affiliated to the TUC; Gen. Sec. KINGSLEY OFEI-NKANSAH.

Ghana Mineworkers' Union (GMWU): Hall of Trade Unions Bldg, off Barnes and Liberia Roads, Tudu, POB 701, Accra; tel. (21) 665563; e-mail admin@gmwu.org; internet www.gmwu.org; f. 1944; Chair. JOHN KOJO BRIMPONG; Gen. Sec. PRINCE WILLIAM ANKRAH.

Teachers and Educational Workers' Union (TEWU): Hall of Trade Unions, Liberia Road, POB 701, Accra; tel. (30) 2663050; fax (30) 2671544; e-mail tewu@ghana.com; mem. of TUC; Chair. Alhaji H. I. KAMBASI; Sec.-Gen. DANIEL AYIM ANTWI.

Transport

RAILWAYS

Ghana has a railway network of 977 km, which connects Accra, Kumasi and Takoradi. In late 2004 OPEC provided a loan of US $5m. to upgrade the Accra–Tema railway. In 2006 the Government was undertaking negotiations to contract out the upgrading and operation of the rail network, and plans were underway regarding the construction of a rail link with Burkina Faso. In 2010 a concessionary loan of US $4,000m. was secured from the Export-Import Bank of China to extend the Takoradi-Kumasi railway to Paga on the border with Burkina Faso.

Ghana Railway Co Ltd (GRC): POB 251, Takoradi; f. 1901; responsible for the operation and maintenance of all railways; to be run under private concession from April 2004; 947 km of track in use in 2003; Chair Dr CLEMENT HAMMAH; Acting Man. Dir K. B. AMOFA.

Ghana Railway Development Authority (GRDA): Ministry of Transport, PMB, Accra; tel. (21) 681780; fax (21) 681781; internet grda.gov.gh; f. 2005; regulatory and devt authority; Chair. DAN MARKIN; Man. Dir EMMANUEL OPOKU.

ROADS

In 2005 Ghana had a total road network of approximately 57,614 km, of which just 15% was paved. Construction work on 36 bridges nation-wide, funded by the Japanese Government, commenced in 2003. In 2005 €11m. was pledged by the European Union for upgrading the road network in key cocoa-producing areas.

Ghana Highway Authority: POB 1641, Accra; tel. (30) 2666591; fax (30) 2665571; e-mail eokonadu@highways.mrt.gov.gh; internet www.highways.gov.gh; f. 1974 to plan, develop, administer and maintain trunk roads and related facilities; Chair. JOE GIDISU (acting); Chief Dir ANTHONY ESSILFIE (acting).

Intercity State Transport Company (STC) Coaches Ltd: POB 7384, 1 Adjuma Cres., Ring Rd West Industrial Area, Accra; tel. (30) 2221912; fax (30) 2221945; e-mail stc@ghana.com; f. 1965; fmrly State Transport Co; transferred to private sector ownership in 2000 and renamed Vanef STC; above name adopted in 2003; regional and international coach services; Man. Dir EDWARD LORD ATTIVOR.

SHIPPING

The two main ports are Tema (near Accra) and Takoradi, both of which are linked with Kumasi by rail. There are also important inland ports on the Volta, Ankobra and Tano rivers. At 31 December 2009 the merchant fleet comprised 236 vessels, totalling 116,000 grt.

Ghana Maritime Authority (GMA): E354/3 Third Ave, East Ridge, PMB 34, Ministries, Accra; tel. (30) 2662122; fax (30) 2677702; e-mail info@ghanamaritime.org; internet www.ghanamaritime.org; f. 2002; policy-making body; part of Ministry of Transport; regulates maritime industry; Dir-Gen. ISSAKA PETER AZUMA.

Ghana Ports and Harbour Authority (GPHA): POB 150, Tema; tel. (30) 3202631; fax (30) 3202812; e-mail headquarters@ghanaports.net; internet www.ghanaports.gov.gh; f. 1986; holding co for the ports of Tema and Takoradi; Dir-Gen. NESTER PERCY GALLEY.

Alpha (West Africa) Line Ltd: POB 451, Tema; operates regular cargo services to West Africa, the United Kingom, the USA, the Far East and northern Europe; shipping agents; Man. Dir AHMED EDGAR COLLINGWOOD WILLIAMS.

Liner Agencies and Trading (Ghana) Ltd: POB 214, Tema; tel. (30) 3202987; fax (30) 3202989; e-mail enquiries@liner-agencies.com; international freight services; shipping agents; Dir J. OSSEI-YAW.

Maersk Ghana Ltd: Obourwe Bldg, Torman Rd, Fishing Harbour Area, POB 8800, Community 7, Tema; tel. (30) 3218700; fax (30) 3202048; e-mail gnamkt@maersk.com; internet www.maerskline.com/ghana; f. 2001; owned by Maersk Line (Denmark); offices in Tema, Takoradi and Kumasi; Man. Dir JEFF GOSCINIAK.

Scanship (Ghana) Ltd: Mensah Utreh Rd, Commercial Warehouse Area, POB 64, Tema; tel. (30) 3202561; fax (30) 3202571; e-mail scanship.ghana@gh.dti.bollore.com; shipping agents.

Shipping Association

Ghana Shippers' Council: Enterprise House, 5th Floor, High St, POB 1321, Accra; tel. (30) 2555915; fax (30) 2668768; e-mail scouncil@shippers-gh.com; internet www.ghanashipperscouncil.org; f. 1974; represents interests of 28,000 registered Ghanaian shippers; also provides cargo-handling and allied services; Chief Exec. KOFI MBIAH.

CIVIL AVIATION

The main international airport is at Kotoka (Accra). There are also airports at Kumasi, Takoradi, Sunyani, Tamale and Wa. The construction of a dedicated freight terminal at Kotoka Airport was completed in 1994. In 2001 622,525 passengers and 44,779 metric tons of freight passed through Kotoka Airport. The rehabilitation of Kumasi Airport began in 2006, while there were also plans to construct a further international airport at Kumasi.

Ghana Civil Aviation Authority (GCAA): PMB, Kotoka International Airport, Accra; tel. (30) 2776171; fax (30) 2773293; e-mail info@gcaa.com.gh; internet www.gcaa.com.gh; f. 1986; Chair. ALBAN SUMANA BAGBIN; Dir-Gen. KWAME MAMPHEY.

Afra Airlines Ltd: 7 Nortei St, Airport Residential Area, Accra; tel. 244932488 (mobile); e-mail lukebutler@afraairlines.com; f. 2005; CEO LUKE BUTLER.

Antrak Air: 50 Senchi St, Airport Residential Area, Accra; tel. (30) 2782814; fax (30) 2782816; e-mail info@antrakair.com; internet www.antrakair.com; f. 2003; passenger and cargo services for domestic and international routes; Chair. ASOMA BANDA.

Gemini Airlines Ltd (Aero Gem Cargo): America House, POB 7238, Accra-North; tel. (30) 2771921; fax (30) 2761939; e-mail aerogemcargo@hotmail.com; f. 1974; operates weekly cargo flight between Accra and London; Gen. Man. ENOCH ANAN-TABURY.

Tourism

Ghana's attractions include fine beaches, game reserves, traditional festivals, and old trading forts and castles. In 2009 some 803,000 tourists visited Ghana; revenue from tourism totalled US $968m. in that year

Ghana Tourist Board: POB GP3106, Accra-North; tel. (30) 2222153; fax (30) 2244611; e-mail gtb@africaonline.com.gh; internet www.touringghana.com; f. 1968; Exec. Dir JULIUS DEBRAH.

Ghana Association of Tourist and Travel Agencies (GATTA): Swamp Grove, Asylum Down, POB 7140, Accra-North; tel. (30) 2222398; fax (30) 2231102; e-mail info@gattagh.com; internet www.gattagh.com; Pres. HILLARIUS MCCASH AKPAH; Exec. Sec. TINA OSEI.

Ghana Tourist Development Co Ltd: POB 8710, Accra-North; tel. (30) 2770720; fax (30) 2770694; e-mail info@ghanatouristdevelopment.com; internet www.ghanatouristdevelopment.com; f. 1974; develops tourist infrastructure, incl. hotels, restaurants and casinos; operates duty-free shops; Man. Dir ALFRED KOMLADZEI.

Defence

As assessed at November 2011, Ghana's total armed forces numbered 15,500 (army 11,500, navy 2,000 and air force 2,000). In March 2000 the Government restructured the armed forces; the army was subsequently organized into north and south commands, and the navy into western and eastern commands. In January 2004 a peacekeeping training centre, which was primarily to be used by ECOWAS, was established in Accra. In 2011 a total of 2,598 Ghanaian troops were stationed abroad, of which 25 were observers.

Defence Expenditure: Estimated at 198,000m. cedis in 2011.

Commander-in-Chief of the Armed Forces: Pres. JOHN EVANS ATTA MILLS.

Chief of Defence Staff and Commander of the Navy: Maj.-Gen. PETER AUGUSTINE BLAY.

Chief of Air Staff: Air Vice-Marshall MICHAEL SAMSON-OJE.

Chief of Army Staff: Maj.-Gen. JOSEPH NARH ADINKRAH.

Chief of Naval Staff: Rear Adm. MATTHEW QUARSHIE.

Education

Education is officially compulsory and free of charge for eight years, between the ages of six and 14. Primary education begins at the age of six and lasts for six years, comprising two cycles of three years each. Secondary education begins at the age of 12 and lasts for a further seven years, comprising a first cycle of three years and a second of four years. Following three years of junior secondary education, pupils are examined to determine admission to senior secondary school courses, or to technical and vocational courses. In 2008/09, according to UNESCO, primary enrolment included 77% of children in the relevant age-group (boys 76%; girls 77%), while the comparable ratio for secondary enrolment in that year was estimated at 47% (boys 49%; girls 45%). Some 203,400 students were enrolled in tertiary education in 2008/09. There are seven universities in Ghana. Tertiary institutions also included 38 teacher-training colleges, eight polytechnics and 61 technical colleges.

GREECE

Introductory Survey

LOCATION, CLIMATE, LANGUAGE, RELIGION, FLAG, CAPITAL

The Hellenic Republic lies in south-eastern Europe. The country consists mainly of a mountainous peninsula between the Mediterranean Sea and the Aegean Sea, bounded to the north by Albania, the former Yugoslav republic of Macedonia and Bulgaria, and to the east by Turkey. To the south, east and west of the mainland lie numerous Greek islands, of which the largest is Crete. The climate is Mediterranean, with mild winters and hot summers. The average temperature in the capital is 28°C (82°F) in July and 9°C (48°F) in January. The language is Greek, of which there are two forms—the formal language (katharevoussa) and the language commonly spoken and taught in schools (demotiki). Almost all of the inhabitants profess Christianity, and the Greek Orthodox Church, to which about 97% of the population adhere, is the established religion. The national flag (proportions 2 by 3) displays nine equal horizontal stripes of blue and white, with a white cross throughout a square canton of blue at the upper hoist. The capital is Athens (Athinai).

CONTEMPORARY POLITICAL HISTORY

Historical Context

The liberation of Greece from the German occupation (1941–44) was followed by a civil war, which lasted until 1949. The communist forces were defeated, and the constitutional monarchy re-established. King Konstantinos (Constantine) II acceded to the throne on the death of his father, King Pavlos (Paul), in 1964. A succession of weak governments and conflicts between the King and his ministers, and an alleged conspiracy involving military personnel, culminated in a coup, led by right-wing army officers, in April 1967. An attempted counter-coup, led by the King, failed, and he went into exile. Col Georgios Papadopoulos dominated the new regime, becoming Prime Minister in December 1967 and Regent in March 1972. All political activity was banned, and political opponents were expelled from all positions of influence.

Following an abortive naval mutiny, Greece was declared a republic in June 1973, and Papadopoulos was appointed President. Martial law was ended, and a civilian Government was appointed in preparation for a general election. A student uprising in Athens in November was violently suppressed by the army, and Papadopoulos was overthrown by another military coup. Lt-Gen. Phaidon Ghizikis was appointed President, and a mainly civilian Government, led by Adamantios Androutsopoulos, was installed, but effective power lay with a small group of officers and the military police under Brig.-Gen. Demetrios Ioannides. As a result of the failure of the military junta's attempt to overthrow President Makarios of Cyprus, and its inability to prevent the Turkish invasion of the island (see the chapter on Cyprus), the Androutsopoulos administration collapsed in July 1974. Ghizikis summoned from exile a former Prime Minister, Konstantinos Karamanlis, who was invited to form a civilian Government of National Salvation. Martial law was ended, the press was released from state control and political parties, including the communists, were allowed to operate freely. A general election in November resulted in victory for Karamanlis' New Democracy (ND), which won 220 of the 300 parliamentary seats. A referendum in December rejected proposals for a return to constitutional monarchy, and in June 1975 a new republican Constitution, providing for a parliamentary democracy, was promulgated. In the same month Prof. Konstantinos Tsatsos was elected President by the Vouli (Parliament).

At legislative elections in November 1977 ND was returned to power. In May 1980 Karamanlis was elected President; Georgios Rallis subsequently assumed the leadership of ND and was appointed Prime Minister. Rallis encountered considerable opposition from the increasingly popular Panhellenic Socialist Movement (PASOK). On 1 January 1981 Greece acceded to the European Community (EC, now the European Union—EU, see p. 276). PASOK secured an absolute majority at elections to the Vouli in October 1981, and the PASOK leader, Andreas Papandreou, became Prime Minister.

In March 1985 Papandreou unexpectedly withdrew support for President Karamanlis's candidature for a further five-year term. The Prime Minister planned to amend the 1975 Constitution to relieve the President of all executive power and render the Head of State's functions largely ceremonial. Karamanlis resigned in protest, and the Vouli elected Christos Sartzetakis, a judge, as President, in a vote that was widely considered to be unconstitutional. Legislative elections were held in June 1985 to enable the Government to secure support for the proposed constitutional changes. PASOK was returned to power, winning 161 seats in the 300-member Vouli. In October the Government introduced a programme of economic austerity, provoking widespread industrial unrest, which continued throughout 1986. In March 1986 the Vouli approved a series of constitutional amendments limiting the powers of the President. In May 1987, in response to ND accusations of mismanagement and corruption within the Government, Papandreou sought and won a parliamentary vote of confidence in his Government. However, in November 1988 several prominent ministers, having been implicated in a financial scandal, were forced to resign.

In January 1989 the Greek Left Party, led by Leonidas Kyrkos, formed an electoral alliance with the 'Exterior' faction of the Communist Party of Greece (KKE), under the leadership of Charilaos Florakis, to create the Coalition of the Left and Progress (the Left Coalition). At elections in June, ND won the largest proportion of the votes cast, but failed to attain an overall majority in the Vouli. The Left Coalition eventually agreed to form an interim administration with ND, on the condition that ND leader Konstantinos Mitsotakis renounced his claim to the premiership. Accordingly, Tzannis Tzannetakis, an ND deputy, was appointed Prime Minister of a Government that included two communist ministers. The conservative-communist coalition announced its intention to govern for only three months, during which time it aimed to implement a *katharsis* (campaign of purification) of Greek politics. The administration duly resigned in October, having initiated investigations into the involvement of officials of the former socialist Government, including Papandreou, in a number of scandals involving banking, armaments and financial transactions. (In 1991 Papandreou and three of his former ministers were tried on charges of complicity in large-scale embezzlement during their terms of office. In 1992 Papandreou was acquitted, and two of the former ministers received minor sentences; the third had died during the trial.) The President of the Supreme Court, Ioannis Grivas, was appointed Prime Minister of an interim Government comprising non-political figures, which was to oversee the second legislative elections of the year. The results of the elections, conducted in November 1989, were again inconclusive. In mid-November ND, PASOK and the Left Coalition agreed to form an interim coalition. However, following a dispute over military promotions in February 1990, the Government collapsed, and the former administration was reinstated to govern until the new general election. Further elections, conducted in April, resolved the impasse; ND secured 150 seats in the Vouli. Mitsotakis secured the support of Konstantinos Stefanopoulos, the leader (and the sole parliamentary representative) of the Party of Democratic Renewal, thereby enabling him to form the first single-party Government since 1981. In May 1990 Karamanlis took office as President for a five-year term, following his election by 153 of the 300 members of the Vouli. Stefanopoulos formally joined ND in June. In November reforms to the electoral law were ratified, which required political parties to obtain a minimum of 3% of the votes in elections in order to secure parliamentary representation.

Domestic Political Affairs

In August 1991 Mitsotakis effected a comprehensive reorganization of the Government. In April 1992 the Prime Minister successfully sought a vote of confidence from the Vouli, following the dismissal of the Minister of Foreign Affairs, Antonis Samaras, and Mitsotakis's assumption of the portfolio in order to address attempts by the former Yugoslav republic of Macedonia (FYRM—q.v.) to achieve international recognition as the Republic of Macedonia (see below). In August Michalis Papakonstantinou, a defender of national territorial integrity, was allocated the foreign affairs portfolio. Industrial unrest continued throughout 1992 and 1993, in protest against government austerity measures.

In September 1993 two ND deputies resigned, following an appeal for support by Political Spring (POLAN), a centre-right party that had been established in July by Samaras. The consequent loss of Mitsotakis's one-seat majority in the Vouli obliged him to offer the Government's resignation and schedule early legislative elections. At the elections, conducted in October, PASOK obtained 46.9% of the total votes cast and 170 of the 300 parliamentary seats, while ND received 39.3% of the votes and 111 seats, and POLAN 4.9% of the votes and 10 seats. In October Mitsotakis resigned as leader of ND. In June 1994 Papandreou undertook a government reorganization.

In March 1995 Stefanopoulos was elected President by 181 of the 300 members of the Vouli. From mid-1995 tensions within the governing PASOK became increasingly evident. Konstantinos Simitis, together with Theodoros Pangalos, Vasiliki Papandreou and Paraskevas Avgerinos, constituted a group of 'dissident' PASOK deputies (referred to as the Group of Four) who urged the resignation of Andreas Papandreou, and the implementation of further reforms within the party. In November the Prime Minister was admitted to hospital; Apostolos-Athanassios (Akis) Tsohatzopoulos assumed Papandreou's prime ministerial duties, in an acting capacity. On 15 January Papandreou submitted his resignation as Prime Minister. Three days later, Simitis was elected to the premiership by the PASOK parliamentary faction. Simitis awarded Pangalos the foreign affairs portfolio, while pro-European ministers, who supported Simitis's desire for economic reform, replaced the majority of Papandreou's former associates.

Almost immediately, Simitis was confronted by a sharp escalation in hostilities with Turkey (see below). Following his acceptance of a US-mediated compromise to defuse the situation, Simitis was condemned by all opposition parties. In February 1996 he dismissed the Chief of the General Staff of the armed forces. Following Papandreou's death in June, Simitis was elected leader of PASOK, defeating Tsohatzopoulos. In early legislative elections, held on 22 September, PASOK won 162 of the 300 parliamentary seats, with 41.5% of the votes cast, while ND obtained 108 seats (38.2%); POLAN failed to obtain parliamentary representation. Principal ministers in the outgoing Government were retained in the new PASOK administration. Despite a general strike in November 1996, Simitis continued to implement austerity policies in accordance with his commitment to meeting the 'convergence' criteria of the EU's economic and monetary union (EMU). In March 1997 Konstantinos (Kostas) Karamanlis (a nephew of the former President and ND party leader) was elected leader of ND.

In February 1999 it emerged that Abdullah Öcalan, the leader of the proscribed Kurdistan Workers' Party (PKK), accused by Turkey of a number of charges of terrorism, had been given refuge at the Greek embassy in Kenya, before being captured by the Turkish authorities. The Ministers of the Interior, Public Administration and Decentralization, of Foreign Affairs, and of Public Order subsequently resigned, prompting a government reorganization. Vasiliki Papandreou was appointed Minister of the Interior, Public Administration and Decentralization, and Georgios Papandreou (the son of the late Andreas Papandreou) replaced Pangalos as Minister of Foreign Affairs.

In early February 2000 Simitis announced that early legislative elections were to be held on 9 April. On 9 February Stefanopoulos was re-elected President by 269 of the 300 members of the Vouli. At the legislative elections PASOK was returned to office, winning 43.8% of the votes cast and 158 parliamentary seats, narrowly defeating ND, with 42.7% of the votes and 125 seats. On 12 April Simitis formed a new Government. In April 2001 government plans to raise the retirement age and reform the pension system precipitated public protests, including a general strike. In October Simitis reorganized the Government, following his re-election as PASOK party leader.

In January 2004 Simitis announced his resignation from the leadership of PASOK, and scheduled early legislative elections for 7 March, asserting that an administration with a new mandate was necessary to address developments on the issue of Cyprus (see below). On 8 February Georgios Papandreou was elected unopposed as the President of PASOK.

The 2004 elections: ND Government

At the legislative elections held on 7 March 2004, ND secured 45.4% of the votes cast, thereby removing PASOK, which won 40.6% of the votes, from government. A new administration, headed by Karamanlis, was installed on 10 March. Although there were reports that many construction projects greatly exceeded cost projections, Greece's hosting of the summer Olympic Games in August was widely considered to be a success for the Government. However, in November the Government publicly conceded that the PASOK administration had significantly understated public debt and budgetary deficit figures for several years in order for Greece to qualify for membership of EMU in January 2001, after evidence to that effect emerged; it appeared that continued misrepresentation of defence expenditure had partially caused the discrepancies. The statement provoked a dispute between the ruling ND and PASOK, which criticized the revision of past official figures. The Government subsequently pledged to restrain the budgetary deficit to within the stipulated limit by the end of 2006, in compliance with EU criteria. On 8 February 2005 Karolos Papoulias, a member of PASOK and a former Minister of Foreign Affairs, was elected unopposed as President, receiving 279 votes in the 300-member Vouli; Papoulias was inaugurated as President on 12 March.

In early February 2006 the Government revealed that mobile cellular telephones belonging to Karamanlis, to prominent government and opposition members, and to public officials had been clandestinely monitored between June 2004 and March 2005. A judicial inquiry was subsequently announced into the illegal surveillance (thought to be linked to security concerns relating to the holding of the summer Olympic Games in 2004). Later in February 2006 Karamanlis announced an extensive reorganization of the Government, which included the appointment of Dora Bakoyannis, a member of ND, the hitherto Mayor of Athens, and the daughter of former Prime Minister Mitsotakis, as Minister of Foreign Affairs and of Evangelos Meimarakis as Minister of National Defence. Georgios Voulgarakis, who, as Minister of Public Order, had been held responsible for the controversy surrounding the illegal surveillance, was transferred to the Ministry of Culture. Local government elections took place on 15 and 22 October. ND retained control of some 30 prefectural councils and the municipalities of Athens and Thessaloníki, while PASOK increased its representation from 19 to 22 councils and gained control of the port towns of Piraeus and Patras. In December, following an independent inquiry, the mobile cellular telecommunications operator Vodafone Greece was ordered to pay €76m., after being held responsible for the clandestine surveillance and for obstructing the subsequent investigations.

In early 2007 mass protests were organized by students and education sector staff, in opposition to proposals to allow the establishment of private universities from 2008. The proposed reforms, which were supported by PASOK but opposed by other opposition parties, required an amendment to the national Constitution. In February 2007 PASOK withdrew from a parliamentary committee session during the constitutional debate, after accusing the Government of pressurizing ND dissenters to support reforms, and demanded the organization of early elections.

On 25 August 2007 Karamanlis declared a state of emergency after fires, exacerbated by drought conditions, resulted in the deaths of some 65 people. More than 30 suspects were subsequently detained, and seven were charged. In late August an estimated 10,000 people held a protest in Athens at the Government's response to the emergency; it was alleged that poor control of forests had prompted arsonists to take action to clear land for unauthorized building, while opposition leaders accused the authorities of failing to organize effective efforts to combat the fires. At legislative elections conducted on 16 September ND was returned to power, securing 41.8% of the votes cast and 152 seats in the Vouli. PASOK, with 38.1% of the votes, won a reduced number of seats (102), followed by the KKE (with 8.2% of votes and 22 seats) and the Coalition of the Radical Left (5.0% of votes and 14 seats); an extreme nationalist organization, Popular Orthodox Rally (LAOS), received 3.8% of the votes and 10 seats, obtaining parliamentary representation for the first time. The rate of participation by the electorate was some 74.1%. Karamanlis subsequently established a smaller administration; following the criticism of the Government's management of the fires, the Ministry of Public Order was merged into the Ministry of the Interior.

PASOK's return to power

The international financial crisis from late 2008 exacerbated economic hardship and public discontent, and there were widespread skirmishes between police and disaffected youths. On 6 December a 15-year-old student was shot and killed in Exarchia, an impoverished district of Athens. Two police officers were charged in connection with the killing, which precipitated rioting in Athens, Thessaloníki and other towns. Students occupied some 15 universities and 100 high schools in Athens and Thessaloníki, benefiting from a constitutional provision that prohibited police from entering the grounds of certain educational establishments. A one-day national strike by public sector unions in protest against the Government's economic policies proceeded on 10 December, and developed into more general protests against further austerity measures planned by the Government. In early January 2009 a protest, organized mainly by students and teachers against the education reforms, police repression and the social system, was violently suppressed by police; some 60 people were arrested.

In January 2009 Karamanlis announced an extensive ministerial reorganization, in an effort to restore public confidence in the Government; Pavlopoulos, Bakoyannis and Meimarakis retained their posts, while new appointments included that of Ioannis Papathanasiou as Minister of the Economy and Finance. At elections to the European Parliament on 7 June, PASOK secured 36.7% of the votes cast and eight seats, ND obtained 32.3% of the votes and eight seats, the KKE 8.4% and two seats, and LAOS 7.2% and two seats; 52.6% of the registered electorate participated in the elections. On 2 September Karamanlis requested the dissolution of the Vouli, and announced that the legislative elections (due in September 2011) would be brought forward to October 2009. The Vouli was officially dissolved on 9 September.

In the legislative elections held on 4 October 2009 PASOK secured victory, with 43.9% of the votes cast and 160 seats, while ND received 33.5% of the votes and 91 seats; the KKE received 7.5% and 21 seats, LAOS 5.6% and 15 seats, and the Coalition of the Radical Left 4.6% and 13 seats. The rate of participation was recorded at 70.9% of the registered electorate. In response to the party's defeat, Karamanlis resigned as President of ND; he was succeeded, in November, by Samaras, who had rejoined the party in 2004. President of PASOK Georgios Papandreou appointed a new Government on 7 October 2009; Papandreou assumed the foreign affairs portfolio, in addition to the premiership, while former Minister of Foreign Affairs Theodoros Pangalos received the new position of Deputy Chairman of the Government, responsible for Co-ordination of the Foreign Policy and Defence Committee and the Economic and Social Policy Committee. The new administration, which also included two new ministries, of the Environment, Energy and Climate Change, and of Civic Protection, won a motion of confidence in the Vouli on 19 October. Later that month the Minister of Civic Protection announced that, under an extensive review of immigration policies, some 20,000 children of migrants who had themselves been born and resided in Greece without having been officially recognized as Greek nationals would be granted Greek citizenship. In December anti-Government demonstrations on the anniversary of the killing of the student in the previous year resulted in violence in central Athens and Thessaloníki; more than 150 people were arrested. Later in December the adoption of an austerity budget by the Vouli prompted further public protests and days of national strike; these intensified from late February 2010. A new programme of spending reductions and tax increases (which was opposed by ND) was adopted by the Vouli on 5 March; a large protest by trade union members in central Athens was disrupted by members of extremist groups, resulting in violent clashes.

Meanwhile, on 3 February 2010 President Papoulias was elected, again unopposed, by the Vouli for a further term of office, obtaining the support of 266 deputies. On 2 May the EU, the IMF and the European Central Bank (ECB) reached agreement with Greece on an austerity programme intended to stabilize the Greek economy, which was adopted by the Vouli four days later. (Three PASOK deputies who had opposed the motion were subsequently expelled from the party, thereby reducing its representation in the legislature to 157 seats.) Meanwhile, on 5 May, when a national strike was scheduled, a large-scale demonstration in Athens against the planned measures escalated into violence, and protesters attempted to occupy the parliamentary building; three people died in a fire at a bank that had been attacked. Papandreou condemned the violence.

In June 2010 trade unions organized a one-day strike against austerity measures (which included further extensive changes to the pension system and labour legislation), and a large-scale demonstration took place in Athens. Nevertheless, on 8 July (when a further one-day strike was held) the pension reforms were adopted, with the support of 159 votes in the Vouli. A subsequent strike by truck drivers from late July, in protest at government plans to issue cheaper truck licences, resulted in nation-wide fuel shortages and the suspension of transport services, including international flights. The strike action was suspended on 1 August, after protesters agreed to enter into dialogue with the Government.

On 7 September 2010 Prime Minister Papandreou implemented an extensive government reorganization that was intended to support efforts to combat the debt crisis. Minister of Finance Georgios Papaconstantinou was retained, but new appointments were made to other principal posts, while Papandreou's additional portfolio of foreign affairs was reallocated to Deputy Prime Minister Pangalos. In the same month truck drivers resumed strike action, as the Vouli adopted legislation liberalizing licensing regulations in the sector. Meanwhile, a police officer was sentenced to life imprisonment for the intentional killing of the student in December 2008, while his patrol partner received a custodial term of 10 years for complicity. The outcome of local elections, which were scheduled for November 2010 (prior to an extensive restructuring of the country's administrative system at the beginning of 2011), was regarded as an indication of public opinion of the Government's economic programme and Papandreou declared that he would dissolve the Vouli if the Government failed to receive sufficient support. In the event, when the elections took place on 7 and 14 November 2010, PASOK won about 34.6% of the votes cast nation-wide, narrowly defeating ND (which received 32.8% of the votes), despite registering a significant loss of support compared with the 2009 legislative elections; PASOK secured governorships in eight of the 13 regions and ND in five. (However, an exceptionally high rate of abstention was reported.)

In early December 2010 protesters clashed with police during rallies to mark the second anniversary of the death of the student killed in 2008. Public transport workers staged one-day strikes in protest at salary reductions and the planned restructuring of state-owned transport companies, and a further one-day general strike in mid-December degenerated into violent altercations between demonstrators and police. Later that month the adoption of the austerity budget for 2011 precipitated further protests in Athens. Public transport strikes continued in early 2011, despite a court order ruling the action to be illegal. Nevertheless, on 16 February the Vouli adopted legislation providing for the reform of the public transport system. On 23 February, when a national strike was organized, police dispersed violent protesters who had gathered at the parliamentary building in Athens; the Vouli approved legislation liberalizing licensing regulations in a large number of professions.

Recent developments: deepening fiscal crisis and new rescue plan

On 17 June 2011 Papandreou again reorganized the Government; notably, Georgios Papaconstantinou was removed from his position as Minister of Finance and replaced by Evangelos Venizelos, hitherto the Minister of National Defence, who also became a Deputy Chairman of the Government. Panos Beglitis was appointed as Minister of National Defence, and Stavros Lambrinidis replaced Dimitris Doutras as Minister of Foreign Affairs. At the end of June, amid a two-day national strike and violent protests outside the parliament building, the Vouli approved a programme of austerity measures, deemed necessary by the EU and the IMF in order to mitigate the deepening financial crisis and provide for the release of further emergency funds; lending was duly approved by EU Ministers of Finance in early July, temporarily alleviating the threat of default. On 21 July, at an emergency summit meeting, held in Brussels, Belgium, euro area leaders agreed the terms of a new, three-year rescue plan, totalling €159,000m., for Greece.

At the beginning of October 2011 the Government indicated that it would not satisfy budget deficit targets agreed with the EU and the IMF for 2011 and 2012, and as part of its draft 2012 budget agreed further harsh austerity measures, which, *inter alia*, threatened some 30,000 jobs in the state sector. On the following day, Ministers of Finance of the euro area, meeting in Luxembourg, agreed to postpone until November a decision on Greece's eligibility for continued funding under the EU-IMF emergency package. On 20 October, amid a further two-day national strike and a protest staged by some 100,000 people outside the parliamentary building that escalated into violent clashes, the Vouli (by 154 votes to 144) adopted the new austerity measures, thereby allowing the disbursement of rescue funds to proceed. At a summit meeting in Brussels on 26–27 October, leaders of the countries of the euro area reached a new agreement intended to reverse the escalating sovereign debt crisis. An emergency funding plan of €130,000m. for Greece was conditionally approved (since it had become evident that the programme agreed in July was no longer adequate to prevent a Greek debt default). Notably, the arrangement made provision for losses of 50% on the part of private banks holding Greek debt, with the aim of reducing Greece's liabilities to 120% of GDP by 2020.

At the end of October 2011, however, Papandreou unexpectedly announced that the new rescue plan and accompanying economic measures would require endorsement at a national referendum. Papandreou's decision precipitated a further dramatic loss of confidence in international financial markets, and euro area leaders demanded that he attend emergency discussions in Cannes, France; disbursement of funds was again suspended, pending adoption of the rescue plan. The proposed referendum also prompted criticism and demands for Papandreou's resignation from within the Government and PASOK, with one PASOK parliamentarian resigning from the party. At the beginning of November the Minister of Defence replaced the joint chiefs of the general staff, prompting concerns of an imminent military coup. Convening an emergency cabinet meeting on 3 November, Papandreou agreed to abandon the planned referendum and to enter into dialogue with ND on the creation of an interim administration. On 5 November Papandreou's Government narrowly survived a vote of confidence in the Vouli. Since ND remained unwilling to participate in a transitional government headed by Papandreou, however, he announced his resignation on the following day.

On 10 November 2011 Lucas Papademos, a former Governor of the Greek Central Bank and Vice-President of the ECB, received a mandate from President Papoulias to establish a transitional coalition administration, which was to begin to implement the measures demanded by the rescue plan. Several members of the outgoing PASOK Government remained in the cabinet, including Venizelos, who retained his position as Deputy Chairman and Minister of Finance. Stavros Dimas of ND was appointed as the new Minister of Foreign Affairs, and Dimitris Avramopoulos, also of ND, was appointed as Minister of National Defence. The Government also included Mavroudis Voridis, a member of the nationalist LAOS, as Minister of Infrastructure, Transport and Networks. Early legislative elections, initially scheduled for February 2012, were later postponed until May.

A general strike in protest at the austerity measures was organized by trade unions at the beginning of December 2011, and a protest, which resulted in clashes with police, was staged to coincide with the adoption of the 2012 budget by the Vouli on 6 December. In early 2012 the agreement of government party leaders to the implementation of spending reductions amounting to 1.5% of GDP and labour market reforms became an urgent priority in order to permit the rescue plan to proceed, and thereby avert a default on its debt by Greece. On 10 February (as a 48-hour strike began) LAOS withdrew its four representatives from the governing coalition and a PASOK deputy minister resigned, in protest against the austerity measures; however, Voridis subsequently reclaimed his cabinet post, returning to the Government as a member of ND. Following government approval, the measures were formally adopted by 199 votes to 74 in the Vouli on 12 February, while violent protests, with a number of arson attacks against shops and banks, took place in central Athens. On 21 February euro area ministers of finance formally approved the €130,000m. rescue plan, with a number of additional preconditions, including an undertaking by Greece to reduce its debt from 160% to 120.5% of GDP within eight years, and to accept a permanent EU economic monitoring mission. Amid continuing anti-austerity protests, the Vouli subsequently began to adopt reforms in accordance with EU requirements for the disbursement of funds under the plan. After agreement was reached on debt restructuring, on 9 March euro area Ministers of Finance announced that conditions had been met for the country to receive funds. In mid-March Venizelos announced his resignation as Minister of Finance, following his election as PASOK leader, in order to focus on preparing the party for the upcoming legislative elections.

Domestic extremism

Throughout the 1990s and early 2000s numerous bomb attacks against military and commercial targets (particularly those associated with the USA) in Greece were carried out by dissident groups, in particular the extremist left-wing November 17 Revolutionary Organization (active since 1975) and the Revolutionary People's Struggle (ELA). In June 2000 a British defence attaché, Brig. Stephen Saunders, was assassinated by the November 17 group. The first arrest of a member of November 17, Savvas Xiros, took place in June 2002, and the police subsequently arrested the movement's leader, Alexandros Giotopoulos, and two of Xiros's brothers, one of whom had reportedly confessed to the assassination of Saunders. Shortly afterwards the Government announced that November 17 had been disbanded. In September Dimitris Koufodinas, the second highest-ranking member of November 17, surrendered to police in Athens. By January 2003 a total of 19 suspected members of November 17 had been apprehended, and in February the police arrested four suspected members of the ELA. The trial of all 19 alleged members of November 17 was concluded in December; Giotopoulos, Koufodinas and four others were sentenced to life imprisonment, and eight defendants received lesser custodial sentences. In October five members of the ELA, including the movement's leader, were each sentenced to 25 years' imprisonment on charges relating to more than 100 bomb attacks.

Meanwhile, another extremist left-wing organization, Revolutionary Struggle (EA), which had emerged in 2003, claimed responsibility for numerous bomb attacks, including an assassination attempt against the Minister of Culture, Georgios Voulgarakis, in May 2006 and a rocket attack against the US embassy in Athens in January 2007. Following the killing of a teenager by a police officer in December 2008 (see above), public disorder also gave rise to a resurgence in extremist activity. A group believed to be affiliated to the EA, the Sect of Revolutionaries (SE), also issued a series of threats to attack police and government facilities, and in June claimed responsibility for the killing of a police officer. In September four terrorist suspects, alleged to be members of the previously unknown Conspiracy of Fire Nuclei (SPF), were arrested on charges related to a bomb attack at the residence of a former Minister of Public Order in July and against a PASOK parliamentary deputy earlier in September. In June 2010 an employee at the Ministry of Civic Protection was killed by a parcel bomb. At the beginning of November some 14 parcel bombs were posted from Greece to foreign government headquarters and embassies; a number of explosive devices were also dispatched to embassies in Athens. The SPF subsequently claimed responsibility for the parcel bombs. Following a number of arrests in a police operation in December, six suspects were formally charged with belonging to a terrorist organization and with possession of armaments and explosives. In January 2011 the trial began of 13 suspected members of the SPF (four *in absentia*) in connection with the parcel bombs and other attacks in Athens. In March a bomb exploded at the offices of the Ministry of Health and Social Solidarity.

Regional Affairs

Relations with Turkey have been characterized by long-standing disputes concerning Cyprus (q.v.) and sovereignty over the continental shelf beneath the Aegean Sea. The difficulties in relations with Turkey were exacerbated by the unilateral declaration of an 'independent' Turkish Cypriot state in Cyprus in November 1983 (the 'Turkish Republic of Northern Cyprus'—'TRNC'), together with various minor sovereignty disputes over islands in the Aegean Sea, which led to Greece's withdrawal from North Atlantic Treaty Organization (NATO, see p. 370) military exercises in August 1984 and to a boycott of manoeuvres in subsequent years. In March 1987 a disagreement between Greece and Turkey over petroleum-prospecting rights in disputed areas of the Aegean Sea almost resulted in military conflict. In January 1988, however, the Greek and Turkish Prime Ministers, meeting (in the first formal contact between Greek and Turkish Heads of Government for 10 years) in Davos, Switzerland, agreed that the two countries' premiers should meet annually in order to improve bilateral relations, and that joint committees should be established to negotiate peaceful solutions to disputes.

In 1994 the issue of the demarcation of territorial waters in the Aegean Sea re-emerged as a major source of tension. Greece's stated intention of exercising its right, enshrined in the international Convention on the Law of the Sea (the International

Seabed Authority, see p. 354), to extend its territorial waters from six to 12 nautical miles, was strongly condemned by Turkey, which feared the loss of shipping access, via the Aegean Sea, to international waters. The dispute intensified prior to the scheduled entry into force of the Convention in mid-November, with both countries conducting concurrent military exercises in the Aegean. The concern surrounding the international Convention on the Law of the Sea resurfaced in June 1995, when the Vouli ratified the treaty. In early 1996 tensions were exacerbated by conflicting claims of sovereignty over Imia (Kardak), a group of uninhabited islands in the Aegean Sea. In February Greece delayed the implementation of a financial protocol of the EU-Turkey customs union, claiming that Turkey's aggressive action in the Aegean violated the terms of the customs union agreement. In July Greece finally withdrew its opposition to Turkey's participation in an EU-Mediterranean assistance programme, in response to a joint statement by EU Heads of Government urging an end to Turkey's 'hostile policy' towards Greece; however, the block on funds from the customs union agreement remained in effect.

In July 1997 the Greek Prime Minister, Konstantinos Simitis, and the Turkish President, Süleyman Demirel, held direct talks, which led to an agreement, the Madrid Declaration, pledging not to use violence or the threat of violence to resolve bilateral disputes. However, relations remained strained, particularly concerning Greek support for Cyprus' application for membership of the EU. As Cyprus began accession talks with the EU in March 1998, Greece reiterated its intention to veto the admission of other applicant countries if Cyprus were rejected, and maintained its refusal to lift its veto on EU financial aid to Turkey. Relations between the two countries improved in August 1999, however, when Greece offered both financial and material assistance to Turkey, following a severe earthquake in the north-west of that country; Greece also announced its intention to lift its veto on EU financial aid to Turkey. Turkey reciprocated Greece's provision of emergency assistance when an earthquake struck Athens in September. At an EU summit, held in Helsinki, Finland, in December, a diplomatic impasse was finally ended when Greece formally lifted its objections to Turkey's membership of the EU, although the conditions for its accession depended on the resolution of both the Cyprus issue and of its dispute with Greece in the Aegean. In January 2000 the Greek Minister of Foreign Affairs, Georgios Papandreou, visited Ankara, the Turkish capital, for talks with his Turkish counterpart, İsmail Cem, and the Turkish Prime Minister, in the first official visit by a Greek Minister of Foreign Affairs to Turkey since 1962. In February 2000 the rapprochement between Greece and Turkey continued with an official visit to Athens by the Turkish Minister of Foreign Affairs, during which further co-operation agreements (primarily relating to economic affairs) were signed.

In November 2001 Greece and Turkey signed an agreement that allowed Greece to repatriate illegal Turkish immigrants. (The Greek Government believed that as many as 750,000 illegal immigrants had entered the country from Turkey since 1998.) None the less, the issue of Cyprus continued to overshadow bilateral relations. In February 2002 the Greek and Turkish Ministers of Foreign Affairs recommenced talks, following the resumption of negotiations between the Greek and Turkish Cypriot sides over the issue of Cyprus. In April 2003, after further efforts towards reaching a peace settlement ended in failure, the newly elected Cypriot President, Tassos Papadopoulos, signed Cyprus' Treaty of Accession to the EU in Athens, thereby confirming that Cyprus would join the organization on 1 May 2004. In February 2004 agreement was reached on proposals for the resolution of the reunification issue, which would provide for Cyprus' accession to the EU as a single state. The final plan for reunification, submitted for approval in both the Republic of Cyprus and the 'TRNC' at referendums on 24 April, was endorsed in the latter with 64.9% of the votes cast, but rejected in the former with 75.8% of the votes (with the result that only that part of Cyprus administered by the principally Greek Cypriot Republic of Cyprus joined the EU). In early May the Turkish Prime Minister, Reçep Tayyip Erdoğan, made an official visit to Greece (the first by a Turkish premier in 16 years). In July the Greek Minister of Public Order and his Turkish counterpart signed a security co-operation agreement in İstanbul, Turkey. The EU opened accession talks with Turkey in October 2005.

Following the installation of a new Greek Government in October 2009, Erdoğan contacted the Greek Prime Minister and Minister of Foreign Affairs, Georgios Papandreou, with proposals for the establishment of a bilateral working group at ministerial level in an effort to resolve outstanding issues of contention. In May 2010 Erdoğan made an official two-day visit to Greece, where a joint government meeting, attended by 10 Turkish ministers travelling with him, was conducted, and 21 co-operation accords were signed. In November, following a request from the Greek Government, the European Commission dispatched more than 150 border guards from EU member countries to assist in controlling Greece's border with Turkey, in response to an increasing flow of migrants entering the country. In March 2011 the Turkish Minister of Foreign Affairs and his Greek counterpart, meeting in Athens for discussions, pledged continued improvement in bilateral relations.

In 1985 Greece and Albania reopened their borders, which had remained closed since 1940, and Greece formally annulled claims to North Epirus (southern Albania), where there is a sizeable Greek minority. In 1987 the Greek Government put a formal end to a legal vestige of the Second World War by proclaiming that it no longer considered Greece to be at war with Albania. In 1988 the two countries signed an agreement to promote trade between their border provinces. During the early 1990s, however, bilateral relations were severely strained by concerns over the treatment of ethnic Greeks residing in Albania (numbering an estimated 300,000) and over the illegal immigration of several thousand Albanians to Greece. In March 1996 President Stefanopoulos signed a treaty of friendship and co-operation with Albania's President, Sali Berisha. Albania agreed to provide Greek-language education in schools serving the ethnic Greek population, and Greece declared its willingness to issue temporary work permits for seasonal workers from Albania. Following a revolt in southern Albania in 1997, Greece agreed to legitimize the status of large numbers of illegal Albanian immigrants by granting them temporary work permits, in exchange for assistance from Albania in combating cross-border crime. A new border crossing was opened between Greece and Albania in May 1999. However, following the stabilization of the political situation in Albania, the influx of Albanians into Greece decreased considerably.

Attempts after 1991 by the FYRM to achieve international recognition as an independent state were strenuously opposed by the Greek Government, which insisted that 'Macedonia' was a purely geographical term (delineating an area that included a large part of northern Greece) and expressed fears that the adoption of such a name could imply ambitions on the Greek province of Macedonia. In early 1993 the Greek administration withdrew its former objection to the use of the word 'Macedonia', and its derivatives, as part of a fuller name for the new republic. At the end of March the Greek Government accepted a UN proposal that the title 'the former Yugoslav republic of Macedonia' should be used temporarily and agreed to hold direct talks with the FYRM to consider confidence-building measures. In late 1993 the newly elected PASOK Government strongly criticized recognition of the FYRM by several EU members, and in February 1994 also condemned a decision by the USA (the final permanent member of the UN Security Council to do so) to recognize the FYRM. At an emergency meeting in mid-February, the Government agreed to prevent any movement of goods, other than humanitarian aid, into the FYRM via the Greek port of Thessaloníki. The initiative was widely criticized by the international community as effectively constituting an illegal trade embargo. In April the European Commission commenced legal proceedings against Greece at the Court of Justice of the European Communities. In April 1995 a preliminary opinion of the Court determined that the embargo was not in breach of Greece's obligations under the Treaty of Rome. In September the ministers responsible for foreign affairs of Greece and the FYRM, meeting in New York, under UN auspices, signed an interim accord to normalize relations between the two countries, which included recognition of the existing international border. Under the terms of the agreement, Greece was to grant access to the port facilities at Thessaloníki and to remove all obstructions to the cross-border movement of people and goods, while the FYRM was to approve a new state flag; the measures were successfully implemented by October. Negotiations were to be pursued regarding the issue of a permanent name for the FYRM. In March 1997 the Greek Minister of Foreign Affairs visited the FYRM for the first time since its independence.

Greece strongly objected to the decision by the USA, announced in November 2004, that it would henceforth recognize the FYRM by its constitutional name of 'the Republic of

Macedonia'. Negotiations on the issue, mediated by the UN, continued, while the Greek Government repeatedly threatened to obstruct the FYRM's aspirations to NATO and EU accession, if it failed to agree to a compromise resolution. In January 2007 Greece protested at a decision by the FYRM Government to rename the international airport near Skopje after Alexander 'the Great' (who was considered by Greece to be integral to its cultural heritage). At a NATO conference convened in Bucharest, Romania, in April 2008, Greece vetoed the FYRM's application for membership, threatening similarly to obstruct the country's application to join the EU. In November the FYRM Government submitted legal proceedings against Greece to the International Court of Justice (ICJ, see p. 25) at The Hague, Netherlands, claiming that it had violated the terms of a UN-mediated interim accord regulating relations between the two countries, which stipulated that Greece would not veto the FYRM's accession to international institutions under that provisional name. Discussions were resumed in February 2009, but continued to be unproductive. In April the Greek Government reacted favourably to a proposal by Matthew Nimetz, the UN Special Representative, for the appellation 'Republic of Northern Macedonia'. On 5 December 2011 the ICJ ruled that Greece had contravened the interim accord by vetoing the FYRM's application to join NATO in 2008 and dismissed Greece's counterclaim that the FYRM had previously breached the accord (but rejected a court order sought by the FYRM to prevent Greece from violating the accord in the future).

CONSTITUTION AND GOVERNMENT

Under the Constitution of June 1975, and as subsequently revised, Greece is a parliamentary republic. The unicameral Vouli (Parliament) has 300 members, directly elected by universal adult suffrage for four years. The President is Head of State and is elected by the Vouli for a five-year term. The President formally appoints the leader of the party with an absolute majority of seats in the Vouli, or where no such party exists, the party with a plurality of seats, as Prime Minister and, upon his recommendation, the other members of the Government. Judicial power is exercised by the Supreme Court of Civil and Penal Law, courts of first instance and courts of justice of the peace. Greece comprises seven decentralized administrations, 13 administrative regions (perifereia) and 325 municipalities.

REGIONAL AND INTERNATIONAL CO-OPERATION

Greece is a member of the North Atlantic Treaty Organization (NATO, see p. 370), the Organisation for Economic Co-operation and Development (OECD, see p. 379) and the Organization of the Black Sea Economic Co-operation (see p. 402). Greece became a full member of the EC (now the European Union—EU, see p. 276) in 1981, having signed the Treaty of Accession in 1979.

Greece is a founding member of the UN. As a contracting party to the General Agreement on Tariffs and Trade, Greece joined the World Trade Organization (see p. 433) on its establishment in 1995.

ECONOMIC AFFAIRS

In 2010, according to estimates by the World Bank, Greece's gross national income (GNI), measured at average 2008–10 prices, was US $308,596m., equivalent to $27,260 per head (or $27,380 per head on an international purchasing-power parity basis). During 2001–10, it was estimated, the population increased at an average annual rate of 0.4%, while gross domestic product (GDP) per head increased, in real terms, at an average annual rate of 1.8%. Overall GDP increased, in real terms, at an average annual rate of 2.2% in 2001–10. Real GDP declined by 4.5% in 2010.

Agriculture (including hunting, forestry and fishing) contributed some 3.1% of GDP in 2010, according to provisional figures, and engaged 12.4% of the employed labour force in 2011. The principal cash crops are vegetables and fruit (which, together, accounted for 8.8% of total export earnings in 2009), cereals, sugar beet and tobacco. According to the World Bank, real agricultural GDP declined at an average annual rate of 0.4% during 2001–09; however, the GDP of the sector increased by 9.8% in 2009.

Industry (including mining, manufacturing, utilities and construction) provided 18.8% of GDP in 2010, according to provisional figures, and engaged 18.4% of the employed labour force in 2011. According to the World Bank, during 2001–09 real industrial GDP declined at an average annual rate of 0.2%; the GDP of the industrial sector decreased by 6.0% in 2009.

Mining and quarrying provisionally contributed 0.4% of GDP in 2010, and engaged 0.3% of the employed labour force in 2011. Mineral fuels and lubricants, iron and steel, and aluminium and aluminium alloys are the major mineral and metal exports. At the end of 2010, proven coal reserves stood at 3,020m. metric tons. Lignite, magnesite, silver ore and marble are also mined. In addition, Greece has small reserves of uranium, natural gas and gold.

Manufacturing provided 10.0% of GDP in 2010, according to provisional figures, and engaged 10.5% of the employed labour force in 2011. According to the World Bank, the GDP of the manufacturing sector increased, in real terms, by an average annual rate of 1.7% in 2001–09; manufacturing GDP increased by 4.3% in 2009.

Construction provided 5.3% of GDP in 2010, according to provisional figures, and engaged 6.4% of the employed labour force in 2011.

Energy is derived principally from lignite, which accounted for 53.0% of production in 2008, followed by petroleum (15.9%) and natural gas (21.9% in 2008). Greece is exploiting an offshore petroleum deposit in the north-eastern Aegean Sea. In April 2008 an agreement was signed on Greece's participation in the planned South Stream natural gas pipeline, which is intended to supply Russian natural gas to Europe by 2015. Solar power resources are also being developed. Mineral fuels represented 14.9% of the total value of imports in 2009.

The services sector contributed 78.0% of GDP in 2010, according to provisional figures, and engaged 69.2% of the employed labour force in 2011. Tourism is an important source of foreign exchange. There were 15.0m. visitor arrivals in 2009, according to provisional figures, when, according to World Tourism Organization estimates, receipts from the tourist sector totalled US $12,741m. in 2010 (excluding passenger transport). According to the World Bank, during 2001–09 the GDP of the services sector increased, in real terms, at an average annual rate of 4.4%; sectoral GDP declined by 1.1% in 2009.

In 2010 Greece recorded a visible trade deficit of US $37,537m., and there was a deficit of $32,335m. on the current account of the balance of payments. In 2009 the principal source of imports was Germany (12.2%), followed by Italy; other major sources were the People's Republic of China, France, the Netherlands, the Republic of Korea and Russia. The principal market for exports in that year was also Germany (11.1%); other major purchasers were Italy, Cyprus and Bulgaria. The principal exports in that year were basic manufactures (in particular, non-ferrous metals), constituting 19.6% of total exports. Other major exports were food and live animals, chemicals, machinery and transport equipment, miscellaneous manufactured articles (especially clothing and accessories), and mineral fuels and lubricants. The principal imports were machinery and transport equipment (30.4%), chemicals, mineral fuels and lubricants (mainly petroleum and petroleum products), miscellaneous manufactured articles, basic manufactures, and food and live animals.

According to official estimates, the budgetary deficit amounted to €21,712m. in 2011. Greece's general government gross debt was €328,588m. in 2010, equivalent to 142.8% of GDP. Greece's total external debt was estimated at €182,702m. at the end of 2004 (equivalent to 110.5% of that year's GDP). In 2001–10 the average annual rate of inflation was 3.3%; consumer prices increased by 4.7% in 2010. The rate of unemployment was 15.9% in the first quarter of 2011.

In October 2009 the Government announced that the budgetary deficit for that year would reach more than 12% of GDP, while GDP had contracted. In early May 2010 the European Union (EU, see p. 276), the IMF and the European Central Bank (ECB) reached agreement with Greece on an economic stabilization programme, for which funding of €110,000m. was to be provided over a period of three years, while Greece was required to undertake further budget cuts, increase taxation, and implement substantial public sector reforms (including wage reductions). None the less, the Government admitted that the 2010 targets for the fiscal deficit and increases in tax revenue would not be met. At an emergency summit meeting in July 2011, the EU agreed an emergency funding plan totalling €159,000m. for Greece, which provided for the disbursement of funds from the new European Financial Stability Facility (EFSF), lower rates of interest and extended repayment terms. After it became evident that the programme agreed in July was no longer adequate to prevent a Greek debt default, on 27 October the EU conditionally approved a renegotiated second rescue plan, totalling €130,000m., whereby €100,000m. would be lent to the country through the EFSF and the IMF until 2014 in new funding, and an additional €30,000m. would be used to support Greek debt restructuring. In addition to the stipulated austerity measures, Greece would be required to raise €15,000m. in privatization revenue to reinvest in the EFSF. In early 2012 the approval of spending reductions amounting to 1.5% of GDP and labour market reforms became an urgent priority in order for the rescue plan to proceed. The austerity measures, which included a 22% reduction in the minimum wage (32% for workers under 25) and some 150,000 public sector job cuts, were adopted by the Vouli on 12 February. On 21 February the €130,000m. rescue plan was formally approved, with a number of additional preconditions, including undertakings by Greece to reduce its debt from 160% to 120.5% of GDP within eight years, and to accept a permanent EU economic monitoring mission; private sector holders of Greek sovereign bonds were required to accept a loss of 53.5% of the value of their investments. The Vouli began to adopt further reforms in accordance with EU criteria, while agreement on the debt restructuring was reached on 9 March; the first instalment of funds under the plan was disbursed on 20 March, thereby averting a default by Greece on its debt.

PUBLIC HOLIDAYS

2013: 1 January (New Year's Day), 6 January (Theophany), 18 March (Clean Monday), 25 March (Independence Day), 1 May (Labour Day), 3–6 May (Greek Orthodox Easter), 24 June (Whit Monday), 15 August (Assumption of the Virgin Mary), 28 October ('Ochi' Day, anniversary of Greek defiance of Italy's 1940 ultimatum), 25–26 December (Christmas).

Statistical Survey

Source (unless otherwise stated): National Statistical Service of Greece, Odos Lykourgou 14–16, 101 66 Athens; tel. (210) 4852084; fax (210) 4852552; e-mail info@statistics.gr; internet www.statistics.gr.

Area and Population

AREA, POPULATION AND DENSITY

Area (sq km)	131,957*
Population (census results)†	
18 March 2001	10,964,020
10–24 May 2011 (provisional)	
Males	5,303,690
Females	5,484,000
Total	10,787,690
Density (per sq km) at 2011 census	81.8

* 50,949 sq miles.

† Including armed forces stationed abroad, but excluding foreign forces stationed in Greece.

POPULATION BY AGE AND SEX

(official estimates at 1 January 2010)

	Males	Females	Total
0–14	836,860	786,899	1,623,759
15–64	3,816,392	3,723,181	7,539,573
65 and over	944,213	1,197,573	2,141,786
Total	5,597,465	5,707,653	11,305,118

ADMINISTRATIVE DIVISIONS

(population at 2011 census, provisional)

Regions	Area (sq km)	Population	Density (per sq km)
Attica	3,808	3,812,330	1,001.1
East Macedonia and Thrace	14,156	606,170	42.8
Central Macedonia	18,810	1,874,590	99.7
Epirus	9,203	336,650	36.6
West Macedonia	9,451	282,120	29.9
Thessaly	14,036	730,730	52.1
Central Greece	15,549	546,870	35.2
Peloponnese	15,491	581,980	37.6
West Greece	11,350	680,190	59.9
Ionian Islands	2,307	206,470	89.5
North Aegean	5,286	308,610	58.4
South Aegean	3,836	197,810	51.6
Crete	8,336	621,340	74.5
Autonomous Monastic State			
'Holy Mountain' (Mount Athos)	336	1,830	5.5
Total	131,957	10,787,690	81.8

PRINCIPAL TOWNS

(population at 2011 census, provisional)

Athinai (Athens, the capital)	655,780	Larissa	163,380
Thessaloníki (Salonika)	322,240	Pésterion	138,920
Patras (Patrai)	214,580	Níkaia-Ágios Ioánnis Réndis	105,230
Iraklion	173,450	Kordelió-Évosmos	101,010
Piraeus	163,910	Calithèa	100,050

BIRTHS, MARRIAGES AND DEATHS

	Registered live births		Registered marriages		Registered deaths	
	Number	Rate (per 1,000)	Number	Rate (per 1,000)	Number	Rate (per 1,000)
2002	103,569	9.4	57,872	5.3	103,915	9.5
2003	104,420	9.5	61,081	5.5	105,529	9.6
2004	105,655	9.6	51,377	4.6	104,942	9.5
2005	107,545	9.7	61,043	5.5	105,091	9.5
2006	112,042	10.1	57,802	5.2	105,476	9.5
2007	111,926	10.0	61,377	5.5	109,895	9.8
2008	118,302	10.5	53,500	4.8	107,979	9.6
2009	117,933	10.5	59,212	5.3	108,316	9.6

Life expectancy (years at birth, WHO estimates): 80 (males 78; females 83) in 2009 (Source: WHO, *World Health Statistics*).

ECONOMICALLY ACTIVE POPULATION

(sample surveys, '000 persons aged 15 years and over, January–March*)

	2009	2010	2011
Agriculture, hunting, forestry and fishing	520.0	562.4	519.0
Mining and quarrying	13.5	13.4	11.1
Manufacturing	529.0	481.9	440.7
Electricity, gas and water supply	59.3	58.3	51.9
Construction	367.7	340.4	267.2
Wholesale and retail trade; repair of motor vehicles, motorcycles and personal and household goods	837.2	785.5	782.0
Hotels and restaurants	279.7	288.0	272.3
Transport, storage and communications	293.0	305.7	286.3
Financial intermediation	111.7	114.5	113.7
Real estate, renting and business activities	317.4	302.4	302.7
Public administration and defence; compulsory social security	372.8	373.2	373.2

—continued	2009	2010	2011
Education	326.5	331.2	308.8
Health and social work	229.4	243.9	244.6
Other community, social and personal service activities	144.4	132.8	134.3
Private households with employed persons	82.5	90.1	84.6
Extra-territorial organizations and bodies	1.5	1.8	2.1
Total employed	4,485.8	4,425.6	4,194.4
Unemployed	462.3	586.8	792.6
Total labour force	4,948.1	5,012.4	4,987.0
Males	2,908.2	2,924.2	2,888.0
Females	2,040.0	2,088.2	2,099.1

* Including members of the regular armed forces, but excluding persons on compulsory military service.

Note: Totals may not be equal to the sum of components, owing to rounding.

Health and Welfare

KEY INDICATORS

Total fertility rate (children per woman, 2009)	1.4
Under-5 mortality rate (per 1,000 live births, 2009)	4
HIV/AIDS (% of persons aged 15–49, 2009)	0.1
Physicians (per 1,000 head, 2006)	5.0
Hospital beds (per 1,000 head, 2005)	4.7
Health expenditure (2008): US $ per head (PPP)	3,010
Health expenditure (2008): % of GDP	10.1
Health expenditure (2008): public (% of total)	60.9
Total carbon dioxide emissions ('000 metric tons, 2007)	98,037.6
Carbon dioxide emissions per head (metric tons, 2007)	8.8
Human Development Index (2011): ranking	29
Human Development Index (2011): value	0.861

For sources and definitions, see explanatory note on p. vi.

Agriculture

PRINCIPAL CROPS
('000 metric tons)

	2008	2009	2010
Wheat	1,939	1,830	1,600*
Rice, paddy	209	205	230
Barley	380	280	318
Maize	2,472	2,352	2,195†
Oats	170	110	116
Potatoes	848	848	792
Sugar beet	903	1,600	762
Olives	2,575	2,285	1,810
Cabbages	188	182*	188
Lettuce	90*	90†	115
Tomatoes	1,339	1,561	1,406
Cauliflowers and broccoli	62	64†	73
Pumpkins, squash and gourds	76	76†	73
Cucumbers and gherkins	124	124†	110†
Aubergines (Eggplants)	85	82	71
Chillies and peppers, green	120	120†	141
Onions, dry	200	192	188
Beans, green	65	65†	58†
Watermelons	629*	623*	493
Cantaloupes and other melons	167*	166*	167†
Oranges	802	800†	770†
Tangerines, mandarins, clementines and satsumas	104	119†	130
Lemons and limes	75	75	75†
Apples	235	260	239
Pears	73	74	94*
Apricots	77	62	77
Peaches and nectarines	734	749	639
Grapes	853	880†	1,003
Figs	18	20†	17†
Tobacco, unmanufactured	21	23	22

* Unofficial figure.

† FAO estimate.

Aggregate production ('000 metric tons, may include official, semi-official or estimated data): Total cereals 5,238 in 2008, 4,820 in 2009, 4,499 in 2010; Total roots and tubers 851 in 2008–09, 795 in 2010; Total vegetables (incl. melons) 3,444 in 2008, 3,646 in 2009, 3,376 in 2010; Total fruits (excl. melons) 3,189 in 2008, 3,260 in 2009, 3,230 in 2010.

Source: FAO.

LIVESTOCK
('000 head, year ending 30 September)

	2008	2009	2010
Horses*	27	27	27
Asses*	40	40	40
Mules*	20	20	20
Cattle	624	620*	625*
Pigs	922	942†	950†
Sheep	8,897	8,994	8,966
Goats	5,346	4,178†	4,200†
Chickens†	31,800	31,800	31,800

* FAO estimate(s).

† Unofficial figure(s).

Source: FAO.

LIVESTOCK PRODUCTS
('000 metric tons)

	2008	2009	2010
Cattle meat*	68.0	68.8	70.0
Sheep meat*	90.5	89.6	89.3
Goat meat	55.5*	54.2*	53.7†
Pig meat*	105.0	103.7	100.2
Horse meat†	2.7	2.7	2.7
Chicken meat*	111.5	111.8	114.3
Cows' milk*	820.0	784.0	774.6
Sheep's milk*	785.0	779.0	855.0
Goats' milk*	490.0	484.0	470.0
Hen eggs	101.8	108.8	99.8
Honey	15.7	16.0	14.3†
Wool, greasy†	8.0	7.4	7.6

* Unofficial figure(s).

† FAO estimate(s).

Source: FAO.

Forestry

ROUNDWOOD REMOVALS
('000 cubic metres, excl. bark)

	2005	2006	2007
Sawlogs, veneer logs and logs for sleepers	420	384	756
Other industrial wood	99	78	192
Fuel wood	1,004	1,100	795
Total	1,523	1,562	1,743

2008–10: Production assumed to be unchanged from 2007 (FAO estimates).

Source: FAO.

SAWNWOOD PRODUCTION
('000 cubic metres, incl. railway sleepers)

	2005	2006	2007
Coniferous (softwood)	74	64	64
Broadleaved (hardwood)	117	44	44
Total	191	108	108

2008–10: Production assumed to be unchanged from 2007 (FAO estimates).

Source: FAO.

Fishing

('000 metric tons, live weight)

	2007	2008	2009
Capture	96.1	89.4	83.3
European pilchard (sardine)	9.4	10.5	10.1
European anchovy	16.0	16.3	14.5
Aquaculture	113.3	114.9	122.0
European seabass	34.8	35.0	33.6
Gilthead seabream	50.0	52.0	60.5
Mediterranean mussel	22.2	21.1	22.4
Total catch	209.4	204.3	205.3

Note: Figures exclude corals and sponges (metric tons, capture only): 3.8 in 2007; 4.8 in 2008; 5.9 in 2009.

Source: FAO.

Mining

('000 metric tons, unless otherwise indicated)

	2007	2008	2009
Lignite	73,092	64,521	62,730
Crude petroleum ('000 barrels)	660*	478*	628
Natural gas (million cu m)	15*	14*	11
Iron ore†*	575	570	560
Bauxite	2,126	2,176	1,935
Zinc†	17.7	20.3*	18.1
Lead†	15.0*	23.3	17.0
Nickel†	21.2*	16.6	8.3
Silver (metric tons)†*	38.3	35.5	36.0
Magnesite (crude)	351	455	250
Salt (unrefined)	195*	220	189*
Bentonite	950*	1,500	845
Kaolin	40*	4	n.a.
Gypsum and anhydrite	865*	865*	730
Feldspar	100*	62	29
Perlite (crude)*	1,100	1,100	1,100
Pozzolan	1,400	1,059	830
Pumice	900*	828*	381
Marble ('000 cu m)	250*	348	256

* Estimate(s).

† Figures refer to the metal content of ores and concentrates.

Source: US Geological Survey.

Industry

SELECTED PRODUCTS
('000 metric tons unless otherwise indicated)

	2007	2008	2009
Olive oil, virgin	318	328	305
Wine	350	400	337*
Beer of barley*	415	460	445
Liquefied petroleum gas ('000 barrels)†	8,000	8,000	8,000
Naphthas ('000 barrels)†	8,400	8,400	8,400
Motor spirit (petrol) ('000 barrels)†	32,000	32,000	32,000
Jet fuels ('000 barrels)†	16,000	16,000	16,000
Distillate fuel oils ('000 barrels)†	42,000	42,000	42,000
Residual fuel oils ('000 barrels)†	50,000	50,000	50,000
Cement (hydraulic)†	15,000	14,000	12,000
Crude steel (incl. alloys)	2,554	2,477	2,082
Aluminium (primary, unwrought)	166.3	162.3	134.7

* Unofficial figure(s).

† Estimates.

2010 (unofficial figures): Olive oil, virgin 353; Wine 303; Beer of barley 405.

Sources: FAO; US Geological Survey.

2003 (metric tons, unless otherwise indicated): Cigarettes (million) 26,249; Cotton yarn 93,980; Woven cotton fabrics 14,000; Wool yarn 3,300; Yarn of artificial material 7,950; Leather footwear ('000 pairs) 3,563; Wrapping and packaging paper and paperboard ('000 metric tons) 94; Sulphuric acid ('000 metric tons) 484; Polyvinyl chloride (metric tons) 77,270 (Source: UN Industrial Commodity Statistics Database).

2004 (metric tons, unless otherwise indicated): Cigarettes (million) 28,048; Cotton yarn 76,420 (Source: UN Industrial Commodity Statistics Database).

Finance

CURRENCY AND EXCHANGE RATES

Monetary Units
100 cent = 1 euro (€).

Sterling, Dollar and Euro Equivalents (30 December 2011)
£1 sterling = 1.195 euros;
US $1 = 0.773 euros;
€10 = £8.37 = $12.94.

Average Exchange Rate (euros per US $)
2009 0.7198
2010 0.7550
2011 0.7194

Note: The national currency was formerly the drachma. Greece became a member of the euro area on 1 January 2001, after which a fixed exchange rate of €1 = 340.75 drachmae was in operation. Euro notes and coins were introduced on 1 January 2002. The euro and local currency circulated alongside each other until 28 February, after which the euro became the sole legal tender.

CENTRAL GOVERNMENT BUDGET
(€ million)*

Revenue	2010	2011†	2012‡
Ordinary budget	56,178	56,308	58,234
Tax revenue	51,266	49,703	53,301
Direct taxes	20,224	20,619	24,213
Personal income tax	9,398	8,272	10,682
Corporate income tax	3,167	2,765	2,157
Indirect taxes	31,042	29,084	29,088
Consumption taxes	8,611	4,681	4,950
Value-added tax	17,374	16,900	16,560
Non-tax revenue	4,912	6,605	4,933
Investment budget	3,072	3,365	4,750
Total	59,250	59,673	62,984

Expenditure§	2010	2011†	2012‡
Ordinary budget	72,254	74,495	72,324
Salaries and pensions	24,072	23,112	20,534
Interest payments	13,223	16,380	17,900
Investment budget	8,454	6,890	7,700
Total	80,708	81,385	80,024

* Figures refer to the budgetary transactions of the central Government, excluding the operations of social security funds and public entities (such as hospitals, educational institutions and government agencies) with individual budgets.

† Provisional figures.

‡ Budget figures; expenditure figures exclude potential adjustments arising from the implementation of private sector investment in national debt servicing (PSI).

§ Excluding amortization payments (€ million): 19,549 in 2010; 28,851 in 2011 (provisional figure); n.a. in 2012. Also excluded is expenditure on military procurement (€ million): 1,017 in 2010; 600 in 2011 (provisional figure); 1,000 in 2012 (budget figure).

Source: Bank of Greece.

INTERNATIONAL RESERVES

(US $ million at 31 December)*

	2008	2009	2010
Gold†	3,128.7	3,991.0	5,060.0
IMF special drawing rights	23.8	1,088.3	938.0
Reserve position in IMF	161.3	267.7	263.3
Foreign exchange	158.7	198.8	108.2
Total	3,472.5	5,545.8	6,369.5

* Figures exclude deposits made with the European Monetary Institute.

† Gold reserves are valued at market-related prices.

Source: IMF, *International Financial Statistics*.

MONEY SUPPLY

(incl. shares, depository corporations, national residency criteria, € '000 million at 31 December)

	2008	2009	2010
Currency issued	19.00	21.63	22.52
Bank of Greece	21.48	21.72	30.44
Demand deposits	90.08	102.42	90.30
Other deposits	141.91	140.40	123.74
Securities other than shares	3.04	2.49	3.43
Money market fund shares	2.49	1.77	1.18
Shares and other equity	29.32	40.45	45.45
Other items (net)	–11.12	–12.34	–15.08
Total	274.71	296.82	271.52

Source: IMF, *International Financial Statistics*.

COST OF LIVING

(Consumer Price Index; base: 2000 = 100)

	2007	2008	2009
Food	125.9	132.6	135.1
Fuel and light	147.3	172.8	147.5
Clothing	126.1	129.5	133.4
Rent	137.5	142.8	148.0
All items (incl. others)	125.5	130.7	132.3

2010: Food 135.3; All items (incl. others) 138.5.

Source: ILO.

NATIONAL ACCOUNTS

(€ million at current prices, provisional)

National Income and Product

	2008	2009	2010
Compensation of employees	83,828	86,381	81,976
Gross operating surplus	123,045	122,403	120,582
Gross domestic product (GDP) at factor cost	206,872	208,785	202,558
Taxes on production and imports	29,548	26,605	28,099
Less Subsidies	3,500	3,748	3,339
GDP in market prices	232,920	231,642	227,318
Primary incomes received from abroad	9,039	7,966	7,003
Less Primary incomes paid abroad	16,635	13,609	13,200
Gross national income (GNI)	225,324	225,999	221,120
Less Consumption of fixed capital	29,846	32,618	35,647
Net national income	195,478	193,381	185,473
Current transfers from abroad	3,046	2,367	1,957
Less Current transfers paid abroad	3,616	3,564	3,605
Net national disposable income	194,908	192,184	183,825

Expenditure on the Gross Domestic Product

	2008	2009	2010
Final consumption expenditure	211,336	215,518	210,689
Households	165,923	164,646	165,762
Non-profit institutions serving households	3,202	3,523	3,601
General government	42,211	47,349	41,326
Gross capital formation	55,149	42,421	36,808
Gross fixed capital formation	51,568	44,141	37,771
Changes in inventories	3,581	–1,720	–962
Total domestic expenditure	266,485	257,939	247,497
Exports of goods and services	56,238	44,457	48,880
Less Imports of goods and services	89,803	70,754	69,059
GDP in purchasers' values	232,920	231,642	227,318

Gross Domestic Product by Economic Activity

	2008	2009	2010
Agriculture, hunting and forestry	5,529	5,690	5,610
Fishing	668	681	687
Mining and quarrying	851	769	746
Manufacturing	18,724	20,538	20,012
Electricity, gas and water supply	6,522	6,370	6,290
Construction	12,286	11,970	10,716
Wholesale and retail trade; repair of motor vehicles and household goods	31,866	27,766	25,121
Hotels and restaurants	11,301	11,276	13,699
Transport, storage and communications	24,819	23,630	24,945
Financial intermediation	8,990	9,191	8,786
Real estate, renting and business activities	36,726	38,208	36,312
Public administration and defence; compulsory social security	17,388	19,835	18,381
Education	10,294	11,732	11,038
Health and social work	9,680	8,789	7,787
Other service activities	7,775	8,650	8,911
Private households with employed persons	1,454	1,517	1,589
Gross value added in basic prices	204,873	206,610	200,629
Taxes, less subsidies, on products	28,047	25,032	26,689
GDP in market prices	232,920	231,642	227,318

BALANCE OF PAYMENTS
(US $ million)

	2008	2009	2010
Exports of goods f.o.b.	29,163	21,361	22,628
Imports of goods f.o.b.	-94,209	-64,197	-60,165
Trade balance	-65,046	-42,836	-37,537
Exports of services	50,473	37,789	37,465
Imports of services	-24,903	-20,007	-20,187
Balance on goods and services	-39,477	-25,054	-20,259
Other income received	8,427	5,933	5,031
Other income paid	-24,442	-18,449	-17,226
Balance on goods, services and income	-55,492	-37,570	-32,454
Current transfers received	10,189	7,328	6,053
Current transfers paid	-6,010	-5,670	-5,935
Current balance	-51,313	-35,913	-32,335
Capital account (net)	5,995	2,818	2,776
Direct investment abroad	-2,776	-2,097	-1,262
Direct investment from abroad	5,304	2,419	2,250
Portfolio investment assets	144	-4,146	17,078
Portfolio investment liabilities	24,891	43,145	-43,932
Financial derivatives assets	-661	-1,151	416
Other investment assets	-40,679	-32,753	10,245
Other investment liabilities	58,021	29,678	30,926
Net errors and omissions	1,113	-788	-99
Overall balance	39	1,213	-13,936

Source: IMF, *International Financial Statistics*.

External Trade

PRINCIPAL COMMODITIES
(US $ million)

Imports c.i.f.	2007	2008	2009
Food and live animals	6,831.1	7,713.0	6,714.4
Meat and meat preparations	1,391.5	1,643.6	1,559.0
Crude materials (inedible) except fuels	2,169.5	2,457.9	1,414.8
Mineral fuels, lubricants, etc.	11,508.7	17,834.4	10,016.4
Petroleum, petroleum products, etc.	10,247.2	15,671.2	8,757.2
Crude petroleum oils, etc.	8,326.4	11,644.5	6,250.9
Chemicals and related products	10,572.9	12,210.6	10,730.8
Medicinal and pharmaceutical products	4,568.9	5,377.7	5,490.4
Medicaments (incl. veterinary medicaments)	3,863.9	4,502.0	4,579.9
Basic manufactures	11,049.5	11,791.2	7,293.7
Textile yarn, fabrics, etc.	1,380.9	1,372.8	989.5
Iron and steel	2,542.4	2,975.2	1,385.1
Machinery and transport equipment	22,579.8	24,244.4	20,448.4
Machinery specialized for particular industries	1,808.1	1,919.9	1,141.1
General industrial machinery equipment and parts	2,390.1	2,819.3	1,971.3
Office machines and automatic data-processing machines	1,453.7	1,619.7	1,296.0
Telecommunications and sound equipment	2,725.9	2,684.8	2,024.0
Other electrical machinery, apparatus, etc.	2,326.5	2,602.1	2,149.3
Road vehicles and parts*	7,017.6	6,887.5	4,953.0
Passenger motor cars (excl. buses)	4,508.2	4,360.1	3,206.9
Other transport equipment*	4,055.4	4,230.2	5,937.8
Ships, boats and floating structures	3,628.0	3,406.1	5,231.9
Miscellaneous manufactured articles	9,472.3	11,316.7	8,910.7
Clothing and accessories (excl. footwear)	2,868.1	3,292.2	2,800.0
Total (incl. others)	76,099.2	89,301.6	67,192.0

* Excluding tyres, engines and electrical parts.

Exports f.o.b.	2007	2008	2009
Food and live animals	3,450.9	3,988.5	3,794.3
Vegetables and fruit	1,786.7	1,972.5	1,771.3
Fresh or dried fruit and nuts (excl. oil nuts)	626.8	761.6	721.1
Preserved fruit and fruit preparations	492.3	506.8	407.5
Beverages and tobacco	686.5	851.2	821.0
Tobacco and manufactures	485.6	611.1	586.1
Unmanufactured tobacco (incl. refuse)	300.2	383.1	380.3
Crude materials (inedible) except fuels	1,055.8	1,141.1	991.7
Textile fibres and waste	256.3	357.9	431.1
Cotton	245.2	346.7	425.4
Raw cotton (excl. linters)	227.5	329.4	402.9
Mineral fuels, lubricants, etc.	2,856.4	2,800.5	1,897.6
Refined petroleum products	2,666.6	2,577.3	1,690.6
Animal and vegetable oils, fats and waxes	482.0	487.7	397.9
Fixed vegetable oils and fats	453.0	440.6	373.5
Olive oil	420.2	380.5	339.9
Chemicals and related products	3,237.4	3,391.7	2,914.4
Basic manufactures	5,113.7	5,778.8	3,939.1
Textile yarn, fabrics, etc.	745.7	763.0	611.3
Non-metallic mineral manufactures	490.1	608.9	554.8
Lime, cement, etc.	331.8	411.8	404.7
Non-ferrous metals	1,881.4	1,848.2	1,089.3
Aluminium	1,018.3	1,062.1	757.1
Worked aluminium and aluminium alloys	736.0	798.5	613.6
Machinery and transport equipment	3,189.5	3,595.3	2,719.8
Electrical machinery, apparatus, etc.	955.9	945.8	677.3
Miscellaneous manufactured articles	2,645.0	2,802.5	2,194.1
Clothing and accessories (excl. footwear)	1,575.6	1,519.8	1,101.1
Total (incl. others)	23,504.2	25,509.4	20,052.5

Source: UN, *International Trade Statistics Yearbook*.

PRINCIPAL TRADING PARTNERS
(US $ million)*

Imports c.i.f.	2007	2008	2009
Austria	975.1	1,151.7	820.1
Belgium	2,911.9	3,149.2	2,650.4
Bulgaria	1,180.5	1,711.0	1,342.8
China, People's Republic	3,830.3	4,926.0	4,241.6
Denmark	650.8	719.6	740.7
Finland	711.1	856.0	553.6
France (incl. Monaco)	4,222.2	4,559.4	3,640.1
Germany	9,751.3	10,652.4	8,187.3
Iran	2,726.7	2,983.5	1,512.2
Italy	8,877.5	10,181.8	7,585.3
Japan	1,710.0	1,354.1	965.9
Korea, Republic	2,584.5	2,112.3	3,456.2
Netherlands	3,796.6	4,131.0	3,589.5
Russia	4,290.5	6,555.1	3,450.4
Saudi Arabia	1,288.6	1,952.6	864.9
Spain	2,742.4	3,140.2	2,427.6
Sweden	758.5	769.1	571.6
Switzerland-Liechtenstein	1,458.9	1,245.5	1,078.5
Turkey	2,287.5	2,492.0	1,806.8
United Kingdom	2,739.9	2,879.4	2,293.7
USA	1,728.0	2,437.7	1,959.4
Total (incl. others)	76,099.2	89,301.6	67,192.0

Exports f.o.b.	2007	2008	2009
Albania	620.8	556.8	542.7
Belgium	379.4	327.7	310.0
Bulgaria	1,521.3	1,820.5	1,348.7
Cyprus	1,524.0	1,623.3	1,460.5
France (incl. Monaco)	981.6	983.7	750.3
Germany	2,714.2	2,680.4	2,230.2
Italy	2,523.5	2,946.2	2,218.0
Macedonia, former Yugoslav republic	534.5	650.7	552.4
Netherlands	471.7	591.7	520.9
Romania	1,061.8	1,136.8	777.0
Russia	488.6	616.5	326.7
Serbia	394.4	439.2	337.0
Spain	795.5	742.9	503.6
Sweden	244.9	229.8	165.4
Turkey	850.1	914.9	845.8
United Kingdom	1,277.8	1,206.9	881.2
USA	976.8	1,303.1	996.1
Total (incl. others)	23,504.2	25,509.4	20,052.5

* Imports by country of first consignment; exports by country of consumption.

Source: UN, *International Trade Statistics Yearbook*.

Transport

RAILWAYS
(estimated traffic)

	2002	2003	2004
Passenger-kilometres (million)	1,836	1,574	1,669
Net ton-kilometres (million)	327	457	592

Source: UN, *Statistical Yearbook*.

2005 (million): Passenger-kilometres 1,854; Net ton-kilometres 613 (Source: World Bank, World Development Indicators database).

ROAD TRAFFIC
(motor vehicles in use at 31 December)

	2008	2009	2010
Passenger cars	5,023,944	5,131,960	5,216,873
Buses and coaches	27,186	27,324	27,311
Lorries and vans	1,289,525	1,302,430	1,318,768
Motorcycles	1,388,607	1,448,851	1,499,133
Total	7,729,262	7,910,565	8,062,085

SHIPPING

Merchant Fleet
(registered at 31 December)

	2007	2008	2009
Number of vessels	1,478	1,498	1,517
Total displacement ('000 grt)	35,704.5	36,822.3	38,910.6

Source: IHS Fairplay, *World Fleet Statistics*.

International Sea-borne Freight Traffic
('000 metric tons)

	2007	2008	2009
Goods loaded	24,588	26,412	23,436
Goods unloaded	56,196	52,176	46,752

Source: UN, *Monthly Bulletin of Statistics*.

CIVIL AVIATION
(traffic on scheduled services)

	2007	2008	2009
Kilometres flown (million)	91	95	76
Passengers carried ('000)	10,155	10,721	8,745
Passenger-kilometres (million)	9,535	10,194	7,543
Total ton-kilometres (million)	964	1,053	764

Source: UN, *Statistical Yearbook*.

Tourism

FOREIGN TOURIST ARRIVALS BY NATIONALITY
(arrivals of non-resident tourists at national borders)

Country	2007	2008	2009
Albania	213,725	242,999	234,276
Austria	377,341	354,748	352,223
Belgium	408,654	420,748	334,240
Bulgaria	701,666	623,476	657,130
Czech Republic	269,774	267,596	267,833
Denmark	267,648	245,946	264,040
France	991,117	910,021	962,435
Germany	2,711,662	2,469,151	2,364,486
Hungary	201,703	180,914	70,894
Italy	1,251,779	1,099,983	935,011
Netherlands	737,771	756,940	651,440
Norway	213,349	277,303	315,595
Poland	227,363	270,039	203,487
Romania	350,723	327,261	307,596
Spain	182,644	219,917	164,461
Sweden	311,358	382,922	356,154
Switzerland	310,293	339,808	352,514
United Kingdom	2,508,651	2,278,014	2,112,149
USA	617,478	612,825	531,276
Total (incl. others)	16,165,265	15,938,806	14,914,534

2010: Total tourist arrivals ('000) 15,007 (provisional).

Tourism receipts (US $ million, incl. passenger transport, unless otherwise indicated): 17,586 in 2008; 14,796 in 2009; 12,741 in 2010 (excl. passenger transport, provisional).

Source: World Tourism Organization.

Communications Media

	2008	2009	2010
Telephones ('000 main lines in use)	5,253.7	5,248.1	5,203.3
Mobile cellular telephones ('000 subscribers)	13,799.3	13,295.1	12,292.7
Internet subscribers ('000)	1,744.1	1,980.0	2,282.7
Broadband subscribers ('000)	1,506.6	1,916.6	2,257.1

Personal computers: 1,045,000 (93.7 per 1,000 persons) in 2006.

Television receivers ('000 in use): 5,500 in 2001.

Radio receivers ('000 in use): 5,020 in 1997.

Daily newspapers (1997): 207 (average circulation 1,389,000 copies).

Non-daily newspapers (2000): 14 (average circulation 441,000 copies).

Books (titles published): 4,225 in 1996.

Sources: UN, *Statistical Yearbook*, UNESCO, *Statistical Yearbook*, and International Telecommunication Union.

Education

(2005/06)

	Institutions	Teachers	Students
Pre-primary	5,672	12,334	143,637
Primary	5,675	64,416	643,200
Secondary: General	3,308	62,149	569,887
Secondary: Technical, vocational and ecclesiastical	654	22,124	125,067
Higher: Universities	21*	12,684	170,629*
Higher: Technical, vocational and ecclesiastical	75	11,557	142,114

* Excluding data from the Medical School of Athens.

Pupil-teacher ratio (primary education, UNESCO estimate): 10.3 in 2006/07 (Source: UNESCO Institute for Statistics).

Adult literacy rate (UNESCO estimates): 97.2% (males 98.3%; females 96.1%) in 2009 (Source: UNESCO Institute for Statistics).

Directory

The Government

HEAD OF STATE

President: KAROLOS PAPOULIAS (elected by vote of the Vouli 8 February 2005, inaugurated 12 March; re-elected by vote of the Vouli 3 February 2010, inaugurated 12 March).

GOVERNMENT

(April 2012)

An interim coalition Government, principally comprising members of the Panhellenic Socialist Movement (PASOK) and New Democracy (ND), remained in place, pending legislative elections on 6 May.

Prime Minister and Chairman of the Government: LUCAS PAPADEMOS (Independent).

Deputy Chairman of the Government: THEODOROS PANGALOS (PASOK).

Minister of Finance: FILIPPOS SACHINIDIS (PASOK).

Minister for Administrative Reform and e-Governance: DIMITRIS REPPAS (PASOK).

Minister of Foreign Affairs: STAVROS DIMAS (ND).

Minister of the Interior: ANASTASIOS GIANNITSIS (PASOK).

Minister of National Defence: DIMITRIS AVRAMOPOULOS (ND).

Minister of Regional Development, Competitiveness and Shipping: ANNA DIAMANTOPOULOU (PASOK).

Minister of the Environment, Energy and Climate Change: GEORGIOS PAPACONSTANTINOU (PASOK).

Minister of Education, Lifelong Learning and Religion: GEORGE BABINIOTIS (Independent).

Minister of Infrastructure, Transport and Communications: MAVROUDIS VORIDIS (ND).

Minister of Labour and Social Protection: GEORGIOS KOUTROUMANIS (PASOK).

Minister of Health and Social Solidarity: ANDREAS LOVERDOS (PASOK).

Minister of Rural Development and Food: KOSTAS SKANDALIDIS (PASOK).

Minister of Justice, Transparency and Human Rights: MILTIADIS PAPAIOANNOU (PASOK).

Minister of Civic Protection: MIHALIS CHRYSOHOIDES (PASOK).

Minister of Culture and Tourism: PAVLOS GEROULANOS (PASOK).

Minister of State at the Office of the Prime Minister: GIORGOS STAVROPOULOS (Independent).

MINISTRIES

Office of the President: Odos Vassileos Georgiou 2, 100 28 Athens; tel. (210) 7283111; fax (210) 7248938; e-mail publicrelationsoffice@presidency.gr; internet www.presidency.gr.

Office of the Prime Minister: Maximos Mansion, Herodou Atticou 19, 106 74 Athens; tel. (210) 3385491; fax (210) 3238129; e-mail primeminister@primeminister.gr; internet www.primeminister.gr.

Ministry of Administrative Reform and e-Governance: Athens; internet www.ydmed.gov.gr.

Ministry of Civic Protection: P. Khanellopoulou 4, 101 77 Athens; tel. (210) 6924558; fax (210) 6929764; e-mail pressoffice@yptp.gr; internet www.ydt.gr.

Ministry of Culture and Tourism: Odos Mpoumpoulinas 20–22, 106 82 Athens; tel. (213) 1322100; fax (210) 8201138; e-mail grplk@culture.gr; internet www.culture.gr.

Ministry of Education, Lifelong Learning and Religion: Andreas Papandreou 37, 151 80 Maroussi; tel. (210) 3442505; e-mail webmaster@ypepth.gr; internet www.minedu.gov.gr.

Ministry of the Environment, Energy and Climate Change: Odos Amalia 17, 115 23 Athens; tel. (210) 1515000; fax (210) 6447608; e-mail service@dorg.minenv.gr; internet www.minenv.gr.

Ministry of Finance: Odos Nikis 5–7, Syntagma Sq., 101 80 Athens; tel. (210) 3332602; fax (210) 3332608; e-mail minister@mnec.gr; internet www.minfin.gr.

Ministry of Foreign Affairs: Odos Sofias 1, 106 71 Athens; tel. (210) 3681000; fax (210) 3624195; e-mail mfa@mfa.gr; internet www.mfa.gr.

Ministry of Health and Social Solidarity: Odos Aristotelous 17, 101 87 Athens; tel. (210) 5232821; e-mail secretary.gen@yyka.gov.gr; internet www.yyka.gov.gr.

Ministry of Infrastructure, Transport and Communications: Odos Anastaseos 2, 101 91 Athens; tel. (210) 6508000; fax (210) 6508088; e-mail press@yme.gov.gr; internet www.yme.gr.

Ministry of the Interior: Odos Stadiou 27, 101 83 Athens; tel. (210) 3744000; fax (210) 3240631; e-mail info@ypes.gr; internet www.ypes.gr.

Ministry of Justice, Transparency and Human Rights: Odos Mesogeion 96, 115 27 Athens; tel. (210) 7711019; fax (210) 7759879; e-mail minjust@otenet.gr; internet www.ministryofjustice.gr.

Ministry of Labour and Social Protection: Odos Pireos 40, 104 37 Athens; tel. (210) 5295248; fax (210) 5249805; e-mail info@ypakp.gr; internet www.ypakp.gr.

Ministry of National Defence: Odos Mesogeion 227–231, 154 51 Athens; tel. (210) 6598100; fax (210) 6443832; e-mail minister@mod.mil.gr; internet www.mod.mil.gr.

Ministry of Regional Development, Competitiveness and Shipping: Odos Mesogeion 119, 101 92 Athens; tel. (210) 6974802; fax (210) 6969604; e-mail polites@mindev.gov.gr; internet www.mindev.gov.gr.

Ministry of Rural Development and Food: Odos Acharnon 2, 104 32 Athens; tel. (210) 2124000; fax (210) 5240475; e-mail info@minagric.gr; internet www.minagric.gr.

President

In voting by members of the Vouli (Parliament), held on 8 February 2005, the sole candidate for the presidency, KAROLOS PAPOULIAS, was elected to a five-year term of office, having obtained the support of 279 of the 300 legislative deputies. He was inaugurated on 12 March. He was elected, again unopposed, to a second five-year term on 3 February 2010, with the support of 266 legislative deputies. His inauguration took place on 12 March.

Legislature

Vouli
(Parliament)

Parliament Bldg, Leoforos Vassilissis Sofias 2, 100 21 Athens; tel. (210) 3707000; fax (210) 3733566; e-mail infopar@parliament.gr; internet www.hellenicparliament.gr.

President: PHILIPPOS PETSALNIKOS.

General Election, 4 October 2009

Parties	Votes	% of votes	Seats
Panhellenic Socialist Movement	3,012,373	43.92	160
New Democracy	2,295,967	33.48	91
Communist Party of Greece	517,154	7.54	21
Popular Orthodox Rally	386,152	5.63	15
Coalition of the Radical Left*	315,627	4.60	13
Ecologist Greens	173,449	2.53	—
Others	157,620	2.30	—
Total	6,858,342	100.00	300

* A coalition of left-wing parties, led by the Coalition of the Left of Movements and Ecology.

Election Commission

National Election Commission: 155 61 Athens; tel. (210) 6535522; fax (210) 6546886; controlled by the Ministry of the Interior.

Political Organizations

Coalition of the Left of Movements and Ecology (SYN) (Synaspismós Tis Aristerás Ton Kinimáton Kai Tis Oikologias): Pl. Eleftherias 1, 105 53 Athens; tel. (210) 3378400; fax (210) 3217003; e-mail info@syn.gr; internet www.syn.gr; f. 1991 on the basis of an alliance (f. 1989) of the nine political groups comprising the Greek Left Party and the Communist Party of Greece ('of the Exterior'); present name adopted 2003; contested Oct. 2009 legislative elections as part of the Coalition of the Radical Left; Pres. ALEXIS TSIPRAS.

Coalition of the Radical Left (SYRIZA) (Synaspismós Rizospastikís Aristerás): Odos Valtetsiou 39, 106 81 Athens; tel. (210) 3829910; fax (210) 3829911; e-mail info@syriza.gr; internet www.syriza.gr; f. 2004; comprises Active Citizens, Coalition of the Left of Movements and Ecology (SYN, q.v.), Communist Organization of Greece (KOE), Democratic Social Movement (DIKKI, q.v.), Ecosocialists Greece (OE), Group Roza, Internationalist Workers Left (DEA), Movement for Unity of Action of the Left (KEDA), Red (Kokkino), Renewing Communist Ecological Left (AKOA) and Start (Xekinima); Leader ALEXIS TSIPRAS.

Communist Party of Greece (KKE) (Kommunistiko Komma Ellados): Leoforos Irakliou 145, Perissos, Nea Ionia, 142 31 Athens; tel. (210) 2592111; fax (210) 2592298; e-mail cpg@int.kke.gr; internet inter.kke.gr; f. 1918; banned 1947, re-emerged 1974; Gen. Sec. ALEKA PAPARIGA.

Democratic Social Movement (DIKKI) (Dimokratiko Koinoniko Kinima): Odos Karolou 28, 104 37 Athens; tel. (210) 5234288; fax (210) 5239856; e-mail info@dikki.org; internet www.dikki.org; f. 1995; leftist; contested Oct. 2009 legislative elections as part of the Coalition of the Radical Left; Co-ordinator, Steering Committee PANTAGIOTIS MANTAS.

Ecologist Greens (Oikologoi Prasinoi—OP): Plateia Eleytherias 14, 105 53 Athens; tel. (210) 3306301; fax (210) 3834390; e-mail ecogreen@otenet.gr; internet www.ecogreens-gr.org; f. 2002; mem. of European Green Party; Mems. of Executive Secretarial Committee IOANNIDOU ELEANA, ZOTOU ELEONORA, KROMMYDAS TASOS, DIMITRIOS GEORGE, TSEKOS GEORGE, GIANNIS CHARALAMPAKIS.

New Democracy (ND) (Nea Demokratia): Leoforos Syngrou 340, 176 73 Kallithea, Athens; tel. (210) 9444000; fax (210) 7251491; e-mail ndpress@nd.gr; internet www.nd.gr; f. 1974; broadly-based centre-right party advocating social reform in the framework of a liberal economy; supports European integration and enlargement; Pres. ANTONIS SAMARAS; Sec. of the Policy Committee ANTONIS SAMARAS.

Panhellenic Socialist Movement (PASOK) (Panellinio Sosialistiko Kinima): Odos Hippocrates 22, 106 80 Athens; tel. (210) 3665000; fax (210) 3665209; e-mail pasok@pasok.gr; internet www.pasok.gr; f. 1974; incorporates Democratic Defence and Panhellenic Liberation Movement resistance orgs; supports social welfare, decentralization and self-management, aims for Mediterranean socialist devt through international co-operation; Pres. EVANGELOS VENIZELOS; Sec. of the Nat. Council MICHAEL KARCHIMAKIS; 500 local orgs, 30,000 mems.

Popular Orthodox Rally (LAOS) (Laikos Orthodoxos Synagermos): Leoforos Kallirrois 52, 117 45 Athens; tel. (210) 3665000; fax (210) 3665209; e-mail pr@laos.gr; internet www.laos.gr; f. 2000; nationalist; Pres. GEORGIOS KARATZAFERIS.

Diplomatic Representation

EMBASSIES IN GREECE

Albania: Odos Vekiareli 7, Filothei, 152 37 Athens; tel. (210) 6876200; fax (210) 6876223; e-mail embassy.athens@mfa.gov.al; Ambassador DASHNOR DERVISHI.

Algeria: Leoforos Vassileos Konstantinou 14, 116 35 Athens; tel. (210) 7564191; fax (210) 7018681; e-mail embalg@otenet.gr; Ambassador TEDJINI SALAOUANDJI.

Angola: Odos El. Venizelou 24, 152 37 Filothei-Athens; tel. (210) 6898681; fax (210) 6898683; e-mail info@angolaembassy.gr; internet www.angolanembassy.gr; Ambassador ISABEL MERCEDES DA SILVA FEIJÓ.

Argentina: Leoforos Vassilissis Sofias 59, 115 21 Athens; tel. (210) 7224753; fax (210) 7227568; e-mail politica@embar.gr; Ambassador JORGE ALEJANDRO MASTROPIETRO.

Armenia: Leoforos Konstantinou Paleologou 95, 152 32 Khalandri; tel. (210) 6831130; fax (210) 6831183; e-mail embassy.athens@mfa.am; Ambassador GAGIK GHALATCHIAN.

Australia: Thon Bldg, Odos Kifisias & Odos Alexandras, Ambelokipi, POB 14070, 115 23 Ambelokipi-Athens; tel. (210) 8704000; fax (210) 8704111; e-mail ae.athens@dfat.gov.au; Ambassador JENNY BLOOMFIELD.

Austria: Leoforos Vassilissis Sofias 4, 106 74 Athens; tel. (210) 7257270; fax (210) 7257292; e-mail athen-ob@bmeia.gv.at; internet www.bmeia.gv.at/botschaft/athen; Ambassador Dr MICHAEL LINHART.

Azerbaijan: Leoforos Vassilissis Sofias 25, 106 74 Athens; tel. (210) 3632721; fax (210) 3639087; e-mail embassy@azembassy.gr; internet www.azembassy.gr; Ambassador RAHMAN MUSTAFAYEV.

Bangladesh: Akti Miaouli 81, 185 38 Piraeus; tel. (210) 6720250; fax (210) 6754513; e-mail mission.athens@mofa.gov.bd; Ambassador MIZANUR RAHMAN.

Belgium: Odos Sekeri 3, 106 71 Athens; tel. (210) 3617886; fax (210) 3604289; e-mail athens@diplobel.fed.be; internet www.diplomatie.be/athens; Ambassador MARK VAN DEN REEK.

Bosnia and Herzegovina: Odos Filaellinon 25, 105 57 Athens; tel. (210) 6410788; fax (210) 6411978; e-mail ambasbih@otenet.gr; Ambassador BORO BRONZA.

Brazil: Plateia Philikis Etairias 14, 3rd Floor, 106 73 Athens; tel. (210) 7213039; fax (210) 7244731; e-mail embragre@embratenas.gr; Ambassador OTO AGRIPINO MAIA.

Bulgaria: Odos Stratigou Kallari 33A, Palaio Psychiko, 154 52 Athens; tel. (210) 6748105; fax (210) 6748130; e-mail embassy.athens@mfa.bg; internet www.mfa.bg/bg/26/; Ambassador ANDREI KARASLAVOV.

Canada: Odos Ioannou Ghennadiou 4, 115 21 Athens; tel. (210) 7273400; fax (210) 7273480; e-mail athns@international.gc.ca; internet www.canadainternational.gc.ca/greece-grece; Ambassador ROBERT PECK.

Chile: Leoforos Kifissias 317A, 145 61 Athens; tel. (210) 7252574; fax (210) 7252536; e-mail embajada@embachile.gr; Ambassador CARMEN PATRICIA IBANEZ SOTO.

China, People's Republic: Odos Demokratias 10–12, Palaio Psychiko, 154 52 Athens; tel. (210) 6723282; fax (210) 6723819; e-mail chinaemb_gr@mfa.gov.cn; internet gr.chineseembassy.org; Ambassador DU QIWEN.

Congo, Democratic Republic: Odos Kodrou 20, 152 31 Halandri; tel. (210) 6776123; fax (210) 6776124; e-mail ambardcathenes@yahoo.fr; Chargé d'affaires a.i. HENRI BENJAMIN NTIKALA BOOTO.

Croatia: Odos Tzavela 4, 154 51 Psychiko; tel. (210) 6777033; fax (210) 6711208; e-mail croemb.athens@mvpei.hr; Ambassador Dr VESNA CVJETKOVIĆ-KURELAC.

Cuba: Odos Sofokleos 5, 152 37 Filothei; tel. (210) 6855550; fax (210) 6842807; e-mail secretaria@embacuba.gr; internet www.cubadiplomatica.cu/grecia/en/Home.aspx; Ambassador LUIS PRADO GARCIA.

Cyprus: Odos Xenofontos 2A, 105 57 Athens; tel. (210) 3734800; fax (210) 7258886; e-mail cyempkl@hol.gr; Ambassador Prof. JOSEPH JOSEPH.

Czech Republic: Odos Georgiou Seferis 6, 154 52 Palaio Psychiko; tel. (210) 6713755; fax (210) 6710675; e-mail athens@embassy.mzv.cz; internet www.mzv.cz/athens; Ambassador HANA ŠEVČÍKOVÁ.

Denmark: Odos Mourouzi 10, 106 74 Athens; tel. (210) 7256440; fax (210) 7256473; e-mail athathen@um.dk; internet www.graekenland.um.dk; Ambassador TOM HELGE NØRRING.

Egypt: Leoforos Vassilissis Sofias 3, 106 71 Athens; tel. (210) 3618612; fax (210) 3603538; e-mail emb.egypt@yahoo.gr; Ambassador TAREK AHMED IBRAHIM ADEL.

Estonia: Leoforos Messoghion 2–4, Athens Tower, 23rd Floor, 115 27 Athens; tel. (210) 7475660; fax (210) 7475661; e-mail embassy.athens@mfa.ee; internet www.estemb.gr; Ambassador ANDRES TALVIK.

Finland: Odos Hatziyianni Mexi 5, 115 28 Athens; POB 18123, 116 10 Athens; tel. (210) 7255860; fax (210) 7255864; e-mail sanomat.ate@formin.fi; internet www.finland.gr; Ambassador PEKKA LINTU.

France: Leoforos Vassilissis Sofias 7, 106 71 Athens; tel. (210) 3391000; fax (210) 3391009; e-mail info@ambafrance-gr.org; internet www.ambafrance-gr.org; Ambassador JEAN-LOUP KUHN-DELFORGE.

Georgia: Odos Taygetou 27 & Marathonodromou, 154 52 Palaio Psychiko, Athens; tel. (210) 6742186; fax (210) 6716722; e-mail athens.emb@mfa.gov.ge; internet greece.mfa.gov.ge; Ambassador IRAKLI TAVARTKILADZE.

Germany: Odos Karaoli & Dimitriou 3, Kolonaki, 106 75 Athens; tel. (210) 7285111; fax (210) 7285335; e-mail info@athen.diplo.de; internet www.athen.diplo.de; Ambassador WOLFGANG DOLD.

Holy See: POB 65075, Odos Mavili 2, 154 52 Palaio Psychiko; tel. (210) 6722728; fax (210) 6742849; e-mail nunate@ath.forthnet.gr; Apostolic Nuncio EDWARD JOSEPH ADAMS.

Hungary: Odos Karneadou 25–29, Kolonaki, 106 75 Athens; tel. (210) 7256800; fax (210) 7256840; e-mail mission.ath@kum.hu; internet www.mfa.gov.hu/emb/athens; Ambassador ESZTER SÁNDORFI.

India: Odos Kleanthous 3, 106 74 Athens; tel. (210) 7216227; fax (210) 7211252; e-mail embassy@indianembassy.gr; internet www.indianembassy.gr; Ambassador TSEWANG TOPDEN.

Indonesia: Odos Marathonodromou 99, 154 52 Palaio Psychiko; tel. (210) 6742345; fax (210) 6756955; e-mail indathgr@otenet.gr; internet www.indonesia.gr; Ambassador AHMAD RUSDI.

Iran: Odos Stratigou Kalari 16, 154 52 Palaio Psychiko; tel. (210) 6471436; fax (210) 6477945; e-mail irembatn@otenet.gr; internet www.iranembassy.gr; Ambassador BEHROUZ BEHNAM.

Iraq: Odos Strait 17–19, Palaio Psychiko, 152 37 Filothei; tel. (210) 6722330; fax (210) 6717185; e-mail iraqath@otenet.gr; Ambassador BURHAN JAF.

Ireland: Leoforos Vassileos Konstantinou 7, 106 74 Athens; tel. (210) 7232771; fax (210) 7293383; e-mail athensembassy@dfa.ie; internet www.embassyofireland.gr; Ambassador CHARLES SHEEHAN.

Israel: Odos Marathonodromou 1, 154 52 Palaio Psychiko; tel. (210) 6705502; fax (210) 6705555; e-mail ambassadorsec@athens.mfa.gov.il; internet athens.mfa.gov.il; Ambassador ARYE MEKEL.

Italy: Odos Sekeri 2, 106 74 Athens; tel. (210) 3617260; fax (210) 3617330; e-mail ambasciata.atene@esteri.it; internet www.ambatene.esteri.it; Ambassador CLAUDIO GLAENTZER.

Japan: Odos Ethnikis Antistasseos 46, Halandri, 152 31 Athens; tel. (210) 6709900; fax (210) 6709980; e-mail embjapan@otenet.gr; internet www.gr.emb-japan.go.jp; Ambassador HIROSHI TODA.

Jordan: Odos Papadiamanti 21, 154 52 Palaio Psychiko; tel. (210) 6744161; fax (210) 6740578; e-mail jor_emb1@otenet.gr; internet www.jordanembassy.gr; Ambassador ZAID ABDULLAH ZURAIKAT.

Kazakhstan: Odos Imittou 122, 15 669 Papagou; tel. (210) 6515643; fax (210) 6516362; e-mail athens@kazembassy.gr; Ambassador SERGEI NURTAEV.

Korea, Republic: Leoforos Messoghion 2–4, Athens Tower, A-Building, 19th Floor, 115 27 Athens; tel. (210) 6984080; fax (210) 6984083; e-mail gremb@mofat.go.kr; Ambassador TAE-SHIN JANG.

Kuwait: Odos Marathonodromou 27, 154 52 Palaio Psychiko; tel. (210) 6743593; fax (210) 6775875; e-mail kuwemath@otenet.gr; Ambassador RAED ABDULLAH AL-RIFAI.

Latvia: Odos Vassilissis Constantinou 38, 116 35 Athens; tel. (210) 7294483; fax (210) 7294479; e-mail embassy.greece@mfa.gov.lv; Ambassador (vacant).

Lebanon: Odos 25 Maritou 6, 154 52 Palaio Psychiko; tel. (210) 6755873; fax (210) 6755612; e-mail grlibemb@yahoo.com; Ambassador GÉBRAN MICHEL SOUFAN.

Libya: Odos Vyronos 13, 154 52 Palaio Psychiko; tel. (210) 6472120; fax (210) 6742761; Chargé d'affaires a.i. ADEL B. H. EROUBI.

Lithuania: Leoforos Vassilissis Konstantinous 38, 116 35 Athens; tel. (210) 7294356; fax (210) 7294347; e-mail amb.gr@urm.lt; internet gr.mfa.lt; Chargé d'affaires a.i. DALIA AMBRAZEVIČIŪTE.

Luxembourg: Leoforos Vassilissis Sofias 23A & Odos Neophytou Vamva 2, Kolonaki, 106 74 Athens; tel. (210) 7256400; fax (210) 7256405; e-mail athenes.amb@mae.etat.lu; internet athenes.mae.lu; Ambassador RONALD DOFING.

Malta: Leoforos Vassilissis Sofias 96, 115 28 Athens; tel. (210) 7785138; fax (210) 7785242; e-mail maltaembassy.athens@gov.mt; Ambassador WALTER BALZAN.

Mexico: Plateia Filikis Etairias 14, 5th Floor, 106 73 Athens; tel. (210) 7294780; fax (210) 7294783; e-mail embgrecia@sre.gob.mx; Ambassador RICARDO-TARCISIO NAVARRETE-MONTES DE OCA.

Moldova: Odos Georgiou Bacu 20, 115 24 Athens; tel. (210) 6990372; fax (210) 6990660; e-mail atena@mfa.md; internet www.grecia.mfa.gov.md; Ambassador MIHAI BALAN.

Montenegro: Odos Loukianou 5, Kolonaki, 106 75 Athens; tel. (210) 7241212; fax (210) 7241076; e-mail greece@mfa.gov.me; Ambassador IVO ARMENKO.

Morocco: Odos Marathonodromou 5, 154 52 Palaio Psychiko; tel. (210) 6744209; fax (210) 6749480; e-mail sifamath@otenet.gr; Ambassador ABDELKADER AL-ANSARI.

Netherlands: Leoforos Vassileos Konstantinou 5–7, 106 74 Athens; tel. (210) 7254900; fax (210) 7254907; e-mail ath@minbuza.nl; internet www.dutchembassy.gr; Ambassador CORNELIS VAN RIJ.

Nigeria: Odos Dolianis 65, Maroussi, 151 24 Athens; tel. (210) 8021168; fax (210) 8024208; e-mail ngrathen@otenet.gr; Ambassador Dr ETIM UDO UYE.

Norway: Leoforos Vassilissis Sofias 23, 106 74 Athens; tel. (210) 7246173; fax (210) 7244989; e-mail emb.athens@mfa.no; internet www.norway.gr; Ambassador SJUR LARSEN.

Pakistan: Odos Loukianou 6, Kolonaki, 106 75 Athens; tel. (210) 7290122; fax (210) 7257641; e-mail info@pak-embassy.gr; Ambassador IRFAN UR-REHMAN RAZA.

Panama: Odos Praxitelous 192 & Odos II Merarchias, 185 35 Piraeus; tel. (210) 4286441; fax (210) 4286448; e-mail info@panamaconsulate.gr; Ambassador FELICIA DUSHKA PAPADIMITRIU.

Peru: Odos Koumbari 2, 115 28 Athens; tel. (210) 7792761; fax (210) 7792905; e-mail lepruate@otenet.gr; Ambassador JULIO EDUARDO MARTINETTI MACEDO.

Philippines: Odos Antheon 26, 154 52 Palaio Psychiko; tel. (210) 6721883; fax (210) 6721872; e-mail athenspe@otenet.gr; Ambassador MEYNARDO L. B. MONTEALEGRE.

Poland: Odos Chryssanthemon 22, 154 52 Palaio Psychiko; tel. (210) 6797700; fax (210) 6797711; e-mail ambpol@otenet.gr; internet www.poland-embassy.gr; Ambassador MICHAL KLINGER.

Portugal: Leoforos Vassilissis Sofias 23, 106 74 Athens; tel. (210) 7290096; fax (210) 7245122; e-mail embportg@otenet.gr; Ambassador (vacant).

Qatar: Odos Rigillis 16A, 106 74 Athens; tel. (210) 7255031; fax (210) 7255024; Ambassador HAMAD BIN ABDULLA ALI AM-MISNAD.

Romania: Odos Emmanuel Benaki 7, 154 52 Palaio Psychiko; tel. (210) 6728875; fax (210) 6728883; e-mail secretariat@romaniaemb.gr; internet www.atena.mae.ro; Ambassador GEORGE CIAMBA.

Russia: Odos Nikiforou Litra 28, 154 52 Palaio Psychiko; tel. (210) 6725235; fax (210) 6479708; e-mail embraf@otenet.gr; internet www.greece.mid.ru; Ambassador VLADIMIR I. CHKHIKVISHVILI.

Saudi Arabia: Odos Marathonodromou 71, Palaio Psychiko, 154 52 Athens; tel. (210) 6716911; fax (210) 6749833; e-mail gremb@mofa.gov.sa; Ambassador (vacant).

Serbia: Leoforos Vassilissis Sofias 106, 115 27 Athens; tel. (210) 7774344; fax (210) 7796436; e-mail beograd@hol.gr; internet www.embassyofserbia.gr; Ambassador DRAGAN ŽUPANJEVAC.

Slovakia: Odos Georgiou Seferis 4, 154 52 Palaio Psychiko; tel. (210) 6771980; fax (210) 6776765; e-mail emb.athens@mzv.sk; internet www.mzv.sk/athens; Ambassador JÁN VODERADSKÝ.

Slovenia: Leoforos Kifissias 280 & Odos Dimokratias 1, 154 52 Palaio Psychiko; tel. (210) 6720090; fax (210) 6775680; e-mail vat@gov.si; Ambassador ROBERT BASEJ.

South Africa: Leoforos Kifissias 60, 151 25 Maroussi; tel. (210) 6178020; fax (210) 6106640; e-mail athens.info@foreign.gov.za; Ambassador SOPHONIA RAPULANE MAKGETLA.

Spain: Odos D. Areopagitou 21, 117 42 Athens; tel. (210) 9213123; fax (210) 9213090; e-mail emb-esp@otenet.gr; Ambassador MIGUEL FUERTES SUAREZ.

Sudan: Odos Mousson 6, 154 52 Palaio Psychiko, Athens; tel. (210) 6742520; fax (210) 6742521; Ambassador ALI EL-SADIG ALI EL-HUSEIN.

Sweden: Leoforos Vassileos Konstantinou 7, 106 74 Athens; tel. (210) 7266100; fax (210) 7266150; e-mail ambassaden.athen@foreign.ministry.se; internet www.swedenabroad.com/athen; Ambassador HÅKAN MALMQVIST.

Switzerland: Odos Iassiou 2, 115 21 Athens; tel. (210) 7230364; fax (210) 7249209; e-mail ath.vertretung@eda.admin.ch; internet www.eda.admin.ch/athens; Ambassador LORENZO AMBERG.

Syria: Diamandidou 61, 154 52 Palaio Psychiko; tel. (210) 6725577; fax (210) 6716402; e-mail syrembas@otenet.gr; internet www.syrianembassy.gr; Ambassador HOUDA AL-HOUMSI.

Thailand: Odos Marathonodromou 25 & Odos Kyprou, 154 52 Palaio Psychiko; tel. (210) 6710155; fax (210) 6749508; e-mail thaiath@otenet.gr; Ambassador PREUDTIPONG KULTHANAN.

Tunisia: Odos Antheon 2 & Odos Marathonodromou, 154 52 Palaio Psychiko; tel. (210) 6717590; fax (210) 6713432; e-mail atathina@otenet.gr; Ambassador SAMIA ZOUARI.

Turkey: Odos Vassileos Gheorghiou II 8, 106 74 Athens; tel. (210) 7263000; fax (210) 7229597; e-mail info@turkishembassy.ondsl.gr; Ambassador KERIM URAS.

Ukraine: Odos Stefanou Delta 2, 152 37 Filothei; tel. (210) 6800230; fax (210) 6854154; e-mail emb_gr@mfa.gov.ua; internet www.mfa.gov.ua/greece; Ambassador VOLODYMYR SHKUROV.

United Arab Emirates: Leoforos Kifissias 290 & Odos N. Paritsi 2, Neo Psychiko, 154 51, Athens; tel. (210) 6770220; fax (210) 6770274; Ambassador ABDELHADI ABDELWAHID AL-KHAJAH.

United Kingdom: Odos Ploutarchou 1, 106 75 Athens; tel. (210) 7272600; fax (210) 7272723; e-mail information.athens@fco.gov.uk; internet ukingreece.fco.gov.uk; Ambassador DAVID MAURICE LANDSMAN.

Uruguay: Odos Menandrou 1, 145 61 Kifissia; tel. (210) 3602635; fax (210) 3613549; e-mail urugrec@otenet.gr; Ambassador JOSÉ LUIS POMBO MORALES.

USA: Leoforos Vassilissis Sofias 91, 106 10 Athens; tel. (210) 7212951; fax (210) 6456282; e-mail usembassy@usembassy.gr; internet athens.usembassy.gov; Ambassador DANIEL BENNETT SMITH.

Venezuela: Odos Marathonodromou 19, 154 52 Palaio Psychiko; tel. (210) 6729169; fax (210) 6727464; e-mail emvenath@hol.gr; internet www.embavenez.gr; Ambassador RODRIGO OSWALDO CHAVES SAMUDIO.

Viet Nam: 50 Yakinthon, Palaio Psychiko, 154 52 Athens; tel. (210) 6128733; fax (210) 6128734; e-mail vnemb.gr@mofa.gov.vn; internet www.mofa.gov.vn/vnemb.gr; Ambassador BINH VU.

Judicial System

SUPREME ADMINISTRATIVE COURTS

Special Supreme Tribunal: Odos Patision 30, Athens; has final jurisdiction in matters of constitutionality.

Council of State

Odos Panepistimiou 47-49, 105 64 Athens; tel. (210) 2132102; fax (210) 3710097; e-mail s-epikr@otenet.gr; internet www.ste.gr.

Has appellate powers over acts of the administration and final rulings of administrative courts; has power to rule upon matters of judicial review of laws.

President: PIKRAMMENOS PANAGIOTIS.

Supreme Court of Civil and Penal Law

Leoforos Alexandros 121, 115 10 Athens; tel. (210) 6411506; fax (210) 6433799; e-mail areios@otenet.gr; internet www.areiospagos.gr.

Supreme court in the State, also having appellate powers; consists of six sections (four Civil, two Penal) and adjudicates in quorum.

President: GEORGIOS KALAMIDAS.

COURTS OF APPEAL

There are 12 Courts of Appeal with jurisdiction in cases of Civil and Penal Law of second degree, and, in exceptional penal cases, of first degree.

COURTS OF FIRST INSTANCE

There are 59 Courts of First Instance with jurisdiction in cases of first degree, and, in exceptional cases, of second degree. They function both as Courts of First Instance and as Criminal Courts. For serious crimes the Criminal Courts function with a jury.

In towns where Courts of First Instance sit, there are also Juvenile Courts. Commercial Tribunals do not function in Greece, and all commercial cases are tried by ordinary courts of law. There are, however, Tax Courts in some towns.

OTHER COURTS

There are 360 Courts of the Justice of Peace throughout the country. There are 48 Magistrates' Courts (or simple Police Courts).

In all the above courts, except those of the Justice of Peace, there are District Attorneys. In Courts of the Justice of Peace, the duties of District Attorney are performed by the Public Prosecutor.

Religion

CHRISTIANITY

The Eastern Orthodox Church

The Greek branch of the Eastern Orthodox Church is the officially established religion of the country, to which nearly 97% of the population profess adherence.

Within the Greek State, there is also the semi-autonomous Church of Crete, which is under the spiritual jurisdiction of the Ecumenical Patriarchate of Constantinople (based in İstanbul, Turkey).

There are also four Metropolitan Sees of the Dodecanese, which are dependent on the Ecumenical Patriarchate, and, finally, the peninsula of Athos, which constitutes the region of the Holy Mountain (Mount Athos) and comprises 20 monasteries. These are dependent on the Ecumenical Patriarchate of Constantinople, but are autonomous and are safeguarded constitutionally.

The Orthodox Church of Greece: Odos Ioannou Gennadiou 14, 115 21 Athens; tel. (210) 7218381; e-mail contact@ecclesia.gr; internet www.ecclesia.gr; f. 1850.

Primate of Greece: IERONYMOS II (LIAPIS).

Archbishop of Crete: Archbishop IRENAIOS (whose See is in Heraklion).

The Roman Catholic Church

Greece comprises four archdioceses (including two, Athens and Rhodes, directly responsible to the Holy See), four dioceses, one Apostolic Vicariate and one Apostolic Exarchate for adherents of the Byzantine Rite. There is also an Ordinariate for Armenian Catholics. At 31 December 2008 there were an estimated 180,637 adherents in the country, including 2,500 of the Byzantine Rite and 300 of the Armenian Rite.

Latin Rite

Bishops' Conference: G. Papandreou 15, 841 00 Syros; tel. (22) 81084783; fax (22) 8108684781; e-mail syrensis@otenet.gr; f. 1967; Pres. Rt Rev. FRAGKISKOS PAPAMANOLIS (Bishop of Syros and Milos, and of Santorini).

Archbishop of Athens: Archbishop Most Rev. NIKÓLAOS FÓSKOLOS, Odos Homirou 9, 106 72 Athens; tel. (210) 3624311; fax (210) 3618632.

Archbishop of Corfu, Zante and Cefalonia: Most Rev. IOANNIS SPITERIS, Montzeníkhou 3, 491 00 Kérkyra; tel. (26610) 30277; fax (26610) 31675; e-mail cathepco@otenet.gr.

Archbishop of Naxos, Andros, Tinos and Mykonos: Most Rev. NIKÓLAOS PRINTESIS, 842 00 Tinos; tel. (22830) 22382; fax (22830) 24769; e-mail kamipai@cathecclesia.gr.

Archbishop of Rhodes: (vacant), Odos Ionos Dragoumi 5, 851 00 Rhodes; tel. (22410) 21845; fax (22410) 26688.

Apostolic Vicariate of Thessaloníki: Kolokotroni 19B, 564 30 Thessaloníki; tel. (2310) 654256; fax (2310) 835780; e-mail ioas17@otenet.gr; Apostolic Vicar JOANNIS SPITERIS.

Byzantine Rite

Apostolic Exarchate for Greek Catholics of the Byzantine Rite: Odos Akarnon 246, 112 53 Athens; tel. (210) 8670170; fax (210) 8677039; e-mail grcathex@hol.gr; 3 parishes; 3,500 adherents (31 Dec. 2006); Apostolic Exarch Most Rev. DIMITRIOS SALACHAS (Titular Bishop of Carcabia).

Armenian Rite

Ordinariate for Catholics of the Armenian Rite in Greece: Odos René Pyo 2, 117 44 Athens; tel. (210) 9014089; fax (210) 9012109; 350 adherents (31 Dec. 2006); Ordinary (vacant); Apostolic Administrator Most Rev. NECHAN KARAKAHIAN (Titular Archbishop of Adana of the Armenian Rite).

Protestant Church

Greek Evangelical Church: Odos Markon Botsari 24, 117 41 Athens; tel. (210) 3231079; fax (210) 3316577; e-mail info@gec.gr;

internet www.gec.gr; f. 1858; comprises 32 organized churches; 5,000 adherents (1996); Moderator Rev. MELETIS MELETIADIS.

ISLAM

The law provides as religious head of the Muslims a Chief Mufti; the Muslims in Greece possess a number of mosques and schools.

JUDAISM

The Jewish population of Greece, estimated in 1943 at 75,000 people, was severely reduced as a result of the Nazi German occupation. In 1994 there were about 5,000 Jews in Greece.

Central Board of the Jewish Communities of Greece: Odos Voulis 36, 105 57 Athens; tel. (210) 3244315; fax (210) 3313852; e-mail info@kis.gr; internet www.kis.gr; f. 1945; officially recognized representative body of the Jewish communities of Greece; Pres. DAVID SALTIEL.

The Press

PRINCIPAL DAILY NEWSPAPERS

Morning papers are not published on Mondays, nor afternoon papers on Sundays. The afternoon papers generally enjoy a wider circulation than do the morning ones.

Adesmeftos Typos (Rizos): Thiseseos 218, Kallithea, 176 75 Athens; tel. (210) 9405888; fax (210) 9407173; e-mail info@adesmeytos.gr; internet www.adesmeytos.gr; f. 1998; afternoon; publ. by Makedonikes Publications; Dir DIMITRIS RIZOS; Editor KOSTAS SARRIKOSTAS; circ. weekdays 12,973, Sun. 11,837 (2009).

Apogevmatini (The Afternoon): Odos Phidiou 12, 106 78 Athens; tel. (210) 6430011; fax (210) 3304800; e-mail info@apogevmatini.gr; internet www.apogevmatini.gr; f. 1956; independent; Editor MIHAIL VASILIADIS; circ. 12,815 (2009).

Avgi (Dawn): Odos Ag. Konstantiou 12, 104 31 Athens; tel. (210) 5231831; fax (210) 5231822; e-mail editors@avgi.gr; internet www.avgi.gr; f. 1952; morning; independent newspaper of the left; Dir NIKOS PHILES; circ. 2,741 (2009).

Eleftherotypia (Press Freedom): Odos Minou 10–16, 117 43 Athens; tel. (210) 9296001; fax (210) 9028311; e-mail elef@enet.gr; internet www.enet.gr; f. 1974; afternoon; Publr THANASSIS TEGOPOULOS; Editor SIFIS POLIMILIS; circ. daily 41,511, Sun. 148,652 (2009).

Espresso: C. Averof 26–28, 142 32 Nea Ionia; tel. (210) 2503100; e-mail contact@espressonews.gr; internet www.espressonews.gr; f. 2000; afternoon; publ. by Daily Press; Publr ANTONIS LIMBERIS; circ. daily 22,693, Sun. 34,017 (2009).

Ethnos (Nation): Odos Benaki 152, Metamorfosi Halandriou, 152 38 Athens; tel. (210) 6061000; fax (210) 6396515; e-mail editor@ethnos.gr; internet www.ethnos.gr; f. 1981; afternoon; Dir GIORGOS CHARVALIAS; Editor THANASIS TSEKOURAS; circ. daily 39,712, Sun. 114,993 (2009).

Exedra Ton Sports: Michalakopoulou 80, 115 28 Athens; tel. (211) 3657000; fax (211) 3659301; e-mail info@exedrasports.gr; internet www.exedrasports.gr; f. 2008; sport; circ. Tue.–Sun. 17,388, Mon. 18,199 (2009).

Express: 46 Leoforos Lavrion, POB 4814, Keratea, 190 01 Attica; tel. (213) 0161700; fax (213) 0161734; e-mail info@express.gr; internet www.express.gr; f. 1963; morning; financial; publ. by Kalofolia Group SA; Publr D. G. KALOFOLIAS; Editor G. DIAMANTOPOULOS; circ. 28,000.

Filathlos: Odos Dimitros 31, 177 78 Athens; tel. (210) 3486000; fax (210) 3486450; e-mail info@filathlos.gr; internet www.filathlos.gr; f. 1982; morning; sports; Publr and Editor G. KOLOKOTRONIS; circ. 8,879.

Goal News: Odos Benaki & Ag. Nektariou, Halandriou, 152 38 Athens; tel. (210) 6061800; fax (210) 6061801; internet www.sentragoal.gr; f. 2002; sport; publ. by Pegasus Publishing SA; circ. Tue.–Sun. 23,371, Mon. 26,459 (2009).

Imerissia (Daily): Odos Benaki & Ag. Nektariou, Metamorfosi Halandriou, 152 38 Athens; tel. (210) 6061000; fax (210) 6014636; e-mail imerissia@pegasus.gr; internet www.imerisia.gr; f. 1947; morning; financial; Dir ANTONIS DALIPIS; Editor ALEX KASIMATIS; circ. 39,000.

Kathimerini (Every Day): Ethnarchou Makariou & Odos Falireos 2, Neo Faliro, 185 47, Piraeus, Athens; tel. (210) 4808000; fax (210) 4808055; e-mail info@ekathimerini.com; internet www.kathimerini.gr; f. 1919; morning; conservative; Editor NIKOS KONSTADARAS; circ. 46,086 (2009).

Kerdos (Profit): Odos Vas. George 44 & Odos Kalvou, Halandri, 152 33 Athens; tel. (210) 6747881; fax (210) 6747893; e-mail mail@kerdos.gr; internet www.kerdos.gr; f. 1985; morning; financial; Editor G. STEVIS; circ. 18,000.

Naftemporiki (Daily Journal): Odos Lenorman 205, 104 42 Athens; tel. (210) 5198000; fax (210) 5146013; e-mail info@naftemporiki.gr; internet www.naftemporiki.gr; f. 1924; morning; non-political journal of finance, commerce and shipping; Dir NIKOS FRANTZIS; Editor DIMITRIS PLAKOUTSIS; circ. 20,000.

Peloponnesos: Maizonos 206, 262 22 Patras; tel. (2610) 312530; fax (2610) 312535; internet www.peloponnisos.com.gr; f. 1886; independent; conservative; Publr and Editor S. DOUKAS; circ. 7,000.

Protathlitis (Champions): Dimokratias 34, Melissia, 151 27 Athens; tel. (210) 8109000; fax (210) 8040149; e-mail info@championsday.gr; internet www.championsday.gr; f. 1998; sport; circ. Tue.–Sun. 24,452, Mon. 24,651 (2009).

Rizospastis (Radical): Vitiligo 134, Krioneri, 145 68 Athens; tel. (210) 6297000; fax (210) 6297999; e-mail mailbox@rizospastis.gr; internet www.rizospastis.gr; f. 1974; morning; publ. by Modern Age-Publishing SA; Editor PAVLOS ALEPIS; circ. 10,108 (2009).

Sport Day: Davaki 58, Kallithea, 176 72 Athens; tel. (210) 9508100; fax (210) 9508155; e-mail info@sday.gr; internet www.sday.gr; f. 2005; sport; circ. Tue.–Sun. 31,099, Mon. 32,216 (2009).

Ta Nea (News): Odos Michalakopoulou 80, 115 28 Athens; tel. (211) 3657000; fax (211) 3658301; e-mail info@tanea.gr; internet www.tanea.gr; f. 1944; liberal; afternoon; publ. by Lambrakis Press SA; Dir and Editor PANTELIS KAPSIS; circ. 56,543.

To Fos Ton Spor: Athinon 122, 104 42 Athens; tel. (210) 5154000; fax (210) 5141330; e-mail fos@otenet.gr; f. 1968; sport; circ. Tue.–Sun. 23,693, Mon. 24,918 (2009).

To Vima (Tribune): Odos Michalakopoulou 80, 115 28 Athens; tel. (210) 3657000; fax (210) 3658004; e-mail tovima@dolnet.gr; internet www.tovima.gr; f. 1922; liberal; publ. by Lambrakis Press SA; Dir and Editor STAVROS R. PSYCHARIS; circ. daily 38,712, Sun. 172,368 (2009).

WEEKLY PUBLICATIONS

Athens News: Odos Doiranis 181, Kallithea, 176 73 Athens; tel. (213) 0087150; fax (210) 9431110; e-mail athensnews@athensnews.eu; internet www.athensnews.gr; f. 1952; weekly; in English; owned by NEP Publishing Company SA; Editor IOANNA PAPADIMITROPOULOU; circ. 10,000.

I Aksia (Value): 3 Septemvriou 144, 112 51 Athens; tel. (210) 8254811; fax (210) 8814229; f. 1998; Publr ANTONIS PIKOULAS; circ. 13,165 (2009).

Kathimerini Tis Kiriakis (Every Day on Sunday): Minoos 10–16, 117 43 Athens; tel. (210) 9296001; fax (210) 9028311; e-mail ke@enet.gr; internet www.enet.gr; f. 1919; Dir JOHN VLASTARIS; Editors ALEXANDRA DALIANI, VAGELIS SIAFAKAS; circ. 134,665 (2009).

O Kosmos Tou Ependiti (The World of Investors): Leoforos 174, Kallithea, 176 71 Athens; tel. (210) 3721100; fax (210) 3721110; e-mail ependitis@kte.gr; internet www.kte.gr; f. 2002; politics, economics and social; Chair. and Man. Dir KOSTAS A. GIANNIKOS; Editor NIKOS FELEKIS; circ. 80,397 (2009).

Proto Thema (One Topic): Apostolou Pavlou 6, 15 123 Marousi; tel. (210) 6834444; fax (210) 6892778; e-mail protothema@protothema.gr; internet www.protothema.gr; f. 2005; Sunday; circ. 179,782 (2009).

Real News: Leoforos Kifisias 215, 151 24 Athens; tel. (211) 2008300; fax (211) 2008399; e-mail news@realnews.gr; internet www.realnews.gr; f. 2008; Sunday; Editor and Dir NIKOS HATZINIKOLAOU; circ. 101,491.

Sto Karfi Tou Savvatokyriakou (The Weekend Nail): Krimeas 2 & Mesogion 125, 115 26 Athens; tel. (210) 6901000; fax (210) 6915741; e-mail info@stokarfi.gr; internet digital.stokarfi.gr; f. 2004; Saturdays; left-wing; Dir KOSTAS GIANNOPOULOS; circ. 23,344 (2009).

Xrisi Efkeria (Golden Opportunity): Golden Opportunity Publ., Sakasomouli Hekataios 95 & 73, 117 44 Athens; tel. (210) 9091333; fax (210) 9091420; e-mail contact@xe.gr; internet www.xe.gr; f. 1993; publ. by Golden Opportunity Publications; CEO AVGOUSTINIATOS HARRIS; circ. 41,293 (2009).

SELECTED PERIODICALS

Aktines (Rays): Odos Karytsi 14, 105 61 Athens; f. 1938; monthly; Christian publication on current affairs, science, philosophy, arts; circ. 10,000.

Asfalistikn Agora (The Insurance Market): Dionysus 126, 151 24 Maroussi; tel. (210) 6196879; fax (210) 6196943; e-mail aagora@aagora.gr; internet www.aagora.gr; monthly; Dir and Editor DIMITRIS ROUCHOTAS.

Computer Gia Olous (Computers for All): Capt. Dedousi 1 & Mesogion 304, Holargos, 155 62 Athens; tel. (210) 9238672; fax (210) 9216847; e-mail cpress@compupress.gr; internet www.cgomag.gr; monthly; Editor FORTIS KARATZIAS.

Deltion Diikiseos Epichiriseon Euro-Unial (Euro-Unial Business Administration Bulletin): Odos Rhigillis 26, 106 74 Athens; fax (210) 7240000; e-mail info@dde.gr; internet www.dde.gr; monthly; Editor I. PAPAMICHALAKIS; circ. 26,000 (2006).

Ebdomi (Seventh): Kanari 18, 153 51 Pallini; tel. (210) 6030655; fax (210) 9658949; e-mail scarabe@hol.gr; internet www.ebdomi.com; weekly; political-economic and cultural journal of Eastern Attica; Publr ANNA VENETSANOU.

Economiki Epitheorissi (Economic Review): Odos Vlahava 6–8, 105 51 Athens; tel. (210) 3314714; fax (210) 3230338; e-mail info@economia.gr; internet www.economia.gr; f. 1934; monthly; economy, business and politics; publ. by Group Economia-Kerkyra Publications; Dir and Publr ALEXANDRA VOVOLINI; Editors ANDREAS PETSINIS, SPYROS A. VRETOS; circ. 45,000.

Electrologos (Electrician): Odos Pileos & Leoforos Pentelis 3, Vrilissia, 152 35 Athens; tel. (210) 6800470; fax (210) 6800476; e-mail technoekdotiki@technoekdotiki.gr; internet www.electrologos.gr; f. 1991; monthly; technical; Publr VOULA MOURTA; Editor CHRISTINA SOURRA; circ. 11,500 (2009).

Elnavi (Greek Shipping Industry): Odos Aristidou 19, 185 31 Piraeus; tel. (210) 4522100; fax (210) 4282467; e-mail elnavi@elnavi.gr; internet www.elnavi.gr; f. 1974; monthly; shipping; Publr ELIAS KALAPOTHARAKOS; Dirs STEFANOS PAPANDREOU, THEANO KALAPOTHARAKOU; circ. 4,000 (2009).

Epiloghi (Selection): Theophanous 19–21, 115 23 Athens; tel. (210) 6401852; e-mail press@allmedia.gr; internet www.epilogimag.gr; f. 1962; weekly; economics; publ. by All Media Publications; Dir CHRISTOS PAPAIOANNOU; Editor MELIDOU THOMI.

Greek Diplomatic Life: Giving Fountain 5, 106 78 Athens; tel. (210) 3806534; fax (210) 3818983; e-mail diplomat@otenet.gr; f. 1978; bi-monthly; Publr BOUTSIKOS NIKOLAOS; circ. 5,500 (2009).

Gynaika (Women): Odos Fragoklissias 7, Marousi, 151 25 Athens; tel. (210) 6199149; fax (210) 6104707; e-mail admin@e-gynaika.com; internet www.e-gynaika.gr; f. 1950; monthly; Publr CHRISTOS TERZOPOULOS; circ. 45,000.

Idaniko Spiti (Ideal Home): Odos Benaki 5, Halandri, 152 38 Athens; tel. (210) 6061777; fax (210) 6061891; e-mail idanikospiti@pegasus.gr; internet www.idanikospiti.gr; f. 1990; monthly; interior decoration; Editor ALEXANDRA VAGENA; circ. 13,000 (2009).

Klik: Odos Fragoklisias 7, 151 25 Athens; fax (210) 6899153; internet www.klik.gr; f. 1987; monthly; popular music, media and fashion; Editor ARIS TERZOPUOLOS.

Kynigos Kai Fysi (Hunter and Nature): Kallirrois 85, 117 45 Athens; tel. (210) 7755464; fax (210) 7785776; e-mail onel@onel.gr; internet www.go-outdoor.gr; publ. by Onel SA; Publr KAKAVOULIS ELEFTHERIOS.

Mastoremata (Do-it-yourself): Odos Thorikou, Viopa Kalyvion, Kalyvia, 190 10 Attica; tel. (229) 9021360; fax (229) 9021359; e-mail info@mastoremata.gr; internet www.mastoremata.gr; monthly; publ. by Stefanos Karidakis SA; Publr PROKOPIS KARIDAKIS; Editor DIMITRIS GEORGOPOULOS.

Pantheon: Odos Christou Lada 3, 102 37 Athens; fax (210) 3228797; every two weeks; Publr and Dir N. THEOFANIDES.

Ptisi & Diastima (Flight & Space): Ioannou Metaxa 80, Koropi, 194 00 Athens; tel. (210) 9792500; fax (210) 9792528; e-mail ptisi@ptisi.gr; internet www.ptisi.gr; f. 1979; monthly; Editor FAITHON KARAIOSSIFIOIS; circ. 1,467.

Radiotileorasi (Radio-TV): Odos Rhigillis 4, 106 74 Athens; tel. (210) 7407252; fax (210) 7224812; e-mail radiotileorasi@ert.gr; internet www.radiotileorasi.gr; weekly; Editor DIMITRIS KOCHLATZIS; circ. 55,000.

Stigmes (Moments): Psaromiligkon 17, Heraklion, 712 02 Crete; tel. (281) 0288333; fax (281) 0301927; e-mail spiti@stigmes.gr; internet www.stigmes.gr; six a year; Cretan culture; Editor NIKOS KARELLIS.

Technika Chronika (Technical Times): Odos Nikis, Syndagma, 102 48 Athens; tel. (210) 3291200; fax (210) 3221772; e-mail tee@central.tee.gr; internet www.tee.gr; f. 1932; weekly; general technical subjects; Editor IOANNIS ALAVANOS; circ. 100,000.

Tilerama: Odos Voukourestiou 18, 106 71 Athens; tel. (210) 3607160; fax (210) 3607032; f. 1977; weekly; radio and television; circ. 189,406.

To Pontiki (The Mouse): Odos Massalias 10, 106 81 Athens; fax (210) 6898226; e-mail asfalistiko@topontiki.gr; internet www.topontiki.gr; weekly; humour; Dir and Editor K. PAPAIOANNOU.

NEWS AGENCY

Athens News Agency (ANA): Odos Tsoha 36, 115 21 Athens; tel. (210) 6400560; fax (210) 6400581; e-mail press@ana-mpa.gr; internet www.ana-mpa.gr; f. 1895; correspondents in leading capitals of the world and towns throughout Greece; Man. Dir NIKOLAS VOULELIS; Gen. Dir GEORGE TAMBAKOPOULOS.

PRESS ASSOCIATIONS

Enosis Antapokriton Xenou Tipou (Foreign Press Association of Greece): Odos Akademias 23, 106 71 Athens; tel. (210) 3637318; fax (210) 3605035; e-mail fpa@fpa.gr; internet www.fpa.gr; f. 1916; Pres. VASSILIS TRIANDAFYLLOU; Gen. Sec. IOANNA KOURELA; 300 mems.

Enosis Demosiograpson Idioktiton Periodikou Tipou (Union of Journalists and Proprietors of the Periodical Press—EDIPT): Leoforos Vas Sofias 25, Athens; tel. (210) 7220875; fax (210) 7215128; e-mail info@edipt.gr; internet www.edipt.gr; f. 1939; Pres. BAIOS ELIAS SELLOUNTOS; Gen. Sec. KONSTANTINOS KALYVAS; 250 mems (2009).

Enosis Idioktiton Imerission Ephimeridon Athinon (Athens Daily Newspaper Publishers' Association): Mourouzi 14, 106 74 Athens; tel. (210) 7209810; e-mail postmaster@eihea.gr; internet www.eihea.gr; f. 1951; Pres. DIMITRIS KALOFOLIAS; Sec. DIMITRIS RIZOS.

Enosis Syntakton Imerission Ephimeridon Athinon (Journalists' Union of Athens Daily Newspapers): Odos Akademias 20, 106 71 Athens; tel. (210) 3632601; fax (210) 3632608; e-mail info@esiea.gr; internet www.esiea.gr; f. 1914; Pres. PANOS SOMPOLOS; Gen. Sec. KOSTAS BETINAKIS; 1,400 mems.

Enosis Syntakton Periodikou Tipou (Journalists' Union of the Periodical Press): Odos Valaoritou 9, 6th Floor, 106 71 Athens; tel. (210) 3633427; fax (210) 3638627; e-mail espt@otenet.gr; internet www.espit.gr; f. 1959; Pres. JOHN PLACHOURAS; Gen. Sec. THEMISTOKLES BEREDIMAS; 835 mems.

Publishers

Agkyra Publications: Odos Lamprou Katsoni 271, Aghi Anargyri, 135 62 Athens; tel. (210) 2693800; fax (210) 2693806; internet www.agyra.gr; f. 1890; general; Man. Dir DIMITRIOS PAPADIMITRIOU.

Akritas: Odos Chalkokondili 36, 104 32 Athens; tel. (210) 9334554; fax (210) 9404950; e-mail akritas@pkbooks.gr; internet www.akritas.net.gr; f. 1978; history, Orthodox Christianity, children's books.

A. Arsenides & Co: Odos Akadimias 57, 106 79 Athens; tel. (210) 3629538; fax (210) 3618707; e-mail tarsen@otenet.gr; f. 1952; philosophy, psychology, sociology, history, biography, literature, children's books; Man. Dir AIKATERINI ARSENIDES.

Ekdotike Athenon: Odos Hippokratous 13, 106 79 Athens; tel. (210) 3608911; fax (210) 3608914; e-mail info@ekdotikeathenon.gr; internet www.ekdotikeathenon.gr; f. 1962; history, archaeology, art.

Exandas Publications: Odos Didotou 57, 106 81 Athens; tel. (210) 3804885; fax (210) 3813065; e-mail info@exandasbooks.gr; internet www.exandasbooks.gr; f. 1974; fiction, literature, social sciences; Pres. MAGDA N. KOTZIA.

Govostis Publishing: Zoodohou Pigis 73, 106 81 Athens; tel. (210) 3815433; fax (210) 3816661; e-mail cotsos@govostis.gr; internet www.govostis.gr; f. 1926; arts, fiction, politics; Pres. COSTAS GOVOSTIS.

Denise Harvey: Katounia, 340 05 Limni, Evia; tel. and fax (22270) 31154; e-mail dhp@dharveypublisher.gr; internet www.deniseharveypublisher.gr; f. 1972; books concerned with post-Byzantine Greek culture, incl. literature, theology, history, music, anthropology and sociology (English and Greek); Man. Dir DENISE HARVEY.

Hestia-I.D. Kollaros S.A. & Co: Odos Evripidou 84, 105 53 Athens; tel. (210) 3213704; fax (210) 220821; e-mail info@hestia.gr; internet www.hestia.gr; f. 1885; literature, history, politics, psychoanalysis, philosophy, children's books, political and philosophical essays; Gen. Dir EVA-MARIA KARAITIDI.

Kastaniotis Editions: Odos Zalogou 11, 106 78 Athens; tel. (210) 3301208; fax (210) 3822530; e-mail info@kastaniotis.com; internet www.kastaniotis.com; f. 1968; fiction and non-fiction, incl. arts, social sciences and psychology, children's books; Man. Dir ATHANASIOS KASTANIOTIS.

Kritiki Publishing: Odos Patission 75, 104 34 Athens; tel. (210) 8211811; fax (210) 8211026; e-mail biblia@kritiki.gr; internet www.kritiki.gr; f. 1987; economics, politics, literature, philosophy, business management, popular science; Publr THEMIS MINOGLOU.

Livani Publishing Organization: Odos Solonos 98, 106 80 Athens; tel. (210) 3661200; fax (210) 3617791; e-mail rights@livanis.gr; internet www.livanis.gr; f. 1972; fiction, non-fiction, children's books; Publr A. A. LIVANI.

Minoas: Odos Davaki Konstantinou 34, 144 51 Metamorfosi; tel. (210) 2711222; fax (210) 2711056; e-mail info@minoas.gr; internet www.minoas.gr; f. 1952; fiction, art, history; Man. Dir IOANNIS KONSTANTAROPOULOS.

Papazissis Publishers: Nikitara 2, 106 78 Athens; tel. (210) 3822496; fax (210) 3809150; e-mail papazisi@otenet.gr; internet www.papazisi.gr; f. 1929; economics, politics, law, history, school books; Man. Dir ALEXANDROS PAPAZISSIS.

Patakis Publishers: Pan. Tsaldari 38, 104 37 Athens; tel. (210) 3650000; fax (210) 3811940; e-mail bookstore@patakis.gr; internet www.patakis.gr; f. 1974; art, reference, fiction, educational, philosophy, psychology, sociology, religion, music, children's books, audiobooks; Pres. STEFANOS PATAKIS.

PUBLISHERS' ASSOCIATIONS

Book Publishers' Association of Athens: Odos Themistokleus 73, 106 83 Athens; tel. (210) 3303268; fax (210) 3823222; e-mail seva@otenet.gr; internet www.seva.gr; f. 1945; Pres. STELIOS ELLINIADIS; Sec. LOUCAS RINOPOULOS.

Hellenic Federation of Publishers and Booksellers: Odos Themistokleus 73, 106 83 Athens; tel. (210) 3804760; fax (210) 3301617; e-mail secretary@poev.gr; internet www.poev.gr; f. 1961; Pres. RAGIA ANNIE; Gen. Sec. STATHATOS NICHOLAS.

Broadcasting and Communications

TELECOMMUNICATIONS

By the end of 2009 531 licensed service providers were operating in the main electronic communications market of voice telephony and fixed-line networks (178), voice telephony (141), fixed-line networks (87), satellite networks (34), 2G and 3G mobile technology (13), terrestrial trunk radio (TETRA—five) and wireless local area network (W-LAN—73).

Hellenic Telecommunications and Post Commission: Leoforos Kifissias 60, 151 25 Athens; tel. (210) 6151000; fax (210) 6105049; e-mail info@eett.gr; internet www.eett.gr; regulatory body; Chair. LEONIDAS KANELLOS.

Ericsson Hellas S.A.: Odos Attiki 40/2, Peania, Athens; tel. (210) 6695100; fax (210) 6695328; internet www.ericsson.com; f. 1876; parent co based in Sweden; CEO HANS VESTBERG.

Forthnet: Atthidon 4, 176 71 Kallithea; tel. (211) 9559000; fax (211) 9559333; e-mail info@forthnet.gr; internet www.forthnet.gr; broadband and satellite telecommunications services; CEO PANAYIOTIS PAPADOPOULOS.

Hellenic Telecommunications Organization (OTE) (Organismos Telepikoinonion tis Elladas): Leoforos Kifissias 99, 151 24 Maroussi, Athens; tel. (210) 6117434; fax (210) 6115825; e-mail media-office@ote.gr; internet www.ote.gr; f. 1949; 20% owned by the Government, 30% by Deutsche Telekom (Germany); Chief Exec. and Chair. MICHAEL TSAMAZ.

COSMOTE: Leoforos Kifissias 44, 151 25 Athens; tel. (210) 6177777; fax (210) 6177594; e-mail mediarelations@cosmote.gr; internet www.cosmote.gr; f. 1998; 59% owned by OTE; mobile cellular telecommunications; Pres. and CEO MICHAEL TSAMAZ.

Maritel: Odos Egaleo 8, 185 45 Piraeus; tel. (210) 4599500; fax (210) 4599600; e-mail maritel@maritel.gr; internet www.otesat-maritel.com; OTE subsidiary; marine telecommunications; Chair. THEODOROS VENIAMIS; CEO GEORGE POLYCHRONOPOULOS.

Vodafone Greece: 1–3 Tzavella, 152 31 Halandri; tel. (210) 6702000; fax (210) 6703200; internet www.vodafone.gr; 55% owned by Vodafone Europe Holdings (United Kingdom); mobile cellular telecommunications; Chair. NICHOLAS SOPHOCLEOUS.

WIND Hellas Telecommunications: Leoforos Kifissias 66, 151 25 Athens; tel. (210) 6158000; fax (210) 5100001; internet www.wind.com.gr; f. 1992 as Telestet; renamed as above in 2007; fixed and mobile cellular telecommunications, internet services; Chair. and CEO NASSOS ZARKALIS.

RADIO

In addition to the seven national radio stations operated by Elliniki Radiophonia Tileorasi (ERT), there are approximately 1,079 registered radio stations broadcasting from across the country.

Elliniki Radiophonia Tileorasi (ERT) (Greek Radio-Television): Leoforos Messoghion 432, 106 74 Athens; tel. (210) 6066000; fax (210) 6009325; e-mail president@ert.gr; internet www.ert.gr; state-controlled; Man. Dir LAMBIS TAGMATARCHIS.

Elliniki Radiophonia (ERA) (Greek Radio): Leoforos Messoghion 432, 153 42 Aghia Paraskevi, Athens; tel. (210) 7298853; fax (210) 7292826; e-mail ntheleriti@ert.gr; internet www.ert.gr/radio; Dir-Gen. DIMITRIS PAPADIMITRIOU.

ERT3—Macedonia Radio Station: Odos Angelaki 2, 546 21 Thessaloníki; tel. (2310) 299400; fax (2310) 299451; e-mail info@ert3.gr; internet www.ert3.gr.

TELEVISION

In June 2011, in addition to the publicly owned four national analogue terrestrial TV stations, three national digital TV stations and one satellite TV station, there were seven main national private TV networks and approximately 150 local and regional TV stations broadcasting across the country.

State Stations

Elliniki Radiophonia Tileorassi (ERT) (Greek Radio-Television): see Radio.

Elliniki Tileorassi 1 (ET1) (Greek Television 1): Leoforos Messoghion 136, 115 27 Athens; tel. (210) 7758824; fax (210) 7797776; e-mail kalavanos@ert.gr; internet www.ert.gr/et1; Dir-Gen. KONSTANTINOS ALAVANOS.

ET2: Leoforos Messoghion 136, 115 25 Athens; tel. (210) 7701911; fax (210) 7797776; Dir-Gen. PANAYOTIS PANAYOTOU.

ERT3: Aggelaki 2, 546 36 Thessaloníki; tel. (2310) 299610; fax (2310) 299655; e-mail pr@ert3.gr; internet www.ert.gr; Dir-Gen. KOSTAS BLIATKAS.

Private Stations

Antenna TV: Leoforos Kifissias 10–12, Maroussi, 151 25 Athens; tel. (210) 6886100; fax (210) 6834349; e-mail webmaster@antenna.gr; internet www.antenna.gr; f. 1989; Chair. M. X. KYRIAKOU.

City Channel: Leoforos Kastoni 14, 412 23 Larissa; tel. (241) 232839; fax (241) 232013.

Mega Channel: Leoforos Messoghion 117, 115 26 Athens; tel. (210) 6903000; fax (210) 6983600; e-mail ngeorgiou@megatv.com; internet www.megatv.com; f. 1989; Man. Dir ELIAS TSIGAS.

Serres TV: Nigritis 27, 621 24 Serres.

Star Channel: Odos Thermopylon 87, 351 00 Lamia; tel. (22310) 46725; fax (22310) 46728; e-mail starch@lam.forthnet.gr; internet www.lamiastar.gr; f. 1988; Pres. NIKE CHEIMONIDIS.

Tele City: Praxitelous 58, 176 74 Athens; tel. (210) 9429222; fax (210) 9413589.

Traki TV: Central Sq., 671 00 Xanthi; tel. (25410) 20670; fax (25410) 27368.

TRT: Ferron 65, 383 34 Volos; tel. (24210) 28801; fax (24210) 36888; e-mail commercial@trttv.com; internet www.trttv.com; f. 1990; Pres. and CEO EVANGELOS ANTONIOU.

TV-100: Odos Aggelaki 16, 546 21 Thessaloníki; tel. (2310) 265828; fax (2310) 267532.

Finance

(cap. = capital; res = reserves; dep. = deposits; m. = million; brs = branches; amounts in euros, unless otherwise stated; SDR = Special Drawing Rights)

BANKING

In 2006 there were 62 banks in Greece, of which 24 were foreign-owned.

Central Bank

Bank of Greece: Leoforos E. Venizelos 21, 102 50 Athens; tel. (210) 3201111; fax (210) 3232239; e-mail sec.secretariat@bankofgreece.gr; internet www.bankofgreece.gr; f. 1927; cap. 111.2m., res 694.1m., dep. 10,266.6m. (Dec. 2009); Gov. GEORGIOS A. PROVOPOULOS; 18 branches, 8 counters and 38 agencies.

Commercial Banks

Agricultural Bank of Greece: Odos Panepistimiou 23, 105 64 Athens; tel. (210) 3298911; fax (210) 3298322; e-mail ategt@ate.gr; internet www.atebank.gr; f. 1929; state-owned; cap. 1,326.9m., res 65.6m., dep. 30,098.1m. (Dec. 2009); Pres. and Gov. THEODORE PANTALAKIS; 505 brs; under restructuring in 2011.

Alpha Bank: Stadiou 40, 102 52 Athens; tel. (210) 3260000; fax (210) 3265052; e-mail secretariat@alpha.gr; internet www.alpha.gr; f. 1879; present name adopted 2000; cap. 3,451.1m., res 609.2m., dep. 61,583.9m. (Dec. 2009); Chair. and Gen. Man. IOANNIS S. COSTOPOULOS; 431 brs.

Bank of Attica: Odos Omirou 23, 106 72 Athens; tel. (210) 3669000; fax (210) 3667253; e-mail info@atticabank.gr; internet www.atticabank.gr; f. 1925; cap. 185.9m., res 366.5m., dep. 4,610.6m. (Dec. 2009); Exec. Dir IOANNIS GAMVRILIS; 62 brs.

Black Sea Trade and Development Bank: Odos Komninon 1, 546 24 Thessaloníki; tel. (2310) 290400; fax (2310) 221796; e-mail info@bstdb.org; internet www.bstdb.org; f. 1997; owned by 11 member states: Greece, Russian Federation, Turkey (16.5% each); Bulgaria, Romania, Ukraine (13.5% each); Albania, Armenia,

Azerbaijan, Georgia, Moldova (2.0% each); cap. SDR 301.5m., res SDR 27.7m., dep. SDR 1.1m. (Dec. 2009); Pres. ANDREY KONDAKOV.

EFG Eurobank Ergasias SA: Odos Leoforos Amalias 20, 105 57 Athens; tel. (210) 3337688; fax (210) 3337256; e-mail info@eurobank.gr; internet www.eurobank.gr; f. 1990; present name adopted 2000; cap. 2,430m., res 3,609m., dep. 76,195m. (Dec. 2009); Pres. EYTHYMIOS N. CHRISTODOULOU; CEO NIKOLAS NANOPOULOS; 400 brs.

Emporiki Bank of Greece SA: Odos Sophokleous 11, 102 35 Athens; tel. (210) 3284000; fax (210) 3253746; e-mail pubrel@emporiki.gr; internet www.emporiki.gr; f. 1907; present name adopted 2003; 86.5% owned by Crédit Agricole SA (France); cap. 1,577.7m., res 122.7m., dep. 25,086.7m. (Dec. 2009); Chair. NIKOLAOS EMPEOGLOY; CEO ALAIN STRUB; 340 brs.

Geniki Bank—General Bank of Greece: Odos Messogeion 109–111, 115 10 Athens; tel. (210) 6975200; fax (210) 6975910; e-mail intdiv@geniki.gr; internet www.geniki.gr; f. 1937; present name adopted 1998; controlling stake acquired by Société Générale (France) in 2004; cap. 255.6m., res 21.4m., dep. 4,370.9m. (Dec. 2009); Chair. TRYFON KOUTALIDIS; 141 brs.

Marfin Egnatia Bank: Leoforos Kifissias 24, 151 25 Athens; tel. (210) 9304811; fax (210) 6896306; e-mail info@marfinegnatiabank.gr; internet www.marfinegnatiabank.gr; f. 1991 as Egnatia Bank; present name adopted July 2007, after merger of Laiki Bank (Hellas) and Marfin Bank with Egnatia Bank; cap. 366.8m., res 592.3m., dep. 19,181.3m. (Dec. 2009); Pres. and Chair. VASSILIOS THEOCHARAKIS; 157 brs.

National Bank of Greece (NBG): Odos Aeolou 86, 102 32 Athens; tel. (210) 3341000; fax (210) 4806510; e-mail contact.center@nbg.gr; internet www.nbg.gr; f. 1841; state-controlled, but operates independently of the Govt; cap. 3,392.7m., res 5,577.4m., dep. 96,026.7m. (Dec. 2009); CEO APOSTOLOS TAMVAKAKIS; 601 brs.

Piraeus Bank: Odos Amerikis 4, 105 64 Athens; tel. (210) 3335000; fax (210) 3335080; e-mail investor-relations@piraeusbank.gr; internet www.piraeusbank.gr; f. 1916; cap. 1,604.0m., res 1,219.4m., dep. 45,046.1m. (Dec. 2009); Chair. MICHALIS G. SALLAS; 86 brs.

TBank: Odos Omirou 22, 106 72 Athens; tel. (210) 3364000; fax (210) 9986215; e-mail aspis@aspisbank.gr; internet www.tbank.com.gr/tbank; f. 1992; fmrly Aspis Bank; renamed as above after acquisition by TT Hellenic Postbank in May 2010; cap. 173.6m., res –37.1m., dep. 2,273.4m. (Dec. 2008); Chair. of Bd PAPADOPOULOS KLEANTHIS.

STOCK EXCHANGE

Athens Stock Exchange: Odos Sophokleous 10, 105 59 Athens; tel. (210) 3211301; fax (210) 3213938; e-mail webmaster@ase.gr; internet www.ase.gr; f. 1876; Pres. CAPRALOS SPYROS; Vice-Pres. LAZARIDIS SOKRATIS.

PRINCIPAL INSURANCE COMPANIES

In 2005 there were 95 insurance companies operating in Greece, of which 18 provided life insurance, 64 provided non-life insurance, and 13 provided both life and non-life insurance.

Agrotiki Hellenic Insurance Co: Leoforos Syngrou 163, 171 21 Kallithea, Athens; tel. (210) 9379100; fax (210) 9358924; e-mail info@agroins.com; internet www.agroins.com; Pres. THEODORE PANTALAKIS.

Aspis Pronia General Insurance SA: Leoforos Kifissias 62, 151 25 Maroussi, Athens; tel. (210) 6198960; fax (210) 6176165; e-mail info@aspis.gr; internet www.aspis.gr; f. 1941; Pres. and Chief Exec. PAUL PSOMIADES.

Atlantiki Enosis/Atlantic Union: Odos Messoghion 71 & Ilidos 36, 115 26 Athens; tel. (210) 7454000; fax (210) 7794446; e-mail atlantiki@atlantiki.gr; internet www.atlanticunion.gr; f. 1970; subsidiary of La Baloise (Switzerland); Pres. STASINOPOULOS SARANDOS.

Axa Insurance: Odos Michalakopoulou 48, 115 28 Athens; tel. (210) 7268311; fax (210) 7268408; e-mail info@axa-insurance.gr; internet www.axa-insurance.gr; fmrly Alpha Insurance; Man. Dir ERIC KLEIJNEN.

Commercial Value: Odos Sofias 60, 115 28 Athens; tel. (210) 6389200; fax (210) 6106038; e-mail admin@nch.gz; internet www.commercialvalue.gr; f. 2002; Pres. D. VIDALIS; Sec. V. APOSTOLOPOULOS.

Dynamis: Leoforos Syngrou 320, 176 73 Kallithea, Athens; tel. (210) 9006900; fax (210) 9237768; e-mail info@dynamis.gr; internet www.dynamis.gr; f. 1977; Man. Dir NIKOLAS STAMATOPOULOS.

Emporiki Life: Odos Mitropoleos 45, 105 56 Athens; tel. (210) 3283583; fax (210) 3283503; e-mail dkalimeri@emporikilife.gr; f. 1940; Chair. PANAYIOTIS VARELAS; Man. Dir BERNARD CHAUVEL.

Ethniki Hellenic General Insurance Co SA: Odos Karageorgi Servias 8, 102 10 Athens; tel. (210) 3299000; fax (210) 3236101; internet www.ethniki-asfalistiki.gr; f. 1891; Gen. Man. C. PHILIPOU.

Horizon General Insurance Co: Leoforos Amalias 26A, 105 57 Athens; tel. (210) 3227932; fax (210) 3225540; e-mail info@horizonins.gr; f. 1965; Gen. Man THEODORE ACHIS.

Imperial Hellas: Leoforos Syngrou 253, N. Smirni, 171 22 Athens; tel. (210) 9426352; fax (210) 9426202; internet www.imperial.gr; f. 1971; Gen. Man. G. TZANIS.

Interamerican Hellenic Life Insurance Co: Odos Sygrou 124–126, 176 80 Athens; tel. (210) 9461111; fax (210) 9461008; e-mail moissism@interamerican.gr; internet www.interamerican.gr; f. 1971; 79.4% owned by Eureko (Netherlands); subsidiary cos provide medical, property, casualty, and automobile insurance; Chair. ADRIAN HEGARTY.

Phoenix General Insurance Co of Greece: Odos Omirou 2, 105 64 Athens; tel. (210) 3295111; fax (210) 3239135; e-mail phoenix@phoenix.gr; internet www.phoenix.gr; f. 1928; general.

Sideris Insurance Co: Odos Lekka 3–5, 105 63 Athens; tel. (281) 0301678; fax (281) 0301679; e-mail info@sideris-insurance.gr; internet www.sideris-insurance.gr; Dir G. SIDERIS.

Syneteristiki General Insurance Co: Leoforos Syngrou 367, 175 64 Kallithea, Athens; tel. (210) 9491280; fax (210) 9403148; e-mail com@syneteristiki.gr; internet www.syneteristiki.gr; Gen. Man. DIMITRIS ZORBAS.

Victoria General Insurance Co SA: Odos Sofias 97, 115 21 Athens; tel. (210) 3705550; fax (210) 3705300; e-mail victoria@victoria.gr; internet www.victoria.gr; f. 1972; Man. Dir G. ANDONIADIS.

Insurance Association

Hellenic Association of Insurance Companies: Odos Xenophontos 10, 105 57 Athens; tel. (210) 3334100; fax (210) 3334149; e-mail info@eaee.gr; internet www.eaee.gr; f. 1907; 71 mem cos; Gen. Man. MARGARITA ANTONAKI.

Trade and Industry

CHAMBERS OF COMMERCE

Athens Chamber of Commerce and Industry: Odos Akademias 7, 106 71 Athens; tel. (210) 3604815; fax (210) 3616464; e-mail info@acci.gr; internet www.acci.gr; f. 1919; Pres. CONSTANTINOS MICHALOS; Sec.-Gen. NIKOS SOFIANOS; 70,000 mems.

Athens Chamber of Small and Medium-sized Industries: Odos Akademias 18, 106 71 Athens; tel. (210) 3680700; fax (210) 3614726; e-mail info@acsmi.gr; internet www.acsmi.gr; f. 1940; Pres. RAVANIS PAUL; Gen. Sec. LIAMETIS VASILIOS; c. 60,000 mems.

Piraeus Chamber of Commerce and Industry: Odos Loudovikou 1, Pl. Odessa, 185 31 Piraeus; tel. (210) 4177241; fax (210) 4178680; e-mail evep@pcci.gr; internet www.pcci.gr; f. 1919; Pres. GEORGE KASSIMATIS; Gen. Sec. DIMITRIOS MARKOMICHALIS.

Piraeus Chamber of Industry: Odos Karaiscou 111, 185 32 Piraeus; tel. (210) 4110443; fax (210) 4179495; e-mail info@bep.gr; internet www.bep.gr; f. 1925; Pres. ANDRIANOS MIHALARIAS; Gen. Sec. GERASIMOS MICHALAKIS.

Thessaloníki Chamber of Commerce and Industry (TCCI): Odos Tsimiski 29, 546 24 Thessaloníki; tel. (231) 0370100; fax (231) 0370166; e-mail root@ebeth.gr; internet www.ebeth.gr; f. 1918; Pres. DIMITRIOS BAKATSELOS; Sec.-Gen. MARIA CHATZAKOU; 18,000 mems.

INDUSTRIAL AND TRADE ASSOCIATIONS

Federation of Industries of Northern Greece (FING): Morihovou 1, 546 25 Thessaloníki; tel. (231) 0539817; fax (231) 0541933; e-mail info@sbbe.gr; internet www.sbbe.gr; f. 1915; Pres. NIKOS PENTOZ; Gen. Sec. ATHANASIOS SAVAKIS.

Hellenic Cotton Board: Leoforos Syngrou 150, 176 71 Kallithea, Athens; tel. (210) 9225011; fax (210) 9243676; f. 1931; state org.; Pres. P. K. MYLONAS.

Hellenic Federation of Enterprises (SEV): Odos Xenophontos 5, Syntagma, 105 57 Athens; tel. (211) 5006000; fax (210) 3222929; e-mail info@sev.org.gr; internet www.sev.org.gr; f. 1907; Chair. DIMITRIS DASKALOPOULOS.

Hellenic Organization of Small and Medium Enterprises and Handicrafts (EOMMEX): Odos Xenias 16, 115 28 Athens; tel. (210) 7491100; fax (210) 7491146; e-mail interel@eommex.gr; internet www.eommex.gr; f. 1977; Pres. CHRIS PITELIS.

UTILITIES

Regulatory Authority

Regulatory Authority for Energy (RAE): Leoforos Piraeus 132, 118 54 Athens; tel. (210) 3727400; fax (210) 3255460; e-mail info@rae.gr; internet www.rae.gr; f. 2000; Chair. Dr NIKOS VASILAKOS.

Electricity

Hellenic Transmission System Operator SA (HTSO): Kastoros 72, 18545 Piraeus; tel. (210) 9466700; fax (210) 9466766; e-mail contact@desmie.gr; internet www.desmie.gr; electric energy transmission; Pres. MICHAEL PAPADOPOULOS.

Public Power Corpn (DEI): Odos Chalkokondili 30, 104 32 Athens; tel. (210) 5293417; fax (210) 5238445; e-mail info@dei.com.gr; internet www.dei.gr; f. 1950; 51% state-owned; generating capacity of 96 power stations: 12,843 MW (2008); generation, transmission and distribution of electricity; Chair. and CEO ARTHOUROS ZERVOS.

Gas

Public Gas Corpn (DEPA): Marinou Antipa 92, Leoforos Antipa, 141 21 Athens; tel. (210) 2701000; fax (210) 2701010; e-mail pr@depa.gr; internet www.depa.gr; f. 1988; 35% owned by Hellenic Petroleum SA, 65% state-owned; began gas imports 1997, initially for industrial use; Chair. and CEO HARRIS SACHINIS.

Water

In 1980 a law was approved, creating Municipal Enterprises for Water Supply and Sewerage (DEYA) to manage drinking water and sewerage throughout Greece. Since then some 90 DEYA have been established.

The Hellenic Union of Municipal Enterprises for Water Supply and Sewerage (EDEYA): Odos Papakyriazi 37–43, 412 22 Larissa; tel. (241) 0258261; fax (241) 0532347; e-mail info@edeya.gr; internet www.edeya.gr; f. 1989; Dir GEORGE MARINAKIS; 155 mems.

TRADE UNIONS

There are about 5,000 registered trade unions, grouped together in 82 federations and 86 workers' centres, which are affiliated to the Greek General Confederation of Labour.

Greek General Confederation of Labour (GSEE): Odos Patission 69 & Aenian 2, 104 34 Athens; tel. (210) 8202100; fax (210) 8202186; e-mail info@gsee.gr; internet www.gsee.gr; f. 1918; Pres. IOANNIS PANAGOPOULOS; Sec.-Gen. KOSTAS POUPAKIS; 700,000 mems.

Pan-Hellenic Federation of Seamen's Unions (PNO): Akti Miaouli 47–49, 185 36 Piraeus; tel. (210) 4292958; fax (210) 4293040; e-mail info@pno.gr; internet www.pno.gr; f. 1920; confederation of 14 marine unions; Pres. IOANNIS CHELAS; Gen. Sec. JOHN HALAS.

Supreme Administration of Greek Civil Servants' Trade Unions (ADEDY): Odos Psylla Philellinon 2, 105 57 Athens; tel. (210) 3246109; fax (210) 3246165; e-mail adedyed@adedy.gr; internet www.adedy.gr; Pres. COSTAS TSIKRIKAS; Gen. Sec. HLIAS HLIOPOULOS.

Transport

RAILWAYS

In 2009 there were 1,552 km of railway track in use. Construction of a 26.3-km electrified extension to the Athens–Piraeus line, in order to provide a three-line urban railway system for Athens, designated Metro Line 1, was completed in 2000. Metro Lines 2 and 3, each measuring some 9 km, opened prior to the holding of the Summer Olympic Games in 2004.

Attiko Metro: Leoforos Messoghion 191–93, 115 25 Athens; tel. (210) 6792399; fax (210) 6726126; e-mail info@ametro.gr; internet www.ametro.gr; f. 1991; operates lines 2 and 3 of underground railway in Athens; Chair. GEORGE IOANNIS.

Ilektriki Sidirodromi Athinon–Pireos (ISAP) (Athens–Piraeus Electric Railways): Odos Athinas 67, 105 52 Athens; tel. (210) 3248311; fax (210) 3223935; internet www.isap.gr; state-owned; 25.6 km of electrified track; Chair. GEORGE PAPAVASSILIOU; Man. Dir DIONISSIOS RAPPOS.

Organismos Sidirodromon Ellados (OSE) (Hellenic Railways Organization Ltd): Odos Karolou 1–3, 104 37 Athens; tel. (210) 5248395; fax (210) 5243290; internet www.ose.gr; f. 1971; state railways; Chair. NIKOLAOS BALTAS; Dir-Gen. A. LAZARIS.

ROADS

In 2008 there were 116,711 km of roads in Greece. Of this total, an estimated 9,299 km were main roads, and 948 km were motorways. The construction of the 680-km Egnatia highway, extending from the Adriatic coast to the Turkish border, was one of the largest road projects in Europe and was completed in 2009.

INLAND WATERWAYS

There are no navigable rivers in Greece.

Corinth Canal: built 1893; over six km long, links the Corinthian and Saronic Gulfs; shortens the journey from the Adriatic to Piraeus by 325 km; spanned by three single-span bridges, two for road and one for rail; can be used by ships of a maximum draught of 22 ft and width of 60 ft; managed since June 2001 by Sea Containers Group (United Kingdom).

SHIPPING

At the end of 2009 the Greek merchant fleet totalled 1,517 vessels, with a combined aggregate displacement of 38.9m. grt. Greece controls one of the largest merchant fleets in the world. The principal ports are Piraeus, Patras and Thessaloníki.

Union of Greek Shipowners: Akti Miaouli 85, 185 38 Piraeus; f. 1916; Pres. NICOS EFTHYMIOU.

Port Authorities

Patras Port Authority: South Patras Port, Akti Dimeon, 26333 Patras; tel. and fax (261) 0365134; e-mail programsecr@patrasport.gr; internet www.patrasport.gr; Pres. KOSTAS PLATIKOSTAS.

Piraeus Port Authority: Piraeus Port Authority, Akti Miaouli 10, 185 38 Piraeus; tel. (210) 4550000; fax (210) 4550280; e-mail ceo@olp.gr; internet www.olp.gr; f. 1930; 25% privatized; CEO GEORGE ANOMERITIS.

Port of Thessaloníki: Thessaloníki Port Authority, POB 10467, 541 10 Thessaloníki; tel. (231) 0593128; fax (231) 0510500; e-mail secretariat@thpa.gr; internet www.thpa.gr; Pres. and CEO STYLIANOS AGGELOUDIS.

Shipping Companies

The following are among the largest or most important shipping companies.

Anangel Shipping Enterprises: Akti Miaouli, POB 80004, 185 10 Piraeus; tel. (210) 4224500; fax (210) 4224819; f. 1971; subsidiary of Agelef Shipping Group (United Kingdom); Man. Dir J. PLATSIDAKIS.

Attica Holdings: Leoforos Syngrou 123–25 & Odos Torva 3, 117 45 Athens; tel. (210) 8919500; fax (210) 8919509; internet www.attica-group.com; f. 1918; subsidiary cos include Blue Star Ferries and Superfast.com; Chair. CHARALAMBOS S. PASCHALIS.

Blue Star Ferries: Leoforos Syngrou 123–25 & Odos Torva 3, 117 45 Athens; tel. (210) 8919800; fax (210) 8919829; e-mail bluestarferries@bluestarferries.com; internet www.bluestarferries.com; subsidiary of Attica Holdings (q.v.); operates passenger and cargo ferry services between the Greek mainland and islands, and between Greece and Italy.

Chandris (Hellas) Co: POB 80067, Akti Miaouli 95, 185 38 Piraeus; tel. (210) 4584000; fax (210) 4290256; e-mail chandris-hellas@chandris-group.gr; internet www.chandris-hellas.gr; f. 1915; Man. Dirs A. C. PIPERAS, M. G. SKORDIAS.

Costamare Shipping Co: Odos Zephyrou 60, Kallithea, 175 64 Athens; tel. (210) 9390000; fax (210) 9409051; f. 1974; container-shipping; Pres. Capt. VASSILIS C. KONSTANTAKOPOULOS.

Golden Union Shipping Co: Odos Aegales 8, 185 45 Piraeus; tel. (210) 4061000; fax (210) 4061199; e-mail infgusc@goldenunion.gr; internet www.goldenunion.gr; f. 1977; dry cargo bulk operations; Chair. and Man. Dir THEODORE VENIAMIS.

Marmaras Navigation Co: Odos Filellinon 4–6, 185 36 Piraeus; tel. (210) 4589000; fax (210) 4589037; e-mail crew@marmaras-nav.gr; internet www.marmaras-nav.gr; Dir D. DIAMANTIDES.

Minoan Lines Shipping Co: Odos 25 August 17, 712 02 Heraklion; tel. (2810) 399800; fax (2810) 330308; e-mail info@minoan.gr; internet www.minoan.gr; f. 1972; operate passenger and cargo ferry services between the Greek mainland and Crete, and between Greece and Italy; Man. Dir ANTONIS MANIADAKIS.

Naftomar Shipping and Trading Co: Leoforos C. Karamanlis 243, 166 73 Voula; tel. (210) 8914200; fax (210) 8914235; e-mail naftomar@naftomar.gr; internet www.naftomar.gr; f. 1972; specializes in the shipping of liquid petroleum gas; Man. Dir RIAD ZEIN.

Thenamaris Ships Management Co: Odos Athinas 16 & Odos Vorreou, Kavouri, 166 71 Athens; tel. (210) 8909000; fax (210) 8909653; e-mail op@thenamaris.com; internet www.thenamaris.gr; Dir K. MARTINOS.

Tsakos Group: Macedonia House, Leoforos Syngrou 367, POB 79141, Paleon Faliron, 175 64 Athens; tel. (210) 9480700; fax (210) 9480710; e-mail mail@tsakoshellas.gr; internet www.tsakosgroup.com; f. 1970; subsidiary cos include: Tsakos Shipping and Trading; Tsakos Energy Navigation; Tsakos Industrias Navales; Dir Capt PANAGIOTIS N. TSAKOS.

CIVIL AVIATION

There are international airports at Athens, Eleftherios Venizelos-Spata, Thessaloníki, Alexandroupolis, Corfu, Lesbos, Andravida,

Rhodes, Kos and Heraklion/Crete, and 24 domestic airports (of which 13 are authorized to receive international flights).

Aegean Airlines: Leoforos Vouliagmenis 572, 164 51 Athens; tel. (210) 9988350; fax (210) 9957598; internet www.aegeanair.com; f. 1987; domestic and international services; merger into Olympic Air (q.v.) proposed in 2010; Pres. and Chief Exec. THEODOROS VASSILAKIS.

Olympic Air: Eleftherios Venizelos Athens International Airport, Bldg 97, 190 19 Athens; tel. (210) 3569111; fax (210) 9267154; e-mail ebusms@olympicairlines.com; internet www.olympicair.com; f. 2009 in succession to state-owned Olympic Airways (f. 1957); owned by Marfin Investment Group; merger with Aegean Airlines (q.v.) proposed in 2010; Chair. ANDREAS VGENOPOULOS.

Tourism

The sunny climate, the natural beauty of the country, and its history and traditions attract tourists to Greece. There are numerous islands and many sites of archaeological interest. The number of tourists visiting Greece increased from 1m. in 1968 to 15.0m. in 2010, according to provisional data, in which year receipts from tourism amounted to an estimated US $12,741m. (excluding passenger transport).

Ellinikos Organismos Tourismou (EOT) (Greek National Tourist Organization): Odos Tsoha 7, 115 21 Athens; tel. (210) 8707000; e-mail info@gnto.gr; internet www.visitgreece.gr; Pres. Dr ARISTIDIS S. CALOGEROPOULOS-STRATIS.

Defence

Greece returned to the military structure of the North Atlantic Treaty Organization (NATO) in 1980, after an absence of six years. Military service is compulsory, and lasts for up to nine months. As assessed at November 2011, the armed forces numbered 145,647 (including conscripts), with an army of 87,441, a navy of 20,000, an air force of 26,606 and 11,600 joint-service troops; in addition, there were paramilitary forces of 4,000. Reservists, which included a national guard of 32,988, totalled 216,650. The USA occupied three military bases in Greece, with a total of 378 troops stationed there at November 2011.

Defence Expenditure: Budgeted at €4,730m. in 2012.

Chief of the General Staff of the National Defence: Lt-Gen. MICHALIS KOSTARAKOS.

Chief of the General Staff of the Army: Lt-Gen. KONSTANTINOS ZAZIAS.

Chief of the General Staff of the Navy: Rear-Adm. KOSMAS CHRISTIDIS.

Chief of the General Staff of the Air Force: Air Marshal ANTONIS TSANTIRAKIS.

Education

Education is available free of charge at all levels, and is officially compulsory for all children between the ages of six and 15 years. Primary education begins at the age of six and lasts for six years. Secondary education, beginning at the age of 12, is generally for six years, divided into two equal cycles. The vernacular language (demotiki) has replaced the formal version (katharevoussa) in secondary education. Pre-primary enrolment in 2006/07 included 68% of children in the relevant age-group. The comparable ratio in the same year at primary schools was 99%, and that at secondary schools was 91%. In 2003/04 the equivalent of 70% of the relevant age-group were enrolled in tertiary education (males 60%; females 79%). There were 21 universities in 2005, excluding the Medical School of Athens. In 2006 budgetary spending on education represented an estimated 9.9% of total expenditure, according to preliminary figures.

GRENADA

Introductory Survey

LOCATION, CLIMATE, LANGUAGE, RELIGION, FLAG, CAPITAL

Grenada, a mountainous, heavily forested island, is the most southerly of the Windward Islands, in the West Indies. The country also includes some of the small islands known as the Grenadines, which lie to the north-east of Grenada. The most important of these are the low-lying island of Carriacou and its neighbour, Petit Martinique. The climate is semi-tropical, with an average annual temperature of 28°C (82°F) in the lowlands. Annual rainfall averages about 1,500 mm (60 ins) in the coastal area and 3,800 mm to 5,100 mm (150–200 ins) in mountain areas. Most of the rainfall occurs between June and December. The majority of the population speak English, although a French patois is sometimes spoken. According to the census of 1991, 82% of Grenada's population were of African descent, while 13% were of mixed ethnic origins. Most of the population profess Christianity, and the main denominations are Roman Catholicism (to which some 45% of the population adhered in 2006) and Anglicanism (about 14% of the population). The national flag (proportions 1 by 2) consists of a diagonally quartered rectangle (yellow in the upper and lower segments, green in the right and left ones) surrounded by a red border bearing six five-pointed yellow stars (three at the upper edge of the flag, and three at the lower edge). There is a red disc, containing a large five-pointed yellow star, in the centre, and a representation of a nutmeg (in yellow and red) on the green segment near the hoist. The capital is St George's.

CONTEMPORARY POLITICAL HISTORY

Historical Context

Grenada was initially colonized by the French but was captured by the British in 1762. The Treaty of Versailles recognized British control in 1783. Grenada continued as a British colony until 1958, when it joined the Federation of the West Indies, remaining a member until the dissolution of the Federation in 1962. Full internal self-government and statehood in association with the United Kingdom were achieved in March 1967. During this period, the political life of Grenada was dominated by Herbert Blaize, the leader of the Grenada National Party (GNP), and Eric Gairy, a local trade union leader, who in 1950 founded the Grenada United Labour Party (GULP), with the support of an associated trade union. Gairy became Premier after the elections of 1967 and again after those of 1972, which he contested chiefly on the issue of total independence.

Domestic Political Affairs

Grenada became independent, within the Commonwealth, on 7 February 1974, with Gairy as Prime Minister. Domestic opposition to Gairy was expressed in public unrest, and the formation by the three opposition parties—the GNP, the United People's Party and the New Jewel Movement (NJM)—of the People's Alliance, which contested the 1976 general elections and reduced GULP's majority in the lower house.

The opposition regarded the rule of Sir Eric Gairy, as he became in 1977, as increasingly autocratic and corrupt, and in 1979 he was replaced in a bloodless coup by the leader of the left-wing NJM, Maurice Bishop. The new People's Revolutionary Government (PRG) suspended the Constitution and announced the imminent formation of a People's Consultative Assembly to draft a new constitution. Meanwhile, Grenada remained a monarchy, with the British Queen as Head of State, represented in Grenada by a Governor-General. During 1980–81 there was an increase in repression, against a background of mounting anti-Government violence and the PRG's fears of an invasion by US forces.

By mid-1982 relations with the USA, the United Kingdom and the more conservative members of the Caribbean Community and Common Market (CARICOM, see p. 227) were becoming increasingly strained: elections had not been arranged, restrictions against the privately owned press had been imposed, many detainees were still awaiting trial, and Grenada was aligning more closely with Cuba and the USSR. Cuba was contributing funds and construction workers for the airport at Point Salines, a project that further strengthened the US Government's conviction that Grenada was to become a centre for Soviet manoeuvres in the area.

In June 1983 Bishop sought to improve relations with the USA, and announced the appointment of a commission to draft a new constitution. The more left-wing members of the PRG denounced this attempt at conciliation as an ideological betrayal. A power struggle developed between Bishop and his deputy, Bernard Coard. In October Bishop was placed under house arrest, allegedly for his refusal to share power with Coard. The commander of the People's Revolutionary Army (PRA), Gen. Hudson Austin, subsequently announced that Bishop had been expelled from the NJM. On 19 October thousands of Bishop's supporters stormed the house, freed Bishop, and demonstrated outside the PRA headquarters. PRA forces responded by firing into the crowd. Later in the day, Bishop, three of his ministers and two trade unionists were executed by the PRA. The Government was replaced by a 16-member Revolutionary Military Council (RMC), led by Gen. Austin and supported by Coard. The remaining NJM ministers were arrested and imprisoned, and a total curfew was imposed.

Regional and international outrage at the assassination of Bishop, in addition to fears of a US military intervention, was so intense that after four days the RMC relaxed the curfew, reopened the airport and promised a swift return to civilian rule. However, the Organisation of Eastern Caribbean States (OECS, see p. 465) resolved to intervene in an attempt to restore democratic order, and asked for assistance from the USA, which readily complied. (It is unclear whether the decision to intervene preceded or followed a request for help to the OECS by the Grenadian Governor-General, Sir Paul Scoon.) On 25 October 1983 some 1,900 US military personnel invaded the island, accompanied by 300 troops from Jamaica, Barbados and member countries of the OECS. Fighting continued for some days, and the USA gradually increased its troop strength, with further reinforcements waiting offshore with a US naval task force. The RMC's forces were defeated, while Coard, Austin and others who had been involved in the coup were detained.

In November 1983 Scoon appointed a non-political interim Council to assume responsibility for the government of the country until elections could be held. Nicholas Brathwaite, a former Commonwealth official, was appointed Chairman of this Council in December. The 1974 Constitution was reinstated and an electoral commission was created. By mid-December the USA had withdrawn all its forces except 300 support troops, who remained until September 1985.

Several political parties that had operated clandestinely or from exile during the rule of the PRG re-emerged and announced their intention of contesting the elections for a new House of Representatives. Sir Eric Gairy returned to Grenada in January 1984 to lead GULP, but did not stand as a candidate himself. In May three former NJM ministers formed the Maurice Bishop Patriotic Movement (MBPM). A number of centrist parties emerged or re-emerged, including Blaize's GNP. Fears that a divided opposition would allow GULP to win a majority of seats in the new House resulted in an agreement by several of these organizations, in August 1984, to form the New National Party (NNP), led by Blaize. The NNP achieved a convincing victory in the December election, and Blaize became Prime Minister.

The trial of 19 detainees (including Coard, his wife, Phyllis, and Gen. Austin), accused of murder and conspiracy against Bishop and six of his associates, opened in November 1984, although there were repeated adjournments. One of the detainees agreed to give evidence for the State in return for a pardon. Eventually, in December 1986, the jury returned verdicts on 196 charges of murder and conspiracy to murder. Fourteen of the defendants were sentenced to death, three received prison sentences of between 30 and 45 years, and one was acquitted. In 1991 the Court of Appeal upheld the original verdicts on the defendants in the Bishop murder trial, and further pleas for clemency were rejected. Preparations for the imminent hanging of the 14, however, provoked international outrage, and in

August Brathwaite announced that the death sentences were to be commuted to life imprisonment.

In 1987 breakaway members of the NNP launched a new party, the National Democratic Congress (NDC), led by George Brizan, who had earlier been appointed parliamentary opposition leader. In January 1989 Blaize was replaced as party leader by his cabinet colleague, Dr Keith Mitchell, although he remained Prime Minister. In July, however, following allegations of corruption by the NDC, Blaize announced the dismissal of Mitchell and the Chairman of the NNP. Amid uncertainty as to whether the Blaize faction had formed a separate party, two more members of the Government resigned, thus reducing support for the Government to only five of the 15 members of the House of Representatives. Blaize did not officially announce the formation of a new party, the National Party, until late August, by which time he had advised the acting Governor-General to prorogue Parliament. Blaize died in December, and the Governor-General appointed Ben Jones, Blaize's former deputy, as Prime Minister. At the general election, held in March 1990, no party achieved an absolute majority in the House of Representatives, although the NDC achieved a working parliamentary majority. Nicholas Brathwaite became Prime Minister and appointed a new Cabinet. Brathwaite resigned as Prime Minister in February 1995, and was succeeded by Brizan.

The NNP's political domination

The NNP secured eight of the 15 seats in the House of Representatives at the general election of June 1995, while the NDC's representation was reduced to five seats. The remaining two seats were secured by GULP. Mitchell became Prime Minister.

In late November 1998 the resignation of the Minister of Foreign Affairs, Raphael Fletcher, from the Government and NNP in order to join GULP, resulted in an early general election being called. The NNP obtained all of the 15 seats in the House of Representatives in the subsequent ballot, held in January 1999, constituting the first time in the country's history that a political party had been given two successive terms in government.

In October 1999 Bernard Coard, serving a term of life imprisonment with 16 others for the 1983 murder of Prime Minister Maurice Bishop and a number of his associates (see above), issued a statement in which he accepted full responsibility for the crimes. In 2002 it was announced that three former soldiers gaoled in 1986 for Bishop's murder and that of seven others during the 1983 coup were to be released. Furthermore, in March 2004 the Court of Appeal ruled that the 17 prisoners would be resentenced, since the life sentences imposed on them were unconstitutional. However, the day before the resentencing, the Court of Appeal of the Eastern Caribbean Supreme Court, based in Saint Lucia, overturned the ruling. This decision was confirmed after a further hearing in 2005; lawyers for the men appealed against the judgment to the Privy Council, based in the United Kingdom, occasioning a ruling in February 2007 for the resentencing of 13 of the prisoners (three of their original number had been released in 2006, while Phyllis Coard had secured early release in 2000 in order to seek life-saving medical treatment). Subsequently, in June 2007 the Supreme Court ordered the release of three of the prisoners and reduced the sentences of the remaining 10. Three further prisoners secured an early release in December 2008, and in September 2009 the remaining seven, including Bernard Coard, were set free, prompting expressions of disapproval from large sections of the population.

The NNP secured a third successive term in office in the general election of November 2003, although its parliamentary majority was reduced to just one seat. The NDC won the seven remaining seats in the 15-seat House of Representatives. Keith Mitchell was sworn in again as Prime Minister.

Grenada was devastated by Hurricane Ivan in September 2004, which killed 39 Grenadians and destroyed 90% of the housing stock. According to the OECS, full rehabilitation would cost at least US $814m. Opposition deputies strenuously criticized the Government's relief efforts and the country's perceived slow recovery progress. In October the Agency for Reconstruction and Development was established to implement and monitor reconstruction projects and to manage the receipt of grants from international donors. Widespread looting and violent crime was brought under relative control after intervention from regional (primarily Trinidadian) security forces. The island was struck by another huge storm, Hurricane Emily, in July 2005. The cost of the damage was estimated at $200m.; the misfortune was compounded by the impact of Emily upon the recovery process from Hurricane Ivan. In January 2006 Mitchell announced that a 5% salary tax to help finance rebuilding efforts would be introduced. The levy was strenuously opposed by the Grenada Trade Union Congress.

Recent developments: the NDC in office

The NNP failed to secure an unprecedented fourth successive term in office in a general election held on 8 July 2008, with the NDC winning 11 of the 15 legislative seats and 51.2% of the valid votes cast. The NNP won the remaining four seats and 48.0% of the ballot. Electoral participation was high, with some 80.3% of eligible voters participating in the poll, and election observers from the Organization of American States reported positively upon the procedure of the election. Tillman Thomas, the NDC leader, was sworn in as Prime Minister and the new Cabinet duly installed: notable appointments included Nazim Burke as Minister of Finance, Planning, Economy, Energy and Co-operatives, and Peter David as Minister of Foreign Affairs. The Attorney-General, James Bristol, resigned in July 2009 after it emerged that he had used his position to appeal to the US authorities for leniency when considering charges of drugs-dealing against his stepson; Bristol was replaced by Rohan Phillip in the following month.

In October 2009 the High Court of Justice effected the liquidation of *Grenada Today*, following the newspaper's inability to pay compensation to former Prime Minister Keith Mitchell. Mitchell had successfully sued the newspaper for libel following the publication in 2001 of material deemed defamatory by the Court. The compensation award, at US $71,000, was generally viewed as excessive, and press freedom advocates appealed for a limit on libel damages.

Thomas implemented a cabinet reorganization in November 2010. Karl Hood became Minister of Foreign Affairs and of the Environment, Foreign Trade and Export Development, Peter David was given responsibility for tourism, and Glynis Roberts was awarded the labour portfolio. Michael Church was removed from the environment ministry and assigned a lower-level position in the Ministry of Works, Physical Development and Public Utilities as punishment for taking an unauthorized trip to Switzerland to attend a trade meeting. David, Roberts and Church failed to attend the official ceremony to be sworn in to office, raising questions about the unity of the Government. Church submitted his resignation shortly afterwards. Press reports alleged that the reorganization had led to divisions within the Cabinet, although Thomas rejected these claims.

Building upon earlier efforts to effect constitutional reform, in December 2010 a draft constitution was published, which advocated the removal of the British monarch as Head of State and the creation of a republic; the document also stipulated that the Privy Council would be replaced by the Caribbean Court of Justice as the nation's final appellate court. Consultations were ongoing in early 2012, in advance of a proposed referendum on the draft constitution.

Thomas reorganized the Cabinet again in September 2011. Denneth Modeste became the new Minister of Works, Physical Development and Public Utilities, while Joseph Gilbert was appointed as Minister of the Environment, Foreign Trade and Export Development. Thomas added the newly created national mobilization portfolio to his other ministerial responsibilities and transferred the culture portfolio to the Ministry of Tourism and Civil Aviation. However, amid press reports of rising factionalism within the ruling party, in January 2012 Gilbert was dismissed from his post after allegedly concluding an unauthorized agreement with a US firm in relation to the establishment of a casino on the island.

Foreign Affairs

Regional relations

Negotiations on the delimitation of Grenada's maritime border with Trinidad and Tobago had been in abeyance since 1993. However, a treaty demarcating the boundary was finally ratified in April 2010, allowing for the initiation of offshore petroleum and gas exploration. Discussions on possible joint exploration operations took place in September 2011.

In September 2005 Grenada became one of 13 Caribbean nations to sign the PetroCaribe accord, under which Grenada would be allowed to purchase petroleum from Venezuela at reduced prices. Grenada received its first shipment—20,000 barrels of diesel oil—under this accord in October 2007.

Improved relations with Cuba, which had been severely strained since 1983 when diplomatic ties were suspended, resulted in offers of assistance with education, health and agriculture in Grenada in 1997. Diplomatic relations between the two countries were restored in December 1999, and in January 2003 a new hospital was opened in St George's, partly financed by the Cuban Government.

Other external relations

In May 1996 Grenada signed two treaties with the USA, relating to mutual legal assistance and extradition, as part of a regional campaign to combat drugs-trafficking. An agreement on maritime security co-operation was signed by Grenada and the USA in March 2011.

In 2000 Grenada restored diplomatic relations with Libya, suspended in 1983. From 1983 Grenada had maintained diplomatic relations with Taiwan instead of the People's Republic of China; however, in 2004 Taiwan recalled its ambassador to Grenada after Mitchell visited mainland China. It had been reported that the Chinese Government had promised Mitchell substantial funds for development projects in Grenada. Mitchell emphasized that the destruction caused by Hurricane Ivan had forced the Government to reconsider its international relationships and in January 2005 Grenada duly established official ties with the People's Republic of China. One week later Taiwan severed its relations with Grenada. In June 2009 the Chinese Government provided Grenada with aid and loans amounting to some US $6m. and expressed interest in further co-operation in the tourism, education and agricultural sectors. Taiwan commenced legal proceedings against Grenada during 2011 to reclaim outstanding loan repayments totalling $28m. Major airlines and cruise lines operating in Grenada were court ordered to deposit fees owed to the island's authorities into an escrow account, depriving the Government, which launched a legal challenge against Taiwan's actions, of an important revenue source. Taiwan had earlier rejected Grenadian proposals to restructure the debt.

CONSTITUTION AND GOVERNMENT

The Constitution of Grenada was adopted upon independence in 1974. Grenada has dominion status within the Commonwealth. The British monarch is Head of State and is represented locally by a Governor-General. The Cabinet, led by the Prime Minister, holds executive power. Parliament comprises the Senate, made up of 13 Senators appointed by the Governor-General on the advice of the Prime Minister and the Leader of the Opposition, and the 15-member House of Representatives, elected by universal adult suffrage. The Cabinet is responsible to Parliament. Judicial power is vested in the Eastern Caribbean Supreme Court, although in certain cases further appeal can be made to the Privy Council in the United Kingdom.

REGIONAL AND INTERNATIONAL CO-OPERATION

Grenada is a member of the Caribbean Community and Common Market (CARICOM, see p. 227). It is also a member of the Economic Commission for Latin America and the Caribbean (ECLAC, see p. 44), the Organization of American States (OAS, see p. 394), the Association of Caribbean States (see p. 448), and of the Community of Latin American and Caribbean States (see p. 462), which was formally inaugurated in December 2011. Grenada is a member of the Eastern Caribbean Securities Exchange (based in Saint Christopher and Nevis), and of the Eastern Caribbean Central Bank (ECCB, see p. 453). On 18 June 2010 Grenada was a signatory to the Revised Treaty of Basseterre, establishing an Economic Union among the member nations of the Organisation of Eastern Caribbean States (OECS, see p. 465). The Cabinet ratified the Treaty in mid-January 2011, and the Economic Union, which involved the removal of barriers to trade and the movement of labour as a step towards a single financial and economic market, came into effect on 21 January. Freedom of movement between the signatory states was granted to OECS nationals on 1 August.

Grenada acceded to the UN in 1974, upon independence. It joined the World Trade Organization (see p. 433) in February 1996. The country is a member of the Commonwealth (see p. 239). Grenada is a signatory to the Cotonou Agreement (see p. 328), the successor arrangement to the Lomé Conventions between the African, Caribbean and Pacific (ACP) countries and the European Union. The country is also a member of the Group of 77 (see p. 450) organization of developing states.

ECONOMIC AFFAIRS

In 2010, according to estimates by the World Bank, Grenada's gross national income (GNI), measured at average 2008–10 prices, was US $580m., equivalent to US $5,550 per head (or $7,550 per head on an international purchasing-power parity basis). During 2001–10 Grenada's population increased at an average rate of 0.3% per year, while gross domestic product (GDP) per head increased, in real terms, by an average of 0.6% per year. Overall GDP increased, in real terms, at an average annual rate of 0.9% in 2001–10. Real GDP decreased by an estimated 8.3% in 2009 and by a further 1.1% in 2010.

Agriculture (including hunting, forestry and fishing) contributed 5.1% of GDP in 2010. The sector engaged an estimated 19.6% of the employed labour force in 2012, according to FAO estimates. Grenada is one of the world's largest producers of nutmeg (although Indonesia produces some 75% of the world's total). In 2008 sales of nutmeg, mace (the pungent red membrane around the nut) and cardamom accounted for an estimated 8.5% of Grenada's domestic export earnings. The importance of bananas to the economy has fallen in recent years; by 2010 FAO estimated output at only 1,600 tons. Livestock production, for domestic consumption, is important on Carriacou. There are extensive timber reserves on the island of Grenada; forestry development is strictly controlled and involves a programme of reafforestation. Exports of fish contributed an estimated 8.5% of domestic export earnings in 2008. According to preliminary figures from the Eastern Caribbean Central Bank (ECCB, see p. 453), agricultural GDP decreased at an average annual rate of 1.6% in 2001–10; the sector grew by 12.1% in 2009, but decreased by 6.0% in 2010.

Industry (mining, manufacturing, construction and utilities) provided an estimated 16.8% of GDP in 2010 and engaged 23.9% of the employed labour force in 1998. According to preliminary figures from the ECCB, industrial GDP increased by an annual average of 0.5% during 2001–10; the sector's GDP declined by 19.3% in 2009 and by a further 3.7% in 2010.

The mining and quarrying sector accounted for only 0.2% of employment in 1998 and 0.4% of GDP in 2010. Mining GDP decreased by an annual average of 4.8% in 2001–10; the sector contracted by 19.6% in 2009 and by 44.1% in 2010.

Manufacturing, which contributed 4.4% of GDP in 2010 and employed 7.7% of the working population in 1998, consists mainly of the processing of agricultural products and of cottage industries producing garments and spice-based items. Rum, soft drinks, paints and varnishes, household paper products and the tyre-retreading industries are also important. According to the ECCB, manufacturing GDP declined by an average of 0.4% per year in 2001–10; the sector's GDP declined by 5.3% in 2009, but expanded by 3.9% in 2010.

The construction sector contributed 7.5% of GDP in 2010 and engaged 15.4% of the labour force in 1998. Construction GDP remained constant in 2001–10, according to preliminary figures from the ECCB, the sector's GDP declined by 31.6% in 2009 and by a further 6.3% in 2010.

Grenada is dependent upon imports for its energy requirements, and in 2009 mineral fuels and lubricants accounted for an estimated 14.5% of the total cost of imports, according to the World Bank. Electricity generation totalled 182.9m. kWh in 2009.

The services sector contributed 78.0% of GDP in 2010. Tourism and financial and business services were the main contributors to GDP. Receipts from tourism totalled EC $259.8m. in 2010, a decrease on the previous year. Tourist arrivals decreased in 2010, by 3.3%, although this was mainly driven by a fall in cruise ship arrivals. These totalled 333,765, compared with 342,852 in 2009. The more lucrative stop-over market actually contracted in 2010, by 4.3%, mainly owing to the world-wide economic downturn. Financial and business services contributed 7.8% to the economy in 2010. The 'offshore' financial sector has become more economically significant in recent years. According to preliminary figures from the ECCB, the GDP of the services sector increased at an average annual rate of 2.9% in 2001–10; the sector decreased by 3.2% in 2009 and by 0.2% in 2010.

In 2010 Grenada reported a deficit on merchandise trade of EC $686.2m. and there was a deficit of $622.2m. on the current account of the balance of payments. In 2008 the principal source of imports was the USA, accounting for 30.9% of the total. The USA is also the principal market for exports, taking 16.4% of the total in 2008, along with Dominica. The principal export was milling products, malt and starches, accounting for 24.9% of total exports in 2008. The principal imports in that year were mineral fuels, oils and distillation products, nuclear reactors, boilers and machinery, and electrical and electronic equipment. The trade deficit is partly offset by earnings from tourism, capital receipts and remittances from the large numbers of Grenadians working abroad.

In 2010 there was an overall budgetary deficit of EC $102.8m. Grenada's general government gross debt was EC $2,102m. in 2010, equivalent to 98.6% of GDP. Grenada's total external debt was US $531m. in 2009, of which US $462m. was public and publicly guaranteed debt. In 2008 the cost of servicing long-term public and publicly guaranteed debt and repayments to the IMF was equivalent to 10.7% of the value of exports of goods, services and income (excluding workers' remittances). The average annual rate of inflation was 3.8% in 2004–10; consumer prices declined by 0.3% in 2009, but increased by 3.4% in 2010, according to the IMF. According to estimates, 10.9% of the labour force were unemployed at the end of 2003, although the rate was presumed to have increased to over 25% in 2005 after Hurricane Ivan destroyed much of the island's economic infrastructure.

Grenada's economy is heavily dependent upon the tourism industry, which is vulnerable to external economic conditions. Agriculture, particularly the production of bananas and nutmeg, is also a significant sector, although pest infestations, drought and hurricanes present serious challenges. In April 2010 the IMF approved a US $13.7m. Extended Credit Facility, which, combined with EC $21m. of financial assistance allocated to Grenada by the European Commission in December 2009, aimed to alleviate the negative effects of the global economic downturn on the island: during 2009 the economy contracted by 8.3%. In an attempt to improve the fiscal position, a value-added tax (VAT) came into effect in February 2010, resulting in increased revenues, although this was tempered in September by a reduction in VAT rates for key economic sectors. The tourism and construction sectors remained depressed throughout 2010, and, despite a manufacturing recovery and an increase in agricultural output, the economy contracted by a further 1.1% during the year. Higher visitor numbers during the first half of 2011 suggested that the tourism industry was starting to recover, and the agricultural sector was also performing strongly, with rising banana and nutmeg production. However, construction activity was still slow, and the IMF estimated that there was zero growth in the economy as a whole during 2011. A number of tourism initiatives were under way in early 2012 in an attempt to attract more investment into the sector and to boost tourist arrivals. The IMF forecast real GDP expansion of 1.0% in 2012.

PUBLIC HOLIDAYS

2013: 1 January (New Year's Day), 7 February (Independence Day), 29 March (Good Friday), 1 April (Easter Monday), 1 May (Labour Day), 20 May (Whit Monday), 30 May (Corpus Christi), 1 August (Emancipation Holiday), 5–6 August (Carnival), 25 October (Thanksgiving Day), 25–26 December (Christmas).

Statistical Survey

AREA AND POPULATION

Area: 344.5 sq km (133.0 sq miles).

Population: 94,806 (males 46,637, females 48,169) at census of 12 May 1991 (excluding 537 persons in institutions and 33 persons in the foreign service); 100,895 at census of 25 May 2001 (preliminary). *Mid-2012* (UN estimate) 105,299 (Source: UN, *World Population Prospects: The 2010 Revision*).

Density (mid-2012): 305.7 per sq km.

Population by Age and Sex (UN estimates at mid-2012): *0–14:* 28,409 (males 14,546, females 13,863); *15–64:* 69,445 (males 35,181, females 34,264); *65 and over:* 7,445 (males 2,997, females 4,448); *Total* 105,299 (males 52,724, females 52,575) (Source: UN, *World Population Prospects: The 2010 Revision*).

Principal Town (population at 2001 census, preliminary): St George's (capital) 3,908. *Mid-2009* (UN estimate, incl. suburbs): St George's 40,400 (Source: UN, *World Urbanization Prospects: The 2009 Revision*).

Births and Deaths (registrations, 2001, provisional): Live births 1,899 (birth rate 18.8 per 1,000); Deaths 727 (death rate 7.2 per 1,000); *2011*: Birth rate 17.0 per 1,000; Death rate 7.9 per 1,000 (Source: Pan American Health Organization).

Life Expectancy (years at birth, WHO estimates): 73 (males 69; females 77) in 2009. Source: WHO, *World Health Statistics*.

Employment (employees only, 1998): Agriculture, hunting, forestry and fishing 4,794; Mining and quarrying 58; Manufacturing 2,579; Electricity, gas and water 505; Construction 5,163; Wholesale and retail trade 6,324; Restaurants and hotels 1,974; Transport, storage and communications 2,043; Financing, insurance and real estate 1,312; Public administration, defence and social security 1,879; Community services 3,904; Other services 2,933; *Sub-total* 33,468; Activities not adequately defined 1,321; *Total employed* 34,789 (males 20,733, females 14,056). *Mid-2012* (estimates): Agriculture, etc. 9,000; Total labour force 46,000 (Source: FAO).

HEALTH AND WELFARE

Key Indicators

Total Fertility Rate (children per woman, 2011): 2.2.

Under-5 Mortality Rate (per 1,000 live births, 2009): 14.

Physicians (per 1,000 head, 2009): 0.8.

Hospital Beds (per 1,000 head, 2009): 2.4.

Health Expenditure (2008): US $ per head (PPP): 593.

Health Expenditure (2008): % of GDP: 6.7.

Health Expenditure (2008): public (% of total): 48.9.

Access to Water (% of persons, 2004): 95.

Access to Sanitation (% of persons, 2008): 98.

Total Carbon Dioxide Emissions ('000 metric tons, 2007): 241.8.

Total Carbon Dioxide Emissions Per Head (metric tons, 2007): 2.3.

Human Development Index (2011): ranking: 67.

Human Development Index (2011): value: 0.748.

For sources and definitions, see explanatory note on p. vi.

AGRICULTURE, ETC.

Principal Crops ('000 metric tons, 2010, FAO estimates): Sugar cane 7.2; Pigeon peas 0.5; Coconuts 5.5; Bananas 1.6; Plantains 0.8; Oranges 0.7; Grapefruit and pomelos 1.8; Apples 0.6; Plums and sloes 0.8; Mangoes, mangosteens and guavas 2.1; Avocados 1.7; Cocoa beans 0.3; Nutmeg, mace and cardamom 1.9. *Aggregate Production* ('000 metric tons, may include official, semi-official or estimated data, 2010): Roots and tubers 3.6; Vegetables (incl. melons) 2.5; Fruits (excl. melons) 14.6.

Livestock ('000 head, year ending September 2010, FAO estimates): Cattle 4.5; Pigs 2.7; Sheep 13.2; Goats 7.2; Chickens 270.

Livestock Products ('000 metric tons, 2010, FAO estimates): Chicken meat 0.7; Cows' milk 0.7; Hen eggs 1.4.

Fishing (metric tons, live weight, 2009): Red hind 148; Coney 84; Snappers and jobfishes 104; Parrotfishes 107; Blackfin tuna 187; Yellowfin tuna 630; Atlantic sailfish 162; Swordfish 31; Common dolphinfish 195; *Total catch* (incl. others) 2,615.

Source: FAO.

INDUSTRY

Production (1994 unless otherwise indicated): Rum 300,000 litres; Beer 2,400,000 litres; Wheat flour 4,000 metric tons (1996); Cigarettes 15m.; Electricity 182.9 million kWh (2009). Sources: UN, *Industrial Commodity Statistics Yearbook*; Eastern Caribbean Central Bank.

FINANCE

Currency and Exchange Rates: 100 cents = 1 Eastern Caribbean dollar (EC $). *Sterling, US Dollar and Euro Equivalents* (30 December 2011): £1 sterling = EC $4.174; US $1 = EC $2.700; €1 = EC $3.494; EC $100 = £24.00= US $37.04 = €28.62. *Exchange Rate:* Fixed at US $1 = EC $2.70 since July 1976.

Budget (EC $ million, 2010, preliminary figures): *Revenue:* Tax revenue 379.9 (Taxes on income and profits 87.2, Taxes on property 18.8, Taxes on domestic goods and services 76.0, Taxes on international trade and transactions 197.9); Other current revenue 21.9; Total 401.8 (excluding grants received 29.2). *Expenditure:* Current expenditure 416.7 (Personal emoluments 191.2, Goods and services

86.0, Interest payments 45.3, Transfers and subsidies 94.1); Capital expenditure and net lending 117.1; Total 533.8. Source: Eastern Caribbean Central Bank.

International Reserves (US $ million at 31 December 2010): IMF special drawing rights 16.39; Foreign exchange 102.76; Total 119.15. Source: IMF, *International Financial Statistics*.

Money Supply (EC $ million at 31 December 2010): Currency outside depository corporations 98.82; Transferable deposits 374.92; Other deposits 1,597.02; *Broad money* 2,070.76. Source: IMF, *International Financial Statistics*.

Cost of Living (Consumer Price Index; base: 2005 = 100): 117.0 in 2008; 116.6 in 2009; 120.6 in 2010. Source: IMF, *International Financial Statistics*.

Gross Domestic Product (EC $ million at constant 1990 prices): 1,026.16 in 2007; 1,035.42 in 2008; 965.13 in 2009 (preliminary estimate). Source: Eastern Caribbean Central Bank.

Expenditure on the Gross Domestic Product (EC $ million at current prices, 2010, preliminary estimates): Government final consumption expenditure 347.06; Private final consumption expenditure 1,890.09; Gross capital formation 447.98; *Total domestic expenditure* 2,685.13; Exports of goods and services 451.90; *Less* Imports of goods and services 1,021.30; *GDP in purchasers' values* 2,115.73. Source: Eastern Caribbean Central Bank.

Gross Domestic Product by Economic Activity (EC $ million at current prices, 2010, preliminary estimates): Agriculture and fishing 94.36; Mining and quarrying 6.61; Manufacturing 82.11; Electricity and water 83.19; Construction 139.02; Wholesale and retail trade 140.62; Hotels and restaurants 77.26; Transport and communications 233.16; Housing, real estate and business activities 244.77; Financial services 144.55; Public administration and defence 151.27; Other services 448.80; *Sub-total* 1,845.72; *Less* Financial intermediation services indirectly measured (FISIM) 29.29; *GDP at factor cost* 1,816.42; Taxes on products, less subsidies 299.31; *GDP in market prices* 2,115.73. Source: Eastern Caribbean Central Bank.

Balance of Payments (EC $ million, 2010): Goods (net) –686.22; Services (net) 116.82; *Balance of goods and services* –569.40; Other income (net) –138.91; Current transfers (net) 86.08; *Current balance* –622.23; Capital account (net) 160.20; Direct investment 162.55; Portfolio investment –2.05; Other investments 214.81; Net errors and omissions 60.73; *Overall balance* –25.99. Source: Eastern Caribbean Central Bank.

EXTERNAL TRADE

Principal Commodities (US $ million, 2008): *Imports c.i.f.:* Meat and edible meat offal 12.0; Mineral fuels, oils, distillation products, etc. 71.2; Wood, articles of wood and wood charcoal 13.8; Iron and steel articles 12.5; Nuclear reactors, boilers, machinery, etc. 26.9; Electrical and electronic equipment 26.5; Vehicles other than railway, tramway 19.4; Furniture, lighting, signs, prefabricated buildings 9.4; Total (incl. others) 363.3. *Exports f.o.b:* Fish, crustaceans, molluscs, aquatic invertebrates 3.0; Coffee, tea, mate and spices 2.7; Milling products, malt, starches, etc. 7.6; Residues, wastes of food industry, animal fodder 1.5; Paper, paperboard and pulp, paper and board articles 3.0; Electrical and electronic equipment 0.9; Total 30.5. Source: Trade Map-Trade Competitiveness Map, International Trade Centre, www.intracen.org/marketanalysis.

Principal Trading Partners (US $ million, 2008): *Imports c.i.f.:* Barbados 6.5; Brazil 9.2; Canada 10.1; China, People's Republic 12.0; France (incl. Monaco) 3.2; Germany 5.2; Guyana 3.9; Japan 13.0; Netherlands 4.8; Trinidad and Tobago 90.3; United Kingdom 16.1; USA 112.2; Venezuela 25.5; Total (incl. others) 363.3. *Exports f.o.b.:* Antigua and Barbuda 1.0; Barbados 2.9; Belgium 1.0; Canada 0.9; Dominica 5.0; France (incl. Monaco) 0.3; Guyana 0.6; Jamaica 0.5; Japan 6.5; Netherlands 1.1; Saint Christopher and Nevis 2.6; Saint Lucia 3.4; Saint Vincent and the Grenadines 1.0; Trinidad and Tobago 0.6; USA 5.0; Total (incl. others) 30.5. Source: Trade Map-Trade Competitiveness Map, International Trade Centre, www.intracen.org/marketanalysis.

TRANSPORT

Road Traffic ('000 motor vehicles in use, 2001): Passenger cars 15.8; Commercial vehicles 4.2. Source: UN, *Statistical Yearbook*.

Shipping: *Merchant Fleet* (registered at 31 December 2009) 10 vessels (total displacement 2,401 grt) (Source: IHS Fairplay, *World Fleet Statistics*). *International Sea-borne Freight Traffic* (estimates, '000 metric tons, 1995): Goods loaded 21.3; Goods unloaded 193.0. *Ship Arrivals* (1991): 1,254. *Fishing Vessels* (registered, 1987): 635.

Civil Aviation (aircraft arrivals, 1995): 11,310.

TOURISM

Visitor Arrivals: 426,900 (incl. 123,770 stop-over visitors and 292,712 cruise ship passengers) in 2008; 459,391 (incl. 109,474 stop-over visitors and 342,852 cruise ship passengers) in 2009; 444,427 (incl. 104,732 stop-over visitors and 333,765 cruise ship passengers) in 2010.

Tourism Receipts (EC $ million): 293.6 in 2007; 293.2 in 2008; 267.2 in 2009; 259.8 in 2010.

Source: Eastern Caribbean Central Bank.

COMMUNICATIONS MEDIA

Radio Receivers (1997): 57,000 in use*.

Television Receivers (1999): 35,000 in use*.

Telephones (2010): 28,369 main lines in use†.

Mobile Cellular Telephones (2010): 121,946 subscribers†.

Personal Computers (2005): 16,000 in use*.

Internet Subscribers (2008): 10,874†.

Broadband Subscribers (2010): 10,573†.

Non-daily Newspapers (2004): 4; circulation 14,000 (1996)*.

* Source: UNESCO, *Statistical Yearbook*.
† Source: International Telecommunication Union.

EDUCATION

Pre-primary (2009/10 unless otherwise indicated): 74 schools (1994); 246 teachers; 3,562 pupils.

Primary (2009/10 unless otherwise indicated): 57 schools (1995); 851 teachers; 13,663 pupils.

Secondary (2009/10 unless otherwise indicated): 20 schools (2002); 566 teachers; 11,500 pupils.

Higher (excl. figures for the Grenada Teachers' Training College, 1993): 66 teachers; 651 students.

Source: partly UNESCO Institute for Statistics.

Pupil-teacher Ratio (primary education, UNESCO estimate): 16.1 in 2009/10 (Source: UNESCO Institute for Statistics).

Adult Literacy Rate: 96.0% in 2003. Source: UN Development Programme, *Human Development Report*.

Directory

The Government

HEAD OF STATE

Queen: HM Queen ELIZABETH II.

Governor-General: CARLYLE GLEAN, Sr (appointed 27 November 2008).

THE CABINET
(May 2012)

Prime Minister and Minister of National Security, Public Administration, Information, Information Communications Technology, Legal Affairs and National Mobilization: TILLMAN THOMAS.

Minister of Foreign Affairs: KARL HOOD.

Minister of Finance, Planning, Economy, Energy and Co-operatives: NAZIM BURKE.

Minister of the Environment, Foreign Trade and Export Development: (vacant).

Minister of Youth Empowerment and Sports: PATRICK SIMMONS.

Minister of Housing, Lands and Community Development: ALLEYNE WALKER.

Minister of Works, Physical Development and Public Utilities: DENNETH MODESTE.

Minister of Labour, Social Security and Ecclesiastical Affairs: GLYNIS ROBERTS.

Minister of Social Development: SYLVESTER QUARLESS.

Minister of Tourism, Civil Aviation and Culture: GEORGE VINCENT.

Minister of Agriculture, Forestry and Fisheries: MICHAEL DENIS LETT.

Minister of Carriacou and Petit Martinique Affairs: GEORGE PRIME.

Minister of Education and Human Resource Development: FRANKA ALEXIS-BERNADINE.

Minister of Health: ANN PETERS.

Attorney-General: ROHAN A. PHILLIP.

Minister of State in the Prime Minister's Office with responsibility for Information and National Mobilization: GLEN NOEL.

Minister of State responsible for Culture: ARLEY GILL.

MINISTRIES

Office of the Governor-General: Government House, Bldg 5, Financial Complex, The Carenage, St George's; tel. 440-6639; fax 440-6688; e-mail pato@spiceisle.com.

Office of the Prime Minister and Ministry of National Security, Public Administration, Information, Information Communications Technology, Legal Affairs and National Mobilization: Ministerial Complex, 6th Floor, Botanical Gardens, Tanteen, St George's; tel. 440-2255; fax 440-4116; e-mail pmsec@gov.gd; internet www.pmoffice.gov.gd.

Ministry of Agriculture, Forestry and Fisheries: Ministerial Complex, 3rd Floor, Botanical Gardens, Tanteen, St George's; tel. 440-2708; fax 440-4191; e-mail agriculture@gov.gd; internet www.agriculture.gov.gd.

Ministry of Carriacou and Petit Martinique Affairs: Beauséjour, Carriacou; tel. 443-6026; fax 443-6040; e-mail minccoupm@spiceisle.com.

Ministry of Education and Human Resource Development: Ministry of Education Bldg, Ministerial Complex, Botanical Gardens, Tanteen, St George's; tel. 440-2737; fax 440-6650; internet www.grenadaedu.com.

Ministry of the Environment, Foreign Trade and Export Development: Financial Complex, The Carenage, St George's; tel. 440-2731; fax 440-4115; e-mail michael.church@gov.gd.

Ministry of Finance, Planning, Economy, Energy and Cooperatives: Financial Complex, The Carenage, St George's; tel. 440-2731; fax 440-4115; e-mail finance@gov.gd; internet finance.gov.gd.

Ministry of Foreign Affairs: Ministerial Complex, 4th Floor, Botanical Gardens, Tanteen, St George's; tel. 440-2640; fax 440-4184; e-mail foreignaffairs@gov.gd.

Ministry of Health: Ministerial Complex, Southern Wing, 1st and 2nd Floors, Botanical Gardens, Tanteen, St George's; tel. 440-2649; fax 440-4127; e-mail min-healthgrenada@spiceisle.com.

Ministry of Housing, Lands and Community Development: Ministerial Complex, 2nd Floor, Botanical Gardens, Tanteen, St George's; tel. 440-2103; fax 435-5864; e-mail mofhlcd@gov.gd.

Ministry of Labour, Social Security and Ecclesiastical Affairs: Ministerial Complex, 1st Floor, Botanical Gardens, Tanteen, St George's; tel. 440-2269; fax 440-7990.

Ministry of Social Development: Ministerial Complex, West Wing, 1st Floor, Botanical Gardens, Tanteen, St George's; tel. 440-7952; fax 440-7990; e-mail ministrysod@yahoo.com.

Ministry of Tourism, Civil Aviation and Culture: Ministerial Complex, 4th Floor, Botanical Gardens, Tanteen, St George's; tel. 440-0366; fax 440-0443; e-mail tourism@gov.gd; internet www.grenada.mot.gd.

Ministry of Works, Physical Development and Public Utilities: Ministerial Complex, 4th Floor, Botanical Gardens, Tanteen, St George's; tel. 440-2271; fax 440-4122; e-mail ministryofworks@gov.gd.

Ministry of Youth Empowerment and Sports: Ministerial Complex, 3rd Floor, Botanical Gardens, Tanteen, St George's; tel. 440-6917; fax 440-6924; e-mail sports@gov.gd.

Legislature

PARLIAMENT

Houses of Parliament: Office of the Houses of Parliament, Botanical Gardens, Tanteen, POB 315, St George's; tel. 440-2090; fax 440-4138; e-mail order.order@spiceisle.com.

Senate

President: Sen. JOAN PURCELL.

There are 13 appointed members.

House of Representatives

Speaker: GEORGE JAMES MCGUIRE.

General Election, 8 July 2008

	Votes	%	Seats
National Democratic Congress (NDC)	28,998	51.15	11
New National Party (NNP)	27,188	47.97	4
United Labour Platform (ULP)*	479	0.85	—
Total (incl. others)	56,677	100.00	15

* A coalition of the Grenada United Labour Party and the People's Labour Movement.

Political Organizations

Grenada United Labour Party (GULP): St George's; tel. 438-1234; e-mail gulp@spiceisle.com; f. 1950; merged with United Labour Congress in 2001; right-wing; formed a coalition with the People's Labour Movt, the United Labour Platform, to contest the 2008 elections; Pres. WILFRED HAYES.

National Democratic Congress (NDC): NDC Headquarters, Lucas St, St George's; tel. 440-3769; e-mail ndcgrenada@ndcgrenada.org; internet www.ndcgrenada.org; f. 1987 by fmr mems of the NNP and merger of Democratic Labour Congress and Grenada Democratic Labour Party; centrist; Leader TILLMAN THOMAS; Gen.-Sec. PETER DAVID.

New National Party (NNP): Upper Lucas St, Mount Helicon, POB 646, St George's; tel. 440-1875; fax 440-1876; e-mail nnpadmin@spiceisle.com; internet www.nnpnews.com; f. 1984 following merger of Grenada Democratic Movt, Grenada National Party and National Democratic Party; centrist; Leader Dr KEITH MITCHELL; Dep. Leader GREGORY BOWEN.

People's Labour Movement (PLM): St George's; f. 1995 by fmr mems of the NDC; fmrly known as the Democratic Labour Party; formed a coalition with the Grenada United Labour Party, the United Labour Platform, to contest the 2008 elections; Leader Dr FRANCIS ALEXIS.

Diplomatic Representation

EMBASSIES IN GRENADA

Brazil: Mount Cinnamon Hill, Morne Rouge, POB 1226, Grand Anse, St George's; tel. 439-7162; fax 439-7165; e-mail brasemb.saintgeorges@mre.gov.br; Ambassador RICARDO ANDRE VIEIRA DINIZ.

China, People's Republic: Azar Villa, Calliste St, St George's; tel. 439-6230; fax 439-6231; internet gd.china-embassy.org; Ambassador XU JIANGUO.

Cuba: L'Anse aux Epines, St George's; tel. 444-1884; fax 444-1877; e-mail embacubagranada@caribsurf.com; Ambassador ANGEL NARCISO REIGOSA DE LA CRUZ.

USA: L'Anse aux Epines, POB 54, St George's; tel. 444-1173; fax 444-4820; e-mail usembgd@caribsurf.com; Chargé d'affaires a.i. BERNARD LINK.

Venezuela: Upper Lucas St, Belmont, POB 201, St George's; tel. 440-1721; fax 440-6657; e-mail vennes@caribsurf.com; Ambassador CARLOS AMADA PEREZ SILVA.

Judicial System

Justice is administered by the Eastern Caribbean Supreme Court, based in Saint Lucia, composed of a High Court of Justice and a Court of Appeal. The Itinerant Court of Appeal consists of three judges and sits three times a year; it hears appeals from the High Court and the Magistrates' Court. Three judges of the High Court are resident in Grenada. The Magistrates' Court administers summary jurisdiction.

High Court Judges: FRANCIS MORTIMER CUMBERBATCH, CLAIRE HENRY, MARGARET PRICE FINDLAY.

Registrar: ROBERT BRANCH.

Office of the Attorney-General: Communal House, 414 H. A. Blaize St, St George's; tel. 440-2050; fax 435-2964; e-mail legalaffairs@spiceisle.com; Attorney-Gen. ROHAN PHILLIP.

Religion

CHRISTIANITY

The Roman Catholic Church

Grenada comprises the single diocese of Saint George's, suffragan to the archdiocese of Castries (Saint Lucia). The Bishop participates in the Antilles Episcopal Conference (based in Port of Spain, Trinidad and Tobago). Some 45% of the population are Roman Catholics.

Bishop of St George's in Grenada: Rev. VINCENT DARIUS, Bishop's House, Morne Jaloux, POB 375, St George's; tel. 443-5299; fax 443-5758; e-mail bishopgrenada@caribsurf.com; internet www.stgdiocese.org.

The Anglican Communion

Anglicans in Grenada are adherents of the Church in the Province of the West Indies. The country forms part of the diocese of the Windward Islands (the Bishop, the Rt Rev. CALVERT LEOPOLD FRIDAY, resides in Kingstown, Saint Vincent).

Other Christian Churches

The Presbyterian, Methodist, Plymouth Brethren, Baptist, Salvation Army, Jehovah's Witness, Pentecostal and Seventh-day Adventist faiths are also represented.

The Press

NEWSPAPERS

Barnacle: Mt Parnassus, St George's 3530; tel. 435-0981; fax 435-5685; e-mail barnacle@spiceisle.com; internet www.barnaclegrenada.com; f. 1991; business journal; once every 2 weeks; Editor IAN GEORGE.

Government Gazette: St George's; weekly; official; Man. ERIC BRATHWAITE.

The Grenada Informer: Market Hill, POB 622, St George's; tel. 440-1530; fax 440-4119; e-mail grenadainformer@yahoo.com; f. 1985; weekly; Editor CARLA-RAE A. BRIGGS; circ. 6,000.

The Grenadian Voice: Frequente Industrial Park, Bldg 1B, Maurice Bishop Hwy, POB 633, St George's; tel. 440-1498; fax 440-4117; e-mail gvoice@spiceisle.com; weekly; Man. Editor LESLIE PIERRE; circ. 3,000.

PRESS ASSOCIATION

Press Association of Grenada: St George's; f. 1986; Pres. LESLIE PIERRE.

Publishers

Anansi Publications: Woodlands, St George's; tel. 440-0800; e-mail aclouden@spiceisle.com; f. 1986; Man. Dir ALVIN CLOUDEN.

Caribbean Publishing Co: Suite 5, Le Marquis Complex, POB 1744, Grand Anse, St George's; tel. 439-5000; fax 439-5003; e-mail vcharlemagne@globaldirectories.com; internet www.grenadayp.com; print and online directories.

St George's University Publications: Office of University Publications, University Centre, St George's; tel. 665-8500; e-mail mlambert@sgu.edu; internet www.sgu.edu/university-communications; f. 2007; Dir MARGARET LAMBERT.

Broadcasting and Communications

TELECOMMUNICATIONS

Regulatory Authorities

Eastern Caribbean Telecommunications Authority: Vide Boutielle, Castries, POB 1886, Saint Lucia; tel. 458-1701; fax 458-1698; e-mail ectel@ectel.int; internet www.ectel.int; f. 2000 to regulate telecommunications in Grenada, Dominica, Saint Christopher and Nevis, Saint Lucia and Saint Vincent and the Grenadines.

National Telecommunications Regulatory Commission (NTRC): Suite 7, Grand Anse Shopping Centre, POB 854, St George's; tel. 435-6872; fax 435-2132; e-mail gntrc@ectel.int; internet www.ntrc.gd; Chair. Dr SPENCER THOMAS; Co-ordinator ALDWYN FERGUSON.

Major Service Providers

Digicel Grenada Ltd: Point Salines, POB 1690, St George's; e-mail grenadacustomercare@digicelgroup.com; internet www.digicelgrenada.com; tel. 439-4463; fax 439-4464; f. 2003; began operating cellular telephone services in Oct. 2003; owned by an Irish consortium; Chair. DENIS O'BRIEN; Gen. Man. GERALDINE PITT (OECS South).

Grenada Postal Corporation (GPC): Burns Point, St George's; tel. 440-2526; fax 440-4271; e-mail grenadapost@grenadapost.net; internet www.grenadapost.net; Chair. ADRIAN FRANCIS; Dir of Post LEO ROBERTS.

LIME: POB 119, The Carenage, St George's; tel. 440-1000; fax 440-4134; e-mail cwcares@candw.gd; internet www.time4lime.com; f. 1989; fmrly Cable & Wireless Grenada Ltd; name adopted as above 2008; until 1998 known as Grenada Telecommunications Ltd (Grentel); 30% govt-owned; CEO DAVID SHAW.

BROADCASTING

Grenada Broadcasting Network (GBN): Observatory Rd, POB 535, St George's; tel. 444-5521; fax 440-4180; e-mail gbn@spiceisle.com; internet www.klassicgrenada.com; f. 1972; 60% owned by One Caribbean Media Ltd, 40% govt-owned; Chair. CRAIG REYNALD; Gen. Man. RUEL EDWARDS.

Radio

City Sound FM: River Road, St George's; tel. 440-9616; e-mail citysound97i5@yahoo.com; internet www.citysoundfm.com; f. 1996.

Grenada Broadcasting Network (Radio): see Broadcasting.

HOTT FM: Observatory Rd, POB 535, St George's; tel. 444-5521; fax 440-4180; e-mail gbn@spiceisle.com; internet www.klassicgrenada.com; f. 1999; contemporary music.

Klassic AM: Observatory Rd, POB 535, St George's; tel. 435-2041; fax 440-4180; e-mail gbn@spiceisle.com; internet www.klassicgrenada.com.

Harbour Light of the Windwards: Carriacou; tel. and fax 443-7628; e-mail harbourlight@spiceisle.com; internet www.harbourlightradio.org; f. 1991; owned by Aviation Radio Missionary Services; Christian radio station; Station Man. Dr RANDY CORNELIUS.

KYAK 106: Church St, Hillsborough, Carriacou; tel. 443-6262; e-mail info@kyak106.com; internet www.kyak106.com; f. 1996; Office Man. DOREEN STANISLAUS.

Sister Isle Radio: Fort Hill, Hillsborough, Carriacou; tel. 443-8141; fax 443-8142; e-mail sisterisle@gmail.com; internet www.sisterisleradio.com; f. 2005.

Spice Capital Radio FM 90: Springs, St George's; tel. 440-0162.

WeeFM: Cross St, POB 555, St George's; tel. 440-4933; e-mail weefmradio@hotmail.com; internet www.weefmgrenada.com.

Television

Television programmes from Trinidad and Tobago and Barbados can be received on the island.

Grenada Broadcasting Network (Television): see Broadcasting; two channels.

Finance

(cap. = capital; res = reserves; dep. = deposits; brs = branches; amounts in Eastern Caribbean dollars)

The Eastern Caribbean Central Bank, based in Saint Christopher, is the central issuing and monetary authority for Grenada.

Eastern Caribbean Central Bank—Grenada Office: Monckton St, St George's; tel. 440-3016; fax 440-6721; e-mail eccbgnd@spiceisle.com; Country Dir LINDA FELIX-BERKLEY.

BANKING

Regulatory Authority

Grenada Authority for the Regulation of Financial Institutions (GARFIN): POB 3973, Queens Park, St George's; tel. 440-6575; fax 440-4780; e-mail angus.smith@garfin.org; internet www.garfingrenada.org; f. 1999 as Grenada International Financial Services Authority; name changed to above in Feb. 2007; revenue 4.2m. (2002); Chair. TIMOTHY ANTOINE; Exec. Dir ANGUS SMITH.

Commercial Banks

FirstCaribbean International Bank (Barbados) Ltd: Church St, POB 37, St George's; tel. 440-3232; fax 440-4103; internet www

.firstcaribbeanbank.com; f. 2002; 83.0% owned by Canadian Imperial Bank of Commerce (CIBC), after Barclays Bank PLC (United Kingdom) sold its 43.7% stake to CIBC in 2006; Chair. MICHAEL MANSOOR; CEO JOHN D. ORR; 4 brs.

Grenada Co-operative Bank Ltd: 8 Church St, POB 135, St George's; tel. 440-2111; fax 440-6600; e-mail info@grenadaco-opbank.com; internet www.grenadaco-opbank.com; f. 1932; cap. 24.8m., res 11.2m., dep. 460.8m. (Sept. 2010); Chair. DERICK STEELE; Man. Dir and Sec. RICHARD W. DUNCAN; brs in St Andrew's, St George's, St Patrick's and Hillsborough.

Grenada Development Bank: Melville St, POB 2300, St George's; tel. 440-2382; fax 440-6610; e-mail gdbbank@spiceisle.com; internet www.grenadadevelopmentbank.com; f. 1965; govt-owned; Chair. MICHAEL ARCHIBALD.

RBTT Bank Grenada Ltd: Cnr of Cross and Halifax Sts, POB 4, St George's; tel. 440-3521; fax 440-4153; e-mail RBTTLTD@caribsurf.com; internet www.rbtt.com; f. 1983 as Grenada Bank of Commerce; name changed as above 2002; 10% govt-owned; national insurance scheme 15%; public 13%; RBTT Bank Caribbean Ltd, Castries 62%; cap. 11.0m., res 5.3m., dep. 487.8m. (Oct. 2010); Country Man. CHAMPA RAMPERSAD-BARNES; Regional Dir DAVID HACKETT.

Republic Bank (Grenada) Ltd: Republic House, Maurice Bishop Hwy, Grand Anse, POB 857, St George's; tel. 444-2265; fax 444-5500; e-mail republichouse@republicgrenada.com; internet www.republicgrenada.com; f. 1979; fmrly National Commercial Bank of Grenada; name changed as above in 2006; 51% owned by Republic Bank Ltd, Port of Spain, Trinidad and Tobago; cap. 15.0m., res 19.3m., dep. 636.1m. (Sept. 2010); Chair. RONALD HARFORD; Man. Dir KEITH A. JOHNSON; 8 brs.

STOCK EXCHANGE

Eastern Caribbean Securities Exchange: Bird Rock, Basseterre, Saint Christopher and Nevis; tel. (869) 466-7192; fax (869) 465-3798; e-mail info@ECSEonline.com; internet www.ecseonline.com; f. 2001; regional securities market designed to facilitate the buying and selling of financial products for the eight member territories—Anguilla, Antigua and Barbuda, Dominica, Grenada, Montserrat, Saint Christopher and Nevis, Saint Lucia, and Saint Vincent and the Grenadines; Chair. Sir K. DWIGHT VENNER; Gen. Man. TREVOR E. BLAKE.

INSURANCE

Several foreign insurance companies operate in Grenada and the other islands of the group. Principal locally owned companies include the following:

Gittens Insurance Brokerage Co Ltd: Benoit Bldg, Grand Anse, POB 1695, St George's; tel. 439-4408; fax 439-4462; internet www.cisgrenada.com/gittensinsurance; f. 2003; Chair. PHILLIP MCLAWRENCE GITTENS; CEO PHILLIP ARTHUR GITTENS.

Grenada Motor and General Insurance Co Ltd: Scott St, POB 152, St George's; tel. 440-3379; fax 440-7977; e-mail g500z@spiceisle.com; Gen. Man. GABRIEL OLOUYNE.

Grenadian General Insurance Co Ltd: Cnr of Young and Scott Sts, POB 47, St George's; tel. 440-2434; fax 440-6618; e-mail ggicoltd@spiceisle.com; internet www.grenadiangeneralinsurance.com; Dir KEITH RENWICK.

Trade and Industry

CHAMBER OF COMMERCE

Grenada Chamber of Industry and Commerce, Inc (GCIC): Bldg 11, POB 129, Frequente, St George's; tel. 440-2937; fax 440-6627; e-mail info@grenadachamber.org; internet www.grenadachamber.org; f. 1921; inc. 1947; 170 mems; Pres. CEDRIC MITCHELL; Exec. Dir HAZELANN HUTCHINGS.

INDUSTRIAL AND TRADE ASSOCIATIONS

Grenada Cocoa Association (GCA): Lagoon Rd, POB 3649, St George's; tel. 440-2234; fax 440-1470; e-mail gca@spiceisle.com; f. 1964; Chair. RAMSEY RUSH; Man. ANDREW HASTICK.

Grenada Co-operative Nutmeg Association (GCNA): Lagoon Rd, POB 160, St George's; tel. 440-2117; fax 440-6602; e-mail gcna.nutmeg@caribsurf.com; f. 1947; processes and markets all the nutmeg and mace grown on the island; includes the production of nutmeg oil; Chair. VICTOR ASHBY; Gen. Man. MARLON CLYNE.

Grenada Industrial Development Corporation (GIDC): Frequenté Industrial Park, Frequente, St George's; tel. 444-1035; fax 444-4828; e-mail invest@grenadaidc.com; internet www.grenadaidc.com; f. 1985; Chair. R. ANTHONY JOSEPH; Gen. Man. SONIA RODEN.

Marketing and National Importing Board (MNIB): Young St, POB 652, St George's; tel. 440-1791; fax 440-4152; e-mail mnib@spiceisle.com; internet www.mnib.gd; f. 1974; govt-owned; imports basic food items, incl. sugar, rice and milk; also exports fresh produce; Chair. CLAUDIA ALEXIS; Gen. Man. FITZROY JAMES.

EMPLOYERS' ORGANIZATION

Grenada Employers' Federation: Bldg 11, Frequenté Industrial Park, Grand Anse, POB 129, St George's; tel. 440-1832; fax 440-6627; e-mail gef@spiceisle.com; internet www.grenadaemployers.com; Pres. MICHAEL PHILBERT; Exec. Dir CECIL EDWARDS; 60 mems.

UTILITIES

Electricity

Grenada Electricity Services Ltd (Grenlec): Halifax St, POB 381, St George's; tel. 440-2097; fax 440-4106; e-mail customersupport@grenlec.com; internet www.grenlec.com; generation and distribution; 90% privately owned, 10% govt-owned; Chair. G. ROBERT BLANCHARD, Jr; Man. Dir and CEO VERNON LAWRENCE.

Water

National Water and Sewerage Authority (NAWASA): The Carenage, POB 392, St George's; tel. 440-2155; fax 440-4107; e-mail nawasa@caribsurf.com; internet www.spiceisle.com/nawasa; f. 1969; Chair. TERRENCE SMITH; Gen. Man. CHRISTOPHER HUSBANDS.

TRADE UNIONS

Grenada Trade Union Council (GTUC): Green St, POB 411, St George's; tel. and fax 440-3733; e-mail gtuc@caribsurf.com; Pres. MADONNA HARFORD; Gen. Sec. RAY ROBERTS; 8,000 mems (2011).

Bank and General Workers' Union (BGWU): Bain's Alley, POB 329, St George's; tel. and fax 440-3563; e-mail bgwu@caribsurf.com; Pres. JUSTIN CAMPBELL; Gen. Sec. EDMOND CALLISTE.

Commercial and Industrial Workers' Union: Bain's Alley, Grand Anse, POB 1791, St George's; tel. and fax 440-3423; e-mail cominwu@caribsurf.com; Pres. GEORGE MASON; Gen. Sec. BARBARA FRASER; 492 mems.

Grenada Manual, Maritime and Intellectual Workers' Union (GMMIWU): c/o Birchgrove, POB 1927, St Andrew's; tel. and fax 442-7724; Pres. BERT LATOUCHE; Gen. Sec. OSCAR WILLIAMS.

Grenada Public Workers' Union (GPWU): Tanteen, POB 420, St George's; tel. 440-2203; fax 440-6615; e-mail gpwu@spiceisle.com; f. 1931 as Civil Service Asscn; Pres. MADONNA HARFORD; Exec. Sec. AUGUSTINE DAVID.

Grenada Technical and Allied Workers' Union (GTAWU): Green St, POB 405, St George's; tel. 440-2231; fax 440-5878; e-mail tawu@gtawu.org; internet spicy-design.net/~gtawu; f. 1958; Pres.-Gen. Sen. CHESTER HUMPHREY; Gen. Sec. BERT PATERSON.

Grenada Union of Teachers (GUT): Marine Villa, POB 452, St George's; tel. 440-2992; fax 440-9019; e-mail gut@caribsurf.com; internet gutgrenada.org; f. 1913; Pres. KENNY A. M. JAMES; Gen. Sec. TESSA MCQUILKIN; 1,300 mems.

Media Workers' Association of Grenada (MWAG): St George's; e-mail mwagrenada@yahoo.com; f. 1999; Pres. RAWLE TITUS.

Seamen and Waterfront Workers' Union: Ottway House, POB 154, St George's; tel. 440-2573; fax 440-7199; e-mail swwu@caribsurf.com; f. 1952; Pres. ALBERT JULIEN; Gen. Sec. LYLE SAMUEL; 350 mems.

Transport

RAILWAYS

There are no railways in Grenada.

ROADS

In 2001 there were approximately 1,127 km (700 miles) of roads, of which 61% were paved. Public transport is provided by small private operators, with a system covering the entire country. Following the completion of the first phase of the Agricultural Feeder Roads Project funded by the OPEC Fund for International Development (OFID), the Government secured US $8.5m. each from OFID and the Kuwait Fund for Arab Economic Development as loans for the second phase of the project, expected to be completed by the end of 2012.

SHIPPING

The main port is St George's, with accommodation for two ocean-going vessels of up to 500 ft. A number of shipping lines call at St George's. Grenville, on Grenada, and Hillsborough, on Carriacou, are used mostly by small craft. The port at St George's was expanded in 2003, to enable the harbour to accommodate modern super-sized cruise ships, while the Melville Street Cruise Terminal phase became operational in 2004. An ambitious EC $1,600m. development at Port Louis, to include a 350-slipway marina with yachting facilities, was completed in 2009.

Grenada Ports Authority: POB 494, The Pier, St George's; tel. 440-7678; fax 440-3418; e-mail grenport@caribsurf.com; internet www.grenadaports.com; f. 1981; state-owned; Chair. NIGEL JOHN; Gen. Man. AMBROSE PHILLIP.

CIVIL AVIATION

Maurice Bishop International Airport (formerly Point Salines International Airport), 10 km (6 miles) from St George's, was opened in 1984, and has scheduled flights to most East Caribbean destinations, including Venezuela, and to the United Kingdom and North America. There is an airfield at Pearls, 30 km (18 miles) from St George's, and Lauriston Airport, on the island of Carriacou, offers regular scheduled services to Grenada, Saint Vincent and Palm Island (Grenadines).

Grenada is a shareholder in the regional airline, LIAT (see Antigua and Barbuda).

Grenada Airports Authority: Maurice Bishop Int. Airport, POB 385, St George's; tel. 444-4101; fax 444-4838; e-mail gaa@mbiagrenada.com; e-mail www.mbiagrenada.com; f. 1985; Chair. RODNEY GEORGE.

Tourism

Grenada has the attractions of both white sandy beaches and a scenic, mountainous interior with an extensive rainforest. There are also sites of historical interest, and the capital, St George's, is a noted beauty spot. In 2010 there were 104,732 stop-over arrivals and 333,765 cruise ship passengers. In that year tourism earned a preliminary EC $259.8m.

Grenada Board of Tourism: Burns Point, POB 293, St George's; tel. 440-2279; fax 440-6637; e-mail gbt@spiceisle.com; internet www.grenadagrenadines.com; f. 1991; Chair. COLIN DOWE; Dir SIMON STEILL.

Grenada Hotel and Tourism Association Ltd: Ocean House Bldg, Morne Rouge Rd, Grand Anse, POB 440, St George's; tel. 444-1353; fax 444-4847; e-mail mail@ghta.org; internet www.gogrenada.gd; f. 1961; Pres. RUSSELL FIELDEN; Exec. Dir PANCY CHANDLER CROSS.

Defence

A regional security unit was formed in 1983, modelled on the British police force and trained by British officers. A paramilitary element, known as the Special Service Unit and trained by US advisers, acts as the defence contingent and participates in the Regional Security System, a defence pact with other East Caribbean states.

Commissioner of Police: JAMES CLARKSON.

Education

Education is free and compulsory for children between the ages of five and 16 years. Primary education begins at five years of age and lasts for seven years. Secondary education, beginning at the age of 12, lasts for a further five years. In 2007/08 enrolment at primary schools included 93% of children in the relevant age-group; there were 57 primary schools in 1995. There were 20 public secondary schools in 2002, with 11,500 pupils registered in 2009/10; enrolment at all secondary schools included 89% of pupils in the relevant age-group in 2007/08. In 2006 there were 2,710 full-time enrolled students at the T. A. Marryshow Community College. Technical Centres have been established in St Patrick's, St David's and St John's, and the Grenada National College, the Mirabeau Agricultural School and the Teachers' Training College have been incorporated into the Technical and Vocational Institute in St George's. The Extra-Mural Department of the University of the West Indies has a branch in St George's. In 2011 plans to open a teaching hospital in Grenada were announced. The combined capital expenditure on education and human resources development was budgeted at EC $115.7m. in 2011 (equivalent to 14.8% of total capital expenditure).

GUATEMALA

Introductory Survey

LOCATION, CLIMATE, LANGUAGE, RELIGION, FLAG, CAPITAL

The Republic of Guatemala lies in the Central American isthmus, bounded to the north and west by Mexico, with Honduras and Belize to the east and El Salvador to the south. It has a long coastline on the Pacific Ocean and a narrow outlet to the Caribbean Sea. The climate is tropical in the lowlands, with an average temperature of 28°C (83°F), and more temperate in the central highland area, with an average temperature of 20°C (68°F). The official language is Spanish, but more than 20 indigenous languages are also spoken. Almost all of the inhabitants profess Christianity: the majority are Roman Catholics, while an estimated 40% are Protestants. A large proportion of the population also follows traditional Mayan beliefs. The national flag (proportions 5 by 8) has three equal vertical stripes, of blue, white and blue, with the national coat of arms (depicting a quetzal, the 'bird of freedom', and a scroll, superimposed on crossed rifles and sabres, encircled by a wreath) in the centre of the white stripe. The capital is Guatemala City.

CONTEMPORARY POLITICAL HISTORY

Historical Context

Under Spanish colonial rule, Guatemala was part of the Viceroyalty of New Spain. Independence was obtained from Spain in 1821, from Mexico in 1824 and from the Federation of Central American States in 1838. Subsequent attempts to revive the Federation failed and, under a series of dictators, there was relative stability, tempered by periods of disruption. A programme of social reform was begun by Juan José Arévalo (President in 1944–50) and his successor, Col Jacobo Arbenz Guzmán, whose policy of land reform evoked strong opposition from landowners. In 1954 President Arbenz was overthrown in a coup led by Col Carlos Castillo Armas, who invaded the country with US assistance. Castillo became President but was assassinated in July 1957. The next elected President, Gen. Miguel Ydigoras Fuentes, took office in March 1958 and ruled until he was deposed in 1963 by a military coup, led by Col Enrique Peralta Azurdia. He assumed full powers as Chief of Government, suspended the Constitution and dissolved the legislature. A Constituent Assembly, elected in 1964, introduced a new Constitution in 1965. Dr Julio César Méndez Montenegro was elected President in 1966, and in 1970 the candidate of the Movimiento de Liberación Nacional (MLN), Col (later Gen.) Carlos Araña Osorio, was elected President. Despite charges of fraud in the elections of March 1974, Gen. Kjell Laugerud García of the MLN took office as President in July.

President Laugerud sought to discourage extreme right-wing violence and claimed some success, although it was estimated that 50,000–60,000 people were killed in political violence between 1970 and 1979. In March 1978 Gen. Fernando Romeo Lucas García was elected President. The guerrilla movement increased in strength in 1980–81, while the Government was accused of the murder and torture of civilians and, particularly, persecution of the country's indigenous Indian inhabitants, who comprise 60% of the population.

Domestic Political Affairs

In the presidential election of March 1982, from which the left-wing parties were absent, the Government's candidate, Gen. Angel Aníbal Guevara, was declared the winner; however, the election was denounced as fraudulent by the other candidates. A coup followed on 23 March, in which a group of young right-wing military officers installed Gen. José Efraín Ríos Montt as leader of a three-man junta. The Congreso Nacional (National Congress) was closed, and the Constitution and political parties suspended. In June Gen. Ríos Montt dissolved the junta and assumed the presidency. He attempted to fight corruption, reorganized the judicial system and disbanded the secret police. The number of violent deaths diminished. However, after initially gaining the support of the national university, the Roman Catholic Church and the labour unions, Ríos Montt declared a state of siege and imposed censorship of the press. The war against the guerrillas intensified, and a civil defence force of Indians was established. Villages were burned, and many inhabitants killed, in order to deter the Indians from supporting the guerrillas. Ríos Montt's fragile hold on power was threatened in 1982 by several attempted coups, which he managed to forestall.

In January 1983 the US Government announced the resumption of arms sales to Guatemala, which had been suspended in 1977 as a result of human rights violations. However, independent reports claimed that the human rights situation had deteriorated, and revealed that 2,600 people had been killed during the first six months of Ríos Montt's rule. In March the army was implicated in the massacre of 300 Indian peasants at Nahulá, and there was a resurgence in the activity of both left- and right-wing 'death squads'. The President declared a 30-day amnesty for guerrillas and political exiles, and lifted the state of siege. The Government's 'guns and beans' policy provided food and medicine in exchange for recruitment to the Patrullas de Autodefensa Civil (PAC), a pro-Government peasant militia.

By mid-1983 opposition to the President was widespread. In August Gen. Oscar Humberto Mejía Victores, the Minister of Defence, led a successful coup against Ríos Montt. President Mejía ended press censorship and announced an amnesty for guerrillas. Urban and rural terrorism continued to escalate, however. Following the murder in northern Guatemala of six US aid workers, the USA suspended US $50m. in aid to the country in 1984. In accordance with Mejía's assurance of electoral reform, elections for a Constituent Assembly were held in July, at which the centre groups, including the newly formed Unión del Centro Nacional (UCN), obtained the greatest number of votes. Under the system of proportional representation, however, the right-wing coalition of the MLN and the Central Auténtica Nacionalista obtained a majority of seats in the Assembly.

Guatemala's new Constitution was promulgated in 1985. Eight candidates participated in the presidential election in November, but the main contest was between Jorge Carpio Nicolle, the candidate of the UCN, and Mario Vinicio Cerezo Arévalo, the candidate of the Partido Democracia Cristiana Guatemalteca (PDCG). As neither of the leading candidates obtained the requisite majority, a second round of voting was held in December, which Cerezo won. The PDCG won the majority of seats in the concurrent election to the new Congreso. The US Administration increased economic aid and resumed military aid to Guatemala, in support of the new civilian Government.

Immediately prior to the transfer of power in January 1986, the outgoing military Government decreed a general amnesty to encompass those suspected of involvement in abuses of human rights since 1982. In 1987 the creation of a government commission to investigate 'disappearances' was announced. Nevertheless, by mid-1988 there were frequent reports of torture and killings by right-wing 'death squads' as discontent with the Government's liberal policies increased. In 1989 the Consejo Nacional de Desplazados de Guatemala was created to represent the 1m. refugees who had fled their homes since 1980. According to the UN Commission for Human Rights, almost 3,000 complaints of human rights abuses were lodged in 1989.

In August 1987 a peace plan for the region was signed in Guatemala City by the Presidents of Costa Rica, El Salvador, Guatemala, Honduras and Nicaragua. Subsequently, a Commission of National Reconciliation (CNR) was formed in compliance with the terms of the accord. In October representatives of the Guatemalan Government and the main guerrilla grouping, the Unidad Revolucionaria Nacional Guatemalteca (URNG), met in Spain, but the peace negotiations ended without agreement. Right-wing pressure on the Government, and an attempted coup in May 1988, forced Cerezo to postpone further negotiations with the URNG.

During 1989 guerrilla activity intensified. Many political figures and labour leaders fled the country after receiving death threats from paramilitary groups. Meanwhile, Cerezo refused to negotiate with the URNG for as long as its members remained armed. In September the URNG made further proposals for negotiations, following the signing of the Tela Agreement (the Central American peace plan accord), but these were rejected.

Despite Cerezo's promise to restrict the unlawful activities of the armed forces and right-wing 'death squads', the number of politically motivated assassinations and 'disappearances' escalated in 1990. The URNG and the CNR held discussions, as a result of which the URNG pledged not to disrupt the upcoming elections and agreed to participate in a constituent assembly to reform the Constitution.

In the presidential election of November 1990 none of the presidential nominees obtained an absolute majority in the first round. A second ballot, held in January 1991, between the two leading candidates was won by Jorge Serrano Elías of the Movimiento de Acción Solidaria (MAS). The MAS failed to secure a majority in the legislative election, however, and Serrano invited the Partido de Avanzada Nacional (PAN) and the Partido Socialista Democrático (PSD) to participate in the formation of a coalition Government.

In April 1991 direct talks between the URNG and the Government began in Mexico City. However, in an attempt to destabilize efforts at national reconciliation, members of the state security forces, believed to be acting independently of their superiors, launched a campaign of violence, directing death threats against leaders of trade unions and human rights organizations, and murdering a PSD politician. In late 1991 the ombudsman, Ramiro de León Carpio, secured the resignation of the Director of the National Police, Col Mario Enrique Paíz Bolanos, who was alleged to be responsible for the use of torture. Further peace talks at the end of the year failed to produce any agreement.

Further negotiations in Mexico City in 1992 led to concessions by the Government, which agreed to curb the expansion of the PAC. The URNG, which maintained that *campesinos* (peasants) were forcibly enlisted into the PAC, included in its conditions for a peace agreement the immediate dissolution of the patrols, which were accused of human rights abuses. In November the Government accepted renewed proposals by the URNG for the establishment of a commission on past human rights violations, but only on the condition that the rebels sign a definitive peace accord. Talks stalled in March 1993, owing principally to government demands that the URNG disarm as a precondition to the implementation of procedures for the international verification of human rights in Guatemala, and were suspended in May, owing to the constitutional crisis (see below).

The URNG announced a unilateral cease-fire as a gesture of goodwill to the incoming President, Ramiro de León Carpio, in June 1993 (see below). In August, in a concession to the URNG, de León announced the reform of the Estado Mayor Presidencial, a military body widely accused of human rights offences. However, in September the army announced a resumption of military operations against the rebels. A revised peace plan was rejected by the rebels. Preliminary talks were finally resumed in Mexico in January 1994.

Constitutional coup of 1993

Unrest at economic austerity measures escalated in May 1993. With the MAS no longer able to effect a constructive alliance in the Congreso, on 25 May Serrano, with the support of the military, suspended parts of the Constitution and dissolved the Congreso and the Supreme Court. A ban was imposed on the media and Serrano announced that he would rule by decree pending the drafting of a new constitution by a constituent assembly, to be elected within 60 days. The constitutional coup provoked almost unanimous international condemnation, with the USA immediately suspending aid. The military reappraised its position and forced the resignation of Serrano, who fled to El Salvador. (He was later granted political asylum in Panama.) The Minister of National Defence, Gen. José Domingo García Samayoa, assumed control of the country pending the election of a new President. The entire Cabinet, excluding García and the Minister of the Interior, Francisco Perdomo Sandoval, resigned on 3 June. Two days later the Congreso reconvened to conduct a presidential ballot. The Instancia Nacional de Consenso (INC), a broad coalition of political parties, business leaders and trade unions, elected Ramiro de León Carpio, the former human rights ombudsman, as President. The USA subsequently restored its aid programme to Guatemala.

In August 1993, as an initial measure in a campaign to eradicate corruption from state institutions, de León requested the voluntary resignation of the Congreso and the Supreme Court. The request caused a serious division in the legislature, which separated into two main factions, the Gran Grupo Parlamentario (GGP), which included some 70 members of the MAS, UCN, PAN and the Frente Republicano Guatemalteco (FRG) and supported the dismissal of 16 deputies identified by the INC as corrupt, and a group of 38 deputies, including members of the PDCG and independents, who supported the resignation of all 116 deputies. In September, following the suspension of a congressional session by the President of the Congreso, Fernando Lobo Dubón (a member of the PDCG), the GGP defied the decision and elected a new congressional President. Although Lobo was temporarily reinstated by the Constitutional Court, the GGP threatened to boycott any further sessions convened by him. In November a compromise was reached between the Government and the legislature, involving a series of constitutional reforms. These were subsequently approved by a referendum, although less than 20% of the electorate participated in the voting, reflecting popular concern that more extensive reforms were necessary. The reforms took effect in April 1994, and fresh legislative elections were to be held in August. The new Congreso, which was to serve until 14 January 1996, was to appoint the members of a new, enlarged Supreme Court of Justice. Other reforms included a reduction in the terms of office of the President, legislature and municipal authorities, and of the Supreme Court justices, and a reduction in the number of seats in the Congreso.

In March 1994 the Government and the URNG agreed a timetable of formal negotiations aimed at achieving a definitive peace agreement by the end of the year. In addition, a general human rights agreement was signed, providing guarantees, including a government commitment to eliminate illegal security corps, strengthen national human rights institutions and cease obligatory military recruitment. Agreement was also reached on the establishment of a UN deputation, the Human Rights Verification Mission in Guatemala (MINUGUA), to verify the implementation of the accord. Further talks resulted in the signing, in June, of agreements on the resettlement of people displaced by the civil war (estimated to number some 1m.), and on the establishment of a Comisión para el Esclarecimiento Histórico (CEH—Commission for Historical Clarification) to investigate human rights violations committed during the 33-year conflict.

In August 1994 the URNG withdrew from the peace negotiations and accused the Government of failing to observe the agreed human rights provisions. Talks remained deadlocked until February 1995, when a new timetable for negotiations, achieved with UN mediation, was announced. The new agenda provided for a cease-fire agreement by June and the signing of a definitive peace accord in August. The issue of the identity and rights of indigenous peoples was finally resolved, but talks continued beyond the agreed deadline without agreement on other substantive issues, including socio-economic reform and the incorporation of URNG guerrillas into civilian life.

At the legislative election of August 1994 only some 20% of the electorate exercised their vote, again reflecting widespread scepticism about the reforms instigated by de León. Despite winning the greatest number of seats in the 80-seat legislature, the FRG, led by Gen. (retd) José Efraín Ríos Montt, was excluded from the 12-member congressional directorate by an alliance of the PAN, PDCG, MLN and Unión Democrática. However, in December the PDCG transferred its allegiance to the FRG and Ríos Montt was subsequently elected President of the Congreso. His inauguration in January 1995 provoked demonstrations by human rights organizations, which considered him responsible for the deaths of as many as 15,000 civilians as a result of counter-insurgency operations conducted during his period as de facto ruler in 1982–83.

The presidential and legislative elections of November 1995 were notable for the return to the electoral process, for the first time for more than 40 years, of the left wing, which was represented by the Frente Democrático Nueva Guatemala (FDNG). In addition, the URNG declared a unilateral cease-fire to coincide with the electoral campaign and urged people to exercise their vote. The two leading presidential candidates, Alvaro Enrique Arzú Irigoyen of the PAN and Alfonso Antonio Portillo Cabrera of the FRG, contested a second round of voting in January 1996, at which Arzú secured a narrow victory. At the legislative election the PAN also secured a majority of seats in the Congreso.

Shortly after assuming office in January 1996, Arzú implemented a comprehensive reorganization of the military high command, replacing those officers who were not in favour of a negotiated peace settlement. In March the Congreso ratified the International Labour Organization's Convention on the rights of indigenous peoples. However, the document had been amended by the Congreso, prompting protests by Indian organizations. On 20 March the URNG announced an indefinite unilateral ceasefire. Arzú immediately ordered the armed forces to suspend counter-insurgency operations. In May the Government and the URNG signed an agreement on agrarian and socio-economic reforms. In the following month the Congreso adopted legislation that made members of the armed forces accountable to civilian courts for all but strictly military crimes. In September the Government and the URNG signed an agreement on the strengthening of civilian power and the role of the armed forces. Under the terms of the accord, all military and intelligence services were to be placed under the authority of the Government. The police force was to be reorganized, with the creation of a new National Civilian Police force (Policía Nacional Civil—PNC). Also confirmed in the accord was the abolition of the PAC. A general amnesty law was approved by the Congreso in December.

1996 peace treaty

On 29 December 1996 the Government and the URNG signed the definitive peace treaty in Guatemala City, bringing to an end some 36 years of civil war, during which an estimated 140,000 people had died. The demobilization of URNG guerrillas, estimated to number some 3,250, was supervised by MINUGUA and completed in May 1997. In the following month the URNG registered as a political party in formation and, in December 1998, formally engaged as a political party.

In April 1998 the auxiliary bishop of the metropolitan diocese of Guatemala City, Juan José Gerardi Conedera, was murdered. Gerardi had been a founder of the Roman Catholic Church's Oficina de Derechos Humanos del Arzobispado (ODHA—Archbishopric's Human Rights Office), and a prominent critic of the armed forces. Days before his death Gerardi had presented a report by the ODHA documenting human rights abuses committed during the civil conflict, of which army personnel were found responsible for some 80%. In what the Church and human rights groups interpreted as an attempt to conceal the truth, a priest, Mario Orantes Nájera, was arrested and formally charged with Gerardi's murder in October. In February 1999 the presiding judge in the case, Henry Monroy, ordered the release of Orantes on grounds of insufficient evidence; Monroy withdrew from the case in the following month after allegedly receiving death threats. In 2001 former intelligence chief Col (retd) Disrael Lima Estrada, his son, Capt. Byron Lima Oliva, and a former member of the presidential guard, José Obdulio Villanueva, were convicted of Gerardi's murder; Orantes was convicted of conspiring in his death. However, in 2002 a Court of Appeal overturned the convictions and ordered a retrial after accepting the defence's argument that there had been irregularities in the testimony of a key witness. At the retrial in 2003 the sentences were upheld by the Supreme Court. Nevertheless, in March 2005 a Court of Appeal amended the convictions of Lima Estrada and Lima Oliva to accessory to murder, reducing their sentences from 30 years' to 20 years' imprisonment.

In August 1999, in what was widely regarded as a test case for the judicial system, 25 members of the armed forces convicted of the massacre in 1995 of 11 civilians in Xamán, Alta Verapaz, received minimum sentences of five years' imprisonment. The case was the first in which military personnel accused of killing civilians had been tried by a civilian court, and the decision, which provoked public outrage, served greatly to undermine confidence in the courts' ability to administer justice in the remaining 625 cases of massacres attributed to the security forces. By contrast, in 1998 death sentences had been passed on three members of the PAC found guilty of participating in massacres of civilians. In December 1999 MINUGUA issued a report stating that commitments made by the Arzú administration under the 1996 peace treaty to reduce the influence of the military remained unfulfilled. A MINUGUA report in the following year stated that the number of extra-judicial executions had doubled between 1996 and 2000.

In February 1999 the CEH published its final report, in which it attributed more than 93% of human rights violations committed during the civil conflict to the armed forces and state paramilitaries. It announced that 200,000 people had been killed or had 'disappeared' between 1962 and 1996, the majority of them Mayan Indians. It also concluded that the USA had financed and trained Guatemalan forces responsible for atrocities. The report recommended that compensation be provided for the families of victims, that prosecutions be brought against those suspected of crimes against humanity and that a purge of the armed forces be implemented. The Government described the Commission's findings as 'controversial', and did not express any intention of pursuing its recommendations.

In October 1998 the Congreso approved constitutional reforms provided for in the 1996 peace accords. The reforms, which concerned the rights of indigenous peoples, the role of the armed forces and the police, and the strengthening of the courts, were subject to ratification in a referendum. However, at the referendum, in May 1999, 55.6% of participating voters rejected the constitutional amendments. The turn-out was extremely low, at 18.6%, and observers attributed the result to a lack of information and to mistrust of the political establishment rather than to the rejection of the peace accords themselves. At presidential and legislative elections, conducted in November, voter participation, at some 40%, was greatly improved. The two leading presidential candidates, Alfonso Portillo of the FRG and Oscar Berger Perdomo of the PAN, contested a second round of voting on 26 December, in which Portillo secured victory. The FRG secured an outright majority in the election to the newly enlarged legislature.

The Portillo Government

The new Government of President Portillo, which took office on 14 January 2000, immediately undertook the promised demilitarization of the upper echelons of government. A Governability Pact was introduced, intended to build consensus between the representatives of the state and the country's political and social leaderships. However, disputes between the Government and the Congreso resulted in virtual paralysis in policy-making throughout 2001. Furthermore, throughout the year the Government was beset by allegations of corruption. In March 2002 a congressional commission was formed to investigate claims that President Portillo and Vice-President Francisco Reyes López had established bank accounts in Panama for the purpose of money-laundering. The allegations provoked mass protests in Guatemala City. However, the Auditor-General's Office declared that evidence used to support the claims had been fabricated, and in June the investigation by the congressional commission collapsed, owing to a lack of evidence.

Meanwhile, violent attacks against public figures continued in 2002. In March the leader of the opposition Partido Patriótico, Jorge Rosal Zea, was assassinated. The US Government expressed its concern at levels of corruption, drugs-trafficking and continuing human rights abuses in Guatemala. President Portillo subsequently announced a number of reforms to the security forces, including the dissolution of the Departamento de Operaciones Antinarcóticos (Department of Anti-Narcotics Operations) and the creation of a new unit, Unidades Móviles Operativas, to combat drugs-trafficking and terrorism. Nevertheless, in February 2003 the USA added Guatemala to the list of nations it considered unco-operative in combating drugs-trafficking.

In May 2003 Oscar Berger Perdomo, hitherto the PAN's candidate in the forthcoming presidential election, announced that he would stand as the nominee of the Gran Alianza Nacional (GANA), a small, centre-right alliance supported by the private sector and comprising the Partido Patriota (PP), the Movimiento Reformador and the Partido Solidaridad Nacional. Nine PAN deputies followed suit. President Portillo supported the nomination of Ríos Montt as the FRG's nominee. Nevertheless, in July the Supreme Court subsequently barred his candidacy, prompting violent protests. At the end of the month the Constitutional Court again overruled the supreme court decision and instructed the Electoral Tribunal to register Ríos Montt as a candidate.

Presidential and legislative elections of 2003

Presidential and legislative elections took place in November 2003. Berger and Alvaro Colom Caballeros of the Unidad Nacional de la Esperanza (UNE) contested a second round of voting in December, in which Berger narrowly secured the presidency. In the legislative elections, GANA secured the largest number of seats in the expanded assembly, although it failed to secure a majority. In January 2004 GANA agreed a two-year governability pact with the UNE and the PAN. President Berger took office on 14 January.

In February 2004 the Constitutional Court lifted the parliamentary immunity Ríos Montt had hitherto enjoyed. The following month Ríos Montt was charged with premeditated murder, coercion and threats in connection to the violence outside the Supreme Court in July 2003 and placed under house arrest; the charges were dismissed in 2006. Also in February 2004, former President Portillo and former Vice-President Reyes similarly lost their parliamentary immunity from prosecution. Shortly afterwards, Portillo left the country for Mexico. An injunction for his arrest on charges of money-laundering and misuse of public funds was subsequently requested and the US embassy revoked his visa. Reyes was arrested in July and charged with fraud, embezzlement and abuse of authority. In July 2005 Portillo was accused of embezzling over US $15m. of public funds during his presidency and a warrant for his arrest was confirmed. However, in May 2007 the Constitutional Court ordered that the case against Portillo be abandoned. Nevertheless, in October 2008 Portillo surrendered himself to Mexican authorities to be extradited. On arrival in Guatemala, however, he was controversially released on bail of just $132,000, a move that provoked outcry given the severity and number of corruption charges against him. Portillo was arrested in January 2010, after an extradition request by the USA (on money-laundering charges) was approved by a court in Guatemala City. In August, however, Portillo was ordered to stand trial in Guatemala on the embezzlement charges. The trial of Portillo, together with his former Minister of National Defence, Eduardo Arévalo, and his former Minister of Public Finance, Manuel Maza, commenced in January 2011. Owing to a lack of evidence, all three men were exonerated in May, prompting criticism from CICIG (see below). Nevertheless, in November Portillo's extradition to the USA was ratified by President Colom, confirming an earlier ruling by the Constitutional Court.

Domestic security was one of the most pressing problems facing the Berger Government. Gang rivalry and vigilante groups were widely held to be responsible for the rising rates of murder and violent crime. In the first six months of 2004 the incidence of violent crime increased by 13% on the previous year, prompting the resignation of the Minister of the Interior in July. Following the exposure of several senior police officers with links to criminal groups, in June Berger dismissed the head of the PNC. He also ordered the deployment of some 4,000 police and military officers in areas with particularly high crime rates. In spite of these initiatives, the murder rate increased by 25% in 2004. In October 2005 19 inmates escaped from a prison in Escuintla; it was alleged that prison guards were privy to the security breach. In response, the Minister of Defence, Gen. Carlos Aldana Villanueva, announced that the armed forces would assume responsibility for the external security surrounding prisons. Berger subsequently dismissed Aldana Villanueva.

Internal political conflicts and the defection of congressional deputies impeded the Berger Government's efforts to implement its legislative agenda. In an attempt to secure opposition support for proposed fiscal reforms, in May 2004 President Berger met with Ríos Montt. However, the meeting prompted the withdrawal of the UNE and the PAN from the governability pact and the PP left GANA in protest. Despite some success in addressing the problems of corruption, in late 2004 a MINUGUA report noted that government efforts to reform the criminal justice system had been largely ineffective and that the state remained unable to ensure that laws were observed. Upon its withdrawal from Guatemala in December, MINUGUA reported that the Government still had to overcome three major challenges: public security, judicial reform and discrimination against indigenous peoples. Following legislative approval, an office of the UN's High Commission for Human Rights was opened in Guatemala in 2005.

Political tensions escalated into violence in early 2006. A number of political activists were assassinated, including a UNE deputy and the co-ordinator of the nascent political party Encuentro por Guatemala, Eleaza Tebalan. The lynching of four people in two separate attacks in April prompted the mobilization of 11,000 members of the armed forces to assist the police in maintaining order. In September the Government disclosed that the controversial deployment of the armed forces to support the police was expected to continue for at least two further presidential terms.

In February 2007 the creation of an auxiliary police unit, composed of former members of the armed forces, to be deployed in areas experiencing the highest rates of violent crime, was announced. In the same month three Salvadorean deputies were found murdered on the outskirts of Guatemala City. Three days later four Guatemalan police officers who had confessed to the murders were arrested and imprisoned; however, they too were later killed. Following the incident 22 prison employees were arrested on suspicion of complicity in the crime. The Minister of the Interior, Carlos Vielmann, and PNC Director Erwin Sperissen tendered their resignations, but these were rejected by Berger. Notwithstanding the arrest of four further suspects in relation to the assassinations, a vote of no confidence in Vielmann was approved by the Congreso in March.

The crisis provoked by the assassinations facilitated, in August 2007, the overwhelming approval by the Congreso of legislation to create the International Commission against Impunity in Guatemala (CICIG—Comisión Internacional contra la Impunidad en Guatemala), in fulfilment of an agreement between the Government and the UN signed in December 2006. The independent body was to comprise a panel of international experts who would assist the Guatemalan authorities in the investigation and dismantling of paramilitary security forces and other criminal organizations linked to state institutions. CICIG officially began its operations in January 2008.

Presidential and legislative elections of 2007

Security issues dominated the campaign for the presidential and legislative elections held on 9 September 2007. The vote was preceded by the most violent electoral campaign since the end of the civil war, in which more than 40 people were killed. In the presidential ballot, the UNE's Colom—contesting his third consecutive election—secured 28% of valid votes cast, followed by Gen. (retd) Otto Fernando Pérez Molina, the PP candidate, with 24%, and Alejandro Eduardo Giammattei Falla, representing GANA, who received 17%. At a second round of voting on 4 November, Colom defeated Pérez Molina, with 53% of valid votes. In elections to the Congreso the UNE increased its representation to 50 seats, becoming the largest party in the legislature. Colom was sworn in on 14 January 2008, becoming the first centre-left President since 1954.

Upon assuming office, Colom introduced the 'Plan Cuadrante', intended to reduce high crime rates. In February 2008 the Congreso approved a PP proposal to restore the death penalty, suspended since 2002. The legislation, however, was vetoed by Colom in March. (Colom again vetoed legislation providing for the reinstatement of capital punishment in November 2010.) Investigations into the 2007 murders of the three Salvadorean deputies also progressed in 2008, with the arrest of two more suspects. In July a state prosecutor investigating the case was shot dead. The shooting took place the week after 13 gang members were acquitted of killing the police officers who had confessed to the murders.

There were several changes in key personnel in Colom's first year in government. In May 2008 the Minister of the Economy, José Carlos García Macal, resigned and was replaced by Rómulo Caballeros. In the following month Carlos Vinicio Gómez Ruiz, the interior minister, was killed in a helicopter crash; he was succeeded by Francisco Jiménez Irungaray. In July Colom dismissed his Ministers of Public Health and Social Welfare and of Agriculture, Livestock and Food. The upheaval continued in August with the resignation of the Attorney-General, Juan Luis Florido. Florido's departure was welcomed by CICIG, which had pressed for a change of personnel in the Attorney-General's office better to combat impunity. Furthermore, in August Eduardo Meyer Maldonado, the legislative speaker and a close ally of the President, was obliged to resign over his alleged involvement in the unauthorized transfer of congressional funds. (In January 2010 Meyer was charged with embezzlement, dereliction of duty and failure to report a crime.)

Colom's electoral campaign included a pledge to improve internal security and reduce impunity. To this effect, in February 2008 the President announced that he planned gradually to decrease army participation in civilian security operations. In a decision welcomed by human rights activists, Colom also declared that previously unseen military archives would be released to the public. Reluctance from military personnel, however, led to delays in the files becoming available. (In June 2011 over 99% of the military's archives were finally declassified, although it had earlier been revealed that the documents covering 1980–85 had disappeared.) Nevertheless, in September 2008, the President announced plans to increase the size of the army to 25,000. The increase was intended to bolster the police force, with the proviso that army numbers could later be reduced as the PNC gained strength. Public uncertainty about military power increased further in the same month when Colom summoned the army to guard the presidential palace after bugging devices were discovered in his office. The crisis precipitated a complete restructuring of presidential security. In a further step to enhance security, Colom inaugurated a new security council, the Consejo Nacional de Seguridad, in November, to co-ordinate and supervise Guatemala's security institutions. In December Colom undertook further changes to the Guatemalan military with the dismissal of many important army officials and the replacement of the Minister of National Defence, Brig.-Gen. Marco Tulio García Franco, with Gen. Abraham Valenzuela González.

Efforts to improve security

CICIG's 2008 report conceded a lack of tangible progress in reducing crime and levels of impunity, largely owing to opposition from Guatemalan authorities. Colom replaced Jiménez Irungaray at the Ministry of the Interior with a more hard-line candidate, Salvador Gándara, in January 2009 and made renewed promises to improve security. In March the President announced the creation of an anti-impunity commission intended to complement CICIG's investigations, and in April he signed a national security and justice accord with the President of the Congreso and the acting President of the Supreme Court. Notable provisions of the accord included the creation of a public security ministry and the extension of CICIG's mandate. Meanwhile, at the end of March the Congreso approved long-awaited gun control legislation.

The President's efforts to reduce violent crime were overshadowed in May 2009 by allegations that he was involved in the killing of a prominent lawyer, Rodrigo Rosenberg Marzano, who, in a video recording made prior to his death, had claimed that Colom and other senior officials were plotting his murder. Colom requested that CICIG conduct an investigation into the allegations, which he vehemently denied, accusing his opponents of attempting to destabilize his Government. Thousands of people subsequently participated in protests in Guatemala City to demand Colom's resignation, while demonstrations in support of the President were also well attended. In January 2010 CICIG exonerated Colom, concluding that Rosenberg had orchestrated his own assassination, although the commission was to continue examining other claims made by Rosenberg, including alleged corruption at the Banco de Desarrollo Rural. In July eight people were convicted in connection with Rosenberg's killing.

Meanwhile, CICIG continued to encounter resistance from officials while conducting its investigations. In June 2009 the commission filed a formal complaint against a judge who was seeking to terminate its involvement in the case against former President Portillo. The Congreso approved a two-year extension of CICIG's mandate in July. With the violent murder rate continuing to rise, Gándara resigned as Minister of the Interior in July 2009; he was succeeded by Raúl Antonio Velásquez Ramos. Gándara's decision to replace the leadership of the PNC with retired police officials in the previous month had been criticized by human rights groups. In August Velásquez dismissed the PNC officials appointed by Gándara for alleged involvement in drugs-trafficking. Following objections by CICIG to several of the Congreso's nominees to the Supreme Court, as well as criticism from UN officials over a lack of transparency, in October the legislature revised the list of new judges. CICIG achieved a significant victory in January 2010, when it facilitated the arrest of Portillo (see above).

In the first such conviction since the end of the civil war, in August 2009 Felipe Cusanero Coj, a former member of the PAC, was found guilty of the forced 'disappearances' of six Mayan citizens in 1982–84 and sentenced to 150 years' imprisonment. In December a retired army officer, Marco Antonio Sánchez, received a 53-year prison sentence for the 'disappearances' of eight farm workers.

Further changes were made to the Cabinet and to the leadership of the PNC in 2010. Three ministers were dismissed in February: the Minister of Agriculture, Livestock and Food, Mario Aldana, owing to irregularities in the tendering process for the supply of fertilizers; the Minister of Education, Bienvenido Argueta, for failing to reveal information about the beneficiaries of Mi Familia Progresa, a social programme that some opposition members suspected had been used to reward government supporters; and Minister of the Interior Velásquez as a result of corruption allegations. Carlos Menocal, hitherto co-ordinator of the presidential anti-impunity commission, was appointed to replace Velásquez, becoming Colom's fifth Minister of the Interior. In March the PNC Director, Baltázar Gómez Barrios, the head of the PNC's counter-narcotics division, Nelly Bonilla, and the latter's deputy were arrested on suspicion of alleged collusion with drugs-traffickers. The resignation of Rubén Morales as Minister of the Economy in mid-June was followed later that month by those of the Minister of Energy and Mines, Carlos Meany, and the Minister of Public Finance, Juan Alberto Fuentes Knight. Fuentes cited disappointment with the Congreso's repeated refusal to approve fiscal reforms aimed at increasing tax revenue. Fuentes' replacement, Edgar Balsells, was removed from the Government in November, owing to his failure to communicate with other ministers, although he reportedly claimed that he had been dismissed for seeking to reduce expenditure on social programmes overseen by Colom's wife, Sandra Torres de Colom. The Government's ability to pursue its legislative agenda had been severely hampered by the UNE's lack of a majority in the Congreso, the party's position having been weakened further since the 2007 elections by the defection of a number of its deputies to Libertad Democrática Renovada (LIDER), a dissident legislative bloc created in 2009.

The continuing difficulties encountered by CICIG in fulfilling its mandate were again apparent in June 2010, when Carlos Castresana Fernández resigned as its director, expressing frustration with the Government's failure to co-operate in the commission's efforts and urging Colom to dismiss the recently appointed Attorney-General, Conrado Reyes, whom he alleged had strong links to organized crime. The Constitutional Court subsequently ruled that the selection process leading to the appointment of Reyes had been unconstitutional, resulting in his removal from the post. Meanwhile, in August arrest warrants were issued for 19 former officials of the Ministry of the Interior and the PNC who were accused by CICIG of involvement in the extrajudicial execution of 10 prisoners in 2005–06, among other serious crimes. Several of those sought were swiftly detained, including Alejandro Giammattei, a former director of the prison system who had unsuccessfully contested the 2007 presidential election, while in May 2011 the extradition to Guatemala of former Minister of the Interior Carlos Vielmann, who had been arrested in Spain in October 2010, was authorized by a Spanish judge. (Giammattei was exonerated in May 2011, owing to a lack of evidence.) The appointment of Claudia Paz y Paz Bailey, a lawyer and human rights activist, as Attorney-General in December 2010 was welcomed by civil society groups; she pledged to ensure effective co-ordination with CICIG. Also in that month, a further extension of CICIG's mandate, to 2013, was approved by the UN.

President Colom declared a 30-day state of siege in the northern department of Alta Verapaz in December 2010, in response to reports that much of the department was under the control of a Mexican drugs cartel, Los Zetas. The state of siege, which suspended constitutional guarantees, allowing the army to detain suspects without warrants and curtail public gatherings, among other measures, was ended in early February 2011. However, a further state of siege was enforced in Petén in May following the massacre of 27 people by suspected Los Zetas members. Also in that month, Brig.-Gen. Juan José Ruiz Morales was appointed as the new Minister of Defence.

The arrest in mid-2011 of several former high-ranking members of the security forces indicated that progress was being made in bringing to justice the alleged perpetrators of serious human rights violations during the civil conflict. Moreover, in an unprecedented ruling, four ex-soldiers were sentenced to life imprisonment in August after being found guilty of massacring over 200 villagers in 1982.

Recent developments: the 2011 elections

Despite a constitutional provision barring those related to the incumbent President by blood or 'affinity' from contesting the presidency, in March 2011 Colom's wife, Sandra Torres de Colom, announced that she intended to compete in the upcoming election as the candidate of the UNE and GANA. Ostensibly to facilitate this objective, Torres and Colom divorced in the following month. However, the Supreme Electoral Tribunal regarded this move as a fraudulent attempt to bypass the Constitution and in June rejected Torres' candidacy. This ruling was endorsed by the Supreme Electoral Court and the Supreme Court in July and the Constitutional Court in August. With Torres' legal options exhausted and the registration deadline expired, the UNE-GANA coalition was unable to field a presidential candidate in the 11 September poll.

The presidential and legislative polls took place peacefully, although the pre-election period had been marred by political violence. In the general election, the PP gained control of 56 seats in the 158-seat Congreso, while the UNE-GANA (which terminated their alliance later that month) secured 48, LIDER and the Unión del Cambio Nacional 14 each, and Compromiso, Renovación y Orden 12; the remaining 14 seats were distributed among six smaller parties and coalitions. No candidate secured an outright victory in the presidential contest, so a second round of voting between the two leading contenders—the PP's Gen. (retd) Otto Fernando Pérez Molina (who had won 36.1% of the first round ballot) and Manuel Antonio Baldizón Méndez of LIDER (22.7%)—was scheduled for 6 November. In the event, Pérez Molina triumphed in the run-off election, receiving 53.7% of the valid votes cast. The rate of participation by the electorate was recorded at 69.3% in the legislative poll and 69.4% and 60.8% in the first and second rounds, respectively, of the presidential election. Pérez Molina was sworn in as President on 14 January 2012, becoming the first head of state with a military background since the end of the civil conflict. His new Government was dominated by the PP, although the foreign affairs and agriculture portfolios were allocated to members of the Visión con Valores-Encuentro por Guatemala. A new Ministry of Social Development was also established, which was to focus on poverty reduction initiatives.

To address the country's crime problems, in January 2012 Pérez Molina announced plans for the involvement of the military in police operations, in spite of the fact that this was in breach of the 1996 peace treaty. In addition, he proposed recruiting an additional 10,000 police officers. Later that month Ríos Montt, whose immunity from prosecution had expired with the inauguration of the new Congreso, was charged with genocide and other serious crimes dating from his 1982–83 presidency. This development, along with the concurrent ratification of the Rome Statute of the International Criminal Court, alleviated some of the concerns expressed by Pérez Molina's critics, who feared that the new President might obstruct the ongoing investigations into military abuses committed during the civil war.

Pérez Molina encountered opposition in the legislature in March 2012 after LIDER summoned the Minister of Public Finance, Pavel Centeno, to appear before the Congreso to answer questions on the Government's tax reform plans. The opposition originally issued its demand in February, barely a month after the minister had taken office. Centeno ignored the request, but following a further summons he stepped down from his post on 20 March to avoid submitting to the order. Pérez Molina refused to accept his resignation, however. LIDER argued that as Centeno was still in charge of the public finance ministry, he should appear before the Congreso. The dispute led to a congressional impasse that continued into April.

Foreign Affairs

Until the return to civilian government in 1986, Guatemala remained steadfast in its claims to the neighbouring territory of Belize. However, Guatemala's new Constitution, which took effect in 1986, did not include Belize in its delineation of Guatemalan territory. In 1991 Guatemala and Belize signed an accord under the terms of which Belize pledged to legislate to reduce its maritime boundaries and to allow Guatemala access to the Caribbean Sea and use of its port facilities. In return, Guatemala officially recognized Belize as an independent state and established diplomatic relations. Nevertheless, in 1994 Guatemala formally reaffirmed its territorial claim to Belize. The Standing Committee of Ministers of Foreign Affairs of the Caribbean Community and Common Market (CARICOM, see p. 227) again confirmed its support for Belizean sovereignty. In 2000 the Organization of American States (OAS, see p. 394) established a panel of negotiators to supervise the process of bilateral negotiations. Talks in 2001 focused on the issue of Guatemalans living in the disputed border area; an agreement was later reached to relocate the families.

In 2002 relations with Belize appeared to improve following further OAS-mediated discussions on the border issue; proposals were outlined for a solution to the dispute. These included the provision that Guatemala would recognize Belize's land boundary as set out in the Treaty of 1859, and the creation of a model settlement for peasants and landless farmers in the disputed area. The two countries were to hold simultaneous public referendums on the agreement. However, the fatal shooting of a Guatemalan on the Belizean side of the border in October delayed the plebiscites. In 2003 the foreign ministers of both countries signed a co-operation agreement pending a final settlement of the dispute. In 2004 delegations from the two countries participated in OAS-sponsored negotiations to establish a series of initiatives designed to promote mutual confidence, and in 2005 Guatemala and Belize signed an Agreement on a Framework of Negotiation and Confidence Building Measures. Following almost two years of negotiations, in 2006 representatives of the two countries signed a partial free trade accord, which entered into force in October 2009. In December 2008 the foreign ministers of Guatemala and Belize signed an agreement, subject to ratification by referendum, to submit the Belizean territory dispute to the International Court of Justice (ICJ) for resolution. In September 2010 the Guatemalan Congreso approved the agreement. In November 2011 the ministers responsible for foreign affairs of Guatemala and Belize agreed that concurrent referendums on the issue would be conducted by the end of 2013.

CONSTITUTION AND GOVERNMENT

Under the 1986 Constitution (revised in 1994), legislative power is vested in the unicameral Congreso de la República (Congress), with 158 members elected for four years by universal adult suffrage. Of the total seats, 127 are filled by departmental representation and 31 according to national listing. Executive power is held by the President (also directly elected for four years), assisted by a Vice-President and an appointed Cabinet. Judicial power is exercised by the Supreme Court of Justice and other tribunals. For the purposes of local administration the country comprises 22 departments, which are divided into 330 municipalities.

REGIONAL AND INTERNATIONAL CO-OPERATION

Guatemala is a member of the Central American Common Market (see p. 232), of the Organization of American States (see p. 394), and of the Community of Latin American and Caribbean States (see p. 462), which was formally inaugurated in December 2011. Guatemala, El Salvador and Honduras signed a free trade agreement with Mexico in 2000. In 2004 the Presidents of Guatemala, El Salvador, Honduras and Nicaragua signed an agreement creating a Central American customs union. The Dominican Republic-Central American Free Trade Agreement (DR-CAFTA), between Guatemala, Costa Rica, El Salvador, Honduras, Nicaragua, the Dominican Republic and the USA, came into effect in 2006. DR-CAFTA entailed the gradual elimination of tariffs on most industrial and agricultural products over a period of 10 and 20 years, respectively. An accord partially liberalizing trade between Guatemala and Belize entered into force in October 2009; it was hoped that this would eventually lead to the signature of a full free trade agreement. Bilateral free trade accords with Panama and Colombia took effect in 2009, and in February 2010 the Presidents of Guatemala and Chile ratified a free trade agreement between their two countries.

Guatemala was a founder member of the UN in 1945. The country was elected as a non-permanent member of the UN Security Council in October 2011 and commenced its two-year mandate on 1 January 2012. As a contracting party to the General Agreement on Tariffs and Trade, Guatemala joined the World Trade Organization (see p. 433) shortly after its establishment in 1995.

ECONOMIC AFFAIRS

In 2010, according to estimates by the World Bank, Guatemala's gross national income (GNI), measured at average 2008–10 prices, was US $39,345m., equivalent to $2,730 per head (or $4,600 per head on an international purchasing-power parity basis). During 2001–10, it was estimated, the population increased by an average of 2.5% per year, while gross domestic product (GDP) per head increased, in real terms, by an average of 0.9% per year. Overall GDP increased, in real terms, at an average annual rate of 3.4% in 2001–10; according to official figures, GDP grew by an estimated 2.8% in 2010.

Agriculture, including hunting, forestry and fishing, contributed an estimated 12.6% of GDP in 2010 and engaged 33.2% of the employed population in 2006. The principal cash crops are sugar cane (which accounted for 8.9% of export earnings in 2010), coffee and bananas. Exports of shrimps are also significant. In recent years the country has successfully expanded production of less traditional crops, such as mangoes, berries and green beans. During 2001–10 agricultural GDP increased, in real terms, by an estimated average of 2.9% per year. Growth in agricultural GDP was an estimated 0.6% in 2010.

Industry, including mining, manufacturing, construction and power, contributed an estimated 27.4% of GDP in 2010 and engaged 22.8% of the working population in 2006. Industrial GDP increased by an estimated average of 2.2% per year in 2001–10. Industrial GDP declined by an estimated 2.1% in 2009, but grew by an estimated 0.7% in 2010.

Mining contributed an estimated 2.0% of GDP in 2010 and employed 0.1% of the working population in 2006. The most important mineral exports are precious metals and stones, which accounted for 6.2% of total export earnings in 2010, and petroleum, which contributed 2.7% of the value of exports in 2010. In addition, copper, antimony, lead, zinc and tungsten are mined on a small scale. There are also deposits of nickel, gold and silver. It was estimated that mining GDP increased by an average of 2.4% per year during 2001–10. The sector increased by an estimated 4.2% in 2009 and by a meagre 0.1% in 2010.

Guatemala's industrial sector is the largest in Central America. Manufacturing contributed an estimated 18.9% of GDP in 2010 and employed 15.9% of the working population in 2006. Manufacturing GDP increased by an estimated average of 2.5% per year in 2001–10.The sector's GDP declined by 0.9% in 2009, but grew by an estimated 3.3% in 2010. Guatemala's *maquila*, or clothing assembly sector, was an important economic contributor, accounting for 13.6% of the value of exports in 2010.

The construction sector contributed an estimated 4.3% of GDP in 2010 and engaged 6.6% of the employed labour force in 2006. During 2001–10 the GDP of the sector increased at an estimated average annual rate of 0.2%. Construction GDP declined by an estimated 10.8% in 2009 and by a further estimated 11.8% in 2010.

Energy is derived principally from mineral fuels and hydroelectric power. Petroleum provided 26.6% of electric energy in 2008. However, hydroelectric power was responsible for a decreasing proportion of total power output, accounting for 42.6% of electricity generation in 2008, compared with 57.6% in 1997, while power generation from coal sources increased from 0.7% in 1999 to 13.0% in 2008. Guatemala is a marginal producer of petroleum and, in 2010, produced on average 13,073 barrels per day. According to estimates, proven petroleum reserves amounted to 83m. barrels in January 2011, while reserves of natural gas totalled some 109,000m. cu ft in 2006. Imports of mineral products comprised 19.4% of the value of total imports in 2009. In 2008 the Government of Alvaro Colom Caballeros announced a new energy policy aimed at reducing Guatemala's dependency on oil. To this end, US $1,800m. was to be invested in the construction of three coal-based generators and five hydroelectric plants by 2014.

In 2010 the services sector contributed an estimated 60.1% of GDP and in 2006 the sector employed 44.0% of the working population. The GDP of the services sector increased by an estimated average of 4.8% per year in 2001–10; growth in the sector was an estimated 4.1% in 2010.

In 2010 Guatemala recorded a visible trade deficit of US $4,292.3m., and there was a deficit of $878.3m. on the current account of the balance of payments. In 2010 the principal source of imports (37.0%) was the USA; other major suppliers were Mexico, the People's Republic of China and El Salvador. The USA was the principal market for exports (taking 38.5% of exports in that year); other significant purchasers were El Salvador, Honduras and Mexico. The main exports in 2010 were clothing, sugar, coffee and bananas. The principal imports were electrical machinery and apparatus, chemical and pharmaceutical products, vehicles and transport equipment, and diesel oil. Remittances from citizens working abroad represented the second largest hard currency inflow into the country, after non-traditional exports. According to the central bank, Banco de Guatemala, in 2011 remittances from the USA totalled $4,378.0m.

In 2009 there was a budgetary deficit of 4,276.4m. quetzales, equivalent to some 1.3% of GDP. Guatemala's general government gross debt was 80,271m. quetzales in 2010, equivalent to 24.2% of GDP. In 2009 Guatemala's total external debt stood at US $13,801m., of which $4,931m. was public and publicly guaranteed debt. In that year, the cost of servicing long-term public and publicly guaranteed debt and repayments to the IMF was equivalent to 5.5% of the value of exports of goods, services and income (excluding workers' remittances). In 2000–10 the average annual rate of inflation was 7.5%. Consumer prices declined by an average of 0.3% in 2009, but increased by an average of 5.4% in 2010. An estimated 3.5% of the labour force were unemployed in 2010, and a further 59.5% were described as underemployed.

The Dominican Republic-Central American Free Trade Agreement (DR-CAFTA) with the USA was considered vital to the future development of the Guatemalan economy, which suffered from large trade deficits. The implementation of DR-CAFTA was expected to bring greater access to US markets and encourage economic diversification. Given the price volatility of agricultural goods exported by Guatemala, the steady inflow of remittances from abroad tended to offset shortfalls in foreign exchange earnings. A major obstacle to economic growth was the high rate of violent crime in the country, which deterred foreign investment. The administration of Otto Fernando Pérez Molina, which took office in January 2012, pledged to address insecurity. The global financial crisis impeded Guatemala's development, and in April 2009 the IMF approved a precautionary 18-month stand-by arrangement worth some US $935m. The country's main economic indicators improved in 2010, with real GDP growth recorded at 2.8%, despite the devastation caused by a tropical storm in May and particularly heavy rains later in the year. At a conference held in October to raise funds to cover the costs of reconstruction (estimated at $1,550m.), international donors pledged a total of $590m. Exports, remittances and tax revenues all rose during 2011, and the IMF estimated that real GDP expanded by 2.8% in that year, with growth of 3.0% projected in 2012. Fiscal reform was one of Pérez Molina's immediate economic priorities, and in early 2012 the Congreso approved legislation to restructure the taxation system, which was expected to lead to a further increase in tax receipts. Measures were also introduced to reduce the high levels of tax evasion.

PUBLIC HOLIDAYS

2013: 1 January (New Year's Day), 28 March–31 March (Easter), 1 May (Labour Day), 30 June (Anniversary of the Revolution), 15 August (Assumption, Guatemala City only), 15 September (Independence Day), 12 October (Columbus Day), 20 October (Revolution Day), 1 November (All Saints' Day), 24 December (Christmas Eve, afternoon only), 25 December (Christmas Day), 31 December (New Year's Eve, afternoon only).

Statistical Survey

Sources (unless otherwise stated): Banco de Guatemala, 7a Avda 22-01, Zona 1, Apdo 365, Guatemala City; tel. 2429-6000; fax 2253-4035; internet www.banguat.gob.gt; Instituto Nacional de Estadística, Edif. América, 4°, 8a Calle 9-55, Zona 1, Guatemala City; tel. 2232-6212; e-mail info-ine@ine.gob.gt; internet www.ine.gob.gt.

Area and Population

AREA, POPULATION AND DENSITY

Area (sq km)	
Land	108,429
Inland water	460
Total	108,889*
Population (census results)†	
17 April 1994	8,322,051
24 November 2002	
Males	5,496,839
Females	5,740,357
Total	11,237,196
Population (official estimates at mid-year)	
2010	14,361,666
2011	14,713,763
2012	15,073,375
Density (per sq km) at mid-2012	138.4

* 42,042 sq miles.

† Excluding adjustments for underenumeration.

POPULATION BY AGE AND SEX

(official estimates at mid-2010)

	Males	Females	Total
0–14	3,027,304	2,941,373	5,968,677
15–64	3,682,854	4,089,170	7,772,024
65 and over	293,177	327,788	620,965
Total	7,003,335	7,358,331	14,361,666

DEPARTMENTS

(official estimates at mid-2012)

Alta Verapaz	1,147,593	Quetzaltenango	807,571
Baja Verapaz	277,380	Quiché	985,690
Chimaltenango	630,609	Retalhuleu	311,167
Chiquimula	379,359	Sacatepéquez	323,283
El Progreso	160,754	San Marcos	1,044,667
Escuintla	716,204	Santa Rosa	353,261
Guatemala	3,207,587	Sololá	450,471
Huehuetenango	1,173,977	Suchitepéquez	529,096
Izabal	423,788	Totonicapán	491,298
Jalapa	327,297	Zacapa	225,108
Jutiapa	444,434		
Petén	662,779	**Total**	15,073,375

PRINCIPAL TOWNS

(population at census of November 2002)

Guatemala City	942,348	Cobán	144,461
Mixco	403,689	Quetzaltenango	127,569
Villa Nueva	355,901	Escuintla	119,897
San Juan Sacatepéquez	152,583	Jalapa	105,796
San Pedro Carcha	148,344	Totonicapán	96,392

Mid-2010 ('000, incl. suburbs, UN estimate): Guatemala City 1,104 (Source: UN, *World Urbanization Prospects: The 2009 Revision*).

BIRTHS, MARRIAGES AND DEATHS

	Registered live births		Registered marriages		Registered deaths	
	Number	Rate (per 1,000)	Number	Rate (per 1,000)	Number	Rate (per 1,000)
2001	415,338	35.6	54,722	4.7	68,041	5.8
2002	387,287	32.3	51,857	4.3	66,089	5.5
2003	375,092	31.0	51,247	4.2	66,695	5.5
2004	383,704	31.0	53,860	4.3	66,991	5.4
2005	374,066	29.5	52,186	4.1	71,039	5.6
2006	368,399	28.3	57,505	4.4	69,756	5.4
2007	366,128	26.8	57,003	4.3	70,030	5.2
2008	369,769	26.4	52,315	3.8	70,233	5.1

2009: Live births 351,628.

Sources: partly UN, *Demographic Yearbook* and *Population and Vital Statistics Report*.

Life expectancy (years at birth, WHO estimates): 69 (males 66; females 73) in 2009 (Source: WHO, *World Health Statistics*).

ECONOMICALLY ACTIVE POPULATION

(at census of November 2002)

	Males	Females	Total
Agriculture, forestry, hunting and fishing	1,278,739	178,364	1,457,103
Mining and quarrying	5,313	756	6,069
Manufacturing	301,222	164,725	465,947
Construction	186,611	21,266	207,877
Electricity, gas, water and sanitary services	23,518	10,135	33,653
Commerce	343,586	228,114	571,700
Transport, storage and communications	96,410	16,913	113,323
Financial and property services	82,644	42,839	125,483
Public administration and defence	60,853	25,137	85,990
Education	42,366	59,796	102,162
Community and personal services	68,165	197,794	265,959
Sub-total	2,507,427	927,839	3,435,266
Activities not adequately described	18,256	9,875	28,131
Total	2,525,683	937,714	3,463,397

2006 ('000 persons aged 10 years and over, labour force survey): Agriculture, forestry, hunting and fishing 1,791.4; Mining and quarrying 7.5; Manufacturing 854.8; Electricity, gas and water 12.4; Construction 354.9; Wholesale and retail trade; repair of motor vehicles, motorcycles and personal and household goods; restaurants and hotels 1,226.9; Transport, storage and communications 160.7; Finance, real estate, renting and business activities 176.1; Public administration, defence and compulsory social security 115.5; Education 219.8; Health, social work and other community, social and personal service activities 457.4; Extra-territorial organizations and bodies 13.2; *Total employed* 5,390.5 (Source: ILO).

2010 (persons aged 10 years and over, labour force survey, September-October): Total employed 5,566,386; Unemployed 202,876; Total labour force 5,769,262 (males 3,677,831, females 2,091,431).

Health and Welfare

KEY INDICATORS

Total fertility rate (children per woman, 2009)	4.0
Under-5 mortality rate (per 1,000 live births, 2009)	40
HIV/AIDS (% of persons aged 15–49, 2009)	0.8
Physicians (per 1,000 head, 1999)	0.9
Hospital beds (per 1,000 head, 2005)	0.7
Health expenditure (2008): US $ per head (PPP)	308
Health expenditure (2008): % of GDP	6.5
Health expenditure (2008): public (% of total)	35.7
Access to water (% of persons, 2008)	94
Access to sanitation (% of persons, 2008)	81
Total carbon dioxide emissions ('000 metric tons, 2007)	12,919.3
Carbon dioxide emissions per head (metric tons, 2007)	1.0
Human Development Index (2011): ranking	131
Human Development Index (2011): value	0.574

For sources and definitions, see explanatory note on p. vi.

Agriculture

PRINCIPAL CROPS
('000 metric tons)

	2008	2009	2010*
Maize	1,566.2	1,686.9	2,035.4
Potatoes	449.2	460.4	472.6
Sugar cane	16,226.4	18,391.7	18,391.7
Oil palm fruit*	1,233.3	1,233.3	1,233.3
Tomatoes	355.5	364.9	358.1
Watermelons*	127.4	131.4	138.9
Cantaloupes and other melons	436.1	455.6	477.7
Bananas	2,448.4	2,544.2	2,621.5
Plantains	195.1	203.6	202.6
Lemons and limes	107.3	117.8	110.6
Guavas, mangoes and mangosteens	108.2	108.9	124.9
Pineapples	200.4	201.4	207.8
Coffee, green	248.5	249.3	257.0
Tobacco, unmanufactured*	199.4	201.6	184.0

* FAO estimates.

Aggregate production ('000 metric tons, may include official, semi-official or estimated data): Total cereals 1,643.4 in 2008, 1,761.5 in 2009, 2,122.5 in 2010; Total pulses 229.6 in 2008, 230.8 in 2009, 222.4 in 2010; Total roots and tubers 466.0 in 2008, 477.7 in 2009, 489.9 in 2010; Total vegetables (incl. melons) 1,580.1 in 2008, 1,626.6 in 2009, 1,679.4 in 2010; Total fruits (excl. melons) 3,711.4 in 2008, 3,840.6 in 2009, 3,951.7 in 2010.

Source: FAO.

LIVESTOCK
('000 head, year ending September)

	2008	2009	2010*
Horses*	125	125	125
Asses*	9.9	9.9	9.9
Mules*	38.7	38.7	38.7
Cattle	3,040	3,061	3,061
Sheep	594	598	600
Pigs	2,736	2,677	2,750
Goats	124	125	128
Chickens*	31,430	31,430	31,430

* FAO estimates.

LIVESTOCK PRODUCTS
('000 metric tons)

	2008	2009	2010*
Cattle meat	74.2	75.0*	75.3
Pig meat*	57.5	55.0	56.4
Chicken meat*	166.3	166.0	167.0
Cows' milk*	338.0	340.0	354.6
Hen eggs*	95.0	89.4	97.3
Honey	3.4	3.5	3.5

* FAO estimate(s).

Source: FAO.

Forestry

ROUNDWOOD REMOVALS
('000 cubic metres, excl. bark, FAO estimates)

	2007	2008	2009
Sawlogs, veneer logs and logs for sleepers	439	439	439
Other industrial wood	15	15	15
Fuel wood	16,960	17,319	17,685
Total	17,414	17,773	18,139

2010: Production assumed to be unchanged from 2009 (FAO estimates).

Source: FAO.

SAWNWOOD PRODUCTION
('000 cubic metres, incl. railway sleepers, FAO estimates)

	2008	2009	2010
Coniferous (softwood)	251	251	251
Broadleaved (hardwood)	128	128	115
Total	379	379	366

Fishing

('000 metric tons, live weight)

	2007	2008	2009
Capture*	17.6	22.8	19.9
Freshwater fishes	2.3*	2.3	2.3*
Skipjack tuna	7.5	10.5	7.6
Yellowfin tuna	4.6	5.7	5.9
Bigeye tuna	1.1	2.2	2.5
Penaeus shrimps	0.6	0.5	0.5
Pacific seabobs	0.8	0.8	0.1
Aquaculture	16.4*	18.7	16.6
Other tilapias	2.9	3.0	3.0
Penaeus shrimps	13.5*	15.7	13.6
Total catch*	34.0	41.6	36.6

* FAO estimate(s).

Source: FAO.

Mining

('000 metric tons, unless otherwise indicated, estimates)

	2007	2008	2009
Crude petroleum ('000 42-gallon barrels)	5,584	5,158	4,933
Gold (kg)	7,497	7,837	8,897
Silver (kg)	88,250	99,923	128,420
Limestone	8,470*	5,470*	6,090
Sand and gravel ('000 cubic metres)	140	192	174

* Estimate.

Source: US Geological Survey.

Industry

SELECTED PRODUCTS

('000 metric tons unless otherwise indicated)

	2004	2005	2006
Sugar (raw)	2,092	2,015	1,961
Cement*	2,200	2,365	2,500
Electric energy (million kWh)	7,009	7,550	7,916

* Estimates from US Geological Survey.

2000 (million): Cigarettes 4,262.

2002 ('000 metric tons): Motor spirit (petrol) 111.

2007: Electric energy (million kWh) 8,755; Cement ('000 metric tons) 2,500 (US Geological Survey estimate).

2008: Electric energy (million kWh) 8,717; Cement ('000 metric tons) 2,500 (US Geological Survey estimate).

2009: Cement ('000 metric tons) 1,500 (US Geological Survey estimate).

Source (unless otherwise indicated): UN Industrial Commodity Statistics Database.

Finance

CURRENCY AND EXCHANGE RATES

Monetary Units

100 centavos = 1 quetzal.

Sterling, Dollar and Euro Equivalents (30 December 2011)

£1 sterling = 12.070 quetzales;
US $1 = 7.807 quetzales;
€1 = 10.101 quetzales;
10,000 quetzales = £8.39 = $12.81 = €9.90.

Average Exchange Rate (quetzales per US dollar)

2009 8.1616
2010 8.0578
2011 7.7854

Note: In December 2000 legislation was approved to allow the circulation of the US dollar and other convertible currencies, for use in a wide range of transactions, from 1 May 2001.

GOVERNMENT FINANCE

(budgetary central government operations, cash basis, million quetzales)

Summary of Balances

	2007	2008	2009
Revenue	33,521.5	35,448.3	33,968.1
Less Expense	32,608.3	34,564.5	38,244.5
Net cash inflow from operating activities	913.2	883.8	–4,276.4
Less Net cash outflow from investments in non-financial assets	4,664.3	5,567.9	5,405.0
Cash surplus/deficit	–3,751.1	–4,684.1	–9,681.4

Revenue

	2007	2008	2009
Taxation	31,566.6	33,356.0	31,829.9
Taxes on income, profits and capital gains	8,653.9	9,698.4	9,705.8
Taxes on goods and services	19,623.4	20,610.2	19,155.4
Social contributions	658.6	746.5	922.1
Grants	419.7	362.9	489.7
Other revenue	876.6	982.9	726.4
Total (incl. grants)	33,521.5	35,448.3	33,968.1

Expense/Outlays

Expense by economic type	2007	2008	2009
Compensation of employees	8,180.0	9,202.1	11,103.1
Use of goods and services	3,447.1	5,255.5	5,708.0
Interest	3,831.3	3,961.8	4,295.4
Subsidies	78.5	564.9	170.1
Grants	9,716.3	9,777.2	9,484.0
Social benefits	2,058.0	2,415.0	2,835.9
Other expense	5,297.1	3,388.0	4,648.1
Total	32,608.3	34,564.5	38,244.5

Outlays by function of government*	2007	2008	2009
General public services	7,183.3	7,442.7	10,199.1
Defence	868.1	903.8	922.0
Public order and safety	3,620.2	4,415.5	4,375.5
Economic affairs	6,853.9	7,047.9	5,938.8
Environmental protection	649.8	309.0	345.0
Housing and community amenities	4,837.8	4,858.4	5,370.2
Health	2,645.7	2,957.1	3,844.5
Recreation, culture and religion	574.9	600.7	657.4
Education	6,925.9	7,848.3	9,203.3
Social protection	3,113.7	3,749.3	5,008.4
Statistical discrepancy	–0.7	–0.2	–2,214.6
Total	37,272.6	40,132.5	43,649.5

* Including purchases of non-financial assets.

Source: IMF, *Government Finance Statistics Yearbook*.

INTERNATIONAL RESERVES

(US $ million at 31 December)

	2008	2009	2010
Gold (national valuation)	191.0	244.9	312.9
IMF special drawing rights	3.5	273.3	267.4
Foreign exchange	4,458.4	4,690.3	5,369.4
Total	4,652.9	5,208.5	5,949.7

Source: IMF, *International Financial Statistics*.

MONEY SUPPLY

(million quetzales at 31 December)

	2008	2009	2010
Currency outside depository corporations	16,695.1	18,108.5	19,736.5
Transferable deposits	39,737.8	42,557.9	48,104.3
Other deposits	66,382.8	76,172.8	82,367.5
Securities other than shares	4,857.4	5,319.2	4,835.8
Broad money	127,673.0	142,158.4	155,044.1

Source: IMF, *International Financial Statistics*.

COST OF LIVING

(Consumer Price Index at December; base: December 2000 = 100)

	2008	2009	2010
Food and non-alcoholic beverages	219.7	213.5	230.0
Clothing and footwear	136.4	138.5	141.9
Housing, water and power	157.2	160.2	166.9
Health	157.7	164.7	173.0
Transport and communications	171.0	176.7	184.6
Recreation and culture	166.5	171.3	173.6
Education	163.6	156.4	160.1
All items (incl. others)	183.0	182.4	192.3

NATIONAL ACCOUNTS

(million quetzales at current prices)

Expenditure on the Gross Domestic Product

	2008	2009*	2010*
Government final consumption expenditure	26,667.7	31,303.0	34,279.9
Private final consumption expenditure	264,134.4	264,651.2	285,054.6
Increase in stocks	−4,527.3	−6,451.8	−1,950.3
Gross fixed capital formation	53,056.4	46,128.8	50,614.5
Total domestic expenditure	339,331.2	335,631.2	367,998.7
Exports of goods and services	73,134.3	73,922.2	83,287.7
Less Imports of goods and services	116,594.0	102,001.2	119,415.9
GDP in purchasers' values	295,871.5	307,552.3	331,870.5
GDP at constant 2001 prices	192,894.9	193,950.6	199,309.7

Gross Domestic Product by Economic Activity

	2008	2009*	2010*
Agriculture, hunting, forestry and fishing	32,991.1	35,925.0	40,211.2
Mining and quarrying	5,370.7	5,062.8	6,423.5
Manufacturing	54,629.1	57,279.1	60,575.2
Electricity, gas and water	6,667.3	6,906.2	7,088.7
Construction	15,177.9	14,184.3	13,673.3
Trade, restaurants and hotels	48,787.8	50,504.8	55,981.9
Transport, storage and communications	22,236.5	23,510.3	24,674.9
Finance, insurance and real estate	9,345.5	9,973.3	10,850.9
Ownership of dwellings	26,121.8	27,606.4	29,200.7
General government services	18,500.1	21,801.8	24,029.3
Other community, social and personal services	43,955.2	44,727.3	47,658.4
Sub-total	283,783.0	297,481.3	320,368.0
Less Financial intermediation services indirectly measured (FISIM)	8,220.8	9,032.7	9,710.3
Gross value added in basic prices	275,562.2	288,448.6	310,657.9
Taxes on imports, less subsidies	20,309.4	19,107.3	21,212.6
GDP in purchasers' values	295,871.5	307,552.3	331,870.5

* Preliminary figures.

BALANCE OF PAYMENTS

(US $ million)

	2008	2009	2010
Exports of goods f.o.b.	7,846.4	7,294.9	8,565.9
Imports of goods f.o.b.	−13,421.2	−10,643.1	−12,858.2
Trade balance	−5,574.8	−3,348.2	−4,292.3
Exports of services	1,872.9	1,925.0	2,216.3
Imports of services	−2,149.0	−2,083.6	−2,369.9
Balance on goods and services	−5,850.3	−3,506.8	−4,445.9
Other income received	544.5	352.1	288.1
Other income paid	−1,482.1	−1,463.2	−1,488.0
Balance on goods, services and income	−6,788.5	−4,617.9	−5,645.8
Current transfers received	5,056.7	4,584.5	4,792.0
Current transfers paid	−19.0	−18.4	−24.5
Current balance	−1,751.0	−51.8	−878.3
Direct investment abroad	−16.4	−26.3	−23.5
Direct investment from abroad	753.9	600.0	686.9
Portfolio investment assets	−10.4	23.2	−15.4
Portfolio investment liabilities	−118.3	−281.4	−27.6
Other investment assets	−2.4	−260.6	82.8
Other investment liabilities	667.0	15.6	580.8
Net errors and omissions	547.2	257.7	156.5
Overall balance	70.6	277.4	563.3

Source: IMF, *International Financial Statistics*.

External Trade

PRINCIPAL COMMODITIES

(US $ million)

Imports c.i.f.	2008	2009	2010
Transmitting and receiving apparatus	361.7	270.7	429.1
Threads and yarns	336.9	290.1	373.6
Paper and cardboard products	364.9	329.9	354.9
Electrical machinery and apparatus	1,179.3	956.3	1,152.3
Plastics and manufactures thereof	818.4	639.0	796.6
Textile materials (cloth or fabric)	644.6	506.4	581.4
Chemical and pharmaceutical products	1,041.4	912.0	988.0
Vehicles and transport equipment	1,084.1	728.7	961.6
Diesel oil	1,027.3	768.1	878.2
Motor gasoline	827.1	707.3	797.8
Iron and steel	556.7	242.8	365.4
Total (incl. others)	14,546.5	11,531.3	13,837.9

Exports f.o.b.	2008	2009	2010
Coffee	646.2	582.3	713.9
Sugar	378.1	507.7	726.7
Bananas	317.1	414.8	353.3
Articles of clothing	1,206.0	1,023.0	1,154.9
Plastics and manufactures thereof	221.7	177.1	223.5
Pharmaceutical products	175.4	169.7	190.7
Petroleum	373.7	191.7	227.8
Precious metals and stones	261.6	345.5	523.7
Total (incl. others)	7,737.4	7,213.7	8,462.0

PRINCIPAL TRADING PARTNERS

(US $ million, preliminary)

Imports c.i.f.	2008	2009	2010
Argentina	142.4	119.9	114.7
Brazil	268.1	233.5	232.9
Canada	174.8	95.8	103.8
Chile	268.2	132.9	93.9
China, People's Republic	839.4	607.7	983.6
Colombia	289.2	325.7	393.9
Costa Rica	422.7	394.2	427.7
Ecuador	124.1	205.2	178.2
El Salvador	692.1	590.0	676.1
Germany	215.0	172.0	24.8
Honduras	353.4	262.3	307.0
Hong Kong	164.3	137.0	144.7
Italy	108.0	75.3	84.3
Japan	365.4	173.9	276.6
Korea, Republic	365.0	317.8	387.5
Mexico	1,411.6	1,185.6	1,542.6
Netherlands Antilles	460.8	300.0	159.0
Panama	412.5	363.9	440.4
Puerto Rico	96.8	30.3	21.6
Spain	183.9	142.2	151.4
Taiwan	110.3	85.9	93.3
USA	5,242.4	4,209.3	5,123.9
Total (incl. others)	14,546.5	11,531.3	13,837.9

Exports f.o.b.	2008	2009	2010
Canada	110.8	110.6	135.9
Costa Rica	318.9	283.7	347.1
Dominican Republic	113.8	107.2	134.0
El Salvador	973.3	817.3	994.7
Germany	78.2	73.5	94.0
Honduras	737.1	606.4	700.2
Korea, Republic	31.8	68.0	79.3
Mexico	509.2	425.7	448.5
Netherlands	107.3	108.3	106.2
Nicaragua	327.6	281.8	352.7
Panama	161.6	184.5	222.0
Switzerland	35.2	13.7	6.7
USA	3,014.4	2,941.6	3,258.6
Total (incl. others)	7,737.4	7,213.7	8,462.0

Transport

RAILWAYS
(traffic)

	1994	1995	1996
Passenger-km (million)	991	0	0
Freight ton-km (million)	25,295	14,242	836

Source: UN, *Statistical Yearbook*.

ROAD TRAFFIC
(motor vehicles in use at 31 December)

	1997	1998	1999
Passenger cars	470,016	508,868	578,733
Buses and coaches	9,843	10,250	11,017
Lorries and vans	34,220	37,057	42,219
Motorcycles and mopeds	111,358	117,536	129,664

2007: Total vehicles 1,558,145.

Source: IRF, *World Road Statistics*.

SHIPPING

Merchant Fleet
(registered at 31 December)

	2007	2008	2009
Number of vessels	12	10	12
Total displacement ('000 grt)	5.9	3.6	3.9

Source: IHS Fairplay, *World Fleet Statistics*.

International Sea-borne Freight Traffic
('000 metric tons)

	1992	1993	1994
Goods loaded	2,176	1,818	2,096
Goods unloaded	3,201	3,025	3,822

CIVIL AVIATION
(traffic on scheduled services)

	1997	1998	1999
Kilometres flown (million)	5	7	5
Passengers carried ('000)	508	794	506
Passenger-km (million)	368	480	342
Total ton-km (million)	77	50	33

Source: UN, *Statistical Yearbook*.

Tourism

TOURIST ARRIVALS BY COUNTRY OF ORIGIN

	2007	2008	2009
Belize	34,572	31,803	37,191
Canada	32,206	36,079	47,675
Costa Rica	40,436	41,545	46,504
El Salvador	617,798	647,568	507,802
France	19,835	21,539	28,022
Germany	18,587	19,630	21,334
Honduras	138,944	155,063	211,456
Italy	14,932	14,746	12,630
Mexico	86,466	92,905	105,456
Nicaragua	40,298	47,171	77,688
Spain	24,581	24,806	25,863
USA	377,565	386,921	451,682
Total (incl. others)	1,627,551	1,715,426	1,776,868

Tourism receipts (US $ million, excl. passenger transport): 1,055 in 2007; 1,068 in 2008;1,179 in 2009.

Source: World Tourism Organization.

Communications Media

	2008	2009	2010
Telephones ('000 main lines in use)	1,448.9	1,413.2	1,498.6
Mobile cellular telephones ('000 subscribers)	14,948.6	17,307.5	18,068.0
Internet users ('000)	1,959.9	2,279.4	n.a.
Broadband subscribers ('000)	94.5	156.0	259.0

Personal computers: 262,000 (20.6 per 1,000 persons) in 2005.

Source: International Telecommunication Union.

Radio receivers ('000 in use): 835 in 1997.

Television receivers ('000 in use): 680 in 1999 (Source: UN, *Statistical Yearbook*).

Daily newspapers (number): 7 in 1996.

Education

(2009/10 unless otherwise indicated)

	Institutions	Teachers	Students
Pre-primary	11,859*	24,394	584,833
Primary	17,499*	95,194	2,659,776
Secondary	4,874*	61,472	982,650
Tertiary	1,946†	3,843*	233,885‡

* 2005/06.
† 2003/04.
‡ 2006/07.

Source: mainly UNESCO Institute for Statistics.

Pupil-teacher ratio (primary education, UNESCO estimate): 27.9 in 2009/10 (Source: UNESCO Institute for Statistics).

Adult literacy rate (UNESCO estimates): 74.5% (males 80.0%; females 69.5%) in 2009 (Source: UNESCO Institute for Statistics).

Directory

The Government

HEAD OF STATE

President: Gen. (retd) OTTO FERNANDO PÉREZ MOLINA (took office 14 January 2012).

Vice-President: INGRID ROXANA BALDETTI ELÍAS.

CABINET
(May 2012)

The Government is formed by the Partido Patriota (PP) and the Visión con Valores-Encuentro por Guatemala (VIVA-EG) coalition.

Minister of Foreign Affairs: HAROLD OSBERTO CABALLEROS LÓPEZ (VIVA-EG).

Minister of the Interior: MAURICIO LÓPEZ BONILLA (PP).

Minister of National Defence: Col. ULISES NOÉ ANZUETO (PP).

Minister of Public Finance: PAVEL CENTENO.

Minister of the Economy: SERGIO DE LA TORRE (PP).

Minister of Public Health and Social Welfare: (vacant).

Minister of Communications, Infrastructure, Transport and Housing: ALEJANDRO SINIBALDI (PP).

Minister of Agriculture, Livestock and Food: EFRAÍN MEDINA (VIVA-EG).

Minister of Education: CYNTHIA DEL AGUILA (PP).

Minister of Employment and Social Security: CARLOS CONTRERAS (PP).

Minister of Energy and Mines: ERICK ARCHILA (PP).

Minister of Culture and Sport: CARLOS BATZÍN (PP).

Minister of the Environment and Natural Resources: ROXANA SOBENES (PP).

Minister of Social Development: LUZ LAINFIESTA.

Minister of Labour and Social Security: CARLOS CONTRERAS SOLÓRZANO (PP).

MINISTRIES

Ministry of Agriculture, Livestock and Food: Edif. Monja Blanca, Of. 306, 3°, 7a Avda 12-90, Zona 13, Guatemala City; tel. 2413-7351; fax 2413-7352; e-mail infoagro@maga.gob.gt; internet www.maga.gob.gt.

Ministry of Communications, Infrastructure, Transport and Housing: Edif. Antiguo Cocesna, 8a Avda y 15 Calle, Zona 13, Guatemala City; tel. 2362-6051; fax 2362-6059; e-mail relpublicas@micivi.gob.gt; internet www.civ.gob.gt.

Ministry of Culture and Sport: Calle 7, entre Avda 6 y 7, Centro Histórico, Palacio Nacional de la Cultura, Zona 1, Guatemala City; tel. 2239-5100; fax 2253-0540; e-mail info@mcd.gob.gt; internet www.mcd.gob.gt.

Ministry of the Economy: 8a Avda 10-43, Zona 1, Guatemala City; tel. 2412-0200; e-mail infonegocios@mineco.gob.gt; internet www.mineco.gob.gt.

Ministry of Education: 6a Calle 1-87, Zona 10, Guatemala City; tel. 2411-9595; fax 2361-0350; e-mail info@mineduc.gob.gt; internet www.mineduc.gob.gt.

Ministry of Employment and Social Security: Edif. Torre Empresarial, 7a Avda 3-33, Zona 9, Guatemala City; tel. 2422-2500; fax 2422-2507; e-mail ministro@mintrabajo.gob.gt; internet www.mintrabajo.gob.gt.

Ministry of Energy and Mines: Diagonal 17, 29-78, Zona 11, Las Charcas, Guatemala City; tel. 2419-6363; fax 2476-2007; e-mail informatica@mem.gob.gt; internet www.mem.gob.gt.

Ministry of the Environment and Natural Resources: Edif. MARN, 20 Calle 28-58, Zona 10, Guatemala City; tel. 2423-0500; e-mail rpublicas@marn.gob.gt; internet www.marn.gob.gt.

Ministry of Foreign Affairs: 2a Avda La Reforma 4-17, Zona 10, Guatemala City; tel. 2410-0010; fax 2410-0011; e-mail webmaster@minex.gob.gt; internet www.minex.gob.gt.

Ministry of the Interior: Antiguo Palacio de la Policía Nacional Civil, 6a Avda 13-71, Zona 1, Guatemala City; tel. 2413-8888; fax 2413-8587; internet www.mingob.gob.gt.

Ministry of Labour and Social Security: Edif. Torre Empresarial, 7 Avda 3-33, Zona 9, Guatemala City; tel. 2422-2500; fax 2422-2503; internet www.mintrabajo.gob.gt.

Ministry of National Defence: Antiguas Instalaciones de la Escuela Politécnica, Avda La Reforma 1-45, Zona 10, Guatemala City; tel. 2269-4924; fax 2360-9919; e-mail dip@mindef.mil.gt; internet www.mindef.mil.gt.

Ministry of Public Finance: Centro Cívico, 8a Avda y 21 Calle, Zona 1, Guatemala City; tel. 2248-5005; fax 2248-5054; e-mail info@minfin.gob.gt; internet www.minfin.gob.gt.

Ministry of Public Health and Social Welfare: Escuela de Enfermería, 3°, 6a Avda 3-45, Zona 1, Guatemala City; tel. 2475-2121; fax 2475-1125; e-mail info@mspas.gob.gt; internet www.mspas.gob.gt.

Ministry of Social Development: Guatemala City.

President and Legislature

PRESIDENT

Presidential Election, 11 September and 6 November 2011

Candidate	First round % of votes	Second round % of votes*
Gen. (retd) Otto Fernando Pérez Molina (PP)	36.10	53.74
Manuel Antonio Baldizón Méndez (LIDER)	22.68	46.26
José Eduardo Suger Cofiño (CREO)	16.62	—
Mario Amilcar Estrada Orellana (UCN)	8.72	—
Harold Osberto Caballeros López (VIVA-EG)	6.24	—
Rigoberta Menchú Tum (WINAQ-URNG—MAIZ-ANN)	3.22	—
Juan Guillermo Gutiérrez Strauss (PAN)	2.76	—
Patricia de Arzú (Partido Unionista)	2.19	—
Alejandro Eduardo Giammattei Falla (CASA)	1.05	—
Adela Camacho de Torrebiarte (ADN)	0.42	—
Total valid votes	100.00	100.00

* Preliminary results.

CONGRESO DE LA REPÚBLICA

President: GUDY RIVERA.

General Election, 11 September 2011

	% of votes	Seats*
Partido Patriota	26.37	56
Unidad Nacional de la Esperanza-Gran Alianza Nacional	22.24	48
Unión del Cambio Nacional	9.48	14
Libertad Democrática Renovada	8.66	14
Compromiso, Renovación y Orden	8.77	12
Visión con Valores-Encuentro por Guatemala	7.84	6
WINAQ-Unidad Revolucionaria Nacional Guatemalteca—Movimiento Amplio de Izquierdas-Alternativa Nueva Nación	3.20	3
Partido de Avanzada Nacional	3.08	2
Frente Republicano Guatemalteco	2.72	1
Partido Unionista	2.67	1
VICTORIA	1.62	1
Centro de Acción Social	1.10	—
Acción de Desarrollo Nacional	0.88	—
Frente de Convergencia Nacional	0.53	—
Total valid votes (incl. others)	100.00	158

* Seats are distributed according to a combination of national lists and departmental and proportional representation.

Election Commission

Tribunal Supremo Electoral: 6a Avda 0-32, Zona 2, Guatemala City; tel. 2413-0303; e-mail tse@tse.org.gt; internet www.tse.org.gt; f. 1983; independent; Pres. MARIA EUGENIA VILLAGRÁN DE LEÓN.

Political Organizations

Acción de Desarrollo Nacional (ADN): Vía 7, 5-33 Zona 4, Guatemala City; tel. 2339-4000; internet www.adn.com.gt; Sec.-Gen. ADELA CAMACHO DE TORREBIARTE.

Alternativa Nueva Nación (ANN): Avda 1-31, 8°, Zona 1, Guatemala City; tel. 2251-2514; e-mail corriente@intelnet.net.gt; contested the 2011 elections in coalition with the URNG—MAIZ (q.v.) and the Movimiento Político WINAQ (q.v.); Sec.-Gen. PABLO MONSANTO.

Bienestar Nacional (BIEN): 8a Avda 6-40, Zona 2, Guatemala City; tel. 2254-1458; internet www.bienestarnacional.org; Sec.-Gen. FIDEL REYES LEE.

Compromiso, Renovación y Orden (CREO): Vía 3, 5–27 Zona 4, Antiguo Edif. Manuel, Guatemala City; tel. 2339-4942; internet creo.org.gt; Pres. JOSÉ EDUARDO SUGER COFIÑO; Sec.-Gen. JOSÉ RODOLFO NEUTZE AGUIRRE.

Encuentro por Guatemala (EG): 9 Avda 0-71, Zona 4, Guatemala City; tel. 2231-9859; fax 2230-6463; e-mail izaveliz@yahoo.es; internet www.encuentroporguatemala.org; f. 2006; centre-left; promotes indigenous interests; contested the 2011 elections in coalition with Visión con Valores (q.v.); Sec.-Gen. NINETH VERENCA MONTENEGRO COTTOM.

Frente de Convergencia Nacional (FCN): Avda Centroamérica 13-45, Zona 1, Guatemala City; tel. 5908-7848; e-mail soporte@partidofcn.com; internet www.partidofcn.com; Sec.–Gen. JOSÉ LUIS QUILO AYUSO.

Frente Republicano Guatemalteco (FRG): 3a Calle 5-50, Zona 1, Guatemala City; tel. 2238-0826; internet www.frg.org.gt; f. 1988; right-wing group; Sec.-Gen. LUIS FERNANDO PÉREZ MARTÍNEZ.

Gran Alianza Nacional (GANA): 6a Avda, 3-44, Zona 9, Guatemala City; tel. 2331-4811; fax 2362-7512; e-mail info@gana.com.gt; internet www.gana.com.gt; f. 2003 as electoral alliance of PP, Movimiento Reformador and Partido Solidaridad Nacional; registered as a party in 2005 following withdrawal of PP; Sec.-Gen. JAIME ANTONIO MARTÍNEZ LOHAYZA.

Libertad Democrática Renovada (LIDER): 13 Calle, 2-52 Zona 1, Guatemala City; tel. 2463-4942; Sec.-Gen. EDGAR AJCIP.

Movimiento Político WINAQ: 33 Avda 3–57, Zona 4 de Mixco Bosques de San Nicolás, Guatemala City; tel. 2436-0939; internet winaq.org.gt; promotes indigenous interests; contested the 2011 elections in coalition with the URNG—MAIZ (q.v.) and the Alternativa Nueva Nación (q.v.); Sec.-Gen. RIGOBERTA MENCHÚ TUM.

Partido de Avanzada Nacional (PAN): 3a Avda 18-28, Zona 14, Guatemala City; tel. 2366-1509; fax 2337-2001; e-mail pan.partidodeavanzadanacional@gmail.com; internet www.pan-gt.com; Sec.-Gen. JUAN GUILLERMO GUTIÉRREZ STRAUSS.

Partido Patriota (PP): 11 Calle 11-54, Zona 1, Guatemala City; tel. 2311-6886; e-mail comunicacion@partidopatriota.org; internet www.partidopatriota.com; f. 2002; contested 2003 elections as part of GANA (q.v.); withdrew from GANA in May 2004; right-wing; Leader Gen. (retd) OTTO FERNANDO PÉREZ MOLINA; Sec.-Gen. INGRID ROXANA BALDETTI ELÍAS.

Partido Unionista: 5a Avda 'A' 13-43, Zona 9, Guatemala City; tel. 2331-7468; fax 2331-6141; e-mail info@unionistas.com; internet www.unionistas.org; f. 1917; Sec.-Gen. ALVARO ENRIQUE ARZÚ IRIGOYEN.

Unidad Nacional de la Esperanza (UNE): 6a Avda 8-72, Zona 9, Guatemala City; tel. 2334-3451; e-mail ideas@une.org.gt; internet www.une.org.gt; f. 2001 following a split within the PAN; centre-left; Sec.-Gen. JAIRO JOAQUÍN FLORES DIVAS.

Unidad Revolucionaria Nacional Guatemalteca—Movimiento Amplio de Izquierdas (URNG—MAIZ): 12a Avda 'B' 6-00, Zona 2, Guatemala City; tel. 2254-0704; fax 2254-7062; e-mail debate@urng-maiz.org.gt; internet www.urng-maiz.org.gt; f. 1982 following unification of principal guerrilla groups engaged in the civil war; formally registered as a political party in 1998; contested the 2011 elections in coalition with the Movimiento Político WINAQ (q.v.) and the Alternativa Nueva Nación (q.v.); Sec.-Gen. HÉCTOR ALFREDO NUILA ERICASTILLA.

Unión del Cambio Nacional (UCN): 5a Calle 5-27, Zone 9, Guatemala City; tel. 2361-6729; e-mail administracion.ucn@gmai.com; f. 2006; Sec.-Gen. MARIO AMILCAR ESTRADA ORELLANA.

Unión Democrática (UD): Casa 9, 5 Calle 12-00, Zona 14, Guatemala City; tel. 2363-5013; fax 2369-3062; e-mail info@uniondemocratica.info; f. 1983; Sec.-Gen. MANUEL EDUARDO CONDE ORELLANA.

Los Verdes (LV): 3a Avda 3-72, Zona 1, Guatemala City; tel. 2570-3420; e-mail losverdesguatemala@gmail.com; Sec.-Gen. RODOLFO ROSALES GARCÍA SALAS.

VICTORIA: Edif. Crece Condado el Naranjo, Of. 607, 6°, 23 Calle 14–58, Zona 4 de Mixco, Guatemala City; Sec.-Gen. EDGAR ABRAHAM RIVERA SAGASTUME.

Visión con Valores (VIVA): 41 Calle 3-45, Zona 8, Guatemala City; tel. 2243-2999; e-mail contacto@visionconvalores.com; internet www.visionconvalores.com; contested the 2011 elections in coalition with Encuentro por Guatemala (q.v.); Sec.-Gen. HAROLD OSBERTO CABALLEROS LÓPEZ.

Diplomatic Representation

EMBASSIES IN GUATEMALA

Argentina: Edif. Europlaza 1703, 17°, Torre I, 5a Avda 5-55, Zona 14, Apdo 120, Guatemala City; tel. and fax 2385-3786; e-mail eguat@mrecic.gov.ar; Ambassador ERNESTO JUSTO LÓPEZ.

Belize: Edif. Europlaza Torre II, Of. 1502, 5a Avda 5-55, Zona 14, Guatemala City; tel. 2367-3883; fax 2367-3884; e-mail infobelice@embajadadebelice.org; internet www.embajadadebelice.org; Ambassador ALFREDO MARTÍN MARTÍNEZ.

Brazil: Edif. Los Arcos, 2a Avda 20-13, Zona 10, Apdo 196-A, Guatemala City; tel. 2321-6800; fax 2366-1762; e-mail brascom@intelnet.net.gt; internet guatemala.itamaraty.gov.br; Ambassador JOSÉ ROBERTO DE ALMEIDA PINTO.

Canada: Edif. Edyma Plaza, 8°, 13a Calle 8-44, Zona 10, Apdo 400, Guatemala City; tel. 2363-4348; fax 2365-1210; e-mail gtmla@international.gc.ca; internet www.canadainternational.gc.ca/guatemala; Ambassador HUGUES RÉAL ROUSSEAU.

Chile: 14a Calle 15-21, Zona 13, Guatemala City; tel. 2334-8273; fax 2334-8276; e-mail echilegu@intelnet.net.gt; Ambassador JUAN ALFONSO MANUEL MASFERRAR PELLIZARI.

Colombia: Edif. Europlaza, Torre I, Of. 1603, 5a Avda 5-55, Zona 14, Guatemala City; tel. 2385-3432; fax 2385-3438; e-mail embacolombia@intelett.com; internet www.embajadaenguatemala.gov.co; Ambassador JUAN GUILLERMO ANGEL MEJÍA.

Costa Rica: 5a Avda 9-33, Zona 14, Guatemala City; tel. 2366-4215; fax 2337-1969; e-mail embacosta.gt@gmail.com; internet www.embajadacostaricaguatemala.com; Ambassador FERNANDO BORBÓN ARIAS.

Cuba: Avda las Américas 20-72, Zona 13, Guatemala City; tel. 2332-5521; fax 2332-5525; e-mail embajador@gt.embacuba.cu; internet www.cubadiplomatica.cu/guatemala; Ambassador ROBERTO BLANCO DOMÍNGUEZ.

Dominican Republic: Centro Empresarial 'Zona Pradera', Torre II, Of. 1606, 18 Calle 24-69, Zona 10, Guatemala City; tel. 2261-7016; fax 2261-7017; e-mail embardgt@gmail.com; Ambassador RENÉ BIENVENIDO SANTANA GONZÁLEZ.

Ecuador: 4a Avda 12-04, Zona 14, Guatemala City; tel. 2337-2994; fax 2368-1831; e-mail embecuad@itelgua.com; Ambassador GALO ANDRÉS YÉPEZ HOLGUÍN.

Egypt: Edif. Cobella, 5°, 5a Avda 10-84, Zona 14, Apdo 502, Guatemala City; tel. 2333-6296; fax 2368-2808; e-mail embassy.gautemala@mfa.gov.eg; internet www.mfa.gov.eg/Guatemala_Emb; Ambassador MOSTAFA MAHMOUD MAHER ELREMALY.

El Salvador: Avda las Américas 16-40, Zona 13, Guatemala City; tel. 2360-7660; fax 2332-1228; e-mail emsalva@intelnet.net.gt; Ambassador CLAUDIA IVETTE CANJURA DE CENTENO.

France: Edif. Cogefar, 5a Avda 8-59, Zona 14, Apdo 971-A, 01014 Guatemala City; tel. 2421-7370; fax 2421-7372; e-mail courrier@ambafrance-gt.org; internet www.ambafrance-gt.org; Ambassador PHILIPPE BASTELICA.

Germany: Edif. Plaza Marítima, 2°, 20 Calle 6-20, Zona 10, Guatemala City; tel. 2364-6700; fax 2333-6906; e-mail embalemana@intelnet.net.gt; internet www.guatemala.diplo.de; Ambassador THOMAS SCHÄFER.

Holy See: 10a Calle 4-47, Zona 9, Apdo 3041, Guatemala City (Apostolic Nunciature); tel. 2332-4274; fax 2334-1918; e-mail nuntius@itelgua.com; Apostolic Nuncio Most Rev. PAUL RICHARD GALLAGHER (Titular Archbishop of Hodelm).

Honduras: 19 Avda 'A' 20-19, Zona 10, Guatemala City; tel. 2366-5640; fax 2368-0062; e-mail embhond@intelnet.net.gt; Ambassador JORGE MIGUEL GABRIE LAGOS.

Israel: 13a Avda 14-07, Zona 10, Guatemala City; tel. 2333-4624; fax 2333-6950; e-mail info@guatemala.mfa.gov.il; internet guatemala.mfa.gov.il; Ambassador ELIYAHU LOPEZ.

Italy: Edif. Santa Bárbara, 12a Calle 6-49, Zona 14, Guatemala City; tel. 2366-9271; fax 2367-3916; e-mail ambasciata.guatemala@esteri.it; internet www.ambguatemala.esteri.it; Ambassador MAINARDO BENARDELLI DE LEITENBURG.

Japan: Edif. Torre Internacional, 10°, Avda de la Reforma 16-85, Zona 10, Guatemala City; tel. 2382-7300; fax 2382-7310; e-mail info@japon.net.gt; internet www.gt.emb-japan.go.jp; Ambassador TERUAKI NAGASAKI.

Korea, Republic: Edif. Europlaza, Torre III, 7°, 5a Avda 5-55, Zona 14, Guatemala City; tel. 2382-4051; fax 2382-4057; e-mail korembsy@mofat.go.kr; internet gtm.mofat.go.kr; Ambassador NAM SANG-JUNG.

Mexico: 2a Avda 7-57, Zona 10, Apdo 1455, Guatemala City; tel. 2420-3400; fax 2420-3410; e-mail embamexguat@itelgua.com; internet www.sre.gob.mx/guatemala; Ambassador EDUARDO IBARROLA NICOLÍN.

Netherlands: Edif. Torre Internacional, 13°, 16a Calle 0-55, Zona 10, Guatemala City; tel. 2381-4300; fax 2381-4350; e-mail gua@minbuza.nl; internet www.embajadadeholanda-gua.org; Ambassador JOHAN JACOB VAN DE VELDE.

Nicaragua: 13 Avda 14-54, Zona 10, Guatemala City; tel. 2368-2284; fax 2333-4636; e-mail embaguat@terra.com.gt; Ambassador SILVIO MORA MORA.

Norway: Edif. Murano Center, 15°, Of. 1501, 14 Calle 3-51, Zona 10, Apdo 1764, Guatemala City; tel. 2366-5908; fax 2366-5823; e-mail emb.guatemala@mfa.no; internet www.noruega.org.gt; Ambassador LARS OLE VAAGEN.

Panama: 12a Calle 2-65, Zona 14, Apdo 929-A, Guatemala City; tel. 2366-3336; fax 2366-3338; e-mail panaguate@hotmail.com; internet www.panamaenelexterior.gob.pa/guatemala; Ambassador IRVING ORLANDO CENTENO SANSON.

Peru: 15a Avda 'A' 20-16, Zona 13, Guatemala City; tel. 2331-7841; fax 2361-8542; e-mail embajadadelperu@yahoo.com; Ambassador NILO JÉSUS FIGUEROA CORTAVARRIA.

Russia: 2a Avda 12-85, Zona 14, Guatemala City; tel. 2367-2765; fax 2367-2766; e-mail embajadarusa@gmail.com; internet www.guat.mid.ru; Ambassador VLADIMIR TIKHONOVICH KURAEV (resident in San José, Costa Rica).

Spain: 6a Calle 6-48, Zona 9, Guatemala City; tel. 2379-3530; fax 2379-3533; e-mail emb.guatemala@maec.es; internet www.maec.es/embajadas/guatemala; Ambassador MANUEL MARÍA LEJARRETA LOBO.

Sweden: Edif. Reforma 10, 11°, Avda de la Reforma 9-55, Zona 10, Apdo 966-A, Guatemala City; tel. 2384-7300; fax 2384-7350; e-mail ambassaden.guatemala@foreign.ministry.se; internet www.swedenabroad.com/guatemala; Ambassador JAN ANDERS MICHAEL FRUHLING.

Switzerland: Edif. Torre Internacional, 14°, 16a Calle 0-55, Zona 10, Apdo 1426, Guatemala City; tel. 2367-5520; fax 2367-5811; e-mail vertretung@gua.rep.admin.ch; internet www.eda.admin.ch/guatemala; Ambassador THOMAS KOLLY.

Taiwan (Republic of China): 4a Avda 'A' 13-25, Zona 9, Apdo 897, Guatemala City; tel. 2339-0711; fax 2332-2668; e-mail gtm@mofa.gov.tw; internet www.taiwanembassy.org/gt; Ambassador ADOLFO SUN.

United Kingdom: Edif. Torre Internacional, 11°, Avda de la Reforma, 16a Calle, Zona 10, Guatemala City; tel. 2380-7300; fax 2380-7339; e-mail embassy@intelnett.com; internet ukinguatemala.fco.gov.uk; Ambassador JULIE CHAPPELL.

USA: Avda de la Reforma 7-01, Zona 10, Guatemala City; tel. 2326-4000; fax 2326-4654; internet guatemala.usembassy.gov; Ambassador ARNOLD A. CHACON.

Uruguay: Edif. Plaza Marítima, 3°, Of. 342, 6a Avda 20-25, Zona 10, Guatemala City; tel. 2368-0810; fax 2333-7553; e-mail uruguate@gmail.com; Ambassador CARMEN FROS DONINELLI.

Venezuela: Edif. Atlantis, Of. 601, 13a Calle 3-40, Zona 10, Apdo 152, Guatemala City; tel. 2366-9832; fax 2366-9838; e-mail embavene@concyt.gob.gt; Ambassador ORLANDO TORREALBA JÍMENEZ.

Judicial System

Corte Suprema de Justicia

Centro Cívico, 21 Calle 7-70, Zona 1, Guatemala City; internet www.oj.gob.gt.

The members of the Supreme Court are appointed by Congress.

President of the Supreme Court of Justice: THELMA E. ALDANA HERNÁNDEZ.

Members: Dr C. R. C. BARRIENTOS PELLECER, Dr G. A. MEDRANO VALENZUELA, G. A. MENDIZÁBAL MAZARIEGOS, H. M. MALDONADO MÉNDEZ, Dr R. ZARCEÑO GAITÁN, L. A. PINEDA ROCA, M. C. FRANCO FLORES, E. G. GÓMEZ MÉNDEZ, J. A. SIERRA GONZÁLEZ, A. R. ARCHILA LERAYEES, G. BONILLA; 1 vacancy.

Civil Courts of Appeal: 20 courts, located in Guatemala City, Quetzaltenango, Jalapa, Zacapa, Antigua Guatemala, Retalhuleu, Cobán and Mazatenango.

Courts of the First Instance: 10 civil and 12 penal in Guatemala City, and at least one civil and one penal in each of the 21 remaining Departments of the Republic.

Attorney-General: CLAUDIA PAZ Y PAZ BAILEY.

Religion

Almost all of the inhabitants profess Christianity, with a majority belonging to the Roman Catholic Church. In recent years the Protestant churches have attracted a growing number of converts.

CHRISTIANITY

The Roman Catholic Church

For ecclesiastical purposes, Guatemala comprises two archdioceses, 10 dioceses and the Apostolic Vicariates of El Petén and Izabal. Some 60% of the population are Roman Catholics.

Bishops' Conference

Conferencia Episcopal de Guatemala, Secretariado General del Episcopado, Km 15, Calzada Roosevelt 4-54, Zona 7, Mixco, Apdo 1698, Guatemala City; tel. 2433-1832; fax 2433-1834; e-mail ceguatemala@gmail.com; internet www.iglesiacatolica.org.gt.

f. 1973; Pres. Rev. PABLO VIZCAÍNO PRADO (Bishop of Suchitepéquez-Retalhuleu).

Archbishop of Guatemala City: OSCAR JULIO VIAN MORALES, Arzobispado, 7a Avda 6-21, Zona 1, Apdo 723, Guatemala City; tel. 2232-9707; fax 2251-5068; e-mail curiaarzobispal@intelnet.net.gt.

Archbishop of Los Altos, Quetzaltenango-Totonicapán: MARIO ALBERTO MOLINA PALMA, Arzobispado, 11a Avda 6-27, Zona 1, Apdo 11, 09001 Quetzaltenango; tel. 7761-2840; fax 7761-6049.

The Anglican Communion

Guatemala comprises one of the five dioceses of the Iglesia Anglicana de la Región Central de América.

Bishop of Guatemala: Rt Rev. ARMANDO ROMÁN GUERRA SORIA, Avda Castellana 40-06, Zona 8, Apdo 58-A, Guatemala City; tel. 2473-6828; fax 2472-0764; e-mail diocesis@infovia.com.gt; diocese founded 1967.

Protestant Churches

The largest Protestant denomination in Guatemala is the Full Gospel Church, followed by the Assembly of God, the Central American Church, and the Prince of Peace Church. The Baptist, Presbyterian, Lutheran and Episcopalian churches are also represented.

The Baptist Church: Convention of Baptist Churches of Guatemala, 12a Calle 9-54, Zona 1, Apdo 322, 01901 Guatemala City; tel. and fax 2232-4227; e-mail cibg@intelnet.net.gt; f. 1946; Pres. JOSÉ MARROQUÍN R.; 43,876 mems.

Church of Jesus Christ of Latter-day Saints: 12a Calle 3-37, Zona 9, Guatemala City; e-mail contactos@mormones.org.gt; internet www.mormones.org.gt; 17 bishoprics, 9 chapels; Pres. THOMAS S. MONSON.

Conferencia de Iglesias Evangélicas de Guatemala (CIEDEG) (Conference of Protestant Churches in Guatemala): 7a Avda 1-11, Zona 2, Guatemala City; tel. 2232-3724; fax 2232-1609; Pres. VITALINO SIMILOX.

Congregación Luterana La Epifanía (Evangelisch-Lutherische Epiphanias-Gemeinde): 2a Avda 15-31, Zona 10, 01010 Guatemala City; tel. 2368-0301; fax 2366-4968; e-mail schweikle@web.de; mem. of Lutheran World Federation; Pres. ROLF MEIER; 200 mems.

Divine Saviour Lutheran Church: Zacapa; tel. 7941-0254; e-mail hogarluterano@hotmail.com; f. 1946; Pastor GERARDO VENANCIO VÁSQUEZ SALGUERO.

Iglesia Evangélica Nacional Presbiteriana de Guatemala: Avda Simeón Cañas 7-13, Zona 2, Apdo 655, Guatemala City; tel. 2288-4441; fax 2254-1242; e-mail ienpg@yahoo.com; f. 1962; mem. of World Alliance of Reformed Churches; Sec. Pastor ISAÍAS GARCÍA CITALÁN; 25,000 mems.

Iglesia Nacional Evangélica Menonita Guatemalteca: Guatemala City; tel. 2339-0606; e-mail AlvaradoJE@ldschurch.org; Contact JULIO ALVARADO; 210,000 mems (2003).

Union Church: 12a Calle 7-37, Zona 9, 01009 Guatemala City; tel. 2361-2037; fax 2362-3961; e-mail unionchurch@guate.net.gt; internet careministryucg.org; f. 1943; English-speaking church; Pastor DAVID GINTER.

The Press

PRINCIPAL DAILIES

Diario de Centroamérica: 18a Calle 6-72, Zona 1, Guatemala City; tel. 2222-4418; e-mail info@dca.gob.gt; internet www.diariodecentroamerica.gob.gt; f. 1880; morning; official; Dir-Gen. GUSTAVO RENÉ SOBERANIS MONTES; Editor-in-Chief BYRON BARILLAS.

Guía Interamericana de Turismo: Edif. Plaza los Arcos, 3°, 20 Calle 5-35, Zona 10, Guatemala City; tel. 2450-6431; e-mail info@guiainter.org; internet www.guiainter.org; f. 1989; online journal; Dir-Gen. MARIO ORINI; Editor ALFREDO MAYORGA.

La Hora: 9a Calle 'A' 1-56, Zona 1, Apdo 1593, Guatemala City; tel. 2423-1800; fax 2423-1837; e-mail lahora@lahora.com.gt; internet www.lahora.com.gt; f. 1920; evening; independent; Dir-Gen. OSCAR CLEMENTE MARROQUÍN; Editor-in-Chief MARIO CORDERO; circ. 18,000.

Nuestro Diario: 15 Avda 24-27, Zona 13, Guatemala City; tel. and fax 2379-1600; fax 2379-1621; e-mail opinion@nuestrodiario.com.gt; internet www.nuestrodiario.com; Gen. Man. JORGE SPRINGMÜHL; Gen. Editor RODRIGO CASTILLO DEL CARMEN.

El Periódico: 15a Avda 24-51, Zona 13, Guatemala City; tel. 2427-2300; fax 2427-2361; e-mail redaccion@elperiodico.com.gt; internet www.elperiodico.com.gt; f. 1996; morning; independent; Pres. José Rubén Zamora; Editor Ana Carolina Alpírez; circ. 30,000.

Prensa Libre: 13a Calle 9-31, Zona 1, Apdo 2063, Guatemala City; tel. 2230-5096; fax 2251-8768; e-mail nacional@prensalibre.com.gt; internet www.prensalibre.com.gt; f. 1951; morning; independent; Gen. Man. Luis Enrique Solórzano; Editor Gonzalo Marroquín Godoy; circ. 120,000.

Siglo Veintiuno: 12a Avda 4-33, Zona 1, Guatemala City; tel. 2423-6101; fax 2423-6346; e-mail buzon21@sigloxxi.com; internet www.sigloxxi.com; f. 1990; morning; Dir Guillermo Fernández; Gen. Man. Luciana Cisneros; circ. 65,000.

PERIODICALS

Amiga: 13 Calle 9-31, Zona 1, Guatemala City; tel. 2412-5000; fax 2220-5123; e-mail revistas@prensalibre.com.gt; internet www.revistaamiga.com; health; Dir Carolina Vásquez Araya; Editor Alejandra Cardona.

Gerencia: Torre Citigroup, Of. 402, 3a Avda 13-78, Zona 14, Guatemala City; tel. 2427-4900; fax 2427-4971; e-mail agg@guate.net; internet www.agg.org.gt; f. 1967; monthly; official organ of the Asscn of Guatemalan Managers; Man. Ileana López Avila.

El Metropolitano: Plaza Morumbi 7 y 8, 2°, 3a Calle 15-29, Zona 8, San Cristóbal, Guatemala City; e-mail info@elmetropolitano.net; internet www.elmetropolitano.net; Editor Jorge García Montenegro.

Mundo Motor: 13a Calle 9-31, Zona 1, Guatemala City; tel. 2412-5000; fax 2220-5123; e-mail evasquez@prensalibre.com.gt; internet www.mundoymotor.com; Dir Carolina Vásquez; Editor Néstor A. Larrazábal B.

Revista Data Export: 15 Avda 14-72, Zona 13, Guatemala City; tel. 2422-3431; fax 2422-3434; e-mail portal@export.com.gt; internet www.revistadataexport.com; monthly; foreign trade affairs; organ of the Asociacíon Guatemalteca de Exportadores; Editor Fulvia Donis.

Revista Industria y Negocios: 6a Ruta 9-21, Zona 4, Guatemala City; tel. 2380-9000; e-mail contactemos@industriaguate.com; internet www.revistaindustria.com; monthly; official organ of the Chamber of Industry; Dir Javier Zapeda.

Revista Mundo Comercial: 10a Calle 3-80, Zona 1, 01001 Guatemala City; e-mail mundo@guatemala-chamber.org; internet www.negociosenguatemala.com; monthly; business; official organ of the Chamber of Commerce; circ. 11,000.

Viaje a Guatemala: 13a Calle 9-31, Zona 1, Guatemala City; tel. 2412-5000; fax 2220-5123; internet www.viajeaguatemala.com; Dir-Gen. Carolina Vásquez; Editor-in-Chief Silvia Lanuza.

PRESS ASSOCIATIONS

Asociación de Periodistas de Guatemala (APG): 14a Calle 3-29, Zona 1, Guatemala City; tel. 2232-1813; fax 2238-2781; e-mail apege@intelnet.net.gt; f. 1947; affiliated to International Freedom of Expression Exchange and Fed. Latinoamericana de Periodistas; Pres. Miguel Angel Albizures; Sec. Ana Julieta Cárdenas.

Círculo Nacional de Prensa (CNP): 2 Avda 10-52, Zona 1, Guatemala City; tel. 2251-4363; internet www.circuloprensa.org; f. 1963; Pres. Sergio Roberto Lima Morales; Sec.-Gen. Jorge Roberto Chan Pedro.

NEWS AGENCY

Inforpress Centroamericana: Calle Mariscal o Diagonal 21, 6-58, Zona 11, 0100 Guatemala City; tel. and fax 2473-1704; e-mail inforpre@guate.net; internet www.inforpressca.com; f. 1972; independent news agency; publishes 2 weekly news bulletins, in English and Spanish.

Publishers

Cholsamaj: Calle 5, 2-58, Zona 1, Iximulew, Guatemala City; tel. 2232-5402; fax 2232-5959; e-mail editorialcholsamaj@yahoo.com; internet www.cholsamaj.org; Mayan language publs; Pres. Kikab' Gerber Mux; Exec. Dir Ulmil Joel Mejía.

Ediciones Legales Comercio e Industria: 12a Avda 14-78, Zone 1, Guatemala City; tel. 2253-5725; fax 2220-7592; Man. Dir Luis Emilio Barrios.

Editorial Cultura: Avda 12 11-11, Zona 1, Guatemala City; tel. 2232-5667; fax 2230-0591; e-mail kaxin@tutopia.com; internet www.mcd.gob.gt/editorial-cultura; f. 1987; part of the Ministry of Culture and Sport; Chief Editor Francisco Morales Santos.

Editorial Palo de Hormigo: 0 Calle 16-40, Zona 15, Col. El Maestro, Guatemala City; tel. 2369-3089; fax 2369-8858; e-mail eph_info@palodehormigo.com; f. 1990; Man. Dir Ricardo Ulysses Cifuentes.

Editorial Santillana, SA: 7 Avda 11-11, Zona 9, Guatemala City; tel. 2429-4300; fax 2429-4301; e-mail santillana@santillana.com.gt; internet www.gruposantillana.com/gr_gu.htm; f. 1995; subsidiary of Grupo Santillana (Spain); Dir-Gen. Alberto Polanco.

Editorial Universitaria: Universidad de San Carlos de Guatemala, Ciudad Universitaria, Zona 12, Guatemala City; tel. and fax 2476-9616; e-mail editorialusac@usac.edu.gt; internet editorial.usac.edu.gt; literature, social sciences, health, pure and technical sciences, humanities, secondary and university educational textbooks; Dir Anacleto Medina Gómez.

F & G Editores: 31a Avda 'C' 5-54, Zona 7, 01007 Guatemala City; tel. and fax 2439-8358; e-mail informacion@fygeditores.com; internet www.fygeditores.com; f. 1990 as Figueroa y Gallardo; changed name in 1993; law, literature and social sciences; Editor Raúl Figueroa Sarti.

Piedra Santa: 37 Avda 1-26, Zona 7, Guatemala City; tel. 2422-7676; fax 2422-7610; e-mail info@piedrasanta.com; internet www.piedrasanta.com; f. 1947; education, culture; Man. Dir Irene Piedra Santa.

PUBLISHERS' ASSOCIATION

Consejo Nacional del Libro (CONALIBRO): 11 Avda 11-07, Zona 1, Guatemala City; tel. 2253-0536; fax 2253-0544; e-mail conalibro@gmail.com; f. 1989; Pres. Luis Eduardo Morales.

Broadcasting and Communications

TELECOMMUNICATIONS

Regulatory Authority

Superintendencia de Telecomunicaciones de Guatemala: 2 Avda 3-87, Zona 10, Guatemala City; tel. 2321-1000; fax 2321-1074; e-mail supertel@sit.gob.gt; internet www.sit.gob.gt; f. 1996; Supt Oscar Stuardo Chinchilla.

Major Service Providers

Comcel Guatemala (Tigo): Edif. Plaza Tigo, 3°, Km 9.5, Carretera al Salvador, Guatemala City; tel. 2428-0000; fax 2428-1140; e-mail sugerencias@comcel.com.gt; internet www.tigo.com.gt; f. 1990; provider of mobile telecommunications; 55% owned by Millicom International Cellular (Luxembourg).

Telecomunicaciones de Guatemala, SA (Claro): Edif. Central Telgua, 7a Avda 12-39, Zona 1, Guatemala City; tel. 2230-2098; fax 2251-1799; e-mail clientes@claro.com.gt; internet www.claro.com.gt; fmrly state-owned Empresa Guatemalteca de Telecomunicaciones (Guatel); name changed as above to facilitate privatization; 95% share transferred to private ownership in 1998; owned by América Móvil, SA de CV (Mexico); Dirs Julio Belizario Montepeque, Marvin Emilio Par-González López.

Telefónica MoviStar Guatemala, SA: Edif. Iberoplaza, 1°, Blvd Los Próceres 20-09, Zona 10, Guatemala City; tel. 2379-7979; e-mail servicioalcliente@telefonica.com.gt; internet www.movistar.com.gt; owned by TelefónicaMóviles, SA (Spain); acquired BellSouth Guatemala in 2004; wireless, wireline and radio paging communications services; 298,000 customers; CEO Mario Bermúdez.

BROADCASTING

Dirección General de Radiodifusión y Televisión Nacional: Edif. Tipografía Nacional, 3°, 18 de Septiembre 6-72, Zona 1, Guatemala City; tel. 2323-8282; e-mail radiotgw@radiotgw.gob.gt; internet www.radiotgw.gob.gt; f. 1931; govt supervisory body; Dir-Gen. Carlos Enrique Morales Monzón.

Radio

Radio Cultural TGN: 4a Avda 30–09 Zona 3, Apdo 601, 01901 Guatemala City; tel. 2471-4378; fax 2440-0260; e-mail tgn@radiocultural.com; internet www.radiocultural.com; f. 1950; religious and cultural station; programmes in Spanish and English, Cakchiquel, Kekchi, Quiché and Aguacateco; Dir Anthony Wayne Berger Wiseman.

Radio Nacional TGW (La Voz de Guatemala): 18a Calle 6-72, Zona 1, Guatemala City; tel. 2323-8282; fax 2323-8310; e-mail info@radiotgw.gob.gt; internet www.radiotgw.gob.gt; f. 1930; govt station; Dir Jorge Manuel Jiménez Terrón.

There are some 80 commercial stations, of which the most important are:

Emisoras Unidas de Guatemala: 4a Calle 6-84, Zona 13, Guatemala City; tel. 2421-5353; fax 2475-3870; e-mail patrullajeinformativo@emisorasunidas.com; internet www.emisorasunidas.com; f. 1964; 6 stations: Yo Sí Sideral, Emisoras-

Unidas, Kiss, Atmósfera, Fabustereo and La Grande; Vice-Pres. and Gen. Man. ROLANDO ARCHILA DEHESA MARROQUÍN.

La Marca: 30a Avda 3-40, Zona 11, Guatemala City; tel. 2410-3150; fax 2410-3151; e-mail lamarca@94fm.com.gt; internet www.94fm.com.gt.

Metro Stereo: 14a Avda 14-78, Zona 10, Guatemala City; tel. 2277-7686; fax 2368-2040; e-mail metrored@metrostereo.net; internet www.metrostereo.net; f. 1980; Dir RUGGIERO MAURO-RHODIO.

Television

Guatevisión: Guatemala City; tel. 2328-6000; e-mail info@guatevision.com; internet www.guatevision.com; f. 1975; adopted present name in 1985.

Radio-Televisión Guatemala, SA: Edif. Canal 3, 30 Avda 3-40, Zona 11, Apdo 1367, Guatemala City; tel. 2410-3000; e-mail telediario@canal3.com.gt; internet www.canal3.com.gt; f. 1956; commercial; operates channels 3 and 10; Pres. MAX KESTLER FARNÉS; Vice-Pres. J. F. VILLANUEVA.

Teleonce: 20 Calle 5-02, Zona 10, Guatemala City; tel. 2368-2532; fax 2368-2221; e-mail jcof@canalonce.tv; f. 1968; commercial; channel 11; Gen. Dir JUAN CARLOS ORTIZ.

Televisiete, SA: 30 Avda 3-40, Zona 11, Apdo 1242, Guatemala City; tel. 2410-3000; fax 2369-1393; internet www.canal7.com.gt; f. 1988; commercial; channel 7; Dir ABDÓN RODRÍGUEZ ZEA.

Trecevisión, SA (Canales 11 y 13): 20 Calle 5-02, Zona 10, Guatemala City; tel. 2368-2221; e-mail escribanos@canal7.com.gt; f. 1978; commercial; channel 13; f. 1978; Dir FERNANDO VILLANUEVA; Gen. Man. JUAN CARLOS GONZÁLEZ.

Finance

(cap. = capital; res = reserves; dep. = deposits; m. = million; brs = branches; amounts in quetzales)

BANKING

Superintendencia de Bancos: 9a Avda 22-00, Zona 1, Apdo 2306, Guatemala City; tel. 2232-0001; fax 2232-0002; e-mail info@sib.gob.gt; internet www.sib.gob.gt; f. 1946; Supt VÍCTOR MANUEL MANCILLA CASTRO.

Central Bank

Banco de Guatemala: 7a Avda 22-01, Zona 1, Apdo 365, Guatemala City; tel. 2429-6000; fax 2253-4035; e-mail webmaster@banguat.gob.gt; internet www.banguat.gob.gt; f. 1946; state-owned; cap. and res 504.1m., dep. 34,384.7m. (Dec. 2009); Pres. EDGAR BALTAZAR BARQUÍN DURÁN; Gen. Man. SERGIO FRANCISCO RECINOS RIVERA.

State Commercial Bank

Crédito Hipotecario Nacional de Guatemala (CHN): 7a Avda 22-77, Zona 1, Apdo 242, Guatemala City; tel. 2223-0333; fax 2238-2041; e-mail mercadeo@chn.com.gt; internet www.chn.com.gt; f. 1980; govt-owned; cap. 15m., res –131.8m., dep. 2,384.2m. (Dec. 2009); Pres. OSCAR ERASMO VELASQUEZ RIVERA; Gen. Man. GUSTAVO ADOLFO DÍAZ LEÓN; 44 agencies.

Private Commercial Banks

Banco Agromercantil de Guatemala, SA: 7a Avda 7-30, Zona 9, 01009 Guatemala City; tel. 2338-6565; fax 2388-6566; e-mail agromercantil@bam.com.gt; internet www.agromercantil.com.gt; f. 2000 as Banco Central de Guatemala; changed name to Banco Agrícola Mercantil in 1948; name changed as above in 2000, following merger with Banco del Agro; cap. 765.3m., res 325.5m., dep. 12,634.1m. (Dec. 2010); Pres. JOSÉ LUIS VALDÉS; Man. RAFAEL ANTONIO E. VIEJO RODRÍGUEZ; 237 brs.

Banco de América Central, SA (BAC): Local 6-12, 1º, 7a Avda 6-26, Zona 9, Guatemala City; tel. 2360-9440; fax 2331-8720; internet www.bac.net; Gen. Man. JUAN JOSÉ VIAUD PÉREZ; 20 brs.

Banco Citibank de Guatemala, SA: Torre Citibank, 1°, 3a Avda 13-78, Zona 10, 01010 Guatemala City; tel. 2333-6574; fax 2333-6860; internet www.latinamerica.citibank.com/guatemala; Citi acquired Banco Cuscatlan and Banco Uno in 2007.

Banco de Desarrollo Rural, SA: Avda La Reforma 9-30, Zona 9, Guatemala City; tel. 2339-8888; fax 2360-9740; e-mail internacional4@banrural.com.gt; internet www.banrural.com.gt; f. 1971 as Banco de Desarrollo Agrícola; name changed as above in 1998; cap. 1,080.5m., res 1,363.9m., dep. 23,427.2m. (Dec. 2010); Pres. JOSÉ ANGEL LÓPEZ CAMPOSECO; Gen. Man. ADOLFO FERNANDO PEÑA PÉREZ; 640 brs.

Banco G & T Continental, SA: Plaza Continental, 6a Avda 9-08, Zona 9, Guatemala City; tel. 2338-6801; fax 2332-2682; e-mail subanco@gytcontinental.com.gt; internet www.gytcontinental.com.gt; f. 2000 following merger of Banco Continental and Banco Granai y Townson; total assets 11.4m. (2000); 151 brs.

Banco Industrial, SA (BAINSA): Edif. Centro Financiero, Torre 1, 7a Avda 5-10, Zona 4, Apdo 744, Guatemala City; tel. 2420-3000; fax 2331-9437; e-mail webmaster@bi.com.gt; internet www.bi.com.gt; f. 1964 to promote industrial devt; merged with Banco del Quetzal in 2007; cap. 1,376.9m., res 1,005.5m., dep. 33,633.3m. (Dec. 2009); Gen. Man. DIEGO PULIDO ARAGÓN; 350 brs.

Banco Inmobilario, SA: 7a Avda 11-59, Zona 9, Apdo 1181, Guatemala City; tel. 2339-3777; fax 2332-1418; e-mail info@bcoinmob.com.gt; internet www.bancoinmobiliario.com.gt; f. 1958; cap. 77.6m., res 0.4m., dep. 738.6m. (Dec. 2002); Pres. ADEL ABED ANTON TURJUMAN; 44 brs.

Banco Internacional, SA: Torre Internacional, Avda Reforma 15-85, Zona 10, Apdo 2588, Guatemala City; tel. 2277-3666; fax 2366-6743; e-mail info@bco.inter.com; internet www.bancointernacional.com.gt; f. 1976; cap. 217.7m., res 66.6m., dep. 3,408.1m. (Dec. 2010); Pres. CÉSAR JOSÉ ANTONIO CORRALES AGUILAR; Gen. Man. FRANCISCO NARANJO MARTÍNEZ; 44 brs.

Banco Promerica Guatemala: Edif. Reforma 10, 2°, Avda 9-55Z, 01010 Guatemala City; tel. 2413-9400; e-mail servicio@bancopromerica.com.gt; internet www.bancopromerica.com.gt; f. 1991 as Banco de la Producción, SA (BANPRO), adopted present name in 2007 following merger with Bancasol.

Banco Reformador, SA: 7a Avda 7-24, Zona 9, 01009 Guatemala City; tel. 2362-0888; fax 2362-0847; internet www.bancoreformador.com; cap. 392.5m., res 177.6m., dep. 6,369.4m. (Dec. 2009); merged with Banco de la Construcción in 2000, acquired Banco SCI in 2007; Pres. LUIS MIGUEL AGUIRRE FERNÁNDEZ; Gen. Man. RAYMOND PUCCINI; 100 brs.

Banco de los Trabajadores: Avda Reforma 6-20, Zona 9, 01001 Guatemala City; tel. 2410-2600; fax 2410-2616; e-mail webmaster@bantrab.net.gt; internet www.bantrab.com.gt; f. 1966; deals with loans for establishing and improving small industries as well as normal banking business; cap. 460.4m., dep. 2,119.5m., total assets 2,897.6m. (Dec. 2005); Pres. SERGIO HERNÁNDEZ; Gen. Man. RONALD GIOVANNI GARCIA NAVARIJO; 52 brs.

Banking Association

Asociación Bancaria de Guatemala: Edif. Margarita 2, Of. 502, Diagonal 6, Zona 10, Guatemala City; tel. 2336-6080; fax 2336-6094; internet www.abg.org.gt; f. 1961; represents all state and private banks; Pres. LUIS LARA GROJEC.

STOCK EXCHANGE

Bolsa de Valores Nacional, SA: Centro Financiero, Torre 2, 9°, 7a Avda 5-10, Zona 4, Guatemala City; tel. 2338-4400; fax 2332-1721; e-mail bvn@bvnsa.com.gt; internet www.bvnsa.com.gt; f. 1987; the exchange is commonly owned (1 share per associate) and trades stocks from private companies, govt bonds, letters of credit and other securities.

INSURANCE

National Companies

Aseguradora La Ceiba, SA: 20 Calle 15-20, Zona 13, Guatemala City; tel. 2379-1800; fax 2334-8167; e-mail aceiba@aceiba.com.gt; internet www.aceiba.com.gt; f. 1978; Man. ALEJANDRO BELTRANENA.

Aseguradora General, SA: 10a Calle 3-71, Zona 10, Guatemala City; tel. 2285-7200; fax 2334-2093; e-mail servicio@generali.com.gt; internet www.aseguresemejor.com; f. 1968; subsidiary of Grupo Generali, Trieste, Italy; Pres. ENRIQUE NEUTZE AYCINENA; Man. ENRIQUE NEUTZE TORIELLO.

Aseguradora Guatemalteca, SA (ASEGUA): Edif. Torre Azul, 10º, 4a Calle 7-53, Zona 9, Guatemala City; tel. 2361-0206; fax 2361-1093; e-mail aseguate@guate.net; internet www.aseguate.com; f. 1974; Pres. Gen. FERNANDO ALFONSO CASTILLO RAMÍREZ; Man. JOSÉ GUILLERMO H. LÓPEZ CORDÓN.

Chartis Seguros Guatemala, SA: Edif. Etisa, 7a Avda 12-23, Plazuela España, Zona 9, Guatemala City; tel. 2285-5900; fax 2361-3032; e-mail cmg.servicios@chartisinsurance.com; internet www.chartisinsurance.com; f. 1967 as La Seguridad de Centroamérica; present name adopted 2010; Gen. Man. JUAN MANUEL FRIEDERICH LOPEZ.

Cía de Seguros El Roble, SA: Torre 2, 7a Avda 5-10, Zona 4, Guatemala City; tel. 2420-3333; fax 2361-1191; e-mail rerales@elroble.com; internet www.elroble.com; f. 1973; Pres. JUAN MIGUEL TORREBIARTE; Gen. Man. HERMANN GIRON.

Departamento de Seguros y Previsión del Crédito Hipotecario Nacional: Centro Cívico, 7a Avda 22-77, Zona 1, Guatemala City; tel. 2223-0333; fax 2253-8584; e-mail vjsc@chn.com.gt; internet www.chn.com.gt; f. 1942; Pres. OSCAR ERASMO VELASQUEZ RIVERA; Man. GUSTAVO ADOLFO DÍAZ LEÓN.

Mapfre Seguros Guatemala, SA: Edif. Europlaza, Torre IV, 5a Avda 5-55, Zona 14, Guatemala City; tel. 2328-5000; fax 2328-5001; e-mail roberto.ewel@mapfre.com.gt; internet www.mapfre.com.gt; Gen. Man. JOSÉ TULIO URRUTIA.

Pan-American Life Insurance de Guatemala Cía de Seguros, SA: Edif. Plaza Panamericana, 10º, Avda la Reforma 9-00, Zona 9, Guatemala City; tel. 2338-9800; e-mail servicioalclientegt@panamericanlife.com; internet www.palig.com/Regions/guatemala; f. 1968; Country Man. SALVADOR LEIVA MADRID.

Seguros Columna, SA: 5a. Calle 0-55, Zona 9, Apdo 01009, Guatemala City; tel. 2419-2020; e-mail info@seguroscolumna.com; internet www.seguroscolumna.com; f. 1994; part of Corporación Financiera Cooperativa FENACOAC; Pres. JOSÉ GUILLERMO PERALTA ROSA; Gen. Man. BORIS ESTUARDO QUIRDA PINTO.

Seguros G & T, SA: Edif. Mini, 6a Avda 1-73, Zona 4, Guatemala City; tel. 2338-5778; e-mail erodriguez@gyt.com.gt; internet www.segurosgyt.com.gt; f. 1947; Pres. MARÍO GRANAI ANDRINO; Gen. Man. ENRIQUE RODRÍGUEZ MHAR.

Seguros de Occidente, SA: Edif. Corporación de Occidente, 7a Avda 7-33, Zona 9, Guatemala City; tel. 2279-7000; e-mail seguros@occidentecorp.com.gt; internet www.occidente.com.gt/cdo; f. 1979; Pres. JOSÉ GÚZMAN; Gen. Man. MARIO ROBERTO VALDEAVELLANO MUÑOZ.

Seguros Universales, SA: 4a Calle 7-73, Zona 9, Apdo 01009, Guatemala City; tel. 2384-7400; fax 2332-3372; e-mail info@segurosuniversales.net; internet www.segurosuniversales.net; f. 1962; Pres. PEDRO NOLASCO SICILIA VALLS; Gen. Man. FELIPE SICILIA.

Insurance Association

Asociación Guatemalteca de Instituciones de Seguros (AGIS): Edif. Torre Profesional I, Of. 703, 4°, 6a Avda 0-60, Zona 4, Guatemala City; tel. 2335-2140; fax 2335-2357; e-mail info@agis.com.gt; internet www.agis.com.gt; f. 1953; 12 mems; Pres. JUAN RAÚL AGUILAR KAEHLER; Exec. Dir ENRIQUE MURILLO C.

Trade and Industry

DEVELOPMENT ORGANIZATIONS

Instituto de Fomento de Hipotecas Aseguradas (FHA): Edif. Aristos Reforma, 2°, Avda Reforma 7-62, Zona 9, Guatemala City; tel. 2323-5656; fax 2362-9491; e-mail promocion@fha.com.gt; internet www.fha.com.gt; f. 1961; insured mortgage institution; Pres. JORGE FIDEL FRANCO SUCHINNI; Man. GUIDO RODAS.

Instituto Nacional de Administración Pública (INAP): Blvd Los Próceres 16-40, Zona 10, Apdo 2753, Guatemala City; tel. 2419-8181; fax 2366-2655; e-mail informacion@inap.gob.gt; internet www.inap.gob.gt; f. 1964; provides technical experts to assist in administrative reform programmes; provides training for govt staff; research programmes in administration, sociology, politics and economics; Pres. FERNANDO FUENTES MOHR; Man. HÉCTOR HUGO VÁSQUEZ BARREDA.

Secretaría de Planificación y Programación (SEGEPLAN): 9a Calle 10-44, Zona 1, Guatemala City; tel. 2232-6212; fax 2253-3127; e-mail segeplan@segeplan.gob.gt; internet www.segeplan.gob.gt; f. 1954; oversees implementation of the national economic devt plan; Sec. Dr KARIN SLOWING UMAÑA.

CHAMBERS OF COMMERCE AND INDUSTRY

Cámara de Comercio de Guatemala: 10a Calle 3-80, Zona 1, Guatemala City; tel. 2417-2700; fax 2220-9393; e-mail info@camaradecomercio.org.gt; internet www.negociosenguatemala.com; f. 1894; Pres. JORGE EDUARDO BRIZ ABULARACH; Exec. Dir RICARDO RODRÍGUEZ AMADO.

Cámara de Industria de Guatemala: 6a Ruta 9-21, 12°, Zona 4, Apdo 214, Guatemala City; tel. 2380-9000; e-mail info@industriaguate.com; internet www.industriaguate.com; f. 1959; Pres. ANDRÉS CASTILLO; Exec. Dir JAVIER ZEPEDA.

Cámara Oficial Española de Comercio de Guatemala: Edif. Paladium, 14°, 4 Avda 15-70, Zona 10, Guatemala City; tel. 2470-3301; fax 2470-3304; e-mail gerencia@camacoes.org.gt; internet www.camacoes.org.gt; f. 1928; Pres. Dr RAFAEL BRIZ; Gen. Man. SILVIA CAROLINA TAMAYAC MÁRQUEZ.

Comité Coordinador de Asociaciones Agrícolas, Comerciales, Industriales y Financieras (CACIF): Edif. Cámara de Industria de Guatemala, 6a Ruta 9-21, Zona 4, Guatemala City; tel. 2231-0651; fax 2334-7025; e-mail informacion@cacif.org.gt; internet www.cacif.org.gt; 6 mem. chambers; Pres. MARCO AUGUSTO GARCÍA NORIEGA; Exec. Dir ROBERTO ARDÓN.

INDUSTRIAL AND TRADE ASSOCIATIONS

Asociación de Azucareros de Guatemala (ASAZGUA): Edif. Europlaza, 178°, 5a Avda 5-55, Zona 14, Guatemala City; tel. 2386-2299; fax 2386-2020; e-mail asazgua@azucar.com.gt; internet www.azucar.com.gt; f. 1957; sugar producers' asscn; 15 mems; Pres. MARCO AUGUSTO GARCÍA; Gen. Man. ARMANDO BOESCHE.

Asociación General de Agricultores (AGA): Edif. Rodseguros, 6°, Via 1, 1-67, Zona 4, Guatemala City; tel. 2361-0654; fax 2332-4817; e-mail asistente@aga.org.gt; internet www.aga.org.gt; f. 1920; general farmers' asscn; Pres. PETER FRANK; 350 mems.

Asociación Guatemalteca de Exportadores (AGEXPORT): 15a Avda 14-72, Zona 13, Guatemala City; tel. 2422-3400; fax 2422-3434; e-mail portal@export.com.gt; internet www.export.com.gt; f. 1982; exporters' asscn; Pres. FRANCISCO MENENDEZ.

Asociación Nacional de Avicultores (ANAVI): Edif. El Reformador, 4°, Of. 401, Avda La Reforma 1-50, Zona 9, Guatemala City; tel. 2360-3384; fax 2360-3161; e-mail anavi@anaviguatemala.org; internet www.anaviguatemala.com; f. 1964; national asscn of poultry farmers; 60 mems; Pres. MARIA DEL ROSARIO DE FALLA; Gen. Man. PEGGY CONTRERAS.

Asociación Nacional del Café—Anacafé: 5a Calle 0-50, Zona 14, Guatemala City; tel. 2421-3700; e-mail info@email.anacafe.org; internet www.anacafe.org; f. 1960; national coffee asscn; Pres. RICARDO VILLANUEVA CARRERA; Sec. MARTÍN ARÉVALO DE LEÓN.

Cámara del Agro: Edif. Géminis 10, Torre Norte, 9°, Of. 909, 12 Calle, 1-25, Zona 10, Guatemala City; tel. 2219-9021; e-mail camagro@intelnet.net.gt; internet www.camaradelagro.org; f. 1973; Pres. OTTO KUSIEK; Exec. Dir CARLA CABALLEROS.

Gremial de Huleros de Guatemala: 6a Avda A 12-37, Zona 9, Guatemala City; tel. 2339-1752; fax 2339-1755; e-mail gremhuleger@guate.net.gt; internet www.gremialdehuleros.org; f. 1970; rubber producers' guild; 125 mems; Pres. JOSÉ MIGUEL EIZAGUIRRE; Gen. Man. CARLOS ALFREDO NÁJERA CASTILLO.

UTILITIES

Regulatory Authority

Comisión Nacional de Energía Eléctrica (CNEE): Edif. Paladium, 12°, 4 Avda 15-70, Zona 10, Guatemala City; tel. 2321-8000; fax 2321-8002; e-mail cnee@cnee.gov.gt; internet www.cnee.gob.gt; f. 1996; Pres. CARLOS EDUARDO COLOM BICKFORD.

Electricity

Empresa Eléctrica de Guatemala, SA: 6a Avda 8-14, Zona 1, Guatemala City; tel. 2277-7000; e-mail consultas@eegsa.net; internet www.eegsa.com; f. 1972; state electricity producer; 80% privatized in 1998; Gen. Man. JORGE ALONZO; subsidiaries include:

Comercializadora Eléctrica de Guatemala, SA (COMEGSA): Avda 6, 8-14, Zona 1, Guatemala City; tel. 2420-4200; fax 2230-5628; e-mail comegsaonline@comegsa.net; internet www.comegsa.com.gt; f. 1998; Gen. Man. ANGEL GARCÍA.

Trelec, SA: 2 Avda 9-27, Zona 1, Guatemala City; tel. 2420-4235; fax 2420-0409; e-mail trelec@trelec.net; f. 1999; Gen. Man. LEONEL FRANCISCO SANTIZO GONZÁLEZ.

Instituto Nacional de Electrificación (INDE): Edif. La Torre, 7a Avda 2-29, Zona 9, Guatemala City; tel. (2) 2422-1800; e-mail gerencia.general@inde.gob.gt; internet www.inde.gob.gt; f. 1959; fmr state agency for the generation and distribution of hydroelectric power; principal electricity producer; privatized in 1998; Pres. ERICK ESTUARDO ARCHILA DEHESA; Gen. Man. MARINUS ARIE BOER JOHANNESSEN.

CO-OPERATIVE

Instituto Nacional de Cooperativas (INACOP): Via 6, 6-72, Zona 4, Guatemala City; tel. 2339-1627; fax 2339-1648; e-mail macoadministrativa@inacop.gob.gt; internet www.inacop.gob.gt; technical and financial assistance in planning and devt of co-operatives; Gen. Man. LUIS ALBERTO MONTENEGRO.

TRADE UNIONS

Asamblea Nacional del Magisterio (ANM): Guatemala City; teachers' union; Co-ordinator JOVIEL ACEVEDO.

Central de Trabajadores del Campo y la Ciudad (CTC): 12a Calle 'A' 12-44, Zona 1, Guatemala City; tel. and fax 2232-6947; e-mail centracampo@yahoo.com; Sec.-Gen. MIGUEL ANGEL LUCAS GÓMEZ.

Confederación General de Trabajadores de Guatemala (CGTG): 3a Avda 13-22, Zona 1, Guatemala City; tel. 2232-1010; fax 2251-3212; e-mail cgtg@turbonett.com; f. 1987; Sec.-Gen. JOSÉ E. PINZÓN SALAZAR; 60,000 mems (2007).

Federación Sindical de Trabajadores de la Alimentación Agro-Industrias y Similares de Guatemala (FESTRAS): 16a

Avda 13-52, Zona 1, Guatemala City; tel. and fax 2251-8091; e-mail festras@terra.com.gt; internet festras.homestead.com; Sec.-Gen. JOSÉ DAVID MORALES C.

Unidad de Acción Sindical y Popular (UASP): 10a Avda 'A' 5-40, Zona 1, Guatemala City; f. 1988; broad coalition of leading labour and peasant orgs; Pres. NERY BARRIOS; includes:

Comité de la Unidad Campesina (CUC) (Committee of Peasants' Unity): 31a Avda 'A' 14-46, Zona 7, Ciudad de Plata II, Apdo 1002, Guatemala City; tel. 2434-9754; fax 2438-1424; e-mail cuc@intelnett.com; internet www.cuc.org.gt; f. 1978; Gen. Co-ordinator DANIEL PASCUAL HERNÁNDEZ.

Confederación de Unidad Sindical de Guatemala (CUSG): 12a Calle 'A', Zona 1, Guatemala City; tel. and fax 2232-8154; e-mail cusg@itelgua.com; f. 1983; Sec.-Gen. CARLOS ENRIQUE MANCILLA GARCÍA; 30,000 mems (2011).

Federación Nacional de Sindicatos de Trabajadores del Estado de Guatemala (FENASTEG): 10a Avda 5-40, Zona 1, Guatemala City; tel. and fax 2232-2772; Sec. ARTURO MESÍAS.

Unión Sindical de Trabajadores de Guatemala (UNSITRAGUA): 9a Avda 1-43, Zona 1, Guatemala City; tel. 2220-4121; fax 2238-2272; e-mail unsitragua02@yahoo.com; f. 1985; Sec.-Gen. AMPARO LOCÁN; 17,500 mems (2011).

Unión Guatemalteca de Trabajadores (UGT): 13a Calle 11-40, Zona 1, Guatemala City; tel. and fax 2251-1686; e-mail ugt.guatemala@yahoo.com; Sec.-Gen. ADOLFO LACS.

Transport

RAILWAYS

In 2007 there were 885 km of railway track in Guatemala.

Ferrovías Guatemala: 24 Avda 35-91, Zona 12, 01012 Guatemala City; tel. 2412-7200; fax 2412-7205; e-mail info@ferroviasgt.com; internet www.rrdc.com/op_guatemala_fvg.html; f. 1968 as Ferrocarriles de Guatemala (FEGUA); 50-year concession awarded in 1997 to the US Railroad Devt Corpn (RDC); 784 km from Puerto Barrios and Santo Tomás de Castilla on the Atlantic coast to Tecún Umán on the Mexican border, via Zacapa, Guatemala City and Santa María; in 2007 services were suspended after arbitration claim filed by the RDC under the terms of the DR-CAFTA free trade agreement; Pres. WILLIAM J. DUGGAN.

ROADS

In 2005 there were 14,283 km of roads, of which about 6,500 km were paved in 2008. The Guatemalan section of the Pan-American highway is 518.7 km long and totally asphalted. In 2009 construction began of the 362-km Franja Transversal del Norte highway, linking the departments of Huehuetenango and Izabal. The Banco Centroamericano de Integración Económica approved a US $203m. loan for the project.

SHIPPING

Guatemala's major ports are Puerto Barrios and Santo Tomás de Castilla on the Gulf of Mexico, San José and Champerico on the Pacific Ocean, and Puerto Quetzal.

Comisión Portuaria Nacional: 6 Avda A 8-66, Zona 9, Apdo 01009, Guatemala City; tel. 2419-4800; fax 2360-5457; e-mail info@cpn.gob.gt; internet www.cpn.gob.gt; f. 1972; Pres. VIOLETA LUNA; Exec. Dir CARLOS ENRIQUE DE LA CERDA.

Dacotrans de Centroamerica, SA: 24 Avda 41-81, Zona 12, Interior Almacenadora Integrada, Apdo 40, Guatemala City; tel. 2381-1200; fax 2381-1244; e-mail dacotrans@dacotrans.com.gt; internet www.dacotrans.com.gt; f. 1969; part of Grupo Dacotrans Grosskopf GMBH & Co (Germany); Gen. Man. MATHIAS REHE.

Empresa Portuaria Nacional de Champerico: Avda del Ferrocarril, frente a la playa, 1000101 Champerico, Retalhuleu; tel. 7773-7223; fax 7773-7221; e-mail vallejo.l@gmail.com; internet www.epnac.blogspot.com; f. 1955; Pres. LUIS ENRIQUE PRADO LUARCA; Man. MARGARITO FLORIAN ESCOBEDO.

Empresa Portuaria Nacional Santo Tomás de Castilla (EMPORNAC): Calle Real de la Villa, 17 Calle 16-43, Zona 10, Guatemala City; tel. 7720-4040; fax 7960-0584; e-mail mercadeo@santotomasport.com.gt; internet www.santotomasport.com.gt; Pres. JOSÉ ROBERTO DÍAZ-DÚRAN QUEZADA; Gen. Man. JORGE ESTUARDO VARGAS.

Empresa Portuaria Quetzal: Edif. Torre Azul, 1°, Of. 105, 4 Calle 7-53, Zona 9, 01009 Guatemala City; tel. 2312-5000; fax 2334-8172; e-mail mercadeo@puerto-quetzal.com; internet www.puerto-quetzal.com; port and shipping co; Pres. FELIPE CASTAÑEDA; Gen. Man. RODOLFO KUSHIEK.

Seaboard Marine Ltda: Edif. Galerias Reforma, 4°, Of. 411, Avda La Reforma 8-60, Zona 9, Guatemala City; tel. 2384-3900; fax 2334-0077; e-mail Guillermo_Ortiz@seaboardmarine.com.gt; internet www.seaboardmarine.com; subsidiary of Seaboard Corpn (USA); Rep. GUILLERMO ORTIZ.

Transmares, SA: Torre 2, 8°, Centro Gerencial Las Margaritas, Diagonal 6, 10-01, Zona 10, 01010 Guatemala City; tel. 2429-8100; fax 2429-8148; e-mail henneke.sieveking@transmares.net; internet www.transmares.org; ocean liner and cargo shipping; logistics services under Translogística, SA; Gen. Man. HENNEKE SIEVEKING.

CIVIL AVIATION

There are two international airports, La Aurora in Guatemala City and Mundo Maya in Santa Elena, El Petén.

Dirección General de Aeronáutica Civil: Aeropuerto La Aurora, Zona 13, 01013 Guatemala City; tel. 2362-0216; e-mail direccion@dgac.gob.gt; internet www.dgacguate.com; f. 1929; administers and regulates aviation services; Dir JUAN JOSÉ CARLOS SUÁREZ.

Aviones Comerciales de Guatemala (Avcom): Aeropuerto 'La Aurora', Avda Hincapié 18, Zona 13, Guatemala City; tel. 2331-5821; fax 2332-4946; domestic charter passenger services.

TACA: Aeropuerto 'La Aurora', Avda Hincapié 12-22, Zona 13, Guatemala City; tel. 2470-8222; e-mail scastillo@taca.com; internet www.taca.com; f. 1945 as Aerolíneas de Guatemala (AVIATECA); privatized in 1989; domestic services and services to the USA, Mexico, and within Central America; Gen. Man. MYNOR CORDON.

Transportes Aéreos Guatemaltecos, SA (TAG): Avda Hinapie y 18 Calle, Zona 13, Guatemala City; tel. 2380-9494; fax 2334-7205; e-mail tagsa@tag.com.gt; internet www.tag.com.gt; f. 1969; domestic and int. charter services; Gen. Man. JONATHAN LAYTON.

Tourism

Guatemala's main attraction lies in the ancient Mayan ruins. Other tourism highlights include its active steaming volcanos, mountain lakes, pristine beaches and a rich indigenous culture. After the end of the civil war in 1996 the number of tourist arrivals rose steadily. By 2009 arrivals had reached 1,776,868. In the same year receipts from tourism were estimated at US $1,179m.

Instituto Guatemalteco de Turismo (INGUAT) (Guatemala Tourist Institute): Centro Cívico, 7a Avda 1-17, Zona 4, Guatemala City; tel. 2421-2800; fax 2331-4416; e-mail informacion@inguat.gob.gt; internet www.inguat.gob.gt; f. 1967; policy and planning council: 11 mems representing the public and private sectors; Dir PEDRO PABLO DUCHEZ.

Defence

As assessed in November 2011, Guatemala's active armed forces numbered an estimated 15,212: army 13,444, navy 897 and air force 871. Reserve forces totalled 63,863. In addition, there were paramilitary forces of 19,000. Military service is by selective conscription for 30 months.

Defence Budget: an estimated 1,610m. quetzales in 2012.

Chief of Staff of National Defence: Brig.-Gen. ANÍBAL FLORES ESPAÑA.

Education

Elementary education is free and, in urban areas, compulsory between seven and 14 years of age. Primary education begins at the age of seven and lasts for six years. Secondary education, beginning at 13 years of age, lasts for up to six years, comprising two cycles of three years each. Enrolment at primary schools in 2008 included 95% of children in the relevant age-group (males 97%; females 94%). The comparable ratio for secondary education in that year was 40% (males 41%; females 39%). There are 12 universities, of which 11 are privately run. In 2012 expenditure on education by the central Government was projected at 11,097.7m. quetzales, equivalent to 18.6% of total spending.

GUINEA

Introductory Survey

LOCATION, CLIMATE, LANGUAGE, RELIGION, FLAG, CAPITAL

The Republic of Guinea lies on the west coast of Africa, with Sierra Leone and Liberia to the south, Senegal and Guinea-Bissau to the north, and Mali and Côte d'Ivoire inland to the east. The climate on the coastal strip is hot and moist, with temperatures ranging from about 32°C (90°F) in the dry season to about 23°C (73°F) in the wet season (May–October). The interior is higher and cooler. The official language is French, but Soussou, Manika and six other national languages are widely spoken. Most of the inhabitants are Muslims, but some follow traditional animist beliefs. Around 3% are Roman Catholics. The national flag (proportions 2 by 3) consists of three equal vertical stripes, of red, yellow and green. The capital is Conakry.

CONTEMPORARY POLITICAL HISTORY

Historical Context

The Republic of Guinea (formerly French Guinea, part of French West Africa) became independent on 2 October 1958, after 95% of voters rejected the Constitution of the Fifth Republic under which the French colonies became self-governing within the French Community. The new state was the object of punitive reprisals by the outgoing French authorities: all aid was withdrawn, and the administrative infrastructure destroyed. The Parti démocratique de Guinée—Rassemblement démocratique africain (PDG—RDA) became the basis for the construction of new institutions. Its leader, Ahmed Sékou Touré, became President, and the PDG—RDA the sole political party.

Sékou Touré pursued vigorous policies of socialist revolution. Opposition was ruthlessly crushed, and Sékou Touré perpetuated rumours of a 'permanent conspiracy' by foreign powers to overthrow his regime. Notably, an abortive invasion by Portuguese troops and Guinean exiles in 1970 prompted the execution of many of those convicted of involvement.

In November 1978 it was announced that the functions of the PDG—RDA and the State were to be merged, and the country was renamed the People's Revolutionary Republic of Guinea. There was, none the less, a general move away from rigid Marxism and a decline in relations with the USSR, as Guinea sought a political and economic rapprochement with its African neighbours, with France and with other Western powers.

Domestic Political Affairs

In March 1984 Sékou Touré died while undergoing surgery in the USA. On 3 April, before a successor had been chosen by the ruling party, the armed forces seized power in a bloodless coup. A Comité militaire de redressement national (CMRN) was appointed, headed by Col (later Gen.) Lansana Conté, the PDG—RDA and the legislature were dissolved, and the Constitution was suspended. In May the 'Second Republic of Guinea' was proclaimed.

In December 1984 Conté, as President, assumed the posts of Head of Government and Minister of Defence. In May 1987 it was announced that 58 people, including nine former government ministers, had been sentenced to death in secret trials for crimes committed under Sékou Touré or following an abortive coup attempt in 1985. The announcement did little to allay international suspicions that many detainees had been executed in the aftermath of the failed coup.

In late 1989 Conté announced that, following a referendum on a proposed new constitution, a joint civilian and military Comité transitoire de redressement national (CTRN) would replace the CMRN. After a transitional period of not more than five years, civilian rule would be established, with an executive and legislature directly elected within a two-party system. The draft Constitution of what was designated the Third Republic was reportedly endorsed by 98.7% of the 97.4% of the electorate who voted in a referendum on 23 December 1990; the CTRN was inaugurated in February 1991 under Conté's chairmanship.

In October 1991 Conté announced that a law authorizing the registration of an unlimited number of political parties would come into effect in April 1992, and that legislative elections would be held before the end of 1992. The Constitution was promulgated on 23 December 1991, and in January 1992 Conté ceded the presidency of the CTRN, in conformity with the constitutional separation of powers. In February most military officers and all those who had returned from exile after the 1984 coup (known as *Guinéens de l'extérieur*) were removed from the Council of Ministers.

In April 1992 some 17 political parties, including the Rassemblement du peuple de Guinée (RPG), led by Alpha Condé, were legalized; it was subsequently rumoured that the pro-Conté Parti pour l'unité et du progrès (PUP), established by prominent *Guinéens de l'extérieur*, was benefiting from state funds. In December the Government postponed indefinitely the legislative elections, which had been scheduled for later that month.

In October 1993 the Supreme Court approved eight candidates for the forthcoming presidential election. The official rate of participation by voters in the election, held on 19 December, was 78.5%. According to official results, Conté was elected with 51.7% of the votes cast; Condé took 19.6% of the votes, Mamadou Boye Bâ of the Union pour la nouvelle République (UNR) 13.4% and Siradiou Diallo of the Parti pour le renouveau et le progrès (PRP) 11.9%. Conté was inaugurated as President on 29 January 1994.

Some 846 candidates, from 21 parties, contested the 114 seats in the Assemblée nationale at the delayed legislative elections, held on 11 June 1995. As preliminary results indicated that the PUP had won an overwhelming majority in the legislature, the so-called 'radical' opposition (the RPG, the PRP and the UNR) announced their intention to boycott the assembly, protesting that voting had been conducted fraudulently. According to the final results, which were verified by the Supreme Court in July, the PUP won 71 seats—having taken 30 of the 38 single-member constituencies and 41 of the 76 seats elected on the basis of national lists. Of the eight other parties to win representation, the RPG secured 19 seats, while the PRP and the UNR each won nine seats. The rate of participation was reported to be 63%. In July the RPG, the PRP and the UNR joined with nine other organizations in a Coordination de l'opposition démocratique (Codem), which indicated its willingness to enter into a dialogue with the authorities. The Assemblée nationale was officially inaugurated on 30 August.

In February 1996 Conté was reportedly seized as he attempted to flee the presidential palace during a mutiny by disaffected elements of the military, and was held by rebels for some 15 hours until he made concessions including a doubling of salaries and immunity from prosecution for those involved in the uprising. The Minister of Defence, Col Abdourahmane Diallo, was dismissed, and Conté assumed personal responsibility for defence. In March it was announced that eight members of the military, including four senior officers, had been charged with undermining state security in connection with the coup attempt. In July Conté announced the appointment of a non-partisan economist, Sidya Touré, as Prime Minister, the first time that position had existed under the Third Republic. (The Constitution made no explicit provision for such a post.)

In June 1997 it was announced that a State Security Court was to be established to deal with matters of exceptional jurisdiction, and that its first task would be to try the alleged leaders of the 1996 mutiny, including Cmmdr Joseph Gbago Zoumanigui, a former member of the CMRN. In September the State Security Court sentenced 38 of those charged with offences related to the 1996 attempted coup to custodial sentences of up to 15 years, some with hard labour, while 51 defendants were acquitted.

The official results of the presidential election held on 14 December 1998 confirmed a decisive victory for Conté, with 56.1% of the valid votes cast; Bâ, contesting the election for the Union pour le progrès et le renouveau (UPR, formed in 1998 by a merger of the UNR and the PRP), won 24.6% and Condé (who had been outside Guinea since April 1997, owing to fears for his safety, for the RPG) 16.6%. The rate of participation by registered voters was 71.4%. In March 1999 Lamine Sidimé, hitherto Chief Justice of the Supreme Court, was appointed Prime Minister of a new Government.

Opposition groups and human rights organizations campaigned throughout 1999 and 2000 for the release of Condé and other activists detained at the time of the 1998 presidential election. In September 2000 Condé was found guilty of sedition by the State Security Court and sentenced to five years' imprisonment, while a further seven defendants were given custodial sentences of between 18 months and three years; 40 other defendants were acquitted.

In early September 2000 an armed rebellion in the forest region of south-east Guinea reportedly resulted in at least 40 deaths. Instability subsequently intensified in regions near the borders with Sierra Leone and Liberia. Fighting between armed groups and Guinean soldiers was reported to have led to around 360 deaths between early September and mid-October. The Government attributed the upsurge in violence to forces supported by the Governments of Liberia and Burkina Faso, and to members of the Sierra Leonean rebel group, the Revolutionary United Front (RUF, see Sierra Leone), in alliance with Guinean dissidents. In November a series of cross-border attacks were reportedly conducted by former members of a faction of a dissolved Liberian dissident group, the United Liberation Movement of Liberia for Democracy (ULIMO), ULIMO—K (see iberia), which President Conté had previously supported. In December rebel attacks on the southern towns of Guéckédou and Kissidougou led to more than 230 deaths, and the almost complete destruction of Guéckédou. The Government estimated that some 94,000 people had been displaced as a result of fighting in the region, and aid agencies withdrew from south-east Guinea later in the month, as a result of the heightened instability.

As rebel attacks continued, it was reported that Guinean planes had launched minor air offensives on rebel-held border areas of Sierra Leone. In January–February 2001 more than 130 deaths were reported in a series of attacks around Macenta. Allegations persisted that an unofficial alliance between former ULIMO—K rebels and Guinean government forces had broken down, with the result that ULIMO—K forces were now attacking Guinean military and civilian targets. Renewed clashes around Guéckédou prevented the proposed deployment by the Economic Community of West African States (ECOWAS, see p. 264) of an ECOMOG force, which had been intended to monitor stability and border security in the region from mid-February. Meanwhile, in February the death penalty, which had been suspended in 1984, was officially restored, and four of five defendants sentenced to death in 1995 were executed by firing squad (the fifth had died in detention).

Constitutional changes

A constitutional referendum took place on 11 November 2001, following violent clashes between security forces and those opposed to the referendum. According to official results, 98.4% of those who voted approved the amendments (which removed the restriction on the number of terms the President could serve, allowed candidates aged over 70 years to contest the presidency and extended the presidential term of office from five years to seven, with effect from the presidential election due in 2003) and 87.2% of the registered electorate participated. Opposition members disputed the results, alleging that less than 20% of the electorate had voted.

In April 2002 President Conté issued a decree, scheduling repeatedly postponed elections to the Assemblée nationale for 30 June; a further presidential decree, issued later in April, established a Conseil national electoral, to be responsible for the supervision of the elections. However, concern was expressed that the short period between the establishment of the Conseil and the holding of elections would be insufficient to ensure transparency in the conduct of the polls, and the European Union (EU, see p. 276) subsequently withheld funding towards the elections. In May four opposition parties, which had announced their intention to boycott the legislative elections, including the RPG and the Union des forces républicaines (UFR), announced the formation of a political alliance, the Front de l'alternance démocratique (FRAD). Notably, Boubacar Biro Diallo, who was not affiliated to any party, and Bâ, the honorary President of the UPR, pledged allegiance to the FRAD, and a split in the UPR became increasingly apparent between those, led by Siradiou Diallo, the President of the party, who sought to engage with the electoral process, and those, led by Bâ, who rejected any such engagement.

At elections to the Assemblée nationale, held on 30 June 2002, the PUP increased its majority in the legislature, winning a total of 85 seats. The party was unopposed in all 38 single-member constituency seats, and obtained 47 of the 76 seats allocated by proportional representation. Other pro-presidential parties secured five seats, while the UPR became the second largest party in the Assemblée, with 20 seats. Opposition parties, both those of the FRAD and those that contested the elections, alleged that fraudulent practice had been widespread in the conduct of the elections, and the US ambassador to Guinea expressed concern at apparent irregularities in the poll. In October Bâ was elected as President of a new party, the Union des forces démocratiques de Guinée (UFDG), which largely comprised the faction of the UPR that had boycotted the elections to the Assemblée nationale.

In September 2003, several days after the formal nomination of Conté as the presidential candidate of the PUP, the FRAD announced that negotiations between the Government and opposition parties on the conduct of the presidential election had broken down. In November the FRAD announced that it was to boycott the polls and later that month the UPR also announced that it would boycott the election. Meanwhile, the Assemblée nationale approved legislation providing for an amnesty for those convicted of political crimes, including, most notably, Condé, who would thereby be permitted to contest the presidential election. However, in the event, the sole candidate approved to contest the election, apart from Conté, was Mamadou Bhoye Barry, the leader of the Union pour le progrès national—Parti pour l'unité et le développement. It was reported that the Supreme Court had rejected on technical grounds the nominations of six other candidates.

Voting in the presidential election proceeded, as scheduled, on 21 December 2003. In the absence of any significant opposition, Conté was re-elected to a further seven-year term of office, receiving 95.3% of the votes cast, according to official figures. Although the opposition claimed that turn-out had been as low as 15% of the electorate, official figures indicated a rate of participation of approximately 82%. Barry, meanwhile, alleged that the official results were fraudulent, and that he had, in fact, received a majority of the votes cast. On 23 February 2004 Conté dismissed Sidimé and appointed a substantially reorganized Government, headed by François Lonsény Fall as Prime Minister.

In late April 2004 it was announced that Fall had resigned as Prime Minister and had fled Guinea; the former premier subsequently claimed that his Government had been obstructed in its attempts to implement economic and judicial reforms. The post of Prime Minister remained vacant until the appointment in December of Cellou Dalein Diallo, previously Minister of Fisheries and Aquaculture and a government minister since 1996. Diallo pledged to reopen dialogue with opposition parties.

Domestic unrest

During 2005 President Conté's continuing ill-health continued to be a major source of concern, as did the lack of a clear process of succession for the appointment of a new leader in the event of his death. In May further sharp increases in the prices of rice and, in particular, of fuel products precipitated a series of protests in Conakry and several other cities.

Prime Minister Diallo announced the implementation of a comprehensive governmental reorganization in April 2006, nominating new appointees to the overwhelming majority of ministerial positions. Notably, responsibility for the economy and finance, for planning and international co-operation and for economic and financial control was to be transferred to the office of the Prime Minister, with three minister-delegates appointed to assume responsibilities over these matters. However, it emerged that President Conté (who was constitutionally Head of Government as well as Head of State) had not authorized the reorganization, and on 5 April he dismissed Diallo, and issued a decree restoring the Government that had been in place prior to the aborted reorganization.

In late May 2006 Conté restructured the Government, nominating six ministers of state—responsible for the key portfolios, including foreign affairs, economy and finance, and presidential affairs—but, notably, no Prime Minister was appointed. In early June the country's two principal trade unions, the Confédération Nationale des Travailleurs de Guinée (CNTG) and the Union Syndicale des Travailleurs de Guinée (USTG), organized a widely observed general strike and demanded the reduction of the prices of fuel and rice. Clashes were subsequently reported between protesters and the security forces resulting in the deaths of some 20 people. The strike was brought to an end after nine days, following the Government's decision to increase public sector salaries and allowances for rent and transportation, as well as to lower the cost of rice.

On 10 January 2007 the CNTG and the USTG commenced a further general strike, which was supported by a number of opposition parties, and several non-governmental organizations

(NGOs) and civil society groups. Initially, their demands again focused on the lowering of the cost of basic foodstuffs and fuel, as well as the return to gaol of two former prominent politicians accused of financial impropriety whose release had been secured by the President in the previous month. However, following violent clashes between demonstrators and the security forces in mid-January, during which five people were killed and several hundred were arrested, the unions insisted on the resignation of Conté and his Government. The President's proposals to reduce the duty on fuel and to increase the salaries of teachers were rejected as insufficient by the union leaders. On 19 January Conté dismissed the Minister of State for Presidential Affairs, El Hadj Fodé Bangoura, but protests continued and further deaths were reported across the country. The Government's response to the strike was condemned by the UN and the African Union (AU, see p. 189), and both organizations urged the Government to commence negotiations with the trade unions. On 23 January the leaders of the CNTG, the USTG and the Organisation Nationale des Syndicats Libres de Guinée were briefly detained. They were released the following day and invited to talks with Conté, following which he indicated his willingness to appoint a 'consensus' Prime Minister. Nevertheless, nation-wide disturbances continued, and it was reported that as many as 60 people had been killed since the beginning of the strike.

On 27 January 2007 the trade unions ended the general strike after President Conté agreed to nominate a new Prime Minister, although they threatened the commencement of further industrial action if the premier was not selected by 11 February. On 9 February Conté announced that he had chosen Eugène Camara, who had succeeded Bangoura as Minister of State for Presidential Affairs, as Prime Minister. The President's decision was rejected by the trade unions and the political opposition; on 12 February the unions recommenced the general strike and demanded the resignation of Conté, who, in response, declared a 'state of siege' and imposed martial law and a nation-wide curfew the following day. Negotiations between the Government and the trade unions took place on 19 February, at which the unions refused to acquiesce to Conté's proposal to maintain Camara as Prime Minister for a period of three months. As the strike continued, on 23 February the Assemblée nationale voted to terminate martial law and the curfew with effect from the end of that day, and, following further negotiations facilitated by an ECOWAS delegation led by former Nigerian President Gen. Ibrahim Babangida, on 26 February Conté announced that he would select a Prime Minister from a list of candidates supplied by the trade unions and opposition parties. Lansana Kouyaté, a career diplomat and the former Executive Secretary of ECOWAS, was duly appointed as Prime Minister and the industrial action was brought to an end on 27 February.

Kouyaté was sworn in as Prime Minister on 1 March 2007 and later that month announced a new, 22-member Council of Ministers, composed largely of technocrats and which did not include any ministers from the previous administration. Ousmane Doré, a senior IMF official, was appointed Minister of the Economy, Finance and Planning, while the former Deputy Chief of Staff of the Armed Forces, Gen. Arafan Camara, assumed the national defence portfolio. In May members of the armed forces launched a widespread campaign of intimidation against civilians in protest against salary arrears, in some cases dating back as far as 11 years, and the appointment of several senior defence personnel earlier in the year. The two-week uprising was finally suppressed when Arafan Camara and Kerfalla Camara (the Chief of Staff of the Armed Forces) were dismissed. Gen. Bailo Diallo was subsequently named as the new Minister of National Defence, while Brig.-Gen. Diarra Camara replaced Kerfalla Camara.

In early January 2008 Conté dismissed the Minister of Communication and Information Technology, Justin Morel Junior, and appointed in his place Issa Condé, hitherto the head of the state news agency; Morel Junior had criticized the content of the President's New Year's address in which he referred to Kouyaté's administration as a 'disappointment'. The trade unions demanded Morel Junior's reinstatement, and maintained that his replacement was contrary to the agreement that had brought an end to the violence of early 2007. On 9 January 2008 Kouyaté and a delegation of government ministers held lengthy negotiations with representatives from the trade unions and civil society organizations in an attempt to avert further industrial action that would threaten economic recovery. An accord was reached whereby the unions postponed a planned general strike until 31 March, pending the further discussion of a presidential decree issued in December 2007, which resulted in a reduction in the powers of the Prime Minister. It was widely believed that Conté intended to reclaim a number of the responsibilities that had passed to Kouyaté following his appointment to the premiership, and, in a controversial move, Conté dismissed Kouyaté in May 2008, replacing him with Ahmed Tidiane Souaré, who was known to be a close ally of the President. Souaré announced the composition of an enlarged administration the following month.

Meanwhile, in late May 2008 President Conté dismissed Gen. Bailo Diallo, following a protest by soldiers demanding the payment of salary arrears, and appointed Almany Kabèle Camara as his replacement. At least three people were killed in Conakry during demonstrations and it was reported that the Army Chief of Staff had been taken hostage. Further clashes took place in June. In August and October Conté effected a series of further governmental reorganizations, which included the dismissal of Doré, while the much-delayed parliamentary elections scheduled for November were again postponed in October, owing to insufficient funds and incomplete preparations; at that time voter registration had yet to begin. Civil unrest continued throughout late 2008 and the conduct of Guinea's security forces was condemned by numerous NGOs after they forcibly dispersed protesters demanding lower fuel prices in early November, resulting in the deaths of four people.

The death of Conté

On 23 December 2008 it was announced that Conté had died following a recent deterioration in his health. Although Aboubacar Somparé, the Speaker of the Assemblée nationale, stated that he should assume the presidency pending an election, a group of junior army officers, led by Capt. Moussa Dadis Camara, swiftly seized power. Camara proclaimed the formation of a 32-member Conseil national pour la démocratie et le développement (CNDD), the suspension of the Constitution and the dissolution of all state institutions. The CNDD also imposed a ban on all political and trade union activities and demoted all military generals of the former regime. The coup was widely condemned by the international community and on 29 December the AU announced the suspension of Guinea's membership, pending the return of constitutional order; membership of ECOWAS was suspended in January 2009. On 30 December 2008 Camara appointed an economist, Kabiné Komara, to the post of Prime Minister and on 5 January 2009 pledged to hold legislative and presidential elections within 12 months; Camara declared that he did not intend to contest the latter, and pledged to eradicate corruption and improve living standards.

A new Government was named on 14 January 2009, which included Gen. Sékouba Konaté as Minister at the Presidency, in charge of National Defence, while Morel Junior was notably reassigned to his former portfolio. In February the ban on political and trade union activity was lifted. Meanwhile, in January a number of former ministers, including Doré, and several prominent business executives appeared before a commission charged with investigating corruption during the Conté era. In late April two army officers were detained on suspicion of plotting a coup as Camara prepared to leave the country for the first time since taking power.

Despite an earlier agreement that members of the military were not to be allowed to stand in the forthcoming elections, in August 2009 Camara indicated his intention to contest the presidential election. (A revised election timetable had been announced in that month according to which the presidential election was to be held in January 2010, followed by legislative elections in March.) Tensions had been increasing in the country since the military's seizure of power, and, in response to Camara's decision, opposition parties staged a protest rally in Conakry in September 2009, attended by some 10,000 people, during which security forces opened fire leaving 157 dead and more than 1,000 people wounded. International observers severely condemned the actions, and several governments advised foreign nationals to leave the country. ECOWAS imposed an arms embargo on Guinea, declaring the attack by security forces an 'irresponsible' use of power. A UN commission of inquiry was to investigate the incident and the AU, the EU and the USA imposed targeted sanctions against members of the CNDD. Camara responded to the events by visiting the victims in hospital and expressing his regret and sympathy, claiming that the shootings had been carried out by 'uncontrollable elements in the military'; he later appealed for the establishment of a government of national unity to lead the country to forthcoming elections, with talks between political parties to be mediated by ECOWAS. Several ministers resigned from office in October in an expression of their disapproval of the September massacre and although Camara insisted that the presidential election would proceed as planned, this was subsequently rescheduled to take place in July 2010, with the legislative elections to follow at an unspecified date.

A significant rift within the military junta began to emerge shortly after the shootings of September 2009. Camara's decision to delay elections, and his suggestion that he himself would stand as a candidate, coupled with international pressure on Camara to bring to justice those believed to be responsible for the Conakry killings, led to growing disaffection. On 4 December this culminated in an assassination attempt against Camara by Lt Abubakar 'Toumba' Diakite, who, it was subsequently reported, was to have been handed over to the authorities to be prosecuted for his role in the events of September. Camara, who suffered a gunshot wound to the head, was transferred to Morocco for medical treatment, while Toumba evaded capture and fled abroad. Gen. Konaté was immediately installed as Interim President; however, attempts by the international community to dispatch peace-keeping forces to Guinea were greeted with hostility by senior members of the junta. In late December a UN report indicated that there was sufficient evidence that Camara had been directly responsible for the Conakry massacre, and stated that the killings were considered as crimes against humanity. (In early February 2012 Col Moussa Tiegboro Camara, a minister in the Presidency responsible for combating drugs-trafficking and organized crime, was charged by investigative judges in Guinea with involvement in the violence of September 2009, the highest-ranking official to date to be so charged.)

In January 2010 Konaté pledged to restore civilian rule and indicated the CNDD's willingness to appoint a transitional government of national unity headed by an opposition Prime Minister. Although Camara was transferred from Morocco to Burkina Faso in mid-January and stated his intention to return to Guinea, following negotiations mediated by the Burkina President, Blaise Compaoré, involving Camara, senior members of the CNDD and representatives of the Guinean political opposition, it was agreed that Camara would remain outside the country on a 'leave of absence' to continue his convalescence. On 26 January Jean-Marie Doré, the leader of the Union pour le progrès de la Guinée, was sworn in as Prime Minister, and in mid-February he appointed a new 34-member Government. A number of military members of the outgoing administration were reappointed to ministerial positions, while representatives of opposition political parties, trade unionists and members of civil society were also awarded portfolios.

Meanwhile, in late January 2010 Konaté installed the Secretary-General of the CNTG, Rabiatou Serah Diallo, as President of a Conseil national de transition (CNT), charged with overseeing the transition from military to civilian rule, comprising representatives of civil society, political parties, and religious groups, as well as members of the CNDD. In early March Konaté announced that the presidential election would be held on 27 June (confirming that he would not take part in the poll), and also appointed the 155 members of the CNT.

In late April 2010 the CNT presented a draft Constitution (replacing that suspended in December 2008) to Konaté. On 7 May 2010 Konaté signed a decree adopting the new Constitution, under which a new President and legislature were to be elected for a term of five years, the presidential mandate was renewable only once, and the minimum age to seek the presidency was 35. Campaigning for the presidential election officially began on 17 May, after the Supreme Court approved a total of 24 candidates, including long-standing opposition leader Alpha Condé, and four former Prime Ministers under Conté—Cellou Dalein Diallo, Sidya Touré, François Lonsény Fall and Lansana Kouyaté.

Recent developments: Condé elected President

The first round of the presidential election proceeded without incident on 27 June 2010. The following day the Commission électorale nationale indépendante (CENI) acknowledged widespread technical failings, but ECOWAS confirmed that the election had been conducted without malpractice. In early July the CENI released provisional results indicating that Diallo and Condé would contest the second round. Protests at the results from several presidential candidates, in particular from Touré (who had been placed third in the poll) and his supporters, ensued; Konaté threatened to resign, after Touré reportedly accused him of involvement in alleged malpractice, but agreed to remain in office following international intervention. On 20 July the Supreme Court declared revised election results, according to which Diallo, with about 43.7% of the votes, and Condé, with 18.3%, were to contest the second round; Touré remained third placed, with 13.0% of the votes. Voter turn-out was recorded at about 52% of the registered electorate, significantly lower than earlier estimates. Touré subsequently urged his supporters to vote for Diallo, while Kouyaté, who had been placed fourth in the first round, declared support for Condé. In early August Konaté announced that the second round of the presidential election (originally scheduled for 18 July) would take place on 19 September.

In early September 2010 the President of the CENI, Ben Sékou Sylla, and its Director of Planning, Boubacar Diallo, were found guilty of fraudulent activity during the first round of the election, and sentenced to one year's imprisonment. (Sylla died in Paris, France, later that month.) The announcement of their convictions precipitated violent clashes between supporters of Diallo and Condé, in which one person was killed and at least 50 others were injured. The authorities suspended the election process and banned all demonstrations. In October the second round was again postponed, after Diallo accused the newly appointed President of the CENI, Lounceny Camara, of favouring Condé, prompting his replacement by a Malian general, Siaka Toumany Sangaré. The poll was finally deferred to 7 November by the CENI, which cited technical difficulties.

International electoral observers declared that the second round of the presidential election, which duly took place on 7 November 2010, had been conducted successfully. In mid-November the CENI announced that Condé had been elected to the presidency, with about 52.5% of votes cast. Diallo repeated allegations of electoral malpractice and announced that he would challenge the results at the Supreme Court. Following the declaration of the election results, violent clashes erupted between supporters of the two candidates in Conakry and the western cities of Pita and Labé, in which some 10 people were killed and 200 injured, obliging Konaté to impose a national state of emergency on 17 November. The election of Condé, who was of the Malinké ethnic group, was reported to have exacerbated long-standing tensions between the Malinké and Peul (Diallo's ethnic group).

The results of the presidential election were confirmed by the Supreme Court on 2 December 2010. The AU subsequently restored Guinea's membership, which had been suspended following the coup in December 2008, and ended all other sanctions in force. The state of emergency was ended on 10 December 2010, and Konaté relinquished the presidency, urging the country's armed forces to support Condé (who had announced plans to establish a truth and reconciliation commission in the country). Condé was inaugurated on 21 December, becoming the country's first democratically elected President. He subsequently nominated members of his new administration, including Fall, who became Secretary of State to the Presidency. A hitherto relatively unknown economist, Mohamed Saïd Fofana, was appointed Prime Minister. Kerfala Yansané, the Minister of the Economy and Finance in the transitional Government was retained in the post, while Condé assumed responsibility for defence.

In early April 2011 in anticipation of the return of Diallo to Conakry, Condé placed a ban upon demonstrations. Demonstrators defied the ban, leading to violent clashes with security forces in which, according to the UFDG, three activists were killed and 60 wounded. Diallo left Guinea and went into exile in May.

On 18 July 2011 in an apparent assassination attempt against Condé, a rocket-propelled grenade landed in the president's residence, killing at least one bodyguard and wounding several others. Shooting also occurred in the vicinity. The Government attributed the attacks to former senior officers in the army.

Meanwhile, in mid-June 2011 the CENI stated that legislative elections would be held by the end of the year, contingent on the Government and opposition reaching agreement on the issue of the voters' list. The Government sought to compile a completely new list, while the opposition preferred a revision of the current list, and claimed that the Government would seek to manipulate a new list to their electoral advantage. In September it was announced that the poll would be held on 29 December. Opposition groups objected that the proposed date would not provide sufficient time to instigate the electoral reforms they believed to be necessary. On 27 September, on the eve of what had been planned as a day of national reconciliation in remembrance of the violent events of September 2009, opposition supporters clashed with police in demonstrations over the issues of the timing of the election and voters' list reform. At least two demonstrators were reported to have been killed, while prosecution authorities stated that 322 people had been arrested. The events were condemned by international observers, including Amnesty International and the Government of the USA. In early October it was announced that voter list reform had been postponed.

In October 2011 the formation was announced of a coalition of political parties, the Front d'union pour la démocratie et le progrès (FDP). Mamadou Baadikko Bah, President of the Union des forces démocratiques (UFD), assumed the responsibility of co-ordinator of the FDP committee. In early December numerous casualties were reported when security forces dispersed a meeting of Kouyaté's Parti de l'espoir pour le développement national (PEDN) in Kankan. On 20 December it was announced that the scheduled legislative elections would be postponed. At the same time, 15 opposition activists convicted for their involvement in the events of 27 September were pardoned, while the enforced retirement of some 4,600 soldiers in late December was considered by some to be a significant gesture towards reform on the part of Condé. Nevertheless, talks scheduled for early January 2012 to agree a date for elections were subsequently boycotted by the opposition. In mid-January at least one person was reportedly killed during riots caused by power outages in the bauxite mining town of Kamsar, some 300 km north-west of Conakry.

Although it had been stated in February 2012 that the legislative elections would take place in May, in early March Lounceny Camara confirmed 8 July as the election date. Leading opposition figures again maintained that electoral lists could not successfully be updated prior to this date, and in late April President Condé announced the postponement of the elections, although no new date for their holding was given.

Foreign Affairs

Regional relations

Relations between Guinea and several of its neighbours, most notably Sierra Leone and Liberia, have repeatedly been strained. In August 1999 the Liberian Government declared a state of emergency, claiming that an invasion force had entered Liberia from Guinea, and the border between the two countries was closed. None the less, at an extraordinary summit meeting of ECOWAS leaders in mid-September, Conté and President Charles Taylor of Liberia made pledges of good neighbourliness and non-aggression. The functions of the Mano River Union (MRU, see p. 451), comprising Guinea, Liberia and Sierra Leone, were to be reactivated, and a joint committee on border security was to be established.

Liberia reopened the border with Guinea in February 2000, but in July the Liberian Government reported renewed fighting, apparently following an attack by rebel groups allegedly based in Guinea. In January 2001 Liberia accused the Guinean Government of having supported the recent shelling of towns in its Foya district and recalled its ambassador from Conakry. Conté boycotted an ECOWAS conference in Abuja, Nigeria, in April, which had been organized to discuss the conflict in the countries of the MRU, in protest against Taylor's attendance: Liberia had recently expelled the ambassadors of Guinea and Sierra Leone and also sealed its borders with the two countries. As the peace process in Sierra Leone advanced in mid-2001, violent unrest in Guinea also abated. In June the Sierra Leone President, Ahmed Tejan Kabbah, and Conté met in Kambia, in northern Sierra Leone, to discuss regional tensions; following the discussions it was announced that the commercial highway between Conakry and the Sierra Leonean capital, Freetown, closed since 1998, was to reopen. In August 2001 the Liberian authorities withdrew all restrictions imposed on the Guinean and Sierra Leonean diplomatic presences in the Liberian capital, Monrovia, and the ambassadors of the two countries resumed their duties. At the end of September Taylor announced that Liberia was to reopen its borders with Guinea and Sierra Leone.

In February 2002, as violence by rebel groups in Liberia escalated and extended to the outskirts of Monrovia, the Guinean authorities denied allegations, made by Taylor (and subsequently reiterated by Guinean opposition leader Jean-Marie Doré), that Guinea supported rebels of the Liberians United for Reconciliation and Democracy (LURD—see Liberia). In late February Taylor, Conté and Kabbah participated in a summit in Rabat, Morocco, to discuss the cross-border insurgencies affecting the three countries. Following further meetings of ministers from the three countries, agreement was reached on the deployment of joint defence and security troops along the common borders to facilitate the return of refugees and to monitor the movement of small arms in the region. Relations with Liberia improved markedly from August 2003, when Taylor was forced into exile and the incumbent Government, rebel factions, political opposition and civil organizations in Liberia reached a peace agreement providing for the formation of a transitional power-sharing government and legislature. Sékou Damate Conneh, the Chairman of LURD, who was reported to be an associate of President Conté, returned to Liberia from Guinea in September.

Relations between Guinea and Sierra Leone were complicated in the early 2000s by the ongoing dispute over ownership of the border town of Yenga, in a reportedly diamond-rich region of Sierra Leone, which Guinean troops had occupied in 1998. In a joint statement in September 2004, signed by Presidents Conté and Kabbah, it was announced that both countries recognized Yenga as belonging to Sierra Leone, on the basis of a border agreement of 1912 between the British and French colonial powers.

The protracted conflicts in Liberia and Sierra Leone, and the civil conflict in Côte d'Ivoire from 2002, have resulted in the presence in Guinea of large numbers of refugees, variously estimated to number 5%–15% of the total population. In December 2010 further political violence in Côte d'Ivoire caused a mass flight of civilians to neighbouring countries, several hundred taking refuge in Guinea. In that year the office of the UN High Commissioner for Refugees assessed that it was providing assistance to some 15,800 refugees in Guinea, of which the majority were from Liberia.

In September 2011 President Alpha Condé claimed that the assassination attempt made against him that July had been planned in Dakar, the capital of Senegal, and accused the Governments of The Gambia and Senegal of complicity in the attack. Both governments denied the accusations.

Other external relations

Relations with both the Government of France and with private French interests strengthened considerably in the 1990s: official assistance from, and trade with, France is of great importance to the Guinean economy, as is French participation in the mining sector and in newly privatized organizations. However, in the early 2000s military assistance from France to Guinea was reduced and, to some extent, supplanted by support from other sources: Guinea signed a pact of military co-operation with Russia in 2001, and received military aid from the People's Republic of China in 2002, while in mid-2002 the US military participated in the training of Guinean troops. Franco-Guinean relations were strained in late 2009, after a spokesperson for the military junta accused the French Minister of Foreign and European Affairs, Bernard Kouchner, of involvement in the attempted assassination of Capt. Moussa Dadis Camara (see above). Following the installation of a new transitional Government in February 2010 (see above), France announced the resumption of civilian and military co-operation with Guinea.

CONSTITUTION AND GOVERNMENT

The Constitution adopted on 7 May 2010 defines the clear separation of the powers of the executive, the legislature and the judiciary. The President of the Republic, who is Head of State, must be elected by an absolute majority of the votes cast, and a second round of voting is held should no candidate obtain such a majority at a first round. The duration of the presidential mandate is five years, renewable only once, and elections are by universal adult suffrage. The President appoints a Prime Minister, who is Head of Government, and proposes the structure and composition of the Government for approval by the President. Legislative power is vested in the Assemblée nationale. The legislature is elected, by universal suffrage, with a five-year mandate.

Local administration is based on eight administrative entities (the city of Conakry and seven administrative regions) each under the authority of an appointed Governor; the country is sub-divided into 33 prefectures. Conakry, which comprises a separate administrative unit, is divided into five communes. The 33 prefectures outside of Conakry are sub-divided into 303 communes.

REGIONAL AND INTERNATIONAL CO-OPERATION

Guinea is a member of the African Union (see p. 189) and of the Economic Community of West African States (ECOWAS, see p. 264). Guinea is also a member of the Gambia River Basin Development Organization (OMVG, see p. 450), of the Africa Rice Center (AfricaRice, see p. 444) and of the Mano River Union (see p. 451).

Guinea became a member of the UN in 1958 and was admitted to the World Trade Organization (WTO, see p. 433) in 1995.

Guinea participates in the Group of 77 (G77, see p. 450) developing countries and is a member of the International Coffee Organization (see p. 445).

ECONOMIC AFFAIRS

In 2010, according to estimates by the World Bank, Guinea's gross national income (GNI), measured at average 2008–10 prices, was US $3,972m., equivalent to $400 per head (or $1,020 on an international purchasing-power parity basis). During 2001–10, it was estimated, the population increased at an average annual rate of 1.8%, while gross domestic product (GDP) per head increased, in real terms, by an average of 1.0% per year during 2001–10. Overall GDP increased, in real terms, at an average annual rate of 2.8% in 2001–10; it declined by 0.3% in 2009, but growth of 1.9% was recorded in 2010.

According to the African Development Bank (AfDB), agriculture (including hunting, forestry and fishing) contributed 22.5% of GDP in 2010. About 78.9% of the labour force were employed in the agricultural sector in mid-2012, according to FAO estimates. The principal cash crops are fruits, oil palm, groundnuts and coffee. Important staple crops include rice, cassava, maize and plantains. The attainment of self-sufficiency in rice and other basic foodstuffs remains a priority. The food supply is supplemented by the rearing of cattle and other livestock. The Government has made efforts towards the commercial exploitation of Guinea's forest resources (forests cover about two-thirds of the country's land area) and substantial fishing stocks. According to the World Bank, during 2001–10 agricultural GDP increased at an average annual rate of 3.8%; according to the AfDB, growth in agricultural GDP in 2010 was 3.2%.

Industry (including mining, manufacturing, construction and power) contributed an estimated 44.5% of GDP in 2010, according to the AfDB. An estimated 5.8% of the employed labour force were engaged in the industrial sector at the time of the 1996 census. According to the World Bank, industrial GDP increased at an average annual rate of 4.8% in 2001–10; growth in 2010 was 6.8%.

According to the AfDB, mining contributed an estimated 26.0% of GDP in 2010. Only 1.1% of the employed labour force were engaged in the sector at the time of the 1996 census. Guinea is the world's foremost exporter of bauxite and the second largest producer of bauxite ore (from which aluminium is extracted), possessing between one-quarter and one-third of known reserves of the mineral. In 2008 aluminium ores and concentrates accounted for 51.3% of the country's total export earnings. In recent years a greater proportion of bauxite output has been processed into alumina in Guinea; various plans to increase the production of alumina have been proposed. Exploitation of valuable reserves of high-grade iron ore at Mt Nimba, near the border with Liberia, has been impeded by political instability in the region. Of Guinea's other known mineral deposits, only granite is exploitable on a commercial scale. The GDP of the mining sector increased at an average annual rate of 2.0% in 2000–06, according to the IMF. According to the AfDB, the sector's GDP increased by 1.1% in 2010.

The manufacturing sector remains largely undeveloped, contributing only an estimated 7.0% of GDP in 2010, according to the AfDB. At the time of the 1996 census, 2.8% of the employed labour force were engaged in the manufacturing sector. Other than the country's one alumina smelter, most industrial companies are involved in import-substitution, including the processing of agricultural products and the manufacture of construction materials. According to the World Bank, manufacturing GDP increased at an average annual rate of 3.4% in 2001–08. It increased by 1.2% in 2010, according to the AfDB.

The construction sector contributed 11.0% of GDP in 2010, according to the AfDB. At the time of the 1996 census, the sector engaged 1.8% of the employed labour force. According to AfDB figures, the sector grew by 4.5% in 2010.

Electricity generation is, at present, insufficient to meet demand, and power failures outside the mining and industrial sectors (in which the largest operators generate their own power supplies) have been frequent. However, Guinea possesses considerable hydroelectric potential. The 75-MW Garafiri dam project was inaugurated in 1999, and a further major scheme, at Kaléta, was scheduled for completion in the early 2010s. In the mean time, some 600,000 metric tons of hydrocarbons are imported annually, and in 2008 imports of petroleum products accounted for 32.7% of the value of total merchandise imports.

According to the AfDB, the services sector contributed an estimated 33.1% of GDP in 2010. According to the World Bank, during 2001–10 the sector's GDP decreased at an average annual rate of 1.9%; it increased by 16.6% in 2009, but decreased by 7.1% in 2010.

In 2010 Guinea recorded a visible trade surplus of US $66.3m., but there was a deficit of $329.2m. on the current account of the balance of payments. The principal suppliers of imports in 2008 were the Netherlands (which supplied 20.6% of the total), France, the United Kingdom, the People's Republic of China, Belgium and the USA. The principal markets for exports in that year were France (which took 24.5% of exports), Switzerland-Liechtenstein, Russia, Spain, Ireland, the USA and Germany. The principal exports in 2008 were aluminium ore and concentrate, and gold. The principal imports included refined petroleum products, machinery and transport equipment, food and live animals, and chemicals and related products.

In 2008 Guinea's overall budget deficit was projected at 200,000m. FG. Guinea's general government gross debt was 16,767,330m. FG in 2009, equivalent to 77.0% of GDP. The country's total external debt was US $2,926m. at the end of 2009, of which $2,827m. was public and publicly guaranteed debt. In that year the cost of debt-servicing long-term public and publicly guaranteed debt and repayments to the IMF was equivalent to 11.2% of the value of exports of goods, services and income (excluding workers' remittances). Annual inflation averaged 17.5% in 2001–10, according to the AfDB; consumer prices increased by an average of 15.8% in 2010.

Guinea's potential for the attainment of wealth is substantial, owing to its valuable mineral deposits (particularly bauxite, gold, and iron ore), water resources and generally favourable climate; however, the economy remains over-dependent on revenue from bauxite reserves and on external assistance, while the country's infrastructure is inadequate and its manufacturing base narrow. Economic growth was modest in the early 2000s, chiefly as a result of insecurity in the region, a decline in the price of bauxite (Guinea's principal export) and an increase in the international prices of imports, most significantly petroleum products. The death of President Lansana Conté in December 2008 precipitated the assumption of power by a military junta, and a period of political and economic uncertainty. The military takeover was widely condemned by the international community, and resulted in the suspension of all non-humanitarian aid by the USA and the EU, and relations with the IMF (which had previously supported Poverty Reduction and Growth Facility arrangements). The inauguration of former opposition leader Alpha Condé as President in December 2010, however, was accompanied by Guinea's return to membership of the African Union that same month, and the country was expected to benefit further from regional and international recognition of its new Government. The new administration declared that it would investigate the alleged corruption of the previous military regime, and in early 2011 the new Prime Minister, Mohamed Saïd Fofana (an economist), deplored the economic situation inherited from the preceding Government, citing growth of only 1.2% in 2010 (following a contraction in 2009), a rise in inflation to about 21% and substantial debt arrears. In September 2011 significant reforms to mining legislation were implemented that granted the Government a free shareholding of 15% in any mining enterprise undertaken in Guinea, with the option to purchase additional shares up to a total of 35%. The new legislation also instituted heightened standards of transparency and local community development responsibilities for mining companies operating within Guinea. The Government subsequently announced its intention to review all contracts made with foreign companies for mineral extraction. Although the consequences of these reforms were not immediately clear, it appeared likely that these legislative changes would not deter foreign-owned companies seeking to exploit Guinea's considerable mineral resources, which, besides bauxite, included significant reserves of iron ore recently discovered within the country's territory.

PUBLIC HOLIDAYS

2013: 1 January (New Year's Day), 23 January* (Mouloud, Birth of Muhammad), 1 April (Easter Monday), 1 May (Labour Day), 7 August* (Id al-Fitr, end of Ramadan), 27 August (Anniversary of Women's Revolt), 28 September (Referendum Day), 2 October (Republic Day), 1 November (All Saints' Day), 22 November (Day of 1970 Invasion), 25 December (Christmas).

* These holidays are determined by the Islamic lunar calendar and may vary by one or two days from the dates given.

Statistical Survey

Source (unless otherwise stated): Direction Nationale de la Statistique, BP 221, Conakry; tel. 21-33-12; e-mail dnstat@biasy.net; internet www.stat-guinea.org/.

Area and Population

AREA, POPULATION AND DENSITY

Area (sq km)	245,857*
Population (census results)	
4–17 February 1983	4,533,240†
31 December 1996‡	
Males	3,497,551
Females	3,658,855
Total	7,156,406
Population (UN estimates at mid-year)§	
2010	9,981,590
2011	10,221,804
2012	10,480,709
Density (per sq km) at mid-2012	42.6

* 94,926 sq miles.
† Excluding adjustment for underenumeration.
‡ Including refugees from Liberia and Sierra Leone (estimated at 640,000).
§ Source: UN, *World Population Prospects: The 2010 Revision*.

POPULATION BY AGE AND SEX

(UN estimates at mid-2012)

	Males	Females	Total
0–14	2,272,860	2,187,288	4,460,148
15–64	2,868,360	2,806,848	5,675,208
65 and over	155,644	189,709	345,353
Total	5,296,864	5,183,845	10,480,709

Source: UN, *World Population Prospects: The 2010 Revision*.

ETHNIC GROUPS

1995 (percentages): Peul 38.7; Malinké 23.3; Soussou 11.1; Kissi 5.9; Kpellé 4.5; Others 16.5 (Source: La Francophonie).

ADMINISTRATIVE DIVISIONS

(1996 census)

Region	Area (sq km)	Population	Density (per sq km)	Principal city
Conakry	450	1,092,936	2,428.7	Conakry
Basse-Guinée	47,063	1,460,577	31.0	Kindia
Moyenne-Guinée	52,939	1,639,617	31.0	Labé
Haute-Guinée	99,437	1,407,734	14.2	Kankan
Guinée Forestière	45,968	1,555,542	33.8	N'Zérékoré
Total	245,857	7,156,406	29.1	

Note: The regions were subsequently reorganized. The new regions (which in each case share their name with the regional capital) are: Boké; Conakry; Faranah; Kankan; Kindia; Labé; Mamou; and N'Zérékoré.

PRINCIPAL TOWNS

(population at 1996 census)

Conakry (capital)	1,092,936	Kindia	96,074
N'Zérékoré	107,329	Guéckédou	79,140
Kankan	100,192	Kamsar	61,526

Mid-2009 (incl. suburbs, UN estimate): Conakry 1,653,495 (Source: UN, *World Urbanization Prospects: The 2009 Revision*).

BIRTHS AND DEATHS

(annual averages, UN estimates)

	1995–2000	2000–05	2005–10
Birth rate (per 1,000)	43.4	41.5	39.9
Death rate (per 1,000)	18.1	15.7	13.9

Source: UN, *World Population Prospects: The 2010 Revision*.

Life expectancy (years at birth, WHO estimates): 52 (males 49; females 55) in 2009 (Source: WHO, *World Health Statistics*).

ECONOMICALLY ACTIVE POPULATION

('000 persons at 1996 census)

	Males	Females	Total
Agriculture, hunting and forestry	1,140,775	1,281,847	2,422,622
Fishing	9,969	889	10,858
Mining and quarrying	26,599	8,376	34,975
Manufacturing	84,974	5,911	90,885
Electricity, gas and water supply	4,366	324	4,690
Construction	59,802	724	60,526
Wholesale and retail trade; repair of motor vehicles and motorcycles and personal and household goods	176,527	191,230	367,757
Restaurants and hotels	3,162	2,790	5,952
Transport, storage and communications	75,374	1,696	77,070
Financial intermediation	1,728	626	2,354
Real estate, renting and business activities	877	209	1,086
Public administration and defence; compulsory social security	50,401	12,791	63,192
Education	15,044	3,773	18,817
Health and social work	4,762	3,522	8,284
Other community, social and personal service activities	44,897	48,292	93,189
Private households with employed persons	5,553	6,202	11,755
Extra-territorial organizations and bodies	3,723	1,099	4,822
Total employed	1,708,533	1,570,301	3,278,834

Mid-2012 ('000 persons): Agriculture, etc. 3,999; Total labour force 5,070 (Source: FAO).

Health and Welfare

KEY INDICATORS

Total fertility rate (children per woman, 2009)	5.3
Under-5 mortality rate (per 1,000 live births, 2009)	142
HIV/AIDS (% of persons aged 15–49, 2009)	1.3
Physicians (per 1,000 head, 2004)	0.1
Hospital beds (per 1,000 head, 2005)	0.3
Health expenditure (2008): US $ per head (PPP)	58
Health expenditure (2008): % of GDP	5.5
Health expenditure (2008): public (% of total)	13.6
Access to water (% of persons, 2008)	71
Access to sanitation (% of persons, 2008)	19
Total carbon dioxide emissions ('000 metric tons, 2007)	1,388.7
Carbon dioxide emissions per head (metric tons, 2007)	0.1
Human Development Index (2011): ranking	178
Human Development Index (2011): value	0.344

For sources and definitions, see explanatory note on p. vi.

Agriculture

PRINCIPAL CROPS

('000 metric tons)

	2008	2009	2010
Rice, paddy	1,534.1	1,499.0*	1,614.9*
Maize	952.2	565.7*	580.1*
Fonio	341.2	329.9*	388.6*
Sweet potatoes	204.6	194.5*	174.6*
Cassava (Manioc)	1,122.2	989.3*	1,030.8*
Taro (Cocoyam)*	31.2	27.8	17.5
Yams	27.4	24.0*	24.4*
Sugar cane*	283	283	283
Pulses*	63	50	56
Groundnuts, with shell	315.1	277.0†	291.7†

—continued	2008	2009	2010
Coconuts	48.4†	37.3†	39.0*
Oil palm fruit*	830.0	830.0	830.0
Bananas*	162.0	179.6	201.5
Plantains*	449.7	479.9	461.7
Guavas, mangoes and mangosteens*	166.0	165.0	163.9
Pineapples*	109.0	108.0	107.5
Seed cotton*	42	39	40
Coffee, green†	30.2	34.0	27.0

* FAO estimate(s).
† Unofficial figure(s).

Aggregate production ('000 metric tons, may include official, semi-official or estimated data): Total cereals 3,187.1 in 2008, 2,659.5 in 2009, 2,858.9 in 2010; Total roots and tubers 1,397.5 in 2008, 1,246.4 in 2009, 1,258.1 in 2010; Total vegetables (incl. melons) 515.5 in 2008, 410.5 in 2009, 536.9 in 2010; Total fruits (excl. melons) 1,153.2 in 2008, 1,228.1 in 2009, 1,218.7 in 2010.

Source: FAO.

LIVESTOCK
('000 head, year ending September)

	2008	2009*	2010*
Cattle	4,409	4,652	4,907
Sheep	1,419	1,500	1,586
Goats	1,696	1,800	1,910
Pigs	86.4	90.7	95.2
Chickens*	18,900	20,050	22,500

* FAO estimates.

Source: FAO.

LIVESTOCK PRODUCTS
('000 metric tons)

	2008	2009*	2010*
Cattle meat	49.4	52.0	55.0
Chicken meat*	6.8	7.2	8.1
Sheep meat	5.6	6.0	6.3
Goat meat	8.4	8.9	9.0
Game meat*	4.7	5.0	5.4
Cows' milk*	106.0	111.9	115.0
Goats' milk*	11.5	12.2	12.7
Hen eggs*	22.2	23.5	23.5

* FAO estimates.

Source: FAO.

Forestry

ROUNDWOOD REMOVALS
('000 cubic metres, excl. bark, FAO estimates)

	2007	2008	2009
Sawlogs, veneer logs and logs for sleepers	138	138	138
Other industrial wood	513	513	513
Fuel wood	11,791	11,845	11,901
Total	12,442	12,496	12,552

2010: Production assumed to be unchanged from 2009 (FAO estimates).

Source: FAO.

SAWNWOOD PRODUCTION
('000 cubic metres, incl. railway sleepers, FAO estimates)

	2007	2008	2009
Total (all broadleaved)	30.0	30.0	30.0

2010: Production assumed to be unchanged from 2009 (FAO estimate).

Source: FAO.

Fishing

('000 metric tons, live weight)

	2007	2008	2009*
Freshwater fishes*	4.0	4.0	4.0
Sea catfishes	3.9	8.9	8.8
Bobo croaker	4.6	7.7	7.6
West African croakers	3.4	3.9	3.9
Sardinellas	2.5	1.7	1.7
Bonga shad	27.9	32.9	32.9
Total catch (incl. others)*	76.1	86.5	86.1

* FAO estimates.

Source: FAO.

Mining

('000 metric tons unless otherwise indicated)

	2008	2009	2010
Bauxite (dry basis)*	16,000	13,600	15,100
Gold (kilograms)	19,945	18,091	15,217
Salt (unrefined)	15	15	15†
Diamonds ('000 carats)‡	3,098	697	374

* Estimated to be 7% water.
† Estimate.
‡ Including artisanal production.

Source: US Geological Survey.

Industry

SELECTED PRODUCTS
('000 metric tons unless otherwise indicated)

	2006!	2007!	2008!
Palm oil (unrefined)*†	50	50	50
Beer of barley*†	15.6	12.7	16.7
Raw sugar‡	25	25	20
Alumina (calcined equivalent)§	530	527	593
Electric energy (million kWh)‡	872	973	1,000

* Data from FAO.
† Estimates.
‡ Data from UN Industrial Commodity Statistics Database.
§ Data from the US Geological Survey.

Salted, dried or smoked fish ('000 metric tons, FAO estimates): 11.0 in 2000–02 (Source: FAO).

2009: Alumina (calcinated equivalent) 530 (Source: US Geological Survey); Palm oil (unrefined) 50 (unofficial figure; Source: FAO); Beer of barley 16.7 (FAO estimate; Source: FAO).

2010: Alumina (calcinated equivalent) 597; (Source: US Geological Survey); Palm oil (unrefined) 50 (unofficial figure; Source: FAO); Beer of barley 16.7 (FAO estimate; Source: FAO).

Finance

CURRENCY AND EXCHANGE RATES

Monetary Units
100 centimes = 1 franc guinéen (FG or Guinean franc).

Sterling, Dollar and Euro Equivalents (30 November 2011)
£1 sterling = 10,995.418 Guinean francs;
US $1 = 7,044.732 Guinean francs;
€1 = 9,452.622 Guinean francs;
100,000 Guinean francs = £9.09 = $14.20 = €10.58.

Average Exchange Rate (Guinean francs per US $)
2008 4601.7
2009 4801.1
2010 5726.1

BUDGET

('000 million Guinean francs)

Revenue*	2006†	2007†	2008‡
Mining-sector revenue	675	572	758
Other revenue	1,497	1,905	2,472
Tax revenue	1,337	1,775	2,229
Taxes on domestic production and trade	620	875	1,079
Taxes on international trade	436	473	681
Non-tax revenue	161	130	243
Total	2,172	2,477	3,230

Expenditure§	2006†	2007†	2008‡
Current expenditure	2,188	1,954	2,676
Wages and salaries	444	607	881
Other goods and services	810	559	872
Subsidies and transfers	397	375	402
Interest due on external debt	274	220	217
Interest due on domestic debt	263	193	304
Capital expenditure	672	608	1,136
Domestically financed	295	294	334
Externally financed	377	314	802
Total	2,860	2,562	3,812

* Excluding grants received ('000 million Guinean francs): 225 in 2006 (estimate); 143 in 2007 (estimate); 390 in 2008 (projection).

† Estimates.

‡ Projections.

§ Excluding lending minus repayments ('000 million Guinean francs): 11 in 2006 (estimate); 5 in 2007 (estimate); 8 in 2008 (projection).

Source: IMF, *Guinea: First Review Under the Three-Year Arrangement Under the Poverty Reduction and Growth Facility, Request for Waiver of Nonobservance of Performance Criteria, Modification of Performance Criteria, Augmentation of Access, and Financing Assurances Review - Staff Report; Staff Statement; Press Release on the Executive Board Discussion; and Statement by the Executive Director for Guinea* (August 2008).

INTERNATIONAL RESERVES

(US $ million at 31 December)

	2004	2005
Gold (national valuation)	1.29	1.27
IMF special drawing rights	—	0.02
Reserve position in IMF	0.12	0.11
Foreign exchange	110.37	94.93
Total	111.78	96.33

2006 (US $ million at 31 December): Reserve position in IMF 0.11.

2007 (US $ million at 31 December): IMF special drawing rights 12.20; Reserve position in IMF 0.12.

2008 (US $ million at 31 December): IMF special drawing rights 2.43; Reserve position in IMF 0.12.

2009 (US $ million at 31 December): IMF special drawing rights 128.88; Reserve position in IMF 0.12.

2010 (US $ million at 31 December): IMF special drawing rights 116.16; Reserve position in IMF 0.12.

Source: IMF, *International Financial Statistics*.

MONEY SUPPLY

(million Guinean francs at 31 December)

	2003	2004	2005
Currency outside banks	478,133	536,169	786,587
Demand deposits at commercial banks	386,359	518,469	590,420
Total (incl. others)	893,055	1,143,312	1,394,203

Source: IMF, *International Financial Statistics*.

COST OF LIVING

(Consumer Price Index for Conakry; base: 2002 = 100)

	2004	2005	2006
Foodstuffs, beverages and tobacco	147.1	201.6	287.3
Clothing and shoes	109.8	121.9	151.6
Housing, water, electricity and gas	114.0	142.7	174.7
All items (incl. others)	130.1	170.9	230.2

Source: IMF, *Guinea: Selected Issues and Statistical Appendix* (January 2008).

Cost of Living (Consumer Price Index; base: 2000 = 100): 313.1 in 2007; 370.6 in 2008; 388.0 in 2009; 449.3 in 2010 (Source: African Development Bank).

NATIONAL ACCOUNTS

('000 million Guinean francs at current prices)

Expenditure on the Gross Domestic Product

	2008	2009	2010
Government final consumption expenditure	1,270.8	1,889.1	3,324.5
Private final consumption expenditure	16,253.0	17,896.4	20,554.9
Gross fixed capital formation	4,429.2	3,631.8	4,851.7
Changes in inventories	140.9	−8.5	4.8
Total domestic expenditure	22,093.9	23,408.8	28,735.9
Exports of goods and services	7,009.0	5,357.0	8,864.5
Less Imports of goods and services	8,322.4	6,640.7	10,591.9
GDP at market prices	20,780.4	22,125.0	27,008.5

Gross Domestic Product by Economic Activity

	2008	2009	2010
Agriculture, livestock, forestry and fishing	4,741.2	5,232.1	5,490.6
Mining and quarrying	4,611.3	4,258.2	6,359.7
Manufacturing	1,297.7	1,492.4	1,715.8
Electricity, gas and water	78.1	90.7	104.2
Construction	2,063.7	2,304.9	2,695.3
Trade, restaurants and hotels	3,240.9	3,579.8	4,179.7
Transport and communications	1,067.3	1,193.7	1,388.3
Public administration and defence	1,458.6	1,511.5	1,839.2
Other services	447.4	559.4	673.8
GDP at factor cost	19,006.2	20,222.7	24,446.6
Indirect taxes	1,774.3	1,902.0	2,562.0
GDP at purchasers' values	20,780.4	22,125.0	27,008.5

Note: Deduction for imputed bank service charge assumed to be distributed at origin.

Source: African Development Bank.

BALANCE OF PAYMENTS

(US $ million)

	2008	2009	2010
Exports of goods f.o.b.	1,342.0	1,049.7	1,471.2
Imports of goods f.o.b.	−1,366.1	−1,060.1	−1,404.9
Trade balance	−24.1	−10.4	66.3
Exports of services	102.9	72.2	62.4
Imports of services	−444.3	−330.7	−395.5
Balance on goods and services	−365.5	−268.8	−266.9
Other income received	9.9	22.2	14.9
Other income paid	−101.1	−190.4	−92.0
Balance on goods, services and income	−456.7	−437.1	−344.0
Current transfers received	102.6	61.9	81.5
Current transfers paid	−86.0	−51.5	−66.8
Current balance	−440.1	−426.7	−329.2

—continued	2008	2009	2010
Capital account (net)	34.8	16.4	16.9
Direct investment abroad	–63.6	—	—
Direct investment from abroad	381.9	49.8	101.4
Portfolio investment assets	—	—	0.1
Other investment assets	–44.1	56.1	–77.4
Other investment liabilities	162.4	409.9	289.5
Net errors and omissions	–16.2	48.6	38.7
Overall balance	15.0	154.1	39.8

Source: IMF, *International Financial Statistics*.

External Trade

PRINCIPAL COMMODITIES
(US $ million)

Imports c.i.f.	2006	2007	2008
Food and live animals	211.3	168.4	187.5
Cereals and cereal preparations	163.3	114.0	113.0
Rice	133.5	76.3	75.3
Rice, semi-milled or wholly milled	133.4	76.3	67.4
Rice, broken	131.9	70.8	64.7
Sugar, sugar preparations and honey	19.8	20.6	31.3
Sugar and honey	18.5	19.6	28.7
Beverages and tobacco	40.8	32.1	37.9
Tobacco and tobacco manufactures	39.3	29.8	32.8
Cigarettes	39.1	29.7	32.8
Mineral fuels, lubricants, etc.	261.5	334.4	605.0
Petroleum products, refined	257.4	331.0	601.1
Chemicals and related products	87.1	87.7	136.3
Inorganic chemicals	32.8	21.3	56.2
Inorganic chemical elements, oxides and halogen salts	27.8	14.6	41.8
Medicinal and pharmaceutical products	17.2	25.0	25.8
Medicaments (incl. veterinary medicaments)	15.6	24.6	25.1
Basic manufactures	144.8	155.1	233.3
Non-metallic mineral manufactures	36.9	36.4	87.0
Lime, cement and fabricated construction materials	31.6	30.8	76.3
Cement	28.3	23.4	68.4
Iron and steel	40.3	27.9	45.8
Machinery and transport equipment	246.2	427.1	538.6
Machinery specialized for particular industries	75.8	144.7	161.4
Road vehicles	52.7	72.2	120.8
Passenger motor vehicles (excl. buses)	17.5	33.5	48.9
Miscellaneous manufactured articles	41.6	54.2	70.9
Total (incl. others)	1,063.9	1,281.5	1,835.5

Exports f.o.b.	2006	2007	2008
Crude materials (inedible) except fuels	456.4	792.2	785.1
Aluminium ore and concentrate	429.9	775.3	734.5
Chemicals and related products	0.3	12.5	6.2
Aluminium hydroxide	0.0	12.3	5.5
Miscellaneous manufactured articles	2.7	21.6	119.5
Unused postage; stamp-impressed papers; stock; cheque books, etc.	0.0	18.8	112.7
Gold, non-monetary (excl. gold ores and concentrates), unwrought or semi-manufactured	207.0	181.2	458.0
Total (incl. others)	770.5	1,059.0	1,430.5

Source: UN, *International Trade Statistics Yearbook*.

PRINCIPAL TRADING PARTNERS
(US $ million)

Imports c.i.f.	2006	2007	2008
Australia	12.0	19.4	71.7
Belgium	78.1	197.4	95.6
Brazil	16.4	20.8	53.8
China, People's Republic	80.1	74.7	123.4
Côte d'Ivoire	169.3	55.2	31.1
France (incl. Monaco)	110.7	109.0	185.4
Gabon	7.3	2.9	37.6
Germany	13.4	14.9	21.7
India	83.1	63.7	48.4
Indonesia	19.9	12.2	11.5
Italy	8.2	8.7	27.8
Japan	34.4	58.4	47.4
Morocco	14.5	9.0	14.9
Netherlands	59.4	174.8	377.6
South Africa	28.5	31.0	45.2
Spain	12.5	58.7	41.0
Thailand	21.0	14.2	28.1
Turkey	7.4	19.5	15.4
Ukraine	15.0	7.7	11.4
United Arab Emirates	9.9	22.8	39.4
United Kingdom	34.2	36.0	144.3
USA	57.6	78.5	95.1
Total (incl. others)	1,063.9	1,281.5	1,835.5

Exports f.o.b.	2006	2007	2008
Belgium	8.7	0.4	6.9
Canada	24.3	50.9	57.7
China, People's Republic	13.6	1.3	19.9
France (incl. Monaco)	51.2	187.0	349.8
Germany	61.9	84.4	83.9
Ireland	69.7	196.1	106.3
Morocco	2.3	0.8	2.7
Netherlands	1.6	7.4	2.4
Romania	12.0	14.7	0.0
Russia	0.0	98.7	151.3
Spain	88.7	163.8	141.5
Switzerland-Liechtenstein	11.5	34.3	278.4
Ukraine	18.8	14.6	40.7
United Kingdom	0.2	6.5	0.3
USA	79.6	145.5	96.1
Total (incl. others)	770.5	1,059.0	1,430.5

Source: UN, *International Trade Statistics Yearbook*.

Transport

RAILWAYS
(estimated traffic)

	1991	1992	1993
Freight ton-km (million)	660	680	710

Source: UN Economic Commission for Africa, *African Statistical Yearbook*.

ROAD TRAFFIC
('000, motor vehicles in use, estimates)

	2001	2002	2003
Passenger cars	41.6	43.1	47.5
Buses and coaches	24.8	20.5	20.9
Lorries and vans	11.1	10.5	15.7

SHIPPING

Merchant Fleet
(registered at 31 December)

	2007	2008	2009
Number of vessels	42	42	44
Total displacement ('000 grt)	19.5	19.5	23.3

Source: IHS Fairplay, *World Fleet Statistics*.

International Sea-borne Freight Traffic
('000 metric tons)

	2001	2002	2003
Goods loaded	2,424	2,595	2,828
Goods unloaded	2,043	2,178	2,453

CIVIL AVIATION
(traffic on scheduled services)

	1997	1998	1999
Kilometres flown (million)	1	1	1
Passengers carried ('000)	36	36	59
Passenger-km (million)	55	55	94
Total ton-km (million)	6	6	10

Source: UN, *Statistical Yearbook*.

Tourism

FOREIGN VISITOR ARRIVALS*

Country of origin	2005	2006	2007
Belgium	1,126	970	685
Canada	1,135	1,023	798
China, People's Repub.	1,575	1,696	1,874
Côte d'Ivoire	2,453	1,261	1,103
France	7,984	7,376	4,488
Germany	1,029	1,114	603
Mali	1,295	818	870
Senegal	4,523	3,406	2,171
Sierra Leone	1,328	1,620	802
USA	3,237	380	911
Total (incl. others)†	45,330	46,096	30,194

* Arrivals of non-resident tourists at national borders, by country of residence.

† Air arrivals at Conakry airport.

Receipts from tourism (US $ million, incl. passenger transport): 1.1 in 2007; 4.0 in 2008; 4.9 in 2009.

Source: World Tourism Organization.

Communications Media

	2008	2009	2010
Telephones ('000 main lines in use)	27	22	18
Mobile cellular telephones ('000 subscribers)	2,750	3,489	4,000
Internet users ('000)	90	95	n.a.
Broadband subscribers ('000)	n.a.	n.a.	0.5

Personal computers: 45,000 (4.9 per 1,000 persons) in 2005.

Source: International Telecommunication Union.

Television receivers ('000 in use): 351 in 2000 (Source: UNESCO, *Statistical Yearbook*).

Radio receivers ('000 in use): 380 in 1999 (Source: UNESCO, *Statistical Yearbook*).

Daily newspapers: 2 titles in 2004 (Source: UNESCO, *Statistical Yearbook*).

Non-daily newspapers: 1 title in 1996 (average circulation 20,000) (Source: UNESCO, *Statistical Yearbook*).

Education

(2009/10 unless otherwise indicated)

			Students ('000)		
	Institutions*	Teachers	Males	Females	Total
Pre-primary	202	3,599	61.7	59.0	120.7
Primary	5,765	34,451	802.9	650.5	1,453.4
Secondary†	557	17,564	357.1	203.4	560.5
General	n.a.	16,988	361.1	212.0	573.1
Tertiary‡	7	2,163	60.6	19.6	80.2

* 1996/97.

† 2008/09.

‡ 2007/08.

Source: mainly UNESCO Institute for Statistics.

Pupil-teacher ratio (primary education, UNESCO estimate): 42.2 in 2009/10 (Source: UNESCO Institute for Statistics).

Adult literacy rate (UNESCO estimates): 39.5% (males 50.8%; females 28.1%) in 2009 (Source: UNESCO Institute for Statistics).

Directory

The Government

HEAD OF STATE

President and Minister of National Defence: ALPHA CONDÉ (inaugurated 21 December 2010).

COUNCIL OF MINISTERS
(May 2012)

Prime Minister: MOHAMED SAÏD FOFANA.

Minister of State, in charge of Public Works and Transport: OUSMANE BAH.

Minister of State, in charge of Energy and the Environment: PAPA KOLY KOUROUMA.

Minister of State, in charge of Security and Civil Protection: Gen. MAMADOUBA TOTO CAMARA.

Minister of the Economy and Finance: KERFALA YANSANÉ.

Minister of Foreign Affairs and Guineans Abroad: EDOUARD GNAKOÏ LAMAHET.

Minister of Justice and Keeper of the Seals: CHRISTIAN SOW.

Minister of Information: DIRIS DIANÉ DORÉ.

Minister of Mines and Geology: MOHAMED LAMINE FOFANA.

Minister of Telecommunications and ICT: HOYÉ GUILAVOGUI.

Minister of the Promotion of Women and Children: NANTÉNIN CHÉRIF KONATÉ.

Minister of Urban Development, Housing and Construction: Gen. MATHURIN BANGO.

Minister of Youth and Youth Employment: SANOUSSI BANTAMA SOW.

Minister of Sport: ABOUBACAR TITI CAMARA.

Minister of Literacy and the Promotion of National Languages: BAMBA CAMARA.

Minister of Industry and Small and Medium-sized Enterprises: RAMATOULAYE BAH.

Minister of Tourism, Hotels and Handicrafts: MARIAMA BALDÉ.

Minister of Stockbreeding: Gen. MAMADOU KORKA DIALLO.

Minister of Employment, Technical Education and Vocational Training: DAMANTANG ALBERT CAMARA.

Minister of Labour and the Civil Service: FATOUMATA TOUNKARA.

Minister of Territorial Decentralization and Political Affairs: ALASSANE CONDÉ.

Minister of Agriculture: JEAN-MARC TELLIANO.

Minister of Commerce: MOHAMED DORVAL DOUMBOUYA.

Minister of Higher Education and Scientific Research: MORIKÉ DAMARO CAMARA.

Minister of Culture and Heritage: AHMED TIDIANE CISSÉ.

Minister of Health and Public Hygiene: Dr NAMAN KÉITA.

Minister of Planning: SOULEYMANE CISSÉ.

Minister of International Co-operation: KOUTOUBOU MOUSTAPHA SANOH.

Minister of Auditing and Economic and Financial Control: ABOUBACAR SIDIKI COULIBALY.

Minister of Pre-university Education: IBRAHIMA KOUROUMA.

Minister of Fisheries and Aquaculture: MOUSSA CONDÉ.

Minister-delegate, in charge of Transport: TIDIANE TRAORÉ.

Minister-delegate, in charge of the Environment: SARAMADY TOURÉ.

Minister-delegate for the Budget: MOHAMED DIARÉ.

Minister-delegate for the Promotion of Women and Children and Social Affairs: DIAKA DIAKITÉ.

Minister-delegate, in charge of Guineans Abroad: ROUGUI BARRY.

Minister-delegate for National Defence: Commdr ABDOUL KABÈLÈ CAMARA.

Minister-delegate to the Minister of Security and Civil Protection, in charge of the Reform of Security Services: MOURAMANI CISSÉ.

MINISTRIES

Office of the President: BP 1000, Boulbinet, Conakry; tel. 30-41-10-16; fax 30-41-16-73.

Office of the Prime Minister: BP 5141, Conakry; tel. 30-41-51-19; fax 30-41-52-82.

Office of the Secretary-General at the Presidency: Conakry.

Ministry of Agriculture: face à la Cité du Port, BP 576, Conakry; tel. 30-41-11-81; fax 30-41-11-69; e-mail dourasano@hotmail.com.

Ministry of Auditing and Economic and Financial Control: Conakry.

Ministry of Commerce: Conakry.

Ministry of Culture and Heritage: Conakry.

Ministry of Decentralization and Local Development: Conakry.

Ministry of the Economy and Finance: Boulbinet, BP 221, Conakry; tel. 30-45-17-95; fax 30-41-30-59.

Ministry of Employment, Technical Education and Vocational Training: Conakry.

Ministry of Energy and the Environment: route du Niger, Coléah, Conakry; tel. 60-22-50-54 (mobile).

Ministry of Fisheries and Aquaculture: face à la Cité du Port, BP 307, Conakry; tel. 30-41-12-58; fax 30-41-43-10; e-mail minipaq.jpl@eti-bull.net; internet www.fis.com/guinea.

Ministry of Foreign Affairs and Guineans Abroad: face au Port, ex-Primature, BP 2519, Conakry; tel. 30-45-12-70; fax 30-41-16-21; internet www.mae.gov.gn.

Ministry of Health and Public Hygiene: blvd du Commerce, BP 585, Conakry; tel. 30-41-20-32; fax 30-41-41-38.

Ministry of Higher Education and Scientific Research: face à la Cathédrale Sainte-Marie, BP 964, Conakry; tel. 30-45-12-17; fax 30-41-20-12.

Ministry of Industry and Small and Medium-sized Enterprises: Conakry.

Ministry of Information: Conakry.

Ministry of International Co-operation: Conakry.

Ministry of Justice: face à l'Immeuble 'La Paternelle', Almamya, Conakry; tel. 30-41-29-60.

Ministry of Labour and the Civil Service: Boulbinet, Conakry; tel. 30-45-20-01.

Ministry of Literacy and the Promotion of National Languages: Conakry.

Ministry of Mines and Geology: BP 295, Conakry; tel. 30-41-38-33; fax 30-41-49-13.

Ministry of National Defence: Camp Samory-Touré, Conakry; tel. 41-11-54.

Ministry of Planning: BP 221, Conakry; tel. 30-44-37-15; fax 30-41-43-50.

Ministry of Pre-university Education: Boulbinet, BP 2201, Conakry; tel. 30-45-19-17.

Ministry of the Promotion of Women and Children: Corniche-Ouest, face au Terminal Conteneurs du Port de Conakry, BP 527, Conakry; tel. 30-45-45-39; fax 30-41-46-60.

Ministry of Public Works and Transport: BP 715, Conakry; tel. 30-41-36-39; fax 30-41-35-77.

Ministry of Security and Civil Protection: Coléah-Domino, Conakry; tel. 30-41-45-50.

Ministry of Sport: Conakry.

Ministry of Stockbreeding: Conakry.

Ministry of Telecommunications and New Information Technologies: BP 3000, Conakry; tel. 30-43-17-81; fax 30-45-18-96.

Ministry of Territorial Decentralization and Political Affairs: face aux Jardins du 2 Octobre, Tombo, BP 2201, Conakry; tel. 30-41-15-10; fax 30-45-45-07.

Ministry of Tourism, Hotels and Handicrafts: BP 1304, Conakry; tel. 30-44-26-06; fax 30-44-49-90.

Ministry of Urban Development, Housing and Construction: Conakry.

Ministry of Youth and Youth Employment: ave du Port Secrétariat, BP 262, Conakry; tel. 30-41-19-59; fax 30-41-19-26.

President and Legislature

PRESIDENT

Presidential Election, First Round, 27 June 2010

Candidate	% of votes
Cellou Dalein Diallo (UFDG)	43.69
Alpha Condé (RPG)	18.25
Sidya Touré (UFR)	13.02
Lansana Kouyaté (PEDN)	7.04
Papa Koly Kouroumah (RDR)	5.74
Ibrahima Abe Sylla (NGR)	3.23
Jean-Marc Telliano (RDIG)	2.33
Others*	6.70
Total	100.00

* There were 17 other candidates.

Presidential Election, Second Round, 7 November 2010

Candidate	Votes	% of votes
Alpha Condé (RPG)	1,474,973	52.52
Cellou Dalein Diallo (UFDG)	1,333,666	47.48
Total	2,808,639	100.00

LEGISLATURE

Assemblée nationale

Palais du Peuple, BP 414, Conakry; tel. 30-41-28-04; fax 30-45-17-00; e-mail s.general@assemblee.gov.gn; internet www.assemblee.gov.gn.

Speaker: Aboubacar Sompare.

General Election, 30 June 2002

Party	% of votes	Seats
Parti de l'unité et du progrès (PUP)	61.57	85
Union pour le progrès et le renouveau (UPR)	26.63	20
Union pour le progrès de la Guinée (UPG)	4.11	3
Parti démocratique de Guinée—Rassemblement démocratique africain (PDG—RDA)	3.40	3
Alliance nationale pour le progrès (ANP)	1.98	2
Union pour le progrès national—Parti pour l'unité et le développement (UPN—PUD)	0.69	1
Others	1.61	—
Total	100.00	114*

* Comprising 76 seats allocated by proportional representation from national party lists and 38 seats filled by voting in single-member constituencies, all of which were won by the PUP.

Election Commission

Commission électorale nationale indépendante (CENI): Villa 17, Cité des Nations, Conakry; tel. 64-24-22-06; e-mail bensekou@ceniguinee.org; internet www.ceniguinee.org; f. 2005; comprises seven representatives of the parliamentary majority, seven representatives of the parliamentary opposition, five representatives of the state administration and three representatives of civil society; Pres. Gen. Siaka Toumany Sangaré.

Advisory Council

Conseil Économique et Social: Immeuble FAWAZ, Corniche Sud, Coléaah, Matam, BP 2947, Conakry; tel. 30-45-31-23; fax 30-45-31-24; e-mail ces@sotelgui.net.gn; f. 1997; 45 mems; Pres. Michel Kamano; Sec.-Gen. Mamadou Bobo Camara.

Political Organizations

There were 65 officially registered parties in mid-2010.

Alliance nationale pour le progrès (ANP): Conakry; Leader Dr Sagno Moussa.

Front uni pour la démocratie et le changement (FUDEC): Ratoma, Conakry; tel. 60-22-76-71 (mobile); fax 66-87-28-62 (mobile); internet www.fudec.org; f. 2009; Pres. François Lonsény Fall.

Nouvelle génération pour la République (NGR): Kissosso; tel. 64-29-05-72; Leader Ibrahima Abe Sylla.

Parti démocratique de Guinée—Rassemblement démocratique africain (PDG—RDA): Conakry; f. 1946; revived 1992; Sec.-Gen. El Hadj Ismaël Mohamed Gassim Ghussein.

Parti Dyama: Conakry; e-mail mansourkaba@yahoo.fr; internet www.guinea-dyama.com; moderate Islamist party; Pres. Mohamed Mansour Kaba.

Parti écologiste de Guinée (PEG—Les Verts): BP 3018, Quartier Boulbinet, 5e blvd, angle 2e ave, Commune de Kaloum, Conakry; tel. 30-44-37-01; Leader Oumar Sylla.

Parti de l'espoir pour le développement national (PEDN): Commune Ratoma, BP 1403, Conakry; tel. 65-55-00-00; e-mail info@pednespoirl.org; internet pednespoir.org; Pres. Lansana Kouyaté.

Parti du peuple de Guinée (PPG): BP 1147, Conakry; socialist; boycotted presidential election in 2003, following the Supreme Court's rejection of its nominated candidate; Leader Charles-Pascal Tolno.

Parti de l'unité et du progrès (PUP): Camayenne, Conakry; internet www.pupguinee.org; Pres. (vacant); Sec.-Gen. El Hadj Dr Sékou Konaté.

Rassemblement pour la défense de la République (RDR): Leader Papa Koly Kourouma.

Rassemblement pour le développement intégré de la Guinée (RDIG): Leader Jean-Marc Telliano.

Rassemblement du peuple de Guinée (RPG): Conakry; e-mail admin@rpgguinee.org; internet www.rpgguinee.org; f. 1980 as the Rassemblement des patriotes guinéens; socialist; Pres. Alpha Condé.

Union démocratique de Guinée (UDG): Dixinn Centre, Conakry; tel. 60-52-40-26; f. 2009; Leader El Hadj Mamadou Sylla.

Union des forces démocratiques (UFD): BP 3050, Conakry; tel. 30-34-50-20; e-mail ufdconakry@yahoo.fr; internet www.ufd-conakry.com; Pres. Mamadou Baadikko Bah.

Union des forces démocratiques de Guinée (UFDG): BP 3036, Conakry; e-mail baggelmalal@yahoo.fr; internet www.ufdg.org; f. 2002 by faction of UPR (q.v.) in protest at that party's participation in elections to Assemblée nationale; Pres. Cellou Dalein Diallo.

Union des forces républicaines (UFR): Immeuble 'Le Golfe', 4e étage, BP 6080, Conakry; tel. 64-30-47-50 (mobile); fax 30-45-42-31; e-mail ufrguinee@yahoo.fr; internet www.ufrguinee.org; f. 1992; liberal-conservative; Pres. Sidya Touré; Sec.-Gen. Bakary G. Zoumanigui.

Union pour le progrès de la Guinée (UPG): Conakry; Leader Jean-Marie Doré.

Union pour le progrès et le renouveau (UPR): BP 690, Conakry; tel. 30-25-26-01; e-mail basusmane@mirinet.net.gn; internet www.uprguinee.org; f. 1998 by merger of the Parti pour le renouveau et le progrès and the Union pour la nouvelle République; boycotted presidential election in 2003; Pres. Ousmane Bah.

Union pour le progrès national—Parti pour l'unité et le développement (UPN—PUD): Conakry; Leader Mamadou Bhoye Barry.

Diplomatic Representation

EMBASSIES IN GUINEA

Algeria: Cité des Nations, Quartiers Kaloum, BP 1004, Conakry; tel. 30-44-15-05; fax 30-41-15-35; Ambassador Rabah Fassi.

Angola: Conakry; Ambassador Eduardo Ruas de Jesus Manuel.

China, People's Republic: Quartier Donka, Cité Ministérielle, Commune de Dixinn, BP 714, Conakry; tel. 60-25-32-94 (mobile); fax 30-46-95-83; e-mail chinaemb_gn@mfa.gov.cn; internet gn.chineseembassy.org; Ambassador Zhao Lixing.

Congo, Democratic Republic: Quartier Almamya, ave de la Gare, Commune du Kaloum, BP 880, Conakry; tel. 30-45-15-01.

Côte d'Ivoire: blvd du Commerce, BP 5228, Conakry; tel. 30-45-10-82; fax 30-45-10-79; e-mail acign@ambaci-guinee.org; Ambassador Diarrassouba M. Youssouf.

Cuba: Cité Ministérielle, Quartier Donka, Commune de Dixinn, Conakry; tel. 30-46-95-25; fax 30-46-95-28; e-mail embagcon@sotelgui.net.gn; Ambassador Carlos Gutiérrez Corrales.

Egypt: Corniche Sud 2, BP 389, Conakry; tel. 30-46-85-08; fax 30-46-85-07; e-mail ambconakry@hotmail.com; Ambassador Bahaa Eldin Mohatar Wahafi.

France: ave du Commerce, BP 373, Conakry; tel. 30-47-10-00; fax 30-47-10-15; e-mail ambafrance.conakry@diplomatie.gouv.fr; internet www.ambafrance-gn.org; Ambassador Bertrand Cochery.

Germany: 2e blvd, Kaloum, BP 540, Conakry; tel. 30-41-15-06; fax 30-45-22-17; e-mail amball@sotelgui.net.gn; internet www.conakry.diplo.de; Ambassador HARTMUT KRAUSSER.

Ghana: Immeuble Ex-Urbaine et la Seine, BP 732, Conakry; tel. 30-44-15-10; Ambassador DOMINIC ABOAGYE.

Guinea-Bissau: Quartier Bellevue, Commune de Dixinn, BP 298, Conakry; Ambassador MALAM CAMARA.

Holy See: c/o Archevêché de Conakry, BP 2016, Conakry; tel. 64-58-49-59; e-mail nunziaturaguinea@gmail.com; Apostolic Nuncio Most Rev. MARTIN KREBS (Titular Archbishop of Taborenta).

Iran: Donka, Cité Ministérielle, Commune de Dixinn, BP 310, Conakry; tel. 30-01-03-19; fax 30-47-81-84; e-mail ambiran@yahoo.com; Ambassador BAKHTIAR ASADZADEH SHEIKHJANI.

Japan: Lanseboundji, Corniche Sud, Commune de Matam, BP 895, Conakry; tel. 30-46-85-10; fax 30-46-85-09; Ambassador NAOTSUGU NAKANO.

Korea, Democratic People's Republic: BP 723, Conakry; Ambassador RI KYONG SON.

Liberia: Cité Ministérielle, Donka, Commune de Dixinn, BP 18, Conakry; tel. 30-42-26-71; Chargé d'affaires a.i. SIAKA FAHNBULLEH.

Libya: Commune de Kaloum, BP 1183, Conakry; tel. 30-41-41-72; Ambassador B. AHMED.

Malaysia: Quartier Mafanco, Corniche Sud, BP 5460, Conakry; tel. 30-22-17-54; e-mail malconakry@kln.gov.my; Ambassador (vacant).

Mali: rue D1–15, Camayenne, Corniche Nord, BP 299, Conakry; tel. 30-46-14-18; fax 30-46-37-03; e-mail ambamaliguinee@yahoo.fr; Ambassador HASSANE BARRY.

Morocco: Cité des Nations, Villa 12, Commune du Kaloum, BP 193, Conakry; tel. 30-41-36-86; fax 30-41-38-16; e-mail sifamgui@biasy.net; Ambassador MAJID HALIM.

Nigeria: Corniche Sud, Quartier de Matam, BP 54, Conakry; tel. 30-46-13-41; fax 30-46-27-75; Ambassador Dr AISHA LARABA ABDULLAHI.

Russia: Matam-Port, km 9, BP 329, Conakry; tel. 30-40-52-22; fax 30-47-84-43; e-mail ambrus@biasy.net; internet www.guinee.mid.ru; Ambassador DMITRII V. MALEV.

Saudi Arabia: Quartier Camayenne, Commune de Dixinn, BP 611, Conakry; tel. 30-46-24-87; fax 30-46-58-84; e-mail gnemb@mofa.gov.sa; Ambassador AMJAD BIN HOSAIN BIN ABDUL HAMEED BDAIWI.

Senegal: bâtiment 142, Coleah, Corniche Che Sud, BP 842, Conakry; tel. 30-44-61-32; fax 30-46-28-34; Ambassador YAKHAM DIOP.

Sierra Leone: Quartier Bellevue, face aux cases présidentielles, Commune de Dixinn, BP 625, Conakry; tel. 30-46-40-84; fax 30-41-23-64; Ambassador ADIKALIE FODAY SUMAH.

South Africa: Coleah, Mossoudougou, Conakry; tel. 30-49-08-75; fax 30-49-08-79; e-mail conakrys@foreign.gov.za; Ambassador (vacant).

Ukraine: Commune de Dixinn, Corniche Nord, Cité Ministérielle, Rue DI 256, BP 1350, Conakry; tel. 62-35-38-01 (mobile); fax 62-35-38-03 (mobile); e-mail ambukra@gmail.com; internet www.mfa.gov.ua/guinea; Ambassador ANDRIY ZAYATS.

United Kingdom: BP 6729, Conakry; tel. 63-35-53-29 (mobile); fax 63-35-90-59 (mobile); e-mail britembconakry@hotmail.com; Ambassador GRAHAM CHARLES TRAYTON STYLES.

USA: Koloma, Ratoma, BP 603, Conakry; tel. 65-10-40-00 (mobile); fax 65-10-42-74 (mobile); e-mail Consularconkr@state.gov; internet conakry.usembassy.gov; Ambassador PATRICIA NEWTON MOLLER.

Judicial System

The Constitution of 7 May 2010 embodies the principle of the independence of the judiciary, and delineates the competencies of each component of the judicial system, including the Supreme Court and the Revenue Court.

Supreme Court

Corniche-Sud, Camayenne, Conakry; tel. 30-41-29-28; Pres. MAMADOU SYLLA

Director of Public Prosecutions: ANTOINE IBRAHIM DIALLO.

Religion

It is estimated that 85% of the population are Muslims and 8% Christians, while 7% follow animist beliefs.

ISLAM

National Islamic League: BP 386, Conakry; tel. 30-41-23-38; f. 1988; Sec.-Gen. (vacant).

CHRISTIANITY

The Roman Catholic Church

Guinea comprises one archdiocese and two dioceses. About 3% of the population are Roman Catholics.

Bishops' Conference

Conférence Episcopale de la Guinée, BP 1006 bis, Conakry; tel. and fax 30-41-32-70; e-mail dhewara@eti.met.gn; Pres. Most Rev. VINCENT COULIBALY (Archbishop of Conakry).

Archbishop of Conakry: Most Rev. VINCENT COULIBALY, Archevêché, BP 2016, Conakry; tel. and fax 30-43-47-04; e-mail conakriensis@yahoo.fr.

The Anglican Communion

Anglicans in Guinea are adherents of the Church of the Province of West Africa, comprising 12 dioceses. The diocese of Guinea was established in 1985 as the first French-speaking diocese in the Province. The Archbishop and Primate of the Province is the Bishop of Koforidua, Ghana.

Bishop of Guinea: Rt Rev. ALBERT D. GÓMEZ, Cathédrale Toussaint, BP 1187, Conakry; tel. 30-45-13-23; e-mail agomezd@yahoo.fr.

BAHÁ'Í FAITH

Assemblée spirituelle nationale: BP 2010, Conakry 1; e-mail asngunee@yahoo.fr; Sec. MAMMA TRAORE.

The Press

REGULATORY AUTHORITY

Haute Autorité de la Communication (HAC): en face Primature, BP 2955, Conakry; tel. 30-45-54-82; fax 30-41-23-85; f. 2010; regulates the operations of the press, and of radio and television; regulates political access to the media; nine mems; Pres. MARTINE CONDÉ.

NEWSPAPERS AND PERIODICALS

In early 2004 there were more than 200 periodicals and newspapers officially registered with the National Council of Communication, although only around 60 were believed to be in operation at that time.

Le Démocrate: Quartier Ratoma Centre, Commune de Ratoma, BP 2427, Conakry; tel. 60-20-01-01; e-mail mamadoudianb@yahoo.fr; weekly; Dir HASSANE KABA; Editor-in-Chief MAMADOU DIAN BALDÉ.

Le Diplomate: BP 2427, Conakry; tel. and fax 30-41-23-85; f. 2002; weekly; Dir SANOU KERFALLAH CISSÉ.

L'Enquêteur: Conakry; e-mail habib@boubah.com; internet enqueteur.boubah.com; f. 2001; weekly; Editor HABIB YAMBERING DIALLO.

L'Evénement de Guinée: BP 796, Conakry; tel. 30-44-33-91; monthly; independent; f. 1993; Dir BOUBACAR SANKARELA DIALLO.

Fonike: BP 341, Conakry; daily; sport and general; state-owned; Dir IBRAHIMA KALIL DIARE.

La Guinée Actuelle: Sans Fils, près Le Makity, BP 3618, Conakry; tel. 30-69-36-20.

Horoya (Liberty): BP 191, Conakry; tel. 30-47-71-17; fax 30-45-10-16; e-mail info@horoyaguinee.net; govt daily; Dir OUSMANE CAMARA.

L'Indépendant: Quartier Ratoma Centre, Commune de Ratoma, BP 2427, Conakry; tel. 60-20-01-01; e-mail lindependant@afribone.net.gn; internet www.lindependant-gn.info; weekly; also *L'Indépendant Plus*; Publr ABOUBACAR SYLLA; Dir HASSANE KABA; Editor-in-Chief MAMADOU DIAN BALDÉ.

Journal Officiel de Guinée: BP 156, Conakry; fortnightly; organ of the Govt.

La Lance: Immeuble Baldé Zaïre, BP 4968, Conakry; tel. and fax 30-41-23-85; weekly; general information; Dir SOULEYMANE E. DIALLO.

Le Lynx: Immeuble Baldé Zaïre Sandervalia, BP 4968, Conakry; tel. 30-41-23-85; fax 30-45-36-96; e-mail le-lynx@afribone.net.gn; internet www.afribone.net.gn/lynx; f. 1992; weekly; satirical; Editor SOULEYMANE DIALLO.

La Nouvelle Tribune: blvd Diallo Tally, entre 5e et 6e ave, BP 35, Conakry; tel. 30-22-33-02; e-mail abdcond@yahoo.fr; internet www.nouvelle-tribune.com; weekly, Tuesdays; independent; general information and analysis; Dir of Publ. and Editing ABDOULAYE CONDÉ.

L'Observateur: Immeuble Baldé, Conakry; tel. 30-40-05-24; e-mail ibrahimanouhou@yahoo.fr; internet www.observateur-guinee.com; weekly; independent; Dir NOUHOU BALDÉ.

L'Oeil du Peuple: BP 3064, Conakry; tel. 30-67-23-78; weekly; independent; Dir of Publishing ISMAËL BANGOURA.

Sanakou: Labé, Foutah Djallon, Moyenne-Guinée; tel. 30-51-13-19; e-mail sanakoulabe@yahoo.fr; f. 2000; monthly; general news; Publr

IDRISSA SAMPIRING DIALLO; Editor-in-Chief YAMOUSSA SOUMAH; circ. 1,000.

3-P Plus (Parole-Plume-Papier) Magazine: 7e ave Bis Almamyah, BP 5122, Conakry; tel. 30-45-22-32; fax 30-45-29-31; e-mail 3p-plus@mirinet.net.gn; internet www.mirinet.net.gn/3p_plus; f. 1995; journal of arts and letters; supplements *Le Cahier de l'Economie* and *Mag-Plus: Le Magazine de la Culture*; monthly; Pres. MOHAMED SALIFOU KEÏTA; Editor-in-Chief SAMBA TOURÉ.

NEWS AGENCY

Agence Guinéenne de Presse: BP 1535, Conakry; tel. 30-41-14-34; e-mail info@agpguinee.net; internet www.agpguinee.net; f. 1960; Man. Dir NÈTÈ SOVOGUI.

PRESS ASSOCIATION

Association Guinéenne des Editeurs de la Presse Indépendante (AGEPI): Conakry; f. 1991; an asscn of independent newspaper publishers; Chair. BOUBACAR SANKARELA DIALLO.

Publishers

Les Classiques Guinéens (SEDIS sarl): 545 rue KA020, Mauquepas, BP 3697, Conakry; tel. 11-21-18-57; fax 13-40-92-62; e-mail cheick.sedis@mirinet.net.gn; f. 1999; art, history, youth literature; Dir CHEICK ABDOUL KABA.

Editions du Ministère de l'Education Nationale: Direction nationale de la recherche scientifique et technique, BP 561, Conakry; tel. 30-43-02-66; e-mail dnrst@mirinet.net.gn; f. 1959; general and educational; Deputy Dir Dr TAMBA TAGBINO.

Editions Ganndal (Knowledge): BP 542, Conakry; tel. and fax 30-46-35-07; e-mail ganndal@mirinet.net.gn; f. 1992; educational, youth and children, general literature and books in Pular; Dir MAMADOU ALIOU SOW.

Société Africaine d'Edition et de Communication (SAEC): Belle-Vue, Commune de Dixinn, BP 6826, Conakry; tel. 30-29-71-41; e-mail dtniane@yahoo.fr; social sciences, reference, literary fiction; Editorial Assistant OUMAR TALL.

Broadcasting and Communications

TELECOMMUNICATIONS

In 2011 there were five providers of mobile cellular telephone services and one provider of fixed line telephone services in Guinea.

Regulatory Authority

Autorité de Régulation des Postes et des Télécommunications (ARPT): BP 1500, Conakry; e-mail contact@arptguinee.org; internet www.arptguinee.org; f. 2008; Dir-Gen. DIABY MOUSTAPHA MAMY.

Service Providers

Areeba Guinée: Quartier Almamya, Commune de Kaloum, BP 3237, Conakry; tel. 64-22-22-22; fax 64-33-33-33; internet www.areeba.com.gn; f. 2005; mobile cellular telephone provider; 75% owned by MTN (South Africa); Dir-Gen. P. J. PHIKE.

Cellcom Guinée: Immeuble WAQF-BID, Almamya, C/Kaloum, BP 6567, Conakry; tel. 65-10-01-00; fax 65-10-01-01; e-mail info@gn.cellcomgsm.com; internet www.gn.cellcomgsm.com; f. 2008; Dir-Gen. HANOCH DOMBEK.

Intercel: Quartier Coleah Larseboundji, près du pont du 8 novembre, Immeuble le Golfe, BP 965, Conakry; tel. 30-45-57-44; fax 30-40-92-92; e-mail info@gn.intercel.net; mobile cellular telephone operator; fmrly Telecel Guinée; acquired by Sudatel (Sudan) in 2011; Dir-Gen. DJIBRIL TOBE.

Orange Guinée: Conakry; tel. 62-77-00-00 (mobile); internet www.orange-guinee.com; f. 2007; 85% owned by the Groupe Sonatel (Senegal); Dir-Gen. ALASSANE DIÈNE.

Société des Télécommunications de Guinée (SOTELGUI): 4e blvd, BP 2066, Conakry; tel. 30-45-27-50; fax 30-45-03-06; e-mail vickycu@sotelgui.net.gn; internet www.sotelgui.net; f. 1992; state-owned; provides fixed line services; 12,000 landline subscribers and 549,713 subscribers (2010); Dir-Gen. MOUSSA KEITA.

Lagui: Conakry; wholly owned subsidiary of SOTELGUI providing mobile telephone services.

BROADCASTING

Regulatory Authority

Haute Autorité de la Communication (HAC): see The Press.

In mid-2005 a presidential decree permitted the creation of private radio and television stations in Guinea, subject to certain conditions. Political parties and religious organizations were to be prohibited from creating broadcast media, however, while restrictions were to be placed on foreign ownership of radio and television stations.

Radio

Espace FM: Quartier Matoto, Immeuble Mouna, BP 256, Conakry; tel. 64-20-20-92; e-mail services@espacefmguinee.info; internet espacefmguinee.info.

Milo FM: BP 215, Kankan; tel. 30-72-00-82; e-mail info@milo-fm.com; internet www.milo-fm.com; Dir-Gen. LANCINÉ KABA.

Radiodiffusion-Télévision Guinéenne (RTG): BP 391, Conakry; tel. 30-44-22-01; fax 30-41-50-01; broadcasts in French, English, Créole-English, Portuguese, Arabic and local languages; Dir-Gen. IBRAHIMA AHMED BARRY; Dir of Radio ISSA CONDÉ.

Radio Rurale de Guinée: BP 391, Conakry; tel. 30-42-11-09; fax 30-41-47-97; e-mail ruralgui@mirinet.net.gn; network of rural radio stations.

Television

Radiodiffusion-Télévision Guinéenne (RTG): see Radio; transmissions in French and local languages; one channel; f. 1977.

Finance

(cap. = capital; res = reserves; dep. = deposits; m. = million; brs = branches; amounts in Guinean francs)

BANKING

Central Bank

Banque Centrale de la République de Guinée (BCRG): 12 blvd du Commerce, BP 692, Kaloum, Conakry; tel. 30-41-26-51; fax 30-41-48-98; e-mail gouv.bcrg@eti-bull.net; internet www.bcrg-guinee.org; f. 1960; bank of issue; cap. 50,000m., res 20,881m., dep. 7,171,432m. (Dec. 2009); Gov. LOUCENY NABÉ; First Deputy Gov. YÉRO BALDÉ BALDÉ.

Commercial Banks

Banque Internationale pour le Commerce et l'Industrie de la Guinée (BICIGUI): ave de la République, BP 1484, Conakry; tel. 30-41-45-15; fax 30-41-39-62; e-mail dg.bicigui@africa.bnpparibas.com; internet www.bicigui.com; f. 1985; 30.8% owned by BNP Paribas BDDI Participations (France), 15.1% state-owned; cap. and res 37,989.3m., total assets 315,689.5m. (Dec. 2003); Pres. IBRAHIMA SOUMAH; Dir-Gen. MANGA FODÉ TOURÉ; 20 brs.

Banque Populaire Maroco-Guinéenne (BPMG): Immeuble BPMG, blvd du Commerce, Kaloum, BP 4400, Conakry 01; tel. 30-41-36-93; fax 30-41-32-61; e-mail bpmg@sotelgui.net.gn; f. 1991; 55% owned by Crédit Populaire du Maroc, 42% state-owned; cap. and res 9,936m., total assets 65,549m. (Dec. 2004); Pres. EMMANUEL GNAN; Dir-Gen. AHMED IRAQUI HOUSSAINI; 3 brs.

Ecobank Guinée: Immeuble Al Iman, ave de la République, BP 5687, Conakry; tel. 30-45-57-77; fax 30-45-42-41; e-mail ecobankgn@ecobank.com; internet www.ecobank.com; f. 1999; wholly owned by Ecobank Transnational Inc. (Togo); cap. 25,000.0m., res 27,667.3m., dep. 975,266.4m. (Dec. 2009); Pres. SAIKOU BARRY; Man. Dir MAMADOU MOUSTAPHA FALL; 9 brs.

First American Bank of Guinea: blvd du Commerce, angle 9e ave, BP 4540, Conakry; tel. 30-41-34-32; fax 30-41-35-29; f. 1994; jtly owned by Mitan Capital Ltd (Grand Cayman) and El Hadj Haidara Abdourahmane Chérif (Mali).

International Commercial Bank SA: Ex-cité Chemin de Fer, Immeuble Mamou, BP 3547, Conakry; tel. 30-41-25-90; fax 30-41-54-50; e-mail enquiry@icbank-guinea.com; internet www.icbank-guinea.com; f. 1997; total assets 19.6m. (Dec. 1999); Pres. JOSÉPHINE PREMLA; Man. Dir HAMZA BIN ALIAS; 3 brs.

Société Générale de Banques en Guinée (SGBG): Immeuble Boffa, Cité du Chemin de Fer, BP 1514, Conakry; tel. 30-45-60-00; fax 30-41-25-65; e-mail contact@sgbg.net.gn; internet www.sgbg.net; f. 1985; 53% owned by Société Générale (France); cap. and res 13,074m., total assets 228,196m. (Dec. 2003); Pres. GÉRALD LACAZE; Dir-Gen. JEAN-PHILIPPE EQUILBECQ; 8 brs.

Union Internationale de Banques en Guinée (UIBG): 6e ave de la République, angle 5e blvd, BP 324, Conakry; tel. 62-35-90-90; fax 30-97-26-30; e-mail info-gn@orabank.net; f. 1988; fmrly the Union Internationale de Banques en Guinée, present name adopted in 2011; 54.0% owned by Oragroup SA (Togo), 14.3% owned by Orabank Tchad; cap. 25,000m., res –1,139.1m., dep. 259,713.9m. (Dec. 2009); Pres. ALPHA AMADOU DIALLO; Dir-Gen. MAMADOU SENE.

Islamic Bank

Banque Islamique de Guinée: Immeuble Nafaya, 6 ave de la République, BP 1247, Conakry; tel. 30-41-21-08; fax 30-41-50-71; e-mail info@big-banque.com; internet www.big-banque.com; f. 1983; 50.01% owned by Dar al-Maal al-Islami Trust (Switzerland), 49.99% owned by Islamic Development Bank (Saudi Arabia); cap. and res 2,368.5m., total assets 26,932.1m. (Dec. 2003); Pres. Aderraouf Benessaiah; Dir-Gen. Lyagoubi Abdouilah.

INSURANCE

Gras Savoye Guinée: 4e ave, angle 4e blvd, Quartier Boulbinet, Commune de Kaloum, BP 6441, Conakry; tel. 30-45-58-43; fax 30-45-58-42; e-mail gsguinee@sotelgui.net.gn; affiliated to Gras Savoye (France); Man. Chérif Bah.

International Insurance Co: Conakry; tel. 62-03-81-05; f. 2007; Dir-Gen. Kabinet Kondé.

Société Guinéenne d'Assurance Mutuelle (SOGAM): Immeuble Sonia, BP 434, Conakry; tel. 30-44-50-58; fax 30-41-25-57; f. 1990; Chair. Dr M. K. Bah; Man. Dir P. I. Ndao.

Société Nouvelle d'Assurance de Guinée (SONAG): BP 3363, Conakry; tel. 30-41-49-77; fax 30-41-43-03.

Union Guinéenne d'Assurances et de Réassurances (UGAR): pl. des Martyrs, BP 179, Conakry; tel. 30-41-48-41; fax 30-41-17-11; e-mail ugar@ugar.com.gn; f. 1989; 40% owned by AXA (France), 35% state-owned; cap. 2,000m.; Man. Dir Raphaël Y. Touré.

Trade and Industry

GOVERNMENT AGENCIES

Agence de Promotion des Investissements Privés-Guichet Unique (APIP–GUINEE): BP 2024, Conakry; tel. 30-41-49-85; fax 30-41-39-90; e-mail dg@apiguinee.org; internet www.apiguinee.org; f. 1992; promotes private investment; Dir-Gen. Mohamed Lamine Bayo.

Centre de Promotion et de Développement Miniers (CPDM): BP 295, Conakry; tel. 30-41-15-44; fax 30-41-49-13; e-mail cpdm@mirinet.net.gn; f. 1995; promotes investment and co-ordinates devt strategy in mining sector; Dir Mociré Sylla.

Entreprise Nationale Import-Export (IMPORTEX): BP 152, Conakry; tel. 30-44-28-13; state-owned import and export agency; Dir Mamadou Bobo Dieng.

Office de Développement de la Pêche Artisanale et de l'Aquaculture en Guinée (ODEPAG): 6 ave de la République, BP 1581, Conakry; tel. 30-44-19-48; devt of fisheries and fish-processing.

DEVELOPMENT ORGANIZATIONS

Agence Française de Développement (AFD): 5e ave, KA022, BP 283, Conakry; tel. 30-41-25-69; fax 30-41-28-74; e-mail afdconakry@groupe-afd.org; internet www.afd.fr; Country Dir Philippe Michaud.

France Volontaires: BP 570, Conakry; tel. 30-35-08-60; internet www.france-volontaires.org; f. 1987; name changed as above in 2009; devt and research projects; Nat. Delegate Franck Dagois.

Service de Coopération et d'Action Culturelle: BP 373, Conakry; tel. 30-41-23-45; fax 30-41-43-56; administers bilateral aid; Dir in Guinea Tobie Nathan.

CHAMBERS OF COMMERCE

Chambre de Commerce, d'Industrie et de l'Artisanat de la Guinée (CCIAG): Quartier Tombo, Commune de Kaloum, BP 545, Conakry; tel. 60-26-02-31; fax 30-47-70-58; e-mail cciag@sotelgui.net.gn; internet www.cciag.org; f. 1985; Pres. Morlaye Diallo.

Chambre Economique de Guinée: BP 609, Conakry.

TRADE AND EMPLOYERS' ASSOCIATIONS

Association des Commerçants de Guinée: BP 2468, Conakry; tel. 64-21-92-42; fax 30-45-31-66; e-mail thouca_acic@yahoo.fr; f. 1976; Pres. Thierno Oumar Camara.

Association des Femmes Entrepreneurs de Guinée (AFEG): BP 104, Kaloum, Conakry; tel. 60-28-02-95; e-mail afeguine@yahoo.fr; f. 1987; Pres. Hadja Ramatoulaye Sow.

Conseil National du Patronat Guinéen (CNPG): Dixinn Bora, BP 6403, Conakry; tel. and fax 30-41-24-70; e-mail msylla@leland-gn.org; f. 1992; Pres. El Hadj Mamadou Sylla.

Fédération Patronale de l'Agriculture et de l'Elevage (FEPAE): BP 5684, Conakry; tel. 30-22-95-56; fax 30-41-54-36; Pres. El Hadj Mamadou Sylla; Sec.-Gen. Mamady Camara.

Groupement des Importateurs Guinéens (GIG): BP 970, Conakry; tel. 30-42-18-18; fax 30-42-19-19; Pres. Fernand Bangoura.

UTILITIES

Electricity

Barrage Hydroélectrique de Garafiri: BP 1770, Conakry; tel. 30-41-50-91; inaugurated 1999.

Electricité de Guinée (EDG): BP 1463, Conakry; tel. 30-45-18-56; fax 30-45-18-53; e-mail di.sogel@biasy.net; f. 2001 to replace Société Guinéenne d'Electricité; majority state-owned; production, transport and distribution of electricity; Dir-Gen. Sékou Sanfina Diakité.

Water

Service National d'Aménagement des Points d'Eau (SNAPE): BP 2064, Conakry; tel. 30-41-18-93; fax 30-41-50-58; e-mail snape@mirinet.net.gn; supplies water in rural areas; Dir-Gen. Ibrahima Sory Sankon.

Société Nationale des Eaux de Guinée (SONEG): Belle-vue, BP 150, Conakry; tel. 30-45-44-77; e-mail oaubot@seg.org.gn; f. 1988; national water co; Dir-Gen. Dr Ousmane Aribot; Sec.-Gen. Mamadou Diop.

TRADE UNIONS

Confédération Nationale des Travailleurs de Guinée (CNTG): Bourse du Travail, Corniche Sud 004, BP 237, Conakry; tel. 30-41-50-44; fax 11-45-49-96; e-mail cntg60@yahoo.fr; f. 1984; Sec.-Gen. Amadou Diallo.

Organisation Nationale des Syndicats Libres de Guinée (ONSLG): BP 559, Conakry; tel. 30-41-52-17; fax 30-43-02-83; e-mail onslguinee@yahoo.fr; 27,000 mems (1996); Sec.-Gen. Yamoudou Touré.

Union Syndicale des Travailleurs de Guinée (USTG): BP 1514, Conakry; tel. 30-41-25-65; fax 30-41-25-58; e-mail fofi1952@yahoo.fr; independent; 64,000 mems (2001); Sec.-Gen. Ibrahima Fofana.

Transport

RAILWAYS

There are 1,086 km of railways in Guinea, including 662 km of 1-m gauge track from Conakry to Kankan in the east of the country, crossing the Niger at Kouroussa. The contract for the first phase of the upgrading of this line was awarded to a Slovak company in early 1997. Three lines for the transport of bauxite link Sangaredi with the port of Kamsar in the west, via Boké, and Conakry with Kindia and Fria, a total of 383 km. In 2011 plans were under way for the reconstruction of the 662-km Conakry-Kankan line, which has not been in operation since 1983.

Office National des Chemins de Fer de Guinée (ONCFG): BP 589, Conakry; tel. 30-44-46-13; fax 30-41-35-77; f. 1905; Man. Dir Morel Marguerite Camara.

Chemin de Fer de Boké: BP 523, Boké; operations commenced 1973.

Chemin de Fer Conakry–Fria: BP 334, Conakry; operations commenced 1960; Gen. Man. A. Camara.

Chemin de Fer de la Société des Bauxites de Kindia: BP 613, Conakry; tel. 30-41-38-28; operations commenced 1974; Gen. Man. K. Keita.

ROADS

The road network comprised 44,348 km of roads (of which 4,342 km were paved) in 2003. In 2009 an estimated 35% of all roads were paved. An 895-km cross-country road links Conakry to Bamako, in Mali, and the main highway connecting Dakar (Senegal) to Abidjan (Côte d'Ivoire) also crosses Guinea. The road linking Conakry to Freetown (Sierra Leone) forms part of the Trans West African Highway, extending from Morocco to Nigeria.

La Guinéenne-Marocaine des Transports (GUIMAT): Conakry; f. 1989; owned jtly by Govt of Guinea and Hakkam (Morocco); operates nat. and regional transport services.

Société Générale des Transports de Guinée (SOGETRAG): Conakry; f. 1985; 63% state-owned; bus operator.

SHIPPING

Conakry and Kamsar are the international seaports. Guinea handled 5.3m. metric tons of foreign trade in 2003. The country's registered merchant fleet at 31 December 2009 numbered 44 vessels, totalling 23,300 grt.

Getma Guinée: Immeuble KASSA, Cité des Chemins de Fer, BP 1648, Conakry; tel. 30-41-26-66; fax 30-41-42-73; e-mail info@getmaguinee.com.gn; internet www.getma.com; f. 1979; fmrly Société Guinéenne d'Entreprises de Transports Maritimes et

Aeriens; marine transportation; cap. 1,100m. FG; Chair. and CEO JEAN-JACQUES GRENIER; 135 employees.

Port Autonome de Conakry (PAC): BP 805, Conakry; tel. 30-41-27-28; fax 30-41-26-04; e-mail pac@eti-bull.net; internet www.biasy.net/~pac; haulage, porterage; Gen. Man. MAMADOUBA SAKHON.

Société Navale Guinéenne (SNG): BP 522, Conakry; tel. 30-44-29-55; fax 30-41-39-70; f. 1968; state-owned; shipping agents; Dir-Gen. MAMADI TOURÉ.

SOAEM: Immeuble Zaidan, blvd du Commerce, BP 3177, Conakry; tel. 30-41-24-57; fax 30-41-20-25; e-mail jean-jacques.corneille@smtp.saga.fr.

SOTRAMAR: Kamsar; e-mail sotramar@sotramar.com; f. 1971; exports bauxite from mines at Boké through port of Kamsar.

Transmar: 33 blvd du Commerce, Kaloum, BP 3917, Conakry; tel. 30-43-05-41; fax 30-43-05-42; e-mail elitegn@gmail.com; shipping, stevedoring, inland transport.

CIVIL AVIATION

There is an international airport at Conakry-Gbessia, and smaller airfields at Labé, Kankan and Faranah. Facilities at Conakry have been upgraded, at a cost of US $42.6m.; the airport handled some 300,000 passengers in 1999. In 2010 plans were under way for the construction of a new international airport at Matakang.

Air Guinée International: Conakry; f. 2010 to replace Air Guinée (f. 1960); regional and internal services; Dir-Gen. MOHAMED EL-BORAÏ.

Guinée Air Service: Aéroport Conakry-Gbessia; tel. 30-41-27-61.

Guinée Inter Air: Aéroport Conakry-Gbessia; tel. 30-41-37-08.

Société de Gestion et d'Exploitation de l'Aéroport de Conakry (SOGEAC): BP 3126, Conakry; tel. 30-46-48-03; f. 1987; manages Conakry-Gbessia int. airport; 51% state-owned.

Union des Transports Aériens de Guinée (UTA): scheduled and charter flights to regional and int. destinations.

Tourism

Some 30,194 tourists visited Guinea in 2007; receipts from tourism in 2009 totalled US $4.9m.

Office National du Tourisme: Immeuble al-Iman, 6e ave de la République, BP 1275, Conakry; tel. 30-45-51-63; fax 30-45-51-64; e-mail ibrahimabakaley@yahoo.fr; internet www.ontguinee.com; f. 1997; Dir-Gen. IBRAHIM A. DIALLO.

Defence

As assessed at November 2011, Guinea's active armed forces numbered 12,300, comprising an army of 8,500, a navy of 400 and an air force of 800. Paramilitary forces comprised a republican guard of 1,600 and a 1,000-strong gendarmerie, as well as a reserve 'people's militia' of 7,000. Military service is compulsory (conscripts were estimated at some 7,500 in 2001) and lasts for two years.

Defence Expenditure: Estimated at 275,000m. Guinean francs in 2010.

Chief of Staff of the Armed Forces: Gen. KÈLÈFA DIALLO.

Chief of Staff of the Army: Commdr MORIBA ABEL MARA.

Chief of Staff of the Air Force: Maj. MAMADY MARA.

Chief of Staff of the Navy: Capt. MOHAMED CAMARA.

Chief of Staff of the National Gendarmerie: Maj. IBRAHIMA BALDE.

Education

Education is provided free of charge at every level in state institutions. Primary education, which begins at seven years of age and lasts for six years, is officially compulsory. According to UNESCO estimates, in 2009/10 enrolment in primary education included 77% of children in the relevant age-group (males 83%; females 70%), while in 2008/09 enrolment at secondary schools included 29% of children in the appropriate age-group (boys 36%; girls 22%). Secondary education, from the age of 13, lasts for seven years, comprising a first cycle (collège) of four years and a second (lycée) of three years. There are universities at Conakry and Kankan, and other tertiary institutions at Manéyah, Boké and Faranah; some 80,200 students were enrolled at these institutions in 2007/08. In 2008 spending on education represented 19.2% of total budgetary expenditure.

GUINEA-BISSAU

Introductory Survey

LOCATION, CLIMATE, LANGUAGE, RELIGION, FLAG, CAPITAL

The Republic of Guinea-Bissau lies on the west coast of Africa, with Senegal to the north and Guinea to the east and south. The climate is tropical, although maritime and Sahelian influences are felt. The average temperature is 20°C (68°F). The official language is Portuguese, of which the locally spoken form is Creole (Crioulo). There are 19 local languages, of which the most widely spoken are Balanta-Kentohe, Pulaar (Fula), Mandjak, Mandinka and Papel. The principal religious beliefs are animism and Islam. There is a small minority of Roman Catholics and other Christian groups. The national flag (proportions 1 by 2) has two equal horizontal stripes, of yellow over light green, and a red vertical stripe, with a five-pointed black star at its centre, at the hoist. The capital is Bissau.

CONTEMPORARY POLITICAL HISTORY

Historical Context

Portuguese Guinea (Guiné) was colonized by Portugal in the 15th century. Nationalist activism began to emerge in the 1950s. Armed insurgency commenced in the early 1960s, and by 1972 the Partido Africano da Independência da Guiné e Cabo Verde (PAIGC) was in control of two-thirds of the country. The independence of the Republic of Guinea-Bissau was unilaterally proclaimed in September 1973, with Luís Cabral (the brother of the founder of the PAIGC, Amílcar Cabral) as President of the State Council. Hostilities ceased following the military coup in Portugal in April 1974, and on 10 September Portugal recognized the independence of Guinea-Bissau under the leadership of Luís Cabral.

The PAIGC regime introduced measures to establish a single-party socialist state. At elections in December 1976 and January 1977 voters chose regional councils from which a new National People's Assembly (Assembleia Nacional Popular—ANP) was later selected. In 1978 the Chief State Commissioner, Francisco Mendes, died; he was succeeded by Commdr João Vieira, hitherto State Commissioner for the Armed Forces and President of the ANP.

The PAIGC initially supervised both Cape Verde and Guinea-Bissau, the Constitutions of each remaining separate but with a view to eventual unification. These arrangements were terminated in November 1980, when President Cabral was deposed in a coup organized by Vieira, who was installed as Chairman of the Council of the Revolution. Diplomatic relations between Guinea-Bissau and Cape Verde were restored after the release of Cabral from detention in 1982.

Domestic Political Affairs

In May 1983 the ANP, which had been dissolved following the 1980 coup, was re-established, and the Council of the Revolution was replaced by a 15-member Council of State (Conselho de Estado), selected from among the members of the ANP. Vieira was subsequently elected as President of the Conselho de Estado and Head of State. The ANP immediately ratified a new Constitution, and formally abolished the position of Prime Minister.

In December 1990 the Central Committee of the PAIGC agreed to the adoption of a multi-party system, following a period of transition, and the holding of a presidential election in 1993. In May 1991 a series of constitutional amendments ending one-party rule were approved by the ANP, terminating the political monopoly of the PAIGC. In addition, all links between the PAIGC and the armed forces were severed, and the introduction of a free-market economy was guaranteed. New legislation in October accorded greater freedom to the press and permitted the formation of new trade unions. In November the Frente Democrática (FD) became the first opposition party to obtain official registration.

In December 1991 a major government reshuffle took place, in which the office of Prime Minister was restored. Carlos Correia was appointed to the post. In late 1991 and early 1992 three further opposition parties obtained legal status: the Resistência da Guiné-Bissau—Movimento Bah-Fatah (RGB—MB); the Frente Democrática Social (FDS); and the Partido Unido Social Democrático (PUSD). Following a split in the FDS, a further party, the Partido para a Renovação Social (PRS), was established in January 1992 by the former Vice-Chairman of the FDS, Kumba Yalá. In the same month four opposition parties—the PUSD, FDS, RGB—MB and the Partido da Convergência Democrática (PCD), led by Vítor Mandinga—agreed on the establishment of a 'democratic forum', whose demands included the dissolution of the political police, the creation of an electoral commission and an all-party consultation on the setting of election dates. Legislation preparing for the transition to a multi-party democracy was approved by the ANP in February 1993, and in the following month a commission was appointed to supervise the forthcoming elections. In July Vieira announced that multi-party presidential and legislative elections would be held in March 1994.

However, one week before the designated date of the elections, Vieira announced their postponement, owing to financial and technical difficulties. In May 1994 it was announced that the elections would be held in July. In May six opposition parties, the FD, the FDS, the Movimento para a Unidade e a Democracia, the Partido Democrático do Progresso, the Partido de Renovação e Desenvolvimento and the Liga Guinéense de Protecção Ecológica (LIPE), formed a coalition, the União para a Mudança (UM). The elections took place on 3 July, although voting was extended for two days, owing to logistical problems. The PAIGC secured a clear majority in the ANP, winning 62 of the 100 seats, while in the presidential election Vieira obtained 46.3% of the votes, and his nearest rival, Yalá, secured 21.9% of the votes. The two candidates contested a second round of polling on 7 August in which Yalá was narrowly defeated, securing 48.0% of the votes, compared with Vieira's 52.0%. International observers later declared the elections to have been free and fair. Vieira was inaugurated as President on 29 September and appointed Manuel Saturnino da Costa (the Secretary-General of the PAIGC) as Prime Minister in late October. The Council of Ministers was appointed in November, comprising solely members of the PAIGC.

Guinea-Bissau attained membership of the Union économique et monétaire ouest-africaine (see p. 333) in March 1997 and entered the Franc Zone in April. The national currency was replaced by the franc CFA, and the Banque centrale des états de l'Afrique de l'ouest assumed central banking functions. In May da Costa was dismissed. Carlos Correia was subsequently again appointed Prime Minister, and a new 14-member Council of Ministers was inaugurated in June. In March 1998, following protests by opposition parties at delays in the organization of legislative elections, an independent national elections commission was established. The elections were due to be held in July. In April a new political party, the União Nacional para Democracia e Progresso (UNDP) was established.

Attempted coup

In June 1998 rebel troops, led by Brig. (later Gen.) Ansumane Mané, who had recently been dismissed as Chief of Staff of the Armed Forces, seized control of the Bra military barracks in the capital and the international airport. Mané subsequently formed a military junta and demanded the resignation of Vieira and his administration. With the support of Senegalese and Guinean soldiers, troops loyal to the Government attempted unsuccessfully to regain control of rebel-held areas of the city, and heavy fighting ensued. Over the following days more than 3,000 foreign nationals were evacuated from the capital to Senegal. An estimated further 200,000 residents of Bissau fled the city. Fighting continued into July, with many members of the Guinea-Bissau armed forces reportedly defecting to the side of the rebels.

On 26 July 1998, following mediation by a delegation from the lusophone commonwealth body, the Comunidade dos Países de Língua Portuguesa (CPLP, see below), the Government and the rebels agreed to implement a truce. In August representatives of the Government and the rebels met, under the auspices of the CPLP and the Economic Community of West African States (ECOWAS, see p. 264), and an agreement was reached to transform the existing truce into a cease-fire. The accord provided for the deployment of international forces to maintain and supervise the cease-fire. In September talks between the Government and the rebels resumed. However, the rebels' demand that all Senegalese and Guinean forces be withdrawn from the country as a prerequisite to a definitive peace agreement was rejected by the Government and the following month the cease-fire collapsed. On 20 October the Government imposed a nationwide curfew, and on the following day Vieira declared a unilateral cease-fire. By that time almost all of the government troops had joined forces with the rebels, who were thought to control some 99% of the country. On 23 October Mané agreed to conform to a 48-hour truce, and agreement was subsequently reached for direct talks to be held. Further negotiations, held under the aegis of ECOWAS, resulted in the signing of a peace accord on 1 November. Under the terms of the accord, the two sides reaffirmed the cease-fire of 25 August, and resolved that the withdrawal of Senegalese and Guinean troops from Guinea-Bissau be conducted simultaneously with the deployment of an ECOMOG (ECOWAS Cease-fire Monitoring Group) interposition force, which would guarantee security on the border with Senegal. It was also agreed that a government of national unity would be established, to include representatives of the rebel junta, and that presidential and legislative elections would be held no later than March 1999. In November 1998 agreement was reached on the composition of a Joint Executive Commission to implement the peace accord. In December Francisco Jose Fadul was appointed Prime Minister, and Vieira and Mané reached agreement on the allocation of portfolios to the two sides.

In January 1999 agreement was reached between the Government, the rebel military junta and ECOWAS on the strength of the ECOMOG interposition force, which was to comprise some 710 troops. A timetable for the withdrawal of Senegalese and Guinean troops from the country was also established. However, at the end of January hostilities resumed in the capital. In February talks between the Government and the rebels produced agreement on a cease-fire and provided for the immediate withdrawal of Senegalese and Guinean troops. On 20 February the new Government of National Unity was announced. The disarmament of rebel troops and those loyal to the President began in March and the withdrawal of Senegalese and Guinean troops was completed that month. On 30 April the UN Secretary-General established the UN Peace-building Support Office in Guinea-Bissau (UNOGBIS), with a mandate to aid peace-building efforts, support the consolidation of democracy and the rule of law, encourage friendly relations with the country's neighbours and assist in the electoral process; its mandate was regularly extended in subsequent years. An extension until December 2008 was approved in late 2007 and Guinea-Bissau also became the third country on the agenda of the Peace-building Commission, the UN advisory body set up to help countries emerging from conflict avoid returning to war.

Vieira overthrown

In early May 1999 Vieira announced that the elections would take place on 28 December. However, on 7 May, to widespread condemnation by the international community, Vieira was overthrown by the rebel military junta, which claimed that their actions had been prompted by Vieira's refusal to allow his presidential guard to be disarmed. Vieira signed an unconditional surrender and the President of the ANP, Malam Bacai Sanhá, was appointed acting President of the Republic pending a presidential election. At a meeting in late May of representatives of the Government, the military junta and the political parties, agreement was reached that Vieira should stand trial for his involvement in the trafficking of arms to separatists from the Senegalese region of Casamance and for political and economic crimes relating to his terms in office. ECOMOG forces were withdrawn from the country in June. That month Vieira went into exile in Portugal where he was offered political asylum. In July constitutional amendments were introduced limiting the tenure of presidential office to two terms and abolishing the death penalty. It was also stipulated that the country's principal offices of state could only be held by Guinea-Bissau nationals born of Guinea-Bissau parents. In September an extraordinary congress of the PAIGC voted to expel Vieira and six others from the party. The incumbent Minister of Defence and Freedom Fighters, Francisco Benante, was appointed President of the party. In October the Attorney-General, Amine Michel Saad, announced that he had sufficient evidence to prosecute Vieira for crimes against humanity and expressed his intention to seek Vieira's extradition from Portugal.

Presidential and legislative elections took place on 28 November 1999. Of the 102 seats in the enlarged legislature, the PRS secured 38, the RGB—MB 28, the PAIGC 24, the Aliança Democrática (AD, an alliance of the FD and the PCD) four, the UM three, the Partido Social Democrata (PSD) three, and the FDS and the UNDP one each. As no candidate received the necessary 50% of the votes to win the presidential election outright, the leading candidates, Yalá of the PRS and Sanhá of the PAIGC, contested a second round of voting on 16 January 2000, at which Yalá secured victory with 72% of the votes cast. Yalá was inaugurated on the following day and installed a new Council of Ministers, which included members of several former opposition parties, later that month. Caetano N'Tchama of the PRS was appointed Prime Minister. The election was subsequently judged by international observers to have been 'free and fair'. In May tensions were reported between Yalá and certain elements in the army who viewed Mané as the rightful leader of the country, on the grounds that it was he who had ousted Vieira from power. In October Yalá appointed a State Council, comprising members of all parliamentary political parties, which was to have an advisory role.

Demonstrations organized by the PAIGC, in support of demands for the resignation of the Government, took place in Bissau in November 2000. In late November Mané declared himself Commander-in-Chief of the armed forces, following renewed violence in Bissau, instigated by soldiers loyal to him. However, government troops quickly suppressed the insurgency, and a number of opposition leaders were arrested. Mané fled the capital, and was subsequently killed by the security forces.

In October 2001 a motion of no confidence in Yalá was approved by the ANP; the vote had been instigated by opposition parties in response to what they considered to be increasingly unconstitutional actions by the President. A demonstration against Yalá in Bissau, attended by some 10,000 people, followed further demands for the President's resignation by a coalition of opposition parties. Prime Minister Faustino Fadut Imbali was dismissed in December and was replaced by Almara Nhassé, a member of the PRS and hitherto Minister of Internal Administration. Nhassé immediately formed a new Government, composed solely of members of the ruling coalition. Nhassé was subsequently elected President of the PRS, in place of Yalá.

The developing political uncertainty in the country intensified in November 2002, when Yalá dissolved the ANP and dismissed the Government, citing its incompetence in coping with the economic crisis. Legislative elections were scheduled for February 2003. Mario Pires was appointed as Prime Minister, to head a transitional Government, which was dominated by the PRS. Several political coalitions opposing the PRS were formed in late 2002 and early 2003 in preparation for the legislative elections, which had been postponed until 20 April. In December 2002 the PSD, the LIPE, the Partido da Renovação e Progresso and the Partido Socialista Guinéense created the União Eleitoral (UE). In February 2003 the Plataforma Unida—Mufunessa Larga Guiné was formed by the AD, the FDS, the Frente para a Libertação e Independência da Guiné and the Grupo de Democratas Independentes, which had been established by former members of the RGB—MB.

In March 2003 Yalá announced that the elections were to be further delayed, until 6 July. In May the army demanded the resignation of Prime Minister Pires, on the grounds that they had not been paid for six months. In an attempt to broaden support for his increasingly isolated presidency, in June Yalá appointed five opposition-affiliated ministers to the Government. In the same month the elections were postponed until 12 October. The elections were again postponed in early September.

Seabra deposes Yalá

On 14 September 2003 President Yalá was detained by the armed forces in a bloodless *coup d'état*, which was widely welcomed within Guinea-Bissau. The Chief of Staff of the Armed Forces, Gen. Veríssimo Correia Seabra, who led the coup, stated that the seizure of power had been in response to the worsening political and economic situation. Seabra proclaimed himself interim President of Guinea-Bissau, and President of a Comité Militar para a Recuperação da Ordem Constitucional e Democrática (Military Committee for the Restoration of Constitutional and Democratic Order). On 17 September Yalá officially resigned the presidency, and on 28 September Henrique Pereira Rosa, a business executive, and Artur Sanhá were sworn in as interim President and Prime Minister, respectively. On 2 October a transitional civilian Government was appointed, in accordance with an agreement signed by political organizations and the military authorities. It was envisaged that elections to the ANP would be held within six months, and a presidential election within 18 months. A 56-member National Transition Council (NTC), composed of representatives of political and civil groups and the army, was to monitor government policy.

In October 2003 President Rosa dismissed ex-President Yalá's close aides and appointed five new advisers, with the rank of minister. In November the Government resumed payment of civil servants' salaries, and schools were reopened, having been closed for much of the previous two years owing to a series of strikes by unpaid teachers, after the World Bank provided a loan of US $2.5m. to pay salaries. In early December the NTC announced that legislative elections would be held on 28 March 2004, with the presidential election expected to be held one year later (in accordance with the Transitional Charter drafted in October 2003).

Elections to the ANP took place on 28 and 30 March 2004 and voter turn-out was estimated at 74.6%. The PAIGC won 45 of the 100 seats while the PRS secured 35 and the PUSD 17. The PAIGC reached an agreement with the PRS, whereby the latter undertook to support the Government in return for senior positions in the ANP, governmental departments and other state institutions. The ANP was inaugurated on 7 May, and PAIGC President Carlos Gomes Júnior took office as Prime Minister on 10 May. The new Council of Ministers was sworn in on 12 May.

On 6 October 2004 Seabra and another senior military official were taken hostage and killed by a group of disaffected soldiers, led by Maj. Buate Yanta Namam, in protest against their non-payment for a peace-keeping operation undertaken in Liberia. On 6 and 7 October the soldiers, who emphasized that they were not seeking to overthrow the Government, presented their demands, which included an improvement in army conditions, a salary increase and the payment of salary arrears. Gomes Júnior attributed the unrest to political forces dissatisfied with the outcome of the April elections (widely assumed as referring to members of the PRS). On 10 October a Memorandum of Understanding was signed by Gomes Júnior, Yanta Naman and Maj.-Gen. Baptista Tagmé Na Wai, representing the armed forces, according to which the soldiers would return to their barracks and salary arrears would be paid. An amnesty was to be granted to the mutineers and later in October Gomes Júnior announced that nearly all salary arrears had been settled. A new military high command, reportedly chosen by the mutineers, was also installed. Na Wai became Chief of Staff of the Armed Forces, while José Americo Bubo Na Tchuto was appointed Navy Chief of Staff.

It was announced in March 2005 that a presidential election would take place on 19 June and the registration of voters proceeded later that month. Malam Bacai Sanhá, who served as acting President in 1999, was chosen as the candidate for the PAIGC. Meanwhile, both Vieira (who was standing as an independent) and Yalá, representing the PRS, announced their candidacies. According to the Transitional Charter, both Yalá and Vieira were subject to five-year bans from political activity; however, in April their candidacies were approved by the Supreme Court. Also in that month, Gomes Júnior effected a major reorganization of the Council of Ministers.

The return of Vieira

The presidential election took place, as scheduled, on 19 June 2005. Sanhá secured 35.5% of the votes cast, while Vieira took 28.9% and Yalá 25.0%. As none of the candidates had won an outright majority there followed on 24 July a second round of voting, contested by Sanhá and Vieira, at which Vieira received 52.4% of valid votes cast, while Sanhá took 47.7%. The rate of voter participation was recorded at 87.6% in the first round and 78.6% in the second round, and international observers declared the election to have been free and fair.

Despite allegations of widespread electoral fraud and Sanhá's demands that the results of the election be annulled, the outcome was upheld by the Supreme Court and Vieira took office on 1 October 2005. Tensions continued, however, among the pro-Vieira members of the PAIGC and the pro-Sanhá, governing faction of the party, which announced that it would accept the election result only days before Vieira's inauguration. In mid-October 14 PAIGC deputies resigned from the party and declared themselves independents, and several members of that party, together with the PRS and the PUSD, formed a pro-Vieira alliance, the Forúm de Convergência para o Desenvolvimento (FCD), with the intention of precipitating the collapse of Gomes Júnior's Government. Members of the FCD claimed to have a majority in the ANP, while the PAIGC could count on the support of only 31 of the 100 members of the legislature.

In late October 2005, following continued demands by the FCD for the dismissal of the Prime Minister, Vieira dissolved the Government. Aristides Gomes, the former Vice-President of the PAIGC, was appointed Prime Minister on 2 November. Meanwhile, civil unrest and criticism of the current political situation by non-governmental organizations exacerbated tensions, resulting in the temporary allocation to Aristides Gomes of the economy and finance portfolios, in order to facilitate the payment of civil service salaries. The new 19-member Government was sworn in on 9 November and comprised members of five parties (the PAIGC, the PRS, the PUSD, the PCD and the UE) and independents, the majority of whom were former members of the PAIGC. Notably, Issufo Sanhá of the PAIGC was reappointed as Minister of the Economy, the only member of the previous Government to remain in office. Vítor Mandinga, the leader of the PCD, was named Minister of Finance, and an independent, Ernesto de Carvalho, was subsequently appointed Minister of the Interior. The PAIGC challenged the constitutional legitimacy of the appointment of Aristides Gomes, claiming that as the party that held the largest number of seats in the legislature, it had the right to propose the new Prime Minister; however, in January 2006 the Supreme Court ruled that Vieira had acted in accordance with the Constitution.

In November 2006 Kumba Yalá was re-elected as leader of the PRS, following one year's absence from the country; he announced that he no longer recognized the FCD and sought early elections. In the same month the President dismissed the Minister of the Interior, de Carvalho (a close associate of Yalá). In mid-March 2007 the PAIGC, the PRS and the PUSD announced that they had signed a National Stability Pact (NSP), which aimed to precipitate the formation of a new government of national unity. The PRS and the PUSD also confirmed their withdrawal from the FCD. President Vieira initially refused to accede to demands to dismiss the Government; however, on 19 March 54 deputies approved a motion of no confidence in Prime Minister Gomes, who tendered his resignation 10 days later. Also in late March it was reported that the PUSD had withdrawn its support for the NSP. On 10 April Vieira nominated Martinho N'Dafa Cabi, a senior member of the PAIGC, who had held the positions of Deputy Prime Minister and Minister of National Defence in the Gomes Júnior administration, as the new Prime Minister. A new 29-member unity Government was installed in mid-April. Legislative elections were subsequently scheduled for November 2008 and the registration of voters commenced in July.

In early August 2008 a number of senior ministers were dismissed, prompting the PAIGC to withdraw from the government of national unity. In anticipation of the forthcoming elections Vieira dissolved the ANP and appointed Carlos Correia as Prime Minister at the head of a new Government composed largely of former PAIGC members loyal to him. Political tensions remained high and later that month it was revealed that an attempted coup to overthrow the President had been averted. Nevertheless, preparations for the legislative elections continued and the ballot duly took place as scheduled on 16 November. According to official results, the PAIGC won 67 seats in the ANP, securing 49.8% of the votes cast, while the PRS took 28 seats with 25.3% of the votes. The newly formed Partido Republicano para a Independência e o Desenvolvimento, led by Aristides Gomes, took three seats and the Partido para a Nova Democracia and the AD won one seat each. Voter participation was reported to have been high and international observers praised the 'political maturity' of the voters. However, a further failed coup attempt in late November—a number of mutinous soldiers were reported to have forced their way into the presidential palace, killing one member of the presidential guard—highlighted the growing instability in the country.

In late December 2008 a new Council of Ministers was named, with Gomes Júnior returning to the post of Prime Minister. Key appointments included Maj. Lúcio Soares, who was named as Minister of the Interior and Artur Silva, who became Minister of National Defence; José Mário Vaz assumed responsibility for the finance portfolio.

The assassination of Vieira

President Vieira was assassinated in an attack on his private residence in the early hours of 2 March 2009, which was reported to have been carried out by soldiers seeking to avenge the killing of Na Wai, allegedly ordered by Vieira just hours earlier.

Relations between the two had deteriorated in January when Na Wai ordered the disarming of the 400-member militia that had been recruited to protect the President after the November 2008 coup attempt. Na Wai had, in January 2009, reportedly escaped unharmed following an outbreak of gunfire at the presidential palace; three soldiers were held for questioning by military investigators, although it was strenuously denied that any attempt on Na Wai's life had been made. In the days immediately after Vieira's death senior army figures insisted that no coup had been carried out and stated that the armed forces reaffirmed their respect for the democratically elected institutions of state and the Constitution. On 3 March Raimundo Pereira, President of the ANP, was sworn in as Interim President, pending a presidential election that was, in accordance with the Constitution, to be held within 60 days. The Government subsequently announced that it would hold a judicial inquiry into the deaths of Na Wai and Vieira. The events in Guinea-Bissau were condemned by the African Union (AU), the UN, the European Union (EU, see p. 276) and ECOWAS, and the latter declared that it was to deploy a multi-disciplinary group to monitor and co-ordinate security sector reform in the country. In April Pereira issued a decree stipulating that the presidential election would take place on 28 June.

On 5 June 2009 Baciro Dabo, a close ally of Vieira and a former government minister who had announced his intention to contest the forthcoming presidential election as an independent candidate, was shot dead in his residence by armed men, and a second candidate, former Prime Minister Imbali, was reportedly abducted. With the security situation worsening—the former Minister of Defence Helder Proenca was also killed in early June—Pedro Nfanda withdrew from the presidential poll. Requests were filed with the Supreme Court for the election to be postponed and while the Constitution stipulated that the ballot should be delayed in the event of the death of a candidate, Interim President Pereira announced that the poll would proceed as scheduled. Malam Bacai Sanhá, again representing the PAIGC, won 39.6% of votes cast, while Mohamed Yalá Embaló (as Kumba Yalá, who had converted to Islam in 2008 had become known) took 29.4% and Henrique Rosa secured 24.2%. At a second round of voting, which took place on 26 July, Sanhá secured 63.3% of the votes cast, while Yalá Embaló, took 36.7%. Shortly after the election results were announced, Commdr José Zamora Induta, formerly the Navy Chief of Staff, was confirmed as Chief of Staff of the Armed Forces.

Sanhá was sworn in as President on 8 September 2009 and a new Council of Ministers, again headed by Gomes Júnior, was appointed in late October. The number of government ministers was reduced from 21 to 16 and Maria Adiatú Djaló Nandingna, Minister of Foreign Affairs in the outgoing administration, was appointed Minister of the Presidency of the Council of Ministers, Social Communication and Parliamentary Affairs, the most senior cabinet post after the Prime Minister. Adelino Mano Quetá assumed responsibility for the foreign affairs portfolio, while Aristedes Ocante da Silva, hitherto Minister of National Education, Culture and Science, became Minister of National Defence and Fighters for the Country's Freedom. In February 2010 Sanhá carried out a government reorganization in which the ministers of agriculture and of energy and natural resources (associates of Gomes Júnior) were both replaced.

In late December 2009 former Navy Chief of Staff Na Tchuto, who had fled to The Gambia following his alleged involvement in the coup attempt of August 2008 (see above), returned to the country, prompting the Government to order that he be arrested and prosecuted. Claiming to fear for his personal safety, Na Tchuto was granted refuge in the headquarters of UNOGBIS (which upon completion of its mandate was formally replaced on 1 January 2010 by UNIOGBIS, the UN Integrated Peace-Building Office in Guinea-Bissau).

Attempted military coup and continuing instability

On 1 April 2010 dissident members of the armed forces, led by the Deputy Army Chief of Staff, Gen. (later Maj.-Gen.) António Indjai, staged a coup attempt. Early that day rebel soldiers entered the UNIOGBIS compound to release Na Tchuto, who joined Indjai, subsequently causing many commentators to question the extent to which he may have been involved in the planning of the coup. Induta was seized, together with the head of military intelligence, Samba Djaló, and a number of other officers, after which he was transferred to a military compound outside of Bissau, where he remained in detention. After assuming control over the armed forces, Indjai and his entourage arrested Prime Minister Gomes Júnior at the government headquarters. Upon news of his detention, demonstrations were staged in the capital to express support for Gomes Júnior and rejection of the attempted coup. Indjai responded by announcing in a radio broadcast that he would kill Gomes Júnior unless his supporters dispersed. Shortly afterwards, however, the Prime Minister was released, and returned to his office. The international community condemned the attempted coup and urged that the Constitution be respected. On 8 April the US Department of State issued a statement accusing Na Tchuto and Ibraima Papá Camara, the Chief of Staff of the Air Force, of involvement in drugs-trafficking, and announced the freezing of the two men's assets in the USA. Although both Na Tchuto and Camara denied the accusations, the decision increased speculation that the coup attempt might have been linked to resistance within some elements of the armed forces to efforts to reform the country's security forces, which potentially jeopardized their control over illegal sources of revenue.

Throughout April 2010 there were rumours of further attempts to arrest the Prime Minister. After reportedly seeking refuge in foreign embassies on more than one occasion, Gomes Júnior fled the country and remained abroad for over one month, allegedly for health reasons, returning in June. In late June Sanhá appointed Indjai as the new Chief of Staff of the Armed Forces (the post having been left officially vacant since the ousting of Induta). In the same month the EU announced that it was to end its security sector reform mission in Guinea-Bissau (with effect from the end of September), in view of Na Tchuto and Camara's alleged involvement in narcotics-trafficking and Indjai's appointment. On 1 June Na Tchuto was formally acquitted by a military court of all the charges pending against him, and in October he was reinstated by Sanhá as Navy Chief of Staff (prompting criticism from the USA). In October Gomes Júnior suspended the Minister of the Interior, Hadja Satu Camara Pinto, from office, after she appointed police officers in defiance of a decree issued by the Prime Minister prohibiting this on the grounds that it would disrupt reforms in the armed and security forces. In December Camara Pinto tendered her resignation, complaining that President Sanhá (who had been admitted to hospital in Paris, France) had failed to support her in the dispute with Gomes Júnior. (Dinis Na Fantchamena was subsequently appointed as the new Minister of the Interior.)

In November 2010 the UN Security Council approved a resolution authorizing the extension of UNIOGBIS's mandate in the country until the end of 2011 (subsequently renewed until February 2013), expressing its concern at continuing instability in Guinea-Bissau, including a lack of control of the armed forces and continued summary detentions. The Government had also requested the deployment of an international stabilization force, which was to be established by the AU and ECOWAS to assist in post-conflict reconstruction and development. In December Induta, together with Djaló, were released from detention, shortly after the EU threatened to impose sanctions against the Government.

Following the withdrawal of EU support for Guinea-Bissau's security sector reform programme, a replacement plan devised by ECOWAS and the CPLP was finalized in November 2010 (and endorsed by the Council of Ministers in March 2011). In particular, the ECOWAS-CPLP 'roadmap' envisaged a reduction in the size of the military, and hence a concomitant reduction in its power and influence. To achieve this goal, a military pension fund was to be established to encourage servicemen to retire from the armed forces, while others were to be helped to reintegrate into civilian society. Although legislation facilitating the implementation of the roadmap was approved during 2011, by early 2012 little substantive progress had been made. Meanwhile, in March 2011 Angola, which had assumed a leading role in the ECOWAS-CPLP mission, transferred some 200 troops to Guinea-Bissau to assist in the training and restructuring of the security forces—representing the first phase of an expected deployment of 600 ECOWAS-CPLP personnel.

In May 2011 the official investigation into the June 2009 murders of Dabo and Proenca was suspended, ostensibly because of insufficient evidence, while the judicial inquiry examining the deaths of Na Wai and Vieira in March 2009 had only made limited headway by mid-2011. Opposition parties organized several anti-Government demonstrations during July to protest against this lack of progress and also to express concern about recent increases in the prices of staple foodstuffs. Sanhá effected an extensive cabinet reorganization in the following month, but rejected opposition demands to replace Gomes Júnior as Prime Minister. Most notably, the President appointed Baciro Djá as

Minister of National Defence and Fighters for the Country's Freedom.

Recent developments: the death of Sanhá

Sanhá travelled to Senegal in September 2011, reportedly to receive medical treatment for diabetes. He returned to Guinea-Bissau three weeks later, but in late November was again hospitalized in Senegal, before being transferred to a French hospital shortly thereafter. Amid growing concern for Guinea-Bissau's stability, on 26 December reports emerged from the capital of intra-military clashes. Gomes Júnior fled to the Angolan embassy during the unrest, and at least one fatality was recorded. The Government declared on the following day that Na Tchuto and a number of his associates had been arrested after attempting to stage a coup. However, other sources claimed that a military pay dispute had precipitated the violence, rather than an attempt to overthrow the Government. There were also suspicions that the fighting had been related to the illegal drugs trade. The Government announced its intention to launch an inquiry into the alleged uprising. Sanhá died in Paris on 9 January 2012. In compliance with the Constitution, ANP President Raimundo Pereira again became Interim President. Pereira subsequently proclaimed that a presidential election would be held on 18 March.

In early February 2012 Gomes Júnior resigned the premiership and announced his intention to stand for the presidency as the candidate of the PAIGC; Djaló Nandingna was appointed Acting Prime Minister. Among the other eight candidates to contest the presidential election, which was duly held on 18 March, were Yalá Embaló and Henrique Rosa. According to official results, Gomes Júnior won 49.0, while Yalá Embaló was placed second with 23.4% and Manuel Serifo Nhamadjo took 15.7%. The rate of voter participation was put at 55% of the registered electorate. As no candidate had secured an overall majority, a run-off election was scheduled to be held on 22 April. However, Yalá Embaló maintained that he would boycott the second round of voting, in protest at alleged irregularities that took place during the first round.

On 12 April 2012 members of the military seized power and detained Pereira and Gomes Júnior. It was reported that the coup was carried out in reaction to plans by Gomes Júnior to use Angolan troops to remove certain elements of the Guinea-Bissau armed forces. A 'Military Command' (Comando Militar) was formed, under the leadership of the army Deputy Chief of Staff, Gen. Mamadu Ture Kuruma, and on 18 April the establishment of a National Transitional Council (NTC—Conselho Nacional de Transição) was announced, after 22 political parties, although notably excluding the PAIGC, and the military junta agreed upon a timeframe towards new elections. The Government was dissolved. The NTC was to govern for two years and nominated Nhamadjo to the position of Transitional President; however, on 20 April Nhamadjo rejected his appointment to that post. Meanwhile, the African Union announced the suspension of Guinea-Bissau from the organization, pending the restoration of democratic rule, while the World Bank and the African Development Bank also suspended their development programmes. On 21 April the junta stated that the transitional period would be reduced to just one year. Nevertheless, in late April ECOWAS, which also suspended Guinea-Bissau's membership, issued the junta with a 72-hour deadline by which they were to have restored 'constitutional order', and maintained that failure to do so would invoke further sanctions and the dispatch of a military contingent to the country. Despite the release from custody of Pereira and Gomes Júnior on 27 April, ECOWAS confirmed the imposition of diplomatic and financial sanctions on Guinea-Bissau on 30 April. Although it was reported that Indjai had also been arrested in the immediate aftermath of the coup, by late April he had become a key figure in the negotiations between the junta and the regional community, and was believed to have masterminded the overthrow of the institutions of state.

Foreign Affairs

Regional relations

In 1989 a dispute arose between Guinea-Bissau and Senegal over the demarcation of maritime borders. Guinea-Bissau began proceedings against Senegal in the International Court of Justice (ICJ) after rejecting an international arbitration tribunal's ruling in favour of Senegal. In November 1991 the ICJ ruled that a 1960 agreement regarding the demarcation of maritime borders between Guinea-Bissau and Senegal remained valid. In December 1992, in retaliation for the deaths of two Senegalese soldiers, the Senegalese air force and infantry bombarded alleged Casamance separatist bases in the São Domingos area of Guinea-Bissau. In October 1993 the Presidents of Guinea-Bissau and Senegal signed an agreement providing for the joint management and exploitation of the countries' maritime zones. Petroleum resources were to be divided, with Senegal receiving an 85% share and Guinea-Bissau the remaining 15%. Fishing resources were to be divided according to the determination of a joint management agency. The agreement was renewable after a period of 20 years. In December 1995 the legislature authorized the ratification of the October 1993 accord. In the previous month the ICJ announced that Guinea-Bissau had halted all proceedings regarding the border dispute with Senegal.

In February 1995 the Senegalese air force bombarded a village in Guinea-Bissau, close to the border with Senegal. Despite an acknowledgement by the Senegalese authorities that the bombing had occurred as a result of an error, the Senegalese armed forces conducted a similar attack later that month. In March President Abdou Diouf of Senegal visited Guinea-Bissau to provide a personal apology for the two recent incidents and to offer a commitment that Senegal would respect Guinea-Bissau's sovereignty. In September agreement was reached on strengthening co-operation and establishing dialogue concerning security on the countries' joint border. However, a further attack by the Senegalese air force in October prompted the Guinea-Bissau legislature to form a commission of inquiry to investigate such border incidents.

In April 2000 there were renewed reports of incidents on the border between Senegal and Guinea-Bissau. In August an agreement was signed by Yalá and President Abdoulaye Wade of Senegal providing for the establishment of a joint military force to patrol the border area. Following the signing of a peace accord between the Senegalese Government and the Casamance separatists in December 2004, security in the region improved. However, a dissident faction of the separatists renewed disruption and from mid-March 2006 further skirmishes occurred with Guinea-Bissau troops, causing the displacement of civilian population. Tensions between the two countries mounted again in October 2009, when a minor border dispute related to the construction of a hotel by a Guinean construction company in territory claimed by the two countries led to the deployment of troops, but were defused soon afterwards.

Relations between Guinea-Bissau and The Gambia were severely strained in June 2002, when President Yalá accused the Government of The Gambia of harbouring and training Casamance rebels and former associates of Gen. Mané, the leader of the coup of 1998 and attempted coup of 2000. With specific reference to the alleged attempted coup of May 2002, Yalá threatened invasion of The Gambia if support for the rebels continued; President Jammeh of The Gambia denied any such support was being provided. A visit to The Gambia by Guinea-Bissau's Minister of Foreign Affairs in mid-June eased tensions somewhat, and was followed by UN intervention in July, which recommended the reactivation of a joint commission of the two countries. An improvement in relations was signalled by a visit by Yalá to The Gambia in October.

Other external relations

The People's Republic of China has been active in promoting good economic relations with Guinea-Bissau since the mid-2000s and funded various public projects, such as the construction of a new parliament building in 2005. This was regarded as undermining the unified approach of the rest of the international donor community in eliciting commitments to reform in return for aid. China benefited from maritime treaties and fishing rights in Guinea-Bissau territorial waters.

In July 1996 Guinea-Bissau was among the five lusophone African nations that, along with Brazil and Portugal, officially established the CPLP, a lusophone grouping intended to benefit each member state by means of joint co-operation in technical, cultural and social matters. Portugal provided Guinea-Bissau with considerable funding and other aid. Guinea-Bissau was a signatory to the 'Luanda Declaration' in November 2011, which pledged greater co-operation between the CPLP member states in the fields of, *inter alia*, security, crime prevention and immigration.

CONSTITUTION AND GOVERNMENT

Under the terms of the 1984 Constitution (revised in 1991, 1996 and 1999), Guinea-Bissau is a multi-party state, although the formation of parties on a tribal or geographical basis is prohibited. Legislative power is vested in the Assembleia Nacional

Popular, which comprises 100 members, elected by universal adult suffrage for a term of four years. Executive power is vested in the President of the Republic, who is Head of State and who governs with the assistance of an appointed Council of Ministers, led by the Prime Minister. The President is elected by universal adult suffrage for a term of five years.

REGIONAL AND INTERNATIONAL CO-OPERATION

Guinea-Bissau is a member of the African Union (see p. 189), of the Economic Community of West African States (ECOWAS, see p. 264) and of the West African organs of the Franc Zone (see p. 333). In 2004 Guinea-Bissau became a member of the Community of Sahel-Saharan States (see p. 449).

Guinea-Bissau became a member of the UN in 1974 and was admitted to the World Trade Organization (WTO, see p. 433) in 1995. Guinea-Bissau participates in the Group of 77 (G77, see p. 450) developing countries.

ECONOMIC AFFAIRS

In 2010, according to estimates by the World Bank, Guinea-Bissau's gross national income (GNI), measured at average 2008–10 prices, was US $890m., equivalent to $590 per head (or $1,180 on an international purchasing-power parity basis). During 2001–10, it was estimated, the population increased at an average annual rate of 2.0%, while during 2001–10 gross domestic product (GDP) per head decreased, in real terms, by an average of 0.7% per year. Overall GDP increased, in real terms, at an average annual rate of 1.4% in 2001–10; it increased by 3.5% in 2010.

Agriculture (including forestry and fishing) contributed 43.8% of GDP in 2010, according to the African Development Bank (AfDB) and the sector engaged an estimated 78.7% of the economically active population in mid-2012, according to FAO. The main cash crops are cashew nuts (production of which in 2010 was estimated by FAO at 91,100 metric tons, with export earnings in 2010 totalling 47m. francs CFA) and cotton. Other crops produced include rice, oil palm fruit, millet, coconuts, cassava, plantains and maize. Livestock and timber production are also important. The fishing industry developed rapidly during the 1990s, and earnings from fishing exports and the sale of fishing licences are a significant source of government revenue (revenue from fishing licences was 7,515m. francs CFA in 2005, equivalent to 26.9% of total revenue). A study conducted in 2004 revealed that the potential annual fishing catch was 96,000 tons, although in 2009 the total catch recorded by FAO amounted to only 6,800; in early 2006 the Minister of Fisheries and the Maritime Economy estimated that 40,000 tons of fish were stolen from Guinea-Bissau waters annually. According to the World Bank, agricultural GDP increased, in real terms, by an average of 3.9% per year in 2000–08; it increased by 3.5% in 2008.

Industry (including mining, manufacturing, construction and power) employed an estimated 4.1% of the economically active population at mid-1994 and, according to the AfDB, provided 13.7% of GDP in 2010. According to the World Bank, industrial GDP grew, in real terms, by an average of 4.2% per year in 2000–08; growth of 3.8% was recorded in 2008.

The mining sector is underdeveloped, although Guinea-Bissau possesses reserves of bauxite, phosphates, diamonds and gold. A Canadian company was attempting to develop phosphate mining at Farim, in the north of the country, in the early 2000s. In 2003 recoverable petroleum reserves were estimated at 2,000m. barrels per day.

The sole branches of the manufacturing sector are food-processing, brewing and timber- and cotton-processing, while there are plans to develop fish-processing. According to the AfDB, manufacturing contributed 11.8% of GDP in 2010. According to the World Bank, manufacturing GDP increased, in real terms, by an average of 4.1% per year in 2000–08; growth of 4.0% was recorded in 2008.

The construction sector contributed 1.5% of GDP in 2010. According to estimates by the AfDB, the sector recorded a massive decline in 2008, decreasing by 33.3%, but recovered and grew by 10.0% in both 2009 and in 2010.

Energy is derived principally from thermal and hydroelectric power. Imports of refined petroleum products comprised 20.8% of the value of total imports in 2010. Energy production since 1999 has been insufficient to supply demand in Bissau, mainly owing to fuel shortages caused by government-set low prices, and to equipment failures caused by poor maintenance. As a result, most energy is currently supplied by private generators.

Services employed an estimated 19.4% of the economically active population at mid-1994, and, according to the AfDB, provided 42.5% of GDP in 2010. According to the World Bank, the combined GDP of the service sectors increased by 1.4% in 2000–08; services GDP grew by 4.0% in 2008.

In 2010 Guinea-Bissau recorded a trade deficit of 37.8m. francs CFA, and there was a deficit of 27.7m. francs CFA on the current account of the balance of payments, according to the IMF. In 2010 the principal source of imports was Senegal (12.3%). In that year India was the principal market for exports (58.8%). In 2010 the principal export was cashew nuts. The principal imports in that year were refined petroleum products and rice.

According to the IMF, in 2010 there was a budgetary deficit of 900m. francs CFA. Guinea Bissau's general government gross debt was 643,762m francs CFA in 2009, equivalent to 163.8% of GDP. Guinea-Bissau's total external debt was US $1,111m. at the end of 2009, out of which $950m. was public and publicly guaranteed debt. In that year the cost of servicing long-term public and publicly guaranteed debt and repayments to the IMF was equivalent to 3.4% of the value of exports of goods, services and income (excluding workers' remittances). In 2003–2010 the average annual rate of inflation was 2.9%. Consumer prices decreased by 1.7% in 2009, but increased by 1.2% in 2010.

Guinea-Bissau is one of the world's poorest, and most indebted, countries. Its economy is largely dependent on the traditional rural sector, which employs the vast majority of the labour force and produces primarily for subsistence. Revenue from the export of cashew nuts is vital to the country's economy and foreign financing accounts for a significant part of budget revenue. Relations with donors have, however, been uneasy since the early 2000s and support has periodically been withheld. The economy has also been negatively affected by chronic political instability and the growing use of the country as a route for the trafficking of illegal narcotics between South America and Europe. According to the IMF, in 2010 GDP growth (assisted by higher prices for cashew nuts, a recovery in the construction sector and increased remittances) rose to 3.5%. In May the Fund approved a three-year Extended Credit Facility of US $33.3m. to support the Government's economic programme, and in December Guinea-Bissau was pronounced by the IMF to have met the requirements to reach completion point under the initiative for heavily indebted poor countries (which had begun in 2000). The IMF and the World Bank subsequently announced their decision to support $1,200m. in debt relief for Guinea-Bissau, which also became eligible for further assistance under a Multilateral Debt Relief Initiative. In May 2011 the 'Paris Club' of creditor nations announced debt relief totalling $283m., while Angola, Brazil, France, the European Union (see p. 276) and the African Development Bank also cancelled large proportions of Guinea-Bissau's debt during that year. The IMF estimated that economic growth increased to 5.3% in 2011, supported predominantly by further rises in cashew output and prices. Activity in the construction sector also contributed to this improvement in GDP expansion. Guinea-Bissau's economic outlook appeared encouraging in the short term, and the IMF projected GDP growth of 4.5% in 2012, again driven by the cashew and construction sectors. However, the economy remained undiversified, leaving it vulnerable to fluctuations in the global price of cashew nuts, and there were fears of renewed political instability following an alleged coup attempt in December 2011 and the death of President Malam Bacai Sanhá in January 2012.

PUBLIC HOLIDAYS

2013: 1 January (New Year's Day), 20 January (Death of Amílcar Cabral), 8 March (International Women's Day), 1 May (Labour Day), 3 August (Anniversary of the Killing of Pidjiguiti), 7 August* (Korité, end of Ramadan), 24 September (National Day), 14 October* (Tabaski, Feast of the Sacrifice), 14 November (Anniversary of the Movement of Readjustment), 25 December (Christmas Day).

* These holidays are dependent on the Islamic lunar calendar and may vary by one or two days from the dates given.

Statistical Survey

Source (unless otherwise stated): Instituto Nacional de Estatística Guiné-Bissau, Av. Amílcar Cabral, CP 6, Bissau; tel. 3225457; e-mail inec@mail.gtelecom.gw; internet www.stat-guinebissau.com.

Area and Population

AREA, POPULATION AND DENSITY

Area (sq km)	36,125*
Population (census results)	
1 December 1991	983,367
15–29 March 2009	
Males	737,634
Females	783,196
Total	1,520,830
Population (UN estimates at mid- year)†	
2010	1,515,224
2011	1,547,049
2012	1,579,631
Density (per sq km) at mid-2012	43.7

* 13,948 sq miles.
† Source: UN, *World Population Prospects: The 2010 revision*.

POPULATION BY AGE AND SEX
(UN estimates at mid-2012)

	Males	Females	Total
0–14	323,784	322,423	646,207
15–64	435,401	445,501	880,902
65 and over	23,779	28,743	52,522
Total	782,964	796,667	1,579,631

Source: UN, *World Population Prospects: The 2010 Revision*.

ETHNIC GROUPS

1996 (percentages): Balante 30; Fulani 20; Mandjak 14; Mandinka 12; Papel 7; Other 16 (Source: Comunidade dos Países de Língua Portuguesa).

POPULATION BY REGION
(2009 census)

Bafatá	210,007	Quinará	63,610
Biombo	97,120	Sector Autónomo Bissau (SAB)	387,909
Bolama/Bijagós	34,563	Tombali	94,939
Cacheu	192,508	**Total**	1,520,830
Gabú	215,530		
Oio	224,644		

PRINCIPAL TOWNS
(population at 2009 census)

Bissau (capital)	365,097*	Bigene	51,412
Gabú†	81,495	Farim	48,264
Bafatá	68,956	Mansôa	46,046
Bissorã	56,585	Pitche	45,594

* Figure for Sector Autónomo Bissau (SAB) administrative division.
† Formerly Nova Lamego.

BIRTHS AND DEATHS

	2008	2009	2010
Birth rate (per 1,000)	41.2	42.0	41.8
Death rate (per 1,000)	17.2	16.0	16.0

Source: African Development Bank.

Life expectancy (years at birth, WHO estimates): 53 (males 53; females 54) in 2009 (Source: WHO, *World Health Statistics*).

ECONOMICALLY ACTIVE POPULATION
('000 persons at mid-1994)

	Males	Females	Total
Agriculture, etc.	195	175	370
Industry	15	5	20
Services	80	14	94
Total	290	194	484

Source: UN Economic Commission for Africa, *African Statistical Yearbook*.

Mid-2012 (estimates in '000): Agriculture, etc. 463; Total labour force 588 (Source: FAO).

Health and Welfare

KEY INDICATORS

Total fertility rate (children per woman, 2009)	5.7
Under-5 mortality rate (per 1,000 live births, 2009)	193
HIV/AIDS (% of persons aged 15–49, 2009)	2.5
Physicians (per 1,000 head, 2004)	0.1
Hospital beds (per 1,000 head, 2007)	0.7
Health expenditure (2008): US $ per head (PPP)	48
Health expenditure (2008): % of GDP	8.6
Health expenditure (2008): public (% of total)	17.7
Access to water (% of persons, 2008)	60
Access to sanitation (% of persons, 2008)	21
Total carbon dioxide emissions ('000 metric tons, 2007)	285.8
Carbon dioxide emissions per head (metric tons, 2007)	0.2
Human Development Index (2011): ranking	176
Human Development Index (2011): value	0.353

For sources and definitions, see explanatory note on p. vi.

Agriculture

PRINCIPAL CROPS
('000 metric tons)

	2008	2009	2010
Rice, paddy	148.8	181.9	177.0*
Maize	16.7	6.6	12.3*
Millet	31.4	12.3	28.1*
Sorghum	18.3	14.6	17.6
Cassava	47.7	27.7	88.8*
Sugar cane†	6.0	6.0	6.0
Cashew nuts†	81.0	64.7	91.1
Groundnuts, with shell	46.5	30.7	69.7
Coconuts	45.5*	39.5*	40.1†
Oil palm fruit†	80.0	80.0	80.0
Plantains†	41.3	44.0	42.4
Oranges†	6.1	6.7	6.5

* Unofficial figure.
† FAO estimate(s).

Aggregate production ('000 metric tons, may include official, semi-official or estimated data): Total cereals 217.0 in 2008, 217.2 in 2009, 237.0 in 2010; Total roots and tubers 130.2 in 2008, 100.4 in 2009, 161.9 in 2010; Total vegetables (incl. melons) 32.9 in 2008, 26.1 in 2009, 34.2 in 2010; Total fruits (excl. melons) 82.4 in 2008, 89.6 in 2009, 87.1 in 2010.

Source: FAO.

LIVESTOCK
('000 head, year ending September, FAO estimates)

	2008	2009	2010
Cattle	599	620	642
Pigs	401	410	419
Sheep	389	420	454
Goats	393	416	441
Chickens	1,750	1,925	2,000

Source: FAO.

LIVESTOCK PRODUCTS
('000 metric tons, FAO estimates)

	2008	2009	2010
Cattle meat	6.7	6.1	6.4
Pig meat	12.5	12.8	12.8
Cows' milk	16.3	16.9	17.3
Goats' milk	3.6	3.8	4.0

Source: FAO.

Forestry

ROUNDWOOD REMOVALS
('000 cubic metres, excluding bark)

	2008	2009	2010
Sawlogs, veneer logs and logs for sleepers	1.9	1.9*	1.9*
Other industrial wood*	130.0	130.0	130.0
Fuel wood*	2,523.1	2,561.3	2,600.0
Total*	2,655.0	2,693.2	2,731.9

* FAO estimate(s).

Source: FAO.

SAWNWOOD PRODUCTION
('000 cubic metres, including railway sleepers, FAO estimates)

	1970	1971	1972
Total	10	16	16

1973–2010: Production assumed to be unchanged since 1972 (FAO estimates).

Source: FAO.

Fishing

(metric tons, live weight, FAO estimates)

	2007	2008	2009
Freshwater fishes	150	150	150
Marine fishes	2,650	2,866	2,862
Sea catfishes	340	385	385
Meagre	240	240	240
Mullets	1,500	1,500	1,500
Sompat grunt	200	230	230
Lesser African threadfin	370	420	420
Total catch (incl. others)	6,500	6,804	6,800

Source: FAO.

Industry

SELECTED PRODUCTS
('000 metric tons, unless otherwise indicated)

	2001	2002	2003
Hulled rice	69.1	68.4	67.7
Groundnuts (processed)	6.8	6.7	6.6
Bakery products	7.6	7.7	7.9
Frozen fish	1.7	1.7	1.7
Dry and smoked fish	3.6	3.7	3.8
Vegetable oils (million litres)	3.6	3.6	3.7
Beverages (million litres)	3.5	0.0	0.0
Dairy products (million litres)	1.1	0.9	0.9
Wood products	4.7	4.5	4.4
Soap	2.6	2.5	2.4
Electric energy (million kWh)	18.9	19.4	15.8

Source: IMF, *Guinea-Bissau: Selected Issues and Statistical Appendix* (March 2005).

Electric energy (million kWh, estimates): 66 in 2006; 70 in 2007; 70 in 2008 (Source: UN Industrial Commodity Statistics Database).

Finance

CURRENCY AND EXCHANGE RATES

Monetary Units
100 centimes = 1 franc de la Communauté financière africaine (CFA).

Sterling, Dollar and Euro Equivalents (30 December 2011)
£1 sterling = 783.813 francs CFA;
US $1 = 506.961 francs CFA;
€1 = 655.957 francs CFA;
10,000 francs CFA = £12.76 = $19.73 = €15.24.

Average Exchange Rate (francs CFA per US $)
2009 472.186
2010 495.277
2011 471.866

Note: An exchange rate of 1 French franc = 50 francs CFA, established in 1948, remained in force until January 1994, when the CFA franc was devalued by 50%, with the exchange rate adjusted to 1 French franc = 100 francs CFA. This relationship to French currency remained in effect with the introduction of the euro on 1 January 1999. From that date, accordingly, a fixed exchange rate of €1 = 655.957 francs CFA has been in operation. Following Guinea-Bissau's admission in March 1997 to the Union économique et monétaire ouest-africaine, the country entered the Franc Zone on 17 April. As a result, the Guinea peso was replaced by the CFA franc, although the peso remained legal tender until 31 July. The new currency was introduced at an exchange rate of 1 franc CFA = 65 Guinea pesos. At 31 March 1997 the exchange rate in relation to US currency was $1 = 36,793.3 Guinea pesos.

BUDGET

Revenue (million francs CFA)	2003	2004	2005
Tax revenue	11,941	11,830	18,334
Income taxes	2,907	2,838	4,074
Corporate tax	2,139	1,596	1,973
Individual taxes	587	605	1,338
Consumption taxes	1,437	1,420	2,148
General sales tax	3,568	3,192	5,649
Taxes on international trade and transactions	3,745	4,047	6,429
Import duties	2,583	2,347	3,754
Export duties	1,171	1,699	2,010
Port service charges	—	—	662
Other taxes	—	50	77
Non-tax revenue	8,903	12,699	9,644
Fees and duties	8,142	9,101	7,558
Fishing licences	7,977	8,988	7,515
Other non-tax revenues	760	3,597	2,087
Total	20,844	24,529	27,978

Source: IMF, *Guinea-Bissau: Selected Issues and Statistical Appendix* (August 2006).

2007 ('000 million francs CFA): Total revenue and grants 53.8 (Tax revenue 18.8, Non-tax revenue 7.8, Grants 27.2). Source: IMF, *Guinea-Bissau: Use of Fund Resources—Request for Third Purchase Under Emergency Post-Conflict Assistance—Staff Report; Staff Supplement; Press Release; and Statement by the Executive Director for Guinea-Bissau* (July 2009).

2008 ('000 million francs CFA): Total revenue and grants 65.3 (Tax revenue 20.9, Non-tax revenue 13.7, Grants 30.7). Source: IMF, *Guinea-Bissau: First Review Under the Three-Year Arrangement Under the Extended Credit Facility and Financing Assurances Review—Staff Report; Staff Statement; Press Release on the Executive Board Discussion; and Statement by the Executive Director for Guinea-Bissau* (December 2010).

2009 ('000 million francs CFA): Total revenue and grants 97.5 (Tax revenue 26.6, Non-tax revenue 8.8, Grants 62.1). Source: IMF, *Guinea-Bissau: First Review Under the Three-Year Arrangement Under the Extended Credit Facility and Financing Assurances Review—Staff Report; Staff Statement; Press Release on the Executive Board Discussion; and Statement by the Executive Director for Guinea-Bissau* (December 2010).

2010 ('000 million francs CFA): Total revenue and grants 84.6 (Tax revenue 33.1, Non-tax revenue 11.5, Grants 40.0). Source: IMF, *Guinea-Bissau: Third Review Under the Three-Year Arrangement Under the Extended Credit Facility and Financing Assurances Review—Staff Report; Joint IMF/World Bank Debt Sustainability Analysis; Informational Annex; Press Release on the Executive Board Discussion; and Statement by the Executive Director for Guinea-Bissau* (December 2011).

2011 ('000 million francs CFA, programmed): Total revenue and grants 88.8 (Tax revenue 37.9, Non-tax revenue 11.9, Grants 38.9). Source: IMF, *Guinea-Bissau: Third Review Under the Three-Year Arrangement Under the Extended Credit Facility and Financing Assurances Review—Staff Report; Joint IMF/World Bank Debt Sustainability Analysis; Informational Annex; Press Release on the Executive Board Discussion; and Statement by the Executive Director for Guinea-Bissau* (December 2011).

2012 ('000 million francs CFA, projections): Total revenue and grants 101.6 (Tax revenue 46.7, Non-tax revenue 15.1, Grants 39.8). Source: IMF, *Guinea-Bissau: Third Review Under the Three-Year Arrangement Under the Extended Credit Facility and Financing Assurances Review—Staff Report; Joint IMF/World Bank Debt Sustainability Analysis; Informational Annex; Press Release on the Executive Board Discussion; and Statement by the Executive Director for Guinea-Bissau* (December 2011).

Expenditure ('000 million francs CFA)	2010	2011*	2012†
Current expenditure	49.3	55.3	61.8
Wages and salaries	20.7	23.8	26.3
Goods and services	8.6	9.1	11.0
Transfers	10.7	12.6	12.5
Other current expenditures	8.6	9.0	11.8
Scheduled interest payments	0.7	0.8	0.3
Capital expenditure and net lending	36.2	42.5	44.6
Total	85.5	97.9	106.4

* Programmed figures.

† Projections.

Source: IMF, *Guinea-Bissau: Third Review Under the Three-Year Arrangement Under the Extended Credit Facility and Financing Assurances Review—Staff Report; Joint IMF/World Bank Debt Sustainability Analysis; Informational Annex; Press Release on the Executive Board Discussion; and Statement by the Executive Director for Guinea-Bissau* (December 2011).

CENTRAL BANK RESERVES
(US $ million at 31 December)

	2008	2009	2010
IMF special drawing rights	0.08	18.64	19.09
Reserve position in IMF	0.08	0.15	0.20
Foreign exchange	124.40	149.80	137.15
Total	124.56	168.59	156.43

Source: IMF, *International Financial Statistics*.

MONEY SUPPLY
(million francs CFA at 31 December)

	2008	2009	2010
Currency outside banks	53,320	56,318	64,086
Demand deposits at deposit money banks	27,181	30,850	40,400
Total money (incl. others)	80,688	87,483	104,871

Source: IMF, *International Financial Statistics*.

COST OF LIVING
(Consumer Price Index; base: 2003 = 100)

	2006	2007	2008
Food, beverages and tobacco	105.2	111.3	129.1
Clothing	108.0	112.0	104.0
Rent, water, electricity, gas and other fuels	105.8	111.6	121.5
All items (incl. others)	106.4	111.2	122.9

2009: Food, beverages and tobacco 128.3; All items (incl. others) 120.8.

2010: Food, beverages and tobacco 99.4; All items (incl. others) 122.2.

Source: ILO.

NATIONAL ACCOUNTS

Expenditure on the Gross Domestic Product
(US $ million at current prices)

	2008	2009	2010
Government final consumption expenditure	45,986	53,297	55,196
Private final consumption expenditure	357,433	364,196	368,527
Gross capital formation	32,526	31,212	39,818
Change in inventories	378	400	422
Total domestic expenditure	436,323	449,105	463,963
Exports of goods and services	58,627	60,502	73,360
Less Imports of goods and services	117,499	114,523	118,523
GDP in purchasers' values	377,451	395,084	418,800

Gross Domestic Product by Economic Activity
(million francs CFA at current prices)

	2008	2009	2010
Agriculture, hunting, forestry and fishing	173,021	165,500	166,792
Mining and quarrying	105	110	116
Manufacturing	43,207	44,142	44,877
Electricity, gas and water	1,502	1,636	1,670
Construction	3,469	5,154	5,739
Trade, restaurants and hotels	72,874	79,184	80,173
Finance, insurance and real estate	1,487	1,491	1,495
Transport, storage and communications	15,941	20,028	21,142
Public administration and defence	33,623	41,712	41,724
Other services	18,007	17,487	17,500
Sub-total	363,236	376,444	381,228
Indirect taxes	14,932	24,422	26,376
Less Imputed bank service charge	717	5,782	4,803
Statistical discrepancy	—	—	15,999
GDP at purchasers' values	377,451	395,084	418,800

Source: African Development Bank.

BALANCE OF PAYMENTS
('000 million francs CFA)

	2008	2009	2010
Exports of goods f.o.b.	54.5	55.5	59.5
Imports of goods f.o.b.	–89.0	–95.5	–97.3
Trade balance	–34.5	–40.0	–37.8
Exports of services	5.4	5.4	5.7
Imports of services	–23.9	–30.8	–25.2
Balance on goods and services	–53.0	–65.3	–57.3
Other income (net)	–6.0	–4.8	–0.5
Balance on goods, services and income	–59.0	–70.1	–57.8
Official current transfers	24.3	31.5	14.5
Private current transfers	16.4	13.7	15.5
Current balance	–18.3	–25.0	–27.7
Capital account (net)	38.4	34.6	30.8
Financial account (net)	–39.0	–11.4	–457.9
Statistical discrepancy	11.4	6.0	–3.3
Overall balance	–7.5	4.2	–458.1

Source: IMF, *Guinea-Bissau: Third Review Under the Three-Year Arrangement Under the Extended Credit Facility and Financing Assurances Review—Staff Report; Joint IMF / World Bank Debt Sustainability Analysis; Informational Annex; Press Release on the Executive Board Discussion; and Statement by the Executive Director for Guinea-Bissau* (December 2011).

External Trade

PRINCIPAL COMMODITIES
(US $ million)

Imports c.i.f.	2003	2004	2005*
Foodstuffs	25.8	19.1	15.1
Rice	18.2	12.7	10.8
Wheat flour	2.5	1.8	0.9
Oil	2.1	1.0	1.2
Beverages and tobacco	5.5	4.9	6.0
Other consumer goods	5.0	9.8	15.0
Petroleum and petroleum products	8.7	12.4	15.8
Diesel fuel and gasoline	7.7	8.8	13.7
Construction materials	7.2	12.5	20.6
Transport equipment	4.9	10.2	13.2
Passenger vehicles	3.4	7.5	8.2
Freight vehicles	1.1	2.1	3.5
Electrical equipment and machinery	6.0	10.6	12.0
Non-registered trade	6.1	3.3	15.7
Total (incl. others)	70.8	83.0	119.1

* Estimates.

Exports f.o.b.	2003	2004	2005
Agricultural products	56.7	73.2	94.4
Cashew nuts	55.7	72.8	93.5
Total (incl. others)	62.2	75.8	100.8

Source: IMF, *Guinea-Bissau: Selected Issues and Statistical Appendix* (August 2006).

2006 (million francs CFA): *Imports:* Rice 11,024; Wheat flour 3,616; Beverages 3,475; Refined petroleum products 18,611; Construction materials 4,218; Total (incl. others) 75,731. *Exports:* Cashew nuts 28,902; Total (incl. others) 38,766 (Source: African Development Bank).

2007 (million francs CFA): *Imports:* Rice 9,395; Wheat flour 4,214; Beverages 3,510; Refined petroleum products 19,278; Construction materials 3,296; Total (incl. others) 91,736. *Exports:* Cashew nuts 32,113; Total (incl. others) 51,299 (Source: African Development Bank).

2008 (million francs CFA): *Imports:* Rice 9,769; Wheat flour 2,251; Beverages 4,451; Refined petroleum products 20,000; Construction materials 3,400; Total (incl. others) 89,010. *Exports:* Cashew nuts 46,213; Total (incl. others) 57,421 (Source: African Development Bank).

2009 (million francs CFA): *Imports:* Rice 9,876; Wheat flour 2,376; Beverages 4,546; Refined petroleum products 18,531; Construction materials 3,516; Total (incl. others) 93,916. *Exports:* Cashew nuts 45,863; Total (incl. others) 56,418 (Source: African Development Bank).

2010 (million francs CFA): *Imports:* Rice 8,963; Wheat flour 1,731; Beverages 3,731; Refined petroleum products 20,000; Construction materials 4,013; Total (incl. others) 96,121. *Exports:* Cashew nuts 46,812; Total (incl. others) 57,021 (Source: African Development Bank).

PRINCIPAL TRADING PARTNERS
(percentage of trade)

Imports	2003	2004	2005
France	2.7	2.2	2.5
India	2.0	0.8	0.6
Italy	8.0	3.7	20.4
Netherlands	2.9	4.0	3.0
Pakistan	0.3	1.9	1.4
Portugal	13.3	13.8	12.7
Senegal	36.2	44.5	34.6
Spain	4.4	2.3	1.2

Exports	2003	2004	2005
Guinea	1.9	0.2	0.3
India	62.3	52.2	67.4
Nigeria	15.7	13.2	19.0
Portugal	2.6	0.8	1.1
Senegal	0.9	1.1	1.5
USA	2.6	22.2	0.2

Source: IMF, *Guinea-Bissau: Selected Issues and Statistical Appendix* (August 2006).

2006 (million francs CFA): *Imports:* China, People's Republic 1,075; France 1,025; India 1,314; Portugal 2,428; Senegal 15,745; Total (incl. others) 75,731. *Exports:* India 20,002; Singapore 8,827; Total (incl. others) 38,766 (Source: African Development Bank).

2007 (million francs CFA): *Imports:* China, People's Republic 1,295; France 987; India 1,425; Portugal 2,369; Senegal 10,815; Total (incl. others) 91,736. *Exports:* India 34,183; Singapore 1,204; Total (incl. others) 51,299 (Source: African Development Bank).

2008 (million francs CFA): *Imports:* China, People's Republic 1,278; India 70; Portugal 3,251; Senegal 11,351; Total (incl. others) 89,010. *Exports:* India 35,351; Singapore 1,123; Total (incl. others) 57,421 (Source: African Development Bank).

2009 (million francs CFA): *Imports:* China, People's Republic 1,233; India 1,426; Portugal 2,132; Senegal 9,321; Total (incl. others) 93,916. *Exports:* India 34,213; Singapore 1,093; Total (incl. others) 56,418 (Source: African Development Bank).

2010 (million francs CFA): *Imports:* China, People's Republic 900; India 1,236; Portugal 3,031; Senegal 11,821; Total (incl. others) 96,121. *Exports:* India 33,512; Singapore 1,216; Total (incl. others) 57,021 (Source: African Development Bank).

Transport

ROAD TRAFFIC
(motor vehicles in use, estimates)

	1994	1995	1996
Passenger cars	5,940	6,300	7,120
Commercial vehicles	4,650	4,900	5,640

2008 (motor vehicles in use): Passenger cars 42,222; Buses and coaches 289; Vans and lorries 9,323; Motorcycles and mopeds 4,936.

Source: International Road Federation, *World Road Statistics*.

SHIPPING

Merchant Fleet
(registered at 31 December)

	2007	2008	2009
Number of vessels	25	25	24
Total displacement (grt)	6,627	6,627	6,141

Source: IHS Fairplay, *World Fleet Statistics*.

International Sea-Borne Freight Traffic
(UN estimates, '000 metric tons)

	1991	1992	1993
Goods loaded	40	45	46
Goods unloaded	272	277	283

Source: UN Economic Commission for Africa, *African Statistical Yearbook*.

CIVIL AVIATION
(traffic on scheduled services)

	1996	1997	1998
Kilometres flown (million)	1	0	0
Passengers carried ('000)	21	21	20
Passenger-km (million)	10	10	10
Total ton-km (million)	1	1	1

Source: UN, *Statistical Yearbook*.

Tourism

TOURIST ARRIVALS BY NATIONALITY

	2005	2006	2007
Cape Verde	159	401	1,498
China, People's Republic	46	659	1,488
Cuba	29	329	309
France	599	834	2,984
Italy	213	343	1,871
Korea, Republic	36	523	1,289
Portugal	1,552	2,599	2,245
Senegal	235	921	2,798
Spain	324	231	1,458
USA	57	320	265
Total (incl. others)	4,978	11,617	30,092

Receipts from tourism (US $ million, excl. passenger transport): 2.8 in 2006; 28.4 in 2007; 38.2 in 2008.

Source: World Tourism Organization.

Communications Media

	2008	2009	2010
Telephones ('000 main lines in use)	4.6	4.8	5.0
Mobile cellular telephones ('000 subscribers)	500.2	560.3	594.1
Internet subscribers ('000)	0.7	0.7	n.a.

Personal computers: 3,000 (2.0 per 1,000 persons) in 2005.

Radio receivers ('000 in use): 49 in 1997.

Daily newspapers: 1 (average circulation 6,200 copies) in 1998.

Sources: UNESCO Institute for Statistics; UNESCO, *Statistical Yearbook*; UN, *Statistical Yearbook*; International Telecommunication Union.

Education

(2009/10 unless otherwise indicated, UNESCO estimates)

	Teachers	Students		
		Males	Females	Total
Pre-primary	309	4,360	4,590	8,950
Primary	5,371	144,075	134,815	278,890
Secondary: general	1,913*	46,445	31,581	78,026
Secondary: technical and vocational		656†	239†	895†
Tertiary†	32	399	74	473

* 1999.

† 2000/01.

Institutions (1999): Pre-primary 54; Primary 759.

Students (2005/06): Primary 269,287; Secondary 55,176; Tertiary 3,689.

Teachers (2005/06): Primary 4,327; Secondary 1,480; Tertiary 25.

Pupil-teacher ratio (primary education, UNESCO estimate): 51.9 in 2009/10 (Source: UNESCO Institute for Statistics).

Adult literacy rate (UNESCO estimates): 52.2% (males 66.9%; females 38.0%) in 2009.

Source: UNESCO Institute for Statistics.

Directory

The Government

HEAD OF STATE

President: (vacant).

COUNCIL OF MINISTERS
(May 2012)

Following the assumption of power by members of the military on 12 April 2012, the Government of Guinea-Bissau was dissolved. On 18 April the formation of a National Transitional Council (Conselho Nacional de Transição) was announced.

President of the National Transitional Council: BRAIMA SORI DJALO.

MINISTRIES

Office of the President: Bissau; internet www.presidencia-gw.org.

Office of the Prime Minister: Av. dos Combatentes da Liberdade da Pátria, CP 137, Bissau; tel. 3211308; fax 3201671.

Ministry of Agriculture and Rural Development: Av. dos Combatentes da Liberdade da Pátria, CP 102, Bissau; tel. 3221200; fax 3222483.

Ministry of the Civil Service, Employment and Modernization: Bissau.

Ministry of the Economy, Planning and Regional Integration: Av. dos Combatentes da Liberdade da Pátria, CP 67, Bissau; tel. 3203670; fax 3203496; e-mail info@mail.guine-bissau.org; internet www.guine-bissau.org.

Ministry of Energy, Industry and Natural Resources: CP 311, Bissau; tel. 3215659; fax 3223149.

Ministry of Finance: Rua Justino Lopes 74A, CP 67, Bissau; tel. 3203670; fax 3203496; e-mail info@mail.guine-bissau.org.

Ministry of Fisheries: Av. Amílcar Cabral, CP 102, Bissau; tel. 3201699; fax 3202580.

Ministry of Foreign Affairs and Communities: Av. dos Combatentes da Liberdade da Pátria, Bissau; tel. 3204301; fax 3202378.

Ministry of Infrastructure: Av. dos Combatentes da Liberdade da Pátria, CP 14, Bissau; internet www.minisinfraestruturas-gov.com; tel. 3206575; fax 3203611.

Ministry of the Interior: Av. Unidade Africana, Bissau; tel. 3203781.

Ministry of Justice: Av. Amílcar Cabral, CP 17, Bissau; tel. 3202185; internet mj-gb.org.

Ministry of National Defence: Amura, Bissau; tel. 3223646.

Ministry of National Education, Culture and Science: Rua Areolino Cruz, Bissau; tel. 3202244.

Ministry of the Presidency of the Council of Ministers: Bissau.

Ministry of Public Health: CP 50, Bissau; tel. 3204438; fax 3201701.

Ministry of Social Communication and Parliamentary Affairs: Bissau.

Ministry of Territorial Administration: Bissau.

Ministry of Trade, Tourism and Crafts: 34A Av. Pansau na Isna, Bissau; tel. and fax 3206062; e-mail turismom@yahoo.com; internet www.minturgb-gov.com.

Ministry of War Veterans: Bissau.

Ministry of Women, Families, Social Cohesion and the Fight against Poverty: Av. dos Combatentes da Liberdade da Pátria, Bissau; tel. 3204785.

Ministry of Youth and Sports: Bissau.

President and Legislature

PRESIDENT

Presidential Election, First Round, 18 March 2012*

Candidate	Votes	% of votes
Carlos Gomes Junior	154,797	48.97
Mohamed Yalá Embaló (PRS)	73,842	23.36
Manuel Serifo Nhamadjo	49,767	15.74
Henrique Rosa	17,070	5.40
Others†	20,631	6.53
Total	316,107	100.00

* Under the terms of the Constitution, a second round of the presidential election was scheduled to take place on 29 April in order to determine which of the two leading candidates from the first round would be elected. However, on 12 April members of the military seized power and announced the dissolution of the organs of state and their intention to form a National Transitional Council (Conselho Nacional de Transição).

† There were five other candidates.

LEGISLATURE

Assembleia Nacional Popular: Palácio Colinas de Boé, Bissau; tel. 3201991; fax 3206725.

President: RAIMUNDO PEREIRA.

General Election, 16 November 2008

Party	Votes	% of votes	Seats
Partido Africano da Independência da Guiné e Cabo Verde (PAIGC)	227,036	49.75	67
Partido para a Renovação Social (PRS)	115,409	25.29	28
Partido Republicano para a Independência e o Desenvolvimento (PRID)	34,305	7.52	3
Partido para a Nova Democracia (PND)	10,721	2.35	1
Partido dos Trabalhadores (PT)	10,503	2.30	—
Partido Unido Social Democrático (PUSD)	7,695	1.69	—
Partido para Democracia, Desenvolvimento e Cidadania (PADEC)	7,073	1.55	—
Aliança Democrática (AD)	6,321	1.39	1
Partido Social Democrata (PSD)	6,315	1.38	—
Total (incl. others)	456,312	100.00	100

Election Commission

Comissão Nacional de Eleições (CNE): Av. 3 de Agosto 44, CP 359, Bissau; tel. 3203600; fax 3203601; e-mail cne-info@guinetel.com; internet www.cne-guinebissau.org; Pres. DESEJADO LIMA DA COSTA.

Political Organizations

The legislative elections of November 2008 were contested by the 19 parties and two coalitions listed below

Aliança Democrática (AD): c/o Assembleia Nacional Popular, Bissau; f. 2008; Leader VÍTOR FERNANDO MANDINGA.

Frente Democrática (FD): Bissau; f. 1991; officially registered in Nov. 1991; Pres. JORGE FERNANDO MANDINGA.

Partido da Convergência Democrática (PCD): Bissau; Leader VÍTOR FERNANDO MANDINGA.

Aliança de Forças Patrióticas (AFP): Bissau; f. 2008; Pres. AMINE MICHEL SAAD.

Forum Cívico Guinéense-Social Democracia (FCG-SD): Bissau; Pres. ANTONIETA ROSA GOMES; Sec.-Gen. CARLOS VAIMAN.

Frente Democrática Social (FDS): c/o Assembleia Nacional Popular, Bissau; f. 1991; Pres. LUCAS DA SILVA.

Partido de Solidariedade e Trabalho (PST): Bissau; f. 2002; Leader IANCUBA INDJAI; Sec.-Gen. ZACARIAS BALDÉ.

União para a Mudança (UM): Bissau; f. 1994; Leader AMINE MICHEL SAAD.

Centro Democrático (CD): Bissau; tel. and fax 452517; e-mail empossaie@centrodemocratico.com; internet www.cd.empossaie.com; f. 2006; Sec.-Gen. VICTOR DJELOMBO.

Liga Guinéense de Protecção Ecológica (LIPE): Bairro Missirá 102, CP 1290, Bissau; tel. and fax 3252309; f. 1991; ecology party; Interim Pres. MAMADU MUSTAFA BALDÉ.

Movimento Democrático Guinéense (MDG): Bissau; f. 2003; Pres. SILVESTRE CLAUDINHO ALVES.

Partido Africano da Independência da Guiné e Cabo Verde (PAIGC): CP 106, Bissau; internet www.paigc.org; f. 1956; fmrly the ruling party in both Guinea-Bissau and Cape Verde; although Cape Verde withdrew from the PAIGC following the coup in Guinea-Bissau in Nov. 1980, Guinea-Bissau has retained the party name and initials; Pres. CARLOS DOMINGOS GOMES JÚNIOR; Sec. AUGUSTO OLIVAIS.

Partido para Democracia, Desenvolvimento e Cidadania (PADEC): Bissau; f. 2005; Leaders FRANCISCO JOSE FADUL.

Partido Democrático Guinéense (PDG): f. 2007; Pres. EUSEBIO SEBASTIAO DA SILVA.

Partido Democrático Socialista (PDS): Bissau; f. 2006; Pres. JOÃO SECO MAMADÚ MANÉ.

Partido para a Nova Democracia (PND): Bissau; f. 2007; Pres. IBRAIMA DJALÓ.

Partido Popular Democrático (PPD): Bissau; f. 2006; Pres. BRAIMA CORCA EMBALÓ.

Partido de Progresso (PP): Bissau; f. 2004; Pres. IBRAHIMA SOW.

Partido da Reconciliação Nacional (PRN): Bissau; f. 2004; Leader ALMARA NHASSÉ; Sec.-Gen. OLUNDO MENDES.

Partido para a Renovação Social (PRS): c/o Assembleia Nacional Popular, Bissau; f. 1992; Pres. MOHAMED YALÁ EMBALÓ.

Partido Republicano para a Independência e o Desenvolvimento (PRID): Bissau; f. 2008; Pres. ARISTIDES GOMES.

Partido Social Democrata (PSD): c/o Assembleia Nacional Popular, Bissau; f. 1995 by breakaway faction of the RGB—MB; Pres. ANTONIO SAMBA BALDÉ.

Partido Socialista-Guiné Bissau (PS-GB): Bissau; f. 1994; Pres. CIRILO OLIVEIRA RODRIGUES.

Partido dos Trabalhadores (PT): Bissau; e-mail contact@nodjuntamon.org; internet www.nodjuntamon.org; f. 2002; left-wing; Pres. ARREGADO MANTENQUE TÉ.

Partido Unido Social Democrático (PUSD): Bissau; f. 1991; officially registered in Jan. 1992; Pres. AUGUSTO BARAI MANGO.

União Nacional para Democracia e Progresso (UNDP): Bissau; f. 191998; Pres. ABUBACAR BALDÉ.

União Patriótica Guinéense (UPG): Bissau; f. 2004 by dissident members of the RGB; Pres. FRANCISCA VAZ TURPIN.

Diplomatic Representation

EMBASSIES IN GUINEA-BISSAU

Angola: Bissau; Ambassador FELICIANO DOS SANTOS.

Brazil: Rua São Tomé, Esquina Rua Moçambique, CP 29, Bissau; tel. 3212549; fax 3201317; e-mail emb_brasil_bxo@hotmail.com; Ambassador JORGE GERALDO KADRI.

China, People's Republic: Av. Francisco João Mendes, Bissau; tel. 3203637; fax 3203590; e-mail chinaemb_gw@mail.mfa.gov.cn; Ambassador LI BAOJUN.

Cuba: Rua Joaquim N'Com 1, y Victorino Costa, CP 258, Bissau; tel. 3213579; fax 3201301; e-mail embcuba@sol.gtelecom.gw; Ambassador PEDRO FÉLIZ DOÑA SANTANA.

France: Bairro de Penha, Av. dos Combatentes da Liberdade da Pátria, Bissau; tel. 3257400; fax 3257421; e-mail cad.bissao-amba@diplomatie.gouv.fr; internet www.ambafrance-gw.org; Ambassador MICHEL FLESCH.

The Gambia: 47 Victorino Costa, Chao de Papel, CP 529, 1037 Bissau; tel. 3205085; fax 3251099; e-mail gambiaembbissau@hotmail.com; Ambassador CHERNO B. TOURAY.

Guinea: Rua 14, no. 9, CP 396, Bissau; tel. 3212681; Ambassador TAMBA TIENDO MILLIMONO.

Korea, Democratic People's Republic: Bissau; Ambassador KIM KYONG SIN.

Libya: Rua 16, CP 362, Bissau; tel. 3212006; Representative DOKALI ALI MUSTAFA.

Portugal: Av. Cidade de Lisboa, CP 76, 1021 Bissau; tel. 3201261; fax 3201269; e-mail embaixada@bissau.dgaccp.pt; Ambassador Dr ANTÓNIO MANUEL RICOCA FREIRE.

Russia: Av. 14 de Novembro, CP 308, Bissau; tel. 3251036; fax 3251028; e-mail russiagb@eguitel.com; Chargé d'affaires a.i. VIACHELAV ROZHNOV.

Senegal: Rua Omar Torrijos 43A, Bissau; tel. 3212944; fax 3201748; Ambassador Gen. ABDOULAYE DIENG.

South Africa: c/o Bissau Palace Hotel, Rm No. 9, Av. 14 de Novembro, CP 1334, Bissau; tel. 6678910; e-mail bissau@foreign.gov.za; Ambassador LOUIS MNGUNI.

Spain: Praza Dos Hèroes Naçionais; tel. 6722246; fax 3207656; e-mail emb.bissau@maec.es; Ambassador D. ANGEL BALLESTEROS GARCÍA.

Judicial System

The Supreme Court is the final court of appeal in criminal and civil cases and consists of nine judges. Nine Regional Courts serve as the final court of appeal for the 24 Sectoral Courts, and deal with felony cases and major civil cases. The Sectoral Courts hear minor civil cases.

President of the Supreme Court: MARIA DO CÉU SILVA MONTEIRO.

Religion

According to the 1991 census, 45.9% of the population were Muslims, 39.7% were animists and 14.4% were Christians, mainly Roman Catholics.

ISLAM

Associação Islâmica Nacional: Bissau; Sec.-Gen. Alhaji ABDÚ BAIO.

Conselho Superior dos Assuntos Islâmicos da Guiné-Bissau (CSAI-GB): Bissau; Exec. Sec. MUSTAFA RACHID DJALÓ.

CHRISTIANITY

The Roman Catholic Church

Guinea-Bissau comprises two dioceses, directly responsible to the Holy See. The Bishops participate in the Episcopal Conference of Senegal, Mauritania, Cape Verde and Guinea-Bissau, currently based in Senegal. Approximately 10% of the total population are adherents of the Roman Catholic Church.

Bishop of Bafatá: Rev. CARLOS PEDRO ZILLI, CP 17, Bafatá; tel. 3411507; e-mail domzilli@yahoo.com.br.

Bishop of Bissau: JOSÉ CÂMNATE NA BISSIGN, Av. 14 de Novembro, CP 20, 1001 Bissau; tel. 3251057; fax 3251058; e-mail diocesebissau@yahoo.it.

The Press

REGULATORY AUTHORITY

Conselho Nacional de Comunicação Social (CNCS): Bissau; f. 1994; dissolved in 2003, recreated in November 2004; Pres. AUGUSTO MENDES.

NEWSPAPERS AND PERIODICALS

Banobero: Rua José Carlos Schwarz, CP 760, Bissau; tel. 3230702; fax 3230705; e-mail banobero@netscape.net; weekly; Dir FERNANDO JORGE PEREIRA.

Comdev Negócios (Community Development Business): Av. Domingos Ramos 21, 1° andar, Bissau; tel. 3215596; f. 2006; independent; business; Editor FRANCELINO CUNHA.

Correio-Bissau: Bissau; weekly; f. 1992; Editor-in-Chief JOÃO DE BARROS; circ. 9,000.

Diário de Bissau: Rua Vitorino Costa 29, Bissau; tel. 3203049; daily; Owner JOÃO DE BARROS.

Expresso de Bissau: : Rua Vitorino Costa 30, Bissau; tel. 6666647; e-mail expressobissau@hotmail.com.

Fraskera: Bairro da Ajuda, 1ª fase, CP 698, Bissau; tel. 3253060; fax 3253070; weekly.

Gazeta de Notícias: Av. Caetano Semeao, CP 1433, Bissau; tel. 3254733; e-mail gn@eguitel.com; internet www.gaznot.com; f. 1997; weekly; Dir HUMBERTO MONTEIRO; circ. 1,000.

Journal Nô Pintcha: Av. do Brasil, CP 154, Bissau; tel. 3213713; internet www.jornalnopintcha.com; Dir SRA CABRAL; circ. 6,000.

Kansaré: Edifico Sitec, Rua José Carlos Schwarz, Bissau; e-mail kansare@eguitel.com; internet www.kansare.com; f. 2003; Editor FAFALI KOUDAWO.

Última Hora: Av. Combatentes da Liberdade da Pátria (Prédio Suna Ker), Bissau;; tel. 5932236; e-mail damil@portugalmail.com; Dir ATHIZAR PEREIRA; circ: 500.

Voz de Bissau: Rua Eduardo Mondlane, Apdo 155, Bissau; tel. 3202546; twice weekly.

Wandan: Rua António M'Bana 6, CP 760, Bissau; tel. 3201789.

NEWS AGENCIES

Agência Bissau Media e Publicações: Rua Eduardo Mondlane 52, CP 1069, Bissau; tel. 3206147; e-mail agenciabissau@agenciabissau.com; internet www.agenciabissau.com.

Agência Noticiosa da Guiné-Bissau (ANG): Av. Domingos Ramos, CP 248, Bissau; tel. 3212151; fax 3202155.

Publisher

Ku Si Mon: Bairro d'Ajuda, Rua José Carlos Schwarz, CP 268, Bissau; tel. 3203704; e-mail kusimon@eguitel.com; internet www.guine-bissau.net/kusimon; f. 1994; privately owned; Portuguese language; Dir ABDULAI SILA.

Broadcasting and Communications

TELECOMMUNICATIONS

Regulatory Authority

Autoridade Reguladora Nacional das Tecnologias de Informação (ARN): Av. Domingos Ramos 53, Praça Cheguevara, CP 1372, Bissau; tel. 3204874; fax 3204876; e-mail geral@arn-gb.com; internet arn-gb.com; f. 2010 to replace Instituto das Comunicações da Guiné-Bissau; also manages radio spectrum; Pres. GIBRIL MANÉ.

Service Providers

Guiné Telecom (GT): Bissau; tel. 3202427; internet www.gtelecom.gw; f. 2003 to replace the Companhia de Telecomunicações da Guiné-Bissau (Guiné Telecom—f. 1989); state-owned; privatization pending.

Guinetel: Bissau; f. 2003; mobile operator; CEO JOÃO FREDERICO DE BARROS.

MTN Guinea Bissau: 7 Av. Unidade Africana, CP 672, Bissau; tel. 3207000; fax 6600111; e-mail contact@mtn-bissau.com; internet www.mtn-bissau.com; f. 2007; CEO ANTHONY MASOZERA; 110 employees.

Orange Bissau: Praça dos Herois Nacionais, BP 1087, Bissau; tel. 5603030; e-mail abdul.dapiedadeTMP@orange-sonatel.com; internet orange-bissau.com; f. 2007; provides fixed line and mobile telecommunications services.

RADIO AND TELEVISION

An experimental television service began transmissions in 1989. Regional radio stations were to be established at Bafatá, Cantchungo and Catió in 1990. In 1990 Radio Freedom, which broadcast on behalf of the PAIGC during Portuguese rule and had ceased operations in 1974, resumed transmissions. Other radio stations included Radio Televisão Portuguesa Africa (RTP/Africa), which broadcast from Bissau, and Rádio Sintchã Oco.

Radiodifusão Nacional da República da Guiné-Bissau (RDN): Av. Domingos Ramos, Praça dos Martires de Pindjiguiti, CP 191, Bissau; tel. 3212426; fax 3253070; e-mail rdn@eguitel.com; f. 1974; govt-owned; broadcasts in Portuguese on short-wave, MW and FM; Dir-Gen. LAMINE DJATA.

Rádio Bafatá: CP 57, Bafatá; tel. 3411185.

Rádio Bombolom: Bairro Cupelon, CP 877, Bissau; tel. 3201095; f. 1996; independent; Dir AGNELO REGALA.

Rádio Mavegro: Rua Eduardo Mondlane, CP 100, Bissau; tel. 3201216; fax 3201265.

Rádio Pindjiguiti: Bairro da Ajuda, 1ª fase, CP 698, Bissau; tel. 3253070; f. 1995; independent.

Televisão da Guiné-Bissau (TGB): Bairro de Luanda, CP 178, Bissau; tel. 3221920; fax 3221941; internet www.televisao-gb.net; f. 1997; Dir-Gen. LUÍS DOMINGOS CAMARÁ DE BARROS.

Finance

(cap. = capital; res = reserves; m. = million; amounts in francs CFA)

BANKING

Central Bank

Banque centrale des états de l'Afrique de l'ouest (BCEAO): Av. dos Combatentes da Liberdade da Pátria, Brá, CP 38, Bissau; tel. 3256325; fax 3256300; internet www.bceao.int; HQ in Dakar, Senegal; f. 1955; bank of issue for the mem. states of the Union économique et monétaire ouest-africaine (UEMOA, comprising Benin, Burkina Faso, Côte d'Ivoire, Guinea-Bissau, Mali, Niger, Senegal and Togo); cap. 134,120m., res 1,474,195m., dep. 2,124,051m. (Dec. 2009); Gov. KONÉ TIÉMOKO MEYLIET; Dir in Guinea-Bissau JOÃO ALAGE MAMADU FADIA.

Other Banks

Banco da África Ocidental, SARL: Rua Guerra Mendes 18, CP 1360, Bissau; tel. 3203418; fax 3203412; e-mail bao-info@eguitel.com; internet bancodaafricaocidental.com; f. 2000; International Finance Corporation 15%, Grupo Montepio Geral (Portugal) 15%, Carlos Gomes Júnior 15%; cap. and res 1,883m. (Dec. 2003); Chair. ABDOOL VAKIL; Man. Dir RÓMULO PIRES.

Banco Regional de Solidariedade: Rua Justino Lopes, Bissau; tel. 3207112.

Banco da União (BDU): Av. Domingos Ramos 3, CP 874, Bissau; tel. 3207160; fax 3207161; internet www.bdu-sa.com; f. 2005; 30% owned by Banque de Développement du Mali; CEO HUGO DOS REIS BORGES.

Caixa de Crédito da Guiné: Bissau; govt savings and loan institution.

Caixa Económica Postal: Av. Amílcar Cabral, Bissau; tel. 3212999; postal savings institution.

Ecobank Guinea-Bissau: Av. Amílcar Cabral, BP 126, Bissau; tel. 3207360; fax 3207363; e-mail info@ecobankgw.com; Chair. JOÃO JOSÉ SILVA MONTEIRO; Man. Dir GILLES GUERARD.

STOCK EXCHANGE

In 1998 a regional stock exchange, the Bourse Régionale des Valeurs Mobilières, was established in Abidjan, Côte d'Ivoire, to serve the member states of the UEMOA.

INSURANCE

GUINEBIS—Guiné-Bissau Seguros: Rua Dr Severino Gomes de Pina 36, Bissau; tel. 211458; fax 201197.

Instituto Nacional de Previdência Social: Av. Domingos Ramos 12, CP 62, Bissau; tel. and fax 3211331; fax 3204396; e-mail inps_informatica@hotmail.com; internet www.inps-gb.com; state-owned; Dir-Gen. MAMADU IAIA DJALÓ.

Trade and Industry

DEVELOPMENT ORGANIZATION

Ajuda de Desenvolvimento de Povo para Povo ná Guiné Bissau (ADPP): CP 420, Bissau; tel. 6853323; e-mail adppartemisa@eguitel.com.

CHAMBER OF COMMERCE

Câmara de Comércio, Indústria, Agricultura e Serviços da Guiné-Bissau (CCIAS): Av. Amílcar Cabral 7, CP 361, Bissau; tel. 3212844; fax 3201602; f. 1987; Pres. BRAIMA CAMARÁ; Sec.-Gen. SALIU BA.

INDUSTRIAL AND TRADE ASSOCIATIONS

Associação Comercial, Industrial e Agricola (ACIA): CP 88, Bissau; tel. 3222276.

Direcção de Promoção do Investimento Privado (DPIP): Rua 12 de Setembro, Bissau Velho, CP 1276, Bissau; tel. 3205156; fax 3203181; e-mail dpip@mail.bissau.net.

Fundaçao Guineense para o Desenvolvimento Empresarial Industrial (FUNDEI): Rua Gen. Omar Torrijos 49, Bissau; tel. 3202470; fax 3202209; e-mail fundei@fundei.bissau.net; internet www.fundei.net; f. 1994; industrial devt org.; Pres. MACÁRIA BARAI.

Procajú: Bissau; private sector association of cashew producers.

UTILITIES

Gas

Empresa Nacional de Importação e Distribuição de Gás Butano: CP 269, Bissau; state gas distributor.

TRADE UNIONS

Confederação Geral dos Sindicatos Independentes da Guiné-Bissau (CGSI-GB): Rua nº10, Bissau Apartado 693, Bissau; tel. 204110; fax 204114; e-mail cgsi-gb@hotmail.com; internet http://www.lgdh.org/CONFEDERACAOGERALDOSSINDICATOSINDEPENDENTES.htm; Sec.-Gen. FILOMENO CABRAL.

Sindicato Nacional dos Marinheiros (SINAMAR): Bissau.

Sindicato Nacional dos Professores (SINAPROF): CP 765, Bissau; tel. and fax 3204070; e-mail ict@mail.bissau.net; Pres. LUÍS NANCASSA.

União Nacional dos Trabalhadores da Guiné (UNTG): 13 Av. Ovai di Vievra, CP 98, Bissau; tel. and fax 3207138; e-mail untgcs.gb@hotmail.com; Pres. DESEJADO LIMA DA COSTA; Sec.-Gen. ESTÊVÃO GOMES CÓ.

Transport

RAILWAYS

There are no railways in Guinea-Bissau. However, the proposed construction of a railway line by Bauxite Angola, linking the bauxite extraction site in Boé with the future deep-water port at Buba, has been announced.

ROADS

According to the Minister of Infrastructure, there are 2,755 km of 'classified' roads in Guinea-Bissau, of which 770 km are paved. There are plans in place for a further 300 km to be paved by 2020.

SHIPPING

Plans have been announced to build a major deep-water port at Buba, the capacity of which will make it one of the largest in West Africa. At 31 December 2009 the merchant fleet comprised 24 vessels, totalling 6,141 grt. In mid-2004 plans were announced to improve links with the Bijagós islands, by providing a regular ferry service.

Empresa Nacional de Agências e Transportes Marítimos: Rua Guerva Mendes 4–4A, CP 244, Bissau; tel. 3212675; fax 3213023; state shipping agency; Dir-Gen. M. LOPES.

CIVIL AVIATION

There is an international airport at Bissau, which there are plans to expand, and 10 smaller airports serving the interior. TAP Portugal and Transportes Aéreos de Cabo Verde (TACV) fly to Bissau.

Tourism

There were 30,092 tourist arrivals in 2007. Receipts from tourism totalled US $38.2m. in 2008.

Central de Informação e Turismo: CP 294, Bissau; tel. 213905; state tourism and information service.

Direcção Geral do Turismo: CP 1024, Bissau; tel. 202195; fax 204441.

Defence

As assessed at November 2011, the armed forces officially totalled an estimated 6,458 men (army 4,000, navy 350, air force 100 and paramilitary gendarmerie 2,000). Military service was made compulsory from 2007, as part of a programme of reform for the armed forces. Following the military uprising of April 2010, the EU decided to suspend, and then not to renew, the mandate of its Security Sector Reform (SSR) mission in Guinea-Bissau, which ended on 30 September 2010. Subsequently, a new joint SSR roadmap was approved by ECOWAS and the Lusophone Community CPLP in November 2010 and is currently under way. In this context, a two-year Angolan Armed Forces Security Mission in Guinea-Bissau (MISSANG) was launched in January 2011, one of the aims of which was to reduce the number of army troops to 2,500.

Defence Expenditure: Budgeted at 9,520m. francs CFA in 2011.

Chief of Staff of the Armed Forces: Maj.-Gen. ANTÓNIO INDJAI.

Army Chief of Staff: Brig.-Gen. ARMANDO GOMES.

Navy Chief of Staff: JOSÉ AMERICO BUBO NA TCHUTO.

Chief of Staff of the Air Force: IBRAIMA PAPÁ CAMARA.

Education

Education is officially compulsory only for the period of primary schooling, which begins at six years of age and lasts for seven years. Secondary education, beginning at the age of 13, lasts for up to five years (a first cycle of three years and a second of two years). According to UNESCO estimates, in 2009/10 enrolment at primary schools included 74% of children in the relevant age-group (males 75%; females 72%), while enrolment at secondary schools in 2005/06 was equivalent to only 36% of children in the relevant age-group. In 2000/01 473 students were enrolled in tertiary education. There are three tertiary level institutions in Guinea-Bissau: the Universidade Amílcar Cabral (public); the Universidade Colinas do Boé (private); and the Faculdade de Direito de Bissau (a law school funded and run within the ambit of Portuguese co-operation). According to the 2005 budget, expenditure on education was forecast at 15.0% of total spending.

GUYANA

Introductory Survey

LOCATION, CLIMATE, LANGUAGE, RELIGION, FLAG, CAPITAL

The Co-operative Republic of Guyana lies on the north coast of South America, between Venezuela to the west and Suriname to the east, with Brazil to the south. The narrow coastal belt has a moderate climate with two wet seasons, from April to August and from November to January, alternating with two dry seasons. Inland, there are tropical forests and savannah, and the dry season lasts from September to May. The average annual temperature is 27°C (80°F), with average rainfall of 1,520 mm (60 ins) per year inland, rising to between 2,030 mm (80 ins) and 2,540 mm (100 ins) on the coast. English is the official language but Hindi, Urdu and Amerindian dialects are also spoken. The principal religions are Christianity (which is professed by about 50% of the population), Hinduism (about 28%) and Islam (7%). The national flag (proportions 3 by 5 when flown on land, but 1 by 2 at sea) is green, with a white-bordered yellow triangle (apex at the edge of the fly) on which is superimposed a black-bordered red triangle (apex in the centre). The capital is Georgetown.

CONTEMPORARY POLITICAL HISTORY

Historical Context

Guyana was formerly British Guiana, a colony of the United Kingdom, formed in 1831 from territories finally ceded to Britain by the Dutch in 1814. A new Constitution, providing for universal adult suffrage, was introduced in 1953. The elections of April 1953 were won by the left-wing People's Progressive Party (PPP), led by Dr Cheddi Bharat Jagan. In October, however, the British Government, claiming that a communist dictatorship was threatened, suspended the Constitution. An interim administration was appointed. The PPP split in 1955, and in 1957 some former members founded a new party, the People's National Congress (PNC), under the leadership of Forbes Burnham. The PNC drew its support mainly from the African-descended population, while PPP support came largely from the (Asian-descended) 'East' Indian community.

Domestic Political Affairs

A revised Constitution was introduced in December 1956 and an election was held in August 1957. The PPP won and Jagan became Chief Minister. Another Constitution, providing for internal self-government, was adopted in July 1961. The PPP won an election in August and Jagan was appointed premier. In the election of December 1964, held under the system of proportional representation, the PPP won the largest number of seats in the Legislative Assembly, but not a majority. A coalition Government was formed by the PNC and The United Force (TUF), with Burnham as Prime Minister. This coalition led the colony to independence, as Guyana, on 26 May 1966.

The PNC won elections in 1968 and in 1973, although the results of the latter, and every poll thenceforth until the defeat of the PNC in 1992, were disputed by the opposition parties. Guyana became a co-operative republic on 23 February 1970, and Arthur Chung was elected non-executive President in March. In 1976 the PPP, which had boycotted the National Assembly since 1973, offered the Government its 'critical support'. Following a referendum in July 1978 that gave the Assembly power to amend the Constitution, elections to the Assembly were postponed for 15 months. The legislature assumed the role of a constituent assembly, established in November 1978, to draft a new constitution. In October 1979 elections were postponed for a further year. In October 1980 Forbes Burnham declared himself executive President of Guyana, and a new Constitution was promulgated.

Internal opposition to the PNC Government had increased after the assassination in 1980 of Walter Rodney, leader of the Working People's Alliance (WPA). The Government was widely believed to have been involved in the incident; an official inquest in 1988 produced a verdict, rejected by the opposition, of death by misadventure. All opposition parties except the PPP and TUF boycotted the December 1980 elections to the National Assembly. The PNC received 78% of the votes, according to official results, although allegations of substantial electoral malpractice were made, both within the country and by international observers. None the less, Burnham was inaugurated as President in January 1981.

In 1981 arrests and trials of opposition leaders continued, and in 1982 the Government's relations with human rights groups, and especially the Christian churches, deteriorated further. Editors of opposition newspapers were threatened, political violence increased, and the Government was accused of interference in the legal process. Industrial unrest and public discontent continued in 1983 and 1984, as Guyana's worsening economic situation increased opposition to the Government, and led to growing disaffection within the trade union movement and the PNC.

Burnham died in August 1985 and was succeeded as President by Desmond Hoyte, hitherto the First Vice-President and Prime Minister. The PNC won the December election, although opposition groups, including the PPP and WPA, denounced the poll as fraudulent. In January 1986 five of the six opposition parties formed the Patriotic Coalition for Democracy (PCD).

Outside the formal opposition of the political parties, the Government also experienced pressure from members of the Guyana Human Rights Association, business leaders and prominent religious figures. This culminated, in 1990, in the formation of a movement for legal and constitutional change, Guyanese Action for Reform and Democracy (Guard), which initiated a series of mass protests, urging the Government to accelerate the process of democratic reform. To counter this civic movement, the PNC began mobilizing its own newly established Committees to Re-elect the President (Creeps). Guard accused the Creeps of orchestrating violent clashes at Guard's rallies, and of fomenting racial unrest in the country in an attempt to regain support from the Afro-Guyanese population.

In January 1991 the date of the forthcoming general election was postponed, following the approval of legislation by the PNC extending the term of office of the National Assembly by two months after its official dissolution date of 2 February. In March a further two-month extension of the legislative term provoked the resignation of TUF and PPP members from the National Assembly (WPA members had resigned a month earlier). Similar extensions followed in May and July, owing to alleged continuing problems relating to electoral reforms. The National Assembly was finally dissolved in late September. The publication of a revised electoral register in that month, however, revealed widespread inaccuracies, including the omission of an estimated 100,000 eligible voters. In November several opposition parties announced a boycott of the general election, which had been rescheduled for mid-December. However, on 28 November Hoyte declared a state of emergency (subsequently extended until June 1992) in order to legitimize a further postponement of the election. A further revised electoral register was finally approved by the Elections Commission in August 1992. The election finally took place on 5 October and resulted in a narrow victory for the PPP in alliance with the Civic movement (a social and political movement of businessmen and professionals). The result, which signified an end to the PNC's 28-year period in government, provoked riots by the mainly Afro-Guyanese PNC supporters in Georgetown. International observers were, however, satisfied that the elections had been fairly conducted, and on 9 October Dr Cheddi Bharat Jagan took office as President. Jagan appointed Samuel Hinds, an industrialist who was not a member of the PPP, as Prime Minister.

In August 1995 a serious environmental incident resulted in the temporary closure of Omai Gold Mines Ltd (OGML). The company, which began production in the Omai District of Essequibo province in 1993, was responsible for an increase of some 400% in Guyana's gold production in subsequent years and was Guyana's largest foreign investor. However, a breach in a tailings pond (a reservoir where residue from the gold extraction process is stored) resulted in the spillage of some 3.5m. cu m of cyanide-tainted water, of which a large volume flowed into the Omai river, a tributary of the Essequibo river. OGML resumed operations in February 1996 following the implementation of government-approved environmental safeguards.

In March 1997, following the death of Jagan, Prime Minister Hinds succeeded to the presidency, in accordance with the provisions of the Constitution. Hinds subsequently appointed Janet Jagan, the widow of the former President, to the post of Prime Minister. Following the PPP/Civic's success in the December general election, Jagan, who was that alliance's nominee, was inaugurated as President on 19 December.

In January 1998 the Government accepted a proposal by private sector leaders for an international audit of the election to be conducted. The PNC, however, rejected the proposal and demanded instead the holding of fresh elections. In mid-January the Chief Justice ruled that it was beyond the jurisdiction of the High Court to prohibit Jagan from exercising her presidential functions pending a judicial review of the election. The ruling provoked serious disturbances in Georgetown. Public protests by PNC supporters continued in defiance of a ban on demonstrations in the capital. However, following mediation by a three-member Caribbean Community and Common Market (CARICOM, see p. 227) commission, it was announced that an accord (the Herdmanston Agreement) had been signed by Jagan and PNC leader Desmond Hoyte, which provided for the organization of fresh elections within 36 months and the creation of a constitutional commission to make recommendations on constitutional reform, subsequently to be submitted to a national referendum and a legislative vote. The agreement also made provision for an independent audit of the December election. Meanwhile, the PNC continued to boycott the National Assembly. In June the CARICOM commission upheld the published results of the December poll. Nevertheless, Hoyte continued publicly to question the legitimacy of the Jagan administration.

In January 1999 a 20-member Constitutional Reform Commission was established, comprising representatives of the country's principal political parties and community groups. The Commission's report included proposals (submitted by the PPP/Civic alliance) that the country should be renamed the Republic of Guyana, that the President should be limited to two consecutive terms of office, and that the President should no longer be empowered to dissolve the National Assembly should he/she be censured by the Assembly. The Commission further proposed that the President should no longer have the power to dismiss a public officer in the public interest, and the President and Cabinet should be collectively responsible to the National Assembly and should resign if defeated in a vote of no confidence.

President Jagan announced her retirement on the grounds of ill health in August 1999. She was replaced as head of state by the erstwhile Minister of Finance, Bharrat Jagdeo. The appointment of Jagdeo, whose relative youth (he was 35 years of age), reported willingness to reach across the political divide, and strong background in economics all contributed to his popularity, was widely welcomed in Guyana and by the international community.

In December 1999 the National Assembly approved the establishment of a committee to supervise the revision of the Constitution prior to the general election scheduled for January 2001. In July 2000 the National Assembly approved legislation creating a permanent electoral institution, the Guyana Elections Commission. In October the legislature unanimously approved a constitutional amendment establishing a mixed system of proportional representation combining regional constituencies and national candidate lists. Also approved was the abolition of the Supreme Congress of the People of Guyana and the National Congress of Local Democratic Organs. In December an Ethnic Relations Commission was officially established.

The general and regional elections of 19 March 2001 were preceded by demonstrations over the late distribution of voter identification cards. The PPP/Civic obtained a majority in the National Assembly, with 34 seats, while the PNC (which contested the elections as the PNCReform) won 27 seats. Some 90% of the registered electorate participated. International observers declared the elections to be generally free and fair, and on 23 March it was officially declared that Jagdeo had regained the presidency, although continued allegations of irregularities by the PNCReform resulted in the postponement of the presidential inauguration until the end of March.

A period of social unrest, accompanied by a high incidence of violent crime began in 2002, as a result of ongoing hostilities between the Government and opposition. During that period large numbers of people were killed or 'disappeared'. The disorder culminated on 3 July in an attack by opposition protesters on the presidential offices during a meeting of CARICOM heads of government. The security forces opened fire on the protesters, killing two and wounding 15. While condemning the violence, the PNCReform leadership announced their support for the demonstrators' grievances of racial discrimination and police brutality.

Robert Corbin was elected as the new leader of the PNCReform in February 2003 following the unexpected death of Hoyte in December 2002. Corbin pledged a policy of 'constructive engagement' with the PPP and in May 2003 Jagdeo and Corbin signed an agreement on a number of issues, including local government reform and opposition representation on state bodies, particularly the government-owned media. In the same month the PNCReform ended its boycott of the National Assembly. A 'stakeholder group' was established to monitor the implementation of the accord. Progress was slow and acrimonious throughout the year; none the less, in December agreement was reached by the two parties on the establishment of four constitutional commissions to oversee reform of the judiciary, the police, the civil service and the teaching sector.

Crime, in particular violent crime, continued to increase under Jagdeo's presidency. Following an increase in the number of abductions in the first months of 2003, in June the National Assembly approved legislation to extend the terms of imprisonment for those convicted of kidnap. In December a parliamentary report by the Disciplined Forces Commission referred to the possible existence of a clandestine, government-run paramilitary group. It was claimed that the group targeted suspected criminals and persons linked to known criminals. The allegations were supported in the following month by George Bacchus, who claimed he had been an informant for the so-called 'death squad', which had been allegedly responsible for more than 40 extra-judicial killings in 2003. Bacchus alleged that the Minister of Home Affairs, Ronald Gajraj, had orchestrated the group's operations. The Canadian and US Governments revoked Gajraj's visas in response to the claims. In May 2004 a three-member commission was appointed to investigate the allegations. However, on 24 June, the day that he was scheduled to testify before the commission, Bacchus was shot and killed. The murder of Bacchus led to increased calls by the opposition for an independent inquiry into the matter. In April 2005 a Presidential Commission of Inquiry cleared Gajraj of involvement in the activities of the 'death squads'. He was immediately reinstated to his cabinet post; however, following international pressure and vociferous criticism from the opposition PNCReform, at the end of the month Gajraj stepped down from office.

Heightened criminal activity continued to affect the business sector in 2005, discouraging investment and increasing the rate of migration of skilled workers. In an attempt to prevent attacks on private businesses, in September the Guyana Revenue Authority introduced tax concessions for companies that imported security and surveillance equipment to protect their premises. Despite a slight fall in the number of murders in 2005 the problem of violent crime remained a pressing concern in the months preceding the general election of August 2006. The high incidence of violent crime was brought into dramatic focus in April when Minister of Agriculture Satyadeow Sawh was shot dead at his home.

The re-election of Jagdeo

The PPP/Civic secured a comfortable victory at the general election on 28 August 2006. The party increased its representation in the National Assembly to 36 seats, having secured a majority 54.3% of the votes cast, while the People's National Congress Reform-One Guyana (PNCR-1G, as PNCReform was restyled ahead of the elections) obtained 22 seats and 34.0% of the ballot. The recently formed Alliance for Change (AFC) won five seats, with 8.3% of the votes cast. The rate of voter participation, at 69%, was the lowest since independence.

Jagdeo was inaugurated as President on 2 September 2006. In the new Cabinet, which included nine new ministerial appointments, Jagdeo appointed two ministers to each of the Ministries of Finance, Health and Education. President Jagdeo pledged that the new executive would give priority to reforming the police force and addressing social problems.

During the trial in mid-2009 in the USA of notorious Guyanese drugs-trafficker Shaheed 'Roger' Khan on several charges of cocaine-trafficking, witness-tampering and illegal firearms possession, evidence was presented linking his activities to the Government of Guyana. The Minister of Health, Leslie Ramsammy, was urged by some observers to resign after specific allegations were made against him. The Government denied any wrongdoing and any involvement with Khan (who had been arrested by the authorities in Suriname rather than those in Guyana). However, in November the opposition parties published a dossier that alleged widespread human rights abuses, including the torture and murder of citizens carried out with state support. The dossier was passed to foreign diplomats and the US Department of State.

A series of strikes, reportedly involving up to 10,000 sugar industry workers, were organized during 2010 by the Guyana Agricultural and General Workers' Union (GAWU) to demand a 15% pay increase from the state-owned Guyana Sugar Corpn (GuySuCo). After negotiations between GAWU and GuySuCo stalled in late 2010, in December the Government proposed a one-time 5% pay raise, which was viewed as an acceptable compromise by most sugar workers. GuySuCo claimed that the strike action had resulted in the lowest levels of sugar output for almost 20 years.

In December 2010 the National Assembly adopted legislation to postpone the local elections (last held in 1994 and due since 1997) for one year. Jagdeo argued that the state did not have the resources necessary to stage both the local elections and the national elections, and that as a result he had to prioritize the latter. He also blamed the opposition deputies in the National Assembly for the delay, holding them responsible for a lack of progress on local government reform—a prerequisite for the staging of fresh local elections.

Efforts by the PNCR (as the party was known from 2006) to create an opposition coalition to challenge the PPP/Civic at the upcoming presidential and legislative elections, eventually held in November 2011 (see below), were frustrated in July 2010, when the AFC announced that it would stand alone at the elections. None the less, in July 2011 a coalition of opposition parties—the PNCR, the Guyana Action Party, the National Front Alliance and the Working People's Alliance—formed A Partnership for National Unity (APNU) to contest the ballot. Retired brigadier in the Guyana Defence Force David Granger, who had been chosen as the PNCR's presidential nominee in February, became the coalition's candidate. As the Constitution prevented Jagdeo from running for a third term in office, the PPP/Civic in early April selected General Secretary Donald Ramotar as its presidential contender in the election that was constitutionally due by the end of the year. In early October Jagdeo ended months of speculation by announcing that the ballot would be held on 28 November.

Recent developments: the November 2011 elections

The PPP/Civic secured a narrow victory at the general election held on 28 November 2011, its fifth consecutive electoral victory. However, the party lost its overall majority in the National Assembly, securing 32 seats (four fewer than in the previous parliament). It garnered 48.6% of votes cast, while the APNU—the coalition of opposition parties formed to contest the elections—obtained 26 seats and 40.8% of the ballot. The AFC won seven seats, with 10.3% of the votes cast. The rate of voter participation was 73%, slightly higher than in 2006.

Donald Ramotar was inaugurated as President on 3 December 2011. Given that the PPP/Civic would be forming a minority government (the first minority government in Guyana), President Ramotar emphasized in his inauguration speech the importance of national unity and of working together for the country's benefit, which raised expectation he might include members of opposition parties in his Cabinet. However, the new administration, announced on 5 December, included only PPP/Civic members. The Cabinet also remained largely unchanged compared to that of Jagdeo, with only a small number of new appointments. The Prime Minister and Ministers of Foreign Affairs, Finance and Home Affairs all remained unchanged from the previous Government, indicating policy continuity within the main portfolios. Significantly, the President created a new ministry—of Natural Resources and the Environment—to which he appointed former agriculture minister Robert Persaud.

Opposition supporters protested against the election results, leading to the police firing rubber bullets and injuring some demonstrators in the capital on 6 December 2011. Granger alleged irregularities in the election process, while the APNU called on the Chairman of the Guyana Elections Commission and the Chief Elections Officer to resign for failing to release the preliminary results on the day after the ballot, despite earlier pledges.

Because the two main opposition parties obtained a combined majority of one seat over the PPP/Civic in the November 2011 elections, they could control the legislative branch of government. Thus, in January 2012 the AFC leader Raphael Trotman was installed as parliamentary speaker.

Foreign Affairs

Guyana has been involved in long-running border disputes with Venezuela and Suriname, although Suriname restored diplomatic representation in Guyana in 1979. In 1983 relations improved further as a result of increased trade links between the countries. However, in May 2000 Suriname formally claimed that Guyana had violated its territorial integrity by granting a concession to a Canadian company to explore for petroleum and gas. Negotiations to settle the dispute ended inconclusively, so in January 2002 the Presidents of the two countries met to discuss the possibility of a production-sharing agreement. However, relations deteriorated when, in June, the Surinamese navy forcibly ejected a rig that had been authorized by Guyana to drill in waters disputed by the two countries. Guyana referred the dispute to arbitration at the UN's International Tribunal for the Law of the Sea (ITLOS), in Hamburg, Germany, and in September 2007 the Tribunal ruled in favour of Guyana, granting sovereignty over 33,152 sq km (12,800 sq miles) of coastal waters; Suriname was awarded 17,891 sq km (6,900 sq miles).

In October 2008 the seizure by the Surinamese military of a Guyanese ship provoked serious confrontation between the two countries. The crew of the ship, which had been transporting sugar up the Corentyne river along the border between the two countries, was detained for allegedly being in Suriname illegally. The ship and its crew were eventually released after payment of a small fine. In September 2010 new Surinamese President Desiré (Desi) Bouterse travelled to Guyana for talks with Jagdeo. The two leaders agreed to put aside any unresolved border issues and concentrate instead on enhancing bilateral co-operation in areas of mutual interest such as trade and security. Relations continued to improve in late 2010 following further amicable discussions, during which plans were formulated to build a bridge across the Corentyne river. Construction work had not begun by early 2012, as Guyana and Suriname sought financing for the project from the Inter-American Development Bank.

In 1962 Venezuela renewed its claim to 130,000 sq km (50,000 sq miles) of land west of the Essequibo river (nearly two-thirds of Guyanese territory). The area was accorded to Guyana in 1899, on the decision of an international tribunal, but Venezuela based its claim on a papal bull of 1493, referring to Spanish colonial possessions. The Port of Spain Protocol of 1970 put the issue in abeyance until 1982. Guyana and Venezuela referred the dispute to the UN in 1983, and in 1989 the two countries agreed to a mutually acceptable intermediary, suggested by the UN Secretary-General. In 1999 Guyana and Venezuela established a joint commission, the High Level Bi-national Commission, which was intended to expedite the resolution of the territorial dispute and to promote mutual co-operation. However, in October President Hugo Chávez of Venezuela, speaking on the 100th anniversary of the international tribunal's decision, announced his Government's intention to reopen its claim to the territory. In 2004 President Chávez visited Guyana and met President Jagdeo with the aim of increasing bilateral co-operation. In 2005 Guyana signed the PetroCaribe energy accord with Venezuela, which extended the financing arrangements introduced by the Caracas agreement on special energy concessions and offered favourable terms should the price of petroleum exceed US $40 per barrel. Moreover, Guyana could settle its debt to Venezuela for energy imports by exporting crops such as rice, for which Venezuela was dependent. Under the agreement, which began in late 2010, Guyana used funds from its PetroCaribe account to pay those farmers who supplied Venezuela with rice, then deduct the equivalent amount owed to Venezuela for petroleum products.

Relations were strained in November 2007 when Guyana accused Venezuelan troops of crossing into its territory and blowing up two gold-mining dredges. The Venezuelan Government subsequently expressed regret for the incident and talks took place between the two countries to establish measures to prevent another military incursion. In July 2010 Jagdeo and Chávez concluded a number of trade agreements and agreed to restart UN-mediated negotiations on their territorial dispute, which had been in abeyance since 2007.

In September 2011 relations between Guyana and Venezuela were strained further after Guyana made an application to the UN to extend its continental shelf by 150 nautical miles. The UN's Commission on the Limits of the Continental Shelf notified Venezuela of the application, to which Venezuela objected on two fronts: that Guyana had not informed it of the application beforehand; and that Guyana had claimed that the area of the extension was not under dispute. The Guyanese Government rejected both accusations. Guyana wanted to extend its underwater shelf to conduct seismic surveys, which could lead to wider access to potential mineral and hydrocarbon deposits.

Guyana's relations with Brazil continued to improve through trade and military agreements. In 2003 the Government approved a request by the Brazilian authorities for a partial abolition of visas for both countries. On a visit to Guyana in February 2005, Brazil's President, Lula da Silva, reiterated his Government's commitment to the construction of a bridge across the Takutu river between the two countries. During the visit bilateral agreements on health and education were also signed, as was a three-year agreement aimed at facilitating improved training and qualifications for foreign service personnel in both countries. Joint-venture oil and gas exploration was also announced. The Takutu Bridge was completed in mid-2009.

In January 2010 President Jagdeo held talks in Moscow with his Russian counterpart. The negotiations were aimed at furthering political dialogue, as well as extending trade, economic and humanitarian co-operation between the two countries. In the same month Jagdeo made an official visit to Iran during which he signed two co-operation agreements with that country; Iranian officials travelled to Guyana for further discussions in November.

CONSTITUTION AND GOVERNMENT

Guyana became a republic, within the Commonwealth, on 23 February 1970. A new Constitution was promulgated in October 1980, and amended in 1998, 2000 and 2001. Legislative power is held by the unicameral National Assembly, with 65 members: 53 elected for five years by universal adult suffrage, on the basis of proportional representation; 40 members are elected from national lists, and a further 25 members are elected from regional constituency lists. Executive power is held by the President, who leads the majority party in the Assembly and holds office for its duration. The President appoints and heads a Cabinet, which includes the Prime Minister, and may include up to four Ministers who are not elected members of the Assembly. The Cabinet is collectively responsible to the National Assembly. Guyana comprises 10 regions.

REGIONAL AND INTERNATIONAL CO-OPERATION

Guyana is a founder member of CARICOM (see p. 227). It was also one of the six founder members of CARICOM's Caribbean Single Market and Economy (CSME), established in 2006. Guyana was a member of the Community of Latin American and Caribbean States (see p. 462), which was formally inaugurated in December 2011. Guyana became a member of the UN in 1966. As a contracting party to the General Agreement on Tariffs and Trade, Guyana joined the World Trade Organization (see p. 433) on its establishment in 1995. The country is a member of the Commonwealth (see p. 239). Guyana is also a member of the Group of 77 (see p. 450) organization of developing states. In 2001 Guyana was one of 11 Caribbean states to sign an agreement establishing a jointly administered regional court. The Caribbean Court of Justice (CCJ), inaugurated in Trinidad and Tobago in April 2005, replaced the Privy Council in the United Kingdom as Guyana's highest appellate body. Guyana also participated in the third meeting of South American Presidents in Cusco, Peru, in December 2004, which created the Comunidad Sudamericana de Naciones (South American Community of Nations, which was renamed Unión de Naciones Suramericanas, UNASUR—Union of South American Nations—in April 2007), intended to promote greater regional economic integration. In February 2011 Guyana was a signatory to the Caribbean Basin Security Initiative between CARICOM and the USA.

ECONOMIC AFFAIRS

In 2010, according to estimates by the World Bank, Guyana's gross national income (GNI), measured at average 2008–10 prices, was US $2,491m., equivalent to US $3,300 per head (or US $3,560 per head on an international purchasing-power parity basis). During 2001–10, it was estimated, the population increased at an average annual rate of 0.3%, while gross domestic product (GDP) per head increased, in real terms, by an average of 1.1% per year during 2001–10. Overall GDP increased, in real terms, at an average annual rate of 1.4% in 2000–10; real GDP increased by 4.4% in 2010.

Agriculture (including forestry and fishing) provided an estimated 17.4% of GDP in 2010 and employed an estimated 14.0% of the total labour force in mid-2012. The principal cash crops are rice (17.6%) and sugar cane (sugar provided an estimated 11.8% of the value of total domestic exports in 2010). In the 21st century the sugar industry, which accounted for 2.2% of GDP in 2010, was threatened by the disappearing preferential markets and the increasing cost of employment. In 2006 long-anticipated changes were implemented to the European Union's (EU) sugar regime, ending the preferential prices paid to Guyanese producers. Guyana and the other sugar-producing members of the African, Caribbean and Pacific (ACP) group of countries condemned the changes, noting that they would adversely impact on rural development, employment and investment. In 2009 a US $180m. project, to be jointly financed by the Government, the state sugar company GuySuCo (Guyana Sugar Corpn Inc) and international lending institutions, to upgrade the Skeldon sugar refinery in Berbice and to construct a 30-MW co-generation facility, was officially inaugurated. Vegetables and fruit are cultivated for the local market, and livestock-rearing is being developed. Fishing is also important (particularly shrimp fishing), and accounted for an estimated 1.8% of GDP in 2010. Agricultural production increased by 0.2% during 2001–10. The sector's GDP increased by 5.5% in 2010.

Timber resources in Guyana are extensive and underdeveloped. In 2010 the forestry sector contributed 3.2% of GDP. About three-quarters of the country's total land area consists of forest and woodland. In 2010 timber shipments provided an estimated 5.5% of total domestic exports. Although foreign investment in Guyana's largely undeveloped interior continued to be encouraged by the Government, there was much popular concern at the extent of the exploitation of the rainforest. The forestry sector's GDP declined at an average annual rate of 0.7% in 2000–09; the output from the sector increased by 1.4% in 2010.

Industry (including mining, manufacturing, construction and power) provided an estimated 34.2% of GDP in 2010 and engaged 25.4% of the employed labour force in 2002. Industrial GDP (excluding power) decreased at an average annual rate of 0.6% in 2001–10. Industrial GDP increased by 3.4% in 2010.

Mining contributed an estimated 15.1% of GDP in 2010, and employed 4.1% of the total working population in 2002. Bauxite, which is used for the manufacture of aluminium, is one of Guyana's most valuable exports. The value of bauxite exports decreased significantly following the withdrawal in 2002 of the US-based aluminium company Alcoa from the Aroaima bauxite and aluminium mine. In 2010 a total of 114.6m. metric tons of bauxite was exported, generating 13.1% of the value of exports. The registered production of gold accounted for 41.5% of domestic exports in 2010 (compared with 36.7% in the previous year). In 2000 the gold industry was estimated directly to employ some 32,000 people. In March 2011 Guyana Goldfields Inc announced it had discovered up to 6m. troy ounces of high-quality gold in Aurora, in the north-west of the country. There are also some petroleum reserves and significant diamond resources. In 2010 diamond production stood at 49,920 metric carats, compared with 143,982 metric carats in 2009. The GDP of the mining sector was estimated to have declined by an average of 3.9% per year in 2000–09; the sector increased by 0.9% in 2010.

Manufacturing accounted for an estimated 6.6% of GDP in 2010 and, in 2002, employed 13.3% of the total working population. The main activities are the processing of bauxite, sugar, rice and timber. Manufacturing GDP increased at an average annual rate of 2.0% in 2001–10. Output from the sector increased by 4.2% in 2010.

Construction accounted for an estimated 10.2% of GDP in 2010 and, in 2002, employed 7.0% of the total working population. According to official figures, construction GDP (including engineering) increased at an average annual rate of 4.9% in 2000–09. Output from the sector increased by 10.8% in 2010.

Energy requirements are almost entirely met by imported hydrocarbon fuels. In 2010 fuels and lubricants constituted 27.8% of the total value of imports (mainly from Venezuela and Trinidad and Tobago). In 2005 Guyana was one of 13 Caribbean countries that signed the PetroCaribe agreement, under which Venezuela accorded petroleum concessions.

The services sector contributed an estimated 48.4% of GDP in 2010 and engaged 52.4% of the employed labour force in 2002. The GDP of the services sector increased by an average of 4.8% per year in 2001–10. Services GDP increased, in real terms, by 4.4% in 2010.

In 2010 Guyana recorded a visible trade deficit of US $525.8m. and a deficit of US $239.0m. on the current account of the balance of payments. In 2009 the principal source of imports was the USA (28.8%), followed by Trinidad and Tobago, Venezuela, and Suriname. In the same year Canada was the principal market for exports (26.4% of total exports), followed by the United Kingdom, the USA and Ukraine. The principal exports in 2010 were gold, rice, sugar and bauxite, and the principal imports were consumer goods and fuel and lubricants.

In 2010 the overall budget deficit was an estimated $ G13,404.2m. (equivalent to 3.0% of GDP). Guyana's general government gross debt was $ G276,867m. in 2010, equivalent to 60.2% of GDP. According to World Bank estimates, by the end of 2009 Guyana's external debt totalled US $1,036m., of which US $781.0m. was public and publicly guaranteed debt. In that year, the cost of servicing long-term public and publicly guaranteed debt and repayments to the IMF was equivalent to 1.3% of the value of exports of goods, services and income (excluding workers' remittances). According to the ILO, the annual rate of inflation averaged 6.3% in 2001–10. Consumer prices increased by some 3.7% in 2010. According to census figures, the rate of unemployment in 2002 was 11.7%.

The global economic crisis from late 2008 led to a decline in remittances, foreign direct investment and tourism receipts in Guyana. The Guyanese economy's reliance on sugar meant that the gradual withdrawal of the EU's Sugar Protocol in 2009 (combined with the removal of sugar duties in 2008) posed an enormous challenge to the authorities. However, the centrepiece of the Government's strategy to modernize the sector, the sugar-processing factory at Skeldon, which opened in 2009, was still not operating at full capacity by mid-2012, while strike action, management problems, technical difficulties and adverse weather conditions had also undermined progress. Nevertheless, compared with most of its neighbours in the region, Guyana demonstrated an impressive resilience when confronted by the global economic downturn, registering its fifth consecutive year of GDP growth in 2010. Moreover, the IMF projected real GDP growth of 5.3% in 2011, underpinned by rising gold production and renewed services sector expansion. The country's fiscal position was bolstered in December 2010 by the disbursement of US $30m. from the Norwegian Government as part of an environmental mechanism to reward Guyana for the preservation of its rainforests, potentially worth up to $250m. over four years. However, in March 2011 it was reported that deforestation rates had increased dramatically over the previous year—by some 300%—as a result of an inaccurate baseline target in the Norwegian agreement. The IMF also noted that road projects and construction work on the Amaila Falls hydroelectric power project would maintain similar levels of growth over the medium term. Guyana is believed to possess substantial petroleum deposits, so the development of the nascent hydrocarbons sector could be an important factor in stimulating future economic growth. Economic policy was expected to remain largely unchanged following the inauguration of Donald Ramotar as Guyana's new President in late 2011.

PUBLIC HOLIDAYS

2013: 1 January (New Year's Day), 25 January* (Yum an-Nabi, birth of the Prophet), 23 February (Mashramani, Republic Day), 29 March (Good Friday), 1 April (Easter Monday), 1 May (Labour Day), 5 May (Indian Heritage Day), 2 July (CARICOM Day), 5 August (Freedom Day), 8 August* (Id al-Fitr, end of Ramadan), 15 October* (Id al-Adha, feast of the Sacrifice), 25–26 December (Christmas).

* These holidays are dependent on the Islamic lunar calendar and may vary by one or two days from the dates given.

In addition, the Hindu festivals of Holi Phagwah (usually in March) and Diwali (October or November) are celebrated. These festivals are dependent on sightings of the moon and their precise date is not known until two months before they take place.

Statistical Survey

Sources (unless otherwise stated): Bank of Guyana, 1 Church St and Ave of the Republic, POB 1003, Georgetown; tel. 226-3250; fax 227-2965; e-mail communications@bankofguyana.org.gy; internet www.bankofguyana.org.gy; Bureau of Statistics, Ministry of Finance, Main and Urquhart Sts, Georgetown; tel. 227-1114; fax 226-1284; internet www.statisticsguyana.gov.gy.

AREA AND POPULATION

Area: 214,969 sq km (83,000 sq miles).

Population: 759,567 (males 376,381, females 383,186) at census of 12 May 1980; 723,673 (males 356,540, females 367,133) at census of 12 May 1991; 751,223 (males 376,034, females 375,189) at census of 15 September 2002. *2010* (official projection): 784,894 (males 393,059, females 391,835).

Density (2010): 3.7 per sq km.

Population by Age and Sex (official projections in 2010): *0–14:* 210,824 (males 106,785, females 104,039); *15–64:* 529,809 (males 266,850, females 262,959); *65 and over:* 44,262 (males 19,425, females 24,837); *Total* 784,894 (males 393,059, females 391,835).

Ethnic Groups (at 2002 census): 'East' Indians 326,277; Africans 227,062; Mixed 125,727; Amerindians 68,675; Portuguese 1,497; Chinese 1,396; White 477; Total (incl. others) 751,223.

Regions (population at 2002 census): Barima–Waini 24,275; Pomeroon–Supenaam 49,253; Essequibo Islands–West Demerara 103,061; Demerara–Mahaica 310,320; Mahaica–Berbice 52,428; East Berbice–Corentyne 123,695; Cuyuni–Mazaruni 17,597; Potaro–Siparuni 10,095; Upper Takutu–Upper Essequibo 19,387; Upper Demerara–Berbice 41,112; Total 751,223.

Principal Towns (population at 2002 census): Georgetown (capital) 134,497; Linden 29,298; New Amsterdam 17,033; Corriverton 11,494. *Mid-2009* ('000, incl. suburbs, UN estimate): Georgetown 132 (Source: UN, *World Urbanization Prospects: The 2009 Revision*).

Births, Marriages and Deaths (2010): Birth rate 19.2 per 1,000; Marriages 4,239 (marriage rate 5.4 per 1,000); Deaths 4,649 (death rate 6.4 per 1,000).

Life Expectancy (years at birth, WHO estimates): 67 (males 64; females 70) in 2009. Source: WHO, *World Health Statistics*.

Economically Active Population (persons aged 15 years and over, census of 2002): Agriculture, hunting and forestry 45,378; Fishing 5,533; Mining and quarrying 9,374; Manufacturing 30,483; Electricity, gas and water 2,246; Construction 16,100; Trade, repair of motor vehicles and personal and household goods 37,690; Restaurants and hotels 5,558; Transport, storage and communications 16,790; Financial intermediation 3,074; Real estate, renting and business services 7,384; Public administration, defence and social security 14,995; Education 13,015; Health and social work 5,513; Other community, social and personal service activities 9,599; Private households with employed persons 6,156; Extra-territorial organizations and bodies 477; *Sub-total* 229,365; Activities not adequately defined 1,489; *Total employed* 230,854. *2009:* Central government 10,094; Rest of the public sector 17,410; Total public sector employment 27,504. *Mid-2012* ('000, estimates): Agriculture, etc. 49; Total labour force 349 (Source: FAO).

HEALTH AND WELFARE

Key Indicators

Total Fertility Rate (children per woman, 2009): 2.3.

Under-5 Mortality Rate (per 1,000 live births, 2009): 35.

HIV/AIDS (% of persons aged 15–49, 2009): 1.2.

Physicians (per 1,000 head, 2000): 0.5.

Hospital Beds (per 1,000 head, 2005): 2.8.

Health Expenditure (2008): US $ per head (PPP): 247.

Health Expenditure (2008): % of GDP: 8.1.

Health Expenditure (2008): public (% of total): 87.3.

Access to Water (% of persons, 2008): 94.

Access to Sanitation (% of persons, 2008): 81.

Total Carbon Dioxide Emissions ('000 metric tons, 2007): 1,505.9.

Total Carbon Dioxide Emissions Per Head (metric tons, 2007): 2.0.

Human Development Index (2011): ranking: 117.

Human Development Index (2011): value: 0.633.

For sources and definitions, see explanatory note on p. vi.

AGRICULTURE, ETC.

Principal Crops ('000 metric tons, 2010): Rice, paddy 507 (FAO estimate); Cassava (Manioc) 18 (FAO estimate); Sugar cane 2,766; Coconuts 71 (FAO estimate); Bananas 6 (FAO estimate); Plantains 4 (FAO estimate). *Aggregate Production* ('000 metric tons, may include official, semi-official or estimated data): Total cereals 513.4; Vegetables (incl. melons) 29.2; Fruits (excl. melons) 33.6.

Livestock ('000 head, year ending September 2010, FAO estimates): Horses 2.4; Asses 1.0; Cattle 110; Sheep 130; Pigs 14; Goats 79; Chickens 19,900.

Livestock Products ('000 metric tons, 2010, FAO estimates): Cattle meat 1.8; Sheep meat 0.6; Pig meat 0.8; Chicken meat 23.1; Cows' milk 43.1; Hen eggs 1.0.

Forestry ('000 cubic metres, 2010, FAO estimates): *Roundwood Removals:* Sawlogs, veneer logs and logs for sleepers 339, Pulpwood 100, Other industrial wood 19, Fuel wood 851; Total 1,309. *Sawnwood Production:* Total (all broadleaved) 73.

Fishing ('000 metric tons, live weight, 2009): Capture 43.6 (FAO estimate—Marine fishes 23.9; Atlantic seabob 15.4; Whitebelly prawn 1.3); Aquaculture 0.5; *Total catch* 44.1 (FAO estimate). Note: Figures exclude crocodiles: the number of spectacled caimans caught in 2009 was 28,000.

Source: FAO.

MINING

Production (2010): Bauxite 1,087,000 metric tons; Gold 9,543 kg; Diamonds 49,920 metric carats.

INDUSTRY

Selected Products (2010): Raw sugar 220,819 metric tons; Rice 360,996 metric tons; Rum 33,000 hl; Beer and stout 144,000 hl; Logs 318,242 cu m; Margarine 2,135 metric tons; Biscuits 1,182,100 kg; Paint 25,002 hl; Electricity 627m. kWh.

FINANCE

Currency and Exchange Rates: 100 cents = 1 Guyana dollar ($ G). *Sterling, US Dollar and Euro Equivalents* (30 November 2011): £1 sterling = $ G319.184; US $1 = $ G204.500; €1 = $ G274.398; $ G1,000 = £3.13 = US $4.89 = €3.64. *Average Exchange Rate* ($ G per US $): 203.633 in 2008; 203.950 in 2009; 203.636 in 2010.

Budget ($ G million, 2010): *Revenue:* Tax revenue 100,958.6 (Income tax 39,455.3; Value-added tax 27,070.0; Trade taxes 9,731.8); Other current revenue 6,916.7; Capital revenue (incl. grants) 11,820.7; Total 119,696.0. *Expenditure:* Current expenditure 86,381.5 (Personnel emoluments 28,367.3, Other goods and services 50,134.8, Interest 7,879.4); Capital expenditure 46,718.7; *Total* 133,100.2.

International Reserves (US $ million at 31 December 2010): IMF special drawing rights 2.04; Foreign exchange 780.02; *Total* 782.06. Source: IMF, *International Financial Statistics*.

Money Supply ($ G million at 31 December 2010): Currency outside depository corporations 45,835; Transferable deposits 51,465; Other deposits 207,720; *Broad money* 305,020. Source: IMF, *International Financial Statistics*.

Cost of Living (Consumer Price Index; base: 2000 = 100): All items 166.0 in 2008; 170.9 in 2009; 177.3 in 2010. Source: ILO.

Expenditure on the Gross Domestic Product ($ G million at current prices, 2010): Government final consumption expenditure 69,533; Private final consumption expenditure 392,923; Gross capital formation 116,839; *Total domestic expenditure* 579,294; Net imports of goods and services –126,078; *GDP in purchasers' values* 453,216.

Gross Domestic Product by Economic Activity ($ G million at current prices, 2010): Agriculture, forestry and fishing 71,400 (Sugar 8,915); Mining and quarrying 61,842; Manufacturing 27,209; Construction 41,604; Electricity, gas and water 9,391; Wholesale and retail trade 59,780; Transport, storage, information and communications 44,504; Finance and insurance 17,054; Real estate and renting 4,486; Public administration 34,843; Education 16,819; Health and social welfare 6,446; Other services 14,191; *Sub-total* 409,569; *Less* Financial intermediation services indirectly measured 15,438; *Gross value added in basic prices* 394,131; Indirect taxes, less subsidies 59,084; *GDP in purchasers' values* 453,216.

Balance of Payments (US $ million, 2010): Exports of goods f.o.b. 891.9; Imports of goods f.o.b. –1,417.7; *Trade balance* –525.8; Services (net) –84.0; *Balance on goods and services* –609.8; Transfers (net) 370.8; *Current balance* –239.0; Capital account (net) 339.2; Net errors and omissions 16.3; *Overall balance* 116.5.

EXTERNAL TRADE

Principal Commodities (US $ million, 2010): *Imports c.i.f.:* Capital goods 291.0; Consumer goods 376.8; Fuel and lubricants 394.1; Other intermediate goods 347.3; Total (incl. others) 1,417.7. *Exports f.o.b.:* Bauxite 114.6; Sugar 104.0; Rice 154.6; Gold 346.4; Shrimps 43.2; Timber 48.0; Total (incl. others, excl. re-exports) 878.1.

Principal Trading Partners (US $ million, 2009): *Imports:* Canada 26.0; China, People's Republic 59.3; Finland 28.1; Japan 42.2; Suriname 61.4; Trinidad and Tobago 227.3; United Kingdom 43.5; USA 334.0; Venezuela 79.7; Total (incl. others) 1,161.0. *Exports:* Barbados 15.9; Belgium 13.8; Canada 203.1; Germany 31.9; Jamaica 37.4; Trinidad and Tobago 28.5; Ukraine 48.4; United Kingdom 105.6; USA 94.8; Total (incl. others) 768.2. *2010:* Total imports 1,417.7; Total exports 878.1.

TRANSPORT

Road Traffic (vehicles in use, 2008): Passenger cars 44,739; Lorries and vans 28,122; Motorcycles and mopeds 37,069. Source: IRF, *World Road Statistics*.

Shipping: *International Sea-borne Freight Traffic* ('000 metric tons, estimates, 1990): Goods loaded 1,730; Goods unloaded 673 (Source: UN, *Monthly Bulletin of Statistics*). *Merchant Fleet* (at 31 December 2009): Vessels 122; Displacement 41,362 grt (Source: IHS Fairplay, *World Fleet Statistics*).

Civil Aviation (traffic on scheduled services, 2001): Kilometres flown (million) 1; Passengers carried ('000) 48; Passenger-km (million) 175; Total ton-km (million) 17. Source: UN, *Statistical Yearbook*.

TOURISM

Tourist Arrivals: 134,057 (USA 69,823) in 2007; 129,595 (USA 66,350) in 2009; 141,281 (USA 76,955) in 2010.

Tourism Receipts (US $ million, excl. passenger transport): 37 in 2006; 50 in 2007; 59 in 2008.

Source: World Tourism Organization.

COMMUNICATIONS MEDIA

Radio Receivers (1999): 400,000 in use.

Television Receivers (2000): 70,000 in use.

Telephones (2010): 149,900 main lines in use.

Mobile Cellular Telephones (2010): 555,400 subscribers.

Personal Computers (2005): 29,000 (38.0 per 1,000 persons) in use.

Internet Subscribers (2010): 16,400.

Broadband Subscribers (2010): 11,200.

Daily Newspapers (2000): 2; estimated circulation 56,750.

Non-daily Newspapers (2000): 4; estimated circulation 47,700.

Book Production (1997): 25.

Sources: mainly UNESCO, *Statistical Yearbook*; UN, *Statistical Yearbook*; International Telecommunication Union.

EDUCATION

Pre-primary (1999/2000): Institutions 320; Teachers 2,218 (males 22, females 2,196); Students 36,955 (males 18,768, females 18,187).

Primary (1999/2000): Institutions 423; Teachers 3,951 (males 561, females 3,390); Students 105,800 (males 54,105, females 51,695).

General Secondary (1999/2000): Institutions 70; Teachers 1,972 (males 715, females 1,257); Students 36,055 (males 16,000, females 20,055).

Special Education (1999/2000): Institutions 6; Teachers 64 (males 14, females 50); Students 617 (males 420, females 197).

Technical and Vocational (1999/2000): Institutions 6; Teachers 215 (males 144, females 71); Students 4,662 (males 2,585, females 2,077).

Teacher Training (1999/2000): Institutions 1; Teachers 297 (males 121, females 176); Students 1,604 (males 246, females 1,358).

University (1999/2000): Institutions 1; Teachers 371 (males 256, females 115); Students 7,496 (males 2,455, females 5,041).

Private Education (1999/2000): Institutions 7; Teachers 120 (males 27, females 93); Students 1,692 (males 831, females 861).

Institutions (2007/08, estimates): Pre-primary 425; Primary 441; Secondary 332.

Source: Ministry of Education.

2009/10 (estimates): *Pre-primary:* 25,470 pupils; 1,811 teachers. *Primary:* 99,241 pupils; 4,031 teachers. *Secondary:* 80,676 pupils; 3,766 teachers. *Tertiary:* 7,939 students; 752 teachers (Source: UNESCO Institute for Statistics).

Pupil-Teacher Ratio (primary education, UNESCO estimate): 24.6 in 2009/10 (Source: UNESCO Institute for Statistics).

Adult Literacy Rate (UNESCO estimates): 98.6% (males 99.0%; females 98.2%) in 2001. Source: UN Development Programme, *Human Development Report*.

Directory

The Government

HEAD OF STATE

President: DONALD RAMOTAR (sworn in 3 December 2011).

CABINET
(May 2012)

The PPP/Civic alliance forms the Government.

Prime Minister and Minister of Parliamentary Affairs and Energy: SAMUEL A. HINDS.

Minister of Foreign Affairs: Dr CAROLYN RODRIGUES-BIRKETT.

Minister of Finance: Dr ASHNI K. SINGH.

Minister of Agriculture: Dr LESLIE RAMSAMMY.

Minister of Amerindian Affairs: PAULINE CAMPBELL-SUKHAI.

Minister of Home Affairs: CLEMENT J. ROHEE.

Minister of Legal Affairs and Attorney-General: ANIL NANDLALL.

Minister of Education: PRIYA DEVI MANICKCHAND.

Minister of Health: Dr BHERI S. RAMSARAN.

Minister of Housing and Water: IRFAAN ALI.

Minister of Labour: Dr NANDA K. GOPAUL.

Minister of Human Services and Social Security: JENNIFER I. M. WEBSTER.

Minister of Local Government and Regional Development: GANGA PERSAUD.

Minister of Public Service: Dr JENNIFER WESTFORD.

Minister of Public Works: BRINDLEY H. R. BENN.

Minister of Culture, Youth and Sport: Dr FRANK C. S. ANTHONY.

Minister of Natural Resources and Environment: ROBERT M. PERSAUD.

Head of the Presidential Secretariat: Dr ROGER LUNCHEON.

Minister in the Ministry of Finance: JUAN A. EDGHILL.

Minister in the Ministry of Local Government and Regional Development: NORMAN WHITTAKER.

Minister in the Ministry of Agriculture: ALLI BAKSH.

MINISTRIES

Office of the President: New Garden St, Bourda, Georgetown; tel. 225-3130; fax 227-3050; e-mail opmed@op.gov.gy; internet www.op.gov.gy.

Office of the Prime Minister: Oranapai Towers, Wights Lane, Kingston, Georgetown; tel. 226-6955; fax 226-7573; e-mail opm@networksgy.gy.

Ministry of Agriculture: Regent and Vlissengen Rds, POB 1001, Georgetown; tel. 226-5165; fax 227-2978; e-mail minister@agriculture.gov.gy; internet www.agriculture.gov.gy.

Ministry of Amerindian Affairs: Thomas and Quamina Sts, Georgetown; tel. 227-5067; fax 225-7072; e-mail ministryofamerindian@networksgy.com.

Ministry of Culture, Youth and Sport: 71–72 Main St, South Cummingsburg, Georgetown; tel. 227-7867; fax 225-5067; e-mail mincys@guyana.net.gy.

Ministry of Education: 26 Brickdam, Stabroek, POB 1014, Georgetown; tel. 226-3094; fax 225-5570; e-mail moegyweb@yahoo.com; internet www.moe.gov.gy.

Ministry of Finance: Main and Urquhart Sts, Kingston, Georgetown; tel. 225-6088; fax 226-1284; e-mail minister@finance.gov.gy; internet www.finance.gov.gy.

Ministry of Foreign Affairs: 254 South Rd and Shiv Chanderpaul Dr., Bourda, Georgetown; tel. 226-1606; fax 225-9192; e-mail minfor@guyana.net.gy; internet www.minfor.gov.gy.

Ministry of Health: Brickdam, Stabroek, Georgetown; tel. 226-5861; fax 225-4505; e-mail moh@sdnp.org.gy; internet www.health.gov.gy.

Ministry of Home Affairs: 60 Brickdam, Stabroek, Georgetown; tel. 225-7270; fax 227-4806; e-mail homemin@guyana.net.

Ministry of Housing and Water: 41 Brickdam, Stabroek, Georgetown; tel. 225-7192; fax 227-3455; e-mail mhwps@sdnp.org.gy.

Ministry of Labour, Human Services and Social Security: 1 Water St and Corhill St, Stabroek, Georgetown; tel. 225-0655; fax 227-1308; e-mail psmlhsss@yahoo.com; internet www.mlhsss.gov.gy.

Ministry of Legal Affairs and Office of the Attorney-General: 95 Carmichael St, North Cummingsburg, Georgetown; tel. 226-2616; fax 226-9721; e-mail legalaffairsps@yahoo.com; internet www.agmla.gov.gy.

Ministry of Local Government and Regional Development: De Winkle Bldg, Fort St, Kingston, Georgetown; tel. 225-8621; fax 226-5070; e-mail mlgrdps@telsnetgy.net.

Ministry of Natural Resources and Environment: Georgetown.

Ministry of Public Service: 164 Waterloo St, North Cummingsburg, Georgetown; tel. 226-6528; fax 225-7899; e-mail psm@sdnp.org.gy.

Ministry of Public Works: Wights Lane, Kingston, Georgetown; tel. 226-1875; fax 225-6954; e-mail minoth@networksgy.com.

President and Legislature

NATIONAL ASSEMBLY

Speaker: RAPHAEL TROTMAN.

Deputy Speaker: DEBORAH BACKER.

Clerk: SHERLOCK ISAACS.

Election, 28 November 2011, preliminary results

Party	% of votes	Seats
People's Progressive Party/Civic	48.6	32
A Partnership for National Unity*	40.8	26
Alliance for Change	10.3	7
The United Force	0.2	—
Total	100.0	65

* A coalition comprising the Guyana Action Party, the National Front Alliance, the People's National Congress Reform and the Working People's Alliance.

Under Guyana's system of proportional representation, the nominated candidate of the party receiving the most number of votes is elected to the presidency. Thus, on 3 December 2011 the candidate of the PPP/Civic alliance, DONALD RAMOTAR, was inaugurated as President.

Election Commission

Guyana Elections Commission (GECOM): 41 High and Cowan Sts, Kingston, Georgetown; tel. 225-0277; e-mail gecomfeedback@webworksgy.com; internet www.gecom.org.gy; f. 2000; appointed by the Pres., partly in consultation with the leader of the opposition; Chair. Dr STEVE SURUJBALLY; Chief Elections Officer GOCOOL BOODHOO.

Political Organizations

Alliance for Change (AFC): 77 Hadfield St, Werk-en-Rust, Georgetown; tel. 231-8183; fax 225-0455; e-mail office@voteafc.com; internet www.afcguyana.com; f. 2005; Leader RAPHAEL TROTMAN; Chair. KHEMRAJ RAMJATTAN.

Guyana National Congress (GNC): Georgetown; Leader SAMUEL HAMER.

Justice For All Party (JFAP): 43 Robb and Wellington Sts, Lacytown, Georgetown; tel. 226-5462; fax 227-3050; e-mail cnsharma@guyana.net.gy; Leader CHANDRANARINE SHARMA.

A Partnership for National Unity (APNU): 121 Regent Rd, Bourda, Georgetown; e-mail info@apnuguyana.com; internet www.apnuguyana.com; f. 2011; fmrly the Joint Opposition of Political Parties (JOPP); coalition formed to contest the 2011 elections; presidential candidate Brig.-Gen. (retd) DAVID GRANGER; comprises the following parties.

Guyana Action Party (GAP): Georgetown; allied with ROAR in 2006 elections; Leader EVERALL FRANKLIN.

National Front Alliance: Georgetown; f. 2000; comprises the National Democratic Movt and National Republican Party; Leader KEITH SCOTT; Sec. FIESAL FEROSE ALI.

People's National Congress Reform (PNCR): Congress Place, Sophia, POB 10330, Georgetown; tel. 225-7852; fax 225-2704; e-mail pnc@guyana-pnc.org; internet www.guyanapnc.org; f. 1957 as People's National Congress following split with the PPP; present name adopted in 2006; Reform wing established in 2000; Leader ROBERT H. O. CORBIN; Chair. BISHWAISHWAR RAMSAROOP; Gen. Sec. OSCAR E. CLARKE.

Working People's Alliance (WPA): Walter Rodney House, 80 Croal St, Stabroek, Georgetown; tel. and fax 225-3679; originally popular pressure group, became political party 1979; independent Marxist; Collective Leadership Dr CLIVE THOMAS, Dr RUPERT ROOPNARINE.

People's Democratic Party of Guyana (PDP): e-mail admin@guyanapdp.org; internet www.guyanapdp.org; f. 2008.

People's Progressive Party/Civic (PPP/Civic): Freedom House, 41 Robb St, Lacytown, Georgetown; tel. 227-2095; fax 227-2096; e-mail pr@ppp-civic.org; internet www.ppp-civic.org; f. 1950; Marxist-Leninist; Gen. Sec. DONALD RAMOTAR.

Rise, Organize and Rebuild Guyana Movement (ROAR): 186 Parafield, Leonora, West Coast Demerara, POB 101409, Georgetown; tel. 268-2452; fax 268-3382; e-mail guyroar@yahoo.com; f. 1999; allied with GAP in 2006 elections; Leader RAVI DEV; Sec. ROY SINGH.

The United Force (TUF): Unity House, 95 Robb and New Garden Sts, Bourda, Georgetown; tel. 226-2596; fax 225-2973; f. 1960; right-wing; advocates rapid industrialization through govt partnership and private capital; allied with the PPP/Civic since 2001 but contested 2006 election under its own auspices; Leader MANZOOR NADIR; Dep. Leader MICHAEL ANTHONY ABRAHAM.

Unity Party: 77 Hadfield St, Georgetown; tel. 227-6744; fax 227-6745; e-mail info@unityparty.net; internet www.unitypartyguyana.com; f. 2005; promotes private enterprise and coalition politics; Pres. CHEDDI (JOEY) JAGAN, Jr.

Diplomatic Representation

EMBASSIES AND HIGH COMMISSIONS IN GUYANA

Brazil: 308 Church St, Queenstown, POB 10489, Georgetown; tel. 225-7970; fax 226-9063; e-mail brasemb@networksgy.com; Ambassador LUIZ GILBERTO SEIXAS DE ANDRADE.

Canada: High and Young Sts, POB 10880, Georgetown; tel. 227-2081; fax 225-8380; e-mail grgtn@international.gc.ca; internet www.canadainternational.gc.ca/guyana; High Commissioner DAVID DEVINE.

China, People's Republic: Lot 2, Botanic Gardens, Mandella Ave, Georgetown; tel. 227-1651; fax 225-9228; e-mail prcemb@networks.gy.com; internet gy.china-embassy.org/eng; Ambassador YU WENZHE.

Cuba: 46 High St, POB 10268, Kingston, Georgetown; tel. 225-1883; fax 226-1824; e-mail emguyana@networksgy.com; internet www.cubanembassy.org.gy; Ambassador RAUL GORTÁZAR MARRERO.

India: 307 Church St, Queenstown, Georgetown; tel. 226-3996; fax 225-7012; e-mail hoc.georgetown@mea.gov.in; High Commissioner PURAN MAL MEENA (designate).

Mexico: 44 Brickdam, Stabroek, Georgetown; tel. 226-3987; fax 226-3722; e-mail mexicoembassygy@gmail.com; internet embamex.sre.gob.mx/guyana; Ambassador FRANCISCO OLGUIN.

Russia: 3 Public Rd, Kitty, Georgetown; tel. 226-9773; fax 227-2975; e-mail embrus.guyana@mail.ru; internet www.rusembassyguyana.org.gy; Ambassador NIKOLAY SMIRNOV.

Suriname: 171 Peter Rose and Crown Sts, Queenstown, Georgetown; tel. 226-7844; fax 225-0759; e-mail surnmemb@gol.net.gy; Ambassador MANORMA SOEKNANDAN.

United Kingdom: 44 Main St, POB 10849, Georgetown; tel. 226-5881; fax 225-3555; e-mail bhcguyana@networksgy.com; internet ukinguyana.fco.gov.uk; High Commissioner ANDREW AYRE.

USA: 100 Young and Duke Sts, POB 10507, Kingston, Georgetown; tel. 225-4900; fax 225-8497; e-mail usembassy@hotmail.com; internet georgetown.usembassy.gov; Ambassador BRENT HARDT.

Venezuela: 296 Thomas St, South Cummingsburg, Georgetown; tel. 226-1543; fax 225-3241; e-mail embveguy@gol.net.gy; Ambassador DARÍO MORANDY.

Judicial System

The Judicature of Guyana comprises the Supreme Court of Judicature, which consists of the Court of Appeal and the High Court (both of which are superior courts of record), and a number of Courts of Summary Jurisdiction.

The Court of Appeal consists of the Chancellor as President, the Chief Justice, and such number of Justices of Appeal as may be prescribed by the National Assembly.

The High Court of the Supreme Court consists of the Chief Justice as President of the Court and Puisne Judges. Its jurisdiction is both original and appellate. It has criminal jurisdiction in matters brought before it on indictment. The High Court of the Supreme Court has unlimited jurisdiction in civil matters and exclusive jurisdiction in probate, divorce and admiralty and certain other matters. In April 2005 the Caribbean Court of Justice was inaugurated, in Port of Spain, Trinidad and Tobago, as Guyana's highest court of appeal.

A magistrate has jurisdiction to determine claims where the amount involved does not exceed a certain sum of money, specified by law. Appeal lies to the Full Court.

Chancellor of Justice: CARL SINGH (acting).

Chief Justice: IAN CHANG.

Justices of Appeal: YONETTE CUMMINGS-EDWARDS, B. S. ROY, CHARLES RAMSON.

High Court Justices: WINSTON HORATIO PATTERSON, ROXANNE GEORGE, BRASSINGTON REYNOLDS.

Religion

CHRISTIANITY

Guyana Council of Churches: 26 Durban St, Lodge, Georgetown; tel. 227-5126; e-mail bishopedghill@hotmail.com; f. 1967 by merger of the Christian Social Council (f. 1937) and the Evangelical Council (f. 1960); 15 mem. churches, 1 assoc. mem.; Chair. Rev. ALPHONSO PORTER; Sec. Rev. NIGEL HAZEL.

The Anglican Communion

Anglicans in Guyana are adherents of the Church in the Province of the West Indies, comprising eight dioceses. The Archbishop of the Province is the Bishop of the North Eastern Caribbean and Aruba, resident in St John's, Antigua. The diocese of Guyana also includes French Guiana and Suriname. According to the latest available census figures (2002), Anglicans constitute 7% of the population.

Bishop of Guyana: Rt Rev. RANDOLPH OSWALD GEORGE, The Church House, 49 Barrack St, POB 10949, Georgetown 1; tel. and fax 226-4183; e-mail dioofguy@networksgy.com; internet www.anglican.bm/G/01.html.

The Baptist Church

The Baptist Convention of Guyana: POB 10149, Georgetown; tel. 226-0428; 33 mem. churches, 1,823 mems.

The Lutheran Church

The Evangelical Lutheran Church in Guyana: Lutheran Courts, Berbice, POB 40, New Amsterdam; tel. and fax 333-6479; e-mail lcg@guyana.net.gy; internet www.elcguyana.org; f. 1947; 13,000 mems; Pres. Rev. PAUL D. MOONU.

The Roman Catholic Church

Guyana comprises the single diocese of Georgetown, suffragan to the archdiocese of Port of Spain, Trinidad and Tobago. According to the 2002 census, some 8% of the population are Roman Catholics. The

Bishop participates in the Antilles Episcopal Conference Secretariat, currently based in Port of Spain, Trinidad.

Bishop of Georgetown: Francis Dean Alleyne, Bishop's House, 27 Brickdam, POB 101488, Stabroek, Georgetown; tel. 226-4469; fax 225-8519; e-mail rcbishop@networksgy.com; internet www .rcdiocese.org.gy.

Seventh-day Adventists

According to the 2002 census, 5% of the population are Seventh-day Adventists. The Guyana Conference is a member of the Caribbean Union Conference and comprises two congregations and 137 churches.

Guyana Conference: 222 Peter Rose and Almond Sts, Queenstown, POB 10191, Georgetown; tel. 226-3313; fax 223-8142; e-mail hgarnett@guyanaconference.org; internet guyanaconference.org; 50,291 mems in 2007; 173 churches in 23 pastoral districts; Pres. Pastor Hilton Garnett.

Other Christian Churches

According to the 2002 census, 17% of the population are Pentecostal Christians. Other denominations active in Guyana include the African Methodist Episcopal Church, the African Methodist Episcopal Zion Church, the Church of God, the Church of the Nazarene, the Ethiopian Orthodox Church, the Guyana Baptist Mission, the Guyana Congregational Union, the Guyana Presbyterian Church, the Hallelujah Church, the Methodist Church in the Caribbean and the Americas, the Moravian Church and the Presbytery of Guyana.

HINDUISM

According to the 2002 census, Hindus constitute 28% of the population.

Guyana Hindu Dharmic Sabha (Hindu Religious Centre): 162 Lamaha St, POB 10576, Georgetown; tel. 225-7443; f. 1934; Pres. Reepu Daman Persaud.

ISLAM

Muslims in Guyana comprise 7% of the population, according to the 2002 census.

The Central Islamic Organization of Guyana (CIOG): M.Y.O. Bldg, Woolford Ave, Thomas Lands, POB 10245, Georgetown; tel. 225-8654; fax 227-2475; e-mail contact@ciog.org.gy; internet www .ciog.org.gy; Pres. Haji S. M. Nasir; Dir of Education Qays Arthur.

Guyana United Sad'r Islamic Anjuman: 157 Alexander St, Kitty, POB 10715, Georgetown; tel. 226-9620; e-mail khalid@gusia.org; f. 1936; 120,000 mems; Pres. Haji A. Hafiz Rahaman.

BAHÁ'Í FAITH

National Spiritual Assembly: 220 Charlotte St, Bourda, Georgetown; tel. and fax 226-5952; e-mail secretariat@gy.bahai.org; internet gy.bahai.org; incorporated in 1976; National Sec. Kala Seegopaul.

The Press

DAILIES

Guyana Chronicle: 2A Lama Ave, Bel Air Park, POB 11, Georgetown; tel. 227-5204; fax 227-5208; e-mail gm@guyanachronicle.com; internet www.guyanachronicle.com; f. 1881; govt-owned; also produces weekly *Sunday Chronicle* (tel. 226-3243); Editor-in-Chief Mark Ramotar; circ. 23,000 (weekdays), 43,000 (Sun.).

Guyana Times: 238 Camp and Quamina Sts, Georgetown; tel. 225-5128; fax 225-5134; e-mail news@guyanatimesgy.com; internet www .guyanatimesgy.com; f. 2008; owned by Queen's Atlantic Investment Inc; Editor Nigel Williams.

Kaieteur News: 24 Saffon St, Charlestown, Georgetown; tel. 225-8465; fax 225-8473; e-mail kaieteurnews@yahoo.com; internet www .kaieteurnewsonline.com; f. 1994; independent; Editor-in-Chief Adam Harris; Publr Glenn Lall; daily circ. 19,000, Fri. 25,000, Sun. 32,000.

Stabroek News: E1/2 46–47 Robb St, Lacytown, Georgetown; tel. 227-5197; fax 226-2549; e-mail stabroeknews@stabroeknews.com; internet www.stabroeknews.com; f. 1986; also produces weekly *Sunday Stabroek*; liberal independent; Editor-in-Chief Anand Persaud; circ. 14,100 (weekdays), 26,400 (Sun.).

WEEKLIES AND PERIODICALS

The Catholic Standard: 222 South & Wellington Sts, Queenstown, POB 10720, Georgetown; tel. 226-1540; e-mail colinsmith@gmail .com; f. 1905; organ of the Roman Catholic church; weekly; Editor Colin Smith; circ. 4,000.

Diocesan Magazine: 49 Barrack St, Kingston, Georgetown; e-mail dioofguy@networksgy.com; quarterly.

Guyana Review: 143 Oronoque St, POB 10386, Georgetown; tel. 226-3139; fax 227-3465; e-mail guyrev@networksgy.com; f. 1993; taken over by Guyana Publs Inc in Jan. 2007; monthly.

Mirror: Lot 8, Industrial Estate, Ruimveldt, Greater Georgetown; tel. 226-2471; fax 226-2472; e-mail ngmirror@guyana.net.gy; internet www.mirrornewsonline.com; owned by the New Guyana Co Ltd; Sun.; Editor David de Groot; circ. 25,000.

The Official Gazette of Guyana: Guyana National Printers Ltd, Lot 1, Public Rd, La Penitence; govt-owned; weekly; circ. 450.

Thunder: Freedom House, 41 Robb St, Lacytown, Georgetown; tel. 227-2095; fax 227-2096; e-mail ppp@guyana.net.gy; internet www .ppp-civic.org; organ of the People's Progressive Party/Civic; quarterly; Editor (vacant).

PRESS ASSOCIATION

Guyana Press Association (GPA): 82C Duke St, Kingston, Georgetown; tel. 623-5430; fax 223-6625; e-mail gpaexecutive@gmail .com; internet www.gpa.org.gy; f. 1945; affiliated with the Association of Caribbean Media Workers; Pres. Denis Chabrol.

NEWS AGENCY

Guyana Information Agency: Area B, Homestretch Ave, D'Urban Backlands, Georgetown; tel. 225-3117; fax 226-4003; e-mail gina@ gina.gov.gy; internet www.gina.gov.gy; f. 1993; Dir Dr Prem Misir.

Publishers

Guyana Free Press: POB 10386, Georgetown; tel. 226-3139; fax 227-3465; e-mail guyrev@networksgy.com; books and learned journals.

Guyana National Printers Ltd: 1 Public Rd, La Penitence, POB 10256, Greater Georgetown; tel. 225-3623; e-mail gnpl@guyana.net .gy; f. 1939; govt-owned printers and publishers; privatization pending.

Guyana Publications Inc: E 1/2 46–47 Robb St, Lacytown, Georgetown; tel. 226-5197; fax 226-3237; e-mail info@stabroeknews.com; internet www.stabroeknews.com; publrs of *Stabroek News* and *Sunday Stabroek*; Chair. Dr Ian McDonald.

Broadcasting and Communications

TELECOMMUNICATIONS

Digicel Guyana: Fort & Barrack St, Kingston, Georgetown; tel. 669-2677; fax 227-8184; e-mail guy_ccfrontoffice@digicelgroup.com; internet www.digicelguyana.com; f. 1999 as Trans-World Telecom; acquired Cel Star Guyana in 2003; acquired by Digicel Group in Nov. 2006; GSM cellular telecommunications network; operates Celstar and U-Mobile brands; CEO Gregory Dean.

Guyana Telephones and Telegraph Company (GT & T): 79 Brickdam, POB 10628, Georgetown; tel. 226-0053; fax 226-7269; e-mail pubcomm@gtt.co.gy; internet www.gtt.co.gy; f. 1991; fmrly state-owned Guyana Telecommunications Corpn; 80% ownership by Atlantic Tele-Network (USA); CEO Yog Mahadeo.

BROADCASTING

National Communications Network (NCN): Homestretch Ave, D'Urban Park, Georgetown; tel. 227-1566; fax 226-2253; e-mail feedback@ncnguyana.com; internet www.ncnguyana.com; f. 2004 following merger of Guyana Broadcasting Corpn (f. 1979) and Guyana Television and Broadcasting Co (f. 1993); govt-owned; operates three radio channels and six TV channels; CEO Desmond Mohamed Sattaur; Editor-in-Chief Michael Gordon.

Radio

National Communications Network (NCN): see Broadcasting; operates three channels: Hot FM, Radio Roraima and Voice of Guyana.

Television

CNS Television Six (CNS6): 43 Robb and Wellington Sts, Lacytown, Georgetown; tel. 226-5462; fax 227-3050; e-mail sharma@cns6 .tv; internet www.cns6.tv; f. 1992; privately owned; Man. Dir Chandranarine Sharma.

National Communications Network (NCN): see Broadcasting; TV network covers channels 8, 11, 13, 15, 21 and 26.

Finance

(cap. = capital; res = reserves; dep. = deposits; m. = million; brs = branches; amounts in Guyana dollars)

BANKING

Central Bank

Bank of Guyana: 1 Church St and Ave of the Republic, POB 1003, Georgetown; tel. 226-3250; fax 227-2965; e-mail communications@bankofguyana.org.gy; internet www.bankofguyana.org.gy; f. 1965; cap. 1,000m., res 1,125.8m., dep. 140,694.3m. (Dec. 2009); central bank of issue; acts as regulatory authority for the banking sector; Gov. LAWRENCE T. WILLIAMS.

Commercial Banks

Bank of Baroda (Guyana) Inc (India): 10 Ave of the Republic and Regent St, POB 10768, Georgetown; tel. 226-6423; fax 225-1691; e-mail bobinc@networksgy.com; f. 1966; Man. Dir P. K. KALA.

Citizens' Bank Guyana Inc (CBGI): 201 Camp St, Lacytown, Georgetown; tel. 226-1705; fax 226-1719; internet www.citizensbankgy.com; f. 1994; 51% owned by Banks DIH; total assets 18,773m. (Sept. 2007); Chair. CLIFFORD B. REIS; Man. Dir ETON M. CHESTER (acting); 4 brs.

Demerara Bank Ltd: 230 Camp and South Sts, POB 12133, Georgetown; tel. and fax 225-0610; e-mail banking@demerarabank.com; internet www.demerarabank.com; f. 1994; cap. 450.0m., res 345.7m., dep. 17,899.9m. (Sept. 2007); Chair. YESU PERSAUD; CEO PRAVINCHANDRA S. DAVE.

Guyana Bank for Trade and Industry Ltd (GBTI): High and Young Sts, Georgetown; tel. 231-4401; fax 231-1075; e-mail banking@gbtibank.com; internet www.gbtibank.com; f. 1987 to absorb the operations of Barclays Bank; cap. 800m., res 4,669.3m., dep. 53,741.9m. (Dec. 2010); Chair. ROBIN STOBY; CEO JOHN TRACEY; 9 brs.

Republic Bank (Guyana): Promenade Court, 155–156 New Market St, Georgetown; tel. 223-7938; fax 227-2921; e-mail email@republicguyana.com; internet www.republicguyana.com; f. 1984; 51% owned by Republic Bank Ltd, Port of Spain, Trinidad and Tobago; acquired Guyana National Co-operative Bank in 2003; name changed from National Bank of Industry and Commerce in 2006; cap. 300m., res 828.3m., dep. 84,357.6m. (Sept. 2010); Chair. DAVID DULAL-WHITEWAY; Man. Dir EDWIN H. GOODING; 5 brs.

Merchant Bank

Guyana Americas Merchant Bank Inc (GAMBI): GBTI Bldg, 138 Regent St, Lacytown, Georgetown; tel. 223-5193; fax 223-5195; e-mail gambi@networksgy.com; f. 2001; fmrly known as Guyana Finance Corpn Ltd; Man. Dir Dr GRAHAM SCOTT.

STOCK EXCHANGE

The Guyana Association of Securities Companies and Intermediaries Inc. (GASCI): Hand-in-Hand Bldg, 1 Ave of the Republic, Georgetown; tel. 223-6176; fax 223-6175; e-mail info@gasci.com; internet www.gasci.com; f. 2001; Chair. NIKHIL RAMKARRAN; Gen. Man. GEORGE EDWARDS.

INSURANCE

Supervisory Body

Office of the Commissioner of Insurance: Privatisation Unit Bldg, 126 Barrack St, Kingston, Georgetown; tel. 225-0318; fax 226-6426; e-mail mvanbeek@insurance.gov.gy; internet www.insurance.gov.gy; regulates insurance and pensions industries; Commr MARIA VAN BEEK.

Companies

Caricom General Insurance Co Inc: Lot A, Ocean View Dr., Ruimzeight Gardens, Ruimzeight, West Coast Demerara; tel. 269-0020; fax 269-0022; e-mail mail@guyanainsurance.com; internet www.guyanainsurance.com; f. 1997; fmrly Guyana Fire, Life & General Insurance Co Ltd; CEO SAISNARINE KOWLESSAR.

Demerara Mutual Life Assurance Society Ltd: 61–62 Robb St and Ave of the Republic, Georgetown; tel. 225-8991; fax 225-8995; e-mail demlife@demeraramutual.com; internet demeraramutual.net; f. 1891; Chair. RICHARD B. FIELDS; CEO KEITH CHOLMONDELEY.

Diamond Fire and General Insurance Inc: 44B High St, Kingston, Georgetown; tel. 223-9771; fax 223-9770; e-mail diamondins@solutions2000.net; f. 2000; privately owned; Man. TARA CHANDRA; cap. 100m.

Guyana Co-operative Insurance Service (GCIS): 47 Main St, Georgetown; tel. 225-9153; f. 1976; 67% owned by the Hand-in-Hand Group; Area Rep. SAMMY RAMPERSAUD.

Guyana and Trinidad Mutual Fire & Life Insurance Co Ltd: 27–29 Robb and Hinck St, Georgetown; tel. 225-7910; fax 225-9397; e-mail gtmgroup@gtm-gy.com; internet www.gtm-gy.com; f. 1925; affiliated co: Guyana and Trinidad Mutual Fire Insurance Co Ltd; Chair. HAROLD B. DAVIS; Gen. Man. ROGER YEE.

Hand-in-Hand Mutual Fire and Life Group: Hand-in-Hand Bldg, 1–4 Ave of the Republic, POB 10188, Georgetown; tel. 225-1865; fax 225-7519; e-mail info@hihgy.com; internet www.hihgy.com; f. 1865; fire and life insurance; Chair. JOHN G. CARPENTER; CEO KEITH EVELYN.

Association

Insurance Association of Guyana: South 0.5, 14 Pere St, Kitty, Georgetown; tel. 226-3514; f. 1968.

Trade and Industry

GOVERNMENT AGENCIES

Environmental Protection Agency, Guyana: Ganges St, Sophia, Georgetown; tel. 225-5467; fax 225-5481; e-mail epa@epaguyana.org; internet www.epaguyana.org; f. 1988 as Guyana Agency for the Environment; renamed 1996; formulates, implements and monitors policies on the environment; Exec. Dir INDARJIT RAMDASS.

Guyana Energy Agency (GEA): 295 Quamina St, POB 903, South Cummingsburg, Georgetown; tel. 226-0394; fax 226-5227; e-mail gea@gea.gov.gy; internet www.gea.gov.gy; f. 1998 as successor to Guyana National Energy Authority; CEO MAHENDRA SHARMA.

Guyana Marketing Corporation: 87 Robb and Alexander Sts, Lacytown, POB 10810, Georgetown; tel. 226-8255; fax 227-4114; e-mail newgmc@networksgy.com; internet www.newgmc.com; Gen. Man. NIZAM HASSAN.

Guyana Office for Investment (Go-Invest): 190 Camp and Church Sts, Georgetown; tel. 225-0653; fax 225-0655; e-mail goinvest@goinvest.gov.gy; internet www.goinvest.gov.gy; f. 1994; CEO GEOFFREY DA SILVA.

DEVELOPMENT ORGANIZATION

Institute of Private Enterprise Development (IPED): 253–254 South Rd, Bourda, Georgetown; tel. 225-8949; fax 226-4675; e-mail iped@solutions2000.net; internet www.ipedgy.com; f. 1986 to help establish small businesses; total loans provided $ G1,400m. (2007); Chair. YESU PERSAUD; Exec. Dir RAMESH PERSAUD.

CHAMBER OF COMMERCE

Georgetown Chamber of Commerce and Industry: 156 Waterloo St, North Cummingsburg, POB 10110, Georgetown; tel. 225-5846; fax 226-3519; e-mail gtchambe@networksgy.com; internet www.georgetownchamberofcommerce.org; f. 1889; Pres. KOMAL RAMNAUTH; 90 mems.

INDUSTRIAL AND TRADE ASSOCIATIONS

Guyana Rice Development Board: 116–17 Cowan St, Kingston, Georgetown; tel. 225-8717; fax 225-6486; internet www.grdb.gy; f. 1994 to assume operations of Guyana Rice Export Board and Guyana Rice Grading Centre; Gen. Man. JAGNARINE SINGH.

National Dairy and Development Programme (NDDP): c/o Lands and Surveys Bldg, 22 Upper Hadfield St, Durban Backlands, POB 10367, Georgetown; tel. 225-7107; fax 226-3020; e-mail nddp@sdnp.org.gy; f. 1984; aims to increase domestic milk and beef production; Programme Dir MEER BACCHUS.

EMPLOYERS' ASSOCIATIONS

Consultative Association of Guyanese Industry Ltd: 157 Waterloo St, POB 10730, North Cummingsburg, Georgetown; tel. 225-7170; fax 227-0725; e-mail info@cagi.org.gy; internet www.cagi.org.gy; f. 1962; Chair. YESU PERSAUD; Exec. Dir SAMUEL JERRY GOOLSARRAN; 54 mems.

Forest Products Association of Guyana: 157 Waterloo St, Cummingsburg, Georgetown; tel. 226-9848; fax 226-2832; e-mail fpasect@sdnp.org.gy; internet www.fpaguyana.org; f. 1944; 62 mem. cos; Pres. HILBERTUS CORT; Exec. Officer WARREN PHOENIX.

Guyana Manufacturing and Services Association Ltd (GMSA): National Exhibition Centre, Sophia, Georgetown; tel. 219-0072; fax 219-0073; e-mail gma_guyana@yahoo.com; f. 1967 as the Guyana Manufacturers' Asscn; name changed in 2005 to reflect growth in services sector; 190 mems; Pres. CLINTON WILLIAMS.

Guyana Rice Producers' Association (GRPA): 126 Parade and Barrack St, Georgetown; tel. 226-4411; fax 223-7249; e-mail grpa.riceproducers@networksgy.com; f. 1946; non-govt org.; 18,500 mems; Pres. LEEKHA RAMBRICH; Gen. Sec. DHARAMKUMAR SEERAJ.

UTILITIES

Electricity

Guyana Power and Light Inc (GPL): 40 Main St, POB 10390, Georgetown; tel. 225-4618; fax 227-1978; e-mail enquiries@gplinc.com; internet www.gplinc.com; f. 1999; fmrly Guyana Electricity Corpn; state-owned; Chair. WINSTON BRASSINGTON; CEO BHARAT DINDYAL; 1,200 employees.

Water

Guyana Water Inc (GWI): Vllissengen Rd and Church St, Bel Air Park, Georgetown; tel. 225-0471; fax 225-0478; e-mail pro@gwi.gy; internet www.gwiguyana.com; f. 2002 following merger of Guyana Water Authority (GUYWA) and Georgetown Sewerage and Water Comm.; operated by Severn Trent Water International (United Kingdom); Chair. Dr CYRIL SOLOMON; CEO NIGEL NILES (acting).

CO-OPERATIVE SOCIETY

Chief Co-operatives Development Officer: Ministry of Labour, Human Services and Social Security, 1 Water and Cornhill Sts, Stabroek, Georgetown; tel. 225-8644; fax 227-1308; e-mail coopdept@telsnet.gy.net; f. 1948; Dir KAREEM ABDUL-JABAR.

TRADE UNIONS

Federation of Independent Trade Unions of Guyana (FITUG): f. 1988; c. 35,000 mems; Gen. Sec. KENNETH JOSEPH.

Clerical and Commercial Workers' Union (CCWU): Clerico House, 140 Quamina St, South Cummingsburg, POB 101045, Georgetown; tel. 225-2822; fax 227-2618; e-mail ccwu@guyana.net.gy; Pres. ROY HUGHES; Gen. Sec. GRANTLEY L. CULBARD.

Guyana Agricultural and General Workers' Union (GAWU): 59 High St and Wights Lane, Kingston, Georgetown; tel. 227-2091; fax 227-2093; e-mail gawu@bbgy.com; internet www.gawu.net; f. 1977; Pres. KOMAL CHAND; Gen. Sec. SEEPAUL NARINE; 20,000 mems.

Guyana Labour Union (GLU): 198 Camp St, Cummingsburg, Georgetown; tel. 227-1196; fax 225-0820; e-mail glu@solutions2000.net; Pres. SAMUEL WALKER; Gen. Sec. CARVIL DUNCAN; 6,000 mems.

National Association of Agricultural, Commercial and Industrial Employees (NAACIE): 64 High St, Kingston, Georgetown; tel. 227-2301; f. 1946; Gen. Sec. KENNETH JOSEPH; c. 2,000 mems.

Guyana Public Service Union (GPSU): 160 Regent Rd and Shiv Chanderpaul Dr., Bourda, Georgetown; tel. 225-0518; fax 226-5322; e-mail gpsu@networksgy.com; internet gpsu.org; f. 1923; Pres. PATRICK YARDE; Gen. Sec. LAWRENCE MENTIS; 11,600 mems.

Guyana Trades Union Congress (GTUC): Critchlow Labour College, Woolford Ave, Non-pareil Park, Georgetown; tel. 226-1493; fax 227-0254; e-mail gtucorg@yahoo.com; f. 1940; national trade union body; 13 affiliated unions; c. 15,000 mems; affiliated to the International Trade Union Confederation; Pres. NORRIS WITTER; Gen. Sec. LINCOLN LEWIS.

Amalgamated Transport and General Workers' Union: Transport House, 46 Urquhart St, Georgetown; tel. 226-6243; fax 225-6602; Pres. CLAIRMONT PEARSON; Gen. Sec. VICTOR JOHNSON.

Guyana Bauxite and General Workers' Union: 180 Charlotte St, Georgetown; tel. 225-4654; Pres. LESLIE GONSALVES; Gen. Sec. LEROY ALLEN (acting).

Guyana Local Government Officers' Union: Woolford Ave, Georgetown; tel. 227-7209; fax 227-7376; e-mail daleantford@yahoo.com; f. 1954; Pres. ANDREW GARNETT; Gen. Sec. DALE BERESFORD.

Guyana Mining, Metal and General Workers' Union: 56 Wismar St, Linden, Demerara River; tel. 204-6822; Pres. ERIC TELLO; Gen. Sec. LESLIE GONSALVES; 5,800 mems.

Guyana Postal and Telecommunication Workers' Union: Postal House, 310 East St, POB 10352, Georgetown; tel. 226-7920; fax 225-1633; Pres. HAROLD SHEPHERD; Gen. Sec. GILLIAN BURTON.

Guyana Teachers' Union: Woolford Ave, POB 738, Georgetown; tel. 226-3183; fax 227-0403; Pres. COLLIN BYNOE; Gen. Sec. CORETTA MCDONALD.

National Union of Public Service Employees: 4 Fort St, Kingston, Georgetown; tel. 227-1491; Pres. ROBERT JOHNSON; Gen. Sec. RUDOLPH WELCH.

Printing Industry and Allied Workers' Union: c/o Guyana TUC, Georgetown; tel. 226-8968; Gen. Sec. PATRICIA HODGE (acting).

Public Employees' Union: Regent St, Georgetown; Pres. REUBEN KHAN.

Union of Agricultural and Allied Workers (UAAW): 10 Hadfield St, Werk-en-Rust, Georgetown; tel. 226-7434; Pres. JEAN SMITH; Gen. Sec. SEELO BAICHAN.

University of Guyana Workers' Union: POB 841, Turkeyen, Georgetown; tel. 222-3586; e-mail adeolaplus@yahoo.com; supports Working People's Alliance; Pres. CLIVE Y. THOMAS; Gen. Sec. A. ESOOP.

Transport

RAILWAY

There are no public railways in Guyana. Until the early 21st century the 15-km Linmine Railway was used for the transportation of bauxite from Linden to Coomaka.

ROADS

The coastal strip has a well-developed road system. In 2001 there were an estimated 7,970 km (4,952 miles) of paved and good-weather roads and trails. In 2009 a bridge across the Takutu river, linking Guyana to Brazil, was officially inaugurated. Construction of a bridge over the Berbice river was completed in 2008. In 2010 a feasibility study of construction of a bridge across the Corentyne river was begun by Guyana and Suriname. In November of that year the Inter-American Development Bank granted a US $20m. loan to expand the East Bank Demerara Main Road and improve pedestrian safety. In the 2011 budget some $10,100m. was allocated for the construction and maintenance of roads and bridges.

SHIPPING

Guyana's principal ports are at Georgetown and New Amsterdam. The port at Linden serves for the transportation of bauxite products. A ferry service is operated between Guyana and Suriname. Communications with the interior are chiefly by river, although access is hindered by rapids and falls. There are 1,077 km (607 miles) of navigable rivers. The main rivers are the Mazaruni, the Potaro, the Essequibo, the Demerara and the Berbice. The 2011 budget allocated some US $555m. for the maintenance of port facilities and construction of the Kumaka wharf.

Transport and Harbours Department: Water St, Stabroek, Georgetown; tel. 225-9350; fax 227-8445; e-mail t&hd@solutions2000.net; Gen. Man. MARCLENE MERCHANT.

Shipping Association of Guyana Inc (SAG): 10–11 Lombard St, Werk-en-Rust, Georgetown; tel. 226-2169; fax 226-9656; e-mail saginc@networksgy.com; internet www.shipping.org.gy; f. 1952; non-governmental forum; Chair. ANDREW ASTWOOD; Sec. IAN D'ANJOU; members:

Guyana National Industrial Company Inc (GNIC): 1–9 Lombard St, Charlestown, POB 10520, Georgetown; tel. 225-5398; fax 226-0432; e-mail gnicadmin@futurenetgy.com; metal foundry, shipbuilding and repair, agents for a number of international transport cos; privatized 1995; CEO CLINTON WILLIAMS; Port Man. ALBERT SMITH.

Guyana National Shipping Corporation Ltd: 5–9 Lombard St, La Penitence, POB 10988, Georgetown; tel. 226-1840; fax 225-3815; e-mail agencydivision@gnsc.com; internet www.gnsc.com; fmrly Bookers Shipping Transport and Wharves Ltd; govt-owned since 1976; Man. Dir ANDREW ASTWOOD (acting).

John Fernandes Ltd: 24 Water St, POB 10211, Georgetown; tel. 227-3344; fax 226-1881; e-mail philip@jf-ltd.com; internet www.jf-ltd.com; f. 1959; ship agents, pier operators and stevedore contractors; part of the John Fernandes Group of Cos; Chair. and CEO CHRIS FERNANDES.

CIVIL AVIATION

The main airport, Cheddi Jaggan International Airport, is at Timehri, 42 km (26 miles) from Georgetown. In 2009 Ogle International Airport, located six miles east of Georgetown, became the second airport in the country to accept international flights; construction of a 4,000-ft runway was expected to be completed in 2011. The regional airline LIAT (based in Antigua and Barbuda, and in which Guyana is a shareholder) provides scheduled passenger and cargo services.

Roraima Airways: R8 Epring Ave, Bel Air Park, Georgetown; tel. 225-9650; fax 225-9648; e-mail ral@roraimaairways.com; internet www.roraimaairways.com; f. 1992; flights to Venezuela and 4 domestic destinations; Man. Dir Capt. GERALD GOUVEIA.

Trans Guyana Airways: Ogle Aerodrome, Ogle, East Coast Demerara; tel. 222-2525; e-mail commercial@transguyana.net; internet www.transguyana.net; f. 1956; internal flights to 22 destinations; Dir Capt. GERARD GONSALVES.

Tourism

Despite the beautiful scenery in the interior of the country, Guyana has limited tourist facilities, although during the 1990s the country began to develop its considerable potential as an 'eco-tourism' destination. The total number of visitors to Guyana in 2010 was 141,281, of whom 54.5% were from the USA. In 2008 expenditure by tourists amounted to some US $59m.

Guyana Tourism Authority: National Exhibition Centre, Sophia, Georgetown; tel. 219-0094; fax 219-0093; e-mail info@guyana-tourism.com; internet www.guyana-tourism.com; f. 2003; state-owned; Dir INDRANAUTH HARALSINGH.

Tourism and Hospitality Association of Guyana (THAG): 157 Waterloo St, Georgetown; tel. 225-0807; fax 225-0817; e-mail thag@networksgy.com; internet www.exploreguyana.com; f. 1992; Pres. PAUL STEPHENSON; Exec. Dir TREINA BUTTS.

Defence

The armed forces are united in a single service, the Combined Guyana Defence Force, which consisted of some 1,100 men (of whom 900 were in the army, 100 in the air force and about 100 in the navy), as assessed at November 2011. In addition there were reserve forces numbering some 670 (army 500, navy 170). The Guyana People's Militia, a paramilitary reserve force, totalled about 1,500. The President is Commander-in-Chief.

Defence Budget: An estimated $ G6,100m. (US $30m.) in 2011.

Chief-of-Staff: Cdre GARY BEST.

Education

Education is free and compulsory for children aged between five years at the beginning of the school year and 15 years of age. Children receive primary education for a period of six years; enrolment at primary schools in 2009 included 95% of children in the relevant age-group. Secondary education, beginning at 12 years of age, lasts for up to seven years in a general secondary school, comprising an initial cycle of five years, followed by a cycle of two years. In 2009/10 an estimated 80,676 pupils were enrolled in secondary schools. Higher education is provided by five technical and vocational schools, one teacher-training college and one school for home economics and domestic crafts, in all of which 7,939 students were enrolled in 2009/10. An estimated $ G31,175m. was allocated to the Ministry of Education from the central Government's current expenditure in 2011, equivalent to 19.3% of the total budget.

HAITI

Introductory Survey

LOCATION, CLIMATE, LANGUAGE, RELIGION, FLAG, CAPITAL

The Republic of Haiti occupies the western part of the Caribbean island of Hispaniola (the Dominican Republic occupies the remaining two-thirds) and some smaller offshore islands. Cuba, to the west, is less than 80 km away. The climate is tropical but the mountains and fresh sea winds mitigate the heat. Temperatures vary little with the seasons, and the annual average in Port-au-Prince is about 27°C (80°F). The rainy season is from May to November. The official languages are French and Creole. About 65% of the population belong to the Roman Catholic Church, the country's official religion, and other Christian churches are also represented. The folk religion is Voodoo (vodou), a fusion of beliefs originating in West Africa involving communication with the spirit-world through the medium of trance. The national flag (proportions variable) has two equal vertical stripes, of dark blue and red. The state flag (proportions 3 by 5) has, in addition, a white rectangular panel containing the national coat of arms (a palm tree, surmounted by a Cap of Liberty and flanked by flags and cannons) in the centre. The capital is Port-au-Prince.

CONTEMPORARY POLITICAL HISTORY

Historical Context

Haiti was first colonized in 1659 by the French, who named the territory Saint-Domingue. French sovereignty was formally recognized by Spain in 1697. Following a period of internal unrest, a successful uprising, begun in 1794 by African-descended slaves, culminated in 1804 with the establishment of Haiti as an independent state, ruled by Jean-Jacques Dessalines, who proclaimed himself Emperor. Hostility between the negro population and the mulattos continued throughout the 19th century until, after increasing economic instability, the USA intervened militarily and supervised the government of the country from 1915 to 1934. Mulatto interests retained political ascendancy until 1946, when a negro President, Dumarsais Estimé, was installed following a military coup. Following the overthrow of two further administrations, Dr François Duvalier, a country physician, was elected President in 1957.

Domestic Political Affairs

The Duvalier administration soon became a dictatorship, maintaining its authority by means of a notorious private army, popularly called the Tontons Macoutes (Creole for 'Bogeymen'), who used extortion and intimidation to crush opposition to the President's rule. In 1964 Duvalier became President-for-Life, and at his death in April 1971 he was succeeded by his 19-year-old son and designated successor, Jean-Claude Duvalier.

At elections held in February 1979 almost all seats were won by the official government party, the Parti de l'Unité Nationale. The first municipal elections for 25 years, which took place in 1983, were overshadowed by allegations of electoral fraud and Duvalier's obstruction of opposition parties. No opposition candidates were permitted to contest the general election of February 1984.

In April 1985 Duvalier announced a programme of constitutional reforms, including the eventual appointment of a Prime Minister and the formation of political parties, subject to certain limiting conditions. In September Roger Lafontant, the minister most closely identified with the Government's acts of repression, was dismissed. However, protests organized by the Roman Catholic Church and other religious groups gained momentum, and further measures to curb continued disorder were adopted in January 1986. Duvalier imposed a state of siege and declared martial law.

In February 1986, following intensified public protests, Duvalier fled to exile in France, leaving a National Council of Government (Conseil National Gouvernemental—CNG), led by the Chief of Staff of the army, Gen. Henri Namphy, to succeed him. The military-civilian CNG appointed a new Cabinet. The National Assembly was dissolved, the Constitution was suspended, and the Tontons Macoutes were disbanded.

In April 1986 Gen. Namphy announced a proposed timetable for elections to restore constitutional government by February 1988. The first of these, to select members of a Constituent Assembly to revise the Constitution, took place in October 1986, but the level of participation was very low. The new Constitution was approved by 99.8% of voters in a referendum held on 29 March 1987. An independent Provisional Electoral Council (Conseil Electoral Provisoire—CEP) was subsequently appointed.

Presidential and legislative elections were cancelled three hours after voting had begun on 29 November 1987, owing to renewed violence and killings, for which former members of the Tontons Macoutes were believed to be responsible. A new CEP was appointed by the Government in December, and elections were rescheduled for 17 January 1988. Leslie Manigat of the Rassemblement des Démocrates Nationaux et Progressistes (RDNP) was declared the winner of the presidential ballot. Opposition leaders alleged that there had been extensive fraud and malpractice.

The Manigat Government was overthrown by disaffected members of the army in June 1988. Gen. Namphy, whom Manigat had attempted to replace as army Chief of Staff, assumed the presidency and appointed a Cabinet comprising members of the armed forces. The Constitution of 1987 was abrogated, and Duvalier's supporters returned to prominence, as did the Tontons Macoutes.

In September 1988 Gen. Namphy was ousted in a coup, led by Brig.-Gen. Prosper Avril (who became President), who advocated the introduction of radical reforms. In March 1989 Avril partially restored the Constitution of 1987 and restated his intention to hold democratic elections. In the following month the Government survived two coup attempts by the Leopard Corps, the country's élite anti-subversion squadron, and the Dessalines battalion, based in Port-au-Prince. Both battalions were subsequently disbanded.

Avril resigned as President in March 1990 in response to sustained popular opposition, together with diplomatic pressure from the USA. Power was ceded to the Chief of the General Staff, Hérard Abraham, who subsequently transferred authority to Ertha Pascal-Trouillot, a member of the Supreme Court. Pascal-Trouillot shared power with a 19-member Council of State.

Presidential and legislative elections took place in December 1990. Fr Jean-Bertrand Aristide, a left-wing Roman Catholic priest representing the Front National pour le Changement et la Démocratie (FNCD), won an overwhelming victory in the presidential election. His closest rival was Marc Bazin, the candidate of the centre-right Mouvement pour l'Instauration de la Démocratie en Haïti (MIDH), who obtained about 14% of the poll. However, the FNCD failed to win a majority of seats in either the Sénat (Senate) or the Chambre des Députés (Chamber of Deputies).

Aristide was inaugurated as President in February 1991. The new Head of State subsequently initiated proceedings to secure the extradition from France of Duvalier to face charges that included embezzlement, abuse of power and murder. Aristide also undertook the reform of the armed forces and in July Gen. (later Lt-Gen.) Raoul Cédras replaced Abraham as Commander-in-Chief and René Garcia Préval was appointed Prime Minister.

Military coup of 1991

On 30 September 1991 a military junta, led by Gen. Cédras, overthrew the Government. Following international diplomatic intervention, Aristide was allowed to go into exile. The coup received international condemnation, and an economic embargo was imposed on Haiti by the Organization of American States (OAS, see p. 394). Many hundreds of people were reported to have been killed during the coup. On 7 October military units assembled 29 members of the legislature and coerced them into approving the appointment of Joseph Nerette as interim President; several days later a new Cabinet was announced.

During the following months the OAS, which continued to recognize Aristide as the legitimate head of state, attempted to negotiate a settlement. However, the two sides remained deadlocked over the conditions for Aristide's return. In February 1992, following OAS-supervised talks in Washington, DC, USA, between Aristide and members of a Haitian legislative delegation, an agreement was signed providing for the installation of René Théodore, leader of the Mouvement pour la Reconstruction Nationale, as Prime Minister. He was to govern in consultation with the exiled Aristide and facilitate his return. However, in March 1992 politicians opposed to the accord withdrew from a joint session of the legislature, leaving it inquorate. In late March, following an appeal by Nerette, the Supreme Court declared the agreement null and void, on the grounds that it violated the Constitution by endangering the country's sovereignty. In response, the OAS increased economic sanctions against Haiti.

In May 1992 an agreement providing for the appointment of a new Prime Minister and a multi-party government of national consensus was ratified by the Sénat. In June the legislature, in the absence of the FNCD, approved the nomination of Bazin to be Prime Minister. The presidency was left vacant, ostensibly to allow for Aristide's return. A Cabinet, comprising members of most major parties (with the exception of the FNCD), was installed, with the army retaining control of the interior and defence. The appointment of the new Government provoked world-wide condemnation. In September the Government agreed to allow the presence of an 18-member OAS commission in Haiti to help to guarantee human rights, reduce violence and assess progress towards a resolution of the prevailing political crisis.

In June 1993 the USA imposed sanctions against Haiti. Shortly afterwards Bazin resigned as Prime Minister following a loss of support in the legislature. In July, following OAS- and UN-sponsored talks between Cédras and Aristide, a peace accord was signed, delineating a 10-point agenda for Aristide's reinstatement. Under the terms of the accord, the embargo was to be revoked following the installation of a new Prime Minister (to be appointed by Aristide), Cédras would retire and a new Commander-in-Chief of the armed forces would be appointed by Aristide, who would return to Haiti by 30 October. The accord was approved by Haiti's main political parties. Legislation providing for a series of political and institutional reforms, as required by the accord, was to be enacted, including provision for the transfer of the police force to civilian control.

In August 1993 the legislature ratified the appointment by Aristide of Robert Malval as Prime Minister. In September a concerted campaign of political violence and intimidation by police auxiliaries, known as 'attachés', threatened to undermine the accord. With the upsurge of a Duvalierist tendency, largely embodied by the attachés, a new political party, the Front Revolutionnaire pour l'Avancement et le Progrès d'Haïti (FRAPH), was founded in opposition to any attempt to reinstate Aristide. In late September the UN Security Council approved a resolution providing for the immediate deployment of a lightly armed UN Mission in Haiti. Cédras refused to resign his post in October. In that month the campaign of political violence by the attachés escalated. In response, the US Government ordered six warships into Haitian territorial waters to enforce the reimposed UN embargo. Malval officially resigned as Prime Minister in December.

A National Reconciliation Conference, proposed by Aristide and excluding the military, took place in Miami, Florida, USA, in mid-January 1994. Following the military regime's failure to meet the revised UN deadline of 15 January to comply with the terms of the July 1993 accord, the USA unilaterally imposed further sanctions. In April the US Government abandoned its attempts to effect a compromise solution to the crisis in Haiti in favour of the implementation of more rigorous economic sanctions with a view to forcing the military regime to relinquish power. In May the UN Security Council approved a resolution introducing sanctions banning all international trade with Haiti, excluding food and medicine, reducing air links with the country and preventing members of the regime from gaining access to assets held outside Haiti.

In early 1994 the Sénat declared the presidency of the Republic vacant, invoking Article 149 of the Constitution, which provides that, in case of prolonged absence by the Head of State, the position may be assumed by the President of the Court of Cassation. In May, with the support of the armed forces, an inquorate legislature appointed the President of the Court of Cassation, Emile Jonassaint, provisional President of the Republic. The appointment by Jonassaint of a new Cabinet was denounced as illegal by the international community and by the outgoing acting Prime Minister, Malval. In the following month the USA increased sanctions against Haiti.

In July 1994 the Haitian junta issued an order providing for the expulsion of the UN/OAS international civil commission. On 31 July the UN Security Council approved a resolution authorizing 'all necessary means' to remove the military regime from power and providing for the deployment of a UN peace-keeping force once stability had been achieved, to remain in Haiti until February 1996, when Aristide's presidential term expired. In August leaders of the Caribbean Community and Common Market (CARICOM, see p. 227) agreed to support a US-led military invasion.

Agreement on a return to civilian rule, 1994

On 19 September 1994 a nominally multinational force composed almost entirely of US troops began a peaceful occupation of Haiti. Under a compromise agreement, the Haitian security forces were to co-operate with the multilateral force in effecting a transition to civilian rule. All sanctions were to be lifted and the military junta granted 'early and honourable retirement' following legislative approval of a general amnesty law, or by 15 October at the latest (the date when Aristide was to return from exile to resume his presidency). The agreement did not, however, require the junta's departure from Haiti. In late September the USA announced the suspension of its unilateral sanctions. A few days later the UN Security Council approved a resolution ending all sanctions against Haiti with effect from the day after the return of Aristide.

In early October 1994 Aristide signed a decree authorizing the amnesty of those involved in the coup of September 1991. Later that month the USA formally ended its freeze on the assets of the Haitian military regime. On 12 October Robert Malval resumed office as interim Prime Minister following the resignation of the Jonassaint administration.

Aristide returned to Haiti on 15 October 1994 and on 25 October appointed Smarck Michel as premier. A new Cabinet, comprising mainly members of the pro-Aristide Organisation Politique Lavalas (OPL), was inaugurated in November. Later that month the legislature approved the separation of the police from the army. In December the formation of a new CEP was completed. In the following month two commissions were established for the restructuring of the armed forces and the new civilian police force.

In January 1995 the UN Security Council adopted a resolution authorizing the deployment of a UN force of 6,000 troops and 900 civil police to succeed the multinational force. The UN Mission in Haiti (UNMIH), which was to be led by a US commander and include some 2,400 US troops, was to be responsible for reducing the strength of the army and training both the army and the 4,000-strong (subsequently increased to 6,000) civilian police force, as well as maintaining the 'secure and stable' environment. On 31 March authority was officially transferred from the multinational force to UNMIH.

The first round of legislative, local and municipal elections, which was held on 25 June 1995, was marred by administrative failures and isolated incidents of violence and intimidation. The official election results indicated that all of the seats so far decided had been won by the Plateforme Politique Lavalas (PPL), a three-party electoral alliance comprising the OPL, the Mouvement d'Organisation du Pays (MOP) and the Pati Louvri Baryè (PLB). The results were rejected by the majority of opposition parties, which announced a boycott of the electoral process. In early August the FNCD, MIDH and the Parti National Progressiste Révolutionnaire withdrew their respective representatives from the Government, in protest at the absence of a resolution to the electoral dispute. On 13 August complementary elections for voters who had been denied the opportunity to vote on 25 June were conducted in 21 districts. The PPL won all of the seats available; the party made further large gains in a second round of voting on 17 September. In October Michel resigned as Prime Minister, and was succeeded by Claudette Werleigh.

Presidential election of 1995

At a presidential election held on 17 December 1995, which was boycotted by all the main opposition parties, the candidate endorsed by Aristide, René Préval, was elected with some 88% of the votes cast. He was inaugurated as President on 7 February 1996, and later that month the legislature approved the appointment of Rosny Smarth as Prime Minister.

In November 1996 Aristide established a new political party, La Fanmi Lavalas (FL), which, it was anticipated, would promote his candidacy for the next presidential election. Aristide had openly expressed his opposition to Préval's adoption of economic policies proposed by the IMF, notably the privatization of state enterprises. In January 1997 a general strike, in support of demands for the resignation of the Smarth administration and the reversal of the planned divestment of state enterprises, received considerable support.

On 6 April 1997 partial legislative elections were held, as well as elections to local councils. The elections were boycotted by many opposition parties, and less than 5% of the electorate participated in the poll. Of the legislative seats contested, only two, in the Sénat, were decided, both of which were secured by the FL. The OPL, the majority party in the governing coalition, alleged that members of the CEP had manipulated the election results in favour of Aristide's party. OAS observers supported the claims of electoral irregularities, and, following strong international pressure, the CEP postponed indefinitely the second round ballot.

On 9 June 1997 Smarth resigned from office, criticizing the CEP for failing to annul the results of the April elections. However, Préval's nomination of Ericq Pierre as Smarth's replacement was rejected by the Chambre des Députés, and in October Smarth announced that he was to cease his role as caretaker Prime Minister. In November Préval nominated Hervé Denis, an economist and former minister in the Malval Government, as Prime Minister and announced the establishment of an electoral commission, comprising three independent legal experts, to resolve the electoral deadlock, and the resignation of six of the nine members of the CEP. In January 1998 the legislature formally rejected the nomination of Denis. In March, following negotiations with the Anti-Neoliberal Bloc, a group of supporters of Aristide in the lower house, the OPL (renamed the Organisation du Peuple en Lutte in February) withdrew its demands for the annulment of the April 1997 elections as a precondition for the approval of a new Prime Minister, and proposed three candidates. However, Préval renominated Denis: his candidacy was again rejected by the legislature in April. In July Préval finally agreed to OPL demands to replace the CEP, subsequently receiving the party's support for the nomination of the Minister of National Education, Jacques-Edouard Alexis, as Prime Minister. Conversely, the Anti-Neoliberal Bloc opposed the nomination of Alexis. In August the FL announced that it had formally gone into opposition to the Préval administration.

In November 1998 the Sénat voted to extend the legislature's term to October 1999; under electoral legislation adopted in 1995, the term of office of legislators elected in that year's delayed vote had been shortened by one year in order to restore the constitutional timetable of elections, and was thus scheduled to end in January 1999. In December 1998 Alexis was finally declared eligible to assume the office of Prime Minister, subject to his nomination being approved by the legislature (which did not occur until November 2000). On 11 January 1999 Préval announced that he would no longer recognize the legislature, rejecting the Sénat's earlier decision to extend its mandate. In mid-January Préval withdrew parliamentary funding, prompting the legislature to seek a Supreme Court ruling on the constitutionality of the 1995 electoral law. In February the Supreme Court postponed indefinitely a decision concerning the electoral law.

On 25 March 1999 Préval appointed by decree a new Cabinet headed by Alexis and including representatives of five small opposition parties that had negotiated an agreement with the President to end the political impasse. The OPL, which had ceased negotiations following the murder, in early March, of one of its leaders, was not included in the new administration. In May the Supreme Court refused to rule on the legality of Préval's decision to end the funding of the outgoing parliament. The OPL subsequently announced that it had accepted that the parliamentary term had ended and that it would participate in the forthcoming elections. In June a new CEP announced that it would disregard the results of the flawed partial legislative elections of April 1997; Préval signed a decree annulling the elections in July.

Disputed legislative and presidential elections of 2000

On 21 May 2000 the first round of legislative and municipal elections was held; an estimated 60% of the electorate participated. Opposition parties alleged that the results had been manipulated in favour of the FL and demanded the conduct of a fresh ballot. The CEP rejected these claims, but in June the CEP President, Léon Manus, fled to the Dominican Republic, claiming that he had received death threats following his refusal to validate the first round results. His flight prompted demonstrations by Aristide supporters, demanding the publication of the results. According to official first round results, the FL won 16 of the 19 contested seats in the Sénat, and 26 of the 83 seats in the lower house. The results were criticized as inaccurate by the UN, the OAS and numerous foreign governments. Nevertheless, a second round of voting went ahead on 9 July. A boycott by the 15-party opposition coalition, the Convergence Démocratique (CD), resulted in a low rate of voter participation (an estimated 10%). According to official results, the FL won 72 seats in the Chambre des Députés and 18 of the 19 seats contested in the 27-seat upper house. The party also secured control of some 80% of the local councils.

Elections to the presidency and to renew the remaining eight senate seats were held on 20 November 2000 and boycotted by the CD. Aristide was elected President with some 92% of the votes cast. According to official estimates, some 61% of the electorate voted, although the only official observer mission, from CARICOM, estimated a 30% rate of voter participation. The FL also won the eight seats contested in the Sénat, and the one remaining seat in the Chambre des Députés.

An eight-member Transition Committee was established in December 2000 to oversee the transfer of power to Aristide, who was to take office on 7 February 2001. However, on 7 December the CD announced the formation of an alternative, provisional Government, the Front Alternatif, with the intention of holding fresh elections within two years, provoking widespread violent demonstrations by Aristide supporters. On 15 February 2001 seven of the senators controversially awarded seats in the May 2000 elections resigned. President Aristide named Jean-Marie Chérestal as Prime Minister, and in early March a new Cabinet was appointed. In the same month, in an attempt to end the political impasse, Aristide appointed a new nine-member CEP to investigate the results of the disputed May 2000 elections. The CD was not represented on the Council. In March it was announced that legislative elections would be held one year early, in November 2002, in order to satisfy international and opposition criticism and to restore the flow of foreign aid, suspended since May 2000. Three days later violent protests broke out in Port-au-Prince, in which three people died and dozens were injured. Violence continued over the following months, and a number of opposition party members were arrested on treason and terrorism charges. In July, following further OAS mediation, the Government stated that legislative and local elections would be held in 2002; an accord was also reached on the composition of the new CEP. The CEP would additionally organize an election to the seven Sénat seats vacated in February.

Political violence continued throughout 2001. In October the FL announced the resumption of OAS-mediated talks with the opposition, but these again ended without a resolution. In December an armed group, allegedly composed of former members of the armed forces, attacked the presidential palace. At least four people were killed in the coup attempt, which prompted further outbreaks of violence. The Government announced that former police chief Guy Philippe was wanted in connection with the palace attack; he subsequently fled the country. The opposition claimed that the coup attempt had been staged by the Government in order to justify further repression, and demanded that a UN mission be deployed to monitor the situation. In July 2002 an OAS Commission of Inquiry reported that no attempted coup had taken place and chastised the Government for its reluctance to punish those of its supporters who engaged in violence against the opposition.

On 23 January 2002 Prime Minister Chérestal resigned his post, following allegations of corruption, and criticism over his inability to resolve the crisis. On 15 March Aristide appointed Sénat speaker and prominent FL member Yvon Neptune as Prime Minister. Neptune subsequently reorganized his Cabinet, appointing Marc Bazin as Minister without Portfolio with specific responsibility for negotiations with the opposition. In June Aristide met opposition leaders for the first time in two years, but the talks achieved little progress. Further OAS-mediated dialogue in the following month also failed to make any significant headway. Bazin resigned from office in September, claiming that his job had become impossible. Meanwhile, Haiti's accession to full membership of CARICOM in July increased international pressure on Aristide to bring about an end to political instability in the country.

Intensification of political unrest

In late 2002 political unrest intensified as the November deadline for the creation of a new CEP passed unfulfilled. On 17 November some 15,000 people in Cap-Haïtien participated in an anti-Government rally. Shortly afterwards supporters of Aristide rioted in Port-au-Prince to protest against the anti-Government demonstrations. President Aristide refused to resign, stating that he believed the crisis could best be resolved through the formation of a CEP and the holding of new elections. Five of the nation's civil groups chose representatives to the CEP in November, although the opposition continued to refuse to do so. In early December a general strike led by the opposition was joined by members of Haiti's private sector. Opposition parties united in demanding the resignation of Aristide as the demonstrations continued. In December, frustrated by the continued political instability, some 184 business and civil society organizations formed the 'Group of 184', which subsequently emerged as a major element of the opposition to Aristide.

The political stalemate between the Government and the opposition remained unresolved in 2003, despite further mediatory efforts by the OAS. Most nominees to the nine-member CEP refused to assume their posts, claiming that they were unconvinced that the Government would not resort to fraudulent practices in future legislative elections, as it had done in 2000. The CD and other opposition groups continued to insist that their participation in any elections would be conditional upon the resignation of President Aristide. In October at least four people died as a result of violent clashes between police and anti-Government demonstrators in Gonaïves. In December three ministers resigned in protest at the Government's increasing use of violence to suppress the continuing demonstrations.

On 12 January 2004 the mandates of all the members of the Chambre des Députés and 12 of the 27 members of the Sénat expired, leaving Haiti effectively without a legislature and entitling President Aristide to rule by decree. The President subsequently pledged to hold legislative elections within six months, an offer quickly rejected by the Haitian opposition. Meanwhile, two general strikes were held as public demonstrations demanding the President's resignation continued. CARICOM threatened to impose economic sanctions on Haiti unless President Aristide satisfied a number of conditions, including the formation of a new electoral council and the holding of legislative elections. Following a meeting between Aristide, opposition members and CARICOM leaders, which was held in Kingston, Jamaica, Aristide agreed to implement a number of reforms within the following two months, including: nominating an independent Prime Minister; reforming the police force; creating a neutral electoral council; releasing illegally imprisoned members of the opposition; and disarming his supporters.

In February 2004 Prime Minister Neptune accused the opposition of attempting to orchestrate a coup and demanded that opposition parties actively discourage the ongoing demonstrations. However, as violent protests escalated, anti-Government forces took control of Gonaïves and, subsequently, several other cities in the north of the country. Shortly afterwards, former members of the Haitian armed forces, led by ex-police chief Guy Philippe and the former deputy commander of the FRAPH, Louis-Jodel Chamblain, joined the insurrection, enlisting with the rebels to form the Front pour la Libération et la Reconstruction Nationales (FLRN). President Aristide appealed to the international community for assistance in suppressing the rebellion. A plan to end the violence, proposed by France, CARICOM and the OAS, was rejected by the opposition as it failed to provide for the President's departure. Meanwhile, the uprising continued to gather momentum as the insurgents advanced towards Port-au-Prince, insisting that they would attack unless Aristide resigned. Cap-Haïtien had been brought under rebel control on 22 February. At a meeting of the UN Security Council in late February, Caribbean nations called for a multilateral force to be sent to the country in an attempt to bring an end to the violence. However, the USA and France insisted that a political settlement would have to be reached before any forces were deployed to Haiti.

President Aristide finally resigned on 29 February 2004, largely owing to international pressure, and fled to the Central African Republic, where he claimed he had been unconstitutionally removed from office by the USA. The USA maintained that Aristide had requested assistance to leave Haiti. In accordance with the Constitution, the President of the Supreme Court, Boniface Alexandre, was sworn in as interim President. On the same day the UN Security Council, acting in response to a request from Alexandre, authorized the establishment of a Multinational Interim Force (MIF) to help to secure law and order prior to the deployment of a larger peace-keeping mission. The MIF eventually comprised around 3,600 troops from the USA, France, Canada and Chile. On 9 March Alexandre and the recently established Council of Elders appointed Gérard Latortue as Prime Minister. The installation of a new Cabinet, composed of independents and technocrats, was generally welcomed by the international community, although CARICOM refused to recognize the Latortue Government. In mid-March Aristide arrived in Jamaica at the invitation of the Government; his arrival prompted Latortue to suspend diplomatic relations with Jamaica in protest.

In April 2004 Latortue, the seven members of the Council of Elders, representatives of the main political organizations (with the exception of the FL) and leaders of civil society organizations signed an agreement on political transition, which provided for the organization of presidential, legislative and municipal elections in 2005, leading to the inauguration of a new administration by February 2006. The agreement also provided for a new CEP, which was inaugurated in May 2004. The FL refused to designate a representative to the CEP, demanding that alleged persecution and repression of its supporters cease. In the same month Jocelerme Privert, the former Minister of the Interior, was arrested on suspicion of having ordered the killing of a number of anti-Aristide protesters in February.

In a report to the UN Security Council presented in April 2004, the UN Secretary-General, Kofi Annan, accused Aristide of having formed an alliance with armed groups, known as *chimères*, in order to reinforce his position in power and of having condoned their engagement in organized crime, including drugs-smuggling. Aristide went into exile in South Africa at the end of May.

UN peace-keeping force established, 2004

A UN peace-keeping force, the UN Stabilization Mission in Haiti (MINUSTAH), was officially established on 1 June 2004 and replaced the MIF later that month. MINUSTAH, which had an authorized strength of 6,700 military personnel and 1,622 civilian police, was to assist the interim administration with preparations for elections and the disarmament and demobilization of armed militias. Meanwhile, the OAS General Assembly approved a resolution declaring Aristide's removal from power to be unconstitutional, although it continued to recognize Latortue's Government. In mid-June Latortue announced the Government's intention to hold local and legislative elections in September 2005, followed by a presidential election in November of that year.

Former Prime Minister Neptune was arrested in June 2004 in connection with the deaths of demonstrators in the uprising against Aristide's administration in February. In July the Latortue Government issued a deadline of 15 September for armed groups to surrender their weapons. The disarmament of the rebels was one of CARICOM's principal demands, and a five-member ministerial delegation from the Community arrived in Port-au-Prince the day after the deadline was announced to discuss developments in Haiti, but the deadline for the surrender of weapons passed unfulfilled.

At the end of September 2004 violence broke out between the police and supporters of Aristide at a rally in Port-au-Prince in support of the former President's return from exile. Clashes continued, and by early November at least 80 people had been killed. Tensions were exacerbated by the arrival in the capital of more than 200 former soldiers, who demanded to be allowed to confront the so-called *chimères*. Three members of the FL, including the former President of the Sénat, Yvon Feuillé, were arrested in early October on suspicion of inciting the violence and possessing illegal firearms, and 75 suspected members of the *chimères* were also detained by the national police and MINUSTAH troops in a joint operation. Latortue accused Aristide of co-ordinating the uprising from exile. By mid-October only around 2,100 troops of the 6,700-strong authorized MINUSTAH force had actually been deployed.

In November 2004 the President of the CEP, Roselaure Julien, resigned, claiming that considerable pressure had been exerted on her, particularly by the 'Group of 184', to allow manipulation of the electoral process. Later that month a five-member Anti-Corruption Commission was established within the Ministry of the Economy and Finance to investigate alleged corruption between February 2001 and February 2004, as envisaged in the agreement on political transition signed in April. Also in November, following a meeting in Trinidad and Tobago, CARICOM issued a 'consensus statement' reaffirming its decision not to recognize Latortue's Government. Later in the month the UN Security Council approved the extension of MINUSTAH's mandate until 1 June 2005. In December 2004, amid continuing political violence and civil unrest, MINUSTAH troops entered the Cité Soleil area of Port-au-Prince, a stronghold of the pro-Aristide gangs, and successfully seized control of two police stations and other official buildings that had been occupied by the *chimères* for several months. Meanwhile, following pressure from the UN Secretary-General to free politicians detained without formal charge, the authorities provisionally released the three FL members arrested in early October.

In early January 2005 CARICOM announced that Haiti's participation in the Community's councils would not resume until elections had been held and democracy restored. In late January the CEP announced a timetable for the forthcoming elections: the municipal elections were to take place on 9 October, followed by legislative and presidential elections in two rounds, on 13 November and 18 December. A permanent register of voters was to be compiled prior to the elections, and national identity cards were to be issued. It was hoped that proposed mediation by the African Union (see p. 189) would result in the participation of the FL, which continued to demand the release of former officials of the Aristide administration, such as Neptune and Privert, and other 'political' prisoners. Latortue had earlier announced that he and his cabinet ministers would not contest the presidency. In February the Government created a National Disarmament Commission to facilitate and monitor the recovery of illegal weapons.

Escalation of violence

A sharp escalation in fighting between MINUSTAH troops and rebel groups was evident from March 2005. Many of the rebels who had helped to oust Aristide from power had subsequently turned against the interim Government. A number of UN peace-keeping troops and rebels were killed in confrontations in the following months. The interim Government denied claims from local residents and human rights organizations that there had been civilian fatalities. In a report published in May, the UN Security Council stated that the security situation had 'gradually improved' since 2004, but highlighted the need for continued international assistance if social and political progress were to be maintained.

In May 2005 Neptune was formally charged, 11 months after being arrested, for his alleged role in political killings during the uprising against Aristide's administration; in the previous month Neptune had begun a hunger strike to protest against his detention without charge. Human rights organizations claimed that hundreds of Aristide supporters had similarly been detained without charge for almost a year.

In June 2005 Paul-Henri Mourral, the French honorary consul, was shot dead and numerous others were also killed as gangs ran amok in the capital. Later that month the UN Security Council decided both to extend MINUSTAH's mandate by a further eight months and to deploy an additional 1,000 peace-keeping troops to the country. MINUSTAH subsequently intensified military operations against the rebel gangs and denied allegations that civilians had been killed by UN troops. In July about 1,000 demonstrators marched through the capital to protest against the interim Government, MINUSTAH and the collective failure of both to address adequately the security situation within Haiti. (The protest was catalysed by the murder earlier that month of the prominent Haitian journalist Jacques Roche, at whose funeral the Minister of Culture and Communications, Magalie Comeau Denis, had alleged that Aristide supporters had orchestrated the killing in an attempt to disrupt the electoral process.)

In August 2005 local elections, scheduled to take place in October, were postponed until December, so as to allow the authorities to concentrate on preparations for legislative and presidential elections, the scheduled date of which was brought forward by a week, to 6 November. In September, however, the legislative and presidential elections were delayed until 20 November, on account of extremely low voter registration, divisions in the electoral council and general disorganization. The elections were further postponed on three subsequent occasions, with a revised date of 7 February 2006 eventually being announced; at the same time Latortue also announced that he was to resign as Prime Minister on 7 February, regardless of when elections were finally held.

Meanwhile, in October 2005 the CEP published its final list of 35 presidential candidates; one notable absentee from the list was Gérard Jean-Juste, a Roman Catholic priest imprisoned for his alleged role in the murder of Jacques Roche; the FL's attempt to register Jean-Juste as its presidential nominee had been denounced as 'unconstitutional' by the CEP as Jean-Juste had been unable to register in person. The FL had threatened to withdraw from the electoral process if Jean-Juste was not released. However, Marc Bazin, supported by the FL leadership, and former President Préval, representing Fwon Lespwa (Front de l'Espoir)—a self-created party—but supported by the FL's grassroots, were both included on the CEP's list of accepted candidates. In January 2006 Jean-Juste was temporarily released from prison to receive medical treatment in the USA; the murder charges against him were dismissed, but he still faced charges of involvement in illegal gang activity and of possessing illegal weapons.

Presidential and legislative elections of 2006

On 7 February 2006 presidential and legislative elections were finally held. Voter participation was higher than expected, at 60% of the total electorate, in the presidential poll. Initial reports suggested that the favourite, Préval, had secured a convincing victory; however, after all the votes had been counted it was announced that he had obtained 49% of the vote—far more than any other candidate, but marginally short of the overall majority required to avoid a second round of voting. Incensed by what they perceived to be an attempt by the interim Government to force a run-off vote, and with tempers further inflamed by the discovery of thousands of burnt ballot papers (many of which were reported to be marked in favour of Préval) in a dump near Port-au-Prince, thousands of Préval supporters marched through the capital in protest. Préval warned of more violent protests from his supporters if a second poll was required. Following calls from the UN Security Council, and amid allegations of vote manipulation from two members of the CEP itself, the interim Government ordered that the publication of official results be halted until a full inquiry could be held into the allegations of electoral fraud. However, it was announced on 16 February that Préval had in fact secured an outright victory and was consequently to be declared President. The announcement followed emergency talks between the interim Government and electoral officials, during which it was agreed to share out the 91,219 blank ballots (4.4% of the total votes cast) proportionately among the candidates, thereby increasing Préval's percentage of the vote to 51.2%. The RDNP representative, former President Leslie Manigat—the second-placed candidate (with only 12.4% of the vote)—denounced the outcome, as did the third-placed Respè nominee, Charles Henri Baker. The international community—including, significantly, the UN, CARICOM, the OAS and the USA—did, however, recognize Préval's victory. Préval was formally sworn into office on 14 May.

Elections to a newly enlarged 30-seat Sénat and 99-seat Chambre des Députés were also held on 7 February 2006. However, most of the results were inconclusive, necessitating a second round of voting, to be held on 19 March. This was subsequently postponed until 21 April, a delay attributed by the CEP to the need to investigate numerous claims of voting irregularities from the first round. According to partial, provisional results following the second round of voting, Préval's Fwon Lespwa won the largest number of seats in both legislative chambers (13 in the Sénat and 24 in the Chambre des Députés), although the party failed to secure a majority in either house. The Fusion des Sociaux-Démocrates Haïtiens alliance was placed second, with four seats in the upper house and 18 in the lower chamber, while the OPL won three senate seats and 11 seats in the Chambre des Députés.

Shortly after his inauguration, President Préval nominated Jacques-Edouard Alexis as Prime Minister. The proposed return of Alexis to his former role was subsequently approved by both legislative chambers, and on 9 June 2006 a new 18-member coalition cabinet, with representatives from six political parties, was sworn into office. Alexis declared that he would give consideration to the plight of political prisoners enduring lengthy detentions without being put on trial. A few days later it was announced that Jocelerme Privert had been released on parole, and in July Yvon Neptune was released on health and humanitarian grounds (the charges against Neptune were withdrawn in September 2009). Meanwhile, the period of relative calm that had followed Préval's election victory was fractured in June 2006, during which month a severe intensification of street violence and kidnappings prompted MINUSTAH to increase its presence in Port-au-Prince. Between June and August approximately 100 people were reported to have been killed in the capital, with a further 400 people thought to have been wounded. In mid-August the President and the Prime Minister issued an ultimatum to the gang leaders thought to be responsible for much of the violence, ordering them to hand in their weapons or be killed. In September the Government appointed a new commission designed to disarm gang members by offering them food, financial support and training.

In August 2006 the UN Security Council voted unanimously to extend MINUSTAH's mandate until February 2007. In November and December 2006 angry protesters amassed in the streets of Cité Soleil to demonstrate against the continued presence of MINUSTAH in the country, accusing UN troops of using indiscriminate force to quell civil unrest and alleging that many innocent civilians had been killed or injured in the crossfire, claims that the UN mission denied. Despite the opposition, MINUSTAH's mandate was extended until October 2008. The Principal Deputy Special Representative of the UN Secretary-General in Haiti, Luiz Carlos da Costa, stated in July 2007 that MINUSTAH would need a further four years in order to guarantee the process of stabilization, including reform of the judicial and prison system and consolidation of the police force. Joint operations by MINUSTAH and Haitian police contributed to a significant improvement in security in Port-au-Prince during 2007, with a reported 70% reduction in kidnappings compared with the previous year. MINUSTAH's mandate was extended for a further 12 months in October 2008.

Continuing political unrest

In early April 2008 several days of violent demonstrations by thousands of protesters against a sharp increase in the cost of food resulted in the deaths of five people and the murder of a Nigerian MINUSTAH peace-keeper. (It was reported that the prices of food staples had increased by some 50% in the previous year.) On 12 April President Préval announced a 15.7% reduction in the price of rice. On the same day the Sénat approved a motion to dismiss Alexis as Prime Minister over his handling of the crisis. In late April Préval nominated Ericq Pierre as Prime Minister, for which role he had previously been designated in 1997 under Préval's first administration. Pierre was subsequently rejected once again by the Chambre des Députés, as was Préval's subsequent nomination, Robert Manuel. In June Préval nominated Michèle Pierre-Louis, an economist and director of a charitable foundation, and, following approval in both the Sénat and the Chambre des Députés, she was eventually sworn in on 29 August, bringing to an end some four months without a functioning Government.

In mid-2008 Haiti was struck by four tropical storms, which resulted in the deaths of at least 800 people and damage estimated at US $1,000m. (equivalent to about 15% of gross domestic product—GDP), while an estimated 1m. people lost their homes. This, in conjunction with the steep increases in food prices and the ongoing political deadlock, prompted a humanitarian crisis and widespread appeals for international aid.

It was announced in November 2008 that the delayed elections to renew one-third of the seats in the Sénat would be held in April 2009. In February 2009 it was revealed by the CEP that all candidates from former President Aristide's FL were to be excluded from the elections on the grounds that it was not clear which nominees of the party were legitimate, as two rival FL factions had both submitted lists of candidates. Thousands of FL supporters took to the streets on 28 February in protest at the decision, which had also prompted expressions of concern from the OAS and the US embassy, and to mark the fifth anniversary of Aristide's exile. The first round of the elections, held on 19 April, was marked by a low rate of voter participation, of only 11.8%, and violent demonstrations caused polling to be cancelled in the Centre department. As no candidate obtained the required 50% majority, a second round of voting was eventually conducted on 21 June. Fwon Lespwa won five of the 11 seats contested, giving the party a total of 12 of the Sénat's 30 seats, with the remaining six seats divided between five parties and an independent. However, the turn-out was reported to be even lower than in the first round, prompting the FL, which had urged a boycott of the polls, to declare that the results should be annulled.

At a conference held in Washington, DC, in April 2009, international donors pledged to disburse US $324m. in development aid for Haiti over the following two years. Following continued improvement in security in 2008–09, the UN began to broaden the focus of its activities in Haiti, and in May the UN Secretary-General, Ban Ki-Moon, appointed former US President Bill Clinton as his first Special Envoy for the country in May 2009, with a remit to secure further international support for economic and social recovery. In October the UN Security Council extended MINUSTAH's mandate for a further year, maintaining its overall strength but amending its composition slightly to reflect the changing security situation, with an increase of 120 in the maximum number of civilian police officers to be deployed and a corresponding reduction in the military contingent.

The Sénat adopted a motion to dismiss Pierre-Louis as Prime Minister on 30 October 2009, on the grounds that her Government's efforts to address Haiti's economic difficulties had been insufficient. Noting that Pierre-Louis had succeeded in securing the support of bilateral and multilateral donors during her 14 months in office, observers speculated that her removal was in fact politically motivated. Préval acted swiftly to replace Pierre-Louis, nominating Jean-Max Bellerive on the same day. Following the ratification of his appointment by both legislative chambers, Bellerive was sworn into office on 11 November, together with his new Cabinet, in which 11 of the 18 ministers from the outgoing administration were retained. Bellerive remained Minister of Planning and External Co-operation, thus providing continuity in relations with foreign donors and investors, and little change in government policy was expected.

In late November 2009 the CEP announced that the FL would not be permitted to contest legislative elections scheduled to be held on 28 February and 3 March 2010, citing the party's alleged failure to meet the legal requirements for registration; 16 more minor organizations were also disqualified from participating. Meanwhile, following the dissolution of Fwon Lespwa (at Préval's behest), a new movement in support of the President, Inite (Unité), was formed by several organizations, including the MOP, the PLB and the Union Nationale Chrétienne pour la Reconstruction d'Haïti. Inite's main opposition was expected to come from the Alternative pour le Progrès et la Democratie (Altenativ), a new electoral alliance created by Alyans, the Fusion des Sociaux-Démocrates Haïtiens and the OPL. In mid-December several thousand supporters of the FL demonstrated in Port-au-Prince to demand the return of Aristide from exile and to protest against the party's exclusion from the forthcoming elections.

Earthquake of January 2010

More than 220,000 people were estimated to have been killed and more than 300,000 injured in Port-au-Prince and surrounding areas on 12 January 2010 in an earthquake with a magnitude of 7.0. Damage to buildings and infrastructure was also extensive: the UN estimated that some 10% of the buildings in the capital had been destroyed, while at least 1.5m. people had been made homeless. On 15 January the UN appealed for US $562m. (subsequently raised to $577m.) in emergency relief to assist an estimated 3m. affected people over a period of six months; one-half of this amount was to be used to provide food aid. The Government's response to the disaster was hampered by the destruction of the presidential palace, the parliament building, the police headquarters and many of its ministries, as well as by the death of public officials and civil servants. International organizations based in the capital were similarly affected: the headquarters of MINUSTAH collapsed and the head of the mission and his deputy were among those killed. Logistical difficulties, resulting from the damage to transport infrastructure and also from the scale of the aid required, delayed the distribution of supplies, and there were reports of widespread looting. A state of emergency was declared on 17 January (and extended for a further 18 months in April). A resolution approved by the UN Security Council on 19 January authorized the deployment to Haiti of an additional 2,000 military personnel and 1,500 police officers. In late January FAO appealed to international donors to support an 18-month plan for the investment of $700m. in the Haitian agricultural sector in order to repair infrastructure, to stimulate food production and to create employment for people (subsequently estimated to number 661,000) fleeing the Port-au-Prince area. Those who did not leave the capital settled in more than 1,300 camps created around the earthquake-affected area.

A government report published in mid-March 2010 estimated the total value of damage and losses caused by the earthquake at $7,860m. (equivalent to around 120% of GDP) and the cost of the long-term reconstruction of the country at $11,500m., one-half of which would be required for the basic social services, such as health, education, nutrition, water and sanitation. The report also advocated a development strategy focused on greater decentralization, noting that 65% of Haiti's economic activity had hitherto been located in the Port-au-Prince area. At a conference held in New York at the end of March, international donors pledged $9,900m. in support of the Haitian Government's Action Plan for National Recovery and Development, including some $996m. in debt relief and $4,500m. in funding to be disbursed during 2010–11. An Interim Haiti Recovery Commission, co-chaired by Prime Minister Bellerive and Bill Clinton, was established in April to co-ordinate the implementation of the Plan and to monitor the distribution of funds.

The legislative elections were postponed indefinitely in February 2010. In May the Chambre des Députés and the Sénat approved legislation allowing President Préval, whose term was due to end on 7 February 2011, to remain in office until 14 May of that year if the presidential election had to be delayed. The extension of Préval's term prompted demands for the President's resignation at opposition-organized demonstrations in Port-au-Prince attended by some 2,000 people. In June 2010, however, Préval signed a decree scheduling both the legislative and the presidential elections for 28 November.

The UN Security Council approved a resolution authorizing the deployment of an additional 680 police officers in Haiti in June 2010, recognizing the need for MINUSTAH to assist the Haitian national police force in protecting the population, amid reports of increased crime and sexual violence in the temporary settlements for displaced people, particularly those adjacent to traditional slum areas such as Cité Soleil. There were also concerns about a rise in the activity of criminal gangs, which was partly linked to the escape following the earthquake of 5,409 prisoners, several hundred of whom had been detained on charges related to gang activity. (Joint operations between MINUSTAH and the Haitian police resulted in at least 629 prisoners being recaptured during 2010.) The UN Security Council extended MINUSTAH's mandate for a further year in October, maintaining its authorized strength at a military component of up to 8,940 troops and a police component of up to 4,391 officers.

Haiti suffered a further severe set-back in October 2010, with the confirmation of an outbreak of cholera in the Artibonite and Centre departments, which subsequently spread throughout the country. Allegations that Nepalese peace-keepers were the source of the outbreak (after tests indicated that the strain of cholera affecting Haiti was most similar to one found in South Asia) led to unrest and demonstrations against MINUSTAH's presence in Haiti in November. One protester was killed in clashes with UN troops in the northern city of Cap-Haïtien, although the UN suggested that the violence had been orchestrated by those seeking to disrupt the forthcoming elections. In December Ban Ki-Moon announced the establishment of an independent panel to investigate the source of the cholera outbreak; the panel's report, issued in May 2011, concluded that the cholera outbreak had originated from the contamination of the Artibonite river, near the base where the Nepalese peace-keepers were stationed, although a variety of factors had caused the disease to spread. Meanwhile, the UN appealed for some US $175m. in international aid to combat the cholera epidemic. By February 2012 more than 526,000 cases of cholera, including more than 7,000 fatalities, had been recorded.

Two years after the 2010 earthquake, in January 2012, progress on reconstruction efforts remained slow, with almost 520,000 people still displaced. According to the office of the UN Special Envoy for Haiti, only 52.9% of the US $4,500m. pledged to assist Haiti during 2010–11 at the international donor conference held in New York in March 2010 had been disbursed, although almost all the rest of the total had been committed for a specific purpose.

2010 and 2011 elections

The presidential and legislative elections were held, as scheduled, on 28 November 2010. Voter participation was extremely low, at just 22.8%. Immediately after the elections, 12 of the 19 presidential candidates alleged that fraud had been perpetrated in favour of Inite's candidate, Jude Célestin, but a joint OAS-CARICOM mission concluded that the irregularities that its officials had observed were not sufficiently serious to invalidate the vote. According to preliminary results released by the CEP on 7 December, the RDNP candidate, Mirlande Manigat, an academic and wife of former President Leslie Manigat, secured the largest share of the presidential ballot, with 31.4%, followed by Célestin, with 22.5%, and Michel Martelly, a musician representing Repons Peyizan (Réponse des Paysans), with 21.8%. A second round of voting between the two leading nominees was to be held on 16 January 2011. However, the US embassy cast doubt on the CEP's preliminary results, noting that they were 'inconsistent' with those published by a national election observation organization, which placed Martelly in second place, and violent protests by supporters of Martelly resulted in five deaths. In mid-December 2010, in response to increasing international pressure, President Préval requested OAS assistance in reviewing the disputed results. The second round of voting (in both the presidential and legislative elections) was consequently suspended by the CEP. The OAS electoral experts issued their report in January 2011, concluding that Martelly was the second-placed presidential candidate, ahead of Célestin. In early February, without releasing detailed results of the first round, the CEP announced that Manigat and Martelly would contest the run-off presidential ballot, which was to be held on 20 March, concurrently with the second round of the legislative elections (only four of the 11 seats contested in the Sénat and 18 of the 99 seats in the lower house having thus far been filled). Meanwhile, former President Duvalier unexpectedly returned to Haiti in January, after 25 years in exile; he was swiftly charged with corruption and misappropriation of funds. Moreover, on the eve of the run-off ballot, Aristide, whose FL had been excluded from the elections, also returned from exile.

International observers asserted that the run-off presidential ballot of 20 March 2011 was better conducted than the first round of voting. Martelly defeated Manigat, winning 67.6% of the valid votes cast, his victory reflecting his popularity among younger voters and public disenchantment with more traditional politicians. The electoral turn-out was again very low, at only 22.5%. Following voting in the second round of the legislative election, Inite was by far the largest party in the legislature, holding 17 of the 30 seats in the Sénat and 46 of the 99 seats in the Chambre des Députés, according to final, official results released on 20 April. Martelly's Repons Peyizan took only three seats in the Chambre des Députés and failed to gain representation in the upper chamber. However, the results of 19 legislative seats (17 in the lower house and two in the Sénat), 16 of which had been allocated to Inite, were subsequently disputed. In late April, having examined each case at the request of President Préval, the joint OAS-CARICOM electoral observation mission recommended the reinstatement of preliminary results issued on 4 April, which had attributed 33 seats in the Chambre des Députés to Inite. On 11 May the CEP announced the reversal of 15 of the 19 challenged results, with Inite retaining just four of the seats in question. Later that month the Sénat established a committee of inquiry to consider allegations of electoral wrongdoing, while a second round of voting finally took place in three constituencies in which the first round had not been held until 20 March owing to the cancellation of polling on 28 November 2010.

Recent developments: Martelly in office

President Martelly took office on 14 May 2011, pledging to accelerate stalled reconstruction efforts, to address the cholera epidemic, to restore security, to boost employment and to introduce free education, which would be financed by the imposition of taxes on international telephone calls and money transfers to Haiti. More controversially, he also proposed the re-establishment of the armed forces, which had been disbanded by Aristide in 1995, suggesting that it could eventually replace MINUSTAH, and mooted granting amnesty to Aristide and Duvalier. Meanwhile, the legislature adopted a number of amendments to the Constitution, notably voting against a proposed change that would have allowed Presidents to serve two consecutive five-year terms, but in favour of a revision according dual nationality to Haitians living abroad, thereby allowing them to vote and own land in Haiti and to hold lower public office. However, despite having expressed support for the latter measure, Martelly subsequently vetoed the amendments, after it emerged that that there were discrepancies between the constitutional text to be published in the official gazette and that adopted by parliament. The issue had not been resolved by early 2012, and the unamended Constitution remained in force, pending the publication of the corrected version of the revisions adopted in May 2011.

The President's ability to implement his plans was constrained during his first few months in office by his weak position in the legislature and consequent failure to secure approval for his choice of Prime Minister. On the day after his inauguration Martelly designated businessman Daniel-Gérard Rouzier as premier, but this was rejected in June 2011 by the Chambre des Députés, in which Inite had joined with other parties to form the Groupe des parlementaires pour le renouveau, an alliance claiming to comprise some 70 deputies. His second nominee, Bernard Gousse, a former Minister of Justice in the administration of Gérard Latortue (2004–06), was rejected by the Sénat in early August. As tensions mounted between the President and the legislature, with a number of deputies criticizing Martelly for failing to seek consensus on a suitable candidate for premier, the

Secretary-General of the OAS, José Miguel Insulza, and other international donors expressed concern regarding the continued stalemate. Finally, on 4 October, the appointment of Martelly's third nominee, Garry Conille, an official at the UN Development Programme and until recently chief of staff to UN Special Envoy Bill Clinton, was endorsed by the Sénat, having been accepted by the Chambre des Députés on 16 September. On 15 October the lower house approved Conille's programme for government—including plans to attract foreign aid and investment, to resettle the homeless, to modernize infrastructure, to establish urban and rural development zones, and to create 1.5m. jobs over a period of five years—as well as the composition of his Cabinet, which took office three days later. Prior to the vote on the Government, Conille and Martelly attempted to foster a sense of reconciliation, holding talks with members of the parliamentary alliance led by Inite, which provided three cabinet ministers, while the President also met with Aristide, Duvalier and Prosper Avril, President in 1988–90.

Meanwhile, in September 2011 further details emerged regarding President Martelly's intention to re-establish the military, when it was reported that he proposed recruiting and training 3,500 troops by late 2014. However, Inite, together with the USA and several other donor countries, advocated spending the funds required to create a new army (estimated at some US $95m.) on improving the police force instead. Nevertheless, Martelly subsequently appointed a civilian commission to consider the issue. In January 2012 he announced that the commission had recommended the restoration of the army with a remit to safeguard territorial integrity, respond to natural disasters and combat drugs-trafficking and terrorism. However, concerns remained within the opposition and the international community regarding the financial burden involved and the poor human rights record of the previous military.

The mandate of the Interim Haiti Recovery Commission officially expired in October 2011; although Martelly and Conille favoured an extension of its mandate, this had not been approved by the legislature by early 2012. In August 2011 the Commission had notably approved a US $78m. project, proposed by the President and expected to create some 4,500 jobs, to rehabilitate 16 neighbourhoods of Port-au-Prince to allow the return of some 30,000 people from six particularly vulnerable camps. In September President Martelly announced the creation of a 32-member Presidential Advisory Council on Economic Growth and Investment, comprising eight former heads of state of various countries, as well as business executives with expertise in a wide range of areas; co-chaired by Bill Clinton, the Council was charged with helping to attract foreign investment to Haiti and to revitalize the country's economy. In early December the World Bank announced funding of $255m. for a new 12-month programme for Haiti, which, *inter alia*, aimed to protect the population from natural disasters, facilitate the return of 22,500 people to safe housing and finance free schooling for 100,000 children.

The UN Security Council approved an extension of MINUSTAH's mandate for a further year in October 2011, but reduced its maximum authorized strength to pre-earthquakes levels (some 7,340 troops and 3,241 police officers), in view of the completion of the presidential and legislative elections and the gradual curtailment of large-scale humanitarian operations. The Council none the less acknowledged the continued humanitarian challenges confronting Haiti, not least the fact that more than 600,000 remained internally displaced and dependent on assistance for their survival. In the previous month, meanwhile, clashes had occurred in Port-au-Prince between police and hundreds of protesters who were demanding MINUSTAH's withdrawal from Haiti, following allegations that Uruguayan peace-keepers had sexually assaulted a Haitian man and amid growing anger regarding the possibility that Nepalese peace-keepers had been the source of the ongoing cholera epidemic.

The Minister of Justice and Public Security, Josué Pierre-Louis, was forced to resign from office in November 2011, after he ordered the arrest of Arnel Bélizaire, an opposition member of the Chambre des Députés, thereby further damaging relations between the legislative and executive branches of government. Legislators were angered by the Government's failure to request the removal of Bélizaire's immunity from prosecution, also noting that the deputy had been highly critical of Martelly. Pierre Michel Brunache was appointed to replace Pierre-Louis in December, while Pierre Raymond Dumas became Minister of Culture and Communication, following the death, prior to taking office, of Choiseul Henriquez. Also in December, the Sénat established a committe of inquiry into the nationality of Martelly and members of his Government, following allegations that the President and several ministers held foreign citizenship, in contravention of the Constitution.

In late December 2011 President Martelly dismissed all nine members of the discredited CEP. Municipal polls and elections to renew one-third of the members of the Sénat were to be held in 2012. Although the mandates of 10 senators were due to expire in May 2012, at mid-March no date had been set for the elections, and a new electoral council had yet to be appointed.

In late January 2012, in a report to the Attorney-General's office, the judge handling the case against Duvalier recommended that the former dictator should be tried on charges of embezzlement of public funds, but that the statute of limitations had expired with regard to human rights abuses committed during his regime. However, domestic and international human rights groups declared that they would appeal against the latter recommendation, arguing that, under international law, the statute of limitations did not apply to crimes against humanity.

Prime Minister Conille resigned from office on 24 February 2012. His departure followed a deterioration in relations with President Martelly, particularly after Conille's decision to establish a commission to examine the awarding of construction contracts in the wake of the 2010 earthquake. Conille was also one of the ministers facing the senate inquiry into allegations that he held dual nationality. On 1 March Martelly nominated close ally and Minister of Foreign Affairs and Religion Laurent Lamothe to succeed Conille; he received senate approval in April, and was overwhelmingly endorsed by the Chambre des Députés on 3 May.

Foreign Affairs

Regional relations

Relations between Haiti and its neighbour on the island of Hispaniola, the Dominican Republic, have traditionally been tense owing to the use of the border area by anti-Government guerrillas, smugglers and illegal migrants, resulting in the periodic closure of the border. In March 1996, following an official visit to the Dominican Republic by Préval, the first by a Haitian President since 1935, a joint communiqué was issued establishing a bilateral commission to promote improved co-operation between the two countries. In 1998 agreement was reached to establish joint border patrols to combat the traffic of drugs and other contraband between the two countries. In November 1999 Préval submitted a formal protest to the Dominican Republic following a spate of summary deportations of Haitians from the neighbouring country; according to human rights observers, some 8,000 Haitians were forcibly repatriated in the first three weeks of that month. Following a direct meeting between representatives of the two Governments, a protocol was signed in December limiting the repatriations. Despite this, the number of Haitians entering the Dominican Republic continued to increase.

Relations between Haiti and the Dominican Republic suffered a marked deterioration in 2005. The Dominican Republic's army forcibly repatriated thousands of Haitian immigrants, a process that was intensified following the murder of a Dominican woman, allegedly at the hands of two Haitian men, in May of that year. Human rights organizations alleged that the Dominican army was acting indiscriminately and had deported not only illegal immigrants but also many Haitians of legal status and Dominicans of Haitian origin; the army strenuously denied such claims. In December a visit to Haiti by Dominican President Leonel Fernández was abruptly curtailed after violent demonstrations in protest at the alleged abuse of Haitians in the Dominican Republic broke out around the presidential palace. In January 2006 at least 25 Haitians died from asphyxiation while being smuggled into the Dominican Republic in the back of a truck; however, some survivors of the incident alleged that the truck in which they were travelling came under fire from a passing vehicle. The Dominican authorities returned the bodies of the Haitians to UN forces in Haiti, but the vehicle carrying the coffins was shot at by Haitian protesters, who demanded a full explanation for the circumstances surrounding the deaths. Tensions rose again in 2009, following the decapitation of a Haitian migrant in the Dominican capital. The murder prompted protests outside the Dominican embassy in Port-au-Prince. Following the earthquake in Haiti in January 2010, the Dominican authorities provided humanitarian assistance to the country and suspended the repatriation of Haitian immigrants. In January 2011, however, the Dominican Government resumed deportations of illegal immigrants and tightened border controls, in an attempt to curtail the spread of cholera from Haiti, where several thousand deaths from the disease had been recorded (see Domestic Political Affairs). President-elect Martelly visited the Dominican Republic in May 2011, shortly before his inauguration. Talks with President Fernández focused on border security issues and the status of the estimated 1m. undocumented Haitians living in the Dominican Republic.

Other external relations

Following the 1991 coup, the USA came under international criticism for its forced repatriation of Haitian refugees fleeing the repressive military regime. While a small percentage of refugees were considered for political asylum, the US Government insisted that the majority were economic refugees and therefore not eligible. In 1994 a change in US policy regarding Haitian refugees (it agreed to hold hearings for all asylum applications, rather than repatriating all refugees intercepted at sea) prompted a renewed exodus of thousands of refugees, forcing a further change of policy in July, under which refugees granted asylum were henceforth to be held indefinitely in safe havens outside the USA. The USA contributed some 1,900 troops to the MIF deployed in Haiti following the resignation of Aristide in February 2004. In March 2006 President-elect Préval made a three-day visit to the USA, during which he met with US President George W. Bush and addressed the UN Security Council. In October, in recognition of the Alexis Government's efforts to introduce peace and stability to the country, the USA partially lifted its arms embargo against Haiti, imposed in 1991. The Haitian Government would henceforth be able to obtain licences for the purchase of high-powered weapons and other items required by the national police force. Préval swiftly sought to promote strong relations with the US Administration of Barack Obama that took office in January 2009, meeting Secretary of State Hillary Clinton in February during a week-long visit to Washington, DC. Clinton emphasized the Obama Administration's commitment to assisting Haiti during talks with Préval in Port-au-Prince in April. Following the earthquake of January 2010, the USA dispatched more than 22,000 military personnel to the country to assist in the distribution of relief supplies and temporarily to assume control of the international airport. The majority of US troops had been withdrawn by June. Clinton expressed strong support for President-elect Martelly when he visited Washington, DC, in April 2011, prior to his inauguration in May. During his three-day visit to the USA Martelly also met senior officials from the World Bank, the IMF and the Inter-American Development Bank in an attempt to secure support for an acceleration in reconstruction efforts.

CONSTITUTION AND GOVERNMENT

The Constitution, approved by referendum in 1987, provided for a bicameral legislature. Both houses were elected by universal adult suffrage. Executive power was held by the President, who was elected by universal adult suffrage for a five-year term and could not stand for immediate re-election. However, the Constitution was interrupted by successive coups, in 1988 and 1991. A return to constitutional rule was finally effected in 1994. In January 2004, owing to the country's failure to hold legislative elections, the mandates of the legislature expired, entitling the President to rule by decree. Constitutional rule was re-established in May 2006.

There are 10 departments, subdivided into arrondissements and communes.

REGIONAL AND INTERNATIONAL CO-OPERATION

Haiti is a member of the Caribbean Community and Common Market (see p. 227), the Association of Caribbean States (see p. 448), of the Latin American Economic System (see p. 451), and of the Community of Latin American and Caribbean States (see p. 462), which was formally inaugurated in December 2011. Haiti is also a member of the International Coffee Organization (see p. 445). Haiti was a founder member of the UN in 1945. Having been a contracting party to the General Agreement on Tariffs and Trade since 1950, Haiti joined the World Trade Organization (see p. 433) in 1996. Haiti is also a signatory to the European Union's Cotonou Agreement (see p. 328), which replaced the Lomé Convention from June 2000.

ECONOMIC AFFAIRS

In 2010, according to estimates by the World Bank, Haiti's gross national income (GNI), measured at average 2008–10 prices, was US $6,464m., equivalent to $650 per head (or $1,110 per head on an international purchasing-power parity basis). In 2001–10 the population increased at an average annual rate of 1.4%, while gross domestic product (GDP) per head decreased, in real terms, by an average of 1.2% per year. Overall GDP increased, in real terms, at an average annual rate of 0.9% in 2006/07–10/11; according to official estimates, real GDP increased by 5.6% in 2010/11.

Agriculture (including hunting, forestry and fishing) contributed an estimated 24.2% of GDP, at constant prices, in 2010/11. About 57.8% of the total labour force were engaged in agricultural activities in mid-2012, according to FAO estimates. The principal cash crop, traditionally, was coffee, although production decreased significantly from the late 1990s. In 2008/09 coffee accounted for only 0.4% of export earnings. The export of mangoes and of essential oils for cosmetics and pharmaceuticals has become increasingly important, and cocoa exports remain significant. Crayfish are also an important export commodity. The main food crops are sugar, bananas, maize, sweet potatoes and rice. The World Bank released US $50m. in aid for the agriculture sector in January 2012. During 1995–2004, according to the World Bank, the real GDP of the agricultural sector increased at an average annual rate of 1.7%; according to official estimates, agricultural GDP decreased at an average annual rate of 0.4% during 2006/07–2010/11. The sector's GDP increased by 1.1% in 2010/11.

Industry (including mining, manufacturing, construction and power) contributed an estimated 17.9% of GDP, at constant prices, in 2010/11. About 9.7% of the employed labour force were engaged in the sector in 2003. According to official estimates, industrial GDP increased at an average annual rate of 4.7% during 2006/07–2010/11; sectoral GDP increased by 5.9% in 2010/11.

Mining contributed 0.1% of GDP, at constant prices, in 2010/11. About 0.3% of the employed labour force were engaged in extractive activities in 2003. Marble, limestone and calcareous clay are mined. There are also unexploited copper, silver and gold deposits.

Manufacturing contributed a provisional 7.8% of GDP, at constant prices, in 2010/11. Some 6.5% of the employed population were engaged in the sector in 2003. The most important branches of manufacturing were food-processing, textiles (including apparel, leather and fur products, and footwear), chemicals (including rubber and plastic products) and tobacco. According to official estimates, manufacturing GDP increased at an average annual rate of 1.1% during 2006/07–2010/11; the sector's GDP decreased by 14.7% in 2009/10, but increased by 18.0% in 2010/11.

Construction contributed an estimated 9.3% of GDP, at constant prices, in 2010/11. Some 2.7% of the employed population were engaged in the sector in 2003. According to official estimates, manufacturing GDP increased at an average annual rate of 5.4% during 2006/07–2010/11; the sector's GDP increased by 9.2% in 2010/11.

In 2008 some 62.8% of the country's public electricity came from petroleum, while 37.2% came from hydroelectric power. Overall electricity production was believed to amount to just one-10th of the capital's requirements. Imports of mineral fuels and related products accounted for 17.6% of the total value of imports in 2008/09.

The services sector contributed an estimated 57.9% of GDP, at constant prices, in 2010/11 and engaged 44.6% of the employed labour force in 2003. According to official estimates, services GDP increased by an average annual rate of 1.1% during 2006/07–2010/11; the sector's GDP decreased by 5.4% in 2009/10, but decreased by 4.2% in 2010/11.

In 2009/10 Haiti recorded a visible trade deficit of US $2,247.7m., and there was a deficit of $1,955.6m. on the current account of the balance of payments. In 2004 the principal source of imports (35%) was the USA; the USA was also the principal market for exports (81%) in that year. Other significant trading partners in recent years include France, Canada, Japan and the Dominican Republic. The principal export in 2008/09 was manufactured goods (34.8%); agricultural products were also significant, predominantly mangoes (1.9%). The principal imports in 2008/09 were food products (24.6%) and mineral fuels and lubricants (18.4%). The re-export, to the USA, of assembled goods (valued at $425.1m. in 2007/08) has become a significant source of revenue, with income rivalling that derived from domestic exports. Smuggling was estimated to have accounted for two-thirds of Haiti's imports in 2000.

In the financial year ending 30 September 2010 there was an estimated budgetary deficit of 6,521.7m. gourdes, equivalent to 2.5% of GDP in that year. Haiti's general government gross debt was 45,244m. gourdes in 2010, equivalent to 17.1% of GDP. At the end of 2009 Haiti's total external debt was US $1,244m., of which $1,078m. was public and publicly guaranteed debt. In that year the cost of servicing long-term public and publicly guaranteed debt and repayments to the IMF was equivalent to 4.7% of the total value of exports of goods, services and income (excluding workers' remittances). The annual rate of inflation averaged 14.3% per year in 2001–10. Consumer prices remained stable in 2009, but increased by an average of 5.7% in 2010. Some 60% of the labour force were estimated to be unemployed in 2001. Remittances from Haitians living abroad amounted to approximately $1,499m. in 2010 (equivalent to 11.7% of GDP in that year).

In terms of average income, Haiti is the poorest country in the Western hemisphere, and there is extreme inequality of wealth. More than one-half of the population lives on less than US $1 a day. Economic progress has been impeded by political instability and a series of natural disasters, most notably an earthquake in January 2010, which caused severe damage to Port-au-Prince and surrounding areas, with the total value of damage and losses estimated at $7,860m., equivalent to more than 120% of GDP in 2009. Substantial emergency assistance was pledged to Haiti, and the IMF announced the immediate disbursement of $102m., on highly concessionary terms, under its Extended Credit Facility (ECF). In February, moreover, the Group of Seven most industrialized nations agreed to cancel all Haiti's bilateral debts, and in March international donors pledged to provide aid of more than $5,300m. by 2013. In July the IMF approved the cancellation of Haiti's outstanding liabilities to the Fund, as well as a new three-year ECF arrangement. In January 2011, in a significant move towards economic decentralization, the Government signed an agreement with a South Korean garment manufacturer on the creation of an industrial park in Caracol, near Cap-Haïtien, which would employ an estimated 20,000 workers. The park was scheduled to commence operations in March 2012. Following a contraction of an estimated 5.4% in 2009/10, GDP increased by an estimated 5.6% in 2010/11. However, the rate of growth in 2010/11 was considerably lower than had been projected for the year, mainly owing to slow progress with reconstruction activity and a deceleration in donor disbursements, in part prompted by concerns regarding disputed elections in 2010 and 2011 and the subsequent delay in forming a government. The attraction of foreign investment was a key priority of President Michel Martelly and the Government that finally took office in October 2011. The new Government announced that further investments by South Korean companies would create some 20,000 jobs in 2012, in addition to those at the Caracol industrial park. The IMF forecast GDP growth of 7.8% for 2011/12.

PUBLIC HOLIDAYS

2013: 1 January (Independence Day), 2 January (Heroes of Independence), 11 February (Shrove Monday, half-day), 12 February (Shrove Tuesday), 29 March (Good Friday), 14 April (Pan-American Day), 1 May (Labour and Agriculture Day), 18 May (Flag and University Day), 30 May (Corpus Christi), 15 August (Assumption), 17 October (Death of J.-J. Dessalines), 24 October (United Nations Day), 1 November (All Saints' Day), 2 November (All Souls' Day), 18 November (Army Day and Commemoration of the Battle of Vertières), 25 December (Christmas Day).

Statistical Survey

Sources (unless otherwise stated): Banque de la République d'Haïti, angle rues du Pavée et du Quai, BP 1570, Port-au-Prince; tel. 2299-1200; fax 2299-1045; e-mail brh@brh.net; internet www.brh.net; Institut Haitien de Statistique et d'Informatique, Ministère de l'Economie et des Finances, 1, angle rue Joseph Janvier et boulevard Harry S Truman, Port-au-Prince; tel. 2514-3789; fax 2221-5812; e-mail info@ihsi.ht; internet www.ihsi.ht.

Area and Population

AREA, POPULATION AND DENSITY

Area (sq km)	27,065*
Population (census results)	
30 August 1982†	5,053,792
7 July 2003	
Males	4,039,272
Females	4,334,478
Total	8,373,750
Population (official projections at mid-year)	
2007	9,602,304
2008	9,761,927
2009	9,923,243
Density (per sq km) at mid-2009	366.6

* 10,450 sq miles.

† Excluding adjustment for underenumeration.

Note: It was estimated that as many as 230,000 people were killed as a result of a powerful earthquake that devastated the country's capital, Port-au-Prince, in January 2010. No reliable official estimates of total population have been published since the earthquake.

POPULATION BY AGE AND SEX

(official projections at mid-2009)

	Males	Females	Total
0–14	1,832,933	1,767,764	3,600,697
15–64	2,886,307	3,007,789	5,894,095
65 and over	193,273	235,177	428,451
Total	4,912,513	5,010,730	9,923,243

DEPARTMENTS

(official population projections at mid-2009)

	Area (sq km)	Population	Density (per sq km)	Capital
L'Artibonit (Artibonite)	4,886.9	1,571,020	321.5	Gonaïves
Centre	3,487.4	678,626	194.6	Hinche
Grand'Anse	1,911.9	425,878	222.8	Jérémie
Nippes	1,267.8	311,497	245.7	Miragoâne
Nord	2,115.2	970,495	458.8	Cap-Haïtien
Nord-Est	1,622.9	358,277	220.8	Fort Liberté
Nord-Ouest	2,102.9	662,777	315.2	Port-de-Paix
Ouest	4,982.6	3,664,620	735.5	Port-au-Prince
Sud	2,653.6	704,760	265.6	Les Cayes
Sud-Est	2,034.1	575,293	282.8	Jacmel
Total	27,065.3	9,923,243	366.6	—

PRINCIPAL TOWNS

(official projected population at mid-2009)

Port-au-Prince (capital)	897,859	Delmas	359,451
Carrefour	465,019		

BIRTHS AND DEATHS

(UN estimates)

	1995–2000	2000–05	2005–10
Crude birth rate (per 1,000)	32.5	29.5	27.6
Crude death rate (per 1,000)	10.6	10.1	9.2

Source: UN, *World Population Prospects: The 2010 Revision*.

Life expectancy (years at birth, WHO estimates): 62 (males 60; females 63) in 2009 (Source: WHO, *World Health Statistics*).

ECONOMICALLY ACTIVE POPULATION
(official estimates, persons aged 10 years and over, mid-1990)

	Males	Females	Total
Agriculture, hunting, forestry and fishing	1,077,191	458,253	1,535,444
Mining and quarrying	11,959	12,053	24,012
Manufacturing	83,180	68,207	151,387
Electricity, gas and water	1,643	934	2,577
Construction	23,584	4,417	28,001
Trade, restaurants and hotels	81,632	271,338	352,970
Transport, storage and communications	17,856	2,835	20,691
Financing, insurance, real estate and business services	3,468	1,589	5,057
Community, social and personal services	81,897	73,450	155,347
Sub-total	1,382,410	893,076	2,275,486
Activities not adequately defined	33,695	30,280	63,975
Total employed	1,416,105	923,356	2,339,461
Unemployed	191,333	148,346	339,679
Total labour force	1,607,438	1,071,702	2,679,140

Source: ILO, *Yearbook of Labour Statistics*.

2003 (national survey of living conditions, sample survey of persons aged 10 years and over, primary occupation, percentage distribution): Agriculture 44.6; Fishing 1.2; Mining and quarrying 0.3; Manufacturing 6.5; Electricity, gas and water 0.2; Construction 2.7; Wholesale and retail trade, vehicle repairs 27.7; Hotels and restaurants 1.5; Transport, storage and communications 2.1; Financial intermediation 0.2; Real estate, renting and other business activities 1.4; Public administration and compulsory social security 1.7; Education 3.8; Health and social welfare 1.3; Other community, social and personal services 2.5; Other services 2.4; Total employed 100.0.

Mid-2012 (estimates in '000): Agriculture, etc. 2,323; Total labour force 4,022 (Source: FAO).

Health and Welfare

KEY INDICATORS

Total fertility rate (children per woman, 2009)	3.4
Under-5 mortality rate (per 1,000 live births, 2009)	87
HIV/AIDS (% of persons aged 15–49, 2009)	1.3
Physicians (per 1,000 head, 1998)	0.3
Hospital beds (per 1,000 head, 2000)	0.8
Health expenditure (2008): US $ per head (PPP)	69
Health expenditure (2008): % of GDP	6.1
Health expenditure (2008): public (% of total)	22.1
Access to water (% of persons, 2008)	63
Access to sanitation (% of persons, 2008)	17
Total carbon dioxide emissions ('000 metric tons, 2007)	2,396.3
Carbon dioxide emissions per head (metric tons, 2007)	0.2
Human Development Index (2011): ranking	158
Human Development Index (2011): value	0.454

For sources and definitions, see explanatory note on p. vi.

Agriculture

PRINCIPAL CROPS
('000 metric tons)

	2008	2009*	2010*
Rice, paddy	110	128	125
Maize	210	220	234
Sorghum	100	105	79
Sweet potatoes	230	272	248
Cassava (Manioc)	435	468	600
Yams	235	307	353
Sugar cane	1,110	1,110	1,100
Avocados*	45	44	47
Bananas*	245	284	335
Plantains	200	229	239
Guavas, mangoes and mangosteens*	245	245	218

* FAO estimates.

Aggregate production ('000 metric tons, may include official, semi-official or estimated data): Total cereals 420 in 2008, 453 in 2009, 437 in 2010; Total roots and tubers 964 in 2008, 1,098 in 2009, 1,265 in 2010; Total vegetables (incl. melons) 162 in 2008, 167 in 2009, 145 in 2010; Total fruits (excl. melons) 861 in 2008, 949 in 2009, 977 in 2010.

Source: FAO.

LIVESTOCK
('000 head, year ending September, FAO estimates)

	2006	2007	2008
Horses	500	500	500
Asses	210	210	210
Mules	80	80	80
Cattle	1,450	1,450	1,455
Pigs	1,000	1,001	1,001
Sheep	153	153	154
Goats	1,900	1,900	1,910
Chickens	5,500	5,500	5,600
Turkeys	195	195	195
Ducks	190	190	190

2009–10: Figures assumed to be unchanged from 2008 (FAO estimates).

Source: FAO.

LIVESTOCK PRODUCTS
('000 metric tons, FAO estimates)

	2008	2009	2010
Cattle meat	43.5	43.5	45.0
Goat meat	7.3	6.5	5.5
Pig meat	33.0	33.0	35.0
Horse meat	5.6	5.6	5.6
Chicken meat	8.0	8.0	8.0
Cows' milk	55.3	59.9	63.4
Goats' milk	25.8	27.7	28.1
Hen eggs	4.5	4.7	5.0

Source: FAO.

Forestry

ROUNDWOOD REMOVALS
('000 cubic metres, excl. bark, FAO estimates)

	2008	2009	2010
Sawlogs, veneer logs and logs for sleepers*	224	224	224
Other industrial wood*	15	15	15
Fuel wood	2,024	2,033	2,041
Total	2,263	2,272	2,280

* Production assumed to be unchanged since 1971.

Source: FAO.

SAWNWOOD PRODUCTION
('000 cubic metres, incl. railway sleepers)

	1969	1970	1971
Coniferous (softwood)	5	8	8
Broadleaved (hardwood)	10	5	6
Total	14	13	14

1972–2010: Annual production as in 1971 (FAO estimates).

Source: FAO.

Fishing

('000 metric tons, live weight, FAO estimates)

	2006	2007	2008
Freshwater fishes	0.3	0.3	0.3
Marine fishes	5.7	5.7	5.7
Marine crabs	0.3	0.3	0.3
Caribbean spiny lobster	1.0	1.0	1.0
Natantian decapods	0.8	0.8	0.8
Stromboid conchs	0.3	0.3	0.3
Total catch	8.3	8.4	8.4

2009: Catch assumed to be unchanged from 2008 (FAO estimates).

Note: Figures exclude corals and madrepores (FAO estimates, metric tons): 10 in 2006–09.

Source: FAO.

Industry

SELECTED PRODUCTS
(metric tons, unless otherwise indicated, year ending 30 September)

	1999/2000
Edible oils	38,839.6
Butter	2,972.2
Margarine	2,387.4
Cornflour	104,542.6
Soap	30,069.9
Detergent	4,506.1
Beer ('000 cases of 24 bottles)	784.5
Beverages ('000 cases of 24 bottles)	1,807.7
Rum ('000 750ml bottles)	2,009.5
Electric energy (million kWh)	698.0

Cement ('000 metric tons, estimates): 290.0 in 2004–10 (Source: US Geological Survey).

Electric energy (million kWh): 535 in 2003; 547 in 2004; 556 in 2005; 570 in 2006; 469 in 2007; 486 in 2008 (Source: UN Industrial Commodity Statistics Database).

Finance

CURRENCY AND EXCHANGE RATES

Monetary Units
100 centimes = 1 gourde.

Sterling, Dollar and Euro Equivalents (30 December 2011)
£1 sterling = 63.355 gourdes;
US $1 = 40.977 gourdes;
€1 = 53.021 gourdes;
1,000 gourdes = £15.78 = $24.40 = €18.86.

Average Exchange Rate (gourdes per US $)
2009 41.198
2010 39.797
2011 40.523

Note: The official rate of exchange was maintained at US $1 = 5 gourdes until September 1991, when the central bank ceased all operations at the official rate, thereby unifying the exchange system at the 'floating' free market rate.

BUDGET
(million gourdes, year ending 30 September)

Current revenue	2008	2009	2010
Internal receipts	18,025.5	19,948.1	19,489.6
Customs	7,917.3	9,013.3	10,493.8
Total (incl. others)	26,673.7	31,303.6	31,445.3

Expenditure	2008	2009	2010
Current expenditure	24,300.2	29,605.5	28,259.0
Wages and salaries	12,855.6	14,465.0	13,437.2
Capital expenditure	6,066.0	5,949.1	9,708.0
Total	30,366.1	35,554.6	37,967.0

INTERNATIONAL RESERVES
(US $ million at 31 December)

	2008	2009	2010
IMF special drawing rights	7.0	108.0	106.1
Reserve position in IMF	0.1	0.1	0.1
Foreign exchange	534.3	680.4	1,288.8
Total	541.4	788.6	1,395.0

Source: IMF, *International Financial Statistics*.

MONEY SUPPLY
(million gourdes at 31 December)

	2008	2009	2010
Currency outside depository corporations	15,304.8	15,854.7	20,347.8
Transferable deposits	25,133.4	32,879.3	48,759.8
Other deposits	51,377.4	55,549.6	62,397.0
Broad money	91,815.6	104,283.6	131,504.6

Source: IMF, *International Financial Statistics*.

COST OF LIVING
(Consumer Price Index, year ending 30 September; base: 2000 = 100, metropolitan areas)

	2007	2008	2009
Food	324.5	388.6	378.5
Clothing and footwear	250.0	278.4	298.1
Rent	309.6	350.4	341.3
All items (incl. others)	311.3	359.6	359.6

2010: Food 397.4; All items (incl. others) 380.1.

Source: ILO.

NATIONAL ACCOUNTS
(million gourdes, year ending 30 September)

Expenditure on the Gross Domestic Product
(at current prices)

	2008/09*	2009/10†	2010/11†
Final consumption expenditure	269,640	328,993	337,701
Gross capital formation	73,161	67,154	83,338
Total domestic expenditure	342,801	396,147	421,039
Exports of goods and services	37,806	32,346	40,693
Less Imports of goods and services	114,048	164,454	164,045
GDP in purchasers' values	266,559	264,039	297,687
GDP at constant 1986/87 prices	14,014	13,255	13,996

Gross Domestic Product by Economic Activity
(at constant 1986/87 prices)

	2008/09*	2009/10†	2010/11†
Agriculture, hunting, forestry and fishing	3,288	3,289	3,326
Mining and quarrying	17	17	18
Manufacturing	1,067	910	1,074
Electricity and water	68	69	88
Construction	1,118	1,167	1,274
Trade, restaurants and hotels	3,911	3,600	3,766
Transport, storage and communications	991	963	1,034
Business services	1,654	1,536	1,577
Other services	1,518	1,540	1,586
Sub-total	13,633	13,091	13,743
Less Imputed bank service charge	689	839	810
Taxes, less subsidies, on products.	1,071	1,003	1,063
GDP in purchasers' values	14,014	13,255	13,996

* Provisional figures.
† Estimates.

BALANCE OF PAYMENTS
(US $ million, year ending 30 September)

	2007/08	2008/09	2009/10
Exports of goods f.o.b.	490.2	551.0	561.5
Imports of goods f.o.b.	–2,107.8	–2,032.1	–2,809.1
Trade balance	–1,617.6	–1,481.1	–2,247.7
Exports of services	339.5	375.5	238.0
Imports of services	–756.6	–772.1	–1,274.9
Balance on goods and services	–2,034.8	–1,877.7	–3,284.6
Other income received	28.2	31.1	32.6
Other income paid	–12.2	–18.3	–10.4
Balance on goods, services and income	–2,018.8	–1,864.9	–3,262.4
Current transfers received	1,369.8	1,375.5	1,473.8
Current transfers paid	–117.1	–134.8	–167.0
Current balance	–766.1	–624.2	–1,955.6
Direct investment from abroad	29.8	38.0	150.0
Capital account (net)	–	910.1	1,205.0
Other investment assets	–75.0	36.0	58.8
Other investment liabilities	350.6	–594.4	–313.0
Net errors and omissions	83.1	–188.6	161.4
Overall balance	–377.5	–423.1	–693.4

Source: IMF, *International Financial Statistics*.

External Trade

PRINCIPAL COMMODITIES
(US $ million, year ending 30 September, provisional figures)

Imports c.i.f.	2006/07	2007/08	2008/09
Food products	369.8	553.6	484.0
Mineral fuels, lubricants, etc.	406.0	618.3	384.6
Basic manufactures	276.3	217.3	350.9
Machinery and transport equipment	224.8	187.0	196.6
Miscellaneous manufactured goods	169.7	173.0	278.1
Total (incl. others)	1,851.7	2,148.2	2,185.1

Exports f.o.b.*	2006/07	2007/08	2008/09
Coffee	2.0	3.7	2.7
Cocoa	6.2	7.4	7.4
Mangoes	7.9	10.0	11.1
Crayfish	4.4	4.8	3.4
Essential oils	13.8	17.2	9.8
Manufactured goods	180.6	158.7	191.6
Total (incl. others)	522.8	472.4	551.0

* Excluding re-export of assembled goods to USA (US $ million, year ending 30 September, provisional figures): 463.4 in 2006/07; 425.1 in 2007/08; n.a. in 2008/09.

Source: Administration Générale des Douanes, Port-au-Prince.

PRINCIPAL TRADING PARTNERS
(US $ million, year ending 30 September)*

Imports c.i.f.	1989/90	1990/91	1991/92
Belgium	3.4	3.7	2.9
Canada	22.0	31.9	15.2
France	24.5	32.4	17.2
Germany, Federal Republic	14.6	19.2	10.0
Japan	23.6	31.2	17.7
Netherlands	11.2	13.9	8.7
United Kingdom	5.6	6.7	4.2
USA	153.1	203.2	126.7
Total (incl. others)	332.2	400.5	277.2

Exports f.o.b.†	1989/90	1990/91	1991/92
Belgium	15.9	19.5	6.0
Canada	4.5	4.7	2.3
France	17.4	21.6	6.1
Germany, Federal Republic	5.4	6.6	2.4
Italy	16.5	20.7	8.7
Japan	2.4	2.9	0.9
Netherlands	3.4	4.3	1.4
United Kingdom	2.3	2.3	0.7
USA	78.3	96.3	39.7
Total (incl. others)	163.7	198.7	74.7

* Provisional figures.
† Excluding re-exports.

Source: Administration Générale des Douanes, Port-au-Prince.

Transport

ROAD TRAFFIC
('000 motor vehicles in use)

	1994	1995	1996
Passenger cars	30.0	49.0	59.0
Commercial vehicles	30.0	29.0	35.0

1999 ('000 motor vehicles in use): Passenger cars 93.0; Commercial vehicles 61.6.

Source: UN, *Statistical Yearbook*.

SHIPPING

Merchant Fleet
(registered at 31 December)

	2007	2008	2009
Number of vessels	6	7	5
Total displacement ('000 grt)	1.8	2.4	1.6

Source: IHS Fairplay, *World Fleet Statistics*.

International Sea-borne Freight Traffic
('000 metric tons)

	1988	1989	1990
Goods loaded	164	165	170
Goods unloaded	684	659	704

Source: UN, *Monthly Bulletin of Statistics*.

CIVIL AVIATION

Traffic (international flights, 1995): Passengers arriving 367,900; Passengers departing 368,330.

Tourism

TOURIST ARRIVALS BY COUNTRY OF ORIGIN

	2006	2007	2008
Canada	8,733	30,046	23,661
Dominican Republic	2,785	n.a.	n.a.
France	2,787	10,246	8,068
Jamaica	1,936	n.a.	n.a.
USA	79,247	266,793	210,099
Total (incl. others)	107,783	386,060	304,021

Receipts from tourism (US $ million, excl. passenger transport): 190 in 2007; 276 in 2008; 315 in 2009.

Source: World Tourism Organization.

Communications Media

	2008	2009	2010
Telephones ('000 main lines in use)	108.0	108.3	50.0
Mobile cellular telephones ('000 subscribers)	3,200	3,648	4,000
Internet users ('000)	1,000	1,000	n.a.

Personal computers: 16,000 (1.7 per 1,000 persons) in 2005.

Source: International Telecommunication Union.

Radio receivers ('000 in use): 415 in 1997.

Television receivers ('000 in use): 42 in 1999.

Daily newspapers: 4 in 1996 (total circulation 20,000 copies); 2 in 2004.

Book production: 340 titles published in 1995.

Sources (unless otherwise indicated): UNESCO, *Statistical Yearbook*; UN, *Statistical Yearbook*.

Education

(1994/95)

	Institutions	Teachers	Students
Pre-primary	n.a.	n.a.	230,391*
Primary	10,071	30,205	1,110,398
Secondary	1,038	15,275	195,418
Tertiary	n.a.	654*	6,288*

* 1990/91 figure.

Adult literacy rate (UNESCO estimates): 62.1% (males 60.1%; females 64.0%) in 2007 (Source: UNESCO Institute for Statistics).

Directory

The Government

HEAD OF STATE

President: MICHEL JOSEPH MARTELLY (took office on 14 May 2011).

CABINET
(May 2012)

Following the resignation of Prime Minister Garry Conille on 24 February 2012, Minister of Foreign Affairs and Religion Laurent Lamothe was designated head of government by President Michel Martelly. His nomination was approved by the legislature on 3 May.

Prime Minister and Minister of Foreign Affairs and Religion: LAURENT LAMOTHE.

Minister of Justice and Public Security: PIERRE MICHEL BRUNACHE.

Minister of Agriculture, Natural Resources and Rural Development: HÉBERT DOCTEUR.

Minister of the Economy and Finance: ANDRÉ LEMERCIER GEORGES.

Minister of Education and Professional Training: RÉGINALD PAUL.

Minister of the Environment: JOSEPH RONALD TOUSSAINT.

Minister to the Presidency in charge of Haitians Residing Abroad: DANIEL SUPPLICE.

Minister of Culture and Communication: PIERRE RAYMOND DUMAS.

Minister of the Interior and Territorial Collectivities and National Defence: THIERRY MAYARD-PAUL.

Minister of Public Health and the Population: FLORENCE DUPERVAL GUILLAUME.

Minister of Public Works, Transport, Energy and Communications: JACQUES ROUSSEAU.

Minister of Social Affairs and Labour: FRANÇOIS RICHEL LAFAILLE.

Minister of Tourism: STÉPHANIE BALMIR VILLEDROUIN.

Minister of Trade and Industry: WILSON LALEAU.

Minister of Women's Affairs and Women's Rights: YANICK MÉZIL.

Minister of Youth, Sports and Civic Action: RENÉ JEAN ROOSEVELT.

Minister of Planning and External Co-operation: JUDE HERVÉ DAY.

Minister-delegate to the Prime Minister, in charge of Parliamentary Relations: RALPH RICARDO THÉANO.

MINISTRIES

Many ministerial buildings were destroyed in the earthquake of January 2010.

Office of the President: Palais National, rue de la République, Port-au-Prince; tel. 2222-3024; e-mail webmestre@palaisnational.info.

Office of the Prime Minister: Villa d'Accueil, 1 rue Prosper, Musseau, Port-au-Prince; tel. 2228-6000; e-mail primature@primature.gouv.ht; internet www.primature.gouv.ht.

Ministry of Agriculture, Natural Resources and Rural Development: BP 2162, Route Nationale 1, Damien, Port-au-Prince; tel. 2222-3599; fax 2222-3591; internet www.agriculture.gouv.ht.

Ministry of Culture and Communication: Champ de Mars, Port-au-Prince; tel. 2221-3238; fax 2221-7318; e-mail dg1@haiticulture.org.

Ministry of the Economy and Finance: Palais des Ministères, rue Mgr Guilloux, Port-au-Prince; tel. 2223-7113; fax 2223-1247; e-mail mef@mefhaiti.gouv.ht; internet www.mefhaiti.gouv.ht.

Ministry of Education and Professional Training: rue Dr Audain, Port-au-Prince; tel. 2222-1036; fax 2245-3400; internet www.eduhaiti.gouv.ht.

Ministry of the Environment: 181 ave Jean-Paul II, Port-au-Prince; tel. 2245-7585; fax 2245-7360.

Ministry of Foreign Affairs and Religion: blvd Harry S Truman, Cité de l'Exposition, Port-au-Prince; tel. 2222-8482; fax 2223-1668; e-mail webmaster@maehaitiinfo.org; internet www.mae.gouv.ht.

Ministry of Haitians Residing Abroad: 87 ave Jean-Paul II, Turgeau, Port-au-Prince; tel. 2245-1116; fax 2245-0287; e-mail info@mhave.gouv.ht; internet www.mhave.gouv.ht.

Ministry of the Interior and Territorial Collectivities and National Defence: Palais des Ministères, rue Mgr Guilloux, Port-au-Prince; tel. 2222-6490; fax 2222-8057.

Ministry of Justice and Public Security: Port-au-Prince; tel. 2245-9737; fax 2245-0474; internet www.mjsp.gouv.ht; bldg destroyed in Jan. 2010 earthquake.

Ministry of Planning and External Co-operation: Palais des Ministères, rue Mgr Guilloux, Port-au-Prince; tel. 2228-2512; fax 2222-0226; e-mail info@mpce.gouv.ht; internet www.mpce.gouv.ht.

Ministry of Public Health and the Population: Palais de Ministères, rue Mgr Guilloux, Port-au-Prince; tel. 2223-6248; fax 2222-4066.

Ministry of Public Works, Transport and Communications: Palais des Ministères, rue Mgr Guilloux, Port-au-Prince; tel. 2222-2528; fax 2223-4519; e-mail secretariat.directiongenerale@mtptc.gouv.ht; internet www.mtptc.gouv.ht.

Ministry of Social Affairs and Labour: 16 rue de la Révolution, Port-au-Prince; tel. 2222-1244; fax 2221-0717.

Ministry of Tourism: 8 rue Légitime, Port-au-Prince; tel. 2223-2135; fax 2223-5359; e-mail pdelatour@yahoo.com.

Ministry of Trade and Industry: rue Légitime, Champ de Mars, BP 200, Port-au-Prince; tel. 2222-2125; fax 2223-8402.

Ministry of Women's Affairs and Women's Rights: ave Magny 4, Port-au-Prince; tel. 2224-9152; e-mail contact@mcfdf.gouv.ht; internet www.mcfdf.gouv.ht.

Ministry of Youth, Sports and Civic Action: angle rues Garoute et Pacot, Turgeau, BP 2339, Port-au-Prince; tel. 2245-5794.

Office of the Minister-delegate to the Prime Minister, in charge of Parliamentary Relations: Delmas 48, 5 rue François, Port-au-Prince; tel. 2246-9912.

President and Legislature

PRESIDENT

Election, first round, 28 November 2010*

Candidates	Valid votes cast	%
Mirlande Manigat (RDNP)	336,878	31.37
Jude Celéstin (Inite)	241,462	22.48
Michel Joseph Martelly (Repons Peyizan)	234,617	21.84
Jean Henry Ceant (Renmen Ayiti)	87,834	8.18
Jacques Edouard Alexis (MPH)	32,932	3.07
Charles Henri Baker (Respè)	25,512	2.38
Total (incl. others)	1,074,056	100.00

* Preliminary results from the Conseil Electoral Provisoire (CEP). A report issued by the Organization of American States in January 2011 stated that Martelly, not Celéstin, was the second-placed candidate. In February the CEP announced that Manigat would face Martelly in the run-off ballot, held on 20 March.

Election, second round, 20 March 2011

Candidates	Valid votes cast	%
Michel Joseph Martelly (Repons Peyizan)	716,986	67.57
Mirlande Manigat (RDNP)	336,747	31.74
Total*	1,061,089	100.00

* Including 7,356 blank ballots.

LEGISLATURE

Sénat
(Senate)

President: SIMON DIEUSEUL DESRAS (LAVNI).

Vice-President: ANDRIS RICHÉ (Altenativ).

Distribution of Seats, March 2012*

	Seats
Inite/Lespwa	15
Alternative pour le Progrès et la Democratie (Altenativ)	5
Fusion des Sociaux-Démocrates Haïtiens	3
Ayiti an Aksyon (AAA)	2
Konbit pou Bati Ayiti (KONBA)	1
Pou Nou Tout (PONT)	1
Organisation du Peuple en Lutte (OPL)	1
La Fanmi Lavalas	1
Oganizasyon Lavni	1
Total	30

* The Sénat has 30 members, three from each province. One-third of these seats are renewable every two years. The last elections to the Sénat were held on 28 November 2010 and 20 March 2011.

Chambre des Députés
(Chamber of Deputies)

President: LEVAILLANT LOUIS JEUNE (Inite).

Vice-President: OCINJAC BENJAMIN (INITE).

Elections, 28 November 2010 and 20 March 2011

	Seats
Inite	32
Alternative pour le Progrès et la Democratie (Altenativ)	11
Ansanm Nou Fò	10
Ayiti an Aksyon (AAA)	8
Oganizasyon Lavni	7
Rasanble	4
Repons Peyizan	3
Konbit pou Refè Haïti (KONBIT)	3
Pou Nou Tout (PONT)	3
Mouvement Chrétien pour une Nouvelle Haïti (MOCHRENHA)	3
Plateforme Liberation	2
Plateforme des Patriotes Haïtiens (PLAPH)	2
Mouvement Action Socialiste (MAS)	2
Mouvement Démocratique pour la Libération d'Haïti-Parti Revolutionnaire Démocratique d'Haïti (MODELH-PRDH)	1
Respè	1
Veye Yo	1
Independent	2
Vacant	4
Total	99

Election Commission

The Conseil Electoral Provisoire was dissolved by a presidential decree on 29 December 2011. A new permanent electoral commission was scheduled to be formed in 2012, pending a constitutional amendment. According to the Constitution, the nine-member Conseil Electoral Permanent would be composed of three representatives from each of the three branches of government.

Political Organizations

Some 52 political parties and movements were registered to contest the legislative elections of November 2010 and March 2011. Many addresses in Port-au-Prince and surrounding areas were destroyed in the earthquake of January 2010.

Action Démocratique pour Bâtir Haïti (ADEBHA): 509 route de Delmas, entre Delmas 103 et 105, Port-au-Prince; tel. 2256-6739; fax 3446-6161; e-mail versun_etatdedroit@yahoo.fr; internet www.adebha.populus.org; f. 2004; Pres. RENÉ JULIEN.

Alliance Chrétienne Citoyenne pour la Reconstruction d'Haïti (ACCRHA): Port-au-Prince; Leader JEAN CHAVANNES JEUNE.

Alliance pour la Libération et l'Avancement d'Haïti (ALAH): Haut Turgeau 95, BP 13350, Port-au-Prince; tel. 2245-0446; fax 2257-4804; e-mail reynoldgeorges@yahoo.com; f. 1975; Leader REYNOLD GEORGES.

Alternative pour le Progrès et la Democratie (Altenativ): f. 2010 to contest the legislative elections; grouping of more than 70 legislative candidates; Mems of Exec. Cttee ROSNY SMART, EDGARD LEBLANC FILS, VICTOR BENOÎT, SERGE GILLES, EVANS PAUL.

Alyans (Alliance Démocratique): Port-au-Prince; centre-left coalition of Konvansyon Inite Demokratik (KID) and Popular Party for the Renewal of Haïti (PPRH); formed an alliance with the Fusion des Sociaux-Démocrates Haïtiens and the OPL in late 2009 to contest the 2010 legislative elections; Leader EVANS PAUL.

Ansanm Nou Fò: contested the 2010 elections; Leader LESLIE VOLTAIRE.

Ayisyen pou Ayiti: Port-au-Prince; contested the 2010 presidential election; Leader YVON NÉPTUNE.

Ayiti an Aksyon (AAA): Port-au-Prince; internet ayitianaksyon .net; contested the 2010 legislative elections; Pres. YOURI LATORTUE.

Congrès National des Mouvements Démocratiques (KONAKOM): 101 Bois Verna, Port-au-Prince; tel. 2245-6228; f. 1987; social-democratic; Leader VICTOR BENOÎT.

La Fanmi Lavalas (FL): blvd 15 Octobre, Tabarre, Port-au-Prince; tel. 2256-7208; internet www.hayti.net; f. 1996 by Jean-Bertrand Aristide; barred from contesting the 2010 elections.

Force 2010 (Fos 2010): Delmas; f. 2010; contested the 2010 presidential election; Leader WILSON JEUDI.

Front pour la Reconstruction Nationale (FRN): Gonaïves; f. 2004; Sec.-Gen. GUY PHILIPPE.

Fusion des Sociaux-Démocrates Haïtiens: POB 381056, Miami, FL 33138, USA; e-mail fusion@pfsdh.org; internet www.pfsdh.org; formed an alliance with Alyans and the OPL in late 2009 to contest the 2010 legislative elections; Leader SERGE GILLES.

Inite (Unité): Port-au-Prince; f. 2009 to replace Lespwa (l'Espoir, f. 2005); supported Pres. René Préval; Nat. Co-ordinator LEVAILLANT LOUIS-JEUNE.

Konbit pou Bati Ayiti (KONBA): Port-au-Prince; f. 2005.

Konbit pou Refè Haïti (KONBIT): Port-au-Prince; contested the 2010 legislative elections.

Mobilisation pour le Progrès Haïtien (MPH): Port-au-Prince; contested the 2010 presidential election; Leader JACQUES EDOUARD ALEXIS.

Mouvement Action Socialiste (MAS): Hinche; contested the 2010 legislative elections.

Mouvement Chrétien pour une Nouvelle Haïti (MOCHRENHA): rue M 7 Turgeau, Carrefour, Port-au-Prince; tel. 3443-3120; e-mail mochrenha@hotmail.com; f. 1998; contested the 2010 legislative elections; Leaders LUC MÉSADIEU, GILBERT N. LÉGER.

Mouvement Démocratique pour la Libération d'Haïti-Parti Revolutionnaire Démocratique d'Haïti (MODELH-PRDH): contested the 2010 legislative elections; Leader FRANÇOIS LATORTUE.

Mouvement Indépendant pour la Réconciliation Nationale (MIRN): Port-au-Prince; mem. of Inite; Leader LUC FLEURINORD.

Mouvement pour l'Instauration de la Démocratie en Haïti (MIDH): 114 ave Jean Paul II, Port-au-Prince; tel. 2245-8377; f. 1986; centre-right; contested the 2010 legislative elections.

Nouveau Parti Communiste Haïtien (NPCH): Grand Rue 1, Nan Gonmye; e-mail vanialubin@yahoo.fr; internet www.npch.net; Marxist-Leninist.

Oganizasyon Lavni (LAVNI): contested the 2010 presidential election; Leader YVES CHRISTALIN.

Organisation du Peuple en Lutte (OPL): 105 ave Lamartinière, Bois Verna, Port-au-Prince; tel. 2245-4214; e-mail info@oplpeople .com; internet www.oplpeople.com/home.html; f. 1991 as Organisation Politique Lavalas; name changed as above 1998; formed an alliance with Alyans and the Fusion des Sociaux-Démocrates Haïtiens in late 2009 to contest the 2010 legislative elections; Leader SAUVEUR PIERRE ETIENNE.

Parti Agricole Industriel National (PAIN): f. 1956; Pres. HÉBERT DOCTEUR.

Parti du Camp Patriotique et de l'Alliance Haïtienne (PACAPALAH): Port-au-Prince; contested the 2010 legislative elections.

Parti pour l'Evolution Nationale d'Haïti (PENH): Port-au-Prince; contested the 2010 elections; Leader ERIC SMARKI CHARLES.

Parti des Industriels, Travailleurs, Agents du Développement et Commercants d'Haïti (PITACH): Port-au-Prince.

Parti Social Rénové (PSR): Port-au-Prince; Leader BONIVERT CLAUDE.

Plateforme Liberation: Port-au-Prince; contested the 2010 legislative elections.

Plateforme des Patriotes Haïtiens (PLAPH): Cap-Haïtien; contested the 2010 legislative elections.

Pou Nou Tout (PONT): Port-au-Prince; contested the 2010 legislative elections.

Rasanble: contested the 2010 legislative elections.

Rassemblement des Démocrates Nationaux Progressistes (RDNP): 234 route de Delmas, Delmas, Port-au-Prince; tel. 2246-3313; f. 1979; centre party; Sec.-Gen. MIRLANDE MANIGAT.

Regwoupman Sitwayen pou Espwa (Respè): Port-au-Prince; f. 2005; party of the wealthy élite; Leader CHARLES HENRI BAKER.

Renmen Ayiti: Port-au-Prince; e-mail info@renmenayiti.org; internet www.renmenayiti.org; Leader JEAN HENRY CEANT.

Repons Peyizan (Réponse des Paysans): Port-au-Prince; Leader MICHEL JOSEPH MARTELLY.

Solidarité: contested the 2010 elections; Leader GÉNARD JOSEPH.

Union de Citoyens Ayisyen pour la Démocratie, le Développement et l'Education (UCADDE): Miragoâne; contested the 2010 legislative elections.

Veye Yo: Cap-Haïtien; contested the 2010 legislative elections.

Viv Ansanm: Port-au-Prince; Leader DANIEL JEAN JACQUES.

Diplomatic Representation

EMBASSIES IN HAITI

Many addresses in Port-au-Prince and surrounding areas were destroyed in the earthquake of January 2010.

Argentina: 48 rue Metellus, Pétionville, BP 1755, Port-au-Prince; tel. 2256-6711; fax 2256-6714; e-mail ehait@mrecic.gov.ar; Ambassador MARCELO RAUL SEBASTE.

Bahamas: 12 rue Boyer, Pétionville, Port-au-Prince; tel. 2256-4407; fax 2256-5729; e-mail bahamasembassy@hainet.net; Ambassador CLIFFORD SCAVELLA.

Brazil: Immeuble Héxagone, 3ème étage, angle des rues Clerveaux et Darguin, Pétionville, BP 15845, Port-au-Prince; tel. 2256-9662; fax 2256-0900; e-mail brasemb1@accesshaiti.com; internet portoprincipe.itamaraty.gov.br; Ambassador IGOR KIPMAN.

Canada: route de Delmas, entre Delmas 71 et 75, BP 826, Port-au-Prince; tel. 2249-9000; fax 2249-9920; e-mail prnce@international.gc .ca; internet www.canadainternational.gc.ca/haiti; Ambassador HENRI-PAUL NORMANDIN.

Chile: 2 rue Coutilien et Rue Delmas 60, Musseau, Port-au-Prince; tel. 2813-1613; fax 2813-1708; e-mail embajadachile_haiti@hotmail .com; internet chileabroad.gov.cl/haiti; Ambassador MAURICIO LEONE BRAVO.

Cuba: 3 rue Marion, Peguy Ville, Pétionville, POB 15702, Port-au-Prince; tel. 3701-3815; fax 2257-8566; e-mail secretaria@ht .embacuba.cu; internet www.cubadiplomatica.cu/haiti; Ambassador RICARDO SOTERO GARCÍA NÁPOLES.

Dominican Republic: rue Panaméricaine 121, BP 56, Pétionville, Port-au-Prince; tel. 3257-9215; fax 3257-0383; e-mail embrepdomhai@yahoo.com; Ambassador RUBÉN SILIÉ VALDEZ.

France: 51 rue de Capois, BP 1312, Port-au-Prince; tel. 2999-9000; fax 2999-9001; e-mail ambafrance@hainet.net; internet www .ambafrance-ht.org; Ambassador DIDIER LE BRET.

Germany: 2 impasse Claudinette, Bois Moquette, Pétionville, BP 1147, Port-au-Prince; tel. 2949-0202; fax 2257-4131; e-mail info@ port-au-prince.diplo.de; internet www.port-au-prince.diplo.de; Ambassador JENS-PETER VOSS.

Holy See: rue Louis Pouget, Morne Calvaire, BP 326, Port-au-Prince; tel. 2257-6308; fax 2257-3411; e-mail nonciatureap@hughes .net; Apostolic Nuncio Most Rev. BERNARDITO CLEOPAS AUZA (Titular Archbishop of Suacia).

Japan: Hexagone, 2ème étage, angle rues Clerveaux et Darguin, Pétionville, Port-au-Prince; tel. 2256-3333; fax 2256-9444; internet www.ht.emb-japan.go.jp; Ambassador KENTARO MINAMI (resident in the Dominican Republic).

Mexico: rue Métélus 48, Pétionville, BP 327, Port-au-Prince; tel. 2813-0089; fax 2256-6528; e-mail embhaiti@sre.gob.mx; Ambassador LUIS MANUEL LÓPEZ MORENO.

Panama: 73 rue Grégoire, Pétionville, Port-au-Prince; tel. 3828-5471; fax 3864-4881; e-mail panaembahaiti@yahoo.com; internet www.panamaenelexterior.gob.pa/Hait; Ambassador FLOREAL GARRIDO.

Spain: 54 rue Metellus, Pétionville, BP 386, Port-au-Prince; tel. 2940-0952; fax 2940-1098; e-mail Emb.PuertoPrincipe@maec.es; internet www.maec.es/embajadas/puertoprincipe; Ambassador MANUEL HERNÁNDEZ RUIGÓMEZ.

Taiwan (Republic of China): 22 rue Lucien Hubert, Morne Calvaire, Pétionville, Port-au-Prince; tel. 2257-2899; fax 2256-8067; e-mail haiti888@gmail.com; internet www.taiwanembassy .org/HT; Ambassador LIU BANG-ZYH.

USA: Tabarre 41, blvd 15 Octobre, Port-au-Prince; tel. 2229-8000; fax 2229-8028; internet haiti.usembassy.gov; Ambassador KENNETH H. MERTEN.

Venezuela: blvd Harry S Truman, Cité de l'Exposition, BP 2158, Port-au-Prince; tel. 3443-4127; fax 2223-7672; e-mail embavenezhaiti@hainet.net; Ambassador PEDRO ANTONIO CANINO GONZÁLEZ.

Judicial System

Law is based on the French Napoleonic Code, substantially modified during the presidency of François Duvalier.

Courts of Appeal and Civil Courts sit at Port-au-Prince and the three provincial capitals: Gonaïves, Cap-Haïtien and Port de Paix. In principle each commune has a Magistrates' Court. Judges of the Supreme Court and Courts of Appeal are appointed by the President.

Cour de Cassation (Supreme Court): Port-au-Prince; the Cour de Cassation building was destroyed in the 2010 earthquake; court proceedings resumed in mid-April from a temporary location; Pres. ANEL ALEXIS JOSEPH; Vice-Pres. JULES CANTAVE.

Citizens' Rights Defender: FLORENCE ÉLIE.

Religion

Roman Catholicism and the folk religion Voodoo (vodou) are the official religions. There are various Protestant and other denominations.

Many addresses in Port-au-Prince and surrounding areas were destroyed in the earthquake of January 2010.

CHRISTIANITY

The Roman Catholic Church

For ecclesiastical purposes, Haiti comprises two archdioceses and eight dioceses. Some 65% of the population are Roman Catholics.

Bishops' Conference

Conférence Episcopale de Haïti, angle rues Piquant et Lammarre, BP 1572, Port-au-Prince; tel. 222-5194; fax 223-5318; e-mail ceh56@hotmail.com.

f. 1977; Pres. Most Rev. LOUIS KÉBREAU (Archbishop of Cap-Haïtien).

Archbishop of Cap-Haïtien: Most Rev. LOUIS KÉBREAU, Archevêché, rue 19–20 H, BP 22, Cap-Haïtien; tel. 262-0071; fax 262-1278.

Archbishop of Port-au-Prince: GUIRE POULARD, Archevêché, rue Dr Aubry, BP 538, Port-au-Prince; tel. 222-2045; e-mail archevechepap@globalsud.com.

The Anglican Communion

Anglicans in Haiti fall under the jurisdiction of a missionary diocese of Province II of the Episcopal Church in the USA.

Bishop of Haiti: Rt Rev. JEAN ZACHÉ DURACIN, Eglise Episcopale d'Haïti, BP 1309, Port-au-Prince; tel. 2257-1624; fax 2257-3412; e-mail epihaiti@egliseepiscopaledhaiti.org; internet www.egliseepiscopaledhaiti.org.

Protestant Churches

Baptist Convention: Route Nationale 1, Cazeau BP 2601, Port-au-Prince; tel. 2262-0567; e-mail conventionbaptiste@yahoo.com; f. 1964; Gen. Sec. EMMANUEL PIERRE.

Evangelical Lutheran Church of Haiti: Eglise Evangélique Luthérienne d'Haiti, 144 rue Capitale, BP 15, Les Cayes; tel. 2286-3398; f. 1975; Pres. THOMAS BERNARD; 9,000 mems.

Other denominations active in Haiti include Methodists and the Church of God 'Eben-Ezer'.

VOODOO

Konfederasyon Nasyonal Vodou Ayisyen (KNVA): f. 2008; Supreme Leader FRANÇOIS MAX GESNER BEAUVOIR.

The Press

Many addresses in Port-au-Prince and surrounding areas were destroyed in the earthquake of January 2010.

DAILY

Le Nouvelliste: 198 rue du Centre, Port-au-Prince; tel. 2222-4754; fax 2224-2061; e-mail manigapier@lenouvelliste.com; internet www.lenouvelliste.com; f. 1898; evening; French; suspended print edn following Jan. 2010 earthquake; recommenced daily edn in April; independent; Editor-in-Chief PIERRE MANIGAT, Jr; Publr MAX CHAUVET; circ. 10,000.

PERIODICALS

Ayiti Fanm: Centre National et International de Documentation, d'Information et de Défense des Droits des Femmes en Haïti, 16 rue de La Ligue Féminine, BP 6114, Port-au-Prince; tel. 2245-0346; fax 2244-1841; e-mail ayitifanm@enfofanm.net; internet www.ayitifanm.org; f. 1991; monthly; publ. by ENFOFANM; Creole; Founder and Editor-in-Chief CLORINDE ZÉPHIR; Dir MYRIAM MERLET.

Bulletin de Liaison: Centre Pedro-Arrupe, BP 1710, Port-au-Prince; tel. and fax 2245-3132; e-mail gillesbeaucheminsj@hotmail.com; internet liaison.lemoyne.edu; f. 1996; 4 a year; Editors ANDRÉ CHARBONNEAU, GILLES BEAUCHEMIN, DONALD MALDARI.

Haïti en Marche: 74 bis, rue Capois, Port-au-Prince; tel. 3454-0126; e-mail melodiefm@gmail.com; internet www.haitienmarche.com; f. 1986; weekly; Editors MARC GARCIA, ELSIE ETHÉART.

Haïti Observateur: 98 ave John Brown, 3ème étage, Port-au-Prince; tel. 2223-0782; e-mail contact@haiti-observateur.net; internet www.haiti-observateur.net; f. 1971; weekly; Editor LÉO JOSEPH; circ. 75,000.

Haïti Progrès: 6 Impasse Dupuy, ruelle Chrétien, Port-au-Prince; tel. 3446-1957; fax 3680-9397; e-mail editor@haiti-progres.com; internet www.haiti-progres.com; f. 1983; weekly; French, English and Creole; Dir KIM IVES.

Liaison: Centre Pedro-Arrupe, CP 1710, 6110 Port-au-Prince; tel. 2245-3132; fax 2245-3629; e-mail gillesbeaucheminsj@hotmail.com; internet liaison.lemoyne.edu; French; available in Creole as *Aksyon*; Editors ANDRÉ CHARBONNEAU, DONALD MALDARI, GILLES BEAUCHEMIN.

Le Matin: 3 rue Goulard, Pétionville, Port-au-Prince; tel. 2256-4461; e-mail info@lematinhaiti.com; internet www.lematinhaiti.com; f. 1907; French; suspended daily publication following Jan. 2010 earthquake; publ. every other week from Jan. 2010; independent; Editor-in-Chief CLARENS FORTUNÉ; Publr RÉGINALD BOULOS; circ. 5,000.

Le Moniteur: Presses Nationales d'Haïti, rue Hammerton Killick 231, BP 1746 bis, Port-au-Prince; tel. 2222-1744; fax 2223-1026; e-mail pndh-moniteur@hainet.net; f. 1845; 2 a week; French; official state gazette; Dir-Gen. WILLEMS EDOUARD; circ. 2,000.

Le Septentrion: Cap-Haïtien; weekly; independent; Editor NELSON BELL; circ. 2,000.

Superstar Détente: 3 ruelle Chériez, Port-au-Prince; tel. 2245-3450; fax 2222-6329; cultural magazine; Dir CLAUDEL VICTOR.

NEWS AGENCIES

Agence Haïtienne de Presse (AHP): 6 rue Fernand, Port-au-Prince; tel. 2245-7222; fax 2245-5836; e-mail ahp@yahoo.com; internet www.ahphaiti.org; f. 1989; publishes daily news bulletins in French and English; continued to publish following Jan. 2010 earthquake; Dir-Gen. GEORGES VENEL REMARAIS.

AlterPresse: 38 Delmas 8, BP 19211, Port-au-Prince; tel. 2249-9493; e-mail alterpresse@medialternatif.org; internet www.alterpresse.org; f. 2001; independent; owned by Alternative Media Group; still publishing online following Jan. 2010 earthquake; Dir GOTSON PIERRE.

Haiti Press Network: 14 rue Lamarre, Pétionville, Port-au-Prince; tel. 2511-6555; fax 2256-6197; e-mail hpnhaiti@yahoo.fr; internet www.hpnhaiti.com; still online following Jan. 2010 earthquake; Dir CLARENS RENOIS.

Publishers

Many addresses in Port-au-Prince and surrounding areas were destroyed in the earthquake of January 2010.

Editions des Antilles: route de l'Aéroport, Delmas, Port-au-Prince; tel. 2940-0217; fax 2249-1225; e-mail editiondesantilles@yahoo.com.

Editions Caraïbes, SA: 57 rue Pavée, BP 2013, Port-au-Prince; tel. 2222-0032; e-mail piereli@yahoo.fr; Man. PIERRE J. ELIE.

Editions CUC-Université Caraïbe: 7, Delmas 29, Port-au-Prince; tel. 2246-5531; e-mail editions@universitecaraibe.com; internet www.editionsuniversitecaraibe.com.

Editions Les Presses Nationales d'Haïti: 223 rue du Centre, BP 1746, Port-au-Prince; tel. 2222-1744; fax 2223-1026; e-mail pnd-moniteur@hainet.net.

Imprimerie Roland Theodore, SA: Delmas 1A, No 19, Delmas; tel. 2940-7200; e-mail info@imprimerie-theodore.com; internet www.imprimerie-theodore.com; Gen. Man. HENRI THEODORE.

Maison Henri Deschamps—Les Entreprises Deschamps Frisch, SA: 25 rue Dr Martelly Seïde, BP 164, Port-au-Prince; tel. 2223-2215; fax 2223-4976; e-mail entdeschamps@gdfhaiti.com; internet www.maisonhenrideschamps.com; f. 1898; education and literature; divisions include *Editions Hachette-Deschamps* and *Imprimerie Henri Deschamps*; Man. Dir JACQUES DESCHAMPS, Jr; CEO HENRI R. DESCHAMPS.

Broadcasting and Communications

Many addresses in Port-au-Prince and surrounding areas were destroyed in the earthquake of January 2010.

TELECOMMUNICATIONS

Regulatory Body

Conseil National des Télécommunications (CONATEL): 16 ave Marie Jeanne, Cité de l'Exposition, BP 2002, Port-au-Prince; tel. 2224-0748; fax 2223-9229; e-mail info@conatel.gouv.ht; internet www.conatel.gouv.ht; f. 1969; govt communications licensing authority; Dir-Gen. JEAN MARIE GUILLAUME.

Major Operators

Digicel Haiti: 151 angle ave John Paul II et Impasse Duverger, BP 15516, Port-au-Prince; tel. 3711-3444; e-mail customercarehaiti@digicelgroup.com; internet www.digicelhaiti.com; f. 2005; owned by Digicel (Ireland); mobile telephone network provider; bldg badly damaged by Jan. 2010 earthquake; Group Chair. DENIS O'BRIEN; CEO, Haiti MAARTEN BOUTE.

Haiti Telecommunications International, SA (HaiTel): 17 rue Darguin, 3ème étage, Pétionville, Port-au-Prince; tel. 3510-1201; fax 3510-6273; internet www.haitelonline.com; f. 1999; part-owned by US-based MCI WorldCom; mobile telecommunications provider; Pres. FRANCK CINÉ.

Natcom (Téléco-NatCom): blvd Jean-Jacques Dessalines, BP 814, Port-au-Prince; tel. 2245-2200; fax 223-0002; e-mail info@haititeleco.com; fmrly Télécommunications d'Haiti; renamed as above in 2010; 60% owned by Viettel (Viet Nam), 40% govt-owned; landline provider; Dir MICHEL PRÉSUMÉ.

Voilà: Port-au-Prince; e-mail customer-care@comcelhaiti.com; internet www.voila.ht; f. 1998 as Communication Céllulaire d'Haïti (ComCEL); fmrly owned by US-based Western Wireless, bought by Trilogy (USA) in 2005; mobile telecommunications provider; CEO JOHN STANTON.

BROADCASTING

Following the earthquake in January 2010, many radio and television stations were unable to broadcast, or were able to broadcast only at a low capacity. According to the Association of Haitian Journalists, of the approximately 50 radio stations in Port-au-Prince, only around 12 were back on the air by February. Most television stations were still unable to broadcast, although Télé Métropole and Télé Caraïbe were broadcasting via foreign stations.

Radio

La Brise FM 105.3: Camp Perrin, Les Cayes, Sud; tel. 2942-1938; e-mail contact@labrisefm.com; internet www.labrisefm.com; music station; Dir, Public Relations CARMELIE MONTUMA.

Radio Antilles International: 75 rue du Centre, BP 2335, Port-au-Prince; tel. 3433-0712; fax 2222-0260; e-mail jacquessampeur@yahoo.com; f. 1984; independent; Dir-Gen. JACQUES SAMPEUR.

Radio Caraïbes: 45 rue Chavannes, Port-au-Prince; tel. 3558-9110; e-mail radiocaraibesfm@yahoo.fr; internet www.caraibesfm.com; f. 1949; independent; Dir PATRICK MOUSSIGNAC.

Radio Galaxie: 17 rue Pavée, Port-au-Prince; tel. 3727-7725; e-mail info@radiogalaxiehaiti.com; internet www.radiogalaxiehaiti.com; f. 1990; independent; Dir YVES JEAN-BART.

Radio Ginen: 21 bis, Delmas 31, Port-au-Prince; tel. 2511-1738; e-mail jeanlborges@radioteleginenhaiti.com; internet radioteleginenhaiti.com; f. 1994; Dir JEAN LUCIEN BORGES.

Radio Ibo: 51 route du Canapé-Vert, BP 15174, Pétionville, Port-au-Prince; tel. 3557-5214; fax 2245-9850; e-mail info@radioiboht.com; internet radioiboht.com; broadcasting from Dir's private residence following Jan. 2010 earthquake; Dir HÉROLD JEAN FRANÇOIS.

Radio Kiskeya: 42 rue Villemenay, Boisverna, Port-au-Prince; tel. 2244-6605; e-mail admin@radiokiskeya.com; internet radiokiskeya.com; f. 1994; Dir MARVEL DANDIN.

Radio Lumière: Côte-Plage 16, Carrefour, BP 1050, Port-au-Prince; tel. 2234-0331; fax 2234-3708; e-mail rlumiere@radiolumiere.org; internet www.radiolumiere.org; f. 1959; Protestant; independent; Dir VARNEL JEUNE.

Radio Megastar: 106 rue de la Réunion, Port-au-Prince; tel. 3711-1197; e-mail jcharleus0@yahoo.com; internet megastarfmhaiti.com; f. 1991; Dir JEAN-EDDY CHARLEUS.

Radio Mélodie: 74 bis, rue Capois, Port-au-Prince; tel. 2452-0428; e-mail melodiefm@gmail.com; internet radiomelodiehaiti.com; f. 1998.

Radio Metropole: Delmas 52, BP 62, Port-au-Prince; tel. 2246-2626; fax 2249-2020; e-mail informations@naskita.com; internet www.metropolehaiti.com; f. 1970; independent; resumed normal programming in Feb. 2010 following Jan. earthquake; Pres. HERBERT WIDMAIER; Dir-Gen. RICHARD WIDMAIER.

Radio Nirvana FM: Cap-Haïtien; tel. 2431-5784; e-mail pdg@radionirvanafm.com; internet www.radionirvanafm.com; Dir-Gen. RAPHAEL ABRAHAM.

Radio Port-au-Prince Plus: Stade Sylvio Cator, BP 863, Port-au-Prince; tel. 3927-3182; e-mail contactus@radioportauprinceplus.com; internet www.radioportauprinceplus.com; f. 1979; independent; broadcasts in Creole and English; religious programming; Dir-Gen. MAX PRINCE.

Radio Sonic Plus: rue Duplan 42, Saint-Marc; tel. 2279-4943; e-mail sonicplus@peoplepc.com; internet radiosonicplus.com; Dir-Gen. WILSON PAUL.

Radio Superstar: Delmas 68, angle rues Safran et C. Henri, Pétionville, Port-au-Prince; tel. 3734-2254; fax 2257-3015; e-mail info@radiosuperstarhaiti.com; internet www.superstarhaiti.com; f. 1987; independent; Dir ALBERT CHANCY, Jr.

Radio Télé Venus: 106 rue 5 et 6 E, Cap-Haïtien; tel. 2262-2742; fax 3780-8053; internet www.radiotelevenushaiti.com; f. 1994.

Radio Tropic FM: 6 ave John Brown, 3ème étage, Lalue, Port-au-Prince; tel. 2224-0571; e-mail tropicradio@yahoo.fr; internet www.radiotropichaiti.com; f. 1991; independent; Dir GUY JEAN.

Radio Vision 2000: 184 ave John Brown, Port-au-Prince; tel. 2245-4914; e-mail info@radiovision2000.com; internet www.radiovision2000haiti.net; f. 1991; Dir LÉOPOLD BERLANGER.

Sans Souci FM: rue Républicaine, km 18 milot, Cap-Haïtien; tel. 2813-1874; fax 3701-5913; e-mail sanssoucifm@radiosanssouci.com; internet www.radiosanssouci.com; f. 1998; Dir IVES-MARIE CHANEL.

Signal FM: 127 rue Louverture, Pétionville, BP 391, Port-au-Prince; tel. 2256-4368; fax 2256-4396; e-mail info@signalfmhaiti.com; internet www.signalfmhaiti.com; f. 1991; independent; Dir-Gen. MARIO VIAU.

Television

PVS Antenne 16: 137 rue Mgr Guilloux, Port-au-Prince; tel. and fax 2222-1277; f. 1988; independent; religious; Dir-Gen. RAYNALD DELERME.

Société Haïtienne de Télévision par Satellites, SA (Télé Haïti): blvd Harry S Truman, BP 1126, Port-au-Prince; tel. 2222-3887; fax 2222-9140; e-mail telhaiti@hotmail.com; internet www.telehaiti.com; f. 1959; independent; pay-cable station with 38 channels; broadcasts in French, Spanish and English; Dir MARIE CHRISTINE MOURRAL BLANC.

Télé Caraïbe: Port-au-Prince; broadcasts continued following earthquake of Jan. 2010.

Télé Eclair: 526 route de Delmas, Port-au-Prince; tel. 2256-4505; fax 2256-3828; f. 1996; independent; Dir PATRICK ANDRÉ JOSEPH.

Télé Metropole: 18 Delmas 52, BP 62, Port-au-Prince; tel. 2246-2626; fax 2249-2020; e-mail informations@naskita.com; internet www.metropolehaiti.com; f. 1970; independent; broadcasts continued following Jan. 2010 earthquake; Pres. HERBERT WIDMAIER; Dir-Gen. RICHARD WIDMAIER.

Télémax: 3 Delmas 19, Port-au-Prince; tel. 246-2002; fax 2246-1155; f. 1994; independent; Dir ROBERT DENIS.

Télévision Nationale d'Haïti: Delmas 33, BP 13400, Port-au-Prince; tel. 2246-2325; fax 2246-0693; e-mail info@tnh.ht; internet www.tnh.ht; f. 1979; merged with Radio Nationale d'Haïti in 1987; govt-owned; cultural; 4 channels in Creole, French and Spanish; administered by 4-mem. board; Dir PRADEL HENRIQUEZ.

Trans-America: ruelle Roger, Gonaïves; tel. 2274-0113; f. 1990; independent; Dir-Gen. HÉBERT PELISSIER.

Finance

(cap. = capital; m. = million; res = reserves; dep. = deposits; brs = branches; amounts in gourdes)

Many addresses in Port-au-Prince and surrounding areas were destroyed in the earthquake of January 2010.

BANKING

Central Bank

Banque de la République d'Haïti: angle rues du Pavée et du Quai, BP 1570, Port-au-Prince; tel. 2299-1200; fax 2299-1045; e-mail brh@brh.net; internet www.brh.net; f. 1911 as Banque Nationale de la République d'Haïti; name changed as above in 1979; bank of issue; administered by 5-mem. board; cap. 50m., res 3,053.4m., dep. 55,355.2m. (Sept. 2009); Gov. CHARLES CASTEL; Dir-Gen. MARC HÉBERT IGNACE.

Commercial Banks

Banque Nationale de Crédit: angle rues du Quai et des Miracles, BP 1320, Port-au-Prince; tel. 2299-4081; fax 2299-4076; internet www.bnconline.com; f. 1979; cap. 25m., dep. 729.9m. (Sept. 1989); Pres. (vacant); Dir-Gen. JOSEPH EDY DUBUISSON.

Banque Populaire Haïtienne: angle rues des Miracles et du Centre, Port-au-Prince; tel. 2299-6080; fax 2299-6076; e-mail bphinfo@brh.net; f. 1973; state-owned; cap. and res 72.9m., dep. 819m. (Mar. 2007); Dir-Gen. ANDRE DAUPHIN; Pres. RODNÉE DESCHINEAUX; 3 brs.

Banque de l'Union Haïtienne: angle rues du Quai et Bonne Foi, BP 275, Port-au-Prince; tel. 2299-8500; fax 2299-8517; e-mail buh@buhsa.com; internet www.buh.ht; f. 1973; cap. 30.1m., res 6.2m. (Sept. 1997), dep. 1,964.3m. (Sept. 2004); Pres. MARCEL FONTIN; 12 brs.

Capital Bank: 38 rue Flaubert, BP 2464, Port-au-Prince; tel. 2299-6700; fax 2299-6519; e-mail capitalbank@brh.net; internet www.capitalbankhaiti.com; f. 1986; fmrly Banque de Crédit Immobilier, SA; Pres. BERNARD ROY; Gen. Man. LILIANE C. DOMINIQUE.

Sogebank, SA (Société Générale Haïtienne de Banque, SA): route de Delmas, BP 1315, Port-au-Prince; tel. 2229-5000; fax 2229-5022; internet www.sogebank.com; f. 1986; part of Groupe Sogebank; cap. 647.3m., dep 1,117.7m., res. 28,256.9m. (Sept. 2009); Pres. RALPH PERRY; 35 brs.

Unibank: 157 rue Flaubert, Pétionville, BP 46, Port-au-Prince; tel. 2299-2057; fax 2299-2070; e-mail info@unibankhaiti.com; internet www.unibankhaiti.com; f. 1993; cap. 1,098m., res 500.9m., dep. 35,296.4m. (Sept. 2010); Pres. F. CARL BRAUN; Dir-Gen. FRANCK HELMCKE; 20 brs.

INSURANCE

Principal Companies

Alternative Insurance, SA: 4 rue Jean Gilles, blvd Toussaint Louverture, Port-au-Prince; tel. 2229-6300; fax 2250-1461; e-mail info@aic.ht; internet www.aic.ht; Dir-Gen. OLIVIER BARREAU.

Les Assurances Léger, SA (ALSA): 40 rue Lamarre, BP 2120, Port-au-Prince; tel. 2222-3451; fax 2223-8634; e-mail alsa@alsagroup.com; f. 1994; headquarters in France; Pres. (vacant).

Compagnie d'Assurances d'Haïti, SA (CAH): étage Dynamic Entreprise, route de l'Aéroport, BP 1489, Port-au-Prince; tel. 2250-0700; fax 2250-0236; e-mail info@groupedynamic.com; internet www.groupedynamic.com/cah.php; f. 1978; subsidiary of Groupe Dynamic SA; Group Chair. and CEO PHILIPPE R. ARMAND.

Excelsior Assurance, SA: rue 6, no 24, Port-au-Prince; tel. 2245-8881; fax 2245-8598; e-mail ingesanon@yahoo.fr; Dir-Gen. EMMANUEL SANON.

Haïti Sécurité Assurance, SA: 352 Ave John Brown, BP 1754, Bourdon, Port-au-Prince; tel. 3489-3444; fax 3489-3423; e-mail admin@haiti-securite.com; internet www.haiti-securite.com; f. 1985; Dir-Gen. WILLIAM PHIPPS.

MAVSA Multi Assurances, SA: étage Dynamic Entreprise, route de l'Aéroport, BP 1489, Port-au-Prince; tel. 2250-0700; fax 2250-0236; e-mail info@groupedynamic.com; internet www.groupedynamic.com/mavsa.php; f. 1992; subsidiary of Groupe Dynamic SA; credit life insurance and pension plans; Group Chair. and CEO PHILIPPE R. ARMAND.

National d'Assurance, SA (NASSA): 25 rue Ferdinand Canapé-Vert, BP 532, Port-au-Prince, HT6115; tel. 2245-9800; fax 2245-9701; e-mail nassa@nassagroup.com; internet www.nassagroup.com; f. 1989; specializing in property, medical and life insurance; Pres. FRITZ DUPUY.

National Western Life Insurance: 13 rue Pie XII, Cité de l'Exposition, Port-au-Prince; tel. 2223-0734; e-mail intlmktg@globalnw.com; headquarters in USA; Chair. and CEO ROBERT L. MOODY; Agent VORBE BARRAU DUPUY.

Office National d'Assurance Vieillesse (ONA): 21 angle des rue Gregoire et Villate, Petion-Ville, Port-au-Prince; tel. 2256-6272; fax 2256-6274; e-mail ona@ona.ht; internet www.ona.ht; f. 1965; Dir-Gen. BERNARD DEGRAFF.

Société de Commercialisation d'Assurance, SA (SOCOMAS): étage Complexe STELO, 56 route de Delmas, BP 636, Port-au-Prince; tel. 2246-4768; fax 2246-4874; e-mail socomashaiti@hotmail.com; Dir-Gen. JEAN DIDIER GARDÈRE.

Insurance Association

Association des Assureurs d'Haïti: 153 rue des Miracles, POB 1754, Port-au-Prince; tel. 3449-1737; fax 2223-8634; e-mail fdecat@hotmail.com; Dir FRITZ DE CATALOGNE.

Trade and Industry

Many addresses in Port-au-Prince and surrounding areas were destroyed in the earthquake of January 2010.

GOVERNMENT AGENCIES

Centre de Facilitation des Investissements (CFI): 8 rue Légitime, Champs de Mars, BP 6110, Port-au-Prince; tel. 2514-5792; fax 2224-8990; e-mail info@cfihaiti.net; internet www.cfihaiti.net; f. 2006; investment promotion; Dir-Gen. GUY G. LAMOTHE.

Centre National des Équipements (CNE): Port-au-Prince; state-run construction co; Dir-Gen. JUDE CÉLESTIN.

Conseil de Modernisation des Entreprises Publiques (CMEP): Palais National, Port-au-Prince; tel. 2222-4111; fax 2222-7761; f. 1996; oversees modernization and privatization of state enterprises; Dir-Gen. YVES BASTIEN.

DEVELOPMENT ORGANIZATIONS

Fonds de Développement Industriel (FDI): 12 angle rue Butte et impasse Chabrier, BP 2597, Port-au-Prince; tel. 2244-9728; fax 2244-9727; e-mail fdi@fdihaiti.com; internet www.fdihaiti.com; f. 1981; Dir-Gen. LHERMITE FRANÇOIS.

Mouvman Peyizan Papay (MPP): Papaye, Hinche; internet www.mpphaiti.org; f. 1973; peasant org., chiefly concerned with food production and land protection; Leader CHAVANNES JEAN-BAPTISTE.

Société Financière Haïtienne de Développement, SA (SOFIHDES): 11 Blvd Harry S Truman, BP 1399, Port-au-Prince; tel. 2250-1427; fax 2250-1436; e-mail info@sofihdes.com; internet www.sofihdes.com; f. 1983; industrial and agro-industrial project-financing, accounting, data-processing, management consultancy; Chair. FRANTZ BERNARD CRAAN; Man. Dir MICHÈLE CÉSAR JUMELLE.

CHAMBERS OF COMMERCE

Chambre Américaine de Commerce en Haïti (AMCHAM): 6 rue Moïse, Pétionville, Delmas, BP 13486, Port-au-Prince; tel. 2511-3024; e-mail info@amcham.ht; internet www.amcham.ht; f. 1979; Pres. RENÉ MAX AUGUSTE; Exec. Dir CHANTAL SALOMON-JEAN.

Chambre de Commerce et d'Industrie d'Haïti (CCIH): blvd Harry S Truman, Cité de l'Exposition, BP 982, Port-au-Prince; tel. and fax 3512-5141; e-mail ccih@ccih.ht; internet www.ccih.org.ht; f. 1895; 10 departmental chambers nation-wide; Pres. HERVÉ DENIS; Sec. JOVENEL MOISE.

Chambre de Commerce et d'Industrie Haitiano-Canadienne (CCIHC): rue des Nimes, Port-au-Prince; tel. 2250-5452; e-mail direction@ccihc.com; internet ccihc.com; Pres. FRANTZ LIAUTAUD; Sec. GAMIL HECHEMA.

Chambre Franco-Haïtienne de Commerce et d'Industrie (CFHCI): 5 rue Goulard, Pétionville, 6140 Port-au-Prince; tel. and fax 2510-8965; e-mail cfhci@yahoo.fr; internet www.chambrefrancohaitienne.com; f. 1987; Pres. GRÉGORY BRANDT; Exec. Dir KETTLY FOURON; 109 mems.

INDUSTRIAL AND TRADE ORGANIZATIONS

Association des Exportateurs de Café (ASDEC): rue Barbancourt, BP 1334, Port-au-Prince; tel. 2249-2919; fax 2249-2142; e-mail incahaiti@hotmail.com; Pres. JULIEN ETIENNE.

Association Haïtienne pour le Développement des Technologies de l'Information et de la Communication (AHTIC): 18 rue Moise, Pétionville, Port-au-Prince; tel. 2454-1498; e-mail sbruno@websystems.ht; promotes technological devt; Pres. MATHIAS PIERRE; Vice-Pres. STÉPHANE BRUNO.

Association Haïtienne des Economistes (AHE): rue Lamarre, 26 étage, BP 15567, Pétionville; tel. 2512-4605; e-mail haiti_economistes@yahoo.fr; asscn of economists; Pres. EDDY LABOSSIÈRE.

Association des Industries d'Haïti (ADIH): 21 rue Borno, Pétionville, BP 15199, Port-au-Prince; tel. 3776-1211; fax 2514-0184; e-mail administration@adih.ht; internet www.adih.ht; f. 1980; Pres. NORMA POWELL; Exec. Dir GRÉGOR AVRIL.

Association Nationale des Distributeurs de Produits Pétroliers (ANADIPP): Centre Commercial Dubois, route de Delmas, Bureau 401, BP 1379, Port-au-Prince; tel. 2246-1414; fax 2245-0698; e-mail moylafortune@hotmail.com; f. 1979; asscn of petroleum product distributors; Pres. MAURICE LAFORTUNE.

Association Nationale des Exporteurs de Mangues (ANEM): 5 Santo 20, Route Nationale 3, Croix des Bouquets; tel. 2510-2636; e-mail anem@mango-haiti.com; group of 10 mango exporters; Pres. JEAN-MAURICE BUTEAU; Man. BERNARD CRAAN.

Association Nationale des Importateurs et Distributeurs de Produits Pharmaceutiques (ANIDPP): Blvd Harry S Truman,

Port-au-Prince; tel. 2222-0268; fax 2222-7887; e-mail anidpp@direcway.com; Pres. RALPH EDMOND.

Association Nationale des Institutions de Microfinance d'Haïti (ANIMH): 87 rue Wallon, Plc Boyer, BP 15321, Pétionville; tel. 2257-3405; e-mail info@animhaiti.org; internet www.animhaiti.org; f. 2002; group of 17 institutions for developing the microfinance sector; Pres. SINIOR RAYMOND; Exec. Dir WINDSOR CALIXTE.

Association Professionnelles des Banques (APB): 133 rue Faubert, Pétionville; tel. 2299-3298; fax 2257-2374; e-mail apbhaiti@yahoo.com; asscn of bank professionals; Pres. MAXIME CHARLES; Exec. Dir VLADIMIR FRANÇOIS.

UTILITIES

Electricity

Electricité d'Haïti (Ed'H): rue Dante Destouches, Port-au-Prince; tel. 2222-4600; state energy utility company; recommenced energy production (10 MW) in Feb. 2010 following Jan. earthquake; Gen. Man. SERGE RAPHAEL.

Péligre Hydroelectric Plant: Artibonite Valley.

Saut-Mathurine Hydroelectric Plant: Les Cayes.

Water

Service Nationale d'Eau Potable (SNEP): 1 Delmas 45, Port-au-Prince; tel. 2246-3044; fax 2246-0881; e-mail snep_eau_potable@hotmail.com; Dir-Gen. PÉTION ROY.

TRADE UNIONS

Association des Journalistes Haïtiens (AJH): f. 1954; Sec.-Gen. JACQUES DESROSIERS.

Batay Ouvriye (Workers' Struggle): Delmas, BP 13326, Port-au-Prince; tel. 2222-6719; e-mail batay@batayouvriye.org; internet www.batayouvriye.org; f. 2002; independent umbrella org. providing a framework for various autonomous trade unions and workers' asscns.

Centrale Autonome des Travailleurs Haïtiens (CATH): 37 route Delmas, Port-au-Prince (bldg destroyed in Jan. 2010 earthquake); tel. 3401-5820; e-mail fignole2000@yahoo.fr; f. 1980; Sec.-Gen. FIGNOLE SAINT-CYR.

Confédération Nationale des Educateurs d'Haïti (CNEH): impasse Noë 17, ave Magloire Ambroise, BP 482, Port-au-Prince; tel. 3421-5777; fax 3812-4576; e-mail cneh@yahoo.fr; f. 1986; Sec.-Gen. JOLIBOIS RENE.

Confédération des Travailleurs Haïtiens (CTH): 138 route de Fréres, Pétionville; tel. 2424-5959; fax 2256-7268; e-mail cthhaiti@googlemail.com; internet haiticth.org; f. 1989; Sec.-Gen. LOULOU CHÉRY.

Fédération des Ouvriers Syndiques (FOS): angle rues Dr Aubry et des Miracles 115, BP 785, Port-au-Prince; tel. 2222-0035; f. 1984; Pres. PIERRE CHARLES JOSEPH.

Organisation Générale Indépendante des Travailleurs et Travailleuses d'Haïti (OGITH): 2–3 étage, 121 angle route Delmas et Delmas 3, BP 1212, Port-au-Prince; tel. 2249-0575; e-mail pnumas@yahoo.fr; f. 1988; Gen. Sec. PATRICK NUMAS.

Syndicat des Employés de l'EDH (SEEH): c/o EDH, rue Joseph Janvier, Port-au-Prince; tel. 2222-3367; Pres. DUCKENS RAPHAËL.

Transport

RAILWAYS

The railway service closed in the early 1990s.

ROADS

In 1999, according to International Road Federation estimates, there were 4,160 km (2,585 miles) of roads, of which 24.3% was paved. There are all-weather roads from Port-au-Prince to Cap-Haïtien, on the northern coast, and to Les Cayes, in the south.

SHIPPING

The two principal ports are Port-au-Prince and Cap-Haïtien. There are also 12 minor ports.

Autorité Portuaire Nationale: Blvd La Saline, BP 616, Port-au-Prince; tel. 2223-2440; fax 2221-3479; e-mail apnpap@hotmail.com; internet www.apn.gouv.ht; f. 1978; Dir-Gen. JEAN EVENS CHARLES.

Adeko Enterprises: 33–35 Blvd Harry S Truman, Ave Marie-Jeanne, Port-au-Prince; tel. 3445-0617; e-mail info@adeko-ht.com; internet www.adeko-ht.com; air and sea freight forwarders and maritime agency; Pres. JEAN MARC ANTOINE; Gen. Man. MARC KINSON ANTOINE.

AI Shipping International: Apt No 1, Sonadim Bldg, Blvd Toussaint Louverture and Patrice Lumumba, Port-au-Prince; tel. 2940-5476; fax 2941-5476; e-mail info@aishippingintl.com; internet www.aishippingintl.com; f. 1981; freight forwarder and maritime agency; Pres. ANTOINE ILANES.

CIVIL AVIATION

The international airport, situated 8 km (5 miles) outside Port-au-Prince, is the country's principal airport. Although the airport was badly damaged by the earthquake of January 2010, it reopened to commercial flights in the following month. There is also an airport at Cap-Haïtien, which was scheduled to open to international flights in 2013 following an upgrade. There are smaller airfields at Jacmel, Jérémie, Les Cayes and Port-de-Paix.

Autorite Aéroportuaire Nationale (AAN): Aéroport International Toussaint Louverture, Port-au-Prince; tel. 3443-0250; fax 2250-5866; e-mail dgaan@haitiworld.com; internet papaeroportauthority.org; Dir-Gen. PIERRE ANDRÉ LAGUERRE.

Office National de l'Aviation Civile (OFNAC): Aéroport International Toussiant Louverture, Delmas, BP 1346, Port-au-Prince; tel. 2246-0052; fax 2246-0998; e-mail lpierre@ofnac.org; Dir-Gen. JEAN MARC FLAMBERT.

Tourism

Tourism was formerly Haiti's second largest source of foreign exchange. However, as a result of political instability, the number of cruise ships visiting Haiti declined considerably. In 2008 tourist arrivals totalled 304,021. Receipts from tourism in 2009 totalled US $315m. In November 2011 it was announced that Marriot Hotels and Resorts was to build a 173-room hotel in Port-au-Prince; construction would begin in 2012 and the hotel was expected to be ready in 2014.

Association Haïtienne des Agences de Voyages (ASHAV): 17 rue des Miracles, Port-au-Prince; tel. 3445-5903; fax 2511-2424; e-mail ashav@hainet.net; f. 1988; Pres. PIERRE CHAUVET, Fils.

Association Touristique d'Haïti (ATH): rue Moise 18, Pétion-Ville, BP 2562, Port-au-Prince; tel. 2510-4746; fax 3906-8484; e-mail ath_haiti@yahoo.com; internet www.haiticherie.ht; Pres. MARYSE CHANCY; Exec. Dir GILIANE C. JOUBERT.

Defence

In 1995 the armed forces were effectively dissolved, although officially they remained in existence pending an amendment to the Constitution providing for their abolition. As assessed at November 2011, the national police force numbered an estimated 2,000. There was also a coastguard of 30. In June 2004 a UN security force—the UN Stabilization Mission in Haiti (MINUSTAH)—assumed peacekeeping responsibilities in the country. Following the earthquake of January 2010, MINUSTAH's authorized capacity was increased, standing at a maximum of 8,940 military personnel and 4,391 police officers in June 2010. As of February 2011, MINUSTAH comprised 8,743 troops, 3,312 civilian police, 1,724 international and local civilian staff, and 209 UN Volunteers. The MINUSTAH budget for 2010/11 was an estimated US $853.8m.

Director-General of the Police Nationale: MARIO ANDRESOL.

Education

Education is provided by the state, by the Roman Catholic Church and by other religious organizations. Teaching is based on the French model, and French is the language of instruction. Primary education, which normally begins at six years of age and lasts for six years, is officially compulsory. Secondary education usually begins at 12 years of age and lasts for a further six years, comprising two cycles of three years each. According to UNICEF estimates, in 2005 the primary school attendance ratio included 48% of male and 52% of female children in the relevant age-group, while attendance ratio at secondary schools included 18% of male and 21% of female students in the relevant age-group. Higher education is provided by 18 technical and vocational centres, 42 domestic science schools, and by the Université d'Etat d'Haïti. More than 1,300 educational institutions were destroyed in the January 2010 earthquake. In 2011 the National Fund for Education (FNE) was launched to provide more than 500,000 children with access to education. Some US $70m. was made available in January 2012 to the FNE. In the budget of 2010/11 an estimated 8,504m. gourdes was allocated to education, representing 8% of the total spending.

HONDURAS

Introductory Survey

LOCATION, CLIMATE, LANGUAGE, RELIGION, FLAG, CAPITAL

The Republic of Honduras lies in the middle of the Central American isthmus. It has a long northern coastline on the Caribbean Sea and a narrow southern outlet to the Pacific Ocean. Its neighbours are Guatemala to the west, El Salvador to the south-west and Nicaragua to the south-east. The climate ranges from temperate in the mountainous regions to tropical in the coastal plains: temperatures in the interior range from 15°C (59°F) to 24°C (75°F), while temperatures in the coastal plains average about 30°C (86°F). There are two rainy seasons in upland areas, May–July and September–October. The national language is Spanish. Almost all of the inhabitants profess Christianity, and about 82% of the population are adherents of the Roman Catholic Church. The national flag (proportions 1 by 2) has three horizontal stripes, of blue, white and blue, with five blue five-pointed stars, arranged in a diagonal cross, in the centre of the white stripe. The capital is Tegucigalpa.

CONTEMPORARY POLITICAL HISTORY

Historical Context

Honduras was ruled by Spain from the 16th century until 1821 and became a sovereign state in 1838. From 1939 the country was ruled as a dictatorship by Gen. Tiburcio Carías Andino, leader of the Partido Nacional (PN), who had been President since 1933. In 1949 Carías was succeeded as President by Juan Manuel Gálvez, also of the PN. In 1954 the leader of the Partido Liberal (PL), Dr José Ramón Villeda Morales, was elected President, but was immediately deposed by Julio Lozano Díaz, himself overthrown by a military junta in 1956. The junta organized elections in 1957, when the PL secured a majority in Congress and Villeda was re-elected President. He was overthrown in 1963 by Col (later Gen.) Oswaldo López Arellano, who, following elections held on the basis of a new Constitution, was appointed President in June 1965.

A presidential election in 1971 was won by Dr Ramón Ernesto Cruz Uclés, the PN candidate. In December 1972, however, Cruz was deposed in a bloodless coup, led by former President López. In 1974 President López was replaced as Commander-in-Chief of the Armed Forces by Col (later Gen.) Juan Melgar Castro, who was appointed President in 1975. President Melgar was forced to resign in August 1978, and was replaced by a military junta. The Commander-in-Chief of the Armed Forces, Gen. Policarpo Paz García, assumed the role of Head of State.

Domestic Political Affairs

Military rule was ended officially when, in April 1980, elections to a Constituent Assembly were held. The PL won 52% of the votes but was unable to assume power. Gen. Paz was appointed interim President. At a general election in 1981 the PL, led by Dr Roberto Suazo Córdova, secured an absolute majority in the Congreso Nacional (National Congress). Suazo was sworn in as President in January 1982. However, real power lay in the hands of Col (later Gen.) Gustavo Alvarez Martínez, who became Commander-in-Chief of the Armed Forces. Alvarez suppressed increasing political unrest by authorizing the arrests of trade union activists and left-wing sympathizers; 'death squads' were allegedly also used to eliminate 'subversive' elements of the population. In 1984 Gen. Alvarez was deposed as Commander-in-Chief by a group of army officers.

At the November 1985 presidential election the leading candidate of the PN, Rafael Leonardo Callejas Romero, obtained 42% of the votes cast, but the PL's leading candidate, José Simeón Azcona del Hoyo (who had obtained only 27% of the votes cast), was declared the winner because, in accordance with a new electoral law, the combined votes of the PL's candidates secured the requisite majority of 51% of the total votes cast.

In February 1988 a report by the human rights organization Amnesty International gave evidence of an increase in violations of human rights by the armed forces and by right-wing 'death squads'. The Inter-American Court of Human Rights (an organ of the Organization of American States—OAS, see p. 394) found the Honduran Government guilty of the 'disappearances' of Honduran citizens during 1981–84. The PL secured a majority of seats in the Congreso Nacional at the November general election, while Callejas of the PN won the concurrent presidential election. The Callejas administration promptly adopted economic austerity measures, provoking widespread social unrest.

In 1993, in response to increasing pressure by human rights organizations, the Government established a special commission to investigate allegations of human rights violations by the armed forces. The commission recommended, *inter alia*, the replacement of the armed forces' much-criticized secret counter-intelligence organization, the División Nacional de Investigaciones (DNI), with a body under civilian control. Legislation replacing the DNI with a new ministry, the Dirección de Investigación Criminal, was approved in December.

At presidential and legislative elections in November 1993 Carlos Roberto Reina Idiáquez, the candidate of the PL, was elected President. The PL also obtained a clear majority in the Congreso. Reina, a former President of the Inter-American Court of Human Rights, expressed his commitment to the reform of the judicial system and the armed forces. In May 1994 the Congreso Nacional approved a constitutional reform abolishing compulsory military service (the amendment was ratified in April 1995). Also approved was the transfer of the police from military to civilian control. In July 4,000 members of indigenous organizations occupied the Congreso building and succeeded in securing an agreement with the Government granting rights and social assistance to the country's indigenous community. The following months were characterized by growing social and political tension. Concern was raised by human rights organizations that instability was being fomented by the armed forces in an attempt to stem the rapid diminution of its powers. An increase in the incidence of crime and violent demonstrations forced the Government to declare a state of national emergency in August and to deploy the armed forces to maintain order.

In May 1997, following the killing of two ethnic minority leaders in the previous month, more than 3,000 members of the indigenous community conducted a march from the western departments of Copán and Ocotepeque to the capital to protest outside the presidential palace. As a result, Reina agreed to conduct a full investigation into the killings and to accelerate the distribution of some 7,000 ha of land to the indigenous community. However, the killing of a further two ethnic minority leaders later that month led to accusations by human rights groups that attempts were being made to eliminate minority autonomous organizations.

At the general election held in November 1997 Carlos Roberto Flores Facussé, the candidate of the ruling PL, was elected President. The PL also obtained a majority in the Congreso Nacional. In May 1998 control of the police force was transferred from the military to the civilian authorities. The Fuerza de Seguridad Pública, which had been under military control since 1963 and was widely suspected of perpetrating human rights abuses, was replaced by a new force, the Policía Nacional. Nevertheless, reports of human rights abuses continued.

Legislative and presidential elections were held in November 2001. Five candidates contested the presidential election; the PN candidate, Ricardo Maduro Joest, emerged victorious. The PN also gained a majority in the Congreso Nacional.

The Maduro presidency

On taking office in January 2002 Maduro announced that the armed forces would play a greater role in the anti-crime effort, a declaration that was met with opposition domestically and internationally. Maduro affirmed his intention to reorganize the police force and to reform the criminal justice system, including the depoliticization of the selection of judges.

President Maduro faced increasing industrial unrest during his term in office. Public dissatisfaction with reductions in public expenditure culminated with a 'March for Dignity', in which some 10,000 people converged on Tegucigalpa in August 2003 in protest at, *inter alia*, the decentralization of water services and plans for civil service reform. In October some 30,000 public sector employees held a one-day strike in protest at the Government's economic austerity measures. Intermittent unrest continued in 2004.

Despite the implementation of increased security measures by the Maduro administration, Honduras experienced rising levels of violent crime in the 2000s. In January 2003, in response to increasing conflict between street gangs (*maras*), 10,000 army troops had been deployed on to the streets of several cities. Controversial legislation approved in August introduced prison sentences of between nine and 12 years for members of the *maras*, which were held responsible for much of the crime in Honduras. However, the continued high incidence of kidnappings of businessmen and foreigners in 2004–05 prompted many to flee the country. In December 2004 the Government introduced further legislation, increasing the maximum prison sentence for gang membership and extending the period of detention without charge. However, President Maduro's strict policies towards criminals also raised fears of human rights abuses. In May more than 100 inmates, mainly gang members, died in a fire at a prison in San Pedro Sula. Representatives of the deceased claimed that police and prison guards started the fire and subsequently refused to free the prisoners. The incident echoed another in the previous April when 69 people, mainly *mara* members, died in a riot and subsequent fire at a prison in La Ceiba. A government inquiry into the deaths at La Ceiba later concluded that 51 of the victims had been summarily executed by prison officials, who then set the fire to conceal their actions.

The 2005 elections

The presidential election held on 27 November 2005 was narrowly won by the PL's José Manuel (Mel) Zelaya Rosales. In the concurrent legislative election the PL won 62 of the 128 seats in the Congreso Nacional, while the PN secured 55 seats. The delay in announcing the final results was severely criticized by observers, who denounced the electoral process as the worst in 25 years of democracy. Zelaya assumed the presidency on 27 January 2006 and a new Government was installed.

The assassination, in March 2007, of Rigoberto Aceituno, the second most senior police official in Honduras, served as a stark reminder of the continuing influence of the country's drugs gangs. Violent crime persisted as a serious problem in 2008, with the assassination of several political figures, including the Vice-President of the Congreso Nacional, Mario Fernando Hernández, in November.

In April 2008 demonstrators began a hunger strike outside the Congreso Nacional to protest against government corruption and impunity. They demanded a review of case files involving prominent figures from politics and business, accusing the Attorney-General of failing to investigate corruption charges. The Congreso agreed to an audit of the cases, and the strike ended after 38 days.

The ratification, in October 2008, of Honduras's accession to the Bolivarian Alliance for the Americas (Alianza Bolivariana para las Américas—ALBA), a Venezuelan-led economic and social integration initiative, created some tension within the Congreso Nacional. In order to win the support of the legislature, President Zelaya agreed to endorse the campaign of the speaker, Roberto Micheletti Baín, for the presidential election due in November 2009, and created a development fund worth US $19.5m. to support the congressional campaigns of PL deputies who voted in favour of ratification. The PN decried the misuse of public funds and abstained from voting.

The 2009 constitutional crisis

President Zelaya provoked considerable controversy in March 2009 when he ordered the Instituto Nacional de Estadística to organize a referendum on convening a constituent assembly to revise the Constitution. The PN and several prominent members of the PL opposed the proposal, amid speculation that Zelaya was seeking a reform that would allow him to remain in office beyond the expiry of his term in January 2010, while the office of the Attorney-General insisted that only the Tribunal Supremo Electoral (TSE) had the power to conduct a referendum.

On 23 June 2009, five days before the plebiscite was scheduled to be held, political tensions escalated when the Congreso Nacional attempted to thwart Zelaya's plans by approving legislation prohibiting the holding of referendums 180 days before or after a general election. The Chairman of the Joint Chiefs of Staff, Gen. Romeo Vásquez Velásquez, consequently refused to provide logistical support for the vote on the grounds that it was unlawful, leading to his dismissal by Zelaya, which, in turn, prompted the resignation of several senior military officials and of Edmundo Orellana as Minister of National Defence. The Supreme Court, meanwhile, insisted that Vásquez be reinstated. However, Zelaya refused to comply with the Court's demand and proceeded with preparations for the non-binding referendum, without the support of the military and in defiance of both the judiciary and the legislature, which commenced discussions on the possibility of impeaching the President.

Shortly before voting was due to begin, on 28 June 2009, President Zelaya was seized at his residence by members of the armed forces and forced into exile in Costa Rica; it subsequently emerged that the Supreme Court had authorized the detention of Zelaya on 18 charges, including treason and abuse of authority. Later that day the Congreso Nacional voted to remove Zelaya from the presidency, on the grounds that he had repeatedly violated the Constitution and failed to observe court orders, and Micheletti was sworn in to act as President until the end of the current term in January 2010; prior to the vote, the Congreso Nacional had been read an alleged letter of resignation from Zelaya (which he denied having signed). An interim Cabinet was appointed on 29 June. Micheletti, who maintained that Zelaya had been legally removed from office in what he termed a 'constitutional succession', declared that the presidential and legislative elections would be conducted, as scheduled, on 29 November. However, the ousting of Zelaya was denounced internationally, with both the UN General Assembly and the OAS adopting resolutions condemning what they deemed to be a coup and demanding the restoration of Zelaya to the presidency. The OAS also suspended the right of Honduras to participate in the Organization and designated Costa Rican President Oscar Arias Sánchez to lead diplomatic efforts to mediate a resolution to the country's political crisis. Meanwhile, demonstrations both for and against Zelaya's reinstatement as President took place nation-wide. Zelaya attempted to return to Honduras on 5 July, but the aircraft in which he was travelling was prevented from landing; at least two people were reportedly killed in clashes between the security forces and supporters of the deposed President.

Arias brokered talks between the two sides in Costa Rica, in July 2009, but Micheletti's representatives repeatedly rejected a proposed arrangement that would involve Zelaya returning to serve the remainder of his presidential term as head of a unity government. An OAS delegation of foreign ministers visited Tegucigalpa in late August, but failed to persuade Micheletti's de facto Government to accept the US-supported accord devised by Arias, which also provided for the general election to be conducted a month earlier than scheduled, for Micheletti to resume the office of President of the Congreso Nacional, and for a political amnesty to be offered to both sides. The Honduran Supreme Court also rejected the terms of the accord.

As campaigning for the general election officially commenced at the end of August 2009, three months before the scheduled ballot on 29 November, the OAS and the US Department of State both announced that they would not recognize the outcome of polls conducted under Micheletti's administration. Zelaya made an unexpected return to Honduras on 21 September, taking refuge in the Brazilian embassy in Tegucigalpa, outside which thousands of his supporters subsequently gathered before being dispersed by the security forces. The de facto Government imposed a temporary curfew and, on the following day, adopted a decree suspending five constitutional articles, including those guaranteeing freedom of expression, freedom of association and of assembly, and freedom of movement, for a period of 45 days. The decree proved divisive, prompting widespread condemnation, not only internationally, but also from domestic political and business figures, many of whom had previously supported Zelaya's removal from office, including the two main presidential candidates, Porfirio Lobo Sosa of the PN and Elvin Santos for the PL. Micheletti repealed the decree in October.

Representatives of Micheletti and Zelaya held a series of talks in Tegucigalpa in October 2009, under the auspices of the OAS. The main point of contention was Zelaya's proposed restitution to office. On 30 October, following the intervention of the US Department of State, which insisted that international support for the general election depended on the conclusion of an agreement aimed at ending the political crisis, the Tegucigalpa/San José Accord was signed. Under the terms of the Accord, an interim government of unity and national reconciliation was to be formed by 5 November to oversee the election on 29 November and the transition to a new administration on 27 January 2010. Also, a congressional vote was to be held on the restoration of executive power to those in office prior to 28 June 2009, taking into account an 'opinion' on the matter to be issued by the Supreme Court. A Verification Commission was established to monitor compliance with the commitments contained in the Accord, and a Truth and Reconciliation Commission was to be created. However, amid dissent regarding the timing of the legislative vote on the potential reinstatement of Zelaya (which had not been specified by the Accord), Micheletti announced on 5 November that he was proceeding unilaterally with the appointment of the new interim government owing to the failure of the deposed President to nominate ministers. The US Department of State adopted a different approach from the OAS, meanwhile, stating that the Honduran state institutions should determine how to implement the agreement and confirming that it would recognize the forthcoming elections.

Lobo was victorious in the presidential election held on 29 November 2009, securing 56.6% of the valid votes cast, compared with 38.1% for Santos. In the concurrent legislative elections, Lobo's PN also won a large majority in the Congreso Nacional, taking 71 of the 128 seats, while the PL obtained 45 seats, the Partido Demócrata Cristiano de Honduras (PDCH) five, the Partido de Unificación Democrática (PUD) four and the Partido Innovación y Unidad—Social Demócrata (PINU—SD) three. The PN's strong performance was largely attributed to public disenchantment with the divided PL, the party of both Micheletti and Zelaya. A turn-out of some 50% of registered voters was recorded. The results were recognized by the USA and a number of Latin American countries, including Colombia, Costa Rica and Panama, although the OAS, ALBA, the Mercado Común del Sur (Mercosur) and other members of the international community refused to accept the legitimacy of the vote.

President-elect Lobo's most immediate challenge was to secure international support for his incoming administration, particularly in view of the urgent need for a resumption of foreign aid and lending to Honduras, largely suspended since June 2009. This task was made more difficult on 2 December, when the legislature voted overwhelmingly against the reinstatement of Zelaya (who remained in the Brazilian embassy), pending Lobo's inauguration in January 2010. Lobo subsequently came under significant international pressure to persuade Micheletti to resign as acting President in order to allow the formation of a government of national unity and reconciliation, and to secure a safe passage out of Honduras for Zelaya. However, Micheletti resolutely refused to stand down before Lobo's investiture and insisted that Zelaya would only be permitted to leave Honduras without answering the charges against him if he accepted political asylum in a country outside Central America. In early January the Chairman of the Joint Chiefs of Staff, Gen. Vásquez, and five other senior military officials were charged with abuse of authority in connection with the forced expulsion of Zelaya from Honduras. On 20 January Lobo signed an agreement with President Leonel Fernández Reyna of the Dominican Republic on the safe passage of the deposed President to that country following Lobo's investiture; Zelaya accepted the arrangement.

Recent developments: Lobo in office

Lobo was sworn in as President on 27 January 2010. The new Congreso Nacional approved a decree granting amnesty for any political offences committed by Zelaya and those involved in his removal from power, while the Supreme Court acquitted the six senior military officials charged with abuse of authority. Lobo's Cabinet included the defeated presidential candidates of the PDCH, the PUD and the PINU—SD, although the most senior posts were allocated to members of the PN: notably, Mario Canahauti, a prominent businessman and former ambassador to the USA, was appointed as Minister of Foreign Affairs, and William Chong Wong returned to the position of Minister of Finance, which he had formerly held during Maduro's presidency.

The primary focus of President Lobo's first months in office was the restoration of relations with the international community. To this end, he continued efforts to fulfil the requirements of the Tegucigalpa/San José Accord, appointing a working group in February 2010 to formulate guidelines for the creation of the Truth and Reconciliation Commission. The World Bank and the US Government subsequently announced that they would resume the provision of aid to Honduras. However, a number of human rights groups, including the Inter-American Commission on Human Rights (an organ of the OAS), expressed concern in March over the murder of several journalists and a series of attacks on political activists, particularly members of the Frente Nacional de Resistencia Popular (FNRP), a broad alliance of organizations and movements that had opposed Zelaya's removal from office. Lobo subsequently sought to demonstrate his commitment to protecting human rights by creating a new government post of Minister Adviser on Human Rights. Meanwhile, Zelaya and four former ministers and officials from his administration were charged in February with fraud, falsification of documents and abuse of authority in relation to the alleged misuse of 30m. lempiras from the Honduran social investment fund. The charges against Zelaya complicated Lobo's efforts to gain recognition of his administration from the countries of ALBA and Mercosur, which demanded that the former President be permitted to return to political life in Honduras. (The charge of abuse of authority was later dismissed, in accordance with the recently approved amnesty decree, which did not, however, cover the corruption charges.)

The Truth and Reconciliation Commission commenced work in May 2010. The FNRP, which continued to seek Zelaya's return and to advocate the creation of a constituent assembly to amend the Constitution, questioned the independence of the Commission, claiming that its purpose was to exonerate the coup leaders, and established an alternative truth commission in June. An OAS commission tasked with assessing the political situation in Honduras issued its report in July. It recommended the termination of legal proceedings involving Zelaya and his associates; the application by Zelaya for membership of the Central American Parliament (Parlacen) in order to secure recognition of his status as Lobo's predecessor as constitutional President of Honduras; the adoption of measures to protect journalists, members of the FNRP and judges who had opposed the coup; the cessation of impunity for human rights violations; and the organization of a national dialogue with the participation of all political sectors. In May the Supreme Court had provoked controversy by dismissing four judges who had criticized the removal of Zelaya from office and the Court's role in this.

Meanwhile, in June 2010 a joint committee of the TSE and the Congreso Nacional was established to consider, and consult the public on, a range of proposed political reforms, including a constitutional amendment to ease the conditions for holding a referendum. In October Lobo initiated a national dialogue to discuss the convening of a constituent assembly to reform the Constitution. Despite the formation of such an assembly being one of the principal demands of the FNRP, its leaders rejected the President's invitation to participate in the dialogue on the grounds that they would not engage with a Government that they did not recognize. However, several members of the FNRP did hold discussions with Lobo, who also met representatives of trade unions, civic groups, business associations, churches and political parties. The President of the Congreso, Juan Hernández, subsequently announced the creation of a commission charged with drafting reforms to the article of the Constitution regulating referendums. In February 2011 the Congreso Nacional adopted the proposed constitutional amendments, which not only eased the conditions both for initiating a referendum or plebiscite and for validating the results of such a vote, but also removed a restriction preventing referendums on a provision that forbade the revision of a number of other constitutional articles, including those relating to the length of the presidential term and the ban on presidential re-election. Despite favouring constitutional reform, the FNRP expressed opposition to the amendments, continuing to demand that a constituent assembly be convened. Also approved was the creation of a judicial council, which would assume responsibility for appointing and dismissing judges from the Supreme Court.

Amid mounting concern regarding increasing insecurity in Honduras, in early 2011 Lobo ordered some 2,000 troops to participate in joint patrols with the police force in an effort to combat organized crime, particularly drugs-trafficking. The murder rate had risen to 82 per 100,000 persons in 2010. In November 2011 the Government announced a further joint police-military deployment, and measures were introduced to address endemic police corruption. Nevertheless, the declining security situation led the Government in December to declare a 90-day state of emergency, which, in accordance with a controversial constitutional amendment adopted by the legislature in the previous month, granted the military extensive powers to carry out policing duties. Some observers raised questions about the appropriateness of using soldiers to perform functions usually conducted by trained police officers. Also in December, the Congreso Nacional approved legislation authorizing electronic surveillance, while in the following month the Constitution was modified again to permit the extradition of Hondurans accused of committing offences related to drugs-trafficking, organized crime and terrorism. In spite of these efforts, the murder rate increased to an estimated 86 per 100,000 persons in 2011.

In early May 2011, following pressure from the Government, the Supreme Court revoked the corruption charges against Zelaya, and shortly thereafter Lobo and Zelaya, with Colombian-Venezuelan mediation, concluded a formal reconciliation agreement. As a result, the former President returned to Honduras at the end of the month. This successful process of reconciliation fulfilled a key demand of Lobo's critics in the region, precipitating Honduras' readmission to the OAS in June and the normalization of the country's diplomatic relations. In July the Truth and Reconciliation Commission released its report on the events of 28 June 2009, concluding that Zelaya's letter of resignation had been fabricated and that his deposition had constituted a coup. The Commission therefore adjudged Micheletti's administration to have been illegal, but also criticized Zelaya for having increased institutional tensions prior to the coup by defiantly proceeding with his constitutional referendum. The report recommended that the Constitution be amended to permit presidential impeachment, thus providing the Honduran institutions with a legitimate alternative to military intervention in cases where the head of state is suspected of acting unlawfully. Six senior military officers accused of abuse of authority for their involvement in the 2009 coup were controversially exonerated by the Supreme Court in October 2011. Zelaya denounced this decision, claiming that those responsible for deposing him were being 'protected'.

With support from the FNRP and defectors from the PL, in October 2011 Zelaya established a new political party, the Partido Libertad y Refundación (LIBRE). However, even though the former President had been removed from power before the completion of his full term of office, the Constitution prohibited him from contesting another presidential election. As a result, it was announced in November that Zelaya's wife, Xiomara Castro Zelaya, would stand as LIBRE's candidate in the 2013 election. Also in that month, the Alianza Patriótica Hondureña was founded, with Gen. Vásquez, the former Chairman of the Joint Chiefs of Staff and a central figure in the ouster of Zelaya, as the party's presidential nominee.

With violent crime still prevalent, in September 2011 Lobo replaced Minister of Public Security Oscar Alvarez with Pompeyo Bonilla Reyes. In the same government reorganization, Arturo Corrales Alvarez was appointed Minister of Foreign Affairs. Further cabinet changes were implemented in February 2012: Héctor (Tito) Guillén received the finance portfolio, Marlon Oniel Escoto Valerio became the new Minister of Education, and José Adonis Lavaire was given responsibility for industry and commerce. A fire at Comayagua prison in mid-February killed 359 inmates. Reports that it was several hours before guards released prisoners from their cells in the overcrowded gaol highlighted the poor domestic security situation in the country and prompted calls for prison reform. The director of the prison service, Danilo Orellana, was dismissed following the tragedy.

Foreign Affairs

Regional relations

From the early 1980s former members of the Nicaraguan National Guard (so-called 'Contras') established bases in Honduras, from which they conducted raids across the border between the two countries, allegedly with support from the Honduran armed forces. In return for considerable military assistance from the USA, the Honduran Government permitted US military aid to be supplied to the Contras based in Honduras. Public opposition to US military presence in Honduras increased from 1984, and in December, following revelations that the USA had secretly sold weapons to the Government of Iran and that the proceeds had been used to finance the activities of the Contra rebels, President José Simeón Azcona requested the departure of the Contras from Honduras.

In 1987 Honduras, Costa Rica, El Salvador, Guatemala and Nicaragua signed a Central American peace plan, the 'Esquipulas agreement', the crucial provisions of which included the implementation of simultaneous cease-fires in Nicaragua and El Salvador, a halt to foreign assistance to rebel groups, and the establishment of national reconciliation commissions in each of the Central American nations. The Government agreed to the establishment by the UN and the OAS of an international commission to oversee the voluntary repatriation or removal to a third country of the rebel forces; in return, the Nicaraguan Government agreed to abandon the action that it had initiated against Honduras at the International Court of Justice (ICJ).

In 1995 Honduras and Nicaragua signed an accord providing for the visible demarcation of each country's territorial waters in the Gulf of Fonseca, and the establishment of a joint naval patrol to police the area. However, in 1999 Nicaragua, severed commercial ties with, and imposed import taxes on, Honduras following a dispute over the Caribbean Sea Maritime Limits Treaty, which granted Colombia territorial rights to areas of the Caribbean historically claimed by Nicaragua. In 2000, following OAS mediation, the two countries agreed to establish a maritime exclusion zone in the disputed area. Representatives of Honduras and Nicaragua also signed an accord on joint patrols in the Caribbean, pending a ruling by the ICJ, and on combined operations in the Gulf of Fonseca, as well as the withdrawal of forces from the land border area. Following further talks under OAS auspices, in 2001 the two countries agreed to allow monitors into the disputed area to verify troop deployment. In 2002, however, the situation deteriorated when the Nicaraguan Government announced plans to sell oil-drilling rights in the disputed area. The ICJ brought an end to the dispute in October 2007, ruling on a revised maritime border approximately midway between the two countries.

A long-standing dispute between Honduras and El Salvador, regarding the demarcation of the two countries' common border and rival claims to three islands in the Gulf of Fonseca, caused hostilities to break out between the two countries in 1969. Although armed conflict soon subsided, the Honduran and Salvadorean Governments did not sign a peace treaty until 1980. In 1992 the ICJ awarded Honduras sovereignty over some two-thirds of the disputed mainland territory and over one of the disputed islands in the Gulf of Fonseca. A convention governing the acquired rights and nationality of those people was finally signed by the Presidents of both countries in 1998. In 2006 President Zelaya met his Salvadorean counterpart to ratify the border demarcation.

In 2002 Honduras restored diplomatic relations with Cuba, suspended since 1961. President Zelaya visited Cuba in October 2007, when he met the country's then acting President, Raúl Castro, and in March 2009, when he held talks with both Raúl Castro and former President Fidel Castro.

Relations with other Latin American countries, in particular Venezuela, were strengthened by the admission of Honduras, in December 2007, to the PetroCaribe initiative (whereby Caribbean countries were able to purchase petroleum from Venezuela on preferential terms), and by the country's accession to ALBA (see above) in October 2008. Petroleum supplies to Honduras under the PetroCaribe initiative were suspended in July 2009, however, in response to the removal from office of President Zelaya, which was condemned by regional leaders, most vigorously by Venezuelan President Hugo Chávez. Moreover, ALBA refused to recognize the elections conducted in November, at which Porfirio Lobo Sosa was elected President. In January 2010 the outgoing Congreso Nacional ratified a decree issued by de facto President Micheletti withdrawing Honduras from ALBA. President Lobo swiftly succeeded in gaining recognition for his administration from other Central American countries, with the notable exception of Nicaragua, but many South American countries, including Argentina, Brazil and Venezuela, continued to withhold their support for the restoration of OAS membership rights to Honduras, insisting that Zelaya should be allowed to return to Honduras and participate freely in political activities. Following Venezuelan and Colombian mediation, in May 2011 a reconciliation agreement was signed by Lobo and Zelaya, which precipitated the latter's return to Honduras later that month. This breakthrough led to the re-establishment of diplomatic relations between Honduras and its regional neighbours (excluding Ecuador), and the country was permitted to rejoin the OAS in June. Moreover, it was reported that Lobo met with Venezuelan representatives in December to discuss Honduras' potential readmission to the PetroCaribe programme.

Other external relations

The US Administration of President Barack Obama condemned the removal from power of Zelaya in 2009, demanding his reinstatement and suspending all military co-operation and some development aid in response. In September further US aid to Honduras was cancelled and the visas of Micheletti, several other senior officials in his administration and the members of the Supreme Court were revoked. None the less, the USA opted to recognize the elections held in Honduras in November 2009. In March 2010 the US Secretary of State, Hillary Clinton, announced the resumption of US aid to Honduras and urged Latin American states to restore normal relations with Honduras. In the following month the USA agreed to provide the Honduran police force with US $4.4m. in assistance to combat organized crime and drugs-trafficking, and a new naval base, constructed with US funding and intended to be used for counter-trafficking operations, was inaugurated in the north-eastern department of Gracias a Dios. Nevertheless, in September the USA included Honduras for the first time on its list of major illicit drugs-transit or drugs-producing countries.

CONSTITUTION AND GOVERNMENT

Following the elections of April 1980, the 1965 Constitution was revised. The new Constitution was approved by the legislature in November 1982, and amended in 1995. Under the provisions of the 1982 Constitution, the President is elected by a simple majority of the voters. The President holds executive power and has a single four-year mandate. Legislative power is vested in the Congreso Nacional (National Congress), with 128 members elected by universal adult suffrage for a term of four years. Judicial power is exercised by the Supreme Court, the Courts of Appeal and various lesser tribunals. The country is divided into 18 local departments, which are subdivided into 298 autonomous municipalities.

REGIONAL AND INTERNATIONAL CO-OPERATION

Honduras is a member of the Central American Common Market (see p. 232), of the Organization of American States (OAS, see p. 394), of the Association of Caribbean States (see p. 448), and of the Community of Latin American and Caribbean States (see p. 462), which was formally inaugurated in December 2011. The Dominican Republic-Central American Free Trade Agreement (DR-CAFTA), between the Dominican Republic, the Central American countries of Costa Rica, Honduras, El Salvador, Guatemala and Nicaragua, and the USA, entered force in Honduras in 2006. DR-CAFTA, which aims to foster export-orientated growth in the region, was to entail the gradual elimination of tariffs on most industrial and agricultural products over a period of 10 and 20 years, respectively. In 2010 an association agreement, covering trade, political dialogue and co-operation, was concluded between Costa Rica, El Salvador, Guatemala, Honduras, Nicaragua and Panama and the European Union. Honduras was a founder member of the UN in 1945. As a contracting party to the General Agreement on Tariffs and Trade, Honduras joined the World Trade Organization (see p. 433) on its establishment in 1995. The country is also a member of the Group of 77 (see p. 450) organization of developing states.

ECONOMIC AFFAIRS

In 2010, according to estimates by the World Bank, Honduras' gross national income (GNI), measured at average 2008–10 prices, was US $14,302m., equivalent to $1,880 per head (or $3,740 per head on an international purchasing-power parity basis). During 2001–10, it was estimated, the population increased at an average annual rate of 2.0%, while gross domestic product (GDP) per head increased, in real terms, by an average of 2.1% per year. Overall GDP increased, in real terms, at an average annual rate of 4.2% in 2001–10; real GDP declined by 2.1% in 2009, but increased by 2.8% in 2010, according to central bank estimates.

Agriculture (including hunting, forestry and fishing) contributed an estimated 11.8% of GDP and employed 35.1% of the economically active population in 2010. The principal cash crop is traditionally coffee, which contributed 27.1% of the total value of exports (excluding gold and *maquila* exports) in 2010. Exports of bananas contributed 12.6% of total export earnings in 2010. The main subsistence crops include maize, plantains, beans, rice, sugar cane and citrus fruit. Exports of shellfish make a significant contribution to foreign earnings (lobsters and prawns provided 6.5% of total export earnings in 2010). According to official estimates, agricultural GDP increased at an average annual rate of 3.0% during 2001–10; the sector declined by 1.4% in 2009, but increased by 1.8% in 2010.

Industry (including mining, manufacturing, construction and power) contributed an estimated 25.1% of GDP and employed 20.2% of the economically active population in 2010. According to official estimates, industrial GDP increased at an average annual rate of 3.1% during 2001–10; it declined by 7.9% in 2009, but increased by 2.3% in 2010.

Mining contributed an estimated 0.7% of GDP and employed 0.2% of the economically active population in 2010. In 2008 gold was the major mineral export, contributing an estimated 1.8% of total export earnings. Lead, zinc, silver, copper and low-grade iron ore are also mined. In addition, small quantities of petroleum derivatives are exported. The GDP of the mining sector decreased by an average of 3.9% per year in 2001–10; it declined by an estimated 2.4% in 2010.

Manufacturing contributed an estimated 17.4% of GDP and employed 14.0% of the economically active population in 2010. Value added by the *maquila* sector contributed an estimated 16,502m. lempiras to the economy in 2010. According to official estimates, manufacturing GDP increased at an average annual rate of 3.7% during 2001–10. The sector's GDP ideclined by -8.0% in 2009, but increased by 4.0% in 2010.

Construction contributed an estimated 5.5% of GDP and employed 5.5% of the economically active population in 2010. According to official estimates, the GDP of the construction sector decreased at an average annual rate of 0.6% during 2001–10; it declined by 6.7% in 2010.

Petroleum accounted for 61.9% of electrical energy output in 2008, while the remainder was derived from hydroelectric power. Imports of mineral fuels and lubricants accounted for 21.4% of the value of total imports in 2010. In 2009 the Brazilian firm Odebrecht was awarded a contract to build two hydroelectric dams on sections of the Ulua river in the north-western province of Santa Bárbara. The project, valued at around US $600m., was to be jointly financed by international and regional aid donors, the Brazilian Banco Nacional do Desenvolvimento Econômico e Social and the state-owned electricity company, Empresa Nacional de Energía Eléctrica. The new facilities were projected to become operational in 2014.

The services sector contributed an estimated 63.1% of GDP and engaged 44.7% of the working population in 2010. The GDP of the services sector increased by an average of 6.7% per year in 2001–10, according to official estimates; it increased by 3.3% in 2010.

In 2010 Honduras recorded a visible trade deficit of US $2,807.6m., while there was a deficit of $954.8m. on the current account of the balance of payments. Workers' remittances from abroad constitute an important source of income: according to central bank estimates, remittances totalled some $2,594.1m. in 2010. The majority of remittances came from the USA. The USA was the principal market for exports (34.5%, excluding *maquila* goods) in 2010; other significant purchasers were Germany, El Salvador and Guatemala. In the same year the principal source of imports (42.5%) was the USA; other major suppliers were Guatemala, Mexico and El Salvador. The principal exports (excluding *maquila* goods) in 2010 were coffee (27.1%), bananas, lobsters and prawns and palm oil. The principal imports in that year were mineral fuels and lubricants (21.4%), machinery and electrical equipment, and chemicals and related products.

In 2009 there was an estimated budgetary deficit of 10,864.5m. lempiras (equivalent to 4.0% of GDP). Honduras's general government gross debt was 76.652m. lempiras in 2010, equivalent to 26.3% of GDP. Honduras's external debt totalled US $3,675m. at the end of 2009, of which $2,446m. was public and publicly guaranteed debt. In 2008 the cost of debt-servicing long-term public and publicly guaranteed debt and repayments to the IMF was equivalent to 1.6% of the value of the exports of goods, services and income (excluding workers' remittances). The annual rate of inflation averaged 8.1% in 2001–11. Consumer prices increased by an annual average of 6.8% in 2011. Some 3.9% of the labour force were registered as unemployed in May 2010; it was estimated that around one-quarter of the work-force was underemployed.

In terms of average income, Honduras is among the poorest nations in the Americas. According to official figures, poverty affected 66% of the population in 2011. The Honduran economy contracted in 2009, owing to a sharp decline in consumer spending and investment, exacerbated by political instability. Adverse global conditions, particularly in the USA, resulted in a marked decrease in Honduran exports, as well as lower levels of remittances (which traditionally account for a significant portion of GDP). Substantial amounts of financial assistance to Honduras were also suspended both by bilateral donors, and by multilateral institutions. After taking office in January 2010, President Porfirio Lobo Sosa secured a resumption of credit from multilateral lenders, although many Latin American countries continued to withhold recognition of his administration's legitimacy. IMF-recommended fiscal measures aimed at increasing tax revenue were approved, as was IMF financing of US $202m. in support of the Government's economic programme, which aimed primarily to restore macroeconomic stability and to strengthen public finances. Renewed growth of an estimated 2.8% was recorded in 2010, as the value of exports rose, partly owing to higher prices for coffee and bananas. Remittances increased by 5.3% as a result of improved conditions in the USA. According to IMF estimates, real GDP expanded by a further 3.5% in 2011. The economy benefited from continued high prices for export commodities, while the restoration of diplomatic relations with the country's regional trading partners in mid-2011 was also a positive development. However, inflation, already high owing to rising international petroleum and food prices, continued to rise. The IMF forecast real GDP growth of 3.6% in 2012, although the economy remained vulnerable to instability on global markets. Honduras was reportedly attempting to rejoin the PetroCaribe programme during early 2012; regaining access to cheaper Venezuelan petroleum would alleviate some of the pressure on the current account.

PUBLIC HOLIDAYS

2013: 1 January (New Year's Day), 28–30 March (Easter), 14 April (Pan-American Day/Bastilla's Day), 1 May (Labour Day), 15 September (Independence Day), 3 October (Morazán Day), 12 October (Columbus Day), 21 October (Army Day), 25 December (Christmas).

Statistical Survey

Sources (unless otherwise stated): Department of Economic Studies, Banco Central de Honduras, Avda Juan Ramón Molina, 1a Calle, 7a Avda, Apdo 3165, Tegucigalpa; tel. 2237-2270; fax 2237-1876; e-mail jreyes@bch.hn; internet www.bch.hn; Instituto Nacional de Estadística, Edif. Gómez, Blvd Suyapa, Col. Florencia Sur, Apdo 9412, Tegucigalpa; e-mail info@ine.online.hn.

Area and Population

AREA, POPULATION AND DENSITY

Area (sq km)	112,492*
Population (census results)†	
29 May 1988	4,614,377
1 August 2001	
Males	3,230,958
Females	3,304,386
Total	6,535,344
Population (official estimates at mid-year)	
2008	7,706,907
2009	7,876,662
2010	8,045,990
Density (per sq km) at mid-2010	71.5

* 43,433 sq miles.

† Excluding adjustments for underenumeration, estimated to have been 10% at the 1974 census.

POPULATION BY AGE AND SEX

(UN estimates at mid-2012)

	Males	Females	Total
0–14	1,439,226	1,381,754	2,820,980
15–64	2,354,290	2,388,636	4,742,926
65 and over	162,857	185,272	348,129
Total	3,956,373	3,955,662	7,912,035

Source: UN, *World Population Prospects: The 2010 Revision*.

PRINCIPAL TOWNS

('000 in 2010, official population estimates)

Tegucigalpa—Distrito Central (capital)	1,126.5	Juticalpa	119.5
San Pedro Sula	719.4	Comayagua	118.4
Choloma	276.9	Puerto Cortés	115.2
El Progreso	204.4	Catacamas	112.9
La Ceiba	185.8	Siguatepeque	85.2
Danlí	181.2	Tocoa	81.2
Choluteca	169.1	La Lima	63.2
Villanueva	137.7		

BIRTHS AND DEATHS

(UN estimates)

	1995–2000	2000–05	2005–10
Birth rate (per 1,000)	33.4	30.0	27.7
Death rate (per 1,000)	5.5	5.2	5.0

Source: UN, *World Population Prospects: The 2010 Revision*.

Life expectancy (years at birth, WHO estimates): 69 (males 67; females 73) in 2009 (Source: WHO, *World Health Statistics*).

EMPLOYMENT

('000 persons)

	2008	2009	2010
Agriculture, hunting, forestry and fishing	1,049	1,162	1,205
Mining and quarrying	8	8	8
Manufacturing	425	412	482
Electricity, gas and water	12	12	12
Construction	191	206	190
Trade, restaurants and hotels	643	693	777
Transport, storage and communications	101	105	123
Financing, insurance, real estate and business services	97	95	108
Community, social, personal and other services	428	444	527
Total employed	2,953	3,135	3,432

Health and Welfare

KEY INDICATORS

Total fertility rate (children per woman, 2009)	3.2
Under-5 mortality rate (per 1,000 live births, 2009)	30
HIV/AIDS (% of persons aged 15–49, 2009)	0.8
Physicians (per 1,000 head, 2000)	0.6
Hospital beds (per 1,000 head, 2002)	1.0
Health expenditure (2008): US $ per head (PPP)	248
Health expenditure (2008): % of GDP	6.3
Health expenditure (2008): public (% of total)	58.6
Access to water (% of persons, 2008)	86
Access to sanitation (% of persons, 2008)	71
Total carbon dioxide emissions ('000 metric tons, 2007)	8,826.6
Carbon dioxide emissions per head (metric tons, 2007)	1.2
Human Development Index (2011): ranking	121
Human Development Index (2011): value	0.625

For sources and definitions, see explanatory note on p. vi.

Agriculture

PRINCIPAL CROPS

('000 metric tons)

	2008	2009	2010
Maize	536	587	509
Sorghum	36	37	45
Sugar cane	6,082	6,895	7,819
Beans, dry	67	71	69
Oil palm fruit	1,433	1,579	1,556
Tomatoes	161	142	158
Melons	302	250	283
Bananas	690	719	751
Plantains	68	78	82
Oranges	237	245	266
Pineapples	132	115	125
Coffee, green	190	191	229

Aggregate production ('000 metric tons, may include official, semi-official or estimated data): Total cereals 623.3 in 2008, 670.4 in 2009, 589.3 in 2010; Total vegetables (incl. melons) 734.1 in 2008, 633.2 in 2009, 687.8 in 2010; Total fruits (excl. melons) 1,258.3 in 2008, 1,289.4 in 2009, 1,357.2 in 2010.

Source: FAO.

LIVESTOCK

('000 head, year ending September)

	2008	2009	2010
Cattle	2,545	2,673	2,695
Sheep*	15	15	15
Goats*	25	25	25
Pigs	449	463	470
Horses*	181	181	181
Mules*	70	70	70
Chickens	39,273	38,645	40,000*

* FAO estimate(s).

Source: FAO.

LIVESTOCK PRODUCTS

('000 metric tons)

	2008	2009	2010
Cattle meat	74.4	55.8	58.6
Pig meat	11.6	14.1	9.6
Chicken meat	142.0	145.3	152.5
Cows' milk	796.5	703.9	739.4
Hen eggs	49.6	47.4	44.2

Source: FAO.

Forestry

ROUNDWOOD REMOVALS

('000 cubic metres, excl. bark)

	2008	2009	2010
Sawlogs, veneer logs and logs for sleepers	662	483	483
Fuel wood*	8,617	8,595	8,575
Total	9,279	9,078	9,058

* FAO estimates.

Source: FAO.

SAWNWOOD PRODUCTION

('000 cubic metres, incl. railway sleepers)

	2007	2008	2009
Coniferous (softwood)	370	342	267
Broadleaved (hardwood)	9	7	10
Total	379	349	277

2010: Production assumed to be unchanged from 2009 (FAO estimates).

Source: FAO.

Fishing

('000 metric tons, live weight)

	2007	2008	2009
Capture*	14.8	12.9	11.3
Marine fishes	3.7	2.3	2.0
Caribbean spiny lobster	2.8	3.0	2.1
Penaeus shrimps	1.2	1.7	1.4
Stromboid conchs	0.4	—	1.6
Aquaculture	54.7	47.1	28.9
Nile tilapia	28.4	20.5	14.2
Penaeus shrimps	26.3	26.6	14.6
Total catch*	69.5	60.0	40.2

* FAO estimates.

Source: FAO.

Mining

(metal content)

	2008	2009	2010*
Lead (metric tons)	12,545	14,471	16,900
Zinc (metric tons)	28,462	36,370	36,370
Silver (kilograms)	59,934	57,697	48,614
Gold (kilograms)	2,965	2,590	4,900

* Estimates.

Source: US Geological Survey.

Industry

SELECTED PRODUCTS

	2008	2009	2010
Raw sugar ('000 quintales)	8,340	8,531	9,336
Cement ('000 bags of 42.5 kg)	41,966	38,335	35,779
Cigarettes ('000 packets of 20)	307,170	308,942	268,665
Beer ('000 12 oz bottles)	294,958	253,413	236,196
Soft drinks ('000 12 oz bottles)	1,604,007	1,867,888	1,991,811
Wheat flour ('000 quintales)	3,017	3,239	3,274
Fabric ('000 yards)	204,853	171,054	208,468
Liquor and spirits ('000 litres)	13,883	14,267	14,794
Vegetable oil and butter ('000 libras)	213,359	199,057	193,493
Electric energy (million kWh)	6,605	6,581	6,729

Finance

CURRENCY AND EXCHANGE RATES

Monetary Units

100 centavos = 1 lempira.

Sterling, Dollar and Euro Equivalents (30 December 2011)

£1 sterling = 29.214 lempiras;
US $1 = 18.895 lempiras;
€1 = 24.448 lempiras;
1,000 lempiras = £34.23 = $52.92 = €40.90.

Average Exchange Rate (lempiras per US $)

2009 18.8951
2010 18.8951
2011 18.8951

GOVERNMENT FINANCE

(general government transactions, non-cash basis, million lempiras, preliminary)

Summary of Balances

	2007	2008	2009
Revenue	56,048.6	68,092.3	64,621.8
Less Expense	50,279.9	57,476.9	65,855.5
Gross operating balance	5,768.7	10,615.5	−1,233.7
Less Net acquisition of non-financial assets	8,483.9	11,315.0	12,176.1
Net lending/borrowing	−2,715.2	−699.5	−13,409.8

Revenue

	2007	2008	2009
Taxes	38,867.5	44,007.6	40,919.4
Taxes of income, profits and capital gains	11,845.6	13,163.5	12,502.8
Taxes of goods and services	23,067.8	25,646.7	24,076.3
Social contributions	6,036.6	7,307.6	8,122.1
Grants	3,718.8	5,520.1	5,096.6
Other revenue	7,425.7	11,257.0	10,483.7
Total	56,048.6	68,092.3	64,621.8

Expense by economic type*

	2007	2008	2009
Compensation of employees	25,994.3	30,735.4	37,197.4
Wages and salaries	23,914.4	28,300.5	36,243.6
Social contributions	2,079.9	2,434.9	953.8
Use of goods and services	9,048.3	10,016.4	12,900.8
Interest	1,458.5	1,630.6	1,780.4
Subsidies	3,037.4	857.4	363.3
Grants	256.9	245.6	209.8
Social benefits	262.5	252.7	387.0
Other expense	10,222.1	13,738.8	13,016.9
Total	50,279.9	57,476.9	65,855.5

* Including purchases of non-financial assets.

Source: IMF, *Government Finance Statistics Yearbook*.

CENTRAL BANK RESERVES

(US $ million at 31 December)

	2008	2009	2010
Gold (national valuation)	19.11	24.04	31.15
IMF special drawing rights	0.09	164.26	159.60
Foreign exchange	2,460.00	1,908.70	2,497.90
Reserve position in IMF	13.29	13.52	13.29
Total	2,492.49	2,110.52	2,701.94

Source: IMF, *International Financial Statistics*.

MONEY SUPPLY

(million lempiras at 31 December)

	2008	2009	2010
Currency outside depository corporations	11,857	12,971	14,686
Transferable deposits	24,032	24,476	28,422
Other deposits	100,328	100,912	108,322
Securities other than shares	2,876	1,514	2,135
Broad money	139,093	139,873	153,565

Source: IMF, *International Financial Statistics*.

COST OF LIVING

(Consumer Price Index, base: 1999 = 100)

	2007	2008	2009
Food and non-alcoholic beverages	164.8	193.1	200.0
Alcohol and tobacco	200.5	214.0	228.7
Rent, water, fuel and power	198.8	217.1	232.0
Clothing and footwear	172.4	181.9	192.8
Health	207.6	220.1	236.7
Transport	202.0	226.6	222.7
Communications	78.2	74.0	72.8
Culture and recreation	147.6	154.1	160.0
Education	267.6	285.6	306.4
Restaurants and hotels	179.4	201.0	222.0
All items (incl. others)	179.0	199.4	210.3

2010: All items 220.2.

2011: All items 235.1.

NATIONAL ACCOUNTS

(million lempiras at current prices)

Expenditure on the Gross Domestic Product

	2008	2009*	2010†
Government final consumption expenditure	44,912	49,498	52,903
Private final consumption expenditure	209,717	215,897	231,634
Changes in inventories	6,286	−7,202	−1,332
Gross fixed capital formation	88,357	60,359	68,131
Total domestic expenditure	349,272	318,552	351,336
Exports of goods and services	134,686	109,178	127,661
Less Imports of goods and services	221,542	159,879	188,006
GDP in purchasers' values	262,417	267,851	290,991
GDP at constant 2000 prices	157,919	154,555	158,841

Gross Domestic Product by Economic Activity

	2008	2009*	2010†
Agriculture, hunting, forestry and fishing	31,884	29,458	33,739
Mining and quarrying	2,036	1,978	2,132
Manufacturing	46,724	45,135	49,650
Electricity, gas and water	2,904	3,376	3,950
Construction	16,432	15,927	15,809
Wholesale and retail trade	37,917	36,061	38,970
Hotels and restaurants	7,637	8,429	9,088
Transport and storage	9,067	8,887	9,686
Communications	8,931	10,127	10,844
Finance and insurance	16,801	17,245	18,095
Owner-occupied dwellings	13,818	15,145	16,231
Business activities	11,857	12,836	13,795
Education services	18,928	21,558	23,283
Health	8,256	9,832	10,935
Public administration and defence	16,365	18,844	20,579
Other services	6,930	7,950	8,509
Sub-total	256,487	262,788	285,295
Less Financial intermediation services indirectly measured	13,292	14,737	15,769
GDP at factor cost	243,193	248,049	269,526
Indirect taxes, *less* subsidies	19,223	19,802	21,465
GDP in purchasers' values	262,417	267,851	290,991

* Preliminary.

† Estimates.

BALANCE OF PAYMENTS
(US $ million)

	2008	2009	2010
Exports of goods f.o.b.	6,347.0	4,824.6	5,741.9
Imports of goods f.o.b.	−10,323.2	−7,299.2	−8,549.5
Trade balance	−3,976.2	−2,474.5	−2,807.6
Exports of services	885.4	953.4	1,021.6
Imports of services	−1,213.1	−1,103.4	−1,331.3
Balance on goods and services	−4,303.9	−2,624.4	−3,117.4
Other income received	148.1	73.9	54.6
Other income paid	−605.3	−603.9	−625.5
Balance on goods, services and income	−4,761.1	−3,154.5	−3,715.3
Current transfers received	3,049.5	2,697.0	2,818.0
Current transfers paid	−69.9	−57.9	−57.5
Current balance	−1,781.6	−515.5	−954.8
Capital account (net)	89.8	130.4	84.4
Direct investment abroad	1.0	−0.7	1.4
Direct investment from abroad	929.3	523.2	797.4
Portfolio investment assets	−26.8	6.0	−15.0
Portfolio investment liabilities	—	50.0	—
Other investment assets	17.6	77.6	88.3
Other investment liabilities	434.6	−176.9	375.7
Net errors and omissions	205.1	−510.5	192.2
Overall balance	−130.9	−416.4	569.5

Source: IMF, *International Financial Statistics*.

External Trade

PRINCIPAL COMMODITIES
(US $ million)

Imports c.i.f.*	2008	2009	2010
Vegetables and fruit	385.6	271.9	309.2
Mineral fuels and lubricants	1,999.3	1,141.4	1,525.1
Chemicals and related products	1,117.3	915.5	1,055.5
Plastic and manufactures	451.8	338.7	442.8
Paper, paperboard and manufactures	377.5	307.4	369.4
Textile yarn, fabrics and manufactures	198.3	162.3	196.5
Metal and manufactures	706.4	373.7	423.5
Food products	722.4	650.4	713.5
Machinery and electrical appliances	1,562.3	992.0	1,074.0
Transport equipment	612.5	395.7	408.3
Total (incl. others)	8,813.5	6,069.8	7,133.5

* Excluding imports destined for the *maquila* sector (US $ million): 2,293.1 in 2008; 1,659.9 in 2009; 1,951.0 in 2010.

Exports f.o.b.*	2008	2009	2010
Bananas	383.8	327.2	335.4
Cigars and cigarettes	96.2	66.9	73.6
Coffee	617.9	531.5	722.6
Lead and zinc	47.1	43.6	71.5
Melons and watermelons	44.5	42.3	42.9
Palm oil	216.7	125.4	140.5
Lobsters and prawns	145.1	134.3	172.9
Soaps and detergents	52.3	48.4	59.6
Tilapia	63.0	55.8	56.8
Wood	36.3	19.9	19.9
Total (incl. others)	2,783.4	2,238.2	2,664.8

* Excluding exports of gold, and of *maquila* goods (US $ million): 3,350.2 in 2008; 2,506.8 in 2009; 2,979.1 in 2010.

PRINCIPAL TRADING PARTNERS
(US $ million, excluding *maquila* goods)

Imports c.i.f.	2008	2009	2010
Brazil	133.4	104.5	77.6
Colombia	93.2	167.4	160.1
Costa Rica	349.2	281.2	336.5
El Salvador	482.2	380.8	401.9
Germany	142.1	72.6	65.3
Guatemala	763.9	643.7	768.9
Japan	150.0	101.6	94.4
Mexico	482.7	416.5	415.1
Nicaragua	122.8	111.0	86.1
Spain	92.9	62.6	47.2
USA	3,538.6	2,040.9	3,030.4
Venezuela	145.3	132.4	5.5
Total (incl. others)	8,813.5	6,069.8	7,133.5

Exports f.o.b.*	2008	2009	2010
Belgium	158.4	99.6	128.7
Canada	53.7	43.3	56.3
Costa Rica	70.5	56.5	80.9
El Salvador	254.1	197.5	213.2
France	24.4	30.5	52.5
Germany	151.2	160.4	223.3
Guatemala	210.7	165.4	193.9
Italy	21.4	34.4	52.3
Japan	26.5	19.3	24.2
Mexico	181.0	51.1	88.0
Netherlands	35.2	25.1	46.3
Nicaragua	137.4	105.3	118.9
Spain	38.5	53.2	52.0
United Kingdom	51.5	71.0	48.2
USA	1,057.4	872.0	920.2
Total (incl. others)	2,783.4	2,238.2	2,664.8

* Excluding exports of gold.

Transport

ROAD TRAFFIC
(licensed vehicles in use)

	2001	2002	2003
Passenger cars	345,931	369,303	386,468
Buses and coaches	20,380	21,814	22,514
Lorries and vans	81,192	86,893	91,230
Motorcycles and bicycles	36,828	39,245	41,852

2008 (vehicles in use): Passenger cars 213,643; Buses and coaches 51,233; Vans and lorries 427,503; Motorcycles and mopeds 122,397 (Source: IRF, *World Road Statistics*).

SHIPPING

Merchant Fleet
(registered at 31 December)

	2007	2008	2009
Number of vessels	1,052	1,041	997
Total displacement ('000 grt)	712.4	704.5	643.1

Source: IHS Fairplay, *World Fleet Statistics*.

International Sea-borne Freight Traffic
('000 metric tons)

	1988	1989	1990
Goods loaded	1,328	1,333	1,316
Goods unloaded	1,151	1,222	1,002

Source: UN, *Monthly Bulletin of Statistics*.

CIVIL AVIATION
(traffic on scheduled services)

	1993	1994	1995
Kilometres flown (million)	4	5	5
Passengers carried ('000)	409	449	474
Passenger-km (million)	362	323	341
Total ton-km (million)	50	42	33

Source: UN, *Statistical Yearbook*.

Tourism

TOURIST ARRIVALS BY COUNTRY OF ORIGIN

	2007	2008	2009
Canada	18,184	19,812	20,140
Costa Rica	25,031	25,415	22,317
El Salvador	165,901	167,590	148,225
Guatemala	126,645	128,559	113,639
Italy	8,462	17,629	19,253
Mexico	23,412	24,505	24,771
Nicaragua	119,569	120,018	108,962
Panama	9,071	9,223	8,109
Spain	6,260	13,053	14,297
USA	276,547	293,708	297,468
Total (incl. others)	831,433	899,319	869,805

Receipts from tourism (US $ million, excl. passenger transport): 619 in 2008; 611 in 2009; 650 in 2010.

Source: World Tourism Organization.

Communications Media

	2008	2009	2010
Telephones ('000 main lines in use)	825.8	716.3	669.5
Mobile cellular telephones ('000 subscribers)	6,210.7	8,390.8	9,505.1
Internet subscribers ('000)	58.9	72.4	n.a.
Broadband subscribers ('000)	n.a.	n.a.	76.0

Radio receivers ('000 in use): 2,450 in 1997 (Source: UN, *Statistical Yearbook*).

Television receivers ('000 in use): 640 in 2001 (Source: UN, *Statistical Yearbook*).

Daily newspapers: 4 in 2002; 4 in 2003.

Weekly newspapers: 3 in 2002; 3 in 2003.

Personal computers: 181,875 (24.9 per 1,000 persons) in 2008 (Source: International Telecommunication Union).

Education

(2006/07 unless otherwise indicated)

	Institutions	Teachers	Students
Pre-primary	8,178	8,925	216,438
Primary (grades 1 to 6)	11,277	45,685	1,272,499
Secondary (grades 7 to 9)			304,959
High school	938	24,048	163,767
Higher (incl. university)*	16	6,457	145,171

* Figures for 2005/06.

Pupil-teacher ratio (primary education, UNESCO estimate): 33.9 in 2008/09 (Source: UNESCO Institute for Statistics).

Adult literacy rate (UNESCO estimates): 83.6% (males 83.7%; females 83.5%) in 2007 (Source: UNESCO Institute for Statistics).

Directory

The Government

HEAD OF STATE

President: Porfirio Lobo Sosa (took office 27 January 2010).

First Vice-President: María Antonieta Guillén de Bográn.

Second Vice-President: Samuel Armando Reyes Rendón.

Third Vice-President: Víctor Hugo Barnica Alvarado.

CABINET
(May 2012)

A coalition of the Partido Nacional, the Partido Liberal, the Partido de Unificación Democrática and the Partido Demócrata Cristiano de Honduras.

Minister of the Interior and Justice: Africo Madrid.

Minister of the Presidency: María Antonieta Guillén de Bográn.

Minister of Foreign Affairs: Arturo Corrales Alvarez.

Minister of Industry and Commerce: José Adonis Lavaire.

Minister of Finance: Héctor (Tito) Guillén.

Minister of Labour and Social Welfare: Felícito Avila.

Minister of Health: Arturo Bendaña.

Minister of Public Security: Pompeyo Bonilla Reyes.

Minister of Public Works, Transport and Housing: Miguel Pastor.

Minister of Education: Marlon Escoto.

Minister of Culture, Art and Sports: Tulio Mariano González.

Minister of Agriculture and Livestock: Jacobo Regalado Weizemblut.

Minister of the National Agrarian Institute: César Ham.

Minister of National Defence: Marlon Pascua Cerrato.

Minister of Natural Resources and the Environment: Rigoberto Cuéllar.

Minister of Tourism: Nelly Jerez.

Minister of the Technical Secretariat for Planning and External Co-operation: Julio Raudales.

Minister of Communications and Strategy: Miguel Angel Bonilla.

Minister of Social Development: Hilda Hernández.

Minister of the National Institute for Women's Affairs: María Antonieta Botto.

MINISTRIES

Office of the President: Palacio José Cecilio del Valle, Blvd Juan Pablo II, Tegucigalpa; tel. 2232-6282; fax 2231-0097; internet www.presidencia.gob.hn.

Ministry of Agriculture and Livestock: Blvd Miraflores, Avda La FAO, Tegucigalpa; tel. 2232-4105; fax 2231-0051; e-mail infoagro@sag.gob.hn; internet www.sag.gob.hn.

Ministry of Communications and Strategy: Tegucigalpa.

Ministry of Culture, Art and Sports: Col. Palmira, Edif. Castillo y Poujol, Tegucigalpa; tel. 2235-4700; fax 2235-6717; e-mail binah@sdnhon.org.hn.

Ministry of Education: 1a Avda, entre 2a y 3a Calle, Comayagüela, Tegucigalpa; tel. 2238-4325; fax 2222-8571; e-mail webmaster@se.gob.hn; internet www.se.gob.hn.

Ministry of Finance: Edif. SEFIN, Avda Cervantes, Barrio El Jazmín, Tegucigalpa; tel. 2222-0111; fax 2238-2309; e-mail sgeneral@sefin.gob.hn; internet www.sefin.gob.hn.

Ministry of Foreign Affairs: Centro Cívico Gubernamental, Antigua Casa Presidencial, Blvd Kuwait, Contiguo a la Corte Suprema de Justicia, Tegucigalpa; tel. 2234-1962; fax 2234-1484; e-mail consultas.sre@gmail.com; internet www.sre.hn.

Ministry of Health: 2a Calle, Avda Cervantes, Tegucigalpa; tel. 2222-8518; fax 2238-6787; e-mail info@secretariadesaludhn.com; internet www.salud.gob.hn.

Ministry of Industry and Commerce: Edif. San José, Col. Humuya, Blvd José Cecilio del Valle, Tegucigalpa; tel. 2235-3699; fax 2235-3686; e-mail info@sic.gob.hn; internet www.sic.gob.hn.

Ministry of the Interior and Justice: Residencia La Hacienda, Calle La Estancia, Tegucigalpa; tel. 2232-1373; fax 2232-0226; e-mail atencionalpublico@gobernacion.gob.hn; internet www.gobernacion.gob.hn.

Ministry of Labour and Social Welfare: Blvd Hacienda, frente a Auto Excel, Tegucigalpa; tel. 2232-3918; fax 2235-3456; e-mail info@trabajo.gob.hn; internet www.trabajo.gob.hn.

Ministry of National Defence: Barrio Concepción, Paseo El Obelisco, Comayagüela, Tegucigalpa; tel. 2238-2890; fax 2238-0238; internet www.ffaah.mil.hn.

Ministry of Natural Resources and the Environment: 100 m al sur del Estadio Nacional, Apdo 1389, Tegucigalpa; tel. 2232-1386; fax 2232-6250; e-mail sdespacho@yahoo.com; internet www.serna.gob.hn.

Ministry of Public Security: Cuartel General de Casamata, subida al Picacho, Tegucigalpa; tel. 2220-4298; fax 2220-1711; e-mail info@seguridad.gob.hn; internet www.seguridad.gob.hn.

Ministry of Public Works, Transport and Housing: Barrio La Bolsa, Comayagüela, Tegucigalpa; tel. 2225-2690; fax 2225-5003; e-mail info@soptravi.gob.hn; internet www.soptravi.gob.hn.

Ministry of Social Development: Edif. Ejecutivo, frente Casa Presidencial, Blvd Juan Pablo II, Tegucigalpa; e-mail transparencia@desarrollosocial.gob.hn; internet desarrollosocial.gob.hn.

Ministry of Tourism: Edif. Europa, Col. San Carlos, Apdo 3261, Tegucigalpa; tel. and fax 2222-2124; e-mail tourisminfo@iht.hn; internet www.iht.hn.

National Agrarian Institute: see Instituto Nacional Agrario, Trade and Industry.

National Institute for Women's Affairs: Tegucigalpa; tel. 2221-3637; fax 2221-4827; e-mail dtecnica@inam.gob.hn; internet www.inam.gob.hn.

Technical Secretariat for Planning and External Co-operation: Edif. El Sol, Col. Puerta del Sol, Blvd San Juan Bosco, Apdo 1327, Tegucigalpa; tel. 2239-5545; fax 2239-5277; e-mail a_corrales@seplan.gob.hn; internet www.seplan.gob.hn.

President and Legislature

PRESIDENT

Election, 29 November 2009

Candidate	Valid votes cast	% of valid votes
Porfirio Lobo Sosa (PN)	1,213,695	56.56
Elvin Santos (PL)	817,524	38.09
Bernard Martínez (PINU—SD)	39,960	1.86
Felícito Avila (PDCH)	38,413	1.79
César Ham (PUD)	36,420	1.70
Total	2,146,012	100.00

In addition, there were 61,440 blank votes and 92,604 invalid votes

CONGRESO NACIONAL

President: JUAN ORLANDO HERNÁNDEZ ALVARADO.

General Election, 29 November 2009

	Seats
Partido Nacional (PN)	71
Partido Liberal (PL)	45
Partido Demócrata Cristiano de Honduras (PDCH)	5
Partido de Unificación Democrática (PUD)	4
Partido Innovación y Unidad—Social Demócrata (PINU—SD)	3
Total	128

Election Commission

Tribunal Supremo Electoral (TSE): Col. El Prado, frente a Edif. Syre, Tegucigalpa; tel. 2239-1058; fax 2239-3060; e-mail centroinformacion@tse.hn; internet www.tse.hn; f. 2004 as successor to Tribunal Nacional de Elecciones; Pres. JOSÉ SAÚL ESCOBAR.

Political Organizations

Alianza Patriótica Hondureña (La Alianza): Tegucigalpa; tel. 2213-8091; fax 2213-2367; e-mail contacto@laalianza.hn; internet www.laalianza.hn; f. 2011; right-wing; Pres. Gen. (retd) ROMEO VÁSQUEZ VELÁSQUEZ.

Partido Anticorrupción (PAC): Tegucigalpa; e-mail honduras@salvadornasralla.com; f. 2012; Pres. SALVADOR NASRALLA.

Partido Demócrata Cristiano de Honduras (PDCH): Col. San Carlos, Tegucigalpa; tel. 2236-5969; fax 2236-9941; e-mail pdch@hondutel.hn; internet www.pdch.hn; legally recognized in 1980; Pres. FELICITO AVILA ORDÓÑEZ; Sec.-Gen. MARCO ANTONIO REYES.

Partido Innovación y Unidad—Social Demócrata (PINU—SD): 2a Avda, entre 9 y 10 calles, Apdo 105, Comayagüela, Tegucigalpa; tel. 2220-4224; fax 2220-4232; e-mail pinusd@amnettgu.com; internet pinusd.hn; f. 1970; legally recognized in 1978; Pres. JORGE RAFAEL AGUILAR PAREDES; Sec. IRIS ELIZABETH VIGIL.

Partido Liberal (PL): Col. Miramontes, atrás de Supermercado la Col. No 1, Tegucigalpa; tel. 2232-0822; e-mail info@partidoliberaldehonduras.hn; f. 1891; factions within the party include the Movimiento Pinedista (Leader Dr RAFAEL PINEDA PONCE), the Movimiento LIBRE (Leader JAIME ROSENTHAL OLIVA) and the Movimiento Esperanza Liberal (Leader JOSÉ MANUEL (MEL) ZELAYA ROSALES); has a youth organization called the Frente Central de Juventud Liberal de Honduras (Pres. EDUARDO RAINA GARCÍA); Pres. ELVIN SANTOS.

Partido Libertad y Refundación (LIBRE): Tegucigalpa; internet libertadyrefundacion.tumblr.com; f. 2011; presidential candidate for 2013 elections Xiomara Castro de Zelaya; Pres. JOSÉ MANUEL ZELAYA ROSALES.

Partido Nacional (PN): Paseo el Obelisco, Comayagüela, Tegucigalpa; tel. 2237-7310; fax 2237-7365; e-mail partidonacional@partidonacional.net; internet www.partidonacional.hn; f. 1902; traditional right-wing party; Pres. RICARDO ANTONIO ALVAREZ ARIAS; Sec.-Gen. JUAN ORLANDO HERNÁNDEZ.

Partido de Unificación Democrática (PUD): Barrio La Plazuela, Avda Cervantes, Tegucigalpa; tel. and fax 2238-2498; e-mail colectivoparlud@hotmail.com; f. 1993; left-wing coalition comprising Partido Revolucionario Hondureño, Partido Renovación Patriótica, Partido para la Transformación de Honduras and Partido Morazanista; Leaders CÉSAR HAM, MARVIN PONCE.

Diplomatic Representation

EMBASSIES IN HONDURAS

Argentina: Calle Palermo 302, Col. Rubén Darío, Apdo 3208, Tegucigalpa; tel. 2232-3376; fax 2231-0376; e-mail ehond@mrecic.gov.ar; Ambassador GUILLERMO ROBERTO ROSSI.

Belize: Area Comercial del Hotel Honduras Maya, Col. Palmira, Tegucigalpa; tel. 2238-4614; fax 2238-4617; e-mail vesahonduras@gmail.com; Chargé d'affaires a.i. RICHARD CLARK VINELLI REISMAN.

Brazil: Col. Palmira, Calle República del Brasil, Apdo 341, Tegucigalpa; tel. 2221-4432; fax 2236-5873; e-mail brastegu@sigmanet.hn; internet tegucigalpa.itamaraty.gov.br; Ambassador ZENIK KRAWCTSCHUK.

Chile: Calle Oslo C-4242, Col. Lomas del Guijarro, Tegucigalpa; tel. 2232-4106; fax 2232-2114; e-mail embachilehonduras@clarotv.com.hn; internet chileabroad.gov.cl/honduras; Ambassador RODRIGO PÉREZ MANRÍQUEZ.

Colombia: Edif. Palmira, 3°, Col. Palmira, Apdo 468, Tegucigalpa; tel. 2239-9709; fax 2232-9324; e-mail ehonduras@cancilleria.gov.co; internet www.embajadaenhonduras.gov.co; Ambassador FRANCISCO CANOSSA GUERRERO.

Costa Rica: Residencial El Triángulo, Calle 3451, Lomas del Guijarro, Apdo 512, Tegucigalpa; tel. 2232-1768; fax 2232-1054; e-mail embacori@amnettgu.com; internet www.embajadadecostaricaenhonduras.com; Chargé d'affaires a.i. MARÍA DE LOS ANGELES GUTIÉRREZ VARGAS.

Cuba: Col. Loma Linda Norte, Calle Diangonal Huri 2255, contiguo a Residencial Torres Blancas, Tegucigalpa; tel. 2239-3778; fax 2235-7624; e-mail secretaria@hn.embacuba.cu; internet www

.cubadiplomatica.cu/honduras; Chargé d'affaires a.i. JUAN CARLOS-SERGIO OLIVA GUERRA.

Dominican Republic: Plaza Miramontes, 2°, Local No 6, Col. Miramontes, Tegucigalpa; tel. 2239-0130; fax 2239-1594; e-mail joacosta@serex.gov.do; Chargé d'affaires a.i. JOSÉ MARTÍNEZ MANZUETA.

Ecuador: Bloque F, Casa 2968, Sendero Senecio, Col. Lomas del Castaños Sur, Apdo 358, Tegucigalpa; tel. 2221-4906; fax 2221-1049; e-mail mecuahon@multivisionhn.net; Chargé d'affaires a.i. CRISTINA GRANDA MENDOZA.

El Salvador: Col. Altos de Miramontes, Casa 2952, Diagonal Aguan, Tegucigalpa; tel. 2232-4947; fax 2239-6556; e-mail embasalhonduras@rree.gob.sv; internet embajadahonduras.rree.gob.sv; Ambassador CARLOS POZO.

France: Col. Palmira, Avda Juan Lindo, Callejón Batres 337, Apdo 3441, Tegucigalpa; tel. 2236-6800; fax 2236-8051; e-mail info@ambafrance-hn.org; internet www.ambafrance-hn.org; Ambassador PHILIPPE ARDANAZ.

Germany: Avda República Dominicana 925, Callejón Siria, Col. Lomas del Guijarro, Apdo 3145, Tegucigalpa; tel. 2232-3161; fax 2239-9018; e-mail info@tegucigalpa.diplo.de; internet www.tegucigalpa.diplo.de; Ambassador KARL-HEINZ RODE.

Guatemala: Calle Arturo López Rodezno 2421, Col. Las Minitas, Tegucigalpa; tel. 2232-5018; fax 2232-1580; e-mail embhondurasgt@gmail.com; Ambassador STEPHANIE HOCHSTETTER SKINNER-KLÉE.

Holy See: Palacio de la Nunciatura Apostólica, Col. Palmira, Avda Santa Sede 412, Apdo 324, Tegucigalpa; tel. 2232-6613; fax 2239-8869; e-mail nunciature@amnettgu.com; Apostolic Nuncio Most Rev. LUIGI BIANCO (Titular Archbishop of Falerone).

Italy: Edif. Plaza Azul, 4°, Col. Lomas del Guijarro Sur, Apdo U-9093, Tegucigalpa; tel. 2239-5790; fax 2239-5737; e-mail ambasciata.tegucigalpa@esteri.it; internet www.ambtegucigalpa.esteri.it; Ambassador GIOVANNI ADORNI BRACCESI CHIASSI.

Japan: Col. San Carlos, Calzada Rep. Paraguay, Apdo 3232, Tegucigalpa; tel. 2236-5511; fax 2236-6100; e-mail keikyo1@multivisionhn.net; internet www.hn.emb-japan.go.jp; Ambassador SHISEI KAKU.

Korea, Republic: Edif. Plaza Azul, 5°, Col. Lomas del Guijarro Sur, Tegucigalpa; tel. 2235-5561; fax 2235-5564; e-mail coreaembajada@mofat.go.kr; internet hnd.mofat.go.kr; Ambassador WON CHONG-ON.

Mexico: Col. Lomas del Guijarro, Avda Eucalipto 1001, Tegucigalpa; tel. 2232-4039; fax 2232-4719; e-mail embamexhonduras@gmail.com; internet www.sre.gob.mx/honduras; Ambassador VÍCTOR HUGO MORALES.

Nicaragua: Col. Tepeyac, Bloque M-1, Avda Choluteca 1130, Apdo 392, Tegucigalpa; tel. 2231-1966; fax 2231-1412; e-mail embanic@amnettgu.com; Ambassador MARIO JOSÉ DUARTE ZAMORA.

Panama: Edif. Palmira, 2°, Col. Palmira, Apdo 397, Tegucigalpa; tel. 2239-5508; fax 2232-8147; e-mail ephon@multivisionhn.net; Ambassador MARIO RUÍZ DOLANDE.

Peru: Col. Linda Vista, Calle Principal 3301, Tegucigalpa; tel. 2236-7994; fax 2221-4596; e-mail embajadadelperu@cablecolor.hn; Ambassador HELÍ PELÁEZ CASTRO.

Spain: Col. Matamoros, Calle Santander 801, Apdo 3221, Tegucigalpa; tel. 2236-6875; fax 2236-8682; e-mail emb.tegucigalpa@maec.es; internet www.maec.es/Embajadas/Tegucigalpa; Ambassador LUIS BELZUZ DE LOS RÍOS.

Taiwan (Republic of China): Col. Lomas del Guijarro, Calle Eucaliptos 3750, Apdo 3433, Tegucigalpa; tel. 2239-5837; fax 2232-0532; e-mail hnd@mofa.gov.tw; internet www.taiwanembassy.org/hn; Ambassador JOSEPH Y. L. KUO.

USA: Avda La Paz, Apdo 3453, Tegucigalpa; tel. 2236-9320; fax 2236-9037; internet honduras.usembassy.gov; Ambassador LISA KUBISKE.

Venezuela: Col. Rubén Darío, 2116 Circuito Choluteca, Apdo 775, Tegucigalpa; tel. 2232-1879; fax 2232-1016; e-mail info@venezuelalabolivariana.com; internet venezuelalabolivariana.com; Chargé d'affaires a.i. ARIEL NICOLAS VARGAS ARDENCO.

Judicial System

Justice is administered by the Supreme Court (which has 15 judges), five Courts of Appeal and departmental courts (which have their own local jurisdiction).

Tegucigalpa has two Courts of Appeal, the first of which has jurisdiction in the department of Francisco Morazán, and the second of which has jurisdiction in the departments of Choluteca Valle, El Paraíso and Olancho.

The Appeal Court of San Pedro Sula has jurisdiction in the department of Cortés; that of Comayagua has jurisdiction in the departments of Comayagua, La Paz and Intibucá; and that of Santa Bárbara in the departments of Santa Bárbara, Lempira and Copán.

Supreme Court: Edif. Palacio de Justicia, contiguo Col. Miraflores, Centro Cívico Gubernamental, Tegucigalpa; tel. 2233-9208; fax 2233-6784; internet www.poderjudicial.gob.hn; Pres. JORGE RIVERA AVILÉS.

Attorney-General: ETHEL S. DERAS.

Religion

The majority of the population are Roman Catholics; the Constitution guarantees toleration to all forms of religious belief.

CHRISTIANITY

The Roman Catholic Church

Honduras comprises one archdiocese and seven dioceses. Some 82% of the population are Roman Catholics.

Bishops' Conference

Conferencia Episcopal de Honduras, Blvd Estadio Suyapa, Apdo 3121, Tegucigalpa; tel. 2229-1111; fax 2229-1144; e-mail ceh@unicah.edu.

f. 1929; Pres. Cardinal OSCAR ANDRÉS RODRÍGUEZ MARADIAGA (Archbishop of Tegucigalpa).

Archbishop of Tegucigalpa: Cardinal OSCAR ANDRÉS RODRÍGUEZ MARADIAGA, Arzobispado, 3a y 2a Avda 1113, Apdo 106, Tegucigalpa; tel. 2237-0353; fax 2222-2337; e-mail orodriguez@unicah.edu.

The Anglican Communion

Honduras comprises a single missionary diocese, in Province IX of the Episcopal Church in the USA.

Bishop of Honduras: Rt Rev. LLOYD EMMANUEL ALLEN, Apdo 586, San Pedro Sula; tel. 2556-6155; fax 2556-6467; e-mail emmanuel@anglicano.hn.

The Baptist Church

Convención Nacional de Iglesias Bautistas de Honduras (CONIBAH): Apdo 2176, Tegucigalpa; tel. and fax 2221-4024; internet www.ublaonline.org/paises/honduras.htm; Pres. Pastor TOMÁS MONTOYA; 24,142 mems.

Other Churches

Iglesia Cristiana Luterana de Honduras (Lutheran): Barrio Villa Adela, 19 Calle entre 5a y 6a Avda, Apdo 2861, Tegucigalpa; tel. 2225-4464; fax 2225-4893; e-mail iclh@cablecolor.hn; internet www.iglesialuteranadehonduras.com; Pres. Rev. JOSÉ MARTIN GIRÓN; 1,500 mems.

BAHÁ'Í FAITH

National Spiritual Assembly: Sendero de los Naranjos 2801, Col. Castaños, Apdo 273, Tegucigalpa; tel. 2232-6124; fax 2231-1343; internet www.bahaihon.org; Co-ordinator SOHEIL DOOKI; 40,000 mems resident in more than 500 localities.

The Press

DAILIES

La Gaceta: Empresa Nacional de Artes Gráficas, Col. Miraflores, Tegucigalpa; tel. 2230-4956; fax 2230-3026; f. 1830; morning; official govt paper; Gen. Man. MARTA GARCÍA CASCO; Co-ordinator MARCO ANTONIO RODRÍGUEZ CASTILLO; circ. 3,000.

El Heraldo: Avda los Próceres, Frente al Pani, Barrio San Felipe, Apdo 1938, Tegucigalpa; tel. 2236-6000; e-mail contactos@elheraldo.hn; internet www.elheraldo.hn; f. 1979; morning; independent; Editor FERNANDO BERRÍOS; circ. 50,000.

La Prensa: Guamilito, 3a Avda, 6–7 Calles No 34, Apdo 143, San Pedro Sula; tel. 2553-3101; fax 2553-0778; e-mail redaccion@laprensa.hn; internet www.laprensahn.com; f. 1964; morning; independent; Editor NELSON GARCÍA; Exec. Dir MARÍA ANTONIA FUENTES; circ. 50,000.

El Tiempo: 1 Calle, 5a Avda 102, Barrio Santa Anita, Cortés, Apdo 450, San Pedro Sula; tel. 2553-3388; fax 2553-4590; e-mail web.tiempo@continental.hn; internet www.tiempo.hn; f. 1960; morning; left-of-centre; Pres. JAIME ROSENTHAL OLIVA; Editor MANUEL GAMERO; circ. 35,000.

La Tribuna: Col. Santa Bárbara, Carretera al Primer Batallón de Infantería, Comayagüela, Apdo 1501, Tegucigalpa; tel. 2234-3206; fax 2234-3050; e-mail tribuna@latribuna.hn; internet www.latribuna.hn; f. 1976; morning; independent; Dir ADÁN ELVIR FLORES; Gen. Man. MANUEL ACOSTA MEDINA; circ. 45,000.

PERIODICALS

Comercio Global: Cámara de Comercio e Industrias de Tegucigalpa, Blvd Centroamérica, Apdo 3444, Tegucigalpa; tel. 2232-4200; fax 2232-0759; e-mail mercadeo@ccit.hn; internet www.ccit.hn; f. 1970; 4 a year; commercial and industrial news; Publr DANIELA ZELAYA.

Hablemos Claro: Edif. Torre Libertad, Blvd Suyapa, Residencial La Hacienda, Tegucigalpa; tel. 2232-8058; fax 2239-7008; e-mail rwa@hablemosclaro.com; internet www.hablemosclaro.com; f. 1990; weekly; Editor RODRIGO WONG ARÉVALO; circ. 9,000.

Honduras Weekly: Centro Comercial Villa Mare, Blvd Morazán, Apdo 1323, Tegucigalpa; tel. 2239-0285; fax 2232-2300; e-mail editor@hondurasweekly.com; internet www.hondurasweekly.com; f. 1988; weekly; English language; tourism, culture and the environment; Bureau Chief NICOLE MARRDER; Editor MARCO CÁCERES.

El Libertador: Tegucigalpa; internet www.ellibertador.hn; Dir JHONY LAGOS; Editor DELMER MEMBREÑO.

Poder Ciudadano: Residencial Las Lomas del Guijarro Sur, Calle Madrid, Casa 39, Tegucigalpa; tel. 2239-4945; e-mail poderciudadanohn@yahoo.com; internet www.poderciudadano.info; f. 2007; weekly; govt-owned.

PRESS ASSOCIATION

Asociación de Prensa Hondureña: Casa del Periodista, Avda Gutemberg 1525, Calle 6, Barrio El Guanacaste, Apdo 893, Tegucigalpa; tel. 2239-2970; fax 2237-8102; f. 1930; Pres. MIGUEL OSMUNDO MEJÍA; Sec.-Gen. FELA ISABEL DUARTE.

Publishers

Centro Editorial: Apdo 1683, San Pedro Sula; tel. and fax 2558-1282; e-mail escoto@globalnet.hn; f. 1987; Dir JULIO ESCOTO.

Ediciones Ramses: Edif. Chiminike, 2°, Blvr Fuerzas Armadas de Honduras, Tegucigalpa; tel. 2225-6630; fax 2225-6633; e-mail servicioalcliente@edicionesramses.hn; internet www.edicionesramses.hn; educational material.

Editorial Coello: Avda 9, Calle 4, 64a, Barrio El Benque, San Pedro Sula; tel. 2553-1680; fax 2557-4362; e-mail tcoello@globalnet.hn; Dir AUGUSTO C. COELLO.

Editorial Pez Dulce: 143 Paseo La Leona, Barrio La Leona, Tegucigalpa; tel. and fax 222-1220; e-mail pezdulce@yahoo.com; Dir RUBÉN IZAGUIRRE.

Editorial Universitaria de la Universidad Nacional Autónoma de Honduras: Blvd Suyapa, Tegucigalpa; tel. and fax 2232-4772; f. 1847; Dir SEGISFREDO INFANTE.

Guaymuras: Avda Zaragoza, Apdo 1843, Barrio La Leona, Tegucigalpa; tel. 2237-5433; fax 2238-4578; e-mail ediguay@123.hn; internet www.guaymuras.hn; f. 1980; Dir ISOLDA ARITA MELZER.

Broadcasting and Communications

TELECOMMUNICATIONS

Regulatory Authority

Comisión Nacional de Telecomunicaciones (Conatel): Edif. Conatel, Col. Modelo, 6a Avda Suroeste, Apdo 15012, Tegucigalpa; tel. 2234-8600; fax 2234-8611; e-mail conatel@conatel.gob.hn; internet www.conatel.hn; Pres. LIDIA ESTELA CARDONA.

Major Service Providers

The monopoly of the telecommunications sector by Hondutel ceased at the end of 2005, when the fixed line and international services market was opened to domestic and foreign investment. In 2010 there were, in addition to Hondutel, three private mobile cellular telephone providers in operation.

Claro Honduras: Col. San Carlos, Avda República de Colombia, Tegucigalpa; tel. 2205-4222; fax 2205-4337; e-mail recepciontgu@claro.com.hn; internet www.claro.com.hn; f. 2003; operated by Servicios de Comunicaciones de Honduras (Sercom Honduras), a subsidiary of América Móvil, SA de CV (Mexico) since 2004; mobile cellular telephone operator.

Digicel Honduras: Col. Castaño Sur, 1 ½ cuadra al Sur de Reasa, Blvd Morazán, Tegucigalpa; tel. 2281-7000; e-mail servicioalcliente.hn@digicelgroup.com; internet www.digicel.hn; f. 2007; negotiations under way in Aug. 2011 to sell Digicel to América Móvil, SA de CV (Mexico); mobile cellular telephone operator; Gen. Man. DAMIAN BLACKBURN.

Empresa Hondureña de Telecomunicaciones (Hondutel): Edif. Gerencia Hondutel, Blvd Morazán, Atrás Canchas de Bigos, Col. San Carlos, Apdo 1794, Tegucigalpa; tel. 2221-1452; fax 2221-1454; e-mail miguel.velez@hondutelnet.hn; internet www.hondutel.hn; f. 1976; scheduled for privatization; Gen. Man. Gen. (retd) ROMEO VÁSQUEZ VELÁSQUEZ.

Multifon: Tegucigalpa; tel. 206-0607; e-mail sac@multifon.net; f. 2003; subsidiary of MultiData; awarded govt contract with UT Starcom (q.v.) for fixed telephone lines in 2003; Pres. JOSÉ RAFAEL FERRARI; CEO JOSÉ LUIS RIVERA.

Telefónica Celular (CELTEL) (Tigo): Edif. Celtel, contiguo a la Iglesia Episcopal, Blvd Suyapa, Col. Florencia Norte Hondureña, Tegucigalpa; tel. 2235-7966; fax 2220-7060; e-mail info@mail.celtel.net; internet www.tigo.com.hn; f. 1996; mobile cellular telephone company; wholly owned subsidiary of Millicom International Cellular (Luxembourg); Pres. ANTONIO TAVEL OTERO.

UT Starcom (USA): Edif. Plaza Azul, 6°, Calle Viena, Avda Berlin, Col. Lomas del Guijarro Sur, Tegucigalpa; tel. 2239-8289; fax 2239-9161; e-mail services@utstar.com; internet www.utstar.com; awarded govt contract with Multifon (q.v.) for fixed telephone lines in 2003; Pres. and CEO JACK LU.

BROADCASTING

Radio

Estereo McIntosh: La Ceiba, Atlántida; tel. 2440-0326; fax 2440-0325; commercial channel.

HRN, La Voz de Honduras: Blvd Suyapa, Apdo 642, Tegucigalpa; tel. 2232-5100; internet www.radiohrn.hn; commercial station; f. 1933; broadcasts 12 channels; 23 relay stations; Gen. Man. NAHÚN VALLADARES.

Power FM: Edif. Power FM, Blvd del Norte, Apdo 868, San Pedro Sula; tel. 2552-4898; fax 2553–3214; e-mail info@powerfm.hn; internet www.powerfm.hn; Gen. Man. XAVIER SIERRA.

Radio América: Col. Alameda, frente a la Droguería Mandofer, Apdo 259, Tegucigalpa; tel. 2290-4960; fax 2232-4938; e-mail info@americamultimedios.net; internet www.radioamericahn.net; commercial station; broadcasts Radio San Pedro, Radio Continental, Radio Monderna, Radio Universal, Cadena Radial Sonora, Super Cien Stereo, Momentos FM Stereo and 3 regional channels; f. 1948; 13 relay stations; Gen. Man. CHRIS MÜLLER.

Radio Club Honduras: Salida Chamelecon, Apdo 273, San Pedro Sula; tel. 2556-6173; fax 2617-1151; e-mail hr2rch@yahoo.com; internet www.hr2rch.org; f. 1958; amateur radio club; Pres. MARCO VINICIO DE LEÓN.

Radio Esperanza: La Esperanza, Intibucá; tel. 2783-0025; fax 2783-0644; internet www.honducontact.com/Radio%20Esperanza.htm; Dir J. M. DEL CID.

Radio Juticalpa: Juticalpa, Olancho; tel. 2785-2277; internet www.radiojuticalpa.com; Gen. Man. MARTHA ELENA RUBÍ.

Radio Nacional de Honduras: Avda La Paz, Col. Lomas Del Mayab, detras del edif. del Ministerio de la Presidencia, Tegucigalpa; tel. 2235-6723; fax 2235-6678; e-mail radio@rnh.hn; internet www.rnh.hn; f. 1976; official station, operated by the Govt; Exec. Dir FILIBERTO DIAZ SOLIS.

Radio la Voz del Atlántico: 12a Calle, 2a–3a Avda, Barrio Copen, Puerto Cortés; tel. 2665-5166; fax 2665-2401; e-mail administracion@lavozdelatlantico.com; internet www.lavozdelatlantico.com; f. 1955.

Television

Televicentro: Edif. Televicentro, Blvd Suyapa, Col. Florencia, Apdo 734, Tegucigalpa; tel. 2207-5514; fax 2232-5514; internet www.televicentrotv.net; f. 1987; 11 relay stations; Pres. JOSÉ RAFAEL FERRARI SAGASTUME.

Canal 5: tel. 2232-7835; fax 2232-0097; f. 1959; Gen. Man. JOSÉ RAFAEL FERRARI SAGASTUME.

Telecadena 7 y 4: tel. 2239-2081; fax 2232-0097; f. 1959; Pres. JOSÉ RAFAEL FERRARI SAGASTUME; Gen. Man. RAFAEL ENRIQUE VILLEDA.

Telesistema Hondureño, Canal 3 y 7: tel. 2232-7064; fax 2232-5019; f. 1967; Gen. Man. RAFAEL ENRIQUE VILLEDA.

VICA Television: 9a Calle, 10a Avda 64, Barrio Guamilito, Apdo 120, San Pedro Sula; tel. 2552-4478; fax 2557-3257; e-mail info@mayanet.hn; internet www.vicatv.hn; f. 1986; operates regional channels 2, 9 and 13; Pres. BLANCA SIKAFFY.

Finance

(cap. = capital; res = reserves; dep. = deposits; m. = million; brs = branches; amounts in lempiras unless otherwise stated)

BANKING

Central Bank

Banco Central de Honduras (BANTRAL): Avda Juan Ramón Molina, 7a Avda y 1a Calle, Apdo 3165, Tegucigalpa; tel. 2237-2270; fax 2237-1876; e-mail Carlos.Espinoza@bch.hn; internet www.bch.hn; f. 1950; bank of issue; cap. 212.5m., res 1,192m., dep. 39,232.9m. (Dec. 2009); Pres. María Elena Mondragón; Gen. Man. Héctor Mendéz.

Commercial Banks

BAC Honduras: Blvd Suyapa, frente a Emisoras Unidas, Apdo 116, Tegucigalpa; tel. 2216-0200; fax 2239-4509; internet www.bac.net/honduras; bought by Grupo Aval de Colombia in Dec. 2010; fmrly Banco Mercantil, SA, then BAC BAMER.

Banco Atlántida, SA (BANCATLAN): Plaza Bancatlán, Blvd Centroamérica, Apdo 3164, Tegucigalpa; tel. 2232-1050; fax 2232-6120; e-mail webmaster@bancatlan.hn; internet www.bancatlan.hn; f. 1913; cap. 3,500m., res 22.7m. dep. 27,009.7m. (Dec. 2010); Exec. Pres. Guillermo Bueso Anduray; Exec. Vice-Pres Gustavo Oviedo, Ildoira G. de Bonilla; 179 brs.

Banco Continental, SA (BANCON): 9–10 Avda NO, Blvd Morazán, San Pedro Sula; tel. 2550-0880; fax 2550-2750; e-mail imontoya@continental.hn; internet www.bancon.hn; f. 1974; cap. 500.0m., res 11.2m., dep. 4,001.4m. (Dec. 2010); Pres., Chair. and Gen. Man. Jaime Rosenthal Oliva; 77 brs.

Banco Financiera Comercial Hondureña (Banco FICOHSA): Edif. Plaza Victoria, Col. Las Colinas, Blvd Francia, Tegucigalpa; tel. 2239-6410; fax 2239-6420; e-mail ficobanc@ficohsa.hn; internet www.ficohsa.com; Pres. Leonel Giannini; 101 brs.

Banco de Honduras, SA: Blvd Suyapa, Col. Loma Linda Sur, Tegucigalpa; tel. 2232-6122; fax 2232-6167; internet www.bancodehonduras.citibank.com; f. 1889; subsidiary of Citibank NA (USA); cap. 250.0m., res 6.8m., dep. 1,940.9m. (2008); Gen. Man. Máximo R. Vidal; 2 brs.

Banco HSBC Honduras, SA: Intersección Blvd Suyapa y Blvd Juan Pablo II, Apdo 344, Tegucigalpa; tel. 2240-0909; internet www.hsbc.com.hn; bought by Banco Davivienda (Colombia) in 2012; Exec. Pres. Jonathan Hartley.

Banco de Occidente, SA (BANCOCCI): 6a Avda, Calle 2–3, Apdo 3284, Tegucigalpa; tel. 2226-0027; fax 2263-8240; internet www.bancocci.hn; f. 1951; cap. 800.0m., res 315.1m., dep. 17,297.4m. (2006); Pres. and Gen. Man. Jorge Bueso Arias; Vice-Pres. Emilio Medina R.; 146 brs.

Banco del País (BANPAIS): San Pedro Sula; internet www.banpais.hn; f. 1969; acquired Banco Sogerin and client portfolio of Banco de las Fuerzas Armadas in 2003; Pres. Juan Miguel Torrebiarte; 109 brs.

Banco de los Trabajadores, SA (BANCOTRAB): 3a Avda, 13a Calle, Comayagüela, Apdo 3246, Tegucigalpa; tel. 2238-0017; fax 2238-0077; internet www.btrab.com; f. 1967; cap. 204.8m. (Dec. 2002); Pres. Rolando del Cid Velásquez; 6 brs.

Development Banks

Banco Centroamericano de Integración Económica: Edif. Sede BCIE, Blvd Suyapa, Apdo 772, Tegucigalpa; tel. 2240-2243; fax 2228-2185; e-mail cmartine@bcie.hn; internet www.bcie.org; f. 1960 to finance the economic devt of the Central American Common Market and its mem. countries; mems: Costa Rica, El Salvador, Guatemala, Honduras, Nicaragua; cap. and res US $1,020.0m. (June 2003); Dir Tania Lobo de Quiñónez.

Banco Financiera Centroamericana, SA (FICENSA): Edif. FICENSA, Blvd Morazán, Apdo 1432, Tegucigalpa; tel. 2238-1661; fax 2238-1630; e-mail rrivera@ficensa.com; internet www.ficensa.com; f. 1974; private org. providing finance for industry, commerce and transport; Pres. Oswaldo López Arellano.

Banco Hondureño del Café, SA (BANHCAFE): Calle República de Costa Rica, Blvd Juan Pablo II, Col. Lomas del Mayab, Apdo 583, Tegucigalpa; tel. 2232-8370; fax 2232-8782; e-mail bcaferhu@hondutel.hn; internet www.banhcafe.com; f. 1981 to help finance coffee production; owned principally by private coffee producers; cap. 280.5m., res 69.1m., dep. 2,352.3m. (Dec. 2009); Pres. Miguel Alfonso Fernández Rápalo; 50 brs.

Banco Nacional de Desarrollo Agrícola (BANADESA): 4a Avda y 5a Avda, 13a y 14a Calles, Barrio Concepción, Apdo 212, Tegucigalpa; tel. 2237-2201; fax 2237-5187; e-mail banadesa@banadesa.hn; internet www.banadesa.hn; f. 1980; govt devt bank; loans to agricultural sector; cap. 354m., res 3.7m., dep. 841.3m. (Dec. 2008); Gen. Man. Enrique Alberto Castellon; 37 brs.

Banking Associations

Asociación Hondureña de Instituciones Bancarias (AHIBA): Edif. AHIBA, Blvd Suyapa, Apdo 1344, Tegucigalpa; tel. 2235-6770; fax 2239-0191; e-mail ahiba@ahiba.hn; internet www.ahiba.hn; f. 1957; 21 mem. banks; Pres. Roque Ribera Rivas; Exec. Dir María Lydia Solano.

Comisión Nacional de Bancos y Seguros (CNBS): Edif. Santa Fé, Col. Castaño Sur, Paseo Virgilio Zelaya Rubí Bloque C, Apdo 20074, Tegucigalpa; tel. 2290-4500; fax 2237-6232; e-mail rbarahona@cnbs.gov.hn; internet www.cnbs.gov.hn; Pres. Milton Jiménez Puerto.

STOCK EXCHANGE

Bolsa Centroamericana de Valores: Edif. Torre Alianza 2, 5°, Frente a Gasolinera Puma, Blvd San Juan Bosco, Col. Lomas del Guijarro Sur, Apdo 3885, Tegucigalpa; tel. 2271-0400; fax 2271-0403; internet www.bcv.hn; Pres. José Arturo Alvarado.

INSURANCE

American Home Assurance Co (Chartis Honduras): Edif. Los Castaños, 4°, Blvd Morazán, Apdo 3220, Tegucigalpa; tel. 2232-3938; fax 2239-9169; e-mail ask.chartis@chartisinsurance.com; internet www.chartisinsurance.com; f. 1958; Gen. Man. José Edgardo Flores Riveiro.

Ficohsa Seguros, SA: Edif. Plaza Victoria, Torre II, Col. Las Colinas, Blvd Francia, Tegucigalpa; tel. 2232-4747; fax 2232-2255; internet www.ficohsaseguros.com; f. 1957; fmrly Interamericana de Seguros, SA; part of Grupo Financiero Ficohsa; Gen. Man. Luis Alberto Atala Faraj.

HSBC Seguros: Edif. Torre Imperial Colonia Palmira, Avda República de Panamá, Tegucigalpa; tel. 2237-8219; fax 2237-4780; internet www.hsbc.com.hn; f. 1917; Exec. Dir Marcelo Pedemonte.

Mapfre Honduras, SA: Edif. El Planetario, 4°, Avda París, Col. Lomas del Guijarro Sur, Calle Madrid, Apdo 312, Tegucigalpa; tel. 2216-2672; fax 2231-0982; e-mail info@mapfre.com.hn; internet www.mapfre.com.hn; f. 1954; fmrly Aseguradora Hondureña, SA; Gen. Man. Gerardo Corrales.

Pan American Life Insurance Co (PALIC): Edif. PALIC, Avda República de Chile 804, Col. Palmira, Apdo 123, Tegucigalpa; tel. 2216-0909; fax 2239-3437; e-mail servicioalclientehn@panamericanlife.com; internet www.palig.com/Regions/honduras; f. 1944; Pres. Salvador Ortega (Central America); Gen. Man. María del Rosario Alvarez.

Seguros Atlántida: Edif. Sonisa, Costado Este de Plaza Bancatlan, Tegucigalpa; tel. 2232-4014; fax 2232-3688; e-mail info@seatlan.com; internet www.segurosatlantida.com; f. 1985; Pres. Robert Vinelli; Gen. Man. Juan Miguel Orellana.

Seguros Continental, SA: Edif. Continental, 4°, 3a Avda SO, 2a y 3a Calle, Apdo 605, San Pedro Sula; tel. 2550-0880; fax 2550-2750; e-mail seguros@continental.hn; internet www.seguros.continental.hn; f. 1968; Pres. Jaime Rolando Rosenthal Oliva; Gen. Man. Mario Roberto Solís Dacosta.

Seguros Crefisa: Edif. Banco Ficensa, 1°, Blvd Morazán, Apdo 3774, Tegucigalpa; tel. 2238-1750; fax 2238-1714; e-mail info@crefisa.com; internet www.crefisa.com; f. 1993; Gen. Man. Mario Batres Pineda.

Seguros del País: Edif. IPM Anexo, 4°, Blvd Centroamérica, Tegucigalpa; tel. 2239-7077; fax 2232-4216; internet www.segpais.com; f. 2000; Gen. Man. Gerardo Rivera.

Insurance Association

Cámara Hondureña de Aseguradores (CAHDA): Edif. Casa Metromedia, 3°, Col. San Carlos, Apdo 3290, Tegucigalpa; tel. 2221-5354; fax 2221-5356; e-mail info@cahda.org; internet www.cahda.org; f. 1974; Pres. Pedro Barquero; Gen. Man. Tethey Martinez.

Trade and Industry

GOVERNMENT AGENCY

Fondo Hondureño de Inversión Social (FHIS): Antiguo Edif. I.P.M., Col. Godoy, Comayagüela, Apdo 3581, Tegucigalpa; tel. 2234-5231; fax 2534-5255; e-mail dgarcia@fhis.hn; internet www.fhis.hn; social investment fund; Exec. Dir Gunther Bustamente.

DEVELOPMENT ORGANIZATIONS

Dirección Ejecutiva de Fomento a la Minería (DEFOMIN): Edif. DEFOMIN, 3°, Blvd Miraflores, Avda la FAO, Apdo 981, Tegucigalpa; tel. 2232-6721; fax 2232-6044; e-mail miguel.mejia@

defomin.gob.hn; internet www.defomin.gob.hn; promotes the mining sector; Exec. Dir ALDO SANTOS.

Instituto Hondureño del Café (IHCAFE): Edif. El Faro, Col. Las Minitas, Apdo 40-C, Tegucigalpa; tel. 2237-3130; fax 2238-2368; e-mail gerencia@ihcafe.2hn.com; internet www.cafedehonduras.org; f. 1970; coffee devt programme; Pres. ASTERIO REYES; Gen. Man. VICTOR HUGO MOLINA.

Instituto Hondureño de Mercadeo Agrícola (IHMA): Apdo 727, Tegucigalpa; tel. 2235-3193; fax 2235-5719; internet ihmahn.org; f. 1978; agricultural devt agency; Gen. Man. CARLOS GIRÓN.

Instituto Nacional Agrario (INA): Col. La Almeda, 4a Avda, entre 10a y 11a Calles, No 1009, Apdo 3391, Tegucigalpa; tel. 2232-4893; fax 2232-7398; e-mail transparencia@ina.hn; internet www.ina.hn; agricultural devt programmes; Exec. Dir CÉSAR HAM PEÑA.

Instituto Nacional de Conservación Forestal (INCF): Salida Carretera del Norte, Zona El Carrizal, Col. Brisas de Olancho, CComayagüela, Apdo 1378, Tegucigalpa; tel. 2223-7303; fax 2223-8587; e-mail direccion@icf.gob.hn; internet www.icf.gob.hn; f. 2008 to replace Corporación Hondureña de Desarrollo Forestal (f. 1974); control of the forestry industry and conservation of forest resources; Dir JOSÉ TRINIDAD SUAZO.

CHAMBERS OF COMMERCE

Cámara de Comercio e Industrias de Copán: Edif. Comercial Romero, 2°, Barrio Mercedes, Santa Rosa de Copán; tel. 2662-0843; fax 2662-1783; e-mail info@camaracopan.com; internet www.camaracopan.com; f. 1940; Pres. RAMÓN DE JESÚS FLORES.

Cámara de Comercio e Industrias de Cortés (CCIC): Barrio Las Brisas, 22 y 24 Calle, Apdo Postal 14, San Pedro Sula; tel. 2566-0345; fax 2553-3777; e-mail ccic@ccichonduras.org; internet www.ccichonduras.org; f. 1931; 812 mems; Pres. LUIS NAPOLEON LARACH; Dir RAÚL REINA CLEAVES.

Cámara de Comercio e Industrias de Tegucigalpa (CCIT): Blvd Centroamérica, Apdo 3444, Tegucigalpa; tel. 2232-4200; fax 2232-5764; e-mail asuservicio@ccit.hn; internet www.ccit.hn; Pres. ALINE FLORES; Exec. Dir MARIO BUSTILLO.

Cámara Hondureña de la Industria de la Construcción (Chico): Casa 2525, 2da Calle, entre 1era y 2da Avda, al par de Kinder Happy Faces, Col. Florencia Sur, Tegucigalpa; tel. 2239-2039; internet www.chicoorg.org; f. 1968; Pres. JOSÉ ALEJANDRO ALVAREZ ALVARADO; Gen. Man. SILVIO LARIOS BONES.

Federación de Cámaras de Comercio e Industrias de Honduras (FEDECAMARA): Edif. Castañito, 2°, 6a Avda, Col. Los Castaños, Apdo 3393, Tegucigalpa; tel. 2232-1870; fax 2232-6083; e-mail fedecamara.direccion@amnettgu.com; internet www.fedecamara.org; f. 1948; 1,200 mems; Pres. AMÍLCAR BULNES; Coordinator JUAN FERRERA LÓPEZ.

Fundación para la Inversión y Desarrollo de Exportaciones (FIDE) (Foundation for Investment and Export Development): Col. La Estancia, Plaza Marte, final del Blvd Morazán, Apdo 2029, Tegucigalpa; tel. 2221-6304; fax 2221-6318; internet www.hondurasinfo.hn; f. 1984; private, non-profit agency; Pres. VILMA SIERRA DE FONSECA.

Honduran American Chamber of Commerce (Amcham Honduras): Commercial Area Hotel Honduras Maya, POB 1838, Tegucigalpa; tel. 2232-6035; fax 2232-2031; e-mail amcham@amchanhonduras.org; internet www.amchamhonduras.org; f. 1981; Pres. JOSÉ EDUARDO ATALA; Exec. Dir PATRICIA LÓPEZ.

INDUSTRIAL AND TRADE ASSOCIATIONS

Asociación Hondureña de Maquiladores (AHM): Altia Business Park, 12°, Blvd Armenta, San Pedro Sula; tel. 2516-9100; internet www.ahm-honduras.com; f. 1991; non-profit asscn for the maquila industry; Pres. DANIEL FACUSSÉ.

Consejo Hondureño de la Empresa Privada (COHEP): Edif. 8, Calle Yoro, Col. Tepeyac, Apdo 3240, Tegucigalpa; tel. 2235-3336; fax 2235-3345; e-mail consejo@cohep.com; internet www.cohep.com; f. 1968; represents 52 private sector trade asscns; Pres. SANTIAGO RUÍZ; Exec. Dir ARMANDO URTECHO.

Asociación Hondureña de Productores de Café (AHPROCAFE) (Coffee Producers' Association): Edif. AHPROCAFE, Avda La Paz, Apdo 959, Tegucigalpa; tel. 2236-8286; fax 2236-8310; e-mail ahprocafe@amnet.tgu.com; Pres. ASTERIO REYES.

Asociación Nacional de Acuicultores de Honduras (ANDAH) (Aquaculture Association of Honduras): Calle Vicente Williams, Barrio La Esperanza, Apdo 229, Choluteca; tel. 2782-0986; fax 2782-3848; e-mail andahn@hondutel.hn; f. 1986; 136 mems; Pres. JACOBO PAZ.

Asociación Nacional de Exportadores de Honduras (ANEXHON) (National Association of Exporters): Industrias Panavisión, salida nueva a la Lima Frente a Sigmanet, San Pedro Sula; tel. 2553-3029; fax 2557-0203; e-mail roberto@ipsa.hn; comprises 104 private enterprises; Pres. ROBERTO PANAYOTTI.

Asociación Nacional de Industriales (ANDI) (National Association of Manufacturers): Edif. Fundación Covelo, 3°, Col. Castaño Sur, Blvd Morazán, Apdo 3447, Tegucigalpa; tel. 2239-1238; fax 2221-5199; e-mail andi@andi.hn; internet www.andi.hn; Pres. ADOLFO FACUSSÉ; Exec. Dir FERNANDO GARCÍA MERINO.

Federación Nacional de Agricultores y Ganaderos de Honduras (FENAGH) (Farmers' and Livestock Breeders' Association): Col. Miramontes, Avda Principal, 7a Calle 1557, Tegucigalpa; tel. 2239-1303; fax 2231-1392; e-mail jlizardo@fenagh.net; internet www.fenagh.net; Pres. LEOPOLDO DÚRAN; Exec. Dir JOSÉ LIZARDO REYES.

UTILITIES

Electricity

Empresa Nacional de Energía Eléctrica (ENEE) (National Electrical Energy Co): Edif. EMAS, 4°, Bo El Trapiche, Tegucigalpa; tel. 2235-2934; fax 2235-2969; e-mail informatica@enee.hn; internet www.enee.hn; f. 1957; state-owned electricity co; Pres. RIGOBERTO CUELLAR; Man. EMIL HAWIT.

Luz y Fuerza de San Lorenzo, SA (LUFUSSA): Edif. Comercial Los Próceres, Final Avda Los Próceres 3917, Tegucigalpa; tel. 2236-6545; fax 2236-5826; e-mail lufussa@lufussa.com; internet www.lufussa.com; f. 1994; generates thermoelectric power; Pres. EDUARDO KAFIE.

TRADE UNIONS

Central General de Trabajadores de Honduras (CGTH) (General Confederation of Labour of Honduras): Barrio La Granja, antiguo Local CONADI, Apdo 1236, Comayagüela, Tegucigalpa; tel. 2239-7383; fax 2225-2525; e-mail cgt@123.hn; f. 1970; legally recognized from 1982; attached to Partido Demócrata Cristiano de Honduras; Sec.-Gen. DANIEL A. DURÓN; 250,000 mems (2011).

Federación Auténtica Sindical de Honduras (FASH): Barrio La Granja, antiguo Local CONADI, Apdo 1236, Comayagüela, Tegucigalpa; tel. 2225-2509.

Federación Sindical del Sur (FESISUR): Barrio La Ceiba, 1 c. al norte del Instituto Santa María Goretti, Apdo 256, Choluteca; tel. 2882-0328; Pres. REINA DE ORDÓÑEZ.

Unión Nacional de Campesinos (UNC) (National Union of Farmworkers): antiguo Local CONADI, Barrio La Granja, Comayagüela, Tegucigalpa; tel. 2225-1005; Sec.-Gen. MARCIAL REYES CABALLERO.

Confederación Hondureña de Cooperativas (CHC): Edif. I.F.C., 3001 Blvd Morazán, Apdo 3265, Tegucigalpa; tel. 2232-2890; fax 2231-1024; f. 1971; Pres. JOSÉ FRANCISCO ORDÓÑEZ.

Confederación de Trabajadores de Honduras (CTH) (Workers' Confederation of Honduras): Edif. Beige, 2°, Avda Juan Ramón Molina, Barrio El Olvido, Apdo 720, Tegucigalpa; tel. 2220-1757; fax 2237-8575; e-mail organizacioncth@yahoo.es; f. 1964; Sec.-Gen. JOSÉ HILARIO ESPINOZA; 55,000 mems (2007).

Asociación Nacional de Campesinos Hondureños (ANACH) (National Association of Honduran Farmworkers): Edif. Chávez Mejía, 2°, Calle Juan Ramón Molina, Barrio El Olvido, Tegucigalpa; tel. 2238-0558; f. 1962; Pres. RAMÓN NAVARRO; Sec.-Gen. FRANCISCO GARCÍA; 80,000 mems.

Federación Central de Sindicatos de Trabajadores Libres de Honduras (FECESITLIH) (Honduran Federation of Free Trade Unions): antiguo Edif. EUKZKADI, 3a Avda, 3a y 4a Calle No 336, Comayagüela, Tegucigalpa; tel. 2237-3955; Pres. (vacant).

Federación Sindical de Trabajadores Nacionales de Honduras (FESITRANH) (Honduran Federation of Farmworkers): 10a Avda, 11a Calle, Barrio Los Andes, Apdo 245, Cortés, San Pedro Sula; tel. 2557-2539; f. 1957; Sec.-Gen. JOSÉ DOLORES VALENZUELA.

Sindicato Nacional de Motoristas de Equipo Pesado de Honduras (SINAMEQUIPH) (National Union of HGV Drivers): Avda Juan Ramón Molina, Barrio El Olvido, Tegucigalpa; tel. 2237-4415; Pres. ERASMO FLORES.

Confederación Unitaria de Trabajadores de Honduras (CUTH): Barrio Bella Vista, 10a Calle, 8a y 9a Avda, Casa 829, Tegucigalpa; tel. and fax 2220-4732; e-mail sgeneral@cuth.hn; f. 1992; Sec.-Gen. JOSÉ LUIS BAQUEDANO; 295,000 mems (2011).

Asociación Nacional de Empleados Públicos de Honduras (ANDEPH) (National Association of Public Employees of Honduras): Barrio Los Dolores, Avda Paulino Valladares, frente Panadería Italiana, atrás Iglesia Los Dolores, Tegucigalpa; tel. 2237-4393; Pres. DULCE MARÍA ZAVALA.

Federación Unitaria de Trabajadores de Honduras (FUTH): Barrio La Granja, contiguo Banco Atlántida, Casa

3047, frente a mercadito La Granja, Apdo 1663, Comayagüela, Tegucigalpa; tel. 2225-1010; f. 1981; Pres. JUAN ALBERTO BARAHONA MEJÍA; 45,000 mems.

Federación de Cooperativas de la Reforma Agraria de Honduras (FECORAH): Casa 2223, antiguo Local de COAPALMA, Col. Rubén Darío, Tegucigalpa; tel. 2232-0547; fax 2225-2525; f. 1970; legally recognized from 1974; Pres. ELÍAS VILLALTA.

Federación de Organizaciones Magisteriales (FOMH): Tegucigalpa; teachers' union; Sec.-Gen. EDWIN OLIVA.

Transport

RAILWAYS

The railway network is confined to the north of the country and most lines are used for fruit cargo. There are 995 km of railway track in Honduras, of which 349 km are narrow gauge. In 2010 the Government allocated 15m. lempiras to revive three railway routes serving San Pedro Sula, Choloma, Villanueva and Puerto Cortés. There are plans to restructure the train stations and coaches, as well as to set up additional railway routes to serve banana plantations.

Ferrocarril Nacional de Honduras (National Railway of Honduras): 1a Avda entre 1a y 2a Calle, Apdo 496, San Pedro Sula; tel. and fax 2552-8001; f. 1870; govt-owned; Gen. Man. LESTER AGUILAR.

ROADS

According to Fondo Vial de Honduras, in 2011 there were an estimated 14,044 km of roads in Honduras, of which only 21.2% were paved. A further 3,156 km of roads have been constructed by the Fondo Cafetero Nacional, and some routes have been built by the Corporación Hondureña de Desarrollo Forestal in order to facilitate access to coffee plantations and forestry development areas. In 2010 the Inter-American Development Bank approved a US $30m. loan for a rapid bus transit system in Tegucigalpa.

Dirección General de Carreteras: Barrio La Bolsa, Comayagüela, Tegucigalpa; tel. 2225-1703; fax 2225-2469; e-mail dgc@soptravi.gob.hn; internet www.soptravi.gob.hn/Carreteras; f. 1915; highways board; Dir WALTER MALDONADO.

SHIPPING

The principal port is Puerto Cortés on the Caribbean coast, which is the largest and best-equipped port in Central America. Other ports include Tela, La Ceiba, Trujillo/Castilla, Roatán, Amapala and San Lorenzo; all are operated by the Empresa Nacional Portuaria. There are several minor shipping companies. A number of foreign shipping lines call at Honduran ports.

Empresa Nacional Portuaria (National Port Authority): Apdo 18, Puerto Cortés; tel. 665-0987; fax 665-1402; e-mail gerencia@enp.hn; internet www.enp.hn; f. 1965; has jurisdiction over all ports in Honduras; a network of paved roads connects Puerto Cortés and San Lorenzo with the main cities of Honduras, and with the principal cities of Central America; Gen. Man. JOSÉ DARÍO GÁMEZ PANCHAMÉ.

CIVIL AVIATION

Local airlines in Honduras compensate for the deficiencies of road and rail transport, linking together small towns and inaccessible districts. There are four international airports: Golosón airport in La Ceiba, Ramón Villeda Morales airport in San Pedro Sula, Toncontín airport in Tegucigalpa and Juan Manuel Gálvaz airport in Roatán. A new airport at Río Amarillo, Copán, near the Copán Ruinas archaeological park, commenced operations in 2011.

Dirección General Aeronáutica Civil: Apdo 30145, Tegucigalpa; tel. 2234-0263; fax 2233-0258; e-mail contactos@dgachn.org; internet www.dgachn.org; airport infrastucture and security; Dir-Gen. MANUEL ENRIQUE CÁCERES.

Isleña Airlines: Edif. Taragon, 2°, Avda Circunvalacion, San Pedro Sula; tel. 2552-9910; fax 2552-9964; e-mail info.islena@taca.com; internet www.flyislena.com; subsidiary of TACA, El Salvador; domestic service and service to the Cayman Islands; Pres. and CEO ARTURO ALVARADO WOOD.

Tourism

Tourists are attracted by the Mayan ruins, the fishing and boating facilities in Trujillo Bay and Lake Yojoa, near San Pedro Sula, and the beaches on the northern coast. There is an increasing eco-tourism industry. Honduras received 869,500 tourists (excluding excursionists) in 2009, and in 2010 tourism receipts totalled US $650m.

Asociación Hotelera y Afines de Honduras (AHAH): Hotel Escuela Madrid, Suite 402, Col. 21 de Octubre-Los Girasoles, Tegucigalpa; tel. 2221-5805; fax 2221-4789; e-mail asociacionhotelerahn@yahoo.com; Pres. LUZ MEJÍA AMADOR; Exec. Dir NORMA MENDOZA.

Asociación Nacional de Agencias de Viajes y Turismo de Honduras: Blvd Morazán, frente a McDonald's, Tegucigalpa; tel. 2232-2308; e-mail scarlethmoncada@yahoo.com; Pres. SCARLETH DE MONCADA.

Asociación de Operadores de Turismo Receptivo de Honduras (OPTURH): Col. San Carlos, Avda Ramon E Cruz, Tegucigalpa; tel. 2236-9704; e-mail secretaria@opturh.com; internet www.opturh.com; f. 1996; Pres. ROBERTO BANDES.

Cámara Nacional de Turismo de Honduras: Calle Paris, Avda Niza, Casa 1233, Col. Lomas del Guijarro Sur, Tegucigalpa; tel. 2232-1937; fax 2235-8355; e-mail canaturh@canaturh.org; internet www.canaturh.org; f. 1976; Pres. JUAN BENDECK.

Instituto Hondureño de Turismo: Edif. Europa, 5°, Col. San Carlos, Apdo 3261, Tegucigalpa; tel. and fax 2222-2124; e-mail tourisminfo@iht.hn; internet www.iht.hn; f. 1972; Exec. Vice-Pres. SYNTIA BENNETT SALOMON; Sec.-Gen. MÓNICA HÍDALGO.

Defence

Military service is voluntary. Active service lasts eight months, with subsequent reserve training. As assessed at November 2011, the armed forces numbered 12,000: army 8,300, navy 1,400 and air force some 2,300. Paramilitary public security and defence forces numbered 8,000. There were also 60,000 joint reserves. In addition, some 358 US troops were based in Honduras.

Defence Budget: 2,680m. lempiras (US $140m.) in 2011.

Chairman of the Joint Chiefs of Staff: Brig.-Gen. RENÉ ARNOLDO OSORIO CANALES.

Commander-General of the Army: Col WILFREDO EFRAHÍN OLIVA LÓPEZ.

Commander-General of the Air Force: Col RUIZ PASTOR LANDA.

Commander-General of the Navy: Capt. RIGOBERTO ESPINOZA POSADAS.

Education

Primary education, beginning at six years of age and comprising three cycles of three years, is officially compulsory and is provided free of charge. Secondary education, which is not compulsory, begins at the age of 15 and lasts for three years. In 2007/08 enrolment at primary schools included 97% of children in the relevant age-group, while enrolment at secondary schools in that year was equivalent to 65% of children (57% of boys; 72% of girls) in the appropriate age-group. There are eight universities, including the Autonomous National University in Tegucigalpa. Estimated spending on education in 2012 was 23,000m. lempiras, representing 15.9% of the total budget.

HUNGARY

Introductory Survey

LOCATION, CLIMATE, LANGUAGE, RELIGION, FLAG, CAPITAL

The Republic of Hungary (renamed Hungary in the Constitution that took effect on 1 January 2012) lies in central Europe, bounded to the north by Slovakia, to the east by Ukraine and Romania, to the south by Serbia and Croatia, and to the west by Slovenia and Austria. Its climate is continental, with long, dry summers and severe winters. Temperatures in Budapest are generally between −3°C (27°F) and 28°C (82°F). The language is Hungarian (Magyar). There is a large Romany community (numbering between 500,000 and 700,000 people), and also Croat, German, Romanian, Serb, Slovak, Slovene and Jewish minorities. Most of the inhabitants profess Christianity, and the largest single religious denomination is the Catholic Church, representing about 58% of the population. Other Christian groups include Calvinists (20%), Lutherans (5%), Pentecostals, and the Eastern Orthodox Church. The national flag (proportions 2 by 3) consists of three equal horizontal stripes, of red, white and green. The capital is Budapest.

CONTEMPORARY POLITICAL HISTORY

Historical Context

Although Hungary co-operated with Nazi Germany before the Second World War and obtained additional territory when Czechoslovakia was partitioned in 1938 and 1939, when it sought to break the alliance in 1944 the country was occupied by German forces. In January 1945 Hungary was invaded by Soviet troops and signed an armistice, restoring the pre-1938 frontiers. It became a republic in February 1946. Nationalization measures began in December, despite opposition from the Catholic Church. In the 1947 elections, the communists became the largest single party, with 22.7% of the votes. The communists merged with the Social Democrats to form the Hungarian Workers' Party in June 1948. A People's Republic was established in August 1949.

As First Secretary of the Workers' Party, Mátyás Rákosi became the leading political figure, and opposition was removed by means of purges and political trials. Rákosi became Prime Minister in 1952, but, after the death of the Soviet leader Stalin (Iosif V. Dzhugashvili) in 1953, he was replaced by the more moderate Imre Nagy, and a short period of liberalization followed. Rákosi, however, remained as First Secretary, and in 1955 forced Nagy's resignation. Dissension between the Rákosi and Nagy factions increased in 1956; in July Rákosi was forced to resign but was replaced by a close associate, Ernő Gerő. The consequent discontent provoked demonstrations against communist domination, and in October fighting broke out. Nagy was reinstated as Prime Minister; he renounced membership of the Warsaw Pact (the defence grouping of the Soviet bloc) and promised other controversial reforms. In November Soviet troops, stationed in Hungary under the 1947 peace treaty, intervened, and the uprising was suppressed. A new Soviet-supported Government, led by János Kádár, was installed. Some 20,000 participants in the uprising were arrested, of whom 2,000 were subsequently executed, including Nagy and four associates. Many opponents of the regime were deported to the USSR. Kádár, who was appointed the leader of the renamed Hungarian Socialist Workers' Party (HSWP), held the premiership until January 1958, and from September 1961 until July 1965.

In March 1985 Kádár was re-elected as leader of the HSWP, with the new title of General Secretary of the Central Committee. The legislative elections in June gave voters a wider choice of candidates under the system of mandatory multiple nominations. In May 1988 Kádár was replaced as General Secretary of the Central Committee by Károly Grósz (Chairman of the Council of Ministers since June 1987), and promoted to the new and purely ceremonial post of HSWP President; he lost his membership of the Politburo (Political Bureau). About one-third of the members of the Central Committee were replaced by younger politicians. Grósz declared his commitment to radical economic and political change, but excluded the immediate possibility of a multi-party political system. In June 1988 Dr Brunó Ferenc Straub, who was not a member of the HSWP, was elected to the largely ceremonial post of President of the Presidential Council. In November Miklós Németh, a prominent member of the HSWP, replaced Grósz as Chairman of the Council of Ministers.

Following Grósz's appointment as leader of the HSWP, there was a relaxation of censorship laws, and independent political groups were formally established. In January 1989 the right to strike was fully legalized. In the same month the Országgyülés (National Assembly) enacted legislation guaranteeing the right to demonstrate and to form associations and political parties independent of the HSWP. In February the HSWP agreed to abandon the constitutional clause upholding the party's leading role in society. In March an estimated 100,000 people took part in a peaceful anti-Government demonstration in Budapest.

During 1989 there was increasing evidence of dissension within the HSWP between conservative and reformist members. (At least 100,000 members had tendered their resignations between late 1987 and early 1989.) In April the Politburo was replaced by a smaller body. In May the Council of Ministers declared its independence from the HSWP; Kádár was removed from the presidency and the Central Committee of the party, officially for health reasons. In June a radical restructuring of the HSWP was effected; although Grósz remained as General Secretary, the newly elected Chairman, Rezső Nyers, effectively emerged as the party's leading figure. At a provincial by-election in July 1989, a joint candidate of the centre-right Hungarian Democratic Forum (HDF), the liberal Alliance of Free Democrats (AFD) and the Federation of Young Democrats (FYD) became the first opposition deputy since 1947 to win representation in the legislature. Four further by-elections were won by opposition candidates in July–September 1989. At an HSWP Congress in October, delegates voted to reconstitute the party as the Hungarian Socialist Party (HSP).

Domestic Political Affairs

On 23 October 1989 (the anniversary of the 1956 uprising) the Republic of Hungary was proclaimed. In preparation, the Országgyülés approved fundamental amendments to the Constitution, including the removal of the clause guaranteeing one-party rule. A new electoral law was approved, and the Presidential Council was replaced by the post of President of the Republic. Mátyás Szűrös, the President (Speaker) of the Országgyülés, was named President of the Republic, on an interim basis.

Hungary's first free multi-party elections since 1945 were held, in two rounds, on 25 March and 8 April 1990. The HDF received the largest proportion of the total votes cast (42.7%) and 165 of the 386 seats in the Országgyülés, followed by the AFD, with 23.8% of the votes and 92 legislative seats. The Independent Smallholders' Party (ISP, which advocated the restoration to its original owners of land collectivized after 1947) and the Christian Democratic People's Party (CDPP), both of which contested the second round of polling in alliance with the HDF, secured 43 and 21 seats, respectively. The HSP secured 33 seats, while the FYD (which was closely aligned with the AFD) obtained 21 seats. The HSWP failed to secure the 4% of the votes required for representation.

A coalition Government was formed in May 1990, comprising members of the HDF (which held the majority of posts), the ISP, the CDPP and three independents. József Antall, the Chairman of the HDF, had earlier been elected to chair the new Council of Ministers. Among the declared aims of the new Government were membership of the European Community (now European Union—EU, see p. 276) and a full transition to a market economy. In the same month Gyula Horn, the outgoing Minister of Foreign Affairs, replaced Nyers as leader of the HSP. In August Árpád Göncz, a writer and member of the AFD, was elected President of the Republic by the legislature. At municipal and local elections in September and October, a coalition of the AFD and the FYD won control of Budapest and many other cities, while in rural areas independent candidates obtained a majority of the votes.

In May 1991 the Országgyülés approved legislation to provide compensation for persons killed, imprisoned or deported, or whose property had been expropriated for political reasons in 1939–89. Further legislation was approved in early 1993 allowing for prosecutions in connection with crimes committed under the communist regime.

In February 1992 the Chairman of the ISP, József Torgyán, announced that his party was to withdraw from the Government, in frustration at the party's perceived lack of political influence. However, most ISP deputies refused to withhold their support for the Government, thus causing divisions in the party. In April some 20,000 people reportedly attended an anti-Government demonstration organized by Torgyán in Budapest. The split in the party was formalized in June, when members loyal to the Government formed what became the United Historic Smallholders' Party; the ISP renamed itself the Independent Smallholders' and Peasants' Party (ISPP).

In September 1992 some 50,000 people demonstrated in Budapest against extreme right-wing figures within the HDF, including the Vice-Chairman of the party, István Csurka. Csurka was expelled from the HDF in July 1993, and subsequently founded the Hungarian Justice and Life Party (HJLP). Antall died in December, and was succeeded as Prime Minister by Dr Péter Boross, an independent and hitherto the Minister of the Interior. In February 1994 Lajos Für was elected Chairman of the HDF.

Democratic consolidation

Elections to the Országgyülés, held on 8 and 29 May 1994, resulted in a parliamentary majority for the HSP, which received 33.0% of the votes cast for regional party lists and won 209 of the 386 legislative seats. The AFD won 19.8% of the votes and 70 seats, while the HDF won only 11.7% of the votes and 37 seats. The ISPP, the CDPP and the FYD also secured parliamentary seats. The HSP and the AFD signed a coalition agreement in June. Horn was invested as Prime Minister in July.

In January 1995 the Minister of Finance, László Bekesi, resigned, following disagreements with Horn regarding economic reform; he was replaced by Lajos Bokros. Economic austerity measures, adopted in March, prompted strong domestic criticism, and the ministers responsible for public health and for national security resigned shortly afterwards. On 19 June Göncz was re-elected President of the Republic by the Országgyülés. In late July the Országgyülés approved adjustments to the austerity programme, to comply with the requirements of the Constitution. The economic programme continued to cause dissent within the Government, and the Minister of Labour tendered her resignation in October. Bokros resigned in February 1996, and a banker, Péter Medgyessy, was appointed as the new Minister of Finance. Following the election of Sándor Lezsák to the HDF leadership, a split in the party ensued in March, with the departure of those who discerned an increasingly nationalistic tendency in the party. In December the HDF established an electoral alliance with the Federation of Young Democrats—Hungarian Civic Party (FYD—HCP, which had been reconstituted from the FYD) and the Hungarian Christian Democratic Federation, a newly formed association of breakaway members of the CDPP.

Legislative elections took place, in two rounds, on 10 and 24 May 1998. The FYD—HCP, with 147 seats, obtained the largest representation in the Országgyülés; the HSP received 134 seats, the ISPP 48, the AFD 24, the HDF 18 and the HJLP 14. In June the FYD—HCP signed an agreement with the HDF and the ISPP, providing for the formation of a new coalition government. In July the Országgyülés elected Viktor Orbán, the Chairman of the FYD—HCP, as Prime Minister; his Government comprised 11 representatives of the FYD—HCP, four of the ISPP (later renamed the Independent Smallholders', Agrarian Workers' and Civic Party—ISCP), one of the HDF and one of the Hungarian Christian Democratic Federation. In September, following the resignation of Horn from the leadership of the HSP, a former minister, László Kovács, was elected Chairman. In January 2000 László Kövér replaced Orbán as leader of the FYD—HCP. On 6 June 2000 Ferenc Mádl, the sole candidate, secured the requisite two-thirds' majority to be elected President of the Republic. He took office on 4 August.

In June 2001 the Országgyülés approved legislation that, with effect from January 2002, granted ethnic Hungarians living in adjacent countries education, employment and medical rights in Hungary. This legislation, widely referred to as the 'status' or 'benefit' law, prompted protests from Romania and Slovakia (see below) that the law discriminated against their non-ethnic Hungarian populations and constituted a violation of sovereignty.

In the legislative elections held on 7 and 21 April 2002, although an alliance of the FYD and the HCP-HDF won 48.7% of the total votes cast (188 seats), a left-wing coalition of the HSP (46.1% of the votes and 178 seats) and the AFD (5.2% of the votes and 20 seats) secured an overall majority in the Országgyülés. Péter Medgyessy of the HSP was sworn in as Prime Minister on 27 May; the Council of Ministers comprised eight further members of the HSP, four members of the AFD and three independents.

In June 2002 media allegations prompted the new Prime Minister to reveal that he had served as a counter-intelligence agent at the Ministry of Finance in 1977–82. Medgyessy insisted that he had worked to protect sensitive economic information from the KGB (the Soviet secret service), in order to negotiate Hungarian membership of the IMF (which it joined in 1982); the AFD subsequently retracted a threat to withdraw from the governing coalition. In July 2002 two parliamentary commissions were established to investigate the past role of Medgyessy and the alleged links of other post-communist government officials with the Soviet-era security service. Meanwhile, in early July the leader of the FYD—HCP, Zoltán Pokorni, who had led demands for Medgyessy's resignation, had relinquished his own party and parliamentary posts, after his father's role as a communist informer was revealed. It subsequently emerged that several members of the FYD—HCP (which had emphasized its anti-communist past during campaigning for the legislative elections) had counter-intelligence associations, thereby severely damaging the party's reputation. Local elections took place on 20 October, in which the governing coalition consolidated its position.

In December 2002 the Országgyülés voted to adopt a number of constitutional amendments, which were required to permit the country to become a full member of the EU (see below). In May 2003 the FYD—HCP re-formed as a new right-wing alliance, Fidesz—Hungarian Civic Alliance (Fidesz), with former premier Orbán as its leader.

In January 2004 the Minister of Finance, Csaba László, left office when it was revealed that the fiscal results for 2003 had exceeded government targets. Tibor Draskovics (a non-partisan candidate) succeeded László in February, and implemented a financial austerity plan shortly afterwards. On 1 May Hungary acceded to full membership of the EU.

On 18 August 2004 Medgyessy resigned as Prime Minister following a decline in support and a severe dispute with the AFD over proposed changes to the Council of Ministers. On 24 August the HSP nominated one of the country's wealthiest business executives, Ferenc Gyurcsány, hitherto the Minister of Children, Youth and Sports, as Prime Minister. Following Gyurcsány's inauguration as Prime Minister on 4 October, he appointed seven new ministers, including a further Minister without Portfolio, Etele Baráth, with responsibility for EU issues. The Council of Ministers comprised 12 members of the HSP, four AFD politicians and two independents. In February 2005 Gyurcsány appointed Andras Bozoki as Minister of Cultural Heritage to replace István Hiller, who had resigned from his ministerial duties after having been appointed Chairman of the HSP in October 2004. Gyurcsány made further adjustments to the Council of Ministers in April 2005. Draskovics was dismissed as Minister of Finance, and replaced by János Veres, a member of the executive committee of the HSP. On 7 June László Sólyom, an independent politician endorsed by the main opposition parties, was elected as President, after three rounds of legislative voting. Sólyom took office on 5 August.

Left-wing coalition elected to second term

At the legislative elections, which were held on 9 and 23 April 2006, the governing HSP-AFD coalition secured 210 of the 386 seats in the Országgyülés and 54.4% of the votes. A coalition of Fidesz and the CDPP, with 42.5% of the votes, secured 164 seats, the HDF took 11 seats (with 2.9% of the votes) and one seat was won by an independent candidate. In early June, after several weeks of coalition negotiations, a new Government, led by Gyurcsány and comprising members of the HSP and the AFD, was formed. On the following day Gyurcsány announced stringent fiscal adjustment measures, which aimed to reduce the considerable budget deficit.

On 17 September 2006 the media broadcast of a clandestine recording of a post-election speech by Gyurcsány to his party members, in which he admitted having repeatedly misled the electorate during the campaign over the country's fiscal situation, precipitated mass anti-Government riots in Budapest. Protesters surrounded government buildings and temporarily seized control of the state television headquarters; some 300 people were injured in the rioting and the ensuing confrontations with the police. On 27 September Gyurcsány issued a public apology at the Government's delay in addressing the economic situation. At municipal elections on 2 October, Fidesz made significant gains, securing mayoralties in 15 of Hungary's 23 largest cities and majorities in 18 of the 19 county councils. Nevertheless, in early October a parliamentary motion of confidence in the Government, proposed by Gyurcsány, was supported by 207 votes in the Országgyülés.

Official celebrations on 23 October 2006, the 50th anniversary of the 1956 uprising against Soviet rule, were marred by anti-Government demonstrations, organized by the leadership of Fidesz, which boycotted commemorations attended by Gyurcsány and demanded his resignation. Security forces suppressed ensuing violent riots, in which about 170 people were injured, and a total of 130 protesters were arrested. Gyurcsány subsequently accused Orbán of inciting the rioting, and the Budapest municipal authorities implemented measures to restrain continuing protests. In February 2007 a commission investigating the rioting issued a report strongly criticizing Fidesz's increasingly populist stance for implying support for the protesters, who were predominantly associated with extreme nationalist groups, and also concluding that the police had employed excessive force in suppressing the violence.

In April 2007 the Minister of Health tendered his resignation, following increasing criticism of planned health care reforms, to be introduced as part of the Government's fiscal austerity plan. In May the Minister of Justice and Law Enforcement also resigned; he was replaced by Albert Takács. In June Gyurcsány reorganized the Government in support of his reform programme. In December Csaba Kákossy became the new Minister of Economy and Transport, following the resignation of János Kóka, who had been elected Chairman of the AFD in March. In February 2008 Tibor Draskovics succeeded Takács as Minister of Justice and Law Enforcement.

In November 2007 one of the principal trade union federations, the Democratic Confederation of Free Trade Unions, organized a widely observed strike by public sector workers in protest against the Government's proposed health care reforms. In December legislation on the disputed reforms was approved in the Országgyülés, but was vetoed by President Sólyom on the grounds that many issues remained unresolved. On 11 February 2008 demonstrations were staged outside parliament to coincide with the repeated approval by the Országgyülés of the health care legislation, which Sólyom was constitutionally obliged to endorse. Fidesz organized a national referendum to seek support for the abolition of newly introduced fees for doctors' visits and hospital stays and in support of state-subsidized university fees. At the referendum, held on 9 March, more than 80% of the votes, cast by some 50.5% of the electorate, were in favour of the abolition of fees. Gyurcsány duly announced that the fees would be abandoned from 1 April.

Minority Government

At the end of March 2008 Gyurcsány dismissed the Minister of Health, who was an AFD representative, prompting the party to withdraw from the governing coalition (which henceforth lacked a parliamentary majority). An extensive government reorganization was approved by 200 votes in the Országgyülés in May. The appointment of Gordon Bajnai, a close associate of Gyurcsány and hitherto the Minister of Local Government and Regional Development, as Minister of National Development and the Economy was viewed as a demonstration of the Government's commitment to implementing measures aimed at reducing the budget deficit. In June Gábor Fodor was elected as the new Chairman of the AFD, following divisions within the party and the emergence of a faction opposed to Kóka (who, however, remained leader of the party's parliamentary caucus).

The international financial crisis, which intensified in late 2008 and which had a marked impact in Hungary, further exacerbated anti-Government sentiment. However, in February 2009 a parliamentary motion proposed by Fidesz to seek support for the organization of early elections was defeated. In mid-March several thousand extreme nationalist supporters demonstrated against the Government in Budapest; some 35 protesters were arrested following clashes with the police. Later that month, at a congress of the HSP, Gyurcsány announced his intention to resign as Prime Minister, citing concern that he had become an 'obstacle' to further economic reform, and relinquished the party leadership. (On 5 April he was succeeded as party leader by Ildikó Lendvai.) Bajnai, an independent candidate nominated by the HSP, was formally elected Prime Minister by the Országgyülés on 14 April; he affirmed his commitment to austerity measures, and subsequently formed a new Council of Ministers. However, Fidesz boycotted the parliamentary vote, and a demonstration was staged in Budapest to demand early legislative elections, as the unpopularity of the HSP became increasingly apparent.

At elections to the European Parliament, held on 7 June 2009, Fidesz, in coalition with the CDPP, secured 56.4% of the votes cast and 14 of the 22 contested seats, the HSP 17.4% of the votes cast and four seats, an extreme nationalist movement, Movement for a Better Hungary (Jobbik), obtained 14.8% of votes and three seats, and the HDF 5.3% of votes and one seat; the rate of electoral participation was recorded at 36.3% of the electorate. The relative success of Jobbik at these polls generated concern both domestically and internationally, partly because of the close association of the party with a proscribed nationalist group, the Hungarian Guard (see Minority Affairs, below), and also because of the frequent public expression of anti-Semitic and anti-Roma sentiments by numerous senior party officials. (The party also incorporated a substantial presence of former members of the HJLP). Fodor resigned as Chairman of the AFD following the party's failure to obtain European representation; in mid-July a congress of the party elected Attila Retkes as his successor. Upon taking office, Retkes urged Kóka's resignation from the leadership of the party's parliamentary faction, and denounced several policies of the Government that were supported by the AFD's parliamentary group. However, Kóka remained in his post; during subsequent months a number of prominent members announced their withdrawal from the party. Meanwhile, Katalin Szili resigned as Chairman of the Országgyülés in September, and was succeeded by Béla Katona of the HSP. In December Draskovics resigned as Minister of Justice and Law Enforcement; he was succeeded by Imre Forgács.

Fidesz returns to power

In the elections to the Országgyülés on 11 and 25 April 2010, Fidesz, again in coalition with the CDPP, secured 263 of the 386 elective seats (enabling it to adopt constitutional amendments). The HSP was the second-placed party, with 59 seats, followed by Jobbik (which secured national representation for the first time), with 47 seats; a recently formed environmentalist party, Politics Can Be Different!, obtained 16 seats. Later in April President Sólyom confirmed the nomination of Orbán as Prime Minister. In early May Orbán appointed a new Government, in which the number of ministries was reduced from 12 to eight. Tibor Navracsics of Fidesz became Deputy Prime Minister and Minister of Public Administration and Justice, and Zsolt Semjén of the CDPP Deputy Prime Minister and Minister without Portfolio. Other principal new appointments included János Martonyi of Fidesz as Minister of Foreign Affairs, the independent Sándor Pintér as Minister of the Interior and György Matolcsy of Fidesz as Minister of the National Economy. The new administration, which was approved by the Országgyülés on 29 May, announced that it intended to introduce legislation to reduce the number of parliamentary deputies by one-half and to rationalize structures of local government. On 29 June the Országgyülés voted to elect Pál Schmitt of Fidesz (the parliamentary Chairman since May), as President of the Republic, in succession to Sólyom. On 10 July Attila Mesterházy was elected as leader of the HSP, replacing Lendvai. Schmitt formally assumed office on 6 August. In municipal elections, which were conducted on 3 October, Fidesz secured 22 of the 23 mayoralties, including in Budapest (where the long-standing AFD Mayor was replaced by a Fidesz-supported candidate, István Tarlós), and majorities in all 19 county councils.

In October 2010 a dispute erupted between the Government, which had adopted a number of controversial fiscal measures through its parliamentary majority, and the Constitutional Court, after the Court reversed new legislation retroactively imposing a 98% tax on large public-sector severance payments. In November the Országgyülés adopted controversial legislation restricting the powers of the Constitutional Court to rule on the state budget, taxes and other financial matters. (Despite its reduced powers, the Constitutional Court ruled again, in May 2011, that the imposition of retroactive tax demands was unconstitutional.) Also in October 2010 legislation was introduced that greatly reduced funding for an independent fiscal council (established in 2008), which had criticized the Government's budget proposals, effectively indicating its abolition. In December 2010 new media legislation, whereby a regulatory authority, comprising five members nominated by the ruling coalition, was empowered to impose large fines on print, broadcast and internet outlets for violating 'public interest, public morals or order', prompted a protest by students in Budapest. The legislation, which entered into effect at the beginning of 2011, coinciding with Hungary's assumption of the EU presidency for a six-month period (see below), continued to attract strenuous criticism from civil liberty organizations and from other EU member states. Following a review of the legislation by the European Commission, which stated that it was in violation of EU regulations on freedom of expression, the Government announced in February that it was to revise its wording. In December the Constitutional Court vetoed parts of the new media legislation.

Recent developments: constitutional reform and the resignation of President Schmitt

On 18 April 2011 the Országgyülés approved a new Constitution, with 262 votes cast in favour, 44 against and one abstention. The text renamed the country 'Hungary', rather than the 'Republic of Hungary', with effect from January 2012. The Constitution included a new preamble, protecting human life from the moment of conception, and reaffirming the traditional definition of marriage as the union of one man and one woman. The opposition expressed concern that the new Constitution might prompt additional legislation to be introduced on contentious issues such the legal position of minority citizens, and lead to a potential ban or strong restrictions on abortion. Described as fiscally conservative, the new basic law also introduced financial restrictions, including a legal limit, equivalent to 50% of GDP, on the permitted level of national debt (see below), causing further concern among political opponents. The non-governmental organization, Human Rights Watch, urged President Schmitt to refer the text back to the Országgyülés for reconsideration; nevertheless, Schmitt signed the new Constitution on 25 April.

A series of legislative reforms were introduced by the ruling party in 2011, alongside the new Constitution, as Fidesz attempted to consolidate its balance of power. In December new legislation was approved significantly reducing the number of members of the Országgyülés from 386 to 199. A new two-tier (hitherto three-tier) parliamentary election system was introduced, providing for 106 seats to be filled in single-member districts and 93 from national party lists. Voters were to have two votes, one for the single-member district and one for the national list. Voting rights were introduced for Hungarian citizens not permanently resident in Hungary. In addition, new legislation on religion acknowledged 14 recognized faiths, including the Catholic, Lutheran and Calvinist churches and three Jewish denominations; the new bill stipulated that only churches that had been active for at least a century were eligible for recognition. As a result, at December 2011 some 300 formerly registered churches were no longer recognized by the State.

Meanwhile, in October 2010 Gyurcsány had announced the launch of a platform known as the Democratic Coalition (DK), within the HSP, following the latter's defeat in the legislative elections. The split within the HSP deepened, and in October 2011 the DK formally withdrew from the HSP and became a political party in its own right. Gyurcsány announced his party's commitment to the welfare state and to reviving 'civic centre-left politics', while declaring his opposition to the new Constitution. Orbán was re-elected as Chairman of Fidesz in July.

With the entry into force of the new Constitution on 1 January 2012, thousands of people protested in the streets of Budapest. In February the European Parliament adopted a resolution expressing serious concerns about the new Constitution and announced that it was investigating whether the new legislation was in breach of 'common European values of freedom and democracy'. The European Commission asked Hungary to submit proposals for amendments to three specific laws affecting the independence of the central bank and the national data office, and imposing a mandatory retirement age on judges and prosecutors, by 17 February. The Commission also opened an inquiry against the Hungarian authorities, citing political interference in the judiciary, the central bank and data protection laws. In early March the Commission announced that Hungary could be referred to the European Court of Justice if it did not expedite the reform of the laws deemed to be in breach of EU standards. Later in the month, at a rally to commemorate the anniversary of the 1848 uprising against Austrian rule, reportedly attended by some 100,000 people, Orbán denounced what he termed the 'colonialism' of the EU, shortly after the European Commission had announced that it was to suspend funding to Hungary (see Economic Affairs). In late April, after the Government announced that it was to amend legislation concerning the central bank, the Commission announced that it was willing to re-open negotiations on financial assistance.

Meanwhile, in late 2011 allegations emerged (which were denied by Schmitt) that the President had committed plagiarism in the composition of his doctoral thesis, which had been awarded by Semmelweis University in Budapest in 1992. Following newspaper reports that a substantial proportion of the text comprised translations of previously published manuscripts, the university conducted an investigation, and at the end of March 2012 announced that it had withdrawn Schmitt's doctoral award. On 2 April Schmitt, while continuing to deny the allegations, resigned as President. In accordance with constitutional norms, the legislative President, Kövér, became acting President. Later in the month Orbán nominated János Áder, a Fidesz member of the European Parliament, and former President of the Országgyülés, as presidential candidate. A presidential election took place in the Országgyülés on 2 May, and Áder was duly elected as President.

Minority affairs

There has been considerable activism within Hungary by the country's ethnic minorities for the protection of their rights. In July 1993 the Országgyülés adopted legislation guaranteeing the cultural, civil and political rights of 12 minority groups and prohibiting ethnic discrimination. Following the approval of this legislation, minority rights activists launched a new campaign to change Hungary's electoral law, with the aim of securing the direct representation of ethnic groups in the legislature. In the 1994 municipal elections, ethnic minorities were able to elect their own local ethnic authorities, with consultative roles on cultural and educational issues affecting the community. In February 1995 Hungary signed the Council of Europe (see p. 256) Convention on the Protection of National Minorities. In April the Roma of Hungary elected their own governing body, the National Autonomous Authority of the Romany Minority (the first such body in the former Eastern bloc), which was empowered to administer funds and deliberate issues affecting the Roma. In December 2008 the Metropolitan Court in Budapest ordered the dissolution of the extreme nationalist Hungarian Guard (established, with the support of Jobbik, in August 2007), which was responsible for attacks and discriminatory behaviour against the Roma community. This dissolution of the Hungarian Guard was confirmed by the Supreme Court in December 2010. (However, former Hungarian Guard members continued to convene, and attempted to reconstitute the movement as a civil service association.)

In March 2010 legislation that criminalized the denial or 'questioning' of the Holocaust (*shoah*) of the Jews during the Second World War was signed into law in Hungary. Although the law was widely supported among the Jewish community of Hungary (and similar legislation existed in numerous neighbouring countries), concern was expressed that the legislation might become a focus of extreme nationalist agitation, and represent an unacceptable prohibition on free speech.

Foreign Affairs

Regional relations

A principal factor governing Hungary's relations with several neighbouring states since the 1990s—particularly Romania and Slovakia—has been the presence in those countries of a substantial population of ethnic Hungarians, including over 1m. permanently resident in Romania and around 500,000 in Slovakia. In September 1996 Hungary and Romania signed a bilateral treaty, guaranteeing the inviolability of the joint border between the two countries and the rights of minority ethnic groups. In May 1997 President Árpád Göncz made an official visit to Romania (the first by a Hungarian Head of State). In August 2001 a meeting between Viktor Orbán and Prime Minister Adrian Năstase of Romania failed to resolve the tensions arising from Hungarian legislation pertaining to the rights of the ethnic Hungarian diaspora (see Democratic consolidation, above). However, a memorandum of understanding was signed by the two Prime Ministers in December, which extended the short-term employment rights offered to ethnic Hungarians under the terms of the law to all Romanian citizens. Finally, in September 2003 a bilateral agreement on the implementation of the status law in Romania was signed in the Romanian capital, Bucharest, by Péter Medgyessy and Năstase.

Apart from issues arising from the presence of a large ethnic Hungarian minority in Slovakia, relations between Hungary and Slovakia were strained by a dispute over the Gabčíkovo-Nagymaros hydroelectric project (a joint Hungarian-Czechoslovak scheme initiated in 1977). In November 1989 Hungary announced that it was to abandon the scheme, following pressure from environmentalists. In July 1991 Czechoslovakia decided to proceed unilaterally with the project; the resumption of work, in February 1992, prompted the Hungarian Government to abrogate the 1977 treaty. In April 1993 it was agreed to refer the case to the International Court of Justice (ICJ).

In March 1995 Prime Minister Horn and his Slovak counterpart, Vladimír Mečiar, signed a Treaty of Friendship and Co-operation, according to which the two countries undertook to guarantee the rights of minority ethnic groups and to recognize the inviolability of their common border. The Treaty came into effect in May 1996, following its ratification by the Slovak President. In August 1997 discussions between Horn and Mečiar resulted in an agreement that a joint committee be established to monitor the standard of human rights of ethnic Hungarians resident in Slovakia and the Slovak community in Hungary. In September the ICJ concluded proceedings regarding the dispute over the Gabčíkovo-Nagymaros hydroelectric project, ruling that both countries had contravened international law. Both Hungary and Slovakia were required to pay compensation for damages incurred, and to resume negotiations regarding the further implementation of the agreement. In February 2006 it was announced that Slovakia and Hungary had agreed to implement the 1997 ICJ ruling on the Gabčíkovo-Nagymaros hydroelectric project.

The entry into force of the Hungarian 'status' law (see above) in January 2002 threatened to damage relations with Slovakia, although that country had in place a similar law, which granted privileges to the Slovak diaspora. In March 2003 the Council of Europe drafted a resolution urging the Hungarian Government to amend the status law. Also in March Hungary agreed to suspend the application of the law in Slovakia, pending the approval by the Országgyülés of a draft amendment stipulating that the legislation was not to apply in EU member countries (Slovakia acceded to the EU in May 2004, along with Hungary—see below). Finally, in December 2003 the Ministers of Foreign Affairs of Hungary and Slovakia signed a bilateral agreement on the implementation of the status law in Slovakia.

Tensions between Hungary and Slovakia were again apparent in August 2009, when the Hungarian President, László Sólyom, was prohibited from entering Slovakia on the instructions of the Slovak Ministry of Foreign Affairs, despite EU regulations on freedom of movement between member states. Sólyom's visit, which was to have been in a private capacity, to unveil a statue to St István (Stephen), the first King of Hungary, in a predominantly ethnically Hungarian town in southern Slovakia, Komárno, was condemned by the President, Prime Minister and legislative Chairman, on the grounds that it took place on 21 August, the anniversary of the 1968 invasion of Czechoslovakia by Warsaw Pact (including Hungarian) troops. The growth in support, in both Hungary and Slovakia, for extreme nationalist parties (Jobbik and the Slovak National Party, respectively) from the late 2000s was also a cause of mutually hostile accusations between elements in both countries. Several days after Sólyom had been prevented from entering Slovakia, two small bombs were detonated outside the Slovak embassy in Budapest. Legislation that took effect in Slovakia from 1 September placing restrictions on the use of languages in an official context other than Slovak was a further source of controversy. In early September 2009 some 10,000 people, believed to be mainly ethnic Hungarians, attended a rally in the southern town of Dunajská Streda to demand that the legislation be amended. Concern was expressed that the legislation might criminalize the use of minority languages in private, as well as official, conversation. Slovakia and Hungary subsequently agreed that the Organization for Security and Co-operation in Europe (OSCE, see p. 388) would oversee the implementation of the law to ensure that it complied with international norms.

On 26 May 2010 the Országgyülés approved controversial legislation, regarded as an extension of the 'status' law, which would permit ethnic Hungarians resident outside the country to apply for Hungarian citizenship with effect from January 2011. The Prime Minister of Slovakia, Robert Fico, described the legislation as representing a security threat to his country, and prompted the amendment, on the same day, of that country's law on citizenship, with the proposed effect that anyone applying for citizenship of a second country would have their Slovak citizenship removed. The Slovakian Government further condemned legislation, adopted by the Országgyülés at the end of May, declaring 4 June, the date of the signing of the Treaty of Trianon in 1920, as 'National Unity Day'. At January 2011 the status law stipulated that ethnic Hungarians residing permanently in neighbouring states, with Hungarian as their first language, would remain eligible for benefits, regardless of whether they held Hungarian citizenship. The amendment was passed to avoid discrimination against those who wished to apply for Hungarian citizenship under new legislation that became effective that month.

In November 1990 Hungary was the first former Eastern bloc, European country to become a member of the Council of Europe. In March 1996 Hungary was admitted to the Organisation for Economic Co-operation and Development (OECD, see p. 379). Meanwhile, Hungary's associate membership of the EU came into effect on 1 February 1994, and in April Hungary became the first post-communist state to apply for full EU membership. In December 2002 Hungary was one of 10 countries formally invited to join the EU in May 2004. At a national referendum, held on 12 April 2003, Hungarian membership of the EU was endorsed by 83.8% of votes cast (with 45.6% of the electorate participating). In December 2007 Hungary, together with eight other nations, implemented the EU's Schengen Agreement, enabling its citizens to travel to and from other member states without border controls. In the same month Hungary became the first EU member state to ratify the draft Treaty of Lisbon by parliamentary vote. In January 2011 Hungary assumed control of the six-month rotational presidency of the EU Council.

Other external relations

Following a North Atlantic Treaty Organization (NATO, see p. 370) summit meeting in Madrid, Spain, in July 1997, Hungary was invited to enter into discussions regarding its application for membership of the Alliance. A national referendum on the country's entry into NATO was conducted in November, at which its accession was approved by 85.3% of the votes cast, with the participation of 49% of the electorate. Hungary was formally admitted to NATO in March 1999 (although it was subsequently subject to some criticism for failing to fulfil its financial commitments). In early 2003 an air base at Taszar, in south-western Hungary, was used by the USA for the training of Iraqi opposition forces, in relation to the US-led military campaign in Iraq. Hungary subsequently contributed 300 soldiers to the international peace-keeping force in Iraq. Following considerable public and political opposition, these were withdrawn from the region in March 2005. Prior to a visit to the Russian capital, Moscow, in March 2007, Prime Minister Ferenc Gyurcsány declared support for plans of the Russian gas producer Gazprom to extend its 'South Stream' pipeline, linking Novorossiisk in southern Russia, to Ankara, Turkey, further to central Europe, which would allow the wider expansion of Russian gas exports. In February 2008 Gyurcsány signed an agreement with Russian government leaders in Moscow, which provided for the construction of the 'South Stream' gas pipeline through Hungary. In March 2009 Gazprom signed an agreement in Moscow with the Hungarian Development Bank, in the presence of Gyurcsány and Russian premier Vladimir Putin, on the establishment of a joint venture for the 'South Stream' pipeline project on Hungarian territory. On the same occasion, the Hungarian Oil and Gas Company (MOL) signed an accord with Gazprom on the construction of a gas storage facility in Hungary. However, in July 2009 Hungary was one of five countries to sign an agreement on the establishment of the EU- and US-supported Nabucco pipeline, which would eventually supply gas from various Central Asian states, by way of Turkey, to Central and South-Eastern Europe.

CONSTITUTION AND GOVERNMENT

On 1 January 2012 a new Constitution entered into force, removing references to the 'Republic of Hungary' and referring only to 'Hungary'. Controversial new laws (see above) were introduced on social and fiscal issues. Legislative power is held by the unicameral Országgyülés (National Assembly), which, under the new Constitution was to comprise 199 members, rather than the previous 386, elected for a term of four years by universal adult suffrage, under a mixed system of proportional and direct representation. The President of the Republic (Head of State) is elected by the Országgyülés for a term of five years. The President may be re-elected for a second term. The Council of Ministers, the highest organ of state administration, is elected by the Assembly on the recommendation of the President. Judicial power is exercised by local courts, labour courts, county courts (or the Metropolitan Court) and the Supreme Court. All judicial offices are filled by election. For local administrative purposes, Hungary is divided into 19 counties (*megyei*) and the capital city (with 23 districts). A 53-member National Autonomous Authority of the Romany Minority, first elected in April 1995, is empowered to administer funds disbursed by the central Government.

REGIONAL AND INTERNATIONAL CO-OPERATION

Hungary became a full member of the European Union (EU, see p. 276) in May 2004. It is also a member of the North Atlantic Treaty Organization (NATO, see p. 370), the Council of Europe, the Organization for Security and Co-operation in Europe (OSCE, see p. 388) and the Organisation for Economic Co-operation and Development (OECD, see p. 379).

Hungary joined the UN in 1955 and became a member of the World Trade Organization (WTO, see p. 433) in 1995.

ECONOMIC AFFAIRS

In 2010, according to estimates by the World Bank, Hungary's gross national income (GNI), measured at average 2008–10 prices, was US $129,923m., equivalent to $12,980 per head (or $19,270 per head on an international purchasing-power parity basis). During 2001–10, it was estimated, the population decreased at an average annual rate of 0.2%, while gross domestic product (GDP) per head increased, in real terms, by an average of 1.7% per year. Overall GDP increased, in real terms, at an average annual rate of 1.5% during 2001–10; real GDP declined by 6.7% in 2009, but increased by 1.2% in 2010.

Agriculture (including hunting, forestry and fishing) contributed 3.8% of GDP in 2010 and engaged 4.5% of the employed labour force in 2008. The principal crops are maize, wheat, sugar beet, barley and sunflower seeds. Viticulture is also important. During 2001–08, according to World Bank estimates, real agricultural GDP increased at an average annual rate of 5.7%. The GDP of the sector declined by 21.0% in 2007, owing to an extremely poor crop harvest caused by higher than average temperatures in the summer of that year. However, the sector showed signs of significant recovery in 2008, when real GDP increased by 50.6%.

Industry (including mining, manufacturing, construction and power) contributed 31.3% of GDP in 2010 and engaged 32.1% of the employed labour force in 2008. The World Bank estimated that real industrial GDP increased at an average annual rate of 3.3% in 2001–08. Industrial GDP decreased by 0.8% in 2008.

Mining and quarrying accounted for 0.2% of GDP in 2009 and engaged 1.7% of the employed labour force in 2008. Hungary's most important mineral resources are lignite (brown coal) and natural gas. Petroleum, bauxite and hard coal are also exploited. At the end of 2010 Hungary's proven coal reserves stood at 1,660m. metric tons.

The manufacturing sector contributed 22.3% of GDP in 2010 and engaged 22.4% of the employed labour force in 2008. According to World Bank estimates, manufacturing GDP increased, in real terms, at an average annual rate of 4.7% in 2001–08. Manufacturing GDP increased by 7.7% in 2007, but decreased by 1.0% in 2008.

The construction sector contributed 4.4% of GDP in 2010 and engaged 8.0% of the labour force in 2008.

In 2008 some 37.0% of Hungary's electricity production was generated by nuclear power, 37.9% by natural gas and 18.0% by coal. Imports of fuels and electricity represented 10.7% of the value of total imports in 2010.

The services sector has a significant role in the Hungarian economy, contributing 64.9% of GDP in 2010, and engaging 63.4% of the employed labour force in 2008. According to the World Bank, the GDP of the services sector increased, in real terms, at an average rate of 2.9% per year in 2001–08. The GDP of the services sector increased by 0.9% in 2007, but decreased by 1.4% in 2008.

In 2010 Hungary recorded a visible trade surplus of US $6,212m., but there was a deficit of $3,049m. on the current account of the balance of payments. In that year the principal source of imports was Germany (accounting for 24.0% of the total); other major sources were Russia, the People's Republic of China, Austria and Poland. Germany was also the principal market for exports in that year (25.1%); other important purchasers were Italy, the United Kingdom, Romania, Slovakia and France. The principal exports in 2010 were machinery and transport equipment (accounting for 60.2% of the total), basic manufactures, and food, beverages and tobacco. The main imports in that year were machinery and transport equipment (accounting for 50.4% of the total), basic manufactures and fuels and electricity.

According to official figures, in 2010 Hungary's overall budgetary surplus amounted to 6,212m. forint. Hungary's general government gross debt was 21,749,420m. forint in 2010, equivalent to 80.2% of GDP. The country's total external debt was an estimated US $107,677m. at the end of 2006, of which $28,017m. was long-term public debt. In that year the cost of debt-servicing was equivalent to 33.1% of the value of exports of goods and services. The annual rate of inflation averaged 5.3% in 2001–09; consumer prices increased by 4.2% in 2009. The average rate of unemployment between December 2011 and February 2012 was 11.6%, according to official figures.

Hungary acceded to the European Union (EU, see p. 276) in 2004, but the country's failure to reduce its budgetary deficit (the largest among EU member nations in 2006) to a level consistent with EU requirements (equivalent to no more than 3% of GDP for two consecutive years) meant that by early 2012 there was no target date for adopting the euro. Legislative elections in April 2010 resulted in the establishment of a new Government with a substantial parliamentary majority, which announced an economic action plan that included a reduction in public sector wage costs, the introduction of a uniform personal income tax rate of 16% and a reduction in the corporate tax burden on small companies. In October the Government, after deciding to withdraw from further IMF funding, announced the imposition of a three-year 'crisis' tax on the banking, telecommunications, energy and retail sectors. In April 2011 a package of fiscal measures and policy reforms, referred to as the Széll Kálmán Plan, was introduced with the aim of reducing the national deficit. Following the introduction of the new Constitution (which entered into force in January 2012), the Constitutional Court's tax and budgetary remit was restricted until national debt was reduced to less than 50% of GDP. Other controversial reforms were also introduced: the President was to be afforded the power to dissolve the Országgyülés (the national legislature) if the national budget was not approved; the powers of the Governor of the central bank were to be restricted; and modifications to tax and pension laws were to require a two-thirds' majority. The EU and the IMF found Hungary to be in breach of European law, and in December 2011 suspended discussions on the provision of precautionary credit, which had been requested by Hungary. In January 2012 the European Commission announced that Hungary had not taken sufficient action to reduce the country's deficit, and in March the EU suspended the release of funds of €495m. to the country on the grounds that its budgetary deficit and debt levels exceeded acceptable levels. Following a contraction in real GDP of about 6.7% in 2009, modest GDP growth, of around 1.2%, resumed in 2010. Growth remained relatively stable in 2011, but in the medium term prospects continued to be threatened by the ongoing financial crisis in the euro area.

PUBLIC HOLIDAYS

2013: 1 January (New Year's Day), 15 March (Anniversary of 1848 uprising against Austrian rule), 1 April (Easter Monday), 1 May (Labour Day), 20 May (Whit Monday), 15 August (Assumption), 20 August (Constitution Day), 23 October (Day of the Proclamation of the Republic), 1 November (All Saints' Day), 25–26 December (Christmas).

Statistical Survey

Source (unless otherwise stated): Központi Statisztikai Hivatal (Hungarian Central Statistical Office), 1525 Budapest, Keleti Károly u. 5–7; tel. (1) 345-6136; fax (1) 345-6378; e-mail erzsebet.veto@office.ksh.hu; internet www.ksh.hu.

Area and Population

AREA, POPULATION AND DENSITY

Area (sq km)	93,027*
Population (census results)	
1 January 1990	10,374,823
1 February 2001	
Males	4,850,650
Females	5,347,665
Total	10,198,315
Population (official estimates at 1 January)	
2009	10,030,975
2010	10,014,324
2011†	9,985,722
Density (per sq km) at 1 January 2011	107.3

* 35,918 sq miles.
† Preliminary figure.

Languages (2001 census): Magyar (Hungarian) 98.6%; Romany 0.5%; German 0.3%; Slovak 0.1%; Croatian 0.1%; Ukrainian 0.1%; Others 0.2%.

POPULATION BY AGE AND SEX
('000, official estimates at 1 January 2011)

	Males	Females	Total
0–14	746	710	1,456
15–64	3,385	3,131	6,516
65 and over	612	1,402	2,014
Total	4,743	5,243	9,986

ADMINISTRATIVE DIVISIONS
(population at 1 January 2011)

	Area (sq km)	Population	Density (per sq km)	County town (with population)
Counties:				
Bács-Kiskun	8,445	524,841	62.1	Kecskemét (113,275)
Baranya	4,430	391,455	88.4	Pécs (157,721)
Békés	5,630	361,802	64.3	Békéscsaba (64,074)
Borsod-Abaúj-Zemplén	7,250	684,793	94.5	Miskolc (168,075)
Csongrád	4,263	421,827	99.0	Szeged (170,285)
Fejér	4,358	426,120	97.8	Székesfehérvár (101,943)
Győr-Moson-Sopron	4,208	449,967	106.9	Győr (131,267)
Hajdú-Bihar	6,211	539,674	86.9	Debrecen (208,016)
Heves	3,637	307,985	84.7	Eger (56,530)
Jász-Nagykun-Szolnok	5,582	386,752	69.3	Szolnok (74,544)
Komárom-Esztergom	2,265	311,411	137.5	Tatabánya (70,164)
Nógrád	2,546	201,919	79.3	Salgótarján (37,166)
Pest	6,391	1,237,561	193.6	Érd (65,043)
Somogy	6,036	317,947	52.7	Kaposvár (67,979)
Szabolcs-Szatmár-Bereg	5,937	555,496	93.6	Nyíregyháza (117,852)
Tolna	3,703	231,183	62.4	Szekszárd (33,720)
Vas	3,336	257,688	77.2	Szombathely (79,590)
Veszprém	4,493	356,573	79.4	Veszprém (64,339)
Zala	3,784	287,043	75.9	Zalaegerszeg (61,970)
Capital city				
Budapest*	525	1,733,685	3,302.3	—
Total	93,027	9,985,722	107.3	—

* Budapest has separate county status.

PRINCIPAL TOWNS
(estimates at mid-2007)

Budapest (capital)	1,699,213	Győr	128,537
Debrecen	204,604	Nyíregyháza	116,586
Miskolc	171,867	Kecskemét	110,082
Szeged	165,961	Székesfehérvár	101,678
Pécs	156,657		

Source: UN, *Demographic Yearbook*.

2011 (official estimate at 1 January): Budapest 1,733,685.

BIRTHS, MARRIAGES AND DEATHS

	Registered live births		Registered marriages		Registered deaths	
	Number	Rate (per 1,000)	Number	Rate (per 1,000)	Number	Rate (per 1,000)
2003	94,647	9.3	45,398	4.5	135,823	13.4
2004	95,137	9.4	43,791	4.3	132,492	13.1
2005	97,496	9.7	44,234	4.4	135,732	13.5
2006	99,871	9.9	44,528	4.4	131,603	13.1
2007	97,613	9.7	40,842	4.1	132,938	13.2
2008	99,149	9.9	40,105	4.0	130,027	13.0
2009	96,442	9.6	36,730	3.7	130,414	13.0
2010	90,335	9.0	35,520	3.6	130,456	13.0

Life expectancy (years at birth, WHO estimates): 74 (males 70; females 78) in 2009 (Source: WHO, *World Health Statistics*).

ECONOMICALLY ACTIVE POPULATION
(labour force surveys, '000 persons aged 15 years to 74 years)

	2006	2007	2008
Agriculture, hunting, forestry and fishing	190.8	182.9	174.1
Mining and quarrying	15.0	14.6	9.0
Manufacturing	865.2	872.0	870.8
Electricity, gas and water supply	67.6	64.2	57.4
Construction	321.6	330.5	309.5
Wholesale and retail trade; repair of motor vehicles, motorcycles and personal and household goods	582.0	591.5	585.0
Hotels and restaurants	157.2	156.1	157.2
Transport, storage and communications	301.3	301.7	287.4
Financial intermediation	80.3	83.8	94.7
Real estate, renting and business activities	282.8	282.9	306.6
Public administration and defence; compulsory social security	299.2	285.3	288.6
Education	322.9	316.3	310.7
Health and social work	269.5	260.4	249.1
Other community, social and personal service activities	174.7	184.0	176.9
Households with employed persons	—	—	1.9
Extra-territorial organizations and bodies	—	—	0.5
Total employed	3,930.1	3,926.2	3,879.4
Unemployed	316.8	311.9	329.2
Total labour force	4,246.9	4,238.1	4,208.6
Males	2,302.0	2,307.2	2,285.1
Females	1,944.9	1,930.9	1,923.5

Source: ILO.

Health and Welfare

KEY INDICATORS

Total fertility rate (children per woman, 2009)	1.4
Under-5 mortality rate (per 1,000 live births, 2009)	6.0
HIV/AIDS (% of persons aged 15–49, 2009)	<0.1
Physicians (per 1,000 head, 2006)	3.0
Hospital beds (per 1,000 head, 2006)	7.9
Health expenditure (2008): US $ per head (PPP)	1,506
Health expenditure (2008): % of GDP	7.2
Health expenditure (2008): public (% of total)	68.9
Total carbon dioxide emissions ('000 metric tons, 2007)	56,425.6
Carbon dioxide emissions per head (metric tons, 2007)	5.6
Human Development Index (2011): ranking	38
Human Development Index (2011): value	0.816

For sources and definitions, see explanatory note on p. vi.

Agriculture

PRINCIPAL CROPS
('000 metric tons)

	2008	2009	2010
Wheat	5,630.8	4,419.2	3,763.7
Barley	1,467.1	1,063.9	965.7
Maize	8,897.1	7,528.4	6,967.2
Rye	112.5	72.5	79.4
Oats	181.8	111.1	122.8
Triticale (wheat-rye hybrid)	503.4	360.7	371.9
Potatoes	683.9	560.6	439.9
Sugar beet	573.2	737.0	818.9
Peas, dry	46.0	32.5	36.6
Soybeans (Soya beans)	74.1	71.6	85.4
Sunflower seed	1,468.1	1,256.2	969.7
Rapeseed	654.7	579.4	530.6
Cabbages and other brassicas	103.2	100.2	76.6
Tomatoes	205.6	192.8	134.3
Cucumbers and gherkins	55.4	51.7	38.0
Chillies and peppers, green	166.6	168.9	122.4
Onions, dry	67.4	61.2	40.9
Peas, green	117.8	98.5	61.1
Carrots and turnips	75.2	65.6	58.5
Maize, green	536.6	421.7	302.8
Watermelons	224.4	220.4	141.1
Apples	568.6	575.4	496.9
Sour (Morello) cherries	68.2	78.8	51.9
Peaches and nectarines	47.5	61.4	54.2
Plums and sloes	56.0	51.5	70.9
Grapes	570.5	550.0	294.8
Tobacco, unmanufactured	9.7	6.7	7.8

Aggregate production ('000 metric tons, may include official, semi-official or estimated data): Total cereals 16,840.7 in 2008, 13,590.4 in 2009, 12,304.2 in 2010; Total roots and tubers 683.9 in 2008, 560.6 in 2009, 439.9 in 2010; Total vegetables (incl. melons) 1,817.7 in 2008, 1,614.3 in 2009, 1,144.6 in 2010; Total fruits (excl. melons) 1,428.3 in 2008, 1,452.3 in 2009, 1,124.3 in 2010.

Source: FAO.

LIVESTOCK
('000 head, year ending September)

	2008	2009	2010
Cattle	705	701	700
Pigs	3,871	3,383	3,247
Sheep	1,231	1,236	1,223
Goats	67	66	58
Horses	60	58	61
Chickens	29,866	31,165	32,128
Ducks	2,230	2,904	3,713
Geese	1,817	2,120	1,425
Turkeys	4,368	3,527	3,018

Source: FAO.

LIVESTOCK PRODUCTS
('000 metric tons)

	2008	2009	2010
Cattle meat	32.1	30.2	27.6
Sheep meat	0.9	0.8	0.8
Pig meat	461.2	453.5	452.1
Chicken meat	217.2	213.3	221.4
Duck meat	42.6	52.3	52.4
Rabbit meat	2.8	3.6	5.4
Cows' milk	1,840.5	1,758.2	1,684.9
Sheep's milk	2.0	1.4	1.8
Goats' milk	3.2	3.3	3.8
Hen eggs	159.9	155.9	151.8
Other poultry eggs*	4.4	4.0	3.9
Honey	22.4	22.5	16.5
Wool, greasy	4.5	4.4	4.3*

* FAO estimate(s).

Source: FAO.

Forestry

ROUNDWOOD REMOVALS
('000 cu metres, excl. bark)

	2008	2009	2010
Sawlogs, veneer logs and logs for sleepers	1,635	979	1,079
Pulpwood	832	853	954
Other industrial wood	248	533	713
Fuel wood	2,561	2,879	2,994
Total	5,276	5,244	5,740

Source: FAO.

SAWNWOOD PRODUCTION
('000 cu metres, incl. railway sleepers)

	2008	2009	2010
Coniferous (softwood)	89	9	13
Broadleaved (hardwood)	118	130*	160*
Total	207	139*	173*

* Unofficial figure.

Source: FAO.

Fishing

(metric tons, live weight)

	2007	2008	2009
Capture	7,024	7,394	6,366
Common carp	3,554	3,913	3,238
Silver carp	583	578	367
Other cyprinids	1,344	1,340	1,257
Aquaculture	15,864	15,687	14,825
Common carp	9,570	10,485	9,931
Grass carp	591	578	480
Silver carp	2,484	1,493	1,567
North African catfish	1,911	1,839	1,716
Freshwater fishes	823	761	743
Total catch	22,888	23,081	21,191

Source: FAO.

Mining

('000 metric tons, unless otherwise indicated)

	2007	2008	2009
Brown coal	1,392	1,373	1,370*
Lignite	8,352	8,041	8,000
Crude petroleum	839	775	743
Bauxite	546	511	317
Natural gas (million cu metres)†	2,653	2,691	2,517

* Estimate.
† Marketed production.

Source: US Geological Survey.

Industry

SELECTED PRODUCTS

('000 metric tons unless otherwise indicated)

	2006	2007	2008
Crude steel*	2,144	2,317	2,160
Cement*	3,724	3,552	3,544
Nitrogenous fertilizers†	302	223	n.a.
Refined sugar	493	346	188
Non-rubber footwear ('000 pairs)	1,580	5,346	n.a.
Electric energy (million kWh)	35,859	39,960	40,025
Radio receivers ('000)	2,258	2,341	1,926

* Source: US Geological Survey.
† Production in terms of nitrogen (Source: FAO).

Source: mainly UN Industrial Commodity Statistics Database.

2009 ('000 metric tons): Crude steel 1,401; Cement 3,200 (estimate) (Source: US Geological Survey).

Finance

CURRENCY AND EXCHANGE RATES

Monetary Units

100 fillér = 1 forint.

Sterling, Dollar and Euro Equivalents (30 December 2011)

£1 sterling = 372.115 forint;
US $1 = 240.680 forint;
€1 = 311.416 forint;
1,000 forint = £2.69 = $4.15 = €3.21.

Average Exchange Rate (forint per US dollar)

2009 202.342
2010 207.944
2011 201.055

BUDGET

('000 million forint)

Revenue	2009	2010	2011*
Payments of economic units	1,017.5	1,125.8	1,182.6
Corporate taxes	385.5	323.4	288.0
Special tax on business	156.9	–32.4	—
Simplified business tax	169.7	181.9	180.1
Gambling tax	66.7	53.4	51.3
Other central payments	111.6	44.1	109.8
Taxes on consumption	3,070.9	3,200.1	3,402.4
Value-added tax	2,168.5	2,313.6	2,489.0
Excises and tax on consumption	902.4	886.6	913.4
Payments of households†	2,020.2	1,860.5	1,446.2
Personal income tax revenue of the central budget	1,899.7	1,773.9	1,363.0
Fees	112.2	83.5	81.9
Central budgetary institutions and chapter-administered appropriations	1,624.8	1,878.2	1,794.7
Payments of general government sub-systems	226.4	77.0	32.8
Payments of extra-budgetary funds	146.1	8.0	—
Payments related to state property	143.4	66.4	43.5
Revenue related to debt service	184.3	257.0	83.6
Other revenues	—	—	95.6
Transfers from the European Union	36.8	–0.1	29.2
Total	8,324.2	8,464.7	8,110.6

Expenditure	2009	2010	2011*
Subsidies to economic units	178.6	201.4	214.9
Supports to the media	53.7	45.8	58.7
Consumer price subsidy	107.4	107.3	109.0
Housing grants	199.3	147.4	126.0
Family benefits and social subsidies	641.0	632.4	628.3
Family benefits	464.6	460.8	456.2
Income-supplement benefits	149.9	144.8	145.6
Payments of central budgetary institutions and chapter-administered appropriations	4,047.2	4,204.7	4,082.5
Transfers to general government sub-systems†	2,262.8	2,424.4	1,897.4
Contribution to social-security funds	913.8	1,147.5	637.4
Transfers to local governments	1,308.5	1,259.4	1,173.3
Transfer to non-profit organizations	5.3	5.0	3.8
Expenditures of international transactions	9.5	—	—
Debt service related expenditures and interest expenditures	1,180.2	1,136.4	1,067.2
Reserves	—	—	123.9
Reserve for interest risk	—	—	—
State property expenditures	99.3	80.8	594.4
Extraordinary and other expenditures	38.0	51.0	48.6
Government guarantees redeemed	20.4	33.5	35.4
Debt assumptions	1.6	0.1	0.4
Contribution to the European Union budget	223.7	230.2	258.1
Total	9,067.9	9,300.5	9,248.7

* Budget estimates.
† Including personal income tax ceded to local governments.

INTERNATIONAL RESERVES

(US $ million at 31 December)

	2008	2009	2010
Gold (national valuation)	86	109	139
IMF special drawing rights	54	1,479	1,154
Reserve position in IMF	114	116	114
Foreign exchange	33,620	42,479	43,581
Total	33,874	44,183	44,988

Source: IMF, *International Financial Statistics*.

MONEY SUPPLY

('000 million forint at 31 December)

	2008	2009	2010
Currency outside depositary corporations	2,137.2	2,039.3	2,218.3
Transferable deposits	4,024.8	4,082.3	4,416.7
Other deposits	8,111.7	8,277.4	7,758.1
Securities other than shares	1,368.2	1,756.2	2,440.7
Broad money	15,641.8	16,155.2	16,833.7

Source: IMF, *International Financial Statistics*.

COST OF LIVING

(Consumer Price Index; base: 2000 = 100)

	2006	2007	2008
Food	144.8	161.5	177.9
Fuel and power	160.9	200.6	225.9
Clothing	116.1	117.2	117.1
Rent	168.4	181.2	197.5
All items (incl. others)	138.3	149.3	158.4

2009: Food 185.7; All items (incl. others) 165.0.

Source: ILO.

NATIONAL ACCOUNTS

('000 million forint at current prices)

Expenditure on the Gross Domestic Product

	2008	2009	2010
Government final consumption expenditure	2,674.5	2,695.8	2,849.9
Private final consumption expenditure*	17,501.2	17,087.4	17,236.4
Changes in inventories	489.4	–700.4	116.1
Gross fixed capital formation	5,760.0	5,295.2	4,806.3
Total domestic expenditure	26,425.1	24,378.1	25,008.7
Exports of goods and services	21,677.1	19,881.0	23,148.8
Less Imports of goods and services	21,556.6	18,636.2	21,409.8
GDP in purchasers' values	26,545.6	25,622.9	26,747.7

* Includes non-profit institutions serving households.

Gross Domestic Product by Economic Activity

	2008	2009	2010
Agriculture, hunting, forestry and fishing	912.0	746.6	852.7
Mining, quarrying and utilities	897.2	975.1	1,042.2
Manufacturing	4,881.4	4,360.5	5,036.0
Construction	1,112.6	1,054.9	995.8
Wholesale and retail trade; repair of motor vehicles, accommodation and food service activities, etc.	2,943.2	2,558.7	2,541.3
Transport, storage and communications	2,472.1	2,502.0	2,559.1
Financial intermediation	937.9	1,046.6	1,071.9
Real estate, renting and business activities	3,738.7	3,782.9	3,862.7
Public administration, defence and compulsory social security; education; human health and social work activities	4,071.9	3,994.5	3,999.2
Other community, social and personal service activities	679.0	635.3	653.9
Gross value added in basic prices	22646.0	21,657.1	22,614.8
Taxes *less* subsidies on products	3,899.5	3,965.6	4,132.8
GDP in market prices	26,545.6	25,622.9	26,747.7

BALANCE OF PAYMENTS

(US $ million)

	2008	2009	2010
Exports of goods f.o.b.	107,239	81,563	93,294
Imports of goods f.o.b.	–108,031	–76,780	–87,082
Trade balance	–792	4,782	6,212
Exports of services	20,277	18,578	19,056
Imports of services	–18,822	–16,669	–15,879
Balance on goods and services	663	6,691	9,389
Other income received	16,296	16,982	15,552
Other income paid	–27,232	–23,711	–22,389
Balance on goods, services and income	–10,273	–38	2,552
Current transfers received	2,657	3,401	3,410
Current transfers paid	–3,500	–2,890	–2,913
Current balance	–11,116	473	3,049
Capital account (net)	1,649	1,493	2,295

—continued	2008	2009	2010
Direct investment abroad	–70,261	–3,482	45,187
Direct investment from abroad	72,257	3,354	–41,989
Portfolio investment assets	–3,854	–1,061	–437
Portfolio investment liabilities	910	–3,724	604
Financial derivatives assets	12,981	7,766	6,518
Financial derivatives liabilities	–14,044	–6,732	–5,679
Other investment assets	–3,574	–1,049	–906
Other investment liabilities	22,719	7,702	–1,220
Net errors and omissions	–3,493	–775	–3,259
Overall balance	4,173	3,965	4,162

Source: IMF, *International Financial Statistics*.

External Trade

PRINCIPAL COMMODITIES

('000 million forint)

Imports c.i.f.	2008	2009	2010
Food, beverages and tobacco	861.2	853.5	901.0
Crude materials	357.0	251.0	382.1
Fuels and electricity	2,359.4	1,690.2	1,948.6
Basic manufactures	5,847.0	5,017.7	5,790.1
Machinery and transport equipment	9,078.9	7,705.1	9,152.5
Total	18,503.5	15,517.5	18,174.3

Exports f.o.b.	2008	2009	2010
Food, beverages and tobacco	1,234.6	1,201.1	1,365.3
Crude materials	434.0	365.8	477.4
Fuels and electricity	691.8	425.8	558.6
Basic manufactures	4,894.7	4,573.6	5,435.5
Machinery and transport equipment	11,185.4	10,007.7	11,853.4
Total	18,440.4	16,574.0	19,690.0

PRINCIPAL TRADING PARTNERS

('000 million forint)*

Imports c.i.f.	2008	2009	2010
Austria	1,145.1	1,008.5	1,124.9
Belgium	429.2	372.9	401.5
China, People's Republic	1,050.4	1,000.9	1,284.5
Czech Republic	699.3	525.0	588.3
France	804.5	681.1	671.8
Germany	4,711.9	3,848.8	4,360.6
Italy	781.5	642.4	777.9
Japan	478.3	390.6	394.5
Korea, Republic	312.2	401.5	595.4
Netherlands	841.8	734.5	821.0
Poland	732.0	633.4	958.4
Romania	397.4	362.5	474.0
Russia	1,718.5	1,132.2	1,419.1
Slovakia	654.5	651.6	754.9
Spain	270.9	233.0	228.2
Sweden	165.0	132.9	165.6
Switzerland	163.9	127.6	136.7
Ukraine	262.5	139.7	182.4
United Kingdom	363.7	306.4	341.5
USA	337.1	309.9	327.8
Total (incl. others)	18,503.5	15,517.5	18,174.3

Exports f.o.b.	2008	2009	2010
Austria	903.2	754.6	965.3
Belgium	311.6	290.5	296.0
Croatia	290.4	242.4	238.5
Czech Republic	736.8	539.8	682.1
Finland	94.2	59.4	69.2
France	868.3	901.7	984.9
Germany	4,911.4	4,235.9	4,941.8
Italy	982.1	949.0	1,089.2
Netherlands	530.7	615.1	622.4
Poland	729.0	613.8	725.2

Exports f.o.b.—*continued*	2008	2009	2010
Romania	980.5	871.0	1,060.5
Russia	661.8	590.1	704.0
Slovakia	876.3	825.3	1,053.1
Slovenia	214.1	180.6	208.1
Spain	512.6	558.0	625.2
Sweden	187.5	174.3	197.2
Switzerland	232.8	191.3	193.1
Ukraine	366.8	250.7	401.5
United Kingdom	865.4	877.7	1,070.5
USA	422.4	380.3	401.3
Total (incl. others)	18,440.4	16,574.0	19,690.0

* Imports by country of origin; exports by country of destination.

Transport

RAILWAYS
(traffic)

	2008	2009	2010
Passengers carried (million)	144.9	142.8	140.5
Passenger-kilometres (million)	8,293	8,073	7,692
Freight carried ('000 metric tons)	51,542	42,277	45,794
Net ton-kilometres (million)	9,874	7,673	8,809

ROAD TRAFFIC
(motor vehicles in use at 31 December)

	2008	2009	2010
Passenger cars	3,055,427	3,013,719	2,984,063
Buses and coaches	17,995	17,720	17,641
Lorries and vans	424,452	419,416	416,672
Motorcycles and mopeds	141,540	141,956	142,251
Road tractors	46,303	47,304	48,207

SHIPPING

Merchant Fleet
(registered at 31 December)

	2001	2002	2003
Number of vessels	1	1	2
Total displacement (grt)	1,901	3,784	7,568

Source: Lloyd's Register-Fairplay, *World Fleet Statistics*.

INLAND WATERWAYS
(traffic)

	2008	2009	2010
Freight carried ('000 metric tons)	8,829	7,744	9,951
Freight ton-km (million)	2,250	1,831	2,393

CIVIL AVIATION
(traffic)

	2004	2005	2006
Kilometres flown (million)	52	54	57
Passengers carried ('000)	2,546	2,735	3,073
Passenger-km (million)	3,510	3,806	4,140
Total ton-km	344	368	401

Source: UN, *Statistical Yearbook*.

Tourism

TOURISTS BY COUNTRY OF ORIGIN
('000 arrivals, including visitors in transit)

	2008	2009	2010
Austria	6,397	6,437	6,696
Croatia	990	971	868
Germany	3,103	3,130	3,135
Poland	1,526	1,566	1,540
Romania	8,079	7,783	7,614
Serbia	2,279	2,203	2,329
Slovakia	8,142	9,095	8,404
Ukraine	1,371	1,685	1,819
Total (incl. others)	39,554	40,624	39,904

Tourist receipts (million forint): 1,087,161 in 2008; 1,200,637 in 2009; 1,189,819 in 2010.

Communications Media

	2008	2009	2010
Telephones ('000 main lines in use)	3,094.0	3,068.7	2,977.2
Mobile cellular telephones ('000 subscribers)	12,224.2	11,792.5	12,011.8
Internet subscribers ('000)	1,705.9	1,902.5	1,971.4
Broadband subscribers ('000)	1,681.1	1,880.0	1,956.2
Book production: titles	15,255	13,562	12,997
Book production: copies ('000)	44,500	37,626	34,416

Radio receivers ('000 in use): 7,245 in 1998; 7,231 in 1999.

Television receivers ('000 in use): 4,377 in 1998; 4,519 in 1999; 4,451 in 2000.

Daily newspapers: 34 titles (average daily circulation 2,195,000) in 2004.

Non-daily newspapers: 97 titles (average daily circulation 1,368,000) in 2004.

Personal computers: 2,571,660 (255.7 per 1,000 persons) in 2007.

Sources: partly UNESCO, *Statistical Yearbook*, and International Telecommunication Union.

Education

(2010/11, full- and part-time education, preliminary)

	Institutions	Teachers	Students
Pre-primary	4,358	30,359	338,162
Primary	3,306	73,565	758,566
Vocational	802	10,832	147,340
Secondary	1,815	38,121	515,468
General	876	18,292	241,872
Vocational	939	19,829	273,596
Tertiary	69	21,495	361,347

Pupil-teacher ratio (primary education, UNESCO estimate): 10.5 in 2008/09 (Source: UNESCO Institute for Statistics).

Adult literacy rate (UNESCO estimates): 99.4% (males 99.4%; females 99.3%) in 2009 (Source: UNESCO Institute for Statistics).

Directory

The Government

HEAD OF STATE

President of the Republic: JÁNOS ÁDER.

COUNCIL OF MINISTERS

(May 2012)

Comprising members of Fidesz—Hungarian Civic Alliance (Fidesz), the Christian Democratic People's Party (CDPP) and Independents.

Prime Minister: VIKTOR ORBÁN (Fidesz).

Deputy Prime Minister, Minister of Public Administration and Justice: TIBOR NAVRACSICS (Fidesz).

Deputy Prime Minister, Minister without Portfolio: ZSOLT SEMJÉN (CDPP).

Minister of Foreign Affairs: JÁNOS MARTONYI (Fidesz).

Minister of Defence: CSABA HENDE (Fidesz).

Minister of Rural Development: Dr SÁNDOR FAZEKAS (Fidesz).

Minister of the Interior: SÁNDOR PINTÉR (Independent).

Minister of National Development: ZSUZSA NÉMETH (Independent).

Minister of the National Economy: GYÖRGY MATOLCSY (Fidesz).

Minister of National Resources: MIKLÓS RÉTHELYI (Independent).

Minister without Portfolio, responsible for Liaison with certain International Financial Organizations: TAMÁS FELLEGI (Independent).

MINISTRIES

Office of the President: 1014 Budapest, Szent György tér 1; tel. (1) 224-5000; fax (1) 784-9181; e-mail ugyfelkapu@keh.hu; internet www.keh.hu.

Office of the Prime Minister: 1357 Budapest, pf. 6; tel. (1) 795-5000; fax (1) 795-0381; e-mail titkarsag@me.gov.hu; internet www.kormany.hu.

Ministry of Defence: 1055 Budapest, Balaton u. 7–11; tel. (1) 236-5111; fax (1) 474-1335; e-mail hmugyfelszolgalat@hm.gov.hu; internet www.kormany.hu/hu/honvedelmi-miniszterium.

Ministry of Foreign Affairs: 1027 Budapest, Bem rakpart 47; tel. (1) 458-1000; fax (1) 212-5918; e-mail kozkapcsolat@kum.gov.hu; internet www.kormany.hu/hu/kulugyminiszterium.

Ministry of the Interior: 1051 Budapest, József Attila u. 2–4; tel. (1) 441-1000; fax (1) 441-1437; e-mail ugyfelszolgalat@bm.gov.hu; internet www.kormany.hu/hu/belugyminiszterium.

Ministry of National Development: 1011 Budapest, Fő u. 44–50; tel. (1) 795-1700; fax (1) 795-0697; e-mail ugyfelszolgalat@nfm.gov.hu; internet www.kormany.hu/hu/nemzeti-fejlesztesi-miniszterium.

Ministry of the National Economy: 1051 Budapest, József Nádor tér 2–4; tel. (1) 374-2700; fax (1) 374-2925; e-mail ugyfelszolgalat@ngm.gov.hu; internet www.kormany.hu/hu/nemzetgazdasagi-miniszterium.

Ministry of National Resources: 1055 Budapest, Szalay u. 10–14; tel. (1) 795-1200; fax (1) 795-0012; e-mail info@nefmi.gov.hu; internet www.kormany.hu/hu/nemzeti-eroforras-miniszterium.

Ministry of Public Administration and Justice: 1055 Budapest, Kossuth Lajos tér 4; tel. (1) 795-1000; fax (1) 795-0002; e-mail lakossag@kim.gov.hu; internet www.kormany.hu/hu/kozigazgatasi-es-igazsagugyi-miniszterium.

Ministry of Rural Development: 1055 Budapest, Kossuth Lajos tér 11; tel. (1) 795-2000; fax (1) 795-0200; e-mail miniszter@vm.gov.hu; internet www.kormany.hu/hu/videkfejlesztesi-miniszterium.

President

Following the resignation of PÁL SCHMITT on 2 April 2012, a presidential election was conducted in the Országgyűlés on 2 May. JÁNOS ÁDER was duly elected as President.

Legislature

Országgyűlés (National Assembly)

1055 Budapest, Kossuth Lajos tér 1–3; 1357 Budapest, POB 2; tel. (1) 441-4000; fax (1) 441-5000; internet www.mkogy.hu.

President: LÁSZLÓ KÖVÉR.

General Election, 11 and 25 April 2010

Parties	Seats			
	A*	B*	C*	Total
Fidesz—Hungarian Civic Alliance-Christian Democratic People's Party (Fidesz-CDPP) coalition†	173†	87	3	263†
Hungarian Socialist Party (HSP)	2	28	29	59
Movement for a Better Hungary (Jobbik)	—	26	21	47
Politics Can Be Different!	—	5	11	16
Independent	1	—	—	1
Total	176	146	64	386

* The 386 seats of the Országgyűlés comprise 176 elected in single-mandate constituencies (A), 146 elected on the basis of regional lists (B) and 64 compensatory seats (C) that take account of the share of the national vote allocated to parties or coalitions that are under-represented in proportion to their share of the vote in categories A and B.

† Including one seat won in coalition, additionally, with the Entrepreneurs' Party.

Election Commission

Országos Választási Iroda (OVI) (National Election Office): 1357 Budapest, pf. 2; tel. (1) 795-3303; fax (1) 795-0143; e-mail visz@otm.gov.hu; internet www.valasztas.hu; Chair. VILMOS BORDÁS.

Political Organizations

Alliance of Free Democrats (AFD) (Szabad Demokraták Szövetsége—SzDSz): 1092 Budapest, Ráday u. 50; tel. (1) 223-2050; fax (1) 222-3599; e-mail szerkesztoseg@szdsz.hu; internet www.szdsz.hu; f. 1988; formed an electoral alliance with the Hungarian Socialist Party (q.v.) to contest the 2006 legislative elections; Exec. Chair. VIKTOR SZABADAI.

Christian Democratic People's Party (CDPP) (Kereszténydemokrata Néppárt—KDNP): 1141 Budapest, Bazsarózsa u. 69; tel. (1) 489-0880; fax (1) 489-0879; e-mail kdnp@kdnp.hu; internet www.kdnp.hu; f. 1989 as revival of pre-communist-era party; formed an electoral alliance with the Fidesz—Hungarian Civic Alliance (q.v.) to contest the 2010 legislative elections; Chair. SEMJÉN ZSOLT.

Civil Movement (Civil Mozgalom): 1426 Budapest, POB 122; tel. (70) 231-6933; e-mail civilek@civilmozgalom.hu; internet www.civilmozgalom.hu; seeks to reduce government bureaucracy and eliminate corruption, and the strengthening of civil society; Leader MÁRIA SERES.

Democratic Community of Welfare and Freedom (Jólét és Szabadság Demokrata Közösség—JESZ): 1026 Budapest, Szilágyi Erszébet fasor 73; tel. (1) 225-2280; fax (1) 225-2290; e-mail kis.jozsef@jesz.hu; internet www.mdf.hu; f. 1987; fmrly Hungarian Democratic Forum; present name 2011; centre-right; Chair. ZSOLT MAKAY.

Entrepreneurs' Party (Vállalkozók Pártja): 6000 Kecskemét, Csány János körút 12; tel. (76) 509-527; f. 1989; established an electoral pact with Fidesz—Hungarian Civic Alliance (q.v.) and the Christian Democratic People's Party in advance of the 2006 legislative elections, and contested a number of seats in alliance with these two parties at the 2010 legislative elections; Chair. ANTAL CSÁSZÁR.

Fidesz—Hungarian Civic Alliance (Fidesz) (Fidesz—Magyar Polgári Szöevetség): 1062 Budapest, Lendvay u. 28; tel. (1) 555-2000; fax (1) 441-5463; e-mail fidesz@fidesz.hu; internet www.fidesz.hu; f. 1988 as the Federation of Young Democrats; renamed April 1995; re-formed as an alliance in 2003, with a new charter; Chair. VIKTOR ORBÁN; 10,000 mems.

Hungarian Justice and Life Party (Magyar Igazság és Élet Pártja): 1085 Budapest, Rökk Szilárd u. 19; tel. (1) 309-0393; fax (1) 309-0394; e-mail miep@vipmail.hu; internet www.miep.hu; f. 1993; contested 2006 legislative elections as Third Way, in alliance with Movement for a Better Hungary (Jobbik, q.v.); extreme right-wing, nationalist party; Chair. ISTVÁN CSURKA.

Hungarian Social Democratic Party (HSDP) (Magyarországi Szociáldemokrata Párt—MSzDP): 1535 Budapest; tel. (1) 214-9496; fax (1) 214-9497; e-mail mszdp@mszdp.hu; internet www.mszdp.hu; f. 1890; absorbed by the Communist Party in 1948; revived 1988;

affiliated with the Social Democratic Youth Movement; Chair. LÁSZLÓ KAPOLYI.

Hungarian Socialist Party (HSP) (Magyar Szocialista Párt—MSzP): 1066 Budapest, Jókai u. 6; tel. (1) 459-7200; fax (1) 210-0081; e-mail info@mszp.hu; internet www.mszp.hu; f. 1989 to replace the Hungarian Socialist Workers' Party; Pres. ATTILA MESTERHÁZY.

Movement for a Better Hungary (Jobbik) (Jobbik Magyarországért Mozgalom): 1113 Budapest, Villányi út 20A; tel. and fax (1) 365-1488; e-mail jobbik@jobbik.hu; internet www.jobbik.hu; f. 2003; extreme nationalist; Pres. GÁBOR VONA.

Politics Can Be Different! (Lehet Más a Politika!): 1065 Budapest, Bajcsy-Zsilinszky u. 37; 1386 Budapest, POB 959; tel. and fax (30) 302-0022; e-mail info@lehetmas.hu; internet www.lehetmas.hu; f. 2009; environmentalist; Sec. JÁNOS BARTA.

Diplomatic Representation

EMBASSIES IN HUNGARY

Albania: 1062 Budapest, Andrássy u. 132; tel. and fax (1) 336-1098; e-mail embassy.budapest@mfa.gov.al; Ambassador MIRA HOXHA.

Algeria: 1121 Budapest, Zugligeti u. 27; tel. (1) 200-6860; fax (1) 200-6781; e-mail ambalbud@t-online.hu; Ambassador LOUNES MAGRAMANE.

Angola: 1123 Budapest, Alkotás u. 50; tel. (1) 487-7680; fax (1) 325-3006; e-mail embanhun@angolaembassy.hu; internet www.angolaembassy.hu; Ambassador JOÃO MIGUEL VAHEKENI.

Argentina: 1023 Budapest, Vérhalom u. 12–16; tel. (1) 325-0492; fax (1) 326-0494; e-mail eungr@mrecic.gov.ar; Ambassador DOMINGO SANTIAGO CULLEN.

Australia: 1126 Budapest, Királyhágó tér 8–9; tel. (1) 457-9777; fax (1) 201-9792; e-mail ausembbp@mail.datanet.hu; internet www.hungary.embassy.gov.au/btps/home.html; Ambassador JOHN GRIFFIN.

Austria: 1068 Budapest, Benczúr u. 16; tel. (1) 479-7010; fax (1) 352-8795; e-mail budapest-ob@bmeia.gv.at; internet www.austrian-embassy.hu; Ambassador Dr MICHAEL ZIMMERMANN.

Azerbaijan: 1067 Budapest, Eötvös u. 14; tel. (1) 374-6070; fax (1) 302-3535; e-mail budapest@azembassy.hu; internet www.azembassy.hu; Ambassador VILAYAT GULIYEV.

Belarus: 1126 Budapest, Agárdi u. 3B; tel. (1) 214-0553; fax (1) 214-0554; e-mail hungary@belembassy.org; internet www.hungary.mfa.gov.by; Ambassador ALENA KUPCHYNA.

Belgium: 1015 Budapest, Toldy Ferenc u. 13; tel. (1) 457-9960; fax (1) 375-1566; e-mail budapest@diplobel.fed.be; internet www.diplomatie.be/budapest; Ambassador JOHAN INDEKEU.

Bosnia and Herzegovina: 1026 Budapest, Verseghy Ferenc u. 4; tel. (1) 212-0106; fax (1) 212-0109; e-mail bihambud@yahoo.com; Ambassador NIKOLA ĐUKIĆ.

Brazil: 1123 Budapest, Alkotás u. 50; tel. (1) 351-0060; fax (1) 351-0066; e-mail embassy@brazil.hu; internet budapeste.itamaraty.gov.br; Ambassador SÉRGIO EDUARDO MOREIRA LIMA.

Bulgaria: 1062 Budapest, Andrássy u. 115; tel. (1) 322-0824; fax (1) 322-5215; e-mail bgembhu@axelero.hu; Ambassador DIMITAR K. IKONOMOV.

Canada: 1027 Budapest, Ganz u. 12–14; tel. (1) 392-3360; fax (1) 392-3390; e-mail bpest@international.gc.ca; internet www.canadainternational.gc.ca/hungary-hongrie; Ambassador TAMARA GUTTMAN.

Central African Republic: 1056 Budapest, Molnár u. 19; tel. (1) 484-7590; fax (1) 421-8558; e-mail ambassaderca@yahoo.fr; internet www.centrafricaine.info/hu; Ambassador BERNARD LECLERC.

Chile: 1024 Budapest, Rózsahegy u. 1B; tel. (1) 326-3054; fax (1) 326-3056; e-mail echilehu@embachile.hu; internet chileabroad.gov.cl/hungria; Ambassador RODRIGO NIETO MATURANA.

China, People's Republic: 1068 Budapest, Városligeti fasor 20–22; tel. (1) 413-2400; fax (1) 413-2451; e-mail protocol@knnk.ehc.hu; internet hu.chineseembassy.org; Ambassador GAO JIAN.

Croatia: 1063 Budapest, Munkácsy Mihály u. 15; tel. (1) 354-1315; fax (1) 354-1319; e-mail hrvhu1@mail.euroweb.hu; internet hu.mvp.hr; Ambassador IVAN BANDIĆ.

Cuba: 1026 Budapest, Harangivrág u. 5; tel. (1) 325-7290; fax (1) 438-5956; e-mail prensa@embacuba.hu; internet www.embacuba.hu; Ambassador SORAYA ELENA ÁLVAREZ NÚÑEZ.

Cyprus: 1051 Budapest, Dorottya u. 3; tel. (1) 266-1330; fax (1) 266-0538; e-mail cypembhu@axelero.hu; Ambassador VASSOS CHAMBERLEN.

Czech Republic: 1064 Budapest, Rózsa u. 61; tel. (1) 462-5011; fax (1) 351-9189; e-mail budapest@embassy.mzv.cz; internet www.mzv.cz/budapest; Ambassador HELENA BAMBASOVÁ.

Denmark: 1122 Budapest, Határőr u. 37; tel. (1) 487-9000; fax (1) 487-9045; e-mail budamb@um.dk; internet www.ambbudapest.um.dk; Ambassador MADS SANDAU-JENSEN.

Ecuador: 1023 Budapest, Levél u. 4; tel. (1) 315-2124; fax (1) 315-2104; e-mail embajada@ecuador.hu; internet www.ecuador.hu; Ambassador JAIME AUGUSTO BARBERIS MARTINEZ.

Egypt: 1124 Budapest, Istenhegyi u. 7B; tel. (1) 225-2150; fax (1) 225-8596; e-mail egyptembassybudapest@yahoo.com; Ambassador ALI EL-HEFNY.

Estonia: 1025 Budapest, Áldás u. 3; tel. (1) 354-2570; fax (1) 354-2571; e-mail embassy.budapest@mfa.ee; internet www.estemb.hu; Ambassador PRIIT PALLUM.

Finland: 1118 Budapest, Kelenhegyi u. 16A; tel. (1) 279-2500; fax (1) 385-0843; e-mail sanomat.bud@formin.fi; internet www.finland.hu; Ambassador JARI VILÉN.

France: 1062 Budapest, Lendvay u. 27; tel. (1) 374-1100; fax (1) 374-1140; e-mail cad.budapest-amba@diplomatie.gouv.fr; internet www.ambafrance-hu.org; Ambassador ROLAND GALHARAGUE.

Georgia: 1125 Budapest, Virányos u. 6B; tel. (1) 202-3390; fax (1) 214-3299; e-mail budapest.emb@mfa.gov.ge; internet www.hungary.mfa.gov.ge; Ambassador ZVIAD CHUMBURIDZE.

Germany: 1014 Budapest, Úri u. 64–66; tel. (1) 488-3500; fax (1) 488-3505; e-mail info@budapest.diplo.de; internet www.budapest.diplo.de; Ambassador MATEI I. HOFFMANN.

Greece: 1063 Budapest, Szegfű u. 3; tel. (1) 413-2600; fax (1) 342-1934; e-mail greekemb@axelero.hu; internet www.greekembassy.hu; Ambassador SPYRIDON GEORGILES.

Holy See: 1126 Budapest, Gyimes u. 1–3; tel. (1) 355-8979; fax (1) 355-6987; e-mail nuntbud@communio.hcbc.hu; Apostolic Nuncio JULIUSZ JANUSZ (Titular Archbishop of Opitergium).

India: 1025 Budapest, Búzavirág u. 14; tel. (1) 325-7742; fax (1) 325-7745; e-mail chancery@indianembassy.hu; internet www.indianembassybudapest.org; Ambassador GAURI SHANKAR GUPTA.

Indonesia: 1068 Budapest, Városligeti fasor 26; tel. (1) 413-3800; fax (1) 322-8669; e-mail embassy@indonesianembassy.hu; internet www.indonesia.hu; Ambassador MARULI TUA SAGALA.

Iran: 1143 Budapest, Stefánia u. 97; tel. (1) 460-9260; fax (1) 460-9430; e-mail embiran@nextra.hu; internet www.iranembassy.hu; Ambassador Dr SAYED BANIHESHEMI.

Iraq: 1146 Budapest, Bölöni György u. 3; tel. (1) 392-5120; fax (1) 392-5133; e-mail budemb@iraqmofamail.net; Ambassador QASIM ASKAR.

Ireland: 1054 Budapest, Szabadság tér, Bank Center; tel. (1) 301-4960; fax (1) 302-9599; e-mail budapestembassy@dfa.ie; internet www.embassyofireland.hu; Ambassador KEVIN DOWLING.

Israel: 1026 Budapest, Fullánk u. 8; tel. (1) 392-6200; fax (1) 200-0783; e-mail info@budapest.mfa.gov.il; internet budapest.mfa.gov.il; Ambassador ILAN MOR.

Italy: 1143 Budapest, Stefánia u. 95; tel. (1) 460-6200; fax (1) 460-6260; e-mail ambasciata.budapest@esteri.it; internet www.ambbudapest.esteri.it; Ambassador Dr GIOVAN BATTISTA CAMPAGNOLA.

Japan: 1125 Budapest, Zalai u. 7; tel. (1) 398-3100; fax (1) 275-1281; e-mail administration@japanembassy.hu; internet www.hu.emb-japan.go.jp; Ambassador ITO TECUO.

Kazakhstan: 1025 Budapest, Kapy u. 59; tel. (1) 275-1300; fax (1) 275-2092; e-mail kazak@t-online.hu; internet www.kazembassy.hu; Ambassador RASHID T. IBRAYEV.

Korea, Republic: 1062 Budapest, Andrássy u. 109; tel. (1) 462-3080; fax (1) 351-1182; e-mail hungary@mofat.go.kr; internet hun.mofat.go.kr; Ambassador NAM GWAN-PYO.

Kosovo: 1054 Budapest, Szabadság tér 7; tel. (1) 688-7872; fax (1) 688-7875; e-mail embassy.hungary@ks-gov.net; Ambassador SHKENDIJE SHERIFI.

Kuwait: 1122 Budapest, Székács u. 16; tel. (1) 202-3335; fax (1) 202-3387; e-mail kuwait.emb@kuwaitembassy.hu; Ambassador ABD AL-HAMID AL-FAILAKAWI.

Latvia: 1124 Budapest, Vas Gereben u. 20; tel. (1) 310-7262; fax (1) 249-2901; e-mail embassy.hungary@mfa.gov.lv; Ambassador VERONIKA ERTE.

Lebanon: 1112 Budapest, Sasadi u. 160; tel. (1) 249-0900; fax (1) 249-0901; e-mail amblib@t-online.hu; Ambassador CHARBEL STEPHAN.

Libya: 1143 Budapest, Stefánia u. 111; tel. (1) 364-9336; fax (1) 364-9330; Ambassador AHMED MENESI.

Lithuania: 1121 Budapest, Hóvirág u. 44; tel. (1) 224-7910; fax (1) 202-3995; e-mail amb.hu@urm.lt; internet hu.mfa.lt; Ambassador RENATAS JUŠKA.

Macedonia, former Yugoslav republic: 1022 Budapest, Balogvar u. 9; tel. (1) 336-0510; fax (1) 315-1921; e-mail budapest@mfa.gov.mk;

internet www.missions.gov.mk/budapest; Ambassador DARKO ANGELOV.

Malaysia: 1026 Budapest, Pasaréti u. 29; tel. (1) 488-0810; fax (1) 488-0824; e-mail malbdpest@kln.gov.my; internet www.kln.gov.my/perwakilan/budapest; Ambassador Dato' KAMILAN MAKSOM.

Mexico: 1024 Budapest, Rómer Flóris u. 58; tel. (1) 326-0447; fax (1) 326-0485; e-mail embamexhu@t-online.hu; internet www.sre.gob.mx/hungria; Ambassador ISABEL BÁRBARA TÉLLEZ ROSETE.

Moldova: 1024 Budapest, Ady Endre u. 16; tel. (1) 336-3450; fax (1) 209-1195; e-mail budapesta@mfa.md; internet www.ungaria.mfa.md; Ambassador ALEXANDRU CODREANU.

Mongolia: 1022 Budapest II, Bogár u. 14C; tel. (1) 212-5904; fax (1) 212-5731; e-mail mongolemb@t-online.hu; Ambassador TÖGSJARGALYN GANDI.

Montenegro: 1051 Budapest, Arany Janos 15; tel. (1) 373-0300; fax (1) 269-4475; e-mail ambasada@cg.t-online.hu; Ambassador VANJA BRAILO.

Morocco: 1026 Budapest, Sodrás u. 11; tel. (1) 391-4310; fax (1) 275-1437; e-mail sifamabudap@t-online.hu; Ambassador NOUREDDINE BENOMAR.

Netherlands: 1022 Budapest, Füge u. 5–7; tel. (1) 336-6300; fax (1) 326-5978; e-mail bdp@minbuza.nl; internet www.netherlandsembassy.hu; Ambassador ROBERT MILDERS.

Nigeria: 1023 Budapest, Rómer Flóris u. 57; tel. (1) 212-2021; fax (1) 212-2025; e-mail embassy@nigerianembassy.hu; internet www.nigerianembassy.hu; Ambassador CHARLES ONONYE.

Norway: 1015 Budapest, Ostrom u. 13, POB 32; tel. (1) 325-3300; fax (1) 325-3399; e-mail emb.budapest@mfa.no; internet www.norvegia.hu; Ambassador SIRI ELLEN SLETNER.

Pakistan: 1125 Budapest, Adonis u. 3A; tel. (1) 355-8017; fax (1) 375-1402; e-mail parepbudapest@yahoo.com; internet www.mofa.gov.pk/hungary; Ambassador QASIM RAZA MUTTAQI.

Philippines: 1026 Budapest, Gábor Áron u. 58; tel. (1) 391-4300; fax (1) 200-5528; e-mail pe.budapest@dfa.gov.ph; Ambassador ELEANOR JAUCIAN.

Poland: 1068 Budapest, Városligeti fasor 16; tel. (1) 413-8200; fax (1) 351-1722; e-mail budapeszt.amb.sekretariat@msz.gov.pl; internet www.budapeszt.polemb.net; Ambassador ROMAN KOWALSKI.

Portugal: 1123 Budapest, Alkotás u. 53, MOM Park Bldg C, 4th Floor; tel. (1) 201-7617; fax (1) 201-7619; e-mail embport@t-online.hu; Ambassador ANTÓNIO AUGUSTO JORGE MENDES.

Qatar: 1025 Budapest, Cseppkő u. 27B; tel. (1) 392-1010; fax (1) 392-1019; e-mail info@qatarembassy.hu; internet www.qatarembassy.hu; Ambassador MUBARAK RASHID AL-BOAININ.

Romania: 1146 Budapest, Thököly u. 72; tel. (1) 384-8394; fax (1) 384-5535; e-mail postmaster@roembbud.axelero.net; internet budapest.mae.ro; Ambassador VICTOR MICULA.

Russia: 1062 Budapest, Bajza u. 35; tel. (1) 302-5230; fax (1) 353-4164; e-mail rusemb@t-online.hu; internet www.hungary.mid.ru; Ambassador ALEKSANDR A. TOLKACH.

Saudi Arabia: 1037 Budapest, Szépvölgyi Business Park, Szépvölgyi út 37, 3rd Floor; tel. (1) 436-9500; fax (1) 453-3554; e-mail huemb@mofa.gov.sa; internet www.saudiembassy.org.hu; Ambassador NABIL BIN KHALAF BIN AHMAD ASHOOR.

Serbia: 1068 Budapest, Dózsa György u. 92 B; tel. (1) 322-9838; fax (1) 322-1438; e-mail budapest@amb.srbije.net; internet budapest.mfa.gov.rs; Ambassador DEJAN ŠAHOVIĆ.

Slovakia: 1143 Budapest, Stefánia u. 22–24; tel. (1) 460-9010; fax (1) 460-9020; e-mail emb.budapest@mzv.sk; internet www.budapest.mfa.sk; Ambassador PETER WEISS.

Slovenia: 1025 Budapest, Cseppkő u. 68; tel. (1) 438-5600; fax (1) 325-9187; e-mail vbp@gov.si; internet budimpesta.veleposlanistvo.si; Ambassador DARJA BAVDAŽ KURET.

South Africa: 1026 Budapest, Gárdonyi Géza u. 17; tel. (1) 392-0999; fax (1) 200-7277; e-mail saembassy.budapest@dirco.gov.za; Ambassador TAKALANI E. NETSHITENZHE.

Spain: 1067 Budapest, Eötvös u. 11B; tel. (1) 202-4006; fax (1) 202-4206; e-mail emb.budapest@maec.es; internet www.maec.es/embajadas/budapest/es/home; Ambassador D. ENRIQUE PASTOR Y DE GANA.

Sweden: 1027 Budapest, Kapás u. 6–12; tel. (1) 460-6020; fax (1) 460-6021; e-mail ambassaden.budapest@foreign.ministry.se; internet www.swedenabroad.com/budapest; Ambassador KARIN OLOFSDOTTER.

Switzerland: 1143 Budapest, Stefánia u. 107; tel. (1) 460-7040; fax (1) 384-9492; e-mail bud.vertretung@eda.admin.ch; internet www.swissembassy.hu; Ambassador CHRISTIAN MÜHLETHALER.

Syria: 1026 Budapest, Budakeszi u. 47D; tel. (1) 200-8046; fax (1) 200-8048; e-mail hungary@syrianembassy.hu; internet www.syrianembassy.hu; Chargé d'affaires a.i. MOHAMMED AMIR SMADI.

Thailand: 1025 Budapest, Verecke u. 79; tel. (1) 438-4020; fax (1) 438-4023; e-mail info@thaiembassy.hu; internet www.thaiembassy.org/budapest; Chargé d'affaires a.i. SIRIPORN PANUPNG.

Tunisia: 1021 Budapest, Pusztaszeri u. 24A; tel. (1) 336-1616; fax (1) 325-7291; e-mail at.budapest@t-online.hu; Chargé d'affaires a.i. ADNENE DAMERGI.

Turkey: 1062 Budapest, Andrássy u. 123; tel. (1) 478-9100; fax (1) 344-5143; e-mail embassy.budapest@mfa.gov.tr; internet budapest.emb.mfa.gov.tr; Ambassador KEMAL GÜR.

Ukraine: 1125 Budapest, Istenhegyi u. 84B; tel. (1) 422-4120; fax (1) 220-9873; e-mail uakovetseg@t-online.hu; internet www.mfa.gov.ua/hungary; Ambassador YURIY MUSHKA.

United Kingdom: 1051 Budapest, Harmincad u. 6; tel. (1) 266-2888; fax (1) 266-0907; e-mail info@britemb.hu; internet ukinhungary.fco.gov.uk; Ambassador JONATHAN KNOTT.

USA: 1054 Budapest, Szabadság tér 12; tel. (1) 475-4400; fax (1) 475-4764; e-mail pa@usembassy.hu; internet hungary.usembassy.gov; Ambassador ELENI TSAKOPOULOS KOUNALAKIS.

Venezuela: 1051 Budapest, József Nádor tér 5–6; tel. (1) 326-0460; fax (1) 326-0450; e-mail embavenezhu@t-online.hu; Chargé d'affaires a.i. MARÍA TERESA GONZÁLEZ.

Viet Nam: 1146 Budapest, Thököly u. 41; tel. (1) 342-5583; fax (1) 352-8798; e-mail vp-budapest@mofa.gov.vn; internet www.vietnamembassy-hungary.org; Ambassador NGÔ DUY NGO.

Yemen: 1026 Budapest, Bimbó út 179/a; tel. (1) 212-3991; fax (1) 212-3883; e-mail yemen22may@t-online.hu.

Judicial System

The system of court procedure in Hungary is based on an act that came into effect in 1953 and that has since been updated frequently. The system of jurisdiction is based on the local courts (district courts in Budapest, city courts in other cities), labour courts, county courts (or the Metropolitan Court) and the Supreme Court. In the legal remedy system of two instances, appeals against the decisions of city and district courts can be lodged with the competent county court and the Metropolitan Court of Budapest, respectively. Against the judgment of first instance of the latter, appeal is to be lodged with the Supreme Court. The Chief Public Prosecutor and the President of the Supreme Court have the right to submit a protest on legal grounds against the final judgment of any court.

By virtue of the 1973 act, effective from 1974 and modified in 1979, the procedure in criminal cases is differentiated for criminal offences and for criminal acts. In the first instance, criminal cases are tried, depending on their character, by a professional judge, and where justified by the magnitude of the criminal act, by a council composed of three members, a professional judge and two lay assessors, while in major cases the court consists of five members, two professional judges and three lay assessors. In the Supreme Court, second instance cases are tried only by professional judges. The President of the Supreme Court is elected by the Országgyűlés. Judges are appointed by the President of the Republic for an indefinite period. Assessors are elected by the local municipal councils.

In the interest of ensuring legality and a uniform application of the law, the Supreme Court exercises a principled guidance over the jurisdiction of courts. In the Republic of Hungary, judges are independent and subject only to the law and other legal regulations.

The Minister of Public Administration and Justice supervises the general activities of courts. The Chief Public Prosecutor is elected by the Országgyűlés. The Chief Public Prosecutor and the Prosecutor's Office provide for the consistent prosecution of all acts violating or endangering the legal order of society or the safety and independence of the state, and for the protection of citizens.

The prosecutors of the independent prosecuting organization exert supervision over the legality of investigations and the implementation of punishments, assist with specific means in ensuring that legal regulations should be observed by state, economic and other organs and citizens, and they support the legality of court procedures and decisions.

Supreme Court (Legfelsőbb Bíróság): 1055 Budapest, Markó u. 16; tel. (1) 268-4500; fax (1) 268-4740; e-mail kuria@kuria.birosag.hu; internet www.kuria-birosag.hu; Pres. Dr PÉTER DARÁK.

Chief Public Prosecutor: PÉTER POLT.

Constitutional Court (Alkotmánybíróság): 1015 Budapest, Donáti u. 35–45; tel. (1) 488-3100; fax (1) 212-1170; internet www.mkab.hu; Pres. Dr PÉTER PACZOLAY.

Religion

CHRISTIANITY

The Roman Catholic Church

Hungary comprises four archdioceses, nine dioceses (including one for Catholics of the Byzantine Rite), one apostolic exarchate of the Byzantine Rite and one territorial abbacy (directly responsible to the Holy See). The Church has an estimated 6,054,088 adherents in Hungary, equivalent to 58.5% of the total population. Of this number, 290,000 are adherents of the Byzantine Rite.

Bishops' Conference

1071 Budapest, Városligeti fasor 45, POB 79; tel. (1) 342-6959; fax (1) 342-6957; e-mail pkt@katolikus.hu; internet www.katolikus.hu; Pres. Cardinal PÉTER ERDŐ (Archbishop of Esztergom-Budapest).

Archbishop of Eger: Most Rev. CSABA TERNYÁK, 3301 Eger, Széchenyi u. 1; tel. (36) 517-589; fax (36) 517-751.

Archbishop of Esztergom-Budapest: Cardinal PÉTER ERDŐ, 1014 Budapest, Uri u. 62; tel. (33) 225-2590; fax (33) 202-5458; e-mail egombp@katolikus.hu.

Archbishop of Kalocsa-Kecskemét: Most Rev. BALÁZS BÁBEL, 6301 Kalocsa, Szentháromság tér 1; tel. (78) 462-166; fax (78) 465-279; e-mail hivatal@asztrik.hu.

Archbishop of Veszprém: Most Rev. GYULA MÁRFI, 8201 Veszprém, Vár u. 19; tel. (88) 462-088; fax (88) 466-287; e-mail ersekseg@ersekseg.veszprem.hu.

Apostolic Exarch of Miskolc for Catholics of the Byzantine Rite in the Hungarian Territories: OROSZ ATANÁZ (Titular Bishop of Panium), 4400 Nyíregyháza, Bethlen Gábor u. 5; tel. (42) 415-901; fax (42) 415-911.

Protestant Churches

Evangelical Lutheran Church in Hungary (Magyarországi Evangélikus Egyház): 1085 Budapest, Üllői u. 24; tel. (1) 483-2260; fax (1) 486-3554; e-mail szerkesztoseg@lutheran.hu; internet www.lutheran.hu; Presiding Bishop PÉTER GÁNCS; 213,125 mems (2010).

Faith Church (Hit Gyülekezete): 1103 Budapest, Gyömrői u. 63; 1143 Budapest, POB 219; tel. (1) 432-2700; fax (1) 432-3717; e-mail hit@hit.hu; internet www.hit.hu; f. 1979; charismatic pentecostal church; Senior Pastor SÁNDOR NÉMETH.

Reformed Church in Hungary—Presbyterian (Magyarországi Református Egyház): 1146 Budapest, Abonyi u. 21; tel. (1) 343-7870; e-mail info@reformatus.hu; internet www.reformatus.hu; Pres. of Gen. Synod Bishop Dr GUSZTÁV BÖLCSKEI.

The Eastern Orthodox Church

The Bulgarian, Romanian, Russian and Serbian Orthodox Churches are all represented in Hungary.

ISLAM

There are about 3,000 Muslims in Hungary.

Hungarian Islamic Community (Magyar Iszlám Közösség): Budapest, Róbert Karoly krt. 104; tel. (1) 177-7602; internet www.magyariszlam.hu; Leader Dr BALÁZS MIHÁLFFY.

JUDAISM

The Jewish community in Hungary is estimated to number between 100,000 and 120,000 people. Some 80% of Hungary's Jewish community resides in Budapest.

Federation of Jewish Communities in Hungary (Magyarországi Zsidó Hitközségek Szövetsége): 1075 Budapest, Síp u. 12; tel. and fax (1) 413-5504; internet mazsihisz.hu; 120,000 mems; 40 active synagogues; Orthodox and Conservative; Pres. Dr PÉTER FELDMAJER; Chief Rabbi of Hungary ROBERT DEUTSCH.

The Press

Budapest dailies circulate nationally. The most popular are: *Népszabadság*, *Nemzeti Sport* and *Népszava*. *Népszabadság*, the most important daily, was formerly the central organ of the Hungarian Socialist Workers' Party, but is now independent.

PRINCIPAL DAILIES

24 Óra (24 Hours): 2800 Tatabánya, Fő tér 4; tel. (34) 514-010; fax (34) 514-011; e-mail kemma@kemma.hu; internet www.24ora.hu; Editor-in-Chief ZOLTÁN TAKÁCS; circ. 17,023 (2010).

Békés Megyei Hírlap (Békés County News): 5600 Békéscsaba, Kiss Ernő u. 3; tel. (66) 527-226; e-mail beol@beol.hu; fax (66) 527-231; internet www.bmhirlap.hu; f. 1945; Editor-in-Chief JÁNOS NÁNÁSI; circ. 23,279 (2010).

Blikk: 1082 Budapest, Futó u. 35–37; tel. (1) 460-2400; fax (1) 460-2501; e-mail online@blikk.hu; internet www.blikk.hu; f. 1994; colour tabloid; Editor-in-Chief GERGELY KOMÁROMI; circ. 192,182 (2010).

Déli Hírlap (Midday Journal): 3527 Miskolc, Tabódy Ida tér 15; tel. (46) 42-694; Editor-in-Chief DEZSŐ BEKES; circ. 20,000.

Délmagyarország (Southern Hungary): 6740 Szeged, Szabadkai 20; tel. (62) 567-888; fax (62) 567-881; e-mail szerkesztoseg@delmagyar.hu; internet www.delmagyar.hu; Editor-in-Chief CSABA NYERGES; circ. 27,199 (2010).

Észak-Magyarország (Northern Hungary): 3526 Miskolc, Zsolcai kapu 3; tel. (46) 502-900; fax (46) 501-262; e-mail laszlo.kiss@inform.hu; internet www.eszak.hu; Editor-in-Chief LÁSZLÓ KISS; circ. 44,615 (2010).

Fejér Megyei Hírlap (Fejér County Journal): 8000 Székesfehérvár, Ady Endre u. 15; tel. (22) 542-703; fax (22) 542-719; e-mail elekes.andras@fmh.plt.hu; internet www.fmh.hu; Editor-in-Chief ELEKES ANDRÁS; circ. 37,053 (2010).

Hajdú-Bihari Napló (Hajdú-Bihar Diary): 4031 Debrecen, Balmazújvárosi út 11; tel. and fax (52) 523-400; e-mail info@naplo.hu-ra; internet www.naplo.hu; f. 1944; Editor-in-Chief MIKLÓS SZABÓ; circ. 60,000.

Heves Megyei Hírlap (Heves County Journal): 3301 Eger, Trinitárius u. 1; tel. (36) 513-600; e-mail heol@heol.hu; internet www.hevesmegyeihirlap.hu; Editor-in-Chief OTTÓ VARGA; circ. 15,276 (2010).

Hirportal: 1122 Budapest, Városmajor u. 11; tel. (1) 488-5564; fax (1) 488-5615; e-mail adatkezelo@axelspringer.hu; internet www.reggel.hu; f. 2005; publ. by Axel Springer (of Germany); Publr JÓZSEF BAYER.

Kisalföld: 9021 Győr, Újlak u. 4A; tel. (96) 504-555; fax (96) 504-414; e-mail szerkesztoseg@kisalfold.hu; internet www.kisalfold.hu; Editor-in-Chief CSABA NYERGES; circ. 70,257 (2010).

Magyar Hírlap (Hungarian Journal): 1145 Budapest, Thököly u. 105–107; tel. (1) 887-3230; fax (1) 887-3253; e-mail levelezes@magyarhirlap.hu; internet www.magyarhirlap.hu; f. 1968; Editor-in-Chief ISTVÁN STEFKA; circ. 13,858 (2010).

Magyar Nemzet (Hungarian Nation): Budapest; tel. (1) 476-2131; fax (1) 215-3197; e-mail szerk@mno.hu; internet www.mno.hu; Editor-in-Chief GÁBOR LISZKAY; circ. 48,877 (2010).

Metropol: 1134 Budapest, Tüzér u. 39-41; tel. (1) 431-6422; fax (1) 431-6401; e-mail g.izbeki@metropol.hu; internet www.metropol.hu; fmrly *Metro*, current name adopted in Aug. 2008; five issues a week; distributed free of charge; Editor-in-Chief GÁBOR IZBÉKI; circ. 274,105 (2010).

Napló (Diary): 8200 Veszprém, Almádi u. 3; 8201 Veszprém, POB 161; tel. (88) 579-420; fax (88) 579-432; e-mail bartak.peter@naplo.plt.hu; internet naplo-online.hu; Editor-in-Chief PÉTER BARTÁK; circ. 40,744 (2010).

Nemzeti Sport (National Sport): 1082 Budapest, Futó u. 35-37; tel. (1) 460-2600; fax (1) 460-2601; e-mail szerkesztoseg@nemzetisport.hu; internet www.nemzetisport.hu; Editor-in-Chief JÓZSEF BUZGÓ; circ. 69,607 (2010).

Népszabadság (People's Freedom): 1960 Budapest, Bécsi u. 122–124; tel. (1) 436-4444; fax (1) 387-8945; e-mail szerkesztoseg@nepszabadsag.hu; internet www.nol.hu; f. 1942; independent; Editor-in-Chief T. KÁROLY VÖRÖS; circ. 72,502 (2010).

Népszava (Voice of the People): 1087 Budapest, Könyves Kálmán 76; tel. (1) 688-7030; fax (1) 688-7031; e-mail nemethp@nepszava.hu; internet www.nepszava.hu; f. 1873; Editor PÉTER NÉMETH; circ. 19,099 (2010).

Petőfi Népe: 6000 Kecskemét, Széchenyi 29; tel. (76) 518-200; e-mail baon@baon.hu; internet www.petofinepe.hu; Editor-in-Chief ERNŐ KIRÁLY; circ. 27,938 (2010).

Somogyi Hírlap (Somogy Journal): 7400 Kaposvár, Kontrássy u. 2A; tel. (82) 528-104; fax (82) 528-155; e-mail sonline@sonline.hu; internet www.somogyihirlap.hu; Editor ATTILA CZENE; circ. 25,478 (2010).

Tolnai Népújság (Tolna News): 7100 Szekszárd, Liszt Ferenc tér 3; tel. (74) 511-510; fax (74) 511-500; e-mail teol@teol.hu; internet www.tolnainepujsag.hu; Editor-in-Chief JÁNOS LENGYEL; circ. 16,601 (2010).

Új Dunántúli Napló: 1122 Budapest, Városmajor u. 12–14/2; tel. (72) 505-026; fax (72) 505-034; internet www.dunantulinaplo.hu; f. 1948; Editor FERENC NIMMERFROH; circ. 34,677.

Új Néplap (New People's Paper): 5000 Szolnok, Mészáros Lőrinc út 2; tel. (56) 516-753; e-mail szoljon@szoljon.hu; internet www.ujneplap.hu; Editor-in-Chief JÁNOS BÁN; circ. 22,338 (2010).

Vas Népe (Vas People): 9700 Szombathely, Moszkva tér 40; tel. (94) 522-563; fax (94) 522-596; e-mail vasnepe@vn.plt.hu; internet www.vasnepe.hu; Editor-in-Chief MIKLÓS HALMÁGYI; circ. 48,672 (2010).

Zalai Hírlap (Zala Journal): 8901 Zalaegerszeg, Ady Endre u. 62; tel. (92) 502-231; fax (92) 502-240; e-mail zalaihirlap@zh.plt.hu; internet www.zalaihirlap.hu; Editor-in-Chief ZSOLT VIRRASZTÓ; circ. 47,979 (2010).

WEEKLIES

The Budapest Times/Budapester Zeitung: 1037 Budapest, Kunigunda útja 18; tel. (1) 453-0752; fax (1) 240-7583; e-mail editor@budapesttimes.hu; internet www.budapesttimes.hu; internet www.budapester.hu; f. 1999 (*Budapester Zeitung*); f. 2003 (*The Budapest Times*); English and German edns; Editors ALLAN BOYKO (*The Budapest Times*), ÁGNES LUKÁCS (*Budapester Zeitung*).

Élet és Irodalom (Life and Literature): 1089 Budapest, Rezsö tér 15; tel. (1) 303-9211; fax (1) 303-9241; e-mail es@es.hu; internet www.es.hu; f. 1957; literary and political; Editor ZOLTÁN KOVÁCS; circ. 22,000.

Élet és Tudomány (Life and Science): 1428 Budapest, POB 47; tel. (1) 327-8950; fax (1) 327-8979; e-mail eltud@eletestudomany.hu; internet www.eletestudomany.hu; f. 1946; popular science; Editor-in-Chief ÁKOS GÓZON; circ. 20,000.

Evangélikus Élet (Evangelical Life): 1085 Budapest, Üllői u. 24; tel. (1) 317-1108; fax (1) 486-1195; e-mail evelet@lutheran.hu; internet www.evangelikuselet.hu; f. 1933; Evangelical Lutheran Church newspaper; Editor KÁROLY T. PINTÉR; circ. 4,000 (2012).

Figyelő (Observer): 1037 Budapest, Montevideo u. 9; tel. (1) 437-1413; fax (1) 437-1420; e-mail figyelo@sanomabp.hu; internet www.fn.hu; f. 1957; Thursdays; business; Editor-in-Chief ERNŐ SIMON; circ. 15,932 (2010).

Heti Világgazdaság (World Economy Weekly): 1037 Budapest, Montevideo u. 14; tel. (1) 436-2000; fax (1) 436-2045; e-mail hvg.hu@hvg.hu; internet www.hvg.hu; f. 1979; Editor RICHARD HERSCHLER.

Képes Újság (Illustrated News): 1085 Budapest, Könyves Kálmán krt. 76; tel. (1) 236-4534; internet www.kepesujsag.com; f. 1960; Editor MIHÁLY KOVÁCS; circ. 400,000.

Ľudové Noviny (People's News): 1135 Budapest, Csata u. 17; tel. (1) 878-1431; fax (1) 878-1432; e-mail ludove@luno.hu; internet www.luno.hu; in Slovak; for Slovaks in Hungary; Editor ALŽBETA H. RAČKOVÁ; circ. 1,700.

Magyar Mezőgazdaság (Hungarian Agriculture): 1141 Budapest, Mírtusz u. 2; 1591 Budapest, POB 294; tel. (1) 470-0411; fax (1) 470-0410; e-mail kiado@magyarmezogazdasag.hu; internet www.magyarmezogazdasag.hu; f. 1946; Editors LÁSZLÓ BÁRDOS, DÁNIEL HAFNER; circ. 24,000.

Magyarország (Hungary): Budapest; tel. (1) 138-4644; f. 1964; news magazine; Editor DÉNES GYAPAY; circ. 200,000.

Neue Zeitung (New Paper): 1062 Budapest, Lendvay u. 22; tel. (1) 302-6784; fax (1) 302-6877; e-mail neueztg@hu.inter.net; internet www.neue-zeitung.hu; f. 1957; in German; for Germans in Hungary; Editor JOHANN SCHÜTH; circ. 3,000 (2010).

Reformátusok Lapja: 1113 Budapest, Tas vezér u. 13; tel. (1) 217-6809; fax (1) 217-8386; e-mail szerk@reflap.hu; internet www.reflap.hu; f. 1957; Reformed Church paper for the laity; Editor-in-Chief and Publr LÁSZLÓ T. NÉMETH.

RTV Részletes (Radio and TV News): 1801 Budapest; tel. (1) 328-8114; fax (1) 328-7349; e-mail info@rtvreszletes.hu; internet www.rtvreszletes.hu; f. 1924; Editor JANOS CSILLAG; circ. 70,000 (2010).

Szabad Föld (Free Earth): 1036 Budapest, Lajos u. 48–66; tel. (1) 489-8800; internet www.szabadfold.hu; f. 1945; Editor LÁSZLÓ HORVÁTH; circ. 720,000.

Új Ember (New Man): 1053 Budapest, Kossuth Lajos u. 1; tel. (1) 317-3933; fax (1) 317-3471; e-mail ujember@katolikus.hu; internet ujember.katolikus.hu; f. 1945; weekly; Roman Catholic; Editor TAMÁS PAPP; circ. 40,000.

OTHER PERIODICALS

(published monthly, unless otherwise indicated)

Beszélő (The Speaker): 1016 Budapest, Naphegy tér 8; tel. and fax (1) 302-2912; e-mail beszelo@enternet.hu; internet beszelo.c3.hu; f. 1981; political and cultural; Editor-in-Chief LÁSZLÓ NEMÉNYI.

Budapest Business Journal (BBJ): 1022 Budapest, Alsó-Törökvész u. 9; tel. (1) 398-0344; fax (1) 398-0345; e-mail circulation@bbj.hu; internet www.bbj.hu; biweekly; English; Editor-in-Chief MELINDA TÜNDE DÓRA; circ. 9,226 (2010).

Ezermester 2000 (Handyman 2000): 1145 Budapest, Mexikói u. 35A; tel. (1) 222-6392; fax (1) 220-9065; e-mail ezermester@ezermester.hu; internet www.ezermester2000.hu; f. 1957; do-it-yourself magazine; Editor JÓZSEF PERÉNYI; circ. 50,000.

Gramofon—Klasszikus: 1023 Budapest, Borbolya u. 9; tel. (1) 430-2870; fax (1) 436-0101; e-mail info@gramofon.hu; internet www.gramofon.hu; f. 1996; classical, jazz and 'world' music; 4 a year; Editor-in-Chief TAMÁS VÁRKONYI; circ. 3,000 (2009).

Közgazdasági Szemle (Economic Review): 1112 Budapest, Budaörsi u. 45; tel. (1) 319-3165; fax (1) 319-3166; e-mail kszemle@econ.core.hu; internet www.kszemle.hu; f. 1954; publ. by Cttee for Economic Sciences of Hungarian Academy of Sciences; Editor-in-Chief TAMÁS HALM; circ. 1,000.

Magyar Közlöny (Official Gazette): 1055 Budapest, Kossuth Lajos tér 4; tel. (1) 112-1236; e-mail info@magyarorszag.hu; internet kozlony.magyarorszag.hu; publ. by Office of the Prime Minister; Chief of Editorial Bd Dr ANDRÁS LEVENTE GÁL; circ. 90,000.

Magyar Tudomány (Hungarian Science): Hungarian Academy of Sciences, 1051 Budapest, Nádor u. 7; tel. and fax (1) 317-9524; e-mail matud@hefka.iif.hu; internet www.matud.iif.hu; f. 1846; multi-disciplinary science review; Chief Editor VILMOS CSÁNYI.

Új Élet (New Life): Magyarországi Zsidó Hitközségek Szövetsége, 1075 Budapest, Síp u. 12; tel. (1) 413-5564; fax 413-5504; f. 1945; every two weeks; Jewish interest; Editor Dr PÉTER KARDOS; circ. 5,000.

Új Technika (New Technology): Budapest; tel. (1) 155-7122; f. 1967; popular industrial quarterly; circ. 35,000.

NEWS AGENCIES

HavariaPress News Agency: 1068 Budapest, Benczúr u. 1; tel. (1) 321-5538; e-mail havaria@havaria.hu; internet www.havariapress.hu; f. 1994; independent.

Hungarian News Agency Co (Magyar Távirati Iroda Rt—MTI): 1016 Budapest, Naphegy tér 8; tel. (1) 441-9000; fax (1) 318-8297; e-mail mti@mti.hu; internet www.mti.hu; f. 1880; 20 brs in Hungary; 10 bureaux abroad; CEO CSABA BELÉNESSY.

Independent News Agency (Független Hírügynökség—FH): 1137 Budapest, Szent István Park 3; tel. (1) 382-0310; fax (1) 382-0309; e-mail info@fuggetlenhir.hu; internet www.fuggetlenhir.hu; f. 2004; Editor-in-Chief PÉTER KÖVESDI.

PRESS ASSOCIATIONS

Hungarian Newspaper Publishers' Association: 1016 Budapest, Naphegy tér 8; tel. (1) 368-8674; fax (1) 212-5025; e-mail mle@t-online.hu; internet www.mle.org.hu; f. 1990; Gen. Sec. KATALIN HAVAS; 40 mems.

National Association of Hungarian Journalists (Magyar Újságírók Országos Szövetsége—MÚOSZ): 1064 Budapest, Vörösmarty u. 47A; tel. (1) 478-9057; e-mail info@muosz.hu; internet www.muosz.hu; f. 1896; Pres. PÁL EÖTVÖS; 7,000 mems.

Publishers

PRINCIPAL PUBLISHING HOUSES

Akadémiai Kiadó: 1117 Budapest, Prielle Kornélia u. 19/D; tel. (1) 464-8200; fax (1) 464-8201; e-mail ak@akkrt.hu; internet www.akkrt.hu; f. 1828; economics, humanities, social, political, natural and technical sciences, dictionaries, textbooks and journals; Hungarian and English; Dir BUCSI SZABÓ ZSOLT.

Corvina Kiadó: 1086 Budapest, Dankó u. 4–8; tel. (1) 411-2410; fax (1) 318-4410; e-mail corvina@lira.hu; internet www.corvinakiado.hu; f. 1955; art and educational books, fiction and non-fiction, tourist guides, cookery books and musicology; Dir LÁSZLÓ KUNOS.

EMB Music Publisher: 1132 Budapest, Victor Hugo u. 11–15; tel. (1) 236-1100; fax (1) 236-1101; e-mail emb@emb.hu; internet www.emb.hu; f. 1950; music publishing and books on musical subjects; Dir ANTAL BORONKAY.

Európa Könyvkiadó: 1055 Budapest, Kossuth Lajos tér 13–15; tel. (1) 353-2328; fax (1) 331-4162; e-mail info@europakiado.hu; internet www.europakiado.hu; f. 1946; world literature translated into Hungarian; Dir IMRE BARNA.

Helikon Kiadó: 1027 Budapest, Horvát u. 14–24/V; tel. (1) 225-4300; fax (1) 225-4320; e-mail helikon@helikon.hu; internet www.helikon.hu; bibliophile books; Dir KATALIN BERGER.

Kossuth Kiadó: 1043 Budapest, Csányi László u. 36; tel. (1) 370-0607; fax (1) 370-0602; f. 1944; social sciences, educational and philosophy publs, information technology books; Man. ANDRÁS SÁNDOR KOCSIS.

Közgazdasági és Jogi Könyvkiadó: Budapest; tel. (1) 112-6430; fax (1) 111-3210; f. 1955; business, economics, law, sociology, psychology, tax, politics, education, dictionaries; Man. Dir DAVID G. YOUNG.

Magvető Könyvkiadó: 1806 Budapest, Dankó u. 4–8; 1086 Budapest, POB 123; tel. (1) 235-5032; e-mail magveto@lira.hu; internet www.lira.hu/kiado/magveto; f. 1955; literature; Dir GÉZA MORCSÁNYI.

Medicina Könyvkiadó: 1072 Budapest, Rákóczi u. 16; tel. (1) 312-2650; fax (1) 312-2450; e-mail medicina@euroweb.eu; internet www.medicina-kiado.hu; f. 1957; books on medicine, health-care, tourism; Dir BORBÁLA FARKASVÖLGYI.

Mezőgazda Kiadó: 1165 Budapest, Koronafürt u. 44; tel. (1) 407-1018; fax (1) 407-1012; e-mail mezoig@mezogazdakiado.hu; internet www.mezogazdakiado.hu; ecology, natural sciences, environmental protection, food industry; Man. Dr LAJOS LELKES.

Móra Könyvkiadó Zrt: 1134 Budapest, Váci u. 19; tel. (1) 320-4740; fax (1) 320-5382; e-mail mora@mora.hu; internet www.mora.hu; f. 1950; fiction and non-fiction; Pres. Dr JÁNOS JANIKOVSZKY.

Műszaki Könyvkiadó: 1033 Budapest, Szentendre u. 89–93; tel. (1) 437-2405; fax (1) 437-2404; e-mail lakatosz@muszakikiado.hu; internet www.muszakikiado.hu; f. 1955; scientific and technical, vocational, and general textbooks; Man. SÁNDOR BÉRCZI.

Nemzeti Tankönyvkiadó (National Textbook Publishing House): 1143 Budapest, Szobránc u. 6–8; tel. (1) 460-1800; fax (1) 460-1869; e-mail public@ntk.hu; internet www.ntk.hu; f. 1949; school and university textbooks, pedagogical literature and language books; Gen. Man. JÓZSEF PÁLFI.

PUBLISHERS' ASSOCIATION

Hungarian Publishers' and Booksellers' Association (Magyar Könyvkiadók és Könyvterjesztők Egyesülése): 1073 Budapest, Kertész u. 41 I/4; 1367 Budapest, POB 130; tel. (1) 343-2540; fax (1) 343-2541; e-mail mkke@mkke.hu; internet www.mkke.hu; f. 1795; Pres. LÁSZLÓ PÉTER ZENTAI; Sec.-Gen. MARTINA BUDAY.

Broadcasting and Communications

National Media and Communications Authority (Nemzeti Média- és Hírközlési Hatóság): 1525 Budapest, POB 75; tel. (1) 457-7100; fax (1) 356-5520; e-mail info@nmhh.hu; internet www.nmhh.hu; f. 2010, by the merger of the National Communications Authority and the National Radio and Television Commission; responsible to the legislature; Pres. ANNAMÁRIA SZALAI.

TELECOMMUNICATIONS

In May 2011 there were 11 fixed-line telephone operators and three providers of mobile cellular telecommunications services in Hungary. At that time 60.4% of households had a fixed-line telephone, while the rate of mobile network subscription was equivalent to 118% of the population.

Service Providers

Magyar Telekom: 1013 Budapest, Krisztina krt 55; tel. (1) 458-0000; fax (1) 458-7176; e-mail investor.relations@telekom.hu; internet www.telekom.hu; f. 1991 as Matáv Hungarian Telecommunications Co; name changed as above in May 2005; 59.2% owned by Deutsche Telekom AG (Germany); merged with T-Mobile Magyarország in Dec. 2005; telecommunications service provider; Chair. and Chief Exec. CHRISTOPHER MATTHEISEN; 10,170 employees (2011).

Telenor Magyarorszag (Telenor Hungary): 2045 Törökbálint, Pannon u. 1; e-mail sajto@telenor.hu; internet www.telenor.hu; f. 1993 as Pannon GSM Telecommunications; 100% stake acquired by Telenor (Norway) in 2002; rebranded as above in May 2010; mobile telecommunications; CEO CHRISTOPHER LASKA.

Vodafone Hungary: 1476 Budapest, POB 350; e-mail ugyfelszolgalat.hu@vodafone.com; internet www.vodafone.hu; f. 1999; mobile cellular telecommunications; owned by Vodafone (United Kingdom); Chief Exec. GYÖRGY BECK; more than 2m. subscribers (May 2007).

BROADCASTING

Antenna Hungária Rt: 1119 Budapest, Petzvál József u. 31–33; tel. (1) 203-6060; fax (1) 203-6093; internet www.ahrt.hu; f. 1989; radio and television; 100% owned by TDF, SAS (France); Chief Exec. JEAN FRANCOIS FENECH; 405 employees.

Radio

Hungarian Radio (Magyar Rádió zrt): 1088 Budapest, Bródy Sándor u. 5–7; tel. (1) 328-7000; fax (1) 328-7332; e-mail info@radio.hu; internet www.radio.hu; f. 1925; stations: Radio Kossuth, Radio Petőfi, Radio Bartók (classical music), MR4 (regional and minority interest), MR5 (parliamentary sessions) and MR6 (regional programmes); CEO ISTVÁN JÓNÁS.

Neo FM: 1025 Budapest, Csévi u. 7B; tel. (1) 555-1001; fax (1) 555-1002; e-mail web@neofm.hu; internet neofm.hu; f. 2009.

Radio C: 1086 Budapest, Teleki László tér 7; tel. (1) 492-0240; fax (1) 459-0094; e-mail radioc@radioc.hu; internet www.radioc.hu; f. 2001; Roma radio station; Man. Dir FÁTYOL TIVADAR.

Television

Hungarian Television Rt (Magyar Televízió): 1054 Budapest, Naphegy tér 8; tel. (1) 441-9353; fax (1) 373-4133; e-mail ujmedia@mti.hu; internet premier.mtv.hu; f. 1957; owned by parliament; two channels; Editor ALEXANDER KORDA.

Finance

(cap. = capital; res = reserves; dep. = deposits; m. = million; brs = branches; amounts in forint)

In 2010 there were 30 commercial banks in operation in Hungary. Responsibility for bank supervision is divided between the Central Bank of Hungary and the Hungarian Financial Supervisory Authority. The supervisory responsibilities of the Central Bank are restricted to areas relating to the operation of monetary policy and the foreign-exchange system.

BANKING

Central Bank

Central Bank of Hungary (Magyar Nemzeti Bank): 1850 Budapest, Szabadság tér 8–9; tel. (1) 428-2600; fax (1) 428-2500; e-mail info@mnb.hu; internet www.mnb.hu; f. 1924; bank of issue; conducts international transactions; supervises banking system; cap. 10,000m., res 261,768m., dep. 4,912,097m. (Dec. 2009); Gov. ANDRÁS SIMOR; 2 regional directorates.

Other Banks

Bank of Hungarian Savings Co-operatives (Magyar Takarékszövetkezeti Bank): 1122 Budapest, Pethényi köz 10, POB 775; tel. (1) 457-8907; fax (1) 225-4280; e-mail info@tbank.hu; internet www.takarekbank.hu; f. 1989; 63.72% owned by savings co-operatives, 31.27% owned by DZ Bank AG (Germany); cap. 2,367m., res 10,356m., dep. 345,743m. (Dec. 2009); Chair. of Bd IMRE HARTMANN; CEO PÉTER CSICSÁKY.

Budapest Credit and Development Bank: 1138 Budapest, POB 1852, Váci u. 188; tel. (1) 450-6000; fax (1) 450-6001; e-mail info@budapestbank.hu; internet www.budapestbank.hu; f. 1987; cap. 19,346m., res 75,456m., dep. 761,670m. (Dec. 2009); 99.7% owned by GE Capital International Financing Corpn (USA); Pres. and CEO SEAN MORRISSEY; 65 brs.

CIB Bank Ltd: 1027 Budapest, Medve u. 4–14, POB 394; tel. (1) 423-1000; fax (1) 489-6500; e-mail cib@cib.hu; internet www.cib.hu; f. 1979; 89.1% owned by Intesa Holding International, SA (Luxembourg); name changed as above Jan. 2008, following merger with Inter-Európa Bank Zrt; cap. 105,000m., res 30,504m., dep. 2,408,740m. (Dec. 2009); Chair. Dr GYÖRGY SURÁNYI; CEO TOMAS SPURNY.

Citibank Zrt: 1367 Budapest, POB 123; tel. (1) 374-5000; fax (1) 374-5100; internet www.citibank.hu; f. 1985; wholly owned by Citibank Overseas Investment Corpn (USA); cap. 13,005m., res 7,295m., dep. 364,493m. (Dec. 2006); Country Chief Officer SAJJAD RAZVI.

Commerzbank Zrt: 1054 Budapest, Széchenyi rkp 8; tel. (1) 374-1000; fax (1) 269-4574; e-mail info.budapest@commerzbank.hu; internet www.commerzbank.hu; f. 1993; cap. 2,466.9m., res 22,276.1m., dep. 211,659.4m. (Dec. 2009); Pres. and Chair. of Supervisory Bd WILHELM NÜSE; Chair. and Chief Exec. KOZMA ANDRÁS.

Erste Bank Hungary Zrt: 1138 Budapest, Népfürdo u. 24–26; tel. (1) 298-0221; fax (1) 272-5160; e-mail uszolg@erstebank.hu; internet www.erstebank.hu; f. 1987; present name adopted 1998; absorbed Postbank and Savings Bank Corpn—Postabank in 2004; 99.9% owned by Erste Group Bank (Austria); cap. 60,910m., res 72,404m., dep. 2,486,210m. (Dec. 2009); CEO EDIT PAPP; 186 brs.

Hungarian Export-Import Bank (EXIMBANK): 1065 Budapest, Nagymezö u. 46–48; tel. (1) 374-9100; fax (1) 269-4476; e-mail eximh@eximbank.hu; internet www.eximbank.hu; f. 1994; state-owned; cap. 10,100m., res 6,055m., dep. 197,713m. (Dec. 2009); CEO Dr ZOLTÁN BODNAR.

K&H Bank Zrt: 1051 Budapest, Vigadó tér 1; tel. (1) 328-9000; fax (1) 328-9696; e-mail bank@kh.hu; internet www.kh.hu; f. 1987 as Kereskedelmi és Hitelbank Nyrt; name changed as above 2008; owned by KBC Bank NV (Belgium); dep. 2,767,677m., total assets 3,064,497m. (2009); Pres. and Chair. BÉLA SINGLOVICS; CEO MARKO VOLJC; 206 brs.

MFB Hungarian Development Bank (Magyar Fejlesztési Bank): 1051 Budapest, Nádor u. 31; tel. (1) 428-1400; fax (1) 428-1490; e-mail ugyfelszolgalat@mfb.hu; internet www.mfb.hu; f. 1991 as an investment company; authorized as a bank 1993; name changed as above 2007; state-owned; cap. 87,570m., res 26,935m., dep. 989,342m. (Dec. 2009); Pres. LÁSZLÓ BARANYAY.

MKB Bank Nyrt: 1056 Budapest, Váci u. 38; tel. (1) 327-8600; fax (1) 327-8700; e-mail mkb@mkb.hu; internet www.mkb.hu; f. 1950; commercial banking; 89.6% owned by Bayerische Landesbank (Germany); absorbed Konzumbank in 2003; present name adopted 2005; cap. 14,094m., res 102,892m., dep. 2,248,406m. (Dec. 2008); Chair. and CEO TAMÁS ERDEI; 68 brs.

OTP Bank (Országos Takarékpénztár Bank): 1051 Budapest, Nádor u. 16; tel. (1) 473-5000; fax (1) 473-5955; e-mail otpbank@otpbank.hu; internet www.otpbank.hu; f. 1949 as Hungarian National Savings Bank; name changed as above 2006; savings deposits, credits, foreign transactions; privatized in 1996; cap. 28,000m., res 1,157,454m., dep. 8,020,452m. (Dec. 2008); Chair. and Chief Exec. Dr SÁNDOR CSÁNYI; 408 brs.

Raiffeisen Bank Zrt: 1054 Budapest, Akadémia u. 6; tel. (1) 484-4400; fax (1) 484-4444; e-mail info@raiffeisen.hu; internet www.raiffeisen.hu; f. 1986; present name adopted 1999; 100% owned by Raiffeisen Banking Group (Austria); cap. 45,129m., res 26,705m., dep. 2,120,091m. (Dec. 2009); Pres. Dr HERBERT STEPIC; Man. Dir Dr PÉTER FELCSUTI; 126 brs.

UniCredit Bank Hungary Zrt: 1054 Budapest, Szabadság tér 5–6; tel. (1) 269-0812; fax (1) 353-4959; e-mail info@unicreditbank.hu; internet www.unicreditbank.hu; f. 2001 by merger of Bank Austria Creditanstalt Hungary RT and Hypovereinsbank Hungary RT; name changed as above 2007; 100% owned by Bank Austria Creditanstalt AG; cap. 24,118m., res 118,885m., dep. 1,523,307m. (Dec. 2009); CEO Dr MIHALY PATAI.

WestLB Hungaria Bank: 1075 Budapest, Madách Imre u. 13–14; tel. (1) 235-5900; fax (1) 235-5906; e-mail public@westlb.hu; internet www.westlb.de; f. 1985; owned by WestLB AG (Germany); cap. 4,485.8m., res 4,718.8m., dep. 35,498.8m. (Dec. 2008); Chair. and Man. Dir GÁBOR KURUTZ.

Supervisory Authority

Hungarian Financial Supervisory Authority (HFSA) (Pénzügyi Szervezetek Állami Felügyelete—PSZAF): 1535 Budapest, POB 777; tel. (1) 489-9100; fax (1) 489-9102; e-mail pszaf@pszaf.hu; internet www.pszaf.hu; Chair. of Supervisory Bd ISTVÁN FARKAS; Dir-Gen. CSABA VARGA.

STOCK EXCHANGE

Budapest Stock Exchange (Budapesti Értéktőzsde—BET): 1062 Budapest, Andrássy u. 93; tel. (1) 429-6700; fax (1) 429-6800; e-mail info@bse.hu; internet www.bse.hu; f. 1991; partly owned by a consortium comprising: UniCredit Bank Hungary (25.2%), Wiener Börse (Vienna Stock Exchange, Austria, 12.5%) and Österreichische Kontrollbank AG (Austria, 12.5%); allied with the Wiener Börse from May 2004; Pres. MIHÁLY PATAI; Chief Exec. GYÖRGY MOHAI.

INSURANCE

In 2010 there were 33 insurance companies. The following are among the most important:

AB-AEGON Általános Biztosító: 1091 Budapest, Üllői u. 1; tel. (1) 476-5765; fax (1) 476-5838; internet www.aegon.hu; f. 1949; present name adopted 1992; pensions, life and property insurance, insurance of agricultural plants, co-operatives, foreign insurance, etc.; Gen. Man. Dr GÁBOR KEPECS.

Allianz Hungária Insurance Co (Hungária Biztosító): 1054 Budapest, Bajcsy u. 52; tel. (1) 301-6565; fax (1) 301-6100; e-mail ugyfelszolgalat@allianz.hu; internet www.allianz.hu; f. 1986; handles international insurance, industrial and commercial insurance, and motor car, marine, life, household, accident and liability insurance; cap. 4,266m.; Chair. and Chief Exec. Dr MIHÁLY PATAI.

Aviva Életbiztosító Zrt: 1138 Budapest, Népfürdő u. 22; tel. (40) 444-445; fax (1) 391-1660; e-mail info@aviva.hu; internet www.aviva.hu; f. 1996; 100% owned by Aviva PLC (United Kingdom).

ERSTE Vienna Insurance Group Biztosító Zrt: 1138 Budapest, Népfürdő u. 24-26; tel. (1) 484-1700; fax (1) 484-1799; e-mail info@erstebiztosito.hu; internet www.esb.hu; f. 2000.

Generali Esoport: 1066 Budapest, Teréz 39; tel. (40) 200-250; fax (1) 452-3570; e-mail egeszsegpenztar@generali.hu; internet www.generali.hu; f. 1832; Exec. Dir TORNYOS CSABA.

Grawe Életbiztosító Zrt: 1126 Budapest, Istenhegyi u. 9B; tel. (1) 202-1211; fax (1) 355-5530; internet www.grawe.hu; Pres. Dr OTHMAR EDERER.

ING Biztosító Zrt: 1068 Budapest, Dózsa György u. 84B; tel. (1) 235-8870; fax (1) 267-4833; e-mail ing@ing.hu; internet www.ing.hu; f. 2003.

QBE Atlasz Insurance Co (QBE Atlasz Biztosító): 1143 Budapest, Stefánia u. 51; tel. (1) 460-1400; fax (1) 460-1499; e-mail info.hungary@gbeatlasz.com; internet www.qbeatlasz.hu; f. 1988; cap. 1,000m.; CEO FRANK O'HALLORAN.

UNION Biztosító: 1082 Budapest, Baross u. 1; tel. (1) 486-4200; fax (1) 486-4390; e-mail info@unionbiztosito.hu; internet www.unionbiztosito.hu; f. 2000; Pres. and CEO MIKLÓS ZSOLDOS.

UNIQA Biztosító Zrt: 1134 Budapest, Róbert Károly 70–74; tel. (1) 544-5555; fax (1) 238-6060; e-mail info@uniqa.hu; internet www.uniqa.hu; f. 1999; CEO OTHMAR MICHL.

Trade and Industry

GOVERNMENT AGENCY

Hungarian State Holding Co (Magyar Nemzeti Vagyonkezelő Zrt.—MNV Zrt): 1133 Budapest, Pozsonyi u. 56; tel. (1) 237-4400; fax (1) 237-4100; e-mail info@mnv.hu; internet www.mnv.hu; f. 2008; Chair. Dr HALASI TIBOR.

NATIONAL CHAMBERS OF COMMERCE AND OF AGRICULTURE

Hungarian Chamber of Agriculture (Magyar Agrárkamara): 1119 Budapest, Fehérvári u. 89-95; tel. (1) 802-6100; fax (1) 802-0600; e-mail info@agrarkamara.hu; internet www.agrarkamara.hu; f. 1994; Pres. Dr FORGÁCS BARNA.

Hungarian Chamber of Commerce and Industry (Magyar Kereskedelmi és Iparkamara): 1055 Budapest, Kossuth Lajos tér 6–8; tel. (1) 474-5100; fax (1) 474-5105; e-mail hcci@hcci.com; internet www.mkik.hu; f. 1850; central org. of the 23 Hungarian county chambers of commerce and industry; based on a system of voluntary membership; over 46,000 mems; Pres. Dr LÁSZLÓ PARRAGH; Sec.-Gen. PÉTER DUNAI.

REGIONAL CHAMBERS OF COMMERCE

There are regional chambers of commerce in each of the 20 principal administrative divisions of Hungary (comprising the 19 counties and the City of Budapest). The following are among the most important:

Borsod-Abaúj-Zemplén County Chamber of Commerce and Industry (Borsod-Abaúj-Zemplén Kereskedelmi és Iparkamara): 3525 Miskolc, Szentpáli u. 1; tel. (46) 501-090; fax (46) 501-099; e-mail bokik@bokik.hu; internet www.bokik.hu; f. 1990; membership of 1,100 cos; Pres. TAMÁS BIHALL.

Budapest Chamber of Industry and Commerce (Budapesti Kereskedelmi és Iparkamara): 1016 Budapest, Krisztina krt 99; tel. (1) 488-2000; e-mail ugyfelszolgalat@bkik.hu; internet www.bkik.hu; f. 1850; Chair. KRISTÓF SZATMÁRY; Sec.-Gen. ERVIN KISS.

Csongrád County Chamber of Commerce and Industry: 6721 Szeged, Párizsi krt 8-12; tel. (62) 426-343; fax (62) 426-149; e-mail info@csmkik.com; internet kamara.dravanet.hu; Pres. PÁL NEMESI; Sec. ZSUZSANNA TRÁSERNÉ OLÁH.

Hajdú-Bihar County Chamber of Commerce and Industry: 4025 Debrecen, Petőfi tér 10; tel. (52) 500-710; fax (52) 500-720; e-mail hbkik@hbkik.hu; internet www.hbkik.hu; Chair. FERENC MIKLÓSSY; Sec. Dr EVA SKULTÉTI.

Pécs-Baranya Chamber of Commerce and Industry: 7625 Pécs, Dr Majorossy I. u. 36; tel. (72) 507-148; fax (72) 507-152; e-mail pbkik@pbkik.hu; internet www.pbkik.hu; Pres. ISTVÁN KÉRI; Sec. TAMÁS SÍKFÔI.

Pest County Chamber of Commerce and Industry (Pest Megyei Kereskedelmi és Iparkamara): 1056 Budapest, Vàci u. 40; tel. (1) 317-7666; fax (1) 317-7755; e-mail titkarsag@pmkik.hu; internet www.pmkik.hu; Chair. Dr ZOLTÁN VERECZKEY; Sec.-Gen. Dr LAJOS KUPCSOK.

EMPLOYERS' ASSOCIATIONS

Confederation of Hungarian Employers and Industrialists (Munkaadók és Gyáriparosok Országos Szövetsége—MGYOSZ): 1055 Budapest, Kossuth L. tér 6–8; tel. (1) 474-2044; fax (1) 474-2065; e-mail mgyosz@mgyosz.hu; internet www.mgyosz.hu; f. 1902; re-est. 1990; 64 member orgs; Sec.-Gen. ISTVÁN WIMMER.

National Assn of Entrepreneurs and Employers (Vállalkozók és Munkáltatók Országos Szövetsége—VOSZ): 1107 Budapest, Mázsa tér 2–6; tel. (1) 414-2181; fax (1) 414-2180; e-mail center@vosz.hu; internet www.vosz.hu; f. 1988; Sec.-Gen. DÁVID FERENC.

INDUSTRIAL AND TRADE ASSOCIATIONS

Hungarian Industrial Assn (Magyar Iparszövetség—OKISZ): 1146 Budapest, Thököly u. 58–60; tel. (1) 343-5181; fax (1) 343-5521; e-mail okisz@okiszinfo.hu; internet www.okisz.hu; safeguards interests of over 1,100 mem. enterprises (all private); Pres. ISTVÁN TOKÁR.

HUNICOOP Foreign Trade Co for Industrial Co-operation: 1036 Budapest, Galagonya u. 7; tel. (1) 250-8117; fax (1) 250-8121;

e-mail hunicoop@axelero.hu; internet www.hunicoop.hu; agency for foreign cos in Hungary, export and import; Dir Gábor Tombácz.

National Assen of Industrial Corporations (Ipartestületek Országos Szövetsége—IPOSZ): 1054 Budapest, Kálmán Imre u. 20; tel. (1) 354-3140; e-mail titkarsag@iposz.hu; internet www.iposz.hu; Chair. György Szűcs; 230 mem. orgs.

Agricultural Cooperatives and Producers' Association (Mezőgazdasági Szövetkezők és Termelők Országos Szövetsége—MOSZ): 1125 Budapest, Istenhegyi u. 59–61; tel. (1) 332-1163; fax (1) 353-2552; e-mail mosztit@mosz.agrar.hu; internet www.mosz.agrar.hu; f. 1967; as National Council of Producer Cooperatives; renamed as above in 1989; Pres. Tamás Nagy; Sec.-Gen. Gábor Horváth; c. 1,300 mem. orgs.

UTILITIES

Supervisory Organization

Hungarian Energy Office (Magyar Energia Hivatal): 1081 Budapest, II János Pál Pápa tér 7; tel. (1) 459-7777; fax (1) 459-7766; e-mail eh@eh.gov.hu; internet www.eh.gov.hu; f. 1994; regulation and supervision of activities performed by gas and electricity cos, price regulation and protection of consumer interest; Pres. Péter Horváth.

Electricity

Budapest Electricity Co (Budapesti Elektromos Művek—ELMŰ): 1132 Budapest, Váci u. 72–74; tel. (1) 238-1000; fax (1) 238-2822; e-mail elmu@elmu.hu; internet www.elmu.hu; f. 1949; transmission and distribution of electricity; Chair. Dr Marie-Theres Thiell; Pres. Emmerich Endresz; 2,700 employees.

Démász (South Hungarian Power Supply Co): 6720 Szeged, Klauzál tér 9; tel. (62) 565-565; fax (62) 482-500; e-mail info@edf.hu; internet www.edfdemasz.hu; f. 1951; distributes electricity to south-eastern Hungary; Pres. Thierry Le Boucher.

EDF Émász (North Hungarian Electricity Supply Co): 3525 Miskolc, Dózsa Gy, u. 13; tel. (46) 411-875; fax (46) 411-871; e-mail emasz@emasz.hu; internet www.emasz.hu; majority share owned by EDF (France); Chair. Dr Marie-Theres Thiell.

E.ON Hungária Rt: 1051 Budapest, Széchenyi tér 7-8; tel. (1) 472-2300; e-mail info@eon-hungaria.com; internet www.eon-hungaria.com; f. 2000; 85.98% owned by E.ON Energie AG (Germany); subsidiary electicity supply cos incl. E.ON Del-dunántúli Áramszolgáltató (South-West Hungary), E.ON Észak-dunántúli Áramszolgáltató (North-West Hungary), E.ON Tiszántúli Áramszolgáltató (North-East Hungary); Chair. of Bd of Dirs Konrad Krauser.

Hungarian Power Companies Co (Magyar Villamos Művek Rt—MVM): 1031 Budapest, Szentendrei u. 207-209; tel. (1) 304-2000; fax (1) 202-1246; e-mail mvm@mvm.hu; internet www.mvm.hu; electricity wholesaler and power-system controller; CEO Baji Csaba.

Mátrai Power Plant (Erőmű Részvénytársaság) Co: H-3271 Visonta, Erőmű u. 11; tel. (37) 334-000; fax (37) 334-016; e-mail matra@mert.hu; internet www.mert.hu; f. 1965; electricity generation; Chair. József Valaska; 3,645 employees.

Paks Nuclear Plant Co (Paksi Atomerőmű): 7031 Paks, POB 71; tel. (75) 508-833; fax (75) 506-662; e-mail uzemlatogatas@npp.hu; internet www.npp.hu; f. 1992; electrical energy production; CEO Hamvas István László; 2,800 employees.

Vértesi Power Plant (Erőmű) Co: 2841 Oroszlány, POB 23; tel. (34) 360-255; fax (34) 360-882; e-mail vert@vert.hu; internet www.vert.hu; electricity and heat generation; CEO Kovács András Zoltán.

Gas

Főgáz—Fővárosi Gázművek (Budapest Gas) Co: 1081 Budapest, II János Pál Pápa tér 20; tel. (1) 477-1111; fax (1) 477-1277; e-mail kommunikacio@fogaz.hu; internet www.fogaz.hu; f. 1856; gas distribution; Pres. Dr Bán Tamás.

GDF SUEZ Energia Magyarorzság Zrt.: 6724 Szeged, Pulz u. 44; tel. (62) 569-600; fax (63) 473-943; e-mail ugyfel@degas.hu; internet www.gdfsuez-energia.hu; fmrly Égáz-Dégáz Zrt; present name adopted 2010; gas supply and services; 99.6% owned by Gaz de France (France); CEO Patrick Eeckelers.

MOL Hungarian Oil and Gas PLC: 1117 Budapest, Október huszonharmadika u. 18; tel. (1) 209-0000; fax (1) 209-0005; e-mail webmaster@mol.hu; internet www.mol.hu; f. 1991; privatized in 1995; petroleum and gas exploration, processing, transportation and distribution; 34,000 employees; Chair. and CEO. Zsolt Hernádi.

Tigáz—Tiszántúli Gázszolgáltató (Tiszá Gas) Co: 4200 Hajdúszoboszló, Rákóczi u. 184; tel. (52) 333-338; fax (52) 361-149; e-mail titkarsaga@tigaz.hu; internet www.tigaz.com; f. 1950; majority share owned by ENI S.p.A (Italy); gas distribution in north-eastern regions of Hungary; Chair. of Bd Cesare Cuniberto.

TRADE UNIONS

From 1988, and particularly after the restructuring of the former Central Council of Hungarian Trade Unions (SzOT) as the National Confederation of Hungarian Trade Unions (MSzOSz) in 1990, several new union federations were created. Several unions are affiliated to more than one federation, and others are completely independent.

Trade Union Federations

Association of Hungarian Free Trade Unions (Magyar Szabad Szakszervezetek Szövetsége): 1068 Budapest, Városligeti fasor 46–48; tel. (1) 323-2686; fax (1) 323-2651; internet www.mszosz.com; f. 1994; Pres. Béla Balogh.

Autonomous Trade Union Confederation (Autonóm Szakszervezetek Svövetsége): 1068 Budapest, Benczúr u. 45; tel. (1) 413-1934; fax (1) 461-2480; e-mail autonom@t-online.hu; internet www.autonomok.hu; Pres. Lajos Főcze; 137,000 mems (2007).

Democratic League of Independent Trade Unions—LIGA (Független Szakszervezetek Demokratikus Ligája): 1146 Budapest, Ajtósi Dürer sor 27/A; tel. (1) 321-5262; fax (1) 321-5405; e-mail info@liganet.hu; internet www.liganet.hu; f. 1988; Pres. István Gaskó; 110,000 mems (2011).

Federation of Unions of Intellectual Workers (Értelmiségi Szakszervezeti Tömörülés—ÉSzT): 1066 Budapest, Jókai u. 2; tel. (1) 473-1429; fax (1) 331-4577; e-mail eszt@eszt.hu; internet www.eszt.hu; Pres. Dr László Kuti.

National Confederation of Hungarian Trade Unions (Magyar Szakszervezetek Országos Szövetsége—MSzOSz): 1086 Budapest, Magdolna u. 5–7; tel. (1) 323-2660; fax (1) 323-2662; e-mail gykiss@mszosz.hu; internet www.mszosz.hu; f. 1898; reorganized 1990; Pres. Dr László Sándor; 400,000 mems (2007).

Transport

RAILWAYS

In 2009 the rail network in Hungary totalled 7,793 km in length. There is an underground railway in Budapest, which has a network of three lines totalling 33 km. A fourth line was under construction in 2011 and was expected to become operational in 2014.

Budapest Transport Company (BKV): 1072 Budapest, Akácfa u. 15; tel. (1) 461-6500; fax (1) 461-6557; e-mail bkvzrt@bkv.hu; internet www.bkv.hu; f. 1968; operates metro system, suburban railway network, trams, trolley buses and conventional buses; Chief Exec. István Kocsis.

Hungarian State Railways Co (Magyar Államvasutak—MÁV): 1940 Budapest, Andrássy u. 73–75; tel. (1) 322-0660; fax (1) 342-8596; internet www.mav.hu; f. 1868; Pres. and Chief Exec. Gyula Gaal; Gen. Dir Márton Kukely.

ROADS

In 2008 there were 197,534 of roads in Hungary, of which 1,274 km were motorways and 6,793 km were main roads.

SHIPPING AND INLAND WATERWAYS

MAHART—Magyar Hajózás (Hungarian Shipping) Co: 1366 Budapest, POB 58; tel. (1) 484-6421; fax (1) 484-6422; e-mail freeport@mahart.hu; f. 1895; transportation of goods on the Rhine–Main–Danube waterway; carries passenger traffic on the Danube; operates port activities at Budapest Csepel National and Free Port (port agency service, loading, storage, handling goods); management of multi-modal and combined transport (cargo-booking, oversized goods, chartering); shipbuilding and ship-repair services; Dir-Gen. Capt. László Somlóvári.

CIVIL AVIATION

Budapest Ferenc Liszt International Airport (formerly Budapest Ferihegy International Airport) and Balatonkiliti airport, near Siófok, serve international traffic. Other airports are located at Nyíregyháza, Debrecen, Szeged, Pécs, Szombathely and Győr.

Civil Aviation Authority (Polgári Légiközlekedésigyi Hatóság): Budapest; tel. (1) 296-9502; fax (1) 296-8808; e-mail info@caa.hu; internet www.caa.hu; controls civil aviation; Dir-Gen. Zoltán Antal.

Malév Hungarian Airlines: 1097 Budapest, Könyves Kálmán körút 12, Lurdy Ház; tel. (1) 235-3646; fax (1) 235-3255; e-mail sajto@malev.hu; internet www.malev.hu; f. 1946; regular services from Budapest to Europe, North Africa, North America, Asia and the Middle East; 95% state-owned; Chair. of Bd János Berényi.

Wizz Air Hungary: 2220 Vecsés, Lorinci u. 59; tel. (22) 351-9499; e-mail info@wizzair.com; internet www.wizzair.com; f. 2004; wholly owned subsidiary of Wizz Air (United Kingdom); mem. of European Low Fares Airline Asscn; Chair. and Chief Exec. József Váradi.

Tourism

Tourism has developed rapidly and is an important source of foreign exchange. Lake Balaton is the main holiday centre for boating, bathing and fishing. Hungary's cities have great historical and recreational attractions, and the annual Budapest Spring Festival is held in March. Budapest has numerous swimming pools watered by thermal springs, which are equipped with modern physiotherapy facilities. There were 39.9m. foreign visitors in 2010, when revenue from tourism amounted to 1,189,819m. forint.

Hungarian Tourism Office: 1052 Budapest, Sütő u. 2; tel. (1) 317-9800; fax (1) 317-9656; e-mail info@hungarytourism.hu; internet www.hungarytourism.hu; Gen. Man. Dr Gábor Galla.

Defence

Compulsory military service was abolished in November 2004. As assessed at November 2011, the active armed forces numbered 22,587, including an army of 9,911, an air force of 5,039 and 7,637 joint-forces troops. Reservists totalled 44,000. Paramilitary forces comprised 12,000 border guards. In 1999 Hungary became a member of the North Atlantic Treaty Organization (NATO).

Defence Expenditure: Budgeted at 275,000m. forint in 2011.

Chief of the Defence Staff: Gen. Tibor Benkő.

Education

Children under the age of three years attend crèches (bölcsődék), and those between the ages of three and six years attend kindergartens (óvodák). Education is compulsory between the ages of six and 16 years. Children attend basic or primary school (általános iskola) until the age of 14. In 2008/09 pre-primary enrolment included 85% of children in the relevant age-group. The comparable ratio in the same year for primary education was 91% and that for secondary education was 92%. In southern Hungary, bilingual schools have been established to promote the languages of the national minorities. The majority of children continue with their education after 16 years of age. The most popular types of secondary school are the grammar school (gimnázium) and the vocational school (szakközépiskola). The gimnázium provides a four-year course of mainly academic studies, although some vocational training does feature on the curriculum. The szakközépiskola offers full vocational training together with a general education, emphasis being laid on practical work. Apprentice training schools (szakmunkásképző intézetek) are attached to factories, agricultural co-operatives, etc., and lead to full trade qualifications. In 1999–2000 the system of higher education underwent a major reorganization, as a result of which from 1 January 2000 there were 30 state-run universities and colleges, 26 church universities and colleges, and six colleges administered by foundations. In 2009/10 370,331 students attended 69 institutions of tertiary education. Expenditure on education in 2003 was some 1,070,400m. forint (equivalent to 12.2% of total government expenditure).

ICELAND

Introductory Survey

LOCATION, CLIMATE, LANGUAGE, RELIGION, FLAG, CAPITAL

The Republic of Iceland comprises one large island and numerous smaller ones, situated near the Arctic Circle in the North Atlantic Ocean. The main island lies about 300 km (190 miles) south-east of Greenland, about 1,000 km (620 miles) west of Norway and about 800 km (500 miles) north of Scotland. The Gulf Stream keeps Iceland warmer than might be expected, with average temperatures ranging from 10°C (50°F) in the summer to 1°C (34°F) in winter. Icelandic is the official language. Almost all of the inhabitants profess Christianity: the Evangelical Lutheran Church is the established church and embraces about 79% of the population. The civil flag (proportions 18 by 25) displays a red cross, bordered with white, on a blue background, the upright of the cross being towards the hoist; the state flag (proportions 9 by 16) bears the same design, but has a truncated triangular area cut from the fly. The capital is Reykjavík.

CONTEMPORARY POLITICAL HISTORY

Historical Context

Iceland became independent on 17 June 1944, when the Convention that linked it with Denmark, under the Danish crown, was terminated. Iceland became a founder member of the North Atlantic Treaty Organization (NATO, see p. 370) in 1949, joined the Council of Europe (see p. 256) in 1950, and has belonged to the Nordic Council (see p. 464) since its foundation in 1952. Membership of the European Free Trade Association (EFTA, see p. 450) was formalized in 1970.

From 1959 to 1971 Iceland was governed by a coalition of the Independence Party (IP) and the Social Democratic Party (SDP). Following the general election of June 1971, Ólafur Jóhannesson, the leader of the Progressive Party (PP), formed a coalition Government with the left-wing People's Alliance (PA) and the Union of Liberals and Leftists. At the general election held in June 1974 voters favoured right-wing parties, and in August the IP and the PP formed a coalition Government under the leader of the IP, Geir Hallgrímsson. However, failure adequately to address economic difficulties resulted in a decline in the coalition's popularity and prompted the Government's resignation in June 1978, following extensive electoral gains by the PA and the SDP. In September Jóhannesson formed a coalition of the PP with the PA and the SDP, but this Government, after addressing immediate economic necessities, resigned in October 1979, when the SDP withdrew from the coalition. An interim administration was formed by Benedikt Gröndal, the leader of the SDP. The results of a general election, held in December, were inconclusive, and in February 1980 Gunnar Thoroddsen of the IP formed a coalition Government with the PA and the PP.

Domestic Political Affairs

In June 1980 Vigdís Finnbogadóttir, a non-political candidate who was favoured by left-wing groups owing to her opposition to the US military airbase at Keflavík, achieved a narrow victory in the election for the mainly ceremonial office of President. She took office on 1 August 1980, becoming the world's first popularly elected female Head of State. The coalition Government lost its majority in the Lower House of the Althingi (Alþingi—parliament) in September 1982, and a general election took place in April 1983. The IP received the largest share of the votes cast, and a centre-right coalition was subsequently formed by the IP and the PP, with Steingrímur Hermannsson (the leader of the PP) as Prime Minister. In May 1985 the Althingi unanimously approved a resolution declaring the country a 'nuclear-free zone', thus banning the entry of nuclear weapons.

A general election for an enlarged, 63-seat Althingi was held in April 1987. Both parties of the outgoing coalition suffered losses: the IP's representation decreased from 24 to 18 seats, and the PP lost one of its 14 seats. The SDP secured 10 seats, and the newly formed, right-wing Citizens' Party (CP) won seven. A coalition of the IP, the PP and the SDP was formally constituted in July. Thorsteinn Pálsson, the leader of the IP and hitherto the Minister of Finance, was appointed Prime Minister.

In June 1988 President Finnbogadóttir (who had begun a second term in office, unopposed, in August 1984) was elected for a third term, receiving more than 90% of the votes cast. In June 1992 Finnbogadóttir was elected unopposed for a fourth term of office.

In September 1988 the SDP and the PP withdrew from the Government, following disagreements over economic policy. Later that month Hermannsson became Prime Minister in a centre-left coalition of the PP, the SDP and the PA. The new Government committed itself to a series of devaluations of the króna, and introduced austerity measures, with the aim of lowering the rate of inflation and stimulating the fishing industry. In September 1989 a new Government, based on a coalition agreement between the PP, the SDP, the PA, the CP and the Association for Equality and Social Justice, was formed. Hermannsson remained as Prime Minister.

In March 1991 Davíð Oddsson, the mayor of Reykjavík, successfully challenged Pálsson for the leadership of the IP. At a general election in April the IP emerged as the largest single party, securing 26 seats, mostly at the expense of the CP. Although the incumbent coalition would have retained an overall majority of seats, the SDP decided to withdraw from the coalition, chiefly as a result of the failure to reach agreement on Iceland's position in the discussions between EFTA and the European Community (EC, now European Union—EU, see p. 276), with regard to the creation of a European Economic Area (EEA). A new coalition Government was formed in late April by the IP and the SDP, with Oddsson as Prime Minister; the new administration promised economic liberalization and a strengthening of links with the USA and Europe, but was faced with a deteriorating economic situation.

In 1991 Iceland's Constitution was amended, ending the system whereby the Althingi was divided into an Upper House (one-third of the members) and a Lower House.

Although the IP secured the largest number of seats (25) at a general election in April 1995, the SDP obtained only seven seats, three fewer than in the previous election. Later in the month a new coalition Government was formed, comprising the IP and the PP, with Oddsson continuing as Prime Minister. Halldór Ásgrímsson, the Chairman of the PP, became Minister of Foreign Affairs.

Ólafur Ragnar Grímsson, a former leader of the PA, was victorious at a presidential election held in June 1996, winning 41% of the votes cast. (Finnbogadóttir had decided not to seek re-election.) Grímsson duly took office as President in August. He began a second term of office in August 2000, his candidacy being unopposed.

At a general election held in May 1999 the governing coalition retained its majority in the Althingi: the IP won 26 seats, while the PP won 12 seats. The Social Democratic Alliance (SDA), a left-wing electoral grouping composed of the PA, the SDP, the People's Movement and the Women's List, won 17 seats. Two new parties also secured representation in the legislature: the Left-Green Movement, established by three former PA deputies, won six seats, while the Liberal Party, founded by a former IP minister, won two. A new coalition Government comprising the IP and the PP, was formed under Oddsson.

At the general election held on 10 May 2003, the IP remained the party with the largest representation in the Althingi, winning 22 seats. The IP renewed its coalition with the PP, which had won 12 seats, with Oddsson remaining as Prime Minister. The two parties agreed that Oddsson would relinquish the premiership in September 2004 in favour of Ásgrímsson, who had been reappointed as Minister of Foreign Affairs. The SDA won 20 seats, the Left-Green Movement five, and the Liberal Party four.

In May 2004 the Althingi narrowly approved a bill to limit media ownership. Although the legislation was drafted following the publication of a report by a government-appointed committee that expressed concerns regarding the increased consolidation of media corporations, it provoked uncharacteristic public protests as many perceived the bill to be directed against a particular company, the Baugur Group, whose media outlets had been openly critical of Oddsson. In the first use of the presidential power of veto in the 60-year history of the Republic, President Grímsson refused to sign the bill, stating that it lacked the necessary consensus. Grímsson was re-elected President for a third term on 26 June, with 85.6% of the votes cast. The Althingi rejected an amended version of the media bill in July.

On 15 September 2004, in accordance with the post-election agreement between the IP and PP, Oddsson stood down as Prime Minister in favour of Ásgrímsson, whose post Oddsson assumed. Oddsson resigned from politics in September 2005 and assumed the chairmanship of the Central Bank of Iceland. He was replaced as Minister of Foreign Affairs by Geir Haarde, hitherto the Minister of Finance, who was also elected leader of the IP in October.

In June 2006 Ásgrímsson resigned as Prime Minister, following the PP's poor performance in municipal elections, and was succeeded by Haarde. Ásgrímsson also announced that he would resign as Chairman of the PP following the party conference in August; he was replaced by Jón Sigurðsson, whom Haarde had appointed Minister of Industry and Commerce in June.

At the general election of 12 May 2007 the IP remained the largest party in the Althingi, securing 25 seats. The PP, however, won just seven seats. The SDA won 18 seats, while the Left-Green Movement became the third largest party in the legislature, increasing its representation from five to nine seats. On 24 May a new coalition Government comprising the IP and the SDA, which commanded the support of 43 of the 63 members of the Althingi, was sworn in. Haarde retained the post of Prime Minister, while the leader of the SDA, Ingibjörg Sólrún Gísladóttir became Minister of Foreign Affairs. Meanwhile, Sigurðsson resigned as Chairman of the PP; he was succeeded by Guðni Agústsson.

Collapse of the banking sector

The economic situation in Iceland had declined significantly by mid-2008. The sharp contraction of credit on the global financial markets had severely weakened confidence in Iceland's banking sector, which held assets reported to be worth 10 times the country's annual gross domestic product (GDP); meanwhile, the value of the króna declined rapidly during 2008, and the country experienced high levels of inflation. On 6 October the Althingi approved an emergency bill to give the Icelandic Financial Supervisory Authority (Fjármálaeftirlitið—FME) extensive powers to intervene in the country's financial system. By the second week in October the Government had taken control of Iceland's three largest banks—Glitnir Banki, Landsbanki Íslands and Kaupþing Banki—and placed all three in receivership. Relations between the United Kingdom and Iceland were strained when it emerged that, as a consequence of the action taken by the FME, the accounts of some 400,000 British and Dutch savers who had invested in Icesave, a savings brand operated by Landsbanki in the United Kingdom and the Netherlands, had been frozen. Amid strong doubts that the Icelandic Depositors' and Investors' Guarantee Fund had sufficient assets to compensate Landsbanki's foreign creditors, the British Government invoked anti-terrorism legislation in order to seize Landsbanki's assets in the United Kingdom. The measure, which was described by Haarde as 'hostile', caused significant popular resentment in Iceland. In an effort to resolve the dispute, delegates from the two countries held talks in Reykjavík; the Bank of England subsequently granted Landsbanki a loan of £100m. to assist Iceland in repaying British Icesave account holders. Negotiations between government officials from the two countries were held in Reykjavík later in October to discuss the possibility of the United Kingdom granting Iceland a further loan to help the country honour its obligations to British savers. The IMF approved a loan of US $2,100m. to Iceland in November, following an announcement that Iceland and EU member states had finally reached an agreement over compensation for Icesave account holders in the United Kingdom and the Netherlands.

In November 2008 the Government defeated a motion of no confidence proposed by the opposition in the Althingi over its handling of the economic crisis. However, this did little to increase public confidence in the administration. A series of demonstrations were staged around Iceland throughout late 2008 and early 2009 calling for the Government to resign, with as many as 6,000 people attending the protests held periodically in Reykjavík. Moreover, tensions were increasing within the coalition itself. In January Haarde scheduled an early general election for 9 May, and announced that he did not intend to seek re-election to the IP leadership at the party conference scheduled for late March, owing to ill health. Two days later the Minister of Business Affairs, Björgvin Sigurðsson, resigned, citing his resolve to take responsibility for the political role he had played in the country's financial decline. Prior to his resignation, he dismissed the director of the FME. The following day Haarde announced the resignation of the Government. On 1 February Jóhanna Sigurðardóttir of the SDA, hitherto Minister of Social Affairs, was sworn in as Iceland's first female Prime Minister and a minority interim coalition Government comprising the SDA, the Left-Green Movement and independents was appointed, pending the general election, which was brought forward to 25 April.

On assuming the premiership, Sigurðardóttir immediately began implementing a series of measures aimed at alleviating Iceland's acute financial situation. In February 2009 the Althingi approved a bill on the reorganization of the senior management of the Central Bank of Iceland, facilitating the immediate dismissal of the bank's Governor, Oddsson, whom many considered responsible for exacerbating the country's economic problems. In the event, Oddsson resigned. In March Gísladóttir resigned as leader of the SDA for health reasons; Sigurðardóttir was elected her successor. Meanwhile, Bjarni Benediktsson was appointed Chairman of the IP, replacing Haarde.

At the general election held on 25 April 2009 the interim coalition parties, the SDA and the Left-Green Movement, won 34 of the 63 seats in the Althingi, the first time left-wing parties had won a majority in parliament. The SDA replaced the IP as the largest party in the Althingi, winning 20 seats, while the Left-Green Movement won 14 seats. The IP won 16 seats, defying the predictions of many political analysts by coming ahead of the increasingly popular Left-Green Movement. The success of the newly formed Citizens' Movement also confounded expectations; founded in February by activists involved in the protests against the Government's handling of the economic crisis, the party won four seats. The PP, meanwhile, increased its representation from seven seats to nine.

The SDA-Left-Green Movement Coalition

On 10 May 2009 a new Government, led by Sigurðardóttir and largely unchanged from the outgoing interim coalition, formally took office. Steingrímur J. Sigfússon, the leader of the Left-Green Movement, remained as Minister of Finance. The new administration declared its principal aim to be to achieve a balanced state budget by 2013. The coalition parties also agreed to allow the Althingi to vote on whether to apply for accession to the EU (which had gained increasing popular support since the onset of the economic crisis and which had been a central policy of the SDA), despite the fact that the Left-Green Movement remained opposed to EU membership. Accordingly, in July the Althingi voted narrowly in favour of applying for accession. A formal application was duly submitted later in the month to the European Council. The Government emphasized that, should Iceland be admitted to the EU, the accession treaty would be subject to approval in a referendum.

Meanwhile, negotiations continued with the United Kingdom and the Netherlands over the consequences of the collapse of Landsbanki Íslands. In June 2009 it was agreed that the Icelandic Government would guarantee loans of some £2,350m. from the United Kingdom and €1,200m. from the Netherlands to the Depositors' and Investors' Guarantee Fund in respect of the compensation that the two countries' Governments had issued to savers who had lost deposits held in Icesave accounts; the loans were to be repaid by 2024, with repayment, at an interest rate of 5.55%, to commence in 2016. The agreement encountered strong domestic opposition on the grounds that it placed an unduly harsh burden on the Icelandic economy, the amount loaned being equivalent to some US $17,000 per head. None the less, in August 2009 the Althingi approved a bill to ratify the loan agreement, but added stipulations to the effect that Iceland would repay no more than 4% of its annual GDP growth to the United Kingdom and 2% to the Netherlands in any one year, and that any portion of the debt not repaid by 2024 would effectively be cancelled. The British and Dutch Governments objected to the amended bill (which was signed into law in September 2009) and demanded further negotiations with Iceland, prompting the resignation of the Minister of Health, Ögmundur Jónasson, who cited disagreement with his cabinet colleagues over the Government's approach to the talks. A revised agreement with the United Kingdom and the Netherlands was concluded in October, which retained the Althingi's annual limits on repayment but allowed for payments to continue beyond the 2024 deadline if necessary. The new agreement was narrowly approved by the Althingi in December 2009.

However, by 2 January 2010 more than 56,000 people—some 23% of the electorate—had signed a petition urging President Grímsson to veto the bill. In response, on 5 January Grímsson announced that he would not sign the legislation, and that, in accordance with the Constitution, it would thus be subject to a referendum, which was subsequently scheduled for 6 March.

In anticipation of a referendum defeat for the Icesave compensation bill, the Government held further talks with the British and Dutch authorities in February 2010. However, the talks collapsed after Iceland rejected as insufficient a British and Dutch offer, estimated to be worth €450m., to waive interest payments for the first two years and to replace the fixed interest rate of 5.55% with a variable one. Further negotiations in early March also ended without agreement. Sigurðardóttir maintained that the Government remained committed to dialogue and urged electors not to vote in the referendum, arguing that the offer of revised terms for the loans had already made the bill of December 2009 obsolete. None the less, 62.7% of registered voters participated in the referendum (the first since Iceland's independence) on 6 March 2010, at which 93.2% of votes cast were against the bill. As a result, the payment terms authorized in September 2009 were to remain in force pending further negotiations with the United Kingdom and the Netherlands.

A commission established by the Althingi to investigate the collapse of the banking sector in 2008 presented its report in April 2010, accusing the Icelandic Government and regulators of the financial sector of 'extreme negligence' in the period preceding the crisis and concluding that the failure of the banking system had become inevitable as early as the end of 2006. Seven former officials were specifically criticized: from the Government, then Prime Minister Geir Haarde, Minister of Finance, Árni Mathiesen, and Minister of Business Affairs, Björgvin Sigurðsson; from the Central Bank, former Governor, Davíð Oddsson, and two other officials; and from the FME, former Director-General Jónas Jónsson. The report was also highly critical of the management and largest shareholders of the three banks that failed, noting that the owners had 'abnormally easy access to loans in these banks' and were, indeed, their largest borrowers. In September the nine-member commission voted in favour of a recommendation to convene the Landsdómur, a special court for hearing cases against elected officials, to try Haarde, Mathiesen and Sigurðsson, as well as former Minister of Foreign Affairs Ingibjörg Gísladóttir. Later that month the Althingi voted to pursue charges of negligence against Haarde, but not the other three erstwhile ministers.

The Landsdómur was duly convened, for the first time since its establishment in 1905, in February 2011. In June Haarde was formally charged by the Landsdómur on six counts of violating the laws on ministerial responsibility. Appearing before the Landsdómur in September, Haarde sought the dismissal of the charges against him, all of which he denied, claiming that they were a result of a 'political vendetta' against him by the current Government. The Landsdómur withdrew two of the six charges against Haarde in the following month. His trial on the remaining charges of negligence took place in March 2012, after the Althingi rejected a motion proposed by the IP that the charges should be revoked. In April Haarde was found guilty of a minor charge, for which he faced no punishment, and was cleared of more serious charges. Meanwhile, a special prosecutor appointed in early 2009 to investigate the collapse of the banking sector in 2008 began to file charges against former bank executives, including Lárus Welding, the former CEO of Glitnir Banki, in December 2011 and Hreiðar Már Sigurðsson and Sigurður Einarsson, respectively the former CEO and Chairman of Kaupþing Banki, in February 2012; Sigurjón Árnason, the former CEO of Landsbanki Íslands, was also under investigation.

Recent developments: the second Icesave referendum

The municipal elections held on 29 May 2010 were notable for the relatively high percentage of blank and invalid votes cast, 6.3% compared with 2.4% at the 2006 elections. Public discontent with the traditional parties was also indicated by the success in Reykjavík of a new, satirical political organization, the Best Party, which had been established by a comedian, Jón Gnarr, in November 2009. The party narrowly won the largest number of seats on Reykjavík's city council, with Gnarr subsequently becoming mayor.

At a summit held in Brussels, Belgium, in June 2010, EU leaders agreed to open membership negotiations with Iceland, although it was made clear that accession would not be possible while the dispute with the United Kingdom and the Netherlands over compensation for savers who had lost Icesave deposits remained unresolved. In the previous month the EFTA Surveillance Authority had ruled that Iceland was obliged to ensure payment of the minimum compensation (€20,000) to British and Dutch savers. Negotiations on Iceland's accession to the EU formally opened in Brussels in July. However, support for EU membership within Iceland appeared to have weakened, with 57.6% of respondents in an opinion poll conducted in June favouring the withdrawal of the application.

The number of ministers was reduced from 12 to 10 in a government reorganization effected in September 2010. Ögmundur Jónasson returned to the Cabinet to head the Ministries of Justice and Human Rights and of Transport, Communications and Local Government (which were merged as the Ministry of the Interior from January 2011), while Guðbjartur Hannesson of the SDA was appointed Minister of Social Affairs and Social Security and of Health (Minister of Welfare from January 2011). Four ministers left the Government, including the two non-affiliated ministers, Gylfi Magnússon, who was replaced as Minister of Economic Affairs by Árni Páll Árnason of the SDA, and Ragna Árnadóttir, hitherto responsible for justice. Continued public discontent with the Government was evident in the following month, when an estimated 8,000 people demonstrated outside the Althingi while Sigurðardóttir was addressing the chamber.

Direct elections to a constitutional parliament, which was to propose revisions to the Constitution, took place on 27 November 2010, but were marked by an extremely low turn-out of only around 36%. Of the 525 candidates, 25 secured representation in the parliament (among them academics, doctors and lawyers), which was to convene by mid-February 2011 and to complete its mission two months later. However, the Supreme Court declared the elections void in January, owing to a number of irregularities in the organization of the vote. In February a legislative committee recommended that, instead of holding new elections, the 25 people elected to the constitutional parliament should be appointed by the Althingi to a Constitutional Council, which would have a similar role to the planned parliament. The Constitutional Council was duly appointed and convened for its first meeting at the beginning of April.

In December 2010 Iceland reached a new agreement with the Netherlands and the United Kingdom on the repayment of loans related to the compensation of savers who had lost deposits held in Icesave accounts. From Iceland's perspective, the terms of this accord represented a significant improvement on those of the previous one: repayments were to commence in 2016 and to be completed by 2046, while interest was to be paid at a fixed rate of 3.0% to the Netherlands and 3.3% to the United Kingdom (reflecting the differing cost to each country of raising funds). Annual repayments would also be limited to no more than the equivalent of 5% of government revenue in the preceding year or 1.3% of GDP (whichever was higher). In February 2011 the Althingi approved the ratification of the agreement and decided against the need for a public vote on the issue, but President Grímsson again vetoed the accord, thus triggering the organization of a referendum, which was subsequently scheduled for 9 April. At the referendum the repayment agreement was rejected by 58.9% of those who voted. Those opposing the agreement were expressing their opposition to the principle that the Icelandic taxpayer should be responsible for the debt. It was expected in any case that the sale of the assets of Landsbanki Íslands would cover much of the debt. The dispute reverted to the EFTA Surveillance Authority, which decided in mid-December to refer the matter to the Court of Justice of the European Free Trade Association States (EFTA Court). Meanwhile, payments from the estate of Landsbanki Íslands to the Governments of the United Kingdom and the Netherlands and to other priority creditors, including British and Dutch local authorities, commenced earlier in December, following a ruling by the Supreme Court in October upholding emergency legislation adopted in 2008 that had given depositors priority status over other creditors for compensation.

The Government narrowly defeated a motion of no confidence proposed by the IP in April 2011. Three Left-Green Movement members of the Althingi had left the party's parliamentary group in March and April, owing to their opposition to the austerity measures being introduced by the Government, leaving the ruling coalition with a very slim majority in the Althingi.

Iceland and the EU commenced formal negotiations on the first four of the 35 negotiating chapters of the *acquis communautaire*, the EU's body of law, on 27 June 2011. Two of the chapters were completed that day, an unprecedented development within the EU's enlargement history, which was attributed to the fact that Iceland already largely complied with some two-thirds of EU law through its membership of the EEA. Following further meetings in October and December, negotiations had been initiated on a total of 11 chapters, of which eight had been provisionally completed. Although a majority of respondents in successive opinion polls continued to oppose accession to the Union, a significant percentage were unsure, and the percentage favouring the withdrawal of the application for membership declined to 51.0% and to 43.6% in polls conducted in June 2011 and February 2012, respectively.

In late July 2011 the Constitutional Council presented its draft bill on a new constitution to the Althingi, recommending that, following further consultation, it be subject to a referendum, prior to a final parliamentary vote. The bill notably provided for increased public participation in decision-making (allowing 10% of the electorate to demand a referendum on laws adopted by the Althingi and 2% to submit a legislative proposal); a strengthening of the role of the Althingi; the creation of a Law Council (Lögrétta) to examine the constitutionality of new legislation; and greater autonomy for local authorities. In addition, the President would be limited to serving a maximum of three terms in office and government ministers to holding the same office for eight years, while the Prime Minister would be directly elected by the Althingi following legislative elections. The Council's proposals remained under consideration by the Althingi's constitutional and supervisory committee in early 2012.

The Minister of Fisheries and Agriculture, Jón Bjarnason of the Left-Green Movement, and the Minister of Economic Affairs, Árni Páll Árnason of the SDA, were dismissed in a cabinet reorganization effected at the end of December 2011. Bjarnason's particularly vocal opposition to Iceland's proposed membership of the EU had exacerbated tensions within the governing coalition, with the Left-Green Movement being officially against accession and the SDA in favour. Sigfússon, the leader of the Left-Green Movement, became Minister of Fisheries and Agriculture and of Economic Affairs, being replaced as Minister of Finance by Oddný G. Harðardóttir of the SDA. The changes, which reduced the number of ministers to nine, followed a failed attempt to increase the Government's majority in the Althingi by securing the support of the three deputies of the opposition party The Movement (which had been created in 2009 by former members of the Citizens' Movement).

Three new political parties were formed in early 2012, with a view to contesting the legislative elections due to be held in April 2013: the Civil Freedom Party, a right-wing party advocating membership of the EU; Bright Future, established by members of the Best Party and Guðmundur Steingrímsson, an independent deputy formerly belonging to the PP; and Solidarity, created by Lilja Mósesdóttir, an independent deputy who had left the Left-Green Movement's parliamentary group in March 2011.

In March 2012 President Grímsson announced that he would contest the presidential election scheduled to take place on 30 June, reversing an earlier decision not stand, in response to a petition signed by more than 30,000 supporters urging him to seek a fifth term. He also cited uncertainty regarding the future role of the President, resulting from the ongoing process to draft a new constitution, as a factor in his decision. Ástþór Magnússon, a businessman and peace activist, who had unsuccessfully contested the 1996 and 2004 presidential poll, had announced his candidacy two days earlier.

Foreign Affairs

Regional relations

Iceland has strong links to the EU through its participation in the EEA and its membership of the Schengen Agreement on border controls. Negotiations on Iceland's accession to the EU formally opened in July 2010, one year after the country applied for membership, and discussions on the first four of the 35 negotiating chapters of the *acquis communautaire*, the EU's body of legislation, commenced in July 2011. Accession to the Union was not expected before 2013, and would be subject to the approval of the Icelandic electorate in a referendum (which was far from assured). Discussions on fisheries were expected to prove particularly difficult, with disputes over fishing rights having frequently strained Iceland's relations with EU member states. Accession was also contingent on the resolution of Iceland's dispute with the United Kingdom and the Netherlands regarding the compensation of savers who had lost deposits in the collapsed Landsbanki Islands (see Contemporary Political History).

The importance of fishing to Iceland's economy, and fears of excessive exploitation of the fishing grounds near Iceland by foreign fleets, caused the Icelandic Government to extend its territorial waters to 12 nautical miles (22 km) in 1964 and to 50 nautical miles (93 km) in 1972. British opposition to these extensions resulted in two 'cod wars'. In October 1975 Iceland unilaterally introduced a fishing limit of 200 nautical miles (370 km), both as a conservation measure and to protect Icelandic interests. The 1973 agreement on fishing limits between Iceland and the United Kingdom expired in November 1975, and failure to reach a new agreement led to the third and most serious 'cod war'. Casualties occurred, and in February 1976 Iceland temporarily severed diplomatic relations with the United Kingdom, the first diplomatic break between two NATO countries. In June the two countries reached an agreement, and in December the British trawler fleet withdrew from Icelandic waters. In June 1979 Iceland declared its exclusive rights to the 200-mile fishing zone. Following negotiations between the EC and EFTA on the creation of the EEA, an agreement was reached (in October 1991) allowing tariff-free access to the EC for 97% of Iceland's fisheries products by 1997, while Iceland was to allow EC vessels to catch 3,000 metric tons of fish per year in its waters, in return for some access to EC waters. The EEA agreement was ratified by the Althingi in January 1993 and entered into force in January 1994.

In August 1993 a dispute developed between Iceland and Norway over fishing rights in an area of the Barents Sea fished by Iceland, over which Norway claimed jurisdiction. The dispute continued throughout 1994, and in June the Norwegian coastguards cut the nets of Icelandic trawlers fishing for cod in the disputed region. Iceland's case was weakened in January 1995, when Canada officially recognized Norway's sovereign rights over the disputed area (a fisheries protection zone extending 200 km around the Svalbard archipelago). A similar dispute arose in August 1996 between Iceland and Denmark over fishing rights in an area of the Atlantic Ocean between Iceland and Greenland (a self-governing province of Denmark). The Danish Government claimed that an agreement had been concluded in 1988 to allow fishing boats that were in possession of a licence issued in Greenland to operate in the area. Iceland, however, denied the existence of such an agreement, and announced that Danish boats would not be permitted to fish in the disputed area.

Iceland's relations with the EU and Norway were strained during the second half of 2010 and early 2011 by a dispute over fishing quotas for mackerel in the north-east Atlantic Ocean. In April 2010 Iceland had unilaterally set itself a mackerel quota of 130,000 metric tons for that year, in the absence of an agreement on the issue between the interested states. Iceland and the Faroe Islands, which also set its own quota in July, maintained that they had been forced to take this action having been excluded from a bilateral quota arrangement between the EU and Norway and that stocks of mackerel had become more plentiful in their waters as a result of changing migration patterns. Three rounds of negotiations between officials from the four parties, held in October and November, failed to reach a resolution on quotas for 2011. Having opted not to participate in further talks in December 2010 (which again ended without agreement), the Icelandic Government announced that its mackerel quota for 2011 would be 146,818 tons, prompting threats of sanctions from the European Commission. However, Icelandic officials claimed that the EU and Norway would be primarily responsible for overfishing of mackerel in 2011, having allocated themselves more than 90% of the recommended total allowable catch. Officials from the EU, Norway, Iceland and the Faroe Islands engaged in five rounds of negotiations on quotas for 2012 between October 2011 and February 2012, but these again ended without agreement. Meanwhile, as a result of the ongoing dispute, the EU was considering the adoption of a regulation to restrict imports of fish from countries deemed to be engaging in unsustainable fishing practices.

Other external relations

Iceland has developed close relations with the USA, which was the first country officially to recognize Icelandic independence in 1944. Having joined NATO at its foundation in 1949, in 1951 Iceland concluded a bilateral defence agreement with the USA, which provided for the territorial defence of Iceland by the USA and led to the establishment of the Iceland Defence Force (IDF) at Keflavík airbase, near Reykjavík.

In May 2003 it emerged that the USA was planning to withdraw the four remaining fighter jet aircraft stationed at Keflavík, following a review of its international military commitments. The IDF, which, in mid-2003, was composed of 1,658 US troops, was traditionally viewed as providing protection for Iceland, which had no military of its own; moreover, many Icelanders in the nearby town of Reykjanesbær depended on the Keflavík airbase for their livelihood. Oddsson suggested that if the USA withdrew the aircraft it would have to end its military presence in Iceland altogether—an unpalatable proposition for the USA, which still regarded its reconnaissance of the North Atlantic as a high priority. Concern among Icelanders was such that the Government requested that the Secretary-General of NATO, Lord Robertson of Port Ellen, intervene on their behalf. Following Lord Robertson's subsequent non-partisan representations in July 2003, the US authorities announced that they had delayed their decision with regard to the aircraft at Keflavík. The USA had previously withdrawn eight fighter aircraft from Iceland in 1994, but had agreed to retain four aircraft on a permanent basis at the Keflavík airbase.

In March 2006 the USA announced its intention to withdraw the remaining US troops from Keflavík airbase by October of that year; the decision was received unfavourably by the Government. A subsequent offer by the Government to contribute one-half of the annual cost of maintaining the US mission was rejected. In September the new coalition Government signed an agreement with the USA, under which the USA reaffirmed its commitment to defend Iceland as a NATO ally and agreed to return the Keflavík airbase to Icelandic ownership. For its part, Iceland would pay up to 5,000m. krónur to clean contaminated land at the former US airbase and return the site to civilian use. On 30 September the USA completed the withdrawal of its troops from Iceland.

At a meeting of the North Atlantic Council in July 2007 NATO members signed an agreement over the protection of Icelandic airspace, which had been proposed by the Prime Minister, Geir Haarde, in November 2006. Under the accord, the air forces of NATO member countries would undertake military exercises and patrols in Iceland on a rotating basis at intervals of no more than four months, while the Icelandic Government would pay for technical assistance and the use by visiting forces of the facilities at the Keflavík airbase. In May 2008 the Ministry of Foreign Affairs established the Iceland Defence Agency (IDA) to co-ordinate the country's security and defence policy and supervise all NATO matters pertaining to Iceland. In January 2011, however, the IDA was dissolved, with its duties integrated into the new Ministry of the Interior, although relations with NATO were to remain the responsibility of the Ministry for Foreign Affairs.

Iceland strongly criticized the moratorium on commercial whaling, imposed (for conservation purposes) by the International Whaling Commission (IWC, see p. 442) in 1986, and continued to catch limited numbers of whales for scientific purposes. However, in 1989 Iceland halted whaling, following appeals by environmental organizations for an international boycott of Icelandic products. In 1991 Iceland announced its withdrawal from the IWC (with effect from June 1992), claiming that certain species of whales were not only too plentiful to be in danger of extinction, but were also threatening Iceland's stocks of cod and other fish. In March 1999 the Althingi voted to end the self-imposed 10-year ban on whaling and requested the Government to implement the ruling swiftly.

Iceland's application to rejoin the IWC, with an unprecedented exemption that would allow it to disregard the moratorium on commercial whaling, was rejected in July 2001. However, it was granted permission to attend discussions as an observer without voting rights. Its bid for full membership was rejected again in May 2002, but in October of that year Iceland was readmitted, when the Government undertook not to allow the resumption of commercial whaling until at least 2006 and after that not to resume commercial whaling while negotiations on a revised management plan were in progress. In August 2003, however, Iceland resumed whaling for research purposes, provoking widespread international criticism. Furthermore, in October 2006 Iceland resumed commercial whaling. However, whaling was halted following the killing of seven minke whales and seven fin whales, owing to a lack of consumer demand. In August 2007 the Minister of Fisheries and Agriculture, Einar Kristinn Guðfinnsson, announced the suspension of commercial whaling quotas during the forthcoming fishing season, since meat from the 2006/07 season remained unsold. By early 2008, however, all of the minke meat from the previous year had reportedly been sold, and in May Guðfinnsson licensed the capture of 40 minke whales for the impending fishing season. In January 2009 Guðfinnsson issued an annual whaling quota of 150 fin whales and 100 minke whales over a five-year period. The number of fin whales actually caught reportedly increased to 148 in 2010, compared with 125 in 2009. Meanwhile, at its annual meeting in June 2010, the IWC failed to reach agreement on a proposal that would have lifted the moratorium on commercial whaling but allowed the Commission to set quotas for whaling countries; the deep divisions between pro- and anti-whaling members were again evident at the largely inconclusive annual meeting held in June 2011. Iceland's whaling quota for 2011 was 216 minke whales and 154 fin whales. In May 2011, however, the only company involved in capturing fin whales, Hvalur, suspended hunting for that year, owing to weak demand from Japan, its main export market.

CONSTITUTION AND GOVERNMENT

The Constitution came into force in June 1944, when Iceland became an independent republic. Executive power is vested in the President (elected for four years by universal adult suffrage) and the Cabinet, consisting of the Prime Minister and other ministers appointed by the President. In practice, however, the President performs only nominally the functions ascribed in the Constitution to this office, and it is the Cabinet alone that holds real executive power. Legislative power is held jointly by the President and the unicameral Althingi (parliament), with 63 members elected by universal suffrage for four years (subject to dissolution by the President), using a system of proportional representation in eight multi-member constituencies. The Cabinet is responsible to the Althingi. Iceland is divided into 76 municipalities, each with a municipal council and executive. Municipal governments are responsible for education, infrastructure and social services.

REGIONAL AND INTERNATIONAL CO-OPERATION

Iceland is a member of the Nordic Council (see p. 464), the Arctic Council (see p. 448) and the European Free Trade Association (EFTA, see p. 450). It participates in the European Economic Area, and is thus integrated into the internal market of the European Union (EU, see p. 276); it is also a member the EU's Schengen Agreement on border controls by virtue of its membership of the Nordic passport union. Iceland applied for full membership of the EU in July 2009 and accession negotiations formally opened in July 2010. It is also participates in the Council of Europe (see p. 256) and the Organization for Security and Co-operation in Europe (OSCE, see p. 388).

Iceland joined the UN in 1946. As a contracting party to the General Agreement on Tariffs and Trade, it joined the World Trade Organization (WTO, see p. 433) on its establishment in 1995. Iceland was a founder member of the North Atlantic Treaty Organization (NATO, see p. 370) and is a member of the Organisation for Economic Co-operation and Development (OECD, see p. 379).

ECONOMIC AFFAIRS

In 2010, according to estimates by the World Bank, Iceland's gross national income (GNI), measured at 2008–10 prices, was US $10,787m., equivalent to $33,900 per head (or $28,720 per head on an international purchasing-power parity basis). During 2001–10, it was estimated, the population increased at an average annual rate of 1.2%, while gross domestic product (GDP) per head increased, in real terms, by an average of 0.8% per year. Iceland's overall GDP increased, in real terms, at an average annual rate of 2.0% during 2001–10; GDP increased by 1.4% in 2008, but declined by 6.9% in 2009 and by 3.5% in 2010.

Agriculture (including fishing) contributed 6.9% of GDP in 2009 (fishing contributed 5.8% of GDP and agriculture alone only 1.1%); in 2010 5.9% of the employed labour force were engaged in the agricultural and fishing sectors, with a further 2.2% employed in fish processing. The principal agricultural products are dairy produce and lamb. Marine products accounted for 32.5% of total export earnings in 2008. A cod quota system is in place to avoid the depletion of fish stocks through overfishing as happened in previous years. The decline in the catch of cod has been offset by an increase in the catch of other species, such as haddock and redfish. However, cod remains the most valuable species, accounting for 16.8% of the value of the total catch in 2010, followed by capelin (9.6%) and herring (6.3%). According to the World Bank, during 2001–08 agricultural GDP (including fishing) decreased at an average annual rate of 0.1%; the sector declined by 0.1% in 2008.

Industry (including mining, manufacturing, construction and power) contributed 22.9% of GDP in 2009 and engaged 18.6% of the employed labour force (including the 2.2% employed in fish processing) in 2010. Mining activity is negligible. During 2001–08, according to the World Bank, industrial GDP decreased at an average annual rate of 3.9%; industrial GDP increased by 1.2% in 2008.

Manufacturing contributed 12.5% of GDP in 2009, and employed 9.2% of the labour force in 2010. The most important sectors are fish processing (which contributed 3.0% of GDP in 2008), the production of aluminium, medical equipment, pharmaceuticals and ferrosilicon. Basic metal processing contributed 2.8% of GDP in 2008. A new aluminium smelter, Alcoa Fjardaál, fuelled by hydroelectric power plants, opened in 2007, with a production capacity of 322,000 metric tons per year. Construction of an aluminium smelter at Helguvík, with a planned production capacity of 360,000 tons, was halted in late 2008 as a consequence of the global financial crisis.

The construction sector contributed 5.0% of GDP in 2009 and engaged 6.3% of the employed labour force in 2010.

Iceland is potentially rich in hydroelectric and geothermal power, although both energy sources have yet to be fully exploited. Hydroelectric power has promoted the development of the aluminium industry, while geothermal energy provides nearly all the country's heating and hot water. In 2010 hydroelectric power provided 73.8% of the country's electricity and geothermal energy 26.2%. Fuel imports comprised 12.4% of the value of merchandise imports in 2009. In 2001 Iceland announced its intention to develop the world's first economy free of carbon dioxide emissions by using hydrogen or methanol-powered fuel cells. Two new hydroelectric power plants in the east of the country, the Kárahnjúkar Hydroelectric Project, built amid much controversy to fuel the Alcoa Fjardaál smelter, were officially opened in June 2007.

Services contributed 70.3% of GDP in 2009 and employed 69.2% of the labour force in 2010. Banking was an important sector in Iceland, with the financial sector providing 8.7% of GDP in 2007; however, the sector effectively collapsed in October 2008, when the three largest banks, Glitnir Banki, Landsbanki Íslands and Kaupþing Banki, were placed in receivership. The tourism sector is becoming an increasingly significant source of revenue; the number of overnight stays by foreign visitors in hotels and guest houses totalled 1,620,597 in 2010; receipts from tourism totalled US $881m. in 2008.

In 2010 Iceland recorded a visible trade surplus of US $983m., while there was a deficit of $1,417m. on the current account of the balance of payments. In 2010 the principal sources of imports were Norway (providing 9.1% of total imports), Netherlands, the USA, Germany, China, Finland, Sweden and the United Kingdom; the principal market for exports was the Netherlands (accounting for 34.0% of total exports), followed by Germany and the United Kingdom. In 2008 member countries of the European Economic Area (EEA, see p. 450) provided 69.6% of Iceland's merchandise imports and took 84.6% of its exports. The principal imports in 2009 were machinery and transport equipment (29.9%, including road vehicles, which accounted for 3.2% of the total value of imports), inedible crude materials and mineral fuels and lubricants. The principal exports in the same year were food and live animals (41.4%), aluminium and machinery and transport equipment.

In 2010 there was a budgetary deficit of 154,600m. krónur, equivalent to 10.1% of GDP. Iceland's total external debt was 13,696,852m. krónur at the end of 2010. Iceland's general government gross debt was 1,422,080m. krónur in 2010, equivalent to 92.4% of GDP. The annual rate of inflation averaged 6.0% in 2001–11; consumer prices increased by 4.0% in 2011. The unemployment rate was 7.6% in 2010.

From the late 1990s the Icelandic economy expanded rapidly: the financial sector benefited from the liberalization of capital flows and a series of privatizations, while significant high-technology industries were developed and the tourism sector grew strongly. However, by 2008 Iceland, more than any other nation, was adversely affected by the international financial crisis. The over-extended banking sector experienced major difficulties as a result of the lack of availability of credit, and in October the Government was forced to assume control of the three largest commercial banks. In November the IMF approved a US $2,100m. loan for the country, making Iceland the first Western nation to receive such assistance since 1976, and the Nordic countries agreed to lend a further €1,775m.; the key priority of the IMF-supported programme of economic recovery was the stabilization of the currency, which had depreciated drastically. The Government that took office in May 2009 aimed to eliminate the fiscal deficit by 2013 and to seek accession to the European Union (see p. 276). The fiscal deficit was reduced from 13.5% of GDP in 2008 to 10.0% in 2009 and to a preliminary 4.4% in 2011 (following a slight rise to 10.1% in 2010), while the inflation rate decreased rapidly, from 18.6% in January 2009 to 1.8% in January 2011, and the currency stabilized, as the central bank lowered interest rates and imposed restrictions on capital flows. However, unemployment rose significantly, peaking at 9.1% in the second quarter of 2009, and remained fairly high in 2011, at 6.0% in the fourth quarter. Following contractions of 6.9% in 2009 and 3.5% in 2010, GDP increased by a preliminary 3.1% in 2011. Iceland returned to the international credit markets in June 2011, in its first bond issue since 2006, and successfully completed its IMF-supported programme in August 2011. In March 2012 the Government announced the early repayment of some of its loans from the IMF and the Nordic countries. The country's relatively rapid recovery was attributed in part to its refusal (and inability) to bail out the failed banks and their foreign creditors and its exchange rate flexibility, which allowed the devaluation of the currency, thereby increasing export competitiveness. Challenges at early 2012 included the removal of the capital controls imposed in 2008 and the need to complete household and corporate debt restructuring, while the rising inflation rate (which reached 6.5% in January 2012) was of some concern.

PUBLIC HOLIDAYS

2013: 1 January (New Year's Day), 28 March (Maundy Thursday), 29 March (Good Friday), 1 April (Easter Monday), 25 April (First Day of Summer), 1 May (Labour Day), 9 June (Ascension Day), 20 May (Whit Monday), 17 June (National Day), 5 August (Bank Holiday), 24*–26 December (Christmas), 31 December (New Year's Eve)*.

* Afternoon only.

Statistical Survey

Sources (unless otherwise stated): Statistics Iceland, Borgartúni 21A, 150 Reykjavík; tel. 5281000; fax 5281099; e-mail statice@statice.is; internet www.statice.is; Seðlabanki Íslands (Central Bank of Iceland), Kalkofnsvegur 1, 150 Reykjavík; tel. 5699600; fax 5699605; e-mail sedlabanki@sedlabanki.is; internet www.sedlabanki.is.

AREA AND POPULATION

Area: 103,000 sq km (39,769 sq miles).

Population: 319,622 (males 160,698, females 158,924) at 1 January 2012 (national population register).

Density (at 1 January 2012): 3.1 per sq km.

Population by Age and Sex (national population register at 1 January 2012): *0–14:* 66,683 (males 34,083, females 32,600); *15–64:* 212,730 (males 108,034, females 104,696); *65 and over:* 40,209 (males 18,581, females 21,628); *Total* 319,622 (males 160,698, females 158,924).

Principal Towns (population at 1 January 2011): Reykjavík (capital) 118,898; Kópavogur 30,779; Hafnarfjörður 26,099; Akureyri 17,754; Reykjanesbær 13,971.

Births, Marriages and Deaths (2010): Live births 4,907 (birth rate 15.5 per 1,000); Marriages 1,547 (marriage rate 4.9 per 1,000); Deaths 2,020 (death rate 6.4 per 1,000).

Life Expectancy (years at birth, WHO estimates): 82 (males 80; females 83) in 2009. Source: WHO, *World Health Statistics*.

Economically Active Population (2010, figures rounded to nearest 100 persons): Agriculture 4,800; Fishing 5,000; Manufacturing (excl. fish-processing) 15,400; Fish-processing 3,600; Electricity and water supply 1,500; Construction 10,600; Wholesale and retail trade, repairs 20,600; Restaurants and hotels 8,000; Transport, storage and communications 10,800; Financial intermediation 7,900; Real estate and business services 17,500; Public administration 8,600; Education 20,400; Health services and social work 28,300; Other services not specified 4,500; *Total employed* (incl. unclassified) 167,300; Unemployed 13,700; *Total labour force* 181,000. Note: Totals may not be equal to the sum of components, owing to rounding.

HEALTH AND WELFARE

Key Indicators

Total Fertility Rate (children per woman, 2009): 2.1.

Under-5 Mortality Rate (per 1,000 live births, 2009): 3.

HIV/AIDS (% of persons aged 15–49, 2009): 0.3.

Physicians (per 1,000 head, 2006): 3.8.

Hospital Beds (per 1,000 head, 2002): 7.5.

Health Expenditure (2008): US $ per head (PPP): 3,583.

Health Expenditure (2008): % of GDP: 9.2.

Health Expenditure (2008): public (% of total): 81.8.

Total Carbon Dioxide Emissions ('000 metric tons, 2007): 2,337.6.

Carbon Dioxide Emissions Per Head (metric tons, 2007): 7.5.

Human Development Index (2011): ranking: 14.

Human Development Index (2011): value: 0.898.

For sources and definitions, see explanatory note on p. vi.

AGRICULTURE, ETC.

Principal Crops (metric tons, 2010): Cereals 13,175; Carrots 612; Cabbages 425; Tomatoes 1,652; Cucumbers 1,458; Cauliflower 114; Turnips 833; Peppers 187; Chinese cabbages 164; Mushrooms 579.

Livestock (2010): Cattle 73,781; Sheep 479,841; Horses 77,164; Goats 729; Pigs 3,615; Hens 173,419; Other poultry 44,493; Mink 37,409; Foxes 5.

Livestock Products (metric tons, unless otherwise indicated, 2010): Sheep meat 9,166; Cattle meat 3,895; Horse meat 799; Pig meat 6,158; Chicken meat 6,905; Milk ('000 litres, processed) 123,218; Eggs 2,741. Source: FAO.

Fishing (metric tons, live weight, 2010): Atlantic cod 178,438; Saithe 53,900; Haddock 64,972; Atlantic redfish 56,307; Capelin 102,196; Atlantic herring 66,602; Total (incl. others) 1,063,605.

INDUSTRY

Selected Products ('000 metric tons, 2009, unless otherwise indicated): Frozen fish 462.8 (demersal catch); Salted, dried or smoked fish 875.6 (2007); Cement 138.0 (estimated figure); Ferrosilicon 81.0 (estimated figure); Aluminium (unwrought) 785.0 (estimated figure); Electric energy 17,059 million kWh (2010). Source: partly US Geological Survey.

FINANCE

Currency and Exchange Rates: 100 aurar (singular: eyrir) = 1 new Icelandic króna (plural: krónur). *Sterling, Dollar and Euro Equivalents* (30 December 2011): £1 sterling = 189.722 krónur; US $1 = 122.710 krónur; €1 = 158.774 krónur; 1,000 krónur = £5.27 = $8.15 = €6.30. *Average Exchange Rate* (krónur per US $): 123.638 in 2009; 122.242 in 2010; 115.954 in 2011.

Budget (general government finances, '000 million krónur, 2010): *Revenue:* Tax revenue 474.1 (Taxes on income, profits and capital gains 239.7, Taxes on payroll and work-force 2.8, Taxes on property 35.5, Taxes on goods and services 184.2, Taxes on international trade 6.0, Other taxes 6.0); Social contributions 63.6; Grants 2.4; Other revenue 97.2; Total 637.3. *Expenditure:* Current expenditure 780.8 (Compensation of employees 227.1, Use of goods and services 186.9, Consumption of fixed capital 33.6, Interest 84.8, Subsidies 27.5, Grants 4.9, Social benefits 120.6, Other expenditure 95.4); Non-financial assets 11.1; Total 791.9.

International Reserves (US $ million at 31 December 2010): Gold (national valuation) 90.6; Reserve position in IMF 28.7; Foreign exchange 5,557.0; Total 5,676.3. Source: IMF, *International Financial Statistics*.

Money Supply (million krónur at 31 December 2010): Currency outside banks 34,666; Transferable deposit 491,340; Other deposit 934,411; *Broad money* 1,460,417. Source: IMF, *International Financial Statistics*.

Cost of Living (Consumer Price Index; base: 2005 = 100): All items 126.3 in 2008; 141.4 in 2009; 149.1 in 2010. Source: IMF, *International Financial Statistics*.

Gross Domestic Product (million krónur at constant 2000 prices): 947,186 in 2008; 883,985 in 2009; 848,626 in 2010. Source: IMF, *International Financial Statistics*.

Expenditure on the Gross Domestic Product (million krónur at current prices, 2010, preliminary): Government final consumption expenditure 398,618; Private final consumption expenditure 787,724; Changes in inventories –3,373; Gross fixed capital formation 199,891; *Total domestic expenditure* 1,382,860; Exports of goods and services 861,272; *Less* Imports of goods and services 707,026; *Gross domestic product in market prices* 1,537,106.

Gross Domestic Product by Economic Activity (million krónur at current prices, 2009): Agriculture, hunting and forestry 14,285; Fishing 76,729; Mining and quarrying 762; Manufacturing 165,661; Electricity, gas and water supply 69,823; Construction 66,804; Wholesale and retail trade and repair of vehicles and household goods 120,678; Hotels and restaurants 24,896; Transport, storage and communications 124,631; Financial intermediation 111,228; Real estate, renting and business services 202,955; Public administration and compulsory social security 72,242; Education 69,619; Health and social work 132,603; Other community, social and personal services 70,819; Private households with employed persons 1,306; *Sub-total* 1,325,040; Correction item, taxes and subsidies on products 13,842; *Gross value added at basic prices* 1,338,882; Taxes on production and imports 172,509; *Less* Subsidies 13,719; *GDP in market prices* 1,497,672.

Balance of Payments (US $ million, 2010): Exports of goods f.o.b. 4,603; Imports of goods f.o.b. –3,620; *Trade balance* 983; Exports of services 2,464; Imports of services –2,183; *Balance on goods and services* 1,264; Other income received –420; Other income paid –2,190; *Balance on goods, services and income* –1,346; Current transfers received 7; Current transfers paid –78; *Current balance* –1,417; Capital account (net) –3; Direct investment abroad 2,630; Direct investment from abroad 488; Portfolio investment assets –22; Portfolio investment liabilities –10,540; Other investment assets 2,438; Other investment liabilities 9,898; Net errors and omissions –1,811; *Overall balance* 1,660. Source: IMF, *International Financial Statistics*.

EXTERNAL TRADE

Principal Commodities (distribution by SITC, million krónur, 2009): *Imports c.i.f.:* Food and live animals 41,898.4; Crude materials, inedible 60,512.4 (Metalliferous ores and metal scrap 59,138.1); Mineral fuels and lubricants 55,443.2 (Petroleum and petroleum products 50,866.7); Chemicals and related products 46,040.6 (Medicinal and pharmaceutical products 15,171.4); Basic manufactures 50,987.9 (Metal products 13,036.4); Machinery and transport equipment 130,645.5 (Machinery specialized for particular industries 4,836.0; General industrial machinery and equipment 13,827.9; Office machines and computers 7,729.4; Other electrical machinery, apparatus and appliances 54,611.8; Road vehicles 14,460.7; Other transport equipment 20,966.8); Miscellaneous manufactured articles 51,289.1 (Apparel and clothing accessories 12,985.6); Total (incl. others) 446,128.2. *Exports f.o.b.:* Food and live animals 207,152.2 (Fish, crustaceans, molluscs and preparations thereof 186,637.1; Animal feeds, excl. unmilled cereals 16,922.6); Chemicals and related products 13,675.3 (Medicinal and pharmaceutical products 11,986.0); Basic manufactures 196,137.1 (Aluminium 173,278.1); Machinery and transport equipment 50,151.9; Total (incl. others) 500,854.5. *2010:* Total imports 477,222.3; Total exports 561,032.2.

Principal Trading Partners (million krónur, country of consignment, 2010): *Imports c.i.f.:* Belgium 6,514.3; Canada 8,147.7; China, People's Republic 28,731.4; Finland 25,291.8; France 8,718.1; Germany 35,837.4; Ireland 3,892.7; Italy 14,177.4; Japan 11,027.8; Netherlands 40,618.7; Norway 43,217.1; Poland 5,876.6; Russia 2,731.6; Spain 5,459.1; Suriname 4,042.7; Sweden 24,918.8; Switzerland 6,602.3; United Kingdom 24,393.7; USA 37,792.9; Total (incl. others) 477,222.3. *Exports f.o.b.:* Belgium 9,415.9; Denmark (incl. Faroe Islands and Greenland) 19,682.3; France 17,594.7; Germany 78,320.7; Japan 14,283.4; Netherlands 190,631.7; Nigeria 10,378.8; Norway 23,787.4; Portugal 6,924.7; Russia 11,593.3; Spain 26,588.3; United Kingdom 56,712.3; USA 25,429.0; Total (incl. others) 561,032.2.

TRANSPORT

Road Traffic (registered motor vehicles, 2008): Passenger cars 209,740; Buses and coaches 1,955; Goods vehicles 31,819; Motorcycles 9,009.

Shipping: *Merchant Fleet* (registered vessels, 31 December 2009): Vessels 226; Displacement 161,607 grt (Source: IHS Fairplay, *World Fleet Statistics*). *International Freight Traffic* ('000 metric tons, 2006): Goods loaded 1,858.4; Goods unloaded 4,058.4.

Civil Aviation (scheduled traffic, 2009): Kilometres flown (million) 28; Passengers ('000) 1,365; Passenger-km (million) 3,632; Total ton-km (million) 431. Source: UN, *Statistical Yearbook*.

TOURISM

Foreign Visitors by Country of Origin (overnight stays in hotels and guesthouses, 2010): Denmark 102,836; France 109,192; Germany 294,395; Italy 47,633; Netherlands 76,123; Norway 87,306; Spain 45,807; Sweden 78,692; Switzerland 42,169; United Kingdom 231,306; USA 142,072; Total (incl. others) 1,620,597.

Receipts from Tourism (US $ million, incl. passenger transport): 702 in 2006; 848 in 2007; 881 in 2008 (Source: World Tourism Organization).

COMMUNICATIONS MEDIA

Radio Receivers (2002): 94,840 licensed.

Television Receivers (2002): 91,952 licensed.

Telephones (2010): 193,600 main lines in use. Source: International Telecommunication Union.

Mobile Cellular Telephones ('000 subscribers, 2010): 341.1 Source: International Telecommunication Union.

Personal Computers: 160,000 (526.7 per 1,000 persons) in 2005. Source: International Telecommunication Union.

Internet Subscribers ('000, 2010): 114.2. Source: International Telecommunication Union.

Broadband Subscribers ('000, 2010): 109.2. Source: International Telecommunication Union.

Books (published, 2008): 1,637 titles (incl. new editions).

Daily Newspapers (2007, unless otherwise specified): 5 (combined circulation 278,154 copies per issue in 2008).

Non-daily Newspapers (2008): 20 (combined circulation 58,305 copies).

EDUCATION

Institutions (2009 unless otherwise indicated): Pre-primary 282; Primary and secondary (lower level) 175; Secondary (higher level) 53 (2005); Tertiary (universities and colleges) 24 (2005).

Teachers (incl. part-time, 2009): Pre-primary 3,362; Primary and secondary (lower level) 4,978; Secondary (higher level) 1,926; Tertiary 2,138.

Students (2009): Pre-primary 18,716; Primary and Secondary (lower level) 42,929; Secondary (higher level) 29,698; Tertiary 18,226.

Pupil-teacher Ratio (primary education, UNESCO estimate): 10.3 in 2006/07 (Source: UNESCO Institute for Statistics).

Directory

The Government

HEAD OF STATE

President: ÓLAFUR RAGNAR GRÍMSSON (took office 1 August 1996; began a second term in August 2000; re-elected 26 June 2004; commenced a fourth term in August 2008).

THE CABINET
(May 2012)

A coalition of the Social Democratic Alliance (SDA) and the Left-Green Movement (LG).

Prime Minister: JÓHANNA SIGURÐARDÓTTIR (SDA).

Minister of Finance and acting Minister of Industry, Energy and Tourism: ODDNÝ G. HARÐARDÓTTIR (SDA).

Minister for Foreign Affairs and External Trade: ÖSSUR SKARPHÉÐINSSON (SDA).

Minister of Education, Science and Culture: KATRÍN JAKOBSDÓTTIR (LG).

Minister of the Interior: ÖGMUNDUR JÓNASSON (LG).

Minister of Fisheries and Agriculture and of Economic Affairs: STEINGRÍMUR J. SIGFÚSSON (LG).

Minister of Industry, Energy and Tourism: KATRÍN JÚLÍUSDÓTTIR (SDA) (on maternity leave).

Minister of Welfare: GUÐBJARTUR HANNESSON (SDA).

Minister of the Environment: SVANDÍS SVAVARSDÓTTIR (LG).

MINISTRIES

Office of the President: Stadastaður, Sóleyjargötu 1, 101 Reykjavík; tel. 5404400; fax 5624802; e-mail forseti@forseti.is; internet www.forseti.is.

Prime Minister's Office: Stjórnarráðshúsinu við Lækjartorg, 150 Reykjavík; tel. 5458400; fax 5624014; e-mail postur@for.stjr.is; internet www.forsaetisraduneyti.is.

Ministry of Economic Affairs: Skuggasundi 3, 150 Reykjavík; tel. 5458800; fax 5111161; e-mail postur@evr.is; internet www.efnahagsraduneyti.is.

Ministry of Education, Science and Culture: Sölvhólsgötu 4, 150 Reykjavík; tel. 5459500; fax 5623068; e-mail postur@mrn.stjr.is; internet www.menntamalaraduneyti.is.

Ministry for the Environment: Skuggasund 1, 150 Reykjavík; tel. 5458600; fax 5624566; e-mail postur@environment.is; internet www.environment.is.

Ministry of Finance: Arnarhvoli við Lindargötu, 150 Reykjavík; tel. 5459200; fax 5628280; e-mail postur@fjr.stjr.is; internet www.ministryoffinance.is.

Ministry of Fisheries and Agriculture: Skúlagötu 4, 150 Reykjavík; tel. 5458300; fax 5521160; e-mail postur@slr.stjr.is; internet www.sjavarutvegsraduneyti.is.

Ministry for Foreign Affairs: Rauðarárstígur 25, 150 Reykjavík; tel. 5459900; fax 5622373; e-mail external@utn.stjr.is; internet www.mfa.is.

Ministry of Industry, Energy and Tourism: Arnarhvoli, 150 Reykjavík; tel. 5458500; fax 5621289; e-mail postur@idn.stjr.is; internet www.idnadarraduneyti.is.

Ministry of the Interior: Skuggasund, 150 Reykjavík; tel. 5459000; fax 5527340; e-mail postur@irr.is; internet www.innanrikisraduneyti.is.

Ministry of Welfare: Hafnarhúsinu við Tryggvagötu, 150 Reykjavík; tel. 5458100; fax 5519165; e-mail postur@vel.is; internet www.velferdarraduneyti.is.

President and Legislature

PRESIDENT

Presidential Election, 26 June 2004

	% of votes
Ólafur Ragnar Grímsson	85.6
Baldur Ágústsson	12.3
Ástþór Magnússon	1.9

Ólafur Ragnar Grímsson was re-elected unopposed as President in June 2008; he was sworn in for his fourth term on 1 August

LEGISLATURE

Althingi
(Alþingi)

v/Austurvöll, 150 Reykjavík; tel. 5630500; fax 5630920; e-mail editor@althingi.is; internet www.althingi.is.

Speaker of the Althingi: ÁSTA R. JÓHANNESDÓTTIR.

Secretary-General (Clerk) of the Althingi: HELGI BERNÓDUSSON.

General Election, 25 April 2009

Party	Votes	% of votes	Seats
Samfylkingin (Social Democratic Alliance)	55,758	29.79	20
Sjálfstæðisflokkurinn (Independence Party)	44,369	23.70	16
Vinstrihreyfingin–grænt framboð (Left-Green Movement)	40,580	21.68	14
Framsóknarflokkurinn (Progressive Party)	27,699	14.80	9
Borgarahreyfingin (Citizens' Movement)	13,519	7.22	4
Frjálslyndi flokkurinn (Liberal Party)	4,148	2.22	—
Lýðræðishreyfingin (Democracy Party)	1,107	0.59	—
Total	187,180	100.00	63

Political Organizations

Besti Flokkurin (Best Party): Laugavegi 40, 101 Reykjavík; e-mail bestiflokkurinn@bestiflokkurinn.is; internet www.bestiflokkurinn.is; f. 2009; satirical; won the largest number of seats on Reykjavík city council at municipal elections in 2010; Leader JÓN GNARR.

Borgarahreyfingin (Citizens' Movement): Höfðatúni 12, 105 Reykjavík; tel. 5111944; e-mail info@borgarahreyfingin.is; internet www.xo.is; f. 2009; advocates economic reform and membership of the European Union; 3 mems of parliamentary group left the party in Sept. 2009 to form Hreyfingin (The Movement, q.v.); Leader FRIÐRIK ÞÓR GUÐMUNDSSON.

Framsóknarflokkurinn (Progressive Party—PP): Hverfisgötu 33, POB 453, 101 Reykjavík; tel. 5404300; fax 5404301; e-mail framsokn@framsokn.is; internet www.framsokn.is; f. 1916 with a programme of social liberalism and co-operation; Chair. SIGMUNDUR DAVÍÐ GUNNLAUGSSON; Parliamentary Leader GUNNAR BRAGI SVEINSSON.

Frjálslyndi flokkurinn (Liberal Party): Lyngháls 3, 110 Reykjavík; tel. 5522600; e-mail xf@xf.is; internet www.xf.is; f. 1998 by Sverrir Hermannsson, a former IP cabinet minister; incorporated fmr mems of defunct Nýtt Afl (New Force) in 2006; Leader SIGURJÓN ÞÓRÐARSON.

Hreyfingin (The Movement): Austurstræti 8–10, 150 Reykjavík; tel. 5630484; e-mail hreyfingin@hreyfingin.is; internet www.hreyfingin.is; f. 2009 by fmr mems of Borgarahreyfingin (Citizens' Movement); Parliamentary Leader BIRGITTA JÓNSDÓTTIR.

Lýðræðishreyfingin (Democracy Party): Vogasel 1, 109 Reykjavík; tel. 4500500; e-mail postur@lydveldi.is; internet www.lydveldi.is; Leader ÁSTÞÓR MAGNÚSSON.

Samfylkingin (Social Democratic Alliance—SDA): Hallveigarstíg 1, 101 Reykjavík; tel. 4142200; fax 4142201; e-mail samfylking@samfylking.is; internet www.samfylking.is; f. 1999 by merger of Alþýðubandalagið (People's Alliance, f. 1956), Alþýðuflokkurinn (Social Democratic Party, f. 1916), Samtök um kvennalista (Women's List, f. 1983) and Þjóðvaki—hreyfing fólksins (Awakening of the Nation—People's Movement, f. 1994); Chair. JÓHANNA SIGURÐARDÓTTIR; Parliamentary Leader ÞÓRUNN SVEINBJARNARDÓTTIR.

Sjálfstæðisflokkurinn (Independence Party—IP): Háaleitisbraut 1, 105 Reykjavík; tel. 5151700; fax 5151717; e-mail xd@xd.is; internet www.xd.is; f. 1929 by an amalgamation of the Conservative and Liberal Parties; advocates social reform within the framework of private enterprise and the furtherance of national and individual independence; Leader BJARNI BENEDIKTSSON; Parliamentary Leader RAGNHEIÐUR E. ÁRNADÓTTIR; Sec.-Gen. JÓNMUNDUR GUÐMARSSON.

Vinstrihreyfingin–grænt framboð (Left-Green Movement): Suðurgötu 3, POB 175, 101 Reykjavík; tel. 5528872; e-mail vg@vg.is; internet www.vg.is; f. 1999 by dissident mems of the People's Alliance, the Women's List, the Greens and independent left-wingers; around 3,000 mems; Leader STEINGRÍMUR J. SIGFÚSSON; Parliamentary Leader THURÍDUR BACKMANN; Sec.-Gen. SÓLEY TÓMASDÓTTIR.

Diplomatic Representation

EMBASSIES IN ICELAND

Canada: POB 1510, 121 Reykjavík; Túngata 14, 101 Reykjavík; tel. 5756500; fax 5756501; e-mail rkjvk@international.gc.ca; internet www.canadainternational.gc.ca/iceland-islande; Ambassador ALAN BONES.

China, People's Republic: Víðimelur 29, 107 Reykjavík; tel. 5526751; fax 5626110; e-mail chinaemb_is@mfa.gov.cn; internet is.china-embassy.org; Ambassador SU GE.

Denmark: Hverfisgata 29, 101 Reykjavík; tel. 5750300; fax 5750310; e-mail rekamb@um.dk; internet www.ambreykjavik.um.dk; Ambassador SØREN HASLUND.

Finland: POB 1060, 121 Reykjavík; Túngata 30, 101 Reykjavík; tel. 5100100; fax 5623880; e-mail sanomat.rey@formin.fi; internet www.finland.is; Ambassador IRMA ERTMAN.

France: Túngata 22, 101 Reykjavík; tel. 5759600; fax 5759604; e-mail ambafrance@ambafrance.is; internet ambafrance-is.org; Ambassador MARC BOUTEILLER.

Germany: Laufásvegur 31, 101 Reykjavík; tel. 5301100; fax 5301101; e-mail info@reykjavik.diplo.de; internet www.reykjavik.diplo.de; Ambassador HERMANN SAUSEN.

India: Skúlagata 17, 101 Reykjavík; tel. 5349955; fax 5349959; e-mail gen@indianembassy.is; internet www.indianembassy.is; Ambassador (vacant).

Japan: Laugavegur 182, POB 5380, 105 Reykjavík; tel. 5108600; fax 5108605; e-mail japan@itn.is; internet www.is.emb-japan.go.jp; Ambassador AKIO SHIROTA (resident in Oslo, Norway).

Norway: Fjólugötu 17, 101 Reykjavík; tel. 5200700; fax 5529553; e-mail emb.reykjavik@mfa.no; internet www.noregur.is; Ambassador DAG WERNØ HOLTER.

Russia: POB 380, Garðastræti 33, 101 Reykjavík; tel. 5515156; fax 5620633; e-mail russemb@itn.is; internet www.iceland.mid.ru; Ambassador ANDREY V. TSYGANOV.

Sweden: POB 8136, 128 Reykjavík; Lágmúla 7, 108 Reykjavík; tel. 5201230; fax 5201235; e-mail ambassaden.reykjavik@foreign.ministry.se; internet www.swedenabroad.com/reykjavik; Ambassador ANDERS LJUNGGREN.

United Kingdom: POB 460, 121 Reykjavík; Laufásvegur 31, 101 Reykjavík; tel. 5505100; fax 5505105; e-mail britemb@centrum.is; internet ukiniceland.fco.gov.uk; Ambassador IAN WHITTING.

USA: Laufásvegur 21, 101 Reykjavík; tel. 5629100; fax 5629110; e-mail reykjavikprotocol@state.gov; internet iceland.usembassy.gov; Ambassador LUIS E. ARREAGA.

Judicial System

All cases are heard in Ordinary Courts except those specifically within the jurisdiction of Special Courts. The Ordinary Courts include both a lower division of urban and rural district courts presided over by the district magistrates, and the Supreme Court.

Justices of the Supreme Court are appointed by the President and cannot be dismissed except by the decision of a court. The Justices elect the Chief Justice for a period of two years.

Supreme Court

Dómhúsið v. Arnarhól, 150 Reykjavík; tel. 5103030; fax 5623995; e-mail haestirettur@haestirettur.is; internet www.haestirettur.is.

Chief Justice: MARKÚS SIGURBJÖRNSSON.

Justices: ÁRNI KOLBEINSSON, GARÐAR GÍSLASON, HJÖRDÍS HÁKONARDÓTTIR, JÓN STEINAR GUNNLAUGSSON, MARKÚS SIGURBJÖRNSSON, ÓLAFUR BÖRKUR ÞORVALDSSON, PÁLL HREINSSON, GUNNLAUGUR CLAESSEN.

Religion

In 2010 79.2% of the total population were members of the Þjoðkirkja Íslands (Evangelical Lutheran Church of Iceland). The Free Lutheran Churches had a total membership of 4.3% of the population, and 7.1% were members of 30 other recognized and registered religious organizations, including the Roman Catholic Church. A further 6.2% belonged to 'other or unspecified religious organizations' (including religions, such as Judaism, that have been practised in the country for years without requesting official recognition), while 3.3% were not part of any religious organization.

CHRISTIANITY

Protestant Churches

Þjoðkirkja Íslands (Evangelical Lutheran Church of Iceland): Biskupsstofa, Laugavegur 31, 150 Reykjavík; tel. 5284000; fax 5284098; e-mail kirkjan@kirkjan.is; internet www.kirkjan.is; the national church, endowed by the state; Iceland forms 1 diocese, with 2 suffragan sees; 272 parishes, 150 pastors and 247,245 mems (2011); Bishop KARL SIGURBJÖRNSSON.

A further 19 Protestant churches are officially registered, the largest of which are the following:

Fríkirkjusöfnuðurinn í Hafnarfirði (Hafnarfjörður Free Lutheran Church): Linnetsstíg 6-8, 220 Hafnarfjörður; tel. 5653430; e-mail einar@frikirkja.is; internet www.frikirkja.is; 5,364 mems (2010); Head EINAR EYJÓLFSSON.

Fríkirkjusöfnuðurinn í Reykjavík (Reykjavík Free Lutheran Church): POB 1671, 121 Reykjavík; Laufásvegi 13, 101 Reykjavík; tel. 5527270; fax 5527287; e-mail frikirkjan@frikirkjan.is; internet www.frikirkjan.is; f. 1899; Free Lutheran denomination; 8,227 mems (2010); Head HJÖRTUR MAGNI JÓHANNSSON.

Hvítasunnukirkjan á Íslandi (Pentecostal Assemblies): Hátúni 2, 105 Reykjavík; tel. 5354700; e-mail filadelfia@filadelfia.is; internet www.filadelfia.is; f. 1936; 2,109 mems (2010); Head JÓN ÞÓR EYJÓLFSSON.

Óháði söfnuðurinn (Independent Congregation): Háteigsvegi 56, 105 Reykjavík; tel. 551099; e-mail postur@ohadisofnudurinn.is; internet www.ohadisofnudurinn.is; Free Lutheran denomination; 2,906 mems (2010); Head Rev. PÉTUR ÞORSTEINSSON.

The Roman Catholic Church

Iceland comprises a single diocese, directly responsible to the Holy See. In 2010 there were 9,672 adherents in the country (3.1% of the total population).

Bishop of Reykjavík: Rt Rev. PIERRE BÜRCHER, POB 490, 121 Reykjavík; Biskupsstofa, Hávallagata 14, 101 Reykjavík; tel. 5525388; fax 5623878; e-mail catholica@catholica.is; internet www.catholica.is.

ISLAM

Félag múslima á Íslandi (Muslim Asscn of Iceland): Ármúli 38, 3 hæð, 108 Reykjavík; tel. 8951967; e-mail salmannt@gmail.com; internet www.islam.is; f. 1997; 373 mems (2010); Head SALMAN TAMIMI.

BAHÁ'Í FAITH

Bahá'í samfélagið á Íslandi (Bahá'í Community of Iceland): Öldugötu 2, 101 Reykjavík; tel. 5670344; e-mail nsa@bahai.is; internet www.bahai.is; 398 mems (2010); Sec. INGIBJÖRG DANÍELSDÓTTIR.

BUDDHISM

Búddistafélag Íslands (Buddhist Association of Iceland): Víghólastíg 21, 200 Kópavogur; 880 mems (2010); Head PHAMAHAPRASIT BOONKAM.

Trúfélagið Zen á Íslandi, Nátthagi (Soto Zen Buddhist Asscn of Iceland): Grensásvegur 8, 105 Reykjavík; e-mail mikhaelaaron@gmail.com; internet www.zen.is; 75 mems (2010); Head HELGA JÓAKIMSDÓTTIR.

The Press

PRINCIPAL DAILIES

DV (Dagblaðið-Vísir): Útgáfufélagið DV ehf, Skaftahlíð 24, POB 5480, 105 Reykjavík; tel. 5127000; e-mail ritstjorn@dv.is; internet www.dv.is; f. 1981; independent; Editors REYNIR TRAUSTASON, JÓN TRAUSTI REYNISSON; circ. 13,100 (2008).

Fréttablaðið (The Newspaper): Skaftahlíð 24, 105 Reykjavík; tel. 5125000; fax 5125301; e-mail ritstjorn@frettabladid.is; internet www.visir.is; f. 2001; distributed free of charge; owned by 365 hf; Editor-in-Chief ÓLAFUR Þ. STEPHENSEN; circ. 88,000 (2010).

Morgunblaðið (Morning News): Hádegismóum 2, 110 Reykjavík; tel. 5691100; fax 5691110; e-mail morgunbladid@mbl.is; internet www.mbl.is; f. 1913; owned by Árvakur hf; Editors DAVÍÐ ODDSSON, HARALDUR JOHANNESSEN; circ. 43,250 (2010).

WEEKLIES

Bæjarins besta (BB): Sólgötu 9, 400 Ísafjörður; tel. 4564560; fax 4564564; e-mail bb@bb.is; internet www.bb.is; f. 1984; local; Editor SIGURJÓN J. SIGURÐSSON.

Fiskifréttir: Nóatúni 17, 105 Reykjavík; tel. 5116622; fax 5696692; e-mail vb@vb.is; internet www.fiskifrettir.is; f. 1983; weekly; for the fishing industry; Editor GUÐJÓN EINARSSON; circ. 6,000.

Séð & Heyrt: Lyngás 17, 210 Garðabær; tel. 5155500; fax 5155599; e-mail birtingur@birtingur.is; internet www.birtingur.is; showbusiness and celebrities; Editor LILJA KATRÍN GUNNARSDÓTTIR; circ. 23,000.

Skessuhorn: Kirkjubraut 56, 300 Akranesi; tel. 4335500; fax 4335501; e-mail skessuhorn@skessuhorn.is; internet www.skessuhorn.is; f. 1998; local; Editor MAGNÚS MAGNÚSSON.

Sunnlenska Fréttablaðið: Austurvegi 22, 800 Selfoss; tel. 4823074; fax 4823084; e-mail sunnlenska@sunnlenska.is; internet www.sunnlenska.is; f. 1991; local newspaper; Editor SIGMUNDUR SIGURDÓRSSON; circ. 6,300.

Vikan: Lyngháls 17, 210 Garðabær; tel. 5155500; fax 5155599; e-mail birtingur@birtingur.is; internet www.birtingur.is; f. 1938; publ. by Birtíngur; women's weekly; Editor ELÍN ARNAR; circ. 17,000.

Víkurfréttir: Grundarvegur 23, 260 Reykjanesbær; tel. 4210000; fax 4210020; e-mail pket@vf.is; internet www.vf.is; f. 1983; local newspaper; Editor PÁLL KETILSSON; circ. 8,700.

Viðskiptablaðið: Nóatún 17, 105 Reykjavík; tel. 5116622; fax 5116692; e-mail mottaka@vb.is; internet www.vb.is; f. 1994; publ. by Framtíðarsýn hf; business weekly in collaboration with the *Financial Times* (United Kingdom); Editor-in-Chief HARALDUR JOHANNESSEN.

OTHER PERIODICALS

Atlantica: Borgartún 23, 105 Reykjavík; tel. 5617575; fax 5618646; e-mail atlantica@heimur.is; internet www.heimur.is; f. 1967; 6 a year; in-flight magazine of Icelandair; Editor BJARNI BRYNJÓLFSSON.

Bændablaðið: POB 7080, 127 Reykjavík; tel. 5630300; fax 5623058; e-mail bbl@bondi.is; f. 1995; fortnightly; organ of the Icelandic farmers' union; Editor TJÖRVI BJARNASON; circ. 6,400.

Bíllinn: Reykjavík; tel. 5526090; fax 5529490; internet www.billinn.is; f. 1982; 3–4 a year; cars and motoring equipment; circ. 4,000.

Eiðfaxi: Dugguvogur 10, 104 Reykjavík; tel. 5882525; fax 5882528; e-mail frettir@eidfaxi.is; internet www.eidfaxi.is; f. 1977; monthly (Icelandic edn, English and German edns every 2 months); horse-breeding and horsemanship; Editor TRAUSTI ÞÓR GUÐMUNDSSON; circ. 7,000.

Fjármálatíðindi: Kalkofnsvegur 1, 150 Reykjavík; tel. 5699600; fax 5699608; e-mail sedlabanki@sedlabanki.is; internet www.sedlabanki.is; 2 a year; economic journal published by the Central Bank; circ. 1,600.

Freyr, búnaðarblað: Bændahöllin við Hagatorg, 107 Reykjavík; tel. 5630300; fax 5623058; e-mail freyr@bondi.is; internet www.bondi.is; monthly; agriculture; Editor TJORVI BJARNASON; circ. 1,600.

Frjáls Verslun (Free Trade): Borgartún 23, 105 Reykjavík; tel. 5617575; fax 5618646; e-mail jgh@heimur.is; internet www.heimur.is; f. 1939; 10 a year; business magazine; Editor JÓN G. HAUKSSON; circ. 6,000–9,000.

Gestgjafinn: Héðinshúsið, Seljavegur 2, 101 Reykjavík; tel. 5155506; fax 5155599; e-mail gestgjafinn@frodi.is; internet www.gestgjafinn.is; f. 1981; 12 a year; food and wine; Editors SÓLVEIG BALDURSDÓTTIR, GUÐRÚN HRUND SIGURÐARDÓTTIR; circ. 13,000–16,000.

Hár og Fegurð (Hair and Beauty Magazine): Skúlagata 54, 105 Reykjavík; tel. and fax 5628141; e-mail pmelsted@vortex.is; f. 1980; 3 a year; hair, beauty, fashion; Editor PÉTUR MELSTEÐ.

Heilbrigðismál: 105 Reykjavík; tel. 5621414; fax 5621417; f. 1949; quarterly; public health; Editor JÓNAS RAGNARSSON; circ. 6,000.

Heima er Bezt: Jöklafold 22, 112 Reykjavík; tel. 5538200; fax 5155201; e-mail heimaerbezt@simnet.is; internet www.heimaerbezt.net; f. 1951; monthly; general interest; Editor GUÐJÓN BALDVINSSON; circ. 3,000.

Hús og Híbýli: Lyngháls 5, 110 Reykjavík; tel. 5155500; fax 5155599; e-mail hogh@birtingur.is; internet www.birtingur.is/hus-og-hibyli; f. 1973; 17 a year; architecture, homes and gardens; Editor SIGRÍÐUR ELÍN ÁSMUNDSDÓTTIR; circ. 15,000–17,000.

Húsfreyjan (The Housewife): Túngata 14, 101 Reykjavík; tel. 5517044; f. 1949; quarterly; the organ of the Federation of Icelandic Women's Societies; Editor HRAFNHILDUR VALGARÐS; circ. 4,000.

Iceland Review: Borgartún 23, 105 Reykjavík; tel. 5127575; e-mail icelandreview@icelandreview.com; internet www.icelandreview.com; f. 1963; quarterly, in English; general; Editor PÁLL STEFÁNSSON.

Lifandi vísindi: Klapparstíg 25, 105 Reykjavík; tel. 5708300; fax 5703809; e-mail lifandi@visindi.is; internet www.visindi.is; popular science; Editor GUÐBJARTUR FINNBJÖRNSSON.

Mannlíf: Lynghás 5, 110 Reykjavík; tel. 5155500; fax 5155599; e-mail mannlif@frodi.is; internet www.birtingur.is; f. 1984; 10 a year; general interest; Editor GERDUR KRISTNÝ GUÐJÓNSDÓTTIR; circ. 16,000.

Myndbönd mánaðarins (Videos of the Month): Reykjavík; tel. 5811280; fax 5811286; f. 1993; monthly; Editor GUÐBERGUR ÍSLEIFSSON; circ. 26,000.

Nýtt Líf: Seljavegur 2, 101 Reykjavík; tel. 5155660; fax 5155599; e-mail nyttlif@birtingur.is; f. 1978; 11 a year; fashion; Editor KOLBRÚN PÁLÍNA HELGADÓTTIR; circ. 13,000–17,000.

Peningamál: Kalkofnsvegur 1, 150 Reykjavík; tel. 5699600; fax 5699605; e-mail publish@centbk.is; internet www.sedlabanki.is; f. 1999; 2 a year; bulletin published by the Central Bank; circ. 1,600.

The Reykjavík Grapevine: Hafnarstræti 15, 101 Reykjavík; tel. 5403600; fax 5403609; e-mail grapevine@grapevine.is; internet www.grapevine.is; f. 2003; 18 a year; in English; distributed free of charge; owned by Fröken ehf; Publr HILMAR STEINN GRÉTARSSON; Editor HAUKUR S. MAGNÚSSON; circ. 30,000.

Skírnir: Skeifan 3B, 108 Reykjavík; tel. 5889060; e-mail hib@islandia.is; internet www.hib.is; f. 1827; journal of Hið íslenska bókmenntafélag (Icelandic Literary Society); Editor HALLDÓR GUÐMUNDSSON.

Skutull (Harpoon): Miðtun 16, 400 Isafjörður; tel. 8958270; e-mail skutull@skutull.is; internet skutull.is; f. 1923; monthly; organ of the Social Democratic Alliance; Editor SIGURÐUR PÉTURSSON.

Ský: Borgartún 23, 105 Reykjavík; tel. 5127575; fax 5618646; e-mail benedikt@heimur.is; internet www.heimur.is; complimentary in-flight magazine of Air Iceland; Editors BENEDIKT JÓHANNESSON, JÓN G. HAUKSSON.

Tölvuheimur (PC World Iceland): Borgartún 23, 105 Reykjavík; tel. 5127575; fax 5618646; e-mail tolvuheimur@heimur.is; internet www.heimur.is; in collaboration with International Data Group; computers; Editor ÓLI KRISTJÁN ÁRMANNSSON.

Veiðimaðurinn (The Angler): Borgartún 23, 105 Reykjavík; tel. 5127575; fax 5618646; e-mail heimur@heimur.is; internet www.heimur.is; f. 1984; 3 a year; angling; Editor BJARNI BRYNJÓLFSSON; circ. 5,000–7,000.

Vinnan (Labour): Sætún 1, 105 Reykjavík; tel. 5355600; fax 5355601; e-mail gra@asi.is; internet www.asi.is; 2 a year; f. 1943; publ. by Icelandic Federation of Labour; Editor Dr GUÐMUNDUR RÚNAR ÁRNASON; circ. 5,000.

Vísbending: Borgartún 23, 105 Reykjavík; tel. 5127575; fax 5618646; e-mail heimur@heimur.is; internet www.heimur.is; f. 1983; business.

Ægir: Hafnarstræti 82, 600 Akureyri; tel. 5155220; e-mail johann@athygli.is; internet www.athygli.is; f. 1905; owned by Athygli ehf; publ. by the Fisheries Asscn of Iceland; monthly; Editor JÓHANN ÓLAFUR HALLDÓRSSON; circ. 2,500.

Publishers

Birtíngur útgáfufélag: Lynghals 5, 110 Reykjavík; tel. 5155500; fax 5155599; e-mail birtingur@birtingur.is; internet www.birtingur.is; f. 2007; publ. 9 popular magazines: *Gestgjafinn*, *GOLFblaðið*, *Hús & Híbýli*, *Mannlíf*, *Nýtt Líf*, *Sagan Öll*, *Séð & Heyrt*, *Skakki Turninn* and *Vikan*; and 2 other magazines: *Leifur* and *Lifið heil*; Dir SVERRIR ARNGRÍMSSON.

Bjartur: Bræðraborgarstíg 9, 101 Reykjavík; tel. 4141450; e-mail bjartur@bjartur.is; internet www.bjartur.is; f. 1990; contemporary fiction, illustrated and children's books; Dir GUÐRÚN VILMUNDARDÓTTIR; Publr PÉTUR MÁR ÓLAFSSON.

Bókaútgáfan Björk: Birkivöllum 30, 800 Selfoss; tel. 4821394; fax 4823894; e-mail bokbjork@simnet.is; f. 1941; children's; Dir ERLENDUR DANIELSSON.

Bókaútgáfan Æskan ehf: Húsalind 7, 201 Kópavogur; tel. 5305400; e-mail karl@aeskanbok.is; f. 1930; general, children's books; Dir KARL HELGASON.

Edda Publishing: Síðumúla 28, 108 Reykjavík; tel. 5222000; fax 5222022; e-mail edda@edda.is; internet www.edda.is; imprints: Almenna bókafélagið, Forlagið, Iðunn, Mál og menning, Nýja bókafélagið-Þjoðsaga, Vaka-Helgafell; Icelandic fiction and non-fiction, translated fiction, biography, illustrated books, children's books on Iceland, maps; Man. Dir HEIÐDÍS ELLEN RÓBERTSDÓTTIR; Editor GRÉTA BJÖRG JAKOBSDÓTTIR.

Forlagið: Bræðraborgarstíg 7, 101 Reykjavík; tel. 5755600; fax 5755601; e-mail forlagid@forlagid.is; internet www.forlagid.is; general, fiction, biography, reference, illustrated; Dir JÓHANN PÁLL VALDIMARSSON.

Háskólaútgáfan (University of Iceland Press): Dunhagi 18, 107 Reykjavík; tel. 5254003; fax 5255255; e-mail hu@hi.is; internet www.haskolautgafan.hi.is; f. 1988; non-fiction, science, culture, history; Man. Dir JÖRUNDUR GUÐMUNDSSON.

Hið íslenska bókmenntafélag (Icelandic Literary Society): Skeifan 3B, 108 Reykjavík; tel. 5889060; fax 5814088; e-mail hib@islandia.is; internet www.hib.is; f. 1816; literary criticism; Pres. SIGURÐUR LÍNDAL; Dir SVERRIR KRISTINSSON.

Hið íslenska Fornritafélag: Skeifan 3B, 108 Reykjavík; tel. 5889060; fax 5814088; e-mail hib@islandia.is; internet www.hib.is; f. 1928; Pres. J. NORDAL.

Hólar: Hagasel 14, 109 Reykjavík; tel. 5872619; fax 5871180; e-mail holar@holabok.is; internet www.holabok.is; f. 1995; general; Dir GUDJÓN INGI EIRÍKSSON.

Hörpuútgáfan: Dalbraut 17, 300 Akranes; tel. 4312860; fax 4313309; f. 1960; fiction, biography, poetry, reference; Dir BRAGI ÞÓRÐARSON.

Jentas ehf: Austurströnd 10, 170 Seltjarnarnes; tel. 5687054; fax 5687053; e-mail info@jentas.com; internet www.jentas.com; f. 1997; formerly PP Forlag ehf Ísland; general; Dir SIGRÚN HALLDÓRS.

Krydd í tilveruna: Heiðarhjalli 5, 200 Kópavogur; tel. 8923334; e-mail krydd@simnet.is; f. 1989; children's, cookery; Dir ÆVAR GUÐMUNDSSON.

Myndabókaútgáfan ehf: Vorduberg 18, 221 Hafnarfjörður; tel. 5653690; fax 5659966; e-mail andrea@myndabokautgafan.is; children's; Dir ANDREA ÍSÓLFSDÓTTIR.

Námsgagnastofnun (National Centre for Educational Materials): Víkurhvarf 3, 203 Kópavogur; tel. 5350400; fax 5350401; e-mail simi@nams.is; internet www.nams.is; f. 1979; state-owned; Man. Dir INGIBJÖRG ÁSGEIRSDÓTTIR.

Ormstunga: Ránargötu 20, 101 Reykjavík; tel. 5610055; e-mail books@ormstunga.is; internet www.ormstunga.is; f. 1992; Icelandic and foreign fiction and non-fiction; Dir GÍSLI MÁR GÍSLASON.

Pjaxi ehf: Suðurlandsbraut 6, 108 Reykjavík; tel. 5659320; fax 5659325; Dir ÓMAR SKAPTI GÍSLASON.

Salka: Skipholti 50C, 105 Reykjavík; tel. 5222250; e-mail salka@salka.is; internet www.salka.is; f. 2000; non-fiction, books for, by and about women; Dir HILDUR HERMÓÐSDÓTTIR.

Samhjálp: Stangarhyl 3A, 110 Reykjavík; tel. 5611000; fax 5610050; e-mail heidar@samhjalp.is; internet www.samhjalp.is; religious, pentecostal; Dir HEIÐAR GUÐNASON.

Setberg: Freyjugötu 14, POB 619, 101 Reykjavík; tel. 5517667; fax 5526640; e-mail setberg@setberg.is; internet www.setberg.is; f. 1950; fiction, cookery, juvenile, picture books, activity books and children's books; Dir ARNBJÖRN KRISTINSSON.

Skálholtsútgáfan (National Church Publishing): Laugavegi 31, 101 Reykjavík; tel. 5284200; fax 5621595; e-mail skalholtsutgafan@skalholtsutgafan.is; internet www.skalholtsutgafan.is; f. 1981; non-fiction, religion, children's; Man. Dir EDDA MÖLLER.

Skjaldborg ehf: Mörkin 1, POB 8427, 108 Reykjavík; tel. 5521090; fax 5621595; e-mail skjaldborg@skjaldborg.is; internet www.skjaldborg.is; general; Dir BJÖRN EIRÍKSSON.

Skrudda: Eyjarslóð 9, 101 Reykjavík; tel. 5528866; fax 5528870; e-mail skrudda@skrudda.is; internet www.skrudda.is; fiction, non-fiction, translated fiction, biography, children's.

Sögufélagið: Fischersundi 3, 101 Reykjavík; tel. 5514620; e-mail sogufelag@sogufelag.is; internet www.sogufelag.is; f. 1902; non-fiction, history; Dir RAGNHEIÐUR ÞORLÁKSDÓTTIR.

Stofnun Árna Magnússonar í íslenskum fræðum: Árnagarður, Suðurgötu, 101 Reykjavík; tel. 5254010; fax 5254035; e-mail arnastofnun@hi.is; internet www.arnastofnun.is; f. 1972; state-owned; non-fiction; Dir GUÐRÚN NORDAL.

Útgáfufélagið Heimur: Borgartún 23, 105 Reykjavík; tel. 5127575; fax 5618646; e-mail heimur@heimur.is; internet www.heimur.is; f. 2000; magazines, travel books; Man. Dir BENEDIKT JÓHANNESSON.

PUBLISHERS' ASSOCIATION

Félag íslenskra bókaútgefenda (Icelandic Publishers' Asscn): Barónsstíg 5, 101 Reykjavík; tel. 5118020; fax 5115020; e-mail baekur@simnet.is; internet www.bokautgafa.is; f. 1889; Pres. KRISTJÁN JÓNASSON; Man. BENEDIKT KRISTJANSSON.

Broadcasting and Communications

TELECOMMUNICATIONS

Supervisory Authority

Póst- og Fjarskiptastofnun (Post and Telecom Administration): Suðurlandsbraut 4, 108 Reykjavík; tel. 5101500; fax 5101509; e-mail pfs@pfs.is; internet www.pfs.is; supervisory authority; Man. Dir HRAFNKELL V. GÍSLASON.

Service Providers

IceCell ehf: Skulagata 19, 101 Reykjavík; tel. 6666330; fax 6666331; e-mail info@icecell.is; internet www.icecell.is; mobile telecommunications; CEO ANDREAS FINK.

IMC Island ehf: Borgartún 31, 105 Reykjavík; tel. 6618540; e-mail info@worldcell.com; GSM mobile service provider; wholly owned subsidiary of WorldCell Inc., USA; CEO JEFFREY STARK.

Nova ehf: Lágmúla 9, 108 Reykjavík; tel. 5191000; fax 5190001; e-mail nova@nova.is; internet www.nova.is; f. 2006; mobile telecommunications and broadband internet access; Chair. TÓMAS OTTO HANSSON.

Síminn hf: Ármúla 25, 108 Reykjavík; tel. 5506000; fax 5506009; e-mail siminn@siminn.is; internet www.siminn.is; f. 1998 as Iceland Telecom Ltd; present name adopted 2005 following privatization; offers fixed-line telecommunications, digital television services and broadband internet access; Pres. and CEO SÆVAR FREYR ÞRÁINSSON.

Vodafone Iceland: Skútuvogi 2, 104 Reykjavík; tel. 5999000; fax 5999001; e-mail vodafone@vodafone.is; internet www.vodafone.is; f. 2003 as Og Vodafone by merger of Tal, Íslandssími and Halló; renamed as above in 2006; provides mobile and fixed-line telecommunications; CEO ÓMAR SVAVARSSON.

BROADCASTING

Ríkisútvarpið (Icelandic National Broadcasting Service—RÚV): Broadcasting Centre, Efstaleiti 1, 150 Reykjavík; tel. 5153000; fax 5153010; e-mail istv@ruv.is; internet www.ruv.is; f. 1930; Dir-Gen. PÁLL MAGNÚSSON.

Skjárinn: Skipholt 31, 105 Reykjavík; tel. 5956000; e-mail info@skjarinn.is; internet www.skjarinn.is; f. 2005; owned by Síminn hf; multi-channel digital television service; also operates 3 television channels: Skjáreinn, Skjárbíóand and Skjárheimur; Man. FRIÐRIK FRIÐRIKSSON.

365 miðlar ehf: Skaftahlíð 24, 105 Reykjavík; tel. 5125000; e-mail askrft@stod2.is; internet www.365.is; f. 2005; owns fmr broadcasting assets of Íslenska Sjónvarpsfélagið hf, as well as the daily newspaper *DV*; Chair. INGIBJÖRG STEFANÍA PÁLMADÓTTIR.

Radio

Ríkisútvarpið—Útvarpi (Icelandic National Broadcasting Service—Radio): Radio Division, Efstaleiti 1, 150 Reykjavík; tel. 5153000; fax 5153010; e-mail radionews@ruv.is; internet www.ruv.is; f. 1930; Programmes 1 and 2 are broadcast over a network of 89 transmitters each; Programme 1 is broadcast for 112 hours a week, with the remaining hours simulcast with Programme 2; Programme 2 is broadcast 168 hours a week; 2 long-wave transmitters broadcast the same programme, alternating between Programme 1 and Programme 2; Dir SIGRÚN STEFÁNSDÓTTIR.

Akraneskaupstaður: Stillholt 16–18, 300 Akranes; tel. 4331000; fax 4331090; e-mail akranes@akranes.is; internet www.akranes.is; broadcasts only in Akranes; Dir BJÖRN LÁRUSSON.

Bylgjan: Skaftahlíð 24, 105 Reykjavík; tel. 5125000; fax 5156900; e-mail ritstjorn@visir.is; internet bylgjan.visir.is; owned by 365 miðlar ehf; Dir ÁGÚST HEÐINSSON.

FM957: Skaftahlíð 24, 110 Reykjavík; tel. 5110957; e-mail fm957@fm957.is; internet www.fm957.is; owned by 365 miðlar ehf.

Kristilega útvarpsstöðin Lindin: Krókháls 4A, 110 Reykjavík; tel. 5671818; fax 5671824; e-mail lindin@lindin.is; internet lindin.is; Dir MICHAEL E. FITZGERALD.

Létt Bylgjan: Skaftahlíð 24, 105 Reykjavík; tel. 5125000; fax 5156830; e-mail lettbylgjan@lettbylgjan.is; internet www.bylgjan.is; owned by 365 miðlar ehf; Dir AGUST HEÐINSSON.

Útvarp Saga: Nóatún 17, 105 Reykjavík; tel. 5333943; fax 5881994; e-mail saga@utvarpsaga.is; internet www.utvarpsaga.is; Dir ARNÞRÚÐUR KARLSDÓTTIR.

Útvarp Vestmannaeyjar: Brekkugata 1, 900 Vestmannaeyjar; tel. 4811534; fax 4813475; broadcasts only in Vestmannaeyjar; Dir BJARNI JÓNASSON.

X 97.7: Skaftahlíð 24, 105 Reykjavík; tel. 5125000; e-mail x977@x977.is; internet www.x977.is; owned by 365 miðlar ehf.

Television

Ríkisútvarpið—Sjónvarp (Icelandic National Broadcasting Service—Television): Efstaleiti 1, 150 Reykjavík; tel. 5153000; fax 5153010; e-mail istv@ruv.is; internet www.ruv.is; f. 1966; covers 99% of the population; broadcasts daily, total 70 hours a week; Dir SIGRÚN STEFÁNSDÓTTIR.

Bíórásin: Skaftahlíð 24, 105 Reykjavík; tel. 5125000; owned by 365 miðlar ehf.

Kristniboðskirkjan: Grensásvegur 8, 108 Reykjavík; tel. 5683131; fax 5683741; f. 1995; broadcasts only in the Reykjavík area; religious; Dir EIRÍKUR SIGURBJÖRNSSON.

PoppTíví: Skaftahlíð 24, 105 Reykjavík; tel. 5156000; f. 1998; owned by 365 miðlar ehf; music station.

Stöð 2: Skaftahlíð 24, 105 Reykjavík; tel. 5125000; fax 5125100; e-mail askrift@stod2.is; internet www.stod2.is; f. 1986; owned by 365 miðlar ehf; 'pay-TV' station.

Sýn (Vision): Skaftahlíð 24, 105 Reykjavík; tel. 5125000; owned by 365 miðlar ehf.

Finance

(cap. = capital; res = reserves; dep. = deposits; m. = million; amounts in krónur; brs = branches)

BANKING

Iceland's banking and finance system has undergone substantial transformation. In 1989–90 the number of commercial banks was reduced from seven to three, by amalgamating four banks to form Íslandsbanki as the only remaining major commercial bank in private ownership. A further restructuring of the banking sector commenced in 2000 with the merger of Íslandsbanki with the recently privatized investment bank FBA. Íslandsbanki was renamed Glitnir Banki in 2006. By early 2003 the Icelandic Government had withdrawn completely from the country's commercial banking sector, having sold its controlling stakes in Bunarðarbanki Íslands and Landsbanki Íslands.

In 2008 the banking sector suffered severe difficulties resulting from a reduction in the availability of credit on global financial markets, and the Icelandic Government was forced to intervene in an attempt to stabilize the economy. On 1 October the Government acquired a 75% stake in Iceland's third largest retail bank, Glitnir Banki, and announced days later that it would guarantee the security of all domestic bank deposits held in Icelandic banks. On 6 October the Althingi (parliament) approved legislation that granted wide-ranging powers to the Financial Supervisory Authority (Fjármálaeftirlitið—FME, see below), allowing it to take control of financial institutions. The FME subsequently assumed control of Landsbanki Íslands, Glitnir Banki and Kaupþing Banki. Three new banks—Nýi Glitnir Banki (renamed Íslandsbanki in February 2009), Nýi Kaupþing Banki (renamed Arion Banki in November) and NBI (Landsbankinn)—which were fully owned by the Icelandic Government, were created to take control of domestic assets, ensure the provision of normal banking services and safeguard domestic deposits, while the foreign assets and liabilities were retained by the former banks, which were in receivership.

Central Bank

Seðlabanki Íslands (Central Bank of Iceland): Kalkofnsvegur 1, 150 Reykjavík; tel. 5699600; fax 5699605; e-mail sedlabanki@sedlabanki.is; internet www.sedlabanki.is; f. 1961; cap. 57,501m., res 11,878.2m., dep. 1,019,162.5m. (Dec. 2010); Chair., Supervisory Bd LÁRA V. JÚLÍUSDÓTTIR; Gov. MÁR GUÐMUNDSSON.

Principal Banks

Arion Banki: Borgartún 19, 105 Reykjavík; tel. 4446000; fax 4446009; e-mail info@kaupthing.is; internet www.arionbanki.is; f. 2008 as Nýi Kaupþing Banki hf to assume responsibility for domestic assets and deposits of Kaupþing Banki (f. 2003) after it was nationalized; adopted current name Nov. 2009; 87% owned by creditors of Kaupþing Banki, 13% by Icelandic Govt; cap. 2,000m., res 75,386m., dep. 553,527m. (Dec. 2010); Chair. MONICA CANEMAN; CEO HÖSKULDUR H. ÓLAFSSON; 35 brs.

Íslandsbanki hf: Kirkjusandur, 155 Reykjavík; tel. 4404000; fax 4404001; e-mail islandsbanki@islandsbanki.is; internet www.islandsbanki.is; f. 2008 as Nýi Glitnir Banki to assume responsibility for domestic assets and deposits of Glitnir Banki (f. 1990) after it was nationalized in Oct. 2008; adopted current name Feb. 2009; 95% owned by creditors of Glitnir Banki, 5% by Icelandic Govt; cap. 10,000m., res 57,498m., dep. 423,802m. (Dec. 2010); Chair. FRIÐRIK SOPHUSSON; CEO BIRNA EINARSDÓTTIR; 29 brs.

Landsbankinn hf (Nýi Landsbanki Íslands—Landsbankinn): Austurstræti 11, 155 Reykjavík; tel. and fax 5606600; e-mail info@landsbank.is; internet www.landsbanki.is; f. 2008; 81.3% owned by Icelandic Govt; established to assume responsibility for domestic assets and deposits of Landsbanki Íslands (f. 1885) after it was nationalized in Oct. 2008; present name adopted 2011; cap. 24,000m., res 126,830m., dep. 371,558m. (Dec. 2010); Chair GUNNAR HELGI HÁLFDÁNARSON; CEO STEINÞÓR PÁLSSON; 27 brs.

MP Banki hf: Ármúli 13A, 108 Reykjavík; tel. 5403230; fax 5403201; e-mail info@mp.is; internet www.mp.is; f. 1999 as a brokerage firm under name MP Verdbref; status changed to investment bank in 2003 and name changed to MP Fjárfestingarbanki; granted a commercial licence in Oct. 2008 and adopted current name; cap. 1,171m., res 1,314m., dep. 51,393m. (Dec. 2009); Chair. ÞORSTEINN PÁLSSON; CEO SIGURÐUR ATLI JÓNSSON.

STOCK EXCHANGE

NASDAQ OMX Nordic Exchange Iceland: Laugavegur 182, 105 Reykjavík; tel. 5252800; fax 5252888; internet www.nasdaqomx.com; f. 2006 by merger of Kauphöll Íslands and OMX AB (Sweden); part of OMX Nordic Exchange with Copenhagen (Denmark), Helsinki (Finland) and Stockholm (Sweden) exchanges; acquired by NASDAQ Stock Market, Inc (USA) in 2008; Group CEO ROBERT GREIFELD.

INSURANCE

Tryggingastofnun ríkisins (Social Insurance Administration): Laugavegi 114, 105 Reykjavík; tel. 5604400; fax 5604451; e-mail tr@tr.is; internet www.tr.is; f. 1936; Chair. STEFAN OLAFSSON; Dir-Gen. SIGRIÐUR LILLÝ BALDURSDÓTTIR.

Private Insurance Companies

Íslensk Endurtrygging hf (Icelandic Reinsurance Co Ltd): Síðumuli 24, 108 Reykjavík; tel. 5152000; fax 5152050; e-mail hjalmar@tm.is; f. 1939; Gen. Man. HJÁLMAR SIGURÞÓRSSON.

Líftryggingafélag Íslands hf (Lífís): Ármúla 3, 108 Reykjavík; tel. 5605060; fax 5605100; internet www.lifis.is; f. 1990; owned by holding co. of Vátryggingafélag Íslands hf (VÍS); life.

Líftryggingamiðstöðin hf: Aðalstræti 6–8, 101 Reykjavík; tel. 5152000; fax 5152020; f. 2002; subsidiary of Tryggingamiðstöðin hf (TM); Gen. Man. HJÁLMAR SIGURÞÓRSSON.

Sjóvá-Almennar tryggingar hf (Marine-General Insurance Co): Kringlan 5, 103 Reykjavík; tel. 4402000; fax 4402020; e-mail sjova@sjova.is; internet www.sjova.is; f. 1988; all branches except life; Chair. BENEDIKT SVEINSSON; Gen. Mans EINAR SVEINSSON, ÓLAFUR B. THORS.

Tryggingamiðstöðin hf (TM): Síðumúla 24, 108 Reykjavík; tel. 5152000; fax 5152020; e-mail tm@tm.is; internet www.tm.is; f. 1956; acquired Trygging hf in 1999; Chair. JÚLÍUS ÞORFINNSSON.

Vátryggingafélag Íslands hf (VÍS): Ármúla 3, 108 Reykjavík; tel. 5605000; fax 5605108; e-mail vis@vis.is; internet www.vis.is; f. 1989; non-life; Chair. AXEL GISLASON; CEO SIGRÚN RAGNA ÓLAFSDÓTTIR.

Viðlagatrygging Íslands: Borgartún 6, 105 Reykjavík; tel. 5753300; fax 5753303; e-mail vidlagatrygging@vidlagatrygging.is; internet www.vidlagatrygging.is; Chair. GUÐRÚN ERLINGSDÓTTIR.

Vörður tryggingar hf: Borgartún 25, 105 Reykjavík; tel. 5141000; fax 5141001; e-mail vordur@vordur.is; internet www.vordur.is; f. 1926; as Vörður; life and non-life; Chair. JENS ERIK CHRISTENSEN.

Supervisory Authority

Fjármálaeftirlitið (FME) (Financial Supervisory Authority): Höfðatún 2, 105 Reykjavík; tel. 5203700; fax 5203727; e-mail fme@fme.is; internet www.fme.is; f. 1999 by merger of Insurance Supervisory Authority and Bank Inspectorate of the Central Bank of Iceland; Chair. AÐALSTEINN LEIFSSON; Dir-Gen. HALLDÓR S. MAGNÚSSON.

Trade and Industry

GOVERNMENT AGENCIES

Orkustofnun (National Energy Authority): Grensásvegur 9, 108 Reykjavík; tel. 5696000; fax 5688896; e-mail os@os.is; internet www.os.is; f. 1967; 2 main divisions: hydrological research unit and energy administration unit; contracts and supervises energy research projects financed by the national budget, monitors energy consumption and publishes forecasts for energy market; operates United Nations Geothermal Training Programme as independent entity; licenses and monitors exploration for oil and gas in Icelandic waters; Dir-Gen. Prof. GUÐNI A. JOHANNESSON.

Útflutningsráð Íslands (Trade Council of Iceland): POB 1000, 121 Reykjavík; Borgartún 35, 105 Reykjavík; tel. 5114000; fax 5114040; e-mail icetrade@icetrade.is; internet www.icetrade.is; promotes Icelandic exports; Man. Dir JÓN ÁSBERGSSON.

Invest in Iceland Agency: POB 1000, 121 Reykjavík; Borgartún 35, 105 Reykjavík; tel. 5615200; fax 5114040; e-mail info@invest.is; internet www.invest.is; f. 1995; promotes foreign investment; managed by the Trade Council of Iceland and Ministry of Industry, Energy and Tourism; Man. Dir ÞÓRÐUR H. HILMARSSON.

CHAMBER OF COMMERCE

Viðskiptaráð Íslands (Iceland Chamber of Commerce): Hús verslunarinnar, Kringlan 7, 103 Reykjavík; tel. 5107100; fax 5686564; e-mail info@vi.is; internet www.vi.is; f. 1917; fmrly Verslunarráð Íslands; Man. Dir FINNUR ODDSSON; 370 mems.

INDUSTRIAL AND TRADE ASSOCIATIONS

Fiskifélag Íslands (Fisheries Asscn of Iceland): POB 8214, 128 Reykjavík; tel. 5910308; fax 5910301; e-mail fi@fiskifelag.is; internet www.fiskifelag.is; f. 1911; conducts technical and economic research and services for the fishing vessels and for fishing industry; Chair. KRISTJÁN LOFTSSON.

Landssamband Íslenskra Útvegsmanna (Icelandic Fishing Vessel Owners' Federation): Borgartúni 35, 105 Reykjavík; tel. 5910300; fax 5910301; e-mail liu@liu.is; internet www.liu.is; f. 1939; Chair. ADOLF GUÐMUNDSSON; Man. FRIÐRIK JÓN ARNGRÍMSSON.

Samtök Iðnaðarins (SI) (Federation of Icelandic Industries): Borgartúni 35, 105 Reykjavík; tel. 5910100; fax 5910101; e-mail mottaka@si.is; internet www.si.is; f. 1993 by merger of Federation of Icelandic Industries (f. 1933), Federation of Icelandic Crafts and Industries (f. 1932) and 4 other employers' orgs; Chair. HELGI MAGNUSSON; Dir-Gen. JÓN STEINDÓR VALDIMARSSON; 1,160 mems.

EMPLOYERS' ORGANIZATION

Samtök atvinnulífsins (SA) (Confederation of Icelandic Employers): Borgartúni 35, 105 Reykjavík; tel. 5910000; fax 5910050; e-mail sa@sa.is; internet www.sa.is; f. 1934; 8 mem. asscns; Chair. VILMUNDUR JÓSEFSSON; Man. Dir Dr VILHJÁLMUR EGILSSON.

UTILITIES

Electricity

HS Orka hf: Brekkustíg 36, POB 225, 260 Reykjanesbær; tel. 4225200; fax 4214727; e-mail hs@hs.is; internet www.hsorka.is; f. 2008 by division of Hitaveita Suðurnesja hf (HS, f. 1974) into HS Orka hf and HS Veitur hf; produces and sells geothermal electricity; transfer of majority stake to Magma Energy Corp. (Canada) agreed May 2010; Chair. ALEXANDER GUÐMUNDSSON; Man. Dir JÚLÍUS JÓNSSON.

HS Veitur hf: Brekkustíg 36, POB 225, 260 Reykjanesbær; tel. 4225200; fax 4214727; e-mail hs@hs.is; internet www.hsveitur.is; f. 2008 by division of Hitaveita Suðurnesja hf (HS); produces and distributes hot-water heating and electricity for the Suðurnes region; Chair. ÁRNI SIGFÚSSON.

Landsvirkjun (National Power): Háaleitisbraut 68, 103 Reykjavík; tel. 5159000; fax 5159007; e-mail landsvirkjun@lv.is; internet www.landsvirkjun.com; f. 1965; state-owned; generates and sells electric power wholesale to public distribution systems and industrial enterprises; Chair. BRYNDÍS HLÖDVERSDÓTTIR; Man. Dir HÖRDUR ARNARSON.

Orkubú Vestfjarða hf (Westfjord Power Co): Stakkanesi 1, 400 Isafjördur; tel. 4503211; fax 4563204; e-mail orkubu@ov.is; internet www.ov.is; f. 1977; produces, distributes and sells electrical energy in the Westfjords area; state-owned; Chair. GUÐMUNDUR JÓHANNSSON; Man. Dir KRISTJÁN HARALDSSON.

Orkuveita Reykjavíkur (OR) (Reykjavík Energy): Bæjarháls 1, 110 Reykjavík; tel. 5166000; fax 5166709; e-mail or@or.is; internet www.or.is; f. 1999; produces and distributes geothermal hot-water central heating, cold water and electricity for the city of Reykjavík and regions in south-western Iceland; owned by city of Reykjavík and other local authorities; Chair. HARALDUR FLOSI TRYGGVASON; CEO HJÖRLEIFUR B. KVARAN.

RARIK ohf (Iceland State Electricity): Bíldshöfða 9, 110 Reykjavík; tel. 5289000; fax 5289009; e-mail rarik@rarik.is; internet www.rarik.is; f. 1947 as Rafmagnsveitur Ríkisins; produces, procures, distributes and sells electrical energy; also provides consultancy services; Chair. ÁRNI STEINAR JOHANNSSON; Man. Dir TRYGGVI ÞÓR HARALDSSON.

TRADE UNIONS

Althýðusamband Íslands (ASÍ) (Icelandic Confederation of Labour): Sætún 1, 105 Reykjavík; tel. 5355600; fax 5355601; e-mail asi@asi.is; internet www.asi.is; f. 1916; affiliated to ITUC, ETUC and the Council of Nordic Trade Unions; Pres. and Gen. Sec. GYLFI ARNBJÖRNSSON; c. 109,000 mems.

Bandalag Háskólamanna (BHM) (Asscn of Academics): Borgartún 6, 105 Reykjavík; tel. 5812090; fax 5889239; e-mail bhm@bhm.is; internet www.bhm.is; f. 1958; asscn of 25 trade unions; publishes *BHM-tíðindi* (3 a year); Chair. GUÐLAUG KRISTJÁNSDÓTTIR; 9,800 mems.

Bandalag Starfsmanna Ríkis og Bæja (BSRB) (Municipal and Government Employees' Asscn): Grettisgötu 89, 105 Reykjavík; tel. 5658300; fax 5258309; e-mail bsrb@bsrb.is; internet www.bsrb.is; f. 1942; Chair. ELÍN BJÖRG JÓNSDÓTTIR; 20,000 mems.

Blaðamannafélag Íslands (Union of Icelandic Journalists): Síðumúla 23, 108 Reykjavík; tel. 5539155; fax 5539177; e-mail bi@press.is; internet www.press.is; f. 1897; Chair. HJÁLMAR JÓNSSON; 570 mems.

Transport

RAILWAYS

There are no railways in Iceland.

ROADS

Much of the interior is uninhabited and the main road follows the coastline. Regular motor coach services link the main settlements. In 2008 Iceland had 13,048 km of roads, of which 4,224 km were main roads. Approximately one-third of the main roads are paved.

Vegagerðin (Icelandic Road Administration—ICERA): Borgartún 7, 105 Reykjavík; tel. 5221000; e-mail vegagerdin@vegagerdin.is; internet www.vegagerdin.is; part of the Ministry of Transport, Communications and Local Government; oversees the construction and maintenance of roads; Man. Dir JÓN HELGASON.

Bifreiðastöð Íslands hf (BSÍ) (Iceland Motor Coach Service): Umferðarmiðstöðinni, Vatnsmýrarveg 10, 101 Reykjavík; tel. 5621011; e-mail bsi@bsi.is; internet www.bsi.is; f. 1936; 45 scheduled bus lines throughout Iceland; also operates sightseeing tours and excursions; Chair. ÓSKAR SIGURJÓNSSON; Man. Dir GUNNAR SVEINSSON.

SHIPPING

Heavy freight is carried by coastal shipping. The principal seaport for international shipping is Reykjavík. At 31 December 2009 the Icelandic merchant fleet numbered 226 vessels, with a combined displacement of 161,607 grt.

Port Authority

Faxaflóahafnir sf (Associated Icelandic Ports): POB 382, 121 Reykjavík; Harbour Bldg, Tryggvagata 17, 101 Reykjavík; tel. 5258900; fax 5258990; e-mail hofnin@faxaports.is; internet www.faxaports.is; f. 2005 by merger of ports of Akranes, Borgarnes, Grundartangi and Reykjavík; Chair. HJALMAR SVEINSSON; Dir GISLI GISLASON.

Principal Companies

Atlantsskip ehf: Cuxhavengata 1, 220 Hafnarfjörður; tel. 5913000; fax 5913001; e-mail atlantsskip@atlantsskip.is; internet www.atlantsskip.is; f. 1998; Chair. and CEO GUÐMUNDUR KJÆRNESTED; Gen. Man. DAVÍÐ BLÖNDAL.

Eimskip (Iceland Steamship Co Ltd): Korngörðum 2, 104 Reykjavík; tel. 5257000; fax 5257009; e-mail info@eimskip.com; internet www.eimskip.com; f. 1914 as Eimskipafélag Íslands; subsidiary of Avion Group; transportation and logistics services incl. ground operation, warehousing, coastal service, trucking and intermodal transportation between Iceland and the United Kingdom, Scandinavia, the rest of Europe, the USA and Canada; Chair. SINDRI SINDRASON; Pres. and CEO GYLFI SIGFÚSSON.

Nesskip hf: Austurstrond 1, 172 Seltjarnarnes; tel. 5639900; fax 5639919; e-mail operations@nesskip.is; internet www.nesskip.is; f. 1974; bulk cargo shipping services to the USA, Canada, Russia, Scandinavia, the Baltic countries and other parts of Europe; agency and chartering for vessels in all Icelandic ports; Chair. Capt. GUÐMUNDUR ÁSGEIRSSON; Man. Dir GARÐAR JÓHANNSSON.

Samskip hf: Kjalarvogur, 104 Reykjavík; tel. 4588000; fax 4588100; e-mail samskip@samskip.is; internet www.samskip.is; services to Europe, the USA, South America and the Far East; Chair ÓLAFUR ÓLAFSSON.

CIVIL AVIATION

Air transport is particularly important to Iceland and is used to convey both people and agricultural produce from remote districts. More than 90% of passenger traffic between Iceland and other countries is by air. There are regular air services between Reykjavík and outlying townships. There is an international airport at Keflavík, 47 km from Reykjavík.

Flugmálastjórn Íslands (ICAA) (Icelandic Civil Aviation Administration): Skogarhlid 12, 105 Reykjavík; tel. 5694100; fax 5623619; e-mail fms@caa.is; internet www.caa.is; f. 1945; under Ministry of the Interior; regulatory authority; Dir-Gen. PÉTUR K. MAACK.

Air Atlanta Icelandic: Hlíðasmára 3, 201 Kópavogur; tel. 4584000; fax 4584001; e-mail info@airatlanta.com; internet www.airatlanta.com; f. 1986; leases cargo and passenger aircraft; Pres. and CEO HANNES HILMARSSON.

Air Iceland: Reykjavík Airport, 101 Reykjavík; tel. 5703000; fax 5703001; e-mail service@airiceland.is; internet www.airiceland.is; part of Icelandair Group; scheduled regional flights; 96% owned by Icelandair; Man. Dir ÁRNI GUNNARSSON.

Eagle Air (Flugfélagið Ernir ehf): Reykjavík Airport, 101 Reykjavík; tel. 5624200; fax 5624202; e-mail info@eagleair.is; internet www.eagleair.is; f. 1970; charter and domestic scheduled services; Pres. and CEO HÖRÐUR GUÐMUNDSSON.

Iceland Express ehf: Grímsbær, Efstaland 26, 108 Reykjavík; tel. 5500650; fax 5500601; e-mail info@icelandexpress.is; internet www.icelandexpress.com; f. 2002; low-cost airline offering daily scheduled flights between Iceland and 17 destinations in Europe; Chair. THORSTEINN ÖRN GUÐMUNDSSON; Man. Dir MATTHÍAS IMSLAND.

Icelandair (Flugleiðir hf): Reykjavík Airport, 101 Reykjavík; tel. 5050757; fax 5050758; e-mail pr@icelandair.is; internet www.icelandair.is; f. 1973 as the holding co for the 2 principal Icelandic airlines, Flugfélag Islands (f. 1937) and Loftleiðir (f. 1944); in 1979 all licences, permits and authorizations previously held by Flugfélag Íslands and Loftleiðir were transferred to it; operates flights from Reykjavík to 9 domestic airfields and more than 20 destinations in Europe and North America; CEO BIRKIR HÓLM GUÐNASON.

Tourism

Iceland's main attraction for tourists lies in the rugged beauty of the interior, with its geysers and thermal springs. In 2008 receipts from tourism, including passenger transport, totalled US $881m. Overnight stays by foreign visitors in hotels and guesthouses amounted to 1.6m. in 2010.

Iceland Tourist Board: Borgartún 35, 105 Reykjavík; tel. 5114000; fax 5114040; e-mail info@promoteiceland.is; internet www.visiticeland.com; Gen. Dir ÓLÖF ÝRR ATLADÓTTIR.

Höfuðborgarstofa (Visit Reykjavík): Aðalstræti 2, 101 Reykjavík; tel. 5901500; fax 5901501; e-mail info@visitreykjavik.is; internet www.visitreykjavik.is; tourism marketing and events for the city of Reykjavík; Dir SIF GUNNARSDÓTTIR.

Defence

Apart from a 130-strong coastguard, Iceland has no defence forces of its own, but it is a member of the North Atlantic Treaty Organization (NATO). Until 2006 there were units of US forces at Keflavík airbase, which was used for observation of the North Atlantic Ocean, under a bilateral agreement made in 1951 between Iceland and the USA. In September 2006 the USA withdrew its forces from Iceland, but maintained its commitment to defend Iceland as a fellow member of NATO.

Defence Expenditure: Budgeted at 4,000m. krónur (coastguard only) for 2009.

Education

Education starts at the pre-primary level, which is non-compulsory for pupils aged between one and six years of age. Education is compulsory and free for 10 years between six and 16 years of age (primary and lower secondary levels). Upper secondary education begins at 16 years of age and usually lasts for four years. In 2008/09, enrolment in pre-primary schools included 98% of children in the relevant age-group. In the same year, enrolment in primary schools included 98% of children in the relevant age-group, while enrolment in secondary education included 89% of children in the relevant age-group. Higher education is provided by universities and select institutions offering a limited number of study programmes. Iceland had 23 institutions providing tertiary-level education in 2010. In 2011 there were 29,389 students registered at the upper secondary level at the beginning of the school year and 19,334 students enrolled in tertiary-level education. General government expenditure on education was 8.5% of total public expenditure in 2009. Local communities finance compulsory education.

INDIA

Introductory Survey

LOCATION, CLIMATE, LANGUAGE, RELIGION, FLAG, CAPITAL

The Republic of India forms a natural sub-continent, with the Himalaya mountain range to the north. Two sections of the Indian Ocean—the Arabian Sea and the Bay of Bengal—lie to the west and east, respectively. India's neighbours are Tibet (the Xizang Autonomous Region of the People's Republic of China), Bhutan and Nepal to the north, Pakistan to the north-west and Myanmar (formerly Burma) to the north-east, while Bangladesh is surrounded by Indian territory except for a short frontier with Myanmar in the east. Near India's southern tip, across the Palk Strait, is Sri Lanka. India's climate ranges from temperate to tropical, with an average summer temperature on the plains of approximately 27°C (85°F). Annual rainfall varies widely, but the summer monsoon brings heavy rain over much of the country in June and July. The official language is Hindi, spoken by about 30% of the population. English is used as an associate language for many official purposes. The Indian Constitution also recognizes 18 regional languages, of which the most widely spoken are Telugu, Bengali, Marathi, Tamil, Urdu and Gujarati. In addition, many other local languages are used. According to the 2001 census, about 81% of the population are Hindus and 13% Muslims. There are also Christians, Sikhs, Buddhists, Jains and other minorities. The national flag (proportions 2 by 3) has three equal horizontal stripes, of saffron, white and green, with the Dharma Chakra (Wheel of the Law), in blue, in the centre of the white stripe. The capital is New Delhi.

CONTEMPORARY POLITICAL HISTORY

Historical Context

After a prolonged struggle against British colonial rule, India became independent, within the Commonwealth, on 15 August 1947. The United Kingdom's Indian Empire was partitioned, broadly on a religious basis, between India and Pakistan. The principal nationalist movement that had opposed British rule was the Indian National Congress (later known as the Congress Party). At independence the Congress leader, Jawaharlal Nehru, became India's first Prime Minister. Sectarian violence, the movement of 12m. refugees, the integration of the former princely states into the Indian federal structure and a territorial dispute with Pakistan over Kashmir presented major problems to the new Government.

India became independent as a dominion, with the British monarch as Head of State, represented by an appointed Governor-General. In November 1949, however, the Constituent Assembly approved a republican Constitution, providing for a President (with mainly ceremonial functions) as head of state. Accordingly, India became a republic on 26 January 1950, although remaining a member of the Commonwealth. France transferred sovereignty of Chandernagore to India in May 1950, and ceded its four remaining Indian settlements in 1954.

In December 1961 Indian forces overran the Portuguese territories of Goa, Daman and Diu, which were immediately annexed by India. Border disputes with the People's Republic of China escalated into a brief military conflict in 1962. Nehru died in May 1964 and was succeeded by Lal Bahadur Shastri. India and Pakistan fought a second war over Kashmir in 1965. Following mediation by the USSR, Shastri and President Ayub Khan of Pakistan signed a joint declaration, aimed at a peaceful settlement of the Kashmir dispute, on 10 January 1966. However, Shastri died on the following day and Nehru's daughter, Indira Gandhi, became Prime Minister.

Domestic Political Affairs

Indira Gandhi dominates Indian politics (1966–84)

Following the presidential election of August 1969, when two factions of Congress supported different candidates, the success of Indira Gandhi's candidate split the party. The Organization (Opposition) Congress, led by Morarji Desai, emerged in November, but at the next general election to the lower house of the legislature, the Lok Sabha (House of the People), held in March 1971, Indira Gandhi's wing of Congress won 350 of the 515 elective seats.

Border incidents led to a 12-day war with Pakistan in December 1971. The Indian army rapidly occupied East Pakistan, which India recognized as the independent state of Bangladesh. Indira Gandhi and President Zulfikar Ali Bhutto of Pakistan held a summit conference at Shimla in June–July 1972, when the two leaders agreed that their respective forces should respect the cease-fire line in Kashmir, and that India and Pakistan should resolve their differences through bilateral negotiations or other peaceful means. In 1975 the former protectorate of Sikkim became the 22nd state of the Indian Union, leading to tensions in India's relations with Nepal.

A general election to the Lok Sabha was held in March 1977, when the number of elective seats was increased to 542. The election resulted in victory for the Janata (People's) Party, chaired by Morarji Desai, who became Prime Minister. The Janata Party and an allied party, the Congress for Democracy, together won 298 of the 540 seats where polling took place. Congress obtained 153 seats. In January 1978 Indira Gandhi became leader of a new breakaway political group, the Congress (Indira) Party, known as Congress (I).

In 1979 the Government's ineffectual approach to domestic problems provoked a wave of defections by Lok Sabha members of the Janata Party. Many joined Raj Narain, who formed a new party, the Lok Dal, the policies of which were based on secularism. Congress (I) lost its position as official opposition party after defections from its ranks to the then official Congress Party by members who objected to Indira Gandhi's perceived authoritarianism. The resignation of Desai's Government in July was followed by the departure from the Janata Party of Charan Singh, who became the leader of the Lok Dal and, shortly afterwards, Prime Minister in a coalition with both Congress parties. When Congress (I) withdrew its support, Singh's 24-day administration collapsed, and Parliament was dissolved. A general election to the Lok Sabha was held in January 1980. Congress (I) won an overwhelming majority (352) of the elective seats; the Janata Party and the Lok Dal won only 31 and 41 seats, respectively. Indira Gandhi was reinstated as Prime Minister. Presidential rule was imposed in nine states, hitherto governed by opposition parties, in February. At elections to state assemblies in June, Congress (I) won majorities in eight of them.

By-elections in June 1981 for the Lok Sabha and state assemblies were notable because of the overwhelming victory that Rajiv Gandhi, the Prime Minister's son, obtained in the former constituency of his late brother (killed in an air crash in 1980) and because of the failure of the fragmented Janata Party to win any seats. In February 1983 Rajiv Gandhi became a General Secretary of Congress (I).

Indira Gandhi's Government faced serious problems, as intercommunal disturbances in several states (particularly Assam and Meghalaya) continued in 1982–83, with violent protests against the presence of Bengali immigrants. Election defeats in Andhra Pradesh, Karnataka and Tripura represented a series of set-backs for Indira Gandhi. Alleged police corruption and the resurgence of caste violence (notably in Bihar and Gujarat) caused further problems for the Government.

There was also unrest in the Sikh community of the Punjab, despite the election to the Indian presidency in July 1982 of Giani Zail Singh, the first Sikh to hold the position. Demands were made for greater religious recognition, for the settlement of grievances over land and water rights, and over the sharing of the state capital at Chandigarh with Haryana; in addition, a minority called for the creation of a separate Sikh state ('Khalistan'). In October 1983 the state was brought under presidential rule. However, the violence continued, and followers of an extremist Sikh leader, Jarnail Singh Bhindranwale, established a terrorist stronghold inside the Golden Temple (the Sikh holy shrine) at Amritsar. The Government sent in troops to dislodge the terrorists and the assault resulted in the death of Bhindranwale and hundreds of his supporters, and serious damage to sacred buildings.

Rajiv Gandhi assumes power (1984–89)

In October 1984 Indira Gandhi was assassinated by militant Sikh members of her personal guard. Her son, Rajiv Gandhi, was immediately sworn in as Prime Minister, despite his lack of ministerial experience. The widespread communal violence that erupted throughout India, resulting in more than 2,000 deaths, was curbed by prompt government action. Congress (I) achieved a decisive victory in elections to the Lok Sabha in December. Including the results of the January 1985 polling, the party received 49.2% of the total votes and won 403 of the 513 contested seats.

In February 1986 there were mass demonstrations and strikes throughout India in protest against government-imposed increases in the prices of basic commodities. The opposition parties united against Rajiv Gandhi's policies, and Congress (I) suffered considerable reversals in the indirect elections to the upper house of the legislature, the Rajya Sabha (Council of States), in March. In April Rajiv Gandhi attempted to purge Congress (I) of critics calling themselves 'Indira Gandhi loyalists', and, in a major government reorganization, he appointed Sikhs to two senior positions. The Prime Minister survived an assassination attempt by three Sikhs in October.

In June 1986 Laldenga, the leader of the Mizo National Front (MNF), signed a peace agreement with Rajiv Gandhi, thus ending Mizoram's 25 years of rebellion. The accord granted Mizoram limited autonomy in the drafting of local laws, independent trade with neighbouring foreign countries and a general amnesty for all Mizo rebels. In February 1987 Mizoram and Arunachal Pradesh were officially admitted as the 23rd and 24th states of India, and in May the Union Territory of Goa became India's 25th state.

During 1987 Congress (I) experienced serious political setbacks. It sustained defeats in a number of state elections, and political tensions were intensified by an open dispute between the Prime Minister and the outgoing President, Giani Zail Singh. Public concern was aroused by various accusations of corruption and financial irregularities made against senior figures in the ruling party. Several ministers resigned from the Government, among them the Minister of Defence, Vishwanath Pratap (V. P.) Singh, who was also, with three other senior politicians, expelled from Congress (I) in July for 'anti-party activities'. V. P. Singh soon emerged as the leader of the Congress (I) dissidents, and in October formed a new political group, the Jan Morcha (People's Front), advocating radical social change.

In 1988 a more confrontational style was adopted by the central administration towards non-Congress (I) state governments, and presidential rule was imposed in states suffering political instability. The opposition forces attained a degree of unity when four major centrist parties, the Indian National Congress (S), the Jan Morcha, the Janata Party and the Lok Dal, and three major regional parties formed a coalition National Front (Rashtriya Morcha), to oppose Congress (I) at the next election. Three of the four centrist parties formed a new political grouping, the Janata Dal (People's Party), which was to work in collaboration with the National Front. V. P. Singh, who was widely regarded as Rajiv Gandhi's closest rival, was elected President of the Janata Dal.

The Janata Dal Government (1989–91)

At the general election to the Lok Sabha held in November 1989, Congress (I) lost its overall majority. Of the 525 contested seats, it won 193, the Janata Dal and its electoral allies in the National Front won 141 and three, respectively, and the right-wing Hindu nationalist Bharatiya Janata Party (BJP) won 88. In December, after the National Front had been promised the support of the communist parties and the BJP, V. P. Singh was sworn in as the new Prime Minister. He appointed Devi Lal, the populist Chief Minister of Haryana and President of Lok Dal (B), as Deputy Prime Minister, and a Kashmiri Muslim, Mufti Mohammed Sayeed, as Minister of Home Affairs. This latter appointment was widely seen as a gesture of reconciliation to the country's Muslims and as reaffirmation of the Government's secular stance. A few weeks later V. P. Singh's Government won a vote of confidence in the Lok Sabha, despite the abstention of all the Congress (I) members. In January 1990 the Government ordered the mass resignation of all the state governors; the President then appointed new ones. In February elections were held to 10 state assemblies, all formerly controlled by Congress (I). Congress (I) lost power in eight of the 10 assemblies and there was a notable increase in support for the BJP.

In July 1990 Devi Lal was dismissed from his post as Deputy Prime Minister, for nepotism and disloyalty and for making unsubstantiated accusations of corruption against ministerial colleagues. In August there were violent demonstrations in many northern Indian states against the Government's populist decision to implement the recommendations of the 10-year-old Mandal Commission and to raise the quota of government and public sector jobs reserved for deprived sections of the population. In October the Supreme Court directed the Government to halt temporarily the implementation of the quota scheme, in an attempt to curb the caste violence.

In October 1990 the BJP withdrew its support for the National Front, following the arrest of its President, Lal Krishna (L. K.) Advani, as he led a controversial procession of Hindu devotees to the holy town of Ayodhya, in Uttar Pradesh, to begin the construction of a Hindu temple on the site of a disused ancient mosque. V. P. Singh accused the BJP leader of deliberately inciting inter-communal hatred by exhorting Hindu extremists to join him in illegally tearing down the mosque. Paramilitary troops were sent to Ayodhya, and thousands of Hindu activists were arrested, in an attempt to prevent a Muslim–Hindu confrontation. However, following repeated clashes between police and crowds, Hindu extremists stormed and slightly damaged the mosque and laid siege to it for several days.

In November 1990 one of the Prime Minister's leading rivals in the Janata Dal, Chandra Shekhar (with the support of Devi Lal), formed his own dissident faction, known as the Janata Dal (Socialist) or Janata Dal (S) (which merged with the Janata Party in April 1991 to become the Samajwadi Party). The Lok Sabha convened for a special session, at which the Government overwhelmingly lost a vote of confidence. V. P. Singh immediately resigned, and the President invited Rajiv Gandhi, as leader of the party holding the largest number of seats in the Lok Sabha, to form a new government. Gandhi refused the offer, in favour of Chandra Shekhar. Although the strength of the Janata Dal (S) in the Lok Sabha comprised only about 60 deputies, Congress (I) had earlier offered it unconditional parliamentary support. On 10 November 1990 Chandra Shekhar was sworn in as Prime Minister. Devi Lal became Deputy Prime Minister and President of the Janata Dal (S). Shekhar won a vote of confidence in the Lok Sabha and a new Council of Ministers was appointed. Although Shekhar succeeded in initiating talks between the two sides in the Ayodhya dispute, violence between Hindus and Muslims increased throughout India in December.

In January 1991 the Prime Minister imposed direct rule in Tamil Nadu, claiming that this was necessitated by the increased activity of Sri Lankan Tamil militants in the state, which had led to the breakdown of law and order. In the resultant riots more than 1,000 arrests were made. In February five members of the Council of Ministers were forced to resign when they lost their seats in the Lok Sabha for violating India's anti-defection laws: they had left the Janata Dal to join the Janata Dal (S). The fragility of the parliamentary alliance between the Janata Dal (S) and Congress (I) became apparent in March, when the Congress (I) deputies boycotted Parliament, following the revelation that Rajiv Gandhi's house had been kept under police surveillance. In an unexpected counter-move, Chandra Shekhar resigned, but accepted the President's request that he remain as head of an interim Government until the holding of a fresh general election.

The return of Congress to power (1991–96)

As the general election, which was scheduled to take place over three days in May 1991, approached, it seemed likely that no party would win an outright majority and that the political stalemate would continue. On 21 May, however, after the first day's polling had taken place, Rajiv Gandhi was assassinated, allegedly by members of the Tamil separatist group, the Liberation Tigers of Tamil Eelam (LTTE), while campaigning in Tamil Nadu. Consequently, the remaining elections were postponed until June. The final result gave Congress (I) 227 of the 511 seats contested. The BJP, which almost doubled its share of the vote compared with its performance in the 1989 general election, won 119 seats, and the Janata Dal, the popularity of which had considerably declined, gained only 55 seats. P. V. Narasimha Rao, who had been elected as acting President of Congress (which had gradually shed its (I) suffix) following Rajiv Gandhi's assassination, assumed the premiership and appointed a new Council of Ministers. The new Government's main priority on assuming power was to attempt to solve the country's severe economic crisis, caused by an enormous foreign debt, high inflation, a large deficit on the current account of the balance of payments and an extreme shortage of foreign exchange reserves. The new Minister of Finance, Dr Manmohan Singh (an experienced economist and former Governor of the Reserve Bank of India), launched a far-reaching programme of economic liberalization and reform, including the dismantling of bureaucratic regulations and the encouragement of private and foreign investment. In September the Government announced the adoption of the recommendations of the Mandal Commission that 27% of government jobs and institutional places be reserved for certain lower castes, in addition to the 22.5% already reserved for those from a Dalit ('untouchable') background and tribal people. (In November 1992 the Supreme Court ruled that non-Hindus, such as Christians and Sikhs, who were socially disadvantaged were also entitled to job reservations.) Meanwhile, in July the Congress candidate, Dr Shankar Dayal Sharma, was elected, with no serious opposition, to the presidency.

In January 1992 the BJP increased communal tension between Hindus and Muslims by hoisting the national flag on Republic Day in Srinagar, the capital of Kashmir. Following the collapse of talks in November 1992 between the Vishwa Hindu Parishad (VHP—World Hindu Council) and the All India Babri Masjid Action Committee regarding the Ayodhya dispute—see The Janata Dal Government (1989–91)—the VHP and the BJP appealed for volunteers to begin the construction of a Hindu temple on the site of the existing mosque in early December. As thousands of Hindu militants assembled in Ayodhya, paramilitary troops were dispatched to the town. However, despite the armed presence, the temple/mosque complex was stormed by the Hindu volunteers, who proceeded to tear down the remains of the ancient mosque. This highly inflammatory action provoked widespread communal violence throughout India (Bombay, or Mumbai as it was later renamed, being one of the worst affected areas), which resulted in more than 1,200 deaths, and prompted world-wide condemnation, notably from the neighbouring Islamic states of Pakistan and Bangladesh, where violent anti-Hindu demonstrations were subsequently held. The central Government also strongly condemned the desecration and demolition of the holy building and pledged to rebuild it. The leaders of the BJP, including L. K. Advani and the party's President, Dr Murli Manohar Joshi, and the leaders of the VHP were arrested. The BJP Chief Minister of Uttar Pradesh resigned, the state legislature was dissolved and Uttar Pradesh was placed under presidential rule. The security forces took full control of Ayodhya, including the disputed complex, meeting with little resistance. The Government banned five communal organizations, including the VHP and two Muslim groups, on the grounds that they promoted disharmony among different religious communities. In mid-December the Government established a commission of inquiry into the events leading to the demolition of the mosque. In an attempt to prevent any further acts of Hindu militancy, the central Government dismissed the BJP administrations in Madhya Pradesh, Rajasthan and Himachal Pradesh and placed these three states under presidential rule. In late December the Government announced plans to acquire all the disputed areas in Ayodhya. The land would be made available to two trusts, which would be responsible for the construction of a new Hindu temple and a new mosque and for the planned development of the site.

However, in January 1993 there was a resurgence of Hindu–Muslim violence in India's commercial centre, Mumbai, and in Ahmedabad, necessitating the imposition of curfews and the dispatch of extra paramilitary troops to curb the serious unrest. Despite a government ban on communal rallies, thousands of Hindu militants attempted to converge on the centre of New Delhi to attend a mass rally organized by the BJP in February. In an effort to prevent the proposed rally taking place, thousands of BJP activists were arrested throughout India and the crowds that did gather in the capital were dispersed by the security forces. In March there were a number of bomb explosions in Mumbai, resulting in some 250 casualties.

In July 1993 Narasimha Rao narrowly survived a vote of no confidence, which was proposed in the Lok Sabha by virtually all the opposition parties. However, in November, in the state assembly elections in the four northern states where BJP state administrations had been dismissed by the central Government in December 1992, the BJP regained power in only one state, Rajasthan, while Congress obtained outright majorities in Himachal Pradesh and Madhya Pradesh. These results appeared to highlight a definite decline in the popularity of the BJP. In December 1993 Congress's political standing was strengthened when a small faction of the Janata Dal led by Ajit Singh merged with the ruling party, thus giving the latter a parliamentary majority.

During 1994 the extensive economic reforms continued to show positive results and Narasimha Rao's premiership appeared fairly secure, with the opposition suffering from fragmentation. Nevertheless, in late 1994 Congress suffered crushing defeats in elections to the state assemblies in its former strongholds of Andhra Pradesh and Karnataka; it was also defeated in state elections in Sikkim. The ruling party enjoyed mixed results in the state elections held in February–March 1995.

In January 1996 accusations of corruption came to the fore in Indian politics when the Central Bureau of Investigation (CBI) charged seven leading politicians, including L. K. Advani and Devi Lal, and sought the prosecution of three Union ministers (who subsequently resigned) for allegedly accepting large bribes from a Delhi-based industrialist, Surendra Jain. The sheer scale of the scandal (known as the Hawala—illegal money transfer—case), in terms of the sums involved and the number of people implicated, led to widespread public disillusionment with politicians in general. At the end of January another high-ranking political figure, the President of the Janata Dal, S. R. Bommai, was implicated in the scandal; Bommai subsequently resigned from his post. In February Congress's hopes of retaining power in the forthcoming general election appeared increasingly fragile when three more ministers resigned from the Council of Ministers after their names had been linked to the Hawala case.

Political instability under the United Front (1996–98)

The results of the general election, which was held in April–May 1996, gave no party or group an overall majority. The largest party in terms of seats was the BJP, which won 160 seats and, with the support of Shiv Sena (a right-wing Hindu nationalist party based in Mumbai) and other smaller allies, could count on an overall legislative strength of 194 seats. Congress secured 136 seats. The National Front (comprising the Janata Dal and its allies) and Left Front (representing the two major communist parties) together obtained 179 seats, with the remainder won by minor parties and independents. On 15 May the President asked the BJP under its new parliamentary leader, Atal Bihari Vajpayee, to form the new Government and to prove its majority support within two weeks. Given the antagonism felt towards the BJP by the majority of other political parties, the latter task proved impossible, and Vajpayee resigned on 28 May in anticipation of his Government's inevitable defeat in a parliamentary vote of confidence. In the mean time, the National and Left Fronts had merged to form an informal coalition known as the United Front (UF), which comprised a total of 13 parties, with the Janata Dal, the Samajwadi Party, the two communist parties and the regional Dravida Munnetra Kazhagam (DMK) and Telugu Desam as its major components. With Congress prepared to lend external support, the UF was able to form a Government at the end of May. A former Chief Minister of Karnataka, H. D. Deve Gowda, was selected to lead the UF and the new Government.

In September 1996 Narasimha Rao resigned from the leadership of Congress after he was ordered to stand trial on charges of cheating and criminal conspiracy, in a case that also involved Chandraswami, a controversial faith healer and spiritual adviser to numerous political leaders, including Narasimha Rao himself; the party presidency was assumed by the veteran politician Sitaram Kesri. Later that month separate charges of forgery and criminal conspiracy (dating back to the former Prime Minister's tenure of the external affairs ministry in the 1980s) were made against the beleaguered Narasimha Rao; he resigned as Congress's parliamentary leader in December 1996 and was replaced in the following month by Kesri.

In March 1997 Deve Gowda was faced with a serious political crisis when Congress threatened to withdraw its parliamentary support for the UF Government. On 11 April the Prime Minister resigned following the defeat of the UF administration in a vote of confidence. Inder Kumar Gujral, the Minister of External Affairs in the outgoing Government, was chosen by the UF to replace Deve Gowda as leader of the coalition; Gujral was sworn in as Prime Minister on 22 April. In May Sonia Gandhi, the widow of the former Prime Minister Rajiv Gandhi, joined Congress as a 'primary member', and in the following month Kesri was re-elected President of the party in Congress's first contested leadership poll since 1977. In July 1997 Kocheril Raman Narayanan was elected as India's new President; this appointment was particularly notable in that Narayanan was the first Indian President to originate from a Dalit background. In September the results of a five-year investigation into the destruction of the mosque at Ayodhya in 1992 led to charges of criminal conspiracy and incitement to riot being filed against senior BJP and religious leaders, including L. K. Advani and the leader of Shiv Sena, Balashaheb 'Bal' Thackeray.

Prime Minister Gujral was forced to resign on 28 November 1997 when Congress withdrew its support for the Government, following Gurjal's refusal to expel the Tamil Nadu-based DMK (which was alleged to be indirectly implicated in the 1991 assassination of Rajiv Gandhi) from the coalition. This constituted the third government collapse in less than two years. In early December President Narayanan dissolved the Lok Sabha following the inability of both Congress and the BJP to form an alternative coalition government. Gujral retained the premiership in an acting capacity pending the holding of a fresh general election in early 1998.

During December 1997 Congress suffered a series of internal splits and defections in at least six states. In an apparent attempt to halt the fragmentation of the ailing party, Sonia Gandhi agreed to campaign on behalf of Congress in the run-up to the general election. After a low-key start Sonia Gandhi gained in confidence and popularity during the campaign and attracted ever larger crowds; she steadfastly refused, however, to stand for actual parliamentary office. In January 1998 26 Tamil militants implicated in the murder of Rajiv Gandhi were sentenced to death by a court in Chennai (Madras). (In May 1999, however, the Supreme Court in New Delhi acquitted 19 defendants and commuted the sentences of three others.)

The BJP heads coalition governments (1998–2004)

In the general election held in February–March 1998, the BJP emerged as the largest party, with 182 of the 545 seats in the Lok Sabha, but failed to win an overall majority. Congress secured 142 seats, and shortly after the election Sonia Gandhi replaced Kesri as the party's President. On 19 March President Narayanan appointed BJP parliamentary leader Atal Bihari Vajpayee as Prime Minister and asked him to form a coalition government and to seek a legislative vote of confidence within the next 10 days. This he did (by 274 votes to 261) on 28 March, with the support of the All-India Anna Dravida Munnetra Kazhagam (AIADMK), the Telugu Desam (which eventually left the UF) and a number of other minor groups. None the less, it was apparent from the very outset that Vajpayee's 14-party coalition Government had a fragile hold on power and that the Prime Minister would be required to use both skill and tact to retain his position.

In May 1998 the Government shocked both India and the rest of the world by ordering the carrying out of a series of underground nuclear test explosions. This provocative action was initially greeted with massive popular enthusiasm, but Pakistan's retaliatory tests and a rapid realization of the negative international consequences (particularly the imposition of economic sanctions by the USA) soon led to a more measured domestic assessment.

In early April 1999 Prime Minister Vajpayee rejected demands by the AIADMK (whose controversial leader, Jayalalitha Jayaram, was faced with ongoing investigations into corruption allegations) to reinstate the Chief of Staff of the Navy and to dismiss the Minister of Defence, George Fernandes; the following day the two AIADMK ministers resigned from the Government. The President resolved the resultant political stalemate by forcing Vajpayee to seek a parliamentary vote of confidence. The Government narrowly lost the motion (by 270 votes to 269) and the President then invited Sonia Gandhi to assemble a new coalition. Following her failure to do so, the Lok Sabha was dissolved on 26 April and fresh elections were called. Vajpayee and his Government remained in power, in an acting capacity, pending the holding of the polls.

In May 1999 Congress's erstwhile parliamentary leader, Sharad Pawar, who had earlier publicly criticized Sonia Gandhi's foreign (Italian) origins, announced the formation of a breakaway party, entitled the Nationalist Congress Party (NCP); the NCP absorbed the Indian National Congress (S) in the following month. Meanwhile, the assertion of Indian military dominance following an outbreak of hostilities between Indian and Pakistani troops in the Kargil area of Kashmir in mid-1999 (see Foreign Affairs) had a positive effect on the nationalist BJP's standing and, in particular, on that of Vajpayee, who, as acting Prime Minister, was widely perceived to have responded with dignity, firmness and commendable restraint in the face of Pakistani provocation.

The BJP contested the general election, held in September–October 1999, at the head of a 24-member alliance, known as the National Democratic Alliance (NDA), which comprised numerous and diverse minor regional and national parties with little shared ideology. The NDA won an outright majority in the Lok Sabha, with 299 of the 545 seats, while Congress and its electoral allies obtained 134 seats. Although Sonia Gandhi won both of the seats that she herself contested in Karnataka and Uttar Pradesh, her lack of political experience, her weak grasp of Hindi and her foreign birth all contributed to Congress's worst electoral defeat since India's independence. Following his appointment as leader of the NDA, Vajpayee was sworn in as Prime Minister, for a third term, at the head of a large coalition Government.

In May 2000 the Government introduced three items of legislation in the Lok Sabha to establish the states of Chhattisgarh, Jharkhand and Uttaranchal, and amended versions were finally approved by both parliamentary Houses in August. The three new states came into being in November. In the previous month former Prime Minister P. V. Narasimha Rao was convicted of corruption and sentenced to three years' imprisonment. (In March 2002, however, his conviction was overturned by the High Court in New Delhi.)

The head of the Roman Catholic Church, Pope John Paul II, conducted a state visit to India, amid tight security, in November 1999. During the pontiff's meetings with senior Indian politicians, he broached the subject of a recent upsurge in anti-Christian persecution and called for greater religious tolerance. However, there was a resurgence in violent attacks against Christians in mid-2000. In July Indian Christians held protests across South India, demanding protection against the attacks. In October the leader of the fundamentalist Hindu group Rashtriya Swayamsevak Sangh (RSS—National Volunteer Organization) urged the Government to replace 'foreign' churches with a national church and to expel all Christian missionaries. The RSS campaign caused embarrassment for the Government, in particular Vajpayee, who requested the newly appointed BJP President, Bangaru Laxman, to declare that the views of the RSS did not represent those of the BJP.

In December 2000 communal tension between Hindus and Muslims increased, following Vajpayee's statement that the construction of the Ram Janmabhoomi, the Hindu temple, in Ayodhya was an expression of 'national sentiment that has yet to be realized' and part of the 'unfinished agenda' of his Government. Although the Prime Minister later attempted to downplay his remarks, declaring that he did not support the destruction of the Muslim Babri Masjid mosque, the opposition demanded an immediate apology and forced the abrupt adjournment of Parliament. In February 2001 an Indian high court ruled that around 40 people could be brought to trial in connection with the destruction of the mosque in Ayodhya, but that senior BJP leaders would not be among the defendants, owing to certain technicalities. In January plans for a negotiated settlement over the religious site in Ayodhya suffered a set-back when the All India Babri Masjid Action Committee ruled out negotiations with the VHP. A religious parliament, the Dharma Sansad, was convened by the VHP leaders at the Maha Kumbh Mela (the largest ever Hindu gathering) in January–February. The Dharma Sansad stated that all obstacles impeding the construction of the temple should be removed by the relevant organizations by March 2002. Meanwhile, following the occurrence in January 2001 of a devastating earthquake in Gujarat, which claimed the lives of more than 30,000 people and rendered more than 1m. people homeless, the central Government and the state government of Gujarat were criticized for their tardy reaction to the disaster—a delay that reportedly led to greater loss of life.

In 2001 a new series of political and financial scandals exposed continuing corruption at the highest levels of government and commerce, and further undermined popular confidence in the BJP. In March videotaped evidence emerged of senior Government and army officials accepting bribes from journalists posing as facilitators seeking to secure a bogus defence contract. Both Bangaru Laxman, President of the BJP, and Jaya Jaitly, leader of the Samata Party, resigned from their posts following the revelations, as did the Minister of Defence, George Fernandes. (Laxman was charged in connection with the case in mid-2006; in April 2012 he was convicted of bribery and sentenced to four years' imprisonment.) Elections to four state assemblies and one union territory assembly in May resulted in major gains for Congress and its electoral allies (in Kerala and Assam) at the expense of the parties of the NDA coalition. In July the chairman of India's largest investment fund, the Unit Trust of India (UTI), was arrested on charges of financial misappropriation. Once again, Vajpayee was alleged to have been loosely connected to the affair. In September the Prime Minister expanded and reorganized the Council of Ministers, and in October George Fernandes (now the leader of the Samata Party) was reappointed Minister of Defence.

In January 2002 Prime Minister Vajpayee resumed efforts to resolve the dispute over the religious site in Ayodhya. However, the All India Babri Masjid Action Committee continued to refuse to enter negotiations with the uncompromising VHP. As the mid-March deadline set by the Dharma Sansad to begin building the temple approached, hundreds of Hindu activists assembled in Ayodhya to take part in the illegal construction. Despite warnings by the Government that it would enforce the law, the VHP announced that the movement of building material to the site would begin on 15 March. In late February communal violence broke out in Gujarat after a train carrying members of the VHP returning from Ayodhya was attacked by a suspected group of Muslims in the town of Godhra. The attack, in which 60 Hindu activists were killed, provoked a cycle of communal violence throughout Gujarat that lasted for several weeks and resulted in the deaths of up to 2,000 people, the majority of whom were Muslims. The Indian army was drafted in to quell the riots. Opposition members demanded the resignation of the Minister of Home Affairs, L. K. Advani, and the Chief Minister of Gujarat, Narendra Modi, for failing to control the riots, amid claims that the Government had deliberately prevented the police from controlling the Hindu activists. In April the European Union's report on the situation in Gujarat, which corroborated a number of other reports published in the same month, concluded that the riots and killings had been, contrary to the official account, not in reaction to the attack on the train, but in fact an organized massacre of Muslims, and that the security forces had been under orders not to intervene. Modi eventually resigned and recommended the dissolution of the state assembly in July; he was requested to continue as leader of an interim administration until state elections were held in December. (The trial of 94 people charged with criminal conspiracy and murder in connection with the attack on the train, which commenced in June 2009, concluded in February 2011: 31 people were convicted, of whom 11 were sentenced to death and 20 were imprisoned for life, while the remaining 63 defendants were acquitted. In November a further 31 people were sentenced to life imprisonment, upon being convicted of having killed 33 Muslims during the riots that had erupted in Gujarat's Mehsana district in the aftermath of the train attack; 42 other defendants were acquitted owing to a lack of evidence. In April 2012 23 people were convicted of involvement in the killing of 23 Muslims in the village of Ode during the riots; of these, 18 received life sentences. In the same month a special investigation team, appointed by the Supreme Court in 2008, announced that it had found no evidence to support allegations that Modi and more than 60 other Gujarat state officials bore responsibility for the deaths of 69 mainly Muslim residents of the Gulbarg housing complex in Ahmedabad, including Ehsan Jafri, a Congress member of Parliament.) Meanwhile, in March 2002 security forces prevented Hindu nationalists from defying a court order and entering the disputed religious site in Ayodhya. In March 2003 the Allahabad High Court ordered the Archaeological Survey of India to carry out an excavation at the disputed site to ascertain whether an earlier Hindu temple existed beneath the Babri mosque. Meanwhile, the VHP continued its campaign to build a temple at the site.

In April 2002 the federal Minister of Coal and Mines, Ram Vilas Paswan, resigned and withdrew his Lok Jan Shakti party from the NDA in protest against the Government's handling of the situation in Gujarat. In June Minister of Home Affairs L. K. Advani was assigned the additional portfolio of Deputy Prime Minister, prompting speculation that he had been nominated as Vajpayee's eventual successor. In the following month the Government's candidate, Aavul Pakkiri Jainulabidin Abdul Kalam, a South Indian Muslim who was closely involved in the development of the country's missile and nuclear programme, won a convincing victory in the presidential election.

Elections to the Gujarat state assembly took place on 12 December 2002. The BJP won 51% of the vote, securing 126 of the 182 seats in the state legislature. Congress, criticized for selecting only five Muslim candidates and for attempting to attract the Hindu nationalist vote (albeit at a lesser level than the BJP), despite being a secular party, won only 51 seats. Interim Chief Minister Narendra Modi was confirmed in the post. Meanwhile, controversy over the Gujarat riots continued as communal tensions persisted. In September two armed assailants forced entry into a Hindu temple in Gujarat and shot dead 29 worshippers and injured 74 people; three commandos were also killed in the attack, which was believed to have been carried out in retaliation for the deaths of Gujarati Muslims in the riots earlier in the year. The gunmen were shot dead by security forces, ending a night-long siege of the temple. The Indian Government accused the Pakistani Government of orchestrating the attack, an allegation strongly rejected by the latter. In September 2003, amid allegations of witness intimidation and inadequate police investigations, the Supreme Court openly challenged the Government of Gujarat's competence and integrity to pursue any case against alleged rioters.

In the mean time, in January 2003 the Government established a Nuclear Command Authority to manage India's nuclear weapons, giving sole authority to launch a nuclear strike to the Prime Minister and his advisers. The Government also stated that it would forgo its 'no first use' policy on nuclear weapons if India were the target of a major attack using chemical or biological weapons.

In August 2003 the Archaeological Survey of India issued its report on the disputed site in Ayodhya to the Lucknow High Court. The report indicated that there was evidence of a massive temple-like structure existing from the 10th century, supporting claims that a Hindu temple once stood on the site. However, the report was challenged by a group of independent archaeologists and historians, claiming that the Survey had misused or falsified evidence for political reasons. Meanwhile, in May the CBI filed new charges against L. K. Advani and seven other leading politicians in connection with the destruction of the mosque in Ayodhya in December 1992. In September 2003 a special court exonerated Advani of any role in inciting crowds, provoking the demolition of the mosque and encouraging communal agitation, but sustained the charges against the seven other defendants.

In January 2004, encouraged by the BJP's victory in state elections in November–December 2003, and buoyed by a surging economy and an improvement in relations with Pakistan, Vajpayee announced that a general election would be held by the end of April, five months earlier than scheduled. In the mean time, in December 2003 the DMK withdrew its support for the ruling NDA, owing to the BJP's recent support for the AIADMK (the DMK's rival) and to differences over the 2001 Prevention of Terrorism Act (POTA—see Internal Unrest and the Threat of Terrorism). The regional Marumalarchi Dravida Munnetra Kazhagam (MDMK) also withdrew from the NDA; Pattali Makkal Katchi followed suit in January 2004, announcing that it was to form an alliance with the DMK and Congress. The AIADMK, meanwhile, announced that it would form an alliance with the BJP to contest the forthcoming general election. In the same month the NCP split into two factions; the faction led by Sharad Pawar entered into an alliance with Congress, while Purno Shangma's group agreed to support the NDA.

Congress returned to power (2004–)

At the general held in April–May 2004, Congress defeated the NDA, securing, together with its allies, a total of 222 seats in the 545-member Lok Sabha, compared with 186 for the NDA. Congress alone won 145 seats, while the BJP secured 138. Left Front parties also performed well at the polls, with the Communist Party of India—Marxist (CPI—M) winning 43 seats. Shortly after the election Sonia Gandhi, who had been unanimously endorsed as a prime-ministerial candidate by Congress, its allies and the Left Front (which had offered its support to a Congress-led Government), announced that she did not intend to stand for the office. However, she remained President of Congress, and was elected as Chairwoman of the newly formed Congress-led coalition, the United Progressive Alliance (UPA). The respected Sikh economist Dr Manmohan Singh, a former Minister of Finance and member of the Rajya Sabha, was subsequently appointed as India's first non-Hindu Prime Minister by President Kalam on Gandhi's recommendation, assuming office on 22 May. Following the election, former Prime Minister Vajpayee stood down as parliamentary leader of the BJP; he was replaced by L. K. Advani. Elections to four state legislative assemblies also took place in May. Congress secured a dramatic victory in Andhra Pradesh, comprehensively defeating the Telugu Desam, which had previously held a majority in the state.

At the first session of the newly elected Lok Sabha, held in June 2004, the BJP disrupted the meeting by protesting against the UPA's appointment of three ministers—all members of the Bihar-based Rashtriya Janata Dal—who had been charged variously with corruption and attempted murder, most notably the new Minister of Railways, Lalu Prasad Yadav, who continued to face corruption charges related to his tenure as Chief Minister of Bihar in 1997. (In April 2005 Yadav was formally charged with having been involved in embezzlement during his tenure as Chief Minister.) In the following month the Government dismissed the Governors of Goa, Gujarat, Haryana and Uttar Pradesh, owing to their alleged links to the RSS Hindu fundamentalist group. In September the Council of Ministers approved the repeal of the controversial POTA and stated its intention to amend the Unlawful Activities (Prevention) Act, 1967, by adding another ordinance in order to incorporate legislative provisions against terrorism. The Rajya Sabha gave its assent to the amended legislation in December.

Meanwhile, in October 2004 state legislative elections took place in Maharashtra, resulting in another victory for Congress. Following the BJP's removal from office in the state, the party's President, Venkaiah Naidu, resigned and L. K. Advani was elected to succeed him. Congress also secured a majority at legislative elections in the state of Arunachal Pradesh.

India was one of the countries worst affected by the devastating tsunami generated by a huge earthquake in the Indian Ocean on 26 December 2004. The states of Tamil Nadu, Kerala and Andhra Pradesh and the Union Territory of Pondicherry on the east coast were all affected, together with the Andaman and Nicobar Islands, which were severely damaged. The disaster resulted in the loss of around 16,000 lives and numerous homes and livelihoods. The Government was able to provide aid to those affected in India without requesting any international assistance, and also provided emergency relief to other countries affected by the disaster, notably Sri Lanka and the Maldives.

In June 2005 divisions emerged within the BJP, following comments made by its President, L. K. Advani, during a trip to Pakistan that were perceived to be in praise of Mohammed Ali Jinnah, the founder of Pakistan. Advani's comments attracted harsh criticism from certain elements of his party, which claimed that he had betrayed its *Hindutva* ('Hinduness') ideology. In July charges were brought against Advani (and seven others) in connection with the riots at Ayodhya in 1992, overturning the ruling in September 2003 that had exonerated him of blame. Advani's resignation from the leadership of the party in December 2005 was believed to be largely a result of pressure from the RSS, which had close links with the BJP. Rajnath Singh, a former Chief Minister of Uttar Pradesh and a federal minister in the Government of Atal Bihari Vajpayee, was subsequently appointed as Advani's successor.

In November 2005 the Minister of External Affairs, K. Natwar Singh, was forced to resign from his post, having been implicated as a beneficiary of corrupt practices following an investigation into the UN's 'oil-for-food' programme in Iraq; Prime Minister Manmohan Singh subsequently assumed the external affairs portfolio. In December a total of 11 legislators (10 from the Lok Sabha and one from the Rajya Sabha) were expelled from Parliament, having been filmed in the process of accepting bribes, apparently in exchange for asking certain questions in the chamber. Six of those expelled were BJP legislators. The expulsion was the largest to have taken place in India since independence.

In February 2006 the BJP assumed a position in government in a southern Indian state for the first time when, in coalition with the Janata Dal (Secular), it came to power in Karnataka. In March Sonia Gandhi resigned as a member of the Lok Sabha and as Chairperson of the National Advisory Council (NAC), following assertions made by her opponents regarding the alleged illegality of her holding both positions simultaneously (the latter was viewed as an 'office of profit' and therefore untenable for a member of parliament). A wider government debate about the issue of such offices ensued, and in May the Parliament (Prevention of Disqualification) Amendment Bill was presented for presidential approval. This piece of legislation categorized 56 posts as non-'office of profit' positions, including the chairmanship of the NAC. In the same month Sonia Gandhi was re-elected to the Lok Sabha in a by-election in Rae Bareilly. In April and May legislative elections were held in four states and in the Union Territory of Pondicherry (now Puducherry). Congress retained power (albeit in alliance with smaller parties) in Assam (Asom) and in Puducherry, but the Congress-led coalition government in Kerala was soundly defeated by a left-wing alliance of parties headed by the CPI—M. The coalition government headed by the CPI—M in West Bengal won a second term in office.

In August 2006 one of Congress's coalition partners, the regional party Telangana Rashtra Samithi (TRS), withdrew from the UPA, expressing its dissatisfaction with the Government's apparent lack of commitment to creating an independent Telangana state in Andhra Pradesh; the leader of the TRS, K. Chandrasekhar Rao, resigned from his post as Minister of Labour and Employment. In October Prime Minister Manmohan Singh instigated a ministerial reorganization, including the allocation of the external affairs portfolio to the erstwhile Minister of Defence, Pranab Mukherjee.

In early 2007 state legislative elections were held in Manipur, Punjab and Uttarakhand. Although the Congress coalition secured a victory in Manipur, the party was defeated by an alliance of the Shiromani Akali Dal and the BJP in the Punjab and by the BJP in Uttarakhand. In late 2007 the BJP defeated the incumbent Congress party at elections in Himachal Pradesh, and continued to dominate Gujarati politics with a victory in that state; the latter result in particular was held to bode well for a resurgence of the BJP on a national scale. In May 2008 the BJP expanded its power base, winning the state elections in the southern state of Karnataka. This represented a significant victory since, for the first time, the party headed a government of its own (i.e. not a coalition) in the south of the country. However, in late 2008 Congress unexpectedly defeated both the incumbent BJP government in Rajasthan, albeit without an absolute majority, and the ruling Mizo National Front in Mizoram, and retained power in the National Capital Territory of Delhi, while the BJP remained in government in the states of Chhattisgarh and Madhya Pradesh. Following elections in the troubled state of Jammu and Kashmir in November–December, Congress formed another coalition government with the moderate Jammu and Kashmir National Conference in January 2009.

Meanwhile, the federal Government suffered a set-back in February 2007, when the Samajwadi Party withdrew from the UPA central coalition; this was followed by the withdrawal of the MDMK in March and the Bahujan Samaj Party (BSP) in June 2008. In July 2007, upon the expiry of A. P. J. Abdul Kalam's presidential term, the UPA candidate and erstwhile Governor of Rajasthan, Pratibha Patil, was sworn in to succeed him. Although Patil's election as the first female President of India represented a milestone in the country's history, the UPA's choice of nominee was not without controversy, with critics objecting to a perceived politicization of the office and Patil's reportedly unexceptional record. However, despite a challenge from the incumbent Vice-President, Bhairon Singh Shekhawat, who presented himself as an independent candidate (while having the unofficial support of the NDA), Patil received the larger proportion of votes in Parliament, almost twice as many as Shekhawat. In September the rapid rise to political prominence of Rahul Gandhi, the son of Sonia Gandhi and Rajiv Gandhi, continued with his appointment as a General Secretary of Congress.

In July 2008 the Left Front bloc withdrew its parliamentary support from the UPA Government in protest against the ratification of a nuclear co-operation agreement with the USA (see Foreign Affairs). Prime Minister Singh swiftly called for the scheduling of a parliamentary vote of confidence, which took place later in the month amid an atmosphere of uncertainty and allegations of bribery. Ultimately the Government was able to ensure its survival, gaining the support of the Samajwadi Party and others to secure a total of 275 votes against the opposition's 256 votes.

Meanwhile, in 2007 the establishment of Special Economic Zones (SEZs) was a major point of controversy in a number of states, including West Bengal, where activists and local residents protested against the forcible seizure of land for industrial development. In March these protests escalated into violence in the Nandigram region of the state, resulting in some 14 fatalities. Land reform became the subject of protests in October, when thousands of rural demonstrators entered Delhi, having marched across the country; among their demands was the formation of a supervisory body. In response, the Government pledged to appoint a panel, including indigenous citizens and representatives of the landless, to assess what action should be taken in the area of land reform. Meanwhile, government plans to introduce larger quotas in higher education for the so-called 'Other Backward Classes' (a category that included numerous under privileged and low-caste groups) were suspended by the Supreme Court in March, owing to an apparent lack of recent data on the relevant populations. The proposed measures had prompted both praise and criticism, along with large-scale demonstrations. However, the Supreme Court lifted its suspension in April 2008. In May protests staged by Gujjar tribespeople in Rajasthan against their official caste status escalated into violence, resulting in the deaths of more than 40 people and causing disruption in other states; the dispute was resolved in June following a series of talks held between the state government and Gujjar tribal leaders. Violence against Christians increased dramatically in 2008, with attacks on churches in Orissa and Karnataka and the displacement of thousands of people.

In the general election held over five phases during April–May 2009, the UPA won a decisive victory, taking 262 seats in the 543-seat Lok Sabha, while the NDA achieved 159 seats and the Third Front (a newly formed electoral alliance comprising the Left Front and a number of major regional parties—including the AIADMK, the BSP and the Telugu Desam) garnered a disappointing 79 seats. Many observers interpreted Congress's comfortable victory as a sign of the Indian public's overriding wish for stability and continuity at a time of world-wide economic crisis. Manmohan Singh was reappointed Prime Minister (the first Indian premier since Jawaharlal Nehru to be returned to office following a full five-year term) and a new coalition Government, which was dominated by Congress members, was installed on 22 May. Following state legislative elections in Maharashtra, Haryana and Arunachal Pradesh in October, Congress retained power in all three states.

In December 2009 the Government announced that it intended to commence the process of granting statehood to the northern Telangana region of Andhra Pradesh. Although welcomed by some (including the TRS), the announcement prompted the immediate criticism of the Congress-led state legislature, which claimed not to have been consulted regarding the decision. As the federal Government subsequently appeared reluctant to further the process of creating the new state and stated that it needed more time to discuss the matter under the auspices of a special committee, there was a series of violent protests for and against the proposal in Andhra Pradesh during the course of 2010.

In March 2010 the Women's Reservation Bill—a groundbreaking piece of legislation that had first been proposed in 1996, and which stipulated that one-third of all seats in the federal Parliament and in the state legislatures be reserved for women—was approved by the Rajya Sabha; however, at early 2012 it had yet to be discussed by the Lok Sabha, amid arguments from those opposed to the draft legislation that its provisions would discriminate against those from disadvantaged castes and the Muslim minority. Meanwhile, an historic piece of legislation came into effect in April 2010, which made free and elementary education a fundamental right for all children in India between the ages of six and 14 years.

Angered by the Government's perceived failure adequately to address the issue of rising food prices, the opposition called a 12-hour general strike in April 2010, which severely affected transport services and business operations in a number of states, including West Bengal and Kerala. Another 12-hour strike, over rising fuel prices, was called by the opposition in July; the action followed the Government's decision in the previous month to eliminate state petrol subsidies in a bid to tackle the fiscal deficit. The announcement in August that parliamentarians' salaries were to be almost tripled, from Rs 16,000 a month to Rs 50,000, while their parliamentary expenses allowances were to be doubled, to Rs 40,000, further exacerbated the sense of public anger. Further protests against food price inflation and unemployment took place in February 2011, with at least 100,000 trade union members reported to have marched through the streets of New Delhi—the largest public demonstration to have been staged in the capital in recent years.

In September 2010 Allahabad High Court ruled that the disputed Ayodhya holy site should be divided equally between Hindus and Muslims within three months, and that the razed mosque should not be rebuilt, appearing to accept the findings of the August 2003 Archaeological Survey of India report—see The Bharatiya Janata Party heads coalition governments (1998–2004). The ruling was summarily rejected by both sides, with Hindu and Muslim groups both filing appeals; Hindu groups were seeking to claim the share of the disputed site allotted to Muslims, while Muslim leaders denounced the ruling as being unfairly biased in favour of Hindus. In May 2011 the Supreme Court suspended the High Court's verdict, ruling that it was 'very strange and surprising' since neither party had sought the partitioning of the site. Pending a final ruling, a date for which had not been set as of early 2012, both sides were to be prohibited from engaging in any construction activities at the disputed site.

Recent developments: mounting corruption scandals put pressure on the Congress-led Government

During 2010–11 the Government was beset by a number of corruption scandals that diminished public confidence in the Congress-led administration. In April 2010 allegations emerged that the Government had covertly monitored the mobile telephone calls of prominent political figures, including the Minister of Agriculture and of Food Processing Industries, Sharad Pawar, without the required authorization. Furore over the allegations, which the Government adamantly denied, precipitated the adjournment of both legislative chambers in late April. In December, following further revelations concerning the widespread use of telephone surveillance measures by government agencies, Prime Minister Singh defended the use of telephone tapping as being essential to the protection of national security and in the prevention of money-laundering and tax evasion; none the less, the premier ordered an inquiry into the use of telephone surveillance by law enforcement agencies.

The Government was criticized by the Supreme Court in October 2010 for alleged inaction in response to claims that in 2008 the Minister of Communications and Information Technology, Andimuthu Raja of the DMK, had sold mobile telephone licences at grossly undervalued rates to a select group of companies, instead of organizing appropriate commercial bidding processes. Critics claimed that the Prime Minister's reluctance to intervene was borne out of a fear of alienating the DMK, one of Congress's main coalition partners. A leaked report by the office of the Comptroller and Auditor General in November 2010 deemed Raja to be personally responsible for the scandal, which it alleged had cost the Government as much as US $37,000m. in lost revenue; the report accused the minister of manipulating the licence application process, employing a 'first come, first served' means of selection, which, it claimed, had favoured a specific group of companies. Raja resigned later in November, but denied the accusations against him, insisting that he had merely sought to introduce new companies to India's lucrative telecommunications industry and thereby to increase competition and reduce tariff prices. The Government resisted opposition demands for a full, joint inquiry into the allegations, underlining that impartial agencies—the CBI and the Supreme Court—were already investigating the case. Meanwhile, further adding to the growing sense of crisis, a report published by the US-based Global Financial Integrity in November 2010 claimed that India had lost some US $462,000m. in illegal capital outflows since acceding to independence in 1947, outflows that the report alleged had increased markedly since economic liberalization began in 1991.

Prime Minister Singh effected a minor cabinet reorganization in January 2011 in what was generally perceived as an attempt to promulgate an image of change and renewal amid rising public anger in response to the corruption scandals and food price inflation. The most prominent portfolios remained unchanged, however, and critics of the Government argued that the reorganization failed to remove ageing, ineffectual ministers or those most complicit in state corruption. During a rare press conference in February Singh denied rumours that he was planning to resign owing to the ongoing corruption allegations against his Government and reiterated his commitment to eradicating corruption at all levels of the political system. In a *volte-face* that was welcomed by the opposition, on the following day the Prime Minister announced that a joint parliamentary committee was to be launched to investigate the circumstances surrounding the telecommunications scandal. In a parliamentary address to both legislative chambers in mid-February President Patil pledged the Government's ongoing commitment to improving the quality of governance and enhancing public transparency, and underscored India's intention to ratify the UN Convention Against Corruption (UNCAC), following the signing, in November 2010, of the Group of Twenty (G20) Anti-Corruption Action Plan, which required all signatories to ratify and fully implement the UNCAC. In her address, Patil also announced that the Government had established a committee on electoral reforms to expedite efforts to build consensus on an acceptable reforms agenda.

In a further setback for the Government, in March 2011 the Supreme Court ruled that the appointment of P. J. Thomas as head of the Central Vigilance Commission, an organization charged with monitoring public corruption, had been inappropriate, in light of corruption allegations against him dating back to 1992, as well as his having worked in the Ministry of Communications and Information Technology during the telecommunications scandal. Thomas duly tendered his resignation, while refuting the charges against him as baseless. Further controversy was provoked following the online release, in mid-March 2011, by WikiLeaks—an organization publishing leaked private and classified content—of a US diplomatic cable in which it was alleged that an aide to a senior Congress leader had shown a US embassy official cash that was intended to buy votes in advance of a vote of no confidence in 2008 over a controversial nuclear agreement with the USA (see Foreign Affairs). The opposition had claimed at the time that the Government had bought votes, but an investigation subsequently found insufficient evidence to corroborate the allegations. Two men were arrested in connection with the allegations in July 2011; in the same month the Supreme Court dismissed the police investigation into the scandal as a 'shoddy probe'. In August four members of Parliament were charged with each having accepted bribes worth US $2.5m. in return for their support in the vote of no confidence, and in September a former aide of the BJP's L. K. Advani was arrested in connection with the scandal; all denied having committed any wrongdoing.

In April 2011 Raja—who had been arrested, together with two former subordinates at the Ministry of Communications and Information Technology, by the CBI in February—was formally indicted on a series of charges including conspiracy, forgery and abuse of official position; eight other individuals, including the two ministry officials arrested in February and senior executives from the telecommunications companies Reliance Telecoms, Swan Telecom and Unitech Wireless, were also indicted on similar charges. The trial of Raja and his co-accused commenced in November, with the proceedings expected to continue for many months; if convicted, the accused faced a maximum sentence of life imprisonment. Meanwhile, the scandal claimed its second ministerial scalp in July, when the Minister of Textiles, Dayanidhi Maran of the DMK, had tendered his resignation amid allegations of coercion in relation to the mis-selling of the mobile telephone licences during his tenure as Minister of Communications and Information Technology in 2004–08. The Government was further embarrassed in February 2012, when the Supreme Court ordered the cancellation of 122 licences awarded by Raja during 2008; the ruling was expected to cause considerable disruption to the telecommunications sector.

Meanwhile, an estimated 100,000 people gathered at an anti-corruption rally staged in New Delhi in February 2011 by Swami Ramdev (popularly known as Baba Ramdev), a well-known yoga guru who had become increasingly renowned for his political and social activism. In April a social campaigner, Kisan Baburao Hazare (popularly known as Anna Hazare), launched a hunger strike in protest against what he contended were endemic levels of public corruption. Hazare's protest action ended peacefully after the Government promised to address his concerns; however, an anti-corruption hunger strike initiated by Ramdev in June, which attracted thousands of his supporters, prompted the authorities to forcibly evict the activist from Delhi. Ramdev pledged to continue his hunger strike in his hometown of Haridwar, while Hazare staged a new hunger strike in protest against the treatment of Ramdev.

In response to growing public protests against corruption, the Government approved draft legislation in July 2011 that would provide for the establishment of an independent ombudsman—the Lokpal—which would have the authority to investigate and prosecute public officials suspected of corruption; however, to the consternation of the anti-corruption movement, neither serving Prime Ministers, senior members of the judiciary nor the conduct of legislators within Parliament would fall within its remit. Hazare, who denounced the draft legislation as 'unacceptable', pledged to stage a new hunger strike at a rally in Delhi in mid-August in support of more comprehensive anti-corruption reforms; however, he was arrested by the authorities shortly prior his planned protest, prompting hundreds of his supporters to stage a vigil outside the prison in which he was detained. The authorities stated that Hazare's arrest had been in response to his refusal to limit his fast to three days and to restrict the number of people attending the rally to no more than 5,000. Hazare was released after three days in custody, whereupon he commenced a 15-day hunger strike in the capital, again urging the Government to implement more stringent anti-graft legislation or to resign. In late August Hazare ended his hunger strike, on its 12th day, after members of Parliament, apparently taken aback by the outpouring of public support for the activist, with many thousands of people taking to the streets in cities across the country, approved a resolution in favour of tabling tougher anti-corruption legislation.

Meanwhile, the 2010 Commonwealth Games, which were hosted by New Delhi in October of that year (the largest international sporting event ever to be held in India), were plagued by poor planning and delays in the construction of stadia and other amenities, highlighting India's infrastructural deficiencies and wreaking not inconsequential damage to its international reputation. In June Minister of State for Youth Affairs and Sport Dr M. S. Gill had announced that the projected cost of staging the Games had increased from Rs 6,500m. to Rs 115,000m. A number of accidents at sites related to the event, as well as media reports of ill-prepared facilities, added to the sense of urgency and chaos in the immediate run-up to the Games. Amid claims by some foreign sports officials that the accommodation for competitors was 'uninhabitable', a number of high-profile athletes threatened to withdraw from the Games, while the shooting of two Taiwanese tourists by suspected militants near a mosque in New Delhi in September prompted concerns about the safety of athletes and spectators alike. In the event, the concerns proved largely unfounded and the Games passed off relatively smoothly. However, immediately after the event, Prime Minister Singh announced the creation of a special investigating committee that was to examine the allegations of corruption and mismanagement surrounding the Games. (In August the Government's anti-corruption agency had identified 16 projects related to the Games in which financial irregularities were suspected.) A number of senior officials, including the treasurer of the organizing committee for the Games, M. Jayachandran, were arrested in November amid corruption allegations pertaining to the supply of contracts for the tournament. In February 2011 the secretary-general and director-general of the organizing committee, Lalit Bhanot and V. K. Verma, respectively, were arrested in connection with the ongoing investigations, and in April the chairman of the organizing committee, Suresh Kalmadi, who had been dismissed as the President of the Indian Olympic Association in January, was also arrested. Kalmadi, Bhanot, Verma and Jayachandran were granted bail in January 2012, pending the filing of formal charges by the CBI.

Legislative elections were held in April–May 2011 in the states of Assam, Kerala, Tamil Nadu and West Bengal and in the Union Territory of Puducherry. Congress retained power in Assam, while the Congress-led United Democratic Front ousted the CPI—M in Kerala. In West Bengal the All India Trinamool Congress (AITC) comfortably defeated the CPI—M, thereby ending the longest-serving democratically elected Communist government in the world; the CPI—M had enjoyed an uninterrupted period of rule in the state since 1977. Mamata Banerjee, Chairwoman of the AITC, became West Bengal's inaugural female Chief Minister, heading a coalition government that also comprised Congress. In Tamil Nadu the AIADMK defeated the DMK to gain control of the state assembly. In Puducherry Congress was defeated by the All India N. R. Congress (a new regional party founded in February 2011 by N. Rangasamy, who had served as Chief Minister of the Union Territory in 2001–08); Rangasamy was returned to the territory's premiership.

A cabinet reorganization effected in July 2011 included the appointment of Dinesh Trivedi of the AITC as the new Minister of Railways, replacing Mamata Banerjee who had stood down in order to become Chief Minister of West Bengal, while Veerappa Moily of Congress was transferred from the law and justice portfolio to that of corporate affairs; Moily was replaced in his former post by Salman Khursheed of Congress, who retained concurrent responsibility for the minority affairs portfolio. The key portfolios of defence, external affairs, finance and home affairs were unaffected by the reorganization.

Rahul Gandhi's rise to political prominence continued in August 2011, when he was appointed to a four-member committee charged with assuming the leadership of Congress while Sonia Gandhi underwent medical treatment in the USA; the committee also comprised Congress General Secretary Janardan Dwivedi, Minister of Defence A. K. Antony and Sonia Gandhi's private secretary, Ahmed Patel. Moreover, following Sonia Gandhi's return to India, and to the helm of Congress, in September, Rahul Gandhi was named as one of five new appointees to Congress's Central Election Committee, which was responsible for finalizing the party's nominations for parliamentary and state assembly elections. With Singh's reputation increasingly tainted by the ongoing corruption allegations, many observers anticipated that the beleaguered premier would step aside at the legislative elections due in 2014, paving the way for Rahul Gandhi to assume the premiership should Congress be returned to a third term in office.

Corruption allegations against the Chief Minister of Karnataka, B. S. Yeddyurappa of the BJP, who in November 2010 had been accused of undervaluing state-owned land that had subsequently been purchased by his sons, intensified during 2011, and, following his indictment on charges pertaining to his alleged involvement in illegal mining operations in Karnataka, Yeddyurappa finally tendered his resignation, at the request of his party, in July. Yeddyurappa adamantly denied any connection with the fraudulent operations, which were estimated to have cost the treasury in excess of US $3,000m. during 2006–10. In September 2011 Shivaraj Patil, the Karnataka ombudsman and former Supreme Court judge, was forced to resign amid allegations that he had breached land ownership laws.

In mid-September 2011 six people were killed when police in Tamil Nadu opened fire on a group of Dalit protesters in the town of Paramakudi who were demanding the release of the Tamizhaga Makkal Munnetra Kazhagam (TMMK—Tamil People's Progressive Federation) leader, John Pandian, who had been arrested earlier in the month en route to Paramakudi to commemorate the anniversary of the death of another Dalit leader, Immanuel Sekaran. State authorities insisted that the police had acted in self-defence after coming under attack by the protesters. Later in the month 17 police and government officials were convicted of rape while 252 others were convicted of 'atrocities against Dalits', in connection with an incident in the Tamil Nadu village of Vachathi in June 1992, when officials had raided the village following reports that villagers were involved in sandalwood-smuggling; more than 100 Dalits were reported to have been abused, 18 women were raped, and homes and livestock destroyed. Twelve of those convicted were imprisoned for 10 years, five received seven-year gaol terms, while the remainder were each sentenced to between two and five years' imprisonment.

Meanwhile, representatives from Telangana boycotted the Andhra Pradesh assembly in February 2011 in protest at the state government's failure to introduce a bill on the formation of the proposed new state of Telangna—see Congress returned to power (2004–). Amid mounting protests, the majority of the elected representatives from Telangana and 12 Telangana members of the national Parliament tendered their resignations in July, demanding that the new state be created as a matter of urgency; the fact that the resignations cut across party lines served further to augment the increasing pressure on the state and federal governments to address the issue. In the same month pro-Telangana activists staged a 48-hour strike in support of their demands for the new state, bringing Andhra Pradesh's capital city, Hyderabad, and other towns and cities in the state to a virtual standstill. In November the Speaker of the Lok Sobha rejected the resignations submitted by the 12 Telangana members of Parliament in July on the stated grounds that their resignation letters had not followed the correct format prescribed by parliamentary rules.

A session of the Lok Sabha in November 2011 was disrupted by angry protests following the approval by the Uttar Pradesh state assembly of a resolution, introduced by Chief Minister Kumari Mayawati, in support of the division of Uttar Pradesh into four smaller states—Avadh Pradesh, Bundelkhand, Paschim Pradesh and Purvanchai. Disagreements over the proposal, which was widely interpreted as an attempt by the ruling BSP to bolster its popular support in advance of state legislative elections due to be held in February–March 2012, led to the temporary adjournment of both the Lok Sabha and the Rajya Sabha, and were expected to compound the heated atmosphere of parliamentary sessions during 2012, with tensions already running high over a number of controversial bills, including, notably, draft anti-corruption legislation (see above) and proposals to allow foreign investment in the retail sector. Meanwhile, with effect from 1 November 2011, the state of Orissa was officially redesignated as Odisha, with the Oriya language henceforth to be known as Odia; the formal renaming of the state followed approval of the proposal by the state assembly in November 2009, by the Lok Sabha in November 2010 and by the Rajya Sabha in March 2011.

Elections to five state assemblies were held during January–March 2012. With a general election scheduled for mid-2014, the state polls were expected to provide an indication of the political prospects for Congress and its main rivals. Despite running a lengthy and intensive election campaign, which was led by Rahul Gandhi, Congress achieved disappointing results in Uttar Pradesh, India's most populous state. The left-wing Samajwadi Party registered a convincing victory, securing an overall majority of 224 seats in the 404-seat Uttar Pradesh assembly, ousting Mayawati's BSP, which saw its representation fall from 206 seats in 2007 to 80 in 2012; the BJP won 47 seats, while Congress recorded only a marginal increase, to 28 seats (from 22 in the previous election), and remained a minor party in the state. Akhilesh Yadav of the Samajwadi Party was sworn in as Chief Minister on 15 March, becoming, at 38 years of age, the state's youngest ever Chief Minister. In Goa, the BJP replaced Congress in power, securing 21 out of 40 seats; Congress's representation fell to 9 seats, from 16 at the previous election. Manohar Parrikar of the BJP was sworn in as Chief Minister on 9 March. Congress emerged as the largest party in Uttarakhand, securing 32 seats in the 70-seat assembly, one seat more than the incumbent BJP party. The support of several independent candidates enabled Congress to form a state administration, led by Vijay Bahuguna. Congress increased its representation in Manipur, securing an overall majority (42 out of 60 seats) and retaining power for a third consecutive term. In the Punjab, the ruling Shiromani Akali Dal-BJP coalition retained control of the state assembly. Congress also failed to register any significant gains in municipal elections in the capital, Delhi, in April; the BJP secured control of 138 of the city's 272 wards, while Congress won 77 wards.

Meanwhile, in mid-March 2012, following objections from within his own party to the announcement of passenger fare increases, Dinesh Trivedi of the AITC resigned as federal Minister of Railways. Mukul Roy, also of the AITC, was appointed as his replacement, and it was expected that the proposed fare rises would be lessened. The incident provided a further illustration of the ability of junior partners in the UPA coalition to wield a disproportionate influence on government policy.

Internal Unrest and the Threat of Terrorism

In the aftermath of the devastating terrorist attacks on the US mainland on 11 September 2001, for which the USA held the militant Islamist al-Qa'ida organization responsible, the Indian Government sought to emphasize its own uncompromising response to the activities of illegal organizations. In late September national security forces clashed with members of the outlawed Students' Islamic Movement of India (SIMI—which was alleged to be linked to both al-Qa'ida and the militant Hizbul Mujahideen, see Foreign Affairs) in Lucknow, Uttar Pradesh. Three SIMI supporters were killed during the altercation, following which some 240 SIMI activists were arrested across the country. In October the Government promulgated the Prevention of Terrorism Act 2001 (POTA), which broadened the definitions of terrorist activity and the preventative and retaliatory powers of the Government, and proscribed indefinitely 23 organizations engaged in principally separatist activities. A series of audacious terrorist attacks perpetrated by Kashmiri separatists severely tested the resolve of the Government in late 2001 and early 2002 (see Foreign Affairs), resulting in an unexpected consolidation of popular and political support for the ruling coalition.

A number of bomb explosions occurred in Mumbai in December 2002–January 2003, killing at least two people and injuring almost 90. Another bomb explosion was carried out in the city in March, killing at least 12 people. No group claimed responsibility for any of the attacks. In August two car-bombs exploded in Mumbai, killing 52 people and injuring 150. In June 2004 five people were charged under the POTA in connection with the bombings.

During 2005–08 there was a series of terrorist attacks against civilian targets in various locations across India. In October 2005 a number of bomb attacks in the national capital, New Delhi, resulted in the deaths of more than 60 people. In November police announced that they had arrested a man suspected of having financed and planned the bombings; he was believed to be a member of the Pakistan-based militant group Lashkar-e-Taiba, which had previously denied responsibility for the attacks. In March 2006 a number of bombs exploded at a Hindu temple and a railway station in the holy city of Varanasi in Uttar Pradesh, leading to the deaths of at least 14 people. Several suspects, allegedly linked to the Bangladesh-based Islamist militant group Harakat-ul-Jihad-i-Islami, were subsequently arrested. On 11 July about 180 people were killed and hundreds more injured in a series of bomb blasts on the Mumbai train network. In October 28 people were charged with involvement in the bombings, including 15 suspects who had not yet been apprehended. Among those charged *in absentia* was Azam Cheema, who was reported to be a member of Lashkar-e-Taiba (although in July Lashkar-e-Taiba had denied responsibility for the attacks). Another series of bomb explosions, at a Muslim cemetery in Malegaon, Maharashtra, killed at least 37 people in September. By the end of November several suspects, with alleged links to the banned SIMI, had been arrested. In August 2007 two bomb explosions in the southern city of Hyderabad killed some 42 people. Six bomb explosions targeting three courts in Uttar Pradesh, at Varanasi, Lucknow and Faizabad, claimed the lives of 18 people and injured more than 80 others in November; a previously little known group, the Indian Mujahideen (which was believed to comprise junior members of SIMI), claimed responsibility for the attacks.

Further attacks were carried out in May 2008 in Jaipur, Rajasthan, resulting in the deaths of more than 80 people. In July bombings in Bangalore, Karnataka, which caused two fatalities, were followed by a series of explosions in the Gujarati city of Ahmedabad, killing some 50 people. In September, a month after Prime Minister Singh had identified 'terrorism, extremism, communalism and fundamentalism' as the 'major challenges to the unity and integrity' of the country, bomb attacks resulted in the deaths of more than 20 people in Delhi. The Indian Mujahideen claimed responsibility for each of the four series of attacks.

In November 2008 some 166 people were killed in co-ordinated offensives carried out by 10 gunmen against public targets in Mumbai, including two hotels, a hospital, a railway station and a Jewish centre. Following the attacks and subsequent siege, which lasted for several days in some locations, and in which all but one of the gunmen were killed, the Minister of Home Affairs, Shivraj V. Patil, resigned on 30 November; he was replaced by the incumbent Minister of Finance, P. Chidambaram. As public criticism of the Government's handling of the attacks increased, in December the Chief Minister of Maharashtra, Vilasrao Deshmukh, was also forced to step down. In the same month the establishment of the National Investigation Agency was announced as part of a government campaign for greater internal security; anti-terrorism legislation was also expected to be reviewed.

The trial of the sole surviving gunman of the 2008 Mumbai attacks, Pakistani national Mohammed Ajmal Amir Kasab, began in April 2009, with the defendant initially pleading not guilty. While giving testimony in June, Kasab unexpectedly changed his plea to guilty, declared that he deserved to be hanged, and gave a detailed account of his alleged recruitment and training by Lashkar-e-Taiba; however, he subsequently retracted this confession, which he claimed he had fabricated following sustained torture at the hands of the Indian police. Kasab was convicted in May 2010 on five charges, including murder, terrorist activity and waging war against the nation, and he was sentenced to the death penalty a few days later. Following an unsuccessful appeal, the death sentence was upheld by Mumbai High Court in February 2011; however, Kasab filed an appeal against the ruling at the Supreme Court in July, claiming that he had not received a fair trial and had been denied access to a legal counsel. While acknowledging his guilt on the counts of murder and terrorist activity, Kasab claimed that he had been 'brainwashed' into participating in the attacks, insisted that he was not guilty of waging war against the nation, and appealed for the death penalty to be commuted to life imprisonment. The appeal opened in January 2012.

From December 2008 the authorities in Pakistan arrested several militants suspected of involvement in planning the Mumbai attacks; these included Zaki-ur-Rehman Lakhvi, a senior leader of Lashkar-e-Taiba who was alleged to have orchestrated the 2008 attacks. However, Pakistan resisted Indian demands for the suspects to be extradited to India. Seven suspects, including Lakhvi, were charged in connection with the attacks under Pakistani anti-terrorism laws in November 2009; all seven denied the charges against them. Nine others were charged *in absentia*. In December the Indian Government announced plans to overhaul and strengthen its security services by recruiting 400,000 more police officers, establishing a national intelligence database and creating a national counter-terrorism centre.

Three co-ordinated bomb explosions in busy districts of Mumbai in July 2011 claimed the lives of 26 people and injured around 130 others. No individuals or groups claimed responsibility for the attacks. In August Minister of Home Affairs P. Chidambaram disclosed that ongoing investigations into the bombings appeared to indicate the involvement of an 'Indian module', with some officials attributing the blame for the attacks to the Indian Mujahideen. However, some contended that the attacks had been orchestrated by Lashkar-e-Taiba or other elements seeking to derail the Indian-Pakistani peace process, while others argued that the attacks were linked to the Indian underworld, following the fatal shooting in Mumbai in mid-June by four men on motorcycles of prominent journalist Jyotirmoy Dey, who had written a number of damning articles about the activities of India's 'oil mafia'—criminal gangs that pilfered oil in transit, before diluting it and selling it on the black market.

In early September 2011, while Prime Minister Singh was on a state visit to Bangladesh (see Foreign Affairs), a bomb explosion outside the High Court in Delhi claimed the lives of 12 people and injured 76 others. (The Court had previously been the target of a bomb attack in May, although on that occasion there were not reported to have been any casualties.) The Indian Mujahideen and Harakat-ul-Jihad-e-al-Islami (HUJI—the Movement for Islamic Jihad, which was founded in 1984 and believed to have links to al-Qa'ida) both claimed responsibility for the September attack; HUJI's senior leader, Ilyas Kashmiri, was reported to have been killed by a US unmanned drone strike in north-western Pakistan in June. Five men were arrested in connection with the bombing on the day after the attack. Responding to the latest terrorist attack, Singh acknowledged that there were 'weaknesses' in India's security system and that the authorities needed comprehensively to address these. However, Nitin Gadkari, President of the BJP, accused the Singh administration of having failed to adopt a sufficiently firm stance both in its efforts to combat home-grown terrorism and in negotiations with Pakistan, and argued that the Government's approach was tantamount to 'appeasement of terrorism'. Later in September the Indian Mujahideen became the first Indian-based group to be formally designated as a foreign terrorist organization by the US Department of State.

The car of an Israeli diplomat's wife was the target of a bomb attack outside the Israeli embassy in New Delhi in mid-February 2012, on the same day as a the car of a driver for the Israeli embassy in Tbilisi, Georgia, was targeted in another bomb explosion. (The intended target of a bomb attack in Bangkok, Thailand, on the following day also appeared to have been an Israeli diplomat.) The series of attacks, which was reported to have injured at least nine people, including four in New Delhi, was attributed by the Israeli authorities to 'Iran and its protégé, Hezbollah'; Iran adamantly denied any involvement. The Indian Government, which enjoyed amicable relations with both Israel and Iran, refused to comment on the Israeli accusations, with Minister of Home Affairs Chidambaram stating only that the attack appeared to have been carried out by well-trained assailants.

Gurkha Separatist Movement

Regional issues continue to play an important role in Indian political affairs. In 1986 the Gurkhas (of Nepalese stock) in West Bengal launched a campaign for a separate autonomous homeland in the Darjiling (Darjeeling) region and the recognition of Nepali as an official language. The violent separatist campaign, led by the Gurkha National Liberation Front (GNLF), was prompted by the eviction of about 10,000 Nepalis from the state of Meghalaya, where the native residents feared that they were becoming outnumbered by immigrants. When violent disturbances and a general strike were organized by the GNLF in June 1987, the central Government agreed to hold tripartite talks with the GNLF's leader, Subhas Ghising, and the Chief Minister of West Bengal. The Prime Minister rejected the GNLF's demand for an autonomous Gurkha state, but Ghising agreed to the establishment of a semi-autonomous Darjiling Gorkha Hill Council (DGHC), which was inaugurated in August 1988. Following elections to the DGHC in November, the GNLF won 26 of the 28 elective seats (the 14 remaining members of the Council were to be nominated) and Ghising was elected Chairman of the Council. However, the GNLF continued to demand the establishment of a fully autonomous Gurkha state. In 1992 a constitutional amendment providing for the recognition of Nepali as an official language was adopted.

In February 2008 a splinter group of the GNLF, the Gorkha Janmukti Morcha (GJM), blockaded entry routes into Darjiling to protest against a new autonomy agreement drawn up between the DGHC and the state and federal authorities. Following the resignation and enforced exile from the region of Ghising in March, the GJM rapidly became the dominant force representing Gurkha separatism. A series of GJM-orchestrated strikes and protests severely disrupted the key tourism and tea industries in the area. In August 2009 the central Government initiated a series of tripartite talks involving the GJM and the West Bengal state authorities, following which the Government agreed to repeal the legislation creating the DGHC, while the GJM pledged to remain 'peaceful and democratic'. Following the West Bengal legislative elections in April–May 2011, as a result of which Mamata Banerjee of the AITC became Chief Minister (see Domestic Political Affairs), talks regarding the establishment of an interim council to replace the DGHC were held between the state government and the GJM. (Banerjee had pledged during her electoral campaign to conclude an agreement regarding the formation of a new administrative authority to replace the DGHC within three months of assuming office.) An agreement was signed between the two sides in July providing for the creation of a semi-autonomous Gorkhaland Territorial Administration (GTA), which was to comprise Darjiling, Kalimpong and Kurseong and which was to have various administrative, executive and financial powers, as well as the authority to regulate its tea plantations; legislative and tax levying responsibilities would remain vested in the central Government. The agreement was ratified by the West Bengal state assembly in September. In October the GJM proposed the enlargement of the GTA to include a number of subdivisions in Terai and Dooars inhabited primarily by Gurkhas or Adivasis (also of Nepalese stock); the GJM thus also mooted the amendment of the GTA's official designation to the Gorkhaland and Adivasi Territorial Administration. Meanwhile, in May 2011, violence erupted in West Bengal in the aftermath of the AITC's electoral success, resulting in the deaths of at least eight people (predominantly communist activists); armed mobs raided the local offices of the CPI—M, while police officers were reported to have confiscated hundreds of weapons and explosive devices in various southern districts in the state.

Unrest in Assam

In December 1985 an election for the state assembly in Assam was won by the Asom Gana Parishad (AGP—Assam People's Council), a newly formed regional party. This followed the signing, in August, of an agreement between the central Government and two groups of Hindu activists, concluded after five years of sectarian violence, which limited the voting rights of immigrants (mainly Bangladeshis) to Assam. When the accord was announced, Bangladesh stated that it would not take back Bengali immigrants from Assam and denied that it had allowed illegal refugees to cross its borders into Assam. Another disaffected Indian tribal group, the Bodos of Assam, demanded a separate state of Bodoland within India. In February 1989 the Bodos, under the leadership of the All Bodo Students' Union (ABSU), intensified their separatist campaign by organizing strikes, bombings and violent demonstrations. The central Government dispatched armed forces to the state. In August the ABSU held peace talks with the state government and central government officials, agreeing to suspend its violent activities, while the Assam government agreed to suspend emergency security measures. The situation became more complicated in 1989, when a militant Maoist group, the United Liberation Front of Assam (ULFA), re-emerged. The ULFA demanded the outright secession of the whole of Assam from India. In 1990 the ULFA claimed responsibility for about 90 assassinations, abductions and bombings. In November, when the violence began to disrupt the state's tea industry, the central Government placed Assam under direct rule, dispatched troops to the state and outlawed the ULFA. In the 1991 state elections the AGP was defeated, and Congress (I) took power. In September, following the breakdown of prolonged talks with the ULFA, the Government launched a new offensive against the separatist guerrillas and declared the entire state a disturbed area. Meanwhile, following the suspension of violence by the ABSU, the Bodo Security Force assumed the leading role in the violent campaign for a separate state of Bodoland. The Bodo Security Force was outlawed by the central Government in November 1992. At a tripartite meeting attended by the Minister of State for Home Affairs, the Chief Minister of Assam and the President of the ABSU in Guwahati in February 1993, a memorandum was signed providing for the establishment of a 40-member Bodoland Autonomous Council, which would be responsible for the socio-economic and cultural affairs of the Bodo people. However, attacks leading to substantial loss of life were made by Bodo and ULFA activists in the second half of the 1990s, both on the security forces and on non-tribal groups in the area. In March 2000 the Government and the Bodo Liberation Tigers (BLT—a group that had waged a violent campaign for a separate state for the Bodo people since 1996) agreed to a cease-fire.

In February 2002 it was reported that the Assam state assembly had passed a resolution granting a degree of autonomy to the Bodo people through the creation of a territorial council for the Bodos of four western districts of the state. One year later, the Union Government, state government and BLT signed a pact formally agreeing upon the introduction of a Bodoland Territorial Council. The Council was established in December 2003 and the Bodo militants surrendered their weapons to mark the formal disbanding of the BLT. However, the ULFA continued its campaign of violence and inter-tribal clashes also occurred in the state. In August 2004 the ULFA was believed to have been responsible for an explosion at a parade held in the town of Dhemaji to commemorate Independence Day, which killed 16 people, many of whom were children. In October a series of violent incidents in Assam and neighbouring Nagaland was attributed to the ULFA and the National Democratic Front of Bodoland (NDFB), one of the militant groups operating in the region. In May 2005 the NDFB signed a cease-fire agreement with both the government of Assam and the Union Government, with all parties pledging to suspend hostile operations for one year. In September the ULFA agreed to conduct peace negotiations with the Union Government, on the condition that the army halted the counter-insurgency operation that it was conducting in the state. Talks between the two sides were held for the first time in February 2006; by September, however, negotiations had collapsed, and the following months witnessed an escalation of violence, with the Government dispatching further troops to the region to deal with the insurgents. There was also an increase in attacks on migrant workers in Assam, allegedly perpetrated by the ULFA, together with the new strategy of targeting Congress officials, the most notable example of which was the murder of a senior regional Congress leader in the eastern district of Golaghat in February 2007, which was blamed on the separatist group. In September a senior military leader of the ULFA, Prabal Neog, was reportedly arrested by the Indian security forces. Co-ordinated bomb attacks, most of them in Guwahati, resulted in more than 80 fatalities in October 2008. In the same month violence between Bodos and settlers caused dozens of deaths in the state. In early 2009 it was reported that the ULFA had split into two rival factions. In November several senior ULFA leaders were arrested by the Bangladeshi Government authorities and transferred into Indian custody. A marked reduction in militant activity was evident from 2010, and, to facilitate peace talks with the central Government, the ULFA announced a unilateral cease-fire in July 2011.

Nagaland

Elsewhere in north-eastern India, violence—separatist, inter-tribal (particularly against ethnic Bengali settlers) and anti-Government—continued in Nagaland, Tripura, Bihar, Mizoram and Manipur during the 2000s, leading to an alarming increase in the number of civilian deaths caused by unrest. In 1997 the central Government entered a cease-fire agreement with the National Socialist Council of Nagaland—Issak Muivah (NSCN—IM), a rebel organization that advocated the creation of a 'greater Nagaland', which, in addition to the state of Nagaland, would include districts in Assam, Manipur and Arunachal Pradesh. In June 2001 the Government extended the scope of the existing cease-fire in Nagaland to include the National Socialist Council of Nagaland (Khaplang)—NSCN (K), along with all underground organizations in north-eastern India, and offered to involve the NSCN (K) and the NSCN (Issak-Muivah—IM) in peace negotiations. The decision to extend the cease-fire to Naga groups in the neighbouring states of Assam, Manipur and Arunachal Pradesh gave rise to fears of the creation of a 'greater Nagaland' as part of an eventual settlement at the expense of the other states. Strikes and violent protests took place in Manipur. In July, in an effort to curb the violence, the national Government agreed to limit the cease-fire arrangement to the state of Nagaland. In November 2002 the central Government lifted its ban on the NSCN—IM and agreed to hold negotiations on the political status of Nagaland. In February 2007, at India's request, security forces in Myanmar took action against NSCN (K) bases inside Myanma territory. During April–June 2010 there was renewed conflict between Naga and non-Naga groups in Manipur, with a Naga student group linked to the NSCN (IM) conducting a blockade of all roads leading into Manipur.

Naxalite Insurgency

The Naxalites are a myriad group of Maoist insurgents who emerged in the late 1960s in West Bengal. Since then the rebels, who claim to be fighting for the rights of the rural poor, have spread into less developed areas of central and eastern India (popularly known as the 'Red Corridor'). According to India's intelligence agency, the Research and Analysis Wing, the total number of regular Naxalite cadres is estimated at around 50,000 and armed cadres at about 20,000.

In mid-2004 the state government of Andhra Pradesh agreed a cease-fire with the People's War Group, a faction of the Communist Party of India (Marxist-Leninist), which had been waging a sporadic violent campaign in the state since 1980. The Naxalite rebels demanded the creation of a communist state comprising tribal areas in Andhra Pradesh, Maharashtra, Orissa, Bihar and Chhattisgarh. In September 2004 the People's War Group merged with another militant separatist group, the Maoist Communist Centre, to become the Communist Party of India (Maoist)—CPI (Maoist). Peace negotiations commenced between the rebels and the Andhra Pradesh state authorities in October. However, negotiations collapsed in early 2005, leading to escalating violence in the region. In August the state government imposed a fresh ban on the CPI (Maoist), after rebels murdered nine people in the town of Narayanpet.

In September 2005 an Inter-State Joint Task Force was established following an agreement among the chief ministers of 13 states affected by ongoing Naxalite insurgencies. The Force was intended to co-ordinate operations against guerrillas across state borders, and was to have the assistance of the Union Government. In the same month the government of Chhattisgarh outlawed all Naxalite organizations, following a recent increase in insurgent activity in the state. In April 2006 Prime Minister Manmohan Singh stated that the Naxalite insurgency posed the 'single biggest internal security challenge' to India, and called for further co-operation between the main affected states. In 2007 insurgents were allegedly involved in the road blockades and attacks on infrastructure staged in protest against the establishment of SEZs in states such as West Bengal (see Domestic Political Affairs). During 2006–07 Naxalite attacks and clashes between rebels and security forces in Chhattisgarh reportedly resulted in several hundred deaths, including many civilians. In 2008 it was reported that Naxalites were operating in as many as 16 states and that the CPI (Maoist) remained active in at least seven states. In February 2009, in the run-up to the general election, the Union Government announced plans to launch simultaneous, co-ordinated counter-operations in all of the states that were worst affected by Naxalite violence—Chhattisgarh, Orissa, Andhra Pradesh, Maharashtra, Jharkhand, Bihar, Uttar Pradesh and West Bengal—in an attempt to block all possible escape routes of the insurgents. In June the Government banned the CPI (Maoist) as a terrorist organization. Despite this concerted action, the number of deaths resulting from Naxalite violence increased from 794 in 2008 to 1,134 in 2009. By early 2010 it was estimated that Naxalite insurgency unrest had spread to at least 20 of India's 28 states. In April more than 70 paramilitary troops were killed by Naxalite rebels in Chhattisgarh.

Following a landmine detonation in Chhattisgarh in May 2010, which claimed the lives of more than 30 people (the majority of whom were civilians), the Government announced that it was reviewing its strategy against Naxalite rebels. Minister of Home Affairs P. Chidambaram claimed that the Government needed recourse to enhanced powers, including the use of air force, against the rebels. In an apparent case of sabotage by rebels later that month, a train travelling from Calcutta to Mumbai derailed and hit a freight train travelling in the opposite direction; the incident claimed the lives of more than 80 people, rendering it the most deadly attack of the Naxalites' 43-year insurgency. Naxalite leaders denied involvement in the derailment, but pledged to launch an investigation and to punish any 'rogue' rebels found to have been involved; police claimed to have substantial evidence indicating the responsibility of a local Naxalite militia. In June Chidambaram set out the Government's preconditions for initiating peace talks with Naxalite rebels, demanding the total cessation of violent activities for a 72-hour period, following which security forces would refrain from targeting them. The initiative was reported to have been cautiously welcomed by Naxalite rebels. However, the violence continued unabated, including a rebel ambush of a security patrol in Chhattisgarh at the end of the month, in which more than 25 police officers were killed. Two days later a senior Naxalite leader, Cherukuri Rajkumar (alias Azad), was killed during a security raid; a number of other rebels were also reported to have been killed during July–August. In mid-August a senior Naxalite rebel leader demanded that the Government commit to a simultaneous cease-fire prior to the holding of peace talks, a demand that was rebuffed by the Government, and the violence continued unabated; the number of deaths resulting from Naxalite violence increased further to 1,169 in 2010. In May 2011 Naxalite rebels killed and dismembered 10 police officers in Chhattisgarh, and in August a further 11 police officers and one civilian were killed in the same state when a police patrol was ambushed by Naxalites. Meanwhile, a bomb explosion that destroyed a bridge in Chhattisgarh, killing four people and wounding five others, in July was also attributed to Naxalite rebels. Nevertheless, government officials noted a marked decline, to 584 persons, in the total number of fatalities arising from Naxalite violence during 2011, and attributed this to the Government's ongoing counter-insurgency efforts; enhanced co-operation between the various authorities across state borders and significant improvements in intelligence-gathering were believed to have played key roles in the significant reduction of casualties. Meanwhile, in November a senior CPI—M leader, Koteswara Rao (alias Kishenji), was killed by security forces in West Bengal.

Foreign Affairs

Relations with Pakistan and the Kashmir issue

Relations with Pakistan had deteriorated in the late 1970s and early 1980s, owing to Pakistan's potential capability for the development of nuclear weapons and as a result of major US deliveries of armaments to Pakistan. The Indian Government believed that such deliveries would upset the balance of power in the region and precipitate an 'arms race'. Pakistan's President, Gen. Mohammad Zia ul-Haq, visited India in 1985, when he and Rajiv Gandhi announced their mutual commitment not to attack each other's nuclear installations and to negotiate the sovereignty of the disputed Siachen glacier region in Kashmir. Pakistan continued to demand a settlement of the Kashmir problem in accordance with earlier UN resolutions, prescribing a plebiscite under the auspices of the UN in the two parts of the state, now divided between India and Pakistan. India argued that the problem should be settled in accordance with the Shimla Agreement of 1972, which required that all Indo–Pakistani disputes be resolved through bilateral negotiations. The Indian decision to construct a barrage on the River Jhelum in Jammu and Kashmir, in an alleged violation of the 1960 Indus Waters Treaty, also created concern in Pakistan. Relations between India and Pakistan reached a crisis in late 1989, when the outlawed Jammu and Kashmir Liberation Front (JKLF) and several other militant Islamic groups intensified their campaigns of civil unrest, strikes and terrorism, demanding an independent Kashmir or unification with Pakistan. The Indian Government dispatched troops to the region and placed the entire Srinagar valley under curfew. Pakistan denied India's claim that the militants were trained and armed in Pakistan-held Kashmir (known as Azad Kashmir). In January 1990 Jammu and Kashmir was placed under Governor's rule, and in July under President's rule. By 1996 the total death toll resulting from the conflict in Jammu and Kashmir, including civilians, security force personnel and militants, was estimated at up to 20,000. However, the situation in Kashmir improved somewhat when elections for the national parliamentary seats were held in the troubled state shortly after the general election in April–May 1996. State elections (the first to be held since 1987) were conducted in Jammu and Kashmir in September and attracted a turn-out of more than 50%, despite being boycotted by the majority of the separatist groups. The moderate Jammu and Kashmir National Conference (JKNC), led by Dr Farooq Abdullah, won the majority of seats in the state assembly, and, on assuming power, immediately offered to instigate talks with the separatist leaders.

Meanwhile, in June 1994 the Indian army had begun to deploy a new missile, *Prithvi*, which had the capacity to reach most of Pakistan. While the 'arms race' between the two countries continued, with claims on both sides concerning the other's missile programmes, talks (which had been suspended since 1994) were resumed in March 1997. Tension increased in September when a large-scale outbreak of artillery exchanges along the Line of Control (LoC) in Kashmir (a cease-fire line drawn up in 1949) resulted in about 40 civilian deaths. After a hiatus of more than one year (during which time both countries carried out controversial nuclear test explosions—see Domestic Political Affairs), Indo-Pakistani talks at foreign secretary level regarding Kashmir and other issues were resumed in Islamabad in October 1998. In February 1999 relations appeared to improve considerably when Prime Minister Vajpayee made an historic bus journey (inaugurating the first passenger bus service between India and Pakistan) over the border to Lahore, following which he and his Pakistani counterpart, Mohammad Nawaz Sharif, held a summit meeting (the first to be conducted in Pakistan for 10 years), at which they signed the Lahore Declaration; the Declaration, with its pledges regarding peace and nuclear security, sought to allay world-wide fears of a nuclear confrontation in South Asia, and committed the two sides to working towards better relations and to implementing a range of confidence-building measures. The contentious subject of Jammu and Kashmir was, however, largely avoided.

Despite the apparent rapprochement between India and Pakistan, in April 1999 both countries carried out separate tests on their latest missiles, which were capable of carrying nuclear warheads. In early May the situation deteriorated drastically when the Indian army discovered that Islamist guerrilla groups, reinforced by regular Pakistani troops, had occupied strategic positions on the Indian side of the LoC in the Kargil area of Kashmir. Air-strikes launched by the Indian air force at the end of the month failed to dislodge the so-called 'infiltrators', and the army was forced to wage an expensive and lengthy campaign, during which more than 480 Indian soldiers were killed and two Indian military aircraft were shot down. In July, however, Indian military dominance combined with US diplomatic pressure led to a Pakistani withdrawal. In August there was renewed tension when India shot down a Pakistani naval reconnaissance aircraft near Pakistan's border with Gujarat, killing all 16 personnel on board; Pakistan retaliated the following day by opening fire on Indian military aircraft in the same area.

In July 1999 one of the main Kashmiri militant groups, the Hizbul Mujahideen, declared a three-month cease-fire. The gesture obtained a quick and positive response from the Indian Government: the Indian Army suspended all offensive operations against the militants for the first time in 11 years. However, other militant groups denounced the cessation of hostilities as a betrayal and continued their violent campaign in an attempt to disrupt the peace process. The Hizbul Mujahideen ended the cease-fire at the beginning of August owing to the Indian Government's opposition to instigating tripartite negotiations including representatives of Pakistan. Consequently, Pakistan appeared relatively moderate and India somewhat intransigent. Vajpayee accused Pakistan of orchestrating the events, of encouraging divisions among militant leaders and of turning the Kashmir issue into a pan-Islamic movement.

In April 2000 there were indications that the Indian Government was willing to re-establish dialogue with Kashmiri militants. Leaders of the All-Party Hurriyat Conference (APHC), an organization that, to an extent, acted as the political voice for some of the militant groups, were released in April and May. However, following the collapse of a short-lived cease-fire in July–August, violence in the region intensified. In November the Indian Government declared the suspension of combat operations against Kashmiri militants during the Muslim holy month of Ramadan. The unilateral cease-fire began at the end of November (and was subsequently extended, at intervals, until the end of May 2001); Indian security forces were authorized to retaliate if fired upon. The majority of national parties and foreign governments supported the cessation of hostilities, although the Pakistani authorities described the cease-fire as 'meaningless' without simultaneous constructive dialogue. The APHC welcomed the development and offered to enter negotiations with Pakistani authorities in order to prepare for tripartite discussions. However, the militant groups rejected the offer and continued their campaign of violence, extending their activities as far as the Red Fort in Old Delhi, where three people were shot dead in December 2000. In January 2001 the Indian High Commissioner to Pakistan visited the Pakistani President, Gen. Pervez Musharraf. This meeting constituted the first high-level contact between the two countries since the military coup in Pakistan in 1999. The two officials urged an early resumption of negotiations on the Kashmir question. At the end of May 2001 the Government announced the end of its unilateral cease-fire; more than 1,000 people were estimated to have been killed in violence related to the crisis in the region since the cease-fire was first announced in November 2000.

Relations with Pakistan appeared to improve following the earthquake in Gujarat in January 2001, when Pakistan offered humanitarian relief to India and the leaders of the two countries thus established contact. In May Vajpayee issued an unexpected invitation to Gen. Musharraf to attend bilateral negotiations in Agra in July. However, hopes for a significant breakthrough on the issue of Kashmir were frustrated by the failure of the two leaders to agree to a joint declaration at the conclusion of the dialogue; the divergent views of the two sides on the priority issue in the dispute (cross-border terrorism according to India, and Kashmiri self-determination in the opinion of Pakistan) appeared to be more firmly entrenched than ever. Violence increased in the region following the disappointment engendered by the meeting, and in August the Indian Government extended its official 'disturbed area' designation (invoking the 1990 Armed Forces Special Powers Act) to cover all districts of the state of Jammu and Kashmir (only Ladakh was unaffected). Tension with Pakistan was heightened considerably following a guerrilla-style attack on the state assembly building in Srinagar on 1 October. An estimated 38 people (including two of the four assailants) were killed and around 70 were wounded in the attack and in the subsequent confrontation with security forces. The Indian Government attributed responsibility for the attack to the Pakistan-based Jaish-e-Mohammed and Lashkar-e-Taiba groups.

On 13 December 2001 five armed assailants gained access to the grounds of the Union Parliament in New Delhi and attempted to launch an apparent suicide attack on the parliament building. Although no parliamentary deputies were hurt in the attack, 14 people (including the five assailants, a number of policemen, some security officials and a groundsman) were killed and some 25 were injured. The Indian authorities again attributed responsibility for the attack to Jaish-e-Mohammed and Lashkar-e-Taiba, and suggested that the assailants appeared to be of Pakistani origin. Pakistan, which had been among the many countries to express immediate condemnation of the attack (which was popularly described as an assault on democracy), now demanded to see concrete proof to support the allegations made by the Indian Government, while the US Administration urged the Indian authorities to exercise restraint in their response. Tensions between India and Pakistan continued to mount when Mohammed Afzal, a member of Jaish-e-Mohammed arrested in Kashmir on suspicion of complicity in the incident, admitted his involvement and alleged publicly that Pakistani security and intelligence agencies had provided support to those directly responsible for the attack. India recalled its High Commissioner from Islamabad and announced that overground transport services between the two countries would be suspended from 1 January 2002. As positions were reinforced with troops and weapons (including missiles) on both sides of the LoC, there was considerable international concern that such brinkmanship might propel the two countries (each with nuclear capabilities) into renewed armed conflict. Mindful of the potential detriment to security at Pakistan's border with Afghanistan that could result from an escalation in conflict in Kashmir, the USA applied increased pressure on the beleaguered Pakistani Government (already facing vociferous domestic opposition to its accommodation of US activities in Afghanistan) to adopt a more conciliatory attitude towards India's security concerns, and in late December 2001 the Pakistani authorities followed the US Government's lead in freezing the assets of the two groups held responsible for the attack on India. The leaders of the two groups were later detained by the Pakistani authorities, but, despite evident satisfaction at this development, the Indian Government continued to dismiss much of the Pakistani response as superficial and demanded that the two leaders be extradited to stand trial in India. However, in December 2002 Pakistan freed one of the leaders, Maulana Masood Azhar, from house arrest. Later that month a special court established under the POTA (see Domestic Political Affairs) convicted three Kashmiri Muslims—two of whom were reportedly members of Jaish-e-Mohammed and the third a member of the JKLF—of organizing the attack on the Union Parliament and sentenced them to death. (However, a High Court ruling overturned the convictions of two of the men following an appeal in October 2003.)

In January 2002 Musharraf yielded to relentless international pressure by publicly condemning the activities of militant extremists based in Pakistan and announcing the introduction of a broad range of measures to combat terrorist activity and religious zealotry, including the proscription of five extremist organizations (among them Jaish-e-Mohammed and Lashkar-e-Taiba). An armed attack by four suspected Islamist militants on a US cultural centre in Kolkata (Calcutta) on 22 January, in which five Indian policeman were killed and more than 20 were injured, placed relations between the two countries under renewed strain when the Indian authorities attempted to link the unidentified assailants to the Pakistani intelligence services.

Tensions between the two countries rose again, following a suspected Islamist militant attack on an army camp in Jammu and Kashmir in May, in which 34 people were killed, including 19 civilians. India identified the gunmen as Pakistani nationals and a few days later requested the withdrawal of Pakistan's High Commissioner to India. The two countries appeared to be on the brink of war again as positions were reinforced with troops and weapons on both sides of the LoC, and exchanges of gunfire intensified. Relations deteriorated further following the assassination of Abdul Ghani Lone, the leader of the APHC, on 21 May, by suspected Islamist militants. As a result of international efforts to ease tensions between the two neighbours, in June India withdrew five naval ships from patrol of the coast of Pakistan and allowed Pakistani civilian aircraft to enter its airspace, in response to Pakistani pledges to halt cross-border infiltration. In October the Minister of Defence stated that India would withdraw a large number of troops from the international border with Pakistan; however, the number of troops along the LoC would remain unchanged. Pakistan responded by withdrawing a portion of its troops.

Meanwhile, the APHC declared that it would boycott the state elections in Jammu and Kashmir (which were due to be held in September–October 2002), regarding them as meaningless unless a referendum on independence was held first. Violence continued throughout the election period, with at least 730 people reportedly being killed. Following the elections, in which no single party won an outright majority, Congress and the regional People's Democratic Party (PDP) reached a power-sharing arrangement, under which PDP leader Mufti Mohammed Sayeed was to be appointed Chief Minister for a three-year term, followed by local Congress President Ghulam Nabi Azad for the next three years. Sayeed pledged to seek a resolution to the Kashmir issue through a programme of dialogue and reconciliation. The state government also announced that it would disband the Special Operations Group of the police, which had been accused in the past of serious human rights violations.

Indo-Pakistani relations deteriorated in early 2003 amid mutual accusations of diplomatic espionage. Tensions were exacerbated by India's latest round of 'routine' ballistic missile tests without advance warning (Pakistan responded in kind), the violence in Kashmir, and India's recently signed military agreement with Russia (see Other external relations). In March separatist violence in Jammu and Kashmir escalated. The killing of 24 Kashmiri Hindus, including women and children, in a remote village south of Srinagar by suspected Islamists at the end of the month provoked widespread condemnation and posed a set-back to Sayeed's reconciliation programme. Nevertheless, in May the Indian and Pakistani premiers agreed to restore the recently severed diplomatic relations and civil aviation links. Two months later the bus service between the Pakistani city of Lahore and New Delhi was restored.

From July 2003 militant activity, including suicide attacks, and the exchange of gunfire across the LoC increased. The assassination of the militant leader Ghazi Baba at the end of August provoked a surge in violence in September. In the same month the APHC openly split after the new leadership of Maulvi Abbas Ansari, the first Shi'a Muslim to chair the organization, was challenged by a significant faction, which proceeded to elect former Chairman Syed Ali Shah Geelani instead. In October the Indian Minister of External Affairs, Yashwant Sinha, announced 12 confidence-building measures to improve and normalize relations with Pakistan, while emphasizing, however, that no direct talks on Kashmir between India and Pakistan would take place until the latter put a stop to cross-border infiltration by Islamist militants. In November a bilateral cease-fire along the LoC came into effect. In December Indian and Pakistani officials signed a three-year agreement on the restoration from mid-January 2004 of a passenger and freight train service between New Delhi and Lahore. Direct aviation links between the two countries were resumed on 1 January 2004.

At a ground-breaking South Asian Association for Regional Cooperation (SAARC, see p. 420) summit meeting in Islamabad in January 2004, Musharraf assured Vajpayee that he would not permit any territory under Pakistan's control to be used to support terrorism; in return Vajpayee agreed to begin negotiations on all bilateral issues, including Kashmir, in February. However, Islamist militants who were unhappy with what they perceived as a betrayal by Musharraf continued their violent campaign. The APHC called for a boycott of the general election, held in April–May, and a series of violent attacks directed at all politicians campaigning in Jammu and Kashmir over the election period resulted in several deaths. Overall electoral turn-out in Kashmir was 35%, although this declined to less than 19% in Srinagar. In June several rounds of discussions took place between Indian and Pakistani officials in New Delhi during which both sides agreed to restore their diplomatic missions to full strength. An agreement was also reached that each country would, in future, notify the other of any forthcoming missile tests. In September India and Pakistan held their first, official, ministerial-level talks in more than three years in New Delhi. As a result, the two sides agreed to implement a series of confidence-building measures, including the restoration of bilateral transport links.

In November 2004 Prime Minister Manmohan Singh ordered a 'substantial' reduction in the number of Indian troops deployed in Kashmir, a move welcomed by Pakistan. In early 2005 Jammu and Kashmir held its first municipal elections in 27 years. At the same time, tensions resurfaced between India and Pakistan, with each side accusing the other of violating the ongoing cease-fire along the LoC. However, in February the two countries agreed to open a bus service across the LoC, linking Srinagar with Muzaffarabad. In April Musharraf travelled to India for the first time since 2001 and met with Manmohan Singh in New Delhi for further peace talks.

In June 2005 a delegation of leaders from the APHC crossed the LoC and travelled to Muzaffarabad, where they held talks with Pakistani Kashmiri leaders. The visit represented the first time since 1946 that Indian Kashmiri politicians had been permitted to traverse the LoC. In September Manmohan Singh held talks with APHC leaders in New Delhi. In the same month, in a symbolic gesture, the Government began to withdraw paramilitary Border Security Force (BSF) troops from Srinagar; responsibility for security in the city was subsequently assumed by the Central Reserve Police Force.

In October 2005 the devastating consequences of a massive earthquake centred in Azad Kashmir had implications for the ongoing peace process. In the aftermath of the disaster, which resulted in widespread loss of life and destruction, particularly on the Pakistani side of the LoC, Pakistan accepted an Indian offer of aid. Following a series of negotiations, the two countries subsequently agreed to open a number of crossing-points on the LoC, in order to permit the reunification of divided families. However, fears on the part of both countries that the other would take advantage of the situation to conduct military surveillance hampered the prospect of more extensive co-operation. Nevertheless, in February 2006 a second rail link was opened between India and Pakistan, linking the town of Munabao in Rajasthan to the Pakistani town of Khokrapar in Sindh.

Relations between India and Pakistan were strained by the Mumbai train bombings in July 2006 (see Internal Unrest and the Threat of Terrorism). Although President Musharraf condemned the attacks, Prime Minister Singh suggested that those responsible had links to Pakistan. Bilateral peace talks were postponed, and in September the Mumbai police claimed that Lashkar-e-Taiba was responsible for the July bombings and had apparently been aided in the attacks by Pakistan's Inter-Services Intelligence agency (an accusation swiftly denied by the Pakistani authorities). In November India and Pakistan agreed to establish an information-sharing panel to co-operate on anti-terrorism measures. In February 2007, however, explosions on the Samjhauta Express train, which was bound for Lahore, Pakistan, from Delhi, caused a devastating fire on board, killing at least 67 passengers, the majority of whom were Pakistani nationals. The attack was viewed by many as an attempt to hinder the peace process between the two countries. None the less, later in the month India and Pakistan signed an agreement designed to prevent inadvertent nuclear conflict between the two countries, and the planning and implementation of other confidence-building measures continued in areas such as trade and transport.

In mid-2008 a decision by the state government of Jammu and Kashmir to transfer land (on a permanent basis) to a board managing a popular Hindu shrine precipitated considerable unrest in the region. Following large-scale protests, the government rescinded its offer, but the issue had already served to intensify hostility between Muslim separatists and Hindu nationalists. The episode culminated in the resignation of Chief Minister Ghulam Nabi Azad and the placement of the state under federal rule. Legislative elections were held in November, in which the JKNC emerged as the party with the largest number of seats, but was forced to form a coalition with Congress in order to secure a majority. Omar Abdullah, the son of Dr Farooq Abdullah, was sworn in as Chief Minister in January 2009. According to official statistics, militancy-related violence in Jammu and Kashmir in 2009 fell to its lowest level in 20 years; the number of militancy-related deaths totalled 386, compared with 3,035 in 1995.

While India accused Pakistan of border incursions in Kashmir, terrorist attacks on Indian targets were also a source of strain in relations with Pakistan in 2008. In July a suicide bombing at the Indian embassy in Kabul, Afghanistan, resulted in more than 40 fatalities; the Indian Government intimated that the plot had originated in Pakistan. In the aftermath of the November Mumbai attacks (see Internal Unrest and the Threat of Terrorism), the Indian Government suggested that the perpetrators were all from Pakistan, a claim that the Pakistani authorities initially denied; however, they subsequently conceded that the sole gunman captured alive was indeed a Pakistani national. Moreover, in an unexpected turnaround, a senior official of the Pakistan Government publicly admitted in February 2009 that the Mumbai attacks had been partly planned in Pakistan and stated that seven suspects belonging to Lashkar-e-Taiba had been arrested. The Indian Government welcomed the admission as a 'positive development' and demanded that the suspects be extradited to India; however, Pakistan insisted that any prosecutions be carried out internally.

In February 2010 India and Pakistan held their first high-level direct talks since the 2008 Mumbai attacks; however, the discussions, which were held in New Delhi, proved fruitless, with both sides accusing each other of supporting terrorism and of tolerating human rights abuses. A meeting between the two countries' respective Prime Ministers at a nuclear security summit in Washington, DC, USA, in April 2010 proved similarly ineffectual. In June the Indian Minister of Home Affairs, P. Chidambaram, visited Islamabad, becoming the first Indian minister to visit Pakistan since the Mumbai attacks. During his stay, Chidambaram urged the Pakistani Government to intensify its efforts against Lashkar-e-Taiba members thought to have been involved in the planning of the attacks. In July a visit to Islamabad by a senior-level Indian delegation headed by the Indian Minister of External Affairs, S. M. Krishna, was initially hailed by both sides as having been a 'constructive' resumption of high-level cross-border talks, but Krishna's Pakistani counterpart subsequently accused the Indian delegation of being ill-prepared for the talks and refusing to discuss the Kashmir issue; the summit culminated in mutual recriminations. An accusation issued on the eve of the talks, by Indian Home Secretary G. K. Pillai, in which he claimed that Pakistan's intelligence agency had co-ordinated the 2008 Mumbai attacks, the first time that an Indian official had accused the Pakistani authorities of a direct, controlling role in the attacks, had done little to dissipate bilateral tensions.

In February 2011 it was announced that the two countries had agreed to a formal resumption of bilateral discussions, with the two ministers responsible for foreign affairs agreeing to reconvene in July, in New Delhi. In late March an international cricket match between India and Pakistan, the semi-final of the Cricket World Cup, was utilized by Prime Minister Singh to expedite progress in Indo-Pakistani relations. Accepting an invitation from Singh, Pakistani Prime Minister Yousaf Raza Gilani made his first official visit to India to attend the match in Mohali, in the state of Punjab. During Gilani's visit, the premiers held discussions that apparently encompassed 'all outstanding issues' concerning bilateral relations. Following the summit, both leaders emphasized the positive outcome of the discussions, expressing their commitment to resolve all bilateral problems through dialogue and to promote peace and prosperity in the region. Meanwhile, following a two-day meeting involving the Indian and Pakistani Home Secretaries, held in New Delhi in advance of the prime-ministerial summit, agreement was reportedly reached on a range of measures to enhance co-operation in counter-terrorism; furthermore, security officials from India and Pakistan were to be granted access to each other's countries to facilitate investigations into the 2008 Mumbai attacks. However, a planned visit by a Pakistani judicial commission to Delhi to meet with Indian officials involved in the investigations was cancelled by the Pakistani authorities at short notice in February 2012, with no explanation for the cancellation reported to have been offered. The development further added to the consternation of the Indian Government, which had previously expressed increasing dissatisfaction with the failure of the Pakistani authorities to open trial proceedings against any of the seven Lashkar-e-Taiba members arrested in 2009 in connection with the attacks. The Pakistani authorities insisted that they needed to conduct interviews with the sole surviving gunman, Ajmal Amir Qasab, as part of their investigations—a demand rejected by the Indian authorities, which continued to suspect Pakistani state involvement in the planning of the attacks, and which insisted that they had already handed over enough evidence to secure convictions.

Nevertheless, a significant amelioration in bilateral relations was evident during 2011. During a meeting in the Indian capital in July, the Indian and Pakistani ministers responsible for foreign affairs reaffirmed the mutual commitment of their respective Governments to resolve all outstanding bilateral issues through dialogue. Meanwhile, in April 2011 India's Commerce Secretary, Rahul Khullar, and his Pakistani counterpart convened in Islamabad for the first bilateral trade talks to be held since the 2008 Mumbai attacks. During the meeting, Khullar affirmed the Indian Government's commitment to a policy of 'constructive engagement' in order to facilitate an increase in bilateral trade, which the two countries pledged to double (to around US $6,000m.) within three years following a meeting in New Delhi between the two countries' respective ministers responsible for trade in September 2011. The decision by Pakistan to confer the status of 'most favoured nation' upon India in November (having previously insisted that this would require a resolution to the ongoing dispute over Kashmir) was hailed by both countries as a reflection of improving ties, and later in the month, during sideline talks at the SAARC summit meeting in the Maldives, Prime Ministers Singh and Gilani pledged to open a 'new chapter' in bilateral relations; the two leaders acknowledged 'positive movement' but stressed that further sustained effort would be required by both sides if a long-lasting, mutually beneficial working relationship was to be secured. In April 2012, during what was ostensibly a private visit to India, Pakistani President Asif Ali Zardari met with Prime Minister Singh for informal discussions on bilateral issues. It was hoped that the meeting might serve as a precursor to formal, substantive dialogue between the respective leaders in the near future.

Other regional relations

In 1986 India and Bangladesh signed an agreement on measures to prevent 'cross-border terrorism'. In 1988 the two countries established a joint working committee to examine methods of averting the annual devastating floods in the Ganga (Ganges) delta. In 1992 the Indian Government, under the provisions of an accord signed with Bangladesh in 1974, formally leased the Tin Bigha Corridor (a small strip of land covering an area of only 1.5 ha) to Bangladesh for 999 years. India maintained sovereignty over the Corridor, but the lease gave Bangladesh access to its enclaves of Dahagram and Angarpota. The transfer of the Corridor occasioned protests from right-wing quarters in India, who also made an issue over the presence in Delhi and other cities of illegal immigrants from Bangladesh and claimed that the Bangladeshi Government had done little to protect its Hindu minority. In December 1996 India signed an 'historic' treaty with Bangladesh, which was to be in force for 30 years, regarding the sharing of the Ganga waters. The worst fighting between the two countries since 1976 took place in April 2001 on the Bangladeshi border with the Indian state of Meghalaya. Some 16 members of the Indian BSF and three members of the Bangladesh Rifles were killed. The situation was brought under control and the two sides entered border negotiations in June, as a result of which two joint working groups were established to review the undemarcated section of the border.

In September 2004 senior Indian and Bangladeshi officials held talks in Dhaka, the Bangladeshi capital, concerning security issues and water-sharing. While some agreement was reached on water-sharing and the two countries agreed to co-ordinate their border patrols, relations remained strained into 2005. Tensions were exacerbated by India's decision not to attend a planned summit of SAARC in Bangladesh in February, citing security concerns; this forced the postponement of the meeting until later that year. Further clashes occurred between the border patrols of the two countries in March and, later that month, talks were held in an attempt to resolve the ongoing problems, which had been exacerbated by India's continued construction of a fence along the joint border, in contravention of its obligations under a 1974 treaty. The Indian Government claimed that the fence was intended to prevent Bangladeshi insurgents and illegal immigrants from crossing the border. Several further clashes occurred in the following months, as relations remained tense. In October 2007 military officials from

Bangladesh and India held talks in Dhaka with the aim of resolving outstanding border issues; the two countries reiterated their commitment to sharing information and co-operating in their fight against militants and criminals in border areas. A direct train link between Kolkata (Calcutta) and Dhaka began operating in April 2008.

Relations between India and Bangladesh improved following the return to power of the Bangladesh Awami League in December 2008, one of the main reasons for this being the fact that the new Bangladeshi Government began to take action against the Indian groups that maintained bases in Bangladesh (including the arrest and the transfer to the Indian authorities of a number of ULFA leaders). Following a successful visit to New Delhi by the Bangladeshi Prime Minister, Sheikh Hasina, in January 2010, it was reported that Bangladesh and India aimed to remove all barriers to mutual trade in an effort to improve bilateral economic co-operation and as a precursor to the conclusion of a bilateral free trade agreement. The two countries announced an agreement in August providing for a US $1,000m. loan by India to Bangladesh, to be disbursed on infrastructural development in the latter country, and the two countries were to improve road and rail connectivity with one another to facilitate the transit of goods and people. In October India eliminated tariffs on 61 local products imported by Bangladesh, including textiles. In November the two countries held the first bilateral border talks in five years, which was interpreted by some observers as a tacit acknowledgement from India of the importance of ensuring continued growth and development in Bangladesh in order to safeguard the development and security of India's north-eastern states. A joint border survey of disputed frontier areas commenced in December and was concluded in early 2011. In August 2011 Bangladesh and India began the process of approving border maps, officially recognizing their 4,156-km frontier; however, a 6.5-km stretch of the border had yet to be demarcated and remained disputed. Meanwhile, in October 2010 reports emerged that a prominent separatist leader in Manipur, Rajkumar Meghen, had been arrested in Dhaka in the previous month by the Bangladeshi authorities and handed over to India; the reports were confirmed when Meghen, the leader of the militant United National Liberation Front appeared in court in Bihar in December.

An interim bilateral agreement on the sharing of waters from the Teesta river was one of several significant deals that had been expected to be concluded during an official visit to Dhaka in September 2011 by Prime Minister Singh—the first state visit to Bangladesh by an Indian Prime Minister in 12 years. Mamata Banerjee, the Chief Minister of West Bengal, was to have joined the Indian delegation in Dhaka; however, shortly prior to the visit, she announced her refusal to participate in the proceedings owing to her anger over the proposed water-sharing agreement, which would have provided for a 50:50 share of the waters from the Teesta river; Banerjee argued that this was too great a share for India to cede to Bangladesh and would have been to the detriment of farmers in West Bengal, who also depended on the river's water supply. Reportedly owing to Banerjee's objections, Singh withdrew the deal during his two-day visit. The two countries also failed to reach agreement on a land transit agreement that would have granted India overland access to its landlocked north-eastern states through Bangladeshi territory. (Bangladesh had insisted that the latter agreement was dependent upon a successful conclusion to the water-sharing deal.) Nevertheless, a land border agreement, resolving demarcation of the remaining 6.5-km stretch on the bilateral frontier, and an agreement providing for the exchange of 111 Indian enclaves within Bangladesh and 51 Bangladeshi enclaves within India, were signed, formally concluding a dispute dating back to 1947. (For further details on these and other agreements signed during Singh's visit, see the chapter on Bangladesh.) Despite the failure to conclude the water-sharing and land transit agreements, both countries' respective Governments hailed Singh's visit as a success and pledged to continue discussions on all remaining bilateral issues. During a two-day visit to Tripura in January 2012, Bangladeshi Prime Minister Sheikh Hasina urged the Indian Government to be more flexible and open to compromise in order to facilitate the resolution of outstanding bilateral issues, including the issue of water-sharing, a view that was reiterated by the Tripura Chief Minister, Manik Sarkar.

Relations between India and Nepal deteriorated in 1989, when India decided not to renew two bilateral treaties determining trade and transit, insisting that a common treaty covering both issues be negotiated. Nepal refused, stressing the importance of keeping the treaties separate on the grounds that Indo-Nepalese trade issues were negotiable, whereas the right of transit was a recognized right of landlocked countries. India responded by closing most of the transit points through which Nepal's trade was conducted. The dispute was aggravated by Nepal's acquisition of Chinese-made military equipment, which, according to India, violated the Treaty of Peace and Friendship of 1950. However, in June 1990 India and Nepal signed an agreement restoring trade relations and reopening the transit points. Chandra Shekhar visited Kathmandu in February 1991 (the first official visit to Nepal by an Indian Prime Minister since 1977), shortly after it was announced that the first free elections in Nepal were to be held in May. In June 1997 the Indian Prime Minister, Inder Kumar Gujral, made a visit to Nepal and announced the opening of a transit route through north-eastern India between Nepal and Bangladesh. Gujral and the Nepalese Prime Minister, Lokendra Bahadur Chand, also agreed that there should be a review of the 1950 treaty between the two countries. In February 2005 relations with Nepal were seriously affected when the Nepalese King orchestrated a coup, dismissing the Government and declaring a state of emergency in the country. It was feared that a significant number of Maoist rebels from Nepal might infiltrate the country's border with India's fractious north-eastern states, a concern borne out to an extent by a reported decision by the CPI (Maoist) and Nepalese rebels to co-operate in promoting the spread of communism in both countries. India subsequently ceased provision of all military aid to Nepal and intensified security along the shared border. In July India resumed non-lethal military aid to Nepal. In January 2006 the bilateral transit treaty expired; in order to allow time for a review of the agreement, India subsequently extended the term of the treaty. The bilateral trade treaty expired in March 2007, but was automatically renewed pending its review by the two sides. Meanwhile, in June 2006, following the reinstatement of Parliament, the newly appointed Nepalese Prime Minister, G. P. Koirala, paid an official visit to India, during which India pledged to increase aid to Nepal. In August 2009 the two countries signed a trade treaty and India pledged to assist its neighbour with development projects such as road and rail links and the establishment of a police academy. During a visit to New Delhi in October 2011, Baburam Bhattarai, who had assumed the Nepalese premiership in August, met with Prime Minister Singh, whereupon the two leaders discussed a range of issues including plans to expand bilateral economic co-operation, to which end a 10-year Bilateral Investment Promotion and Protection Agreement was signed, under the terms of which investors of one country would be compensated in the event of sustaining investment losses in the other country as a result of riots, insurrections and armed conflict.

Since 1983 India's relations with Sri Lanka have been threatened by conflicts between the latter's Sinhalese and Tamil communities, in which India has sought to arbitrate. In July 1987 Rajiv Gandhi and the Sri Lankan President, Junius Jayewardene, signed an accord aimed at settling the conflict. An Indian Peace-Keeping Force (IPKF) was dispatched to Sri Lanka but encountered considerable resistance from the Tamil separatist guerrillas. Following the gradual implementation of the peace accord, the IPKF troops completed their withdrawal in March 1990. However, violence flared up again and the flow of Sri Lankan refugees into Tamil Nadu increased considerably; by late 1991 the number of Sri Lankans living in refugee camps in the southern Indian state was estimated at more than 200,000. The assassination of Rajiv Gandhi in May 1991, allegedly by members of the LTTE, completed India's disenchantment with the latter organization. Measures were subsequently taken by the state government in Tamil Nadu to suppress LTTE activity within the state, and also to begin the process of repatriating refugees. The repatriation programme (allegedly conducted on a voluntary basis) proved a slow and difficult process. In May 1992 the LTTE was officially banned in India. In December 1998 the Indian Prime Minister and Sri Lankan President signed a bilateral free trade agreement, which finally came into effect in March 2000. During the 2000s India refrained from any direct involvement in the Sri Lankan conflict. However, the escalation in hostilities in 2008 following the collapse of a cease-fire was a cause of considerable concern to the Indian authorities, which insisted that a negotiated political settlement rather than a military solution should be sought. In May of that year India extended the ban on the LTTE by a further two years; the ban was extended for a further two years in May 2010.

Following the defeat of the LTTE in 2009, India has played a major role in the resettlement and rehabilitation of thousands of displaced Tamil civilians and in the reconstruction of the war-ravaged north-east of Sri Lanka. India opened two new consulates in Sri Lanka during 2010—one in Hambantota, and the other in Jaffna. During an official visit to India by Sri Lankan President Mahinda Rajapakse in June 2010, an agreement was signed regarding the possibility of Sri Lanka supplying India with electricity. The extension by India of an invitation to Rajapakse to attend the closing ceremony of the Commonwealth Games hosted by New Delhi in October—the only invitation to be extended to a foreign head of state—was widely interpreted as being symptomatic of improved relations between the two countries. Bilateral relations were threatened by the shooting, allegedly by members of the Sri Lankan navy, of two Indian fishermen in separate incidents in January 2011. Nevertheless, in a sign of burgeoning ties, the first passenger boat service to operate between the two countries in nearly three decades was inaugurated in June, linking the southern Indian port of Tuticorin and the Sri Lankan capital, Colombo, across the Palk Strait. (Ferry services between the two countries had been suspended in the 1980s as a result of the Sri Lankan conflict.) However, in March 2012 bilateral relations were undermined following a decision by India to support a US-sponsored resolution at the UN Human Rights Council (UNHRC), which urged the Sri Lankan Government to investigate allegations of human rights violations in the final stages of the Sri Lankan civil conflict. India's stance, which appeared to contravene a traditional policy of abstaining on country-specific UNHRC resolutions, was widely interpreted as a response to pressure exerted on the federal Government by its political partners in Tamil Nadu.

During 1981 there was an improvement in India's relations with the People's Republic of China. Both countries agreed to attempt to find an early solution to their Himalayan border dispute and to seek to normalize relations, and a number of working groups were subsequently established. In February 1991 a major breakthrough occurred when a draft protocol for 1991/92, including the proposed resumption of border trade between the two countries for the first time in three decades, was signed. All six border posts had been closed since the brief border war in 1962. Following an official visit to India by the Chinese Premier, Li Peng, in December 1991 (the first such visit by a Chinese Premier for 31 years), bilateral border trade was resumed in July 1992. Sino-Indian relations were further strengthened as a result of a three-day visit to India conducted by the Chinese President, Jiang Zemin, in November 1996 (the first ever visit by a Chinese head of state to India). However, despite the gradual improvement in relations India has frequently expressed concern over the nuclear asymmetry between the two countries and what it perceives as China's willingness to transfer missiles and missile technology to Pakistan. Sino-Indian relations deteriorated following India's 1998 nuclear tests, partly because China believed that India was using a fabricated threat from China to justify its actions. In June 1999 the Indian Minister of External Affairs visited Beijing to restore Sino-Indian dialogue. During border negotiations in November 2000, India and China exchanged detailed maps of the middle sector of the Line of Actual Control: a significant step towards resolving differences. In April 2003 the Indian Minister of Defence paid a week-long visit to Beijing to discuss outstanding bilateral issues, including China's support for Pakistan, and Chinese observation posts in the Bay of Bengal. Prime Minister Vajpayee made a state visit to China in June 2003 (the first by an Indian premier in 10 years), during which a number of agreements were signed, the most significant being India's official recognition of Chinese sovereignty over Tibet (the Xizang Autonomous Region). China also agreed to trade with the north-eastern Indian state of Sikkim, thus implicitly acknowledging India's control of that area. In January 2005 India and China held their first-ever strategic dialogue, in New Delhi, agreeing, *inter alia*, to attempt to resolve their boundary dispute in a fair and mutually satisfactory manner. In April of that year Chinese Premier Wen Jiabao visited India. During his stay he signed a series of agreements with Indian Prime Minister Manmohan Singh; these included plans for the resolution of the boundary dispute and the expansion of bilateral trade. In July 2006 the reopening of the historic border trading post of Nathu La (which was once part of the ancient Silk Road) highlighted the ongoing improvement in Sino-Indian relations, which was further strengthened when the Chinese President, Hu Jintao, paid an official visit to India in November, during which the two countries agreed to co-operate in several fields, including nuclear energy. Prime Minister Singh reciprocated with a visit to China in January 2008, meeting with President Hu and Premier Wen in order to discuss issues such as trade and defence. Although the year 2010 was designated a 'Year of Friendship' between the two countries, a number of issues continued to undermine cordial relations, including India's deepening relations with the USA, and in August India suspended all bilateral defence exchanges, in protest at the refusal by the Chinese authorities to grant a visa to an Indian army general from Kashmir—China has long maintained a claim to the Shaksam Valley and Aksai Chin areas of Kashmir. Furthermore, during a three-day state visit to India in December, Premier Wen refused to condemn the 2008 Mumbai attacks, a refusal that was widely interpreted as reflecting a wish not to alienate China's other firm ally in South Asia, Pakistan (for further details, see Relations with Pakistan); in response, India refused to reiterate its adherence to the 'one China' policy. Nevertheless, during Wen's visit 48 bilateral commercial contracts, collectively worth an estimated US $16,000m., were signed and the two leaders pledged to increase bilateral trade to some $100,000m. by 2015. In April 2011 India and China agreed to resume bilateral defence exchanges, and in January 2012 an agreement was signed providing for the establishment of a joint border management mechanism, which was to convene once or twice annually and was intended to bolster border co-operation and to prevent border incidents from escalating into major confrontations. In the same month the two countries held a new round of talks intended to resolve their long-running Himalayan border dispute.

In October 2004 the Chairman of Myanmar's ruling body, the State Peace and Development Council, Field Marshal Than Shwe, paid the first visit to India by a Myanma head of state in 24 years. The visit was illustrative of improving relations between the two countries, deemed necessary if India was to combat successfully the problem of insurgents in north-eastern India establishing bases across the border in Myanmar. In April 2008 India signed an agreement worth US $120m. to construct a seaport at Sittway in north-western Myanmar and to improve roads and waterways elsewhere in the country. In return for its help with infrastructure development, it was widely believed that India was hoping for preferential access (as was China) to Myanmar's reserves of petroleum and natural gas. Than Shwe visited India for a second time in July 2010, whereupon he met with President Pratibha Patil and Prime Minister Singh; during the visit India and Myanmar signed five bilateral agreements intended to enhance co-operation in the fields of energy, defence, counter-terrorism and transnational crime prevention. In October 2011 Singh hosted a visit to India from Myanma President Thein Sein, who had been inaugurated in March, following controversial legislative elections in Myanmar (q.v.) in November 2010. During Thein Sein's visit, a series of agreements intended to bolster bilateral trade and investment, including the provision by India of a $500m. grant for infrastructural development projects in Myanmar, was signed; the two leaders also pledged to enhance co-operation in the field of oil and gas exploration.

As relations between Afghanistan and Pakistan deteriorated amid Afghan allegations of Pakistani support for a series of violent attacks against the Afghan authorities during 2011 (see the chapter on Afghanistan), India appeared keen to enhance its own ties with Afghanistan. In May, during his first visit to the Afghan capital, Kabul, since August 2005, Prime Minister Singh announced that India was to grant US $500m. over a six-year period (in addition to the $1,500m. that it had already pledged) to Afghanistan, to be disbursed on a range of development projects, with a focus on agriculture, infrastructure and social programmes. Bilateral relations were further consolidated during a reciprocal visit to India by Afghan President Hamid Karzai in October 2011 by the signing of a strategic partnership agreement, which was intended to enhance co-operation in the fields of trade, counter-terrorism, and political and cultural engagement. Under the terms of the accord, India also pledged to provide security training and equipment to support the Afghan authorities as they prepared to assume full responsibility for national security by 2014, and to undertake efforts to facilitate Afghanistan's economic integration within the South Asian region as a whole.

Other external relations

Prior to its disintegration in December 1991, the USSR was a major contributor of economic and military assistance to India. The President of Russia, Boris Yeltsin, made an official visit to India in 1993, during which he signed an Indo-Russian Treaty of Friendship and Co-operation. In October 1996 India and Russia signed a defence co-operation agreement (later extended to 2010 and subsequently, in September 2008, until 2020), and in December India signed a US $1,800m. contract to purchase 40 fighter aircraft from Russia. In June 1998 Russia defied a Group of Eight (G8) ban on exporting nuclear technology to India by agreeing to supply the latter with two nuclear reactors. In October 2000 the newly elected Russian President, Vladimir Putin, visited India. The two countries signed a declaration of 'strategic partnership', which involved co-operation on defence, economic matters and international terrorism issues. India signed a contract to purchase a further 50 fighter aircraft from Russia, with a licence to manufacture around 150 more. The agreement was reportedly worth more than $3,000m. In February 2001 India agreed to buy 310 Russian tanks, at an estimated cost of $700m. In June the two countries successfully conducted tests of a new, jointly developed supersonic cruise missile, the PJ-10, which was believed to be globally unique. In November it was announced that Russia had been awarded a contract to construct a nuclear power reactor in Kudankulam in Tamil Nadu (this was later extended to two reactors). During a visit to India by the Russian President in January 2007, Putin and Prime Minister Singh focused on the key bilateral issues of energy and trade, and announced that Russia was to assist India with the construction of four more nuclear power reactors at Kudankulam. A formal agreement on these additional reactors was included in a civil nuclear co-operation declaration that was signed by Prime Minister Singh and by the new Russian President, Dmitrii Medvedev, during the latter's official visit to New Delhi in December 2008. In March 2010 Putin, in his new role as Russia's Prime Minister, paid an official visit to India, during which an important agreement was signed by the two countries regarding Russia's pledge to construct 16 new nuclear reactors in India. A further 30 bilateral deals were signed during a visit to India by President Medvedev in December, including two framework agreements that provided for the construction of two additional nuclear reactors in India; Medvedev also offered Russian support for Indian aspirations to gain a permanent seat on the UN Security Council. (In October India, together with Colombia, Germany, Portugal and South Africa, had secured election to the 15-member Council for a two-year term; as a result of India's election, all four of the 'BRIC' emerging countries—Brazil, Russia, India and China—were for the first time seated together on the Council.) Following talks between Medvedev and Singh in Moscow in December 2011, the former expressed the support of the Russian Government for India's bid to secure full membership of the Shanghai Co-operation Organization (SCO), and urged the SCO's existing member states to accelerate the accession process.

Meanwhile, in mid-1996, in a move that provoked widespread international condemnation, India decided not to be party to the Comprehensive Test Ban Treaty (CTBT), which it had earlier supported, so long as the existing nuclear powers were unwilling to commit themselves to a strict timetable for full nuclear disarmament. In May 1998 India's controversial decision to explode five nuclear test devices and to claim thereby its new status as a nuclear-weapons state led to a rapid escalation in the 'arms race' with Pakistan (which responded with its own series of nuclear tests). The USA, with limited support from other countries, subsequently imposed economic sanctions on both India and Pakistan until such time as they had signed the Nuclear Non-Proliferation Treaty (NPT) and the CTBT and taken steps to reverse their nuclear programmes. Immediately after the tests, India announced a self-imposed moratorium on further testing and launched itself into intense diplomatic activity. During 1998–99 the USA lifted some of the sanctions imposed on India and Pakistan, while reiterating its requests that the two countries sign the CTBT and exercise restraint in their respective missile programmes.

Following the collapse of the USSR, the Indian Government sought to strengthen its ties with the USA. In January 1992 discussions were held between Indian and US officials regarding military co-operation and ambitious joint defence projects. However, the USA remained concerned about the risks of nuclear proliferation in the South Asia region as a whole, and India's ongoing refusal to sign the NPT contributed to the two countries' failure to come to an understanding on the issue, a position not resolved until mid-2005 (see below). In addition, despite India's adoption of a programme of economic liberalization, conflicts over trade and related issues remained. During a visit to India by the US Secretary of Defense in January 1995, a 'landmark' agreement on defence and security co-operation was signed by the two countries. US President Bill Clinton made an official six-day state visit to India in March 2000 (the first by a US President since 1978), which was widely considered as the launch of a new era in bilateral relations. President Clinton appeared to endorse India's opinion that the Kashmir dispute was a regional issue and did not directly concern the international community. In September Prime Minister Vajpayee visited the USA. He continued to assert that consensus among Indian ministers had to be reached before a decision on the CTBT could be made. In late September 2001 US President George W. Bush announced an end to the military and economic sanctions imposed against India and Pakistan in 1998. The decision followed the renewal of high-level military contacts between the USA and India in April and May and Pakistan's co-operation with US counter-terrorism initiatives against neighbouring Afghanistan in the aftermath of the terrorist attacks carried out on US mainland targets on 11 September 2001. In July 2003 India declined a request by the USA to contribute peace-keeping troops to the US-led forces in Iraq.

In July 2005 Prime Minister Manmohan Singh visited the USA, where he signed an historic outline agreement with President Bush regarding future nuclear co-operation between the two countries. In return for an Indian pledge to separate its civilian and military nuclear programmes, to allow international monitoring of its civilian nuclear programme, and not to conduct further nuclear weapons tests or to transfer nuclear technology to other countries, the US Government proposed to share civilian nuclear technology with India. The agreement represented a reversal of previous US policy, and reflected the considerable recent improvement in bilateral relations. The agreement was finalized during a visit to India by President Bush in March 2006. In August 2007, however, the agreement met with opposition not only from the BJP, but from the UPA coalition's allies, the left-wing parties comprising the Left Front, which feared the possibility of US intervention in India's foreign policy and other areas. As the dispute intensified, the future of the agreement appeared increasingly uncertain, while the UPA parliamentary majority itself seemed to be under threat. In early 2008 progress on the implementation of the agreement slowed to a virtual halt; however, despite the withdrawal of support by the Left Front, in July the Government was able to win a parliamentary vote of confidence and to proceed with the agreement, which, having subsequently received the endorsement of the International Atomic Energy Agency and the Nuclear Suppliers Group, as well as the approval of the US Congress, was signed into law by President Bush in October. In November 2010, during his first state visit to India following his inauguration as US President in January 2009, Barack Obama furthered the promises of the civilian nuclear pact by announcing that export controls on sensitive dual-use technologies—those that have both civilian and military uses—were to be lifted, assuaging Indian concerns that the momentum built up during Bush's two presidential terms might be lost under the Obama Administration; the controls were formally rescinded in January 2011. In addition, Obama reiterated the US view that the Kashmir issue was an internal affair and pledged not to intervene unless requested to do so by India. A series of relatively minor bilateral agreements was signed during the visit, but Obama hailed the breadth and sheer number of deals, collectively estimated to be worth some US $10,000m., as a sign of burgeoning bilateral relations. During his visit, Obama also expressed US support for India's quest to attain a permanent seat on the UN Security Council—an endorsement that was denounced as 'incomprehensible' by Pakistan, which contended that India's record of observing UN charter principles and international law was 'at best chequered'. Counter-terrorism operations, bilateral trade and investment, and Indian concerns about the USA's withdrawal from Afghanistan formed the focus of a visit to New Delhi by US Secretary of State Hillary Clinton in July 2011. During her stay, Clinton appealed for a deepening of bilateral security and nuclear energy co-operation, while noting the US Government's positive response to the renewed dialogue between India and Pakistan.

During a four-day state visit to Delhi in December 2010 by French President Nicolas Sarkozy, whereupon he held negotiations with Prime Minister Singh, India and France signed a co-operation deal providing for the construction by the French company Areva of two nuclear reactors, each worth approximately US $10,000m., and for a new nuclear plant in Jaitapur, in the western Indian state of Maharashtra. A range of other deals were signed between the two countries during Sarkozy's visit, including agreements pertaining to atomic energy, civil aviation and defence. Meanwhile, India and Canada signed a nuclear co-operation deal in June 2010, which provided for the opening up of the Indian market to Canadian nuclear exports, as well as enhanced co-operation in the field of nuclear waste management.

CONSTITUTION AND GOVERNMENT

The Constitution of India, adopted by the Constituent Assembly on 26 November 1949, was inaugurated on 26 January 1950. India is a federal republic. Legislative power is vested in Parliament, consisting of the President and two Houses. The Council of States (Rajya Sabha) has 245 members, most of whom are indirectly elected by the state assemblies for six years (one-third retiring every two years), the remainder being nominated by the President for six years. The House of the People (Lok Sabha) has up to 550 elected members, serving for five years (subject to dissolution). A small number of members of the Lok Sabha may be nominated by the President to represent the Anglo-Indian community, while the 550 members are directly elected by universal adult suffrage in single-member constituencies. The President is a constitutional head of state, elected for five years by an electoral college comprising elected members of both Houses of Parliament and the state legislatures. The President exercises executive power on the advice of the Council of Ministers, which is responsible to Parliament. The President appoints the Prime Minister and, on the latter's recommendation, other ministers.

India contains 28 self-governing states, each with a governor (appointed by the President for five years), a legislature (elected for five years) and a council of ministers headed by the chief minister. Bihar, Jammu and Kashmir, Karnataka, Maharashtra and Uttar Pradesh have bicameral legislatures, the other 23 state legislatures being unicameral. Each state has its own legislative, executive and judicial machinery, corresponding to that of the Indian Union. In the event of the failure of constitutional government in a state, presidential rule can be imposed by the Union. There are also six Union Territories and one National Capital Territory, administered by lieutenant-governors or administrators, all of whom are appointed by the President. The territories of Delhi and Puducherry also have elected chief ministers and state assemblies.

REGIONAL AND INTERNATIONAL CO-OPERATION

India is a member of the Asian Development Bank (ADB, see p. 210), the South Asian Association for Regional Cooperation (SAARC, see p. 420) and the Colombo Plan (see p. 449).

Having joined the UN on its foundation in 1945, India is a member of the Economic and Social Commission for Asia and the Pacific (ESCAP, see p. 40) and was elected a non-permanent member of the UN Security Council for a two-year term commencing on 1 January 2011. As a contracting party to the General Agreement on Tariffs and Trade (GATT), India joined the World Trade Organization (WTO, see p. 433) on its establishment in 1995.

ECONOMIC AFFAIRS

In 2010, according to estimates by the World Bank, India's gross national income (GNI), measured at average 2008–10 prices, was US $1,566,636m., equivalent to $1,340 per head (or $3,560 per head on an international purchasing-power parity basis). During 2001–10, it was estimated, the population increased at an average annual rate of 1.4%, while gross domestic product (GDP) per head grew, in real terms, by an average of 6.5% per year. Overall GDP increased, in real terms, at an average annual rate of 8.0% in 2001–10. According to official figures, the rate of growth was 4.7% in 2008/09 and 8.3% in 2009/10.

Agriculture (including forestry and fishing) contributed 17.8% of GDP in 2009/10. According to FAO estimates, about 53.5% of the economically active population were expected to be engaged in agriculture in mid-2012. The principal cash crops are cotton (which accounted for 2.7% of total export earnings in 2010/11), tea, rice, spices, sugar cane and groundnuts. Coffee and jute production are also important. According to the World Bank, the average annual growth rate in the output of the agricultural sector was 2.5% in 2001–10; agricultural GDP increased by 6.3% in 2007/08, but decreased by 0.6% in 2008/09 and by 0.1% in 2009/10, according to official figures.

Industry (including mining, manufacturing, power and construction) contributed 27.0% of GDP in 2009/10. According to World Bank estimates, about 12.9% of the working population were employed in the industrial sector in 1995. According to the World Bank, industrial GDP increased at an average annual rate of 8.6% in 2001–10; the rate of growth of the GDP of the industrial sector reached 4.4% in 2008/09 and 8.0% in 2009/10, according to official figures.

Mining contributed 2.5% of GDP in 2009/10, and employed 0.6% of the working population in 1991. Iron ore and cut diamonds are the major mineral exports. Coal, limestone, zinc and lead are also mined. In 2010 India was the third largest coal producer in the world after the People's Republic of China and the USA. It was reported in July 2011 that uranium deposits recently discovered in Andhra Pradesh had proven reserves of 49,000 metric tons; according to the Atomic Energy Commission of India, following the completion of exploratory work (which remained ongoing at early 2012) total reserves at the Tumalapalli mine were expected to amount to some 150,000 tons, which would render it the largest uranium mine in the world. According to official figures, mining GDP increased at an estimated average annual rate of 4.1% during 2005–10; sectoral GDP increased by an estimated 1.3% in 2008/09 and by 6.9% in 2009/10.

Manufacturing contributed 14.8% of GDP in 2009/10, and employed 10.0% of the working population in 1991. According to the World Bank, the GDP of the manufacturing sector increased at an average annual rate of 8.7% during 2001–10; according to official figures manufacturing GDP rose by an estimated 4.2% in 2008/09 and by 8.8% in 2009/10.

Construction contributed 8.2% of GDP in 2009/10, and employed 1.9% of the working population in 1991. According to official figures, the GDP of the manufacturing sector increased at an average annual rate of 9.2% during 2005–10; manufacturing GDP rose by an estimated 5.4% in 2008/09 and by 7.0% in 2009/10.

Production of electricity rose from 746,626m. kWh in 2008/09 to 796,281m. kWh in 2009/10. In 2009/10 thermal plants (incl. renewable energy sources) accounted for an estimated 84.3% of total power generation and hydroelectric plants (often dependent on monsoons) for 13.4%. Nuclear plants accounted for 2.3% of total power generation. However, the Government has proposed plans to increase this to 25% of total power generation by 2050, which would involve the establishment of 30 nuclear reactors. Imports of mineral fuels, lubricants, etc., comprised 31.4% of the cost of total imports in 2010/11.

The services sector, which is dominated by the rapidly expanding data-processing business, the growing number of business call centres and the tourism industry, contributed an estimated 55.3% of GDP in 2009/10, and engaged 20.5% of the economically active population in 1991. By the early 2000s business call centres had become the fastest growing industry in India and an increasing number of multinational companies were transferring their call centre operations to the country, largely owing to cheaper labour costs and low long-distance telephone charges. More than 415,000 people were employed in the outsourcing industry in 2005/06. According to the World Bank, the GDP of the services sector increased by an average of 9.5% per year in 2001–10; the rate of growth reached 10.1% in 2008/09 and remained constant in 2009/10.

In 2010/11 India reported an estimated trade deficit of US $130,467m. and there was a deficit of $44,281m. on the current account of the balance of payments. In that year the principal source of imports was the People's Republic of China (providing 11.8% of total imports), followed by the United Arab Emirates (UAE), Switzerland, Saudi Arabia and the USA. The principal market for exports (accounting for 13.7% of total exports) was the UAE. Other major trading partners were the USA, China, Hong Kong and Singapore. The principal exports in 2010/11 were mineral fuels, mineral oils and products of their distillation, natural or cultured pearls, precious and semi-precious stones and precious metals, vehicles other than railway or tramway rolling stock and their parts, electrical machinery and their parts, iron and steel, organic chemicals, and nuclear reactors, boilers, machinery, mechanical appliances, etc. The principal imports in that year were mineral fuels and lubricants, pearls, precious and semi-precious stones, and nuclear reactors, boilers, machinery and mechanical appliances.

In the financial year ending 31 March 2012 there was a projected budgetary deficit of Rs 4,128,168m. In 2006, according to the UN Development Programme, India received a total of US $1,378.9m. in official development assistance. India's general government gross debt was Rs 50,522,170m. in 2010, equivalent to 64.1% of GDP. India's total external debt was $237,692m. at the end of 2009, of which $76,531m. was public and publicly-guaranteed debt. According to the ADB, the cost of debt-servicing in 2009 was equivalent to 5.5% of earnings from the exports of goods and services. The average annual rate of inflation was 6.5% in 2001–10; according to the ADB, consumer prices rose by 12.4% in 2008/09 and by 9.0% in 2009/10. A labour force survey for 2009/10 indicated that the rate of unemployment stood at about 9.4% (with the rate in urban areas at 7.3%, and that in rural areas in excess of 11%).

The process of wide-ranging economic reform initiated in 1991, including trade and investment liberalization, industrial deregulation, gradual privatization of public enterprises, and financial and tax reforms, has continued despite several changes in government. Following the creation in November 2004 of an Investment Commission for the purpose of encouraging domestic and foreign investment, total foreign direct investment (FDI) inflows, according to data published by the Department of Industrial Policy and Promotion, reached US $37,800m. in both 2008/09 and 2009/10, up from $4,300m. in 2003/04, but declined significantly, to $25,900 in 2010/11; however, FDI inflows were forecast to increase to around $35,000m. in 2011/12. Meanwhile, ongoing attempts to address India's unwieldy fiscal deficit (traditionally exacerbated by the country's modest tax base and cumbersome local government apparatus) have been largely frustrated by the repeated stalling of the divestment programme, internal security concerns, volatile foreign relations and the costs associated with natural disasters; nevertheless, the deficit declined to an estimated 4.8% of GDP in 2010/11, from in excess of 6% in 2009/10, with a further decline—to 4.6% of GDP—projected for 2011/12. Recognizing the need for significant infrastructural development in order to maintain the accelerated rate of economic growth, the 2012/13 national budget allocated increased funding to infrastructure. Despite a concomitant increase in budgetary funding for agriculture, which continues to provide employment for most of the working population, data released by the Government in early 2012 indicated that the sector was forecast to expand by just 2.5% in 2011/12 (down from 7.0% in 2010/11). Similarly poor performances were anticipated for the manufacturing and mining sectors, with manufacturing growth projected to decelerate to 3.9% (from 7.6% in 2010/11) and the mining sector forecast to contract by 2.2% (compared with positive growth of 5.0% in 2010/11). This, combined with global market uncertainties—particularly within the euro area—and the effects of the imposition of some 13 separate increases to the national interest rate between March 2010 and February 2012 (in which month the rate stood at 8.5%), in an effort to control rising inflation, led the Government in March 2012 to revise its GDP growth forecasts for 2011/12, from an initial projection of 8.5% to 6.9% (compared with growth of 8.4% in 2010/11). Inflation reached a 13-month high of 9.78% in August 2011; however, falling food prices in the latter stages of 2011 led to a subsequent decline in overall inflation, with the rate standing at 6.55% in January 2012. As a result, the central bank was widely expected to announce a reduction in the national interest rate later in the year, which, it was hoped, would facilitate efforts to boost economic growth. Meanwhile, in October 2011 a major new manufacturing development programme was approved by the Council of Ministers, which aimed to increase the sector's contribution to GDP to around 25% by 2022. The initiative, which was to include the establishment of a number of Special Economic Zones, also envisaged the creation of some 100m. new employment opportunities.

PUBLIC HOLIDAYS

The public holidays observed in India vary locally. The dates given below apply to Delhi.

2013: 23 January (Milad-un-Nabi, Birth of the Prophet), 26 January (Republic Day), 10 March (Maha Shivaratri), 27 March (Holi), 29 March (Good Friday), 23 April (Mahavir Jayanti), 25 May (Buddha Purnima), 7 August (Id al-Fitr, end of Ramadan), 15 August (Independence Day), 28 August (Janmashtami), 2 October (Mahatma Gandhi's Birthday), 14 October (Dussehra; Id ul-Zuha, Feast of the Sacrifice), 3 November (Diwali), 4 November (Muharram, Islamic New Year), 17 November (Guru Nanak Jayanti), 25 December (Christmas).

Note: A number of Hindu, Muslim and Buddhist holidays depend on lunar sightings.

Statistical Survey

Source (unless otherwise stated): Central Statistical Organization, Ministry of Statistics and Programme Implementation, Sardar Patel Bhavan, Patel Chowk, New Delhi 110 001; tel. (11) 23742150; fax (11) 23344689; e-mail moscc@bol.net.in; internet mospi.nic.in.

Area and Population

AREA, POPULATION AND DENSITY*

Area (sq km)	3,166,414†
Population (census results)	
1 March 2001‡	1,028,610,328
1 March 2011 (provisional)	
Males	623,724,248
Females	586,469,174
Total	1,210,193,422
Population (official estimate at mid-year)§	
2012	1,213,370,000
Density (per sq km) at mid-2012	383.2

* Including the Indian-held part of Jammu and Kashmir.

† 1,222,559 sq miles.

‡ Including estimates for certain areas in the states of Gujarat and Himachal Pradesh where the census could not be conducted owing to recent natural disasters, but excluding data for Mao-Maram, Paomata and Purul sub-divisions of Senapati district of Manipur.

§ Official projection; data rounded to nearest thousand persons.

Source: Office of the Registrar General of India, Ministry of Home Affairs, New Delhi.

POPULATION BY AGE AND SEX

('000 persons at 2001 census)

	Males	Females	Total
0–14	189,488	174,123	363,611
15–64	316,987	296,168	613,155
65 and over	24,182	24,924	49,106
Total*	530,657	495,215	1,025,872

* Excluding persons of unknown or undeclared age: 2,738,000 (males 1,500,000, females 1,238,000).

2011 census (provisional): *0–6:* 158,789,287 (males 82,952,135, females 75,837,152); *7 and over:* 1,051,404,135 (males 540,772,113, females 510,632,022); *Total:* 1,210,193,422 (males 623,724,248, females 586,469,174).

STATES AND TERRITORIES

(population at 2011 census, provisional)

	Area (sq km)	Population ('000)	Density (per sq km)	Capital
States				
Andhra Pradesh	275,045	84,666	307.8	Hyderabad
Arunachal Pradesh	83,743	1,383	16.5	Itanagar
Assam	78,438	31,169	397.4	Dispur
Bihar	94,163	103,805	1,102.4	Patna
Chhattisgarh	135,191	25,540	188.9	Raipur
Goa	3,702	1,458	393.8	Panaji
Gujarat	196,024	60,384	308.0	Gandhinagar
Haryana	44,212	25,353	573.4	Chandigarh*
Himachal Pradesh	55,673	6,857	123.2	Shimla
Jammu and Kashmir†	101,387	12,549	123.8	Srinagar/Jammu
Jharkhand	79,714	32,966	413.6	Ranchi
Karnataka	191,791	61,131	318.7	Bangalore
Kerala	38,863	33,388	859.1	Thiruvananthapuram (Trivandrum)
Madhya Pradesh	308,245	72,598	235.5	Bhopal
Maharashtra	307,713	112,373	365.2	Mumbai (Bombay)
Manipur	22,327	2,722	121.9	Imphal
Meghalaya	22,429	2,964	132.2	Shillong
Mizoram	21,081	1,091	51.8	Aizawl
Nagaland	16,579	1,981	119.5	Kohima
Orissa‡	155,707	41,947	269.4	Bhubaneswar
Punjab	50,362	27,704	550.1	Chandigarh*
Rajasthan	342,239	68,621	200.5	Jaipur
Sikkim	7,096	608	85.7	Gangtok
Tamil Nadu	130,058	72,139	554.7	Chennai (Madras)
Tripura	10,486	3,671	350.1	Agartala
Uttarakhand§	53,483	10,117	189.2	Dehradun
Uttar Pradesh	240,928	199,581	828.4	Lucknow
West Bengal	88,752	91,348	1,029.3	Kolkata (Calcutta)
Territories				
Andaman and Nicobar Islands	8,249	380	46.1	Port Blair
Chandigarh*	114	1,055	9,254.4	Chandigarh
Dadra and Nagar Haveli	491	343	698.6	Silvassa
Daman and Diu	112	243	2,169.6	Daman
Delhi	1,483	16,753	11,296.7	Delhi
Lakshadweep	32	64	2,000.0	Kavaratti
Puducherry (Pondicherry)	479	1,244	2,591.7	Puducherry (Pondicherry)
Total‖	3,166,414	1,210,193	382.2	—

* Chandigarh forms a separate Union Territory, not within Haryana or the Punjab. As part of a scheme for a transfer of territory between the two states, Chandigarh was due to be incorporated into the Punjab on 26 January 1986, but the transfer was postponed.

† Figures refer only to the Indian-held part of the territory.

‡ Renamed Odisha from November 2011.

§ Uttaranchal prior to 2007.

‖ Area data exclude contested area of Jammu and Kashmir (120,849 sq km), a disputed area between Puducherry and Andhra Pradesh (13 sq km) and two as yet undemarcated areas of Madhya Pradesh (7 sq km) and Chhattisgarh (3 sq km).

Source: Office of the Registrar General of India, Ministry of Home Affairs, New Delhi.

PRINCIPAL TOWNS

(population at 2011 census, provisional*)

Greater Mumbai (Bombay)	12,478,447	Tiruchirappalli	846,915
Delhi	11,007,835	Bhubaneswar	837,737
Bangalore	8,425,970	Salem	831,038
Hyderabad	6,809,970	Mira-Bhayander	814,655
Ahmedabad	5,570,585	Thiruvananthapuram	752,490
Chennai (Madras)	4,681,087	Bhiwandi	711,329
Kolkata (Calcutta)	4,486,679	Saharanpur	703,345
Surat	4,462,002	Gorakhpur	671,048
Pune (Poona)	3,115,431	Guntur	651,382
Jaipur (Jeypore)	3,073,350	Bikaner	647,804
Lucknow	2,815,601	Amravati	646,801
Kanpur (Cawnpore)	2,767,031	Noida	642,381
Nagpur	2,405,421	Jamshedpur	629,659
Indore	1,960,631	Bhilai Nagar	625,697
Thane	1,818,872	Warangal	620,116
Bhopal	1,795,648	Cuttack	606,007
Visakhapatnam (Vizag)	1,730,320	Firozabad	603,797
Pimpri-Chinchwad	1,729,359	Kochi (Cochin)	601,574
Patna	1,683,200	Bhavnagar	593,768
Vadodara (Baroda)	1,666,703	Dehradun	578,420
Ghaziabad	1,636,068	Durgapur	566,937
Ludhiana	1,613,878	Asansol	564,491
Agra	1,574,542	Nanded Waghala	550,564
Nashik	1,486,973	Kolapur	549,283
Faridabad Complex	1,404,653	Ajmer	542,580
Meerut	1,309,023	Gulbarga	532,031
Rajkot	1,286,995	Jamnagar	529,308
Kalyan-Dombivli	1,246,381	Ujjain	515,215
Vasai Virar	1,221,233	Loni	512,296
Varanasi (Banaras)	1,201,815	Siliguri	509,709
Srinagar	1,192,792	Jhansi	507,293
Aurangabad	1,171,330	Ulhasnagar	506,937
Dhanbad	1,161,561	Nellore	505,258
Amritsar	1,132,761	Jammu	503,690
Navi Mumbai	1,119,477	Sangli Miraj Kupwad	502,697
Allahabad	1,117,094	Belgaum	488,292
Ranchi	1,073,440	Mangalore	484,785
Haora	1,072,161	Ambattur	478,134
Coimbatore	1,061,447	Tirunelveli	474,838
Jabalpur (Jubbulpore)	1,054,336	Malegoan	471,006
Gwalior	1,053,505	Gaya	463,454
Vijayawada (Vijayavada)	1,048,240	Jalgaon	460,468
Jodhpur	1,033,918	Udaipur	451,735
Madurai	1,016,885	Maheshtala	449,423
Raipur	1,010,087	Tiruppur	444,543
Kota	1,001,365	Davanagere	435,128
Guwahati	963,429	Kozhikode (Calicut)	432,097
Chandigarh	960,787	Akola	427,146
Solapur	951,118	Kurnool	424,920
Hubli-Dharwad	943,857	Rajpur Sonarpur	423,806
Bareilly	898,167	Bokaro Steel City	413,934
Moradabad	889,810	South Dum Dum	410,524
Mysore	887,446	Bellary	409,644
Gurgaon	876,824	Patiala	405,164
Aligarh	872,575	Rajarhat Gopalpur	404,991
Jalandhar	862,196		

* Figures refer to the city proper in each case.

Capital: New Delhi, provisional population 249,998 at 2011 census.

Population of principal urban agglomerations at 2011 census, provisional: Greater Mumbai 18,414,288; Delhi 16,314,838; Kolkata 14,112,536; Chennai 8,696,010; Bangalore 8,499,399; Hyderabad 7,749,334; Ahmedabad 6,352,254; Pune 5,049,968; Surat 4,585,367; Kanpur 2,920,067; Lucknow 2,901,474; Nagpur 2,497,777; Ghaziabad 2,358,525; Indore 2,167,447; Coimbatore 2,151,466; Kochi 2,117,990; Patna 2,046,652; Kozhikode 2,030,519; Bhopal 1,883,381; Thrissur 1,854,783; Vadodara 1,817,191; Agra 1,746,467; Malappuram 1,698,645; Thiruvananthapuram 1,687,406; Kannur 1,642,892; Nashik 1,562,769; Vijayawada 1,491,202; Madurai 1,462,420; Varanasi 1,435,113; Meerut 1,424,908; Rajkot 1,390,933; Jamshedpur 1,337,131; Srinagar 1,273,312; Jabalpur 1,267,564; Asansol 1,243,008; Allahabad 1,216,719; Dhanbad 1,195,298; Aurangabad 1,189,376; Amritsar 1,183,705; Jodhpur 1,137,815; Ranchi 1,126,741; Raipur 1,122,555; Kollam 1,110,005; Gwalior 1,101,981; Durg-Bhilainagar 1,064,077; Chandigarh 1,025,682; Tiruchirappalli 1,021,717.

BIRTHS AND DEATHS

(estimates based on Sample Registration Scheme)

	2007	2008	2009
Birth rate (per 1,000)	23.1	22.8	22.5
Death rate (per 1,000)	7.4	7.4	7.3

Life expectancy (years at birth, WHO estimates): 65 (males 63; females 66) in 2009 (Source: WHO, *World Health Statistics*).

ECONOMICALLY ACTIVE POPULATION
(persons aged five years and over, 1991 census, excluding Jammu and Kashmir)

	Males	Females	Total
Agriculture, hunting, forestry and fishing	139,361,719	51,979,110	191,340,829
Mining and quarrying	1,536,919	214,356	1,751,275
Manufacturing	23,969,433	4,702,046	28,671,479
Construction	5,122,468	420,737	5,543,205
Trade and commerce	19,862,725	1,433,612	21,296,337
Transport, storage and communications	7,810,126	207,620	8,017,746
Other services	23,995,194	5,316,428	29,311,622
Total employed	221,658,584	64,273,909	285,932,493
Marginal workers	2,705,223	25,493,654	28,198,877
Total labour force	224,363,807	89,767,563	314,131,370

Unemployment (work applicants at 31 December, '000 persons aged 14 years and over): 41,466 (males 29,685, females 11,781) in 2006; 39,974 (males 27,972, females 12,002) in 2007; 39,112 (males 26,785, females 12,327) in 2008 (Source: ILO).

2001 census: Cultivators 127,312,851 (males 85,416,498, females 41,896,353); Agricultural labourers 106,775,330 (males 57,329,100, females 49,446,230); Household industry workers 16,956,942 (males 8,744,183, females 8,212,759); Other 151,189,601 (males 123,524,695, females 27,664,906); Total employed 402,234,724 (incl. 89,229,741 marginal workers).

Mid-2012 (official estimates in '000): Agriculture, etc. 275,633; Total labour force 515,200 (Source: FAO).

Health and Welfare

KEY INDICATORS

Total fertility rate (children per woman, 2009)	2.7
Under-5 mortality rate (per 1,000 live births, 2009)	66
HIV/AIDS (% of persons aged 15–49, 2007)	0.3
Physicians (per 1,000 head, 2005)	0.6
Hospital beds (per 1,000 head, 2002)	0.7
Health expenditure (2008): US $ per head (PPP)	122
Health expenditure (2008): % of GDP	4.2
Health expenditure (2008): public (% of total)	32.4
Access to water (% of persons, 2008)	88
Access to sanitation (% of persons, 2008)	31
Total carbon dioxide emissions ('000 metric tons, 2007)	1,611,042.5
Carbon dioxide emissions per head (metric tons, 2007)	1.4
Human Development Index (2011): ranking	134
Human Development Index (2011): value	0.547

For sources and definitions, see explanatory note on p. vi.

Agriculture

PRINCIPAL CROPS
('000 metric tons, year ending 30 June)

	2008/09	2009/10	2010/11*
Total cereals	219,900	203,450	223,470
Rice, milled	99,180	89,090	95,320
Sorghum (Jowar)	7,240	6,700	6,740
Cat-tail millet (Bajra)	8,890	6,510	10,080
Maize	19,730	16,720	21,280
Finger millet (Ragi)	2,040	1,890	2,170
Small millets	440	380	380
Wheat	80,680	80,800	85,930
Barley	1,690	1,350	1,570
Chick-peas (Gram)	7,060	7,480	8,250
Pigeon-peas (Tur)	2,270	2,460	2,890
Dry beans, dry peas, lentils and other pulses	5,240	4,720	6,950
Total food grains	234,470	218,110	241,560
Groundnuts (in shell)	7,168	5,429	7,538
Sesame seed	640	588	876
Rapeseed and mustard	7,201	6,608	7,667
Linseed	169	154	137
Castorseed	1,171	1,009	1,337
Total edible oilseeds (incl. others)	27,719	24,882	31,101
Cotton lint†	22,276	24,225	33,425
Jute and kenaf‡	10,365	11,817	10,582
Sugar cane: production cane	285,029	292,302	339,168

* Estimates.
† Production in '000 bales of 170 kg each.
‡ Production in '000 bales of 180 kg each.

Sources: Directorate of Economics and Statistics, Ministry of Agriculture.

Tea ('000 metric tons): 987 in 2008; 973 in 2009; 991 in 2010 (Source: FAO).

Tobacco, unmanufactured ('000 metric tons): 490 in 2008; 620 in 2009; 756 in 2010 (FAO estimate) (Source: FAO).

Potatoes ('000 metric tons): 34,658 in 2008; 34,391 in 2009; 36,577 in 2010 (Source: FAO).

LIVESTOCK
('000 head, year ending September, FAO estimates)

	2008	2009	2010
Cattle	202,700	206,400	210,200
Sheep	72,360	73,172	73,991
Goats	145,000	149,000	154,000
Pigs	10,606	10,104	9,630
Horses	581	552	524
Asses	397	359	326
Mules	128	120	112
Buffaloes	107,300	109,300	111,300
Camels	492	468	446
Chickens	666,000	810,000	866,000
Ducks	27,100	26,600	26,000

Source: FAO.

LIVESTOCK PRODUCTS
('000 metric tons)

	2008	2009	2010
Cattle meat*	1,036.6	1,055.8	1,086.5
Buffalo meat*	1,436.0	1,462.7	1,462.7
Sheep meat*	275.3	285.9	289.2
Goat meat*	550.0	567.5	586.5
Pig meat*	367.5	350.0	332.5
Chicken meat	1,815.0	2,026.0	2,300.0*
Duck meat*	36.4	37.7	37.7
Cows' milk	47,006	47,825	50,300†
Buffaloes' milk	57,549	59,201	62,400†
Goats' milk	3,983	3,910	4,300†
Hen eggs	3,077	3,324	3,414
Wool, greasy	42.9	43.2	43.0*

* FAO estimate(s).
† Unofficial figure.

Source: FAO.

Forestry

ROUNDWOOD REMOVALS
('000 cubic metres, excl. bark, FAO estimates)

	2008	2009	2010
Sawlogs, veneer logs and logs for sleepers	22,390	22,390	22,390
Pulpwood	624	624	624
Other industrial wood	178	178	178
Fuel wood	307,782	308,545	309,307
Total	330,975	331,737	332,499

Source: FAO.

SAWNWOOD PRODUCTION
('000 cubic metres, incl. railway sleepers)

	2003	2004	2005
Coniferous sawnwood	7,990	9,300	9,900
Broadleaved sawnwood	3,890	4,361	4,889
Total	11,880	13,661	14,789

2006–10: Figures assumed to be unchanged from 2005 (FAO estimates).

Source: FAO.

Fishing

('000 metric tons, live weight)

	2007	2008	2009
Capture	3,859.3	4,099.2	4,053.2
Bombay-duck (Bummalo)	211.9	234.6	195.7
Croakers and drums	224.8	233.1	247.4
Indian oil-sardine (Sardinella)	279.2	318.6	320.1
Giant tiger prawn	199.2	221.5	182.5
Aquaculture	3,112.2	3,851.1*	3,791.9*
Roho labeo	386.1	504.7	495.7
Mrigal carp	145.3	281.5	304.8
Catla	1,920.5	2,160.7	2,191.8
Silver carp	209.5	281.0	285.6
Total catch	6,971.5	7,950.3*	7,845.1*

* FAO estimate.

Source: FAO.

Mining

('000 metric tons, unless otherwise indicated)

	2007/08	2008/09	2009/10*
Coal	457,082	492,757	532,062
Lignite	33,980	32,421	34,080
Iron ore†	213,250	212,960	218,639
Manganese ore†	2,697	2,789	2,440
Bauxite	22,625	15,460	13,952
Chalk (Fireclay)	195	203	184
Kaolin (China clay)	1,466	2,084	2,578
Dolomite	5,852	5,504	5,182
Gypsum	3,400	3,877	3,422
Limestone	193,089	221,563	228,934
Crude petroleum	34,118	33,506	33,691
Chromium ore†	4,873	4,073	3,413
Phosphorite	1,849	1,804	1,547
Kyanite	5	5	5
Magnesite	253	253	286
Steatite	923	888	835
Copper ore†	3,242	3,452	3,228
Lead concentrates†	126	134	136
Zinc concentrates†	1,036	1,224	1,277
Mica—crude (metric tons)	4,578	1,462	1,213
Gold (kilograms)	2,969	2,438	2,106
Diamonds (carats)	586	536	16,810
Natural gas (million cu m)‡	32,417	32,849	47,510

* Provisional figures.

† Figures refer to gross weight. The estimated metal content is: Iron 63%; Manganese 40%; Chromium 30%; Copper 1.2%; Lead 70%; Zinc 60%.

‡ Figures refer to gas utilized.

Source: Indian Bureau of Mines.

Industry

SELECTED PRODUCTS
('000 metric tons unless otherwise indicated)

	2008/09	2009/10	2010/11
Refined sugar*	18,407	17,303	22,535
Cotton cloth (million sq metres)	26,898	28,517	30,659
Paper and paper board	6,543	7,067	n.a.
Soda ash	1,989	2,051	2,298
Fertilizers	14,334	16,224	n.a.
Motor spirit	16,020	15,970	17,509
Cement	181,400	200,651	209,660
Pig-iron	6,206	5,796	5,585
Stainless steel	2,680	2,881	3,737
Aluminium ingots (metric tons)	784,755	745,542	n.a.
Diesel engines—stationary (number)	3,337,682	3,377,819	n.a.
Television receivers (number)	7,574,271	9,622,186	n.a.
Electric fans (number)	11,541,791	14,074,284	n.a.
Passenger cars	1,516,791	1,910,465	2,452,819
Commercial vehicles (number)	416,491	566,585	752,597
Motorcycles, mopeds and scooters (number)	8,361,411	10,510,331	13,376,451
Bicycles (number)	11,123,734	12,651,846	n.a.

* Figures relate to crop year (beginning November) and are in respect of cane sugar only.

Finance

CURRENCY AND EXCHANGE RATES

Monetary Units

100 paise (singular: paisa) = 1 Indian rupee (R).

Sterling, Dollar and Euro Equivalents (30 December 2011)

£1 sterling = Rs 82.345;
US $1 = Rs 53.260;
€1 = Rs 68.913;
1,000 Indian rupees = £12.14 = $18.78 = €14.51.

Average Exchange Rate (rupees per US $)

2009 48.405
2010 45.726
2011 46.671

UNION BUDGET
(Rs million, rounded, year ending 31 March)

Revenue	2009/10	2010/11*	2011/12†
Tax revenue (net)	4,565,360	5,636,850	6,644,570
Customs receipts	833,240	1,318,000	1,517,000
Union excise duties	1,036,210	1,377,780	1,641,160
Corporation tax	2,447,250	2,963,770	3,599,900
Other taxes on income	1,323,150	1,490,660	1,720,260
Other taxes and duties	605,420	718,670	846,080
Less States' share of tax revenue	1,648,310	2,193,030	2,634,580
Less Surcharge transferred to National Calamity Contingency Fund	31,600	39,000	45,250
Other current revenue	1,162,750	2,201,480	1,254,350
Interest receipts (net)	217,560	197,280	195,780
Dividends and profits	502,480	487,270	426,240
Receipts of Union Territories	12,180	11,430	11,690
External grants	31,410	27,560	21,730
Other receipts (net)	399,120	1,477,940	598,910
Non-debt capital revenue	331,940	317,450	550,200
Total	6,060,050	8,155,780	8,449,120

Expenditure	2009/10	2010/11*	2011/12†
Central Ministries/Departments	9,358,137	11,162,382	11,477,262
Agriculture and co-operation (incl. agricultural research and education)	120,599	174,542	163,159
Atomic energy	89,007	81,575	93,525
Defence	1,800,183	1,897,473	2,025,723
Drinking water supply	92,000	105,849	110,052
Economic affairs	2,408,836	2,730,408	3,174,198
External affairs	62,085	71,200	71,060
Fertilizers	606,158	552,150	502,450
Food and public distribution	591,490	680,211	616,060
Health and family welfare	195,541	233,000	268,970
Home affairs	353,108	402,681	467,899
Education and literacy	244,661	363,420	414,510
Petroleum and natural gas	159,661	385,585	237,162
Railways	169,108	181,333	200,000
Road transport and highways	17,162	19,355	21,593
Rural development	566,371	763,782	741,437
Urban development	76,483	81,547	85,415
State plans	791,572	929,790	1,012,348
Union territories	95,166	73,586	87,679
Total	10,244,875	12,165,757	12,577,288
Current‡	9,118,091	10,536,768	10,971,622
Capital	1,126,784	1,628,989	1,605,666

* Estimates.

† Forecasts.

‡ Including interest payments (Rs million): 2,130,930 in 2009/10; 2,407,570 in 2010/11 (estimate); 2,679,860 in 2011/12 (forecast).

Source: Government of India, Union Budget 2011/12.

INTERNATIONAL RESERVES

(US $ million at 31 December)

	2008	2009	2010
Gold (national valuation)	6,605	9,486	22,470
IMF special drawing rights	3	5,169	5,078
Reserve position in IMF	813	1,430	2,385
Foreign exchange	246,603	258,583	267,814
Total	254,024	274,668	297,747

Source: IMF, *International Financial Statistics*.

MONEY SUPPLY

(Rs million, last Friday of year ending 31 March)

	2008/09	2009/10	2010/11*
Currency with the public	6,654,500	7,67,493	9,141,970
Demand deposits with banks	5,886,880	7,17,970	7,176,600
Other deposits with Reserve Bank	55,700	38,390	37,130
Time deposits	35,351,050	41,13,430	48,639,790
Broad money	47,948,120	56,02,731	64,995,480

* Provisional.

Note: Totals may not be equal to the sum of components, owing to rounding.

Source: Reserve Bank of India.

COST OF LIVING

(Consumer Price Index for Industrial Workers; base: 2000 = 100)

	2006	2007	2008
Food (incl. beverages)	125.0	137.0	152.0
Fuel and light	140.0	144.0	154.0
Clothing (incl. footwear)	114.0	118.0	123.0
Rent	137.0	142.0	147.0
All items (incl. others)	128.0	136.0	147.0

2009: Food (incl. beverages) 173.0; All items (incl. others) 163.2.

2010: Food (incl. beverages) 194.2; All items (incl. others) 182.8.

Source: ILO.

NATIONAL ACCOUNTS

(Rs '000 million at current prices, year ending 31 March)

National Income and Product

	2007/08	2008/09	2009/10
Domestic factor incomes	40,968.64	47,187.96	54,775.57
Consumption of fixed capital	4,845.58	5,632.90	6,556.73
Gross domestic product at factor cost	45,814.22	52,820.86	61,332.30
Indirect taxes	5,793.27	5,999.47	6,900.89
Less Subsidies	1,743.23	2,994.10	2,730.48
GDP in purchasers' values	49,864.26	55,826.23	65,502.71
Net factor income from abroad	–205.12	–329.23	–380.00
Gross national product	49,659.14	55,497.00	65,122.71
Less Consumption of fixed capital	4,845.58	5,632.90	6,556.73
National income in market prices	44,813.56	49,864.10	58,565.98

Expenditure on the Gross Domestic Product

	2007/08	2008/09	2009/10
Government final consumption expenditure	5,130.21	6,164.30	7,854.43
Private final consumption expenditure	28,404.21	32,578.00	37,820.13
Increase in stocks	2,014.56	1,125.19	2,146.19
Gross fixed capital formation	16,415.15	17,888.03	20,161.86
Acquisitions, less disposals, of valuables	535.92	722.13	1,133.74
Total domestic expenditure	52,500.05	58,477.65	69,116.35
Exports of goods and services	10,189.07	13,287.65	12,983.71
Less Imports of goods and services	12,191.09	16,140.40	16,398.72
Statistical discrepancy	–633.77	201.33	–198.63
GDP in purchasers' values	49,864.26	55,826.23	65,502.71
GDP at constant 2004/05 prices	42,531.84	44,629.67	48,693.17

Gross Domestic Product by Economic Activity

	2007/08	2008/09	2009/10
Agriculture	7,162.76	7,995.17	9,399.22
Forestry and logging	813.11	861.58	904.84
Fishing	389.31	432.68	588.91
Mining and quarrying	1,248.12	1,386.49	1,542.69
Manufacturing	7,327.20	8,162.17	9,052.24
Electricity, gas and water supply	838.30	841.64	926.71
Construction	3,889.14	4,514.14	5,017.06
Trade, hotels and restaurants	7,827.38	8,944.98	10,004.47
Transport, storage and communications	3,666.36	4,141.42	4,770.09
Banking and insurance	2,511.95	2,989.31	3,310.10
Real estate and business services	4,402.69	5,502.62	6,961.48
Public administration and defence	2,349.92	3,075.82	3,888.94
Other services	3,387.98	3,972.84	4,965.55
GDP at factor cost	45,814.22	52,820.86	61,332.30
Indirect taxes	5,793.27	5,999.47	6,900.89
Less Subsidies	1,743.23	2,994.10	2,730.48
GDP in market prices	49,864.26	55,826.23	65,502.71

BALANCE OF PAYMENTS
(US $ million)

	2008/09	2009/10	2010/11*
Exports of goods f.o.b.	189,001	182,235	250,468
Imports of goods f.o.b.	–308,521	–300,609	–380,935
Trade balance	–119,520	–118,374	–130,467
Services (net)	53,916	35,726	47,664
Balance on goods and services	–65,604	–82,648	–82,803
Other income (net)	–7,110	–8,040	–14,863
Balance on goods, services and income	–72,714	–90,688	–97,666
Current transfers (net)	44,798	52,305	53,385
Current balance	–27,915	–38,383	–44,281
Direct investment abroad	37,672	33,124	23,364
Direct investment from abroad	–17,855	–14,353	–16,222
Portfolio investment assets	–13,854	32,376	31,471
Portfolio investment liabilities	–177	20	–1,179
Net loans	8,318	13,259	27,859
Banking capital (net)	–3,246	2,084	4,963
Rupee debt service	–100	–97	–69
Other capital (net)	–3,990	–13,016	–10,440
Net errors and omissions	1,067	–1,573	–2,416
Overall balance	–20,080	13,441	13,050

* Preliminary figures.

Note: Totals may not be equal to the sum of components, owing to rounding.

Source: Reserve Bank of India.

OFFICIAL DEVELOPMENT ASSISTANCE
(US $ million)

	1998	1999	2000
Bilateral donors	896.4	826.7	638.7
Multilateral donors	713.2	664.6	848.5
Total	1,609.6	1,491.3	1,487.2
Grants	802.6	772.2	775.3
Loans	807.0	719.1	711.9
Per caput assistance (US $)	1.7	1.5	1.5

Source: UN, *Statistical Yearbook for Asia and the Pacific*.

External Trade

PRINCIPAL COMMODITIES
(Rs million, year ending 31 March)

Imports c.i.f.	2008/09	2009/10	2010/11
Animal and vegetable oils, fats and waxes	160,891	266,973	300,562
Mineral fuels, mineral oils and products of their distillation	4,667,474	4,551,788	5,277,877
Organic chemicals	388,528	445,055	575,498
Natural or cultured pearls, precious and semi-precious stones, precious metals and articles thereof; imitation jewellery; coin	1,970,150	2,182,485	3,503,964
Iron and steel	469,173	417,465	501,332
Nuclear reactors, boilers, machinery, mechanical appliances and parts thereof	1,211,542	1,136,828	1,321,619
Electrical machinery and equipment and parts thereof; sound and television apparatus	1,150,622	1,047,658	1,238,592
Aircraft, spacecraft, and parts thereof	246,254	235,209	156,756
Total (incl. others)	13,744,356	13,637,355	16,834,670

Exports f.o.b.	2008/09	2009/10	2010/11
Cereals	150,864	142,281	144,059
Ores, slag and ash	248,150	313,024	264,191
Mineral fuels, mineral oils and products of their distillation	1,273,241	1,368,536	1,933,861
Organic chemicals	340,579	352,413	415,692
Iron and steel	336,431	213,063	429,913
Articles of iron or steel	264,959	193,635	348,445
Cotton	142,243	216,230	304,225
Articles of apparel and clothing accessories, knitted or crocheted	232,641	217,766	217,180
Articles of apparel and clothing accessories, not knitted or crocheted	271,256	290,555	293,511
Natural or cultured pearls, precious and semi-precious stones, precious metals and articles thereof; imitation jewellery; coin	1,288,269	1,381,483	1,823,347
Nuclear reactors, boilers, machinery, mechanical appliances and parts thereof	364,968	340,996	407,759
Vehicles other than railway or tramway rolling stock, and parts and accessories thereof	274,971	291,475	514,010
Total (incl. others)	8,407,551	8,455,336	11,426,490

Source: Ministry of Commerce and Industry.

PRINCIPAL TRADING PARTNERS
(Rs million, year ending 31 March)

Imports c.i.f.	2008/09	2009/10	2010/11
Australia	504,965	586,620	491,876
Belgium	260,579	284,658	391,787
China, People's Republic	1,476,056	1,460,486	1,980,791
France	211,652	198,289	168,666
Germany	549,224	488,858	541,360
Hong Kong	297,325	223,167	428,251
Indonesia	307,513	410,088	451,363
Iran	558,218	546,356	497,246
Iraq	342,850	332,727	409,772
Italy	199,836	182,741	193,947
Japan	358,328	318,938	393,093
Korea, Republic	396,582	405,506	477,125
Kuwait	431,994	389,880	469,760
Malaysia	325,916	244,940	297,459
Nigeria	399,955	343,771	490,051
Oman	54,644	164,431	181,843
Qatar	158,947	220,100	310,358
Russia	197,874	169,239	164,167
Saudi Arabia	897,470	806,643	928,549
Singapore	345,614	306,233	325,458
South Africa	248,823	269,002	325,251
Switzerland	527,032	692,320	1,127,396
Thailand	123,527	138,885	194,599
United Arab Emirates	1,059,264	917,989	1,491,234
United Kingdom	267,677	211,254	245,617
USA	848,183	805,843	913,585
Venezuela	184,792	135,069	237,482
Total (incl. others)	13,744,356	13,637,355	16,834,670

Exports f.o.b.	2008/09	2009/10	2010/11
Bangladesh	113,172	115,011	163,854
Belgium	203,094	177,570	286,679
Brazil	118,744	113,648	180,961
China, People's Republic	426,613	547,139	889,326
France	137,767	179,994	230,501
Germany	291,948	256,329	307,556
Hong Kong	303,907	373,005	470,820
Indonesia	115,778	146,046	283,877
Iran	115,652	88,074	124,680
Israel	65,843	92,894	137,799
Italy	173,649	160,722	206,900
Japan	138,077	171,428	236,305
Korea, Republic	183,536	161,268	188,267
Malaysia	157,804	135,039	180,666
Netherlands	288,900	303,009	352,874
Saudi Arabia	229,401	185,523	237,554
Singapore	377,569	359,483	469,061

Exports f.o.b.—*continued*	2008/09	2009/10	2010/11
South Africa	89,943	97,513	182,147
Spain	113,879	96,038	116,450
Sri Lanka	108,950	102,896	183,618
Thailand	87,240	82,276	126,821
Turkey	63,703	72,778	125,493
United Arab Emirates	1,102,291	1,133,479	1,562,565
United Kingdom	303,446	294,763	325,214
USA	964,584	924,165	1,163,625
Viet Nam	79,495	86,740	120,823
Total (incl. others)	8,407,551	8,455,336	11,426,490

Source: Ministry of Commerce and Industry.

Transport

RAILWAYS
(million, year ending 31 March)

	2007/08	2008/09	2009/10
Passengers	6,524	6,920	7,246
Passenger-km	769,956	838,032	903,465
Freight (metric tons)	804.1	836.6	892.2
Freight (metric ton-km)	523,196	552,002	601,290

Source: Railway Board, Ministry of Railways and Indian Railways.

ROAD TRAFFIC
('000 motor vehicles in use at 31 March)

	2007	2008	2009*
Private cars, jeeps and taxis	12,649	13,950	15,313
Buses and coaches	1,350	1,427	1,486
Goods vehicles	5,119	5,601	6,041
Motorcycles and scooters	69,129	75,336	82,401
Others	8,460	9,039	9,710
Total	96,707	105,353	114,951

* Provisional figures.

Source: Ministry of Road Transport and Highways.

SHIPPING

Merchant Fleet
(registered at 31 December)

	2007	2008	2009
Vessels	1,417	1,460	1,349
Displacement ('000 grt)	9,168.0	9,283.2	9,026.9

Source: IHS Fairplay, *World Fleet Statistics*.

International Sea-borne Traffic
(year ending 31 March)

	2003/04	2004/05	2005/06
Vessels ('000 nrt):			
entered	68,111	66,943	44,320
cleared	88,733	41,634	23,891
Freight ('000 metric tons):			
loaded	n.a.	143,071	154,045
unloaded	n.a.	157,593	175,162

2006/07 ('000 nrt): Vessels entered 67,404; Vessels cleared 40,700.

CIVIL AVIATION
(all Indian carriers, traffic on scheduled services)

	2007/08	2008/09	2009/10
Passengers carried ('000)	53,493	49,516	56,949
Passenger-km (million)	77,847	78,445	89,443
Freight carried (metric tons)	422,509	423,703	513,706
Freight ton-km (million)	1,041	1,196	1,427
Mail carried (metric tons)	22,957	27,997	33,361
Mail ton-km (million)	43	49	58

Source: Directorate General of Civil Aviation.

Tourism

FOREIGN VISITORS BY COUNTRY OF ORIGIN

	2008	2009	2010
Australia	146,209	149,074	169,647
Bangladesh	541,884	468,899	431,962
Canada	222,364	224,069	242,372
France	207,802	196,462	225,232
Germany	204,344	191,616	227,720
Japan	145,352	124,756	168,019
Malaysia	115,794	135,343	179,077
Pakistan	85,529	53,137	51,739
Sri Lanka	218,805	239,995	266,515
United Kingdom	776,530	769,251	759,494
USA	804,933	827,140	931,292
Total (incl. others)	5,282,603	5,167,699	5,775,692

Receipts from tourism (US $ million, estimates): 11,747 in 2008; 11,394 in 2009; 14,193 in 2010.

Source: Ministry of Tourism.

Communications Media

	2008	2009	2010
Telephones ('000 main lines in use)	37,900	37,060	35,090
Mobile cellular telephones ('000 subscribers)	346,890	525,090	752,190
Internet subscribers ('000)	12,850	15,240	18,690
Broadband subscribers ('000)	5,280.0	7,745.7	10,990.0

1997: Radio receivers ('000 in use) 116,000; Facsimile machines ('000 in use, year ending 31 March) 100.

Personal computers: 37,000,000 (32.9 per 1,000 persons) in 2007.

Television receivers ('000 in use): 79,000 in 2000; 85,000 in 2001.

Daily newspapers (2008/09): 8,475 (circulation 135,805,000 copies).

Non-daily newspapers and other periodicals (2008/09): 64,671 (circulation 122,149,000 copies).

Sources: International Telecommunication Union; UN, *Statistical Yearbook*; Register of Newspapers for India; Ministry of Information and Broadcasting.

Education

(2009/10 unless otherwise indicated, provisional)

	Institutions	Teachers	Students
Pre-primary	67,822	n.a.	5,799,329
Primary	823,162	2,480,414	135,669,843
Middle	367,745	1,912,585	59,421,002
Secondary (high school); Higher secondary (new pattern); Intermediate/pre-degree/junior college	190,643	2,339,072	48,265,863
Higher education*	33,634†	699,000‡	26,223,000‡

* Includes colleges for general and professional education, universities and institutions of national importance.

† At August 2011.

‡ Rounded figure.

Source: Ministry of Human Resource Development.

Pupil-teacher ratio (primary education, UNESCO estimate): 40.2 in 2003/04 (Source: UNESCO Institute for Statistics).

Adult literacy rate (UNESCO estimates): 66.0% (males 76.9%; females 54.5%) in 2007 (Source: UNESCO Institute for Statistics).

Directory

The Government

HEAD OF STATE

President: PRATIBHA DEVISINGH PATIL (sworn in 25 July 2007).

Vice-President: MOHAMMAD HAMID ANSARI (sworn in 12 August 2007).

COUNCIL OF MINISTERS

(May 2012)

The Government is formed by the United Progressive Alliance, a coalition of the Indian National Congress (Congress), the Nationalist Congress Party (NCP), Dravida Munnetra Kazhagam (DMK), the All India Trinamool Congress (AITC), the Jammu and Kashmir National Conference (JKNC) and the Rashtriya Lok Dal (RLD).

Prime Minister and Minister-in-charge of Personnel, Public Grievances and Pensions, of Planning, of Atomic Energy, and of Space: Dr MANMOHAN SINGH (Congress).

Minister of Finance: PRANAB MUKHERJEE (Congress).

Minister of Agriculture and of Food Processing Industries: SHARAD PAWAR (NCP).

Minister of Defence: A. K. ANTONY (Congress).

Minister of Home Affairs: P. CHIDAMBARAM (Congress).

Minister of External Affairs: S. M. KRISHNA (Congress).

Minister of Micro, Small and Medium Enterprises: VIRBHADRA SINGH (Congress).

Minister of Science and Technology, and of Earth Sciences: VILASRAO DESHMUKH (Congress).

Minister of Health and Family Welfare: GHULAM NABI AZAD (Congress).

Minister of Power: SUSHILKUMAR SHINDE (Congress).

Minister of Corporate Affairs: VEERAPPA MOILY (Congress).

Minister of New and Renewable Energy: Dr FAROOQ ABDULLAH (JKNC).

Minister of Petroleum and Natural Gas: S. JAIPAL REDDY (Congress).

Minister of Urban Development: KAMAL NATH (Congress).

Minister of Overseas Indian Affairs: VAYALAR RAVI (Congress).

Minister of Civil Aviation: AJIT SINGH (RLD).

Minister of Information and Broadcasting: AMBIKA SONI (Congress).

Minister of Labour and Employment: MALLIKARJUN KHARGE (Congress).

Minister of Human Resource Development, and of Communications and Information Technology: KAPIL SIBAL (Congress).

Minister of Commerce and Industry, and of Textiles: ANAND SHARMA (Congress).

Minister of Road Transport and Highways: C. P. JOSHI (Congress).

Minister of Housing and Urban Poverty Alleviation, and of Culture: KUMARI SELJA (Congress).

Minister of Tourism: SUBODH KANT SAHAY (Congress).

Minister of Shipping: G. K. VASAN (Congress).

Minister of Social Justice and Empowerment: MUKUL WASNIK (Congress).

Minister of Tribal Affairs, and of Panchayati Raj: KISHORE CHANDRA DEO (Congress).

Minister of Steel: BENI PRASAD VERMA (Congress).

Minister of Railways: MUKUL ROY (AITC).

Minister of Chemicals and Fertilizers: M. K. ALAGIRI (DMK).

Minister of Coal: SHRIPRAKASH JAISWAL (Congress).

Minister of Law and Justice, and of Minority Affairs: SALMAN KHURSHEED (Congress).

Minister of Parliamentary Affairs, and of Water Resources: PAWAN KUMAR BANSAL (Congress).

Minister of Heavy Industries and Public Enterprises: PRAFUL PATEL (NCP).

Minister of Rural Development, and of Drinking Water and Sanitation: JAIRAM RAMESH (Congress).

Ministers of State with Independent Charge

Minister of State for Mines: DINSHA PATEL (Congress).

Minister of State for Women and Child Development: KRISHNA TIRATH (Congress).

Minister of State for Youth Affairs and Sports: AJAY MAKEN (Congress).

Minister of State for Consumer Affairs, Food and Public Distribution: Prof. K. V. THOMAS.

Minister of Statistics and Programme Implementation, and of Chemicals and Fertilizers: SRIKANT JENA.

Minister of State for Environment and Forests: JAYANTHI NATARAJAN (Congress).

Minister of State for Development of North Eastern Region: PABAN SINGH GHATOWAR (Congress).

There are, in addition, 37 Ministers of State without independent charge.

MINISTRIES AND GOVERNMENT OFFICES

President's Office: Rashtrapati Bhavan, New Delhi 110 004; tel. (11) 23015321; fax (11) 23017290; e-mail presidentofindia@rb.nic.in; internet www.presidentofindia.nic.in.

Vice-President's Office: 6 Maulana Azad Rd, New Delhi 110 011; tel. (11) 23016344; fax (11) 23018124; e-mail vpindia@nic.in; internet vicepresidentofindia.nic.in.

Prime Minister's Office: South Blk, Raisina Hill, New Delhi 110 011; tel. (11) 23012312; fax (11) 23016857; internet www.pmindia.nic.in.

Ministry of Agriculture: Krishi Bhavan, Dr Rajendra Prasad Rd, New Delhi 110 001; tel. (11) 23383370; fax (11) 23384129; e-mail am.krishi@nic.in.

Ministry of Chemicals and Fertilizers: Shastri Bhavan, Dr Rajendra Prasad Rd, New Delhi 110 001; tel. (11) 23386519; fax (11) 23384020; e-mail mincf.cpc@sb.nic.in; internet chemicals.gov.in; internet fert.nic.in.

Ministry of Civil Aviation: Rajiv Gandhi Bhavan, Safdarjung Airport, New Delhi 110 023; tel. (11) 24610350; fax (11) 24613054; e-mail secy.moca@nic.in; internet civilaviation.nic.in.

Ministry of Coal: Shastri Bhavan, Dr Rajendra Prasad Rd, New Delhi 110 001; tel. (11) 23384884; fax (11) 23381678; e-mail secy.moc@nic.in; internet coal.nic.in.

Ministry of Commerce and Industry: 45C Udyog Bhavan, New Delhi 110 011; tel. (11) 23063086; fax (11) 23019947; e-mail ikeshari@gmail.com; internet commerce.nic.in.

Ministry of Communications and Information Technology: Electronic Niketan, CGO Complex, Lodhi Rd, New Delhi 110 003; tel. (11) 24369191; fax (11) 24362333; e-mail webmaster@mit.gov.in; internet www.mit.gov.in.

Ministry of Consumer Affairs, Food and Public Distribution: Krishi Bhavan, New Delhi 110 001; tel. (11) 23383370; fax (11) 23384129; e-mail secy-food@nic.in; internet fcamin.nic.in.

Ministry of Corporate Affairs: 'A' Wing, Shastri Bhavan, Dr Rajendra Prasad Rd, New Delhi 110 001; tel. (11) 23384660; fax (11) 23073806; e-mail hq.delhi@mca.gov.in; internet www.mca.gov.in.

Ministry of Culture: 'C' Wing, Shastri Bhavan, Dr Rajendra Prasad Rd, New Delhi 110 001; tel. (11) 23386995; fax (11) 23384093; e-mail pvtsecymoc@gmail.com; internet indiaculture.gov.in.

Ministry of Defence: South Blk, New Delhi 110 011; tel. (11) 23019030; fax (11) 23015403; e-mail ak.antony@sansad.nic.in; internet www.mod.nic.in.

Ministry of Development of North Eastern Region: Vigyan Bhavan Annexe, Maulana Azad Rd, New Delhi 110 011; tel. (11) 23022020; fax (11) 23022024; e-mail secydoner@nic.in; internet mdoner.gov.in.

Ministry of Drinking Water and Sanitation: 9th Floor, Paryavaran Bhavan, CGO Complex, Lodhi Rd, New Delhi 110 003; tel. (11) 24361043; fax (11) 24364113; e-mail jstm@nic.in; internet ddws.gov.in.

Ministry of Earth Sciences: Blk 12, CGO Complex, Lodhi Rd, New Delhi 110 003; tel. (11) 24360874; fax (11) 2432644; e-mail secretary@moes.gov.in; internet moes.gov.in.

Ministry of Environment and Forests: Paryavaran Bhavan, CGO Complex, Lodhi Rd, New Delhi 110 003; tel. (11) 24361727; fax (11) 24362222; e-mail envisect@nic.in; internet moef.nic.in.

Ministry of External Affairs: South Blk, New Delhi 110 011; tel. (11) 23011127; fax (11) 23013254; e-mail eam@mea.gov.in; internet meaindia.nic.in.

Ministry of Finance: North Blk, 1st Floor, New Delhi 110 001; tel. (11) 23092611; fax (11) 23094075; e-mail secy-dea@nic.in; internet finmin.nic.in.

Ministry of Food Processing Industries: Panchsheel Bhavan, August Kranti Marg, New Delhi 110 049; tel. (11) 26492475; fax (11) 26493228; e-mail ajitji@nic.in; internet mofpi.nic.in.

Ministry of Health and Family Welfare: Nirman Bhavan, Maulana Azad Rd, New Delhi 110 011; tel. and fax (11) 23061647; e-mail resp-health@hub.nic.in; internet mohfw.nic.in.

Ministry of Heavy Industries and Public Enterprises: Udyog Bhavan, New Delhi 110 011; tel. (11) 23061854; fax (11) 23062633; e-mail shioff@nic.in; internet dhi.nic.in.

Ministry of Home Affairs: North Blk, Central Secr., New Delhi 110 001; tel. (11) 23092011; fax (11) 23093750; e-mail websitemhaweb@nic.in; internet mha.nic.in.

Ministry of Housing and Urban Poverty Alleviation: Nirman Bhavan, Maulana Azad Rd, New Delhi 110 108; tel. (11) 23061444; fax (11) 23061991; e-mail secy-muepa@nic.in; internet mhupa.gov.in.

Ministry of Human Resource Development: Shastri Bhavan, Dr Rajendra Prasad Rd, New Delhi 110 001; tel. (11) 23383936; fax (11) 23381355; e-mail dsel-mhrd@nic.in; internet mhrd.gov.in.

Ministry of Information and Broadcasting: 'A' Wing, Shastri Bhavan, Dr Rajendra Prasad Rd, New Delhi 110 001; tel. (11) 23382639; fax (11) 23386530; e-mail secy-in@nic.in; internet mib.gov.in.

Ministry of Labour and Employment: Shram Shakti Bhavan, Rafi Marg, New Delhi 110 001; tel. (11) 23710265; fax (11) 23718730; e-mail laborweb@nic.in; internet labour.nic.in.

Ministry of Law and Justice: 'A' Wing, 4th Floor, Shastri Bhavan, Dr Rajendra Prasad Rd, New Delhi 110 001; tel. (11) 23387557; fax (11) 23384241; e-mail vnathan@nic.in; internet lawmin.nic.in.

Ministry of Micro, Small and Medium Enterprises: Udyog Bhavan, Rafi Marg, New Delhi 110 011; tel. (11) 23062107; fax (11) 23063045; e-mail secretary-msme@nic.in; internet msme.gov.in.

Ministry of Mines: 'A' Wing, 3rd Floor, Shastri Bhavan, Dr Rajendra Prasad Rd, New Delhi; tel. (11) 23385173; fax (11) 23384682; e-mail secy-mines@nic.in; internet mines.nic.in.

Ministry of Minority Affairs: 11th Floor, Paryavaran Bhavan, CGO Complex, Lodhi Rd, New Delhi 110 003; tel. (11) 24364271; fax (11) 23017999; e-mail vm@nic.in; internet minorityaffairs.gov.in.

Ministry of New and Renewable Energy: Blk 14, CGO Complex, Lodhi Rd, New Delhi 110 003; tel. (11) 24361298; fax (11) 24361830; e-mail secymnes@nic.in; internet mnes.nic.in.

Ministry of Overseas Indian Affairs: Akbar Bhavan, Chanakya Puri, New Delhi 110 021; tel. (11) 24197900; fax (11) 24197919; e-mail info@moia.nic.in; internet moia.gov.in.

Ministry of Panchayati Raj: Krishi Bhavan, Dr Rajendra Prasad Rd, New Delhi 110 001; tel. (11) 23074309; fax (11) 23389028; e-mail secy-mopr@nic.in; internet panchayat.gov.in.

Ministry of Parliamentary Affairs: 87 Parliament House, New Delhi 110 001; tel. (11) 23017663; fax (11) 23017726; e-mail secympa@nic.in; internet mpa.nic.in.

Ministry of Personnel, Public Grievances and Pensions: North Blk, New Delhi 110 001; tel. (11) 23094848; fax (11) 23382848; e-mail secy_mop@nic.in; internet persmin.nic.in.

Ministry of Petroleum and Natural Gas: Shastri Bhavan, Dr Rajendra Prasad Rd, New Delhi 110 001; tel. (11) 23382889; fax (11) 23382673; e-mail jse.png@nic.in; internet petroleum.nic.in.

Ministry of Power: Shram Shakti Bhavan, Rafi Marg, New Delhi 110 001; tel. (11) 23710271; e-mail harisankar@nic.in; internet powermin.nic.in.

Ministry of Railways: Rail Bhavan, Raisina Rd, New Delhi 110 001; tel. (11) 23386645; fax (11) 23387333; e-mail secyrb@rb.railnet.gov.in; internet www.indianrailways.gov.in.

Ministry of Road Transport and Highways: Parivahan Bhavan, 1 Parliament St, New Delhi 110 001; tel. (11) 23719955; fax (11) 23719023; e-mail ifcmost@nic.in; internet morth.nic.in.

Ministry of Rural Development: Krishi Bhavan, Dr Rajendra Prasad Rd, New Delhi 110 001; tel. (11) 23382230; fax (11) 23382408; e-mail secyrd@nic.in; internet rural.nic.in.

Ministry of Science and Technology: Technology Bhavan, New Mehrauli Rd, New Delhi 110 016; tel. (11) 26567373; fax (11) 26864570; e-mail dstinfo@nic.in; internet dst.gov.in.

Ministry of Shipping: Transport Bhavan, 1 Parliament St, New Delhi 110 001; tel. (11) 23710220; fax (11) 23716656; e-mail dsadmn-ship@nic.in; internet shipping.gov.in.

Ministry of Social Justice and Empowerment: Shastri Bhavan, Dr Rajendra Prasad Rd, New Delhi 110 001; tel. (11) 23385180; fax (11) 23382683; e-mail secywel@nic.in; internet socialjustice.nic.in.

Ministry of Statistics and Programme Implementation: Sardar Patel Bhavan, Patel Chowk, New Delhi 110 001; tel. (11) 23340884; fax (11) 23340138; e-mail bajajvk@nic.in; internet mospi.gov.in.

Ministry of Steel: Udyog Bhavan, New Delhi 110 107; tel. (11) 23062052; fax (11) 23063236; e-mail ric-steel@nic.in; internet steel.nic.in.

Ministry of Textiles: Udyog Bhavan, New Delhi 110 011; tel. (11) 23061338; fax (11) 23063711; e-mail secy-ub@nic.in; internet texmin.nic.in.

Ministry of Tourism: Transport Bhavan, Rm 123, 1 Parliament St, New Delhi 110 001; tel. and fax (11) 23715084; e-mail amitabhk@nic.in; internet tourism.gov.in.

Ministry of Tribal Affairs: Shastri Bhavan, Dr Rajendra Prasad Rd, New Delhi 110 001; tel. (11) 23388482; fax (11) 23356318; e-mail dirit@tribal.nic.in; internet tribal.gov.in.

Ministry of Urban Development: Nirman Bhavan, Maulana Azad Rd, New Delhi 110 011; tel. (11) 23062377; fax (11) 23061459; e-mail secyurban@nic.in; internet urbanindia.nic.in.

Ministry of Water Resources: Shram Shakti Bhavan, Rafi Marg, New Delhi 110 001; tel. and fax (11) 23710343; e-mail jsadm-mowr@nic.in; internet wrmin.nic.in.

Ministry of Women and Child Development: Shastri Bhavan, Dr Rajendra Prasad Rd, New Delhi; tel. (11) 23383586; fax (11) 23381495; e-mail secy.wcd@nic.in; internet wcd.nic.in.

Ministry of Youth Affairs and Sports: Shastri Bhavan, Dr Rajendra Prasad Rd, New Delhi 110 001; tel. (11) 23384183; e-mail minister.yas@nic.in; internet yas.nic.in.

Department of Atomic Energy: Anushakti Bhavan, Chatrapathi Shivaji Maharaj Marg, Mumbai 400 001; tel. (22) 22862500; fax (22) 22048476; e-mail info@dae.gov.in; internet www.dae.gov.in.

Department of Space: 3rd Floor, Lok Nayak Bhavan, Prithviraj Lane, New Delhi 110 003; tel. (11) 24694745; fax (11) 24693871.

Legislature

PARLIAMENT

Rajya Sabha
(Council of States)

Most of the members of the Rajya Sabha are indirectly elected by the State Assemblies for six years, with one-third retiring every two years. The remaining members are nominated by the President.

Chairman: Mohammad Hamid Ansari.

Deputy Chairman: K. Rahman Khan.

Distribution of Seats, April 2012

Party	Seats
Congress*	70†
Bharatiya Janata Party	49
Bahujan Samaj Party	15
Communist Party of India (Marxist)	11
All India Trinamool Congress	9
Janata Dal (United)	9
Samajwadi Party	8
Biju Janata Dal	7
Dravida Munnetra Kazhagam	7
Nationalist Congress Party	7
All-India Anna Dravida Munnetra Kazhagam	5
Telugu Desam	5
Shiv Sena	4
Communist Party of India	3
Shiromani Akali Dal	3
Asom Gana Parishad	2
Jammu and Kashmir National Conference	2
Rashtriya Janata Dal	2
Independents and others	14
Nominated	5
Total	237

* Formerly known as the Indian National Congress (Indira) or Congress (I); name gradually changed to the Indian National Congress or Congress Party in the early to mid-1990s.

† Including three nominated members.

Lok Sabha
(House of the People)

Speaker: MEIRA KUMAR.

Deputy Speaker: KARIYA MUNDA.

General Election, 16, 22, 23 and 30 April and 7 and 13 May 2009

Party	Seats
United Progressive Alliance	262
Congress	206
Dravida Munnetra Kazhagam	18
Nationalist Congress Party	9
All India Trinamool Congress	19
Jharkhand Mukti Morcha	2
Jammu and Kashmir National Conference	3
Viduthali Chiruthaigal Katch	1
All India Majlis-e-Ittehadul Muslimeen	1
Muslim League Kerala State Committee	2
Kerala Congress (Mani)	1
National Democratic Alliance	159
Bharatiya Janata Party	116
Shiv Sena	11
Rashtriya Lok Dal	5
Shiromani Akali Dal	4
Janata Dal (United)	20
Telangana Rashtra Samithi	2
Asom Gana Parishad	1
Third Front	79
Communist Party of India (Marxist)	16
Communist Party of India	4
All India Forward Bloc	2
Revolutionary Socialist Party	2
Bahujan Samaj Party	21
Biju Janata Dal	14
All-India Anna Dravida Munnetra Kazhagam	9
Telugu Desam Party	6
Janata Dal (Secular)	3
Haryana Janhit Congress	1
Marumalarchi Dravida Munnetra Kazhagam	1
Fourth Front	27
Samajwadi Party	23
Rashtriya Janata Dal	4
Independents and others	16
Nominated	2*
Total	545

* Nominated by the President to represent the Anglo-Indian community.

State Governments
(May 2012)

ANDHRA PRADESH
(Capital—Hyderabad)

Governor: E. S. L. NARASIMHAN.

Chief Minister: KIRAN KUMAR REDDY (Congress).

Legislative Assembly: 295 seats (Congress 156, Telugu Desam 91, Praja Rajyam Party 18, Telangana Rashtra Samithi 11, All India Majlis-e-Ittehadul Muslimeen 7, Communist Party of India 4, Bharatiya Janata Party 2, Communist Party of India—Marxist 1, Lok Satta Party 1, independents 3, nominated 1).

Legislative Council: revived April 2007; 90 seats (Congress 38, Telugu Desam 16, Telangana Rashtra Samithi 2, Communist Party of India 2, Communist Party of India—Marxist 1, All-India Majlis-e-Ittehadul Muslimeen 1, independents 15, nominated 12, vacant 3).

ARUNACHAL PRADESH
(Capital—Itanagar)

Governor: Gen. (retd) JOGINDER JASWANT SINGH.

Chief Minister: NABAM TUKI.

Legislative Assembly: 60 seats (Congress 42, Nationalist Congress Party 5, All India Trinamool Congress 5, People's Party of Arunachal 4, Bharatiya Janata Party 3, independent 1).

ASSAM (ASOM)
(Capital—Dispur)

Governor: JANAKI BALLAV PATNAIK.

Chief Minister: TARUN GOGOI (Congress).

Legislative Assembly: 126 seats (Congress 78, All India United Democratic Front 18, Bodoland Peoples Front 12, Asom Gana Parishad 10, Bharatiya Janata Party 5 and others 3).

BIHAR
(Capital—Patna)

Governor: DEVANAND KONWAR.

Chief Minister: NITISH KUMAR (Janata Dal—United).

Legislative Assembly: 243 seats (Janata Dal—United 115, Bharatiya Janata Party 91, Rashtriya Janata Dal 22, Lok Jan Shakti Party 3, Congress 4, independents 6, others 2).

Legislative Council: 75 seats.

CHHATTISGARH
(Capital—Raipur)

Governor: SHEKHAR DUTT.

Chief Minister: Dr RAMAN SINGH (Bharatiya Janata Party).

Legislative Assembly: 91 seats (Bharatiya Janata Party 50, Congress 38, Bahujan Samaj Party 2, nominated 1).

GOA
(Capital—Panaji)

Governor: B. V. WANCHOO.

Chief Minister: MANOHAR PARRIKAR (Bharatiya Janata Party).

Legislative Assembly: 40 seats (Bharatiya Janata Party 21, Congress 9, Maharashtrawadi Gomantak Party 3, Goa Vikas Party 2, independents 5).

GUJARAT
(Capital—Gandhinagar)

Governor: Dr KAMLA BENIWAL.

Chief Minister: NARENDRA DAMODARDAS MODI (Bharatiya Janata Party).

Legislative Assembly: 182 seats (Bharatiya Janata Party 117, Congress 59, Nationalist Congress Party 3, Janata Dal—United 1, independents 2).

HARYANA
(Capital—Chandigarh)

Governor: JAGANNATH PAHADIA.

Chief Minister: BHUPINDER SINGH HOODA (Congress).

Legislative Assembly: 90 seats (Congress 40, Indian National Lok Dal 31, Haryana Janhit Congress 6, Bharatiya Janata Party 4, Bahujan Samaj Party 1, Shiromani Akali Dal 1, others 7).

HIMACHAL PRADESH
(Capital—Shimla)

Governor: URMILA SINGH.

Chief Minister: Prof. PREM KUMAR DHUMAL (Bharatiya Janata Party).

Legislative Assembly: 68 seats (Bharatiya Janata Party 41, Congress 23, Bahujan Samaj Party 1, independents 3).

JAMMU AND KASHMIR
(Capitals—Srinagar (Summer), Jammu (Winter))

Governor: NARENDRA NATH VOHRA.

Chief Minister: OMAR ABDULLAH (Jammu and Kashmir National Conference).

Legislative Assembly: 87 seats (Jammu and Kashmir National Conference 28, People's Democratic Party 21, Congress 17, Bharatiya Janata Party 11, Panther's Party 3, Communist Party of India—Marxist 1, People's Democratic Front 1, Jammu and Kashmir Democratic Party Nationalist 1, independents 4).

Legislative Council: 36 seats.

JHARKHAND
(Capital—Ranchi)

Governor: Dr SYED AHMED.

Chief Minister: ARJUN MUNDA (Bharatiya Janata Party).

Legislative Assembly: 81 seats (Bharatiya Janata Party 18, Jharkhand Mukti Morcha 18, Congress 14, Jharkhand Vikas Morcha (Prajatantrik) 11, Rashtriya Janata Dal 5, Janata Dal—United 2, independents and others 13).

KARNATAKA
(Capital—Bangalore)

Governor: HANS RAJ BHARDWAJ.

Chief Minister: D. V. SADANANDA GOWDA.

Legislative Assembly: 224 seats (Bharatiya Janata Party 110, Congress 80, Janata Dal—Secular 28, independents 6).

Legislative Council: 75 seats.

KERALA
(Capital—Thiruvananthapuram)

Governor: HANS RAJ BHARDWAJ (acting) (also Governor of Karnataka).

Chief Minister: OOMMEN CHANDY (Congress).

Legislative Assembly: 140 seats (Communist Party of India (Marxist) 45, Congress 38, Muslim League Kerala State Committee 20, Communist Party of India 13, Kerala Congress (M) 9, Janata Dal (Secular) 4, National Congress Party 2, Revolutionary Socialist Party 2 and others 7).

MADHYA PRADESH
(Capital—Bhopal)

Governor: RAM NARESH YADAV.

Chief Minister: SHIVRAJ SINGH CHAUHAN (Bharatiya Janata Party).

Legislative Assembly: 230 seats (Bharatiya Janata Party 143, Congress 71, Bahujan Samaj Party 7, Bharatiya Jan Shakti 5, Samajwadi Party 1, independents 3).

MAHARASHTRA
(Capital—Mumbai)

Governor: KATEEKAL SANKARANARAYANAN.

Chief Minister: PRITHVIRAJ CHAVAN (Congress).

Legislative Assembly: 288 seats (Congress 82, Nationalist Congress Party 62, Bharatiya Janata Party 46, Shiv Sena 44, Maharashtra Navnirman Sena 13, Samajwadi Party 4, Peasants' and Workers' Party of India 4, Bahujan Vikas Aghadi 2, Communist Party of India—Marxist 1, others 30).

Legislative Council: 78 seats.

MANIPUR
(Capital—Imphal)

Governor: GURBACHAN JAGAT.

Chief Minister: OKRAM IBOBI SINGH (Congress).

Legislative Assembly: 60 seats (Congress 42, All India Trinamool Congress 7, Manipur State Congress Party 5, Naga People's Front 4, Lok Jan Shakti Party 1, Nationalist Congress Party 1).

MEGHALAYA
(Capital—Shillong)

Governor: RANJIT SHEKHAR MOOSHAHARY.

Chief Minister: Dr MUKUL M. SANGMA (Congress).

Legislative Assembly: 60 seats (Congress 25, Nationalist Congress Party 15, United Democratic Party 11, Hill State People's Democratic Party 2, Bharatiya Janata Party 1, independents and others 6).

MIZORAM
(Capital—Aizawl)

Governor: VAKKOM PURUSHOTHAMAN.

Chief Minister: LAL THANHAWLA (Congress).

Legislative Assembly: 40 seats (Congress 32, Mizo National Front 3, Mizo People's Conference 2, Zoram Nationalist Party 2, Maraland Democratic Front 1).

NAGALAND
(Capital—Kohima)

Governor: NIKHIL KUMAR.

Chief Minister: NEIPHIU RIO (Nagaland People's Front).

Legislative Assembly: 60 seats (Nagaland People's Front 26, Congress 24, Bharatiya Janata Party 2, Nationalist Congress Party 2, independents 6).

ODISHA
(Capital—Bhubaneswar)

Governor: MURLIDHAR CHANDRAKANT BHANDARE.

Chief Minister: NAVEEN PATNAIK (Biju Janata Dal).

Legislative Assembly: 147 seats (Biju Janata Dal 103, Congress 27, Bharatiya Janata Party 6, Nationalist Congress Party 4, Communist Party of India 1, independents 6).

THE PUNJAB
(Capital—Chandigarh)

Governor: SHIVRAJ VISHWANATH PATIL (also Governor of Rajasthan and Administrator of Chandigarh ex officio).

Chief Minister: PARKASH SINGH BADAL (Shiromani Akali Dal).

Legislative Assembly: 117 seats (Shiromani Akali Dal 56, Congress 46, Bharatiya Janata Party 12, independents 3).

RAJASTHAN
(Capital—Jaipur)

Governor: MARGARET ALVA; also Governor of Punjab.

Chief Minister: ASHOK GEHLOT (Congress).

Legislative Assembly: 200 seats (Congress 96, Bharatiya Janata Party 79, Bahujan Samaj Party 6, Communist Party of India—Marxist 3, Janata Dal—United 1, Loktantrik Samajwadi Party 1, Samajwadi Party 1, independents 13).

SIKKIM
(Capital—Gangtok)

Governor: BALMIKI PRASAD SINGH.

Chief Minister: PAWAN KUMAR CHAMLING (Sikkim Democratic Front).

Legislative Assembly: 32 seats (Sikkim Democratic Front 32).

TAMIL NADU
(Capital—Chennai)

Governor: KONIJETI ROSAIAH.

Chief Minister: J. JAYALALITHAA (All India Anna Dravida Munnetra Kazhagam).

Legislative Assembly: 234 seats, (All India Anna Dravida Munnetra Kazhagam 150, Desiya Murpokku Dravida Kazhagam 29, Dravida Munnetra Kazhagam 23, Communist Party of India (Marxist) 10, Communist Party of India 9, Congress 5, Pattali Makkal Katchi 3, All India Forward Bloc 1 and others 4).

TRIPURA
(Capital—Agartala)

Governor: D. Y. PATIL.

Chief Minister: MANIK SARKAR (Communist Party of India—Marxist).

Legislative Assembly: 60 seats (Communist Party of India—Marxist 46, Congress 10, Revolutionary Socialist Party 2, others 2).

UTTAR PRADESH
(Capital—Lucknow)

Governor: B. L. JOSHI.

Chief Minister: AKHILESH YADAV (Samajwadi Party).

Legislative Assembly: 404 seats (Samajwadi Party 224, Bahujan Samaj Party 80, Bharatiya Janata Party 47, Congress 28, Rashtriya Lok Dal 9, Peace Party 4, Qaumi Ekta Dal 2, Apna Dal 1, Nationalist Congress Party 1, Ittehad-e-Millat Council 1, independents 6, nominated 1).

Legislative Council: 100 seats.

UTTARAKHAND
(Capital—Dehradun)

Governor: AZIZ QURESHI.

Chief Minister: VIJAY BAHUGUNA.

Legislative Assembly: 70 seats (Congress 32, Bharatiya Janata Party 31, Bahujan Samaj Party 3, Uttarakhand Kranti Dal 1, independents 3).

WEST BENGAL
(Capital—Kolkata)

Governor: MAYANKOTE KELATH NARAYANAN.

Chief Minister: MAMATA BANERJEE (All India Trinamool Congress).

Legislative Assembly: 294 seats (All India Trinamool Congress 184, Congress 42, Communist Party of India—Marxist 40, All India Forward Bloc 11, Revolutionary Socialist Party 7, Gorkha Janmukti Morcha 3, Communist Party of India 2, and others 5).

UNION TERRITORIES

Andaman and Nicobar Islands (Headquarters—Port Blair): Lt-Gov. Lt-Gen. (retd) BHOPINDER SINGH.

Chandigarh (Headquarters—Chandigarh): Administrator SHIVRAJ VISHWANATH PATIL (Governor of Punjab *ex officio*).

Chandigarh was to be incorporated into the Punjab state on 26 January 1986, but the transfer was postponed indefinitely.

Dadra and Nagar Haveli (Headquarters—Silvassa): Administrator NARENDRA KUMAR.

Daman and Diu (Headquarters—Daman): Administrator NARENDRA KUMAR.

Lakshadweep (Headquarters—Kavaratti): Administrator J. K. DADOO.

Puducherry (Capital—Puducherry): Lt-Gov. IQBAL SINGH; Chief Minister THIRU. N. RANGASAMY (All India NR Congress).

Assembly: 30 seats (Congress 7, All India Anna Dravida Munnetra Kazhagam 5, Dravida Munnetra Kazhagam 2 and others 16).

NATIONAL CAPITAL TERRITORY

Delhi (Headquarters—Delhi): Lt-Gov. TEJENDRA KHANNA; Chief Minister SHEILA DIXIT (Congress).

Assembly: 70 seats (Congress 43, Bharatiya Janata Party 23, Bahujan Samaj Party 2, Lok Jan Shakti Party 1, independent 1).

Election Commission

Election Commission of India: Nirvachan Sadan, Ashoka Rd, New Delhi 110 001; tel. (11) 23717391; fax (11) 23717075; e-mail feedbackeci@gmail.com; internet eci.nic.in; f. 1950; independent; Chief Election Commr SHAHABUDDIN YAQOOB QURAISHI.

Political Organizations

MAJOR NATIONAL POLITICAL ORGANIZATIONS

Bahujan Samaj Party (Majority Society Party): c/o Lok Sabha, New Delhi; internet www.bspindia.org; f. 1984; promotes the rights of the *Harijans* ('Untouchables') of India; Founder KANSHI RAM; Pres. KUMARI MAYAWATI.

Bharatiya Janata Party (BJP) (Indian People's Party): 11 Ashok Rd, New Delhi 110 001; tel. (11) 23005700; fax (11) 23005787; e-mail webmaster@bjp.org; internet www.bjp.org; f. 1980 as a breakaway group from Janata Party; right-wing Hindu party; Pres. NITIN GADKARI; Chair. of Parliamentary Party L. K. ADVANI; Gen. Secs RAM LAL, ANANTH KUMAR, THAWARCHAND GEHLOT, VIJAY GOEL; 10.5m. mems.

Communist Party of India (CPI): 15 Ajoy Bhavan, Indrajit Gupta Marg, New Delhi 110 002; tel. (11) 23235546; fax (11) 23235543; e-mail nationalcouncil@communistparty.in; internet www.communistparty.in; f. 1925; advocates the establishment of a socialist society led by the working class, and ultimately of a communist society; nine-mem. cen. secr; Leader GURUDAS DASGUPTA; Gen. Sec. ARDHENDU BHUSHAN BARDHAN; 486,578 mems (2004).

Communist Party of India—Marxist (CPI—M): A. K. Gopalan Bhavan, 27–29 Bhai Vir Singh Marg, New Delhi 110 001; tel. (11) 23344918; fax (11) 23747483; e-mail cc@cpim.org; internet www.cpim.org; f. 1964; est. after split in the CPI; maintains an ind. position; managed by a cen. cttee of 87 mems and a politburo of 14 mems; Leaders BUDDHADEV BHATTACHARYA, PRAKASH KARAT, SITARAM YECHURY; Gen. Sec. PRAKASH KARAT; 1,040,967 mems (2011).

Communist Party of India (Marxist-Leninist): U-90, Shakarpur, New Delhi 110 092; tel. and fax (11) 22521067; fax (11) 22442790; e-mail mail@cpiml.org; internet www.cpiml.org; f. 1969; Gen. Sec. DIPANKAR BHATTACHARYA.

Indian National Congress (Congress): 24 Akbar Rd, New Delhi 110 011; tel. (11) 23019080; fax (11) 23017047; e-mail aicc@congress.org.in; internet www.aicc.org.in; f. in 1885 as a forum for political debate; subsequently played an active role in the struggle for independence; following independence in 1947, the party remained the dominant force in Indian politics for three decades, under the leadership of Jawaharlal Nehru, Indira Ghandi and others; following a split in the party in 1969, a separate faction was est. under Indira Gandhi, originally known as Indian National Congress (R), then as Indian National Congress (I); name of party gradually reverted to Indian National Congress or, simply, Congress in the early to mid-1990s; Pres. SONIA GANDHI; Gen. Secs MUKUL WASNIK, JANARDAN DWIVEDI, DIGVIJAYA SINGH, B. K. HARIPRASAD, RAHUL GANDHI, BIRENDER SINGH, GHULAM NABI AZAD, MADHUSUDAN MISTRY, OSCAR FERNANDES, VILAS MUTTEMWAR; 35m. mems (1998).

Nationalist Congress Party (NCP): 10 Dr Bishambhar Das Marg, New Delhi 110 001; tel. (11) 23314414; fax (11) 23352112; e-mail mail@ncp.org.in; internet www.ncp.org.in; f. 1999; est. as breakaway faction of Congress Party; split into two factions—one headed by Sharad Pawar and the other by Purno Sangma—in Jan. 2004, but was reunified in 2006; Pres. SHARAD PAWAR; Gen. Secs PURNO AGITOK SANGMA, TARIQ ANWAR, T. P. PEETHAMBARAN MASTER, Prof. DEVI PRASAD TRIPATHI, Dr V. RAJESHWARAN, GOVINDRAO ADIK.

MAJOR REGIONAL POLITICAL ORGANIZATIONS

Akhil Bharat Hindu Mahasabha: Hindu Mahasabha Bhavan, Mandir Marg, New Delhi 110 001; tel. and fax (11) 23365354; e-mail info@akhilbharathindumahasabha.org; internet www.akhilbharathindumahasabha.org; f. 1915; seeks the establishment of a democratic Hindu state; Pres. CHANDRA PRAKASH KAUSHIK; Gen. Sec. MUNNA KUMAR SHARMA; 525,000 mems.

All-India Anna Dravida Munnetra Kazhagam (AIADMK) (All-India Anna Dravidian Progressive Asscn): 226 Awai Shanmugam Salai, Roayapettah, Chennai 600 014; tel. (44) 28132266; fax (44) 28133510; e-mail aiadmk.tn@hotmail.com; internet www.aiadmkallindia.org; f. 1972; breakaway group from the DMK; Leader and Gen. Sec. JAYARAM JAYALALITHA.

All India Forward Bloc: 28 Gurudwara Rakab Ganj Rd, New Delhi 110 001; tel. and fax (11) 23714131; e-mail biswasd@sansad.nic.in; internet www.forwardbloc.org; f. 1940; socialist aims, incl. nationalization of major industries, land reform and redistribution, and the establishment of a union of socialist republics through revolution; Chair. N. VELAPPAN NAIR; Gen. Sec. DEBABRATA BISWAS; 900,000 mems (1999).

All India Trinamool Congress (AITC): 30B Harish Chatterjee St, Kolkata 700 026; tel. (33) 24540881; fax (33) 24540880; e-mail aitmc@aitmc.org; internet aitmc.org; Chair. MAMATA BANERJEE; Gen. Secs MUKUL ROY, DINESH TRIBEDI.

Asom Gana Parishad (AGP) (Assam People's Council): Gopinath Bordoloi Rd, Guwahati 781 001; tel. and fax (361) 2600536; internet www.asomganaparishad.in; f. 1985; draws support from All-Assam Gana Sangram Parishad and All-Assam Students' Union (Pres. SANKAR PRASAD ROY; Gen. Sec. TAPAN KUMAR GOGOI); advocates the unity of India in diversity and a united Assam; Pres. CHANDRA MOHAN PATOWARY.

Biju Janata Dal: 6R/3, Unit 6, Forest Park, Bhubaneswar 751 006; tel. and fax (674) 2395979; e-mail president@bijujanatadal.net; internet www.bijujanatadal.net; f. 1997; Pres. NAVEEN PATNAIK.

Dravida Munnetra Kazhagam (DMK): Anna Arivalayam, 367–369 Anna Salai, Chennai 600 018; e-mail thedmk@vsnl.com; internet www.dmk.in; f. 1949; aims at full autonomy for states (primarily Tamil Nadu) within the Union; Pres. MUTHUVEL KARUNANIDHI; Gen. Sec. K. ANBAZHAGAN; more than 4m. mems.

Indian National Lok Dal: 18 Janpath, New Delhi 110 001; internet inld.in; fmrly mem. of the National Democratic Alliance; promotes the cause of farmers and labourers of Haryana; Nat. Pres. OM PRAKASH CHAUTALA; Sec.-Gen. AJAY SINGH CHAUTALA.

Jammu and Kashmir National Conference (JKNC): Mujahid Manzil, Nawa-i-Subh Complex Zero Bridge, Srinagar 190 002; tel. (194) 2452326; e-mail contact@jknc.in; internet www.jknc.in; fmrly All Jammu and Kashmir Nat. Conference; f. 1931; renamed 1939, reactivated 1975; state-based party campaigning for internal autonomy and responsible self-govt; Pres. Dr FAROOQ ABDULLAH; Gen. Sec. SHEIKH NAZIR AHMED; 1m. mems.

Janata Dal—Secular (People's Party—Secular): 14A, Ferozeshah Rd, New Delhi 110 001; tel. (11) 23321455; e-mail info@janatadalsecular.org.in; internet www.janatadalsecular.org.in; f. 2000 following split of Janata Dal; Pres. H. D. DEVE GOWDA; Sec.-Gen. KUNWAR DANISH ALI.

Janata Dal—United (People's Party—United): 7 Jantar Mantar Rd, New Delhi 110 001; tel. (11) 23368833; fax (11) 23368138; e-mail info@janatadalunited.org; internet www.janatadalunited.org; f. 2000; est. following split of Janata Dal; merged with Samata Party in 2003; mem. of National Democratic Alliance; advocates non-alignment, eradication of poverty, unemployment and wide disparities in wealth, and protection of minorities; Pres. SHARAD YADAV; Leader NITISH KUMAR.

Jharkhand Mukti Morcha: Bariatu Rd, Ranchi 834 008; tel. and fax (651) 2542009; aligned with national ruling coalition, the United Progressive Alliance; Leader SHIBU SOREN.

Lok Jan Shakti Party (LJSP): 12 Janpath, Firoz Shah Marg, New Delhi, 110 001; tel. (11) 23017681; fax (11) 23015249; e-mail lokjanshaktiparty@gmail.com; internet www.lokjanshaktiparty.org.in; f. 2000; est. as breakaway faction of Janata Dal—United; left-wing; Pres. RAM VILAS PASWAN.

Marumalarchi Dravida Mennetra Kazhagam: Thayagam, Chennai; internet mdmk.org.in; f. 1994; Leader VAIKO.

Pattali Makkal Katchi (PMK): 63 Nattumuthu Naicken St, Teynampet, Chennai 600 118; internet www.pmkparty.org; f. 1989; Tamil; Leader Dr ANBUMANI RAMDOSS; Pres. G. K. MANI.

Rashtriya Janata Dal (RJD) (National People's Party): 13 V. P. House, Rafi Marg, New Delhi 110 001; tel. (11) 23357182; e-mail rjdal@rediffmail.com; f. 1997; est. by breakaway mems of Janata Dal; Leader LALU PRASAD YADAV.

Rashtriya Lok Dal: 12 Tughlaq Rd, New Delhi 110 011; tel. (11) 23016892; fax (11) 23792037; e-mail rld@rashtriyalokdal.com; internet rashtriyalokdal.com; Leader AJIT SINGH.

Republican Party of India (RPI): Ensa Hutments, I Blk, Azad Maidan, Fort, Mumbai 400 001; tel. (22) 22621888; f. 1952; by 2003 the group had split into 10 factions; the three main factions were led by PRAKASH RAO AMBEDKAR, RAMDAS ATHAVALE and R. S. GAVAI, respectively.

Revolutionary Socialist Party: 17 Feroz Shah Rd, New Delhi 110 001; tel. (11) 23782167; fax (11) 23782342; f. 1940; Marxist-Leninist; Leader ABANI ROY; Gen. Sec. T. J. CHANDRACHOODAN.

Samajwadi Party (Socialist Party): 18 Copernicus Lane, New Delhi; tel. (11) 23386842; fax (11) 23382430; e-mail contact@samajwadipartyindia.com; internet www.samajwadiparty.in; f. 1991; Pres. MULAYAM SINGH YADAV; Gen. Secs RAM GOPAL YADAV, MOHAN SINGH, VISHAMBHAR PRASAD NISHAD, RAMASARE KUSHWAHA.

Shiromani Akali Dal (SAD): Block 6, Madhya Marg, Sector 28, Chandigarh; e-mail contact@shiromaniakalidal.org.in; internet www.shiromaniakalidal.org.in; f. 1920; largest of six splinter groups, each of which claims to be the 'real' Akali Dal; Pres. (Shiromani Akali Dal—Badal) SUKHBIR SINGH BADAL; Sec.-Gen. SUKHDEV SINGH DHINDSA.

Shiv Sena (Army of Shiv): Shiv Sena Bhavan, Ram Ganesh Gadkari Chowk, Dadar, Mumbai 400 028; tel. (22) 24328181; e-mail mazamaharashtra@shivsena.org; internet www.shivsena.org; f. 1966; militant Hindu group; Bharatiya Kamgar Sena (Indian Workers' Army) affiliated to the party; Leader BAL THACKERAY, Exec. Pres. UDDHAV THACKERAY.

Sikkim Democratic Front: Upper Deorali, Gangtok, East Sikkim; internet sikkimdemocraticfront.org; f. 1993; Pres. Dr PAWAN KUMAR CHAMLING.

Telangana Rashtra Samithi: Telangana Bhavan, Rd 10, Banjara Hills, Hyderabad; f. 2001; Pres. K. CHANDRASEKHAR RAO.

Telugu Desam (Telugu Nation): NTR Bhavan, Rd 2, Banjara Hills, Hyderabad 500 034; tel. (40) 30699999; fax (40) 23542108; e-mail contact@telugudesam.org; internet www.telugudesam.org; f. 1983; state-based party (Andhra Pradesh); Pres. N. CHANDRABABU NAIDU; 8m. mems.

Diplomatic Representation

EMBASSIES AND HIGH COMMISSIONS IN INDIA

Afghanistan: 5/50F Shanti Path, Chanakyapuri, New Delhi 110 021; tel. (11) 24103331; fax (11) 26875439; e-mail afghanspirit@yahoo.com; Ambassador Dr NANGUYULAI TARZI.

Albania: B2, West End, New Delhi 110 021; tel. and fax (11) 46108285; e-mail embassy.delhi@mfa.gov.al; Ambassador FATOS KERCIKU.

Algeria: E-6/5 Vasant Vihar, New Delhi 110 057; tel. (11) 26147036; fax (11) 26147033; Ambassador MOHAMMED HACENE ECHARIF.

Angola: 5 Poorvi Marg, Vasant Vihar, New Delhi 110 057; tel. (11) 26146195; fax (11) 26146184; e-mail angolaembassyindia@gmail.com; internet www.angolaembassyindia.org; Ambassador MANUEL EDUARDO DOS SANTOS E SILVA BRAVO.

Argentina: A-2/6 Vasant Vihar, New Delhi 110 057; tel. (11) 41661982; fax (11) 41661988; Ambassador ERNESTO CARLOS ALVAREZ.

Armenia: D-133 Anand Niketan, New Delhi 110 057; tel. (11) 24112851; fax (11) 24112853; e-mail armemb@vsnl.com; Ambassador ARA HAKOBYAN.

Australia: 1/50G Shanti Path, Chanakyapuri, POB 5210, New Delhi 110 021; tel. (11) 41399900; fax (11) 41494490; e-mail austhighcom.newdelhi@dfat.gov.au; internet www.india.embassy.gov.au; High Commissioner PETER JOSEPH NOOZHUMURRY VARGHESE.

Austria: EP-13 Chandragupta Marg, Chanakyapuri, New Delhi 110 021; tel. (11) 24192700; fax (11) 26886929; e-mail new-delhi-ob@bmeia.gv.at; internet www.aussenministerium.at/newdelhi; Ambassador Dr FERDINAND MAULTASCHL.

Azerbaijan: 8 Golf Links, New Delhi 110 003; tel. (11) 24652228; fax (11) 24652227; e-mail azembassy@airtelmail.in; Ambassador IBRAHIM ASSAD OGLU HAJIYEV.

Bahrain: 4 Olof Palme Marg, Vasant Vihar, New Delhi 110 057; tel. (11) 26154153; fax (11) 26146731; e-mail bahrainembindia@yahoo.com; internet www.bahrainembassyindia.com; Ambassador MOHAMMED GHASSAN SHAIKHO.

Bangladesh: EP-39 Dr S. Radhakrishnan Marg, Chanakyapuri, New Delhi 110 021; tel. (11) 24121389; fax (11) 26878953; e-mail bdhcdelhi@gmail.com; internet www.bhcdelhi.org; High Commissioner TARIQ AHMAD KARIM.

Belarus: 163 Jor Bagh, New Delhi 110 003; tel. (11) 24694518; fax (11) 24697029; e-mail india@belembassy.org; Ambassador VLADIMIR GOSHIN.

Belgium: 50N Shanti Path, Chanakyapuri, New Delhi 110 021; tel. (11) 42428000; fax (11) 42428002; e-mail newdelhi@diplobel.fed.be; internet www.diplomatie.be/newdelhi; Ambassador PIERRE VAESEN.

Benin: New Delhi; Ambassador ANDRE SANRA.

Bhutan: Chandragupta Marg, Chanakyapuri, New Delhi 110 021; tel. (11) 26889807; fax (11) 26876710; Ambassador Maj.-Gen. VETSOP NAMGYEL.

Bosnia and Herzegovina: E-9/11 Vasant Vihar, New Delhi 110 057; tel. (11) 41662481; fax (11) 41662482; e-mail abhind@gmail.com; Ambassador Dr SEAD AVDIĆ.

Botswana: F-8/3 Vasant Vihar, New Delhi 110 057; tel. (11) 46537000; fax (11) 46036191; e-mail botind@gov.bw; High Commissioner LESEGO ETHEL MOTSUMI.

Brazil: 8 Aurangzeb Rd, New Delhi 110 011; tel. (11) 23017301; fax (11) 23793684; e-mail brasindi@eth.net; internet www.brazilembassy.in; Ambassador CARLOS SERGIO SOBRAL DUARTE.

Brunei: 4 Poorvi Marg, Vasant Vihar, New Delhi 110 057; tel. (11) 26148340; fax (11) 26142101; e-mail newdelhi.india@mfa.gov.bn; High Commissioner Haji SIDEK BIN Haji ALI.

Bulgaria: 16/17 Chandragupta Marg, Chanakyapuri, New Delhi 110 021; tel. (11) 26115549; fax (11) 26876190; e-mail bulemb@bulgariaembindia.com; internet www.bulgariaembindia.com; Ambassador BORISLAV KOSTOV.

Burkina Faso: F-3/1 Vasant Vihar, New Delhi 110 057; tel. (11) 26140641; fax (11) 26140630; e-mail embassy@burkinafasoindia.org; internet www.burkinafasoindia.org; Ambassador IDRISS RAOUA OUEDRAOGO.

Burundi: C-1/24 Vasant Vihar, New Delhi 110 057; tel. (11) 46151947; e-mail ambabudelhi@yahoo.fr; Ambassador RUBUKA ALOYS.

Cambodia: W-112 Greater Kailash Part II, New Delhi 110 048; tel. (11) 29214435; fax (11) 46016117; e-mail cambodiaembassykapoor@yahoo.com; Ambassador YOUS MAKANA.

Canada: 7/8 Shanti Path, Chanakyapuri, New Delhi 110 021; tel. (11) 41782000; fax (11) 41782020; e-mail delhi@international.gc.ca; internet www.canadainternational.gc.ca/india-inde; High Commissioner STEWART BECK.

Chile: A-16/1 Vasant Vihar, New Delhi 110 057; tel. (11) 43100400; fax (11) 43100431; e-mail embchile@airtelmail.in; internet chileabroad.gov.cl/india; Ambassador CRISTIAN BARROS MELET.

China, People's Republic: 50D Shanti Path, Chanakyapuri, New Delhi 110 021; tel. (11) 26112345; fax (11) 26885486; e-mail chinaemb_in@mfa.gov.cn; internet www.chinaembassy.org.in; Ambassador ZHANG YAN.

Colombia: 85 Poorvi Marg, Vasant Vihar, New Delhi 110 057; tel. (11) 41662106; fax (11) 41662108; e-mail edelhi@minrelext.gov.co; Ambassador JUAN ALFREDO PINTO SAAVEDRA.

Congo, Democratic Republic: B-3/61 Safdarjung Enclave, New Delhi 110 029; tel. (11) 41660976; fax (11) 41663152; e-mail congoembassy@yahoo.co.in; Ambassador BALUMUENE NKUNA FRANCOIS.

Costa Rica: C-25, Anand Niketan, New Delhi 110 021; tel. (11) 41080810; fax (11) 41080809; e-mail embajadacostarica.india@gmail.com; Ambassador JUAN FERNANDO CORDERO.

Côte d'Ivoire: B-9/6 Vasant Vihar, New Delhi 110 057; tel. (11) 46043000; fax (11) 46043031; e-mail embassy@amb2ci-inde.org; internet www.amb2ci-inde.org/en/accueil.php; Ambassador SAINY TIEMELE.

Croatia: A-15 West End, New Delhi 110 021; tel. (11) 41663101; fax (11) 24116873; e-mail croemb.new-delhi@mvpei.hr; Ambassador BORIS VELIĆ.

Cuba: W-124A Greater Kailash Part I, New Delhi 110 048; tel. (11) 29242467; fax (11) 26232469; e-mail embcuind@del6.vsnl.net.in; internet embacuba.cubaminrex.cu/Default.aspx?tabid=4294; Ambassador ABELARDO RAFAEL CUETO SOSA.

Cyprus: 106 Jor Bagh, New Delhi 110 003; tel. (11) 24697503; fax (11) 24628828; e-mail delhihc@mfa.gov.cy; internet www.mfa.gov.cy/mfa/highcom/highcom_newdelhi.nsf; High Commissioner MARIA MICHAEL.

Czech Republic: 50M Niti Marg, Chanakyapuri, New Delhi 110 021; tel. (11) 26110205; fax (11) 26886221; e-mail newdelhi@embassy.mzv.cz; internet www.mfa.cz/newdelhi; Ambassador MILOSLAV STAŠEK.

Denmark: 11 Aurangzeb Rd, New Delhi 110 011; tel. (11) 42090700; fax (11) 23792019; e-mail delamb@um.dk; internet www.ambnewdelhi.um.dk; Ambassador FREDDY SVANE.

Djibouti: A-2/20 Safdarjung Enclave, New Delhi 110 029; tel. (11) 41354491; fax (11) 41354490; e-mail info@embassyofdjibouti.org; internet embassyofdjibouti.org/EmbasyNewDelhi.htm; Ambassador YOUSSOUF OMAR DOUALEH.

Dominican Republic: B–1/20, Vasant Vihar, New Delhi 110 057; tel. (11) 43425000; fax (11) 43425050; e-mail info@dr-embassy-india.com; internet www.dr-embassy-india.com; Ambassador FRANK HANS DANNENBERG CASTELLANOS.

Ecuador: D-3/1 Vasant Vihar, New Delhi 110 057; tel. (11) 46011801; fax (11) 46011804; e-mail eecuindia@mmrree.gov.ec; internet www.embassyofecuadortoindia.com; Ambassador CARLOS ABAD ORTIZ.

Egypt: 1/50M Niti Marg, Chanakyapuri, New Delhi 110 021; tel. (11) 26114096; fax (11) 26885355; e-mail egyptdel@spectranet.com; internet www.mfa.gov.eg/missions/india/delhi/embassy/en-gb; Ambassador KHALED EL-BAKLY.

El Salvador: E-5/1 Vasant Vihar, New Delhi 110 057; tel. (11) 46088400; fax (11) 46011688; e-mail embasalva-ndelhi@rree.gob.sv; Ambassador RUBEN I. ZAMORA.

Eritrea: C-7/9 Vasant Vihar, New Delhi 110 057; tel. (11) 26146336; fax (11) 26146337; e-mail eriindia@yahoo.co.in; internet www.eritreaembindia.com; Ambassador ALEM TSEHAYE WOLDEMARIAM.

Ethiopia: 7/50G Satya Marg, Chanakyapuri, New Delhi 110 021; tel. (11) 26119513; fax (11) 26875731; e-mail delethem@yahoo.com; internet www.ethiopiaembassy.in; Ambassador GENET ZEWDIE.

Fiji: N-57 Panchsheel Park, New Delhi 110 017; tel. (11) 41751092; fax (11) 41751095; e-mail info@fijihc.in; internet www.fijihc.in; High Commissioner YOGESH KARAN.

Finland: E-3 Nyaya Marg, Chanakyapuri, New Delhi 110 021; tel. (11) 41497500; fax (11) 41497555; e-mail sanomat.nde@formin.fi; internet www.finland.org.in; Ambassador TERHI HAKALA.

France: 2/50E Shanti Path, Chanakyapuri, New Delhi 110 021; tel. (11) 24196100; fax (11) 24196169; e-mail webmaster@france-in-india.org; internet www.ambafrance-in.org; Ambassador FRANÇOIS RICHIER.

Gabon: 26 Poorvi Marg, Vasant Vihar, New Delhi 110 057; tel. (11) 26731600; fax (11) 26731611; e-mail embassygabonindia@yahoo.fr; Ambassador DESIRE KOUMBA.

The Gambia: 7 Olof Palme Marg, 1st Floor, Vasant Vihar, New Delhi 110 057; tel. (11) 46120472; fax (11) 46120471; e-mail gamhighcomdel@hotmail.com; High Commissioner DEMBO BADJIE (designate).

Georgia: 115 Jor Bagh, New Delhi 110 003; tel. (11) 47078602; fax (11) 47078602; e-mail delhi.emb@mfa.gov.ge; internet india.mfa.gov.ge; Ambassador ZURAB KACHKACHISHVILI.

Germany: 6/50G Shanti Path, Chanakyapuri, POB 613, New Delhi 110 021; tel. (11) 44199199; fax (11) 26873117; e-mail info@new-delhi.diplo.de; internet www.new-delhi.diplo.de; Ambassador MICHAEL STEINER (designate).

Ghana: 50N Satya Marg, Chanakyapuri, New Delhi 110 021; tel. (11) 26883298; fax (11) 26883202; e-mail ghstarin@vsnl.net; High Commissioner ROBERT TACHIE-MENSON.

Greece: EP-32 Dr S. Radhakrishnan Marg, Chanakyapuri, New Delhi 110 021; tel. (11) 26880700; fax (11) 26888010; e-mail gremb.del@mfa.gr; internet www.greeceinindia.com; Ambassador IOANNIS E. RAPTAKIS.

Guyana: B-3/20 Vasant Vihar, New Delhi 110 057; tel. (11) 41669717; fax (11) 41669714; e-mail hcommguy.del@gmail.com; High Commissioner JAIRAM RONALD GAJRAJ.

Holy See: 50C Niti Marg, Chanakyapuri, New Delhi 110 021 (Apostolic Nunciature); tel. (11) 26889187; fax (11) 26874286; e-mail nuntius@apostolicnunciatureindia.com; internet www.apostolicnunciatureindia.com; Nuncio Most Rev. SALVATORE PENNACCHIO (Titular Archbishop of Montemarano).

Hungary: Plot 2, 50M Niti Marg, Chanakyapuri, New Delhi 110 021; tel. (11) 26114737; fax (11) 26886742; e-mail mission.del@mfa.gov.hu; internet www.mfa.gov.hu/emb/newdelhi; Ambassador Dr JÁNOS TERÉNYI.

Iceland: 11 Aurangzeb Rd, New Delhi 110 011; tel. (11) 43530300; fax (11) 42403001; e-mail emb.newdelhi@mfa.is; internet www.iceland.org/in; Ambassador GUDMUNDUR EIRIKSSON.

Indonesia: 50A Kautilya Marg, Chanakyapuri, New Delhi 110 021; tel. (11) 26118642; fax (11) 26886763; e-mail administrasi@indonesianembassy.in; internet www.indonesianembassy.in; Ambassador Lt-Gen. (retd) ANDI MUHAMMAD GHALIB.

Iran: 5 Barakhamba Rd, New Delhi 110 001; tel. (11) 23329600; fax (11) 23325493; e-mail info@iran-embassy.org.in; internet www.iran-embassy.org.in; Ambassador SAYED MAHDI NABIZADEH.

Iraq: L-1/2 Hauz Khas, New Delhi 110 016; tel. (11) 26535593; fax (11) 26535236; e-mail dlh1emb@iraqmfamail.com; Ambassador AHMAD TAHSIN AHMAD BERWARI.

Ireland: 230 Jor Bagh, New Delhi 110 003; tel. (11) 24626733; fax (11) 24697053; e-mail newdelhiembassy@dfa.ie; internet www.embassyofireland.in; Ambassador FEILIM MCLAUGHLIN.

Israel: 3 Aurangzeb Rd, New Delhi 110 011; tel. (11) 30414500; fax (11) 30414555; e-mail info@newdelhi.mfa.gov.il; internet delhi.mfa.gov.il; Ambassador ALON USHPIZ.

Italy: 50E Chandragupta Marg, Chanakyapuri, New Delhi 110 021; tel. (11) 26114355; fax (11) 26873889; e-mail ambasciata.newdelhi@esteri.it; internet www.ambnewdelhi.esteri.it; Ambassador GIACOMO SANFELICE DI MONTEFORTE.

Japan: Plots 4–5, 50G Shanti Path, Chanakyapuri, New Delhi 110 021; tel. (11) 26876581; fax (11) 26885587; e-mail jpembjic@bol.net.in; internet www.in.emb-japan.go.jp; Ambassador AKITAKA SAIKI.

Jordan: 30 Golf Links, New Delhi 110 003; tel. (11) 24653318; fax (11) 24653353; e-mail jordan@jordanembassyindia.org; internet www.jordanembassyindia.org; Ambassador Dr MUHAMMAD SHARARI AL-FAYEZ.

Kazakhstan: 61 Poorvi Marg, Vasant Vihar, New Delhi 110 057; tel. (11) 46007700; fax (11) 46007701; e-mail office@kazembassy.in; internet www.kazembassy.in; Chargé d'affaires a.i. DOULAT KUANYSHAEV.

Kenya: F-3/12 Vasant Vihar, New Delhi 110 057; tel. (11) 26146537; fax (11) 26146550; e-mail info@kenyahicom-delhi.com; internet www.kenyahicom-delhi.com; High Commissioner Prof. FESTUS KABERIA.

Korea, Democratic People's Republic: E-455 Greater Kailash Part II, New Delhi 110 048; tel. (11) 29219644; fax (11) 29219645; e-mail dprk194899@yahoo.com; Ambassador RIM HOE SONG.

Korea, Republic: 9 Chandragupta Marg, Chanakyapuri Ext., New Delhi 110 021; tel. (11) 42007000; fax (11) 26884840; e-mail india@mofat.go.kr; internet ind.mofat.go.kr; Ambassador KIM JOONG-KEUN.

Kuwait: 5A Shanti Path, Chanakyapuri, New Delhi 110 021; tel. (11) 24100791; fax (11) 26873516; e-mail new_delhi@mofa.gov.kw; Ambassador SAMI MOHAMMAD AL-SULAIMAN.

Kyrgyzstan: C-93 Anand Niketan, New Delhi 110 021; tel. (11) 24118008; fax (11) 24118009; e-mail delhi@kgzembind.in; internet www.kgzembind.in; Ambassador OROLBAYEVA IRINA ABDYEVNA.

Laos: A-104/7 Parmanand Estate, Maharani Bagh, New Delhi 110 065; tel. (11) 41327352; fax (11) 41327353; e-mail boualyrone_delhi@yahoo.com; Ambassador THONGPHANH SYACKHAPHOM.

Lebanon: H-1 Anand Niketan, New Delhi 110 021; tel. (11) 24110919; fax (11) 24110818; e-mail lebemb@airtelmail.in; Ambassador KHALED SALMAN.

Lesotho: B-8/19 Vasant Vihar, New Delhi 110 057; tel. (11) 41660713; fax (11) 26141636; e-mail lesothonewdelhi@airtelmail.in; High Commissioner Dr SHABBIR HOOSEN PEERBHAI.

Libya: 22 Golf Links, New Delhi 110 003; tel. (11) 24697717; fax (11) 24633005; e-mail libya_bu_ind@yahoo.com; Ambassador (vacant).

Lithuania: D-129 Anand Niketan, New Delhi 110 021; tel. (11) 43132200; fax (11) 43132222; e-mail amb.in@urm.lt; Ambassador PETRAS SIMELIUNAS.

Luxembourg: 730 Gadaipur Rd, Branch Post Office, Gadaipur, New Delhi 110 030; tel. (11) 26801966; fax (11) 26801971; e-mail newdelhi.amb@mae.etat.lu; internet newdelhi.mae.lu; Ambassador GASTON STRONCK.

Macedonia, former Yugoslav republic: K-80A Hauz Khaz Enclave, New Delhi 110 016; tel. (11) 46142603; fax (11) 46142604; e-mail delhi@mfa.gov.mk; Ambassador SLOBODAN TASHOVSKI.

Madagascar: 781 Nikka Singh Block, Asian Games Village, New Delhi 110 049; fax (11) 66173222; e-mail contact@madagascar-embassy.in; Ambassador ANDRIANARISON SAHOBISOA OLIVIER ACHILLE.

Malawi: F-63 Poorvi Marg, Vasant Vihar, New Delhi 110 057; tel. (11) 46078800; fax (11) 46078810; e-mail malawindia@airtelbroadband.in; internet www.malawi-india.org; High Commissioner Dr CHRISSIE CHAWANJE MUGHOGHO.

Malaysia: 50M Satya Marg, Chanakyapuri, New Delhi 110 021; tel. (11) 26111291; fax (11) 26881538; e-mail maldelhi@kln.gov.my; internet www.kln.gov.my/perwakilan/newdelhi; High Commissioner Dato' TAN SENG SUNG.

Maldives: B-2 Anand Niketan, New Delhi 110 021; tel. (11) 41435701; fax (11) 41435709; e-mail admin@maldiveshighcom.in; internet www.maldiveshighcom.in; High Commissioner ABDUL AZEEZ YOOSUF.

Malta: N-60 Panchsheel Park, New Delhi 110 017; tel. (11) 47674900; fax (11) 47674949; e-mail maltahighcommission.newdelhi@gov.mt; High Commissioner THERESA CUTAJAR.

Mauritius: EP-41 Jesus and Mary Marg, Chanakyapuri, New Delhi 110 021; tel. (11) 24102161; fax (11) 24102194; e-mail mhcnd@bol.net.in; High Commissioner ARYE KUMAR JAGESSUR.

Mexico: C-8 Anand Niketan, New Delhi 110 021; tel. (11) 24107182; fax (11) 24117193; e-mail embamexindia@airtelmail.in; internet www.sre.gob.mx/india; Ambassador JAIME NUALART.

Mongolia: 34 Archbishop Makarios Marg, New Delhi 110 003; tel. (11) 24631728; fax (11) 24633240; e-mail mongemb@vsnl.net; Ambassador SANJAASÜRENGIIN BAYARA.

Morocco: 46 Sunder Nagar, New Delhi 110 003; tel. (11) 24355582; fax (11) 24355579; e-mail embassyofmorocco@rediffmail.com;

internet www.moroccoembassyin.org; Ambassador EL ARBI RAFFOUH.

Mozambique: B-3/24 Vasant Vihar, New Delhi 110 057; tel. (11) 26156663; fax (11) 26156665; e-mail hcmoz@hclinfinet.com; High Commissioner JOSÉ MARÍA DA SILVA VIEIRA MORAIS.

Myanmar: 3/50F Nyaya Marg, Chanakyapuri, New Delhi 110 021; tel. (11) 24121132; fax (11) 24678824; e-mail myandelhi@gmail.com; Ambassador ZIN YAW.

Namibia: B-8/9 Vasant Vihar, New Delhi 110 057; tel. (11) 26140389; fax (11) 26146120; e-mail nam@nhcdelhi.com; internet www.nhcdelhi.com; High Commissioner Dr SAMUEL KAVETO MBAMBO.

Nepal: Barakhamba Rd, New Delhi 110 001; tel. (11) 23327361; fax (11) 23329647; e-mail nepembassydelhi@airtelmail.in; Ambassador RAM KARKI.

Netherlands: 6/50F Shanti Path, Chanakyapuri, New Delhi 110 021; tel. (11) 24197600; fax (11) 24197710; e-mail nde@minbuza.nl; internet india.nlembassy.org; Ambassador BOB H. HIENSCH.

New Zealand: Sir Edmund Hillary Marg, Chanakyapuri, New Delhi 110 021; tel. (11) 26883170; fax (11) 26883165; e-mail newzealandhc@bol.net.in; internet www.nzembassy.com/india; High Commissioner JAN HENDERSON.

Nigeria: EP-4 Chandragupta Marg, Chanakyapuri, New Delhi 110 021; tel. (11) 24122142; fax (11) 24122138; e-mail nigeria.newdelhi@mfa.gov.ng; internet www.nigeriahcindia.com; High Commissioner OYEBOLA KUKU.

Norway: 50C Shanti Path, Chanakyapuri, New Delhi 110 021; tel. (11) 41779200; fax (11) 41680145; e-mail emb.newdelhi@mfa.no; internet www.norwayemb.org.in; Ambassador ANN OLLESTAD.

Oman: EP-10/11 Chandragupta Marg, Chankyapuri, New Delhi 110 021; tel. (11) 26885622; fax (11) 26885621; e-mail omandelhi@vsnl.com; Ambassador Sheikh HUMAID BIN ALI BIN SULTAN AL-MA'ANI.

Pakistan: 2/50G Shanti Path, Chanakyapuri, New Delhi 110 021; tel. (11) 26110601; fax (11) 26872339; e-mail pakhc@nda.vsnl.net.in; internet www.mofa.gov.pk/india; High Commissioner SALMAN BASHIR (designate).

Panama: 3D Palam Marg, Vasant Vihar, New Delhi 110 057; tel. (11) 26148268; fax (11) 26148261; e-mail panaind@bol.net.in; Ambassador JULIO DE LA GUARDIA ARROCHA.

Papua New Guinea: B-2/19 Vasant Vihar, 1st Floor, New Delhi 110 057; tel. (11) 46012813; fax (11) 46012812; e-mail kundund@yahoo.com; High Commissioner TARCISIUS A. ERI.

Paraguay: B-11 Vasant Marg, Vasant Vihar, New Delhi 110 057; tel. (11) 42705671; fax (11) 42705672; e-mail gpemparaindia@airtelbroadband.in; Ambassador GENARO VICENTE PAPPALARDO AYALA.

Peru: A-9/5 Bucharest Marg, Vasant Vihar, New Delhi 110 057; tel. (11) 46163333; fax (11) 46163301; e-mail admin@embassyperuindia.in; internet www.embassyperuindia.in; Ambassador JAVIER MANUAL PAULINICH VELARDE.

Philippines: 50N Nyaya Marg, Chanakyapuri, New Delhi 110 021; tel. (11) 26889091; fax (11) 26876401; e-mail newdelhipe@bol.net.in; internet www.newdelhipe.com; Ambassador RONALD B. ALLAREY.

Poland: 50M Shanti Path, Chanakyapuri, New Delhi 110 021; tel. (11) 41496900; fax (11) 26871914; e-mail info@newdelhi.polemb.net; internet www.newdelhi.polemb.net; Ambassador Prof. PIOTR KLODKOWSKI.

Portugal: 4 Panchsheel Marg, Chanakyapuri, New Delhi 110 021; tel. (11) 46071001; fax (11) 4607103; e-mail embportin@ndf.vsnl.net.in; internet www.embportindia.co.in; Ambassador JORGE ROZA DE OLIVEIRA.

Qatar: EP-31A Chandragupta Marg, Chanakyapuri, New Delhi 110 021; tel. (11) 26117988; fax (11) 26886080; e-mail newdelhi@mofa.gov.qa; Ambassador HASSAN MUHAMMAD RAFEH AL-EMADI.

Romania: A-47 Vasant Marg, Vasant Vihar, New Delhi 110 057; tel. (11) 26140447; fax (11) 26140611; e-mail embrom@airtelmail.in; internet www.newdelhi.mae.ro; Ambassador VALERICA EPURE.

Russia: Shanti Path, Chanakyapuri, New Delhi 110 021; tel. (11) 26873799; fax (11) 26876823; e-mail emb@rusembassy.in; internet www.india.mid.ru; Ambassador ALEXANDER M. KADAKIN.

Rwanda: 41 Paschimi Marg, Vasant Vihar, New Delhi 110 057; tel. (11) 28661604; fax (11) 28661605; e-mail rwandaembassy@yahoo.com; internet india.embassy.gov.rw; High Commissioner WILLIAM NKURUNZIZA.

Saudi Arabia: 2 Paschimi Marg, Vasant Vihar, New Delhi 110 057; tel. (11) 26144102; fax (11) 22187272; e-mail inemb@mofa.gov.sa; Ambassador SAUD BIN MOHAMMED AL-SATI.

Senegal: C-6/11 Vasant Vihar, New Delhi 110 057; tel. (11) 26147687; fax (11) 26142422; e-mail embassy@senindia.org; internet www.embsenindia.org; Ambassador AMADOU MOUSTAPHA DIOUF.

Serbia: 3/50G Niti Marg, Chanakyapuri, New Delhi 110 021; tel. (11) 26873661; fax (11) 26885535; e-mail office@embassyofserbiadelhi.net.in; internet www.embassyofserbiadelhi.net.in; Ambassador JOVAN MIRILOVIĆ.

Seychelles: A-4, Westend, New Delhi 110 021; tel. (11) 47875500; fax (11) 47875502; e-mail seychelleshighcommission@gmail.com; High Commissioner WAVEN WILLIAM.

Singapore: E-6 Chandragupta Marg, Chanakyapuri, New Delhi 110 021; tel. (11) 46000800; fax (11) 46016413; e-mail singhc_del@sgmfa.gov.sg; internet www.mfa.gov.sg/newdelhi; High Commissioner KAREN TAN.

Slovakia: 50M Niti Marg, Chanakyapuri, New Delhi 110 021; tel. (11) 26889071; fax (11) 26877941; e-mail emb.delhi@mzv.sk; internet www.newdelhi.mfa.sk; Ambassador MARIÁN TOMÁŠIK.

Slovenia: 46 Poorvi Marg, Vasant Vihar, New Delhi 110 057; tel. (11) 41662891; fax (11) 41662895; e-mail vnd@mzz-dkp.gov.si; internet newdelhi.embassy.si; Ambassador JANEZ PREMOÄE.

Somalia: Sector 12, Plot 27, A-702 Sunny Valley Apt, Dwarka, New Delhi 110 075; tel. (11) 24335026; e-mail somaliembassyindia@yahoo.com; Ambassador EBYAN MAHAMED SALAH.

South Africa: B-18 Vasant Marg, Vasant Vihar, New Delhi 110 057; tel. (11) 26149411; fax (11) 26143605; e-mail highcommissioner@sahc-india.com; High Commissioner HARRIS MAJEKE.

Spain: 12 Prithviraj Rd, New Delhi 110 011; tel. (11) 51293000; fax (11) 51293020; e-mail emb.nuevadelhi@maec.es; Ambassador FRANCISCO JAVIER ELORZA CAVENGT.

Sri Lanka: 27 Kautilya Marg, Chanakyapuri, New Delhi 110 021; tel. (11) 23010201; fax (11) 23793604; e-mail lankacomnd@bol.net.in; internet www.slhcindia.org; High Commissioner PRASAD KARIYAWASAM.

Sudan: Plot 3, Shanti Path, Chanakyapuri, New Delhi 110 021; tel. (11) 26873785; fax (11) 26883758; e-mail sudanembassy@yahoo.com; internet www.sudanembassyindia.org; Ambassador KHIDER HAROUN AHMED ABDULRAZIG.

Suriname: C-15 Malcha Marg, New Delhi 110 021; tel. (11) 26888543; fax (11) 26888450; e-mail embsurnd123@rediffmail.com; internet www.embsurnd.com; Ambassador AASHNA WANDANI RADHA KANHAI.

Sweden: 4–5 Nyaya Marg, Chanakyapuri, New Delhi 110 021; tel. (11) 44197100; fax (11) 26885401; e-mail ambassaden.new-delhi@foreign.ministry.se; internet www.swedenabroad.se/newdelhi; Ambassador LARS-OLOF LINDGREN.

Switzerland: Nyaya Marg, Chanakyapuri, New Delhi 110 021; tel. (11) 26878372; fax (11) 26873093; e-mail vertretung@ndh.rep.admin.ch; Ambassador LINUS VON CASTELMUR.

Syria: D-5/8 Vasant Vihar, New Delhi 110 057; tel. (11) 26140233; fax (11) 26143107; Ambassador RIAD KAMEL ABBAS.

Tajikistan: E-13/2 Vasant Vihar, New Delhi 110 057; tel. and fax (11) 26154282; fax 26154282; e-mail tajembindia@gmail.com; internet www.tajikembassy.in; Ambassador SAIDOV SAIDBEG BOYKHONOVICH.

Tanzania: EP-15C Chanakyapuri, New Delhi 110 021; tel. (11) 24122864; fax (11) 24122862; e-mail tanzrep@del2.vsnl.net.in; High Commissioner JOHN W. H. KIJAZI.

Thailand: 56N Nyaya Marg, Chanakyapuri, New Delhi 110 021; tel. (11) 26118103; fax (11) 26872029; e-mail thaidel@mfa.go.th; internet www.thaiemb.org.in; Ambassador PISAN MANAWAPAT.

Trinidad and Tobago: B-3/26 Vasant Vihar, New Delhi 110 057; tel. (11) 46007500; fax (11) 46007505; e-mail info@hctt.in; internet www.hctt.net; High Commissioner CHANDRADATH SINGH.

Tunisia: B-1/2 Vasant Vihar, New Delhi 110 057; tel. (11) 26145346; fax (11) 26145301; e-mail tunisiaembassy@airtelbroadband.in; Ambassador TAREK AZOUZ.

Turkey: 50N Nyaya Marg, Chanakyapuri, New Delhi 110 021; tel. (11) 26889054; fax (11) 24101974; e-mail tbd@vsnl.net; internet yenidelhi.be.mfa.gov.tr; Ambassador Dr BURAK AKCAPAR.

Turkmenistan: C-11 West End Colony, Chanakyapuri, New Delhi 110 021; tel. (11) 24116527; fax (11) 24116526; e-mail turkmen_embassy@starith.net; internet www.turkmenembassy.in; Ambassador PARAHAT HOMMADOVICH DURDYEV.

Uganda: B-3/26 Vasant Vihar, New Delhi 110 057; tel. (11) 26144413; fax (11) 26144405; e-mail newdelhiuganda highcommission@yahoo.in; High Commissioner NIMISHA MADHVANI.

Ukraine: E-1/8 Vasant Vihar, New Delhi 110 057; tel. (11) 26146041; fax (11) 26146043; e-mail embassy@bol.net.in; internet www.mfa.gov.ua/india; Ambassador OLEKSANDR D. SHEVCHENKO.

United Arab Emirates: EP-12 Chandragupta Marg, Chanakyapuri, New Delhi 110 021; tel. (11) 26111111; fax (11) 26873272; e-mail info.newdelhi@mofa.gov.ae; internet www.uaeembassy-newdelhi.com; Ambassador MUHAMMAD SULTAN ABDULLA AL-OWAIS.

United Kingdom: Shanti Path, Chanakyapuri, New Delhi 110 021; tel. (11) 26872161; fax (11) 26870065; e-mail web.newdelhi@fco.gov.uk; internet ukinindia.fco.gov.uk; High Commissioner JAMES BEVAN.

USA: Shanti Path, Chanakyapuri, New Delhi 110 021; tel. (11) 24198000; fax (11) 24190017; e-mail ndcentral@state.gov; internet newdelhi.usembassy.gov; Ambassador NANCY J. POWELL.

Uruguay: B-8/3 Vasant Vihar, New Delhi 110 057; tel. (11) 26151991; fax (11) 26144306; e-mail uruind@del3.vsnl.net.in; Ambassador CÉSAR FERRER.

Uzbekistan: EP-40 Dr S. Radhakrishnan Marg, Chanakyapuri, New Delhi 110 021; tel. (11) 24670774; fax (11) 24670773; e-mail info@uzbekembassy.in; internet www.uzbekembassy.in; Ambassador Dr SALIKH INAGAMOV.

Venezuela: E-106 Malcha Marg, Chanakyapuri, New Delhi 110 021; tel. (11) 41680218; fax (11) 41750743; e-mail embassy@embaveneindia.com; internet www.embaveneindia.com; Ambassador MILENA SANTANA-RAMÍREZ.

Viet Nam: 17 Kautilya Marg, Chanakyapuri, New Delhi 110 021; tel. (11) 23019818; fax (11) 23017714; e-mail sqdelhi@del3.vsnl.net.in; Ambassador NGUYEN THANH TAN.

Yemen: D2/5 Vasant Vihar, New Delhi 110 057; tel. (11) 42705723; fax (11) 42705725; e-mail info@yemeninindia.com; internet www.yemeninindia.com; Ambassador (vacant).

Zambia: D5/4 Vasant Vihar, New Delhi 110 057; tel. (11) 26145883; fax (11) 26145764; e-mail zambiand@sify.com; High Commissioner SUSAN YOYO SIKANETA.

Zimbabwe: 4 Aradhana Enclave, Sector 13, R. K. Puram, New Delhi 110 066; tel. (11) 26110430; fax (11) 26114316; e-mail info@zimdelhi.com; Ambassador JONATHAN WUTAWUNASHE.

Judicial System

THE SUPREME COURT

The Supreme Court, consisting of a Chief Justice and 28 other judges appointed by the President, exercises exclusive jurisdiction in any dispute between the Union and the states (although there are certain restrictions where an acceding state is involved). It has appellate jurisdiction over any judgment, decree or order of the High Court where that Court certifies that either a substantial question of law or the interpretation of the Constitution is involved. The Supreme Court can enforce fundamental rights and issue writs covering habeas corpus, mandamus, prohibition, quo warranto and certiorari. The Supreme Court is a court of record and has the power to punish for its contempt.

Provision is made for the appointment by the Chief Justice of India of judges of High Courts as ad hoc judges at sittings of the Supreme Court for specified periods, and for the attendance of retired judges at sittings of the Supreme Court. The Supreme Court has advisory jurisdiction in respect of questions which may be referred to it by the President for opinion. The Supreme Court is also empowered to hear appeals against a sentence of death passed by a State High Court in reversal of an order of acquittal by a lower court, and in a case in which a High Court has granted a certificate of fitness.

The Supreme Court also hears appeals which are certified by High Courts to be fit to be heard, subject to rules made by the Court. Parliament may, by law, confer on the Supreme Court any further powers of appeal.

The judges hold office until the age of 65 years.

Supreme Court: Tilak Marg, New Delhi 110 001; tel. (11) 23388942; fax (11) 23383792; e-mail supremecourt@nic.in; internet supremecourtofindia.nic.in.

Chief Justice of India: SAROSH HOMI KAPADIA.

Attorney-General: GOOLAM ESSAJI VAHANVATI.

HIGH COURTS

The High Courts are the Courts of Appeal from the lower courts, and their decisions are final except in cases where appeal lies with the Supreme Court.

LOWER COURTS

Provision is made in the Code of Criminal Procedure for the constitution of lower criminal courts called Courts of Session and Courts of Magistrates. The Courts of Session are competent to try all persons duly committed for trial, and inflict any punishment authorized by the law. The President and the local government concerned exercise the prerogative of mercy.

The constitution of inferior civil courts is determined by regulations within each state.

Religion

BUDDHISM

The Buddhists in Ladakh (Jammu and Kashmir) are followers of the Dalai Lama. The Buddhists in Sikkim are also followers of Mahayana Buddhism. In 2001 there were 8.0m. Buddhists in India, representing 0.8% of the population.

Mahabodhi Society of India: 4-A, Bankim Chatterjee St, Kolkata 700 073; tel. and fax (33) 22415214; internet www.mahabodhiindia.com; 11 centres in India, 5 centres world-wide; Pres. Dr BHUPENDRA KUMAR MODI; Gen. Sec. Dr D. REWATHA THERO.

HINDUISM

In 2001 there were 827.6m. Hindus in India, representing 80.5% of the population.

Rashtriya Swayamsevak Sangh (RSS) (National Volunteer Organization): Keshav Kunj, Jhandewala, D. B. Gupta Marg, New Delhi 110 055; tel. (11) 23611372; fax (11) 23611385; e-mail rss@rss.org; internet www.rss.org; f. 1925; 934,000 service centres in tribal, rural and urban slum areas; 58,000 working centres; Pres. MOHAN BHAGWAT; Gen. Sec. SURESH SONI.

Sarvadeshik Arya Pratinidhi Sabha: 3/5 Asaf Ali Rd, Near Ram Lila Maidan, New Delhi 110 002; tel. (11) 23274771; f. 1875 by Maharishi Dayanand Saraswati; the international body for Arya Samaj temples propagating reforms in all fields on the basis of Vedic principles; Pres. Capt. DEV RATNA ARYA; Sec. VIMAL WADHAWAN.

Vishwa Hindu Parishad (VHP) (World Hindu Council): Sankat Mochan Ashram, Ramakrishna Puram Sector 6, New Delhi 110 022; tel. (11) 26178992; fax (11) 26195527; e-mail vishwahindu@gmail.com; internet www.vhp.org; f. 1964, banned in Dec. 1992–June 1993 for its role in the destruction of the Babri mosque in Ayodhya; Pres. ASHOK SINGHAL; Sec.-Gen. Dr PRAVINBHAI TOGADIYA.

ISLAM

Muslims are divided into two main sects, Shi'as and Sunnis. Most of the Indian Muslims are Sunnis. At the 2001 census Islam had 138.2m. adherents (13.4% of the population).

Jamiat Ulama-i-Hind (Assembly of Muslim Religious Leaders of India): 1 Bahadur Shah Zafar Marg, New Delhi 110 002; tel. (11) 23311455; fax (11) 23316173; e-mail jamiat@vsnl.com; internet www.jamiatulamaihind.net; f. 1919; Pres MAULANA QARI MOHAMMAD USMAN MANSOORPURI; Leader MAULANA MAHMOOD.

SIKHISM

In 2001 there were 19.2m. Sikhs (comprising 1.9% of the population), the majority living in the Punjab.

Shiromani Gurdwara Parbandhak Committee: Darbar Sahab, Amritsar 143 001; tel. (183) 2553956; fax (183) 2553919; e-mail info@sgpc.net; internet www.sgpc.net; f. 1925; highest authority in Sikhism; Pres. Jathedar AVTAR SINGH; Sec. SARDAR DALMEGH SINGH.

CHRISTIANITY

According to the 2001 census, Christians represented 2.3% of the population in India.

National Council of Churches in India: Christian Council Lodge, Civil Lines, POB 205, Nagpur 440 001; tel. (712) 2561464; fax (712) 2520554; e-mail ncci@nccindia.in; internet www.nccindia.in; f. 1914; mems: 30 protestant and orthodox churches, 17 regional Christian councils, 17 All-India ecumenical orgs, 7 related agencies and 3 autonomous bodies; represents c. 13m. mems; Pres. Bishop Dr TARANATH S. SAGAR; Gen. Sec. Bishop Dr ROGER GAIKWAD.

Orthodox Churches

Malankara Orthodox Syrian Church: Devalokam, Kottayam 686 038; tel. (481) 2578500; fax (481) 2570569; e-mail catholicos@mosc.in; internet malankaraorthodoxchurch.in; c. 2.5m. mems (2009); 22 bishops, 23 dioceses, 1,540 parishes; Catholicos of the East and Malankara Metropolitan HH BASELIOS MARTHOMA DIDYMOS I.

Mar Thoma Syrian Church of Malabar: Tiruvalla 689 101; tel. (469) 2630449; fax (469) 2630327; e-mail sabhaoffice@marthoma.in; internet www.marthomasyrianchurch.org; c. 1m. mems (2001); Valia Metropolitan Most Rev. Dr JOSEPH MAR THOMA; Sec. Rev. KUTTIKATTU MAMMEN MAMMEN.

The Malankara Jacobite Syrian Orthodox Church is also represented.

Protestant Churches

Church of North India (CNI): CNI Bhavan, 16 Pandit Pant Marg, New Delhi 110 001; tel. (11) 23731079; fax (11) 43214006; e-mail alwanmasih@cnisynod.org; internet www.cnisynod.org; f. 1970 by merger of the Church of India (Anglican—fmrly known as the

Church of India, Pakistan, Burma and Ceylon), the Council of the Baptist Churches in Northern India, the Methodist Church (British and Australasian Conferences), the United Church of Northern India (a union of Presbyterians and Congregationalists, f. 1924), the Church of the Brethren in India, and the Disciples of Christ; comprises 27 dioceses; c. 1.2m. mems (1999); Moderator Most Rev. Dr PHILIP P. MARANDIH (Bishop of Patna); Gen. Sec. ALWAN MASIH.

Church of South India (CSI): CSI Centre, 5 Whites Rd, Chennai 600 014; tel. (44) 28521566; fax (44) 28523528; e-mail info@csisynod.com; internet www.csisynod.com; f. 1947 by merger of the Weslyan Methodist Church in South India, the South India United Church (itself a union of churches in the Congregational and Presbyterian/Reformed traditions) and the 4 southern dioceses of the (Anglican) Church of India; comprises 22 dioceses (incl. one in Sri Lanka); c. 3.8m. mems (2009); Moderator Most Rev. J. W. GLADSTONE (Bishop of Medak); Gen. Sec. Rev. MOSES JEYAKUMAR.

Methodist Church in India: Methodist Centre, 21 YMCA Rd, Mumbai 400 008; tel. (22) 23094316; fax (22) 23074137; e-mail gensecmci@vsnl.com; f. 1856 as the Methodist Church in Southern Asia; 648,000 mems (2005); Gen. Sec. Rev. SUBODH C. MONDAL.

Samavesam of Telugu Baptist Churches: A. B. M. Compound, Kavali 524 201; tel. (8626) 241201; fax (8626) 241847; e-mail stbcpabc@yahoo.com; f. 1962; comprises 856 independent Baptist churches; 578,295 mems (1995); Functional Adviser Dr G. DEVADANAM.

United Evangelical Lutheran Churches in India: Martin Luther Bhavan, 95 Purasawalkam High Rd, Kilpauk, Chennai 600 010; tel. (44) 26430008; fax (44) 26611364; e-mail augustinejkumar@uelci.org; internet www.uelci.org; f. 1975; 12 constituent denominations: Andhra Evangelical Lutheran Church, Arcot Lutheran Church, Evangelical Lutheran Church in Madhya Pradesh, Evangelical Lutheran Church in the Himalayan States, Good Shepherd Evangelical Lutheran Church, Gossner Evangelical Lutheran Church in Chotanagpur and Assam (Asom), India Evangelical Lutheran Church, Jeypore Evangelical Lutheran Church, Nepal Northern Evangelical Lutheran Church, Northern Evangelical Lutheran Church, South Andhra Lutheran Church and Tamil Evangelical Lutheran Church; more than 4.5m. mems; Pres. Rt Rev. GODWIN NAG; Exec. Sec. Rev. Dr A. G. AUGUSTINE JEYAKUMAR.

Other denominations active in the country include the Assembly of the Presbyterian Church in North East India, the Bengal-Odisha-Bihar Baptist Convention (6,000 mems), the Chaldean Syrian Church of the East, the Convention of the Baptist Churches of Northern Circars, the Council of Baptist Churches of North East India, the Council of Baptist Churches of Northern India, the Hindustani Convent Church and the Mennonite Church in India.

The Roman Catholic Church

India comprises 30 archdioceses and 134 dioceses. These include five archdioceses and 23 dioceses of the Syro-Malabar rite, and two archdioceses and six dioceses of the Syro-Malankara rite. The archdiocese of Goa and Daman is also the seat of the Patriarch of the East Indies. The remaining archdioceses are metropolitan sees. In 2011 there were an estimated 15.5m. adherents of the Roman Catholic faith in the country.

Catholic Bishops' Conference of India (CBCI): CBCI Centre, 1 Ashok Place, nr Gole Dakkhana, New Delhi 110 001; tel. (11) 23344470; fax (11) 23364615; e-mail cbci@vsl.com; internet www.cbcisite.com; f. 1944; Pres. Cardinal OSWALD GRACIAS (Archbishop of Bombay); Sec.-Gen. Most Rev. STANISLAUS FERNANDES (Archbishop of Gandhinagar).

Latin Rite

Conference of Catholic Bishops of India (CCBI): CCBI Centre, 2nd Cross, Hutchins Rd, POB 8490, Bangalore 560 084; tel. (80) 25498282; fax (80) 25498180; e-mail ccbi@airtelmail.in; internet www.ccbi.in; f. 1994; Pres. Cardinal TELESPHORE TOPPO (Archbishop of Ranchi).

Syro-Malabar Rite

Major Archbishop of Ernakulam-Angamaly: Most Rev. MAR GEORGE ALENCHERRY, Archdiocesian Curia, Mount St Thomas, POB 2580, Kakkand, Kochi 682 031; tel. (484) 2352629; fax (484) 2355010; e-mail secretary@ernakulamarchdiocese.org; internet www.ernakulamarchdiocese.org.

Archbishop of Changanasserry: Most Rev. MAR JOSEPH PERUMTHOTTAM, Archbishop's House, POB 20, Changanasserry 686 101; tel. (481) 2420040; fax (481) 2422540; e-mail abpchry@sancharnet.in; internet www.archdiocesechanganacherry.org.

Archbishop of Kottayam: Most Rev. MATHEW MOOLAKKATTU, Archbishop's House, POB 71, Kottayam 686 001; tel. (481) 2563527; fax (481) 2563327; e-mail cbhktym@hotmail.com; internet www.kottayamad.org.

Archbishop of Tellicherry: Most Rev. GEORGE VALIAMATTAM, Archbishop's House, POB 70, Tellicherry 670 101; tel. (490) 2341058; fax (49) 2341412; e-mail archbishopgeorgev@gmail.com; internet www.archdioceseoftellicherry.org.

Archbishop of Trichur: Most Rev. MAR ANDREWS THAZHATH, Archbishop's House, Trichur 680 005; tel. (487) 2333325; fax (487) 2338204; e-mail carbit@sancharnet.in; internet www.trichurarchdiocese.org.

Syro-Malankara Rite

Archbishop of Trivandrum: Most Rev. BASELIOS CLEEMIS THOTTUNKAL, Major Archbishop's House, Pattom, Thiruvananthapuram 695 004; tel. (471) 2541643; fax (471) 2541635; e-mail mabd@dataone.in; internet www.malankara.net.

BAHÁ'Í FAITH

National Spiritual Assembly: Bahá'í House, 6 Shrimant Madhavrao Scindia Rd, POB 19, New Delhi 110 001; tel. (11) 23387004; fax (11) 23782178; e-mail admin@bahai.in; internet www.bahai.in; f. 1923; c. 2m. mems; Sec.-Gen. Dr A. K. MERCHANT.

OTHER FAITHS

Jainism: 4.2m. adherents (2001 census), 0.4% of the population.

Zoroastrianism: In 2001 69,601 Parsis practised the Zoroastrian religion, compared with 76,382 in 1991.

The Press

Freedom of the press was guaranteed under the 1950 Constitution. In 1979 a Press Council was established (its predecessor was abolished in 1975), the function of which was to uphold the freedom of the press and maintain and improve journalistic standards.

The growth of a thriving press has been inhibited by cultural barriers caused by religious, social and linguistic differences. Consequently the English-language press, with its appeal to the educated middle-class urban readership throughout the states, has retained its dominance. The English-language metropolitan dailies are some of the widest circulating and most influential newspapers. The main Indian-language dailies, by paying attention to rural affairs, cater for the increasingly literate non-anglophone provincial population. Most Indian-language papers have a relatively small circulation.

The majority of publications in India are under individual ownership (75% in 2002/03), and they claim a large part of the total circulation (60% in 1999). The most powerful groups, owned by joint stock companies, publish most of the large English dailies and frequently have considerable private commercial and industrial holdings. Four of the major groups are as follows:

Ananda Bazar Patrika Group: controlled by AVEEK SARKAR and family; dailies: the *Ananda Bazar Patrika* (Kolkata) and the English *The Telegraph* (Guwahati, Kolkata and Siliguri); periodicals include: *Business World*, Bengali weekly *Anandamela*, Bengali fortnightly *Desh*, Bengali monthly *Anandalok* and the Bengali monthly *Sananda*.

Hindustan Times Group: controlled by the K. K. BIRLA family; dailies: the *Hindustan Times* (published from 6 regional centres), *Pradeep* (Patna) and the Hindi *Hindustan* (published from 13 regional centres); periodicals: the weekly *Overseas Hindustan Times* and the Hindi monthlies *Nandan* and *Kadambini* (New Delhi).

Indian Express Group: controlled by the family of the late RAMNATH GOENKA; publishes 9 dailies including the *Indian Express*, the Marathi *Lokasatta*, the Tamil *Dinamani*, the Telugu *Andhra Prabha*, the Kannada *Kannada Prabha* and the English *Financial Express*; 6 periodicals including the English weeklies the *Indian Express* (Sunday edition), *Screen*, the Telugu *Andhra Prabha Illustrated Weekly* and the Tamil *Dinamani Kadir* (weekly).

Times of India Group: controlled by family of the late ASHOK JAIN; dailies: *The Times of India* (published in 10 regional centres), *Economic Times*, the Hindi *Navbharat Times* and *Sandhya Times*, the Marathi *Maharashtra Times* (Mumbai); periodicals: the English fortnightly *Femina* and monthly *Filmfare*.

PRINCIPAL DAILIES

Circulation figs are for 2009, unless otherwise stated.

Delhi (incl. New Delhi)

The Asian Age: S-7, Green Park, Main Market, New Delhi 110 016; tel. (11) 26530001; fax (11) 26530027; e-mail delhidesk@asianage.com; internet www.asianage.com; f. 1994; morning; English; also publ. from Ahmedabad, Bangalore, Kolkata, Mumbai and London; Editor-in-Chief VENKATTRAM REDDY; circ. 46,895.

Business Standard: Nehru House, 4 Bahadur Shah Zafar Marg, New Delhi 110 002; tel. (11) 23720202; fax (11) 23720201; e-mail letters@business-standard.com; internet www.business-standard.com; morning; English; also publ. from Kolkata, Ahmedabad, Bangalore, Chennai, Hyderabad, Chandigarh, Pune, Kochi, Lucknow, Bhubaneswar and Mumbai; Editor Dr SANJAYA BARU; circ. 26,390.

Daily Milap: Milap Niketan, 8A Bahadur Shah Zafar Marg, New Delhi 110 002; tel. (11) 23317651; fax (11) 23319166; e-mail yogi@milap.com; internet www.milap.com; f. 1923; Urdu; nationalist, also published in Hindi; published from Jullundur and Hyderabad as well; Man. Editor PUNAM SURI; Editor NAVIN SURI; circ. 36,295.

Daily Pratap: Pratap Bhavan, 5 Bahadur Shah Zafar Marg, New Delhi 110 002; tel. (11) 23317938; fax (11) 41509555; e-mail admin@dailypratap.com; internet www.dailypratap.com; f. 1919; Urdu; Chief Editor K. NARENDRA; CEO S. M. AFIF AHSEN; circ. 65,866.

The Economic Times: 7 Bahadur Shah Zafar Marg, New Delhi 110 002; tel. (11) 23492234; fax (11) 23491248; internet economictimes.indiatimes.com; f. 1961; English; also publ. from Kolkata, Ahmedabad, Bangalore, Hyderabad, Chennai and Mumbai; Exec. Editor ROHIT SARAN; circ. 175,438.

Financial Express: Express Bldg, The Indian Express Online Media (Pvt) Ltd, 9–10 Bahadur Shah Zafar Marg, New Delhi 110 002; tel. 2370210007 (mobile); fax (11) 26530114; e-mail editor@expressindia.com; internet www.financialexpress.com; f. 1961; morning; English; also publ. from Ahmedabad (in Gujarati), Mumbai, Bangalore, Kolkata and Chennai; Editor MYTHILI BHUSNURMATH; circ. 31,383.

The Hindu: 3rd Floor, PTI Bldg, 4 Parliament St, New Delhi 110 001; tel. (11) 43579797; fax (11) 23723808; e-mail letters@thehindu.co.in; internet www.thehindu.com; f. 1878; morning; English; also publ. from 12 other regional centres; Editor-in-Chief N. RAM; circ. 65,847 (2011).

Hindustan: 18–20 Kasturba Gandhi Marg, New Delhi 110 001; tel. (11) 23704600; fax (11) 66561445; e-mail feedback@hindustantimes.com; internet www.livehindustan.com; f. 1936; morning; Hindi; also publ. from Patna, Muzaffarpur, Bhagalpur, Ranchi, Jamshedpur, Dhanbad, Lucknow, Varanasi, Meerut, Agra, Kanpur and Chandigarh; Editor-in-Chief SHASHI SHEKHAR; circ. 429,759.

Hindustan Times: 18–20 Kasturba Gandhi Marg, New Delhi 110 001; tel. (11) 23361234; fax (11) 66561270; e-mail feedback@hindustantimes.com; internet www.hindustantimes.com; f. 1924; morning; English; also publ. from Mumbai, Lucknow, Patna, Ranchi and Kolkata; Editor-in-Chief SANJOY NARAYAN; circ. 993,349.

Indian Express: Express Bldg, The Indian Express Online Media (Pvt) Ltd, 9–10 Bahadur Shah Zafar Marg, New Delhi 110 002; tel. (11) 2370210007; fax (11) 23702141; e-mail editor@expressindia.com; internet www.indianexpress.com; f. 1953; English; also publ. from 9 other cities; Chair. and Man. Dir VIVEK GOENKA; Editor-in-Chief SHEKHAR GUPTA; circ. 71,585.

Jansatta: 9–10 Bahadur Shah Zafar Marg, New Delhi 110 002; tel. (11) 23702100; fax (11) 23702141; e-mail jansatta@expressindia.com; f. 1983; Hindi; also publ. from Kolkata and Raipur; Editor OM THANVI; circ. 43,612.

Navbharat Times: 7 Bahadur Shah Zafar Marg, New Delhi 110 002; tel. (11) 23492041; fax (11) 23492168; internet navbharattimes.indiatimes.com; f. 1947; Hindi; also publ. from Mumbai; Editor RAM KRIPAL SINGH; circ. 409,584.

The Pioneer: Link House, 3 Bahadur Shah Zafar Marg, New Delhi 110 002; tel. (11) 23755271; fax (11) 23755275; e-mail info@dailypioneer.com; internet www.dailypioneer.com; f. 1865; also publ. from Lucknow, Bhopal, Bhubaneswar, Ranchi, Kochi, Chandigarh and Dehradun; Editor CHANDAN MITRA; circ. 96,332.

Punjab Kesari: Plot No. 2, Printing Press Complex, Ring Rd, nr Wazirpur Bus Depot, Delhi 110 035; tel. (11) 27193719; fax (11) 27194470; e-mail sales@punjabkesari.com; internet www.punjabkesari.com; f. 1983; Hindi; also publ. from Jalandhar and Ambala; circulated in Haryana, Rajasthan, Uttar Pradesh, Uttarakhand, Madhya Pradesh, Punjab, Himachal Pradesh, Maharashtra, Bihar and Gujarat; Resident Editor ASHWANI KUMAR; circ. 348,890.

Rashtriya Sahara: 12th Floor, Navrang House, 21 Kasturba Gandhi Marg, New Delhi 110 001; tel. (11) 43596017; fax (11) 23352370; e-mail rsahara@saharasamay.com; internet rashtriyasahara.samaylive.com; morning; Hindi; also publ. from Lucknow, Gorakhpur, Kanpur, Dehradun and Patna; Resident Editor AZIZ BURNEY; circ. 97,625 (2011).

Sandhya Times: 7 Bahadur Shah Zafar Marg, New Delhi 110 002; tel. (11) 23492162; fax (11) 23492047; f. 1979; Hindi; evening; Editor SAT SONI; circ. 34,756.

The Statesman: Statesman House, 148 Barakhamba Rd, New Delhi 110 001; tel. (11) 23315911; fax (11) 23315295; e-mail thestatesman@vsnl.com; internet www.thestatesman.net; f. 1931; English; also publ. from Bhubaneswar, Kolkata and Siliguri; Editor and Man. Dir RAVINDRA KUMAR; circ. 7,598.

The Times of India: 7 Bahadur Shah Zafar Marg, New Delhi 110 002; tel. (11) 23492049; fax (11) 23351606; internet timesofindia.indiatimes.com; f. 1838; English; also publ. from 9 other towns (Mumbai, Pune, Ahmedabad, Bangalore, Chennai, Hyderabad, Jaipur, Kolkata and Lucknow); Editor-in-Chief JAIDEEP BOSE; circ. 1,190,772.

Andhra Pradesh

Hyderabad

Andhra Jyothi: Andhra Jyothi Bldg, Plot No. 76, HUDA Heights, Rd No. 70, Journalist Colony, Jubilee Hills, Hyderabad 500 033; tel. (40) 23558233; fax (40) 23558288; e-mail editor@andhrajyothy.com; internet www.andhrajyothy.com; f. 1960; Telugu; also publ. from 13 other regional centres; Editor K. SRINIVAS; combined circ. 91,896.

Andhra Prabha: 16-1-28, Kolandareddy Rd, Poornanandampet, Vijayawada 520 003; tel. (866) 2571351; e-mail info@andhraprabha.com; internet www.andhraprabha.in; f. 1938; Telugu; also publ. from Bangalore, Hyderabad, Chennai and Visakhapatnam; Editor VASUDEV DEKSHITILU; circ. 68,590.

Deccan Chronicle: 36 Sarojini Devi Rd, Hyderabad 500 003; tel. (40) 27803930; fax (40) 27803870; e-mail thomas@deccanmail.com; internet www.deccanchronicle.com; f. 1938; English; also publ. from 6 other regional centres; Editor-in-Chief A. T. JAYANTI; circ. 45,748.

Eenadu: Somajiguda, Hyderabad 500 082; tel. (40) 23318181; fax (40) 23392530; e-mail editor@eenadu.net; internet www.eenadu.net; f. 1974; Telugu; also publ. from 22 other towns; Chief Editor RAHUL KUMAR; circ. 34,459.

Rahnuma-e-Deccan: 12-2-837/A/3, Asif Nagar, Hyderabad 500 028; tel. (40) 23534943; fax (40) 23534945; e-mail jameelnews@gmail.com; f. 1949; morning; Urdu; independent; Chief Editor SYED VICARUDDIN; circ. 26,293.

Siasat Daily: Jawaharlal Nehru Rd, Hyderabad 500 001; tel. (40) 24744180; fax (40) 24603188; e-mail contact@siasat.com; internet www.siasat.com; f. 1949; morning; Urdu; Editor ZAHID ALI KHAN; circ. 44,073.

Vijayawada

New Indian Express: 29-28-39, Dasarivari St, Suryaraopet, Vijayawada; tel. (866) 2444163; internet www.expressbuzz.com; English; also publ. from 7 other cities; Man. Editor MANOJ KUMAR SONTHALIA; circ. 9,588.

Assam (Asom)

Guwahati

Amar Asom: G. S. Rd, Ulubari, Guwahati 781 007; tel. (361) 2458395; fax (361) 2521620; e-mail glpghy2009@hotmail.com; internet amarasom.glpublications.in; f. 1997; Assamese; also publ. from Jorhat and Lakhimpur; Editor HOMEN BORGOHAIN; circ. 59,995.

Asomiya Pratidin: Maniram Dewan Rd, Chandmari, Guwahati 781 003; tel. (361) 2660420; fax (361) 2666377; e-mail pratidinedi@vsnl.net; internet www.asomiyapratidin.co.in; morning; Assamese; also published from Dibrugarh, Barpari and Kamrup; Editor HAIDAR HUSSAIN; circ. 74,460.

Assam Tribune: GNB Rd, Guwahati 781 003; tel. (361) 2661357; fax (361) 2666398; e-mail editoratribune@gmail.com; internet www.assamtribune.com; f. 1939; English; also publishes Assamese edn, Dainik Assam; Man. Dir and Editor P. G. BARUAH; circ. 90,815 (2011).

Dainik Agradoot: Agradoot Bhavan, Dispur, Guwahati 781 006; tel. (361) 2261923; fax (361) 2260655; e-mail agradoot@sify.com; internet www.dainikagradoot.com; f. 1995; Assamese; Editor K. S. DEKA; circ. 66,409.

Dainik Jugasankha: 13 Green Path, G. S. Rd, Guwahati 781 007; tel. (361) 2526670; fax (361) 2450496; e-mail dainikjugasankha@yahoo.com; f. 1950; Bengali; also publ. from Silchar; Editor-in-Chief BIJOY KRISHNA NATH; Editor AMAL GUPTA; circ. 75,650.

The North East Times: G.S. Rd, Ulubari, Guwahati 781 007; tel. (361) 2458395; fax (361) 2521620; e-mail guwahatiglpghy@hotmail.com; internet net.glpublications.in; English; Editor G. L. AGARWALLA; circ. 34,891.

The Sentinel: G. S. Rd, Six Mile, Dispur, Guwahati 781 022; tel. (361) 2229330; fax (361) 2229110; e-mail thesentinel@satyam.net.in; internet www.sentinelassam.com; f. 1983; English; Editor SHANKAR RAJKHEWA; circ. 58,751.

Jorhat

Dainik Janmabhumi: Tulsi Narayan Sarma Rd, Jorhat 785 001; tel. (376) 2320033; fax (376) 2321713; e-mail editordj@sify.com; internet www.dainikjanambhumi.co.in; f. 1972; Assamese; also published from Tinsukia, Guwahati and Tezpur; Editor HEMANTA BARMAN; Man. Partner SUBROTO SHARMA; circ. 29,163.

Bihar

Patna

Dainik Jagran: 172/92/11 B/2, 5th Floor, Rashmi Complex, Kidwaipuri, Patna 800001; tel. (612) 2520671; fax (612) 2534386; internet in.jagran.yahoo.com; f. 1942; Hindi; also publ. from 25 other cities; Man. Editor MAHENDRA MOHAN GUPTA; circ. 356,328.

Hindustan Times: Buddha Marg, Patna 800 001; tel. (612) 2223434; fax (612) 2226120; internet www.hindustantimes.com; f. 1918; morning; English; also publ. from 5 regional centres; Editor SHEKHAR BHATIA; circ. 17,285.

Chhattisgarh

Raipur

Dainik Bhaskar: Press Complex, Rajbandha Maidan, G. E. Rd, Raipur 492 001; tel. (771) 2535277; fax (771) 2535255; e-mail editorbhaskar@bhaskar.com; internet www.bhaskar.com; Hindi; morning; also publ. from 18 other regional centres; Editor RAMESH CHANDRA AGRAWAL; circ. 184,587.

Deshbandhu: Deshbandhu Complex, Ramsagar Para, Raipur 492 001; tel. (771) 4288888; e-mail deshbandhuraipur@gmail.com; internet www.deshbandhu.co.in; f. 1959; Hindi; also publ. from Jabalpur, Satna, Bilaspur, Indore, New Delhi and Bhopal; publishes an evening edn, Highway Channel, from Raipur, Jabalpur and Bilaspur; Chief Editor LALIT SURJAN; circ. 84,357 (Raipur), 24,289 (Satna), 46,785 (Bhopal), 50,468 (Jabalpur), 59,013 (Bilaspur).

Nava Bharat: Nava Bharat Bhavan Press Complex, G. E. Rd, Raipur 492 001; tel. (771) 2535544; fax (771) 2534936; internet www.navabharat.biz; Hindi; also publ. from 6 other regional centres; Editor PRAKASH MAHESHWARI; circ. 189,186 (2011).

Goa

Panaji

Gomantak Times: Gomantak Bhavan, St Inez, Panaji, Goa 403 001; tel. (832) 2422700; fax (832) 2422701; internet www.dainikgomantak.com; f. 1962; morning; Marathi and English edns; Exec. Editor DERRICK ALMEIDA; circ. 24,906 (Marathi).

Navhind Times: Navhind Bhavan, Rua Ismail Gracias, POB 161, Panaji, Goa 403 001; tel. (832) 6651111; fax (832) 2224258; e-mail advt@navhindtimes.com; internet www.navhindtimes.in; f. 1963; morning; English; Editor ARUN SINHA; circ. 34,835.

Panjim

O Heraldo: Herald Publications Pvt Ltd, POB 160, Rua St Tome, Panjim 403 001; tel. (832) 2224202; fax (832) 2225622; e-mail info@oheraldo.in; internet www.heraldgoa.in; f. 1900; English; Editor-in-Chief R. F. FERNANDES; Editor SUJAY GUPTA; circ. 61,587 (2011).

Gujarat

Ahmedabad

Gujarat Samachar: Gujarat Samachar Bhavan, Khanpur, Ahmedabad 380 001; tel. (79) 30410000; fax (79) 5502000; e-mail editor@gujaratsamachar.com; internet www.gujaratsamachar.com; f. 1930; morning; Gujarati; also publ. from Surat, Rajkot, Baroda, Bhavnagar, Mumbai, London and New York; Editor SHREYANSH SHAH; circ. 537,029.

Indian Express: 5th Floor, Sanidhya Bldg, Ashram Rd, Ahmedabad 380 009; tel. (79) 26583023; fax (79) 26575826; e-mail praman@express2.indexp.co.in; internet www.indianexpress.com; f. 1968; English; also publ. in 10 other towns; Man. Editor VIVECK GOENKA; Chief Editor SHEKHAR GUPTA; circ. 18,203.

Lokasatta—Janasatta: Mirzapur Rd, POB 188, Ahmedabad 380 001; tel. (79) 25507307; fax (79) 25507708; f. 1953; morning; Gujarati; also publ. from Rajkot and Vadodara; Man. Editor VIVEK GOENKA; circ. 49,161.

Sandesh: Sandesh Bhavan, Lad Society Rd, Ahmedabad 380 054; tel. (79) 40004000; fax (79) 40004242; e-mail advt@sandesh.com; internet sandesh.com; f. 1923; Gujarati; also publ. from Bhavnagar, Vadodara, Rajkot and Surat; Editor FALGUNBHAI C. PATEL; circ. 346,553.

The Times of India: 139 Ashram Rd, POB 4046, Ahmedabad 380 009; tel. (79) 26553300; fax (79) 26583758; internet timesofindia.indiatimes.com; f. 1968; English; also publ. from 9 other towns; Chief Editor RAJESH KALRA; circ. 199,612.

Western Times: 301, 3rd Floor, Gala Argos, nr Kalgi Char Rasta, Gujarat College Rd, Ellisbridge, Ahmedabad 380 006; tel. (79) 26402880; fax (79) 26402882; e-mail gujarati@westerntimes.co.in; internet www.westerntimes.co.in; f. 1967; English and Gujarati edns; also publ. (in Gujarati) from 8 other towns; Editor NIKUNJ PATEL; total circ. more than 200,000.

Bhuj

Kutchmitra: Kutchmitra Bhavan, nr Indirabai Park, Bhuj 370 001; tel. (2832) 252090; fax (2832) 250271; e-mail info@kutchmitradaily.com; internet www.kutchmitradaily.com; f. 1947; Gujarati; Propr Saurashtra Trust; Editor KIRTI J. KHATRI; circ. 47,882 (2011).

Rajkot

Jai Hind: Jai Hind Press Bldg, Babubhai Shah Rd, POB 59, Rajkot 360 001; tel. (281) 3048684; fax (281) 2448677; e-mail editor@jaihinddaily.com; internet www.jaihinddaily.com; f. 1948; morning and evening (in Rajkot as Sanj Samachar); Gujarati; also publ. from Ahmedabad; Editor Y. N. SHAH; combined circ. 107,300.

Phulchhab: Phulchhab Bhavan, Phulchhab Marg, Rajkot 360 001; tel. (281) 2444611; fax (281) 2448751; e-mail editor@janmabhoominewspapers.com; internet phulchhab.janmabhoominewspapers.com; f. 1950; morning; Gujarati; Propr Saurashtra Trust; Editor DINESH RAJA; circ. 84,500.

Surat

Gujaratmitra and Gujaratdarpan: Gujaratmitra Bhavan, nr Old Civil Hospital, Sonifalia, Surat 395 003; tel. (261) 2599992; fax (261) 2599990; e-mail mitra@gujaratmitra.in; internet www.gujaratmitra.in/web; f. 1863; morning; Gujarati; Editor B. P. RESHAMWALA; circ. 91,000.

Haryana

Rohtak

Bharat Janani: Sonipat Rd, Rohtak; tel. and fax (1262) 427191; f. 1971; Hindi; morning; also publ. from Rewari; Editor Dr R. S. SANTOSHI; circ. 56,360.

Himachal Pradesh

Shimla

Dainik Himachal Sewa: Hans Kutir, Khalini, Shimla 171 002; tel. (177) 2224119; fax (177) 2260187; f. 1986; Hindi; Editor-in-Chief Dr R. S. SANTOSHI; circ. 60,000.

Himachal Times: Himachal Times Complex, 64–66 The Mall, Shimla 171 001; tel. and fax (177) 2811555; e-mail devkpandhi@gmail.com; internet himachaltimesgroup.com; f. 1948; English; Chief Editor VIJAY PANDHI.

Jammu and Kashmir

Jammu

Daily Excelsior: Excelsior House, Excelsior Lane, Janipura, Jammu Tawi 180 007; tel. (191) 2537055; fax (191) 2537831; e-mail editor@dailyexcelsior.com; internet www.dailyexcelsior.com; f. 1965; English; Publr and Editor S. D. ROHMETRA.

Kashmir Times: Residency Rd, Jammu 180 001; tel. (191) 2543676; fax (191) 2542028; e-mail jmt_prabodh@sancharnet.in; internet www.kashmirtimes.com; f. 1955; morning; English and Hindi; Editor-in-Chief PRABODH JAMWAL.

Srinagar

Greater Kashmir: 6 Pratap Park, Residency Rd, Srinagar 190 001; tel. (194) 2455435; fax (194) 2477782; e-mail editor@greaterkashmir.com; internet www.greaterkashmir.com; f. 1993; English; Chief Editor FAYAZ AHMED KALOO; circ. 79,370.

Jharkhand

Ranchi

Aaj: 15–16 Namkum Industrial Area, Ranchi; Hindi; morning; also publ. from 8 other cities; Publr AMITAV CHAKRAVORTHY; circ. 59,267 (Ranchi).

Hindustan: Circular Court, Circular Rd, Ranchi 834 001; tel. (651) 2205811; Hindi; morning; also publ. from Patna, Delhi, Bhagalpur, Lucknow, Varanasi and Muzaffarpur; Editor MRINAL PANDE; circ. 295,934 (2011).

Prabhat Khabar: 15-P, Kokar Industrial Area, Kokar, Ranchi 834 001; tel. (651) 3053100; fax (651) 254006; e-mail ranchi@prabhatkhabar.in; internet www.prabhatkhabar.com; f. 1984; Hindi; also publ. from Dhanbad, Kolkata, Jamshedpur, Siliguri, Deoghar and Patna; Chief Editor HARIVANSH; circ. 120,162 (Ranchi).

Ranchi Express: 55 Baralal St, Ranchi 834 001; tel. (651) 2206320; fax (651) 2206213; e-mail news@ranchiexpress.com; internet ranchiexpress.com; f. 1963; Hindi; morning; Editor AJAY MAROO; circ. 57,959.

Karnataka

Bangalore

Deccan Herald: 75 Mahatma Gandhi Rd, POB 5331, Bangalore 560 001; tel. (80) 25588000; fax (80) 25580523; e-mail ads@deccanherald.co.in; internet www.deccanherald.com; f. 1948; morning; English; also publ. from Hubli-Dharwar, Mangalore, Dhavangere and Gulbarga; Editor K. N. Tilak Kumar; circ. 163,221.

Kannada Prabha: Express Bldgs, 1 Queen's Rd, Bangalore 560 001; tel. (80) 22866893; fax (80) 22866617; e-mail anisikeprabha@gmail.com; internet www.kannadaprabha.com; f. 2005; morning; Kannada; also publ. from Belgaum, Mangalore, Gulbarga, Hubali and Shimoga; Editor Vishweshwar Bhat; circ. 96,485 (2011).

New Indian Express: 1 Queen's Rd, Bangalore 560 001; tel. (80) 22256998; fax (80) 22256617; f. 1965; English; also publ. from Bhubaneswar, Kochi, Hyderabad, Chennai, Madurai, Vijayawada and Vizianagaram; Chair. and Man. Editor Manoj Kumar Sonthalia; circ. 27,634.

Prajavani: 75 M.G. Rd, POB 5331, Bangalore 560 001; tel. (80) 25880000; fax (80) 25880165; e-mail ads@deccanherald.co.in; internet www.prajavani.net; f. 1948; morning; Kannada; also publ. from Mysore, Gulbarga, Mangalore and Dharwad; Editor-in-Chief K. N. Shanth Kumar; circ. 56,240.

Hubli-Dharwar

Samyukta Karnataka: POB 30, Koppikar Rd, Hubli 580 020; tel. (836) 2364303; fax (836) 2362760; e-mail skhubli@gmail.com; internet www.samyukthakarnataka.com; f. 1933; Kannada; also publ. from Bangalore, Davangere, and Gulbarga; Editor A. C. Gopal; circ. 100,337.

Vijay Karnataka: Giriraj Annexe, Circuit House Rd, Hubli 580 029; tel. (836) 2237556; fax (836) 2253630; internet www.vijaykarnatakaepaper.com; f. 1999; Kannada; also publ. from Bangalore, Gangavati, Gulbarga, Mangalore, Mysore, Bagalkot, Chitradurga and Shimoga; Printer and Publr Vijay Sankeshwar; circ. 69,201.

Manipal

Udayavani: Manipal Media Network, New Udayavani Bldg, Manipal 576 119; tel. (820) 2571151; fax (820) 2570563; e-mail udayavanionline@manipalmedia.com; internet www.udayavani.com; f. 1970; Kannada; also publ. from Manipal-Udupi and Mumbai; Editor T. Satish U. Pai; Regional Editors N. Guraj (Manipal), R. Poornima (Bangalore), T. Satish (Mumbai); circ. 21,739.

Kerala

Kottayam

Deepika: POB 7, Kottayam 686 001; tel. (481) 3012001; fax (481) 3012222; e-mail editor@deepika.com; internet www.deepika.com; f. 1887; Malayalam; independent; also publ. from Kannur, Kochi, Kozhikode, Thiruvananthapuram and Thrissur; Chief Editor Fr Alexander Paikada; circ. 47,520.

Malayala Manorama: K. K. Rd, POB 26, Kottayam 686 001; tel. (481) 2563646; fax (481) 2562479; e-mail editor@malayalamanorama.com; internet www.manoramaonline.com; f. 1890; Malayalam; also publ. from 16 other regional centres; morning; Man. Dir and Editor Mammen Mathew; circ. 308,985.

Kozhikode

Deshabhimani: Deshabhimani Bldg, Kaloor, Kochi 682 017; tel. (484) 253034; fax (484) 2530006; e-mail kochi@deshabhimani.com; internet www.deshabhimani.com; f. 1946; Malayalam; morning; publ. by the CPI (M); also publ. from Kochi, Kottayam, Thrissur, Calicut, Malappuram and Thiruvananthapuram; Chief Editor V. V. Dakshinamoorthy; circ. 57,530.

Mathrubhumi: M. J. Krishnamohan Memorial Bldg, K. P. Kesava Menon Rd, POB 46, Kozhikode 673 001; tel. (495) 2366655; fax (495) 2366656; e-mail mbiclt@mpp.co.in; internet www.mathrubhumi.com; f. 1923; Malayalam; also publ. from Thiruvananthapuram, Kozhikode, Kannur, Thrissur, Kollam, Malappuram, Pallakad, Alappuzha, Kottayam, Kochi, Bangalore, Chennai, New Delhi and Mumbai; Editor M. Kesava Menon; circ. 157,040 (2011).

Thiruvananthapuram

Kerala Kaumudi: Kaumudi Bldgs, Pettah, Thiruvananthapuram 695 024; tel. (471) 2461010; fax (471) 2461985; e-mail editor@ekaumudi.com; internet news.keralakaumudi.com; f. 1911; Malayalam; also publ. from Kollam, Alappuzha, Kochi, Kannur, Kozhikode and Bangalore; Editor-in-Chief M. S. Mani; Man. Editor Deepu Ravi; circ. 60,036.

Madhya Pradesh

Bhopal

Dainik Bhaskar: 6 Dwarka Sadan, Press Complex, M. P. Nagar, Bhopal; tel. (755) 3988884; fax (755) 270466; e-mail editorbhaskar@bhaskar.com; internet www.bhaskar.com; f. 1958; morning; Hindi; also publ. from 18 other regional centres; Chief Editor Shravan Garg; circ. 265,474.

Indore

Naidunia: 60/1 Babu Labhchand Chhajlani Marg, Indore 452 009; tel. (731) 4711000; fax (731) 4711111; e-mail response@naidunia.com; internet www.naidunia.com; f. 1947; morning; Hindi; also publ. from Jabalpur, Gwalior and Bhopal; CEO Vinay Chhajlani; combined circ. 412,904.

Maharashtra

Kolhapur

Pudhari: 2318, 'C' Ward, Kolhapur 416 002; tel. (231) 2543111; fax (231) 2543124; e-mail news.kop@pudhari.co.in; internet www.pudhari.com; f. 1974; Marathi; Editor P. S. Jadhav; circ. 361,176 (2011).

Mumbai (Bombay)

Afternoon Despatch & Courier: 3rd Floor, Janmabhoomi Bhavan, Janmabhoomi Marg, Fort, Mumbai 400 001; tel. (22) 40768999; fax (22) 40768916; e-mail afternoonnews@gmail.com; internet www.afternoondc.in; evening; English; Editor Carol Andrade.

Bombay Samachar: Red House, S. A. Brelvi Rd, Horniman Circle, Fort, Mumbai 400 001; tel. (22) 22045531; fax (22) 22046642; e-mail samachar.bombay@gmail.com; internet www.bombaysamachar.com; f. 1822; morning and Sun.; Gujarati; political, social and commercial; Editor Pinky Dalal; circ. 77,774 (2011).

Daily News and Analysis (DNA): First Floor, Oasis Bldg, Lower Parel, Mumbai 400 013; tel. (22) 39888888; fax (22) 39801000; internet www.dnaindia.com; f. 2005; English; also publ. from Bangalore, Pune, Ahmedabad, Surat and Jaipur; Exec. Editor Aditya Sinha; circ. 397,147.

Dainik Saamana: Sadguru Darshan, Nagu Sayaji Wadi, Dainik Saamana Marg, Prabhadevi, Mumbai 400 028; tel. (22) 24370591; fax (22) 24224181; f. 1989; Marathi; Exec. Editor Sanjay Raut; circ. 102,900.

The Economic Times: Times of India Bldg, Dr Dadabhai Naoroji Rd, Mumbai 400 001; tel. (22) 22733535; fax (22) 22731344; e-mail etbom@timesgroup.com; internet economictimes.indiatimes.com; f. 1961; also publ. from New Delhi, Kolkata, Ahmedabad, Hyderabad, Chennai and Bangalore; English; Editor (Mumbai) Sudeshna Sen; combined circ. 461,900, circ. 241,617 (Mumbai).

Financial Express: Express Towers, Nariman Point, Mumbai 400 021; tel. (22) 6740000; fax (11) 22022139; e-mail editor@expressindia.com; internet www.financialexpress.com; f. 1961; morning; English; also publ. from New Delhi, Bangalore, Kolkata, Coimbatore, Ahmedabad (Gujarati) and Chennai; Man. Editor Viveck Goenka; Editor Shobhana Subramanian; circ. 22,427(English).

The Free Press Journal: Free Press House, 215 Free Press Journal Rd, Nariman Point, Mumbai 400 021; tel. (22) 22874566; fax (22) 22874688; e-mail mail@fpj.co.in; internet www.freepressjournal.in; f. 1930; English; also publ. from Indore, Kolkata, Bhopal, Chennai and New Delhi; Man. Editor G. L. Lakhotia.

Hindustan Times: 2nd Floor, Mahalaxmi Industrial Estate, L. J. Coross Rd No. 1, Mumbai 400 016; tel. (22) 24368012; fax (22) 24303625; e-mail feedback@hindustantimes.in; internet www.hindustantimes.com; f. 1923; also publ. from Delhi, Lucknow, Bhopal, Kolkata and Chandigarh; Editor Soumya Bhattacharya; circ. 279,372.

Indian Express: Express Tower, 1st and 2nd Floors, Nariman Point, Mumbai 400 021; tel. (22) 67440000; fax (22) 22022139; f. 1940; English; also publ. from 8 regional centres; Man. Editor Viveck Goenka; Chief Editor Shekhar Gupta; circ. 75,020.

Inquilab: 156 D. J. Dadajee Rd, Tardeo, Mumbai 400 034; tel. (22) 23522586; fax (22) 23510226; e-mail inquilab@mid-day.com; internet www.inquilab.com; f. 1938; morning; Urdu; Editor Shahid Latif; circ. 31,640.

Janmabhoomi: Janmabhoomi Bhavan, Janmabhoomi Marg, Fort, POB 62, Mumbai 400 001; tel. (22) 22870831; fax (22) 22874097; e-mail jbhoomi@yahoo.com; internet www.janmabhoominewspapers.com; f. 1934; evening; Gujarati; Propr Saurashtra Trust; Editor Kundan Vyas; circ. 18,464.

Lokasatta: 3/50 Lalbaug Industrial Estate, Dr B. Ambedkar, Lalbaug, Mumbai 400 012; tel. (22) 24717677; fax (22) 24717654; e-mail pratikriya@expressindia.com; internet www.loksatta.com; f. 1948;

morning (incl. Sun.); Marathi; also publ. from Pune, Nagpur and Ahmednagar; Editor GIRISH KUBER; circ. 206,975.

Maharashtra Times: Dr Dadabhai Naoroji Rd, POB 213, Mumbai 400 001; tel. (22) 22733636; fax (22) 22731175; internet maharashtratimes.indiatimes.com; f. 1962; Marathi; Editor ASHOK PANVALKAR; circ. 312,614.

Mid-Day: Peninsula Centre, Dr S. S. Rao Rd, opp. Mahatma Gandhi Hospital, Parel, Mumbai 400 012; tel. (22) 67017171; fax (22) 24150009; e-mail cs@mid-day.com; internet www.mid-day.com; f. 1979; daily and Sun.; English; also publ. from New Delhi, Pune and Bangalore; Editor AVIROOK SEN; circ. 121,342.

Mumbai Mirror: The Times of India Bldg., Dr D. N. Rd, Mumbai 400 001; tel. (22) 26005555; e-mail mumbai.mirror@timesgroup.com; internet www.mumbaimirror.com; f. 2005; English; Editor MEENAL BAGHEL; circ. 708,687.

Navakal: 13 Shenviwadi, Khadilkar Rd, Girgaun, Mumbai 400 004; tel. (22) 23860978; fax (22) 23860989; f. 1923; Marathi; Editor N. Y. KHADILKAR; circ. 172,466.

Navbharat Times: Dr Dadabhai Naoroji Rd, Mumbai 400 001; tel. (22) 22733535; fax (22) 22731144; internet navbharattimes .indiatimes.com; f. 1950; Hindi; also publ. from New Delhi, Jaipur, Patna and Lucknow; Chief Editor VISHWANATH SACHDEV; circ. 159,578 (Mumbai).

Navshakti: Free Press House, 215 Nariman Point, Mumbai 400 021; tel. (22) 22853335; fax (22) 22874688; e-mail editor@navshakti.co.in; internet navshakti.co.in; f. 1932; Marathi; Chief Editor PRAKASH KULKARNI; circ. 16,719.

Sakal: Sakal Bhavan, Plot No. 42-B, Sector No. 11, CBD Belapur, Navi Mumbai 400 614; tel. (22) 66843000; fax (22) 27574280; e-mail editor.mumbai@esakal.com; internet www.esakal.com; f. 1970; Marathi; also publ. from Pune, Aurangabad, Nasik, Kolhapur and Solapur; Chief Editor SANJEEV LATKAR; circ. 88,094.

The Times of India: The Times of India Bldg, Dr Dadabhai Naoroji Rd, Mumbai 400 001; tel. (22) 56353535; fax (22) 22731444; e-mail toieditorial@timesgroup.com; internet www.timesofindia.com; f. 1838; morning; English; also publ. from 9 regional centres; Exec. Editor ARINDAM SENGUPTA; circ. 763,758.

Nagpur

The Hitavada: Pandit Jawaharlal Nehru Marg, POB 201, Dhantoli, Nagpur 440 012; tel. (712) 2435737; fax (712) 2422362; e-mail hitavada_ngp@sancharnet.in; internet www.ehitavada.com; f. 1911; morning; English; also publ. from Raipur and Jabalpur; Man. Editor BANWARILAL PUROHIT; Editor V. PHANSHIKAR; circ. 73,550.

Lokmat: Lokmat Bhavan, Wardha Rd, Nagpur 440 012; tel. (712) 2523527; fax (712) 2445555; e-mail lokmat@bom2.vsnl.net.in; internet onlinenews.lokmat.com; also publ. from Jalgaon, Pune and Nasik; Marathi; Lokmat Samachar (Hindi) publ. from Nagpur, Akola and Aurangabad; Lokmat Times (English) publ. from Nagpur and Aurangabad; Chair. VIJAY DARDA; circ. 205,990 (Marathi), 93,744 (Hindi).

Nava Bharat: Nava Bharat Bhavan, Cotton Market, Nagpur 440 018; tel. (712) 2726677; fax (712) 2723444; internet www.navabharat .biz; f. 1938; morning; Hindi; also publ. from 10 other cities; Editor-in-Chief R. G. MAHESWARI; circ. 133,495.

Tarun Bharat: 28 Farmland, Ramdaspeth, Nagpur 440 010; tel. (712) 6653102; fax (712) 2531758; e-mail ibharat_ngp@sancharnet .in; internet tarunbharat.net; f. 1941; Marathi; independent; also publ. from Belgaum; Man. Editor ANIL DANDEKAR; Chief Editor SUDHIR PATHAK; circ. 53,617 (Nagpur).

Pune

Kesari: 569 Narayan Peth, Pune 411 030; tel. (20) 4459250; fax (20) 4451677; e-mail kesari@giaspn01.vsnl.net.in; internet www .dailykesari.com; f. 1881; Marathi; also publ. from Solapur, Chiplun, Ahmednagar and Sangli; Editor ARVIND VYANKATESH GOKHALE; circ. 41,191.

Sakal: 595 Budhawar Peth, Pune 411 002; tel. (20) 24455500; fax (20) 24450583; e-mail webeditor@esakal.com; internet www.esakal.com; f. 1932; daily; Marathi; also publ. from 10 other regional centres; Chief Editor NAVNEET DESHPANDE (Pune); Man. Editor PRATAP PAWAR; circ. 410,932.

Manipur

Imphal

Naharolgi Thoudang: Keishampat Airport Rd, Imphal 795 001; tel. (38) 52449086; fax (38) 52440353; e-mail nthoudang@yahoo.co .in; internet www.naharolgithoudang.com; f. 1996; daily; Manipuri; Editor LOYALAKPA KHOIROM; circ. 27,420.

Pokmapham: Keishampat Junction, Keishampat Thiyam Leirak, Imphal 795 001; tel. (38) 52459175; fax (38) 52442981; e-mail poknafamdaily@rediffmail.com; internet www.poknapham.in; f. 1975; daily; Manipuri; also publ. from Silchar; Editor ROBINDRO SHARMA A.; Assoc. Editor BIJOY KAKCHINGTABAM; circ. 32,566.

The Sangai Express: Sega Rd, Thouda Bhabok Leikai, Imphal 795 001; tel. (38) 52458133; fax (38) 52444881; e-mail sangaiinfo@gmail .com; internet www.thesangaiexpress.com; f. 1999; daily; Manipuri and English; Editor RAJESH HIJAM; circ. 27,513 (Manipuri) and 11,817 (English).

Meghalaya

Shillong

Mawphor: Mawkhar, Mavis Dunn Rd, Shillong 793 002; tel. (364) 2548433; e-mail mawphordailynews@yahoo.com; internet mawphor .com; f. 1989; Khasi; Editor D. L. SIANGSHAI; circ. 53,972.

The Shillong Times: Rilbong, Shillong 793 004; tel. (364) 2223488; fax (364) 2229488; e-mail letters@theshillongtimes.com; internet www.theshillongtimes.com; f. 1945; English; Editor PATRICIA MUKHIM; circ. 30,899.

Nagaland

Dimapur

The Morung Express: 4 Duncan Basti, Dimapur 797 112; tel. (386) 236871; fax (386) 235194; e-mail morung@gmail.com; internet www .morungexpress.com; f. 2005; Man. Dir AKUM LONGCHARI; Editor ALONG LONGKUMER; circ. 25,593.

Nagaland Post: Nagaland Post Bldg, POB 59, Circular Rd, Dimapur 797 112; tel. (386) 2230748; fax (386) 2225366; e-mail info@ nagalandpost.com; internet www.nagalandpost.com; f. 1990; English; Editor GEOFFREY YADEN; circ. 50,450 (2011).

Odisha

Bhubaneswar

Dharitri: 26B, Industrial Estate, POB 144, Bhubaneswar 751 010; tel. (674) 2580101; fax (674) 2586854; e-mail advt@dharitri.com; internet www.dharitri.com; f. 1974; evening and morning; Oriya; Editor TATHAGATA SATPATHY; circ. 210,986.

Pragativadi: 178B, Mancheswar Industrial Estate, Bhubaneswar 751 010; tel. (674) 2588297; fax (674) 2582709; e-mail pragativadi@ yahoo.com; internet www.pragativadi.com; f. 1973; Exec. Editor SAMAHIT BAL; circ. 215,388.

The Samaya: Plot No. 44 and 54, Sector A, Zone D, Mancheswar Industrial Estate, Bhubaneswar 751 017; tel. (674) 2585740; fax (674) 2582565; e-mail thesamaya@yahoo.com; internet www .orissasamaya.com; f. 1966; Oriya; Editor SATAKADI HOTA; circ. 226,668.

Sambad: B-27 Industrial Estate, Rasulgarh, Bhubaneswar 751 010; tel. (674) 2585351; fax (674) 2588517; e-mail sambadadvt@ easternmedia.in; internet sambadepaper.com; f. 1984; Oriya; also publ. from 7 other regional centres; Editor S. R. PATNAIK; circ. 94,903.

The Punjab

Chandigarh

The Tribune: Sector 29C, Chandigarh 160 030; tel. (172) 2655066; fax (172) 2651293; e-mail letters@tribuneindia.com; internet www .tribuneindia.com; f. 1881 (English edn), f. 1978 (Hindi and Punjabi edns); Editor-in-Chief RAJ CHENGAPPA; Editor (Hindi edn) NARESH KAUSHAL; Editor (Punjabi edn) VARINDER WALIA; circ. 161,231–English, 59,846–Punjabi, 1,010–Hindi (2011).

Jalandhar

Ajit: Ajit Bhavan, Nehru Garden Rd, Jalandhar 144 001; tel. (181) 2455961; fax (181) 2455960; internet www.ajitjalandhar.com; f. 1955; Punjabi; Chief Editor SADHU SINGH HAMDARD; CEO SARVINDER KAUR; circ. 369,474.

Hind Samachar: Civil Lines, Jalandhar 144 001; tel. (181) 2280104; fax (181) 2280113; e-mail punjabkesari@vsnl.com; internet hindsamachar.in; f. 1948; morning; Hindi; also publ. from Ambala Cantt and Jammu; Editor-in-Chief VIJAY KUMAR CHOPRA; combined circ. 30,041.

Jag Bani: ER-129 Pucca Bagh, Jalandhar; tel. (181) 2280104; fax (181) 2280111; e-mail contact@thepunjabkesari.com; internet www .jagbani.in; f. 1978; morning; Punjabi; also publ. from Ludhiana; Publr JAGAT NARAIN; circ. 302,988.

Punjab Kesari: Civil Lines, Pucca Bagh, Jalandhar 144 001; tel. (181) 2280104; fax (181) 2280111; e-mail contact@thepunjabkesari .com; internet www.thepunjabkesari.com; f. 1965; morning; Hindi; also publ. from Ludhiana, Ambala, Panipat, Hisar, Palampur and Jammu; Editor-in-Chief VIJAY KUMAR CHOPRA; Jt Editor AVINASH CHOPRA; circ. 10,093 (2011).

Rajasthan

Jaipur

Rajasthan Patrika: Kesargarh, Jawaharlal Nehru Marg, Jaipur 302 004; tel. (141) 39404142; fax (141) 2566011; e-mail info@epatrika.com; internet www.rajasthanpatrika.com; f. 1956; Hindi edn also publ. from 17 other towns; Chief Editor GULAB KOTHARI; circ. 345,382 (Hindi).

Rashtradoot: M.I. Rd, POB 30, Jaipur 302 001; tel. (141) 2372634; fax (141) 2373513; f. 1951; Hindi; also publ. from Kota, Udaipur, Ajmer, Bikaner, Jalore, Hindaun and Churu; CEO SOMESH SHARMA; Chief Editor RAJESH SHARMA; circ. 204,878.

Tamil Nadu

Chennai (Madras)

Daily Thanthi: 86 E.V.K. Sampath Rd, POB 467, Chennai 600 007; tel. (44) 26618661; fax (44) 26618676; e-mail managerms@dt.co.in; internet www.dailythanthi.com; f. 1942; Tamil; also publ. from 13 other regional centres; Gen. Man. RENGASAMY CHANDRASEKARAN; Editor V. SUNDARESON; circ. 33,321.

Dinakaran: 229 Kutchery Rd, Mylapore, POB 358, Chennai 600 004; tel. (44) 42209191; fax (44) 24951008; e-mail dotcom@dinakaran.com; internet www.dinakaran.com; f. 1977; Tamil; also publ. from Madurai, Tiruchirapalli, Vellore, Tirunelveli, Salem, Coimbatore and Puducherry (Pondicherry); Man. Dir KALANIDHI MARAN; Editor R. M. R. RAMESH; circ. 246,487.

Dinamalar: 219 Anna Salai, Chennai 600 002; tel. (44) 28413553; fax (44) 28523695; e-mail dmrae@dinamalar.in; internet www.dinamalar.com; f. 1951; Tamil; also publ. from 10 other towns; Editor Dr R. KRISHNAMURTHY; circ. 128,436.

Dinamani: Express Estates, Mount Rd, Chennai 600 002; tel. (44) 8520751; fax (44) 8524500; e-mail webmani@dinamani.com; internet www.dinamani.com; f. 1934; morning; Tamil; also publ. from Madurai, Coimbatore, Thiruchirapalli, Vellore, Tirunelveli and Bangalore; Editor K. VAIDYANATHAN; circ. 37,981.

Financial Express: Vasanthi Medical Center, 30/20 Pycrofts Garden Rd, Chennai 600 006; tel. (44) 28231112; fax (44) 28231489; e-mail editor@expressindia.com; internet www.financialexpress.com; f. 1961; morning; English; also publ. from Mumbai, Ahmedabad (in Gujarati), Bangalore, Kochi, Kolkata and New Delhi; Man. Editor VIVECK GOENKA; combined circ. 13,909.

The Hindu: Kasturi Bldgs, 859/860 Anna Salai, Chennai 600 002; tel. (44) 28576300; fax (44) 28415325; e-mail letters@thehindu.co.in; internet www.thehindu.com; f. 1878; morning; English; independent; also publ. from 12 other regional centres; Editor-in-Chief SIDDHARTH VARADARAJAN; circ. 1,420,368.

The Hindu Business Line: 859 Anna Salai, Chennai 600 002; tel. (44) 28413344; fax (44) 28415325; e-mail bleditor@thehindu.co.in; internet www.thehindubusinessline.com; f. 1994; morning; English; also publ. from 12 other regional centres; Editor-in-Chief SIDDHARTH VARADARAJAN; circ. 178,520.

Murasoli: 93 Kodambakkam High Rd, Chennai 600 034; tel. (44) 28270044; fax (44) 28217515; internet www.murasoli.in; f. 1960; organ of the DMK; Tamil; Editor S. SELVAM; circ. 54,000.

New Indian Express: 29 Express Gardens, Ambattur Industrial Estate, Chennai 600 058; tel. (44) 23457601; fax (44) 23457619; e-mail info@expressbuzz.com; internet expressbuzz.com; f. 1932 as Indian Express; morning; English; also publ. from 7 other cities; Chair. and Man. Dir MANOJ KUMAR SONTHALIA; circ. 103,247.

Tripura

Agartala

Dainik Sambad: 11 Jagannath Bari Rd, POB 2, Agartala 799 001; tel. (381) 2326676; fax (381) 2324845; e-mail dainik2@sanchar.net.in; internet www.dainiksambad.net; f. 1966; Bengali; morning; Editor SANJAY GUPTA; circ. 56,922.

Uttarakhand

Dehradun

Amar Ujala: Shed 2, Patel Nagar Industrial Estate, Dehradun 248 003; tel. (135) 2720378; fax (135) 2721776; e-mail editor@amarujala.com; internet www.amarujala.com; Hindi; morning; also publ. from 10 other cities; Editor AJAY K. AGRAWAL; circ. 112,778.

Uttar Pradesh

Agra

Amar Ujala: Sikandra Rd, Agra 282 007; tel. (562) 2321600; fax (562) 2322181; e-mail editor@amarujala.com; internet www.amarujala.com; f. 1948; Hindi; also publ. from Bareilly, Allahabad, Jhansi, Kanpur, Moradabad, Chandigarh and Meerut; Editor AJAY K. AGARWAL; circ. 131,688.

Kanpur

Dainik Jagran: Jagran Bldg, 2 Sarvodaya Nagar, Kanpur 208 005; tel. (512) 2216161; fax (512) 2216972; e-mail jpl@jagran.com; internet in.jagran.yahoo.com; f. 1942; Hindi; also publ. from 26 other cities; Chair. and Man. Editor MAHENDRA MOHAN GUPTA; Editor SANJAY GUPTA; combined circ. 3,200,000.

I Next: Jagran Bldg, 2 Sarvodaya Nagar, Kanpur 208005; tel. (512) 2216161; fax (512) 2216972; internet epaper.inextlive.com; f. 2006; Hindi daily in bilingual format.

Lucknow

Hindustan: Vibhuti Khand, nr Picup Bhawan, Gomti Nagar, Lucknow 226 010; tel. (522) 6663296; e-mail hindustan.lucknow@gmail.com; internet www.livehindustan.com; f. 1996; Hindi; also publ. from Delhi, Muzaffarpur, Bhagalpur, Ranchi, Jamshedpur, Dhanbad, Varanasi, Meerut, Agra, Kanpur and Chandigarh; Editor NAVEEN JOSHI; circ. 214,928 (2011).

The Pioneer: Sahara Shopping Centre, Faizabad Rd, Lucknow 226 016; tel. (522) 2346444; fax (522) 2345582; internet www.dailypioneer.com; f. 1865; English; also publ. from Bhopal, Chandigarh, Dehradun, Ranchi and New Delhi; Editor CHANDAN MITRA; circ. 86,913.

Swatantra Bharat: 2nd Floor, 1 Jopling Rd, Lucknow 226 001; tel. (522) 2204306; fax (522) 2208071; e-mail swatantrabharat47@gmail.com; internet swatantrabharat.com; f. 1947; Hindi; also publ. from Kanpur; Editor K. K. SRIVASTAVA; circ. 73,317 (Lucknow), 73,689 (Kanpur).

The Times of India: 16 Rana Pratap Marg, Lucknow 226 001; tel. (522) 2206081; internet timesofindia.indiatimes.com; f. 1838; also publ. from 9 other towns (Mumbai, Pune, Ahmedabad, Bangalore, Chennai, Hyderabad, Jaipur, Kolkata and Delhi); Editor-in-Chief JAIDEEP BOSE; circ. 107,503 (2011).

Varanasi

Aj: Aj Bhavan, Sant Kabir Rd, Kabirchaura, Varanasi 221 001; tel. (542) 2393981; fax (542) 2393989; e-mail ajhindidaily@gmail.com; f. 1920; Hindi; also publ. from Gorakhpur, Patna, Allahabad, Ranchi, Agra, Bareilly, Lucknow, Jamshedpur, Haldwani and Kanpur; Editor SHARDUL VIKRAM GUPTA; circ. 45,314.

West Bengal

Kolkata (Calcutta)

Aajkaal: BP-7, Sector 5, Bidhannagar, Kolkata 700 091; tel. (33) 30110800; fax (33) 23675502; e-mail aajkaal@cal.vsnl.net.in; internet www.aajkaal.net; f. 1981; morning; Bengali; also publ. from Agartala and Siliguri; Chief Editor ASHOK DASGUPTA; circ. 152,123.

Ananda Bazar Patrika: 6 Prafulla Sarkar St, Kolkata 700 001; tel. (33) 22374880; fax (33) 22253241; internet www.anandabazar.com; f. 1922; morning; Bengali; also publ. from Mumbai; Chief Editor AVEEK SARKAR; circ. 1,263,259.

Bartaman: Bartaman Pvt Ltd, 6 J. B. S Haldane Ave, Kolkata 700 105; tel. (33) 23000291; fax (33) 23234030; e-mail info@bartamanpatrika.com; internet www.bartamanpatrika.com; f. 1984; also publ. from Barddhaman and Siliguri; Editor SUBHA DUTTA; circ. 534,603.

Business Standard: Saraf Bldg, 3rd Floor, 4/1 Red Cross Place, Kolkata 700 001; tel. (33) 22101314; fax (33) 22101599; e-mail letters@business-standard.com; internet www.business-standard.com; f. 1975; morning; also publ. from Mumbai, Delhi, Patna, Lucknow, Bhopal and Chandigarh; English; Editor A. K. BHATTACHARYA; circ. 13,217.

Financial Express: 83 B. K. Pal Ave, Kolkata 700 005; e-mail editor@expressindia.com; internet www.financialexpress.com; morning; English; also publ. from Mumbai, Ahmedabad, Bangalore, Coimbatore, Kochi, Chennai and New Delhi; Man. Editor VIVECK GOENKA; circ. 12,312.

Ganashakti: 74A A. J. C. Bose Rd, Kolkata 700 016; tel. (33) 22278950; fax (33) 2278090; e-mail mail@ganashakti.co.in; internet www.ganashakti.com; f. 1967; owned by Communist Party of India (Marxist), West Bengal State Cttee; morning; Bengali; also publ. from Durgapur and Siliguri; Editor NARAYAN DATTA; circ. 176,812.

Sandhya Aajkaal: BP-7, Sector 5, Salt Lake City, Kolkata 700 091; tel. (33) 30110800; fax (33) 23675502; e-mail aajkaal@cal.vsnl.net.in; internet www.aajkaal.net; evening; Bengali; Chief Editor ASHOK DASGUPTA; circ. 12,815.

Sangbad Pratidin: 20 Prafulla Sarkar St, Kolkata 700 072; tel. (33) 22128400; fax (33) 22126031; e-mail mail@sangbadpratidin.org; internet sangbadpratidin.in; f. 1992; morning; Bengali; also publ. from Ranchi and Siliguri; Chief Editor SRINJOY BOSE; circ. 299,876.

Sanmarg: 160B Chittaranjan Ave, Kolkata 700 007; tel. (33) 30615000; fax (33) 22415087; e-mail sanmarghindi@gmail.com; internet www.sanmarg.in; f. 1948; Hindi; also publ. from Varanasi, Patna, Ranchi and Bhubaneswar; Editor HARI RAM PANDEY; circ. 115,049.

The Statesman: Statesman House, 4 Chowringhee Sq., Kolkata 700 001; tel. (33) 22127070; fax (33) 22126181; e-mail thestatesman@vsnl.com; internet www.thestatesman.net; f. 1875; morning; English; independent; also publ. from New Delhi, Siliguri and Bhubaneswar; Editor RAVINDRA KUMAR; circ. 177,113.

The Telegraph: 6 Prafulla Sarkar St, Kolkata 700 001; tel. (33) 22345374; fax (33) 22253243; e-mail ttedit@abpmail.com; internet www.telegraphindia.com; f. 1982; English; also publ. from Guwahati, Jamshedpur, Ranchi and Siliguri; Editor AVEEK SARKAR; circ. 555,869.

Uttar Banga Sambad: 7 Old Court House St, Kolkata 700 001; tel. (33) 22435663; fax (33) 22435618; e-mail uttarmail@sify.com; internet www.uttarbangasambad.com; f. 1980; Bengali; circ. 143,177.

Vishwamitra: 74 Lenin Sarani, Kolkata 700 013; tel. (33) 22651139; fax (33) 22656393; e-mail vismtra@vsnl.com; f. 1915; morning; Hindi; commercial; Editor PRAKASH CHANDRA AGRAWALLA; circ. 99,911.

SELECTED PERIODICALS

Delhi and New Delhi

Alive: Delhi Press Bldg, E-3 Jhandewala Estate, Rani Jhansi Rd, New Delhi 110 055; tel. (11) 23529557; fax (11) 23625020; e-mail delpress@bol.net.in; internet www.caravanalive.com; f. 1940 as *Caravan*; monthly; English; men's interests; Editor, Publr and Printer PARESH NATH; circ. 4,049.

Bal Bharati: Patiala House, Publications Division, Ministry of Information and Broadcasting, New Delhi; f. 1948; monthly; Hindi; for children; Editor VEDPAL; circ. 60,425.

Business Today: Videocon Towers, E-1 Jhandelwalan Extn, New Delhi 110 055; tel. (11) 23684800; fax (11) 23684819; e-mail Mukta.Saigal@intoday.com; internet businesstoday.intoday.in; f. 1992; fortnightly; English; Editor CHAITANYA KALBAG; circ. 111,806.

Catholic India: CBCI Centre, 1 Ashok Place, Goldakkhana, New Delhi 110 001; tel. and fax (11) 23344470; fax (11) 23364615; e-mail editor@cbci.in; internet cbci.in; bi-annual; Fr GEORGE PLATHOTTAM.

Champak: Delhi Press Bldg, E-3 Jhandewala Estate, Rani Jhansi Rd, New Delhi 110 055; tel. (11) 41398888; fax (11) 23625020; e-mail editorial@delhipressgroup.com; f. 1968; fortnightly (Hindi, English, Gujarati, Tamil, Telugu, Malayalam, Marathi and Kannada edns); children's; Editor, Publr and Printer PARESH NATH; circ. 65,220 (Hindi), 47,225 (English), 13,155 (Marathi), 5,812 (Gujarati), 1,934 (Malayalam), 1,652 (Telugu), 992 (Tamil), 8,393 (Kannada).

Children's World: Nehru House, 4 Bahadur Shah Zafar Marg, New Delhi 110 002; tel. (11) 23316970; fax (11) 23721090; e-mail cbtnd@cbtnd.com; internet www.childrensbooktrust.com; f. 1968; monthly; English; Editor NAVIN MENON; circ. 25,000.

Competition Refresher: 4739/23 UGF, Ansari Rd, Daryaganj, New Delhi 110 002; tel. (11) 23283226; fax (11) 23269227; e-mail editorial@brightpublications.com; internet www.brightpublications.com; f. 1984; monthly; English; Chief Editor, Publr and Man. Dir PRITAM SINGH BRIGHT; circ. 175,000.

Competition Success Review (CSR): 604 Prabhat Kiran Bldg, Rajendra Place, Delhi 110 008; tel. (11) 45113300; fax (11) 25825391; e-mail info@competitionreview.com; internet www.competitionreview.com; monthly; English; f. 1964; Editor S. K. SACHDEVA; circ. 185,955.

Cosmopolitan: 5th Floor, Videocon Tower, E-1 Jhandewalan Extn, New Delhi 110 055; tel. (11) 23684800; e-mail nandini.bhalla@intoday.com; internet cosmo.intoday.in; monthly; English; women's lifestyle; Editor NANDINI BHALLA; circ. 31,149.

Cricket Samrat: A6/1 Mayapuri Phase–1, New Delhi 110 064; tel. (11) 28115835; fax (11) 25469581; internet www.dewanpublications.com/magazine/index.php; f. 1978; monthly; Hindi; Editor ANAND DEWAN; circ. 9,645 (2011).

Employment News: Government of India, East Block IV, Level 5, R. K. Puram, New Delhi 110 066; tel. (11) 26174975; fax (11) 26105875; e-mail empnews@bol.net.in; internet www.employmentnews.gov.in; f. 1976; weekly; Hindi, Urdu and English edns; Gen. Man. and Chief Editor VISHWANATH RAMESH; Editor HASAN ZIA; combined circ. 301,868.

Filmi Duniya: B-10 Shiv Apt, 7 Rajnarain Marg, Civil Lines, New Delhi 110 054; tel. (11) 23278087; fax (11) 23279341; e-mail filmiduniyaonline@yahoo.com; f. 1958; monthly; Hindi; Publr V. K. CHOPRA; circ. 35,550.

Grihshobha: Delhi Press Bldg, E-3 Jhandewala Estate, Rani Jhansi Rd, New Delhi 110 055; tel. (11) 51398888; fax (11) 51540714; e-mail editorial@delhipressgroup.com; internet www.grihshobhaindia.com; f. 1979; fortnightly Hindi and Bangla edns; monthly Tamil, Telugu, Kannada, Marathi, Malayalam and Gujarati edns; women's interests; Editor, Publr and Printer PARESH NATH; circ. 68,355 (Kannada), 41,334 (Gujarati), 88,119 (Marathi), 286,031 (Hindi), 11,111 (Telugu), 3,569 (Tamil), 4,700 (Malayalam), 3,144 (Bangla).

India Perspectives: Room 149B, 'A' Wing, Shastri Bhavan, New Delhi 110 001; tel. (11) 23389471; fax 23385549; internet meaindia.nic.in/mystart.php?id=2701; f. 1988; culture; publ. by Ministry of External Affairs; Editor NAVDEEP SURI.

India Today: F-14/15, Connaught Place, New Delhi 110 001; tel. (11) 23315801; fax (11) 23316180; e-mail ratnam@intoday.com; internet www.india-today.com; f. 1975; weekly; English, Tamil, Telugu, Malayalam, Bengali and Hindi; Editor M. J. AKBAR; Editor-in-Chief AROON PURIE; circ. 336,460 (English), 130,574 (Hindi), 28,355 (Tamil), 18,850 (Malayalam), 16,974 (Telugu), 4,981 (Bengali).

Indian Railways: 411 Rail Bhavan, Raisina Rd, New Delhi 110 001; tel. (11) 23384481; fax (11) 23383540; e-mail editorir@rb.railnet.gov.in; f. 1956; monthly; English; publ. by the Ministry of Railways (Railway Board); Editor M. R. KALYANI; circ. 7,000.

Junior Science Refresher: 4739/23 UGF, Ansari Road, Daryaganj, New Delhi 110 002; tel. (11) 23282226; fax (11) 23269227; e-mail editorial@brightpublications.com; internet www.brightpublications.com; f. 1987; monthly; English; Chief Editor, Publr and Man. Dir PRITAM SINGH BRIGHT; circ. 118,000.

Kadambini: Hindustan Times House, 18–20 Kasturba Gandhi Marg, New Delhi 110 001; tel. (11) 66561234; fax (11) 66561270; e-mail vnagar@hindustantimes.com; f. 1960; monthly; Hindi; Editor VIJAY KISHORE MANAV; Exec. Editor VISHNU NAGAR; circ. 31,530.

Krishak Samachar: Bharat Krishak Samaj, Dr Panjabrao Deshmukh Krishak Bhavan, A-1 Nizamuddin West, New Delhi 110 013; tel. (11) 24619508; fax (11) 24359509; e-mail publication@bks.org.in; f. 1957; monthly; English and Hindi edns; agriculture; Editor Dr KRISHAN BIR CHAUDHARY; circ. 6,970 (English), 22,728 (Hindi).

Kurukshetra: Soochna Bhawan, CGO Complex, Lodhi Rd, New Delhi 110 003; tel. (11) 23015014; fax (11) 23386879; monthly; English and Hindi; rural development; Publr KAILASH CHAND MEENA; circ. 18,056 (English), 21,146 (Hindi).

Liberation: U-90 Shakarpur, New Delhi 110 092; tel. and fax (11) 22521067; fax (11) 22442790; e-mail mail@cpiml.org; internet www.cpiml.org; f. 1967; monthly; organ of Communist Party of India (Marxist-Leninist).

Mainstream: 145/1D Shahpur Jat, 1st Floor, nr Asiad Village, New Delhi 110 049; tel. (11) 26497188; fax (11) 26569382; e-mail mainlineweekly@yahoo.com; internet www.mainstreamweekly.net; English; weekly; politics and current affairs; Editor SUMIT CHAKRAVARTTY.

Maxim India: Media Transasia (India) Ltd, K-35, Green Park, New Delhi 110 016; tel. (11) 26862687; fax (11) 26867641; internet www.maximindia.in; f. 2005; monthly; English; men's lifestyle; CEO and Publr PIYUSH SHARMA; Editor-in-Chief ANUP KUTTY.

Mayapuri: A-5, Mayapuri Phase 1, New Delhi 110 064; tel. (11) 28116120; fax (11) 41833139; e-mail info@mayapurigroup.com; internet www.mayapurigroup.com/mayapuri.htm; f. 1974; weekly; Hindi; cinema; Editor A. P. BAJAJ; circ. 146,144.

Nandan: Hindustan Times House, 18–20 Kasturba Gandhi Marg, New Delhi 110 001; tel. (11) 23361234; fax (11) 66561270; e-mail kshamasharma@hindustantimes.com; f. 1963; monthly; Hindi; children's; Publr RAKESH SHARMA; circ. 57,694.

New Age Weekly: Ajoy Bhavan, 15 Comrade Indrajeet Gupta Marg, Delhi 110 002; tel. (11) 23230762; fax (11) 23235543; e-mail cpindia@del2.vsnl.net.in; internet www.newageweekly.com; f. 1953; main organ of the Communist Party of India; weekly; English; Editor SHAMEEM FAIZEE; Man. N. S. NEGI; circ. 215,000.

Organiser: Sanskriti Bhavan, D. B. Gupta Rd, Jhandewala, New Delhi 110 055; tel. (11) 47642022; fax (11) 47642023; e-mail editor@organiserweekly.com; internet www.organiser.org; f. 1947; weekly; English; Editor R. BALASHANKAR; circ. 44,100.

Outlook: AB-10 Safdarjung Enclave, New Delhi 110 029; tel. (11) 26191421; fax (11) 26191420; e-mail outlook@outlookindia.com; internet www.outlookindia.com; f. 1995; weekly; Hindi and English edns; Publr MAHESHWER PERI; Editor-in-Chief VINOD MEHTA; circ. 62,880.

Panchjanya: Sanskriti Bhavan, Deshbandhu Gupta Marg, Jhandewala, New Delhi 110 055; tel. (11) 47642013; fax (11) 47642015; e-mail editor.panchjanya@gmail.com; internet www.panchjanya

.com; f. 1947; weekly; Hindi; general interest; nationalist; Editor BALDEV BHAI SHARMA; circ. 41,573.

Punjabi Digest: 209 Hemkunt House, 6 Rajendra Place, POB 2549, New Delhi 110 008; tel. (11) 25715225; fax (11) 25761053; e-mail info@punjabidigest.com; internet www.punjabidigest.com; f. 1971; literary monthly; Gurmukhi; Chief Editor Sardar S. B. SINGH; circ. 55,000.

Sainik Samachar: Blk L-1, Church Rd, New Delhi 110 001; tel. (11) 23094668; e-mail einc-ss@nic.in; internet sainiksamachar.nic.in; f. 1909; pictorial fortnightly for India's armed forces; English, Hindi, Urdu, Tamil, Punjabi, Telugu, Marathi, Kannada, Gorkhali, Malayalam, Bengali, Assamese and Oriya edns; Editor-in-Chief DHIRENDRA OJHA; circ. 20,000.

Saras Salil: Delhi Press Bldg, E-3 Jhandewala Estate, Rani Jhansi Rd, New Delhi 110 055; tel. (11) 41398888; fax (11) 41540714; e-mail editorial@delhipressgroup.com; internet www.delhipress.in; f. 1993; fortnightly; Hindi, Telugu, Tamil, Gujarati and Marathi edns; Editor, Publr and Printer PARESH NATH; circ. 677,503 (Hindi), 4,066 (Marathi), 1,092 (Gujarati), 1,015 (Telugu).

Sarita: Delhi Press Bldg, E-3 Jhandewala Estate, Rani Jhansi Rd, New Delhi 110 055; tel. (11) 41398888; fax (11) 23625020; e-mail editorial@delhipressgroup.com; internet www.delhipress.in; f. 1945; fortnightly; Hindi; family magazine; Editor, Publr and Printer PARESH NATH; circ. 75,735.

Vigyan Pragati: NISCAIR (CSIR), Dr K. S. Krishnan Marg, New Delhi 110 012; tel. (11) 25843359; fax (11) 25847062; e-mail vp@niscair.res.in; internet www.niscair.res.in; f. 1952; monthly; Hindi; popular science; Editor PRADEEP SHARMA; circ. 33,000.

Woman's Era: Delhi Press Bldg, E-3 Jhandewala Estate, Rani Jhansi Rd, New Delhi 110 055; tel. (11) 41398888; fax (11) 23625020; e-mail delpress@bol.net.in; internet www.womansera.com; f. 1973; fortnightly; English; women's interests; Editor, Publr and Printer PARESH NATH; circ. 66,200.

Yojana: Yojana Bhavan, Sansad Marg, New Delhi 110 001; tel. (11) 23717910; fax (11) 23359578; e-mail yojana@techpilgrim.com; internet www.yojana.gov.in; f. 1957; monthly; English, Tamil, Bengali, Marathi, Gujarati, Assamese, Malayalam, Telugu, Kannada, Punjabi, Urdu, Oriya and Hindi edns; Chief Editor RINA SONOWAL KOULI; circ. 29,032 (English).

Andhra Pradesh

Andhra Bhoomi Sachitra Masa Patrika: 36 Sarojini Devi Rd, Secunderabad 500 003; tel. (842) 27802346; fax (842) 27805256; f. 1977; fortnightly; Telugu; Editor T. VENKATRAM REDDY; circ. 34,817.

Andhra Jyoti Sachitra Vara Patrika: Vijayawada 520 010; tel. (866) 2474532; f. 1967; weekly; Telugu; Editor PURANAM SUBRAMANYA SARMA; circ. 59,000.

Andhra Prabha Weekly: 591 Lower Tank Bund Rd, Express Centre, Domalaguda, Hyderabad 500 029; tel. (40) 2233586; e-mail info@apweekly.com; internet www.apweekly.com; weekly; Telugu; publ. by Indian Express Group.

Swati Saparivara Patrika: Anil Bldgs, Suryaraopet, POB 339, Vijayawada 520 002; tel. (866) 2431862; fax (866) 2430433; e-mail advt_swati@sify.com; internet www.swatipublications.com; f. 1984; weekly; Telugu; Editor VEMURI BALARAM; circ. 252,100.

Assam (Asom)

Agradoot: Agradoot Bhavan, Dispur, Guwahati 781 006; tel. (361) 2261923; fax (361) 2260655; e-mail agradoot@sify.com; f. 1971; bi-weekly; Assamese; Editor KANAK SEN DEKA; circ. 29,463.

Asam Bani: Tribune Bldg, Guwahati 781 003; tel. (361) 2661356; fax (361) 2660594; e-mail assam@assamnet.org; internet www.assamtribune.com; f. 1955; weekly; Assamese; Editor DILEEP CHANDAN; circ. 6,153.

Sadin: Maniram Dewan Rd, Chandmari, Guwahati 781 003; tel. (361) 2524594; fax (361) 2524634; e-mail sadin@pratidinassam.com; internet www.pratidinassam.com/sadin; weekly; Assamese; Editor ANURADHA SHARMA PUJARI; circ. 33,082.

Bihar

Hamara Dinmaan: Trading Co Pvt Ltd, Bandhuk Bhawan, Station Rd, Patna; monthly; Hindi; Publr MAHESH KUMAR SINGH; circ. 53,700.

Kewal Sach: East Ashok Nagar, 14 Kankarbagh Rd, Patna 800 020; tel. (612) 3240075; e-mail info@kewalsach.com; internet www.kewalsach.com; monthly; Hindi; Publr BRAJESH MISHRA; circ. 24,035.

Ubharta Bihar: C-49 Housing Colony, Lohiya Nagar, Kankadbagh, Patna 800020; internet ubhartabihar.com; monthly; Hindi; Publr RAJIV RANJAN; circ. 23,550.

Chhattisgarh

Krishak Jagat: LIG-163, Sector 2, Shankar Nagar, Raipur; tel. (771) 2420449; e-mail info@krishakjagat.org; internet www.krishakjagat.org; f. 1946; weekly; Hindi; agricultural devt; Chief Editor VIJAY KUMAR BONDRIYA; circ. 35,460.

Gujarat

Akhand Anand: Anand Bhavan, Relief Rd, POB 123, Ahmedabad 380 001; tel. (79) 2357482; e-mail innitadi@sancharnet.in; f. 1947; monthly; Gujarati; Pres. ANAND AMIN; Editor Dr DILAVARSINH JADEJA; circ. 10,000.

Chitralok: Gujarat Samachar Bhavan, Khanpur, POB 254, Ahmedabad 380 001; tel. (79) 5504010; fax (79) 5502000; e-mail editor@gujaratsamachar.com; internet www.gujaratsamachar.com/20110624/purti/chitralok/chlokhome.html; f. 1952; weekly; Gujarati; films; Man. Editor SHREYANS S. SHAH; circ. 20,000.

Parmarth: Jai Hind Publications, Jai Hind Press Bldg, Babubhai Shah Marg, Rajkot 360 001; tel. (281) 2440511; fax (281) 2448677; e-mail info@jaihinddaily.com; monthly; Gujarati; philosophy and religion; Editor Y. N. SHAH; circ. 8,000.

Sakhi: Sakhi Publications, Jai Hind Press Bldg, nr Gujarat Chamber, Ashram Rd, Navrangpura, Ahmedabad 380 009; tel. (79) 26581734; fax (79) 26587681; f. 1984; fortnightly; Gujarati; women's; Man. Editor NITA Y. SHAH; Editor Y. N. SHAH; circ. 10,000.

Stree: Sandesh Bhavan, Lad Society Rd, Ahmedabad 380 054; tel. (79) 26765480; fax (79) 26753587; e-mail stree@sandesh.com; internet www.sandesh.com; f. 1962; weekly; Gujarati; Editor RITABEN PATEL; circ. 42,000.

Zagmag: Gujarat Samachar Bhavan, Khanpur, Ahmedabad 380 001; tel. (79) 30410000; fax 25502000; f. 1952; weekly; Gujarati; for children; Editor BAHUBALI S. SHAH; circ. 38,000.

Karnataka

Mayura: 75 Mahatma Gandhi Rd, Bangalore 560 001; tel. (80) 25588999; fax (80) 25587179; e-mail ads@deccanherald.co.in; f. 1968; monthly; Kannada; Editor-in-Chief K. N. SHANTH KUMAR; circ. 20,512 (2011).

Sudha: 75 Mahatma Gandhi Rd, Bangalore 560 001; tel. (80) 25588999; fax (80) 25587179; e-mail ads@deccanherald.co.in; f. 1965; weekly; Kannada; Editor-in-Chief K. N. HARI KUMAR; circ. 61,300.

Taranga: New Udayavani Bldg, Press Corner, Manipal 576 104; tel. (820) 2571151; fax (820) 2570563; e-mail tarangaonline@manipalmedia.com; internet www.udayavani.com; f. 1983; weekly; Kannada; Editor-in-Chief SANDHYA S. PAI; circ. 69,510.

Kerala

Arogya Masika: Mathrubhumi Bldgs, K. P. Kesava Menon Rd, Kozhikode 673 001; tel. (495) 2765381; fax (495) 2760138; e-mail arogyamasika@mpp.co.in; internet www.mathrubhumi.com; owned by Mathrubhumi Printing and Publishing Co Ltd; monthly; Malayalam; health; Man. Editor P. V. CHANDRAN; circ. 193,391 (2011).

Balabhumi: Matrabhumi Bldgs, K. P. Kesava Menon Rd, Kozhikode 673 001; tel. (495) 2366655; fax (495) 2366656; e-mail balabhumi@mpp.co.in; internet www.mathrubhumi.com; f. 1996; weekly; Malayalam; children's; Editor K. K. SREEDHARAN NAIR; circ. 126,580.

Balarama: MM Publications Ltd, POB 226, Kottayam 686 001; tel. (481) 2563721; fax (481) 2564393; e-mail childrensdivision@mmpublications.com; f. 1972; children's weekly; Malayalam; Chief Editor BINA MATHEW; Senior Gen. Man. V. SAJEEV GEORGE; circ. 245,898.

Chithrabhumi: Mathrubhumi Bldgs, K. P. Kesava Menon Rd, Kozhikode 673 001; tel. (495) 2366655; fax (495) 2366656; e-mail cinema@mpp.co.in; internet www.mathrubhumi.org; f. 1982; owned by Mathrubhumi Printing and Publishing Co; weekly; Malayalam; films; Editor K. K. SREEDHARAN NAIR; circ. 23,260.

Grihalakshmi: Mathrubhumi Bldgs, K. P. Kesava Menon Rd, POB 46, Kozhikode 673 001; tel. (495) 2366655; fax (495) 2366656; e-mail mathrclt@md2.vsnl.net.in; internet www.mathrubhumi.org; f. 1979; monthly; Malayalam; women's; Editor K. K. SREEDHARAN NAIR; circ. 204,674.

Kalakaumudi: Kaumudi Bldgs, Pettah, Thiruvananthapuram 695 024; tel. (471) 2443531; fax (471) 2442895; e-mail vellinakshatram@gmail.com; internet www.kalakaumudi.com; f. 1975; weekly; Malayalam; Chief Editor M. S. MANI; Editor N. R. S. BABU; circ. 73,000.

Kerala Sabdam: Andamukkam, Kollam 691 001; tel. (474) 2745772; fax (474) 2751010; e-mail sabdam@vsnl.com; internet www.nanaonline.in; f. 1962; weekly; Malayalam; Man. Editor B. A. RAJAKRISHNAN; circ. 66,600.

Malayala Manorama: K. K. Rd, POB 26, Kottayam 686 001; tel. (481) 2563646; fax (481) 2565398; e-mail editorial@mm.co.in; internet www.manoramaonline.com; f. 1937; weekly; Malayalam; also publ. from Kozhikode; Editor-in-Chief MAMMEN MATHEW; circ. 518,542 (2011).

Mathrubhumi Sports Masika: Mathrubhumi Bldgs, K. P. Kesava Menon Rd, Kozhikode 673 001; tel. (495) 2366655; fax (495) 2366656; e-mail sports@mpp.co.in; internet www.mathrubhumi.com/sports; monthly; Malayalam; sport; Editor M. KESAVA MENON; circ. 46,933 (2011).

Thozhilvartha: Mathrubhumi Bldgs, K. P. Kesava Menon Rd, Kozhikode 673 001; tel. (495) 2366655; fax (495) 2366656; e-mail mbiclt@mpp.co.in; internet www.mathrubhumi.org; f. 1992; weekly; Malayalam; employment; Editor K. K. SREEDHARAN NAIR; circ. 313,131.

Vanitha: MM Publications Ltd, POB 226, Kottayam 686 001; tel. (481) 2563721; fax (481) 2564393; e-mail vanitha@mmp.in; f. 1975; women's fortnightly; Malayalam (monthly) and Hindi editions; Chief Editor PREMA MAMMEN MATHEW, MARIAM MAMMEN MATHEW; Gen. Man. V. SAJEEV GEORGE; circ. 586,609 (Malayalam), 209,188 (Hindi).

Vellinakshatram: Kaumudi Bldgs, Pettah, Thiruvananthapuram 695 024; tel. (471) 2443531; fax (471) 2442895; e-mail kalakaumudi@vsnl.net; internet www.vellinakshatram.com; f. 1987; film weekly; Malayalam; Editor PRASAD LAKSHMANAN; Chief Editor SUKUMARAN MANI; circ. 65,000.

The Week: Malayala Manorama Buildings, POB 4278, Kochi 682 036; tel. (484) 2316285; fax (484) 2315745; e-mail editor@the-week.com; internet week.manoramaonline.com; f. 1982; weekly; English; current affairs; Man. Editor PHILIP MATHEW; circ. 235,667.

Madhya Pradesh

Krishak Jagat: 14 Indira Press Complex, M. P. Nagar, POB 37, Bhopal 462 011; tel. (755) 2768452; fax (755) 2760449; e-mail info@krishakjagat.org; internet www.krishakjagat.org; f. 1946; weekly; Hindi; agriculture; also published in Jaipur and Raipur; Chief Editor VIJAY KUMAR BONDRIYA; Editor SUNIL GANGRADE; circ. 73,950.

Maharashtra

Mumbai (Bombay)

Abhiyaan: Sambhaav Media Ltd, 4 AB, Government Industrial Estate, Charkop, Kandivli (W), Mumbai 400 067; tel. (22) 28687515; fax (22) 28680991; e-mail rajeshpathak@sambhaav.com; internet www.sambhaav.com; f. 1986; weekly; Gujarati; Chief Man. Dir KIRAN VADODARIA; Group Editor DEEPAL TREVEDIE; circ. 68,883.

Arogya Sanjeevani: C-14 Royal Industrial Estate, 5-B Naigaum Cross Rd, Wadala, Mumbai 400 031; tel. (22) 24138723; fax (22) 24133610; e-mail woman17@zediffmail.com; f. 1990; quarterly; Hindi; Editor RAM KRISHNA SHUKLA; circ. 12,204 (2011).

Auto India: Nirmal, Nariman Point, Mumbai 400 021; tel. (22) 22883946; fax (22) 22883940; e-mail editor@auto-india.com; f. 1994; monthly; Editor RAJ WARRIOR; circ. 31,845.

Bhavan's Journal: Kulapati Dr K. M. Munshi Marg, Chowpatty, Mumbai 400 007; tel. (22) 23631261; fax (22) 23630058; e-mail bhavan@bhavans.info; internet www.bhavans.info; f. 1954; fortnightly; English; literature, philosophy, culture and spirituality; Exec. Sec. H. N. DASTUR; Editor V. N. NARAYANAN; circ. 40,000.

Bombay Samachar: Red House, Sayed Abdulla Brelvi Rd, Mumbai 400 001; tel. (22) 22045531; fax (22) 22046642; e-mail samachar.bombay@gmail.com; internet bombaysamachar.com; f. 1822; weekly; Gujarati; Editor P. D. DALAL (acting); circ. 77,774 (2011).

Business India: Nirmal, 14th Floor, Nariman Point, Mumbai 400 021; tel. (22) 22883943; fax (22) 22883940; e-mail biedit.mumbai@businessindiagroup.com; internet www.businessindiagroup.com; f. 1978; fortnightly; English; Publr ASHOK ADVANI; circ. 75,700.

Business World: B-2/C-2, Paragon Condominium Assen, P. Budhkar Marg, Worli, Mumbai 400 013; tel. (22) 24962587; fax (22) 24962596; e-mail bwonline@bworldmail.com; internet www.businessworld.in; f. 1980; weekly; English; Editor PROSENJIT DATTA; circ. 146,500.

Chitralekha: 62 Vaju Kotak Marg, Fort, Mumbai 400 001; tel. (22) 40347777; fax (22) 22615895; e-mail mumbai@chitralekha.com; internet www.chitralekha.com; f. 1950 (Gujarati), f. 1989 (Marathi); weekly; Gujarati and Marathi; Editors BHARAT GHELANI, GYANESH MAHARAO; circ. 114,587 (Gujarati), 21,763 (Marathi).

Cine Blitz Film Monthly: A/3, Sangam Bhavan, Ground Floor, Brahma Kumaris Rd, nr Strand Cinema, Colaba, Mumbai 400 005; tel. (22) 22830668; fax (22) 22830672; e-mail cbedit@sify.com; f. 1974; fortnightly; English; Editor NISHI PREM; circ. 41,611.

Economic and Political Weekly: 320–321, A to Z Industrial Estate, Ganapatrao Kadam Marg, Lower Parel, Mumbai 400 013; tel. (22) 40638282; fax (22) 24934515; e-mail epw.mumbai@gmail.com; internet epw.in; f. 1966; English; Editor C. RAMMANOHAR REDDY; circ. 12,500.

Femina: Times of India Bldg, Dr Dadabhai Naoroji Rd, Mumbai 400 001; tel. and fax (22) 22733535; fax (22) 22731585; e-mail contactfemina@wwm.co.in; internet www.femina.in; f. 1959; fortnightly (English), monthly (Hindi); Editor-in-Chief PETTY S. FATIMAH; circ. 138,644 (English), 39,575 (Hindi).

Filmfare: 4th Floor, Times of India Bldg, Dr Dadabhai Naoroji Rd, Mumbai 400 001; tel. (22) 22733535; fax (22) 22731585; e-mail rahul.nanda@wwm.co.in; internet www.filmfare.com; f. 1952; monthly; English; Exec. Editor SHASHI BALIGA; circ. 93,127.

Janmabhoomi-Pravasi: Janmabhoomi Bhavan, Janmabhoomi Marg, Fort, POB 62, Mumbai 400 001; tel. (22) 22870831; fax (22) 22874097; e-mail bhoomi@bom3.vsnl.net.in; internet pravasi.janmabhoominewspapers.com; f. 1939; weekly; Gujarati; Propr Saurashtra Trust; Editor KUNDAN VYAS; circ. 27,709.

Meri Saheli: C-14 Royal Industrial Estate, 5-B Naigaum Cross Rd, Wadala, Mumbai 400 031; tel. (22) 24182797; fax (22) 24133610; e-mail woman17@zediffmail.com; internet www.merisaheli.com; f. 1987; monthly; Hindi; women's lifestyle; Editor HEMA MALINI; circ. 369,446.

New Woman: C-14 Royal Industrial Estate, 5-B Naigaum Cross Rd, Wadala, Mumbai 400 031; tel. (22) 43448000; fax (22) 43448080; e-mail newwomanmag@gmail.com; f. 1996; monthly; English; Editor HEMA MALINI; circ. 72,800.

Onlooker: Free Press House, 215 Free Press Journal Marg, Nariman Point, Mumbai 400 021; tel. (22) 22874566; f. 1939; fortnightly; English; news magazine; Exec. Editor K. SRINIVASAN; circ. 61,000.

Reader's Digest: 45 Vaju Kotak Marg, Ballard Estate, Mumbai 400 001; tel. (22) 66522500; fax (22) 22650643; e-mail editor.india@rd.com; internet readersdigest.co.in; f. 1954; monthly; English; Editor-in-Chief AROON PURIE; circ. 389,378.

Savvy: Magna Publishing Co Ltd, Magna House, 100E Old Prabhadevi Rd, Prabhadevi, Mumbai 400 025; tel. (22) 24362270; fax (22) 24306523; e-mail savvy@magnamags.com; internet www.magnamags.com; f. 1984; monthly; English; Editor FAHEEM RUHANI; circ. 25,994.

Screen: Express Tower, Nariman Point, Mumbai 400 021; tel. (22) 22022627; fax (22) 22022139; e-mail iemumbai@expressindia.co.in; internet www.screenindia.com; f. 1950; film weekly; English; circ. 8,379.

Society: Magna Publishing Co Ltd, Magna House, 100E Old Prabhadevi Rd, Prabhadevi, Mumbai 400 025; tel. (22) 24362270; fax (22) 24306523; e-mail society@magnamags.com; internet www.magnamags.com; f. 1979; monthly; English; Editorial Dir FAHEEM RUHANI; circ. 29,302.

Stardust: Magna Publishing Co Ltd, Magna House, 100E Old Prabhadevi Rd, Prabhadevi, Mumbai 400 025; tel. (22) 24362270; fax (22) 24306523; e-mail stardust@magnamags.com; internet www.magnamags.com; f. 1985; monthly; English and Hindi; Editor FAHEEM RUHANI; circ. 84,186.

Vyapar: Janmabhoomi Bhavan, Janmabhoomi Marg, POB 62, Fort, Mumbai 400 001; tel. (22) 22870831; fax (22) 22874097; e-mail jbhoomi@yahoo.com; internet www.janmabhoominewspapers.com/Vyapar/Default.aspx; f. 1949; (Gujarati), 1987 (Hindi); Gujarati (2 a week) and Hindi (weekly); commerce; propr Saurashtra Trust; Editor RAJESH M. BHAYANI; circ. 8,933 (Gujarati), 5,017 (Hindi), 1,438 (English).

Nagpur

All India Reporter: AIR Ltd, Congress Nagar, POB 209, Nagpur 440 012; tel. (712) 2534321; fax (712) 2526283; e-mail info@airwebworld.com; internet www.airwebworld.com; f. 1914; weekly and monthly; English; law journals and court reports; Chief Editor V. R. MANOHAR; circ. 55,500.

Manipur

The Eastern Frontier: Kwakeithel Thiyam Leikai, Imphal; monthly; Manipuri; Editor LOITONGBAM BINODKUMAR SINGH.

Image: Keishampat Leimajam Leikai, Imphal 795001; tel. 9856114682 (mobile); e-mail imagemag@live.com; f. 2007; monthly; Manipuri; film; Editor RANJAN SALAM; circ. 5,500.

Rajasthan

Balhans: Kesargarh, Jawahar Lal Nehru Marg, Jaipur 302 004; tel. (141) 39404142; fax (141) 2566011; e-mail info@patrika.com; internet www.rajasthanpatrika.com; Hindi; children's fortnightly; circ. 345,382.

Itwari Patrika: Kesargarh, Jawahar Lal Nehru Marg, Jaipur 302 004; tel. (141) 2561582; fax (141) 2566011; e-mail ads@rajasthanpatrika.com; weekly; Hindi; circ. 12,000.

Krishak Jagat: F-47, Ghiya Marg, Bani Park, Jaipur 302 016; tel. (141) 2282680; e-mail info@krishakjagat.org; internet www.krishakjagat.org; f. 2002; Hindi; agricultural and rural devt; weekly; Editor VIJAY BONDRIYA; circ. 41,633.

Rashtradoot Saptahik: M.I. Rd, POB 30, Jaipur 302 001; tel. (141) 2372634; fax (141) 2373513; e-mail info@rashtradoot.com; f. 1983; Hindi; also publ. from Kota and Bikaner; Chief Editor and Man. Editor RAJESH SHARMA; CEO SOMESH SHARMA; combined circ. 324,721.

Tamil Nadu

Chennai (Madras)

Ananda Vikatan: 757 Anna Salai, Chennai 600 002; tel. (44) 28524074; fax (44) 28523819; e-mail ennangal@vikatan.com; internet www.vikatan.com; f. 1924; weekly; Tamil; Editor R. KANNAN; Man. Dir B. SRINIVASAN; circ. 359,936.

Aval Vikatan: 757 Anna Salai, Chennai 600 002; tel. (44) 28524074; fax (44) 28523819; e-mail aval@vikatan.com; internet www.vikatan.com; f. 1998; fortnightly; Tamil; Editor and Man. Dir B. SRINIVASAN; circ. 233,560.

Chandamama: No. 2, Ground Floor,Rms 5 & 6, Swathi Enclave, Amman Koil St, Vadapalani,Chennai 600 026; tel. (44) 43992828; e-mail editor@chandamama.com; internet www.chandamama.com; f. 1947; children's monthly; publ. in 13 languages incl. Hindi, Gujarati, Telugu, Kannada, English, Tamil, Malayalam; Editor B. VISWANATHA REDDI; combined circ. 420,000.

Chutti Vikatan: 757 Anna Salai, Chennai 600 002; tel. (44) 28524074; fax (44) 28523819; e-mail chutti@vikatan.com; internet www.vikatan.com; f. 1999; fortnightly; Tamil; children's; Editor N.V. SANKARAN; Man. Dir B. SRINIVASAN; circ. 24,215.

Devi: 727 Anna Salai, Chennai 600 006; tel. (44) 28521428; f. 1979; weekly; Tamil; Editor B. RAMACHANDRA ADITYAN; circ. 24,498.

Frontline: Kasturi Bldgs, 859/860 Anna Salai, Chennai 600 002; tel. (44) 28413344; fax (44) 28415325; e-mail frontline@thehindu.co.in; internet www.flonnet.com; f. 1984; fortnightly; English; current affairs; independent; Editor and Publr N. RAM; circ. 73,442.

Junior Vikatan: 757 Anna Salai, Chennai 600 002; tel. (44) 28524074; fax (44) 28523819; e-mail junior@vikatan.com; internet www.vikatan.com; f. 1983; twice a week; Tamil; Editor and Man. Dir B. SRINIVASAN; circ. 180,447.

Kalki: Bharathan Publications (P) Ltd, Kalki Bldgs, 47-NP Jawaharlal Nehru Rd, Ekkatuthangal, Chennai 600 032; tel. (44) 43438888; fax (44) 43438899; e-mail onlines@kalkiweekly.com; internet www.kalkionline.com; f. 1941; weekly; Tamil; literary and cultural; circ. 25,933.

Kumudam: 151 Purasawalkam High Rd, Chennai 600 010; tel. (44) 26422146; fax (44) 26425041; e-mail kumudam@hotmail.com; internet www.kumudam.com; f. 1947; weekly; Tamil; Editor Dr S. A. P. JAWAHAR PALANIAPPAN; circ. 286,109.

Kungumam: 93A Kodambakkam High Rd, Chennai 600 034; tel. (44) 28268177; e-mail hariharan@dinakaran.com; internet www.kungumam.co.in; f. 1978; weekly; Tamil; Editor PARASAKTHI; circ. 184,323.

Rani Muthu: 86 Periyar E.V.R. High Rd, Chennai 600 007; tel. (44) 25324771; fax (44) 26426884; e-mail raniweekly@vsnl.net; f. 1969; fortnightly; Tamil; Editor RAGUPATHY BASKARAN; circ. 35,175.

Rani Weekly: 86 Periyar E.V.R. High Rd, Chennai 600 007; tel. (44) 25324771; fax (44) 26426884; e-mail raniweekly@vsnl.net; f. 1962; Tamil; Editor RAGUPATHY BASKARAN; circ. 141,911.

Sportstar: Kasturi Bldgs, 859/860 Anna Salai, Chennai 600 002; tel. (44) 28413344; fax (44) 28415325; e-mail wsvcs@thehindu.co.in; internet www.tssonnet.com; f. 1978; weekly; English; independent; Publr S. RANGARAJAN; Editor N. RAM; circ. 48,900.

Thuglak: 46 Greenways Rd, Chennai 600 028; tel. (44) 42606228; fax (44) 24936915; e-mail webmaster@thuglak.com; internet www.thuglak.com; f. 1970; weekly; Tamil; Editor CHO S. RAMASWAMY; circ. 66,087.

Uttar Pradesh

Manohar Kahaniyan: 1A Tagore Town, Hashimpur Rd, Allahabad 211 002; tel. (532) 2415549; fax (532) 2415533; f. 1940; monthly; Hindi; Editor ASHOK MITRA; circ. 34,130.

Nutan Kahaniyan: 15 Sheo Charan Lal Rd, Allahabad 211 003; tel. (532) 2400612; f. 1975; monthly; Hindi; Chief Editor K. K. BHARGAVA; circ. 31,655.

Satya Katha: 1A Tagore Town, Hashimpur Rd, Allahabad 211 002; f. 1974; monthly; Hindi; Editor ALOK MITRA; circ. 15,785.

West Bengal

Kolkata (Calcutta)

All India Appointment Gazette: 7 Old Court House St, Kolkata 700 001; tel. (33) 22435663; fax (33) 22435618; e-mail sambadmail@sify.com; f. 1973; weekly; English; circ. 22,713.

Anandalok: 6 Prafulla Sarkar St, Kolkata 700 001; tel. (33) 22374880; fax (33) 22253241; f. 1975; fortnightly; Bengali; film; Editor DULENDRA BHOWMIK; circ. 71,707.

Anandamela: 6 Prafulla Sarkar St, Kolkata 700 001; tel. (33) 22216600; fax (33) 22253240; f. 1975; weekly; Bengali; for children; Editor PAULAMI SENGUPTA SARKAR; circ. 56,721.

Contemporary Tea Time: c/o Contemporary Brokers Pvt Ltd, 1 Old Court House Corner, POB 14, Kolkata 700 001; tel. (33) 22307241; fax (33) 22435753; e-mail webmaster@contemporary.co.in; internet www.contemporarybrokers.com; f. 1988; quarterly; English; tea industry; Editor SAMAR SIRCAR; circ. 5,000.

Desh: 6 Prafulla Sarkar St, Kolkata 700 001; tel. (33) 22374880; fax (33) 22253240; e-mail desh@abpmail.com; f. 1933; fortnightly; Bengali; literary; Editor HARSHA DATTA; circ. 99,881.

Global Reach Newsletter: 7W The Millennium, 235/2A A. J. C. Bose Rd, Kolkata 700 020; tel. (33) 22835537; fax (33) 22835538; e-mail global.reach@vsnl.com; internet www.globalreach.in; f. 1991; monthly; English; education magazine for those planning to study abroad; Editor RAVI LOCHAN; circ. 4,500.

Naba Kallol: 11 Jhamapookur Lane, Kolkata 700 009; tel. (33) 23504294; f. 1960; monthly; Bengali; Editor P. K. MAZUMDAR; circ. 29,500.

Prabuddha Bharata (Awakened India): 5 Dehi Entally Rd, Kolkata 700 014; tel. (33) 22640898; e-mail mail@advaitaashrama.org; internet www.advaitaashrama.org; f. 1896; monthly; art, culture, religion, humanities and philosophy; Publr Swami BODHASARANANDA; Editor Swami SATYAMAYANANDA; circ. 7,500.

Sananda: 6 Prafulla Sarkar St, Kolkata 700 001; tel. (33) 22374880; fax (33) 22253241; f. 1986; monthly; Bengali; Editor MADHUMITA CHATTOPADHYAY; circ. 16,460.

Saptahik Bartaman: 6 J. B. S. Haldane Ave, Kolkata 700 105; tel. (33) 23000101; fax (33) 23234030; e-mail bartaman@satyam.net.in; f. 1988; weekly; Bengali; Editor KAKOLI CHAKRABORTY; circ. 120,025.

Suktara: 11 Jhamapukur Lane, Kolkata 700 009; tel. (33) 23504294; e-mail dev_sahityer@rediffmail.com; f. 1948; monthly; Bengali; juvenile; Editor ARUN CHANDRA MAZUMDER; circ. 41,541.

Unish-Kuri: 6 Prafulla Sarkar St, Kolkata 700 001; f. 2004; fortnightly; Bengali; youth; Editor PAULAMI SENGUPTA SARKAR; circ. 55,128.

NEWS AGENCIES

Press Trust of India Ltd: PTI Bldg, 4 Parliament St, New Delhi 110 001; tel. (11) 23716621; fax (11) 23718714; e-mail trans@pti.in; internet www.ptinews.com; f. 1947; re-established 1978; Editor-in-Chief and CEO M. K. RAZDAN.

United News of India (UNI): 9 Rafi Marg, New Delhi 110 001; tel. (11) 23710522; fax (11) 23355841; e-mail uninet@uniindia.com; internet www.uniindia.com; f. 1959; national and international news service in English, Hindi (UNIVARTA) and Urdu; photograph and graphics service; brs in 67 centres in India; Chair. DIPANKAR DAS PURKAYASTHA; Chief Editor and Gen. Man. ARUN KUMAR BHANDARI.

CO-ORDINATING BODIES

Press Information Bureau: Shastri Bhavan, Dr Rajendra Prasad Rd, New Delhi 110 001; tel. (11) 23383643; fax (11) 23383203; e-mail pib@alpha.nic.in; internet www.pib.nic.in; f. 1946 to co-ordinate press affairs for the govt; represents newspaper managements, journalists, news agencies, parliament; has power to examine journalists under oath and may censor objectionable material; Prin. Information Officer DEEPAK SANDHU.

Registrar of Newspapers for India: Ministry of Information and Broadcasting, West Block 8, Wing 2, Ramakrishna Puram, New Delhi 110 066; tel. (11) 26107504; fax (11) 26189801; e-mail rni.hub@nic.in; internet rni.nic.in; f. 1956 as a statutory body to collect press statistics; maintains a register of all Indian newspapers; Press Registrar AMITABHA CHAKRABARTI.

PRESS ASSOCIATIONS

All-India Newspaper Editors' Conference: 36–37 Northend Complex, Rama Krishna Ashram Marg, New Delhi 110 001; tel. (11) 23364519; fax (11) 23317947; f. 1940; c. 300 mems; Pres. VISHWA BANDHU GUPTA; Sec.-Gen. BISHAMBER NEWAR.

All India Small and Medium Newspapers' Federation: 26-F Rajiv Gandhi Chowk (Connaught Pl.), New Delhi 110 001; tel. (11) 23326000; fax (11) 23320906; e-mail indian.observer@gmail.com; c.

9,200 mems; Pres. GURINDER SINGH; Gen. Secs B. C. GUPTA, B. M. SHARMA.

The Foreign Correspondents' Club of South Asia: AB-19 Mathura Rd, opp. Pragati Maidan Gate 3, New Delhi 110 001; tel. (11) 23385118; fax (11) 23385517; e-mail fccsouthasia@gmail.com; internet www.fccsouthasia.net; f. 1992; over 400 mems; Pres. JOHN ELLIOTT.

Indian Federation of Working Journalists: A-4/199 Basant Lane, nr Connaught Pl., New Delhi 110 055; tel. and fax (11) 23418871; e-mail ifwj.media@gmail.com; internet www.ifwj.in; f. 1950; 31,000 mems; Pres. K. VIKRAM RAO; Sec.-Gen. PARMANAND PANDEY.

Indian Journalists' Association: New Delhi; Pres. VIJAY DUTT; Gen. Sec. A. K. DHAR.

Indian Languages Newspapers' Association: Janmabhoomi Bhavan, Janmabhoomi Marg, POB 10029, Fort, Mumbai 400 001; tel. (22) 22870537; f. 1941; 320 mems; Pres. VIJAY KUMAR BONDRIYA; Hon. Gen. Secs PRADEEP G. DESHPANDE, KRISHNA SHEWDIKAR, LALIT SHRIMAL.

Indian Newspaper Society: INS Bldg, Rafi Marg, New Delhi 110 001; tel. (11) 23715401; fax (11) 23723800; e-mail indnews@sify.com; internet www.indiannewspapersociety.org; f. 1939; 685 mems; Pres. HORMUSJI N. CAMA.

National Union of Journalists (India): 7 Jantar Mantar Rd, 2nd Floor, New Delhi 110 001; tel. and fax (11) 23368610; e-mail nujindia@ndf.vsnl.in; internet education.vsnl.com/nujindia; f. 1972; 12,000 mems; Pres. J. K. GUPTA; Sec.-Gen. M. D. GANGWAR.

Press Club of India: 1 Raisina Rd, New Delhi 110 001; tel. (11) 23719844; fax (11) 23357048; internet www.pressclubofindia.org; f. 1958; Pres. PARVEZ AHMED; 4,500 mems.

Press Council of India: Soochna Bhavan, 8 C. G. O. Complex, Ground Floor, Lodhi Rd, New Delhi 110 003; tel. (11) 24366746; e-mail pcibpp@gmail.com; internet www.presscouncil.nic.in; est. under an Act of Parliament to preserve the freedom of the press and maintain and improve the standards of newspapers and news agencies in India; 28 mems; Chair. Justice GANENDRA NARAYAN RAY; Sec. VIBHA BHARGAVA.

Press Institute of India: Rind Premises, Second Main Rd, Taramani, CPT Campus, Chennai 600 113; tel. (44) 22542344; fax (44) 22542323; e-mail arunchacko@pressinstitute.org; internet www.pressinstitute.org; f. 1963; 32 mem. newspapers and other orgs; Chair. O. P. BHATT; Dir and Editor V. MURALI.

Publishers

DELHI AND NEW DELHI

Affiliated East-West Press (Pvt) Ltd: G-1/16 Ansari Rd, Daryaganj, New Delhi 110 002; tel. (11) 23264180; fax (11) 23260538; e-mail affiliat@vsnl.com; internet www.aewpress.com; textbooks and reference books; also represents scientific societies; Dirs SUNNY MALIK, KAMAL MALIK.

All India Publishers & Distributors: 4380/4B, Ansari Rd, Kaushalya Bldg, Daryaganj, New Delhi 110 002; tel. (11) 22324429; fax (11) 22467613; e-mail aipdraj@vsnl.com; CEO ARYA RAJENDER.

Amerind Publishing Co (Pvt) Ltd: c/o Mohan Primlani, A-61, Mayfair Gardens, New Delhi 110 016; tel. (11) 23324578; fax (11) 23710090; e-mail mohanprimlani@hotmail.com; f. 1970; offices at Kolkata, Mumbai and New York; scientific and technical; Dirs MOHAN PRIMLANI, GULAB PRIMLANI.

Arnold Heinman Publishers (India) Pvt Ltd: New Delhi; f. 1969 as Arnold Publishers (India) Pvt Ltd; literature and general; Man. Dir G. A. VAZIRANI.

Atma Ram and Sons: 1376 Kashmere Gate, POB 1429, Delhi 110 006; tel. (11) 23946466; fax (11) 23973082; e-mail atmaram_books@hotmail.com; f. 1909; scientific, technical, humanities, medical; Man. Dir S. PURI; Dir Y. PURI.

B. I. Publications Pvt Ltd: B. I. House, 54 Janpath, New Delhi 110 001; tel. (11) 46209999; fax (11) 23323138; e-mail bipgroup@vsnl.com; internet www.bipgroup.com; f. 1959; academic, general and professional; Man. Dir SHASHANK BHAGAT.

Book Circle: 19A Ansari Rd, Daryaganj, New Delhi 110 002; tel. (11) 23264444; fax (11) 23263050; e-mail bookcircle@vsnl.net; f. 2001; social sciences, art and architecture, technical, medical, scientific; Propr and Dir HIMANSHU CHAWLA.

S. Chand and Co Ltd: 7361 Ram Nagar, Qutab Rd, nr New Delhi Railway Station, New Delhi 110 055; tel. (11) 23672080; fax (11) 23677446; e-mail info@schandgroup.com; internet www.schandgroup.com; f. 1917; educational and general in English and Hindi; also book exports and imports; Man. Dir RAVINDRA KUMAR GUPTA.

Children's Book Trust: Nehru House, 4 Bahadur Shah Zafar Marg, New Delhi 110 002; tel. (11) 23316970; fax (11) 23721090; e-mail cbtnd@vsnl.com; internet www.childrensbooktrust.com; f. 1957; children's books in English and other languages of India; Editor C. G. R. KURUP; Gen. Man. RAVI SHANKAR.

Concept Publishing Co: A/15–16, Commercial Block, Mohan Garden, New Delhi 110 059; tel. (11) 25351794; fax (11) 25357109; e-mail publishing@conceptpub.com; internet www.conceptpub.com; f. 1974; social sciences, management, psychology, community development; Chair. and Man. Dir ASHOK KUMAR MITTAL; CEO NITIN MITTAL.

Frank Bros & Co (Publishers) Ltd: 4675A Ansari Rd, 21 Daryaganj, New Delhi 110 002; tel. (11) 23263393; fax (11) 23269032; e-mail connect@frankbros.com; internet www.frankbros.com; f. 1930; children's, educational and management; Chair. and Man. Dir R. C. GOVIL.

Heritage Publishers: 19A Ansari Rd, Daryaganj, New Delhi 110 002; tel. (11) 23266633; fax (11) 23263050; e-mail heritage@nda.vsnl.net.in; internet www.meditechbooks.com; f. 1973; social sciences, art and architecture, technical, medical, scientific; Propr and Dir B. R. CHAWLA.

Hindustan Publishing Corpn (India): 4805/24 Bharat Ram Rd, 102, Daryaganj, New Delhi 110 002; tel. (11) 43580512; e-mail hpcedu@rediffmail.com; archaeology, anthropology, business management, demography and population dynamics, economics, pure and applied sciences, geology, mathematics, physics, sociology; publ. *Demography India* and *Journal of Economic Geology and Georesource Management*; exporter of Indian journals and periodicals, Indian and foreign books; Man. Partner B. B. JAIN.

Lalit Kala Akademi: Rabindra Bhavan, New Delhi 110 001; tel. (11) 23387241; fax (11) 23782485; e-mail lka@lalitkala.org.in; internet www.lalitkala.gov.in; books on Indian art; CEO Dr SUDHAKAR SHARMA.

Lancers Books: POB 4236, New Delhi 110 048; tel. (11) 26241617; fax (11) 26992063; e-mail lancersbooks@hotmail.com; internet www.lancersbooks.net; f. 1977; politics (with special emphasis on north-east India), defence; Propr S. KUMAR.

Motilal Banarsidass Publishers (Pvt) Ltd: 41 U. A. Bungalow Rd, Jawahar Nagar, Delhi 110 007; tel. (11) 23851985; fax (11) 25797221; e-mail mlbd@vsnl.com; internet www.mlbd.com; f. 1903; religion, philosophy, astrology, yoga, linguistics, history, art, architecture, literature, music and dance, alternative medicine; English and Sanskrit; offices in Bangalore, Chennai, Kolkata, Mumbai, Patna, Pune and Varanasi; Man. Dir N. P. JAIN.

Munshiram Manoharlal Publishers Pvt Ltd: 54 Rani Jhansi Rd, POB 5715, New Delhi 110 055; tel. (11) 23671668; fax (11) 23612745; e-mail info@mrmlonline.com; internet www.mrmlonline.com; f. 1952; Indian art, architecture, archaeology, religion, music, law, medicine, dance, dictionaries, travel, history, politics, numismatics, Buddhism, philosophy, sociology, etc.; Man. Dir ASHOK JAIN.

National Book Trust: 5 Institutional Area, Vasant Kunj, Phase 2, New Delhi 110 070; tel. (11) 26707700; fax (11) 26121883; e-mail nbtindia@ndb.vsnl.net.in; internet www.nbtindia.org.in; f. 1957; autonomous organization established by the Ministry of Human Resources Development to produce and encourage the production of good literary works; Chair. Prof. BIPAN CHANDRA.

National Council of Educational Research and Training (NCERT): Sri Aurobindo Marg, New Delhi 110 016; tel. (11) 26560620; fax (11) 26868419; e-mail directorncert@vsnl.com; internet www.ncert.nic.in; f. 1961; school textbooks, teachers' guides, research monographs, journals, etc.; Dir Prof. KRISHNA KUMAR.

Neeta Prakashan: A-4 Ring Rd, South Extension Part I, POB 3853, New Delhi 110 049; tel. (11) 24636010; fax (11) 24636011; e-mail neetabooks@vsnl.com; internet www.neetaprakashan.com; f. 1960; educational, children's, general; Dir RAJESH GUPTA.

New Age International Pvt Ltd: 4835/24 Ansari Rd, Daryaganj, New Delhi 110 002; tel. (11) 23276802; fax (11) 23267437; e-mail info@newagepublishers.com; internet www.newagepublishers.com; f. 1966; science, engineering, technology, management, humanities, social sciences; Man. Dir SAUMYA GUPTA.

Oxford University Press: YMCA Library Bldg, 1st Floor, 1 Jai Singh Rd, POB 43, New Delhi 110 001; tel. (11) 43600300; fax (11) 23360897; e-mail admin.in@oup.com; internet www.oup.co.in; f. 1912; educational, scientific, medical, general, humanities and social sciences, dictionaries and reference; Man. Dir MANZAR KHAN.

Penguin Books India (Pvt) Ltd: 11 Community Centre, Panchsheel Park, New Delhi 110 017; tel. (11) 26494401; fax (11) 26494403; e-mail penguin@del2.vsnl.net.in; internet www.penguinbooksindia.com; f. 1987; Indian literature and general non-fiction in English; Chair. JOHN MAKINSON; Pres. THOMAS ABRAHAM.

Pitambar Publishing Co Pvt Ltd: 888 East Park Rd, Karol Bagh, New Delhi 110 005; tel. (11) 23676058; fax (11) 23676058; e-mail pitambar@bol.net.in; internet www.pitambarbooks.com; academic, children's books, textbooks and general; Man. Dir ANAND BHUSHAN; 5 brs.

Prentice-Hall of India (Pvt) Ltd: M-97 Connaught Circus, New Delhi 110 001; tel. (11) 22143344; fax (11) 23417179; e-mail phi@phindia.com; internet www.phindia.com; f. 1963; university-level text and reference books; Man. Dir A. K. GHOSH.

Pustak Mahal: J-3/16 Daryaganj, New Delhi 110 002; tel. (11) 23272783; fax (11) 23260518; e-mail info@pustakmahal.com; internet www.pustakmahal.com; children's, general, computers, religious, encyclopaedias; Chair. R. A. GUPTA; Man. Dir ASHOK GUPTA.

Rajkamal Prakashan (Pvt) Ltd: 1B Netaji Subhas Marg, Daryaganj, New Delhi 110 002; tel. (11) 23274463; fax (11) 23278144; e-mail info@rajkamalprakashan.com; internet www.rajkamalprakashan.com; f. 1947; Hindi; literary; also literary journal and monthly trade journal; Man. Dir ASHOK KUMAR MAHESHWARI.

Rajpal and Sons: 1590 Madrasa Rd, Kashmere Gate, Delhi 110 006; tel. (11) 23865483; fax (11) 23867791; e-mail sales@rajpalpublishing.com; internet www.rajpalpublishing.com; f. 1891; humanities, social sciences, art, juvenile; Hindi; Chair. MEERA JOHRI.

Research and Information System for Developing Countries: Zone IV-B, 4th Floor, India Habitat Centre, Lodhi Rd, New Delhi 100 003; tel. (11) 24682177; fax (11) 24682173; e-mail publication@ris.org.in; internet www.ris.org.in; f. 1983; trade and development issues; Dir-Gen. Dr BISWAJIT DHAR.

Rupa & Co: 7/16 Ansari Rd, Daryaganj, POB 7017, New Delhi 110 002; tel. (11) 23278586; fax (11) 23277294; e-mail info@rupapublications.com; internet www.rupapublications.com; f. 1936; Chief Exec. R. K. MEHRA.

Sage Publications India Pvt Ltd: B-1/I-1, Mohan Co-operative Industrial Estate, Mathura Rd, Post Bag 7, New Delhi 110 044; tel. and fax (11) 26491290; e-mail info@sagepub.in; internet www.sagepub.in; f. 1981; social sciences, development studies, business and management studies; Man. Dir VIVEK MEHRA.

Sahitya Akademi: Rabindra Bhavan, 35 Ferozeshah Rd, New Delhi 110 001; tel. (11) 23386626; fax (11) 23382428; e-mail secy@ndb.vsnl.net.in; internet www.sahitya-akademi.gov.in; f. 1954; bibliographies, translations, monographs, encyclopaedias, literary classics, etc.; Pres. SUNIL GANGOPADHYAY; Sec. A. KRISHNA MURTHY.

Scholar Publishing House (Pvt) Ltd: 85 Model Basti, New Delhi 110 005; tel. (11) 23541299; fax (11) 23676565; e-mail info@scholar.ws; internet www.scholar.ws; f. 1968; educational; Man. Dir RAMESH RANADE.

Shiksha Bharati: 1590 Madrasa Rd, Kashmere Gate, Delhi 110 006; tel. (11) 23869812; fax (11) 23867791; e-mail sales@rajpalpublishing.com; f. 1955; textbooks, creative literature, popular science and juvenile in Hindi and English; Editor MEERA JOHRI.

Sterling Publishers (Pvt) Ltd: A-59 Okhla Industrial Area, Phase II, New Delhi 110 020; tel. (11) 26387070; fax (11) 26383788; e-mail mail@sterlingpublishers.com; internet www.sterlingpublishers.com; f. 1964; academic books on the humanities and social sciences, children's books, trade paperbacks; Chair. and Man. Dir S. K. GHAI; Dirs VIKAS GHAI, GAURAV GHAI.

Tata McGraw-Hill Publishing Co Ltd: 7 West Patel Nagar, New Delhi 110 008; tel. (11) 25882743; fax (11) 25885154; e-mail prakash_tiwari@mcgraw-hill.com; internet www.tatamcgrawhill.com; f. 1970; engineering, computers, sciences, medicine, management, humanities, social sciences; Chair. Dr F. A. MEHTA; Man. Dir Dr N. SUBRAHMANYAM.

Taylor & Francis Books India Pvt Ltd: 15–17 Tolstoy Marg, 912 Tolstoy House, New Delhi 110 001; tel. (11) 23712131; fax (11) 23712132; e-mail inquiry@tandfindia.com; internet www.taylorandfrancisgroup.com; f. 2004; Man. Dir SHAMMI MANIK.

Vitasta Publishing: 2/15 Ansari Rd, New Delhi 110 002; tel. (11) 23283024; fax (11) 23263522; e-mail info@vitastapublishing.com; internet www.vitastapublishing.com; f. 2004; science, technology and management; Man. Dir SUDESH KUMAR.

A. H. Wheeler & Co Ltd: 411 Surya Kiran Bldg, 19 K. G. Marg, New Delhi 110 001; tel. (11) 23312629; fax (11) 23357798; e-mail wheelerpub@mantraonline.com; f. 1958; textbooks, reference books, computer science and information technology, electronics, management, telecommunications, social sciences, etc.; Exec. Pres. ALOK BANERJEE.

Women Unlimited: K-36, Hauz Khas Enclave, Ground Floor, New Delhi 110 016; tel. (11) 26964947; fax (11) 26496597; e-mail womenunltd@vsnl.net; internet www.womenunlimited.net; f. 2003; feminism; Head RITU MENON.

Zubaan: 128B, First Floor, Shahpur Jat, New Delhi 110 019; tel. (11) 26494617; e-mail contact@zubaanbooks.com; internet www.zubaanbooks.com; f. 2003; women's studies, social sciences, humanities, general non-fiction, fiction, etc.; Dir URVASHI BUTALIA; Editor PREETI GILL.

CHENNAI (MADRAS)

Emerald Publishers: 15A Casa Major Rd, 1st Floor, Egmore, Chennai 600 008; tel. (44) 28193206; fax (44) 28192380; e-mail info@emeraldpublishers.com; internet www.emeraldpublishers.com; English textbooks, self-help and examination skills; CEO G. OLIVANNAN.

Eswar Press: Archana Arcade, 27 Natesan St, T. Nagar, Chennai 600 017; tel. (44) 24345902; e-mail enquiry@eswar.com; internet www.eswar.com; science and technology; CEO M. PERIYASAMY.

Minerva Publications: 6 Pycrofts Rd, 1st Floor, Triplicane, Chennai 600 005; tel. (44) 28445674; fax (44) 28445674; e-mail minerva@hathway.com; children's books and dictionaries; CEO T. NAZIBUDEEN.

Scitech Publications (India) (Pvt) Ltd: 7/3-C Madley Rd, T. Nagar, Chennai 600 017; tel. (44) 24328737; e-mail scitech@md5.vsnl.net.in; internet www.scitechpublications.com; f. 1998; science, technology, management, reference, etc.; Man. Dir M. R. PURUSHOTHAMAN.

Sura Books (Pvt) Ltd: 1620 J Block, 16th Main Rd, Anna Nagar, Chennai 600 040; tel. (44) 26161099; fax (44) 26162173; e-mail subashvks@surabooks.com; internet www.surabooks.com; children's books, dictionaries, examinations guides, tourist guides, Indology, etc.; Man. Dir V. K. SUBBURAJ.

T. R. Publications Pvt Ltd: PMG Complex, 2nd Floor, 57 South Usman Rd, T. Nagar, Chennai 600 017; tel. (44) 24340765; fax (44) 24348837; e-mail trpubs@md5.vsnl.net.in; internet www.trpublications.com; Chief Exec. S. GEETHA.

JAIPUR

Aavishkar Publishers, Distributors: 807 Vyas Bldg, Chaura Rasta, Jaipur 302 003; tel. (141) 2708286; fax (141) 2578159; e-mail aavishkarbooks@hotmail.com; internet www.pointerpublishers.com; f. 1984; general and reference books on humanities, arts, science, commerce, agriculture and biotechnology; CEO PREM C. BAKLIWAL.

Mangal Deep Publications: Duggar Bldg, M. I. Rd, Jaipur 302 001; tel. (141) 2365086; fax (141) 5102022; e-mail mdpbk@sancharnet.net; humanities, social sciences, science, technology; Propr B. K. MANGAL.

Pointer Publishers: 807 Vyas Bldg, Chaura Rasta, Jaipur 302 003; tel. and fax (141) 2578159; e-mail pointerpub@hotmail.com; internet www.pointerpublishers.com; f. 1986; sciences, commerce, economics, education, literature, history, journalism, law, philosophy, psychology, sociology, tourism; in English and Hindi; Contact VIPIN JAIN.

Publication Scheme: C 12/13, 1st Floor, Ganga Mandir, Sansar Chandra Rd, Jaipur 302 001; tel. (141) 5104038; fax (141) 2376922; e-mail parampsj@datainfosys.net; internet www.pubscheme.com; social sciences, humanities, Ayurveda, Indology; Propr S. S. NATANI.

Rajasthan Hindi Granth Akademi: Plot No. 1, Jhalana Institutional Area, Jaipur 302 004; tel. (141) 2711129; fax (141) 2710341; e-mail hindigranth@indiatimes.com; internet www.rajhga.com; engineering, agriculture, science, social sciences, law, education, fine arts and journalism; Dir Dr R. D. SAINI.

Shyam Prakashan: Film Colony, Chaura Rasta, Jaipur 302 003; tel. (141) 2317659; fax (141) 2326554; e-mail ankit_146@sify.com; internet www.shyamprakashan.com; Propr OM PRAKASH AGRAWAL.

KOLKATA (CALCUTTA)

Academic Publishers: 5A Bhawani Dutta Lane, Kolkata 700 073; tel. (33) 22414857; fax (33) 22572489; e-mail acabooks@cal.vsnl.net.in; internet www.acabooks.net; f. 1958; textbooks, management, medical, technical; Man. Partner B. K. DHUR.

Advaita Ashrama: 5 Dehi Entally Rd, Kolkata 700 014; tel. (33) 22164000; e-mail mail@advaitaashrama.org; internet www.advaitaashrama.org; f. 1899; religion, philosophy, spiritualism, Vedanta; publication centre of Ramakrishna Math and Ramakrishna Mission; Publication Man. Swami BODHASARANANDA.

Ananda Publishers (Pvt) Ltd: 45 Beniatola Lane, Kolkata 700 009; tel. (33) 22414352; fax (33) 22193856; e-mail ananda@cal3.vsnl.net.in; internet www.anandapub.com; literature, general; Man. Dir S. MITRA.

Assam Review Publishing Co: 27A Waterloo St, 1st Floor, Kolkata 700 069; tel. (33) 22482251; fax (33) 22482251; e-mail assamrev@yahoo.co.in; f. 1926; publrs of *The Assam Review and Tea News* (monthly) and *The Assam Directory and Tea Areas Handbook* (annually); Chief Exec. GOBINDALAL BANERJEE.

Dev Sahitya Kutir: 21 Jhamapukur Lane, Kolkata 700 009; tel. (33) 23507887; e-mail dev_sahitya@rediffmail.com; children's, general; Dir ARUN CHANDRA MAZUMDER.

Dey's Publishing: 13 Bankim Chatterjee St, Kolkata 700 073; tel. (33) 22412330; fax (33) 22192041; e-mail deyspublishing@hotmail

.com; academic books, religion, philosophy, general; Dir SUDHANGSHU KUMAR DEY.

Eastern Law House (Pvt) Ltd: 54 Ganesh Chunder Ave, Kolkata 700 013; tel. (33) 22151989; fax (33) 22150491; e-mail elh.cal@gmail.com; internet www.easternlawhouse.com; f. 1918; legal, commercial and accountancy; Dir ASOK DE; br. in New Delhi.

Firma KLM Private Ltd: 257B B. B. Ganguly St, Kolkata 700 012; tel. and fax (33) 22217294; e-mail info@firmaklm.net; internet www.firmaklm.net; f. 1950; Indology, scholarly in English, Bengali, Sanskrit and Hindi, alternative medicine; Man. Dir S. MUKHERJI.

Indian Museum: 27 Jawaharlal Nehru Rd, Kolkata 700 016; tel. (33) 22499902; fax (33) 22495696; e-mail imbot@cal12.vsnl.net.in; internet www.indianmuseumkolkata.org; social sciences and humanities; Dir SAKTI KALI BASU.

Naya Udyog: 206 Bidhan Sarani, Kolkata 700 006; tel. (33) 22413540; e-mail nayaudyog@yahoo.in; f. 1992; books in English and Bengali; agriculture, horticulture, social sciences, history, botany; distributes Naya Prokash publications; Man. Dir PARTHA SANKAR BASU.

Punthi Pustak: 136/4B Bidhan Sarani, Kolkata 700 004; tel. and fax (33) 25555573; e-mail info@punthipustak.com; f. 1956; religion, history, philosophy; Propr P. K. BHATTACHARYA.

Samya: 16 Southern Ave, Kolkata 700 026; tel. (33) 24660812; fax (33) 24644614; e-mail stree@vsnl.com; internet www.stree-samyabooks.com; f. 1996; owned by joint partnership, Bhatkal and Sen; social change, cultural studies, caste studies and Dalit writings; Dir MANDIRA SEN.

M. C. Sarkar and Sons (Pvt) Ltd: 14 Bankim Chatterjee St, Kolkata 700 073; f. 1910; reference; Dir SAMIT SARKAR.

Seagull Books (Pvt) Ltd: 26 Circus Ave, Kolkata 700 017; tel. (33) 22403636; fax (33) 22805143; e-mail seagullfoundation@vsnl.com; internet www.seagullindia.com; academic, literary, general; CEO NAVIN KISHORE.

Shishu Sahitya Samsad: 32A Acharya Prafulla Chandra Rd, Kolkata 700 009; tel. (33) 23507669; fax (33) 23603508; e-mail ss_samsad@yahoo.in; internet www.samsadbooks.com; f. 1951; children's, reference, science, literature; Man. Dir DEBAJYOTI DATTA.

Stree-Samya: 16 Southern Ave, Kolkata 700 026; tel. (33) 24660812; fax (33) 24644614; e-mail stree@cal2.vsnl.net.in; internet www.stree-samyabooks.com; f. 1990 (Stree), 1996 (Samya); imprints publ. by joint venture of Harsha Bhatkal, Popular Prakashan and Mandira Sen; social and women's issues and caste writings in English and Bengali; Dir MANDIRA SEN.

Visva-Bharati: 6 Acharya Jagadish Bose Rd, Kolkata 700 017; tel. (33) 22479868; f. 1923; literature; Dir Prof. KUKUM BHATTACHARYA.

MUMBAI (BOMBAY)

Allied Publishers (Pvt) Ltd: 15 J. N. Heredia Marg, Mumbai 400 001; tel. (22) 42126969; fax (22) 22617928; e-mail mumbai.books@alliedpublishers.com; internet alliedpublishers.com; f. 1934; academic and general; Man. Dir ARJUN SACHDEV.

Bharatiya Vidya Bhavan: Munshi Sadan, Kulapati K. M. Munshi Marg, Mumbai 400 007; tel. (22) 23631261; fax (22) 23630058; e-mail bhavans@bhavans.info; internet www.bhavans.info; f. 1938; art, literature, culture, education, philosophy, religion, history of India; various periodicals in English, Hindi, Sanskrit and other Indian languages; Pres. SURENDRALAL G. MEHTA; Dir-Gen. H. N. DASTUR.

Himalaya Publishing House: Dr Bhalerao Marg (Kelewadi), Girgaon, Mumbai 400 004; tel. (22) 23860170; fax (22) 23877178; e-mail himpub@vsnl.com; internet www.himpub.com; f. 1976; textbooks and research work; Publr MEENA PANDEY.

India Book House (Pvt) Ltd: 412 Tulsiani Chambers, Nariman Point, Mumbai 400 021; tel. (22) 22840165; fax (22) 22835099; e-mail info@ibhworld.com; internet www.ibhworld.com; Man. Dir DEEPAK MIRCHANDANI.

International Book House (Pvt) Ltd: Indian Mercantile Mansions (Extension), Madame Cama Rd, Mumbai 400 039; tel. (22) 66242222; fax (22) 22851109; e-mail ibh@vsnl.com; internet www.ibhbookstore.com; f. 1941; children's, general, educational, scientific, technical, engineering, social sciences, humanities and law; Dir ROHIT GUPTA; Dir SANJEEV GUPTA.

Jaico Publishing House: A2, Jash Chambers, Sir P. M. Rd, Fort, Mumbai 400 001; tel. (22) 40306767; fax (22) 22656412; e-mail jaicowbd@vsnl.com; internet www.jaicobooks.com; f. 1947; general paperbacks, management, computer and engineering books, etc.; imports scientific, medical, technical and educational books; Man. Dir ASHWIN J. SHAH.

Popular Prakashan (Pvt) Ltd: 35C Pandit Madan Mohan Malaviya Marg, Tardeo, opp. Crossroads, Mumbai 400 034; tel. (22) 23265245; fax (22) 24945294; e-mail sales@popularprakashan.com; internet www.popularprakashan.com; f. 1968; sociology, biographies, religion, philosophy, fiction, arts, music, current affairs, medicine, history, politics and administration in English and Marathi; CEO HARSHA BHATKAL.

Sheth Publishing House: G-12 Suyog Industrial Estate, nr LBS Marg, Vikhroli (W), Mumbai 400 083; tel. (22) 25773707; fax (22) 25774200; e-mail no.sph@bom5.vsnl.net.in; educational, children's; Propr NILESH M. SHETH.

Somaiya Publications (Pvt) Ltd: 45–47 Mahatma Gandhi Rd, Fazalbhoy Bldg, POB 384, Fort, Mumbai 400 001; tel. (22) 24130230; fax (22) 22047297; e-mail somaiyabooks@rediffmail.com; internet www.somaiya.com; f. 1967; economics, sociology, history, politics, mathematics, sciences, language, literature, education, psychology, religion, philosophy, logic; Chair. Dr S. K. SOMAIYA.

Taraporevala, Sons and Co (Pvt) Ltd D.B.: 210 Dr Dadabhai Naoroji Rd, Fort, Mumbai 400 001; tel. (22) 22071433; f. 1864; Indian art, culture, history, sociology, scientific, technical and general in English; Chief Exec. R. J. TARAPOREVALA.

N. M. Tripathi (Pvt) Ltd: Jal Vihar, Juhu Tara Rd, Mumbai 400 049; tel. (22) 32934769; e-mail mistertripathi@rediffmail.com; f. 1888; general in English and Gujarati; Chair. Dr PRAKASH TRIVEDI; Man. Dir KARTIK R. TRIPATHI.

K. M. Varghese Co: Hind Rajasthan Bldg, Dada Saheb Phalke Rd, Dadar, Mumbai 400 014; tel. (22) 24149074; fax (22) 24146904; e-mail km@varghese.net; internet www.varghese.net; f. 1960; medicine, pharmacy, nursing, physiotherapy; Propr K. M. VARGHESE.

Vora Medical Publications: 6 Princess Bldg, E. R. Rd, Mumbai 400 003; tel. (22) 23754161; fax (22) 23704053; e-mail voramedpub@yahoo.co.in; medicine, nursing, management, spiritualism, general knowledge; Propr R. K. VORA.

OTHER TOWNS

Anada Prakashan (Pvt) Ltd: 1756 Gandhi Rd, Ahmedabad 380 001; tel. (79) 2169956; fax (79) 2139900; e-mail anadaad1@sancharnet.in; internet www.anada.com; children's, educational, dictionaries; Man. Dir B. R. ANADA.

Bharati Bhawan: Thakurbari Rd, Kadamkuan, Patna 800 003; tel. (612) 2671356; fax (612) 2670010; e-mail bbpdpat@sancharnet.in; f. 1942; educational and juvenile; Man. Partner TARIT KUMAR BOSE.

Bishen Singh Mahendra Pal Singh: 23A New Connaught Place, POB 137, Dehradun 248 001; tel. (135) 2715748; fax (135) 2715107; e-mail bsmps@vsnl.com; f. 1957; botany, forestry, agriculture; Dirs GAJENDRA SINGH GAHLOT, ABHIMANYU GAHLOT.

Books for Change: 139 Richmond Rd, Bangalore 560 025; tel. (80) 25580346; fax (80) 25321747; e-mail bfc@bookforchange.info; internet www.booksforchange.info; f. 1997; operated by ActionAid Karnataka Projects; publr and distributor of books and other media relating to social issues; Publr and Chief Editor SHOBA RAMACHANDRAN.

DC Books: POB 214, DC Kizhakemuri Edam, Good Shepherd St, Kottayam 686 001; tel. (481) 2563114; fax (481) 2564758; e-mail ceo@dcbooks.com; internet www.dcbooks.com; f. 1974; fiction, general and reference books in Malayalam; CEO RAVI DEECEE.

Hind Pocket Books (Pvt) Ltd: B-13, Sector 81, Phase II, Noida 201305; tel. (120) 3093992; fax (120) 2563983; e-mail gbp@del2.vsnl.net.in; f. 1958; fiction and non-fiction paperbacks in English, Hindi, Punjabi, Malayalam and Urdu; Chair DINA NATH MALHOTRA; Man. Dir SHEKHAR MALHOTRA.

Indica Books: D-40/18 Godowlia, Varanasi 221 001; tel. (542) 3094999; fax (542) 2452258; e-mail infoindica@indicabooks.com; internet www.indicabooks.com; Indology, philosophy, religion, culture; Propr DILIP KUMAR JAISWAL.

Jnan Bichitra: Jogendranagar, Vidyasagar Chowmuhani, Agartala, West Tripura 799 001; tel. (381) 2323781; e-mail jnanbichitra@rediffmail.com; f. 1976; general, science; Propr DEBANANDA DAM.

Kalyani Publishers: 1/1 Rajinder Nagar, Civil Lines, Ludhiana 141 008; tel. (161) 2745756; fax (161) 2745872; e-mail kalyanibooks@yahoo.co.in; textbooks; Dir RAJ KUMAR.

Krishna Prakashan Media (Pvt) Ltd: Krishna House, 11 Shivaji Rd, Meerut 250 001; tel. (121) 2644766; fax (121) 2645855; e-mail info@krishnaprakashan.com; internet www.krishnaprakashan.com; f. 1942; textbooks; Exec. Dir SUGAM RASTOGI; Dir S. K. RASTOGI.

Law Publishers: Sardar Patel Marg, Civil Lines, POB 1004, Allahabad 211 001; tel. (532) 2622758; fax (532) 2622781; e-mail lawpub@vsnl.com; internet www.law-publishers.com; f. 1929; legal texts in English; Dir NARESH SAGAR.

Macmillan Publishers India Ltd: 315/316 Raheja Chambers, 12 Museum Rd, Bangalore 560 001; tel. (80) 25586563; fax (80) 25588713; e-mail rberi@macmillan.co.in; internet www.macmillanindia.com; school and university books in English; general; Pres. and Man. Dir RAJIV BERI.

Madhubun Educational Books: E-28, Sector 8, Noida 201 301; tel. (120) 4078900; fax (120) 4078999; e-mail info@madhubunbooks.com;

internet madhubunbooks.com; f. 1969; school books, children's books; Dir SAJILI SHIRODKAR.

Mapin Publishing (Pvt) Ltd: 10B Vidyanagar Society Part I, Usmanpura, Ahmedabad 380 014; tel. (79) 27545390; fax (79) 27545392; e-mail mapin@mapinpub.com; internet www.mapinpub .com; f. 1984; illustrated books on Indian art, culture, history, architecture, photography, crafts and literature; collaborates with art book publrs and museums to provide custom packaging services; Man. Dir BIPIN SHAH.

Navajivan Publishing House: PO Navajivan, Ahmedabad 380 014; tel. (79) 7540635; f. 1919; Gandhiana and related social sciences; in English, Hindi and Gujarati; Man. Trustee JITENDRA DESAI; Sales Man. KAPIL RAWAL.

Neelkamal Publications (Pvt) Ltd: NN Complex, Hyderabad 500 095; tel. (40) 24757140; fax (40) 24757951; e-mail suresh@ neelkamalpub.com; education, psychology, dictionaries, encyclopaedias; Man. Dir SURESH CHANDRA SHARMA.

Orient Blackswan (Pvt) Ltd: 3-6-752 Himayat Nagar, Hyderabad 500 029; tel. (40) 27665466; fax (40) 27645046; e-mail centraloffice@ orientblackswan.com; f. 1948 as Orient Longman (Pvt) Ltd; educational, technical, general and children's in English and almost all Indian languages; Chair. SHANTA RAMESHWAR RAO; Dirs Dr NANDINI RAO, J. KRISHNADEV RAO.

Parikalpana Prakashan: D-68 Nirala Nagar, Lucknow 226 010; tel. (522) 2786782; fax (11) 27296559; e-mail janchetna@rediffmail .com; f. 1996; fiction, poetry, literary criticism, history, political sciences, philosophy; Hindi and English; Pres. KATYAYANI.

Pilgrims Publishing: Pilgrims Book House, B27/98-A-8 Nawabganj Rd, Durga Kund, Varanasi 221 001; tel. (542) 2314060; fax (542) 2312456; e-mail pilgrims@satyam.net.in; internet www .pilgrimsbooks.com; f. 1986; publishes fiction and reference books on subjects including history, travel, Nepal, Tibet, India and the Himalayas; also operates Pilgrims Book House in India and Nepal; Editor CHRISTOPHER N. BURCHETT.

Publication Bureau: Panjab University, Chandigarh 160 014; tel. (172) 2541782; f. 1948; textbooks, academic and general; CEO DARSHAN SINGH; Man. H. R. GROVER.

Publication Bureau: Punjabi University, Patiala 147 002; tel. (175) 3046093; fax (175) 2283073; internet www.universitypunjabi .org; f. 1966; university-level text and reference books, and other general interest books; Punjabi, English and other languages; CEO Dr B. S. MANGAT.

Ram Prasad and Sons: Hospital Rd, Agra 282 003; tel. (562) 2461904; fax (562) 2460920; e-mail rpsons@sancharnet.in; f. 1905; agricultural, arts, history, commerce, education, general, computing, engineering, pure and applied science, economics, sociology; Man. S. N. AGARWAL; br. in Bhopal.

Random House India: Windsor IT Park, 7th Floor, Tower-B, A-1, Sector 125, Noida 201 301; tel. (120) 4607500; fax (120) 4607518; e-mail contact@randomhouse.co.in; internet www.randomhouse.co .in; f. 2005; part of United Kingdom-based Random House Group; Man. Dir GAURAV SHRINAGESH.

Sahitya Bhawan Publications: Hospital Rd, Agra 282 003; tel. (562) 2151665; fax (562) 2151568; e-mail info@sbpagra.com; internet www.sbpagra.com; social sciences, humanities; Propr RAHUL BANSAL.

Sahitya Sangam: New 100, Lukerganj, Allahabad 211 001; Hindi literature, communication, journalism, political science, art, history, etc.; Propr ALOK CHATURVEDI.

Samvad Prakashan: 233 Rajlaxmi Society, nr Shivmahal Palace, Old Padra Rd, Vadodara 390015; tel. (265) 2312747; e-mail samvadprakashan@yahoo.co.in; internet www.samvadprakashan .com; books and magazines in Gujarati; Propr YUYUTSU PANCHAL.

Simon and Schuster India: 2316, Tower A, The Corenthum, A-41, Sector 62, Noida 201 301; tel. (91) 9810173662 (mobile); e-mail rahul .srivastava@simonandschuster.com; f. 2011; Dir RAHUL SRIVASTAVA.

Universities Press (India) (Pvt) Ltd: 3-6-747/1/A & 3-6-754/1 Himayat Nagar, Hyderabad 500 029; tel. (40) 27662849; fax (40) 27645046; e-mail info@universitiespress.com; internet www .universitiespress.com; academic and educational books on science, technology, management; Man. Dir MADHU REDDY.

Vikas Publishing House Pvt Ltd: A-22, Sector 4, Noida 201 301; tel. (120) 4078900; fax (120) 4078999; e-mail helpline@ vikaspublishing.com; internet www.vikaspublishing.com; f. 1969; computers, management, commerce, sciences, engineering textbooks; Dir PIYUSH CHAWLA.

Vishwavidyalaya Prakashan: Vishalakshi Bldg, POB 1149, Chowk, Varanasi 221 001, Uttar Pradesh; tel. (542) 2413741; fax (542) 2413082; e-mail vvp@vsnl.com; internet www.vvpbooks.com; f. 1950; Hindu and Sanskrit literature, Indology, history, art and culture, spiritualism, religion, philosophy, education, sociology, psychology, music, journalism, mass communication, science and social science; Partner ANURAG KUMAR MODI.

GOVERNMENT PUBLISHING HOUSE

Publications Division: Ministry of Information and Broadcasting, Govt of India, Patiala House, New Delhi 110 001; tel. and fax (11) 24366670; e-mail dpd@sb.nic.in; internet publicationsdivision.nic .in; f. 1941; culture, art, literature, planning and development, general; also 21 periodicals in English and 13 Indian languages; Dir-Gen K. GANESAN.

PUBLISHERS' ASSOCIATIONS

Bombay Booksellers' and Publishers' Association: No. 25, 6th Floor, Bldg No. 3, Navjivan Commercial Premises Co-op Society Ltd, Dr Bhadkamkar Marg, Mumbai 400 008; tel. (22) 23088691; e-mail bbpassn@yahoo.co.in; f. 1961; 400 mems; Pres. T. M. SATISH; Hon. Gen. Sec. B. S. FERNANDES.

Delhi State Booksellers' and Publishers' Association: 4760-61/ 23 Ansari Rd, Daryaganj, New Delhi 110 002; tel. (11) 43502211; fax (11) 43502212; e-mail info@dsbpa.in; internet www.dsbpa.in; f. 1941; 450 mems; Pres. PARMIL MITTAL; Sec. K. K. SAXENA.

Federation of Educational Publishers in India: X-39, Institutional Area, Karkardoma, New Delhi 110 092; tel. (11) 22377017; f. 1987; 14 affiliated asscns; 150 life mems; 45 annual mems; Pres. R. K. GUPTA; Sec.-Gen. KAMAL ARORA.

Federation of Indian Publishers: Federation House, 18/1-C Institutional Area, nr JNU, New Delhi 110 067; tel. (11) 26964847; fax (11) 26864054; e-mail fipl@satyam.net.in; internet www.fipindia .org; 18 affiliated asscns; 190 mems; Pres. ANAND BHUSHAN; Hon. Gen. Sec. SHAKTI MALIK.

Akhil Bharatiya Hindi Prakashak Sangh: A-2/1, Krishna Nagar, Delhi 110 051; tel. (11) 2219398; f. 1954; 400 mems; Pres. KRISHNAN DEV SHARMA; Gen. Sec. ARUN KUMAR SHARMA.

Akhil Bharatiya Marathi Prakashak Sangha: c/o Dilipraj Prakashan (Pvt) Ltd, 251-C, Shaniwar Peth, Pune 411 030; Pres. SHARAD GOGATE.

All Assam Publishers' and Booksellers' Association: Chancellor Bldg, H. B. Rd, Panbazar, Guwahati 781 001; tel. (361) 2634790; fax (361) 2513886; e-mail devchowdhurygp@rediffmail .com; Pres. GIRIPADA DEV CHOWDHURY; Sec. BIDYUT GUHA.

All India Urdu Publishers' and Booksellers' Association: 3243 Kuchatarachand, Daryaganj, New Delhi 110 002; tel. (11) 23257189; fax (11) 23265480; e-mail aakif@del3.vsnl.net.in; internet www.aakif.com; f. 1988; 175 mems; Pres. Dr KHALIQ ANJUM; Gen. Sec. S. M. ZAFAR ALI.

All Kerala Publishers' and Booksellers' Association: D. C. Kizhakemuri Edam, Good Shepherd St, Kottayam 686 001; tel. (481) 2563114; fax (481) 2564758; e-mail info@dcbooks.com; Pres. E. N. NANTHAKUMAR.

Booksellers' and Publishers' Association of South India: 8, 2nd Floor, Sun Plaza, G. N. Chetty Rd, Chennai 600 006; 251 mems; Pres. GANDHI KANNADASAN; Sec. R. S. SHANMUGAM.

Gujarati Publishers' Association: Navajivan Trust, PO Navajivan, Ahmedabad 380 014; tel. (79) 7540635; 125 mems; Pres. JITENDRA DESAI; Sec. K. N. MADRASI.

Karnataka Publishers' Association: c/o Ankita Pustaka, 53 Sham Singh Complex, Gandhi Bazar Main Rd, Bangalore 560 004; tel. (80) 26617100; Pres. Dr RAMAKANT JOSHI.

Odisha Publishers' and Booksellers' Association: Binodbihari, Cuttack 753 002; tel. (671) 2620637; f. 1973–74; 280 mems; Pres. PITAMBAR MISHRA; Sec. SUBHENDU SEKHAR RATHA.

Paschimbanga Prakasak Sabha: 206 Bidhan Sarani, Kolkata 700 006; tel. (33) 23506720; fax (33) 22413852; Pres. BIPLAB BHOWAL; Gen. Sec. SOMENATH MUKHERJEE.

Publishers' and Booksellers' Association of Bengal: 93 Mahatma Gandhi Rd, Kolkata 700 007; tel. (33) 22411993; f. 1912; 4,500 mems; Pres. KHIMANGSHU BANDYOPADHYAY; Gen. Sec. CHITTA SINGHA ROY.

Publishers' Association of West Bengal: 6-B, Ramanath Mazumder St, Kolkata 700 009; tel. (33) 2325580; 164 mems; Pres. MOHIT KUMAR BASU; Gen. Sec. SHANKARI BHUSAN NAYAK.

Punjabi Publishers' Association: Bazar Mai Sewan, Amritsar 143 006; tel. (183) 2545787; fax (183) 2543965; Pres. KULWANT SINGH SURI; Gen. Sec. PARAMJIT SINGH.

Vijayawada Publishers' Association: 27-1-68, Karl Marx Rd, Vijayawada 520 002; tel. (866) 2433353; fax (866) 2426348; 41 mems; Pres. DUPATI VIJAY KUMAR; Sec. U. N. YOGI.

Federation of Publishers' and Booksellers' Associations in India: 2nd Floor, 84 Daryaganj, New Delhi 110 002; tel. (11) 23272845; fax (11) 23281227; e-mail fpbai@vsnl.net; internet www

.fpbai.org; f. 1955; 12 affiliated asscns; 507 mems; Pres. A. S. CHOWDHRY; Hon. Sec. BALDEV VERMA.

Publishers' and Booksellers' Guild: Guild House, 2B Jhamapukur Lane, Kolkata 700 009; tel. (33) 23544417; fax (33) 23604566; e-mail guildpb@gmail.com; internet www.kolkatabookfaironline.com; f. 1975; 39 mems; organizes annual internationally recognized Kolkata Book Fair; Pres. JAYANT MANAKTALA; Hon. Gen. Sec. TRIDIB KR. CHATTERJEE.

UP Publishers' Association: Bharati Bhavan, Western Kutchery Rd, Meerut 250 001; Pres. RAJENDRA AGARWAL.

Broadcasting and Communications

TELECOMMUNICATIONS

The telecommunications sector has expanded rapidly in recent years. Mobile cellular subscriptions increased from 52.2m. in 2004 to 903.7m. at the end of January 2012 (representing the second largest market in the world in terms of subscribers); of these, 660.0m. were described as active subscriptions. The mobile telephone penetration rate was measured at 74.9% of the population. At this time, there were 32.4m. fixed-line telephone subscribers. There has been an increase in the number of companies providing 3G services, though its usage was still not extensive by early 2012.

Regulatory Authority

Telecom Regulatory Authority of India (TRAI): Mahanagar Doorsanchar Bhavan (next to Zakir Hussain College), Jawaharlal Nehru Marg (Old Minto Rd), New Delhi 110 002; tel. (11) 23236308; fax (11) 23213294; e-mail ap@trai.gov.in; internet www.trai.gov.in; f. 1997; Chair. J. S. SARMA.

Service Providers

Aircel Ltd: Dishnet Wireless Ltd, Bldg 10A, 2nd Floor, DLF Cyber City, Phase II, Gurgaon 122 022; tel. (124) 4765000; fax (124) 4290524; e-mail care.haryana@aircel.co.in; internet www.aircel.com; f. 1999; 74% owned by Maxis Communications Bhd (Malaysia); 58m. subscribers (July 2011); Chair. SUNEETA REDDY.

Bharat Sanchar Nigam Ltd (BSNL): Bharat Sanchar Bhavan, Harish Chandra Mathur Lane, Janpath, New Delhi 110 001; tel. (11) 23372424; fax (11) 23372444; e-mail cmdbsnl@bsnl.co.in; internet www.bsnl.co.in; f. 2000; fmrly Dept of Telecom Operations; state-owned; 104.2m. subscribers (Jan. 2011); Chair. and Man. Dir R. K. UPADHYAY.

Bharti Airtel Ltd: Bharti Crescent, 1 Nelson Mandela Rd, Vasant Kunj, Phase 2, New Delhi 110 070; tel. (11) 46666100; fax (11) 41666137; internet www.airtel.in; f. 1995; India's first privately owned telephone network; provides mobile, fixed-line, direct-to-home and internet protocol TV services; 200m. subscribers (July 2011); Chair. and Man. Dir SUNIL BHARTI MITTAL.

Idea Cellular: Idea Cellular Ltd, 5th Floor, Windsor CST Rd, Kalina Santa Cruz (East), Mumbai 400 098; tel. 9594004000 (mobile); fax 9594003182 (mobile); e-mail rajat.mukarji@idea.adityabirla.com; internet www.ideacellular.com; f. 1995; 100m. subscribers (Sept. 2011); Chair. KUMAR MANGALAM BIRLA; Man. Dir HIMANSHU KAPANIA.

Mahanagar Telephone Nigam Ltd (MTNL): Jeevan Bharati Bldg, 124 Connaught Circus, New Delhi 110 001; tel. (11) 23719020; fax (11) 23314243; e-mail cmd@bol.net.in; internet www.mtnl.net.in; f. 1986; 56% state-owned; owns and operates telecommunications and information technology services in Mumbai and Delhi; 8.8m. subscribers (Jan. 2011); Chair. and Man. Dir A. K. GARG.

Reliance Communications Ltd: Blk H, 1st Floor, Dhirubhai Ambani Knowledge City, Navi Mumbai 400 709; tel. (22) 30373333; fax (22) 30388005; e-mail customercare@relianceada.com; internet www.rcom.co.in; f. 1999; provides mobile and fixed-line telephony services throughout India; 150m. subscribers (July. 2011); Chair. and Man. Dir ANIL D. AMBANI.

Sistema Shyam TeleServices Ltd: MTS Towers, 334 Udyog Vihar, Phase IV, Gurgaon 122 001; tel. (12) 44812500; e-mail ceo@mtsindia.in; internet www.mtsindia.in; f. 1993; offers services under the brand MTS; 9.1m. subscribers (Jan. 2011); Pres. and CEO VSEVOLOD ROZANOV.

Tata Group: operates Tata Teleservices Ltd, Tata Communications (fmrly VSNL) and Tatanet; 87.2m. subscribers (Jan 2011); Chair. RATAN TATA.

Tata Communications: Plots C-21 & C-36, Blk G, Bandra Kurla Complex, Bandra (East), Mumbai 400 098; tel. (22) 66578765; fax (22) 66591912; e-mail ravindran.s@tatacommunications.com; internet www.tatacommunications.com; f. 1986 as Videsh Sanchar Nigam Ltd (VSNL); enterprise data services and overseas communications; Man. Dir VINOD KUMAR.

Tata Teleservices Ltd: A, E & F Blks, Voltas Premises, T. B. Kadam Marg, Chinchpokli, Mumbai 400033; tel. (22) 66671414; fax (22) 66605335; internet www.tatateleservices.com; f. 1996; Chair. RATAN N. TATA; Man. Dir and CEO SRINATH NARASIMHAN.

Uninor: Unitech Wireless (Tamil Nadu) Pvt Ltd, Ground Floor, Masterpiece, Sector 54, DLF Golf Course Rd, Gurgaon 122 002; tel. (12) 43329000; e-mail sharad.goswami@uninor.in; internet www.uninor.in; f. 2009; 20.3m. subscribers (Jan. 2011); Man. Dir SIGVE BREKKE.

Videocon Telecommunications Ltd: 248 Udyog Vihar, Phase IV, Gurgaon 122 015; e-mail 121@videocon.com; internet www.videocon.com; f. 2010; 6m. subscribers (Jan. 2011); Chair. VENUGOPAL DHOOT.

Vodafone Essar Ltd (Hutch): Peninsula Corporate Park, Ganpatrao Kadam Marg, Lower Parel, Mumbai 400 013; tel. 9619215000 (mobile); fax (22) 24963645; e-mail vodafonecare.mum@vodafone.com; internet www.vodafone.in; f. 1994; Vodafone (United Kingdom) acquired controlling 67% share from Hutchison Telecommunications International (Hong Kong) in Feb. 2007, 33% owned by Essar Group; 127.3m. subscribers (Jan 2011); CEO MARTEN PIETERS.

Other mobile telephone operators include: Loop Mobile, HFCL and S Tel.

Other Companies

ITI Ltd: ITI Bhavan, Doorvaninagar, Bangalore 560 016; tel. (80) 25614466; fax (80) 25617525; e-mail secretary@itiltd.co.in; internet www.itiltd-india.com; f. 1948; govt undertaking; mfrs of all types of telecommunication equipment, incl. telephones, automatic exchanges and long-distance transmission equipment; also produces optical fibre equipment and microwave equipment; will manufacture all ground communication equipment for the 22 earth stations of the Indian National Satellite; in conjunction with the Post and Telegraph Department, a newly designed 2,000-line exchange has been completed; Chair. and Man. Dir K. L. DHINGRA.

BROADCASTING

Prasar Bharati (Broadcasting Corpn of India): Doordarshan Bhavan, Copernicus Marg, New Delhi 110 001; tel. (11) 23737603; fax (11) 23352549; e-mail webadmin@dd.nic.in; internet www.ddindia.gov.in/Prasar+Bharati; f. 1997; autonomous body; oversees operations of state-owned radio and television services; Chair. MRINAL PANDE; CEO RAJIV TAKRU.

Radio

In 2005 the Government adopted a policy that sought to expand radio services through private agencies, opening up the sector to foreign investment. Since then, satellite, internet and community radio have proliferated rapidly. By 2011 there were more than 245 privately owned FM radio channels in operation.

All India Radio (AIR): Akashvani Bhavan, Sansad Marg, New Delhi 110 001; tel. (11) 23710300; fax (11) 23421956; e-mail dgair@air.org.in; internet allindiaradio.org; broadcasting is controlled by the Ministry of Information and Broadcasting and is primarily govt-financed; operates a network of 208 stations and 380 transmitters (grouped into four zones—north, south, east and west), covering almost the entire population and over 90% of the total area of the country; Dir-Gen. NOREEN NAQVI; The News Services Division of AIR, centralized in New Delhi, is one of the largest news organizations in the world. It has 45 regional news units, which broadcast 469 bulletins daily in 75 languages. Daily broadcasts include: 178 bulletins in 33 languages in the Home Services; 187 regional bulletins in 65 languages and dialects; and 66 bulletins in 26 languages in the External Services.

Big FM: 401, 4th Floor, Infinity Mall, New Link Rd, Oshiwara, Andheri (West), Mumbai 400 053; tel. (22) 30689444; fax (22) 39888927; internet www.big927fm.com; f. 2006; covers 45 cities; owned by Reliance Broadcast Network Ltd; CEO TARUN KATIAL.

Fever 104: 17th Floor, HT Bldg, K. G. Marg, New Delhi 110 001; tel. (11) 43104104; e-mail fever104@fever.fm; internet www.fever.fm; f. 2006; owned by HT Media; covers Delhi, Mumbai, Bangalore and Kolkata; music and entertainment programmes; CEO RAJIV VERMA; Head HARSHAD JAIN.

Oye! FM: Shlok House, Bldg 25, Off Link Rd, Oshiwara, Andheri (West), Mumbai 400 053; tel. (22) 42451000; fax (22) 42451002; internet oyefm.in; owned by the India Today Group; fmrly Meow FM, renamed as above 2010; CEO G. KRISHNAN.

Radio City: 5th Floor, RNA Corporate Park, Off Western Express Highway, Kala Nagar, Bandra (East), Mumbai 400 051; tel. and fax (22) 66969100; e-mail reshmak@myradiocity.com; internet www.planetradiocity.com; f. 2001; 20 cities; music and entertainment; owned by IVF Holdings Pvt. Ltd; CEO APURVA PUROHIT.

Radio Mirchi: Trade Gardens, Ground Floor, Kamala Mills Compound, Senapati Bapat Marg, Lower Parel (West), Mumbai 400 013; tel. (22) 67536983; fax (22) 67536900; e-mail sheeza@radiomirchi

.com; internet www.radiomirchi.com; f. 1993; fmrly Times FM, renamed as above 2000; owned by Entertainment Network (India) Ltd; contemporary music; CEO Prashant Panday.

Radio One: internet www.radioone.in; f. 2006; Man. Dir Vineet Singh Hukmani.

Red FM: Murasoli Maran Towers, 73 Main Rd, MRC Nagar, Chennai 600 028; tel. (44) 44676767; fax (22) 24346814; e-mail queries935@redfm.in; internet www.redfm.in; f. 2002; over 40 cities; Hindi music; privately owned; CEO Kulwinder Sanghera.

Television

In late 2011 the Government introduced legislation that required the entire industry to convert to digital infrastructure by the end of 2014. The total number of television channels grew from 461 in 2009 to 626 in 2011. Cable and satellite penetration across the country had reached 80% by 2012.

Doordarshan India (Television India): Mandi House, Doordarshan Bhavan, Copernicus Marg, New Delhi 110 001; tel. (11) 23385958; fax (11) 23386507; e-mail webadmin@dd.nic.in; internet www.ddindia .gov.in; f. 1976; broadcasting is controlled by the Ministry of Information and Broadcasting and is govt-financed; programmes: 280 hours weekly; 5 all-India channels, 11 regional-language satellite channels, 5 state networks and 1 international channel; Dir-Gen. Tripurari Sharan.

NDTV Network: NDTV Ltd, 207 Okhla Industrial Estate, Phase III, New Delhi 110 020; tel. (11) 26446666; fax (11) 41037119; e-mail feedback@ndtv.com; internet www.ndtv.com; f. 1988; 3 news channels: NDTV 24x7 (English), NDTV India (Hindi) and NDTV Profit (Business); also NDTV Lifestyle, NDTV Convergence and NDTV Good Times; 23 offices and studios; Chair. and Dir Dr Prannoy Roy; CEO Vikramaditya Chandra.

Network 18 Group: 503, 504 & 507, 5th Floor, Mercantile House, 15 Kasturba Gandhi Marg, New Delhi 110 001; tel. (11) 41506112; fax (11) 41506115; internet www.network18online.com; f. 1993; owns news channels, incl. CNN-IBN, CNBC-TV18, IBN 7 and IBN Lokmat (Marathi); also operates, in a joint venture with Viacom, Inc. of the USA, entertainment channels incl. Colors, MTV, VH1 and Nick; Chair. and Man. Dir Raghav Bahl; Exec. Dir Sanjay Ray Chaudhuri.

Sony Entertainment Television (Multi Screen Media Pvt. Ltd): Multi Screen Media Pvt. Ltd, 3rd Floor, Bldg No. 7, Malad Link Rd, Malad (West), Mumbai 400 064; tel. (22) 67081111; fax (22) 66434748; e-mail feedback.set@setindia.com; internet www .setindia.com; f. 1995; channels incl. Sony Entertainment Television, SAB TV, SET Max, Sony Aath, SET PIX, Sony MIX, AXN and Animax India; owned by MSM Pvt. Ltd, fmrly SET India Pvt. Ltd; CEO Man Jit Singh.

Star TV: Star India Pvt. Ltd, Star House, Dr E. Moses Rd, Mahalaxmi, Mumbai 400 011; tel. (22) 66305555; fax (22) 66305050; e-mail info@startv.com; internet www.startv.com; f. 1991; 35 channels in 7 languages, incl. Star World, Star Movies, Star Plus, Star One, Star Utsav, Star Gold, Star News, ESPN, Star Sports, Channel [V], National Geographic Channel, etc.; CEO Uday Shankar.

TV Today Network: 8th Floor, Videocon Tower, E-1 Jhandewalan Extn, New Delhi 110 055; tel. (11) 23684878; fax (11) 23684895; e-mail info@aajtak.com; internet www.indiatodaygroup.com; f. 1975; owns news channels incl. Aaj Tak (Hindi), Headlines Today (English), Tez (Hindi) and Dilli Aaj Tak (Hindi) news channel; Chair. Aroon Purie; CEO Joy Chakraborthy.

Zee Entertainment Enterprises Ltd: 135 Continental Bldg, Dr Annie Beasant Rd, Worli, Mumbai 400 018; tel. (22) 66971234; fax (22) 24900302; e-mail inquiry@zeenetwork.com; internet www .zeetelevision.com; f. 1992; owns more than 30 news and entertainment channels, incl. Zee TV, Zee Cinema, Ten Sports, Zee Studio, Zee News, Zee Business, 9X, etc.; Chair. Subhash Chandra; CEO Punit Goenka.

Finance

(cap. = capital; p.u. = paid up; res = reserves; dep. = deposits; m. = million; brs = branches; amounts in rupees unless otherwise stated)

BANKING

State Banks

Reserve Bank of India: Central Office Bldg, Shahid Bhagat Singh Rd, POB 10007, Mumbai 400 001; tel. (22) 22661602; fax (22) 22658269; e-mail helpprd@rbi.org.in; internet www.rbi.org.in; f. 1934; nationalized 1949; sole bank of issue; cap. 50m., res 65,000m., dep. 3,754,115m. (June 2010); Gov. Dr D. Subbarao; Dep. Govs Dr K. C. Chakrabarty, Anand Sinha, Dr Subir Gokarn; 22 regional offices.

State Bank of India: Corporate Centre, Madame Cama Rd, POB 10121, Mumbai 400 021; tel. (22) 22022426; fax (22) 22851391; e-mail gm.gbu@sbi.co.in; internet www.statebankofindia.com; f. 1955; cap. 6,349.9m., res 720,927m., dep. 12,555,624.8m. (March 2011); 7 associates, 7 domestic subsidiaries/affiliates, 3 foreign subsidiaries, 4 jt ventures abroad; Chair. Pratip Chaudhuri; Man Dirs Hemant Contractor, Diwakar Gupta, A. Krishna Kumar; 9,593 brs (incl. 52 overseas brs and rep. offices in 34 countries).

State-owned Commercial Banks

Fourteen of India's major commercial banks were nationalized in 1969 and a further six in 1980. They are managed by 15-member boards of directors (two directors appointed by the central Government, one employee director, one representing employees who are not workmen, one representing depositors, three representing farmers, workers, artisans, etc., five representing persons with special knowledge or experience, one Reserve Bank of India official and one Government of India official). The Department of Banking of the Ministry of Finance controls all banking operations.

There were 87,768 branches of public sector and other commercial banks in March 2010.

Aggregate deposits of all scheduled commercial banks amounted to an estimated Rs 41,186,030m. in September 2009.

Allahabad Bank: 2 Netaji Subhas Rd, Kolkata 700 001; tel. (33) 22319144; fax (33) 22107425; e-mail gmpd@allahabadbank.in; internet www.allahabadbank.com; f. 1865; nationalized 1969; cap. 4,762m., res 65,559m., dep. 1,318,821m. (March 2011); Chair. and Man. Dir J. P. Dua; Exec. Dirs Debabrata Sarkar, M. R. Nayak; 2,020 brs.

Andhra Bank: Andhra Bank Bldgs, Saifabad, 5-9-11 Secretariat Rd, Hyderabad 500 004; tel. (40) 23230001; fax (40) 23211050; e-mail customerser@andhrabank.co.in; internet www.andhrabank.in; f. 1923; nationalized 1980; cap. 5,595m., res 44,950m., dep. 921,431m. (March 2011); Chair. and Man. Dir B. A. Prabhakar; Exec. Dirs K. K. Misra, A. A. Taj; 1,128 brs and 113 extension counters.

Bank of Baroda: Baroda Corporate Centre, C-26, G Block, Bandra-Kurla Complex, Bandra (East), Mumbai 400 051; tel. (22) 26985000; fax (22) 26523000; e-mail customerservice@bankofbaroda.com; internet www.bankofbaroda.com; f. 1908; nationalized 1969; merged with Benares State Bank in 2002; cap. 3,928m., res 168,636m., dep. 3,116,032m. (March 2011); Chair. and Man. Dir M. D. Mallya; Exec. Dirs Rajiv Kumar Bakshi, N. S. Srinath; 2,773 brs in India, 38 brs overseas.

Bank of India: Star House, C-5, G Block, 3rd Floor, Bandra-Kurla Complex, Bandra (East), Mumbai 400 051; tel. (22) 66684444; fax (22) 56684558; e-mail headoffice.god@bankofindia.co.in; internet www .bankofindia.com; f. 1906; nationalized 1969; cap. 5,472m., res 145,464m., dep. 2,995,594m. (March 2011); Chair. and Man. Dir Alok Kumar Misra; 2,883 brs in India, 21 brs overseas.

Bank of Maharashtra: 'Lokmangal', 1501 Shivajinagar, Pune 411 005; tel. (20) 25532731; fax (20) 25533246; e-mail bomcopln@mahabank.co.in; internet www.bankofmaharashtra.in; f. 1935; nationalized 1969; cap. 10,697m., res 22,935.7m., dep. 668,388.9m. (March 2011); Chair. and Man. Dir Narendra Singh; Exec. Dir C. V. R. Rajendran; 1,291 brs.

Canara Bank: 112 Jayachamarajendra Rd, POB 6648, Bangalore 560 002; tel. (80) 22221581; fax (80) 22223168; internet www .canarabank.com; f. 1906; nationalized 1969; cap. 4,430m., res 159,249m., dep. 2,937,939m. (March 2011); Chair. and Man. Dir S. Raman; Exec. Dirs Archana S. Bhargava, Ashok Kumar Gupta; 2,744 brs.

Central Bank of India: Chandermukhi, Nariman Point, Mumbai 400 021; tel. (22) 66387777; fax (22) 22044336; e-mail chairman@centralbank.co.in; internet www.centralbankofindia.co.in; f. 1911; nationalized 1969; cap. 20,211m., res 88,303m., dep. 1,793,785m. (March 2011); Chair. and Man. Dir M. V. Tanksale; Exec. Dirs Vijayalakshmi R. Iyer, Rajiv Kishore Dubey; 3,130 brs.

Corporation Bank: Mangaladevi Temple Rd, POB 88, Mangalore 575 001; tel. (824) 2426416; fax (824) 2440964; e-mail query@corpbank.co.in; internet www.corpbank.com; f. 1906; nationalized 1980; cap. 1,481m., res 56,332m., dep. 1,167,391m. (March 2011); Chair. and Man. Dir Ajai Kumar; Exec. Dirs Amar Lal Daultani, Ashwani Kumar; 617 brs.

Dena Bank: C-10, G Block, Bandra-Kurla Complex, Bandra (East), Mumbai 400 051; tel. (22) 26545035; fax (22) 26545761; e-mail cmd@denabank.co.in; internet www.denabank.com; f. 1938 as Devkaran Nanjee Banking Co Ltd; nationalized 1969; cap. 3,333.8m., res 27,109m., dep. 642,096m. (March 2011); Chair. and Man. Dir Nupur Mitra; Exec. Dir A. K. Dutt; 1,122 brs.

Indian Bank: 66 Rajaji Salai, POB 1384, Chennai 600 001; tel. (44) 25233231; fax (44) 25231278; e-mail indianbank@vsnl.com; internet www.indian-bank.com; f. 1907; nationalized 1969; cap. 8,297.7m., res 70,118.7m., dep. 1,057,184m. (March 2011); Chair. and Man. Dir T. M. BHASIN; Exec. Dirs B. RAJ KUMAR, RAJEEV RISHI; 1,376 brs.

Indian Overseas Bank: 763 Anna Salai, POB 3765, Chennai 600 002; tel. (44) 28524212; fax (44) 28523595; e-mail investor@iobnet.co.in; internet www.iob.in; f. 1937; nationalized 1969; merged with Bharat Overseas Bank Ltd in 2007; cap. 6,187m., res 76,336m., dep. 1,452,287m. (March 2011); Chair. and Man. Dir M. NARENDRA; Exec. Dirs A. D. M. CHAVALI, A. K. BANSAL; 1,496 brs.

Oriental Bank of Commerce: Harsha Bhavan, E Blk, Connaught Place, POB 329, New Delhi 110 001; tel. (11) 47651186; fax (11) 23321514; e-mail bdncmd@obcindia.com; internet www.obcindia.co.in; f. 1943; nationalized 1980; cap. 2,917m., res 93,017m., dep. 1,390,542m. (March 2011); Chair. and Man. Dir S. L. BANSAL; Exec. Dirs V. KANNAN, S. C. SINHA; 1,130 brs.

Punjab & Sind Bank: Bank House, 21 Rajendra Place, New Delhi 110 008; tel. (11) 25719082; fax (11) 25723793; e-mail ho.pr@psb.org.in; internet www.psbindia.com; f. 1908; nationalized 1980; cap. 4,230m., res 22,074m., dep. 597,231.9m. (March 2011); Chair. and Man. Dir DEVINDER PAL SINGH; Exec. Dir PARVEEN KUMAR ANAND; 866 brs.

Punjab National Bank: 7 Bhikaiji Cama Place, Africa Ave, New Delhi 110 066; tel. (11) 26102303; fax (11) 26196456; e-mail cmd@pnb.co.in; internet www.pnbindia.com; f. 1895; nationalized 1969; merged with New Bank of India in 1993; cap. 3,168m., res 173,636m., dep. 3,162,319m. (March 2011); Chair. and Man. Dir Dr K. R. KAMATH; Exec. Dirs USHA ANANTHASUBRAMANIAN, RAKESH SETHI; 3,833 brs.

Syndicate Bank: POB 1, Manipal 576 119; tel. (825) 2571181; fax (825) 2570266; e-mail idcb@syndicatebank.com; internet www.syndicatebank.com; f. 1925; est. as Canara Industrial and Banking Syndicate Ltd; name changed as above 1964; nationalized 1969; cap. 5,732.8m., res 54,316m., dep. 1,355,931m. (March 2011); Chair. and Man. Dir MADHUKANT GIRDHARLAL SANGHVI; Exec. Dirs M ANJANEYA PRASAD, RAVI CHATTERJEE; 2,127 brs.

UCO Bank: 10 Biplabi Trailokya Maharaj Sarani (Brabourne Rd), POB 2455, Kolkata 700 001; tel. (33) 22254120; fax (33) 22253986; e-mail ucobank@vsnl.net; internet www.ucobank.com; f. 1943; est. as United Commercial Bank Ltd; name changed as above 1985; nationalized 1969; cap. 24,505m., res 32,835m., dep. 1,452,776m. (March 2011); Chair. and Man. Dir ARUN KAUL; Exec. Dirs S. CHANDRASEKHARAN, N. R. BADRINARAYANAN; 1,849 brs.

Union Bank of India: Union Bank Bhavan, 239 Vidhan Bhavan Marg, Nariman Point, Mumbai 400 021; tel. (22) 22892000; fax (22) 22824689; e-mail ibd@unionbankofindia.com; internet www.unionbankofindia.co.in; f. 1919; nationalized 1969; cap. 6,353m., res 102,306m., dep. 2,024,000m. (March 2011); Chair. and Man. Dir DEBABRATA SARKAR; Exec. Dirs SURESH KUMAR JAIN, S. S. MUNDRA; 2,082 brs.

United Bank of India: 16 Old Court House St, Kolkata 700 001; tel. (33) 2487471; fax (33) 2485852; e-mail homail@unitedbank.co.in; internet www.unitedbankofindia.com; f. 1950; nationalized 1969; cap. 11,444m., res 33,532.8m., dep. 778,448m. (March 2011); Chair. and Man. Dir BHASKAR SEN; Exec. Dir D. NARANG; 1,354 brs.

Vijaya Bank: 41/2 Mahatma Gandhi Rd, Bangalore 560 001; tel. (80) 25584066; fax (80) 25584142; e-mail ibd@vijayabank.co.in; internet www.vijayabank.com; f. 1931; nationalized 1980; cap. 16,726m., res 26,205m., dep. 732,483m. (March 2011); Chair. and Man. Dir UPENDRA KAMATH; Exec. Dir SHUBHALAKSHMI PANSE; 1200 brs.

Principal Private Banks

Bombay Mercantile Co-operative Bank Ltd: 78 Mohammed Ali Rd, Mumbai 400 003; tel. (22) 23425961; fax (22) 23482387; e-mail bmcit@vsnl.net; internet bmcbankltd.com; f. 1939; cap. 382m., res 959.9m., dep. 21,150.7m. (March 2011); Man. Dir SHAIKH MUSHTAQUE ALI AHMED; 52 brs.

Catholic Syrian Bank Ltd: St Mary's College Rd, POB 502, Trichur 680 020; tel. (487) 2333020; fax (487) 2333435; e-mail pdd@csb.co.in; internet www.csb.co.in; f. 1920; cap. 313m., res 5,015m., dep. 87,256m. (March 2011); Chair. S. SANTHANAKRISHNAN; Man. Dir and CEO V. P. ISWARDAS; 267 brs.

City Union Bank Ltd: 149 TSR (Big) St, Kumbakonam 612 001; tel. (435) 2432322; fax (435) 2431746; e-mail co@cityunionbank.com; internet www.cityunionbank.com; f. 1904; cap. 405m., res 7,455m., dep. 129,142.8m. (March 2011); Chair. S. BALASUBRAMANIAN; Man. Dir and CEO N. KAMAKODI; 125 brs.

The Federal Bank Ltd: Federal Towers, POB 103, Alwaye 683 101; tel. (484) 2623620; fax (484) 2622672; e-mail nrihelp@federalbank.co.in; internet www.federalbank.co.in; f. 1931; cap. 1,710.4m., res 43,281m., dep. 429,884m. (March 2011); Man. Dir and CEO SHYAM SRINIVASAN; Exec. Dirs P. C. JOHN, ABRAHAM CHACKO; 606 brs.

HDFC Bank: HDFC Bank House, Senapati Bapat Marg, Lower Parel, Mumbai, 400 013; tel. (22) 66521000; fax (22) 24960739; e-mail corporatecommunications@hdfcbank.com; internet www.hdfcbank.com; merged with Centurion Bank of Punjab in 2008; cap. 4,652m., res 165,031m., dep. 2,082,872m. (March 2011); Chair. C. M. VASUDEV; Man. Dir ADITYA PURI; 1,412 brs.

ICICI Bank Ltd: ICICI Towers, South Tower, 4th Floor, Bandra-Kurla Complex, Bandra (East), Mumbai 400 051; tel. (22) 26531414; fax (22) 26531124; e-mail info@icicibank.com; internet www.icicibank.com; f. 1994; cap. 15,018m., res 463,687m., dep. 2,598,079.7m. (March 2011); merged with Sangli Bank in 2007 and with The Bank of Rajasthan Ltd in 2010; CEO and Man. Dir CHANDA D. KOCHHAR; Chair. K. V. KAMATH; 1,400 brs.

IndusInd Bank Ltd: One Indiabulls Centre, Tower 1, 8th Floor, 841 S. B. Marg, Elphinstone Rd, Mumbai 400 013; tel. (22) 24231999; fax (22) 24231998; e-mail mktg@indusind.com; internet www.indusind.com; f. 1994; cap. 4,659m., res 26,154m., dep. 343,653.7m. (March 2011); Chair. R. SESHASAYEE; Man. Dir ROMESH SOBTI; 209 brs.

ING Vysya Bank Ltd: 22 M. G. Rd, Bangalore 560 001; tel. (80) 25005000; fax (80) 25588442; e-mail ingvysyabank@ingvysyabank.com; internet www.ingvysyabank.com; f. 1930; cap. 1,209.8m., res 18,569m., dep. 329,689.9m. (March 2011); Chair. ARUN THIAGARAJAN; Man. Dir and CEO SHAILENDRA BHANDARI; 404 brs.

Jammu and Kashmir Bank Ltd: Corporate Headquarters, M. A. Rd, Srinagar 190 001; tel. (194) 2481930; fax (194) 2481923; e-mail jkbcosgr@jkbmail.com; internet jkbank.net; f. 1938; cap. 484.9m., res 28,151m., dep. 446,704m. (March 2011); Chair. MUSHTAQ AHMAD; 556 brs.

Karnataka Bank Ltd: POB 599, Kodialbail, Mangalore 575 003; tel. (824) 2228222; fax (824) 2228284; e-mail info@ktkbank.com; internet www.karnatakabank.com; f. 1924; cap. 1,882m., res 20,362m., dep. 273,364m. (March 2011); Chair. and CEO ANANTHAKRISHNA; Man. Dir and CEO P. JAYARAMA BHAT; 370 brs.

The Karur Vysya Bank Ltd: Erode Rd, POB 21, Karur, Tamil Nadu 639 002; tel. (4324) 226520; fax (4324) 225700; e-mail kvbpdd@kvbmail.com; internet www.kvb.co.in; f. 1916; cap. 1,169m., res 16,026m., dep. 247,218m. (March 2011); Chair. K. P. KUMAR; Man. Dir and CEO K. VENKATARAMAN; 312 brs.

Lakshmi Vilas Bank Ltd: Kathaparai, Salem Rd, POB 2, Karur 639 006; tel. (4324) 220051; fax (4324) 220068; e-mail info@lvbank.com; internet www.lvbank.com; f. 1926; cap. 975m., res 6,413m., dep. 94,093m. (March 2010); Man. Dir and CEO P. R. SOMASUNDARAM; Exec. Dirs K. S. R. ANJANEYULU; 234 brs.

South Indian Bank Ltd: SIB House, T. B. Rd, Mission Quarters, Thrissur 680 001; tel. (487) 2420020; fax (487) 2442021; e-mail sibcorporate@sib.co.in; internet www.southindianbank.com; f. 1929; cap. 1,130m., res 14,246.7m., dep. 297,210.7m. (March 2011); Man. Dir and CEO V. A. JOSEPH; 450 brs.

Tamilnad Mercantile Bank Ltd: 57 Victoria Extension Rd, Tuticorin 628 002; tel. (461) 2321932; fax (461) 2322994; e-mail ttn_tmbankhi@sancharnet.in; internet www.tmb.in; f. 1921; est. as Nadar Bank; name changed as above 1962; cap. 2.8m., res 11,148m., dep. 137,932.9m. (March 2011); Man. Dir and CEO A. K. JAGANNATHAN; 173 brs.

Banking Organizations

Indian Banks' Association: World Trade Centre Complex, Centre I Bldg, 6th Floor, Cuffe Parade, Mumbai 400 005; tel. (22) 22174040; fax (22) 22184222; e-mail webmaster@iba.org.in; internet www.iba.org.in; 156 mems; Chair. O. P. BHATT.

Indian Institute of Banking and Finance: 'The Arcade', World Trade Centre, 2nd Floor, East Wing, Cuffe Parade, Mumbai 400 005; tel. (22) 22187003; fax (22) 22185147; e-mail mem-services@iibf.org.in; internet www.iibf.org.in; f. 1928; 343,202 mems; Pres. O. P. BHATT; four zonal offices.

National Institute of Bank Management: NIBM Post Office, Kondhwe Khurd, Pune 411 048; tel. (20) 26833080; fax (20) 26834478; e-mail director@nibmindia.org; internet www.nibmindia.org; f. 1969; Gov. Dr D. SUBBARAO; Dir Dr ASHISH SAHA.

DEVELOPMENT FINANCE ORGANIZATIONS

Agricultural Finance Corporation Ltd: Dhanraj Mahal, 1st Floor, Chhatrapati Shivaji Maharaj Marg, Mumbai 400 001; tel. (22) 22028924; fax (22) 22028966; e-mail afcl@afcindia.org.in; internet www.afcindia.org.in; f. 1968; est. by consortium of 45 public and private sector commercial banks incl. devt finance institutions; aims to increase the flow of investment and credit into agriculture and rural devt projects; provides project consultancy services to commercial banks, Union and state govts, public sector corpns, the World Bank, the ADB, FAO, the International Fund for Agricultural Development and other institutions and to individuals; undertakes techno-economic and investment surveys in agriculture and agro-industries etc.; publishes quarterly journal *Financing Agriculture*; Chair. Y. C. NANDA; Man. Dir A. K. GARG; 3 regional offices and 9 br. offices.

Export-Import Bank of India: Centre One Bldg, Floor 21, World Trade Centre Complex, Cuffe Parade, Mumbai 400 005; tel. (22) 22172600; fax (22) 22182572; e-mail cag@eximbankindia.in; internet www.eximbankindia.com; f. 1982; cap. 19,999.9m., res 28,315m., dep. 32,410m. (March 2011); Chair. and Man. Dir T. C. A. RANGANATHAN; 14 offices world-wide.

Housing Development Finance Corpn Ltd (HDFC): Ramon House, 169 Backbay Reclamation, Churchgate, Mumbai 400 020; tel. (22) 66316000; fax (22) 22048834; e-mail info@hdfc.com; internet www.hdfc.com; f. 1977; provides loans to individuals and corporate bodies; cap. p.u. 2,844.5m., res 128,529.4m., dep. 193,746.7m. (March 2009); Chair. DEEPAK S. PAREKH; Man. Dir RENU SUD KARNAD; 173 brs (incl. one overseas br.).

IDBI Bank Ltd (Industrial Development Bank of India): IDBI Tower, World Trade Centre Complex, Cuffe Parade, Mumbai 400 005; tel. (22) 66553355; fax (22) 22188137; e-mail pro@idbi.co.in; internet www.idbi.com; f. 1964; reorg. 1976; merged with The United Western Bank Ltd in 2006; 52.68% govt-owned; provides direct finance, refinance of industrial loans and bills, finance to large- and medium-sized industries, extends financial services, such as merchant banking and forex services, to the corporate sector; cap. 9,845m., res 117,771m., dep. 1,804,443m. (March 2011); Chair. and Man. Dir R. M. MALLA; 5 zonal offices and 36 br. offices.

Small Industries Development Bank of India: SIDBI Tower, 15 Ashok Marg, Lucknow 226 001; tel. (522) 2288547; fax (522) 2288548; e-mail cmdsecttlho@sidbi.com; internet www.sidbi.in; f. 1990; wholly owned subsidiary of IDBI; promotes, finances and develops small-scale industries; cap. 4,500m., res 53,872.7m., dep. 144,734m. (March 2011); Chair. and Man. Dir SUSHIL MUHNOT; 39 offices.

IFCI Ltd: IFCI Tower, 61 Nehru Place, New Delhi 110 019; tel. (11) 41792800; fax (11) 26488471; e-mail helpdesk@ifciltd.com; internet www.ifciltd.com; f. 1948, as Industrial Finance Corpn of India; renamed as above in 1999; CEO and Man. Dir ATUL K. RAI.

Industrial Investment Bank of India: 19 Netaji Subhas Rd, Kolkata 700 001; tel. (33) 22209941; fax (33) 22208049; e-mail iibiho@vsnl.com; Chair. and Man. Dir BHASKAR SEN; Exec. Dir V. K. DHINGRA.

National Bank for Agriculture and Rural Development: Plot C-24, G Blk, Bandra-Kurla Complex, Bandra (East), Mumbai 400 051; tel. (22) 26525068; fax (22) 26530050; e-mail contact@nabard.org; internet www.nabard.org; f. 1982; est. to provide credit for agricultural and rural devt through commercial, co-operative and regional rural banks; cap. p.u. 20,000m., res 52,910m. (March 2004); held 50% each by cen. Govt and Reserve Bank; Man. Dir K. G. KARMAKAR; Chair. RAKESH SINGH; 28 regional offices, 10 sub-offices and 6 training establishments.

STOCK EXCHANGES

There are 23 stock exchanges (with a total of more than 9,985 listed companies) in India, including:

National Stock Exchange of India Ltd: Exchange Plaza, Bandra-Kurla Complex, Bandra (East), Mumbai 400 051; tel. (22) 26598100; fax (22) 26598120; e-mail cc_nse@nse.co.in; internet www.nseindia.com; f. 1994; New York Stock Exchange, Goldman Sachs, General Atlantic (all of the USA) and SoftBank Asian Infrastructure Fund (Hong Kong) each acquired a 5% share in Jan. 2007; Chair. S. B. MATHUR; Man. Dir RAVI NARAIN.

Ahmedabad Stock Exchange: Kamdhenu Complex, opp. Sahajanand College, Panjarapole, Ambawadi, Ahmedabad 380 015; tel. (79) 26307971; fax (79) 26308877; e-mail info@aselindia.org; internet www.aselindia.org; f. 1894; 2,000 mems; Administrator P. K. GHOSH; Exec. Dir V. V. RAO.

Bangalore Stock Exchange Ltd: 51 Stock Exchange Towers, 1st Cross, J. C. Rd, Bangalore 560 027; tel. (80) 41575234; fax (80) 41575232; e-mail bgse@bgse.co.in; internet www.bgse.co.in; 241 mems; Chair. A. MURALI; Exec. Dir V. RAVI KUMAR.

Bombay Stock Exchange: Phiroze Jeejeebhoy Towers, 25th Floor, Dalal St, Fort, Mumbai 400 001; tel. (22) 22721233; fax (22) 22721919; e-mail info@bseindia.com; internet www.bseindia.com; f. 1875; 4,482 listed cos; Chair. JAGDISH CAPOOR; Man. Dir and CEO MADHU KANNAN.

Calcutta Stock Exchange Association Ltd: 7 Lyons Range, Kolkata 700 001; tel. (33) 22104470; fax (33) 22104486; e-mail cseadmn@cse-india.com; internet www.cse-india.com; f. 1908; 917 mems; Chair. UDAYAN BOSE; Man. Dir and CEO MOLLY THAMBI.

Delhi Stock Exchange Association Ltd: DSE House, 3/1 Asaf Ali Rd, New Delhi 110 002; tel. (11) 23292182; fax (11) 23292174; e-mail info@dseindia.org.in; internet www.dseindia.org.in; f. 1947; some 3,000 listed cos (March 2007); Exec. Dir H. S. SIDHU.

Ludhiana Stock Exchange Association Ltd: Feroze Gandhi Market, Ludhiana 141 001; tel. (161) 4612317; fax (161) 2401645; e-mail lse@satyam.net.in; internet lse.co.in; f. 1981; 292 mems; Chair. PADAM PARKASH KANSAL.

Madras Stock Exchange Ltd: Exchange Bldg, 30 Second Line Beach, POB 183, Chennai 600 001; tel. (44) 25228951; fax (44) 25244897; e-mail info@mseindia.in; internet www.madrasstockexchange.in; f. 1937; 210 mems; Co Sec. V. BALASUBRAMONIAM.

Uttar Pradesh Stock Exchange Association Ltd: Padam Towers, 14/113 Civil Lines, Kanpur 208 001; tel. (512) 2293115; fax (512) 2293175; e-mail upse@vsnl.net.in; 540 mems; Pres. R. K. AGARWAL; Exec. Dir Dr J. N. GUPTA.

The other recognized stock exchanges are: Hyderabad, Madhya Pradesh (Indore), Kochi, Pune, Guwahati, Jaipur, Bhubaneswar (Odisha), Coimbatore, Saurashtra, Meerut, Vadodara and Magadh (Patna).

INSURANCE

In January 1973 all Indian and foreign insurance companies were nationalized. The Insurance Regulatory and Development Authority Bill, approved by the legislature in December 1999, established a regulatory authority for the insurance sector and henceforth permitted up to 26% investment by foreign companies in new domestic, private sector insurance companies.

Bajaj Allianz: GE Plaza, Airport Rd, Yerawada, Pune 411 006; tel. (20) 30587888; fax (20) 40111502; e-mail info@bajajallianz.co.in; internet www.bajajallianz.com; f. 2001; life and general insurance; private sector; Chair. RAHUL BAJAJ; Man. Dir and CEO HEMANT KAUL.

General Insurance Corpn of India (GIC): 'Suraksha', 170 J. Tata Rd, Churchgate, Mumbai 400 020; tel. (22) 22867000; fax (22) 22899600; e-mail info@gicofindia.com; internet www.gicofindia.com; f. 1972; Chair. and Man. Dir YOGESH LOHIYA.

HDFC ERGO General: 6th Floor, Leela Business Park, Andheri Kurla Rd, Andheri (East), Mumbai 400 059; tel. (22) 66383600; fax (22) 66383699; e-mail care@hdfcergo.com; internet www.hdfcergo.com; f. 2002; general insurance; private sector; Chair. DEEPAK S. PAREKH; Man. Dir and CEO RITESH KUMAR; 78 brs.

ICICI Lombard: 401 and 402, Interface Bldg, 11 Link Rd, Malad (West), Mumbai 400 064; internet www.icicilombard.com; f. 2001; general insurance; private sector; Chair. CHANDA KOCHHAR; Man. Dir and CEO BHARGAV DASGUPTA; 350 brs.

ICICI Prudential: ICICI Pru Life Towers, 1,089 Appasaheb Marathe Marg, Prabhadevi, Mumbai 400 025; tel. (22) 40391600; e-mail lifeline@iciciprulife.com; internet www.iciciprulife.com; f. 2000; life insurance; private sector; Chair. CHANDA KOCHHAR; Man. Dir and CEO SANDEEP BAKHSHI.

IFFCO—Tokio: IFFCO Tower, 4th and 5th Floors, Plot 3, Sector 29, Gurgaon 122 001; internet www.iffcotokio.co.in; f. 2000; general insurance; private sector; Man. Dir S. NARAYANAN.

Life Insurance Corpn of India (LIC): 'Yogakshema', Jeevan Bima Marg, Mumbai 400 021; tel. (22) 26137545; fax (22) 22810680; e-mail co_pgs@licindia.com; internet www.licindia.in; f. 1956; leading insurance co; public sector; Chair. T. S. VIJAYAN; Man. Dirs THOMAS MATTHEW, A. K. DASGUPTA, D. K. MEHROTRA; 109 divisional offices, 2,048 brs, 8 zonal offices and 992 satellite offices.

National Insurance Co Ltd: 3 Middleton St, Kolkata 700 071; tel. (33) 22831705; fax (33) 22831712; e-mail website.administrator@nic.co.in; internet www.nationalinsuranceindia.com; f. 1906; general insurance; public sector; Chair. and Man. Dir N. S. R. CHANDRA PRASAD; 1,000 brs.

New India Assurance Co Ltd: 87 Mahatma Gandhi Rd, Fort, Mumbai 400 001; tel. (22) 22708220; fax (22) 22652811; e-mail cmd.nia@newindia.co.in; internet www.newindia.co.in; f. 1919; general insurance; public sector; 26 regional offices, 393 divisional offices, 614 br. offices, 34 direct agent brs and 19 overseas brs; Chair. and Man. Dir A. R. SEKAR (acting).

The Oriental Insurance Co Ltd: Oriental House, A-25/27 Asaf Ali Rd, New Delhi 110 002; tel. (11) 23279221; internet www.orientalinsurance.org.in; general insurance; public sector; Chair. and Man. Dir Dr R. K. KAUL.

Sahara India Life Insurance Co Ltd: Sahara India Centre, 2 Kapoorthala Complex, Lucknow 226 024; tel. (522) 2337777; fax (522) 2332683; e-mail life@life.sahara.co.in; internet www.saharalife.com; f. 2004; was the first wholly Indian-owned insurance co; pvt sector; Chair. SUBRATA ROY SAHARA; Dir and CEO N. P. BALI.

SBI Life Insurance Co Ltd: Natraj, M.V. Rd and Western Express Highway Junction, Andheri (East), Mumbai 400 069; e-mail info@sbilife.co.in; internet www.sbilife.co.in; f. 2001; jt venture between State Bank of India and BNP Paribas Assurance; Man. Dir and CEO M. N. RAO; 430 brs.

United India Insurance Co Ltd: 24 Whites Rd, Chennai 600 014; tel. (44) 28520161; internet www.uiic.co.in; f. 1938; general insurance; public sector; Chair. and Man. Dir G. SRINIVASAN GARG; 1,340 brs.

Trade and Industry

GOVERNMENT AGENCIES AND DEVELOPMENT ORGANIZATIONS

Coal India Ltd: 10 Netaji Subhas Rd, Kolkata 700 001; tel. (33) 22488099; fax (33) 22435316; e-mail chairman@coalindia.in; internet www.coalindia.in; f. 1975; cen. govt holding co with 8 subsidiaries; responsible for almost total (more than 90%) exploration for, planning and production of coal mines; owns 471 coal mines throughout India; marketing of coal and its products; cap. p.u. Rs 63,163.6m., net sales Rs 32,6338.6m. (2007/08); Chair. and Man. Dir ZOHRA CHATTERJI; 383,347 employees (2012).

Cotton Corpn of India Ltd: Plot No. 3A, Sector No. 10, CBD Belapur, Navi Mumbai 400 614; tel. (22) 27579217; fax (22) 27576030; e-mail headoffice@cotcorp.com; internet www.cotcorp.gov.in; f. 1970 as an agency in the public sector for the purchase, sale and distribution of home-produced cotton and imported cotton staple fibre; exports long staple cotton; cap. p.u. Rs 250m., res and surplus Rs 2772.0m., sales Rs 16,386.1m. (2007/08); Chair. and Man. Dir B. K. MISHRA.

Export Credit Guarantee Corpn of India Ltd (ECGC): Express Towers, 10th Floor, Nariman Point, POB 11677, Mumbai 400 021; tel. (22) 66590500; fax (22) 66590517; e-mail webmaster@ecgc.in; internet www.ecgc.in; f. 1957 to insure for risks involved in exports on credit terms and to supplement credit facilities by issuing guarantees, etc.; cap. Rs 9,000.0m., res Rs 9134.2m. (2007/08); Chair. and Man. Dir N. SHANKAR; 29 brs.

Fertilizer Corpn of India Ltd: A-14, 5th Floor, PDIL Bhavan, Sector 1, Noida 201 301; tel. (120) 2530023; fax (120) 2537613; e-mail fertcorpindia@nic.in; internet fertcorpindia.nic.in; f. 1961; fertilizer factories at Sindri (Jharkhand), Gorakhpur (Uttar Pradesh), Talcher (Odisha) and Ramagundam (Andhra Pradesh), producing nitrogenous and some industrial products; cap. Rs 7,547.3m., sales Rs 1,262m. (March 2002).

Food Corpn of India: DDA Complex, Ground Floor, Rajendra Pl., Rajendra Bhavan, New Delhi 110 008; tel. (11) 25710962; fax (11) 25750670; e-mail fci-gmhq@lsmgr.nic.in; internet www.fciweb.nic.in; f. 1965 to undertake trading in food grains on a commercial scale but within the framework of an overall govt policy; to provide farmers an assured price for their produce; to supply food grains to the consumer at reasonable prices; also purchases, stores, distributes and sells food grains and other foodstuffs and arranges imports and handling of food grains and fertilizers at the ports; distributes sugar in a number of states and has set up rice mills; Man. Dir SIRAJ HUSSAIN; 59,800 employees (2002).

Handicrafts and Handlooms Exports Corpn of India Ltd: Jawahar Vyapar Bhavan Annexe, 5th Floor, 1 Tolstoy Marg, New Delhi 110 001; tel. (11) 23701086; fax (11) 23701051; e-mail hhecnd@bol.net.in; internet www.hhecworld.com; f. 1958; govt undertaking dealing in export of handicrafts, handloom goods, ready-to-wear clothes, carpets, jute, leather and precious jewellery, and import of bullion and raw silk; promotes exports and trade development; cap. p.u. Rs 138.2m. (2007/08); Chair. and Man. Dir NIRMAL SINHA.

Housing and Urban Development Corpn Ltd: HUDCO Bhavan, India Habitat Centre, Lodhi Rd, New Delhi 110 003; tel. (11) 24649610; fax (11) 24625308; e-mail mail@hudco.org; internet www.hudco.org; f. 1970 to finance and undertake housing and urban development programmes including the establishment of new or satellite towns and building material industries; cap. p.u. Rs 20,019.0m., res Rs 17,735.0m., sales Rs 37,359.9m. (Jan. 2007); 21 brs; Chair. and Man. Dir V. P. BALIGAR.

India Trade Promotion Organisation (ITPO): Pragati Bhavan, Pragati Maidan, Lal Bahadur Shastri Marg, New Delhi 110 001; tel. (11) 23371540; fax (11) 23371492; e-mail info@itpo-online.com; internet www.indiatradefair.com; f. 1992 following merger; promotes selective development of exports of high quality products; arranges investment in export-orientated ventures undertaken by India with foreign collaboration; organizes trade fairs; operates Trade Information Centre; cap. p.u. Rs 2.5m., res and surplus Rs 2,311.8m., sales Rs 818.4m. (March 2002); regional offices in Bangalore, Mumbai, Kolkata and Chennai, and international offices in Frankfurt, New York, Moscow, São Paulo and Tokyo; Chair. and Man. Dir RITA MENON; Exec. Dir NEERAJ KUMAR GUPTA.

Jute Corpn of India Ltd: 15-N, Nellie Sengupta Sarani, 7th Floor, Kolkata 700 087; tel. (33) 22527027; fax (33) 22526771; e-mail jutecorp@vsnl.net; internet www.jci.gov.in; f. 1971; objects: (i) to undertake price support operations in respect of raw jute; (ii) to ensure remunerative prices to producers through efficient marketing; (iii) to operate a buffer stock to stabilize raw jute prices; (iv) to handle the import and export of raw jute; (v) to promote the export of jute goods; cap. p.u. Rs 50.0m., sales Rs 1193.8m. (2006/07); Chair. and Man. Dir ARUN KUMAR CHAKRABORTY.

Minerals and Metals Trading Corpn of India Ltd (MMTC): Scope Complex, Core-1, 7 Institutional Areas, Lodhi Rd, New Delhi 110 003; tel. (11) 24362200; fax (11) 24360724; e-mail cpmr@mmtclimited.com; internet www.mmtclimited.com; f. 1963; export of iron and manganese ore, ferro-manganese, finished stainless steel products, engineering, agricultural and marine products, textiles, leather items, chemicals and pharmaceuticals, mica, coal and other minor minerals; import of steel, non-ferrous metals, rough diamonds, fertilizers, etc. for supply to industrial units in the country; sales Rs 265,030.0m.; res Rs 9,800.0m. (2007/08); 13 regional offices in India; foreign offices in Japan, the Republic of Korea, Jordan and Romania; Chair. and Man. Dir SANJIV BATRA; 2,378 employees (2002).

National Co-operative Development Corpn: 4 Siri Institutional Area, Hauz Khas, New Delhi 110 016; tel. (11) 26569246; fax (11) 26962370; e-mail editor@ncdc.in; f. 1963 to plan, promote and finance country-wide programmes through co-operative societies for the production, processing, marketing, storage, export and import of agricultural produce, foodstuffs and notified commodities and minor forest produce; also programmes for the development of poultry, dairy, fish products, coir, handlooms, distribution of consumer articles in rural areas, industrial and service co-operatives, water conservation work, irrigation, micro-irrigation, animal care, health, disease prevention, agricultural insurance and credit, rural sanitation etc.; 18 regional directorates; Pres. SHARAD PAWAR; Dir V. K SURI.

National Mineral Development Corpn Ltd: Khanij Bhavan, 10-3-311/A Castle Hills, Masab Tank, POB 1352, Hyderabad 500 028; tel. (40) 23538713; fax (40) 23538711; e-mail hois@nmdc.co.in; internet www.nmdc.co.in; f. 1958; cen. govt undertaking; to exploit minerals (excluding coal, atomic minerals, lignite, petroleum and natural gas) in public sector; may buy, take on lease or otherwise acquire mines for prospecting, development and exploitation; iron ore mines at Bailadila-11C, Bailadila-14 and Bailadila-5 in Madhya Pradesh, and at Donimalai in Karnataka State; new 5m. metric ton iron ore mine under construction at Bailadila-10/11A; diamond mines at Panna in Madhya Pradesh; research and development laboratories and consultancy services covering all aspects of mineral exploitation at Hyderabad; investigates mineral projects; cap. p.u. Rs 1,321.6m., res and surplus Rs 81,574.9m., sales Rs 57,091.6m. (March 2008); Chair. and Man. Dir N. K. NANDA.

National Productivity Council: Utpadakta Bhavan, 5–6 Institutional Area, Lodhi Rd, New Delhi 110 003; tel. (11) 24690331; fax (11) 24615002; e-mail info@npcindia.org; internet www.npcindia.org; f. 1958 to increase productivity and to improve quality by improved techniques which aim at efficient and proper utilization of available resources; autonomous body representing national orgs of employers and labour, govt ministries, professional orgs, local productivity councils, small-scale industries and other interests; 13 regional professional management groups, one training institute; 75 mems; Chair. AJAY SHANKAR; Sec. G. S. KRISHNAN.

National Research Development Corpn: 20–22 Zamroodpur Community Centre, Kailash Colony Extension, New Delhi 110 048; tel. (11) 29240401; fax (11) 29240409; e-mail write2@nrdcindia.com; internet www.nrdcindia.com; f. 1953 to stimulate development and commercial exploitation of new inventions with financial and technical aid; finances development projects to set up demonstration units in collaboration with industry; exports technology; cap. p.u. Rs 44.2m., res and surplus Rs 47.6m. (March 2002); Chair. and Man. Dir SOMENATH GHOSH.

National Seeds Corpn Ltd: Beej Bhavan, Pusa, New Delhi 110 012; tel. (11) 25846292; fax (11) 25846462; e-mail nsc@indiaseeds.com; internet www.indiaseeds.com; f. 1963 to improve and develop the seed industry; cap. p.u. Rs 206.2m., res and surplus Rs 20.8m., sales Rs 1,532.6m. (March 2007); Chair. and Man. Dir S. K. ROONGTA.

National Small Industries Corpn Ltd: NSIC Bhavan, Okhla Industrial Estate, New Delhi 110 020; tel. (11) 26926275; fax (11) 26932075; e-mail pro@nsic.co.in; internet www.nsic.co.in; f. 1955 to aid, advise, finance and promote the interests of small industries; establishes and supplies machinery for small industries in other developing countries on turnkey basis; cap. p.u. Rs 2,329.9m., res and surplus Rs 150.2m., sales Rs 4,022.9m. (March 2008); all shares held by the Govt; Chair. and Man. Dir H. P. KUMAR.

PEC Ltd: 'Hansalaya', 15 Barakhamba Rd, New Delhi 110 001; tel. (11) 23316397; fax (11) 23314797; e-mail pec@peclimited.com; internet www.peclimited.com; f. 1971; export of engineering, industrial and railway equipment; undertakes turnkey and other projects and management consultancy abroad; countertrade, trading in agrocommodities, construction materials (steel, cement, clinkers, etc.) and fertilizers; cap. p.u. Rs 20.0m., res and surplus Rs 1,240.7m., sales Rs 56,715.6m. (March 2008); Chair. and Man. Dir A. K. MIRCHANDANI.

Power Finance Corpn Ltd: Urjanidhi Bldg, 1 Barakhamba Lane, Connaught Pl., New Delhi 110 001; tel. (11) 23456000; internet www.pfcindia.com; f. 1986; provides funding for power sector projects; Chair. SATNAM SINGH.

State Farms Corpn of India Ltd: Farm Bhavan, 14–15 Nehru Place, New Delhi 110 019; tel. (11) 26446903; fax (11) 26226898; e-mail sfci-moa@nic.in; internet sfci.nic.in; f. 1969 to administer the central state farms; activities include the production of quality seeds of high-yielding varieties of wheat, paddy, maize, bajra and jowar; advises on soil conservation, reclamation and development of waste and forest land; consultancy services on farm mechanization; auth. cap. Rs 1,486.1m., res and surplus Rs 638.0m., sales Rs 1,952.7m. (March 2009); Chair. and Man. Dir Brig. VINOD KUMAR GAUR.

State Trading Corpn of India Ltd: Jawahar Vyapar Bhavan, Tolstoy Marg, New Delhi 110 001; tel. (11) 23313177; fax (11) 23701191; e-mail co.stc@gov.in; internet stc.gov.in; f. 1956; govt undertaking dealing in exports and imports; cap. p.u. Rs 600.0m., res and surplus Rs 4,648.8m., sales Rs 155,741.2m. (March 2008); 10 regional brs, 6 sub-brs and 1 office overseas; Chair. and Man. Dir N. K. MATHUR; 1,069 employees (2002).

Steel Authority of India Ltd (SAIL): Ispat Bhavan, Lodhi Rd, POB 3049, New Delhi 110 003; tel. (11) 24367481; fax (11) 24367015; e-mail sail.co@vsnl.com; internet www.sail.co.in; f. 1973 to provide co-ordinated development of the steel industry in the public sector; integrated steel plants at Bhilai, Bokaro, Durgapur, Rourkela; stainless and alloy steel plants at Chhattisgarh, West Bengal, Odisha, Jharkhand, Tamil Nadu and Karnataka; five jt venture power- and steel-related cos; 86% govt-owned; subsidiaries: Bhilai Oxygen Ltd (Chhattisgarh), Indian Iron and Steel Co (West Bengal), Maharashtra Elektrosmelt Ltd; combined crude steel capacity is 12m. metric tons annually; equity cap. Rs 41,300m., res and surplus Rs 188,874m., sales Rs 455,550m. (March 2008); Chair. CHANDRA SHEKHAR VERMA; 131,910 employees (March 2004).

Tea Board of India: 14 B. T. M. Sarani (Brabourne Rd), POB 2172, Kolkata 700 001; tel. (33) 22351411; fax (33) 22215715; internet teaboard.gov.in; provides financial assistance to tea research stations; sponsors and finances independent research projects in universities and tech. institutions to supplement the work of tea research establishments; also promotes tea production and export; Chair. M. G. V. K. BHANU.

CHAMBERS OF COMMERCE

Associated Chambers of Commerce and Industry of India (ASSOCHAM): 1 Community Centre, Zamrudpur Kailash Colony, New Delhi 110 048; tel. (11) 46550555; fax (11) 46536481; e-mail assocham@nic.in; internet www.assocham.org; f. 1920; central org. of 350 chambers of commerce and industry and industrial asscns representing more than 100,000 cos throughout India; five promoter chambers, 115 ordinary mems, 45 patron mems and 500 corporate associates; Pres. SWATI PIRAMAL; Sec.-Gen. D. S. RAWAT.

Federation of Indian Chambers of Commerce and Industry (FICCI): Federation House, Tansen Marg, New Delhi 110 001; tel. (11) 23738760; fax (11) 23320714; e-mail ficci@ficci.com; internet www.ficci.com; f. 1927; more than 1,500 corporate mems, 500 chamber of commerce and business asscn mems; Pres. RAJAN BHARTI MITTAL; Sec.-Gen. Dr AMIT MITRA.

ICC India: Federation House, Tansen Marg, New Delhi 110 001; tel. (11) 23322472; fax (11) 23320714; e-mail iccindia@iccindiaonline.org; internet www.iccindiaonline.org; f. 1929; 43 org. mems, 375 corporate mems, 8 patron mems, 130 cttee mems; Pres. SUSHIL KUMAR JIWARAJKA; Exec. Dir AMIT MITRA.

Associated Chambers of Commerce and Industry of Uttar Pradesh: 2/302 Vikas Khand, Gomti Nagar, POB 17, Lucknow 226 010; tel. (522) 2301957; fax (522) 2301958; e-mail asochamup@yahoo.com; internet asochamup.org.in; f. 1994; 405 mems; Pres. ANIL RATHI; Sec.-Gen. S. B. AGRAWAL.

Bengal Chamber of Commerce and Industry: 6 Netaji Subhas Rd, Kolkata 700 001; tel. (33) 22303711; fax (33) 22301289; e-mail bencham@bengalchamber.com; internet www.bengalchamber.com; f. 1853; more than 270 mems; Pres. SANDIPAN CHAKRABORTY.

Bengal National Chamber of Commerce and Industry: BNCCI House, 23 Sir R. N. Mukherjee Rd, Kolkata 700 001; tel. (33) 22482951; fax (33) 22487058; e-mail bncci@bncci.com; internet www.bncci.com; f. 1887; 500 mems, 35 affiliated industrial and trading asscns; Pres. SUNIL DASGUPTA; Sec. D. P. NAG.

Bharat Chamber of Commerce: 9 Park Mansions, 2nd Floor, 57-A Park Street, Kolkata 700 016; tel. (33) 22299591; fax (33) 22294947; e-mail bcc@cal2.vsnl.net.in; internet www.bharatcham.com; f. 1900; c. 500 mems; Pres. PAVAN PODDAR; Sec.-Gen. K. SARMA.

Bihar Chamber of Commerce: Judges Court Rd, Patna 800 001; tel. (612) 2673505; fax (612) 2689505; e-mail bcc_chamber@rediffmail.com; f. 1926; 552 ordinary mems; Pres. O. P. SAH.

Bombay Chamber of Commerce and Industry: Mackinnon Mackenzie Bldg, 4 Shoorji Vallabhdas Rd, Ballard Estate, POB 473, Mumbai 400 001; tel. (22) 22614681; fax (22) 22621213; e-mail einfo@bombaychamber.com; internet www.bombaychamber.com; f. 1836; 935 ordinary mems, 650 assoc. mems, 75 hon. mems; Pres. RAVIJ B. LALL; Vice-Pres. BHARAT DOSHI.

Calcutta Chamber of Commerce: 18H Park St, Stephen Court, Kolkata 700 071; tel. (33) 22290758; fax (33) 22298236; e-mail calchamb@bsnl.in; internet www.calcuttachamber.com; 300 mems; Pres. ALKA BANGUR; Sr Vice-Pres. R. K. CHHAJER.

Chamber of Commerce and Industry (Regd): OB 31, Rail Head Complex, Jammu 180 012; tel. (191) 2472266; fax (191) 2472255; e-mail ccijammu@yahoo.com; f. 1932; 1,069 mems; Pres. Y. V. SHARMA; Sec.-Gen. SATISH GUPTA.

Cochin Chamber of Commerce and Industry: Bristow Rd, Willingdon Island, POB 503, Kochi 682 003; tel. (484) 2668650; fax (484) 2668651; e-mail cochinchamber@eth.net; internet www.cochinchamber.org; f. 1857; 206 mems; Pres. ANAND MENON; Vice-Pres. P. NARAYANAN.

Delhi Chamber of Commerce: 49 Rani Jhansi Rd, New Delhi 110055; tel. (11) 23616421; fax (11) 23628847; e-mail dccnd@nda.vsnl.net.in; internet www.delhichamber.com; f. 1949; Pres. S. K. MITTAL; Sec.-Gen. RAVINDER S. SODHBANS.

Federation of Andhra Pradesh Chambers of Commerce and Industry: Federation House, 11-6-841, Red Hills, POB 14, Hyderabad 500 004; tel. (40) 23395515; fax (40) 23395525; e-mail info@fapcci.in; internet www.fapcci.in; f. 1917; 2,940 mems; Pres. SHEKHAR AGARWAL; Sec. V. S. RAJU.

Federation of Karnataka Chambers of Commerce and Industry: Federation House, K. G. Rd, POB 9996, Bangalore 560 009; tel. (80) 22262355; fax (80) 22251826; e-mail president@fkcci.in; internet www.fkcci.org; f. 1916; 2,100 mems; Pres. N. S. SRINIVASA MURTHY; Vice Pres. J. R. BANGERA.

Federation of Madhya Pradesh Chambers of Commerce and Industry: Udyog Bhavan, 129A Malviya Nagar, Bhopal 462 003; tel. (755) 2573612; fax (755) 2551451; e-mail fmpcci@yahoo.co.in; internet fmpcci.com; f. 1975; 500 ordinary mems, 58 asscn mems; Pres. RANJIT VITHALDAS.

Goa Chamber of Commerce and Industry: Narayan Rajaram Bandekar Bhavan, Rua de Ormuz, POB 59, Panaji 403 001; tel. (832) 2422635; fax (832) 2425560; e-mail goachamber@goachamber.org; internet www.goachamber.org; f. 1908 as Associacao Commercial da India Portuguesa; more than 500 mems; Pres. MANGUIRISH PAI RAIKAR; Dir-Gen. Air Cmmdr (retd) P. K. PINTO.

Gujarat Chamber of Commerce and Industry: Shri Ambica Mills, Gujarat Chamber Bldg, Ashram Rd, POB 4045, Ahmedabad 380 009; tel. (79) 26582301; fax (79) 26587992; e-mail gcci@gujaratchamber.org; internet www.gujaratchamber.org; f. 1949; 7,713 mems; Pres. CHINTANBHAI N. PARIKH; Sr Vice-Pres. MAHENDRABHAI N. PATEL.

Indian Chamber of Commerce: ICC Towers, 4 India Exchange Place, Kolkata 700 001; tel. (33) 22203242; fax (33) 22213377; e-mail info@indianchamber.net; internet www.indianchamber.org; f. 1925; 500 corporate group mems, more than 1,200 mem. cos; Pres. JAYANTA ROY; Dir-Gen. Dr RAJEEV SINGH.

Indian Chamber of Commerce and Industry—Cochin: POB 236, Indian Chamber Rd, Mattancherry, Kochi 682002; tel. (484) 2224335; fax (484) 2224203; e-mail info@iccicochin.com; internet www.iccicochin.com; f. 1897; Sec. RAMAKRISHNAN S.

Indian Merchants' Chamber: IMC Bldg, IMC Marg, Churchgate, Mumbai 400 020; tel. (22) 22046633; fax (22) 22048508; e-mail imc@imcnet.org; internet www.imcnet.org; f. 1907; 185 asscn mems, 2,915 mem. firms; Pres. DILIP DANDEKAR; Sec.-Gen. ARVIND PRADHAN.

Karnataka Chamber of Commerce and Industry: G. Mahadevappa Karnataka Chamber Bldg, Jayachamraj Nagar, Hubli 580 020; tel. (836) 2218234; fax (836) 2360933; e-mail kccihble@sify.com; internet www.kccihubli.org; f. 1928; 2,500 mems; Pres. MRUTYUNJAY HIREMATH; Hon. Sec. KARABASAPPA KOTEKAR.

Madhya Pradesh Chamber of Commerce and Industry: Chamber Bhavan, Sanatan Dharam Mandir Marg, Gwalior 474 009; tel. (751) 2382917; fax (751) 2323844; e-mail info@mpcci.com; internet www.mpcci.com; f. 1906; 1,705 mems; Pres. VISHNUPRASAD GARG; Hon. Sec. BHUPENDRA JAIN.

Madras Chamber of Commerce and Industry: Karumuttu Centre, 634 Anna Salai, Chennai 600 035; tel. (44) 24349452; fax (44) 24349164; e-mail madraschamber@madraschamber.in; internet www.madraschamber.in; f. 1836; 374 mem. firms, 20 affiliated, 8 hon.; Pres. T. T. SRINIVASARAGHAVAN; Sec.-Gen. K. SARASWATHI.

Maharashtra Chamber of Commerce, Industry and Agriculture: Oricon House, 6th Floor, 12 K. Dubhash Marg, Fort, Mumbai 400 001; tel. (22) 22855859; fax (22) 22855861; e-mail maccia@maccia.org.in; internet www.maccia.org.in; f. 1927; more than 3,500 mems;

more than 800 affiliated trade asscns and professional bodies; Pres. MANSINGH PAWAAR; Vice Pres. ASHISH PEDNEKAR.

Mahratta Chamber of Commerce, Industries and Agriculture: MCCIA Trade Tower, 505, A-Wing, ICC Complex, 403 Senapati Pabat Rd, Pune 411 016; tel. (20) 25709000; fax (20) 25709021; e-mail info@mcciapune.com; internet www.mcciapune.com; f. 1934; more than 2,000 mems; Pres. Dr ABHAY FIRODIA; Hon. Secs SATISH D. MAGAR, P. C. NAMBIAR.

Merchants' Chamber of Uttar Pradesh: 14/76 Civil Lines, Kanpur 208 001; tel. (512) 2530877; fax (512) 2531306; e-mail info@merchantschamber-up.com; internet www.merchantschamber-up.com; f. 1932; 222 mems; Pres. S. K. JHUNJHUNWALA; Sec. A. K. SINHA.

North India Chamber of Commerce and Industry: 9 Gandhi Rd, Dehra Dun; tel. (935) 223479; f. 1967; 105 ordinary mems, 29 asscn mems, seven mem. firms, 91 assoc. mems; Pres. DEV PANDHI; Hon. Sec. ASHOK K. NARANG.

Oriental Chamber of Commerce: 6A Dr Rajendra Prasad Sarani (Clive Row), Kolkata 700 001; tel. (33) 22302120; fax (33) 22303609; e-mail orientchamb@vsnl.net; f. 1932; 250 ordinary mems, 3 assoc. mems; Pres. N. D. MEHTA; Sec. Kazi ABU ZOBER.

PHD Chamber of Commerce and Industry (PHDCCI): PHD House, 4/2 Siri Institutional Area, August Kranti Marg, New Delhi 110 016; tel. (11) 26863801; fax (11) 26863135; e-mail phdcci@phdcci.in; internet www.phdcci.in; f. 1905; 1,760 mems, 150 asscn mems; Pres. SALIL BHANDARI; Sec.-Gen. KRISHAN KALRA.

Rajasthan Chamber of Commerce and Industry: Rajasthan Chamber Bhavan, M. I. Rd, Jaipur 302 002; tel. (141) 2565163; fax (141) 2561419; e-mail info@rajchamber.com; internet www.rajchamber.com; 575 mems; Pres. Dr MAHENDRA S. DAGA; Hon. Sec.-Gen. Dr K. L. JAIN.

Southern India Chamber of Commerce and Industry (SICCI): Indian Chamber Bldgs, 6 Esplanade, POB 1208, Chennai 600 108; tel. (44) 25342228; fax (44) 25341876; e-mail sicci@md3.vsnl.net.in; internet sicci.in; f. 1909; 1,000 mems; Pres. A. VELLAYAN; Sec. S. RAGHAVAN.

Upper India Chamber of Commerce: 113/47, Swaroop Nagar, POB 63, Kanpur 208 002; tel. (512) 2543905; fax (512) 2531684; f. 1888; 52 mems; Pres. DILIP BHARGAVA; Sec. S. P. SRIVASTAVA.

Utkal Chamber of Commerce and Industry Ltd: N/6, IRC Village, Nayapalli, Bhubaneswar 751 015; tel. (674) 3296035; fax (674) 2557598; e-mail contact@utkalchamber.com; internet utkalchamber.com; f. 1963; 250 mems; Pres. RAMESH MOHAPATRA; Hon. Sec. KHALID AHMED.

INDUSTRIAL AND TRADE ASSOCIATIONS

Ahmedabad Textile Mills' Association: Ashram Rd, Navrangpura, POB 4056, Ahmedabad 380 009; tel. (79) 26582273; fax (79) 26588574; e-mail shukla@atmaahd.com; f. 1891; 12 mems; Pres. CHINTAN N. PARIKH; Sec.-Gen. ABHINAVA SHUKLA.

All India Federation of Master Printers: 605 Madhuban, 6th Floor, 55 Nehru Place, New Delhi 110 019; tel. (11) 26451742; fax (11) 26451743; e-mail fopaid11@gmail.com; internet www.aifmp.com; f. 1953; 59 affiliates, 900 mems; Pres. RANJAN KUTHARI; Hon. Gen. Sec. ASOK KUMAR PAL.

All India Manufacturers' Organization (AIMO): Jeevan Sahakar, 4th Floor, Sir P.M. Rd, Fort, Mumbai 400 001; tel. (22) 22661016; fax (22) 22660838; e-mail aimoindia@mtnl.net.in; f. 1941; 800 mems; Pres. AMITKUMAR SEN; Sr Vice-Pres. JAGDISH TODI.

All India Plastics Manufacturers' Association: AIPMA House, A-52, St No. 1, MIDC, Andheri (East), Mumbai 400 093; tel. (22) 28216390; fax (22) 28252295; e-mail office@aipma.net; internet www.aipma.net; f. 1947; 2,500 mems; Pres. JAYESH RAMBHIA.

All India Shippers' Council: Federation House, Tansen Marg, New Delhi 110 001; tel. (11) 23487492; fax (11) 23320736; e-mail aisc.india@gmail.com; internet www.aisc.in; f. 1967; 82 mems; Chair. RAMU S. DEORA; CEO and Sec. MANAB MAJUMDAR.

Association of Man-made Fibre Industry of India: Resham Bhavan, 78 Veer Nariman Rd, Mumbai 400 020; tel. (22) 22040009; fax (22) 22049172; e-mail amfiirayon@hotmail.com; internet www.viscoserayonindia.com; f. 1954; seven mems; Pres. K. K. MAHESHWARI; Sec. M. P. JOSEPH.

Automotive Component Manufacturers' Association of India: 6th Floor, The Capital Court, Olof Palme Marg, Munirka, New Delhi 110 067; tel. (11) 26160315; fax (11) 26160317; e-mail acma@acma.in; internet www.acmainfo.com; 600 mems; Pres. ARVIND KAPUR; Exec. Dir VINNIE MEHTA.

Automotive Tyre Manufacturers' Association: PHD House, opp. Asian Games Village, Siri Fort Institutional Area, New Delhi 110 016; tel. (11) 26851187; fax (11) 26864799; e-mail atma@vsnl.in; internet www.atmaindia.org; f. 1975; 10 mems; Chair. NEERAJ KANWAR; Dir-Gen. RAJIV BUDHRAJA.

Bharat Krishak Samaj (Farmers' Forum, India): Dr Panjabrao Deshmukh Krishak Bhavan, A-1 Nizamuddin West, New Delhi 110 013; tel. (11) 46121708; fax (11) 24359509; e-mail ho@bks.org.in; internet www.farmersforum.in; f. 1954; national farmers' org.; 5m. ordinary mems, 100,000 life mems; Chair. AJAY JAKHAR; Pres. RAM NIWAS MIRDHA.

Bombay Metal Exchange Ltd: 1st Floor, 88/90 Kika St, Gulalwadi, Mumbai 400 004; tel. (22) 22421964; fax (22) 22422640; e-mail bme@bom8.vsnl.net.in; internet www.bme.in; f. 1950; promotes trade and industry in non-ferrous metals; 386 mems; Pres. ASHOK G. BAFNA; Sr Vice-Pres MAHENDRA H. SHAH.

Bombay Shroffs Association: 250 Sheikh Memon St, Mumbai 400 002; tel. (22) 23425588; f. 1910; 325 mems; Pres SEVANTILAL P. SHAH, KAMLESH C. SHAH.

Calcutta Tea Traders' Association: 6 Netaji Subhas Rd, Kolkata 700 001; tel. (33) 22301574; fax (33) 22301289; e-mail info@cttacal.org; internet www.cttacal.org; f. 1886; 1,300 mems; Chair. SANGEETA KICHLU; Vice-Chair. L. N. GUPTA.

Cement Manufacturers' Association: CMA Tower, A-2E, Sector 24, Noida 201 301; tel. (95120) 2411955; fax (95120) 2411956; e-mail cmand@vsnl.com; internet cmaindia.org; f. 1961; 54 mems; 126 major cement plants; Pres. M. A. M. R. MUTHIAH; Sec.-Gen. N. A. VISWANATHAN.

Confederation of Indian Industry (CII): 23 Institutional Area, Lodi Rd, New Delhi 110 003; tel. (11) 24629994; fax (11) 24626149; e-mail info@cii.in; internet www.cii.in; f. 1974; 7,500 mem. cos; Pres. B. MUTHURAMAN; Dir-Gen. CHANDRAJIT BANERJEE.

Consumer Electronics and Appliances Manufacturers' Association (CEAMA): 5th Floor, PHD House, 4/2 Siri Institutional Area, August Kranti Marg, New Delhi 110 016; tel. (11) 46070335; fax (11) 46070336; e-mail ceama@airtelmail.in; internet www.ceama.in; f. 1978; 106 mems; Pres. ANIRUDH V. DHOOT; Sec.-Gen. VIKAS MOHAN.

Cotton Association of India: 2nd Floor, Cotton Exchange Bldg, Cotton Green, Mumbai 400 033; tel. (22) 30063400; fax (22) 23700337; e-mail cai@caionline.in; internet www.caionline.in; f. 1921; 400 mems; Pres. DHIREN N. SHETH; Sec. AMAR SINGH.

Darjeeling Tea Association: Royal Exchange, 6 Netaji Subhas Rd, Kolkata 700 001; tel. and fax (33) 22102408; fax (33) 22102408; internet www.darjeelingtea.com; Chair. S. S. BAGARIA.

ELCINA Electronic Industries Association of India: ELCINA House, 422 Okhla Industrial Estate, New Delhi 110 020; tel. (11) 26924597; fax (11) 26923440; e-mail elcina@vsnl.com; internet www.elcina.com; f. 1967; fmrly Electronic Component Industries Association; 255 mems; Pres. T. VASU; Sec.-Gen. RAJOO GOEL.

Federation of Automobile Dealers Associations: 805 Surya Kiran, 19 Kasturba Gandhi Marg, New Delhi 110 001; tel. (11) 23320095; fax (11) 23320093; e-mail fada@airtelmail.in; internet www.fadaweb.com; f. 1964; Pres. NIKUNJ SANGHI; Hon. Sec. K. V. S PRAKASH RAO; 1,072 mems.

Federation of Gujarat Industries: Gotri-Sevasi Rd, Khanpur, Vadodara 390 101; tel. (265) 2372901; fax (265) 2372904; e-mail info@fgi.co.in; internet www.fgibaroda.com; f. 1918; 350 mems; Pres. GEETA GORADIA.

Federation of Hotel and Restaurant Associations of India (FHRAI): B-82 Himalaya House, 23 Kasturba Gandhi Marg, New Delhi 110 001; tel. (11) 40780780; fax (11) 40780777; e-mail fhrai@vsnl.com; internet www.fhrai.com; f. 1955; 3,961 mems; Pres. KAMLESH BAROT; Sec.-Gen. M. D. KAPOOR.

Federation of Indian Export Organisations: Niryat Bhavan, Rao Tula Ram Marg, opp. Army Hospital Research and Referral, New Delhi 110 057; tel. (11) 46042222; fax (11) 26148194; e-mail fieo@nda.vsnl.net.in; internet www.fieo.org; f. 1965; 8,000 mems; Pres. M. RAFEEQUE AHMED; Dir-Gen. G. BALACHANDHRAN.

Federation of Indian Mineral Industries (FIMI): B-311, Okhla Industrial Area, Phase 1, New Delhi 110 020; tel. (11) 26814596; fax (11) 26814593; e-mail fimi@fedmin.com; internet www.fedmin.com; f. 1966; 350 mems; Pres. P. K. MUKHERJEE.

The Fertiliser Association of India: 10 Shaheed Jit Singh Marg, New Delhi 110 067; tel. (11) 26567144; fax (11) 26960052; e-mail general@faidelhi.org; internet www.faidelhi.org; f. 1955; 1,414 mems; Chair. A. VELLAYEN; Dir-Gen. S. NAND.

Indian Drug Manufacturers' Association: 102B Poonam Chambers, Dr A. B. Rd, Worli, Mumbai 400 018; tel. (22) 24944624; fax (22) 24950723; e-mail idma1@idmaindia.com; internet www.idma-assn.org; f. 1961; 800 mems; Pres. MANISH U. DOSHI; Hon. Sec.-Gen. BAL KISHAN GUPTA.

Indian Electrical and Electronics Manufacturers' Association (IEEMA): 501 Kakad Chambers, 132 Dr Annie Besant Rd, Worli, Mumbai 400 018; tel. (22) 24930532; fax (22) 24932705; e-mail mumbai@ieema.org; internet www.ieema.org; f. 1948; 650 mems; Pres. RAMESH CHANDAK; Dir-Gen. P.V. KRISHNA.

Indian Jute Mills Association: Royal Exchange, 6 Netaji Subhas Rd, Kolkata 700 001; tel. (33) 22309918; fax (33) 22313836; e-mail ijma@cal2.vsnl.net.in; sponsors and operates export promotion, research and product development; regulates labour relations; 35 mems; Chair. MANISH PODDAR; Exec. Vice-Chair. S.K. BHATTACHARYA.

Indian Leather Products Association: Suite 6, Chatterjee International Centre, 14th Floor, 33-A, Jawaharlal Nehru Rd, Kolkata 700 071; tel. (33) 22267102; fax (33) 22468339; e-mail ilpa@cal2.vsnl.net.in; internet www.ilpaindia.org; 150 mems; Pres. DARSHAN SINGH SABHARWAL; Exec. Dir P. P. RAY CHAUDHURI.

Indian Machine Tool Manufacturers' Association: 10th Mile, Tumkur Rd, Madavara Post, Bangalore 562 123; tel. (80) 66246600; fax (80) 66246661; e-mail imtma@imtma.in; internet www.imtma.in; 400 mems; Pres. LOKESWARA RAO; Sec. and Exec. Dir V. ANBU.

Indian Motion Picture Producers' Association: IMPPA House, Dr Ambedkar Rd, Bandra (West), Mumbai 400 050; tel. (22) 26486344; fax (22) 26480757; e-mail imppa1937@gmail.com; f. 1938; 12,038 mems; Pres. T. P. AGGARWAL; Sec. DINKAR CHOWDHARY.

Indian National Shipowners' Association: 22 Maker Tower F, Cuffe Parade, Mumbai 400 005; tel. (22) 22182105; fax (22) 22182104; e-mail insa@insa.org.in; internet insa.in; f. 1929; 36 mems; Pres. S. HAJARA; Sec.-Gen. S. S. KULKARNI.

Indian Oilseeds & Produce Export Promotion Council (IOPEA): 78/79 Bajaj Bhavan, Nariman Point, Mumbai 400 021; tel. (22) 22023225; fax (22) 22029236; e-mail info@iopepc.org; internet www.iopepc.org; f. 1956; export promotion council; 350 mems; Chair. RAJESH BHEDA; CEO SURESH RAMRAKHIANI.

Indian Refractory Makers' Association: 5 Lala Lajpat Rai Sarani, 4th Floor, Kolkata 700 020; tel. (33) 22810868; fax (33) 22814357; e-mail irmaindia@hotmail.com; internet www.irmaindia.org; 85 mems; Chair. A. K. CHATTOPADHYAY; Exec. Dir P. DAS GUPTA.

Indian Soap and Toiletries Makers' Association: 614 Raheja Centre, 6th Floor, Free Press Journal Marg, Nariman Point, Mumbai 400 021; tel. (22) 22824115; fax (22) 22853649; e-mail istmamum@gmail.com; internet istma.internetindia.com/index.htm; f. 1937; 29 mems; Pres. GOPAL VITTAL; Sec.-Gen. O. P. AGARWAL.

Indian Sugar Mills' Association: 2nd Floor, Ansal Plaza, C-Blk, Andrews Ganj, New Delhi 110 049; tel. (11) 26262294; fax (11) 26263231; e-mail isma@indiansugar.com; internet www.indiansugar.com; f. 1932; 181 mems; Pres. GAUTAM GOEL.

Indian Tea Association: Royal Exchange, 6 Netaji Subhas Rd, Kolkata 700 001; tel. (33) 22102474; fax (33) 22434301; e-mail ita@indiatea.org; internet www.indiatea.org; f. 1881; 210 mem. cos; 420 tea estates; Chair. C. S. BEDI.

Indian Woollen Mills' Federation: Churchgate Chambers, 7th Floor, 5 New Marine Lines, Mumbai 400 020; tel. (22) 22624372; fax (22) 22624675; e-mail mail@iwmfindia.com; internet www.iwmfindia.com; f. 1963; 50 mems; Chair. RAJ K. KHANNA; Sec.-Gen. MAHESH N. SANIL.

Industries and Commerce Association: ICO Association Rd, POB 70, Dhanbad 826 001; tel. (326) 2303147; fax (326) 2303787; e-mail ica_dnb_1@hotmail.com; f. 1933; represents manufacturers of metallurgical coke; 78 mems; Pres. B. N. SINGH; Sec. PRADEEP CHATTERJEE.

Millowners' Association, Mumbai: Elphinstone Bldg, 10 Veer Nariman Rd, Fort, Mumbai 400 001; tel. (22) 22040411; fax (22) 22832611; f. 1875; 23 mem. cos; Chair. R. K. DALMIA; Sec.-Gen. V. Y. TAMHANE.

Mumbai Textile Merchants' Mahajan: 250 Sheikh Memon St, Mumbai 400 002; tel. (22) 22411686; fax (22) 22400311; f. 1879; 1,900 mems; Pres. SURENDRA TULSIDAS SAVAI.

National Association of Software and Service Companies (NASSCOM): International Youth Centre, Teen Murti Marg, Chanakyapuri, New Delhi 110 021; tel. (11) 23010199; fax (11) 23015452; e-mail info@nasscom.in; internet www.nasscom.in; 1,200 mems; Pres. SOM MITTAL; Chair. RAJENDRA SINGH PAWAR.

Organisation of Pharmaceutical Producers of India (OPPI): Peninsular Corporate Park, Peninsular Chambers, Ground Floor, Ganpatrao Kadam Marg, Lower Parel, Mumbai 400 013; tel. (22) 24918123; fax (22) 24915168; e-mail indiaoppi@vsnl.com; internet www.indiaoppi.com; f. 1965; 74 mems; Pres. RANJIT SHAHANI; Dir-Gen. TAPAN RAY.

Society of Indian Automobile Manufacturers: Core 4B, 5th Floor, India Habitat Centre, Lodhi Rd, New Delhi 110 003; tel. (11) 24647810; fax (11) 24648222; e-mail siam@vsnl.com; internet www.siamindia.com; f. 1960; 36 mems; Pres. S. SANDILYA; Dir-Gen. VISHNU MATHUR.

Southern India Mills' Association: 41 Race Course, Coimbatore 641 018; tel. (422) 2211391; fax (422) 4225366; e-mail info@simamills.com; internet www.simamills.com; f. 1933; 360 mems; Chair. S. DINAKARAN; Sec.-Gen. Dr K. SELVARAJAU.

Surgical Manufacturers' and Traders' Association: 60 Darya Ganj, New Delhi 110 002; tel. (11) 23271027; fax (11) 23258576; e-mail info@smta.in; internet www.smta.in; f. 1951; Pres. RAVI AWASTHI; Sec. S. B. SAWHNEY.

Synthetic and Art Silk Mills' Research Association Ltd (SASMIRA): Sasmira Bldg, Sasmira Marg, Worli, Mumbai 400 030; tel. (22) 24935351; fax (22) 24930225; e-mail sasmira@vsnl.com; internet www.sasmira.org; f. 1950; 100 mems; Pres. MAGANLAL H. DOSHI; Exec. Dir .K. GANGOPADHYAY.

Telecom Equipment Manufacturers' Association of India (TEMA): PHD House, 4th Floor, Khel Gaon Marg, Hauz Khas, New Delhi 110 016; tel. (11) 26859621; fax (11) 26859620; e-mail tema@eth.net; internet tematelecom.in; f. 1990; Pres. RAJIV MEHROTRA; Sec.-Gen. SANJAY BAKAYA.

Travel Agents' Association of India: 2D Lawrence and Mayo House, 276 Dr D. N. Rd, Mumbai 400 001; tel. (22) 22074022; fax (22) 40836767; e-mail taai@taai.in; internet www.travelagentsofindia.com; 1,692 mems; Pres. IQBAL MULLA; Hon. Sec.-Gen. R. SUNIL KUMAR.

The United Planters' Association of Southern India (UPASI): Glenview, POB 11, Coonoor 643 101; tel. (423) 2230270; fax (423) 2232030; e-mail upasi@upasi.org; internet www.upasi.org; f. 1893; 850 mems; Pres. D. HEGDE; Sec.-Gen. ULLAS MENON.

EMPLOYERS' ORGANIZATIONS

Council of Indian Employers: Federation House, Tansen Marg, New Delhi 110 001; tel. (11) 23316121; fax (11) 23320714; e-mail secretariat@aioe.com; f. 1956; Pres. SAROJ KUMAR PODDAR; comprises:

All India Organisation of Employers (AIOE): Federation House, Tansen Marg, New Delhi 110 001; tel. (11) 23316121; fax (11) 23320714; e-mail aioe@ficci.com; internet www.aioe.in; f. 1932; 50 affiliated asscns and 149 corporate mems; Pres. Dr JYOTSNA SURI; Exec. Dir Dr B. P. PANT.

Employers' Federation of India (EFI): Army and Navy Bldg, 148 Mahatma Gandhi Rd, Mumbai 400 001; tel. (22) 22844232; fax (22) 22843028; e-mail efisolar@mtnl.net.in; internet www.efionline.in; f. 1933; 28 asscn mems, 182 ordinary mems, 18 hon. mems; Pres. B. SANTHANAM; Sec.-Gen. SHARAD S. PATIL.

Standing Conference of Public Enterprises (SCOPE): 1st Floor, Core 8, SCOPE Complex, 7 Lodhi Rd, New Delhi 110 003; tel. (11) 24362604; fax (11) 24361371; e-mail scope_dg@yahoo.co.in; internet www.scopeonline.in; f. 1973; representative body of all central public enterprises in India; advises the Govt and public enterprises on matters of major policy and co-ordination; trade enquiries, regarding imports and exports of commodities, carried out on behalf of mems; 211 mems; Chair. ARUP ROY CHOUDHURY; Vice-Chair. K. L. DHINGRA.

Employers' Association of Northern India: 14/113 Civil Lines, POB 344, Kanpur 208 001; tel. (512) 2210513; f. 1937; 190 mems; Chair. RAJIV KEHR; Sec.-Gen. P. DUBEY.

Employers' Federation of Southern India: 33 Hindi Prachar Sabha St, T Nagar, Chennai 600 017; tel. (44) 24320801; fax (44) 24322750; e-mail efsi@vsnl.net; internet www.efsi.org.in; f. 1920; 735 mems; Pres. S. GOAPA KUMAR; Sec. T. M. JAWAHARLAL.

UTILITIES

Electricity

Central Electricity Authority (CEA): Sewa Bhavan, R. K. Puram, New Delhi 110 066; tel. (11) 26108476; fax (11) 26105619; e-mail cea-edp@hub.nic.in; internet www.cea.nic.in; responsible for technical co-ordination and supervision of electricity programmes; advises Ministry of Power on all technical, financial and economic issues; Chair. GURDIAL SINGH.

Bangalore Electricity Supply Co Ltd: K. R. Circle, 4th Floor, Bangalore 560 001; tel. (80) 22354939; e-mail gmca.work@gmail.com; internet www.bescom.org; Man. Dir P. MANIVANNAN.

Calcutta Electricity Supply Corpn Ltd (CESC): CESC House, Chouringhee Sq., Kolkata 700 001; tel. (33) 22256040; fax (33) 22256334; internet cesc.co.in; f. 1978; generation and supply of electricity; Chair. R. P. GOENKA; Man. Dir SUMANTRA BANERJEE.

Damodar Valley Corpn: DVC Towers, VIP Rd, Kolkata 700 054; tel. (33) 23551935; fax (33) 23551937; e-mail dvchq@wb.nic.in; internet www.dvcindia.org; f. 1948 to administer the first multipurpose river valley project in India, the Damodar Valley Project, which aims at unified development of irrigation, flood control and power generation in West Bengal and Jharkhand; operates nine power stations, incl. thermal, hydel and gas turbine; power generating capacity 3,070 MW (2010); Chair. DEVENDRA SINGH.

Essar Power Ltd: Essar House, 11 Keshavrao Khadye Marg, Mahalaxmi, Mumbai 400 034; tel. (22) 56601100; fax (22)

24954787; e-mail essarpower@essar.com; internet www.essar.com/power; Chair. S. N. Ruia; Man. Dir A. K. Srivastava.

Jaipur Vidyut Vitran Nigam Ltd: Vidyut Bhawan, Janpath, Jaipur 302 005; tel. (141) 2747064; internet www.jaipurdiscom.in; Chair. Kuldeep Ranka.

National Hydroelectric Power Corporation: Sector 33, Faridabad 121 003; tel. (129) 2278421; fax (129) 2277941; e-mail webmaster@nhpc.nic.in; internet www.nhpcindia.com; f. 1975; Chair and Man. Dir A. B. L. Srivastava.

Noida Power Co Ltd: Commercial Complex, H Blk, Alpha Sector II, Greater Noida 201 308; tel. (120) 2326559; fax (120) 2326448; e-mail npcl@noidapower.com; internet www.noidapower.com; f. 1993; distribution of electricity; Chair. and Man. Dir Usha Chatrath; CEO P. Neogi.

NTPC Ltd: Core-7, SCOPE Complex, Lodhi Rd, New Delhi 110 003; tel. (11) 24360100; fax (11) 24361018; e-mail info@ntpc.co.in; internet www.ntpc.co.in; f. 1975 as National Thermal Power Corpn; renamed as above 2005; operates 11 coal-fired and five gas-fired power stations throughout India; Chair. and Man. Dir Arup Roy Choudhury; 24,000 employees.

Nuclear Power Corporation of India Ltd: 16th Floor, Commerce Center-1, World Trade Centre, Cuffe Parade, Mumbai 400 005; tel. (22) 22182171; fax (22) 22180109; e-mail info@npcil.co.in; internet www.npcil.org; Chair. and Man. Dir Shreyans Kumar Jain.

Power Grid Corporation of India Ltd: Saudamani, Plot No. 2, Sector 29, Gurgaon 122 001; tel. (124) 2571700; fax (124) 2571760; internet www.powergridindia.com; f. 1989; responsible for formation of national power grid; Chair. and Man. Dir R. N. Nayak.

Ratnagiri Gas and Power Pvt Ltd: NTPC Bhavan, SCOPE Complex, 7 Institutional Area, Lodhi Rd, New Delhi 110 003; tel. (11) 24367089; fax (11) 24361003; internet www.rgppl.com; f. 2005; established to take over assets and revive operations of Dabhol Power Co; 28% owned by National Thermal Power Corpn Ltd, 28% by Gas Authority of India Ltd, 15% by Maharashtra State Electricity Board (MSEB) and 29% by Indian banking institutions; operates plant with 3 units with a total combined power-generating capacity of 2,150 MW; Chair. D. K. Jain; Man. Dir Manash Sarkar.

Reliance Energy: Reliance Energy Centre, Santacruz (East), Mumbai 400 055; tel. (22) 30099999; fax (22) 30099536; e-mail rel.website@rel.co.in; internet www.rel.co.in; f. 1929 as Bombay Suburban Electric Supply Ltd, merged with the Reliance Group in Jan. 2003; generates, transmits and distributes power in Maharashtra, Goa and Andhra Pradesh; Chair. and Man. Dir Anil Ambani.

Rural Electrification Corpn Ltd: Core-4, SCOPE Complex, 7 Lodhi Rd, New Delhi 110 003; tel. (11) 24365161; fax (11) 24360644; e-mail recorp@recl.nic.in; internet www.recindia.com; f. 1969; provides support to rural electrification projects; Chair. and Man. Dir H. D. Khunteta.

Tata Power Co Ltd: Bombay House, 24 Homi Mody St, Mumbai 400 001; tel. (22) 56658282; fax (22) 56658801; internet www.tatapower.com; generation, transmission and distribution of electrical energy; Chair. Ratan N. Tata; Man. Dir Firdose Vandrewala.

Thana Electric Supply Co Ltd: Asian Bldg, 1st Floor, 17 Ramji Kamani Marg, Ballard Estate, Mumbai 400 001; tel. (22) 22615444; fax (22) 22611069; e-mail thanaele@bom2.vsnl.net.in; f. 1927; Man. Dir Suresh S. Hemmady.

Torrent Power Ltd (TPL): Torrent House, off Ashram Road, Ahmedabad 380 009; tel. (79) 26583060; fax (79) 26589581; e-mail tpld@torrentpower.com; internet www.torrentpower.com; generation and distribution of electricity; f. 1996; Exec. Chair. Sudhir Mehta.

Gas

Gas Authority of India Ltd: 16 Bhikaji Cama Place, R. K. Puram, Delhi 110 066; tel. (11) 26172580; fax (11) 26185941; internet gail.nic.in; f. 1984; 80% state-owned; transports, processes and markets natural gas; constructing gas-based petrochemical complex; subsidiaries incl.: GAIL Gas Ltd, GAIL Global (Singapore) Pte Ltd; Chair. and Man. Dir B. C. Tripathi; 3,480 employees (2009).

Gujarat Gas Co Ltd: 2 Shanti Sadan Society, Ellis Bridge, Ahmedabad 380 006; tel. (79) 26462980; fax (79) 26466249; internet www.gujaratgas.com; Chair. Hasmukh Shah; Man. Dir Shaleen Sharma.

Indraprastha Gas Ltd: IGL Bhavan Plot No. 4, Community Centre Sector 9, R. K. Puram, New Delhi 110 022; tel. (11) 46074607; internet www.iglonline.net; Chair. B. C. Tripathi; Man. Dir Rajesh Vedvyas.

Water

Central Water Commission: Sewa Bhavan, R. K. Puram, New Delhi 110 606; tel. (11) 26108855; fax (11) 26195516; e-mail secy-cwc@nic.in; internet cwc.gov.in; responsible for co-ordination of nat. water policy and projects; provision of research, promotion and advice on water resources devt; Chair. A. K. Bajaj.

Brihanmumbai Municipal Corporation (Hydraulic Engineers' Department): Municipal Corporation Head Offices, Ground Floor, Annex Bldg, Mahapalika Marg, Mumbai 400 001; tel. (22) 22620251; fax (22) 22634329; Head Eng. Vinay Deshpande.

Chennai Metropolitan Water Supply and Sewerage Board: No. 1 Pumping Station Rd, Chintadripet, Chennai 600 002; tel. (44) 28451300; fax (44) 28458181; internet www.chennaimetrowater.tn.nic.in; f. 1978; Man. Dir Shiv Das Meena.

Delhi Jal Board: Varunalaya Phase II, Karol Bagh, New Delhi 110 005; tel. and fax (11) 23516261; e-mail prodjb306@gmail.com; internet www.delhijalboard.nic.in; f. 1957 as Delhi Water Supply and Sewage Disposal Undertaking, reconstituted as above in 1998; part of the Delhi Municipal Corporation; production and distribution of potable water and treatment and disposal of waste water in Delhi; Chair. Sheila Dixit.

Karnataka Rural Water Supply and Sanitation Agency: 2nd Floor, E Blk, KHB Complex, Cauvery Bhavan, K. G. Rd, Bangalore 560 009; tel. (80) 22246508; fax (80) 22240509; e-mail krwssa@gmail.com; internet www.jalnirmal.org; Chair. and Man. Dir L. Shanthakumari.

Karnataka Urban Water Supply and Drainage Board: 6 Jalabhavan 1st Stage, 1st Phase, BTM Layout, Bannerghatta Rd, Bangalore 560 029; tel. (80) 41106504; fax (80) 26539206; internet www.kuwsdb.org; Chair. S. N. Krishnaiah Setty.

Kolkata Municipal Corporation (Water Supply Department): 5 S. N. Banerjee Rd, Kolkata 700 013; tel. (33) 22861212; fax (33) 22861444; e-mail dgwskmc@rediffmail.com; internet www.kolkatamycity.com; f. 1870; Dir-Gen. (Water Supply) Bibhas Kumar Maiti.

TRADE UNIONS

In 2008 there were 11 Central Trade Union Organizations (CTUO) recognized by the Indian Ministry of Labour and Employment. The major unions were:

All-India Trade Union Congress (AITUC): 24 Canning Lane, New Delhi 110 001; tel. (11) 23387320; fax (11) 23386427; e-mail aitucong@bol.net.in; internet www.aituc.org; f. 1920; affiliated to WFTU; 4.6m. mems, 2,272 affiliated unions; 28 state brs, 21 national feds; Pres. J. Chitharanjan; Gen. Sec. Gurudas Dasgupta.

All India United Trade Union Centre: 77/2/1 Lenin Sarani, Kolkata 700 013; tel. (33) 22659085; fax (33) 22645605; e-mail aiutuc@gmail.com; f. 1958; fmrly the United Trade Union Centre—Lenin Sarani (UTUC—LS); changed to present name in 2008; labour wing of the Socialist Unity Party of India; 600 affiliated unions; 1.3m. members in 2002; Pres. Krishna Chakraborty; Gen. Sec. Shankar Saha.

Bharatiya Mazdoor Sangh: Dattopant Thengadi Bhawan, 27 Deen Dayal Upadhyay Marg, New Delhi 110 002; tel. (11) 23562654; fax (11) 23582648; e-mail bms@bms.org.in; internet www.bms.org.in; f. 1955; 4,700 affiliated unions with a total membership of 8.5m.; 27 state brs; 34 nat. feds; Pres. C. K. Sajinarayanan; Gen. Sec. Baij Nath Rai.

Major affiliated unions:

Bharatiya Jute Mazdoor Sangh: 10 Kiran Shankar Roy Rd, Kolkata 700 001; tel. (33) 22489210; f. 1970; Pres. Shiv Prasad Singh.

Bharatiya Parivahan Mazdoor Mahasangh (Transport Workers' Union): 542 Dr Munje Marg, Congress Nagar, Nagpur 440 012; tel. (712) 2534464; Pres. Waman Rao Khedkar; Gen. Sec. Chetan Kumar Desai.

Kendriya Karmachari Mahasangh: Ram Naresh Bhavan, Tilak Gali, Paharganj, New Delhi 110 055; tel. (11) 23620654; Pres. K. K. Poddar; Gen. Sec. Chandra Mohan.

National Organisation of Bank Workers (NOBW): 542 Dr Munje Marg, Congress Nagar, Nagpur 440 012; tel. (712) 2560808; fax (712) 2542442; f. 1965; Pres. Dinesh Kulkarni.

National Organisation of Insurance Workers (NOIW): 3-AB, Hashim Bldg, 40 Veer Nariman Rd, Mumbai 400 023; tel. (22) 22040958; fax (22) 66348136; internet www.noiw.in; f. 1969; Pres. Manoj J. Gandhi; Gen. Sec. Atul Deshpande.

Centre of Indian Trade Unions: BTR Bhavan, 13 A Rouse Ave, New Delhi 110 002; tel. (11) 23221288; fax (11) 23221284; e-mail citu@bol.net.in; internet www.citucentre.org; f. 1970; 3.37m. mems; 25 state and union territory brs; 4,300 affiliated unions, 12 nat. feds; Pres. A. K. Padmanabhan; Gen. Sec. Tapan Sen.

Major affiliated unions:

All India Coal Workers' Federation: Koyla Shramik Bhavan, N. S. B. Rd, Raniganj 713 347; Gen. Sec. Jibon Roy.

All India Road Transport Workers' Federation (AIRTWF): Rm No. 402, Balaji Residency, Bangalore 560 035; tel. 9916479486 (mobile); e-mail airtwf.com; internet airtwf.com; Pres. MOHAMMAD AMEEN; Gen. Sec. K. K. DIVAKARAN.

Steel Workers' Federation of India: 1 Vidyasagar Ave, Durgapur 713 205; Gen. Sec. P. K. DAS.

Water Transport Workers' Federation of India: 55 Moore St, 1st Floor, Chennai 600 001; Pres. T. NARENDRA RAO.

Hind Mazdoor Sabha (HMS): 120 Babar Rd, New Delhi 110 001; tel. (11) 23413519; fax (11) 23411037; e-mail hms1gs@gmail.com; internet www.hmsindia.org.in; f. 1948; affiliated to ITUC; 5.8m. mems from more than 2,775 affiliated unions; 25 state councils; 16 nat. industrial feds; Pres. SHARAD RAO; Gen. Sec. UMRAOMAL PUROHIT.

Major affiliated unions:

Mumbai Port Trust Dock and General Employees' Union: Port Trust Kamgar Sadan, Nawab Tank Rd, Mazgaon, Mumbai 400 010; tel. (22) 23776320; fax (22) 23754794; e-mail mbptdgeu@vsnl.net; 7,448 mems; Pres. Dr SHANTI PATEL; Gen. Sec. MARUTI VISHWASRAO.

South Central Railway Mazdoor Union: 7C Railway Bldg, Accounts Office Compound, Secunderabad 500 371; tel. (40) 27821351; fax (40) 27821351; e-mail scrmu@rediffmail.com; internet www.scrmu.org; f. 1966; 88,900 mems; Pres. V. P. R. PILLAI; Gen. Sec. C.SANKARA RAO; 135 brs.

Transport and Dock Workers' Union: P. D. Mello Bhavan, Carnec Bunder, Mumbai 400 038; tel. (22) 22616951; fax (22) 22659087; 25,979 mems; Pres. S. R. KULKARNI.

Western Railway Employees' Union: Grant Road Railway Station Bldg, Grant Rd (East), Mumbai 400 007; tel. (22) 23088102; fax (22) 23003185; 150,000 mems; Pres. UMRAOMAL PUROHIT; Gen. Sec. C. S. MENON.

Indian National Trade Union Congress (INTUC): 4 Bhai Veer Singh Marg, New Delhi 110 001; tel. (11) 23747767; fax (11) 23364244; e-mail info@intuc.net; internet www.intuc.net; f. 1947; 4,411 affiliated unions with a total membership of 7.93m.; affiliated to ICFTU; 32 state brs and 29 nat. feds; Pres. G. SANJEEVA REDDY; Gen. Sec. RAJENDRA PRASAD SINGH.

Major affiliated unions:

Indian National Cement Workers' Federation: Mazdoor Karyalaya, Congress House, Mumbai 400 004; tel. (22) 23870804; fax (22) 2622286; e-mail nanjappanintuc@dataone.in; f. 1947; 49,000 mems; 42 affiliated unions; Pres. H. N. TRIVEDI; Gen. Sec. NACHIMUTHU NANJAPPAN.

Indian National Chemical Workers' Federation: Tel Rasayan Bhavan, Tilak Rd, Dadar, Mumbai 400 014; tel. (22) 24121742; fax (22) 24130950; 35,000 mems; Pres. RAJA KULKARNI; Gen. Sec. R. D. BHARADWAJ.

Indian National Electricity Workers' Federation: 392 Sector 21-B, 452 Kotwaliward, Jabalpur 482 002; tel. (129) 2215089; fax (129) 2215868; e-mail inef@ndf.vsnl.net.in; f. 1950; 187,641 mems; 146 affiliated unions; Pres. D. P. PATHAK; Sec.-Gen. S. L. PASSEY.

Indian National Metal Workers' Federation: Shramik Kendra, 4 Bhai Veer Singh Marg, New Delhi 110 001; tel. (661) 24646611; Pres. N. K. BHATT; Gen. Sec. RAJSEKHAR MANTRI.

Indian National Mineworkers' Federation: CJ 49 Salt Lake, Kolkata 700 091; tel. and fax (33) 23372158; e-mail imme@vsnl.com; f. 1949; 351,454 mems in 139 affiliated unions; Pres. RAJENDRA P. SINGH; Sec.-Gen. S. Q. ZAMA.

Indian National Paper Mill Workers' Federation: 6/B, LIGH, Barkatpura, Hyderabad 500 027; tel. (40) 27564706; Pres. G. SANJEEVA REDDY; Gen. Sec. R. CHANDRASEKHARAN.

Indian National Port and Dock Workers' Federation: 15 Coal Dock Rd, Kolkata 700 043; tel. (33) 22455929; f. 1954; 18 affiliated unions; 81,000 mems; Pres. JANAKI MUKHERJEE; Gen. Sec. G. KALAN.

Indian National Sugar Mills Workers' Federation: A-176, Darulsafa Marg, Lucknow 226 001; tel. (522) 2282719; 100 affiliated unions; 40,000 mems; Pres. ASHOK KUMAR SINGH; Gen. Sec. P. K. SHARMA.

Indian National Textile Workers' Federation: 27 Burjorji Bharucha Marg, Fort, Mumbai 400 023; tel. (22) 22671577; f. 1948; 400 affiliated unions; 363,790 mems; Pres. SACHINBHAU AHIR; Gen. Sec. P. L. SUBHAIH.

Indian National Transport Workers' Federation: Bus Mazdoor Karyalaya, L/1, Hathital Colony, Jabalpur 482 001; tel. (761) 2429210; 357 affiliated unions; 379,267 mems; Pres. G. SANJEEVA REDDY; Gen. Sec. K. S. VERMA.

National Federation of Petroleum Workers: Tel Rasayan Bhavan, Tilak Rd, Dadar, Mumbai 400 014; tel. (22) 24181742; fax (22) 24130950; f. 1959; 22,340 mems; Pres. RAJA KULKARNI; Gen. Sec. S. N. SURVE.

Self-Employed Women's Association (SEWA): SEWA Reception Centre, opp. Victoria Garden, Bhadra, Ahmedabad 380 001; tel. (79) 25506444; fax (79) 25506446; e-mail mail@sewa.org; internet www.sewa.org; f. 1972; 12,56,944 mems (2009); Pres. BHANUBEN DANABHAI SOLANKI; Gen. Sec. ELABEN BHATT.

United Trades Union Congress (UTUC): 1st Floor, 249 Bipin Behari Ganguly St, Kolkata 700 012; tel. (33) 22259234; fax (33) 22375609; f. 1949; 1.2m. mems from 387 affiliated unions; 12 state brs and 6 nat. feds; Pres. SHANKARAN NAIR; Gen. Sec. ABANI ROY.

Major affiliated unions:

Bengal Provincial Chatkal Mazdoor Union: Kolkata; textile workers; 28,330 mems.

Dooars Cha Bagan Union: Jalpaiguri; tel. (3564) 255220; 94,532 mems; Pres. SURESH TALUKDAR; Gen. Sec. MANOHAR TIRKEY.

Other principal trade unions:

All India Bank Employees' Association (AIBEA): Prabhat Nivas, Singapore Plaza, 164 Linghi Chetty St, Chennai 600 001; tel. (44) 25351522; fax (44) 25358853; e-mail aibeahq@gmail.com; internet www.bankunionaibea.in; 32 state units, 710 affiliated unions, 525,000 mems; Pres. RAJEN NAGAR; Gen. Sec. C. H. VENKATACHALAM.

All India Defence Employees' Federation (AIDEF): Survey No. 81, Elphinstone Rd, Khadki, Pune 411 003; tel. (20) 25818761; f. 1953; 358 affiliated unions; 200,000 mems; Pres. S. N. PATHAK; Gen. Secs S. BHATTACHARYA, C. SRIKUMAR.

All India Port and Dock Workers' Federation: 9 Second Line Beach, Chennai 600 001; tel. (44) 25224222; fax (44) 25225983; f. 1948; 100,000 mems in 34 affiliated unions; Pres. S. R. KULKARNI; Gen. Sec. S. C. C. ANTHONY PILLAI.

All India Railwaymen's Federation (AIRF): 4 State Entry Rd, New Delhi 110 055; tel. (11) 65732357; fax (11) 23363167; e-mail airfindia@gmail.com; internet www.airfindia.com; f. 1924; 1,0007,709 mems (2010); 24 affiliated unions; Pres. UMRAOMAL PUROHIT; Gen. Sec. SHIVA GOPAL MISHRA.

Assam Chah Karmachari Sangha: POB 13, Dibrugarh 786 001; tel. 20870; 13,553 mems; 20 brs; Pres. G. C. SARMAH; Gen. Sec. A. K. BHATTACHARYA.

Confederation of Central Government Employees and Workers: Manishinath Bhavan, A-2-95 Rajouri Garden, New Delhi 110 027; tel. (11) 25105324; e-mail confederation06@yahoo.co.in; internet confederationhq.blogspot.com; 1.2m. mems; Pres. S. MADHUSUDAN; Sec.-Gen. K. K. N. KUTTY.

Affiliated union:

National Federation of Postal Employees (NFPE): D-7, North Ave Post Office Bldg, 1st Floor, New Delhi 110 001; tel. and fax (11) 23092771; e-mail nfpehq@gmail.com; internet nfpe.blogspot.com; f. 1954 as National Federation of Post and Telegraph Employees, reconstituted as above in 1986; 400,000 mems from seven affiliated unions; Pres. R. N. CHAUDHARY; Sec.-Gen. M. KRISHNAN.

Electricity Employees' Federation of India (EEFI): B. T. R. Bhavan, 13A Rouse Ave, New Delhi 110 002; tel. 9830264170 (mobile); fax (11) 3219670; e-mail eefederation@gmail.com; internet www.eefi.org; f. 1984; largest electricity union in India; 45 affiliated unions; Pres. K. O. HABIB; Gen. Sec. PRASANTA N. CHOWDHURY.

National Federation of Indian Railwaymen (NFIR): 3 Chelmsford Rd, New Delhi 110 055; tel. (11) 23343305; fax (11) 23744013; e-mail nfir@satyam.net.in; f. 1953; 26 affiliated unions; 925,500 mems (2003); Pres. GUMAN SINGH; Gen. Sec. M. RAGHAVAIAH.

Transport

RAILWAYS

India's railway system is the largest in Asia and the fourth largest in the world. In 2009/10 the total length of the railways was 63,974 route-km; in that year the network carried 7,246m. passengers and 887.7m. metric tons of freight traffic. The Government exercises direct or indirect control over all railways through the Railway Board. India's largest railway construction project of the 20th century, the 760-km Konkan railway line (which took seven years and almost US $1,000m. to build), was officially opened in January 1998. The construction of a 345-km Jammu–Udhampur–Srinagar–Baramulla line, linking Jammu and Kashmir with the national rail network, was declared a project of national importance in 2002. By early 2010 two of the project's four phases had been completed. However, owing to technical challenges presented by the difficult terrain, the project was unlikely to be completed before 2016.

A 16.5-km underground railway was completed in Kolkata in 1995 and extended to 22.2 km in 2009. The network carries more than 1m. people daily. The country's second metro system, in New Delhi, became operational in 2004. Following the completion of work on the

second phase of the system in early 2011, the network comprised 142 stations across a route length of 189 km, carrying 1.3m. people daily.

Ministry of Railways (Railway Board): Rail Bhavan, Raisina Rd, New Delhi 110 001; tel. (11) 23384010; fax (11) 23384481; e-mail crb@rb.railnet.gov.in; internet www.indianrailways.gov.in; Chair. VINAY MITTAL.

Zonal Railways

The railways are grouped into 17 zones:

Central Railway: Chhatrapati Shivaji Terminus (Victoria Terminus), Mumbai 400 001; tel. (22) 22697311; fax (22) 22612354; e-mail gmcr@bom2.vsnl.net.in; internet www.cr.indianrailways.gov.in; Gen. Man. S. K. JAIN.

East Central Railway: Hajipur 844 101; tel. (6224) 274728; fax (6224) 274738; internet www.ecr.indianrailways.gov.in; f. 1996; Gen. Man. VARUN BHARTHUAR.

East Coast Railway: Rail Vihar, Chandrasekhar Pur, Bhubaneswar 751 023; tel. (674) 2300773; fax (674) 2300196; e-mail gm@eastcoastrailway.gov.in; internet www.eastcoastrail.indianrailways.gov.in; f. 1996; Gen. Man. INDRA GHOSH.

Eastern Railway: 17 Netaji Subhas Rd, Kolkata 700 001; tel. (33) 22307596; fax (33) 22480370; internet www.er.indianrailways.gov.in; Gen. Man. G. C. AGARWAL.

Metro Railway, Kolkata: Metro Rail Bhavan, 8th Floor, 33/1 J. L. Nehru Rd, Kolkata 700 071; tel. (33) 22267280; fax (33) 22264581; e-mail com@mtp.railnet.gov.in; internet www.mtp.indianrailways.gov.in; f. 1995; Gen. Man. P. B. MURTY.

North Central Railway: Allahabad 211 001; tel. (532) 2230200; fax (532) 2603900; e-mail secy@ncr.railnet.gov.in; internet www.ncr.indianrailways.gov.in; f. 1996; Gen. Man. H. C. JOSHI.

North Eastern Railway: Gorakhpur 273 012; tel. (551) 2201041; fax (551) 2201299; e-mail gm@ner.railnet.gov.in; internet www.ner.indianrailways.gov.in; Gen. Man. OM PRAKASH.

North Western Railway: Nr Jawahar Circle, Jaipur; tel. (141) 2725800; fax (141) 2222936; e-mail gm@nwr.railnet.gov.in; internet www.nwr.indianrailways.gov.in; Gen. Man. ASHOK KUMAR GUPTA.

Northeast Frontier Railway: Maligaon, Guwahati 781 011; tel. (361) 2676000; fax (361) 2570580; e-mail gm@nfr.railnet.gov.in; internet www.nfr.indianrailways.gov.in; f. 1958; Gen. Man. K. CHANDRA.

Northern Railway: NOCR Bldg, State Entry Rd, New Delhi 110 001; tel. (11) 23363469; fax (11) 23363469; e-mail gm@nr.railnet.gov.in; internet www.nr.indianrailways.gov.in; Gen. Man. B. N. RAJASEKHAR.

South Central Railway: Rm 312, 3rd Floor, Rail Nilayam, Secunderabad 500 071; tel. (40) 27822874; fax (40) 27833203; e-mail gm@scr.railnet.gov.in; internet www.scr.indianrailways.gov.in; Gen. Man. G. N. ASTHANA.

South East Central Railway: R. E. Complex, Bilaspur 495 004; tel. (7752) 47102; e-mail webmaster@secr.railnet.gov.in; internet www.secr.indianrailways.gov.in; Gen. Man. ARUNENDRA KUMAR.

South Eastern Railway: 11 Garden Reach Rd, Kolkata 700 043; tel. (33) 24393532; fax (33) 24397831; e-mail cpro@ser.railnet.gov.in; internet www.ser.indianrailways.gov.in; Gen. Man. A. K. VERMA.

South Western Railway: Club Rd, Keshwapur, Hubli 580 023; tel. (836) 2360747; fax (836) 2365209; e-mail gm@southwesternrailway.in; internet www.swr.indianrailways.gov.in; f. 1996; Gen. Man. ASHOK KUMAR MITAL.

Southern Railway: Park Town, Chennai 600 003; tel. (44) 25353455; fax (44) 25354950; e-mail srailway@gmail.com; internet www.sr.indianrailways.gov.in; Gen. Man. DEEPAK KRISHAN.

West Central Railway: Jabalpur 482 001; tel. (761) 2627444; fax (761) 2607555; e-mail osdwcr@yahoo.com; internet www.wcr.indianrailways.gov.in; f. 1996; Gen. Man. S. V. ARYA.

Western Railway: Churchgate, Mumbai 400 020; tel. (22) 22005670; fax (22) 22068545; e-mail secygm@wr.railnet.gov.in; internet www.wr.indianrailways.gov.in; Gen. Man. MAHESH KUMAR.

ROADS

In 2010 there were an estimated 4.2m. km of roads in India, 221,276 km of which were national or state highways. In 2008 49.3% of the total road network was paved. In January 1999 the Government launched the ambitious Rs 500,000m. National Highways Development Project, which included plans to build a circuit of roads linking the four main cities of Mumbai, Chennai, Kolkata and New Delhi (Phase I), as well as an east–west corridor linking Silchar with Porbandar and a north–south corridor linking Kashmir with Kanyakumari (Phase II). The majority of work on the first two phases had been completed by March 2010. The third phase of the project, the widening and upgrading of an estimated 12,000 km of national highways, was scheduled for completion by 2013. Under four other organized plans (Phases III to VI), the Government has approved construction work on expressways and highways across the country. In May 2007 the Government pledged Rs 480,000m. for the upgrade of India's rural road network by 2009 with the stated aim of connecting 66,000 villages; the allocation represented part of the four-year Bharat Nirman initiative (at an estimated cost of Rs 1,740,000m.) to enhance infrastructure and rural incomes by increasing connectivity with roads, telecommunications and drinking water.

Ministry of Road Transport and Highways: Parivahan Bhavan, 1 Sansad Marg, New Delhi 110 001; tel. (11) 23753991; fax (11) 23719023; e-mail nr.gokarn@nic.in; internet morth.nic.in; responsible for the planning, development and maintenance of India's system of national highways connecting the state capitals and major ports and linking with the highway systems of neighbouring countries. This system includes 172 national highways, which constitute the main trunk roads of the country.

Border Roads Organisation: Seema Sadak Bhavan, Ring Road Naraina, Delhi 110 010; e-mail bro-edp@nic.in; internet www.bro.nic.in; f. 1960 to accelerate the economic development of the north and north-eastern border areas; it has constructed 31,061 km and improved 37,077 km of roads, and built permanent bridges totalling a length of 19,544 m in the border areas.

National Highways Authority of India: G-5 and 6, Sector 10, Dwarka, New Delhi 110 075; tel. (11) 25074100; fax (11) 25093507; e-mail chairman@nhai.org; internet www.nhai.org; f. 1995; planning, designing, construction and maintenance of national highways; implementation of the National Highways Development Project; under Ministry of Shipping, Road Transport and Highways; Chair. A. K. UPADHYAY.

INLAND WATERWAYS

About 14,500 km of rivers are navigable by power-driven craft, and 3,700 km by large country boats. Services are mainly on the Ganga and Brahmaputra and their tributaries, the Godavari, the Mahanadi, the Narmada, the Tapti and the Krishna. About 55m. metric tons of cargo is moved annually by certified vessels. In addition, a substantial volume of cargo and passengers is transported in the unorganized sector.

Central Inland Water Transport Corpn Ltd: 4 Fairlie Place, Kolkata 700 001; tel. (33) 22435718; fax (33) 22436164; e-mail ciwtc@cal3.vsnl.net.in; internet www.ciwtcltd.com; f. 1967; inland water transport services in Bangladesh and the east and north-east Indian states; also shipbuilding and repairing, general engineering, lightering of ships and barge services; Chair. and Man. Dir PRAFUL TAYAL.

Inland Waterways Authority of India: A-13, Sector 1, Noida 201 301; tel. (120) 2544036; fax (120) 2544041; e-mail iwainoi@nic.in; internet iwai.nic.in; f. 1986; devt and regulation of inland waterways for shipping and navigation; under Ministry of Shipping, Road Transport and Highways; Chair. S. P. GAUR.

SHIPPING

The major ports are Chennai, Haldia, Jawaharlal Nehru (at Nhava Sheva near Mumbai), Kandla, Kochi, Kolkata, Mormugao, Mumbai, New Mangalore, Paradip (Paradeep), Tuticorin and Visakhapatnam. At December 31 2010 India's merchant fleet had a total of 1,007 ships, with a total displacement of 9.61m. grt.

Port Authorities and Supervisory Bodies

Chennai Port Trust: 1 Rajaji Salai, Chennai 600 001; tel. (44) 25362201; fax (44) 25361228; e-mail info@chennaiport.gov.in; internet www.chennaiport.gov.in; f. 1881; under the Ministry of Shipping; Chair. ATULYA MISRA.

Cochin Port Trust: Willingdon Island, Cochin 682 009; tel. (484) 2668200; fax (484) 2666417; e-mail mail@cochinport.gov.in; internet www.cochinport.com; f. 1926; owned by the Ministry of Shipping; manages infrastructure around Ernakulam and Mattancherry wharfs; Chair. PAUL ANTONY.

Indian Ports Association: First Floor, South Tower, NBCC Place, Bhisham Pitamah Marg, Lodi Rd, New Delhi 110 003; fax (11) 24365866; e-mail ipa@nic.in; internet ipa.nic.in; f. 1966; supervisory and advisory body; Man. Dir A. JANARDHANA RAO.

Indian Register of Shipping: 72 Maker Tower-F, 7th Floor, Cuffe Parade, Mumbai 400 005; tel. (22) 40804080; fax (22) 22181241; e-mail mumbai@irclass.org; internet www.irclass.org; f. 1975; ship classification society; provides technical inspection and certification services for marine craft and structures; Chair. Capt. J. C. ANAND.

Kolkata Port Trust: 15 Strand Rd, Kolkata 700 001; tel. (33) 22303451; fax (33) 22304901; e-mail calport@vsnl.com; internet www.kolkataporttrust.gov.in; f. 1870; operates Kolkata and Haldia dock systems; handles cargo and maintains vessel traffic; Chair. M. L. MEENA.

Mumbai Port Trust: Port House, S. V. Marg, Mumbai 400 001; tel. (22) 22621234; fax (22) 66564011; e-mail chairman@mbptmail.com;

internet www.mumbaiport.gov.in; f. 1873; works to improve infrastructure facilities and manages port traffic; Chair. RAJEEV GUPTA.

Visakhapatnam Port Trust: Port Area, Visakhapatnam 530 035; tel. (891) 2876001; fax (891) 2565023; e-mail info@vizagport.com; internet www.vizagport.com; f. 1964; handles 3 harbours: outer (200 ha with 6 berths), inner (100 ha with 18 berths) and a fishing harbour; Chair. AJEYA KALLAM.

Shipping Companies

Kolkata (Calcutta)

Apeejay Shipping Ltd: Apeejay House, 15 Park St, Kolkata 700 016; tel. (33) 44035455; fax (33) 22179596; e-mail solcal@apeejaygroup.com; internet www.apeejayshipping.com; f. 1948; shipowners; Chair. KARAN PAUL; CEO S. S. MAHAPATRA.

India Steamship Co Ltd: 9th Floor, Birla Bldg, 9/1 R. N. Mukherjee Rd, Kolkata 700 001; tel. (33) 71071000; fax (33) 22624191; e-mail iss@indiasteamship.com; internet www.indiasteamship.com; f. 1928; cargo services; Pres. K. SATISHCHANDRA; br in Delhi.

Mumbai (Bombay)

Chowgule Brothers (Pvt) Ltd: POB 1770, Malhotra House, 3rd Floor, Mumbai 400 001; tel. (22) 22675579; fax (22) 22610659; e-mail mumbai.cb@chowgule.co.in; internet www.chowgulebros.com; Dir JAYWANT CHOWGULE.

Essar Shipping Ltd: Essar House, 11 Keshavrao Khadye Marg, Mahalaxmi, Mumbai 400 034; tel. (22) 24950606; fax (22) 24954312; e-mail contactshipping@essar.com; internet www.essar.com; f. 1969; Chair. SHASHI RUIA; Man. Dir A. R. RAMAKRISHNAN.

The Great Eastern Shipping Co Ltd: Ocean House, 134A Dr Annie Besant Rd, Worli, Mumbai 400 018; tel. (22) 66613000; fax (22) 24920200; e-mail marketing@greatshipglobal.com; internet www.greatshipglobal.com; f. 1948; shipping; Exec. Chair. BHARAT K. SHETH; Man. Dir RAVI K. SHETH; brs in Singapore, Mauritius, Australia and the UK.

Mercator Ltd: 3rd Floor, Mittal Tower, B-wing, Nariman Point, Mumbai 400 021; tel. (22) 66373333; fax (22) 66373344; e-mail mercator@mercator.in; internet www.mercator.in; f. 1983; cargo shipping; fmrly Mercator Lines Ltd; Chair. H. K. MITTAL; Man. Dir ATUL J. AGARWAL.

Shipping Corpn of India Ltd: Shipping House, 245 Madame Cama Rd, Mumbai 400 021; tel. (22) 22026666; fax (22) 22026905; e-mail mail@sci.co.in; internet www.shipindia.com; f. 1961 as a govt undertaking; Chair. and Man. Dir S. HAJARA; brs in Kolkata, New Delhi, Chennai and London.

Tolani Shipping Co Ltd: 10A Bakhtawar, Nariman Point, Mumbai 400 021; tel. (22) 56568989; fax (22) 22870697; e-mail tmi@tolani.edu; internet www.tolanigroup.com; f. 1974; Chair. and Man. Dir Dr NANDLAL PRIBHDAS TOLANI.

Varun Shipping Co Ltd: Laxmi Bldg, 3rd Floor, 6 Shoorji Vallabhdas Marg, Ballard Estate, Mumbai 400 001; tel. (22) 66350100; fax (22) 66350274; e-mail isd@varunship.com; internet www.varunship.com; f. 1971; Chair. and Man. Dir ARUN MEHTA.

CIVIL AVIATION

There are 11 designated international airports, 81 domestic airports, 25 civil enclaves and eight customs airports under the jurisdiction of the Airports Authority of India (AAI). Overall passenger-handling capacity of AAI airports increased from 101.2m. in 2009 to 233m. in 2012. Net air traffic increased from 48.8m. in 2004 to 142.4m. in 2010. Since 2006 contracts to manage and modernize several international airports, including Mumbai, New Delhi and Hyderabad, have been awarded to public-private partnerships. A major new terminal at Indira Gandhi International Airport in New Delhi was inaugurated in July 2010, increasing the airport's annual handling capacity to 37m. passengers.

Airports Authority of India: Rajiv Gandhi Bhavan, Safdarjung Airport, New Delhi 110 003; tel. (11) 24632950; fax (11) 24641088; e-mail aaichmn@vsnl.com; internet www.aai.aero; f. 1972; responsible for air traffic management and devt of airport infrastucture; manages 125 international and domestic airports; Chair. V. P. AGRAWAL.

Air-India: Air-India Bldg, 218 Backbay Reclamation, Nariman Point, Mumbai 400 021; tel. (22) 22023031; fax (22) 22021096; e-mail eCommerce@airindia.in; internet www.airindia.in; f. 1932 as Tata Airlines; renamed Air-India in 1946; in 1953 became a state corpn responsible for international flights; merged with Indian Airlines in Aug. 2007 to form the National Aviation Company of India, operating as Air-India; services to 46 online stations (incl. 2 cargo stations) and 84 offline offices throughout the world; operates domestic flights under the brand name Air India Regional and low-cost services under the Air India Express brand (internet www.air-indiaexpress.in); Chair. and Man. Dir ROHIT NANDAN.

Blue Dart Express: 88–89 Old International Terminal, Meenambakkam Airport, Chennai 600 027; tel. (44) 22568200; fax (44) 22568385; e-mail radhag@bluedart.com; internet www.bluedart.com; f. 1983 as Blue Dart Courier Services; name changed as above in 1990; air express transport co; operates a fleet of 7 aircraft; Chair. SHARAD UPASANI; Man. Dir ANIL KHANNA.

Go Air: 1st Floor, C-1, Wadia Int. Centre, Pandurang Budhkar Marg, Worli, Mumbai 400 025; tel. (22) 67410000; fax (22) 67420001; e-mail feedback@goair.in; internet www.goair.in; f. 2005; low-cost passenger services to domestic destinations; Man. Dir JEHANGIR 'JEH' WADIA.

Indigo Airlines: Level 1, Tower C, Global Business Park, Mehrauli-Gurgaon Road, Gurgaon 122 002; tel. (124) 4352500; fax (124) 4068536; e-mail sakshi.batra@bm.com; internet www.goindigo.in; f. 2005; private co; passenger services to domestic destinations; int. services to Oman, Singapore, Thailand and the United Arab Emirates launched in 2011; Chair. RAHUL BHATIA; Pres. ADITYA GHOSH.

Jagson Airlines: Vandana Bldg, 3rd Floor, 11 Tolstoy Marg, New Delhi 110 001; tel. (11) 23721594; fax (11) 23324693; e-mail jagson-id@eth.net; f. 1991; scheduled and charter passenger services to domestic destinations; Chair. JAGDISH GUPTA.

Jet Airways (India) Ltd: Siroya Centre, Sahar Airport Rd, Andheri (East), Mumbai 400 099; tel. (22) 61211000; fax (22) 29201313; internet www.jetairways.com; f. 1992; commenced operations 1993; acquired Air Sahara in April 2007; private co; scheduled passenger services to domestic and regional destinations; operates flights to 50 domestic and international destinations; also operates low-cost JetLite service; Chair. and Man. Dir NARESH GOYAL; CEO NIKOS KARDASSIS.

JetLite: Siroya Centre, Sahar Airport Rd, Andheri (East), Mumbai 400 099; tel. (11) 61211000; fax (11) 23755510; internet www.jetlite.com; f. 1991 as Sahara India Airlines; name changed as above when acquired by Jet Airways (India) in April 2007; private co; scheduled passenger and cargo services to domestic and regional destinations; Chair. NARESH GOYAL.

Kingfisher Airlines: Kingfisher House, Western Express Highway, Vile Parle (East), Mumbai 400 099; tel. (22) 26262200; fax (22) 67020625; e-mail info@flykingfisher.com; internet www.flykingfisher.com; f. 2005; 100% owned by UB Group; national and international passenger service; also operates Kingfisher Red, a low-cost domestic passenger service; in March 2012, owing to ongoing financial difficulties, the airline announced that it was to suspend all international operations until further notice; Chair. and Man. Dir VIJAY MALLYA.

SpiceJet: 319 Udyog Vihar, Phase IV, Gurgaon 122 016; tel. 9871803333 (mobile); e-mail custrelations@spicejet.com; internet www.spicejet.com; f. 2005; low-cost domestic passenger service; Chair. KALANITHI MARAN; CEO NEIL RAYMOND MILLS.

Trans Bharat Aviation Ltd: 212–213, Somdutt Chamber I, 2nd Floor, Bhikaji Cama Place, Delhi 110 066; tel. (11) 26181824; fax (11) 26160146; e-mail qcmtba@rediffmail.com; f. 1990; commenced operations 1991; provides helicopter charter services throughout India; CEO PRADIP BISWAS.

Tourism

The tourist attractions of India include sub-Himalayan scenery in the north and the east; diverse fauna, including the Bengal tiger, the peacock and the Asiatic elephant; myriad wildlife sanctuaries and national parks; historic monuments, including forts, palaces and temples; various cultural and religious festivals; and many other vibrant urban and rural attractions. India possesses 28 UNESCO World Heritage sites, including the Taj Mahal. Tourism infrastructure has recently been expanded by the provision of additional luxury hotels and improved means of transport. In 2010 there were an estimated 5.8m. foreign visitors to India, an increase of 11.8% compared with the previous year. The USA and the United Kingdom were the most important sources of tourist arrivals, providing 16.1% and 13.2% of total arrivals, respectively. In 2010 revenue from tourism rose by 24.6%, compared with the previous year, to reach an estimated US $14,190m.

Ministry of Tourism: (see Ministries and Government Offices); formulates and administers govt policy for promotion of tourism; plans the org. and devt of tourist facilities; operates tourist information offices in India and overseas; Sec. RAJEN HABIB KHWAJA.

India Tourism Development Corpn Ltd: Core-8, Scope Complex, 7 Lodhi Rd, New Delhi 110 003; tel. (11) 24360303; fax (11) 24360233; e-mail contact@itdc.com; internet www.theashokgroup.com; f. 1966; operates Ashok Group of hotels, resort accommodation, tourist transport services, duty-free shops and a travel agency and provides consultancy and management services; Chair. and Man. Dir Dr LALIT K. PANWAR.

Defence

As assessed at November 2011, India's total armed forces numbered 1,325,000: army 1,129,900, navy 58,350 (incl. naval air force), air force 127,200, coast guard 9,550. Active paramilitary forces totalled 1,300,586 members, including the 208,422-strong Border Security Force (based mainly in the troubled state of Jammu and Kashmir). Military service is voluntary, although the Constitution states that every citizen has a fundamental duty to perform national service when called upon to do so.

Defence Budget (2011/12): Estimated at Rs 1,470,000m.

Chief of Staff of the Air Force: Air Chief Marshal N. A. K. Browne.

Chief of Staff of the Army: Gen. Vijay Kumar Singh.

Chief of Staff of the Navy: Adm. Nirmal Verma.

Education

Under the Constitution, education in India is primarily the responsibility of the individual state governments, although the central Government has several direct responsibilities, some specified in the Constitution, as, for example, responsibility for the Central Universities, all higher institutions, promotion and propagation of Hindi, co-ordination and maintenance of higher education standards, scientific and technological research and welfare of Indian students abroad.

Education in India is administered centrally by the Ministry of Human Resources Development (Department of Education). At state level, there is an Education Minister. There are facilities for free primary education (lower and upper stages) in all the states. Priority has been given to an expansion in elementary and community education as well as in education for girls. An amendment to the Constitution, which came into effect in April 2010, ensures free and compulsory education for children from the age of six to 14. In addition, the historic legislation seeks to ensure universal education by requiring private schools to reserve no less than one-quarter of placements for children from impoverished backgrounds, by creating new state-run neighbourhood schools, by removing school admission fees and by providing for the creation of schools for children with disabilities. Budgetary expenditure on education and literacy for 2010/11 was estimated at Rs 363,420m. (equivalent to 3.0% of total spending).

ELEMENTARY EDUCATION

The notable characteristic of elementary education in India is the use of what is known as basic education. There is an activity-centred curriculum which educates through socially useful, productive activities such as spinning, weaving, gardening, leather work, book craft, domestic crafts, pottery, elementary engineering, etc. The emphasis is on introducing important features of basic education in non-basic schools. Basic education is the national pattern of all elementary education and all elementary schools will ultimately be brought over to the basic system.

In pre-primary and primary classes, for children between six and 11 years of age, the total number of pupils increased from 50m. in 1965 to an estimated 141.5m. in 2009/10. Enrolment in higher primary or middle schools (age-group 11–14 years) in that year was 59.4m. Similarly, the number of primary (lower and higher) schools increased from 466,862 in 1965/66 to more than 1.2m. in 2009/10. Enrolment at primary schools in 2007/08 included 92% of pupils in the relevant age-group.

SECONDARY EDUCATION

Education at this level is provided for those between the ages of 14 and 18. There were an estimated 190,643 secondary schools, higher secondary schools and junior colleges in 2009/10, with some 48.3m. pupils and 2.3m. teachers. In 2007/08 enrolment at secondary schools was equivalent to 60% of pupils in the relevant age-group (64% of boys; 56% of girls).

Most schools follow what is known as the 'three-language formula', which comprises teaching of the regional language or dialect, Hindi and English. Much emphasis is now also being laid on physical training, which has become a compulsory subject.

HIGHER AND ADULT EDUCATION

The universities are for the most part autonomous as regards administration. The University Grants Commission is responsible for the promotion and co-ordination of university education and has the authority to make appropriate grants and to implement development schemes.

India had a total of 564 universities and institutions with university status in 2010/11, and some 31,234 colleges of higher education. In that year, by some estimates, university enrolment was equivalent to some 14.1% of students in the relevant age-group. In 2009/10 an estimated 26.2m. students were enrolled in institutions of higher education.

INDONESIA

Introductory Survey

LOCATION, CLIMATE, LANGUAGE, RELIGION, FLAG, CAPITAL

The Republic of Indonesia consists of a group of about 18,108 islands (including rocks, reefs, sandbanks, etc.), lying between the mainland of South-East Asia and Australia. The archipelago is the largest in the world, and it stretches from the Malay peninsula to New Guinea. The principal islands are Java, Sumatra, Kalimantan (comprising more than two-thirds of the island of Borneo), Sulawesi (Celebes), Papua (formerly Irian Jaya, comprising the western part of the island of New Guinea), Maluku (the Moluccas) and West Timor (comprising part of the island of Timor). Indonesia's only land frontiers are with Papua New Guinea, to the east of Papua, with the Malaysian states of Sarawak and Sabah, which occupy northern Borneo, and with Timor-Leste (formerly East Timor), to the east of West Timor. The climate is tropical, with an average annual temperature of 26°C (79°F) and heavy rainfall during most seasons. Rainfall averages 706 mm (28 ins) annually in Indonesia, although there are large variations throughout the archipelago; the heaviest annual rainfall (2,286 mm or 90 ins) is along the equatorial rain belt, which passes through Sumatra, Borneo and Sulawesi. The official language is Bahasa Indonesia (a form of Malay); there are an estimated 583 other languages and dialects spoken in the archipelago, including Javanese, Sundanese, Arabic and Chinese. An estimated 88% of the inhabitants profess adherence to Islam. About 10% of the population are Christians, while most of the remainder are either Hindus or Buddhists. The national flag (proportions 2 by 3) has two equal horizontal stripes, of red and white. The capital is Jakarta, on the island of Java.

CONTEMPORARY POLITICAL HISTORY

Historical Context

Indonesia was formerly the Netherlands East Indies (except for the former Portuguese colony of East Timor, which became known as Timor-Leste following its accession to independence in 2002—see Provincial Affairs and Separatist Tensions). Dutch occupation began in the 17th century and gradually extended over the whole archipelago. Nationalist opposition to colonial rule began in the early 20th century. During the Second World War the territory was occupied by Japanese forces from March 1942. On 17 August 1945, three days after the Japanese surrender, a group of nationalists proclaimed the independence of Indonesia. The first President of the self-proclaimed republic was Dr Sukarno, a leader of the nationalist movement since the 1920s. The declaration of independence was not recognized by the Netherlands, which attempted to restore its pre-war control of the islands. After four years of intermittent warfare and negotiations between the Dutch authorities and the nationalists, agreement was reached on a formal transfer of power. On 27 December 1949 the United States of Indonesia became legally independent, with Sukarno continuing as President. Initially, the country had a federal Constitution, which gave limited self-government to the 16 constituent regions. In August 1950, however, the federation was dissolved, and the country became the unitary Republic of Indonesia. The 1949 independence agreement excluded West New Guinea (subsequently Irian Jaya and known as Papua from 1 January 2002), which remained under Dutch control until October 1962; however, following a brief period of UN administration, it was transferred to Indonesia in May 1963.

Domestic Political Affairs

Sukarno followed a policy of extreme nationalism, and his regime became increasingly dictatorial. His foreign policy was sympathetic to the People's Republic of China but, under his rule, Indonesia also played a leading role in the Non-aligned Movement (see p. 464). Inflation and widespread corruption provoked opposition to Sukarno's regime; in September–October 1965 there was an abortive military coup, in which the Partai Komunis Indonesia (PKI—Indonesian Communist Party) was strongly implicated. A massacre of alleged PKI members and supporters ensued. In March 1966 Sukarno was forced to transfer emergency executive powers to military commanders, led by Gen. Suharto, Chief of Staff of the Army, who outlawed the PKI. In February 1967 Sukarno transferred full power to Suharto. In March the Majelis Permusyawaratan Rakyat (MPR—People's Consultative Assembly) removed Sukarno from office and named Suharto acting President. He became Prime Minister in October 1967 and, following his election by the MPR, he was inaugurated as President in March 1968. In July 1971, in the first general election since 1955, the government-sponsored Sekretariat Bersama Golongan Karya (Joint Secretariat of Functional Groups), known as Golkar, won a majority of seats in the Dewan Perwakilan Rakyat (DPR—House of Representatives). Suharto was re-elected to the presidency in March 1973.

Under Suharto's 'New Order', real power passed from the legislature and the Cabinet to a small group of army officers and to the Operation Command for the Restoration of Order and Security (Kopkamtib), the internal security organization. Left-wing movements were suppressed, and a liberal economic policy was adopted. A general election in May 1977 gave Golkar a majority in the legislature, and Suharto was re-elected President (unopposed) in March 1978. Golkar won an increased majority in the elections in May 1982. In March 1983 Suharto was re-elected, again unopposed, as President.

During 1984 Suharto's attempt to introduce legislation requiring all political, social and religious organizations to adopt *Pancasila*, the five-point state philosophy (belief in a supreme being; humanitarianism; national unity; democracy by consensus; social justice), as their only ideology encountered violent opposition, allegedly instigated by Muslim opponents of the proposed legislation; many Muslims were tried and sentenced to long terms of imprisonment. All the political parties had accepted *Pancasila* by July 1985. At the April 1987 general election, despite international allegations of corruption and of abuses of human rights, Golkar won 299 of the 500 seats in the DPR.

In February 1988 new legislation reaffirmed the *dwifungsi*, or 'dual (i.e. military and socio-economic) function', of the Indonesian Armed Forces (ABRI). In March Suharto was again re-elected unopposed as President. Lt-Gen. (retd) Sudharmono, the Chairman of Golkar, was subsequently appointed Vice-President, to the consternation of ABRI since, under Sudharmono's chairmanship of Golkar, there had been a shift away from military dominance in the grouping. In October Sudharmono resigned as party Chairman and was replaced by Gen. (retd) Wahono.

In 1989 Suharto promoted legislation whereby decisions made by Islamic courts no longer required confirmation by civil courts, and in December 1990 the President opened the symposium of the newly formed Association of Indonesian Muslim Intellectuals (ICMI), an organization that united a broad spectrum of Islamic interests. ABRI was opposed to the establishment of ICMI because it regarded the polarization of politics by religion as a threat to stability.

During 1991 several new organizations were formed to promote freedom of expression and other democratic values. As labour unrest grew, arrests and the alleged intimidation of political activists curbed expressions of dissent, and political campaigns were banned on university campuses. In September Suharto removed several of the most outspoken members of Golkar from the list of candidates to contest the next legislative elections. During the campaign period, political parties were prohibited from addressing religious issues, the question of the dominant role of the ethnic Chinese community in the economy, or any subject that might present a threat to national unity. However, the opposition parties did exploit the increasing public resentment about the rapidly expanding businesses of Suharto's children. On 9 June 1992 90.4% of the electorate participated in the election to the DPR; Golkar secured 282 of the 400 elective seats, the Partai Persatuan Pembangunan (PPP—United Development Party) won 62 seats (a gain of one seat from the 1987 election) and the Partai Demokrasi Indonesia (PDI—Indonesian Democratic Party) won 56 seats (a gain of 16).

In March 1993 the DPR elected Suharto and Gen. Try Sutrisno, the former Commander-in-Chief of the Armed Forces, to the posts of President and Vice-President, respectively, the election of the latter appearing to consolidate ABRI's position following considerable public debate over its active involvement in political affairs and, in particular, concern over whether the appointment of 100 members of ABRI to the DPR remained justifiable. However, Suharto's new 41-member Cabinet reduced ABRI representation from 11 to eight members, and included several members of ICMI, whose Chairman, Prof. Dr Ir Bucharuddin Jusuf (B. J.) Habibie, was deeply unpopular with ABRI. Those primarily responsible for the country's economic policy since 1988—Prof. Dr Johannes B. Sumarlin, Adrianus Mooy and Radius Prawiro (all western-educated Christians)—were replaced, leaving only three Christians in the Cabinet.

In October 1993, at the party Congress, the Minister of Information, Harmoko, became the first civilian to be elected to the chairmanship of Golkar. In an unprecedented development, Suharto had openly endorsed Harmoko's candidacy. Also at the Congress, Suharto's family entered active national politics; his son, Bambang Trihatmodjo, and daughter, Siti Hardijanti Rukmana (known as Mbak Tutut), who had both been appointed to the MPR in 1992, were elected to positions of responsibility within Golkar.

Meanwhile, in July 1993 the incumbent Chairman of the PDI, Soerjadi, was re-elected to the post at a fractious party Congress. However, the Government invalidated the election of Soerjadi, who had campaigned during the 1992 elections for a limited presidential term of office, and appointed a 23-member 'caretaker board' pending new elections. An extraordinary Congress of the PDI ended inconclusively in December owing to the unexpected candidacy for the chairmanship of Megawati Sukarnoputri, the daughter of former President Sukarno. Despite government pressure to elect Budi Hardjono, a senior party official, Megawati received overwhelming support from the participants in the Congress, and the 'caretaker board' prevented a vote from taking place. The Government then ordered the holding of a new PDI Congress, at which Megawati was elected Chairman.

Suppression of political and civil unrest, 1993–98

In June 1993 the USA imposed a deadline of February 1994 for Indonesia to improve workers' rights or lose trade privileges under the Generalized System of Preferences. The Government adopted reforms to the only officially recognized trade union, the Serikat Pekerja Seluruh Indonesia (All Indonesia Workers' Union), introduced a substantial increase in the minimum wage and revoked the controversial 1986 Labour Law, which allowed the intervention of the armed forces in labour disputes. Workers subsequently went on strike, accusing employers of failing to pay the new minimum wage and demanding improved working conditions. In February 1994 the unrecognized Serikat Buruh Sejahtera Indonesia (SBSI—Indonesian Prosperous Labour Union) appealed for a one-hour national work stoppage. The General Secretary of the SBSI, Muchtar Pakpahan, was charged with inciting hatred against the Government and temporarily detained. In April 1994 riots broke out in Medan, Sumatra, over workers' demands for improved factory conditions and the implementation of the new minimum wage, rapidly degenerating into attacks on ethnic Chinese property and business executives, who were widely perceived to have benefited disproportionately from the country's rapid economic growth. Three members of the SBSI surrendered to the authorities in May and admitted to having organized the protest. Further strikes took place in other parts of northern Sumatra. In August Pakpahan was rearrested; he was given a three-year prison sentence in November for inciting labour unrest (which was later extended to four years).

In January 1995 it was announced by the armed forces that 300 members of the PDI were to be investigated for links to the 1965 coup attempt, following allegations that many members had relatives or contacts in the banned PKI. This apparent attempt to discredit the opposition grouping was followed in May 1995 by a ban on the presence of Megawati at the commemoration, in June, of the 25th anniversary of the death of her father, Sukarno. The authorities attempted to ascribe social unrest to communist subversion. In September the Chief of Staff of the Armed Forces named several prominent dissidents, including Muchtar Pakpahan (whose conviction for incitement had been rescinded by the Supreme Court in that month), as members of 'formless organizations', which, he claimed, had infiltrated pressure groups to promote the revival of communism. In November 300 alleged subversives were arrested in Java.

In July 1995, in response to widespread condemnation of Indonesia's human rights violations, Suharto announced that three prisoners detained for their complicity in the 1965 coup attempt would be released to coincide with the 50th anniversary of independence in August. The administration also subsequently announced that the code ET (which stood for *Eks Tahanan Politik*—former political prisoner) was to be removed from identity papers following the anniversary. The measure affected about 1.3m. citizens, most of whom had been arrested following the 1965 coup attempt, but released without trial; ET status had subjected them to certain restrictions (for example, in employment) and to widespread discrimination. In October 1995 30 members of an extreme right-wing group, the Islamic State of Indonesia, were arrested in western Java for attempting to overthrow 'the unitary state of Indonesia'. In January 1996 in Bandung, West Java, thousands took part in demonstrations against the disproportionately wealthy ethnic Chinese.

In January 1996 the Government abolished permit requirements for political meetings (police permission was still necessary for public gatherings and demonstrations). In March a group of political activists established an Independent Election Monitoring Committee, which was declared unconstitutional by the Government. In April the Government restored voting rights to 1,157,820 people who had been associated with the PKI, leaving a further 20,706 still ineligible to vote. However, the Government's increasing concern over potential opposition resulted in a return to more authoritarian practices. In May 1996 Sri Bintang Pamungkas, an outspoken member of the PPP expelled from the DPR in March 1995, received a custodial sentence of 34 months for insulting Suharto; the High Court upheld the verdict against him in December.

In June 1996 the Government responded to the increasing popularity of Megawati's leadership of the PDI: government supporters within the PDI organized a party Congress in the northern Sumatran town of Medan, which removed Megawati as leader, and installed the former Chairman, Soerjadi. PDI members loyal to Megawati organized demonstrations in her support. In July members of Soerjadi's PDI faction and the armed forces forcibly removed Megawati and her supporters from the PDI headquarters, prompting violence in which five people were killed. The Government declared the minor, Marxist-influenced Partai Rakyat Demokrasi (PRD) to be responsible for the rioting, and renewed its campaign against communism. In September the Government disbanded the PRD, declaring it to be a proscribed organization, and Megawati's new party headquarters in eastern Jakarta was closed.

In October 1996 Suharto ordered ABRI to suppress all political dissent. In November the Government declared that it would take action against non-governmental organizations (NGOs) that violated Indonesian law and the *Pancasila* ideology. In December the DPR ratified legislation granting the Government extensive powers to revoke the broadcasting permits of private television and radio stations. In the same month a government decree banned mass rallies during campaigning for the forthcoming legislative election. In February 1997 the Government announced that all proposed campaign speeches were to be examined to ensure their adherence to the *Pancasila*. In April thousands of supporters of Megawati rallied outside the DPR to protest against the exclusion from the final list of candidates of those nominated by her faction.

In the worst incident of pre-election violence, 125 people were killed when a shopping centre was set alight during clashes between supporters of Golkar and the PPP in the provincial capital of Kalimantan, Banjarmasin; more than 150 others were killed in various other incidents across the country. The election was held on 29 May 1997. However, riots in Madura, as a result of PPP claims that ballots had not been counted, resulted in an unprecedented repeat of voting at 86 polling stations on 4 June. The final results of the election, which continued to attract allegations of fraud, revealed that Golkar had secured 74.3% of the vote (compared with 68.1% in 1992), giving it control of 325 seats; the PPP had won 89 seats, while Soerjadi's PDI had secured only 11 seats (compared with 56 in 1992).

Widespread social unrest continued throughout 1997, as a result of religious tension, income disparity between social and ethnic groups and the repercussions of the central Government's transmigration programme, which had been initiated in 1971 in an effort to reduce population pressure on the most densely populated islands, particularly Java.

In August 1997 two Muslim leaders, Abdurrahman Wahid and Amien Rais, the head of the second largest Islamic grouping, Muhammadiyah, were excluded from the list of 500 civilian and military appointees to the MPR. Amien Rais had been forced to resign from a board of experts in ICMI in February for publicly criticizing the controversial Freeport mine in Irian Jaya (now Papua).

Following a massive decline in the value of the Indonesian currency between August and October 1997, President Suharto was forced to accept a rescue programme from the IMF. However, he subsequently failed to implement the requisite reforms, fearing that they would provoke unrest and adversely affect the business interests of his family and friends. An unprecedented gathering of Muslim leaders and intellectuals included members of ICMI; participants rejected Suharto's leadership and rallied around Amien Rais, who had already offered himself as a presidential candidate. Wahid subsequently joined Amien Rais and Megawati (who had entered an informal alliance) in demanding Suharto's resignation. In a largely symbolic gesture, Megawati also presented herself as a presidential candidate.

Nevertheless, at the presidential election, held on 10 March 1998, Suharto was re-elected unopposed. He then endorsed the nomination of Habibie as the new Vice-President. Suharto's new Cabinet included a number of members of his immediate circle of friends and family. (Prior to his re-election, Suharto had also appointed his son-in-law, Lt-Gen. Prabowo Subianto, as Commander of Kostrad—the Indonesian army's strategic reserve.) In May riots erupted in Jakarta, precipitated by the announcement of a 70% increase in the price of fuel. A report published by Indonesia's leading human rights group in June stated that at least 1,188 people had died in Jakarta alone, while hundreds were thought to have perished during unrest elsewhere. Indonesia's ethnic Chinese minority was the target for much of the violence: an uncertain number of Chinese were murdered, numerous Chinese women were raped, and Chinese homes and businesses were looted and burned.

The presidencies of Habibie and Wahid

On 21 May 1998, following sustained pressure (including an unprecedented demand for his resignation by Golkar Chairman Harmoko, and the resignation of the 14 economic ministers in the Cabinet), Suharto stepped down as President. Vice-President Habibie was sworn in as Suharto's successor, and subsequently appointed a new 'reform Cabinet', which nevertheless retained some ministers from the previous administration. The new President also announced the release of a number of political prisoners (including Muchtar Pakpahan and Sri Bintang Pamungkas), encouraged government departments to sever links with enterprises owned by Suharto's family, and supported the dismissal of Suharto's son-in-law, Lt-Gen. Prabowo, from his position as Commander of Kostrad. In June 1998 an investigation into the assets of Suharto and other government officials was announced, and Habibie expelled 41 members of the MPR, including several close associates of Suharto, on account of alleged corruption, nepotism and collusion. Seven members of Suharto's family were removed from their seats in the MPR the following month.

Unrest continued across the archipelago throughout the latter half of 1998, exacerbated by dissatisfaction at the pace of change under the new administration and at severe food shortages. During a four-day special session of the MPR in Jakarta in November at least 16 people were killed and more than 400 injured when students and other civilians clashed with soldiers outside the building. At least 14 people died during clashes between Muslims and Catholics in further riots. In the same month a report was published containing the findings of a panel appointed by the Government to investigate the riots that had occurred in May. The panel found that elements of the military had acted as provocateurs during the riots, with particular suspicion falling on Kostrad. Lt-Gen. Prabowo had been formally dismissed from the army in August owing to the role that he had played as the then Commander of the unit. In December former President Suharto was questioned at the Higher Prosecutor's Office over allegations of corruption.

In December 1998 it was announced that a legislative election would be held on 7 June 1999; it was also announced that the MPR (including 200 additional delegates) would convene on 29 August to elect a new President, although this was subsequently postponed until November. Under a new electoral system, combining both district and proportional voting, seats in the DPR were to be allocated proportionally, but only parties presenting candidates in the requisite number of districts would be permitted to contest the election. Civil servants were no longer to be obliged to support Golkar; the number of seats in the DPR allocated to the military was to be reduced from 75 to 38; and the membership of the MPR was to be reduced from 1,000 to 700.

At least 159 people were killed during clashes between Muslims and Christians on the island of Ambon, in the province of Maluku, in early 1999. The Habibie Government continued to pursue an extensive programme of reform. Several new laws benefited the provinces, including one providing for the election of district heads (*bupati*) by the district assemblies. In April the police force—part of the Indonesian military since 1962—was formally separated from the armed forces (while remaining under the control of the Ministry of Defence), and the armed forces resumed their revolutionary-era name, Tentara Nasional Indonesia (TNI—the Indonesian National Defence Forces), instead of ABRI (the Armed Forces of the Republic of Indonesia). The Subversion Law, introduced in 1963 and previously applied in the suppression of political dissidents, was repealed by the MPR (although some prohibitions were retained). In May 1999 a presidential decree removed a ban on the use and teaching of the Mandarin Chinese language and also outlawed discrimination on the grounds of ethnic origin.

President Habibie was nominated as the sole presidential candidate of the Golkar party in May 1999, despite some concerns regarding his close association with former President Suharto. The three leading opposition parties—Megawati's Partai Demokrasi Indonesia Perjuangan (PDI—P, Indonesian Democratic Struggle Party), Abdurrahman Wahid's Partai Kebangkitan Bangsa (PKB—National Awakening Party), and Amien Rais's Partai Amanat Nasional (PAN—National Mandate Party)—agreed to create an informal electoral alliance against Golkar; however, the alliance exhibited instability from an early stage. On 7 June approximately 118m. people voted (a turn-out of 91%). As expected, PDI—P was victorious, winning 34% of the votes cast (securing 154 seats); the second largest share of the vote was unexpectedly won by Golkar, which received 20% (120 seats), performing poorly in the cities but achieving a strong result in the outer islands. The PKB secured 59 seats, while the PAN won just 35 seats.

Megawati and Habibie thus emerged initially as the main candidates for the presidency. However, in October 1999, following the rejection of his presidential record by the MPR in a secret ballot, Habibie withdrew his candidacy. Contrary to the expectations of many, Megawati failed to win the presidential contest, receiving 313 votes, compared with the 373 secured by Abdurrahman Wahid, the only other serious candidate, who had received the endorsement of a number of Islamic parties, as well as the support of Golkar. The announcement of Wahid's victory provoked outrage among Megawati's supporters, and violent protests ensued in Jakarta and elsewhere. The MPR voted to appoint Megawati as Vice-President. The new Cabinet reflected the conciliatory and inclusive approach of the incoming President, incorporating both Islamist and nationalist representatives, as well as representatives of non-Javanese groups. Gen. Wiranto was appointed Co-ordinating Minister for Political, Legal and Security Affairs, and was replaced as Minister of Defence by the former Minister of Education and Culture, Juwono Sudarsono, the first civilian to hold the post.

The newly appointed Attorney-General, Marzuki Darusman, announced that the investigation into the allegations of corruption made against former President Suharto was to be reopened. The apparent commitment of the new administration to addressing corruption was further emphasized in November 1999, when Wahid urged the investigation of three government ministers, one of whom, the Co-ordinating Minister for People's Welfare and leader of the PPP, Hamzah Haz, subsequently resigned from the Cabinet.

Following Wahid's election to the presidency, there was further unrest across the archipelago. Ethnic violence continued on the island of Ambon in Maluku province where, according to official estimates in December 1999, more than 750 people had died and many thousands more had fled the region, since the renewal of violent clashes between Muslims and Christians in the region in January. (Aid agencies estimated the total number of dead to be much higher.) In mid-December President Wahid and Vice-President Megawati (who was criticized for her failure to address the crisis, despite having been charged by Wahid with special responsibility for Maluku) visited the region and appealed for an end to the conflict. Hundreds of additional troops were sent to Ambon to supplement the 2,500 already deployed in Maluku, following the occurrence of dozens more deaths.

Although the predominantly Muslim northern districts of Maluku were formally separated as the new province of North Maluku in late 1999, at least 265 people were believed to have been killed in clashes between Christians and Muslims on the island of Halmahera at the end of December, with violence also reported on other islands.

In January 2000 Indonesia's National Human Rights Commission released the results of its investigation into the role of the Indonesian armed forces in human rights abuses in the former Indonesian province of East Timor (now Timor-Leste—see Provincial Affairs and Separatist Tensions). Thirty-three military officers, including Gen. Wiranto, who had been Commander-in-Chief of the armed forces in 1998–99, were implicated. In February 2000 Wahid suspended Wiranto from his cabinet position and in May Wiranto resigned. In January, meanwhile, a reorganization took place within the TNI, in which officers loyal to Wiranto were apparently removed from positions of influence. A second reorganization of senior military personnel was announced in February, in which Maj.-Gen. Agus Wirahadikusumah was appointed as the head of Kostrad. In August doubts concerning the commitment of the Indonesian Government to the trial of military personnel suspected of involvement in gross human rights violations in East Timor were provoked when the MPR introduced a constitutional amendment that excluded military personnel from prosecution for crimes committed prior to the enactment of the relevant legislation. In September, furthermore, Wiranto was not included on the Attorney-General's list of 19 suspects.

In April 2000 President Wahid dismissed from the Cabinet the Minister of State for Investment and Development of State Enterprises, Laksamana Sukardi of the PDI—P, and the Minister of Trade and Industry, Muhammad Jusuf Kalla of the pro-Habibie wing of Golkar, subsequently suggesting that both were guilty of corruption. In July Wahid encountered intense criticism from the DPR when he refused to explain the reasons for his dismissal of the two Ministers. Meanwhile, general misgivings about Wahid's style of government also increased. In August Wahid announced that he was to delegate the daily administration of the Government to Vice-President Megawati. Amendments to the Constitution approved by the MPR in August included articles defining explicitly the authority of the DPR, particularly in relation to the body's questioning and investigating of government activities; legislation was also enacted to extend military representation in the MPR until 2009, four years after the date at which the military had been scheduled to lose its remaining 38 seats in the chamber. President Wahid announced the formation of a new 26-member Cabinet. The incoming Cabinet included considerably fewer representatives of Megawati's PDI—P, and two of the most influential cabinet posts were allocated to Wahid loyalists: Gen. (retd) Susilo Bambang Yudhoyono was appointed Co-ordinating Minister for Political, Legal and Security Affairs, while Rizal Ramli was designated Co-ordinating Minister for Economic Affairs.

In August 2000 former President Suharto was formally charged with corruption. In September, however, the charges against him were dismissed after an independent team of doctors declared him mentally and physically unfit to stand trial, provoking violent protests in Jakarta. (In May 2006 criminal charges against Suharto were formally abandoned on account of his deteriorating health, but a civil case was subsequently instigated—see The first direct presidential election.) In September 2000 President Wahid announced that he had ordered the arrest of Suharto's youngest son, Hutomo Mandala Putra (commonly known as Tommy Suharto), in connection with a series of bomb threats and explosions in Jakarta. In one such attack in September at least 15 people were killed when a bomb exploded at the Jakarta Stock Exchange; two men were subsequently convicted of carrying out the bombing and were both sentenced to 20 years' imprisonment. At the end of September the Supreme Court overruled Tommy Suharto's previous acquittal from an unrelated charge of fraudulent activity in 1999, and sentenced him to 18 months' imprisonment. In July 2001 the judge who had presided over the proceedings, Justice Syafiuddin Kartasasmita, was shot dead. Two suspects subsequently confessed to the murder, but admitted in custody that Suharto's son had financed them and supplied the weapons used in the attack; both were convicted and sentenced to life imprisonment, while a third man was sentenced to a four-year prison term for his involvement in planning the assassination. In an unexpected development, a three-judge Supreme Court panel rescinded the original corruption charge in October. However, Tommy Suharto was arrested in the following month in connection with the murder of Syafiuddin. In July 2002 he was convicted of arranging Syafiuddin's murder, illegal possession of a weapon and attempting to evade justice, and was sentenced to 15 years' imprisonment. Following a successful appeal, this was subsequently reduced to a 10-year term, and in October 2006 he was granted conditional early release. Several further corruption cases against him were dismissed in 2008–09.

The transfer of power to Megawati

In September 2000 the DPR appointed a commission to investigate two financial scandals with which President Wahid had been linked: the first involved the irregular diversion of US $4.1m. from the funds of the Badan Urusan Logistic (BULOG—the National Logistics Agency), allegedly to finance the Golkar party election campaign in 1999, while the second concerned a donation of $2m. made by Sultan Hassanal Bolkiah of Brunei. The President's refusal to be questioned on either matter provoked intense frustration among legislators. In January 2001 the commission concluded that Wahid 'could be suspected of playing a role' in the theft of BULOG funds by his personal masseur and that the President had been deliberately inconsistent in his explanations of how the donation from the Sultan (originally intended for social welfare) had been spent; however, the commission was unable to present clear evidence that Wahid had personally benefited from either situation. In February the DPR voted by 393 votes to four for the formal censure of Wahid over his alleged involvement in the scandals. Wahid was given three months in which to provide a satisfactory explanation of his actions to the DPR. The President continued to deny any wrongdoing and stated his intention to complete his term of presidential office. Tens of thousands of pro-Wahid demonstrators took to the streets in Surabaya and elsewhere in East Java (President Wahid's home province), and protesters set fire to the regional offices of Golkar, which had supported the vote to censure Wahid. Later in the same month Wahid offered himself for questioning by police investigating the two scandals.

In March 2001 more than 12,000 students held a demonstration in Jakarta to demand the President's resignation. In view of Wahid's unsatisfactory reply to his first censure, in April the DPR issued a second censure and requested that the MPR convene a special session to begin impeachment proceedings. Violent pro-Wahid demonstrations took place in East Java. Despite the abandonment of all charges against Wahid in May, following the ruling by Attorney-General Marzuki Darusman that there was no evidence to suggest the President had been involved in either of the financial scandals, later that month the DPR voted by a huge majority to instruct the MPR to instigate an impeachment hearing. In response, in June the President reorganized his Cabinet, dismissing the Co-ordinating Minister for Political, Legal and Security Affairs, Yudhoyono. The Chief of Police, Gen. Surojo Bimantoro, was suspended. In July the President threatened to declare a state of emergency if no compromise had been reached, and effected another reorganization of the Cabinet. He also appointed a new Chief of Police without the support of the legislature. A special session of the MPR was convened to which the President was summoned to give an account of his 21 months in power. President Wahid deemed the session illegal and refused to attend. He suspended the legislature, declaring a state of civil emergency, and urged that new elections be held in one year's time. However, the military refused to support the declaration, and the MPR stated that the President did not have the constitutional authority to dissolve it.

On 23 July 2001 Wahid was deposed as President following an impeachment hearing. He was replaced by Vice-President Megawati. Legislators elected the leader of the PPP, Hamzah Haz, to act as the new President's deputy, and in August Megawati announced the composition of her first Cabinet. Of its 32 members, only four were former military men, in sharp contrast to previous practice, and Yudhoyono was reinstated as Co-ordinating Minister for Political, Legal and Security Affairs.

In October 2001 President Megawati assented to a prosecution request to question the Speaker of the DPR, Akbar Tandjung, over the alleged misappropriation of BULOG funds. Tandjung admitted that he had handled the money on the orders of President Habibie, but had passed it on to an Islamic charity to fund food supplies for the poor. However, Attorney-General Muhammad Abdul Rachman claimed that investigations showed that such contributions had never taken place. In December state prosecutors questioned Habibie, and in January 2002 Tandjung was formally declared to be a suspect. In March approximately 1,500 protesters gathered outside the DPR building to demand Tandjung's resignation and the establishment of an independent inquiry. In September Tandjung was convicted of corruption and sentenced to a three-year prison term, but in February 2004 the Supreme Court overruled his conviction.

The first direct presidential election

In August 2002 a series of constitutional amendments was approved at the annual session of the MPR. These provided for the direct election of both the President and Vice-President at the next national poll, scheduled to be held in 2004, and for the abolition of all seats held by non-elected representatives, effectively terminating military involvement in the legislature five years earlier than originally intended. The legislation also provided for a bicameral legislature through the creation of the Dewan Perwakilan Daerah (DPD—House of Representatives of the Regions), which, together with the DPR, would form the MPR. A total of 14 amendments received legislative assent; these constituted the 'Fourth Amendment' to the Constitution. The DPR ratified the amendments in 2003.

A total of 24 parties contested the 2004 legislative elections, which were held on 5 April; turn-out was estimated at 84% of the electorate. The Golkar party secured 128 of the 550 seats in the expanded DPR, replacing the PDI—P, which won 109 seats, as the largest parliamentary grouping. Of the smaller parties, the PPP won 58 seats, the PD 57, and the PAN and the PKB each secured 52 seats.

At the inaugural direct presidential and vice-presidential election held on 5 July 2004, the presidential candidate of Partai Democrat (PD—Democratic Party), Yudhoyono, whose election campaign had focused on pledges to stimulate the economy and to combat corruption and terrorism, secured 33.6% of the votes cast, followed by the incumbent Megawati, with 26.6%, and Golkar's candidate, Gen. (retd) Wiranto, with 22.2%; Amien Rais and Vice-President Hamzah Haz also contested the election on behalf of their respective parties, the PAN and the PPP. As no candidate won more than 50% of the votes, Yudhoyono and Megawati proceeded to a second round of voting, which was held on 20 September: despite Golkar's declared support for the incumbent, Yudhoyono (whose vice-presidential candidate was Jusuf Kalla, the Co-ordinating Minister for People's Welfare) emerged victorious, securing 60.6% of the votes cast. Estimated voter turn-out in the second round was 75%, compared with 78% in the first. The new President was inaugurated on 20 October, and on the following day announced the composition of his Cabinet, which included representatives of several political organizations. Notable new appointees included Adm. (retd) Widodo Adi Sutjipto, the former Commander-in-Chief of the TNI, as Co-ordinating Minister for Political, Legal and Security Affairs, and Aburizal Bakrie, of Golkar, as Co-ordinating Minister for Economic Affairs; Hassan Wirajuda, the Minister of Foreign Affairs, was one of five ministers retained from Megawati's administration.

Vice-President Jusuf Kalla was elected as Chairman of Golkar in December 2004, defeating the incumbent, Akbar Tandjung. As a result, it was anticipated that Golkar would henceforth broadly support the Government, enabling Yudhoyono to secure legislative approval for his policies. In late December Abdullah Puteh, the Governor of Aceh, became the first person to be prosecuted by the recently formed Komisi Pemberantasan Korupsi (KPK—Corruption Eradication Commission). Puteh, who was suspended from office by Yudhoyono, was charged with corruption in relation to the purchase of a Russian helicopter in 2002. He was convicted in April 2005 and was sentenced to 10 years' imprisonment; he was also ordered to repay the Rp. 3,600m. that he was deemed to have embezzled from state funds and was fined an additional Rp. 500m.

Meanwhile, in August 2004 an Indonesian court acquitted the head of the Kopassus special forces regiment, Maj.-Gen. Sriyanto Muntrasan, who had been accused of human rights violations in connection with the shooting of several Muslim activists near Jakarta's Tanjung Priok port in 1984, despite sentencing Sriyanto's immediate superior, Maj.-Gen. (retd) Rudolf Butar-Butar, to 10 years' imprisonment in April for failing to prevent the shooting; later in August 11 soldiers received prison terms, having been found guilty in the same case of systematic attacks against civilians. However, in July 2005 the convictions of Butar-Butar and the 11 soldiers were overruled on appeal by the High Court, which deemed the shootings to have been accidental.

In November 2004 it emerged that Munir Said Thalib, a leading Indonesian human rights activist who had died during a flight to the Netherlands in September, had been poisoned with arsenic. Munir had been an outspoken critic of Indonesia's military and State Intelligence Agency (Badan Inteligen Negara—BIN). In March 2005 Pollycarpus Priyanto, an airline pilot of the state-owned Garuda Indonesia who had been on Munir's flight while off duty, was arrested and charged with the activist's murder. Pollycarpus was convicted and sentenced to 14 years' imprisonment in December, but was acquitted on appeal by the Supreme Court in September 2006. However, the case was reopened after prosecutors argued that Indra Setiawan, the former CEO of Garuda, had played a significant part in the murder of Munir by allowing the off-duty pilot the opportunity to carry out the poisoning. In January 2008 Pollycarpus was convicted of pre-meditated murder and forgery, and sentenced to 20 years' imprisonment, and in February Setiawan was convicted of assisting in Munir's murder and given a 12-month sentence; both men claimed to have been carrying out orders issued to them by BIN. Independent investigators had previously identified links between Pollycarpus and BIN, and in August Maj.-Gen. Muchdi Purwopranjono, the deputy head of BIN at the time of Munir's murder, went on trial, charged with ordering the killing of Munir. Human rights groups welcomed the development, which represented the first prosecution of a senior BIN official. However, Purwopranjono was acquitted in December owing to a lack of evidence; the failure of a significant number of prosecution witnesses to appear in court prompted allegations that BIN had intimidated witnesses in order to protect Purwopranjono and its own reputation.

Meanwhile, Indonesia, in particular the province of Aceh, was devastated by a series of tsunamis caused by a massive earthquake in the Indian Ocean on 26 December 2004. The provincial capital, Banda Aceh, was severely damaged, while the town of Meulaboh, 150 km from the epicentre of the earthquake, was completely destroyed. UN agencies and other organizations commenced operations to distribute food, medical supplies and shelter to survivors. Aceh had been under emergency rule prior to the disaster, owing to a separatist insurgency (see Provincial Affairs and Separatist Tensions), and largely closed to foreign agencies and the international media. Most official estimates subsequently concurred that in Aceh alone as many as 170,000 had died; more than 400,000 were made homeless. In March 2005 a massive after-shock precipitated by the original earthquake in December struck off the Sumatran coast, killing approximately 300 people.

In July 2005 the Indonesian Ulama Council (Majelis Ulama Indonesia—MUI) issued 11 *fatwa* (religious edicts), the most controversial of which outlawed secularism, pluralism and liberal Islamic teachings. The issue of the *fatwa* was thought to be in response to the activities of two moderate, progressive Islamic organizations: the Liberal Islam Network (Jaringan Islam Liberal—JIL) and the Muhammadiyah Youth Intellectuals Network. Meanwhile, ongoing criticism of the Ahmadiyah sect (which maintained that its founder, Mirza Ghulam Ahmad, rather than the Prophet Muhammad, was the final prophet) continued; although deemed an heretical group, the sect was believed to have attracted 200,000 followers. In July thousands of members of the so-called Indonesian Muslim Solidarity group attacked the Ahmadiyah compound in Jakarta, citing an edict issued in 1980 by the MUI, which had declared members of Ahmadiyah to be deviants. The edict was renewed in August 2005. Ahmadis in Bandung and other Javanese cities were also targeted. In April 2008, after a government panel recommended that the group be banned, a large protest was held in Jakarta; demonstrators demanded the expulsion from Indonesia of Ahmadis. A series of attacks on Ahmadiyah mosques in the country prompted the Government to demand that Ahmadis cease 'spreading interpretations and activities which deviate from the principal teachings of Islam' and to warn of prison terms for offenders. It was subsequently reported that the police had helped local Islamic extremists forcibly to shut down several mosques owned by the sect in the West Javan village of Manislor. The leniency of sentences handed down by an Indonesian district court in July 2011 to 12 men who had participated in a violent mob attack against a group of about 20 Ahmadis at a mosque in another West Javan village, Cikeusik, during which three Ahmadis had been bludgeoned to death, elicited much criticism from human rights groups and the wider international community. The defendants, none of whom were charged with murder, received prison terms ranging between three and six months, having been convicted only of relatively minor offences, including being in possession of a weapon. By contrast, in the following month Deden Sudjana, an Ahmadi who had been present during the attack, was imprisoned for six months for disobeying a police order to leave the scene of the attack and assaulting a member of the violent mob, despite video footage of the incident appearing to corroborate Sudjana's claim that he was merely acting in self-defence. The same footage also showed police officers failing to intervene as members of the mob, some of them wielding machetes, beat the small group of Ahmadis. The US-based international organization Human Rights Watch expressed its concern at the sentence, which, it argued, suggested that 'the Ahmadiyah face blatant discrimination not just from Islamic militant mobs, but also from an Indonesian court'.

In December 2005, meanwhile, President Yudhoyono effected a long-anticipated cabinet reorganization, which focused predominantly on economic personnel. Co-ordinating Minister for Economic Affairs Aburizal Bakrie, who had attracted much criticism for his failure to halt the rapid decline in the value of the rupiah, was transferred to the position of Co-ordinating Minister for People's Welfare; Bakrie was replaced by Prof. Dr Boediono, Minister of Finance during Megawati's presidency. Minister of State for National Development Planning Dr Sri Mulyani Indrawati was transferred to the finance portfolio, in place of Jusuf Anwar. Various ministerial portfolios were re-allocated in May 2007. Changes included the dismissal of the Minister of Justice and Human Rights Affairs, Hamid Awaludin, and State Secretary Yusril Ihza Mahendra, as a result of their alleged involvement in the illegal transfer of US $10m. to Tommy Suharto, son of the former President, from a bank account located in the United Kingdom.

In July 2007 a civil case was filed against former President Suharto, in the hope of recovering some US $440m. that prosecutors claimed he had misappropriated from funds ostensibly allocated to an educational foundation; the Government was also seeking damages of $1,400m. Suharto died in January 2008, prompting the Government to declare a week of mourning. He was posthumously acquitted in March; however, his charitable foundation, Supersemar, was found guilty and directed to reimburse some $100m. to the State. In August the Government seized $150m. from Timor Putra Nasional, a now-defunct motor vehicle company belonging to Tommy Suharto, amid ongoing investigations into allegations that he had illegally sold assets from Timor Putra Nasional to five of his other companies. The Supreme Court subsequently ruled that the action was not lawful and ordered the Government to return the funds to Tommy Suharto. In July 2010, however, the Supreme Court rescinded its previous ruling on the basis of new evidence provided by the Ministry of Finance.

Meanwhile, Jakarta's first ever direct gubernatorial election took place in August 2007. The election was won by the incumbent Deputy Governor, Fauzi Bowo, who received nearly 58% of the votes cast, there being only one other candidate. The level of participation reached 65% of those eligible to vote. It was announced in June 2008 that Minister of Finance and State Enterprises Development Dr Indrawati was to assume concurrent responsibility for the economic affairs portfolio, following the departure of Prof. Dr Boediono from the Cabinet.

In October 2008 Burhanuddin Abdullah, the former Governor of Bank Indonesia, was sentenced to five years' imprisonment and ordered to pay a fine in excess of US $25,000, after being convicted of embezzling funds in order to bribe legislators and to engage lawyers in his attempts to defend officials of the central bank against corruption allegations. In January 2009 House of Representatives member Al-Amin Nasution was sentenced to eight years in prison, having been found guilty of accepting bribes from local officials on Bintan Island, in the province of Riau, in return for granting development rights for the construction of a new provincial capital on protected forest land. Also in January, the MUI issued a *fatwa* forbidding Muslims to practise yoga exercises that incorporated Hindu influences such as chanting.

The 2009 legislative and presidential elections

In April 2008 it was announced that the legal status of 24 new political parties had been recognized. A total of 38 national parties were deemed eligible to participate in the 2009 legislative election. Under new legislation approved in October 2008, political parties were required to secure at least 20% of the seats or 25% of the votes cast in the legislative election in order to nominate a presidential candidate. Vice-President Jusuf Kalla announced in February 2009 that he would not stand as Yudhoyono's vice-presidential candidate again, and would challenge Yudhoyono, if nominated by Golkar as its presidential candidate.

At the legislative election held on 9 April 2009, the number of seats in the DPR was increased from 550 to 560. For the first time, under Indonesia's system of proportional representation, electors were able to vote for specific candidates within each party. Polling for the 132 (hitherto 128) regional delegates of the MPR also took place, along with local elections. A major issue was the rapid deterioration in the country's economy. The PD won 20.8% of the votes cast (nearly tripling its share of the votes received at the 2004 election) to secure 148 of the 560 seats in the DPR, thereby enabling the incumbent President Yudhoyono formally to present his candidacy for the presidential election scheduled for 8 July. Golkar secured 108 seats (14.4% of the vote), reduced from 128 at the last election, while the PDI—P won only 93 seats (14.0%), in comparison with 109 five years previously. Turn-out was estimated at 71% of the 171m. registered voters, a decline of 13 percentage points from that recorded in 2004, although still comparatively high by international standards.

In May 2009, having failed to secure the required 20% of the seats or 25% of the popular vote to nominate a presidential candidate, Golkar and PDI—P announced the formation of a 10-party electoral coalition, thus enabling them to nominate Kalla and Megawati as their respective candidates for the presidential election, which was held on 8 July. Incumbent President Yudhoyono, with Prof. Dr Boediono as his vice-presidential candidate, achieved a resounding victory, attracting 60.8% of the votes cast. Megawati and Lt-Gen. Prabowo secured 26.8% of the ballot, while Kalla and Gen. (retd) Wiranto obtained just 12.4%. Yudhoyono was sworn in for his second consecutive term as President in mid-October, and immediately inaugurated his new Cabinet. The incoming Government retained 10 ministers from the previous administration, including Dr Sri Mulyani Indrawati as Minister of Finance. Notable new appointees included Air Chief Marshal (retd) Djoko Suyanto as Co-ordinating Minister for Political, Legal and Security Affairs and Hatta Radjasa as Co-ordinating Minister for Economic Affairs.

Aburizal Bakrie was elected as the new Chairman of Golkar at a party Congress held in October 2009; the former Co-ordinating Minister for People's Welfare attracted 296 out of 536 delegates' votes to defeat three other candidates, among them Tommy Suharto (who failed to secure a single vote).

Recent developments: declining support for Yudhoyono

An alleged plot to sabotage the KPK was a significant contributory factor in a rapid decline in the popularity of President Yudhoyono from late 2009. In October the integrity of the KPK had been called into question when two of its Deputy Chairmen, Chandra Hamzah and Bibit Samad Rianto, were detained by the police on suspicion of bribery. However, both were released in November, and the charges against them were withdrawn in December, after the pair submitted covert recordings of conversations between several people widely accepted to have been senior members of the police force and the Attorney-General's office, which revealed that those speaking, angered by the KPK's successful investigation and charging of numerous officials, intended to destroy the reputation of the anti-corruption commission. Two of the officials linked to the plot, Deputy Attorney-General Abdul Hakim Ritonga and Chief Detective Susno Duadji, tendered their resignations, following numerous protests demanding the dismissal of those involved. In March 2011 Susno Duadji was sentenced to three-and-a-half years' imprisonment, having been convicted of accepting bribes and embezzling public funds; the verdict was upheld by the Jakarta High Court in November. However, as of early 2012, no proceedings appeared to have been instigated against Susno—or any other individual—in connection with the alleged plot against the KPK. Many Indonesians who had voted for Yudhoyono in the presidential election were disillusioned by his perceived failure to intervene, and questioned his commitment to his pre-election pledge to take firm action against vice and corruption. Yudhoyono's reputation as an anti-graft reformist had already been dented by the conviction on corruption charges of Aulia Pohan, the father-in-law of Yudhoyono's son and a former Deputy Governor of Bank Indonesia, in June 2009. Together with three other central bank Deputy Governors, Aulia Pohan was found to have embezzled Rp 100,000m. from the Yayasan Pengembangan Perbankan Indonesia (Indonesian Banking Development Foundation) in 2003, and was sentenced to four-and-a-half-years' imprisonment and ordered to pay a fine of Rp. 200m.

Meanwhile, the controversy surrounding the alleged plot against the KPK intensified further in February 2010 when the former head of the commission, Antasari Azhar, was convicted of arranging the murder of Indonesian businessman Nasrudin Zulkarnaen and sentenced to 18 years' imprisonment. KPK Chairman at the time of his arrest in May 2009, Antasari was alleged to have been romantically involved with Zulkarnaen's wife and to have arranged for Zulkarnaen to be killed to stop him from exposing details of the affair. Antasari's conviction came despite testimony given during the trial by former South Jakarta police chief Wiliardi Wizard, in which Wiliardi recanted his original testimony against Antasari, claiming that he had been forced to co-operate with a police-instigated plot to incriminate the former KPK head. An appeal lodged by Antasari was rejected by the Supreme Court in September 2010. However, his many supporters continued to insist that he had been the victim of an ongoing attempt by the police to discredit the KPK and obstruct anti-corruption efforts.

The Government's controversial rescue programme for a failing financial institution, PT Bank Century Tbk, was another source of considerable contention. Legislators and the general public alike were angered by the revelation in late 2009 that the takeover of the bank in November 2008 had cost taxpayers the equivalent of US $720m., more than four times the amount originally agreed by the Government and the DPR. Opposition parliamentarians argued that Vice-President Boediono (Governor of Bank Indonesia at the time of the intervention) and Minister of Finance Indrawati had abused their positions to protect the interests of Bank Century, which was renamed PT Bank Mutiara Tbk in October 2009, without first securing the approval of the DPR. (Subsequently, many of the bank's wealthy clients were alleged to have made sizeable donations to the election campaign of Yudhoyono and Boediono.) A parliamentary inquiry into 'Centurygate', as the scandal had become known, was initiated in late 2009. In March 2010 the committee published its final report: although it stated that it had found no evidence of Bank Century money being used to support any political campaign, it did criticize the decision-making process, including the actions of Boediono and Indrawati, and urged the Government to pursue the possibility of prosecutions. However, Yudhoyono contested that the rescue programme had been 'essential to saving the banking system' and declared that he saw no need for any action to be taken against Boediono or Indrawati, who both denied any wrongdoing. A forensic audit of the bank was carried out by the Badan Pemeriksa Keuangan (BPK—Supreme Audit Agency) in mid-2011 at the request of the House of Representatives. In December the BPK submitted to the House a report detailing its findings. However, the report was widely criticized, on account of a lack of new evidence and, crucially, its perceived failure fully to explain how all of the rescue programme funding had been spent, with some legislators alleging interference in the audit process. A KPK investigation into the scandal, launched in January 2010, was widely expected to prove similarly inconclusive, although the appointment in December 2011 of Abraham Samad, a lawyer and rights activist with a strong anti-corruption reputation, as Chairman of the KPK for the period 2012–15 did engender hope in some quarters that prosecutions might be forthcoming. (However, critics of the appointment noted Samad's alleged links in the past to hardline Islamist groups and individuals, including the Muslim cleric Abu Bakar Bashir—see The Threat of Terrorism.)

Meanwhile, the public grief displayed in response to the death, in December 2009, of former President Wahid served further to augment the increasing dissatisfaction with Yudhoyono, and in January 2010 large-scale anti-Government protests were held in several Indonesian cities, including Jakarta, to mark the 100th day of the President's second term in office.

In April 2010 Megawati secured re-election to a third consecutive five-year term as PDI—P Chairperson, but failed to deliver on a pledge to introduce a new generation of PDI—P members to the party's senior leadership. Tjahjo Kumolo, a veteran PDI—P member, was appointed Secretary-General, and other important posts were similarly awarded to well-established senior party members. The decision attracted much criticism, with many observers contending that the PDI—P's poor performance in the 2009 elections had been largely attributable to the party's 'old guard', and that the conservative nature of the appointments would likely damage the party's chances at the next legislative elections, due to be held in 2014.

Also in April 2010 the Constitutional Court rejected appeals to overrule controversial legislation implemented in 1967 allowing for criminal penalties and bans on individuals or groups that 'distort' the central tenets of Indonesia's six officially recognized religions—Buddhism, Christianity (both Catholicism and Protestantism), Confucianism, Hinduism and Islam—declaring that the law was in accordance with the Constitution and was vital to religious harmony. It had been hoped that the legislation might be reviewed to allow the official establishment of new religions and sects. Human Rights Watch condemned the ruling as a 'real threat to the beliefs of Indonesia's religious minorities'. According to a local human rights organization, Setara Institute for Peace and Democracy, there were 28 reported attacks on religious freedom in Indonesia during the first seven months of 2010, compared with 18 in the whole of 2009 and 17 in 2008; many of the attacks were attributed to the Islamic Defenders Front (FPI), which demanded the implementation of Islamic law (*Shari'a*) across the archipelago. Critics of the Yudhoyono Government claimed that the President had failed to intervene since Islamic parties formed the core of his parliamentary support. In August 2010 crowds gathered at an inter-faith rally organized in Jakarta to protest against the harassment of religious minorities, urging the Government to adopt a stronger stance against those responsible.

In May 2010 Indrawati, who was widely credited for the macroeconomic reforms that had helped Indonesia to withstand the effects of the international financial crisis, tendered her resignation as Minister of Finance in order to take up a senior position at the World Bank; she was replaced as Minister of Finance by Agus Martowardojo, hitherto chief executive of PT Bank Mandiri. There were concerns that the resignation of Indrawati, who was perceived by many as a strong reformist in a corrupt system, might lead to a further increase in public corruption, as well as a concomitant decline in foreign investment. Some observers speculated that Indrawati had effectively been forced to resign by Yudhoyono's perceived lack of support for her and for Boediono during the opposition campaign for a criminal investigation into the pair's conduct during Centurygate.

A proposal to amend the Constitution, put forward by DP legislator Ruhut Sitompul in August 2010, in order to allow Yudhoyono to seek re-election for a third term as President elicited an angry response from many Indonesians, who contested that it represented a serious affront to the principles of democracy. Ruhut, by contrast, argued that there were no suitable candidates to replace Yudhoyono at the 2014 election. The President subsequently sought to distance himself from the comments, stating that he would not support any such attempts to amend the Constitution. In October the first anniversary of Yudhoyono's inauguration into his second presidential term prompted renewed demands for his resignation.

Yudhoyono's reputation as an anti-corruption reformist suffered a further reverse during the trial of former tax official Gayus Tambunan, who in January 2011 was convicted on four counts of corruption and sentenced to seven years' imprisonment: during court proceedings, Gayus, who was found to have gained more than Rp. 100,000m. through tax fraud, confessed to having assisted public officials to evade tax charges, bribing prosecutors and police officials, and even to having bribed his way out of prison while awaiting trial; the defendant's testimony suggested endemic levels of corruption among the authorities. The prosecution filed an appeal against the sentence, arguing that it was too lenient, while Gayus appealed against the verdict, attesting that he had merely been 'a pawn' in the extensive political disputes over several high-profile corruption cases, including that of former KPK head Antasari. During his trial, Gayus had alleged that the chief prosecutor in Antasari's case, Cirus Sinaga, had been involved in the falsification of documents pertaining to that case, and suggested that the police's 'failure' to investigate Cirus constituted evidence of institutional-level corruption. An investigation was subsequently initiated, and Cirus was arrested in April and charged with obstruction of justice and abuse of authority. Following a brief trial, he was convicted in October, and was sentenced to five years' imprisonment and ordered to pay a Rp. 150m. fine.

In January 2011 the Minister of Home Affairs, Gamawan Fauzi, expressed concern at the apparent escalation in corruption, noting that some 155 regional leaders had been named as suspects in investigations since 2004; of these, 17 were either current or former governors. Among this number were: the former Governor of Riau Islands, Ismeth Abdullah, who in August 2010 was sentenced to two years' imprisonment upon conviction of involvement in a procurement scandal that cost the Government nearly Rp. 99,000m.; the Governor of North Sumatra, Syamsul Arifin, who was arrested in October in connection with allegations pertaining to his tenure as the Langkat district leader between 2000 and 2007, during which it was claimed that Syamsul had caused losses of more than Rp. 100,000m. for the local administration; and the Governor of Bengkulu, Agusrin Najamuddin, who, it was alleged, had embezzled Rp. 20,200m. from the provincial administration.

In a more positive development, in October 2010 the Constitutional Court revoked legislation that allowed the Attorney-General's office unilaterally to prohibit the publication and supply of books that were deemed to be 'offensive' or a 'threat to public order', ruling that the power to impose such bans should henceforth be accorded to the judicial system. The overruling of the legislation, which had been implemented in 1963 and had been used to silence opposition during the Suharto era, was welcomed as symbolically significant.

Also in October 2010 the Government came under intense criticism following a tsunami that claimed the lives of more than 400 people and left some 13,000 homeless. Indonesia's early warning system, which had been implemented at great expense after the 2004 disaster, failed to alert the authorities to the impending tsunami, generated by a major earthquake off the coast of Sumatra; the system was reported to have fallen into disrepair owing to inadequate maintenance. Yudhoyono curtailed a state visit to Viet Nam and returned to Indonesia to oversee the subsequent rescue operation, together with a separate operation to provide relief to those affected by the eruption of a volcano one day after the tsunami; a series of eruptions by Mount Merapi over the course of several weeks killed more than 200 people. However, the authorities' perceived mishandling of the response to the tsunami disaster, with reports of many people who had sustained only superficial injuries none the less dying some days after the incident owing to a shortage of basic medical and food supplies, prompted widespread anger.

New legislation to combat human-trafficking was approved by the legislature in April 2011. Under the new laws, those convicted of transporting illegal migrants into the country could be sentenced to up to 15 years in prison and a US $170,000 fine; previously, they could be charged only with relatively minor immigration offences. The development was widely welcomed, both domestically and further afield, particularly by the Australian Government, which had for some time been pressing Indonesia to adopt a firmer stance on the issue, with many thousands of migrants and asylum-seekers using Jakarta as a transit point en route to Australia. None the less, concerns were raised as to how the new legislation might be effectively implemented, amid widespread reports of Indonesian immigration officials accepting bribes on a frequent basis.

Further corruption allegations emerged in April 2011, with the Treasurer of the PD, Muhammad Nazaruddin, accused of soliciting bribes amounting to US $2.8m. from a construction company, in exchange for a contract to build athletes' accommodation for the Southeast Asian Games, which Indonesia hosted in November. However, Nazaruddin refuted the claims, alleging that other legislators and PD officials—including Yudhoyono's son and the Secretary-General of the PD, Edhie 'Ibas' Baskoro Yudhoyono, and PD Chairman Anas Urbaningrum—had been involved in the scandal. Further allegations against Nazaruddin were subsequently made, including a claim that he had paid $120,000 to the Secretary-General of the Constitutional Court for unspecified purposes. The question of how best to respond to the allegations against Nazaruddin fomented division with the PD leadership. Nazaruddin was eventually dismissed from his role as PD Treasurer, although he was allowed to retain his parliamentary seat pending further investigation by the KPK. He fled the country in May, but was arrested in Colombia in August and was extradited to Indonesia. Following the conclusion of the KPK investigation, Nazaruddin was formally charged with bribery in December. Having been found guilty in April 2012, he was sentenced to four years and 10 months in prison and fined Rp. 200m. The episode, and particularly concerns regarding how Nazaruddin had been able to flee the country despite the gravity of the claims against him, wreaked considerable damage upon the reputation of both the PD and the Yudhoyono administration, and cast further doubt on the latter's commitment to tackling corruption.

Meanwhile, the appointment in June 2011 of Gen. Pramono Edhie Wibowo, Yudhoyono's brother-in-law, as Chief of Staff of the Army provoked accusations of nepotism and prompted speculation that the President might be preparing his relative to replace him at the presidential election due in 2014. Of further concern to critics of the appointment was the alleged involvement of Gen. Wibowo, who replaced the retiring Gen. George Toisutta, in human rights abuses in East Timor in 1999 (see Provincial Affairs and Separatist Tensions).

A cabinet reorganization effected by Yudhoyono in October 2011 was widely interpreted as an attempt to restore public confidence in the President's administration, particularly its handling of economic concerns. Gita Wirjawan, the well-respected Chairman of the Badan Koordinasi Penanaman Modal (Investment Co-ordinating Board), was allocated the additional post of Minister of Trade, while Dahlan Iskan, hitherto President Director of the state-owned electricity distribution company, PT Perusahaan Listrik Negara, was named Minister of State for State Enterprises. However, critics described the ministerial changes as 'superficial', with around two-thirds of the incumbent ministers retaining their positions—including, notably, Co-ordinating Minister for Economic Affairs Hatta Rajasa and Minister of Finance Agus Martowardojo. Opinion polls conducted in that month suggested that Yudhoyono's popularity had sunk to its lowest ebb, with approval ratings of just 46%, down from 61% one year previously, and from 85% at the time of his re-election in July 2009; the President's perceived failure effectively to combat corruption and to address the country's economic challenges were two of the principal factors cited in the decline.

In December 2011 a student activist, Sondang Hutagalung, set himself on fire outside the presidential buildings; he subsequently died from his injuries. While Sondang's motivation remained unclear, the local press was quick to speculate that the student's self-immolation had been driven by deep discontent with the Government and the 'corrupted' state of Indonesian society. The Deputy Speaker of the MPR, Hajriyanto Tohar, warned that if the incident did not elicit an appropriate response from the Government, social conflict might ensue, drawing an explicit parallel with the situation in Tunisia, where the self-immolation of a lone individual in December 2010 precipitated widespread popular protests that ultimately led to the ousting of that country's President, Zine al-Abidine Ben Ali, in January 2011. Addressing a PDI—P meeting in December 2011, held to formulate a party strategy for regional elections scheduled to take place during the course of 2012 and the presidential poll due in 2014, Megawati, referring to Sondang's death, professed that 'the message was clear . . . that there is something wrong with the management of this country'. The opposition leader insisted that Yudhoyono should be held fully responsible for the prevailing culture of corruption and 'money politics' within Indonesia, and claimed that he and his close associates had inappropriately used public funds to gain electoral support. Megawati also criticized what she deemed to be the country's over-reliance on foreign investment, claiming that Indonesia had become 'subjugated' to external powers and depended too heavily on imported goods and services instead of focusing on improving local output levels.

The Threat of Terrorism

An ongoing challenge for successive Indonesian governments was the threat posed by terrorist activity, at both a domestic and regional level. In October 2002 the Government's response to this threat was tested when two bombs exploded in the tourist resort of Kuta, on the island of Bali. An explosion outside a night-club resulted in the deaths of 202 people, many of whom were Australian tourists. In its first admission that Islamist fundamentalists were operative within Indonesia, the Government initially attributed the attack to the international network of al-Qa'ida, which it believed had collaborated with local terrorists. The DPR authorized two emergency decrees, bringing into effect several previously delayed anti-terrorism measures, including a law permitting suspects to be detained for up to seven days without charge. The Muslim cleric Abu Bakar Bashir, commander of the Majelis Mujahidin Indonesia (MMI—Indonesian Mujahideen Council) and alleged to be the spiritual head of the regional Islamist organization Jemaah Islamiah (JI), was detained in connection with the attacks. (He had been questioned by police in January over alleged links to al-Qa'ida but had been released without charge.) The USA and the UN announced that they had designated JI a terrorist entity and frozen its financial assets. The police made several further arrests as the investigation into the bombings proceeded and in November 2002 one of the suspects, Amrozi bin Nurhasyim, confessed to his involvement and to having strong links to JI, as well as implicating several others in the attack. Later in the same month Imam Samudra was arrested on suspicion of having organized the attacks. He confessed to being a member of JI and to having planned earlier attacks, including the bombing of churches across the archipelago in December 2000 (see Provincial Affairs and Separatist Tensions), together with the operational leader of JI, Riduan Isamuddin (alias Hambali). In December 2002 Ali Gufron (alias Mukhlas), who apparently had succeeded Hambali as JI operational leader, was also arrested and confessed to having helped to plan the Bali attack.

In March 2003 the DPR gave its assent to legislation specifically designating terrorism as a crime and providing for detention without trial for terrorist suspects. The legislation was enacted retrospectively in order to cover the Bali bombings. In April the trial of Abu Bakar Bashir on charges of, *inter alia*, subversion, immigration violations, and involvement in several terrorist attacks, including the December 2000 church bombings, began in Jakarta. In August 2003 more than 3,000 Islamist militants attended a demonstration organized by the MMI in the capital to signal their support for Bashir. In the following month Bashir was convicted of the subversion charges against him but, owing to insufficient evidence, was acquitted of any involvement in terrorist attacks and of being the spiritual leader of JI. He was sentenced to a four-year prison term, which on appeal was later reduced to three years, although the remaining charges against him were upheld. Bashir's sentence was further reduced to 18 months by the Supreme Court in March 2004. In the following month, immediately after his release from prison, Bashir was rearrested on suspicion of terrorism. Meanwhile, Idris (alias Jhoni Hendrawan), suspected of involvement in the Bali bombings, was reported to have been arrested in June 2003, and in August the Thai authorities announced that they had finally captured Hambali, who was subsequently taken into custody by the USA. Also in August Amrozi became the first person to be convicted in connection with the Bali bombings; his appeal against the death sentence was subsequently rejected. In the following month Imam Samudra was also convicted and sentenced to death; a further suspect, Ali Imron, was sentenced to life imprisonment, having expressed some remorse for his actions. In October Mukhlas was convicted of having helped to plan the attacks and was sentenced to death. A further 13 suspects had been sentenced to prison terms for having played minor parts in the bombings. (Amrozi, Imam Samudra and Mukhlas were executed in November 2008, their final appeals against the death sentence having been rejected by the Supreme Court during 2007.) In July 2004 the Constitutional Court declared that the counter-terrorism legislation approved in 2003 and used to convict a number of those responsible for the Bali bombings should not have been applied retroactively. The Minister of Justice and Human Rights Affairs stated that the ruling did not rescind the convictions already secured, but made it impossible to apply the law in future cases for crimes committed before its enactment.

In April 2003 a bomb exploded at the Sukarno-Hatta International Airport, injuring 11 people, and in July an explosion outside the DPR building caused minor damage. In August an explosive device detonated by a suicide bomber outside the Marriott Hotel in Jakarta resulted in the deaths of 12 people. The police apprehended a number of suspects, all of whom were believed to be members of JI. In February 2004 Sardono Siliwangi was convicted of involvement in the Marriott bombing; he was sentenced to a 10-year prison term. A second suspect, Mohammed Rais, was convicted in May and sentenced to seven years in prison. In June two alleged Acehnese separatists were sentenced to prison terms for the bombing of the DPR building. In August Idris was sentenced to 10 years' imprisonment for his part in the hotel bombing, but charges against him in connection with the Bali bombings were withdrawn, owing to the Constitutional Court's July ruling, despite an earlier confession of his involvement.

A bomb exploded outside the Australian embassy in Jakarta in September 2004, killing nine people, mostly Indonesians, and injuring more than 180 others. JI was held responsible for the attack, and a number of suspects were subsequently detained. In October the trial of Bashir on charges of conspiring and inciting acts of terrorism, including the Bali and Marriott bombings, commenced in Jakarta; he was again accused of being the spiritual leader of JI. In relation to the Bali attacks, Bashir was to be tried under the criminal code. In March 2005 Bashir was found guilty of conspiracy over the Bali attacks and sentenced to a prison term of two-and-a-half years, although he was acquitted of involvement in the Marriott bombing. Australia and the USA immediately expressed their disappointment at the leniency of the sentence. An appeal by Bashir against the verdict was rejected by the Supreme Court in August. However, Bashir's sentence was reduced as part of Indonesia's 60th independence celebrations, and he was released from prison in June 2006. He again appealed against the original verdict, and in January 2007 his conviction was overruled by the Supreme Court on the grounds of insufficient evidence. Meanwhile, in July 2005 the first suspect to be tried in connection with the bombing of the Australian embassy in September 2004, the Islamist militant Irun Hidayat, was convicted of being an accessory to the attack and was sentenced to three-and-a-half years' imprisonment. In September three men, Iwan 'Rois' Darmawan, Ahmad Hasan and Syaiful Bahri, were found guilty of helping to organize the attack; Darmawan and Hasan both received the death penalty, while Bahri was sentenced to 10 years' imprisonment.

In October 2005 Bali was again seriously affected by terrorist activity. Three bombs were detonated at tourist locations on the island, killing 23 people, including the bombers, and injuring more than 100 others. In November one of JI's senior leaders, the Malaysian bomb-maker Azahari Husin, who was suspected of organizing the previous month's bombings with fellow Malaysian Noordin Mohammad Top, was killed during an Indonesian police operation in Batu, near Malang, in East Java. In January 2006 Noordin released a statement claiming responsibility for the 2005 Bali attacks. In his message, Noordin also claimed to have formed a new South-East Asian Islamist militant organization, Tanzim Qaedat al-Jihad (Organization for the Basis of Jihad). In the same month six people were arrested in relation to the 2005 Bali bombings. In September 2006 four suspects were convicted of involvement in the attacks and were sentenced to between eight and 18 years' imprisonment. In November eight members of JI were found guilty of carrying out and supporting terrorist activity; they received prison terms of between six years and life. In March 2007 police arrested several suspected JI members in the Javanese city of Yogyakarta; the militants were believed to have links to Abu Dujana, who according to some reports had become the commander of JI's military operations. In June Abu Dujana was one of eight suspects apprehended by the authorities in Central Java. On the same day, Zarkasih (also known as Nuaim or Mbah, among other aliases), who had acted as the head of JI since 2004, was also arrested. Both members of JI admitted their involvement with the organization and in April 2008 were sentenced to 15 years' imprisonment: Abu Dujana on charges of plotting terrorist activities and of sheltering other militants; and Zarkasih on charges of conspiring to commit terrorism and of supplying weapons and training to JI members. Meanwhile, two senior members of JI—Abdul Rohim, who was alleged to have replaced Zarkasih as JI leader following the latter's arrest, and Agus Purwanto—were apprehended in Malaysia in January and subsequently extradited to Indonesia.

In July 2009 the Marriott Hotel suffered a second terrorist attack when suicide bombers launched near-simultaneous strikes on the Marriott and Ritz-Carlton hotels. In the first serious attacks in Indonesia since 2005, six foreign tourists and one Indonesian were killed, as well as the two bombers themselves; more than 50 others were seriously injured. The bombers were widely believed to have links to JI, although no claim of responsibility was reported. In September the Indonesian authorities announced that Noordin Mohammad Top had been killed during a police operation in Central Java; DNA tests conducted on the recovered body were reported to have confirmed that it was that of Noordin. The trials of three men accused of involvement in the Marriott and Ritz-Carlton bombings, Amir Abdillah, Mohammed Jibril Abdurahman and Saudi-citizen Al-Khelawi Ali Abdullah, commenced in February 2010. In June Abdillah was sentenced to eight years' imprisonment for involvement in the bombings, as well as plotting to kill President Yuhoyono and having provided shelter to Noordin, while Abdurahman was convicted of falsifying documents and withholding information about terrorist crimes, and received a five-year prison term. Abdullah was acquitted of involvement in any terrorist activity, although he was sentenced to 18 months' imprisonment for violation of Indonesian immigration law.

In July 2010 the Government formally established a new national anti-terrorism agency, which was to be responsible for all existing anti-terrorism divisions across the Government, the police force and the military. It was hoped that the creation of the new agency would lead to greater security co-operation both on an operational level and in terms of policy. Meanwhile, in early 2010 the authorities announced the discovery in Aceh of a military training camp with purported links to Jemaah Ansharut Tauhid (JAT), a new terrorist network thought to have been established by Amar Usman (alias Dulmatin), a senior JI leader suspected of involvement in the 2002 Bali bombings. In

February members of the cell were reported to have fatally shot three police officers, and in the following month three suspected militants (one of whom was later confirmed to be Dulmatin) were killed in two separate police operations near Jakarta. Abdullah Sonata was subsequently reported to have replaced Dulmatin as leader of JAT, but was arrested in Java, together with two other suspected militants, in June. More than 100 other individuals had already been detained on suspicion of connection with the network. In August Abu Bakar Bashir was rearrested on suspicion of having helped to establish and fund JAT; in December he was charged with multiple counts of terrorist involvement, including inciting others to commit terrorist offences, a crime that carried the death sentence. Following a four-month trial, he was convicted in June 2011 and sentenced to 15 years' imprisonment. Bashir's lawyer filed an appeal against the verdict, and in October the Jakarta High Court reduced Bashir's prison term to nine years 'on humanitarian grounds', prompting widespread anger. However, in February 2012 the Supreme Court overturned the High Court ruling, reinstating Bashir's 15-year sentence.

One of the main suspects in the 2002 Bali bombings, Umar Patek, an Indonesian national, was arrested in Abbottabad, north-western Pakistan, in January 2011, and was extradited to Indonesia in August. (Following the killing of Osama bin Laden in the same Pakistani town in May, claims emerged that Patek had been in Abbottabad to meet the Saudi-born Islamist fundamentalist; however, US counter-terrorism officials insisted that the US Administration had found no evidence to support such assertions.) Following his extradition, Patek, who was alleged to have made the explosives used in the Bali attacks and to have had close links with Dulmatin, was charged with murder rather than terrorism in connection with the 2002 bombings, owing to the Constitutional Court's outlawing of the retroactive use of the 2003 counter-terrorism legislation (see above). However, he was also charged with, *inter alia*, assisting JAT in terrorist activities and with falsifying documents in order to obtain passports for himself and his Filipino wife. Patek's wife was also charged with the latter offence, and in January 2012 she was convicted and imprisoned for two years and three months. The trial of Patek commenced in February, with the more serious of the charges against him carrying the death penalty.

Another suspect in the 2002 Bali bombings, Heru Kuncoro, was arrested in Central Java in June 2011, after the authorities uncovered a new terrorist plot against the police force, in which cyanide was to have been used to poison officers. Kuncoro was one of a number of militants arrested in connection with the plot in mid-2011; some of those detained declared that they were waging *jihad* against the police for killing prominent terrorist leaders, including Noordin Mohammad Top. Attacks against the police force were certainly becoming increasingly prevalent. In April a suicide bomb attack on a mosque in a police compound in Cirebon, West Java, had injured 28 people, including around a dozen police officers. The incident, which occurred during Friday prayers, was reported to have been the first time that a suicide bomber had targeted a mosque in Indonesia, appearing to indicate a hardening of militants in the predominantly Muslim country. In May two police officers were killed in a militant attack in Central Sulawesi, and in the same month Ahmad Abdul Rabani was convicted of carrying out an attempted suicide attack on a police command post near Jakarta; the militant was sentenced to a five-year prison term. Meanwhile, 19 people were arrested in April on suspicion of planning a terrorist attack on Good Friday, following the discovery of a 150-kg bomb buried beneath a gas pipeline close to a Catholic church in Jakarta. A suicide bomb attack at a church in Solo, Central Java, in September claimed the lives of at least two people and injured several others.

Provincial Affairs and Separatist Tensions

From 2000 a major challenge confronting successive governments was the escalation of communal violence across the archipelago, together with separatist tensions in individual regions such as Aceh and Irian Jaya (now Papua). Some of the worst such violence occurred in the provinces of Maluku and North Maluku, arising from the ongoing conflict between the region's Christian and Muslim populations. By mid-2000 more than 4,000 people were reported to have been killed and some 300,000 displaced. In June President Wahid declared a state of civil emergency in the two provinces and it was announced that around 1,400 of the 10,200 members of the armed forces in the region were to be replaced because they had become involved in the conflict. In the case of at least one outbreak of serious violence it was reported that evidence had emerged of the military's collusion with elements of the militant Muslim paramilitary organization Laskar Jihad, which had travelled to the region to participate in the campaign of violence. On 24 December 18 people were reported to have been killed and more than 80 others injured in a series of bombings of Christian churches in nine towns and cities across Indonesia, including Jakarta. (In June 2002 an Iraqi citizen, Omar al-Faruq, who claimed to be the South-East Asian representative of al-Qa'ida, was arrested and allegedly confessed to having participated in carrying out the bombings. Following the bombings in Bali, a senior operative of JI also confessed to involvement in the attacks. In a television broadcast in April 2004 four Malaysians detained in Indonesia admitted involvement in the church bombings and membership of JI. However, human rights groups claimed that the statements had been obtained through coercion.) In February 2001 violence also broke out in the province of Central Kalimantan, where fierce resentment of Madurese transmigrants remained rife among the indigenous Dayak tribespeople. At least 428 Madurese were murdered by native Dayaks, and many of the victims were beheaded in accordance with traditional Dayak practices; many thousands more fled their homes.

Following negotiations between the warring Muslim and Christian factions in Maluku and North Maluku, the 'Malino II Agreement', which urged the expulsion of external groups such as Laskar Jihad from the area, was signed in February 2002. A series of bombings in the city of Ambon between February and April was condemned by the Government, but it insisted that they did not signify the failure of the peace agreement. In the latter month Alex Manuputty, the leader of the Christian separatist organization Front Kedaulatan Maluku (FKM—the Maluku Sovereignty Front), was arrested and charged with treason for planning to raise a flag to commemorate the 52nd anniversary of the proclamation of the South Maluku Republic. On 25 April FKM members raised flags in Ambon in remembrance of the anniversary, prompting the leader of Laskar Jihad, Ja'far Umar Thalib, to urge all Muslims in the region to renew their war against the Christian community. (In October 14 FKM members were sentenced to terms of imprisonment for raising the flags.) Violence broke out again in Ambon at the end of April, resulting in the deaths of 14 Christians. In May Thalib was arrested for allegedly inciting the violence and was subsequently charged with inciting hatred and rebellion and defaming the President and Vice-President. In October, following the Bali bombings, Laskar Jihad reportedly disbanded and left the region; Thalib claimed that the decision had been taken owing to the group's increasing political involvement and denied that it had any connection to events in Bali. In January 2003 Manuputty and another Christian leader, Samuel Waileruny, were convicted of subversion and sentenced *in absentia* to three-year prison terms, later increased to four years. However, Thalib was acquitted of the charges against him. In late 2003, following the rejection of his appeal against his conviction by the Supreme Court, Manuputty fled to the USA; the Government later requested his deportation to Indonesia but this was rejected.

In April 2003 supporters of the separatist movement in Maluku were again alleged to have flown flags in commemoration of the anniversary of the South Maluku Republic. An estimated 129 such supporters were arrested, and in the following month it was announced that they were to be prosecuted on charges of subversion. However, owing to the relative peace that had been maintained in the province since the signing of the Malino II Agreement, in September it was reported that the Government had revoked the state of civil emergency in Maluku; several battalions of peace-keeping troops would continue to be stationed in the province. The civil emergency status in North Maluku had been revoked in the previous year. In January 2004 nine men were sentenced to prison terms of up to 15 years for membership of the FKM. At least 40 people were killed and around 150 injured in violent clashes in Ambon in April, following a rally by a predominantly Christian separatist group on the island. More than 1,000 police officers and troops were dispatched in an attempt to quell the unrest. In May one person was killed and at least 22 others injured in a series of bomb explosions on Ambon. Observers thus questioned the long-term success of the peace treaty. In November Moses Tuanakotta, an FKM leader, was convicted of subversion and sentenced to nine years in prison for instigating the rally in April.

Meanwhile, in late 2001 violence also broke out in the province of Sulawesi, where ongoing religious tensions had caused approximately 1,000 deaths in the previous two years. In the first week of December at least seven people were killed and thousands left homeless following clashes between armed Muslim groups and Christians. The violence was believed to have been precipitated by the recent arrival of members of Laskar Jihad on the island, and more than 2,000 police and troop reinforcements were sent to the area. A peace agreement was concluded between the involved parties in late December, but explosions at four churches in the provincial capital, Palu, during New Year celebrations highlighted the continuing political instability in the province. In June 2002 a bomb exploded on a bus travelling towards Poso, Central Sulawesi, killing four people, and in December, two bombs exploded in Makassar, the capital of South Sulawesi, resulting in the deaths of three people.

In October 2003 an estimated 11 people died as a result of an outbreak of sectarian violence in Poso. There was speculation that the renewal of violence in the province had been co-ordinated by JI to coincide with the anniversary of the bombings in Bali. In the following month at least four more people died following an outbreak of anti-Christian violence in the city. In January 2004 a bomb exploded in the town of Palopo, South Sulawesi, killing four people. In October the new province of West Sulawesi, formed from five former regencies of South Sulawesi, was inaugurated. A series of attacks in Central Sulawesi in 2004–05 included a bomb explosion on a bus in Poso in November, which killed six people, two explosions in a busy market in the predominantly Christian town of Tentena, which claimed the lives of 21 people and injured dozens more; the town's only mosque was subsequently stoned by Christian demonstrators. In July a total of 24 alleged members of JI were arrested in connection with these attacks, as well as with the Bali bombings of 2002. In October 2005 religious tensions were further exacerbated in Central Sulawesi by the beheading, allegedly by Islamist militants, of three Christian schoolgirls who had been ambushed while on their way to a Christian school near Poso. In March 2007 three suspected Islamist militants were convicted in connection with the attack; one man was sentenced to 20 years' imprisonment, and two of his accomplices received sentences of 14 years. In December three further convictions were made in connection with the beheadings: Rahman Kalale received a 19-year prison sentence and Yudi Heryanto a 14-year sentence, with another defendant being sentenced to a term of 10 years; Kalale and Heryanto were also found guilty of injuring two other schoolgirls in a separate shooting incident in Poso.

In September 2006 three Christian men were executed following their convictions on charges of inciting an attack on an Islamic school in Poso, in which approximately 200 people had been killed in May 2000. Many Christians alleged that the three men were not the perpetrators of the attack, and demonstrations ensued, during which rioters stormed a prison in Atambua, West Timor (the home town of one of the executed men), and reportedly released approximately 200 inmates. In the following month a Christian priest, well known locally for leading protests against the executions, was shot dead in Palu. In late 2007 several other Muslim militants were convicted of carrying out attacks in Central Sulawesi. Abdul Muis was sentenced to 19 years' imprisonment, having been convicted of the murder of the Christian priest in Palu in October 2006 and also of a bomb attack on a market in 2005, in which eight people had been killed. Syaiful Anam (alias Brekele) was found guilty of organizing the Tentena bomb attacks and was sentenced to 18 years' imprisonment. Amril Niode and Ardin Djanatu were also convicted of involvement in that attack, and both received long prison sentences.

Meanwhile, on 1 January 2001 new legislation took effect devolving increased financial and administrative control to Indonesia's regional governments. The central Government was to retain control over justice, defence, foreign affairs and monetary policy.

East Timor

During 1974, meanwhile, several parties emerged within the small Portuguese colony of East Timor (which became known as Timor-Leste following its accession to independence on 20 May 2002), with aims ranging from full independence to integration with Indonesia or Australia. Indonesia, which had never presented a claim to East Timor, initially showed little interest in the territory. In 1975 Portuguese forces withdrew from the colony, and the territory's capital, Dili, was occupied by the forces of the left-wing Frente Revolucionária do Timor Leste Independente (Fretilin), which advocated independence for East Timor. To prevent Fretilin from gaining full control of the territory, Indonesian troops intervened and established a provincial government. (In December 2001 the declassification of US state papers relating to the Indonesian occupation revealed that the US Government had endorsed the invasion in the belief that it would curb the spread of communism in the region.) In July 1976 East Timor was declared the 27th province of Indonesia. Human rights organizations subsequently claimed that as many as 200,000 people, from a total population of 650,000, might have been killed by the Indonesian armed forces during the annexation. The UN continued officially to recognize Portugal as the administrative power in East Timor. In February 1983 the UN Commission on Human Rights adopted a resolution affirming East Timor's right to independence and self-determination. In November 1990 the Indonesian Government rejected proposals by the military commander of Fretilin, José Alexandre (Xanana) Gusmão, for unconditional peace negotiations aimed at ending the armed struggle in East Timor. In August 1992 the UN General Assembly adopted its first resolution condemning Indonesia's violations of human rights in East Timor.

Following the downfall of President Suharto, in August 1998 it was announced that Indonesia and Portugal had agreed to hold discussions on the possibility of 'wide-ranging' autonomy for East Timor. In January 1999, the Indonesian Government unexpectedly announced that, if the East Timorese were to vote to reject Indonesia's proposals for autonomy, it would consider granting independence to the province. Although the Government was initially opposed to a referendum on the issue of independence for East Timor, it signed an agreement with Portugal in May, giving its assent to a process of 'popular consultation' to take the form of a UN-supervised poll. The referendum proceeded on 30 August, and resulted in an overwhelming rejection, by 78.5% of voters, of the Indonesian Government's proposals for autonomy and in an endorsement of independence for East Timor. The announcement of the result of the referendum led to a rapid deterioration in the territory's security situation. In late September Indonesia and Portugal reiterated their agreement for the transfer of authority in East Timor to the UN. Also in late September the Indonesian armed forces formally relinquished responsibility for security in the territory to the UN peace-keeping force, the International Force for East Timor (Interfet); the last Indonesian troops left East Timor in late October. In October the result of the referendum was ratified by the Indonesian MPR, thus permitting East Timor's accession to independence to proceed (see Timor-Leste). In September 2000 Indonesia drew criticism from the UN and the international community following the murder of three UN aid workers by pro-Jakarta militias in West Timor. The militia groups were believed by many to be receiving the support of the Indonesian military. In December 2001 10 members of a pro-Indonesia militia became the first individuals to be convicted of crimes against humanity in connection with the violence of 1999. However, the Indonesian Government continued to obstruct efforts to bring all those culpable to justice, blocking attempts to extradite an 11th suspect, a special forces officer, to stand trial.

In January 2002 the Government established a special court in Jakarta to try those suspected of contravening human rights in East Timor in 1999. A total of 18 pro-Jakarta militiamen and Indonesian soldiers were prosecuted by the tribunal, the first trials of which began in March. Prior to its disbandment the tribunal passed just six convictions, prompting widespread international condemnation, with many observers insisting that the acquittal of 12 of the 18 defendants represented a gross miscarriage of justice. The six convicted men included former Governor of East Timor Abílio Soares, who was found guilty of two charges of 'gross rights violations' for his failure to prevent violence involving those subordinate to him and was sentenced to a three-year prison term; Eurico Guterres, head of the youth wing of President Megawati's PDI—P, who was convicted of crimes against humanity and sentenced to 10 years' imprisonment; Lt-Col Soejarwo, Indonesia's military commander in Dili in 1999, who in December 2002 became the first Indonesian officer to be found guilty of the charges against him, and was sentenced to a five-year prison term; and Maj.-Gen. Adam Damiri, the most senior military officer to have been charged, who was convicted of crimes against humanity and sentenced to a three-year prison term in August 2003. However, all six convictions were subsequently overruled.

Meanwhile, in February 2003 the UN-sponsored Special Panel for Serious Crimes (SPSC) in Dili indicted Gen. (retd) Wiranto, Abílio Soares and 56 other Indonesian generals for crimes committed in East Timor; the Indonesian Government continued to refuse to hand over any of those indicted for trial. The SPSC issued an arrest warrant for Wiranto in May 2004. In December Indonesia and Timor-Leste announced the establishment of a joint Commission of Truth and Friendship (CTF) to investigate human rights violations during the violence in East Timor in 1999. In the previous month the UN Security Council had expressed concern at Indonesia's failure to punish those responsible. The first hearing of the CTF opened on Bali in February 2007. Its 10 members were drawn from both Indonesia and Timor-Leste and included experts in the fields of law and human rights. In its final report, which was published in July 2008, the CTF concluded that the Indonesian Government, military and police bore 'institutional responsibility for gross human rights violations'. President Yudhoyono responded by stating his remorse, but critics were dissatisfied with the lack of a clear apology and of punishment for the perpetrators. In April 2008, following the attempted assassination of the Timorese President, José Ramos Horta, three Timorese men were apprehended in Indonesia. (For details of the attempted assassination and the subsequent court proceedings, see Timor-Leste.)

Aceh

In the mid-1970s dissent re-emerged in Aceh, which, at the end of the war of independence, had held the status of a full province of the Republic of Indonesia but which had subsequently had this status removed before being made a special territory (Daerah Istimewa) with considerable autonomy in religious and educational affairs. The dissent was provoked by the central Government's exploitation of Aceh's natural resources and the subsequent lack of benefits from these operations received by the region itself. A sense of the erosion of Aceh's autonomy was heightened by the migration and transmigration of other Indonesians into the region and by the increasing power of the central Government, and in 1976 the Gerakan Aceh Merdeka (GAM—Free Aceh Movement) was formed by Hasan di Tiro, who declared independence in 1977. This small rebellion was swiftly suppressed by the armed forces; Tiro later established a government-in-exile in Sweden.

In 1989 opposition to the central Government rose again, this time led by the National Liberation Front Acheh Sumatra. The region was made a 'military operations zone' in 1990, thus allowing the armed forces far greater freedom to counter the uprising. By mid-1991 the rebellion had been largely suppressed; however, it was estimated that about 1,000 Acehnese had been killed in the process, as a result of the use of excessive and indiscriminate force by the military. The number of deaths continued to rise in subsequent years, and in 1993 Amnesty International estimated that about 2,000 Acehnese had been killed since 1989, with hundreds of others having 'disappeared'.

Aceh's status as a 'military operations zone' was revoked in June 1998, following the downfall of President Suharto in May, and an apology for past military excesses was made by Gen. Wiranto. However, the subsequent intended withdrawal of Indonesian troops from the province was suspended following rioting in Aceh in September. Decentralization measures introduced by President Habibie failed to defuse resentment in the province, and public opinion in Aceh became increasingly sympathetic towards the notion of independence. In 1999 the discovery of several mass graves of people killed by the armed forces during security operations further exacerbated tension in the province. Violence continued to escalate following the legislative elections of 9 June as GAM guerrillas intensified their campaign for independence for Aceh.

In early November 1999, following the rejection by legislators in the provincial assembly of demands for the holding of a referendum on self-determination for Aceh, a provincial government building in western Aceh was set on fire during a demonstration by 5,000 protesters. While much of the ongoing widespread violence in the province was attributed to the separatist movement, it was believed by observers that some unrest was initiated by so-called 'provocateurs' acting to destabilize the province and undermine the separatist movement. Later in that month the newly appointed President of Indonesia, Abdurrahman Wahid, confirmed an unexpected statement that the holding of a referendum in Aceh was a possibility; however, the suggested poll would not include the option of independence, but would instead offer Aceh a broad degree of autonomy. Wahid's proposals angered the military, which reportedly feared that, unless brought under control, the separatist movement in Aceh could potentially incite rebellion across the archipelago, while the offer of increased autonomy, rather than independence, also failed to satisfy Acehnese separatists. In May 2000 the Indonesian Government and Acehnese rebel negotiators agreed upon a cease-fire, which took effect from 2 June and was subsequently extended for an indefinite period. However, violence continued throughout the province, and it was estimated by Acehnese human rights groups that more than 1,000 civilians had died in clashes between the Indonesian military and Acehnese rebels during 2000. In December thousands of Acehnese protesters rallied peacefully in Banda Aceh, demanding independence for the province. However, it was reported that at least 34 (and possibly as many as 200, according to human rights groups) unarmed civilians had been killed in the days preceding the rally as the result of military action to target Acehnese en route to the demonstration. Acehnese separatists withdrew from peace talks with the Indonesian Government, stating that they would resume negotiations only when the military ceased killing Acehnese civilians. In January 2001 peace talks recommenced.

In April 2001 President Wahid signed a decree authorizing the security forces to assist the military in restoring law and order in Aceh by targeting armed separatist organizations. This brought an end to the uneasy truce prevailing in the region. In July one of President Megawati's first official actions was to sign into law a special autonomy plan for Aceh intended to assuage separatism. However, while generous in its scope, the legislation was criticized for failing to address the problems posed by the continued military presence in the area. Critics' concerns were borne out when an estimated 30 civilians were massacred on an Aceh palm oil plantation in August. According to GAM, the military had carried out the attack as retribution for a previous assault on a military post that had left several soldiers dead.

In January 2002 the commander of GAM, Abdullah Syafei, was killed during a gun battle with security forces on Sumatra; six other GAM members also died. Further fighting prompted the Government to resume a separate military command for Aceh, a decision denounced by both GAM and human rights groups. In the following month fighting between separatists and government troops in the province resulted in the deaths of at least 23 people. In May, following discussions in Geneva, Switzerland, the Government and GAM agreed to work towards a cease-fire, signing an agreement that was to act as a mandate for future negotiations. However, the violence continued. At the end of June GAM issued a statement in support of the ongoing peace negotiations taking place in Geneva and in July it released 18 hostages whom it had been holding since the previous month. Meanwhile, following a trip to Aceh, Yudhoyono, then the Co-ordinating Minister for Political, Legal and Security Affairs, declared his support for the regional military commander's request to increase the military presence in the area if GAM did not accept the conditions outlined in May. Aceh's Legal Aid Institute reportedly claimed that 771 people had been killed in the region's conflict during the first six months of 2002.

In December 2002 government and GAM representatives finally signed a peace agreement in Geneva. As well as establishing an immediate cease-fire, the deal provided for free elections (to be held in 2004), which would establish an autonomous, although not independent, government. The new provincial government would retain 70% of all fuel revenues. In return, all rebels in the province would disarm in designated areas. Following the signing of the peace accord, international peace monitors arrived in the region. In February 2003 GAM rebels began surrendering their weapons in compliance with the terms of the peace accord, but by April of that year the agreement had come close to collapse. Offices occupied by the international monitors for the Joint Security Committee had been attacked and, in one instance, burned down. In May peace talks were held in Tokyo, Japan, with the support of the host country, the European Union (EU) and the USA. However, GAM negotiators were unable to accept the Government's demands that it abandon its goal of independence, accept a special autonomy agreement and immediately begin to disarm its forces. President Megawati immediately authorized the imposition of martial law in Aceh, initially for a six-month period, and the commencement of military action against GAM. Owing to the restrictions placed on media reporting of the conflict, little independent information was available as to its progress throughout the succeeding months. In June, however, three government soldiers were sentenced to brief prison terms, having been found guilty of committing human rights violations during the military campaign. In November the Government announced that it would extend its military operations in Aceh indefinitely, prompting international criticism. In December a bomb exploded at a market in the eastern town of Pereulak, killing 10 people.

The Government downgraded the status of martial law in Aceh to a state of civil emergency in May 2004, restoring power to the civilian Governor. The security forces, which were to remain in the province, claimed to have killed some 2,000 suspected GAM rebels and arrested a further 3,000 since commencing the military offensive against the separatist movement a year earlier. Human rights groups alleged that at least 300 of those killed had been civilians. In June Indonesia welcomed Sweden's decision to arrest two senior GAM leaders who were in exile in that country. (GAM's founder, Hasan di Tiro, evaded arrest because of ill health.) However, the two were later released owing to insufficient evidence, although investigations were to continue. In November Yudhoyono, now the country's President, extended the state of civil emergency in Aceh by up to six months and, during a visit to the province, offered an amnesty to all GAM rebels who surrendered their weapons.

Following the tsunami disaster that devastated Aceh in December 2004, GAM and the Government agreed to an informal cease-fire to facilitate relief efforts. In mid-January 2005, however, the Chief of Staff of the Army, Gen. Ryamizard Ryacudu, announced that in the previous two weeks the security forces had killed 120 GAM rebels who had been stealing aid intended for victims of the tsunamis; GAM dismissed these claims. None the less, the natural disaster appeared to have provided a new impetus for GAM and the Indonesian Government to seek a resolution to their conflict, and in late January formal talks between the two sides were held in Helsinki, Finland. After several rounds of negotiations brokered by former Finnish President Martti Ahtisaari, the two sides reached agreement in July upon the terms of a draft accord, which was formally signed on 15 August. GAM agreed to discard its long-standing claims for independence and the Indonesian Government was to allow GAM to operate as an official political party, a concession that would require constitutional change (current laws decreed that all political parties be based in Jakarta and that branches be maintained in at least half of the country's 33 provinces). Furthermore, Aceh was to be allocated as much as 70% of the revenues arising from the exploitation of its natural resources. In late August the Indonesian authorities released approximately 200 Acehnese detainees, including four senior GAM members, and the Indonesian Government began a phased withdrawal of its 24,000 troops based in the province; by the end of 2005 almost 10,000 troops had departed. Meanwhile, GAM effected a process of complete disarmament within three months of the signing of the agreement. In July 2006 legislation was introduced that granted Aceh partial autonomy and allowed for the formation of political parties in the province. Although GAM agreed to its terms, critics argued that the law was strongly biased in favour of the central Government, which was to monitor all the affairs of the Acehnese administration; furthermore, management of oil and gas in Aceh was to be conducted jointly by the provincial administration (which was to control 70% of production revenues) and the central Government.

In December 2006 Aceh held its first-ever direct gubernatorial and district elections, formally marking the culmination of the peace process. The polls passed without incident. Irwandi Yusuf, an independent candidate and former GAM spokesman, secured the position of provincial Governor, attracting 38% of the total votes cast along with his deputy gubernatorial candidate, Muhammad Nazar. The level of participation in the polls was high, at approximately 85% of the total electorate. In the same month the Indonesian Government finalized draft regulation providing for the establishment of local political parties in Aceh, although candidates would only be allowed to stand for seats within the House of Representatives in Jakarta if they secured the support of national parties and would be required to relinquish membership of their local party once nominated. At his inauguration ceremony in February 2007, the new Governor of Aceh declared his intention to focus on the economic recovery of the province. In October 2008 Hasan di Tiro, the founder of GAM, returned to Aceh, thereby ending three decades of self-imposed exile; he died in June 2010. Zaini Abdullah, the former GAM 'foreign minister', was elected as Aceh's second Governor in gubernatorial and district elections held in April 2012, securing nearly 56% of the votes cast, together with his deputy gubernatorial candidate, Muzakir Manaf, and defeating the incumbent Yusuf (who won some 30% of the vote) and three other candidates.

Papua

In May 1977 a rebellion in the province of Irian Jaya (annexed to Indonesia in 1963—see Historical Context) was said to have been organized by the Organisasi Papua Merdeka (OPM—Free Papua Movement), which sought unification with Papua New Guinea. Fighting continued until December 1979, when Indonesia and Papua New Guinea finalized a new border administrative agreement. However, frequent border incidents followed, and in early 1984 fighting broke out in Jayapura, the capital of Irian Jaya. As a result, about 10,000 refugees fled over the border into Papua New Guinea. In October 1984 Indonesia and Papua New Guinea signed a five-year agreement establishing a joint border security committee; by the end of 1985 Indonesians were continuing to cross into Papua New Guinea, but a limited number of repatriations took place in 1986. There was also concern among native Irian Jayans (who are of Melanesian origin) at the introduction of large numbers of Javanese into the province, under the central Government's transmigration scheme. This was interpreted as an attempt to reduce the Melanesians to a minority and thus to stifle opposition. In 1986 it was announced that the Government intended to resettle 65m. people over a 20-year period, in spite of protests from human rights and conservation groups. Relations with Papua New Guinea improved when the Prime Minister, Paias Wingti, visited Suharto in January 1988. However, cross-border action by the Indonesian armed forces during October and November, in an attempt to capture Melanesian separatists operating on the border, led to renewed tension between the two countries. In October 1990 the Governments of Indonesia and Papua New Guinea renewed the basic accord on border arrangements, which included an agreement on the formation of a joint defence committee and a formal commitment to share border intelligence. In September 1992 the two countries agreed to facilitate the passage of border trade, and in the following month an Indonesian consulate was established in Vanimo, Papua New Guinea.

In April 1995 the Australian Council for Overseas Aid (ACFOA) alleged that 37 Irian Jayans had been killed by security forces near the Freeport copper and gold mine between June 1994 and February 1995. In August the ACFOA's claims were reiterated by NGOs, which lodged a complaint with the National Commission on Human Rights in Jakarta about summary executions, arbitrary detentions and torture in the province between mid-1994 and mid-1995. In November 1995 four members of the Indonesian armed forces were arrested in an investigation into the killing in May of 11 unarmed civilians at a prayer meeting. Also in November the Overseas Private Investment Corporation (a US government agency) cancelled political risk insurance valued at US $100m. for Freeport (a subsidiary of a US enterprise), citing environmental concerns. Freeport's perceived responsibility for the situation in Irian Jaya arose from its role as civil administrator in the area of the mine and also because the indigenous inhabitants' campaigns against Freeport's indiscriminate exploitation of natural resources in the area often resulted in their being killed by security forces as suspected members of the OPM.

In December 1995 clashes between Indonesian forces and the OPM intensified, forcing hundreds of refugees to cross into Papua New Guinea. Four people were killed in riots in Jayapura in March 1996. Riots near the Grasberg mine in the same month were the result of problems similar to those experienced by residents in the Freeport area (relating principally to the lack of any benefit from the mining project to the local community and to the potential impact of the project on the local environment). There were also tensions among the local Irianese, Indonesians from other provinces and commercial operators. In April Freeport agreed to allocate 1% of revenue over a period of 10 years to community development programmes for tribal groups living around the mine, and to improve environmental safeguards.

Seven people were reported to have been killed in outbreaks of violence in Jayapura and the island of Biak in July 1998. In October the Government revoked the status of Irian Jaya as a 'military operations zone' following the conclusion of a cease-fire agreement with the OPM in September, but this was not followed by the withdrawal of troops from the region. In February 1999 Irian Jayan tribal leaders raised the issue of independence for the province at a meeting with President Habibie. (A referendum on self-determination for the province had been promised by the Indonesian Government prior to the territory's annexation in 1963; however, while a vote was eventually held in 1969, only tribal chiefs selected by Jakarta were allowed to participate and the result was widely discredited.) The independence movement in the province continued to strengthen throughout 1999, and was encouraged by the achievements of the East Timorese independence movement. In December independence demonstrations took place throughout Irian Jaya. A delegation from the DPR visited the province and announced that the administration of the newly elected President Abdurrahman Wahid had agreed to the popular demand that the province's name be changed from Irian Jaya to West Papua, although it was emphasized that this decision should not be construed as implying the Government's approval of any action towards the province's secession from Indonesia. (However, it was subsequently reported that the proposed change had failed to receive the requisite approval of the Indonesian legislature.)

In mid-2000 the Papuan People's Congress, held in Jayapura, adopted a five-point resolution reinstating a declaration of independence for West Papua originally made in 1961, before the province's annexation to Indonesia. However, the declaration was immediately rebuffed by the Indonesian Government. In October 2000 between 30 and 40 people were killed and many others injured in clashes between police and West Papuan separatists in the town of Wamena when police attempted to remove a Morning Star independence flag being flown by the separatists. Although President Wahid had previously decreed that the flying of the Morning Star flag was allowed, provided that the flag was flown alongside, and slightly lower than, the Indonesian flag, following the violence the Government introduced a ban on the flying of the flag. In November and early December the Indonesian military took severe action against separatists; seven people were shot dead by the armed forces in an outbreak of violence in the town of Merauke, and dozens of separatist sympathizers, including the pro-independence leader of the Presidium Dewan Papua (PDP—Papua Presidium Council), Theys Eluay, were arrested. On 1 December pro-independence supporters rallied in the province to mark the 39th anniversary of the first unilateral declaration of West Papua's independence.

In March 2001 five West Papuan separatist leaders, including Theys Eluay, were released on bail to await trial on charges of treason. In October the DPR gave its assent to legislation giving greater autonomy to the province, in an effort to defuse the separatist tensions that had given rise to more than 40 years of sporadic violence. As well as giving Irian Jaya more autonomy and a larger share of tax revenues, the so-called Special Autonomy Law for Papua also proposed that the region be officially known as Papua and made provision for a bicameral Papuan People's Council, intended to safeguard indigenous interests. However, the separatist PDP swiftly rejected the deal as it failed to grant Irian Jaya complete independence. In November 2001 Theys Eluay was found dead in his car. He was believed to have been assassinated; some military involvement was suspected. In December hundreds of students occupied the parliament building in Jayapura to demand a referendum on independence and to express their anger at the authorities' failure to find the killer of Theys Eluay. The protest came days before the autonomy reforms came into force on 1 January 2002, when the province officially became known as Papua.

In August 2002 two US citizens and an Indonesian were killed following an ambush near the Freeport mine. In November it was alleged by police that Kopassus soldiers had been involved in the attack. (In June 2004 the US authorities indicted *in absentia* Anthonius Wamang, an Indonesian, for murdering the two US citizens, describing him as an operational commander for the OPM, although human rights groups reportedly claimed that Wamang had close links to the Kopassus special forces.) In April 2003 four Kopassus officers and three soldiers were convicted of the abduction, torture and murder of Theys Eluay and were sentenced to brief prison terms. However, the trial was criticized both for the leniency of the verdicts and for its failure to investigate the reasons behind the murder of Eluay. Meanwhile, the central Government gave its approval in January 2003 to an initiative that would lead to the division of Papua into three smaller provinces—Central Papua, East Papua (or Papua) and West Papua (known initially as West Irian Jaya, but formally renamed in April 2007). The proposal angered local leaders, who claimed that such action would threaten the region's autonomy. Following reports that six people had died during fighting in Timika, the designated capital of Central Papua, since the inauguration of the new province in August 2003, the creation of Central Papua was postponed. However, the appointment of a Governor for West Papua was approved in November. In the same month the Government announced provisional plans for the creation of two further provinces in Papua. Meanwhile, it was reported that 10 members of the OPM had been killed in clashes with government troops in East Papua. In December the appointment of Brig.-Gen. Timbul Silaen to the post of regional police commander was criticized by the USA, owing to Silaen's indictment for crimes against humanity in East Timor. In March 2004 it was reported that Leo Warisman, a leader of the OPM, had been killed in a gunfight with security forces in Papua. Another OPM leader, Yance Hembring, was sentenced to 10 years' imprisonment by a court in Jayapura in August for advocating Papua's independence. In December at least five people were injured and 18 arrested during violent clashes between protesters and police at a pro-independence rally in Jayapura.

In October 2005 the Papuan People's Council (Majelis Rakyat Papua—MRP) was formally established; it was charged primarily with the issue of the partition of Papua and with the forthcoming gubernatorial elections. Originally scheduled to be held in November, the elections were twice postponed, owing to poor administrative planning, but finally proceeded on 11 March. Barnabas Suebu and his co-candidate, Alex Hessegem, were subsequently pronounced Governor and Deputy Governor, respectively, of Papua. In January 2006 more than 200 demonstrators forced their way into the local legislative building and demanded the immediate withdrawal of all Indonesian military personnel from the province. In February the Minister of Defence, Juwono Sudarsono, conceded that some members of the Indonesian military and police force had been committing human rights abuses, including incidents of torture and rape, against local residents in Papua. In the same month the Constitutional Court officially reaffirmed the legitimacy of West Irian Jaya's status as a province, maintaining that the 2001 Special Autonomy Law for Papua could not be applied retroactively. In February 2006 protests by unlicensed miners operating in the area resulted in a temporary suspension of production at the Freeport mine, which continued to be regarded locally as a symbol of oppression. In the following month five members of the security forces were killed in Jayapura by demonstrators reiterating demands for the closure of the mine, and in April four people, including two soldiers, were killed in an assault on an army post in the province.

In February 2007 Human Rights Watch drew attention to the continued imprisonment of 18 Papuan activists, who were reported to have received substantial sentences following their peaceful protests in support of self-determination for the province. Human Rights Watch urged the Indonesian Government to release these prisoners and to abandon charges against other political detainees who had yet to be brought to trial. In July Human Rights Watch accused the Papuan police force of perpetrating, with apparent impunity, extra-judicial killings and other serious abuses. A number of people were killed and dozens injured during several days of fighting in October between rival tribal groups near the Freeport mine. In March 2008 several protesters were arrested in Manokwari for displaying the Morning Star flag.

The Freeport mine was the scene of another attack in July 2009, when an Indonesian police officer and an Australian security guard were fatally shot in an attack attributed by the police to the OPM; however, autopsies on the two bodies, which suggested that the evidence had been tampered with, together with the revelation that the bullets used had been of military issue, cast doubt on this theory. A senior leader of the OPM, Kelly Kwalik, denied any involvement, insisting that the OPM had neither the inclination nor the equipment to carry out such an attack. In December Kwalik, who the authorities claimed had been involved in a series of attacks, including the 2002 Freeport ambush, was killed during a police operation in Timika; his death prompted a series of anti-Indonesian protests and demands for self-determination for Papuans. A three-month strike by employees at the Freeport mine in late 2011, which had a severely debilitating effect on production, was finally concluded in December after the company's management agreed to a 37% increase in staff wages, together with improved housing and retirement savings benefits. The industrial action was reported to have been called after workers discovered how much their counterparts earned at Freeport's other mines around the world; in exchange for the wage concessions, union leaders agreed that future wage negotiations were to be based on living costs and wage competitiveness within Indonesia.

Meanwhile, in June 2010 the MRP voted to reject Special Autonomy status. In July an estimated 50,000 Papuans took to the streets of Jayapura, and urged the upper house of the provincial legislature to endorse the MRP's decision. Demands for full autonomy intensified following the release on the internet in October of a video recording purporting to show two men in military uniforms torturing indigenous Papuan civilians; the central Government subsequently confirmed that the aggressors in the footage were members of the Indonesian army, and in January 2011 a military tribunal sentenced the two men to prison terms of eight and nine months, respectively, while their sergeant was sentenced to 10 months' imprisonment. Meanwhile, in December 2010 four Indonesian soldiers were sentenced to up to seven months' imprisonment after being convicted of torturing Papuan civilians in a separate incident.

At least 17 people were killed in a violent clash between supporters of rival local politicians in the Papuan district of Puncak in late July 2011, prompting the local government to deploy riot police and military troops to the area. The dispute, between supporters of Simon Alom, who led the transitional administration during the establishment of the district, and Elvis Satuni, the speaker of the district legislative council—both of whom had announced their intention to stand for the position of district head at inaugural elections due to have been held in November—led to the postponement of the elections, and further confrontations took the collective death toll to in excess of 30 people by January 2012. Meanwhile, at the beginning of August 2011 a further four people (including a military officer) were killed, and at least seven others injured, when unidentified assailants ambushed a minibus in Abepura, near Jayapura; the authorities believed the incident to be linked to the OPM. On the following day thousands of Papuans marched on the parliament building in Jayapura, demanding the holding of a referendum on the question of Papuan self-determination. In October Indonesian troops fired tear gas and warning shots at members of the Papuan People's Congress gathered in Abepura and arrested dozens of those in attendance; the authorities claimed that the Congress had issued a declaration of independence and announced the formation of a transitional government for Papua. Human Rights Watch stated that it had received reports of at least one person having been killed; however, the authorities denied that there had been any casualties. The trial of five activists accused of treason in connection with the incident began in January 2012. Meanwhile, addressing the Council on Foreign Relations—an influential US 'think tank'—in September, the Indonesian Minister of Foreign Affairs, Marty Natalegawa, professed the central Government's awareness of ongoing human rights abuses in Papua and suggested that greater autonomy might, potentially, prove to be the solution. A comprehensive review of Papua's Special Autonomy status was carried out by the central Government in late 2011, the results of which were expected to be announced in early 2012.

Foreign Affairs

Regional relations

Indonesia's foreign policy has focused on its leading role in the regional grouping of the Association of Southeast Asian Nations (ASEAN, see p. 214), which it founded, together with Malaysia, the Philippines, Singapore and Thailand, in 1967. Indonesia supported the organization's opposition to Viet Nam's military presence in Cambodia and played a prominent role in attempts to find a political solution to the situation in Cambodia (q.v.). The Indonesian Minister of Foreign Affairs and his French counterpart were appointed Co-Chairmen of the Paris International Conference on Cambodia, which first met in August 1989. In October 1994 Indonesia underscored its pivotal regional role through hosting its fifth informal meeting to resolve peacefully the dispute over the conflicting claims of six Asian countries to sovereignty over parts of the South China Sea, particularly the Spratly Islands. Moreover, in November the Asia-Pacific Economic Cooperation (APEC, see p. 204) summit meeting took place in Bogor, West Java. Indonesia had been one of the founding members of APEC, which had been established in 1989. In 1997, following Second Prime Minister Hun Sen's assumption of sole power in Cambodia, Indonesia led ASEAN attempts to resolve the crisis. In August 2001 President Megawati Sukarnoputri embarked on a tour of all ASEAN member states on her first overseas trip since assuming the presidency. In October 2008 Indonesia became the final member state to ratify the ASEAN charter, which declared among its purposes the promotion of democracy and good governance, and the creation of a single market. Indonesia assumed the annually rotating chair of ASEAN in 2011. At the ASEAN summit meeting held in Bali in November, President Susilo Bambang Yudhoyono asserted that the regional grouping had recorded a number of positive developments under Indonesia's chairmanship, including the signing of the Bali Declaration on the ASEAN Community in a Global Community of Nations (commonly known as the Bali Concord III), which pledged increased co-operation in the fields of, *inter alia*, politics, security, economics and culture, at both regional and global levels; the agreement also defined development issues pertaining to the implementation, by 2015, of an ASEAN Economic Community and the promotion of ASEAN's full integration into the global economy.

Diplomatic relations with China, suspended since 1967 owing to its alleged complicity in the 1965 attempted coup in Indonesia, were finally restored in August 1990 following an Indonesian undertaking to settle financial debts incurred with China by the Sukarno regime. Bilateral relations suffered a reverse in 1998 following the violence perpetrated against ethnic Chinese Indonesians at the time of the removal of President Suharto in May. China issued a strong diplomatic protest; President Habibie publicly expressed his sympathy for the plight of the ethnic Chinese victims of violence. Subsequently, in May 1999, as part of a programme of general reform, Habibie removed a ban that had existed on the use and teaching of the Mandarin Chinese language within Indonesia. The two countries signed a strategic partnership agreement, intended to promote bilateral trade, investment and maritime co-operation, in April 2005; a further agreement, intended to enhance co-operation in the political, legal and security fields, was signed in January 2010. The year 2010 was designated the 'Year of China-Indonesia Friendship' to commemorate the 60th anniversary of the establishment of diplomatic relations; artistic and cultural exchange programmes were organized during the year to mark the occasion and further consolidate bilateral relations.

Indonesia and Australia restored defence co-operation links in April 1990, following a four-year disruption. In September 1994 Vice-President Sutrisno became the first senior Indonesian official to visit Australia since Suharto's last visit in 1975. In July 1995 Indonesia withdrew the nomination of Lt-Gen. Herman Mantiri, a former Chief of the General Staff, as ambassador to Australia, owing to widespread protests there concerning his defence of the actions of the Indonesian armed forces in the 1991 Dili massacre of unarmed civilians (see Timor-Leste). Relations with Australia were also strained by, *inter alia*, Australia's decision to investigate claims of new evidence about the killing of six Australia-based journalists, in two separate incidents, during the annexation of East Timor in 1975. The Indonesian Government claimed that the journalists had died in cross-fire. However, separate reports published by the Australian Government, in June 1996, and by Switzerland-based human rights organization International Commission of Jurists, in 1998, concluded that the journalists had been killed by Indonesian troops, in order to conceal Indonesia's invasion of East Timor; in October of that year it was announced that Australia was to reopen a judicial inquiry into the killings. In late 2000 newly declassified documents provided conclusive evidence that Australian officials had been aware of Indonesia's plans to invade East Timor. In November 2007 the Deputy State Coroner of New South Wales ruled that five of the Australia-based journalists (the 'Balibo five') had been deliberately killed by Indonesian special forces, declaring that there was sufficient evidence for the case to constitute a war crime.

Meanwhile, in October 1996 the Australia-Indonesia Development Area was created to develop bilateral economic links, and in March 1997 Indonesia and Australia signed a treaty defining permanent maritime boundaries between the two countries. Following the downfall of Suharto in May 1998, relations between Indonesia and Australia continued to be affected by the issue of East Timor. In January 1999 the Indonesian Government expressed its 'deep regret' at Australia's announcement earlier in that month that it was to change its policy on East Timor and actively promote 'self-determination' in the territory. Following the vote in favour of independence held in East Timor in August, Australia committed 4,500 peace-keeping troops to Interfet, which was formed by the UN to restore order in the territory following the violence perpetrated by pro-Jakarta militias after the announcement of the result of the poll. A military co-operation agreement signed between Indonesia and Australia in December 1995 was reported, in October 1999, to have been cancelled as a result of the Indonesian Government's displeasure at Australia's leading involvement in the peace-keeping operation.

In November 2000 the Australian ambassador to Indonesia, John McCarthy, was physically attacked by a pro-Jakarta mob in Makassar, Sulawesi. The Australian Government accepted the Indonesian Government's apology for the incident. In June 2001, following several postponements, President Wahid paid an official visit to Australia, the first by an Indonesian head of state for

26 years. In August the Australian Prime Minister, John Howard, became the first foreign leader to make an official visit to Indonesia following President Megawati's assumption of power.

However, relations were strained once again later in August 2001 when a cargo ship carrying hundreds of mainly Afghan asylum-seekers became stranded in the international waters between the two countries. Neither country agreed to accept responsibility for the refugees. In September the Australian Minister for Foreign Affairs, Alexander Downer, arrived in Jakarta for discussions with Indonesian ministers on the problems raised by illegal trafficking of immigrants. In October more than 350 refugees, believed to be heading for Australia, drowned when their boat sank off the Indonesian coast, and in the same month a missing boat carrying approximately 170 Iraqi and Afghan asylum-seekers was found on the Indonesian island of Wera. In February 2002 Indonesia and Australia co-hosted the inaugural 'Bali Process' regional ministerial summit on people-smuggling and transnational crime; two further summit meetings were co-hosted by Indonesia and Australia in April 2003 and April 2009, respectively.

Both the Speaker of the DPR and the Speaker of the MPR cancelled scheduled meetings with Howard during his visit to Indonesia in February 2002; during the Australian Prime Minister's stay, students protested in response to allegations that Australia was providing funding for separatist groups in Aceh and Papua. Howard denied such charges and signed an agreement with President Megawati concerning counter-terrorism measures. In May, following an initiative proposed during Howard's visit, the inaugural Australia-Indonesia dialogue was held in Bogor, where Minister of Foreign Affairs Hassan Wirajuda met with his Australian counterpart, Downer.

In October 2002 Indonesia's relations with Australia were seriously affected by the bomb attacks on the island of Bali, a popular destination for Australian tourists, which resulted in the deaths of almost 90 Australian citizens. While the Australian Government immediately offered assistance to Indonesia, a subsequent series of raids on the homes of Indonesian Muslims resident in Australia prompted Vice-President Hamzah Haz to warn that such an offensive could damage bilateral relations. In November 2002 Howard appeared to jeopardize Australia's relations with several South-East Asian countries, including Indonesia, when he stated that Australia was prepared to launch pre-emptive attacks against perceived terrorist threats in other Asian countries. In February 2004 Australia and Indonesia co-hosted the Bali Regional Ministerial Meeting on Counter-Terrorism on Bali, which was intended to bolster regional co-operation over the threat posed by terrorism; a second conference was co-hosted by the two countries in Jakarta in March 2007. In August 2004, however, the Indonesian Government expressed concern at Australia's stated intention to arm its fighter aircraft with a cruise missile system, and in December relations were further strained by the Australian Government's announcement that it was to create a coastal security zone extending five times as far as its territorial waters.

Following the tsunami disaster of December 2004, Australia dispatched some 1,000 troops to assist with relief operations in the province of Aceh and pledged US $773m. in aid to the Indonesian Government, to be disbursed over a five-year period. Prime Minister Howard visited Aceh in February 2005. In the same month, however, the lenience of Abu Bakar Bashir's sentence for his role in the 2002 Bali bombings (see The Threat of Terrorism) provoked much criticism from the Australian Government. In April 2005 President Yudhoyono and Prime Minister Howard signed a Comprehensive Partnership Agreement, which addressed economic, trade, security and reconstruction issues. In July a bilateral memorandum of understanding relating to science, research and technology was signed.

Indonesia's relations with Australia were threatened in May 2005 following the imposition by an Indonesian court of a 20-year prison sentence on an Australian woman who had been arrested in Bali on drugs-smuggling charges. Further tension was provoked by the conviction in February 2006 of the 'Bali nine'—a group of nine Australians who had been arrested by the Indonesian authorities in April 2005 for attempting to smuggle a large quantity of heroin into Australia from the Indonesian island. The two ring-leaders of the group, Andrew Chan and Myuran Sukumaran, were sentenced to death by firing squad, while the seven drugs couriers were all sentenced to life imprisonment. The terms of three of the seven—Matthew Norman, Si Yi Chen and Tan Duc Thanh Nguyen—were reduced in April 2006 to 20 years; however, following an appeal by prosecutors, in September the Supreme Court ruled that the death penalty should be imposed on all three, together with a fourth member of the group, Scott Rush. Chan, Sukumaran and Rush lodged appeals against the death penalty in 2007, but this was rejected by the Indonesian Constitutional Court in October of that year. However, appeals lodged with the Supreme Court by Norman, Si Yi Chen and Tan Duc Thanh Nguyen were more successful, and in February 2008 the death sentences of all three were commuted to life imprisonment. Rush lodged a final appeal against his death sentence in August 2010; following a judicial review, his sentence was commuted to life imprisonment in May 2011. Chan and Sukumaran were also granted judicial reviews upon lodging their respective final appeals in September 2010; however, their final appeals were dismissed in May and July 2011, respectively. At early 2012 appeals for clemency by the Australian Government on behalf of the pair were not expected to be successful.

In January 2006 a dispute arose over the case of 43 Papuans who had fled to Australia by boat in search of asylum from alleged human rights abuses; the refugees claimed that they had been tortured while imprisoned without charge, and that they had witnessed the shooting of friends and relatives. Following the Australian Government's announcement in March that all but one of the asylum-seekers were to be granted temporary visas, Indonesia recalled its ambassador from Canberra, accusing Australia of giving tacit support to the Papuan separatist movement. The ambassador returned to Australia in June, prior to Prime Minister Howard's visit to the Indonesian island of Batam to meet with President Yudhoyono, and in July the remaining detainee was finally granted a temporary visa. In November Indonesian Minister of Foreign Affairs Wirajuda and his Australian counterpart, Downer, signed a security pact, which it was hoped would promote co-operation in law enforcement and counter-terrorism. Yudhoyono met with the new Australian Prime Minister, Kevin Rudd, during the latter's visit to Indonesia in June 2008, when the two leaders agreed to collaborate in the areas of defence, the economy and the environment. Relations were further consolidated by a number of senior-level bilateral visits during 2010, including that of Yudhoyono to Australia in March, and reciprocal visits by the Australian Minister for Foreign Affairs and Trade, Stephen Smith, in July and by Prime Minister Julia Gillard (who had replaced Rudd in June) in November. During Gillard's visit it was announced that Indonesia and Australia had commenced negotiations on an economic partnership. During a meeting between Gillard and Yudhoyono on the sidelines of the East Asia Summit, held in Bali in November 2011, Gillard was reported to have offered reassurances to the Indonesian President about Australia's growing military ties with the USA, insisting that Australian-US defence co-operation would have no impact upon Australia's regional neighbours. Under the terms of a disaster management plan agreed between the two countries in late 2011, Australia was to provide US $1m. towards a secretariat in Jakarta to help to co-ordinate the region's response to natural disasters and to supply Indonesia with four aircraft intended to help that country's humanitarian assistance efforts.

The forced repatriation in early 1998 of thousands of Indonesian workers from Malaysia as a result of the regional economic crisis placed a strain on relations between the two countries. Relations were further strained in October when the Indonesian Government condemned the treatment received in custody by the former Malaysian Deputy Prime Minister and Minister of Finance, Anwar Ibrahim (see Malaysia), breaking with a tradition among ASEAN countries of non-interference in the internal affairs of other member countries. In May 2002 Indonesia signed a trilateral security pact with Malaysia and the Philippines, enabling the signatories to exchange intelligence and launch joint police operations in an attempt to combat terrorism in the region; Cambodia and Thailand later also acceded to the agreement. In November 2006 Indonesia and the Philippines signed an additional security treaty, which was intended further to increase co-operation in addressing transnational crime and terrorism. Indonesia also concluded agreements relating to extradition and defence co-operation with Singapore in April 2007.

Meanwhile, in August 2002 relations with Malaysia were further affected by that country's introduction of stringent anti-immigration laws, which resulted in the forced deportation of many illegal immigrants, most of whom were Indonesian, and provoked protests outside the Malaysian embassy in Jakarta. At the beginning of February 2005 Malaysia extended an amnesty for illegal immigrants to leave the country if they were to avoid legal action, in response to a written request from President Yudhoyono. In the same month Yudhoyono visited both Malaysia and Singapore to meet with Malaysian Prime Minister Abdullah Badawi and Singaporean Prime Minister Lee Hsien Loong; this was the first visit to Singapore by an Indonesian head of state since 1974. In February 2006 Yudhoyono embarked upon a four-day tour of Brunei, Cambodia and Myanmar.

Meanwhile, in May 2002 President Megawati attracted criticism when she attended celebrations in Timor-Leste to mark the territory's official accession to nation status; in February Indonesia and East Timor had agreed to establish full diplomatic relations following independence. The inaugural meeting of the Indonesia-Timor-Leste Joint Ministerial Commission for Bilateral Co-operation took place in Jakarta in October. In April 2005, during an official visit to Timor-Leste, President Yudhoyono met with Timorese President Kay Rala (Xanana) Gusmão; the two heads of state signed a border agreement resolving the demarcation of approximately 96% of the land borders between the two countries. In May the UN-sponsored three-member Commission of Experts opened its investigation into human rights abuses allegedly perpetrated by Indonesian troops during the period of the Timorese vote for independence in 1999.

Indonesia signed an important free trade agreement with Japan in August 2007 during a state visit by Prime Minister Shinzo Abe to Jakarta. The agreement envisaged the eventual removal of most bilateral import taxes (with the notable exception of Japanese imports of rice). Indonesia also confirmed its supplies of liquefied natural gas to Japan. The Japan-Indonesia Economic Partnership Agreement entered into force in July 2008.

Other external relations

In response to the Dili massacre in November 1991, the US Congress imposed a ban on International Military Education and Training (IMET) to Indonesia in 1992; in March 1996 the ban was relaxed to allow members of the ABRI, excluding military officers, to attend IMET courses. However, in September 1999 US President Bill Clinton announced the suspension of military assistance to Indonesia following the ABRI's 'campaign of destruction' in East Timor. Later that month the US Senate Foreign Relations Committee passed legislation banning all military co-operation, including IMET, for Indonesia until that country honoured the results of the August 1999 referendum and allowed independence to be granted to East Timor. In October 2000, relations between Indonesia and the USA deteriorated still further, partly owing to the perceived 'interference' in Indonesian domestic affairs of the recently appointed US ambassador to Indonesia, Robert Gelbard. In late October and early November Muslim groups rallied outside the US embassy in Jakarta, calling for *jihad*; threats were made against US citizens in Indonesia; US companies in the country were attacked; and it was reported that the Indonesian Government had requested Gelbard's immediate removal and replacement.

President Megawati visited Washington, DC, in mid-September 2001, becoming the first leader of a predominantly Muslim country to meet with US President George W. Bush in the aftermath of the terrorist attacks of 11 September 2001; the two heads of state issued a joint statement in which they agreed to 'strengthen bilateral co-operation on counter-terrorism'. However, following the commencement of air-strikes against the Taliban regime in Afghanistan in October, fundamentalist Muslims threatened violence if the Indonesian Government did not sever diplomatic relations with the USA. In October the Front Pembela Islam (FPI—Islamic Defenders' Front) warned that if British and US citizens did not leave the country immediately their safety could not be guaranteed. Megawati, under pressure from Muslim groups and Vice-President Hamzah Haz, indirectly condemned the US attacks in Afghanistan for the first time.

In April 2002 Indonesia and the USA held sensitive security talks, during which measures to combat terrorism and to strengthen civilian control over the armed forces were discussed. In July the US Congress approved legislation awarding US $16m. to the Indonesian police forces; this included $12m. for the establishment of a dedicated anti-terrorism unit, and followed a vote by the Senate Appropriations Committee to remove restrictions on the provision of IMET to Indonesia, pending Congress approval. In August, during a two-day visit to Indonesia, US Secretary of State Colin Powell granted some $50m. of funding for Indonesia's police and counter-terrorism units over a three-year period. However, following the murders in the same month of two US citizens in Papua and the 'insufficient co-operation' with the resultant investigation on the part of the Indonesian Government and military, the US Congress voted against the restoration of normal military relations, including any further relaxation of the IMET. In early 2003 the USA placed Indonesia on a list of countries whose citizens were required to register with the US immigration authorities if they visited the country. Nevertheless, in October President Bush visited Indonesia and announced plans for a $157m. programme to improve education in the country in an attempt to create a system that would discourage the development of Islamist extremism.

The USA took an active part in relief operations in Indonesia following the tsunami disaster of December 2004, notably deploying some 13,000 military personnel in the region. The brevity of the 30-month prison sentence given to Abu Bakar Bashir in February 2005, following his conviction on charges pertaining to the Bali bombings of 2002, attracted much US criticism. In the same month US Secretary of State Condoleezza Rice announced a full resumption of IMET for Indonesia (although this excluded the training of Indonesia's élite special forces, Kopassus), stating that Indonesian co-operation in the investigation of the two murdered US citizens in Papua had 'met the conditions set by Congress'. In May President Yudhoyono made an official visit to the USA, during which he met with President Bush. In a joint communiqué, the two heads of state stressed their common commitment to work towards the establishment of normal military relations; to improve economic co-operation and trade relations; and to strengthen co-operation and investment in the fields of counter-terrorism, energy and education. Bush reiterated the US Administration's support for Indonesia's territorial integrity and its opposition to secessionist movements within the archipelago. In the same month the USA resumed the export of non-lethal defence articles to Indonesia. In November the USA resumed the export of lethal defence articles and Foreign Military Financing (FMF) for Indonesia, with a view to modernizing the Indonesian military and supporting joint objectives, thereby achieving the normalization of military bilateral relations. In May 2008 the US Government concluded that Indonesia had experienced 'objective improvements' in its security situation and therefore rescinded the travel warning to its citizens, issued in 2000.

The election in November 2008 of US President Barack Obama, who had lived in Indonesia for several years during childhood, was warmly welcomed by the Indonesian Government and public alike. In February 2009 the new US Secretary of State, Hillary Clinton, visited Indonesia, holding discussions with Indonesian Minister of Foreign Affairs Wirajuda on a range of issues, including security, trade and counter-terrorism. Marty Natalegawa, Wirajuda's replacement as Minister of Foreign Affairs in Yudhoyono's second Cabinet, praised the US President for bringing 'fresh momentum' to Indonesian-US relations and for adopting a more consultative approach to bilateral relations than that engendered by the Bush Administration. In June 2010 Indonesia and the USA signed the Framework Arrangement on Cooperative Activities in the Field of Defense, a wide-ranging agreement that was intended to integrate existing collaboration between the two countries. Meanwhile, owing to domestic issues, Obama was obliged to postpone a planned tour of Asia, initially from March until June, and subsequently from June to November.

The US President finally embarked upon his 10-day tour of Asia in November 2010, less than 24 hours of which were spent in Indonesia—a source of considerable disquiet to many in the country. Nevertheless, Obama was warmly welcomed by the Indonesian public during his visit, and an address given by the US President at the University of Indonesia, in which he hailed Indonesia as an example to the rest of the world of how both democracy and diversity could thrive in a developing nation, was well received. Obama also emphasized Indonesia's global importance as a rising economic power, and stressed his desire to forge 'a deep and enduring partnership', appealing in particular for increased co-operation on efforts to address the challenge posed by religious extremism. Meanwhile, in July US Secretary of Defense Robert Gates announced that the USA was gradually to resume the training of Kopassus, owing to positive reforms within Indonesia's military and assurances that further such reforms were to be implemented. Human Rights Watch and other rights organizations expressed reservations about the announcement, claiming that individuals still active within Kopassus were guilty of human rights transgressions and did not appear likely ever to be brought to justice.

Meanwhile, in December 1999, with the issue of the status of East Timor having been resolved, Indonesia and Portugal formally re-established full diplomatic relations. In August 1995 Queen Beatrix of the Netherlands, the former colonial power in Indonesia, visited Indonesia (the first Dutch monarch to do so for 24 years) and spoke of her regret for the suffering caused to Indonesians by Dutch rule. In March 2010 Indonesia and the Netherlands signed a formal commitment to intensify bilateral co-operation in the field of trade and investment; the two countries also discussed bilateral relations in the energy, agriculture, and research and technology sectors. However, relations deteriorated somewhat following the decision by President Yudhoyono to cancel a three-day official visit to the Netherlands in October, owing to indications that human rights organizations in the European country had been planning to raise human rights issues against Indonesia during his stay. The decision to cancel the President's visit was made despite repeated assurances from the Dutch Government regarding Yudhoyono's safety. There was a significant amelioration in relations in December 2011, when the Dutch Government extended a formal apology for a massacre perpetrated by its soldiers in the Indonesian village of Rawagede (subsequently renamed Balongsari) in 1947, which claimed the lives of several hundred Indonesian men, and pledged a total of €180,000 in compensation for the surviving widows of those killed in the atrocity.

During a visit to Moscow in April 2003 President Megawati signed an agreement to buy Russian defence equipment to the value of US $197m., which was to be partly financed by the bartering of Indonesian palm oil. In September 2007 President Vladimir Putin of Russia visited Jakarta, where he concluded an agreement with President Yudhoyono providing for further purchases of Russian armaments and fighter aircraft. This arrangement was to be financed by a 10-year loan of $1,000m. from Russia. Various other agreements, relating to co-operation in economic relations, counter-terrorism measures and environmental protection, were also signed. In 2010, to commemorate the 60th anniversary of the establishment of diplomatic relations, the Indonesian Cultural Festival was staged in three Russian cities, Moscow, St Petersburg and Tver, in May of that year; the Russian Minister of Culture expressed his hope that the festival, together with other forms of co-operation in the fields of culture and tourism, would help to foster closer relations between the two countries.

Indonesia has appeared keen in recent years to develop its relations with a number of Middle Eastern and South Asian countries. In October 2005 King Abdullah of Jordan undertook a state visit to Jakarta where he had discussions with President Yudhoyono on bilateral relations and issues pertaining to the international Islamic community. In the following month Yudhoyono paid an official visit to Pakistan, during which he signed a framework agreement on bilateral economic co-operation with his Pakistani counterpart, Pervez Musharraf. The two Presidents also held discussions regarding the challenge of countering tendencies to associate Islam with terrorism. During a 10-day tour of the Middle East in April–May 2006, Yudhoyono reached preliminary energy and investment agreements, worth many millions of dollars, and expressed Indonesia's support for the creation of an independent Palestinian state. In July demonstrations were held outside the US embassy in Jakarta in protest at Israel's ongoing military activity against the Palestinians in Gaza, while Muslim protesters accused the US Administration of bias towards Israel.

Relations with Saudi Arabia were threatened in November 2010 by the publicizing of the case of Sumiati, an Indonesian maid working in Saudi Arabia who had received horrific injuries, reportedly inflicted by her employer. Later in November the body of another Indonesian maid employed in Saudi Arabia, Kikim Komalasari, was found in the Saudi town of Abha; the maid had allegedly been tortured to death by her employer. Following the resultant display of public anger, President Yudhoyono expressed his desire for the law to be upheld by the Saudi authorities. Bilateral tensions were exacerbated by the execution in June 2011 of Ruyati binti Sapubi, an Indonesian maid who had been convicted of murdering her Saudi employer, after allegedly suffering months of abuse at her hands and having been denied permission to leave her employment and return to her family in Indonesia. The Minister of Foreign Affairs, Marty Natalegawa, expressed particular displeasure at the Saudi Government's failure to inform the Indonesian Government or the woman's family that she was to be executed until after the event, which Yudhoyono described as a contravention of the 'norms and manners' of international relations, and the Indonesian ambassador in the Saudi capital, Riyadh, was recalled for consultations. During a meeting with Yudhoyono, the Saudi ambassador in Jakarta offered the apologies of his Government for the lack of notification as well as an assurance that such an occurrence would not be repeated. Another Indonesian maid due to be executed after being convicted in Riyadh in 2009 of murdering her Yemeni employee was spared the death penalty after the Indonesian Government agreed to pay *diyat* ('compensation') amounting to £338,000; the maid, Darsem, had pleaded that she had acted in self-defence when her employer had attempted to rape her. Also in June 2011 a lawsuit filed against a Saudi diplomat in Berlin, Germany, by his Indonesian maid—who claimed that he had effectively enslaved her, withholding payment and physically assaulting her over a period of many months before she escaped from his residence in October 2010—was rejected by the Berlin Labour Court on the grounds of diplomatic immunity. The German Institute for Human Rights announced its intention to appeal against the ruling to Germany's Federal Court of Justice, in a case that potentially stood to have far-reaching implications for diplomats' immunity from prosecution within the Western European country. The allegations also served further to strain Indonesian-Saudi relations. At the end of June 2011 the Indonesian Government announced a moratorium prohibiting its nationals from working as domestic servants in Saudi Arabia, effective from 1 August. In response, the Saudi Government announced that it was to cease issuing work permits to Indonesian workers, effective from 2 July. Some 22 Indonesian maids were known to be awaiting execution in Saudi Arabia at mid-2011, although human rights groups claimed that the actual figure was significantly higher.

CONSTITUTION AND GOVERNMENT

Executive power rests with the President, who is elected for five years by the Majelis Permusyawaratan Rakyat (MPR—People's Consultative Assembly), which is the highest authority of the State. The President governs with the assistance of an appointed Cabinet; the Cabinet is responsible to the President. In 2002 the MPR approved a series of amendments to the Constitution. These provided for: the direct election of the President and Vice-President; the termination of all non-elected representation in the Dewan Perwakilan Rakyat (DPR—House of Representatives) and the MPR; and the creation of the Dewan Perwakilan Daerah (DPD—House of Representatives of the Regions), which, together with the DPR, henceforth comprised the MPR. The MPR consists of 692 members serving for five years. The MPR incorporates all 560 (increased in 2009 from 550) members of the DPR, the country's legislative organ, and the 132 (previously 128) elected regional representatives.

There are 33 provinces, and local government is through a three-tier system of provincial, regency and village assemblies. Each province is headed by a Governor, who is elected to a five-year term of office by the Provincial Assembly. Provincial Governors must be confirmed by the President. The Governor of Jakarta, which is designated as a 'special district' (as are Aceh and Yogyakarta), was chosen by direct election for the first time in August 2007.

REGIONAL AND INTERNATIONAL CO-OPERATION

Indonesia is a member of the Association of Southeast Asian Nations (ASEAN, see p. 214), of the Asian Development Bank (ADB, see p. 210) and of Asia-Pacific Economic Cooperation (APEC, see p. 204). It is also a member of the UN's Economic and Social Commission for Asia and the Pacific (ESCAP, see p. 40) and of the Colombo Plan (see p. 449), which promotes economic and social development in Asia and the Pacific.

Indonesia became a member of the UN in 1950. As a contracting party to the General Agreement on Tariffs and Trade (GATT), Indonesia joined the World Trade Organization (WTO, see p. 433) upon its establishment in 1995. The country participates in the Group of 77 (G77, see p. 450) developing countries and Developing Eight (D-8, see p. 449), and it is a member of the International Labour Organization (ILO see, p. 141) and of the Non-aligned Movement (see p. 464). In January 2009 Indonesia suspended its membership of the Organization of the Petroleum Exporting Countries (OPEC, see p. 408).

ECONOMIC AFFAIRS

In 2010, according to estimates by the World Bank, Indonesia's gross national income (GNI), measured at average 2008–10 prices, was US $599,148m., equivalent to $2,500 per head (or $4,170 per head on an international purchasing-power parity basis). During 2001–10, it was estimated, the population increased at an average annual rate of 1.2%, while gross domestic product (GDP) per head increased, in real terms, by an average of 4.2% per year. Overall GDP increased, in real terms, by an average of 5.4% per year in 2001–10. GDP expanded by 6.5% in 2011, according to the Asian Development Bank (ADB).

Agriculture, forestry and fishing contributed 15.3% of GDP in 2010, and engaged 38.2% of the employed labour force in February 2011. Principal crops for domestic consumption include rice, cassava and maize. Although Indonesia remains a major exporter of rubber and palm oil, the respective contributions to the country's total export earnings have declined. Other important cash crops are coffee, spices, tea, cocoa, tobacco, bananas, coconuts and sugar cane. A large percentage of Indonesia's land area remains covered by tropical rainforests. However, illegal logging practices have been widespread, leading to serious environmental damage. During 2001–10, according to figures from the ADB, agricultural GDP increased by an average of 3.5% per year. The GDP of the agricultural sector expanded by 3.0% in 2011.

Industry (including mining, manufacturing, construction and utilities) provided 47.0% of GDP in 2010, and engaged 18.8% of the employed labour force in February 2011. During 2001–10, according to ADB data, industrial GDP increased by an average of 4.2% per year. The GDP of the industrial sector increased by 5.3% in 2011.

Mining contributed 11.2% of GDP in 2010, but engaged just 1.2% of the employed labour force in February 2011. Indonesia's principal mineral resource is petroleum, and the country is a leading exporter of liquefied natural gas. At the end of 2010 proven reserves of petroleum amounted to 4,200m. barrels, sufficient to sustain production at that year's rate for nearly 12 years. Indonesia suspended its membership of the Organization of the Petroleum Exporting Countries (OPEC) in January 2009 on the grounds that the country was no longer a net oil exporter. Prior to that Indonesia was subject to annual quotas for petroleum production as agreed within OPEC. The Government aimed to increase crude petroleum production from an estimated 978,000 barrels per day (b/d) in 2008 to 1.1m. b/d by 2015. In 2010, according to industry sources, natural gas production was 82,000m. cu m, from proven reserves amounting to 310,000m. cu m at the end of that year, sufficient to sustain production at that year's rate for more than 37 years. In 2010 coal production reached 305.9m. metric tons. Indonesia is one of the world's largest producers of tin, with output of ore reaching an estimated 55,000 tons in 2009. Bauxite, nickel, copper, gold and silver are also mined. During 2001–10, according to figures from the ADB, mining GDP increased at an average annual rate of only 1.1%. The GDP of the sector increased by 1.4% in 2011.

Manufacturing contributed 24.8% of GDP in 2010, and engaged 12.3% of the employed labour force in February 2011. Apart from petroleum refineries, the main branches of the sector include food products, textiles, clothing and footwear, transport equipment, electrical machinery and electronic equipment. According to ADB data, manufacturing GDP increased by an average of 4.6% per year in 2001–10. Sectoral GDP increased by 6.2% in 2011.

Construction contributed 10.3% of GDP in 2010, and engaged 5.0% of the employed labour force in February 2011. According to figures from the ADB, construction GDP increased by an average of 7.2% per year in 2001–10. The sector's GDP increased by 7.0% in 2010.

From the 1980s Indonesia broadened the base of its energy supplies to include gas, coal, hydroelectricity and geothermal energy, in addition to the traditional dependence on petroleum. In 2008, of total electricity produced, coal accounted for 41.1%, petroleum for 28.8% and natural gas for 16.9%. In 2010 imports of mineral fuels and lubricants comprised 20.3% of the total value of merchandise imports. Plans for the construction of a nuclear power plant on the island of Bangka, to the east of Sumatra, were confirmed in 2011. It was anticipated that construction work on the plant, which was expected to supply 40% of electricity needs in Sumatra, Java and Bali, would commence in 2015.

Services (including trade, transport and communications, finance and tourism) provided 37.6% of GDP in 2010, and engaged 43.1% of the employed labour force in February 2011. Tourism is normally a major source of foreign exchange. Revenue from tourism (including passenger transport) reached a provisional US $6,980m. in 2010. The number of tourist arrivals exceeded 7.0m. in 2010. According to figures from the ADB, the GDP of the services sector expanded by an average of 7.3% per year in 2001–10. The sector's GDP increased by 8.5% in 2011.

In 2010 Indonesia recorded a visible trade surplus of US $30,628m. In the same year a surplus of $5,643m. was recorded on the current account of the balance of payments. In 2010 the principal source of imports was the People's Republic of China (which supplied 15.1% of the total), followed by Singapore, Japan, the USA, Malaysia, the Republic of Korea and Thailand. Japan was the principal market for exports in 2010 (purchasing 16.3%). Other major purchasers were China, the USA, Singapore and the Republic of Korea. The principal exports in 2010 were mineral fuels and lubricants, animal and vegetable fats, electrical and electronic equipment, and rubber and rubber products. The principal imports were mineral fuels and lubricants, machinery, nuclear reactors and boilers, electrical and electronic equipment, and vehicles (excluding railway and tramway).

The draft budget for 2012 projected revenue of Rp. 1,292,053,000m. and expenditure of Rp. 954,137,000m. According to the ADB, the budget deficit was equivalent to 1.1% of GDP in 2011. Indonesia's general government gross debt was Rp.1,762,067,090m. in 2010, equivalent to 27.4% of GDP. According to the ADB, Indonesia's external debt was estimated at US $224,757m. at the end of 2011. In that year the cost of servicing external public debt was equivalent to 22.5% of the value of exports of goods and services. The annual rate of inflation averaged 8.2% in 2001–10. Consumer prices increased by 5.4% in 2011. The rate of unemployment at February 2011 was 6.8% of the labour force. The level of underemployment (those working fewer than 35 hours a week) also remained very high, at almost 28% in early 2008, according to the ADB.

Amid declining international commodity prices and export demand resulting from the emerging global financial crisis, in February 2009 the Government announced a Rp. 73,300,000m. stimulus programme, which aimed to maintain consumer spending and to create employment opportunities through infrastructure projects. Although the value of merchandise exports increased by 27.5% in 2011, the cost of imports rose by 30.3%. Following a sharp decline in foreign direct investment (FDI), from US $9,318m. in 2008 to $4,877m. in 2009, FDI rose to $13,371m. in 2010 and to an estimated $18,200m. in 2011. Indonesia has a large domestic market, and consumer demand strengthened during 2010, while the rupiah appreciated in value. However, with the costs of essential commodities rising, inflationary pressures began to increase once again in early 2011. In February the central bank's key monetary policy rate was raised from 6.50% to 6.75%; however, it had been reduced to 5.75% by February 2012, with the aim of maintaining strong economic growth amid a poor global outlook. Although GDP contracted in the fourth quarter of 2008, for the year as a whole the economy showed positive growth, which was maintained in 2009 and 2010. GDP increased by 6.5% in 2011, and the ADB envisaged growth of 6.4% in 2012. Meanwhile, however, income inequality was reported to have risen. Under its medium-term plan, therefore, the Government aimed to reduce the incidence of poverty to less than 10% by 2014. According to Statistics Indonesia, the number of impoverished people in Indonesia declined from 31m. in 2010 to 30m. in 2011. However, the Government's official poverty line of Rp. 233,740 (approximately $28) per caput per month—less than $1 per day—was widely criticized as being too low to reflect the true scale of poverty in the country, with some 100m. people estimated to be living on $2 per day. Furthermore, international observers warned that economic development could not be achieved through poverty alleviation alone, and urged the Yudhoyono administration to increase public spending on infrastructural projects. The improvement of basic infrastructure was a key priority of the 2012 national budget. The Government estimated that more than $150,000m. should be disbursed on improving basic infrastructure during Yudhoyono's second presidential term (2009–14); however, in the event, it had allocated only around $50,000m. to this end, hoping to secure private investment to meet its target.

PUBLIC HOLIDAYS

2013: 1 January (New Year's Day), 23 January* (Mouloud, Prophet Muhammad's Birthday), 10 February (Chinese New Year), 29 March (Good Friday), 9 May (Ascension Day), 25 May (Waisak Day), 5 June* (Ascension of the Prophet Muhammad), 7 August* (Id al-Fitr, end of Ramadan), 17 August (Independence Day), 14 October* (Id al-Adha, Feast of the Sacrifice), 4 November* (Muharram, Islamic New Year), 25 December (Christmas Day).

* These holidays are dependent on the Islamic lunar calendar and may vary by one or two days from the dates given.

Statistical Survey

Source (unless otherwise stated): Badan Pusat Statistik (Central Bureau of Statistics/Statistics Indonesia), Jalan Dr Sutomo 6–8, Jakarta 10710; tel. (21) 3507057; fax (21) 3857046; e-mail bpshq@bps.go.id; internet www.bps.go.id.

Note: Unless otherwise stated, figures for East Timor (now Timor-Leste, occupied by Indonesia between July 1976 and October 1999) are not included in the tables.

Area and Population

AREA, POPULATION AND DENSITY

Area (sq km)	1,910,931*
Population (census results)	
30 June 2000	206,264,595
31 May 2010	
Males	119,507,580
Females	118,048,783
Total	237,556,363
Population (UN estimates at mid-year)†	
2011	242,325,637
2012	244,769,111
Density (per sq km) at mid-2012	128.1

* 737,814 sq miles.

† Source: UN, *World Population Prospects: The 2010 Revision*; estimates not adjusted to take account of results of the 2010 census.

POPULATION BY AGE AND SEX

(UN estimates at mid-2012)

	Males	Females	Total
0–14	32,957,764	31,725,232	64,682,996
15–64	82,925,420	83,189,526	166,114,946
65 and over	6,129,751	7,841,418	13,971,169
Total	122,012,935	122,756,176	244,769,111

Note: Estimates not adjusted to take account of results of the 2010 census.

Source: UN, *World Population Prospects: The 2010 Revision*.

ISLANDS AND PROVINCES

(population at census of May 2010)*

	Area (sq km)	Population ('000)	Density (per sq km)
Jawa (Java) and Madura	129,438	136,563.1	1,055.0
DKI Jakarta†	664	9,588.2	14,440.1
Jawa Barat	35,378	43,021.8	1,216.1
Jawa Tengah	32,801	32,380.7	987.2
DI Yogyakarta†	3,133	3,452.4	1,101.9
Jawa Timur	47,800	37,476.0	784.0
Banten	9,663	10,644.0	1,101.5
Sumatera (Sumatra)	480,793	50,613.9	105.3
Nanggroe Aceh Darussalem†	57,956	4,486.6	77.4
Sumatera Utara	72,981	12,985.1	177.9
Sumatera Barat	42,013	4,846.0	115.3
Riau	87,024	5,543.0	63.7
Jambi	50,058	3,088.6	61.7
Sumatera Selatan	91,592	7,446.4	81.3
Bangkulu	19,919	1,713.4	86.0
Lumpung	34,624	7,596.1	219.4
Kepulauan Bangka-Belitung	16,424	1,223.0	74.5
Kepulauan Riau	8,202	1,685.7	205.5
Sulawesi (Celebes)	188,522	17,359.4	92.1
Sulawesi Utara	13,852	2,265.9	163.6
Sulawesi Tengah	61,841	2,633.4	42.6
Sulawesi Selatan	46,717	8,032.6	171.9
Sulawesi Tenggara	38,068	2,230.6	58.6
Gorontalo	11,257	1,038.6	92.3
Sulawesi Barat	16,787	1,158.3	69.0
Kalimantan	544,150	13,772.5	25.3
Kalimantan Barat	147,307	4,393.2	29.8
Kalimantan Tengah	153,565	2,202.6	14.3
Kalimantan Selatan	38,744	3,626.1	93.6
Kalimantan Timur	204,534	3,550.6	17.4
Nusa Tenggara and Bali‡	73,070	13,067.6	178.8
Nusa Tenggara Barat	18,572	4,496.9	242.1
Nusa Tenggara Timur	48,718	4,679.3	96.0
Bali	5,780	3,891.4	673.3
Maluku (Moluccas) and Papua§	494,957	6,179.8	12.5
Maluku	46,914	1,531.4	32.6
Maluku Utara	31,983	1,035.6	32.4
Papua Barat†	97,024	760.9	7.8
Papua†	319,036	2,852.0	8.9
Total	1,910,931	237,556.4	124.3

* Figures refer to provincial divisions, organized according to geography, island or island groupings.

† Province with special status.

‡ The Nusa Tenggara provinces comprise most of the Lesser Sunda Islands, principally Flores, Lombok, Sumba, Sumbawa and part of Timor.

§ The Papua provinces were formerly known as Irian Jaya (West Papua).

PRINCIPAL TOWNS

(estimated population at 31 December 1996)

Jakarta (capital)	9,341,400	Malang	775,900
Surabaya	2,743,400	Padang	739,500
Bandung	2,429,000	Banjarmasin	544,700
Medan	1,942,000	Surakarta	518,600
Palembang	1,394,300	Pontianak	459,100
Semarang	1,366,500	Yogyakarta (Jogjakarta)	421,000
Ujung Pandang (Makassar)	1,121,300		

Mid-2010 (incl. suburbs, UN estimates): Jakarta 9,210,211; Surabaya 2,508,768; Bandung 2,412,271; Medan 2,131,060; Ujung Pandang 1,294,366; Palembang 1,244,144; Bogor 1,044,123 (Source: UN, *World Urbanization Prospects: The 2009 Revision*).

BIRTHS AND DEATHS

(annual averages, UN estimates)

	1995–2000	2000–05	2005–10
Birth rate (per 1,000)	24.5	21.9	21.0
Death rate (per 1,000)	7.6	7.4	7.2

Source: UN, *World Population Prospects: The 2010 Revision*.

Birth rate (per 1,000): 22.9 in 1997; 22.8 in 1998; 22.4 in 1999 (Source: UN, *Statistical Yearbook for Asia and the Pacific*).

Death rate (per 1,000): 7.5 in 1997; 7.7 in 1998; 7.5 in 1999 (Source: UN, *Statistical Yearbook for Asia and the Pacific*).

Life expectancy (years at birth, WHO estimates): 68 (males 66; females 71) in 2009 (Source: WHO, *World Health Statistics*).

ECONOMICALLY ACTIVE POPULATION

(persons aged 15 years and over, at February)

	2009	2010	2011
Agriculture, hunting, forestry and fishing	43,029,493	42,825,807	42,475,329
Mining and quarrying	1,139,495	1,188,634	1,352,219
Manufacturing	12,615,440	13,052,521	13,696,024
Electricity, gas and water	209,441	208,494	257,270
Construction	4,610,695	4,844,689	5,591,084
Trade, restaurants and hotels	21,836,768	22,212,885	23,239,792
Transport, storage and communications	5,947,673	5,817,680	5,585,124
Financing, insurance, real estate and business services	1,484,598	1,639,748	2,058,968
Public services	13,611,841	15,615,114	17,025,934
Total employed	104,485,444	107,405,572	111,281,744
Unemployed	9,258,964	8,592,490	8,117,631
Total labour force	113,744,408	115,998,062	119,399,375

Health and Welfare

KEY INDICATORS

Total fertility rate (children per woman, 2009)	2.1
Under-5 mortality rate (per 1,000 live births, 2009)	39
HIV/AIDS (% of persons aged 15–49, 2009)	0.2
Physicians (per 1,000 head, 2003)	0.10
Hospital beds (per 1,000 head, 1998)	0.60
Health expenditure (2008): US $ per head (PPP)	91
Health expenditure (2008): % of GDP	2.3
Health expenditure (2008): public (% of total)	54.4
Access to water (% of persons, 2008)	80
Access to sanitation (% of persons, 2008)	52
Total carbon dioxide emissions ('000 metric tons, 2007)	396,818.5
Carbon dioxide emissions per head (metric tons, 2007)	1.8
Human Development Index (2011): ranking	124
Human Development Index (2011): value	0.617

For sources and definitions, see explanatory note on p. vi.

Agriculture

PRINCIPAL CROPS

('000 metric tons, incl. East Timor)

	2008	2009	2010
Rice, paddy	60,251	64,399	66,412
Maize	16,324	17,630	18,364
Potatoes	1,045	1,176	1,061
Sweet potatoes	1,877	2,058	2,051
Cassava (Manioc)	21,593	22,039	23,909
Beans, dry	298	314	292
Sugar cane	26,000*	26,500†	26,500†
Cashew nuts, with shell	157	145†	174†
Soybeans (Soya beans)	777	975	908
Groundnuts, with shell	774	778	780
Coconuts	19,500*	21,447*	20,655†
Oil palm fruit†	85,000	86,000	86,000
Cabbages and other brassicas	1,324	1,358	1,385
Tomatoes	726	853	892
Pumpkins, squash and gourds	394	321	370
Cucumbers and gherkins	540	583	547
Aubergines (Eggplants)	427	452	482
Chillies and peppers, green	1,092	1,379	1,332
Onions, dry	854	965	1,048
Beans, green	838	880	885†
Carrots and turnips	367	358	408
Oranges	2,468	2,132	2,033
Avocados	225	258	224
Mangoes, mangosteens and guavas	2,105	2,243	1,314
Pineapples	1,433	1,558	1,390
Bananas	6,005	6,374	5,815
Papayas	718	773	695
Coffee, green	683	791*	801*
Cocoa beans	793	800†	810†
Tea	151	146*	150†
Cinnamon†	64	67	60
Cloves	81	81†	57†
Ginger	192	155	109
Tobacco, unmanufactured	170	181†	195†
Natural rubber	2,922	2,790†	2,788†

* Unofficial figure.

† FAO estimate(s).

Aggregate production ('000 metric tons, may include official, semi-official or estimated data): Total cereals 76,575.0 in 2008, 82,028.6 in 2009, 84,775.9 in 2010; Total roots and tubers 24,874.5 in 2008, 25,636.7 in 2009, 27,410.1 in 2010; Total vegetables (incl. melons) 8,834.6 in 2008, 9,533.0 in 2009, 95,865.0 in 2010; Total fruits (excl. melons) 16,753.5 in 2008, 17,287.7 in 2009, 14,867.8 in 2010.

Source: FAO.

LIVESTOCK

('000 head)

	2008	2009	2010
Cattle	12,257	12,760	13,633
Sheep	9,605	10,200	10,932
Goats	15,147	15,815	16,821
Pigs	6,338	6,975	7,212
Horses	393	399	409
Buffaloes	1,931	1,933	2,005
Chickens	1,253,430	1,341,780	1,622,750
Ducks	39,840	42,367	45,292

Source: FAO.

LIVESTOCK PRODUCTS

('000 metric tons)

	2008	2009	2010*
Cattle meat	392.5	408.1	420.6
Buffalo meat	39.0	34.8	40.2
Sheep meat	47.0	54.2	55.4
Goat meat	66.0	74.1	75.7
Pig meat*	636.8	636.8	636.8
Chicken meat	1,349.6	1,408.8	1,650.0
Cows' milk	647	882	913
Goats' milk*	264	276	281
Hen eggs	1,122.6	1,059.3	1,117.8
Other poultry eggs	201.0	247.1	260.7
Wool, greasy*	22.2	21.4	23.8

* FAO estimates.

Note: Figures for meat refer to inspected production only, i.e. from animals slaughtered under government supervision.

Source: FAO.

Forestry

ROUNDWOOD REMOVALS

('000 cubic metres, excl. bark, FAO estimates)

	2007	2008	2009
Sawlogs, veneer logs and logs for sleepers	21,602	26,855	22,405
Pulpwood	9,500	10,700	10,700
Other industrial wood	3,249	3,249	3,249
Fuel wood	67,825	65,034	62,341
Total	102,176	105,838	98,695

2010: Production assumed to be unchanged from 2009 (FAO estimates).

Source: FAO.

SAWNWOOD PRODUCTION

('000 cubic metres, incl. railway sleepers)

	2006	2007	2008
Total (all broadleaved)	4,330	4,330	4,169

2009–10: Production assumed to be unchanged from 2008 (FAO estimates).

Source: FAO.

Fishing

('000 metric tons, live weight)

	2007	2008	2009
Capture	5,050.3	5,002.3	5,099.4
Scads	305.5	327.4	330.7
Goldstripe sardinella	169.8	174.4	175.8
'Stolephorus' anchovies	175.5	199.7	207.5
Skipjack tuna	303.9	293.8	297.0
Indian mackerels	13.1	16.9	18.2
Aquaculture	1,392.9*	1,690.1*	1,733.4
Common carp	264.4	242.3	249.3
Milkfish	263.1	277.5	328.3
Total catch	6,443.2*	6,692.6*	6,832.8

* FAO estimate.

Note: Figures exclude aquatic plants ('000 metric tons): 1,733.1 (capture 4.6, aquaculture 1,728.5) in 2007; 2,148.0 (capture 2.9, aquaculture 2,145.1) in 2008; 2,965.9 (capture 2.3, aquaculture 2,963.6) in 2009. Also excluded are crocodiles, recorded by number rather than by weight. The number of crocodiles caught was: 17,910 in 2007; 16,306 in 2008; 12,251 in 2009.

Source: FAO.

Mining

('000 metric tons unless otherwise indicated)

	2007	2008	2009*
Crude petroleum (million barrels)†	305.0	311.0	280.0
Natural gas (million cubic metres)	79,410	81,842	85,000
Bauxite	1,251	1,152	1,200
Coal (bituminous)	178,791	188,717	190,000
Nickel‡	229.2	192.6	202.8
Copper‡	796.9	632.6	610.0
Tin ore (metric tons)‡	66,137	53,228	55,000
Gold (kg)§	117,851	64,390	65,000
Silver (kg)§	268,967	226,051	215,000

* Estimates.

† Including condensate.

‡ Figures refer to the metal content of ores and concentrates.

§ Including gold and silver in copper concentrate.

Source: US Geological Survey.

Industry

SELECTED PRODUCTS

('000 metric tons unless otherwise indicated)

	2001	2002	2003
Raw sugar (centrifugal)[1]	2,025	1,902	1,780
Refined sugar[1,2]	2,023	1,750	2,431
Palm oil[1]	8,080[3]	9,350	10,530
Veneer sheets ('000 cubic metres)[1]	94	45[2]	289
Plywood ('000 cubic metres)[1]	7,300	7,550	6,111
Jackets (men's and boys', '000)	55,849	32,777	n.a.
Trousers (men's and boys', '000)	42,403	45,168	n.a.
Shirts (men's and boys', '000)	18,069	76,897	n.a.
Underwear (men's and boys', '000)	76,232	48,154	n.a.
Underwear (women's and girls', '000)	55,769	145,284	n.a.
Blouses (women's and girls', '000)	25,259	22,540	n.a.
Footwear ('000 pairs, excl. rubber)	325,169	306,761	n.a.
Newsprint	1,022	1,022	1,022
Other printing and writing paper[2]	5,394	5,394	5,394
Other paper and paperboard	3,620	3,612	3,612
Nitrogenous fertilizers[1,4]	2,549	n.a.	n.a.
Jet fuel	1,087	1,175	1,349
Motor spirit (petrol)	8,997	8,592	8,584
Naphthas	2,432	1,986	2,221
Kerosene	7,492	7,274	7,565
Gas-diesel oil	14,137	13,791	13,786
Residual fuel oils	12,009	11,951	11,755
Lubricating oils	382	318	404
Liquefied petroleum gas	1,684	1,833	2,316
Rubber tyres ('000)[5]	20,500[2]	n.a.	n.a.
Cement (hydraulic)[6]	n.a.	34,640	35,000
Aluminium (unwrought)[2,6,7]	209	160	200
Tin (unwrought, metric tons)[6,7]	53,470	67,455	65,000
Passenger motor cars ('000)[8]	74	n.a.	n.a.
Television receivers (colour, '000)	21,519	23,680	n.a.
Electric accumulators (for motor vehicles, '000)	49,496	22,510	n.a.
Batteries and cells (primary, millions)	14,059	14,800	n.a.
Electric energy (million kWh)	101,647	108,206	112,944
Gas from gasworks (terajoules)	30,400	30,000[2]	n.a.

Cigarettes (million): 254,276 in 1999.

2007 ('000 metric tons unless otherwise stated): Raw sugar 2,814; Palm oil 16,760[1,3]; Veneer sheets ('000 cubic metres) 299[1]; Plywood ('000 cubic metres) 3,454[1]; Cement (hydraulic) 36,000[6]; Aluminium (unwrought) 242[6]; Tin (unwrought, metric tons) 64,127[6]; Gas-diesel oil 11,368; Residual fuel oils 10,173; Jet fuel 1,087; Naphthas 3,017; Kerosene 6,894; Electric energy (million kWh) 142,236.

2008 ('000 metric tons unless otherwise stated): Raw sugar 3,263; Palm oil 18,910[1,3]; Veneer sheets ('000 cubic metres) 427[1]; Plywood ('000 cubic metres) 3,353[1]; Cement (hydraulic) 37,000[6]; Aluminium (unwrought) 243[6]; Tin (unwrought, metric tons) 53,471[6]; Gas-diesel oil 12,766; Residual fuel oils 9,471; Jet fuel 1,445; Naphthas 2,663; Kerosene 6,182; Electric energy (million kWh) 149,437.

2009 ('000 metric tons unless otherwise stated): Palm oil 20,550[1,3]; Veneer sheets ('000 cubic metres) 685[1]; Plywood ('000 cubic metres) 2,996[1]; Cement (hydraulic) 38,000[2,6]; Aluminium (unwrought) 250[2,6]; Tin (unwrought, metric tons) 54,000[2,6].

[1] Source: FAO.

[2] Provisional or estimated production.

[3] Unofficial figure.

[4] Production in terms of nitrogen.

[5] For road motor vehicles, excluding bicycles and motorcycles.

[6] Source: US Geological Survey.

[7] Primary metal production only.

[8] Vehicles assembled from imported parts.

Source (unless otherwise indicated): UN Industrial Commodity Statistics Database.

Finance

CURRENCY AND EXCHANGE RATES

Monetary Units

100 sen = 1 rupiah (Rp.).

Sterling, Dollar and Euro Equivalents (30 December 2011)

£1 sterling = 14,020.0 rupiah;
US $1 = 9,068.0 rupiah;
€1 = 11,733.1 rupiah;
100,000 rupiah = £7.13 = $11.03 = €8.52.

Average Exchange Rate (rupiah per US $)

2009 10,389.9
2010 9,090.4
2011 8770.4

GOVERNMENT FINANCE

(central government operations, '000 million rupiah)

Summary of Balances

	2005	2006*	2007*
Revenue and grants	495,444	637,799	723,058
Less Expenditure and net lending	509,419	669,880	763,571
Overall balance	–13,975	–32,081	–40,513

Revenue and Grants

	2005	2006*	2007*
Tax revenue	346,834	409,020	509,462
Income tax	175,380	208,834	261,698
Value added tax (VAT) on goods and services, and tax on sales of luxury goods	16,184	20,684	21,267
Tax of rights in land and building	3,429	3,179	5,390
Excise duties	33,256	37,772	42,035
Import duties	14,921	12,142	14,417
Export taxes	318	1,094	453
Other taxes	2,051	2,287	3,158
Non-tax revenue	147,314	226,906	210,927
Grants	1,296	1,873	2,669
Total	495,444	637,799	723,058

Expenditure and Net Lending

	2005	2006*	2007*
Central government expenditure	358,903	443,509	504,776
Personnel expenditure	55,589	72,238	101,202
Material expenditure	33,060	46,944	72,186
Interest payments	57,651	78,910	85,087
Domestic interest	43,496	54,778	n.a.
External interest	14,155	24,132	n.a.
Subsidies	120,708	107,463	102,924
Oil subsidies	95,661	64,212	61,838
Non-oil subsidies	25,047	43,251	41,086
Social expenditure	24,247	43,254	51,409
Capital expenditure	36,854	59,605	73,130
Other expenditure	30,794	35,095	18,838
Regional expenditure	150,516	226,371	258,795
Balance funds	143,301	222,322	250,343
Specific autonomous fund	7,215	4,049	8,452
Total	509,419	669,880	763,571

* Preliminary figures.

2010 (central government operations, '000 million rupiah, preliminary figures): Tax revenue 723,307; Non-tax revenue 268,942; Total 992,249. *Expenditure:* Personnel expenditure 148,078; Material expenditure 97,597; Interest payment 88,383; Subsidies 192,707; Social expenditure 68,611; Capital expenditure 80,287; Other expenditure 21,673; Grant expenditures 70; Total 697,406.

2011 (central government operations, '000 million rupiah, budget proposals): Tax revenue 878,685; Non-tax revenue 286,568; Total 1,165,253. *Expenditure:* Personnel expenditure 182,875; Material expenditure 142,826; Interest payment 106,584; Subsidies 237,195; Social expenditure 81,810; Capital expenditure 140,952; Other expenditure 15,596; Grant expenditures 405; Total 908,243.

2012 (central government operations, '000 million rupiah, budget proposals): Tax revenue 1,019,333; Non-tax revenue 272,720; Total 1,292,053. *Expenditure:* Personnel expenditure 215,725; Material expenditure 138,482; Interest payment 123,072; Subsidies 208,850; Social expenditure 63,572; Capital expenditure 168,126; Other expenditure 34,513; Grant expenditures 1,797; Total 954,137.

INTERNATIONAL RESERVES

(US $ million at 31 December)

	2008	2009	2010
Gold (market prices)	2,044	2,556	3,303
IMF special drawing rights	34	2,763	2,714
Reserve position in IMF	224	228	224
Foreign exchange	49,339	60,572	89,970
Total	51,641	66,119	96,211

Source: IMF, *International Financial Statistics*.

MONEY SUPPLY

('000 million rupiah at 31 December)

	2008	2009	2010
Currency outside depository corporations	209,747	226,006	260,227
Transferable deposits	359,890	414,211	484,312
Other deposits	1,322,922	1,497,663	1,717,592
Securities other than shares	3,279	3,504	9,075
Broad money	1,895,839	2,141,384	2,471,206

Source: IMF, *International Financial Statistics*.

COST OF LIVING

(Consumer Price Index; base: 2000 = 100)

	2008	2009	2010
Food	210.9	225.7	247.0
All items (incl. others)	207.2	216.1	227.2

Source: ILO.

NATIONAL ACCOUNTS

('000 million rupiah at current prices)

Expenditure on the Gross Domestic Product

	2008	2009	2010
Government final consumption expenditure	416,867	537,589	581,921
Private final consumption expenditure	2,999,957	3,290,843	3,641,997
Changes in inventories	5,822	–7,264	21,448
Gross fixed capital formation	1,370,717	1,744,381	2,065,181
Total domestic expenditure	4,793,363	5,565,549	6,310,547
Exports of goods and services	1,475,119	1,354,409	1,580,818
Less Imports of goods and services	1,422,902	1,197,093	1,475,834
Statistical discrepancy	103,109	–118,995	7,388
GDP in purchasers' values	4,948,689	5,603,871	6,422,918
GDP at constant 2000 prices	2,082,456	2,177,742	2,310,690

Gross Domestic Product by Economic Activity

	2008	2009	2010
Agriculture, forestry and fishing	716,656	857,241	985,144
Mining and quarrying	541,334	591,913	716,391
Manufacturing	1,376,442	1,477,674	1,594,330
Electricity, gas and water	40,889	47,166	50,042
Construction	419,712	555,201	660,968
Trade, hotels and restaurants	691,488	744,122	881,109
Transport, storage and communications	312,190	352,423	417,466
Finance, insurance, real estate and business services	368,130	404,013	462,789
Public administration	257,548	318,581	354,155
Other services	224,301	255,536	300,525
Total	4,948,688	5,603,871	6,422,918

Source: Asian Development Bank.

BALANCE OF PAYMENTS

(US $ million)

	2008	2009	2010
Exports of goods f.o.b.	139,606	119,646	158,074
Imports of goods f.o.b.	–116,691	–88,714	–127,447
Trade balance	22,915	30,932	30,628
Exports of services	15,247	13,155	16,766
Imports of services	–28,245	–22,896	–26,090
Balance on goods and services	9,917	21,191	21,303
Other income received	3,592	1,921	1,890
Other income paid	–18,747	–17,061	–22,181
Balance on goods, services and income	–5,238	6,051	1,012
Current transfers received	7,352	7,241	7,571
Current transfers paid	–1,989	–2,663	–2,941
Current balance	125	10,628	5,643

—continued	2008	2009	2010
Capital account (net)	294	96	50
Direct investment abroad	–5,900	–2,249	–2,664
Direct investment from abroad	9,318	4,877	13,371
Portfolio investment assets	–1,294	–144	–2,511
Portfolio investment liabilities	3,059	10,480	15,713
Other investment assets	–10,755	–12,002	–1,725
Other investment liabilities	3,446	3,794	3,968
Net errors and omissions	–212	–2,975	–1,559
Overall balance	–1,918	12,506	30,284

Source: IMF, *International Financial Statistics*.

External Trade

PRINCIPAL COMMODITIES
(distribution by HS, US $ million)

Imports c.i.f.	2008	2009	2010
Mineral fuels, oils, distillation products, etc.	30,682.4	19,090.4	27,530.7
Crude petroleum oils	10,061.5	7,362.2	8,531.3
Non-crude petroleum oils	19,963.6	10,841.0	17,654.3
Organic chemicals	5,132.5	3,940.4	5,325.8
Plastics and articles thereof	3,949.7	3,216.1	4,827.0
Iron and steel	8,281.9	4,356.6	6,371.6
Machinery, nuclear reactors, boilers, etc.	18,305.0	14,724.0	20,506.1
Electrical and electronic equipment	14,188.4	11,087.8	15,089.5
Vehicles other than railway and tramway	6,655.7	3,886.6	7,377.2
Aircraft, spacecraft, and parts thereof	2,036.9	3,241.5	3,528.1
Helicopters, aeroplanes and satellites	1,852.5	3,125.5	3,140.8
Total (incl. others)	129,244.1	96,829.2	135,663.3

Exports f.o.b.	2008	2009	2010
Animal, vegetable fats and oils, cleavage products, etc.	15,624.0	12,219.5	16,312.2
Palm oil and its fraction	12,375.6	10,367.6	13,469.0
Ores, slag and ash	4,295.6	5,804.8	8,148.0
Copper ores and concentrates	3,344.6	5,101.3	6,882.2
Mineral fuels, oils, distillation products, etc.	39,782.5	32,952.3	46,765.3
Solid fuels manufactured from coal	10,488.9	13,799.1	18,169.7
Crude petroleum oils	12,418.7	7,820.3	10,402.9
Petroleum gases	13,160.5	8,935.7	13,669.5
Rubber and articles thereof	7,637.3	4,912.8	9,373.4
Natural rubber, balata, gutta-percha, etc.	6,058.2	3,244.0	7,329.1
Machinery, nuclear reactors, boilers, etc.	5,211.6	4,709.3	5,071.2
Electrical and electronic equipment	8,265.9	8,148.1	10,432.5
Total (incl. others)	137,020.4	116,510.0	157,779.1

Source: Trade Map-Trade Competitiveness Map, International Trade Centre, www.intracen.org/marketanalysis.

PRINCIPAL TRADING PARTNERS
(US $ million)*

Imports c.i.f.	2008	2009	2010
Australia	4,005.3	3,436.0	4,099.0
Brazil	1,375.7	1,087.0	1,717.5
Brunei	2,416.6	639.6	666.2
Canada	1,871.7	992.5	1,108.4
China, People's Republic	15,249.2	14,002.2	20,424.2
France (incl. Monaco)	1,692.5	1,634.2	1,340.9
Germany	3,069.0	2,373.4	3,006.7
Hong Kong	2,367.6	1,698.1	1,860.4
India	2,905.4	2,209.4	3,294.8
Japan	15,129.2	9,843.7	16,965.8
Korea, Republic	6,925.8	4,742.3	7,703.0
Kuwait	1,857.1	1,442.3	1,372.7
Malaysia	8,923.1	5,688.4	8,648.7
Russian Federation	1,325.2	458.8	1,076.2
Saudi Arabia	4,805.0	3,135.8	4,360.8
Singapore	21,790.1	15,550.4	20,240.8
Thailand	6,336.1	4,612.9	7,470.7
USA	7,898.0	7,094.4	9,416.0
Total (incl. others)	129,244.1	96,829.2	135,663.3

Exports f.o.b.	2008	2009	2010
Australia	4,111.0	3,264.2	4,244.4
China, People's Republic	11,636.5	11,499.3	15,692.6
Germany	2,465.2	2,326.7	2,984.7
Hong Kong	1,808.8	2,111.8	2,501.4
India	7,163.3	7,432.9	9,915.0
Italy	1,900.9	1,651.5	2,370.5
Japan	27,743.9	18,574.7	25,781.8
Korea, Republic	9,116.8	8,145.2	12,574.6
Malaysia	6,432.6	6,811.8	9,362.3
Netherlands	3,926.4	2,909.1	3,722.5
Philippines	2,053.6	2,405.9	3,180.7
Singapore	12,862.0	10,262.7	13,723.3
Spain	1,665.3	1,830.5	2,328.7
Thailand	3,661.3	3,233.8	4,566.6
United Arab Emirates	1,652.1	1,265.8	1,475.3
United Kingdom	1,546.9	1,459.4	1,693.2
USA	13,079.9	10,889.1	14,301.9
Viet Nam	1,672.9	1,454.2	1,946.2
Total (incl. others)	137,020.4	116,510.0	157,779.1

* Imports by country of production, exports by country of consumption; figures include trade in gold.

Source: Trade Map-Trade Competitiveness Map, International Trade Centre, www.intracen.org/marketanalysis.

Transport

RAILWAYS
(traffic)

	2006	2007	2008
Passengers embarked ('000)	159,419	150,407	194,076
Passenger-km (million)	15,579	15,872	n.a.
Freight loaded ('000 tons)	17,275	17,078	19,444
Total ton-km (million)	4,474	4,425	n.a.

2009: Passengers embarked ('000) 203,070; Freight loaded ('000 tons) 18,924.

2010: Passengers embarked ('000) 203,270; Freight loaded ('000 tons) 19,113.

ROAD TRAFFIC
(motor vehicles registered)

	2007	2008	2009
Passenger cars	8,864,961	9,859,926	10,364,125
Trucks	4,845,937	5,146,674	5,187,740
Buses	2,103,423	2,583,170	2,729,572
Motorcycles	41,955,128	47,683,681	52,433,132
Total	57,769,449	65,273,451	70,714,569

SHIPPING

Merchant Fleet
(registered at 31 December)

	2007	2008	2009
Number of vessels	4,469	4,464	5,205
Displacement ('000 grt)	5,669.8	5,810.2	8,093.1

Source: IHS Fairplay, *World Fleet Statistics*.

Sea-borne Freight Traffic
('000 metric tons)

	1999	2000	2001*
International:			
goods loaded	139,340	141,528	143,750
goods unloaded	43,477	45,040	46,659
Domestic:			
goods loaded	113,633	127,740	163,685
goods unloaded	122,368	137,512	138,667

* Preliminary figures.

CIVIL AVIATION
(traffic on scheduled services)

	2007	2008	2009
Kilometres flown (million)	295	310	291
Passengers carried ('000)	29,564	30,723	27,421
Passenger-km (million)	33,052	34,952	31,873
Total ton-km (million)	3,249	3,548	3,258

Source: UN, *Statistical Yearbook*.

Tourism

FOREIGN TOURIST ARRIVALS

Country of residence	2008	2009	2010
Australia	450,178	584,437	771,792
Germany	137,854	128,649	145,244
Japan	546,713	475,766	418,971
Korea, Republic	320,808	256,522	274,999
Malaysia	1,117,454	1,179,366	1,277,476
Netherlands	140,771	143,485	151,836
Singapore	1,397,056	1,272,862	1,373,126
Taiwan	224,194	203,239	213,442
United Kingdom	150,412	169,271	192,259
USA	174,331	170,231	180,361
Total (incl. others)	6,234,497	6,323,730	7,002,944

Receipts from tourism (US $ million, excl. passenger transport): 7,378 in 2008; 5,598 in 2009; 6,980 in 2010 (provisional) (Source: World Tourism Organization).

Communications Media

	2008	2009	2010
Telephones ('000 main lines in use)	30,378.1	33,957.9	37,959.6
Mobile cellular telephones ('000 subscribers)	140,578*	159,248	220,000
Internet subscribers ('000)	1,707.2	n.a.	n.a.
Broadband subscribers ('000)	981.6	1,700.0	1,900.3

* Subscription as at September.

Television receivers ('000 in use): 31,700 in 2000 (Source: UN, *Statistical Yearbook*).

Radio receivers ('000 in use): 31,500 in 1997 (Source: UN, *Statistical Yearbook*).

Daily newspapers: 225 (average circulation 4,782,000) in 1999; 863 in 2005 (Source: UN, *Statistical Yearbook*).

Non-daily newspapers: 433 (average circulation 7,838,000) in 1998; 349 (average circulation 5,617,000) in 2004 (Source: UN, *Statistical Yearbook*).

Book production: 6,000 titles in 2003.

Personal computers: 4,510,000 (20.3 per 1,000 persons) in 2006.

Source (unless otherwise indicated): mostly International Telecommunication Union.

Education

(2008/09 unless otherwise indicated)

	Institutions	Teachers	Pupils and Students
Kindergarten*	63,444	233,563	2,783,413
Primary schools	144,228	1,569,326	26,984,824
General junior secondary schools	28,777	629,036	8,992,619
General senior secondary schools	10,762	314,389	3,857,245
Vocational senior secondary schools	7,592	246,018	3,095,704
Tertiary institutions	2,975	228,781	4,281,695

* 2007/08 figure.

Source: Ministry of National Education.

Pupil-teacher ratio (primary education, UNESCO estimate): 16.6 in 2008/09 (Source: UNESCO Institute for Statistics).

Adult literacy rate (UNESCO estimates): 92.2% (males 95.4%; females 89.1%) in 2008 (Source: UNESCO Institute for Statistics).

Directory

The Government

HEAD OF STATE

President: Gen. (retd) SUSILO BAMBANG YUDHOYONO (elected 5 July 2004; re-elected 8 July 2009).

Vice-President: Prof. Dr BOEDIONO.

CABINET
(May 2012)

The Government includes members of the Partai Demokrat (PD), Golkar, Partai Amanat Nasional (PAN), Partai Damai Sejahtera (PDS), Partai Persatuan Pembangunan (PPP) and Partai Kebangkitan Bangsa (PKB), along with numerous unaffiliated members.

Co-ordinating Minister for Political, Legal and Security Affairs: Air Chief Marshal (retd) DJOKO SUYANTO.

Co-ordinating Minister for Economic Affairs: HATTA RAJASA.

Co-ordinating Minister for People's Welfare: Dr AGUNG LAKSONO.

Minister of Home Affairs: GAMAWAN FAUZI.

Minister of Foreign Affairs: Dr RADEN (MARTY) MOHAMMAD MULIANA NATALEGAWA.

Minister of Defence: Dr Ir PURNOMO YUSGIANTORO.

Minister of Justice and Human Rights: AMIR SYAMSUDDIN.

Minister of Finance: AGUS MARTOWARDOJO.

Minister of Energy and Mineral Resources: Ir JERO WATJIK.

Minister of Industry: MOHAMAD S. HIDAYAT.

Minister of Trade: GITA WIRJAWAN.

Minister of Agriculture: Ir H. SUSWONO.

Minister of Forestry: ZULKIFLI HASAN.

Minister of Transportation: E. E. MANGINDAAN.

Minister of Marine Affairs and Fisheries: SYARIF C. SUTARDJO.

Minister of Manpower and Transmigration: Drs MUHAIMIN ISKANDAR.

Minister of Public Works: Ir DJOKO KIRMANTO.

Minister of Health: (vacant).

Minister of Education and Culture: Dr Ir MUHAMMAD NUH.

Minister of Social Affairs: Dr SALIM SEGAF AL-JUFRIE.

Minister of Religious Affairs: Drs SURYADHARMA ALI.

Minister of Tourism and Creative Economy: Dr MARI ELKA PANGESTU.

Minister of Communications and Information Technology: Ir TIFATUL SEMBIRING.

Minister of State for Research and Technology: Dr Ir GUSTI MUHAMMAD HATTA.

Minister of State for Co-operatives and Small and Medium-Sized Businesses: Dr SYARIFUDDIN HASAN.

Minister of State for the Environment: BALTAZAR KAMBUAYA.

Minister of State for Women's Empowerment: LINDA AMALIA SARI.

Minister of State for Administrative Reform: AZWAR ABUBAKAR.

Minister of State for State Enterprises: DAHLAN ISKAN.

Minister of State for Development of Disadvantaged Regions: Ir AHMAD HELMI FAISAL ZAINI.

Minister of State for National Development Planning: Dr ARMIDA ALISJAHBANA.

Minister of State for Public Housing: DJAN FARIDZ.

Minister of State for Youth and Sports Affairs: ANDI ALIFIAN MALLARANGENG.

Officials with the rank of Minister of State:

Attorney-General: BASRIEF ARIEF.

State Secretary: Lt-Gen. (retd) SUDI SILALAHI.

MINISTRIES

Office of the President: Istana Merdeka, 2nd Floor, Jakarta 10110; tel. (21) 3840946; internet www.presidenri.go.id.

Office of the Vice-President: Istana Wakil Presiden, Jalan Medan Merdeka Selatan 14, Jakarta 10110; tel. (21) 3844676; fax (21) 3446122; e-mail tirta_hidayat@yahoo.co.id; internet www.setwapres.go.id.

Office of the Attorney-General: Jalan Sultan Hasanuddin 1, Kebayoran Baru, Jakarta Selatan; tel. (21) 7221269; fax (21) 7392576; e-mail webmaster@kejaksaan.go.id; internet www.kejaksaan.go.id.

Office of the Cabinet Secretary: 4th Floor, Jalan Veteran 18, Jakarta Pusat 10110; tel. (21) 3846463; fax (21) 3866579; e-mail itcp@setkab.go.id; internet www.setkab.go.id.

Office of the Co-ordinating Minister for Economic Affairs: Jalan Lapangan Banteng Timur 2–4, Jakarta 10710; tel. (21) 3521974; fax (21) 3521985; e-mail humas@ekon.go.id; internet www.ekon.go.id.

Office of the Co-ordinating Minister for People's Welfare: Jalan Merdeka Barat 3, Jakarta Pusat; tel. (21) 3459444; fax (21) 3453289; internet www.menkokesra.go.id.

Office of the Co-ordinating Minister for Political, Legal and Security Affairs: Jalan Medan Merdeka Barat 15, Jakarta 10110; tel. (21) 3521121; fax (21) 3450918; e-mail dkpt@polkam.go.id; internet www.polkam.go.id.

Office of the State Secretary: Jalan Veteran 17–18, Jakarta 10110; tel. (21) 3849043; fax (21) 3452685; e-mail webmaster@setneg.go.id; internet www.setneg.go.id.

Ministry of Agriculture: Gedung D, 4th Floor, Jalan Harsono R. M. 3, Ragunan, Pasar Minggu, Jakarta Selatan 12550; tel. (21) 7822803; fax (21) 7816385; e-mail baran@deptan.go.id; internet www.deptan.go.id.

Ministry of Communication and Information Technology: Jalan Medan Merdeka Barat 9, Jakarta Pusat 10110; tel. (21) 3844227; fax (21) 3867600; e-mail info@depkominfo.go.id; internet www.depkominfo.go.id.

Ministry of Defence: Jalan Medan Merdeka Barat 13–14, Jakarta Pusat 10200; tel. (21) 3456184; fax (21) 3440023; e-mail postmaster@dephan.go.id; internet www.dephan.go.id.

Ministry of Education and Culture: Jalan Jenderal Sudirman, Senayan, Jakarta Pusat 12041; tel. (21) 57950226; fax (21) 5733125; e-mail pengaduan@kemdikbud.go.id; internet www.kemdiknas.go.id.

Ministry of Energy and Mineral Resources: Jalan Medan Merdeka Selatan 18, Jakarta 10110; tel. and fax (21) 3519881; e-mail pusdatin@esdm.go.id; internet www.esdm.go.id.

Ministry of Finance and State Enterprises Development: Jalan Lapangan Banteng Timur 2–4, Jakarta 10710; tel. (21) 3841067; fax (21) 3808395; e-mail helpdesk@depkeu.go.id; internet www.depkeu.go.id.

Ministry of Foreign Affairs: 10th Floor, Jalan Taman Pejambon 6, Jakarta Pusat 10110; tel. (21) 3441508; fax (21) 3857316; e-mail infomed@deplu.go.id; internet www.deplu.go.id.

Ministry of Forestry: Gedung Manggala Wanabakti, Blok I, 3rd Floor, Jalan Jenderal Gatot Subroto, Senayan, Jakarta 10270; tel. (21) 5704501; fax (21) 5720216; e-mail pusdata@dephut.go.id; internet www.dephut.go.id.

Ministry of Health and Social Welfare: Blok X5, Jalan H. R. Rasuna Said, Kav. 4–9, Jakarta 12950; tel. (21) 5201590; fax (21) 5201591; e-mail webadmin@depkes.go.id; internet www.depkes.go.id.

Ministry of Home Affairs and Regional Autonomy: Gedung Utama, 4th Floor, Jalan Medan Merdeka Utara 7, Jakarta Pusat 10110; tel. (21) 3450038; fax (21) 3851193; e-mail pusdatinkomtel@depdagri.go.id; internet www.depdagri.go.id.

Ministry of Industry: Jalan Jenderal Gatot Subroto, Kav. 52–53, Jakarta Selatan 12950; tel. (21) 5252194; fax (21) 5261086; e-mail pusdatin@depperin.go.id; internet www.depperin.go.id.

Ministry of Justice and Human Rights: Jalan H. R. Rasuna Said, Kav. 6–7, Kuningan, Jakarta Selatan; tel. (21) 5253004; fax (21) 5253139; e-mail pullahta@depkumham.go.id; internet www.depkumham.go.id.

Ministry of Manpower and Transmigration: Jalan T. M. P Kalibata 17, Jakarta Selatan; tel. (21) 5255683; fax (21) 515669; e-mail redaksi_balitfo@nakertrans.go.id; internet www.nakertrans.go.id.

Ministry of Marine Affairs and Fisheries: Gedung Humpus, Jalan Medan Merdeka Timur 16, Jakarta 10110; tel. (21) 3500023; fax (21) 3519133; e-mail pusdatin@kkp.go.id; internet www.kkp.go.id.

Ministry of Public Works: Jalan Pattimura 20, Kebayoran Baru, Jakarta Selatan 12110; tel. (21) 7392262; fax (21) 7200793; e-mail dkirmanto@pu.go.id; internet www.pu.go.id.

Ministry of Religious Affairs: Jalan Lapangan Banteng Barat 3–4, Jakarta Pusat 10710; tel. (21) 3843005; fax (21) 3812306; e-mail pinmas@depag.go.id; internet www.depag.go.id.

Ministry of Social Affairs: Jalan Salemba Raya 28, Jakarta 10430; tel. (21) 3103591; fax (21) 3103783; e-mail pusdatin@depsos.go.id; internet www.depsos.go.id.

Ministry of Tourism and Creative Economy: Gedung Sapta Pesona, Jalan Medan Merdeka Barat 17, Jakarta Pusat 10110; tel. (21) 3838167; fax (21) 3849715; e-mail pusdatin@budpar.go.id; internet www.budpar.go.id.

Ministry of Trade: Blok I, 3rd Floor, Jalan Merdeka Ikhwan Ridwan Rais 5, Jakarta Pusat; tel. (21) 3840138; fax (21) 3846106; internet www.depdag.go.id.

Ministry of Transportation: Jalan Medan Merdeka Barat 8, Jakarta 10110; tel. (21) 3811308; fax (21) 3862371; e-mail pusdatin@dephub.go.id; internet www.dephub.go.id.

Office of the Minister of State for Co-operatives and Small and Medium-Sized Businesses: Jalan H. R. Rasuna Said, Kav. 3–5, POB 177, Jakarta Selatan 12940; tel. (21) 52992999; fax (21) 5204378; e-mail datin@depkop.go.id; internet www.depkop.go.id.

Office of the Minister of State for the Environment: Gedung A, 6th Floor, Jalan D. I. Panjaitan, Kav. 24, Kebon Nanas, Jakarta 13410; tel. and fax (21) 8517184; e-mail edukom@menlh.go.id; internet www.menlh.go.id.

Office of the Minister of State for Research and Technology: Gedung BPP Teknologi II, 5th–8th Floors, Jalan M. H. Thamrin 8, Jakarta Pusat 10340; tel. (21) 3169119; fax (21) 3101952; e-mail webmstr@ristek.go.id; internet www.ristek.go.id.

Office of the Minister of State for State Enterprises: Jalan Medan Merdeka Selatan 13, Jakarta 10110; e-mail sekretariat@bumn.go.id; internet www.bumn-ri.com.

Office of the Minister of State for Women's Empowerment: Jalan Medan Merdeka Barat 15, Jakarta 10110; tel. (21) 3805563; fax (21) 3805562; e-mail biroren@menegpp.go.id; internet www.menegpp.go.id.

Office of the Minister of State for Youth and Sports Affairs: Jalan Gerbang Pemuda Senayan, Jakarta 10270; internet www.kemenpora.go.id.

OTHER GOVERNMENT BODY

Badan Pemeriksa Keuangan (BPK) (Supreme Audit Board): Jalan Gatot Subroto 31, Jakarta 10210; tel. (21) 25549000; fax (21) 57854096; e-mail webmaster@bpk.go.id; internet www.bpk.go.id; Chair. Drs HADI POERNOMO; Vice-Chair. Dr HERMAN WIDYANANDA.

President and Legislature

PRESIDENT

Presidential Election, 8 July 2009

Candidate	Votes	% of votes
Gen. (retd) Susilo Bambang Yudhoyono (PD)	73,874,562	60.80
Megawati Sukarnoputri (PDI—P)	32,548,105	26.79
Muhammad Jusuf Kalla (Golkar)	15,081,814	12.41
Total	121,504,481	100.00

LEGISLATURE

Majelis Permusyawaratan Rakyat (MPR) (People's Consultative Assembly)

Jalan Jenderal Gatot Subroto 6, Jakarta 10270; tel. (21) 5715773; fax (21) 5734526; e-mail kotaksurat@mpr.go.id; internet www.mpr.go .id.

In late 2002 the Constitution was amended to provide for the direct election of all members of the Majelis Permusyawaratan Rakyat (MPR—People's Consultative Assembly) at the next general election, held in 2004. The MPR thus became a bicameral institution comprising the Dewan Perwakilan Daerah (DPD—House of Representatives of the Regions) and the Dewan Perwakilan Rakyat (DPR—House of Representatives). The MPR subsequently consisted of the 550 members of the DPR and 128 regional delegates, increasing to 560 and 132 respectively at the 2009 election.

Speaker: TAUFIK KIEMAS.

	Seats
Members of the Dewan Perwakilan Rakyat	560
Regional representatives	132
Total	692

Dewan Perwakilan Rakyat (DPR) (House of Representatives)

Jalan Gatot Subroto 16, Jakarta; tel. (21) 586833; e-mail humas@dpr .go.id; internet www.dpr.go.id.

Speaker: MARZUKI ALIE.

General Election, 9 April 2009

	Seats
Partai Demokrat (PD)	148
Partai Golongan Karya (Golkar)	108
Partai Demokrasi Indonesia Perjuangan (PDI—P)	93
Partai Keadilan Sejahtera (PKS)	59
Partai Amanat Nasional (PAN)	42
Partai Persatuan Pembangunan (PPP)	39
Partai Gerakan Indonesia Raya (Gerindra)	30
Partai Kebangkitan Bangsa (PKB)	26
Partai Hati Nurani Rakyat (Hanura)	15
Total	560

Election Commission

Komisi Pemilihan Umum (KPU): Jalan Imam Bonjol 29, Jakarta 10310; tel. (21) 31937223; fax (21) 3157759; e-mail redaktur@kpu.go .id; internet www.kpu.go.id; f. 1999; govt body; Chair. ABDUL HAFIZ ANSHARY.

Political Organizations

All parties must adhere to the state philosophy of *Pancasila* and reject communism. A total of 38 national parties contested the legislative elections of April 2009.

Barisan Nasional (National Front): Jalan Gunawarman 32, Kebayoran Baru, Jakarta Selatan 12810; tel. (21) 7269588; fax (21) 7243081; f. 1998; committed to ensuring that Indonesia remains a secular state; merger with Gerindra announced in early 2011; Sec.-Gen. RACHMAT WITOELAR.

Koalisi Kebangsaan (Nationhood Coalition): Jakarta; f. 2004; coalition formed to contest the presidential election of 2004 in support of Megawati Sukarnoputri, comprising Golkar, PDI—P, PDS, PKB and PPP; PPP defected to Koalisi Kerakyatan following the election.

Koalisi Kerakyatan (People's Coalition): Jakarta; f. 2004; coalition formed in support of Gen. (retd) Susilo Bambang Yudhoyono to contest the presidential election of 2004, centred around PD, PAN and PKS; PPP joined after defecting from Koalisi Kebangsaan following the election.

Partai Amanat Nasional (PAN) (National Mandate Party): Rumah PAN, Jalan Raya Warung Buncit 17, Jakarta Selatan; tel. (21) 7975588; fax (21) 7975632; f. 1998; aims to achieve democracy, progress and social justice, to limit the length of the presidential term of office and to increase autonomy in the provinces; Chair. HATTA RAJASA; Sec.-Gen. TAUFIK KURNIAWAN.

Partai Bintang Reformasi (PBR) (Reform Star Party): Jalan K. H. Abdullah Syafei 2, Tebet, Jakarta Selatan; tel. (21) 8311715; f. 2002; est. by fmr PPP mems; Islamic party; merger with Gerindra announced in early 2011; Chair. BARUSA ZARNUBI; Sec.-Gen. RUSMAN ALI.

Partai Bulan Bintang (PBB) (Crescent Moon and Star Party): Jalan Raya Pasar Minggu 1B, Km 18, Jakarta Selatan; tel. (21) 79180734; fax (21) 79180765; f. 1998; Leader M. S. KABAN; Sec.-Gen. SAHAR HASSAN.

Partai Buruh (Labour Party): Jalan Kramat Raya 91A, Jakarta Pusat; tel. (21) 3154092; fax (21) 3909834; f. 2001; est. as Partai Buruh Sosial Demokrat (PBSD—Socialist Democratic Labour Party); present name adopted 2005; merger with Gerindra announced in early 2011; Chair. MUCHTAR PAKPAHAN; Sec.-Gen. DIAH INDRIASTUTI.

Partai Damai Sejahtera (PDS) (Prosperous Peace Party): Jalan S. Parman G6, Bundaran Slipi, Jakarta Barat 11480; tel. (21) 5307488; fax (21) 5367039; e-mail pds_2014@yahoo.com; internet www .partaidamaisejahtera.com; f. 2001; merger with Gerindra announced in early 2011; Chair. RUYANDI MUSTIKA HUTASOIT; Sec.-Gen. FERRY B. REGAR.

Partai Demokrasi Indonesia Perjuangan (PDI—P) (Indonesian Democratic Struggle Party): Jalan Lenteng Agung 99, Jakarta Selatan; tel. (21) 7806028; fax (21) 7814472; est. by Megawati Sukarnoputri, fmr PDI leader, following her removal from PDI leadership by Govt in 1996; Chair. MEGAWATI SUKARNOPUTRI; Sec.-Gen. TJAHJO KUMOLO.

Partai Demokrat (PD): Jalan Pemuda 712A, Jakarta Timur 13220; tel. (21) 4755146; fax (21) 4757957; internet www.demokrat.or.id; f. 2001; Chair. of Advisory Bd Gen. (retd) SUSILO BAMBANG YUDHOYONO; Gen. Chair. ANAS URBANINGRUM; Sec.-Gen. EDHIE 'IBAS' BASKORO YUDHOYONO.

Partai Gerakan Indonesia Raya (Gerindra) (Great Indonesia Movement Party): Jalan Brawijaya IX 1, Kebayoran Baru, Jakarta Selatan 12160; tel. (21) 7279547; fax (21) 7395154; e-mail info@ partaigerindra.or.id; internet www.partaigerindra.or.id; f. 2008; Chair. SUHARDI; Sec.-Gen. AHMAD MUZANI.

Partai Golongan Karya (Golkar) (Party of Functional Groups): Jalan Anggrek Nellimurni, Jakarta 11480; tel. (21) 5302222; fax (21) 5303380; e-mail info@golkar.or.id; internet www.golkar.or.id; f. 1964; reorg. 1971; Pres. and Chair. ABURIZAL BAKRIE; Sec.-Gen. IDRUS MARHAM.

Partai Hati Nurani Rakyat (Hanura) (People's Conscience Party): Jalan Diponegoro 1, Menteng, Jakarta; tel. (21) 31935334; fax (21) 3922054; e-mail info@hanura.or.id; internet www.hanura .com; f. 2006; Chair. WIRANTO; Sec.-Gen. YUS USMAN SUMANEGARA.

Partai Karya Peduli Bangsa (PKPB) (Concern for the Nation Functional Party): Jalan Cimandiri 30, Raden Saleh Cikini, Jakarta Pusat 13033; tel. (21) 31927421; fax (21) 31937417; internet www .pkpb.net; f. 2002; Chair. R. HARTONO; Sec.-Gen. H. ARY MARDJONO.

Partai Kasih Demokrasi Indonesia (PKDI) (The Indonesian Democratic Party of Devotion): Jalan Panglima Polim I 32, Jakarta Selatan; tel. and fax (21) 7230731; f. 2006; est. by merger of seven Christian parties.

Partai Keadilan dan Persatuan Indonesia (PKPI) (Justice and Unity Party): Jalan Raya Cilandak KKO 32, Pasar Minggu, Jakarta Selatan; tel. (21) 7807653; fax (21) 7807655; f. 2002; Chair. MEUTIA FARIDA HATTA; Sec.-Gen. HAYONO ISMAN.

Partai Keadilan Sejahtera (PKS) (Prosperous Justice Party): Jalan Mampang Prapatan Raya 98 D–F, Jakarta Selatan 12720; tel. (21) 7995425; fax (21) 7995433; e-mail partai@pks.or.id; internet www.pk-sejahtera.org; f. 2002; Islamic party; Chair. MUSTAFA KAMAL; Sec.-Gen. ANIS MATTA.

Partai Kebangkitan Bangsa (PKB) (National Awakening Party): Jalan Sukabumi 23, Jakarta Selatan 12740; tel. and fax (21) 3155138; e-mail dpp@dpp-pkb.or.id; internet www.dpp-pkb.or.id; nationalist Islamic party; f. 1998; Chair. MUHAIMIN ISKANDAR; Sec.-Gen. LUKMAN EDY.

Partai Kebangkitan Nasional Ulama (PKNU) (Scholars' National Awakening Party): Jalan Kramat VI 8, Jakarta Pusat 10430; tel. (21) 31923717; fax (21) 3905686; f. 2006; breakaway faction of PKB; Chair. CHOIRUL ANAM.

Partai Merdeka (Freedom Party): Jalan Mampang Prapatan XII 6, Jakarta Selatan 12790; tel. (21) 7991439; e-mail info@partaimerdeka.or.id; f. 2002; merger with Gerindra announced in early 2011; Chair. ADI SASONO; Sec.-Gen. DHARMA SETIAWAN.

Partai Nasional Benteng Kerakyatan (PNBK) (National Populist Fortress Party): Jalan Penjernihan I 50, Jakarta Utara; tel. (21) 5739550; fax (21) 5739519; f. 2002; est. as Partai Nasional Banteng Kemerdekaan; renamed as above prior to 2009 legislative election; Chair. EROS DJAROT; Sec.-Gen. SOEHARDI SOEDIRO.

Partai Nasional Indonesia Marhaenisme (PNI Marhaenisme): Jalan Gudang Peluru Raya B1 7B, Kebon Baru, Tebet, Jakarta Selatan; tel. and fax (21) 83795157; f. 2002; merger with Gerindra announced in early 2011; Chair. SUKMAWATI SUKARNOPUTRI; Sec.-Gen. ARDY MUHAMMAD.

Partai Patriot Pancasila (Pancasila Patriot Party): Jalan Manggis 12A, Ciganjur, Jakarta Selatan 12630; tel. (21) 7261522; f. 2001; Chair. YAPTO SULISTIO SOERJOSOEMARNO; Sec.-Gen. MAX BOBOY.

Partai Peduli Rakyat Nasional (PPRN) (National People's Concern Party): Jalan Pahlawan Revolusi 148, Pondok Bambu, Jakarta Timur 13140; tel. (21) 86600284; fax (21) 86614140; e-mail dpp.pprn@gmail.com; internet www.pprn.or.id; f. 2006; Chair. AMELIA ACHMAD YANI; Sec.-Gen. ALBERT SIMANJUNTAK.

Partai Pelopor (Pioneer Party): Jalan Pegangsaan Timur 17, Cikini, Jakarta Pusat; tel. and fax (21) 31903634; f. 2002; Chair. RACHMAWATI SUKARNOPUTRI; Sec.-Gen. EKO SURYO SANTJOJO.

Partai Penegak Demokrasi Indonesia (PPDI) (Indonesian Democratic Vanguard Party): Jalan Amil 26, RT-02/RW-05, Kalibata Pulo, Jakarta; tel. (21) 7992758; f. 2003; Chair. ENDUNG SUTRISNO; Sec.-Gen. V. JOES PRANANTO.

Partai Perhimpunan Indonesia Baru (PIB) (New Indonesia Alliance Party): Jalan Teuku Cik Ditiro 31, Menteng, Jakarta Pusat 10310; tel. (21) 3108057; e-mail partaipib@yahoo.com; f. 2002; Chair. Dr SYAHRIR; Sec.-Gen. AMIR KARAMOY.

Partai Persatuan Demokrasi Kebangsaan (PPDK) (National Democratic Unity Party): Jalan Ampera Raya 99, Jakarta Selatan 12560; tel. (21) 7807432; fax (21) 7817341; f. 2002; Chair. Dr RYAAS RASYID; Sec.-Gen. RIVAI PULUNGAN.

Partai Persatuan Nahdlatul Ummah Indonesia (PPNUI) (Indonesian Nahdlatul Community Party): Jalan K. H. Abdullah Syafi'i 5, RT-04/RW-06, Bukit Duri, Tebet, Jakarta Selatan; tel. (21) 70006444; f. 1998; est. as Partai Nahdlatul Ummah; present name adopted 2003; Islamic party; merger with Gerindra announced in early 2011; Chair. SYUKRON MA'MUN; Sec.-Gen. ACHMAD SJATARI.

Partai Persatuan Nasional (National United Party): Jalan Dr Satrio C-4 18, Jakarta Selatan 12940; tel. (21) 5273250; fax (21) 5273249; e-mail sekretariatppn@yahoo.co.id; internet www.partaipersatuannasional.or.id; f. 2002; Chair. OESMAN SAPTA; Sec.-Gen. RATNA ESTER LUMBAN TOBING.

Partai Persatuan Pembangunan (PPP) (United Development Party): Jalan Diponegoro 60, Jakarta Pusat 10310; tel. (21) 31936338; fax (21) 3142558; e-mail dpp@ppp.or.id; internet www.ppp.or.id; f. 1973; est. by merger of four Islamic parties; Leader SURYADHARMA ALI; Sec.-Gen. IRGAN CHAERUL MAHFIZ.

Partai Rakyat Demokratik (PRD) (People's Democratic Party): Jalan Tebet Barat Dalam VIII Nomor 4, Jakarta Selatan 12820; tel. and fax (21) 8296467; e-mail prd@centrin.net.id; internet www.prd.4-all.org; f. 1996; Chair. BUDIMAN SUDJATMIKO.

Partai Reformasi Tionghoa Indonesia (Chinese Indonesian Reform Party): Jakarta; e-mail parti_id@usa.net; f. 1998; Chinese.

Partai Sarikat Indonesia (PSI) (Indonesia Unity Party): Jalan Kemang Utara 6, Jakarta Selatan; tel. (21) 4199110; e-mail dpppsi@indosat.net.id; f. 2002; merger with Gerindra announced in early 2011; Chair. Drs H. MARDINSYAH; Sec.-Gen. NAZIR MUHAMMAD.

Partai Uni Demokrasi Indonesia (PUDI) (Democratic Union Party of Indonesia): Jalan Raya Tanjung Barat 81, Jakarta 12530; tel. (21) 7817565; fax (21) 7814765; e-mail pudi@pudi.or.id; f. 1996; Chair. Sri BINTANG PAMUNGKAS; Sec.-Gen. ESA HARUMAN.

Other groups with political influence include:

Ikatan Cendekiawan Muslim Indonesia (ICMI) (Association of Indonesian Muslim Intellectuals): Gedung BPPT, Jalan M. H. Thamrin 8, Jakarta; tel. (21) 3410382; internet www.icmi.or.id; f. 1990; est. with govt support; Chair. AZYUMARDI AZRA; Sec.-Gen. AGUS SALIM DASUKI.

Partai Syarikat Islam Indonesia 1905: Jalan Prof. Dr Latumenten, Brt 16, Jakarta; tel. (21) 5659790.

The following groups are, or have been, in conflict with the Government:

Gerakan Aceh Merdeka (GAM) (Free Aceh Movement): based in Aceh; e-mail info@asnlf.net; internet www.asnlf.net; f. 1976; signed a peace deal with the Indonesian Govt in July 2005, under the terms of which GAM agreed to relinquish its claims for independence and the Govt agreed to facilitate the establishment of Aceh-based political parties; Military Commdr MUZZAKIR MANAF.

Organisasi Papua Merdeka (OPM) (Free Papua Movement): based in Papua; e-mail opmpapua@yahoo.com; internet www.geocities.com/opm-irja; f. 1963; seeks unification with Papua New Guinea; Chair. MOZES WEROR; Military Commdr Gen. JECK KEMONG.

Presidium Dewan Papua (PDP) (Papua Presidium Council): based in Papua; e-mail pdp@westpapua.net; internet www.melanesianews.org/pdp/org; seeks independence from Indonesia; Chair. TOM BEANAL.

Diplomatic Representation

EMBASSIES IN INDONESIA

Afghanistan: Jalan Dr Kusuma Atmaja 15, Jakarta Pusat 10310; tel. (21) 3143169; fax (21) 31935390; e-mail afghanembassy_jkk@yahoo.com; Ambassador FAZLURRAHMAN FAZIL.

Algeria: Jalan H. R. Rasuna Said, Kav. 10-1, Kuningan, Jakarta 12950; tel. (21) 5254719; fax (21) 5254654; e-mail ambaljak@cbn.net.id; Ambassador ABDELKRIM BELARBI.

Argentina: Menara Thamrin, Suite 1602, 16th Floor, Jalan M. H. Thamrin, Kav. 3, Jakarta 10250; tel. (21) 2303061; fax (21) 2303962; e-mail embargen@cbn.net.id; Ambassador JAVIER A. SANZ DE URQUIZA.

Australia: Jalan H. R. Rasuna Said, Kav. C15–16, Kuningan, Jakarta 12940; tel. (21) 25505555; fax (21) 25505467; e-mail public-affairs-jakt@dfat.gov.au; internet www.indonesia.embassy.gov.au; Ambassador GREG MORIARTY.

Austria: Jalan Terusan Denpasar Raya 1, Kuningan, Jakarta 12950; tel. (21) 2593037; fax (21) 52920651; e-mail jakarta-ob@bmeia.gv.at; internet www.austrian-embassy.or.id; Ambassador Dr KLAUS WOELFER.

Azerbaijan: Jalan Mas Putih D, Persil 29, Grogol Utara Kebayoran Lama, Jakarta Selatan 12430; tel. (21) 5491939; fax (21) 5491745; e-mail jakarta@mission.mfa.gov.az; internet www.azembassy.or.id; Ambassador TAMERLAN GARAYEV.

Bangladesh: Jalan Taman Ubud 1, 5 Kuningan Timur, Jakarta Selatan 12950; tel. (21) 52921271; fax (21) 5251143; e-mail bdootjak@yahoo.com; internet sites.google.com/site/bangladeshembassyjakarta; Ambassador GOLAM MOHAMMED.

Belarus: Jalan Patra Kuningan VII 3, Kuningan, Jakarta Selatan 12950; tel. (21) 5251388; fax (21) 52960207; e-mail indonesia@mfa.gov.by; Ambassador VLADIMIR LOPATO-ZAGORSKY.

Belgium: Deutsche Bank Bldg, 16th Floor, Jalan Imam Bonjol 80, Jakarta 10310; tel. (21) 3162030; fax (21) 3162035; e-mail jakarta@diplobel.fed.be; internet www.diplomatie.be/jakarta; Ambassador CHRISTIAAN TANGHE.

Bosnia and Herzegovina: Menara Imperium, 11th Floor, Suite D-2, Metropolitan Kuningan Super Blok, Kav. 1, Jalan H. R. Rasuna Said, Jakarta 12980; tel. (21) 83703022; fax (21) 83703029; Ambassador TARIK BUKVIC.

Brazil: Menara Mulia, Suite 1602, Jalan Jenderal Gatot Subroto, Kav. 9–11, Jakarta 12390; tel. (21) 5265656; fax (21) 5265659; e-mail embrasil@cbn.net.id; Ambassador MANUEL INNOCENCIO DE LACERDA SANTOS, Jr.

Brunei: Jalan Teuku Umar 9, Menteng, Jakarta Pusat 10350; tel. (21) 31906080; fax (21) 31905070; e-mail kbjindo@cbn.net.id; Ambassador Dato' Paduka MAHMUD Haji SAIDIN.

Bulgaria: Jalan Imam Bonjol 34–36, Menteng, Jakarta Pusat 10310; tel. (21) 3904048; fax (21) 3904049; e-mail bgemb.jkt@centrin.net.id; internet www.mfa.bg/bg/33/; Chargé d'affaires KATINA NOVKOVA.

Cambodia: Jalan T. B. Simatupang, Kav. 13, Jakarta Selatan 12520; tel. (21) 7812523; fax (21) 7812524; e-mail recjkt@indo.net.id; Ambassador KAN PHARITH.

Canada: World Trade Center, 6th Floor, Jalan Jenderal Sudirman, Kav. 29–31, POB 8324/JKS.MP, Jakarta 12920; tel. (21) 25507800; fax (21) 25507811; e-mail canadianembassy.jkrta@international.gc.ca; internet www.canadainternational.gc.ca/indonesia-indonesie; Ambassador MACKENZIE CLUGSTON.

Chile: Bina Mulia I, 7th Floor, Jalan H. R. Rasuna Said, Kav. 10, Kuningan, Jakarta 12950; tel. (21) 2525021; fax (21) 5201955; e-mail emchijak@indosat.net.id; internet chileabroad.gov.cl/indonesia; Ambassador EDUARDO RUIZ ASMUSSEN.

China, People's Republic: Jalan Mega Kuningan 2, Karet Kuningan, Jakarta 12950; tel. (21) 5761038; fax (21) 5761034; e-mail chinaemb_id@mfa.gov.cn; internet id.china-embassy.org/eng; Ambassador LIU JIANCHAO.

Colombia: Plaza Central Building, lantai 16, Jalan Sudirman, Kav. 47, Jakarta 12190; tel. (21) 57903560; fax (21) 52905217; e-mail ejakarta@cancilleria.gov.co; Ambassador ALFONSO GARZÓN MÉNDEZ.

Croatia: Menara Mulia, Suite 2801, Jalan Gatot Subroto, Kav. 9–11, Jakarta 12930; tel. (21) 5257822; fax (21) 5204073; e-mail croemb@rad.net.id; internet www.croatemb.or.id; Ambassador ŽELJKO ČIMBUR.

Cuba: Taman Puri, Jalan Opal, Blok K-1, Permata Hijau, Jakarta 12210; tel. (21) 5304293; fax (21) 53676906; e-mail cubaindo@cbn.net.id; internet embacuba.cubaminrex.cu/indonesia; Ambassador ENNA ESTHER VIANT VALDÉS.

Cyprus: c/o Jalan Purwakarta 8, Menteng, Jakarta Pusat; tel. (21) 3106367; fax (21) 3919256; e-mail nicpanayi@yahoo.com; Ambassador NICOS PANAYI.

Czech Republic: Jalan Gereja Theresia 20, Menteng, Jakarta Pusat 10350; tel. (21) 3904075; fax (21) 3904078; e-mail jakarta@embassy.mzv.cz; internet www.mfa.cz/jakarta; Ambassador TOMAS SMETANKA.

Denmark: Menara Rajawali, 25th Floor, Jalan Mega Kuningan, Lot 5.1, Jakarta 12950; tel. (21) 5761478; fax (21) 5761535; e-mail jktamb@um.dk; internet www.ambjakarta.um.dk; Ambassador BØRGE PETERSEN.

Ecuador: World Trade Center, 16th Floor, Jalan Jenderal Sudirman, Kav. 31, Jakarta 12920; tel. (21) 5211484; fax (21) 5226954; e-mail ecuadorinindonesia@gmail.com; Ambassador EDUARDO ALBERTO CALDERÓN LEDESMA.

Egypt: Jalan Teuku Umar 68, Menteng, Jakarta Pusat 10310; tel. (21) 3143440; fax (21) 3145073; e-mail egypt@indosat.net.id; internet www.mfa.gov.eg/Jakarta_Emb; Ambassador AHMED EL-KEWAISNY.

Fiji: Menara Topaz, 14th Floor, Jalan M. H. Thambrin, Kav. 9, Jakarta 10350; tel. (21) 3902543; fax (21) 3902544; Ambassador SEREMAIA TUI CAVUILATI.

Finland: Menara Rajawali, 9th Floor, Lot 5.1, Jalan Mega Kuningan, Kawasan Mega Kuningan, Jakarta 12950; tel. (21) 5761650; fax (21) 5761631; e-mail sanomat.jak@formin.fi; internet www.finland.or.id; Ambassador KAI SAUER.

France: Jalan M. H. Thamrin 20, Jakarta Pusat 10350; tel. (21) 23557600; fax (21) 23557601; e-mail ambassade@ambafrance-id.org; internet www.ambafrance-id.org; Ambassador BERTRAND LORTHOLARY.

Germany: Jalan M. H. Thamrin 1, Jakarta Pusat 10310; tel. (21) 39855000; fax (21) 3901757; e-mail kontakt-pr@jaka.diplo.de; internet www.jakarta.diplo.de; Ambassador Dr NORBERT BAAS.

Greece: Plaza 89, 12th Floor, Suite 1203, Jalan H. R. Rasuna Said, Kav. X-7 No. 6, Kuningan, Jakarta Selatan 12940; tel. (21) 5207776; fax (21) 5207753; e-mail grembas@cbn.net.id; internet www.greekembassy.or.id; Ambassador GEORGIOS VEIS.

Holy See: Jalan Merdeka Timur 18, POB 4227, Jakarta Pusat (Apostolic Nunciature); tel. (21) 3841142; fax (21) 3841143; e-mail vatjak@cbn.net.id; Apostolic Nuncio ANTONIO GUIDO FILIPAZZI (Titular Archbishop of Sutrium).

Hungary: Jalan H. R. Rasuna Said 36, Kav. X-3, Kuningan, Jakarta 12950; tel. (21) 5203459; fax (21) 5203461; e-mail mission.jkt@kum.hu; internet www.mfa.gov.hu/kulkepviselet/id; Ambassador SZILVESZTER BUS.

India: Jalan H. R. Rasuna Said, Kav. S-1, Kuningan, Jakarta 12950; tel. (21) 5204150; fax (21) 5204160; e-mail ambasador@net-zap.com; internet www.indianembassyjakarta.com; Ambassador GURJIT SINGH.

Iran: Jalan Hos Cokroaminoto 110, Menteng, Jakarta Pusat 10310; tel. (21) 31931378; fax (21) 3107860; e-mail irembjkt@indo.net.id; internet www.iranembassy.or.id; Ambassador MAHMOUD FARAZANDEH.

Iraq: Jalan Teuku Umar 38, Jakarta 10350; tel. (21) 3904067; fax (21) 3904066; e-mail iraqembi@rad.net.id; Ambassador ISMAEL SHAFIQ MUHSIN.

Italy: Jalan Diponegoro 45, Menteng, Jakarta Pusat 10310; tel. (21) 31937445; fax (21) 31937422; e-mail ambasciata.jakarta@esteri.it; internet www.ambjakarta.esteri.it; Ambassador ROBERTO PALMIERI.

Japan: Jalan M. H. Thamrin 24, Jakarta Pusat 10350; tel. (21) 31924308; fax (21) 31925460; internet www.id.emb-japan.go.jp; Ambassador YOSHINORI KATORI.

Jordan: Artha Graha Tower, 9th Floor, Sudirman Central Business District, Jalan Jenderal Sudirman, Kav. 52–53, Jakarta 12190; tel. (21) 5153483; fax (21) 5153482; e-mail jordanem@scbd.net.id; internet www.jordanembassy.or.id; Ambassador MOHAMMAD HASSAN DAWODIEH.

Korea, Democratic People's Republic: Jalan Teluk Betung 1–2, Jakarta Pusat 12050; tel. (21) 31908425; fax (21) 31908427; e-mail dprkorea@rad.net.id; Ambassador RI JONG RYUL .

Korea, Republic: Jalan Jenderal Gatot Subroto 57, Jakarta Selatan; tel. (21) 5201915; fax (21) 5254159; e-mail koremb_in@mofat.go.kr; internet idn.mofat.go.kr; Ambassador KIM YOUNG-SUN.

Kuwait: Jalan Mega Kuningan Barat III, Kav. 16–17, Jakarta; tel. (21) 5764159; fax (21) 5764561; e-mail jakarta@mofa.gov.kw; Ambassador NASER BAREH SHAHER EL-ENEZI.

Laos: Jalan Patra Kuningan XIV 1A, Kuningan, Jakarta 12950; tel. (21) 5229602; fax (21) 5229601; e-mail laoemjktof@hotmail.com; Ambassador PRASITH SAYASITH.

Lebanon: Jalan YBR V 82, Kuningan, Jakarta 12950; tel. (21) 5253074; fax (21) 5207121; e-mail lebanon_embassy_jkt@yahoo.com; Ambassador VICTOR ZMETER.

Libya: Jalan Kintamani Raya II, Blok C-17, Kav. 6–7, Kuningan Timur, Jakarta Selatan 12950; tel. (21) 52920033; fax (21) 52920036; e-mail gsplaj@cbn.net.id; Chargé d'affaires ABDUSSAMEE HARB.

Malaysia: Jalan H. R. Rasuna Said, Kav. X-6 Nos 1–3, Kuningan, Jakarta 12950; tel. (21) 5224947; fax (21) 5224974; e-mail maljakarta@kln.gov.my; internet www.kln.gov.my/web/idn_jakarta; Ambassador Dato' SYED MUNSHE AFDZARUDDIN BIN SYED HASSAN.

Mexico: Menara Mulia, Suite 2306, Jalan Jenderal Gatot Subroto, Kav. 9–11, Jakarta Selatan 12930; tel. (21) 5203980; fax (21) 5203978; e-mail embmexic@rad.net.id; Ambassador MARY MELBA PRIA OLAVARRIETA.

Morocco: Jalan Denpasar Raya, Blok A-13, Kav. 1, Kuningan, Jakarta 12950; tel. (21) 5200773; fax (21) 5200586; e-mail sifamaind@gmail.com; Ambassador MOHAMED MAJDI.

Mozambique: Wisma GKBI, 37th Floor, Suite 3709, Jalan Jenderal Sudirman 28, Jakarta 10210; tel. (21) 5740901; fax (21) 5740907; e-mail embamoc@cbn.net.id; Ambassador CARLOS AGUSTINHO DO ROSÁRIO.

Myanmar: Jalan Haji Agus Salim 109, Menteng, Jakarta 10350; tel. (21) 327684; fax (21) 327204; e-mail myanmar@cbn.net.id; Ambassador NYAN LYNN.

Netherlands: Jalan H. R. Rasuna Said, Kav. S-3, Kuningan, Jakarta 12950; tel. (21) 5248200; fax (21) 5700734; e-mail jak@minbuza.nl; internet indonesia.nlembassy.org; Ambassador TJEERD DE ZWAAN.

New Zealand: Sentral Senayan 2, 10th Floor, Jalan Asia Afrika 8, Gelora Bung Karno, Jakarta Pusat 10270; tel. (21) 29955800; fax (21) 57974578; e-mail nzembjak@cbn.net.id; internet www.nzembassy.com/indonesia; Ambassador DAVID TAYLOR.

Nigeria: Jalan Taman Patra XIV 11, Kuningan Timur, POB 3649, Jakarta Selatan 12950; tel. (21) 5260922; fax (21) 5260924; e-mail embnig@centrin.net.id; Ambassador Alhaji IBRAHIM BABA MAI-SULE.

Norway: Menara Rajawali, 25th Floor, Kawasan Mega Kuningan, Jakarta 12950; tel. (21) 5761523; fax (21) 5761537; e-mail emb.jakarta@mfa.no; internet www.norway.or.id; Ambassador EIVIND HOMME.

Pakistan: Jalan Mega Kuningan, Blok E-3.9, Kav. 5–8, Kawasan Mega Kuningan, Jakarta Selatan 12950; tel. (21) 57851836; fax (21) 57851645; e-mail embassy@parepjakarta.com; internet www.mofa.gov.pk/indonesia; Ambassador SANAULLAH.

Panama: World Trade Center, 13th Floor, Jalan Jenderal Sudirman, Kav. 29–31, Jakarta 12920; tel. (21) 5711867; fax (21) 5711933; e-mail panaemb@net2cyber.web.id; Ambassador ROSEMARY SACETH DE LEÓN.

Papua New Guinea: Panin Bank Centre, 6th Floor, Jalan Jenderal Sudirman 1, Jakarta 10270; tel. (21) 7251218; fax (21) 7201012; e-mail kdujkt@cbn.net.id; Ambassador Cdre PETER ILAU.

Peru: Menara Rajawali, 12th Floor, Jalan Mega Kuningan, Lot 5.1, Kawasan Mega Kuningan, Jakarta Selatan 12950; tel. (21) 5761820; fax (21) 5761825; e-mail embaperu@cbn.net.id; Ambassador JUAN JOSÉ ALVAREZ VITA.

Philippines: Jalan Imam Bonjol 6–8, Jakarta Pusat 10310; tel. (21) 3100334; fax (21) 3151167; e-mail phjkt@indo.net.id; Ambassador MARIA ROSARIO C. AGUINALDO.

Poland: Jalan H. R. Rasuna Said, Blok IV-3, Kav. X, Jakarta Selatan 12950; tel. (21) 2525938; fax (21) 2525958; e-mail poljkt@dnet.net.id; internet www.jakarta.polemb.net; Ambassador GRZEGORZ WIŚNIEWSKI.

Portugal: Jalan Indramayu 2A, Menteng, Jakarta 10310; tel. (21) 31908030; fax (21) 31908031; e-mail porembjak@cbn.net.id; internet www.embassyportugaljakarta.or.id; Ambassador CARLOS MANUEL LEITÃO FROTA.

Qatar: Lot E 2.3, Jalan Mega Kuningan Barat, Kawasan Mega Kuningan, Jakarta 12950; tel. (21) 57906065; fax (21) 57906564;

e-mail qataremj@indosat.net.id; Chargé d'affaires a.i. JASSIM YOUSUF ALABDULJABBAR.

Romania: Jalan Teuku Cik Di Tiro 42A, Menteng, Jakarta Pusat; tel. (21) 3900489; fax (21) 3106241; e-mail romind@cbn.net.id; Ambassador GHEORGHE VÎLCU.

Russia: Jalan H. R. Rasuna Said, Kav. X-7 Nos 1–2, Jakarta 12940; tel. (21) 5222912; fax (21) 5222916; e-mail rusemb.indonesia@gmail.com; internet www.indonesia.mid.ru; Ambassador ALEKSANDR A. IVANOV.

Saudi Arabia: Jalan M. T. Haryono, Kav. 27, Cawang Atas, Jakarta 13630; tel. (21) 8011533; fax (21) 8011527; e-mail idemb@mofa.gov.sa; Ambassador ABDULLAH BIN ABDULRAHMAN A'ALIM AL-KHAYYAT.

Serbia: Jalan Hos Cokroaminoto 109, Jakarta Pusat 10310; tel. (21) 3143560; fax (21) 3143613; e-mail ambajaka@rad.net.id; Ambassador JOVAN JOVANOVIĆ.

Singapore: Jalan H. R. Rasuna Said, Blok X-4, Kav. 2, Kuningan, Jakarta 12950; tel. (21) 5201489; fax (21) 5201486; e-mail singemb_jkt@sgmfa.gov.sg; internet www.mfa.gov.sg/jkt; Ambassador ASHOK MIRPURI.

Slovakia: Jalan Prof. Mohammed Yamin 29, POB 1368, Menteng, Jakarta Pusat 10310; tel. (21) 3101068; fax (21) 3101180; e-mail emb.jakarta@mzv.sk; internet www.mzv.sk/jakarta; Ambassador ŠTEFAN ROZKOPÁL.

Somalia: Jalan Salak 5, Guntur, Jakarta Selatan 12980; tel. (21) 8311506; fax (21) 8352586; e-mail somalirep_jkt@yahoo.com; internet www.indonesia.somaligov.net; Ambassador MOHAMED OLOW BAROW.

South Africa: Wisma GKBI, Suite 705, Jalan Jenderal Sudirman 28, Jakarta 10210; tel. (21) 5740660; fax (21) 5740655; e-mail saembpol@centrin.net.id; internet www.southafricanembassy-jakarta.or.id; Ambassador NOEL NOA LEHOKO.

Spain: Jalan H. Agus Salim 61, Jakarta 10350; tel. (21) 3142355; fax (21) 31935134; e-mail emb.yakarta@mae.es; Ambassador RAFAEL CONDE DE SARO.

Sri Lanka: Jalan Diponegoro 70, Jakarta 10320; tel. (21) 3161886; fax (21) 3107962; e-mail lankaemb@rad.net.id; Ambassador Maj.-Gen. (retd) NANDA MALLAWAARACHCHI.

Sudan: Jalan Lembang 7, Menteng, Jakarta Pusat 10310; tel. (21) 3908234; fax (21) 3908235; e-mail sudanind@cbn.net.id; Ambassador IBRAHIM BUSHRA MOHAMED ALI.

Suriname: Jalan Padalarang 9, Menteng, Jakarta Pusat 10310; tel. (21) 3154437; fax (21) 3154556; e-mail ambassador@surinameembassyjakarta.org; Ambassador ANGELIC C. ALIHUSAIN-DEL CASTILHO.

Sweden: Menara Rajawali, 9th Floor, Jalan Mega Kuningan, Lot 5.1, Kawasan Mega Kuningan, Jakarta Selatan 12950; tel. (21) 55535900; fax (21) 5762691; e-mail ambassaden.jakarta@foreign.ministry.se; internet www.swedenabroad.com/jakarta; Ambassador EWA POLANO.

Switzerland: Jalan H. R. Rasuna Said, Blok X-3 No. 2, Kuningan, Jakarta Selatan 12950; tel. (21) 5256061; fax (21) 5202289; e-mail jak.vertretung@eda.admin.ch; internet www.eda.admin.ch/jakarta; Ambassador HEINZ WALKER-NEDERKOORN.

Syria: Jalan Karang Asem I 8, Jakarta 12950; tel. (21) 5255991; fax (21) 5202511; e-mail syrianemb@cbn.net.id; Chargé d'affaires BASSAM AL-KHATIB.

Thailand: Jalan Imam Bonjol 74, Jakarta Pusat 10310; tel. (21) 3904052; fax (21) 3107469; e-mail thaijkt@indo.net.id; internet www.thaiembassy.org/jakarta; Ambassador THANATIP UPATISING.

Timor-Leste: Gedung Surya, 11th Floor, Jalan M. H. Thamrin, Kav. 9, Jakarta Pusat 10350; tel. (21) 3902678; fax (21) 3902660; e-mail tljkt@yahoo.com; Ambassador MANUEL SERRANO.

Tunisia: Jalan Karang Asem Tengah, Blok C-5, Kav. 15, Kuningan, Jakarta Selatan 12950; tel. (21) 52892328; fax (21) 5255889; e-mail atjkt@uninet.net.id; Ambassador MOHAMED ANTAR.

Turkey: Jalan H. R. Rasuna Said, Kav. 1, Kuningan, Jakarta 12950; tel. (21) 5256250; fax (21) 5226056; e-mail cakartabe@telkom.net; internet cakarta.be.mfa.gov.tr; Ambassador MURAT ADALI.

Ukraine: World Trade Center, 8th Floor, Jalan Jenderal Sudirman, Kav. 29–31, Jakarta 12084; tel. (21) 5211700; fax (21) 5211710; e-mail emb_id@mfa.gov.ua; internet www.mfa.gov.ua/indonesia; Chargé d'affaires SERHIY TARHONIY.

United Arab Emirates: Jalan Prof. Dr Satrio, Blok C-4, Kav. 16–17, Jakarta 12950; tel. (21) 5206518; fax (21) 5206526; e-mail uaeemb@indo.net.id; Ambassador YOUSUF OMER AL-SHARHAN.

United Kingdom: Jalan M. H. Thamrin 75, Jakarta 10310; tel. (21) 23565200; fax (21) 23565351; e-mail commercial@dnet.net.id; internet ukinindonesia.fco.gov.uk; Ambassador MARK CANNING.

USA: Jalan Medan Merdeka Selatan 4–5, Jakarta 10110; tel. (21) 34359000; fax (21) 34359922; e-mail jakconsul@state.gov; internet jakarta.usembassy.gov; Ambassador SCOT ALAN MARCIEL.

Uzbekistan: Menara Mulia, 19th Floor, Suite 1901, Jalan Jenderal Gatot Subroto, Kav. 9–11, Jakarta Selatan 12930; tel. (21) 5222581; fax (21) 5222582; e-mail registan@indo.net.id; Ambassador SHAVKAT DJAMOLOV.

Venezuela: Menara Mulia, 20th Floor, Suite 2005, Jalan Jenderal Gatot Subroto, Kav. 9–11, Jakarta Selatan 12930; tel. (21) 5227547; fax (21) 5227549; e-mail evenjakt@indo.net.id; Chargé d'affaires a.i. MARÍA VIRGINIA MENZONES LICCIONI.

Viet Nam: Jalan Teuku Umar 25, Jakarta Pusat 10350; tel. (21) 3100358; fax (21) 3149615; e-mail embvnam@uninet.net.id; internet www.vietnamembassy-indonesia.org; Ambassador NGUYEN XUAN THUY.

Yemen: Jalan Subang 18, Menteng, Jakarta Pusat 10310; tel. (21) 3108029; fax (21) 3904946; e-mail yemenemb@rad.net.id; Ambassador ALI AL-SOSWA.

Zimbabwe: Jalan Patra Kuningan VII 15, Jakarta Selatan 12950; tel. (21) 5221378; fax (21) 5250365; e-mail zimjakarta@yahoo.com; Ambassador ALICE MAGEZA.

Judicial System

There is one codified criminal law for the whole of Indonesia. In December 1989 the Islamic Judicature Bill, giving wider powers to *Shari'a* courts, was approved by the Dewan Perwakilan Rakyat (House of Representatives). The new law gave Muslim courts authority over civil matters, such as marriage. Muslims may still choose to appear before a secular court. Europeans are subject to the Code of Civil Law published in the State Gazette in 1847. Alien orientals (i.e. Arabs, Indians, etc.) and Chinese are subject to certain parts of the Code of Civil Law and the Code of Commerce. The work of codifying this law has started, but, in view of the great complexity and diversity of customary law, it may be expected to take a considerable time to achieve. In June 2005 a judicial commission was established; the seven-member body, appointed by the House of Representatives, was charged with reforming the judiciary and with nominating Supreme Court justices, including the Chief Justice. In February 2006 the Judicial Commission announced that it was drafting a government regulation in lieu of law urging the re-evaluation of all justices as part of a wider process of judicial reform intended to address the issue of corruption within the legal system.

SUPREME COURT

The Supreme Court (Mahkamah Agung) is the final court of appeal. In February 2006 there were 49 Supreme Court justices.

Chief Justice: HATTA ALI, Jalan Merdeka Utara 9–13, Jakarta 10110; tel. (21) 3843348; fax (21) 3811057; e-mail info@ma-ri.go.id; internet www.mahkamahagung.go.id.

Deputy Chief Justices: Drs AHMAD KAMIL, Dr ABDUL KADIR MAPPONG.

CONSTITUTIONAL COURT

The Constitutional Court was established in 2003 and is composed of nine justices, of whom three each are appointed by, respectively, the President, the Supreme Court and the House of Representatives. The Court adjudicates the following matters: constitutionality of a law; impeachment; dissolution of a political party; disputes between state agencies; and disputes concerning election results.

Chief Justice: MOHAMMAD MAHFUD, Jalan Medan Merdeka Barat 6, Jakarta 10110; tel. (21) 23529000; fax (21) 3520177; e-mail humas@mahkamahkonstitusi.go.id; internet www.mahkamahkonstitusi.go.id.

OTHER COURTS

High Courts in Jakarta Surabaya, Medan, Makassar, Banda Aceh, Padang, Palembang, Bandung, Semarang, Banjarmasin, Menado, Denpasar, Ambon and Jayapura deal with appeals from the District Courts. District Courts deal with marriage, divorce and reconciliation.

Religion

All citizens are required to state their religion. The Ministry of Religion accords official status to six religions—Islam, the Christian faiths of Protestantism and Catholicism, Hinduism, Buddhism and Confucianism. According to a survey in 2000, 88.2% of the population were Muslims, while 5.9% were Protestant, 3.1% were Roman Catholic, 1.8% were Hindus, 0.8% were Buddhists and 0.2% professed adherence to other religions, such as other Christian denominations and Judaism, which remains unrecognized.

National religious councils—representing the official religious traditions—were established to serve as liaison bodies between religious adherents and the Government and to advise the Government on the application of religious principles to various elements of national life.

ISLAM

Indonesia has the world's largest Muslim population.

Majelis Ulama Indonesia (MUI) (Indonesian Ulama Council): Jalan Proklamasi 51, Menteng, Jakarta Pusat; tel. (21) 31902666; fax (21) 31905266; e-mail mui-online@mui.or.id; internet www.mui.or.id; central Muslim org.; Chair. Dr SAHAL MAHFUDH; Sec.-Gen. ICHWAN SAM.

Muhammadiyah: Jalan Menteng Raya 62, Jakarta Pusat 10340; tel. (21) 3903021; fax (21) 3903024; e-mail pp_muhammadiyah@yahoo.com; internet www.muhammadiyah.or.id; f. 1912; 28m. mems; second largest Muslim org. in Indonesia; incorporates the Muhammadiyah Youth Asscn and 'Aisyiyah, a women's org.; religious, charitable and educational activities; has established more than 5,000 Islamic schools; Chair. Dr DIN SYAMSUDDIN; Sec.-Gen. Dr AGUNG DANARTO.

Nahdlatul Ulama (NU) (Council of Scholars): Jalan Kramat Raya 164, Jakarta 10430; tel. (21) 3914014; fax (21) 3914013; internet www.nu.or.id; f. 1926; 30m. mems; largest Muslim org. in Indonesia; promotes Islamic teachings, as well as culture, education and economic devt; directly involved in politics from the mid-1950s until 1984; Chair. Dr SAID AQIL SIRADJ; Sec.-Gen. Dr MARSUDI SYUHUD.

CHRISTIANITY

Persekutuan Gereja-Gereja di Indonesia (Communion of Churches in Indonesia): Jalan Salemba Raya 10, Jakarta Pusat 10430; tel. (21) 3150451; fax (21) 3150457; e-mail pgi@bit.net.id; internet www.pgi.or.id; f. 1950; 81 mem. churches; Chair. Rev. ROYKE OCTAVIAN RORING; Gen. Sec. GOMAR GULTOM.

The Roman Catholic Church

Indonesia comprises 10 archdioceses and 27 dioceses. At 31 December 2007 there were an estimated 6,537,062 adherents in Indonesia, representing 3.9% of the population.

Bishops' Conference: Konferensi Waligereja Indonesia (KWI), Jalan Cut Meutia 10, POB 3044, Jakarta 10340; tel. and fax (21) 31925757; e-mail dokpen@kawali.org; internet www.kawali.org; f. 1973; Pres. MARTINUS D. SITUMORANG.

Archbishop of Ende: Most Rev. VICENTIUS SENSI, Keuskupan Agung, POB 210, Jalan Katedral 5, Ndona-Ende 86312, Flores; tel. (381) 21176; fax (381) 21606; e-mail uskup@ende.parokinet.org.

Archbishop of Jakarta: Most Rev. IGNATIUS SUHARYO HARDJOATMODJO, Keuskupan Agung, Jalan Katedral 7, Jakarta 10710; tel. (21) 3813345; fax (21) 3855681.

Archbishop of Kupang: Most Rev. PETER TURANG, Keuskupan Agung Kupang, Jalan Thamrin, Oepoi, Kupang 85111, Timor NTT; tel. (380) 826199; fax (380) 833331.

Archbishop of Makassar: Most Rev. JOHANNES LIKU ADA', Keuskupan Agung, Jalan Thamrin 5–7, Makassar 90111, Sulawesi Selatan; tel. (411) 315744; fax (411) 326674; e-mail sekr_kams@yahoo.com.

Archbishop of Medan: Most Rev. BONGSU ANTONIUS SINAGA, Jalan Imam Bonjol 39, POB 1191, Medan 20152, Sumatra Utara; tel. (61) 4519768; fax (61) 4145745; e-mail sekrkam@hotmail.com.

Archbishop of Merauke: Most Rev. NICOLAUS ADI SEPTURA, Keuskupan Agung, Jalan Mandala 30, Merauke 99602, Papua; tel. (971) 321011; fax (971) 321311.

Archbishop of Palembang: Most Rev. ALOYSIUS SUDARSO, Keuskupan Agung, Jalan Tasik 18, Palembang 30135; tel. (711) 350417; fax (711) 314776; e-mail alva@mdp.net.id.

Archbishop of Pontianak: Most Rev. HIERONYMUS HERCULANUS BUMBUN, Keuskupan Agung, Jalan A. R. Hakin 92A, POB 1119, Pontianak 78011, Kalimantan Barat; tel. (561) 732382; fax (561) 738785; e-mail kap@pontianak.wasantara.net.id.

Archbishop of Samarinda: Most Rev. FLORENTINUS SULUI HAJANG HAU, Keuskupan Agung, POB 1062, Jalan Gunung Merbabu 41, Samarinda 75010; tel. (541) 741193; fax (541) 203120.

Archbishop of Semarang: Most Rev. JOHANNES MARIA TRILAKSYANTA PUJASUMARTA, Keuskupan Agung, Jalan Pandanaran 13, Semarang 50244; tel. (24) 8312276; fax (24) 8414741; e-mail uskup@semarang.parokinet.org.

Other Christian Churches

Protestant Church in Indonesia (Gereja Protestan di Indonesia): Jalan Medan Merdeka Timur 10, Jakarta 10110; tel. (21) 3519003; fax (21) 34830224; consists of 12 churches of Calvinistic tradition; 3,047,300 mems, 4,808 congregations; Chair. Rev. Dr SAMUEL B. HAKH.

Numerous other Protestant communities exist throughout Indonesia, mainly organized on a local basis.

BUDDHISM

All-Indonesia Buddhist Association: Jakarta.

Indonesian Buddhist Council: Jakarta.

HINDUISM

Hindu Dharma Council: Jakarta.

The Press

PRINCIPAL DAILIES

Bali

Harian Pagi Umum (Bali Post): Jalan Kepundung 67A, Denpasar 80232; tel. (61) 225764; fax (61) 249483; e-mail iklan@balipost.co.id; internet www.balipost.co.id; f. 1948; daily (Indonesian edn), weekly (English edn); Editor K. NADHA; circ. 25,000.

Java

Angkatan Bersenjata: Jalan Kramat Raya 94, Jakarta Pusat; tel. (21) 46071; fax (21) 366870; armed forces newspaper.

Bandung Post: Jalan Lodaya 38A, Bandung 40264; tel. (22) 305124; fax (22) 302882; f. 1979; Chief Editor AHMAD SAELAN; Dir AHMAD JUSACC.

Berita Buana: Jalan Tahah Abang Dua 33–35, Jakarta 10110; tel. (21) 5487175; fax (21) 5491555; f. 1970; relaunched 1990; Indonesian; circ. 150,000.

Bisnis Indonesia: Wisma Bisnis Indonesia, Jalan K. H. Mas Mansyur 12A, Karet, Jakarta 10220; tel. (21) 57901023; fax (21) 57901025; e-mail redaksi@bisnis.co.id; internet www.bisnis.com; f. 1985; available online; Indonesian; Editor SUKAMDANI S. GITOSARDJONO; circ. 60,000.

Harian Pelita: Jalan Minangkabau 35B-C Manggarai, Jakarta Selatan 12970; tel. (21) 83706765; fax (21) 83706771; e-mail redaksi@pelitaonline.com; internet www.harianpelita.com; f. 1974; Indonesian; Muslim; 6 a week; Chief Editor A. BASORI.

Harian Terbit: Jalan Pulogadung 15, Kawasan Industri Pulogadung, Jakarta 13920; tel. (21) 4603973; fax (21) 4603970; e-mail terbit@harianterbit.com; internet www.harianterbit.com; f. 1972; Indonesian; Editor-in-Chief TARMAN AZZAM; circ. 125,000.

Harian Umum AB: CTC Bldg, 2nd Floor, Kramat Raya 94, Jakarta Pusat; f. 1965; official armed forces journal; Dir GOENARSO; Editor-in-Chief N. SOEPANGAT; circ. 80,000.

The Jakarta Post: Jalan Palmerah Barat 142–143, Jakarta 10270; tel. (21) 5300476; fax (21) 5350050; e-mail editorial@thejakartapost.com; internet www.thejakartapost.com; f. 1983; English; Chief Editor MEIDYATAMA SURYODININGRAT; circ. 60,000.

Jawa Pos: Graha Pena Bldg, 4th Floor, Achmad Yani 88, Surabaya 60234; tel. (31) 8202216; fax (31) 8285555; e-mail editor@jawapos.co.id; internet www.jawapos.co.id; f. 1949; Indonesian; CEO DAHLAN ISKAN; Chief Editor LEAK KUSTIYA; circ. 400,000.

Kedaulatan Rakyat: Jalan P. Mangkubumi 40–44, Yogyakarta; tel. (274) 565685; fax (274) 563125; f. 1945; Indonesian; independent; Chief Editor OCTO LAMPITO; circ. 50,000.

Kompas: Gedung Kompas Gramedia, Unit II, Lantai 5, Jalan Palmerah Selatan 26–28, Jakarta 10270; tel. (21) 5350377; fax (21) 5360678; e-mail redaksikcm@kompas.co.id; internet www.kompas.com; f. 1965; Indonesian; Man. Editor M. SUPRIHADI; circ. 523,453.

Koran Tempo: Gedung Tempo, Jalan H. R. Rasuna Said, Kav. C-17, Kuningan, Jakarta 10270; tel. (21) 5201022; fax (21) 5200092; e-mail interaktif@tempo.co.id; internet www.korantempo.com; f. 2001; Indonesian; Editor-in-Chief BAMBANG HARYMURTI.

Media Indonesia Daily: Jalan Pilar Mas Raya, Kav. A–D, Kedoya Selatan, Kebon Jeruk, Jakarta 11520; tel. (21) 5812088; fax (21) 5812105; e-mail miol@mediaindonesia.co.id; internet www.mediaindo.co.id; f. 1989; fmrly Prioritas; Indonesian; Publr SURYA PALOH; Editor DJAFAR H. ASSEGAFF; circ. 2,000.

Pikiran Rakyat: Jalan Asia-Afrika 77, Bandung 40111; tel. (22) 51216; e-mail pdr@pikiran-rakyat.com; internet www.pikiran-rakyat.com; f. 1950; Indonesian; independent; Editor BRAM M. DARMAPRAWIRA; circ. 150,000.

Pos Kota: Yayasan Antar Kota, Jalan Gajah Mada 100, Jakarta 10130; tel. and fax (21) 5652603; e-mail redaksi@poskota.co.id; internet www.poskota.co.id; f. 1970; Indonesian; Editor-in-Chief H. JOHNNY LESTER; circ. 500,000.

Rakyat Merdeka: Graha Pena, 9th Floor, Jalan Raya Kebayoran Lama 12, Jakarta Selatan 12210; tel. (21) 5348460; fax (21) 53671716; e-mail redaksi@rakyatmerdeka.co.id; internet www.rakyatmerdeka.co.id; f. 1945; Indonesian; independent; Chief Editor TEGUH SANTOSA; circ. 130,000.

Republika: Jalan Warung Buncit Raya 37, Jakarta Selatan 12510; tel. (21) 7803747; fax (21) 7800649; e-mail sekretariat@republika.co.id; internet www.republika.co.id; f. 1993; organ of the Asscn of Indonesian Muslim Intellectuals (ICMI); Chief Editor NASIHIN MASHA.

Sin Chew Indonesia: Jalan Toko Tiga Seberang 21, POB 4755, Jakarta 11120; tel. (21) 6295948; fax (21) 6297830; internet www.sinchew-i.com/indonesia; f. 1966; Chinese; fmrly Harian Indonesia; Editor W. D. SUKISMAN; Dir HADI WIBOWO; circ. 42,000.

Solo Pos: Griya SOLOPOS, Jalan Adisucipto 190, Solo 57145; tel. (271) 724811; fax (271) 724833; internet www.solopos.co.id; Editor-in-Chief SUNYOTO YA.

Suara Karya: Jalan Bangka Raya 2, Kebayoran Baru, Jakarta Selatan 12720; tel. (21) 7192656; fax (21) 71790746; e-mail redaksi@suarakarya-online.com; f. 1971; Indonesian; Chief Editor RICKY RACHMADI; circ. 100,000.

Suara Merdeka: Jalan Pandanaran 30, Semarang 50241; tel. (24) 8412600; fax (24) 8411116; e-mail redaksi@suaramerdeka.info; internet www.suaramerdeka.com; f. 1950; Indonesian; Publr Ir H. TOMMY HETAMI; Editor-in-Chief HENDRO BASUKI; circ. 200,000.

Suara Pembaruan: The Aryaduta Suites Tower A, Lantai 1, Jalan Garnisun Dalam 8, Karet Semanggi, Jakarta 12930; tel. (21) 57851555; fax (21) 57851554; e-mail koransp@suarapembaruan.com; internet www.suarapembaruan.com; f. 1987; Chief Editor PRIMUS DORIMULU.

Surabaya Post: Ruko Rich Palace, Kav. 19–20, Jalan Mayjend Sungkono 149–150, Surabaya; tel. (31) 5667000; fax (31) 5635000; e-mail redaksi@surabayapost.co.id; internet www.surabayapost.co.id; f. 1953; independent; afternoon; Chief Editor and Dir BAMBANG HARIAWAN; Man. Editor AGUSTINA WIDYAWATI; circ. 115,000.

Surya: Jalan Rungkut Industri III, 68 & 70 SIER, Surabaya 60293; tel. (31) 8419000; fax (31) 8414024; e-mail redaksi@surya.co.id; internet www.surya.co.id; Editor-in-Chief RUSDI AMRAL.

Kalimantan

Banjarmasin Post: Gedung HJ Djok Mentaya, Jalan AS Musyaffa 16, Banjarmasin 70111; tel. (511) 3354370; fax (511) 4366123; e-mail redaksi@banjarmasinpost.co.id; internet www.banjarmasinpost.co.id; f. 1971; Indonesian; Editor-in-Chief YUSRAN PARE; circ. 50,000.

Harian Umum Akcaya: Pontianak Post Group, Jalan Gajah Mada 2–4, Pontianak 78121; tel. (561) 735071; fax (561) 736607; e-mail redaksi@pontianakpost.com; internet www.pontianakpost.com; Editor B. SALMAN.

Kaltim Post: Jalan Jenderal Sudirman RT XVI 82, Balikpapan 76144; tel. (542) 736459; fax (542) 730353; e-mail redaksi@kaltimpost.net; internet www.kaltimpost.co.id; f. 1988; fmrly *Manuntung*; Editor-in-Chief Drs H. BAMBANG ISNOTO (acting).

Lampung Post: Jalan Pangkal Pinang, Lampung; e-mail webmaster@metrotvnews.com; internet www.lampungpost.com; Editor DJADJAT SUDRADJAT.

Maluku

Pos Maluku: Jalan Raya Pattimura 19, Ambon; tel. (911) 44614.

Suara Maluku: Komplex Perdagangan Mardikas, Blok D3/11A, Ternate; tel. (911) 44590.

Nusa Tenggara

Pos Kupang: Jalan Kenari 1, Kupang 85115; tel. (380) 833820; fax (380) 831801; e-mail poskpg@yahoo.com; internet kupang.tribunnews.com; Chief Editor DION D. B. PUTRA.

Papua

Cenderawasih Post: Jalan Cenderawasih 10, Kelapa II, Entrop, Jayapura 99013; tel. (967) 532417; fax (967) 532418; e-mail cepos_jpr@yahoo.com; internet www.cenderawasihpos.com; Editor-in-Chief DAUD SONY.

Teropong: Jalan Halmahera, Jayapura.

Riau

Batam Pos: Gedung Graha Pena, Lt. 2, Jalan Raya Batam Centre, Batam 29461; tel. (778) 460000; fax (778) 462162; e-mail redaksi@batampos.co.id; internet www.harianbatampos.com; Editor-in-Chief CANDRA IBRAHIM.

Riau Pos: Jalan H. R. Subrantas, Km 10.5, Pekanbaru, Riau 28294; tel. (761) 64633; fax (761) 64640; e-mail redaksi@riaupos.com; internet www.riaupos.co.id; Editor-in-Chief RAJA ISYAM AZWAR; circ. 40,000.

Sulawesi

Bulletin Sulut: Jalan Korengkeng 38, Lt. II, Manado 95114, Sulawesi Utara.

Cahaya Siang: Jalan Kembang II 2, Manado 95114, Sulawesi Utara; tel. (431) 61054; fax (431) 63393.

Fajar (Dawn): Gedung Graha Pena, Lantai 4, Jalan Urip Sumoharjo 21, Makassar 90231; tel. (411) 441441; fax (411) 441224; e-mail redaksi@fajar.co.id; internet www.fajar.co.id; Editor-in-Chief ALWI HAMU; circ. 35,000.

Manado Post: Manado Post Centre, Manado Town Sq., Blok B, Kav. 14–15, Manado; tel. (431) 855558; fax (431) 860398; e-mail editor@mdopost.com; internet www.mdopost.com; Editor-in-Chief SUHENDRO BOROMA.

Pedoman Rakyat: Jalan H. A. Mappanyukki 28, Makassar; f. 1947; independent; Editor M. BASIR; circ. 30,000.

Suluh Merdeka: Jalan R. W. Mongsidi 4/96, POB 1105, Manado 95110; tel. and fax (431) 866150.

Tegas: Jalan Mappanyukki 28, Makassar; tel. (411) 3960.

Sumatra

Harian Analisa: Jalan Balaikota 2, Medan 20111; tel. (61) 4154711; fax (61) 4151436; internet www.analisadaily.com; f. 1972; Indonesian; Editor H. ALI SOEKARDI; circ. 75,000.

Harian Berita Sore: Jalan Letjen Suprapto 1, Medan 20151; tel. (61) 4158787; fax (61) 4150383; e-mail redaksi@beritasore.com; internet www.beritasore.com; Indonesian; Publr SAID PRABUDI SAID; Editor-in-Chief H. TERUNA JASA SAID.

Harian Haluan: Jalan Damar 59 C/F, Padang; f. 1948; Editor-in-Chief Drs ASRIL KASOEMA; circ. 40,000.

Harian Umum Nasional Waspada: Jalan Brigjenderal 1 Katamso, Medan 20151; tel. (61) 4150858; fax (61) 4510025; e-mail redaksi.online@waspada.co.id; internet www.waspada.co.id; f. 1947; Indonesian; Editor-in-Chief AVIAN E. TUMENGKOL.

Mimbar Umum: Merah, Medan; tel. (61) 517807; f. 1947; Indonesian; independent; Editor MOHD LUD LUBIS; circ. 55,000.

Padang Ekspres: Jalan Proklamasi 5D Tarandam, Padang, Sumatra Barat; tel. (751) 841300; fax (751) 841904; e-mail redaksi@padang-today.com; internet www.padang-today.com; Indonesian; Editor SHI MUSLIM.

Serambi Indonesia: Jalan Raya Lambaro, Km 4.5, Tanjung Permai, Manyang PA, Banda Aceh; tel. (651) 635544; fax (651) 637180; e-mail redaksi@serambinews.com; internet www.serambinews.com; Editor-in-Chief MAWARDI IBRAHIM.

Sinar Indonesia Baru: Jalan Brigjenderal Katamso 66, Medan 20151; tel. (61) 4512530; fax (61) 4538150; e-mail redaksi@hariansib.com; internet www.hariansib.com; f. 1970; Indonesian; Chief Editor G. M. PANGGABEAN; circ. 150,000.

Sriwijaya Post: Jalan Jenderal Basuki Rahmat 1608 B–D, Palembang; tel. (711) 310088; fax (711) 312888; e-mail redaksi@sripoku.com; internet palembang.tribunnews.com; f. 2002; Editor-in-Chief HADI PRAYOGO.

Suara Rakyat Semesta: Jalan K. H. Ashari 52, Palembang; Indonesian; Editor DJADIL ABDULLAH; circ. 10,000.

Waspada: Jalan Letjen Suprapto, cnr Jalan Brigjen Katamso 1, Medan 20151; tel. (61) 4150868; fax (61) 4510025; e-mail waspada@waspada.co.id; internet www.waspada.co.id; f. 1947; Indonesian; Chief Editors ANI IDRUS, PRABUDI SAID; circ. 60,000 (daily), 55,000 (Sun.).

PRINCIPAL PERIODICALS

Amanah: Jalan Garuda 69, Kemayoran, Jakarta; tel. (21) 410254; fortnightly; Muslim current affairs; Indonesian; Man. Dir MASKUN ISKANDAR; circ. 180,000.

Ayahbunda: Jalan H. R. Rasuna Said, Blok B, Kav. 32–33, Jakarta 12910; tel. (21) 5209370; fax (21) 5209366; e-mail langganan@feminagroup.com; internet www.ayahbunda.co.id; fortnightly; family magazine.

Berita Negara: Jalan Pertjetakan Negara 21, Kotakpos 2111, Jakarta; tel. and fax (21) 4207251; f. 1951; 2 a week; official gazette.

Bobo (PT Penerbitan Sarana Bobo): Gramedia Magazine Bldg, 2nd Floor, Jalan Panjang 8A, Kebon Jeruk, Jakarta 11530; tel. (21) 5330150; fax (21) 5320681; f. 1973; subsidiary of Gramedia Group; weekly; children's magazine; Editor KOES SABANDIYAH; circ. 206,000.

Bola: Tunas Bola, Jalan Palmerah Barat 33–37, Jakarta 10270; tel. (21) 53677835; fax (21) 5301952; e-mail redaksi@bolanews.com; internet www.bolanews.com; 2 a week; Tue. and Fri.; sports magazine; Indonesian; Chief Editor IAN SITUMORANG; circ. 715,000.

Buana Minggu: Jalan Tanah Abang Dua 33, Jakarta Pusat 10110; tel. (21) 364190; weekly; Sunday; Indonesian; Editor WINOTO PARTHO; circ. 193,450.

Business News: Jalan H. Abdul Muis 70, Jakarta 10160; tel. (21) 3848207; fax (21) 3454280; f. 1956; 3 a week (Indonesian edn), 2 a week (English edn); Chief Editor SANJOTO SASTROMIHARDJO; circ. 15,000.

Cita Cinta: Jalan H. R. Rasuna Said, Blok B, Kav. 32–33, Jakarta 12910; tel. (21) 5254206; fax (21) 5262131; e-mail citacinta@feminagroup.com; internet www.citacinta.com; f. 2000; teenage lifestyle magazine.

Citra: Gramedia Bldg, Unit 11, 5th Floor, Jalan Palmerah Selatan 24–26, Jakarta 10270; tel. (21) 5483008; fax (21) 5494035; e-mail citra@gramedia-majalah.com; f. 1990; weekly; TV and film programmes, music trends and celebrity news; Chief Editor H. MAMAN SUHERMAN; circ. 239,000.

Depthnews Indonesia: Jalan Jatinegara Barat III/6, Jakarta 13310; tel. (21) 8194994; fax (21) 8195501; f. 1972; weekly; publ. by Press Foundation of Indonesia; Editor SUMONO MUSTOFFA.

Dunia Wanita: Jalan Brigjenderal 1 Katamso, Medan; tel. (61) 4150858; fax (61) 4510025; e-mail waspada@indosat.net.id; internet www.dunia-wanita.com; f. 1949; fortnightly; Indonesian; women's tabloid; Chief Editor Dr RAYATI SYAFRIN; circ. 10,000.

Economic Review: Bank BNI, Strategic Planning Division, Gedung Bank BNI, Jalan Jenderal Sudirman, Kav. 1, POB 2955, Jakarta 10220; tel. (21) 5728692; fax (21) 5728456; e-mail renkek01@bni.co.id; internet www.bni.co.id; f. 1946; 3 a year; English; economic and business research and analysis; Editor-in-Chief DARWIN SUZANDI.

Ekonomi Indonesia: Jalan Merdeka, Timur 11–12, Jakarta; tel. (21) 494458; monthly; English; economic journal; Editor Z. ACHMAD; circ. 20,000.

Eksekutif: Jalan R. S. Fatmawati 20, Jakarta 12430; tel. (21) 7659218; fax (21) 7504018; internet eksekutif.com.

Femina: Jalan H. R. Rasuna Said, Blok B, Kav. 32–33, Jakarta Selatan 12910; tel. (21) 5209370; fax (21) 5209366; e-mail redaksi@feminagroup.com; internet www.femina.co.id; f. 1972; weekly; women's magazine; Publr SVIDA ALISJAHBANA; Editor PETTY S. FATIMAH; circ. 160,000.

Gadis: Jalan H. R. Rasuna Said, Blok B, Kav. 32–33, Jakarta 12910; tel. (21) 5253816; fax (21) 5262131; e-mail palupi.ambardini@feminagroup.com; internet www.gadis.co.id; f. 1973; 3 a month; Indonesian; teenage lifestyle magazine; Editor-in-Chief PALUPI AMBARDINI; circ. 150,000.

Gatra: Gedung Gatra, Jalan Kalibata Timur IV/15, Jakarta 12740; tel. (21) 7973535; fax (21) 79196941; e-mail admin@gatra.com; internet www.gatra.com; est. by fmr employees of Tempo (banned 1994–98); Gen. Man. STEPHEN SIAHAYA; Editor-in-Chief BUDIONO KARTOHADIPRODJO.

Gugat (Accuse): Surabaya; politics, law and crime; weekly; circ. 250,000.

Hai: Jalan Panjang 8A, Kebon Jeruk, Jakarta Barat; tel. (21) 5330170; fax (21) 5220070; e-mail hai_magazine@gramedia-majalah.com; internet www.hai-online.com; f. 1973; weekly; youth magazine; Man. Editor JUNIOR EKA PUTRO; circ. 42,000.

Indonesia Business News: Wisma Bisnis Indonesia, 7th Floor, Jalan K. H. Mas Mansyur 12A, Karet, Jakarta 10220; tel. (21) 57901023; fax (21) 57901025; e-mail redaksi@bisnis.co.id; internet www.bisnis.co.id; Indonesian and English.

Indonesia Business Weekly: Wisma Bisnis Indonesia, Jalan Letjenderal S. Parman, Kav. 12, Slipi, Jakarta 11410; tel. (21) 5304016; fax (21) 5305868; English; Editor TAUFIK DARUSMAN.

Indonesia Magazine: Jalan Merdeka Barat 20, Jakarta; tel. (21) 352015; f. 1969; monthly; English; Chair. G. DWIPAYANA; Editor-in-Chief HADELY HASIBUAN; circ. 15,000.

Intisari (Digest): Gramedia Bldg, Unit II, 5th Floor, Jalan Palmerah Selatan 24–26, Jakarta 10270; tel. (21) 5483008; fax (21) 53696525; e-mail intisari@gramedia-majalah.com; internet www.intisari-online.com; f. 1963; monthly; Indonesian; popular science, health, technology, crime and general interest; Editors AL. HERU KUSTARA, IRAWATI; circ. 141,000.

Jakarta Jakarta: Gramedia Bldg, Unit II, 5th Floor, Jalan Palmerah Selatan 24–26, Jakarta 10270; tel. (21) 5483008; fax (21) 5494035; f. 1985; weekly; food, fun, fashion and celebrity news; circ. 70,000.

Jurnal Indonesia: Jalan Hos Cokroaminoto 49A, Jakarta 10350; tel. (21) 31901774; fax (21) 3916471; e-mail jurnal@cbn.net.id; monthly; political, economic and business analysis.

Keluarga: Jalan Sangaji 11, Jakarta; fortnightly; women's and family magazine; Editor S. DAHONO.

Kontan: Gedung Kontan, Jalan Kebayoran Lama 3119, Jakarta 12210; tel. (21) 5357636; fax (21) 5357633; e-mail red@kontan.co.id; internet www.kontan.co.id; weekly; Indonesian; business newspaper; Editor-in-Chief ARDIAN TAUFIK GESURI.

Majalah Ekonomis: POB 4195, Jakarta; monthly; English; business; Chief Editor S. ARIFIN HUTABARAT; circ. 20,000.

Majalah Kedokteran Indonesia (Journal of the Indonesian Medical Assen): Jalan Kesehatan 111/29, Jakarta 11/16; f. 1951; monthly; Indonesian, English.

Manglé: Jalan Lodaya 19–21, 40262 Bandung; tel. (22) 411438; f. 1957; weekly; Sundanese; Chief Editor Drs OEJANG DARAJATOEN; circ. 74,000.

Matra: Grafity Pers, Kompleks Buncit Raya Permai, Kav. 1, Jalan Warung, POB 3476, Jakarta; tel. (21) 515952; f. 1986; monthly; men's magazine; general interest and current affairs; Editor-in-Chief SRI RUSDY; circ. 100,000.

Mimbar Kabinet Pembangunan: Jalan Merdeka Barat 7, Jakarta; f. 1966; monthly; Indonesian; publ. by Dept of Information.

Mutiara: Jalan Dewi Sartika 136D, Cawang, Jakarta Timur; general interest; Publr H. G. RORIMPANDEY.

Nova: Gedung Kompas Gramedia, Lantai 3, Jalan Panjang 8A, Kebon Jeruk, Jakarta Barat 11530; tel. (21) 5330150; fax (21) 5321020; e-mail admin@tabloidnova.com; internet www.tabloidnova.com; weekly; Wed.; women's interest; Indonesian; Publr SAMINDRA UTAMA; circ. 618,267.

Oposisi: Jakarta; weekly; politics; circ. 400,000.

Otomotif: Gedung Kompas Gramedia, Lantai 7, Jalan Panjang 8A, Kebon Jeruk, Jakarta Barat 11530; tel. (21) 5330170; fax (21) 5330185; e-mail otomotifnet@gramedia-majalah.com; internet www.otomotifnet.com; f. 1990; weekly; automotive specialist tabloid; Editor-in-Chief SONI RIHARTO; circ. 215,763.

PC Magazine Indonesia: Jalan H. R. Rasuna Said, Blok B, Kav. 32–33, Jakarta 12910; tel. (21) 5209370; fax (21) 5209366; computers; Editor-in-Chief SVIDA ALISJAHBANA.

Peraba: Bintaran Kidul 5, Yogyakarta; weekly; Indonesian and Javanese; Roman Catholic; Editor W. KARTOSOEHARSONO.

Pertani PT: Jalan Pasar Minggu, Kalibata, POB 247/KBY, Jakarta Selatan; tel. (21) 793108; f. 1974; monthly; Indonesian; agricultural; Pres. Dir Ir RUSLI YAHYA.

Petisi: Surabaya; weekly; Editor CHOIRUL ANAM.

Rajawali: Jakarta; monthly; Indonesian; civil aviation and tourism; Dir R. A. J. LUMENTA; Man. Editor KARYONO ADHY.

Selecta: Kebon Kacang 29/4, Jakarta; fortnightly; illustrated; Editor SAMSUDIN LUBIS; circ. 80,000.

Swasembada: Jalan Taman Tanah Abang, III/23, Jakarta 10610; tel. (21) 3523839; fax (21) 3457338; internet www.swa.co.id; Editor-in-Chief KEMAL EFFENDI GANI.

Tempo: Gedung Temprint, Lantai 2, Jalan Palmerah Barat 8, Jakarta 12210; tel. (21) 5360409; fax (21) 5360412; e-mail interaktif@tempo.co.id; internet www.tempointeractive.com; f. 1971; weekly; Editor-in-Chief WAHYU MURYADI.

Tiara: Gramedia Bldg, Unit 11, 5th Floor, Jalan Palmerah Selatan 24–26, Jakarta 10270; tel. (21) 5483008; fax (21) 5494035; f. 1990; fortnightly; lifestyles, features and celebrity news; circ. 47,000.

Ummat: Jakarta; Islamic; sponsored by ICMI.

Wenang Post: Jalan R. W. Mongsidi 4/96, POB 1105, Manado 95115; tel. and fax (431) 866150; weekly.

NEWS AGENCIES

ANTARA (Indonesian News Agency): Wisma Antara, Lantai 19, 17 Jalan Medan Merdeka Selatan, POB 1257, Jakarta 10110; tel. (21) 3802383; fax (21) 3522178; e-mail newsroom@antaranews.com; internet www.antaranews.com; f. 1937; 33 brs in Indonesia, five overseas brs; 800 bulletins in Indonesian and in English; monitoring service of stock exchanges world-wide; photo service; CEO AHMAD MUKHLIS YUSUF; Chief Editor SAIFUL HADI.

Kantorberita Nasional Indonesia (KNI News Service): Jalan Jatinegara Barat III/6, Jakarta Timur 13310; tel. (21) 811003; fax (21) 8195501; f. 1966; independent national news agency; foreign and domestic news in Indonesian; Dir and Editor-in-Chief Drs SUMONO MUSTOFFA; Exec. Editor HARIM NURROCHADI.

PRESS ASSOCIATIONS

Aliansi Jurnalis Independen (AJI) (Alliance of Independent Journalists): Jalan Kembang Raya 6 Kwitang, Senen, Jakarta Pusat 10420; tel. (21) 3151214; fax (21) 3151261; e-mail office@ajiindonesia.org; internet www.ajiindonesia.org; f. 1994; unofficial; aims to promote freedom of the press; Pres. EKO MARYADI; Sec.-Gen. SUWARJONO.

Jakarta Foreign Correspondents' Club: Plaza Gani Djemat, Lantai 4, Jalan Imam Bonjol 76–78, Jakarta 10310; tel. (21) 3903628; fax (21) 3917453; e-mail office@jfcc.info; internet www.jfcc.info; more than 400 mems; Pres. JASON TEDJASUKMANA.

Persatuan Wartawan Indonesia (PWI) (Indonesian Journalists' Asscn): Gedung Dewan Pers, Lantai 4, Jalan Kebon Sirih 34, Jakarta 10110; tel. (21) 3453131; fax (21) 3453175; e-mail pwi@pwi.or.id; internet www.pwi.or.id; f. 1946; govt-controlled; 14,000 mems (Feb. 2009); Chair. MARGIONO; Gen. Sec. HENDRY BANGUN.

Serikat Penerbit Suratkabar (SPS) (Indonesian Newspaper Publishers' Asscn): Gedung Dewan Pers, 6th Floor, Jalan Kebon Sirih 34, Jakarta 10110; tel. (21) 3459671; fax (21) 3862373; e-mail spspusat@spsindonesia.or.id; f. 1946; mems: 451 publrs; Exec. Chair. DAHLAN IKSAN; Sec.-Gen. SUKARDI DARMAWAN.

Publishers

JAKARTA

Aries Lima/New Aqua Press PT: Jalan Rawagelan II/4, Jakarta Timur; tel. (21) 4897566; general and children's; Pres. TUTI SUNDARI AZMI.

Aya Media Pustaka PT: Wijaya Grand Centre C/2, Jalan Wijaya II, Jakarta 12160; tel. (21) 7206903; fax (21) 7201401; e-mail ayamedia@cbn.net.id; f. 1985; children's; Dir Drs ARIANTO TUGIYO.

PT Balai Pustaka Peraga: Jalan Gunung Sahari Raya 4, Gedung Balai Pustaka, 7th Floor, Jakarta 10710; tel. (21) 3451616; fax (21) 3855735; e-mail con_bpustaka@bumn-ri.com; f. 1917; children's, school textbooks, literary, scientific publs and periodicals; Dir R. SISWADI.

Bhratara Niaga Media PT: Jalan Cipinang Bali 17, Jakarta Timur 13420; tel. (21) 8520319; fax (21) 8191858; f. 1986; fmrly Bhratara Karya Aksara; university and educational textbooks; Man. Dir ROBINSON RUSDI.

Bina Rena Pariwara PT: Jalan Pejaten Raya 5E, Pasar Minggu, Jakarta 12510; tel. (21) 7901931; fax (21) 7901939; e-mail hasanbas@softhome.net; f. 1988; financial, social science, economic, Islamic, children's; Dir Drs HASAN BASRI.

Bulan Bintang PT: Jalan Kramat Kwitang I/8, Jakarta 10420; tel. (21) 3901651; fax (21) 3901652; e-mail bukubulanbintang@gmail.com; internet www.bulanbintang.co.id; f. 1954; Islamic, social science, natural and applied sciences, art; Man. Dir FAUZI AMELZ.

Bumi Aksara PT: Jalan Sawo Raya 18, Rawamanguu, Jakarta 13220; tel. (21) 4717049; fax (21) 4700989; e-mail info@bumiaksara.co.id; internet www.bumiaksara.co.id; f. 1990; university textbooks; Dir LUCYA ANDAM DEWI.

Cakrawala Cinta PT: Jalan Minyak I/12B, Duren Tiga, Jakarta 12760; tel. (21) 7990725; fax (21) 7974076; f. 1984; science; Dir Drs M. TORSINA.

Centre for Strategic and International Studies (CSIS): Jakarta Post Bldg, 3rd Floor, Jalan Palmerah Barat 142–143, Jakarta 10270; tel. (21) 53654601; fax (21) 53654607; e-mail csis@csis.or.id; internet www.csis.or.id; f. 1971; political and social sciences; Exec. Dir RIZAL SUKMA.

Cipta Adi Pustaka: Graha Compaka Mas Blok C 22, Jalan Cempaka Putih Raya, Jakarta Pusat; tel. (21) 4213821; fax (21) 4269315; f. 1986; encyclopedias; Dir BUDI SANTOSO.

Dian Rakyat PT: Jalan Rawa Girang 8, Kawasan Industri Pulogadung, Jakarta; tel. (21) 4604444; fax (21) 4609115; f. 1966; general; Pres. Dir MARIO ALISJAHBANA.

Djambatan PT: Jalan Paseban 29, Jakarta 10440; tel. (21) 7203199; fax (21) 7227989; e-mail djam@dnet.net.id; f. 1954; children's, textbooks, social sciences, fiction; Dir SJARIFUDIN SJAMSUDIN.

Dunia Pustaka Jaya: Jalan Kramat Raya 5K, Komp. Maya Indah, Jakarta 10450; tel. (21) 3909322; fax (21) 3909320; f. 1971; fiction, religion, essays, poetry, drama, criticism, art, philosophy and children's; Man. A. RIVAI.

EGC Medical Publishers: Jalan Agung Timur 4, No. 39 Blok 0–1, Jakarta 14350; tel. (21) 65306283; fax (21) 6518178; e-mail contact@egc-arcan.com; f. 1978; medical and public health, nursing, dentistry; Dir IMELDA DHARMA.

PT Elex Media Komputindo: Gramedia Bldg, 6th Floor, Jalan Palmerah Selatan 22, Jakarta 10270; tel. (21) 5483008; fax (21) 5326219; e-mail langganan@elexmedia.co.id; internet www.elexmedia.co.id; f. 1985; management, computing, software, children's, parenting, self-development and fiction; Dir AL. ADHI MARDHIYONO.

Erlangga PT: Kami Melayani II, Pengetahuan, Jalan H. Baping 100, Ciracas, Jakarta 13740; tel. (21) 8717006; fax (21) 87794609; internet www.erlangga.co.id; f. 1952; secondary school and university textbooks; Man. Dir GUNAWAN HUTAURUK.

Gaya Favorit Press: Jalan H. R. Rasuna Said. Kav. B 32–33, Jakarta 12910; tel. (21) 5209370; fax (21) 5209366; f. 1971; fiction, popular science, lifestyle and children's; Vice-Pres. MIRTA KARTOHADIPRODJO; Man. Dir WIDARTI GUNAWAN.

Gema Insani Press: Jalan Kalibata Utara II/84, Jakarta 12740; tel. (21) 7984391; fax (21) 7984388; e-mail penerbitan@gemainsani.co.id; internet www.gemainsani.co.id; f. 1986; Islamic; Dir UMAR BASYARAHIL.

Ghalia Indonesia: Jalan Pramuka Raya 4, Jakarta 13140; tel. (21) 8581814; fax (21) 8564784; f. 1972; children's and general science, textbooks; Man. Dir LUKMAN SAAD.

Gramedia Widyasarana Indonesia: Gramedia Bldg, 3rd Floor, Jalan Palmerah Barat 33–37, Jakarta 10270; tel. (21) 53650110; fax (21) 53698095; internet www.grasindo.co.id; f. 1973; university textbooks, general non-fiction, children's and magazines; Man. JAROT YUDHOPRATOMO.

Gunung Mulia PT: Jalan Kwitang 22–23, Jakarta 10420; tel. (21) 3901208; fax (21) 3901633; e-mail publishing@bpkgm.com; internet www.bpkgm.com; f. 1946; general, children's, Christian; Chair. IWAN ARKADY; Pres. Dir STEPHEN Z. SATYAHADI.

Hidakarya Agung PT: Jalan Percetakan Negara D51, Jakarta Pusat; tel. (21) 4219786; fax (21) 4247128; Dir MAHDIARTI MACHMUD.

Ichtiar: Jalan Majapahit 6, Jakarta Pusat; tel. (21) 3841226; f. 1957; textbooks, law, social sciences, economics; Dir JOHN SEMERU.

Indira PT: Jalan Borobudur 20, Jakarta 10320; tel. (21) 3148868; fax (21) 3921079; f. 1953; general science, general trade and children's; Dir BAMBANG P. WAHYUDI.

Kinta CV: Jalan Kemanggisan Ilir V/110, Pal Merah, Jakarta Barat; tel. (21) 5494751; f. 1950; textbooks, social science, general; Man. Drs MOHAMAD SALEH.

Midas Surya Grafindo PT: Jalan Kesehatan 54, Cijantung, Jakarta 13760; tel. (21) 8400414; fax (21) 8400270; f. 1984; children's; Dir Drs FRANS HENDRAWAN.

Mutiara Sumber Widya PT: Gedung Maya Indah, Jalan Kramat 55C, Jakarta 10450; tel. (21) 3909864; fax (21) 3160313; f. 1951; textbooks, Islamic, social sciences, general and children's; Pres. FADJRAA OEMAR.

Penebar Swadya PT: Jalan Gunung Sahari III/7, Jakarta Pusat; tel. (21) 4204402; fax (21) 4214821; agriculture, animal husbandry, fisheries; Dir Drs ANTHONIUS RIYANTO.

Penerbit Universitas Indonesia: Jalan Salemba Raya 4, Jakarta; tel. (21) 335373; f. 1969; science; Man. S. E. LEGOWO.

Pradnya Paramita PT: Jalan Bunga 8–8A, Matraman, Jakarta 13140; tel. (21) 8504944; fax (21) 8583369; e-mail pradnya@centrin.net.id; f. 1973; children's, general, educational, technical and social science; Pres. Dir KONDAR SINAGA.

Pustaka Antara PT: Jalan Perdagangan 99, Bintaro, Jakarta 12330; tel. (21) 7361711; fax (21) 7351079; e-mail nacelod@indo.net.id; f. 1952; textbooks, political, Islamic, children's and general; Man. Dir AIDA JOESOEF AHMAD.

Pustaka Binaman Pressindo: Jalan Kembang Raya 8, Jakarta Pusat 10030; tel. (21) 2303157; fax (21) 2302051; e-mail pustaka@bit.net.id; f. 1981; management; Dir Ir MAKFUDIN WIRYA ATMAJA.

Pustaka LP3ES Indonesia: Jalan Letjen. S. Parman 81, Jakarta 11420; tel. (21) 5663527; fax (21) 56964691; e-mail puslp3es@indo.net.id; f. 1971; general; Dir M. D. MARUTO.

Pustaka Sinar Harapan PT: Jalan Dewi Sartika 136D, Jakarta 13630; tel. and fax (21) 8006982; internet penerbitsinarharapan.co.id; f. 1981; general science, fiction, comics, children's; Dir W. M. NAIDEN.

Pustaka Utma Grafiti PT: 25 Jalan Kramat VI, Jakarta Pusat 10250; tel. (21) 31903006; fax (21) 31906649; f. 1981; social sciences, humanities and children's books; Dir ZULKIFLY LUBIS.

Rajagrafindo Persada PT: Jalan Pelepah Hijau IV TN-1 14–15, Kelapa Gading Permai, Jakarta 14240; tel. (21) 4520951; fax (21) 4529409; f. 1980; general science and religion; Dir Drs ZUBAIDI.

Rineka Cipta PT: Kompang Perkantoran Mitra Matraman, 148 Jalan Matraman Raya B 1–2, Jakarta; tel. (21) 85918080; fax (21) 85918143; f. 1990; est. by merger of Aksara Baru (f. 1972) and Bina Aksara; general science and university texts; Dir Dr H. SUARDI.

Rosda Jayaputra PT: Jalan Kembang 4, Jakarta 10420; tel. (21) 3904984; fax (21) 3901703; f. 1981; general science; Dir H. ROZALI USMAN.

Sastra Hudaya: Jalan Kalasan 1, Jakarta Pusat; tel. (21) 882321; f. 1967; religious, textbooks, children's and general; Man. ADAM SALEH.

Tintamas Indonesia: Jalan Kramat Raya 60, Jakarta 10420; tel. and fax (21) 3911459; f. 1947; history, modern science and culture, especially Islamic; Man. MARHAMAH DJAMBEK.

Tira Pustaka: Jalan Cemara Raya 1, Kav. 10D, Jaka Permai, Jaka Sampurna, Bekasi 17145; tel. (21) 8841277; fax (21) 8842736; e-mail

Tirapus@cbn.net.id; f. 1977; translations, children's; Dir ROBERT B. WIDJAJA.

Toko Buku Walisongo PT: Gedung Idayu, Jalan Kwitang 13, Jakarta 10420; tel. (21) 3154890; fax (21) 3154889; e-mail edp@tokowalisongo.com; f. 1986; fmrly Masagung Group; general, Islamic, textbooks, science; Pres. H. KETUT ABDURRAHMAN MASAGUNG.

Widjaya: Jalan Pecenongan 48C, Jakarta Pusat; tel. (21) 3813446; f. 1950; textbooks, children's, religious and general; Man. DIDI LUTHAN.

Yasaguna: Jalan Minangkabau 44, POB 422, Jakarta Selatan; tel. (21) 8290422; f. 1964; agricultural, children's, handicrafts; Dir HILMAN MADEWA.

BANDUNG

Alma'arif: Jalan Tamblong 48–50, Bandung; tel. (22) 4207177; fax (22) 4239194; e-mail almaarif@bdg.centrin.net.id; f. 1949; textbooks, religious and general; Man. H. M. BAHARTHAH.

Alumni PT: Jalan Bukit Pakar Timur II/109, Bandung 40197; tel. (22) 2501251; fax (22) 2503044; f. 1968; university and school textbooks; Dir EDDY DAMIAN.

Angkasa: Jalan Kiara Condong 437, Bandung; tel. (22) 7320383; fax (22) 7320373; e-mail akspst@centrin.net.id; Dir H. FACHRI SAID.

Armico: Jalan Madurasa Utara 10, Cigereleng, Bandung 40253; tel. (22) 5202234; fax (22) 5201972; f. 1980; school textbooks; Dir Ir ARSIL TANJUNG.

Citra Aditya Bakti PT: Jalan Geusanulun 17, Bandung 40115; tel. (22) 438251; fax (22) 438635; e-mail cab@citraaditya.com; internet www.citraaditya.com; f. 1985; general science; Dir Ir IWAN TANUATMADJA.

Diponegoro Publishing House: Jalan Mohammad Toha 44–46, Bandung 40252; tel. and fax (22) 5201215; fax (22) 5201815; e-mail dpnegoro@indosat.net.id; internet www.penerbitdiponegoro.com; f. 1963; Islamic, textbooks, fiction, non-fiction, general; Dir HADIDJAH DAHLAN.

Epsilon Group: Jalan Marga Asri 3, Margacinta, Bandung 40287; tel. (22) 7567826; f. 1985; school textbooks; Dir Drs BAHRUDIN.

Eresco PT: Jalan Megger Girang 98, Bandung 40254; tel. (22) 5205985; fax (22) 5205984; f. 1957; scientific and general; Man. Drs ARFAN ROZALI.

Ganeca Exact Bandung: Kawasan Industri MM 2100, Jalan Selayar Kav A5, Bekasi 17520; tel. (22) 89981946; fax (22) 89981947; e-mail presdir@ganeca-exact.com; internet www.ganeca-exact.com; f. 1982; school textbooks; Dir Ir KETUT SUARDHARA LINGGIH.

Mizan Pustaka PT: Jalan Cinambo 135, Bandung 40294; tel. (22) 7834310; fax (22) 7834311; e-mail info@mizan.com; internet www.mizan.com; f. 1983; Islamic and general books; Pres. Dir HAIDAR BAGIR.

Penerbit ITB: Jalan Ganesa 10, Bandung 40132; tel. and fax (22) 2504257; e-mail itbpress@bdg.centrin.net.id; f. 1971; academic books; Dir EMMY SUPARKA; Chief Editor SOFIA MANSOOR-NIKSOLIHIN.

Putra A. Bardin: 3 Jalan Kembar Timur II, Bandung 40254; tel. (22) 5208305; fax (22) 7300879; f. 1998; textbooks, scientific and general; Dir NAI A. BARDIN.

Remaja Rosdakarya PT: Jalan Ibu Inggit Garnasih 40, Bandung 40252; tel. (22) 5200287; fax (22) 5202529; e-mail rosda@indosat.net.id; textbooks and children's fiction; Pres. ROZALI USMAN.

Sarana Panca Karya Nusa PT: Jalan Kopo 633, Km 13/4, Bandung 40014; e-mail spkn641@yahoo.com; f. 1986; general; Dir WIMPY S. IBRAHIM.

Tarsito PT: Jalan Guntur 20, Bandung 40262; tel. (22) 7304915; fax (22) 7314630; academic; Dir T. SITORUS.

FLORES

Nusa Indah: Jalan El Tari, Ende 86318, Nusa Tenggara Timur, Flores; tel. (381) 21502; fax (381) 23974; e-mail namkahu@yahoo.com; f. 1970; religious and general; Dir LUKAS BATMOMOLIN.

KUDUS

Menara Kudus: Jalan Menara 4, Kudus 59315; tel. (291) 437143; fax (291) 436474; f. 1958; Islamic; Man. CHILMAN NAJIB.

MEDAN

Hasmar: Jalan Letjenderal Haryono M. T. 1, POB 446, Medan 20231; tel. (61) 4144581; fax (22) 4533673; f. 1962; primary school textbooks; Dir FAUZI LUBIS; Man. AMRAN SAID RANGKUTI.

Impola: Jalan H. M. Joni 46, Medan 20217; tel. (61) 711415; f. 1984; school textbooks; Dir PAMILANG M. SITUMORANG.

Madju Medan Cipta PT: Jalan Amaliun 37, Medan 20215; tel. (61) 7361990; fax (61) 7367753; e-mail koboi@indosat.net; f. 1950; textbooks, children's and general; Pres. H. MOHAMED ARBIE; Man. Dir Drs DINO IRSAN ARBIE.

Masco: Jalan Sisingamangaraja 191, Medan 20218; tel. (61) 713375; f. 1992; school textbooks; Dir P. M. SITUMORANG.

Monora: Jalan Letjenderal Jamin Ginting 583, Medan 20156; tel. (61) 8212667; fax (61) 8212669; e-mail monora_cv@plasa.com; f. 1962; school textbooks; Dir CHAIRIL ANWAR.

SEMARANG

Aneka Ilmu: Jalan Raya Semarang Demak, Km 8.5, Sayung, Demak; tel. (24) 6580335; fax (24) 6582903; e-mail pemasaran@anekailmu.com; internet www.anekailmu.com; f. 1983; general and school textbooks; Dir H. SUWANTO.

Effhar COY PT: Jalan Dorang 7, Semarang 50173; tel. (24) 3511172; fax (24) 3551540; e-mail dahara@indosat.net.id; f. 1976; general books; Dir H. DARADJAT HARAHAP.

Intan Pariwara: Jalan Ki Hajar Dewantoro, Kotak Pos III, Kotif Klaten, Jawa-Tengah; tel. (272) 322441; fax (272) 322607; e-mail intan@intanpariwara.co.id; internet www.intanpariwara.co.id; school textbooks; Pres. CHRIS HARJANTO.

Mandira PT: Jalan Letjenderal M. T. Haryono 501, Semarang 50241; tel. (24) 8316150; fax (24) 8415092; f. 1962; Dir Ir A. HARIYANTO.

Mandira Jaya Abadi PT: Jalan Kartini 48, Semarang 50241; tel. (24) 3519547; fax (24) 3542189; e-mail mjabadi@indosat.net.id; f. 1981; Dir Ir A. HARIYANTO.

SOLO

Pabelan PT: Jalan Raya Solo, Kertasura, Km 8, Solo 57162; tel. (271) 743975; fax (271) 714775; f. 1983; school textbooks; Dir AGUNG SASONGKO.

Tiga Serangkai Pustaka Mandiri, PT: Jalan Dr Supomo 23, Solo 57141, Central Java; tel. (271) 714344; fax (271) 713607; internet www.tigaserangkai.com; e-mail tspm@tigaserangkai.co.id; f. 1959; school textbooks, general textbooks; Pres. Commr ABDULLAH SITI AMINAH.

SURABAYA

Airlangga University Press: Kampus C, Jalan Mulyorejo, Surabaya 60115; tel. (31) 5992246; fax (31) 5992248; e-mail aupsby@rad.net.id; academic; Dir Dr ISMUDIONO.

Bina Ilmu PT: Jalan Tunjungan 53E, Surabaya 60275; tel. (31) 5323214; fax (31) 5315421; f. 1973; school textbooks, Islamic; Pres. ARIEFIN NOOR.

Bintang: Jalan Potroagung III/41C, Surabaya; tel. (31) 3770687; fax (31) 3715941; school textbooks; Dir AGUS WINARNO.

Grip PT: Jalan Rungkut Permai II/C11, Surabaya; tel. (31) 22564; f. 1958; textbooks and general; Man. SURIPTO.

Jaya Baya: Jalan Embong Malang 69H, POB 250, Surabaya 60001; tel. (31) 41169; f. 1945; religion, philosophy and ethics; Man. TADJIB ERMADI.

Sinar Wijaya: Jalan Raya Sawo VII/58, Bringin-Lakarsantri, Surabaya; tel. (31) 7406616; general; Dir DULRADJAK.

YOGYAKARTA

Andi Publishers: Jalan Beo 38–40, Yogyakarta 55281; tel. (274) 561881; fax (274) 588282; e-mail andi_pub@indo.net.id; f. 1980; Christian, computing, business, management and technical; Dir J. H. GONDOWIJOYO.

BPFE PT: Jalan Gambiran 37, Yogyakarta 55161; tel. (274) 373760; fax (274) 380819; f. 1984; university textbooks; Dir Drs INDRIYO GITOSUDARMO.

Centhini Yayasan: Gedung Bekisar UH V/716 E1, Yogyakarta 55161; tel. (274) 383148; f. 1984; Javanese culture; Chair. H. KARKONO KAMAJAYA.

Gadjah Mada University Press: Jalan Grafika 1, Kampus UGM, Bulaksumur, Yogyakarta 55281; tel. and fax (274) 561037; e-mail gmupress@ugm.ac.id; internet www.gmup.ugm.ac.id; f. 1971; university textbooks; Dir S. MUNANDAR.

Indonesia UP: Gedung Bekisar UH V/716 E1, Yogyakarta 55161; tel. (274) 383148; f. 1950; general science; Dir H. KARKONO KAMAJAYA.

Kanisius Printing and Publishing: Jalan Cempaka 9, Deresan, Yogyakarta 55281; tel. (274) 588783; fax (274) 563349; e-mail office@kanisiusmedia.com; internet www.kanisiusmedia.com; f. 1922; philosophy, children's, textbooks, Christian and general; Pres. Dir AUGUSTINUS SARWANTO.

Kedaulatan Rakyat PT: Jalan P. Mangkubumi 40–42, Yogyakarta; tel. (274) 2163; Dir DRONO HARDJUSUWONGSO.

Penerbit Tiara Wacana Yogya: Jalan Kaliurang, Km 7, 8 Kopen 16, Banteng, Yogyakarta 55581; tel. and fax (274) 880683; f. 1986; university textbooks and general science; Dir SITORESMI PRABUNINGRAT.

Government Publishing House

Balai Pustaka PT (Persero) (State Publishing and Printing House): 1 Jalan Pulokambing, Kav. 15, Kawasan Industri Pulogadung, Jakarta; tel. (21) 4613519; fax (21) 4613520; e-mail humas@balaipustaka.co.id; internet balaipustaka.co.id; history, anthropology, politics, philosophy, medical, arts and literature; Pres. Dir ZAIM UCHROWI.

PUBLISHERS' ASSOCIATION

Ikatan Penerbit Indonesia (IKAPI) (Asscn of Indonesian Book Publishers): Jalan Kalipasir 32, Jakarta Pusat 10330; tel. (21) 31902532; fax (21) 31926124; e-mail sekretariat@ikapi.org; internet www.ikapi.org; f. 1950; 1009 mems (July 2011); Pres. LUYA ANDAM DEWI; Gen. Sec. HUSNI SYAWIE.

Broadcasting and Communications

TELECOMMUNICATIONS

Directorate-General of Posts and Informatics Resources (SDPPI): Gedung Sapta Pesona, Jalan Medan Merdeka Barat 17, Jakarta 10110; tel. (21) 3835955; fax (21) 3860754; e-mail admin@postel.go.id; internet www.postel.go.id; Dir-Gen. MUHAMMAD BUDI SETIAWAN.

PT AXIS Telekom Indonesia (AXIS): Jalan Jenderal Gatot Subroto, Kav. 35–36, Jakarta Selatan 12950; tel. (21) 5760880; fax (21) 5760809; e-mail cs@axisworld.co.id; internet www.axisworld.co.id; f. 2001; cellular telephone network operator; provides GSM 1800 and 3G video services; 80.1% owned by Saudi Telecom Co; Pres. Dir and CEO ERIK AAS.

PT Hutchison CP Telecommunications (HCPT): Wisma Barito Pacific, Tower II, 2nd Floor, Jalan Letjenderal S. Parman, Kav. 62–63, Slipi, Jakarta 11410; tel. (21) 53650000; fax (21) 53660000; internet www.three.co.id; f. 2003; est. as PT Cyber Access Communications; present name adopted 2005; 60% owned by Hutchison Telecom Int. Ltd (Hong Kong), 40% owned by Charoen Pokphand Group (Thailand); cellular telephone network operator providing GSM 1800 and third-generation (3G) video services; CEO LAURENTIUS BULTERS.

PT Indonesian Satellite Corporation Tbk (INDOSAT): Jalan Medan Merdeka Barat 21, POB 2905, Jakarta 10110; tel. (21) 54388888; fax (21) 5449501; e-mail publicrelations@indosat.com; internet www.indosat.com; f. 1967; telecommunications; partially privatized in 1994; 41.94% stake sold to Singapore Technologies Telemedia in 2002; 40.81% share sold to QTEL in 2008; Pres. Dir HARRY SASONGKO TIRTOTJONDRO; Pres. Commr Sheikh ABDULLAH BIN MOHAMMED BIN SAUD AL-THANI.

PT Satelit Palapa Indonesia (SATELINDO): Jalan Daan Mogot Km 11, Jakarta 11710; tel. (21) 5455121; fax (21) 5418548; e-mail palapa-c@satelindo.co.id; internet satelindo.boleh.com; f. 1993; owned by INDOSAT; telecommunications and satellite services; Pres. Dir DJOKO PRAJITNO.

PT SmartFren Telecom Tbk: Jalan H. Agus Salim 45, Sabang, Jakarta Pusat 10340; e-mail customercare@smartfren.com; internet www.smartfren.com; f. 2010 by merger of PT Mobile-8 and PT Smart Telecom; Pres. Dir RUDOLFO PANTOJA.

PT Telekomunikasi Indonesia Tbk (TELKOM): Corporate Office, Jalan Japati 1, Bandung 40133; tel. (22) 2500000; fax (22) 4240313; internet www.telkom.co.id; domestic telecommunications; 24.2% of share capital was transferred to the private sector in 1995; Pres. Commr JUSMAN DJAMAL; Pres. Dir RINALDI FIRMANSYAH.

PT Telekomunikasi Selular (TELKOMSEL): Wisma Mulia, 12th Floor, Jalan Jenderal Gatot Subroto, Kav. 42, Jakarta Selatan 12710; tel. (21) 5240811; fax (21) 52906121; e-mail investor@telkomsel.co.id; internet www.telkomsel.com; f. 1995; provides domestic cellular services with international roaming available through 356 network partners; jt venture between PT Telekomunikasi Indonesia Tbk (65%) and Singapore Telecommunications Ltd (35%); Pres. Commr RINALDI FIRMANSYAH; Pres. Dir SARWOTO ATMOSUTARNO.

PT XL Axiata Tbk (Excelcom): Jalan Mega Kuningan Lot E4-7 1, Kawasan Mega Kuningan, Jakarta 12950; tel. (21) 5761881; fax (21) 5761880; e-mail corpcomm@xl.co.id; internet www.xl.co.id; f. 1996; fixed-line and cellular telephone network provider; Pres. Dir HASNUL SUHAIMI.

BROADCASTING

Regulatory Authority

Komisi Penyiaran Indonesia—KPI (Indonesian Broadcasting Commission): Lantai 6, Jalan Gajah Mada 8, Jakarta 10120; tel. (21) 6340713; fax (21) 6340667; internet www.kpi.go.id; f. 2002; ind. broadcasting regulatory authority; Dir-Gen. DADANG RAHMAT HIDAYAT.

Radio

KBR68H: Jalan Utan Kayu 68H, Jakarta Timur 13120; tel. (21) 8513386; fax (21) 8513002; e-mail redaksi@kbr68h.com; internet www.kbr68h.com; Man. Dir TOSCA SANTOSO.

PT Radio Prambors 102.2 FM: Jalan Adityawarman 71, Kebayoran Baru, Jakarta 12160; tel. (21) 7202238; fax (21) 7222058; e-mail info@pramborsfm.com; internet pramborsfm.com; Gen. Man. JUNAS MIRADIARSYAH.

Radio Republik Indonesia (RRI): Jalan Medan Merdeka Barat 4–5, Jakarta 10110; tel. (21) 3846817; fax (21) 3457134; internet rri.co.id; f. 1945; 49 stations; Pres. Dir ROSARITA NIKEN WIDIASTUTI.

Voice of Indonesia: Jalan Medan Merdeka Barat 4–5, POB 1157, Jakarta; tel. (21) 3456811; fax (21) 3500990; e-mail voi@rri-online.com; internet www.voi.co.id; f. 1945; international service provided by Radio Republik Indonesia; daily broadcasts in Arabic, English, French, German, Bahasa Indonesia, Japanese, Bahasa Malaysia, Mandarin, Spanish and Thai.

Television

In March 1989 Indonesia's first private commercial television station began broadcasting to the Jakarta area. In 2008 there were 10 privately owned television stations in operation.

PT Cakrawala Andalas Televisi (ANTEVE): Gedung Sentra Mulia, 18th Floor, Jalan H. R. Rasuna Said, Kav. X-6 No. 8, Jakarta Selatan 12940; tel. (21) 5222086; fax (21) 5229174; e-mail humas@an.tv; internet www.an.tv; f. 1993; private channel; broadcasting to 10 cities; Pres. Commr ANINDYA N. BAKRIE; Pres. Dir DUDI HENDRAKUSUMA.

MNCTV: Jalan Pintu II—Taman Mini Indonesia Indah, Pondok Gede, Jakarta Timur 13810; tel. (21) 8412473; fax (21) 8412470; e-mail info@tpi.tv; internet www.mnctv.com; f. 1991; private channel funded by commercial advertising.

PT Rajawali Citra Televisi Indonesia (RCTI): Jalan Raya Pejuangan 3, Kebon Jeruk, Jakarta 11000; tel. (21) 5303540; fax (21) 5320906; e-mail webmaster@rcti.tv; internet www.rcti.tv; f. 1989; first private channel; 22-year licence; Pres. Dir HARY TANOESOEDIBJO; Vice-Pres. Commr POSMA LUMBAN TOBING.

PT Surya Citra Televisi (SCTV): SCTV Tower, Senayan City, Jalan Asia Afrika, Lot 19, Jakarta 10270; tel. (21) 27935555; fax (21) 27935444; e-mail stephanus@sctv.co.id; internet www.sctv.co.id; f. 1990; private channel broadcasting nationally; Pres. Dir SUTANTO HARTONO.

Televisi Republik Indonesia (TVRI): TVRI Senayan, Jalan Gerbang Pemuda, Senayan, Jakarta 10270; tel. (21) 5704720; fax (21) 5733122; e-mail daffa2000@tvri.co.id; internet www.tvri.co.id; f. 1962; fmrly state-controlled; became independent in 2003; Pres. Dir Maj.-Gen. (retd) I GDE NYOMAN ARSANA.

Finance

(cap. = capital; p.u. = paid up; res = reserves; dep. = deposits; m. = million; brs = branches; amounts in rupiah)

BANKING

Central Bank

Bank Indonesia (BI): Jalan M. H. Thamrin 2, Jakarta Pusat 10350; tel. (21) 2310108; fax (21) 3501867; e-mail humasbi@bi.go.id; internet www.bi.go.id; f. 1828; nationalized as central bank in 1953; cap. 7,610,885m., res 86,906,362m., dep. 503,825,034m. (Dec. 2009); Gov. DARMIN NASUTION; 42 brs.

State Banks

PT Bank Mandiri (Persero): Plaza Mandiri, Jalan Jenderal Gatot Subroto, Kav. 36–38, Jakarta 12190; tel. (21) 52997777; fax (21) 52997735; internet www.bankmandiri.co.id; f. 1998; est. following merger of four state-owned banks—PT Bank Bumi Daya, PT Bank Dagang Negara, PT Bank Ekspor Impor Indonesia and PT Bank Pembangunan Indonesia; cap. 10,485,058m., res 6,765,078m., dep. 331,268,432m. (Dec. 2009); Chair. EDWIN GERUNGAN; Pres. Dir ZULKIFLI ZAINI; 909 local brs; 6 overseas brs.

PT Bank Negara Indonesia (Persero) Tbk: Jalan Jenderal Sudirman, Kav. 1, Jakarta 10220; tel. (21) 2511946; fax (21)

2511214; e-mail hin@bni.co.id; internet www.bni.co.id; f. 1946; commercial bank; specializes in credits to the industrial sector; cap. 7,789,288m., res 6,691,845m., dep. 194,810,525m. (Dec. 2009); Pres. Commr Ery Riyana Hardjapamekas; Pres. Dir Gatot Mudiantoro Suwondo; 919 local brs, 5 overseas brs.

PT Bank Rakyat Indonesia (Persero): Gedung BRI 1, Jalan Jenderal Sudirman, Kav. 44–46, POB 94, Jakarta 10210; tel. (21) 2510244; fax (21) 2500077; internet www.bri.co.id; f. 1895; present name since 1946; commercial and foreign exchange bank; specializes in agricultural smallholdings and rural devt; cap. 6,164,926m., res 3,257,761m., dep. 265,533,166m. (Dec. 2009); Pres. Commr Bunasor Sanim; Pres. Dir Sofyan Basir; 326 brs.

PT Bank Tabungan Negara (Persero): Menara Bank BTN, 10th Floor, Jalan Gajah Mada 1, Jakarta 10130; tel. (21) 6336789; fax (21) 6336704; e-mail webadmin@btn.co.id; internet www.btn.co.id; f. 1964; commercial bank; state-owned; cap. 4,996,655m., res 104,182m., dep. 41,384,482m. (Dec. 2009); Pres. Commr Zaki Baridwan; Pres. Dir Iqbal Latanro; 44 brs.

PT BPD Jawa Timur (Bank Jatim): Jalan Basuki Rachmad 98–104, Surabaya; tel. (31) 5310090; fax (31) 5470159; e-mail humas@bankjatim.co.id; internet www.bankjatim.co.id; f. 1961; cap. 696,420m., res 846,115m., dep. 14,839,631m. (Dec. 2009); Chair. Chairul Djaelani; Pres. Muljanto.

Indonesia Eximbank: Gedung Bursa Efek, Menara II, Lantai 8, Jalan Jenderal Sudirman, Kav. 52–53, Jakarta 12190; tel. (21) 5154638; fax (21) 5154639; e-mail intbank@indonesiaeximbank.go.id; internet www.indonesiaeximbank.go.id; cap. 4,321,586m., dep. 3,174,994m. (Dec. 2009), res 1,020,746m. (Dec. 2008); fmrly PT Bank Ekspor Indonesia (Persero); Chair. Made Gde Erata; Man. Dir Arifin Indra Sulistyanto.

Commercial Banks

PT Bank ANZ Indonesia: Panin Bank Centre, Ground Floor, Jalan Jenderal Sudirman (Senayan), Kav. 33A, Jakarta 10220; tel. (21) 5750300; fax (21) 5727447; e-mail products@anz.com; internet www.anz.com/indonesia; f. 1990; est. as Westpac Panin Bank; present name adopted 1993; 85% owned by Australia and New Zealand Banking Group Ltd; cap. 50,000m., res 10,000m., dep. 13,002,042m. (Dec. 2009); Pres. Dir Joseph Abraham.

PT Bank Artha Graha Internasional Tbk: Bank Artha Graha Tower, 5th Floor, Jalan Jenderal Sudirman, Kav. 52–53, Jakarta 12190; tel. (21) 5152168; fax (21) 5153470; e-mail agraha@rad.net.id; internet www.arthagraha.com; f. 1967; est. as PT Bank Bandung; merged with PT Bank Arta Pratama in 1999 and with PT Bank Inter-Pacific in 2005; cap. 950,804.4m., res 418,462.2m., dep. 13,142,250.7m. (Dec. 2009); Pres. Dir Andy Kasih; Pres. Commr Kiki Syahnakri; 78 brs.

PT Bank Central Asia Tbk (BCA): Menara BCA, Grand Indonesia, Jalan M. H. Thamrin 1, Jakarta 10310; tel. (21) 23588000; fax (21) 23588300; e-mail halobca@bca.co.id; internet www.klikbca.com; f. 1957; 51% share sold to Farallon Capital Management (USA) in March 2002; cap. 1,540,938m., res 3,728,472m., dep. 248,469,919m. (Dec. 2009); Pres. Commr Eugene Keith Galbraith; Pres. Dir Djohan Emir Setijoso; 760 local brs.

PT Bank Chinatrust Indonesia: Wisma Tamara, Lantai 15–17, Jalan Jenderal Sudirman, Kav. 24, Jakarta 12920; tel. (21) 5207878; fax (21) 5206767; e-mail ctcbjak@rad.net.id; internet www.chinatrust.co.id; f. 1995; cap. 150,000m., dep. 2,976,336m. (Dec. 2009); Pres. Dir Peter Liu; Chair. Jeffrey L. S. Koo.

PT Bank CIMB Niaga Tbk: Graha Niaga, Jalan Jenderal Sudirman, Kav. 58, Jakarta 12190; tel. (21) 2505252; fax (21) 2505205; e-mail 14041@bniaga.co.id; internet www.cimbniaga.com; f. 1955; cap. 1,552,420m., res 5,985,935m., dep. 88,029,672m. (Dec. 2009); Pres. Commr Sri Nazir Razak; Pres. Dir Arwin Rasyid; 227 brs.

PT Bank Danamon Indonesia Tbk: Menara Danamon, Jalan Prof. Dr Satrio 6, Kav. E-4, Mega Kuningan, Jakarta 12930; tel. (21) 34358888; fax (21) 34358800; e-mail danamon.access@danamon.co.id; internet www.danamon.co.id; f. 1956; placed under supervision of Indonesian Bank Restructuring Agency in April 1998; merged with PT Bank Tiara Asia, PT Tamara Bank, PT Bank Duta and PT Bank Nusa Nasional in 2000; 51% share sold to consortium led by Singapore's Temasek Holdings in May 2003; cap. 5,303,992m., res 2,760,125m., dep. 75,528,733m. (Dec. 2009); Pres. Commr Ng Kee Choe; Pres. Dir Henry Ho Hon Cheong; 483 brs.

PT Bank ICB Bumiputera Tbk: Menara ICB Bumiputera, Jalan Probolinggo 18, Menteng, Jakarta Pusat 10350; tel. (21) 3919898; fax (21) 3919797; e-mail bank@icbbumiputera.co.id; internet www.icbbumiputera.co.id; f. 1989; cap. 500,000m., res 3,469m., dep. 6,323,738m. (Dec. 2009); Pres. Commr Dato Mat Amir bin Jaffar; Pres. Dir Sridhar Natarajan.

PT Bank Internasional Indonesia Tbk (BII): Plaza BII, Menara I, Lantai 8, Jalan M. H. Thamrin 51, Kav. 22, Jakarta 10350; tel. (21) 2300666; fax (21) 31934609; e-mail cs@bii.co.id; internet www.bii.co.id; cap. 3,226,706m., res 224,705m., dep. 51,190,708m. (Dec. 2009); Pres. Commr Tan Sri Dato' Megat Zaharuddin bin Megat Mohammad Nor; Pres. Dir Ridha Wirakusumah; 246 local brs; 3 overseas brs.

PT Bank KEB Indonesia: Wisma GKBI, Lantai 20, Suite 2002, Jalan Jenderal Sudirman, Kav. 28, Selatan, Jakarta; tel. (21) 5741030; fax (21) 5741031; e-mail contact.center@kebi.co.id; internet www.kebi.co.id; owned by KEB Seoul (99%) and PT Clemont Finance Indonesia (1%); f. 1990; fmrly PT Korea Exchange Bank Danamon; cap. 150,000m., dep. 2,519,337.1m. (Dec. 2009); Pres. Dir Cho Yong Woo; Chair. Ho Sun Yun.

PT Bank Mayapada Internasional Tbk: Menara Mayapada, Jalan Jenderal Sudirman, Kav. 28, Jakarta 12920; tel. (21) 5212288; fax (21) 5211985; e-mail mayapada@bankmayapada.com; internet www.bankmayapada.com; f. 1989; cap. 412,956m., res 453,884m., dep. 6,571,318m. (Dec. 2009); Chair. Dr Tahir; Pres. Dir Hariyono Tjahjarijadi; 41 brs.

PT Bank Mizuho Indonesia: Plaza B11, Lantai 24, Menara 2, Jalan M. H. Thamrin 51, Jakarta 10350; tel. (21) 3925222; fax (21) 3926354; f. 1989; fmrly PT Bank Fuji International Indonesia; name changed as above in 2001; cap. 323,574m., res 117,654m., dep. 8,244,996m. (Dec. 2009); Pres. Dir Jiro Totsu.

PT Bank Muamalat Indonesia (BMI): Gedung Arthaloka, Jalan Jenderal Sudirman 2, Jakarta 10220; tel. (21) 2511414; fax (21) 2511453; internet www.muamalatbank.com; Indonesia's first Islamic bank; cap. 492.7m., res 132.4m., dep. 14,678.4m. (Dec. 2009); Pres. Dir Ir Arviyan Arifin; Pres. Commr Widigdo Sukarman.

PT Bank Mutiara Tbk: Gedung Sentral Senayan II, 22nd Floor, Jalan Asia Afrika 8, Jakarta 10270; tel. (21) 5724180; fax (21) 5724443; e-mail corsec@mutiarabank.co.id; internet www.mutiarabank.co.id; f. 1989 as PT Bank Century Tbk; renamed as above in 2009; Pres. Commr Pontas Riyanto Siahaan; Pres. Dir Maryono.

PT Bank OCBC NISP Tbk: Menara Bank OCBC NISP, Jalan Prof. Dr Satrio, Kav. 25, Jakarta 12940; tel. (21) 25533888; fax (21) 57944000; internet www.ocbcnisp.com; f. 1941; 81.9% owned by OCBC Bank, Singapore; cap. 726,822m., res 1,215,727m., dep. 30,875,568m. (Dec. 2009); Pres. Commr Pramukti Surjaudaja; Pres. Dir Parwati Surjaudaja; 168 brs.

PT Bank Permata Tbk: Menara PermataBank I, Lantai 17, Jalan Jenderal Sudirman, Kav. 27, Jakarta 12920; tel. (21) 5237899; fax (21) 5237253; e-mail isaptono@permatabank.co.id; internet www.permatabank.com; f. 1954; est. as Bank Persatuan Dagang Indonesia; became PT Bank Bali in 1971 and PT Bank Bali Tbk in 1990; name changed as above Sept. 2002 following merger with PT Bank Prima Express, PT Bank Universal Tbk, PT Arthamedia Bank and PT Bank Patriot; cap. 7,127,512m., res 26m., dep. 46,394,206m. (Dec. 2009); Pres. Commr Raymond Ferguson; Pres. Dir David Martin Fletcher; 288 brs.

PT Bank Rabobank International Indonesia: Plaza 89, Lantai 9, Jalan H. R. Rasuna Said, Kav. X-7 No. 6, Jakarta 12940; tel. (21) 2520876; fax (21) 2520875; e-mail indonesia@rabobank.com; internet www.rabobank.co.id; f. 1990; est. as PT Rabobank Duta Indonesia; name changed as above in 2001 when Rabobank Nederland secured sole ownership; cap. 715,000m., res 2,741m., dep. 8,910,657m. (Dec. 2009); Pres. Commr Jan Alexander Pruijs; Pres. Dir Henk Mulder.

PT Bank Sumitomo Mitsui Indonesia: Gedung Summitmas II, Lantai 10, Jalan Jenderal Sudirman, Kav. 61–62, Jakarta 12190; tel. (21) 5227011; fax (21) 5227022; f. 1989; fmrly PT Bank Sumitomo Indonesia; merged with PT Bank Sakura Swadharma in April 2001; cap. 1,502,441m., res –521,365m., dep. 7,906,763.5m. (Dec. 2009); Pres. Commr Masayuki Shimura; Pres. Dir Shuji Fujikawa; 1 br.

PT Bank UOB Buana: UOB Plaza, Jalan M. H. Thamrin 10, Jakarta 10230; tel. (21) 23506000; fax (21) 29936632; e-mail cst.comm@uobbuana.com; internet www.uobbuana.com; f. 1956; fmrly PT Bank Buana Indonesia Tbk; cap. 1,663,339m., res 862,896m., dep. 17,285,563m. (Dec. 2009); Pres. Commr Wee Cho Yaw; Pres. Dir Armand B. Arief; 32 brs.

PT Pan Indonesia Tbk (Panin Bank): Panin Bank Centre, Lantai 11, Jalan Jenderal Sudirman, Kav. 1, Senayan, Jakarta 10270; tel. (21) 2700545; fax (21) 2700340; e-mail panin@panin.co.id; internet www.panin.co.id; f. 1971; est. as a result of the merger of three private national banks; cap. 2,408,765m., res 3,570,446m., dep. 59,168,198m. (Dec. 2009); Pres. Commr Johnny N. Wiraatmadja; Pres. Dir Drs H. Rostian Sjamsudin; 250 local brs, 2 overseas brs.

PT Woori Bank Indonesia: Jakarta Stock Exchange Bldg, Lantai 16, Jalan Jenderal Sudirman, Kav. 52–53, Jakarta 12190; tel. (21) 5151919; fax (21) 5151477; e-mail indonesia@wooribank.com; internet id.wooribank.com; fmrly PT Hanvit Bank Indonesia; cap. 170,000m., dep. 2,395,013m. (Dec. 2008); Pres. Cheul Su Kim.

Banking Association

The Association of Indonesian National Private Commercial Banks (Perhimpunan Bank-Bank Umum Nasional Swasta—PERBANAS): Griya Perbanas, Lantai 1, Jalan Perbanas, Karet Kuningan, Setiabudi, Jakarta 12940; tel. (21) 5223038; fax (21) 5223037; e-mail sekretariat@perbanas.org; internet www.perbanas.org; f. 1952; 78 mems; Chair. SIGIT PRAMONO; Sec.-Gen. FARID RAHMAN.

STOCK EXCHANGE

Indonesia Stock Exchange (IDX): Indonesia Stock Exchange Bldg, Menara 1, Jalan Jenderal Sudirman, Kav. 52–53, Jakarta 12190; tel. (21) 5150515; fax (21) 5150330; e-mail callcenter@idx.co.id; internet www.idx.co.id; fmrly Jakarta Stock Exchange; name changed as above upon merger with Surabaya Stock Exchange in 2007; 128 securities houses constitute the members and the shareholders of the exchange, each company owning one share; Pres. Dir ITO WARSITO.

Regulatory Authority

Badan Pengawas Pasar Modal (BAPEPAM) (Capital Market Supervisory Agency): Gedung Sumitro Djojohadikusumo, Jalan Lapangan Banteng Timur 1–4, Jakarta 10710; tel. (21) 3858001; fax (21) 3857917; e-mail bapepam@bapepam.go.id; internet www.bapepam.go.id; Chair. A. FAUD RAHMANY; Exec. Sec. NGALIM SAWEGA.

INSURANCE

In August 2006 there were 157 insurance companies, including 97 non-life companies, 51 life companies, four reinsurance companies and two social insurance companies.

Insurance Supervisory Authority of Indonesia: Directorate of Financial Institutions, Jalan Dr Wahidin, Jakarta 10710; tel. (21) 3451210; fax (21) 3849504; wing of the Ministry of Finance and State Enterprises Devt; Dir H. FIRDAUS DJAELANI.

Selected Life Insurance Companies

PT AIA Financial: Menara Matahari, Lantai 8, Jalan Bulevar Palem Raya 7, Lippo Karawaci 1200, Tangerang 15811; tel. (21) 54218777; fax (21) 5475409; e-mail id.customer@aia.com; internet www.aia-financial.co.id; f. 1983; CEO and Pres. Dir PETER J. CREWE.

PT Asuransi Allianz Life Indonesia: Gedung Summitmas II, Lantai 1, Jalan Jenderal Sudirman, Kav. 61–62, Jakarta 12190; tel. (21) 25989999; fax (21) 30003400; e-mail contactus@allianz.co.id; internet www.allianz.co.id; f. 1996; CEO JOACHIM WESSLING.

Asuransi Jiwa Bersama Bumiputera 1912: Wisma Bumiputera, Lantai 18–21, Jalan Jenderal Sudirman, Kav. 75, Jakarta 12910; tel. (21) 2512154; fax (21) 2512172; e-mail bp1912@bumiputera.com; internet www.bumiputera.com; Chair. Dr H. SUGIHARTO; Pres. Dir DIRMAN PARDOSI.

PT Asuransi Jiwa Central Asia Raya: Blue Dot Center, Blok A–C, Jalan Gelong Baru Utara 5–8, Jakarta Barat 11440; tel. (21) 56961929; fax (21) 56961939; e-mail lancar@car.co.id; internet www.car.co.id; Chair. SOEDONO SALIM.

PT Asuransi Jiwa 'Panin Putra': Jalan Pintu Besar Selatan 52A, Jakarta 11110; tel. (21) 672586; fax (21) 676354; f. 1974; Pres. Dir SUJONO SOEPENO; Chair. NUGROHO TJOKROWIRONO.

PT Asuransi Jiwasraya (Persero): Jalan H. Juanda 34, Jakarta 10120; tel. (21) 3444444; fax (21) 3862344; e-mail asuransi@jiwasraya.co.id; internet www.jiwasraya.co.id; f. 1959; Pres. Commr DJONNY WIGUNA; Pres. Dir HENDRISMAN RAHIM.

PT Asuransi Panin Life: Panin Life Center, Lantai 6, Jalan Letjenderal S. Parman, Kav. 91, Jakarta 11420; tel. (21) 25566888; fax (21) 25566711; e-mail customer@paninlife.co.id; internet www.paninlife.co.id; Pres. Dir HERU YUWONO.

Bumi Asih Jaya Life Insurance Co Ltd: Jalan Matraman Raya 165–167, Jakarta 13140; tel. (21) 2800700; fax (21) 8509669; e-mail baj@bajlife.com; internet www.bajlife.co.id; f. 1967; Chair. P. SITOMPUL; Pres. VIRGO HUTAGALUNG.

Selected Non-Life Insurance Companies

PT Asuransi Bina Dana Arta Tbk: Plaza ABDA, Lantai 27, Jalan Jenderal Sudirman, Kav. 59, Jakarta 122190; tel. (21) 51401688; fax (21) 51401698; e-mail contactus@abdainsurance.co.id; internet www.abdainsurance.co.id; Pres. Commr TJAN SOEN ENG; Pres. Dir CANDRA GUNAWAN.

PT Asuransi Bintang Tbk: Jalan R. S. Fatmawati 32, Jakarta Selatan 12430; tel. (21) 75902777; fax (21) 7656287; e-mail bintang@asuransibintang.com; internet www.asuransibintang.com; f. 1955; general insurance; Pres. Commr SHANTI POESPOSOETJIPTO; Pres. Dir ZAFAR DINESH IDHAM.

PT Asuransi Buana Independen: Jalan Pintu Besar Selatan 78, Jakarta 11110; tel. (21) 6266286; fax (21) 6263005; e-mail headoffice@buanaindependent.co.id; internet buanaindependent.co.id; Pres. Commr ISHAK SUMARNO; Pres. Dir MADE MARKA.

PT Asuransi Central Asia: Wisma Asia, Lantai 12–15, Jalan Letjenderal S. Parman, Kav. 79, Slipi, Jakarta Barat 11420; tel. (21) 56998288; fax (21) 5638029; e-mail info@aca.co.id; internet www.aca.co.id; Pres. Commr ANTHONY SALIM; Pres. Dir TEDDY HAILAMSAH.

PT Asuransi Dayin Mitra: Jalan Raden Saleh Raya, Kav. 1B–1D, Jakarta 10430; tel. (21) 3153577; fax (21) 3912902; e-mail nuning@dayinmitra.co.id; internet www.dayinmitra.co.id; f. 1982; general insurance; Man. Dir LARSOEN HAKER.

PT Asuransi Indrapura: Menara Chase Plaza, Lantai 4, Jalan Jenderal Sudirman, Kav. 21, Jakarta 12920; tel. (21) 5200338; fax (21) 5200175; e-mail insure@indrapura.co.id; internet www.indrapura.co.id; f. 1954; Pres. Commr A. WAHYUHADI; Pres. Dir MINTARTO HALIM.

PT Asuransi Jasa Indonesia: Jalan Letjenderal M. T. Haryono, Kav. 61, Jakarta 12041; tel. (21) 7994508; fax (21) 7995364; e-mail jasindo@jasindo.co.id; internet www.jasindo.co.id; Pres. Commr MOELYADI; Pres. Dir Drs EKO BUDIWIYONO.

PT Asuransi Jasa Tania: Wisma Jasa Tania, Jalan Teuku Cik Ditiro 14, Jakarta 10350; tel. (21) 3101850; fax (21) 31923089; e-mail ajstania@jasatania.co.id; internet www.jasatania.co.id; Pres. Dir BASRAN DAMANIK (acting).

PT Asuransi Maipark Indonesia: Gedung Setiabudi Atrium, Lantai 4, Suite 408, Jalan H. R. Rasuna Said, Kav. 62, Jakarta 12920; tel. (21) 5210803; fax (21) 5210738; e-mail maipark@maipark.com; internet www.maipark.com; fmrly PT Maskapai Asuransi Indonesia; Chair. and CEO KORNELIUS SIMANJUNTAK.

PT Asuransi Parolamas: Komplek Golden Plaza, Blok G 39–42, Jalan R. S. Farmawati 15, Jakarta 12420; tel. (21) 7508983; fax (21) 7506339; internet www.parolamas.co.id; Chief Commr TJUT ROEKMA RAFFLI; Pres. Dir Drs SYARIFUDDIN HARAHAP.

PT Asuransi Ramayana: Jalan Kebon Sirih 49, Jakarta 10340; tel. (21) 31937148; fax (21) 31934825; e-mail info@ramayanains.com; internet ramayanainsurance.com; f. 1965; Pres. Commr A. WINOTO DOERIAT; Pres. Dir SYAHRIL.

PT Asuransi Tri Pakarta: Jalan Paletehan I/18, Jakarta 12160; tel. (21) 711850; fax (21) 7394748; internet www.tripakarta.co.id; Chair. SAIFUDIEN HASAN; Pres. TEDDY PUSPITO.

PT Asuransi Wahana Tata: Jalan H. R. Rasuna Said, Kav. C-4, Jakarta 12920; tel. (21) 5203145; fax (21) 5203149; e-mail aswata@aswata.co.id; internet www.aswata.co.id; Chair. RUDY WANANDI; Pres. Dir CHRISTIAN WANANDI.

PT Berdikari Insurance: Jalan Merdeka Barat 1, Jakarta 10110; tel. (21) 3440266; fax (21) 3440586; e-mail ho@berdikariinsurance.com; internet www.berdikariinsurance.com; Pres. ANGGIAT ISIDORUS SITOHANG.

PT Tugu Pratama Indonesia: Wisma Tugu I, Jalan H. R. Rasuna Said, Kav. C8–9, Kuningan, Jakarta Selatan 12920; tel. (21) 52961777; fax (21) 52961555; e-mail tpi@tugu.com; internet www.tugu.com; f. 1981; general insurance; Pres. Commr FEREDERICK SIAHAAN; Pres. Dir EVITA M. TAGOR.

Joint Ventures

PT Asuransi AIG Life: Matahari AIG Lippo Cyber Tower, 5th–7th Floors, Jalan Bulevar Palem Raya 7, Lippo Karawaci 1200, Tangerang 15811; tel. (21) 54218888; fax (21) 5475415; e-mail service@aig-life.co.id; internet www.aig-life.co.id; jt venture between American International Group, Inc, and PT Asuransi Lippo Life; life insurance; Dep. Pres. Dir S. BUDISUHARTO.

PT Asuransi Allianz Utama Indonesia: Gedung Summitmas II, 9th Floor, Jalan Jenderal Sudirman, Kav. 61–62, Jakarta Selatan 12190; tel. (21) 2522470; fax (21) 2523246; e-mail general@allianz.co.id; internet www.allianz.co.id; f. 1989; non-life insurance; Chair. EDI SUBEKTI; Pres. Dir VOLKER MISS.

PT Asuransi Jiwa Manulife Indonesia: Menara Selatan, Lantai 3, Jalan Jenderal Sudirman, Kav. 45, Jakarta 12930; tel. (21) 25557788; fax (21) 25557799; e-mail communication_id@manulife.com; internet www.manulife-indonesia.com; f. 1985; life insurance; Pres. Dir ALAN MERTEN.

PT Asuransi Jiwa Sinarmas: Wisma EKA Jiwa, Lantai 8, Jalan Mangga Dua Raya, Jakarta 10730; tel. (21) 6257808; fax (21) 6257837; e-mail cs@sinarmaslife.co.id; internet www.sinarmaslife.com; fmrly PT Asuransi Jiwa EKA Life; Pres. Commr INDRA WIDJAJA; Pres. Dir IVENA WIDJAJA.

PT Asuransi MSIG Indonesia: Gedung Summitmas II, Lantai 15, Jalan Jenderal Sudirman, Kav. 61–62, Jakarta 12190; tel. (21) 2523110; fax (21) 2524307; e-mail msig@id.msig-asia.com; internet www.msig.co.id; f. 1975; est. as PT Asuransi Mitsui Marine Indonesia; name changed to PT Asuransi Mitsui Sumitomo Indonesia in 2003, following merger with PT Asuransi Sumitomo

Marine and Pool; present name adopted 2007; Chair. RUDY WANANDI; Pres. Dir TADASHI MAEKAWA.

PT Asuransi Tokio Marine Indonesia: Sentral Senayan I, Lantai 4, Jalan Asia Afrika 8, Jakarta 10270; tel. (21) 5725772; fax (21) 5724005; e-mail cp@tokiomarine.co.id; internet www.tokiomarine.co .id; jt venture between Tokio Marine Asia Pte Ltd and PT Asuransi Jasa Indonesia; Pres. Dir MITSUTAKA SATO.

PT Chartis Insurance Indonesia: The Indonesia Stock Exchange Bldg, Menara II, Lantai 3A, Jalan Jenderal Sudirman, Kav. 52–53, Jakarta 12190; tel. (21) 52914888; fax (21) 52914889; e-mail contact .us@chartisinsurance.com; internet www.chartisinsurance.co.id; f. 1970; fmrly PT Asuransi AIU Indonesia; Pres. Dir MICHAEL BLAKEWAY.

Insurance Associations

Asosiasi Asuransi Jiwa Indonesia (Indonesia Life Insurance Association): The Plaza Office Tower, Lantai 19, Jalan M. H. Thamrin, Kav. 28–30, Jakarta 10350; tel. (21) 29922929; fax (21) 29922828; e-mail aaji.info@aaji.or.id; internet www.aaji.or.id; f. 2002; 49 mems; Chair. EVELINA PEITRUSCKHA; Exec. Dir STEPHEN JUWONO.

Asosiasi Asuransi Umum Indonesia (General Insurance Association of Indonesia): Jalan Majapahit 34, Blok V-29, Jakarta 10160; tel. (21) 3454387; fax (21) 3454307; e-mail secretary@aaui.or.id; f. 1957; est. as Dewan Asuransi Indonesia (Insurance Council of Indonesia); present name adopted 2003; Chair. KORNELIUS SIMANJUNTAK; Exec. Dir FRANS WIYONO.

Trade and Industry

GOVERNMENT AGENCIES

Badan Pelaksana Kegiatan Usaha Hulu Minyak dan Gas Bumi (BP Migas): Gedung Wisma Mulia, Lantai 22, 42 Jalan Gatot Subroto, Jakarta 12710; tel. (21) 29241607; fax (21) 29249999; e-mail humas@bpmigas.go.id; internet www.bpmigas.go.id; f. 2002; regulates upstream petroleum and natural gas industry; Chair. R. PRIYONO.

Badan Pengatur Hilir Minyak dan Gas Bumi (BPH Migas): Gedung BPH Migas, Jalan Captain P. Tendean 28, Jakarta Selatan 12710; tel. (21) 5255500; fax (21) 5223210; e-mail humas@bphmigas .go.id; internet www.bphmigas.go.id; f. 2002; regulates downstream petroleum and gas industry; Chair. TUBAGUS HARYONO.

Badan Pengembangan Industri Strategis (BPIS) (Agency for Strategic Industries): Gedung Arthaloka, 3rd Floor, Jalan Jenderal Sudirman 2, Jakarta 10220; tel. (21) 5705335; fax (21) 3292516; f. 1989; co-ordinates production of capital goods.

Badan Pengkajian dan Penerapan Teknologi (BPPT) (Agency for the Assessment and Application of Technology): Jalan M. H. Thamrin 8, Jakarta 10340; tel. (21) 3168200; fax (21) 3904573; e-mail humas@bppt.go.id; internet www.bppt.go.id; Chair. Dr Ir MARZAN A. ISKANDAR.

Badan Tenaga Nuklir Nasional (BATAN) (National Nuclear Energy Agency): Jalan Kuningan Barat, Mampang Prapatan, Jakarta 12710; tel. (21) 5251109; fax (21) 5251110; e-mail humas@ batan.go.id; internet www.batan.go.id; Chair. Dr SOEDYARTOMO.

Badan Urusan Logistik (BULOG) (National Logistics Agency): Jalan Jenderal Gatot Subroto, Kav. 49, Jakarta 12950; tel. and fax (21) 5256482; e-mail redaksiweb@bulog.co.id; internet www.bulog.co .id; Dir-Gen. SUTARTO ALIMOESO.

National Agency for Export Development (NAFED): Jalan M. I. Ridwan Rais 5, 3rd Floor, Jakarta 10110; tel. (21) 3858171; fax (21) 23528662; e-mail nafed@nafed.go.id; internet www.nafed.go .id; Chair. HESTI INDAH KRESNARINI.

National Economic Council: Jakarta; f. 1999; 13-mem. council formed to advise the President on economic policy; Chair. EMIL SALIM; Sec.-Gen. Sri MULYANI INDRAWATI.

DEVELOPMENT ORGANIZATIONS

Badan Koordinasi Penanaman Modal (BKPM) (Investment Co-ordinating Board): Jalan Jenderal Gatot Subroto 44, POB 3186, Jakarta 12190; tel. (21) 52921334; fax (21) 5264211; e-mail info@ bkpm.go.id; internet www.bkpm.go.id; f. 1976; Chair. GITA IRAWAN WIRJAWAN.

Badan Perencanaan Pembangunan Nasional (Bappenas) (National Development Planning Board): Jalan Taman Suropati 2, Jakarta 10310; tel. (21) 3905650; fax (21) 3145374; e-mail admin@ bappenas.go.id; internet www.bappenas.go.id; formulates Indonesia's economic devt plans; Chair. Dr ARMIDA ALISJAHBANA.

CHAMBER OF COMMERCE

Kamar Dagang dan Industri Indonesia (KADIN) (Indonesian Chamber of Commerce and Industry): Menara Kadin Indonesia, Lantai 29, Jalan H. R. Rasuna Said X5, Kav. 2–3, Jakarta 12950; tel. (21) 5274484; fax (21) 5274331; e-mail kadin@kadin-indonesia.or.id; internet www.kadin-indonesia.or.id; f. 1968; 33 provincial-level chambers and 442 district-level chambers; Chair. SURYO BAMBANG SULISTO; Exec. Dir Drs RAHARDJO JAMTOMO.

INDUSTRIAL AND TRADE ASSOCIATIONS

Association of Indonesian Automotive Industries (GAIKINDO): Jalan Hos Cokroaminoto 6, Jakarta Pusat 10350; tel. (21) 3157178; fax (21) 3142100; e-mail gaikindo@cbn.net.id; internet www.gaikindo.org; Chair. BAMBANG TRISULO.

Association of Indonesian Beverage Industries (ASRIM): 8/F, Wisma GKBI, Jalan Jenderal Sudirman 28, Jakarta 10210; tel. (21) 5723838; fax (21) 5740817; e-mail sekertariat.asrim@gmail.com; 22 mems; Chair. WILLY SIDHARTA; Sec.-Gen. SUROSO NATAKUSUMA.

Association of Indonesian Coffee Exporters (AIKE): Gedung AIKE, Lantai 3, Jalan R. P. Soeroso 20, Jakarta 10350; tel. (21) 3106765; fax (21) 3144115; e-mail bphaeki@yahoo.com; 800 mems; Chair. HASSAN WIDJAYA; Sec.-Gen. RACHIM KARTABRATA.

Association of State-Owned Companies: CTC Bldg, Jalan Kramat Raya 94–96, Jakarta; tel. (21) 346071; co-ordinates the activities of state-owned enterprises; Pres. ODANG.

BANI Arbitration Center (BANI): Wahana Graha, Lantai 2, Jalan Mampang Prapatan 2, Jakarta 12760; tel. (21) 7940542; fax (21) 7940543; e-mail bani-arb@indo.net.id; internet www.bani-arb .org; f. 1977; resolves business disputes; Chair. Prof. Dr H. PRIYATNA ABDURRASYID; Sec.-Gen. N. KRISNAWENDA.

Electric and Electronic Appliance Manufacturers' Association: Jalan Pangeran, Blok 20A-1D, Jakarta; tel. (21) 6480059.

Importers' Association of Indonesia (GINSI): Wisma Kosgoro Bldg, 8th Floor, Jalan M. H. Thamrin 53, Jakarta 10350; tel. (21) 39832510; fax (21) 39832540; f. 1956; 2,921 mems (1996); Chair. AMIRUDIN SAUD; Sec.-Gen. DEDDY BINTANG.

Indonesia National Shippers' Council (INSC): Jalan Cempaka Putih, Barat 6, Jakarta Pusat 10520; tel. (21) 4254677; fax (21) 4206303; e-mail depalindo@yahoo.com; Chair. SUARDI ZEN; Sec.-Gen. RACHIM KARTABRATA.

Indonesian Cement Association (ICA): Graha Irama Bldg, Lantai 11, Suite 11G, Jalan H. R. Rasuna Said, Blok X-1, Kav. 1–2, Jakarta Selatan 12950; tel. (21) 5261105; fax (21) 5261108; e-mail info@asi.or.id; internet www.asi.or.id; f. 1969; Chair. URIP TIMURYONO.

Indonesian Coal Mining Association (APBI-ICMA): Menara Kuningan, Lantai 1, Jalan H. R. Rasuna Said, Blok X-7, Kav. 5, Jakarta 12940; tel. (21) 30015935; fax (21) 30015936; e-mail apbi-icma@indo.net.id; internet www.apbi-icma.com; 109 mems; Chair. BOB KAMANDANU; Exec. Dir SUPRIATNA SUHALA.

Indonesian Cocoa Association (ASKINDO): Jalan Pungkur 115, Bandung 40262; tel. (22) 4262235; fax (22) 4214084; e-mail info@ askindo.or.id; internet www.askindo.or.id; Chair. ZULHEFI SIKUMBANG.

Indonesian Exporters' Federation: Menara Sudirman, 8th Floor, Jalan Jenderal Sudirman, Kav. 60, Jakarta 12190; tel. (21) 5226522; fax (21) 5203303; Chair. HAMID IBRAHIM GANIE.

Indonesian Food and Beverages Association (GAPMMI): Kantor Pusat Departemen Pertanian, Ground Floor, Lot 2, Jalan Harsono, Rm 3, 224A Ragunan, Pasarminggu, Jakarta 12550; tel. (21) 70322627; fax (21) 7804347; e-mail gapmmi@cbn.net.id; internet www.gapmmi.or.id; f. 1976; 260 mems; Chair. ADHI SISWAJA LUKMAN.

Indonesian Footwear Association (APRISINDO): Gedung Adis Dimension Footwear, Jalan Tanah Abang III/18, Jakarta Pusat 10160; tel. (21) 3447575; fax (21) 3447572; e-mail aprisindo@vision .net.id; internet www.aprisindo.info; 95 mems; Chair. EDDY WIJANARKO; Sec.-Gen. YUDHI KOMARUDIN.

Indonesian Furniture Industry and Handicraft Association (ASMINDO): Jalan Pegambiran 5A, 3rd Floor, Rawamangun Jakarta 13220; tel. (21) 47864028; fax (21) 47864031; e-mail asmindo@indo.net.id; Chair. AMBAR TJAHYONO; Sec.-Gen. TANANGGA KARIM.

Indonesian Nutmeg Exporters' Association: c/o PT Berdirari (Persero) Trading Division, Jalan Yos Sudarso 1, Jakarta; tel. (21) 4301625; e-mail bnuina@indosat.net.id.

Indonesian Palm Oil Producers' Association (GAPKI): Sudirman Park Rukan, Blok B, Jalan K. H. Mas Mansyur 18, Kav. 35, Jakarta 10220; tel. (21) 57943871; fax (21) 57943872; internet www .gapki.or.id; Chair. JOEFLY J. BAHROENY.

Indonesian Precious Metals Association: Galva Bldg, 5th Floor, Jakarta Pusat, Jakarta 10120; tel. (21) 3451202; fax (21) 3812713.

Indonesian Pulp and Paper Association: Jalan Cimandiri 6, Flat I/2, Jakarta 10330; tel. (21) 326084; fax (21) 3140168; Chair. M. MANSUR.

Indonesian Tea Association (ATI): Jalan Polombangkeng 15, Kebayoran Baru, Jakarta; tel. (21) 7260772; fax (21) 7205810; e-mail insyaf@hotmail.com; internet www.indotea.org; Chair. SUGIAT; Gen. Sec. ATIK DHARMADI.

Indonesian Textile Association (API): Panin Bank Centre, 3rd Floor, Jalan Jenderal Sudirman 1, Jakarta Pusat 10270; tel. (21) 7396094; fax (21) 7396341; f. 1974; Sec.-Gen. DANANG D. JOEDONAGORO.

Indonesian Tobacco Association: Jalan H. Agus Salim 85, Jakarta 10350; tel. (21) 3140627; fax (21) 325181; Pres. H. A. ISMAIL.

Masyarakat Perhutanan Indonesia (MPI) (Indonesian Forestry Community): Gedung Manggala Wanabakti, 9th Floor, Wing B, Blok IV, Jalan Jenderal Gatot Subroto, Jakarta Pusat 10270; tel. (21) 5733010; fax (21) 5732564; f. 1974; nine mems; Pres. M. HASAN.

Rubber Association of Indonesia (Gapkindo): Jalan Cideng Barat 62A, Jakarta 10150; tel. (21) 3501510; fax (21) 3500368; e-mail karetind@indosat.net.id; internet www.gapkindo.org; 161 mems; Chair. Drs H. ASRIL SUTAN AMIR; Exec. Dir SUHARTO HONGGOKUSUMO.

UTILITIES

Electricity

PT Perusahaan Listrik Negara (Persero) (PLN): Jalan Trunojoyo, Blok M1/135, Kebayoran Baru, Jakarta Selatan 12160; tel. (21) 7251234; fax (21) 7204929; e-mail kontakkami@pln.co.id; internet www.pln.co.id; state-owned electricity co; Pres. Dir NUR PAMUDJI.

Gas

PT Perusahaan Pertambangan Minyak dan Gas Bumi Negara (PERTAMINA): Jalan Medan Merdeka Timur 1A, Jakarta 10110; tel. (21) 3815111; fax (21) 3843882; e-mail wpurnama@pertamina.com; internet www.pertamina.com; f. 1968; state-owned petroleum and natural gas mining enterprise; Pres. Dir and CEO KAREN AUGUSTIAWAN.

Perusahaan Gas Negara (PGN) (Public Gas Corporation): Jalan K. H. Zainul Arifin 20, Jakarta 11140; tel. (21) 6334838; fax (21) 6333080; e-mail contact.center@pgn.co.id; internet www.pgn.co.id; monopoly of domestic gas distribution; Pres. Dir HENDI PRIO SANTOSO.

Water

PDAM DKI Jakarta (PAM JAYA): Jalan Penjernihan II, Pejompongan, Jakarta 10210; tel. (21) 5704250; fax (21) 5711796; internet www.pamjaya.co.id; f. 1977; responsible for the water supply systems of Jakarta; govt-owned; Pres. Dir SRIWIDAYANTO KADERI.

PDAM Kodya Dati II Bandung: Jalan Badaksinga 10, Bandung 40132; tel. (22) 2509030; fax (22) 2508063; e-mail pdambdg@elga.net.id; f. 1974; responsible for the water supply and sewerage systems of Bandung; Pres. Dir Ir SOENITIYOSO HADI PRATIKTO.

PDAM Tirtanadi Medan: Jalan Sisingamangaraja 1, Medan 20212; tel. (61) 4571666; fax (61) 4572771; e-mail tirtanadi@pdamtirtanadi.co.id; internet www.pdamtirtanadi.co.id; f. 1979; manages the water supply of Medan and nearby towns and cities; Man. Dir Ir AZZAM RIZAL.

TRADE UNIONS

Konfederasi Serikat Pekerja Seluruh Indonesia (KSPSI) (Confederation of All Indonesian Trades Unions): Jalan Raya Pasar Minggu 9, Km 17, Jakarta Selatan 12740; tel. (21) 7974359; fax (21) 7974361; f. 1973; renamed 2001; sole officially recognized Nat. Industrial Union; 5.1m. mems in June 2005; Gen. Chair. JACOB NUWA WEA; Gen. Sec. LATIEF NASUTION.

Konfederasi Serikat Buruh Sejahtera Indonesia (KSBSI) (Confederation of Indonesia Prosperity Trade Union): Jalan Cipinang Muara Raya 33, Jatinegara, Jakarta Timur 13420; tel. (21) 70984671; fax (21) 8577646; e-mail sbsi@pacific.net.id; internet www.ksbsi.or.id; f. 1998; application for official registration rejected in May 1998; 1,228,875 mems in 168 branches in 27 provinces throughout Indonesia; Pres. REKSON SILABAN; Sec.-Gen. IDIN ROSIDIN.

Transport

Directorate-General of Land Transport and Inland Waterways: Ministry of Transportation, Jalan Medan Merdeka Barat 8, Jakarta 10110; tel. (21) 3502971; fax (21) 3503013; e-mail info@hubdat.web.id; internet www.hubdat.web.id; Dir-Gen. ISKANDAR ABUBAKAR.

RAILWAYS

There are railways on Java, Madura and Sumatra. In 2006 the Japanese Government agreed to provide a US $741m. loan to finance a Mass Rapid Transport (MRT) rail system in Jakarta. Construction was due to commence in early 2012, with completion expected by 2016.

Directorate General of Railways: Ministry of Transportation, Jalan Medan Merdeka Barat 8, Jakarta 10110; tel. (21) 3800349; fax (21) 3860758; e-mail bagrenka_dephub@yahoo.com; internet perkeretaapian.dephub.go.id; Head Ir NUGROHO INDRIO.

PT Kereta Api Indonesia (Persero) (KAI): Jalan Perintis Kermedekaan 1, Bandung 40117; tel. (22) 4230031; fax (22) 4241370; e-mail kontak_pelanggan@kereta-api.co.id; internet www.kereta-api.co.id; six regional offices; transferred to the private sector in 1991; Chief Commr BUDHI MULYAWAN SUYITNO; Chief Dir IGNASIUS JONAN.

ROADS

There is an adequate road network on Java, Sumatra, Sulawesi, Kalimantan, Bali and Madura, but on many of the other islands traffic is by jungle track or river boat. In 2009 Indonesia had a total road length of 476,337 km, of which some 57% was asphalted.

SHIPPING

The four main ports are Tanjung Priok (near Jakarta), Tanjung Perak (near Surabaya), Belawan (near Medan) and Makassar (formerly Ujung Pandang, in South Sulawesi). More than 100 of Indonesia's ports and harbours are classified as capable of handling ocean-going shipping.

Directorate General of Sea Communications: Ministry of Transportation, Jalan Medan Merdeka Barat 8, Jakarta 10110; tel. (21) 3456332; internet www.dephub.go.id/ditlaut; Dir-Gen. SOENTORO.

Indonesian National Ship Owners' Association (INSA): Jalan Tanah Abang III, No. 10, Jakarta Pusat; tel. (21) 3850993; fax (21) 3849522; e-mail info@insa.or.id; internet insa.or.id; Chair. JOHNSON W. SUTJIPTO; Sec.-Gen. BUDHI HALIM.

Shipping Companies

PT Admiral Lines: POB 1476, Jakarta 10014; tel. (21) 4247908; fax (21) 4206267; e-mail admiral@uninet.net.id; f. 1966; fmrly PT Pelayaran Samudera Admiral Lines; Pres. Commr DAUHAN SYAMSURI; Pres. Dir MOCHAMAD SOEGIARTO.

PT Djakarta Lloyd: Jalan Senen Raya 44, Jakarta 10410; tel. (21) 3456208; fax (21) 3441401; internet www.djakartalloyd.co.id; f. 1950; services to USA, Europe, Japan, Australia and the Middle East; Pres. Dir Capt. ADRIAN MARTHIANUS.

PT Karana Line: Wisma Kalimanis, 12th and 13th Floors, Jalan M. T. Haryono, Kav. 33, Jakarta 12770; tel. (21) 7985914; fax (21) 7985913; internet www.karana.co.id; Pres. Dir BAMBANG EDIYANTO.

PT Pelayaran Bahtera Adhiguna (Persero): Jalan Kalibesar Timur 10–12, POB 4313, Jakarta 11110; tel. (21) 6912547; fax (21) 6901450; e-mail pelba@bahteradhiguna.co.id; internet www.bahteradhiguna.co.id; f. 1971; Pres. Commr HASUDUNGAN ARITONANG; Pres. Dir DJOKO TAHONO.

PT Pelayaran Nasional Indonesia (PELNI): Jalan Gajah Mada 14, Jakarta 10130; tel. (21) 6334342; fax (21) 63854130; e-mail humas@pelni.co.id; internet www.pelni.co.id; state-owned; national shipping co; Pres. Commr KALALO NUGROHO; Pres. Dir JUSSABELLA SAHEA.

PT Pertamina (Persero): Downstream Directorate for Shipping, Jalan Yos Sudarso 32–34, POB 14020, Tanjung Priok, Jakarta Utara 14320; tel. (21) 43930325; fax (21) 4370161; e-mail pcc@pertaminashipping.com; internet www.pertaminashipping.com; f. 1959; state-owned; maritime business services; Pres. Dir KAREN AGUSTIAWAN.

PT Perusahaan Pelayaran Gesuri Lloyd: Gesuri Lloyd Bldg, Jalan Tiang Bendera IV/45, Jakarta 11230; tel. (21) 6904000; fax (21) 6925987; e-mail operation_agency@gesuri.co.id; internet www.gesuri.co.id; f. 1963; Pres. Dir ANTONIUS NURIMBA.

PT Perusahaan Pelayaran Nusantara (PANURJWAN): Jalan Raya Pelabuhan Nusantara, POB 2062, Jakarta 10001; tel. (21) 494344; internet www.panurjwan.co.id; Pres. Dir A. J. SINGH.

PT Perusahaan Pelayaran Samudera 'Samudera Indonesia': Jalan Yos Sudarso 1, Blok A1-7, Tanjung Priok, Jakarta 14320; tel. (21) 4301150; fax (21) 43930116; internet www.samudera.com; Chair. SHANTI L. POESPOSOETJIPTO; Pres. Dir MASLI MULIA.

PT Perusahaan Pelayaran Samudera Trikora Lloyd: Graha Satria, 4th Floor, Jalan R. S. Fatmawati 5, Jakarta Selatan, Jakarta 12430; tel. (21) 75915381; fax (21) 75915385; internet www.boedihardjogroup.com/shipping/trikora_lloyd.htm; e-mail tkldir@cbn.net.id; f. 1964; Pres. Dir GANESHA SOEGIHARTO; Man. Dir P. R. S. VAN HEEREN.

CIVIL AVIATION

Sukarno-Hatta Airport, at Cengkareng, serves Jakarta. Other international airports include Ngurah Rai Airport at Denpasar (Bali), Polonia Airport in Medan (North Sumatra), Juanda Airport, near Surabaya (East Java), Sam Ratulangi Airport in Manado (North Sulawesi), Hasanuddin Airport, near Makassar (formerly Ujung Pandang, South Sulawesi) and Frans Kaisepo Airport, in Papua (formerly Irian Jaya). There are numerous other commercial airports.

Directorate-General of Civil Aviation: Jalan Medan Merdeka Barat 8, Jakarta Pusat 10110; tel. (21) 3505550; fax (21) 3505139; e-mail hubud@dephub.go.id; internet hubud.dephub.go.id; Dir-Gen. HERRY BAKTI.

PT Batavia Airlines: Jalan Ir H. Juanda 15, Jakarta Pusat 10120; tel. (21) 3864308; fax (21) 3864486; internet www.batavia-air.co.id; f. 2002; scheduled domestic and regional services; Pres. YUDIAWAN TANSARI.

Citilink: Juanda Business Centre, Jalan Juanda 1, Blok C2, Gedangan, Sidoarjo; tel. (31) 8549860; internet www.citilink.co.id; f. 2001; subsidiary of PT Garuda Indonesia; low-cost carrier providing shuttle services between 7 domestic destinations.

Deraya Air Taxi (DRY): Terminal Bldg, 1st Floor, Rm 150/HT, Halim Perdanakusuma Airport, Jakarta 13610; tel. (21) 8093627; fax (21) 8095770; e-mail admderaya@deraya.co.id; internet www.deraya.co.id; f. 1967; scheduled and charter passenger and cargo services to domestic and regional destinations; Pres. Dir SITI RAHAYU SUMADI.

Dirgantara Air Service (DAS): POB 6154, Terminal Bldg, Halim Perdanakusuma Airport, Rm 231, Jakarta 13610; tel. (21) 8093372; fax (21) 8094348; charter services from Jakarta, Barjarmas and Pontianak to destinations in West Kalimantan; Pres. MAKKI PERDANAKUSUMA.

PT Garuda Indonesia: Gedung Garuda Indonesia, Jalan Medan Merdeka Selatan 13, Jakarta 10110; tel. (21) 2311801; fax (21) 2311679; internet www.garuda-indonesia.com; f. 1949; state airline; operates scheduled domestic, regional and international services to destinations in Europe, the USA, the Middle East, Australasia and the Far East; Pres. and CEO EMIRSYAH SATAR; Chair. HADIYANTO.

Lion Air: Lion Air Tower, Jaland Gajah Mada 7, Jakarta Pusat; tel. (21) 63798000; fax (21) 6348744; e-mail info@lionair.co.id; internet www.lionair.co.id; f. 1999; budget carrier providing domestic and international services; Pres. Dir RUSDI KIRANA.

PT Mandala Airlines: Jalan Tomang Raya, Kav. 33–37, Jakarta 11440; tel. (21) 56997000; fax (21) 5663788; e-mail widya@mandalaair.com; internet www.mandalaair.com; f. 1969; privately owned; scheduled regional and domestic passenger and cargo services; Pres. Dir DIONO NURJADIN; CEO WARWICK BRADY.

PT Merpati Nusantara Airlines: Jalan Angkasa, Blok B-15, Kav. 2–3, Jakarta 10720; tel. (21) 6548888; fax (21) 6540620; e-mail marketing@merpati.co.id; internet www.merpati.co.id; f. 1962; subsidiary of PT Garuda Indonesia; domestic and regional services to Australia and Malaysia; Chair. GUNAWAN KOSWARA; Pres. Dir SARDJONO JHONY TJITROKUSUMO.

Pelita Air Service: Jalan Abdul Muis 52–56A, Jakarta 10160; tel. (21) 2312030; fax (21) 2312216; e-mail humas@pelita-air.com; internet www.pelita-air.com; f. 1970; subsidiary of state oil co Pertamina; domestic scheduled and charter passenger and cargo services; Pres. Dir ANDJAR WIBAWANUN.

Premiair: Halim Perdanakusuma Airport Terminal Bldg, Ground Floor, Jakarta 13610; tel. (21) 8091255; fax (21) 8002060; e-mail sales@flypremiair.com; internet www.flypremiair.com; f. 1989; domestic and international charter services; CEO Capt. ARI DARYATA SINGGIH.

Sriwijaya Air: No. 68, Blok C, 15–16, Jalan Pangeran Jayakarta, Jakarta; tel. (21) 6396006; internet www.sriwijayaair-online.com; f. 2003; domestic services; Dir CHANDRA LIE.

Wings Abadi Airlines (Wings Air): Lion Air Tower, Jalan Gajah Mada 7, Jakarta Pusat; tel. (21) 6326039; fax (21) 6348744; f. 2003; subsidiary co of Lion Air; budget carrier providing scheduled domestic passenger services.

Tourism

Indonesia's tourist industry is based mainly on the islands of Java, famous for its volcanic scenery and religious temples, and Bali, renowned for its scenery and Hindu/Buddhist temples and religious festivals. Lombok, Sumatra and Sulawesi are also increasingly popular. Domestic tourism within Indonesia has also increased significantly. Revenue from tourism (excluding passenger transport) was a provisional US $6,980m. in 2010. Average expenditure per visit rose from US $901.7 in 2004 to $1,085.8 in 2010. The number of tourist arrivals exceeded 7.0m. in 2010.

Indonesia Tourism Promotion Board: Wisma Nugra Santana, 9th Floor, Jalan Jenderal Sudirman 8, Jakarta 10220; tel. (21) 5704879; fax (21) 5704855; e-mail itpb@cbn.net.id; private body; promotes national and international tourism; Chair. WIRYANT SUKAMDANI.

Defence

As assessed at November 2011, the total strength of the armed forces was an estimated 302,000: army 233,000, navy 45,000, and air force 24,000; paramilitary forces comprised some 280,000, including a police 'mobile brigade' of 14,000 and an estimated 40,000 trainees of KAMRA (People's Security). Reserve forces numbered 400,000. Military service, which is selective, lasts for two years. In support of international peace-keeping efforts, 1,356 Indonesian troops were stationed in Lebanon in November 2011 and 175 in the Democratic Republic of the Congo.

Defence Expenditure: Rp. 60,500,000m. for 2010.

Commander-in-Chief of the Armed Forces: Gen. AGUS SUHARTONO.

Chief of Staff of the Army: Gen. PRAMONO EDHIE WIBOWO.

Chief of Staff of the Navy: Adm. SOEPARNO.

Chief of Staff of the Air Force: Air Marshal IMAM SUFAAT.

Education

Education is administered mainly by the Ministry of National Education, but the Ministry of Religious Affairs also operates Islamic religious schools (*madrasahs*) at the primary level.

Primary education, beginning at seven years of age and lasting for six years, was made compulsory in 1987. In 1993 it was announced that compulsory education was to be expanded to nine years. Secondary education begins at 13 years of age and lasts for a further six years, comprising three years of junior secondary education and a further three years of senior secondary education. A further three years of academic level or five years of higher education may follow. In May 2010 the Government announced plans to implement compulsory 12-year education for all Indonesian children by 2014.

In 2008/09 there were 26,984,824 pupils enrolled at 144,228 primary schools, 8,992,619 pupils enrolled at 28,777 general junior secondary schools, and 3,857,245 pupils at 10,762 general senior secondary schools. Enrolment at primary level in 2009/10 included 96% of pupils in the relevant age group (males 95%; females 97%); enrolment at secondary level in the same year included 67% of children in the relevant age group (males 68%, females 67%). Vocational subjects have been introduced in the secondary schools. There were 3,095,704 pupils at 7,592 vocational senior secondary schools in 2008/09. In the same year there were 2,975 tertiary institutions, with enrolment totalling 4,281,695. The Government's budget for 2009 allocated Rp. 244,440,000m., representing 20% of total expenditure, to education.

IRAN

Introductory Survey

LOCATION, CLIMATE, LANGUAGE, RELIGION, FLAG, CAPITAL

The Islamic Republic of Iran lies in western Asia, bordered by Armenia, Azerbaijan and Turkmenistan to the north, by Turkey and Iraq to the west, by the Persian (Arabian) Gulf and the Gulf of Oman to the south, and by Pakistan and Afghanistan to the east. The climate is one of great extremes. Summer temperatures of more than 55°C (131°F) have been recorded, but in the winter the great altitude of much of the country results in temperatures of −18°C (0°F) and below. The principal language is Farsi (Persian), spoken by about 50% of the population. Turkic-speaking Azeris form about 27% of the population, and Kurds, Arabs, Baluchs and Turkomans form less than 25%. The great majority of Persians and Azeris are Shi'i Muslims, while the other ethnic groups are mainly Sunni Muslims. There are also small minorities of Christians (mainly Armenians), Zoroastrians and Jews. The Bahá'í faith, which originated in Iran, has been severely persecuted, being denied rights given to other recognized religious minorities. The national flag (proportions 4 by 7) comprises three unequal horizontal stripes, of green, white and red, with the emblem of the Islamic Republic of Iran (the stylized word Allah) centrally positioned in red, and the inscription *'Allaho Akbar'* ('God is Great') written 11 times each in white Kufic script on the red and green stripes. The capital is Tehran.

CONTEMPORARY POLITICAL HISTORY

Historical Context

Iran, called Persia until 1935, was formerly a monarchy, ruled by a Shah (Emperor). In 1927 Reza Khan, a Cossack officer, seized power in a military coup, and was subsequently elected Shah, adopting the title Reza Shah Pahlavi. In 1941 British and Soviet forces occupied Iran, and the Shah (who favoured Nazi Germany) was forced to abdicate in favour of his son, Muhammad Reza Pahlavi. British and US forces left Iran in 1945, but Soviet forces remained in the north-west of the country until 1946. The United Kingdom retained considerable influence through the Anglo-Iranian Oil Co, which controlled much of Iran's extensive petroleum reserves. In March 1951, however, the Majlis (National Consultative Assembly) approved the nationalization of the petroleum industry, despite British and other Western opposition. The leading advocate of nationalization, Dr Muhammad Mussadeq, who became Prime Minister in May 1951, was deposed in August 1953 in a military coup, engineered by the US and British intelligence services.

The Shah gradually increased his personal control of government following the coup, assuming dictatorial powers in 1963 with the so-called 'White Revolution'. Large estates were redistributed to small farmers, and women were granted the right to vote in elections. In 1965 Prime Minister Hassan Ali Mansur was assassinated, reportedly by a follower of Ayatollah Ruhollah Khomeini, a fundamentalist Shi'ite Muslim leader strongly opposed to the Shah. (Khomeini had been deported in 1964 for his opposition activities, and was living in exile in Iraq.) Amir Abbas Hoveida held the office of Prime Minister until 1977.

Between 1965 and 1977 Iran enjoyed political stability and considerable economic growth, based on substantial petroleum revenues which funded expenditure on defence equipment and infrastructure projects. From late 1977, however, public opposition to the regime increased dramatically, largely in response to a declining economy and the repressive nature of the Shah's rule. By the end of 1978 anti-Government protests were widespread, involving both left-wing and liberal opponents of the Shah, as well as Islamist activists. The most effective opposition came from supporters of Ayatollah Khomeini, who was now based in France. The growing unrest forced the Shah to leave Iran in January 1979. Khomeini arrived in Tehran on 1 February and effectively assumed power 10 days later. A 15-member Islamic Revolutionary Council was formed to govern the country, in co-operation with a Provisional Government, and on 1 April Iran was declared an Islamic republic. Supreme authority was vested in the Wali Faqih, a religious leader (initially Khomeini) appointed by the Shi'ite clergy. Executive power was to be vested in a President, to which post Abolhasan Bani-Sadr was elected in January 1980. Elections to a 270-member Majlis (renamed the Islamic Consultative Assembly) took place in two rounds in March and May. The Islamic Republican Party (IRP), which was identified with Khomeini and traditionalist Muslims, won some 60 seats, but subsequently increased its support base.

Domestic Political Affairs

In November 1979 Iranian students seized 63 hostages at the US embassy in Tehran. The original purpose of the siege was to force the USA (where the Shah was undergoing medical treatment) to return the former monarch to Iran to face trial. The Shah died in Egypt in July 1980, by which time Iran had made other demands, notably for a US undertaking not to interfere in its affairs. Intense diplomatic activity led to the release of the 52 remaining hostages in January 1981, others having been freed two weeks into the siege. However, a failed rescue operation by the US military in April 1980 had resulted in the deaths of eight US servicemen.

The hostage crisis had forced the resignation of the moderate Provisional Government, and during 1980 it became clear that a rift was developing between President Bani-Sadr and his modernist allies on the one hand, and the IRP and traditionalist elements on the other. In June 1981 clashes between supporters of the two groups escalated into sustained fighting between members of the Mujahidin-e-Khalq (an Islamist guerrilla group that supported Bani-Sadr) and troops of the Islamic Revolutionary Guards Corps. The Majlis voted to impeach the President, who was subsequently dismissed by Khomeini. Bani-Sadr fled to France, as did the leader of the Mujahidin, Massoud Rajavi. A presidential election in July resulted in victory for the Prime Minister, Muhammad Ali Rajani, who was himself replaced by Muhammad Javar Bahonar. In August, however, both the President and Prime Minister were killed in a bomb attack attributed to the Mujahidin-e-Khalq. A further presidential election, held in October, was won by Hojatoleslam Sayed Ali Khamenei. Mir Hossein Mousavi was appointed Prime Minister.

The resignation or dismissal of five ministers, all 'bazaaris' (members of the merchant class), in August 1983 characterized opposition to the policies of nationalization and land reform advocated by technocrats in the Government. Mousavi's attempts to implement such economic reforms were continually obstructed by the predominantly 'conservative', clerical Majlis. Elections to the second Majlis in April and May 1984 resulted in an easy victory for the IRP. The elections were boycotted by the sole opposition party to have a degree of official recognition, Nehzat-e Azadi-ye Iran (Liberation Movement of Iran), led by Dr Mehdi Bazargan (Prime Minister of the Provisional Government during February–November 1979), in protest against the allegedly undemocratic conditions prevailing in Iran. Three candidates, including the incumbent, contested the August 1985 presidential election. The Council of Guardians (responsible for the supervision of elections) had rejected almost 50 others, among them Bazargan, who opposed the continuation of the war with Iraq (see The Iran–Iraq War). Khamenei was elected President for a second four-year term, with 85.7% of the votes cast. Mousavi was reconfirmed as Prime Minister in October.

The Iran–Iraq War

For most of the 1980s Iran's domestic and foreign policy was dominated by the war with Iraq. In September 1980, ostensibly to assert a claim of sovereignty over the disputed Shatt al-Arab waterway, Iraqi forces invaded Iran along a 500-km front, apparently anticipating a rapid military victory. The Iranian military offered strong resistance, and began a counter-offensive in early 1982; by June Iraq had been forced to withdraw from Iranian territory, and Iranian troops subsequently entered Iraq. A conflict of attrition thus developed, characterized by mutual offensives and the targeting of each other's petroleum reserves, installations and transshipment facilities. From 1984 Iraq began attacking tankers using Iran's Kharg Island oil terminal in the Persian (Arabian) Gulf, and Iran retaliated by targeting Saudi Arabian and Kuwaiti tankers, as well as neutral vessels using

Kuwait. Despite subsequent efforts by the UN to establish a basis for peace negotiations, Iran's conditions for peace were the removal from power of the Iraqi President, Saddam Hussain, in conjunction with agreement by Iraq to pay war reparations. The war had left Iran in virtual diplomatic isolation; however, in late 1986 it emerged that the USA, in contradiction to its active discouragement of arms sales to Iran by other countries, had begun secret negotiations with the country in 1985 and had made shipments of weapons, allegedly in exchange for Iranian assistance in securing the release of US hostages held by Shi'ite groups in Lebanon, and an Iranian undertaking to relinquish involvement in international terrorism.

In April 1988 Iraq recaptured the Faw peninsula (which Iran had taken in 1986), forcing the Iranian military to withdraw across the Shatt al-Arab. In June Iraq also retook Majnoun Island and the surrounding area (which had been captured by Iran in 1984). In July an IranAir passenger flight, apparently mistaken for an attacking fighter jet, was shot down by a US aircraft carrier in the Strait of Hormuz; all 290 people on board were killed. In that month Iraqi troops crossed into Iranian territory for the first time since 1986, and the last Iranian troops on Iraqi territory were dislodged. On 18 July 1988 Iran unexpectedly announced its unconditional acceptance of UN Security Council Resolution 598, adopted one year earlier. This urged an immediate cease-fire, the withdrawal of military forces to international boundaries, and the co-operation of Iran and Iraq in mediation efforts to achieve a peace settlement. More than 1m. people were estimated to have died in the eight-year conflict. A cease-fire came into effect on 20 August, and UN-sponsored peace negotiations began shortly afterwards in Geneva, Switzerland. In the same month a UN Iran-Iraq Military Observer Group (UNIIMOG) was deployed in the region. However, the negotiations soon became deadlocked in disputes regarding the sovereignty of the Shatt al-Arab waterway, the exchange of prisoners of war and the withdrawal of armed forces to within international boundaries. Hopes of a comprehensive peace settlement were raised by a meeting of the Iranian and Iraqi Ministers of Foreign Affairs in Geneva in July 1990, but were swiftly overshadowed by Iraq's invasion of Kuwait at the beginning of August. Saddam Hussain sought an immediate, formal peace with Iran, accepting all the claims that Iran had pursued since the declaration of a cease-fire (including the reinstatement of the Algiers Agreement of 1975, dividing the Shatt al-Arab), and Iraq immediately began to redeploy troops from its border with Iran to Kuwait. Prisoner exchanges took place, and in September 1990 Iran and Iraq restored diplomatic relations. In February 1991 the withdrawal of all armed forces to internationally recognized boundaries was confirmed by UNIIMOG, the mandate of which was terminated shortly afterwards.

Iran denounced Iraq's invasion of Kuwait, and observed the economic sanctions imposed by the UN on Iraq. However, it was unequivocal in its condemnation of the deployment of the US-led multinational force in the Gulf region. Relations between Iran and Iraq deteriorated after the liberation of Kuwait in February 1991. Iran protested strongly against the Baathist regime's suppression of the Shi'a-led rebellion in southern and central Iraq, and renewed its demand for the resignation of President Saddam Hussain. Iraq, in turn, accused Iran of supporting the rebellion. Thus, there was little further progress in implementing the terms of Resolution 598 until late 1993, when high-level bilateral talks recommenced on the exchange of remaining prisoners of war. (See section on Foreign Affairs for further details of Iran's relations with Iraq.)

Political developments following the death of Ayatollah Khomeini

Elections to the Majlis in April and May 1988 apparently provided a stimulus to 'reformist' elements in the Government (identified with Ali Akbar Hashemi Rafsanjani, since 1980 the Speaker of the Majlis, and Prime Minister Mousavi) by producing an assembly strongly representative of their views. (The elections were the Islamic Republic's first not to be contested by the IRP, which had been dissolved in 1987.) In June 1988 Rafsanjani was re-elected as Speaker and Mousavi was overwhelmingly endorsed as Prime Minister. In February 1989, however, Ayatollah Khomeini referred explicitly to a division in the Iranian leadership between 'reformers' (who sought a degree of Western participation in Iran's post-war reconstruction) and 'conservatives' (who opposed such involvement), and declared that he would never permit the 'reformers' to prevail. His intervention was reportedly prompted by Rafsanjani's decision to contest the presidential election scheduled for mid-1989. A number of prominent 'reformers', among them Ayatollah Ali Hossein Montazeri (who had been designated as successor to Khomeini by the Assembly of Experts in 1985), subsequently resigned from the Iranian leadership.

Ayatollah Khomeini died on 3 June 1989. In an emergency session on 4 June the Assembly of Experts elected President Khamenei to succeed Khomeini as Iran's spiritual leader (Wali Faqih). The presidential election, scheduled for mid-August, was brought forward to 28 July, to be held simultaneously with a referendum on proposed amendments to the Constitution. Both 'conservatives' and 'reformers' within the leadership apparently united in support of Rafsanjani's candidacy for the presidency, and Rafsanjani (opposed only by a 'token' candidate) secured an overwhelming victory, with 95.9% of the votes cast. A similar proportion of voters approved the constitutional amendments, the most important of which was the abolition of the post of Prime Minister (and a consequent increase in the powers of the President).

President Rafsanjani appointed a Government balancing 'conservatives', 'reformers' and technocrats, and its endorsement by the Majlis in August 1989 was viewed as a mandate for Rafsanjani to conduct a more conciliatory policy towards the West. Large-scale protests against food shortages and high prices in early 1990 demonstrated the urgent need for economic reform. In October, with the co-operation of Ayatollah Khamenei, Rafsanjani was able to prevent the election of many powerful 'conservatives' to the Assembly of Experts. An estimated 70% of deputies elected to the fourth Majlis in April and May 1992 were, broadly speaking, pro-Rafsanjani. However, economic reform was lowering the living standards of the traditional constituency of the Islamic regime, the urban lower classes, leading to serious rioting in several cities. The extent to which President Rafsanjani had lost popular support became clear when he stood for re-election in June 1993: competing against three ostensibly 'token' candidates, Rafsanjani received only 63.2% of the votes. In May 1994 the Government indicated that it would proceed more cautiously with a plan to reduce economic subsidies applied to basic commodities. Meanwhile, in August 1995 it was reported that political parties, associations and groups were free to conduct political activities in Iran on condition that they honoured the country's Constitution, although Nehzat-e Azadi was subsequently refused formal registration as a political party.

Elections to the fifth Majlis in March and April 1996 provided an important measure of the shifting balance of power between 'reformers', or 'liberals', and 'conservatives' in Iranian politics. At the first round of voting, candidates of the Servants of Iran's Construction, a new pro-Rafsanjani faction, were reported to have won some 70% of the seats. However, the 'conservative' Society of Combatant Clergy, with the unofficial patronage of Ayatollah Khamenei, claimed that its candidates had achieved an equally conclusive victory. After the second round of voting, unofficial sources suggested that the Society of Combatant Clergy would command the loyalty of 110–120 deputies in the new 270-seat Majlis, and the Servants of Iran's Construction that of 90–100 deputies.

President Khatami's first term of office

In March 1997 Rafsanjani, whose presidential mandate was due to expire, was appointed Chairman of the Council to Determine the Expediency of the Islamic Order for a further five-year term. (He was reappointed as head of the Expediency Council—which arbitrates in disputes between the Majlis and the Council of Guardians—in March 2002 and February 2007.) In May 1997 the Council of Guardians approved four candidatures for that month's presidential election, rejecting 234. It had been widely predicted that Ali Akbar Nateq Nouri, the Majlis Speaker favoured by the Society of Combatant Clergy, would secure an easy victory, but Sayed Muhammad Khatami (a presidential adviser and former Minister of Culture and Islamic Guidance) emerged as a strong contender immediately prior to the election. Regarded as a 'liberal', Khatami—supported by the Servants of Iran's Construction as well as by intellectuals, professionals, and women's and youth groups—took some 69.1% of the total votes cast, ahead of Nateq Nouri, with 24.9%.

Taking office in August 1997, President Khatami emphasized his commitment to fostering sustained and balanced growth in the political, economic, cultural and educational spheres. In foreign affairs, the President undertook to promote the principle of mutual respect, but pledged that Iran would stand up to any power seeking to subjugate Iranian sovereignty. Notable among the 'liberal' or 'moderate' appointees in Khatami's first Council of Ministers were Ata'ollah Mohajerani (a former Vice-President) as Minister of Culture and Islamic Guidance, Abdollah Nuri as Minister of the Interior (a post he had previously held in 1989–93), and Dr Massoumeh Ebtekar as Vice-President and Head of the Organization for the Protection of the Environment, the first woman to be appointed to such a senior government post since the Islamic Revolution. In the months following his election President Khatami appeared conciliatory towards the West, while Khamenei continued to denounce the West's military and cultural ambitions, particularly those of the USA and Israel.

During 1998 the Khatami administration moved to formalize its support base, primarily through the registration or establishment of 'reformist' parties such as the Servants of Construction, the Islamic Iran Solidarity Party (Hezb-e Hambastegi-ye Iran-e Islami) and the Islamic Iran Participation Front (Jebbeh-ye Mosharekat-e Iran-e Islami—which counted Vice-President Massoumeh Ebtekar among its leaders). In June 1998 the Majlis voted to dismiss Abdollah Nuri as Minister of the Interior, a group of 'conservative' deputies having initiated impeachment on the grounds that he had made provocative statements and permitted dissident rallies. Khatami subsequently appointed Nuri as Vice-President in charge of Development and Social Affairs. At elections to the Assembly of Experts in October, 'conservatives' retained overwhelming control of the assembly, with an estimated 60% of the 86 seats being won by candidates of the 'radical' right wing; candidates of a 'centrist' grouping apparently associated with ex-President Rafsanjani took about 10% of the seats. Khatami's Government suffered a further setback in February 1999 with the resignation of Qorbanali Dorri Najafabadi, the Minister of Information, after it was admitted that agents of his ministry had (allegedly without his knowledge) been responsible for the murders of several intellectuals and dissident writers (among them Dariush Foruhar, leader of the unauthorized but officially tolerated Iranian People's Party) in late 1998.

Iran's first local government elections since the Islamic Revolution took place in February 1999, when some 60% of the electorate voted to elect representatives in 200,000 council seats. The elections resulted in considerable success for 'reformist' candidates, notably in Tehran, Shiraz and Esfahan, while 'conservatives' secured control of councils in their traditional strongholds of Qom and Mashad.

The issue of press censorship had increasingly become a focus of the political rivalries between 'conservatives' and 'reformists'. During 1998 several prominent journals had been closed, and their journalists prosecuted, and Ayatollah Khamenei had personally sought action against publications that he perceived as abusing freedom of speech to weaken Islamic beliefs. Legislation adopted by the Majlis in June 1999 further curbed the activities of 'liberal' publications. In July the closure of *Salam*, a 'reformist' newspaper with close links to President Khatami, triggered a small demonstration by students at the University of Tehran, which was dispersed with considerable violence by police. This action, in conjunction with a raid on student dormitories by security forces, aided by vigilantes of the semi-official Ansar-e Hezbollah paramilitary group (in which at least one student was killed), provoked five days of rioting in Tehran and other cities, resulting in some 1,400 arrests. Within a year both the national and Tehran chiefs of police had been dismissed, while as many as 100 police officers had been arrested for their role in the campus raid. Abdollah Nuri, who had resigned as Vice-President in order to participate in February's municipal elections, was brought before the Special Clerical Court in October, accused in his capacity as founder and editor of the 'liberal' *Khordad* daily of publishing reports contrary to Islamic fundamentals and refuting the values of Ayatollah Khomeini. Many observers regarded the charges against Nuri as a clear attempt to prevent his standing in the forthcoming elections to the Majlis, where, if elected, he was likely to be a strong contender for the post of Speaker. In November Nuri was convicted on 15 charges and sentenced to five years' imprisonment; he was also fined IR 15m., and the closure of *Khordad* was ordered. However, in November 2002 Nuri was pardoned by Ayatollah Khamenei following the sudden death of his brother, Ali Reza Nuri, a 'reformist' deputy who had achieved success in the 2000 general election (see below).

An estimated 80% of Iran's registered electorate participated in elections to the Majlis held on 18 February 2000, at which the number of seats in the chamber had been increased from 270 to 290. 'Reformist' candidates secured notable victories, including that of Muhammad Reza Khatami (brother of the President and head of the Participation Front's political bureau). By mid-2000 'reformist' or 'liberal' deputies were believed to hold some 200 seats in the new Majlis, with the remaining 90 occupied by 'conservatives'. (By-elections were to take place in mid-2001—concurrently with the scheduled presidential election—for 18 seats where the results of earlier voting had been annulled.)

'Reformist' deputies acted swiftly to draft legislation to replace a further restrictive new press law, endorsed by the outgoing, 'conservative'-controlled Majlis, which made criticism of the Constitution illegal and increased judicial powers to close newspapers. However, in August 2000 Ayatollah Khamenei instructed the new Majlis not to debate proposed amendments to the press law (which would make it more difficult for the judiciary to imprison journalists), on the grounds that such reforms would endanger state security and religious faith. This intervention appeared to sanction a more vigorous campaign against 'liberal' interests, including the closure of several more 'reformist' publications.

In November 2000 the trial opened in Tehran of a group of prominent 'reformists', accused of 'acting against national security and propagandizing against the regime' through their attendance at a conference on Iranian political reform, held in Berlin, Germany, in April. The severity of the sentences, pronounced in January 2001, against seven of the defendants, who were given custodial terms of between four and 10 years, was denounced by 'reformist' politicians within Iran. The renowned investigative journalist Akbar Ganji received the maximum prison term, followed by five years' internal exile, having been found guilty of harming national security, propagandizing against the regime, possessing secret documents and committing offences against senior officials. Following an earlier appeal, Ganji was released from detention in March 2006. Ganji had been investigating the deaths of dissident intellectuals in late 1998 (see above), which he claimed involved senior 'conservatives', but which the authorities maintained had been instigated by 'rogue' agents of the Ministry of Information. In January 2001 three intelligence agents were condemned to death, having been convicted of perpetrating the killings; five received life sentences, and seven others custodial terms of up to 10 years. However, after a retrial in January 2003, at least two of the agents had their death sentences commuted to terms of life imprisonment; of those given life sentences, two now received prison terms of 10 years, while seven of the agents were given gaol terms of between two and 10 years.

Khatami's second presidential term

As had been widely predicted, on 8 June 2001 Khatami was re-elected as President, winning some 76.9% of the total votes cast, compared with 15.6% for his closest rival, Ahmed Tavakkoli, a former Minister of Labour and Social Affairs. Despite Khatami's victory, the rate of participation by voters (at around 67%) was considerably lower than the 88% recorded in 1997. Moreover, although he had received a public endorsement of his programme of political and economic reforms, it soon became apparent that the 'ultra-conservatives' were unwilling to cede control of the Council of Guardians to 'reformist' supporters of Khatami. On 5 August Khatami's scheduled inauguration was postponed after the 'reformist' Majlis refused to approve two of the judiciary's 'conservative' nominees to the Council of Guardians. Ayatollah Khamenei requested, to strenuous 'reformist' opposition, that the dispute be resolved by the 'conservative'-dominated Expediency Council. Two days later, however, the Majlis finally endorsed the two candidates, following a ruling that candidates did not require the support of a majority of deputies in order to be elected to the Council of Guardians. Khatami was duly sworn in for a second presidential term on 8 August.

The judiciary's campaign against 'pro-reform' activists intensified following Khatami's re-election: it included mass arrests, public floggings and even public executions, ordered ostensibly to reduce crime and encourage greater morality. In November 2001 trial proceedings, held in camera, began of more than 30 members of the Nehzat-e Azadi movement who had been arrested on charges including acting against national security and plotting to overthrow the Islamic regime. Among the defendants—in what was reported to be the largest political trial in Iran since 1979—were two former ministers and a former mayor of Tehran. Custodial sentences of up to 10 years were handed down to 33 of the activists by the Revolutionary Court in July 2002, and Nehzat-e Azadi was formally banned.

In September 2002 President Khatami presented draft legislation to the Majlis which was aimed at reducing the powers of

Iran's 'ultra-conservative' establishment in order to accelerate his reform programme. The first bill envisaged transferring the rights of the Council of Guardians to approve or disqualify electoral candidates to the Ministry of the Interior. The second proposed granting Khatami wider powers to enforce adherence to the terms of the Constitution by the judiciary and other government departments. Both bills received preliminary approval by the Majlis in early November. However, in April and May 2003 the Council of Guardians refused to ratify Khatami's two reform bills.

Iran officially opposed the 2003 US-led intervention in Iraq, despite the not unwelcome removal from power of Saddam Hussain and his Baathist regime. The British embassy in Tehran became a focal point for protests against the conflict, and was the target of small arms fire on several occasions during 2003. In March a fuel-laden truck was driven into the embassy gates, killing the driver; however, the Minister of Foreign Affairs, Kamal Kharrazi, described this incident as an 'accident'. There was also a suspicion that three shooting incidents at the British embassy in September might be more closely related to the arrest of the former Iranian ambassador to Argentina by the British authorities (see The 2009 presidential election) than to events in Iraq.

With elections to the seventh Majlis scheduled for February 2004, the Council of Guardians announced in early January that, from a preliminary list of around 8,200 candidates, more than 2,000 candidates would be barred from standing in the polls, including 80 current Majlis deputies. ('Reformists' insisted that at least one-half of the proposed candidates would effectively be disqualified.) President Khatami's brother and the Secretary-General of the Islamic Iran Participation Front, Muhammad Reza Khatami, was perhaps the most notable of these 'reformist' candidates. President Khatami and several of his ministers threatened to resign in protest against the ban, as did all of the country's 27 regional governors, and about 100 deputies staged a 'sit-in' at the Majlis. Although, as a result of two direct interventions by Ayatollah Khamenei, the Council of Guardians reversed its decision in relation to a small number of the barred candidates, in late January the Council vetoed emergency legislation that had been adopted by the Majlis with the intention of weakening the former's control over the election process and thereby reversing the bans on all of the candidates. At the elections to the Majlis, held on 20 February, turn-out by voters was estimated to have been as low as 51%; 229 candidates received enough votes to be elected directly to the Majlis, with the remainder of the 290 seats to be filled at a second round of voting, held on 7 May. The 'reformist' Speaker of the outgoing Majlis, Mahdi Karrubi, withdrew his candidacy after failing to secure re-election at the first round. As had been widely predicted, 'conservatives' were confirmed as having secured a majority in the legislature, and following the second round of voting were estimated to have secured 195 seats in the Majlis and the 'reformists' fewer than 50, with the remainder being held by 'independents'. In early May 2004 a law banning the use of torture in Iran was approved by the Council of Guardians. Later that month the new Majlis took office and nominated Gholam-Ali Haddad-Adel as the first non-clerical Speaker since the Islamic Revolution; Haddad-Adel was elected to the post in June.

It was announced in January 2005 that the vote to elect President Khatami's successor was to take place on 17 June, simultaneously with by-elections in eight parliamentary constituencies where results of the February 2004 elections were overturned by the Council of Guardians and in the city of Bam, which had been almost completely destroyed by an earthquake in December 2003; one undecided seat in the Tehran constituency was also to be filled. In May 2005 the Council of Guardians disqualified all but six out of 1,014 candidacies submitted for the presidential election. The six other eligible candidates included former President Rafsanjani, who attempted to place himself in the middle ground between 'reformers' and 'hardliners' and was broadly considered the likely victor in advance of the election. Among the candidates regarded as 'hardline' were Muhammad Baqir Qalibaf, a former national chief of police, Ali Ardeshir Larijani, former head of the state broadcasting agency, and Mahmoud Ahmadinejad, the mayor of Tehran. The final candidate, former Majlis Speaker Mahdi Karrubi, was considered to be a moderate 'reformist'.

President Ahmadinejad's first term of office

Since none of the seven candidates received 50% or more of the total vote at the first round of the 2005 presidential election, held on 17 June 2005, a second round of voting was required for the first time in the Islamic Republic. As had been widely predicted, Rafsanjani received the most votes at the first round, with 21.0%; more unexpected, however, was the success of Ahmadinejad, who finished in second place, with 19.5% of votes cast. Ahmadinejad's campaign promised greater economic equality, reduced corruption and a return to the values of the 1979 Islamic Revolution, and was thought to be strongly supported by poorer Iranians. Several allegations of electoral fraud were made regarding the poll, most notably by defeated candidate Mahdi Karrubi, who wrote an open letter to the Supreme Leader alleging that Revolutionary Guards and members of the Basij Resistance Force (a large volunteer militia that pledges loyalty to the Supreme Leader) had interfered in the election. The Council of Guardians, however, announced following a partial recount that no evidence of electoral fraud had been uncovered. At the second round, held on 24 June 2005, Ahmadinejad secured 61.7% of the vote, to become the sixth President of the Islamic Republic of Iran. Turn-out at the second round was recorded at 59.6%.

The election of Ahmadinejad led to a major overhaul of political personnel. The President was inaugurated on 6 August 2005, and on 14 August he presented his list of ministerial nominees to the Majlis for approval. The list was widely described as being both 'hardline' and inexperienced, and included only one member of the outgoing cabinet. Among the more prominent nominations were Manouchehr Mottaki as Minister of Foreign Affairs and Moustafa Pour-Muhammadi as Minister of the Interior. The Majlis approved 17 of Ahmadinejad's 21 nominations; three of the four vacant posts were filled in November, but the appointment of a new Minister of Oil proved more contentious. Eventually, Ahmadinejad's fourth nominee for the post, Sayed Kazem Vaziri Hamaneh, who had been caretaker of the Ministry since August, was accepted by the Majlis in December.

There were notable instances of violent tension in ethnic minority-dominated regions of Iran during 2005. In April riots broke out in the town of Ahvaz, in the largely Arab-populated province of Khuzestan, leading to clashes with police in which between three and 20 people died, according to various reports. The unrest was apparently connected to a letter, attributed to the former Vice-President in charge of Legal and Parliamentary Affairs, Muhammad Ali Abtahi, which appeared to describe a deliberate government policy forcibly to relocate much of its historically Arab population. (Abtahi strongly denied the authenticity of the letter.) In June, shortly before the first round of the presidential election, several bombs exploded in Ahvaz, resulting in the deaths of some eight people, while an explosion also occurred in Tehran, killing one person. No group claimed responsibility for the attacks, although government spokesmen blamed Arab separatists acting in conjunction with the Mujahidin-e-Khalq and former members of the Baath Party of deposed Iraqi President Saddam Hussain, while also suggesting the involvement of the United Kingdom and the USA. In August troops were reportedly deployed in the Kurdish regions of north-western Iran in order to suppress weeks of protests and riots, during which up to 20 people were thought to have died.

Ethnic unrest continued in 2006, with two bombs exploding in Ahvaz in January, causing nine deaths. The Government again accused the United Kingdom of involvement in the attacks, and alleged that the bombers had used British military facilities in Basra, Iraq. In February a court in Ahvaz sentenced at least 11 Iranians to death for their alleged involvement in bomb attacks in Khuzestan, although the use of one-day secret trials and forced televised confessions drew the condemnation of international human rights observers. The authorities also accused the United Kingdom and the USA of attempting to provoke ethnic unrest in March, when armed rebels in the south-eastern province of Sistan and Baluchestan ambushed a convoy of government and provincial officials and killed 22 of them. All of the victims were members of the Shi'a community, whom the province's Baluchi Sunni population had long accused of religious discrimination. In February 2007 11 people were believed to have died in an explosion on a bus carrying members of the Revolutionary Guards in the provincial capital, Zahedan. The militant Sunni People's Resistance Movement of Iran (PRMI, formerly Jundallah—Soldiers of God) was widely believed to have orchestrated the explosion, as well as other recent attacks against government and security officials in Sistan and Baluchestan.

In August 2006 the Government banned the Centre for Defence of Human Rights, on the grounds that it was an 'illegal' organization since it had failed to apply for a permit. Under the presidency of Nobel Peace Prize winner Shirin Ebadi, who in

2003 became both the first Iranian and the first Muslim woman to receive a Nobel prize, the Centre provided free legal advice to dissidents and other activists who had been detained for protesting against the authorities or criticizing government policies. Although the Centre was formally closed by the Iranian authorities in December 2008, Ebadi vowed to continue the group's activities.

Meanwhile, the country began to prepare for two important polls to be held on 15 December 2006, to elect members of the Assembly of Experts and more than 113,000 municipal councillors, including those on the 15-seat Tehran municipal council. Both these bodies were dominated by political 'hardliners', and the composition of the former was especially crucial as it is charged with electing the country's Supreme Leader. In September 2006 Ahmadinejad appointed Mojtaba Samare, described by many as the President's closest aide, as deputy of political affairs at the Ministry of the Interior and thus the official responsible for monitoring the elections. By November more than two-thirds of the 500 candidates who had registered for membership of the Assembly of Experts had been disqualified. According to the Council of Guardians, 100 prospective candidates had withdrawn their applications, while all the female candidates had reportedly failed the exam concerning religious interpretation. As a result, in some constituencies there would only be one person running for office. None the less, the results of the municipal election demonstrated an unexpected victory for the 'moderates', the President's allies having failed to win control of any municipal council. Associates of Ahmadinejad secured only two seats on the Tehran council, while allies of the 'hardline' mayor Muhammad Baqir Qalibaf won eight seats, 'reformists' four and an independent one seat. A significant majority of municipal seats were secured by 'reformists', independents, 'moderate conservatives' and other opponents of the President. Particularly notable among those elected to the Assembly of Experts was former President Rafsanjani (who was also elected as Speaker of the Council in September 2007, following the death of Ayatollah Ali Akbar Meshkini in July).

In January 2007 a reported 50 legislators signed a document demanding that President Ahmadinejad answer questions in the Majlis with regard to his increasingly aggressive stance on the nuclear issue. Moreover, 150 Majlis deputies (including former allies of the President) were said to have signed a letter blaming Ahmadinejad for the country's high levels of inflation and unemployment, and condemning him for failing to deliver the state budget on time. In May the Government raised the price of petrol and, in the following month, unexpectedly introduced petrol rationing in order to reduce the fuel subsidies that were contributing to Iran's considerable state budget deficit. The measures resulted in attacks being carried out by angry protesters against a number of petrol stations and other state buildings in Tehran and elsewhere. Several Iranian newspapers reported that President Ahmadinejad had dismissed two prominent members of the Council of Ministers in August; the state news agency, however, insisted that the two men had resigned their posts. Minister of Industries and Mines Ali Reza Tahmasbi was replaced by Ali Akbar Mehrabian, and Minister of Petroleum Sayed Kazem Vaziri Hamaneh by Gholamhossein Nozari (head of the National Iranian Oil Co); Vaziri Hamaneh was said to have been appointed as a special adviser to the President on oil and gas affairs.

Press reports in January 2008 suggested that, in advance of the eighth elections to the Majlis scheduled to be held in March, almost one-half of the 7,168 candidates who had registered for the polls (the majority of these being 'reformists') had been disqualified by either the Ministry of the Interior or the Council of Guardians. It was evident at this time that the popularity of President Ahmadinejad was waning, as the public became increasingly frustrated by their economic hardships, by official repression of their individual freedoms and by the President's handling of foreign affairs. In late January Ahmadinejad's authority was questioned by Ayatollah Khamenei, who overruled his decision not to supply subsidized gas to Iranians in rural areas who were suffering shortages owing to the extreme weather conditions. In early March it was reported that 'conservatives' had split into two separate lists to contest the forthcoming polls: the United Principlist Front was formed by traditionalists who supported President Ahmadinejad's policies, while the Broad Principlist Coalition consisted of those who were more critical of the President's foreign and economic policies (including so-called 'revisionists' Ali Larijani, Mohsen Rezai and Muhammad Baqir Qalibaf).

Although no official results were issued at this stage, 208 of the 290 seats had reportedly been filled at the first legislative ballot, held on 14 March 2008. Several sources indicated that the Majlis would be dominated by 'conservatives', who already controlled an estimated 132 seats in the legislature (with a reported 90 of these being supporters of President Ahmadinejad). However, 'reformists', who won some 31 seats at the first round, asserted that the election had been neither free nor fair, owing to the disqualification by the authorities of at least 1,700 candidates considered to be 'reformists' in advance of the poll (some of those disqualified in early 2008 were subsequently reinstated). Opposition politicians also remarked that Iran's state-controlled media had been noticeably biased in favour of the President's supporters during electoral campaigning. Officials from the USA and the European Union (EU, see p. 276) were strongly critical of the conduct of the election. 'Conservatives' secured 19 of the 30 seats in Tehran, with the remainder to be decided at the run-off election. According to the Ministry of the Interior, almost 60% of eligible voters had participated in the first ballot. A second round of voting for the 82 undecided Majlis seats was held on 25 April. However, three seats remained vacant following both rounds, after election officials had annulled the results for unspecified reasons; by-elections for these seats were to be held at a later date. According to official reports, 'conservatives' had consolidated their control of the legislature, with an estimated 198–200 seats; 'reformists' secured around 46–50 seats, and some 40–43 seats were held by independents'. Only one of the 11 contested seats in Tehran went to a 'reformist' candidate at the second round; thus 29 of the 30 seats in the capital would be controlled by 'conservatives'. However, despite 'conservative' factions being in control of the new Majlis, around one-third of these were said to be members of the Broad Principlist Coalition. It was, therefore, generally assumed that Ahmadinejad would experience greater levels of opposition among Majlis deputies than had been the case in the previous parliament. On 28 May Larijani was elected Speaker of the Majlis, in succession to Gholam-Ali Haddad-Adel; he was subsequently re-elected to the post three times, most recently on 25 May 2011.

Meanwhile, in mid-May 2008 President Ahmadinejad was reported to have dismissed the Minister of the Interior, Moustafa Pour-Muhammadi; he was replaced by Ali Kordan in August, when two other new ministers were approved by the Majlis: Sayed Shamseddin Hosseini became the Minister of Economic Affairs and Finance, and Hamid Behbahani Minister of Roads and Transport. However, Kordan was dismissed from his post in early November, after his impeachment by the Majlis for having admitted to possessing a forged law degree. The disclosure proved to be politically embarrassing for President Ahmadinejad, who had supported Kordan during the impeachment proceedings. Sadeq Mahsouli was sworn in as Minister of the Interior in mid-November.

It was reported in January 2009 that 16 police officers who had been kidnapped from Sistan and Baluchestan province in June 2008 had all been killed by militants of the PRMI; the group had issued the demand that 200 of its members were released from captivity. More than 20 people were killed in a suicide bomb attack on a Shi'a mosque in Zahedan on 28 May 2009. Responsibility for the attack was claimed by the PRMI, which claimed that a secret meeting involving senior members of the Revolutionary Guards was taking place at the mosque. Allegations by Mahsouli and other Iranian officials that the attack had been sponsored by the US Administration were vehemently denied by President Barack Obama. On 30 May three members of the PRMI were publicly executed, having allegedly confessed to involvement in planning the mosque bombing; the men were already in custody at the time of the attack, having been arrested in connection with other militant activity in the area, including the bombing in February 2007 (see above). In June 2009 14 suspected PRMI rebels were extradited from Pakistan, and in mid-July 13 of the suspects were executed on charges of involvement in militant activity (although they were not specifically charged with involvement in the Zahedan mosque bombing). The 14th suspect, Abdolhamid Rigi—brother of the group's leader, Abdolmalek Rigi—was also sentenced to death, and was executed in May 2010. According to reports published in Iran in late July 2009, Abdolhamid Rigi had informed the authorities that his brother had received financial assistance and equipment from US intelligence agents. In February 2010 the Iranian authorities announced that Abdolmalek Rigi had been arrested at Bandar Abbas airport after a commercial aircraft on which he was travelling was forced to land by the Iranian air force. He was executed in June, having been found guilty of 79 charges relating to the PRMI's violent campaign against the Iranian military, police, other establishment figures and civilians.

The 2009 presidential election

In mid-May 2009 it was announced that only four of 475 prospective candidates had been approved by the Council of Guardians to participate in the presidential election due in the following month. These were: Ahmadinejad; Mousavi, the former Prime Minister who was supported by former President Khatami; the 'reformist' former Majlis Speaker, Karrubi; and Mohsen Rezai, a 'conservative' former Revolutionary Guards commander who had been critical of the President's handling of economic affairs. An estimated 85% of registered voters participated in the election on 12 June. Ahmadinejad was pronounced the winner of the contest with 62.6% of the vote; Mousavi, his principal opponent, secured 33.8% of the votes cast, Rezai 1.7% and Karrubi 0.9%, according to figures released by the Ministry of the Interior on 13 June. The official result was disputed by the defeated candidates, who alleged that electoral irregularities had taken place and called for the result to be annulled. Within hours of the results being announced, violent clashes between anti-Government protesters and security forces took place in Tehran; public demonstrations and civil unrest escalated in the following days and spread to other cities, including Shiraz and Esfahan. Despite an official ban on unauthorized demonstrations, large numbers of opposition supporters marched in Tehran on 15 June in protest against what they believed was a rigged election. The rally, which, according to some observers, was attended by hundreds of thousands of people, constituted the largest display of public protest in Iran since the Islamic Revolution in 1979. Many demonstrators wore green items of clothing, a reference to the predominant colour in Mousavi's election campaign material, and the unprecedented wave of public protests in the following weeks subsequently became known as the 'Green movement'. It was reported on 16 June 2009 that seven people had been killed in violent incidents during the previous day's protests. Meanwhile, on 15 June Ayatollah Khamenei ordered the Council of Guardians to instigate an inquiry into the allegations of voting irregularities. Public demonstrations and sporadic violent clashes continued in Tehran for several days amid reports of the increasing deployment of Basij forces to suppress the protests. Foreign journalists were prohibited from reporting on the unrest, and extensive disruption to internet and mobile telecommunications services was reported. Up to 10 protesters were reportedly killed during unrest in the capital on 20 June; amateur footage of the fatal shooting of a young female protester, Neda Agha-Soltan, was broadcast on a social networking website, leading to widespread international condemnation.

Meanwhile, on 19 June 2009 Ayatollah Khamenei declared the validity of the election and ordered an immediate end to the demonstrations; the Supreme Leader also accused foreign powers of fomenting unrest within Iran. The Council of Guardians announced that there had been irregularities in numerous districts, stating that the number of votes cast exceeded the number of eligible voters in up to 50 constituencies. However, the Council ruled that these discrepancies were insufficient to affect the outcome of the election and rejected an annulment of the result. On 24 June Rezai withdrew his opposition to the election result. By this time at least 17 people were reported to have been killed and over 600 arrested during the unrest. Intermittent violent clashes between protesters and security forces continued into July, although the numbers of demonstrators decreased progressively. Long-standing divisions within the Iranian political hierarchy were reportedly deepened as a result of the disputed election: in mid-July former President Rafsanjani, head of both the Expediency Council and the Assembly of Experts, delivered a prayer sermon at Tehran University, in which he alleged that the authorities had lost the trust of the people, and called for the lifting of restrictions on the media and the release of hundreds of detainees.

Ahmadinejad's appointment of a close ally, Esfandiar Rahim-Mashai, to the position of First Vice-President on 17 July 2009 provoked strong disapproval within the political establishment. Rahim-Mashai, a former head of the Cultural Heritage, Handicrafts and Tourism Organization, had attracted severe criticism in 2008 when he was reported to have referred to Iran as being 'a friend of the Israeli people'. Following a letter to the President from the Supreme Leader, which demanded the annulment of the appointment, Rahim-Mashai tendered his resignation on 24 July 2009. Yet despite the controversy, Ahmadinejad retained Rahim-Mashai as an adviser and head of the presidential office. The dismissal, in late July, of the Minister of Intelligence and Security, Gholamhossein Mohseni Ejeie, and the subsequent resignation of the Minister of Culture and Islamic Guidance, Muhammad Hossein Saffar-Harandi, were widely reported to have resulted from the two ministers' strong opposition to the appointment of Rahim-Mashai. Following the formal endorsement of Ahmadinejad's appointment by the Supreme Leader on 3 August, he was sworn in for a second term as President two days later. The inauguration ceremony was not attended by the defeated candidates Mousavi and Karrubi, who continued to reject the legitimacy of the result; several other senior political figures—including former Presidents Rafsanjani and Khatami, and up to 50 parliamentary deputies—also stayed away from the ceremony.

On 3 September 2009 the Majlis approved 18 of President Ahmadinejad's 21 ministerial nominees, five of whom retained the posts they had held in the outgoing cabinet. However, the proposed ministers of Education, Energy, and Welfare and Social Security failed to receive a sufficient number of parliamentary votes to be appointed. Marzieh Vahid Dastjerdi, the new Minister of Health and Medical Education, became the first woman to join the Council of Ministers since the 1979 Revolution. The appointment of Brig.-Gen. Ahmad Vahidi as the Minister of Defence and Armed Forces Logistics provoked international criticism: Vahidi, a former Revolutionary Guards commander, was accused by the authorities in Argentina of involvement in the bombing of a Jewish cultural centre in Buenos Aires in 1994, which resulted in the deaths of 85 people. Crucially, the level of support for the nominees was interpreted as a significant endorsement of Ahmadinejad's tenure. In mid-November 2009 nominees for the three outstanding ministerial positions received parliamentary approval.

Meanwhile, at the beginning of August 2009 a trial took place of more than 100 detainees, including numerous prominent 'reformist' figures such as former Vice-President Abtahi and former Deputy Minister of Foreign Affairs Mohsen Aminzadeh, during which several defendants allegedly confessed to involvement in a plot to foment the recent unrest. Further confessions were elicited in several subsequent televised sessions during August, with defendants, who also included journalists, student activists and lawyers, reading statements giving details of an alleged conspiracy to overthrow the Islamic Republic in collusion with various foreign agencies. During the trials many of Ahmadinejad's critics and political rivals, including Mousavi, Khatami and Rafsanjani, were implicated in the alleged conspiracy. The trials were condemned by opposition leaders and international human rights organizations, who alleged that the confessions had been extracted under duress and that the proceedings were unconstitutional. According to the authorities, 20 people had been killed during the unrest and some 4,000 had been arrested, of whom about 300 were reportedly still in custody in mid-August; however, the number of fatalities was disputed by opposition supporters, who claimed that as many as 69 people had been killed. Following the trials, in October three detainees were reportedly sentenced to death for their role in the unrest; another five defendants received death sentences in mid-November. In late November Abtahi was sentenced to six years' imprisonment on charges including plotting against national security and insulting the President.

Tens of thousands of 'Green movement' supporters participated in anti-Government demonstrations in Tehran on 19 September 2009, to coincide with an official Palestinian solidarity rally. In defiance of an order banning such protests, senior opposition figures, including Mousavi and Khatami, took part in the demonstrations. In early November over 100 people were arrested following violent clashes in Tehran between demonstrators and security forces on the occasion of the 30th anniversary of the storming of the US embassy. As well as demanding the removal of the President, some protesters chanted slogans against the Supreme Leader, in anger at his endorsement of Ahmadinejad and bias towards the 'ultra-conservative' establishment. In mid-November it was revealed that Ayatollah Khamenei, in response to the ongoing civil unrest, had sanctioned the creation of a new intelligence agency under the auspices of the Revolutionary Guards.

It was reported in mid-October 2009 that Karrubi was to be investigated by a special judicial committee after he alleged, in August, that security forces had tortured and sexually abused political prisoners following the post-election unrest. Amid repeated demands from 'hardliners' that the leaders of the anti-Government movement should be put on trial, Mousavi was removed from his post as President of the Iranian Academy of the Arts in late December. On 19 December it was announced that an important advocate of the 'reformist' cause in Iran, Ayatollah Montazeri, had died. Montazeri had publicly questioned the validity of Ahmadinejad's recent election victory, and violent clashes between rival 'reformist' and 'conservative' supporters erupted during his funeral procession. At the end of December the Ashoura festival was marked by large demonstrations by opposition activists in central Tehran; eight people were reported to have been killed, including a nephew of Mousavi, and hundreds were arrested during clashes with security forces.

More than 40 people, including at least five senior Revolutionary Guards commanders, were killed in a suicide bomb attack in Sistan and Baluchestan province on 18 October 2009. Two bombs were reportedly detonated as a convoy of Revolutionary Guards personnel arrived for a meeting with local Shi'a and Sunni leaders. Responsibility for the attack was claimed by the PRMI. Once again, senior Iranian officials accused the USA and the United Kingdom of providing support to the Baluchi militants. The Iranian authorities also claimed that the militants maintained bases across the border in Pakistan and had received assistance from Pakistani intelligence agents. President Ahmadinejad urged Pakistan to apprehend and extradite those responsible for the bombing. On 15 July 2010 a reported 28 people, again including members of the Revolutionary Guards, were killed in a double suicide bomb attack at a Shi'a mosque in Zahedan. The PRMI alleged that it had carried out the attack in revenge for the execution of its leader, Abdolmalek Rigi, in the previous month (see above). Shortly afterwards three Majlis deputies from Sistan and Baluchestan announced their resignations in protest against the authorities' failure to prevent the attack. In November the US Department of State formally designated the PRMI as a terrorist organization.

Two dissidents convicted during the trials in August 2009 were executed in January 2010. The men were alleged to have participated in a pro-royalist plot to overthrow the Islamic Republic. (In January 2011 two further dissidents were executed, having been convicted of distributing footage of the 2009 demonstrations via the internet, and of promoting the proscribed Mujahidin-e-Khalq.) In the second week of February 2010 two prominent opposition figures, Aminzadeh and former minister Mohsen Behzad, were sentenced to six and five years' imprisonment, respectively. A report published by Human Rights Watch in that month accused the Iranian authorities of committing widespread human rights abuses since the presidential election in June 2009, including: arbitrary arrests and detentions of political opponents; torture and sexual abuse of detainees; extrajudicial killings; and repression of citizens' rights to free assembly and expression. Opposition websites reported that at least 55 journalists were in detention in early February 2010.

Representatives of the 'reformist' Islamic Iran Participation Front, which had referred to Ahmadinejad's victory in the 2009 election as a '*coup d'état*', complained in mid-March 2010 that the judiciary had barred them from holding their annual party conference. Marking the Iranian New Year in late March, Mousavi urged his supporters to ensure that 2010/11 would be a 'year of resistance' against the current regime. However, in April 2010 both the Islamic Iran Participation Front and the Organization of the Mujahidin of the Islamic Revolution, which had also supported Mousavi in the presidential election, were said to have been 'dissolved' for reasons of undermining national security. Although, in early June, Ayatollah Khamenei pardoned or commuted the gaol terms of 81 people accused of crimes during the unrest that followed the disputed election, the Iranian opposition believed this merely to be an attempt to prevent any large-scale protests from taking place on the first anniversary of the poll. In the event, security forces managed to contain demonstrations held on 12 June, and no serious violence occurred. In September supporters of Mousavi alleged that the presence of security forces around his office in Tehran meant that the former premier was essentially under house arrest.

In April 2010 the Majlis gave its approval to a bill that reduced the legislature's powers to review orders issued by the appointed Council of Guardians, Assembly of Experts, Expediency Council and Supreme National Security Council (SNSC). According to many Iranian commentators, this proved that these non-elected bodies close to Ayatollah Khamenei now wielded even more influence over Iran's elected parliament than they had done previously. Nevertheless, it became apparent later that year that President Ahmadinejad was facing growing opposition from fellow 'conservative' politicians who were concerned by the increasing authoritarianism of his regime. It was reported in 'conservative' newspapers that some legislators were preparing a petition that would grant them the right to debate the impeachment of the President. Moreover, an article published in the USA's *Wall Street Journal* in late November claimed that four Majlis deputies had accused both Ahmadinejad and his Council of Ministers of irregularities such as a lack of fiscal transparency and the unauthorized withdrawal of funds from the Central Bank's foreign reserves. However, despite widespread concerns within Iran that too much power was centred around the President, Ahmadinejad appeared to retain the support of Ayatollah Khamenei.

At least 33 people were killed and 95 people injured in a bomb attack at a mosque in Chabahar, in the south-east of the country, on 15 December 2010. The PRMI subsequently claimed that it had carried out the attack. Also that month it was announced that Minister of Foreign Affairs Manouchehr Mottaki had been removed from office and replaced on an interim basis by the Vice-President and Head of the Atomic Energy Organization, Ali Akbar Salehi. No official reason was given for Mottaki's departure, although it was reported that he had disagreed with President Ahmadinejad over the ongoing negotiations on Iran's nuclear programme. On 30 January 2011 the formal nomination of Salehi as Minister of Foreign Affairs was approved by the Majlis; on 13 February Fereydoun Abbasi Davani, a leading nuclear scientist who had been the target of an attempted assassination in November 2010, became the new Vice-President and Head of the Atomic Energy Organization. Meanwhile, in early February 2011 the Minister of Roads and Transportation, Hamid Behbahani, was dismissed from office, after a vote of no confidence was approved by the Majlis; Minister of Housing and Urban Development Ali Nikzad assumed responsibility for the portfolio on an interim basis. In late February two people were killed after protests by 'Green movement' activists in Tehran, apparently in support of the popular uprisings in Tunisia and Egypt; it was reported that Karrubi and Mousavi had been placed under house arrest in an attempt to prevent their participation in the protests.

Recent developments: increased tensions within the political establishment

In early March 2011 Ayatollah Muhammad Reza Mahdavi Kani was elected as Speaker of the Assembly of Experts, in place of Rafsanjani, who had declined nomination for the role, citing his concern for national unity. Rafsanjani's replacement followed reports of a campaign against him by supporters of President Ahmadinejad, owing to his equivocal stance in the wake of Ahmadinejad's re-election in 2009. In late April 2011 it was reported that Ahmadinejad had forced the resignation of the Minister of Intelligence and Security, Heydar Moslehi, but that Moslehi had been ordered to remain in office after the intervention of Ayatollah Khamenei, who was thought to retain considerable influence over the allocation of key ministerial posts. In an apparent protest at Khamenei's decision, Ahmadinejad declined to attend meetings of the Council of Ministers for 11 days, before he was persuaded by legislators to return to his presidential duties. Tensions between the President and the Spiritual Leader became increasingly evident as the year progressed. Disagreements between various sections of Iran's 'conservative' establishment were also more prominent in advance of the legislative elections due in March 2012 (see Recent developments) and the presidential election in 2013—when President Ahmadinejad was constitutionally required to stand down.

On 14 May 2011 the Ministers of Petroleum, of Industries and Mines, and of Welfare and Social Security were all dismissed by President Ahmadinejad, who stated that he wished to reduce the number of government ministers; however, many observers assessed the dismissals as being politically motivated. Serving cabinet ministers were given temporary charge of the latter two ministries, but Ahmadinejad angered 'conservative' deputies in the Majlis by naming himself as interim Minister of Petroleum. He was prevented from formally assuming the post, on the grounds that it was an unconstitutional act, by both the Council of Guardians in late May and by a large majority of Majlis deputies in a vote held on 1 June. Despite the obvious setback, Ahmadinejad proceeded with plans approved by the Government on 8 May (as part of its Fifth Five-Year Development Plan for 2010–15) to reduce the number of ministries from 21 to 17 by 2015 through the mergers of eight portfolios into four new ones: of Co-operatives, Labour and Social Welfare; Industries, Mines and Trade; Roads and Urban Development; and Sport and Youth Affairs. The changes were endorsed by the Majlis, despite strong opposition from 'conservative' deputies. On 2 June Ahmadinejad named Mahmoud Aliabadi as acting Minister of Petroleum; however, he was replaced in a permanent capacity by Brig.-Gen. Rostam Ghasemi on 3 August. Ghasemi was a controversial appointment since he is a commander in the Revolutionary Guards and is thus subject to US and EU sanctions. Moreover, since Iran held the OPEC presidency at that time, he would automatically assume the chairmanship of the organization.

Meanwhile, after Ahmadinejad was reputed to have blocked some funds previously allocated to the office of the Supreme Leader in the national budget, in early June 2011 the President finally admitted that serious differences did exist among those at the highest levels of the state. On 21 June the resignation was announced of the newly appointed Deputy Minister of Foreign Affairs, Muhammad Sharif Malekzadeh, a close ally of both the President and of his adviser Rahim-Mashai—who had reportedly been replaced as head of the presidential office by Hamid Baqai in early April. His resignation followed mounting pressure from 'conservative' deputies, who accused him of acting against the clerical hierarchy. Two days later Malekzadeh was arrested on suspicion of involvement in a US $2,600m. financial scandal which reportedly involved some of Iran's largest banks. Similar charges of corruption were also said to have been made in that month against two other pro-Ahmadinejad industrialists. Moreover, on 27 October another close associate of the President, Sayed Hamid Pour-Mohammadi, the Deputy Governor of the Central Bank, was also detained by police on suspicion of involvement in the alleged fraud, which was said to have included the embezzlement of funds from Bank Melli in 2005. On 30 October a number of Majlis deputies formally requested that President Ahmadinejad be questioned by a parliamentary committee in relation to the affair. On 1 November the Minister of Finance, Shamseddin Hosseini, survived a vote in parliament after a number of deputies also requested his impeachment over the banking scandal.

Supporters of Iran's opposition 'Green movement' held a rally in the centre of Tehran on 12 June 2011, the second anniversary of the disputed presidential election. The rally was forcibly disrupted by security forces using tear gas and batons; a number of protesters were reportedly arrested by the authorities. Indeed, several reports in mid-2011 indicated that the Government was continuing with its repressive policy towards opposition activists, apparently to prevent the occurrence of any mass political unrest as seen in many parts of the Middle East and North Africa since the start of the year. Human rights groups also noted a significant increase in the number of executions during the first half of 2011. At the end of August the wife of Mahdi Karrubi—who had been placed under house arrest in February—revealed that he had been held in solitary confinement at an apartment in Tehran for almost two months. On 12 November a bomb attack at a Revolutionary Guards missile base in Bigdaneh, east of Tehran, killed a reported 17 members of the corps, among them Maj.-Gen. Hassan Moghaddam, who was said to be a leading figure in Iran's missiles programme. Although the Iranian authorities stated that the explosion had been an accident, there was widespread speculation as to whether Israel's foreign intelligence agency, Mossad, might have been responsible.

Further arrests of dissidents, journalists and intellectuals were reported in January 2012, in advance of the legislative elections scheduled for 2 March. Moreover, the Government appeared to be attempting to block public access to internet sites that were critical of the regime. On 7 February 2012 the Deputy Speaker of the Majlis, Shahabeddin Sadr, was named as Secretary-General of a new principlist coalition, the Insight and Islamic Awakening Front. On the same day Mahmoud Ahmadinejad became the first serving President since the creation of the Islamic Republic in 1979 to be summoned to the Majlis to be questioned by deputies about a number of issues, principally concerning the Iranian economy but also related to his domestic and foreign policies. It was reported that some legislators intended to question the President about the state of his relationship with Ayatollah Khamenei and on the details of recent disputes regarding the appointment or dismissal of certain government officials.

The Nuclear Issue

Following President Khatami's announcement in February 2003 regarding the discovery and successful extraction of uranium, the USA urged the International Atomic Energy Agency (IAEA) to declare Iran to be in violation of the nuclear non-proliferation treaty (NPT), and appealed for Russia to end its collaboration with Iran on construction of the Bushehr nuclear power plant, in south-western Iran. In June the Director-General of the IAEA, Dr Mohammed el-Baradei, presented a report concerning Iran's nuclear capabilities to the IAEA Board of Governors, in which he called on Iran to open its nuclear programme to a more rigorous system of inspections. Iran responded that it would only comply with this request if it were given access to the nuclear technology it required. Despite assurances by President Khatami that Iran's nuclear programme was 'entirely peaceful', the USA insisted that Iran was in breach of its safeguards obligations, and the IAEA (with US support) adopted a resolution on 12 September giving Iran until 31 October to disclose full details of its nuclear programme and to show evidence that it was not developing nuclear weapons. This followed the discovery of enriched uranium at a processing plant south of Tehran. On 21 October 2003, following visits to the country by officials of the IAEA, France, Germany and the United Kingdom, it was announced that Iran would accept a more rigorous system of inspections at its nuclear facilities.

In February 2004, however, the IAEA reported that it had found evidence of undeclared facilities that could be used for the enrichment of uranium. The Agency adopted a resolution condemning Iran for the secrecy of its nuclear activities in March, and a further resolution on 18 June criticizing Iran for failing to co-operate with the inspections process. In late June the Iranian leadership announced that, although it would adhere to its pledge to suspend actual uranium enrichment, it would resume manufacturing parts for centrifuges and would also recommence the testing and assembly of centrifuges. Moreover, Iran criticized the United Kingdom, France and Germany for not supplying it with the technology and trade they had promised in October 2003 in return for this pledge. In October 2004 Russia and Iran completed the construction of the Bushehr nuclear plant. Russian officials pressed the Islamic regime to cease uranium enrichment, apparently fearing that the sanctions likely to be imposed by the UN Security Council would threaten the Bushehr deal. Iran also tested a long-range satellite-launching rocket, the *Shahab-4*, asserting that it would only use its missiles in self-defence. In November, following further talks with French, German and British officials in Paris, France, Iran complied with IAEA demands to suspend temporarily its enrichment programme.

In August 2005 Iran resumed the conversion of uranium to gas (the stage before enrichment) at the Esfahan conversion facility, having previously rejected as 'worthless' a set of compensatory proposals put forward by the United Kingdom, France and Germany in exchange for abandoning its enrichment programme. The IAEA subsequently adopted a resolution on 11 August expressing 'serious concern' at the resumption of nuclear activities at Esfahan, and urging Iran to revert to suspension. Also in August President Ahmadinejad appointed Ali Larijani (believed to be a close ally of Ayatollah Khamenei) as Secretary of the SNSC and chief nuclear negotiator, replacing the more moderate Hassan Rohani. A further IAEA resolution on 24 September found Iran guilty of 'non-compliance' and asserted that it should increase the transparency of its nuclear programme and reinstate suspension.

However, Iran announced on 10 January 2006 that it had reopened its uranium enrichment research facility at Natanz, south of Tehran, after a moratorium of two years. On 4 February the Board of Governors of the IAEA voted to report Iran to the UN Security Council. Iran confirmed on 14 February that small-scale uranium enrichment work had recommenced at the Natanz plant. On 8 March el-Baradei transmitted his IAEA report on Iran's nuclear programme to the Security Council, which, on 29 March, unanimously approved a statement calling on Iran to suspend all uranium enrichment activities within 30 days. On 11 April President Ahmadinejad responded to this demand by announcing that, two days previously, Iran had successfully enriched uranium for the first time, although he insisted that his country had no intention of developing nuclear weapons. The US Administration revealed at this time that it was allocating US $75m. to fund Iranian dissident groups.

On 28 April 2006 el-Baradei delivered a report to the UN Security Council which concluded that Iran had failed to comply with the 30-day deadline imposed by the Council to halt its uranium enrichment activities, and affirmed that since the country had failed fully to co-operate with the IAEA, there could be no guarantee that its nuclear activities were purely peaceful.

In response, the US ambassador to the UN, John Bolton, called on the Security Council to invoke Chapter VII of the UN Charter, which contained provision for the use of military action—a demand that was immediately rejected by the People's Republic of China and Russia. Meeting in Brussels, Belgium, in mid-May, EU ministers responsible for foreign affairs attempted to find a way out of the impasse by proposing a 'bold' package of trade and technical incentives for Iran to halt its nuclear programme. However, the offer was firmly rejected by the Iranian leadership. Further economic incentives were offered by the EU's High Representative for Common Foreign and Security Policy, Javier Solana, in June, following an agreement reached by the five permanent members of the UN Security Council—China, France, Russia, the United Kingdom and the USA—together with Germany, concerning new proposals to encourage Iran to renounce enrichment. These included an offer of nuclear technical assistance, the removal of certain US economic sanctions and the possible opening of direct discussions between Iran and the USA.

On 31 July 2006 the UN Security Council approved a resolution (No. 1696), which expressed 'serious concern' regarding Iran's refusal to co-operate with the IAEA and warned that the country could face possible sanctions unless it halted its uranium enrichment programme by 31 August. Significantly, however, the text of Resolution 1696 fell short of mentioning specific sanctions (at the request of China and Russia), instead referring to 'appropriate measures' being adopted. On 22 August Iran's chief nuclear negotiator, Ali Larijani, presented a formal response to the package of economic incentives offered by the permanent members of the Security Council plus Germany in June. Despite indicating that the Iranian leadership was prepared to begin serious negotiations with the international community, Larijani described the country's enrichment activities as an 'inalienable right'. The IAEA reported to the UN Security Council on 31 August that Iran had failed to meet its requirement to cease uranium enrichment and that Iranian officials had not co-operated with the Agency's investigators.

On 23 December 2006 the UN Security Council adopted Resolution 1737, which imposed a series of limited sanctions on the Iranian regime owing to its lack of compliance with the terms of Resolution 1696. The sanctions banned the import and export of nuclear-related technology and materials, and froze the assets of leading individuals and companies involved in the nuclear programme. Iran was granted 60 days in which to cease all enrichment activities and thus avoid the imposition of further sanctions. However, President Ahmadinejad rejected the terms of Resolution 1737, and in late December the Majlis adopted legislation that required the Iranian Government to review its co-operation with the IAEA and urged an acceleration of Iran's nuclear energy programme. In January 2007 Iran announced that it was barring 38 IAEA inspectors from the country, in retaliation for the imposition of sanctions.

In his report to the IAEA on 22 February 2007, el-Baradei affirmed that Iran had failed to meet the deadline of the previous day to cease uranium enrichment and that the Islamic regime had actually expanded the programme from 'research-scale' to 'industrial-scale' enrichment. This refusal to halt uranium enrichment resulted in tougher sanctions being imposed by the UN Security Council against Iran. On 24 March the Security Council adopted Resolution 1747, which again required Iran to suspend all uranium enrichment-related and reprocessing activities and to agree to grant IAEA inspectors full access to its nuclear sites. Resolution 1747 imposed, *inter alia*, an embargo on the sale of arms to and from Iran, and a ban on the transfer of funds to Iran by state and international financial institutions except where these were intended for humanitarian or development aid. The UN granted Iran 60 days to comply with the measures or face 'further appropriate measures'.

In a defiant response to the imposition of Resolution 1747, in April 2007 President Ahmadinejad confirmed that Iran had begun the enrichment of uranium on an 'industrial scale' at the Natanz nuclear facility, and boasted that Iran had joined the 'nuclear club of nations'. Following an inspection of the facility, IAEA inspectors agreed that Iran had commenced this process, but asserted that they were uncertain as to whether all of the 1,300 centrifuges at Natanz were actually in operation. The day before the UN Security Council's deadline for Iranian compliance of 24 May (according to the terms of UN Resolution 1747), the IAEA issued a report claiming that Iran remained in defiance of the demands of the international community to suspend its enrichment programme and open its nuclear facilities fully to agency inspectors. El-Baradei subsequently declared that he believed Iran to possess the capability to build a nuclear weapon in between three to eight years. However, the IAEA Director-General asserted that he did not have evidence to support the claim that Iran was seeking to produce such weapons of mass destruction.

Following a meeting between Iranian and IAEA officials in Vienna, Austria, in July 2007, Iran agreed to provide information about previous nuclear experiments, to allow inspectors to visit a plutonium-producing reactor being built at Arak and to decelerate its uranium enrichment programme at Natanz. El-Baradei was reported at the end of August to have agreed a 'work plan' with Iranian officials, whereby Iran was given a three-month deadline by which to end any technical ambiguities concerning its nuclear programme. However, the US Administration continued to demand a complete and immediate cessation of uranium enrichment. President Nicolas Sarkozy of France also indicated that his country was henceforth to adopt a tougher approach to Iranian non-compliance with UN resolutions. In late October Iran's Deputy Foreign Minister for European and American Affairs, Saeed Jalili, was chosen to replace Larijani as Secretary of the SNSC and principal negotiator on the nuclear issue, after Larijani had tendered his resignation. The appointment of Jalili, who was closely affiliated with President Ahmadinejad, was expected to result in Iran taking a firmer stance in the ongoing negotiations with the IAEA and international community. Towards the end of October the USA imposed further unilateral sanctions against Iran, which principally targeted Iranian state-owned banks, organizations and agencies deemed to be involved in a clandestine nuclear programme or to sponsor terrorism abroad, and in particular named affiliates of the Revolutionary Guards and its élite Qods Force.

In November 2007 el-Baradei informed the IAEA that, although there had been improvements as far as transparency in the programme was concerned (as laid out in the 'work plan'), the Iranian authorities were continuing to restrict inspectors' access to nuclear plants. The IAEA Director-General also confirmed that Iran now had an estimated 3,000 centrifuges in operation. The US Administration insisted in December that a joint report (entitled the National Intelligence Estimate—NIE) published by the 16 US intelligence agencies, in which they disclosed their findings that Iran had in fact suspended its nuclear weapons development programme in 2003, would not lead his country to re-evaluate its policy towards the Islamic Republic. This report contradicted an earlier NIE report released in 2005, which assessed that Iran was 'determined' to build nuclear weapons. Although President Ahmadinejad hailed the findings of the report, he reiterated his assertion that Iran had never sought to develop a clandestine nuclear weapons programme.

On 3 March 2008 the UN Security Council adopted Resolution 1803, which tightened the sanctions already imposed on Iran with regard to the financial assets and ability to travel of officials and institutions allegedly involved in nuclear activities. Under the terms of the resolution, UN member states were required to monitor the activities of two state-owned banks with suspected links to nuclear proliferation, Bank Melli and Bank Saderat. The new resolution also prohibited the trade in 'dual-use' goods or technologies (i.e. those that could be employed for civilian or military purposes). In April, however, President Ahmadinejad declared that a further 6,000 centrifuges were being installed at the Natanz nuclear plant. In May the latest IAEA report issued by el-Baradei—as requested by the UN Security Council within 90 days of Resolution 1803—affirmed that Iranian officials had again failed to co-operate with the Agency in answering vital questions about the nature of its nuclear programme, and indeed that 500 centrifuges had been added to the 3,000 already in place at Natanz.

In an effort to resolve the ongoing dispute between Iran and the international community, Solana led a delegation from the United Kingdom, France, Germany, Russia and China (the so-called P5+1 group) to Tehran in mid-June 2008 to offer Iran a new package of incentives. Solana proposed that the UN Security Council would delay any further imposition of sanctions against the Iranian regime in return for Iran's agreement to suspend the installation of extra centrifuges at its nuclear facilities, while continuing current levels of uranium enrichment for a six-week period only. Under the proposals, which sought to ensure that Iran would cease the expansion of its enrichment programme prior to the start of formal negotiations (a precondition which Iranian officials were apparently unwilling to meet), the international community would also provide assistance with the construction of light-water reactors for electricity generation. A few days later the EU imposed new financial sanctions against Iran. Further talks were held by Solana and Jalili in Geneva in mid-July, notably in the presence of the USA's Undersecretary of State for Political Affairs, William Burns—this represented the most senior diplomatic contacts between the USA and Iran since 1979. However, by early August 2008 it became apparent that Iran had not sufficiently clarified its stance towards the incentives offered by the international delegation in June, instead favouring wider discussions on security issues. On 8 August the EU imposed tighter trade restrictions on Iran, and on 12 August the USA extended its unilateral sanctions, targeting five companies with links to the nuclear industry.

On 27 September 2008 the UN Security Council adopted Resolution 1835, requiring Iran to 'comply fully and without delay' with its obligations concerning its nuclear programme as outlined in earlier UN resolutions. This followed a report by the IAEA Director-General five days earlier, in which he maintained that Iran had failed to provide sufficient evidence that it was enriching uranium for peaceful purposes alone. In his subsequent report to the IAEA Board on 19 November, el-Baradei stated that Iran's stockpiles of enriched uranium were growing at a rapid rate, and therefore that by early 2009 the country might achieve nuclear 'breakout capacity'—meaning that in theory it had the capability to produce a sufficient level of enriched uranium to build a nuclear weapon.

In early April 2009, on the occasion of Iran's National Nuclear Day, President Ahmadinejad inaugurated the country's first nuclear fuel manufacturing plant at Esfahan. The new facility was expected to produce uranium fuel pellets for use in the nuclear reactor under construction at Arak. Ahmadinejad also announced that tests had commenced on new centrifuges with enhanced enrichment capacity. During the same week senior officials representing the permanent members of the UN Security Council and Germany held talks in London, United Kingdom, concerning a unified diplomatic response to the Iranian nuclear issue. In early June an IAEA quarterly report on Iran revealed that the number of installed centrifuges had increased to 7,221, with almost 5,000 in operation at that time. A subsequent report, issued on 28 August, revealed that IAEA inspectors had been granted access to the Arak reactor site for the first time in more than a year, and that improved monitoring arrangements had been introduced at the Natanz facility. None the less, the report noted Iran's continuing refusal to suspend its enrichment activity, as required by five Security Council resolutions, and highlighted its failure to co-operate with the Agency in connection with several issues of concern regarding the possibility of a military dimension to its nuclear programme. On 7 September el-Baradei described the IAEA's relations with Iran as having reached a 'stalemate'. On the same day President Ahmadinejad, in his first press conference since the inauguration of his second presidential term, announced his determination to proceed with the nuclear programme.

Tensions between Iran and Western nations increased considerably in late September 2009 following the revelation that a second uranium enrichment facility, the Fordo plant, was close to completion at a site near Qom. The Iranian authorities, who had hitherto concealed the plant, informed the IAEA of its existence just days before the leaders of the USA, the United Kingdom and France planned to disclose details of the facility at a meeting of the Group of 20 leading industrialized and developing nations (G20) in Pittsburgh, USA on 25 September. The site had reportedly been monitored by Western intelligence agencies for two years. Ahmadinejad insisted that, as the facility was more than six months from completion, Iran was not obliged to report its existence to the IAEA; nevertheless, the secretive development of such a significant nuclear plant was viewed by most Western governments as further evidence of Iran's covert nuclear agenda. Moreover, on 28–29 September the Revolutionary Guards test-fired a number of *Shahab-3* and *Sajjil-2* rockets, which have a range of up to 1,200 miles and could thus reach targets in Israel as well as US military bases in the Gulf region.

Direct negotiations involving Jalili and the international negotiating group took place in Geneva on 1 October 2009. The international negotiators stipulated that Iran should immediately suspend its enrichment programme in order to forestall the introduction of a new round of economic sanctions. They also detailed a proposal for the transfer of a large proportion of Iran's stock of low-enriched uranium to Russia and France for conversion into the higher-grade fuel that Iran claimed it required for medical research purposes. Iran's negotiators confirmed that they would facilitate an IAEA inspection of the Fordo enrichment plant and agreed to enter into substantive negotiations on the nuclear issue. However, Jalili reasserted Iran's demand that these should be linked to a broad package of agreements on regional and international security and global nuclear disarmament. In the first direct senior-level engagement between US and Iranian officials since the Islamic Revolution, Jalili held bilateral talks with Burns during the summit. On 3 October the *New York Times* newspaper published details of a confidential IAEA dossier which alleged that Iran was in possession of sufficient knowledge to create an effective nuclear missile. However, during an official visit to Iran on 4 October el-Baradei emphasized that there was still no concrete evidence of an Iranian military nuclear programme. El-Baradei hosted further talks in Vienna on 20–21 October, involving US, Russian, French and Iranian officials, during which a draft agreement on the uranium transfer proposal was finalized. An Iranian counter-proposal was received by the IAEA on 29 October; this involved Iran retaining most of its stock of low-enriched uranium and being granted permission to import higher-grade fuel from abroad—demands that were highly unlikely to be accepted by the international negotiators. Meanwhile, on 26 October the IAEA initiated an inspection of the nuclear facility near Qom, and in its report of 16 November the Agency confirmed that around 3,000 centrifuges had been installed at the plant.

In mid-November 2009 the Presidents of Russia and the USA issued a joint statement in which they urged Iran to expedite an agreement based on the original IAEA uranium transfer proposal. During the same week the Russian Minister of Energy, Sergei Shmatko, announced that, due to technical reasons, the Bushehr nuclear power plant would not be operational by the end of 2009, as previously scheduled. On 18 November the Minister of Foreign Affairs, Manouchehr Mottaki, announced that Iran was not prepared to send its enriched uranium abroad for further processing. However, Mottaki insisted that Iran was prepared to enter into further negotiations on securing fuel for its medical research reactor. On 27 November the IAEA adopted a resolution calling on Iran to suspend construction of the Fordo facility and to confirm whether any other nuclear facilities were under development. In a defiant response, on 29 November President Ahmadinejad announced plans for a major escalation of Iran's nuclear programme; some 10 new uranium enrichment plants, with an annual production capacity of 300 tons, were scheduled for construction. While analysts suggested that Iran lacked the resources to implement such a programme, the claims drew strong criticism from officials in the USA, France, Germany and the United Kingdom. In early February 2010, in response to the stalled uranium transfer negotiations, Salehi confirmed that Iran had commenced production of 20%-enriched uranium. Previously, Iran had processed only 3.5%-enriched uranium, a grade sufficient for the production of nuclear power, while the higher-grade fuel was required for the production of isotopes for use in medical research and diagnosis. (Uranium enriched to 90% would be required for the production of atomic weapons.) In mid-February the new Director-General of the IAEA, Yukiya Amano, issued a report in which he expressed the Agency's concerns that the Iranian nuclear programme had 'possible military dimensions', noting that the regime was still refusing to co-operate as far as IAEA inspections were concerned, and was continuing to expand its uranium enrichment activities in contravention of previous UN and IAEA resolutions. A second report by Amano, published on 31 May, additionally stated that, with further enrichment, Iran now had sufficient nuclear fuel ultimately to produce two atomic weapons.

The acceleration of Iran's nuclear activities resulted in further international pressure on the Government either to accept the terms of the original uranium transfer proposal or to cease enrichment entirely. With Iranian officials remaining defiant, on 17 May 2010 the so-called Tehran Declaration, signed by Iran, Turkey and Brazil, agreed a new uranium transfer proposal whereby Iran would send 1,200 kg of its stockpile of low-enriched uranium to be stored in Turkey, in exchange for 120 kg of nuclear reactor fuel (the uranium having been processed further into fuel rods within one year). Yet the deal, which would still require further agreement to be reached with the Western negotiating governments, failed to prevent a fourth round of sanctions against Iran from being adopted by the UN Security Council on 9 June, by 12 votes to two (Turkey and Brazil opposed the motion, while Lebanon abstained). Resolution 1929, which expressed 'serious concern' regarding Iran's failure to comply with previous resolutions and to stop enriching uranium, involved more stringent military and economic penalties against Iran, focusing on the possible transport by Iranian-owned ships of proscribed materials and on financial institutions suspected of having links with nuclear activities, as well as freezing the assets of, and imposing travel bans on, 41 companies and individuals connected with the Revolutionary Guards and Iran's wider defence establishment. The resolution also asked the UN Secretary-General to establish a panel of experts charged with monitoring Iran's compliance with the new measures. It appeared that China and Russia had been persuaded by other members of the Security Council that by supporting a new round of sanctions they would not jeopardize their bilateral trade relations with the Islamic Republic and that the extended sanctions did not specifically target Iran's oil and gas sector, in which both were investing heavily.

The US Administration, which intended the UN sanctions to encourage Iranian officials to resume negotiations on the nuclear issue, announced further unilateral sanctions against Iran on 16 June 2010; these were promulgated by President Obama on 1 July. The latest US sanctions specifically targeted the Post Bank of Iran (making it the 16th Iranian bank to be blacklisted by the US Administration), shipping and financial companies, and those providing the country with much needed fuel imports. The EU also announced new economic sanctions against Iran on 26 July: these included prohibiting investment in Iran's hydrocarbons sector by EU-based firms and increasing the number of goods which EU governments were prevented from exporting to Iran. On the same day Iran informed the IAEA that it was prepared to resume discussions regarding the proposed transfer of uranium without preconditions. On 3 August the US Administration extended its sanctions to include several institutions suspected of assisting radical organizations in the region such as the Islamic Resistance Movement (Hamas) in the Palestinian territories and Hezbollah in Lebanon.

At the end of November 2010 the Iranian authorities declared that the loading of fuel into the nuclear reactor at the Bushehr power plant was complete, the reactor having finally been launched on 21 August, under the supervision of officials from Iran, Russia and the IAEA. At further talks between negotiators from the five permanent members of the UN Security Council plus Germany and the Iranian team led by Jalili in Geneva on 6–7 December, it was agreed to convene a new round of discussions in Istanbul, Turkey, in the following month. However, no breakthrough was achieved at those talks, held on 20–21 January 2011. Earlier that month Salehi had announced that Iran now possessed the capability to manufacture fuel plates and rods to be used in its nuclear reactors. In Amano's sixth report to the IAEA board on 24 May, the Director-General again reported an expansion of Iran's nuclear programme, and suggested that a weapons programme might be under development; Iran was asked to clarify details of specific nuclear experiments that it was carrying out. In June the authorities revealed that they intended to enrich uranium up to a level of 20% at the Fordo facility near Qom. Iranian officials announced in July that the installation of a new range of centrifuges would accelerate the process by which uranium could be enriched. The declaration further alarmed the leaders of many Western and neighbouring countries, since analysts had already stated that Iran was potentially only months away from enriching uranium to the level required to produce a nuclear weapon. A visit to Iran's nuclear sites by IAEA inspectors in late August brought a generally positive response from the Agency, which talked of more 'transparency' from Iranian officials. On 2 September Amano's seventh report to the IAEA, which again suggested that there remained unanswered questions by Iran concerning a possible military dimension to the country's past and present nuclear programme, prompted Abbasi Davani, Vice-President and Head of the Atomic Energy Organization of Iran, to promise full access to Iran's nuclear sites by IAEA inspectors if the sanctions in place against Tehran were lifted. On 12 September, a week after it had been connected to the national grid, the Bushehr plant was officially opened.

The IAEA issued a report concerning Iran's nuclear programme on 8 November 2011, which used detailed evidence to indicate that the Islamic regime had, as recently as 2010, been involved in research and other testing processes required specifically for the 'development of a nuclear explosive device'. Crucially, the Agency found that some of these actions 'may still be ongoing'. This was the first time that the Agency had indicated directly that Iran was engaged in such efforts. A resolution passed by the IAEA Board on 18 November sought to increase the pressure against Iran by urging it to comply with the terms of previous UN Security Council resolutions and to engage in renewed dialogue with negotiators. Iranian officials were swift in their renewed assertions that the programme was solely for civilian purposes. However, on 22 November both the USA and the United Kingdom announced a new range of sanctions affecting Iranian banks and the energy sector. (For further details on sanctions imposed by the USA, the EU and the United Kingdom in late 2011 and early 2012, see Foreign Affairs.)

Officials of the IAEA confirmed on 9 January 2012 that scientists at the Fordo enrichment plant had begun to enrich uranium to the higher level of 20% and thus were getting closer to reaching weapons-grade capacity. The revelation led the US Administration to describe Iran as 'further escalating' its violation of UN Security Council resolutions. On 26 January President Ahmadinejad surprised some Western observers by offering to resume discussions on its nuclear programme, although he was not specific about the details of such talks. It was reported in mid-February that a resumption of negotiations between Iranian officials and those of the P5+1 group of countries was likely; the Turkish Government had again offered to host the talks. Iran's ambassador to the UN, Muhammad Khazaii, declared on 12 February that Iran would enter new negotiations without preconditions, but he reiterated the fact that his country would not give up any of its 'inalienable rights'. On 15 February President Ahmadinejad was present at a ceremony held at the Tehran research reactor (which manufactures isotopes for medical usage), where for the first time the reactor was loaded with domestically produced nuclear fuel rods.

Foreign Affairs

Relations with the USA

Relations with the USA since the end of the Iran–Iraq War have continued to be characterized by mutual suspicion. In April 1995 US efforts to isolate Iran internationally culminated in the announcement that all US companies and their overseas subsidiaries would be banned from investing in, or trading with, Iran (with the subsequent exception of US oil companies in the Caucasus and Central Asia involved in marketing petroleum from the countries of the former USSR). Russia refused to support the embargo, but announced in May that it would henceforth separate the civilian and military components of an agreement to supply Iran with a nuclear reactor (see The Nuclear Issue). In mid-1996 the US Congress approved legislation (termed the Iran-Libya Sanctions Act—ILSA) to penalize companies operating in US markets that were investing US $40m. (subsequently amended to $20m.) or more in energy projects in prescribed countries deemed to be sponsoring terrorism. However, these 'secondary' economic sanctions received little international support.

A notable development following Khatami's election to the Iranian presidency in mid-1997 was the designation by the USA, in October, of the opposition Mujahidin-e-Khalq as one of 30 proscribed terrorist organizations. (The Mujahidin-e-Khalq's parent organization, the National Council of Resistance of Iran, also based in France, was proscribed by the USA in October 1999.) In December 1997 Khatami expressed his desire to engage in a 'thoughtful dialogue' with the American people. In what was interpreted as a major concession, US President Bill Clinton stated subsequently that the USA would not require Iran (or any other Islamic state) to modify its attitude towards the Middle East peace process. The cautious rapprochement continued in January 1998, when Khatami made a widely publicized address, via a US television news network, emphasizing the need for Iran to develop closer cultural links with the USA.

The announcement, in July 1998, that Iran had successfully test-fired a new ballistic missile, the *Shahab-3*, capable of striking targets at a distance of 1,300 km (thus potentially Israel or US forces in the Gulf), caused renewed tensions. US concerns regarding what it perceived as Iran's efforts to acquire weapons of mass destruction remained a principal cause of mutual suspicion, and there was continuing evidence of efforts by the Clinton Administration to block trading agreements deemed to assist Iran's military programme. Nevertheless, earlier in that year Russia, stating that the plant it had constructed at Bushehr conformed with standards prescribed by the IAEA for the prevention of nuclear weapons proliferation, declared its willingness to provide equipment for the reactor.

Addressing the American-Iranian Council in Washington, DC, in March 2000, US Secretary of State Madeleine Albright announced an end to restrictions on imports from Iran of several non-hydrocarbons items. This substantive step towards the normalization of relations was in recognition of what the US Administration regarded as trends towards democracy under President Khatami. Albright furthermore offered what amounted to an apology for the role played by the USA in the coup of 1953, as well as for US support for Iraq in the Iran–Iraq War. Relations between Iran and the USA deteriorated in June 2001 after 14 men (13 Saudi Arabians and one Lebanese) were indicted *in absentia* by the US Government, having been charged in connection with the bomb attack at al-Khobar, Saudi Arabia in 1996 (see Regional relations). Although no Iranians were among the accused, US officials reiterated allegations that members of the Iranian Government were behind the bombing. In August 2001 the new Administration of President George W. Bush, inaugurated in January, confirmed that ILSA was to be extended for a further five years. Iran's 20th application to enter negotiations regarding membership of the World Trade Organization (WTO) was vetoed by the USA in December 2004. However, in March 2005 President Bush announced a series of economic incentives, including the removal of the ban on Iran's membership of the WTO, provided that Iran agreed permanently to suspend its nuclear energy programme. Subsequently, with Iran still at that time maintaining the suspension of its nuclear activities, the USA abandoned its objection to Iran's WTO application, enabling a working party to be established. Yet by early 2012 Iran had not begun accession negotiations with the WTO.

President Khatami was swift to offer his condolences to the USA following the suicide bombings in New York and Washington, DC, on 11 September 2001. Although Ayatollah Khamenei also condemned the terrorist attacks, he and Iran's 'conservative' press warned against any large-scale US military offensive targeting the Taliban regime and militants of the al-Qa'ida network—then led by the principal suspect for the attacks, the radical Islamist Osama bin Laden—in Afghanistan. In 2002 the Iranian administration denied accusations by the USA that it was permitting fleeing al-Qa'ida and Taliban fighters to cross the Afghan border into Iran. Relations deteriorated abruptly in January, when, in his annual State of the Union address, the US President referred to Iran as forming (together with Iraq and the Democratic People's Republic of Korea—North Korea) an 'axis of evil', explicitly accusing Iran of aggressively pursuing the development of weapons of mass destruction and of 'exporting terror'. President Khatami accused his US counterpart of 'warmongering', and in May urged 'reformist' deputies in the Majlis not to attempt to hold discussions with US officials. Meanwhile, the US Department of State again designated Iran as the world's 'most active' sponsor of terrorism (as the country was also termed during 2003–11), and US officials reiterated claims that Russia was assisting Iran in the manufacture of nuclear weapons. President Khatami, for his part, openly condemned US plans to use military force to bring about 'regime change' in Iraq, warning that such action posed a serious risk to regional stability. The announcement made by Iranian officials in February 2003 that the country was to extract recently discovered deposits of uranium in order to produce nuclear fuel heightened fears within the US Administration that Iran was secretly involved in the manufacture of nuclear weapons. However, the dialogue on Iran's nuclear capabilities was temporarily interrupted in March by the conflict in neighbouring Iraq.

Iran had been host to many Iraqi groups-in-exile, most notably the Shi'ite-dominated Supreme Council for the Islamic Revolution in Iraq (renamed the Islamic Supreme Council of Iraq in 2007) and its military wing, the Badr Brigade (subsequently renamed the Badr Organization). Therefore, following the removal from power of President Saddam Hussain by the US-led coalition in April 2003, the US Administration warned Iran not to get involved in Iraqi affairs, fearing that the Iranian leadership sought a political settlement that would favour the Shi'a Muslim majority and lead to the formation of a Shi'ite bloc in the Middle East antipathetic to US interests. However, in May it became necessary for the USA and Iran to instigate talks in Geneva, under the auspices of the UN, to discuss the return of Iraqi exiles and refugees in Iran, as well as the presence in Iraq of the Mujahidin-e-Khalq and its military wing, the National Liberation Army (NLA—see Regional relations). The talks collapsed after Ayatollah Khamenei described them as 'tantamount to surrender', and when US officials accused Iran of interfering in Iraqi internal affairs and of sheltering al-Qa'ida militants suspected of masterminding suicide bombings at expatriate compounds in Riyadh, Saudi Arabia, earlier that month. Iranian officials subsequently admitted that a group of al-Qa'ida suspects were in Iranian detention and were to stand trial.

After a devastating earthquake in the city of Bam in December 2003, the US Administration agreed to ease financial sanctions and restrictions on the export of technical apparatus to Iran in order to facilitate the reconstruction process. However, President Bush denied that offers of humanitarian aid would in any way influence US policy towards Iran. In April 2004 Iranian officials rejected suggestions that the USA had asked Iran for assistance in its struggle to defeat the insurgency in Iraq or that any Iranian element was supporting the radical Shi'ite movement led by Hojatoleslam Muqtada al-Sadr. An Iranian diplomatic mission, supposedly dispatched upon the request of the United Kingdom to mediate between US troops and al-Sadr's forces around the Iraqi city of Najaf, was withdrawn following the assassination of the first secretary of the Iranian embassy in Baghdad. In July the USA declared a group of 3,800 members of the Mujahidin-e-Khalq interned in Iraq to be protected persons under the Geneva Convention. Iran criticized the USA for supporting 'terrorists', but US officials emphasized that they would not protect any individuals suspected of carrying out terrorist attacks. The introduction to the US Senate in August of the Iran Freedom and Support Act of 2004, which was designed to promote 'regime change' in Iran and to provide US $10m. in support of pro-democracy opposition groups, was seen as further evidence of the desire of the Bush Administration to use military force against Iran. Meanwhile, despite its vehement opposition to the US-led invasion and occupation of Iraq, the Iranian regime undoubtedly benefited from the success of Shi'a parties in the elections to Iraq's new permanent legislature in December 2005.

The election of the 'ultra-conservative' Mahmoud Ahmadinejad to the Iranian presidency in June 2005 caused concern in US political circles. Rumours circulated in the US media that Ahmadinejad had, as a student, been involved in the taking of hostages at the US embassy in Tehran in 1979, although the Iranian Government denied the allegations. Bilateral tensions also increased markedly as a result of Iran's resumption of uranium enrichment. In May 2006 President Ahmadinejad sent an 18-page letter to Bush, proposing 'new solutions' for the two states to settle their differences. The letter was reported to be the first direct communication between an Iranian President and his US counterpart since the 1979 Islamic Revolution. The US response to the letter, which was received as Secretary of State Condoleezza Rice was meeting members of the UN Security Council in New York to formulate a common response to the Iranian regime, was dismissive. In September 2006 the US Administration blacklisted the state-owned Bank Saderat Iran, following accusations that the bank was involved in the transfer of money to terrorist organizations, including Hezbollah in Lebanon.

Renewed tension erupted between Iran and the USA in January 2007, when US troops detained five Iranians during a raid on an Iranian liaison office in the northern Iraqi town of Irbil (Arbil). The USA accused the officials of being linked to the Revolutionary Guards, whom they alleged to be training insurgents within Iraq. The Iranian Government, for its part, accused the USA of having made illegal arrests, stating that, since the liaison office was in the process of being registered as a consulate, the officials enjoyed diplomatic immunity. Also in January the US Administration froze the assets of Iran's Bank Sepah, accusing the bank of acting as the conduit for an agreement with a North Korean organization that allegedly provided missile technology to Iran. Yet despite the considerable tension in Iranian–US relations during mid-2007, exacerbated by military exercises being carried out by US naval forces in the Gulf, three rounds of direct talks concerning the sectarian conflict in Iraq were held by the US and Iranian ambassadors to Baghdad between May and August. (These discussions were halted by the Iranian Ministry of Foreign Affairs in May 2008, amid Iran's displeasure regarding a recent operation by US and Iraqi forces against Shi'a militias in Iraq.)

Upon the inauguration of Barack Obama as US President in late January 2009, it was reported that the Iranian Government had rejected an offer by the Turkish Prime Minister, Recep Tayyip Erdoğan, to mediate in future negotiations with the USA; however, Erdoğan claimed in late February that Iran had sought Turkey's intervention. President Ahmadinejad had stated in early February that he was willing to enter into a dialogue with the new US Administration provided that such a dialogue was based on 'mutual respect'. President Obama had indicated during his election campaign that his Administration would be far more open to constructive discussions with Iran than his predecessor, President Bush, had been. Nevertheless, the new Administration continued with the USA's policy of sanctions against Iran, extending these for another year from mid-March and stating that the Islamic Republic continued to represent a threat to US national security.

On 20 March 2009, on the occasion of the Iranian New Year, President Obama released a video message in which he appealed for a 'new beginning' in relations between the two nations. A rare meeting between US and Iranian officials occurred at the end of March when Richard Holbrooke, the US special representative for Afghanistan and Pakistan, held a 'brief but cordial' discussion with the Iranian Deputy Minister of Foreign Affairs, Mahdi Akhundzadeh, during an international conference on Afghanistan at The Hague, Netherlands. However, the nascent thaw in relations was endangered following the trial in Iran of Roxana Saberi, a journalist with dual US-Iranian citizenship, who was sentenced to eight years' imprisonment on charges of spying on behalf of the USA in April. Senior US officials strongly denied the allegation and demanded her immediate release; the case also drew widespread criticism from international human rights organizations. However, in what was seen as a conciliatory measure, Saberi's sentence was subsequently commuted to a two-year suspended term, and in May she was released from prison and permitted to return to the USA.

President Obama condemned the violent repression of demonstrators during the unrest that followed the presidential election in June 2009 and rejected persistent allegations that the USA was complicit in fomenting the unrest. Nevertheless, the Obama Administration continued to pursue a policy of engagement with Iran and did not dispute the legitimacy of Ahmadinejad's presidency. The USA's engagement policy was most evident in its participation in direct negotiations over Iran's nuclear programme, initiated in October, during which US and Iranian officials held their most senior-level summit since the Islamic Revolution. However, from late 2009, following a lack of progress in the nuclear talks, the Obama Administration actively campaigned for a new package of UN Security Council sanctions against Iran. In mid-February 2010 the US Administration extended its unilateral sanctions against businesses connected to the Revolutionary Guards. Meanwhile, earlier that month Gen. David Petraeus, Commander of the US Central Command, confirmed that the imminent deployment of major new US-manufactured missile defence systems in Bahrain, Kuwait, Qatar and the United Arab Emirates (UAE) was designed to counter the growing threat of a military conflict with Iran. Gen. Petraeus also revealed that US warships equipped with advanced anti-missile systems had been stationed in the Mediterranean and the Gulf. The US Administration rejected the terms of the Tehran Declaration signed by the leaders of Iran, Turkey and Brazil in May, and welcomed the adoption of a fourth round of UN sanctions against the Islamic regime in early June (see The Nuclear Issue). The USA also imposed two further packages of unilateral sanctions against Iran in July and August, as bilateral relations continued to be dominated by US suspicions of a covert Iranian nuclear agenda and objections to Iranian interference in neighbouring Iraq.

In early October 2011 the US Administration accused Iran of having plotted to assassinate Saudi Arabia's ambassador to Washington, DC, and to have planned to detonate bombs at the embassies of both Saudi Arabia and Israel in the US capital; Iranian officials strongly rejected the claims. Following the publication of an IAEA report on Iran's nuclear activities (see The Nuclear Issue), in late November the USA extended its bilateral sanctions against the Islamic regime; these were targeted at firms engaged in business deals with the Iranian oil and petrochemical sectors. Although the Obama Administration was keen to continue pursuing diplomatic means as a way of pressurizing the regime into changing its nuclear policy, some US officials appeared unwilling to rule out the possibility that the USA would engage in military action should Iran persist with the programme's rapid expansion. Further sanctions imposed on 31 December were intended to make it harder for Iran to sell petroleum by placing restrictions on foreign companies that engage in business with the Central Bank. The Central Bank sanctions were further expanded on 6 February 2012, while President Obama also announced the 'freezing' of all Iranian government assets in the USA. Meanwhile, in late January and mid-February the USA sent an aircraft carrier through the Straits of Hormuz, in an apparent gesture of defiance in response to Iran's recent threats that it would close the vital transit route.

Regional relations

In October 2000 Kamal Kharrazi became the first Iranian Minister of Foreign Affairs to visit Iraq for a decade, and the two countries agreed to reactivate a 1975 border and security agreement that had been in abeyance since 1980. Tensions between the two sides increased in April 2001, however, when Iran launched a heavy missile attack against Iraqi military bases used by the Mujahidin-e-Khalq, apparently in response to repeated attacks by the armed opposition group on Iranian targets. By early 2002 a general thaw in bilateral relations was evident, despite a protest lodged with the UN by Iraq in June stating that Iran was continuing to violate agreements reached at the end of the Iran–Iraq War.

Following the removal from power of the Iraqi regime under Saddam Hussain by the US-led coalition in early 2003, large numbers of Iraqis-in-exile returned to their homeland. Indeed, the UN High Commissioner for Refugees (UNHCR) estimated that, by December 2004, an estimated 107,000 Iraqi refugees—more than one-half of the pre-conflict total in Iran—had returned home; a further 56,000 returned to Iraq in 2005. After US-led coalition aircraft had launched attacks against training camps of the NLA, in April 2003 the Mujahidin-e-Khalq and its military wing (which had been based in Iraq since 1986) agreed a ceasefire with the occupying forces in Iraq, a move that was condemned by Iran. In November 2005 President Jalal Talabani became the first Iraqi head of state for over 30 years to visit Iran, and a high-profile reciprocal visit by President Ahmadinejad to Iraq in March 2008 was hailed by the Iranian President as heralding the start of a new era in bilateral relations. In November Iran and Iraq exchanged the remains of 241 troops (200 Iraqi, 41 Iranian) killed in the 1980–88 conflict, after the two sides had held their first direct talks regarding the location of soldiers' remains. However, in December 2009 the Iraqi Government accused Iranian troops of occupying a section of the al-Fakkah oilfield in south-eastern Iraq. Moreover, following Iraq's legislative elections of March 2010, Iran was accused of interference in the protracted negotiations to form a new coalition government in order to guarantee the success of the Shi'a parties which it supported. In late December 2011 an agreement was reached between the Iraqi Government and the UN whereby some 3,000 members of the Mujahidin-e-Khalq who had been living at Camp Ashraf, a refugee camp close to Baghdad, would be relocated to enable officials to verify their refugee status.

Amid the continuing international disquiet over the country's nuclear ambitions in recent years, Iran has fuelled further outrage by its frequent statements about Israel and the Holocaust. Remarks by President Ahmadinejad in October 2005, in which he reiterated the demand of Ayatollah Khomeini that Israel be 'wiped off the map', provoked an international outcry and were condemned in a statement by the UN Security Council. Subsequent public statements by Ahmadinejad in December, to the effect that the Holocaust was a 'fabrication' and that the Jewish state should be moved outside the Middle East, were similarly condemned by Israel, the USA and the EU as illustrating the dangers of allowing Iran to develop military nuclear capabilities. Hostility between Iran and Israel was exacerbated by the victory of Hamas in the Palestinian legislative elections of January 2006 and Iran's subsequent offer of financial support to the Hamas-led administration.

Iran was also viewed as having played a leading role in the conflict between Israel and the militant Lebanese organization Hezbollah in July–August 2006; however, while the Iranian leadership admitted its support for Hezbollah, it denied that Iran was providing the group with military assistance. In November a spokesman from the Iranian Ministry of Foreign Affairs warned that any pre-emptive military strikes launched by Israel against Iran's nuclear facilities would be met with a swift and powerful military response. In July 2008 the Iranian regime conducted a series of missile tests, which included testing a new *Shahab-3* ballistic missile. The tests were viewed by many observers as being Iran's response to Israeli military air exercises that had been held over the Mediterranean Sea in June. A new long-range missile, the *Sajjil*, was test-fired by the Iranian regime in November. Production of the missile was deemed to be significant since it used solid, rather than liquid, fuel and could thus be launched against potential targets more quickly and provide greater resistance against any pre-emptive strike. Further Iranian tests, conducted in May 2009, demonstrated that the

Islamic Republic possessed missiles with sufficient range to target Israel and the USA's military bases in the region.

Meanwhile, following his appointment as Prime Minister of Israel in February 2009, Binyamin Netanyahu indicated that significant progress in the stalled Middle East peace process would not be possible until the threat posed by Iran's nuclear programme had been negated. In November it was announced that Israeli forces had intercepted a cargo ship in the Mediterranean Sea, en route to Syria, which Israel claimed was carrying a large consignment of Iranian armaments destined for Hezbollah militants in Lebanon. During his first official visit to Lebanon in October 2010, President Ahmadinejad provoked controversy—both within Israel and among members of Lebanon's pro-Western coalition Government—by visiting towns near the country's border with Israel, where fighting had been most intense during the war between Israel and Hezbollah in 2006.

Iran has accused Israel's external intelligence service, Mossad, of being responsible for the actual and attempted assassinations of several of its leading nuclear scientists; for example, Mostafa Ahmadi-Roshan, who worked at the Natanz nuclear plant, was killed in a car bomb explosion in Tehran in early January 2012. In mid-February a spokesman for Iran's Ministry of Foreign Affairs denied allegations by Netanyahu that Iran and Hezbollah were jointly responsible for a bomb attack in the Indian capital, New Delhi, and an attempted bombing in the Georgian capital, Tbilisi; in both cases, Israeli diplomats were the apparent targets. Police in the Thai capital, Bangkok, also accused Iran of being behind the attempted assassination of two Israeli diplomats on the following day, in which a suspected Iranian bomber was apparently injured while trying to detonate a device. In early 2012 there were international concerns that, should the expansion of Iran's nuclear programme continue at such a rapid rate—with the possibility of development of an atomic bomb potentially only a few months away—Israel might launch unilateral pre-emptive military action against Iran. Despite suggestions by the Israeli President, Shimon Peres, in early November 2011 that the possibility of such a strike was becoming 'closer and closer', in January 2012 the Deputy Prime Minister and Minister of Defence, Ehud Barak, sought to reassure international leaders that an Israeli military strike was not imminent.

Relations between Iran and Saudi Arabia were frequently strained after the Islamic Revolution of 1979. A period of particularly hostile relations, following the deaths of 275 Iranian pilgrims as a result of clashes with Saudi security forces in the Islamic holy city of Mecca during the *Hajj* (annual pilgrimage) in July 1987, culminated in the suspension of diplomatic relations in April 1988. Links were not restored until March 1991. Allegations of Iranian involvement in the bombing of a US military housing complex at al-Khobar, Saudi Arabia, in June 1996 again strained relations for several months. However, the installation of a new Iranian Government in August 1997 facilitated further rapprochement, perhaps reflecting the desire of the two countries, as the region's principal petroleum producers, to co-operate in maintaining world oil prices and in efforts to curtail overproduction by members of the Organization of the Petroleum Exporting Countries (OPEC). An Iranian delegation led by former President Rafsanjani began a 10-day visit to Saudi Arabia in February 1998, at the end of which the formation of a joint ministerial committee for bilateral relations was announced, and several co-operation agreements were signed following a visit to Iran by the Saudi Minister of State for Foreign Affairs in May. The signing of a Saudi-Iranian security agreement was announced in April 2001. During the latter part of 2003 Iran countered US accusations that certain suspected al-Qa'ida militants who remained in Iranian custody had been involved in plotting suicide attacks against expatriate compounds in Riyadh in May.

In March 2007 President Ahmadinejad undertook his first state visit to Saudi Arabia, where he held discussions with King Abdullah; the meeting was believed to represent an attempt by the two leaders to demonstrate that perceived differences between their countries as a result of recent sectarian tensions in Iraq and Lebanon had been exaggerated and that they were in fact seeking closer diplomatic relations. Nevertheless, Saudi officials have outlined their opposition to Iran's nuclear activities, expressing deep concerns regarding regional security, and have warned that Saudi Arabia would also seek to develop a nuclear weapons capability should it be discovered that Iran had done so. Diplomatic relations were also damaged by the Cooperation Council of the Arab States of the Gulf (Gulf Cooperation Council—GCC)'s dispatch of a contingent of (principally Saudi) military forces to assist the Sunni Muslim authorities in Bahrain in quelling the largely Shi'a anti-Government protests which erupted there in February 2011. Saudi Arabia, for its part, accused Iran of being behind much of the unrest in Bahrain.

Both the Khatami and Ahmadinejad administrations have sought improved relations with Saudi Arabia's fellow members of the GCC, although a long-standing territorial dispute with the UAE remains unresolved. In March 1992 Iran occupied those parts of the Abu Musa islands and the Greater and Lesser Tunbs that had remained under the control of the emirate of Sharjah since the original occupation in 1971. In December 1994 the UAE announced its intention to refer the dispute to the International Court of Justice in The Hague, Netherlands. In early 1995 Iran was reported to have deployed air defence systems on Abu Musa and the Greater and Lesser Tunbs, prompting the USA to warn of a potential threat to shipping. Relations deteriorated further in the first half of 1996, after Iran opened an airport on Abu Musa and a power station on Greater Tunb. In 1997 the UAE protested that Iran was repeatedly violating the emirates' territorial waters, and in June complained to the UN about Iran's construction of a pier on Greater Tunb. During the 2000s the UAE remained an important trading partner of Iran and, although both countries continued to assert their sovereignty over the three disputed areas—with Iran angering the UAE leadership by establishing two maritime offices on Abu Musa in August 2008—political relations were generally improving. In October Iran's Minister of Foreign Affairs, Mottaki, hosted talks with his UAE counterpart, Sheikh Abdullah bin Zayed Al Nahyan, in Tehran, at the end of which an agreement was signed to establish a bilateral commission to encourage political and economic co-operation. Reports in July 2010 that the UAE's ambassador to the USA, Yousuf al-Otaiba, had appeared to encourage the idea of a pre-emptive US military strike against Iran in order to prevent the Islamic regime from building a nuclear weapon precipitated a deterioration in diplomatic relations. Difficulties persisted in 2011, amid allegations of Iranian meddling in Bahrain and the UAE's support for the international sanctions imposed against Iran; however, bilateral relations remained strong and joint economic initiatives continued to be pursued. Despite Iran's extremely close relationship with Syria and its military and financial support for the regime of President Bashar al-Assad, President Ahmadinejad surprised many in the West by urging Assad, in mid-September, to end the violence being perpetrated by Syrian government forces in their crackdown on the political uprising against Assad's regime, and to begin talks with representatives of the opposition.

Victories achieved by the Sunni fundamentalist Taliban in the Afghan civil war in September 1996 prompted Iran, which supported the Government of President Burhanuddin Rabbani, to express fears for its national security, and to accuse the USA of interference in Afghanistan's internal affairs. In June 1997 the Taliban accused Iran of espionage, and ordered the closure of the Iranian embassy in Kabul and the withdrawal of all Iranian diplomats. Iran retaliated by halting all trade across its land border with Afghanistan, prompting Taliban protests that the ban violated international law. In September 1998, as it emerged that nine Iranian diplomats missing since August had been murdered by Taliban militia as they stormed the city of Mazar-i-Sharif, 500,000 Iranian troops were reportedly placed on full military alert in readiness for open conflict with Afghanistan. In an attempt to defuse the crisis, in October the Taliban agreed to free all Iranian prisoners being held in Afghanistan and to punish those responsible for the killing of the nine diplomats. Following the suicide attacks on the USA in September 2001, as the USA began preparations for military action against al-Qa'ida and its Taliban hosts, Iran closed its eastern border with Afghanistan and sent a large contingent of troops there in order to prevent a further influx of Afghan refugees. In October, however, when the US-led military action began, Iran reportedly agreed to the establishment of eight refugee camps within its borders to provide shelter for some 250,000 Afghan refugees. Although Iran refused to give military assistance to the US-led coalition, it actively supported the Western-backed opposition forces, collectively known as the United National Islamic Front for the Salvation of Afghanistan (the Northern Alliance), and welcomed their swift victory over the Taliban.

A programme allowing for voluntary repatriations of Afghan refugees under the auspices of UNHCR was inaugurated by the Iranian and Afghan authorities in April 2002, although UNHCR put the number of 'spontaneous' repatriations prior to that date at 57,000. Iran hosts one of the largest refugee populations in the world: at the end of 2003, according to data published by UNHCR, the number of refugees in Iran was 984,896, of whom 834,699 were from Afghanistan and 150,196 from Iraq. More than 1.5m. Afghan refugees in Iran were estimated by UNHCR to have returned to Afghanistan by November 2005. By the end of 2010 UNHCR estimated that the total number of refugees in Iran had risen slightly, to 1,073,366; those fleeing Afghanistan (1,027,577) now accounted for virtually all of the refugees, with the number of Iraqis totalling 45,708. In August 2002 President Khatami became the first Iranian head of state to visit Afghanistan for 40 years. In mid-June 2011 Brig.-Gen. Ahmad Vahidi, the Minister of Defence and Armed Forces Logistics, undertook an historic visit to Kabul for discussions with his Afghan counterpart, as the Government in Afghanistan was preparing to assume control of some aspects of national security in advance of the planned departure of all foreign forces by the end of 2014.

Closer relations were developed with Turkey during the 1990s, despite periodic tensions arising particularly from Turkish allegations of Iranian support for the Kurdish separatist Kurdistan Workers' Party (Partiya Karkeren Kurdistan—PKK) in its conflict with the armed forces in south-eastern Turkey. In 1997 Iran was a founder member of the Developing Eight (D-8) group of Islamic countries, based in İstanbul. In May 2004 Tehran's Imam Khomeini International Airport, which the Turkish-led consortium Tepe-Akfen-Vie (TAV) was contracted to operate, was closed by the Revolutionary Guards after only one flight had landed because it was seen as a danger to national security, and apparently owing to Iran's hostility towards Turkey for its links with Israel and the USA. The airport reopened in May 2005, following complex negotiations that reportedly resulted in TAV rescinding control of operations to IranAir. Since 2010 the Turkish Government has played a more significant role in attempts to resolve the dispute between Iran and Western countries concerning Iran's nuclear programme, even hosting formal discussions in İstanbul between Iran and international negotiators in January 2011 (see The Nuclear Issue).

Meanwhile, considerable political and economic advantage has been perceived arising from Iran's potential as a transit route for hydrocarbons from the former Soviet republics of Central Asia, and since the early 1990s Iran has sought to strengthen its position in Central Asia through bilateral economic, security and cultural agreements as well as institutions such as the Tehran-based Economic Cooperation Organization. Relations between Iran and Azerbaijan—already tense owing to disagreement over a contested section of the Caspian Basin—deteriorated in July 2001, when Iran ordered a military patrol boat into the disputed waters in order to prevent foreign companies from undertaking oil exploration there. Subsequent meetings of the five littoral states (Iran, Russia, Azerbaijan, Kazakhstan and Turkmenistan) failed to resolve the dispute regarding the legal status of the Caspian. An improvement in relations between Iran and Azerbaijan was evident during the early 2000s, and moves towards the imposition of wider economic sanctions against Iran in the second half of the decade were of concern to Azerbaijan, owing to Iran's large ethnic Azeri population, as well as the energy agreements in place between the two countries. However, in February 2012 relations between the two countries appeared to deteriorate after Azerbaijan announced that it was to purchase arms valued at some US $1,600m. from Israel. The following month the Azerbaijani Government denied reports by international media that it had agreed to allow the Israeli air force access to airfields within Azerbaijan in the event of Israeli military action against Iranian nuclear facilities.

Other external relations

The EU pursued a policy of 'critical dialogue' with Iran during the 1990s, despite US pressure as well as tensions between Iran and certain EU states. Notably, a lengthy period of strained relations with the United Kingdom developed after Ayatollah Khomeini issued a *fatwa* (edict) in February 1989, imposing a death penalty against a British writer, Salman Rushdie, for material deemed offensive to Islam in his novel *The Satanic Verses*. 'Critical dialogue' was suspended in April 1997, after a German court ruled that the Iranian authorities had ordered the assassination of four prominent members of the dissident Democratic Party of Iranian Kurdistan in Berlin in September 1992. Germany announced the withdrawal of its ambassador to Tehran and expelled four Iranian diplomats, while other EU members similarly withdrew their representatives. In November 1997, following the inauguration of President Khatami and the formation of a new Council of Ministers, a compromise arrangement was finally reached allowing the readmission of all EU ambassadors, and in February 1998 EU ministers responsible for foreign affairs agreed to resume senior-level ministerial contacts with Iran. Despite assurances given to the British Secretary of State for Foreign and Commonwealth Affairs, Robin Cook, in September by the Iranian Minister of Foreign Affairs that the Iranian Government had no intention of threatening the life of Rushdie or anyone associated with his work, 'conservative' clerics maintained that the *fatwa* issued by Ayatollah Khomeini was irrevocable, and the Qom-based 15 Khordad Foundation subsequently increased its financial reward offered for the writer's murder. President Khatami became the first Iranian head of state to visit the West since the Islamic Revolution when, in March 1999, he travelled to Italy and the Vatican. In September 2001 the most high-level discussions since 1979 were held between Iranian and EU representatives in Brussels and later Tehran.

In December 2002 the EU commenced negotiations with Iran regarding a trade and co-operation agreement, with the stipulation that the accord be linked with consideration of political issues (notably human rights and terrorism). In May 2003, following the US-led campaign to oust the regime of Saddam Hussain in Iraq, British Prime Minister Tony Blair echoed statements made by the US Administration that Iran should desist from 'interfering' in Iraq's affairs. In June 2004 a crisis erupted in relations with the United Kingdom when Iran captured three British patrol craft and detained eight Royal Navy personnel on the Shatt al-Arab waterway dividing Iran from Iraq. Iran asserted that the vessels had entered Iranian territorial waters, but the sailors, who were released four days later, alleged that they had been 'forcibly escorted' into Iranian waters. In October 2005 British officials accused the Iranians of supplying explosives to and running training camps for Iraqi Shi'a insurgents operating in the British-controlled region of southern Iraq.

In March 2007 15 British Royal Navy and Royal Marines personnel were captured and detained by Iranian Revolutionary Guards while patrolling the Shatt al-Arab waterway. As in 2004, Iran claimed that the sailors had trespassed into Iranian territorial waters; however, British naval officials insisted that the two crews were operating in Iraqi waters at the time of their arrest. The sailors were subsequently transferred to Tehran, where Iranian television broadcast footage of them apparently admitting to their 'intrusion' into Iranian territory. Following high-level discussions between Iranian and British officials in April 2007, the 15 sailors were finally released from detention 13 days after their capture. President Ahmadinejad stated that he had granted them a pardon as a 'gift to the British people', while the British Government denied that a deal had been agreed with Iran to secure the sailors' release. However, several commentators noted that shortly before the pardon five diplomats who had been seized by US forces at the Iranian consulate in Arbil, Iraq, in January 2007 had been granted consular access; moreover, a senior diplomat at the Iranian embassy in Baghdad, who had been abducted by gunmen in February, had also recently been released.

Relations between Iran and the United Kingdom deteriorated in the aftermath of the disputed Iranian presidential election in June 2009. The Iranian authorities alleged that British agents had travelled to Iran prior to the election to plan civil unrest, and that the British Broadcasting Corporation's Persian-language service had encouraged protests against the result of the election. Following allegations that they had engaged in activities 'inconsistent with their diplomatic status', two British diplomats were expelled from Iran on 22 June. The British Government retaliated with the expulsion of two Iranian diplomats. On 27 June nine Iranian employees from the United Kingdom's embassy in Tehran were arrested for their alleged role in the post-election unrest. Although by mid-July all had been released from custody, according to reports in Iran, trial proceedings against at least one of the workers were anticipated. Hossein Rassam, a political counsellor, appeared at a court hearing in early August, during which he admitted collecting and distributing information on the post-election unrest, and reportedly apologized for his actions. The hearing was one of a series of mass trials of political prisoners that took place during August, which were described as 'show trials' by international observers. Meanwhile, Clotilde Reiss, a French student and teaching assistant at Esfahan University, was arrested and detained on espionage charges while attempting to leave Iran at the start of July; she was alleged to have distributed photographs taken during the unrest and submitted a report on post-election events to a French institute of Iranian studies. President Sarkozy of France denounced the charges against her and demanded her immediate release. Reiss was subsequently released from custody but confined to the French embassy in Tehran. In October Rassam was convicted of espionage and fomenting unrest, and sentenced to four years' imprisonment. Trial proceedings against Reiss were adjourned in January 2010, and in May she returned to France, after her 10-year prison sentence was commuted to a fine. Although only days later Ali Vakili Rad, who was serving a life sentence in France for the murder in 1991 of former Iranian Prime Minister Shapour Bakhtiar, was released from French custody and deported to Iran, the French Minister for Foreign and European Affairs, Bernard Kouchner, denied that any secret agreement had been reached between the two countries.

Amid an intensification of the dispute concerning Iran's nuclear programme during 2011, the EU extended its list of Iranian individuals and companies whose assets were frozen on 23 May, on 10 October and again on 1 December. On 29 November 2011, two days after Iranian legislators voted to downgrade Iran's diplomatic ties with the United Kingdom, hundreds of Iranian demonstrators attacked the British embassy in Tehran to protest against the imposition by the British Government on 22 November of further economic sanctions—which included a virtual ban on British banks doing business with Iranian banks and on firms involved in Iran's energy sector. This followed the IAEA's strongly worded report detailing suspicions that Iran was engaged in the development of a nuclear weapons programme (see The Nuclear Issue). In response, on 30 November the United Kingdom closed its embassy, ordered all British diplomatic staff to leave Iran, and gave Iranian diplomats in London two days to leave the country. The British Government expressed outrage that the Iranian authorities had not prevented the protesters from entering the embassy compound. On 23 January 2012 the EU (which accounts for some 20% of Iranian oil exports) banned imports of crude petroleum from the Islamic Republic; however, existing agreements were to be honoured until 1 July. The Union also froze assets belonging to the Central Bank. The Iranian leadership warned that it would close the Straits of Hormuz if the country was 'seriously threatened'.

In March 2001 Russia pledged to assist Iran with the completion of the nuclear plant at Bushehr (see The Nuclear Issue), and in May Russian officials reportedly agreed to supply Iran with advanced ship-borne cruise missiles. The two countries signed a military co-operation pact in October, believed to amount to annual sales to Iran of Russian weapons worth some US $300m. In July 2002 Russia and Iran concluded a draft 10-year development and co-operation accord, which was reported to include the construction of a further three nuclear reactors at Bushehr. Construction of the Bushehr plant was completed in October 2004, and in February 2005 Russia agreed to supply Iran with nuclear fuel for the plant; however, following international pressure, the deal required that Iran return to Russia spent fuel rods, which could be used to produce nuclear weapons, from the site. As the diplomatic crisis over Iran's nuclear programme intensified during that year, Russia developed an alternative proposal whereby the sensitive elements of Iran's nuclear programme, such as uranium enrichment, could be conducted on Russian territory, thereby allaying the concerns of the IAEA, the USA and EU member states that such nuclear activities would lead to the development of a bomb. However, this proposal was rejected by the Iranian administration in early 2006.

It was reported in January 2007 that Russia had recently sold some 30 air defence missile systems to Iran, in a contract that was estimated to be worth US $700m. In March the Russian Government rejected a deadline by which it was to deliver nuclear fuel to the Bushehr plant, claiming that Iran had failed to make the requisite payments; Russia also warned Iran that it would continue to withhold the provision of fuel until Iran agreed to suspend uranium enrichment, as demanded by the UN Security Council. President Vladimir Putin attended a summit meeting of the five littoral states of the Caspian Sea in Tehran in October, at which the Russian leader expressed his opposition to any US-led military strike against Iran's nuclear facilities and all parties asserted Iran's right to develop nuclear energy for peaceful purposes. The first shipment of Russian nuclear fuel to the Bushehr reactor arrived in December, after Russia and Iran had finally agreed on a timetable for completion of the project; however, expectations that the plant would be fully operational by the end of 2009 were not realized. The Bushehr facility finally commenced operations in August, and in November Iranian officials announced that the loading of fuel into its nuclear reactor had been concluded. After a fourth round of UN sanctions were adopted against Iran in June 2010, the Russian Government declared that it was required, under the terms of Resolution 1929, to cancel the planned delivery of an *S-300* air defence missile system to the Iranian regime. By early 2012 senior Russian officials were expressing the view that any new sanctions imposed against Iran would merely harm the Iranian people rather than have the desired effect of urging Tehran to end its nuclear programme.

Political and economic relations between Iran and China have been steadily improving in recent years. Iranian exports to the People's Republic (including oil exports) have risen considerably as Chinese demand has increased, and a growing number of Chinese companies are now investing in large-scale Iranian infrastructure projects, often replacing Western businesses which have withdrawn their interests as a consequence of sanctions imposed by the UN, the USA and the EU. Although China has voted for certain UN Security Council resolutions imposing stricter penalties against the Iranian regime, the Chinese have expressed support for Iran's right to develop a civil nuclear energy programme, and the official Chinese position is that negotiations and constructive dialogue are a more effective way of dealing with international concerns regarding the exact nature of Iranian nuclear ambitions. In 2009 China was reported to have become Iran's largest trading partner, with the value of bilateral trade estimated at US $21,200m. in that year, compared with a mere $400m. 15 years previously.

Iran's relations with South and Central America grew in importance during 2006, not least owing to the election of new leaders in that region who shared President Ahmadinejad's hostility towards the US Administration under President Bush. In January 2007 Ahmadinejad embarked on a four-day tour of Venezuela—whose President, Hugo Chávez, had consistently supported Ahmadinejad's insistence on Iran's right to nuclear energy—together with Nicaragua, Ecuador and Bolivia. During Ahmadinejad's visit the Iranian delegation signed 11 bilateral agreements with its Venezuelan counterpart, with the aim of increasing the price of petroleum and furthering co-operation on energy, trade, industry and construction. Presidents Ahmadinejad and Chávez also agreed to expedite the creation of a US $2,000m. fund to invest in countries joining their anti-US alliance. A further 200 economic co-operation accords were signed when Chávez visited Tehran in September 2009. During a tour of South American countries in November, which also included meetings with Chávez and President Evo Morales of Bolivia, Ahmadinejad met with his Brazilian counterpart Luiz Inácio Lula da Silva in the Brazilian capital, Brasília. The two Presidents declared their intention to increase the volume of bilateral trade to some $25,000m. within the next five years.

CONSTITUTION AND GOVERNMENT

A draft constitution for the Islamic Republic of Iran was published on 18 June 1979. It was submitted to an Assembly of Experts, elected by popular vote on 3 August, to debate the various clauses and to propose amendments. The amended Constitution was approved by a referendum on 2–3 December 1979. A further 45 amendments to the Constitution were approved by a referendum on 28 July 1989.

Legislative power is vested in the Islamic Consultative Assembly (Majlis-e-Shura-e Islami), with 290 members. The chief executive of the administration is the President. The Majlis and the President are both elected by universal adult suffrage for a term of four years. A 12-member Council of Guardians supervises elections and ensures that legislation is in accordance with the Constitution and with Islamic precepts. The Council to Determine the Expediency of the Islamic Order, created in February 1988 and formally incorporated into the Constitution in 1989, rules on legal and theological disputes between the Majlis and the Council of Guardians. In October 2005 the powers of the Expediency Council were extended, allowing it to supervise all branches of government. The executive, legislative and judicial wings of state power are subject to the authority of the Wali Faqih (supreme religious leader). Iran is divided into 30 provinces, each with an appointed Governor.

REGIONAL AND INTERNATIONAL CO-OPERATION

Iran became a member of the UN upon its foundation in October 1945. A working party was established in May 2005 to examine Iran's application to join the World Trade Organization (WTO); however, accession negotiations had not begun by early 2012. Iran is also a member of the Organization of Islamic Cooperation (OIC), of the Organization of the Petroleum Exporting Countries (OPEC), of the Developing Eight group of Islamic countries (D-8), and of the Group of 15 developing countries (G15). The headquarters of the Economic Cooperation Organization (ECO) are located in Tehran.

ECONOMIC AFFAIRS

In 2009, according to estimates by the World Bank, Iran's gross national income (GNI), measured at average 2007–09 prices, was US $330,400m., equivalent to $4,520 per head (or $11,380 per head on an international purchasing-power parity basis). During 2001–10, it was estimated, the population increased at an average annual rate of 1.2%, while gross domestic product (GDP) per head increased, in real terms, by an average of 4.0% per year during 2001–09. Overall GDP increased, in real terms, at an average annual rate of 5.2% in 2001–09; according to the Central Bank of Iran, GDP growth was 6.7% in 2007/08 (Iranian year to March), while the IMF estimated growth of 3.2% in 2010/11.

Agriculture (including forestry and fishing) contributed 9.1% of GDP in 2007/08, according to provisional figures. About 21.2% of the employed labour force were engaged in agriculture in 2008. The principal cash crops are fresh and dried fruit and nuts, which accounted for a provisional 8.1% of non-petroleum export earnings in 2009/10. Wheat, rice, barley, sugar cane and sugar beet are the main subsistence crops. Imports of cereals comprised some 6.4% of the value of total imports in 2009/10. Production of fruit and vegetables is also significant. Agricultural GDP increased by an average of 5.2% per year in 2000–07; according to official figures, the sector's GDP grew by an estimated 6.4% in 2007/08.

Industry (including manufacturing, construction and power, but excluding mining) contributed 17.1% of GDP in 2007/08, according to provisional figures, and engaged some 32.2% of the employed labour force in 2008. During 2000–07 industrial GDP increased by an average of 10.2% per year; growth was recorded at 9.0% in 2007/08.

Mining (including petroleum-refining) contributed 28.0% of GDP in 2007/08, according to provisional figures, although the sector engaged only an estimated 0.6% of the working population in 2008. Metal ores are the major non-hydrocarbon mineral exports, and coal, magnesite and gypsum are also mined. The sector is dominated by the hydrocarbons sector, which contributed some 27.3% of GDP in 2007/08, according to provisional figures. At the end of 2009 Iran's proven reserves of petroleum were estimated at 137,010m. barrels, sufficient to maintain the 2010 rate of production—estimated at 4.2m. barrels per day (b/d)—for almost 88 years. As a member of the Organization of the Petroleum Exporting Countries (OPEC, see p. 408), Iran is subject to production quotas agreed by the Organization's Conference. Iran's proven reserves of natural gas (29,610,000m. cu m at the end of 2009) are the second largest in the world, after those of Russia. Since late 2008 Iran, Russia and Qatar have increased their cooperation on gas projects. A deal was concluded in June 2010 for the construction of a pipeline, at a cost of US $7,600m., through which Iran would export natural gas from its South Pars offshore gasfield (an extension of Qatar's North Field) to Pakistan's southern provinces of Balochistan and Sindh from 2015. An agreement worth $10,000m. was signed by Iran, Iraq and Syria in July 2011; this involved the construction, by 2014–16, of a pipeline that would transport gas from the South Pars field to the latter countries and eventually via Lebanon to the Mediterranean Sea. The GDP of the mining sector increased by an average of 4.2% per year in 2002/03–06/07; according to official figures, mining GDP expanded by 12.1% in 2007/08.

Manufacturing (excluding petroleum-refining) contributed 10.7% of GDP in 2007/08, according to provisional figures, and engaged about 17.1% of the employed labour force in 2008. The most important sectors, in terms of value added, are textiles, food-processing and transport equipment. The sector's GDP increased by an average of 11.5% per year in 2000–07, with official estimates recording growth of 8.3% in 2007/08.

According to provisional official figures, the construction sector contributed 5.1% of GDP in 2007/08, and engaged 13.6% of the employed labour force in 2008. The GDP of the sector increased at an average annual rate of 6.3% during 2000–07; growth was recorded at 11.9% in 2007/08, according to official estimates.

Principal sources of energy are natural gas (providing around 80.8% of total electricity production in 2008) and petroleum (some 16.6% in the same year). Imports of mineral fuels and lubricants comprised just 4.0% of the value of total imports in 2006. The first phase of Iran's South Pars gasfield was brought on stream in 2004, and a total of 29 phases are planned. Gas reserves in the South Pars field are estimated at more than 14,000,000m. cu m, with a production capacity in late 2010 of 75m. cu m of gas per year.

The services sector contributed 45.8% of GDP in 2007/08, according to provisional figures, and engaged an estimated 46.6% of the employed labour force in 2008. During 2000–07 the GDP of the services sector increased by an average of 6.4% per year; according to official figures, growth in the sector was about 6.4% in 2007/08.

According to projected figures, in the year ending March 2010 Iran recorded a visible trade surplus of US $20,935m., and there was a surplus of $10,908m. on the current account of the balance of payments. In 2007/08 the principal source of imports was the United Arab Emirates (UAE, which supplied 23.8% of total imports); other major suppliers included Germany, the People's Republic of China, Switzerland and the Republic of Korea (South Korea). The UAE (which took 14.1%) was also the principal market for exports in 2007/08; Iraq, China, Japan and India were also important markets for Iranian exports. Other than petroleum and natural gas, Iran's principal exports in 2009/10 were chemical products, fruit and nuts, iron and steel, and carpets. Exports of petroleum and gas comprised 76.6% of the value of total exports in that year, according to provisional figures. The principal imports in that year were machinery and transport equipment, basic manufactures, food and live animals, and chemicals and related products.

According to IMF estimates, the budget surplus for the financial year ending March 2011 totalled IR 71,049m. Iran's general government gross debt was IR 490,409,400m. in 2010, equivalent to 11.6% of GDP. Iran's total external debt was US $13,435m. at the end of 2009, of which $7,524m. was public and publicly guaranteed debt. The annual rate of inflation averaged 14.7% in 2004/05–10/11; consumer prices increased by an estimated average of 12.4% in 2010/11. According to the Central Bank, the rate of unemployment was 13.5% in 2010/11.

At the end of 2010 Iran possessed the world's second largest proven reserves of both crude oil and natural gas; nevertheless, in early 2012 significant weaknesses in the economy remained, especially the over-reliance on revenue from the petroleum sector, high rates of inflation and unemployment. Since 2006 international concerns regarding Iran's nuclear energy programme have resulted in the imposition by the UN, the USA and the EU of tighter economic and technological sanctions, which have drastically reduced foreign investment and removed many sources of financing for vital hydrocarbons projects. Inadequate refining capacity, ageing infrastructure and international isolation have contributed to Iran's status as a net importer of both refined petroleum and natural gas. In 2009 the Government announced plans to invest up to $200,000m. over a five-year period, in an attempt to double the level of gas production and achieve self-sufficiency by 2012. Traditionally, the fact that the country maintained high domestic fuel subsidies restricted its capacity to use oil revenue to promote growth. Following President Ahmadinejad's re-election in June 2009, however, the Council of Guardians in January 2010 approved a government reform bill that aimed gradually to reduce fuel and food subsidies over a five-year period. The reduced subsidies were to be partly offset by cash payments to those families deemed to be most in need (although by mid-2011 the population was apparently becoming increasingly frustrated by rising food and fuel prices resulting from the policy). Ahmadinejad presented a reduced budget for 2011/12; however, despite a proposed decrease of 5.6% in government spending, defence expenditure was to more than double, and increased spending on health, scientific research and development projects was also planned. An average annual growth rate of 8% was projected in the Fifth Five-Year Development Plan (FiFYDP, 2010–15). However, according to the IMF, GDP growth was estimated to have slowed from 6.7% in 2007/08 to 3.2% in 2010/11, owing mainly to declining prices and output in the petroleum sector. In June 2011 the IMF praised the authorities for their achievement of non-oil growth and for reducing average annual inflation to 12.4% in 2010/11 from 25.4% in 2008/09. The Fund also noted that the subsidy reform plan was having a positive impact by 'reducing inequalities, improving living standards, and supporting domestic demand'. Nevertheless, the rate of GDP growth was expected to remain much lower than that envisaged by the FiFYDP in the medium term, not least owing to the effects of increased economic sanctions. Further sanctions oil imports imposed by the EU, and US and EU restrictions on firms dealing with Iran's financial institutions, including the Central Bank, were likely to have significant economic repercussions during 2012.

PUBLIC HOLIDAYS

The Iranian year 1391 runs from 20 March 2012 to 20 March 2013, and the year 1392 from 21 March 2013 to 20 March 2014.

2013: 3 January* (Arbain), 11 January (Demise of Prophet Muhammad and Martyrdom of Imam Hassan), 12 January* (Martyrdom of Imam Reza), 29 January (Birth of Prophet Muhammad and Birth of Imam Jafar Sadegh), 31 January (Victory of the Islamic Revolution), 19 March (Day of Oil Industry Nationalization), 21–24 March† (Norouz, Iranian New Year), 1 April (Islamic Republic Day), 2 April (Sizdah-bedar, Nature Day—13th Day of Norouz), 14 April (Martyrdom of Hazrat Fatemeh), 23 May (Birth of Imam Ali), 4 June (Death of Imam Khomeini), 5 June (1963 Uprising), 6 June* (Prophet Muhammad receives his calling), 24 June* (Birth of Imam Mahdi), 29 July* (Martyrdom of Imam Ali), 7 August* (Eid-e Fitr, end of Ramadan), 1 September* (Martyrdom of Imam Jafar Sadeq), 14 October* (Qorban, Feast of the Sacrifice), 23 October* (Eid-e Ghadir Khom), 13 November* (Tassoua), 14 November* (Ashoura).

* These holidays are dependent on the Islamic lunar calendar and may vary by one or two days from the dates given.

† This festival begins on the date of the Spring Equinox.

Statistical Survey

The Iranian year runs from approximately 21 March to 20 March

Sources (except where otherwise stated): Statistical Centre of Iran, POB 14155-6133, Dr Fatemi Ave, Tehran 14144; tel. (21) 88965061; fax (21) 88963451; e-mail sci@sci.org.ir; internet www.sci.org.ir; Bank Markazi Jomhouri Islami Iran (Central Bank), POB 15875-7177, 144 Mirdamad Blvd, Tehran; tel. (21) 29954855; fax (21) 29954780; e-mail g.secdept@cbi.ir; internet www.cbi.ir.

Area and Population

AREA, POPULATION AND DENSITY

Area (sq km)	1,648,195*
Population (census results)†	
25 October 1996	60,055,488
28 October 2006	
Males	35,866,362
Females	34,629,420
Total	70,495,782
Population (official estimate at 20 March)	
2009	72,583,587
2010	73,650,566
2011	74,733,230
Density (per sq km) at 20 March 2011	45.3

* 636,372 sq miles.

† Excluding adjustment for underenumeration.

POPULATION BY AGE AND SEX

(population at 2006 census)

	Males	Females	Total
0–14	9,063,337	8,618,292	17,681,629
15–64	24,874,641	24,282,921	49,157,562
65 and over	1,928,384	1,728,207	3,656,591
Total	35,866,362	34,629,420	70,495,782

PROVINCES

(official estimates at 20 March 2011)*

Province (Ostan)	Area (sq km)†	Population	Density (per sq km)	Provincial capital
Tehran (Teheran)	18,814	14,795,116	786.4	Tehran (Teheran)
Markazi (Central)	29,130	1,392,435	47.8	Arak
Gilan	14,042	2,453,469	174.7	Rasht
Mazandaran	23,701	3,037,336	128.2	Sari
Azarbayejan-e-Sharqi (East Azerbaijan)	45,650	3,691,270	80.9	Tabriz
Azarbayejan-e-Gharbi (West Azerbaijan)	37,437	3,016,301	80.6	Orumiyeh
Bakhtaran (Kermanshah)	24,998	1,905,793	76.2	Bakhtaran
Khuzestan	64,055	4,471,488	69.8	Ahvaz
Fars	122,608	4,528,514	36.9	Shiraz
Kerman	180,836	2,947,346	16.3	Kerman
North Khorasan	28,434	838,781	29.5	Bojnurd
South Khorasan	69,555	676,794	9.7	Birjand
Razavi Khorasan	144,681	5,940,766	41.1	Mashhad
Esfahan	107,029	4,804,458	44.9	Esfahan
Sistan and Baluchestan	181,785	2,733,205	15.0	Zahedan
Kordestan (Kurdistan)	29,137	1,467,585	50.4	Sanandaj
Hamadan	19,368	1,699,588	87.8	Hamadan
Chaharmahal and Bakhtiyari	16,332	892,909	54.7	Shahr-e-Kord
Lorestan	28,294	1,758,226	62.1	Khorramabad
Ilam	20,133	566,332	28.1	Ilam
Kohgiluyeh and Boyerahmad	15,504	669,140	43.2	Yasuj
Bushehr	22,743	943,535	41.5	Bushehr
Zanjan	21,773	983,369	45.2	Zanjan
Semnan	97,491	624,482	6.4	Semnan
Yazd	129,285	1,065,893	8.2	Yazd
Hormozgan	70,669	1,558,878	22.1	Bandar Abbas
Ardebil	17,800	1,242,956	69.8	Ardebil
Qom	11,526	1,127,713	97.8	Qom
Qazvin	15,549	1,212,464	78.0	Qazvin
Golestan	20,195	1,687,086	83.5	Gorgan
Total	1,628,554	74,733,230	45.9	—

* In January 1997 the legislature approved a law creating a new province, Qazvin (with its capital in the city of Qazvin), by dividing the existing province of Zanjan. In June of that year the Council of Ministers approved draft legislation to establish another new province, Golestan (with its capital in the city of Gorgan), by dividing the existing province of Mazandaran. In September 2004 legislation was enacted whereby the province of Khorasan was divided into three new provinces: North Khorasan, South Khorasan and Razavi Khorasan (with their respective capitals in the cities of Bojnurd, Birjand and Mashhad).

† Excluding inland water; densities are calculated on basis of land area only.

PRINCIPAL TOWNS
(population at 2006 census)

Tehran (Teheran, the capital)	7,088,287	Kerman	515,114
Mashad (Meshed)	2,427,316	Hamadan	479,640
Esfahan (Isfahan)	1,602,110	Arak	446,760
Tabriz	1,398,060	Yazd	432,194
Karaj	1,386,030*	Ardabil (Ardebil)	418,262
Shiraz	1,227,331	Bandar Abbas	379,301
Ahvaz	985,614	Eslamshahr (Islam Shahr)	357,389
Qom	964,706	Qazvin	355,338
Bakhtaran (Kermanshah)	794,863	Zanjan	349,713
Orumiyeh	583,255	Khorramabad	333,945
Zahedan	567,449	Sanandaj	316,862
Rasht	557,366		

* Including towns of Rajayishahr and Mehrshahr. Estimated population of Mehrshahr at 1 October 1994 was 413,299 (Source: UN, *Demographic Yearbook*).

Mid-2010 ('000, incl. suburbs, UN estimates): Tehran 7,241; Mashad 2,652; Esfahan 1,742; Karaj 1,584; Tabriz 1,483; Shiraz 1,299; Ahvaz 1,060; Qom 1,042; Kermanshah 837 (Source: UN, *World Urbanization Prospects: The 2009 Revision*).

BIRTHS, MARRIAGES AND DEATHS
(annual averages, UN estimates)

	1995–2000	2000–05	2005–10
Birth rate (per 1,000)	21.1	18.0	17.7
Death rate (per 1,000)	5.4	5.3	5.4

Source: UN, *World Population Prospects: The 2010 Revision*.

Births ('000): 1,172 in 2003/04; 1,154 in 2004/05; 1,239 in 2005/06; 1,254 in 2006/07; 1,287 in 2007/08; 1,300 in 2008/09; 1,349 in 2009/10; 1,364 in 2010/11.

Marriages ('000): 681 in 2003/04; 724 in 2004/05; 788 in 2005/06; 778 in 2006/07; 841 in 2007/08; 882 in 2008/09; 890 in 2009/10; 892 in 2010/11.

Deaths ('000): 369 in 2003/04; 355 in 2004/05; 364 in 2005/06; 409 in 2006/07; 413 in 2007/08; 418 in 2008/09; 394 in 2009/10; 441 in 2010/11.

Life expectancy (years at birth, WHO estimates): 73 (males 70; females 75) in 2009 (Source: WHO, *World Health Statistics*).

ECONOMICALLY ACTIVE POPULATION
('000 persons aged 10 years and over, excl. armed forces, 2008)

	Males	Females	Total
Agriculture, hunting and forestry	3,232	1,034	4,266
Fishing	76	2	78
Mining and quarrying	123	5	128
Manufacturing	2,630	882	3,512
Electricity, gas and water supply	171	9	180
Construction	2,762	27	2,791
Wholesale and retail trade; repair of motor vehicles, motorcycles and personal and household goods	2,821	160	2,981
Hotels and restaurants	194	17	211
Transport, storage and communications	2,021	46	2,067
Financial intermediation	243	41	284
Real estate, renting and business activities	444	77	521
Public administration and defence; compulsory social security	1,216	116	1,332
Education	618	601	1,219
Health and social work	244	204	448
Other community, social and personal service activities	303	140	443
Private households with employed persons	5	14	19
Extra-territorial organizations and bodies	1	1	2
Sub-total	17,105	3,376	20,481
Activities not adequately defined	14	5	19
Total employed	17,119	3,381	20,500
Unemployed	1,715	677	2,392
Total labour force	18,834	4,058	22,892

Source: ILO.

Health and Welfare

KEY INDICATORS

Total fertility rate (children per woman, 2009)	1.8
Under-5 mortality rate (per 1,000 live births, 2009)	31
HIV/AIDS (% of persons aged 15–49, 2009)	0.2
Physicians (per 1,000 head, 2005)	0.9
Hospital beds (per 1,000 head, 2005)	1.7
Health expenditure (2008): US $ per head (PPP)	613
Health expenditure (2008): % of GDP	5.5
Health expenditure (2008): public (% of total)	42.4
Access to water (% of persons, 2004)	94
Access to sanitation (% of persons, 2002)	84
Total carbon dioxide emissions ('000 metric tons, 2007)	495,581.6
Carbon dioxide emissions per head (metric tons, 2007)	7.0
Human Development Index (2011): ranking	88
Human Development Index (2011): value	0.707

For sources and definitions, see explanatory note on p. vi.

Agriculture

PRINCIPAL CROPS
('000 metric tons)

	2008	2009	2010
Wheat	7,956.6	13,484.5	15,028.8
Rice, paddy	2,184.0	2,253.4	2,288.2
Barley	1,547.4	3,446.2	3,209.6
Maize	1,777.5	1,642.7	1,735.9
Potatoes	4,706.7	4,107.6	4,054.5
Sugar cane	3,097.5	2,823.1	5,685.1
Sugar beet	1,829.3	2,015.9	3,896.8
Beans, dry	183.1	181.4	194.1
Chick-peas	113.3	208.9	239.8
Lentils	56.1	84.0	79.2
Almonds, with shell	126.7	140.0*	158.1
Walnuts, with shell*	300.0	300.0	270.3
Pistachios	446.6	446.6	446.6
Soybeans (Soya beans)	197.2	207.5	162.7
Cabbages and other brassicas*	316.0	360.6	371.9
Lettuce and chicory	219.7	390.8	402.8*
Tomatoes	4,826.4	5,887.7	5,256.1
Pumpkins, squash and gourds*	591.1	674.5	695.6
Cucumbers and gherkins	1,459.2	1,603.7	1,811.6
Aubergines (Eggplants)	443.1	862.2	888.5
Chillies and peppers, green	34.0	35.5	36.6
Onions, dry	1,849.3	1,522.2	1,923.0
Garlic	59.9	64.0	66.0*
Watermelons	2,566.7	3,074.6	3,466.9
Cantaloupes and other melons	1,332.1	1,278.5	1,317.6*
Oranges	2,619.7	2,000.0*	1,502.8
Tangerines, mandarins, clementines and satsumas	276.1	276.1	276.1
Lemons and limes	694.9	711.7*	706.8*
Apples	2,718.8	2,000.0*	1,662.4
Pears	115.8	153.4	160.0*
Apricots	487.3	371.8	400.0*
Sweet cherries	198.8	225.0*	255.5*
Peaches and nectarines	575.0	496.1	500.0*
Plums and sloes	269.1	269.1	269.1
Grapes	2,255.7	2,255.7	2,255.7
Figs	76.4	76.4	76.4
Dates	1,023.1	1,023.1	1,023.1
Tea	165.7	165.7	165.7

* FAO estimate(s).

Aggregate production ('000 metric tons, may include official, semi-official or estimated data): Total cereals 13,475.5 in 2008, 20,834.7 in 2009, 22,272.2 in 2010; Total roots and tubers 4,706.7 in 2008, 4,107.6 in 2009, 4,054.5 in 2010; Total vegetables (incl. melons) 15,872.6 in 2008, 18,120.9 in 2009, 18,678.5 in 2010; Total fruits (excl. melons) 13,833.5 in 2008, 12,538.3 in 2009, 12,126.0 in 2010.

Source: FAO.

LIVESTOCK
('000 head, FAO estimates)

	2008	2009	2010
Horses	140	140	140
Asses	1,600	1,600	1,600
Mules	175	175	175
Cattle	8,120	8,400	8,500
Buffaloes	630	630	650
Camels	152	152	152
Sheep	53,800	53,800	54,000
Goats	25,500	25,500	25,700
Chickens	481,000	495,000	507,000
Ducks	1,600	1,600	1,600
Geese and guinea fowl	1,000	1,000	1,000
Turkeys	2,000	2,000	2,000

Source: FAO.

LIVESTOCK PRODUCTS
('000 metric tons)

	2008	2009	2010
Cattle meat	373*	387*	392†
Buffalo meat†	19	19	19
Sheep meat	346*	359*	360†
Goat meat	132*	137*	138†
Chicken meat	1,566	1,610	1,650
Turkey meat†	6	6	6
Cows' milk	5,965.7	6,620.2†	6,391.4†
Buffaloes' milk†	270	279	280
Goats' milk†	420	429	452
Hen eggs	727	725	741†
Honey	41	46	47†
Wool: greasy†	74	75	60

* Unofficial figure.
† FAO estimate(s).

Source: FAO.

Forestry

ROUNDWOOD REMOVALS
('000 cubic metres, excl. bark)

	2006	2007	2008
Sawlogs, veneer logs and logs for sleepers	285	321	321
Pulpwood	235	248	248
Other industrial wood	209	231	250
Fuel wood	65	67	67
Total	794	867	886

2009–10: Production assumed to be unchanged from 2008 (FAO estimates).

Source: FAO.

SAWNWOOD PRODUCTION
('000 cubic metres, incl. railway sleepers)

	2006	2007	2008
Total (all broadleaved)	50	52	50

2009–10: Production assumed to be unchanged from 2008 (FAO estimate).

Source: FAO.

Fishing

('000 metric tons, live weight)

	2007	2008	2009
Capture	403.6	407.8	419.9
Caspian shads	15.4	16.7	25.5
Indian oil sardine	22.3	27.2	21.2
Kawakawa	15.7	20.4	17.8
Skipjack tuna	68.1	42.4	44.8
Longtail tuna	29.5	34.1	49.5
Yellowfin tuna	16.3	19.5	22.6
—continued			
Aquaculture*	158.6	154.7	179.6
Silver carp	53.5	48.2	55.2
Rainbow trout	58.8	62.6	73.6
Total catch*	562.2	562.6	599.5

* FAO estimates.

Source: FAO.

Production of caviar (metric tons, year ending 20 March): 31 in 2006/07; 19 in 2007/08; 14 in 2008/09.

Mining

CRUDE PETROLEUM
('000 barrels per day, year ending 20 March)

	2007/08	2008/09	2009/10
Total production	4,057	3,945	3,557

Total production ('000 barrels per day, estimates): 4,245 in 2010 (Source: BP, *Statistical Review of World Energy*).

NATURAL GAS
(excluding reinjection gas; million cu metres, year ending 20 March)

	2005/06	2006/07	2007/08
Consumption (domestic)*	102,200	109,800	122,500
Flared	15,800	15,100	15,000
Regional uses and wastes	7,400	5,000	7,300
Gas for export	4,800	5,700	5,600
Less Net imports	5,200	6,300	6,200
Total production	125,000	129,300	144,200

* Includes gas for household, industrial, generator and refinery consumption.

Gas injection (year ending 20 March, million cu metres): 26,663 in 2006/07; 25,971 in 2007/08; 28,448 in 2008/09; 28,840 in 2009/10.

OTHER MINERALS
('000 metric tons, unless otherwise indicated, year ending 20 March)

	2006/07	2007/08	2008/09
Iron ore: gross weight*	31,538	32,000	33,000
Iron ore: metal content*	15,000	15,000	16,000
Copper concentrates*†	244	248	260
Bauxite	521	715	700*
Lead concentrates†	20*	27	27
Zinc concentrates†	100*	69	80*
Manganese ore‡	103	115*	115*
Chromium concentrates§	186	269	225
Molybdenum concentrates (metric tons)*†	3,600	3,700	3,700
Silver (metric tons)*†	20	15	15
Gold (kilograms)†	252	400*	400*
Bentonite	254	376	380*
Kaolin*	350	320	320
Other clays*	550	530	530
Magnesite	112	116	115*
Fluorspar (Fluorite)	68	62	65*
Feldspar	512	502	500*
Barite (Barytes)	249	227	240*
Salt (unrefined)	2,565	2,158	2,200*
Gypsum (crude)	12,000*	11,251	13,000*
Pumice and related materials*	1,500	1,500	1,500
Mica (metric tons)	1,800	1,510	1,500*
Talc	91	89	90*
Turquoise (kilograms)*	20,000	19,000	19,000
Coal*	2,000	1,800	1,900

* Estimate(s).
† Figures refer to the metal content of ores and concentrates.
‡ Figures refer to gross weight. The estimated metal content (in '000 metric tons) was: 35 in 2006/07, 40 in 2007/08, 40 in 2008/09.
§ Figures refer to gross weight. The estimated chromic oxide content (in '000 metric tons) was: 90 in 2006/07, 130 in 2007/08, 110 in 2008/09.

Source: US Geological Survey.

Industry

PETROLEUM PRODUCTS
(average cu m per day, year ending 20 March)

	2007/08	2008/09	2009/10
Liquefied petroleum gas	7,723	8,071	8,362
Motor spirit (petrol)	45,080	51,496	59,515
Burning oil (for electricity)	21,680	21,347	18,519
Jet fuel	3,426	3,519	4,188
Gas-diesel (distillate fuel) oil	81,549	84,957	88,702
Residual fuel oils	73,020	77,132	76,101
Petroleum bitumen (asphalt)	976	616	698

OTHER PRODUCTS
(year ending 20 March)

	2005/06	2006/07	2007/08
Refined sugar ('000 metric tons)	1,590	1,319	1,841
Soft drinks (million bottles)	4,896	4,930	4,252
Malt liquor (million bottles)	181	232	356
Cigarettes (million)	23,796	27,050	17,387
Threads ('000 metric tons)	330	552	417
Finished fabrics (million metres)	385	344	325
Machine-made carpets ('000 sq m)	55,119	41,472	30,583
Hand-woven carpets (moquette—'000 sq m)	56,098	54,508	68,510
Paper ('000 metric tons)	378	491	455
Detergent powder ('000 metric tons)	522	562	584
Soap (metric tons)	61,982	68,312	72,616
Cement ('000 metric tons)	33,049	32,831	40,189
Washing machines ('000)	354	418	774
Radio receivers ('000)	562	821	702
Television receivers ('000)	768	620	355
Water meters ('000)	915	618	823
Electricity meters ('000)	803	562	689
Passenger cars and jeeps ('000)	922	917	946
Electric energy (million kWh)	178,072	192,574	203,971

Electric energy (million kWh): 215,763 in 2008/09, 222,256 in 2009/10.

Finance

CURRENCY AND EXCHANGE RATES

Monetary Units
100 dinars = 1 Iranian rial (IR).

Sterling, Dollar and Euro Equivalents (30 December 2011)
£1 sterling = 17,262.2 rials;
US $1 = 11,165.0 rials;
€1 = 14,446.4 rials;
100,000 Iranian rials = £5.79 = $8.96 = €6.92.

Average Exchange Rate (rials per US $)
2009 9,864.30
2010 10,254.18
2011 10,616.31

Note: In March 1993 the former multiple exchange rate system was unified, and since then the exchange rate of the rial has been market-determined. The foregoing information on average exchange rates refers to the base rate, applicable to receipts from exports of petroleum and gas, payments for imports of essential goods and services, debt-servicing costs and imports related to large national projects. There was also an export rate, set at a mid-point of US $1 = 3,007.5 rials in May 1995, which applied to receipts from non-petroleum exports and to all other official current account transactions not effected at the base rate. In addition, a market rate was determined by transactions on the Tehran Stock Exchange: at 31 January 2002 it was US $1 = 7,924 rials. The weighted average of all exchange rates (rials per US $, year ending 20 December) was: 3,206 in 1997/98; 4,172 in 1998/99; 5,731 in 1999/2000. A new unified exchange rate, based on the market rate, took effect from 21 March 2002.

BUDGET
(consolidated accounts of central government and Oil Stabilization Fund—OSF, '000 million rials, year ending 20 March)

Revenue	2007/08	2008/09*	2009/10†
Oil and gas revenue	578,708	569,951	436,159
Budget revenue	444,278	559,589	498,071
Transfers from OSF	209,098	184,235	223,099
Revenues transferred to OSF	134,430	10,362	-61,912
Non-oil budgetary revenue	237,893	283,918	354,315
Tax revenue	162,579	203,042	240,454
Taxes on income, profits and capital gains	97,097	130,453	153,994
Domestic taxes on goods and services	16,663	15,900	29,771
Taxes on international trade and transactions	48,819	56,689	56,689
Non-tax revenue	75,314	80,876	113,861
Non-oil OSF revenues	4,551	6,038	6,223
Total	821,152	859,906	796,697

Expenditure	2007/08	2008/09*	2009/10†
Central government expenditures	710,022	841,093	884,798
Current expenditure	562,306	595,254	676,682
Wages and salaries	151,583	211,000	229,000
Interest payments	7,371	5,982	5,982
Subsidies	62,862	61,000	68,000
Goods and services	39,119	55,000	71,600
Grants	13,823	50,800	28,700
Social benefits	64,492	139,605	181,000
Gasoline imports	33,820	60,867	34,300
Other expenses	189,236	11,000	58,100
Capital expenditure	147,716	245,839	208,116
OSF expenditures	40,289	19,148	—
Total	750,311	860,240	884,798

* Estimates.
† Projections.

Source: IMF, *Islamic Republic of Iran: 2009 Article IV Consultation—Staff Report; Staff Supplement; Public Information Notice on the Executive Board Discussion; and Statement by the Executive Director for Iran* (March 2010).

2010/11 ('000 million rials, estimates): *Revenue:* Tax revenue 272,382 (Taxes on income, profits and capital gains 145,470; Domestic taxes on goods and services 37,894; Taxes on international trade and transactions 77,886); Other revenue 714,731; Total 987,113. *Expenditure:* Current expenditure 710,957 (Compensation of employees 204,463; Goods and services 79,147; Subsidies 118,720; Social benefits 191,272); Net acquisition of non-financial assets 205,107; Total 916,064 (Source: *Islamic Republic of Iran: 2011 Article IV Consultation—Staff Report; Public Information Notice on the Executive Board Discussion; and Statement by the Executive Director for Iran,* August 2011).

INTERNATIONAL RESERVES
(US $ million at 31 December)*

	1993	1994	1995
Gold (national valuation)	229.1	242.2	251.9
IMF special drawing rights	144.0	142.9	133.6
Total	373.1	385.1	385.5

* Excluding reserves of foreign exchange, for which no figures have been available since 1982 (when the value of reserves was US $5,287m.).

IMF special drawing rights (US $ million at 31 December): 436 in 2008; 2,407 in 2009; 2,365 in 2010.

Source: IMF, *International Financial Statistics.*

MONEY SUPPLY
('000 million rials at 20 December)

	2007	2008	2009
Currency outside banks	60,881	122,603	147,878
Non-financial public enterprises' deposits at Central Bank	15,955	16,978	15,496
Demand deposits at commercial banks	351,365	300,451	317,415
Total money	428,201	440,031	480,790

Source: IMF, *International Financial Statistics.*

COST OF LIVING

(Consumer Price Index in urban areas, year ending 20 March; base: 2004/05 = 100)

	2008/09	2009/10	2010/11
Food and beverages	198.9	218.6	254.1
Clothing	163.1	179.7	200.9
Housing, water, electricity, gas, and other fuels	196.2	220.2	236.2
All items (incl. others)	183.3	203.0	228.2

NATIONAL ACCOUNTS

('000 million rials at current prices, year ending 20 March)

Expenditure on the Gross Domestic Product

	2005/06	2006/07*	2007/08*
Final consumption expenditure	1,038,136	1,249,280	1,494,606
Private	786,920	938,888	1,185,508
Public	251,216	310,392	309,098
Changes in inventories	100,651	138,844	231,396
Gross fixed capital formation	474,983	544,249	685,452
Total domestic expenditure	1,613,770	1,932,373	2,411,454
Exports of goods and services	613,102	738,427	944,164
Less Imports of goods and services	441,236	529,766	606,663
Statistical discrepancy	46,101	83,058	133,282
GDP at market prices	1,831,737	2,224,093	2,882,236
GDP at constant 1997/98 prices	433,463	460,387	497,671

* Provisional.

Gross Domestic Product by Economic Activity

	2005/06	2006/07*	2007/08*
Hydrocarbon GDP	522,119	613,213	805,986
Non-hydrocarbon GDP	1,332,593	1,647,316	2,084,361
Agriculture	171,811	207,037	267,679
Industry	323,716	396,979	528,389
Mining	15,924	19,281	23,074
Manufacturing	208,023	252,901	316,127
Construction	74,670	92,746	152,095
Electricity, gas and water	25,099	32,051	37,093
Services	886,024	1,097,052	1,355,096
Transport and communication	151,017	194,968	246,175
Banking and insurance	49,129	59,023	79,576
Trade, restaurants and hotels	210,440	245,381	302,271
Ownership and dwellings	230,250	299,927	405,522
Public services	194,601	235,513	244,032
Private services	50,588	62,241	77,520
Less Imputed bank service charge	48,958	53,752	66,803
GDP at factor prices	1,854,711	2,260,530	2,890,347
Net indirect taxes	–22,974	–36,437	–8,111
GDP at market prices	1,831,737	2,224,093	2,882,236

* Provisional.

BALANCE OF PAYMENTS

(US $ million, year ending 20 March)

	2007/08	2008/09	2009/10
Exports of goods f.o.b.	97,668	101,289	87,534
Petroleum and gas	81,567	82,403	66,210
Non-petroleum and gas exports	16,101	18,886	21,324
Imports of goods f.o.b.	–58,240	–70,199	–66,599
Trade balance	39,428	31,090	20,935
Exports of services and other income received	10,093	11,272	9,403
Imports of services and other income paid	–17,566	–19,821	–19,854
Balance on goods, services and income	31,955	22,541	10,484
Transfers (net)	642	362	424
Current balance	32,597	22,903	10,908

—*continued*	2007/08	2008/09	2009/10
Medium- and long-term debt	–62	–1,282	–1,468
Trade credit	791	–3,292	2,188
Other capital	–2,600	1,134	–11,481
Foreign direct investment and portfolio equity	–299	–247	260
Net errors and omissions	–15,173	–10,987	–5,752
Overall balance	15,254	8,229	–5,345

Source: IMF, *Islamic Republic of Iran: 2011 Article IV Consultation—Staff Report; Public Information Notice on the Executive Board Discussion; and Statement by the Executive Director for Iran* (August 2011).

External Trade

PRINCIPAL COMMODITIES

(US $ million, year ending 20 March)

Imports c.i.f. (distribution by SITC)	2007/08	2008/09	2009/10*
Food and live animals	3,172	6,738	6,394
Cereals and cereal preparations	1,201	4,434	3,514
Crude materials (inedible) except fuels	2,386	2,159	2,052
Animal and vegetable oils and fats	1,000	1,150	988
Vegetable oils and fats	994	1,142	983
Chemicals and related products	6,256	6,343	6,023
Chemical elements and compounds	1,477	1,344	1,247
Plastic, cellulose and artificial resins	2,023	1,811	1,832
Basic manufactures	12,672	13,364	12,559
Iron and steel	8,803	9,307	8,146
Machinery and transport equipment	16,493	19,171	17,984
Non-electric machinery	8,224	9,015	9,509
Electrical machinery, apparatus, etc.	3,800	4,609	3,955
Transport equipment	4,469	5,548	4,519
Miscellaneous manufactured articles	1,465	1,729	1,902
Total (incl. others)	48,439	56,042	55,189

Exports f.o.b.*	2007/08	2008/09	2009/10*
Agricultural and traditional goods	3,482	3,304	3,982
Carpets	398	422	494
Fruits (fresh and dried)	1,826	1,307	1,725
Industrial manufactures	11,548	14,662	16,551
Oil and gas products	2,956	3,819	3,835
Iron and steel	925	679	991
Total (incl. others)	15,312	18,334	21,321

* Preliminary.

† Excluding exports of crude petroleum and associated gas (US $ million): 84,505 in 2007/08; 86,619 in 2008/09; 69,825 in 2009/10 (preliminary).

Note: Imports include registration fee, but exclude defence-related imports and imports of refined petroleum products.

PRINCIPAL TRADING PARTNERS
(US $ million, year ending 20 March)

Imports c.i.f.	2005/06	2006/07	2007/08
Austria	712	800	1,071
Belgium	712	665	536
Brazil	818	787	563
China, People's Republic	2,204	2,753	4,292
France	2,680	2,192	1,894
Germany	5,165	5,076	5,328
India	1,115	1,440	1,457
Italy	2,361	1,717	1,902
Japan	1,311	917	1,325
Korea, Republic	2,136	1,949	2,456
Netherlands	929	915	537
Russia	1,070	708	863
Saudi Arabia	243	596	500
Singapore	463	401	575
Sweden	1,016	571	451
Switzerland	1,274	2,289	2,779
Taiwan	338	390	519
Turkey	867	890	1,246
United Arab Emirates	7,683	9,349	11,509
United Kingdom	983	1,440	2,002
Total (incl. others)	39,248	41,723	48,439

Exports f.o.b.	2005/06	2006/07	2007/08
Afghanistan	497	515	543
Azerbaijan	331	343	350
Belgium	70	182	223
China, People's Republic	529	1,053	1,244
Germany	356	359	374
Hong Kong	231	219	292
India	764	837	837
Indonesia	91	63	206
Iraq	1,224	1,792	1,842
Italy	246	645	522
Japan	539	664	927
Korea, Republic	141	231	552
Kuwait	453	279	319
Netherlands	254	103	234
Pakistan	295	307	274
Russia	183	289	367
Saudi Arabia	257	351	310
Spain	144	161	234
Syria	186	204	330
Taiwan	96	126	205
Tajikistan	110	129	171
Turkey	205	326	566
Turkmenistan	141	144	189
United Arab Emirates	1,545	1,728	2,166
Total (incl. others)	10,474	12,997	15,312

Note: Exports exclude crude petroleum and associated gas.

Transport

RAILWAYS
(traffic, year ending 20 March)

	2008/09	2009/10	2010/11
Passengers carried ('000)	26,225	27,710	28,814
Passenger-km (million)	15,312	16,814	17,611
Freight carried ('000 metric tons)	33,044	32,817	33,458
Freight ton-km (million)	20,540	20,247	21,779

ROAD TRAFFIC
(registered motor vehicles, year ending 20 March)

	2008/09	2009/10	2010/11
Passenger cars*	1,007,403	1,170,581	1,104,304
Pick-ups and light trucks	182,916	202,200	189,302
Motorcycles	654,320	591,318	835,711
Total (incl. others)	1,888,514	2,005,475	2,190,835

* Including ambulances.

SHIPPING

Merchant Fleet
(registered at 31 December)

	2007	2008	2009
Number of vessels	508	503	542
Displacement ('000 grt)	3,576.9	1,096.4	987.6

Source: IHS Fairplay, *World Fleet Statistics*.

International Sea-borne Freight Traffic
(year ending 20 March, '000 metric tons)*

	2008/09	2009/10	2010/11
Goods loaded	30,540	42,230	54,910
Crude petroleum and petroleum products	12,786	14,376	18,011
Goods unloaded	70,708	77,744	72,102
Petroleum products	27,618	29,997	24,045

* Cargo loaded onto and from vessels with a capacity of 1,000 metric tons or greater only.

CIVIL AVIATION
(year ending 20 March)

	2008/09	2009/10	2010/11
Passengers ('000):			
domestic flights	12,836	14,440	16,104
international arrivals	3,706	3,714	3,847
international departures	3,599	3,704	4,053
Freight (excl. mail, metric tons):			
domestic flights	33,971	37,688	47,158
international arrivals	60,517	53,506	65,274
international departures	29,597	29,034	30,762
Mail (metric tons):			
domestic flights	5,726	5,211	5,785
international arrivals	8,011	8,247	8,708
international departures	2,069	2,724	3,038

Tourism

FOREIGN TOURIST ARRIVALS
(year ending 20 March)

Country of nationality	1997/98	1998/99	1999/2000
Afghanistan	69,793	125,189	146,322
Azerbaijan	302,574	383,123	447,797
Kuwait	19,642	26,472	30,941
Pakistan	100,427	115,431	134,916
Russia	16,466*	10,191*	11,911
Saudi Arabia	17,406	21,093	24,654
Turkey	93,105	160,959	188,130
Total (incl. others)	764,092	1,007,597	1,320,905

* Including Belarus.

Total arrivals (year ending 20 March): 1,341,762 in 2000/01; 1,402,160 in 2001/02; 1,584,922 in 2002/03; 1,500,439 in 2003/04; 1,659,479 in 2004/05; 1,160,699 in 2005/06; 1,816,900 in 2006/07; 2,171,699 in 2007/08; 2,027,528 in 2008/09; 2,272,575 in 2009/10; 3,121,283 in 2010/11.

Tourism receipts (US $ million, incl. passenger transport): 1,950 in 2007; 2,202 in 2008; 2,310 in 2009 (Source: World Tourism Organization).

Communications Media

	2008	2009	2010
Telephones ('000 main lines in use)	24,800.0	25,804.1	26,848.9
Mobile cellular telephones ('000 subscribers)	43,000.0	52,555.0	67,500.0
Internet users ('000)	7,507.1	8,213.5	n.a.
Broadband subscribers ('000)	300.0	400.0	500.0
Book production*:			
titles	55,999	60,801	64,606
copies ('000)	219,709	206,161	198,593

* Twelve months beginning 21 March of year stated.

Newspapers and periodicals (number of titles, year ending 20 March 2006): Daily 183; Other 4,528.

Personal computers: 7,420,791 (105.9 per 1,000 persons) in 2006.

Television receivers ('000 in use, year ending 20 March): 11,040 in 2001/02.

Radio receivers ('000 in use, year ending 20 March): 17,400 in 1998/99.

Sources: partly International Telecommunication Union; UN, *Statistical Yearbook*.

Education

(2010/11 unless otherwise indicated)

	Institutions	Teachers	Students ('000)		
			Males	Females	Total
Special*	2,983	10,142	59.5	41.9	101.5
Pre-primary*	16,299	1,848	221.8	230.4	452.3
Primary*	57,115	208,872	2,878.3	2,713.5	5,591.8
Lower secondary:					
mainstream*	26,981	151,935	1,733.9	1,558.3	3,292.2
adult*	278		5.7	11.0	16.8
Upper secondary:					
mainstream*	15,289	169,463	1,552.8	1,429.6	2,982.4
adult	2,761		157.4	130.9	288.3
Pre-university:					
mainstream	8,442	n.a.	170.4	264.7	435.0
adult	1,227		24.0	16.5	40.5
Teacher training*	96	n.a.	2.6	2.3	4.9
Islamic Azad University	n.a.	79,780	940.6	595.6	1,536.2
Other higher	n.a.	125,576	1,138.1	1,442.3	2,580.4

* 2009/10 figures.

Pupil-teacher ratio (primary education, UNESCO estimate): 20.3 in 2008/09 (Source: UNESCO Institute for Statistics).

Adult literacy rate (UNESCO estimates): 85.0% (males 89.3%; females 80.7%) in 2008 (Source: UNESCO Institute for Statistics).

Directory

The Government

SUPREME RELIGIOUS LEADER

Wali Faqih: Ayatollah SAYED ALI KHAMENEI.

HEAD OF STATE

President: MAHMOUD AHMADINEJAD (assumed office 6 August 2005; re-elected 12 June 2009).

First Vice-President: MUHAMMAD REZA RAHIMI.

Executive Vice-President: HAMID BAGHAEI.

Vice-President in charge of Legal Affairs: FATIMA BODAGHI.

Vice-President in charge of Parliamentary Affairs: Hojatoleslam SAYED MUHAMMAD REZA MIR TAJ AL-DINY.

Vice-President for Strategic Planning and Supervision Affairs: EBRAHIM AZIZI.

Vice-President for Management Development and Human Resources Affairs: LOTFOLLAH FOROUZANDEH DEHKORDI.

Vice-President for International Affairs: SAYED ALI SAIDLOO.

Vice-President and Head of the Organization for the Protection of the Environment: MUHAMMAD JAVAD MUHAMMADI ZADEH.

Vice-President and Head of the Cultural Heritage, Handicrafts and Tourism Organization: SEYED HASSAN MOUSAVI.

Vice-President for Science and Technology: NASRIN SOLTANKHAH.

Vice-President and Head of the Atomic Energy Organization: FEREYDOUN ABBASI DAVANI.

Vice-President and Head of the Martyrs' and Self-Sacrificers' Affairs Foundation: MASOUD ZARIBAFAN.

The Head of Presidential Office, ESFANDIAR RAHIM-MASHAI, and the Cabinet Secretary, ALI SADOUGHI, also have full ministerial status.

COUNCIL OF MINISTERS

(May 2012)

Minister of Education: HAMID REZA HAJI BABAIE.

Minister of Communications and Information Technology: REZA TAQIPOUR.

Minister of Intelligence: HEYDAR MOSLEHI.

Minister of Economic Affairs and Finance: SEYED SHAMSEDDIN HOSSEINI.

Minister of Foreign Affairs: ALI AKBAR SALEHI.

Minister of Health and Medical Education: MARZIEH VAHID DASTJERDI.

Minister of Agricultural Jihad: SADEQ KHALILIAN.

Minister of Justice: MORTEZA BAKHTIARI.

Minister of Defence and Armed Forces Logistics: Brig.-Gen. AHMAD VAHIDI.

Minister of Roads and Urban Development: ALI NIKZAD.

Minister of Science, Research and Technology: KAMRAN DANESHJOU.

Minister of Culture and Islamic Guidance: SAYED MUHAMMAD HOSSEINI.

Minister of Co-operatives, Labour and Social Welfare: ABDOLREZA SHEIKHOLESLAMI.

Minister of the Interior: MOSTAFA MUHAMMAD NAJJAR.

Minister of Petroleum: Brig.-Gen. ROSTAM GHASEMI.

Minister of Energy: MAJID NAMJOU.

Minister of Sport and Youth Affairs: MUHAMMAD ABBASI.

Minister of Industries, Mines and Trade: MAHDI GHAZANFARI.

MINISTRIES

Office of the President: POB 1423-13185, Pasteur Ave, Tehran 13168-43311; tel. (21) 64451; e-mail webmaster@president.ir; internet www.president.ir.

Ministry of Agricultural Jihad: 20 Malaei Ave, Vali-e-Asr Sq., Tehran; tel. (21) 81363301; fax (21) 81363345; e-mail pr@maj.ir; internet www.maj.ir.

Ministry of Communications and Information Technology: POB 15875-4415, Shariati St, Tehran 16314; tel. (21) 88114315; fax (21) 88467210; e-mail khajeh@ict.gov.ir; internet www.ict.gov.ir.

Ministry of Co-operatives, Labour and Social Welfare: Azadi St, Tehran; tel. (21) 88977415; fax (21) 88951536; e-mail support@irimlsa.ir; internet www.irimlsa.ir.

Ministry of Culture and Islamic Guidance: POB 5158, Baharestan Sq., Tehran 11365; tel. (21) 38512583; fax (21) 33117535; e-mail info@ershad.gov.ir; internet www.ershad.gov.ir.

Ministry of Defence and Armed Forces Logistics: Shahid Yousuf Kaboli St, Sayed Khandan Area, Tehran; tel. (21) 21401; fax (21) 864008; e-mail info@mod.ir; internet www.mod.ir.

Ministry of Economic Affairs and Finance: Sour Esrafil Ave, Nasser Khosrou St, Tehran 11149-43661; tel. (21) 22553401; fax (21) 22581933; e-mail info@mefa.gov.ir; internet mefa.gov.ir.

Ministry of Education: Si-e-Tir St, Imam Khomeini Sq., Tehran; tel. (21) 32421; fax (21) 675503; e-mail negah@medu.ir; internet www.medu.ir.

Ministry of Energy: POB 19968-32611, Niayesh Highway, Vali-e-Asr Ave, Tehran; tel. (21) 81606757; fax (21) 81606552; e-mail info@moe.org.ir; internet www.moe.org.ir.

Ministry of Foreign Affairs: Imam Khomeini Sq., Tehran; tel. (21) 61151; fax (21) 66743149; e-mail matbuat@mfa.gov.ir; internet www.mfa.gov.ir.

Ministry of Health and Medical Education: POB 310, Jomhouri Islami Ave, Hafez Crossing, Tehran 11344; tel. (21) 88363560; fax (21) 88364111; e-mail webmaster@mohme.gov.ir; internet www.mohme.gov.ir.

Ministry of Industries, Mines and Trade: Shahid Kalantari, Ostad Negatollahi St, Ferdosi Sq., Tehran; tel. (21) 88906563; fax (21) 88903650; e-mail intl@mim.gov.ir; internet www.mim.gov.ir.

Ministry of Intelligence: POB 16765-1947, Second Negarestan St, Pasdaran Ave, Tehran; tel. (21) 233031; fax (21) 23305.

Ministry of the Interior: Jahad Sq., Fatemi St, Tehran; tel. (21) 84866031; fax (21) 88964678; e-mail ravabetomomi@moi.gov.ir; internet www.moi.ir.

Ministry of Justice: Panzdah-e-Khordad Sq., Tehran 14158-55139; tel. (21) 88383201; fax (21) 3904986; e-mail info@justice.ir; internet www.justice.ir.

Ministry of Petroleum: Hafez Crossing, Taleghani Ave, Tehran 15936-57919; tel. (21) 66152606; fax (21) 66154977; e-mail public-relations@nioc.ir; internet www.mop.ir.

Ministry of Roads and Urban Development: Dadman Tower, Africa Blvd, Tehran; tel. (21) 88646130; internet www.mrud.ir.

Ministry of Science, Research and Technology: POB 15875-4375, Central Bldg, Ostad Nejatollahi Ave, Tehran; tel. (21) 82231000; fax (21) 88827234; e-mail zahedi@msrt.ir; internet www.msrt.ir.

Ministry of Sport and Youth Affairs: Tehran.

President and Legislature

PRESIDENT

Presidential Election, 12 June 2009

Candidates	Votes	%
Mahmoud Ahmadinejad	24,527,516	62.63
Mir Hossein Mousavi	13,216,411	33.75
Mohsen Rezai	678,240	1.73
Mahdi Karrubi	333,635	0.85
Total	39,165,191*	100.00

* Including 409,389 invalid votes (1.04% of total votes cast).

Majlis-e-Shura-e Islami—Islamic Consultative Assembly

Baharestan Sq., Tehran; tel. (21) 33440236; fax (21) 33440309; internet www.parliran.ir.

Elections to the eighth Majlis took place in early 2008. Prior to the elections the Council of Guardians and the Ministry of the Interior barred at least 1,700 of the 7,168 registered candidates from standing, including a number of current Majlis deputies. The majority of the barred candidates were recognized as being 'reformists'. At the first round of voting, held on 14 March, 208 deputies received a sufficient number of votes to be elected directly to the Majlis; at the second round, on 25 April, a further 79 deputies were elected. Three seats remained vacant following both rounds, after election officials had annulled the results for unspecified reasons; by-elections for these seats were to be held at a later date. According to official reports, 'conservatives' controlled the eighth Majlis, with an estimated 198–200 seats; 'reformists' secured around 46–50 seats, and some 40–43 seats were held by 'independents'. A reported 29 of the 30 seats in Tehran were filled by 'conservatives', with only one seat going to a 'reformist' candidate. However, despite the 'conservatives' having consolidated their control of the Majlis, some of the new deputies were reported to be critical of President Mahmoud Ahmadinejad's policies. On 2 March 2012 the first round of elections to the ninth Majlis took place. Of the 290 seats, 'conservatives' secured 143 seats, while 'reformists' took 59 seats. Candidates representing religious minorities held 14 seats and nine seats went to 'independents'. The remaining 65 seats were contested at a second round of voting, held on 4 May.

Speaker: ALI ARDESHIR LARIJANI.

First Deputy Speaker: MUHAMMAD REZA BAHONAR.

Second Deputy Speaker: SEYED SHAHABEDDIN SADR.

Shura-ye Ali-ye Amniyyat-e Melli—Supreme National Security Council

Formed in July 1989 (in place of the Supreme Defence Council) to co-ordinate defence and national security policies, the political programme and intelligence reports, and social, cultural and economic activities related to defence and security. The Council is chaired by the President and includes a representative of the Wali Faqih, the Minister of the Interior, the Speaker of the Majlis, the Head of the Judiciary, the Chief of the Supreme Command Council of the Armed Forces, the Minister of Foreign Affairs, the Head of the Management and Planning Organization, and the Minister of Intelligence and Security.

Secretary: SAEED JALILI.

Majlis-e Khobregan—Assembly of Experts

Tehran; internet www.majlesekhobregan.ir.

Elections were held on 10 December 1982 to appoint an Assembly of Experts which was to choose an eventual successor to the Wali Faqih (then Ayatollah Khomeini) after his death. The Constitution provides for a three- or five-man body to assume the leadership of the country if there is no recognized successor on the death of the Wali Faqih. The Council comprises 86 clerics, who are elected to serve an eight-year term. Elections to a fourth term of the Council were held on 15 December 2006.

Speaker: Ayatollah MUHAMMAD REZA MAHDAVI KANI.

First Deputy Speaker: Ayatollah SAYED MAHMOUD HASHEMI SHAHROUDI.

Second Deputy Speaker: Ayatollah MUHAMMAD YAZDI.

Secretaries: Ayatollah AHMAD KHATAMI, Ayatollah QORBANALI DORRI NAJAFABADI.

Shura-e-Nigahban—Council of Guardians

The Council of Guardians, composed of six qualified Muslim jurists appointed by Ayatollah Khomeini and six lay Muslim lawyers, appointed by the Majlis from among candidates nominated by the Head of the Judiciary, was established in 1980 to supervise elections and to examine legislation adopted by the Majlis, ensuring that it accords with the Constitution and with Islamic precepts.

Chairman: Ayatollah AHMAD JANNATI.

Shura-ye Tashkhis-e Maslahat-e Nezam—Council to Determine the Expediency of the Islamic Order

Formed in February 1988, by order of Ayatollah Khomeini, to arbitrate on legal and theological questions in legislation approved by the Majlis, in the event of a dispute between the latter and the supervisory Council of Guardians. Its permanent members, defined in March 1997, are Heads of the Legislative, Judiciary and Executive Powers, the jurist members of the Council of Guardians, and the Minister or head of organization concerned with the pertinent arbitration. In October 2005 the powers of the Expediency Council were extended, allowing it to supervise all branches of government. Four new members were appointed to the Expediency Council in February 2007, when Rafsanjani was reappointed as Chairman; the term of the Council is five years.

Chairman: Hojatoleslam ALI AKBAR HASHEMI RAFSANJANI.

Secretary: Maj.-Gen. MOHSEN REZAI.

Hey'at-e Peygiri-ye Qanun Asasi Va Nezarat Bar An—Committee for Ensuring and Supervising the Implementation of the Constitution

Formed by former President Khatami in November 1997; members are appointed for a four-year term. Two new members were appointed to the Committee in April 2002.

Members: Dr GUDARZ EFTEKHAR-JAHROMI, MUHAMMAD ISMAÏL SHOUSHTARI, HASHEM HASHEMZADEH HERISI, Dr HOSSEIN MEHRPUR, Dr MUHAMMAD HOSSEIN HASHEMI.

Political Organizations

Numerous political organizations were registered in the late 1990s, following the election of former President Khatami, and have tended to be regarded as either 'conservative' or 'reformist', the principal factions in the legislature. There are also a small number of centrist political parties. Under the Iranian electoral system, parties do not field candidates *per se* at elections, but instead back lists of candidates, who are allowed to be members of more than one party. In the mid-2000s there were estimated to be more than 100 registered political organizations, some of which are listed below:

Etelaf-e Abadgaran-e Iran-e Islami (Islamic Iran Developers' Council): e-mail info@abadgaran.ir; f. 2003 to contest that year's municipal elections; influential conservative grouping; includes mems of Jame'e-ye Eslaami-e Mohandesin (Islamic Society of Engineers) and fmr officers of the Revolutionary Guards; Leader GHOLAM-ALI HADDAD-ADEL.

Hezb-e Etedal va Toseh (Moderation and Development Party): first congress held 2002; moderate, centrist; Sec.-Gen. MUHAMMAD BAQIR NOBAKHT.

Hezb-e Iran-e Sarfaraz (Proud Iran Party): reformist; Sec.-Gen. RUZBEH MESHKIN.

Hezb-e Islami-ye Kar (Islamic Labour Party): f. 1999 as splinter group of Khaneh-ye Kargar (Workers' House); reformist; Sec.-Gen. ABOLQASEM SARHADIZADEH.

Hezb-e Kargozaran-e Sazandegi (Servants of Construction Party): f. 1996 as Servants of Iran's Construction; authorized as political party in 1998; reformist; Sec.-Gen. GHOLAM HOSSEIN KARBASCHI.

Hezb-e Motalefeh-e Islami (Islamic Coalition Party): f. 1963; also known as Jam'iyat-e Motalefeh-e Islami (Islamic Coalition Society); traditionalist conservative, incl. clerics and merchants; opposed to political reforms, but some mems favour economic reforms; Sec.-Gen. MUHAMMAD NABI HABIBI.

Jamiyat-e Isargaran-e Inqilab-e Islami (Islamic Revolution Devotees' Society): Tehran; hardline conservative; includes fmr officers of the Revolutionary Guards; Co-Founder MAHMOUD AHMADINEJAD.

Khaneh-ye Kargar (Workers' House): reformist, leftist; Sec.-Gen. ALIREZA MAHJUB.

Majma'-e Ruhaniyun-e Mobarez (Militant Clergy Association): f. 1988 as splinter group of the Jam'-ye Ruhaniyat-e Mobarez-i Tehran (Tehran Militant Clergy Association); reformist; Sec.-Gen. Hojatoleslam MUHAMMAD ASQAR MUSAVI-KHOENIHA.

Most of the following are either registered political parties that have boycotted elections to the Majlis-e-Shura-e Islami (Islamic Consultative Assembly) in the 2000s, or are unregistered organizations or guerrilla groups:

Ansar-e Hezbollah (Helpers of the Party of God): internet www.ansarehezbollah.org; f. 1995; militant, ultra-conservative youth movement; pledges allegiance to the Wali Faqih (supreme religious leader).

Daftar-e Tahkim-e Vahdat (Office for Strengthening Unity): Tehran; org. of Islamist university students who supported Khatami in the presidential election of 1997 and reformist candidates in the Majlis elections of 2000; Spokesman ALI NIKUNESBATI.

Democratic Party of Iranian Kurdistan: 17 ave d'Italie, Paris 75013, France; tel. 1-45-85-64-31; fax 1-45-85-20-93; e-mail pdkiran@club-internet.fr; internet www.pdki.org; f. 1945; seeks a federal system of govt in Iran, in order to secure the national rights of the Kurdish people; mem. of the Socialist International; 95,000 mems; Sec.-Gen. MUSTAFA HIJRI.

Fedayin-e-Khalq (Organization of the Iranian People's Fedayeen—Majority): Postfach 260268, 50515 Köln, Germany; e-mail info@fadai.org; internet www.fadai.org; f. 1971; Marxist; Sec. of Int. Dept FARROKH NEGAHDAR.

Fraksion-e Hezbollah: f. 1996 by deputies in the Majlis who had contested the 1996 legislative elections as a loose coalition known as the Society of Combatant Clergy; Leader ALI AKBAR HOSSAINI.

Free Life Party of Kurdistan (PJAK): internet pjak.org; f. 2004; militant org. that operates in mountainous areas of Iran and northern Iraq; apparently has close links with the Partiya Karkeren Kurdistan (Kurdistan Workers' Party) of Turkey; seeks a federal, secular system of govt in Iran, in order to secure the national rights of the Kurdish people; Sec.-Gen. RAHMAN HAJI AHMADI.

Hezb-e Etemad-e Melli (National Confidence Party—NCP): Tehran; tel. (21) 88373305; fax (21) 88373306; e-mail info@etemademelli.ir; internet etemademelli.ir; f. 2005 by Mahdi Karrubi, fmrly of the Militant Clergy Association, shortly after his defeat in the presidential election of June; reformist, centrist; Sec.-Gen. MAHDI KARRUBI.

Hezb-e Hambastegi-ye Iran-e Islami (Islamic Iran Solidarity Party): f. 1998; reformist; Sec.-Gen. EBRAHIM ASGHARZADEH.

Hezb-e-Komunist Iran (Communist Party of Iran): POB 70445, 107 25 Stockholm, Sweden; e-mail cpi@cpiran.org; internet www.cpiran.org; f. 1979 by dissident mems of Tudeh Party; Sec.-Gen. 'AZARYUN'.

Iran National Front (Jebhe Melli Iran): US Section, POB 136, Audubon Station, New York, NY 10032, USA; e-mail contact@jebhemelli.net; internet www.jebhemelli.net; f. late 1940s by the late Dr Muhammad Mussadeq; secular, pro-democracy opposition group, which also seeks to further religious freedom within Iran.

Jame'e-ye Eslaami-e Mohandesin (Islamic Society of Engineers): f. 1988; conservative; mems incl. President Mahmoud Ahmadinejad; Sec.-Gen. MUHAMMAD REZA BAHONAR.

Jebbeh-ye Mosharekat-e Iran-e Islami (Islamic Iran Participation Front): e-mail mail.emrooz@gmail.com; internet www.mosharekat.com; f. 1998; reformist, leftist; reportedly proscribed by the Iranian authorities in March 2010; Sec.-Gen. MOHSEN MIRDAMADI.

Komala Party of Iranian Kurdistan: e-mail secretariat@komala.org; internet www.komala.org; f. 1969; Kurdish wing of the Communist Party of Iran; Marxist-Leninist; Sec.-Gen. ABDULLAH MOHTADI.

Marze Por Gohar (Glorious Frontiers Party): 1351 Westwood Blvd, Suite 111, Los Angeles, CA 90024, USA; tel. (310) 473-4763; fax (310) 477-8484; e-mail info@marzeporgohar.org; internet www.marzeporgohar.org; f. 1998 in Tehran; nationalist party advocating a secular republic in Iran; Chair. ROOZBEH FARAHANIPOUR.

Mujahidin-e-Khalq (Holy Warriors of the People): e-mail mojahed@mojahedin.org; internet www.mojahedin.org; Marxist-Islamist guerrilla group opposed to clerical regime; since June 1987 comprising the National Liberation Army; mem. of the National Council of Resistance of Iran; based in Paris, France 1981–86 and in Baghdad, Iraq, 1986–2003; Leaders MARYAM RAJAVI, MASSOUD RAJAVI.

National Democratic Front: f. March 1979; Leader HEDAYATOLLAH MATINE-DAFTARI (based in Paris, France Jan. 1982–).

Nehzat-e Azadi-ye Iran (Liberation Movement of Iran): e-mail nehzateazadi1340@gmail.com; internet www.nehzateazadi.org; f. 1961; emphasis on basic human rights as defined by Islam; Sec.-Gen. Dr IBRAHIM YAZDI.

Pan-Iranist Party: POB 31535-1679, Karaj; internet www.paniranist.org; calls for a Greater Persia; Gen. Sec. ZAHRA GHOLAMIPOUR.

Sazeman-e Mujahidin-e Enqelab-e Islami (Organization of the Mujahidin of the Islamic Revolution): reformist; Sec.-Gen. MUHAMMAD SALAMATI.

Sazmane Peykar dar Rahe Azadieh Tabaqe Kargar (Organization Struggling for the Freedom of the Working Class): Marxist-Leninist.

Tudeh Party of Iran (Party of the Masses): POB 100644, 10566 Berlin, Germany; tel. (30) 3241627; e-mail mardom@tudehpartyiran.org; internet www.tudehpartyiran.org; f. 1941; declared illegal 1949; came into open 1979; banned again April 1983; First Sec., Cen. Cttee ALI KHAVARI.

The National Council of Resistance (NCR) was formed in Paris, France, in October 1981 by former President Abolhasan Bani-Sadr and Massoud Rajavi, the leader of the Mujahidin-e-Khalq in Iran. In 1984 the Council comprised 15 opposition groups, operating either clandestinely in Iran or from exile abroad. Bani-Sadr left the Council in that year because of his objection to Rajavi's growing links with the Iraqi Government. The French Government asked Rajavi to leave Paris in June 1986 and he moved his base of operations to Baghdad, Iraq. In June 1987 Rajavi, Secretary of the NCR, announced the formation of a 10,000–15,000-strong National Liberation Army as the military wing of the Mujahidin-e-Khalq. However, the status of the Mujahidin was initially uncertain following the invasion of Iraq by the US-led coalition in March 2003 (see the chapter on Iraq) and firmer measures being taken against the activities of the organization by the authorities in Paris in mid-2003. In July 2004 the USA declared a group of 3,800 members of the Mujahidin-e-Khalq interned in Iraq to have 'protected status' under the Geneva Convention. There is also a National Movement of Iranian Resistance, based in Paris.

Diplomatic Representation

EMBASSIES IN IRAN

Afghanistan: Dr Beheshti Ave, cnr of 4th St, Pakistan St, Tehran; tel. (21) 88735040; fax (21) 88735600; e-mail info@afghanembassy.ir; internet www.afghanembassy.ir; Ambassador Dr OBAIDULLAH OBAID.

Algeria: No. 6, 16th Alley, Velenjak Ave, Velenjak, Tehran; tel. (21) 22420015; fax (21) 22420017; e-mail ambalg_teheran@yahoo.fr; Ambassador MIMOUNI SOFIANE.

Argentina: POB 15875-4335, 11 Ghoo Alley, Yar Mohammadi Ave, Darrous, Tehran; tel. (21) 22577433; fax (21) 22577432; e-mail eiran@mrecic.gov.ar; Chargé d'affaires GUILLERMO NICOLÁS.

Armenia: 1 Ostad Shahriar St, Razi St, Jomhouri Islami Ave, Tehran 11337; tel. (21) 66704833; fax (21) 66700657; e-mail emarteh@yahoo.com; Ambassador GRIGOR ARAKELYAN.

Australia: POB 15875-4334, No. 2, 23rd St, Khalid Islambuli Ave, Tehran 15138; tel. (21) 88724456; fax (21) 88720484; e-mail dfat-tehran@dfat.gov.au; internet www.iran.embassy.gov.au; Ambassador MARC INNES-BROWN.

Austria: 6–8 Bahonar St, Moghaddasi St, Ahmadi Zamani St, Tehran; tel. (21) 22750038; fax (21) 22705262; e-mail teheran-ob@bmeia.gv.at; internet www.aussenministerium.at/teheran; Ambassador Dr THOMAS M. BUCHSBAUM.

Azerbaijan: 10 Akdsihi St, Tehran; tel. (21) 22215191; fax (21) 22217504; e-mail info@azembassy.ir; Ambassador JAVANSHIR AKHUNDOV.

Bahrain: 248 Africa Ave, cnr of Joubin Alley, Tehran; tel. (21) 88773383; fax (21) 88779112; e-mail tehran.mission@mofa.gov.bh; internet www.mofa.gov.bh; Ambassador RASHID BIN SAAD AL-DOSARI.

Bangladesh: POB 11365-3711, Bldg 58, cnr Maryam Alley, Vanak St, Tehran; tel. (21) 88063073; fax (21) 88039965; e-mail info@bangladoot.ir; Ambassador KHANDAKAR ABDUS SATTAR.

Belarus: 1 Azar St, Aban St, Shahid Taheri St, Zafaranieyeh Ave, Tehran 19887; tel. (21) 22752229; fax (21) 22751382; e-mail iran@belembassy.org; internet www.iran.belembassy.org; Ambassador VIKTOR RYBAK.

Belgium: POB 11365-115, 155–157 Shahid Fayyaz Bakhsh Ave, Shemiran, Elahieh, Tehran 16778; tel. (21) 22041617; fax (21) 22044608; e-mail teheran@diplobel.fed.be; internet www.diplomatie.be/tehran; Ambassador FRANÇOIS DEL MARMOL.

Bosnia and Herzegovina: No. 485, Aban Alley, 4th St, Iran Zamin Ave, Shahrak-e-Ghods, Tehran; tel. (21) 88086929; fax (21) 88092120; e-mail bhembasy@parsonline.net; Ambassador EMIR HADŽIKADUNIĆ.

Brazil: POB 19886-33854, 26 Yekta St, Zafaranieh, Tehran; tel. (21) 22753010; fax (21) 22752009; e-mail embassy@brazil-iran.org; internet teera.itamaraty.gov.br; Ambassador ANTONIO LUIS ESPINOLA SALGODA.

Brunei: No. 7 Mina Blvd, Africa Ave, Tehran; tel. (21) 88797946; fax (21) 88770162; e-mail bruneiran@hotmail.com; Ambassador Pengiran Haji SAHARI Pengiran Haji SALEH.

Bulgaria: POB 11365-7451, Vali-e-Asr Ave, Dr Abbaspour Ave, 82 Nezami-e-Ganjavi St, Tehran; tel. (21) 88775662; fax (21) 88779680; e-mail bulgr.tehr@neda.net; Ambassador PLAMEN GEORGIEV SHUKYURLIEV.

Canada: POB 11155-4647, 57 Shahid Sarafraz St, Ostad Motahari Ave, Tehran 15868; tel. (21) 81520000; fax (21) 88733200; e-mail teran@international.gc.ca; internet www.canadainternational.gc.ca/iran; Chargé d'affaires DENNIS HORAK.

China, People's Republic: POB 11365-3937, 13 Narenjestan 7th, Pasdaran Ave, Tehran; tel. (21) 22291240; fax (21) 22290690; e-mail chinaemb_ir@mfa.gov.cn; internet ir.china-embassy.org; Ambassador YU HONGYANG.

Comoros: No. 10 Malek St, Shariati Ave, Tehran; tel. (21) 77624400; fax (21) 77624411; e-mail ambacomoresthn@yahoo.fr; Ambassador AHMAD NADJID AL-MARZOUQI.

Croatia: No. 25, 1st Behestan, Pasdaran St, Tehran; tel. (21) 22589923; fax (21) 22549199; e-mail vrhteh@mvpei.hr; Ambassador Dr ESAD PROHIĆ.

Cuba: No. 3, Hast Metro Ghaem Alley, Shahid Maleki, Tehran; tel. and fax (21) 22054383; e-mail embacuba.teheran@accir.com; internet emba.cubaminrex.cu/iranfar; Ambassador WILLIAM CARBO RICARDO.

Cyprus: POB 18348-44681, 328 Shahid Karimi, Dezashib, Tajrish, Tehran; tel. (21) 22219842; fax (21) 22219843; e-mail cyprus@parsonline.net; internet www.mfa.gov.cy/embassytehran; Ambassador (vacant).

Czech Republic: POB 11365-4457, No. 199, Lavasani Ave, cnr of Yas St, Tehran 195376-4358; tel. (21) 22288149; fax (21) 22802079; e-mail teheran@embassy.mzv.cz; internet www.mfa.cz/tehran; Chargé d'affaires a.i. JOSEF HAVLAS.

Denmark: POB 19395-5358, 10 Dashti St, Dr Shariati Ave, Hedayat St, Tehran 1914861144; tel. (21) 22640009; fax (21) 22640007; e-mail thramb@um.dk; internet www.ambteheran.um.dk; Ambassador ANDERS CHRISTIAN HOUGÅRD.

Finland: POB 19395-1733, No. 2, Haddadian St, Mirzapour St, Dr Shariati Ave, Tehran; tel. (21) 22207090; fax (21) 22215822; e-mail sanomat.teh@formin.fi; internet www.finland.org.ir; Ambassador HARRI SALMI.

France: 64–66 Neauphle-le-Château Ave, Tehran; tel. (21) 64094000; fax (21) 64094092; e-mail contact@ambafrance-ir.org; internet www.ambafrance-ir.org; Ambassador BRUNO FOUCHER.

The Gambia: No. 10, Malek St, Shariati Ave, Tehran; tel. (21) 77500074; fax (21) 77529515; e-mail gambiaembassy_tehran@yahoo.co.uk; Ambassador SAEED ZARE.

Georgia: No. 9, 8th Alley, Shahid Qalandari (Dastoor-e Jonoobi) St, Sadr Express Way, Tehran; tel. (21) 22609765; fax (21) 22604154; e-mail tehran.emb@mfa.gov.ge; internet www.iran.mfa.gov.ge; Ambassador GIORGI JANJGAVA.

Germany: POB 11365-179, 320–324 Ferdowsi Ave, Tehran; tel. (21) 39990000; fax (21) 39991890; e-mail info@tehe.diplo.de; internet www.teheran.diplo.de; Ambassador BERND ERBEL.

Greece: POB 11365-8151, Africa Ave, 43 Esfandiar St, Tehran; tel. (21) 22050533; fax (21) 22057431; e-mail gremb.teh@mfa.gr; internet www.mfa.gr/tehran; Ambassador NIKOLAOS GARILIDIS.

Guinea: POB 11365-4716, Dr Shariati Ave, Malek St, No. 10, Tehran; tel. (21) 77535744; fax (21) 77535743; e-mail ambaguinee_thr@hotmail.com; Ambassador OLIA KAMARA.

Holy See: Apostolic Nunciature, POB 11365-178, Razi Ave, 97 Neauphle-le-Château Ave, Tehran; tel. (21) 66403574; fax (21) 66419442; e-mail nuntius.iran@gmail.com; Apostolic Nuncio Most Rev. JEAN-PAUL GOBEL (Titular Archbishop of Galazia in Campania).

Hungary: POB 6363-19395, No. 16, Shadloo St, Hedayat Sq., Darrous, Tehran; tel. (21) 22550460; fax (21) 22550503; e-mail mission.thr@kum.hu; internet www.mfa.gov.hu/kulkepviselet/ir; Ambassador GYULA PETHŐ.

India: POB 15875-4118, 22 Mir-Emad St, cnr of 9th St, Dr Beheshti Ave, Tehran; tel. (21) 88755103; fax (21) 88755973; e-mail indemteh@dpimail.net; internet www.indianembassy-tehran.ir; Ambassador D. P. SRIVASTAVA.

Indonesia: POB 11365-4564, Ghaem Magham Farahani Ave, No. 210, Tehran; tel. (21) 88716865; fax (21) 88718822; e-mail kbritehran@safineh.net; internet www.indonesian-embassy.ir; Ambassador DIAN WIRENGJURIT.

Iraq: Vali-e-Asr Ave, Vali-e-Asr Sq., Tehran; tel. (21) 88938865; fax (21) 88938877; e-mail info@iraqembassy.ir; internet www.iraqembassy.ir; Ambassador MUHAMMAD MAJID ABBAS AL-SHEIKH.

Italy: POB 11365-7863, 81 Neauphle-le-Château Ave, Tehran; tel. (21) 66726955; fax (21) 66726961; e-mail segreteria.teheran@esteri.it; internet www.ambteheran.esteri.it; Ambassador ALBERTO BRADANINI.

Japan: POB 11365-814, Bucharest Ave, cnr of 5th St, Tehran; tel. (21) 88717922; fax (21) 88706093; e-mail infoeoj@neda.net; internet www.ir.emb-japan.go.jp; Ambassador KINICHI KOMANO.

Jordan: No. 1553, 2nd Alley, North Zarafshan, Phase 4, Shahrak-e-Ghods, Tehran; tel. (21) 88088356; fax (21) 88080496; e-mail jordanemb-teh@hotmail.com; Chargé d'affaires JANTI GLAZOGA.

Kazakhstan: 4 North Hedayet St, cnr of Masjed Alley, Darrous, Tehran; tel. (21) 22565933; fax (21) 22546400; e-mail iran@asdc.kz; Ambassador BAGDAD K. AMREYEV.

Kenya: POB 19395-4566, 46 Golshar St, Africa Ave, Tehran; tel. (21) 22059154; fax (21) 22053372; e-mail kenemteh@irtp.com; Ambassador Dr RASHID ALI.

Korea, Democratic People's Republic: 349 Shahid Dastjerdi Ave, Africa Ave, Tehran; tel. (21) 22357300; fax (21) 22089718; Ambassador PARK JAE-HYUN.

Korea, Republic: No. 18, West Daneshvar St, Shaikhbahai Ave, Sheikhbahai Sq., Tehran; tel. (21) 88054900; fax (21) 88064899; e-mail emb-ir@mofat.go.kr; internet irn.mofat.go.kr; Ambassador KIM YOUNG-MOK.

Kuwait: Africa Ave, Mahiyar St, No. 15, Tehran; tel. (21) 88785997; fax (21) 88788257; Ambassador MAJDI AL-DHUFAIRI.

Kyrgyzstan: POB 19579-3511, Bldg 12, 5th Naranjestan Alley, Pasdaran St, Tehran; tel. (21) 22830354; fax (21) 22281720; e-mail krembiri@mydatak.net; Ambassador MEDETKAN SH. SHERIMKULOV.

Lebanon: POB 11365-3753, No. 31, Shahid Kalantari St, Gharani Ave, Tehran; tel. (21) 88908451; fax (21) 88907345; Ambassador ZAIN ALI AL-MOUSSAWI.

Libya: 2 Maryam Alley, South Kamranieh St, Tehran; tel. (21) 22201677; fax (21) 22236649; Ambassador SAAD MOJBAR.

Macedonia, former Yugoslav republic: No. 7, 4th Alley, Intifada Ave, Tehran; tel. and fax (21) 88720810; Ambassador CVETKO SOFKOVSKI.

Malaysia: No. 46, between 18th and 20th Sts, Velenjak Ave, Tehran; tel. (21) 22404081; fax (21) 22417921; e-mail mwtehran@parsonline.net; internet www.kln.gov.my/web/irn_tehran; Ambassador MUHAMMAD SADIK KETHERGANY.

Mali: No. 16, Aroos Alley, Istanbul St, Shariati Ave, Tehran; tel. (21) 22207278; fax (21) 22234631; e-mail malimissiontehran@yahoo.com; Ambassador AMADOU MODY DIALL.

Mexico: POB 19156, No. 12, Golfam St, Africa Ave, Tehran; tel. (21) 22057590; fax (21) 22057589; e-mail embiran@sre.gob.mx; internet embamex.sre.gob.mx/iran; Ambassador CARLOS TIRADO ZAVALA.

Morocco: No. 4, Tchakavak Deadend, Djahanshahi St, North of Niyavaran Palace, Niyavaran Ave, Tehran; tel. (21) 22284845; fax (21) 22813829; e-mail sifamateh@sefaratmaghreb.com; internet www.sefaratmaghreb.com; Ambassador MUHAMMAD LOUAFA.

Netherlands: West Arghavan, 7 Sonbol St, Farmanieh, Tehran; tel. (21) 23660000; fax (21) 23660190; e-mail teh@minbuza.nl; internet iran.nlambassade.org; Ambassador CEES J. KOLE.

New Zealand: POB 15875-4313, 34 North Golestan Complex, cnr of 2nd Park Alley and Sosan St, Aghdasiyeh St, Niavaran, Tehran 11365; tel. (21) 26122175; fax (21) 26121973; e-mail tehran@nzembassy.org; internet www.nzembassy.com/iran; Ambassador BRIAN SANDERS.

Nicaragua: Tehran; Ambassador MARIO BARQUERO.

Nigeria: 11 Sarvestan St, Elahieh, Tehran; tel. (21) 22009119; fax (21) 88799783; e-mail ngrembtehran@yahoo.com; Ambassador ALHAJI ABUBAKAR CIKA.

Norway: No. 201, Dr Lavasani St, cnr of Sonbol St, Tehran; tel. (21) 22291333; fax (21) 22292776; e-mail emb.tehran@mfa.no; internet www.norway-iran.org; Chargé d'affaires a.i. KNUT EILIV LEIN.

Oman: No. 12, Tandis Alley, Africa Ave, Tehran; tel. (21) 22056831; fax (21) 22044672; Ambassador Sheikh YAHYA BIN ABDULLAH AL-FANA AL-ARAIMI.

Pakistan: No. 1, Ahmed Eitmadzadeh Ave, Jamshidabad Shomali, Dr Fatemi Ave, Tehran 14118; tel. (21) 66941388; fax (21) 66944898; e-mail pareptehran@yahoo.com; internet www.mofa.gov.pk/iran; Ambassador (vacant).

Philippines: POB 19395-4797, 5 Khayyam St, Vali-e-Asr Ave, Tehran; tel. (21) 22668774; fax (21) 22668990; e-mail tehranpe@yahoo.com; internet www.philippine-embassy.ir; Chargé d'affaires a.i. MARIANO DUMIA.

Poland: POB 11155-3489, 1–3 Pirouz St, Africa Ave, Tehran; tel. (21) 88787262; fax (21) 88788774; e-mail teheran.amb.sekretariat@msz.gov.pl; internet www.teheran.polemb.net; Ambassador JULIUSZ JACEK GOJŁO.

Portugal: No. 13, Rouzbeh Alley, Hedayat St, Darrous, Tehran; tel. (21) 22543237; fax (21) 22552668; e-mail portugal@mydatak.com; internet www.portugueseembassy.ir; Ambassador Dr JORGE TITO DE VASCONCELOS NOGUEIRA DIAS CABRAL.

Qatar: POB 11365-1631, 4 Golazin Blvd, Africa Ave, Tehran; tel. (21) 22029336; fax (21) 22058478; e-mail gatarembir@hotmail.com; Ambassador IBRAHIM BIN ABD AL-RAHMAN AL-MEGHAISEEB.

Romania: 22 Fakhrabad Ave, Baharestan Ave, Tehran; tel. (21) 77539041; fax (21) 77535291; e-mail ambrotehran@parsonline.net; Ambassador CRISTIAN TEODORESCU.

Russia: 32 Neauphle-le-Château Ave, Tehran; tel. (21) 66728873; fax (21) 66701676; e-mail teheran@dks.ru; internet www.rusembiran.ru; Ambassador LEVAN S. DZHAGARYAN.

Saudi Arabia: No. 1, Niloufar St, Boustan St, Pasdaran Ave, Tehran; tel. (21) 22288543; fax (21) 22294691; e-mail iremb@mofa.gov.sa; Ambassador MUHAMMAD BIN ABBAS AL-KILABI.

Senegal: POB 19395-4743, 76 Sepand West St, Nejatollahi Ave, Tehran; tel. (21) 88881123; fax (21) 88805676; e-mail sandicoly2000@yahoo.fr; Chargé d'affaires MAMADOU DIARRA.

Serbia: POB 11365-118, Velenjak Ave, No. 9, 9th St, Tehran 19858; tel. (21) 22412571; fax (21) 22402869; e-mail serbembteh@parsonline.net; Ambassador ALEXANDER TASIĆ.

Sierra Leone: POB 11365-1689, No. 4, Bukan St, Sadeghi Ghomi St, Bahonar Ave, Niavaran, Tehran; tel. (21) 22721474; fax (21) 22721485; e-mail slembsy_tehran@yahoo.com; Ambassador Alhaji MOHAMED KEMOH FADIKA.

Slovakia: POB 19395-6341, 34 Sarlashgar Fallahi St, Tehran 19887; tel. (21) 22411164; fax (21) 22409719; e-mail emb.tehran@mzv.sk; internet www.tehran.mfa.sk; Ambassador JAN BORY.

Slovenia: POB 19575-459, 30 Narenjestan 8th Alley, Pasdaran Ave, Tehran 19576; tel. (21) 22836042; fax (21) 22290853; e-mail vte@gov.si; internet tehran.embassy.si/en; Chargé d'affaires a.i. KRISTINA RADEJ.

Somalia: 1 Hadaiyan St, Mirzapour St, Dr Shariati Ave, Tehran; tel. and fax (21) 22245146; e-mail safarian@hotmail.com; Ambassador KHALIFA MOUSSA.

South Africa: POB 11365-7476, 5 Yekta St, Bagh-e-Ferdows, Vali-e-Asr Ave, Tehran; tel. (21) 22702866; fax (21) 22719516; e-mail tehran.admin@foreign.gov.za; Ambassador E. SALEY.

Spain: 76 Sarv St, Africa Ave, Tehran 19689; tel. (21) 22568681; fax (21) 22568017; e-mail emb.teheran@maec.es; internet www.maec.es/embajadas/teheran; Ambassador PEDRO ANTONIO VILLENA PÉREZ.

Sri Lanka: No. 25, Jahantab St, Qheytariyeh, Tehran; tel. (21) 22569179; fax (21) 22540924; e-mail info@slembir.com; internet www.slembir.com; Ambassador MOHAMED MOHAMED ZUHAIR.

Sudan: No. 39, Babak Bahrami St, Africa Ave, Tehran; tel. (21) 88781183; fax (21) 88792331; e-mail sundanembassytehran@sap-it.net; internet www.sudanembassyir.com; Ambassador SULAYMAN ABD AL-TOWAB EL-ZEIN.

Sweden: POB 19575-458, 27 Nastaran Ave, Pasdaran Ave, Tehran; tel. (21) 23712200; fax (21) 22296451; e-mail ambassaden.teheran@foreign.ministry.se; internet www.swedenabroad.com/tehran; Ambassador MAGNUS WERNSTEDT.

Switzerland: POB 19395-4683, 13 Yasaman St, cnr of Sharifi Manesh Ave, Elahieh, Tehran 19649; tel. (21) 22008333; fax (21) 22006002; e-mail teh.vertretung@eda.admin.ch; internet www.eda.admin.ch/tehran; Ambassador LIVIA LEU AGOSTI.

Syria: 19 Iraj St, Africa Ave, Tehran; tel. (21) 22052780; fax (21) 22059409; e-mail tehran@mofa.gov.sy; Ambassador Dr HAMED HASSAN.

Tajikistan: No. 10, 3rd Alley, Shahid Zeynali St, Niavaran, Tehran; tel. (21) 22299584; fax (21) 22809299; e-mail tajemb-iran@tajikistanir.com; Ambassador DAVLATALI HOTAMOV.

Thailand: POB 11495-111, 4 Esteghlal Alley, Baharestan Ave, Tehran; tel. (21) 77531433; fax (21) 77532022; e-mail info@thaiembassy-tehran.org; internet www.thaiembassy-tehran.org; Chargé d'affaires a.i. CHAIRAT SIRIVAT.

Tunisia: No. 12, Shahid Lavasani Ave, Farmanieh, Tehran; tel. (21) 2706699; fax (21) 22631994; e-mail at-teheran@neda.net; Ambassador MUHAMMAD AL-HASAYERI.

Turkey: POB 11365-8758, 337 Ferdowsi Ave, Africa Ave, Tehran; tel. (21) 33118997; fax (21) 33117928; e-mail tctahranbe@parsonline.net; internet tehran.emb.mfa.gov.tr; Ambassador ÜMIT YARDIM.

Turkmenistan: 5 Barati St, Vatanpour St, Tehran; tel. (21) 22206731; fax (21) 22206732; e-mail tmnteh@afranet.com; Ambassador AKHMED GURBANOV.

Uganda: 3rd Floor, 10 Malek St, Shariati Ave, Tehran; tel. (21) 77643335; fax (21) 77643337; e-mail uganda_teh@yahoo.com; Ambassador Dr MUHAMMAD AHMAD KISULE.

Ukraine: 101 Vanak St, Vanak Sq., Tehran; tel. (21) 88606171; fax (21) 88007130; e-mail emb_ir@mfa.gov.ua; internet mfa.gov.ua/iran; Ambassador ALEKSANDR SAMARSKY.

United Arab Emirates: POB 19395-4616, No. 355, Vahid Dastjerdi Ave, Vali-e-Asr Ave, Tehran; tel. (21) 88781333; fax (21) 88789084; e-mail uae_emb_thr@universalmail.com; Ambassador SAIF MUHAMMAD OBAID AL-ZAABI.

United Kingdom: POB 11316-91144, 198 Ferdowsi Ave, Tehran 11344; tel. (21) 64052000; fax (21) 64052289; e-mail chancery.tehran@fco.gov.uk; internet ukiniran.fco.gov.uk; Ambassador DOMINICK JOHN CHILCOTT.

Uruguay: POB 19395-4718, No. 6, Mina Blvd, Africa Ave, Tehran; tel. (21) 88679690; fax (21) 88782321; e-mail uruter@uruter.com; Ambassador CARLOS OJEDA.

Uzbekistan: No. 6, Nastaran Alley, Boustan St, Pasdaran Ave, Tehran; tel. (21) 22299780; fax (21) 22299158; Ambassador ILHAM SOLIEVICH AKRAMOV.

Venezuela: No. 25, Golazin Blvd, Africa Ave, Tehran; tel. (21) 22036317; fax (21) 22036351; e-mail embajadavenezuela@emveniran.gob.ve; Ambassador DAVID N. VELÁSQUEZ.

Viet Nam: 6 East Ordibehesht, Mardani Sharestan, 8th St, Pey Syan St, M. Ardabili Vali-e-Asr Ave, Tehran; tel. (21) 22411670; fax (21) 22416045; e-mail vnemb.ir@mofa.gov.vn; internet www.vietnamembassy-iran.org; Ambassador TRAN TRONG KHANH.

Yemen: No. 15, Golestan St, Africa Ave, Tehran; tel. (21) 22042701; e-mail yem.emb.ir@neda.net; Ambassador JAMAL ABDULLAH AL-SOLAL.

Zimbabwe: 6 Shad Avar St, Mogghadas Ardabili, Tehran; tel. (21) 22027555; fax (21) 22049084; e-mail zimtehran@yahoo.com; Ambassador NICHOLAS KITIKITI.

Judicial System

In August 1982 the Supreme Court revoked all laws dating from the previous regime that did not conform with Islam; in October all courts set up prior to the Islamic Revolution of 1979 were abolished. In June 1987 Ayatollah Khomeini ordered the creation of clerical courts to try members of the clergy opposed to government policy. A new system of *qisas* (retribution) was established, placing the emphasis on swift justice. Islamic codes of correction were introduced in 1983, including the dismembering of a hand for theft, flogging for fornication and violations of the strict code of dress for women, and stoning for adultery. The Islamic revolutionary courts try those accused of crimes endangering national security, corruption, drugs-trafficking, and moral and religious offences. The Supreme Court has 33 branches, each of which is presided over by two judges.

Head of the Judiciary: Hojatoleslam SADEQ ARDESHIR LARIJANI.

SUPREME COURT

Chief Justice: Ayatollah MOHSENI GORKANI.

Prosecutor-General: GHOLAMHOSSEIN MOHSENI EJEIE.

Religion

According to the 1979 Constitution, the official religion is Islam of the Ja'fari sect (Shi'ite), but other Islamic sects, including Zeydi, Hanafi, Maleki, Shafe'i and Hanbali, are valid and will be respected. Zoroastrians, Jews and Christians will be recognized as official religious minorities. According to the 2006 census, there were 70,097,741 Muslims, 109,415 Christians (mainly Armenian), 19,823 Zoroastrians and 9,252 Jews in Iran.

ISLAM

The great majority of the Iranian people are Shi'a Muslims, but there is a minority of Sunni Muslims. Persians and Azerbaijanis are mainly Shi'ite, while the other ethnic groups are mainly Sunni.

CHRISTIANITY

The Roman Catholic Church

At 31 December 2007 there were an estimated 19,200 adherents in Iran, comprising 8,000 of the Armenian Rite, 7,000 of the Latin Rite and 4,200 of the Chaldean Rite.

Armenian Rite

Bishop of Esfahan: (vacant), Armenian Catholic Bishopric, POB 11318, Khiaban Ghazzali 65, Tehran; tel. (21) 66707204; fax (21) 66727533; e-mail arcaveso@yahoo.com.

Chaldean Rite

Archbishop of Ahvaz: HANNA ZORA, Archbishop's House, 334 Suleiman Farsi St, Ahvaz; tel. (61) 2224980.

Archbishop of Tehran: RAMZI GARMOU, Archevêché, Enghelab St, Sayed Abbas Moussavi Ave 91, Tehran 15819; tel. (21) 88823549; fax (21) 88308714.

Archbishop of Urmia (Rezayeh) and Bishop of Salmas (Shahpour): THOMAS MERAM, Khalifagari Kaldani Katholiq, POB 338, 7 Mirzaian St, Orumiyeh 57135; tel. (441) 2222739; fax (441) 2236031; e-mail thmeram@yahoo.com.

Latin Rite

Archbishop of Esfahan: IGNAZIO BEDINI, Consolata Church, POB 11155-445, 73 Neauphle-le-Château Ave, Tehran; tel. (21) 66703210; fax (21) 66724749; e-mail latin.diocese@gmail.com.

The Anglican Communion

Anglicans in Iran are adherents of the Episcopal Church in Jerusalem and the Middle East, formally inaugurated in January 1976. The Bishop in Cyprus and the Gulf is resident in Cyprus.

Bishop in Iran: Rt Rev. AZAD MARSHALL, POB 135, 81465 Esfahan; tel. (21) 88801383; fax (21) 88906908; internet dioceseofiran.org; diocese founded 1912.

Presbyterian Church

Synod of the Evangelical (Presbyterian) Church in Iran: POB 14395-569, Assyrian Evangelical Church, Khiaban-i Hanifnejad, Khiaban-i Aramanch, Tehran; tel. (21) 88006135; Moderator Rev. ADEL NAKHOSTEEN.

ZOROASTRIANS

There are an estimated 30,000–60,000 Zoroastrians, a remnant of a once widespread religion.

OTHER COMMUNITIES

Communities of Armenians, and somewhat smaller numbers of Jews, Assyrians, Greek Orthodox Christians, Uniates and Latin Christians are also found as officially recognized faiths. The Bahá'í faith, which originated in Iran, has about 300,000 Iranian adherents, although at least 10,000 are believed to have fled since 1979 in order to escape persecution. The Government banned all Bahá'í institutions in August 1983.

The Press

Tehran dominates the media, as many of the daily papers are published there, and the bi-weekly, weekly and less frequent publications in the provinces generally depend on the major metropolitan dailies as a source of news. A press law announced in August 1979 required all newspapers and magazines to be licensed, and imposed penalties of imprisonment for insulting senior religious figures. Offences against the Act will be tried in the criminal courts. Under the Constitution, the press is free, except in matters that are contrary to public morality, insult religious belief or slander the honour and reputation of individuals. An intense judicial campaign since the late 1990s has sought to curb freedom of the press; some sources estimate that more than 100 publications were closed down during President Khatami's presidency (1997–2005).

PRINCIPAL DAILIES

Aftab-e-Yazd (Sun of Yazd): POB 13145-1134, Tehran; tel. (21) 66495833; fax (21) 66495835; internet www.aftab-yazd.com; f. 2000; Farsi; pro-reform; Chief Editor SAYED MOJTABA VAHEDI; circ. 100,000.

Alik: POB 11365-953, 26 Shahid Mohebi Ave, North Sohrevardi Ave, Tehran 155588; tel. (21) 88768567; fax (21) 88760994; e-mail alikmail@hyenet.ir; internet www.alikonline.com; f. 1931; afternoon; Armenian; political, literary, cultural, social, sport; Editor DERENIK MELIKIAN; circ. over 4,500.

Donya-e-Eqtesad (Economic World): POB 14157-44344, Tehran; tel. (21) 87762511; fax (21) 87762516; e-mail info@donya-e-eqtesad.com; internet www.donya-e-eqtesad.com; Farsi; Editor Dr MOUSA GHANINEJAD.

Entekhab (Choice): 12 Noorbakhsh Ave, Vali-e-Asr Ave, Tehran; tel. (21) 88893954; fax (21) 88893951; e-mail info@tiknews.net; online only; Farsi; centrist; Man. Dir Dr TAHA HASHEMI.

Etemad (Confidence): e-mail info@etemaad.com; internet www.etemaad.ir; Farsi; pro-reform; Man. Dir ELIAS HAZRATI; Editor BEHROUZ BEHZADI.

Ettela'at (Information): Ettela'at Bldg, Mirdamad Ave, South Naft St, Tehran 15499; tel. (21) 29999; fax (21) 22258022; e-mail ettelaat@ettelaat.com; internet www.ettelaat.com; f. 1925; evening; Farsi; political and literary; operates under the direct supervision of *wilayat-e-faqih* (religious jurisprudence); Editor SAYED MAHMOUD DO'AYI; circ. 500,000.

Hambastegi (Solidarity): Tehran; e-mail info@hambastegi-news.com; internet www.hambastegidaily.com; Farsi; pro-reform; Editor SALEH ABADI.

Ham-Mihan (Compatriot): Tehran; e-mail info@hammihan.com; internet www.hammihan.com; f. 2000; Farsi; independent, pro-reform; Founder and Man. Dir GHOLAMHOSSEIN KARBASCHI; Chair. of Bd MUHAMMAD ATRIANFAR; Editor MUHAMMAD GHOUCHANI.

Hamshahri (Citizen): POB 19395-5446, Tehran; tel. (21) 23023453; fax (21) 23023455; e-mail adjigol@hamshahri.org; internet www.hamshahrilinks.org; f. 1993; Farsi; conservative; economics, society and culture; owned by the Municipality of Tehran; Editor-in-Chief HOSSEIN GORBANZADEH; circ. 400,000.

Iran: POB 15875-5388, Tehran; tel. (21) 88761720; fax (21) 88761254; e-mail iran-newspaper@iran-newspaper.com; internet www.iran-newspaper.com; Farsi; conservative; connected to the Islamic Republic News Agency; Man. Dir HOSSEIN ZIYAEI; Editor-in-Chief BIJAN MOGHADDAM.

Iran Daily: Iran Cultural and Press Institute, 208 Khorramshahr Ave, Tehran; tel. (21) 88755761; fax (21) 88761869; e-mail iran-daily@iran-daily.com; internet www.iran-daily.com; English.

Iran News: POB 15875-8551, No. 13, Pajouhesh Lane, Golestan St, Marzdaran Blvd, Tehran; tel. (21) 44253450; fax (21) 44253478; e-mail info@irannewsdaily.com; internet www.irannewsdaily.com; f. 1994; English; Man. Dir MAJID AQAZADEH; circ. 35,000.

Jam-e Jam: Tehran; tel. (21) 22222511; fax (21) 22226252; e-mail info@jamejamonline.ir; internet www.jamejamonline.ir; online only; Farsi, English and French; conservative; linked to Islamic Republic of Iran Broadcasting; Man. Editor B. MOGHADDAM.

Jomhouri-e-Eslami (Islamic Republic): tel. (21) 33916111; fax (21) 33117552; e-mail info@jomhourieslami.com; internet www.jomhourieslami.com; f. 1980; Farsi; conservative; Man. Dir MASIH MOHAJERI.

Kalameh-ye Sabz (Green Word): f. 2009; Man. Dir MIR HOSSEIN MOUSAVI; Editor-in-Chief SAYED ALI REZA BEHESHTI.

Kayhan (Universe): Institute Kayhan, POB 11365-3631, Shahid Shahcheraghi Alley, Ferdowsi Ave, Tehran 11444; tel. (21) 33110251; fax (21) 33111120; e-mail kayhan@kayhannews.ir; internet www.kayhannews.ir; f. 1941; evening; Farsi; political; also publishes *Kayhan International* (f. 1959; daily; English; Editor HAMID NAJAFI), *Kayhan Arabic* (f. 1980; daily; Arabic), *Kayhan Persian* (f. 1942; daily; Farsi), *Zan-e Rooz* (Today's Woman; f. 1964; weekly; Farsi), *Kayhan Varzeshi* (World of Sport; f. 1955; daily and weekly; Farsi), *Kayhan Bacheha* (Children's World; f. 1956; weekly; Farsi), *Kayhan Farhangi* (World of Culture; f. 1984; monthly; Farsi); owned and managed by Mostazafin Foundation from October 1979 until January 1987, when it was placed under the direct supervision of *wilayat-e-faqih* (religious jurisprudence); Editor-in-Chief HOSSEIN SHARIATMADARI; circ. 350,000.

Khorasan: Mashad; Head Office: Khorasan Daily Newspapers, 14 Zohre St, Mobarezan Ave, Tehran; tel. (511) 7634000; fax (511) 7624395; e-mail info@khorasannews.com; internet www.khorasannews.com; f. 1948; Farsi; Propr MUHAMMAD SADEGH TEHERANIAN; Editor MUHAMMAD SAEED AHADI; circ. 40,000.

Quds Daily: POB 91735-577, Khayyam Sq., Sajjad Blvd, Mashad; tel. (51) 7685011; fax (511) 7684004; e-mail info@qudsdaily.com; internet www.qudsdaily.com; f. 1987; Farsi; owned by Astan Quds Razavi, the org. that oversees the shrine of Imam Reza at Mashad; also publ. in Tehran; Man. Dir GHOLAMREZA GHALANDARIAN; Editor-in-Chief MUHAMMAD HADI ZAHEDI.

Resalat (The Message): POB 11365-777, 53 Ostad Nejatollahi Ave, Tehran; tel. (21) 88902642; fax (21) 88900587; e-mail info@resalat-news.com; internet www.resalat-news.com; f. 1985; organ of right-wing group of the same name; Farsi; conservative; political, economic and social; Propr Resalat Foundation; Man. Dir SAYED MORTEZA NABAVI; circ. 100,000.

Shargh (East): Tehran; f. 2003; Farsi; reformist; publ. suspended in in August 2009, allowed to resume in March 2010; Man. Dir MEHDI RAHMANIAN; Editor AHMAD GHOLAMI.

Tehran Times: POB 14155-4843, 32 Bimeh Alley, Ostad Nejatollahi Ave, Tehran; tel. (21) 88800789; fax (21) 88800788; e-mail info@tehrantimes.com; internet www.tehrantimes.com; f. 1979; English; independent; Man. Dir REZA MOGHADASI; Editor-in-Chief ABOLFAZI AMOUEI.

PRINCIPAL PERIODICALS

Acta Medica Iranica: Bldg No. 8, Faculty of Medicine, Tehran University of Medical Sciences, Poursina St, Tehran 14174; tel. (21) 88973667; fax (21) 88962510; e-mail acta@sina.tums.ac.ir; internet acta.tums.ac.ir; f. 1956; bi-monthly; English; Editors-in-Chief AHMAD REZA DEHPOUR, M. SAMINI; circ. 2,000.

Ashur (Assyria): Ostad Motahari Ave, 11–21 Kuhe Nour Ave, Tehran; tel. (21) 622117; f. 1969; Assyrian; monthly; Founder and Editor Dr WILSON BET-MANSOUR; circ. 8,000.

Bukhara: POB 15655-166, Tehran; tel. 9121300147 (mobile); fax (21) 88958697; e-mail dehbashi.ali@gmail.com; internet www.bukharamag.com; bi-monthly; Farsi; arts, culture and humanities; Editor ALI DEHBASHI.

Bulletin of the National Film Archive of Iran: POB 11155, Baharestan Sq., Tehran 11499-43381; tel. (21) 38512583; fax (21) 38512710; e-mail khoshnevis_nfai@yahoo.com; f. 1989; English; Editor M. H. KHOSHNEVIS.

Daneshmand (Scientist): No. 18, 13th St, Khaled Eslamboli Ave, Tehran; tel. (21) 88101576; fax (21) 88101580; e-mail info@daneshmandonline.ir; f. 1963; monthly; Farsi; owned by Mostazafari Foundation; science and technology in Iran and abroad; CEO YAGHOUB MOSHFEGH; Editor-in-Chief ALI A. GHAZVINI.

Donyaye Varzesh (World of Sports): Tehran; tel. (21) 3281; fax (21) 33115530; weekly; sport; Editor G. H. SHABANI; circ. 200,000.

The Echo of Iran: POB 14155-1168, 4 Hourtab Alley, Hafez Ave, Tehran; tel. (21) 22930477; e-mail info@iranalmanac.com; internet www.iranalmanac.com; f. 1952; monthly; English; news, politics and economics; Man. FARJAM BEHNAM; Editor JAHANGIR BEHROUZ.

Echo of Islam: POB 14155-3899, Tehran; tel. (21) 88897663; fax (21) 88902725; e-mail info@echoofsalam.com; internet www.echoofsalam.com; quarterly; English; publ. by the Islamic Thought Foundation; Man. Dir Dr MAHDI GOLJAN; Editor-in-Chief S. MOUSAVI.

Economic Echo: POB 14155-1168, 4 Hourtab Alley, Hafez Ave, Tehran; tel. (21) 22930477; e-mail info@iranalmanac.com; internet www.iranalmanac.com; f. 1998; English; Man. FARJAM BEHNAM.

Ettela'at Haftegi: 11 Khayyam Ave, Tehran; tel. (21) 311238; fax (21) 33115530; f. 1941; general weekly; Farsi; Editor F. JAVADI; circ. 150,000.

Ettela'at Javanan: POB 15499-51199, Ettela'at Bldg, Mirdamad Ave, South Naft St, Tehran; tel. (21) 29999; fax (21) 22258022; f. 1966; weekly; Farsi; youth; Editor M. J. RAFIZADEH; circ. 120,000.

Farhang-e-Iran Zamin: POB 19575-583, Niyavaran, Tehran; tel. (21) 283254; annual; Farsi; Iranian studies.

Film International, Iranian Film Quarterly: POB 11365-875, Tehran; tel. (21) 66709374; fax (21) 66719971; e-mail info@film-international.com; internet www.film-international.com; f. 1993; quarterly; English; Editor-in-Chief MASSOUD MEHRABI; circ. 15,000.

Iran Almanac: POB 14155-1168, 4 Hourtab Alley, Hafez Ave, Tehran; tel. and fax (932) 9139201; e-mail behnam.f@iranalmanac.com; internet www.iranalmanac.com; f. 2000; English; reference; history, politics, trade and industry, tourism, art, culture and society; Researcher and Editor FARJAM BEHNAM.

Iran Tribune: POB 111244, Tehran; e-mail matlab@iran-tribune.com; internet www.iran-tribune.com; monthly; English and Farsi; socio-political and cultural.

Iran Who's Who: POB 14155-1168, 4 Hourtab Alley, Hafez Ave, Tehran; e-mail info@iranalmanac.com; internet www.iranalmanac.com; annual; English; Editor FARJAM BEHNAM.

Iranian Cinema: POB 11155, Baharestan Sq., Tehran 11499-43381; tel. (21) 35812583; fax (21) 35812710; e-mail khoshnevis-nfai@yahoo.com; f. 1985; annual; English.

Kayhan Bacheha (Children's World): Institute Kayhan, POB 11365-3631, Shahid Shahcheraghi Alley, Ferdowsi Ave, Tehran 11444; tel. (21) 33110251; fax (21) 33111120; f. 1956; weekly; illustrated magazine for children; Editor AMIR HOSSEIN FARDI; circ. 150,000.

Kayhan Varzeshi (World of Sport): Institute Kayhan, POB 11365-3631, Shahid Shahcheraghi Alley, Ferdowsi Ave, Tehran 11444; tel. (21) 33110246; fax (21) 33114228; e-mail info@kayhanvarzeshi.com; internet www.kayhanvarzeshi.com; f. 1955; weekly; Farsi; Dir MAHMAD MONSETI; circ. 125,000.

Mahjubah: POB 14155-3899, Tehran; tel. (21) 88897662; fax (21) 88902725; e-mail mahjubah@iran-itf.com; internet www.itf.org.ir; Islamic family magazine; publ. by the Islamic Thought Foundation; Editor-in-Chief TURAN JAMSHIDIAN.

Soroush: POB 15875-1163, Soroush Bldg, Motahari Ave, Mofatteh Crossroads, Tehran; tel. and fax (21) 88847602; e-mail cultural@soroushpress.com; internet www.soroushpress.com; f. 1972; one weekly magazine; four monthly magazines, one for women, two for adolescents and one for children; one quarterly review of philosophy; all in Farsi; Editor-in-Chief ALI AKBAR ASHARI.

Tavoos: POB 19395-6434, 6 Asgarian St, East Farmanieh Ave, Tehran 19546-44755; tel. (21) 22817700; fax (21) 22825447; e-mail info@tavoosmag.com; internet www.tavoosmag.com; quarterly; Farsi and English; arts; Man. Dir MANIJEH MIREMADI; circ. 5,000.

Tchissta: POB 13145-593, Tehran; tel. (21) 678581; e-mail daneshvamardom@tchissta.com; internet tchissta.com; Farsi; politics, society, science and literature; Editor-in-Chief PARVIZ SHAHRIARI.

ZamZam: POB 14155-3899, Tehran; tel. (21) 88897663; fax (21) 88902725; internet www.itf.org.ir; children's magazine; English; publ. by the Islamic Thought Foundation; Man. Dir. Dr MAHDI GOLJAN; Editor-in-Chief SHAGHAYEGH GHANDEHARI.

Zan-e Rooz (Today's Woman): Institute Kayhan, POB 11365-3631, Shahid Shahcheraghi Alley, Ferdowsi Ave, Tehran 11444; tel. (21) 33911575; fax (21) 33911569; e-mail kayhan@istn.irost.com; f. 1964; weekly; women's; circ. over 60,000.

NEWS AGENCIES

Fars News Agency: Tehran; e-mail Info@Farsnews.com; internet www.farsnews.com; f. 2003; independent; news in Farsi and English; Man. Dir HAMID REZA MOQADDAMFAR.

Iranian Quran News Agency (IQNA): 97 Bozorgmehr St, Qods Ave, Tehran; tel. (21) 66470212; fax (21) 66970769; e-mail info@iqna.ir; internet www.iqna.ir; f. 2003; general news and news on Koranic activities.

Islamic Republic News Agency (IRNA): POB 764, 873 Vali-e-Asr Ave, Tehran; tel. (21) 88902050; fax (21) 88905068; e-mail irna@irna.com; internet www.irna.com; f. 1934; state-controlled; Man. Dir ALI AKBAR JAVANFEKR.

Mehr News Agency: 32, Bimeh Alley, Nejatollahi St, Tehran; tel. (21) 88809500; fax (21) 88805801; e-mail info@mehrnews.com; internet www.mehrnews.com; f. 2003; news in Farsi, English and Arabic; Man. Dir PARVIZ ESMAEILI.

PRESS ASSOCIATION

Association of Iranian Journalists: No. 87, 7th Alley, Shahid Kabkanian St, Keshavarz Blvd, Tehran; tel. (21) 88956365; fax (21) 88963539; e-mail generalsecretary@aoij.org; Pres. RAJABALI MAZROOEI; Sec. BADRALSADAT MOFIDI.

Publishers

Amir Kabir Book Publishing and Distribution Co: POB 11365-4191, Jomhouri Islami Ave, Esteghlal Sq., Tehran; tel. (21) 33900751; fax (21) 33903747; e-mail info@amirkabir.net; internet www.amirkabir.net; f. 1948; historical, philosophical, social, literary and children's books; Dir AHMAD NESARI.

Avayenoor Publications: 31 Roshan Alley, Vali-e-Asr Ave, Tehran; tel. (21) 88899001; fax (21) 88907452; e-mail info@avayenoor.com; internet www.avayenoor.com; f. 1988; sociology, politics and economics; Editor-in-Chief SAYED MUHAMMAD MIRHOSSEINI.

Caravan Books Publishing House: POB 186-14145, 18 Salehi St, Sartip Fakouri Ave, Northern Karegar Ave, Tehran 14136; tel. (21) 88007421; fax (21) 88029486; e-mail info@caravan.ir; internet caravan.ir; f. 1997; fiction and non-fiction; Chief Editor ARASH HEJAZI.

Echo Publishers & Printers: POB 14155-1168, 4 Hourtab Alley, Hafez Ave, Tehran; tel. and fax (21) 22930477; e-mail info@

iranalmanac.com; internet www.iranalmanac.com; f. 2000; politics, economics and current affairs; Dir and Man. FARJAM BEHNAM.

Eghbal Publishing Organization: 273 Dr Ali Shariati Ave, Tehran 16139; tel. (21) 77500973; fax (21) 7768113; f. 1903; Man. Dir SAEED EGHBAL.

Farhang Moaser: 43 Khiaban Daneshgah, Tehran 13147; tel. (21) 66402728; fax (21) 66317018; e-mail info@farhangmoaser.com; internet www.farhangmoaser.com; dictionaries.

Gooya Publications: 139 Karimkhan-e Zand Ave, Tehran 15856; tel. (21) 8838453; fax (21) 8842987; e-mail info@goyabooks.com; internet www.gooyabooks.com; f. 1981; art; Dir NASER MIR BAGHERI.

Iran Chap Co: Ettela'at Bldg, Mirdamad Ave, South Naft St, Tehran; tel. (21) 29999; fax (21) 22258022; e-mail ettelaat@ettelaat.com; internet www.ettelaat.com; f. 1966; newspapers, books, magazines, book-binding and colour printing; Man. Dir MAHMOUD DOAEI.

Iran Exports Publication Co Ltd: POB 16315-1773, 41 First Mehr Alley, Mirzapour St, Shariati Ave, Tehran; tel. (21) 22200646; fax (21) 22888505; e-mail info@iranexportsmagazine.com; internet www.iranexportsmagazine.com; f. 1987; business and trade publs in English; Editor-in-Chief and Dir of Int. Affairs AHMAD NIKFARJAM.

Ketab Sara Co: POB 15117-3695, Tehran; tel. (21) 88711321; fax (21) 88717819; e-mail rashti@ketabsara.org; f. 1980; Man. Dir SADEGH SAMII.

Kowkab Publishers: POB 19575-511, Tehran; tel. (21) 22583723; fax (21) 22949834; e-mail info@kkme.com; internet www.kkme.com; engineering, science, medicine, humanities, reference; Man. Dir Dr AHMAD GHANDI.

The Library, Museum and Documentation Center of the Islamic Consultative Assembly (Ketab-Khane, Muze va Markaz-e Asnad-e Majlis-e-Shura-e Islami): POB 11365-866, Ketab-Khane Majlis-e-Shura-e Islami No. 2, Baharestan Sq., Tehran; tel. (21) 33130920; fax (21) 33124339; e-mail info@majlislib.com; internet www.majlislib.com; f. 1912 as Majlis Library; renamed as above in 1996; arts, humanities, social sciences, politics, Iranian and Islamic studies; Dir SAYED MOHAMMAD ALI AHMADI ABHARI.

Ofoq Publishers: 181 Nazari St, 12th Farvardin St, Tehran 13145-1135; tel. (21) 66413367; fax (21) 66414285; e-mail info@ofoqco.com; internet www.ofoqco.com; f. 1990; illustrated books for children and teenagers, adult fiction and non-fiction; Dir REZA HASHEMINEJAD.

Qoqnoos Publishing House: 107 Shohadaye Jandarmeri St, Enghelab Ave, Tehran; tel. (21) 66408640; fax (21) 66413933; e-mail qoqnoos@morva.net; internet www.qoqnoos.ir; f. 1977; fiction, history, philosophy, law, sociology and psychology; privately owned; Owner and Gen. Man. AMIR HOSSEINZADEGAN; Editor-in-Chief ARSALAN FASIHI.

Sahab Geographic and Drafting Institute: POB 11365-617, 30 Somayeh St, Hoquqi Crossroads, Dr Ali Shariati Ave, Tehran 16517; tel. (21) 77535651; fax (21) 77535876; internet www.sahabmap.com; f. 1936; maps, atlases, and books on geography, science, history and Islamic art; Man. Dir MUHAMMAD REZA SAHAB.

Soroush Press: POB 15875-1163, Soroush Bldg, Motahari Ave, Mofatteh Crossroads, Tehran; tel. and fax (21) 88847602; e-mail cultural@soroushpress.com; internet www.soroushpress.com; part of Soroush Publication Group, the publs dept of Islamic Republic of Iran Broadcasting; publishes books, magazines and multimedia products on a wide range of subjects; Man. Dir ALI AKBAR ASHARI.

Tehran University Press: 16th St, North Karegar St, Tehran; tel. (21) 88012076; fax (21) 88012077; e-mail press@ut.ac.ir; internet press.ut.ac.ir; f. 1944; univ. textbooks; Man. Dir Dr MUHAMMAD SHEKARCIZADEH.

Broadcasting and Communications

TELECOMMUNICATIONS

The Mobile Communications Company of Iran, a subsidiary of the Telecommunications Company of Iran, previously had a monopoly over the provision of mobile cellular telecommunications services in the country. However, in February 2004 Iran's second GSM licence was awarded to Irancell, a consortium led by Turkcell (Turkey). The contract was subsequently revised by the Majlis and the Council of Guardians to require that domestic firms hold a majority stake in the consortium, and Turkcell was replaced as the foreign partner by the second-placed bidder, the South African company MTN. The licence award was eventually signed in November 2005, and initial services commenced in October 2006. A consortium led by the Emirates Telecommunications Corpn (Etisalat—United Arab Emirates) was named as the successful bidder for Iran's third GSM licence in January 2009. However, in May the award was revoked by the regulatory authority. In April 2010 the third GSM licence was reallocated to Tamin Telecom, an Iranian company that had formed part of the previous Etisalat-led consortium. Tamin was expected to begin offering services in 2012.

Radio Communications and Regulations Organization: f. 2005; regulatory authority; affiliated to the Ministry of Communications and Information Technology (see Ministries).

Telecommunications Company of Iran (TCI): POB 3316-17, Dr Ali Shariati Ave, Tehran; tel. (21) 88113938; fax (21) 88405055; e-mail info@irantelecom.ir; internet www.irantelecom.ir; fmrly 100% state-owned; 51% stake acquired by Etemad-e-Mobin consortium Sept. 2009; 24.3m. fixed-line subscribers (Sept. 2008); Chair. VAFA GHAFFARIAN; Man. Dir SABER FEIZI.

Mobile Communications Company of Iran (MCCI): Tehran; e-mail info@mci.ir; internet www.mci.ir; f. 2004; wholly owned subsidiary of TCI; 27.8m. subscribers (Sept. 2008); CEO VAHID SADOUGHI.

MTN Irancell: 12 Anahita Alley, Africa St, Tehran; internet www.irancell.ir; f. 2004 as Irancell, name changed as above 2005; mobile telecommunications; consortium of Iran Electronic Devt Co (51%) and MTN (South Africa—49%); 18.2m. subscribers (March 2009); Chair. Dr IBRAHIM MAHMOUDZADEH; Man. Dir ALIREZA GHALAMBOR DEZFOULI.

BROADCASTING

Article 175 of Iran's Constitution prohibits the establishment of private television channels and radio stations that are deemed to be 'un-Islamic'. However, in addition to the channels operated by the state-controlled Islamic Republic of Iran Broadcasting, many Iranians have access to foreign television programmes transmitted via satellite dishes (although ownership of these is officially banned).

Islamic Republic of Iran Broadcasting (IRIB): POB 19395-3333, Jam-e Jam St, Vali-e-Asr Ave, Tehran; tel. (21) 22041093; fax (21) 22014802; e-mail infopr@irib.ir; internet www.irib.com; semi-autonomous authority, affiliated with the Ministry of Culture and Islamic Guidance; non-commercial; operates seven national and 30 provincial television stations, and nine national radio networks; broadcasts world-wide in 27 languages; launched Al-Alam (international Arabic-language news channel) in 2002 and Press TV (English-language satellite channel) in 2007; Pres. SAYED EZZATOLLAH ZARGHAMI.

Radio

Radio Network 1 (Voice of the Islamic Republic of Iran): Covers the whole of Iran and also reaches Europe, Asia, Africa and part of the USA via short-wave and the internet; medium-wave regional broadcasts in local languages: Arabic, Armenian, Assyrian, Azerbaijani, Balochi, Bandari, Dari, Farsi, Kurdish, Mazandarani, Pashtu, Turkish, Turkoman and Urdu; external broadcasts in English, French, German, Spanish, Italian, Turkish, Bosnian, Albanian, Russian, Georgian, Armenian, Azeri, Tajik, Kazakh, Arabic, Kurdish, Urdu, Pashtu, Dari, Hausa, Bengali, Hindi, Japanese, Chinese, Kiswahili, Indonesian and Hebrew.

Television

Television Network 1 (Vision of the Islamic Republic of Iran): 625-line, System B; Secam colour; two production centres in Tehran producing for national networks and 30 local television stations.

Finance

(cap. = capital; res = reserves; dep. = deposits; brs = branches; m. = million; amounts in rials)

BANKING

Banks were nationalized in June 1979 and a revised commercial banking system was introduced consisting of nine banks (subsequently expanded to 11). Three banks were reorganized, two (Bank Tejarat and Bank Mellat) resulted from mergers of 22 existing small banks, three specialize in industry and agriculture, and one, the Islamic Bank of Iran (now Islamic Economy Organization), set up in May 1979, was exempt from nationalization. The 10th bank, the Export Development Bank, specializes in the promotion of exports. Post Bank of Iran became the 11th state-owned bank upon its establishment in 2006. A change-over to an Islamic banking system, with interest (forbidden under Islamic law) being replaced by a 4% commission on loans, began on 21 March 1984. All short- and medium-term private deposits and all bank loans and advances are subject to Islamic rules.

A partial liberalization of the banking sector was implemented by the administration of former President Khatami during 1997–2005, beginning with the establishment of four private banks after 2001. Two further private banks were granted licences to commence operations in 2005. Notable banks included in the Government's privatization programme are Mellat, Refah, Saderat, Tejarat and Post Bank of Iran.

Although the number of foreign banks operating in Iran has decreased dramatically since the Revolution, some 21 are still represented, in the form of representative offices. However, it was announced in 2007 that legislation to enable foreign banks to establish actual branches in Iran was to be presented to the Majlis. During 2007–08 the UN, USA and the European Union imposed various sanctions against Banks Mellat, Melli, Saderat and Sepah, owing to their suspected involvement in nuclear proliferation and/or terrorism-related activities.

Central Bank

Bank Markazi Jomhouri Islami Iran (Central Bank): POB 15875-7177, 144 Mirdamad Blvd, Tehran; tel. (21) 29954855; fax (21) 29954780; e-mail g.secdept@cbi.ir; internet www.cbi.ir; f. 1960; Bank Markazi Iran until Dec. 1983; issuing bank, govt banking; cap. 15,000,000m., res 102,794,098m., dep. 782,499,933m. (March 2009); Gov. Dr MAHMOUD BAHMANI.

State-owned Commercial Banks

Bank Keshavarzi (Agricultural Bank): POB 14155-6395, 129 Patrice Lumumba Ave, Jalal al-Ahmad Expressway, Tehran 14454; tel. (21) 88250135; fax (21) 88262313; e-mail info@agri-bank.com; internet www.agri-bank.com; f. 1980 by merger of Agricultural Co-operative Bank of Iran and Agricultural Devt Bank of Iran; cap. 8,021,118m., res 696,154m., dep. 156,778,929m. (March 2009); Chair. and Man. Dir Dr MUHAMMAD TALEBI; 1,870 brs.

Bank Mellat (Nation's Bank): Head Office Bldg, 327 Taleghani Ave, Tehran 15817; tel. (21) 82962043; fax (21) 88834417; e-mail info@bankmellat.ir; internet www.bankmellat.ir; f. 1980 by merger of 10 fmr private banks; cap. 13,100,000m., res 2,738,489m., dep. 330,584,526m. (March 2009); Chair. and Man. Dir Dr ALI DIVANDARI; 1,905 brs in Iran, 5 abroad.

Bank Melli Iran (National Bank of Iran): POB 11365-171, Ferdowsi Ave, Tehran; tel. (21) 3231; fax (21) 33912813; e-mail intlrel@bankmelli-iran.com; internet www.bankmelli-iran.com; f. 1928; present name since 1943; cap. 22,400,000m., res 9,635,190m., dep. 476,645,005m. (March 2008); Chair. and Man. Dir (vacant); 3,300 brs in Iran, 16 abroad.

Bank Refah Kargaran: 186 Northern Shiraz Ave, Molla Sadra Ave, Vanak Sq., Tehran 19917; tel. and fax (21) 88042875; e-mail info@bankrefah.ir; internet www.refah-bank.ir; f. 1960; cap. 895,000m., res 302,259m., dep. 56,545,320m. (March 2008); Chair. and Man. Dir SAYYED ZIA IMANI; 1,117 brs.

Bank Saderat Iran: POB 15745-631, Bank Saderat Tower, 43 Somayeh Ave, Tehran; tel. (21) 88302699; fax (21) 88839539; e-mail info@bsi.ir; internet www.bsi.ir; f. 1952; cap. 16,803,000m., res 6,968,000m., dep. 355,327,000m. (March 2009); Chair. and Man. Dir Dr MUHAMMAD JAHROMI; 3,300 brs in Iran, 21 abroad.

Bank Sepah: 7 Africa Ave, Argentina Sq., Tehran 15149-47111; tel. (21) 88646980; fax (21) 88646979; e-mail info@banksepah.ir; internet www.banksepah.ir; f. 1925; nationalized in June 1979; cap. 7,821,522m., res 1,420,165m., dep. 186,463,180m. (March 2009); Chair. and Man. Dir RAMIN PASHAEE FAM; 1,891 brs in Iran, 3 abroad.

Bank Tejarat (Commercial Bank): POB 11365-5416, 130 Taleghani Ave, Nejatoullahie, Tehran 15994; tel. (21) 88826690; fax (21) 88893641; internet www.tejaratbank.ir; f. 1979 by merger of 12 banks; cap. 10,437,384.0m., res 4,326,424.7m., dep. 257,236,117.6m. (March 2009); Chair. and Man. Dir Dr MAJID REZA DAVARI; 1,971 brs in Iran, 2 abroad.

Islamic Economy Organization: Ferdowsi Ave, Tehran; f. 1980 as the Islamic Bank of Iran; cap. 2,000m.; provides interest-free loans and investment in small industry; 1,200 funds under its supervision.

Post Bank of Iran (PBI): 237 Motahari Ave, Tehran 15876-18118; tel. (21) 88502024; fax (21) 88502027; e-mail info@postbank.ir; internet www.postbank.ir; f. 2006; cap. 561,143m., res 11,559m., dep. 8,236,617m. (March 2009); Chair. and Man. Dir MAHMOUD AFZALI; 404 brs.

Private Commercial Banks

Bank Pasargad: POB 19697-74511, 430 Mirdamad Ave, Tehran; tel. (21) 88649502; fax 88649501; e-mail info@bankpasargad.com; internet fa.bpi.ir; f. 2005; cap. 7,700,000m., res 1,661,278m., dep. 107,649,964m. (March 2010); Chair. SAYED KAZEM MIRVALAD; CEO Dr MAJID GHASEMI; 233 brs.

Bank Sarmaye: POB 19395-6415, 24 Arak St, Gharani Ave, Tehran; tel. (21) 88803632; fax (21) 88890839; e-mail info@sbank.ir; internet www.sbank.ir; f. 2005; cap. US $363.7m., res $26.4m., dep. $1,614.6m. (March 2009); Chair. M. SHAYESTEH NIA; CEO HAJI REZA ZADEH; 61 brs.

Eghtesad Novin Bank (EN Bank): 28 Esfandiar Blvd, Vali-e-Asr Ave, Tehran 196865-5944; tel. (21) 82330000; fax (21) 88880166; e-mail info@enbank.ir; internet www.en-bank.com; granted operating licence in 2001; cap. 2,000,000m., res 438,482m., dep. 69,879,425m. (March 2008); Chair. MUHAMMAD SADR HASHEMI NEJAD; CEO SAYYED AHMAD TAHERI BEHBEHANI; 244 brs.

Karafarin Bank: POB 15875-4659, No. 97, West Nahid St, Valiasr Ave, Tehran 15137; tel. (21) 26215000; fax (21) 26214999; e-mail info@karafarinbank.com; internet www.karafarinbank.com; f. 1999 as Karafarin Credit Institute; converted into private bank in 2001; cap. 2,000,000.0m., res 485,647.2m., dep. 25,461,034.7m. (March 2009); Chair. ALI A. AFKHAMI; Man. Dir VALIOLLAH SEIF; 78 brs.

Parsian Bank: 65 Keshavarz Blvd, Tehran; tel. (21) 88979333; fax (21) 88979344; e-mail info@parsian-bank.net; internet www.parsian-bank.com; f. 2002; cap. US $762m., res $357m., dep. $19,577m. (March 2010); Chair. ALI SHEIKHI; Man. Dir ALI SOLEIMANI SHAYESTEH; 155 brs.

Saman Bank Corpn: Bldg No. 1, 879 Kaledge Junction, Engheleb St, Tehran; tel. (21) 66959050; fax (21) 26210911; e-mail info@sb24.com; internet www.sb24.com; f. 2001; cap. 900,000m., res 1,057,411m., dep. 36,471,727m. (March 2009); Chair. ALLAHVERDI RAJAEE SALMASI; 54 brs.

Development Banks

Bank of Industry and Mine (BIM): POB 15875-4456, Firouzeh Tower, 2917 Vali-e-Asr Ave (above Park Way Junction), Tehran; tel. (21) 22029838; fax (21) 22029894; e-mail info@bim.ir; internet w3.bim.ir; f. 1979 by merger of Industrial Credit Bank, Industrial and Mining Devt Bank of Iran, Devt and Investment Bank of Iran, and Iranian Bankers Investment Co; state-owned; cap. 20,722,472m., res 2,184,108m., dep. 15,446,443m. (March 2009); Chair. and Man. Dir MUHAMMAD REZA PISHROW; 31 brs.

Export Development Bank of Iran (EDBI): POB 151674-7913, Tose'e Tower, 15th St, Ahmad Ghasir Ave, Argentina Sq., Tehran; tel. (21) 88702130; fax (21) 88798259; e-mail info@edbi.ir; internet www.edbi.ir; f. 1991; state-owned; cap. 16,418,554m., res 2,637,704m., dep. 18,744,334m. (March 2009); Chair. and Man. Dir BAHMAN VAKILI; 34 brs.

Housing Bank

Bank Maskan (Housing Bank): POB 19947-63811, 14 Attar St, Vanak Sq., Tehran; tel. (21) 88797822; fax (21) 82932735; e-mail intl_div@bank-maskan.ir; internet bank-maskan.ir; f. 1979; state-owned; cap. 7,066,657m., res 2,532,592m., dep. 164,523,614m. (March 2009); provides mortgage and housing finance; Chair. and Man. Dir GHODRATOLLAH SHARIFI; 1,214 brs.

STOCK EXCHANGE

Tehran Stock Exchange: 192 Hafez Ave, Tehran 11355; tel. (21) 66719535; fax (21) 66710111; e-mail int@tse.ir; internet www.tse.ir; f. 1966; cap. 150,000m.; 348 listed cos (2011); Chair. HAMID REZA RAFIEI KESHTELI; Man. Dir Dr HASSAN GHALIBAF ASL.

INSURANCE

The nationalization of insurance companies was announced in June 1979. However, as part of the reforms to the financial sector undertaken by the former Khatami administration, four new private insurance companies were licensed to commence operations in May 2003. By the end of 2008 there were 16 privately owned insurance and reinsurance companies operating in Iran. There were also four state-owned insurance companies in operation.

Bimeh Alborz (Alborz Insurance Co): POB 4489-15875, Alborz Bldg, 234 Sepahboad Garani Ave, Tehran; tel. (21) 88803821; fax (21) 88908088; e-mail info@alborzins.com; internet www.alborzinsurance.ir; f. 1959; state-owned; all types of insurance; Chair. and Man. Dir MUHAMMAD EBRAHIM AMIN; 39 brs.

Bimeh Asia (Asia Insurance Co): POB 15815-1885, Asia Insurance Bldg, 299 Taleghani Ave, Tehran; tel. (21) 88800950; fax (21) 88898113; e-mail info@bimehasia.ir; internet www.bimehasia.com; f. 1959; state-owned; all types of insurance; Man. Dir M. ALIPOUR; 83 brs.

Bimeh Dana (Dana Insurance Co): 25 15th St, Ghandi Ave, Tehran 151789-5511; tel. (21) 88770971; fax (21) 88792997; e-mail info@dana-insurance.com; internet www.dana-insurance.com; f. 1988; 56% govt-owned; life, personal accident and health insurance; Chair. and Man. Dir H. O. HOSSEIN.

Bimeh Day (Day Insurance Co): 241 Mirdamad Blvd, Tehran; tel. (21) 22900551; fax (21) 22900516; e-mail info@dayins.com; internet www.dayins.com; f. 2004; privately owned; all types of insurance.

Bimeh Iran (Iran Insurance Co): POB 14155-6363, 107 Dr Fatemi Ave, Tehran; tel. (21) 88954712; e-mail info@iraninsurance.ir; internet www.iraninsurance.ir; f. 1935; state-owned; all types of insurance; Chair. and Man. Dir JAVAD SAHAMIAN MOGHADDAM; 246 brs in Iran, 14 brs abroad.

Bimeh Karafarin (Karafarin Insurance Co): POB 15875-8475, No. 9, 17th St, Ahmad Ghasir Ave, Argentina Sq., Tehran; tel. (21) 88723830; fax (21) 88723840; e-mail karafarin@karafarin-insurance.com; internet www.karafarin-insurance.com; f. 2003; privately owned; all types of insurance; 14 brs; Chair. Dr PARVIZ AGHILI-KERMANI; Man. Dir ABDOLMAHMOUD ZARRABI.

Bimeh Novin (Novin Insurance Co): POB 19119-33183, 11 Behrouz St, Madar (Mohseni) Sq., Mirdamad Blvd, Tehran; tel. (21) 22258046; fax (21) 22923844; e-mail info@novininsurance.com; internet www.novininsurance.com; f. 2006; privately owned; all types of insurance; Chair. Dr GHOLAMALI GHOLAMI.

Bimeh Saman (Saman Insurance Co): 113 Khaled Eslamboli Ave, Tehran 15138-13119; tel. (21) 88700205; fax (21) 88700204; e-mail info@samaninsurance.com; internet www.samaninsurance.com; f. 2005; privately owned; Chair. MUHAMMAD ZRABYH.

Bimeh Sina (Sina Insurance Co): 343 Beheshti Ave, Tehran; tel. (21) 88706701; fax (21) 88709654; e-mail info@sinainsurance.com; internet www.sinainsurance.com; f. 2003; privately owned.

Mellat Insurance Co: 48 Shahid Haghani Expressway, Vanak Sq., Tehran; tel. and fax (21) 88878814; e-mail info@mellatinsurance.com; internet www.mellatinsurance.com; privately owned; property, life, engineering, aviation and marine insurance; Chair. ABDOLHOSSEIN SABET; Man. Dir MASOUD HAJJARIAN KASHANI.

Regulatory Authority

Bimeh Markazi Iran (Central Insurance of Iran): POB 19395-5588, 72 Africa Ave, Tehran 19157; tel. (21) 22050001; fax (21) 22054099; e-mail pr@centinsur.ir; internet www.centinsur.ir; f. 1971; regulates and supervises the insurance market and tariffs for new types of insurance cover; the sole state reinsurer for domestic insurance cos, which are obliged to reinsure 50% of their direct business in life insurance and 25% of business in non-life insurance with Bimeh Markazi Iran; Pres. Dr JAVAD FARSHBAF MAHERIYAN.

Trade and Industry

CHAMBERS OF COMMERCE

Iran Chamber of Commerce, Industries and Mines: 254 Taleghani Ave, Tehran 15875-4671; tel. (21) 88308327; fax (21) 88810524; e-mail dsg@iccim.ir; internet www.iccim.ir; supervises the affiliated 32 local chambers; Pres. Dr MUHAMMAD NAHAVANDIAN.

Esfahan Chamber of Commerce, Industries and Mines: POB 81656-336, Feyz Sq., Tehran; tel. (311) 6615097; fax (311) 6613636; e-mail m.eslamian@eccim.com; internet www.eccim.com; Chair. MAHMOUD ESLAMIAN.

Shiraz Chamber of Commerce, Industries and Mines: Zand St, Shiraz; tel. (711) 6294901; fax (711) 6294910; e-mail info@sccim.org; internet www.sccim.ir; Chair. FERIDOUN FORGHANI.

Tabriz Chamber of Commerce, Industries and Mines: 65 North Artesh Ave, Tabriz; tel. (411) 5264104; fax (411) 5264115; e-mail expo@tzccim.ir; internet www.tzccim.ir; f. 1906; privately owned; Chair. RAHIM SADEGHIAN.

Tehran Chamber of Commerce, Industries and Mines: 285 Motahari Ave, Tehran; tel. (21) 88701912; fax (21) 88715661; e-mail into@tccim.ir; internet www.tccim.ir; Chair. Dr YAHYA ALE-ESHAGH.

INDUSTRIAL AND TRADE ASSOCIATIONS

National Iranian Industries Organization (NIIO): POB 15875-1331, No. 11, 13th Alley, Miremad St, Tehran; tel. (21) 88744198; fax (21) 88757126; f. 1979; owns 400 factories in Iran; Man. Dir ALI TOOSI.

National Iranian Industries Organization Export Co (NECO): No. 8, 2nd Alley, Bucharest Ave, Tehran; tel. (21) 44162384; fax (21) 212429.

STATE HYDROCARBONS COMPANIES

The following are subsidiary companies of the Ministry of Petroleum:

National Iranian Gas Co (NIGC): POB 6394-4533, 7th Floor, No. 401, Saghitaman, Taleghani Ave, Tehran; tel. (21) 88133347; fax (21) 88133456; e-mail webmaster@nigc.org; internet www.nigc.ir; f. 1965; Chair. Brig.-Gen. ROSTAM GHASEMI (Minister of Petroleum); Man. Dir JAVAD OJI.

National Iranian Oil Co (NIOC): POB 1863, Taleghani Ave, Tehran 15875-1863; tel. (21) 66154975; fax (21) 66154977; e-mail public-relations@nioc.com; internet www.nioc.com; f. 1948; controls all upstream activities in the petroleum and natural gas industries; incorporated April 1951 on nationalization of petroleum industry to engage in all phases of petroleum operations; in Feb. 1979 it was announced that in future Iran would sell petroleum directly to the petroleum companies, and in Sept. 1979 the Ministry of Petroleum assumed control of the NIOC; Chair. Brig.-Gen. ROSTAM GHASEMI (Minister of Petroleum); Man. Dir SEIFOLLAH JASHNSAZ; subsidiary cos include the following:

Iranian Offshore Oil Co (IOOC): POB 5591, 38 Tooraj St, Vali-e-Asr Ave, Tehran 19395; tel. (21) 22664402; fax (21) 22664216; e-mail M.Khandan@iooc.co.ir; internet www.iooc.co.ir; f. 1980; devt, exploitation and production of crude petroleum, natural gas and other hydrocarbons in all offshore areas of Iran in the Persian (Arabian) Gulf and the Caspian Sea; Chair. Dr MUHAMMAD JAVAD ASEMI POOR; Man. Dir MAHMOUD ZIRAKCHIAN ZADEH.

Pars Oil and Gas Co (POGC): POB 14141-73111, 1 Parvin Etesami Alley, Dr Fatemi Ave, Tehran; tel. (21) 88966031; fax (21) 88989273; e-mail info@pogc.ir; internet www.pogc.ir; f. 1999; Man. Dir ALI VAKILI.

National Iranian Oil Refining and Distribution Co (NIORDC): POB 15815-3499, NIORDC Bldg, 140 Ostad Nejatollahi Ave, Tehran 15989; tel. (21) 88801001; fax (21) 66152138; e-mail info@niordc.ir; internet www.niordc.ir; f. 1992 to assume responsibility for refining, pipeline distribution, engineering, construction and research in the petroleum industry from NIOC; Chair. Brig.-Gen. ROSTAM GHASEMI (Minister of Petroleum); Man. Dir NOUREDDIN SHAHNAZIZADEH.

National Iranian Petrochemical Co (NIPC): POB 19395-6896, North Sheikh Bahaei St, Tehran; tel. (21) 88620000; fax (21) 88059702; e-mail webmaster@nipc.net; internet www.nipc.net; f. 1964; oversees the devt and operation of Iran's petrochemical sector; directs activities of over 50 subsidiaries; Chair. Brig.-Gen. ROSTAM GHASEMI (Minister of Petroleum); Man. Dir ABDOLHOSSEIN BAYAT.

CO-OPERATIVES

Central Union of Rural and Agricultural Co-operatives of Iran: POB 14155-6413, 78 North Palestine St, Opposite Ministry of Energy, Tehran; tel. (21) 88978150; fax (21) 88964166; internet www.trocairan.com; f. 1963; educational, technical, commercial and credit assistance to rural co-operative societies and unions; Chair. and Man. Dir SAYED MUHAMMAD MIRMUHAMMADI.

UTILITIES

Electricity

Iran Power Generation, Transmission and Distribution Co (Tavanir): POB 19988-36111, Tavanir Blvd, Rashid Yasami St, Vali-e-Asr Ave, Tehran; tel. (21) 88774088; fax (21) 88778437; e-mail ceo@tavanir.org.ir; internet www.tavanir.org.ir; f. 1979; state-owned; operates a network of 16 regional electricity cos, 27 generating cos and 42 distribution cos; also responsible for electricity transmission; Man. Dir MUHAMMAD ALI VAHDATI.

Water

Iran Water Resources Management Co: 517 Felestin Ave, Tehran; tel. (21) 88901081; fax (21) 88916600; e-mail waterpr@wrm.ir; internet www.wrm.ir; f. 2003; govt agency reporting to the Ministry of Energy; in charge of Iran's Regional Water Authorities; Chair. MAJID NAMJOU (Minister of Energy).

Transport

RAILWAYS

According to the Statistical Centre of Iran, in 2006/07 (Iranian year to March) the railway network system comprised 8,565 km of mainline track, 1,597 km of side and shunting tracks, and 945 km of industrial/commercial lines. In 2007 it was reported that the Government planned to expand the rail network to 28,000 km by 2020. However, the expansion programme has been severely impeded by a shortage of foreign investment and the impact of US-led sanctions. None the less, construction of a 506-km rail link between Esfahan and Shiraz was completed in June 2009. In the same month a 250-km Zahedan–Kerman line was inaugurated, linking the rail networks of Iran and Pakistan and facilitating the launch of a direct Islamabad (Pakistan)–Tehran–Istanbul (Turkey) freight service in August. Construction of a 1,350-km railway along Iran's eastern border, linking Mashad, in the north-east, with Chabahar on the Persian (Arabian) Gulf, commenced in May 2010. A 51-km railway linking Khorramshahr with Basra in southern Iraq was also under construction. In February 2011 a US $12,860m. contract to build eight new lines—totalling some 5,300 km—was awarded to the People's Republic of China.

Islamic Republic of Iran Railways: Railways Central Bldg, Argentina Sq., Africa Blvd, Tehran; tel. (21) 88646568; fax (21) 88646570; e-mail iranrai@rai.ir; internet www.rai.ir; f. 1934; affiliated to Ministry of Roads and Urban Development; Pres. ABDOL-ALI SAHEB MUHAMMADI.

Raja Passenger Trains Co: POB 15875-1363, 1 Sanaie St, Karimkhan Zand Ave, Tehran; tel. (21) 88310880; fax (21) 88834340; e-mail info@raja.ir; internet www.raja.ir; f. 1996; state-owned; affiliated to Iranian Islamic Republic Railways; Chair. and Man. Dir NASER BAKHTIARI.

Underground Railway

Construction of the Tehran underground railway system commenced in 1977. By early 2012 the system consisted of four lines: Line 1, a 32-km line linking north and south Tehran; Line 2, a 25-km line running east–west across the city; Line 4, an 8.5-km line serving five stations in the city centre; and Line 5, a 41.5-km suburban line, linking Tehran with the satellite city of Karaj. Three other underground lines—3, 6 and 7—were under construction in early 2012. In March 2010 the Tehran Urban and Suburban Railway Company announced plans to construct an additional six lines—8 and 9, and four suburban lines linking central Tehran to satellite cities. It was envisaged that construction work on the additional lines would commence in 2018, following the completion of existing projects.

Tehran Urban and Suburban Railway Co (Tehranmetro) (TUSRC): 37 Mir Emad St, Tehran 15878-13113; tel. (21) 88740110; fax (21) 88740114; e-mail info@tehranmetro.com; internet www.tehranmetro.com; f. 1976; CEO HABIL DARVISH.

ROADS

In 2008 there were an estimated 174,301 km of roads, including 1,429 km of motorways, 27,256 km of highways, main or national roads, and 145,616 km of secondary or regional roads; some 73.3% of the road network was paved. There is a paved highway (A1, 2,089 km) from Bazargan on the Turkish border to the Afghanistan border. The A2 highway runs 2,473 km from the Iraqi border to Mir Javeh on the Pakistan border. A new highway linking the eastern city of Dogharun to Herat in Afghanistan was opened in January 2005.

INLAND WATERWAYS

Lake Urmia (formerly Lake Rezaiyeh): 80 km west of Tabriz in north-western Iran; from Sharafkhaneh to Golmankhaneh there is a regular service of tugs and barges for the transport of passengers and goods.

Karun River: Flowing south through the oilfields into the Shatt al-Arab waterway, and thence to the head of the Persian (Arabian) Gulf near Abadan; there is a regular cargo service, as well as a daily motor-boat services for passengers and goods.

SHIPPING

In December 2009 Iran's merchant fleet comprised 542 vessels, with an aggregate displacement of 987,600 grt.

The main oil terminal on the Persian (Arabian) Gulf is at Kharg Island. The principal commercial non-oil ports are Bandar Shahid Rajai (which was officially inaugurated in 1983 and handles a significant proportion of the cargo passing annually through Iran's Gulf ports), Bandar Imam Khomeini, Bushehr, Bandar Abbas and Chabahar. Bandar Abbas port, which predates the 1979 Islamic Revolution, has undergone considerable development in recent years. The port now comprises a new port, called the Shahid Rajai Port Complex, and the old port, named Shahid Bahonar. A major expansion of Chabahar port, which was expected to increase annual handling capacity from 100,000 to 500,000 20-ft equivalent units, was under way in 2012. Iran's principal ports on the Caspian Sea include Bandar Anzali (formerly Bandar Pahlavi) and Bandar Nowshahr.

Port Authority

Ports and Maritime Organization (PMO): POB 158754574-158753754, South Didar St, Shahid Haghani Highway, Vanak Sq., Tehran; tel. (21) 88809280; fax (21) 88651191; e-mail info@pmo.ir; internet www.pmo.ir; f. 1960 as Ports and Shipping Org.; affiliated to Ministry of Roads and Urban Development; Man. Dir ATAOLLAH SADR.

Principal Shipping Companies

Bonyad Shipping Agencies Co (BOSCO): POB 15875-3794, 24 Gandhi Ave, 15177 Tehran; tel. (21) 88795211; fax (21) 88776951; e-mail bosaco@bosaco.ir; internet www.bosacoir.com; f. 1991; Man. Dir ALI SAFARALI.

Iran Marine Services: 151 Mirdamad Blvd, Tehran 19116; tel. (21) 22222249; fax (21) 22223380; e-mail center@ims-ir.com; internet www.ims-ir.com; f. 1981; Chair. and Man. Dir MUHAMMAD HASSAN ASHRAFIAN LAK.

Irano–Hind Shipping Co (IHSC): POB 15875-4647, 18 Sedaghat St, Vali-e-Asr Ave, Tehran; tel. (21) 22058095; fax (21) 22057739; e-mail admin@iranohind.com; internet www.iranohind.com; f. 1974; jt venture between Islamic Republic of Iran and Shipping Corpn of India; Man. Dir Capt. C. P. ATHAIDE.

Islamic Republic of Iran Shipping Lines (IRISL): POB 19395-1311, 37 Asseman Tower, Sayyad Shirazee Sq., Pasdaran Ave, Tehran; tel. (21) 20100369; fax (21) 20100367; e-mail e-pr@irisl.net; internet www.irisl.net; f. 1967; Man. Dir MUHAMMAD HOSSEIN DAJMAR.

National Iranian Tanker Co (NITC): POB 19395-4833, 67–68 Atefis St, Africa Ave, Tehran; tel. (21) 23803325; fax (21) 22058761; e-mail souri@nitc.co.ir; internet www.nitc.co.ir; Chair. and Man. Dir MUHAMMAD SOURI.

CIVIL AVIATION

The principal international airport is the Imam Khomeini International Airport (IKIA), to the south of Tehran, which, when construction began in the late 1990s, was anticipated to be one of the largest airports in the world. The first phase of the project was completed in early 2001, and the first flights landed in February 2003. However, the airport was closed by the Islamic Revolutionary Guards Corps in May 2004, amid security concerns owing to the fact that it was to be operated by a consortium led by the Turkish company, TAV. The IKIA finally reopened in May 2005, and had taken over all international flights from Mehrabad airport (west of Tehran) by mid-2006. There are several other international airports, including those at Esfahan, Mashad, Shiraz and Tabriz.

Civil Aviation Organization (CAO): POB 13445-1798, Taleghani Ave, Tehran; tel. (21) 66025131; fax (21) 44665496; e-mail info@cao.ir; internet www.cao.ir; affiliated to Ministry of Roads and Urban Development; Pres. HAMID REZA PAHLEVANI.

Caspian Airlines: 5 Sabonchi St, Shahid Beheshti Ave, Tehran; tel. (21) 88751671; fax (21) 887516676; internet www.caspian.aero; f. 1992; operates more than 50 flights per week from Tehran to other cities in Iran, as well as scheduled flights to the United Arab Emirates, Lebanon, Syria, Turkey and several European destinations; rep. offices abroad; Gen. Dir Capt. ASGAR RAZZAGHI.

IranAir (Airline of the Islamic Republic of Iran): POB 13185-755, IranAir HQ, Mehrabad Airport, Tehran; tel. (21) 46624256; fax (21) 46628222; e-mail pr@iranair.com; internet www.iranair.com; f. 1962; serves the Middle East and Persian (Arabian) Gulf area, Europe, Asia and the Far East; partial privatization pending; Chair. and Man. Dir FARHAD PARVARESH.

Iran Airtours: POB 1587997811, 183 Motahari St, Dr Mofatteh Cross Rd, Tehran; tel. (21) 88755535; fax (21) 88755884; e-mail info@iranairtours.com; internet iranairtours.ir; f. 1992; low-cost subsidiary of IranAir, offering flights from Tehran and Mashad; serves domestic routes and the wider Middle East; Chair. ABBAS POUR-MUHAMMADI; Man. Dir SAYED MAHDI SADEGHI.

Iran Aseman Airlines: POB 141748, Mehrabad Airport, Tehran 13145-1476; tel. (21) 66035310; fax (21) 66002810; e-mail public@iaa.ir; internet www.iaa.ir; f. 1980 as result of merger of Air Taxi Co (f. 1958), Pars Air (f. 1969), Air Service Co (f. 1962) and Hoor Asseman; domestic routes and charter services to destinations in Central Asia and the Middle East; Chair. and Man. Dir ALI ABEDZADEH.

Kish Air: POB 19395-4639, 215 Africa Ave, Tehran 19697; tel. (21) 44665639; fax (21) 44665221; e-mail info@kishairline.com; internet www.kishairline.com; f. 1989, under the auspices of the Kish Devt Org.; domestic routes and flights to the United Arab Emirates and Turkey; Chair. and CEO Capt. REZA NAKHJAVANI.

Mahan Air: POB 14515-411, Mahan Air Tower, 21 Azadegan St, Karaj Highway, Tehran 14816-55761; tel. (21) 48041111; fax (21) 48041112; e-mail international@mahanairlines.com; internet www.mahan.aero; f. 1992; domestic routes and charter services to other Middle Eastern, Asian and European destinations; Man. Dir HAMID ARABNEJAD.

Qeshm Air: 17 Ghandi Ave, Tehran; tel. (21) 88776012; fax (21) 88786252; e-mail qeshmair@farazqeshm.com; operates regular flights from Qeshm Island to the Iranian mainland and the United Arab Emirates.

Saha Airline: POB 13865-164, Karadj Old Rd, Tehran 13873; tel. (21) 66696200; fax (21) 66698016; e-mail saha2@iran-net.com; f. 1990; owned by the Iranian Air Force; operates passenger and cargo charter domestic flights and services to Europe, Asia and Africa; Man. Dir Capt. MANSOUR NIKUKAR.

Tourism

Iran's principal attraction for tourists is its wealth of historical sites, notably Esfahan, Shiraz, Persepolis, Tabriz and Shush (Susa). The country also possesses a wide variety of natural landscapes, and skiing or hiking are popular activities in the Alborz Mountains close to Tehran. In 2006 it was announced that Iran was seeking to attract tourists from neighbouring Muslim countries by developing the tourism industry on Kish island, declared a free trade zone in 1992. The Government plans to attract 20m. foreign tourists each year to Iran by 2018. Tourist arrivals totalled 3,121,283 in 2010/11 (year ending 20 March). Receipts from tourism in 2009 were recorded at US $2,310m.

Iran Tourism and Touring Organization (ITTO): 154 Keshavarz Blvd, Tehran; tel. (21) 88737065; fax (21) 88736800; e-mail info@itto.org; internet www.itto.org; f. 1985; administered by Ministry of Culture and Islamic Guidance.

Defence

Secretary of the Supreme National Security Council: SAEED JALILI.

Chief of Staff of the Armed Forces: Maj.-Gen. HASSAN FIROUZABADI.

Commander of the Army: Brig.-Gen. ATAOLLAH SALEHI.

Commander of the Air Force: Brig.-Gen. HASSAN SHAHSAFI.

Commander of the Navy: Rear-Adm. HABIBOLLAH SAYYARI.

Chief of Staff of the Islamic Revolutionary Guards Corps (Pasdaran Inqilab): Brig.-Gen. MUHAMMAD ALI JAFARI.

Commander of the Islamic Revolutionary Guards Corps Ground Forces: Brig.-Gen. MUHAMMAD PAKPOUR.

Commander of the Islamic Revolutionary Guards Corps Air Force: Brig.-Gen. AMIR ALI HEJIZADEH.

Commander of the Islamic Revolutionary Guards Corps Navy: Rear-Adm. ALI FADAVI.

Commander of Basij (Mobilization) War Volunteers Corps: Brig.-Gen. MUHAMMAD REZA NAGHDI.

Budgeted defence expenditure (2011): (year ending 20 March) est. IR 128,000,000m.

Total armed forces: As assessed at November 2011, Iran's regular armed forces totalled an estimated 523,000 (excluding 350,000 reserves): army 350,000 men; navy 18,000; air force 30,000; Islamic Revolutionary Guards Corps (*Pasdaran Inqilab*, which has its own land, navy and marine units) some 125,000; membership of Basij War Volunteers Corps estimated to include up to 1,000,000 combatants; there were also some 40,000 paramilitary forces under the command of the Ministry of the Interior.

Education

PRIMARY AND SECONDARY EDUCATION

Primary education, beginning at the age of six and lasting for five years, is compulsory for all children and provided free of charge. Secondary education, from the age of 11, lasts for up to seven years, comprising a first cycle of three years and a second of four years. According to the Government, 24,000 schools were built between the 1979 Revolution and 1984. According to official figures, 5,591,800 pupils were enrolled in primary education in 2009/10, while 6,274,600 were engaged in secondary education. In 2006/07, according to UNESCO estimates, primary enrolment included 99% of children in the relevant age-group, while in 2008/09 enrolment at secondary schools was equivalent to 83% of the appropriate age-group.

HIGHER EDUCATION

Iran has 39 universities, including 16 in Tehran. Universities were closed by the Government in 1980 but have been reopened gradually since 1983. According to official sources, some 2,335,800 students were enrolled at Iran's public colleges and universities in the 2009/10 academic year, in addition to the 1,536,200 students enrolled at the Islamic Azad University in 2010/11. Apart from Tehran, there are universities in Bakhtaran, Esfahan, Hamadan, Tabriz, Ahwaz, Babolsar, Meshed, Kermanshah, Rasht, Shiraz, Zahedan, Kerman, Shahrekord, Urmia and Yazd. There are c. 50 colleges of higher education, c. 40 technological institutes, c. 80 teacher-training colleges, several colleges of advanced technology, and colleges of agriculture in Hamadan, Zanjan, Sari and Abadan. Vocational training schools also exist in Tehran, Ahwaz, Meshed, Shiraz and other cities. Budgetary expenditure on education by the central Government in the financial year 2004/05 was IR 31,518,000m. (8.2% of total spending).

IRAQ

Introductory Survey

LOCATION, CLIMATE, LANGUAGE, RELIGION, FLAG, CAPITAL

The Republic of Iraq is an almost land-locked state in western Asia, with a narrow outlet to the sea on the Persian (Arabian) Gulf. Its neighbours are Iran to the east, Turkey to the north, Syria and Jordan to the west, and Saudi Arabia and Kuwait to the south. The climate is extreme, with hot, dry summers, when temperatures may exceed 43°C (109°F), and cold winters, especially in the highlands. Summers are humid near the Gulf coast. The official language is Arabic, spoken by about 80% of the population; about 15% speak Kurdish, while there is a small Turkoman-speaking minority. Some 95% of the population are Muslims, of whom about 60% belong to the Shi'i sect. However, the Baath regime that was in power during 1968–2003 was dominated by members of the Sunni sect. In January 2008 the Council of Representatives approved the design of a new, temporary national flag, which was to be replaced by a permanent one within one year; however, by early 2012 no announcement had been made regarding a permanent flag. The temporary flag (proportions 2 by 3) has three equal horizontal stripes, of red, white and black, and the inscription *'Allahu Akbar'* ('God is Great') written in green Kufic script on the central white stripe. The capital is Baghdad.

CONTEMPORARY POLITICAL HISTORY

Historical Context

Iraq was formerly part of Turkey's Ottoman Empire. During the First World War (1914–18), when Turkey was allied with Germany, the territory was captured by British forces. In 1920 Iraq was placed under a League of Nations mandate, administered by the United Kingdom. In 1921 Amir Faisal ibn Hussain, a member of the Hashimi (Hashemite) dynasty of Arabia, was proclaimed King of Iraq. After prolonged negotiations, a 25-year Anglo-Iraqi Treaty of Alliance was signed in 1930. The British mandate ended on 3 October 1932, when Iraq became fully independent.

During its early years the new kingdom was confronted with Kurdish revolts (1922–32) and with border disputes in the south. The leading personality in Iraqi political life under the monarchy was Gen. Nuri al-Said, who became Prime Minister in 1930 and held the office for seven terms over a period of 28 years. He strongly supported Iraq's close links with the United Kingdom and with the West in general. After the death of King Faisal I in 1933, the Iraqi monarchy remained pro-British in outlook, and in 1955 Iraq signed the Baghdad Pact, a British-inspired agreement on collective regional security. However, following the overthrow of King Faisal II (the grandson of Faisal I) during a military revolution on 14 July 1958, which brought to power a left-wing, nationalist regime headed by Brig. (later Lt-Gen.) Abd al-Karim Kassem, the 1925 Constitution was abolished, the legislature was dissolved, and in March 1959 Iraq withdrew from the Baghdad Pact. Kassem, who had become increasingly isolated, was assassinated in February 1963 during a coup by members of the armed forces. The new Government of Col (later Field Marshal) Abd al-Salem Muhammad Aref was more pan-Arab in outlook, and sought closer relations with the United Arab Republic (Egypt). Following his death in March 1966, President Aref was succeeded by his brother, Maj.-Gen. Abd al-Rahman Muhammad Aref, who was deposed on 17 July 1968 by members of the Arab Renaissance (Baath) Socialist Party. Maj.-Gen. (later Field Marshal) Ahmad Hassan al-Bakr, a former Prime Minister, became President and Prime Minister, and supreme authority was vested in the Revolutionary Command Council (RCC), of which President al-Bakr was also Chairman.

Domestic Political Affairs

On 16 July 1979 the Vice-Chairman of the RCC, Saddam Hussain, who had long exercised real power in Iraq, replaced al-Bakr as RCC Chairman and as President of Iraq. Shortly afterwards several members of the RCC were executed for their alleged role in a coup plot. The suspicion of Syrian involvement in the attempted putsch, exacerbated by the rivalry between the Baathist movements of both countries, resulted in the suspension of discussions concerning political and economic union between Iraq and Syria. During 1979 the Iraqi Communist Party (ICP) broke away from the National Progressive Front (NPF), an alliance of Baathists, Kurdish groups and Communists, claiming that the Baathists were conducting a 'reign of terror'. In February 1980 Saddam Hussain announced a National Charter, reaffirming the principles of non-alignment. In June elections took place (the first since the 1958 revolution) for a 250-member legislative National Assembly; these were followed in September by the first elections to a 50-member Kurdish Legislative Council in the Kurdish Autonomous Region (which had been established in 1970).

In 1982 Saddam Hussain consolidated his positions as Chairman of the RCC and Regional Secretary of the Baath Party by conducting a purge throughout the administration. Kurdish rebels became active in northern Iraq, occasionally supporting Iranian forces in the war with Iraq (see below). Another threat was posed by the Supreme Council for the Islamic Revolution in Iraq (SCIRI, renamed the Islamic Supreme Council of Iraq—ISCI—in May 2007), formed in the Iranian capital, Tehran, in November 1982 by the exiled Shi'ite leader Hojatoleslam Muhammad Baqir al-Hakim. None the less, the majority of Iraq's Shi'ite community was not attracted by the fundamentalist Shi'ite doctrine of Ayatollah Khomeini of Iran, remaining loyal to Iraq and its Sunni President, while Iranian-backed militant groups (such as the predominantly Shi'ite Islamic Dawa Party—Hizb al-Da'wa al-Islamiya—which made numerous attempts to assassinate Saddam Hussain) were ineffective.

Relations with Iran, precarious for many years, descended into full-scale war in September 1980. Iraq had become increasingly dissatisfied with the 1975 Algiers Agreement, which had defined the southern border between Iran and Iraq as the mid-point of the Shatt al-Arab waterway, and also sought the withdrawal of Iranian forces from Abu Musa and the Tunb islands, which Iran had occupied in 1971. The Iranian Revolution of 1979 exacerbated these grievances, and conflict soon developed as Iran accused Iraq of encouraging Arab demands for autonomy in Iran's Khuzestan ('Arabistan') region. In September 1980, following clashes on the border, Iraq abrogated the Algiers Agreement and its forces advanced into Iran. Fierce Iranian resistance led to military deadlock until mid-1982, when Iranian counter-offensives led to the retaking of the port of Khorramshahr and the withdrawal of Iraqi troops from territory occupied in 1980. In July 1982 the Iranian army crossed into Iraq. However, the balance of military power in the war moved in Iraq's favour in 1984, and its financial position improved as the USA and the USSR provided aid. (Diplomatic relations between the USA and Iraq were restored in November 1984, having been suspended since the Arab–Israeli War of 1967.) By early 1988 Iraqi forces had begun to recapture land occupied by Iran, and in July they crossed into Iran for the first time since 1986. In that month Iran announced its unconditional acceptance of UN Security Council Resolution 598, and by August a UN-monitored cease-fire was in force. However, negotiations on the full implementation of the resolution had made little progress by the time of Iraq's invasion of Kuwait in August 1990 (see below), at which point Saddam Hussain abruptly sought a formal peace agreement with Iran—accepting all the claims that Iran had pursued since the cease-fire, including the reinstatement of the Algiers Agreement of 1975. (For a fuller account of the 1980–88 Iran–Iraq War and of subsequent bilateral relations, see the chapter on Iran.)

In the second half of the 1980s Saddam Hussain consolidated his control over the country. In 1988 the President announced political reforms, including the introduction of a multi-party system, and in January 1989 declared that these would be incorporated into a new permanent constitution. In April 1989 elections took place to the 250-seat National Assembly, in which one-quarter of the candidates were members of the Baath Party and the remainder either independent or members of the NPF. More than 50% of the newly elected deputies were reported to be Baathists. In July the National Assembly approved a new draft Constitution, under the terms of which a 50-member

Consultative Assembly was to be established; both institutions would assume the duties of the RCC, which was to be abolished after a presidential election.

During the 1980s representatives of Iraq's 2.5m.–3m. Kurds demanded greater autonomy. Resources were repeatedly diverted from the war with Iran to control Kurdish insurgency in the north-east of Iraq. Saddam Hussain sought an accommodation with the Kurds, and a series of discussions began in December 1983, after a cease-fire had been agreed with Jalal Talabani, the leader of the Patriotic Union of Kurdistan (PUK). The talks did not, however, include the other main Kurdish group, the Kurdistan Democratic Party (KDP), led by Masoud Barzani. Negotiations collapsed in May 1984, and armed conflict resumed in Kurdistan in January 1985 between PUK guerrillas and government troops, with Kurdish and Iranian forces repeatedly collaborating in raids against Iraqi military and industrial targets. In February 1988 KDP and PUK guerrillas (assisted by Iranian forces) made inroads into government-controlled territory in Iraqi Kurdistan. In March the Iraqi Government retaliated by using chemical weapons against the Kurdish town of Halabja, killing up to 5,000 people and wounding about 10,000. In May the KDP and the PUK announced the formation of a coalition of six organizations to continue the struggle for Kurdish self-determination and to co-operate militarily with Iran. The cease-fire in the Iran–Iraq War in August allowed Iraq to launch a new offensive to overrun guerrilla bases near the borders with Iran and Turkey, again allegedly employing chemical weapons. Kurdish civilians and fighters fled across the borders, and by September there were reported to be more than 200,000 Kurdish refugees in Iran and Turkey. In that month, with the army effectively in control of the border with Turkey, the Iraqi Government offered a full amnesty to all Iraqi Kurds inside and outside the country, excluding only Jalal Talabani. By October 1989 it had also created a 30-km uninhabited 'security zone' along the whole of Iraq's border with Iran and Turkey by evacuating inhabitants of the Kurdish Autonomous Region to the interior of Iraq, prompting the PUK to announce a nationwide urban guerrilla campaign against the Government. In September elections had proceeded to the legislative council of the Kurdish Autonomous Region.

The 1990–91 Gulf War

In mid-1990 the Iraqi Government criticized countries (principally Kuwait and the United Arab Emirates—UAE) that had persistently produced petroleum in excess of the quotas imposed by the Organization of the Petroleum Exporting Countries (OPEC, see p. 408). Iraq also accused Kuwait of violating the Iraqi border in order to secure petroleum resources, and demanded that Kuwait waive repayments of Iraq's vast debt to the emirate, incurred during the Iran–Iraq War. Direct negotiations between Iraq and Kuwait, with the aim of resolving their disputes over territory and Iraq's war debt, failed, and on 2 August Iraqi forces invaded Kuwait, taking control of the country and establishing a provisional 'free government'. The UN Security Council unanimously adopted, on the day of the invasion, Resolution 660, demanding the immediate and unconditional withdrawal of Iraqi forces from Kuwait. Subsequent resolutions imposed mandatory economic sanctions against Iraq and occupied Kuwait (No. 661), and declared Iraq's annexation of Kuwait null and void (No. 662). At a meeting of the League of Arab States (the Arab League, see p. 364) on 3 August, 14 of the 21 members condemned the invasion and demanded an unconditional withdrawal by Iraq; after Iraq announced its formal annexation of Kuwait on 8 August, 12 member states voted to send an Arab deterrent force to the region of the Persian (Arabian) Gulf. On 7 August the US Government dispatched troops and aircraft to Saudi Arabia, at the request of King Fahd, in order to secure the country's border with Kuwait against a possible Iraqi attack; other countries quickly lent their support to what was designated 'Operation Desert Shield', and a multinational force was formed to defend Saudi Arabia.

In response to Iraq's continued refusal to withdraw its forces from Kuwait, in November 1990 the UN Security Council adopted Resolution 678, authorizing member states to use 'all necessary means' to enforce an Iraqi withdrawal if all Iraqi forces had not left by 15 January 1991. 'Operation Desert Storm'—in effect, war with Iraq—began on the night of 16–17 January, with air attacks on Baghdad by the multinational force, and by the end of January the allied force had achieved air supremacy. Although Iraq managed to launch Scud missiles against Saudi Arabia and Israel, the latter's refusal to retaliate was the result of considerable diplomatic pressure aimed at ensuring Arab unity in the coalition. In February Iraq formally severed diplomatic relations with Egypt, France, Italy, Saudi Arabia, Syria, the United Kingdom and the USA. During the night of 23–24 February the multinational force began a ground offensive for the liberation of Kuwait: Iraqi troops were quickly defeated and surrendered in large numbers. A cease-fire was declared by the US Government on 28 February. Iraq agreed to renounce its claim to Kuwait, to release prisoners of war and to comply with all pertinent UN Security Council resolutions. Resolution 687, adopted in April, provided for the establishment of a commission to demarcate the border between Iraq and Kuwait. The resolution also linked the removal of sanctions imposed on Iraq following its invasion of Kuwait to the elimination of non-conventional weaponry, to be certified by a UN Special Commission (UNSCOM), and required that Iraq accept proposals for the establishment of a war reparation fund to be derived from Iraqi petroleum reserves. Later that month the UN Security Council approved Resolution 689, which established a demilitarized zone between the two countries, to be monitored by the UN Iraq-Kuwait Observation Mission (UNIKOM).

Within Iraq, the war was followed by domestic unrest: in March 1991 rebel forces, including Shi'ite Muslims and disaffected soldiers, were reported to have taken control of Basra and other southern cities, although the rebellion was soon crushed by troops loyal to Saddam Hussain. In the north, Kurdish separatists overran a large area of Kurdistan. However, lacking military support from the multinational force, the Kurdish guerrillas were unable to resist the onslaught of the Iraqi armed forces, which were redeployed northwards as soon as they had crushed the uprising in southern Iraq, and an estimated 1m.–2m. Kurds fled across the northern mountains into Turkey and Iran. UN Security Council Resolution 688, adopted in April 1991, condemned the repression of Iraqi civilians and provided for the establishment of an international repatriation and relief effort—co-ordinated by a multinational task force, designated 'Operation Provide Comfort', and based in south-eastern Turkey to provide relief to displaced persons and to secure designated 'safe havens' on Iraqi territory north of latitude 36°N. In support of Resolution 688, a corresponding air exclusion zone was established by the USA, with the support of France and the United Kingdom.

A second air exclusion zone, south of latitude 32°N, was established by France, Russia, the United Kingdom and the USA in August 1992, with the aim of protecting the southern Iraqi Shi'ite communities, including the semi-nomadic Ma'dan (Marsh Arabs). In July 1993 Iraqi armed forces were reported to have renewed the Government's offensive against the inhabitants of the marshlands. In May 1996 government forces launched a major offensive against the Shi'a opposition and tribes in Basra governorate, which led to armed clashes between Iraqi security forces and the Shi'a opposition throughout the southern regions. SCIRI claimed in April 1998 that a renewed offensive against the Shi'a in southern Iraq had resulted in the execution of some 60 people during March.

Conflict in the Kurdish Autonomous Region

Meanwhile, in April 1991 the PUK leader, Jalal Talabani, announced that President Saddam Hussain had agreed in principle to implement the provisions of a 15-point peace plan concluded by Kurdish leaders and the Iraqi Government in 1970. However, negotiations subsequently became deadlocked over the Kurdish demand for the inclusion of Kirkuk in the Kurdish Autonomous Region. Therefore, in October the Iraqi Government withdrew all services from the region, effectively subjecting the Kurds to an economic blockade. The various Kurdish factions proceeded to organize elections, in May 1992, to a 105-member Iraqi Kurdistan National Assembly, and for a paramount Kurdish leader. The outcome of voting, in which virtually the entire electorate (of some 1.1m.) participated, was that the KDP and the PUK were entitled to an almost equal number of seats in the new assembly. None of the smaller Kurdish parties achieved representation, and the KDP and the PUK subsequently agreed to share equally the seats. The election for an overall Kurdish leader was deemed inconclusive, with Masoud Barzani, the leader of the KDP, receiving 47.5% of the votes cast, and Jalal Talabani 44.9%.

In December 1993 armed conflict broke out between militants of the PUK and the Islamic League of Kurdistan (or Islamic Movement of Iraqi Kurdistan—IMIK). Following mediation by the Iraqi National Congress (INC—a broad coalition of largely foreign-based opposition groups), the two parties signed a peace agreement in February 1994. However, more serious armed conflict between partisans of the PUK and the KDP led, in May, to the division of the northern Kurdish-controlled enclave into two zones. In June 1995 the IMIK withdrew from the INC, and in July there was renewed fighting between PUK and KDP forces, as a result of which scheduled elections to the Iraqi Kurdistan National Assembly were postponed. Peace negotiations under US auspices began in Dublin, Ireland, in August but collapsed in the following month. Subsequent discussions in Tehran in October led to the signing of an agreement by the KDP and the PUK to hold elections to the Iraqi Kurdistan National Assembly in May 1996.

In early 1996 Talabani offered to participate in peace negotiations with the KDP and new elections to the Iraqi Kurdistan National Assembly. However, hostilities escalated in August, as the PUK contested the KDP's monopoly of duties levied on Turkish traders. At the end of the month Iraqi military support for the KDP in the recapture of the PUK-held towns of Irbil (Arbil) and Sulaimaniya in the Kurdish area of northern Iraq provoked a new international crisis. In September the USA unilaterally launched retaliatory 'limited' air-strikes on air defence and communications targets in southern Iraq, and extended the southern air exclusion zone from latitude 32°N to latitude 33°N (thereby incorporating some southern suburbs of Baghdad). Turkey, which had refused to allow the use of its air bases for the US operation, deployed some 20,000 troops to reinforce its border with Iraq. Also in September the KDP gained control of all three Kurdish provinces. The Iraqi Government subsequently announced the restoration of Iraqi sovereignty over Kurdistan, and offered an amnesty to its Kurdish opponents. In late September the KDP formed a coalition administration comprising, among others, the IMIK, the Kurdistan Communist Party and representatives of the northern Assyrian and Turkoman communities. In October PUK fighters were reported to have recaptured much of the territory that they had ceded to the KDP, having regained control of Sulaimaniya and Halabja. Concern that Iran's alleged involvement in the conflict would provoke direct Iraqi intervention in the north prompted renewed diplomatic efforts on the part of the USA and Turkey, and US-sponsored peace talks in Ankara, Turkey, in late October resulted in a truce agreement. Following the termination of Operation Provide Comfort, a new air surveillance programme—'Northern Watch', based in south-eastern Turkey and conducted by British, Turkish and US forces—began in January 1997.

In March 1997 the KDP withdrew from the US-sponsored peace negotiations, and in May as many as 50,000 Turkish troops entered northern Iraq, where, apparently in co-operation with the KDP, they launched a major offensive against bases maintained in northern Iraq by the Kurdistan Workers' Party (Partiya Karkeren Kurdistan—PKK). As Turkey began to withdraw its armed forces in October, the PUK launched a massive military offensive against the KDP, targeting several strategic points along the 1996 cease-fire line. The KDP (which subsequently claimed to have regained most of the territory recently lost to the PUK) alleged that the assault had been co-ordinated by Iran and supported by the PKK. By mid-1998 a fragile cease-fire between the PUK and the KDP appeared to be enduring, and the two organizations agreed to exchange prisoners. In September a formal peace agreement was signed in Washington, DC, USA, which, *inter alia*, provided for: Kurdish legislative elections in 1999 (although these did not take place); a unified regional administration; the sharing of local revenues; and an end to hostilities. A new Kurdish coalition government was appointed by the Iraqi Kurdistan National Assembly in December 1999.

Political developments after the Gulf War

Since Iraq's defeat by the US-led coalition forces in 1991, Saddam Hussain had strengthened his control over the country by placing family members and close supporters in the most important government positions. In September Saddam Hussain was re-elected Secretary-General of the Baath Party's powerful Regional Command at its 10th Congress, and in May 1994 he assumed the post of Prime Minister. Unsuccessful coups reportedly took place in January and March 1995; the latter was instigated by the former head of Iraqi military intelligence and supported by Kurdish insurgents in the north and Shi'ite rebels in the south. In an apparent attempt to re-establish domestic and international recognition of Saddam Hussain's mandate, in September the RCC approved an interim amendment of the Constitution whereby the elected Chairman of the RCC would automatically assume the presidency of the Republic, subject to approval by the National Assembly and endorsement by national plebiscite. Saddam Hussain's candidature was duly approved by the Assembly, and endorsed by 99.96% of the votes cast at a referendum held on 15 October.

The first elections to the Iraqi National Assembly since 1989 took place in March 1996, when 689 candidates (all of whom had received the prior approval of a government selection committee) contested 220 of the Assembly's 250 seats: the remaining 30 seats were reserved for representatives of the Autonomous Regions of Arbil, D'hok and Sulaimaniya, and were filled by presidential decree. The elections were denounced by the INC, based in London, United Kingdom, and by other groups opposed to the Government.

Following reports in late 1997 that Saddam Hussain had ordered the execution of a number of senior military officers, Baath Party members and prisoners, internal unrest continued during 1998. The Special Rapporteur of the UN Commission on Human Rights, Max van der Stoel, denounced the assassination of two senior Shi'a religious leaders, Ayatollah Murtada al-Burujirdi and Grand Ayatollah Mirza Ali al-Gharawi, and expressed fears that the murders were part of a systematic attack on the independent leadership of Iraq's Shi'a community. In February 1999 the killing of Iraq's Shi'a leader, Grand Ayatollah Muhammad Sadiq al-Sadr, provoked demonstrations in Baghdad and other cities. Despite claims by the INC that the unrest marked the beginning of an uprising against the Iraqi regime, it was reported that the demonstrations had been brutally suppressed by units of the Sunni-dominated Iraqi Special Republican Guard.

In October 1998 the US Congress had approved the Iraq Liberation Act, permitting the US President to provide up to US $97m. in military assistance to Iraqi opposition groups in exile. In April 1999 11 opposition groups gathered in London, where they undertook to reform the moribund INC and to prepare a plan of campaign against Saddam Hussain's regime, while several INC leaders relocated to the USA, with a view to lobbying US support for the Iraqi opposition movement.

Elections took place on 27 March 2000 for 220 seats in the National Assembly. Official results stated that 165 seats had been won by members of the Baath Party, and the remaining 55 elective seats by independent candidates; a further 30 independents were nominated by the Government to fill the seats reserved for representatives of the Kurdish areas of the north, where the Iraqi authorities stated it was impossible to organize elections since the region remained 'occupied' by the USA. Saddam Hussain's elder son, Uday, was elected to the legislature for the first time. In May 2001 Saddam Hussain was re-elected Secretary-General of the Baath Party Regional Command at the organization's 12th Congress, while speculation that the Iraqi leader's younger son, Qusay, was being prepared as his successor was further fuelled by his election to the party Command and by his subsequent appointment as a deputy commander of the party's military section.

In August 2002 the National Assembly unanimously endorsed the nomination of President Saddam Hussain to face a national referendum on his remaining in office for a further seven-year term. The referendum was duly held on 15 October, at which the President was officially reported to have received 100% of the votes. A general amnesty for prisoners held in Iraqi gaols was subsequently announced by the authorities; however, opposition groups maintained that there were still thousands of political prisoners in Iraq. This proved to be the last major internal political development under the Baath regime prior to the US-led coalition's military campaign of early 2003, which led to the removal of Saddam Hussain's Government, and which was the de facto culmination of more than a decade of international diplomatic manoeuvring on the issues of 'oil-for-food' and banned weapons programmes.

The UN's sanctions regime and international monitoring of Iraq's weapons programme

Issues of the maintenance of sanctions originally imposed under UN Security Council Resolution 661 and of Iraqi non-compliance with its obligations under Resolution 687 with regard to its weapons capabilities remained inextricably linked in the decade following the Gulf conflict. Resolution 692, adopted in May 1991, provided for the establishment of the UN Compensation Commission (UNCC) for victims of Iraqi aggression (both governments and individuals), to be financed by a levy (subsequently fixed at 30%) on Iraqi petroleum revenues. In August the Security Council adopted Resolution 706 (subsequently approved in Resolution 712 in September), proposing that Iraq should be allowed to sell petroleum worth up to US $1,600m. over a six-month period, the revenue from which would be controlled by the UN. Part of the sum thus realized was to be made available to Iraq for the purchase of food, medicines and supplies for essential civilian needs. Iraq rejected the terms proposed by the UN for the resumption of petroleum exports, and in February 1992 withdrew from further negotiations, but in October Resolution 778 permitted the confiscation of oil-related Iraqi assets to the value of up to $500m.

UN Security Council Resolution 707, adopted in August 1991, condemned Iraq's failure to comply with UN weapons inspectors, and demanded that Iraq: disclose details of all non-conventional weaponry; allow members of UNSCOM and of the International Atomic Energy Agency (IAEA) unrestricted access to necessary areas and records; and halt all nuclear activities. Resolution 715, adopted in October, established the terms under which UNSCOM was to inspect Iraq's weapons capabilities. In February 1994 it was reported that Iraq had agreed to co-operate with UN weapons inspectors under Resolution 715. Thereafter, the Iraqi Government engaged in a campaign of diplomacy to obtain the removal of economic sanctions, and in July the first signs emerged of a division within the Security Council regarding their continuation. Russia, France and the People's Republic of China favoured acknowledging Iraq's increased co-operation with UN agencies, but were unable to obtain the agreement of the other permanent members of the Council—the USA and the United Kingdom. Following a stand-off between Iraq and the US and British military, prompted by the movement of Iraqi forces near the border with Kuwait, the Iraqi National Assembly voted in November to recognize Kuwait within the border defined by the UN in April 1992.

Economic sanctions imposed on Iraq were renewed on a 60-day basis in 1995 (and thereafter). In April the Iraqi Government rejected as a violation of its sovereignty a revised UN proposal (contained in Security Council Resolution 986) for the partial resumption of exports of Iraqi petroleum to generate funds for humanitarian supplies under what was designated an 'oil-for-food' programme. However, in May 1996 Iraq accepted the UN's terms governing a resumption of crude petroleum sales. The memorandum of understanding (MOU) signed by the two sides permitted Iraq to sell some 700,000 barrels per day (b/d) of petroleum over a period of six months, after which the UN would review the situation. Of every US $1,000m. realized through the sales, $300m. would be paid into the UN reparations fund; $30m.–$50m. would contribute to the costs of UN operations in Iraq; and $130m.–$150m. would go towards funding UN humanitarian operations in Iraq's Kurdish governorates. Remaining revenues would be used for the purchase and distribution, under close UN supervision, of humanitarian goods in Iraq. Iraqi officials heralded the MOU as the beginning of the dismantling of the sanctions regime, while the UN emphasized that the embargo on sales of Iraqi petroleum would not be fully revoked until all the country's weapons of mass destruction had been accounted for and destroyed.

In October 1996 UNSCOM rejected Iraq's 'full, final and complete disclosures on its weapons programmes'. In October 1997 the initial report of the new head of UNSCOM, Richard Butler, to the UN Security Council asserted that, although some progress had been made by weapons inspectors in inspecting Iraqi missiles, Iraq had failed to produce a credible account of its biological, chemical and nuclear warfare programmes and was continuing to hinder UNSCOM's work. In November the Security Council unanimously adopted a resolution (No. 1137) that imposed a travel ban on Iraqi officials deemed to be responsible for obstructing UNSCOM inspectors. The confrontation over weapons inspections deepened in January 1998, when Iraq prohibited inspections by an UNSCOM team led by a former US marine officer, Scott Ritter, claiming that Ritter was spying for the US Central Intelligence Agency. The UN Security Council issued a statement deploring Iraq's failure to provide UNSCOM with 'full, unconditional and immediate access to all sites'.

However, the Security Council was essentially divided on the issue of weapons inspections: the USA, supported by the United Kingdom, indicated that it was prepared to respond militarily to Iraq's continued non-co-operation, while China, France and Russia opposed the use of force. Moreover, Kuwait was the only country in the region to announce its approval of force if diplomatic efforts should fail; Saudi Arabia and Bahrain refused to authorize military attacks from their territories, while Egypt and Syria notably signalled their disapproval of such a response. In February 1998 the five permanent members of the UN Security Council approved a compromise formula whereby a group of diplomats, specially appointed by the UN Secretary-General, Kofi Annan, in consultation with experts from UNSCOM and the IAEA, would be allowed unconditional and unrestricted access to the eight so-called presidential sites. The compromise was accepted by Iraq, thus averting the immediate threat of military action. In March the UN Security Council unanimously approved a resolution (No. 1154) endorsing the MOU and warning of 'extreme consequences' should Iraq renege on the agreement. Inspection teams returned to Iraq shortly afterwards, and members of the special group began visiting the presidential sites later in the month. In April the head of UNSCOM concluded that there had been no progress in the disarmament verification process since October 1997, and that the destruction of Iraq's chemical and biological weapons was incomplete. The Security Council responded to Butler's report by voting not to review the sanctions in force against Iraq.

During talks between Butler and Iraqi Deputy Prime Minister Tareq Aziz in Baghdad in June 1990, significant progress was reportedly made on plans for the verification of Iraqi disarmament and the eventual removal of sanctions. However, later in the month the UNSCOM head was said to have informed the UN Security Council that US military tests on weaponry dismantled as part of the inspection process had shown that Iraq had loaded missile warheads with a chemical weapon component prior to the Gulf conflict. In August negotiations between Butler and Aziz collapsed, Iraq suspended arms inspections, and Saddam Hussain announced new terms and conditions for their resumption, including the establishment of a new executive bureau to supervise UNSCOM's operations. In September the Security Council unanimously adopted a resolution (No. 1194) condemning Iraq's action of the previous month, demanding that Iraq co-operate fully with UNSCOM and suspending for an indefinite period the review of the sanctions regime. This prompted the Iraqi Government to halt all co-operation with UNSCOM indefinitely. Reporting to the Security Council in October, Butler asserted that, while Iraq was close to fulfilling its obligations with regard to missiles and chemical weapons programmes, UNSCOM remained concerned about the country's capacity for biological warfare. In November the Security Council unanimously adopted a British-drafted resolution (No. 1205) demanding that Iraq immediately and unconditionally resume co-operation with UNSCOM. US and British military enforcements were again dispatched to the Gulf region to prepare for possible air-strikes against Iraqi targets. Egypt, Saudi Arabia and Syria, while opposing the threat of force, urged Iraq to resume co-operation. Later in November Iraq declared that UNSCOM would be permitted unconditionally to resume the weapons inspection programme, and inspectors subsequently returned to Iraq.

However, Iraq's relations with UNSCOM deteriorated once again in early December 1998, after a weapons inspection team conducting a new series of what were termed 'surprise' or 'challenge' inspections was denied access to the Baath Party headquarters in Baghdad. On the night of 16–17 December, following the withdrawal from Iraq of UNSCOM and IAEA personnel, the USA and the United Kingdom commenced a campaign of air-strikes against Iraqi targets; 'Operation Desert Fox' was terminated on 20 December, with US and British forces claiming to have caused significant damage to Iraqi military installations. France, Russia and China contended that the military action had been undertaken without UN Security Council authorization; however, the USA and the United Kingdom maintained that Resolution 1154, adopted in March, provided sufficient legitimacy. In January 1999 ground-launched Iraqi attacks on US aircraft engaged in policing the air exclusion zone over southern Iraq apparently indicated that Iraq was pursuing a more confrontational policy of refusing to recognize the exclusion zone.

The US Administration of President George W. Bush, which assumed office in January 2001, swiftly adopted an uncompromising stance with regard to Iraq. In February US and British fighter aircraft launched their first attack since Operation Desert Fox on air defence targets near Baghdad, in what Bush described as a 'routine mission' to enforce the northern and southern air exclusion zones. Iraq protested that the air-strikes had targeted residential areas of Baghdad, while Western media reports suggested that three people had been killed in the attacks. US and British military aircraft launched air-strikes against Iraqi air defence installations in both exclusion zones during late 2001 and in September 2002, in response to what they claimed were continuing Iraqi attacks on allied aircraft patrolling the zones; Iraqi officials claimed that a number of civilians had died in the raids.

Meanwhile, the campaign of air-strikes conducted against Iraqi targets in December 1998 was regarded as marking the collapse of UNSCOM's mission. Later that month the Security Council adopted a resolution (No. 1284) providing for the establishment of a UN Monitoring, Verification and Inspection Commission (UNMOVIC) as a successor body to UNSCOM. The resolution also provided for the suspension of the economic sanctions in force against Iraq for renewable 120-day periods (on the condition that Iraq co-operated fully with the new weapons inspectorate and the IAEA throughout such periods), and effectively removed restrictions on the maximum amount of petroleum that Iraq was permitted to sell under the oil-for-food programme. However, it was not approved unanimously, with China, France and Russia, together with Malaysia (a non-permanent member), abstaining. Iraq immediately responded that it would not co-operate with UNMOVIC. In January 2000 the Security Council endorsed the appointment of Hans Blix, a former Director-General of the IAEA, as head of UNMOVIC. Meanwhile, IAEA personnel undertook the first routine inspection of Iraqi facilities since their withdrawal in December 1998. In his first report to the UN Security Council in March 2000, Blix emphasized that, should Iraq permit the return of weapons inspectors, UNMOVIC would resume 'challenge' inspections of Iraqi sites. In the same month Tareq Aziz decisively rejected the terms of Resolution 1284. In March 2001 it was reported that a recent UNMOVIC assessment had concluded that Iraq might still have the ability to build and use biological and chemical weapons, and might possess stocks of mustard gas, biological weapons and anthrax, as well as having the capability to deliver Scud missiles.

The 'oil-for-food' programme

Exports of Iraqi crude petroleum, under the terms of Resolution 986, had recommenced in December 1996, and continued until immediately prior to the US-led military intervention to remove the regime of Saddam Hussain in March 2003 (see below). The first supplies of food purchased with the revenues from these exports arrived in Iraq in March 1997. In February 1998 the UN Security Council raised the maximum permitted revenue from exports of petroleum to US $5,200m. in the six months to the end of July, of which Iraq would be permitted to spend some $3,550m. on humanitarian goods. The remainder would be used to finance reparations and UN operations. Following concerns about the deterioration of its oil production facilities, in June the Security Council approved a resolution allowing Iraq to import essential spare parts to the value of $300m. for the oil sector. In November 1999 Iraq rejected a proposal by the Security Council that the oil-for-food programme should be extended for a further two weeks, pending the revision of the programme's terms of reference. Iraq then temporarily suspended its exports of oil, causing world prices to rise to their highest levels since 1990. Nevertheless, the Security Council continued to vote in favour of extending the oil-for-food programme, and under the ninth phase of the programme from December 2000 Iraq was allocated a maximum of $525m. for the local costs of maintaining the oil industry. In September 2000 the UN Security Council approved the payment to Kuwait of US $15,900m. in compensation for lost production and sales of petroleum as a result of the 1990–91 occupation. However, it was agreed to reduce the levy on Iraq's petroleum revenues destined for reparations under the oil-for-food programme from 30% to 25%.

In early 2001 the Bush Administration emphasized its commitment to ensuring the maintenance of the sanctions regime pending the full implementation of Resolution 1284. The new US Secretary of State, Colin Powell, swiftly undertook to secure implementation of a revised sanctions regime, with a view to resolving humanitarian concerns, by means of allowing the direct sale or supply to Iraq of most consumer goods without prior UN approval, while at the same time maintaining strict controls on the supply to Iraq of goods with potential military applications. In November, shortly before the end of the 10th phase of the oil-for-food programme, the Minister of Foreign Affairs, Naji Sabri, emphasized that Iraq would end its participation in the scheme if revisions to the sanctions regime were adopted; he also reiterated that weapons inspectors would not be permitted to return to Iraq. At the end of November the UN Security Council unanimously approved Resolution 1382—essentially a compromise whereby Russia agreed to adopt an annexed list of embargoed items with military and civilian purposes before the expiry of the new (11th) phase, while the USA consented to review Resolution 1284. The Security Council continued to extend the oil-for-food programme at regular six-monthly intervals. In May 2002 the Security Council implemented a mechanism to accelerate the processing of contracts not subject to inclusion on the Goods Review List, while Resolution 1454, approved in December, expanded the list of goods subject to review to include certain items with a potential military use. In mid-March 2003, immediately prior to the start of the US-led military campaign in Iraq (see below), the UN announced a temporary suspension of the oil-for-food programme. However, amid a sharp deterioration in the living conditions of Iraqi citizens following the outbreak of hostilities, at the end of March the UN Security Council adopted Resolution 1472, granting Secretary-General Kofi Annan the authority to implement existing contracts and to facilitate the delivery of aid for an initial 45-day period, which was subsequently extended until the beginning of June. On 22 May the UN Security Council passed Resolution 1483, which removed sanctions against Iraq; the oil-for-food programme was formally discontinued on 21 November.

Negotiations with UNMOVIC and the increasing threat of military intervention

After the defeat of the Taliban regime in Afghanistan (q.v.) in late 2001, there was considerable speculation that the USA would seek 'regime change' in Iraq as part of its declared 'war on terror'. In response to demands by George W. Bush that Iraq readmit UN inspectors to prove that it was not developing weapons of mass destruction, or otherwise be 'held accountable', the Iraqi authorities reiterated that UN sanctions should first be ended and the air exclusion zones revoked. Tensions were heightened in January 2002 when, in his State of the Union address, President Bush assessed Iraq as forming what he termed an 'axis of evil' (with Iran and the Democratic People's Republic of Korea) seeking to develop weapons of mass destruction, specifically accusing Iraq of plotting to develop anthrax, nerve gas and nuclear weapons.

Following a one-year hiatus in talks between Iraq and the UN, in March 2002 Annan met with Naji Sabri in New York in March (with the head of UNMOVIC, Hans Blix, also in attendance), for talks focusing on the implementation of pertinent Security Council resolutions adopted since 1990, including the return to Iraq of weapons inspectors. In August the UN Security Council declined an offer by the Iraqi Government to resume negotiations on the return of weapons inspectors, stating that Iraq should not impose any preconditions on the resumption of inspections. At the same time the USA continued to give clear signals that it intended to intervene to bring about 'regime change' in Iraq, pursuing attempts to secure a UN resolution that would authorize military action, while indicating that the USA would be prepared to act unilaterally. Both US and British officials greeted with scepticism Iraq's declaration, made in mid-September, of its willingness to readmit weapons inspectors 'without conditions'. In late September the British Government published a dossier outlining its case against the regime of Saddam Hussain and the perceived threat posed by Iraq's 'illicit weapons programmes' to the security of both the West and the Middle East. Shortly afterwards the US Secretary of Defense, Donald Rumsfeld, reiterated US claims that Iraq had provided assistance in the training of militants from the al-Qa'ida network. In early October Blix stated that Iraq had agreed to allow inspectors 'unconditional and unrestricted access' to all relevant sites, but that no new agreement had been reached concerning access to the presidential palaces. The USA and the United Kingdom were keen for the Security Council to approve a new resolution that would strengthen the mandate under which the UN inspectors were to operate. China, France and Russia all maintained that—in the event of Iraq's failure to comply with the terms of a future resolution concerning Iraqi disarmament—a second UN resolution should be adopted prior to any military action being taken against the Iraqi regime.

In mid-October 2002 President Bush signed a resolution approved by the US Congress authorizing the use of force, if necessary unilaterally, to disarm Saddam Hussain's regime. On 8 November, after a compromise had been reached between the five permanent members, the UN Security Council unanimously adopted Resolution 1441, which demanded, *inter alia*, that Iraq permit weapons inspectors from UNMOVIC and the IAEA unrestricted access to sites suspected of holding illegal weapons (including the presidential palaces) and required the Iraqi leadership to make a full declaration of its chemical, biological, nuclear and ballistic weapons, as well as related materials used in civilian industries, within 30 days. The resolution warned that this represented a 'final opportunity' for Baghdad to comply with its disarmament obligations under previous UN resolutions, affirming that Iraq would face 'serious consequences' in the event of non-compliance with the UN inspectors or of any 'false statements and omissions' in its weapons declaration. Despite an initial rejection of Resolution 1441 by the Iraqi National Assembly on 12 November, on the following day the RCC announced its formal and unconditional acceptance of the terms of the resolution. Iraqi officials, however, repeatedly stated that they did not possess any weapons of mass destruction. Personnel from UNSCOM and the IAEA resumed weapons inspections in Iraq in late November.

Iraq presented UNMOVIC officials with a 12,000-page declaration of its weapons programmes in early December 2002. In mid-December, however, the USA stated that Iraq was in 'material breach' of UN Resolution 1441 since it had failed to give a complete account of its weapons capabilities, citing in particular Iraq's failure to account for stocks of biological weapons such as anthrax. In January 2003 UNMOVIC personnel to the south of Baghdad reported the discovery of several empty chemical warheads, which had reportedly not been included in Iraq's recent declaration. Meanwhile, Iraqi officials dismissed suggestions by some Arab states (including Saudi Arabia and Egypt) that Saddam Hussain either stand down or go into exile. At an emergency summit meeting of the Arab League in Cairo, Egypt, at the beginning of March, the UAE presented a plan for the Iraqi President to stand down and for the Arab League and UN to assume temporary control of Iraq.

During January 2003 the USA and the United Kingdom ordered a massive deployment of troops to the Gulf region, while asserting that a conflict was not inevitable if Iraq complied with the UN's disarmament terms. Both the French and German Governments, meanwhile, were vociferous in their opposition to military action and advocated an extension of the UN inspectors' mandate. In late January the ministers responsible for foreign affairs of Turkey, Syria, Iran, Jordan, Egypt and Saudi Arabia, meeting in İstanbul, Turkey, issued a joint communiqué urging Iraq to co-operate fully with UN inspectors in order to avoid a new conflict in the region. On 27 January, 60 days after the resumption of UN weapons inspections in Iraq (as stipulated under Resolution 1441), Blix and the Director-General of the IAEA, Muhammad el-Baradei, briefed the UN Security Council on the progress of inspections. El-Baradei stated that IAEA inspectors had found no evidence that Iraq had restarted its nuclear weapons programme, but requested more time for the organization to complete its research. Blix, for his part, claimed that there was no evidence that Iraq had destroyed known stocks of illegal chemical and long-range ballistic weapons, and announced that he was sceptical about Baghdad's willingness to disarm. Following the briefing, the British Secretary of State for Foreign and Commonwealth Affairs, Jack Straw, declared Iraq to be in 'material breach' of Resolution 1441.

As the likelihood of a US-led military response to the crisis increased, at the end of January 2003 eight European countries (including the United Kingdom, Italy and Spain) signed a joint statement expressing support for the USA's stance with regard to Iraq. In February the British Prime Minister, Tony Blair, accelerated his efforts to secure a second UN Security Council resolution authorizing a US-led campaign in Iraq should inspectors from UNMOVIC continue to report Baghdad's non-compliance. President Bush asserted that, although he favoured the adoption of a second resolution, Resolution 1441 had given the USA the authority to disarm Iraq, if necessary by military means. The US Secretary of State, Colin Powell, had, on 5 February, presented to the Security Council what the USA claimed to be overwhelming evidence of Iraq's possession of weapons of mass destruction, its attempts to conceal such weapons from the UN inspectorate and its links with international terrorist groups, including al-Qa'ida. Despite signs of progress being reported by Hans Blix in his report on UNMOVIC's inspections to the Security Council on 14 February—Iraqi officials had submitted new documents relating to banned materials, had announced an easing of restrictions governing the questioning by UN inspectors of Iraqi scientists, and had agreed to allow aerial reconnaissance flights over Iraq—the UNMOVIC chief stated that the inspections should continue, in order to determine whether Iraq did possess undeclared weapons of mass destruction.

On 24 February 2003 the USA, the United Kingdom and Spain presented a draft resolution to the UN Security Council effectively proposing a US-led military campaign against Saddam Hussain's regime, in response to Baghdad's failure to disarm peacefully. The resolution stated that a deadline of 17 March would be set, by which time Iraq should prove that it was disarming; however, no specific mention was made of consequent military action in the event of the deadline not being met, apparently in an effort by the US-led coalition to persuade France, Russia and China not to exercise their right of veto. Officials from France, Russia and Germany presented an alternative proposal involving an extended timetable of weapons inspections in order to avert a war. At the beginning of March Turkey's Grand National Assembly voted to allow US military aircraft to use Turkish airspace in the event of a campaign being waged against the Iraqi regime; however, the parliament rejected a plan for US forces to use Turkey's military bases, even for refuelling their aircraft. Shortly afterwards France and Russia pledged to veto a second UN resolution authorizing the use of force to disarm Saddam Hussain. On 12 March Tony Blair proposed six new conditions that Iraq must meet in order to prove its intention to disarm: this was seen as an attempt at a compromise that might encourage wavering countries in the Security Council to support an amended resolution. The British proposals came a day after President Bush had rejected a suggested 45-day postponement of any decision to go to war by six countries that had the power to influence the Security Council vote. On 15 March, in anticipation of a probable US-led invasion, Iraq's RCC issued a decree dividing the country into four military commands, under the overall leadership of Saddam Hussain. On 16 March a summit meeting was held in the Azores, Portugal, between Bush, Blair and the Spanish Prime Minister, José María Aznar. On the following day the USA, the United Kingdom and Spain withdrew their draft resolution from the UN, demonstrating that the resolution's co-sponsors had realized the unlikelihood of winning UN support for military action; they stated that they reserved the right to take their own action to ensure Iraqi disarmament. On the same day President Bush issued an ultimatum giving Saddam Hussain and his two sons 48 hours to leave Baghdad or face military action; the Iraqi National Assembly rejected the ultimatum.

The overthrow of Saddam Hussain

Shortly after the expiry of President Bush's 48-hour deadline, on 20 March 2003 US and British armed forces launched a 'broad and concerted campaign' (code-named 'Operation Iraqi Freedom') to oust the regime of Saddam Hussain. An initial series of air-strikes against sites in the suburbs of Baghdad, apparently aimed at leading members of the Iraqi regime, failed to achieve their principal targets. Meanwhile, US-led coalition forces crossed into Iraq from Kuwait and began a steady advance towards the capital. At the same time a concerted campaign of massive air-strikes was launched against the key symbols of the Iraqi regime in and around Baghdad, including selected military bases, communications sites, government buildings and broadcasting headquarters. US and British forces adopted a simultaneous campaign of distributing leaflets and broadcasting radio messages, in an effort to persuade Iraqi citizens to abandon their support for the Baath regime: their declared intention was that Operation Iraqi Freedom would precipitate the disintegration of the regime 'from within'. British troops were principally engaged in securing towns in southern Iraq, including Iraq's second city of Basra, after the US-led coalition had seized control of the key southern port of Umm Qasr and the Al-Faw Peninsula. It was their intention that the Shi'a Muslim population of Basra would quickly initiate an uprising against the regime of Saddam Hussain, as had occurred following the Gulf War in 1991. Although fighting between US-led troops and Iraqi armed forces was often intense, resistance from the Iraqi army and from a number of *fedayeen* (martyrs) and volunteers from other Arab countries was generally lighter than had been anticipated by the allies. Moreover, there were widespread reports of Iraqi soldiers surrendering to the advancing forces. Shortly after the commencement of Operation Iraqi Freedom, in late March 2003 US forces had opened a second front in the Kurdish-controlled regions of northern Iraq, where Kurdish forces joined US troops in targeting bases of Ansar al-Islam, a militant Islamist group suspected of having links with al-Qa'ida.

At an emergency summit meeting of Arab League states in Cairo on 24 March 2003, representatives of the 17 member states in attendance (except Kuwait) issued a resolution condemning the US-led invasion of Iraq and demanding the withdrawal of all foreign forces from Iraqi territory. By 7 April US armed forces had entered central Baghdad, including its presidential palaces. The expected strong resistance from Saddam Hussain's élite Republican Guard did not materialize, and the disintegration of the Baath regime appeared to be complete on 9 April when crowds of Iraqis staged street demonstrations denouncing Saddam Hussain and destroying images and statues of the Iraqi President. Kurdish *peshmerga* fighters gained control of the northern town of Kirkuk on 10 April, while the town of Mosul was seized by Kurdish and US forces on the following day. Also on 11 April the USA issued a 'most wanted' list of 55 members of the deposed regime whom it sought to arrest: one of the most high-profile of these, former Deputy Prime Minister Tareq Aziz, surrendered to US forces two weeks later. The seizure by US troops of Saddam Hussain's birthplace and power base, Tikrit (to the north of Baghdad), on 14 April was widely viewed as the last strategic battle of the US-led campaign to remove the Baathist regime. On 1 May President Bush officially declared an end to 'major combat operations' in Iraq.

The US-led coalition initially acted swiftly to fill the political and administrative vacuum that emerged in the aftermath of the removal of the former regime. On 15 April 2003 a US-sponsored meeting of various Iraqi opposition groups took place in Nasiriya in southern Iraq. However, while the participants produced a 13-point resolution detailing proposals for Iraq's future political development, emphasizing their desire for democratic, sovereign government, it became clear that in the interim period the practical day-to-day responsibilities of repairing, rebuilding and maintaining the material infrastructure of Iraq, as well as combating guerrilla supporters of the ousted regime and emerging 'resistance' groups, would fall to the US-led coalition. Retired US army general Jay Garner, Director of the USA's Office of Reconstruction and Humanitarian Assistance (ORHA), arrived in the country on 21 April to manage the restoration of basic services to the Iraqi population and to enforce law and order. However, after the ORHA was deemed to have failed in this task, it was subsequently replaced by the Coalition Provisional Authority (CPA), headed by US diplomat L. Paul Bremer, III. Bremer assumed his responsibilities on 12 May, his first act being to outlaw the Baath Party and related organizations, and to demobilize the Iraqi armed forces and security apparatus. The Ministries of Defence, of Information and of Military Affairs were all dissolved.

UN Security Council Resolution 1483, adopted on 22 May 2003, recognized the CPA as the legal occupying power in Iraq, and mandated it to establish a temporary Iraqi governing authority. On 13 July the inaugural meeting of the 25-member Iraqi Governing Council was held in Baghdad; members of the Governing Council were appointed by the CPA in direct proportion to the principal ethnic and religious groups in Iraq: 13 Shi'a Arabs, five Sunni Arabs, five Kurds, one Assyrian Christian and one Turkoman. They were mostly drawn from the main parties that had been in opposition to Saddam Hussain's regime, notably Ahmad Chalabi of the INC, Dr Ayad Allawi of the Iraqi National Accord (INA), Jalal Talabani of the PUK, Masoud Barzani of the KDP and Abd al-Aziz al-Hakim of SCIRI. The Governing Council had no executive powers, but could appoint ministers and diplomatic representatives, set a date for the holding of free elections, and formulate a new constitution. At the end of July the Governing Council adopted a system of rotating presidency, based on the EU model, in which nine members would share the presidency, each serving for one month beginning in September. Under this system, Ibrahim al-Ja'fari, previously a spokesman for the predominantly Shi'ite Islamic Dawa Party, was chosen as Iraq's first President of the post-Baathist era. In August the UN Security Council approved a resolution 'welcoming', but not formally recognizing, the establishment of the Iraqi Governing Council. On 1 September the Governing Council announced the formation of a 25-member interim Cabinet, appointed along the same ethnic and religious lines, which was to administer the country until the holding of legislative elections. Finally, on 15 November a timetable for the transition of power to an elected, sovereign government was published by the CPA and the Governing Council. The plan was threefold: these two authorities were to be dissolved and replaced by an Iraqi Transitional National Assembly by 30 June 2004; a constitutional convention was to take place by mid-2005, after which a popular referendum would be held on the new constitution; and, by the end of 2005, national elections were to be held to select a new Iraqi government. This process of democratic development was subject, however, to the extremely volatile security situation in Iraq since the declared end of major combat operations.

Increasing violence following the end of US-led combat operations

The *Fedayeen Saddam*, regarded as the most fanatical of the Baathist partisans, were blamed for many of the early attacks against the US-led coalition forces in the aftermath of the war. However, it soon became clear that the arrest or elimination of the main figures of the old regime was not diminishing the level of armed resistance to coalition forces. Moreover, the UN, diplomatic missions, Shi'ite clergy, members of the interim Cabinet and non-governmental organizations were also being targeted by militant groups. In early August 2003 the Jordanian embassy in Baghdad was severely damaged by a car bomb, which killed up to 19 people. The militant Islamist group Ansar al-Islam was initially held to be responsible. (In November 2007 a military court in Jordan sentenced to death a Jordanian national found to have plotted the embassy bombing on the orders of al-Qa'ida in Iraq.) The UN Special Representative for Iraq, Sergio Vieira de Mello, and some 20 others were killed in late August 2003, when a truck laden with explosives was detonated in front of the UN compound in Baghdad. A previously unknown Islamist group, the Armed Vanguards of the Second Muhammad Army, claimed responsibility for the explosion, which resulted in most of the UN's foreign personnel being withdrawn from Iraq. On 29 August a car bomb exploded in the holy city of Najaf, killing Hojatoleslam Muhammad Baqir al-Hakim and up to 125 of his followers after Friday prayers at which the Shi'ite cleric had presided. The murdered cleric (who had returned to Iraq from exile in mid-2003) was succeeded as leader of SCIRI by his brother Abd al-Aziz al-Hakim, a member of the Governing Council. Evident Shi'ite discord had already given rise to the suspicion that the various Shi'ite factions might be attacking each other in order to establish a dominant position among Iraq's majority Shi'ite population. By early September a reported 139 US troops had been killed since the end of combat operations was announced on 1 May, exceeding the number killed during the conflict itself.

The US-led coalition had initially been unable to apprehend Saddam Hussain and his immediate family after the removal from power of his regime. However, in July 2003, acting on information received from an Iraqi citizen, US special forces shot dead Hussain's two sons, Uday and Qusay, at a house in Mosul where they had apparently been hiding. Finally, in December Saddam Hussain was captured by US special forces in the village of al-Dawr near the former President's hometown of Tikrit; they were also believed to have acted as the result of information provided by an unknown source. Saddam Hussain's identity was formally confirmed by DNA testing and by members of the Governing Council; he was accorded prisoner-of-war status and detained in US military custody. In July 2004 Hussain, along with 11 co-defendants, appeared in front of a special US-appointed court in Baghdad to face seven charges, including the use of chemical weapons against Kurds in Halabja in 1988 and the invasion of Kuwait in 1990. The former Iraqi leader, declaring the proceedings to be illegal, refused to sign the list of charges. In October 2004 US investigators seeking evidence as part of preparations for war crime trials against Saddam Hussain and former senior Iraqi officials found a mass grave in Hatra, near the ancient city of Nineveh, in which they uncovered the bodies of hundreds of Kurds apparently killed in late 1987 or early 1988, when the Iraqi regime was waging a war against the Kurdish resistance movement.

Meanwhile, in September 2004 a report issued by the Iraq Survey Group, a team of experts appointed by the US-led coalition to locate Iraq's alleged weapons of mass destruction, following its 15-month search concluded that the Baathist regime's involvement with chemical or biological agents prior to the 2003 invasion had been restricted to small quantities of poisons, probably for use in assassinations. According to the report, while no illegal stockpiles of weapons had been found, and there was no evidence of any attempts to recommence Iraq's nuclear weapons programme (the last Iraqi factory capable of producing weapons of mass destruction having been destroyed in 1996), there was evidence to suggest that the regime under Saddam Hussain intended to reintroduce its illegal weapons programmes if the UN lifted sanctions against the country. However, subsequent to the release of the report, the IAEA, the monitors of which the

USA had not allowed into Iraq after the war began in March 2003, announced that buildings used during Iraq's nuclear programme prior to the Gulf War in 1991 had been dismantled, and that specialized equipment and material inside them that could be utilized to produce nuclear weapons had disappeared. The US Administration officially announced an end to the search for weapons of mass destruction in January 2005.

By January 2004 US-led forces had apprehended or killed 42 of the 55 'most wanted' former Baathists (with only 10 of these believed to remain at liberty in early 2008). However, during the final weekend of the month some 105 people, mostly Kurds, were killed in suicide bomb attacks directed against the offices of the principal Kurdish parties—the KDP and the PUK—in Arbil. Meanwhile, it appeared that the insurgents now regarded as legitimate targets any Iraqis working with the occupying forces: in February 2004 nearly 100 people were killed in two separate attacks against the Iraqi police and army in Iskandariya and Baghdad, respectively. In early March a series of bombs exploded among crowds of Shi'ites who had gathered in Baghdad and Karbala to celebrate the festival of Ashoura. More than 180 people were killed in the blasts, and, although al-Qa'ida purportedly issued a statement denying involvement, the CPA claimed that Abu Musab al-Zarqawi, a Jordanian national believed to have ties with al-Qa'ida, was responsible for the bombings and was also the mastermind behind the majority of attacks on coalition and civilian targets in Iraq.

Following protracted negotiations and several delays, the Transitional Administrative Law (TAL)—was signed by the Governing Council on 8 March 2004; most notably, it outlined a new timetable for the establishment of a permanent legislature and sovereign government (see Constitution and Government, below), which superseded that previously outlined by the agreement on the transfer of power published on 15 November 2003. This development was interpreted as evidence of the growing influence on the political process of Iraq's most senior Shi'ite cleric, Grand Ayatollah al-Sistani: in particular, plans to elect a transitional national assembly by regional caucuses were abandoned and replaced by proposals to hold national elections to an interim (and likely Shi'a-dominated) legislature.

In May 2004 the Independent Electoral Commission of Iraq (IECI) was formed by the CPA to organize elections to a 275-member Transitional National Assembly (TNA), which were subsequently scheduled for 30 January 2005. Seats within the TNA were to be allocated on the basis of proportional representation. Key functions of the TNA were to draft, by 15 August 2005, a permanent constitution, to be submitted to a popular referendum by 15 October; and to elect a President and two Vice-Presidents, together constituting a state Presidency Council, responsible for appointing a Prime Minister and cabinet. Under the timetable for Iraq's political transition, constitutionally elected organs of government were to be installed by 15 December. Voting for the TNA was to be held simultaneously with elections to 18 provincial assemblies and to a new Iraqi Kurdistan National Assembly. A group of 15 primarily Sunni and secular Iraqi political parties, along with the two principal Kurdish factions, the PUK and the KDP, subsequently signed a manifesto demanding that the Interim Government hold the elections at least six months later than scheduled, in order to ensure that they would take place in a secure environment. In early December 2004 the two main Kurdish parties announced that they had agreed to contest the polls, and to operate in the interim legislature, on a joint list—the Kurdistan Alliance List (or Democratic Patriotic Alliance of Kurdistan). Subsequently, major Shi'ite groups, backed by al-Sistani, announced that they too would be campaigning on a shared list of 228 candidates, to be known as the United Iraqi Alliance (UIA). In late December, after failing to secure a delay in the holding of the ballot, the Sunni Iraqi Islamic Party (IIP—al-Hizb al-Islami al-'Iraqi) and various other Sunni groups and clerics withdrew from the campaign, advocating a boycott of the polls.

In March 2004 Bremer announced the re-establishment of the Ministry of Defence. Meanwhile, the CPA closed down the Baghdad newspaper *Al-Hawza al-Natiqa* for allegedly inciting violence against the US-led coalition. The newspaper was closely associated with Hojatoleslam Muqtada al-Sadr, a Shi'ite cleric whose father had been assassinated by the previous regime in February 1999 (see Political developments after the Gulf War), who was a suspect in the murder of a moderate Shi'ite cleric in Najaf in 2003 and who had become the coalition's most vocal opponent. Several of the cleric's supporters had formed a militia known as the 'Mahdi Army', and protests outside the newspaper offices were the precursor to a nation-wide upsurge in violence against coalition forces. After four US private security contractors were killed in an ambush in the Sunni-dominated town of Fallujah, to the west of Baghdad in Al-Anbar (Anbar) province, in early April 2004, US forces surrounded and effectively blockaded the town; around 450 Iraqis (including many civilians) and 40 US soldiers died in the ensuing violence. Two members of the interim Cabinet, including Minister of the Interior Nuri al-Badran, resigned in protest against the coalition's response to the militant violence. A scandal developed in late April, when photographs taken by US guards of US soldiers coercing Iraqi prisoners into performing degrading sexual and other humiliating acts were broadcast world-wide. One soldier received a 10-year gaol sentence in January 2005 in connection with the abuse of prisoners at the Abu Ghraib prison, west of Baghdad, while other implicated officers received lesser sentences. In early 2005 four British soldiers were discharged from the army and sentenced to prison terms of between five months and two years, having been convicted of the abuse of Iraqi prisoners at a military base near Basra in May 2003.

The transfer of power to the Iraqi Interim Government

In mid-May 2004 Sunni insurgents in central Baghdad assassinated the President of the Governing Council, Izzadine Salim, who was replaced by the Sunni Sheikh Ghazi Mashal Ajil al-Yawar. The INA Secretary-General, Dr Ayad Allawi, was appointed interim Prime Minister of Iraq in late May, and in early June it was announced that Ghazi al-Yawar had been appointed President of the Interim Government, to which power was to be transferred from the CPA on 30 June. However, following an increase in the number of insurgent attacks, and the kidnapping and killing of foreign workers, the date for the granting of sovereignty to the Interim Government was secretly moved forward to 28 June, in order to prevent a major insurgent assault. A low-key ceremony was held in Baghdad, and hours later Paul Bremer left Iraq; the CPA and the Governing Council were both dissolved. Around 140,000 US soldiers remained in Iraq following the handover of power. In August delegates to a national conference in Baghdad declared the appointment of a 100-member transitional national council that was to govern Iraq in conjunction with the Interim Government until the January 2005 elections.

The US military had, in April 2004, arranged for an Iraqi security force, led by one of Saddam Hussain's ex-generals, to replace the US Marine Corps in Fallujah; this initially resulted in a significant decrease in the level of fighting. The CPA's decision to re-employ members of the former Baathist security forces was an important development. However, in May coalition forces launched major assaults against Muqtada al-Sadr's Mahdi Army, and particularly heavy fighting was reported in Sadr City (a predominantly Shi'a suburb of Baghdad previously known as Saddam City), Karbala, Najaf and Kufa. In June nine of Iraq's leading political factions reached agreement with Dr Allawi to disband their militias by January 2005. According to the agreement, some 100,000 fighters (but excluding members of the Mahdi Army) would join the security forces or return to civilian life. Meanwhile, US forces reached an accommodation with al-Sadr to end his insurgency, without pressuring him to reduce his military, and in July 2004 the ban on the newspaper *Al-Hawza al-Natiqa* was lifted. However, a Sunni uprising in Najaf, where the Mahdi Army seized the Imam Ali Mosque, and in other southern cities from early August led to renewed fighting, with almost 80 people reported killed in a single 24-hour period in late August. Grand Ayatollah al-Sistani ordered Iraqi Shi'ites to descend upon Najaf to end the fighting there. Thousands of people accompanied him as he entered the city, where he negotiated a cease-fire with al-Sadr, including an end to the siege of the mosque. Meanwhile, Abu Musab al-Zarqawi had declared that he had managed a spate of co-ordinated attacks across Iraq in June, including five car bomb explosions in Mosul, which had killed about 100 people. In July the Interim Government introduced new legislation granting it wider powers to control the insurgency by enabling the Prime Minister to declare a state of emergency for periods of up to 60 days. The death penalty was reintroduced for certain crimes in August, having been suspended by the CPA following the US-led invasion.

Al-Sadr's Mahdi Army announced a cease-fire in October 2004 and stated that it would begin to disarm, provided that the Interim Government released all the army's prisoners, and agreed not to arrest or harm any of its supporters. In mid-October an incident of particular concern for the security of coalition forces in Iraq was the penetration of and suicide attack on central Baghdad's International Zone—an area still commonly known by its original name, the Green Zone, where a high level of security was maintained, and which contained the headquarters of the Iraqi Government and the US and British embassies. At least 10 people, including four US civilians, were killed during the attack. Al-Zarqawi's group, which had recently named itself Tanzim Qa'idat al-Jihad fi Bilad al-Rafidain (Base of Holy War in Mesopotamia, also known as al-Qa'ida in Iraq), claimed responsibility for the attack, and for the killing in late October of 49 unarmed National Guard soldiers in Diyala province, near the Iranian border. It was estimated later in the month that 100,000 Iraqi civilians had died in the period since the US-led invasion, principally as a result of air-strikes by coalition forces.

Allawi declared a 60-day state of emergency in early November 2004, closing Baghdad airport and imposing martial law across most of the country as an estimated 15,000 US troops and 3,000 Iraqi troops descended upon Fallujah, which was still dominated by insurgents. By mid-November US troops claimed to be in absolute control of the city, having killed an estimated 1,200 insurgents, with losses of a reported 38 US and six Iraqi military. (In November 2005 the US Administration admitted that white phosphorus, a substance classified by some as a chemical weapon, had been used in the assault on Fallujah.) Heavy civilian and military casualties were recorded during a spate of suicide car bomb attacks and insurgent raids in Karbala, Najaf, Mosul and the area around Baghdad in December 2004 and early January 2005. The number of insurgents at this time was estimated at 200,000, greater than the number of coalition troops and many more than had previously been estimated. In response to the growing violence and in advance of the forthcoming legislative elections, in January the Interim Government extended the state of emergency for another month, closed Iraq's borders and imposed a strict curfew. Al-Zarqawi, who had castigated Shi'ites for assisting the occupying forces, vowed in the week before the poll to launch a violent battle against the elections. Five days before the scheduled ballot, 37 US troops were killed—the highest single death toll for US forces since March 2003. In advance of the elections, more than 100,000 Iraqi police and soldiers provided tight security in an attempt to forestall insurgent attacks.

The January 2005 election to the Transitional National Assembly

Despite appeals for a boycott by some, especially Sunni, political groups, insurgents' threats to attack citizens intending to vote, and the general acceptance that some areas of the country were too dangerous for secure polls to be held, the legislative election took place as scheduled on 30 January 2005. At least 44 people died in attacks across the country, although the level of violence was in fact lower than had been widely predicted. In the election to the TNA, the UIA took 47.6% of the total votes, winning 140 of the 275 seats, the Kurdistan Alliance List won 75 seats (with 25.4% of the votes) and the Iraqi List, a bloc led by Dr Allawi, secured 40 seats (with 13.6% of the votes); nine other parties achieved representation in the interim legislature. The rate of participation was put at some 58% of the registered electorate. Voting for the TNA was held simultaneously with elections to 18 provincial assemblies and to a new Iraqi Kurdistan National Assembly, where the Kurdistan Democratic List won 104 of the 111 seats. In what was widely conceived to be an attempt further to aggravate the division between Shi'ite and Sunni communities, militants killed over 30 people as Shi'ites celebrated Ashoura in mid-February. At the end of the month some 125 people were killed in a suicide bomb attack in Hilla.

Following protracted negotiations over the formation of the transitional government, on 6 April 2005 the TNA voted to appoint Jalal Talabani, the leader of the PUK, to the post of President. A Sunni, Ghazi al-Yawar (previously the President of the Interim Government), and a Shi'a, Adil Abd al-Mahdi (hitherto the Minister of Finance), were appointed Vice-Presidents. The three, together constituting a state Presidency Council, were sworn in on 7 April, whereupon they appointed Ibrahim al-Ja'fari (a leading member of the Islamic Dawa Party, and a Vice-President in the Interim Government) to the post of Prime Minister. On 28 April the TNA overwhelmingly approved al-Ja'fari's proposed new Council of Ministers, which was sworn in on 3 May. However, in large part owing to disagreements regarding the level of ministerial representation for Sunnis, seven posts remained unallocated, including those of defence (which was to be assumed on an interim basis by al-Ja'fari) and oil (temporarily allocated to Deputy Prime Minister Ahmad Chalabi). Six of the seven vacancies were filled later in May, when Saadoun al-Dulaimi, a Sunni Arab, was appointed Minister of Defence, while the important oil portfolio was awarded to Dr Ibrahim Bahr al-Ulum, a Shi'a. On 12 June the Iraqi Kurdistan National Assembly voted unanimously to appoint Masoud Barzani, leader of the KDP, to the post of President of the Kurdish Autonomous Region.

By the end of May 2005 more than 1,000 people were reported to have been killed in various insurgent attacks across the country following the approval of the new Transitional Government. In June the US military launched a major offensive centred on the town of Karabila, near the Syrian border, with the intention of disrupting the flow of fighters, supplies and money to the insurgency from across the border. Meanwhile, fears of sectarian tension were exacerbated when al-Zarqawi announced that he would form a special unit, the Omar Brigade, specifically in order to target the Badr Organization, the armed faction of SCIRI (which had been founded in Tehran in 1983 as the Badr Brigade, but was renamed upon its relocation to Iraq following the overthrow of the Baathist regime). In a major suicide bomb attack in July 2005, some 98 people were killed at a marketplace in Musayyib, south of Baghdad.

Meanwhile, the transitional administration was engaged in negotiations to draw up an Iraqi constitution. Under the schedule outlined by the TAL, a draft document was to be agreed by a constitutional committee and submitted to the TNA for approval by 15 August 2005, in order to be put to a nation-wide referendum by 15 October. Although their boycott of January's elections proportionally gave the Sunnis a very minor representation on the constitutional committee, this was increased in an attempt to reach an agreeable consensus. Significant points of disagreement included: the degree of federalism to be incorporated into the new state; the distribution of oil revenue; the question of 'de-Baathification' of the official sphere; and the role of Islam as a source of legislation. The agreed deadline was twice missed, largely because of Sunni objections on these key issues, before a final text was submitted to the TNA for approval on 28 August. The text was subsequently submitted to the UN on 14 September. On the same day a series of car bombings in Baghdad caused the deaths of some 150 people. Al-Zarqawi's al-Qa'ida in Iraq claimed responsibility for the attacks. At a referendum held on 15 October, the Constitution was ratified with the support of 78.6% of votes cast.

The trial of former Iraqi President Saddam Hussain began on 19 October 2005, and was conducted by the new Supreme Iraqi Criminal Tribunal—the body that replaced the Iraqi Special Tribune established by the CPA in December 2003 to adjudicate crimes against humanity committed under the Baathist regime. Together with his seven co-defendants, Hussain was charged with organizing the killing of 148 Iraqi Shi'a in the town of al-Dujail, where he had survived an assassination attempt in 1982. All eight defendants pleaded not guilty to the charges. After a day's proceedings the trial was adjourned until late November 2005, by which time two defence lawyers had been killed. In January 2006 the appointment of a Kurd from Halabja (where chemical weapons had been employed against the population by Saddam Hussain's Government in 1988—see above) as the new presiding judge compounded the objections of the defence team that the trial was incapable of impartiality. (For further details regarding the Dujail trial, see below.)

In October 2005 the toll of fatalities suffered by the US military since the invasion of Iraq passed 2,000. In November US troops discovered more than 170 prisoners, many malnourished and showing signs of torture, in the basement of the Shi'ite-dominated Ministry of the Interior. The IIP, with the support of the USA, demanded an inquiry into the practices of the Ministry's officials. In January 2006 some 28 people were killed in a suicide bomb attack on the Ministry building, which al-Qa'ida in Iraq announced it had carried out in revenge for the maltreatment of Sunni prisoners.

The formation of a permanent Council of Representatives

Following the approval of the Constitution, several Sunni groups that had boycotted the elections of January 2005 decided that it would be in their interests to participate in the elections to the first permanent Council of Representatives, which were now scheduled to be held on 15 December. Three major Sunni groups—the IIP, the General Council for the People of Iraq and the Iraqi National Dialogue Council—formed the Iraqi

Accord Front (IAF—Jabhat al-Tawafuq al-Iraqiya) in October, in a bid to engage the Sunni population in the political process. Another Sunni coalition, the Iraqi Front for National Dialogue (Hewar National Iraqi Front), was formed from parties that declined to join the IAF in protest against the IIP's acceptance of the Constitution. Meanwhile, the UIA announced a 17-party list dominated once more by Shi'ites, including supporters of al-Sadr alongside the Islamic Dawa Party, SCIRI and other groups. However, the INC, which had been transformed since the removal of Saddam Hussain's regime from a multi-party coalition into a political party headed by Ahmad Chalabi, declined to run on the UIA list, creating instead a coalition of its own, the National Congress Coalition. In contrast to his support of the UIA in January, Grand Ayatollah al-Sistani indicated his neutrality in the elections, encouraging Shi'ites to participate but to follow their own judgement. Former Prime Minister Ayad Allawi established a secular coalition, the Iraqi National List (INL), including his own INA, the Iraqis party of Ghazi al-Yawar and the ICP, while the PUK and the KDP maintained their co-operation at the centre of the Kurdistan Alliance List. Voting occurred as scheduled on 15 December, with minor disruptions from violence; turn-out was evaluated at around 70% of the electorate. The final results, released on 10 February 2006, gave the UIA 41.2% of votes cast and 128 of the Council's 275 seats. The Kurdistan Alliance List secured 53 seats with 21.7% of votes cast, while the IAF won 15.1% of the vote and 44 seats. Allawi's INL won 25 seats, and 11 seats were allocated to the Iraqi Front for National Dialogue. (Chalabi's coalition failed to win a seat.)

On 22 February 2006, while negotiations were ongoing over the composition of the new government, two bombs were exploded inside the al-Askari Mosque (or Golden Mosque) in Samarra, destroying the dome of one of the holiest Shi'ite shrines in Iraq. The attack on the mosque caused a sharp increase in sectarian violence across the country, which resulted in the deaths of at least 300 people within a week, according to official sources, although independent media reports suggested that more than 1,000 had died. Sunni mosques were destroyed or damaged in retaliatory attacks, while curfews were extended in Baghdad and elsewhere. Following the upsurge in violence, Kurdish, Sunni and secular factions increased their opposition to the continued premiership of al-Ja'fari, who had narrowly won the nomination of the UIA to the post of Prime Minister in the new government in February. Over 60 people were killed in a series of bomb attacks in Sadr City on 12 March, while some 85 bodies were reportedly discovered the following day by Iraqi police in various parts of Baghdad, apparently the victims of increasingly common execution-style killings by sectarian 'death squads'. The Council of Representatives eventually convened for the first time in Baghdad's Green Zone on 16 March.

On 7 April 2006 three suicide bombers detonated their explosives in an important Shi'ite mosque owned by SCIRI in northern Baghdad. More than 70 people were thought to have been killed. Seeking to resolve the impasse in negotiations over the new government, on 20 April al-Ja'fari withdrew his candidacy for the post of Prime Minister. On the following day the UIA nominated Nuri Kamal (Jawad) al-Maliki, another prominent member of the Islamic Dawa Party, as their replacement candidate, a compromise apparently accepted by Sunni and Kurdish factions. At the second session of the Council of Representatives on 22 April, President Talabani was elected for a second term; two Vice-Presidents, Tariq al-Hashimi of the IIP and incumbent Adil Abd al-Mahdi, were also appointed, and Mahmoud al-Mashhadani was chosen as the chamber's Speaker. Talabani subsequently invited al-Maliki to form a permanent government within 30 days. Meanwhile, a new Kurdish regional government, led by Masoud Barzani, assumed office on 7 May; the new administration represented the Kurdish region's first unified Cabinet.

Following lengthy and difficult negotiations between the various parties, on 20 May 2006 the Council of Representatives approved a list of ministerial nominees submitted by Prime Minister-designate al-Maliki and the Council of Ministers was sworn into office. This Government of national unity represented the first permanent Iraqi Government since the removal of the regime of Saddam Hussain in 2003, and it constituted the first administration since that date to include the principal Sunni factions. However, the portfolios of the interior and defence remained unfilled; Prime Minister al-Maliki assumed the interior portfolio on an interim basis, while Deputy Prime Minister Salam al-Zubaie was to serve as acting Minister of Defence. The appointment of a permanent Minister of State for National Security Affairs was also deferred, the position being filled temporarily by the Deputy Prime Minister, Dr Barham Salih, hitherto Minister of Planning and Development Co-operation. Four other members of the outgoing Transitional Government—including Minister of Foreign Affairs Hoshyar al-Zibari and Minister of the Environment Narmin Uthman—remained in post, while Dr Hussain al-Shahristani (an independent Shi'a member of the UIA) became Minister of Oil. In all, the new Council of Ministers included 20 Shi'a, eight Kurds, eight Sunni Arabs and one Christian. Of the 275 seats in the Council of Representatives, the Government—composed principally of the UIA, the Kurdish Alliance, the IAF and the INL—plus three smaller parties, controlled 240. On 8 June 2006 the Council of Representatives approved al-Maliki's nominations for three key positions: Lt-Gen. Abd al-Qadir Muhammad Jasim Obeidi, a Sunni who had served as a general in Saddam Hussain's armed forces, was appointed Minister of Defence; Jawad al-Bulani and Shirwan al-Waili, both Shi'as, were named as Minister of the Interior and Minister of State for National Security Affairs, respectively.

The security situation, however, remained a serious concern. At the end of May 2006 al-Maliki imposed a month-long state of emergency in Basra, in an effort to prevent a continuation of the violence perpetrated by militants and criminal gangs that had seen at least 100 people killed in that month alone. The new Government appeared initially to have been strengthened by reports on 7 June that Abu Musab al-Zarqawi, the leader of al-Qa'ida in Iraq, had been killed during a US air-strike close to the town of Baquba. It was claimed by the Ministry of Health on the day before al-Zarqawi's death that almost 1,400 civilians had been killed in Baghdad during the previous month. However, neither the imposition of a curfew nor a massive security operation involving thousands of extra troops, ordered by al-Maliki's administration on 14 June, appeared to lessen the violence. The new strategy, code-named 'Operation Together Forward', was a joint offensive by Iraqi and US forces. Meanwhile, it was claimed that Abu Ayyub al-Masri, also known as Abu Hamza al-Muhajir, had been appointed to succeed al-Zarqawi as the leader of al-Qa'ida in Iraq. Al-Maliki also appealed for a dialogue with Sunni insurgents, and on 25 June announced a 'national reconciliation plan' offering an amnesty to members of certain militant groups who renounced violence and outlining plans to disarm the country's various militias.

Nevertheless, the violence perpetrated by both Sunni insurgents and Shi'a militias continued relentlessly, prompting international observers to warn that the situation could develop into civil war if the violence was not brought under control. However, this view was rejected by the Iraqi leadership, and in August President Talabani vowed that Iraqi security forces would be in a position to take full control by the end of the year. As the violence worsened, Grand Ayatollah al-Sistani announced that he would no longer act as a political leader, warning his aides that he was powerless to prevent civil war. Nevertheless, the formal hand-over of control of Iraq's armed forces from the US-led coalition to the Government of Prime Minister al-Maliki did occur on 7 September (five days later than scheduled). First to be transferred to Iraqi control were the small air and naval forces, and one of Iraq's 10 army divisions, while other units were to be transferred during the coming months.

Also in September 2006 the Council of Representatives began to debate the controversial issue of federal devolution, which certain analysts claimed might eventually lead to the dissolution of Iraq along ethnic lines. In the previous month Vice-President Adil Abd al-Mahdi had vowed to bring the issue of a federal Shi'a state before the legislature within two months, amid growing demands for Shi'a autonomy. The UIA, which submitted a draft federalism law to the Council of Representatives, stated that it favoured the division of Iraq into autonomous regions, thereby permitting the oil-rich Shi'a south to rule as an autonomous region along the lines of the Kurdish north. While Sunni politicians had previously opposed the move, fearing that it would leave them only with the resource-poor centre and west of the country, they now hinted that they might support the 'administrative application of federalism' so long as a strong central Government remained in place. By late September a compromise had emerged: a parliamentary committee was to be set up immediately to draft constitutional amendments to ensure that national oil revenues were shared fairly and to limit the potential of regions to secede from the central state. Moreover, the Council of Representatives agreed that any legislation on federalism could only be implemented after an 18-month delay.

On 26 September both Kurdish and Shi'a legislators tabled federalism bills. The Kurdish bill (which showed the disputed, oil-rich city of Kirkuk as belonging to the Kurdish Autonomous Region) was rejected, but the Shi'a-proposed draft was given a first reading. The draft made provisions for Iraq's 18 provinces to hold referendums on whether they wanted to merge with neighbouring areas, thus forming larger areas with powers of self-rule. Legislators were given until 22 October to resolve the issue. In the event, a law was adopted by the Council of Representatives on 11 October; while the vote was unanimous, only 138 of the 275 legislators attended the session, the two largest Sunni blocs and two factions making up the Shi'a alliance having refused to attend.

A UN report issued in late September 2006 showed that almost 3,600 civilians had been killed across Iraq in July, and 3,000 in August. British and Iraqi forces operating in Basra initiated a campaign, code-named 'Operation Sinbad', which was aimed at preventing the infiltration of some of the city's police units by Shi'a militants. In October al-Maliki announced the establishment of local security committees to monitor the violence in their respective areas. Reports, however, suggested that the violence was worsening, with Sunni leaders from Anbar province, west of Baghdad, forming their own security forces. Many Iraqis were fleeing their homes and seeking refuge either in other parts of the country or in neighbouring states (see The execution of Saddam Hussain).

The trial of Saddam Hussain and seven co-defendants accused of involvement in the murder of 148 Iraqi Shi'a in Dujail in 1982 (see above) continued in 2006, albeit marred by numerous setbacks. In June one of the former President's lawyers was murdered, becoming the third defence lawyer to be killed since the start of trial proceedings. In response to what they claimed was inadequate security for his legal team, in July the deposed Iraqi leader and three co-defendants began a hunger strike and boycotted the proceedings, but Hussain was returned to the courtroom later that month. On 5 November Hussain and two of his co-defendants—Awad Hamed al-Bandar (former head of the Revolutionary Court under the Baathist regime) and Barzan Ibrahim al-Tikriti (half-brother of the former President)—were found guilty of crimes against humanity in connection with the killing of the 148 Shi'a, and were sentenced to death. Former Vice-President Taha Yassin Ramadan was sentenced to life imprisonment, while three others received 15-year custodial sentences; one defendant was acquitted owing to a lack of evidence. The verdict provoked a combination of rage and jubilation in Iraq, with thousands defying a curfew to express publicly either their support for Hussain or to celebrate the verdict. Nevertheless, many commentators questioned the impartiality of the trial, with the US-based Human Rights Watch warning that it had been so flawed that the verdict should be considered unsound. Hussain's lawyers lodged an appeal against the verdict.

In November 2006 a series of apparently co-ordinated car bombs and mortar rounds exploded in Sadr City; these were followed by mortar attacks on Sunni areas of the capital. At least 215 people were reported to have died in what was described as one of the worst terrorist attacks since the US-led invasion. Prime Minister al-Maliki, who was scheduled to meet US President Bush in Jordan to discuss Iraq's security situation, imposed an indefinite curfew in the capital, while urging all sides to exercise restraint. However, the killings continued, prompting a group led by Shi'a cleric Muqtada al-Sadr to threaten withdrawal from the unity Government, in which his followers held six cabinet posts. This threat was carried out when al-Maliki flew to the Jordanian capital, Amman, a move that al-Sadr's group described as 'a provocation to the Iraqi people and a violation of their constitutional rights'.

The publication of the US cross-party Iraq Study Group report on 6 December 2006 appeared to herald a change in US policy towards Iraq. This was precipitated partly by the resounding defeat of the Republican Party in US mid-term elections held in the previous month, and the subsequent resignation of Donald Rumsfeld as Secretary of Defense. In its report, the panel demanded 'urgent action', warning that Iraq was sliding towards chaos. Rather than conducting a combat mission, the report recommended that US troops should be used to train Iraqis; it also rejected the idea of a massive increase in troop numbers. The report, which was welcomed by many within the Iraqi Government (although not by President Talabani or the leaders of Iraqi Kurdistan), also appealed for direct dialogue on Iraq's future with Syria and Iran. President Bush's reaction to the report, however, was cautious; while he promised to 'seriously consider' the report's recommendation, he appeared to rule out unconditional dialogue with Iraq's neighbours and phasing out the US combat role in Iraq.

The execution of Saddam Hussain

Saddam Hussain was executed by hanging on 30 December 2006, following the rejection, on 26 December, of his appeal against the death sentence imposed by the Supreme Iraqi Criminal Tribunal in November. The manner of his killing was extremely contentious: news reports apparently revealed that the former Iraqi President had been taunted by onlookers as he approached the gallows, and that his execution had been filmed on a mobile telephone, resulting in footage of the event soon appearing on the internet. Fearing a rise in sectarian violence as a result of this development, the Iraqi Government immediately launched an investigation into the circumstances of Saddam Hussain's execution. While some in Iraq celebrated the death of the deposed leader, Baathist loyalists vowed revenge. Many Sunnis described Saddam Hussain as a martyr, and protests against the hanging were held in Baghdad, Samarra and his hometown of Tikrit. A statement issued by the Baath Party at the start of January 2007 named Izzat Ibrahim al-Douri as its new Secretary-General. In mid-January Saddam Hussain's two aides, al-Bandar and al-Tikriti, were hanged, and in March former Vice-President Ramadan was also executed, after the Court of Appeal had decided that his sentence of life imprisonment was too lenient and recommended that the death sentence be imposed.

At the time of Saddam Hussain's death, trial proceedings (initiated in August 2006) were ongoing against the former President and six co-defendants on charges of genocide and crimes against humanity in relation to an offensive in the Anfal region during 1987–88 in which, according to the prosecution, more than 180,000 Iraqi Kurds were killed. Following the passage of the death sentence against Saddam Hussain, it had initially been hoped that a verdict on these charges could be reached prior to his expected execution; however, when this trial resumed in January 2007 the charges against the former Iraqi leader were abandoned. In June Gen. Ali Hassan al-Majid, a cousin of Saddam Hussain, was sentenced to death by the Supreme Iraqi Criminal Tribunal, having been convicted of genocide, war crimes and crimes against humanity for his role in the Anfal operation, when he was a regional commander of the Baath Party. Two of al-Majid's co-defendants, Gen. Sultan Hashim Ahmad al-Jabouri al-Tai and Hussein Rashid al-Tikriti, were handed down the same sentence, while a further two were sentenced to life imprisonment; the sixth defendant was acquitted owing to a lack of evidence. In August al-Majid received an additional death sentence following his conviction on charges of involvement in the violent suppression of thousands of Shi'a rebels in southern Iraq following the Gulf conflict of 1990–91. Al-Majid received a third death sentence in March 2009 for the killing of Shi'as protesting against the assassination of Grand Ayatollah Muhammad Sadiq al-Sadr in 1999. In mid-January 2010 al-Majid received a further death sentence for his role in the attacks involving chemical weapons that killed thousands of Kurds in Halabja in 1988, and he was executed by hanging on 25 January.

In 2007 there were growing fears concerning the large exodus of Iraqi citizens, both to neighbouring states and through displacement from one region of the country to another. According to estimates by the office of the UN High Commissioner for Refugees (UNHCR), by September between 2.1m. and 2.5m. Iraqis had become refugees in neighbouring countries, notably Syria (1.2m.–1.4m.) and Jordan (500,000–750,000), while around 2.3m. Iraqis were displaced internally. (An estimated 1m. of these had been displaced before the 2003 conflict, and although a reported 300,000 Iraqis did return to their homes from Iran, Jordan, Lebanon and Saudi Arabia, among other countries, an increasing number were choosing to flee the violence.) UNHCR estimated in September 2007 that the number of internally displaced persons (IDPs) had increased markedly in the aftermath of the sectarian violence precipitated by the bombing of the al-Askari Mosque in Samarra in February 2006; more than 1,043,900 new IDPs had been reported during that period. Moreover, displacement of Iraqis was thought to be continuing at a rate of up to 60,000 a month, with Syria, Jordan, Egypt and Lebanon hosting most of the refugees. Aid agencies, meanwhile, warned that many neighbouring countries were starting to impose severe limitations on the number of Iraqi refugees allowed to enter. UNHCR also expressed concern in September 2007 regarding the estimated 13,000 Palestinian refugees who were believed to remain in Iraq, as well as the Christian and other minority communities.

About 50 suspected Sunni insurgents were said to have been killed on 9 January 2007 in the area of Baghdad's Haifa Street, which was attacked by US and Iraqi forces supported by helicopters and fighter jets. The battle took place just hours after Prime Minister al-Maliki had announced a new security plan for the capital, centred on the deployment of additional Iraqi forces, including Kurdish troops, with US backing. Sunni leaders denounced the plan as unconstitutional, noting that it had not been referred to the Council of Representatives for debate. The following day US President Bush confirmed that the USA would send an additional 21,000 troops to Iraq, while warning the Iraqi Government that it would be required to adhere to previously set benchmarks on controlling sectarian violence. Bush's new so-called 'surge' strategy also included the following provisions: the Iraqi Government was to appoint a new military commander for Baghdad; there was to be accelerated training of Iraqi security forces, leading to them being brought under Iraqi control by November; provincial elections were to be held later that year; and increased diplomacy was to be sought with Iraq's neighbours, excluding Iran and Syria.

On 16 January 2007 at least 70 people—most of them female students—were killed in a double bomb attack at Baghdad's Mustansiriyah University. Six days later more than 130 people were killed in and around the capital, including some 88 who were killed in a car bombing at a market. None the less, the ending of the two-month political boycott by followers of al-Sadr (see above) appeared to suggest a greater unity among Iraq's Shi'a factions. The announcement that the boycott was to end came just a day before security forces claimed to have captured 600 members of al-Sadr's reportedly 60,000-strong Mahdi Army. In late January officials announced that some 300 insurgents, reportedly from a militant group called the Army of Heaven, had been killed in battles near Najaf. Some news reports, however, claimed that those killed were innocent Shi'a pilgrims. In early February Iraq experienced its most deadly single bombing since the US-led invasion, with at least 130 people killed in a lorry bombing at a central Baghdad marketplace. It was thought that the attack was deliberately timed to coincide with the launch of the new Iraqi-US security initiative in the capital, 'Operation Law and Order' (or the Baghdad Security Plan). In the second week of February the first anniversary of the bombing of the Samarra shrine saw insurgents again launch a series of explosions in Baghdad, with at least 70 people being killed in Shorja market alone. The Iraqi authorities declared in mid-February that the borders with Iran and Syria were to be closed for a 72-hour period in an attempt to stem the alleged flow of insurgents from these neighbouring states. However, in the first week of March more than 110 Shi'a pilgrims on their approach to Karbala were killed by militants in central Iraq.

It was reported at the end of March 2007 that the Minister of Justice, Hashim al-Shebli, had resigned, citing dissatisfaction over the manner in which the Government was being run and also differences with his party, the INL. (These were believed to concern the future status of Kirkuk, which the party did not wish to join the Kurdish Autonomous Region.) In mid-April the six representatives of Muqtada al-Sadr's faction in the Council of Ministers also resigned their posts, in protest against al-Maliki's failure to agree a timetable for the withdrawal of coalition forces from Iraq. Four days prior to the resignations at least one Iraqi legislator was killed in a suicide bomb attack at a cafeteria inside the Council of Representatives building, adjacent to the heavily fortified Green Zone in the centre of Baghdad.

An international conference to discuss reconstruction and security in Iraq was convened in the Egyptian resort of Sharm el-Sheikh in May 2007. At the conference, which was attended by the UN Secretary-General, a five-year framework for the country's future development, the International Compact with Iraq, was launched by Prime Minister al-Maliki (see Economic Affairs). By June it appeared that Operation Law and Order was not achieving significant results in curbing sectarian violence in Baghdad. Moreover, in that month suspected Sunni insurgents again targeted the al-Askari Mosque in Samarra, destroying two minarets of the Shi'a shrine. During July violence also intensified in the north of the country, particularly in Kirkuk and the surrounding area, where vehicle bomb attacks resulted in a large number of fatalities. In one incident, the headquarters of the PUK were targeted, causing extensive damage to the building. While such bombings were clearly designed to influence any future decision regarding the status of Kirkuk (where tensions between the ethnic Kurdish, Arab and Turkmen communities were growing in advance of a proposed referendum—initially scheduled to be held by 31 December, but later postponed), many commentators noted that the recent tightening of security by joint Iraqi-US forces in Baghdad had led some insurgents to disperse to other parts of the country. Meanwhile, on 29 June 2007 the UN Security Council adopted Resolution 1762, which, *inter alia*, ended the mandate of UNMOVIC, on the grounds that Iraq's known weapons of mass destruction had now been rendered harmless and that the new Iraqi Government had declared itself to be in favour of non-proliferation.

The perilous state of the Iraqi administration was demonstrated on 1 August 2007, when the IAF withdrew its six ministers from the national unity Government, resulting in an even weaker participation by Sunni politicians in the country's decision-making processes. (One of the six, the Minister of Planning and Development Co-operation, Ali Baban, returned to the Council of Ministers in early September and was immediately dismissed by the party.) Moderate Kurdish and Shi'a political parties responded to this announcement by establishing a new alliance aimed at assisting the Prime Minister in pushing forward important legislation; this new grouping included the PUK and the KDP, together with al-Maliki's Islamic Dawa Party and the Islamic Supreme Council of Iraq (ISCI—as SCIRI had been renamed in May).

The UN Security Council voted on 10 August 2007 to expand the organization's operations in Iraq, describing this greater role as to 'advise, support and assist the government and people of Iraq on advancing their inclusive, political dialogue and national reconciliation'. (The UN had played a minimal role in Iraq's political affairs following the attack against its Baghdad headquarters in August 2003. The mandate of the UN Assistance Mission for Iraq was extended for further 12-month periods in August 2008, 2009 and 2010.) On 14 August 2007 an estimated 400–500 people from the minority (primarily Kurdish) Yazidi community in northern Iraq were killed as the result of co-ordinated suicide bombings carried out by militants. US military officials asserted that al-Qa'ida in Iraq had been responsible for the blasts. Muqtada al-Sadr, meanwhile, declared at the end of the month that his Mahdi Army was to suspend its campaign against rival militias and US-led forces for a six-month period. (In July al-Sadr's bloc in the Council of Representatives had chosen to end a boycott of legislative proceedings that it had commenced following the bombing of the al-Askari Mosque in the previous month. The Mahdi Army's truce was extended for a further six months in February 2008.) By the end of November 2007 new Ministers of Agriculture and of Health had been sworn in, thereby filling two of the portfolios left vacant by the departure of al-Sadr's Shi'a faction in April.

The withdrawal of British troops from Basra city

British armed forces withdrew from their remaining base in the city of Basra on 3 September 2007, transferring military control of the city centre to Iraqi troops and police. The formal handover of security from British to Iraqi forces in the remainder of Basra province took place on 16 December; this represented the transfer to Iraqi authority of the last of the four southern provinces controlled by the British military since 2003. However, a few days prior to the British withdrawal some 40 people in the southern town of Amara had been killed in a triple car bombing. An independent monitoring group, Iraq Body Count, estimated that 25,063 civilians had died as a result of violence during 2007, which represented a significant decline from 28,250 in 2006 but nevertheless constituted the second highest annual death toll since the conflict began in 2003. The number of fatalities in Baghdad had declined significantly, which US officials were keen to attribute to the effectiveness of the Bush Administration's 'surge' strategy in Baghdad. Moreover, large numbers of Iraqi refugees were returning to the country, particularly from neighbouring countries such as Syria. In December the UN Secretary-General's Special Representative for Iraq, Staffan de Mistura, launched a plan worth US $11,400m. to provide assistance to thousands of refugees and internally displaced families who had chosen to return home. Nevertheless, it was reported in October 2007 that 22 Iraqi insurgent groups had agreed to establish a new coalition, the Supreme Command for Jihad and Liberation, to be led by the Baath Party's Izzat Ibrahim al-Douri.

The period of relatively reduced violence in Baghdad came to a dramatic end on 1 February 2008, when an estimated 100 people were killed following two large-scale suicide bomb attacks. Despite Basra having been noticeably calmer since the withdrawal of British forces, in March al-Maliki ordered a major offensive—code-named 'Operation Charge of the Knights'—against Shi'a militias in the city (apparently including factions of Muqtada al-Sadr's Mahdi Army) in an effort to reduce levels of criminal and militant activity. Some 210 people were reported to have died and an estimated 600 others were wounded during the operation, which involved more than 40,000 Iraqi troops with the assistance of coalition forces, and was concluded when a truce was agreed on 30 March between the Government and al-Sadr, providing for the withdrawal of the Mahdi Army from the streets of Basra. Meanwhile, fierce fighting was reported in several cities in southern Iraq and also in the Sadr City district of Baghdad. A joint Iraqi-US military operation against the Mahdi Army in Sadr City began on 6 April and, after seven weeks—when al-Sadr again declared a cease-fire—had led to around 1,000 (mainly civilian) deaths. On 12 May al-Sadr agreed to allow Iraqi troops only to enter Sadr City; in response, he pledged that his forces would end mortar and rocket attacks against Baghdad's Green Zone.

By mid-2008, despite further fatal bombings in various Iraqi provinces, it was again noted that, in general, violence across the country had showed a significant decline since the overthrow of Saddam Hussain in 2003. One explanation given for the decline in sectarian killings in Baghdad was that the capital was now essentially divided into separate Shi'a and Sunni districts. Another reason for the lesser violence witnessed in Sunni provinces of Iraq (such as Anbar) was the policy adopted by the US Administration whereby former Sunni militias involved in the insurgency against coalition forces were encouraged to form so-called Awakening Councils, receiving the logistical and financial support of US troops in order to fight extremist Islamist groups such as al-Qa'ida in Iraq. Nevertheless, in June 2008 a car bomb attack launched by militants at a market in the (mainly Shi'a) Hurriya district of the capital resulted in at least 60 deaths, and in the following month suicide attacks carried out by female bombers against Kurds in Kirkuk and Shi'a pilgrims in Baghdad killed more than 48 people.

Meanwhile, on 12 January 2008 the Council of Representatives approved a law permitting former middle- and low-ranking members of the Baath Party who had not been charged with crimes to reclaim positions of public office, effectively repealing the de-Baathification legislation adopted by the CPA in the immediate aftermath of the overthrow of Saddam Hussain's regime in 2003, which had resulted in the dismissal of many thousands of Baathist officials. In July the Council of Representatives accepted the nominations of six IAF ministers who had agreed to rejoin the national unity Government, thereby filling cabinet posts that had been vacant since August 2007. The IAF had reportedly been satisfied by recent government actions such as the approval of an amnesty law involving thousands of Sunni prisoners and the clampdown on Shi'a militias. Moreover, four independent members of the UIA replaced the ministers from al-Sadr's faction, who continued to boycott the Government; thus, only the justice portfolio remained vacant.

Following numerous delays, on 24 September 2008 the Council of Representatives approved legislation stipulating that provincial elections originally scheduled to have taken place by 1 October should now be held in most parts of Iraq by the end of January 2009, and that a parliamentary committee would review the status of Kirkuk. The new law was approved by the Presidency Council on 3 October 2008. Meanwhile, in July 2008 Kirkuk council members voted to permit a referendum to be held among the province's population to decide whether or not the city would join the Kurdish Autonomous Region; Turkmen and Arab members boycotted the vote.

Discussions between US and Iraqi officials were ongoing regarding the proposed Status of Forces Agreement (SOFA), which would determine the long-term status of US troops in the country; Prime Minister al-Maliki affirmed in August 2008 that the USA planned to withdraw its military from Iraq by the end of 2011. President Bush declared in September that some 8,000 US forces would leave Iraq by February 2009—far fewer than the number that had previously been anticipated—with some 138,000 troops remaining after that date. On 1 October 2008 the Iraqi Government assumed responsibility for directing and funding members of the Sunni Awakening Councils in Baghdad, although the former militias continued to be strongly supported by the US authorities. On 9 October Saleh al-Auqaeili, a Shi'a member of the Council of Representatives affiliated with Muqtada al-Sadr, died in a roadside explosion in Sadr City. There was speculation that the Badr Organization might have been responsible for al-Auqaeili's murder, owing to the rivalry between its umbrella group, the ISCI, and al-Sadr's followers. On 15 October US military chiefs claimed recently to have killed Abu Qaswarah (also known as Abu Sara), the second-in-command of al-Qa'ida in Iraq, during a military offensive in Mosul. By the end of October 13 of Iraq's 18 provinces were under the control of the Iraqi Government and security forces; this came after Anbar province was transferred to Iraqi security control on 1 September, Babylon on 23 October and Wasit on 29 October. Nevertheless, an upsurge in violent attacks was reported in Baghdad during November, prompting the Iraqi Government to order another review of security provisions. Meanwhile, in late 2008 al-Sadr was reported to have fled to Iran following the issuing of a warrant for his arrest.

The Status of Forces Agreement

The SOFA was signed by the US ambassador in Baghdad, Ryan Crocker, and the Iraqi Minister of Foreign Affairs, Hoshyar al-Zibari, on 17 November 2008; it was endorsed by the Council of Representatives and the Presidency Council on 27 November and 4 December, respectively. However, the Sadrist bloc remained vehemently opposed to the agreement, insisting that the US military should withdraw from Iraq immediately. Under the terms of the security pact, which was to be put to a nation-wide referendum by the end of July 2009, all US armed forces were to withdraw from urban areas of the country by 30 June 2009; the remaining forces would leave by 31 December 2011. However, this timetable was dependent on the successful assumption of control by Iraqi security forces. On 23 December 2008 the Iraqi parliament agreed to allow the Government to extend the mandate for non-US foreign forces to remain in the country after the expiry on 31 December of the UN mandate for the US-led multinational force; however, it was required that these troops were withdrawn by July 2009. The British Government confirmed at this time that its 4,100 armed forces would leave Iraq by mid-2009. The number of US troops killed in Iraq was reported to have declined to some 314 in 2008, compared with 904 in 2007—an apparent sign that the military's counter-insurgency tactics had experienced some success.

On 1 January 2009, when the SOFA entered effect, control of the Green Zone in Baghdad was handed from the Iraqi to US authorities. At the same time, responsibility for the 145,700 US forces was transferred to the Iraqi Government. On 4 January more than 40 people died in a suicide bombing in the north-west of Baghdad, which seemed to have specifically targeted Iranian pilgrims visiting an important Shi'a shrine; the bombing occurred while the Iraqi Prime Minister was undertaking an official visit to Iran. In February, under the new security provisions agreed by the Iraqi and US authorities, the newly renovated Abu Ghraib prison was officially reopened under the name of Baghdad Central Prison.

At the elections finally held on 31 January 2009 in 14 of Iraq's 18 provinces (the three Kurdish provinces and Kirkuk being excluded from the vote), the official rate of voter participation was just 51%; however, turn-out in certain mainly Sunni areas (such as Nineveh) was higher than expected, and the elections were hailed as demonstrating the return of Sunni Arab political parties to the democratic system, such parties having widely boycotted the 2005 polls. The vote was relatively free of violence, compared with 2005, although six prospective candidates were killed in advance of polling. Allies of Prime Minister Nuri al-Maliki—standing as the State of Law coalition—secured notable successes in the elections, particularly in southern Shi'a areas of Iraq; the poll was widely seen as representing a vote of confidence in the premier's recent policies and in more secular nationalist, as opposed to overtly religious, groupings. While al-Maliki's coalition won a majority of votes in Baghdad and nine other provinces, the ISCI—previously dominant in Shi'a areas—failed to win in any provinces. Ayad al-Samarrai, the Sunni leader of the IAF and a senior member of the IIP, was elected as Speaker of the Council of Representatives on 19 April 2009. The post had remained vacant since the resignation of the chamber's former Speaker, Mahmoud al-Mashhadani, in December 2008.

In February 2009 the recently inaugurated US President, Barack Obama, declared that his Administration intended to withdraw the majority of US troops from Iraq by the end of August 2010, referring to this date as the official end of the USA's combat mission. President Obama stated that between 35,000 and 50,000 US forces would remain in the country after that date in order to advise Iraqi security forces and protect US interests. All US forces would have withdrawn from Iraq by the end of 2011, as stipulated under the terms of the SOFA. On 6 April 2009

Baghdad experienced its most serious incidence of violence for nearly two years: seven car bombings were perpetrated across the Iraqi capital, resulting in some 37 deaths, following the detention by the security forces of a number of alleged Sunni militants; al-Qa'ida in Iraq was blamed by Iraqi officials for what appeared to be co-ordinated attacks. Two suicide bombings in Baquba and Baghdad killed an estimated 56 and 28 people, respectively, on 23 April, while an explosion targeting the revered Shi'a Imam Musa al-Kadhim shrine in the capital caused more than 60 deaths; in both the Baquba and latter Baghdad attack, many Iranian pilgrims were among the victims.

The withdrawal of coalition forces and continuing violent insurgency

On 30 April 2009 the United Kingdom's combat mission in Iraq was officially declared to have been completed. A total of 179 British personnel had been killed in Iraq since the start of the military campaign in March 2003. By the end of July 2009 the withdrawal had been effected of the majority of the 4,100-strong British force in southern Iraq, as well as all other non-US coalition forces in the country. An estimated 400 British troops were to remain to provide specialist training to the Iraqi security forces. A bilateral maritime agreement under which the United Kingdom's navy would protect offshore petroleum facilities and provide training for Iraq's navy entered into force in November. (In May 2011 the last remaining British navy personnel were withdrawn from Iraq, signalling the formal end of the British military's operations in Iraq, during which a total of 179 British troops had been killed.) Meanwhile, on 30 June 2009, according to the terms of the SOFA, US combat forces initiated their withdrawal from Baghdad and other urban centres. Henceforth, US forces would fulfil a non-combative support role in the cities, while serving as a partner in Iraqi-led combat operations elsewhere. At this time the number of fatalities suffered by the US military since the invasion of Iraq had reached 4,321. The Iraqi Government declared 30 June a national holiday and staged a large military parade in Baghdad, the first such display since the overthrow of Saddam Hussain.

In the weeks following the scaling down of the US military presence, frequent attacks and incidents of sectarian violence occurred, particularly in the environs of Baghdad and Mosul. Confidence in the Iraqi security forces was severely undermined following a series of co-ordinated bomb and mortar attacks on 19 August, which targeted official buildings near central Baghdad's Green Zone, including the Ministries of Foreign Affairs and of Finance. At least 101 people were killed and more than 500 injured in the attacks, for which no group initially claimed responsibility. On 23 August a former police officer and Baath party member claimed responsibility for organizing one of the bombs, and alleged that the operation had been directed by two senior Iraqi Baath party officials exiled in Syria, a claim that provoked a diplomatic confrontation with Syria (see Regional relations). Nevertheless, in late August the Islamic State of Iraq, a network of Sunni militant groups suspected of links with al-Qa'ida, claimed that it had perpetrated the attacks. Islamic State of Iraq also alleged that it had organized two suicide car bombs in Baghdad on 25 October, which targeted the Ministry of Justice and a provincial government office. At least 155 people were killed and more than 700 injured in the attacks, which represented the worst incidence of violence in Iraq for more than two years. Amid concerns that the security forces were susceptible to infiltration by insurgents, the authorities launched an investigation to discover in particular how the explosives-laden vehicles had passed undetected through the numerous checkpoints in the capital. At the end of October it was reported that more than 60 security officers had been arrested and questioned in connection with the attacks.

Meanwhile, Prime Minister al-Maliki undertook an official visit to the USA in July 2009. Following a meeting with the Iraqi premier, President Obama reaffirmed his Administration's support for the Iraqi Government and advocated the removal of international sanctions, imposed on Iraq during the regime of Saddam Hussain. Amid reports of divisions in the Shi'ite UIA coalition, the largest parliamentary grouping, in August the formation was announced of a new Shi'ite electoral list, the Iraqi National Alliance. This new grouping, which excluded al-Maliki's Islamic Dawa Party, was dominated by supporters of al-Sadr (who remained in self-imposed exile in Iran) and also included the ISCI. In the same month the death was announced of Abd al-Aziz al-Hakim, leader of the ISCI; Ammar al-Hakim, son of the deceased leader, was confirmed as the party's new head in the following month.

Another co-ordinated series of car bomb attacks occurred in Baghdad on 8 December 2009, one day after the approval of new electoral legislation. Five bombs, three of which were suicide attacks, were directed at targets including the Ministry of the Interior and a university campus; at least 127 people were killed and almost 450 injured in the attacks. Once again, responsibility was claimed by Islamic State of Iraq. Meanwhile, in October 2009 the Ministry of Human Rights issued the first comprehensive Iraqi government report on war casualties. According to the report, 85,694 people had been killed in violence between the beginning of 2004 and October 2008; the report also stated that almost 150,000 people had been injured during the same period and an estimated 10,000 people were missing.

Meanwhile, a draft Constitution for the Kurdish Autonomous Region was approved by the Iraqi Kurdistan Parliament on 24 June 2009. (The National Assembly had adopted the name Parliament in February.) The document, which identified Islamic *Shari'a* as the basis for the region's legal system, also included territorial claims to Kirkuk and other disputed regions. However, a planned referendum on the draft Constitution was subsequently postponed, owing to opposition from the Independent High Electoral Commission (IHEC) and the Iraqi Council of Representatives. Following elections to the Iraqi Kurdistan Parliament held on 25 July, the Kurdistani List—comprising the PUK and the KDP—secured 59 of the 111 seats. In a concurrent election for the regional presidency, Barzani was re-elected with 69.6% of the valid votes cast. In August 2009 Barham Salih, of the PUK, resigned as Deputy Prime Minister in the central Government to assume the post of Prime Minister of the Kurdish Autonomous Region.

The March 2010 legislative elections

Following protracted negotiations, revised legislation concerning the forthcoming national legislative elections was approved by the Council of Representatives on 7 November 2009. The chief obstacle to the approval of the new law had been a disagreement over voter registration in the disputed city of Kirkuk. According to the new legislation, election results from Kirkuk would be subject to review by a parliamentary committee. The law also provided for: an increase in the number of Council seats from 275 to 323, to reflect population growth since 2005 and accommodate competing claims for increased representation, especially from Kurds and Sunnis; an allocation of 5% of seats for representatives of minorities (including Christians) and displaced Iraqis; and the adoption of an open list system, which would allow voters to choose individual candidates from electoral lists. However, on 18 November 2009 Vice-President Tariq al-Hashimi announced a veto of the bill on the grounds that it provided inadequate representation for the vast numbers of Iraqis displaced in Syria and Jordan, many of whom were Sunnis. (According to figures published by the Syrian Government, by January 2010 there were an estimated 1,054,466 Iraqi refugees in Syria, while the Jordanian Government estimated that some 450,756 Iraqi refugees were living in Jordan.) As a result, the IHEC declared that it would not be possible to meet the constitutional deadline for holding the election, which was the end of January 2010. An amended electoral law, which increased the number of seats in the Council to 325 and accorded displaced Iraqis the right to vote for candidates in their province of origin, received parliamentary approval on 7 December 2009. Al-Hashimi rescinded his veto, and the election was subsequently rescheduled for 7 March 2010.

In mid-January 2010 the IHEC announced that it was to bar more than 500 candidates and up to 15 political organizations from participating in the forthcoming election. The proscribed list reportedly included more than 170 candidates who had been identified by the Justice and Accountability Commission (JAC), which oversees Iraq's de-Baathification policy, as having alleged links to the Baath Party or to the former security apparatus of Saddam Hussain. Prominent Sunni politicians affected by the ruling included the Minister of Defence, Abd al-Qadir Muhammad Jasim Obeidi, and Saleh al-Mutlaq, the leader of the influential Iraqi Front for National Dialogue. The ruling was condemned by Sunni Arab leaders, who alleged that it would exacerbate sectarian tensions and diminish the legitimacy of the election. In early February it was announced that a special appeals panel had postponed the ban on candidates with Baath Party associations; instead, such candidates, if elected, were to be scrutinized after the election. However, the Government insisted that candidates be fully investigated on an individual basis prior to the election. On 11 February the JAC announced the reinstatement of 26 of the candidates previously barred. Al-Mutlaq, who remained ineligible, subsequently threatened to withdraw his party from the contest; however, following consultation with his coalition partners, al-Mutlaq acquiesced to the Iraqi Front for National Dialogue's participation.

A day of early voting on 4 March 2010 was marked by three separate attacks on polling stations in Baghdad, in which at least 17 people were reported to have been killed. Nevertheless, some 62.4% of eligible voters participated in the election, which took place as scheduled on 7 March. On 26 March final results were announced by the IHEC. Following the allocation of compensatory seats, the Iraqi National Movement of former interim Prime Minister Ayad Allawi emerged as the largest party, with 89 seats (plus two compensatory seats) in the 325-seat Council of Representatives. This new electoral bloc, widely known as Iraqiya, had replaced Allawi's INL, and included the INA and the Iraqi Front for National Dialogue among its constituent parties. The State of Law alliance of incumbent premier Nuri al-Maliki won 87 seats (plus two compensatory seats). The Shi'ite Iraqi National Alliance secured 68 seats (with an additional two seats subsequently being allocated) and the Kurdistan Alliance list of the PUK and KDP 42 (plus one compensatory seat). UN and other international observers confirmed that the conduct of the poll had been fair. However, al-Maliki, whose State of Law alliance had been ahead at an early stage in the vote count, refused to accept the declared outcome and immediately demanded a full manual recount of the votes. Despite support for the proposal from President Talabani, the IHEC ruled out this possibility. The day before the announcement of the final results the Federal Supreme Court had issued a ruling, in an attempt to clarify the constitutional procedure for forming a new government. Under the terms of the ruling, the leader of the largest coalition in parliament was entitled to form a new administration, leaving open the possibility of a post-election merger of the State of Law alliance with former allies in the Iraqi National Alliance (see below). Owing to the lack of overall majority for either of the leading coalitions, the situation reached an impasse, and coalition negotiations continued for months, as the various factions competed for power.

On 19 April 2010, having reviewed the complaints made by the State of Law alliance, the IHEC announced that a manual recount of votes in the Baghdad electoral area would take place. On 26 April the JAC upheld a ruling that a further 52 candidates should not have been permitted to contest the March elections owing to their links with the former Baathist regime; only two of these, both from Allawi's Iraqiya, had won seats, and their votes were thus declared invalid. However, the decision would not affect the final outcome of the ballot since the candidates would be replaced by other members of Iraqiya.

Meanwhile, the political uncertainty, as well as the approach to the formal end of US combat operations in August 2010 (see below), again prompted an increase in violence. On 4 April at least 40 people were reported to have died when three suicide car bombs were exploded close to foreign embassies in Baghdad; two days later at least 35 people were killed in six bomb attacks against predominantly Shi'ite districts of the capital. The militant Islamic State of Iraq later claimed responsibility for the first set of attacks. On 19 April the leaders of Islamic State of Iraq and of al-Qa'ida in Iraq, Abu Omar al-Baghdadi and Abu Ayyub al-Masri, respectively, were reported to have been killed in a joint security operation by Iraqi and US forces near Tikrit. A third insurgent leader, Ahmad al-Obeidi (also known as Abu Suhaib), who was believed to be in charge of al-Qa'ida's activities in three northern provinces, was also reported killed in Nineveh on 20 April.

The killing of the three al-Qa'ida-affiliated operatives led to an intensification of violence across Iraq, as a wave of apparent 'revenge attacks' were launched and militants appeared to be seeking to widen the divisions between Iraq's Sunni and Shi'a communities. On 23 April 2010 Baghdad was hit by a series of co-ordinated bombings, the targets of which included two Shi'a mosques, al-Sadr's party headquarters in the district of Sadr City and a market; at least 58 people died in the attacks, for which no group formally claimed responsibility. On 10 May more than 100 people were killed and around 350 wounded in various Iraqi cities: three bombs were detonated at a textiles factory in Hilla, killing more than 45 people; gunmen attacked Iraqi soldiers and police officers in Baghdad; and a number of other al-Qa'ida-style attacks were carried out, including in Basra, Fallujah and Mosul. On 14 May Islamic State of Iraq announced the appointment of al-Nasser Lideen Allah Abu Suleiman (also known as Noman Salman), the successor to al-Masri, as its new 'Minister of War', and warned that the organization had begun a new military campaign against Iraqi Shi'a and security forces in revenge for the deaths of al-Qa'ida in Iraq's senior commanders and the alleged abuse of Sunni detainees by the authorities. (On 25 February 2011 Iraqi security forces claimed to have killed Abu Suleiman during a military raid to the west of Baghdad.)

Meanwhile, in an effort to defeat Allawi's winning Iraqiya faction in its attempt to form Iraq's next government, on 4 May 2010 al-Maliki's State of Law alliance agreed to form a unified parliamentary bloc with the Iraqi National Alliance, to be called the National Alliance (NA). The merger of the two alliances of Shi'a parties into a new 'super-bloc' was formally announced on 11 June, shortly before the first session of the new legislature (see below). Al-Maliki was also reported to be participating in coalition discussions with the Kurdistan Alliance. However, despite the formation of the NA, Iraqiya insisted that, as the winner of the largest number of seats, it should be entitled to seek to form an administration first. Moreover, despite commanding a total of 159 seats in the Council of Representatives—and thus requiring only four more seats to hold a parliamentary majority of 163 in the 325-seat legislature—the various parties represented in the NA were unable to agree on a prime ministerial candidate, with the ISCI and the Sadrists refusing to accept al-Maliki continuing in that role.

On 16 May 2010 the IHEC announced that it was upholding the results of the March legislative elections following the recount of votes in the Baghdad area, confirming that it had not found any evidence of fraudulent activity. This permitted the Federal Supreme Court on 1 June to ratify the final results of the election, and an inaugural session of the Council of Representatives took place on 14 June. However, although Iraq's new deputies were officially sworn in, the session was declared to be left open but suspended, pending an agreement between the various political factions on the formation of a new government. (Under the terms of the Constitution, a Speaker must be elected during the first session of parliament, and discussions regarding a potential candidate for that post still formed part of the complex negotiations between the different blocs. On 24 October the Supreme Court ordered the parliament to resume its functions, after a number of Iraqi's civic groups launched legal proceedings claiming that Fouad Masoum, who had replaced Ayad al-Samarrai to become interim Speaker on 14 June, had violated the Constitution by leaving the session open.) Meanwhile, on 17 May 2010 a court of appeal decided to reinstate nine successful electoral candidates, eight of whom belonged to Allawi's faction, after they had previously been barred as part of the JAC's de-Baathification process. On 24 May a deputy from Iraqiya was attacked by unidentified gunmen outside his house in Mosul and subsequently died from his injuries.

The formation of a new Government

On 23 June 2010 the Prime Minister accepted the resignation of the Minister of Electricity, Karim Wahid al-Hasan, who had been the target of violent demonstrations in several cities as a result of his tough approach to power-rationing at a time of soaring summer temperatures. Two people were reported to have been shot dead in Basra on 19 June during clashes between security forces and protesters angered by the ongoing electricity shortages and blackouts. Meanwhile, amid renewed violence perpetrated by militant groups, on 13 June 2010 at least 15 people were killed in an insurgent attack on the Central Bank headquarters in Baghdad, which was claimed by Islamic State of Iraq; it was believed to be an attempt by the group to retrieve funds. On 20 June two suicide car bombs targeted the state-controlled Trade Bank of Iraq building, resulting in some 26 deaths; Islamic State of Iraq was again thought to have been behind the attack. On 7 July a reported 32 pilgrims visiting an important Shi'a Muslim shrine in Baghdad were the victims of a suicide bomb attack planned by Sunni insurgents. A further suicide bombing on 18 July resulted in the deaths of up to 45 members of the Sunni Awakening Councils close to the Iraqi capital. Three days later 28 people died in a car bombing which exploded close to a mosque in Baquba.

As the US Administration sought to exert pressure on the first- and second-placed factions in the polls of March 2010, Allawi's Iraqiya and al-Maliki's State of Law alliance, in order to reach a power-sharing deal before the USA withdrew its combat troops, the agreement between al-Maliki's bloc and the Iraqi National Alliance appeared to be faltering. It was reported on 4 August that the NA was on the verge of collapse since smaller Shi'a movements such as the Sadrists were still refusing to back al-Maliki's renomination as Prime Minister; talks between the two alliances broke down in mid-August. For his part, Allawi—whose Iraqiya coalition was also refusing to join a government under al-Maliki's premiership—had held a meeting with al-Sadr in Damascus, Syria, on 19 July, with the declared aim of accelerating moves towards the formation of a viable administration. On 16 August it was reported that discussions between Iraqiya and the State of Law alliance had been suspended, after the incumbent Prime Minister described Iraqiya in a televised interview as being a 'Sunni bloc'. A spokesman for Allawi insisted that his was a secular nationalist movement, although it had predominantly Sunni support. Moreover, al-Maliki steadfastly refused to step down as Prime Minister in favour of Allawi.

President Obama formally declared the end of the US combat mission in Iraq, known as Operation Iraqi Freedom, on 31 August 2010. The US President confirmed that almost 50,000 US forces would remain in the country in order to 'advise and assist' Iraq's security forces and defend US interests, but that the US military would be completely withdrawn by 31 December 2011, under the terms of the SOFA. (The Iraqi Chief of Staff of the Joint Armed Forces, Lt-Gen. Babakir Zebari, had warned in early August 2010 that Iraqi troops might not be adequately prepared to guarantee the security of Iraq until 2020, and suggested that US forces should in fact remain until that date.) A ceremony was held in Baghdad on 1 September 2010 to commemorate the start of the 'final phase' of the USA's mission in Iraq, code-named 'Operation New Dawn'. The weeks preceding the end of US combat operations had been notably violent in several parts of the country, with a wave of attacks being perpetrated against Iraqi police and security targets, as well as ordinary civilians. In two of the most serious incidents, on 7 August 2010 two car bombings in Basra had resulted in more than 43 deaths, while on 17 August a suicide bombing at an army base in Baghdad killed around 60 soldiers and military recruits.

During the latter part of 2010 the campaign being waged by radical Islamist organizations against Iraq's Christian community intensified, resulting in a further exodus of Christians either to the relative safety of northern Iraq or abroad. On 3 November Islamic State of Iraq issued a statement threatening to 'extirpate and disperse' all Christians from the country, describing all institutions and followers of the Christian religion as 'legitimate targets' for Islamist attacks. This followed the deadliest attack on Iraqi Christians since the start of the conflict in 2003. On 31 October 2010 gunmen entered the Syrian Catholic church in central Baghdad during a mass, holding around 100 worshippers hostage and reportedly demanding the release of al-Qa'ida detainees from Iraqi prisons. Some sources described the militants as originating from other Arab countries, but one of the perpetrators claimed to belong to Islamic State of Iraq. At least 58 people (including two priests, and a reported six militants) were killed, most as a result of suicide bombs detonated by the attackers as security forces entered the church in an attempt to free the hostages.

Meanwhile, on 1 October 2010 it was announced that the NA had finally decided to support al-Maliki's continuing as Prime Minister at the head of a new administration, amid reports that a deal had been brokered by the Government of Iran (see below). On 10 November the leaders of Iraq's principal factions in the Council of Representatives formally signed a power-sharing agreement under which a coalition government would again be led by al-Maliki (a Shi'a), while a new foreign policy and security council, the National Council for Strategic Policies (NCSP), would be run by Allawi (a secular Shi'a). Observers described this as an attempt to dilute some of the Prime Minister's powers. The coalition agreement followed a power-sharing deal which had been reached between the newly formed NA and both the Kurdistan Alliance and Iraqiya in early November. On 11 November a session of the Council of Representatives was duly held, at which Jalal Talabani (a Kurd) was re-elected as President, while a Sunni Arab member of Iraqiya, Osama al-Nujaifi, was elected as the chamber's Speaker. However, around 60 Iraqiya deputies subsequently walked out of the parliamentary session, complaining that the terms of the power-sharing deal had been broken since their demands for an end to what they deemed to be the unfair de-Baathification process had been refused. (Iraqiya reportedly sought the reinstatement of three of the movement's senior members who had been barred prior to the election.) Two days later, after a meeting between the leaders of the three major blocs, it was agreed that the deputies' grievances would be addressed. Al-Maliki was officially named by Talabani as Prime Minister-designate on 25 November and given 30 days to form a new government. Meanwhile, it emerged in late October 2010 that, apparently as part of the Iranian-brokered agreement reached in early October between al-Maliki and al-Sadr, large numbers of militants from the latter's militia, the Mahdi Army, had been released from gaol. Although al-Sadr had previously been fiercely opposed to al-Maliki—the Prime Minister's previous administration having ordered the official crackdown against the Mahdi Army in 2008—the cleric was also believed to have been promised certain ministerial portfolios and had also come under pressure from Iran to agree the terms of a deal. The Mahdi Army was reported to have been dissolved by al-Sadr in mid-2008 and succeeded by a civilian organization, Al-Mumahidun (Supporters of the Mahdi). (Al-Sadr returned to Iraq in January 2011, after more than three years' self-imposed exile in Iran.)

On 17 November 2010 President Talabani refused to approve the execution order for Saddam Hussain's former Deputy Prime Minister, Tareq Aziz, after Aziz had on 26 October been sentenced to death by the Federal Supreme Court for his involvement in the persecution of members of Shi'a political parties during the 1980s; two other senior members of the Baathist regime, including the former Minister of the Interior and Director of Iraqi Intelligence, Saadoun Shaker, were also given a death sentence. (Aziz had already been sentenced to a 15-year gaol term for having ordered the killing of 42 merchants found guilty of profiteering in 1992, and a further seven-year term for the forced displacement of a group of Iraqi Kurds from the north of the country in the 1980s.) Announcing his decision, Talabani cited the fact that Aziz was 74 years old and also a Christian. Nevertheless, a prime-ministerial aide indicated in December 2011 that Aziz would be executed during the course of 2012, following the completion of the withdrawal of US troops (see Recent developments: completion of the withdrawal of US troops and escalating sectarian tensions). The aide also noted that new legislation was under consideration that, if approved, would require all death sentences to be ratified by the President within 15 days of their being handed down. Meanwhile, on 29 November 2010 Shaker was given a further death sentence for his role in the execution of Iraqi Kurds during the 1980s.

Some nine months after elections were held to the Council of Representatives, on 21 December 2010 the legislature finally approved the new Council of Ministers submitted by al-Maliki, in which all of Iraq's major blocs were represented. However, the defence, national security and interior portfolios remained vacant as parties continued to disagree about possible nominees to these crucial ministries, which, it was feared, might be used to reinforce Iraq's sectarian divisions; al-Maliki was to take temporary charge of these portfolios. Of the 42 ministers in the Government, 13 were interim appointments. Saleh al-Mutlaq (a Sunni Arab), who had only been permitted to participate in politics a week earlier after he renounced his former Baathist affiliation, was named as one of three Deputy Prime Ministers; Dr Rozh Nuri Shawais (a Kurd) was named as Deputy Prime Minister and Acting Minister of Trade, while Hussein al-Shahristani (a Shi'a) became Deputy Prime Minister for Energy Affairs. The Minister of Foreign Affairs in the outgoing administration, Hoshyar al-Zibari (a Kurd), retained his post; Abd al-Karim al-Luaibi (a Shi'a) and Dr Rafie al-Issawi (a Sunni Arab) became Ministers of Oil and of Finance, respectively. On 13 February 2011 eight further nominees, including Raad Shallal al-Ani as Minister of Electricity and Khairallah Hassan Babakr Muhammad as Minister of Trade, received parliamentary approval. Ali Yousuf Abd al-Nabi al-Shukri was approved as Minister of Planning in early April, although candidates submitted by al-Maliki for the positions of Minister of Defence and of the Interior were rejected. Agreement was finally reached in mid-May on the appointment of three Vice-Presidents—Tariq al-Hashimi, Dr Adil Abd al-Mahdi and Khudhair al-Khuzai. President Talabani subsequently appointed al-Mahdi as First Vice-President; however, al-Mahdi tendered his resignation from the post at the end of May, citing the hope that his departure might precipitate a streamlining of the cabinet, which, prior to his departure, had numbered 46 ministers; al-Mahdi's resignation was reported to have been accepted in July. In August 12 ministries were disbanded, including those of marsh lands and tribal affairs, following parliamentary approval of a proposal submitted by al-Maliki. However, disagreements between the coalition parties regarding the allocation of the defence, interior and national security portfolios remained unresolved at early 2012.

Meanwhile, in mid-January 2011 the Federal Supreme Court issued a controversial ruling that placed Iraq's independent commissions such as the IHEC and the Central Bank under executive, rather than legislative, control. Despite widespread criticism of the Court's decision, al-Maliki stated that it could not be overruled, leading opponents of the Prime Minister to claim that he would use the change to consolidate his power over several important bodies. Following protracted disagreements between the leading parliamentary groups regarding the precise details of the new body's establishment and the extent of its authority, Allawi announced in early March that he no longer wished to preside over the Council, accusing al-Maliki of 'a lack of commitment to national partnership' and citing the Prime Minister's decision to assume interim responsibility for the crucial defence, national security and interior portfolios, together with the protracted delay in appointing permanent ministers, as evidence of his refusal to share power. Despite an apparent breakthrough in August during negotiations, mediated by President Talabani, between the State of Law alliance and Iraqiya—with al-Maliki reported to have agreed to honour the terms of the power-sharing agreement and to accelerate the formation of the NCSP—the Council had yet to be formed as of early 2012. Moreover, al-Maliki had stated on numerous occasions that affording meaningful powers to the Council would effectively result in the creation of a secondary national government, which would be in violation of the Constitution, casting significant doubt on his stated commitment to facilitating the establishment of the NCSP.

According to Iraq Body Count, an estimated 4,045 civilians had died as a result of violence during 2010, compared with 4,713 in 2009; this represented the lowest annual death toll since conflict began in 2003. However, in a renewed wave of violence in early 2011, some 50 people died in a suicide bomb attack on a police recruitment centre in Tikrit in mid-January, while later that month 48 people were killed when a car bomb exploded at a Shi'a funeral in Baghdad. In late March 58 people were reported to have been killed following an attack on the provincial council building in Tikrit.

Meanwhile, during February 2011, as social and political unrest spread across large parts of the Middle East and North Africa, spontaneous protests were held in several of Iraq's major cities—including Baghdad, Basra, Sulaimaniya and Karbala—by people demonstrating against perceived official corruption, high unemployment, the lack of civil liberties, and the failure of federal and local government institutions to provide for their most basic needs. The protesters called for 25 February to be a 'day of rage'; at least nine people were reportedly killed in clashes with security forces in cities outside the capital, including three people in Mosul. Al-Maliki, who was reported to have described the demonstrations as a 'Baathist plot', had attempted to prevent the uprisings in Tunisia and Egypt—which had resulted in the ouster of both countries' governing regimes—from spreading to Iraq by announcing in early February that he would not stand for a third term of office in 2014. He also pledged to pursue constitutional reform, particularly by implementing legislation to prevent any Prime Minister from serving more than two consecutive terms of office. The Government also agreed to reduce the price of electricity in an apparent gesture to placate the protesters. Grand Ayatollah al-Sistani appealed for the Government to improve public services and to reduce benefits offered to senior government officials—a rare intervention from the religious leader since his withdrawal from the political arena in mid-2006 (see The formation of a permanent Council of Representatives). In late February 2011 al-Maliki issued a warning to members of the Council of Ministers, urging an improvement in ministerial performance and promising that changes would be effected if after a period of 100 days a review did not reveal tangible progress, prompting speculation of imminent ministerial dismissals. Al-Maliki also announced that US $900m. of funds that had been allocated to the purchase of fighter aircraft were to be redirected towards the provision of food for the poor, with a further $400m. reserved for the purchase of generator fuel to power air conditioners during the hot summer months, and initiated a series of infrastructure projects intended to improve Iraq's dilapidated road and sewerage systems.

However, the measures appeared to have little effect on the protests, which continued into March–April 2011, principally in the Kurdish Autonomous Region. In late April around 98 people were injured at a demonstration in Sulaimaniya after security forces opened fire on protesters demanding the resignation of the Kurdish regional administration. Days later Iraqi troops and *peshmerga* fighters entered the city in an attempt to quell the protests. By the end of April it was reported that up to 36 people had been killed across Iraq as a result of the unrest. In June, as al-Maliki's deadline for ministerial improvements approached, the Prime Minister announced that there would be no ministerial dismissals owing to poor performance and claimed that his comments in February had been misconstrued. Hundreds of demonstrators converged in Baghdad following the expiry of al-Maliki's deadline for reform later in June, protesting against the Government's perceived failure to achieve meaningful progress, and demanding an improvement in public services, particularly the supply of electricity.

In early August 2011 Raad Shallal al-Ani tendered his resignation as Minister of Electricity, at the request of al-Maliki, after a government investigation discovered procedural irregularities pertaining to power contracts signed with two foreign firms. A government spokesperson subsequently announced that two power plant contracts, providing for the construction by the Canadian Alliance for Power Generation Equipment and Germany's MBH of at least 10 power plants in Iraq, had been cancelled owing to 'manipulation and misleading information' concerning the firms' legal and financial status as well as their technical capabilities. It had been hoped that the terminated contracts, which were reported collectively to have been worth some US $1,700m., would help to ameliorate the problem of power shortages, which remained a source of considerable popular discontent. Abd al-Karim Aftan al-Jumaili was subsequently awarded responsibility for the electricity portfolio.

Recent developments: completion of the withdrawal of US troops

An escalation of attacks targeting US troops from June 2011 prompted concerns regarding the security situation in Iraq ahead of the scheduled completion of the withdrawal of US troops, due by 31 December under the terms of the SOFA. Some 18 US soldiers were killed in eight separate attacks during a six-week period in June–July, forcing the US military back into active combat despite the formal conclusion of the combat operation in August 2010. In mid-August 2011 13 apparently co-ordinated bomb attacks on the same day, targeting largely Shi'a areas across Iraq as well as government compounds in Karbala and Najaf, killed more than 70 people and injured more than 250 others; the attacks, responsibility for which was widely attributed to Islamic State of Iraq, elicited further expressions of concern about the Iraqi authorities' ability to manage national security in the absence of US assistance.

In an important step in Iraq's progress towards full autonomy, in July 2011 the Iraqi authorities assumed control of the Development Fund for Iraq, which had been established following the ousting of the regime of Saddam Hussain in 2003 and contained billions of dollars of oil revenues set aside by the UN. Responsibility for the Fund was henceforth to be controlled by a panel of Iraqi financial experts operating under terms approved by the Council of Ministers. Meanwhile, in June 2011 a US official investigating the disappearance of US $6,600m. from the Fund, which had been airlifted into Iraq by the Bush Administration during 2003–04 as part of a $20,000m. reconstruction package, suggested that the money may have been stolen by elements within the Iraqi interim administration at the time. The investigator did not speculate on the possible identity of those responsible for the disappearance of the funds.

Speculation that an agreement might be brokered between Iraqi and US officials providing for the continued deployment within Iraq of a contingent of US military personnel beyond the end of 2011 was ended in mid-October, when President Obama announced that all US troops remaining in Iraq were to be withdrawn by 31 December, as scheduled. Protracted negotiations regarding the possibility of US troops remaining in Iraq beyond the end of 2011 were reported to have broken down owing to a refusal by the Iraqi authorities to acquiesce to US demands that any remaining troops be granted immunity from prosecution by Iraqi courts. Bitter disagreements had also been reported on the subject within Iraq. Some elements within the Government had stressed the need for continued US military assistance, training and equipment, and had urged al-Maliki to negotiate an extension to the deadline. However, Muqtada al-Sadr, a vital source of support for al-Maliki, was particularly vociferous in his opposition to any extension of the US mission; in September al-Sadr had ordered his supporters to halt attacks on US troops but threatened to resume such operations if withdrawal was not completed by the year-end deadline.

During a joint press conference held on 12 December 2011, al-Maliki and Obama reaffirmed their mutual commitment to a long-term comprehensive partnership between Iraq and the USA, including plans to bolster co-operation in the fields of counter-terrorism, defence and security, as well as trade and economic development, institution-building, education and energy. Although al-Maliki hailed the imminent completion of the US withdrawal as an indication of the successful defeat of terrorism and the beginning of a 'new chapter' for Iraq, Obama—while claiming that US troops were leaving behind an Iraq with a 'stable and self-reliant' Government and stressing that the US commitment to stability in Iraq would be 'enduring'—cautioned of the heightened risk of attacks in the coming months by elements seeking to 'derail Iraq's progress'. Many observers noted that the withdrawal would herald the beginning of a new stage of struggle within Iraq and across the wider region, with the lack of US military personnel rendering Iraq more susceptible to increasing Iranian influence. Following the completion of the US withdrawal, the USA was to have no military bases within Iraq, although a small number of military personnel would remain in the country to assist with arms sales, together with some 16,000 personnel (comprising around 2,000 diplomatic and federal staff, and 14,000 contractors) to assist in the establishment of effective diplomatic, civilian and military ties. (At early 2012 negotiations were reported to be ongoing with regard to the possible redeployment to Iraq of a small number of US troops to engage in future training missions.)

A ceremony was staged in Baghdad on 15 December 2011 to mark formally the end of the US mission, attended by the US Secretary of Defense, Leon Panetta. On 18 December the final convoy of 500 US troops withdrew from Iraq, crossing the border into Kuwait, and thereby concluding a campaign that had claimed the lives of 4,484 US troops and cost the US Government an estimated US $800,000m. since its inception in March 2003.

According to Iraq Body Count, an estimated 4,087 civilians died as a result of violence during 2011, representing a slight increase on the previous year. In early 2012 the independent monitoring group estimated the number of violent civilian deaths during the entire period since the US-led invasion in 2003 at between 105,052 and 114,731.

As had been feared by the Obama Administration, an escalation in sectarian violence soon became apparent across Iraq. According to Iraqi security officials, by late January 2012 some 434 people had been killed since the completion of the US withdrawal, of whom the majority were killed in attacks targeting the Shi'a community. Some 45 Shi'a pilgrims were killed in a suicide bomb attack in the town of Nasiriya in early January, and in mid-January a further 53 pilgrims were killed en route to a major Shi'a mosque in Zubeir district (20 km south-west of Basra) to mark the festival of Arbain—one of the most important holy days in the Shi'a calendar—when a suicide bomber attacked the checkpoint at which they were waiting. Thirteen people were killed and more than 60 others injured when four car bombs exploded in three primarily Shi'a districts of Baghdad in mid-January, and a further 31 people were killed and 60 others injured in a suicide bomb attack outside a hospital in western Baghdad later in the month. Attacks against the national security forces also appeared to intensify, with a spate of attacks targeting police officers in January, including an attack on a police compound in the city of Ramadi (100 km west of Baghdad) in mid-January, in which at least seven people were killed, and the fatal shooting two days later of five police officers at a checkpoint in the province of Anbar.

Meanwhile, in mid-December 2011, shortly after the completion of the US withdrawal, Prime Minister al-Maliki signed a warrant for the arrest of Vice-President al-Hashimi on charges of terrorism, and issued a concurrent request to the Council of Representatives to remove Deputy Prime Minister al-Mutlaq from office. Al-Hashimi, who fled to northern Iraq following the issuing of the arrest warrant, was alleged by an investigative committee established by the Ministry of the Interior to have ordered bodyguards to carry out terrorist attacks against government and security officials, as well as Shi'a pilgrims, for a number of years. Al-Maliki demanded that the President of the Kurdistan Autonomous Region, Masoud Barzani, and Iraqi President Jalal Talabani transfer al-Hashimi over to the custody of the Iraqi judiciary in Baghdad. In protest at the action taken against two of its members, who were both Sunnis, Iraqiya subsequently withdrew its participation from the Council of Ministers and announced a concomitant boycott of the Council of Representatives. Representatives of Iraqiya, which controlled 82 parliamentary seats and nine cabinet posts, accused al-Maliki of attempting to centralize power, of disregarding the terms of the power-sharing agreement signed in November 2010, and of arbitrarily arresting aides and security guards employed by Iraqiya leaders—an aide of former Prime Minister Ayad Allawi claimed that more than 30 members of his staff had been detained in recent weeks. Iraqiya also blamed al-Maliki for the authorities' failure to stem recent unrest in the largely Sunni province of Diyala. The dispute between the Shi'a Prime Minister and the nominally secular Iraqiya (which remained, however, dominated by Sunnis) threatened further to exacerbate sectarian divisions, prompting the US Government to appeal for calm on both sides in an attempt to defuse mounting tensions. In late January 2012 Iraqiya announced that it was to end its parliamentary boycott, with effect from 31 January, as a 'goodwill gesture', and in early February Iraqiya also resumed its participation in cabinet meetings. In April, however, the Higher Judicial Council announced that al-Hashimi—who was thought to be in Istanbul, Turkey—would be tried *in absentia* on charges of murder from 3 May.

Meanwhile, in late January 2012 the UN Office of the High Commissioner for Human Rights (OHCHR) stated that at least 63 people had been executed by the Iraqi authorities in the preceding two months, including 34 on a single day in mid-January, while the UN High Commissioner for Human Rights, Navi Pillay, expressed reservations about the 'due process and fairness of trials' in Iraq. Pillay's comments echoed concerns expressed by Amnesty International in a report published in late 2011, in which the rights organization had claimed that at least 1,300 prisoners were on death row in Iraq at that time, that trials 'consistently failed to satisfy international standards for fair trial', and that torture and other abuse of detainees within Iraqi prisons—particularly those under the control of the Ministries of Defence and of the Interior—was 'rife'. Despite the increasing international concern about the rate of executions by the Iraqi authorities, at the beginning of February the Ministry of Justice confirmed that a further 17 people had been executed 'according to the law' on 31 January, bringing the total of those confirmed as being executed in Iraq in the first month of 2012 to in excess of 50—although some human rights groups claimed that the actual figure might be significantly higher.

Regional relations

Despite numerous setbacks, a general improvement was perceived in Iraq's relations with other Arab states from late 2000. In October Iraq was represented at a summit meeting of the Arab League for the first time since the 1990–91 Gulf crisis, as Revolutionary Command Council (RCC) Vice-President Izzat Ibrahim al-Douri attended the emergency session convened in Cairo, Egypt, to discuss the Israeli–Palestinian crisis that had erupted in September 2000. Saddam Hussain (to whom an invitation had been issued for the first time since 1990) was represented by senior Iraqi officials at the Arab League summit held in Amman in March 2001. The summit was considered as having made the most comprehensive effort hitherto in addressing divisions arising from the Gulf conflict. None the less, a draft resolution presented by the Iraqi delegation urging an end to UN sanctions and a resumption of civilian flights failed to secure adoption, owing to Iraq's unwillingness to accede to a requirement of a specific guarantee that Iraq would not repeat the invasion of 1990: Iraq contended that it had already made sufficiently clear its recognition of Kuwait's territorial integrity.

The extent of Iraq's rehabilitation among the majority of Arab states was particularly evident as speculation increased, from the latter stages of 2001, regarding potential US-led military action against Iraq. Leaders of influential Arab states, among them Egypt, Jordan and Syria, expressed particular concern at the likely consequences should the Bush Administration's campaign be directed against any Arab state, warning against exacerbating tensions in a region already under great strain because of the Israeli–Palestinian crisis. In January 2002 Saddam Hussain referred specifically to the need to improve relations with Kuwait and Saudi Arabia; later in the month Iraq reportedly announced its preparedness to allow a delegation from Kuwait to visit Iraq to verify that no Kuwaiti prisoners of war were being held (Kuwait continued to assert that Iraq was detaining at least 90 Kuwaiti nationals). At the Arab League summit held in Beirut, Lebanon, in March, it was announced that Kuwait and Iraq had reached agreement on the resolution of outstanding differences (see the chapter on Kuwait). In May Iraq notified the UN of its intention to return to Kuwait the official documents and archives removed during the 1990–91 occupation.

Iraq's relations with Kuwait were significantly affected by the US-led campaign to oust the Baathist regime in March 2003, especially since the coalition forces launched their ground assault from Kuwait. The mandate of UNIKOM was declared to have been completed in October, and in June 2004, when sovereignty was transferred to the Iraqi Interim Government, Kuwait announced the resumption of diplomatic relations with Iraq.

In September 2003 the new Iraqi Minister of Oil, Ibrahim Bahr al-Ulum, was invited to take Iraq's seat at an OPEC meeting in Vienna, Austria. Iraq also attended a summit meeting of the Organization of the Islamic Conference (OIC—now Organization of Islamic Cooperation) in Malaysia during October as a full member. In June 2005 Egypt became the first Arab state to nominate an ambassador to Baghdad since the US-led invasion; however, the abduction and murder of the ambassador, Ihab al-Sherif, in July made other Arab countries unwilling to send envoys to Iraq. Al-Qa'ida in Iraq claimed responsibility for the killing of al-Sherif, together with the subsequent abduction and killing of two Algerian diplomats later in July. The ambassador of Pakistan and the head of Bahrain's mission in Baghdad were also attacked in that month, while the diplomatic staff of the countries in question were withdrawn in reaction to the attacks. However, as the security situation showed considerable signs of improvement by mid-2008, several Arab countries (including Kuwait, Bahrain, the UAE, Jordan and Syria) chose to resume full diplomatic relations with Iraq and to return ambassadors to Baghdad. The UAE also cancelled some US $7,000m. of Iraqi debt in July. In November 2009 the new Egyptian ambassador to Iraq, Sherif Kamal Shahin, arrived in Baghdad, assuming a role that had been vacant since the killing of al-Sherif in 2005.

In October 2008 Ali Muhammad al-Momen arrived in Baghdad to take the role of Kuwaiti ambassador to Iraq, thereby becoming the first person to hold that post since diplomatic relations were abruptly severed in 1990. In February 2010 Ban Ki-Moon, the UN Secretary-General, confirmed that senior UN representatives had recently been engaged in intensive efforts to promote progress on all outstanding issues between Iraq and Kuwait, including the issue of Kuwaiti missing persons. In early March it was reported that Iraq had nominated its first ambassador to Kuwait since the Iraqi invasion in 1990; Muhammad Hussain Bahr al-Ulum arrived in Kuwait City to assume his diplomatic post at the end of May 2010. Earlier that month the Iraqi authorities had announced the gradual dissolution of the national airline, Iraqi Airways, in an effort to avoid paying US $1,200m. in compensation to Kuwait for 10 Kuwait Airways planes that it had appropriated after the 1990 invasion. The Kuwaiti authorities had, on several recent occasions, attempted to seize Iraqi Airways planes when they landed at foreign airports. In May 2011 it was announced that the dissolution of the airline had been halted by the Iraqi Government. Later that month the Kuwaiti authorities seized control of the Iraqi Airways office in Amman, after obtaining a court ruling in Jordan. Meanwhile, by mid-2010 Kuwait had received only $17,500m. of the $41,800m. debt owed by Iraq, according to the UN special compensation fund, and the Iraqi Government indicated that it was unable to complete the payment of reparations. However, despite the removal of Iraq's Baathist regime in 2003, the Kuwaiti Government has consistently refused to agree to the cancellation of this debt.

An official visit to Amman by Iraqi Prime Minister al-Maliki in June 2008 heralded new progress in Jordanian-Iraqi relations. Al-Maliki and King Abdullah discussed diplomatic and economic ties between the two states, and in August the King made a surprise visit to Baghdad for further talks with the Iraqi premier. This was the first visit to Baghdad by an Arab head of state since the fall of Saddam Hussain in 2003. In September 2008 a new deal governing the supply of subsidized Iraqi oil to Jordan was announced. In October Nayef al-Zaidan took up his post as Jordan's ambassador to Iraq—the first such appointment since the withdrawal of the previous ambassador following the bombing of the Jordanian embassy in August 2003. In January 2009 the Iraqi Government welcomed a directive from King Abdullah to ease the restrictions on Iraqis entering and residing in Jordan. Following an official visit to Baghdad by the Jordanian Prime Minister, Marouf al-Bakhit, in June 2011, during which he met with al-Maliki and President Jalal Talabani, it was announced that Iraq had agreed to increase the volume of oil supply to Jordan from 10,000 b/d to 15,000 b/d, with a view to increasing supply to some 30,000 b/d ultimately. The two countries also agreed to increase the volume of bilateral trade.

Iraq and Iran resumed diplomatic relations in September 2004, although many issues relating to the 1980–88 War remained unresolved. Prime Minister al-Ja'fari visited Iran in July 2005, followed by President Talabani in November—the first visit to Tehran by an Iraqi head of state in over 30 years. Also in November an Iraqi passenger flight landed in Tehran for the first time since the outbreak of war in 1980. In February 2005, meanwhile, it was reported that Syria had captured and handed over to Iraqi security forces Sabawi Ibrahim al-Hassan, a half-brother of Saddam Hussain, as a gesture of 'goodwill'; al-Hassan was accused of involvement in the insurgency against coalition forces.

A breakthrough in Iraq's relations with Syria occurred in November 2006, when the two countries declared that they would restore diplomatic ties that had been severed in 1982. Iraqi officials hoped that the resumption in relations with Syria would assist in stemming the flow of insurgents across their joint border. In December 2006 Iraq and Syria formally opened embassies in each other's capitals, and in January 2007 President Talabani became the first Iraqi President to pay an official visit to Syria for nearly three decades. Bilateral relations became strained in the following month, when Iraq accused Syria of harbouring fugitive militants and refusing refuge for genuine Iraqi refugees. Syria finally named an ambassador to Baghdad, Nawaf al-Fares, in September 2008. However, al-Fares and the Iraqi ambassador in Syria were both recalled from their respective embassies in August 2009, following Iraqi allegations, adamantly denied by Syria, that the latter was harbouring two men suspected of involvement in a series of bombings that had targeted government buildings in Baghdad earlier that month, killing more than 100 people (see Domestic Political Affairs). Talks, mediated by Turkey, between the Iraqi and Syrian ministers responsible for foreign affairs in September failed to resolve the dispute. However, following further negotiations during 2010, the two ambassadors were returned to their respective posts in November. Meanwhile, Iraqi Vice-President Tariq al-Hashimi travelled to Syria in March 2010 to examine arrangements for the participation of displaced Iraqis in the forthcoming national election in Iraq. During his visit al-Hashimi also held talks on bilateral relations with President Bashar al-Assad and Mouallem, which were subsequently described as 'successful and constructive'. Despite a number of conciliatory statements and gestures by the Iraqi Government during 2011 in response to mounting international calls for President Assad to tender his resignation amid widespread popular protests in Syria (q.v.), in mid-September Prime Minister al-Maliki urged Assad to step down.

Iran, meanwhile, hosted security talks on Iraq in November 2006, when President Talabani made his second official visit to Tehran. According to Iranian television, Talabani spoke of Iraq's 'dire need of Iran's help in establishing security and stability', while also urging the two sides to raise the profile of bilateral economic, political, security and cultural relations. Although the Iranian leadership pledged to assist Iraq by any possible means, it warned that the restoration of security was dependent on the withdrawal of US troops. In March 2007 the most significant international conference to be held in Baghdad since the Arab League summit meeting of 1990 was attended by representatives from Iraq's neighbouring states, as well as other leading regional powers, the Arab League, the UN and the OIC. The aim of the conference was to find a means of reducing the violence in Iraq and accelerating the handover of the country to full Iraqi control. Two sessions of direct discussions took place between the US and Iranian ambassadors to Baghdad in May and July 2007. The two envoys pledged to co-operate in an effort to end the sectarian violence in Iraq, and the first meeting of their newly established joint sub-committee was held in the Iraqi capital in August. The Iranian President, Mahmoud Ahmadinejad, undertook an official two-day visit to Baghdad in March 2008, where he held cordial discussions with his Iraqi counterpart and signed seven MOUs relating to bilateral co-operation. During the visit Ahmadinejad denied persistent claims by the US Administration that Iran was providing military and financial assistance to Iraqi Shi'a militias. In July 2011 Iranian forces crossed the border into northern Iraq in pursuit of fighters belonging to the separatist group the Party of Free Life in Kurdistan. Several Iraqi Kurds were reported to have been killed and hundreds of others displaced during the offensive. In a more positive development, in the same month Iraq, Iran and Syria signed an MOU providing for the construction of a 6,000-km natural gas pipeline, which upon completion would extend under Iraqi, Syrian and Lebanese territory and transport gas from Assalouyeh, in southern Iran, to the European market. The US $10,000m. pipeline project, construction of which was scheduled to commence in mid-2012 and to be completed in 2015, was expected to result in increased investment and employment opportunities within Iraq, as well as generating significant royalties for the Iraqi Government.

In September 2007 Turkey and Iraq signed a security co-operation pact intended to curb the military activities of the Kurdish separatist organization the Kurdistan Workers' Party (Partiya Karkeren Kurdistan—PKK). However, although the pact did not include Turkey's principal demand that its military be permitted to enter Iraqi territory in pursuit of Kurdish fighters, in December Turkish troops began an offensive against PKK bases in Iraq's northern region, in response to a series of cross-border raids by armed separatists to carry out bomb attacks against Turkish soldiers in south-eastern Turkey. (The Turkish Grand National Assembly—TGNA—had voted in October to authorize its military to carry out cross-border military operations in Iraq.) The Iraqi Government protested to its Turkish counterpart that it had not been consulted over the military action, while the President of the Kurdish Autonomous Region, Masoud Barzani, described Turkey's actions as a violation of Iraqi sovereignty. In February 2008 it was initially reported that up to 10,000 Turkish troops had entered northern Iraq, in what appeared to be a much larger incursion than that of the previous December, and with the additional launching of air-strikes against PKK militant bases; however, it was subsequently reported that only several hundred soldiers had participated in the military campaign. Nevertheless, dozens of PKK militants were killed in the week-long offensive, together with several Turkish soldiers. (The Turkish military claimed by this time to have killed 240 PKK fighters, and to have lost 27 of its soldiers; however, PKK sources alleged that around 90 Turkish soldiers had died in the recent incursion.) Once again, the Iraqi authorities asserted that they had not given their approval for the offensive. However, Turkey's Prime Minister, Recep Tayyip Erdoğan, undertook a visit to Iraq in July, and the two sides agreed to form a strategic co-operation council to improve bilateral relations; several accords on energy and border security were also signed.

At the inaugural meeting of the Iraq-Turkey High-Level Strategic Co-operation Council convened in İstanbul, Turkey, in September 2009 and attended by delegations headed by the respective ministers responsible for foreign affairs, the two nations renewed their commitment to pursue greater co-operation and integration in several areas. During a meeting of the strategic co-operation council in Baghdad later that month, attended by Erdoğan and a Turkish ministerial delegation, al-Maliki appealed to Turkey to respect Iraq's sovereignty and to cease its military incursions into Iraqi territory. None the less, co-operation agreements covering a total of 44 topics, including energy, security, environment, water, border crossings and agriculture, were signed by representatives of the two countries. In late March 2011 Erdoğan became the first Turkish premier to visit the Kurdish Autonomous Region of Iraq, where he held talks with Barzani regarding co-operation in combating the PKK. On the previous day the Turkish Prime Minister had visited Baghdad for discussions with al-Maliki, as well as senior Iraqi politicians and religious leaders, aimed at improving economic and political ties between the two countries. In May the Iraqi Government declared that the Turkish authorities' restriction of water supply from Turkey to Iraq via the Euphrates and Tigris rivers was 'unacceptable', claiming that a series of dams constructed on both rivers allowed Turkey to monopolize the rivers' waters, to the detriment of Iraq and Syria. An Iraqi government spokesperson insisted that the Council of Representatives would not recognize the strategic co-operation council with Turkey until a bilateral water-sharing agreement was successfully concluded. In October the TGNA voted to extend for a further year the decree authorizing cross-border military operations against PKK militants in Iraq (this had previously been extended in October 2009 and again in October 2010).

CONSTITUTION AND GOVERNMENT

Prior to the ousting of Saddam Hussain's regime by the US-led coalition in April 2003, Iraq was divided into 18 governorates (including three Autonomous Regions). In the immediate aftermath of the war, a US-led Coalition Provisional Authority (CPA) was established to govern the country in the absence of an elected sovereign government. UN Security Council Resolution 1483 of 22 May gave legitimacy to the occupying powers in this task. On 13 July a 25-member interim Governing Council was formed, the members of which were selected by the CPA in proportion to Iraq's main ethnic and religious groups. It had no executive power, but could appoint ministers and diplomatic representatives, draw up a new constitution and set a date for free elections. The Governing Council decided upon a rotating presidency, commencing in September, with nine members of the council each serving for one month. In the same month 25 ministers were appointed to serve in an interim Cabinet, also chosen according to ethnicity and creed. On 15 November the CPA and Governing Council jointly published a plan for the creation of a democratically elected, sovereign government and constitution by the end of 2005. However, this plan was superseded by the Transitional Administrative Law (TAL) signed on 8 March 2004. Under the terms of the TAL, an Iraqi Interim Government assumed power on 28 June 2004 (two days earlier than was stipulated), and the CPA and Governing Council were dissolved. The Interim Government was replaced by an Iraqi Transitional Government, consisting of a state Presidency Council (comprising a President and two Vice-Presidents) and a Prime Minister and Cabinet to be appointed by the Council, in April 2005, following elections to the 275-member Transitional National Assembly (TNA), which took place on 30 January. Members of the TNA were required to produce a draft constitution by 15 August 2005, to be approved by national referendum by 15 October. In the event, disagreements over key issues delayed the submission of the draft Constitution to the TNA until 28 August 2005, and a further amended text was presented to the UN on 14 September. The draft Constitution was ratified following its endorsement at a national referendum on 15 October (78.6% of the valid votes cast were in favour). National elections for a permanent legislature, the Council of Representatives, took place on 15 December.

REGIONAL AND INTERNATIONAL CO-OPERATION

Iraq is a member of the League of Arab States (the Arab League, see p. 364) and the Organization of Arab Petroleum Exporting Countries (see p. 401). It joined the UN on 21 December 1945. The country was granted observer status at the World Trade Organization (WTO, see p. 433) in February 2004, and working party discussions to negotiate the country's eventual membership of the WTO began in May 2007. The country also participates in the Organization of Islamic Cooperation (OIC, see p. 404), the Organization of the Petroleum Exporting Countries (OPEC, see p. 408), and the Group of 77 developing countries (G77, see p. 450).

ECONOMIC AFFAIRS

In 2010, according to estimates by the World Bank, Iraq's gross national income (GNI), measured at average 2008–10 prices, was US $74,885m., equivalent to $2,340 per head (or $3,350 per head on an international purchasing-power parity basis). During 2001–10, it was estimated, the population increased at an average annual rate of 2.8%, while gross domestic product (GDP) per head decreased, in real terms, by an average of 3.0% per year. Overall GDP declined, in real terms, at an average annual rate of 0.3% during 2001–10; however, real GDP increased by 4.2% in 2009 and by a further 0.8% in 2010.

Agriculture (including hunting, forestry and fishing) contributed 5.0% of GDP in 2010. According to FAO estimates, 4.9% of the labour force was engaged in agriculture in mid-2012. Dates are the principal cash crop. Other crops include wheat, barley, maize, potatoes, tomatoes, aubergines and melons. Production of eggs, milk and poultry meat is also important. According to official estimates, during 2002–07, the real GDP of the agricultural sector declined by an average of 3.8% per year; agricultural GDP increased by an estimated 38.8% in 2010.

Industry (including mining, manufacturing, construction and power) provided 49.8% of GDP in 2010, according to official figures. During 2000–03 industrial GDP decreased by an average of 17.6% per year; the GDP of the sector contracted by an estimated 37.7% in 2003. The industrial sector experienced a further decline in 2004, when, according to the UN, GDP contracted by around 54.1%. According to official estimates, industrial GDP decreased, in real terms, by an average annual rate of 1.0% in 2002–07; however, the sector's GDP increased by an estimated 5.5% in 2010.

The mining sector accounted for 43.0% of GDP in 2010, with crude petroleum contributing 42.8%. Iraq had proven reserves of 115,000m. barrels of petroleum at the end of 2010 (the fourth largest in the world, after Saudi Arabia, Venezuela and Iran), as well as 3,167,700m. cu m of natural gas. In addition, Iraq is believed to possess considerable undiscovered reserves of petroleum. According to oil industry data, the rate of petroleum production in 2010 was 2.46m. barrels per day (b/d). It was reported by the Ministry of Oil in January 2011 that the production rate had reached 2.65m. b/d. Reserves of phosphates, sulphur, gypsum and salt are also exploited. According to official estimates, during 2002–07 the sector's GDP decreased, in real terms, by an average annual rate of 1.2%; the sector's GDP increased by an estimated 0.1% in 2010.

Manufacturing contributed just 2.3% of GDP in 2010. Since the outbreak of the current conflict in Iraq, the development of the manufacturing sector has been severely hindered by issues such as fuel shortages, damaged and outdated equipment, poor security, and communication problems. According to official estimates, manufacturing GDP decreased, in real terms, at an average annual rate of 8.4% during 2002–07; however, manufacturing GDP increased by an estimated 0.1% in 2010.

Construction contributed 3.5% of GDP in 2010. During 2002–07, according to official estimates, the sector's GDP increased at an average annual rate of 8.3%. As reconstruction efforts increased following the end of the conflict, the sector expanded rapidly; construction GDP increased by some 64.8% in 2010.

Energy is derived principally from petroleum, which accounted for an estimated 98.5% of total electricity generation in 2008. Since 2003 power shortages and rationing have been a persistent feature in Iraq, particularly in Baghdad and the surrounding area. The Ministry of Electricity estimated actual electricity generating capacity at 4,500 MW in early 2006, although Iraq, in theory, had an installed capacity of some 7,000 MW; the shortfall was the result of various factors, such as outdated technology, insurgent attacks on power stations and disruptions in fuel supplies. With ongoing reconstruction of the means of generation, transmission and distribution, the Ministry of Electricity was achieving peak production levels of 6,370 MW by early 2010; however, consumption was increasing at an annual rate of some 15%, and was reported to total around 13,000 MW. In 2010 the Government launched a 20-year strategy for the sector, which involved the renovation of existing power plants and the installation of four new ones to provide an additional 2,750 MW of electricity generating capacity.

The services sector contributed 45.1% of GDP in 2010. During 2000–03 the real GDP of the sector increased by an average annual rate of 6.3%; however, services GDP declined by an estimated 23.7% in 2003. According to UN estimates, sectoral GDP rose by 22.9% in 2004, owing to the improved delivery of community, social and personal services. During 2002–07, according to official estimates, the sector's GDP increased, in real terms, by an average annual rate of 15.9%; services GDP increased by an estimated 10.7% in 2010.

In 2008, according to IMF figures, Iraq recorded a visible trade surplus of US $33,965m., and there was a surplus of $26,973m. on the current account of the balance of payments. Crude petroleum was by far the most important export prior to the imposition of international economic sanctions in 1990. According to the figures from the Central Bank, mineral fuels and lubricants constituted 99.3% of Iraqi exports in 2010. The principal imports in the same year were machinery and transport equipment (38.5% of total imports), miscellaneous manufactured articles, basic manufactures, and mineral fuels and lubricants.

Budget proposals for 2011 forecast expenditure of ID 80,900,000m. and revenue of ID 96,600,000m. Iraq's general government gross debt was ID 113,455,740m. in 2010, equivalent to 119.6% of GDP. According to IMF estimates, Iraq's total external debt was US $89,901m. at the end of 2009, equivalent to 137.9% of GDP. According to the Central Bank, the annual average rate of inflation had declined to just 2.7% in 2008, compared with 30.8% in 2007. Consumer prices declined by 2.3% in 2010, compared with the previous year. Estimates concerning the rate of unemployment in Iraq vary considerably: although in mid-2010 the official rate was recorded at 15.0%, the rate of youth unemployment was reported to be twice this figure, while many sources suggested that the real rate of unemployment was much higher.

By February 2012 the Government's draft hydrocarbons law, proposed in February 2007, had still to be approved by the Iraqi parliament, owing to its complex and politically sensitive nature. Under the legislation, Iraq's oil and gas sector would be opened to foreign investment, in joint venture with Iraqi interests. Regional authorities would be permitted to award contracts for exploration and exploitation, in accordance with procedures and guidelines established by a Federal Oil and Gas Council. Revenues accumulated through the exploitation of Iraq's hydrocarbons reserves would then be pooled and redistributed across the regions according to population. In August 2007 the Kurdish regional government adopted a separate oil law; exports of small quantities of oil from Iraqi Kurdistan commenced in June 2009, but were halted in October following a dispute with the national authorities concerning the legality of contracts awarded by the regional administration. After an agreement was reached in January 2011, Kurdish oil exports resumed in March, although disputes pertaining to exploration rights and revenue between the national authorities and the Kurdish regional government had still to be resolved by early 2012; in November 2011 the national Government had announced that a tentative, 'mutually acceptable' agreement to this end had been reached with the Kurdish regional authorities, although at early 2012 details remained scarce. The opening of the Iraqi oil sector to international oil companies (IOCs) from October 2008 for the first time since nationalization in 1972, including the award in June 2009 of a 20-year development contract for the giant Rumaila oilfield to British-based BP and the China National Petroleum Co, led the Ministry of Oil to forecast that production capacity could be increased from its 2010 level of 2.5m. b/d to around 12m. b/d by 2017. However, many industry analysts claimed that this was an unrealistic target, owing to Iraq's ongoing political, security and infrastructural problems, and in June 2011 the Minister of Oil acknowledged that a target of between 7m. b/d and 8m. b/d was more realistic. In December the Government announced that oil production had exceeded 3m. b/d (around one-third of which was generated by the Rumaila concession) to reach its highest level in two decades; output was projected to increase further to 3.4m. b/d by the end of 2012, while exports were forecast to increase to 2.6m. b/d, from 2.2m b/d at the end of 2011. Meanwhile, in December 2010 the Government outlined details of a US $186,000m., five-year National Development Plan, a principal objective of which was the creation of 3m. new jobs through the completion of some 2,800 projects focusing on the agricultural, hydrocarbons, construction, power and transport sectors. Lower than anticipated oil output in 2010 contributed to a deceleration in GDP growth in 2010, although a strong rate of growth, of some 9.6%, was projected by the IMF for 2011, bolstered by increased oil output coupled with rising global oil prices; growth was forecast to reach, to 12.6%, in 2012. The budget for 2012, approved by the Council of Ministers in December 2011 and awaiting parliamentary approval at early 2012, projected a fiscal deficit of $14,500m., of which $10,000m. was to be funded by the Development Fund for Iraq, responsibility for which had been transferred to the Iraqi authorities in July 2011 (see Contemporary Political History). Notwithstanding predictions of robust growth, increased oil production and exports, and rising inflows of foreign investment, at early 2012 political and security instabilities remained significant obstacles to hopes of sustained economic expansion. A resolution to the ongoing political impasse between the State of Law alliance and Iraqiya, coupled with efforts effectively to address the intensification of insurgent attacks following the formal conclusion of US operations in Iraq in December 2011, would be imperative if a long-term economic recovery was to be realized.

PUBLIC HOLIDAYS

2013: 1 January (New Year's Day), 6 January (Army Day), 23 January* (Mouloud, Birth of Muhammad), 17 April (FAO Day), 1 May (Labour Day), 5 June* (Leilat al-Meiraj, ascension of Muhammad), 14 July (Republic Day, commemorating overthrow of the Hashemite monarchy in 1958), 7 August* (Id al-Fitr, end of Ramadan), 8 August (Cease-fire Day, commemorating end of the Iran–Iraq War in 1988), 3 October (National Iraqi Day, commemorating Iraq joining League of Nations in 1932), 14 October* (Id al-Adha, Feast of the Sacrifice), 4 November* (Muharram, Islamic New Year), 13 November* (Ashoura).

* These holidays are dependent on the Islamic lunar calendar and may vary by one or two days from the dates given.

Statistical Survey

Sources (unless otherwise indicated): Central Organization for Statistics and Information Technology (COSIT), Ministry of Planning and Development Co-operation, 929/29/6 Arrasat al-Hindiya, Baghdad; tel. and fax (1) 885-3653; e-mail ministry@mopdc-iraq.org; internet cosit.gov.iq; Central Bank of Iraq, POB 64, al-Rashid St, Baghdad; tel. (1) 816-5170; fax (1) 816-6802; e-mail cbi@cbi.iq; internet www.cbi.iq.

Area and Population

AREA, POPULATION AND DENSITY

Area (sq km)	434,128*
Population (census results)	
17 October 1987	16,335,199
17 October 1997	
Males	10,987,252
Females	11,058,992
Total	22,046,244
Population (UN estimates at mid-year)†	
2010	31,671,591
2011	32,664,940
2012	33,703,070
Density (per sq km) at mid-2012	77.6

* 167,618 sq miles. This figure excludes 924 sq km (357 sq miles) of territorial waters and also the Neutral Zone, of which Iraq's share is 3,522 sq km (1,360 sq miles). The Zone lies between Iraq and Saudi Arabia, and is administered jointly by the two countries. Nomads move freely through it, but there are no permanent inhabitants.

† Source: UN, *World Population Prospects: The 2010 Revision*.

2009 (official estimate): Total population 32,104,988 (males 16,163,412, females 15,941,576).

POPULATION BY AGE AND SEX

(UN estimates at mid–2012)

	Males	Females	Total
0–14	7,381,895	6,976,092	14,357,987
15–64	9,117,806	9,167,035	18,284,841
65 and over	425,204	635,038	1,060,242
Total	16,924,905	16,778,165	33,703,070

Source: UN, *World Population Prospects: The 2010 Revision*.

GOVERNORATES

(official population estimates at 2009)

	Area (sq km)*	Population	Density (per sq km)
Nineveh	35,899	3,237,918	90.2
Salah al-Din	26,175	1,259,298	48.1
Al-Ta'meem (Kirkuk)	10,282	1,290,072	125.5
Diyala	19,076	1,370,537	71.8
Baghdad	734	7,180,889	9,783.2
Al-Anbar (Anbar)	138,501	1,451,583	10.5
Babylon	6,468	1,727,032	267.0
Karbala	5,034	1,003,516	199.3
Al-Najaf (Najaf)	28,824	1,180,681	41.0
Al-Qadisiya	8,153	1,121,782	137.6
Al-Muthanna	51,740	719,824	13.9
Thi-Qar	12,900	1,846,788	143.2
Wasit	17,153	1,158,033	67.5
Maysan	16,072	1,009,565	62.8
Al-Basrah (Basra)	19,070	2,555,542	134.0
Kurdish Autonomous Region			
D'hok	6,553	968,901	147.9
Irbil (Arbil)	14,471	1,471,053	101.7
Al-Sulaimaniya (Sulaimaniya)	17,023	1,551,974	91.2
Total	434,128	32,104,988	74.0

* Excluding territorial waters (924 sq km).

PRINCIPAL TOWNS

(population at 1987 census)

Baghdad (capital)	3,841,268	Al-Sulaimaniya (Sulaimaniya)	364,096
Al-Mawsil (Mosul)	664,221	Al-Najaf (Najaf)	309,010
Irbil (Arbil)	485,968	Karbala	296,705
Kirkuk	418,624	Al-Hillah (Hilla)	268,834
Al-Basrah (Basra)	406,296	Al-Nasiriyah (Nasiriya)	265,937

Source: UN, *Demographic Yearbook*.

Mid-2010 (incl. suburbs, UN estimates): Baghdad 5,890,677; Mosul 1,446,940; Arbil 1,009,204; Basra 923,237 (Source: UN, *World Urbanization Prospects: The 2009 Revision*).

BIRTHS AND DEATHS

(annual averages, UN estimates)

	1995–2000	2000–05	2005–10
Birth rate (per 1,000)	37.9	37.5	36.6
Death rate (per 1,000)	5.4	5.6	6.3

Source: UN, *World Population Prospects: The 2010 Revision*.

Life expectancy (years at birth, WHO estimates): 66 (males 62; females 70) in 2009 (Source: WHO, *World Health Report*).

EMPLOYMENT

(labour force survey, '000)

	2006	2007	2008
Agriculture, hunting and forestry	1,925.7	1,066.2	1,759.9
Fishing	22.8	10.0	21.7
Mining and quarrying	43.4	84.4	32.4
Manufacturing	376.3	522.3	369.4
Electricity, gas and water	76.6	130.5	161.6
Construction	665.0	797.2	823.5
Wholesale and retail trade; repair of motor vehicles, motorcycles and personal and household goods	961.8	1,117.6	1,167.2
Hotels and restaurants	52.9	105.4	62.6
Transport, storage and communications	616.5	707.5	608.1
Financial intermediation	26.9	26.4	20.8
Real estate, renting and business activities	40.6	285.8	35.1
Public administration and defence; compulsory social security	727.3	677.6	1,003.3
Education	556.1	612.9	686.7
Health and social work	146.2	196.8	218.2
Community, social and personal services	312.7	520.8	618.5
Households with employed persons	1.5	—	9.7
Extra-territorial organizations and bodies	4.7	—	7.3
Sub-total	6,557.2	6,861.4	7,606.1
Activities not adequately defined	—	255.3	—
Total employed	6,557.2	7,116.7	7,606.1

Source: ILO.

Mid-2012 (estimates in '000): Agriculture, etc. 425; Total labour force 8,622 (Source: FAO).

Health and Welfare

KEY INDICATORS

Total fertility rate (children per woman, 2009)	4.0
Under-5 mortality rate (per 1,000 live births, 2009)	44
HIV/AIDS (% of persons aged 15–49, 2003)	<0.1
Physicians (per 1,000 head, 2005)	0.7
Hospital beds (per 1,000 head, 2005)	1.3
Health expenditure (2008): US $ per head (PPP)	107
Health expenditure (2008): % of GDP	3.3
Health expenditure (2008): public (% of total)	70.2
Access to water (% of persons, 2008)	79
Access to sanitation (% of persons, 2008)	73
Total carbon dioxide emissions ('000 metric tons, 2007)	100,045.5
Carbon dioxide emissions per head (metric tons, 2007)	3.3
Human Development Index (2011): ranking	132
Human Development Index (2011): value	0.573

For sources and definitions, see explanatory note on p. vi.

Agriculture

PRINCIPAL CROPS
('000 metric tons)

	2008	2009	2010
Wheat	1,255	1,700	2,749
Rice, paddy	248	173	156
Barley	404	502	1,137
Maize	288	238	267
Potatoes	349	223	205
Sugar cane	4	6	13
Chick peas	2	1	1
Tomatoes	802	913	1,013
Cauliflowers and broccoli	31	37	26
Pumpkins, squash and gourds	116	132	145
Cucumbers and gherkins	381	421	433*
Aubergines (Eggplants)	406	396	387
Onions, dry	117	62	88
Watermelons	456	327	304
Canteloupes and other melons	206	185	177
Grapes	203	195	213
Oranges	93	102	98
Tangerines, mandarins, clementines and satsumas*	30	31	34
Apples	36	37	40
Apricots	19	18	19
Peaches and nectarines*	16	17	18
Plums*	3	3	3
Dates	476	507	567

* FAO estimate(s).

Aggregate production ('000 metric tons, may include official, semi-official or estimated data): Total cereals 2,201 in 2008, 2,616 in 2009, 4,312 in 2010; Total roots and tubers 349 in 2008, 223 in 2009, 205 in 2010; Total vegetables (incl. melons) 3,314 in 2008, 3,193 in 2009, 3,281 in 2010; Total fruits (excl. melons) 971 in 2008, 1,006 in 2009, 1,094 in 2010.

Source: FAO.

LIVESTOCK
('000 head, year ending September)

	2008	2009*	2010*
Horses	47	48	48
Asses*	380	380	380
Mules*	11	11	11
Cattle	1,552	1,600	1,600
Buffaloes	286	275	275
Camels	58	59	59
Sheep	7,722	7,800	7,800
Goats	1,475	1,550	1,500
Chickens*	27,500	27,500	29,000

* FAO estimate(s).

Source: FAO.

LIVESTOCK PRODUCTS
('000 metric tons)

	2008	2009	2010
Cattle meat	43.0	47.5*	49.6*
Buffalo meat*	1.2	1.2	1.2
Sheep meat*	47.0	47.0	47.0
Goat meat*	14.3	15.3	15.3
Chicken meat	49.0	49.0*	50.0*
Cows' milk	174.8	185.0*	191.5*
Buffaloes' milk	24.6	23.0*	23.8*
Sheep's milk	55.0	60.0*	62.1*
Goats' milk	17.8	18.0*	18.4*
Hen eggs	45.8	35.3	35.5*
Wool, greasy	16.8†	17.0*	17.2*
Cattle and buffalo hides*	3.8	3.9	3.9

* FAO estimate(s).
† Unofficial figure.

Source: FAO.

Forestry

ROUNDWOOD REMOVALS
('000 cubic metres, excl. bark)

	1996*	1997*	1998
Sawlogs, veneer logs and logs for sleepers	20.0	20.0	25.0
Other industrial wood	30.0	30.0	34.0
Fuel wood	49.3	110.0	118.0
Total	99.3	161.0	177.0

* FAO estimates.

1999–2010: Annual production assumed to be unchanged from 1998 (FAO estimates).

Source: FAO.

SAWNWOOD PRODUCTION
('000 cu m, incl. railway sleepers)

	1996	1997	1998
Total (all broadleaved)	8	8	12

1999–2010: Annual production as in 1998 (FAO estimates).

Source: FAO.

Fishing

('000 metric tons, live weight)

	2007	2008	2009
Capture	57.8	34.5	34.5
Cyprinids (incl. Common carp)	14.3	14.4	10.0
Freshwater siluroids	1.4	2.0	2.7
Other freshwater fishes	29.8	13.6	9.6
Marine fishes	7.9	2.3	5.8
Aquaculture	15.8*	19.2	18.7
Common carp	12.0*	10.4	15.2
Total catch	73.6*	53.7	53.2

* FAO estimate.

Source: FAO.

Mining

('000 metric tons unless otherwise indicated)

	2008	2009	2010
Crude petroleum	119,491	119,775	120,445
Natural gas (million cu m)*	14,781	16,577	16,885
Ammonia (nitrogen content)	10	30	126
Sulphur†	30	20	20
Salt (unrefined)‡	109	113	102

* Figures refer to gross production.
† Figures refer to native production and by-products of petroleum and natural gas processing.
‡ Estimated figures.

Sources: BP, *Statistical Review of World Energy*; US Geological Survey.

Industry

SELECTED PRODUCTS
('000 metric tons unless otherwise indicated)

	2006	2007	2008
Naphtha	533	364	483
Motor spirit (petrol)	3,233	2,212	2,937
Kerosene	1,112	739	981
Jet fuel	599	409	543
Gas-diesel (distillate fuel) oil	4,838	4,995	6,633
Residual fuel oils	5,988	5,595	7,430
Paraffin wax	94	65	86
Petroleum bitumen (asphalt)	364	340	451
Liquefied petroleum gas:			
from natural gas plants	912	918	954
from petroleum refineries	129	121	161
Cement*†	3,500	4,500	6,453
Electric energy (million kWh)	31,869	33,183	36,779

* Source: US Geological Survey.
† Estimated figures.

2009 (estimate): Cement 6,500 (Source: US Geological Survey).

2010 (estimate): Cement 6,500 (Source: US Geological Survey).

Source (unless otherwise indicated): UN Industrial Commodity Statistics Database.

Finance

CURRENCY AND EXCHANGE RATES

Monetary Units
1,000 fils = 20 dirhams = 1 new Iraqi dinar (ID).

Sterling, Dollar and Euro Equivalents (30 December 2011)
£1 sterling = 1,808.9 Iraqi dinars;
US $1 = 1,170.0 Iraqi dinars;
€1 = 1,513.9 Iraqi dinars;
10,000 Iraqi dinars = £5.53 = $8.55 = €6.61.

Average Exchange rate (Iraqi dinars per US $)
2009 1,170.00
2010 1,170.00
2011 1,170.00

Note: Following the overthrow of the regime of Saddam Hussain in 2003, the new Coalition Provisional Authority established an exchange rate of US $1 = 1,400 dinars. A new dinar currency, the new Iraqi dinar (ID), was introduced on 15 October to replace both the 'Swiss' dinar (at ID 1 = 150 'Swiss' dinars), the currency in use in the Kurdish autonomous regions of northern Iraq since 1991, and the 'Saddam' dinar (at par), the official currency of the rest of Iraq. The new currency was to be fully convertible.

BUDGET
(ID '000 million)

Revenue	2004	2005*	2006*
Oil revenues	18,000.0	27,750.0	28,950.0
Reconstruction levy	450.0	525.0	—
Personal income tax	15.0	45.0	90.0
Corporate income tax	30.0	75.0	150.0
Interest	15.0	—	—
Transfers from state enterprises	562.5	142.5	150.0
Central Bank	75.0	90.0	105.0
Agricultural supplies company	105.0	7.5	—
Al-Rashid Hotel	7.5	22.5	45.0
Fees and charges	96.3	132.5	185.1
Prescription charges	30.0	37.5	45.0
Court fees	7.5	7.5	7.5
Vehicle registration	30.0	45.0	60.0
Fees from emergency services	7.5	15.0	22.5
Flight overpass charges for commercial airlines	15.0	15.0	15.0
Other taxes	90.0	105.0	120.0
Excise tax	15.0	15.0	15.0
Hotel and restaurant service tax	7.5	7.5	7.5
Land tax	15.0	30.0	45.0
Total	19,258.8	28,775.0	29,645.1

Expenditure by department†	2004	2005*	2006*
Ministry of Agriculture	53.2	117.2	120.5
Ministry of Awqaf (Religious Endowments) and Religious Affairs	10.2	2.3	2.3
Board of Supreme Audit	4.5	3.8	3.8
Central Organization of Standards	2.7	1.7	1.7
Ministry of Communications	9.3	231.3	231.3
Ministry of Culture	13.8	31.8	31.8
Ministry of Displacement and Migration	2.4	8.4	15.9
Ministry of Education	815.9	836.2	836.2
Electricity Commission	2.2	2,252.2	2,477.2
Office of the Environment	2.4	30.9	60.9
Ministry of Finance	15,816.7	17,681.4	17,785.4
Ministry of Foreign Affairs	66.6	71.9	71.9
Governing Council	9.6	12.0	15.0
Ministry of Health	1,420.5	1,742.9	1,940.5
Ministry of Higher Education and Scientific Research	183.1	178.6	178.6
Ministry of Housing and Construction	255.3	496.7	496.7
Ministry of Human Rights	2.4	8.4	15.9
Ministry of Industry and Minerals	12.0	10.5	10.5
Ministry of the Interior	187.3	350.0	365.0
Iraqi Media Network	2.2	2.2	2.2
Ministry of Justice	207.9	284.4	284.4
Ministry of Labour and Social Affairs	52.3	59.7	74.7
Ministry of Municipalities, Utilities and Public Works	309.0	812.0	1,059.5
New Iraqi Army	34.8	109.8	109.8
Ministry of Oil	2.7	1,501.9	1,501.9
Ministry of Planning	67.5	54.9	61.6
Ministry of Science and Technology	36.4	46.0	46.0
Ministry of Trade	15.3	6.3	6.3
Ministry of Transport	127.2	758.1	758.1
Ministry of Water Resources	217.5	779.3	779.3
Ministry of Youth and Sport	22.4	93.2	93.2
Unallocated expenditure	180.0	180.0	180.0
Total	20,145.1	28,755.7	29,617.8

* Forecasts.
† Names of departments may have been altered since the publication of the budget proposals in October 2003.

Sources: Ministries of Finance and of Planning; Coalition Provisional Authority.

2008 (ID '000 million, estimates): *Revenues and grants:* Revenues 84,200 (Crude petroleum export revenues 73,900); Grants 2,800; Total 87,000. *Expenditures:* Current 58,300 (Salaries and pensions 20,600; Non-oil goods and services 9,500; Oil sector goods and services 7,300; Transfers 16,000); Capital 27,000 (Non-oil 23,200, Oil 3,800); Total 85,200 (Source: IMF, *Iraq: Staff Report for the 2009 Article IV Consultation and Request for Stand-By Arrangement*—March 2010).

2009 (ID '000 million, estimates): *Revenues and grants:* Revenues 56,500 (Crude petroleum export revenues 45,500); Grants 2,400; Total 58,900. *Expenditures:* Current 60,400 (Salaries and pensions 27,400; Non-oil goods and services 10,800; Oil sector goods and services 4,900; Transfers 14,200); Capital 18,800 (Non-oil 16,100, Oil 2,700); Total (incl. deduction for returned letters of credit) 76,300 (Source: IMF, *Iraq: Staff Report for the 2009 Article IV Consultation and Request for Stand-By Arrangement*—March 2010).

2010 (ID '000 million, budget projections): *Revenues and grants:* Revenues 69,100 (Crude petroleum export revenues 56,100); Grants 1,700; Total 70,800. *Expenditures:* Current 62,900 (Salaries and pensions 28,400; Non-oil goods and services 12,800; Oil sector goods and services 5,500; Transfers 11,900); Capital 25,800 (Non-oil 21,800, Oil 4,000); Total 88,700 (Source: IMF, *Iraq: Staff Report for the 2009 Article IV Consultation and Request for Stand-By Arrangement*—March 2010).

INTERNATIONAL RESERVES
(US $ million at 31 December)

	2008	2009	2010
Gold (national valuation)	163.1	208.2	266.0
IMF special drawing rights	143.1	1,818.3	1,773.9
Reserve position in IMF	263.5	268.2	263.5
Foreign exchange	49,531.1	42,041.0	48,339.6
Total	50,100.9	44,335.7	50,643.0

Source: IMF, *International Financial Statistics*.

MONEY SUPPLY
(ID '000 million at 31 December)

	2008	2009	2010
Currency outside depository corporations	18,492.5	21,775.7	24,342.2
Transferable deposits	13,263.9	18,618.0	30,039.2
Other deposits	5,173.2	6,397.6	7,011.6
Broad money	36,929.6	46,791.2	61,393.1

Source: IMF, *International Financial Statistics*.

COST OF LIVING
(Consumer Price Index; base: 2000 = 100)

	2007	2008	2009
Food (incl. non-alcoholic beverages)	270.4	300.0	323.0
Electricity, gas and other fuel	3,320.9	2,609.9	1,635.8
Clothing	156.6	161.5	155.9
Rent	1,538.1	1,765.3	1,904.2
All items (incl. others)	646.8	664.0	645.4

2010: Food (incl. non-alcoholic beverages) 330.1; All items (incl.others) 660.2.

Source: ILO.

NATIONAL ACCOUNTS

National Income and Product
(ID '000 million at current prices, provisional estimates)

	2004	2005	2006
Compensation of employees	7,866.1	10,394.6	16,573.7
Operating surplus	33,857.9	45,296.7	67,543.7
Domestic factor incomes	41,723.9	55,691.2	84,117.4
Consumption of fixed capital	6,234.6	8,308.9	11,470.6
Gross domestic product (GDP) at factor cost	47,958.6	64,000.1	95,588.0
Indirect taxes (net)	−10,909.3	−14,009.4	−15,128.5
GDP in purchasers' values	37,049.3	49,990.7	80,459.4
Net factor income from abroad*	76.2	1,089.0	1,314.1
Gross national product (GNP)	37,125.5	51,079.7	81,773.6
Less Consumption of fixed capital	6,234.6	8,308.9	11,470.6
National income in market prices	30,890.8	42,770.8	70,303.0

* Figures obtained as residuals.

Gross Domestic Product by Economic Activity
(ID '000 million at current prices, provisional estimates)

	2004	2005	2006
Agriculture, hunting, forestry and fishing	3,539.4	4,248.8	5,569.0
Mining and quarrying	30,543.0	39,366.3	53,030.9
Crude petroleum	30,496.0	39,316.0	n.a.
Manufacturing	770.9	1,220.9	1,473.2
Electricity and water	263.3	393.1	779.4
Construction	468.3	2,932.4	3,449.7
Trade, restaurants and hotels	3,070.5	4,083.5	6,350.0
Transport, storage and communications	3,687.7	4,911.3	6,742.9
Finance, insurance and real estate	663.0	931.4	7,945.8
Government, community, social and personal services	5,200.4	6,139.9	10,726.2
Sub-total	48,206.5	64,227.6	96,067.2
Less Imputed bank service charge	248.0	227.5	479.2
GDP at factor cost	47,958.5	64,000.1	95,588.0
Indirect taxes / *Less* Subsidies	−10,909.3	−14,009.4	−15,128.5
GDP in market prices	37,049.3	49,990.7	80,459.4

2008 (ID '000 million at current prices): Agriculture, hunting, forestry and fishing 5,716.8; Mining and quarrying 86,867.1; Manufacturing 2,331.8; Construction 5,972.7; Electricity and water 1,307.9; Transport, storage and communications 12,030.9; Trade, restaurants and hotels 10,078.1; Finance, insurance and real estate 12,970.2; Government, community, social and personal services 19,394.5; *Sub-total* 156,670.1; *Less* Imputed bank service charge 687.8; *Gross domestic product at factor cost* 155,982.3.

2009 (ID '000 million at current prices): Agriculture, hunting, forestry and fishing 6,132.7; Mining and quarrying 56,654.0; Manufacturing 3,369.4; Construction 7,066.1; Electricity and water 1,686.1; Transport, storage and communications 14,185.9; Trade, restaurants and hotels 11,486.6; Finance, insurance and real estate 14,547.0; Government, community, social and personal services 25,031.3; *Sub-total* 140,159.1; *Less* Imputed bank service charge 828.9; *Gross domestic product at factor cost* 139,330.2.

2010 (ID '000 million at current prices): Agriculture, hunting, forestry and fishing 8,657.4; Mining and quarrying 74,357.2; Manufacturing 3,916.5; Construction 6,010.0; Electricity and water 1,979.8; Transport, storage and communications 19,415.2; Trade, restaurants and hotels 14,940.2; Finance, insurance and real estate 16,310.6; Government, community, social and personal services 27,459.4; *Sub-total* 173,046.3; *Less* Imputed bank service charge 1,089.3; *Gross domestic product at factor cost* 171,957.0.

BALANCE OF PAYMENTS
(US $ million)

	2006	2007	2008
Exports of goods f.o.b.	30,529	39,587	63,726
Imports of goods f.o.b.	−18,708	−16,623	−29,761
Trade balance	11,822	22,965	33,965
Exports of services	357	868	1,969
Imports of services	−5,490	−4,866	−7,969
Balance on goods and services	6,689	18,967	27,964
Other income received	1,206	1,923	4,039
Other income paid	−4,751	−4,990	−1,934
Balance on goods, services and income	3,144	15,900	30,070
Current transfers received	261	89	188
Current transfers paid	−2,153	−1,932	−3,284
Current balance	1,252	14,056	26,973
Capital account (net)	2,769	675	441
Direct investment abroad	−305	−8	−34
Direct investment from abroad	383	972	1,856
Portfolio investment assets	−3,670	−1,774	−2,799
Other investment assets	1,847	−4,939	−850
Other investment liabilities	−1,322	474	−1,320
Net errors and omissions	579	−3,662	−5,777
Overall balance	1,533	5,795	18,491

Source: IMF, *International Financial Statistics*.

External Trade

PRINCIPAL COMMODITIES
(US $ million)

Imports c.i.f.	2008	2009	2010
Food and live animals	1,917	2,076	2,371
Beverages and tobacco	461	500	571
Crude materials (inedible) except fuels	639	692	790
Mineral fuels, lubricants, etc.	3,479	3,767	4,304
Animal and vegetable oils and fats	2,272	2,460	2,811
Chemicals	2,378	2,575	2,942
Basic manufactures	4,047	4,381	5,006
Machinery and transport equipment	13,666	14,798	16,907
Miscellaneous manufactured articles	5,608	6,073	6,939
Total (incl. others)	35,496	38,437	43,915

Exports c.i.f.	2008	2009	2010
Food and live animals	191	110	145
Crude materials (inedible) except fuels	128	59	78
Mineral fuels, lubricants, etc.	63,216	39,131	51,376
Chemicals	—	4	5
Basic manufactures	64	20	26
Machinery and transport equipment	127	95	124
Total (incl. others)	63,726	39,427	51,764

PRINCIPAL TRADING PARTNERS
(US $ million)

Imports c.i.f.	1988	1989	1990
Australia	153.4	196.2	108.7
Austria	n.a.	1.1	50.9
Belgium-Luxembourg	57.6	68.2	68.3
Brazil	346.0	416.4	139.5
Canada	169.9	225.1	150.4
China, People's Republic	99.2	148.0	157.9
France	278.0	410.4	278.3
Germany	322.3	459.6	389.4
India	32.3	65.2	57.5
Indonesia	38.9	122.7	104.9
Ireland	150.4	144.9	31.6
Italy	129.6	285.1	194.0
Japan	533.0	621.1	397.2
Jordan	164.3	210.0	220.3
Korea, Republic	98.5	123.9	149.4
Netherlands	111.6	102.6	93.8
Romania	113.3	91.1	30.1
Saudi Arabia	37.2	96.5	62.5
Spain	43.4	129.0	40.5
Sri Lanka	50.1	33.5	52.3
Sweden	63.0	40.6	64.8
Switzerland	65.7	94.4	126.6
Thailand	22.3	59.2	68.9
Turkey	874.7	408.9	196.0
USSR	70.7	75.7	77.9
United Kingdom	394.6	448.5	322.1
USA	979.3	1,001.7	658.4
Yugoslavia	154.5	182.0	123.1
Total (incl. others)	5,960.0	6,956.2	4,833.9

Exports f.o.b.	1988	1989	1990*
Belgium-Luxembourg	147.5	249.6	n.a.
Brazil	1,002.8	1,197.2	n.a.
France	517.4	623.9	0.8
Germany	122.0	76.9	1.7
Greece	192.5	189.4	0.3
India	293.0	438.8	14.7
Italy	687.1	549.7	10.6
Japan	712.1	117.1	0.1
Jordan	28.4	25.2	101.6
Netherlands	152.9	532.3	0.2
Portugal	120.8	125.8	n.a.
Spain	370.0	575.7	0.7
Turkey	1,052.6	1,331.0	83.5
USSR	835.7	1,331.7	8.9
United Kingdom	293.1	167.0	4.4
USA	1,458.9	2,290.8	0.2
Yugoslavia	425.4	342.0	10.4
Total (incl. others)	10,268.3	12,333.7	392.0

* Excluding exports of most petroleum products.

Source: UN, *International Trade Statistics Yearbook*.

2008 (US $ million): *Imports by regions:* Arab nations 16,399; North and South America 3,976; European Union 2,307; Other Europe 8,590; Asia 4,082; Other countries 142; Total imports 35,496. *Exports by region:* Arab nations 2,294; North and South America 34,922; European Union 15,167; Other Europe 510; Asia 10,005; Other countries 828; Total exports 63,726.

2009 (US $ million): *Imports by regions:* Arab nations 14,068; North and South America 5,001; European Union 3,348; Other Europe 9,475; Asia 5,104; Other countries 1,441; Total imports 38,437. *Exports by region:* Arab nations 871; North and South America 19,571; European Union 10,310; Other Europe 1,124; Asia 5,047; Other countries 2,504; Total exports 39,427.

2010 (US $ million): *Imports by regions:* Arab nations 10,399; North and South America 5,248; European Union 5,885; Other Europe 13,253; Asia 8,432; Other countries 698; Total imports 43,915. *Exports by region:* Arab nations 1,155; North and South America 15,886; European Union 11,155; Other Europe 1,289; Asia 21,953; Other countries 326; Total exports 51,764.

Transport

RAILWAYS
(traffic)

	1995*	1996†	1997†
Passenger-km (million)	2,198	1,169	1,169
Freight ton-km (million)	1,120	931	956

* Source: UN, *Statistical Yearbook*.
† Source: Railway Gazette International, *Railway Directory*.

ROAD TRAFFIC
(estimates, '000 motor vehicles in use)

	1995	1996
Passenger cars	770.1	773.0
Buses and coaches	50.9	51.4
Lorries and vans	269.9	272.5
Road tractors	37.2	37.2

2006: Passenger cars 784,794; Buses and coaches 112,113; Vans and lorries 1,345,361; *Total* 2,242,269.

Source: IRF, *World Road Statistics*.

SHIPPING

Merchant Fleet
(registered at 31 December)

	2007	2008	2009
Number of vessels	89	89	84
Total displacement ('000 grt)	159.1	158.6	142.9

Source: IHS Fairplay, *World Fleet Statistics*.

CIVIL AVIATION
(revenue traffic on scheduled services)

	1991	1992	1994*
Kilometres flown (million)	0	0	0
Passengers carried ('000)	28	53	31
Passenger-km (million)	17	35	20
Freight ton-km (million)	0	3	2

* Figures for 1993 unavailable.

Source: UN, *Statistical Yearbook*.

Tourism

ARRIVALS AT FRONTIERS OF VISITORS FROM ABROAD*

Country of nationality	2008	2009
India	6,031	13,876
Iran	840,362	1,161,541
Lebanon	129	1,916
Pakistan	5,771	18,004
Total (incl. others)	863,657	1,261,921

* Including same-day visitors.

Tourism receipts (incl. passenger transport, US $ million): 186 in 2005; 170 in 2006; 555 in 2007.

Source: World Tourism Organization.

Communications Media

	2008	2009	2010
Telephones ('000 main lines in use)	1,082.3	1,108.4	1,600.0
Mobile cellular telephones (subscribers)	17,529	19,722	24,000
Internet subscribers ('000)	3.1	n.a.	0.3
Broadband subscribers ('000)	100	100	100

Personal computers: 200,000 (7.6 per 1,000 persons) in 2002. Source: International Telecommunication Union.

Radio receivers ('000 in use): 4,850 in 1997 (Source: UN, *Statistical Yearbook*).

Television receivers ('000 in use): 1,750 in 1997; 1,800 in 1998; 1,850 in 1999 (Source: UN, *Statistical Yearbook*).

Education

(2007/08 unless otherwise indicated)

	Institutions	Teachers	Students
Pre-primary	586	5,006	85,592
Primary	12,507	237,130	4,333,154
Secondary:			
academic	4,364	114,745	1,603,623
vocational	288	11,161	63,069
Teacher training	171	4,174	71,372
Higher*	65	14,700	240,000†

* 2002/03.
† Figure for undergraduates only.

Sources: Ministries of Education and Higher Education.

Pupil-teacher ratio (primary education, UNESCO estimate): 17.0 in 2006/07 (Source: UNESCO Institute for Statistics).

Adult literacy rate (UNESCO estimates): 77.6% (males 86.0%; females 69.2%) in 2008 (Source: UNESCO Institute for Statistics).

Directory

As a result of the US-led military campaign to oust the regime of Saddam Hussain in early 2003, and the ensuing insurgency, buildings occupied by a number of government ministries and other institutions were reported to have been damaged or destroyed.

The Government

HEAD OF STATE

President: JALAL TALABANI (assumed office 7 April 2005, re-elected by the Council of Representatives 22 April 2006 and 11 November 2010).

Vice-Presidents: TARIQ AL-HASHIMI, KHUDHAIR AL-KHUZAI.

COUNCIL OF MINISTERS
(May 2012)

Following protracted negotiations between the leading groups within the legislature, on 21 December 2010 the Council of Representatives voted to approve cabinet nominations submitted by Prime Minister-designate Nuri Kamal al-Maliki. In mid-February 2011 eight further nominees, including new Ministers of Electricity and of Trade, were approved by the legislature, while a new Minister of Planning was appointed in early April. Discussions between the coalition parties regarding the allocation of the remaining portfolios remained unresolved. In December it was reported that Prime Minister al-Maliki had signed a warrant for the arrest of Vice-President Tariq al-Hashimi and issued a concurrent request to the Council of Representatives to remove Deputy Prime Minister Saleh al-Mutlaq from office. The Iraqi National Movement (Iraqiya), of which both al-Hashimi and al-Mutlaq were members, subsequently withdrew its participation from both the Council of Ministers and the legislature, citing its disapproval of al-Maliki's actions. However, in early February 2012 it was reported that Iraqiya cabinet members and deputies had resumed their duties.

Prime Minister and Acting Minister of Defence, of the Interior and of National Security Affairs: NURI KAMAL (JAWAD) AL-MALIKI.

Deputy Prime Minister: Dr ROZH NURI SHAWAIS.

Deputy Prime Minister for Energy Affairs: HUSSEIN AL-SHAHRISTANI.

Deputy Prime Minister: SALEH AL-MUTLAQ.

Minister of Agriculture: EZZ AL-DIN AHMAD HUSSEIN AL-DAWLA.

Minister of Communications: MUHAMMAD TAWFIQ ALLAWI.

Minister of Construction and Housing: MUHAMMAD SAHEB AL-DARRAJI.

Minister of Culture: SAADOUN AL-DULAIMI.

Minister of Displacement and Migration and Acting Minister of State for Civil Society Affairs: DINDAR NAJMAN SHAFIQ.

Minister of Education: MUHAMMAD TAMIM.

Minister of Electricity: ABD AL-KARIM AFTAN AL-JUMAILI.

Minister of the Environment: SARKIS SLIWA.

Minister of Finance: Dr RAFIE AL-ISSAWI.

Minister of Foreign Affairs: HOSHYAR AL-ZIBARI.

Minister of Health: MAJID HAMAD AMIN.

Minister of Higher Education and Scientific Research and Acting Minister of State for National Reconciliation: ALI AL-ADIB.

Minister of Human Rights: MUHAMMAD SHAYYAA AL-SUDANI.

Minister of Industry and Minerals: AHMAD NASSER AL-DALI.

Minister of Justice: HASSAN AL-SHUMMARI.

Minister of Labour and Social Affairs: NASSAR AL-RUBAI.

Minister of Municipalities and Public Works: ADEL MHODER AL-RADHI.

Minister of Oil: ABD AL-KARIM AL-LUAIBI.

Minister of Planning: ALI YOUSUF ABD AL-NABI AL-SHUKRI.

Minister of Science and Technology: ABD AL-KARIM YASSIN AL-SAMARRAI.

Minister of Trade: KHAIRALLAH HASSAN BABAKR MUHAMMAD.

Minister of Transportation: AMIR HADI AL-AMIRI.

Minister of Tourism and Antiquities: LIWA SUMAYSIM.

Minister of Water Resources: MUHANNAD SALMAN AL-SAADI.

Minister of Youth and Sports: JASIM MUHAMMAD JA'FAR.

Minister of State for Civil Society Affairs: DAKHIL QASSIM.

Minister of State for Council of Representatives Affairs: SAFA AL-DIN MUHAMMAD AL-SAFI.

Minister of State for Foreign Affairs: ALI AL-SAJRI.

Minister of State for National Reconciliation: AMER HASSAN AL-KHUZAI.

Minister of State for Provincial Affairs: TURHAN MOHSEN.

Minister of State for Tribal Affairs: JAMAL AL-BATIKH.

Minister of State and Government Spokesperson: ALI AL-DABBAGH.

Minister of State for Women's Affairs: IBTIHAL AL-ZAIDI.

Ministers of State: DIYAA NAJEM AL-ASADI, JAMAL AL-BATTIKH, SALAH MUZAHIM DARWISH, YASSIN HASSAN MUHAMMAD, HASSAN AL-MUTAIRI, ABD AL-SAHIB QAHRAMAN, HASSAN AL-RADI, BUSHRA HUSSEIN SALEH.

MINISTRIES

Ministry of Agriculture: Khulafa St, Khullani Sq., Baghdad; tel. (1) 887-3251; e-mail minis_of_agr@moagr.org; internet www.moagr.com.

Ministry of Communications: Baghdad; tel. (1) 717-9440; e-mail iraqimoc@iraqimoc.net; internet www.moc.gov.iq.

Ministry of Construction and Housing: Baghdad; e-mail moch@moch.gov.iq; internet www.moch.gov.iq.

Ministry of Culture: POB 624, Qaba bin Nafi Sq., Sadoun St, Baghdad; tel. (1) 538-3171.

Ministry of Defence: Baghdad; e-mail webmaster@mod.iraqiaf.org.

Ministry of Displacement and Migration: Baghdad; tel. (1) 537-0842; fax (1) 537-2497.

Ministry of Education: Saad State Enterprises Bldg, nr the Convention Centre, Baghdad; tel. (1) 883-2571; e-mail general@moedu.gov.iq; internet www.moedu.gov.iq.

Ministry of Electricity: Baghdad; e-mail infocen@moelc.gov.iq; internet www.moelc.gov.iq.

Ministry of Energy Affairs: Baghdad.

Ministry of the Environment: POB 10026, Baghdad; e-mail enviro_center@yahoo.com; internet www.moen.gov.iq.

Ministry of Finance: Khulafa St, nr al-Russafi Sq., Baghdad; tel. (1) 887-4871; e-mail iraqmof@mof.gov.iq; internet www.mof.gov.iq.

Ministry of Foreign Affairs: opp. State Organization for Roads and Bridges, Karradat Mariam, Baghdad; tel. (1) 537-0091; e-mail press@iraqmfamail.com; internet www.mofa.gov.iq.

Ministry of Health: Baghdad; e-mail hedmoh@moh.gov.iq; internet www.moh.gov.iq.

Ministry of Higher Education and Scientific Research: 52 Rusafa St, Baghdad; tel. and fax (1) 280-6315; e-mail info@mohesr.gov.iq; internet www.mohesr.gov.iq.

Ministry of Human Rights: Baghdad; e-mail minister1@humanrights.gov.iq; internet www.humanrights.gov.iq.

Ministry of Industry and Minerals: POB 5815, Baghdad; tel. (1) 816-2006; e-mail admin@industry.gov.iq; internet www.industry.gov.iq.

Ministry of the Interior: Baghdad; tel. (1) 817-3101; e-mail media@moi.gov.iq; internet www.moi.gov.iq.

Ministry of Justice: Baghdad; fax (1) 537-2269; internet www.moj.gov.iq.

Ministry of Labour and Social Affairs: Baghdad; e-mail info@molsa.gov.iq; internet www.molsa.gov.iq.

Ministry of Municipalities and Public Works: Baghdad; e-mail info@mmpw.gov.iq; internet www.mmpw.gov.iq.

Ministry of National Reconciliation: Baghdad.

Ministry of National Security Affairs: North Gate, Baghdad; tel. (1) 888-9071.

Ministry of Oil: Oil Complex Bldg, Port Said St, Baghdad; tel. (1) 817-7000; e-mail minister.office@oil.gov.iq; internet www.oil.gov.iq.

Ministry of Planning: 929/29/6 Arrasat al-Hindiya, Baghdad; tel. (1) 778-3899; e-mail ministry@mopdc-iraq.org; internet www.mop-iraq.org.

Ministry of Science and Technology: Baghdad; internet www.most.gov.iq.

Ministry of Tourism and Antiquities: Baghdad.

Ministry of Trade: POB 5833, Khullani Sq., Baghdad; tel. (1) 887-2681; fax (1) 790-1907; e-mail motcenter@motiraq.org; internet www.mot.gov.iq.

Ministry of Transportation: nr Martyr's Monument, Karradat Dakhil, Baghdad; tel. (1) 776-6041; e-mail mt_office@motrans.gov.iq; internet www.motrans.gov.iq.

Ministry of Water Resources: Palestine St, Baghdad; tel. (1) 772-0240; fax (1) 774-0672; e-mail waterresmin@yahoo.co.uk; internet www.mowr.gov.iq.

Ministry of Youth and Sports: Baghdad; internet www.moys.gov.iq.

Legislature

Council of Representatives

Baghdad International Zone Convention Center, Baghdad; e-mail press@parliament.iq; internet www.parliament.iq.

Elections to the Council of Representatives were held on 7 March 2010. The rate of participation by eligible voters was recorded at 62.4%. According to final results (including compensatory seats) published by the Independent High Electoral Commission (IHEC) on 26 March, the Iraqi National Movement, led by former interim Prime Minister Dr Ayad Allawi, with 91 seats, emerged as the largest group in the 325-seat legislature. The State of Law coalition of incumbent Prime Minister Nuri al-Maliki won 89 seats. The Iraqi National Alliance obtained 70 seats and the Kurdistan Alliance 43 seats. Meanwhile, the Kurdish Movement for Change won eight seats, the Iraqi Accord six, the Kurdistan Islamic Union List and the Iraqi Unity Coalition each four, and the Islamic Group of Kurdistan two. Of the remaining eight seats, five were reserved for Christian parties and one each for the Sabian, Shebek and Yazidi communities. (On 1 June the declared outcome was ratified by the Higher Judicial Council, following a manual recount of the votes cast in the capital, Baghdad.)

Speaker: OSAMA AL-NUJAIFI.

Kurdish Autonomous Region

A 15-article accord signed by the Iraqi Government and Kurdish leaders in 1970 provided for: the creation of a unified autonomous area for the Kurdish population, comprising the administrative departments of al-Sulaimaniya (Sulaimaniya), D'hok and Irbil (Arbil), and the Kurdish sector of the city of Kirkuk; and the establishment of a 50-member Kurdish Legislative Council. Following the recapture of Kuwait from Iraqi forces by a multinational military coalition in early 1991, renewed negotiations between the Iraqi Government (under Saddam Hussain) and Kurdish groups stalled over the status of Kirkuk, and in October 1991 the Government effectively severed all economic and administrative support to the region. In May 1992 the Kurdish Iraqi Front (KIF), an alliance of several Kurdish factions—including the two largest, the Patriotic Union of Kurdistan (PUK) and the Kurdistan Democratic Party (KDP)—established in 1988, organized elections to a new 105-member Iraqi Kurdistan National Assembly. However, by September 1996 bitter factional disputes had led to the effective disintegration of the KIF, and prompted the Government to reassert full Iraqi sovereignty over the Kurdish areas. At a meeting in Washington, DC, USA, in September 1998, representatives of the PUK and the KDP reached a formal peace agreement, which provided for a unified regional administration, the sharing of local revenues and co-operation in implementing the UN-sponsored 'oil-for-food' programme. In December 1999 the KDP announced the composition of a new 25-member coalition administration (comprising the KDP, the Iraqi Communist Party, the Assyrian Movement, the Independent Workers' Party of Kurdistan, the Islamic Union and independents) for the areas under its control, principally the departments of Arbil and D'hok. Municipal elections (to select 571 officials) were conducted in the KDP-administered region in May 2001; according to official KDP sources, KDP candidates received 81% of votes cast. Negotiations between representatives of the KDP and the PUK for the full implementation of the Washington accord were held during 2002, and resulted in the resumption of a transitional joint session of the Iraqi Kurdistan National Assembly in October. The autonomous regions retained their status following the removal of the regime of Saddam Hussain in early 2003, but the status of Kirkuk remained highly controversial (see Contemporary Political History).

THE GOVERNMENT OF THE KURDISH AUTONOMOUS REGION

President: MASOUD BARZANI.

THE CABINET
(May 2012)

A coalition Government comprising the Kurdistan Democratic Party (KDP), the Patriotic Union of Kurdistan (PUK), the Kurdistan Islamic Movement, Turkmen representatives, the Kurdistan Communist Party and independents.

Prime Minister: NECHIRVAN IDRIS BARZANI.

Deputy Prime Minister: IMAD AHMAD SAYFOUR.

Minister of Agriculture and Water Resources: SERWAN BABAN.

Minister of Culture and Youth: KAWA MAHMOUD SHAKIR.

Minister of Education: ASMAT MUHAMMAD KHALID.

Minister of Electricity: YASIN SHEIKH ABU BAKIR MUHAMMAD MAWATI.

Minister of Endowment and Religious Affairs: KAMIL ALI AZIZ.

Minister of Finance and the Economy: BAYIZ SAEED MUHAMMAD TALABANI.

Minister of Health: REKAWT HAMA RASHEED.

Minister of Higher Education and Scientific Research: ALI SAEED.

Minister of Housing and Reconstruction: KAMARAN AHMAD ABDULLAH.

Minister of Justice: SHERWAN HAIDARI.

Minister for the Interior: ABD AL-KARIM SULTAN SINJARI.

Minister of Labour and Social Affairs: ASOS NAJIB ABDULLAH.

Minister of Martyrs and Anfal Affairs: SABAH AHMAD MUHAMMAD.

Minister of Municipalities and Tourism: DILSHAD SHAHAB.

Minister of Natural Resources: ABDULLAH ABD AL-RAHMAN ABDULLAH.

Minister of Peshmerga Affairs: JAFAR MUSTAFA ALI.

Minister of Planning: ALI SINDI.

Minister of Trade and Industry: SINAN ABD AL-KHALQ AHMAD CHALABI.

Minister of Transport and Communications: JONSON SIYAOOSH.

The President of the Divan of the Council of Ministers, the Secretary of the Cabinet, the Head of the Department of Foreign Relations and the Chairman of the Investment Board also have full ministerial status.

LEGISLATURE

Iraqi Kurdistan Parliament

Erbil (Hewlêr) Kurdistan, Iraq; e-mail office@perleman.org; internet www.perleman.org.

In May 1992, negotiations with the Iraqi Government over the full implementation of the 1970 accord on Kurdish regional autonomy having stalled, the KIF unilaterally organized elections to a 105-member Iraqi Kurdistan National Assembly, in which almost the entire electorate of 1.1m. participated. The KDP and the PUK were the only parties to achieve representation in the new Assembly, and subsequently agreed to share seats equally (50 seats each—five having been reserved for two Assyrian Christian parties). However, the subsequent disintegration of the KIF and prolonged armed conflict between elements of the KDP and the PUK prevented the Assembly from becoming properly instituted. Relations between the KDP and the PUK improved following the Washington, DC, agreement of September 1998, and on 8 September 2002 representatives of the two parties signed an agreement providing for the inauguration of a transitional joint parliamentary session (with representation based on the results of the May 1992 elections) before the end of the year. On 4 October 2002 a joint session of the Iraqi Kurdistan National Assembly was convened for the first time since 1996. Following the removal of the regime of Saddam Hussain by US-led forces in early 2003, elections to a new Iraqi Kurdistan National Assembly took place on 30 January 2005, concurrently with elections to the Transitional National Assembly. The Kurdistan Democratic List won 104 of the 111 seats. On 12 June the new Kurdish legislature voted unanimously to appoint Masoud Barzani, leader of the KDP, to the post of President of the Kurdish Autonomous Region. The Government, led by Barzani, assumed office on 7 May 2006, and represented the region's first unified Cabinet. Prior to a unification agreement signed in January 2006, Sulaimaniya had been governed by the PUK, while Arbil and D'hok were administered by the KDP. In February 2009 the Iraqi Kurdistan National Assembly was renamed the Iraqi Kurdistan Parliament. A draft Constitution for the Kurdish Autonomous Region, which included territorial claims to Kirkuk and other disputed regions, was approved by the Iraqi Kurdistan National Assembly on 24 June 2009. However, a planned referendum on the draft Constitution was subsequently postponed, owing to opposition from the Independent High Electoral Commission and the Iraqi parliament. At elections to the Iraqi Kurdistan Parliament held on 25 July, the Kurdistani List, which comprised the PUK and the KDP, secured 59 of the 111 seats in the legislature. The significant reduction in the two main parties' majority was largely due to the success of the Movement for Change (Gorran), which received 25 seats; the group had been established in 2006 by former members of the PUK, and campaigned on a pro-reform and anti-corruption platform. An alliance of Islamist and left-wing parties, the Service and Reform List, won 13 seats. The Islamic Movement in Iraqi Kurdistan took two seats, and the Freedom and Social Justice List one seat. The remaining 11 seats were reserved for representatives of various minority groups. Meanwhile, in a concurrent election for the regional presidency, Barzani was re-elected with 69.6% of the valid votes cast.

Speaker: Dr KAMAL KIRKUKI.

Election, 25 July 2009

	Seats
Kurdistani List (PUK and KDP)	59
Movement for Change (Gorran)*	25
Service and Reform List†	13
Islamic Movement in Iraqi Kurdistan	2
Freedom and Social Justice List	1
Minority Groups	11
Total	111

* Established in 2006 by former members of the PUK.

† Comprises the Kurdistan Islamic Union, Islamic Group in Kurdistan, Kurdistan Socialist Democratic Party and Future Party.

Election Commission

Independent High Electoral Commission (IHEC): POB 55074, Baghdad; tel. (1) 743-2519; e-mail iheciraq@ihec-iraq.com; internet www.ihec-iq.com; f. 2004 as Independent Electoral Comm. of Iraq by fmr Coalition Provisional Authority; renamed as above 2007; Chair. FARAJ AL-HAYDARI.

Political Organizations

Following the removal from power of the Baathist regime, restrictions were effectively lifted on opposition political organizations that were either previously declared illegal, forced to operate clandestinely within Iraq or were based abroad. Some 306 political parties were reported to have participated in the election to the Council of Representatives held on 7 March 2010.

Arab Baath Socialist Party: revolutionary Arab socialist movement founded in Damascus, Syria, in 1947; governed Iraq during 1968–2003 as principal constituent of ruling coalition, the Nat. Progressive Front (NPF); the NPF was removed from power by US-led forces in May 2003, whereupon membership of the Baath Party was declared illegal and former party mems were barred from govt and military posts; subsequently thought to be involved in insurgent activities in Iraq; in Feb. 2008 new legislation was ratified permitting certain former Baathists to be reinstated to official posts; in Jan. 2007, following the execution of former Iraqi President Saddam Hussain, former Vice-President IZZAT IBRAHIM AL-DOURI was named as the party's new leader.

Assyrian Democratic Movement (Zowaa Dimuqrataya Aturaya —Zowaa): e-mail info@zowaa.org; internet www.zowaa.org; f. 1979; seeks recognition of Assyrian rights within framework of democratic national govt; Sec.-Gen. YOUNADAM YOUSUF KANNA.

Assyrian Socialist Party: Baghdad; e-mail gaboatouraya@yahoo .co.uk; internet asp2.no.sapo.pt; f. 2002 (refounded); advocates the establishment of an Assyrian nation.

Constitutional Party: Baghdad; f. 2004; Shi'ite; contested the March 2010 legislative election as part of the Iraqi Unity Coalition; Founder and Leader JAWAD AL-BULANI.

Al-Ezediah Movement for Progress and Reform: Yazidi grouping; Leader AMIN FARHAN JEJO.

Independent Democratic Gathering: f. 2003; seeks a secular and democratic govt of Iraq; contested March 2010 legislative election as part of the State of Law alliance; Leader MAHDI AL-HAFEZ.

Iraqi Accord (Jabhat al-Tawafuq al-Iraqiya): f. 2005 as the Iraqi Accord Front; reformed to contest the March 2010 legislative elections; mainly Sunni; secular; coalition of the Iraqi Islamic Party and the Nat. Gathering of the People of Iraq.

Iraqi Communist Party (ICP): Baghdad; e-mail iraq@iraqcp.org; internet www.iraqicp.com; f. 1934; became legally recognized in July 1973 on formation of NPF; left NPF March 1979; First Sec. HAMID MAJID MOUSSA.

Iraqi Constitutional Movement: Baghdad; f. 1993; fmrly Constitutional Monarchy Movement; contested March 2010 legislative election as part of Iraqi Nat. Alliance.

Iraqi Front for National Dialogue (Hewar National Iraqi Front): f. 2005 as breakaway party from Iraqi Nat. Dialogue Council; coalition of minor Sunni parties; contested the March 2010 legislative election as part of the Iraqi Nat. Movement list, although al-Mutlaq was himself banned from participating by the Justice and Accountability Comm; Founder and Leader SALEH AL-MUTLAQ.

Iraqi Islamic Party (IIP) (al-Hizb al-Islami al-'Iraqi): e-mail iraqiparty@iraqiparty.com; internet www.iraqiparty.com; f. 1960; Sunni; branch of the Muslim Brotherhood; contested March 2010 legislative election as part of the Iraqi Accord list; Sec.-Gen. OSAMA TIKRITI.

Iraqi National Accord (INA): e-mail wifaq_ina@hotmail.com; internet www.wifaq.com; f. 1990; contested March 2010 legislative election as mem. of Iraqi Nat. Movement; Founder and Sec.-Gen. Dr AYAD ALLAWI.

Iraqi National Alliance: list of mainly Shi'ite parties, incl. the ISCI, the Sadr II Movement, the Iraqi Nat. Congress, the Nat. Reform Movement and the Islamic Virtue Party, which contested the March 2010 legislative elections as a single coalition.

Iraqi National Congress (INC): e-mail info@inciraq.com; internet inciraq.com; f. 1992 in London, United Kingdom, as a multi-party coalition supported by the US Govt; following the removal of the regime of Saddam Hussain, the INC moved to Baghdad and was transformed into a distinct political party; formed Nat. Congress Coalition before 2005 legislative elections, at which it failed to win any seats; contested March 2010 election as part of the Iraqi Nat. Alliance; Leader AHMAD CHALABI.

Iraqi National Foundation Congress (INFC): Baghdad; f. 2004; multi-party coalition incl. Nasserites, pre-Saddam Hussain era Baathists, Kurds, Christians, Sunnis and Shi'ites; seeks secular govt of national unity; opposed to presence of US-led coalition in Iraq, and consequently boycotted the electoral process initiated by the coalition; led by 25-mem. secretariat; Gen. Sec. Sheikh JAWAD AL-KHALISI.

Iraqi National Movement (Iraqiya): secular electoral list formed to contest the March 2010 legislative election, comprising a no. of political orgs, incl. the INA, the Iraqi Front for Nat. Dialogue, the Renewal List and Iraqis; Leader Dr AYAD ALLAWI.

Iraqis (Iraqiyun): f. 2004; moderate; includes both Sunnis and Shi'ites; contested March 2010 legislative election as part of Iraqi National Movement list; Leader Sheikh GHAZI MASHAL AJIL AL-YAWAR.

Iraqi Turkmen Front (Irak Türkmen Cephesi): Arbil; internet www.kerkuk.net; f. 1995; coalition of Turkmen groups; seeks autonomy for Turkmen areas in Iraq and recognition of Turkmen as one of main ethnic groups in Iraq, and supports establishment of multi-party democratic system in Iraq; contests status of Kirkuk with Kurds; Leader SADETTIN ERGEÇ; Sec.-Gen. YUNUS BAYRAKTAR.

Iraqi Unity Coalition: f. 2009 to contest the March 2010 legislative election; electoral alliance comprising 38 parties, incl. the Constitutional Party and the Iraqi Awakening Conference.

Islamic Dawa Party (Hizb al-Da'wa al-Islamiya): Baghdad; e-mail info@islamicdawaparty.org; internet www.islamicdawaparty.org; f. 1957 in Najaf; banned 1980; fmrly based in Tehran, Iran, and London, United Kingdom; re-established in Baghdad 2003; contested March 2010 legislative election as part of State of Law coalition; predominantly Shi'ite, but with Sunni mems; advocates govt centred on the principles of Islam; Gen. Sec. NURI KAMAL (JAWAD) AL-MALIKI.

Islamic Group of Kurdistan (Komaleh Islami): Khurmal; f. 2001; splinter group of IMIK; moderate Islamist, aligned with the PUK; contested March 2010 legislative election independently; Founder and Leader Mullah ALI BAPIR.

Islamic Movement in Iraqi Kurdistan (IMIK): Halabja; e-mail bzotnawa@yahoo.com; f. 1987; Islamist movement seeking to obtain greater legal rights for Iraqi Kurds; Founder and Leader Sheikh UTHMAN ABD AL-AZIZ.

Islamic Supreme Council of Iraq (ISCI): Najaf; e-mail info@almejlis.org; internet www.almejlis.org; f. 1982 as the Supreme Council for the Islamic Revolution in Iraq; name changed as above in 2007; Shi'ite; seeks govt based on principle of *wilayat-e-faqih* (guardianship of the jurisprudent); armed faction, the Badr Organization (fmrly Badr Brigade), assisted coalition forces in Iraq after the removal of Saddam Hussain's regime; contested March 2010 legislative election as part of the Iraqi Nat. Alliance; Leader AMMAR AL-HAKIM.

Islamic Virtue Party (Hizb al-Fadhila al-Islamiya—IVP): Basra; Shi'ite; an offshoot of the Sadrist movement; follows the spiritual leadership of Ayatollah al-Sayyid Muhammad al-Ya'qubi; contested March 2010 legislative election as part of Iraqi Nat. Alliance; Sec.-Gen. ABD AL-RAHIM AHMAD ALI AL-HASINI.

Kurdistan Alliance List (Democratic Patriotic Alliance of Kurdistan—DPAK): f. 2004 as a coalition of the PUK, the KDP and smaller Kurdish parties to contest Jan. 2005 legislative elections; participated in March 2010 legislative election as a two-party coalition of the PUK and the KDP; the PUK and the KDP formed a separate electoral list, the Kurdistan List, to contest elections to the Iraqi Kurdistan National Assembly in July 2009.

Kurdistan Democratic Party (KDP): European Office (Germany), 10749 Berlin, POB 301516; tel. (30) 79743741; fax (30) 79743746; e-mail party@kdp.se; internet www.kdp.se; f. 1946; seeks to protect Kurdish rights and promote Kurdish culture and interests through regional political and legislative autonomy, as part of a federative republic; see also Kurdistan Alliance List; Pres. MASOUD BARZANI; Vice-Pres. NECHIRVAN BARZANI.

Kurdistan Islamic Union (Yakgrtui Islami Kurdistan): e-mail kiucenter@kurdiu.org; internet kurdiu.org; f. 1991; seeks establishment of an Islamic state in Iraq that recognizes the rights of Kurds; branch of the Muslim Brotherhood; contested July 2009 elections to the Iraqi Kurdistan National Assembly as part of the Service and Reform List; participated in the March 2010 legislative election independently; Sec.-Gen. SALAHEDDIN MUHAMMAD BAHAEDDIN.

Kurdistan Socialist Democratic Party (KSDP): Sulaimaniya; e-mail info@psdkurdistan.org; internet www.psdkurdistan.com; f. 1994; splinter group of the KDP, aligned with the PUK; contested July 2009 elections to the Iraqi Kurdistan National Assembly as part of the Service and Reform List; Sec.-Gen. MUHAMMAD HAJI MAHMUD.

Kurdistan Toilers Party (Hizbi Zahmatkeshani Kurdistan): f. 1985; advocates a federal Iraq; closely associated with the KSDP; contested July 2009 elections to the Iraqi Kurdistan Nat. Assembly as part of the Social Justice and Freedom List.

Movement for Change (Gorran): internet www.gorran.org; f. 2006; established by fmr members of the PUK; advocates political and economic reform, anti-corruption measures and the independence of the judiciary; advocates a federal Iraq; contested July 2009 elections to the Iraqi Kurdistan Nat. Assembly as the Change List; contested the March 2010 legislative election independently; Leader NAWSHIRWAN MUSTAFA.

National Gathering of the People of Iraq: f. 2004 as the Iraqi People's Conference; name changed in 2009; Sunni; contested March 2010 legislative elections as part of the Iraqi Accord; Leader KHALED AL-BARAA.

National Rafidain List: e-mail info@alrafedainlist.com; internet www.alrafedainlist.com; f. 2004; Assyrian-Christian list headed by the Assyrian Democratic Movement; Leader YOUNADAM KANA.

National Reform Movement: f. 2008 by fmr mems of Islamic Dawa Party; Shi'ite; contested March 2010 legislative election as part of Iraqi Nat. Alliance; Leader IBRAHIM AL-JA'FARI.

National Tribal Gathering: f. 2007; Sunni; participated in March 2010 election as mem. of the Iraqi Accord list; Leader OMAR AL-HAYKAL.

Patriotic Union of Kurdistan (PUK): European Office (Germany), 10502 Berlin, POB 210213; tel. (30) 34097850; fax (30) 34097849; e-mail puk@puk.org; internet www.puk.org; f. 1975; seeks to protect and promote Kurdish rights and interests through self-determination; see also Kurdistan Alliance List; Pres. JALAL TALABANI.

Reconciliation and Liberation Bloc (Kutla al-Musalaha wa't-Tahrir): Mosul; f. 1995 in Jordan as Iraqi Homeland Party (Hizb al-Watan al-Iraqi); moved to Damascus, Syria, and to Mosul in 2003; liberal, secular Sunni; advocates withdrawal of coalition troops and partial rehabilitation of mems of the former Baathist regime; publishes *Al-Ittijah al-Akhar* newspaper; Leader MISH'AN AL-JUBURI.

Renewal List (Tajdeed): f. 2009 by Vice-Pres. Tariq al-Hashimi, following his resignation from the IIP; Sunni; contested March 2010 legislative election as part of the Iraqi Nat. Movement list; Leader TARIQ AL-HASHIMI.

Sadr II Movement (Jamaat al-Sadr al-Thani): Najaf; f. 2003; Shi'ite; opposes presence of US-led coalition in Iraq; mems of the Movement participated in the March 2010 legislative election as part of the Iraqi Nat. Alliance; military wing is Imam al-Mahdi Army; Leader Hojatoleslam MUQTADA AL-SADR.

Service and Reform List: alliance of Islamist and left-wing parties formed prior to the July 2009 elections to the Iraqi Kurdistan Nat. Assembly, comprising the Islamic Group of Kurdistan, the Kurdistan Islamic Union, the Kurdistan Socialist Democratic Party and the Future Party.

State of Law (Dawlat al-Kanoon): f. prior to 2009 provincial elections; contested March 2010 legislative election as a predominantly Shi‘a alliance of parties and independent candidates, incl. the Islamic Dawa Party, the Independent Arab Movement and the Anbar Salvation Nat. Front.

Major militant groups that have launched attacks against Iraqis and the US-led coalition include: **Fedayeen Saddam** (Saddam's Martyrs; f. 1995 by mems of the former Baathist regime; paramilitary group); **Ansar al-Islam** (f. 1998; splinter group of IMIK; Islamist; suspected of having links with al-Qa‘ida); **Hezbollah** (Shi‘ite Marsh Arab; Leader ABD AL-KARIM MAHMOUD MOHAMMEDAWI—‘ ABU HATEM'); **Ansar al-Sunnah** (f. 2003 by mems of Ansar al-Islam; Islamist); **Imam al-Mahdi Army** (armed wing of the Sadr II Movement—Jamaat al-Sadr al-Thani); **Base of Holy War in Mesopotamia** (Tanzim Qa‘idat al-Jihad fi Bilad al-Rafidain; Sunni insurgent network, also known as al-Qa‘ida in Iraq; Leader AL-NASSER LIDEEN ALLAH ABU SULEIMAN, who was reported to have been killed in Feb. 2011); **Islamic State of Iraq** (Dawlat al-Iraq al-Islamiyya; network of Sunni insurgent groups; suspected of links with al-Qa‘ida in Iraq; Leader ABU BAKR AL-BAGHDADI AL-HUSSEINI AL-QURASHI).

Diplomatic Representation

EMBASSIES IN IRAQ

Algeria: Hay al-Mansour, Baghdad; tel. (1) 543-4137; fax (1) 542-5829; Ambassador MUSTAPHA BOUTORA.

Australia: International Zone, Baghdad; e-mail austemb.baghdad@dfat.gov.au; internet www.iraq.embassy.gov.au; Ambassador LYNDALL SACHS.

Bahrain: 41/6/605 Hay al-Mutanabi, Baghdad; tel. (1) 541-0841; fax (1) 541-2027; Ambassador SALAH AL-MALIKI.

Bangladesh: 6/14/929 Hay Babel, Baghdad; tel. (1) 719-0068; fax (1) 718-6045; Ambassador MUHAMMAD KAMAL EL-DIN.

Bulgaria: 12/25/624 al-Ameriya, Baghdad; tel. (1) 556-8197; fax (1) 556-4182; e-mail bulgemb@uruklink.net; Ambassador VALERI RATCHEV.

China, People's Republic: POB 8020, al-Mansour Hotel Salhiyah, Baghdad; tel. 7901912315 (mobile); e-mail chinaemb_iq@mfa.gov.cn; Ambassador NI JIAN.

Czech Republic: POB 27124, 37/11/601 Hay al-Mansour, Baghdad; tel. (1) 542-4868; fax (1) 214-2621; e-mail baghdad@embassy.mzv.cz; internet www.mzv.cz/baghdad; Ambassador JOZEF VRABEC.

Denmark: al-Jana'a Quarter, Hay al-Tashriya, Baghdad; tel. 7901940847 (mobile); e-mail bgwamb@um.dk; internet www.ambbagdad.um.dk; Ambassador GERT MEINECKE.

Egypt: 103/11/601 Hay al-Mansour, Baghdad; tel. (1) 543-0572; fax (1) 556-6346; e-mail egypt@uruklink.net; Ambassador SHERIF KAMAL SHAHIN.

France: POB 118, 7/55/102 Abu Nawas, Baghdad; tel. (600) 248-477; fax (600) 853-141; e-mail info@ambafrance-iq.org; internet www.ambafrance-iq.org; Ambassador DENYS GAUER.

Germany: POB 2036, Hay al-Mansour, Baghdad; tel. (1) 543-1470; fax (1) 543-5840; e-mail info@bagdad.diplo.de; internet www.bagdad.diplo.de; Ambassador CHRISTIAN KARL GEORG BERGER.

Greece: 63/31/913, Jadriyah University Sq., Hay Babel, Baghdad; tel. (1) 778-2273; e-mail gremb.bag@mfa.gr; Ambassador MIRKORIOZ KARAVOTHIAS.

Holy See: Apostolic Nunciature, POB 2090, 904/2/46 Saadoun St, Baghdad; tel. (1) 719-5183; e-mail nuntiusiraq@yahoo.com; Apostolic Nuncio Most Rev. GIORGIO LINGUA (Titular Archbishop of Tuscania).

India: POB 4114, 6/25/306 Hay al-Maghrib, Adhamiya, Baghdad; tel. (1) 422-5438; fax (1) 422-9549; e-mail eoibaghdad@yahoo.com; Ambassador SURESH K. REDDY.

Iran: POB 39095, Salehiya, Karadeh Maryam, Baghdad; tel. (1) 884-3033; fax (1) 537-5636; Ambassador HASSAN DANAFAR.

Italy: 33/7/15 Hay al-Maghrib, Mahala 304, Baghdad; tel. (1) 425-0720; e-mail ambasciata.baghdad@esteri.it; internet www.ambbaghdad.esteri.it/ambasciata_baghdad; Ambassador GERARDO CARANTE.

Japan: International Zone, Baghdad; tel. (1) 776-6791; e-mail azza_fh@yahoo.com; internet www.iraq.emb-japan.go.jp; Ambassador SUSUMU HASEGAWA.

Jordan: POB 6314, 145/49/617 Hay al-Andalus, Baghdad; tel. (1) 541-2892; fax (1) 541-2009; e-mail jordan@uruklink.net; Ambassador MUHAMMAD TAYSIR AL-MASADEH.

Korea, Republic: POB 2387, Alwiya, Baghdad; e-mail kembiraq@mofat.go.kr; internet irq.mofat.go.kr; Ambassador PARK SUK-BUM.

Kuwait: Baghdad; Ambassador ALI MUHAMMAD AL-MOMEN.

Lebanon: al-Liwadiat, Baghdad; tel. (1) 416-6018; fax (1) 885-6731; e-mail lebemb@hotmail.com; Chargé d'affaires NAWAF SHARIF HAZZA.

Netherlands: International Zone, Baghdad; tel. (1) 778-2571; e-mail bad@minbuza.nl; internet iraq.nlembassy.org; Ambassador JEROEN ROODENBURG.

Nigeria: POB 5933, 45/11/601, Hay al-Mansour, Baghdad; tel. (1) 541-3133; fax (1) 243-4513; Ambassador IBRAHIM MOHAMMED.

Pakistan: 14/7/609 Hay al-Mansour, Baghdad; fax (1) 542-8707; e-mail pakembbag@yahoo.com; Ambassador (vacant).

Philippines: POB 3236, 4/22/915 Hay al-Jamiyah, al-Jadriya, Baghdad; tel. (1) 778-2247; fax (1) 719-3228; e-mail baghdad.pe@dfa.gov.ph; Chargé d'affaires a.i. MARLOWE A. MIRANDA.

Poland: 38/75 Karadat Mariam International Zone, Baghdad; tel. (1) 719-0297; fax (1) 719-0296; e-mail bagdad.amb.sekretariat@msz.gov.pl; Ambassador STANISŁAW SMOLEŃ.

Romania: POB 2571, Arassat al-Hindia St, 452A/31/929 Hay Babel, Baghdad; tel. (1) 778-2860; fax (1) 778-7553; e-mail ambrobagd@yahoo.com; Ambassador IACOB PRADA.

Russia: 4/5/605 Hay al-Mutanabi, Baghdad; tel. and fax (1) 543-4462; e-mail russian_embassy_in_iraq@land.ru; Ambassador VALERYAN V. SHUVAYEV.

Serbia: POB 2061, 16/35/923 Hay Babel, Baghdad; tel. (1) 778-7887; fax (1) 778-0489; e-mail embsrbag@yahoo.com; internet www.baghdad.mfa.rs; Ambassador RADISAV PETROVIĆ.

Slovakia: 94/28/923 Hay Babel, Baghdad; tel. (1) 776-7367; fax (1) 776-7368; Ambassador MILOSLAV NAD.

Spain: POB 2072, 50/1/609 al-Mansour, Baghdad; e-mail emb.bagdad@maec.es; Ambassador JOSÉ TURPÍN MOLINA.

Sweden: POB 3475, Karadat Mariam, Baghdad; tel. 7801987450 (mobile); e-mail ambassaden.bagdad@foreign.ministry.se; internet www.swedenabroad.com/baghdad; Ambassador CARL MAGNUS NESSER.

Syria: Hay al-Mansour, Baghdad; Ambassador NAWAF AL-FARES.

Tunisia: 1/49/617 Hay al-Andalus, Baghdad; tel. (1) 542-4569; Ambassador (vacant).

Turkey: 2/8 Waziriya, Baghdad; tel. (1) 422-0022; fax (1) 422-8353; e-mail turkemb.baghdad@mfa.gov.tr; internet www.baghdad.emb.mfa.gov.tr; Ambassador YUNUS DEMIRER.

Ukraine: POB 15192, 20/1/609 al-Mansour, al-Yarmouk, Baghdad; tel. (1) 542-6677; fax 543-9849; e-mail emb_iq@mfa.gov.ua; Chargé d'affaires ANATOLII MARYNETS.

United Arab Emirates: 81/34/611 Hay al-Andalus (al-Daoudi), Baghdad; tel. (1) 543-9174; fax (1) 543-9093; Ambassador ABDULLAH IBRAHIM AL-SHEHHI.

United Kingdom: International Zone, Baghdad; e-mail britishconsulbaghdad@yahoo.co.uk; tel. 7901911684 (mobile); internet ukiniraq.fco.gov.uk; Ambassador MICHAEL ARON.

USA: APO AE 09316, Baghdad; e-mail BaghdadPressOffice@state.gov; internet iraq.usembassy.gov; Ambassador JAMES JEFFREY.

Yemen: 4/36/904 Hay al-Wahada, Baghdad; tel. (1) 718-6682; fax (1) 717-2318; Ambassador ZAID HASSAN AL-WARITH.

Judicial System

Following the ousting of the Baath regime, the judicial system was subject to a process of review and de-Baathification. In June 2003 the former Coalition Provisional Authority (CPA) established a **Judicial Review Committee**, the task of which was to review and repair the material status of the courts and to assess personnel. In December the Governing Council created the **Iraqi Special Tribune**, in order to bring to trial those senior members of the former regime accused of war crimes, crimes against humanity and genocide. The statute of the Tribune was amended by the former Transitional National Assembly in October 2005, when it was renamed the **Supreme Iraqi Criminal Tribunal**.

In the interim period, a new judicial system was formed. The **Central Criminal Court of Iraq**, consisting of an **Investigative Court** and a **Trial Court**, was created by the CPA in July 2003 as the senior court in Iraq, with jurisdiction over all crimes committed in the country since 19 March 2003. With a few exceptions, the application of justice was to be based upon the 1969 Penal Code of Iraq and the 1971 Criminal Proceedings Code of Iraq.

Higher Judicial Council: tel. (1) 538-4406; fax (1) 537-2267; e-mail iraqinfocenter@yahoo.com; internet www.iraqja.iq; Pres. MEDHAT AL-MAHMOUD.

Religion

ISLAM

About 95% of the population are Muslims, some 60% of whom are of the Shi'ite sect. The Arabs of northern Iraq, the Bedouins, the Kurds, the Turkomans and some of the inhabitants of Baghdad and Basra are mainly of the Sunni sect, while the remaining Arabs south of the Diyali are Shi'a.

CHRISTIANITY

There are Christian communities in all the principal towns of Iraq, but their main villages lie mostly in the Mosul district. The Christians of Iraq comprise three groups: (*a*) the free Churches, including the Nestorian, Gregorian and Syrian Orthodox; (*b*) the churches known as Uniate, since they are in union with the Roman Catholic Church, including the Armenian Uniates, Syrian Uniates and Chaldeans; (*c*) mixed bodies of Protestant converts, New Chaldeans and Orthodox Armenians. There are estimated to be 500,000–700,000 Christians of various denominations in Iraq; however, there has been an exodus to neighbouring countries such as Syria and Jordan since the mid-2000s, as a result of the ongoing sectarian conflict.

The Assyrian Church

Assyrian Christians, an ancient sect having sympathies with Nestorian beliefs, were forced to leave their mountainous homeland in northern Kurdistan in the early part of the 20th century. The estimated 550,000 members of the Apostolic Catholic Assyrian Church of the East are now exiles, mainly in Iraq (about 50,000 adherents), Syria, Lebanon and the USA. Their leader is the Catholicos Patriarch, His Holiness MAR DINKHA IV.

The Orthodox Churches

Armenian Apostolic Church: Diocese of the Armenian Church of Iraq, POB 2280, al-Jadriya, Tayaran Sq., Baghdad; tel. (1) 815-1853; fax (1) 815-1857; e-mail iraqitem@yahoo.com; internet www.iraqitem.org; f. 1639; Primate Archbishop AVAK ASADOURIAN; 13 churches (four in Baghdad); 23,091 mems.

Syrian Orthodox Church: Syrian Orthodox Archbishopric, POB 843, al-Seenah St, Baghdad; tel. (1) 719-6320; fax (1) 719-7583; Archbishop of Baghdad and Basra SEVERIUS JAMIL HAWA; 12,000 adherents in Iraq.

The Greek Orthodox Church is also represented in Iraq.

The Roman Catholic Church

Armenian Rite

At 31 December 2007 the archdiocese of Baghdad contained an estimated 1,600 adherents.

Archbishop of Baghdad: Most Rev. EMMANUEL DABBAGHIAN, 27/903 Archevêché Arménien Catholique, POB 2344, Karrada Sharkiya, Baghdad; tel. (1) 719-2461; e-mail dabbaghianemm@hotmail.com.

Chaldean Rite

Iraq comprises the patriarchate of Babylon, five archdioceses (including the patriarchal see of Baghdad) and five dioceses (all of which are suffragan to the patriarchate). Altogether, the Patriarch has jurisdiction over 21 archdioceses and dioceses in Iraq, Egypt, Iran, Lebanon, Syria, Turkey and the USA, and the Patriarchal Vicariate of Jerusalem. At 31 December 2007 there were an estimated 231,799 Chaldean Catholics in Iraq (including 135,000 in the archdiocese of Baghdad).

Patriarch of Babylon of the Chaldeans: Cardinal EMMANUEL III DELLY, POB 6112, Patriarcat Chaldéen Catholique, al-Mansour, Baghdad; tel. (1) 537-9164; fax (1) 537-8556; e-mail info@st-addayyahoo.com.

Archbishop of Arbil: Most Rev. BASHAR WARDA, Archevêché Catholique Chaldéen, Ainkawa, Arbil; tel. (665) 225-0009.

Archbishop of Baghdad: the Patriarch of Babylon (q.v.).

Archbishop of Basra: Most Rev. IMAD AZIZ AL-BANNA, Archevêché Chaldéen, POB 217, Ashar-Basra; tel. (40) 613427; e-mail efather2006@yahoo.com.

Archbishop of Kirkuk: Most Rev. LOUIS SAKO, Archevêché Chaldéen, POB 490, Kirkuk; tel. (50) 220525; fax (50) 213978; e-mail luis_sako2@yahoo.com.

Archbishop of Mosul: Most Rev. EMIL SHIMOUN NONA, Archevêché Chaldéen, POB 757, Mayassa, Mosul; tel. (60) 815831; fax (60) 816742; e-mail archdioceseofmossul@yahoo.com.

Latin Rite

The archdiocese of Baghdad, directly responsible to the Holy See, contained an estimated 2,500 adherents at 31 December 2007.

Archbishop of Baghdad: Most Rev. JEAN BENJAMIN SLEIMAN, Archevêché Latin, POB 35130, Hay al-Wahda—Mahallat 904, rue 8, Immeuble 44, 12906 Baghdad; tel. (1) 719-9537; fax (1) 717-2471; e-mail jbsleiman@yahoo.com.

Melkite Rite

The Greek-Melkite Patriarch of Antioch (GRÉGOIRE III LAHAM) is resident in Damascus, Syria.

Patriarchal Exarchate of Iraq: Exarchat Patriarchal Grec-Melkite, Karradat IN 903/10/50, Baghdad; tel. (1) 719-1082; 100 adherents (2006); Exarch Patriarchal (vacant).

Syrian Rite

Iraq comprises two archdioceses and the Patriarchal Exarchate of Basra; there were an estimated 59,000 adherents at 31 December 2007.

Archbishop of Baghdad: Most Rev. ATHANASE MATTI SHABA MATOKA, Archevêché Syrien Catholique, 903/2/1 Baghdad; tel. (1) 719-1850; fax (1) 719-0166; e-mail mattishaba@yahoo.com.

Archbishop of Mosul: Most Rev. BOUTROS MOSHE, Archevêché Syrien Catholique, Hosh al-Khan, Mosul; tel. (60) 762160; fax (60) 771439; e-mail syrcam2003@yahoo.com.

The Anglican Communion

Within the Episcopal Church in Jerusalem and the Middle East, Iraq forms part of the diocese of Cyprus and the Gulf. Expatriate congregations in Iraq meet at St George's Church, Baghdad. The Bishop in Cyprus and the Gulf is resident in Cyprus.

JUDAISM

A tiny Jewish community, numbering only eight people in late 2008, remains in Baghdad.

OTHERS

About 550,000 Yazidis and a smaller number of Sabians and Shebeks reside in Iraq.

Sabian Community: al-Nasiriyah (Nasiriya); 20,000 adherents; Mandeans, mostly in Nasiriya; Head Sheikh DAKHIL.

Yazidis: Ainsifni; Leader TASHIN SAID ALI.

The Press

Since the overthrow of the regime of Saddam Hussain by US-led coalition forces in early 2003, the number of publications has proliferated: by the end of 2003 an estimated 250 newspapers and periodicals were in circulation, although only some 100 of these were reportedly still being published in 2008. Many newspapers are affiliated with political or religious organizations; however, the daily *Al-Sabah* is controlled by the Iraqi Government, with coalition backing. Security issues have resulted in severe distribution problems, and some newspaper offices have either relocated or chosen to publish online-only editions following threats being issued against journalists by militant groups, militias and security forces. A selection of publications is given below.

DAILIES

Al-Adala (Justice): Baghdad; e-mail aliisadik@yahoo.com; internet www.aladalanews.net; f. 2004; twice weekly; Arabic; organ of the Islamic Supreme Council of Iraq; publ. by the Al-Adala Group for Press, Printing and Publishing; Owner Dr ADIL ABD AL-MAHDI.

Baghdad: al-Zeitoun St, al-Harthiya, Baghdad; e-mail baghdadwifaq@yahoo.com; f. 1991; organ of the Iraqi Nat. Accord; Publr AYAD ALLAWI.

Al-Bayan (The Manifesto): Baghdad; f. 2003; Arabic; organ of Islamic Dawa Party; Man. Editor SADIQ AL-RIKABI.

Dar al-Salam (House of Peace): Baghdad; Arabic; organ of Iraqi Islamic Party.

Al-Dustur (The Constitution): Baghdad; f. 2003; Arabic; politics; independent; publ. by Al-Dustur Press, Publishing and Distribution House; Chair. BASIM AL-SHEIKH; Editor-in-Chief ALI AL-SHARQI.

Al-Jarida (The Newspaper): Baghdad; f. 2003; Arabic; organ of the Iraqi Arab Socialist Movement; Editor Prof. QAYS AL-AZZAWI.

Kul al-Iraq (All Iraq): Baghdad; e-mail info@kululiraq.com; internet www.kululiraq.com; f. 2003; Arabic; independent; Editor-in-Chief Dr ABBAS AL-SIRAF.

Al-Mada: 41/1 Abu Nuwas St, Baghdad; fax (1) 881-3256; e-mail fakhri_kareem@almadapaper.com; internet www.almadapaper.com; f. 2004; Arabic; independent; publ. by Al-Mada Foundation for Media, Culture and Arts; Editor-in-Chief FAKHRI KARIM.

Al-Mannarah (Minarets): Basra; tel. (40) 315758; e-mail almannarah@almannarah.com; internet www.almannarah.com; Arabic; publ. by South Press, Printing and Publishing Corpn; Editor-in-Chief Dr KHALAF AL-MANSHADI.

Al-Mashriq: Baghdad; internet www.al-mashriq.net; f. 2004; Arabic; independent; publ. by Al-Mashriq Institution for Media and Cultural Investments; circ. 25,000.

Al-Mutamar (Congress): Baghdad; e-mail almutamer@yahoo.com; internet www.inciraq.com/index_paper.php; f. 1993; Arabic; publ. by Iraqi Nat. Congress; Editor-in-Chief LUAY BALDAWI.

Al-Sabah: Baghdad; e-mail sabah@alsabaah.com; internet www.alsabaah.com; f. 2003; Arabic and English; state-controlled; publ. by the Iraqi Media Network; Deputy Editor-in-Chief ADNAN SHERKHAN.

Al-Sabah al-Jadid (New Morning): Baghdad; e-mail info@newsabah.com; internet www.newsabah.com; f. 2004; Arabic; independent; Editor-in-Chief ISMAIL ZAYER.

Sawt al-Iraq (Voice of Iraq): Baghdad; e-mail admin@sotaliraq.com; internet www.sotaliraq.com; online only; Arabic; independent.

Al-Taakhi (Brotherhood): e-mail badirkhansindi@yahoo.com; internet www.taakhinews.org; f. 1967; Kurdish and Arabic; organ of the Kurdistan Democratic Party (KDP); publ. by Al-Taakhi Publishing and Printing House; Editor-in-Chief Dr BADIRKHAN SINDI; circ. 20,000 (Baghdad).

Tariq al-Sha'ab (People's Path): Saadoun St, Baghdad; e-mail altareeq_1934@yahoo.com; internet www.iraqcp.org; f. 1974; Arabic and English; organ of the Iraqi Communist Party; Editor ABD AL-RAZZAK AL-SAFI.

Xebat: Arbil; e-mail info@xebat.net; internet www.xebat.net; f. 1959; Arabic and Kurdish; organ of the KDP; Editor-in-Chief NAZHAD AZIZ SURME.

Al-Zaman (Time): Baghdad; tel. (1) 717-7587; e-mail postmaster@azzaman.com; internet www.azzaman.com; f. 1997 in the United Kingdom, f. 2003 in Baghdad; Arabic, with some news translated into English; Editor-in-Chief SAAD AL-BAZZAZ.

WEEKLIES

Al-Ahali (The People): Baghdad; e-mail info@ahali-iraq.net; internet www.ahali-iraq.net; Arabic; politics; Editor HAVAL ZAKHOUBI.

Alif Baa al-Iraq: Baghdad; Arabic and English; general, social and political affairs.

Habazbuz fi Zaman al-Awlamah (Habazbuz in the Age of Globalization): Baghdad; f. 2003; Arabic; satirical; Editor ISHTAR AL-YASIRI.

Iraq Today: Baghdad; f. 2003; English; current affairs; Founder and Editor-in-Chief HUSSAIN SINJARI.

Al-Iraq al-Yawm (Iraq Today): Baghdad; e-mail iraqtoday@iraqtoday.net; Arabic and English; Editor ISRA SHAKIR.

Al-Ittihad (Union): Baghdad and Sulaimaniya; tel. (1) 543-8954; e-mail alitthad@alitthad.com; internet www.alitthad.com; Arabic and Kurdish; publ. by the Patriotic Union of Kurdistan; Editor ABD AL-HADI; circ. 30,000 (Baghdad).

Al-Ittijah al-Akhar (The Other Direction): Baghdad; tel. (1) 776-3334; fax (1) 776-3332; e-mail alitijahalakhar@yahoo.com; internet www.alitijahalakhar.com; Arabic; organ of Reconciliation and Liberation Bloc; Chair. and Editor MISHAAN AL-JUBOURI.

Kurdish Globe: Salah al-Din Highway, Pirzeen, Arbil; tel. (66) 2526792; e-mail info@kurdishglobe.net; internet www.kurdishglobe.net; f. 2005; English; Kurdish news and issues; Exec. Editor JAWAD QADIR; circ. 40,000.

Majallati: POB 8041, Children's Culture House, Baghdad; Arabic; children's newspaper; Editor-in-Chief Dr SHAFIQ AL-MAHDI.

Al-Muajaha (The Witness): 6/41/901, Karrada Dakhil, Baghdad; e-mail almuajaha@riseup.net; f. 2003; Arabic and English; current affairs; independent; Editor RAMZI MAJID JARRAR.

Al-Nahda (Renaissance): Basra; f. 2003; Arabic; organ of the Independent Democratic Gathering; Publr ADNAN PACHACHI.

Regay Kurdistan: Arbil; e-mail dwalapere@regaykurdistan.com; internet www.regaykurdistan.com; Arabic and Kurdish; organ of the Iraqi and Kurdistan Communist Parties; Editor-in-Chief HANDREN AHMAD.

Al-Sina'i (The Industrialist): Baghdad; Arabic; general; publ. by the Nat. Industrialist Coalition; Editor-in-Chief Dr ZAYD ABD AL-MAJID BILAL.

Al-Waqai al-Iraqiya (Official Gazette of the Republic of Iraq): Ministry of Justice, Baghdad; tel. (1) 537-2023; e-mail Hashim_Jaffar_alsaieg@yahoo.com; f. 1922; Arabic and English; Dir HASHIM N. JAFFAR; circ. 5,000.

PERIODICALS

Hawlati: e-mail hawlati2000@yahoo.com; internet www.hawlati.info; f. 2001; fortnightly; Kurdish, Arabic and English; independent, privately owned; mainly Kurdish politics; Publr TARIQ FATIH; Editor KAMAL RAOUF.

Majallat al-Majma' al-'Ilmi al-Iraqi (Journal of the Academy of Sciences): POB 4023, Waziriya, Baghdad; tel. (1) 422-4202; fax (1) 422-2066; e-mail iraqacademy@yahoo.com; internet www.iraqacademy.org; f. 1950; quarterly; Arabic; scholarly magazine on Arabic Islamic culture; Editor-in-Chief Prof. Dr AHMAD MATLOUB.

Al-Sa'ah (The Hour): Baghdad; twice weekly; Arabic; organ of the Iraqi Unified Nat. Movement; Publr AHMAD AL-KUBAYSI; Editor NI'MA ABD AL-RAZZAQ.

Sawt al-Talaba (Voice of the Students): Baghdad; fortnightly; Arabic; publ. by New Iraq Youth and Students' Org; Editor MUSTAFA AL-HAYIM.

NEWS AGENCIES

Aswat al-Iraq (Voices of Iraq): e-mail aswat.info@gmail.com; internet www.aswataliraq.info; f. 2004; Arabic, English and Kurdish; independent news agency with contributions from Iraqi correspondents and three Iraqi newspapers; Editor-in-Chief ZUHAIR AL-JEZAIRI.

National Iraqi News Agency: Baghdad; tel. (1) 719-3459; e-mail news@ninanews.com; internet www.ninanews.com; f. 2005; Arabic and English; independent; Chair. Dr FARID AYAR; Man. Dir ABD AL-MUHSEN HUSSAIN JAWAD.

PRESS ORGANIZATION

Iraqi Union for Journalists: POB 14101, nr al-Resafah Bldg, al-Waziriya, Baghdad; tel. (1) 537-0762; fax (1) 422-6011; e-mail iraqiju@yahoo.com; Chair. MUAID AL-LAMI.

Publishers

Afaq Arabiya Publishing House: POB 4032, Adamiya, Baghdad; tel. (1) 443-6044; fax (1) 444-8760; publr of literary monthlies, periodicals and cultural books; Chair. Dr MOHSIN AL-MUSAWI.

Dar al-Ma'mun for Translation and Publishing: POB 24015, Karradat Mariam, Baghdad; tel. (1) 538-3171; publr of newspapers and magazines.

Al-Hurriyah Printing Establishment: Karantina, Sarrafiya, Baghdad; f. 1970.

Al-Jamaheer Press House: POB 491, Sarrafiya, Baghdad; tel. (1) 416-9341; fax (1) 416-1875; f. 1963; publr of a number of newspapers and magazines; Pres. SAAD QASSEM HAMMOUDI.

Kurdish Culture and Publishing House: Baghdad; f. 1976.

Al-Ma'arif Ltd: Mutanabi St, Baghdad; f. 1929; publishes periodicals and books in Arabic, Kurdish, Turkish, French and English.

Al-Mada Foundation for Media, Culture and Arts: 41/1 Abu Nuwas St, Baghdad; tel. 7702799999 (mobile); e-mail almada119@hotmail.com; internet www.almadapaper.com; f. 1994; Dir FAKHRI KARIM.

Al-Muthanna Library: POB 14019, Mutanabi St, Baghdad; tel. 770-3649664 (mobile); e-mail mail@almuthannabooks.com; internet www.almuthannabooks.com; f. 1936; booksellers and publrs of books and monographs in Arabic and oriental languages; Propr ANAS AL-RAJAB; Dir IBRAHIM AL-RAJAB.

Al-Nahdah: Mutanabi St, Baghdad; tel. (1) 416-2689; e-mail yehya_azawy@yahoo.com; politics, Arab affairs.

National House for Publishing, Distribution and Advertising: POB 624, al-Jumhuriya St, Baghdad; tel. (1) 425-1846; f. 1972; publishes books on politics, economics, education, agriculture, sociology, commerce and science in Arabic and other Middle Eastern languages; Dir-Gen. M. A. ASKAR.

Al-Thawra Printing and Publishing House: POB 2009, Aqaba bin Nafi's Sq., Baghdad; tel. (1) 719-6161; f. 1970; Chair. (vacant).

PUBLISHERS' ASSOCIATION

Iraqi Publishers' Association: Baghdad; tel. (1) 416-9279; fax (1) 416-7584; e-mail al_nasheren@yahoo.com; Chair. Dr ABD AL-WAHAB AL-RADI.

Broadcasting and Communications

REGULATORY AUTHORITY

Communications and Media Commission (CMC): POB 2044, Hay Babel, al-Masbah, Baghdad; tel. (1) 718-0009; fax (1) 719-5839; e-mail enqiries@cmc.iq; internet www.cmc.iq; f. 2004 by fmr Coalition Provisional Authority; independent telecoms and media regulator; responsibilities include the award and management of telecommunications licences, broadcasting, media and information services, as well as spectrum allocation and management; CEO SAFAA RABEE.

TELECOMMUNICATIONS

Under the former Baathist regime, the Iraqi Telecommunications and Posts Co was the sole provider of telecommunications and postal services. Following the removal from power of Saddam Hussain, in 2003 the Coalition Provisional Authority issued three short-term licences for the provision of mobile telephone services to stimulate competition in the sector. Asiacell, led by the Iraqi Kurdish Asiacell Co for Telecommunication Ltd, was awarded the licence for the northern region; the licence for Baghdad and the central region was won by Orascom Telecom Iraq Corpn (Iraqna), led by Orascom Telecom of Egypt; and Atheer Telecom Iraq (MTC Atheer), led by the Mobile Telecommunications Co of Kuwait, won the licence for Basra and the southern region. In August 2007 Asiacell, Korek Telecom Ltd and MTC Atheer (which subsequently acquired 100% of Iraqna shares and was renamed Zain) won the auction launched by the Government for three new national licences to provide mobile telephone services over a 15-year period; Iraqna withdrew from the bidding process. The Government was expected to award a fourth mobile telephone licence by the end of 2011.

Asiacell: Headquarters Bldg, Sulaimaniya; e-mail customercare@asiacell.com; internet www.asiacell.com; f. 1999; 51% owned by Asiacell Co for Telecommunication Ltd, 40% by Wataniya Telecom (Kuwait) and 9% owned by United Gulf Bank (Bahrain); 6.0m. subscribers (Dec. 2008); Chair. of Bd FAROUK MUSTAFA RASOUL.

Iraqi Telecommunications and Posts Co (ITPC): POB 2450, Abu Nuwas St, Baghdad; tel. (1) 718-0400; fax (1) 718-2125; state-owned; Dir-Gen. KASSIM AL-HASSANI.

Korek Telecom Ltd: Kurdistan St, Pirmam, Arbil; tel. (66) 243-3455; e-mail info@korektel.com; internet korektel.com; f. 2001; 1.5m. subscribers (Dec. 2007); CEO HUMAM AMARA.

Zain: Basra; e-mail info@iq.zain.com; internet www.zain.com; f. 2003 as MTC Atheer, a subsidiary of Mobile Telecommunications Co (Kuwait); acquired Iraqna Co for Mobile Phone Services Ltd (operated by Orascom Telecom Holding—Egypt) in Dec. 2007; name changed to above in Jan. 2008; 9.7m. subscribers (Dec. 2008); CEO EMAD MAKIYA.

BROADCASTING

The **Iraqi Media Network (IMN)** was established by the former Coalition Provisional Authority (CPA) to replace the Ministry of Information following the ousting of the former regime. The IMN established new television and both FM and AM radio stations. In January 2004 the CPA announced that a consortium led by the US-based Harris Corpn had been awarded the contract to take over from the IMN the control of 18 television channels, two radio stations and the *Al-Sabah* daily newspaper.

Iraqi Media Network (IMN): Baghdad; e-mail info@imn.iq; internet www.imn.iq; f. 2003.

Al-Iraqiya Television: Baghdad; internet www.imn.iq/pages/iraqia-tv; terrestrial and satellite television.

Iraq Media Network—Southern Region: internet www.imnsr.com.

Republic of Iraq Radio: Baghdad; e-mail rir.info@iraqimedianet.net; internet www.imn.iq/pages/radio-iraqia.

Radio

Radio Dijla: House 3, Hay al-Jamia Zone 635/52, Baghdad; tel. (1) 555-8787; e-mail post@radiodijla.com; internet www.radiodijla.com; f. 2004; privately owned; first talk radio station to be established in post-invasion Iraq; also broadcasts music programmes; Founder Dr AHMAD AL-RIKABI.

Voice of Iraq: Baghdad; e-mail admin@voiraq.com; internet www.voiraq.com; f. 2003; privately owned AM radio station; broadcasts music, news and current affairs programmes in Arabic, Turkmen and English.

Television

Al-Sharqiya: 10/13/52 Karrada Kharj, Baghdad; tel. (88216) 6775-1380 (satellite); e-mail alsharqiya@alsharqiya.com; internet www.alsharqiya.com; f. 2004; privately owned; independent; broadcasts news and entertainment programming 24 hours a day terrestrially and via satellite; Founder SAAD AL-BAZZAZ; Dir ALAA AL-DAHAN.

Alsumaria TV: Beirut, Lebanon; tel. and fax 9614533344 (mobile); e-mail communication-department@alsumaria.tv; internet www.alsumaria.tv; f. 2004; privately owned, independent satellite network; broadcasts news, entertainment and educational programming 24 hours a day; currently operates from temporary offices in Lebanon.

Finance

(cap. = capital; res = reserves; dep. = deposits; brs = branches; m. = million; amounts in Iraqi dinars, unless otherwise stated)

All banks and insurance companies in Iraq, including all foreign companies, were nationalized in July 1964. The assets of foreign companies were taken over by the state. In May 1991 the Government announced its decision to end the state's monopoly in banking, and during 1992–2000 17 private banks were established; however, they were prohibited by the former regime from conducting international transactions. Following the establishment of the Coalition Provisional Authority in 2003, efforts were made to reform the state-owned Rafidain and Rashid Banks, and in October the Central Bank allowed private banks to begin processing international transactions. In January 2004 the Central Bank of Iraq announced that three foreign banks—HSBC and Standard Chartered (both of the United Kingdom), and the National Bank of Kuwait—had been awarded licences to operate in Iraq, the first such licences awarded for 40 years. A further five foreign banks had also been granted licences by mid-2005. There were six public sector and 37 private sector banks operating in Iraq in 2011.

BANKING

Central Bank

Central Bank of Iraq (CBI): POB 64, al-Rashid St, Baghdad; tel. (1) 816-5170; fax (1) 816-6802; e-mail cbi@cbi.iq; internet www.cbi.iq; f. 1947 as Nat. Bank of Iraq; name changed as above 1956; has the sole right of note issue; cap. 100,000m., res 246,026m., dep. 28,479,125m. (Dec. 2009); Gov. Dr SINAN MUHAMMAD RIDA AL-SHIBIBI; 4 brs.

State-owned Commercial Banks

Rafidain Bank: POB 11360, Banks St, Baghdad; tel. (1) 816-0287; fax (1) 816-5035; e-mail emailcenter9@yahoo.com; internet www.rafidain-bank.org; f. 1941; cap. 25,000m., res 49,730m., dep. 22,638,963m. (Dec. 2007); Dir -Gen. HABIB ZIA ALCKHEON; 147 brs in Iraq, 8 brs abroad.

Rashid Bank: al-Rashid St, Baghdad; tel. (1) 885-3411; fax (1) 882-6201; e-mail natbank@uruklink.net; internet www.rasheedbank.gov.iq; f. 1988; cap. 2,000m., res 6,024m., dep. 815,522m. (Dec. 2001); total assets US $750m. (2003); Chair. KADHIM M. NASHOOR; 161 brs.

Private Commercial Banks

Babylon Bank: al-Amara St, Baghdad; tel. (1) 717-3686; fax (1) 719-1014; e-mail info@babylonbank-iq.com; internet www.babylonbank-iq.com; f. 1999; cap. and res 31,310m., total assets 89,981m. (Dec. 2007); Chair. ABD AL-RAZZAQ AL-MANSOUR; Gen. Dir TARIQ ABD AL-BAKI ABOUD; 6 brs.

Bank of Baghdad: POB 3192, al-Karada St, Alwiya, Baghdad; tel. (1) 717-5007; fax (1) 717-5006; internet www.bankofbaghdad.org; f. 1992; 50.6% stake owned by Burgan Bank (Kuwait); cap. 52,973.3m., res 23,133.7m., total assets 363,724.6m. (Dec. 2007); Chair. IMAD ISMAEL SHARIF; Man. Dir ADNAN AL-CHALABI; 5 brs.

Commercial Bank of Iraq PSC (CBIQ): Saadoun St, Alwiya, Baghdad; tel. (1) 740-5583; fax (1) 718-4312; e-mail cb.iraq@ahliunited.com; internet www.ahliunited.com/bh_aub_cbiq.html; f. 1992; Ahli United Bank BSC (Bahrain) acquired 49% stake in Dec. 2005; cap. US $60m., dep. $59.6m., total assets $124.3m. (2006); Chair. FAHAD AL-RAJAAN; CEO and Man. Dir ADEL A. AL-LABBAN; 10 brs.

Credit Bank of Iraq: POB 3420, Saadoun St, Alwiya, Baghdad; tel. (1) 718-2198; fax (1) 717-0156; e-mail creditbkiq@yahoo.com; f. 1998; 75% owned by Nat. Bank of Kuwait SAK, 10% by World Bank's Int. Finance Corpn and 15% by private investors; cap. 1,250m., res 528m., dep. 16,376.9m. (Dec. 2002); Chair. HIKMET H. KUBBA; Man. Dir FOUAD M. MUSTAFA; 12 brs.

Gulf Commercial Bank: POB 3101, nr Baghdad Hotel, Saadoun St, Alwiya, Baghdad; tel. (1) 719-8534; fax (1) 778-8251; e-mail admn@gulfbankiraq.com; f. 2000; cap. 37,500m. (Jan. 2009); Chair. ABU TALIB HASHIM; 14 brs.

National Bank of Iraq (al-Ahli al-Iraqi Bank): Saadoun St, nr Firdos Sq., Baghdad 11194; tel. (1) 717-7735; fax (6) 569-5942; e-mail

Info@nbirq.com; internet www.nbirq.com; f. 1995; 59% owned by Capital Bank of Jordan; Chair. TALAL FANAR AL-FAISAL; 4 brs.

Sumer Commercial Bank: POB 3876, Hay al-Riad, Section 908, St 16, Baghdad; tel. (1) 719-6472; internet www.sumerbankiq.com; cap. 10,200m., res 531m., dep. 7,500m. (Aug. 2005); Chair. KHALIL KHAIRALLAH S. AL-JUMAILI; Man. Dir FOUAD HAMZA AL-SAEED; 9 brs.

Specialized Banks

Agricultural Co-operative Bank of Iraq: POB 2421, al-Rashid St, Baghdad; tel. (1) 886-4768; fax (1) 886-5047; e-mail agriculturalcoopbank@yahoo.com; internet www.agriculturalbank.gov.iq; f. 1936; state-owned; Dir-Gen. MUHAMMAD H. AL-KHAFAJI; 32 brs.

Basra International Bank for Investment: Watani St, Ashar, Basra; tel. (40) 616955; internet www.basrahbank.net; cap. 55,000m., res 10,320m., dep. 110,850m. (Dec. 2007); Chair. HUSSEIN GHALIB KUBBA; Man. Dir HASSAN GHALIB KUBBA; 12 brs.

Dar el-Salaam Investment Bank: POB 3067, al-Saadoun Park 103/41/3, Alwiya, Baghdad; tel. (1) 719-6488; e-mail info@desiraq.com; internet www.desiraq.com; f. 1999; 70.1% share acquired by HSBC (United Kingdom) in 2005; total assets 35,562m. (Aug. 2005); 14 brs.

Economy Bank for Investment and Finance (EBIF): 14 Ramadan St, al-Mansour Sq., Baghdad; tel. (1) 298-7712; fax (1) 298-7713; e-mail info@economybankiraq.com; internet www.economybankiraq.com; f. 1997; CEO HOUSSAM OBEID ALI; 23 brs.

Industrial Bank of Iraq: POB 5825, al-Sinak, Baghdad; tel. (1) 887-2181; fax (1) 888-3047; e-mail bank2004@maktoob.com; f. 1940; state-owned; total assets US $34.7m. (2003); Dir-Gen. BASSIMA ABD AL-HADDI AL-DHAHIR; 9 brs.

Investment Bank of Iraq: POB 3724, 902/2/27 Hay al-Wahda, Alwiya, Baghdad; tel. (1) 719-9042; fax (1) 719-8505; e-mail chairman@ibi-bankiraq.com; internet www.ibi-bankiraq.com; f. 1993; cap. 29,750m., res 9,200m., total assets 131,112m. (Dec. 2007); Chair. THAMIR RESOUKI ABD AL-WAHAB AL-SHEIKHLY; Gen. Man. HAMZA DAWOUD SALMAN HALBOUN; 18 brs.

Iraqi Islamic Bank for Investment and Development: 609/18/67, al-Mansour, Baghdad; tel. (1) 416-4939; fax (1) 414-0697; e-mail info@iraqiislamicb.com; internet www.iraqiislamicb.com; f. 1992; Chair. Dr TARIQ KHALAF AL-ABDULLAH.

Iraqi Middle East Investment Bank: POB 10379, Bldg 65, Hay Babel, 929 Arasat al-Hindiya, Baghdad; tel. (1) 717-5545; e-mail cendep@iraqimdlestbank.com; internet www.iraqinet.net/com/3/mdlestbank.htm; f. 1993; cap. and res 15,992m., dep. 85,265m., total assets 167,850m. (June 2005); Man. Dir M. F. AL-ALOOSI; Exec. Man. SUDAD A. AZIZ; 19 brs.

Kurdistan International Bank for Investment and Development: 70 Abd al-Salam Barzani St, Arbil; tel. (66) 223-0822; fax (66) 253-1369; e-mail info@kibid.com; internet www.kibid.com; f. 2005; private bank; cap. 50,000m., res 27,933m., dep. 253,712m. (Dec. 2009); Chair. SALAR MUSTAFA HAKIM; 4 brs.

Mosul Bank for Development and Investment: POB 1292, al-Markaz St, Mosul; tel. (60) 813-090; fax (60) 815-411; e-mail mosul_bank@yahoo.com; internet www.mosulbank.com.

Real Estate Bank of Iraq: POB 8118, 29/222 Haifa St, Baghdad; tel. (1) 885-3212; fax (1) 884-0980; e-mail estatebank194@yahoo.com; internet www.reb-iraq.com; f. 1949; state-owned; gives loans to assist the building industry; acquired the Co-operative Bank in 1970; total assets US $10m. (2003); Dir-Gen. ABD AL-RAZZAQ AZIZ; 25 brs.

United Bank for Investment: 906/14/69, al-Wathiq Sq., Hay al-Wehda, Baghdad; tel. (1) 888-112; e-mail unitedbank2004@yahoo.com; internet www.unitedbank–iq.net; f. 1995; Chair. IBRAHIM HASSAN AL-BADRI; Man. Dir ZIAD ABBAS HASHEM; 8 brs.

Warka Bank for Investment and Finance: POB 3559, 902/14/50, Hay al-Wehda, Baghdad; tel. (1) 717-4970; fax (1) 717-9555; e-mail info@warka-bank-iq.com; internet www.warka-bank.com; f. 1999; private bank; cap. 24,000m. (2006); Chair. and CEO SAAD SAADOUN AL-BUNNIA; 130 brs.

Trade Bank

Trade Bank of Iraq (TBI): POB 28445, Bldg 20, St 1, 608 al-Yarmouk District, Baghdad; tel. (1) 543-3561; fax (1) 543-3560; e-mail info@tbiraq.com; internet www.tbiraq.com; f. 2003 by fmr Coalition Provisional Authority to facilitate Iraq's exports of goods and services and the country's reconstruction; independent of Cen. Bank of Iraq; cap. US $427m., res $3m., dep. $11,668m. (Dec. 2009); Chair. HUSSAIN AL-UZRI; Sec. ABD AL-KHALIK MUHAMMAD AL-SHABOUT; 7 brs.

INSURANCE

Iraqi Insurance Diwan: Ministry of Finance, 147/6/47 Hay al-Eloom, Baghdad; tel. (1) 416-8030; e-mail IraqiInsuranceDiwan@iraqinsurance.org; internet www.iraqinsurance.org; f. 2005 as independent regulator for the insurance sector.

Ahlia Insurance Co: al-Tahreeat Sq., Baghdad; tel. (790) 4565829 (mobile); e-mail info@aic-iraq.com; internet www.aic-iraq.com; f. 2001; privately owned; general, marine, engineering, motor, health and life insurance; Chair. SAADOUN KUBBA; Gen. Man. SAADOUN M. KHAMIS AL-RUBAI.

Al-Hamra'a Insurance Co: POB 10491, Karrada, Baghdad; tel. (1) 717-7573; fax (1) 717-7574; e-mail info@alhamraains.com; internet www.alhamraains.com; f. 2001; private co; general and life insurance.

Iraq Insurance Co: POB 989, Khaled bin al-Walid St, Aqaba bin Nafi Sq., Baghdad; tel. (1) 719-2185; fax (1) (1) 719-2606; state-owned; life, fire, accident and marine insurance.

Iraq Reinsurance Co: POB 297, Aqaba bin Nafi Sq., Khalid bin al-Waleed St, Baghdad; tel. (1) 719-5131; fax (1) 719-1497; e-mail iraqre@yahoo.com; f. 1960; state-owned; transacts reinsurance business on the international market; Chair. and Gen. Man. SAID ABBAS M. A. MIRZA.

National Insurance Co: POB 248, National Insurance Co Bldg, al-Khullani St, Baghdad; tel. (1) 885-3026; fax (1) 886-1486; f. 1950; state-owned; cap. 20m.; all types of general and life insurance, reinsurance and investment; Chair. and Gen. Man. MUHAMMAD HUSSAIN JAAFAR ABBAS.

STOCK EXCHANGE

Iraq Stock Exchange (ISX): Baghdad; tel. (1) 717-4484; fax (1) 717-4461; e-mail Info-isx@isx-iq.net; internet www.isx-iq.net; f. 2004, following the closure of the fmr Baghdad Stock Exchange by the Coalition Provisional Authority in March 2003; 91 cos listed in Oct. 2009; CEO TAHA AHMAD ABD AL-SALAM.

Trade and Industry

DEVELOPMENT ORGANIZATION

Iraq Foreign Investment Board: e-mail info@ishtargate.org; internet www.ishtargate.org; seeks to attract inward private sector investment into Iraq and to stimulate domestic capital resources for growth and innovation, as well as promote Iraqi businesses; Senior Advisor WILLIAM C. DAHM.

CHAMBERS OF COMMERCE

Federation of Iraqi Chambers of Commerce: POB 3388, Saadoun St, Alwiya, Baghdad; tel. (1) 717-1798; fax (1) 719-2479; e-mail ficcbaghdad@yahoo.com; internet www.ficciraqbag.org; f. 1969; all 18 Iraqi chambers of commerce are affiliated to the Federation; Chair. JAAFAR AL-HAMADANI.

Arbil Chamber of Commerce and Industry: Chamber of Commerce and Industry Bldg, Aras St, Arbil; tel. (66) 2222014; e-mail erbilchamberofcommerce@yahoo.com; internet www.erbilchamber.org; f. 1966; Chair. DARA JALIL KHAYAT.

Baghdad Chamber of Commerce: POB 5015, al-Sanal, Baghdad; tel. (1) 880-220; fax (1) 816-3347; e-mail baghdad_chamber@yahoo.com; internet www.baghdadchamber.com; f. 1926; Chair. AMJAD ABD AL-KARIM AL-JUBURI.

Basra Chamber of Commerce: Manawi Pasha, Ashar, Basra; tel. (40) 614630; e-mail info@bcoc-iraq.net; internet www.bcoc-iraq.net; f. 1926; Chair. MAKKI HASSAN HAMADI AL-SUDANI.

Kirkuk Chamber of Commerce: Kirkuk; e-mail kirkukchamber@yahoo.com; f. 1957; Chair. SABAH AL-DIN MUHAMMAD AL-SALIHI.

Mosul Chamber of Commerce: POB 35, Mosul; tel. (60) 774771; fax (60) 771359; e-mail mcc19262000@yahoo.com; Chair. MUKBIL SIDIQ AL-DABAGH.

Sulaimaniya Chamber of Commerce and Industry: Sulaimaniya; e-mail info@sulcci.com; internet www.sulcci.com; Chair. HASSAN BAQI HORAMI.

EMPLOYERS' ORGANIZATION

Iraqi Federation of Industries: 191/22/915 al-Zaweya, Karada, Baghdad; tel. (1) 778-3502; fax (1) 776-3041; e-mail info@fediraq.org; internet www.fediraq.org; f. 1956; 35,000 mems; Pres. HASHIM THANOUN AL-ATRAKCHI.

PETROLEUM AND GAS

Ministry of Oil: Oil Complex Bldg, Port Said St, Baghdad; tel. (1) 727-0710; e-mail oilministry@oil.gov.iq; internet www.oil.gov.iq; merged with INOC in 1987; affiliated cos: Oil Marketing Co, Oil Projects Co, Oil Exploration Co, Oil Products Distribution Co, Iraqi Oil Tankers Co, Gas Filling Co, Oil Pipelines Co, Iraqi Drilling Co, North Oil Co, South Oil Co, Missan Oil Co, North Refineries Co,

Midland Refineries Co, South Refineries Co, North Gas Co, South Gas Co.

Iraq National Oil Co (INOC): POB 476, Khullani Sq., Baghdad; tel. (1) 887-1115; f. 1964; reorg. upon nationalization of Iraq's petroleum industry, and became solely responsible for exploration, production, transportation and marketing of Iraqi crude petroleum and petroleum products; merged with Ministry of Oil in 1987, and remained under its authority following the overthrow of the regime of Saddam Hussain in 2003; draft legislation providing for the reconstitution of INOC as an independent entity was approved by the Council of Ministers in July 2009; under the proposed reorganization, INOC would be responsible for the management and development of Iraq's petroleum industry and would assume control of the existing state-run oil and gas cos.

UTILITIES

Electricity

Electricity production in Iraq has been greatly diminished as a result of the US-led military campaign in 2003, subsequent looting and sabotage by Baathist loyalists, and disruptions in fuel supplies to power stations. Power outages are common, especially in Baghdad and the surrounding area, and the Government has resorted to rationing. With ongoing reconstruction of the means of generation, transmission and distribution, the Ministry of Electricity was achieving peak production levels of 6,750 MW by early 2009, supplying intermittent power for only 14 hours a day. In late 2008 the Minister of Electricity stated that Iraq's electricity grid would not be restored to its previous capacity until 2011.

Water

The Ministry of Water Resources manages the supply of water throughout Iraq. Water resources are diminishing, and a large-scale investment programme is currently under way, which includes funding for new dam and irrigation projects, repairs to damaged facilities, and improvements in technology. Following years of neglect during the period of UN sanctions, infrastructure has also been damaged since the US-led military campaign in 2003, largely as a result of vandalism and looting. The Baghdad Water Authority is responsible for the management of water resources in the capital.

TRADE UNIONS

General Federation of Iraqi Workers (GFIW): POB 3049, Tahrir Sq., al-Rashid St, Baghdad; e-mail abdullahmuhsin@iraqitradeunions.org; internet www.iraqitradeunions.org; f. 2005 by merger of Gen. Fed. of Trade Unions, Gen. Fed. of Trade Unions of Iraq (an offshoot of the former) and Iraqi Fed. of Workers' Trade Unions; covers all of Iraq's provinces except the three Kurdish Autonomous Regions; Pres. RASEM AL-AWADI; Vice-Pres. IBRAHIM AL-MASHHADANI.

Iraqi Teachers' Union (ITU): al-Mansour, Baghdad; f. 2003; Pres. JASIM HUSSEIN MUHAMMAD AL-LAMI.

There are also unions of doctors, pharmacologists, jurists, writers, journalists, artists, engineers, electricity and railway workers.

Transport

RAILWAYS

Iraq's railway lines extend over some 2,339 km. A line covers the length of the country, from Rabia, on the Syrian border, via Mosul, to Baghdad (534 km), and from Baghdad to Basra and Umm Qasr (608 km), on the Persian (Arabian) Gulf. A 404-km line links Baghdad, via Radi and Haditha, to Husaibah, near the Iraqi–Syrian frontier. Baghdad is linked with Arbil, via Khanaqin and Kirkuk, and a 252-km line (designed to serve industrial projects along its route) runs from Kirkuk to Haditha, via Baiji (though this was rendered out of action in mid-2006, as a result of bombing by US forces). A 638-km line runs from Baghdad, via al-Qaim (on the Syrian border), to Akashat (with a 150-km line linking the Akashat phosphate mines and the fertilizer complex at al-Qaim). A regular international service between Baghdad and İstanbul, Turkey, was suspended following the US-led invasion in 2003; however, services on a section of the line, between Mosul and Gaziantep, resumed in early 2010. Passenger rail services between Mosul and Aleppo, Syria, resumed in August 2000 after an interruption of almost 20 years, but were closed again in 2004 after repeated insurgent attacks. Passenger rail services between Baghdad and Basra resumed in late 2007, and a Baghdad–Ramadi passenger service recommenced in May 2009. The railway system was due to be repaired and upgraded as part of the reconstruction of Iraq following the removal from power of Saddam Hussain's regime in 2003. Eventually, it was planned that the system would be divided, with the infrastructure being kept as a state asset, while operations were to be privatized. It was reported in 2006 that the Ministry of Transportation hoped to add an additional 2,300 km to the existing rail network, although concerns remained over funding. In May 2010 the Government announced that it had invited bids from eight short-listed foreign consortia for the contract to construct a 25-km, two-line metro system in Baghdad; the French company Alstom signed a memorandum of understanding to undertake the project in January 2011.

General Co for Railways: Ministry of Transportation, nr Martyr's Monument, Karradat Dakhil, Baghdad; e-mail iraqitransport@yahoo.com; internet www.scr.gov.iq.

Iraqi Republic Railways Co (IRRC): West Station, Baghdad; tel. (1) 537-0011; e-mail d1_g_office@iraqrailways.com; internet www.iraqrailways.com; f. 1914; Dir-Gen. RAFIL YUSSEF ABBAS.

ROADS

In 2000, according to estimates by the International Road Federation, Iraq's road network extended over 45,550 km, of which approximately 84.3% were paved.

The most important roads are: Baghdad–Mosul–Tel Kotchuk (Syrian border), 521 km; Baghdad–Kirkuk–Arbil–Mosul–Zakho (border with Turkey), 544 km; Kirkuk–Sulaimaniya, 160 km; Baghdad–Hilla–Diwaniya–Nasiriya–Basra, 586 km; Baghdad–Kut–Nasiriya, 186 km; Baghdad–Ramadi–Rurba (border with Syria), 555 km; Baghdad–Kut–Umara–Basra–Safwan (border with Kuwait), 660 km; and Baghdad–Baqaba–Kanikien (border with Iran). Most sections of the six-lane, 1,264-km international Express Highway, linking Safwan (on the Kuwaiti border) with the Jordanian and Syrian borders, had been completed by June 1990. Studies have been completed for a second, 525-km Express Highway, linking Baghdad and Zakho on the Turkish border. A complex network of roads was constructed behind the war front with Iran in order to facilitate the movement of troops and supplies during the 1980–88 conflict. The road network was included in the US-led coalition's programme of reconstruction following the ousting of the Baathist regime in 2003.

Iraqi Land Transport Co: Baghdad; internet sclt.gov.iq; f. 1988 to replace State Org. for Land Transport; fleet of more than 1,000 large trucks; Dir-Gen. AYSAR AL-SAFI.

State Organization for Roads and Bridges: POB 917, Karradat Mariam, Karkh, Baghdad; tel. (1) 32141; responsible for road and bridge construction projects under the Ministry of Construction and Housing.

SHIPPING

The ports of Basra and Umm Qasr are usually the commercial gateway of Iraq. They are connected by various ocean routes with all parts of the world, and constitute the natural distributing centre for overseas supplies. The Iraqi State Enterprise for Maritime Transport maintains a regular service between Basra, the Persian (Arabian) Gulf and north European ports. There is also a port at Khor al-Zubair, which came into use in 1979.

At Basra, there is accommodation for 12 vessels at the Maqal Wharves and for seven vessels at the buoys. There is one silo berth and two berths for petroleum products at Muftia and one berth for fertilizer products at Abu Flus. There is room for eight vessels at Umm Qasr. There are deep-water tanker terminals at Khor al-Amaya and Faw for three and four vessels, respectively. The latter port, however, was abandoned during the early part of the Iran–Iraq War.

For the inland waterways, there are 1,036 registered river craft, 48 motor vessels and 105 motorboats.

The port at Umm Qasr was heavily damaged during the early part of the US-led coalition's campaign to oust Saddam Hussain. A large-scale project to redevelop the port is under way. In July 2009 contracts to lease and develop new commercial berths at Umm Qasr were awarded to two foreign port operators. In February 2011 the UAE-based firm Gulftainer signed a US $150m. contract to construct and operate a dry port north of Umm Qasr. Meanwhile, the Ministry of Transport indicated that bids were to be invited for the development of a new deep-sea port at Faw in Basra province. It was anticipated that the new $6,300m. facility would, upon completion, replace Umm Qasr as Iraq's main commercial port.

Port and Regulatory Authorities

General Co of Iraqi Ports (IPA): Malik bin Dinar St, Basra; tel. (40) 041-3211; e-mail anmarbasrah@gmail.dom; internet scp.gov.iq; Dir-Gen. SALEH QADIR ABOUD.

State Enterprise for Iraqi Water Transport: POB 23016, Airport St, al-Furat Quarter, Baghdad; f. 1987, when State Org. for Iraqi Water Transport was abolished; responsible for the planning, supervision and control of six nat. water transportation enterprises, incl. General Co for Maritime Transport (see below).

Principal Shipping Companies

Arab Bridge Maritime Navigation Co: Aqaba, Jordan; tel. (3) 2092000; fax (3) 2092001; internet www.abmaritime.com.jo; f. 1987; jt venture by Egypt, Iraq and Jordan to improve economic co-operation; an expansion of the co established a ferry link between the ports of Aqaba, Jordan, and Nuweibeh, Egypt, in 1985; six vessels; cap. US $75m. (2010); Chair. Eng. OSAMA MUHAMMAD AL-SADER; Vice-Chairs. MOHANNAD SALMAN AL-QDAH, HISHAM OMAR AL-SARSAWI; Man. Dir HUSSEIN AL-SOUOB.

General Co for Maritime Transport: POB 13038, al-Jadiriya al-Hurriya Ave, Baghdad; Basra office: POB 766, 14 July St, Basra; tel. (1) 776-3201; e-mail watertrans@motrans.gov.iq; internet scmt.gov.iq; f. 1952 as State Enterprise for Maritime Transport; renamed as above 2009; Dir-Gen. SAMIR ABD AL-RAZZAQ.

Gulf Shipping Co: POB 471, Basra; tel. (40) 776-1945; fax (40) 776-0715; f. 1988; imports and exports goods to and from Iraq.

Al-Masar al-Iraqi Co LLC: Manawi Pasha St, nr Manawi Pasha Hotel, POB 85885, Basra; tel. 7704926113 (mobile); e-mail operation@iraqilogistic.com; internet www.iraqilogistic.com; provides a range of freight and shipping agency services.

CIVIL AVIATION

There are international airports at Baghdad, Basra and Mosul. Baghdad's airport, previously named Saddam International Airport, reopened in August 2000, after refurbishment necessitated by damage sustained during the war with the multinational force in 1991. However, international air links were virtually halted by the UN embargo imposed in 1990. Internal flights, connecting Baghdad to Basra and Mosul, recommenced in November 2000. In April 2003 the capital's airport was renamed Baghdad International Airport by US forces during their military campaign to oust the regime of Saddam Hussain. Following a programme of reconstruction, the airports at Baghdad and Basra were reopened to commercial flights from late 2003; Mosul International Airport reopened for civilian flights in December 2007. The expansion of Arbil International Airport (including the construction of a new passenger terminal and runway) was completed in mid-2010. In July 2008 Al-Hamza airport in Najaf (formerly a military airport) was inaugurated for civilian use, as increasing numbers of pilgrims were visiting the shrines of that holy city. Construction work on a new airport in Karbala, with a projected annual capacity of 30m. passengers, commenced in March 2010.

Iraq Civil Aviation Authority (ICAA): Baghdad; e-mail info@iraqcaa.com; internet www.iraqcaa.com; Dir-Gen. SABAH AL-SHABANI.

Iraqi Airways Co: Baghdad International Airport, Baghdad; tel. (1) 537-2002; e-mail Info@IraqiAirways.co.uk; internet www.iraqiairways.co.uk; f. 1945; partial privatization pending; operates flights to other Arab countries, Iran, Turkey, Greece and Sweden; Dir-Gen. Capt. KIFAH HUSSEIN JABBAR.

Tourism

In 2001 (the last year for which statistics are available) some 126,654 tourists visited Iraq; tourist receipts in 2002 were estimated at US $45m. After the US-led invasion of Iraq in 2003, the site housing the ruins of the ancient civilization of Babylon became part of a US military base; several other places of interest became military or refugee camps, and, amid the protracted period of conflict since 2003, tourists have been deterred from visiting the country's many cultural and religious sites. Nevertheless, in August 2006 the relatively peaceful Kurdish Autonomous Region launched a tourism campaign, with advertisements broadcast on US television. Since 2008 religious tourism has been growing, with increasing numbers of pilgrims using the newly renovated airport in Najaf (see Transport) to visit the Islamic holy shrines of both that city and nearby Karbala.

Iraq Tourism Board: POB 7783, Haifa St, Baghdad; tel. (1) 543-3912; Chair. HAMOUD MOHSEN AL-YACOUBI.

Defence

The US-led Coalition Provisional Authority (CPA) dissolved Iraq's armed forces and security organizations in place under Saddam Hussein in May 2003, following the ousting of the regime in the previous month. In August the CPA promulgated the establishment of the New Iraqi Army.

Chief of Staff of the Joint Armed Forces: Lt-Gen. BABAKIR SHAWKAT ZEBARI.

Commander of the Ground Forces: Lt-Gen. ALI GHAIDAN.

Commander of the Air Force: Lt-Gen. ANWAR AHMAD.

Commander of the Navy: Rear Adm. MUHAMMAD JAWAD KADHAM.

Defence Budget (2011): ID 5,660,000m.

Total Armed Forces (as assessed at November 2011): 271,400: army 193,400; navy 3,600; air force 5,050; plus 69,350 support. In addition, there were 531,000 Ministry of Interior Forces, including 302,000 members of the Iraqi Police Service, 44,000 members of the Iraqi Federal police, 95,000 members of the Facilities Protection Service, 60,000 members of the Border Enforcement forces and 30,000 members of the Oil Police.

Education

After the establishment of the Republic in 1958, there was a marked expansion in education at all levels, and spending on education increased substantially. During the mid-1970s free education was established at all stages from pre-primary to higher, and private education was abolished; all existing private schools were transformed into state schools. However, military conflict and economic sanctions during the 1980s and 1990s undermined much of the progress made in education during the previous two decades. Primary education, beginning at six years of age, lasts for six years. Enrolment at primary schools of children in the relevant age-group had declined to 76% by 1995, but reportedly rose again, to 91%, in 2000/01. According to UNESCO estimates, in 2006/07 enrolment at primary schools included 88% of pupils in the relevant age-group. Secondary education, from 12 years of age and lasting for up to six years, is divided into two cycles of three years each. Enrolment at secondary schools in 2006/07 included some 43% of children in the appropriate age-group, according to UNESCO. Following the change of regime in Iraq in April 2003, a comprehensive reform of the country's education system was implemented. In the 2007/08 academic year there were estimated to be 17,159 primary and secondary schools in Iraq, with a total enrolment of 5,999,846 pupils. There are 43 technical institutes and colleges, two postgraduate commissions and 20 universities. In 2002/03 there were approximately 240,000 undergraduates attending institutions of higher education. In 2010 government expenditure on education amounted to US $4,310m., equivalent to 6.0% of total government spending.

IRELAND

Introductory Survey

LOCATION, CLIMATE, LANGUAGE, RELIGION, FLAG, CAPITAL

Ireland consists of 26 of the 32 historic counties that comprise the island of Ireland. The remaining six counties, in the north-east, form Northern Ireland, which is part of the United Kingdom. Ireland lies in the Atlantic Ocean, about 80 km (50 miles) west of Great Britain. The climate is mild and equable, with temperatures generally between 0°C (32°F) and 21°C (70°F). Irish (Gaeilge) is the official first language, but its use as a vernacular is now restricted to certain areas, collectively known as the Gaeltacht, mainly in the west of Ireland. English is the second official language and is almost universally spoken. The majority of the inhabitants profess Christianity: about 87% of the population are Roman Catholics. The national flag (proportions 1 by 2) consists of three equal vertical stripes, of green, white and orange. The capital is Dublin.

CONTEMPORARY POLITICAL HISTORY

Historical Context

The whole of Ireland was formerly part of the United Kingdom. In 1920 the island was partitioned, the six north-eastern counties remaining part of the United Kingdom, with their own government. In 1922 the 26 southern counties achieved dominion status, under the British Crown, as the Irish Free State. The dissolution of all remaining links with Great Britain culminated in 1937 in the adoption of a new Constitution, which gave the Irish Free State full sovereignty within the Commonwealth. Formal ties with the Commonwealth were ended in 1949, when the 26 southern counties became a republic. The partition of Ireland remained a contentious issue, and in 1969 a clandestine organization, calling itself the Provisional Irish Republican Army (IRA—see United Kingdom), initiated a violent campaign to achieve reunification.

Domestic Political Affairs

In the general election of February 1973, the Fianna Fáil party, which had held office, with only two interruptions, since 1932, was defeated. Jack Lynch, who had been Prime Minister (Taoiseach) since 1966, resigned, and Liam Cosgrave formed a coalition between his own party, Fine Gael, and the Labour Party. The Irish Government remained committed to power-sharing in the six counties, but opposed any British military withdrawal from Northern Ireland. Following the assassination of the British Ambassador to Ireland by the Provisional IRA in July 1976, the Irish Government introduced stronger measures against terrorism. Fianna Fáil won the general election of June 1977 and Lynch again became Prime Minister. Following his resignation in December 1979, he was succeeded by Charles Haughey. In June 1981, following an early general election, Dr Garret FitzGerald of Fine Gael became Prime Minister in a coalition of his own party and the Labour Party. However, the rejection by the Dáil (the lower house of the legislature) of the coalition's budget proposals precipitated a further general election in February 1982, in which Haughey was returned to power. The worsening economic situation, however, made the Fianna Fáil Government increasingly unpopular, and in November Haughey lost the support of two independent members of the Dáil, precipitating an early general election, at which Fianna Fáil failed to gain an overall majority. In December FitzGerald formed a new Fine Gael-Labour Party coalition.

During 1986 FitzGerald's coalition lost support, partly due to the formation of a new party, the Progressive Democrats (PD), by disaffected members of Fianna Fáil. In June a controversial government proposal to end a constitutional ban on divorce was defeated by national referendum. Shortly afterwards, as a result of a series of defections, the coalition lost its parliamentary majority. In January 1987 the Labour Party refused to support Fine Gael's budget proposals and the coalition collapsed. Following a general election in February, Fianna Fáil, led by Haughey, formed a minority Government.

Prior to the general election of June 1989 Fine Gael and the PD concluded an electoral pact to oppose Fianna Fáil. Although the Haughey administration had achieved significant economic improvements, severe reductions in public expenditure and continuing problems of unemployment and emigration adversely affected Fianna Fáil's electoral support, and it obtained only 77 of the 166 seats in the Dáil, while Fine Gael won 55 seats and the PD six seats. Following nearly four weeks of negotiations, a Fianna Fáil-PD coalition Government, led by Haughey, was formed.

In October 1991 the Government narrowly defeated a motion of no confidence, which had been introduced following a series of financial scandals involving public officials. In November, however, a group of Fianna Fáil members of the Dáil proposed a motion demanding Haughey's removal as leader of the party. Albert Reynolds, the Minister for Finance and a former close associate of Haughey, and Pádraig Flynn, the Minister for the Environment, announced their intention to support the motion, and were immediately dismissed from office. The attempt to depose Haughey was defeated by a substantial majority of the Fianna Fáil parliamentary grouping.

In January 1992 allegations arose that, contrary to his previous denials, Haughey had been aware of the secret monitoring, in 1982, of the telephone conversations of two journalists perceived to be critical of the Government. The PD made their continued support of the Government conditional on Haughey's resignation. In February 1992 Reynolds replaced Haughey as leader of Fianna Fáil and assumed the premiership.

In June 1992 the leader of the PD, Desmond O'Malley, criticized Reynolds' conduct as Minister for Industry and Commerce before a parliamentary inquiry into allegations of fraud and political favouritism during 1987–88. In October 1992, in his testimony to the inquiry, the Prime Minister accused O'Malley of dishonesty. Following Reynolds' refusal to withdraw the allegations, in early November the PD left the coalition, and the Government was defeated on the following day in a motion of no confidence. A general election took place in November, concurrent with three constitutional referendums on abortion. Fianna Fáil and Fine Gael both suffered a substantial loss of support, while the Labour Party more than doubled its number of seats; the PD also increased its representation. Following prolonged negotiations, in January 1993 Fianna Fáil and the Labour Party agreed to form a coalition Government. Reynolds retained the premiership, while Dick Spring, the leader of the Labour Party, was allocated the foreign affairs portfolio, as well as the post of Deputy Prime Minister (Tánaiste).

In November 1994 the Labour Party withdrew from the coalition after Reynolds and the Fianna Fáil members of the Cabinet approved the appointment of the Attorney-General, Harry Whelehan, to the High Court, in the absence of the Labour Party ministers, who had opposed Whelehan's nomination. Reynolds, while remaining as Prime Minister of a 'caretaker' Government, relinquished the Fianna Fáil leadership and was succeeded by the Minister for Finance, Bertie Ahern. Whelehan, meanwhile, resigned as President of the High Court. Subsequent discussions between Spring and Ahern over the formation of a new Fianna Fáil-Labour coalition failed to produce an agreement. Following extensive talks, a new coalition of Fine Gael, the Labour Party and a small party, the Democratic Left, took office in December. The leader of Fine Gael, John Bruton, became Prime Minister, while Spring regained the role of Deputy Prime Minister and Minister for Foreign Affairs.

In November 1996 the Minister for Transport, Energy and Communications, Michael Lowry, resigned following allegations that he had received personal financial gifts from a business executive, Ben Dunne. During 1997 an inquiry into other political donations by Dunne, chaired by Justice Brian McCracken, revealed that payments totalling some IR£1.3m. had been made to Haughey during his premiership. Haughey later admitted the allegations, although he insisted that he had no knowledge of the donations until he resigned from office; however, McCracken's report, published in August, condemned Haughey's earlier misleading evidence given to the tribunal and recommended further legal investigation.

The Government of Bertie Ahern

At a general election held in June 1997 none of the main political parties secured an overall majority in the Dáil. Sinn Féin (the political wing of the IRA) won its first ever seat in the Dáil at the election. After Bruton conceded that he could not form a majority coalition administration, Ahern formed a Government composed of Fianna Fáil and the PD. The leader of the PD, Mary Harney, was appointed Deputy Prime Minister. In September the President, Mary Robinson, who had been elected in November 1990 as an independent candidate, resigned from her position in order to assume her new functions as the United Nations High Commissioner for Human Rights. In the ensuing election, conducted on 30 October 1997, the Fianna Fáil candidate, Dr Mary McAleese, was elected President, receiving 45.2% of the first-preference votes cast; McAleese was the country's first head of state from Northern Ireland.

During 2000 independent judicial inquiries investigating corruption among politicians implicated many senior political figures. In April Frank Dunlop, a political lobbyist and former government press secretary, admitted to an inquiry into planning irregularities in County Dublin, headed by Justice Feargus Flood, that in 1991 he had made payments to 15 Dublin county councillors on behalf of a property developer in order to ensure a favourable decision. Dunlop also testified that the Fine Gael leader, Bruton, was aware that a member of Fine Gael had demanded IR£250,000 from Dunlop to secure that member's vote in favour of the decision. Furthermore, Bruton was also accused by Liam Lawlor, a Fianna Fáil member of the Dáil, who himself had received payments from Dunlop, of benefiting from the decision. Bruton vehemently denied both accusations against him. In January 2001 Fine Gael members of the Dáil passed a motion of no confidence in Bruton, who resigned as party leader with immediate effect. He was replaced by Michael Noonan, a former Minister for Health and Children. In March 2001 investigations by the Flood tribunal revealed that Ray Burke, who had resigned as Minister for Foreign Affairs in October 1997, had held money in offshore accounts during the 1980s while a minister, and had conducted international financial transactions without first requesting permission from the Central Bank (as the law stipulated). He also admitted to misleading the Dáil regarding his financial affairs. In September 2002 Justice Flood issued the second interim report into the tribunal's findings thus far in which, most notably, he stated that Burke had received several 'corrupt payments' between 1974 and 1989. A number of prominent figures implicated in the proceedings were criticized for failing to co-operate fully with the tribunal and it was anticipated that criminal proceedings against 15 people, including Burke, would be instigated in 2003. Ahern came under intense political pressure regarding his appointment of Burke as Minister for Foreign Affairs. In December 2003 Burke was formally charged with making false tax returns. In September 2004 Justice Alan Mahon (who had replaced Flood as Chairman of the tribunal in June 2003) rejected Burke's application for assistance with legal costs, estimated to amount to €10m., and in January 2005 Burke was sentenced to six months' imprisonment.

Meanwhile, following McCracken's report in August 1997, a new tribunal chaired by Justice Michael Moriarty was established to investigate further payments made to politicians and the sources of specific 'offshore' bank accounts that had been used by Haughey. In May 2000 the tribunal heard that between 1979 and 1996 Haughey had received payments totalling IR£8.5m., a much larger figure than had previously been acknowledged. In March 2003 Haughey agreed to pay the Revenue Commissioners €5m. in settlement of his outstanding tax liabilities resulting from undisclosed payments made to him. Haughey died in June 2006. In December a report by Justice Moriarty stated that, between 1979 and 1996, funds totalling IR£9.1m. had been made available for Haughey's personal use.

In June 2001 a referendum was held on the ratification of the Treaty of Nice, which proposed structural reforms to the institutions of the European Union (EU, see p. 276) prior to the enlargement of the union from 2004. The endorsement of the treaty was rejected by 53.9% of those who voted, resulting in an embarrassing reverse for the Government, which had campaigned in favour of the treaty. The voter participation rate was only 34.8%. The defeat was attributed to fears that ratification of the treaty would result in Irish participation in the EU's proposed rapid reaction force, thus undermining Ireland's neutrality, and concerns that Ireland would receive reduced funding and assistance from the EU. The Government suffered a further reverse when, at a referendum on abortion held in early March 2002, 50.4% of the electorate voted against proposed changes, which would have removed the constitutional protection accorded by the Supreme Court to the lives of suicidal pregnant women wishing to terminate their pregnancies, and would have made abortion a criminal offence.

The elections of 2002 and 2007

At the general election held on 17 May 2002 Fianna Fáil increased its parliamentary representation to 81 seats, and thus only narrowly failed to achieve an overall majority in the Dáil. Fine Gael suffered a significant loss of support, winning just 31 seats. The PD and Sinn Féin increased their representation to eight seats and five seats, respectively, while the ecologist Green Party obtained six seats. The rate of participation, at 63.0%, was the lowest to be recorded at an Irish general election. Following Fine Gael's poor performance at the election, Michael Noonan resigned as party leader; he was succeeded by Enda Kenny. In the same month Fianna Fáil and the PD concluded a new coalition agreement, following which Ahern was duly re-elected Prime Minister, with Harney continuing as his deputy.

In June 2002 the Government won support at an EU summit meeting for a declaration that formally stated that Ireland's participation in the EU rapid reaction force would be limited to those operations with a UN mandate, approved by the Government and sanctioned by the Dáil. For their part, Ireland's EU partners issued a complementary declaration reiterating that neither the Treaty of Nice nor previous EU treaties compromised Ireland's traditional neutrality and that no member state envisaged the rapid reaction force as a future European army. In September the Irish Government announced that a second constitutional referendum which, as well as providing for the final ratification of the Treaty of Nice, would now explicitly prohibit Irish participation in any future common European defence force, would take place on 19 October. At the referendum, 62.9% of those who voted approved the treaty's ratification, with voter turn-out recorded at 49.5%.

At a referendum held in June 2004 a constitutional amendment removing the automatic entitlement to Irish citizenship of children born in Ireland (including Northern Ireland) was approved by 79.2% of voters. The plebiscite followed a ruling issued in January 2003 by the Irish Supreme Court, which declared that non-national parents of Irish-born children were not entitled to live in Ireland by virtue of having an Irish-born child. The Government had endorsed the amendment, citing the need to deter immigrants from exploiting Irish law to gain entitlement to residency in any EU member state. Ireland was the only EU country with an automatic right to citizenship at birth, which had been enshrined in the Constitution in 1999 as a consequence of the Good Friday Agreement for peace in Northern Ireland. In October 2004, as the sole nominee for the post, McAleese was deemed to be re-elected as President, two other candidates having failed to secure the support of the 20 members of parliament or four local authorities required to stand for election.

At the general election held on 24 May 2007 Fianna Fáil remained the largest party in the Dáil, with its representation declining slightly, to 78 seats. Fine Gael increased its representation substantially, to 51 seats, while the Labour Party won 20 seats and the Green Party six. Despite widespread expectations, in advance of the poll, that Sinn Féin would benefit from increased support, its representation in the Dáil declined from five to four seats. The representation of the PD was reduced from eight seats to only two. Having failed to win re-election, John McDowell—who had replaced Harney as leader of the PD and Deputy Prime Minister in September 2006—was obliged (by the terms of the PD's Constitution) to resign as party leader. He was replaced, initially in an interim capacity, by Harney. In June 2007 a coalition agreement was signed between Fianna Fáil, the PD and (despite an undertaking before the election by the party leader, Trevor Sargent, not to join an administration with Fianna Fáil) the Green Party; Sargent subsequently resigned as party leader. A new Government was formed, again headed by Ahern, and in which many senior appointments in the outgoing administration remained unchanged. Brian Cowen retained the post of Minister of Finance, to which he had been appointed in September 2004, and was concurrently designated Deputy Prime Minister. Harney was reappointed as Minister for Health and Children, as the sole PD minister, while two ministers from the Green Party were appointed: John Gormley as Minister for the Environment, Heritage and Local Government; and Eamon

Ryan as Minister for Communications, Energy and Natural Resources. The only new minister appointed from Fianna Fáil was Brian Lenihan, as Minister for Justice, Equality and Law. Three of the five independent members of the Dáil also agreed to support the new coalition.

In July 2007 Gormley was elected as leader of the Green Party. In September Eamon Gilmore was elected as leader of the Labour Party, succeeding Pat Rabbitte, who had resigned in the previous month. On 25 September a vote of no confidence in Ahern, brought by Fine Gael and the Labour Party in response to concerns about the veracity of evidence he had presented to the Mahon tribunal, concerning his personal finances, was defeated. (From September 2006 the tribunal had investigated allegations that, during his period of office as Minister for Finance between 1991 and 1993, Ahern had granted favours in return for loans or donations.) In January 2008 Ahern criticized the tribunal, alleging that it had not given him a fair hearing and that it had permitted the release of confidential information. Later in that month Kenny and Gilmore, as leaders of the two principal opposition parties, both demanded Ahern's resignation as Prime Minister, while the two parties governing in coalition with Fianna Fáil, the PD and the Green Party, expressed their support for the tribunal.

The Government of Brian Cowen

In early April 2008 Ahern announced that he was to resign from the positions of Prime Minister and leader of Fianna Fáil with effect from 6 May. On 9 April the Deputy Prime Minister and Minister for Finance, Brian Cowen, was elected unopposed to succeed Ahern as leader of Fianna Fáil; he was duly elected as Prime Minister by the Dáil on 7 May. Cowen subsequently effected a substantial reorganization of the Cabinet, reallocating those posts held by members of Fianna Fáil. Most notably, Mary Coughlan (previously Minister for Agriculture, Fisheries and Food) was appointed Deputy Prime Minister and Minister for Enterprise, Trade and Employment, while Brian Lenihan succeeded Cowen as Minister for Finance. Micheál Martin became Minister for Foreign Affairs, replacing Dermot Ahern, who assumed the role of Minister for Justice, Equality and Law Reform.

On 12 June 2008 a referendum was held on the ratification of the Treaty of Lisbon, which sought to reform the institutions of the EU and was intended to supersede the defunct EU constitutional treaty. Despite a campaign in favour of ratification led by Cowen, with the support of all the principal political parties except Sinn Féin, the treaty was rejected by 53.4% of those who voted. The result was attributed to the low rate of participation (53.1% of the electorate), widespread public uncertainty about the implications of the treaty, and concerns that it might compromise Ireland's neutrality or affect its policies on taxation or ethical issues such as abortion. As well as representing a major reverse for the new Prime Minister, the referendum defeat raised questions about the future of the treaty, which required ratification by all 27 EU member states in order to enter into force.

In September 2008 Bertie Ahern appeared before the Mahon tribunal to give evidence regarding allegations that, as Minister for Finance, he had received two separate payments from a Cork-based property developer, Owen O'Callaghan, in return for a favourable decision regarding the tax designation of a rival development. Both Ahern and O'Callaghan, who gave evidence to the tribunal two days later, denied that any payments had been made. The tribunal held its last public hearing in October, nearly 11 years after it had been established, and had yet to deliver its final report in early 2012. Meanwhile, in May 2009 Frank Dunlop, who had been investigated by the tribunal in 2000, was sentenced to two years' imprisonment and fined €30,000 after pleading guilty to bribing county councillors in the 1990s.

In November 2008 the PD voted at its conference to dissolve the party, after the leadership argued that it had no viable future. The PD, which had espoused many controversial liberal policies, on issues such as divorce and contraception, was formally disbanded in November 2009. The sole PD member of the Cabinet, Harney, declined to join any other party and retained her ministerial position as an independent.

During 2008 it became clear that the economic prosperity enjoyed by Ireland over the previous decade was coming to an end. Affected by the international credit crisis and the economic decline that was being experienced throughout much of the developed world, the Irish economy moved into recession, the first country in the euro area to do so. Property prices, which had increased dramatically during the decade to 2006, when Irish banks made large loans to developers and builders for speculative projects, now declined rapidly. In September 2008 the Government announced that it would guarantee the deposits in six banks and building societies. In January 2009 it was obliged to nationalize Anglo Irish Bank (which had specialized in large-scale lending for property development) in order to maintain market confidence, and in February it agreed to provide new capital for Allied Irish Banks and the Bank of Ireland. In April the Government announced the establishment of a National Asset Management Agency (NAMA), which would purchase non-performing loans at a discount. Meanwhile, unpopular austerity measures, announced in October 2008 as part of the budget for 2009, included a controversial proposal to remove automatic entitlement to free medical insurance for those aged over 70 years. The announcement prompted vehement criticism in the Dáil both from opposition members and some Fianna Fáil backbenchers, one of whom resigned from the party in protest. The Government was forced to compromise by amending the proposals to allow a higher income threshold in means tests for eligibility. In February 2009, despite failing to reach an agreement with the Irish Congress of Trade Unions, the Government announced further austerity measures, including a pension levy on the wages of public sector workers, which were intended to reduce government expenditure by €1,800m. by the end of 2009. Public disapproval of the Government's response to the economic crisis continued to increase, and Fianna Fáil and the Green Party both suffered heavy losses in local elections held in June, while Fine Gael performed strongly, becoming the largest party in local government.

Also in June 2009 Cowen announced that a second referendum on the Treaty of Lisbon would be held in October. The announcement followed a meeting of the European Council in Brussels, Belgium, at which EU leaders had agreed on a document intended to address Irish concerns over the treaty; the text included formal guarantees, which were to be given force of law by their incorporation into the next EU accession treaty, to the effect that the Treaty of Lisbon would in no way affect any member state's neutrality or its competencies in relation to taxation or family law. At the referendum, which was held on 2 October, ratification of the treaty was approved by 67.1% of voters; the turn-out, at 59.0%, was somewhat higher than in the previous referendum. It was believed that the economic crisis contributed to the strong increase in support for the treaty since June 2008 by strengthening popular enthusiasm for EU membership.

In October 2009 the Chairman (Ceann Comhairle) of the Dáil, John O'Donoghue of Fianna Fáil, was forced to resign as a result of pressure from the opposition parties over his extravagant official expenses, both in his current capacity and as Minister for Arts, Sport and Tourism in 2002–07. Séumas Kirk, also of Fianna Fáil, was elected to replace him. The incident represented a further loss of authority for the Government, which in August 2009 had lost its official majority in the Dáil after two Fianna Fáil members resigned from the parliamentary party in protest at the closure of a hospital unit in their constituency. Public disaffection with the Government was manifested in November in a strike by some 250,000 public sector workers protesting against proposed pay reductions and other austerity measures. The Government was weakened further in February 2010 by the resignation of two ministers over improprieties: Willie O'Dea resigned as Minister of Defence after it emerged that he had sworn an affidavit in which he had falsely denied making an unfounded allegation against a Sinn Féin councillor in Limerick; and, one week later, the former Green Party leader, Trevor Sargent, resigned as a Minister of State after he admitted unlawfully attempting to influence a police officer in a case involving a constituent. In March Cowen carried out a government reorganization, in which O'Dea was replaced by Tony Killeen; among other changes, Mary Coughlan was appointed Minister of Education and Skills (while retaining the post of Deputy Prime Minister), replacing Batt O'Keeffe, who assumed Coughlan's position at the head of the restyled Ministry of Enterprise, Trade and Innovation.

Financial assistance from the EU and the IMF

During 2010 hopes of an economic recovery proved premature when, after a slight expansion in the first quarter of the year, Ireland's gross domestic product (GDP) again contracted in the second quarter: levels of unemployment, and also of emigration, remained high, and the enormous cost to taxpayers of alleviating the banking crisis, necessitating substantial reductions in other budgetary spending, caused considerable resentment. In September fresh assistance for Allied Irish Banks, Anglo Irish Bank and the Irish Nationwide Building Society brought the total cost of supporting the financial system to at least €45,000m.; in addition, Irish banks owed some €130,000m. to the European Central Bank (ECB). By October the total budgetary deficit for 2010, including support for the banks, was estimated to be equivalent to 32% of GDP (compared with the limit of 3% required by the EU). Meanwhile, the cost to Ireland of borrowing on the international bond markets increased as a result of uncertainty over the country's financial stability. The Minister for Finance, Brian Lenihan, insisted that the programme of support for the banks was now complete and that the cost was manageable, that a four-year austerity programme would restore the budgetary deficit to acceptable levels, and that Ireland was not about to default on its debts. Nevertheless, doubts as to whether the Irish Government would be able to secure legislative approval for the budget for 2011, due to be announced in December 2010, led to persistent speculation that Ireland would be obliged to request emergency assistance from the EU and the IMF, as Greece had done in the previous May.

Under pressure from other EU governments, anxious to ensure the stability of the euro, in late November 2010 the Irish Government finally made a formal application for financial assistance from the EU and the IMF. On 28 November the Government announced that agreement had been reached on the provision of financial support totalling €85,000m. from the EU and the IMF, as well as from the United Kingdom, Sweden and Denmark in the form of bilateral loans. Of this total, Ireland itself was to provide €17,500m. from its National Pension Reserve Fund and from cash reserves. The assistance was conditional upon a reorganization of the banking system, intensifying measures already adopted, and upon the four-year budgetary adjustment programme that had already been proposed by the Government, aiming to save €15,000m. over the period and to reduce the budgetary deficit to less than 3% of GDP by 2015. As part of this programme, the Government's proposed budget for 2011 envisaged savings of €6,000m. for that year alone, with reductions in welfare and other spending, in public sector pensions and in the minimum wage, together with tax increases and the introduction of taxation for the lower-paid. The agreement was widely perceived as a national humiliation and as imposing an unfair burden on the least well-off.

Recent developments: the 2011 general election

In November 2010 the Green Party, deploring the proposed economic adjustment programme, announced that it would leave the coalition by the end of January 2011. Cowen refused to accede to demands by the opposition parties and from within his own party that he should resign before the budget was adopted, but undertook to hold a general election early in the following year. Despite the success of a Sinn Féin candidate in a by-election in late November 2010, further reducing the Government's support in the Dáil, the budget was adopted in early December with the support of independent members. In January 2011 Cowen's principal critic within Fianna Fáil, the Minister for Foreign Affairs, Micheál Martin, resigned from his post and urged Cowen to resign, following revelations about previously undisclosed contacts with Sean Fitzpatrick, the former chairman of Anglo Irish Bank, prior to the Government's controversial guarantee to the banks in September 2008. However, Cowen, who denied any impropriety, retained the leadership of Fianna Fáil in a self-imposed vote of confidence among party members in the legislature. Cowen temporarily assumed responsibility for foreign affairs himself. Later in January Cowen attempted to reorganize the Cabinet, replacing five other ministers who had resigned on the grounds that they would not be candidates in the forthcoming election: his motive was apparently to replace them with less well-known Fianna Fáil members, whose chances of being re-elected would thus be enhanced. He also announced that a general election would be held on 11 March. However, the Green Party, which had not been consulted on the reorganization, refused to accept it, and Cowen was obliged to withdraw the appointments and transfer the former ministers' portfolios to other members of the Cabinet. Following further loss of support within Fianna Fáil, on 22 January he resigned as leader of the party, while stating that he would remain as Prime Minister until the election. The Green Party then withdrew from the coalition, although it undertook to support the remaining budgetary legislation (on which depended the release of funds from the emergency assistance provided by the EU and the IMF). The Labour Party proposed a motion of no confidence in the Government, but withdrew it on condition that the passage of budgetary legislation was accelerated in order to dissolve the Dáil and allow a general election in February. Later in January Martin was elected leader of Fianna Fáil. On 1 February Cowen announced the dissolution of the legislature and the holding of a general election on 25 February.

At the general election on 25 February 2011, Fine Gael won 76 seats, compared with 51 at the previous election in 2007, while the Labour Party increased its representation from 20 to 37 seats. Fianna Fáil secured only 20 seats (having won 78 in 2007), and its former coalition partner, the Green Party, lost all six of the seats it had held. Sinn Féin won 14 seats (compared with four in 2007): the party's President, Gerry Adams (who had resigned as a member of the United Kingdom Parliament) was one of the successful candidates. Negotiations between Fine Gael and the Labour Party concluded on 6 March 2011 with an agreement to form a coalition Government, with Enda Kenny, the leader of Fine Gael, as Prime Minister. Kenny announced the formation of a Cabinet with 10 Fine Gael and five Labour members. Eamon Gilmore, the leader of the Labour Party, became Deputy Prime Minister and Minister for Foreign Affairs and Trade. Michael Noonan (Fine Gael) was appointed Minister for Finance, while some of the previous responsibilities of this post were transferred to a new Ministry for Public Expenditure and Reform, allocated to Brendan Howlin (Labour). Several other departments were reconfigured or combined. The new administration undertook to renegotiate the terms of the assistance programme that had been agreed with the EU and the IMF (in particular the high interest rates being charged on some of the loans), while implementing for at least two years most of the austerity measures introduced by the previous Government in order to reduce the budget deficit.

During 2011 the IMF acknowledged the Irish Government's 'resolute implementation' of the economic adjustment programme, reporting that the reduction of the budgetary deficit and the restructuring of the banking sector were proceeding according to schedule. In July EU ministers agreed to reduce the rate of interest payable by Ireland on the loans it had received, and to allow a longer repayment period. Moderate economic growth was resumed in 2011, although unemployment remained at a high level (see Economic Affairs). In February 2012 it was announced that it would be legally necessary to hold a referendum in Ireland on a proposed EU 'fiscal compact' (the Treaty on Stability, Co-ordination and Governance) whereby participating countries would accept legally binding limits on future budgetary deficits, and incur penalties imposed by the European Court of Justice if they exceeded the limits. It was expected that the referendum would take place in May or June. Kenny urged approval of the agreement (which he signed in early March, as did representatives of all other EU governments except the Czech Republic and the United Kingdom) as being in the national interest, and Fianna Fáil and the Green Party also declared their support, although the deputy leader of Fianna Fáil, Éamon Ó Cuív, resigned from his post in late February because he opposed the agreement.

In July 2011, meanwhile, the latest in a series of reports on the sexual abuse of children by Roman Catholic clergy in Ireland was published. The report, dealing with the Cloyne diocese, stated that diocesan officials, including the former bishop, had not followed the Church's own guidelines on reporting suspected abusers to the police. In the same month, speaking in the Dáil, Kenny strongly criticized the Vatican's alleged role in concealing the extent of the abuse. His speech, and the widespread support that it received, was perceived as indicating a profound change in the nation's traditionally deferential attitude to the Church. The Papal Nuncio (the diplomatic representative of the Holy See in Ireland) was recalled for consultations and later replaced.

In October 2011 a presidential election was held, to replace Mary McAleese after the expiry of her second term of office. The successful candidate was Michael D. Higgins, a former Labour member of the Dáil, who had held the post of Minister for Arts, Culture and the Gaeltacht in 1993–97. Higgins' closest rivals in the election (among a total of seven candidates) were a prominent businessman, Sean Gallagher (a former member of Fianna Fáil standing as an independent candidate), and Martin McGuinness, the Sinn Féin Deputy First Minister of Northern Ireland. Higgins took office on 11 November 2011 for a seven-year term.

The peace process in Northern Ireland

Consultations between the United Kingdom and Ireland on the future of Northern Ireland resulted in November 1985 in the signing of the Anglo-Irish Agreement, which provided for regular participation in Northern Ireland affairs by the Irish Government on political, legal, security and cross-border matters. The Agreement maintained that no change in the status of Northern Ireland would be made without the assent of the majority of its population. The terms of the Agreement were approved by both the Irish and the British Parliaments. Under the provisions of the Agreement, the Irish Government pledged co-operation in enhanced cross-border security, in order to suppress IRA operations. Despite underlying tensions, the ensuing co-ordination between the Garda Síochána (Irish police force) and the Northern Ireland police force, the Royal Ulster Constabulary (RUC), was broadly successful. In February 1989 a permanent joint consultative assembly, comprising 25 British MPs and 25 Irish members of the Dáil, was established. The representatives were selected in October. The assembly's meetings, the first of which began in February 1990, were to take place twice a year, alternately in Dublin and London.

In January 1990 the British Government launched an initiative to convene meetings between representatives from the major political parties in Northern Ireland, and the British and Irish Governments, to discuss the restoration of devolution to Northern Ireland, which had been abandoned in 1974. In May 1990 the unionists agreed to hold direct discussions with the Irish Government, an unprecedented concession. Following extensive negotiations, discussions between the Northern Ireland parties, which were a prelude to the inclusion of the Irish Government, commenced in June 1991. They were suspended several times but did reach the inclusion of the Irish Government in April and September 1992. The principal point of contention was the unionists' demand that Ireland hold a referendum on Articles 2 and 3 of its Constitution, which laid claim to the territory of Northern Ireland. Ireland was unwilling to make such a concession except as part of an overall settlement. The negotiations formally ended in November.

In October 1993 the new Irish Prime Minister, Albert Reynolds, and his British counterpart, John Major, issued a joint statement setting out the principles on which future negotiations were to be based, including, notably, that Sinn Féin permanently renounce violence before being admitted to the negotiations. In December the Prime Ministers issued a joint declaration, known as the Downing Street Declaration, which referred to the possibility of a united Ireland and accepted the legitimacy of self-determination, but insisted on majority consent within Northern Ireland. While Sinn Féin and the unionist parties considered their response to the Declaration, Reynolds received both groups' conditional support for his proposal to establish a 'Forum for Peace and Reconciliation', which was to encourage both sides to end violent action. In August 1994 the IRA announced that it had ceased all military operations; this was followed in October by a similar suspension on the part of loyalist organizations.

An international panel, under the chairmanship of George Mitchell (a former US Senator), began work in December 1995 to consider the merits of decommissioning of arms in Northern Ireland. Its findings, announced in January 1996, recommended that weapons decommissioning should take place in parallel with all-party talks, and that their destruction should be monitored by an independent commission. The British and Irish Governments accepted those recommendations, but the Irish Government deemed unacceptable proposals put forward by the British Government for elections to be held to a Northern Ireland assembly, which would provide the framework for all-party negotiations. In February 1996, following a bomb explosion in London, marking the termination of the IRA's cease-fire, the British and Irish Governments suspended official contacts with Sinn Féin.

In May 1997 a meeting of the Irish Prime Minister, John Bruton, with the newly elected British premier, Tony Blair, and the new Secretary of State for Northern Ireland, Mo Mowlam, generated speculation that significant progress could be achieved in furthering a political agreement. In June the two Governments announced a new initiative to proceed with weapons decommissioning, while simultaneously pursuing negotiations for a constitutional settlement. In July the newly elected Irish Prime Minister, Bertie Ahern, confirmed his commitment to the peace initiative during a meeting with Blair in London. Following the IRA's subsequent restoration of its cease-fire, the Irish Government restored official contacts with Sinn Féin and resumed the policy of considering convicted IRA activists for early release from prison. In September Sinn Féin announced that it would accept the outcome of the peace process and would renounce violence as a means of punishment or resolving problems, providing for the party's participation in all-party talks when they resumed in the middle of that month. A procedural agreement to pursue negotiations in parallel with the decommissioning of weapons (which was to be undertaken by an Independent International Commission on Decommissioning—IICD, led by Gen. John de Chastelain of Canada) was signed by all the main parties later in September.

On 10 April 1998 the two Governments and eight political parties involved in the talks signed the Good Friday (or Belfast) Agreement at Stormont Castle in the Northern Irish capital. Immediately thereafter the two Governments signed a new British-Irish Agreement, replacing the Anglo-Irish Agreement, committing them to enact the provisions of the Good Friday Agreement, subject to its approval at referendums to be held in Ireland and Northern Ireland in May. The peace settlement provided for changes to the Irish Constitution (notably Articles 2 and 3) and to British constitutional legislation to enshrine the principle that a united Ireland could be achieved only with the consent of the majority of the people of both Ireland and Northern Ireland. The Good Friday Agreement provided for a new Northern Ireland Assembly and Executive Committee, together with North/South and British-Irish institutions. In addition, provision was made for the release of paramilitary prisoners affiliated to organizations that established a complete and unequivocal cease-fire. On 22 May, at referendums held simultaneously in Ireland and Northern Ireland, 94.4% and 71.1% of voters, respectively, voted in favour of the Good Friday Agreement.

Elections to the Assembly were conducted in June 1998; the Assembly convened in July and elected the leader of the Ulster Unionist Party (UUP), David Trimble, as First Minister. The peace process was threatened with disruption by sectarian violence in July and by the detonation of an explosive device in August in Omagh, Northern Ireland; the device was planted by a republican splinter group, the Real IRA, and caused 29 deaths, more than any other single incident since the beginning of unrest related to Northern Ireland. Progress was also obstructed by a dispute between unionists and Sinn Féin concerning weapons decommissioning. As a result of the dispute the deadlines for the formation both of the Executive Committee and the North/South body, and for the devolution of powers to the new Northern Ireland institutions, were not met. In June 1999 the two Prime Ministers presented a compromise plan that envisaged the immediate establishment of the Executive Committee prior to the surrender of paramilitary weapons, with the condition that Sinn Féin guarantee that the IRA complete decommissioning by May 2000. Negotiations effectively collapsed in July 1999 and a review of the peace process, headed by George Mitchell, began in September. In November Mitchell succeeded in producing an agreement providing for the devolution of powers to the Executive Committee, after the IRA issued a statement announcing that it would appoint a representative to enter discussions with the IICD. On 2 December power was officially transferred to the new Northern Ireland Executive. On the same day, in accordance with the Good Friday Agreement, the Irish Constitution was amended to remove the state's territorial claim over Northern Ireland.

In December 1999 the Irish Cabinet attended the inaugural meeting, in Armagh, of the North/South Ministerial Council. The British-Irish Council met for the first time later that month. With the failure of the IRA to undertake disarmament threatening to result in the collapse of the peace process the British and Irish Governments engaged in intensive negotiations. Despite assurances given by the IRA that its cease-fire would not be broken, in February legislation came into effect returning Northern Ireland to direct rule. The IRA subsequently announced its withdrawal from discussions with the IICD. Direct talks between the Irish and British Governments and the principal parties resumed in May 2000, with the British Government pledging to restore the Northern Ireland institutions and postpone the deadline for decommissioning until June 2001 subject to a commitment by the IRA on the arms issue. The IRA responded by offering to 'initiate a process that will completely and verifiably put arms beyond use'. On 30 May power was again transferred to the Northern Ireland institutions.

The issue of IRA weapons decommissioning continued to threaten the peace process during 2001. In July Trimble resigned as First Minister in protest at the lack of progress on IRA decommissioning; Sir Reg Empey assumed the role of acting First Minister. In August Ahern and Blair announced that they would formulate a package of non-negotiable proposals to be presented to the pro-Agreement parties. The ensuing proposals did not meet with the approval of the major political parties, and on 10 August the British Government suspended the Assembly for 24 hours in order to delay the necessity to appoint a new First Minister for a further six weeks. Following the temporary suspension the IRA retracted its earlier offer to put arms 'beyond use'. The Assembly was again suspended on 22 September as the deadlock continued, and in October the three UUP ministers and two Democratic Unionist Party (DUP) ministers resigned. Later in the month, however, the IRA announced that it had begun a process of 'putting arms beyond use', and the IICD revealed that it had witnessed the 'significant' disposal of IRA weapons. The unionist ministers therefore reassumed their posts and Trimble was re-elected as First Minister.

In October 2002 Sinn Féin's offices at the Assembly were raided by police, who suspected that the IRA had infiltrated the Northern Ireland Office and gained access to large numbers of confidential documents. In consequence, Northern Ireland was returned to direct rule. In a joint statement, Blair and Ahern announced that the devolved institutions would only be restored if Sinn Féin ended its link with paramilitary organizations. Later in October the IRA announced that it had suspended all contact with the IICD.

Talks aimed at resolving the impasse continued between the major parties during late 2002 and early 2003; however, relations between unionists and nationalists remained strained. The IRA failed to respond to the British Government's demand for a definitive cessation of paramilitary activities, and in May 2003 Blair postponed the elections to the Assembly until an unspecified date. In the same month the British and Irish Governments published a Joint Declaration containing their proposals for reinstating the Northern Ireland institutions and demanding a full and permanent cessation of all paramilitary activity. Blair and Ahern stressed that political talks would continue to address the impasse over the holding of elections and pledged that aspects of the Joint Declaration not conditional upon IRA acts of complete disarmament would be implemented. Talks between the British and Irish Governments and the major Northern Ireland political parties continued during late 2003, and in October, following further acts of decommissioning of IRA weapons, elections to the Assembly were scheduled for the following month. However, the UUP declared that the acts of decommissioning witnessed by de Chastelain had been lacking in the transparency that the UUP required to be convinced of the IRA's desire to commit to peace. The IRA maintained that it had honoured its commitments and that there would be no more acts of weapons decommissioning until the UUP agreed to support the restoration of power-sharing.

At elections to the Assembly, held on 26 November 2003, the anti-Good Friday Agreement DUP secured 30 of the 108 seats, thus becoming the largest party. In talks with Ahern in January 2004 the leader of the DUP, Rev. Ian Paisley, remained insistent that his party would not conduct direct talks with Sinn Féin until the IRA had disbanded. In May Blair and Ahern agreed the basis of a 'roadmap' to restore the suspended Northern Ireland Assembly and Executive by October. In September further talks became deadlocked, following a DUP demand for changes to the functioning of the Assembly and the Executive before it would enter a government with Sinn Féin. In October Paisley met Ahern in Dublin, his first formal political meeting with the Irish Prime Minister, to try to break the impasse. In the following month the British and Irish Governments passed their proposals for restoring the power-sharing Executive to the DUP and Sinn Féin for consultation.

In December 2004 Blair and Ahern met in Belfast to reveal their final proposals to restore devolution, although neither the DUP nor Sinn Féin had agreed to the terms. The following day an IRA statement was released, rejecting a demand made by Paisley for photographic proof of decommissioning and stating that, although the IRA was committed to the peace process, it would not be subjected to humiliation. In January 2005 the Northern Ireland Chief Constable placed the blame for a raid on the Belfast headquarters of the Northern Bank in December 2004, in which £26.5m. was stolen, on the IRA. In February 2005 Ahern and Blair warned the IRA that its failure to demilitarize was the only obstacle to reaching an agreement on power-sharing; the following day the IRA withdrew its commitment to decommissioning. However, in July the IRA announced the end of its armed campaign and renewed its commitment to decommissioning. In September the IICD confirmed that the IRA's weapons had been fully decommissioned. In December the British Secretary of State for Northern Ireland, Peter Hain, warned Sinn Féin and the DUP that the Assembly elections, scheduled for 2007, would be cancelled if they did not reach an agreement on power-sharing in 2006. Hain and the Irish Minister for Foreign Affairs, Dermot Ahern, chaired talks with the Northern Ireland parties in February 2006, while Blair and Bertie Ahern met to discuss plans for the restoration of the institutions in March. Dermot Ahern subsequently announced that if attempts to restore the institutions of Northern Ireland in accordance with the Good Friday Agreement failed, then the British and Irish Governments would adopt an intergovernmental approach.

On 15 May 2006 the Assembly was restored; however, no further progress was made regarding the nomination of candidates for the roles of First Minister and Deputy First Minister. In October the four-member International Monitoring Commission (IMC) reported that the IRA was no longer engaged in terrorist activity and was committed to the peace process, but noted that members both of loyalist and republican paramilitary groups continued to engage in criminal activity. Despite the positive overall tone of the IMC report, the DUP remained sceptical concerning the progress of the disbandment of the IRA. On 13 October, following talks in St Andrews, Scotland, Ahern and Blair announced an agreement (the St Andrews Agreement) that was intended to precipitate the restoration of a power-sharing Executive, and set a deadline of 10 November by which the Northern Ireland main parties were to agree to adhere to its provisions, which included support by all parties for the Police Service of Northern Ireland (PSNI) and the Northern Ireland Policing Board, and the formation of a North-South Inter-parliamentary Forum, including an equal number of representatives from both the Assembly and the Irish Parliament. Devolution was to be restored on 24 November, when the DUP and Sinn Féin would nominate candidates for the posts of First Minister and Deputy First Minister, respectively. The Assembly duly convened on 24 November; however, Paisley refused to accept his nomination as First Minister, while hinting that he would assume the role after elections to the Assembly, scheduled to be held in early March 2007, should Sinn Féin formally signal its support for the PSNI and the Policing Board. Following a long period of consultation among Sinn Féin members, in January 2007 delegates to a special conference voted in favour of a proposal to support the policing institutions. Despite the DUP's scepticism concerning Sinn Féin's commitment, the two Governments insisted that the deadline of 26 March was binding and that, in the absence of an agreement, the Assembly would be dissolved.

In elections to the Assembly, held on 7 March 2007, the DUP secured 36 seats and Sinn Féin 28, thereby confirming their status as the main parties in Northern Ireland. As the deadline approached, the Irish Government and Hain indicated that the deadline could be flexible, should the two parties agree an alternative arrangement. On 26 March Paisley and the Sinn Féin President, Gerry Adams, held their first direct meeting, during which an agreement was reached for a power-sharing Executive, which was duly installed on 8 May. Paisley became First Minister and Sinn Féin's Martin McGuinness was appointed as Deputy First Minister. Meanwhile, in April Bertie Ahern met Paisley in Dublin to discuss arrangements for future co-operation between the Executive and the Irish Government.

From mid-2009 the functioning of the Executive was increasingly disrupted by disagreements between Sinn Féin and the DUP (led since June 2008 by Peter Robinson, who had also succeeded Paisley as First Minister) over a timetable for the transfer of powers over policing and justice, which constituted the final area of responsibility due to be devolved under the Good Friday Agreement. In January 2010, following the collapse of negotiations between the two parties aimed at ending the impasse, Brian Cowen and his British counterpart, Gordon Brown, travelled to Belfast in order to mediate in the dispute. After intensive talks involving Cowen, Brown and all the main parties ended without agreement, the two Prime Ministers indicated that they would publish their own plans for the transfer of powers if the DUP and Sinn Féin had not reached an agreement within 48 hours. Although the deadline was not met, negotiations between the two parties continued, and in February the parties concluded a deal that envisaged the transfer of policing and justice powers to the Executive on 12 April; the agreement also addressed other issues of contention between the parties, including a mechanism for resolving disputes over parades by Protestant orders. The transfer of powers took place as scheduled on 12 April, when the Assembly elected a Minister of Justice to form part of the Executive.

During 2010 and 2011 police in the Irish Republic seized weapons and explosives in a number of raids on suspected dissident republicans who were believed to be planning violent attacks in Northern Ireland in protest at the peace process. The Irish Prime Minister, Enda Kenny, was among senior politicians who attended the funeral of a member of the Northern Ireland police force, Ronan Kerr, a Catholic, who died in an explosion in Omagh in April 2011: former members of the Provisional IRA claimed responsibility for the murder.

Foreign Affairs

Ireland became a member of the European Community (EC—now the European Union—EU, see p. 276) in 1973. In May 1987 the country affirmed its commitment to the EC when, in a referendum, 69.9% of Irish voters supported adherence to the Single European Act, which provided for closer economic and political co-operation between EC member states (including the creation of a single market by 1993). In December 1991 Ireland agreed to the far-reaching Treaty on European Union (the Maastricht Treaty). Ireland secured a special provision within the treaty (which was signed by all parties in February 1992), guaranteeing that Ireland's constitutional position on abortion would be unaffected by any future EC legislation. Despite opposition, from both pro- and anti-abortion campaigners, to the special provision within the treaty and the threat to Ireland's neutrality perceived in the document's proposals for a common defence policy, ratification of the treaty was endorsed at a referendum held in June 1992. A referendum conducted in May 1998 approved the Amsterdam Treaty, which had been signed by EU ministers in October 1997, amending the Maastricht Treaty. The common European currency, the euro, was adopted by Ireland at the beginning of 2002. In October of that year the Treaty of Nice, which provided for the impending enlargement of the EU, was approved in a national referendum, despite having been rejected in an earlier referendum held in 2001. In early 2004 Ahern, as President of the Council of the European Union, led negotiations between the leaders of the member states over a draft constitutional treaty, which was eventually agreed in June. It was formally signed in October, but required ratification by all 25 member states either by parliamentary vote or referendum. Following the treaty's rejection in national referendums in France and the Netherlands in mid-2005, further referendums in EU countries yet to ratify the treaty, including Ireland, were postponed indefinitely. During 2007 agreement was reached on a treaty to replace the constitutional treaty. The resulting Treaty of Lisbon was signed in December, but was rejected at a referendum in Ireland in June 2008. However, the ratification process continued across Europe, and at an EU summit meeting in Brussels in June 2009 Cowen achieved a series of formal guarantees from the European Council addressing Irish concerns regarding certain aspects of the treaty. The treaty was approved by a substantial majority at a second referendum in October, and subsequently entered into force across the EU in December.

In February 2006 the Minister for Defence, Willie O'Dea, reversed a decision made in 2005 and announced that Ireland would participate in EU 'battlegroups', which were to be used for deployment to international crisis areas (see Defence). In July 2006 an amendment to previous defence legislation was promulgated following a vote in the Dáil. Under the amended legislation, Irish troops could join EU battlegroups in emergency humanitarian, reconnaissance and training missions prior to receiving a UN mandate or approval from the Dáil, thus circumventing the so-called 'triple-lock' that required any deployment of Irish troops abroad to be mandated by the UN and approved by the Irish Government and Parliament. However, if either or both declined to approve such a mission, troops would be withdrawn.

In November 2010 the Irish Government accepted emergency assistance from the EU after the country's budgetary deficit exceeded by far the limits stipulated by the EU. In March 2012 the Government signed the EU Treaty on Stability, Co-ordination and Governance (more often referred to as the 'fiscal compact'), but adherence to the treaty, which envisaged legally binding limits on national budgetary spending, was to be submitted to a national referendum later in that year.

In May 2011 Queen Elizabeth II paid a state visit to Ireland, becoming the first British monarch to visit the country since its independence. In acts perceived as being of great symbolic importance, the Queen laid wreaths at memorials to those who had died in the struggle for Irish independence, and in the First World War, and in a speech she expressed 'deep sympathy' with victims of the 'troubled past'. The visit was regarded as indicating the development of a more mature and cordial relationship between the two countries, following the successful outcome of the peace process in Northern Ireland.

Ireland has strong historic links with the USA through emigration, and from 1995 the special envoy of the US President undertook an important diplomatic role in negotiations on the future of Northern Ireland (see The peace process in Northern Ireland). The USA is a major trading partner (Ireland's largest individual export market in 2010) and the country's principal source of foreign direct investment, attracted by a skilled English-speaking labour force and a low corporate tax rate: in early 2011 there were 600 US companies operating in Ireland, employing some 100,000 people. In May 2011 President Barack Obama became the sixth US President to pay an official visit to Ireland since John F. Kennedy in 1963.

A visit by the Chinese Vice-President, Xi Jinping, in February 2012, during which various agreements on trade and investment were concluded, indicated that the Chinese Government regarded Ireland as an important entry point in its dealings with the EU.

CONSTITUTION AND GOVERNMENT

The Constitution took effect in 1937. Legislative power is vested in the bicameral National Parliament (Oireachtas), comprising the Senate (Seanad Éireann) and the House of Representatives (Dáil Éireann). The Senate has 60 members, including 11 nominated by the Prime Minister (Taoiseach) and 49 indirectly elected for five years. The House of Representatives has 166 members, elected by universal adult suffrage for five years (subject to dissolution) by means of the single transferable vote, a form of proportional representation.

The President (Uachtarán) is the constitutional head of state, elected by direct popular vote for seven years; re-election is permitted only once. Executive power is effectively held by the Cabinet, led by the Prime Minister, who is appointed by the President on the nomination of the Dáil. The President appoints other Ministers on the nomination of the Prime Minister with the previous approval of the Dáil. The Cabinet is responsible to the Dáil.

Local government in Ireland consists of a number of democratically elected local and regional authorities at three levels: two regional assemblies, eight regional authorities and 29 county councils, five city councils, five borough councils and 75 town councils.

REGIONAL AND INTERNATIONAL CO-OPERATION

Ireland is a member of the European Union (EU, see p. 276) and uses the single currency, the euro; however, it does not participate in the Schengen Agreement on open borders. It is a member of the Council of Europe (see p. 256) and the Organization for Security and Co-operation in Europe (OSCE, see p. 388).

Ireland joined the UN in 1955. As a contracting party to the General Agreement on Tariffs and Trade, it joined the World Trade Organization (WTO, see p. 433) on its establishment in 1995. Ireland is also a member of the Organisation for Economic Co-operation and Development (OECD, see p. 379) and participates in the Partnership for Peace framework of the North Atlantic Treaty Organization (NATO, see p. 370).

ECONOMIC AFFAIRS

In 2010, according to estimates by the World Bank, Ireland's gross national income (GNI), measured at average 2007–09 prices, was US $182,474m., equivalent to $40,720 per head (or $32,520 on an international purchasing-power parity basis). During 2001–10, it was estimated, the population increased at an average annual rate of 1.7%, while gross domestic product (GDP) per head increased, in real terms, by an average of 0.5% per year. Overall GDP increased, in real terms, at an average annual rate of 2.1% in 2001–10; real GDP declined by 7.6% in 2009 and by 1.0% in 2010.

Agriculture (including forestry and fishing) contributed 2.5% of GDP in 2010 and employed an estimated 4.7% of the working population in 2011. Beef and dairy production dominate Irish agriculture. Principal crops include barley, wheat and potatoes. According to the World Bank, agricultural GDP decreased by an average of 3.1% per year during 2001–09; sectoral GDP increased by 8.4% in 2009.

Industry (comprising mining, manufacturing, construction and utilities) provided 30.9% of GDP in 2010 and employed 18.6% of the working population in 2011. Industrial GDP, according to the World Bank, decreased by an average of 3.1%

per year during 2001–09; it grew by 6.1% in 2007, but decreased by 2.5% in 2008 and by 4.6% in 2009.

Mining (including quarrying and turf production) provided employment to 0.4% of the working population in 2006. Ireland possesses substantial deposits of lead-zinc ore and recoverable peat, both of which are exploited. Natural gas is produced from the Kinsale field off the south coast of Ireland (although production is declining) and from the Seven Heads field that came on stream in 2003. Substantial gas supplies were discovered at the Corrib field situated off the west coast of Ireland; the project was delayed owing to local objections to a proposed pipeline to bring the gas onshore. Small quantities of coal are also extracted. Offshore reserves of petroleum have also been located and several licences awarded to foreign-owned enterprises to undertake further exploration.

According to World Bank estimates, manufacturing contributed 22.3% of GDP in 2007. Manufacturing was estimated to employ 20.3% of the working population in 1997. The manufacturing sector comprises many high-technology, largely foreign-owned, capital-intensive enterprises. In the year to February 2010 the value of manufacturing output declined by 2.6%.

Construction engaged 5.8% of the employed labour force in 2011. The construction sector contracted by 31.8% in 2010, according to official preliminary figures, following a similar decline in the previous year.

Electricity is derived principally from natural gas, which provided 54.7% of total requirements in 2008, while coal provided 17.8% and petroleum 5.9%. There was potential for the further development of wind-generated energy, which was increasing in importance. In 2010 imports of mineral fuels were 12.3% (by value) of total merchandise imports.

Service industries (including commerce, finance, transport and communications and public administration) contributed 66.6% of GDP in 2010 and employed 76.6% of the working population in 2011. The financial sector expanded rapidly in the 2000s. However, in 2008–11 there was a crisis in the banking system, following the global financial crisis and the collapse in domestic property prices. Tourism is one of the principal sources of foreign exchange. Revenue from the tourism and travel sector amounted to an estimated €4,890m. in 2009, but declined to €4,077m. in 2010. The GDP of the services sector increased by an average of 2.8% per year during 2001–09, and by 5.2% in 2007, but declined by 2.2% in 2008 and by 8.3% in 2009, according to the World Bank.

In 2010, according to IMF statistics, Ireland recorded a visible trade surplus of US $48,273m. with a surplus of $954m. on the current account of the balance of payments. In 2010 the principal source of imports was the United Kingdom (32.1%). The European Union (EU, see p. 276) as a whole accounted for 60.7% of imports; the USA, Germany and the People's Republic of China were also important suppliers. The USA was the principal market for exports (23.2%); the EU accounted for 57.9% of exports, while other major purchasers included the United Kingdom, Belgium, Germany and France. In 2010 principal imports included office equipment and other electrical machinery, road vehicles and parts, chemical products and other manufactured items. Principal exports included chemicals, machinery and transport equipment and miscellaneous manufactured articles.

There was an estimated general government deficit of €49,599m. in 2010, equivalent to 31.5% of GDP. Ireland's general government gross debt was €148,074m. at the end of 2010, equivalent to 94.9% of GDP. The annual rate of inflation averaged 2.2% in 2001–10. Consumer prices decreased by 4.5% in 2009 and by 1.0% in 2010. The unemployment rate averaged 14.3% in 2011.

In the late 1990s the Irish economy enjoyed an unprecedentedly high rate of growth, which was attributed largely to prudent fiscal and monetary management and low taxation, aided by a substantial increase in foreign direct investment: numerous multinational companies established bases in Ireland (particularly those engaged in information and communications technology, pharmaceuticals, chemicals and medical equipment). Continuing high levels of growth were sustained in 2004–07 by the rapid expansion of the construction sector (assisted by banks and building societies which provided loans on extremely liberal terms) and high levels of consumer spending, in large part due to migrant workers entering the work-force. However, in 2008 the Irish economy became the first in the euro area to enter recession, as the effects of the global financial crisis coincided with, and exacerbated, a correction in domestic property prices. The subsequent collapse in property prices and marked fall in investment, owing to the decline in building activity, led to a drop in consumer spending, while the fall in external demand and the high value of the euro against the pound sterling resulted in a decline in exports. Moreover, Ireland's banking sector, which was affected by the lack of available credit caused by the global financial crisis, was also exposed to the collapse in domestic property prices, which resulted in borrowers' inability to meet repayment obligations on lending. In September 2008 the Government announced that it would guarantee deposits in six financial institutions, in order to maintain confidence, and over the next two years it was obliged to provide support for the banking system totalling at least €45,000m. Meanwhile, the effects of the downturn led to a rapid deterioration of government finances; the budgetary deficit was equivalent to an estimated 31.9% of GDP in 2010 (compared with the maximum of 3% stipulated by the EU under its Stability and Growth Pact for countries belonging to the euro area). In December 2009 the Government announced reductions in welfare spending and public sector pay in order to reduce the budget deficit. Ireland's GDP declined by 7.6% in 2009, representing one of the most severe recessions of any advanced economy. With continued high unemployment and low consumer demand, GDP continued to contract, by 1.0%, in 2010. During that year uncertainty over the country's financial stability meant that the cost to Ireland of borrowing on the international bond markets increased to levels that were widely regarded as unsustainable. In November, under pressure from fellow members of the EU, concerned for the stability of the euro, the Irish Government was finally obliged to make a formal application for assistance from the EU and the IMF. Under the resulting agreement a total of €85,000m. was made available to Ireland; the total included bilateral loans from the United Kingdom, Denmark and Sweden. Of the total, €10,000m. was for the recapitalization of the banks, with a further €25,000m. as a contingency reserve for the banking system. The assistance was conditional upon the restructuring of the banking system, and the adoption of a four-year programme of austerity measures, involving reductions in expenditure amounting to €10,000m. and increases in taxation totalling €5,000m., in order to reduce the budgetary deficit to the equivalent of 3% of GDP by 2015. The budget for 2011, approved in December 2010, represented the first stage of this programme: it envisaged reductions in spending of €4,000m. (including reductions in child benefit, public sector pay and pensions) and increases in tax income (including the introduction of income tax for the lower-paid). Ireland's traditionally low rate of corporation tax (12.5%) was maintained, however (despite pressure from other EU member states), in order to encourage investment. In January 2012 the Government reported that it had succeeded in reducing the budgetary deficit for 2011 to the equivalent of 9.9% of GDP, a slight improvement on the stipulated target for that year. The budget for 2012, announced in December 2011, continued the austerity measures, envisaging reductions of €2,200m. in government spending (chiefly on social benefits, education, health and infrastructure projects) and increases amounting to some €1,500m. in indirect taxation. In February 2012, moreover, the Government announced plans to raise €3,000m. by the sale of state-owned assets, including gas and electricity suppliers and a stake in the national airline. The country's GDP increased by about 1.0% in 2011, according to the IMF, and there were improvements in agricultural production, tourism income and exports, but unemployment remained high, at around 14%. Growth in GDP in 2012 was not expected to exceed 0.5% (according to the IMF), constrained by weak domestic demand and a decline in demand for exports caused by the economic problems of Ireland's trading partners, particularly in the euro area.

PUBLIC HOLIDAYS

2013: 1 January (New Year), 17 March (St Patrick's Day), 1 April (Easter Monday), 6 May (May Bank Holiday), 3 June (June Bank Holiday), 5 August (August Bank Holiday), 28 October (October Bank Holiday), 25 December (Christmas Day), 26 December (St Stephen's Day).

Statistical Survey

Source (unless otherwise stated): Central Statistics Office, Skehard Rd, Cork; tel. (21) 4535000; fax (21) 4535555; e-mail information@cso.ie; internet www.cso.ie.

Area and Population

AREA, POPULATION AND DENSITY

Area (sq km)	70,182*
Population (census results)	
23 April 2006	4,239,848
28 April 2011 (preliminary)	
Males	2,268,698
Females	2,312,571
Total	4,581,269
Density (per sq km) at 2011 census	65.3

* 27,097 sq miles.

POPULATION BY AGE AND SEX

('000, official preliminary estimates at April 2010)

	Males	Females	Total
0–14	491.6	467.4	959.0
15–64	1,495.2	1,506.9	3,002.1
65 and over	229.3	280.1	509.5
Total	2,216.0	2,254.7	4,470.7

Note: Estimates not adjusted to take account of the results of the 2011 census; totals may not be equal to the sum of components, owing to rounding.

ADMINISTRATIVE DIVISIONS

(2011 census, preliminary)

Province/County	Area (sq km)	Population	Density (per sq km)
Connacht	17,713	542,039	30.6
Galway	6,151	250,541	40.7
Galway City	51	75,414	1,478.7
Galway County	6,010	175,127	29.1
Leitrim	1,589	31,778	20.0
Mayo	5,588	130,552	23.4
Roscommon	2,548	63,898	25.1
Sligo	1,837	65,270	35.5
Leinster	19,774	2,501,208	126.5
Carlow	898	54,532	60.7
Dublin	921	1,270,623	1,379.6
Dublin City	118	525,383	4,452.4
Dún Laoghaire-Rathdown	127	206,995	1,629.9
Fingal	453	273,051	602.8
South Dublin	223	265,174	1,189.1
Kildare	1,694	209,955	123.9
Kilkenny	2,072	95,360	46.0
Laoighis	1,719	80,458	46.8
Longford	1,091	38,970	35.7
Louth	832	122,808	147.6
Meath	2,335	184,034	78.8
Offaly	1,990	76,806	38.6
Westmeath	1,825	85,961	47.1
Wexford	2,365	145,273	61.4
Wicklow	2,033	136,448	67.1
Munster	24,608	1,243,726	50.5
Clare	3,442	116,885	34.0
Cork	7,508	518,128	69.0
Cork City	40	118,912	2,972.8
Cork County	7,468	399,216	53.5
Kerry	4,735	145,048	30.6
Limerick	2,760	191,306	69.3
Limerick City*	20	56,779	2,839.0
Limerick County*	2,740	134,527	49.1
Tipperary	4,304	158,652	36.9
Tipperary North	2,046	70,219	34.3
Tipperary South	2,258	88,433	39.2
Waterford	1,859	113,707	61.2
Waterford City	42	46,747	1,113.0
Waterford County	1,817	66,960	36.9
Ulster (part)	8,087	294,296	36.4
Cavan	1,932	72,874	37.7
Donegal	4,860	160,927	33.1
Monaghan	1,296	60,495	46.7
Total	70,182	4,581,269	65.3

* The boundary of Limerick City was expanded at the 2011 census to include the electoral division Limerick North Rural, but revised area details were not available.

PRINCIPAL TOWNS

(population at 2011 census, preliminary)

Dublin (capital)	525,383	Limerick	56,779
Cork	118,912	Waterford	46,747
Galway	75,414		

Mid-2010 (incl. suburbs, UN estimate): Dublin (capital) 1,098,636 (Source: UN, *World Urbanization Prospects: The 2009 Revision*).

BIRTHS, MARRIAGES AND DEATHS

	Registered live births		Registered marriages		Registered deaths	
	Number	Rate (per 1,000)	Number	Rate (per 1,000)	Number	Rate (per 1,000)
2003	61,529	15.5	20,302	5.1	29,074	7.3
2004	61,972	15.3	20,619	5.1	28,665	7.1
2005	61,372	14.8	21,355	5.2	28,260	6.8
2006	65,425	15.4	22,089	5.2	28,488	6.7
2007	70,620	16.3	22,544	5.2	28,050	6.5
2008	75,065	17.0	22,243	5.0	28,192	6.4
2009	74,278	16.7	21,541	4.8	28,898	6.5
2010	73,724	16.5	20,635	4.6	27,122	6.1

Life expectancy (years at birth, WHO estimates): 80 (males 77; females 82) in 2009 (Source: WHO, *World Health Statistics*).

IMMIGRATION AND EMIGRATION

('000, year ending April, official preliminary estimates)

Immigrants

Country of origin	2008/09	2009/10	2010/11
United Kingdom	10.7	7.4	9.6
Other EU	26.1	11.3	15.5
USA	3.1	1.3	1.0
Rest of the world	17.5	10.8	16.2
Total	57.4	30.8	42.3

Note: Data include large number of Irish nationals returning from permanent residence abroad ('000): 18.4 in 2008/09; 13.3 in 2009/10; 17.1 in 2010/11.

Emigrants

Country of destination	2008/09	2009/10	2010/11
United Kingdom	11.9	14.4	18.9
Other EU	29.5	24.8	22.9
USA	3.7	2.8	4.4
Rest of the world	20.1	23.3	30.1
Total	65.2	65.3	76.4

ECONOMICALLY ACTIVE POPULATION
('000 persons, quarterly labour force survey, April–June, estimates)

	2009	2010	2011
Agriculture, forestry and fishing	97.2	84.9	85.8
Mining and quarrying Manufacturing Electricity, gas and water	258.3	240.1	233.7
Construction	155.4	125.3	105.7
Wholesale and retail trade; repair of motor vehicles and motorcycles	277.7	269.1	265.6
Hotels and restaurants	119.8	119.8	107.2
Transport, storage and communications	168.1	163.8	169.6
Finance, insurance and real estate activities	108.7	103.2	103.9
Professional, scientific and technical activities	102.6	100.9	101.8
Administrative and support service activities	65.9	61.3	66.1
Public administration and defence; compulsory social security	107.7	107.8	100.2
Education	150.4	149.8	146.5
Health and social work	227.8	234.9	237.9
Other services	98.7	98.1	97.2
Total employed	1,938.5	1,859.5	1,821.3
Unemployed	264.6	293.6	304.5
Total labour force	2,203.1	2,152.7	2,125.9

Note: Totals may not be equal to the sum of components, owing to rounding.

Health and Welfare

KEY INDICATORS

Total fertility rate (children per woman, 2009)	2.0
Under-5 mortality rate (per 1,000 live births, 2009)	4
HIV/AIDS (% of persons aged 15–49, 2009)	0.2
Physicians (per 1,000 head, 2006)	2.9
Hospital beds (per 1,000 head, 2005)	5.6
Health expenditure (2008): US $ per head (PPP)	3,796
Health expenditure (2008): % of GDP	8.7
Health expenditure (2008): public (% of total)	76.9
Total carbon dioxide emissions ('000 metric tons, 2007)	44,283.1
Carbon dioxide emissions per head (metric tons, 2007)	10.2
Human Development Index (2011): ranking	7
Human Development Index (2011): value	0.908

For sources and definitions, see explanatory note on p. vi.

Agriculture

PRINCIPAL CROPS
('000 metric tons)

	2008	2009	2010
Wheat	993.0	690.0	669.0
Oats	174.0	146.0	148.0
Barley	1,294.0	1,227.0	1,223.0
Potatoes	371.9	361.3	330.5
Carrots and turnips*	24.6	26.4	25.4
Cabbages and other brassicas*	45.6	49.6	46.0

* FAO estimates.

Aggregate production ('000 metric tons, may include official, semi-official or estimated data): Total cereals 2,468.9 in 2008, 2,070.9 in 2009, 2,047.8 in 2010; Total roots and tubers 371.9 in 2008, 361.3 in 2009, 330.5 in 2010; Total vegetables (incl. melons) 239.8 in 2008, 221.2 in 2009, 222.9 in 2010; Total fruits (excl. melons) 56.0 in 2008, 50.9 in 2009, 48.2 in 2010.

Source: FAO.

LIVESTOCK
('000 head at June)

	2008	2009	2010
Cattle	6,902.1	6,890.7	6,606.6
Sheep	5,061.4	4,778.0	4,641.6
Pigs	1,462.0	1,395.2	1,518.3
Chickens*	13,200	13,500	13,800

* FAO estimates.

Source: FAO.

LIVESTOCK PRODUCTS
('000 metric tons)

	2008	2009	2010
Cattle meat	536.3	513.1	557.9
Sheep meat	58.7	55.0	47.8
Pig meat	203.9	196.5	215.0
Chicken meat*	85.5	86.0	83.2
Cows' milk	5,372.6	5,228.3†	5,237.4
Hen eggs	41.2†	41.6†	45.0*

* FAO estimate(s).
† Unofficial figure.

Source: FAO.

Forestry

ROUNDWOOD REMOVALS
('000 cubic metres, excluding bark)

	2008	2009	2010
Sawlogs, veneer logs and logs for sleepers	1,359	1,497	1,425
Pulpwood	734	678	893
Other industrial wood	87	87	108
Fuel wood	52	167	181
Total	2,232	2,429	2,607

Source: FAO.

SAWNWOOD PRODUCTION
('000 cubic metres, including railway sleepers)

	2008	2009	2010
Coniferous (softwood)	696	772	772
Broadleaved (hardwood)	1	2	0
Total	697	774	772

Source: FAO.

Fishing

('000 metric tons, live weight)

	2007	2008	2009
Capture	214.9	205.3	269.1
Blue whiting	31.1	22.9	9.3
Atlantic herring	30.8	28.1	26.3
Atlantic horse mackerel	30.0	36.6	40.7
Atlantic mackerel	48.8	44.9	61.4
Edible crab	11.5	7.1	5.7
Norway lobster	9.3	9.2	7.2
Aquaculture	57.1	44.9	47.2
Atlantic salmon	9.9	9.2	12.2
Blue mussel	37.4	27.1	26.5
Total catch	272.0	250.2	316.3

Note: Figures exclude marine mammals, recorded by number rather than weight. The number of harbour porpoises caught was: 2 in 2007; nil in 2008–09. Also excluded are aquatic plants ('000 metric tons, FAO estimates): 29.5 (North Atlantic rockweed 28.0) in 2007–09.

Source: FAO.

Mining

('000 metric tons, unless otherwise indicated)

	2007	2008	2009
Natural gas (million cu m)	566	502	413
Lead*	54.1	50.2	43.0
Zinc*	400.9	398.2	357.0
Peat†‡	3,800	3,800	3,800

* Figures refer to the metal content of ores mined.
† Excluding peat for horticultural use ('000 metric tons, estimates): 500 in 2006–08.
‡ Estimates.

Source: US Geological Survey.

Industry

SELECTED PRODUCTS

('000 metric tons, unless otherwise indicated)

	2006	2007	2008
Motor spirit (gasoline)	635	493	570
Gas-diesel oil (distillate fuel oil)	1,121	1,186	1,132
Mazout (residual fuel oil)	1,101	1,250	1,161
Electric energy (million kWh)	27,481	28,226	29,685

Cigarettes (million): 232 in 2003.

Source: UN Industrial Commodity Statistics Database.

Finance

CURRENCY AND EXCHANGE RATES

Monetary Units

100 cent = 1 euro (€).

Sterling and Dollar Equivalents (30 December 2011)

£1 sterling = €1.195
US $1 = €0.773;
€10 = £8.72 = $12.94.

Average Exchange Rate (euros per US $)

2009 0.7198
2010 0.7550
2011 0.7194

Note: The national currency was formerly the Irish pound (or punt). From the introduction of the euro, with Irish participation, on 1 January 1999, a fixed exchange rate of €1 = 78.7564 pence was in operation. Euro notes and coins were introduced on 1 January 2002. The euro and local currency circulated alongside each other until 9 February, after which the euro became the sole legal tender.

BUDGET

(€ million)

Revenue*	2007	2008†	2009†
Current revenue	59,922	57,620	58,891
Taxes on income and wealth	20,897	20,209	21,130
Social insurance and health contributions	9,053	9,476	9,636
Taxes on expenditure	25,155	22,783	22,735
Gross trading and investment income	2,013	2,385	2,499
Current transfers from rest of the world	263	157	138
Miscellaneous receipts	2,540	2,610	2,754
Capital revenue	5,191	4,020	4,247
Taxes on capital	3,498	2,030	2,010
Total	65,113	61,640	63,138

Expenditure‡	2007	2008†	2009†
Current expenditure	54,377	60,193	64,588
National debt interest	1,819	2,072	3,469
Current transfer payments to residents	21,566	24,095	26,907
Current transfer payments to rest of the world	2,173	2,342	2,538
Current expenditure on goods and services (excluding depreciation)	22,159	25,051	24,947
Current expenditure on goods and services by local authorities	5,539	5,539	5,579
Capital expenditure	10,292	11,822	10,713
Gross fixed capital formation	7,812	8,355	7,934
Total	64,669	72,015	75,301

* Excluding loan repayments and equity sales (€ million): 874 in 2007; 843 in 2008 (estimate); 896 in 2009 (estimate). Also excluding borrowing (€ million): –83 in 2007; 10,790 in 2008 (estimate); 12,613 in 2009 (estimate).
† Estimates.
‡ Excluding debt redemption (€ million): 515 in 2007; 538 in 2008 (estimate); 622 in 2009 (estimate). Also excluding loans and purchase of share capital (€ million): 721 in 2007; 721 in 2008–09 (estimates).

Source: Department of Finance.

2010 (€ million, estimates): Total revenue 36,009 (current 34,219, capital 1,789); total expenditure 54,753 (current 47,347, capital 7,406). Note: Expenditure data exclude Social Insurance Fund contributions and financial transactions (Source: Department of Finance, *2011 Estimates of Receipts and Expenditure*).

2011 (€ million, estimates): Total revenue 39,222 (current 36,737, capital 2,485); total expenditure 64,425 (current 48,148, capital 16,277). Note: Expenditure data exclude Social Insurance Fund contributions and financial transactions (incl. capital injections to Irish banks estimated at €17,600m. in 2011) (Source: Department of Finance, *2012 Estimates of Receipts and Expenditure*).

2012 (€ million, estimates): Total revenue 39,905 (current 38,081, capital 1,825); total expenditure 61,471 (current 51,223, capital 10,249). Note: Expenditure data exclude Social Insurance Fund contributions and financial transactions (Source: Department of Finance, *2012 Estimates of Receipts and Expenditure*).

INTERNATIONAL RESERVES

(US $ million at 31 December)

	2008	2009	2010
Gold (Eurosystem valuation)	167	213	272
IMF special drawing rights	98	1,179	1,104
Reserve position in IMF	164	245	237
Foreign exchange	609	517	502
Total	1,038	2,154	2,115

Source: IMF, *International Financial Statistics*.

MONEY SUPPLY

(incl. shares, depository corporations, national residence criteria, € million at 31 December)

	2008	2009	2010
Currency issued	9,645	12,480	12,966
Central Bank of Ireland	24,018	26,085	27,923
Demand deposits	69,956	88,733	85,501
Other deposits	108,078	96,833	84,512
Securities other than shares	187,128	179,182	119,811
Money market fund shares	59,899	56,877	65,192
Shares and other equity	75,113	91,545	112,858
Other items (net)	–26,639	–39,317	–16,956
Total	483,181	486,335	463,884

Source: IMF, *International Financial Statistics*.

COST OF LIVING
(Consumer Price Index; base: December 2006 = 100)

	2008	2009	2010
Food and non-alcoholic beverages	109.3	105.5	100.7
Alcoholic beverages and tobacco	106.4	113.1	110.2
Clothing and footwear	89.4	78.9	71.5
Housing, water, electricity, gas and other fuel	120.5	94.0	95.2
Furnishings, household equipment and routine household maintenance	96.6	93.6	89.8
Health	108.1	111.9	112.6
Transport	107.3	103.0	106.2
Communications	101.4	101.9	103.3
Recreation and culture	102.0	101.7	99.9
Education	108.0	114.9	122.2
Restaurants and hotels	106.2	106.2	103.4
Miscellaneous goods and services	102.7	110.5	111.7
All items	107.0	102.2	101.2

NATIONAL ACCOUNTS
(€ million at current prices)

National Income and Product

	2008	2009	2010
Gross domestic product in market prices	179,990	160,596	155,992
Net factor income from abroad	−25,317	−28,363	−27,785
Gross national product in market prices	154,673	132,233	128,207
Subsidies paid by the EU	1,797	1,719	1,494
Less Taxes paid to the EU	−484	−359	−400
Gross national income in market prices	155,986	133,592	129,301
Net current transfers from abroad (excl. EU subsidies and taxes)	−2,467	−2,567	−2,316
Gross national disposable income	153,519	131,026	126,985

Expenditure on the Gross Domestic Product

	2008	2009	2010
Government final consumption expenditure	29,955	28,503	26,222
Private final consumption expenditure	95,671	85,214	82,592
Changes in inventories	−596	−2,264	−852
Gross fixed capital formation	39,430	25,293	18,074
Total domestic expenditure	164,460	136,746	126,036
Exports of goods and services	150,181	145,902	157,673
Less Imports of goods and services	133,877	121,037	127,901
Statistical discrepancy	−774	−1,105	184
GDP in market prices	179,990	160,596	155,992

Gross Domestic Product by Economic Activity

	2008	2009	2010
Agriculture, forestry and fishing	3,677	3,011	3,491
Mining and quarrying; Manufacturing; Electricity, gas and water supply; Construction	48,406	42,236	43,442
Wholesale and retail trade, repair and hotels and restaurants; Transport, storage and communications	23,967	21,710	20,881
Public administration and defence	6,331	5,954	5,619
Other services	76,864	70,679	67,135
Statistical discrepancy	774	1,015	−184
—continued			
Gross value added at factor cost	160,019	144,605	140,384
Taxes (excl. taxes on products)	2,089	2,185	2,173
Less Subsidies (excl. subsidies on products)	1,826	1,805	1,601
Gross value added in basic prices	160,282	144,986	140,956
Taxes on products	20,618	16,417	15,774
Less Subsidies on products	910	807	738
GDP in market prices	179,990	160,596	155,992

BALANCE OF PAYMENTS
(US $ million)

	2008	2009	2010
Exports of goods f.o.b.	119,038	107,880	109,856
Imports of goods f.o.b.	−84,325	−62,768	−61,583
Trade balance	34,713	45,112	48,273
Exports of services	99,872	93,652	97,833
Imports of services	−110,875	−104,741	−107,270
Balance on goods and services	23,711	34,022	38,837
Other income received	123,774	76,471	76,418
Other income paid	−160,909	−115,253	−112,711
Balance on goods, services and income	−13,424	−4,760	2,544
Current transfers received	8,013	7,552	6,626
Current transfers paid	−9,886	−9,085	−8,215
Current balance	−15,297	−6,293	954
Capital account (net)	74	−1,844	−915
Direct investment abroad	−18,567	−26,836	−18,108
Direct investment from abroad	−16,339	26,551	27,085
Portfolio investment assets	−45,303	−749	28,611
Portfolio investment liabilities	−17,190	35,184	101,137
Financial derivatives assets	6,210	16,553	−8,006
Financial derivatives liabilities	−4,822	−19,921	−8,032
Other investment assets	−106,455	72,037	−21,004
Other investment liabilities	227,766	−103,524	−86,244
Net errors and omissions	−9,921	9,874	−15,520
Overall balance	157	1,034	−42

Source: IMF, *International Financial Statistics*.

External Trade

PRINCIPAL COMMODITIES
(distribution by SITC, € million)

Imports c.i.f.	2008	2009	2010
Food and live animals	4,681.1	4,417.0	4,578.8
Mineral fuels, lubricants, etc.	6,594.5	4,445.3	5,601.7
Petroleum and petroleum products	4,913.2	3,299.0	4,285.1
Chemicals and related products	8,282.1	7,371.8	8,758.2
Organic chemicals	1,748.7	1,679.9	2,100.2
Medicinal and pharmaceutical products	2,867.2	2,848.5	3,463.6
Basic manufactures	5,456.8	3,427.7	3,498.7
Machinery and transport equipment	20,048.5	14,292.2	12,324.0
Office machines and automatic data-processing equipment	6,749.4	3,677.9	2,701.4
Telecommunications and sound equipment	1,762.5	1,275.0	1,129.4
Other electrical machinery, apparatus, etc.	2,886.8	2,306.7	2,146.0
Road vehicles and parts (excl. tyres, engines and electrical parts)	3,228.5	898.5	1,558.0
Other transport equipment	2,299.0	3,918.5	2,618.5
Miscellaneous manufactured articles	6,860.6	6,122.3	6,152.5
Total (incl. others)*	57,584.8	45,061.1	45,507.2

* Including transactions not classified by commodity.

Exports f.o.b.	2008	2009	2010
Food and live animals	7,085.3	6,270.6	6,982.9
Chemicals and related products	44,225.5	47,987.7	52,227.4
Organic chemicals	17,815.8	17,655.9	19,063.9
Medicinal and pharmaceutical products	16,750.5	21,235.7	24,206.5
Essential oils, perfume materials and toilet and cleansing preparations	5,455.1	5,237.0	5,462.3
Machinery and transport equipment	18,364.7	13,585.2	11,001.0
Office machines and automatic data-processing equipment	9,329.1	6,441.8	4,515.6
Telecommunications and sound equipment	1,318.4	1,000.9	829.2
Electrical machinery, apparatus, etc.	4,792.7	3,335.7	3,080.5
Miscellaneous manufactured articles	8,902.5	9,190.0	10,471.1
Professional, scientific and controlling apparatus	2,805.7	3,009.5	3,260.4
Total (incl. others)*	86,394.4	84,238.9	89,391.8

* Including transactions not classified by commodity.

PRINCIPAL TRADING PARTNERS
(€ million)*

Imports c.i.f.	2008	2009	2010
Belgium	1,320.5	917.2	1,079.8
China, People's Republic (incl. Hong Kong and Macao)	4,275.1	2,879.2	2,754.5
Denmark	1,042.3	795.4	771.5
France	2,388.4	2,193.2	1,832.1
Germany	4,640.7	3,045.4	3,499.1
Italy	1,343.6	911.1	766.9
Japan	1,144.4	654.5	798.5
Korea, Republic	507.6	262.2	243.6
Netherlands	2,892.2	2,309.5	2,211.4
Norway	1,306.5	869.0	1,291.0
Singapore	745.9	537.0	507.8
Spain	936.6	568.7	667.1
Sweden	482.9	387.2	339.6
Switzerland	525.2	449.4	846.8
Taiwan	535.8	279.6	163.2
United Kingdom	19,202.7	13,728.1	14,587.5
USA	6,762.8	7,841.8	6,414.1
Total (incl. others)	57,584.8	45,061.1	45,507.2

Exports f.o.b.	2008	2009	2010
Belgium	12,253.1	14,130.4	12,818.8
China, People's Republic (incl. Hong Kong and Macao)	2,324.9	2,330.1	2,502.2
France	5,019.4	4,527.1	4,492.5
Germany	6,089.4	5,974.4	7,214.6
Italy	3,006.6	2,784.4	2,713.2
Japan	1,708.2	1,701.9	1,755.4
Malaysia	1,063.0	819.2	693.0
Netherlands	3,028.4	2,848.4	3,093.1
Spain	3,589.9	3,275.8	3,361.5
Sweden	872.9	684.1	670.2
Switzerland	2,560.8	2,433.4	3,557.4
United Kingdom	15,864.3	13,485.3	13,768.3
USA	16,674.3	18,271.9	20,763.2
Total (incl. others)	86,394.4	84,238.9	89,391.8

* Imports by country of origin; exports by country of final destination.

Transport

RAILWAYS
(traffic, '000)

	2007	2008	2009
Passengers carried	45,511	44,647	38,812
Freight tonnage	825	717	631

ROAD TRAFFIC
(licensed motor vehicles at 31 December)

	2008	2009	2010
Passenger cars	1,924,281	1,902,429	1,872,715
Lorries and vans	351,307	343,940	327,096
Buses and coaches	37,964	36,840	34,925
Motorcycles and mopeds	39,409	39,552	38,145

Source: Department of Transport, Dublin.

SHIPPING

Merchant Fleet
(registered at 31 December)

	2007	2008	2009
Number of vessels	246	229	231
Total displacement (grt)	187,238	185,521	189,189

Source: IHS Fairplay, *World Fleet Statistics*.

Sea-borne Freight Traffic
('000 metric tons)*

	2007	2008	2009
Goods loaded	15,232	15,031	12,839
Goods unloaded	38,907	36,049	28,998

* Figures refer to vessels engaged in both international and coastal trade.

CIVIL AVIATION
(traffic on scheduled services)

	2007	2008	2009
Kilometres flown (million)	442	525	573
Passengers carried ('000)	60,098	69,447	77,747
Passenger-km (million)	67,667	79,498	87,475
Total ton-km (million)	6,223	7,292	8,008

Source: UN, *Statistical Yearbook*.

Tourism

FOREIGN TOURIST ARRIVALS BY ORIGIN
('000)

	2007	2008	2009
United Kingdom*	4,369	4,170	3,665
France	394	412	390
Germany	436	456	408
Netherlands	155	151	134
Other continental Europe	1,592	1,542	1,395
USA	975	849	809
Canada	96	103	82
Other areas	316	343	306
Total	8,333	8,026	7,189

* Including residents of Northern Ireland.

Tourism receipts (€ million, excl. passenger transport, estimates): 6,294 in 2008; 4,890 in 2009; 4,077 in 2010 (provisional).

Source: World Tourism Organization.

Communications Media

	2008	2009	2010
Telephone lines ('000 in use)	2,222.7	2,131.9	2,078.0
Mobile cellular telephones ('000 subscribers)	5,048.1	4,704.5*†	4,701.5
Internet subscribers ('000)	1,128.7	1,104.1*	1,074.6
Broadband subscribers ('000)	769.7	870.6*	941.4

* At December.

† Revised methodology for enumeration, not strictly comparable with previous years.

Personal computers: 2,480,000 (582.1 per 1,000 persons) in 2006.

1997 (estimates): Radio receivers 2,550,000 in domestic use; Television receivers 1,470,000 in domestic use; Facsimile machines 100,000 (in use).

2004: Daily newspapers 7 (average circulation 742,000); Non-daily newspapers 63 (average circulation 2,117,000).

Sources: UNESCO, *Statistical Yearbook*; International Telecommunication Union.

Education

(2010/11 unless otherwise indicated)

	Institutions	Teachers (full-time)	Students (full-time)
National schools*	3,305	32,489	509,652
Secondary schools	383	13,228†	186,622
Vocational schools	254	8,335†	114,761
Community and comprehensive schools	92	4,240†	54,724
Teacher (primary and home economics) training colleges	7†	127‡	6,732†
Technology colleges§	15†	3,347‡	62,114
Universities and other Higher Education Authority Institutions	7†	3,507‡	88,308
Other aided institutions	4†	71‡	2,786

* State-aided primary schools; includes Special National Schools (numbering 140 in 2010/11).

† 2009/10.

‡ 2000/01.

§ Comprising 13 Institutes of Technology, the Tipperary Institute and the Hotel Training and Catering College, Killybegs, Co Donegal.

Sources: Central Statistics Office, and Department of Education and Skills.

Pupil-teacher ratio (primary education, UNESCO estimate): 15.8 in 2008/09 (Source: UNESCO Institute for Statistics).

Directory

The Government

HEAD OF STATE

Uachtarán (President): Michael D. Higgins (assumed office 11 November 2011).

THE CABINET
(May 2012)

A coalition of Fine Gael (FG) and the Labour Party (LP)

Taoiseach (Prime Minister): Enda Kenny (FG).

Tánaiste (Deputy Prime Minister), Minister for Foreign Affairs and Trade: Eamon Gilmore (LP).

Minister for Finance: Michael Noonan (FG).

Minister for Education and Skills: Ruairi Quinn (LP).

Minister for Public Expenditure and Reform: Brendan Howlin (LP).

Minister for Enterprise, Jobs and Innovation: Richard Bruton (FG).

Minister for Social Protection: Joan Burton (LP).

Minister for Arts, Heritage and Gaeltacht Affairs: Jimmy Deenihan (FG).

Minister for Communications, Energy and Natural Resources: Pat Rabbitte (LP).

Minister for the Environment, Community and Local Government: Phil Hogan (FG).

Minister for Justice, Equality and Defence: Alan Shatter (FG).

Minister for Agriculture, Fisheries and Food: Simon Coveney (FG).

Minister for Community, Equality and Gaeltacht Affairs: Frances Fitzgerald (FG).

Minister for Health: Dr James Reilly (FG).

Minister for Transport, Tourism and Sport: Leo Varadkar (FG).

MINISTRIES

Office of the President: Áras an Uachtaráin, Phoenix Park, Dublin 8; tel. (1) 6171000; fax (1) 6171001; e-mail webmaster@president.ie; internet www.president.ie.

Department of the Taoiseach: Government Bldgs, Upper Merrion St, Dublin 2; tel. (1) 6194000; fax (1) 6194297; e-mail webmaster@taoiseach.gov.ie; internet www.taoiseach.gov.ie.

Department of Agriculture, Fisheries and Food: Agriculture House, Kildare St, Dublin 2; tel. (1) 6072000; fax (1) 6616263; e-mail info@agriculture.gov.ie; internet www.agriculture.gov.ie.

Department of Arts, Heritage and Gaeltacht Affairs: 23 Kildare St, Dublin 2; tel. (1) 6313800; fax (1) 6611201; e-mail martincullen@dast.gov.ie; internet www.dast.gov.ie.

Department of Communications, Energy and Natural Resources: 29–31 Adelaide Rd, Dublin 2; tel. (1) 6782000; fax (1) 6782449; e-mail press.office@dcenr.gov.ie; internet www.dcenr.gov.ie.

Department of Defence: Station Rd, Newbridge, Co Kildare; tel. (45) 492000; fax (45) 492017; e-mail info@defence.irlgov.ie; internet www.defence.ie.

Department of Education and Skills: Marlborough St, Dublin 1; tel. (1) 8896714; fax (1) 8896712; e-mail bridie-hogan@education.gov.ie; internet www.education.ie.

Department of Enterprise, Jobs and Innovation: 23 Kildare St, Dublin 2; tel. (1) 6312121; fax (1) 6312827; e-mail info@entemp.ie; internet www.deti.ie.

Department of the Environment, Community and Local Government: Custom House, Dublin 1; tel. (1) 8882000; fax (1) 8882888; e-mail minister@environ.ie; internet www.environ.ie.

Department of Finance: Government Bldgs, Upper Merrion St, Dublin 2; tel. (1) 6767571; fax (1) 6789936; e-mail webmaster@finance.gov.ie; internet www.finance.gov.ie.

Department of Foreign Affairs: 80 St Stephen's Green, Dublin 2; tel. (1) 4780822; fax (1) 4082400; internet www.dfa.ie.

Department of Health: Hawkins House, Hawkins St, Dublin 2; tel. (1) 6354000; fax (1) 6354001; e-mail info@health.gov.ie; internet www.dohc.ie.

Department of Justice and Equality: 94 St Stephen's Green, Dublin 2; tel. (1) 6028202; fax (1) 6615461; e-mail info@justice.ie; internet www.inis.gov.ie/en/jelr.

Department of Public Expenditure and Reform: Government Bldgs, Upper Merrion St, Dublin 2.

Department of Social Protection: Áras Mhic Dhiarmada, Store St, Dublin 1; tel. (1) 7043000; fax (1) 7043870; e-mail info@welfare.ie; internet www.welfare.ie.

Department of Transport, Tourism and Sport: 44 Kildare St, Dublin 2; tel. (1) 6707444; fax (1) 6041185; e-mail info@transport.ie; internet www.transport.ie.

Legislature

OIREACHTAS (NATIONAL PARLIAMENT)

Parliament comprises two Houses: Dáil Éireann (House of Representatives), with 166 members (Teachtaí Dála), elected for a five-year term by universal adult suffrage; and Seanad Éireann (Senate), with 60 members serving a five-year term, of whom 11 are nominated by the Taoiseach (Prime Minister) and 49 elected (six by the universities and 43 from specially constituted panels).

Dáil Éireann

Leinster House, Kildare St, Dublin 2; tel. (1) 6183000; fax (1) 6184118; e-mail communications@oireachtas.ie; internet www.oireachtas.ie.

Ceann Comhairle (Chairman): SEÁN BARRETT.

Leas-Cheann Comhairle (Deputy Chairman): MICHAEL KITT.

General Election, 25 February 2011

Party	Votes*	% of votes*	Seats
Fine Gael	801,628	36.10	76
Labour Party	431,796	19.45	37
Fianna Fáil	387,358	17.45	20†
Independents	279,459	12.58	15
Sinn Féin	220,661	9.94	14
Socialist Party	26,770	1.21	2
People Before Profit Alliance	21,551	0.95	2
Green Party	41,039	1.85	—
Total (incl. others)	2,220,359	100.00	166

* The election was conducted by means of the single transferable vote. Figures refer to first-preference votes.

† Including the Ceann Comhairle (Chairman), who is automatically re-elected.

Seanad Éireann

Leinster House, Dublin 2; tel. (1) 6183000; fax (1) 6184118; e-mail info@oireachtas.ie; internet www.oireachtas.ie.

Cathaoirleach (Chairman): PADDY BURKE.

Leas-Chathaoirleach (Deputy Chairman): DENIS O'DONOVAN.

Elections were held to the Seanad Éireann in April 2011, with the closing date for the receipt of votes from the members of five vocational panels (Administrative, Agricultural, Cultural and Educational, Industrial and Commercial, and Labour) being 26 April, and that for the two university panels (National University of Ireland, and University of Dublin) being 27 April. Following the nomination of 11 members by the Taoiseach (Prime Minister) on 20 May, the strength of the parties was as follows:

Party	Elected	Appointed	Total seats
Fianna Fáil	18	1	19
Fine Gael	14	—	14
Labour Party	9	3	12
Sinn Féin	3	—	3
Independents	5	7	12
Total	49	11	60

Political Organizations

Communist Party of Ireland (Páirtí Cumannach na hÉireann): James Connolly House, 43 East Essex St, Dublin 2; tel. and fax (1) 6708707; e-mail cpoi@eircom.net; internet www.communistpartyofireland.ie; f. 1933; advocates a united, socialist, independent Ireland; Chair. LYNDA WALKER; Gen. Sec. EUGENE MCCARTAN.

Fianna Fáil (The Republican Party) (Soldiers of Destiny): 65–66 Lower Mount St, Dublin 2; tel. (1) 6761551; fax (1) 6785690; e-mail info@fiannafail.ie; internet www.fiannafail.ie; f. 1926; centrist; Pres. and Leader MICHEÁL MARTIN; Gen. Sec. SEÁN DORGAN.

Fine Gael (United Ireland Party) (Family of the Irish): 51 Upper Mount St, Dublin 2; tel. (1) 6198444; fax (1) 6625046; e-mail finegael@finegael.com; internet www.finegael.ie; f. 1933; centrist; Leader ENDA KENNY; Chair CHARLIE FLANAGAN; Gen. Sec. TOM CURRAN.

Green Party (Comhaontas Glas): 16–17 Suffolk St, Dublin 2; tel. (1) 6790012; fax (1) 6797168; e-mail info@greenparty.ie; internet www.greenparty.ie; f. 1981 as the Ecology Party of Ireland; name changed as above in 1983; advocates a humane, ecological society, freedom of information and political decentralization; Leader EAMON RYAN; Chair. RODERIC O'GORMAN; Asst Gen. Sec. ALISON MARTIN.

The Labour Party: 17 Ely Place, Dublin 2; tel. (1) 6784700; fax (1) 6612640; e-mail head.office@labour.ie; internet www.labour.ie; f. 1912; merged with Democratic Left (f. 1992) in 1999; democratic socialist party; affiliated to the Party of European Socialists; Leader EAMON GILMORE; Gen. Sec. ITA MCAULIFFE.

Sinn Féin (We Ourselves): 44 Parnell Sq., Dublin 1; tel. (1) 8726100; fax (1) 8733441; e-mail sfadmin@eircom.net; internet www.sinnfein.ie; f. 1905; advocates the termination of British rule in Northern Ireland; seeks a mandate to establish a democratic socialist republic in a reunified Ireland; Pres. GERRY ADAMS; Chair. DECLAN KEARNEY; Gen. Sec. DAWN DOYLE.

Socialist Party: 141 Thomas St, Dublin 8; tel. (1) 6772686; fax (1) 6772592; e-mail info@socialistparty.net; internet www.socialistparty.net; f. 1996; mem. of the Committee for a Workers' International (CWI); advocates a socialist Ireland as part of a free and voluntary socialist federation of Ireland, Scotland, England and Wales; anti-EU; Leader JOE HIGGINS.

The Workers' Party: 48 North Great George's St, Dublin 1; tel. (1) 8740716; fax (1) 8748702; e-mail wpi@indigo.ie; internet www.workerspartyireland.net; f. 1905; fmrly Sinn Féin The Workers' Party; name changed as above in 1982; aims to establish a unitary socialist state on the island of Ireland; Pres. MICHAEL FINNEGAN; Gen. Sec. JOHN LOWRY.

Diplomatic Representation

EMBASSIES IN IRELAND

Argentina: 15 Ailesbury Dr., Dublin 4; tel. (1) 2691546; fax (1) 2600404; e-mail embassyofargentina@eircom.net; Ambassador Dr MARÍA ESTHER TERESA BONDANZA.

Australia: Fitzwilton House, 7th Floor, Wilton Terrace, Dublin 2; tel. (1) 6645300; fax (1) 6785185; e-mail austremb.dublin@dfat.gov.au; internet www.ireland.embassy.gov.au; Ambassador BRUCE LAWRENCE DAVIS.

Austria: 15 Ailesbury Court, 93 Ailesbury Rd, Dublin 4; tel. (1) 2694577; fax (1) 2830860; e-mail dublin-ob@bmeia.gv.at; Ambassador Dr WALTER HAGG.

Belgium: 2 Shrewsbury Rd, Dublin 4; tel. (1) 2057100; fax (1) 2057106; e-mail dublin@diplobel.fed.be; internet www.diplomatie.be/dublin; Ambassador ROBERT DEVRIESE.

Brazil: Harcourt Centre, Block 8, Charlotte Way, Dublin 2; tel. (1) 4756000; fax (1) 4751341; e-mail info@brazil.ie; internet www.brazil.ie; Ambassador PEDRO FERNANDO BRÊTAS BASTOS.

Bulgaria: 22 Burlington Rd, Dublin 4; tel. (1) 6603293; fax (1) 6603915; e-mail bulgarianembassydublin@eircom.net; internet www.mfa.bg/dublin; Ambassador EMIL SAVOV YALNAZOV.

Canada: 7–8 Wilton Terrace, 3rd Floor, Dublin 2; tel. (1) 2344000; fax (1) 2344001; e-mail dubln@international.gc.ca; internet www.canadainternational.gc.ca/ireland-irlande; Ambassador LOYOLA HEARN.

Chile: 44 Wellington Rd, Dublin 4; tel. (1) 6675094; fax (1) 6675156; e-mail echile.irlanda@minrel.gov.cl; internet www.chileabroad.gov.cl/irlanda; Ambassador LEONEL SEARLE.

China, People's Republic: 40 Ailesbury Rd, Dublin 4; tel. (1) 2691707; fax (1) 2839938; e-mail chinaemb_ie@mfa.gov.cn; internet ie.china-embassy.org; Ambassador LUO LINQUAN.

Croatia: Adelaide Chambers, Peter St, Dublin 8; tel. (1) 4767181; fax (1) 4767183; e-mail croemb.dublin@mvpei.hr; internet ie.mfa.hr; Ambassador JASNA OGNJANOVAC.

Cuba: 2 Adelaide Court, Adelaide Rd, Dublin 2; tel. (1) 4752999; fax (1) 4763674; e-mail trujillo@eircom.net; Ambassador TERESITA TRUJILLO.

Cyprus: 71 Lower Leeson St, Dublin 2; tel. (1) 6763060; fax (1) 6763099; e-mail dublinembassy@mfa.gov.cy; internet www.mfa.gov.cy/embassydublin; Ambassador MICHALIS STAVRINOS.

Czech Republic: 57 Northumberland Rd, Dublin 4; tel. (1) 6681135; fax (1) 6681660; e-mail dublin@embassy.mzv.cz; internet www.mfa.cz/dublin; Ambassador TOMÁŠ KAFKA.

Denmark: Block E, 7th Floor, Iveagh Court, Harcourt Rd, Dublin 2; tel. (1) 4756404; fax (1) 4784536; e-mail dubamb@um.dk; internet www.irland.um.dk; Ambassador NIELS CHRISTEN PULTZ.

Egypt: 12 Clyde Rd, Ballsbridge, Dublin 4; tel. (1) 6606566; fax (1) 6683745; e-mail info@embegyptireland.ie; internet www.embegyptireland.ie; Ambassador SHERIF ELKHOLI.

Estonia: Riversdale House, St Ann's, Ailesbury Rd, Dublin 4; tel. (1) 2196730; fax (1) 2196731; e-mail embassy.dublin@mfa.ee; internet www.estemb.ie; Ambassador MAIT MARTINSON.

Ethiopia: 26 Upper Fitzwilliam St, Dublin 2; tel. (1) 6787062; fax (1) 6787065; e-mail info@ethiopianembassy.ie; internet www

.ethiopianembassy.ie; Ambassador LELA-ALEM GEBREYOHANNES TEDLA.

Finland: Russell House, Stokes Place, St Stephen's Green, Dublin 2; tel. (1) 4781344; fax (1) 4783727; e-mail sanomat.dub@formin.fi; internet www.finland.ie; Ambassador PERTTI MAJANEN.

France: 36 Ailesbury Rd, Ballsbridge, Dublin 4; tel. (1) 2775000; fax (1) 2775001; e-mail chancellerie@ambafrance.ie; internet www.ambafrance-ie.org; Ambassador EMMANUELLE D'ACHON.

Georgia: 32 College Sq., Wainsfort Manor Dr., Terenure, Dublin 6; tel. (1) 4067956; Chargé d'affaires IRAKLI KOPLATADZE.

Germany: 31 Trimleston Ave, Booterstown, Blackrock, Co Dublin; tel. (1) 2693011; fax (1) 2693946; e-mail info@dublin.diplo.de; internet www.dublin.diplo.de; Ambassador Dr ECKHARD LÜBKEMEIER.

Greece: 1 Upper Pembroke St, Dublin 2; tel. (1) 6767254; fax (1) 6618892; e-mail embgr@eircom.net; internet www.ypex.gov.gr/dublin; Ambassador CONSTANTINA ZAGORIANOU-PRIFTI.

Holy See: 183 Navan Rd, Dublin 7; tel. (1) 8380577; fax (1) 8380276; e-mail nuncioirl@eircom.net; Apostolic Nuncio Most Rev. CHARLES J. BROWN (Titular Archbishop of Aquileia).

Hungary: 2 Fitzwilliam Place, Dublin 2; tel. (1) 6612902; fax (1) 6612880; e-mail mission.dub@kum.hu; internet www.mfa.gov.hu/kulkepviselet/ie; Ambassador Dr TAMÁS MAGYARICS.

India: 6 Leeson Park, Dublin 6; tel. (1) 4966792; fax (1) 4978074; e-mail indembassy@eircom.net; internet www.indianembassy.ie; Ambassador DEBASHISH CHAKRAVARTI.

Iran: 72 Mount Merrion Ave, Blackrock, Co Dublin; tel. (1) 2880252; fax (1) 2834246; e-mail iranembassy@indigo.ie; Ambassador HOSSEIN PANAHIAZAR.

Israel: Carrisbrook House, 122 Pembroke Rd, Dublin 4; tel. (1) 2309400; fax (1) 2309446; e-mail info@dublin.mfa.gov.il; internet dublin.mfa.gov.il; Ambassador BOAZ MODAI.

Italy: 63–65 Northumberland Rd, Dublin 4; tel. (1) 6601744; fax (1) 6682759; e-mail ambasciata.dublino@esteri.it; internet www.ambdublino.esteri.it; Ambassador MAURIZIO ZANINI.

Japan: Nutley Bldg, Merrion Centre, Nutley Lane, Dublin 4; tel. (1) 2028300; fax (1) 2838726; e-mail cultural@embjp.ie; internet www.ie.emb-japan.go.jp; Ambassador CHIHIRO ATSUMI.

Kenya: 11 Elgin Rd, Dublin 4; tel. (1) 6136380; fax (1) 6685506; e-mail info@kenyaembassyireland.net; internet www.kenyaembassyireland.net; Ambassador CATHERINE MUIGAI MWANGI.

Korea, Republic: Clyde House, 15 Clyde Rd, POB 2101, Dublin 4; tel. (1) 6608800; fax (1) 6608716; e-mail irekoremb@mofat.go.kr; internet irl.mofat.go.kr; Ambassador KIM CHANG-YEOB.

Latvia: 92 St Stephen's Green, Dublin 2; tel. (1) 4780161; fax (1) 4780162; e-mail embassy.ireland@mfa.gov.lv; internet www.am.gov.lv/en/ireland; Ambassador PĒTERIS KĀRLIS ELFERTS.

Lesotho: 2 Clanwilliam Sq., Grand Canal Quay, Dublin 2; tel. (1) 6762233; fax (1) 6762258; e-mail info@lesothoembassy.ie; Ambassador PARAMENTE PHAMOTSE.

Lithuania: 47 Ailesbury Rd, Ballsbridge, Dublin 4; tel. (1) 6688292; fax (1) 6680004; e-mail amb.ie@urm.lt; internet ie.mfa.lt; Ambassador VIDMANTAS PURLYS.

Malaysia: Level 3A–5A Shelbourne House, Shelbourne Rd, Dublin 4; tel. (1) 6677280; fax (1) 6677283; e-mail mwdublin@mwdublin.ie; Ambassador Dato' RAMLI NAAM.

Malta: 15 Leeson Street Lower, Dublin 2; tel. (1) 6762340; fax (1) 6766066; e-mail maltaembassy.dublin@gov.mt; Chargé d'affaires CHANTAL SCIBERRAS.

Mexico: 19 Raglan Rd, Dublin 4; tel. (1) 6673105; fax (1) 6641013; e-mail info@embamex.ie; internet www.sre.gob.mx/irlanda; Ambassador CARLOS EUGENIO GARCIA DE ALBA.

Morocco: 39 Raglan Rd, Dublin 4; tel. (1) 6609449; fax (1) 6609468; e-mail sifamdub@indigo.ie; Ambassador ANAS KHALES.

Netherlands: 160 Merrion Rd, Dublin 4; tel. (1) 2693444; fax (1) 2839690; e-mail dub-info@minbuza.nl; internet www.netherlandsembassy.ie; Ambassador ROBERT J. H. ENGELS.

Nigeria: 56 Leeson Park, Dublin 6; tel. (1) 6604366; fax (1) 6604092; e-mail enquiries@nigerianembassydublin.org; internet www.nigerianembassydublin.org; Ambassador FELIX YUSUFU PWOL.

Norway: 34 Molesworth St, Dublin 2; tel. (1) 6621800; fax (1) 6621890; e-mail emb.dublin@mfa.no; internet www.norway.ie; Ambassador ROALD NÆSS.

Pakistan: Ailesbury Villa, 1B Ailesbury Rd, Dublin 4; tel. (1) 2613032; fax (1) 2613007; e-mail pakembdublin@yahoo.ie; internet www.pakembassydublin.com; Ambassador NAGHMANA A. HASHMI.

Philippines: Fitzwilliam Business Centre, 77 Sir John Rogerson's Quay, Dublin 2; tel. (1) 6401946; fax (1) 6401945; e-mail dublin.philembassy@gmail.com; Ambassador (vacant).

Poland: 5 Ailesbury Rd, Ballsbridge, Dublin 4; tel. (1) 2830855; fax (1) 2698309; e-mail dublin@msz.gov.pl; internet www.dublin.polemb.net; Ambassador BERNARDO FUTSCHER PEREIRA (designate).

Portugal: 15 Leeson Park, Dublin 6; tel. (1) 4127040; fax (1) 4970299; e-mail embport@dublin.dgaccp.pt; internet www.embassyportugal.ie; Ambassador JOSÉ DUARTE RAMALHO ORTIGÃO.

Romania: 26 Waterloo Rd, Dublin 4; tel. (1) 6681085; fax (1) 6681761; e-mail ambrom@eircom.net; internet dublin.mae.ro; Ambassador IULIAN BUGA.

Russia: 184–186 Orwell Rd, Rathgar, Dublin 14; tel. (1) 4922048; fax (1) 4923525; e-mail russiane@indigo.ie; internet www.ireland.mid.ru; Chargé d'affaires SERGEY PETROVICH.

Saudi Arabia: 6–7 Fitzwilliam Sq. East, Dublin 2; tel. (1) 6760704; fax (1) 6760715; e-mail duemb@mofa.gov.sa; Ambassador ABD AL-AZIZ ABD AL-RAHMAN ALDRISS.

Slovakia: 20 Clyde Rd, Ballsbridge, Dublin 4; tel. (1) 6600012; fax (1) 6600014; e-mail emb.dublin@mzv.sk; internet www.mzv.sk/dublin; Ambassador ROMAN BUŽEK.

Slovenia: Morrison Chambers, 2nd Floor, 32 Nassau St, Dublin 2; tel. (1) 6705240; fax (1) 6705243; e-mail vdb@gov.si; internet dublin.veleposlanistvo.si; Ambassador JASNA GERŠAK.

South Africa: Alexandra House, 2nd Floor, Earlsfort Centre, Earlsfort Terrace, Dublin 2; tel. (1) 6615553; fax (1) 6615590; e-mail redmondh@foreign.gov.za; Ambassador AZWINDINI JEREMIAH DINGAAN NDOU.

Spain: 17A Merlyn Park, Dublin 4; tel. (1) 2691640; fax (1) 2691854; e-mail emb.dublin.inf@maec.es; internet www.maec.es/embajadas/dublin; Ambassador JAVIER GARRIGUES FLÓREZ.

Switzerland: 6 Ailesbury Rd, Dublin 4; tel. (1) 2186382; fax (1) 2830344; e-mail dubvertretung@eda.admin.ch; internet www.eda.admin.ch/dublin; Ambassador BEAT LOELIGER.

Turkey: 11 Clyde Rd, Dublin 4; tel. (1) 6685240; fax (1) 6685014; e-mail turkembassy@eircom.net; Ambassador ALTAY CENGIZER.

Ukraine: 16 Elgin Rd, Ballsbridge, Dublin 4; tel. (1) 6685189; fax (1) 6697917; e-mail ukrembassy@eircom.net; internet www.mfa.gov.ua/ireland; Ambassador SERGII REVA.

United Arab Emirates: Glandore Business Centre, Fitzwilliam Hall, Fitzwilliam Pl., Dublin 2; tel. (1) 6698588; fax (1) 6698557; e-mail dublin@mofa.gov.ae; Ambassador KHALID NASSER RASHID LOOTAH.

United Kingdom: 29 Merrion Rd, Dublin 4; tel. (1) 2053700; fax (1) 2053885; e-mail chancery.dublx@fco.gov.uk; internet www.britishembassy.ie; Ambassador. DOMINICK JOHN CHILCOTT.

USA: 42 Elgin Rd, Dublin 4; tel. (1) 6688777; fax (1) 6689946; e-mail dublinrsvp@state.gov; internet dublin.usembassy.gov; Ambassador DANIEL M. ROONEY.

Judicial System

Justice is administered in public by judges appointed by the President on the advice of the Government. The judges of all courts are completely independent in the exercise of their judicial functions. The jurisdiction and organization of the courts are dealt with in the Courts (Establishment and Constitution) Act, 1961, and the Courts (Supplemental Provisions) Acts, 1961 to 1981.

Attorney-General: MÁIRE WHELAN.

SUPREME COURT

An Chúirt Uachtarach (The Supreme Court)

Four Courts, Inns Quay, Dublin 7; tel. (1) 8886569; fax (1) 8732332; e-mail supremecourt@courts.ie; internet www.supremecourt.ie.

Consisting of the Chief Justice and seven other judges, the Supreme Court has appellate jurisdiction from all decisions of the High Court. The President of Ireland may, after consultation with the Council of State, refer a bill that has been passed by both Houses of the Oireachtas (other than a money bill or certain others) to the Supreme Court to establish whether it or any other provisions thereof are repugnant to the Constitution. The President of the High Court is ex officio a member of the Supreme Court.

Chief Justice: SUSAN DENHAM.

Judges: SUSAN DENHAM, ADRIAN HARDIMAN, NIAL FENNELLY, FIDELMA MACKEN, JOSEPH FINNEGAN, DONAL O'DONNELL, LIAM MCKECHNIE.

COURT OF CRIMINAL APPEAL

The Court of Criminal Appeal, consisting of the Chief Justice or an ordinary judge of the Supreme Court and two judges of the High Court, deals with appeals by persons convicted on indictment, where leave to appeal has been granted. The Court has jurisdiction to review a conviction or sentence on the basis of an alleged miscarriage of justice. The Director of Public Prosecutions may appeal against an unduly lenient sentence. The decision of the Court of Criminal Appeal is final unless the Court or Attorney-General or the Director of Public Prosecutions certifies that a point of law involved should, in the public interest, be taken to the Supreme Court.

HIGH COURT

An Ard-Chúirt (The High Court)

Four Courts, Inns Quay, Dublin 7; tel. (1) 8886000; fax (1) 8886125; e-mail highcourtcentraloffice@courts.ie; internet www.courts.ie.

Consisting of the President of the High Court and 37 ordinary judges, the High Court has full original jurisdiction in, and power to determine, all matters and questions whether of law or fact, civil or criminal. The High Court on circuit acts as an appeal court from the Circuit Court. The Central Criminal Court sits as directed by the President of the High Court to try criminal cases outside the jurisdiction of the Circuit Court. The duty of acting as the Central Criminal Court is assigned to a judge, or judges, of the High Court. The Chief Justice and the President of the Circuit Court are ex officio additional Judges of the High Court.

President: NICHOLAS KEARNS.

Judges: VIVIAN LAVAN, PAUL J. P. CARNEY, DECLAN BUDD, MARY LAFFOY, MICHAEL MORIARTY, PETER KELLY, JOHN QUIRKE, IARFHLAITH O'NEILL, RODERICK MURPHY, DANIEL HERBERT, PAUL BUTLER, HENRY ABBOTT, EAMON DE VALERA, MARY FINLAY GEOGHEGAN, MICHAEL PEART, BARRY WHITE, PAUL GILLIGAN, SEAN RYAN, ELIZABETH DUNNE, MICHAEL HANNA, JOHN MACMENAMIN, FRANK CLARKE, KEVIN FEENEY, BRIAN MCGOVERN, PETER CHARLETON, MAUREEN CLARK, JOHN HEDIGAN, BRYAN MCMAHON, GEORGE BIRMINGHAM, MARY C. IRVINE, JOHN A. EDWARDS, PATRICK J. MCCARTHY, GARRETT SHEEHAN, DANIEL O'KEEFFE, JOHN COOKE, GERARD HOGAN.

Master of the High Court: EDMUND HONOHAN.

CIRCUIT AND DISTRICT COURTS

The civil jurisdiction of the Circuit Court is limited to €38,092.14 in contract and tort and in actions founded on hire-purchase and credit-sale agreements and to a rateable value of €252.95 in equity, and in probate and administration, but where the parties consent the jurisdiction is unlimited. In criminal matters the Court has jurisdiction in all cases except murder, rape, treason, piracy and allied offences. One circuit court judge is permanently assigned to each of the eight circuits with the exception of Dublin, which has 10 judges, and Cork, which has three. The remainder of the 38 judges are not permanently assigned to any circuit. The President of the District Court is ex officio an additional Judge of the Circuit Court. The Circuit Court acts as an appeal court from the District Court, which has a summary jurisdiction in a large number of criminal cases where the offence is not of a serious nature. In civil matters the District Court has jurisdiction in contract and tort (except slander, libel, seduction, slander of title, malicious prosecution and false imprisonment) where the claim does not exceed €6,348.69 and in actions founded on hire-purchase and credit-sale agreements.

All criminal cases, except those dealt with summarily by a judge in the District Court, are tried by a judge and a jury of 12 members. Juries are also used in some civil cases in the High Court. In a criminal case 10 members of the jury may, in certain circumstances, agree on a verdict, and in a civil case the agreement of nine members is sufficient.

President of An Chúirt Chuarda (the Circuit Court): MATTHEW DEERY.

President of An Chúirt Dúiche (the District Court): MIRIAM MALONE.

Religion

CHRISTIANITY

The organization of the churches takes no account of the partition of the island of Ireland into two separate political entities; both Northern Ireland and Ireland are subject to a unified ecclesiastical jurisdiction. The Roman Catholic Primate of All Ireland and the Church of Ireland (Protestant Episcopalian) Primate of All Ireland have their seats in Northern Ireland, at Armagh, and the headquarters of the Presbyterian Church in Ireland is at Belfast, Northern Ireland.

Adherents of the Roman Catholic Church were enumerated at 3,681,446 in the 2006 census, representing some 87% of the population. In the same year there were 125,585 adherents of the Church of Ireland, 23,546 of the Presbyterian Church and 12,160 of the Methodist Church.

Irish Council of Churches: Inter-Church Centre, 48 Elmwood Ave, Belfast, BT9 6AZ, Northern Ireland; tel. (28) 9066-3145; fax (28) 9066-4160; e-mail info@irishchurches.org; internet www.irishchurches.org; f. 1922; present name adopted 1966; 14 mem. churches; Pres. Rev. RICHARD CLARKE; Exec. Officer MERVYN MCCULLAGH.

The Roman Catholic Church

The island of Ireland comprises four archdioceses and 22 dioceses. Numerous Roman Catholic religious orders are strongly established in the state; these play an important role, particularly in the spheres of education, health and social welfare.

Irish Episcopal Conference: Ara Coeli, Cathedral Rd, Armagh, BT61 7QY, Northern Ireland; tel. (28) 3752-2045; fax (28) 3752-6182; e-mail admin@aracoeli.com; Pres. Cardinal SEÁN B. BRADY (Archbishop of Armagh).

Archbishop of Armagh and Primate of All Ireland: Cardinal SEÁN B. BRADY, Ara Coeli, Cathedral Rd, Armagh, BT61 7QY, Northern Ireland; tel. (28) 3752-2045; fax (28) 3752-6182; e-mail admin@aracoeli.com; internet www.armagharchdiocese.org.

Archbishop of Cashel and Emly: Most Rev. DERMOT CLIFFORD, Archbishop's House, Thurles, Co Tipperary; tel. (504) 21512; fax (504) 22680; e-mail office@cashel-emly.ie; internet www.cashel-emly.ie.

Archbishop of Dublin and Primate of Ireland: Most Rev. Dr DIARMUID MARTIN, Archbishop's House, Drumcondra, Dublin 9; tel. (1) 8379253; fax (1) 8360793; e-mail communications@dublindiocese.ie; internet www.dublindiocese.ie.

Archbishop of Tuam: Most Rev. Dr MICHAEL NEARY, Archbishop's House, St Jarlath's, Tuam, Co Galway; tel. (93) 24166; fax (93) 28070; e-mail archdiocesetuam@gmail.com; internet www.tuamarchdiocese.org.

Church of Ireland
(The Anglican Communion)

Ireland (including Northern Ireland) comprises two archdioceses and 10 dioceses.

The Representative Body of the Church of Ireland
Church of Ireland House, Church Ave, Rathmines, Dublin 6; tel. (1) 4978422; fax (1) 4978821; e-mail office@rcbdub.org; internet rcb.ireland.anglican.org; Chief Officer and Sec. DENIS REARDON.

Archbishop of Armagh and Primate of All Ireland and Metropolitan: Most Rev. ALAN HARPER, The See House, Cathedral Close, Armagh, BT61 7EE, Northern Ireland; tel. (28) 37522858; fax (28) 37510596; e-mail office@armagh.anglican.org; internet armagh.anglican.org.

Archbishop of Dublin and Bishop of Glendalough, Primate of Ireland and Metropolitan: Most Rev. Dr JOHN R. W. NEILL, The See House, 17 Temple Rd, Milltown, Dublin 6; tel. (1) 4977849; fax (1) 4976355; e-mail archbishop@dublin.anglican.org; internet www.dublin.anglican.org.

Orthodox Churches

Greek Orthodox Church in Ireland: Sacred Church of the Annunciation, 46 Arbour Hill, Dublin 7; tel. and fax (1) 6779020; Pres. Very Rev. Dr IRENEU IOAN CRACIUN.

Russian Orthodox Church (Moscow Patriarchate) in Ireland: Harold's Cross Rd, Dublin 6; tel. (1) 4969038; fax (1) 4640976; e-mail rvgeorge@utvinternet.com; internet www.stpeterstpaul.net; f. 2001; Parish Priest Very Rev. Fr MICHAEL GOGOLEFF.

Other Christian Churches

Association of Baptist Churches in Ireland: The Baptist Centre, 19 Hillsborough Rd, Moira, BT67 0HG, Northern Ireland; tel. (28) 9261-9267; e-mail abc@thebaptistcentre.org; internet www.baptistsinireland.org; Pres. D. BAXTER.

Lutheran Church in Ireland: Lutherhaus, 24 Adelaide Rd, Dublin 2; tel. and fax (1) 6766548; e-mail info@lutheran-ireland.org; internet www.lutheran-ireland.org; Pres. Pastors Dr JOACHIM DIESTELKAMP, CORINNA DIESTELKAMP.

Methodist Church in Ireland: 1 Fountainville Ave, Belfast, BT9 6AN, Northern Ireland; tel. (28) 9032-4554; fax (28) 9023-9467; e-mail secretary@irishmethodist.org; internet www.irishmethodist.org; Pres. Rev. IAN HENDERSON.

Presbyterian Church in Ireland: Church House, Fisherwick Place, Belfast, BT1 6DW, Northern Ireland; tel. (28) 9032-2284; fax (28) 9041-7301; e-mail info@presbyterianireland.org; internet www.presbyterianireland.org; Moderator of Gen. Assembly Rev. IVAN PATTERSON; Clerk of Assembly and Gen. Sec. Rev. Dr DONALD WATTS.

Religious Society of Friends (Quakers) in Ireland: Quaker House, Stocking Lane, Rathfarnham, Dublin 16; tel. (1) 4998003; fax (1) 4998005; e-mail office@quakers.ie; internet www.quakers.ie; 15

meetings in Ireland and 12 in Northern Ireland; Recording Clerk ROSEMARY CASTAGNER.

ISLAM

The Muslim population of Ireland stood at 32,539 at the 2006 census.

Irish Council of Imams: 19 Roebuck Rd, Clonskeagh, Dublin 14; tel. (1) 2080000; e-mail imamhalawa@islamireland.ie; f. 2006; comprises 14 imams from across Ireland; Chair. Imam Sheikh HUSSEIN HALAWA; Vice-Chair. Sheikh YAHYA AL-HUSSEIN.

Islamic Cultural Centre of Ireland: 19 Roebuck Rd, Clonskeagh, Dublin 14; tel. (1) 2080000; fax (1) 2080001; e-mail info@islamireland.ie; internet www.islamireland.ie; f. 1996; CEO Dr NOOH AL-KADDO; Imam Sheikh HUSSEIN HALAWA.

Islamic Foundation of Ireland: 163 South Circular Rd, Dublin 8; tel. (1) 4533242; fax (1) 4532785; e-mail info@islaminireland.com; internet www.islaminireland.com; f. 1959; religious, cultural, educational and social org.; Imam YAHYA MUHAMMAD AL-HUSSEIN.

Supreme Muslim Council of Ireland: Dublin; e-mail irishmuslimcouncil@gmail.com; f. 2003; seeks to co-operate with educational institutions and state bodies; Chair. Sheikh Dr SHAHEED SATARDIEN.

JUDAISM

At the 2006 census, the Jewish community numbered 1,930. In 2008 there were a total of three synagogues operating, of which two were Orthodox and one was progressive.

Chief Rabbi: (vacant), Herzog House, Zion Rd, Rathgar, Dublin 6; tel. (1) 4923751; fax (1) 4920888; e-mail ofchiefrabbi@jewishireland.org; internet www.jewishireland.org.

The Press

A significant feature of the Irish press is the number of weekly and twice-weekly newspapers published in provincial centres.

DAILIES

(Average net circulation figures, including Ireland and the United Kingdom, as at December 2011, unless otherwise stated)

Cork

Evening Echo: City Quarter, Lapps Quay, Cork; tel. (21) 4272722; fax (21) 4273846; e-mail maurice.gubbins@eecho.ie; internet www.eecho.ie; f. 1892; Chief Exec. DAN LINEHAN; Editor MAURICE GUBBINS; circ. 25,904 (2007).

Irish Examiner: City Quarter, Lapps Quay, Cork; tel. (21) 4272722; fax (21) 4273846; e-mail editor@examiner.ie; internet www.irishexaminer.com; f. 1841; Editor TIM VAUGHAN; circ. 42,083.

Dublin

Evening Herald: Independent House, 27–32 Talbot St, Dublin 1; tel. (1) 7055333; fax (1) 7055497; e-mail hnews@independent.ie; internet www.herald.ie; f. 1891; Editor STEPHEN RAE; circ. 62,411.

Irish Daily Mail: Embassy House, 3rd Floor, Herbert Park Lane, Dublin 4; tel. (1) 6375800; fax (1) 6375880; internet www.dailymail.co.uk; Propr Associated Newspapers (United Kingdom); Editor-in-Chief TED VERITY; circ. 50,486.

Irish Daily Star: Bldg 4, Level 5, Dundrum Town Centre, Sandyford Rd, Dublin 16; tel. (1) 4993400; fax (1) 4902193; e-mail info@thestar.ie; internet www.thestar.ie; Editor MICHAEL O'KANE; circ. 81,105 (Ireland only).

Irish Independent: 27–32 Talbot St, Dublin 1; tel. (1) 7055333; fax (1) 8720304; internet www.independent.ie; f. 1905; Editor GERRY O'REGAN; circ. 131,161.

The Irish Times: Irish Times Bldg, 24–28 Tara St, Dublin 2; tel. (1) 6758000; fax (1) 6758035; e-mail newsdesk@irishtimes.com; internet www.irishtimes.com; f. 1859; Editor KEVIN O'SULLIVAN; circ. 96,150.

Metro Herald: Independent House, 1st Floor, 27–32, Talbot St, Dublin 1; tel. (1) 7055055; fax (1) 7055044; e-mail info@metroherald.ie; internet www.metroherald.ie; f. 2009 by merger of Metro and Herald AM (both f. 2005); distributed free of charge in the Greater Dublin area; Man. Dir PAUL CROSBIE; circ. 60,151.

OTHER NEWSPAPERS

(Average net circulation figures, including Ireland and the United Kingdom, as at December 2011, unless otherwise stated)

An Phoblacht: 58 Parnell Sq., Dublin 1; tel. (1) 8733611; fax (1) 8733074; e-mail editor@anphoblacht.com; internet www.anphoblacht.com; f. 1970; organ of Sinn Féin; monthly; Editor JOHN HEDGES; circ. 15,000 (2007).

Anglo-Celt: Station House, Cavan, Co Cavan; tel. (49) 4331100; fax (49) 4332280; e-mail linda@anglocelt.ie; internet www.anglocelt.ie; f. 1846; Thur.; Editor LINDA O'REILLY; circ. 12,310.

Argus: Partnership Court, Park St, Dundalk, Co Louth; tel. (42) 9334632; fax (42) 9331643; e-mail editorial@argus.ie; internet www.argus.ie; f. 1835; Thurs.; circ. 11,507 (2007).

Clare Champion: Barrack St, Ennis, Co Clare; tel. (65) 6828105; fax (65) 6820374; e-mail editor@clarechampion.ie; internet www.clarechampion.ie; f. 1903; Thurs.; Editor AUSTIN HOBBS; circ. 15,742.

Connacht Tribune: 15 Market St, Galway; tel. (91) 536222; fax (91) 567970; e-mail cormac@ctribune.ie; internet www.galwaynews.ie; f. 1909; Fri.; Group Editor DAVE O'CONNELL; circ. 20,702.

Connaught Telegraph: Cavendish Lane, Castlebar, Co Mayo; tel. (94) 9021711; fax (94) 9024007; e-mail info@con-telegraph.ie; internet www.con-telegraph.ie; f. 1828; Tues.; independent; Editor TOM GILLESPIE; circ. 14,900.

Donegal Democrat: Larkin House, Oldtown Rd, Donegal, Co Donegal; tel. (7491) 28000; e-mail editorial@donegaldemocrat.com; internet www.donegaldemocrat.com; f. 1919; Tues. and Thurs.; Editor MICHAEL DALY; circ. 6,618 (Tues.); 9,191 (Thurs.).

Drogheda Independent: 9 Shop St, Drogheda, Co Louth; tel. (41) 9838658; fax (41) 9834271; e-mail editorial@drogheda-independent.ie; internet www.drogheda-independent.ie; f. 1884; Thurs.; circ. 10,328 (2007).

Dundalk Democrat: 7 Crowe St, Dundalk, Co Louth; tel. (42) 9334058; fax (42) 9331399; e-mail editor@dundalkdemocrat.ie; internet www.dundalkdemocrat.ie; f. 1849; Wed.; Editor ANTHONY MURPHY; circ. 6,500 (2007).

Dungarvan Observer: Shandon, Dungarvan, Co Waterford; tel. (58) 41205; fax (58) 41559; e-mail news@dungarvanobserver.com; f. 1912; Editor JAMES A. LYNCH.

The Echo: Slaney Place, Enniscorthy, Co Wexford; tel. (53) 9259900; fax (53) 9233506; e-mail editor@theecho.ie; internet www.theecho.ie; f. 1902; Wed.; edns for Enniscorthy, Gorey, New Ross and Wexford; Editor TOM MOONEY; circ. 7,210.

Iris Oifigiúil (Official Irish Gazette): Unit 20, Lakeside Retail Park, Claremorris, Co Mayo; tel. (1) 6476636; fax (1) 6476843; e-mail irisoifigiuil@opw.ie; internet www.irisoifigiuil.ie; f. 1922; twice weekly (Tues. and Fri.); Editor DEIRBHLE HEGARTY.

Irish Mail on Sunday: Embassy House, 3rd Floor, Herbert Park Lane, Dublin 4; tel. (1) 6375800; fax (1) 4179830; Propr Associated Newspapers (United Kingdom); fmrly *Ireland on Sunday*; name changed as above in 2006; Editor-in-Chief SEBASTIAN HAMILTON; circ. 122,231.

The Kerryman: Denny St, Tralee, Co Kerry; tel. (66) 7145500; fax (66) 7145572; e-mail dmalone@kerryman.ie; internet www.kerryman.ie; f. 1904; Thurs.; Editor DECLAN MALONE; circ. 26,392 (2007).

Kilkenny People: 34 High St, Kilkenny; tel. (56) 7721015; fax (56) 7721414; e-mail editor@kilkennypeople.ie; internet www.kilkennypeople.ie; f. 1892; weekly; Editor BRIAN KEYES; circ. 11,536.

Leinster Express: Dublin Rd, Portlaoise, Co Laois; tel. (57) 8621666; fax (57) 8620491; e-mail conor.ganly@leinsterexpress.ie; internet www.leinsterexpress.ie; f. 1831; weekly; Editor PAT SOMERS; circ. 11,070 (incl. Offaly Express).

Leinster Leader: 19 South Main St, Naas, Co Kildare; tel. (45) 897302; fax (45) 897647; e-mail editor@leinsterleader.ie; internet www.leinsterleader.ie; f. 1880; Tues.; Editor DAVID POWER; circ. 6,497.

Limerick Leader: 54 O'Connell St, Limerick; tel. (61) 214500; fax (61) 401424; e-mail admin@limerick-leader.ie; internet www.limerick-leader.ie; f. 1889; 4 a week; Editor ALAN ENGLISH; circ. 14,851 (weekend edn).

Limerick Post: 97 Henry St, Limerick; tel. (61) 413322; fax (61) 417684; e-mail news@limerickpost.ie; internet www.limerickpost.ie; f. 1986; Carnbeg Limited; distributed free of charge; Thurs.; Man. Dir JOHN RYAN; circ. 52,817.

Mayo News: The Fairgreen, Westport, Co Mayo; tel. (98) 25311; fax (98) 26108; e-mail info@mayonews.ie; internet www.mayonews.ie; f. 1892; Wed.; Editor MICHAEL DUFFY; circ. 10,569 (2007).

Midland Tribune: Main St, Birr, Co Offaly; tel. (509) 20003; fax (509) 20588; e-mail editor@midlandtribune.ie; internet www.midlandtribune.ie; f. 1881; Wed.; Editor JOHN O'CALLAGHAN; circ. 10,105 (2007).

The Nationalist: Hanover House, Hanover, Carlow; tel. (59) 9170100; fax (59) 9130301; e-mail news@carlow-nationalist.ie; internet www.carlow-nationalist.ie; f. 1883; owned by Thomas Crosbie Holdings; Editor CONAL O'BOYLE.

Offaly Express: Bridge St, Tullamore, Co Offaly; tel. (57) 9321744; fax (57) 9351930; e-mail alan@offalyexpress.ie; internet www

.offalyexpress.ie; weekly; Editor ALAN WALSH; circ. 11,070 (incl. Leinster Express).

Sligo Champion: Connacht House, Markievicz Rd, Sligo; tel. (71) 9169222; fax (71) 9169040; e-mail editor@sligochampion.ie; internet www.sligochampion.ie; f. 1836; Wed.; Editor JIM GRAY; circ. 12,574 (2007).

The Southern Star: Ilen St, Skibbereen, Co Cork; tel. (28) 21200; fax (28) 21071; e-mail info@southernstar.ie; internet www.southernstar.ie; f. 1889; Sat.; Editor CON DOWNING; circ. 14,500 (2007).

Sunday Business Post: 80 Harcourt St, Dublin 2; tel. (1) 6026000; fax (1) 6796496; e-mail info@sbpost.ie; internet www.businesspost.ie; f. 1989; owned by Thomas Crosbie Holdings; Editor CLIFF TAYLOR; circ. 47,849.

Sunday Independent: Independent House, 27–32 Talbot St, Dublin 1; tel. (1) 7055333; fax (1) 7055779; e-mail sunday.letters@independent.ie; internet www.independent.ie; f. 1905; Editor ANNE HARRIS; circ. 250,641.

Sunday World: Independent House, 27–32 Talbot St, Dublin 1; tel. (1) 8848900; fax (1) 8849002; e-mail news@sundayworld.com; internet www.sundayworld.com; f. 1973; Editor COLM MCGINTY; circ. 251,455.

Tipperary Star: Friar St, Thurles, Co Tipperary; tel. (504) 21122; e-mail info@tipperarystar.ie; internet www.tipperarystar.ie; f. 1909; Wed.; Editor ANNE O'GRADY; circ. 7,115.

Tuam Herald: Dublin Rd, Tuam, Co Galway; tel. (93) 24183; fax (93) 24478; e-mail editor@tuamherald.ie; internet www.tuamherald.ie; f. 1837; Wed.; Editor DAVID BURKE; circ. 8,482.

Tullamore Tribune: William St, Tullamore, Co Offaly; tel. (5793) 21152; fax (5793) 21927; e-mail editor@tullamoretribune.ie; internet www.tullamoretribune.ie; f. 1978; Wed.; Editor GERARD SCULLY.

Waterford News & Star: Gladstone House, Gladstone St, Waterford; tel. (51) 874951; fax (51) 855281; e-mail editor@waterford-news.ie; internet www.waterford-news.ie; f. 1848; Thurs.; Editor FRANCES RYAN.

Western People: Tone St, Ballina, Co Mayo; tel. (96) 60999; fax (96) 70208; e-mail info@westernpeople.ie; internet www.westernpeople.ie; f. 1883; Tues.; Editor JAMES LAFFEY; circ. 14,166.

Westmeath Examiner: Blackhall Pl., Mullingar, Co Westmeath; tel. (44) 9346700; fax (44) 9330765; e-mail editor@westmeathexaminer.ie; internet www.westmeathexaminer.ie; f. 1882; weekly; Editor BRIAN O'LOUGHLIN; circ. 5,799.

Wicklow People: Channing House, Upper Row St, Wicklow, Co Wexford; tel. (53) 9140100; fax (53) 9140192; e-mail front.office@peoplenews.ie; internet www.wicklowpeople.ie; weekly; circ. 13,122 (2007).

SELECTED PERIODICALS

Afloat: 2 Lower Glenageary Rd, Dún Laoghaire, Co Dublin; tel. (1) 2846161; fax (1) 2846192; e-mail info@afloat.ie; internet www.afloat.ie; monthly; sailing and boating; Man. Editor DAVID O'BRIEN.

Banking Ireland: 1 North Wall Quay, Dublin 1; tel. (1) 6116500; fax (1) 6116565; e-mail info@bankers.ie; internet www.instbankers.com/bi/index.html; f. 1898; quarterly; journal of the Inst. of Bankers in Ireland; circ. 15,500 (Dec. 2006).

Books Ireland: 11 Newgrove Ave, Dublin 4; tel. (1) 2692185; e-mail booksi@eircom.net; f. 1976; 9 a year; reviews Irish-interest books; Editor JEREMY ADDIS; circ. 2,350 (Dec. 2006).

Business & Finance: Cunningham House, 130 Francis St, Dublin 8; tel. (1) 4167800; fax (1) 4167899; e-mail info@businessandfinance.ie; internet www.businessandfinancetoday.com; f. 1964; monthly; Publr IAN HYLAND; Editor JOHN WALSH; circ. 15,767.

Food & Wine: Rosemount House, Dundrum Rd, Dundrum, Dublin 16; tel. (1) 2405300; fax (1) 6619486; e-mail ross@harmonia.ie; internet www.harmonia.ie; f. 1997; published by Harmonia Ltd; Editor ROSS GOLDEN-BANNON; circ. 8,921.

Hot Press: 13 Trinity St, Dublin 2; tel. (1) 2411500; fax (1) 2411538; e-mail info@hotpress.com; internet www.hotpress.com; fortnightly; music, leisure, current affairs; Editor NIALL STOKES; circ. 19,215.

Image: 22 Crofton Rd, Dún Laoghaire, Co Dublin; tel. (1) 2808415; fax (1) 2808309; e-mail mmorris@image.ie; internet www.image.ie; f. 1975; bi-monthly; women's fashion, lifestyle; Editor MELANIE MORRIS.

Ireland's Own: Channing House, Rowe St, Co Wexford; tel. (53) 40140; fax (53) 40192; e-mail irelands.own@peoplenews.ie; f. 1902; weekly; family interest; Editors PHILIP MURPHY, SEAN NOLAN; circ. 40,305.

The Irish Catholic: St Mary's, Bloomfield Ave, Donnybrook, Dublin 4; tel. (1) 4276400; fax (1) 4276450; e-mail news@irishcatholic.ie; internet www.irishcatholic.ie; f. 1888; publ. by The Agricultural Trust; weekly; Man. Editor GARRY O'SULLIVAN; circ. 32,000 (2012).

Irish Computer: Media House, South County Business Park, Leopardstown, Dublin 18; tel. (1) 2947777; fax (1) 2947799; e-mail cliff.hutton@mediateam.ie; internet www.techcentral.ie; f. 1977; monthly; Editor CLIFF HUTTON; circ. 4,000 (+1,500 to Irish Computer Society members).

Irish Farmers' Journal: Irish Farm Centre, Bluebell, Dublin 12; tel. (1) 4199500; fax (1) 4520876; e-mail edit@farmersjournal.ie; internet www.farmersjournal.ie; f. 1948; weekly; Editor MATTHEW DEMPSEY; weekly circ. 72,046 (July-Dec 2011).

The Irish Field: Irish Farm Centre, Bluebell, Dublin 12; tel. (1) 4051100; fax (1) 4554008; e-mail info@theirishfield.ie; internet www.theirishfield.ie; f. 1870; published by the Agricultural Trust; weekly; horse racing, breeding and equine leisure; Man. Editor LEO POWELL; circ. 15,513 (Dec. 2008).

Irish Historical Studies: c/o Dept of Modern History, Trinity College, Dublin 2; tel. (1) 6081020; e-mail wvaughan@tcd.ie; 2 a year; Editors Dr DAVID HAYTON, Dr JOHN MCCAFFERTY.

Irish Journal of Medical Science: Royal Academy of Medicine in Ireland, Frederick House, 19 South Frederick St, Dublin 2; tel. (1) 6334820; fax (1) 6334918; e-mail ijms@rami.ie; internet www.ijms.ie; f. 1832; quarterly; organ of the Royal Academy of Medicine; Editor DAVID BOUCHIER-HAYES.

Irish Law Times: Thomson Reuters, 43 Fitzwilliam Pl., Dublin 2; tel. (1) 6625301; fax (1) 6625302; e-mail terri.mcdonnell@thomsonreuters.com; internet www.thomsonreuters.com; f. 1983; 20 a year; Editor DAVID BOYLE.

Irish Medical Journal: 10 Fitzwilliam Pl., Dublin 2; tel. (1) 6767273; fax (1) 6612758; e-mail imj@imj.ie; internet www.imj.ie; f. 1967; 10 a year; journal of the Irish Medical Org; Editor Dr JOHN MURPHY.

The Irish Skipper: Unit 5, Teach na Rosann, Anagaire, Letterkenny, Co Donegal; tel. (74) 9548935; fax (74) 9548940; e-mail hugh@maramedia.ie; internet www.irishskipper.net; f. 1964; monthly; journal of the commercial fishing and aquaculture industries; Editor JIM MASON.

Irish Tatler: Rosemount House, Dundrum Rd, Dundrum, Dublin 16; tel. (1) 2405300; fax (1) 6619486; internet www.harmonia.ie/#/7; f. 1890; monthly; Editor ELAINE PRENDEVILLE; circ. 26,873 (2009).

Irish University Review: School of English, Drama and Film, Rm K202, University College Dublin, Belfield, Dublin 4; tel. (1) 7168181; fax (1) 7161174; e-mail john.brannigan@ucd.ie; internet www.irishuniversityreview.ie; f. 1970; 2 a year; literature, history, fine arts, politics, cultural studies; Editor Dr JOHN BRANNIGAN.

Law Society Gazette: Law Society of Ireland, Blackhall Pl, Dublin 7; tel. (1) 6724800; fax (1) 6724801; e-mail general@lawsociety.ie; internet www.lawsociety.ie; monthly; published by the Law Society of Ireland; Editor MARK MCDERMOTT.

Magill: 1–4 Swift's Alley, Francis St, Dublin 8; tel. (1) 4167800; e-mail editor@magill.ie; internet www.magill.ie; published by The Business and Finance Group; monthly; politics and current affairs; Editor EAMON DELANEY; circ. 14,985 (Dec. 2006).

Motoring Life: 48 North Great George's St, Dublin 1; tel. (1) 8780444; fax (1) 8787740; internet www.motoringlife.ie; e-mail info@motoringlife.ie; f. 1946; bi-monthly; Editor GERALDINE HERBERT.

PC Live!: Prospect House, 3 Prospect Rd, Glasnevin, Dublin 9; tel. (1) 8824444; fax (1) 8300888; e-mail info@scope.ie; internet www.techcentral.ie; f. 1994; monthly; computers and the internet; Editor NIALL KITSON.

The Phoenix: 44 Lower Baggot St, Dublin 2; tel. (1) 6611062; fax (1) 6624532; e-mail editor@thephoenix.ie; internet www.phoenix-magazine.com; f. 1983; fortnightly; news and comment, satirical; Editor PADDY PRENDIVILLE; circ. 18,268.

Poetry Ireland Review (Éigse Éireann): 2 Proud's Lane, Dublin 2; tel. (1) 4789974; fax (1) 4780205; e-mail info@poetryireland.ie; internet www.poetryireland.ie; quarterly; Editor CAITRÍONA O'REILLY.

RTÉ Guide: Radio Telefís Éireann, Donnybrook, Dublin 4; tel. (1) 2083111; fax (1) 2083080; internet www.rteguide.ie; weekly; programmes of the Irish broadcasting service; Editor RAY WALSH; circ. 113,033 (2006).

ShelfLife: Media House, South County Business Park, Leopardstown, Dublin 18; tel. (1) 2947767; e-mail shelflife@mediateam.ie; internet www.shelflife.ie; monthly; food, drinks, grocery, FMCG Sectors; owned by Mediatean LTD; Man. Dir JOHN MCDONALD; Editor FIONNUALA CAROLAN; circ. 8,116.

Studies: An Irish Quarterly Review: 35 Lower Leeson St, Dublin 2; tel. (1) 6766785; fax (1) 7758598; e-mail studiesorders@jesuit.ie; internet www.studiesirishreview.ie; f. 1912; published by the Jesuits In Ireland; quarterly review of letters, history, religious and social questions; Editor Fr BRUCE BRADLEY.

U Magazine: Rosemount House, Dundrum Rd, Dundrum, Dublin 16; tel. (1) 2405300; fax (1) 6619757; e-mail jstevens@harmonia.ie; internet www.harmonia.ie/#/20; f. 1979; every 2 weeks; for young women; Editor JEN STEVENS; circ. 28,824 (Dec. 2009).

Village Magazine: 6 Ormond Quay Upper, Dublin 7; tel. (1) 6425050; fax (1) 6425001; e-mail news@villagemagazine.ie; internet www.villagemagazine.ie; f. 2004; monthly; current affairs; Editor MICHAEL SMITH.

Woman's Way: Rosemount House, Dundrum Rd, Dundrum, Dublin 14; tel. (1) 2405300; fax (1) 6628719; e-mail atoner@harmonia.ie; internet www.harmonia.ie/#/21; f. 1963; weekly; Editor AINE TONER; circ. 22,942.

NEWS AGENCY

Ireland International News Agency: 51 Wellington Quay, Dublin 2; tel. (1) 6712442; fax (1) 6796586; e-mail iina@eircom.net; Man. Dir DIARMAID MACDERMOTT.

PRESS ORGANIZATIONS

National Newspapers of Ireland: Clyde Lodge, 15 Clyde Rd, Dublin 4; tel. (1) 6689099; fax (1) 6689872; e-mail nni@cullencommunications.ie; internet www.nni.ie; f. 1985; 19 mems; Chair. MAEVE DONOVAN; Co-ordinating Dir FRANK CULLEN.

Regional Newspapers and Printers Association of Ireland: Latt, Cavan; tel. (1) 6779112; e-mail johanlon@regionalnewspapers.ie; f. 1917; 35 mems; Pres. DAVID HICKEY; Dir JOHNNY O'HANLON.

Publishers

Blackhall Publishing: Lonsdale House, Avoca Ave, Dublin; tel. (1) 2785090; fax (1) 2784800; e-mail info@blackhallpublishing.com; internet www.blackhallpublishing.com; f. 1997; law, business, marketing, management.

Boole Press: 19 Silchester Rd, Glenageary, Co Dublin; e-mail info@boolepress.com; internet www.boolepress.com; f. 1979; scientific, technical, medical, scholarly; Man. Dir Dr J. MILLER.

Cló Iar-Chonnachta: Inverin, Connemara, Co Galway; tel. (91) 593307; fax (91) 593362; e-mail sales@cic.ie; internet www.cic.ie; f. 1985; music, children's books; Gen. Man. DEIRDRE NÍ THUATHAIL.

The Columba Press: 55A Spruce Ave, Stillorgan Industrial Park, Dublin; tel. (1) 2942556; fax (1) 2942564; e-mail info@columba.ie; internet www.columba.ie; f. 1985; spirituality, theology, history; Publr SEÁN O'BOYLE.

Comhairle Bhéaloideas Éireann (Folklore of Ireland Council): c/o Dept of Irish Folklore, University College, Belfield, Dublin 4; tel. (1) 7168216; e-mail cumann@ucd.ie; Editor Prof. SÉAMAS Ó CATHÁIN.

Cork University Press: Youngline Industrial Estate, Pouladuff Rd, Togher, Cork; tel. (21) 4902980; fax (21) 4315329; e-mail corkuniversitypress@ucc.ie; internet www.corkuniversitypress.com; f. 1925; owned by University College Cork; academic, art, music, geography, literature, history; imprints include Attic Press and Atrium; Publications Dir MIKE COLLINS.

Dedalus Press: 13 Moyclare Rd, Baldoyle, Dublin 13; tel. (1) 8392034; e-mail editor@dedaluspress.com; internet www.dedaluspress.com; f. 1985; Irish and some international poetry, occasional prose; Publr and Editor PAT BORAN.

Dominican Publications: 42 Parnell Sq., Dublin 1; tel. (1) 8731355; fax (1) 8731760; e-mail sales@dominicanpublications.com; internet www.dominicanpublications.com; f. 1897; religious affairs in Ireland and the developing world, pastoral-liturgical aids; Man. Rev. BERNARD TREACY.

CJ Fallon: Block B, Ground Floor, Liffey Valley Office Campus, Dublin 22; tel. (1) 6166400; fax (1) 6166499; e-mail editorial@cjfallon.ie; internet www.cjfallon.ie; f. 1927; educational; CEO BRIAN GILSENAN.

Four Courts Press: 7 Malpas St, Dublin 8; tel. (1) 4534668; fax (1) 4534672; e-mail info@fourcourtspress.ie; internet www.fourcourtspress.ie; f. 1970; philosophy, theology, Celtic and Medieval studies, art, literature, modern history; Editorial Dir MARTIN FANNING; Publr MARTIN HEALY.

The Gallery Press: Loughcrew, Oldcastle, Co Meath; tel. and fax (49) 8541779; e-mail contactus@gallerypress.com; internet www.gallerypress.com; f. 1970; poetry, plays, prose by Irish authors; Publr and Editor PETER FALLON.

Gill and Macmillan: Hume Ave, Park West, Dublin 12; tel. (1) 5009500; fax (1) 5009597; e-mail sales@gillmacmillan.ie; internet www.gillmacmillan.ie; f. 1968; literature, biography, history, social sciences, current affairs and textbooks; Man. Dir M. D. O'DWYER.

Goldsmith Press: Newbridge, Co Kildare; tel. (45) 433613; fax (45) 434648; f. 1972; poetry, Irish art, plays, foreign language, general; Dirs DESMOND EGAN, VIVIENNE ABBOTT.

Hachette Ireland: Unit 8, Castlecourt Centre, Dublin 15; tel. (1) 8246288; e-mail info@hbgi.ie; internet www.hachette.ie; f. 2002 as Hodder Headline Ireland; fiction, non-fiction; div. of Hachette UK.

Irish Academic Press: 2 Brookside Dundrum Rd, Dublin 14; tel. (1) 2989937; fax (1) 2982783; e-mail info@iap.ie; internet www.iap.ie; f. 1974; academic, mainly history and Irish studies; Dir STEWART CASS; Man. Editor LISA HYDE.

LexisNexis Butterworths Ireland: 24–26 Upper Ormond Quay, Dublin 7; tel. (1) 8728514; fax (1) 8731378; e-mail customer.services@lexisnexis.ie; internet www.lexisnexis.ie; subsidiary of Reed Elsevier United Kingdom; taxation and law; Chair. H. MUMFORD.

Liberties Press: Guinness Enterprise Centre, Taylor's Lane, Dublin 8; tel. (1) 4151286; fax (1) 4100985; e-mail info@libertiespress.com; internet www.libertiespress.com; f. 2003; sport, health, food, music, history, religion, politics and fiction; Editorial Dir SEAN O'KEEFFE.

Lilliput Press: 62/63 Sitric Rd, Arbour Hill, Dublin 7; tel. (1) 6711647; fax (1) 6711233; e-mail info@lilliputpress.ie; internet www.lilliputpress.ie; f. 1985; ecology and environment, literary criticism, biography, memoirs, fiction, Irish history, general; Publr ANTONY FARRELL.

Mentor Books: 43 Furze Rd, Sandyford Industrial Estate, Dublin 18; tel. (1) 2952112; fax (1) 2952114; e-mail admin@mentorbooks.ie; internet www.mentorbooks.ie; adult and children's fiction and non-fiction, educational; Man. Dir DANIEL MCCARTHY.

Mercier Press Ltd: Unit 3B, Oak House, Bessboro Rd, Blackrock, Co Cork; tel. (21) 4614700; fax (21) 4614802; e-mail info@mercierpress.ie; internet www.mercierpress.ie; f. 1944; folklore, history, biography, current affairs, fiction, politics, humour, religious; Man. Dir CLODAGH FEEHAN.

O'Brien Press Ltd: 12 Terenure Rd East, Rathgar, Dublin 6; tel. (1) 4923333; fax (1) 4922777; e-mail books@obrien.ie; internet www.obrien.ie; f. 1974; biography, history, sport, Celtic, politics, travel, crime, children's; Man. Dir IVAN O'BRIEN; Publr MICHAEL O'BRIEN.

Poolbeg Press: 123 Grange Hill, Baldoyle Industrial Estate, Dublin 13; tel. (1) 8321477; fax (1) 8321430; e-mail info@poolbeg.com; internet www.poolbeg.com; f. 1976; general, poetry, politics, children's; Man. Dir KIERAN DEVLIN.

Royal Irish Academy (Acadamh Ríoga na hÉireann): 19 Dawson St, Dublin 2; tel. (1) 6762570; fax (1) 6762346; e-mail admin@ria.ie; internet www.ria.ie; f. 1785; humanities and sciences; Pres. NICHOLAS P. CANNY; Exec. Sec. PATRICK BUCKLEY.

Thomson Reuters/Round Hall: 43 Fitzwilliam Pl., Dublin 2; tel. (1) 6625301; fax (1) 6625302; e-mail catherine.dolan@thomsonreuters.com; internet www.roundhall.ie; f. 1980 as The Round Hall Press; law books and journals and Westlaw IE online; part of Thomson Reuters; Publr CATHERINE DOLAN.

Veritas Publications: 7–8 Lower Abbey St, Dublin 1; tel. (1) 8788177; fax (1) 8786507; e-mail publications@veritas.ie; internet www.veritas.ie; f. 1969; Christian, religious and educational, theological, liturgical; Dir MAURA HYLAND.

GOVERNMENT PUBLISHING HOUSE

Oifig an tSoláthair/Stationery Office: Government Publications, Unit 20, Lakeside Retail Park, Claremorris, Co Mayo; tel. (1) 6476834; fax (94) 9378964; e-mail pubsales@opw.ie; internet www.opw.ie; Asst Principal Office THOMAS MONAGHAN.

PUBLISHERS' ASSOCIATION

Publishing Ireland/Foilsiú Éireann: 25 Denzille Lane, Dublin 8; tel. (1) 6394868; e-mail info@publishingireland.com; internet www.publishingireland.com; f. 1970 as CLÉ—Irish Book Publishers' Association; 100 mem. publishers; Pres. FRANK SCOTT-LENNON.

Broadcasting and Communications

TELECOMMUNICATIONS

Commission for Communications Regulation (ComReg): Block DEF, Abbey Court, Irish Life Centre, Lower Abbey St, Dublin 1; tel. (1) 8049600; fax (1) 8049680; e-mail info@comreg.ie; internet www.comreg.ie; f. 2002; regulatory authority for Ireland's postal and telecommunications sectors; issues licences to service providers; manages the interconnection of telecommunications networks; approves equipment and oversees national telephone numbering; Chair. ALEX CHISHOLM.

eircom: 1 Heuston South Quarter, St John's Rd, Dublin 8; tel. (1) 6714444; fax (1) 6716916; e-mail press-office@eircom.ie; internet www.eircom.ie; f. 1984; fmrly Telecom Éireann; offers fixed-line telecommunications and internet access; partially privatized in 1999, acquired by BCM Ireland Holdings Ltd in August 2006; Chair. NED SULLIVAN; CEO PAUL DONOVAN.

Meteor Mobile Communications Ltd: 1 Heuston South Quarter, St John's Rd, Dublin 8; tel. (1) 4307085; fax (1) 4307013; e-mail info@meteor.ie; internet www.meteor.ie; f. 2001; mobile cellular telecommunications; subsidiary of eircom; 1,065,000 subscribers (March 2010).

Hutchison 3G Ireland Ltd (3 Ireland): 1 Clarendon Row, 3rd Floor, Dublin 2; tel. (1) 5426300; fax (1) 5426301; e-mail customer.services .ie@3mail.com; internet www.three.ie; f. 2005; mobile cellular telecommunications; owned by Hutchison Whampoa Ltd (Hong Kong); 500,000 subscribers (June 2010); CEO ROBERT FINNEGAN.

Telefónica O_2 Ireland Ltd: 28–29 Sir John Rogerson's Quay, Dublin 2; tel. (1) 6095000; e-mail customercare@o2.ie; internet www.o2.ie; f. 1997; mobile cellular telecommunications and broadband internet access; acquired by Telefónica, SA (Spain) 2006; CEO TONY HANWAY.

Vodafone Ireland: Mountainview, Leopardstown, Dublin 18; tel. (1) 2038232; fax (1) 6708465; e-mail custcare@vodafone.ie; internet www.vodafone.ie; f. 2001, following acquisition of Eircell; mobile cellular telecommunications; subsidiary of Vodafone Group PLC (UK); Chief Exec. JEROEN HOENCAMP.

BROADCASTING

The Radio and Television Act of 1988 provided for the establishment of an independent television station, an independent national radio service and a series of local radio stations (see below).

Broadcasting Authority of Ireland (BAI): 2–5 Warrington Pl., Dublin 2; tel. (1) 6441200; fax (1) 6441299; e-mail info@bai.ie; internet www.bai.ie; f. 2009 to replace the Broadcasting Commission of Ireland (f. 1988) and the Broadcasting Complaints Commission (f. 1977); responsible for regulating public service and independent broadcasting in Ireland; also responsible for the licensing of new broadcasting services, as well as the development of codes of programming and advertising standards for television and radio services; Chair. BOB COLLINS.

Radio

Raidió Teilifís Éireann (RTÉ): Donnybrook, Dublin 4; tel. (1) 2083111; fax (1) 2083080; e-mail info@rte.ie; internet www.rte.ie; national public service broadcasting corpn; f. 1960; financed by net licence revenue and sale of advertising time; governed by Board of 12 mems; operates 4 radio networks (see below); Chair. TOM SAVAGE; Dir-Gen. NOEL CURRAN; Man. Dir of Radio CLAIRE DUIGNAN; Man. Dir of Television GLEN KILLANE; Man. Dir of News (vacant).

RTÉ lyric fm: Cornmarket Sq., Limerick, Co Limerick; tel. (61) 207300; fax (61) 207390; e-mail lyric@rte.ie; internet www.rte.ie/lyricfm; broadcasts classical and traditional music, jazz, opera; Dir AODÁN Ó DUBHGHAILL.

RTÉ Radio 1: Donnybrook, Dublin 4; tel. (1) 2083111; e-mail info@rte.ie; internet www.rte.ie/radio1; music news, drama and entertainment programmes; Dir ANA LEDDY.

RTÉ Raidió na Gaeltachta: Casla, Connemara, Co Galway; tel. (91) 506677; fax (91) 506666; e-mail rnag@rte.ie; internet www.rte .ie/rnag; f. 1972; broadcasts in Irish.

RTÉ 2FM: Donnybrook, Dublin 4; tel. (1) 2083111; e-mail info@rte .ie; internet 2fm.rte.ie; popular music; Head JOHN MCMAHON.

Classic Hits 4FM: Castleforbes House, Ground Floor, Castleforbes Rd, Dublin 1; tel. (1) 4255400; fax (1) 4255444; e-mail info@4fm.ie; internet www.4fm.ie; f. 2009; broadcasting popular music programmes in Co Clare, Co Cork, Co Dublin, Co Galway and Co Limerick; Chief Exec. SEAN ASHMORE.

FM104: Macken House, Mayor St Upper, North Wall, Dublin 1; tel. (1) 5006600; fax (1) 6689401; e-mail sales@fm104.ie; internet www .fm104.ie; broadcasts popular music and entertainment programmes in Co Dublin; owned by UTV (UK); Chief Exec. MARGARET NELSON.

NewsTalk 106–108 FM: Marconi House, Digges Lane, Dublin 2; tel. (1) 6445100; fax (1) 6445101; e-mail info@newstalk.ie; internet www .newstalk.ie; f. 2002; began broadcasting news and talk programmes nationally in 2006; Propr Communicorp Group; Chair. DENIS O'BRIEN; Chief Exec. FRANK CRONIN.

98 FM: South Block, The Malt House, Grand Canal Quay, Dublin 2; tel. (1) 4398800; fax (1) 4398899; e-mail info@98fm.ie; internet www .98fm.com; f. 1989; provides news service to independent local radio stations under contract from the BAI; Propr Communicorp Group; CEO CHRIS DOYLE; Head of News TEENA GATES.

100-102 Today FM: Marconi House, Digges Lane, Dublin 2; tel. (1) 8049000; fax (1) 8049099; e-mail live@todayfm.com; internet www .todayfm.com; f. 1998; national, independent station; acquired by Communicorp Group 2007; Chair. JOHN MCCOLGAN; CEO WILLIE O'REILLY.

There are also local radio stations operating under the supervision of the Independent Radio and Television Commission.

Television

Four television channels, RTÉ 1, RTÉ 2, TV3 and TG4 owned by RTÉ NL (RTÉ Transmissions Network Ltd) transmit free-to-air channels. Broadcasting in Ireland is currently in the process of undergoing a transition from analogue to digital, which was to take place in October 2012.

Raidió Teilifís Éireann (RTÉ): see above; operates 2 television channels: RTÉ 1 and RTÉ 2; Man. Dir of Television GLEN KILLANE.

TG4 (Teilifís na Gaeilge): Baile na hAbhann, Connemara, Co Galway; tel. (91) 505050; fax (91) 505021; e-mail pol.o.gallchoir@tg4.ie; internet www.tg4.ie; f. 1996; national public service Irish-language broadcaster; frmly operated under RTÉ, became an independent statutory authority in April 2007; financed by the Govt and sales of commercial airtime; Chief Exec. PÓL Ó GALLCHÓIR.

TV3: Westgate Business Park, Ballymount, Dublin 24; tel. (1) 4193333; fax (1) 4193300; e-mail info@tv3.ie; internet www.tv3.ie; f. 1998; first national, commercial, independent television network; also broadcasts entertainment channel, 3e; CEO DAVID MCREDMOND; Dir of Programming BEN FROW; Dir of News ANDREW HANLON.

Finance

(cap. = capital; res = reserves; dep. = deposits; m. = million; brs = branches; amounts in euros, unless otherwise indicated)

BANKING

Under the Central Bank Reform Act 2010, which took effect on 1 October, the Central Bank of Ireland was created as a new unitary body responsible for both central banking and financial regulation. The new structure replaced the previous related entities, the Central Bank and the Financial Services Authority of Ireland and the Financial Regulator.

Central Bank

Central Bank of Ireland (Banc Ceannais na hÉireann): Dame St, POB 559, Dublin 2; tel. (1) 2246000; fax (1) 6716561; e-mail enquiries@centralbank.ie; internet www.centralbank.ie; f. 1942; bank of issue; responsible for regulation of the banking and financial services industry; cap. and res 1,740.1m., dep. 108,408.4m. (Dec. 2009); Gov. PATRICK HONAHAN; Dir-Gen. TONY GRIMES; Head of Financial Regulation MATTHEW ELDERFIELD.

Principal Banks

AIB Group (Allied Irish Banks PLC): Bankcentre, POB 452, Ballsbridge, Dublin 4; tel. (1) 6600311; fax (1) 6604715; e-mail aibtoday@aib.ie; internet www.aib.ie; f. 1966; 18.6% shares held by the Govt; nationalized in Dec. 2010; cap. 3,965m., res 4,239m., dep. 53,355m. (Dec. 2010); Exec. Chair. DAVID HODGKINSON; Man. Dir DAVID DUFFY; over 750 brs and offices.

Bank of Ireland Group: Lower Baggot St, Dublin 2; tel. (1) 6615933; fax (1) 6615193; e-mail careline@boimail.com; internet www.bankofireland.ie; f. 1783; cap. 1,210m., res 2,401m., dep. 78,403m. (Dec. 2010); Chair. RICHIE BOUCHER; 357 brs.

DEPFA Bank PLC: 1 Commons St, Dublin 1; tel. (1) 7922222; fax (1) 7922211; e-mail info@depfa.com; internet www.depfa.com; subsidiary of Hypo Real Estate Holding AG (Germany); cap. 1,242m., res 2,583m., dep. 71,222m. (Dec. 2010); CEO TOM GLYNN.

DZ BANK Ireland PLC: International House, 3 Harbourmaster Pl., IFSC, Dublin 1; tel. (1) 6700715; fax (1) 8290298; e-mail info@dzbank.ie; internet www.dzbank.ie; f. 1994; present name adopted 2001; subsidiary of DZ BANK AG Deutsche Zentral-Genossenschaftsbank, (Germany); cap. 7m., res 145.6m., dep. 3,862.7m. (Dec. 2010); Man. Dirs Dr TILMANN GERHARDS, MARK JACOB.

EAA Covered Bond Bank PLC: IFSC House, Dublin 1; tel. (1) 6127133; fax (1) 6127175; e-mail bond@westlb.ie; f. 2002 as WestLB Covered Bond Bank PLC; name changed as above following acquisition in 2010; public sector finance; owned by Erste Abwicklungsanstalt (Germany); cap. 6.4m., res –61.5m., dep. 980.7m. (Dec. 2010); Chair. DIETRICH VOIGTLÄNDER; Man. Dir MICHAEL DOHERTY.

Intesa Sanpaolo Bank Ireland PLC: KBC House, 3rd Floor, 4 St George's Dock, IFSC, Dublin 1; tel. (1) 6726720; fax (1) 6726727; e-mail dublin.ie@intesasanpaolo.com; internet www.intesasanpaolo .com; f. 1987; present name adopted 2007; subsidiary of Intesa Sanpaolo SpA (Italy); cap. 400.5m., res 496.7m., dep. 15,084.1m. (Dec. 2010); Chair. STEFANO DEL PUNTA; Man Dir ENRICO CUCCHIANI.

Irish Bank Resolution Corpn Ltd: Stephen Court, 18–21 St Stephen's Green, Dublin 2; tel. (1) 6162000; fax (1) 6162725;

internet www.ibrc.ie; f. 1964 as City of Dublin Bank; nationalized in Jan. 2009; name changed as above 2011; cap. 4,123m., res 26,327m., dep. 14,208m. (Dec. 2010); Exec. Chair. Alan Dukes; CEO Mike Aynsley; 9 brs.

Irish Life & Permanent PLC: Irish Life Centre, Lower Abbey St, Dublin 1; tel. (1) 7041010; fax (1) 7041900; internet www.irishlifepermanent.ie; f. 1884; present name adopted 1999 following merger; brought under state control in 2011; cap. 89m., res –50m., dep. 30,429m. (Dec. 2010); Chair. Alan Cook; CEO Kevin Murphy.

permanent tsb: 56–59 St Stephen's Green, Dublin 2; tel. (1) 2124101; e-mail info@permanenttsb.ie; internet www.permanenttsb.ie; formed by merger of Irish Permanent and TSB Bank; subsidiary of Irish Life and Permanent PLC; CEO Jeremy Masding; 101 brs.

KBC Bank Ireland PLC: Sandwith St, Dublin 2; tel. (1) 6646000; fax (1) 6646199; e-mail info@kbc.ie; internet www.kbc.ie; f. 1973; fmrly IIB Bank PLC; present name adopted 2008; subsidiary of KBC Bank NV (Belgium); cap. 465m., res 27.7m., dep. 2,471.3m. (Dec. 2010); Chair. Luc Philips; CEO John H. Reynolds; 5 brs.

JP Morgan Bank (Ireland) PLC: JP Morgan House, IFSC, Dublin 1; tel. (1) 6123000; fax (1) 6123123; internet www.chase.com; f. 1968 as Chase and Bank of Ireland (International) Ltd; name changed as above 2001; owned by JP Morgan International Finance Ltd (NJ, USA); cap. US $56.6m., res US $226.5m., dep. US $689.3m. (Dec. 2010); Chair. and CEO James Dimon; 1 br.

National Irish Bank Ltd: National House, Airton Close, Tallaght, Dublin 24; tel. (1) 4840000; fax (1) 6385198; internet www.nationalirishbank.ie; f. 1986 as Northern Bank (Ireland) Ltd; subsidiary of Danske Bank Group (Denmark); cap. €62.6m., res €54.8m., dep. €3,732.8m. (Sept. 2004); Chair. Peter Straarup; CEO Andrew Healy; 61 brs.

Rabobank Ireland PLC: George's Dock House, IFSC, Dublin 1; tel. (1) 6076100; fax (1) 6701724; e-mail fm.ie.dublin.information@rabobank.com; internet www.rabobank.ie; f. 1994; corporate and investment banking; owned by Rabobank International Holding BV (Netherlands); cap. 7.1m., res 164.6m., dep. 13,346.6m. (Dec. 2010); CEO Kevin Knightly.

Ulster Bank Ireland Ltd: Ulster Bank Group Centre, George's Quay, Dublin 2; tel. (1) 6777623; fax (1) 6775035; internet www.ulsterbank.com; merged with First Active PLC in early 2010; mem. of Royal Bank of Scotland Group (United Kingdom); cap. 3,582m., res 605m., dep. 45,859m. (Dec. 2009); Chair. Sean Dorgan; Chief Exec. Jim Brown; 132 brs.

UniCredit Bank Ireland PLC: La Touche House, IFSC, Dublin 1; tel. (1) 6702000; fax (1) 6702100; e-mail enquiry@unicreditgroup.ie; internet www.unicreditbank.ie; f. 1995; present name adopted 2007; subsidiary of UniCredit SpA (Italy); cap. 1,343.1m., res 282.6m., dep. 20,730.4m. (Dec. 2010); Man. Dir and CEO Stefano Vaiani.

Banking Association

Irish Banking Federation: Nassau House, Nassau St, Dublin 2; tel. (1) 6715311; fax (1) 6796680; e-mail ibf@ibf.ie; internet www.ibf.ie; more than 60 mems; CEO Pat Farrell.

STOCK EXCHANGE

Irish Stock Exchange: 28 Anglesea St, Dublin 2; tel. (1) 6174200; fax (1) 6776045; e-mail info@ise.ie; internet www.ise.ie; f. 1793; formed as limited co 1995; operates under supervision of the Central Bank of Ireland; Chair. Padraic O'Connor; CEO Deirdre Somers; 67 listed cos.

INSURANCE

Principal Companies

Allianz PLC: Allianz House, Elm Park, Merrion Rd, Dublin 4; tel. (1) 6133000; fax (1) 6134444; internet www.allianz.ie; f. 1998; 66.4% owned by Allianz AG (Germany), 30.4% by Irish Life and Permanent PLC; Chief Exec. Brendan Murphy.

Aviva Group Ireland PLC: One Park Place, Hatch St, Dublin 2; tel. (1) 8985130; internet www.aviva.ie; f. 1908; subsidiary of Aviva PLC (UK); life and non-life; Chief Exec. Seán Egan.

AXA Insurance Ltd: Wolfe Tone House, Wolfe Tone St, Dublin 1; tel. (1) 8726444; fax (1) 8729703; e-mail axa.dublincity@axa.ie; internet www.axa.ie; f. 1967; Chief Exec. John O'Neill.

Bank of Ireland Life: Nassau House, 33-35 Nassau St, Dublin 2; tel. (1) 7039537; fax (1) 6172049; e-mail info@bankofirelandlife.ie; internet www.bankofirelandlife.ie; f. 1987; present name adopted 2002; part of New Ireland Assurance Co (see below); Man. Dir Brian Forrester.

Canada Life Assurance (Ireland) Ltd: Canada Life House, Temple Rd, Blackrock, Co Dublin; tel. (1) 2102000; fax (1) 2102053; e-mail customerservices@canadalife.ie; internet www.canadalife.ie; f. 1903; Man. Dir Ruairi O'Flynn.

FBD Insurance PLC: FBD House, Bluebell, Dublin 12; tel. (1) 4639820; e-mail info@fbd.ie; internet www.fbd.ie; motor, property, business; Group CEO Andrew Langford.

Irish Life Assurance PLC: Lower Abbey St, POB 129, Dublin 1; tel. (1) 7042000; fax (1) 7041900; e-mail customerservice@irishlife.ie; internet www.irishlife.ie; f. 1939; life and non-life; Chief Exec. Gerry Hassett.

Irish Life & Permanent PLC: see Banking.

Liberty Insurance: Dublin Rd, Cavan, Co Cavan; tel. (1) 8500845; fax (49) 4368101; e-mail info@libertyinsurance.ie; internet www.libertyinsurance.ie; f. 1996 as Quinn Insurance; fmrly Quinn Insurance Ltd; acquired by Liberty Mutual Group, Inc (USA) in 2011 and renamed as above; property, motor, health; Chief Exec. Patrick O'Brien.

New Ireland Assurance Co PLC: 9–12 Dawson St, Dublin 2; tel. (1) 6172000; fax (1) 6172075; e-mail info@newireland.ie; internet www.newireland.ie; f. 1918; wholly owned subsidiary of Bank of Ireland Group; Man. Dir Sean Casey.

RSA Insurance Ireland Ltd: RSA House, Sandyford Rd, Dundrum, Dublin 16; tel. (1) 2901000; fax (1) 2901001; e-mail patrick.nally@ie.rsagroup.com; internet www.rsagroup.ie; fmrly Royal & SunAlliance; International Chief Exec. Simon Lee.

Standard Life Ireland: 90 St Stephen's Green, Dublin 2; tel. (1) 6397300; fax (1) 6397909; e-mail marketing@standardlife.ie; internet www.standardlife.ie; f. 1834; life assurance, pensions, investments and annuities; Chief Exec. David Nish.

Zurich Insurance PLC: Zurich House, Ballsbridge Park, Dublin 4; tel. (1) 6670666; fax (1) 6670644; e-mail customerhelp@zurich.ie; internet www.zurichinsurance.ie; f. 1919 as Eagle Star Insurance; present name adopted 2009; mem. of the Zürich Financial Services Group (Switzerland); CEO Ken Norgrove.

Insurance Associations

Insurance Institute of Ireland: 39 Molesworth St, Dublin 2; tel. (1) 6456600; fax (1) 6772621; e-mail info@iii.ie; internet www.iii.ie; f. 1885; Pres. Philip Smith; CEO Eamon Shackleton; around 10,000 mems.

Irish Brokers' Association: 87 Merrion Sq., Dublin 2; tel. (1) 6613067; fax (1) 6619955; e-mail info@iba.ie; internet www.iba.ie; f. 1990; Pres. (2011–2012) Carl Rainey; CEO Ciaran Phelan; 700 mems.

Irish Insurance Federation: Insurance House, 39 Molesworth St, Dublin 2; tel. (1) 6761820; fax (1) 6761943; e-mail fed@iif.ie; internet www.iif.ie; f. 1986; Pres. Sean Egan; CEO Michael Kemp; 63 mems.

Professional Insurance Brokers' Association (PIBA): Unit 14B, Cashel Business Centre, Cashel Rd, Crumlin, Dublin 12; tel. (1) 4922202; fax (1) 4991569; e-mail info@piba.ie; internet www.piba.ie; f. 1995; Chair. Jarlath Jordan; CEO Diarmuid Kelly; c. 900 mems.

Trade and Industry

GOVERNMENT AGENCIES

An Post (The Post Office): General Post Office, O'Connell St, Dublin 1; tel. (1) 7057000; fax (1) 8723553; e-mail press.office@anpost.ie; internet www.anpost.ie; f. 1984; provides national postal, communications and financial services through c. 1,100 outlets; Chair. John Fitzgerald; CEO Donal Connell.

FÁS—Foras Áiseanna Saothair (National Training and Employment Authority): 27–33 Upper Baggot St, Dublin 4; tel. (1) 6070500; fax (1) 6070600; e-mail info@fas.ie; internet www.fas.ie; f. 1988; responsible for the provision of specific skills training, apprenticeships and traineeships, employment programmes provided by a network of 70 nation-wide, local and regional centres; supports co-operative and community enterprise; offers an industrial advisory service; public recruitment service at all levels of occupations; Chair. Michael Dempsey; Dir-Gen. Paul O'Toole.

Food Safety Authority of Ireland (FSAI): Abbey Court, Lower Abbey Street, Dublin 1; tel. (1) 8171300; fax (1) 8171301; e-mail info@fsai.ie; internet www.fsai.ie; f. 1998; takes all reasonable steps to ensure that food produced, distributed or marketed in Ireland meets the highest standards of food safety and hygiene reasonably available and to ensure that food complies with legal requirements, or, where appropriate, with recognized codes of good practice; Chair. Eamonn Ryan; Chief Exec. Prof. Alan Reilly.

Forfás: Wilton Park House, Wilton Pl., Dublin 2; tel. (1) 6073000; fax (1) 6073030; e-mail info@forfas.ie; internet www.forfas.ie; f. 1994; the national policy advisory board for enterprise, trade, science, technology and innovation; Chair. Eoin O'Driscoll; Chief Exec. Martin Cronin.

National Economic and Social Council (NESC): 16 Parnell Sq., Dublin 1; tel. (1) 8146300; fax (1) 8146301; e-mail info@nesc.ie; internet www.nesc.ie; f. 1973; analyses and reports on strategic issues relating to the efficient development of the economy and the achievement of social justice; Chair. DERMOT MCCARTHY; Dir Dr RORY O'DONNELL.

DEVELOPMENT ORGANIZATIONS

Enterprise Ireland: The Plaza, East Point Business Park, Dublin 3; tel. (1) 7272000; fax (1) 8082020; e-mail client.service@enterprise-ireland.com; internet www.enterprise-ireland.com; f. 1998; combines the activities of the fmr An Bord Tráchtála, Forbairt and the in-company training activities of FÁS (q.v.); Chair. HUGH COONEY; Chief Exec. FRANK RYAN.

IDA Ireland: Wilton Park House, Wilton Pl., Dublin 2; tel. (1) 6034000; fax (1) 6034040; e-mail idaireland@ida.ie; internet www.idaireland.com; f. 1993; govt agency with national responsibility for securing new investment from overseas in manufacturing and international services and for encouraging existing foreign enterprises in Ireland to expand their businesses; Chair. LIAM O'MAHONY; CEO BARRY O'LEARY.

Sustainable Energy Ireland: Wilton Park House, Wilton Pl., Dublin 2; tel. (1) 8082100; fax (1) 8372848; e-mail info@sei.ie; internet www.sei.ie; promotes and assists environmentally and economically sustainable production, supply and use of energy, in support of govt policy, across all sectors of the economy; Chair. BRENDAN HALLIGAN; CEO OWEN LEWIS.

Teagasc (Agriculture and Food Development Authority): Oak Park, Carlow; tel. (59) 9170200; fax (59) 9182097; e-mail info@hq.teagasc.ie; internet www.teagasc.ie; f. 1988; provides research, educational and training services to agri-food sector and rural communities; Chair. Dr NOEL CAWLE; Nat. Dir Prof. GERRY BOYLE.

CHAMBERS OF COMMERCE

Chambers Ireland (CI): 17 Merrion Sq., Dublin 2; tel. (1) 4004300; fax (1) 6612811; e-mail info@chambers.ie; internet www.chambers.ie; f. 1923; represents over 13,000 businesses nation-wide, with 60 chamber mems; Pres. DAVID PIERCE; CEO IAN TALBOT.

Cork Chamber: Fitzgerald House, Summerhill North, Cork; tel. (21) 4509044; fax (21) 4508568; e-mail info@corkchamber.ie; internet www.corkchamber.ie; f. 1819; Pres. GER O'MAHONEY; Chief Exec. CONOR HEALY.

Dublin Chamber of Commerce: 7 Clare St, Dublin 2; tel. (1) 6647200; fax (1) 6766043; e-mail info@dubchamber.ie; internet www.dubchamber.ie; f. 1783; Pres. PETER BRENNAN; Chief Exec. GINA QUIN.

INDUSTRIAL AND TRADE ASSOCIATIONS

Construction Industry Federation: Construction House, Canal Rd, Dublin 6; tel. (1) 4066000; fax (1) 4966953; e-mail cif@cif.ie; internet www.cif.ie; 37 asscns representing 2,000 mems; Pres. MATT GALLAGHER; Dir-Gen. TOM PARLON.

Irish Creamery Milk Suppliers' Association (ICMSA): John Feely House, Dublin Rd, Castletroy, Limerick; tel. (61) 314677; fax (61) 315737; e-mail info@icmsa.ie; internet www.icmsa.ie; f. 1950; Pres. JOHN G. COMER; Gen. Sec. CIARAN DOLAN.

Irish Farmers' Association (IFA): Irish Farm Centre, Bluebell, Dublin 12; tel. (1) 4500266; fax (1) 4551043; e-mail postmaster@ifa.ie; internet www.ifa.ie; Pres. JOHN BRYAN; Gen. Sec. PAT SMITH.

Irish Fishermen's Organisation Ltd: Cumberland House, Fenian St, Dublin 2; tel. (1) 6612400; fax (1) 6612424; e-mail irishfish@eircom.net; f. 1974; representative body for Irish commercial fishermen; Chair. EBBIE SHEEHAN.

Irish Grain and Feed Association: c/o 19 Carrick Hill, Portlaoise, Co Laois; tel. (502) 67022; fax (502) 68690; e-mail info@eorna.ie; internet www.eorna.ie; Pres. JERRY CLIFFORD; Dir DEIRDRE WEBB.

EMPLOYERS' ORGANIZATIONS

Irish Business and Employers Confederation (IBEC): Confederation House, 84–86 Lower Baggot St, Dublin 2; tel. (1) 6051500; fax (1) 6381500; e-mail info@ibec.ie; internet www.ibec.ie; f. 1993; represents c. 7,000 cos and orgs; Pres. LEO CRAWFORD; Dir-Gen. DANNY MCCOY.

Irish Exporters' Association: 28 Merrion Sq., Dublin 2; tel. (1) 6612182; fax (1) 6612315; e-mail iea@irishexporters.ie; internet www.irishexporters.ie; f. 1951; Pres. LIAM SHANAHAN; CEO JOHN WHELAN.

UTILITIES

Regulatory Authority

An Coimisiún um Rialáil Fuinnimh/Commission for Energy Regulation (CER): The Exchange, Belgard Sq. North, Tallaght, Dublin 24; tel. (1) 4000800; fax (1) 4000850; e-mail info@cer.ie; internet www.cer.ie; f. 1999; responsible for licensing and regulating the generation and supply of electricity and natural gas, and authorizing construction of new generating plants; designed and implemented cross-border Single Electricity Market with Northern Ireland Authority for Utility Regulation; Chair. MICHAEL G. TUTTY.

Electricity and Gas

Airtricity: Airtricity House, Ravenscourt Office Park, Sandyford, Dublin 18; tel. (1) 6556400; fax (1) 6556444; e-mail info@airtricity.com; internet www.airtricity.com; f. 1997; generator and supplier of electricity, using renewable sources; acquired by Scottish and Southern Energy PLC (United Kingdom) in 2008; Man. Dir KEVIN GREENHORN.

Bord Gáis Éireann (BGÉ) (The Irish Gas Board): Gasworks Rd, POB 51, Cork, Co Cork; tel. (21) 4534000; fax (21) 4534001; e-mail gasinfo@bge.ie; internet www.bordgais.ie; f. 1976; natural gas transmission and distribution, gas and electricity supply, electricity generation; Chair. ROSE HYNES; CEO JOHN MULLINS.

EirGrid PLC: 160 Shelbourne Rd, Dublin 4; tel. (1) 6771700; fax (1) 6615375; e-mail info@eirgrid.com; internet www.eirgrid.com; f. 2006; manages transmission of Ireland's electricity; state-owned; Chair. BERNIE GRAY; CEO DERMOT BYRNE.

Electricity Supply Board (ESB): 27 Lower Fitzwilliam St, Dublin 2; tel. (1) 6765831; fax (1) 6760727; e-mail service@esb.ie; internet www.esb.ie; f. 1927; reorg. 1988; supplier of electricity and operator of 15 generating stations; 95% state-owned; Chair. LOCHLANN QUINN; CEO PAT O'DOHERTY.

Energia: Mill House, Ashtowngate, Navan Rd, Dublin 15; tel. (1) 850363744; fax (1) 8692050; e-mail customer.service@energia.ie; internet www.energia.ie; f. 1999; generator and supplier of electricity and gas to business customers across Ireland; subsidiary of Viridian Group Ltd (UK); Chief Exec. GARY RYAN.

Flogas Natural Gas Ltd: Dublin Rd, Drogheda, Co Louth; tel. (41) 9831041; fax (41) 9834652; e-mail info@flogasnaturalgas.ie; internet www.flogasnaturalgas.ie; supplier of natural gas to residential customers across Ireland; Man. Dir RICHARD MARTIN.

Water

Responsibility for water supply rests with the City and County councils. The Department of the Environment, Community and Local Government is responsible for improving and maintaining water supply infrastructure.

CO-OPERATIVES

Irish Co-operative Organisation Society (ICOS): 84 Merrion Sq., Dublin 2; tel. (1) 6764783; fax (1) 6624502; e-mail info@icos.ie; internet www.icos.ie; f. 1894; 3 operating divisions; offices in Dublin, Cork and Brussels (Belgium); Pres. PATRICK MCLOUGHLIN; over 130 mem. co-operatives representing c. 150,000 farmers.

Irish Dairy Board: Grattan House, Lower Mount St, Dublin 2; tel. (1) 6619599; fax (1) 6612778; e-mail idb@idb.ie; internet www.idb.ie; f. 1961; reorg. 1973 as a farmers' co-operative; principal exporter of Irish dairy products; Chair. MICHAEL CRONIN; Chief Exec. KEVIN LANE.

TRADE UNIONS

Central Organization

Irish Congress of Trade Unions (ICTU): 31–32 Parnell Sq., Dublin 1; tel. (1) 8897777; fax (1) 8872012; e-mail congress@ictu.ie; internet www.ictu.ie; f. 1894; represents some 770,000 workers in 56 affiliated unions in Ireland and Northern Ireland (2005); Pres. JACK O'CONNOR; Gen. Sec. DAVID BEGG.

Principal Trade Unions Affiliated to the ICTU

Association of Higher Civil and Public Servants: Fleming's Hall, 12 Fleming's Place, Dublin 4; tel. (1) 6686077; fax (1) 6686380; e-mail info@ahcps.ie; internet www.ahcps.ie; more than 50 brs; Gen. Sec. DAVE THOMAS; 3,000 mems.

Building and Allied Trades' Union: Arus Hibernia, 13 Blessington St, Dublin 7; tel. (1) 8301911; fax (1) 8304869; e-mail union@batu.ie; internet www.batu.ie; Pres. MICHAEL MCNALLY; Gen. Sec. PATRICK O'SHAUGHNESSY; 10,020 mems (2002).

Civil, Public & Services Union: Adelaide House, 19–20 Adelaide Rd, Dublin 2; tel. (1) 6765394; fax (1) 6762918; e-mail headoffice@cpsu.ie; internet www.cpsu.ie; f. 1922; Gen. Sec. BLAIR HORAN; 13,810 mems (2004).

Communications Workers' Union: Áras Ghaibréil, 575 North Circular Rd, Dublin 1; tel. (1) 8663000; fax (1) 8663099; e-mail info@cwu.ie; internet www.cwu.ie; f. 1922; Pres. CHARLIE KELLY; Gen. Sec. STEVE FITZPATRICK; 19,600 mems (2003).

Electricity Supply Board Officers' Association: East James's Pl., Baggot St, Dublin 2; tel. (1) 6767444; fax (1) 6789226; e-mail info@esboa.ie; internet www.esboa.ie; f. 1959; Pres. TREASA NI MHURCHU; Gen. Sec. FRAN O'NEILL; 2,000 mems.

Irish Bank Officials' Association: IBOA House, Upper Stephen Street, Dublin 8; tel. (1) 4755908; fax (1) 4780567; e-mail info@iboa.ie; internet www.iboa.ie; Pres. BRIAN DEASY; Gen. Sec. LARRY BRODERICK; over 20,000 mems.

Irish Federation of University Teachers: 11 Merrion Sq., Dublin 2; tel. (1) 6610910; fax (1) 6610909; e-mail generalsecretary@ifut.ie; internet www.ifut.ie; f. 1965; Pres. Dr MARIE CLARKE; Gen. Sec. MIKE JENNINGS; 2,084 mems (2011).

Irish Medical Organization: IMO House, 10 Fitzwilliam Pl., Dublin 2; tel. (1) 6767273; fax (1) 6612758; e-mail imo@imo.ie; internet www.imo.ie; f. 1882; Pres. Prof. SEÁN TIERNEY; CEO GEORGE MCNEICE; 5,814 mems (2008).

Irish Municipal, Public and Civil Trade Union (IMPACT): Nerney's Court, Dublin 1; tel. (1) 8171500; fax (1) 8171501; internet www.impact.ie; f. 1991; Pres. KEVIN O'MALLEY; Gen. Sec. SHAY CODY; over 65,000 mems.

Irish National Teachers' Organization: 35 Parnell Sq., Dublin 1; tel. (1) 8047700; fax (1) 8722462; e-mail feedback@into.ie; internet www.into.ie; f. 1868; Pres. NOREEN FLYNN; Gen. Sec. SHEILA NUNAN; 32,932 mems (March 2011, including 6,627 mems in Northern Ireland).

Irish Nurses and Midwives Organization: Whitworth Bldg, North Brunswick St, Dublin 7; tel. (1) 6640600; fax (1) 6610466; e-mail inmo@inmo.ie; internet www.inmo.ie; Pres. SHEILA DICKSON; Gen. Sec. LIAM DORAN; over 40,000 mems.

Mandate Trade Union: 9 Cavendish Row, Dublin 1; tel. (1) 8746321; fax (1) 8729581; e-mail mandate@mandate.ie; internet www.mandate.ie; f. 1994 by merger of Irish National Union of Vintners', Grocers' & Allied Trades' Assistants and Irish Distributive and Administrative Union; Gen. Sec. JOHN DOUGLAS; 45,000 mems (2006).

Public Service Executive Union: 30 Merrion Sq., Dublin 2; tel. (1) 6767271; fax (1) 6615777; e-mail info@pseu.ie; internet www.pseu.ie; f. 1890; Pres. FIONA LEE; Gen. Sec. TOM GERAGHTY; over 10,000 mems.

Services, Industrial, Professional and Technical Union (SIPTU): Liberty Hall, Dublin 1; tel. (1) 8586300; fax (1) 8749466; e-mail info@siptu.ie; internet www.siptu.ie; f. 1990; Gen. Pres. JACK O'CONNOR; Gen. Sec. JOE O'FLYNN; 200,000 mems (2008).

Teachers' Union of Ireland: 73 Orwell Rd, Rathgar, Dublin 6; tel. (1) 4922588; fax (1) 4922953; e-mail tui@tui.ie; internet www.tui.ie; f. 1955; Pres. BERNIE RUANE; Gen. Sec. PETER MACMENAMIN; 14,500 mems.

Technical, Engineering and Electrical Union: 6 Gardiner Row, Dublin 1; tel. (1) 8747047; fax (1) 8747048; e-mail info@teeu.ie; internet www.teeu.ie; f. 1992 by merger of Electrical Trades Union and National Engineering and Electrical Trades Union; Gen. Sec. EAMON DEVOY; c. 40,000 mems.

Union of Construction, Allied Trades and Technicians: UCATT House, 56 Parnell Sq. West, Dublin 1; tel. (1) 8731599; fax (1) 8731403; e-mail info@ucatt.ie; internet www.ucatt.ie; head office based in London, United Kingdom; Regional Sec. JIM MOORE; over 15,000 mems.

Unite—the Union: 55–56 Middle Abbey St, Dublin 1; tel. (1) 8734577; fax (1) 8734602; internet www.unitetheunion.org/regions/ireland.aspx; head office based in London, United Kingdom; Irish Regional Sec. JIMMY KELLY; 46,750 mems (2002, incl. Northern Ireland).

Unions not Affiliated to the ICTU

Association of Secondary Teachers, Ireland (ASTI): Thomas MacDonagh House, Winetavern St, Dublin 8; tel. (1) 6040160; fax (1) 8972760; e-mail info@asti.ie; internet www.asti.ie; f. 1909; Pres. JOE MORAN; Gen. Sec. JOHN WHITE; 18,000 mems.

National Bus and Rail Union: 54 Parnell Sq., Dublin 1; tel. (1) 8730411; fax (1) 8730137; e-mail nbru@eircom.net; internet www.nbru.ie; f. 1963; Gen. Sec. MICHAEL FAHERTY; 3,700 mems.

Transport

Córas Iompair Éireann (CIÉ) (The Irish Transport Co): Heuston Station, Dublin 8; tel. (1) 6771871; fax (1) 7032276; internet www.cie.ie; f. 1945; state corpn operating rail and road transport services; 3 operating cos: Iarnród Éireann (Irish Rail), Bus Éireann (Irish Bus) and Bus Átha Cliath (Dublin Bus); Chair. VIVIENNE JUPP.

RAILWAYS

In 2009 there were 2,288 km of track. Railway services are operated by Iarnród Éireann.

Iarnród Éireann (Irish Rail): Connolly Station, Dublin 1; tel. (1) 8363333; fax (1) 8364760; e-mail info@irishrail.ie; internet www.irishrail.ie; f. 1987; division of CIÉ; Chair. PHIL GAFFNEY; Man. Dir DICK FEARN.

INLAND WATERWAYS

The Grand and Royal Canals and the canal link into the Barrow Navigation system are controlled by CIÉ. The Grand Canal and Barrow are open to navigation by pleasure craft, and the rehabilitation and restoration of the Royal Canal is proceeding. The River Shannon, which is navigable from Limerick to Lough Allen, includes stretches of the Boyle, Suck, Camlin and Inny Rivers, the Erne Navigation and the Shannon–Erne Waterway. The total length of Irish navigable waterways is about 700 km.

ROADS

At 31 December 2008 there were an estimated 96,424 km of roads, of which 423 km were motorways, 5,010 km were national primary roads and 11,641 km were secondary roads.

National Roads Authority: St Martin's House, Waterloo Rd, Dublin 4; tel. (1) 6602511; fax (1) 6680009; e-mail info@nra.ie; internet www.nra.ie; f. 1994; responsible for the planning, supervision and maintenance of national road network; Chair. PETER MALONE; Chief Exec. FRED BARRY.

Bus Éireann (Irish Buses): Heuston Station, Dublin 8; internet www.buseireann.ie; f. 1987; provides bus and coach services across Ireland, except Dublin area; subsidiary of CIÉ; Chair. PAUL MALLEE; Chief Exec. TIM HAYES.

Dublin Bus (Bus Átha Cliath): 59 Upper O'Connell St., Dublin 1; tel. (1) 8734222; internet www.dublinbus.ie; f. 1987; provides bus services in Dublin area; subsidiary of CIÉ; Chair. KEVIN BONNER; Chief Exec. JOE MEAGHER.

SHIPPING

The principal seaports are Dublin, Dún Laoghaire, Cork, Waterford, Rosslare, Limerick, Foynes, Galway, New Ross, Drogheda, Dundalk, Fenit and Whiddy Island.

Arklow Shipping: North Quay, Arklow, Co Wicklow; tel. (402) 39901; fax (402) 39902; e-mail chartering@asl.ie; internet www.asl.ie; f. 1966; Man. Dir JAMES S. TYRRELL; 37 carriers.

Fastnet Line: Ferry Port, Ringaskiddy, Co Cork; tel. (21) 4378892; fax (21) 4378893; e-mail info@fastnetline.com; internet www.fastnetline.com; f. 2009; owned by West Cork Tourism Co-op; operates car ferry service between Cork and Swansea (Wales, United Kingdom); Chair. CONOR BUCKLEY; CEO PHIL JONES.

Irish Continental Group PLC: Ferryport, Alexandra Rd, Dublin 1; tel. (1) 6075628; fax (1) 8552268; e-mail info@icg.ie; internet www.icg.ie; f. 1972; controls Irish Ferries, operating passenger vehicle and ro-ro freight ferry services between Ireland, the United Kingdom and continental Europe; Chair. JOHN B. MCGUCKIAN; Man. Dir EAMONN ROTHWELL.

Irish Ferries: Ferryport, Alexandra Rd, POB 19, Dublin 1; tel. (81) 8300400; fax (1) 8193942; e-mail info@irishferries.com; internet www.irishferries.com; drive-on/drive-off car ferry and ro-ro freight services between Ireland, the United Kingdom and continental Europe, operating up to 109 sailings weekly; Group Man. Dir EAMONN ROTHWELL.

Stena Line: Ferry Terminal, Dún Laoghaire Harbour, Co Dublin; tel. (1) 2047777; fax (1) 2047620; e-mail info.ie@stenaline.com; internet www.stenaline.ie; services between Dún Laoghaire and Dublin Port—Holyhead (Wales, United Kingdom) including high-speed catamaran, Rosslare–Fishguard (Wales, United Kingdom), Belfast (Northern Ireland) and Stranraer (Scotland, United Kingdom), Larne–Fleetwood (England, United Kingdom), passengers, drive-on/drive-off car ferry, ro-ro freight services; Man. Dir GUNNAR BLOMDAHL.

Associations

Irish Chamber of Shipping: Port Centre, Alexandra Rd, Dublin Port, Dublin 1; tel. (1) 8559011; fax (1) 8559022; e-mail bks@iol.ie; Pres. Capt. D. HOPKINS; Dir B. W. KERR.

Irish Ship Agents' Association: Conway House, East Wall Road, Dublin 3; tel. (1) 8556221; fax (1) 8557234; e-mail info@irishshipagents.com; internet www.irishshipagents.com; Pres. MICHAEL COLLINS.

CIVIL AVIATION

There are international airports at Dublin, Shannon, Cork, Kerry and Knock (Ireland West Airport).

Commission for Aviation Regulation: Alexandra House, 3rd Floor, Earlsfort Terrace, Dublin 2; tel. (1) 6611700; fax (1) 6611269; e-mail info@aviationreg.ie; internet www.aviationreg.ie; f. 2001; responsible for licensing the travel trade in Ireland as well as airlines; approves providers of ground handling services under EU regulations; Commissioner CATHAL GUIOMARD.

Dublin Airport Authority PLC: Dublin Airport, Dublin; tel. (1) 8141111; fax (1) 8415386; internet www.dublinairportauthority.com; state-controlled; responsible for the management of Dublin, Shannon and Cork airports; Chair. DAVID DILGER; Chief Exec. DECLAN COLLIER.

Irish Aviation Authority: The Times Bldg, 11–12 D'Olier St, Dublin 2; tel. (1) 6718655; fax (1) 6792934; e-mail info@iaa.ie; internet www.iaa.ie; f. 1994; provides air traffic management, engineering and communications in airspace controlled by Ireland and related air traffic technological infrastructure; also regulates aircraft airworthiness certification and registration; the licensing of personnel and orgs involved in the maintenance of aircraft, as well as the licensing of pilots and aerodromes; Chair. ANNE NOLAN; Chief Exec. EAMONN BRENNAN.

Airlines

Aer Arann: 1 Northwood Ave, Santry, Dublin 9; tel. (1) 8447700; fax (1) 8447701; e-mail info@aerarann.com; internet www.aerarann.ie; f. 1970; regional airline operating flights on 37 routes throughout Ireland, United Kingdom and France; Exec. Chair. PÁDRAIG Ó CÉIDIGH; CEO PAUL SCHUTZ.

Aer Lingus Group PLC: Dublin Airport, Dublin; tel. (1) 8868202; fax (1) 8863832; internet www.aerlingus.com; f. 1936; reorg. 1993; 29.88% owned by Ryanair Holdings PLC, 25.1% govt-owned; domestic and international scheduled services; Chair. COLM BARRINGTON; CEO CHRISTOPH MUELLER.

CityJet: Swords Business Campus, Balheary Rd, Swords, Co Dublin; tel. (1) 8700100; fax (1) 8700115; e-mail info@cityjet.com; internet www.cityjet.com; f. 1994; operates chartered and scheduled passenger routes between Dublin and Belfast (Northern Ireland), London (United Kingdom) and destinations in continental Western Europe; 100% owned by Air France; CEO CHRISTINE OURMIÈRES.

Ryanair: Dublin Airport, Dublin; tel. (1) 8121212; fax (1) 8121213; internet www.ryanair.com; f. 1985; scheduled and charter passenger services to European and North African destinations; Chair. DAVID BONDERMAN; CEO MICHAEL O'LEARY.

Tourism

Intensive marketing campaigns have been undertaken in recent years to develop new markets for Irish tourism. In addition to many sites of historic and cultural interest, the country has numerous areas of natural beauty, notably the Killarney Lakes and the west coast. In 2009 a total of 7.2m. foreign tourists (including residents of Northern Ireland) visited Ireland, compared with 8.0m. in 2008. Receipts from tourism (including passenger transport) totalled an estimated €4,077m. in 2010, compared with €4,890m. in the previous year.

Dublin Regional Tourism Authority Ltd (Dublin Tourism): Suffolk St, Dublin 2; tel. (1) 6057700; fax (1) 6057757; e-mail reservations@dublintourism.ie; internet www.visitdublin.com; Chair. ANN RIORDAN.

Fáilte Ireland (National Tourism Development Authority): 88–95 Amiens St, Dublin 1; tel. (1) 8847700; fax (1) 8556821; e-mail info@failteireland.ie; internet www.failteireland.ie; f. 2003; Chair. REDMOND O'DONAGHUE; Chief Exec. SHAUN QUINN.

Irish Tourist Industry Confederation: Sandyford Office Park, Unit 5, Ground Floor, Dublin 18; tel. (1) 2934950; fax (1) 2934991; e-mail itic@eircom.net; internet www.itic.ie; Chair. RICHARD BOURKE; CEO EAMONN MCKEON.

Tourism Ireland: Bishop's Sq., 5th Floor, Redmond's Hill, Dublin 2; tel. (1) 4763400; fax (1) 4763666; e-mail corporate.dublin@tourismireland.com; internet www.tourismireland.com; f. 2001; promotes Ireland and Northern Ireland as a tourist destination; jointly funded by the Irish Government and the Northern Ireland Executive; Chief Exec. NIALL GIBBONS.

Defence

As assessed at November 2011, the regular armed forces totalled 9,650. The army comprised 7,850, the navy 1,015 and the air force 785. There was also a reserve of 14,875. Military service is voluntary. In November 2004 the European Union (EU) ministers responsible for defence agreed to create a number of 'battlegroups' (each comprising about 1,500 men), which could be deployed at short notice to crisis areas around the world. The EU battlegroups, two of which were to be ready for deployment at any one time, following a rotational schedule, reached full operational capacity from 1 January 2007. Ireland contributed to the Nordic battlegroup, which was commanded by Sweden, with the participation of Finland, Norway and Estonia. From January 2008 Ireland was a participant in the EUFOR mission to eastern Chad and the Central African Republic and by February 2009 was the second largest contributor to the mission (which was taken over by the UN in March), with 476 troops.

Defence Expenditure: budgeted at €933m. in 2011.

Chief of Staff of the Defence Forces: Maj.-Gen. SEÁN MCCANN.

Education

The Irish state has constitutional responsibility for the national education system. An aided system is in operation: Irish schools are funded by the state, but are under the management (with a few minor exceptions) of community bodies, usually religious groups. Pre-primary education is non-compulsory and aimed at students aged between one and six years. Primary and lower secondary education in Ireland is compulsory for nine years between six and 16 years of age. Primary education may begin at the age of four and lasts for up to eight years, comprising a two-year infant cycle and a six-year primary cycle. In 2005/06 aided primary schools accounted for the education of 98.9% of children in the primary sector. In 2008/09, enrolment at primary level included 96% of children in the relevant age-group, while enrolment at secondary level included 89% of children in the relevant age-group. Post-primary education begins at 12 years of age and lasts for up to six years, comprising a junior cycle of three years and a senior cycle of two or three years. The Junior Certificate examination is taken after three years in post-primary (second-level) education. The Leaving Certificate examination is taken after a further two or three years and is a necessary qualification for entry into university education. Accreditation for higher education is provided by the Department of Education and Skills. There are four universities in Ireland: the University of Dublin (Trinity College); the National University of Ireland (comprising the University Colleges of Cork, Dublin, Maynooth and Galway); Dublin City University; and the University of Limerick (which obtained university status in 1989). In addition, there are 15 technical colleges, providing a range of craft, technical, professional and other courses.

In the 2008 budget €8,498m. (equivalent to 21.0% of total government expenditure) was allocated to education and science.

ISRAEL

Introductory Survey

LOCATION, CLIMATE, LANGUAGE, RELIGION, FLAG, CAPITAL

Israel lies in western Asia, occupying a narrow strip of territory on the eastern shore of the Mediterranean Sea. The country also has a narrow outlet to the Red Sea at the northern tip of the Gulf of Aqaba. All of Israel's land frontiers are with Arab countries, the longest being with Egypt to the west and with Jordan to the east. Lebanon lies to the north, and Syria to the north-east. The climate is Mediterranean, with hot, dry summers, when the maximum temperature in Jerusalem is generally between 30°C and 35°C (86°F to 95°F), and mild, rainy winters, with a minimum temperature in the city of about 5°C (41°F). The climate is sub-tropical on the coast but more extreme in the Negev Desert, in the south, and near the shores of the Dead Sea (a lake on the Israeli–Jordanian frontier), where the summer temperature may exceed 50°C (122°F). The official languages are Hebrew and Arabic. Hebrew is spoken by about two-thirds of the population, including most Jews. About 15% of Israeli residents, including Muslim Arabs, speak Arabic (which is also the language spoken by the inhabitants of the Occupied Territories and the Palestinian Autonomous Areas), while many European languages (notably Russian) are also spoken. Some 75.4% of the population profess adherence to Judaism, the officially recognized religion of Israel, while 17.2% are Muslims. The national flag (proportions 8 by 11) has a white background, with a six-pointed blue star composed of two overlapping triangles (the 'Shield of David') between two horizontal blue stripes near the upper and lower edges. Although the Israeli Government has designated the city of Jerusalem (part of which is Jordanian territory annexed by Israel in 1967) as the country's capital, this is not recognized by the UN, and most foreign governments maintain their embassies in Tel-Aviv.

CONTEMPORARY POLITICAL HISTORY

Historical Context

The Zionist movement emerged in Europe in the 19th century in response to the growing sense of insecurity felt by Jewish minorities in many European countries as a result of the racial and religious persecution known as anti-semitism. The primary objective of Zionism was defined in 1897 at the Basle Congress, when Dr Theodor Herzl stated that Zionism sought 'to create for the Jewish people a home in Palestine secured by public law'. Zionists aimed to re-establish an autonomous community of Jews in what was their historical homeland.

Palestine was almost entirely populated by Arabs and had become part of the Turkish Ottoman Empire in the early 16th century. During the First World War the Ottoman Empire's Arab subjects launched the so-called Arab Revolt and, following the withdrawal of the Turks, in 1917–18 British troops occupied Palestine. In November 1917 the British Foreign Secretary, Arthur Balfour, declared British support for the establishment of a Jewish national home in Palestine, on condition that the rights of 'the existing non-Jewish communities' there were safeguarded; this became known as the Balfour Declaration and was confirmed by the governments of other countries then at war with Turkey. The British occupation of Palestine continued after the war under the terms of a League of Nations mandate, which also incorporated the Balfour Declaration. (In 1920 Palestine had been formally placed under British administration.) British rule in Palestine was hampered by the conflict between the declared obligations to the Jews and the rival claims of the indigenous Arab majority. In accordance with the mandate, Jewish settlers were admitted to Palestine only on the basis of limited annual quotas. There was serious anti-Jewish rioting by Arabs in 1921 and again in 1929. However, attempts to restrict immigration led to Jewish-sponsored riots in 1933. The extreme persecution of Jews by Nazi Germany caused an increase in the flow of Jewish immigrants, both legal and illegal, which intensified the unrest in Palestine. In 1937 a British proposal to establish separate Jewish and Arab states, while retaining a British-mandated area, was accepted by most Zionists but rejected by the Arabs, and by the end of that year hostilities between the two communities had descended into open conflict. A British scheme offering eventual independence for a bi-communal Palestinian state was postponed because of the Second World War, during which the Nazis caused the deaths of an estimated 6m. Jews in central and eastern Europe (more than one-third of the world's total Jewish population). The enormity of the Holocaust greatly increased international sympathy for Jewish claims to a homeland in Palestine.

After the war there was strong opposition by Palestinian Jews to continued British occupation. Numerous terrorist attacks were made by Jewish groups against British targets. In November 1947 the UN approved a plan for the partition of Palestine into two states, one Jewish (covering about 56% of the area) and one Arab. The plan was, however, rejected by Arab states and by Palestinian Arab leaders. Meanwhile, the conflict between the two communities in Palestine escalated into full-scale war.

On 14 May 1948 the United Kingdom terminated its Palestine mandate, and Jewish leaders immediately proclaimed the State of Israel, with David Ben-Gurion as Prime Minister. Despite the absence of recognized borders, the new state quickly received international recognition. Neighbouring Arab countries attempted to conquer Israel by military force, and fighting continued until January 1949, when cease-fire agreements left Israel in control of 75% of Palestine, including West Jerusalem. The de facto territory of Israel was thus nearly one-third greater than the area assigned to the Jewish State under the original UN partition plan. Jordanian forces controlled most of the remainder of Palestine, the area eventually known as the West Bank (or, to Israelis, as Judea and Samaria) and which was fully incorporated into Jordan in April 1950.

By the end of the British mandate the Jewish population of Palestine was about 650,000 (or 40% of the total). The new State of Israel encouraged further Jewish immigration: the Law of Return, adopted in July 1950, established a right of immigration for all Jews, and resulted in a rapid influx of Jewish settlers. Many former Arab residents of Palestine, meanwhile, had become refugees in neighbouring countries, mainly Jordan and Lebanon. About 400,000 Arabs had evacuated their homes prior to May 1948, and a similar number fled subsequently. In 1964 exiled Palestinian Arabs formed the Palestine Liberation Organization (PLO), with the aim, at that time, of overthrowing Israel.

Israel, together with the United Kingdom and France, launched an attack on Egypt in October 1956 following the nationalization of the Suez Canal by President Nasser; Israel seized the Gaza Strip (part of Palestine occupied by Egypt since 1949) and the Sinai Peninsula. After pressure from the UN and the USA, Israeli forces evacuated these areas in 1957, when a UN Emergency Force (UNEF) was established in Sinai. In 1967 the United Arab Republic (Egypt) secured the withdrawal of UNEF from its territory. Egyptian forces immediately reoccupied the garrison at Sharm el-Sheikh, near the southern tip of Sinai, and closed the Straits of Tiran to Israeli shipping, effectively (as in 1956) blockading the Israeli port of Eilat. In retaliation, Israeli forces attacked Egypt, Jordan and Syria, swiftly making substantial territorial gains. The so-called Six-Day War left Israel in possession of all Jerusalem, the West Bank area of Jordan, the Sinai Peninsula in Egypt, the Gaza Strip and the Golan Heights in Syria. East Jerusalem was almost immediately integrated into the State of Israel, while the other conquered areas were regarded as Occupied Territories. In November 1967 the UN Security Council adopted Resolution 242, urging Israel to withdraw from all the recently occupied Arab territories.

Domestic Political Affairs

Ben-Gurion resigned in June 1963 and was succeeded by Levi Eshkol. Three of the parties in the ruling coalition merged to form the Israel Labour Party in 1968. On the death of Eshkol in 1969, Golda Meir was elected Prime Minister. A cease-fire between Egypt and Israel was arranged in August 1970, but other Arab states and Palestinian guerrilla (mainly PLO) groups continued hostilities. Another Arab–Israeli war began on

6 October 1973, as Arab forces invaded Israeli-held territory on Yom Kippur (the Day of Atonement), the holiest day of the Jewish year. Egyptian forces crossed the Suez Canal and reoccupied part of Sinai, while Syrian troops launched an offensive on the Golan Heights. Having successfully repelled these advances, Israel made cease-fire agreements with Egypt and Syria on 24 October. The UN Security Council adopted another resolution (No. 338) in that month, urging a cease-fire and reaffirming the principles of Resolution 242. Gen. Itzhak Rabin succeeded Meir as Prime Minister of a Labour Alignment coalition in 1974. In May 1977 the Labour Alignment was defeated in a general election, and the Likud (Consolidation) bloc, led by Menachem Begin of the Herut (Freedom) Party, formed a Government with the support of minority parties.

In November 1977 the Egyptian President, Anwar Sadat, visited Israel, indicating tacit recognition of the Jewish State. In September 1978 President Jimmy Carter of the USA, President Sadat and Prime Minister Begin met at the US presidential retreat at Camp David, Maryland, and concluded two agreements: a 'framework for peace in the Middle East', providing for autonomy for the West Bank and Gaza Strip after a transitional period of five years; and a 'framework for the conclusion of a peace treaty between Egypt and Israel'; a formal peace treaty was subsequently signed, in March 1979, in Washington, DC, USA. In February 1980 Egypt became the first Arab country to grant diplomatic recognition to Israel. However, approval by the Israeli Knesset (parliament) in that year of legislation stating explicitly that Jerusalem should be forever the undivided capital of Israel, and Israel's formal annexation of the Golan Heights in 1981, subsequently impeded prospects of agreement on Palestinian autonomy.

Israel's phased withdrawal from Sinai was completed in April 1982. In June Israeli forces, under 'Operation Peace for Galilee', advanced through Lebanon and surrounded west Beirut, trapping 6,000 PLO fighters. Egypt withdrew its ambassador from Tel-Aviv in protest. Diplomatic efforts resulted in the evacuation of 14,000–15,000 PLO and Syrian fighters from Beirut to various Arab countries. In September Lebanese Phalangists massacred Palestinian refugees in the Sabra and Chatila camps in Beirut (see the chapter on Lebanon); an official Israeli inquiry found the Israeli leadership to be indirectly responsible through negligence and forced the resignation of Gen. Ariel Sharon as Minister of Defence. In May 1983 Israel and Lebanon concluded a peace agreement, declaring an end to hostilities and envisaging the withdrawal of all foreign forces from Lebanon within three months. Syria's refusal, however, to withdraw some 30,000 troops, and the continued presence of some 7,000 PLO fighters in the Beqa'a valley and northern Lebanon, delayed the Israeli withdrawal, although by the end of 1983 only 10,000 Israeli troops (of the original 30,000) remained in Lebanon.

In August 1983 Itzhak Shamir succeeded Begin as leader of the Likud bloc and Prime Minister. However, economic difficulties further undermined the Government, and the Labour Party forced a general election in July 1984. Neither the Labour Alignment nor Likud could form a viable coalition, so President Chaim Herzog invited the Labour leader, Shimon Peres, to form a government of national unity with Likud.

Israel's forces finally completed their withdrawal from Lebanon in June 1985, leaving responsibility for policing the occupied southern area of Lebanon to the Israeli-controlled 'South Lebanon Army' (SLA). During 1986 rocket attacks on settlements in northern Israel were resumed by Palestinian guerrillas. Israel responded with air assaults on Palestinian targets in southern Lebanon. Meanwhile, the Shi'ite fundamentalist group Hezbollah intensified attacks on SLA positions within the southern buffer zone. The conflict escalated following the abduction, in July 1989, of a local Shi'a Muslim leader by Israeli agents, and again in February 1992, after the assassination by the Israeli air force of the Hezbollah Secretary-General, Sheikh Abbas Moussawi.

In July 1988 King Hussein abrogated Jordan's legal and administrative responsibilities in the West Bank, and declared that he would no longer represent the Palestinians in any international conference on the Palestinian question, which from 1984 had come to dominate the political landscape of the Middle East. King Hussein's decision strengthened the PLO's negotiating position as the sole legitimate representative of the Palestinian people. Since December 1987 international attention had been focused on the Palestinian cause after the outbreak of an *intifada* (uprising) against Israeli rule in the Occupied Territories and Israeli attempts to suppress the rebellion. In November 1988 the PLO declared an independent Palestinian State (notionally the West Bank and Gaza Strip), and endorsed UN Security Council Resolution 242, thereby implicitly granting recognition to Israel. The USA refused to accept PLO proposals for a two-state solution put forward by the Chairman of the PLO, Yasser Arafat, in December, but it did open a dialogue with the organization. However, Prime Minister Itzhak Shamir (the Likud leader had assumed the Israeli premiership in October 1986, in accordance with the 1984 coalition agreement) would not negotiate, distrusting the PLO's undertaking to abandon violence. Instead, he appeared to favour the introduction of limited self-rule for the Palestinians of the West Bank and Gaza, as outlined in the 1978 Camp David accords. At the general election in November 1988 neither Likud nor Labour secured enough seats in the Knesset to form a viable coalition, leading to another Government of national unity being formed under Shamir, with Shimon Peres as Deputy Prime Minister and Minister of Finance.

In April 1989 Shamir presented a peace proposal that would include a reaffirmation by Egypt, Israel and the USA of the Camp David accords, and plans for the holding of free democratic elections in the West Bank and Gaza for Palestinian delegates who could negotiate self-rule under Israeli authority. The proposals, precluding direct talks with the PLO, were unacceptable to the PLO, which did not consider that elections could establish the basis for a political settlement. In September, none the less, President Hosni Mubarak of Egypt invited clarification of Shamir's plans and offered to convene an Israeli-Palestinian meeting in Cairo, Egypt. This was rejected by Likud ministers, on the grounds that it would entail direct contact with PLO delegates. In November Israel provisionally accepted a proposal by the US Secretary of State, James Baker, for a preliminary meeting to discuss the holding of elections in the West Bank and Gaza, on condition that Israel would not be required to negotiate with the PLO and that the talks would concern only Israel's election proposals. However, the PLO continued to demand a direct role, and the Baker initiative foundered.

The fragile Likud-Labour coalition was endangered in early 1990 by disputes and dismissals, and in March the Knesset adopted a motion of no confidence in Prime Minister Shamir. Shimon Peres was unable to form a new coalition, and in June, after several weeks of political bargaining, Shamir formed a new Government—a narrow, right-wing coalition of Likud and five small parties, with three independent members of the Knesset. In a policy document, Shamir emphasized the right of Jews to settle in all parts of 'Greater Israel', his opposition to the creation of an independent Palestinian state and his refusal to negotiate with the PLO—or with any Palestinians other than those resident in the Occupied Territories (excluding East Jerusalem).

In March 1990 US President George Bush opposed the granting to Israel of a loan of some US $400m. for the housing of Jewish immigrants from the USSR, since Israel would not guarantee to refrain from constructing new settlements in the Occupied Territories. Violence erupted throughout Israel and the Occupied Territories in May. The PLO's refusal to condemn the violence caused the USA to suspend its dialogue with the organization and to veto a UN Security Council resolution urging that international observers be dispatched to the Occupied Territories.

In October 1990 some 17 Palestinians were shot dead by Israeli police, following clashes with Jewish worshippers. International outrage at the shootings resulted in a UN Security Council vote to send an investigative mission, although Israel agreed only to receive a UN emissary. The invasion of Kuwait by Iraq in August had engendered an improvement in US-Israeli relations. However, Iraqi missile attacks on Israel in January 1991, shortly after a US-led multinational force had begun its offensive against Iraq, threatened the cohesion of the force. US diplomatic efforts, and the installation in Israel of US air defence systems, averted an immediate Israeli response.

The Madrid Peace Conference and the launch of the Middle East peace process

In March 1991 President Bush identified the resolution of the Arab–Israeli conflict as a priority of his Administration. By August intensive diplomacy by Baker had secured the agreement of the Israeli, Syrian, Egyptian, Jordanian and Lebanese Governments, and of Palestinian representatives, to attend a regional peace conference, the terms of reference for which would be a comprehensive peace settlement based on UN Security Council Resolutions 242 and 338. An initial, 'symbolic' session was held in Madrid, Spain, in October. However, subsequent talks soon became deadlocked over procedural issues. Israel repeatedly questioned the status of the Palestinian-Jordanian delegation and the right of the Palestinian component to participate separately in negotiations; furthermore, Israel's refusal to end construction of new settlements in the Occupied Territories continually jeopardized the peace process. In February 1992, immediately prior to the fourth session of peace talks, to be held in Washington, DC, Baker demanded a complete halt to Israel's settlement-building programme as a precondition for the granting of loan guarantees to the value of US $10,000m. for the housing of Jewish immigrants from the former USSR. A fifth round of negotiations was held in Washington, DC, in April 1992. During talks with the Palestinian component of the Palestinian-Jordanian delegation, Israeli representatives presented proposals for the holding of municipal elections in the West Bank and Gaza, and for the transfer of control of health care provision there to the Palestinian authorities. In May the first multilateral negotiations between the parties to the Middle East peace conference commenced; however, the sessions were boycotted by Syria and Lebanon, considering them futile until progress had been made in the bilateral negotiations.

A general election was held in June 1992, following the collapse of Itzhak Shamir's coalition Government in January. The Labour Party won 44 of the 120 seats in the Knesset, and Likud 32. However, even with the support of Meretz (an alliance of Ratz, Shinui and the United Workers' Party, which had won 12 seats) and the two Arab parties, the Democratic Arab Party and Hadash (which together held five seats), a left-wing coalition would have a majority of only two votes over the so-called 'right bloc' (Likud, Tzomet, Moledet and Tehiya) and the religious parties that had allied themselves with Likud in the previous legislature. The new Chairman of the Labour Party, Itzhak Rabin, was accordingly obliged to solicit support among the religious parties. His Government, presented to the Knesset in July, was an alliance of Labour, Meretz and the ultra-Orthodox Shas; the coalition held a total of 62 Knesset seats, and also commanded the unofficial support of the two Arab parties. Most international observers regarded the installation of the Labour-led coalition as having improved the prospects for peace in the Middle East. However, the sixth and seventh rounds of bilateral negotiations between Israeli, Syrian, Lebanese and Palestinian-Jordanian delegations in September–November 1992 failed to achieve any progress.

An eighth round of bilateral negotiations between Israeli and Arab delegations commenced in Washington, DC, in December 1992, but were soon overshadowed by violent confrontations between Palestinians and the Israeli security forces in the Occupied Territories, which led to the withdrawal of the Arab participants. In mid-December, in response to the deaths in the Territories of five members of the Israeli security forces, and to the abduction and murder by the Islamic Resistance Movement (Hamas) of an Israeli policeman, the Government ordered the deportation to Lebanon of 413 alleged Palestinian supporters of Hamas. The expulsions provoked international outrage, while the UN Security Council approved Resolution 799 condemning the deportations and demanding the return of the deportees to Israel. Despite threats by the Palestinian delegation to boycott future talks until all of the deportees had been readmitted, in February 1993 the Israeli Government insisted that the majority of the deportees would have to serve a period of exile. Consequently, the ninth round of bilateral negotiations was formally suspended; although the Security Council welcomed the Israeli Government's decision to permit the return of 100 deportees, Palestinian delegates insisted on full implementation of Resolution 799 as a precondition for resumed discussions. In March, amid a sharp escalation of violence in the West Bank and Gaza, Israel sealed off the territories indefinitely.

The suspended ninth round of bilateral negotiations in the Middle East peace process resumed in Washington, DC, in April 1993. The Palestinian delegation apparently agreed to attend the sessions following pressure by Arab governments, and after Israel had agreed to allow Faisal Husseini, the nominal leader of the Palestinian delegation and a resident of East Jerusalem, to participate. Israel was also reported to have undertaken to halt punitive deportations, and, with the USA, to have reaffirmed its commitment to Resolutions 242 and 338 as the terms of reference for the peace process. In May Ezer Weizman was inaugurated as Israeli President; Weizman, leader of the Yahad party, had been elected by the Knesset in March. Also in March Binyamin Netanyahu was chosen to replace Shamir as the Likud leader. In July Israeli armed forces mounted the most intensive air and artillery attacks on targets in Lebanon since Operation Peace for Galilee in 1982, in retaliation for attacks by Hezbollah fighters on settlements in northern Israel.

Declaration of Principles on Palestinian Self-Rule (the Oslo accords)

Following the 10th round of bilateral negotiations, convened in Washington, DC, in June 1993, on 13 September Israel and the PLO signed a Declaration of Principles on Palestinian Self-Rule in the Occupied Territories. The agreement, which entailed mutual recognition by Israel and the PLO, had been elaborated during a series of secret negotiations mediated by Norwegian diplomacy (and therefore became known as the Oslo accords). The Declaration of Principles established a detailed timetable for Israel's disengagement from the Occupied Territories, and stipulated that a permanent settlement of the Palestinian question should be in place by December 1998. From 13 October 1993 Palestinian authorities were to assume responsibility for education and culture, health, social welfare, direct taxation and tourism in the Gaza Strip and the Jericho area of the West Bank, and a transitional period of Palestinian self-rule was to begin on 13 December. Although the Declaration of Principles was ratified by the Knesset on 23 September 1993, there was widespread opposition to the agreement, particularly Israel's recognition of the PLO, from right-wing Israelis. The PLO Central Council, meeting in the Tunisian capital, Tunis, approved the accord on 11 October. Itzhak Rabin and Yasser Arafat held their first meeting in the context of the Declaration of Principles in Cairo on 6 October. A joint PLO-Israeli liaison committee subsequently met on 13 October, with delegations headed, respectively, by Mahmud Abbas and Shimon Peres; the committee was to meet frequently to monitor the implementation of the accord.

Meanwhile, in September 1993 allegations of corruption against Shas leader Aryeh Der'i prompted the resignation of Shas ministers from the Government, thus reducing the coalition to an alliance between the Labour Party and Meretz (and the Government's majority in the Knesset to only two). A new coalition agreement was signed with Yi'ud, a breakaway group from the Tzomet Party, in July 1994.

At a meeting in Cairo on 4 May 1994 Israel and the PLO signed an accord detailing arrangements for Palestinian self-rule in the Gaza Strip and Jericho. The accord provided for Israel's military withdrawal from these areas, and for the deployment there of a 9,000-strong Palestinian police force. A nominated Palestinian (National) Authority (PA) was to assume the responsibilities of the Israeli military administration in Gaza and Jericho, although Israeli authorities were to retain control in matters of external security and foreign affairs. Elections for a Palestinian Council, which, under the terms of the Oslo accords, were to have taken place in Gaza and the West Bank in July, were postponed until October. Israel's military withdrawal from Gaza and Jericho was completed on 13 May, and on 17 May the PLO formally assumed control of the Israeli Civil Administration's departments there. On 26–28 May the PA held its inaugural meeting in Tunis, defining a political programme and distributing ministerial portfolios. Arafat made a symbolic return to Gaza City on 1 July—his first visit for 25 years—and the PA was formally inaugurated in Jericho on 5 July. In August Israel and the PLO signed an agreement extending the authority of the PA to include education, health, tourism, social welfare and taxation.

In early October 1994 an Israeli soldier was abducted by Hamas fighters near Tel-Aviv, who subsequently demanded that Israel release the detained Hamas spiritual leader, Sheikh Ahmad Yassin, and other Palestinian prisoners in exchange for his life. Despite Palestinian action to detain some 300 Hamas members in the Gaza Strip, the kidnapped soldier was killed in the West Bank in mid-October. Shortly afterwards an attack by a Hamas suicide bomber in Tel-Aviv, in which 22 people died, prompted Israel to close its borders with the Palestinian territories.

In November 1994 a member of another militant Palestinian organization, Islamic Jihad, was killed in a car bomb attack in Gaza. The attack was blamed on the Israeli security forces by many Palestinians opposed to the Oslo accords. Three Israeli soldiers were subsequently killed in a suicide bombing in the Gaza Strip, for which Islamic Jihad claimed responsibility. It became clear that Israel's security concerns would continue to delay the redeployment of its armed forces in the West Bank and the holding of Palestinian elections, since Rabin stated in

December that the elections would either have to take place in the continued presence of Israeli forces or be postponed for a year. In January 1995 a suicide bombing (responsibility for which was again claimed by Islamic Jihad) at Beit Lid, in which 21 Israeli soldiers and civilians died, seriously jeopardized the peace process. The Government again closed Israel's borders with the West Bank and Gaza, and postponed the planned release of some 5,500 Palestinian prisoners. An emergency meeting of the leaders of Egypt, Israel, Jordan and the PLO was convened in Cairo early the following month; the summit's final communiqué condemned acts of terror and violence, and expressed support for the Declaration of Principles and the wider peace process. On 9 February, meanwhile, Israeli armed forces completed their withdrawal from Jordanian territories, in accordance with the bilateral peace treaty concluded in October 1994.

Despite intensive negotiations, it proved impossible to conclude an agreement on the expansion of Palestinian self-rule in the West Bank by the target date of 1 July 1995. The principal obstacles remained the question of precisely to where Israeli troops in the West Bank would redeploy, and the exact nature of security arrangements for some 130,000 Jewish settlers who were to remain there. On 28 September the Israeli-Palestinian Interim Agreement on the West Bank and the Gaza Strip was finally signed by Israel and the PLO. Its main provisions were the withdrawal of Israeli armed forces from a further six West Bank towns (Nablus, Ramallah, Jenin, Tulkaram, Qalqilya and Bethlehem) and a partial redeployment from the town of Hebron; national Palestinian legislative elections to an 82-member Palestinian Council and for a Palestinian Executive President; and the release, in three phases, of Palestinians detained by Israel. In anticipation of a violent reaction against the Interim Agreement by so-called 'rejectionist' groups within the Occupied Territories, Israel immediately sealed its borders with the West Bank and Gaza.

Meanwhile, bilateral negotiations between Israeli and Syrian delegations resumed in Washington, DC, in January 1994. In September Rabin announced details of a plan for a partial withdrawal of Israeli armed forces from the occupied Golan Heights, after which a three-year trial period of Israeli-Syrian 'normalization' would ensue. The proposals were rejected by President Assad; however, the Syrian leader did state his willingness to work towards peace with Israel. Also in that month Morocco, closely followed by Tunisia, became the second and third Arab states to establish diplomatic ties with Israel, and the six members of the Cooperation Council for the Arab States of the Gulf (the Gulf Cooperation Council, see p. 250) also decided to revoke the subsidiary elements of the Arab economic boycott of Israel. In May 1995 Israel and Syria were reported to have concluded a 'framework understanding on security arrangements', intended to facilitate discussions on security issues. Peres subsequently indicated that Israel had proposed that its forces should withdraw from the Golan Heights over a four-year period; Syria, however, had insisted that the withdrawal be effected over 18 months. Meanwhile, on 25 July 1994 Israel and Jordan signed a joint declaration formally ending the state of war between them and further defining arrangements for future bilateral negotiations. On 26 October Israel and Jordan signed a formal peace treaty, defining their common border and providing for a normalization of relations.

The assassination of Itzhak Rabin

On 4 November 1995 Itzhak Rabin was assassinated in Tel-Aviv by a Jewish student opposed to the peace process, in particular the Israeli withdrawal from the West Bank. The assassination caused a further marginalization of those on the extreme right wing of Israeli politics who had advocated violence as a means of halting the Oslo process, and provoked criticism of the opposition Likud, which, it was widely felt, had not sufficiently distanced itself from such extremist elements. The Minister of Foreign Affairs, Shimon Peres, was, with the agreement of Likud, invited to form a new government. The members of the outgoing administration—Labour, Meretz and Yi'ud—subsequently signed a new coalition agreement, and the Cabinet was formally approved by the Knesset in late November. In February 1996 Peres announced that elections to the Knesset and, for the first time, the direct election of the Prime Minister would take place in May 1996.

In spite of Rabin's assassination, Israeli armed forces completed their withdrawal from the West Bank town of Jenin on 13 November 1995, and in December they withdrew from Tulkaram, Nablus, Qalqilya, Bethlehem and Ramallah. With regard to Hebron, Israel and the PA signed an agreement transferring jurisdiction in some 17 areas of civilian affairs from Israel to the PA. At talks with Arafat at the Erez crossing-point between Israel and Gaza in December, Peres confirmed that Israel would release some 1,000 Palestinian prisoners before the impending Palestinian elections.

Peace negotiations between Israel and Syria resumed in December 1995 in Maryland, USA, followed by a second round in January 1996. However, the talks were quickly undermined by a series of suicide bombings in Israel in early 1996 (see below), and in March the Israeli negotiators returned home. Meanwhile, King Hussein of Jordan made a public visit to Tel-Aviv in January, during which Israel and Jordan signed a number of agreements relating to the normalization of economic and cultural relations.

Palestinian legislative and presidential elections were held in late January 1996, leading in principle to the final stage of the peace process, when Palestinian and Israeli negotiators would address such issues as Jerusalem, the rights of Palestinian refugees and the status of Jewish settlements in the Palestinian territories. In February and March, however, more than 50 Israelis died as a result of suicide bomb attacks in Jerusalem, Ashkelon and Tel-Aviv, and talks were suspended. Israel again ordered the indefinite closure of its borders with the Palestinian territories, and demanded that the PA suppress the activities of Hamas and Islamic Jihad in the areas under its control. A hitherto unknown group, the 'Yahya Ayyash Units', claimed responsibility for the attacks, to avenge the assassination—allegedly by Israeli agents—of Ayyash, a leading Hamas activist, in January 1996. Yasser Arafat, now the elected Palestinian President, condemned the bombings, and in late February more than 200 members of Hamas were detained by Palestinian security forces. Following the attacks, Israel asserted the right of its armed forces to enter PA-controlled areas when Israeli security was at stake. Furthermore, an agreement to redeploy troops from Hebron by 20 March was rescinded.

In April 1996 Israeli armed forces began a sustained campaign of intense air and artillery attacks on alleged Hezbollah positions in southern Lebanon and the southern suburbs of Beirut. The declared aim of the Israeli operation (code-named 'Grapes of Wrath') was to achieve the complete cessation of rocket attacks by Hezbollah on settlements in northern Israel. Some 400,000 Lebanese were displaced northwards, after the Israeli military authorities warned that they would be endangered by the offensive against Hezbollah. Moreover, the shelling by Israeli forces of a base of the UN peace-keeping force at Qana resulted in the deaths of more than 100 Lebanese civilians who had been sheltering there, and of four UN peace-keepers. A cease-fire 'understanding' took effect in late April; this was effectively a compromise confining the conflict to the area of the security zone in southern Lebanon, recognizing both Hezbollah's right to resist Israeli occupation and Israel's right to self-defence; the 'understanding' also envisaged the establishment of an Israel-Lebanon Monitoring Group (ILMG), comprising Israel, Lebanon, Syria, France and the USA, to supervise the cease-fire.

Israel welcomed the decision of the Palestine National Council (PNC) in late April 1996 to amend the Palestinian National Charter (or PLO Covenant), removing all clauses demanding the destruction of Israel: the Israeli Government had demanded that the Covenant be amended as a precondition for participation in the final stage of peace negotiations with the PLO.

The first term of Prime Minister Binyamin Netanyahu

No party gained an outright majority of the 120 seats in the elections to the Knesset, held on 19 May 1996, but the Likud leader, Binyamin Netanyahu, achieved a marginal victory over Peres in the direct prime-ministerial election. Prior to the legislative election a formal alliance between Likud, the Tzomet Party and Gesher had been announced. This alliance secured 32 seats, and Labour 34. The success of the ultra-Orthodox Shas and the National Religious Party (NRP), with 10 seats and nine, respectively, was the key factor in determining that the new Government would be formed by Likud. Netanyahu proceeded to sign agreements between the Likud alliance and Shas, the NRP, Israel B'Aliyah, United Torah Judaism and the Third Way, to form a coalition that would command the support of 66 deputies in the Knesset. The new Government's statement of policy excluded the possibility of granting Palestinian statehood or, with regard to Syria, of relinquishing de facto sovereignty of the occupied Golan Heights. Moreover, Netanyahu reportedly postponed further discussion of the withdrawal of Israeli armed forces from the West Bank town of Hebron, where they provided security for some 400 Jewish settlers. In June a summit meeting of Arab leaders (with the exception of Iraq) was convened in Cairo. The meeting's final communiqué reiterated Israel's withdrawal from all occupied territories (including East Jerusalem) as a basic requirement for a comprehensive Middle East peace settlement. However, in July the likely stance of the new Government was underlined by the appointment as Minister of Infrastructure of Ariel Sharon, who had played a leading role in the creation and expansion of Jewish settlements in the West Bank.

In September 1996 it was announced that Israel's Ministry of Defence had approved plans to construct some 1,800 new homes at existing Jewish settlements in the West Bank. Violent confrontations erupted between Palestinian security forces and civilians and the Israeli armed forces, in which at least 50 Palestinians and 18 Israelis were killed. The direct cause of the disturbances was attributed to the decision of the Israeli Government to open the north end of the Hasmonean tunnel running beneath the al-Aqsa Mosque in Jerusalem, although it appeared to be the inevitable culmination of Palestinian frustration at Israel's failure to implement agreements previously signed with the PA. The Israeli military authorities declared a state of emergency in the Gaza Strip and the West Bank. A special session of the UN Security Council was convened, and intense international diplomacy facilitated a crisis summit in Washington, DC, hosted by US President Bill Clinton and attended by Netanyahu, Arafat and King Hussein. In October Israel agreed to resume negotiations on the partial withdrawal of its armed forces from Hebron.

In January 1997 Israel and the PA finally concluded an agreement on the withdrawal of Israeli forces from Hebron. The principal terms of the accord were that the forces should withdraw from 80% of the town within 10 days, and that the first of three subsequent redeployments from the West Bank should take place six weeks after the signing of the agreement, and the remaining two by August 1998. As guarantor of the Hebron agreement, the USA undertook to obtain the release of Palestinian prisoners, and to ensure that Israel continued to engage in negotiations for a Palestinian airport in the Gaza Strip and on safe passage for Palestinians between the West Bank and Gaza. The USA also undertook to ensure that the PA would continue to combat terrorism, complete the revision of the Palestinian National Charter and consider Israeli requests to extradite Palestinians suspected of involvement in attacks in Israel.

Progress achieved through the agreement on Hebron was severely undermined in February 1997, when Israel announced that it was to proceed with the construction of 6,500 housing units at Har Homa (Jabal Abu Ghunaim in Arabic) in East Jerusalem. Tensions escalated in the following month, after Israel decided unilaterally to withdraw its armed forces from only 9% of the West Bank. Arafat denounced the decision and King Hussein accused Netanyahu of intentionally destroying the peace process. Israeli intransigence over the Har Homa settlement prompted Palestinians to abandon the 'final status' talks on borders, the Jerusalem issue, Jewish settlements and Palestinian refugees, scheduled to begin on 17 March, and on the following day construction at the site began. Riots among Palestinians erupted immediately, and shortly afterwards Hamas carried out a bomb attack in Tel-Aviv, killing four people. In late March the League of Arab States (the Arab League, see p. 364) voted to resume its economic boycott of Israel, suspend moves to establish diplomatic relations and withdraw from multilateral peace talks. (Jordan, the PA and Egypt were excluded from the resolution, owing to their binding bilateral agreements with Israel.)

In June 1997 the US House of Representatives voted in favour of recognizing Jerusalem as the undivided capital of Israel and of transferring the US embassy there, from Tel-Aviv. In the same month Ehud Barak, a former government minister and army chief of staff, was elected to replace Peres as Labour Party Chairman. In July two Hamas suicide bombers killed 14 civilians in Jerusalem, prompting Israel to suspend payment of tax revenues to the PA and again close off the Gaza Strip and the West Bank. Further suicide bombings in West Jerusalem in early September resulted in eight deaths. Following a visit by US Secretary of State Madeleine Albright in mid-September, Israel released further Palestinian assets (one-third of tax revenues owed to the PA had been released in August), while the Palestinians announced the closure of 17 institutions affiliated to Hamas.

Renewed hostilities erupted in northern Israel in August 1997 after Hezbollah launched a rocket attack on civilians in Kiryat Shmona. The attack, made following raids by Israeli commandos in which five Hezbollah members were killed, prompted further air-strikes by Israel in southern Lebanon. Violence escalated, with the shelling by the SLA of the Lebanese port of Sidon resulting in at least six deaths. Domestic pressure for an Israeli withdrawal from southern Lebanon increased after 12 Israeli marines, allegedly on a mission to assassinate Shi'ite leaders, were killed south of Sidon in September. Meanwhile, relations between Jordan and Israel deteriorated, after members of the Israeli intelligence force, Mossad, attempted to assassinate Hamas's political leader, Khalid Meshaal, in Amman. Following intensive negotiations between Netanyahu, Crown Prince Hassan of Jordan and US officials, several agreements regarding the release of prisoners ensued: in October Israel freed the Hamas spiritual leader, Sheikh Ahmad Yassin, in return for the release by Jordan of two Mossad agents arrested in connection with the attack on Meshaal; a further 12 Mossad agents were expelled by the Jordanian authorities following the release of 23 Jordanian and 50 Palestinian prisoners by Israel.

Bilateral negotiations between Israel and the PA resumed in November 1997. Israel offered to decelerate its construction of Jewish settlements in return for Palestinian approval of a plan to delay further redeployments of Israeli troops from the West Bank. At the same time, the Israeli Government announced plans to build 900 new housing units in the area. This prompted several Arab states to boycott the Middle East and North Africa economic conference, held in Doha, Qatar, in mid-November, which an Israeli delegation was scheduled to attend. At the end of November the Israeli Cabinet agreed in principle to a partial withdrawal from the West Bank, but specified neither its timing nor its scale. Conflicting opinions within the coalition Government meant that Netanyahu failed to produce a conclusive redeployment plan to present at talks with Albright in Paris, France, in December. In January 1998 Netanyahu announced that he would not make any further decisions regarding the peace process until the Palestinians had demonstrated further efforts to combat terrorism, reduced their security forces from 40,000 to 24,000 and amended their National Charter to recognize Israel's right to exist.

Addressing the Knesset in March 1998, UN Secretary-General Kofi Annan urged Israel to end 'provocative acts' towards the Palestinians, including the building of Jewish settlements. In June President Weizman (who had been elected for a second presidential term in March) angered Netanyahu by publicly demanding the dissolution of the Knesset and early elections so that Israelis might choose the future direction of peace talks. Meanwhile, further controversy arose when the Cabinet approved Netanyahu's draft plan whereby the municipal boundaries of Jerusalem would be extended to incorporate seven West Bank Jewish settlements—to create a 'Greater Jerusalem' covering six times the current area of the city. Arab leaders accused Netanyahu of seeking formally to annex parts of the West Bank, and the UN Security Council urged Israel to abandon the proposals.

On 23 October 1998, after nine days of intensive talks with President Clinton at the Wye Plantation, Maryland, Netanyahu and Arafat signed an agreement (the Wye River Memorandum) that outlined a three-month timetable for the implementation of the 1995 Interim Agreement and signalled the commencement of 'final status' talks, which should have begun in May 1996. With the mediation of Clinton and King Hussein, Israel agreed to redeploy its troops from 13.1% of the West Bank, while the PA agreed to intensify measures to prevent terrorism and to rewrite the Palestinian National Charter. On 11 November 1998, after the postponement of four scheduled meetings (owing to a bombing by Islamic Jihad in Jerusalem and Israeli fears of further attacks by Palestinian militant groups), the Israeli Cabinet approved the Wye Memorandum by a majority of eight votes to four. Netanyahu subsequently reiterated that a number of conditions would first have to be met by the Palestinians, and threatened effective Israeli annexation of areas of the West Bank if a Palestinian state were to be declared on 4 May 1999. (Arafat continued to reassert his right to declare a Palestinian state on the expiry date of the interim stage defined in Oslo, an act that Netanyahu claimed would fundamentally violate the Oslo accords.) On 17 November 1998 the Knesset ratified the Wye Memorandum by 75 votes to 19. Three days later the Israeli Government implemented the first stage of renewed redeployment from the West Bank, also releasing 250 Palestinian prisoners and signing a protocol allowing for the opening of an international airport at Gaza.

During December 1998 it became increasingly evident that divisions within Netanyahu's coalition over implementation of the Wye Memorandum were making government untenable. The administration effectively collapsed when the Minister of Finance, Yaacov Ne'eman, announced his resignation. Shortly afterwards the Knesset voted to hold elections to the legislature and premiership in the spring of 1999.

In December 1998 President Clinton attended a session of the PNC, at which the removal from the Palestinian National Charter of all clauses seeking Israel's destruction was re-affirmed. Following a meeting between Clinton, Arafat and Netanyahu at the Erez checkpoint, Netanyahu reiterated accusations that the Palestinians had not adequately addressed their security commitments and announced that he would not release Palestinian prisoners considered to have 'blood on their hands'. Netanyahu announced that the second phase of Israeli troop deployment envisaged by the Wye Memorandum, scheduled for 18 December, would not be undertaken. The Knesset subsequently voted to suspend implementation of the Wye Memorandum, thereby effectively suspending the peace process. In late December Arafat freed the Hamas spiritual leader, Sheikh Ahmad Yassin, from house arrest, prompting further Israeli claims that agreed anti-terrorism measures were not being implemented. The US Administration threatened to withhold US $1,200m. promised to Israel to fund its redeployment in the West Bank unless it complied with the terms of the Wye Memorandum. For several months President Clinton refused to hold a private meeting with Netanyahu, while agreeing to meet Arafat in March 1999 to discuss his threatened unilateral declaration of statehood on 4 May; following intense international pressure, the declaration was postponed at the end of April.

Hostilities between Israeli forces and Hezbollah in southern Lebanon persisted throughout 1998. In that year some 23 Israeli soldiers were killed, and there was increasing pressure on Netanyahu, even from some Likud ministers, for a unilateral withdrawal from the territory. On 1 April the Israeli Security Cabinet voted unanimously to adopt UN Resolution 425 urging an immediate withdrawal of Israeli troops from all Lebanese territory, provided that the Lebanese army gave security guarantees. However, both Lebanon and Syria demanded an unconditional withdrawal. In June the first Israeli-Lebanese exchange of prisoners and bodies since July 1996 took place. Fighting escalated when, in August 1998, Hezbollah launched rocket attacks on northern Israel in retaliation for an Israeli helicopter attack in which a senior Lebanese military official died. Seven Israeli soldiers died in two attacks in November, leading Netanyahu to curtail a European tour in order to hold an emergency cabinet meeting on a possible withdrawal. In December an Israeli air attack in which eight Lebanese civilians were killed provoked condemnation from the ILMG, which declared it to be a violation of the cease-fire 'understanding' reached in April 1996. In February 1999 the commander of the Israeli army unit for liaison with the SLA became the most senior Israeli officer to be killed in southern Lebanon since 1982. Israel responded with its heaviest air raids against Lebanon since the 1996 Grapes of Wrath operation, prompting fears of another major conflict.

The election of Ehud Barak as Prime Minister

At the general election held on 17 May 1999, Ehud Barak was elected Prime Minister with 56.1% of the total votes cast. In the elections to the Knesset, Barak's One Israel alliance (including Gesher and the moderate Meimad) secured 26 seats, while Likud's representation declined from 32 seats to 19. Shas, meanwhile, won 17 seats. Netanyahu subsequently resigned from both the Knesset and the Likud leadership, and in September Ariel Sharon was elected as Likud's new Chairman. Although Barak had received a clear mandate to form a government that would attempt to revive the stalled Middle East peace process, Israel's Prime Minister-elect committed himself only to seek a formula for regional peace. Barak stated that he would observe four 'security red lines' concerning negotiations with the Palestinians: Jerusalem would remain under Israeli sovereignty; there would be no return to the pre-1967 borders; most West Bank settlers would remain in settlements under Israeli sovereignty; and no 'foreign armies' would be based west of the Jordan river. Following complex negotiations, Barak forged a broad coalition with the Centre Party, Shas, Meretz, Israel B'Aliyah and the NRP, which was endorsed by the Knesset in July 1999. Barak himself took the defence portfolio, while David Levy, the Gesher leader, became the Minister of Foreign Affairs and Shimon Peres the Minister of Regional Co-operation.

In early September 1999, during a visit to the region by US Secretary of State Albright, Barak and Arafat travelled to Egypt for talks at Sharm el-Sheikh. On 4 September the two leaders signed the Sharm el-Sheikh Memorandum (or Wye Two accords), which outlined a revised timetable for implementation of the outstanding provisions of the original Wye Memorandum in order to facilitate the resumption of 'final status' talks: a new target date—13 September 2000—was set for the conclusion of a comprehensive 'final status' settlement, with a framework agreement to be in place by 13 February. (One important change was the reduction, to 350, of the number of Palestinian prisoners to be released by Israel.) On 8 September 1999 the Knesset ratified the Wye Two accords; the following day Israel released some 200 Palestinian prisoners, and on 10 September a further 7% of the West Bank was transferred to Palestinian civilian control. A further 151 Palestinian prisoners were released from Israeli custody in mid-October. On 25 October a southern 'safe passage' for Palestinians travelling between Gaza and Hebron was finally opened, under the terms of the Wye Memorandum. In late 1999 Barak encountered severe criticism by left-wing groups and Palestinians over his Government's apparent intention to continue to approve the expansion of Jewish settlements in the West Bank. (Since coming to power, the Government had issued tenders for some 2,600 new homes in such settlements.) Barak subsequently angered settler groups with a ruling that several of the 42 'outpost settlements' established in the West Bank under the Likud Government had been built illegally; 12 of the 'outposts' were dismantled in October.

Mauritania became the third member of the Arab League (after Egypt and Jordan) to establish full diplomatic relations with Israel in October 1999. Representatives of Israel and the PA commenced talks on 'final status' issues on 8 November in the West Bank city of Ramallah, although the redeployment of Israeli armed forces from a further 5% of the West Bank (due on 15 November) was delayed owing to a dispute over which areas were to be transferred. In December Barak and Arafat met on Palestinian territory for the first time, and at the end of the month Israel released some 26 Palestinian 'security' prisoners as a 'goodwill' gesture. On 6–7 January 2000 Israeli troops withdrew from a further 5% of the West Bank. However, Israel subsequently announced the postponement of a third redeployment, agreed under Wye Two (and scheduled for 20 January), until Barak had returned from talks with Syrian representatives in the USA (see below). In early February PA officials suspended peace negotiations with Israel, following the decision by the Israeli Cabinet to withdraw its armed forces from a sparsely populated 6.1% of the West Bank. The redeployment from a further 6.1% took place on 21 March, facilitating an official resumption of 'final status' talks. In that month a ruling by Israel's Supreme Court that the allocation of state-owned land on the basis of religion, nationality or ethnicity was illegal allowed Israeli Arabs to purchase land for the first time.

Meanwhile, in June 1999 the SLA completed a unilateral withdrawal from the Jezzine enclave. Later that month Barak was reportedly angered when the outgoing Netanyahu administration launched a series of air attacks on Lebanon, destroying Beirut's main power station and other infrastructure, in response to Hezbollah rocket attacks on northern Israel. In December Israel and Syria reached an 'understanding in principle' to limit the fighting in southern Lebanon; the informal cease-fire did not endure, however, and in January 2000 a senior SLA commander became the first Israeli soldier to be killed there for five months. At the end of January the deaths of another three of its soldiers led Israel to declare that peace talks with Syria would not resume until Damascus took action to restrain Hezbollah, but attacks by the militant Shi'ite group continued, and in February Israel retaliated with a massive series of bombing raids on Lebanese infrastructure. Israel announced a unilateral withdrawal from the 1996 cease-fire agreement, and there were renewed fears of a major conflict. Following the killing of three Israeli soldiers by Hezbollah in the same month, the Israeli Security Cabinet approved wide powers for the Prime Minister to order immediate retaliatory bombing raids into Lebanon.

In March 2000 the Israeli Cabinet voted unanimously to withdraw its forces from southern Lebanon by 7 July, even in the absence of a peace agreement with Syria. The Lebanese Government responded by demanding that Israel also depart from a small area on the Syrian border known as Shebaa Farms. (Shebaa Farms has been designated by the UN as being part of

Syria, and thus subject to the Syrian track of the peace process; Hezbollah, however, considers it to be part of southern Lebanon.) In April Israel released 13 Lebanese prisoners who had been detained without trial for more than a decade, apparently as 'bargaining chips' for Israeli soldiers missing in Lebanon. Fighting between Israeli troops and Hezbollah intensified in May, and on 23 May Israel's Security Cabinet voted to accelerate the withdrawal of its remaining troops from southern Lebanon. By this date Hezbollah had taken control of about one-third of the territory following the evacuation by the SLA of outposts transferred to its control by the Israeli army; moreover, mass defections from the SLA were reported. Meanwhile, Lebanese citizens stormed the al-Khiam prison in the security zone and freed 144 inmates. The rapid departure of all Israeli forces from southern Lebanon was completed on 24 May. Israeli public opinion generally welcomed an end to the occupation, since about 900 Israelis had been killed in southern Lebanon since 1978. After the withdrawal several thousand SLA members and their families fled across the border into northern Israel. In June 2000 the UN Security Council confirmed that Israel had completed its withdrawal from Lebanon in compliance with UN Resolution 425. The mandate of the UN Interim Force in Lebanon (UNIFIL) was extended for a six-month period in July, by which time UNIFIL personnel were patrolling the area vacated by Israeli forces, monitoring the line of withdrawal and providing humanitarian assistance. Further extensions of UNIFIL's mandate were announced at six-monthly intervals.

Meanwhile, a third round of 'final status' discussions opened in Eilat on 30 April 2000, but maps presented by Israeli officials to the PA in early May, defining Barak's interpretation of a future Palestinian state, were firmly rejected by the Palestinians. Two days later Barak and Arafat held a crisis meeting in Ramallah, at which Barak proposed that Israel transfer to full PA control three Arab villages situated close to Jerusalem, on condition that the third West Bank redeployment (scheduled for June) was postponed until after the conclusion of a final peace settlement. The Knesset approved the transfer in mid-May. However, Barak later announced that an Israeli withdrawal from the Arab villages would not be implemented until the PA took appropriate measures to curb unrest in the West Bank, where Palestinians had been protesting in support of gaoled Palestinians on hunger strike.

In early July 2000 the three right-wing parties (Israel B'Aliyah, the NRP and Shas) withdrew from Israel's coalition Government in protest against what they perceived to be Barak's willingness to concede to PA territorial claims. Yet, despite the loss of six ministers (two from Meretz had earlier resigned following a dispute with Shas), Barak survived a motion of no confidence in the Knesset. President Clinton opened the Camp David talks, aimed at reaching a framework agreement for a final peace settlement, on 11 July. However, despite intensive mediation efforts, the summit ended on 25 July without agreement. Progress had reportedly been made on the issues of the borders of a future Palestinian entity (to comprise all of the Gaza Strip and at least 90% of the West Bank) and the status of Palestinian refugees, but the two sides were unable to reach a compromise regarding the future status of Jerusalem. In the summit's final communiqué, both sides vowed to continue the pursuit of a 'final status' settlement and to avoid 'unilateral actions'—thereby implying that Arafat would not declare a Palestinian state on 13 September. (Shortly before that date the Palestinian legislature voted to delay such a declaration for an indefinite period.)

Meanwhile, following an inconclusive police investigation into allegations of fraud, President Weizman stated in May that he would resign in July 2000. In the presidential election held on 31 July, the little-known Moshe Katsav of Likud unexpectedly secured a narrow victory over Barak's nominee, Shimon Peres. Katsav was duly sworn in as the eighth President of Israel on 1 August, to serve an exceptional seven-year term. Immediately after the election Barak survived another no-confidence motion. However, in early August the Minister of Foreign Affairs, David Levy, announced his resignation, citing disagreements with Barak over the peace process, and was subsequently replaced by the Minister of Public Security, Shlomo Ben-Ami.

The al-Aqsa intifada

In late September 2000 Barak and Arafat met for the first time since the Camp David summit. Yet the resumption of contacts was swiftly overshadowed by the escalation of what became known as the al-Aqsa *intifada*, a renewed uprising by Palestinians against Israeli occupation, which resulted in the suspension of the Middle East peace process. On 28 September Likud leader Ariel Sharon made a highly controversial visit to the Temple Mount/Haram al-Sharif compound in Jerusalem (the site of the Dome of the Rock and the al-Aqsa Mosque), provoking protests by stone-throwing Palestinians, which in turn triggered violent unrest throughout the Palestinian territories. For the first time, Israeli Arabs clashed with security forces within Israel, and the uncompromising response of the Israeli security forces to the uprising attracted international criticism. On 7 October the UN Security Council issued a resolution condemning the 'excessive use of force' employed by Israeli security forces against Palestinian demonstrators. Israel closed the borders of the Palestinian territories and Gaza airport, and Barak demanded that Arafat rearrest about 60 militant Islamists who had recently been freed from Palestinian detention. Arafat, for his part, demanded an international inquiry into the causes of the violence.

The crisis escalated in mid-October 2000 after Israeli forces launched rocket attacks on the headquarters of Arafat's Fatah movement in Ramallah and other PA offices, in response to the murders of two Israeli army reservists by a Palestinian crowd. On 16–17 October an emergency summit meeting between Barak and Arafat was convened by President Clinton and hosted by President Mubarak at Sharm el-Sheikh, at which the Israelis and Palestinians agreed upon measures intended to end the fighting (including the formation of an international fact-finding commission to investigate its causes). However, violence intensified, and on 22 October Barak announced that Israel was to take a 'time-out' from the peace process. This declaration came as Barak undertook discussions with Likud on the formation of a national unity government prior to the reconvening of the Knesset for the new parliamentary term; but no compromise was reached, reportedly owing to Ariel Sharon's demand for a veto on all decisions relating to national security. Barak's decision formally to suspend Israel's participation in the peace process was precipitated by the final communiqué issued by Arab leaders after an emergency summit of the Arab League held in Cairo on 21–22 October, declaring that Israel bore full responsibility for the recent violence. Morocco, Tunisia and Oman announced that they had severed relations with Israel, and Qatar broke off ties in November.

A suicide bomb attack perpetrated by Islamic Jihad on an Israeli military target in Gaza at the end of October 2000 led the Israeli army to declare a new strategy of 'initiated attacks' or 'targeted killings' of the leaders of such groups, as well as senior Fatah commanders, whom it held responsible for 'terrorist' actions. In early November the Israeli Minister of Regional Co-operation, Shimon Peres, held crisis talks with Arafat in Gaza, at which the two sides agreed a fragile cease-fire based on the provisions agreed the previous month at Sharm el-Sheikh. The truce was broken almost immediately, however, when a car bomb planted by Islamic Jihad exploded in Jerusalem, killing two Israelis; Barak held the PA responsible for the attack through the recent release of dozens of Islamist militants. In mid-November Israel effectively imposed a complete economic blockade of the Palestinian areas, in an effort to overcome increasing concerns over its national security. Later in the month the explosion of a bomb close to a bus carrying Israeli schoolchildren (as a result of which two people died and several children were injured) provoked public outrage and led Israel to launch further air raids against Fatah targets in Gaza. Egypt responded by announcing that it was recalling its ambassador from Tel-Aviv, and in April 2002 suspended all direct contact with the Israeli Government other than for negotiations aimed at restoring peace in the region. (Egypt did not return an ambassador to Israel until March 2005.)

The accession of Prime Minister Ariel Sharon

At the end of November 2000 Barak unexpectedly called early prime ministerial elections for 2001, in an apparent attempt to secure his increasingly beleaguered Government. The election, held on 6 February 2001, resulted in an overwhelming victory for the Likud leader, Ariel Sharon, with 62.4% of the votes cast. Barak had lost the Israeli Arab vote—as the Arab parties had urged their supporters to boycott or abstain in the poll—and his defeat was interpreted as a decisive rejection of the Oslo peace process by the majority of Israelis. Sharon, whose principal election pledge had been the restoration of domestic and regional stability, immediately sought the formation of a broadly based government of national unity, essentially in an effort to secure a political base in the Knesset (where Likud held only 19 of the 120 seats). Following his defeat, Barak announced his resignation as

Labour leader, and later declared that he would not enter a government under Sharon and was to withdraw from political life 'for some time'. In late February Labour's Central Committee voted to join a coalition administration, enabling Sharon to conclude coalition agreements principally with the religious and right-wing parties. The national unity Government was approved by the Knesset in early March. The 26-member Cabinet included the ultra-Orthodox Shas (the leader of which, Eliyahu Yishai, became Deputy Prime Minister and Minister of the Interior), Israel B'Aliyah and the extreme right-wing National Union-Israel Beytenu bloc.

Following his election victory, Sharon rejected an appeal by the new US Administration of President George W. Bush, who had been inaugurated in January 2011, for Israel to end its blockade on the West Bank and Gaza Strip and to deliver overdue tax transfers to the PA. In March Sharon travelled to Washington, DC, for discussions with President Bush, while Arab League heads of state, meeting in Amman, resolved, *inter alia*, to reinstate the 'secondary' economic boycott of Israel.

It was announced in early April 2001 that the Israeli Government had issued tenders for the construction of a further 708 Jewish housing units in the West Bank. The al-Aqsa *intifada* intensified in that month when Israel took unprecedented action in response to a Palestinian mortar attack on the Israeli town of Sderot. Israeli armed forces imposed road blockades that effectively divided the Gaza Strip into three sections, and sent tanks and bulldozers into the Gazan town of Beit Hanoun; this was Israel's first armed incursion into territory that it had transferred to PA control under the terms of the Oslo accords. Amid heavy pressure from the US Administration, Israel withdrew its forces less than 24 hours later. Hopes of a resumption of the Oslo peace talks were raised in mid-April amid a revival of the so-called 'Egyptian-Jordanian initiative' or Taba plan. The initiative, based on the fragile understanding reached at Sharm el-Sheikh in October 2000, required that the situation on the ground be restored to that prior to the start of the al-Aqsa *intifada*. It also stipulated that negotiations be resumed from the point at which they stalled in January 2001, and that Israel agree to halt its settlement programme in the Occupied Territories. Sharon stated in late April that Israel would endorse the Taba plan provided that the PA end its demand for a complete freeze on the construction of Jewish settlements, and that all Palestinian violence should cease prior to the resumption of peace talks.

In May 2001 the Sharm el-Sheikh Fact-Finding Committee, under the chairmanship of former US senator George Mitchell, published its recommendations relating to the causes of the Israeli–Palestinian clashes. The so-called Mitchell Report referred to the visit of Ariel Sharon to the Islamic holy sites in September 2000 as 'provocative', but declined to single out for blame either Sharon or the PA leadership (which Israeli officials had accused of having orchestrated the violence). The Mitchell Report also demanded that Arafat undertake further measures to curb Palestinian 'terrorist operations', and appealed to Israel to end its economic blockade of the West Bank and Gaza Strip and to halt its settlement expansion programme. At the beginning of June 21 Israelis were killed in an attack by a Palestinian suicide bomber at a Tel-Aviv discothèque. On 12 June proposals for a comprehensive cease-fire, brokered by the USA, were approved by Israel and the PA; however, although Israel began to implement provisions made under the terms of the cease-fire to pull back troops from PA-controlled towns and to ease the economic blockade, the murder of two West Bank settlers by Palestinian gunmen and the killing of two Israeli soldiers in a suicide bombing in the Gaza Strip again hindered moves towards peace.

On several occasions during late 2001 Israel ordered its forces into PA-controlled towns—among them Hebron, Bethlehem, Jenin and Beit Jala—where violent clashes between Israelis and Palestinians were taking place. At the end of July, meanwhile, two leading Hamas members, alleged by Israel to have been involved in the Tel-Aviv nightclub bombing, were killed during an air raid on Hamas media offices in Nablus. In early August the Israeli administration published a 'most wanted' list of seven Palestinians whom it alleged to be prominent in the preparation of 'terrorist' attacks. Only days later at least 15 Israelis (including six children) were killed by a Palestinian suicide bomber at a Jerusalem restaurant. The Israeli Government responded to the bombing by taking temporary control of Orient House, the de facto headquarters of the PA in East Jerusalem. At the end of August Abu Ali Moustafa, leader of the Popular Front for the Liberation of Palestine (PFLP), was killed by Israeli security forces at the party's offices in Ramallah. In September the PFLP claimed responsibility for four bomb attacks in Jerusalem.

The massive suicide attacks apparently perpetrated by members of the al-Qa'ida network against New York and Washington, DC, on 11 September 2001 accelerated US and European Union (EU, see p. 276) efforts to urge Israel and the PA to effect a lasting cease-fire. By the time of the first anniversary of the outbreak of the al-Aqsa *intifada* on 28 September, the Israeli–Palestinian violence had led to the deaths of at least 600 Palestinians and more than 160 Israelis.

In mid-October 2001 the right-wing National Union-Israel Beytenu bloc withdrew from the governing coalition in protest at the Sharon administration's decision to pull back Israeli armed forces from the West Bank town of Hebron; two ministers thus resigned. Two days later one of these ministers, the hardline Minister of Tourism, Rechavam Ze'evi, was assassinated at a hotel in Arab East Jerusalem by a PFLP militant, in apparent retaliation for the recent assassination of the group's leader. Following the murder of Ze'evi—who was the first Israeli cabinet minister to be assassinated by an Arab militant—the National Union-Israel Beytenu bloc maintained its presence in the Government, with the other minister who had resigned, Minister of National Infrastructure Avigdor Lieberman, retaining his post and Rabbi Binyamin Elon subsequently being named as Ze'evi's successor. Sharon held Arafat personally responsible for the minister's death and suspended all contact with the PA. The Israeli Government also decided to reverse its recent moves to ease the economic restrictions on Palestinians in the West Bank and Gaza, and demanded that the PA immediately extradite the PFLP militants implicated in the assassination. Israeli armed forces entered six Palestinian towns in the West Bank (including Ramallah, Jenin, Nablus and Bethlehem), leading US officials to urge Israel to pull back its troops from PA-controlled areas. Although Israeli forces duly withdrew from two of the towns (Bethlehem and Beit Jala) at the end of October, Sharon announced that the withdrawal from the remaining four would not take place until the PA arrested more Islamist militants.

The Israeli–Palestinian crisis escalated in early December 2001 when Palestinian militants launched suicide attacks in Haifa and Jerusalem, in retaliation for the 'targeted killing' of a Hamas leader: in one weekend some 25 Israelis were killed, and scores wounded. Sharon cut short an official visit to the USA, and Israel launched heavy military strikes against Palestinian security targets. Israel escalated its military operations in the Palestinian territories in mid-December after 10 Israelis had died in a bomb attack in the West Bank. The Government demanded 'concrete action' from the PA, despite a recent speech in which Arafat had ordered the Palestinian militant groups to end their armed campaign against Israel. Israeli armed forces staged a 'tactical' withdrawal from areas around Nablus and Ramallah to permit Arafat's security forces to arrest wanted Palestinian militants. However, Arafat remained confined to his headquarters in Ramallah after Israel imposed a travel ban on the Palestinian leader. In late December Ben-Eliezer was elected as the new Labour Party leader.

In early January 2002 the Israeli administration ordered the partial withdrawal of its forces from some West Bank towns and the easing of certain restrictions against Palestinians there. Meanwhile, it was announced that Israeli forces in the Red Sea had intercepted a freighter ship, the *Karine-A*, which Israel claimed was carrying a large consignment of Iranian-made heavy weaponry destined for the Gaza Strip. Israeli and US officials claimed to have evidence of the PA's involvement in the trafficking of arms into the Occupied Territories, leading Arafat to institute an internal inquiry into the *Karine-A* affair, although he denied any knowledge of the shipment. In mid-January Israeli forces assassinated a leader of the Fatah-affiliated Al-Aqsa Martyrs' Brigades, provoking retaliatory attacks by that organization in Hadera and Jerusalem in which six Israelis died. Israeli forces proceeded to tighten the blockade around Arafat's Ramallah offices. At the end of the month Sharon approved a security plan involving the physical 'separation' of Jerusalem from the West Bank, in order to prevent attacks by Palestinian Islamist groups on Israeli territory.

In early March 2002 the UN Security Council adopted Resolution 1397, affirming its 'vision' of both Israeli and Palestinian states 'within secure and recognized borders'. Israel rejected a peace initiative put forward by Crown Prince Abdullah of Saudi Arabia at the Arab League summit held in Beirut in late March, owing to its objection to the proposal that Israel withdraw from all Arab lands occupied since 1967 in exchange for full recognition of the State of Israel by the Arab states. Towards the end of March 2002 a Hamas suicide bombing at a Passover celebration in Netanya resulted in the deaths of 30 Israelis and injured 140 others. The so-called 'Passover massacre' led the Israeli Government, on 29 March, to initiate a massive campaign of military incursions into West Bank towns—code-named 'Operation Defensive Shield'—with the declared aim of dismantling the Palestinian 'terrorist infrastructure'. Arafat's presidential compound at Ramallah was surrounded by Israeli troops, leaving the Palestinian leader isolated.

During the first two weeks of April 2002 intense fighting between the Israeli army and Palestinian militias occurred in the Jenin refugee camp—considered by Israel to be a base for Palestinian militants opposed to the Oslo accords. Some 23 Israeli soldiers and an estimated 53 Palestinians were reportedly killed in ambushes and gun battles at the camp. In mid-April US Secretary of State Powell arrived in Israel in an attempt to negotiate an Israeli-Palestinian cease-fire, and the Bush Administration repeated demands for Israel to withdraw from PA-controlled towns. There was a subsequent redeployment of Israeli forces from areas of the West Bank, and Arafat was freed by the Israeli authorities at the beginning of May, after the PA agreed to hand over five men suspected of involvement in the assassination of Rechavam Ze'evi, four of whom were convicted of direct involvement in Ze'evi's murder by an ad hoc Palestinian court established inside the Ramallah compound and sentenced to various terms of imprisonment. (For further details of events in the West Bank and Gaza Strip in March–May 2002, see the chapter on the Palestinian Autonomous Areas.)

The National Union-Israel Beytenu bloc withdrew from the governing coalition in March 2002, in protest against recent concessions made towards the Palestinians. However, the Government was strengthened a month later by the appointment of David Levy of Gesher and two ministers from the NRP as ministers without portfolio. The Central Committee of Likud voted in May to reject categorically the creation of a Palestinian state; this was interpreted as a reversal for Ariel Sharon, who publicly accepted the possibility of Palestinian independence. In mid-June Israel commenced the construction of a 'security fence', to extend the entire length of its border with the West Bank, with a view to preventing Palestinian militants from infiltrating Israeli territory and perpetrating further attacks. The barrier was to be constructed using sections of barbed wire, electrified metal and concrete wall. Despite international diplomatic efforts aimed at securing a new round of peace talks between Israel and the PA, and reports of a potential US initiative involving the creation of an 'interim' Palestinian state, there was a marked increase in violence at this time: Israel launched a new offensive, code-named 'Operation Determined Path', ordering troops into several West Bank and Gaza towns, in retaliation for another series of suicide attacks by Palestinian militants. Once again, Arafat's headquarters in Ramallah were blockaded by the Israeli military. In late June senior-level talks were resumed between Israel and the PA, while the Quartet group (comprising the USA, Russia, the UN and the EU) held discussions in London, United Kingdom, in a bid to reactivate the Oslo peace process.

Several Israelis died in an attack on a bus near a Jewish settlement in the West Bank in mid-July 2002, for which three Palestinian militant groups all claimed responsibility. The Israeli response to the latest assaults included freezing plans to ease some of the restrictions imposed on Palestinians living in the Territories. Human rights organizations criticized plans by Israel to deport a number of relatives of suspected Palestinian militants to the Gaza Strip; however, a ruling by the Israeli Supreme Court in September declared the expulsions to be legitimate. Meanwhile, in late July an Israeli air-strike on a residential building in Gaza City resulted in the deaths of up to 15 Palestinians (including several children) in addition to their intended target, a leader of Hamas's military wing. The Gaza air-strike precipitated a new round of violence, with four Jewish settlers being killed near Hebron. Israel responded by ordering tanks into the Gaza Strip. At the end of July at least seven Israelis were killed in a suicide bomb attack at the Hebrew University in Jerusalem; Hamas claimed responsibility for the blast. Following at least 15 further Israeli fatalities in early August as a result of Palestinian militant attacks, the Israeli Government ordered a total ban on freedom of movement for Palestinians in most West Bank cities, and targeted a number of leading militants in the Gaza Strip. Israel and the PA agreed at this time to implement a security plan (termed the 'Gaza, Bethlehem First' plan) whereby Israel would withdraw from the Gaza Strip and Bethlehem, in return for Palestinian security guarantees and a crackdown on militants. Israel began to withdraw its forces from Bethlehem on the following day; however, violence continued and further talks were cancelled. In early September the Israeli Ministry of the Interior took the unprecedented step of revoking the citizenship of an Arab Israeli who was accused of assisting Palestinian militants in plotting suicide attacks against Israelis. Two suicide bombings in Um al-Fahm and Tel-Aviv in mid-September led Israeli forces to start to demolish buildings in Arafat's Ramallah compound, claiming that some 20 Palestinian militants were being sheltered there.

Elections to the Knesset were held on 28 January 2003, a few months earlier than scheduled. In October 2002 the Labour Party had withdrawn from Sharon's governing coalition in opposition to provisions in the 2003 budget that allocated funds to Jewish settlements in the West Bank. Sharon and his Likud party won a resounding victory over the left-wing parties at the polls, securing 38 seats in the Knesset. A new coalition Government, comprising Likud, the secularist Shinui party, and the right-wing and religious NRP, National Union and Israel B'Aliyah parties, was announced at the end of February 2003. The former Likud premier, Binyamin Netanyahu, was named as Minister of Finance. In May Amram Mitzna resigned as Labour leader and was subsequently replaced, in an acting capacity, by Shimon Peres.

The 'roadmap' peace plan

President Bush announced in mid-April 2003 that he would publish the Quartet-sponsored 'roadmap' for achieving peace in the Middle East once the new Palestinian Prime Minister, Mahmud Abbas—who had been appointed in March—had announced a new Cabinet. On 29 April, the same day that the Palestinian legislature endorsed the new Palestinian administration, two Britons carried out a suicide bombing at a café in Tel-Aviv, killing five people. Nevertheless, on 30 April the USA presented both the Israeli and Palestinian Prime Ministers with copies of the 'roadmap'. This latest peace initiative envisaged the creation of a sovereign Palestinian state by 2005–06 in a process comprising three phases. The first phase dealt largely with Palestinian issues, namely the cessation of militant operations against Israel and the establishment of a civilian and government infrastructure. Israel would be required to withdraw from areas that it had occupied since 2000 and to dismantle Jewish settlements constructed since 2001. In phase two, Israel would hold peace talks with Lebanon and Syria regarding Palestinian borders, while the third and final phase would deal with the issues of Jerusalem and refugees. The roadmap emphasized the importance of UN Security Council Resolutions 242, 338 and 1397 in establishing a two-state settlement, and also reiterated that the Arab states must recognize Israel's right to exist. On 25 May the Israeli Cabinet accepted the terms of the roadmap, and at the end of the month Sharon made the unprecedented admission that Israel was in occupation of the Palestinian areas.

In early June 2003 Ariel Sharon, Mahmud Abbas and President Bush met in Aqaba, Jordan, to discuss the implementation of the roadmap, particularly the contentious issue of Jewish settlements. On 9 June Israeli troops commenced the dismantlement of settlements in the West Bank, but the nascent peace process was thwarted by a resumption of violence. On 10 June Israel attempted to kill a prominent Hamas leader, Abd al-Aziz al-Rantisi, prompting a suicide attack against a bus in Jerusalem, in which 16 people died. Israeli helicopter gunships were subsequently ordered to attack targets in Gaza. In all, 26 people were killed in the renewed hostilities, and the USA condemned Israel's attempt to assassinate al-Rantisi. However, Israel continued to dismantle the settlements as well as to instigate troop withdrawals from the West Bank and Gaza Strip and release a number of Palestinian prisoners. Though the release of Palestinian prisoners was not a condition of the roadmap, it was regarded as an important expression of support for Abbas. By mid-August more than 400 prisoners had been released, including members of Hamas and Islamic Jihad who had not been involved in planning or executing attacks against Israeli targets. These two militant groups, along with Arafat's Fatah movement, had declared a three-month cease-fire at the end of June.

Following these positive first steps, however, the roadmap was threatened by a resumption of Israeli–Palestinian hostilities in late August 2003 and growing international concerns over Israel's construction of its 'security fence' in the West Bank, which Israel was accused of using to annex Palestinian territory, and it was feared that it would become a permanent border in any future peace settlement. President Bush urged Sharon to remove the 'security fence' when the two leaders met in July, and the US Administration further threatened to withhold nearly US $10,000m. of essential loan guarantees unless construction ceased. Despite international pressure, Israel continued to erect the barrier as well as to maintain its policy of 'initiated attacks' against senior Palestinian militants. On 14 August Israeli forces killed a senior commander of Islamic Jihad in Hebron, and on 19 August a suicide bomber killed 20 Israelis on a bus in Jerusalem, an attack for which both Hamas and Islamic Jihad claimed responsibility. In retaliation, on 22 August Israel reimposed road-blocks on the main north–south highway in the Gaza Strip, reversing one of the earliest roadmap initiatives.

In October 2003 the Israeli Cabinet approved the next phase of the 'security fence'; although this was not contiguous to sections of the barrier already built, it was completely to enclose settlements in the West Bank. Additionally, a tender was issued for the construction of 550 new homes in a Jewish settlement close to Jerusalem. The USA announced in November that it was cutting US $290m. from a loan package guarantee for Israel as a penalty for renewed settlement construction in the West Bank and Gaza. The issue of the settlements was one raised by the authors of a new peace plan, launched by senior Palestinian and Israeli political figures in Geneva, Switzerland, on 1 December. The Geneva Accords, which did not have the official approval of either the Israeli or Palestinian administrations, outlined a two-state solution to the Israeli–Palestinian issue, including proposals that Palestinians would receive compensation for giving up the right of return; that most settlements in the West Bank and Gaza (except those neighbouring Jerusalem) would be dismantled; and that Jerusalem (to become the capital of two states) would be divided administratively rather than physically. On 8 December the UN General Assembly adopted a resolution asking the International Court of Justice (ICJ) in The Hague, Netherlands, to issue a (non-binding) ruling on the legality of Israel's 'security fence'; the hearings began in February 2004.

In December 2003 Sharon issued an ultimatum to the Palestinian leadership warning that, unless the PA started disarming and disbanding Palestinian militant groups, Israel would adopt a 'disengagement plan', which would effectively consist of accelerating the construction of the 'security fence' in the West Bank and physically separating Israel from the Palestinian territories. Sharon's speech attracted criticism from right-wing and ultra-Orthodox settler groups when it became clear that the disengagement plan would involve the evacuation of 17 settlements in the Gaza Strip, considered beyond the reach of the 'security fence'. Under the terms of the roadmap, which Sharon stated he was willing to implement if the Palestinians also carried out their obligations, at least 60 settlements in the West Bank and Gaza would have to be dismantled.

Meanwhile, from late 2003 Ariel Sharon became increasingly embroiled in an investigation into allegations that he had received US $1.5m. in illegal campaign contributions in advance of the Likud leadership contest in 1999. Israel's Supreme Court ordered the Prime Minister's son Gilad to hand over documents relating to a loan from a family friend and South African businessman to repay allegedly illegal donations. In June 2004 the Attorney-General dismissed further corruption charges against Ariel and Gilad pertaining to the circumstances under which Gilad had been employed as a consultant on an Israeli-backed development in Greece (despite the fact that the state prosecutor had presented evidence allegedly proving the premier's guilt), and, in February 2005, dropped the charges against the Prime Minister relating to the laundering of illegal campaign funds, citing insufficient evidence in both cases. In November 2005 another of the Prime Minister's sons, Omri Sharon, a member of the Knesset, pleaded guilty to charges relating to illegal fundraising activity during the 1999 Likud leadership campaign. Omri was sentenced to nine months' imprisonment (subsequently reduced to seven months on appeal) and fined US $64,000 in February 2006.

Sharon's disengagement plan

Meanwhile, Sharon announced in an interview published in the *Ha'aretz* newspaper in February 2004 that he had drawn up a plan to evacuate all Jewish settlements in the Gaza Strip. The evacuation would reportedly affect 7,500 settlers in 17 settlements (although details of the plan were subsequently amended—see below). This news was welcomed by the recently appointed Palestinian Prime Minister, Ahmad Quray. However, the proposed disengagement was overshadowed by the 'targeted killing' of Sheikh Ahmad Yassin, the founder and spiritual leader of Hamas, by Israeli helicopter gunships in March. The decision to kill Yassi, which provoked international condemnation, followed a double suicide bombing at the southern port of Ashdod earlier in March in which 10 Israelis died (responsibility for which was claimed jointly by Hamas and the Al-Aqsa Martyrs' Brigades), and apparently indicated the start of a campaign by the Israeli Government to eliminate the entire leadership of Hamas. Yassin's successor as leader of Hamas in Gaza, Abd al-Aziz al-Rantisi, was killed in mid-April in a rocket attack by Israeli helicopter gunships. In the aftermath of al-Rantisi's death, Hamas kept secret the identity of his successor and reportedly adopted a policy of 'collective leadership' in order to prevent future leaders of the organization from being similarly targeted.

During a meeting in the USA with President Bush in mid-April 2004, Sharon secured the endorsement by Bush of his proposals to 'disengage' from Gaza, which also involved the consolidation of six Jewish settlements in the West Bank. This was regarded as a major diplomatic coup for Sharon, but one which was inimical to the spirit of the roadmap. However, in early May members of his own Likud party overwhelmingly rejected the disengagement plan at a party ballot. The Prime Minister drew up a slightly modified version of the proposals, and in early June dismissed Minister of Transport Avigdor Lieberman and Minister of Tourism Binyamin Elon, both from the far-right National Union party and both opposed to an Israeli disengagement from Gaza. A few days later the NRP Minister of Construction and Housing, Efraim Eitam, resigned after Sharon's broad proposals were approved in principle by a cabinet vote. However, Sharon lost his Knesset majority when National Union's six deputies resigned, and he entered into negotiations with the Labour Party.

Meanwhile, as attacks by Palestinian militants against Israeli soldiers in the Gaza Strip intensified, with a number of fatalities being reported, in May 2004 Israel launched a large military offensive, code-named 'Operation Rainbow'. The aims of the operation were to locate and dismantle tunnels in the Rafah refugee camps through which militants were able to smuggle weapons from Egypt for use in attacks against Israelis, and to arrest Palestinians wanted for involvement in such attacks. Some 40 Palestinians, whom Israel claimed to be terrorists, were reported to have been killed. In June, after a petition had been filed by several Palestinian councils, the Israeli Supreme Court ordered the Government to alter the route of part of the 'security fence', including a 30-km section in a Palestinian village, Beit Sourik. In early July the ICJ advised that the barrier contravened international law and effectively constituted the annexation of Palestinian land, and disrupted thousands of civilians' lives, frustrating Palestinian attempts to achieve self-determination. The ICJ urged Israel to remove parts of the fence and pay compensation to affected Palestinians. Sharon rejected the ruling, which he asserted was politically motivated and detrimental to the US-led 'war on terror'. In late July the UN General Assembly voted to demand that Israel comply with the ICJ ruling and take down the barrier (the USA voted against the resolution). In August Sharon approved the construction of 1,000 new Jewish homes in the West Bank.

In October 2004 the Knesset voted to accept Sharon's proposal to dismantle all 21 settlements in Gaza, and four in the northern West Bank. In November the Cabinet approved a plan to compensate Jewish settlers due to be evacuated from Gaza, and to imprison settlers who resisted evacuation. The NRP's six parliamentary members withdrew from the coalition Government in opposition to Sharon's proposals for the Gaza Strip. In early December Sharon dismissed Shinui's five ministers when they voted against the first reading of the 2005 budget because it pledged US $98m. in subsidies to projects backed by United Torah Judaism. The Prime Minister's Likud party was left with only 40 out of the Knesset's 120 seats. After a period of negotiations, Labour agreed in mid-December 2004 to form a coalition with Likud. In January 2005 the Knesset narrowly approved the new coalition Government, to be composed principally of Likud, Labour and United Torah Judaism, thereby restoring Sharon's parliamentary majority; Labour leader Shimon Peres was awarded the new title of Vice-Premier.

In mid-October 2004 the Israeli army ended a 16-day assault, code-named 'Operation Days of Penitence', in northern and southern Gaza that left 135 Palestinians dead and destroyed an estimated 95 homes, according to UN figures. The operation had been prompted by a Hamas rocket that killed two children in Sderot, close to the Gaza Strip. Egypt pledged to provide 750 border guards to replace Israeli troops along the Egypt–Gaza frontier to attempt to prevent Palestinian arms-smuggling and to stop Hamas and other Palestinian factions from firing rockets into Israel in the event of Israel carrying out its Disengagement Plan.

Following the death of Yasser Arafat in November 2004, Mahmud Abbas was elected Executive President of the PA in January 2005. A summit meeting was convened between Sharon, Abbas, Egypt's President Mubarak and King Abdullah of Jordan in Sharm el-Sheikh on 8 February, amid hopes of a breakthrough in the Middle East peace process following the election of a new Palestinian leadership. Sharon and Abbas shook hands and issued verbal declarations to end hostilities between their two peoples; however, no formal cease-fire was agreed, and the militant groups Hamas and Islamic Jihad refused to be bound by the declaration. Israel agreed to hand over to PA security control the towns of Jericho, Tulkaram, Bethlehem, Qalqilya and Ramallah in the coming weeks; its forces duly withdrew from Jericho and Tulkaram in March. Moreover, shortly after the Sharm el-Sheikh summit Israel allowed 56 deported Palestinians to return to the West Bank, and also transferred the bodies of 15 Palestinian bombers to the PA. In late February Israel began the release of 500 Palestinian prisoners as a 'goodwill' gesture; a further 400 prisoners were to be freed after a three-month period. Meanwhile, in late February the Israeli Cabinet gave its final approval to the Government's planned disengagement from all settlements in the Gaza Strip and four in the West Bank. Jordan also returned an ambassador to Israel. In mid-March 13 armed Palestinian factions, including Hamas and Islamic Jihad, declared a cease-fire until the end of the year, on the condition that Israel refrained from attacks and released 8,000 Palestinian prisoners. The Knesset voted in late March to reject a bill that would require a national referendum to be held prior to any implementation of Sharon's Disengagement Plan, and approved the 2005 budget, thus avoiding the need to call a general election and preventing a delay to the Israeli withdrawal from the Gaza Strip and the four settlements in the West Bank.

In July 2005 Israeli and Palestinian officials were reported to have agreed in principle to the establishment of a 'safe passage' between the West Bank and the Gaza Strip following the implementation of Israel's Disengagement Plan. On 7 August, shortly before the Cabinet voted to implement the first stage of the Disengagement Plan, Minister of Finance Netanyahu announced his resignation. He denounced the disengagement as a threat to the security of the country and the unity of the nation, and criticized the unilateral nature of the withdrawal. Sharon appointed Vice-Prime Minister and Minister of Industry, Trade and Labour Ehud Olmert to the vacated portfolio in an acting capacity. Despite public protests and the need forcefully to evacuate settlers who refused to leave the territories after the deadline of 17 August, the disengagement was completed ahead of schedule, on 12 September, when the last Israeli forces left Gaza. Israel had approved the deployment of Egyptian troops along the Egypt–Gaza frontier in late August. In November Israeli and Egyptian officials agreed to reopen the Rafah border crossing, which was to be managed by the PA with the assistance of European monitors. Meanwhile, on 22 September Israeli forces completed their withdrawal from the northern West Bank.

Soon after the completion of the withdrawal, in response to a series of rocket attacks on Israel by Hamas militants from Gaza, Israel carried out air-strikes on the Gaza Strip in which it targeted militant leaders and carried out a series of arrests of suspected militants. Several fatal attacks carried out by militants against Israelis during October 2005 resulted in the suspension of security contacts with the PA. In November Hamas announced that it would not renew its cease-fire, which was to expire at the end of the year. Sharon continued to assert that Israeli operations against Hamas targets would not cease until Abbas disarmed militants and destroyed the 'terrorist infrastructure'.

Meanwhile, the Israeli Supreme Court voted in September 2005 to reject the non-binding ICJ ruling of July 2004 that the 'security fence' contravened international law, criticizing the verdict for not taking into account Israel's security needs. The Government had approved a controversial plan for the final route of its 'security fence' in July 2005, which was to result in four Arab areas of Jerusalem being separated from local schools and hospitals. However, new amenities were apparently to be built on the Palestinian side, and transport and crossing-points were to be provided. Despite the Supreme Court's decision to reject the ICJ's verdict, justices ordered that a section of the barrier around the Jewish village of Alfei Menashe in the West Bank be removed, asserting that due consideration for the rights of Palestinians living in the area had not been taken during its construction. Moreover, following complaints from residents of Palestinian villages near Qalqilya that the 'security fence' isolated them from the rest of the West Bank, the Supreme Court ordered a review of the route of the barrier. (After the Supreme Court ruled in 2006 that its route around Qalqilya should be revised, in July 2008 the Ministry of Defence agreed to remove a section of the barrier in order to give Palestinian residents greater access to their farmland.)

Following his defeat of Vice-Premier Shimon Peres in an internal ballot for the leadership of the Labour Party in mid-November 2005, the Chairman of the Histadrut trade union confederation, Amir Peretz, announced his decision to seek approval for the withdrawal of his party from the Government, which he claimed had mismanaged the peace process as well as domestic social issues. Eight Labour-Meimad ministers resigned their posts on 21 November, after Peretz's proposal had apparently won the support of an absolute majority of Labour members at a party conference. The ministers, whose resignations came into effect two days later, included Peres and Minister of National Infrastructure Binyamin Ben-Eliezer. Sharon adopted the vacated portfolios on an interim basis, and additionally assumed Peres's responsibilities as Vice-Premier.

Formation of the Kadima party

On 21 November 2005 Prime Minister Ariel Sharon announced that he was leaving Likud to establish a breakaway faction, Kadima (Forward), arguing that his former party could not achieve what he considered to be national objectives owing to the constant distraction of political struggles. The new party, he declared, would aim to pursue a peace agreement with the Palestinians in accordance with the roadmap, and to combat economic and social problems. A total of 14 Knesset members from Likud joined the new grouping, including six ministers and six deputy ministers, most notably Vice-Prime Minister Ehud Olmert and Minister of Immigrant Absorption and of Justice Tzipi Livni. Following a request from the Prime Minister, on 23 November President Katsav issued a decree dissolving the legislature with effect from 8 December, and calling legislative elections (due by November 2006) for 28 March 2006. On 30 November 2005 Shimon Peres announced his decision to leave the Labour Party in order to campaign for Kadima in the forthcoming elections, without stating whether he would actually join the new party. Both acting Chairman of Likud and Minister without Portfolio Tzachi Hanegbi and Minister of Defence Lt-Gen. Shaul Mofaz joined the new party in December. Netanyahu was confirmed as the new Likud Chairman later that month, following an internal ballot, and announced plans to withdraw Likud from the Government.

On 4 January 2006 Sharon suffered his second stroke in a month, which left him in a coma from which he had not emerged by early 2012. Olmert took over as acting Prime Minister following Sharon's incapacitation. Minister of Foreign Affairs Silvan Shalom resigned his post on 13 January 2006, after Netanyahu had asked his ministers to withdraw from the Government. Shalom was the last representative of Likud (and indeed of any party excluding Kadima) in the Cabinet, since the other three Likud ministers had tendered their resignations on the previous day. The Cabinet approved the appointment of three new ministers and the reallocation of various portfolios among existing government members on 18 January. Acting Prime Minister Olmert adopted the interior portfolio (he additionally held those of industry, trade and labour, finance, and social affairs), while Minister of Immigrant Absorption and of Justice Livni replaced Shalom as Minister of Foreign Affairs. Olmert was appointed acting leader of Kadima on the same day.

On 15 January 2006, 10 days prior to the staging of elections to the Palestinian Legislative Council (PLC), the Israeli Cabinet voted unanimously to permit Arab residents of East Jerusalem to participate in the poll. In the event, Hamas, which was contesting the polls as the Change and Reform list in order to circumvent a ban on its direct participation, secured a decisive majority in the new legislature, with 74 of the 132 seats, while President Abbas's Fatah movement won only 45 seats. Abbas subsequently confirmed that he would ask the militant group to form a new cabinet to succeed the administration led by Fatah, which announced that it would not join Hamas in government.

Following the announcement of preliminary results of the poll, Olmert declared that Israel would not deal with what he termed an 'armed terror organization that calls for Israel's destruction'. The Quartet group appealed to Hamas to reject violence and recognize Israel, and President Bush declared that the USA would not negotiate with a Hamas-led administration unless the organization renounced its call to destroy the Jewish State. However, in early February 2006 Russian President Vladimir Putin announced his intention to invite cabinet representatives of Hamas, which Russia did not consider to be a terrorist organization, to visit the Russian capital, Moscow, for talks. Meanwhile, Khalid Meshaal, the head of Hamas's political bureau, declared that his organization would not renounce violence, asserting that it was a legitimate form of resistance to Israeli occupation. Hamas was willing to negotiate a long-term truce only if Israel agreed to certain conditions, including a return to the pre-1967 borders. In an interview on Israeli television, Olmert pledged to separate Israel from the Palestinians within permanent borders, and to preserve a Jewish majority in Israel, should Kadima win the general election: Israel would retain the whole of Jerusalem and the main West Bank settlement blocs of Ma'aleh Adumim, Ariel and Gush Etzion, in addition to the Jordan Valley, but would be willing to relinquish parts of the West Bank where the majority of the population were Palestinian. He added that Israel would attempt to secure an internationally backed peace plan with Hamas, and would only pursue a unilateral solution should such attempts fail, and after giving the militant group time to reform, disarm and observe past interim peace agreements. Meshaal called Olmert's proposals 'a war declaration', dismissing the so-called Convergence Plan as allowing Israel to: illegally retain its possession of the largest section of the West Bank and its 'security fence'; reject concessions on the status of Jerusalem; and thwart the 'right of return' of Palestinian refugees.

Following the inauguration of the new PLC on 18 February 2006, Israel approved a series of measures designed to weaken the future Hamas-led administration, including withholding monthly tax payments to the PA and a ban on the transfer of equipment to Palestinian security forces, but promised not to prevent humanitarian aid from reaching Palestinians. In early March, on its scheduled visit to Moscow, Hamas announced that it would never accept Israel's right to exist, asserting that doing so would negate Palestinian rights, including the right to 'their property' of Jerusalem and the holy sites, and the 'right to return' of Palestinian refugees. However, the militant group pledged to extend the cease-fire that it had agreed with Israel in March 2005 for another year, on the condition that Israel refrained from the use of force throughout the period. The new Palestinian administration was sworn in on 28 March 2006.

Kadima obtained the largest share of the votes cast (22.0% of valid votes) in the elections to the Knesset on 28 March 2006, thereby securing 29 of the 120 seats. Labour-Meimad secured 19 seats, as in 2003, while Shas won 12 seats, Likud only 12, Israel Beytenu 11 and the Pensioners' Party seven. At 63.2% of the eligible electorate, the rate of participation was the lowest in the country's history. The new Knesset was sworn in on 17 April. On the same day a suicide bomber launched an attack in Tel-Aviv, killing himself and nine others; Islamic Jihad claimed responsibility for the attack. Dalia Itzik of Kadima was appointed Speaker of the Knesset on 4 May. Meanwhile, on 11 April the Government voted to change the status of Acting Prime Minister Olmert to Interim Prime Minister. (Israeli legislation stipulates that an interim Prime Minister must be appointed, from the governing faction, if the Prime Minister is unable to discharge the duties of his office for 100 days.)

President Katsav had asked Olmert to form a new coalition government in early April 2006, and in late April Labour-Meimad signed an agreement with Kadima to join the future administration. A coalition agreement with Shas and the Pensioners' Party was signed in early May, giving Olmert and his Government 67 seats in the legislature. Likud, which strongly opposed Olmert's plans for Israel to withdraw from large areas of the West Bank, ruled out the possibility of its joining the Cabinet. The Knesset voted to approve the new Government on 4 May. Olmert was to serve as Prime Minister and Minister of Social Affairs. Other notable appointees from Kadima included Shimon Peres as Vice-Premier and Minister for the Development of the Negev and Galilee, and Tzipi Livni as Vice-Prime Minister and Minister of Foreign Affairs; the Labour leader, Amir Peretz, was appointed Deputy Prime Minister and Minister of Defence.

Olmert spent the initial months of his premiership attempting to secure diplomatic support for his unilateralist Convergence Plan, visiting a number of international leaders to explain his strategy. However, the likely success of such a plan was severely challenged amid the violence that broke out in the Gaza Strip in late June 2006, following the kidnapping of an Israeli soldier, Corporal Gilad Shalit, in a cross-border raid by Hamas militants; two other soldiers were killed during the raid. On the following day Palestinian militant groups issued a statement demanding that Israel release all female Palestinian prisoners and all Palestinian prisoners under 18 years of age in exchange for Shalit. Israel responded by launching air-strikes on Gaza and entering the southern part of the Strip, while Israeli security forces arrested dozens of Hamas officials, including cabinet ministers and parliamentarians, for questioning in relation to their alleged involvement in attacks against Israeli targets. Israel's military operation (code-named 'Summer Rains') to seek to secure the release of Shalit in the Gaza Strip continued despite the conflict that began between Israel and Hezbollah in July.

Israel's military campaign in southern Lebanon

On 12 July 2006 Hezbollah militants kidnapped two Israeli soldiers and killed three others in a raid across Lebanon's border with northern Israel, simultaneously firing rockets at Israeli communities and military posts. A further five Israeli soldiers were killed when troops crossed into Lebanon in an attempt to rescue the kidnapped soldiers. Hezbollah declared that it would free the abducted soldiers in exchange for the release of Lebanese prisoners in Israeli gaols. On the same day Olmert secured the approval of his Cabinet, which held the Lebanese Government responsible for the cross-border raid, to pursue a military campaign against Hezbollah targets and Lebanese infrastructure with the aim of securing the release of the soldiers and forcing the disarmament of Hezbollah and the deployment of the Lebanese army in southern Lebanon. During the course of the month-long conflict Hezbollah launched thousands of rockets into Israeli territory, having declared 'open war' on Israel on 14 July. Israel, meanwhile, systematically targeted Lebanese infrastructure, blockading seaports, destroying numerous roads and bridges, and bombing important strategic targets such as Beirut International Airport. When at least 28 Lebanese (many of them children) died in a bombing raid on an apartment building in Qana on 30 July, Prime Minister Olmert expressed 'deep sorrow'; Israeli military chiefs, however, asserted that Hezbollah had been using the building in order to launch missile attacks against Israel. In early August the Israeli Cabinet approved a plan to send ground troops further into Lebanon, as far as the Litani river—some 30 km north of the Israeli border. (For further details regarding the conflict, see the chapter on Lebanon.)

On 11 August 2006 the UN Security Council adopted Resolution 1701, which, *inter alia*, called for: an immediate and full cessation of hostilities; the extension of the Lebanese Government's authority over the whole country; and the delineation of Lebanon's international boundaries, with particular regard to disputed areas such as Shebaa Farms. Although the Lebanese Government endorsed the resolution on 12 August, and Hezbollah stated that it would honour the demand for a cease-fire, 24 Israeli soldiers were killed on that day. Similarly, despite Israel's Cabinet approving the resolution on 13 August, on the following day Israeli troops launched an attack on a refugee camp in Sidon, killing a worker from the UN Relief and Works Agency for Palestine Refugees in the Near East (UNRWA). Nevertheless, the cease-fire between Israel and Hezbollah did take effect, as stipulated, on 14 August. Lebanese government forces and an enhanced UNIFIL contingent were to be deployed in southern Lebanon, while Israel was simultaneously to withdraw its forces from the territory. In line with former UN resolutions, Resolution 1701 also required that all armed groups in Lebanon disarm in order that the Government extend its sovereignty over the whole state. The resolution urged the parties involved to address the underlying causes of the conflict, including making efforts towards settling the issue of Lebanese prisoners in Israeli gaols, and pressed Hezbollah to release unconditionally the kidnapped Israeli soldiers. By the time that the cease-fire commenced, 43 Israeli civilians and 119 soldiers had been killed in the conflict, and more than 1,000 Lebanese had lost their lives; the number of Hezbollah militants killed was unknown. As international forces began controlling positions at Lebanon's seaports and airports, Israel lifted its naval blockade of Lebanon on 8 September, the day after it had removed restrictions on air travel to and from that country. The last Israeli ground forces were withdrawn from Lebanon on 1 October, in accordance with the terms of the cease-fire.

In August 2006 Deputy Prime Minister and Minister of Defence Amir Peretz appointed a committee of inquiry to investigate Israel's military capabilities and performance before and during the conflict with Hezbollah. However, Prime Minister Olmert refused to order a full judicial inquiry into the war (as demanded by many Israelis), but instead suggested forming two commissions—one political and the other military—to examine how both administrations had acted. In the event, the Cabinet voted in September to establish a joint committee under the chairmanship of a retired judge, Dr Eliyahu Winograd. The Winograd Commission published the initial results of its investigation into Israel's military campaign in Lebanon on 30 April 2007. In this interim report, which covered the period between Israel's withdrawal from southern Lebanon in 2000 to mid-July 2006, the Commission found Olmert and other senior Israeli officials to have demonstrated 'very serious failings' in their handling of the war with Hezbollah, and to have neglected to devise a comprehensive plan before launching the military campaign. The Prime Minister was said to have shown 'a serious failure in exercising judgement, responsibility and prudence' during the early stages of the conflict. The investigative panel also found that the declared aims of the Israeli military—i.e. the defeat of Hezbollah—were 'overly ambitious and impossible to achieve'. Although no specific resignations were recommended by the Winograd Commission, it did single out Peretz and former Chief of Staff of the Armed Forces Lt-Gen. Dan Halutz—who had resigned in January 2007 following the conclusion of military investigations in the Israeli armed forces' conduct during the conflict—as being responsible for Israel's military failures. (Lt-Gen. Gabi Ashkenazi was appointed as the new Chief of Staff of the Armed Forces in February.) Following the publication of the Winograd Commission's interim report, mass protests were held by Israelis demanding the resignation of the Prime Minister and his administration; although Olmert survived three votes of no confidence in the Knesset in May 2007, doubts remained over the long-term viability of his governing coalition.

Political developments after the war in Lebanon

In August 2006 the Minister of Justice, Haim Ramon, who was facing charges of sexual harassment, announced his resignation. Trial proceedings were initiated against Ramon in October, while a former Minister of the Environment, Tzahi Hanegbi, also faced charges in relation to allegations of election bribery, fraud and perjury. Significantly, police also recommended that President Moshe Katsav be charged with a number of serious offences, including rape and sexual harassment, fraud, bribery and obstruction of justice. In January 2007 the Knesset voted to declare Katsav 'temporarily incapacitated' for a three-month period while he was contesting the charges. The Speaker, Dalia Itzik, was named as acting President for this period. In April Katsav's leave of absence was extended by a further three months, or until his presidential term was scheduled to end in July. Itzik thus continued as acting President. Ramon, Hanegbi and Katsav all persistently denied the charges against them.

In October 2006 the Cabinet approved the appointment of ultra-nationalist Avigdor Lieberman of Israel Beytenu as Deputy Prime Minister and Minister of Strategic Affairs. In November the Vice-Prime Minister and Minister of Foreign Affairs, Tzipi Livni, also assumed responsibility for the justice portfolio. In January 2007 the Israeli Cabinet endorsed the appointment of an Arab Israeli member of the Knesset, Rajeb Majadele, as a Minister without Portfolio; he was assigned the science, culture and sport portfolio in March. However, Majadele's appointment to the Cabinet was strongly opposed by members of Israel's right-wing parties.

Meanwhile, in mid-January 2007 police began investigations into the role played by Ehud Olmert in the privatization of Bank Leumi in 2005, when the Prime Minister held the finance portfolio in Ariel Sharon's Government; it was alleged that Olmert had promoted the interests of two foreign businessmen in the sale of a controlling stake in the bank. Haim Ramon was found guilty of sexual harassment at the end of January 2007 and was sentenced to 120 hours of community service in March. In April the Minister of Finance, Abraham Hirchson, declared that he was taking a temporary leave of absence as a result of police investigations into his failure to report an embezzlement of funds by a former employee; Olmert assumed the finance portfolio in an acting capacity. A few days later the State Comptroller recommended that the Prime Minister face a criminal investigation into allegations that he arranged investment opportunities for an associate when he served as Minister of Industry, Trade and Labour. Olmert faced a new police investigation into his personal dealings in September: it was alleged that, while serving as mayor of Jerusalem, Olmert had acquired a property in the city at a price significantly below its market value, in exchange for the accelerated provision of building permits to the property developer involved. The Prime Minister's Office strenuously denied the claims. In November the police recommended that there was insufficient evidence to launch criminal proceedings against Olmert in the case concerning the privatization of Bank Leumi.

Former Prime Minister Ehud Barak won the second round of elections to the Labour Party leadership on 12 June 2007, defeating Ayi Ayalon. (Former Labour leader Amir Peretz had been defeated at the first round of voting in late May.) On 18 June Barak assumed the post of Deputy Prime Minister and Minister of Defence. Meanwhile, on 13 June 2007 Shimon Peres was elected by the Knesset as President of Israel, in succession to Katsav, defeating Reuben Rivlin of Likud and Colette Avital of Labour; he was officially inaugurated as President on 15 July. As part of a government reorganization on 4 July 2007, former Minister of Justice Ramon was returned to the Cabinet as Vice-Premier. Abraham Hirchson was succeeded as Minister of Finance by Ronnie Bar-On, whose post as Minister of the Interior was given to Sheetrit.

Increasing division in the Palestinian leadership

Meanwhile, Israel intensified Operation Summer Rains from October 2006. Much of the military action in November focused on the town of Beit Hanoun, in northern Gaza, which was reported to have become a base for militants who were launching rocket attacks on Israeli communities living close to the border. However, towards the end of November—by which time hundreds of Palestinians had been killed in the military campaign—President Abbas brokered a cease-fire between Palestinian fighters and Israeli forces, resulting in an Israeli withdrawal from Gaza. Shortly afterwards Olmert made it clear that he now favoured the resumption of Middle East peace discussions with a view to the eventual creation of a Palestinian state, rather than any further unilateral Israeli withdrawals from the West Bank, and indicated that Israel was prepared to free a significant number of Palestinian prisoners, in exchange for the release of Corporal Gilad Shalit unharmed. Following an agreement signed between representatives of Hamas and Fatah, in February 2007 to form a Palestinian administration of national unity, Israeli officials maintained that they would refuse to have contact with any cabinet that failed to recognize Israel's right to exist, renounce violence, and respect existing agreements between Israel and the PA. Although Israel persisted with its boycott of the Palestinian administration, the USA and some EU governments revealed that they would initiate contacts with non-Hamas ministers. In April 2007 Abbas and Olmert held discussions regarding a future Palestinian state and a possible prisoner exchange, in what was intended to be the first of a series of regular fortnightly meetings between the two leaders. However, later in the month militants from Hamas declared that the cease-fire brokered in November 2006 was ended, and launched a series of rockets into Israel from the Gaza Strip. Israel responded in May 2007 by conducting a series of air-strikes against alleged militant targets in Gaza; a number of Hamas legislators, ministers and local government officials were also detained by Israeli security forces.

On 14 June 2007 Hamas militants seized control of the Gaza Strip, leading President Abbas to dissolve the national unity Cabinet and appoint an Emergency Cabinet in its place. Although Israel was swift to recognize the new administration, the fact that governance of the Palestinian territories was now effectively divided between a Cabinet backed by President Abbas of Fatah in the West Bank and a Hamas-led administration in Gaza made the likelihood of a resumption of bilateral peace negotiations more remote. The Israeli Government moved quickly to show its support for Abbas by agreeing to transfer tax revenues to the PA that it had withdrawn following Hamas's election victory of January 2006. A meeting was also held in Sharm el-Sheikh on 25 June 2007 between Olmert, Abbas, President Mubarak of Egypt and King Abdullah of Jordan, with the Israeli premier declaring that Israel was to free 250 Fatah activists from gaol as a gesture of 'goodwill' to Abbas. Upon the expiry of the 30-day state of emergency, on 13 July President Abbas had appointed three new ministers to a reorganized Cabinet, which was to function as a caretaker administration under Prime Minister Salam Fayyad. Hamas refused to recognize the legitimacy of this interim administration.

Olmert and Abbas held discussions in the West Bank town of Jericho on 6 August 2007—the first talks to be convened between Israeli and Palestinian leaders on Palestinian territory since May 2000. The two leaders held further talks on 'fundamental issues' later in August 2007 and again in early September. On 16 August Israel and the USA signed a memorandum of understanding concerning the provision to Israel of some US $30,000m. of military assistance during 2008–18. Israel released another 57 Palestinian prisoners to the West Bank and 29 to the Gaza Strip in October. Towards the end of that month the Israeli Government responded to the launching of rockets into northern Israel by Palestinian militants from the Gaza Strip by confirming a policy of reducing fuel and electricity supplies to Gaza, which it now classified as a 'hostile entity'. (An intervention by the Supreme Court prevented the authorities from phasing out electricity supplies until they could prove that this would not impede vital services such as hospitals and sanitation provision, although the fuel sanctions were permitted.)

The Annapolis conference

Following a series of preparatory meetings between US officials and Israeli and Palestinian delegations in the preceding weeks, an international peace meeting intended officially to relaunch the Middle East peace process was held under US auspices in Annapolis, Maryland, on 27 November 2007. Members of the international Quartet group and the Arab League attended the talks, and Syria notably sent a low-level delegation. At the close of the meeting, US President Bush read a statement of Joint Understanding on Negotiations between Olmert and Abbas, who both expressed their commitment to achieving a final settlement of the outstanding issues of contention between Israelis and Palestinians by the end of 2008. However, Palestinians were angered in early December 2007 when an Israeli ministry issued tenders for more than 300 new housing units at the Har Homa settlement in East Jerusalem. Moreover, Olmert appeared to indicate that Israel would not be required to conclude a peace treaty with the PA by the end of 2008 if it considered that the Palestinians had not met their security obligations.

Although Hamas reportedly responded to the Annapolis meeting by pledging that Palestinian 'resistance' to Israeli occupation would continue, the Israeli authorities released a further 429 Palestinian prisoners (none of whom had been involved in attacks against Israelis) at this time as a renewed gesture of support for President Abbas. However, in mid-December 2007 Israeli forces conducted a series of air-strikes against militants in the Gaza Strip, as well as sending tanks into the southern part of the Strip, in an attempt to prevent the continuing rocket fire against Sderot in northern Israel.

Following a Palestinian rocket assault against Ashkelon in early January 2008, Israel intensified its military offensive in the Gaza Strip. In response to international criticism regarding the number of Palestinians killed during the offensive, Israeli officials claimed that militants were deliberately firing on Israeli troops from civilian areas. In the second week of January US President Bush undertook a three-day visit to Israel and the West Bank, where he held discussions with both Olmert and Abbas. Bush assured the Israelis that he understood their security concerns, but he also asserted that a future Palestinian state should be contiguous territory and not a 'Swiss cheese' of separate cantons. The US leader again urged Israel to cease the expansion of existing Jewish settlements in the West Bank and to remove illegal outposts, while he stated that the PA must ensure that militant groups be dismantled. Bush also surprised some commentators by issuing a firm statement urging Israel to withdraw from Arab territory that its forces had occupied in 1967. In mid-January 2008 Israel imposed virtually a complete blockade on the Gaza Strip, which prompted vehement international criticism. Amid concerns about a potential humanitarian crisis in Gaza, the Israeli Prime Minister subsequently agreed to allow food, medicine and necessary fuel to be supplied to Palestinians in Gaza.

Also in mid-January 2008 Deputy Prime Minister and Minister of Strategic Affairs Avigdor Lieberman announced that Israel Beytenu was to withdraw its members from the governing coalition, in protest at Olmert's policy of engaging in peace negotiations with the PA. This left Olmert with a reduced majority in the Knesset and resulted in the resignation of Lieberman and of the Minister of Tourism, Yitzhak Aharonovitch, from the Cabinet.

The long-awaited final report of the Winograd Commission was issued on 30 January 2008. Although the Commission described Israel's ground offensive in Lebanon in mid-2006 as a 'serious failure' in both military and political terms—noting the lack of any clear strategy prior to initiating the 34-day campaign against Hezbollah—it assessed Prime Minister Olmert to have acted 'in the sincere interest of Israel' in ordering the military action. Many observers expressed intense surprise at the lack of any serious personal criticism aimed at Olmert, particularly after he had ordered Israeli armed forces to undertake a large-scale ground offensive in southern Lebanon only hours before an agreed cease-fire was scheduled to take effect; 33 Israeli soldiers had died during this final stage of the war. However, the Winograd Commission notably acknowledged Israel's failure to secure an obvious military victory against Hezbollah. Thus, although Olmert initially survived the aftermath of the report's publication, it was widely acknowledged that he had been weakened by the Commission's findings, at a time when he was already under investigation for alleged corrupt practices.

In early March 2008 eight students died, and several others were wounded, in a shooting at a Jewish religious college in West Jerusalem believed to have been perpetrated by a Palestinian resident of East Jerusalem; the gunman was immediately shot dead by an off-duty Israeli soldier. A spokesperson for Hamas appeared to claim, and later deny, its involvement in the crime, which represented the worst such incident to take place in Jerusalem since 2004. Nevertheless, the Israeli Government affirmed that it would pursue peace negotiations with its Palestinian counterpart, and talks between Olmert and Abbas under the terms agreed at Annapolis resumed in April. However, shortly after the Jerusalem shooting, Olmert approved a plan to construct a further 330 homes for Jewish settlers in the West Bank, and in June 2008 the Israeli Government announced two new settlement-building projects in East Jerusalem, involving the construction of some 2,200 new Jewish homes. The US Secretary of State, Condoleezza Rice, during a visit to Jerusalem in an attempt to reinvigorate peace talks, warned Israel that expanding Jewish settlements on the West Bank threatened to undermine recent progress in the peace process.

In May 2008 the Israeli police began questioning Olmert with regard to the alleged receipt of some US $150,000 in donations from a US businessman to support the Prime Minister's campaign for elections both for the mayoralty of Jerusalem and for the Likud leadership during a 15-year period before he assumed the premiership in 2006. The Prime Minister subsequently admitted that he had received the donations, but insisted that these had not been for personal gain. The police investigation was reportedly widened in July 2008, when investigators stated that they intended to examine allegations that Olmert had been involved in 'serious fraud and other offences'. At the end of the month he officially declared his intention to resign the premiership in September, following the election of a new Kadima leader.

Following several violent incidents in previous weeks, in mid-June 2008 a formal cease-fire was finally agreed between Israel and Hamas representatives in the Gaza Strip, after lengthy negotiations led by Egyptian mediators. Israel was to end its economic blockade of the Strip and cease military action in the territory, on condition that Hamas militants and those of other Palestinian groups refrained from conducting any cross-border attacks on Israeli targets. The truce was to remain in place for at least six months, but to take effect in stages. However, later in June Israeli officials complained of a 'grave violation' of the cease-fire by Palestinian militants who had launched a rocket attack against the town of Sderot, and responded by closing Israel's border crossings into Gaza. The rocket attack was alleged to have been carried out by Islamic Jihad in retaliation for an Israeli military raid in the West Bank, which caused two Palestinian deaths. Hamas spokespersons asserted in early July that, since Israel was not abiding by the terms of the recent truce, it had suspended bilateral negotiations concerning a proposed prisoner exchange involving the release of Corporal Shalit. In the same month three Israelis were killed by a Palestinian militant who deliberately drove a bulldozer through a street in central Jerusalem before being shot dead by security forces.

In August 2008 the Israeli Government released 198 Palestinian prisoners in August 2008 as a 'goodwill' gesture to Abbas. The list included two of the longest-serving Palestinian detainees, who—contrary to Israel's usual policy of not freeing those with 'blood on their hands'—had been responsible for the deaths of two Israeli citizens in the 1970s. Earlier in that month Prime Minister Olmert was reported to have proposed a new peace plan whereby Israel would, *inter alia*, offer Palestinians 93% of the

West Bank, provided that Abbas's security forces regained control of the Gaza Strip from Hamas.

At the election for the Kadima leadership, held on 17 September 2008, Vice-Prime Minister and Minister of Foreign Affairs Livni secured a narrow victory, obtaining 43.1% of the votes and defeating the following rival candidates: Deputy Prime Minister and Minister of Transport and Road Safety Shaul Mofaz (with 42%), Minister of the Interior Meir Sheetrit and Minister of Public Security Abraham Dicter. Since the successor of his ruling party had been elected, on 21 September Olmert formally resigned the premiership in order to contest the various corruption charges against him. Olmert and his Cabinet were to remain in office pending the formation of a new government, a task which on 22 September Livni was asked to undertake by President Shimon Peres. However, the Prime Minister-designate announced on 26 October that negotiations with potential coalition partners had been unsuccessful. A general election was thus scheduled for 10 February 2009.

In November 2008 the first direct clashes between Israeli armed forces and Hamas militants since the cease-fire agreement of June took place in the Gaza Strip. Israel launched a renewed military campaign in the territory and reimposed its blockade in an attempt to prevent what it claimed to be Hamas's attempts to kidnap Israeli soldiers. Hamas and Islamic Jihad fighters responded by firing rockets into northern Israel. Nevertheless, following the first meeting held between Olmert and Abbas for two months, on 15 December 227 Palestinian prisoners (none of whom were from Hamas or Islamic Jihad) were released as a 'confidence-building measure'. On 16 December the UN Security Council approved Resolution 1850, which endorsed the idea of a two-state solution to the Israeli–Palestinian conflict and affirmed that the peace process was 'irreversible'. The resolution urged all parties involved in the negotiations to intensify their efforts to achieve a comprehensive and lasting peace in the Middle East.

'Operation Cast Lead'

On 19 December 2008, following discussions with other Palestinian factions in the Gaza Strip, Hamas formally declared an end to its six-month truce with Israel, asserting that Israel had not adhered to its requirements under the terms of the agreement. Rocket and mortar attacks by Palestinian militants against towns in northern Israel followed, and Israel launched air-strikes against Gaza. Despite initially expressing his unwillingness to launch a large-scale military response to the increased cross-border attacks, on 27 December Prime Minister Olmert ordered a campaign of intensive air-strikes against targets in the Strip, as the first phase of its offensive code-named 'Operation Cast Lead'. The military campaign initially targeted security headquarters and police stations in the Hamas-administered territory, as well as the tunnels used by militants to smuggle weapons used to launch attacks against Israelis. At least 225 Palestinians were reported to have been killed on the first day of the Israeli military operation. The UN Security Council met on 28 December and expressed 'serious concern at the escalation of the situation in Gaza and called for an immediate halt to all violence'. However, a statement issued by the US Administration apportioned the blame for the current situation on the 'completely unacceptable' attacks launched against Israelis by Hamas militants.

Having declared an 'all-out war against Hamas' on 29 December 2008, Minister of Defence Barak sanctioned a wider campaign of Israeli air-strikes, which now targeted government offices (including the Ministry of the Interior), presidential buildings and the Islamic University in Gaza. The Israeli Government subsequently ordered a major ground assault into the Strip on 3 January 2009. The declared aim of the operation, which effectively divided the enclave into two, was to guarantee the long-term security of Israel's citizens by preventing the continued firing of rockets and mortars by Hamas militants against towns in southern Israel; the Israeli military sought to destroy Hamas's infrastructure, weapons factories and supplies. Israeli army reservists were called up to join the ground offensive, and heavy fighting occurred in densely populated districts of Gaza City and other urban centres. There was condemnation from the international community on 6 January, when an Israeli mortar attack close to a UN-administered school in the Jabalia refugee camp resulted in the deaths of 43 Palestinians. Moreover, on 15 January Israeli forces bombed the UNRWA headquarters in Gaza City. Israeli officials insisted that, in both instances, the buildings were being used by Hamas militants in order to fire rockets and mortars into northern Israel.

On 8 January 2009 the UN Security Council adopted Resolution 1860, which called for an immediate and durable cease-fire between Israeli armed forces and Hamas militants, leading to a complete withdrawal of Israeli forces from the Gaza Strip, the unimpeded provision of humanitarian aid within Gaza and intensified international arrangements to prevent the smuggling of weapons into the territory. The USA abstained in the vote. Hostilities continued despite the adoption of the resolution, but on 17 January the Israeli Government declared a unilateral cease-fire, with Prime Minister Ehud Olmert asserting that the objectives of Operation Cast Lead had been achieved. The following day Hamas also announced a week-long cessation of hostilities against Israeli targets, in order to permit Israel to withdraw its armed forces from the Gaza Strip. Palestinian sources claimed that more than 1,400 Palestinians had been killed, and some 5,000 wounded, during the 22-day Israeli offensive; 13 Israelis (including 10 soldiers) were reported to have died. In addition, thousands of Palestinian homes, as well as commercial and industrial buildings had been destroyed by Israeli forces.

During January 2009 several countries, including Mauritania, broke off relations with Israel, while the Qatari Government announced that it was closing Israel's trade office in Doha and was suspending political and economic ties. Meanwhile, international diplomatic efforts were ongoing in the region with the aim of securing a more formal, permanent truce between Israel and Hamas, thereby ensuring that international arrangements would be put in place to prevent the smuggling of weapons into Gaza, and to allow for the unimpeded provision of humanitarian aid within Gaza and the subsequent reconstruction of the territory's infrastructure. On 18 January an international summit was held in Sharm el-Sheikh, hosted by Egypt's President Mubarak and attended principally by leaders of European nations and the Arab League (including President Abbas); on the following day European leaders travelled to Israel, where they held discussions with Olmert.

The Israeli military asserted on 21 January 2009 that its forces had completed their withdrawal from Gaza. Towards the end of January an Israeli soldier patrolling the border with Gaza became the first soldier to be reported killed since the end of Operation Cast Lead, as clashes continued between Israeli armed forces and Hamas militants. The Israeli's death in a militant bomb attack led the Israeli Government to order renewed military action against Hamas targets in Gaza, with at least one Palestinian also being killed.

Netanyahu returns as Prime Minister

At the general election to the Knesset held on 10 February 2009, no party secured a sufficient number of seats in the 120-member legislature automatically to be tasked with forming a new government. However, the leaders of the two parties with the largest number of seats—the outgoing Deputy Prime Minister and Minister of Foreign Affairs, Tzipi Livni (of Kadima, which won 28 seats), and former premier Binyamin Netanyahu (of Likud, standing on a joint list with the right-wing, nationalist Ahi party, which secured 27)—each declared their ability to undertake successful coalition negotiations with other, smaller parties. In general, the election witnessed a notable shift in voting towards the more right-wing, nationalist parties: Israel Beytenu, the right-wing immigrant party led by Avigdor Lieberman, won 15 seats, pushing the Labour Party of Deputy Prime Minister and Minister of Defence Ehud Barak, with 13 seats, into fourth place; the ultra-Orthodox Shas and United Torah Judaism secured 11 and five seats, respectively. A controversial decision made in early January by the Knesset and its Central Elections Committee to prevent two Israeli Arab political groupings—Balad (the National Democratic Assembly) and the United Arab List-Arab Movement for Renewal—from standing in the election was later overturned by the Supreme Court. Both groups had been accused of failing to recognize Israel's right to exist and of supporting 'terrorist' groups after protests held by Israeli Arabs against the Israeli invasion of the Gaza Strip.

Since President Peres, after consultations with the relevant parties, considered that the Likud leader presented the greater chance of forging coalition agreements with the smaller parties, on 20 February 2009 he appointed Netanyahu (who had previously led the Government in 1996–99) as Prime Minister-designate. Members of the 18th Knesset were sworn in on 24 February, and the parliament convened for its first session on 2 March. On 31 March—seven weeks after the general election—Netanyahu presented an expanded, 30-minister Cabinet to the parliament. The incoming Cabinet was a coalition of

Likud, Israel Beytenu, Labour, Shas and Jewish Home—the latter right-wing, nationalist party having been formed in 2008 as a successor to the NRP. (Although United Torah Judaism formed part of the Government, none of its ministers were appointed to cabinet posts.) Livni had earlier ruled out joining a government under Netanyahu and dominated by right-wing parties. Notable appointees included Avigdor Lieberman as Deputy Prime Minister and Minister of Foreign Affairs, and Yuval Steinitz, of Likud, as Minister of Finance. The Labour Chairman, Ehud Barak, retained the posts of Deputy Prime Minister and Minister of Defence, while the Chairman of Shas, Eliyahu Yishai, also remained as a Deputy Prime Minister, additionally assuming the interior portfolio. A new post of Deputy Prime Minister and Minister of Intelligence and Atomic Energy was established, for which Dan Meridor assumed responsibility. Two Vice-Prime Ministers were appointed, including Silvan Shalom as Vice-Prime Minister and Minister for Regional Co-operation and the Development of the Negev and Galilee. Netanyahu was additionally named as Minister of Economic Strategy (a new portfolio), of Pensioner Affairs, of Health, and of Science, Culture and Sport.

Meanwhile, the inauguration of Barack Obama as US President on 20 January 2009, having secured victory at the election held in November 2008, appeared, in the few weeks after his new Democrat-led Administration took office, to result in renewed efforts by the USA to engage constructively in efforts to resolve the Israeli–Palestinian conflict. In early March 2009 the new Secretary of State, Hillary Clinton, declared her support for the creation of a Palestinian state in the West Bank and Gaza, and the Obama Administration also sent senior-level envoys to Syria in an effort to improve relations with that Arab state. In April the UN Human Rights Council appointed a committee led by a South African judge and former war crimes prosecutor, Richard Goldstone, to lead an investigation into 'all violations of international humanitarian law' before, during and in the aftermath of Operation Cast Lead in Gaza.

Prime Minister Netanyahu visited Washington, DC, in May 2009 for his first meeting with President Obama. The US President affirmed his determination to foster a revival of the stalled peace process and declared his commitment to a two-state settlement. Obama also identified the expansion of Israeli settlements as the chief obstacle to the resumption of peace negotiations. Netanyahu declined to respond directly to the President's statements on settlements or the two-state solution; instead, he identified Iran's nuclear ambitions as the main threat to regional peace, and insisted that negation of this threat should form an integral part of any Middle East peace agreement. In a speech at Bar-Ilan University on 14 June, Netanyahu presented his vision for the resolution of the Arab–Israeli conflict. Crucially, Netanyahu indicated, for the first time during his premiership, his acceptance of the idea of a sovereign Palestinian state. However, he insisted that the formation of such a state would be conditional on a complete demilitarization of the Palestinian territories, Arab recognition of Israel as a Jewish state, and an undivided, Israeli capital in Jerusalem. Furthermore, he rejected the 'right of return' of Palestinian refugees. An invitation to resume direct negotiations, issued to Palestinian Executive President Mahmud Abbas in mid-July, was rejected; the Palestinians refused to resume peace talks, frozen since the launch of the Israeli offensive in the Gaza Strip in December 2008, until a complete cessation of Israeli settlement activity was agreed.

Resumption of direct Israeli-Palestinian peace talks

In late July 2009 George Mitchell, the US special envoy to the Middle East, and other senior-level US diplomats visited Israel for discussions on reviving the peace process. Mitchell held further talks with Netanyahu in London in August, during which the principal topic was reported to be the settlements issue. However, the prospects for a revival of peace talks were undermined in early September when the Ministry of Defence announced that approval had been granted for the construction of 455 new housing units in Jewish settlements in the West Bank. President Obama hosted a tripartite meeting involving Netanyahu and Abbas, their first face-to-face meeting of Netanyahu's premiership, during a meeting of the UN General Assembly in New York on 22 September. However, all parties acknowledged that the meeting did not signal the resumption of negotiations and was of limited significance. The US position on settlements appeared to have softened on 31 October, when Secretary of State Hillary Clinton, during a visit to Jerusalem, praised Netanyahu's proposals on restraining settlement activity, describing his proposed concessions as 'unprecedented'. Clinton had met with Abbas earlier that day in Abu Dhabi, United Arab Emirates (UAE), where he again rejected a resumption of talks based on a partial suspension of settlement activity.

The UN Fact Finding Mission on the Gaza Conflict, headed by Richard Goldstone, issued its final report in September 2009. The report concluded that both the Israeli armed forces and the Palestinian militants appeared to have committed war crimes during the conflict, and outlined evidence of possible crimes against humanity committed by both sides. The most serious allegations against the Israeli operation included: the launching of a disproportionate offensive, which aimed to 'punish, humiliate and terrorize' the civilian population of Gaza; the targeting of civilian infrastructure, including schools, hospitals, factories, and water and sewage facilities; and the use of inappropriate armaments, including white phosphorous. On the Palestinian side, the report highlighted indiscriminate rocket attacks against Israel; the possible use of 'human shields' by militants in Gaza; and arbitrary arrests and extra-judicial executions carried out by the authorities in both Gaza and the West Bank. Furthermore, the report proposed that the authorities in Israel and Gaza should conduct fully independent inquiries into the findings within six months. Failure to comply with this proposal would result in the referral of the report's findings to the UN Security Council for further investigation. The Israeli authorities, who had refused to co-operate with the investigation, firmly rejected the report and labelled it as 'propaganda' and 'biased'. While Hamas officials denied the allegations contained within the report pertaining to their own conduct, they supported the document's referral to the Security Council. The Human Rights Council endorsed the Gaza report in October, and in November the UN General Assembly endorsed a resolution demanding that Israel conduct an investigation into allegations that its forces had committed war crimes. In February 2010 the UN Secretary-General confirmed that Israel had submitted a formal response to the Goldstone Report. In an unexpected development, in April 2011 Goldstone expressed misgivings about some of the report's findings, arguing in a column published in US newspaper *The Washington Post* that it had been too harsh on Israel with regard to allegations of war crimes, and declaring, 'If I had known then what I know now, the Goldstone Report would have been a different document'. However, Goldstone, who further contended that the Human Rights Council's 'history of bias against Israel cannot be doubted', did not disclose any new information that appeared significantly to challenge the report's findings. In a statement issued later in April, the other members of the UN Fact Finding Mission affirmed their continued support for the report's conclusions and denounced Israeli appeals for the report to be retracted.

Relations with several Western allies, including the United Kingdom and France, were strained in early 2010 after allegations of Israeli involvement in the assassination in January of a senior member of Hamas in Dubai, UAE. Following the death of Mahmoud al-Mabhouh, the Dubai authorities issued details of 11 individuals suspected of carrying out the assassination, all of whom had travelled to the emirate using false British, Australian, Irish, French and German passports. Hamas accused the Israeli intelligence service, Mossad, of involvement in al-Mabhouh's death, and in June the Polish authorities were reported to have arrested, at Germany's request, a suspected Mossad agent on charges relating to the killing. However, the Israeli Government insisted that there was no proof that its intelligence service had been involved in the incident.

Despite the announcement by Netanyahu in December 2009 of the imposition of a 10-month moratorium on settlement-building activity in the West Bank, in February 2010 the Israeli Ministry of Defence confirmed that construction work had continued in some 29 settlements within the territory. (The moratorium applied only to private homes and excluded up to 3,000 housing units that were already under construction or for which permission had already been granted; crucially, moreover, the initiative did not apply to settlements within East Jerusalem, which Netanyahu described as part of Israel's 'sovereign capital'.) The announcement in March 2010 that two further developments had been approved by the Government, in Bethlehem and East Jerusalem, coincided with a visit to Israel by the US Vice-President, Joseph Biden, who criticized the decision and claimed that it would undermine efforts by the USA to foster the peace process. The postponement later that month of a scheduled visit to Israel by George Mitchell appeared to indicate a further decline in relations, and no progress was reported on the issue of settlement-building following talks between Netanyahu and President Obama during separate visits by the Israeli premier to Washington, DC, in late March and June. In the latter month Israel's ambassador to the USA spoke of a 'tectonic rift' developing between the two long-standing allies.

In February 2010 Hamas announced that it had suspended its role in talks over the release of Gilad Shalit, which had resumed in early 2009, in part owing to the allegations of Israel's involvement in the killing of al-Mabhouh. In June, following five days of popular protests led by relatives of Shalit (who had now attained the rank of staff-sergeant), it was announced that the Israeli authorities had agreed to a prisoner exchange deal, under the terms of which Hamas would release Shalit, and Israel would release some 1,000 Palestinian detainees (on the condition that they were not to be granted entry to the West Bank). However, negotiations broke down following disagreements over which particular detainees would be released; Hamas demanded the release of 450 prisoners detained on suspicion of violent attacks against Israel, a demand to which Israel refused to concede.

In May 2010 Israeli authorities arrested two Arab citizens on suspicion of spying for Hezbollah. Relatives of both men, who were prominent activists who regularly campaigned against discrimination against Israeli Arabs, claimed that their arrests were tantamount to 'political persecution'; the two men were charged later that month. One of the pair, Omar Saeed, was freed in September after the charges against him were reduced in a plea bargain; the other man, Amir Makhoul, was convicted of aggravated espionage in October, and was sentenced to nine years' imprisonment in January 2011. Meanwhile, a further six people were arrested in June 2010 on suspicion of spying for Hezbollah.

Following meetings held in early September 2010 between President Obama, Prime Minister Netanyahu and PA President Abbas, together with King Abdullah of Jordan and Egyptian President Mubarak, direct negotiations between Netanyahu and Abbas commenced in Washington, DC, on the following day. The negotiations—the first direct Israeli-Palestinian talks since December 2008—were chaired by US Secretary of State Clinton, and also attended by George Mitchell. However, Hamas refused to recognize the legitimacy of the talks, which were preceded by further violence in the West Bank in July–August, including one incident in which four Jewish settlers were reported to have been killed by Hamas militants. During September Obama urged the Israeli Government to extend the 10-month moratorium on settlement-building in the West Bank, which was due to expire later that month; however, Netanyahu was unwilling to implement a complete freeze on construction. A second round of direct negotiations took place in Sharm el-Sheikh on 14 September and in Jerusalem on the following day. Limited progress was reported to have been made in some areas (for example, an agreement between the two leaders to hold further fortnightly meetings). However, following the expiry of Israel's temporary settlement ban on 26 September, the PA suspended its involvement in the peace process, stating that it would resume talks only when Israel had agreed to end settlement construction and its blockade of Gaza. (Israel had announced an easing of the blockade in June in response to the international criticism that followed a fatal raid by Israeli soldiers on a Gaza-bound ship in May—see Regional Relations; however, severe restrictions remained.) Following reports in October that construction work had commenced on more than 600 new homes in Israeli settlements in the West Bank, a spokesperson for President Abbas described the development as 'another indicator that Israel is not serious about the peace process'.

Also in October 2010 the Cabinet endorsed controversial draft legislation, promoted by the ultra right-wing Deputy Prime Minister and Minister of Foreign Affairs, Avigdor Lieberman, that would require non-Jewish applicants for Israeli citizenship to pledge their loyalty to Israel as a 'Jewish and democratic state'. The law, which was approved by a margin of 22 to eight, was supported by Netanyahu, with some observers speculating that the premier had lent his support in exchange for Lieberman's acquiescence regarding negotiations with the USA on further limits to settlement expansion. Three Likud ministers—including Deputy Prime Minister and Minister of Intelligence and Atomic Energy Dan Meridor—voted against the bill, along with their Labour colleagues. The Minister of Minority Affairs, Avishai Braverman of Labour, denounced the legislation, which was approved by the Knesset in March 2011, arguing that it would turn world opinion further against Israel and 'incite the Arab minority' within Israel. Furthermore, the approval by the Knesset in November 2010 of legislation requiring any proposed withdrawal from territory under Israeli sovereignty—including East Jerusalem and the Golan Heights—to be endorsed by a two-thirds' parliamentary majority, or, failing that, by a national referendum, was widely regarded as a hindrance to peace efforts. The legislation, which was approved by a majority of 65 votes to 33, was supported by Netanyahu, who contended that it would prevent 'irresponsible agreements'.

Recent developments: increasing criticism of the Netanyahu administration

Following a year-long trial conducted behind closed doors, in December 2010 former President Moshe Katsav was convicted on charges of rape and of sexual assault, which were found to have been perpetrated against former employees during his term of office; Katsav was sentenced to seven years' imprisonment in March 2011, and was ordered to pay compensation costs totalling US $35,000. Netanyahu and opposition leader Livni both hailed the verdict as a demonstration of the strength and independence of the Israeli judiciary. Katsav, who had claimed during his trial that he was a victim of 'lynching' by the prosecution and the media, subsequently filed an appeal against his conviction, but this was rejected in November 2011 by the Supreme Court, which upheld the original sentence.

Meanwhile, in February 2010 the trial began of former premier Ehud Olmert on corruption charges relating to his tenure as Minister of Industry, Trade and Labour during 2003–06 and his two terms as mayor of Jerusalem; the charges included fraud, breach of the public trust and failure to report income. On the opening day of the proceedings, Olmert affirmed his 'certainty' that each of the charges against him would be found by the court to be false. The trial was interrupted in late 2010 owing to industrial action by state prosecutors, but proceedings recommenced in January 2011 and remained ongoing in early 2012. In January 2012 Olmert was indicted on fresh charges pertaining to allegations that he had accepted bribes amounting to nearly US $1m. during his tenure as mayor of Jerusalem, in exchange for amending legislation in order to allow construction of a block of luxury residential apartments. Some 17 others, including Olmert's successor as mayor of Jerusalem, Uri Lupolianski, were also charged with offering or receiving bribes in connection with the real estate scandal.

Reports in mid-2011 indicated that Minister of Foreign Affairs Lieberman was likely to be indicted on charges of fraud, money-laundering, breach of trust and the harassment of witnesses relating to his tenure as a member of the Knesset and later as Minister of Strategic Affairs during 2001–08. Lieberman denied any wrongdoing, dismissing the allegations against him as a politically motivated plot to discredit him. A preliminary hearing was held in January 2012, although the Attorney-General was not expected to announce a final decision on whether or not formal charges were to be filed against Lieberman until later in the year.

Meanwhile, in September 2010 the Cabinet approved the appointment of Maj.-Gen. Yoav Galant to replace Ashkenazi as Chief of Staff of the Armed Forces, upon the expiry of Ashkenazi's term in February 2011. However, allegations subsequently emerged that Galant had improperly seized public land near his home, reports that Galant strenuously denied. The Green Party submitted a petition to the High Court against Galant's appointment, which Galant denounced as the result of 'hideous propaganda' disseminated by the media. In January 2011 Netanyahu and Minister of Defence Barak publicly withdrew their support for Galant, instead endorsing the candidacy of Maj.-Gen. Binyamin (Benny) Gantz, whose appointment was subsequently approved in February.

On 17 January 2011 Deputy Prime Minister and Minister of Defence Ehud Barak tendered his resignation as Labour Chairman in order to form a new party, Ha'atzmaut (Independence). Following Barak's defection, the remaining Labour members of the Cabinet tendered their resignation; Micha Harish assumed the role of Labour Party chairman on an interim basis. A renewed coalition agreement, facilitating the appointment of further Ha'atzmaut representatives to the Government, was approved by the Knesset two days later. The revised Cabinet featured four members of Ha'atzmaut, including Barak, who retained the defence portfolio, and Shalom Simhon, hitherto Minister of Agriculture and Rural Development, who was appointed Minister of Industry, Trade and Labour (in place of Ben-Eliezer) and of Minority Affairs (in place of Braverman). A new Ministry of Home Front Defence was established, headed by

Ha'atzmaut's Matan Vilnai, while the Minister of Communications, Likud's Moshe Kahlon, was awarded concurrent responsibility for the welfare and social services portfolio. Barak's decision to establish a new party followed months of division within the Labour Party, amid proposals to withdraw from the governing coalition in protest at Netanyahu's handling of the peace process. On 22 September Shelly Yachimovich, a former journalist, was announced as the new permanent Labour leader, having defeated former party leader Amir Peretz in a run-off poll with 54% of the ballot. (In the first round of voting, held on 12 September, Isaac Herzog—the son of former President Chaim Herzog, and a former cabinet minister—and former party leader Amram Mitzna had been placed third and fourth, respectively.)

The Government came under further pressure from mid-July 2011 as a series of protests primarily in response to rising housing and other living costs erupted across the country, originating in Tel-Aviv, with makeshift camps of hundreds of protesters' tents being erected along the city's main streets, before swiftly spreading to other towns and cities including Jerusalem, Beersheba and Haifa. House prices were reported to have increased by some 40% between 2007 and mid-2011, principally owing to a lack of available space and a shortage of affordable housing. The Government, seemingly taken aback by the rapid spread of the protests, which were serving effectively to unite the right and left wings of the political spectrum, appeared keen to be seen to be addressing the demonstrators' concerns, announcing in late July a range of emergency measures that included the construction of reduced-cost, long-term rental apartments, public transport subsidies for students to assist those unable to afford city-centre accommodation, and discounts on the price of land for construction companies engaged in the building of affordable housing. However, the proposed measures were summarily dismissed as being insufficient by the protesters, whose agenda had widened to incorporate anti-privatization campaigning and demands for higher public spending on social programmes, including education and health care, as well as the reinstatement of the welfare state. The appointment by the Government in early August of a committee of experts charged with investigating the socioeconomic issues confronting Israeli society similarly failed to diminish the intensity of the protest movement. Mass rallies were staged across the country on 30 July, 6 August, 13 August and 3 September, with an estimated 450,000 protesters taking to the streets on the latter date (of whom some 300,000 gathered in Tel-Aviv), prompting the authorities to dismantle the main encampment in Tel-Aviv shortly thereafter. However, protests continued intermittently during mid-September and October, albeit on a smaller scale than previously.

Meanwhile, reports emerged in September 2011 that, shortly prior to stepping down as US Secretary of Defense, Robert Gates had branded Netanyahu 'an ungrateful ally' and had contested that the Israeli premier was endangering his country's security by 'refusing to grapple with Israel's growing isolation and with the demographic challenges it faces if it keeps control of the West Bank'. Gates was reported further to have claimed that, despite numerous concrete steps adopted by the US Government in order to assist Israel in its security efforts, the Netanyahu administration had offered nothing tangible in return. Netanyahu was subject to further public criticism in November, when, amid elevated tensions between Israel and Iran (see Regional Relations), Israeli opposition leader Tzipi Livni issued a stern rebuke of Netanyahu during a session of the Knesset, claiming that the premier was overly preoccupied with the perceived threat posed to Israel by Iran, and urging him to 'listen to the defence chiefs . . . on the Iranian threat'. Livni's comments appeared to confirm reports that Israel's leading military and security experts had made clear their opposition to an Israeli attack on Iranian nuclear facilities. (In June Meir Dagan, who had served as the head of Mossad until the end of 2010, had branded Netanyahu 'irresponsible and reckless', cautioning that an Israeli attack on Iranian interests would lead to a wider regional conflict that could threaten Israel's very existence; Dagan also criticized the Government's lack of progress towards resuming direct peace talks with the PA, while praising Arab efforts to that end.) Livni's comments—which also included the accusation that Netanyahu remained uncommitted to efforts to negotiate peace with the PA and was inherently unwilling to make the concessions that a peace agreement would inevitably require—followed a media campaign run by *Yedioth Ahronoth*, in which the newspaper had claimed that Netanyahu and Barak were considering concrete plans to initiate a military attack against Iranian nuclear facilities and appealed for the Israeli Government to exercise restraint.

In mid-February 2012 the Histadrut trade union confederation launched a nation-wide general strike to demand that contract workers employed by government agencies henceforth be hired directly, rather than through employment agencies, and that they be afforded the same wages and benefits awarded to regular employees. The strike initially led to the temporary closure of Tel-Aviv's Ben-Gurion International Airport, as well as causing severe disruption to basic services and businesses, including public transport, government offices, banks, the stock exchange, post offices, higher education institutions and hospitals. Following intensive negotiations between representatives of Histadrut and of the Government, an agreement was reached—under the terms of which the minimum wage for contract workers was to be raised, and improved benefits were to be made available, including enhanced employer participation in savings and pension plans, while Histadrut agreed to refrain from initiating any further industrial action over wage concerns for a three-year period—bringing an end to the strike on its fifth day.

With legislative elections due to be held by October 2013, at early 2012 some supporters of the incumbent Netanyahu administration, including some within Likud, were becoming increasingly concerned about its ability to hold on to sufficient popular support to secure re-election. Nevertheless, Netanyahu's standing appeared to improve when he was comfortably re-elected as Likud Chairman at a leadership contest staged at the end of January; Netanyahu secured 77% of the vote to defeat perennial challengers Moshe Feiglin (who won 23% of the vote) and Vladimir Herczberg (less than 1%).

Meanwhile, in May 2011 the Israeli Government announced the temporary suspension of the transfer of tax revenues to the PA (which represented about 70% of the PA's total revenues), in response to the conclusion of a so-called 'unity' agreement between the two main Palestinian political factions. The Netanyahu administration, which condemned the agreement between Hamas and Fatah as a 'tremendous blow to peace and a great victory for terrorism', cited concerns that the funds could be used to finance operations against Israeli interests by Hamas militants. Reports emerged in July that the Israeli Government had threatened to renounce all previous agreements concluded with the Palestinians, including the Oslo accords, in response to Palestinian proposals unilaterally to seek, through the UN, formal recognition of an independent Palestinian state, on the basis of its pre-1967 borders, and with East Jerusalem as its capital. Tensions were further exacerbated in September after the PA formally submitted its application for full membership of the UN as an independent state. The Israeli and US Governments criticized the PA's decision, both insisting that bilateral negotiations were the only means of securing a lasting, peaceful resolution to the Israeli–Palestinian conflict, with the Obama Administration pledging to veto the application (which at early 2012 remained under review) should it proceed to a Security Council vote. (For further details, see the chapter on the Palestinian Autonomous Areas.)

Following UNESCO's decision to admit 'Palestine' as a full member at the end of October 2011, in early November the Israeli and US Governments both announced that they were to freeze their funding for UNESCO, which collectively accounted for about one-quarter of the agency's operating budget. Israel also announced that it was again to halt the transfer of tax and customs revenues to the PA, and further stated that it was to accelerate the construction of 2,000 new homes in Jewish settlements in East Jerusalem and the West Bank, a punitive measure that the PA claimed would 'speed up the destruction of the peace process'. However, responding to international pressure, Israel agreed later in the month to resume the transfer of tax and customs revenues to the PA.

In a more positive development, in mid-October 2011, after more than five years spent in Palestinian detention, Gilad Shalit was finally released and allowed to return to Israel, via Cairo. Shalit (now a sergeant-major, following a promotion on the eve of his release) was freed as part of a prisoner exchange agreement concluded, with Egyptian mediation, between Israel and Hamas, which provided for the release by Israel of 477 predominantly Palestinian prisoners immediately following the release of Shalit, and of a further 550 prisoners (including 300 members of Fatah) in December. Of the 1,027 prisoners in total, around 280 were reported to have been serving life sentences for planning or perpetrating terrorist attacks against Israeli targets. Among those released were Walid Abd al-Aziz Abd al-Hadi Anajas, who had received 36 separate life sentences for his involvement in a series of attacks on Israeli interests, including the July 2002 bombing of the Hebrew University in Jerusalem, and Nasir Sami Abd al-Razzaq Ali al-Nasser Yataima, who had received 29 life sentences for his involvement in the Passover massacre in March 2002 (see The accession of Prime Minister Ariel Sharon). While Shalit's release was widely celebrated within Israel, some observers questioned the sagacity of the prisoner exchange programme, of which many relatives of victims of attacks perpetrated by those released were particularly vociferous in their condemnation. However, Netanyahu insisted that the deal had struck 'the right balance' between the need to secure Shalit's release and the security risks posed by the release of the 1,027 prisoners. PA President Abbas welcomed the exchange, but stressed that the Palestinian authorities would continue to press for the release of all remaining Palestinian prisoners detained within Israel (estimated to number around 5,000 at early 2012), while UN Secretary-General Ban Ki-Moon hailed the agreement as a 'significant humanitarian breakthrough' and expressed the hoped that it might precipitate a resumption of the stalled peace talks.

In early January 2012 the first meetings between Israeli and Palestinian peace negotiators in more than a year were held in Amman, under the auspices of King Abdullah; however, the exploratory talks, which it had been hoped might lead to the resumption of formal direct peace negotiations, were reported to have ended without any significant progress. Nevertheless, at a press conference held shortly afterwards, Secretary-General Ban commended both sides for their participation in the talks, while urging them to cease all provocative acts and to pursue confidence-building measures. However, the PA continued to insist that it would not resume formal peace talks until Israel had suspended all settlement-building activity, while the Israeli Government maintained that it would not participate in such talks until the PA had dropped all preconditions to the resumption of formal negotiations.

In late March 2012 Shaul Mofaz was elected as leader of Kadima, in place of Livni, of whose tenure he had been highly critical during the primary campaign. The following month Livni announced that she was to resign as a member of the Knesset, while pledging to continue in public service.

Regional Relations

In July 1999 Ehud Barak, who had been elected to the Israeli premiership in May, undertook to negotiate a bilateral peace agreement with Syria, based on UN Resolutions 242 and 338: this was interpreted as a signal of his intention to return most of the occupied Golan Heights in exchange for peace and normalized relations. On 20 July Syria ordered a 'cease-fire' with Israel. However, it was not until December that the two sides agreed to a resumption of negotiations from the point at which they had broken off in 1996, reportedly as a result of diplomatic efforts by US President Bill Clinton and secret meetings between Israeli and Syrian officials. The Knesset subsequently approved the decision to resume talks, while Barak reasserted that any agreement concluded with Syria would be put to a national referendum. Clinton inaugurated peace negotiations between Barak and the Syrian Minister of Foreign Affairs, Farouk al-Shara', in Washington, DC, on 15 December 1999. The talks commenced amid rising tensions in southern Lebanon, and resulted only in an agreement to resume discussions in January 2000. Barak, meanwhile, was encountering growing opposition in Israel to a possible return of the Golan Heights to Syria. In late December 1999 Israel and Syria agreed an informal 'cease-fire' to curb hostilities in Lebanon. Barak and al-Shara' attended further discussions (in which President Clinton played an active role) on 3–10 January 2000 in Shepherdstown, West Virginia, USA. As a preliminary to the talks, it was agreed that four committees would be established to discuss simultaneously the issues of borders, security, normalization of relations and water sharing. The US Administration presented a 'draft working document' to both sides as the basis for a framework agreement. However, Syria announced that it required a commitment from Israel to withdraw from the Golan Heights before negotiations could resume. In early January a huge demonstration was held in Tel-Aviv by Israelis opposed to any withdrawal from the Golan Heights, while Israel B'Aliyah and the NRP threatened to leave Barak's coalition in any such event. On 17 January talks between Israel and Syria, which had been scheduled to reconvene two days later, were postponed indefinitely. Amid an intensification of the conflict in southern Lebanon (see above), the Knesset voted in March to change the majority required in the event of a referendum on an Israeli withdrawal from the Golan Heights from 50% of participants to 50% of the registered electorate. In April Barak declared that the Israeli Government would resume the construction of settlements in the Golan Heights (following a declared suspension prior to the December 1999 talks).

The prospect of further peace-making initiatives between Israel and Syria was further distanced by the death of President Assad in June 2000, although Assad's second son, Bashar—who assumed the Syrian presidency in July—promised a continuation of his father's policies towards Israel. The Israeli-Syrian track remained deadlocked following the election of Ariel Sharon as Israel's premier (bilateral tensions being compounded by the USA increasingly referring to Syria as a possible target in the Bush Administration's 'war on terror'). In October 2003 Israel launched an air-strike against an alleged training camp for Palestinian militants in Syria. The attack on the Ein Saheb camp, near Damascus, was prompted by a suicide bombing in Haifa a few days previously that killed 19 Israelis. Syria sought a UN Security Council resolution condemning the attack, while both the PFLP and Islamic Jihad denied having used the training camp.

In late 2003 and early 2004 the Israeli President, Moshe Katsav, issued a proposition to President Bashar al-Assad for Syria to start direct negotiations with Israel 'without preconditions'. However, the Syrian leadership dismissed the Israeli offer as being 'not serious'. In February 2005 Israeli officials stated that they would not resume negotiations with Syria regarding the Golan Heights until Syria had implemented a complete withdrawal of its forces from Lebanon (for further details, see the chapters on Lebanon and Syria). A report published in Israel's *Ha'aretz* newspaper in January 2007 alleged that secret discussions had taken place between Israeli and Syrian representatives between September 2004 and the start of the conflict between Israel and Hezbollah in July 2006, reportedly leading to important mutual understandings having been reached with regard to the Golan Heights and other contentious issues. However, the claim was denied by officials from both countries. Tensions between Israel and Syria worsened in September 2007, after Israel carried out an air-strike on a military installation at al-Kibar in Syria. In April 2008 US intelligence indicated that the Israeli military had targeted a covert nuclear facility that was being built with assistance from the Democratic People's Republic of Korea (North Korea). Representatives from the UN's International Atomic Energy Agency (IAEA) subsequently undertook investigations of the al-Kibar site, and an IAEA report published in February 2009 asserted that there was a 'low probability' that Israeli missiles used to bomb the installation were the source of traces of uranium that had been found there.

Israeli and Syrian officials confirmed in May 2008 that indirect negotiations aimed at concluding a 'comprehensive peace' between their two countries were being held through Turkish intermediaries in the city of İstanbul. By the second week of August four rounds of the Turkish-mediated discussions had taken place, although no significant progress had apparently been reached as far as resolving the principal outstanding issues were concerned. Despite subsequent claims by President Assad that Israel and Syria were within 'touching distance' of reaching a peace deal, a fifth round of talks, scheduled for September, was postponed owing to the political uncertainty in Israel following the recent resignation of both Olmert as premier and also of his chief negotiator in the indirect talks, Yoram Turbowicz. Moreover, apparently in response to Israel's large-scale military offensive against Hamas targets in the Gaza Strip between December 2008 and January 2009 (which also led to tense relations between Israel and Turkey), President Assad formally suspended the talks with Israel. Following the inauguration of a new Government under recently appointed Prime Minister Binyamin Netanyahu on 31 March 2009, the new Minister of Foreign Affairs, Israel Beytenu's Avigdor Lieberman, ruled out any Israeli withdrawal from the Golan Heights. A claim by President Assad in April 2010 that Israel was intent on 'leading the region to war, not peace' prompted an angry response from Lieberman, who stated that the Syrian President's comment 'marked a dramatic change of game, a direct threat on the state of Israel' that 'could not be tolerated'. Hopes for a resumption of direct negotiations were further impeded by the popular uprising that emerged in Syria from early 2011, with the Syrian authorities' attention primarily focused on quelling increasing levels of domestic unrest. In May Israeli troops clashed with hundreds of pro-Palestinian protesters who had broken through a security fence to enter the Golan Heights from Syria. Syrian state media reported in the following month that 12 Palestinians and two Syrians had been killed when Israeli soldiers opened fire at another group of protesters attempting to enter the Golan Heights from across the Syrian border; according to hospital reports, some 225 others were injured in the incident. The Israeli authorities accused the Assad regime of orchestrating the violence as a means of diverting international attention from Syria's domestic unrest.

Following the upgrading of Israeli-Turkish diplomatic relations to ambassadorial level in 1991, strategic and commercial co-operation between the two states intensified. A Security and Secrecy Agreement, concerning increased military and intelligence co-operation, was signed in 1994. During 1996 Israel and Turkey signed a number of military accords, which provided for joint military training exercises, reciprocal access to airspace and co-operation in the provision of armaments—developments condemned by Syria as a threat to its own security and to that of all Arab and Islamic countries. The pacts stemmed from common concerns about Iran, Iraq and Syria, and received support from the USA, a strong ally of both Turkey and Israel. Negotiations on a free trade agreement were also concluded in that year, and the arrangement came into force in 1997. In August 2002 a 20-year agreement was signed, according to which Turkey would supply Israel with an annual 50m. cu m of water. In May 2004 Turkish Prime Minister Recep Tayyip Erdoğan described an Israeli offensive in Gaza as 'state-sponsored terrorism'. None the less, Erdoğan visited Jerusalem in May of the following year, attending the Yad Vashem Holocaust memorial and holding discussions on joint military projects.

Turkey acted as host and mediator for indirect peace talks between Syria and Israel during 2008 (see above). However, negotiations were suspended following the launch of Israel's military offensive against Hamas in Gaza in late December. Turkey, along with most other Muslim countries, voiced strong condemnation of the Israeli operation. In late January 2009 there was an angry exchange between Erdoğan and Israeli President Shimon Peres during a debate on Gaza at the World Economic Forum in Davos, Switzerland. Erdoğan accused Israel of having committed crimes against humanity, and stormed out when he was not afforded the same amount of time to speak on the matter as the Israeli President. There was some evidence of an improvement in relations in March when the foreign ministers of Israel and Turkey held talks on bilateral relations and regional stability during a North Atlantic Treaty Organization (NATO) summit in Brussels, Belgium. Turkish officials subsequently announced their readiness to resume their role as mediator in Syrian-Israeli peace negotiations. However, in October Turkey announced the cancellation of Israel's involvement in a scheduled military exercise, as well as plans for a further bilateral military exercise. (Turkey and Syria conducted their first-ever combined exercise in April.) Despite initial official statements that the cancellation was due to technical issues and not a political measure, Turkey's Minister of Foreign Affairs, Ahmet Davutoğlu, acknowledged in November that disapproval of Israel's operation in Gaza was the reason for the decision. Relations deteriorated further in January 2010 following a meeting between Israel's Deputy Minister of Foreign Affairs, Danny Ayalon, and the Turkish ambassador to Israel, Ahmet Çelikkol. The ambassador had been summoned to the Israeli Ministry of Foreign Affairs to receive an official complaint about the broadcast on Turkish state television of programmes depicting Israeli security forces in a manner considered offensive to Israel. However, during the meeting, which was attended by journalists and cameramen, Ayalon was deemed to have intentionally 'humiliated' the ambassador. The Turkish authorities subsequently threatened to suspend relations unless an unequivocal apology was issued. Following the subsequent issue of two apologies by Ayalon, the dispute was officially declared to be finished. Minister of Defence Ehud Barak made a scheduled visit to the Turkish capital, Ankara, in mid-January for talks on military co-operation, during which he also met with Davutoğlu in an attempt to improve bilateral relations.

However, Israeli–Turkish tensions escalated following a raid, in May 2010, by Israeli naval forces on a ship in international waters, which was part of a flotilla attempting to breach the Israeli blockade of Gaza, purportedly to deliver humanitarian aid and materials to the population therein; nine pro-Palestinian Turkish activists were killed during the clashes, and many more were injured. Foreign governments and international organizations roundly condemned the Israeli soldiers' actions, despite Israeli claims that its forces had acted in self-defence, and opposition to the Israeli blockade of Gaza intensified; the International Committee of the Red Cross described the blockade as 'a collective punishment' of the people of Gaza, which was 'in clear violation of Israel's obligations under international humanitarian law'. An Israeli commission established to investigate the raid subsequently determined that the actions of the Israeli soldiers had 'regrettable consequences of human life losses and physical injuries' but were, none the less, compliant with international law. On the evening of the raid, hundreds of Israelis gathered outside the Turkish embassy in Tel-Aviv to protest at what they perceived to be a Turkish ploy to cast Israel in a negative light, claiming that the flotilla of ships had despatched with the express intention of provoking a response from the Israeli military, allegations that were adamantly denied by the Turkish authorities. In June Turkey suspended its diplomatic and military ties with Israel, withdrawing its ambassador from Tel-Aviv and insisting that it would not restore full relations until Israel publicly apologized for the incident, compensated the relatives of the victims and agreed to the holding of a full and independent international inquiry. Israel refused to acquiesce to the demands. The publication by the UN in early September 2011 of a report detailing the findings of an inquiry into the circumstances surrounding the raid precipitated a significant deterioration in Israeli-Turkish relations. The report criticized the conduct of both countries over the incident, determining that the decision by the Israeli soldiers to board the vessel 'with such substantial force and with no final warning' constituted an 'excessive and unreasonable' action, while recognizing the 'legitimacy' of Israel's blockade as a means of stemming the flow of weapons into Gaza by sea. The Turkish Government was swift to condemn the report's conclusions, and, citing Israel's continued refusal formally to apologize for the incident, both the Israeli ambassador and his deputy were expelled from Ankara while Turkey's remaining senior diplomats were recalled from its embassy in Tel-Aviv, as diplomatic relations with Israel were downgraded to the level of second secretary. Bilateral military and trade ties were also suspended.

Amid the continuing international disquiet over Iran's nuclear ambitions in recent years, Iran has provoked further outrage by its frequent statements about Israel and the Holocaust. Remarks by President Mahmoud Ahmadinejad in October 2005, in which he reiterated the demand of Ayatollah Khomeini that Israel be 'wiped off the map', prompted international condemnation; Ahmadinejad later asserted that he had merely expressed the will of his people. Subsequent public statements by Ahmadinejad in December, to the effect that the Holocaust was a 'fabrication' and that the Jewish state should be moved outside the Middle East, were similarly condemned. Hostility between Iran and Israel was exacerbated by Hamas's victory in the Palestinian legislative elections of January 2006 and Iran's subsequent offer of financial support to the Hamas-led administration. Moreover, Iran was viewed as having played a leading role in the conflict between Israel and Hezbollah in July–August; however, while the Iranian leadership admitted its support for Hezbollah, it denied claims that it was providing the group with military assistance. From 2006 Israeli government officials repeatedly urged international leaders to act in order to prevent Iran from developing a nuclear bomb, consistently maintaining that a military attack against Iran's nuclear facilities remained a strategic option. The Iranian authorities countered with warnings that any pre-emptive military strikes launched by Israel would be met with a swift and powerful military response. Iranian tests, conducted in May 2009, appeared to demonstrate that the Islamic Republic possessed missiles with sufficient range to target Israel and US military bases in the region. In November it was announced that Israeli forces in the Mediterranean Sea had intercepted a cargo ship en route to Syria, the *Francop*, which Israel claimed was carrying a large consignment of Iranian-made weapons destined for Hezbollah militants in Lebanon. In February 2010 the Israeli air force announced the development of a fleet of unmanned aircraft that would be able to launch missile attacks or conduct surveillance operations; Ahmadinejad contested that the aircraft were intended to target Iran, alleging that Israel was 'seeking to start a war next spring or summer', while Netanyahu insisted that Israel had no intention to instigate any military action and denounced the Iranian President's comments as 'manipulations'. The passage of two Iranian warships through the Suez Canal, for the first time since the 1979 Islamic Revolution, sailing past the Israeli coast en route to Syria in February 2011 was heavily condemned as a deliberate act of provocation by the Israeli Government and prompted Minister of Foreign Affairs Lieberman to state that 'the international community must understand that Israel cannot forever ignore these provocations'. Speculation that Israel might be planning to launch a pre-emptive military strike against Iranian nuclear facilities was further fuelled by the decision by the Israeli authorities at the beginning of November to test-fire a ballistic missile from a military base in central Israel, prompting stern criticism of Netanyahu from opposition leader Tzipi Livni during a session of the Knesset a few days later (see Domestic Political Affairs). Amid the elevated state of alert regarding a possible Israeli attack, the Iranian Chief of Staff of the Armed Forces, Maj.-Gen. Hassan Firouzabadi, declared that the Iranian authorities were on 'full alert' and were 'ready to punish [Israel] and make them regret any mistake'. Concerns that Israel might resort to military force were heightened following the publication later in November of a report in which the IAEA noted its 'serious concerns regarding possible military dimensions to Iran's nuclear programme', and cited 'strong indicators of possible weapon development'. (Following the publication of the report, the USA and the EU imposed new sanctions targeting Iranian oil sales in a bid to increase pressure on the Iranian Government to halt its nuclear programme.) Responsibility for a series of bomb explosions in mid-February 2012, apparently targeting those affiliated with the Israeli embassies in New Delhi (India), Tbilisi (Georgia) and Bangkok (Thailand), was attributed by the Israeli authorities to 'Iran and its protégé, Hezbollah'; the Iranian Government adamantly denied any involvement in the attacks, which were reported to have injured at least nine people.

Israeli–Lebanese tensions remained elevated following Israel's military campaign in southern Lebanon in mid-2006. In August 2010 clashes between Israeli and Lebanese soldiers near the 'Blue Line'—the UN's name for the bilateral border—prompted fears of a wider conflict between the two adversaries. A group of Israeli soldiers attempting to cut down a tree in an area on the Lebanese side of the border fence (but on the Israeli side of the Blue Line) were confronted by Lebanese soldiers, who fired warning shots into the air; the Israeli soldiers were reported to have responded by shooting directly at the Lebanese troops, injuring several. Shortly thereafter an Israeli helicopter fired a rocket at a Lebanese military vehicle, killing three soldiers and one journalist; Lebanese troops returned fire, killing an Israeli military officer. More than 15 others were injured in what constituted the most serious clashes between the two countries since the 2006 conflict. The UN subsequently determined that the Israeli soldiers had not veered into Lebanese territory, and urged both sides to exercise the 'utmost restraint' to avoid an escalation of tensions. Notwithstanding an initially bellicose response from the two countries' respective Governments, Israel and Lebanon subsequently acted swiftly to reduce tensions. Israeli Minister of Defence Barak underscored the fact that the clash had not arisen as a result of any orders given by the Lebanese military leadership, nor had it involved Hezbollah. More than 100 people were reported to have been arrested by the Lebanese authorities during 2009–11 on suspicion of spying for Israel. Although several of the accused had been convicted and sentenced to death, as of early 2012 none was reported to have been executed. Meanwhile, bilateral tensions were elevated following the discovery of two huge natural gas reserves in the Mediterranean Sea off the coast of Israel, a short distance from the disputed maritime border with Lebanon—the Tamar gasfield, which was discovered in January 2009, and the Leviathan gasfield, which was discovered in December 2010. Lebanon submitted to the UN its proposal for the delineation of its maritime border with Israel (in August 2010) and with Cyprus (in November). However, the Israeli Government contended that the proposed boundaries encroached upon Israeli territory, and, while not including the Tamar and Leviathan prospects, potentially contained significant oil and gas reserves, and contradicted maritime border agreements previously signed between Israel and Cyprus and between Lebanon and Cyprus. In July 2011 Israel submitted to the UN its own proposal for the maritime border, while rejecting the prospect of indirect negotiations via the UN and insisting that Lebanon agree to the staging of bilateral negotiations on all border issues. In September Lebanon filed a formal complaint with the UN over Israel's proposal for the maritime border, contesting that it infringed upon some 860 sq km of Lebanese sovereign territory and 'puts international peace and security at risk'. Meanwhile, at the beginning of August a brief exchange of gunfire was reported to have taken place between Israeli and Lebanese soldiers along the bilateral land frontier. No injuries were sustained by either side, but the incident, which the Lebanese authorities claimed had been provoked by the encroachment onto Lebanon's side of the Blue Line by the Israeli patrol, served further to highlight increasing border tensions. Concerns of renewed violence between the two countries were exacerbated in November, when four rocket attacks were launched into northern Israel from Lebanon, prompting the Israeli military to fire artillery shells into Lebanese territory. The militant Islamist organization Abdullah Azzam Brigades, which was reported to be affiliated with al-Qa'ida, subsequently claimed responsibility for the rocket attacks. Amid elevated tensions, the Israeli Government was reported in early 2012 to have begun preparations for the construction of a wall along the northern cease-line with Lebanon, in order to bolster border security.

Following the removal from power of Egyptian President Hosni Mubarak in February 2011, there were fears of a significant deterioration in Israeli-Egyptian relations, which had remained generally civil during Mubarak's tenure. In May the Egyptian Islamist organization the Muslim Brotherhood, which had been outlawed under Mubarak but was expected to play a prominent role in the formation of a new government, and which had close links with Hamas, urged a review of the 1978 peace treaty signed between Israel and Egypt, insisting that it be submitted to a 'freely elected' parliament for approval, and appealed for 'an end to normalization [with Israel] which has given our enemy stability'. The arrest in Egypt in June 2011 of Ilan Grapel, a student of dual Israeli and US citizenship, on suspicion of espionage and of working to foment unrest in Egypt in the aftermath of Mubarak's removal from office prompted further fears of a deterioration in bilateral relations. The arrest sparked angry protests in Israel, with relatives of Grapel as well as the Israel Government firmly rejecting the espionage charges, which were widely dismissed within Egypt itself. In late October, following the successful conclusion of the first phase of the prisoner exchange programme involving Sergeant-Major Gilad Shalit, Grapel was released in exchange for 25 Egyptian prisoners detained in Israeli gaols. Meanwhile, following the killing in mid-August of five Egyptian soldiers by Israeli troops during an exchange of gunfire with suspected Palestinian militants close to the Israeli–Egyptian border, Egypt announced that it was to recall its ambassador from Tel-Aviv pending the completion by the Israeli Government of a full investigation into the incident (although, in the event, this did not come to pass), while the Council of Ministers issued a statement in which it contended that the shootings represented a violation of the 1979 peace treaty. Protesters gathered outside the Israeli embassy in Cairo to demand the expulsion of the Israeli ambassador, and minor attacks against the embassy were reported throughout late August. In mid-September protesters penetrated the embassy's security wall, replaced the Israeli flag with that of Egypt and ransacked the premises, forcing the emergency evacuation back to Israel of embassy staff and their relatives. Relations consequently remained strained and were expected further to be undermined by the success of the Freedom & Justice Party (a political organization founded in April by the Muslim Brotherhood) at legislative elections held in Egypt in November 2011–January 2012.

CONSTITUTION AND GOVERNMENT

Israel does not have a formal, written constitution. However, in June 1950 the Knesset (parliament) voted to adopt a state constitution by evolution over an unspecified period. A number of laws, including the Law of Return (1950), the Nationality Law (1952), the State President (Tenure) Law (1952), the Education Law (1953) and the 'Yad-va-Shem' Memorial Law (1953), are considered as incorporated into the state Constitution. Other constitutional laws are: the Law and Administration Ordinance (1948), the Knesset Election Law (1951), the Law of Equal Rights for Women (1951), the Judges Act (1953), the National Service and National Insurance Acts (1953), and the Basic Law (the Knesset—1958).

Supreme authority in Israel rests with the Knesset, with 120 members elected by universal suffrage for four years (subject to dissolution), on the basis of proportional representation. The President, a constitutional head of state, is elected by the Knesset for a maximum of one seven-year term. Executive power lies with the Cabinet, led by a Prime Minister. The Cabinet takes office after receiving a vote of confidence in the Knesset, to which it is responsible. Ministers are usually members of the Knesset, but non-members may be appointed. The country is divided into six administrative districts. Local authorities are elected at the same time as elections to the Knesset. In 2010 there were 75 municipal councils, 125 local councils and 984 regional councils.

REGIONAL AND INTERNATIONAL CO-OPERATION

Israel became a member of the UN on 11 May 1949. As a contracting party to the General Agreement on Tariffs and Trade, Israel joined the World Trade Organization (WTO, see p. 433) on its establishment in 1995. The country officially acceded to the Organisation for Economic Co-operation and Development (OECD, see p. 379) on 7 September 2010.

ECONOMIC AFFAIRS

In 2010, according to estimates by the World Bank, Israel's gross national income (GNI), measured at average 2008–10 prices, was US $207,195m., equivalent to $27,170 per head (or $27,630 per head on an international purchasing-power parity basis). During 2001–10, it was estimated, the population increased at an average annual rate of 1.9%, while gross domestic product (GDP) per head increased, in real terms, by an average of 1.6% per year. Overall GDP increased, in real terms, at an average annual rate of 3.5% in 2001–10; GDP grew by 0.8% in 2009 and by 4.8% in 2010, according to official figures.

Agriculture (including hunting, forestry and fishing) contributed a preliminary 1.9% of GDP in 2011, and in 2010 engaged 1.6% of the employed labour force. Most agricultural workers live in large co-operatives (*kibbutzim*), of which there were 266 at December 2010, or co-operative smallholder villages (*moshavim*), of which there were 442. Israel is largely self-sufficient in foodstuffs. Citrus fruits constitute the main export crop. Other important crops are vegetables (particularly potatoes, chillies and peppers, carrots and turnips, and cucumbers and gherkins), wheat, melons and grapes. The export of exotic fruits, winter vegetables and flowers has increased significantly in recent years. Poultry, livestock and fish production are also important. According to official data, the GDP of the agricultural sector increased at an estimated average annual rate of 3.4% in 2003–09; according to official estimates, it remained constant in 2009.

Industry (comprising mining, manufacturing, construction and power) contributed a preliminary 20.5% of GDP in 2011, and engaged 20.4% of the employed labour force in 2010. According to official figures, in 2003–08 industrial GDP increased at an average annual rate of 6.2%; it expanded by an estimated 4.2% in 2009. The state plays a major role in all sectors of industry, and there is a significant co-operative sector.

The mining and manufacturing sectors together contributed a preliminary 13.6% of GDP in 2011, and engaged 14.3% of the employed labour force in 2010; mining and quarrying employed about 0.2% of the working population in 2008. Israel has small proven reserves of petroleum (of some 3.9m. barrels), from which less than 500 barrels per day are currently produced; however, in 1999 potential new reserves were discovered in central Israel and off the southern coast. Israel's Petroleum Commission has estimated that the country could possess around 5,000m. barrels of oil reserves, most likely located underneath gas reserves, and that offshore gas could supply its short-term energy needs. In December 2010 a US-based oil and gas exploration company confirmed a major offshore gas discovery in December 2010. The 'Leviathan' gas field, located around 80 miles off the coast of Haifa, was estimated to contain some 450,000m. cu m of gas; if confirmed, it would constitute the largest find world-wide in more than 10 years. Phosphates, potash, bromides, magnesium and other salts are mined, and Israel is the world's largest exporter of bromine. According to official estimates, in 2003–09 sectoral GDP increased by an average annual rate of 3.9%; it expanded by 6.2% in 2008, before declining by an estimated 6.2% in 2009. The principal branches of manufacturing, measured by gross revenue, are: food products, beverages and tobacco; chemical, petroleum and coal products; electrical machinery; metal products; scientific, photographic, optical equipment, etc.; paper, publishing and printing; textiles and clothing; non-metallic mineral manufactures; rubber and plastic products; and non-electrical machinery.

The construction sector contributed a preliminary 5.2% of GDP in 2011. In 2010 the sector engaged 5.4% of the employed labour force. During 2003–09 the GDP of the sector increased at an average annual rate of 1.2%; however, construction GDP declined by 1.0% in 2009, according to official estimates.

Energy is derived principally from coal (accounting for 62.7% of total electricity output in 2008) and imported petroleum (10.6%); however, it is intended that natural gas should eventually become Israel's principal energy source. Energy derived from natural gas contributed 26.2% of total electricity output in 2008, up from just 0.1% in 2003. Imports of mineral fuels comprised 17.6% of the total value of imports in 2010.

Services contributed a preliminary 77.6% of GDP in 2011, and engaged 78.1% of the employed labour force in 2010. Tourism is an important source of revenue, although the sector has been severely damaged by regional instability and a series of bomb attacks carried out by militant Islamist groups in recent years. However, a decline in the number of militant attacks in the late 2000s resulted in an increase in tourist numbers: in 2010 some 2.8m. tourists visited Israel (increased from 2.3m. in 2009), while receipts from tourism totalled US $4,332m. in 2010. Financial services are also important: banking, insurance, real estate and business services together contributed a preliminary 28.6% of GDP in 2011, and employed 18.8% of the working population in 2010. According to official data, in 2003–08 the GDP of the services sector increased at an average annual rate of 6.5%; it grew by an estimated 4.4% in 2009.

In 2010 Israel recorded a trade deficit of US $1,945m.; however, there was a surplus of $6,342m. on the current account of the balance of payments. Excluding trade with the West Bank and Gaza Strip, in 2010 the principal source of imports was the USA, which supplied 11.3% of imports to Israel; other major suppliers were the People's Republic of China, Germany, the Belgo-Luxembourg Economic Union (BLEU) and Switzerland-Liechtenstein. The USA was also the principal market for exports, taking 31.6% of Israeli exports in that year; other important purchasers were Hong Kong and the BLEU. Israel is the world's largest supplier of polished diamonds. The principal exports in 2010 were basic manufactures (chiefly non-metallic mineral manufactures), machinery and transport equipment, chemicals and related products, and miscellaneous manufactured articles. The principal imports in that year were machinery and transport equipment, basic manufactures (mainly non-metallic mineral manufactures), mineral fuels and lubricants (mainly petroleum and petroleum products), chemicals and related products, and miscellaneous manufactured articles.

Government revenue each year normally includes some US $3,000m. in economic and military aid from the USA. The Government planned for balanced budgets for 2010, with revenue and expenditure both totalling NIS 325,288m. in that year. Israel's general gross government debt was NIS 596,000m. in 2009, equivalent to 77.6% of GDP. During 2001–10 consumer prices rose at an average annual rate of 2.3%; consumer prices increased by 2.7% in 2010. The unemployment rate was reported to be 6.6% in 2010.

Owing to the effects of the global financial crisis that began in late 2008, Israel's economy recorded negative growth in the last quarter of 2008 (representing its first contraction since 2002), and further weakened in early 2009. However, the economy began to show signs of recovery in the second half of 2009 and renewed growth was recorded in 2010, bolstered by strong exports and consumer demand. In a statement issued in February 2012, the IMF noted that the incidence of poverty within Israel was one of the highest among members of the Organisation for Economic Co-operation and Development (OECD), to which Israel acceded in September 2010. (A report published by OECD in January 2010 estimated that almost 20% of the Israeli population were living in poverty in 2009, with poverty levels particularly elevated among Israel's Arab and ultra-Orthodox Jewish communities, at up to 50% and 60%, respectively.) The IMF also urged the continuation of efforts to reduce the level of public debt to a targeted 60% of GDP over the medium term, and recommended a further tightening of fiscal policy in order to address the budgetary deficit, which was forecast to increase to 3.0%–3.5% of GDP in 2012, despite a targeted ceiling of 2.0% of GDP. Meanwhile, in March 2010 the Cabinet endorsed a US $215m., five-year investment plan intended to improve economic infrastructure, housing, transportation and security, as well as creating significant employment opportunities, in 12 Arab localities. While recognizing this and other initiatives, in early 2012 the IMF urged the Government to implement further measures to boost employment levels, as well as the provision of education, basic child care and transportation, among the Arab and ultra-Orthodox Jewish communities. Unemployment was reported to have declined to 5.5% at mid-2011, its second lowest level since the mid-1980s. Declining demand for exports during 2011, in part owing to modest economic growth in Israel's two main export markets, the USA and the euro area, was expected to continue into 2012. Nevertheless, according to the IMF, the rate of GDP growth accelerated to an estimated 4.7% in 2011, buoyed by an increase in foreign investment inflows; growth was forecast to moderate to 2.8% in 2012 before increasing to 3.8% in 2013.

PUBLIC HOLIDAYS

The Sabbath starts at sunset on Friday and ends at nightfall on Saturday. The Jewish year 5773 begins on 17 September 2012, and the year 5774 on 5 September 2013.

2013: 25–31 March (Pesach, Passover—public holidays on first and last days of festival), 16 April (Yom Ha'atzmaut, Independence Day), 15 May (Shavuot, Feast of Weeks), 5–6 September (Rosh Hashanah, Jewish New Year), 14 September (Yom Kippur, Day of Atonement), 18–24 September (Succot, Feast of the Tabernacles), 26 September (Shemini Atzeret, Assembly of the Eighth Day/Simchat Torah, Celebration of the Torah),

(Observance of the Jewish festivals and fast days begins at sunset in the evening prior to the dates given.)

Islamic holidays are observed by Muslim Arabs, and Christian holidays by the Christian Arab community.

Statistical Survey

Source (unless otherwise indicated): Central Bureau of Statistics, POB 13015, Hakirya, Romema, Jerusalem 91130; tel. 2-6592037; fax 2-6521340; e-mail yael@cbs.gov.il; internet www.cbs.gov.il.

Area and Population

AREA, POPULATION AND DENSITY

Area (sq km)	
Land	21,643
Inland water	429
Total	22,072*
Population (*de jure*; census results)†	
4 November 1995	5,548,523
27 December 2008	
Males	3,663,910
Females	3,748,270
Total	7,412,180
Population (*de jure*; official estimates at 31 December)†	
2009	7,552,000
2010	7,695,100
Density (per sq km) at 31 December 2010	355.5§

* 8,522 sq miles. Area includes East Jerusalem, annexed by Israel in June 1967, and the Golan sub-district (1,154 sq km), annexed by Israel in December 1981.

† Including the population of East Jerusalem and Israeli residents in certain other areas under Israeli military occupation since June 1967. Figures also include non-Jews in the Golan sub-district, an Israeli-occupied area of Syrian territory. Census results exclude adjustment for under-enumeration.

§ Land area only.

POPULATION BY AGE AND SEX

('000, official population estimates at 31 December 2010)

	Males	Females	Total
0–14	1,105.7	1,051.5	2,157.2
15–64	2,370.4	2,404.0	4,774.4
65 and over	331.3	432.1	763.4
Total	3,807.4	3,887.6	7,695.1

Note: Totals may not be equal to the sum of components, owing to rounding.

POPULATION BY RELIGION

(31 December 2010)

	Number	%
Jews	5,802,900	75.4
Muslims	1,321,300	17.2
Christians*	153,100	2.0
Druze	127,600	1.7
Unclassified†	290,200	3.8
Total	7,695,100	100.0

* Including Arab Christians.

† Including Lebanese not classified by religion.

DISTRICTS

(31 December 2010)

	Area (sq km)*	Population (rounded)†	Density (per sq km)
Jerusalem‡	653	945,000	1,447.2
Northern§	4,473	1,279,200	286.0
Haifa	866	913,000	1,054.3
Central	1,294	1,854,900	1,433.5
Tel-Aviv	172	1,285,000	7,470.9
Southern	14,185	1,106,900	78.0
Total	21,643	7,695,100	355.5

* Excluding lakes, with a total area of 474 sq km.

† Components exclude, but total includes, Israelis residing in Jewish localities in the West Bank totalling some 311,100 at 31 December 2010.

‡ Including East Jerusalem, annexed by Israel in June 1967.

§ Including the Golan sub-district (area 1,154 sq km, population an estimated 42,200 at 31 December 2010), annexed by Israel in December 1981.

PRINCIPAL TOWNS

(population at 31 December 2010)

Jerusalem (capital)*	788,100	Beersheba	195,400
Tel-Aviv—Jaffa	404,300	Netanya	186,800
Haifa	268,200	Holon	181,500
Rishon LeZiyyon	231,000	Bene Beraq	158,900
Petach-Tikva	211,100	Ramat-Gan	145,900
Ashdod	210,600	Bat Yam	130,400

* The Israeli Government has designated the city of Jerusalem (including East Jerusalem, annexed by Israel in June 1967) as the country's capital, although this is not recognized by the UN.

BIRTHS, MARRIAGES AND DEATHS*

	Registered live births		Registered marriages		Registered deaths†	
	Number	Rate (per 1,000)	Number	Rate (per 1,000)	Number	Rate (per 1,000)
2003	144,936	21.7	39,154	6.1	38,499	5.7
2004	145,207	21.3	39,855	5.9	37,938	5.6
2005	143,913	20.8	41,029	5.9	39,038	5.6
2006	148,170	21.0	44,685	6.3	38,765‡	5.5‡
2007	151,679	21.1	46,448	6.5	40,081	5.6
2008	156,923	21.5	50,038	6.8	39,484	5.4
2009	161,042	21.5	48,997	6.5	38,812	5.2
2010	166,255	21.8	n.a.	n.a.	39,590	5.2

* Including East Jerusalem.

† Including deaths abroad of Israelis residing outside of Israel less than one year.

‡ Excluding 116 deaths of military personnel resulting from hostilities with militant factions based in Lebanon.

Note: From 2006 data include marriages involving a spouse not resident in Israel and those in which spouses may be of different religions.

Life expectancy (years at birth, WHO estimates): 82 (males 80; females 83) in 2009 (Source: WHO, *World Health Statistics*).

IMMIGRATION*

	2008	2009	2010
Immigrants on immigrant visas	11,784	12,099	13,678
Immigrants on tourist visas†	1,917	2,473	2,955
Total	13,701	14,572	16,633

* Excluding immigrating citizens (4,279 in 2008; 4,845 in 2009; 4,226 in 2010) and Israeli residents returning from abroad.
† Figures refer to tourists who changed their status to immigrants or potential immigrants.

ECONOMICALLY ACTIVE POPULATION
(sample surveys, '000 persons aged 15 years and over, excluding armed forces)*

	2008	2009	2010
Agriculture, hunting, forestry and fishing	47.9	48.0	47.8
Industry†	432.0	415.5	416.7
Electricity, gas and water supply	19.9	18.5	20.3
Construction	150.7	143.6	157.4
Wholesale and retail trade; repair of motor vehicles, motorcycles and personal and household goods	377.9	376.9	388.5
Hotels and restaurants	129.9	131.2	134.7
Transport, storage and communications	174.5	184.9	191.2
Financial intermediation	99.2	109.8	116.1
Real estate, renting and business activities	388.9	412.8	429.2
Public administration and defence; compulsory social security	130.6	131.7	134.6
Education	349.3	356.5	367.5
Health and social work	274.6	288.6	303.7
Other community, social and personal service activities	130.3	142.5	147.2
Private households with employed persons	46.2	52.7	55.3
Extra-territorial organizations and bodies	1.8	2.1	2.3
Sub-total	2,753.7	2,815.3	2,907.9
Not classifiable by economic activity	23.0	25.7	25.8
Total employed	2,776.7	2,841.0	2,938.2
Unemployed	180.4	231.8	208.9
Total labour force	2,957.1	3,072.8	3,147.1
Males	1,579.9	1,625.0	1,664.3
Females	1,377.2	1,447.9	1,482.8

* Figures are estimated independently, so the totals may not be the sum of the component parts.
† Comprising mining and quarrying, and manufacturing.

Health and Welfare

KEY INDICATORS

Total fertility rate (children per woman, 2009)	2.8
Under-5 mortality rate (per 1,000 live births, 2009)	5
HIV/AIDS (% of persons aged 15–49, 2009)	0.2
Physicians (per 1,000 head, 2006)	3.7
Hospital beds (per 1,000 head, 2006)	6.0
Health expenditure (2008): US $ per head (PPP)	2,093
Health expenditure (2008): % of GDP	7.6
Health expenditure (2008): public (% of total)	58.4
Total carbon dioxide emissions ('000 metric tons, 2007)	66,684.8
Carbon dioxide emissions per head (metric tons, 2007)	9.3
Human Development Index (2011): ranking	17
Human Development Index (2011): value	0.888

For sources and definitions, see explanatory note on p. vi.

Agriculture

PRINCIPAL CROPS
('000 metric tons)

	2008	2009	2010
Wheat	75.7	133.0	112.3
Maize	99.3	81.1	84.0
Potatoes	557.9	608.8	548.7
Olives	48.8	30.5	73.5
Cabbages and other brassicas	51.1	56.8	52.4
Lettuce and chicory	26.9	36.3	28.7
Tomatoes	419.0	454.8	446.6
Cucumbers and gherkins	107.7	117.3	115.8
Aubergines (Eggplants)	37.2	46.4	45.3
Chillies and peppers, green	177.9	202.3	294.3
Onions, dry	80.9	75.3	83.3
Carrots and turnips	211.4	233.1	234.3
Watermelons	105.9	111.2	108.8
Cantaloupes and other melons	41.1	39.3	41.5
Bananas	85.2	93.5	101.4
Oranges	118.1	136.1	134.8
Tangerines, mandarins, clementines and satsumas	129.0	130.0	152.2
Grapefruit and pomelos	241.1	249.4	204.4
Apples	97.4	114.7	131.5
Peaches and nectarines	96.5	80.1	65.8
Grapes	96.9	91.2	95.1
Avocados	53.1	85.0	73.2

Aggregate production ('000 metric tons, may include official, semi-official or estimated data): Total cereals 198.8 in 2008, 257.0 in 2009, 238.6 in 2010; Total roots and tubers 602.5 in 2008, 641.1 in 2009, 568.7 in 2010; Total vegetables (incl. melons) 1,516.6 in 2008, 1,620.0 in 2009, 1,681.6 in 2010; Total fruits (excl. melons) 1,217.1 in 2008, 1,319.1 in 2009, 1,278.5 in 2010.

Source: FAO.

LIVESTOCK
('000 head, year ending September)

	2008	2009	2010
Cattle	416	400	430
Pigs	206	224	224
Sheep	430	430	445
Goats	90	91	100
Chickens	39,245	41,095	42,599
Geese and guinea fowls*	1,000	1,000	1,000
Turkeys	3,718	3,396	3,800
Ducks*	200	200	200

* FAO estimates.

Source: FAO.

LIVESTOCK PRODUCTS
('000 metric tons)

	2008	2009	2010
Cattle meat	116.6	104.0	108.1
Sheep meat*	6.0	6.0	6.2
Pig meat	18.2	19.6	18.9
Chicken meat	440.0	436.0	450.0
Goose and guinea fowl meat*	3.8	3.7	3.8
Turkey meat	97.0	92.0	90.0
Cows' milk	1,335.2	1,276.7	1,292.1
Sheep's milk	18.9	18.9	16.8
Goats' milk	21.2	21.8	23.3
Hen eggs	96.3	100.8	102.5
Honey	2.8	3.0	2.5

* FAO estimates.

Source: FAO.

Forestry

ROUNDWOOD REMOVALS
('000 cubic metres, excl. bark)

	1999*	2000†	2001†
Sawlogs, veneer logs and logs for sleepers	36	28	11
Pulpwood	32	22	7
Other industrial wood	32	22	7
Fuel wood	13	8	2
Total	113	81	27

* FAO estimates.
† Unofficial figures.

2002–10: Figures assumed to be unchanged from 2001 (FAO estimates).

Source: FAO.

Fishing

(metric tons, live weight)

	2007	2008	2009
Capture	3,435	2,819*	2,996*
Carps, barbels, etc.	635	164	294
Aquaculture*	21,434	20,017	19,405
Common carp	6,737	6,448	5,892
Tilapias	7,973	6,751	7,789
Gilthead seabream	2,204	2,347	1,072
Flathead grey mullet	1,983	2,121	2,048
Total catch*	24,869	22,836	22,401

* FAO estimate(s).

Source: FAO.

Mining

('000 metric tons unless otherwise indicated)

	2008	2009	2010
Crude petroleum ('000 barrels)	15.7	14.7	12.4
Natural gas (million cu m)	3,436	2,825	3,234
Phosphate rock†	3,088	2,697	3,135
Potash salts‡	2,170	1,900	2,080
Salt (unrefined, marketed)	421	357	421
Gypsum	10	9	99.7
Bromine (elemental)	164	128	185

† Figures refer to beneficiated production; the phosphoric acid content (in '000 metric tons) was: 850 in 2008 (estimate); 740 in 2009 (estimate); 860 in 2010 (estimate).
‡ Figures refer to K_2O content.

Source: US Geological Survey.

Industry

SELECTED PRODUCTS
('000 metric tons, unless otherwise indicated)

	1992	1993	1994
Refined vegetable oils (metric tons)	56,463	57,558	45,447
Margarine	35.1	33.8	24.7
Wine ('000 litres)	12,373	12,733	n.a.
Beer ('000 litres)	51,078	58,681	50,750
Cigarettes (metric tons)	5,742	5,525	5,638
Newsprint (metric tons)	0	247	0
Writing and printing paper (metric tons)	66,334	65,426	65,790
Other paper (metric tons)	32,368	30,446	28,985
Cardboard (metric tons)	92,072	95,108	103,142
Rubber tyres ('000)	892	854	966
Ammonia	41	41	46
Ammonium sulphate (metric tons)	12,444	n.a.	n.a.
Sulphuric acid	138	n.a.	n.a.
Chlorine (metric tons)	33,912	35,241	37,555
Caustic soda (metric tons)	29,459	29,851	32,765
Polyethylene (metric tons)	128,739	144,147	126,979
Paints (metric tons)	58,963	57,429	53,260
Cement	3,960	4,536	4,800
Commercial vehicles (number)	852	836	1,260
Electricity (million kWh)	24,731	26,042	28,327

2008 ('000 metric tons unless otherwise indicated): Wine 6.5 (FAO estimate); Beer ('000 litres) 80,000 (FAO estimate); Cement 4,819 (Source: US Geological Survey); Sulphuric acid (sulphuric content) 620 (Source: US Geological Survey); Electricity (total production, million kWh) 50,161.

2009 ('000 metric tons unless otherwise indicated): Cement 4,759 (Source: US Geological Survey); Sulphuric acid (sulphuric content) 520 (estimate—Source: US Geological Survey); Electricity (total production, million kWh) 53,179.

2010 ('000 metric tons unless otherwise indicated): Cement 5,139 (Source: US Geological Survey); Sulphuric acid (sulphuric content) 630 (estimate—Source: US Geological Survey); Electricity (total production, million kWh) 56,147.

Finance

CURRENCY AND EXCHANGE RATES

Monetary Units

100 agorot (singular: agora) = 1 new sheqel (plural: sheqalim) or shekel (NIS).

Sterling, Dollar and Euro Equivalents (30 December 2011)

£1 sterling = NIS 5.908;
US $1 = NIS 3.821;
€1 = NIS 4.944;
NIS 100 = £16.93 = $26.17 = €20.23.

Average Exchange Rate (NIS per US $)

2009 3.9323
2010 3.7390
2011 3.5781

STATE BUDGET*
(NIS million)

Revenue and grants†	2008	2009‡	2010‡
Current receipts	215,233	225,235	234,195
Taxes and compulsory payments	184,842	173,890	184,435
Income and property taxes	95,715	84,800	85,100
Taxes on expenditure	89,127	89,090	99,335
Interest, royalties, etc.	5,090	5,668	5,154
Transfer from loans and capital account receipts	25,301	45,677	44,607
Receipts from loans and capital account	81,031	91,318	91,093
Collection of principal	6,879	5,479	5,231
Miscellaneous	1,471	244	112
Privatization	1,752	298	500
Domestic loans	82,283	104,920	102,950
Loans and grants from overseas	13,947	26,056	26,907
Less Transfer to current receipts	25,301	45,677	44,607
Total	296,265	316,553	325,288

Expenditure§	2008	2009‡	2010‡
Civilian consumption	52,118	59,194	63,200
Domestic	33,853	36,291	39,101
Defence consumption	56,528	48,934	53,769
Transfer and support payments	83,690	87,941	87,463
Investments and credit granting	14,568	18,547	17,418
Interest payments and credit subsidies	33,137	35,673	38,039
Miscellaneous	6,964	7,423	7,523
Reserves	—	4,811	5,143
Debt repayment (principal)	62,835	68,343	69,245
Less Revenue-dependent expenditure	13,576	14,313	16,513
Total	296,265	316,553	325,288

* Excluding Bank of Israel.

† Revenue includes grants received from abroad (NIS million): 10,037 in 2008; 8,640 in 2009 (forecast); 9,900 in 2010 (forecast).

‡ Forecasts.

§ Expenditure includes the central Government's credit issuance (NIS million): 1,947 in 2008; 3,488 in 2009 (forecast); 2,504 in 2010 (forecast).

Source: Ministry of Finance, Budget Division.

INTERNATIONAL RESERVES
(excluding gold, US $ million at 31 December)

	2008	2009	2010
IMF special drawing rights	13.2	1,231.4	1,323.4
Reserve position in IMF	176.1	288.9	319.0
Foreign exchange	42,324.0	59,091.0	69,265.0
Total	42,513.2	60,611.4	70,907.3

Source: IMF, *International Financial Statistics*.

MONEY SUPPLY
(NIS million at 31 December)

	2007	2008	2009
Currency outside banks	24,021	30,180	35,606
Demand deposits at deposit money banks	52,766	61,564	87,493
Total money (incl. others)	76,948	95,507	127,510

2010: Demand deposits at deposit money banks 88,144.

Source: IMF, *International Financial Statistics*.

COST OF LIVING
(Consumer Price Index, annual averages; base: 2000 = 100)

	2006	2007	2008
Food	115.1	119.5	133.2
Electricity, gas and other fuels	145.9	147.7	168.7
Housing	107.3	105.0	108.5
Clothing (incl. footwear)	77.1	74.8	73.7
All items (incl. others)	111.0	111.5	116.6

2009: Food 135.2; All items (incl. others) 120.5.

2010: Food 138.6; All items (incl. others) 123.7.

Source: ILO.

NATIONAL ACCOUNTS
(NIS million at current prices)

National Income and Product

	2009	2010	2011*
Gross domestic product in market prices	766,273	813,021	863,967
Net income paid abroad	–20,029	–23,502	–21,776
Gross national income (GNI)	746,244	789,519	842,191
Less Consumption of fixed capital	98,175	99,144	105,591
Net national income	648,069	690,376	736,600

Expenditure on the Gross Domestic Product

	2009	2010	2011*
Final consumption expenditure	619,887	667,421	717,563
Private	436,173	472,907	508,833
General government	183,714	194,514	208,730
Changes in inventories	–2,576	–15,244	–13,173
Gross fixed capital formation	130,559	145,040	170,220
Total domestic expenditure	747,870	797,217	874,610
Exports of goods and services	265,733	299,741	318,605
Less Imports of goods and services	247,330	283,937	329,247
GDP in market prices	766,273	813,021	863,967

Gross Domestic Product by Economic Activity

	2009	2010	2011*
Agriculture, hunting, forestry and fishing	15,517	14,444	14,946
Manufacturing, mining and quarrying	100,632	104,917	107,058
Electricity, gas and water supply	12,224	11,361	12,827
Construction	34,451	37,235	41,111
Wholesale, retail trade, repair of motor vehicles, motorcycles and personal and household goods; hotels and restaurants	67,631	72,158	75,290
Transport, storage and communications	50,071	52,863	54,608
Financial intermediation; real estate, renting and business activities	198,123	213,854	224,547
Public administration and community services†	116,480	124,131	133,049
Housing services	89,265	95,683	103,901
Other community, social and personal services	16,259	17,172	18,592
Sub-total	700,653	743,818	785,929
Less Imputed bank service charge	19,881	26,563	26,346
Net taxes on products	85,500	95,765	104,384
GDP in market prices	766,273	813,021	863,967

* Preliminary figures.

† Including non-profit institutions serving households.

BALANCE OF PAYMENTS
(US $ million)

	2008	2009	2010
Exports of goods f.o.b.	57,713	46,333	56,094
Imports of goods f.o.b.	–64,397	–45,993	–58,039
Trade balance	–6,684	339	–1,945
Exports of services	23,917	21,411	24,229
Imports of services	–19,769	–17,089	–18,055
Balance on goods and services	–2,536	4,662	4,229
Other income received	7,242	5,692	5,823
Other income paid	–11,357	–10,781	–12,135
Balance on goods, services and income	–6,651	–428	–2,084
Current transfers received	9,424	8,395	9,481
Current transfers paid	–943	–993	–1,055
Current balance	1,830	6,975	6,342
Capital account (net)	1,109	908	983
Direct investment abroad	–7,210	–1,695	–7,960
Direct investment from abroad	10,874	4,438	5,152
Portfolio investment assets	–1,634	–8,254	–8,901
Portfolio investment liabilities	2,149	3,085	8,602
Financial derivatives (net)	–116	230	30
Other investment assets	10,819	4,499	929
Other investment liabilities	–1,112	3,844	3,392
Net errors and omissions	–1,304	3,407	3,005
Overall balance	15,406	17,437	11,573

Source: IMF, *International Financial Statistics*.

External Trade

PRINCIPAL COMMODITIES
(US $ million)

Imports c.i.f.	2008	2009	2010
Food and live animals	3,528.5	2,875.1	3,457.8
Mineral fuels, lubricants, etc.	11,084.7	6,913.1	10,441.2
Petroleum, petroleum products, etc.	10,864.1	6,558.6	8,700.0
Chemicals and related products	7,171.8	5,687.1	6,843.9
Basic manufactures	16,098.2	10,111.4	14,477.6
Non-metallic mineral manufactures	10,052.6	5,974.7	9,126.9
Machinery and transport equipment	18,082.2	14,452.3	16,751.0
General industrial machinery, equipment and parts	2,022.6	1,591.8	1,974.9
Office machines and automatic data-processing machines	1,764.3	1,561.0	1,844.5
Telecommunications and sound equipment	2,358.4	2,122.0	2,259.9
Other electrical machinery, apparatus, etc.	3,616.0	3,002.2	3,822.2
Road vehicles and parts	4,171.4	3,509.9	4,383.4
Other transport equipment and parts	1,056.6	749.0	717.5
Miscellaneous manufactured articles	5,114.0	4,481.0	5,175.8
Total (incl. others)	65,173.2	47,368.2	59,199.4

Exports f.o.b.	2008	2009	2010
Chemicals and related products	13,187.9	10,096.3	13,477.6
Organic chemicals	1,578.5	1,270.5	1,481.7
Medical and pharmaceutical products	4,843.8	4,563.1	6,475.2
Basic manufactures	23,478.7	14,214.5	19,568.2
Non-metallic mineral manufactures	19,833.2	11,907.5	16,696.3
Machinery and transport equipment	13,761.9	14,717.6	14,710.9
Telecommunications and sound equipment	4,109.3	3,294.5	3,424.2
Other electrical machinery, apparatus, etc.	3,888.6	5,867.9	5,395.3
Road vehicles and other transport equipment and parts	1,517.1	2,428.7	2,294.0
Miscellaneous manufactured articles	5,032.0	4,352.4	4,876.6
Professional, scientific and controlling instruments, etc.	1,990.5	1,680.7	2,354.8
Total (incl. others)	61,339.1	47,935.5	58,415.9

PRINCIPAL TRADING PARTNERS
(US $ million)*

Imports (excl. military goods) c.i.f.	2008	2009	2010
Belgium-Luxembourg	4,424.3	2,684.8	3,576.4
China, People's Republic	4,244.0	3,521.1	4,736.8
France	1,889.2	1,428.7	1,517.2
Germany	3,940.5	3,361.8	3,678.8
Hong Kong	1,813.7	1,111.5	1,398.6
India	1,648.8	1,157.4	1,845.6
Italy	2,553.7	2,126.0	2,425.8
Japan	2,226.7	1,523.7	1,779.6
Korea, Republic	1,103.2	871.1	1,100.7
Netherlands	2,465.3	1,885.4	2,102.1
Russia	1,047.1	488.6	784.6
South Africa	494.2	198.0	101.6
Spain	959.1	880.1	975.4
Sweden	693.6	523.1	552.4
Switzerland-Liechtenstein	3,973.6	3,290.0	3,220.2
Taiwan	712.4	544.4	709.1
Turkey	1,825.3	1,387.7	1,800.1
United Kingdom	2,519.9	1,907.2	2,246.4
USA	8,034.4	5,849.1	6,701.0
Total (incl. others)	65,173.2	47,368.2	59,199.4

Exports	2008	2009	2010
Australia	711.3	432.7	531.4
Belgium-Luxembourg	4,639.1	2,382.6	3,116.8
Brazil	1,172.0	716.5	934.8
Canada	901.7	578.3	749.5
China, People's Republic	1,293.5	1,044.6	2,046.8
France	1,298.0	1,110.6	1,266.5
Germany	1,950.6	1,440.3	1,701.4
Hong Kong	4,140.8	2,874.2	3,915.2
India	2,361.3	1,810.9	2,890.4
Italy	1,668.8	1,103.0	1,253.2
Japan	883.0	527.6	657.2
Korea, Republic	818.5	841.0	850.3
Netherlands	2,035.0	1,550.8	1,818.0
Spain	1,108.0	940.5	1,031.8
Switzerland-Liechtenstein	1,210.4	942.3	1,047.5
Taiwan	473.0	478.2	726.2
Turkey	1,609.9	1,086.0	1,310.7
United Kingdom	1,892.7	1,423.5	2,268.1
USA	19,972.5	16,774.1	18,488.2
Total (incl. others)	61,339.1	47,935.5	58,415.9

* Imports by country of purchase; exports by country of destination.

Transport

RAILWAYS
(traffic)

	2008	2009	2010
Passengers carried ('000 journeys)	35,136	35,934	35,877
Passenger-km (million)	1,968	2,011	1,986
Freight carried ('000 metric tons)	6,837	5,683	7,023
Freight ton-km (million)	1,056	799	1,062

ROAD TRAFFIC
(motor vehicles in use at 31 December)

	2008	2009	2010
Private passenger cars	1,875,765	1,946,749	2,053,248
Taxis	19,138	18,624	18,878
Minibuses	16,017	15,260	15,026
Buses and coaches	13,595	14,113	14,762
Lorries, vans and road tractors	358,673	350,456	347,152
Special service vehicles	3,973	3,967	4,118
Motorcycles and mopeds	103,394	109,547	113,007

SHIPPING

Merchant Fleet
(registered at 31 December)

	2007	2008	2009
Number of vessels	51	43	42
Displacement ('000 grt)	728.1	437.4	400.5

Source: IHS Fairplay, *World Fleet Statistics*.

International Sea-borne Freight Traffic
('000 metric tons)

	2008	2009	2010
Goods loaded	18,132	15,398	19,270
Goods unloaded*	22,856	21,545	24,142

* Including traffic between Israeli ports.

CIVIL AVIATION
(traffic on scheduled services)

	2007	2008	2009
Kilometres flown (million)	111	104	103
Passengers carried ('000)	4,663	4,627	4,606
Passenger-km (million)	18,180	17,404	17,251
Total ton-km (million)	3,099	2,683	2,362

Source: UN, *Statistical Yearbook*.

Tourism

TOURIST ARRIVALS
('000)*

Country of residence	2008	2009	2010
Canada	68.5	59.5	70.2
France	256.3	254.0	274.1
Germany	137.4	139.8	171.5
Italy	120.6	116.5	150.2
Jordan	15.3	15.0	17.8
Netherlands	48.3	44.5	53.4
Russia	205.4	231.4	318.7
Spain	61.0	49.0	59.7
Ukraine	63.9	46.5	55.3
United Kingdom	173.3	163.5	168.8
USA	600.6	538.0	605.1
Total (incl. others)	2,559.6	2,321.4	2,803.1

* Excluding arrivals of Israeli nationals residing abroad.

Tourism receipts (US $ million, incl. passenger transport, unless otherwise indicated): 5,030 in 2008; 4,332 in 2009; 4,768 in 2010 (provisional, excl. passenger transport) (Source: World Tourism Organization).

Communications Media

	2008	2009	2010
Telephones ('000 main lines in use)	3,224.0	3,250.0	3,276.2
Mobile cellular telephones ('000 subscribers)	8,982	9,022	9,875
Internet subscribers ('000)	1,714.0	n.a.	n.a.
Broadband subscribers ('000)	1,684.0	1,850.0	1,864.9

Television receivers ('000 in use): 2,100 in 2000; 2,150 in 2001.

Radio receivers (1997): 3,070,000 in use.

Book production (1998): 1,969 titles.

Daily newspapers (1996): 34 titles (estimated circulation 1,650,000 copies).

Non-daily newspapers (1988): 80 titles.

Other periodicals (1985): 807 titles.

Personal computers: 5,037,000 in 2005.

Sources: International Telecommunication Union; UNESCO, *Statistical Yearbook*; UN, *Statistical Yearbook*; UNESCO Institute for Statistics.

Education

(2010/11 unless otherwise indicated, provisional figures)

	Schools	Pupils	Teachers
Hebrew			
Kindergarten	n.a.	371,149*	15,490
Primary schools	2,106	651,419	57,379
Special needs	190	10,045	n.a.
Intermediate schools†	502	183,414	24,489
Secondary schools	1,394	470,765	62,081
Vocational schools*	112	23,485	n.a.
Teacher training colleges	56*	33,893*	5,359‡
Arab			
Kindergarten	n.a.	98,882*	3,289
Primary schools	546	248,192	19,083
Special needs	57	3,304	n.a.
Intermediate schools†	138	70,463	5,195
Secondary schools	355	159,861	14,414
Vocational schools*	24	4,376	n.a.
Teacher training colleges	4†	2,827†	491‡

* 2008/09 provisional data.
† 2007/08 provisional data.
‡ 2006/07 data.

Pupil-teacher ratio (primary education, UNESCO estimate): 13.1 in 2008/09 (Source: UNESCO Institute for Statistics).

Adult literacy rate (UNESCO estimates): 96.9% (males 98.3%; females 95.6%) in 2003 (Source: UN Development Programme, *Human Development Report*).

Directory

The Government

HEAD OF STATE

President: SHIMON PERES (took office 15 July 2007).

THE CABINET
(May 2012)

A coalition of Likud, Kadima, Israel Beytenu, Ha'atzmaut, Shas and Jewish Home. (Although United Torah Judaism formed part of the Government, none of its ministers were appointed to cabinet posts.)

Prime Minister and Minister for Economic Strategies, for Senior Citizens and of Health: BINYAMIN NETANYAHU (Likud).

Vice-Prime Minister and Minister: SHAUL MOFAZ (Kadima).

Vice-Prime Minister and Minister for Regional Co-operation and the Development of the Negev and Galilee: SILVAN SHALOM (Likud).

Vice-Prime Minister and Minister of Strategic Affairs: MOSHE YA'ALON (Likud).

Deputy Prime Minister and Minister of Defence: EHUD BARAK (Ha'atzmaut).

Deputy Prime Minister and Minister of Foreign Affairs: AVIGDOR LIEBERMAN (Israel Beytenu).

Deputy Prime Minister and Minister of Intelligence and Atomic Energy: DAN MERIDOR (Likud).

Deputy Prime Minister and Minister of the Interior: ELIYAHU YISHAI (Shas).

Minister of Finance: YUVAL STEINITZ (Likud).

Minister of Communications and Minister of Welfare and Social Services: MOSHE KAHLON (Likud).

Minister of Industry, Trade and Labour and Minister of Minority Affairs: SHALOM SIMHON (Ha'atzmaut).

Minister of Religious Services: YAACOV MARGI (Shas).

Minister of Immigrant Absorption: SOFA LANDVER (Israel Beytenu).

Minister of Energy and Water Resources: UZI LANDAU (Israel Beytenu).

Minister of Improvement of Government Services: MICHAEL EITAN (Likud).

Minister of Public Security: YITZHAK AHARONOVITCH (Israel Beytenu).

Minister of Environmental Protection: GILAD ERDAN (Likud).

Minister of Justice: YAACOV NE'EMAN (Likud).

Minister of Construction and Housing: ARIEL ATIAS (Shas).

Minister of Transport, National Infrastructures and Road Safety: YISRAEL KATZ (Likud).

Minister of Agriculture and Rural Development: ORIT NOKED (Ha'atzmaut).

Minister of Tourism: STAS MISEZHNIKOV (Israel Beytenu).

Minister of Education: GIDEON SA'AR (Likud).

Minister of Science and Technology: Rabbi DANIEL HERSHKOWITZ (Jewish Home).

Minister of Culture and Sport: LIMOR LIVNAT (Likud).

Minister of Home Front Defence: MATAN VILNAI (Ha'atzmaut).

Minister of Public Diplomacy and the Diaspora: YULI-YOEL EDELSTEIN (Likud).

Ministers without Portfolio: ZE'EV BINYAMIN BEGIN (Likud), MESHULAM NAHARI (Shas), YOSSI PELED (Likud).

Note: The Prime Minister automatically assumes responsibility for any portfolio which becomes vacant, until a permanent or acting minister is appointed.

MINISTRIES

Office of the President: 3 Hanassi St, Jerusalem 92188; tel. 2-6707211; fax 2-5887225; e-mail president@president.gov.il; internet www.president.gov.il.

Office of the Prime Minister: POB 187, 3 Kaplan St, Kiryat Ben-Gurion, Jerusalem 91950; tel. 2-6705555; fax 2-5664838; e-mail pm_eng@pmo.gov.il; internet www.pmo.gov.il.

Ministry of Agriculture and Rural Development: POB 50200, Agricultural Centre, Beit Dagan 50250; tel. 3-9485555; fax 3-9485858; e-mail pniot@moag.gov.il; internet www.moag.gov.il.

Ministry of Communications: 23 Jaffa St, Jerusalem 91999; tel. 2-6706301; fax 2-6240029; e-mail dovrut@moc.gov.il; internet www.moc.gov.il.

Ministry of Construction and Housing: POB 18110, Kiryat Hamemshala (East), Jerusalem 91180; tel. 2-5847211; fax 2-5847688; e-mail sar@moch.gov.il; internet www.moch.gov.il.

Ministry of Culture and Sport: POB 49100, Kiryat Hamemshala, Hamizrachit, Bldg 3, Jerusalem 91490; tel. 2-5411110; e-mail ministerts@most.gov.il; internet www.mcs.gov.il.

Ministry of Defence: Kirya, Tel-Aviv 64734; tel. 3-6975540; fax 3-6976711; e-mail pniot@mod.gov.il; internet www.mod.gov.il.

Ministry for the Development of the Negev and Galilee: 8 Shaul Hamelech Blvd, Tel-Aviv 64733; tel. 3-6060700; fax 3-6958414; e-mail lilach.nb@gmail.com; internet www.vpmo.gov.il.

Ministry of Education: POB 292, 34 Shivtei Israel St, Jerusalem 91911; tel. 2-5602222; fax 2-5602223; e-mail info@education.gov.il; internet www.education.gov.il.

Ministry of Energy and Water Resources: POB 33541, Haifa 31334; tel. 4-8644024; fax 4-8660189; e-mail pniot@energy.gov.il; internet www.energy.gov.il.

Ministry of Environmental Protection: POB 34033, 5 Kanfei Nesharim St, Givat Shaul, Jerusalem 95464; tel. 2-6553777; fax 2-6495892; e-mail pniot@environment.gov.il; internet www.environment.gov.il.

Ministry of Finance: POB 13195, 1 Kaplan St, Kiryat Ben-Gurion, Jerusalem 91030; tel. 2-5317111; fax 2-5637891; e-mail webmaster@mof.gov.il; internet www.mof.gov.il.

Ministry of Foreign Affairs: 9 Yitzhak Rabin Blvd, Kiryat Ben-Gurion, Jerusalem 91950; tel. 2-5303111; fax 2-5303367; e-mail pniot@mfa.gov.il; internet www.mfa.gov.il.

Ministry of Health: POB 1176, 2 Ben-Tabai St, Jerusalem 91010; tel. 2-6705705; fax 2-5681200; e-mail pniot@moh.health.gov.il; internet www.health.gov.il.

Ministry of Immigrant Absorption: 6 Ester Hamalka St. Tel Aviv; tel. 3-5209127; fax 3-5209143; e-mail sar@moia.gov.il; internet www.moia.gov.il.

Ministry of Industry, Trade and Labour: 5 Bank of Israel St, Jerusalem 91009; tel. 2-6662252; fax 2-6662908; e-mail dover@moit.gov.il; internet www.moit.gov.il.

Ministry of Intelligence and Atomic Energy: Jerusalem.

Ministry of the Interior: POB 6158, 2 Kaplan St, Kiryat Ben-Gurion, Jerusalem 91008; tel. 2-6701411; fax 2-6701628; e-mail info@moin.gov.il; internet www.moin.gov.il.

Ministry of Justice: POB 49029, 29 Salahadin St, Jerusalem 91010; tel. 2-6466521; fax 2-6467001; e-mail pniot@justice.gov.il; internet www.justice.gov.il.

Ministry of Public Diplomacy and the Diaspora: Jerusalem; tel. 2-6587120; fax 2-6587125; e-mail ifat.aloni@pmo.gov.il.

Ministry of Public Security: POB 18182, Bldg 3, Kiryat Hamemshala (East), Jerusalem 91181; tel. 2-5309999; fax 2-5847872; e-mail sar@mops.gov.il; internet www.mops.gov.il.

Ministry of Regional Co-operation: Jerusalem.

Ministry of Religious Services: POB 13059, 7 Kanfei Nesharim St, Jerusalem 95464; tel. 2-5311101; fax 2-5311308; e-mail religion@religion.gov.il; internet www.dat.gov.il.

Ministry of Science and Technology: POB 49100, Kiryat Hamemshala, Hamizrachit, Bldg 3, Jerusalem 91490; tel. 2-5411110; fax 2-5811613; e-mail minister@most.gov.il; internet www.most.gov.il.

Ministry of Social Affairs and Social Services: POB 915, 2 Kaplan St, Kiryat Ben-Gurion, Jerusalem 91008; tel. 2-6752523; fax 2-5666385; e-mail sar@molsa.gov.il; internet www.molsa.gov.il.

Ministry of Strategic Affairs: Jerusalem.

Ministry of Tourism: POB 1018, 5 Bank of Israel St, Jerusalem 91009; tel. 2-6664331; fax 2-6514629; e-mail sarb@tourism.gov.il; internet www.tourism.gov.il.

Ministry of Transport, National Infrastructures and Road Safety: POB 867, Government Complex, 5 Bank of Israel St, Jerusalem 91008; tel. 2-6663333; fax 2-6663195; e-mail sar@mot.gov.il; internet www.mot.gov.il.

GOVERNMENT AGENCY

The Jewish Agency for Israel

POB 92, 48 King George St, Jerusalem 91000; tel. 2-6202222; fax 2-6202303; e-mail pniyottzibor@jafi.org; internet www.jewishagency.org.

f. 1929; reconstituted in 1971 as a partnership between the World Zionist Organization and the fund-raising bodies United Israel Appeal, Inc (USA) and Keren Hayesod.

Organization: The governing bodies are: the Assembly, which determines basic policy; the Board of Governors, which sets policy for the Agency between Assembly meetings; and the Executive, responsible for the day-to-day running of the Agency.

Chairman of Executive: NATAN SHARANSKY.

Chairman of Board of Governors: JAMES S. TISCH.

Director-General: ALAN HOFFMANN.

CEO and President of Jewish Agency International Development: MISHA GALPERIN.

Functions: According to the Agreement of 1971, the Jewish Agency undertakes the immigration and absorption of immigrants in Israel, including: absorption in agricultural settlement and immigrant housing; social welfare and health services in connection with immigrants; education, youth care and training; and neighbourhood rehabilitation through project renewal.

Legislature

Knesset

Kiryat Ben-Gurion, Jerusalem 91950; tel. 2-6753665; fax 2-6753566; e-mail mshenkar@knesset.gov.il; internet www.knesset.gov.il.

Speaker: REUVEN RIVLIN.

General Election, 10 February 2009

Party	Valid votes cast	% of valid votes	Seats
Kadima	758,032	22.47	28
Likud-Ahi	729,054	21.61	27
Israel Beytenu	394,577	11.70	15
Israel Labour Party	334,900	9.93	13
Shas	286,300	8.49	11
United Torah Judaism	147,954	4.39	5
United Arab List-Arab Movement for Renewal	113,954	3.38	4
National Union	112,570	3.34	4
Hadash	112,130	3.32	4
Meretz-New Movement	99,611	2.95	3
Jewish Home-New National Religious Party	96,765	2.87	3
Balad	83,739	2.48	3
Total (incl. others)	3,373,490*	100.00	120

* Excluding 43,097 invalid votes.

Election Commission

Central Elections Committee: Knesset, Kiryat Ben-Gurion, Jerusalem 91950; tel. 2-6753407; e-mail doverd@knesset.gov.il; internet knesset.gov.il/elections17/eng/cec/CecIndex_eng.htm; independent; Supreme Court elects a Justice as Chair; each parliamentary group nominates representatives to the Cttee in proportion to the group's level of representation in the Knesset; Chair. Justice ASHER D. GRUNIS; Dir-Gen. TAMAR EDRI.

Political Organizations

Agudat Israel (Union of Israel): POB 513, Jerusalem; tel. 2-5385251; fax 2-5385145; f. 1912; mainly Ashkenazi ultra-Orthodox Jews; stands for introduction of laws and institutions based on Jewish religious law (the Torah); contested 2009 legislative elections as part of the United Torah Judaism list (with Degel Hatorah); Chair. Rabbi MEIR PORUSH.

Arab Movement for Renewal (Tnua'a Aravit le'Hitkadshut—Ta'al): Jerusalem; tel. 2-6753333; fax 2-6753927; e-mail atibi@knesset.gov.il; f. 1996 following split from Balad; contested March 2006 and Feb. 2009 legislative elections on joint list with United Arab List; Leader Dr AHMAD TIBI.

Balad (National Democratic Assembly): POB 2248, Nazareth Industrial Zone, Nazareth 16000; tel. 4-6455070; fax 4-6463457; e-mail balad@zahav.net.il; internet tajamoa.org; f. 1999; united Arab party; Leader Dr JAMAL ZAHALKA.

Communist Party of Israel (Miflagah Kommonistit Yisraelit—Maki): POB 26205, 5 Hess St, Tel-Aviv 61261; tel. 3-6293944; fax 3-6297263; e-mail info@maki.org.il; internet www.maki.org.il; f. 1948; Jewish-Arab party descended from the Socialist Workers' Party of Palestine (f. 1919); renamed Communist Party of Palestine 1921, Jewish and Arab sections split 1945, reunited as Communist Party of Israel (Maki) 1948; further split 1965: pro-Soviet predominantly Arab anti-Zionist group formed New Communist Party of Israel (Rakah) 1965, while predominantly Jewish bloc retained name Maki; Rakah joined with other leftist orgs as Hadash 1977; name changed to Maki 1989, as the dominant component of Hadash (q.v.); Gen. Sec. MUHAMMAD NAFA'H.

Degel Hatorah (Flag of the Torah): 103 Rehov Beit Vegan, Jerusalem; tel. 2-6438106; fax 2-6418967; f. 1988 by Lithuanian Jews as breakaway faction from Agudat Israel; mainly Ashkenazi ultra-Orthodox (Haredi) Jews; contested 2009 legislative elections as part of the United Torah Judaism list (with Agudat Israel).

Ha'atzmaut (Independence): Jerusalem; tel. 2-6753333; internet www.haatzmaut.org.il; f. Jan. 2011 by Deputy Prime Minister and Minister of Defence Ehud Barak, following his resignation as Chair. of the Israel Labour Party; Leader EHUD BARAK.

Hadash (Hachazit Hademokratit Leshalom Uleshivyon—Democratic Front for Peace and Equality): POB 26205, Tel-Aviv 61261; tel. 3-6293944; fax 3-6297263; internet hadash2009.org.il; f. 1977 by merger of the New Communist Party of Israel (Rakah) with other leftist groups; party list, the principal component of which is the Communist Party of Israel (q.v.); Jewish-Arab membership; aims for a socialist system in Israel and a lasting peace between Israel, Arab countries and the Palestinian Arab people; favours full implementation of UN Security Council Resolutions 242 and 338, Israeli withdrawal from all Arab territories occupied since 1967, formation of a Palestinian Arab state in the West Bank and Gaza Strip (with East Jerusalem as its capital), recognition of national rights of State of Israel and Palestinian people, democratic rights and defence of working-class interests, and demands an end to discrimination against Arab minority in Israel and against oriental Jewish communities; Chair. MUHAMMAD BARAKEH.

Herut (Freedom): 55 Hamasger St, Tel-Aviv; tel. 3-5621521; fax 3-5618699; e-mail herut@herut.org.il; internet www.herut.org.il; f. 1948; reconstituted 1999; right-wing nationalist party; opposed to further Israeli withdrawals from the Occupied Territories; Leader MICHAEL KLEINER.

Israel Beytenu (Israel Is Our Home/Nash dom Izrail): 78 Yirmiyahu St, Jerusalem 94467; tel. 2-5012999; fax 2-5377188; e-mail gdv7191@hotmail.com; internet www.beytenu.org.il; f. 1999; right-wing immigrant party; joined Nat. Union in 2000, but left to contest March 2006 and Feb. 2009 legislative elections alone; seeks resolution of the Israeli–Palestinian conflict through the exchange of territory and population with the Palestinians, incl. the transfer of Arab Israelis to territory under Palestinian control; membership largely drawn from fmr USSR; 18,000 mems (2006); Leader AVIGDOR LIEBERMAN.

Israel Labour Party (Mifleget HaAvoda HaYisraelit): POB 62033, Tel-Aviv 61620; tel. 3-6899444; fax 3-6899420; e-mail inter@havoda.org.il; internet www.havoda.org.il; f. 1968 as a merger of the three Labour groups, Mapai, Rafi and Achdut Ha'avoda; Am Ehad (One Nation) merged with Labour in 2004; a Zionist democratic socialist party; election for permanent chair. due Sept. 2011; Chair. SHELLY YACHIMOVITCH; Sec.-Gen. YECHIEL BAR.

Jewish Home (HaBayit HaYehudi): Jerusalem; f. 2008 by merger of Nat. Religious Party (NRP; f. 1956), Moledet and Tekuma; however, Moledet and some Tekuma mems subsequently withdrew from new party; right-wing nationalist, Zionist; opposes further Israeli withdrawals from the West Bank and the creation of a Palestinian state; favours strengthening of the state and system of religious education; contested Feb. 2009 legislative elections on joint list with New NRP, after dissolution of original NRP in Nov. 2008; Leader Rabbi DANIEL HERSHKOVITZ.

Kadima (Forward): Petach Tikva, Tel-Aviv; tel. 3-9788000; fax 3-9788020; internet www.kadima.org.il; f. 2005; liberal party formed as a breakaway faction from Likud by fmr party Chairman Ariel Sharon; aims to pursue a peace agreement with the Palestinians in accordance with the 'roadmap' peace plan, and to establish Israel's permanent borders, if necessary unilaterally; seeks to combat economic and social problems; Leader SHAUL MOFAZ.

Likud (Consolidation): 38 Rehov King George, Tel-Aviv 61231; tel. 3-5630666; fax 3-5282901; internet www.netanyahu.org.il; f. Sept. 1973; fmrly a parliamentary bloc of Herut (f. 1948), the Liberal Party of Israel (f. 1961), Laam (For the Nation—f. 1976), Ahdut, Tami (f. 1981; joined Likud in June 1987) and an ind. faction led by Itzhak Modai (f. 1990), which formed the nucleus of a new Party for the Advancement of the Zionist Idea; Herut and the Liberal Party formally merged in Aug. 1988 to form the Likud-Nat. Liberal Movement; Israel B'Aliyah merged with Likud in 2003; fmr Prime Minister and Likud Chair. Ariel Sharon established a breakaway faction, Kadima, in 2005; contested Feb. 2009 legislative elections on joint list with Ahi (right-wing nationalist; Leader EFRAIM EITAM); aims: territorial integrity; absorption of newcomers; a social order based on freedom and justice, elimination of poverty and want; economic devt and environmental reforms to improve living standards; Chair. BINYAMIN NETANYAHU.

Meimad: POB 53139, 19 Yad Harutzim St, Jerusalem 91533; tel. 2-6725134; fax 2-6725051; f. 1988; moderate democratic Jewish party; ended alliance with Israel Labour Party and joined list with Green Movement (HaTnuah Hayeruka—f. 2008) prior to Feb. 2009 legislative elections, at which it failed to achieve representation in the Knesset; Leader Rabbi MICHAEL MELCHIOR.

Meretz-Yahad (Vitality–Together—Social Democratic Party of Israel): Beit Amot Mishpat, 8th Shaul Hamelech Blvd, Tel-Aviv 64733; tel. 3-6098998; fax 3-6961728; e-mail orit@myparty.org.il; internet www.myparty.org.il; f. 2003 as Yahad (Together—Social Democratic Israel) from a merger of Meretz (f. 1992; an alliance of Ratz, Shinui and the United Workers' Party) and Shahar (f. 2002; a breakaway faction of the Israel Labour Party); name changed to above in 2005; formed joint list with New Movement (Hatnua Hahadasha) prior to Feb. 2009 legislative elections; Jewish-Arab social democratic party; stands for: civil rights; welfarism; Palestinian self-determination and a return to the 1967 borders, with minor adjustments; a divided Jerusalem, but no right of return for Palestinian refugees to Israel; separation of religion from the state; Chair. ZAHAVA GAL-ON.

Moledet (Homeland): 14 Yehuda Halevi St, Tel-Aviv; tel. 3-654580; e-mail moledet@moledet.org.il; internet www.m-moledet.org.il; f. 1988; right-wing nationalist party; aims include the expulsion ('transfer') of Palestinians living in the West Bank and Gaza Strip; united with Tehiya—Zionist Revival Movement in June 1994 as the

Moledet—the Eretz Israel Faithful and the Tehiya; contested Feb. 2009 legislative elections as part of the Nat. Union; Chair. URI BANK.

National Union (Haichud Haleumi): e-mail info@leumi.org.il; f. 1999 as right-wing coalition comprising Herut, Moledet and Tekuma parties; contested March 2006 legislative elections on joint list with Nat. Religious Party, but stood alone (comprising Moledet, Hatikva, Eretz Yisrael Shelanu and fmr Tekuma mems) in Feb. 2009 elections; believes in a 'Greater Israel'; opposed to further withdrawals from the Occupied Territories; stated aim of joint list was the creation of an Israeli society based on the spiritual and social values of Judaism and the retention of an undivided Israel; Leader YAAKOV DOV KATZ.

Pensioners' Party (Gimla'ey Yisrael LaKneset—Gil) (Pensioners of Israel to the Knesset—Age): 100 Ha' Hashmonaim, Tel-Aviv; tel. 3-5611900; fax 3-5611909; e-mail info@gimlaim.org.il; internet www.gimlaim.org.il; stands for pensioners' rights; failed to achieve representation in the Knesset at Feb. 2009 legislative elections; Leader RAFI EITAN.

Shas (Sephardic Torah Guardians): Beit Abodi, Rehov Hahida, Bene Beraq; tel. 3-579776; internet www.shasnet.org.il; f. 1984 by splinter groups from Agudat Israel; ultra-Orthodox Sephardic party; Spiritual Leader Rabbi OVADIA YOSEF; Chair. ELIYAHU YISHAI.

United Arab List (Reshima Aravit Me'uchedet—Ra'am): Jerusalem; tel. 9–7997088; fax 9-7996295; e-mail media.amc@gmail.com; internet www.a-m-c.org; f. 1996 by merger of the Arab Democratic Party and individuals from the Islamic Movement and Nat. Unity Front (left-wing Arab parties); supports establishment of a Palestinian state, with East Jerusalem as its capital, and equality for all Israeli citizens; contested March 2006 and Feb. 2009 legislative elections on joint list with Arab Movement for Renewal; Chair. IBRAHIM SARSUR.

United Torah Judaism (Yahadut Hatorah): f. prior to 1992 election; electoral list of four minor ultra-Orthodox parties (Moria, Degel Hatorah, Poale Agudat Israel and Agudat Israel) established to overcome the increase in election threshold from 1% to 1.5% and to seek to counter the rising influence of the secular Russian vote; contested 2003 election composed of Degel Hatorah and Agudat Israel, into which constituent parties it split in early 2005; two parties reunited in late 2005 and contested March 2006 and Feb. 2009 legislative elections together; represents Ashkenazi ultra-Orthodox Jews and advocates the application of religious precepts in all areas of life and government; Chair., Parliamentary Group YAAKOV LITZMAN.

Diplomatic Representation

EMBASSIES IN ISRAEL

Albania: 54/26 Pinkas St, Tel-Aviv 62261; tel. 3-5465866; fax 3-5444545; e-mail embassy.telaviv@mfa.gov.al; Ambassador BUJAR SKENDO.

Angola: Beit Amot Mishpat, 13th Floor, 8 Shaul Hamelech Blvd, Tel-Aviv 64733; tel. 3-6912093; fax 3-6912094; e-mail embangi@zahav.net.il; internet www.angolaembassy.org.il; Ambassador JOSÉ JOÃO MANUEL.

Argentina: 85 Medinat Hayehudim St, 3rd Floor, Herzliya Pituach 46120; tel. 9-9702744; fax 9-9702748; e-mail embarg@netvision.net.il; Ambassador CARLOS FAUSTINO GARCÍA.

Australia: POB 29108, Discount Bank Tower, 28th Floor, 23 Yehuda Halevi St, Tel-Aviv 65136; tel. 3-6935000; fax 3-6935002; e-mail telaviv.embassy@dfat.org.au; internet www.israel.embassy.gov.au; Ambassador ANDREA FAULKNER.

Austria: Beit Crystal, 12 Hahilazon, Ramat-Gan 52522; tel. 3-6120924; fax 3-7510716; e-mail tel-aviv-ob@bmeia.gv.at; internet www.aussenministerium.at/telaviv; Ambassador Dr FRANZ JOSEF KUGLITSCH.

Belarus: POB 11129, 3 Reines St, Tel-Aviv 64381; tel. 3-5231069; fax 3-5231259; e-mail israel@mfa.gov.by; internet www.israel.mfa.gov.by; Ambassador IGOR LESHCHENYA.

Belgium: 12 Abba Hillel St, Ramat-Gan 52506; tel. 3-6138130; fax 3-6138160; e-mail telaviv@diplobel.fed.be; internet www.diplomatie.be/telaviv; Ambassador BÉNÉDICTE FRANKINET.

Bosnia and Herzegovina: Yachin Bldg, 10th Floor, 2 Kaplan St, Tel-Aviv; tel. 3-6124499; fax 3-6124488; Ambassador IVANA LEVI.

Brazil: 23 Yehuda Halevi St, 30th Floor, Tel-Aviv 65136; tel. 3-6919292; fax 3-6916060; e-mail ambassador.telaviv@itamaraty.gov.br; internet telaviv.itamaraty.gov.br; Ambassador MARIA ELISA BERENGUER.

Bulgaria: 21 Leonardo da Vinci St, Tel-Aviv 64733; tel. 3-6961379; fax 3-6961430; e-mail telaviv@mfa.bg; internet www.mfa.bg/en/118; Ambassador YURI STERK.

Cameroon: 28 Moshe Sharet St, Ramat-Gan 52425; tel. 3-5298401; fax 3-5270352; e-mail activ50@yahoo.fr; Ambassador HENRI ETOUNDI ESSOMBA.

Canada: POB 9442, 3/5 Nirim St, Tel-Aviv 67060; tel. 3-6363300; fax 3-6363380; e-mail taviv@international.gc.ca; internet international.gc.ca/missions/israel; Ambassador PAUL HUNT.

Chile: Beit Sharbat, 8th Floor, 4 Kaufman St, Tel-Aviv 68012; tel. 3-5102751; fax 3-5100102; e-mail echileil@inter.net.il; internet chileabroad.gov.cl/israel; Ambassador JOAQUÍN MONTES LARRAÍN.

China, People's Republic: POB 6067, 222 Ben Yehuda St, Tel-Aviv 61060; tel. 3-5467277; fax 3-5467251; e-mail chinaemb_il@mfa.gov.cn; internet il.china-embassy.org; Ambassador GAO YANPING.

Colombia: Shekel Bldg, 8th Floor, 111 Arlozovov St, Tel-Aviv 62068; tel. 3-6953384; fax 3-6957847; e-mail emcolis@netvision.net.il; Ambassador Dr ISSAC GILINSKI.

Congo, Democratic Republic: 1 Rachel St, 2nd Floor, Tel-Aviv 64584; tel. 3-5248306; fax 3-5292623; Chargé d'affaires a.i. KIMBOKO MA MAKENGO.

Congo, Republic: POB 12504, 9 Maskit St, Herzliya Pituach 46120; tel. 9-9577130; fax 9-9577216; e-mail guy_itoua@yahoo.fr; Chargé d'affaires a.i. GUY NESTOR ITOUA.

Costa Rica: 14 Abba Hillel St, 15th Floor, Ramat-Gan 52506; tel. 3-6135061; fax 3-6134779; e-mail emcri@netvision.net.il; Ambassador RODRIGO X. CARRERAS.

Côte d'Ivoire: South Africa Bldg, 12 Menachim Begin St, Ramat-Gan 52521; tel. 3-6126677; fax 3-6126688; e-mail ambacita@netvision.net.il; Ambassador RAYMOND KESSIÉ KOUDOU.

Croatia: 2 Weizman St, Migdal Amot, Tel-Aviv 64239; tel. 3-6403000; fax 3-6438503; e-mail croemb.israel@mvep.hr; Ambassador ZORICA MARICA MATKOVIĆ.

Cyprus: Top Tower, 14th Floor, Dizengoff Centre, 50 Dizengoff St, Tel-Aviv 64322; tel. 3-5250212; fax 3-6290535; e-mail cypemb@013net.net; Ambassador DIMITRIS HATZIARGYROU.

Czech Republic: POB 16361, 23 Zeitlin St, Tel-Aviv; tel. 3-6918282; fax 3-6918286; e-mail telaviv@embassy.mzv.cz; internet www.mzv.cz/telaviv; Ambassador TOMÁŠ POJAR.

Denmark: POB 21080, Museum Tower, 11th Floor, 4 Berkowitz St, Tel-Aviv 61210; tel. 3-6085850; fax 3-6085851; e-mail tlvamb@um.dk; internet www.ambtelaviv.um.dk; Ambassador LISELOTTE KJÆRSGAARD PLESNER.

Dominican Republic: Beit Ackerstein, 3rd Floor, 103 Medinat Hayehudim St, Herzliya Pituach 46766; tel. 9-9515529; fax 9-9515528; e-mail embajdom@netvision.net.il; Ambassador ALEXANDER DE LA ROSA.

Ecuador: POB 34002, Asia House, 5th Floor, 4 Weizman St, Tel-Aviv 64239; tel. 3-6958764; fax 3-6913604; e-mail eecuisrael@mmrree.gov.ec; Ambassador GUILLERMO BASSANTE RAMÍREZ.

Egypt: 54 Basel St, Tel-Aviv 62744; tel. 3-5464151; fax 3-5441615; e-mail egypem.ta@zahav.net.il; Ambassador YASSER RIDHA.

El Salvador: 6 Hamada St, 4th Floor, Herzliya Pituach 46733; tel. 9-9556237; fax 9-9556603; e-mail embassy@el-salvador.org.il; internet www.el-salvador.org.il; Ambassador SUZANA GUN DE HASENSON.

Eritrea: 33 Jabotinsky St, 11th Floor, Ramat-Gan 52511; tel. 3-6120039; fax 3-5750133; Ambassador TESFAMARIAM TEKESTE.

Ethiopia: Bldg B, Floor 8B, 48 Darech Menachem Begin, Tel-Aviv 66184; tel. 3-6397831; fax 3-6397837; e-mail ethembis@netvision.net.il; internet www.ethioemb.org.il; Ambassador HELAWE YOSEF.

Finland: POB 39666, Canion Ramat Aviv, 9th Floor, 40 Einstein St, Tel-Aviv 61396; tel. 3-7456600; fax 3-7440314; e-mail sanomat.tel@formin.fi; internet www.finland.org.il; Ambassador LEENA-KAISA MIKKOLA.

France: 112 Tayelet Herbert Samuel, Tel-Aviv 63572; tel. 3-5208300; fax 3-5208340; e-mail diplomatie@ambafrance-il.org; internet www.ambafrance-il.org; Ambassador CHRISTOPHE BIGOT.

Georgia: 3 Daniel Frisch St, Tel-Aviv 64731; tel. 3-6093207; fax 3-6093205; e-mail geoemba@netvision.net.il; internet israel.mfa.gov.ge; Ambassador VAKHTANG JAOSHVILI.

Germany: POB 16038, 3 Daniel Frisch St, 19th Floor, Tel-Aviv 64731; tel. 3-6931313; fax 3-6969217; e-mail info@tel-aviv.diplo.de; internet www.tel-aviv.diplo.de; Ambassador ANDREAS MICHAELIS.

Ghana: 12 Hahilazon St, 3rd Floor, Ramat-Gan 52522; tel. 3-5766000; fax 3-7520827; e-mail chancery@ghanaemb.co.il; internet www.ghanaembassy.co.il; Ambassador HENRY HANSON HALI.

Greece: 3 Daniel Frisch St, Tel-Aviv 64731; tel. 3-6953060; fax 3-6951329; e-mail gremil@netvision.net.il; internet www.mfa.gr/telaviv; Ambassador KYRIAKOS LOUKAKIS.

Guatemala: Beit Ackerstein, 4th Floor, 103 Medinat Hayehudim St, Herzliya Pituach 46766; tel. 9-9577335; fax 9-9518506; e-mail embguate@netvision.net.il; Ambassador JORGE RICARDO PUTZEYS URIGUEN.

Holy See: 1 Netiv Hamazalot, Old Jaffa 68037; tel. 2-6835658; fax 2-6835659; e-mail vatge@netvision.net.il; Apostolic Nuncio Most Rev. ANTONIO FRANCO (Titular Archbishop of Gallese).

Honduras: Baruch Sharoni St, 16 Rishon le Zion 75500; tel. 9-9642092; fax 9-9577457; e-mail honduras@netvision.net.il; Chargé d'affaires DENNIS WEIZENBLUT.

Hungary: POB 21095, 18 Pinkas St, Tel-Aviv 62661; tel. 3-5466985; fax 3-5467018; e-mail mission.tlv@kum.hu; internet www.mfa.gov.hu/emb/telaviv; Ambassador ZOLTÁN SZENTGYÖRGYI.

India: POB 3368, 140 Hayarkon St, Tel-Aviv 61033; tel. 3-5291999; fax 3-5291953; e-mail indemtel@indembassy.co.il; internet www.indembassy.co.il; Ambassador NAVTEJ SINGH SARNA.

Ireland: The Tower, 17th Floor, 3 Daniel Frisch St, Tel-Aviv 64731; tel. 3-6964166; fax 3-6964160; e-mail telavivembassy@dfa.ie; internet www.embassyofireland.co.il; Ambassador BREIFNE O'REILLY.

Italy: Trade Tower, 25 Hamered St, Tel-Aviv 68125; tel. 3-5104004; fax 3-5100235; e-mail info.telaviv@esteri.it; internet www.ambtelaviv.esteri.it; Ambassador LUIGI MATTIOLO.

Japan: Museum Tower, 19th and 20th Floors, 4 Berkowitz St, Tel-Aviv 64238; tel. 3-6957292; fax 3-6910516; e-mail embjpcul@netvision.net.il; internet www.israel.emb-japan.go.jp; Ambassador HIDEO SATO.

Jordan: 14 Abba Hillel, Ramat-Gan 52506; tel. 3-7517722; fax 3-7517712; Ambassador (vacant).

Kazakhstan: 52A Hayarkon St, Tel-Aviv 63432; tel. 3-5163411; fax 3-5163437; e-mail kzisrael@kzisr.com; internet www.kazakhemb.org.il; Ambassador GALYM ORAZBAKOV.

Kenya: 15 Aba Hillel Silver St, Ramat-Gan 52136; tel. 3-5754633; fax 3-5754788; e-mail kenya7@netvision.net; Ambassador Lt-Gen. AUGUSTIONO NJOROGE.

Korea, Republic: 4 Hasadna'ot St, Herzliya Pituach 46728; tel. 9-9510318; fax 9-9569853; e-mail israel@mofat.go.kr; internet isr.mofat.go.kr; Ambassador KIM IL-SOO.

Latvia: Amot Investments Tower, 15th Floor, Weizman St, Tel-Aviv 64239; tel. 3-7775800; fax 3-6953101; e-mail embassy.israel@mfa.gov.lv; Ambassador MĀRTIŅŠ PERTS.

Liberia: 74 Derech Menachim Begin, Tel-Aviv 67215; tel. 3-5611068; fax 3-5610896.

Lithuania: 8 Shaul Ha Meleh, Tel-Aviv 64733; tel. 3-6958685; fax 3-6958691; e-mail lrambizr@netvision.net.il; internet il.mfa.lt; Ambassador DARIUS DEGUTIS.

Macedonia, former Yugoslav republic: Paz Tower, 9th Floor, 5–7 Shoham St, Ramat-Gan 52136; tel. 3-7154900; fax 3-6124789; e-mail telaviv@mfa.gov.mk; internet www.missions.gov.mk/telaviv; Ambassador PETAR JOVANOVSKI.

Mexico: Trade Tower, 5th Floor, 25 Hamered St, Tel-Aviv 68125; tel. 3-5163938; fax 3-5163711; e-mail communication1@embamex.org.il; internet www.sre.gob.mx/israel; Ambassador FEDERICO SALAS.

Moldova: 38 Rembrandt St, Tel-Aviv 64045; e-mail moldova@barak.net.il; internet moldovaembassy.org.il; tel. 3-5231000; fax 3-5233000; Ambassador MIHAI BALAN.

Myanmar: Textile Centre, 12th Floor, 2 Kaufman St, Tel-Aviv 68012; tel. 3-5170760; fax 3-5163512; e-mail suh0n3y@gmail.com; internet www.metelaviv.co.il; Ambassador MYINT SWE.

Nepal: Textile Centre, 2 Kaufman St, Tel-Aviv; tel. 3-5100111; fax 3-5167965; e-mail nepal.embassy@012.net.il; Ambassador BAIJANATH THAPALIYA.

Netherlands: Beit Oz, 13th Floor, 14 Abba Hillel St, Ramat-Gan 52506; tel. 3-7540777; fax 3-7540748; e-mail nlgovtel@012.net.il; internet www.netherlands-embassy.co.il; Ambassador CASPAR VELDKAMP.

Nigeria: POB 3339, 34 Gordon St, Tel-Aviv 61030; tel. 3-5222144; fax 3-5248991; e-mail henigtlv@zahav.net.il; internet www.nigerianembassy.co.il; Ambassador DAVID OLADIPO OBASA.

Norway: POB 17575, Canion Ramat Aviv, 13th Floor, 40 Einstein St, Tel-Aviv 69101; tel. 3-7441490; fax 3-7441498; e-mail emb.telaviv@mfa.no; internet www.norway.org.il; Ambassador SVEIN SEVJE.

Panama: 10/3 Hei Be'Iyar St, Kikar Hamedina, Tel-Aviv 62998; tel. 3-6956711; fax 3-6910045; Ambassador ROBERTO E. ARANGO.

Peru: 60 Medinat Hayehudim St, Entrance A, 2nd Floor, Herzliya Pituach 46766; tel. 9-9578835; fax 9-9568495; e-mail emperu@012.net.il; Ambassador LILIANA CINO (designate).

Philippines: 18 Bnei Dan St, Tel-Aviv 62260; tel. 3-6010500; fax 3-6041038; e-mail filembis@netvision.net.il; internet www.philippine-embassy.org.il; Ambassador GENEROSO DE GUZMAN CALONGE.

Poland: 16 Soutine St, Tel-Aviv 64684; tel. 3-7253111; fax 3-5237806; e-mail embpol@netvision.net.il; internet www.telaviv.polemb.net; Chargé d'affaires a.i. WIESŁAW KUCEŁ.

Portugal: 3 Daniel Frisch St, 12th Floor, Tel-Aviv 64731; tel. 3-6956373; fax 3-6956366; e-mail eptel@012.net.il; Chargé d'affaires a.i. MARIA REGINA ALMEIDA.

Romania: 24 Adam Hacohen St, Tel-Aviv 64585; tel. 3-5229472; fax 3-5247379; e-mail office_romania@bezeqint.net; internet www.telaviv.mae.ro; Ambassador EDWARD IOSIPER.

Russia: 120 Hayarkon St, Tel-Aviv 63573; tel. 3-5290691; fax 3-5101093; e-mail consul@russianembassy.org.il; internet russianembassy.org.il; Ambassador SERGEY YA. YAKOVLEV.

Serbia: 10 Bodenheimer St, Tel-Aviv 62008; tel. 3-6045535; fax 3-6049456; e-mail srbambil@netvision.net.il; internet serbiaembassy-il.org; Ambassador ZORAN BASARABA.

Slovakia: POB 6459, 37 Jabotinsky St, Tel-Aviv 62287; tel. 3-5449119; fax 3-5449144; e-mail slovemb1@barak.net.il; Ambassador RADOVAN JAVORČIK.

Slovenia: POB 23245, Top Tower, 50 Dizengoff St, Tel-Aviv 61231; tel. 3-6293563; fax 3-5282214; e-mail vta@gov.si; internet telaviv.veleposlanistvo.si; Ambassador ALENKA SUHADOLNIK.

South Africa: POB 7138, Top Tower, 16th Floor, 50 Dizengoff St, Tel-Aviv 61071; tel. 3-5252566; fax 3-5256481; e-mail info@saemb.org.il; internet www.safis.co.il; Ambassador ISMAIL COOVADIA.

Spain: Dubnov Tower, 18th Floor, 3 Daniel Frisch St, Tel-Aviv 64731; tel. 3-6958875; fax 3-6965217; e-mail embespil@correo.maec.es; Ambassador ALVARO IRANZO GUTIÉRREZ.

Sri Lanka: 4 Jean Jaurès St, Tel-Aviv 63412; tel. 3-5277635; fax 3-5277634; e-mail srilanka@013.net; Ambassador DONALD PERERA.

Sweden: Asia House, 4 Weizman St, Tel-Aviv 64239; tel. 3-7180000; fax 3-7180005; e-mail ambassaden.tel-aviv@foreign.ministry.se; internet www.swedenabroad.com/telaviv; Ambassador ELINOR HAMMARSKJÖLD.

Switzerland: POB 6068, 228 Hayarkon St, Tel-Aviv 61060; tel. 3-5464455; fax 3-5464408; e-mail vertretung@tel.rep.admin.ch; internet www.eda.admin.ch/telaviv; Ambassador WALTER HAFFNER.

Thailand: Mercazim Bldg 2001, 1 Abba Eban Blvd, Herzliya Pituach 46120; tel. 9-9548412; fax 9-9548417; e-mail thaisr@netvision.co.il; internet www.thaiembassy.org/telaviv; Ambassador NUTTAVUDH PHOTISARO.

Turkey: 202 Hayarkon St, Tel-Aviv 63405; tel. 3-35241101; fax 3-5241390; e-mail turkemb.telaviv@mfa.gov.tr; relations downgraded in Sept. 2011; Ambassador (vacant).

Ukraine: 50 Yirmiyahu St, Tel-Aviv 62594; tel. 3-6040242; fax 3-6042512; e-mail emb_il@mfa.gov.ua; internet www.mfa.gov.ua/israel; Ambassador HENNADII NADOLENKO.

United Kingdom: 192 Hayarkon St, Tel-Aviv 63405; tel. 3-7251222; fax 3-5278574; e-mail webmaster.telaviv@fco.gov.uk; internet ukinisrael.fco.gov.uk; Ambassador MATTHEW GOULD.

USA: 71 Hayarkon St, Tel-Aviv 63903; tel. 3-5197575; fax 3-5108093; e-mail nivtelaviv@state.gov; internet israel.usembassy.gov; Ambassador DANIEL B. SHAPIRO.

Uruguay: G.R.A.P. Bldg, 1st Floor, 4 Shenkar St, Industrial Zone, Herzliya Pituach 46725; tel. 9-9569611; fax 9-9515881; e-mail uruisr@emburuguay.co.il; Ambassador BERNARDO GREIVER.

Uzbekistan: 35 Devorah Haneviya St, Ramot Hachayal, Tel-Aviv 69350; tel. 3-6447746; fax 3-6447748; e-mail admindep@uzbembassy.org.il; internet www.uzbembassy.org.il; Ambassador OYBEK I. ESHONOV.

Viet Nam: 4 Weizman St, Tel-Aviv; tel. 3-6966304; fax 3-6966243; e-mail vnembassy.il@mofa.gov.vn; internet www.vietnamembassy-israel.org; Ambassador DINH XUAN LUU.

Judicial System

The law of Israel is composed of the enactments of the Knesset and, to a lesser extent, of the acts, orders-in-council and ordinances that remain from the period of the British Mandate in Palestine (1922–48). The pre-1948 law has largely been replaced, amended or reorganized, in the interests of codification, by Israeli legislation. This legislation generally follows a very similar pattern to that operating in England and the USA. However, there is no jury system.

Attorney-General: YEHUDA WEINSTEIN.

CIVIL COURTS

The Supreme Court

Sha'arei Mishpat St, Kiryat David Ben-Gurion, Jerusalem 91950; tel. 2-6759666; fax 2-6759648; e-mail marcia@supreme.court.gov.il; internet www.court.gov.il.

This is the highest judicial authority in the state. It has jurisdiction as an Appellate Court over appeals from the District Courts in all matters, both civil and criminal (sitting as a Court of Civil Appeal or as a Court of Criminal Appeal). In addition, it is a Court of First Instance (sitting as the High Court of Justice) in actions against governmental authorities, and in matters in which it considers it necessary to grant relief in the interests of justice and which are not within the jurisdiction of any other court or tribunal. The High Court's exclusive power to issue orders in the nature of *habeas corpus, mandamus*, prohibition and *certiorari* enables the court to review the legality of and redress grievances against acts of administrative authorities of all kinds.

President of the Supreme Court: ASHER D. GRUNIS.

Deputy President of the Supreme Court: ELIEZER RIVLIN.

Justices of the Supreme Court: MIRIAM NAOR, EDMOND E. LEVY, AYALA PROCACCIA, EDNA ARBEL, ESTHER HAYUT, ELYAKIM RUBINSTEIN, SALIM JOUBRAN, HANAN MELTZER, YORAM DANZIGER, UZI FOGELMAN, YITZHAK AMIT, NEAL HENDEL.

Registrars: Judge DANA COHEN-LEKAH, GUY SHANI.

District Courts: There are five District Courts (Jerusalem, Tel-Aviv, Haifa, Beersheba, Nazareth). They have residual jurisdiction as Courts of First Instance over all civil and criminal matters not within the jurisdiction of a Magistrates' Court (e.g. civil claims exceeding NIS 1m.), all matters not within the exclusive jurisdiction of any other tribunal, and matters within the concurrent jurisdiction of any other tribunal so long as such tribunal does not deal with them. In addition, the District Courts have appellate jurisdiction over appeals from judgments and decisions of Magistrates' Courts and judgments of Municipal Courts and various administrative tribunals.

Magistrates' Courts: There are 29 Magistrates' Courts, having criminal jurisdiction to try contraventions, misdemeanours and certain felonies, and civil jurisdiction to try actions concerning possession or use of immovable property, or the partition thereof whatever may be the value of the subject matter of the action, and other civil claims not exceeding NIS 1m.

Labour Courts: Established in 1969. Regional Labour Courts in Jerusalem, Tel-Aviv, Haifa, Beersheba and Nazareth, composed of judges and representatives of the public; a National Labour Court in Jerusalem; the Courts have jurisdiction over all matters arising out of the relationship between employer and employee or parties to a collective labour agreement, and matters concerning the National Insurance Law and the Labour Law and Rules.

RELIGIOUS COURTS

The Religious Courts are the courts of the recognized religious communities. They have jurisdiction over certain defined matters of personal status concerning members of their respective communities. Where any action of personal status involves persons of different religious communities, the President of the Supreme Court decides which Court will decide the matter. Whenever a question arises as to whether or not a case is one of personal status within the exclusive jurisdiction of a Religious Court, the matter must be referred to a Special Tribunal composed of two Justices of the Supreme Court and the President of the highest court of the religious community concerned in Israel. The judgments of the Religious Courts are executed by the process and offices of the Civil Courts. Neither these Courts nor the Civil Courts have jurisdiction to dissolve the marriage of a foreign subject.

Jewish Rabbinical Courts: These Courts have exclusive jurisdiction over matters of marriage and divorce of Jews in Israel who are Israeli citizens or residents. In all other matters of personal status they have concurrent jurisdiction with the District Courts.

Muslim Religious Courts: These Courts have exclusive jurisdiction over matters of marriage and divorce of Muslims who are not foreigners, or who are foreigners subject by their national law to the jurisdiction of Muslim Religious Courts in such matters. In all other matters of personal status they have concurrent jurisdiction with the District Courts.

Christian Religious Courts: The Courts of the recognized Christian communities have exclusive jurisdiction over matters of marriage and divorce of members of their communities who are not foreigners. In all other matters of personal status they have concurrent jurisdiction with the District Courts.

Druze Courts: These Courts, established in 1963, have exclusive jurisdiction over matters of marriage and divorce of Druze in Israel, who are Israeli citizens or residents, and concurrent jurisdiction with the District Courts over all other matters of personal status of Druze.

Religion

JUDAISM

Judaism, the religion of the Jews, is the faith of the majority of Israel's inhabitants. On 31 December 2010 Judaism's adherents totalled 5,802,900, equivalent to 75.4% of the country's population. Its basis is a belief in an ethical monotheism.

There are two main Jewish communities: the Ashkenazim and the Sephardim. The former are the Jews from Eastern, Central or Northern Europe, while the latter originate from the Balkan countries, North Africa and the Middle East.

There is also a community of Ethiopian Jews, the majority of whom have been airlifted to Israel from Ethiopia at various times since the fall of Emperor Haile Selassie in 1974.

The supreme religious authority is vested in the Chief Rabbinate, which consists of the Ashkenazi and Sephardi Chief Rabbis and the Supreme Rabbinical Council. It makes decisions on interpretation of the Jewish law, and supervises the Rabbinical Courts. There are eight regional Rabbinical Courts, and a Rabbinical Court of Appeal presided over by the two Chief Rabbis.

According to the Rabbinical Courts Jurisdiction Law of 1953, marriage and divorce among Jews in Israel are exclusively within the jurisdiction of the Rabbinical Courts. Provided that all the parties concerned agree, other matters of personal status can also be decided by the Rabbinical Courts.

There are over 170 Religious Councils, which maintain religious services and supply religious needs, and about 400 religious committees with similar functions in smaller settlements. Their expenses are borne jointly by the state and the local authorities. The Religious Councils are under the administrative control of the Ministry of Religious Services. In all matters of religion, the Religious Councils are subject to the authority of the Chief Rabbinate. There are 365 officially appointed rabbis. The total number of synagogues is about 7,000, most of which are organized within the framework of the Union of Israel Synagogues.

Head of the Ashkenazi Community: The Chief Rabbi YONA METZGER.

Head of the Sephardic Community: The Chief Rabbi SHLOMO AMAR, Jerusalem; tel. 2-5313131.

Two Jewish sects still loyal to their distinctive customs are:

The Karaites: a sect which recognizes only the Jewish written law and not the oral law of the Mishna and Talmud. The community of about 12,000, many of whom live in or near Ramla, has been augmented by immigration from Egypt.

The Samaritans: an ancient sect mentioned in 2 Kings xvii, 24. They recognize only the Torah. The community in Israel numbers about 500; about one-half of this number live in Holon, where a Samaritan synagogue has been built, and the remainder, including the High Priest, live in Nablus, near Mt Gerazim, which is sacred to the Samaritans.

ISLAM

The Muslims in Israel belong principally to the Sunni sect of Islam, and are divided among the four rites: the Shafe'i, the Hanbali, the Hanafi and the Maliki. Before June 1967 they numbered approximately 175,000; in 1971 some 343,900. On 31 December 2010 the total Muslim population of Israel was 1,321,300, equivalent to 17.2% of the country's population.

Mufti of Jerusalem: POB 17412, Jerusalem; tel. 2-283528; Sheikh MUHAMMAD AHMAD HUSSEIN (also Chair. Supreme Muslim Council for Jerusalem); appointed by the Palestinian (National) Authority (PA).

There was also a total of 127,600 Druzes in Israel at 31 December 2010. The official spiritual leader of the Druze community in Israel is Sheikh MUWAFAK TARIF, but his leadership is not widely recognized.

CHRISTIANITY

The total Christian population of Israel (including East Jerusalem) at 31 December 2010 was 153,100.

United Christian Council in Israel: POB 116, Jerusalem 91000; tel. and fax 2-6259012; e-mail ucci@ucci.net; internet www.ucci.net; f. 1956; member of World Evangelical Alliance; over 30 mems (evangelical churches and social and educational insts); Chair. Rev. CHARLES KOPP.

The Roman Catholic Church

Armenian Rite

The Armenian Catholic Patriarch of Cilicia is resident in Beirut, Lebanon.

Patriarchal Exarchate of Jerusalem and Amman: POB 19546, 36 Via Dolorosa, Jerusalem 91190; tel. 2-6284262; fax 2-6272123; e-mail acpejerusalem@yahoo.com; f. 1885; about 800 adherents

(31 December 2007); Exarch Patriarchal Mgr RAPHAEL FRANÇOIS MINASSIAN.

Chaldean Rite

The Chaldean Patriarch of Babylon is resident in Baghdad, Iraq.

Patriarchal Exarchate of Jerusalem: Chaldean Patriarchal Vicariate, POB 20108, 7 Chaldean St, Saad and Said Quarter, Jerusalem 91200; tel. 2-6844519; fax 2-6274614; e-mail kolin-p@zahav.net.il; Exarch Patriarchal Mgr MICHEL KASSARJI.

Latin Rite

The Patriarchate of Jerusalem covers Palestine, Jordan and Cyprus. At 31 December 2006 there were an estimated 78,215 adherents.

Bishops' Conference: Conférence des Evêques Latins dans les Régions Arabes, Notre Dame of Jerusalem Center, POB 20531, Jerusalem 91204; tel. 2-6288554; fax 2-6288555; e-mail evcat@palnet.com; f. 1967; Pres. His Beatitude FOUAD TWAL (Patriarch of Jerusalem).

Patriarchate of Jerusalem: Latin Patriarchate of Jerusalem, POB 14152, Jerusalem 91141; tel. 2-6282323; fax 2-6271652; e-mail chancellery@latinpat.org; internet www.lpj.org; Patriarch His Beatitude FOUAD TWAL; Auxiliary Bishop of Jerusalem WILLIAM SHOMALI; Vicar-General for Israel GIACINTO-BOULOS MARCUZZO (Titular Bishop of Emmaus Nicopolis); Vicariat Patriarcal Latin, Street 6191/3, Nazareth 16100; tel. 4-6554075; fax 4-6452416; e-mail latinpat@rannet.com.

Maronite Rite

The Maronite community, under the jurisdiction of the Maronite Patriarch of Antioch (resident in Lebanon), has about 7,000 members.

Patriarchal Exarchate of Jerusalem: Maronite Patriarchal Exarchate, POB 14219, 25 Maronite Convent St, Jaffa Gate, Jerusalem 91141; tel. 2-6282158; fax 2-6272821; about 504 adherents (31 December 2007); Exarch Patriarchal Mgr PAUL NABIL SAYAH (also the Maronite Archbishop of Haifa).

Melkite Rite

The Greek-Melkite Patriarch of Antioch and all the East, of Alexandria and of Jerusalem (GRÉGOIRE III LAHAM) is resident in Damascus, Syria.

Patriarchal Vicariate of Jerusalem

Patriarcat Grec-Melkite Catholique, POB 14130, Porte de Jaffa, Jerusalem 91141; tel. 2-6282023; fax 2-6289606; e-mail gcpjer@p-ol.com; about 3,300 adherents (31 December 2007); Protosyncellus Archim. Archbishop GEORGES MICHEL BAKAR.

Archbishop of Akka (Acre): ELIAS CHACOUR, Archevêché Grec-Catholique, POB 9450, 33 Hagefen St, 31094 Haifa; tel. 4-8508105; fax 4-8508106; e-mail chacoure@netvision.net.il; 95,000 adherents at 31 December 2006.

Syrian Rite

The Syrian Catholic Patriarch of Antioch is resident in Beirut, Lebanon.

Patriarchal Exarchate of Jerusalem: Vicariat Patriarcal Syrien Catholique, POB 19787, 6 Chaldean St, Jerusalem 91197; tel. 2-6282657; fax 2-6284217; e-mail st_thomas@bezeqint.net; about 1,550 adherents (31 December 2007); Exarch Patriarchal Mgr GRÉGOIRE PIERRE MELKI.

The Armenian Apostolic (Orthodox) Church

Patriarch of Jerusalem: Archbishop TORKOM MANOOGIAN, Armenian Patriarchate of St James, POB 14235, Jerusalem; tel. 2-6264853; fax 2-6264862; e-mail webmaster@armenian-patriarchate.org; internet www.armenian-patriarchate.org.

The Greek Orthodox Church

The Patriarchate of Jerusalem contains an estimated 260,000 adherents in Israel, the Occupied Territories, Jordan, Kuwait, Saudi Arabia and the United Arab Emirates.

Patriarch of Jerusalem: THEOPHILOS III, POB 14518, Jerusalem 91145; tel. 2-6274941; fax 2-6282048; e-mail secretariat@jerusalem-patriarchate.info; internet www.jerusalem-patriarchate.info.

The Anglican Communion

Episcopal Diocese of Jerusalem and the Middle East: POB 19122, St George's Cathedral Close, Jerusalem 91191; tel. 2-6271670; fax 2-6273847; e-mail info@j-diocese.org; internet www.j-diocese.org; Bishop The Rt Rev. SUHEIL DAWANI (Anglican Bishop in Jerusalem).

Other Christian Churches

Other denominations include the Coptic Orthodox Church, the Russian Orthodox Church, the Ethiopian Orthodox Church, the Romanian Orthodox Church, the Baptist Church, the Lutheran Church and the Church of Scotland.

The Press

Tel-Aviv is the main publishing centre. Largely for economic reasons, no significant local press has developed away from the main cities; hence all newspapers have tended to regard themselves as national. Friday editions, issued on Sabbath eve, are increased to as much as twice the normal size by special weekend supplements, and experience a considerable rise in circulation. No newspapers appear on Saturday.

Most of the daily papers are in Hebrew, and others appear in Arabic, English, Russian, Polish, Hungarian, Yiddish, French and German. The total daily circulation is 500,000–600,000 copies, or 21 papers per hundred people, although most citizens read more than one daily paper.

Most Hebrew morning dailies have strong political or religious affiliations, and the majority of newspapers depend on subsidies from political parties, religious organizations or public funds. The limiting effect on freedom of commentary entailed by this party press system has provoked repeated criticism. There are around 400 other newspapers and magazines, including some 50 weekly and 150 fortnightly; over 250 of them are in Hebrew, the remainder in 11 other languages.

Ha'aretz is the most widely read of the morning papers, exceeded only by the popular afternoon press, *Ma'ariv* and *Yedioth Ahronoth*. *The Jerusalem Post* gives detailed news coverage in English.

DAILIES

Calcalist (Economist): Tel-Aviv; internet www.calcalist.co.il; f. 2008; Hebrew; business; publ. by Yedioth Ahronoth Group; Founder and Publr YOEL ESTERON; CEO STEVE SCHUMACHER.

Globes: POB 5126, Rishon le Zion 75150; tel. 3-9538611; fax 3-9525971; e-mail mailbox@globes.co.il; internet www.globes.co.il; f. 1983; evening; Hebrew; business and economics; owned by the Monitin Group; CEO EITAN MADMON; Editor-in-Chief HAGGAI GOLAN; circ. 45,000.

Ha'aretz (The Land): 21 Schocken St, Tel-Aviv 61001; tel. 3-5121212; fax 3-6810012; e-mail contact@haaretz.co.il; internet www.haaretz.co.il; f. 1919; morning; Hebrew and English; liberal; independent; 25% stake acquired by M. DuMont Schauberg (Germany) in 2006; Man. Dir RAMI GUEZ; Editor-in-Chief ALUF BENN; Publisher AMOS SCHOCKEN; circ. 72,000 (weekdays), 100,000 (Fri.).

Hamodia (The Informer): POB 1306, 5 Yehudah Hamacabi St, Jerusalem 91012; tel. 2-5389255; fax 2-5003384; e-mail english@hamodia.co.il; internet www.hamodia.com; f. 1950; morning; Hebrew, English and French edns; Orthodox; organ of Agudat Israel; Editor HAIM MOSHE KNOPF; international circ. 250,000.

Israel HaYom (Israel Today): 2 Hashlosha St, Tel-Aviv; e-mail hayom@israelhayom.co.il; internet israelhayom.co.il; f. 2007; free daily publ. Sun.–Thur; Hebrew; Publr ASHER BAHARAV; Editor-in-Chief AMOS REGEV; CEO ZIPPI KOREN; circ. 255,000.

Israel Nachrichten (News of Israel): POB 28397, Tel-Aviv 61283; tel. 3-5372059; fax 3-5376166; e-mail info@israelnachrichten.de; f. 1935 as Neueste Nachrichten, renamed as above 1948; morning; German; Editor HELGA MÜLLER-GAZMAWE; circ. 1,500.

Israel Post: 15 HaAchim MeSalvita, Tel-Aviv; f. 2007 as Metro Israel; free daily; afternoon; Hebrew; publ. by Metro Israel Ltd; Co-owners ELI AZUR, DAVID WEISMAN; Editor-in-Chief GOLAN BAR-YOSEF.

Al-Itihad (Unity): POB 104, Haifa; tel. 4-8666301; fax 4-8641407; e-mail aletihad@bezeqint.net; internet www.aljabha.org; f. 1944; Arabic; organ of Hadash; Editor-in-Chief AIDA TOUMA-SLIMAN; circ. 60,000.

The Jerusalem Post: POB 81, The Jerusalem Post Bldg, Romema, Jerusalem 91000; tel. 2-5315666; fax 2-5389527; e-mail feedback@jpost.com; internet www.jpost.com; f. 1932 as The Palestine Post, renamed as above 1950; morning; English; independent; CEO RONIT HASIN-HOCHMAN; Editor-in-Chief STEVE LINDE; circ. 15,000 (weekdays), 40,000 (weekend edn); there is also a weekly international edn (circ. 40,000), and a weekly French edn.

Ma'ariv (Evening Prayer): 2 Carlebach St, Tel-Aviv 61200; tel. 3-5632111; fax 3-5610614; internet www.nrg.co.il; f. 1948; mid-morning; Hebrew; independent; publ. by Modiin Publishing House; Editor-in-Chief YOAV TZUR; circ. 150,000 (weekdays), 250,000 (weekends).

Nasha strana (Our Country): 52 Harakeret St, Tel-Aviv 67770; tel. 3-370011; fax 3-5371921; f. 1970; morning; Russian; Editor S. HIMMELFARB; circ. 35,000.

Novosti nedeli (The Week's News): 15 Ha-Ahim Mi-Slavita St, Tel-Aviv; tel. 3-6242225; fax 3-6242227; Russian; Editor-in-Chief DMITRII LODYZHENSKII.

Al-Quds (Jerusalem): POB 19788, Jerusalem; tel. 2-6272663; fax 2-6272657; e-mail hani@alquds.com; internet www.alquds.com; f. 1968; Arabic; Founder and Publr MAHMOUD ABU ZALAF; Gen. Man. Dr MARWAN ABU ZALAF; circ. 55,000.

Viata Noastra: 49 Tchlenor St, Tel-Aviv 66048; tel. 3-5372059; fax 3-6877142; e-mail viatanoastra2001@yahoo.com; internet viatanoastra.1colony.com; f. 1950; morning; Romanian; Editor NANDO MARIO VARGA; circ. 30,000.

Yated Ne'eman: POB 328, Bnei Brak; tel. 3-6170800; fax 3-6170801; e-mail let-edit@yatedneman.co.il; f. 1986; morning; Hebrew; religious; Editors Rabbi ITZHAK ROTH, Rabbi NOSSON ZE'EV GROSSMAN; circ. 25,000.

Yedioth Ahronoth (The Latest News): 2 Yehuda and Noah Mozes St, Tel-Aviv 61000; tel. and fax 3-6082222; e-mail service@y-i.co.il; internet www.ynet.co.il; f. 1939; evening; Hebrew; independent; Editor-in-Chief SHILO DE BEER; circ. 350,000, Fri. 600,000.

WEEKLIES AND FORTNIGHTLIES

Akhbar al-Naqab (News of the Negev): POB 426, Rahat 85357; tel. 8-9919202; fax 8-9917070; e-mail akhbar@akhbarna.com; internet www.akhbarna.com; f. 1988; weekly; Arabic; educational and social issues concerning the Negev Bedouins; Editor-in-Chief MUHAMMAD YOUNIS.

Aurora: Aurora Ltd, POB 57416, Tel-Aviv 61573; tel. 3-5625216; fax 3-5625082; e-mail aurora@aurora-israel.co.il; internet www .aurora-israel.co.il; f. 1963; weekly; Spanish; Editor-in-Chief ARIE AVIDOR; Director MARIO WAINSTEIN; circ. 20,000.

Bamahane (In the Camp): Military POB 1013, Tel-Aviv; f. 1948; illustrated weekly of the Israel Defence Forces; Hebrew; Editor-in-Chief YONI SHANFELD; circ. 70,000.

B'Sheva: Petach Tikva; internet www.inn.co.il/Besheva; f. 2002; Hebrew; religious Zionist newspaper, distributed freely in religious communities; owned by Arutz Sheva (Channel Seven) media network; Editor EMANUEL SHILO; circ. 140,000.

Etgar (The Challenge): POB 35252, Ha'aliyah St, 2nd Floor, Tel-Aviv 61351; tel. 3-5373268; fax 3-5373269; e-mail nirhanitzoz.org.il; internet www.etgar.info; twice weekly; Hebrew; publ. by Hanitzotz Publishing House; Editor NATHAN YALIN-MOR.

InformationWeek: POB 1161, 13 Yad Harutzim St, Tel-Aviv 61116; tel. 3-6385858; fax 3-6889207; e-mail world@pc.co.il; internet www.pc.co.il; weekly; Hebrew and English; Man. Dirs DAHLIA PELED, PELI PELED; Editor-in-Chief PELI PELED.

The Israeli Tourist Guide Magazine: Tourist Guide Communications Ltd, POB 53333, Tel-Aviv 61533; tel. 3-6486611; fax 3-6486622; e-mail ilan777@gmail.com; internet www.touristguide .org.il; f. 1994; weekly; Hebrew and English; Publr and Editor ILAN SHCHORI; circ. 10,000.

The Jerusalem Post International Edition: POB 81, Romema, Jerusalem 91000; tel. 2-5315666; fax 2-5389527; e-mail liat@jpost .com; internet www.jpost.co.il; f. 1959; weekly; English; overseas edn of *The Jerusalem Post (q.v.)*; circ. 70,000 to 106 countries; Editor LIAT COLLINS.

Jerusalem Report: POB 1805, Jerusalem 91017; tel. 2-5315440; fax 2-5379489; e-mail jrep@jreport.co.il; internet www.jrep.com; f. 1990; bi-weekly; English; publ. under umbrella of *The Jerusalem Post*; Editor-in-Chief ETTA PRINCE-GIBSON.

Laisha (For Women): POB 28122, 35 Bnei Brak St, Tel-Aviv 66021; tel. 3-6386977; fax 3-6386933; e-mail laisha@laisha.co.il; f. 1949; Hebrew; women's magazine; Editor-in-Chief MIRIAM NOFECH-MOSES; circ. 100,000.

Reshumot: Ministry of Justice, POB 1087, 29 Rehov Salahadin, Jerusalem 91010; f. 1948; Hebrew, Arabic and English; official govt gazette.

Al-Sabar: POB 2647, Nazareth 16126; tel. 4-6462156; fax 4-6462152; e-mail alsabar.mag@gmail.com; internet www .alsabar-mag.com; publ. by the Org. for Democratic Action; Arabic; political and cultural Israeli-Palestinian affairs.

Vesti (News): 2 Homa U'Migdal, Tel-Aviv 67771; tel. 3-6383444; fax 3-6383440; f. 1992; publ. Sun.–Thur; Russian; Editor-in-Chief SERGEI PODRAZHANSKII.

OTHER PERIODICALS

Bitaon Heyl Ha'avir (Israel Air Force Magazine): Military POB 01560, Zahal; tel. 3-6067729; fax 3-6067735; e-mail iaf@inter.net.il; internet www.iaf.org.il; f. 1948; bi-monthly; Hebrew and English; Dep. Editor U. ETSION; Editor-in-Chief MERAV HALPERIN; circ. 30,000.

Al-Bushra (Good News): POB 6228, Haifa 31061; tel. 4-8385002; fax 4-8371612; f. 1935; monthly; Arabic; organ of the Ahmadiyya movement; Editor MUSA ASA'AD O'DEH.

Challenge: POB 35252, Tel-Aviv 61351; tel. 3-5373268; fax 3-5373269; e-mail oda@netvision.net.il; internet www.challenge-mag .com; f. 1989; magazine on the Israeli–Palestinian conflict, publ. by Hanitzotz Publishing House; online only; English; Editor-in-Chief RONI BEN EFRAT; Editor STEPHEN LANGFUR.

Diamond Intelligence Briefs: POB 3442, Ramat-Gan 52136; tel. 3-5750196; fax 3-5754829; e-mail office@tacy.co.il; internet www .diamondintelligence.com; f. 1985; English; Publr CHAIM EVEN-ZOHAR.

Eastern Mediterranean Tourism/Travel: Israel Travel News Ltd, POB 3251, Tel-Aviv 61032; tel. 3-5251646; fax 3-5251605; e-mail office@itn.co.il; internet www.itn.co.il; f. 1979; monthly; English; Editor GERRY AROHOW; circ. 20,000.

Hamizrah Hehadash (The New East): Israel Oriental Society, The Hebrew University, Mount Scopus, Jerusalem 91905; tel. 2-5883633; e-mail ios49@hotmail.com; f. 1949; annual of the Israel Oriental Society; Middle Eastern, Asian and African Affairs; Hebrew with English summary; Editors HAIM GERBER, ELIE PODEH; circ. 1,500–2,000.

Harefuah (Medicine): POB 3566, 2 Twin Towers, 35 Jabotinsky St, Ramat-Gan 52136; tel. 3-6100444; fax 3-5753303; e-mail tguvot@ima .org.il; internet www.ima.org.il/harefuah; f. 1920; monthly journal of the Israel Medical Asscn; Hebrew with English summaries; also publishes *Israel Medical Asscn Journal*; Editor Prof. YEHUDA SHOENFELD; circ. 16,000.

Hed Hachinuch (Echoes of Education): 2 Tashach St, Tel-Aviv 62093; tel. 3-6091819; fax 3-6094521; e-mail hed@itu.org.il; internet www.itu.org.il; f. 1926; monthly; Hebrew; also publishes Arabic edn; educational; publ. by the Israel Teachers Union; Editor DALIA LACHMAN; circ. 40,000.

Hed Hagan (Echoes of Kindergarten): 8 Ben Saruk St, Tel-Aviv 62969; tel. 3-6922958; e-mail hedhagan@morim.org.il; internet www .itu.org.il; f. 1935; quarterly; Hebrew; early education issues; publ. by the Israel Teachers Union; Editor ILANA MALCHI; circ. 9,000.

Historia: POB 4179, Jerusalem 91041; tel. 2-5650444; fax 2-6712388; e-mail shazar@shazar.org.il; internet www.shazar.org.il/ historia.htm; f. 1998; bi-annual; Hebrew, with English summaries; general history; publ. by the Historical Society of Israel; Editors Prof. YITZHAK HEN, Prof. ISRAEL SHATZMAN, Prof. GIDEON SHELACH; circ. 1,000.

Israel Environment Bulletin: Ministry of Environmental Protection, POB 34033, 5 Kanfei Nesharim St, Givat Shaul, Jerusalem 95464; tel. 2-6553777; fax 2-6535934; e-mail shoshana@environment .gov.il; internet www.environment.gov.il; f. 1973; bi-annual; English; environmental policy, legislation and news; Editor SHOSHANA GABBAY; circ. 3,500.

Israel Exploration Journal: POB 7041, 5 Avida St, Jerusalem 91070; tel. 2-6257991; fax 2-6247772; e-mail ies@vms.huji.ac.il; internet israelexplorationsociety.huji.ac.il/iej.htm; f. 1950; bi-annual; English; general and biblical archaeology, ancient history and historical geography of Israel and the Holy Land; Editors SHMUEL AHITUV, AMIHAI MAZAR; circ. 2,500.

Israel Journal of Chemistry: POB 34299, Jerusalem 91341; tel. 2-6522226; fax 2-6522277; e-mail info@israelsciencejournals.com; internet www.sciencefromisrael.com; f. 1951; quarterly; English; publ. by Science from Israel; Editor Prof. HAIM LEVANON.

Israel Journal of Earth Sciences: POB 34299, Jerusalem 91341; tel. 2-6522226; fax 2-6522277; e-mail info@israelsciencejournals .com; internet www.sciencefromisrael.com; f. 1951; quarterly; English; publ. by Science from Israel; Editor-in-Chief Y. ENZEL.

Israel Journal of Ecology and Evolution: POB 34299, Jerusalem 91341; tel. 2-6522226; fax 2-6522277; e-mail info@ israelsciencejournals.com; internet www.sciencefromisrael.com; f. 1951 as Israel Journal of Zoology; name changed in 2006; quarterly; English; publ. by Science from Israel; Editors LEON BLAUSTEIN, BURT P. KOTLER.

Israel Journal of Mathematics: The Hebrew University Magnes Press, POB 39099, Jerusalem 91390; tel. 2-6586656; fax 2-5633370; e-mail iton@math.huji.ac.il; internet www.ma.huji.ac.il/~ijmath; f. 1951; bi-monthly; English; Editor-in-Chief AVINOAM MANN.

Israel Journal of Plant Sciences: POB 34299, Jerusalem 91341; tel. 2-6522226; fax 2-6522277; e-mail info@israelsciencejournals .com; internet www.sciencefromisrael.com; f. 1951 as Israel Journal of Botany; quarterly; English; publ. by Science from Israel; Editor-in-Chief EFRAIM LEWINSOHN.

Israel Journal of Psychiatry and Related Sciences: Gefen Publishing House Ltd, 6 Hatzvi St, Jerusalem 94386; tel. 2-

5380247; fax 2-5388423; e-mail ijp@gefenpublishing.com; f. 1963; quarterly; English; Editor-in-Chief Dr DAVID GREENBERG.

Israel Journal of Veterinary Medicine: POB 22, Ra'nana 43100; tel. 9-7419929; fax 9-7431778; e-mail ivma@zahav.net.il; internet www.ijvm.org.il; f. 1943; fmrly *Refuah Veterinarith*; quarterly of the Israel Veterinary Medical Asscn; English; Editor-in-Chief TREVOR WANER.

Israel Law Review: Israel Law Review Asscn, Faculty of Law, Hebrew University of Jerusalem, Mt Scopus, Jerusalem 91905; tel. 2-5881156; fax 2-5819371; e-mail ilr@savion.huji.ac.il; internet law.huji.ac.il/eng/pirsumim.asp; f. 1966; 3 a year; English; Editors-in-Chief Sir NIGEL RODLEY, YUVAL SHANY.

Israel Medical Asscn Journal (IMAJ): POB 3604, 2 Twin Towers, 11th Floor, 35 Jabotinsky St, Ramat-Gan 52136; tel. 3-6100418; fax 3-7519673; e-mail imaj@ima.org.il; internet www.ima.org.il/imaj; f. 1999; monthly English-language journal of the Israel Medical Asscn; also publishes *Harefuah*; Editor-in-Chief Prof. YEHUDA SHOENFELD.

Journal d'Analyse Mathématique: The Hebrew University Magnes Press, POB 39099, Jerusalem 91390; tel. 2-6586656; fax 2-5633370; e-mail magnes@vms.huji.ac.il; internet www.ma.huji.ac.il/jdm; f. 1955; 3 vols a year; French; Exec. Editor A. LINDEN.

Leshonenu: Academy of the Hebrew Language, Givat Ram Campus, Jerusalem 91904; tel. 2-6493555; fax 2-5617065; e-mail acad2u@vms.huji.ac.il; internet hebrew-academy.huji.ac.il; f. 1929; quarterly; Hebrew; for the study of the Hebrew language and cognate subjects; Editor MOSHE BAR-ASHER.

Leshonenu La'am: Academy of the Hebrew Language, Givat Ram Campus, Jerusalem 91904; tel. 2-6493555; fax 2-5617065; e-mail acad2u@vms.huji.ac.il; internet hebrew-academy.huji.ac.il; f. 1945; quarterly; Hebrew; popular Hebrew philology; Editor MOSHE FLORENTIN.

Lilac: Nazareth; f. 2000 for Christian and Muslim Arab women in the region; monthly; Arabic; Israel's first magazine for Arab women; Founder and Editor-in-Chief YARA MASHOUR.

MB-Yakinton (Yakinton): POB 1480, Tel-Aviv 61014; tel. 3-5164461; fax 3-5164435; e-mail info@irgun-jeckes.org; internet www.irgun-jeckes.org; f. 1932; 8 a year; monthly journal of the Irgun Jotsei Merkaz Europa (Asscn of Israelis of Central European Origin); Hebrew and German; Editor MICHA LIMOR.

Moznaim (Balance): POB 7098, Tel-Aviv; tel. 3-6953256; fax 3-6919681; f. 1929; monthly; Hebrew; literature and culture; publ. by Hebrew Writers Asscn; Editors ASHER REICH, AZRIEL KAUFMAN; circ. 2,500.

News from Within: POB 31417, Jerusalem 91313; tel. 2-6241159; fax 2-6253151; e-mail bryan@alt-info.org; internet www.alternativenews.org; monthly; joint Israeli-Palestinian publ; political, economic, social and cultural; publ. by the Alternative Information Centre.

PC Plus: PC Media, POB 11438, 13 Yad Harutzim St, Tel-Aviv 61114; tel. 3-6385810; fax 3-6889207; e-mail editor@pc.co.il; internet www.pc.co.il; f. 1992; monthly; Hebrew; information on personal computers; CEO and Man. Editor DAHLIA PELED; CEO and Editor-in-Chief PELI PELED; circ. 23,000.

Proche-Orient Chrétien: St Anne's Church, POB 19079, Jerusalem 91190; tel. 2-6281992; fax 2-6280764; e-mail mafrpoc@steanne.org; f. 1951; quarterly on churches and religion in the Middle East; publ. in asscn with St Joseph University, Beirut, Lebanon; French; circ. 1,000.

Terra Santa: POB 14038, Jaffa Gate, Jerusalem 91142; tel. 2-6272692; fax 2-6286417; e-mail cicts@netmedia.net.il; f. 1973; bi-monthly; publ. by the Christian Information Centre, which is sponsored by the Custody of the Holy Land (the official custodians of the Holy Shrines); Italian, Spanish, French, English and Arabic edns publ. in Jerusalem by the Franciscan Printing Press, German edn in Munich, Maltese edn in Valletta; Dir Fr JERZY KRAJ.

WIZO Review: Women's International Zionist Organization, 38 Sderot David Hamelech Blvd, Tel-Aviv 64237; tel. 3-6923805; fax 3-6923801; e-mail wreview@wizo.org; internet www.wizo.org; f. 1947; English (3 a year); Editor INGRID ROCKBERGER; Asst Editor PATRICIA SCHWITZER; circ. 10,000.

NEWS AGENCY

Jewish Telegraphic Agency (JTA): Mideast Bureau, Jerusalem Post Bldg, Romema, Jerusalem 91000; tel. 2-610579; fax 2-536635; e-mail info@jta.org; internet www.jta.org; Man. Editor URIEL HEILMAN.

PRESS ASSOCIATIONS

Daily Newspaper Publishers' Asscn of Israel: POB 51202, 74 Petach Tikva Rd, Tel-Aviv 61200; fax 3-5617938; safeguards professional interests and maintains standards, supplies newsprint to dailies; negotiates with trade unions; mems all daily papers; affiliated to International Federation of Newspaper Publishers; Pres. SHABTAI HIMMELFARB; Gen. Sec. BETZALEL EYAL.

Foreign Press Asscn: Beit Sokolov, 4 Kaplan St, Tel-Aviv 64734; tel. 3-6916143; fax 3-6961548; e-mail fpa@netvision.net.il; internet www.fpa.org.il; f. 1957; represents journalists employed by international news orgs who report from Israel, the West Bank and the Gaza Strip; private, non-profit org.; almost 500 mems from 30 countries; Chair. JOE FEDERMAN.

Israel Association of Periodical Press (IAPP): 17 Keilat Venezia St, Tel-Aviv 69400; tel. 3-6449851; fax 3-6449852; e-mail iapp@zahav.net.il; internet www.iapp.co.il; f. 1962; 600 mems; Chair. JOSEPH FRENKEL.

Israel Press Council: Beit Sokolov, 4 Kaplan St, Tel-Aviv; tel. 3-6951437; fax 3-6951145; e-mail moaza@m-i.org.il; internet www.m-i.org.il; f. 1963; deals with matters of common interest to the Press such as drafting the code of professional ethics, which is binding on all journalists; Chair. ORNA LIN; Gen. Sec. AVI WEINBERG.

National Federation of Israeli Journalists (NFIJ): POB 585, 37 Hillet St, Jerusalem 91004; tel. 2-6254351; fax 3-6254353; e-mail office@jaj.org.il; internet www.jaj.org.il; affiliated to International Federation of Journalists; Chair. AHIA HIKA GINOSAR.

Publishers

Achiasaf Publishing House Ltd: POB 8414, Netanya 42504; tel. 9-8851390; fax 9-8851391; e-mail info@achiasaf.co.il; internet www.achiasaf.co.il; f. 1937; general; Pres. MATAN ACHIASAF.

Am Oved Publishers Ltd: 22 Mazeh St, Tel-Aviv 65213; tel. 3-6288500; fax 3-6298911; e-mail info@am-oved.co.il; internet www.am-oved.co.il; f. 1942; fiction, non-fiction, reference books, school and university textbooks, children's books, poetry, classics, science fiction; Man. Dir YARON SADAN.

Amihai Publishing House Ltd: POB 8448, 19 Yad Harutzim St, Netanya Darom 42505; tel. 9-8859099; fax 9-8853464; e-mail ami1000@bezeqint.net; internet www.amichaibooks.co.il; f. 1948; fiction, general science, linguistics, languages, arts; Dir ITZHAK ORON.

Arabic Publishing House: 93 Arlozorof St, Tel-Aviv; tel. 3-6921674; f. 1960; established by the Histadrut; periodicals and books; Gen. Man. GHASSAN MUKLASHI.

Ariel Publishing House: POB 3328, Jerusalem 91033; tel. 2-6434540; fax 2-6436164; e-mail elysch@netvision.net.il; internet www.arielpublishinghouse.com; f. 1976; history, archaeology, religion, geography, folklore; CEO ELY SCHILLER.

Astrolog Publishing House: POB 1231, Hod Hasharon 45111; tel. 3-9190957; fax 3-9190958; e-mail abooks@netvision.net.il; f. 1994; general non-fiction, religion, alternative medicine; Man. Dir SARA BEN-MORDECHAI.

Carta, The Israel Map and Publishing Co Ltd: POB 2500, 18 Ha'uman St, Industrial Area, Talpiot, Jerusalem 91024; tel. 2-6783355; fax 2-6782373; e-mail carta@carta.co.il; internet www.holyland-jerusalem.com; f. 1958; the principal cartographic publr; Pres. and CEO SHAY HAUSMAN.

Rodney Franklin Agency: POB 37727, 53 Mazeh St, Tel-Aviv 65789; tel. 3-5600724; fax 3-5600479; e-mail rodneyf@netvision.net.il; internet www.rodneyagency.com; f. 1974; exclusive representative of various British, other European and US publrs; e-marketing services for academic and professional journal publrs in 15 countries; Dir RODNEY FRANKLIN.

Gefen Publishing House Ltd: 6 Hatzvi St, Jerusalem 94386; tel. 2-5380247; fax 2-5388423; e-mail info@gefenpublishing.com; internet www.israelbooks.com; f. 1981; largest publr of English-language books in Israel; also publishes wide range of fiction and non-fiction; CEO ILAN GREENFIELD.

Globes Publishers: POB 5126, Rishon le Zion 75150; tel. 3-9538611; fax 3-9525971; e-mail mailbox@globes.co.il; internet www.globes.co.il; business, finance, technology, law, marketing; CEO EITAN MADMON; Editor-in-Chief HAGGAI GOLAN.

Gvanim: POB 11138, 29 Bar-Kochba St, Tel-Aviv 61111; tel. 3-5281044; fax 3-6202032; e-mail traklinm@zahav.net.il; f. 1992; poetry, belles lettres, fiction; Man. Dir MARITZA ROSMAN.

Hakibbutz Hameuchad—Sifriat Poalim Publishing Group: POB 1432, Bnei Brak, Tel-Aviv 51114; tel. 3-5785810; fax 3-5785811; e-mail info@kibutz-poalim.co.il; internet www.kibutz-poalim.co.il; f. 1939 as Hakibbutz Hameuchad Publishing House Ltd; subsequently merged with Sifriat Poalim; general; Gen. Dir UZI SHAVIT.

Hanitzotz Publishing House: POB 35252, Tel-Aviv 61351; tel. 3-5373268; fax 3-5373269; e-mail oda@netvision.net.il; internet www.hanitzotz.com; f. 1985; 'progressive' booklets and publications, incl. the periodicals *Challenge* (in English), *Etgar* (Hebrew), and *Al-Sabar*

(Arabic); also produces documentary films on human and workers' rights; Contact RONI BEN EFRAT.

The Hebrew University Magnes Press: The Hebrew University, The Sherman Bldg for Research Management, POB 39099, Givat Ram, Jerusalem 91390; tel. 2-6586656; fax 2-5660341; e-mail info@magnespress.co.il; internet www.magnespress.co.il; f. 1929; academic books and journals on many subjects, incl. biblical, classical and Jewish studies, social sciences, language, literature, art, history and geography; Dir HAI TSABAR.

Hed Arzi (Ma'ariv) Publishing Ltd: 3A Yoni Netanyahu St, Or-Yehuda, Tel-Aviv 60376; tel. 3-5383333; fax 3-6343205; e-mail shimoni@hed-arzi.co.il; f. 1954 as Sifriat-Ma'ariv Ltd; later known as Ma'ariv Book Guild Ltd; general; Man. Dir ELI SHIMONI.

Hod-Ami—Computer Books Ltd: POB 6108, Herzliya 46160; tel. 9-9564716; fax 9-9571582; e-mail info@hod-ami.co.il; internet www.hod-ami.co.il; f. 1984; information technology, management; translations from English into Hebrew and Arabic; CEO ITZHAK AMIHUD.

Israeli Music Publications Ltd: POB 7681, Jerusalem 94188; tel. 2-6251370; fax 2-6241378; e-mail khanukaev@pop.isracom.net.il; f. 1949; music, dance, musical works; Dir of Music Publications SERGEI KHANUKAEV.

Jerusalem Center for Public Affairs: 13 Tel Hai St, Jerusalem 92107; tel. 2-5619281; fax 2-5619112; e-mail jcpa@netvision.net.il; internet www.jcpa.org; f. 1976; Jewish political tradition; publishes *Jerusalem Viewpoints*, *Jerusalem Issue Brief*, *Jewish Political Studies Review* and other books; Pres. DORE GOLD; Chair. Dr MANFRED GERSTENFELD.

The Jerusalem Publishing House: 2B HaGai St, Beit Hakerem, Jerusalem 96262; tel. 2-6537966; fax 2-6529895; e-mail jphgagi@netvision.net.il; internet jerpub.com; f. 1966; biblical research, history, encyclopaedias, archaeology, arts of the Holy Land, cookbooks, guidebooks, economics, politics; CEO MOSHE HELLER; Man. Editor RACHEL GILON.

The Jewish Agency—Department of Jewish Zionist Education: POB 10615, Jerusalem 91104; tel. 2-6202629; fax 2-6204122; e-mail bookshop@jafi.org; internet bookshop.jewishagency.org; f. 1945; education, Jewish philosophy, studies in the Bible, children's books publ. in Hebrew, English, French, Spanish, German, Swedish and Portuguese, Hebrew teaching material; Dir of Publication Division IDA REINMAN.

Jewish History Publications (Israel 1961) Ltd: POB 1232, 29 Jabotinsky St, Jerusalem 92141; tel. 2-5632310; f. 1961; encyclopaedias, World History of the Jewish People series.

Keter Publishing House Ltd: POB 7145, Givat Shaul B, Jerusalem 91071; tel. 2-6557822; fax 2-6536811; e-mail info@keterbooks.co.il; internet www.keterbooks.co.il; f. 1959; original and translated works of fiction, encyclopaedias, non-fiction, guidebooks and children's books; publishing imprints: Israel Program for Scientific Translations, Keter Books, Domino, Shikmona, Encyclopedia Judaica; Man. Dir YIPHTACH DEKEL.

Kinneret Zmora-Bitan Dvir Publishing House: 10 Hataasiya St, Or-Yehuda 60210; tel. 3-6344977; fax 3-6340953; internet www.kinbooks.co.il; f. 2002 following merger between Kinneret and Zmora Bitan-Dvir publishing houses; adult and children's fiction and non-fiction, history, science, sociology, psychology, current affairs and politics, dictionaries, architecture, travel; Man. Dir YORAM ROZ.

MAP-Mapping and Publishing Ltd (Tel-Aviv Books): POB 56024, 17 Tchernikhovski St, Tel-Aviv 61560; tel. 3-6210500; fax 3-5257725; e-mail info@mapa.co.il; internet www.mapa.co.il; f. 1985; maps, atlases, travel guides, textbooks, reference books; Man. Dir HEZI LEVY; Editor-in-Chief (vacant).

Rubin Mass Ltd: POB 990, 7 Ha-Ayin-Het St, Jerusalem 91009; tel. 2-6277863; fax 2-6277864; e-mail rmass@barak.net.il; internet www.rubin-mass.com; f. 1927; Hebraica, Judaica, export of all Israeli books and periodicals; Man. OREN MASS.

Ministry of Defence Publishing House: POB 916, Yaakov Dori Rd, Kiryat Ono 55108; tel. 3-7380738; fax 3-7380645; e-mail minuy@inter.net.il; f. 1958; military literature, Judaism, history and geography of Israel; Dir JOSEPH PERLOVITZ.

M. Mizrachi Publishing House Ltd: 67 Levinsky St, Tel-Aviv 66855; tel. 3-6870936; fax 3-6888185; e-mail mizrahi.co@jmail.com; f. 1960; children's books, fiction, history, medicine, science; Dirs MEIR MIZRACHI, ISRAEL MIZRACHI.

Mosad Harav Kook: POB 642, 1 Maimon St, Jerusalem 91006; tel. 2-6526231; fax 2-6526968; e-mail mosad-haravkook@neto.bezeqint.net; f. 1937; editions of classical works, Torah and Jewish studies; Dir Rabbi YOSEF MOVSHOVITZ.

Otsar Hamoreh: c/o Israel Teachers Union, 8 Ben Saruk, Tel-Aviv 62969; tel. 3-6922983; fax 3-6922988; f. 1951; educational; Man. Dir JOSEPH SALOMAN.

People and Computers Ltd: POB 11438, 53 Derech Asholom St, Givatayim 53454; tel. 3-7330733; fax 3-7330703; e-mail info@pc.co.il; internet www.pc.co.il; information technology; Pres. and CEO PELI PELED; Publr and CEO DAHLIA PELED.

Schocken Publishing House Ltd: POB 2316, 24 Nathan Yelin Mor St, Tel-Aviv 61022; tel. 3-5610130; fax 3-5622668; e-mail gila_g@haaretz.co.il; internet www.schocken.co.il; f. 1938; general; Publr RACHELI EDELMAN.

Science from Israel—A Division of LPP Ltd: POB 34299, Merkaz Sapir 6/36, Givat Shaul, Jerusalem 91341; tel. 2-6522226; fax 2-6522277; e-mail elcya@bezeqint.net; internet www.sciencefromisrael.com; fmrly Laser Pages Publishing Ltd; scientific journals.

Shalem Press: POB 8787, 13 Yehoshua Bin-Nun St, Jerusalem 93102; tel. 2-5605586; fax 2-5605565; e-mail shalempress@shalem.org.il; internet www.shalempress.co.il; f. 1994; economics, political science, history, philosophy, cultural issues; Pres. DANIEL POLISAR.

Sinai Publishing: 24 Rambam St, Tel-Aviv 65813; tel. 3-5163672; fax 3-5176783; e-mail sinaipub@zahav.net.il; internet www.sinaibooks.com; f. 1853; Hebrew books and religious articles; Dir MOSHE SCHLESINGER.

Steinhart-Katzir: POB 8333, Netanya 42505; tel. 9-8854770; fax 9-8854771; e-mail mail@haolam.co.il; internet www.haolam.co.il; f. 1991; travel; Man. Dir OHAD SHARAV.

Tcherikover Publishers Ltd: 12 Hasharon St, Tel-Aviv 66185; tel. 3-6396099; fax 3-6874729; e-mail barkay@inter.net.il; education, psychology, economics, psychiatry, literature, literary criticism, essays, history, geography, criminology, art, languages, management; Man. Editor S. TCHERIKOVER.

Yachdav United Publishers Co Ltd: POB 20123, 29 Carlebach St, Tel-Aviv 67132; tel. 3-5614121; fax 3-5611996; e-mail info@tbpai.co.il; f. 1960; educational; Chair. EPHRAIM BEN-DOR; Exec. Dir AMNON BEN-SHMUEL.

Yavneh Publishing House Ltd: 4 Mazeh St, Tel-Aviv 65213; tel. 3-6297856; fax 3-6293638; e-mail publishing@yavneh.co.il; internet www.yavneh.co.il; f. 1932; general; Man. Dir NIRA PREISKEL.

Yedioth Ahronoth Books: POB 53494, 10 Kehilat Venezia, Tel-Aviv 61534; tel. 3-7683333; fax 3-7683300; e-mail info@ybook.co.il; internet www.ybook.co.il; f. 1952; non-fiction, politics, Judaism, health, music, dance, fiction, education; Man. Dir DOV EICHENWALD.

S. Zack: 31 Beit Hadfus St, Jerusalem 95483; tel. 2-6537760; fax 2-6514005; e-mail zackmt@bezeqint.net; internet www.zack.co.il; f. 1935; fiction, science, philosophy, Judaism, children's books, educational and reference books, dictionaries, languages; Dir MICHAEL ZACK.

PUBLISHERS' ASSOCIATION

The Book Publishers' Association of Israel: POB 20123, 29 Carlebach St, Tel-Aviv 67132; tel. 3-5614121; fax 3-5611996; e-mail info@tbpai.co.il; internet www.tbpai.co.il; f. 1939; mems: 84 publishing firms; Chair. RACHELI EDELMAN; Man. Dir AMNON BEN-SHMUEL.

Broadcasting and Communications

TELECOMMUNICATIONS

013 Netvision: Cibel Industrial Park, 15 Hamelacha St, Rosh Ha'ayin 48091; tel. 3-9001100; fax 3-9001113; e-mail service@netvision013.net.il; internet www.013netvision.net.il; f. 2007 after merger with 013 Barak and GlobCall; CEO RICHARD HUNTER.

Bezeq—The Israel Telecommunication Corpn Ltd: Azrieli Center 2, Tel-Aviv 61620; tel. 3-6262600; fax 3-6262609; e-mail dover@bezeq.co.il; internet www.bezeq.co.il; f. 1984; privatized in May 2005; launched own cellular network, Pelephone Communications Ltd, in 1986; total assets NIS 15,156m. (Dec. 2007); CEO AVI GABBAY; Chair. SHAUL ELOVITCH.

Pelephone Communications Ltd: 33 Hagvura St, Givatayim, Tel-Aviv 53483; tel. 3-5728881; fax 3-5728111; internet www.pelephone.co.il; f. 1986; launched Esc brand in 2003; 2.4m. subscribers (2006); CEO GIL SHARON.

Cellcom Israel: POB 4060, 10 Hagavish St, Netanya 42140; tel. 529989755 (mobile); fax 529989700; e-mail investors@cellcom.co.il; internet www.cellcom.co.il; f. 1994; mobile telecommunications operator; 3.3m. subscribers (Sept. 2009); Chair. AMI EREL; Pres. and CEO AMOS SHAPIRA.

ECI Telecom Ltd: POB 3038, 30 Hasivim St, Petach-Tikva, Tel-Aviv 49133; tel. 3-9266555; fax 3-9266444; e-mail web.inquiries@ecitele.com; internet www.ecitele.com; f. 1961; Pres. and CEO RAFI MAOR.

Partner Communications Co Ltd: POB 435, 8 Amal St, Afeq Industrial Park, Rosh Ha'ayin 48103; tel. 54-7814888; fax 54-7814999; e-mail deborah.margalit@orange.co.il; internet www

.orange.co.il; f. 1999; provides mobile telecommunications and wire-free applications services under the Orange brand name; represents about one-third of the mobile-cellular market in Israel; 2.9m. subscribers (Dec. 2008); Chair. CANNING FOK; CEO DAVID AVNER.

Vocal Tec Communications Ltd (Vocal Tec): 14 Beni Ga'on St, Bldg B2-Rakefet, Netanya 42504; tel. 9-9703888; fax 9-9558175; e-mail info@vocaltec.com; internet www.vocaltec.com; carrier services and telecommunications infrastructure; revenues US $6.1m. (2008); Chair. ILAN ROSEN; Pres. and CEO DANIEL BORISLOW.

BROADCASTING

In 1986 the Government approved the establishment of a commercial radio and television network to be run in competition with the state system.

Radio

Israel Broadcasting Authority (IBA) (Radio): POB 28080, 161 Jaffa Rd, Jerusalem 94342; tel. 2-5015555; e-mail dover@iba.org.il; internet www.iba.org.il; f. 1948; state-owned station in Jerusalem with additional studios in Tel-Aviv and Haifa; broadcasts six programmes for local and overseas listeners on medium-wave, shortwave and VHF/FM in 16 languages: Hebrew, Arabic, English, Yiddish, Ladino, Romanian, Hungarian, Moghrabi, Farsi, French, Russian, Bukharian, Georgian, Portuguese, Spanish and Amharic; Chair. AMIR GILAT; Dir-Gen. YONI BEN-MENACHEM.

Galei Zahal: MPOB, Zahal; tel. 3-5126666; fax 3-5126760; e-mail glz@galatz.co.il; f. 1950; Israel Defence Force broadcasting station, Tel-Aviv, with studios in Jerusalem; broadcasts 24-hour news, current affairs, music and cultural programmes in Hebrew on FM, medium and short waves; Dir ITZHAK TUNIK.

Kol Israel (The Voice of Israel): POB 1082, 21 Heleni Hamalka, Jerusalem 91010; tel. 1-599509510; e-mail radiodirector@iba.org.il; internet www.iba.org.il/kolisrael; broadcasts music, news and multilingual programmes within Israel and overseas on short wave, AM and FM stereo, in 15 languages, incl. Hebrew, Arabic, French, English, Spanish, Ladino, Russian, Yiddish, Romanian, Hungarian, Amharic and Georgian; Dir SHMUEL BEN-ZVI; Gen. Dir YONI BEN-MENACHEM.

Television

Israel Broadcasting Authority (IBA) (Television): 161 Jaffa Rd, Jerusalem; tel. 2-5301333; fax 2-292944; internet www.iba.org.il; broadcasts began in 1968; station in Jerusalem with additional studios in Tel-Aviv; one colour network (VHF with UHF available in all areas); one satellite channel; broadcasts in Hebrew, Arabic and English; Chair. AMIR GILAT; Dir-Gen. YONI BEN-MENACHEM.

The Council of Cable TV and Satellite Broadcasting: 23 Jaffa Rd, Jerusalem 91999; tel. 2-6702210; fax 2-6702273; e-mail inbard@moc.gov.il; f. 1982; Chair. NITZAN CHEN.

Israel Educational Television: Ministry of Education, 14 Klausner St, Tel-Aviv 69011; tel. 3-646227; fax 3-6466164; e-mail webmaster@ietv.gov.il; internet www.ietv.gov.il; f. 1966 by Hanadiv (Rothschild Memorial Group) as Instructional Television Trust; began transmission in 1966; school programmes form an integral part of the syllabus in a wide range of subjects; also adult education; Dir-Gen. ELDAD KOBLENTZ; Dir of Engineering SHLOMO KASIF.

Second Authority for Television and Radio: POB 3445, 20 Beit Hadfus St, Jerusalem 95464; tel. 2-6556222; fax 2-6556287; e-mail rashut@rashut2.org.il; internet www.rashut2.org.il; f. 1991; responsible for providing broadcasts through two principal television channels, Channel 2 and Channel 10, and some 14 radio stations; Chair. NURIT DABUSH.

Finance

(cap. = capital; res = reserves; dep. = deposits; m. = million; brs = branches; amounts in shekels)

BANKING

Central Bank

Bank of Israel: POB 780, Bank of Israel Bldg, Kiryat Ben-Gurion, Jerusalem 91007; tel. 2-6552211; fax 2-6528805; e-mail webmaster@bankisrael.gov.il; internet www.bankisrael.gov.il; f. 1954 as Cen. Bank of the State of Israel; cap. 60m., res 3,925m., dep. 212,688m. (Dec. 2009); Gov. Prof. STANLEY FISCHER; 1 br.

Principal Commercial Banks

Arab-Israel Bank Ltd: POB 207, 48 Bar Yehuda St, Tel Hanan, Nesher 36601; tel. 4-8205222; fax 4-8205250; e-mail aravi@bll.co.il; internet www.bank-aravi-israeli.co.il; dep. 4,099m., total assets 4,759m. (Dec. 2009); subsidiary of Bank Leumi le-Israel BM; Chair. SHMUEL ZUSMAN; Gen. Man. ITZHAK EYAL.

Bank Hapoalim: 50 Rothschild Blvd, Tel-Aviv 61000; tel. 3-5673333; fax 3-5607028; e-mail international@bnhp.co.il; internet www.bankhapoalim.co.il; f. 1921 as Workers' Bank; name changed as above 1961; mergers into the above: American-Israel Bank in 1999, Maritime Bank of Israel in 2003, Mishkan-Hapoalim Mortgage Bank and Israel Continental Bank in 2004; privatized in June 2000; dep. 240,793m., total assets 309,555m. (Dec. 2009); Chair. YAIR SEROUSSI; Pres. and CEO ZION KENAN; 325 brs in Israel and 10 brs abroad.

Bank of Jerusalem Ltd: POB 2255, 2 Herbert Samuel St, Jerusalem 91022; tel. 2-6706018; fax 2-6234043; e-mail webmaster@bankjerusalem.co.il; internet www.bankjerusalem.co.il; private bank; res 8,454m., total assets 9,586m. (Dec. 2009); Chair. JONATHAN IRONI; CEO PAZ URI; 14 brs.

Bank Leumi le-Israel BM: 34 Yehuda Halevi St, Tel-Aviv 65546; tel. 3-5148111; fax 3-5148656; e-mail pniot@bll.co.il; internet www.bankleumi.co.il; f. 1902 as Anglo-Palestine Co; renamed Anglo-Palestine Bank 1930; reincorporated as above 1951; 34.78% state-owned; dep. 255,188m., total assets 321,775m. (Dec. 2009); Chair. DAVID BRODET; Pres. and CEO GALIA MAOR; 242 brs in Israel and 2 abroad.

Bank Otsar Ha-Hayal Ltd: POB 52136, 11 Menachem Begin St, Ramat-Gan 52136; tel. 3-7556000; fax 3-7556007; e-mail ozfrndep@netvision.net.il; internet www.bankotsar.co.il; f. 1946; 68% owned by First Int. Bank of Israel, 24% by Hever Veterans & Pensions Ltd, 8% by Provident Fund of the Employees of IAILTD; dep. 11,214.8m., total assets 13,638m. (Dec. 2008); Chair. SMADAR BARBER-TSADIK; Gen. Man. ISRAEL TRAU.

First International Bank of Israel Ltd (FIBI): 42 Rothschild Blvd, Tel-Aviv 66883; tel. 3-5196111; fax 3-5100316; e-mail zucker.d@fibi.co.il; internet www.fibi.co.il; f. 1972 by merger between Foreign Trade Bank Ltd and Export Bank Ltd; dep. 85,883m., total assets 104,568m. (Dec. 2009); Chair. JACK ELAAD; CEO SMADAR BARBER-TSADIK; 182 brs in Israel and abroad (incl. subsidiaries).

Israel Discount Bank Ltd: POB 456, 27–31 Yehuda Halevi St, Tel-Aviv 61003; tel. 3-5145555; fax 3-5146954; e-mail intidb@discountbank.co.il; internet www.discountbank.co.il; f. 1935; name changed as above in 1957; 20% state-owned; dep. 151,187m., total assets 182,248m. (Dec. 2008); Chair. Dr JOSEPH BACHAR; Pres. and CEO REUVEN SPIEGEL; 126 brs in Israel and abroad.

Mercantile Discount Bank Ltd: POB 1292, 103 Allenby Rd, Tel-Aviv 61012; tel. 3-710550; fax 3-7105532; e-mail fec@mdb.co.il; internet www.mercantile.co.il; f. 1971 as Barclays Discount Bank Ltd, to take over (from Jan. 1972) the Israel brs of Barclays Bank Int. Ltd; Barclays Bank PLC, one of the joint owners, sold its total shareholding to the remaining owner, Israel Discount Bank Ltd, in Feb. 1993, and name changed as above that April; Mercantile Bank of Israel Ltd became branch of the above in March 1997; cap. 51m., res 172m., dep. 18,806m. (Dec. 2009); Chair. Dr JOSEPH BACHAR; Gen. Man. JACOB TENNENBAUM; 66 brs.

Mizrahi Tefahot Bank Ltd: POB 3450, 7 Jabotinsky St, Ramat-Gan 52136; tel. 3-7559468; fax 3-7559121; e-mail lernerh@umtb.co.il; internet www.mizrahi-tefahot.co.il; f. 1923 as Mizrahi Bank Ltd; mergers into the above: Hapoel Hamizrahi Bank Ltd, as United Mizrahi Bank Ltd; Finance and Trade Bank Ltd in 1990; Tefahot Israel Mortgage Bank Ltd in 2005, when name changed as above; Adanim Mortgage Bank merged into above bank in 2009; dep. 97,129m., total assets 118,439m. (Dec. 2009); Chair. JACOB PERRY; Pres. and CEO ELIEZER YONES; 166 brs.

UBank Ltd: POB 677, 38 Rothschild Blvd, Tel-Aviv 61006; tel. 3-5645353; fax 3-5645285; e-mail gsteiger@u-bank.net; internet www.u-bank.net; f. 1934 as Palestine Credit Utility Bank Ltd; renamed Israel General Bank Ltd 1964; ownership transferred to Investec Bank Ltd (South Africa) 1996; name changed to Investec Clali Bank Ltd 1999, and to Investec Bank (Israel) Ltd 2001; control of bank transferred to First Int. Bank of Israel 2004 and name changed as above 2005; dep. 7,205m., total assets 9,218m. (Dec. 2009); Chair. JACK ELAAD; CEO BEDNY RON; 8 brs.

Union Bank of Israel Ltd: 6–8 Ahuzat Bayit St, Tel-Aviv 65143; tel. 3-5191222; fax 3-5191344; e-mail info@ubi.co.il; internet www.ubi.co.il; f. 1951; dep. 26,556m., total assets 30,552m. (Dec. 2009); Chair. ZEEV ABELES; Pres. and CEO HAIM FREILICHMAN; 35 brs.

Mortgage Banks

Discount Mortgage Bank Ltd: POB 2844, 16–18 Simtat Beit Hashoeva, Tel-Aviv 61027; tel. 3-5643311; fax 3-5661704; e-mail contact@discountbank.net; internet www.discountbank.net; f. 1959; subsidiary of Israel Discount Bank Ltd; total assets 10,355m. (Dec. 2005); Chair. SHLOMO ZOHAR; Pres. and CEO GIORA OFFER; 3 brs.

Leumi Mortgage Bank Ltd: POB 69, 31–37 Montefiore St, Tel-Aviv 65201; tel. 3-5648444; fax 3-5648334; f. 1921 as Gen. Mortgage Bank Ltd; subsidiary of Bank Leumi le-Israel BM; dep. 37,342m., total assets 43,975m. (Dec. 2009); Chair. AVI ZELDMAN; Gen. Man. R. ZABAG; 9 brs.

STOCK EXCHANGE

The Tel-Aviv Stock Exchange: 54 Ahad Ha'am St, Tel-Aviv 65202; tel. 3-5677411; fax 3-5105379; e-mail info@tase.co.il; internet tase.co.il; f. 1953; Chair. SAUL BRONFELD; CEO ESTER LEVANON.

INSURANCE

The Israel Insurance Asscn lists 14 member companies; a selection of these are listed below, as are some non-members.

Clal Insurance Enterprise Holdings Ltd: POB 326, 46 Petach Tikva Rd, Tel-Aviv 66184; tel. 3-6387777; fax 3-6387676; e-mail avigdork@clal-ins.co.il; internet www.clalbit.co.il; f. 1962; 55% owned by IDB Group, 10% by Bank Hapoalim and 35% by the public; insurance, pensions and finance; Chair. KAPLAN AVIGDOR.

Dikla Insurance Co Ltd: 1 Ben Gurion Rd, BSR-2 Tower, Bnei Brak 51201; tel. 3-6145555; fax 3-6145566; internet www.dikla.co.il; f. 1976; health and long-term care insurance; Chair. YAIR HAMBURGER.

Eliahu Insurance Co Ltd: 2 Ibn Gvirol St, Tel-Aviv 64077; tel. 3-6920911; fax 3-6952117; e-mail gad.nussbaum@eliahu.com; internet www.eliahu.co.il; f. 1966; Chair. SHLOMO ELIAHU; Man. Dir OFER ELIAHU.

Harel Insurance Investments and Financial Services Ltd: Tel-Aviv; tel. 3-7547000; e-mail infonet@harel-group.co.il; internet www.harel-group.co.il; f. 1935 as Hamishmar Insurance Service; Harel est. 1975, became Harel Hamishmar Investments Ltd 1982, Harel Insurance Investments Ltd 1998 and current name adopted 2007; 39.9% owned by Hamburger family, 20.2% by Sampoerna Capital; Chair. GIDEON HAMBURGER.

Menorah Mivtachim Insurance Co Ltd: POB 927, 15 Allenby St, Tel-Aviv 61008; tel. 3-7107777; fax 3-7107402; e-mail anat-by@bezeqint.net; internet www.menoramivt.co.il; f. 1935; Chair. MENACHEM GUREWITZ; Gen. Man. SHABTAI ENGEL.

Migdal Insurance Co Ltd: POB 37633, 26 Sa'adiya Ga'on St, Tel-Aviv 67135; tel. 3-5637637; fax 3-9295189; e-mail marketing@migdal-group.co.il; internet www.migdal.co.il; 70% owned by Generali Group; 10% by Bank Leumi and 20% by the public; f. 1934; Chair. AHARON FOGEL; CEO YONEL COHEN.

Phoenix Insurance Co Ltd: 53 Derech Hashalom St, Givatayim 53454; tel. 3-7332222; fax 3-5735151; e-mail ir@fnx.co.il; internet www.fnx.co.il; f. 1949; controlled by Delek Group; Pres. and CEO EYAL LAPIDOT.

Trade and Industry

DEVELOPMENT ORGANIZATIONS

Galilee Development Authority: POB 2511, Acco 24316; tel. 4-9552426; fax 4-9552440; e-mail judith@galil.gov.il; internet www.galilee.gov.il; f. 1993; statutory authority responsible for the social and economic devt of the Galilee region; Man. Dir MOSHE DAVIDOVITZ.

Jerusalem Development Authority (JDA): 2 Safra Sq., Jerusalem 91322; tel. 2-6297627; e-mail moty@jda.gov.il; internet www.jda.gov.il; f. 1988; statutory authority responsible for the economic devt of Jerusalem; CEO MOTY HAZAN.

Negev Development Authority: Negev; e-mail negev_de@netvision.net.il; internet www.negev.co.il; f. 1991; statutory authority responsible for the economic and social devt of the Negev region, and co-ordination between govt offices; Chair SHMUEL RIFMAN.

CHAMBERS OF COMMERCE

Federation of Israeli Chambers of Commerce: POB 20027, 84 Ha' Hashmonaim St, Tel-Aviv 67132; tel. 3-5631020; fax 3-5619027; e-mail chamber@chamber.org.il; internet www.chamber.org.il; co-ordinates the Tel-Aviv, Jerusalem, Haifa, Nazareth and Beersheba Chambers of Commerce; Pres. URIEL LYNN.

Israel Federation of Bi-National Chambers of Commerce and Industry with and in Israel: POB 50196, 29 Hamered St, Tel-Aviv 61500; tel. 3-5177737; fax 3-5142881; e-mail felixk@export.gov.il; Chair. JAIME ARON; Man. Dir FELIX KIPPER.

Beersheba Chamber of Commerce: POB 5278, 7 Hamuktar St, Beersheba 84152; tel. 8-6234222; fax 8-6234899; e-mail chamber7@zahav.net.il; internet www.negev-chamber.org.il.

Chamber of Commerce and Industry of Haifa and the North: POB 33176, 53 Ha'atzmaut Rd, Haifa 31331; tel. 4-8302100; fax 4-8645428; e-mail main@haifachamber.org.il; internet www.haifachamber.com; f. 1921; 850 mems; Pres. GAD SCHAFFER; Man. Dir DOV MAROM.

Israel-British Chamber of Commerce: POB 50321, Industry House, 13th Floor, 29 Hamered St, Tel-Aviv 61502; tel. 3-5109424; fax 3-5109540; e-mail info@ibcc.co.il; internet www.ibcc.co.il; f. 1951; 350 mems; annual bilateral trade of more than US $3,000m; Chair. LEN JUDES; Exec. Dir FELIX KIPPER.

Jerusalem Chamber of Commerce: POB 2083, Jerusalem 91020; tel. 2-6254333; fax 2-6254335; e-mail jerccom@inter.net.il; f. 1908; 200 mems; Pres. RAMI MANDEL.

INDUSTRIAL AND TRADE ASSOCIATIONS

Agricultural Export Co (AGREXCO): POB 2061, 121 Ha'Hashmonaim St, Tel-Aviv 61206; tel. 3-5630940; fax 3-5630988; e-mail info@agrexco.com; internet www.agrexco.co.il; state-owned agricultural marketing org.; CEO SHLOMO TIROSH.

The Centre for International Agricultural Development Cooperation (CINADCO): POB 30, Beit Dagan 50250; tel. 3-9485760; fax 3-9485761; e-mail cinadco@moag.gov.il; internet www.cinadco.moag.gov.il; shares agricultural experience through the integration of research and project devt; runs specialized training courses, advisory missions and feasibility projects in Israel and abroad, incl. those in co-operation with developing countries; Dir ZVI A. HERMAN.

Citrus Marketing Board of Israel: POB 54, Beit Dagan 50280; tel. 3-9595654; fax 3-9501495; e-mail info@jaffa.co.il; internet www.jaffa.co.il; f. 1941; central co-ordinating body of citrus growers and exporters in Israel; represents the citrus industry in international orgs; licenses private exporters; controls the quality of fruit; has responsibility for Jaffa trademarks; mounts advertising and promotion campaigns for Jaffa citrus fruit world-wide; carries out research and devt of new varieties of citrus and environmentally friendly fruit.

Fruit Board of Israel: POB 20117, 119 Rehov Ha' Hashmonaim, Tel-Aviv 61200; tel. 3-5632929; fax 3-5614672; e-mail fruits@fruit.org.il; internet www.fruit.org.il.

Israel Dairy Board (IDB): POB 15578, 46 Derech Ha'macabim, Rishon le Zion 75054; tel. 3-9564750; fax 3-9564766; e-mail office@is-d-b.co.il; internet www.israeldairy.com; regulates dairy-farming and the dairy industry; implements govt policy on the planning of milk production and marketing; Man. Dir SHYKE DRORI.

Israel Diamond Exchange Ltd: 3 Jabotinsky Rd, Ramat-Gan 52130; tel. 3-5760300; fax 3-5750652; e-mail ella@isde.co.il; internet www.isde.co.il; f. 1937; production, export, import and finance facilities; exports: polished diamonds US $6,610m., rough diamonds $2,701m. (2006); Pres. and Chair. AVI PAZ; Man. Dir YAIR COHEN-PRIVA.

Israel Export and International Co-operation Institute: POB 50084, 29 Hamered St, Tel-Aviv 68125; tel. 3-5142900; fax 3-5162810; e-mail galit@export.gov.il; internet www.export.gov.il; f. 1958; jt venture between the state and private sectors; Dir-Gen. AVI HEFETZ.

The Israeli Cotton Board: POB 384, Herzlia B 46103; tel. 9-9604000; fax 9-9604030; e-mail cotton@cotton.co.il; internet www.cotton.co.il; f. 1956 as the Israel Cotton Production and Marketing Board.

Kibbutz Industries' Asscn: POB 40012, 13 Leonardo da Vinci St, Tel-Aviv 61400; tel. 3-6955413; fax 3-6951464; e-mail kia@kia.co.il; internet www.kia.co.il; f. 1962; liaison office for marketing and export of the goods produced by Israel's kibbutzim; Chair. JONATHAN MELAMED; Man. Dir AMOS RABIN.

Manufacturers' Asscn of Israel: POB 50022, Industry House, 29 Hamered St, Tel-Aviv 61500; tel. 3-5198832; fax 3-5103154; e-mail leor@industry.org.il; internet www.industry.org.il; 1,700 mem. enterprises employing nearly 85% of industrial workers in Israel; Dir LEOR APPELBAUM; Pres. SHRAGA BROSH.

National Federation of Israeli Journalists: POB 585, Beit Agron, 37 Hillet St, Jerusalem 91004; tel. 2-6254351; fax 3-6254353; e-mail office@jaj.org.il; Chair. AHIA HIKA GINOSAR.

Plants Production and Marketing Board: 46 Derech Ha'macabim, Rishon le Zion 75359; tel. 3-9595666; fax 3-9502211; e-mail plants@plants.org.il; internet www.plants.org.il.

UTILITIES

Israel Electric Corporation Ltd (IEC): POB 8810, 2 Ha' Haganah St, Haifa 31086; tel. 4-6348807; e-mail Tinfo@iec.co.il; internet www.iec.co.il; state-owned; total assets US $21,065m. (Dec. 2009); Chair. MORDECHAI FRIEDMAN; Pres. and CEO ELI GLIKMAN.

Mekorot (Israel National Water Co): POB 2012, 9 Lincoln St, Tel-Aviv 61201; tel. 3-6230555; fax 3-6230833; e-mail m-doveret@mekorot.co.il; internet www.mekorot.co.il; f. 1937; state-owned; sales more than US $700m. (2006); Chair. ALEX WIZNITZER; CEO IDO ROSOLIO.

The Histadrut

Histadrut (General Federation of Labour in Israel): 93 Arlozorof St, Tel-Aviv 62098; tel. 3-6921511; fax 3-6921512; e-mail avitals@histadrut.org.il; internet www.histadrut.org.il; f. 1920; Chair. OFER ENI.

The Histadrut is the largest labour organization in Israel. It strives to ensure the social security, welfare and rights of workers, and to assist in their professional advancement, while endeavouring to reduce the divisions in Israeli society. Membership of the Histadrut is voluntary, and open to all men and women of 18 years of age and above who live on the earnings of their own labour without exploiting the work of others. These include the self-employed and professionals, as well as housewives, students, pensioners and the unemployed. Workers' interests are protected through a number of occupational and professional unions affiliated to the Histadrut (see below). The organization operates courses for trade unionists and new immigrants, as well as apprenticeship classes. It maintains an Institute for Social and Economic Issues and the International Institute, one of the largest centres of leadership training in Israel, for students from Africa, Asia, Latin America and Eastern Europe, which includes the Levinson Centre for Adult Education and the Jewish-Arab Institute for Regional Co-operation. Attached to the Histadrut is Na'amat, a women's organization which promotes changes in legislation, operates a network of legal service bureaux and vocational training courses, and runs counselling centres for the treatment and prevention of domestic violence; women joining the Histadrut automatically become members of Na'amat.

Chairman: OFER EINI.

ORGANIZATION

In 2006 the Histadrut had a membership of 700,000. In addition, over 100,000 young people under 18 years of age belong to the Organization of Working and Student Youth, HaNoar HaOved VeHalomed, a direct affiliate of the Histadrut.

All members take part in elections to the Histadrut Convention (Veida), which elects the General Council (Moetsa) and the Executive Committee (Vaad Hapoel). The latter elects the 41-member Executive Bureau (Vaada Merakezet), which is responsible for day-to-day implementation of policy. The Executive Committee also elects the Secretary-General, who acts as its chairman as well as head of the organization as a whole and chairman of the Executive Bureau. Nearly all political parties are represented on the Histadrut Executive Committee.

The Executive Committee has the following departments: Trade Union, Organization and Labour Councils, Education and Culture, Social Security, Industrial Democracy, Students, Youth and Sports, Consumer Protection, Administration, Finance and International.

TRADE UNION ACTIVITIES

Collective agreements with employers fix wage scales, which are linked with the retail price index; provide for social benefits, including paid sick leave and employers' contributions to sick and pension and provident funds; and regulate dismissals. Dismissal compensation is regulated by law. The Histadrut actively promotes productivity through labour management boards and the National Productivity Institute, and supports incentive pay schemes.

There are unions for the following groups: clerical workers, building workers, teachers, engineers, agricultural workers, technicians, textile workers, printing workers, diamond workers, metal workers, food and bakery workers, wood workers, government employees, seamen, nurses, civilian employees of the armed forces, actors, musicians and variety artists, social workers, watchmen, cinema technicians, institutional and school staff, pharmacy employees, medical laboratory workers, X-ray technicians, physiotherapists, social scientists, microbiologists, psychologists, salaried lawyers, pharmacists, physicians, occupational therapists, truck and taxi drivers, hotel and restaurant workers, workers in Histadrut-owned industry, garment, shoe and leather workers, plastic and rubber workers, editors of periodicals, painters and sculptors, and industrial workers.

Histadrut Trade Union Department: Chair. DANIEL AVI NISSENKORN.

OTHER TRADE UNIONS

Histadrut Haovdim Haleumit (National Labour Federation): 23 Sprintzak St, Tel-Aviv 64738; tel. 3-6958351; fax 3-6961753; e-mail nol@netvision.net.il; f. 1934; 220,000 mems.

Histadrut Hapoel Hamizrachi (National Religious Workers' Party): 166 Ibn Gvirol St, Tel-Aviv 62023; tel. 3-5442151; fax 3-5468942; 150,000 mems in 85 settlements and 15 kibbutzim.

Histadrut Poale Agudat Israel (Agudat Israel Workers' Organization): POB 11044, 64 Frishman St, Tel-Aviv; tel. 3-5242126; fax 3-5230689; 33,000 mems in 16 settlements and 8 educational insts.

Transport

RAILWAYS

In 2010 Israel's active railway network, including sidings, comprised an estimated 1,035 km of track. Freight traffic consists mainly of grain, phosphates, potash, containers, petroleum and building materials. A rail route serves Haifa and Ashdod ports on the Mediterranean Sea, while a combined rail-road service extends to Eilat port on the Red Sea. Passenger services operate between the main towns: Nahariya, Haifa, Tel-Aviv and Jerusalem. Construction of a high-speed rail link between Jerusalem and Tel-Aviv commenced in 2001. However, owing to technical and financial difficulties, completion of the project was not expected before 2017. The first line of a light railway network intended to ease traffic congestion in Jerusalem was inaugurated in August 2011. The project was a source of considerable controversy owing to the incorporation within the network of disputed Jewish developments in East Jerusalem.

Israel Railways (IR): POB 18085, Central Station, Tel-Aviv 61180; tel. 3-5774000; fax 3-6937443; e-mail pniyot@rail.co.il; internet www.rail.co.il; f. 2003 as an ind. govt-owned corpn; prior to that date IR had operated as a unit of the Ports and Railways Authority; CEO YARON RAVID (acting).

Underground Railway

Haifa Underground Funicular Railway: 122 Hanassi Ave, Haifa 34633; tel. 4-8376861; fax 4-8376875; e-mail orna@carmelit.com; internet www.carmelit.com; opened 1959; 2 km in operation.

ROADS

In 2010 there were 18,470 km of paved roads, of which 10,334 km were urban roads, 6,515 km were non-urban roads and 1,621 km were access roads.

Ministry of Transport, National Infrastructures and Road Safety: see The Government—Ministries.

Egged Bus Co-operative: POB 43, Egged Bldg, Airport City 70150; tel. 3-6948888; fax 3-9142237; internet www.egged.co.il; f. 1933; operates 945 bus routes throughout Israel; Chair. GIDEON MIZRACHI.

SHIPPING

At 31 December 2009 Israel's merchant fleet consisted of 42 vessels, with a combined aggregate displacement of 400,500 grt.

Haifa and Ashdod are the main ports in Israel. The former is a natural harbour, enclosed by two main breakwaters and dredged to 45 ft below mean sea level. Haifa handled 22.6m. metric tons of cargo and 1.2m. 20-ft equivalent units (TEUs) in 2011. The deep-water port at Ashdod was completed in 1965. A new NIS 3,000m. container terminal, Eitan Port, was inaugurated at Ashdod in 2005. Ashdod handled 18.6m. tons of cargo and 1.2m. TEUs in 2011. In 2009 the Government approved proposals to sell minority stakes in the Haifa and Ashdod port companies. The three-stage privatization process commenced in early 2010, with 15% of the shares in each company to be sold via a public offering.

The port of Eilat, Israel's gateway to the Red Sea, has storage facilities for crude petroleum. It is a natural harbour, operated from a wharf. In April 2011 the Government announced its intention fully to privatize the Eilat Port Company.

Port Authority and Companies

Israel Ports Development and Assets Co Ltd (IPC): POB 20121, 74 Menachem Begin Rd, Tel-Aviv 61201; tel. 3-5657060; fax 3-5622281; e-mail dovf@israports.co.il; internet www.israports.co.il; f. 1961 as the Israel Ports Authority (PRA); the IPC was established by legislation in 2005 as part of the Israeli Port Reform Program, whereby the PRA was abolished and replaced by four govt-owned cos: the IPC as owner and developer of port and infrastructure and three port-operating cos responsible for handling cargo in each of Israel's three commercial seaports; responsible for devt and management of Israel's port infrastructure on behalf of the Govt and carries out some of the largest infrastructure projects in the country; CEO SHLOMO BRIEMAN.

Ashdod Port Co Ltd: POB 9001, Ashdod 77191; tel. 8-8517605; fax 8-8517632; e-mail igalbz@ashdodport.co.il; internet www.ashdodport.co.il; provides full range of freight and passenger services; handled 18.8m. tons of cargo in 2011; f. 1965; CEO SHUKI SAGIS.

Haifa Port Co Ltd: Haifa; tel. 4-8518365; fax 4-8672872; internet www.haifaport.co.il; handled 22.5m. tons of cargo in 2010; 6.5-km dock, 10.5m–14m draught; f. 1933; CEO MENDI ZALTZMAN.

Principal Shipping Companies

Ofer Shipping Group: POB 15090, 9 Andre Saharov St, Matam Park, Haifa 31905; tel. 4-8610610; fax 4-8501515; e-mail mail@oferg.com; internet www.oferg.com; f. 1956 as shipping agency, Mediterranean Seaways; part of the Ofer Group; runs cargo and container services; Chair. UDI ANGEL.

ZIM Integrated Shipping Services Ltd: POB 1723, 9 Andrei Sakharov St, MATAM Park, Haifa 31016; tel. 4-8652111; fax 4-8652956; e-mail shats.avner@il.zim.com; internet www.zim.co.il; f. 1945; 100% owned by the Israel Corpn; international integrated transportation system providing door-to-door services around the world; operates about 100 vessels; estimated 2m. TEUs of cargo carried in 2006; Chair. of Bd NIR GILAD; Pres. and CEO RAFI DANIELI.

CIVIL AVIATION

The principal airport is Ben-Gurion International Airport, situated about 15 km from the centre of Tel-Aviv. Limited international services also operate from Ovda Airport in the Negev Desert. The busiest domestic airports are located at Eilat, Haifa, Rosh Pina and Sde Dov (Tel-Aviv). In mid-2011 the Government approved a proposal to build a new international airport with a capacity of 1.5m. passengers at Timna, north of Eilat, at a projected cost of NIS 1,700m. Construction of the airport, which was to replace the existing airports at Eilat and Ovda, was expected to be completed in 2014.

Israel Airports Authority: POB 137, Ben-Gurion Airport, Tel-Aviv 70100; tel. 3-9752386; fax 3-9752387; internet www.iaa.gov.il; f. 1977; Chair. ELI OVADIA.

El Al Israel Airlines Ltd: 32 Ben-Yehuda St, Tel-Aviv; tel. 3-9771111; fax 3-6292312; e-mail customer@elal.co.il; internet www.elal.co.il; f. 1948; over 40% owned by Knafaim-Arkia Holdings Ltd; about 31% state-owned; regular services to many European cities, as well as to destinations in North America, Africa and Asia; direct flights to Brazil, with connecting flights to other South American destinations, launched in early 2009; Chair. of Bd AMIKAM COHEN; Pres. and CEO Gen. (retd) ELIEZER SHKEDI.

Arkia Israeli Airlines Ltd: POB 39301, Dov Airport, Tel-Aviv 61392; tel. 3-6902210; fax 3-6903311; e-mail customer.service@arkia.co.il; internet www.arkia.co.il; f. 1980 by merger of Kanaf-Arkia Airlines and Aviation Services; scheduled passenger services linking Tel-Aviv, Jerusalem, Haifa, Eilat, Rosh Pina, Kiryat Shmona and Yotveta; charter services to many European destinations, Turkey and Jordan; CEO GAD TEPPER.

Israir Airlines: POB 26444, 23 Ben Yehuda St, Tel-Aviv 63806; tel. 3-7954038; fax 3-7954051; e-mail israir@israir.co.il; internet www.israir.co.il; f. 1996; domestic flights between Tel-Aviv and Eilat, and international flights to destinations in Europe and the USA; Pres. and CEO DAVID KAMINITZ.

Tourism

Israel possesses a wealth of antiquities and cultural attractions, in particular the historic and religious sites of Jerusalem. The country has a varied landscape, with a Mediterranean coastline, as well as desert and mountain terrain. The Red Sea resort of Eilat has become an important centre for diving holidays, while many tourists visit the treatment spas of the Dead Sea. In 2010 an estimated 2,803,100 tourists visited Israel, compared with some 2,321,400 the previous year. Tourism receipts, including passenger transport, in 2009 totalled US $4,332m.

Ministry of Tourism: See The Government—Ministries; Dir-Gen. NOAZ BAR NIR.

Defence

The General Staff: This consists of the Chiefs of the General Staff, Personnel, Technology and Logistics, Intelligence, Operations, and Plans and Policy Branches of the Defence Forces, the Commanders-in-Chief of the Air Force and the Navy, and the officers commanding the four Territorial Commands (Northern, Central, Southern and Home Front). It is headed by the Chief of Staff of the Armed Forces.

Chief of Staff of the Armed Forces: Lt-Gen. BINYAMIN (BENNY) GANTZ.

Commander of Army Headquarters: Maj.-Gen. SHLOMO (SAMI) TURGEMAN.

Commander-in-Chief of the Air Force: Maj.-Gen. IDO NEHOSHTAN.

Commander-in-Chief of the Navy: Maj.-Gen. RAM ROTHBERG.

Defence Budget (2012): NIS 55,600m.

Military Service (Jewish and Druze population only; Christians, Circassians and Muslims may volunteer): Officers are conscripted for regular service of 48 months, men 36 months, women 24 months. Annual training as reservists thereafter, to age 40 for men (54 for some specialists), 38 (or marriage/pregnancy) for women.

Total Armed Forces (as assessed at November 2011): 176,500: army 133,000 (107,000 conscripts); navy 9,500 (2,500 conscripts); air force 34,000.

Paramilitary Forces (as assessed at November 2011): est. 8,000.

Education

Israel has high standards of literacy and advanced educational services. Free, compulsory education is provided for all children between five and 15 years of age; in 1999 legislation was adopted allowing for the introduction of free education for pre-primary children. Primary education is provided for all those between five and 10 years of age. There is also secondary, vocational and agricultural education. Post-primary education comprises two cycles of three years. According to UNESCO estimates, enrolment at primary schools in 2008/09 included 97% of pupils in the relevant age group, while 86% of pupils in the appropriate age group were enrolled at secondary schools. There are six universities, as well as the Technion (Israel Institute of Technology) in Haifa and the Weizmann Institute of Science in Rehovot. In 2010 general government expenditure on education totalled NIS 55,015m. (some 15.9% of total spending).

OCCUPIED TERRITORIES

THE GOLAN HEIGHTS

LOCATION AND CLIMATE

The Golan Heights, a mountainous plateau that formed most of Syria's Quneitra Province (1,710 sq km) and parts of Dar'a Province, was occupied by Israel after the Arab–Israeli War of June 1967. Following the Disengagement Agreement of 1974, Israel continued to occupy some 70% of the territory (1,176 sq km), valued for its strategic position and abundant water resources (the headwaters of the Jordan river have their source on the slopes of Mount Hermon). The average height of the Golan is approximately 1,200 m above sea level in the northern region and about 300 m above sea level in the southern region, near Lake Tiberias (the Sea of Galilee). Rainfall ranges from about 1,000 mm per year in the north to less than 600 mm per year in the southern region.

ADMINISTRATION

Prior to the Israeli occupation, the Golan Heights were incorporated by Syria into a provincial administration of which the city of Quneitra, with a population at the time of 27,378, was the capital. The Disengagement Agreement that was mediated by US Secretary of State Henry Kissinger in 1974 (after the 1973 Arab–Israeli War) provided for the withdrawal of Israeli forces from Quneitra. Before they withdrew, however, Israeli army engineers destroyed the city. In December 1981 the Israeli Knesset enacted the Golan Annexation Law, whereby Israeli civilian legislation was extended to the territory of Golan, now under the administrative jurisdiction of the Commissioner for the Northern District of Israel. The Arab-Druze community of the Golan responded immediately by declaring a strike and appealed to the UN Secretary-General to force Israel to rescind the annexation decision. At the seventh round of multilateral talks between Israeli and Arab delegations in Washington, DC, USA, in August 1992, the Israeli Government of Itzhak Rabin for the first time accepted that UN Security Council Resolution 242, adopted in 1967, applied to the Golan Heights. In January 1999 the Knesset approved legislation stating that any transfer of land under Israeli sovereignty (referring to the Golan Heights and East Jerusalem) was conditional on the approval of at least 61 of the 120 Knesset members and of the Israeli electorate in a subsequent national referendum. Following the election of Ehud Barak as Israel's Prime Minister in May 1999, peace negotiations between Israel and Syria were resumed in December. However, in January 2000 the talks were postponed indefinitely after Syria demanded a written commitment from Israel to withdraw from the Golan Heights. In July 2001 Israel's recently elected premier, Ariel Sharon, stated that he would be prepared to resume peace talks with Syria, but Sharon also declared that the Israeli occupation of the Golan was 'irreversible'. The withdrawal of Israel from the disputed territory is one of Syria's primary objectives in any future peace agreement with Israel. Following his appointment as Israeli Prime Minister in April 2006, Ehud Olmert expressed his willingness to resume direct peace negotiations with Syria; however, the Israeli Government demanded that the Syrian leadership first end its support for militant Islamist groups in the Palestinian territories and Lebanon. Syrian officials, for their part, continued to insist that Israel commit to a complete withdrawal from the Golan Heights in advance of any resumption of bilateral negotiations, a demand persistently rejected by the Israeli Government. Direct peace negotiations between Israel and Syria had not resumed by early 2012, although Syrian President Bashar al-Assad claimed in March 2007 that Syrian representatives had been conducting secret, unofficial discussions with Israeli officials during recent years. Olmert denied that any such talks had taken place. Nevertheless, in July a spokesman for the Israeli Ministry of Foreign Affairs confirmed that messages had been relayed between Israel and Syria by third parties for some time. Tensions between Israel and Syria worsened in September, after Israel carried out an air-strike on a military installation 'deep within' Syrian territory. Both Israeli and Syrian officials confirmed in May 2008 that indirect negotiations aimed at concluding a 'comprehensive peace' between their two countries were being held through Turkish intermediaries in the city of İstanbul. By the second week of August four rounds of the Turkish-mediated discussions had taken place, although no significant progress had apparently been reached as far as resolving the principal outstanding issues was concerned. Despite subsequent claims by President Assad that Israel and Syria were within 'touching distance' of reaching a peace deal, a fifth round of talks, scheduled for September, was delayed owing to the political uncertainty in Israel following Olmert's resignation as premier. Moreover, President Assad apparently responded to Israel's large-scale military offensive against Hamas targets in the Gaza Strip between December and January 2009 (which also led to tense relations between Israel and Turkey) by formally suspending the indirect discussions with Israel. The inauguration, in March 2009, of a new Israeli Government under Prime Minister Binyamin Netanyahu of Likud, with the right-wing Israel Beytenu leader, Avigdor Lieberman, being appointed as Minister of Foreign Affairs, was widely perceived as an obstacle to hopes of a resumption of bilateral negotiations: both have declared their opposition to the surrender of the Golan Heights as part of any Israeli-Syrian peace agreement. In April 2010 Lieberman reiterated Israel's readiness to engage in peace talks with Syria, provided that President Assad abandon Syrian claims to the Golan Heights; Lieberman's comments followed a claim made by Assad that Israel was intent on 'leading the region to war, not peace'. In November the Knesset approved legislation stating that any Israeli withdrawal from the Golan Heights would require the prior endorsement of Israeli voters in a national referendum. Hopes of further progress towards a resumption of direct negotiations were put on hold as a result of the popular uprising that emerged in Syria (q.v.) from early 2011, with the Syrian Government's attention focused primarily on quelling increasing levels of civil unrest. In May Israeli troops clashed with hundreds of pro-Palestinian protesters who had broken through a security fence to enter the Golan Heights from Syria. Syrian state media reported in the following month that 12 Palestinians and two Syrians had been killed when Israeli soldiers opened fire at another group of protesters attempting to enter the Golan Heights from across the Syrian border; according to hospital reports, some 225 others were injured in the incident. The Israeli authorities accused the Assad regime of orchestrating the violence as a means of diverting international attention from Syria's domestic unrest.

DEMOGRAPHY AND ECONOMIC AFFAIRS

As a consequence of the Israeli occupation, an estimated 93% of the ethnically diverse Syrian population of 147,613, distributed across 163 villages and towns and 108 individual farms, was expelled. The majority were Arab Sunni Muslims, but the population also included Alawite and Druze minorities and some Circassians, Turkmen, Armenians and Kurds. Approximately 9,000 Palestinian refugees from the 1948 Arab–Israeli War also inhabited the area. At the time of the occupation, the Golan was a predominantly agricultural province, 64% of the labour force being employed in agriculture. Only one-fifth of the population resided in the administrative centres. By 1991 the Golan Heights had a Jewish population of about 12,000 living in 21 Jewish settlements (four new settlements had been created by the end of 1992), and a predominantly Druze population of some 16,000 living in the only six remaining villages, of which Majd al-Shams is by far the largest. According to official figures, at the end of 2010 the Golan Heights had a total population of 42,200, of whom 18,100 were Jews, 2,300 were Muslims and 20,700 Druze. The Golan Heights have remained largely an agricultural area, and although many Druze now work in Israeli industry in Eilat, Tel-Aviv and Jerusalem, the indigenous economy relies almost solely on the cultivation of apples, for which the area is famous. The apple orchards benefit from a unique combination of fertile soils, abundance of water and a conducive climate.

EAST JERUSALEM

LOCATION

Greater Jerusalem includes Israeli West Jerusalem (99% Jewish), the Old City and Mount of Olives, East Jerusalem (the Palestinian residential and commercial centre), Arab villages declared to be part of Jerusalem by Israel in 1967 and Jewish neighbourhoods constructed since 1967, either on land expropriated from Arab villages or in areas requisitioned as 'government land'. Although the area of the Greater Jerusalem district is 627 sq km, the Old City of Jerusalem covers just 1 sq km.

ADMINISTRATION

Until the 1967 Arab–Israeli War, Jerusalem had been divided into the new city of West Jerusalem—captured by Jewish forces in 1948—and the old city, East Jerusalem, which was part of Jordan. Israel's victory in 1967, however, reunited the city under Israeli control. Two weeks after the fighting had ended, on 28 June, Israeli law was applied to East Jerusalem and the municipal boundaries were extended by 45 km (28 miles). Jerusalem had effectively been annexed. Israeli officials, however, still refer to the 'reunification' of Jerusalem.

DEMOGRAPHY AND ECONOMIC AFFAIRS

In June 1993 the Deputy Mayor of Jerusalem, Avraham Kahila, declared that the city now had 'a majority of Jews', based on population forecasts that estimated the Jewish population at 158,000 and the Arab population at 155,000. For the Israeli administration this signified the achievement of a long-term objective. Immediately prior to the 1967 Arab–Israeli War, East Jerusalem and its Arab environs had an Arab population of approximately 70,000, and a small Jewish population in the old Jewish quarter of the city. By contrast, Israeli West Jerusalem had a Jewish population of 196,000. As a result of this imbalance, in the Greater Jerusalem district as a whole the Jewish population was in the majority even prior to the occupation of the whole city in 1967. Israeli policy following the occupation of East Jerusalem and the West Bank consisted of encircling the eastern sector of the city with Jewish settlements. In contrast to the more politically sensitive siting of Jewish settlements in the old Arab quarter of Jerusalem, the Government of Itzhak Rabin concentrated on the outer circle of settlement building. Official statistics for the end of 2010 reported that Greater Jerusalem had a total population of 945,000, of whom 635,200 (67.2%) were Jews, 281,900 (29.8%) were Muslims and 15,200 (1.6%) were Christians. The Jerusalem Institute for Israel Studies (JIIS) estimated in August 2007 that the growth rate for the Arab population of Greater Jerusalem was almost double that of the Jewish population. According to the JIIS, if this trend continued, the city's population would have a Jewish-Arab ratio of 60:40 by 2020, and of 50:50 by 2035. In May 2007 the mayor of Jerusalem, Uri Lupolianski, suggested easing the restrictions on family reunification for the estimated 10,000 Christian Arabs in Jerusalem, in order to prevent a further decline in their number.

The Old City, within the walls of which are found the ancient quarters of the Jews, Christians, Muslims and Armenians, is predominantly Arab. In 2003 the Old City was reported to have a population of 31,405 Arabs and 3,965 Jews. In addition, there are some 800 recent Jewish settlers living in the Arab quarter.

Many imaginative plans have been submitted with the aim of finding a solution to the problem of sharing Jerusalem between Arabs and Jews, including the proposal that the city be placed under international trusteeship, under UN auspices. However, to make the implementation of such plans an administrative as well as a political quagmire, the Israeli administration, after occupying the whole city in June 1967, began creating 'facts on the ground'. Immediately following the occupation, all electricity, water and telephone grids in West Jerusalem were extended to the east. Roads were widened and cleared, and the Arab population immediately in front of the 'Wailing Wall' was forcibly evicted. Arabs living in East Jerusalem became 'permanent residents' and could apply for Israeli citizenship if they wished (in contrast to Arabs in the West Bank and Gaza Strip). However, few chose to do so. None the less, issued with identity cards (excluding the estimated 25,000 Arabs from the West Bank and Gaza living illegally in the city), the Arab residents were taxed by the Israeli authorities, and their businesses and banks became subject to Israeli laws and business regulations. Now controlling approximately one-half of all land in East Jerusalem and the surrounding Palestinian villages (previously communally, or privately, owned by Palestinians), the Israeli authorities allowed Arabs to construct buildings on only 10%–15% of the land in the city, and East Jerusalem's commercial district has been limited to three streets.

Since the 1993 signing of the Declaration of Principles on Palestinian Self-Rule, the future status of Jerusalem and the continuing expansion of Jewish settlements in East Jerusalem have emerged as two of the most crucial issues affecting the peace process. In May 1999 the Israeli Government announced its refusal to grant Israeli citizenship to several hundred Arabs living in East Jerusalem, regardless of their compliance with the conditions stipulated under the Citizenship Law. In October, however, Israel ended its policy of revoking the right of Palestinians to reside in Jerusalem if they had spent more than seven years outside the city. Moreover, the Israeli Government announced in March 2000 that Palestinian residents of Jerusalem who had had their identity cards revoked could apply for their restoration.

At the Camp David talks held between Israel and the Palestinian (National) Authority (PA) in July 2000, the issue of who would have sovereignty over East Jerusalem in a future 'permanent status' agreement proved to be the principal obstacle to the achievement of a peace deal. It was reported that the Israeli Government had offered the PA municipal autonomy over certain areas of East Jerusalem (including access to the Islamic holy sites), although sovereignty would remain in Israeli hands; the proposals were rejected by Palestinian President Yasser Arafat. In September the holy sites of East Jerusalem were the initial focal point of a renewed uprising by Palestinians against the Israeli authorities, which became known as the al-Aqsa *intifada* (after Jerusalem's al-Aqsa Mosque). Although the publication of the internationally sponsored 'roadmap' peace plan in April 2003 offered directions for talks on the Jerusalem issue, the resumption of attacks by Palestinian militants against Israeli citizens in mid-2003 and Israeli counter-strikes against Palestinian targets, made any such discussions untenable at that time.

Following a lengthy period during which all negotiations between Israel and the PA were effectively stalled, owing to the continued Israeli–Palestinian violence as well as political instability in the Palestinian territories, some optimism was expressed in August 2007 when the Israeli Prime Minister, Ehud Olmert, held direct talks with the Palestinian President, Mahmud Abbas, in the West Bank town of Jericho in preparation for an international Middle East peace conference, which was convened in Annapolis, Maryland, USA, in November. The US Administration of President George W. Bush declared its intention that a permanent Israeli-Palestinian settlement, including the establishment of a Palestinian state, could be reached by the end of the year. However, an increase in attacks being perpetrated by Palestinian militants from the Gaza Strip into northern Israel from January 2008, and a consequent military campaign by Israeli forces in Gaza, resulted in a stalling of negotiations. In February the Israeli Prime Minister angered Palestinians by declaring that talks concerning the final status of Jerusalem, and the key Palestinian demand that East Jerusalem become their capital, would be the last 'core issue' on the agenda to be negotiated by the two parties. Moreover, the Israeli Government continued to issue tenders for hundreds of new housing units at Jewish settlements in East Jerusalem and the West Bank, thereby contravening its obligations under the terms of the roadmap. Relations between Israelis and Palestinians worsened considerably in December, when the Israeli military initiated its month-long campaign against Hamas militants in Gaza (see Contemporary Political History of Israel). The new US Administration of President Barack Obama made renewed efforts to engage constructively in the Middle East peace process, and a series of senior-level summits between US envoys and Israeli and other Middle Eastern leaders took place from March 2009. However, the Obama Administration's demand for a temporary halt to Israel's settlement-building programme, as a precondition for the resumption of the peace process, remained an obstacle to further progress. While Prime Minister Netanyahu was prepared to discuss temporarily curtailing the expansion of some settlements in the West Bank, he reiterated his refusal to limit the expansion of Jewish settlements in East Jerusalem. In December the Israeli Government announced the imposition of a 10-month moratorium on settlement-building in the West Bank; however, the freeze did not encompass building activity in East Jerusalem. Relations with the Obama Administration appeared to deteriorate in March 2010, following the announcement of plans to allow the construction of some 1,600 new homes at the Ramat Shlomo settlement. In a speech to the American Israel Public Affairs Committee in Washington, DC, USA, that month, Netanyahu asserted that the settlements were an 'integral and inextricable' part of the city and that building activity in all areas of Jerusalem would continue. Despite the commencement of direct talks between Netanyahu and Abbas in Washington, DC, in September, the issue of settlement-building remained a significant obstacle to an agreement. Following the expiry later that month of the temporary ban on Israeli settlement-building, the PA suspended its involvement in the peace process, stating that it would resume talks only when the Israeli Government had agreed to end both settlement construction and the blockade of Gaza. Following reports in October that construction had commenced on more than 600 new homes in Israeli settlements in the West Bank, a spokesperson for

President Abbas described the development as 'another indicator that Israel is not serious about the peace process'. In August 2011 the Israeli Government approved the plans for construction at Ramat Shlomo, announced in March 2010, and also indicated its intention to authorize the construction of some 2,700 new homes at the Givat Hamatos and Pisgat Ze'ev settlements. The announcements came amid increased tensions between Israel and the PA, following the announcement by Abbas that the PA would seek full membership in the UN as the State of Palestine at the annual meeting of the UN General Assembly scheduled to be held in September. Abbas duly presented the application on 23 September (see the chapter on the Palestinian Autonomous Areas). Following the PA's successful bid at the end of October for full membership of UNESCO, in early November the Israeli Government announced that it was to accelerate the construction of around 2,000 new homes in East Jerusalem and the West Bank.

ITALY

Introductory Survey

LOCATION, CLIMATE, LANGUAGE, RELIGION, FLAG, CAPITAL

The Italian Republic comprises a peninsula, extending from southern Europe into the Mediterranean Sea, and a number of adjacent islands. The two principal islands are Sicily, to the south-west, and Sardinia, to the west. The Alps form a natural boundary to the north, where the bordering countries are France to the north-west, Switzerland and Austria to the north and Slovenia to the north-east. The climate is temperate in the north and Mediterranean in the south, with mild winters and long, dry summers. The average temperature in Rome is 7.4°C (45.3°F) in January and 25.7°C (78.3°F) in July. The principal language is Italian. German and Ladin are spoken in the Trentino-Alto Adige (South Tyrol) region on the Austrian border, and French in the Valle d'Aosta region (bordering France and Switzerland), while in southern Italy there are Greek-speaking and Albanian minorities. A dialect of Catalan is spoken in north-western Sardinia. Almost all of the inhabitants profess Christianity: more than 90% are adherents of the Roman Catholic Church. The national flag (proportions 2 by 3) has three equal vertical stripes, of green, white and red. The capital is Rome.

CONTEMPORARY POLITICAL HISTORY

Historical Context

The Kingdom of Italy, under the House of Savoy, was proclaimed in 1861 and the country was unified in 1870. Italy subsequently acquired an overseas empire, comprising the African colonies of Eritrea, Italian Somaliland and Libya. Benito Mussolini, leader of the Fascist Party, became President of the Council (Prime Minister) in October 1922 and assumed dictatorial powers in 1925–26. Relations between the Italian State and the Roman Catholic Church, a subject of bitter controversy since Italy's unification, were codified in 1929 by a series of agreements, including the Lateran Pact, which recognized the sovereignty of the State of the Vatican City (q.v.), a small enclave within the city of Rome, under the jurisdiction of the Pope. Under Mussolini, Italian forces occupied Ethiopia in 1935–36 and Albania in 1939. Italy supported the fascist forces in the Spanish Civil War of 1936–39, and from June 1940 supported Nazi Germany in the Second World War. In 1943, however, as forces from the allied powers invaded Italy, the fascist regime collapsed. In July of that year King Victor Emmanuel III dismissed Mussolini, and the Fascist Party was dissolved.

In April 1945 German forces in Italy surrendered and Mussolini was killed. In June 1946, following a referendum, the monarchy was abolished and Italy became a republic. Until 1963 the Partito della Democrazia Cristiana (DC—Christian Democratic Party) held power continuously, while industry expanded rapidly, supported by capital from the USA. By the early 1960s, however, public discontent was increasing, largely owing to low wage rates and a lack of social reform. In the general election of 1963 the Partito Comunista Italiano (PCI—Italian Communist Party), together with other parties of the extreme right and left, made considerable gains at the expense of the DC. During the next decade there was a rapid succession of mainly coalition Governments, involving the DC and one or more of the other major non-communist parties.

Domestic Political Affairs

Aldo Moro's coalition Government of the DC and the Partito Repubblicano Italiano (PRI—Italian Republican Party), formed in 1974, resigned in 1976, following the withdrawal of support by the Partito Socialista Italiano (PSI—Italian Socialist Party). After the failure of a minority DC administration, the PCI won 228 seats at elections to the 630-member Chamber of Deputies (Camera dei Deputati). The DC remained the largest party, but could no longer govern against PCI opposition in the legislature. However, the DC continued to insist on excluding the PCI from power, and in July formed a minority Government, with Giulio Andreotti as premier. He relied on the continuing abstention of PCI deputies to introduce severe austerity measures in response to the economic crisis. In January 1978 the minority Government was forced to resign under pressure from the PCI, which demanded more active participation in government. However, the new Government that Andreotti subsequently formed with support from the PCI was almost identical to the previous administration. In May Moro was murdered by the extreme left-wing Brigate Rosse (Red Brigades).

The Andreotti administration collapsed in January 1979, when the PCI withdrew from the official parliamentary majority. A new coalition Government, formed by Andreotti in March, lasted only 10 days before being defeated on a vote of no confidence. Following elections in June, at which its representation in the Chamber of Deputies declined to 201 seats, the PCI returned to opposition. In August Francesco Cossiga formed a three-party minority coalition Government. However, the new Government was continually thwarted by obstructionism in Parliament. In April 1980 Cossiga formed a majority coalition, comprising members of the DC, the PRI and the PSI. In September, however, the Government resigned after losing a vote on its economic programme. A four-party coalition Government assembled by Arnaldo Forlani, the Chairman of the DC, was beset with allegations of corruption, and in turn was forced to resign in May 1981 after it was revealed that more than 1,000 of Italy's foremost establishment figures belonged to a secret masonic lodge, P-2 ('Propaganda Due'), which had extensive criminal connections both in Italy and abroad. The lodge was linked with many political and financial scandals and with right-wing terrorism, culminating in 1982 with the collapse of one of Italy's leading banks, Banco Ambrosiano, and the death of its President, Roberto Calvi.

In June 1981 the leader of the PRI, Giovanni Spadolini, formed a coalition Government, thus becoming the first non-DC Prime Minister since 1946. Spadolini resigned in November 1982. Amintore Fanfani, a former DC Prime Minister, assembled a new coalition in December which lasted until the PSI withdrew its support in April 1983. A general election was held in June, at which the DC lost considerable support, winning only 33% of the votes for the Chamber of Deputies. The PSI increased its share of the votes to 11%, and its leader, Bettino Craxi, was subsequently appointed Italy's first socialist Prime Minister, at the head of a coalition. His Government lost a vote of confidence in the Chamber of Deputies in June 1986. Craxi subsequently resigned, and Andreotti began talks to form a new government. However, the refusal of other parties to support Andreotti led to Craxi's return to power in July, on condition that he transfer the premiership to a DC member in March 1987. Craxi accordingly submitted his resignation, and that of his Government, at that time. After several unsuccessful attempts to form a coalition, a general election was held in June, at which the DC won 34% of the votes cast and the PSI 14%. The PCI suffered its worst post-war electoral result, winning 27% of the votes. Giovanni Goria of the DC was appointed Prime Minister of a coalition Government. By the end of the year, however, the Government had lost considerable support, and in March 1988 Goria finally resigned. Ciriaco De Mita, the Secretary-General of the DC, formed a coalition with the same five parties that had served in Goria's administration.

Severe criticism by Craxi of De Mita's premiership led to the collapse of the coalition Government in May 1989. In July the coalition partners of the outgoing Government agreed to form a new administration, with Andreotti as Prime Minister. Andreotti resigned the premiership in March 1991, following criticism from the PSI. President Francesco Cossiga (who had taken office in July 1985) none the less nominated Andreotti to form a new government (Italy's 50th since 1945), which comprised the same coalition partners as the outgoing administration, other than the PRI, whose members had rejected the portfolios they had been allocated.

In early 1991 the PCI was renamed the Partito Democratico della Sinistra (PDS—Democratic Party of the Left), having transformed itself into a social democratic party. A minority of members of the former PCI refused to join the PDS, and in May they formed the Partito della Rifondazione Comunista (PRC—Party of Communist Refoundation).

In September 1991, apparently in response to widespread nationalist fervour in parts of Eastern Europe, German-speaking separatists from the Trentino-Alto Adige region made demands for greater autonomy from Italy. In the same month the Union Valdôtaine, the nationalist party governing the Aosta valley on the borders of France and Switzerland, announced that it was planning a referendum on secession. In January 1992 the Italian Government, in an attempt to end a long-standing dispute with Austria over the Trentino-Alto Adige region, agreed to grant further autonomy to the region.

At the general election held in April 1992, support for the DC declined to less than 30% of the votes cast. The PDS won 16.1% of the votes cast, while the PSI received 13.6%. The Lega Nord (Northern League), a grouping of regionalist parties led by Umberto Bossi, performed well in northern Italy. In May Giuliano Amato of the PSI was appointed Prime Minister.

The 'Tangentopoli' affair

The uncovering of a corruption scandal in Milan in 1992, which became known as *'Tangentopoli'* ('Bribesville'), subsequently assumed wider implications. It was alleged that politicians (mainly of the PSI and DC) and government officials had accepted bribes in exchange for the awarding of large public contracts. In February 1993 the Minister of Justice, Claudio Martelli of the PSI, was obliged to resign, having been placed under formal investigation for alleged complicity in the collapse of Banco Ambrosiano. Shortly afterwards Craxi resigned as Secretary-General of the PSI, although he continued to deny accusations of fraud. In March 1993 five DC politicians, including Andreotti, were placed under investigation over their alleged links with the Mafia.

Despite the collapse of confidence in his Government, Amato agreed to remain in office until after nation-wide referendums had been held in April 1993 on a number of proposed legislative amendments, including a reform of the electoral system for the upper legislative chamber, the Senate of the Republic (Senato della Repubblica), and the end of state funding of political parties. These amendments, intended to prevent electoral malpractice and, in particular, interference by organized crime, were overwhelmingly approved. (In August Parliament endorsed a similar system for elections to the Chamber of Deputies.) Amato resigned as Prime Minister shortly after the referendums, and Carlo Azeglio Ciampi was invited by President Oscar Luigi Scalfaro, who had taken office in May 1992, to form a new government. Ciampi, hitherto Governor of the Banca d'Italia (the central bank), was the first non-parliamentarian to be appointed to the premiership. His coalition comprised the four parties of the outgoing administration and the PRI.

In May 1993 the Chamber of Deputies voted overwhelmingly to abolish parliamentary immunity in cases of corruption and serious crime. Furthermore, the Senate approved the removal of Andreotti's parliamentary immunity, to allow investigations into his alleged association with the Mafia, although his arrest remained prohibited. Meanwhile, investigations began in April into the activities of former DC Prime Minister Forlani. The investigations were subsequently extended to encompass politicians of the PDS and PRI, as arrests of leading political and business figures multiplied. In August the Chamber of Deputies voted to allow Craxi to be investigated by magistrates on four charges of corruption. The following month Andreotti was charged with providing the Sicilian Mafia with political protection in exchange for votes in Sicily, and with complicity in the murder of an investigative journalist, Mario Francese, who had allegedly discovered evidence linking Andreotti with the Mafia.

Ciampi resigned in January 1994. President Scalfaro dissolved the legislature and scheduled a general election for March. In January Silvio Berlusconi, the principal shareholder in and former manager of the media-based Fininvest, Italy's third largest private business group, announced the formation of a right-wing organization, Forza Italia (Come on, Italy!), to contest the election. In subsequent weeks, in response to the collapse in popular support for the previously dominant DC and PSI due to the *'Tangentopoli'* affair, parties of the left, right and centre formed electoral alliances capable of securing a majority in the Chamber of Deputies. Seven left-wing parties—including the PDS and the PRC—formed I Progressisti (the Progressives); the Polo delle Libertà e del Buon Governo (commonly known as the Polo delle Libertà—the Freedom Alliance), under the leadership of Berlusconi, was formed by the Lega Nord, Forza Italia and the Alleanza Nazionale (AN—National Alliance), which incorporated members of the neo-fascist Movimento Sociale Italiano-Destra Nazionale (MSI-DN—Italian Social Movement-National Right); and the centre-right Patto per l'Italia (Pact for Italy) included the Partito Popolare Italiano (PPI—Italian People's Party), formed from the liberal wing of the DC. The Polo delle Libertà won an outright majority in the Chamber of Deputies and was only three seats short of a majority in the Senate. In May Berlusconi formed a new Government, which included members of the AN, the Lega Nord and the MSI-DN.

In July 1994 two Fininvest employees were arrested on charges of bribing the finance police (Guardia di Finanza). In November Berlusconi was placed under investigation for bribery. In the following month Antonio Di Pietro, a high-profile magistrate in Milan who had led the investigation into political corruption in 1992, resigned in protest at increasing government interference in the work of the judiciary. The failure of the Prime Minister to resolve his conflict of business and political interests, together with the growing tension between the Government and the judiciary, precipitated the disintegration of the coalition and Berlusconi's resignation in January 1995. Lamberto Dini, the Minister of the Treasury, formed an interim Government composed of technocrats, and pledged to hold elections once he had implemented a programme to improve public finances, reform the state pension system, introduce new regional electoral laws, and establish controls on media ownership and its use during electoral campaigns. In March it was announced that Berlusconi was to be subject to further investigation on charges of financial irregularities.

In June 1995 12 referendums were held on issues including media ownership, trade union and electoral reform, and crime. Significantly, the majority of the voters who participated in the referendums on media ownership supported the partial privatization of the state broadcasting company, Radiotelevisione Italiana (RAI), control of which had become increasingly contentious since the resignation of its directorate in mid-1994 in protest at increased government control over appointments.

In October 1995 the Minister of Justice, Filippo Mancuso, refused to resign despite a successful motion of no confidence in him, which had been prompted by his alleged vendetta against anti-corruption magistrates in Milan. President Scalfaro revoked Mancuso's mandate, appointing Dini as interim Minister of Justice. Shortly afterwards, the Government narrowly defeated a motion of no confidence proposed by Berlusconi and Mancuso, following an agreement whereby PRC deputies abstained from the vote on condition that Dini resign as premier by the end of the year. Dini's resignation, submitted in late December, was, however, rejected by Scalfaro, pending a parliamentary debate to resolve the political crisis. In January 1996 the AN proposed a resolution demanding Dini's resignation, which it was expected to win with the support of parties of the extreme left. Scalfaro was thus obliged to accept Dini's resignation, which he submitted prior to the vote. In February Scalfaro dissolved Parliament and requested that Dini remain as interim Prime Minister until a general election in April.

Meanwhile, in July 1994 Craxi and the former Deputy Prime Minister and Minister of Justice, Martelli, were both sentenced for fraudulent bankruptcy in relation to the collapse of Banco Ambrosiano. Craxi, who claimed to be too ill to return from his residence in Tunisia, was sentenced *in absentia*; in July 1995 he was formally declared a fugitive from justice. In October all 22 defendants were convicted in a trial concerning illegal funding of political parties. Among those convicted were former Prime Ministers Craxi, who was sentenced *in absentia* to four years' imprisonment, and Forlani, sentenced to 28 months' custody; Bossi received a suspended sentence.

The centre-left in power: 1996–2001

The legislative elections held in April 1996 were won by L'Ulivo (The Olive Tree), a centre-left electoral alliance dominated by the PDS, but also including the PPI and Dini's newly formed, centrist Rinnovamento Italiano (RI—Italian Renewal). The alliance narrowly defeated the Polo per le Libertà (as the Polo delle Libertà had been renamed), securing 284 of the 630 seats in the Chamber of Deputies and 157 of the 315 elective seats in the Senate. President Scalfaro invited Romano Prodi, the leader of L'Ulivo, to form a government.

In December 1997 Silvio Berlusconi and four associates were convicted on charges of false accounting with regard to the purchase of a film group in 1988. Later that month Berlusconi and Cesare Previti, a former Minister of Defence and a lawyer for Fininvest, were ordered to stand trial on charges relating to allegations that they had accumulated funds with the intention of bribing judges. In two separate trials in July 1998 Berlusconi was convicted of bribing tax inspectors involved in Fininvest audits and of making illicit payments to Craxi and the PSI in 1991. The prescribed custodial sentences were not, however, to be enforced as the former Prime Minister (who was awaiting trial on several further charges) was protected by parliamentary immunity.

In June 1998 the Chamber of Deputies approved legislation endorsing the admission to the North Atlantic Treaty Organization (NATO, see p. 370) of Hungary, Poland and the Czech Republic. The vote, which had become an issue of confidence in the Prodi Government as the PRC (on which the coalition relied in parliamentary votes) opposed the eastward expansion of the alliance and thus withdrew its support, was carried with the backing of the new, centrist Unione Democratica per la Repubblica (UDR—Democratic Union for the Republic) and with the abstention of Forza Italia. There was a further political crisis in October, when the PRC again withdrew its support for the Government on the issue of the 1999 budget. The Government lost an ensuing confidence motion by one vote, and Prodi was forced to resign. Massimo D'Alema, the leader of the Democratici di Sinistra (DS—Democrats of the Left—as the PDS had been renamed), was asked to assume the premiership. The new Government comprised members of seven political parties. In May 1999 former Prime Minister Ciampi was elected to succeed Scalfaro as President of the Republic.

In October 1999 Berlusconi's 1998 conviction for making illicit payments to Craxi and the PSI was overturned. In the following month, however, Berlusconi was ordered to stand trial in two cases involving charges of bribery and false accounting; in one of the cases Previti was also to stand trial on a charge of perverting the course of justice. Meanwhile, in June a new trial had been ordered against Craxi on charges of illegal party financing; however, in January 2000 Craxi died in exile in Tunisia.

D'Alema tendered his resignation as Prime Minister in December 1999, following the withdrawal of support by a number of the coalition parties. President Ciampi asked D'Alema to form a new government; D'Alema forged a new coalition of parties of the left and centre, including I Democratici per l'Ulivo (The Democrats for the Olive Tree), founded earlier in that year by Prodi, and the Unione Democratici per l'Europa (UDEUR—Union of Democrats for Europe). However, following the defeat of the new centre-left coalition by a centre-right alliance of Forza Italia and Lega Nord at regional elections in April 2000, D'Alema resigned. In late April a new, eight-party, centre-left coalition Government, led by Amato, was sworn in.

In May 2000, at a first appeal, Berlusconi was acquitted of one charge of bribing tax inspectors involved in Fininvest audits on which he had been convicted in 1998; the appeals court also invoked the statute of limitations (which, under Italian law, continued to apply even after proceedings had begun) to overturn his convictions on three similar counts. In June 2000 Berlusconi was further acquitted at a pre-trial hearing of bribery charges relating to his acquisition of the Mondadori publishing company in 1991. (However, in July 2011 a court in Milan ordered Fininvest to make a compensation payment of €560m. to media group Compagnie Industriali Riunite—CIR—for illegally wresting control of Mondadori from the latter by bribing a judge.)

Berlusconi's second premiership: 2001–06

At the general election held on 13 May 2001, Berlusconi's Casa delle Libertà (House of Freedoms) alliance—the successor to the Polo per le Libertà—won majorities in both legislative chambers. Following his nomination as premier by Ciampi, in June Berlusconi formed a coalition Government composed of Forza Italia, the AN, the Lega Nord, the Cristiani Democratici Uniti (CDU—United Christian Democrats), the Centro Cristiano Democratico (CCD—Christian Democratic Centre) and independents. The AN leader, Gianfranco Fini, became Deputy Prime Minister, while the Government included three members of Lega Nord, including Bossi as Minister without Portfolio, with responsibility for Reforms and Devolution.

The issue of apparent conflict of interest between Berlusconi's political role and business interests was heightened by the general election. Berlusconi's new position as Prime Minister placed him in effective control of the state broadcasting company, RAI, and this, coupled with his ownership of the media company Fininvest (which operated Italy's principal private television concern, Mediaset), potentially gave him control over the majority of the Italian television network. Prior to the election Berlusconi had apparently contradicted earlier indications that, should he become premier, he would relinquish a significant proportion of his media interests—stating that he had no intention of selling any part of Fininvest but that he would introduce legislation addressing conflicts of interest.

In August 2001 legislation to decriminalize fraud associated with false accounting was approved by the Chamber of Deputies. Furthermore, in October legislation was adopted by the Senate which altered regulations governing the use of evidence in criminal cases. Opposition parties protested that Berlusconi would directly benefit from the new regulations, which were likely to invalidate legal proceedings against himself and Previti in respect of allegations that they had bribed judges in return for a favourable court judgment over the sale of a state-owned food company, SME Meridionale. Prior to the trial's commencement, in January 2002, an attempt by the Minister of Justice to remove one of the three judges on the case caused public and judicial consternation. In October 2001 the Supreme Court of Appeal overturned Berlusconi's 1998 conviction on charges of bribing tax inspectors in exchange for favourable audits of Fininvest.

In February 2002 Berlusconi announced his intention to privatize two of the three state-owned RAI television channels. The proposal was heavily criticized by opposition members as well as by the outgoing President of RAI. In April a 'conflict of interest' bill was passed in the Chamber of Deputies. The legislation prohibited a figure in public office from active involvement in running a company, but did not forbid ownership, thus permitting Berlusconi's continued possession of Mediaset. (The bill finally became law in July 2004.)

Following the rejection of an appeal by Berlusconi in May 2002 to have his bribery trial moved from Milan (where, he alleged, the judicial system was dominated by communists), several bills proposing judicial reform provoked controversy in the legislature and the judiciary, most notably a trial bill, which would allow proceedings to be rescheduled and relocated if there was 'legitimate suspicion' of prosecutorial bias on the part of the judge. Nevertheless, the bill was passed by Parliament in November. In the same month Bossi presented a draft bill that provided for the devolution of powers to the regions in matters of education, the health service and the police. Although the opposition attempted to hinder its progress, the devolution bill was passed in December.

Also in November 2002 an appeals court in Palermo overturned the acquittal of Andreotti on charges of conspiracy to murder the journalist Mario Francese in 1979, and sentenced the former Prime Minister to 24 years' imprisonment; the sentence aroused condemnation of the judicial system by a number of politicians, including Berlusconi. The Supreme Court of Cassation overturned this ruling, acquitting Andreotti of the murder in October 2003. Meanwhile, in May of that year an appeals court in Sicily upheld a 1999 ruling exonerating Andreotti of charges of association with the Mafia. In October 2004 Andreotti was acquitted by the Supreme Court of Cassation of collusion with the Mafia while in office.

In January 2003, after a further bid to relocate his bribery trial was rejected by the Supreme Court, Berlusconi announced the possible reintroduction of immunity from prosecution for members of Parliament (abolished in 1993), arousing opposition protest. He also confirmed that he would complete his mandate as Prime Minister even if found guilty. In April Berlusconi's trial opened in Milan. Later that month Previti was sentenced to 11 years' imprisonment for bribing judges to influence two corporate takeovers in the 1990s. In May it was announced that Berlusconi would be tried separately from his co-defendants. However, in June the trial was halted, following the adoption of a bill granting immunity while in office to Italy's five most senior politicians (the President, the Prime Minister, the head of the Constitutional Court and the leaders of the two chambers of Parliament). However, the Constitutional Court declared in January 2004 that the legislation was illegal, thus permitting the resumption in April of Berlusconi's trial on charges of corruption. Berlusconi was acquitted on one charge in December; the court ruled that the statute of limitations had expired on the second charge.

In December 2003 President Ciampi refused to sign legislation designed to reduce restrictions on media ownership. The bill would overturn the High Court's decision requiring Berlusconi to convert one of his three terrestrial television channels (Rete 4) to a satellite channel by January 2004 and would also lift a ban on a single company owning licences to both broadcast television and to publish a newspaper. Opponents of the bill maintained that it would allow Berlusconi—who, through his direct influence over RAI and his Mediaset company, already controlled more than

90% of Italy's television media—to expand his media holdings and thereby reduce further the freedom of the press. Ciampi returned the bill to Parliament for further consideration, and published his opinion that the bill was contrary to rulings of the Constitutional Court regarding the plurality of the media. However, the bill was approved by the Chamber of Deputies in February 2004, as the Government linked the vote to a motion of confidence, and received final approval in the Senate in April; Ciampi was constitutionally obliged to sign it into law in May. The President of RAI consequently resigned.

In November 2004 employees in the legal profession organized a strike to protest against planned judicial reform which, it was claimed, would reduce the independence of the judiciary and the power of the legal professionals to prosecute politicians for corruption. Although it was adopted by Parliament, on 16 December President Ciampi refused to sign the legislation (for the second time in two years), stating that it was unconstitutional. On the same day the Chamber of Deputies passed a bill reducing the statute of limitations for business-related crimes, including fraud and corruption.

The ruling coalition performed poorly at regional elections in April 2005. The Unione dei Democratici Cristiani e di Centro (UDC—Christian Democratic and Centrist Union, formed in 2002 from a merger of the CDU and the CCD) subsequently withdrew from the governing coalition and the AN threatened to do likewise. Berlusconi resigned in order to form a new Government, which was duly inaugurated on 23 April. The new Government comprised representatives of the four parties in the previous Government, the PRI, the Nuovo Partito Socialista Italiano (Nuovo PSI—New Italian Socialist Party) and independents.

Legislation providing for a return to total proportional representation prior to the elections in 2006 and setting a threshold for the percentage of votes a party was required to win to be eligible for seats in Parliament was approved by the Chamber of Deputies in October 2005. The opposition abstained from voting, claiming that the legislation was designed to reduce the representation of L'Unione (a nine-party coalition created by Prodi and incorporating members of L'Ulivo and the PRC) in the next parliament. The legislation was approved by the Senate in December.

In November 2005 the two chambers of Parliament approved legislation reducing the statute of limitations for corruption and similar crimes and lengthening it for Mafia-related crimes. The bill had attracted criticism not only because of the perception that it was designed to protect Previti from a prison sentence (although the bill was subsequently amended to exclude current cases), but also because other legislation had been delayed while it was being debated. In January 2006 President Ciampi refused to sign legislation, approved earlier in the month by Parliament, that abolished the right of prosecutors to appeal against an acquittal, claiming that it was unconstitutional. The legislation was widely regarded as designed to exempt Berlusconi from further prosecution since a court in Milan was due to begin hearing an appeal of a case in which Berlusconi had been acquitted on four charges of bribing judges; the appeal was rejected in April 2007.

In March 2006 Berlusconi went on trial in Milan, along with 13 other defendants, on charges of tax fraud relating to the purchase of television and film rights by Mediaset in the 1990s. In November a separate trial opened involving Berlusconi and his former lawyer, David Mills (the estranged husband of a British government minister, Tessa Jowell), in which Berlusconi was accused of paying Mills at least US $600,000 after the latter gave favourable testimony in two corruption trials involving Berlusconi in 1997 and 1998.

Prodi's second Government

At the general election held on 9–10 April 2006, Prodi's L'Unione coalition won a narrow victory in both houses of Parliament. In the Senate L'Unione obtained 158 seats, while the Casa delle Libertà took 156 seats. New legislation, which automatically awarded 55% of the seats in the lower house to the party or group with the largest number of votes, meant that L'Unione obtained 348 seats in the Chamber of Deputies, while Berlusconi's coalition won 281 seats. In May Giorgio Napolitano of the DS was elected to succeed Ciampi as President of the Republic, following which Prodi was inaugurated as Prime Minister. His Government included two former Prime Ministers: D'Alema as Minister of Foreign Affairs and Amato as Minister of Internal Affairs. Tommaso Padoa-Schioppa, an economist with no party affiliation, was appointed Minister of Economy and Finance.

In June 2006 a referendum was held over controversial constitutional reforms, introduced by the previous administration and approved by Parliament in November 2005, that would have granted greater autonomy to Italy's regions and extended the powers of the Prime Minister. The reforms were rejected by the electorate, with 61.7% of the votes cast against the proposal. President Ciampi and the centre-left had been severely critical of the reforms, claiming that the power of the legislature would be diminished and that the devolution of power to the regions, promoted by the Lega Nord, favoured the more affluent northern regions at the expense of their southern counterparts.

In February 2007 the Government was defeated in the Senate on the continued presence of Italian troops in Afghanistan and the expansion of a US military base near Vicenza, actions which were opposed by far-left and pacifist members of the ruling coalition. Although the vote was not tied to a motion of confidence, it led to Prodi submitting his resignation to the President; however, this was not accepted by Napolitano, who asked the Prime Minister to test his authority by calling confidence votes in Parliament. Prodi went on to win the votes in the Senate in February and the Chamber of Deputies in early March, after persuading all parties in the coalition to agree to a 12-point programme that included support for the peace-keeping mission in Afghanistan, as well as measures to liberalize the economy. In a subsequent vote in late March the Senate approved continued funding for all Italian missions abroad, including Afghanistan.

In October 2007, in an attempt to consolidate support for the main left-wing parties and to promote a more centrist agenda, the two largest parties in L'Unione—the DS and Democrazia è Libertà—La Margherita (Democracy is Freedom—The Daisy)—and a number of smaller parties merged to form the Partito Democratico (PD—Democratic Party). In that month some 3.6m. people nation-wide participated in an open primary election, at which the Mayor of Rome, the former Deputy Prime Minister Walter Veltroni, was elected as National Secretary of the PD. Also in October Berlusconi announced his intention to form a new, centre-right party, under his leadership. Berlusconi urged his former coalition partners to join the new formation, which was named the Popolo della Libertà (People of Freedom) in December. However, both the AN and the Lega Nord initially opposed the creation of a single organization.

The ongoing struggle to maintain stability within L'Unione culminated in January 2008 with the resignation of the Minister of Justice, Clemente Mastella, following the arrest of his wife on charges of corruption. Days later Mastella announced the withdrawal from the governing coalition of his UDEUR party, thereby divesting the Government of its narrow majority in the upper house. On 24 January the Government lost a vote of confidence in the Senate that had been prompted by its response to an ongoing refuse collection crisis in Naples. Immediately after the vote, Prodi submitted the Government's resignation, which was accepted by President Napolitano, who, nevertheless, requested that Prodi remain in office on an interim basis pending the appointment of a new Council of Ministers. Later that month Napolitano asked the President of the Senate, Franco Marini, to lead discussions over the formation of a cross-party interim administration with a mandate to pursue electoral reform. However, the main opposition parties refused to agree such measures, which would have reversed reforms implemented during Berlusconi's second term as Prime Minister, and urged Napolitano to call an early general election. In February Napolitano dissolved Parliament and scheduled a general election for 13–14 April. Berlusconi and Fini announced that Forza Italia and the AN were to present a joint list of candidates at the general election as the Popolo della Libertà, a coalition that was subsequently joined by numerous smaller parties. While ruling out a formal merger, the Lega Nord and the Movimento per l'Autonomia agreed to form an alliance with the Popolo della Libertà. The UDC, however, was to contest the election as part of a new coalition, the Unione di Centro (UdC), which it had formed with other centrist, Christian-democratic parties in December 2007.

Meanwhile, in late January 2008 a court in Milan acquitted Berlusconi on charges of false accounting, on the grounds that, according to the reforms promulgated in 2001 under Berlusconi's premiership, it was no longer a criminal offence. In February 2008 a court in Milan upheld a defence request to suspend the two ongoing trials in which Berlusconi was a defendant, to allow him to campaign as a candidate at the forthcoming general election.

Berlusconi's third premiership: 2008–11

At the general election conducted on 13 and 14 April 2008, the number of parties represented in Parliament was greatly reduced, partly owing to the consolidation of the main, centrist alliances. Berlusconi's Popolo della Libertà and its allies won a majority in both the Chamber of Deputies and the Senate. In the lower house the Popolo della Libertà won 276 seats, while its allies the Lega Nord and the Movimento per l'Autonomia won 60 and eight seats, respectively, compared with 217 seats for the PD. The Popolo della Libertà won 147 seats in the upper chamber, while the Lega Nord and the Movimento per l'Autonomia won 25 and two seats, respectively; the PD won 118 seats. The UdC, Antonio Di Pietro's Italia dei Valori (Italy of Principals) and a number of small parties also gained representation in both houses. A high voter turn-out of 81.4% was recorded. A coalition Government, led by Berlusconi and comprising the Popolo della Libertà and the Lega Nord, was sworn in by President Napolitano on 7 May. Franco Frattini (hitherto European Commissioner for Justice) was appointed as Minister of Foreign Affairs, while Roberto Maroni of the Lega Nord became Minister of the Interior. Other notable appointments included that of Umberto Bossi as Minister without Portfolio for Federal Reform. In total, the Popolo della Libertà was allocated 16 government posts and the Lega Nord four.

On entering office, the Government embarked upon a controversial programme of judicial reform, despite fierce criticism from the centre-left opposition, which claimed that the measures were intended to protect Berlusconi against the possibility of conviction in the two ongoing trials in which he was a defendant. In June 2008 both houses of Parliament approved a bill providing for the suspension of all trials involving crimes committed before 2002 for which the maximum sentence was less than 10 years' imprisonment, which the Government claimed was designed to prioritize cases involving serious or violent crimes. Following the promulgation of the legislation, the proceedings against Berlusconi, begun in 2006, were suspended. In July 2008 legislation was approved by both houses of Parliament that granted immunity from prosecution while in office, for one legislative term, to the President, the Prime Minister, and the Presidents of the Chamber of Deputies and the Senate. The Government maintained that the new law would overcome the objections raised by the Constitutional Court to similar legislation, enacted in 2003, which had been annulled by the court in 2004.

Meanwhile, immigration and crime continued to dominate the political agenda. In June 2008 the EU and several non-governmental organizations denounced the Government's proposals to introduce compulsory fingerprinting for all people of Roma origin, accusing it of racial discrimination. The proposals reflected growing anti-Roma sentiment, which followed a number of widely reported violent incidents involving Roma immigrants. In late July Maroni declared a national state of emergency, citing statistics indicating that the number of migrants arriving in Italy had doubled during the first half of 2008, compared with the same period in the previous year. Earlier in July the Government had proposed measures designed to curb illegal immigration and reduce violent crime, under which illegal immigrants convicted of crimes would receive prison sentences of up to one-third longer than those imposed on Italian and other EU citizens. More controversially, the measures also included powers to deploy up to 3,000 troops to patrol strategic locations in major cities, including railway stations and detention centres for illegal immigrants. The measures received final approval from the Senate later that month; the initial six-month deployment of troops in Rome, Milan, Palermo and Turin commenced in August. In February 2009, following several widely publicized incidents of rape allegedly perpetrated by immigrants, the Government promulgated a decree which provided for a mandatory life sentence for certain categories of rape and introduced other measures relating to sexual violence and harassment; controversially, it also sanctioned the creation by local mayors of civilian street patrols to apprehend criminals, and extended the period for which illegal immigrants could be held in detention centres. The decree secured parliamentary approval in April, but only after amendments had been adopted removing the provisions relating to civilian patrols and detention centres. However, these measures were incorporated into a bill also before Parliament that, in addition, sought to make illegal immigration a criminal offence, punishable by a fine of up to €10,000. This legislation was adopted in July. It was criticized by the opposition, the Roman Catholic Church and human rights groups on the grounds that it was likely to increase the growing number of racist and anti-immigrant attacks, as it was liable to promote the creation of vigilante groups who would target immigrants.

The trend for consolidation among the main parties continued in late 2008, as Forza Italia and the AN prepared to formalize the creation of a single, right-wing party. In November members of the national executive committee of Forza Italia agreed to dissolve the party into a new party to be named the Popolo della Libertà (PdL), after the existing coalition. In March 2009 the AN held a special party conference in the capital, at which delegates confirmed the party's dissolution prior to joining the new party. The PdL was finally established as a single party, under the leadership of Berlusconi, at an inaugural conference held in Rome at the end of the month. Eleven small parties joined the new organization, but the Lega Nord remained independent. Meanwhile, following its defeat at the April 2008 general election, the centre-left opposition struggled to make an impact. In February 2009 Veltroni unexpectedly resigned as National Secretary of the PD, citing his failure to establish the party as an effective opposition movement. Later that month Dario Franceschini, the party's deputy leader, was elected to succeed Veltroni on an interim basis. In an open primary election for a permanent successor held in October, Pier Luigi Bersani defeated Franceschini and one other candidate.

In October 2009 the Constitutional Court overturned the legislation of July 2008 granting immunity from prosecution to the holders of the highest offices of state, principally on the grounds that it violated the constitutional principle that all citizens were equal before the law. The court's ruling was given in response to an appeal by the prosecutors in the two corruption trials in which Berlusconi was a defendant. As a result, both trials (one relating to the purchase of film rights by Mediaset and the other to the alleged bribery of Mills) resumed in November 2009. Meanwhile, the Government introduced draft legislation in that month that sought to limit the length of trials for which the maximum sentence was less than 10 years' imprisonment, by imposing time limits of two years for each of the three stages of a trial (the initial hearing and two appeals). The bill, which would apply retroactively, and which the Government described as a much-needed reform of Italy's notoriously slow judicial system, was approved by the Senate in January 2010, but subsequently stalled in the Chamber of Deputies. The trial involving Berlusconi that related to the bribery of Mills was postponed in January, pending the judgment in Mills' final appeal. (In February 2009 Mills had been found guilty of accepting an illegal payment and sentenced to four-and-a-half years' imprisonment.) In February 2010 the Supreme Court of Appeal overturned Mills' conviction on the grounds that 10 years had elapsed since the alleged crimes and the trial was thus invalid under the statute of limitations. Both trials involving Berlusconi were suspended again in April, pending a ruling from the Constitutional Court on the legitimacy of a law passed by Parliament in March, under which the Prime Minister and members of the Council of Ministers were to be granted the automatic suspension of legal process for a maximum of 18 months if they certified that their official commitments constituted a 'legitimate impediment' to their attendance at a trial. Also in April, in a second case involving Mediaset, Berlusconi was accused of tax fraud and embezzlement related to the purchase of film rights by the company's Mediatrade division.

Regional elections held in March 2010 resulted in gains for the centre-right parties at the expense of the centre-left. The Lega Nord was particularly successful, increasing its share of the vote to 12.7% (compared to 5.6% in the regional elections of 2005); moreover, as a result of its electoral alliance with the PdL, the Lega Nord won the governorships of two regions—Piedmont (Piemonte) and the Veneto—for the first time. Although the PdL's performance declined in relation to recent elections (the party won 26.7% of votes cast, compared to 25.9% for the PD), the popularity of the party and of the Prime Minister appeared not to have been significantly damaged by the recent controversies surrounding Berlusconi's confrontation with the judiciary, nor by a series of sex and corruption scandals in which he had been involved since mid-2009 (including numerous press reports in June of that year alleging that the Prime Minister had hired prostitutes to attend parties at his private residence in Sardinia). None the less, the low rate of voter participation, recorded as 64.2% of the electorate, was interpreted as an indication of popular dissatisfaction with the major political parties.

Internal divisions and a series of corruption scandals threatened the stability of the Government in the months following the regional elections. Differences between Berlusconi and Gianfranco Fini, the leader of the AN prior to its merger with Forza Italia, were aired publicly in April 2010 during a televised conference of the PdL, at which Berlusconi challenged Fini to resign from his post as President of the Chamber of Deputies after Fini criticized the political direction taken by the PdL and the growing influence on government policy of the Lega Nord. Claudio Scajola resigned as Minister of Economic Development in May, following allegations (which he denied) that he had purchased a property with financial assistance from a businessman arrested in February as part of an investigation into alleged corruption in the awarding of public tenders. In June the appointment as a Minister without Portfolio of Aldo Brancher, a former business associate of Berlusconi who had been charged with embezzlement, was widely condemned, particularly after he invoked the so-called 'legitimate impediment' law in order to avoid a court hearing. Brancher resigned in early July, after just 17 days in office, shortly before an opposition-proposed motion of no confidence in him was due to be debated in Parliament. Later that month Nicola Cosentino, an under-secretary in the Ministry of the Economy and Finance, also resigned from the Government, after being placed under investigation in connection with his alleged involvement in a secret association of PdL officials and supporters seeking to influence political appointments and judicial decisions.

A bill intended to restrict the use of telephone-tapping in judicial investigations and to prevent pre-trial reporting of intercepted conversations provoked considerable controversy and further divisions within the PdL in mid-2010. After journalists staged a one-day strike in protest against the measures, which they claimed were designed to shield Berlusconi and other government officials from adverse media coverage rather than to protect the privacy of ordinary citizens, the bill was amended in July to allow the publication of transcripts of intercepted conversations when considered relevant by magistrates. However, the Chamber of Deputies subsequently postponed a vote on the proposed legislation (the unamended version of which had been approved by the Senate in June).

Continued tensions between the Prime Minister and the President of the Chamber of Deputies culminated at the end of July 2010 in the adoption by the executive committee of the PdL of a motion censuring Fini for fomenting internal dissent within the PdL and criticizing party decisions. Legislators loyal to Fini proceeded to form a new parliamentary group, Futuro e Libertà per l'Italia (FLI—Future and Freedom for Italy). The Government was thus deprived of a majority in the Chamber of Deputies, although Fini stated that the FLI would support government proposals that implemented electoral pledges made by the PdL.

In a significant reverse for Berlusconi's administration, the FLI withdrew its four members from the Council of Ministers in mid-November 2010 in response to Berlusconi's rejection of an ultimatum issued by Fini that he should resign to form a new, broader coalition. Opposition demands for the Prime Minister's resignation had been precipitated by further revelations regarding his personal life. In mid-December the Government defeated motions of no confidence in Berlusconi tabled in both chambers of Parliament, but the margin of victory in the Chamber of Deputies was only three votes. Following Berlusconi's narrow survival in the lower house, some 50 police officers and 40 anti-Government protesters were injured during violent clashes in Rome.

In January 2011 the Constitutional Court delivered its verdict on the legitimacy of the law under which the Prime Minister and members of the Council of Ministers were able to avoid legal proceedings for up to 18 months if they certified that their official duties constituted a 'legitimate impediment' to their attendance at a trial, ruling that the suspension of legal process should not be automatic but should be decided by individual judges. The three corruption trials in which Berlusconi was a defendant (one relating to the alleged bribery of Mills and the other two to the acquisition of film rights by Mediaset and its Mediatrade division) resumed in early 2011. Berlusconi attended court in March (for the first time since 2003), and again in April and May, for proceedings relating to the Mediaset and Mediatrade cases. In May he also made his first appearance at the Mills case. In February, moreover, the Prime Minister was ordered to stand trial in Milan in April in a fourth case, in which he was accused of paying for sex with an under-age prostitute and of abusing his power by intervening to seek her release from custody after she was arrested on suspicion of theft in May 2010. Berlusconi denied the charges against him, claiming that they were politically motivated. The Prime Minister's faltering popularity was dramatically illustrated by a co-ordinated series of demonstrations organized by thousands of women throughout Italy on 13 February in protest at what they viewed as Berlusconi's disrespectful behaviour towards women. The trial opened in April 2011, although Berlusconi did not attend, but was immediately adjourned. In the same month the Government suffered a further setback when its proposals regarding amendments to the tax system were rejected by a parliamentary committee.

In April 2011 the Chamber of Deputies passed a bill to shorten the statute of limitations on trials of defendants with no previous convictions. The legislation, which required approval by the Senate, formed part of a broader proposed reform of the judiciary, which Berlusconi insisted was necessary to limit political interference by politically biased magistrates but which critics claimed was to protect Berlusconi from prosecution and would weaken judicial independence. In October the Prime Minister was cleared of all charges in the Mediatrade case; however, his eldest son and the Chairman of Mediaset were among the 11 defendants to be indicted. In February 2012 the Mills case was abandoned having expired under the statute of limitations.

Berlusconi's political future appeared increasingly uncertain following poor performances (at the expense of the centre-left) by the PdL and the Lega Nord in local elections in May 2011; notably, the PdL mayor of Milan was unexpectedly ousted from office by the left-wing candidate, thus ending almost 18 years of centre-right rule in the Prime Minister's home town. Since his return to power in 2008 Berlusconi's approval rating had fallen dramatically and the problems arising from the ongoing sex scandals and trials were compounded by Italy's persistently weak economy and its mounting debt crisis. On 12–13 June the Prime Minister's political standing suffered a further serious blow when the electorate voted against government policy in a referendum tabled by the opposition. Despite Berlusconi's appeals for a boycott of the poll, in the first referendum since 1995 to achieve the requisite quorum of more than 51% of the electorate (actual turn-out was around 57%), the Italian people overwhelmingly rejected the Government's plans to revive nuclear power production and partially to privatize water utilities, and voted to repeal the controversial 'legitimate impediment' law.

In late July 2011 Benedetto Francesco Palma was appointed as the new Minister of Justice, replacing Angelino Alfano, who earlier that month had been elected to the new post of National Political Secretary of the PdL and was widely viewed as Berlusconi's chosen political successor.

Meanwhile, in early July 2011 the Minister of the Economy and Finance, Giulio Tremonti, introduced an austerity package aimed at lowering the country's budget deficit; the proposals, which included a range of expenditure cuts and a new series of privatizations, were approved by the Chamber of Deputies on 15 July. However, later that month Tremonti's political credibility was threatened by his links to a former adviser and a group of businessmen who were under investigation for suspected corruption involving official appointments and state tenders. Also in July, Berlusconi's weakening authority was highlighted by the lower house voting, for the first time, to divest a legislator (Alfonso Papa of the PdL) accused of corruption of his immunity from arrest.

In August concern mounted that Italy's increasing debt would necessitate an EU bail-out or, at worst, lead to the collapse of the euro area. In response to growing pressure from the European Central Bank, an emergency austerity package was approved by the Government on 12 August; however, much internal dissension ensued regarding the details of the proposals and numerous revisions were enacted before a compromise package was agreed upon. In early September there were further damaging revelations regarding Berlusconi's personal life and the Prime Minister's problems were exacerbated by a general strike called by the Confederazione Generale Italiana del Lavoro in protest at the proposed austerity measures. On 14 September the Chamber of Deputies passed the much-amended austerity package (approved earlier by the Senate), which included a pledge to balance the budget by 2013.

Recent developments: Government of technocrats appointed

Amid a widespread lack of conviction that the Prime Minister was capable of resolving Italy's financial crisis (the Government agreed in early November to increased scrutiny of its austerity programme by the IMF and the EU), and following a number of defections from the PdL and the loss of the Government's majority in the Chamber of Deputies in October 2011, Berlusconi—Italy's longest-serving post-war Prime Minister—resigned from office on 12 November. (Parliament had previously approved a stability law comprising the urgent reforms demanded by the EU.) On 13 November President Napolitano appointed Mario Monti, a renowned economist and former EU commissioner, as the country's new Prime Minister. On 16 November Monti announced the formation of a new Council of Ministers, composed of a team of 17 technocrats tasked with addressing the deepening financial crisis. Monti himself assumed responsibility for the economy and finance portfolio. The following month Parliament approved a new package of stringent austerity measures (including a rise in the age of retirement for both men and women) drawn up by Monti. In March 2012, despite trade union opposition, the three main parliamentary groups agreed to support Monti's proposed reforms to the labour market aimed at making the economy more competitive.

Organized Crime

Despite mass trials of Mafia suspects in the late 1980s, the Italian Government continued to experience problems in dealing with organized crime. In 1992 the murders of Salvatore Lima, a Sicilian politician and member of the European Parliament, Giovanni Falcone, a prominent anti-Mafia judge, and Paolo Borsellino, a colleague of Falcone, provoked renewed public outrage, and later that year, following an increase in the powers of the police and the judiciary, hundreds of suspects were detained. In January 1993 the capture of Salvatore Riina, the alleged head of the Sicilian Mafia, was regarded as a significant success in the Government's campaign against organized crime. In 1993 the judiciary mounted a campaign to seize Mafia funds, and in the course of the year several suspects, alleged to be leading figures in the world of organized crime, were arrested. In September 1997 24 influential members of the Mafia, including Riina, were sentenced to life imprisonment for their part in the murder of Falcone. The following July Riina received another conviction, along with 17 others, for complicity in the murder of Salvatore Lima in 1992; this constituted Riina's 13th sentence of life imprisonment. In April 1999 an official of the treasury ministry was arrested on charges of external complicity with the Mafia; he was the first serving government member to be taken into preventive detention. In December 17 Mafia members were sentenced to life imprisonment for the murder of Borsellino. Emergency measures were decreed in November 2000 in an attempt to prevent the early release from prison of those accused of Mafia-related crimes. The laws followed the discharge, on technical grounds, of 10 detainees accused of involvement in murders attributed to the Mafia. Magistrates were granted greater powers in determining the length of preventive detention for suspects and a ban on plea-bargaining was introduced. Benedetto Spera, reputedly the closest colleague of the head of the Sicilian Mafia, Bernardo Provenzano, had also been arrested at the end of January; Spera had been convicted *in absentia* for his role in the murders of Falcone and Borsellino. In April 2001 Riina, along with six others, was sentenced to 30 years' imprisonment for the murder, in 1979, of Mario Francese.

Organized crime continued to be problematic during Berlusconi's second term as Prime Minister. Although a murder charge against Berlusconi was dropped in May 2002, the trial of his close friend Marcello Dell'Utri, one of the founders of Forza Italia, on charges of Mafia collusion resulted in the imposition of a nine-year prison sentence in December 2004. Further allegations about Berlusconi's links with the Mafia emerged during Dell'Utri's trial in January 2003, when it was alleged by a Mafia informer that the Mafia had transferred its allegiance from the DC to Berlusconi's Forza Italia after the latter's formation in 1994. (In June 2010, however, an appeals court in Palermo ruled that there was no evidence that Dell'Utri had colluded with the Mafia after 1992 and reduced his sentence to seven years.) Provenzano's closest accomplice, Antonino Giuffrè, was arrested in April 2002 near Palermo. In December Giuffrè directly implicated Berlusconi in the bribing of the Mafia for votes in Sicily in 1993. In April 2006 Provenzano himself, who had been in hiding since 1963, was arrested in Sicily. Meanwhile, in September 2004 an investigation into the President of the Sicilian regional administration, Salvatore Cuffaro of the UDC, concluded that he had indirectly aided the Mafia by transmitting sensitive information. In January 2008 Cuffaro was convicted and sentenced to five years' imprisonment, although he continued to protest his innocence. Later that month Cuffaro was forced to resign, despite having refused to do so in the aftermath of his conviction. However, Cuffaro was re-elected to the Senate in April. Cuffaro's sentence was increased to seven years in January 2010 by an appeals court in Palermo, which convicted him of the additional charge of favouring the Mafia. This verdict was confirmed by the Supreme Court of Appeal a year later, resulting in Cuffaro's imprisonment and the loss of his seat in the Senate.

During 2010–11 the Italian authorities focused their activities against organized crime on seizing control of the various assets of the Mafia (including properties, bank accounts, land, football clubs, vehicles, etc.) in an attempt to weaken the syndicate's financial structure.

Foreign Affairs

Regional relations

Italy's foreign policy has traditionally been governed by its firm commitment to Europe, notably through its membership of the European Community (now European Union—EU, see p. 276) and NATO (see p. 370). The heads of state and of government of the EU formally approved the Treaty establishing a Constitution for Europe in October 2004, which required ratification by all 25 member states. Italy ratified the constitutional treaty by parliamentary vote in April 2005. However, the process of ratification was stalled, following the treaty's rejection in national referendums in France and the Netherlands in May and June, respectively. A reform treaty, to replace the constitutional treaty, was signed by EU heads of state and of government, including Prodi, at a summit meeting in Lisbon, Portugal, on 13 December 2007. The Treaty of Lisbon was ratified by the Italian Parliament in August 2008 and entered into force in December 2009.

Italy's extended coastline and geographical position attracts many illegal immigrants from South-Eastern Europe and North Africa. Following Italy's accession to the EU's Schengen Agreement on cross-border travel in late October 1997, large numbers of refugees, mainly Turkish and Iraqi Kurds, began arriving in southern Italy, provoking concern from Italy's EU partners. On 1 April 1998 the Schengen Agreement, which had previously only been applicable to air travel between Italy and the other EU member states, was fully implemented, opening the borders with Austria and France. In order to comply with the terms of the agreement, a new law had been promulgated in February, providing for the detention, prior to forcible repatriation, of illegal immigrants. In February 1999 legislation was approved allowing for the detention of illegal immigrants arriving in Italy without making an asylum application. In March 2002 a state of emergency was declared following the arrival of 1,000 Kurdish refugees in Sicily. Berlusconi expressed concern over the rise in the level of immigration into Italy, and in June legislation was passed allowing for the fingerprinting of non-EU nationals and requiring residence permits to be renewed every two years. Further increases in arrivals of immigrants prompted a government decree in June 2003 enabling the Italian navy to board ships carrying illegal immigrants and divert them away from the Italian coast. In August 2004 an agreement was reached with Libya on controlling immigration through that country, and in October the Italian Government commenced returning would-be immigrants to Libya by aircraft. In September 2006 a human rights organization accused the Italian and Libyan Governments of abusing the human rights of African migrants through thousands of forced repatriations. (In February 2012 Italy was censured by the European Court of Human Rights for its treatment of Somali and Eritrean nationals, who were deported by Libya in May 2009.) Italy signed an agreement with Libya in December 2007, with regard to establishing joint maritime patrols, although little progress was initially made. In August 2008, however, Libya and Italy signed an accord under which Italy was to invest US $5,000m. in Libya over the following 20 years, in recognition of the injustices Libyans suffered in the colonial era, for which Berlusconi offered an official apology. In accordance with the terms of the so-called 'friendship agreement', which also provided for enhanced business co-operation between the two countries, in May 2009 it was announced that joint maritime patrols had begun. The number of boats carrying illegal immigrants from Libya to Italy subsequently declined sharply. Bilateral relations were strengthened further during a visit to Italy by the Libyan leader, Col Muammar al-Qaddafi, in August 2010. Given its extensive business and trade links with Libya, the Italian Government's response to an uprising in that country in February 2011 was initially cautious. A threat by Qaddafi to end co-operation with the EU on illegal migration from North Africa if the EU supported anti-Government protesters in Libya was of particular concern to Italy, which had received an influx of some 5,000 migrants from Tunisia that month, in the wake of a revolution there. Nevertheless, the Italian Government condemned the violent repression of the anti-Government demonstrations in Libya and, following the evacuation of its citizens from that country, suspended the 2008 friendship agreement and announced its support for EU sanctions against Qaddafi's regime. In late April 2011 the Government committed Italy to joining France, the United Kingdom and the USA in mounting air strikes against Libya. In retaliation, the Italian embassy in Tripoli was attacked by Qaddafi loyalists in early May. Despite this, talks between 22 countries supporting the rebels in Libya took place in Rome later that month, chaired by Italy and Qatar; it was agreed to establish a non-military fund to help the rebels. Thousands of migrants from Tunisia, Libya and Egypt arrived by boat on the Italian island of Lampedusa following the civil unrest in those countries. Relations between Italy and France deteriorated as France objected to Italy providing thousands of Tunisian migrants with temporary residence permits, which enabled them to travel within the EU (often to France). In April, however, Italy and France resolved their differences and agreed to launch joint sea and air patrols in an attempt to limit the influx from North Africa. Following the collapse of Qaddafi's regime in September and the death of the former dictator the following month, relations between Italy and Libya began to be normalized. Prime Minister Monti visited Tripoli in January 2012 to hold discussions with the transitional administration.

Other external relations

Under the premiership of Berlusconi in 2001–05 increasing emphasis on promoting national interests was accompanied by a repositioning of Italian foreign policy towards support for the USA in its 'war on terror'. The deployment of some 2,700 Italian troops to assist US military efforts following the September 2001 suicide attacks on New York and Washington, DC, was approved by the Italian Parliament in November. An investigation into the existence of terrorist cells possibly connected with the al-Qa'ida organization headed by the Saudi-born dissident Osama bin Laden led to a number of arrests in Italy in 2002–03. Berlusconi's increasing political allegiance with the so-called 'coalition of the willing' (the group of powers, including the USA, the United Kingdom and Spain, which was in favour of military action against the regime of Saddam Hussain in Iraq), gave rise to massive nation-wide protests in February 2003. Owing to the level of popular dissent, the Italian Government did not at this stage agree to supply troops for the US-led military campaign in Iraq; it did, however, offer the USA the use of Italy's bases and airspace for logistical purposes. At the onset of armed conflict in Iraq in March, the anti-war movement in Italy gained momentum. In April the Government approved the provision of humanitarian support for Iraq; however, by November Italy had approximately 2,400 troops stationed in the country. In that month a suicide bombing took place at an Italian base in Nasiriyah, Iraq, killing 19 Italian soldiers; this led to renewed calls from the centre-left for Italy to withdraw. Pressure for the withdrawal of troops from Iraq increased following the kidnapping and murder of an Italian journalist, Enzo Baldoni, in August 2004. In January 2006 the Italian Government announced that all 3,000 Italian troops then stationed in Iraq would be withdrawn by the end of the year; the last Italian troops left Iraq in early December.

Following the conflict in Lebanon between Israeli forces and the militant group Hezbollah in mid-2006, Italy sent some 2,500 peace-keeping troops to form part of the UN Interim Force in Lebanon (UNIFIL). In early 2012 Italy also had around 3,952 troops stationed in Afghanistan as part of the NATO-led peace-keeping force (the International Security Assistance Force—ISAF).

CONSTITUTION AND GOVERNMENT

Under the 1948 Constitution, legislative power was held by the bicameral Parliament (Parlamento), elected by universal suffrage for five years (subject to dissolution) on the basis of proportional representation. A referendum held in 1993 supported the amendment of the Constitution to provide for the election of 75% of the members of the Senate of the Republic (Senato della Repubblica) by a simple plurality and the remainder under a system of proportional representation, and provided for further electoral reform. In August Parliament approved a similar system for elections to the Chamber of Deputies (Camera dei Deputati). In December 2005 new legislation was enacted providing for the return to full proportional representation. The Senate has 315 elected members (seats allocated on a regional basis) and seven life Senators. The Chamber of Deputies has 630 members. The minimum voting age is 25 years for the Senate and 18 years for the Chamber of Deputies. The two houses have equal power.

The President of the Republic is a constitutional head of state elected for seven years by an electoral college comprising both houses of Parliament and 58 regional representatives. Executive power is exercised by the Council of Ministers. The head of state appoints the President of the Council (Prime Minister) and, on the latter's recommendation, other ministers. The Council is responsible to Parliament.

The country is divided into 20 regions, of which five (Sicily, Sardinia, Trentino-Alto Adige, Friuli-Venezia Giulia and Valle d'Aosta) enjoy a special status. There is a large degree of regional autonomy. Each region has a Regional Council elected every five years by universal suffrage and a Giunta Regionale responsible to the Regional Council. The Regional Council is a legislative assembly, while the Giunta holds executive power. The regions are subdivided into a total of 95 provinces.

REGIONAL AND INTERNATIONAL CO-OPERATION

Italy was a founder member of the European Community, now the European Union (EU, see p. 276), and uses the single currency, the euro. It is a member of the Council of Europe (see p. 256), the Central European Initiative (see p. 462) and the Organization for Security and Co-operation in Europe (OSCE, see p. 388).

Italy joined the UN in 1955. As a contracting party to the General Agreement on Tariffs and Trade, Italy joined the World Trade Organization (WTO, see p. 433) on its establishment in 1995. Italy is also a member of the North Atlantic Treaty Organization (NATO, see p. 370), the Organisation for Economic Co-operation and Development (OECD, see p. 379), the Group of Eight major industrialized nations (G8, see p. 463) and the Group of 20 major industrialized and systemically important emerging market nations (G20, see p. 454).

ECONOMIC AFFAIRS

In 2010, according to estimates by the World Bank, Italy's gross national income (GNI), measured at average 2008–10 prices, was US $2,125,845m., equivalent to $35,150 per head (or $31,130 per head on an international purchasing-power parity basis). During 2001–10, it was estimated that the population increased by 0.7%, while Italy's gross domestic product (GDP) per head decreased, in real terms, by an average of 0.6% per year. Overall GDP increased, in real terms, at an average annual rate of 0.1% in 2001–10; GDP declined by 5.1% in 2009 and increased by 1.3% in 2010.

Agriculture (including forestry and fishing) contributed 1.9% of GDP in 2010 and engaged 3.8% of the employed labour force in 2008. The principal crops are sugar beet, maize, grapes, wheat and tomatoes. Italy is a leading producer and exporter of wine. According to the World Bank, during 2001–09 the real GDP of the agricultural sector declined at an average rate of 0.4% per year. According to chain linked methodologies, the agricultural sector shrank 2.5% in 2009, but rose by some 1.1% in 2010.

Industry (including mining, manufacturing, construction and power) contributed 24.9% of GDP in 2010 and engaged 29.7% of the employed labour force in 2008. Real industrial GDP fluctuated during 2001–09 and fell by an average of 1.7% annually. According to chain linked methodologies, the industrial sector contracted by 13.1% in 2009, and increased by 2.8% in 2010.

The mining sector contributed just 0.4% of GDP in 2010 and engaged 0.2% of the employed labour force in 2008. The major product of the mining sector is petroleum, followed by talc, feldspar, rock salt and gypsum. Italy also has reserves of lignite, lead and zinc. Average annual growth in the GDP of the mining sector was negligible in 1990–2000; according to chain linked methodologies, mining GDP decreased by 11.7% in 2009, and by 2.3% in 2010.

Manufacturing contributed 16.0% of GDP in 2010 and engaged 20.5% of the employed labour force in 2008. The most important branches of manufacturing are metals and metal products, non-electric machinery, food, electric machinery, and chemical products. According to the World Bank in 2001–09 the GDP of the manufacturing sector declined, in real terms, at an average annual rate of 2.5%. According to chain linked methodologies, manufacturing GDP decreased by an estimated 16.0% in 2009, but increased by some 5.4% in 2010.

Construction contributed 6.1% of GDP in 2010 and engaged 8.4% of the employed labour force in 2008. According to chain linked methodologies, the construction sector contracted by 8.2% in 2009 and by 4.2% in 2010.

More than 80% of energy requirements are imported. According to World Bank figures, in 2008 natural gas-fired stations provided 55.1% of electricity production, coal-fired electricity generating stations provided 15.5%, petroleum provided 10.0% and hydroelectric power stations provided 13.3%. In 2004 Libya began delivering natural gas to Sicily through a pipeline financed by Ente Nazionale Idrocarburi (Eni), the main—formerly wholly state-owned—gas provider, and its Libyan counterpart. In 2009, according to the World Bank, fuel imports accounted for 17.8% of the value of total merchandise imports.

Services accounted for 73.2% of GDP in 2010 and engaged 66.5% of the employed labour force in 2008. Tourism is an important source of income; in 2009 41.1.m. foreigners visited Italy, compared with 41.8m. in the previous year. Tourism receipts totalled €41,872m. in 2009. According to the World Bank, the combined GDP of the services sector increased, in real terms, at an estimated average rate of 0.5% per year in 2001–09. In 2009 according to the chain linked methodologies, the services sector contracted by 2.5%, but increased by 1.3% in 2010.

In 2010 Italy recorded a visible trade deficit of US $27,278m., along with a deficit of $72,015m. on the current account of the balance of payments. According to official figures, in 2010 the principal source of imports was Germany (15.9%); other major suppliers were France, the People's Republic of China, and the Netherlands. Germany was also the principal market for exports (13.0%); other major purchasers in that year were France, the USA, Spain and the United Kingdom. In 2010 Italy's fellow members of the European Union (EU, see p. 276) were the source for 44.2% of Italy's imports and purchased 43.6% of its exports. The principal exports in 2010 were machinery and mechanical equipment, metal and metal products, textile products, chemicals and artificial fibres, and transport equipment. The principal imports were chemicals and artificial fibres, electrical and precision equipment, transport equipment, metals and metal products and minerals for fuel.

The budgetary deficit for 2010 was €71,211m., equivalent to 4.6% of annual GDP. Italy's general government gross debt was €1,843,020m. in 2010, equivalent to 119.0% of GDP, compared with the EU target of 60%. The average annual rate of inflation in 2001–10 was 2.1%. Consumer prices increased by 2.7% in 2011. The rate of unemployment was 8.7% in the last quarter of 2010.

Italy's economy is the fourth largest in Europe. However, the country suffers from significant structural problems, including an economic disparity between the more industrialized, prosperous north and the impoverished south. Following the deterioration in global economic conditions in 2008, Italy officially entered a recession. GDP contracted by 1.3% in 2008 and by a further 5.1% in 2009, largely owing to declines in domestic demand, in investment and in the value of exports, while the budget deficit widened to 2.7% of GDP in 2008 and to 5.4% in 2009. In contrast to other advanced economies, the Italian Government was able to introduce only limited fiscal stimulus owing to the country's high public debt. Moderate growth of 1.3% in 2010 was driven mainly by an increase in the value of exports, as global demand recovered, and the budget deficit narrowed to 4.6% of GDP in that year. However, the debt-to-GDP ratio continued to rise, reaching 119.0% in 2010 (the second highest in the euro area after Greece), and unemployment remained high, at 8.6% in December. Although a small budget deficit (equivalent to 1.0% of GDP) was recorded in 2011, the rate of overall growth decelerated to an estimated 0.4% and the debt-to-GDP ration increased to 120.1% at the end of the year (the highest level since 1996). A number of austerity packages were drawn up by Berlusconi's Government in 2011 as the financial crisis escalated and Italy's borrowing costs soared to unsustainable levels. The gravity of the situation was compounded by the fact that an EU bail-out of Italy was beyond the existing capacity of the euro area's rescue fund (the European Financial Stability Facility). His apparent inability adequately to address the debt crisis was one of the major reasons for Prime Minister Berlusconi's resignation in November. His successor, Mario Monti, who headed a government of highly qualified technocrats, introduced an emergency package of fiscal adjustments in December (dubbed the 'Save Italy measures'), including new taxes, a rise in fuel costs and controversial changes to the pension system. Monti's rigorous approach to resolving Italy's economic problems was generally met with cautious optimism and the IMF forecast that the target of a balanced budget in 2013 would be achieved.

PUBLIC HOLIDAYS

2013: 1 January (New Year's Day), 6 January (Epiphany), 1 April (Easter Monday), 25 April (Liberation Day), 1 May (Labour Day), 2 June (Republic Day), 15 August (Assumption), 1 November (All Saints' Day), 8 December (Immaculate Conception), 25 December (Christmas Day), 26 December (St Stephen's Day).

There are also numerous local public holidays, held on the feast day of the patron saint of each town.

Statistical Survey

Source (unless otherwise stated): Istituto Nazionale di Statistica, Via Cesare Balbo 16, 00184 Roma; tel. (06) 46731; fax (06) 467313101; e-mail info@istat.it; internet www.istat.it.

Area and Population

AREA, POPULATION AND DENSITY

Area (sq km)	301,336*
Population (census results)†	
21 October 2001	56,995,744
9 October 2011	
Males	28,750,942
Females	30,713,702
Total	59,464,644
Density (per sq km) at 2011 census	197.3

* 116,346 sq miles.

† Census figures are *de jure*, in 2001 the de facto population was 57,110,144 (males 27,617,335, females 29,492,809).

POPULATION BY AGE AND SEX
(official estimates at 1 January 2011)

	Males	Females	Total
0–14	4,377,496	4,135,726	8,513,222
15–64	19,844,836	19,966,847	39,811,683
65 and over	5,190,942	7,110,595	12,301,537
Total	29,413,274	31,213,168	60,626,442

Note: Estimates not adjusted to take account of 2011 census results.

REGIONS

(population at 2011 census, preliminary*)

Region	Area (sq km)	Population	Density (per sq km)	Regional capital(s)
Abruzzo	10,763	1,307,199	121.5	L'Aquila
Basilicata	9,995	579,251	58.0	Potenza
Calabria	15,081	1,956,830	129.8	Catanzaro
Campania	13,590	5,748,555	423.0	Napoli (Naples)
Emilia-Romagna	22,117	4,352,794	196.8	Bologna
Friuli-Venezia Giulia	7,858	1,220,078	155.3	Trieste
Lazio	17,236	5,499,537	319.1	Roma (Rome)
Liguria	5,422	1,577,439	290.9	Genova (Genoa)
Lombardia (Lombardy)	23,863	9,719,520	407.3	Milano (Milan)
Marche	9,694	1,542,156	159.1	Ancona
Molise	4,438	314,560	70.9	Campobasso
Piemonte (Piedmont)	25,402	4,367,394	171.9	Torino (Turin)
Puglia	19,358	4,050,817	209.3	Bari
Sardegna (Sardinia)	24,090	1,642,528	68.2	Cagliari
Sicilia (Sicily)	25,711	4,999,164	194.4	Palermo
Toscana (Tuscany)	22,994	3,673,457	159.8	Firenze (Florence)
Trentino-Alto Adige/Südtirol	13,607	1,031,577	75.8	Bolzano/Trento†
Umbria	8,456	888,482	105.1	Perugia
Valle d'Aosta	3,263	126,982	38.9	Aosta
Veneto	18,399	4,866,324	264.5	Venezia (Venice)
Total	301,336	59,464,644	197.3	—

* Population is *de jure*.

† Bolzano (Bozen) and Trento (Trent) are joint regional capitals of Trentino-Alto Adige/Südtirol.

PRINCIPAL TOWNS

(population at 2011 census, preliminary, measured by *comune**)

Town	Population	Town	Population
Roma (Rome, the capital)	2,612,068	Livorno (Leghorn)	158,127
Milano (Milan)	1,245,660	Ravenna	155,373
Napoli (Naples)	947,764	Cagliari	149,671
Torino (Turin)	872,832	Foggia	146,904
Palermo	653,222	Rimini	139,817
Genova (Genoa)	591,790	Salerno	134,887
Bologna	375,935	Ferrara	133,005
Firenze (Florence)	355,342	Sassari	124,774
Bari	316,692	Monza	119,890
Catania	293,541	Pescara	118,029
Venezia (Venice)	263,996	Latina	116,147
Verona	254,607	Forlí	115,855
Messina	240,116	Siracusa (Syracuse)	115,675
Padova (Padua)	205,573	Bergamo	115,499
Trieste	202,533	Trento (Trent)	114,609
Taranto	195,882	Vicenza	111,681
Brescia	191,465	Terni	109,369
Prato	180,113	Giugliano in Campania	106,591
Modena	180,006	Bolzano	102,869
Reggio di Calabria	176,529	Ancona	100,768
Parma	176,504	Novara	100,517
Perugia	165,128	Piacenza	100,215
Reggio nell'Emilia	162,454		

* Population is *de jure*.

BIRTHS, MARRIAGES AND DEATHS

	Registered live births		Registered marriages		Registered deaths	
	Number	Rate (per 1,000)	Number	Rate (per 1,000)	Number	Rate (per 1,000)
2003	544,063	9.4	264,097	4.6	586,468	10.2
2004	562,599	9.7	248,969	4.3	546,658	9.4
2005	554,022	9.7	247,740	4.2	567,304	9.8
2006	560,010	9.5	245,992	4.2	557,892	9.5
2007	563,933	9.5	250,360	4.2	570,801	9.6
2008	576,659	9.6	246,613	4.1	585,126	9.8
2009	568,857	9.5	230,613	3.8	591,663	9.8
2010	561,944	9.3	n.a.	n.a.	587,488	9.7

2010 (estimate): Marriage rate 3.6 per 1,000.

2011 (estimates): Birth rate 9.1 per 1,000; Marriage rate 3.5 per 1,000; Death rate 9.7 per 1,000.

Life expectancy (years at birth, WHO estimates): 82 (males 79; females 84) in 2009 (Source: WHO, *World Health Statistics*).

IMMIGRATION AND EMIGRATION

Immigrants by country of last residence	1998	1999	2000
European Union (EU)	24,140	24,088	25,955
France	4,160	3,892	4,328
Germany	9,435	9,608	10,054
United Kingdom	3,587	3,604	3,844
Other European countries	49,585	69,650	86,477
Albania	19,973	28,838	32,181
Poland	3,012	3,165	5,086
Romania	7,119	10,986	19,710
Switzerland	5,027	5,507	5,687
former Yugoslavia	7,813	11,926	11,991
Africa	30,930	41,967	48,925
Morocco	12,984	19,526	20,344
Senegal	2,167	3,458	4,681
Middle East and Asia	30,406	25,362	36,513
China, People's Republic	7,224	6,119	9,451
India	3,162	3,607	4,759
Philippines	9,089	4,898	7,003
Sri Lanka	3,463	2,942	4,243
Americas	21,287	23,491	28,485
Peru	4,893	3,935	5,279
USA	3,619	3,631	4,055
Oceania	537	494	613
Total	156,885	185,052	226,968

Emigrants by country of destination	1998	1999	2000
European Union (EU)	19,844	28,595	24,493
France	2,848	4,052	3,394
Germany	9,128	13,372	11,413
United Kingdom	3,187	4,535	3,919
Other European countries	9,881	13,677	12,245
Switzerland	6,127	8,850	7,416
former Yugoslavia	1,102	1,163	1,310
Africa	3,185	4,441	4,149
Middle East and Asia	2,849	3,613	3,423
Americas	9,677	13,912	11,740
Argentina	2,141	3,188	2,685
Brazil	953	1,349	1,168
USA	3,555	4,973	4,156
Oceania	453	635	551
Total	45,889	64,873	56,601

Total immigrants: 326,673 in 2005; 297,640 in 2006; 558,019 in 2007; 534,712 in 2008; 442,940 in 2009;458,856 in 2010.

Total emigrants: 65,029 in 2005; 75,230 in 2006; 65,196 in 2007; 80,947 in 2008; 80,597 in 2009;78,771 in 2010.

ECONOMICALLY ACTIVE POPULATION
('000 persons aged 15 years and over)

	2006	2007	2008
Agriculture, hunting and forestry	948	888	860
Fishing	34	35	35
Mining and quarrying	42	39	36
Manufacturing	4,826	4,870	4,805
Electricity, gas and water	159	139	144
Construction	1,900	1,955	1,970
Wholesale and retail trade; repair of motor vehicles, motorcycles and personal and household goods	3,522	3,541	3,540
Restaurants and hotels	1,114	1,154	1,179
Transport, storage and communications	1,224	1,257	1,294
Financial intermediation	675	664	653
Real estate, renting and business activities	2,434	2,542	2,618
Public administration and defence; compulsory social security	1,443	1,418	1,436
Education	1,597	1,606	1,584
Health and social work	1,570	1,575	1,659
Other community, social and personal service activities	1,164	1,167	1,136
Private households with employed persons	324	349	419
Extra-territorial bodies and organizations	12	22	36
Total employed	22,988	23,222	23,405
Unemployed	1,673	1,506	1,692
Total labour force	24,661	24,728	25,097
Males	14,740	14,779	14,884
Females	9,922	9,949	10,213

Source: ILO.

Health and Welfare

KEY INDICATORS

Total fertility rate (children per woman, 2009)	1.4
Under-5 mortality rate (per 1,000 live births, 2009)	4
HIV/AIDS (% of persons aged 15–49, 2009)	0.3
Physicians (per 1,000 head, 2006)	3.7
Hospital beds (per 1,000 head, 2005)	4.0
Health expenditure (2008): US $ per head (PPP)	2,836
Health expenditure (2008): % of GDP	8.7
Health expenditure (2008): public (% of total)	76.3
Total carbon dioxide emissions ('000 metric tons, 2007)	456,054.4
Carbon dioxide emissions per head (metric tons, 2007)	7.7
Human Development Index (2011): ranking	24
Human Development Index (2011): value	0.874

For sources and definitions, see explanatory note on p. vi.

Agriculture

PRINCIPAL CROPS
('000 metric tons)

	2008	2009	2010
Wheat	8,855	6,341	6,900*
Rice, paddy	1,389	1,500†	1,638†
Barley	1,237	1,049	991
Maize	9,491	7,878	8,828
Oats	356	315	279
Sorghum	226	243	271
Potatoes	1,604	1,774	1,558
Sugar beet	3,521	3,308	3,550
Almonds, with shell	119	114	86
Hazelnuts (Filberts)	112	105	94
Soybeans (Soya beans)	346	468	553
Olives	3,474	3,287	3,171
Sunflower seed	261	280	213
Cabbages	345	338	349
Artichokes	484	487	480
Lettuce	916	845	843
Tomatoes	5,977	6,878	6,025
Cauliflowers and broccoli	416	396	427
Pumpkins, squash and gourds	519	509	508
Aubergines (Eggplants)	322	317	303
Chillies and peppers, green	326	324	294
Onions, dry	404	384	381
Beans, green	197	192	183
Carrots and turnips	595	523	489
Watermelons	435	463	478
Cantaloupes and other melons	653	621	666
Oranges	2,167	2,421	2,394
Tangerines, mandarins, clementines and satsumas	765	827	241
Lemons and limes	519	545	522
Apples	2,210	2,326	2,205
Pears	770	872	737
Apricots	205	215	253
Sweet cherries	134	116	115
Peaches and nectarines	1,589	1,692	1,591
Plums	184	189	207
Strawberries	156	163	154
Grapes	7,793	8,243	7,788
Kiwi fruit	474	448	416
Tobacco, unmanufactured†	121	119	97

* Unofficial figure.

† FAO estimate(s).

Aggregate production ('000 metric tons, may include official, semi-official or estimated data): Total cereals 21,613 in 2008, 17,392 in 2009, 18,996 in 2010; Total roots and tubers 1,612 in 2008, 1,782 in 2009, 1,567 in 2010; Total vegetables (incl. melons) 13,728 in 2008, 14,467 in 2009, 13,499 in 2010; Total fruits (excl. melons) 17,267 in 2008, 18,363 in 2009, 16,908 in 2010.

Source: FAO.

LIVESTOCK
('000 head, year ending September)

	2008	2009	2010
Horses*	300	300	300
Asses*	24	24	24
Mules*	9	9	9
Cattle	6,283	6179	6,103
Buffaloes	294	307	344
Pigs	9,273	9,252	9,157
Sheep	8,237	8,175	8,013
Goats	920	957	961
Chickens*	115,000	120,000	130,000
Turkeys*	25,000	24,400	24,000

* FAO estimates.

Source: FAO.

LIVESTOCK PRODUCTS
('000 metric tons)

	2008	2009	2010
Cattle meat	1,057	1,049	1,069
Buffalo meat	2	6	6
Sheep meat	57	57	52
Pig meat	1,606	1,628	1,673
Horse meat	25	22	18
Chicken meat	790	822	865
Turkey meat	311	305	298
Rabbit meat†	240	248	255
Cows' milk	11,286	10,489	10,500
Buffaloes' milk	217	210†	210†
Sheep's milk	565	600	600†
Goats' milk	49	34	34†
Hen eggs†	750	813	737

* FAO estimate(s).

Source: FAO.

Forestry

ROUNDWOOD REMOVALS
('000 cubic metres, excl. bark)

	2008	2009	2010
Sawlogs, veneer logs and logs for sleepers	1,300	1,236	1,374
Pulpwood	643	594	369
Other industrial wood	1,050	898	672
Fuel wood	5,673	5,352	4,839
Total	8,667	8,080	7,254

SAWNWOOD PRODUCTION
('000 cubic metres, incl. railway sleepers)

	2008	2009	2010
Coniferous (softwood)	684	670	700
Broadleaved (hardwood)	700	550	500
Total	1,384	1,220	1,200

Source: FAO.

Fishing

('000 metric tons, live weight)

	2007	2008	2009
Capture	286.6	235.8	253.0
European hake	14.7	13.1	12.5
European anchovy	61.2	45.0	54.4
Striped venus	28.8	24.9	17.3
Aquaculture	179.0	149.0	162.3
Rainbow trout	37.8	34.1	35.8
Mediterranean mussel	58.5	67.2	76.8
Clams (Carpet shells)	61.8	28.6	32.8
Total catch	465.6	384.7	415.3

Note: Figures exclude aquatic plants (FAO estimates, all capture, '000 metric tons): 1.4 in 2007; 1.4 in 2008; 1.4 in 2009. Also excluded are aquatic mammals (recorded by number rather than weight) and corals. The number of whales and dolphins caught was: 7 in 2007; 9 in 2008; nil in 2009. Corals landed (metric tons): 6.3 in 2007; 7.3 in 2008; 9.8 in 2009.

Source: FAO.

Mining

('000 metric tons unless otherwise indicated)

	2002	2003	2004
Crude petroleum	5,394.2	5,529.9	5,406.7
Natural methane gas (million cu m)	14,941.5	13,735.1	12,915.1
Manganese (metric tons)	867	763	714
Lead (metric tons)*	4,709	4,017	1,226
Gold (kg)*†	600	500	100
Fluorspar (Fluorite)	53.3	26.4	17.9
Barite (Barytes)	10.2	12.2	9.6
Feldspar	3,159.6	2,972.2	2,941.3
Bentonite	463.2	474.5	437.7
Kaolin	175.0	224.8	246.6
Salt: Marine†‡	600	600	600
Salt (rock)	3,343.0	2,922.3	2,876.5
Loam (rock)	13,561.3	14,090.5	13,821.1
Gypsum	1,531.5	1,783.9	1,615.3
Pumice†§	600	600	600
Pozzolan†	4,000	4,000	4,000
Talc and steatite	125.0	122.8	138.4

* Metal content of ores and concentrates.

† Source: US Geological Survey.

‡ Excluding production from Sardinia and Sicily, estimated at 200,000 metric tons per year.

§ Including pumiceous lapilli.

2005 ('000 metric tons unless otherwise indicated): Natural methane gas (million cu m) 12,062; Gold (kg) 100; Salt 3,613; Pumice 28; Pozzolan 4,000 (estimate) (Source: US Geological Survey).

2006 ('000 metric tons unless otherwise indicated): Natural methane gas (million cu m) 10,986; Salt 3,438; Pumice 30 (estimate); Pozzolan 4,000 (estimate) (Source: US Geological Survey).

2007 ('000 metric tons unless otherwise indicated): Natural methane gas (million cu m) 9,713; Salt 2,214; Pumice 30 (estimate); Pozzolan 4,000 (estimate) (Source: US Geological Survey).

2008 ('000 metric tons unless otherwise indicated): Natural methane gas (million cu m) 9,260; Salt 2,200(estimate); Pumice 30 (estimate); Pozzolan 4,000 (estimate) (Source: US Geological Survey).

2009 ('000 metric tons unless otherwise indicated): Natural methane gas (million cu m) 8,127; Salt 3,471; Pumice 30 (estimate); Pozzolan 4,000 (estimate) (Source: US Geological Survey).

Industry

SELECTED PRODUCTS
('000 metric tons, unless otherwise indicated)

	2002	2003	2004
Wine (thousand hl)*	44,604.1	44,086.1	53,135.2
Cotton yarn	231.8	212.0	193.9
Cotton woven fabrics	209.8	197.1	186.9
Wood pulp, mechanical	309.2	341.4	364.8
Newsprint†	175.1	182.0	193.0
Magazine print	780.0	830.0	945.1
Other printing and writing paper	2,104.5	2,091.2	2,164.7
Washing powders and detergents	1,982.0	2,123.8	2,174.5
Jet fuels	2,458.8	2,626.8	2,550.9
Benzene	20,999.1	20,759.4	n.a.
Motor gasoline	37,297.0	38,349.5	38,025.0
Naphthas	3,243.3	4,287.7	3,938.8
Gas-diesel oil	12,286.3	12,166.5	13,278.2
Bitumen	2,942.3	3,274.8	3,496.3
Coke	3,973.9	3,663.1	3,964.6
Tyres for road motor vehicles	258.6	265.4	278.9
Glass bottles and other containers of common glass	2,939.8	3,139.5	3,171.1
Cement	41,722.3	43,580.0	45,342.9
Steel	26,301.4	26,832.1	28,385.4
Rolled iron	24,165.6	25,608.6	28,710.6

—*continued*	2002	2003	2004
Other iron and steel-finished manufactures	3,260.2	3,133.9	3,164.8
Refrigerators for household use ('000 units)	7,088.8	6,715.3	6,444.1
Washing machines for household use ('000 units)	8,884.0	9,666.8	9,679.9
Passenger motor cars ('000 units)	1,125.8	1,026.5	839.2
Lorries (Trucks) ('000 units)	266.4	267.4	283.9
Motorcycles, scooters, etc. ('000 units)	588.9	572.5	622.3
Bicycles ('000 units)	597.7	581.6	501.5
Hydroelectric power (million kWh)‡	47,262	44,277	n.a.
Thermoelectric power (million kWh)‡	231,069	242,784	n.a.
Other electric power (million kWh)‡	6,066	6,799	n.a.

* Provisional data.
† Source: FAO.
‡ Net production.

2005 ('000 metric tons): Newsprint 191.2; Mechanical wood pulp 376.5; Other printing and writing paper 3,279 (Source: FAO); Crude steel 29,061; Cement 40,284 (Source: US Geological Survey).

2006 ('000 metric tons): Newsprint 218.7; Mechanical wood pulp 347.6; Other printing and writing paper 3,162 (Source: FAO); Crude steel 31,624; Cement 43,234 (Source: US Geological Survey).

2007 ('000 metric tons): Newsprint 198.4; Mechanical wood pulp 333.4; Other printing and writing paper 3,260 (Source: FAO); Crude steel 31,990; Cement 47,541 (Source: US Geological Survey).

2008 ('000 metric tons): Newsprint 221.3; Mechanical wood pulp 325.5; Other printing and writing paper 3,006 (Source: FAO); Crude steel 30,600; Cement 43,000 (Source: US Geological Survey).

2009 ('000 metric tons): Newsprint 211.3; Mechanical wood pulp 259.9; Other printing and writing paper 2,635 (Source: FAO); Crude steel 19,848; Cement 36,317 (Source: US Geological Survey).

2010 ('000 metric tons): Newsprint 181.3; Mechanical wood pulp 277.5; Other printing and writing paper 2,852 (Source: FAO).

Electrical energy (million kWh, including San Marino): 303,699 in 2005; 314,121 in 2006; 313,888 in 2007.

Finance

CURRENCY AND EXCHANGE RATES

Monetary Units
100 cent = 1 euro (€).

Sterling, Dollar and Euro Equivalents (30 December 2011)
£1 sterling = 1.195 euros;
US $1 = 0.773 euros;
€10 = £8.37 = $12.94.

Average Exchange Rate (euros per US $)
2009 0.7198
2010 0.7550
2011 0.7194

Note: The national currency was formerly the Italian lira (plural: lire). From the introduction of the euro, with Italian participation, on 1 January 1999, a fixed exchange rate of €1 = 1,936.27 lire was in operation. Euro notes and coins were introduced on 1 January 2002. The euro and local currency circulated alongside each other until 28 February, after which the euro became the sole legal tender.

STATE BUDGET
(€ million, consolidated account)

Revenue	2007	2008	2009
Direct taxation	233,170	239,740	222,655
Indirect taxation	227,103	216,009	206,956
Social security contributions	205,259	215,911	215,003
Other current revenue*	54,350	56,695	57,341
Capital revenue	3,534	3,706	16,099
Total	724,416	732,061	718,054

Expenditure	2007	2008	2009
Public services	304,181	317,281	327,814
General administration	42,758	43,437	45,167
Defence	20,476	22,311	24,152
Public order and safety	26,858	28,316	29,199
Economic affairs	20,542	21,618	22,247
Environmental protection	4,406	4,720	4,921
Housing and community amenities	6,363	6,834	7,018
Health	100,559	107,321	109,560
Recreation, culture and religion	6,580	6,806	7,047
Education	62,460	61,892	63,805
Social protection	13,179	14,026	14,698
Interest payments	77,126	81,161	71,288
Social security and assistance contributions	265,316	278,148	292,284
Other current expenditure	38,468	39,678	41,698
Capital expenditure	62,516	58,368	65,770
Total	747,607	774,636	798,854

* Including foreign aid (€ million): 1,103 in 2007; 969 in 2008; 1,664 in 2009.

INTERNATIONAL RESERVES
(US $ million at 31 December)

	2008	2009	2010
Gold (Eurosystem valuation)	68,187	87,027	111,169
IMF special drawing rights	261	9,414	9,549
Reserve position in IMF	1,520	1,835	2,457
Foreign exchange	35,306	34,521	35,678
Total	105,274	132,797	158,853

Source: IMF, *International Financial Statistics*.

MONEY SUPPLY
(incl. shares, depository corporations, national residency criteria, € '000 million at 31 December)

	2008	2009	2010
Currency issued	129.79	136.61	142.32
Banca d'Italia	129.79	136.61	142.32
Demand deposits	692.60	769.84	757.75
Other deposits	421.82	415.46	642.23
Securities other than shares	740.52	819.60	807.08
Money market fund shares	57.67	54.96	38.41
Shares and other equity	332.82	365.13	442.53
Other items (net)	–263.30	–314.80	–343.87
Total	2,111.92	2,246.79	2,486.44

Source: IMF, *International Financial Statistics*.

COST OF LIVING
(Consumer Price Index; base: 1995 = 100)

	2008	2009	2010
Food (incl. non-alcoholic beverages)	134.8	137.2	137.5
Alcohol and tobacco	174.6	181.2	186.3
Rent and utilities	156.8	156.7	158.6
Clothing (incl. footwear)	135.0	136.7	138.0
Household goods	131.6	134.0	135.5
Health services	121.7	122.4	122.8
Transport	144.9	141.7	147.6
Communications	68.7	68.5	67.9
Recreation, entertainment and culture	122.5	123.2	124.0
Education	139.8	142.9	146.5
Hotels, restaurants and public services	149.8	151.6	154.0
All items (incl. others)	136.6	137.7	139.8

2011 (base: 2010 = 100): Food (incl. non-alcoholic beverages) 102.4; Alcohol and tobacco 103.5; Rent and utilities 105.1; Clothing (incl. footwear) 101.7; Household goods 101.7; Health services 100.5; Transport 106.2; Communications 98.8; Recreation, entertainment and culture 100.3; Education 102.3; Hotels, restaurants and public services 102.2; All items (incl. others) 102.8.

NATIONAL ACCOUNTS

(€ million at current prices)

National Income and Product

	2008	2009	2010
Compensation of employees	658,042	651,015	656,273
Operating surplus and mixed income (net)	462,989	430,796	437,300
Domestic factor incomes	1,121,031	1,081,811	1,093,573
Consumption of fixed capital	254,177	258,617	264,062
Gross domestic product (GDP) at factor cost	1,375,208	1,340,428	1,357,635
Taxes on production and imports	220,960	209,955	220,417
Less Subsidies	21,024	23,593	22,023
GDP in market prices	1,575,144	1,526,790	1,556,029
Net primary income received from abroad	–17,185	–7,012	–7,246
Gross national product	1,557,960	1,519,778	1,548,782
Less Consumption of fixed capital	254,177	258,617	264,062
Net national income	1,303,783	1,261,161	1,284,720
Net current transfers from abroad	–14,934	–14,997	–16,785
Net national disposable income	1,288,848	1,246,164	1,267,935

Expenditure on the Gross Domestic Product

	2008	2009	2010
Final consumption expenditure	1,247,413	1,242,313	1,268,373
Households	925,991	911,097	934,293
Non-profit institutions serving households	6,017	6,227	6,420
General government	315,406	324,989	327,660
Gross capital formation	340,837	292,543	317,368
Changes in inventories	8,006	–4,119	9,105
Acquisitions, less disposals, of valuables	2,182	1,981	2,365
Gross fixed capital formation	330,649	294,681	305,899
Total domestic expenditure	1,588,250	1,534,856	1,585,741
Exports of goods and services	448,227	360,881	414,794
Less Imports of goods and services	461,333	368,946	444,507
GDP in market prices	1,575,144	1,526,790	1,556,029
GDP at constant 2005 prices	1,475,412	1,400,894	1,422,432

Gross Domestic Product by Economic Activity

	2008	2009	2010
Agriculture, hunting, forestry and fishing	28,851	26,180	26,698
Mining and quarrying	5,593	4,969	5,158
Manufacturing	249,873	216,586	223,863
Construction	90,253	87,982	85,201
Electricity, gas and water	33,002	32,829	32,871
Wholesale and retail trade; repair of motor vehicles, motorcycles and personal and household goods	154,180	147,625	150,740
Hotels and restaurants	57,080	57,149	57,176
Transport, storage and communications	139,367	135,810	136,186
Financial intermediation	75,595	71,704	72,941
Real estate, renting and business activities	303,023	308,345	313,011
Public administration and defence; compulsory social security	91,917	93,572	94,554
Education	63,859	65,827	65,854
Health and social work	77,701	78,559	81,285
Other community, social and personal service activities	32,550	33,429	34,035
Private households with employed persons	14,654	15,468	15,644
Gross value added in basic prices	1,417,500	1,376,034	1,395,219
Net taxes on products	157,644	150,756	160,810
GDP in market prices	1,575,144	1,526,790	1,556,029

BALANCE OF PAYMENTS

(US $ million)

	2008	2009	2010
Exports of goods f.o.b.	545,081	407,456	448,374
Imports of goods f.o.b.	–547,921	–405,998	–475,652
Trade balance	–2,841	1,458	–27,278
Exports of services	116,261	94,885	98,575
Imports of services	–128,825	–106,363	–110,758
Balance on goods and services	–15,405	–10,020	–39,461
Other income received	103,496	80,392	74,100
Other income paid	–132,136	–94,644	–85,509
Balance on goods, services and income	–44,045	–24,272	–50,871
Current transfers received	28,993	29,172	24,690
Current transfers paid	–51,200	–45,903	–45,835
Current balance	–66,252	–41,004	–72,015
Capital account (net)	–350	–52	–737
Direct investment abroad	–69,520	–19,760	–32,601
Direct investment from abroad	–9,488	16,572	9,594
Portfolio investment assets	95,626	–55,944	–43,163
Portfolio investment liabilities	11,237	88,664	94,026
Financial derivatives assets	–3,513	12,161	6,939
Financial derivatives liabilities	6,071	–6,370	–13,596
Other investment assets	37,423	58,962	64,899
Other investment liabilities	–14,008	–38,239	29,312
Net errors and omissions	20,978	–5,986	–41,319
Overall balance	8,204	9,003	1,338

Source: IMF, *International Financial Statistics*.

External Trade

Note: Figures refer to the trade of Italy, San Marino and the Vatican City.

PRINCIPAL COMMODITIES

(€ million)

Imports c.i.f.	2008	2009	2010
Agriculture and fishing	10,874	9,706	11,107
Food, beverages and tobacco	24,343	22,653	25,259
Crude petroleum	40,029	24,067	34,746
Natural gas	22,815	17,462	19,731
Textiles, clothing, leather and leather products	24,718	21,842	25,816
Wood and wood products; paper and paper products, printing and publishing	9,897	7,952	9,982
Refined oil products	8,442	5,841	8,549
Chemicals and man-made fibres	46,862	41,912	49,385
Rubber, plastics and non-metal mineral ore products	10,999	9,367	11,295
Metals and metal products	44,407	24,704	36,069
Machinery and mechanical equipment	26,806	18,866	22,373
Electric and precision instruments	37,337	33,348	45,842
Transportation means	44,316	35,464	37,754
Total (incl. others)	382,050	297,609	367,122

Exports f.o.b.	2008	2009	2010
Agriculture and fishing	5,354	4,614	5,598
Food, beverages and tobacco	20,907	20,031	22,168
Textiles, clothing, leather and leather products	40,912	33,093	37,277
Wood and wood products; paper and paper products, printing and publishing	7,136	6,157	7,144

Exports f.o.b.—*continued*	2008	2009	2010
Refined oil products	15,440	9,301	14,703
Chemicals and man-made fibres	34,155	30,007	36,504
Rubber, plastics and non-metal mineral ore manufactures	22,435	18,208	20,823
Metals and metal products	45,342	32,273	39,324
Machinery and mechanical equipment	71,024	55,014	60,040
Electric and precision instruments	33,194	26,911	30,938
Transportation means	39,422	29,501	34,433
Total (incl. others)	369,016	291,733	337,810

PRINCIPAL TRADING PARTNERS
(€ million)*

Imports c.i.f.	2008	2009	2010
Austria	8,999	7,189	9,054
China, People's Republic	23,606	19,334	28,790
France	32,873	26,353	30,527
Germany	61,186	49,701	58,531
Japan	5,018	3,899	4,288
Netherlands	20,519	16,918	19,611
Russia	16,089	12,142	13,053
Spain	16,633	13,141	16,660
United Kingdom	11,897	9,817	12,147
USA	11,683	9,463	11,140
Total (incl. others)	382,050	297,609	367,122

Exports f.o.b.	2008	2009	2010
Austria	8,803	6,961	8,069
Belgium	9,931	8,032	8,665
China, People's Republic	6,432	6,629	8,610
France	41,459	33,984	39,079
Germany	47,110	36,942	43,897
Japan	4,251	3,714	4,032
Netherlands	8,678	7,111	8,359
Poland	9,774	7,922	8,542
Russia	10,468	6,432	7,908
Spain	24,123	16,680	19,581
United Kingdom	19,327	14,953	18,068
USA	23,028	17,099	20,333
Total (incl. others)	369,016	291,733	337,810

* Imports by country of production; exports by country of consignment.

Transport

STATE RAILWAYS
(traffic)

	2005	2006	2007
Passenger journeys (million)	516.8	540.3	557.9
Passenger-km (million)	46,144	46,439	45,985
Freight carried ('000 metric tons)	89,755	102,169	105,314
Freight ton-km (million)	22,761	24,151	25,285

ROAD TRAFFIC
(vehicles in use at 31 December)

	2002	2003	2004
Passenger motor cars	33,706,153	34,310,446	33,973,147
Buses and coaches	91,716	92,701	92,874
Trucks (lorries)	3,751,699	3,933,930	4,015,612
Tractors	132,622	139,402	142,413
Motorcycles (incl. sidecars)	4,405,867	4,746,698	4,917,383

2008 (motor vehicles in use): Passenger cars 35,673,416; Buses 99,750; Lorries and vans 4,467,476; Motorcycles 6,015,606 (Source: IRF, *World Road Statistics*).

2009 (motor vehicles in use): Passenger cars 35,871,854; Buses 98,244; Lorries and vans 4,505,348; Motorcycles 6,309,992 (Source: IRF, *World Road Statistics*).

SHIPPING

Merchant Fleet
(registered at 31 December)

	2007	2008	2009
Number of vessels	1,564	1,588	1,635
Displacement ('000 grt)	12,972	13,600	15,531

Source: IHS Fairplay, *World Fleet Statistics*.

International Sea-borne Traffic

	2002	2003	2004
Goods loaded ('000 metric tons)	73,402	74,479	79,222
Goods unloaded ('000 metric tons)	260,986	266,914	270,811
Passengers embarked ('000)	2,841	2,863	3,041
Passengers disembarked ('000)	2,873	2,831	3,187

Source: Ministry of Transport.

CIVIL AVIATION
(traffic on scheduled and charter services)

	2002	2003	2004
Passengers carried ('000):			
domestic	45,221	49,145	49,026
international	45,777	50,587	57,963
Freight carried ('000 metric tons):*			
domestic	165.5	164.4	135.5
international	570.2	598.8	684.6

* Includes mail.

2006 (traffic on scheduled and charter services, '000): Passengers carried 110,070 (domestic 49,104, international 60,966).

Source: Ministry of Transport.

Tourism

TOURIST ARRIVALS BY COUNTRY OF ORIGIN
(arrivals in registered accommodation establishments)

	2007	2008	2009
Austria	1,833,428	1,774,887	1,948,791
Belgium	916,711	943,350	994,999
France	3,245,682	3,215,689	3,332,807
Germany	8,943,586	8,674,799	9,085,679
Japan	1,474,014	1,307,729	1,298,068
Netherlands	1,682,377	1,792,595	1,836,907
Poland	703,250	840,259	811,024
Russia	954,345	1,046,199	894,659
Spain	1,976,899	1,819,854	1,760,924
Switzerland-Liechtenstein	1,648,892	1,601,515	1,717,083
United Kingdom	3,305,568	3,085,321	2,684,392
USA	4,996,537	4,233,647	3,928,677
Total (incl. others)	42,873,122	41,796,724	41,124,722

Source: mostly World Tourism Organization.

Tourism receipts (US $ million, incl. passenger transport): 46,144 in 2007; 48,757 in 2008; 41,872 in 2009 (Source: World Tourism Organization).

Tourist beds: 4,498,910 in 2006; 4,485,581 in 2007; 4,649,050 in 2008; 4,598,682 in 2009.

Communications Media

	2008	2009	2010
Telephones ('000 main lines in use)	22,039	21,683	21,477
Mobile cellular telephones ('000 in use)	90,341	88,024	90,605
Internet subscribers ('000)	11,283	12,300	13,400
Broadband subscribers ('000)	11,276.3	12,283.4	13,259.4

Personal computers: 21,486,000 (366.6 per 1,000 persons) in 2005.

Book production (number of titles, first editions): 34,496 in 2003.

Television receivers ('000 in use): 28,300 in 2000.

Radio receivers ('000 in use): 50,500 in 1997.

Daily newspapers (2004): Titles 96; Average circulation 8,017,000.

Non-daily newspapers (1995): Titles 274; Average circulation 2,132,000.

Sources: mainly UNESCO Institute for Statistics; UN, *Statistical Yearbook*; International Telecommunication Union.

Education

(state education, 2007/08, unless otherwise indicated)

	Schools	Teachers	Students
Pre-primary	13,629	83,586	975,757
Primary	16,018	245,727	2,579,938
Secondary:			
Scuola Media	7,104	163,159	1,625,651
Scuola Secondaria Superiore	5,128	230,881	2,570,010
of which:			
Technical	1,802	78,411	870,708
Professional	1,425	43,950	540,794
Art Licei and institutes	271	9,261	96,812
Classical, linguistic and scientific Licei	1,630	70,040	1,061,696
Higher*	74	61,929	1,820,221†‡

* Includes private institutions.

† Undergraduates only.

‡ 2006/07 figure.

Source: Ufficio di Statistica, Ministero dell'Istruzione, dell'Università e della Ricerca.

Pupil-teacher ratio (primary education, UNESCO estimate): 10.3 in 2006/07 (Source: UNESCO Institute for Statistics).

Adult literacy rate (UNESCO estimates): 98.9% (males 99.2%; females 98.6%) in 2009 (Source: UNESCO Institute for Statistics).

Directory

The Government

HEAD OF STATE

President of the Republic: GIORGIO NAPOLITANO (took office 15 May 2006).

COUNCIL OF MINISTERS
(May 2012)

On 12 November 2011 Silvio Berlusconi resigned as Prime Minister. The following day the President requested the former European Commissioner Mario Monti to form a government of technocrats.

Prime Minister and Minister of the Economy: MARIO MONTI.

Minister of Foreign Affairs: GIULIO TERZI DI SANTAGATA.

Minister of the Interior: ANNA MARIA CANCELLIERI.

Minister of Justice: PAOLA SEVERINO.

Minister of Defence: GIAMPAOLO DI PAOLA.

Minister of Industry, Infrastructure and Transport: CORRADO PASSERA.

Minister of Agricultural, Food and Forestry Policies: MARIO CATANIA.

Minister of the Environment: CORRADO CLINI.

Minister of Labour, Social Policy and Equal Opportunity: ELSA FORNERO.

Minister of Health: RENATO BALDUZZI.

Minister of Education, Universities and Research: FRANCESCO PROFUMO.

Minister of Culture: LORENZO ORNAGHI.

Minister of European Affairs: ENZO MOAVERO MILANESI.

Minister of Regional Affairs, Tourism and Sport: PIERO GNUDI.

Minister of Regional Relations: FABRIZIO BARCA.

Minister of Relations with Parliament: PIERO GIARDA.

Minister of International Co-operation: ANDREA RICCARDI.

Minister for Public Administration and Legislative Simplification: FILIPPO PATRONI GRIFFI.

MINISTRIES

Office of the President: Palazzo del Quirinale, 00187 Roma; tel. (06) 46991; fax (06) 46993125; internet www.quirinale.it.

Office of the Prime Minister: Palazzo Chigi, Piazza Colonna 370, 00187 Roma; tel. (06) 67791; internet www.governo.it.

Ministry of Agricultural, Food and Forestry Policies: Via XX Settembre 20, 00187 Roma; tel. (06) 46651; fax (06) 4742314; e-mail urp@pec.politicheagricole.gov.it; internet www.politicheagricole.gov.it.

Ministry of Cultural Assets and Activities: Via del Collegio Romano 27, 00186 Roma; tel. (06) 67231; fax (06) 6798441; e-mail urp@beniculturali.it; internet www.beniculturali.it.

Ministry of Defence: Palazzo Baracchini, Via XX Settembre 8, 00187 Roma; tel. (06) 46911; internet www.difesa.it.

Ministry of Economic Development: Via Molise 2, 00187 Roma; tel. (06) 420434000; fax (06) 47887770; e-mail segreteria.ministro@sviluppoeconomico.gov.it; internet www.sviluppoeconomico.gov.it.

Ministry of the Economy and Finance: Via XX Settembre 97, 00187 Roma; tel. (06) 476111; fax (06) 5910993; e-mail ufficio.stampa@tesoro.it; internet www.mef.gov.it.

Ministry of Education, Universities and Research: Piazzale Kennedy 20, 00144 Roma; tel. (06) 97726077; fax (06) 97727351; e-mail urp@miur.it; internet www.miur.it.

Ministry of the Environment, Land Management and the Sea: Via Cristoforo Colombo 44, 00147 Roma; tel. (06) 57221; fax (06) 5728513; e-mail segr.ufficiostampa@minambiente.it; internet www.minambiente.it.

Ministry of Foreign Affairs: Piazzale della Farnesina 1, 00194 Roma; tel. (06) 36911; fax (06) 36918899; e-mail relazioni.pubblico@esteri.it; internet www.esteri.it.

Ministry of Health: Viale Giorgio Ribotta 5, 00144 Roma; tel. (06) 59941; fax (06) 59942376; e-mail urpminsalute@sanita.it; internet www.salute.gov.it.

Ministry of Infrastructure and Transport: Piazzale Porta Pia 1, 00198 Roma; tel. (06) 44121; fax (06) 44123205; e-mail ufficio.stampa@mit.gov.it; internet www.mit.gov.it.

Ministry of the Interior: Piazzale del Viminale, Via Agostino Depretis 7, 00184 Roma; tel. (06) 4651; fax (06) 46549599; e-mail segreteriaufficiostampa@interno.it; internet www.interno.it.

Ministry of Justice: Via Arenula 71, 00186 Roma; tel. (06) 68851; fax (06) 68891493; e-mail ufficio.stampa@giustizia.it; internet www.giustizia.it.

Ministry of Labour and Social Policies: Via Veneto 56, 00187 Roma; tel. (06) 59941; fax (06) 59945320; e-mail ufficiostampa@lavoro.gov.it; internet www.lavoro.gov.it.

President

The President of the Republic is elected by the members of both parliamentary chambers, in addition to representations (Grand Electors) of each administrative region, and is required to receive the support of at least two-thirds of the votes cast in the first three rounds of voting, or a simple majority thereafter. GIORGIO NAPOLITANO was elected President in a fourth round of voting conducted on 10 May 2006, receiving 543 votes (from 1,000 voters present at the session).

Legislature

PARLIAMENT
(Parlamento)

Chamber of Deputies
(Camera dei Deputati)

Palazzo di Montecitorio, Piazza Montecitorio, 00186 Roma; tel. (06) 67601; e-mail dlwebmast@camera.it; internet www.camera.it.

President: GIANFRANCO FINI.

General Election, 13 and 14 April 2008

Parties/Alliances	Total seats
Popolo della Libertà*	276
Partito Democratico†	217
Lega Nord*	60
Unione di Centro (UdC)	36
Italia dei Valori—Lista Di Pietro†	29
Movimento per l'Autonomia*	8
Südtiroler Volkspartei	2
Autonomie Liberté Démocratie	1
Movimento Associativo Italiani all'Estero	1
Total	630

*The Popolo della Libertà coalition, the Lega Nord and the Movimento per l'Autonomia contested the election in alliance.
†The Partito Democratico and Italia dei Valori—Lista Di Pietro contested the election in alliance.

Senate
(Senato)

Piazza Madama, 00186 Roma; tel. (06) 67061; e-mail infopoint@senato.it; internet www.senato.it.

President: RENATO SCHIFANI.

General Election, 13 and 14 April 2008

Parties/Alliances	Elective seats
Popolo della Libertà*	147
Partito Democratico†	118
Lega Nord*	25
Italia dei Valori—Lista Di Pietro†	14
Unione di Centro (UdC)	3
Movimento per l'Autonomia*	2
Südtiroler Volkspartei (SVP)	2
SVP—Insieme per le Autonomie	2
Vallée d'Aoste	1
Movimento Associativo Italiani all'Estero	1
Total‡	315

*The Popolo della Libertà coalition, the Lega Nord and the Movimento per l'Autonomia contested the election in alliance.
†The Partito Democratico and Italia dei Valori—Lista Di Pietro contested the election in alliance.
‡In addition to the 315 elected members, there are seven life members.

Political Organizations

NATIONAL PARTIES AND COALITIONS

Alleanza per l'Italia (ApL) (Alliance for Italy): Largo Fontanella Borghese 84, 00186 Roma; tel. (06) 91712000; fax (06) 68802560; e-mail info@alleanzaperlitalia.it; internet www.alleanzaperlitalia.it; f. 2009; Pres. FRANCESCO RUTELLI; Co-ordinator LORENZO DELLAI.

Federazione dei Liberali Italiani (Federation of Italian Liberals): Studio Sgobbo, Corso Trieste 61, 00198 Roma; tel. (06) 8418007; fax (06) 8416975; e-mail info@liberali.it; internet www.liberali.it; f. 1994; Pres. RAFFAELLO MORELLI.

Federazione dei Verdi (I Verdi) (Green Party): Via Antonio Salandra 6, 00187 Roma; tel. (06) 4203061; fax (06) 42004600; e-mail federazione@verdi.it; internet www.verdi.it; f. 1986; advocates environmentalist and anti-nuclear policies; branch of the European Green movement; Pres. ANGELO BONELLI.

Futuro e Libertà per l'Italia (FLI) (Future and Freedom for Italy): Via Poli 29, 00187 Roma; tel. (06) 69773701; internet www.futuroeliberta.it; f. 2011; liberal; Pres. GIANFRANCO FINI; Nat. Co-ordinator ROBERTO MENIA.

Italia dei Valori—Lista Di Pietro (IdV) (Italy of Principals—Di Pietro List): Via Santa Maria in Via 12, 00187 Roma; tel. (06) 97848144; fax (06) 97848355; e-mail info@italiadeivalori.it; internet www.italiadeivalori.it; anti-corruption; Pres. ANTONIO DI PIETRO.

Liberal Democratici (LD) (Liberal Democrats): Largo della Fontanella di Borghese 84, 00186 Roma; tel. (06) 68808380; fax (06) 68808500; e-mail liberal-democratici@libero.it; internet www.liberal-democratici.it; f. 2007; liberal centrist; Pres. DANIELA MELCHIORRE; Co-ordinator ITALO TANONI.

Lista Consumatori (Consumers' List): Via Tagliamento 3, Ardea, 00040 Roma; tel. (06) 23328286; e-mail info@listaconsumatori.it; internet www.listaconsumatori.it; f. 2004; Pres. RENATO CAMPIGLIA; Nat. Sec. DAVID BADINI.

Movimento Cristiano-Sociali (Christian-Social Movement): Lungotevere dei Mellini 7, 00193 Roma; tel. (06) 3210694; fax (06) 68300539; e-mail info@cristianosociali.it; internet www.cristianosociali.it; f. 1993; Pres. MIMMO LUCÀ.

Movimento Sociale—Fiamma Tricolore (Tricolour Flame): Via Flaminia Vecchia 732I, 00191 Rome; tel. (06) 33221128; fax (06) 33972829; e-mail info@fiammatricolore.com; internet www.fiammatricolore.com; f. 1996; electoral alliance incorporating fmr mems of neo-fascist Movimento Sociale Italiano-Destra Nazionale; Nat. Sec. LUCA ROMAGNOLI.

Partito dei Comunisti Italiani (PdCI) (Party of Italian Communists): Piazza Augusto Imperatore 32, 00186 Roma; tel. (06) 686271; fax (06) 68627230; e-mail direzionenazionale@comunisti-italiani.org; internet www.comunisti-italiani.it; f. 1998; Chair. ANTONINO CUFFARO; Gen. Sec. OLIVIERO DILIBERTO.

Partito Democratico (PD): Piazza Sant'Anastasia 7, 00187 Roma; tel. (06) 675471; fax (06) 67547319; e-mail info@partitodemocratico.it; internet www.partitodemocratico.it; f. 2007 by merger of Democratici di Sinistra, Democrazia è Libertà—La Margherita and other left-wing and centrist parties that had formed part of L'Unione; centre-left; Pres. ROSY BINDI; Nat. Sec. PIER LUIGI BERSANI.

Partito Liberale Italiano (PLI) (Italian Liberal Party): Via Uffici del Vicario 43, 2°, 00186 Rome; tel. (06) 45505081; e-mail segretaria@partitoliberale.it; internet www.partitoliberale.it; Pres. ENZO PALUMBO; Nat. Sec. STEFANO DE LUCA.

Partito Repubblicano Italiano (PRI) (Italian Republican Party): Corso Vittorio Emanuele II 326, 00186 Roma; tel. (06) 6865824; e-mail info@pri.it; internet www.pri.it; Nat. Sec. FRANCESCO NUCARA.

Partito della Rifondazione Comunista (PRC) (Party of Communist Refoundation): Viale del Policlinico 131, 00161 Roma; tel. (06) 441821; fax (06) 44182286; e-mail sitoprc@rifondazione.it; internet www.rifondazione.it; f. 1991 by fmr mems of the Partito Comunista Italiano (Italian Communist Party); Nat. Sec. PAOLO FERRERO.

Partito Socialista (Socialist Party): Piazza S. Lorenzo in Lucina 26, 00186 Roma; tel. (06) 6878688; fax (06) 68307659; e-mail info@partitosocialista.it; internet www.partitosocialista.it; f. 2007 by fmr leadership of Socialisti Democratici Italiani; Nat. Sec. RICCARDO NENCINI.

Patto—Partito dei Liberaldemocratici (The Pact—Liberal Democratic Party): Via Vittorio Veneto 169, 00187 Roma; tel. and fax (06) 4744916; e-mail info@ilpatto.it; internet www.ilpatto.it; f. 1993 as Patto Segni; liberal party, advocating institutional reform; Nat. Sec. Prof. MARIO SEGNI.

Popolari—UDEUR (Alleanza Popolare—Unione Democratici per l'Europa) (Union of Democrats for Europe): Via Dandolo 24, 00153 Roma; tel. (06) 58300; fax (06) 5881538; e-mail info@popolariudeur.it; internet www.popolariudeur.it; f. 1999; Sec. CLEMENTE MASTELLA.

Popolo della Libertà (PdL) (People of Freedom): Via dell'Umiltà 36, 00187 Roma; internet www.ilpopolodellaliberta.it; f. 2009 by merger of Forza Italia, Alleanza Nazionale, Nuovo Partito Socialista Italiano, Partito Repubblicano Italiano, Democrazia Cristiana per le Autonomie, Popolari Liberali, Riformatori Liberali, Azione Sociale and Partito Pensionati; fmrly electoral coalition, contested April 2008 general election in alliance with the Lega Nord and the Movimento per l'Autonomia; Pres. SILVIO BERLUSCONI.

Radicali Italiani: Via di Torre Argentina 76, 00186 Roma; tel. (06) 689791; fax (06) 68805396; e-mail segreteria.roma@radicali.it; internet www.radicali.it; f. 2001 as Partito Radicale; Pres. SILVIO VIALE; Gen. Sec. MARIO STADERINI.

Sinistra Ecologia Libertà (SEL) (Left Ecology Freedom): Via Goito 39, 00185 Roma; tel. (06) 44700403; fax (06) 4455832; e-mail redazione@sxmail.it; internet www.sinistraecologialiberta.it; f. 2010; socialist party advocating social progressivism; Pres. NICHI VENDOLA.

Unione dei Democratici Cristiani e di Centro (UDC) (Union of Christian and Centre Democrats): Via dei Due Macelli 66, 00182 Roma; tel. (06) 69791001; fax (06) 6791574; e-mail info@udc-italia.it; internet www.udc-italia.it; f. 2002 from merger of Centro Cristiano Democratico (f. 1994) and Cristiani Democratici Uniti (f. 1995 after split from Partito Popolare Italiano); mem. of Unione di Centro; Nat. Sec. LORENZO CESA; Pres. ROCCO BUTTIGLIONE.

Unione di Centro (UdC) (Union of the Centre): Via dei Due Macelli 66, 00182 Roma; tel. (06) 69791001; fax (06) 6791574; f. 2008; coalition includes Unione dei Democratici Cristiani e di Centro and Rosa Bianca; Leader PIER FERDINANDO CASINI.

Political organizations for Italians abroad include the **Associazioni Italiane in Sud America**, **Alternativa Indipendente Italiani all'Estero (AIIE)**, the **Movimento Associativo Italiani all'Estero**, the **Partito degli Italiani nel Mondo** and the **Unione Sudamericana Emigranti Italiani**.

REGIONAL PARTIES AND COALITIONS

Autonomie Liberté Démocratie (ALD) (Autonomy Liberty Democracy): f. 2006; coalition of parties active in the Aosta valley.

Lega Nord per l'Indipendenza della Padania (LN) (Northern League for the Independence of Padania): Via Carlo Bellerio 41, 20161 Milano; tel. (02) 662341; fax (02) 6454475; e-mail webmaster@leganord.org; internet www.leganord.org; f. 1991; advocates federalism and transfer of control of resources to regional govts; in 1996 declared the 'Independent Republic of Padania'; opposes immigration; Pres. ANGELO ALESSANDRI; Sec. (vacant).

Liga Veneta Repubblica (Venetian Republic League): Via Antonio Provolo 2B, 37060 Verona; tel. and fax (045) 8014404; e-mail info@ligavenetarepubblica.org; internet www.ligavenetarepubblica.org; f. 2001 by merger of Liga Veneta Repubblica—Veneti d'Europa and Fronte Marco Polo; advocates independence for Veneto region; Pres. GIAN PIETRO PIOTTO; Gen. Sec. FABRIZIO COMENCINI.

Movimento per l'Autonomia (MPA) (Autonomy Movement): Via dell'Oca 27, Roma; tel. (06) 3220836; fax (06) 32647632; e-mail info@mpa-italia.it; internet www.mpa-italia.it; pro-regional autonomy in the south; Fed. Sec. RAFFAELE LOMBARDO.

Partito Autonomista Trentino Tirolese (PATT) (Autonomist Party of Trento and the Tyrol): Corso 3 Novembre, 72/A, 38100 Trento; tel. (0461) 391399; fax (0461) 394940; e-mail info@patt.tn.it; internet www.patt.tn.it; advocates autonomy for South Tyrol region; Pres. WALTER KASWALDER; Pol Sec. UGO ROSSI.

Partitu Sardu—Partito Sardo d'Azione (Sardinian Action Party): Piazza Repubblica 18, 09125 Cagliari; tel. and fax (070) 3481434; e-mail info@partitosardo.eu; internet www.partitosardo.it; Pres. GIACOMO SANNA; Nat. Sec. COLLI GIOVANNI ANGELO.

Südtiroler Volkspartei (SVP) (South Tyrol People's Party): Brennerstr. 7A, 39100 Bozen/Bolzano; tel. (0471) 304040; fax (0471) 981473; e-mail info@svpartei.org; internet www.svpartei.org; regional party of the German and Ladin-speaking people in the South Tyrol; Pres. RICHARD THEINER; Gen. Sec. PHILIPP ACHAMMER.

Union Autonomista Ladina (Autonomist Ladin Movement): Strada Dolomites 111, 38036 Pozza di Fassa; tel. and fax (0462) 763396; e-mail ualdefascia@virgilio.it; internet www.movimentual.it; Pres. MICHELE ANESI; Pol. Sec. LUIGI CHIOCCHETTI.

Union Valdôtaine (Aosta Valley Union): Ave des Maquisards 29, 11100 Aosta; tel. (0165) 235181; fax (0165) 364289; e-mail siegecentral@unionvaldotaine.org; internet www.unionvaldotaine.org; f. 1945; promotes interests of the Aosta valley; Pres EGO PERRON.

Other regional parties and coalitions include the **Alleanza Lombarda**, **Die Freiheitlichen** (South Tyrol), the **Federazione per l'Autodeterminazione della Sicilia-Noi Siciliani**, **iRS—indipendèntzia Repùbrica de Sardigna**, the **Movimento Triveneto**, **Nuova Sicilia**, **Per il Sud**, **Progetto Nordest** and **Sardigna Natzione Indipendentzia**.

Diplomatic Representation

EMBASSIES IN ITALY

Afghanistan: Via Nomentana 120, 00161 Roma; tel. (06) 8611009; fax (06) 86322939; e-mail info@afghanistanembassyitaly.com; Ambassador MUHAMMAD MUSA MAROOFI.

Albania: Via Asmara 3–5, 00199 Roma; tel. (06) 86224110; fax (06) 86224120; e-mail embassy.rome@mfa.gov.al; internet www.ambalbania.it; Ambassador LLESH KOLA.

Algeria: Via Bartolomeo Eustachio 12, 00161 Roma; tel. (06) 44202533; fax (06) 44292744; e-mail embassy@algerianembassy.it; internet www.algerianembassy.it; Ambassador RACHID MARIF.

Angola: Via Druso 39, 00184 Roma; tel. (06) 7726951; fax (06) 77590009; e-mail ambasciata@ambasciatangola.com; internet www.ambasciatangolana.com; Ambassador FLORÊNCIO MARIANO DA CONCEIÇÃO DE ALMEIDA.

Argentina: Piazza dell'Esquilino 2, 00185 Roma; tel. (06) 48073300; fax (06) 4819787; e-mail ambasciata.argentina@ambargentina.mysam.it; internet www.ambasciatargentina.it; Ambassador TORCUATO SALVADOR DI TELLA.

Armenia: Via XX Settembre 98E, scala A, 00187 Roma; tel. (06) 3296638; fax (06) 3297763; e-mail ambarmit@tin.it; Ambassador RUBEN KARAPETIAN.

Australia: Via A. Bosio 5, 00161 Roma; tel. (06) 852721; fax (06) 85272300; e-mail info-rome@dfat.gov.au; internet www.italy.embassy.gov.au; Ambassador DAVID RITCHIE.

Austria: Via G. B. Pergolesi 3, 00198 Roma; tel. (06) 8440141; fax (06) 8543286; e-mail rom-ob@bmeia.gv.at; internet www.austria.it; Ambassador CHRISTIAN BERLAKOVITS.

Azerbaijan: Via Regina Margherita 1, II piano, 00198 Roma; tel. (06) 85305557; fax (06) 85231448; e-mail rome@mission.mfa.gov.az; internet www.azembassy.it; Ambassador VAGIF SADIQOV.

Bangladesh: Via Antonio Bertoloni 14, 00197 Roma; tel. (06) 8078541; fax (06) 8084853; e-mail embangrm@mclink.it; Ambassador MASUD BIN MOMEN.

Belarus: Via delle Alpi Apuane 16, 00141 Roma; tel. (06) 8208141; fax (06) 82002309; e-mail italy@mfa.gov.by; internet italy.mfa.gov.by; Ambassador YEVGENII A. SHESTAKOV.

Belgium: Via dei Monti Parioli 49, 00197 Roma; tel. (06) 3609511; fax (06) 3610197; e-mail rome@diplobel.fed.be; internet www.diplomatie.be/romeit; Ambassador VINCENT MERTENS DE WILMARS.

Belize: Piazza di Spagna 81, 00187 Roma; tel. (06) 69190776; fax (06) 69925794; e-mail ambasciatabelize@yahoo.it; internet www.ambasciatabelize.com; Ambassador NUNZIO ALFREDO D'ANGIERI.

Benin: Via dei Settemetri 11E, 00118 Roma; e-mail ambr201@tiscalinet.it; Ambassador MARIE ROSEMONDE YAKOUBOU.

Bolivia: Via Brenta 2A, int. 18, 00198 Roma; tel. (06) 8840740; fax (06) 8841001; e-mail embolivia-roma@rree.gov.bo; internet www.embajadabolivia.it; Ambassador GROVER ALBERTO TERAN GAMBOA.

Bosnia and Herzegovina: Piazzale Clodio 12, int. 17/18, 00195 Roma; tel. (06) 39742817; fax (06) 39030567; e-mail ambasciata@ambih.191.it; Ambassador BRANKO KESIĆ.

Brazil: Palazzo Pamphili, Piazza Navona 14, 00186 Roma; tel. (06) 683981; fax (06) 6867858; e-mail info@ambrasile.it; internet www.ambasciatadelbrasile.it; Ambassador JOSÉ VIEGAS FILHO.

Bulgaria: Via Pietro Paolo Rubens 21, 00197 Roma; tel. (06) 3224640; fax (06) 3226122; e-mail embassy@bulemb.it; internet www.mfa.bg/en/107; Chargé d'affaires a.i. TODOR STOYANOV.

Burkina Faso: Via XX Settembre 86, 00187 Roma; tel. (06) 42010611; fax (06) 42016701; e-mail ambabf.roma@tin.it; Ambassador RAYMOND BALIMA.

Burundi: Corso Francia 221, 00919 Roma; tel. (06) 36381786; fax (06) 36381511; e-mail ambaburoma@yahoo.fr; Ambassador RÉNOVAT NDAYIRUKIYE.

Cameroon: Via Siracusa 4–6, 00161 Roma; tel. (06) 44291285; fax (06) 44291323; e-mail segreteriaambcam@virgilio.it; internet www.cameroonembassy.it; Ambassador DOMINIQUE AWONO ESSAMA.

Canada: Via Salaria 243, 00199 Roma; tel. (06) 854441; fax (06) 854443947; e-mail rome@international.gc.ca; internet www.canadainternational.gc.ca/italy-italie; Ambassador JAMES A. FOX.

Cape Verde: Via Giosuè Carducci 4, 1°, 00187 Roma; tel. (06) 4744678; fax (06) 4744643; Ambassador JOSÉ EDUARDO DANTAS FERREIRA BARBOSA.

Chile: Via Po 23, 00198 Roma; tel. (06) 844091; fax (06) 8841452; e-mail embajada@chileit.it; internet www.chileit.it; Ambassador OSCAR FRANCISCO ARCAYA.

China, People's Republic: Via Bruxelles 56, 00198 Roma; tel. (06) 8413458; fax (06) 85352891; e-mail chinaemb_it@mfa.gov.cn; internet it.china-embassy.org; Ambassador WEI DING.

Colombia: Via Giuseppe Pisanelli 4, 00196 Roma; tel. (06) 3612131; fax (06) 3225798; e-mail eroma@cancilleria.gov.co; internet www.emcolombia.it; Ambassador JUAN MANUEL PRIETO MONTOYA.

Congo, Democratic Republic: Via Barberini 3, 00187 Roma; tel. and fax (06) 42010779; Ambassador ALBERT TSHISELEKA FEHLA.

Congo, Republic: Via Ombrone 8–10, 00198 Roma; tel. and fax (06) 8417422; e-mail ambacorome@libero.it; Ambassador MAMADOU KAMARA DEKAMO.

Costa Rica: Viale Liegi 2, int. 8, 00198 Roma; tel. (06) 84242853; fax (06) 85355956; e-mail embcr.italia@gmail.com; Ambassador FEDERICO ORTUÑO-VICTORY.

Côte d'Ivoire: Via Guglielmo Saliceto 6–10, 00161 Roma; tel. (06) 44231129; fax (06) 44292531; e-mail info@cotedivoire.it; Ambassador JANINE ADELE TAGLIANTE-SARACINO.

Croatia: Via Luigi Bodio 74–76, 00191 Roma; tel. (06) 36307650; fax (06) 36303405; e-mail vhrim@mvpei.hr; internet it.mfa.hr; Ambassador TOMISLAV VIDOŠEVIĆ.

Cuba: Via Licinia 7, 00153 Roma; tel. (06) 5717241; fax (06) 5745445; e-mail embajada@ecuitalia.it; internet emba.cubaminrex.cu/italia; Ambassador MILAGROS CARINA SOTO AGÜERO.

Cyprus: Via Ludovisi 35, V piano, scala A, 00187 Roma; tel. (06) 8088365; fax (06) 8088338; e-mail emb.rome@flashnet.it; Ambassador LEONIDAS MARKIDES.

Czech Republic: Via dei Gracchi 322, 00192 Roma; tel. (06) 36309571; fax (06) 3244466; e-mail rome@embassy.mzv.cz; internet www.mzv.cz/rome; Ambassador PETR BURIÁNEK.

Denmark: Via dei Monti Parioli 50, 00197 Roma; tel. (06) 9774831; fax (06) 97748399; e-mail romamb@um.dk; internet www.ambrom.um.dk; Ambassador BIRGER RIIS-JØRGENSEN.

Dominican Republic: Via Giuseppe Pisanelli 1, int. 8, 00196 Roma; tel. (06) 45434789; fax (06) 45448452; e-mail embajadadominicana@tiscali.it; Ambassador VINICIO ALFONSO TOBAL URENA.

Ecuador: Via Antonio Bertoloni 8, 00197 Roma; tel. (06) 45439007; fax (06) 8076271; e-mail mecuroma@flashnet.it; Ambassador CARLOS LOPEZ.

Egypt: Villa Savoia, Via Salaria 267, 00199 Roma; tel. (06) 84401921; fax (06) 8554424; e-mail ambegitto@yahoo.com; Chargé d'affaires a.i. MOHAMED FARID MOHAMED MONIB.

El Salvador: Via G. Castellini 13, 00197 Roma; tel. (06) 8076605; fax (06) 8079726; e-mail embasalvaroma@tiscali.it; internet www.embasalvaroma.com; Ambassador AIDA LUZ SANTOS DE ESCOBAR.

Equatorial Guinea: Via Bruxelles 59A, 00198 Roma; tel. (06) 8555428; fax (06) 85305685; Ambassador CECILIA OBONO NDONG.

Eritrea: Via Boncompagni 16B, int. 6, 00187 Roma; tel. (06) 42741293; fax (06) 42741514; e-mail segretaria@embassyoferitrea.it; Ambassador ZEMEDE TEKLE WOLDETATIOS.

Estonia: Viale Liegi 28, int. 5, 00198 Roma; tel. (06) 84407510; fax (06) 84407519; e-mail embassy.rome@mfa.ee; internet www.estemb.it; Ambassador MERIKE KOKAJEV.

Ethiopia: Via Andrea Vesalio 16, 00161 Roma; tel. (06) 4416161; fax (06) 4403676; e-mail embethrm@rdn.it; Ambassador MULUGETA ALEMSEGED GESSESE.

Finland: Via Lisbona 3, 00198 Roma; tel. (06) 852231; fax (06) 8540362; e-mail sanomat.roo@formin.fi; internet www.finlandia.it; Ambassador PETRI TUOMAS TUOMI-NIKULA.

France: Piazza Farnese 67, 00186 Roma; tel. (06) 686011; fax (06) 68601418; internet www.ambafrance-it.org; Ambassador ALAIN LE ROY.

Gabon: Via San Marino 36A, 00198 Roma; tel. (06) 85358970; fax (06) 8417278; e-mail ambassadedugabon1@intefree.it; Ambassador CHARLES ESSONGHE.

Georgia: Corso Vittorio Emanuele II 21, scala A, 00186 Roma; tel. (06) 69925809; fax (06) 69941942; e-mail amgeorgia@libero.it; internet www.italy.mfa.gov.ge; Ambassador KONSTANTINE GABASHVILI.

Germany: Via San Martino della Battaglia 4, 00185 Roma; tel. (06) 492131; fax (06) 49213319; e-mail info@rom.diplo.de; internet www.rom.diplo.de; Ambassador MICHAEL GERDTS.

Ghana: Via Ostriana 4, 00199 Roma; tel. (06) 86217191; fax (06) 86325762; e-mail info@ghanaembassy.it; internet www.ghanaembassy.it; Ambassador EVELYN ANITA STOKES-HAYFORD.

Greece: Viale G. Rossini 4, 00198 Roma; tel. (06) 8537551; fax (06) 8415927; e-mail gremroma@tin.it; Ambassador MICHAEL CAMBANIS.

Guatemala: Via dei Colli della Farnesina 128, 00194 Roma; tel. (06) 36381143; fax (06) 3291639; e-mail embaguate.italia@tin.it; Ambassador ALFREDO TRINIDAD VELASQUEZ.

Guinea: Via Adelaide Ristori, 9B 13, 00197 Roma; tel. (06) 8078989; fax (06) 8077588; e-mail ambaguineerome1@virgilio.it; Chargé d'affaires a.i. El Hadj JEAN BAPTISTE GROVOGUI.

Haiti: Via di Villa Patrizi 7/7A, 00161 Roma; tel. (06) 44254106; fax (06) 44254208; e-mail ambhaiti@haiti2006.191.it; Chargé d'affaires a.i. CARL BENNY RAYMOND.

Holy See: Via Po 27A–29, 00198 Roma; tel. (06) 8546287; fax (06) 8549725; e-mail nunzio@nunziatura.it; Apostolic Nuncio Most Rev. ADRIANO BERNARDINI (Titular Archbishop of Falerii).

Honduras: Via Giambattista Vico 40, int. 8, 00196 Roma; tel. (06) 3207236; fax (06) 3207973; e-mail honduras@embajada.it; Chargé d'Affaires a.i. MAYRA ARACELY REINA ORTEGA DE TITTA.

Hungary: Via dei Villini 12–16, 00161 Roma; tel. (06) 4402032; fax (06) 4403270; e-mail mission.rom@kum.hu; internet www.huembit.it; Ambassador JÁNOS BALLA.

India: Via XX Settembre 5, 00187 Roma; tel. (06) 4884642; fax (06) 4819539; e-mail gen.email@indianembassy.it; internet www.indianembassy.it; Ambassador DEBABRATA SAHA.

Indonesia: Via Campania 53–55, 00187 Roma; tel. (06) 4200911; fax (06) 4880280; e-mail indorom@uni.net; internet www.indonesianembassy.it; Chargé d'Affaires a.i. PRIYO ISWANTO.

Iran: Via Nomentana 361–363, 00162 Roma; tel. (06) 86328485; fax (06) 86328492; Ambassador SEYYED MUHAMMAD ALI HOSSEINI.

Iraq: Via della Camilluccia, 355, 00135 Roma; tel. (06) 3014508; fax (06) 3014445; e-mail iraqembroma@yahoo.it; Ambassador SAYWAN SABIR MUSTAFA BARZANI.

Ireland: Piazza di Campitelli 3, 00186 Roma; tel. (06) 6979121; fax (06) 69791231; e-mail romeembassy@dfa.ie; internet www.embassyofireland.it; Ambassador PAT HENNESSY.

Israel: Via Michele Mercati 14, 00197 Roma; tel. (06) 36198500; fax (06) 36198555; e-mail adm-sec@roma.mfa.gov.il; internet roma.mfa.gov.il; Ambassador NAOR GILON.

Japan: Via Quintino Sella 60, 00187 Roma; tel. (06) 487991; fax (06) 4873316; internet www.it.emb-japan.go.jp; Ambassador MASAHARU KOHNO.

Jordan: Via Giuseppe Marchi 1B, 00161 Roma; tel. (06) 86205303; fax (06) 8606122; e-mail embroma@jordanembassy.it; Ambassador ZAID MUFLEH FALEH AL-LOZI.

Kazakhstan: Via Cassia 471, 00189 Roma; tel. (06) 36301130; fax (06) 36292675; e-mail kazakstan.emb@agora.it; internet www.embkaz.it; Ambassador ALMAZ N. KHAMZAYEV.

Kenya: Via Archimede 164, 00197 Roma; tel. (06) 8082717; fax (06) 8082707; e-mail info@embassyofkenya.it; internet www.embassyofkenya.it; Ambassador JOSEPHINE WANGARI GAITA.

Korea, Democratic People's Republic: Via dell'Esperanto 26, 00144 Roma; tel. (06) 54220749; fax (06) 54210090; e-mail permerepun@hotmail.com; Ambassador HAN TAE SONG.

Korea, Republic: Via Barnaba Oriani 30, 00197 Roma; tel. (06) 802461; fax (06) 802462259; e-mail consul-it@mofat.go.kr; internet ita.mofat.go.kr; Ambassador KIM YOUNG-SEOK.

Kosovo: Via Tolmino 12, 00198 Roma; tel. (06) 85355316; fax (06) 8552212; e-mail embassy.italy@ks-gov.net; Ambassador ALBERT PRENKAJ.

Kuwait: Via Archimede 124–126, 00197 Roma; tel. (06) 8078415; fax (06) 8076651; e-mail kwembrome@hotmail.com; Ambassador JABER DUAJI AL-SABAH.

Latvia: Viale Liegi 42, 00198 Roma; tel. (06) 8841227; fax (06) 8841239; e-mail embassy.italy@mfa.gov.lv; internet www.mfa.gov.lv/rome; Ambassador ELITA KUZMA.

Lebanon: Via Giacomo Carissimi 38, 00198 Roma; tel. (06) 8537211; fax (06) 8411794; e-mail ambalibano@hotmail.com; internet www.liban.it; Chargé d'affaires a.i. KARIM KHALIL.

Lesotho: Via Serchio 8, 00198 Roma; tel. (06) 8542496; fax (06) 8542527; e-mail secretary@lesothoembassyrome.com; Ambassador JONAS SPONKIE MALEWA.

Liberia: Piazzale delle Medaglie d'Oro 7, 00136 Roma; tel. (06) 35453399; fax (06) 35344729; e-mail liberiaembassy@hotmail.com; Chargé d'affaires a.i. MOHAMMED S. L. SHERIFF.

Libya: Via Nomentana 365, 00162 Roma; tel. (06) 86320951; fax (06) 86205473; e-mail allibyaroma@libero.it; Ambassador ABD AL-HAFID GADDUR.

Lithuania: Viale di Villa Grazioli 9, 00198 Roma; tel. (06) 8559052; fax (06) 8559053; e-mail amb.it@urm.lt; internet it.mfa.lt; Ambassador PETRAS ZAPOLSKAS.

Luxembourg: Via Santa Croce in Gerusalemme 90, 00185 Roma; tel. (06) 77201177; fax (06) 77201055; e-mail rome.amb@mae.etat.lu; internet www.ambasciatalussemburgo.it; Ambassador JEAN-LOUIS WOLZFELD.

Macedonia, former Yugoslav republic: Viale Bruxelles 73–75, 00198 Roma; tel. (06) 84241109; fax (06) 84241131; e-mail rome@mfa.gov.mk; Ambassador VELIBOR ATANASOVSKI TOPALOSKI.

Madagascar: Via Riccardo Zandonai 84A, 00194 Roma; tel. (06) 36307797; fax (06) 3294306; e-mail ambamad@hotmail.com; Ambassador JEAN PIERRE RAZAFY ANDRIAMIHAINGO.

Malaysia: Via Nomentana 297, 00162 Roma; tel. (06) 8415764; fax (06) 8555040; e-mail mw.rome@flashnet.it; Ambassador Datin Paduka HALIMAH ABDULLAH.

Mali: Via Antonio Bosio 2, 00161 Roma; tel. (06) 44254068; fax (06) 44254029; e-mail amb.malirome@tiscalinet.it; Ambassador MOHAMED GAOUSSOU DRABO.

Malta: Lungotevere Marzio 12, 00186 Roma; tel. (06) 6879990; fax (06) 6892687; e-mail maltaembassy.rome@gov.mt; Ambassador CARMEL INGUANEZ.

Mauritania: Via Giovanni Paisiello 26, 00198 Roma; tel. (06) 85351530; fax (06) 85351441; Ambassador MOCTAR OULD DAHI.

Mexico: Via Lazzaro Spallanzani 16, 00161 Roma; tel. (06) 441151; fax (06) 4403876; e-mail ofna.embajador@emexitalia.it; internet www.sre.gob.mx/italia; Ambassador MIGUEL RUÍZ-CABAÑAS IZQUIERDO.

Moldova: Via Montebello 8, 00185 Roma; tel. (06) 4740210; fax (06) 47881092; e-mail roma@mfa.md; internet www.italia.mfa.md; Ambassador AUREL BAIESU.

Monaco: Via Antonio Bertoloni 36, 00197 Roma; tel. (06) 8083361; fax (06) 8077692; e-mail monaco@ambasciatadimonaco.it; internet www.ambasciatadimonaco.it; Ambassador PHILIPPE BLANCHI.

Montenegro: Via Antonio Gramsci 9, 00197 Roma; tel. (06) 45471660; fax (06) 45443800; e-mail montenegro-roma@libero.it; Ambassador VOJIN VLAHOVIĆ.

Morocco: Via Lazzaro Spallanzani 8–10, 00161 Roma; tel. (06) 4402524; fax (06) 44004458; e-mail sifamaroma@ambaciatadelmarocco.it; Ambassador HASSAN ABOUYOUB.

Mozambique: Via Filippo Corridoni 14, 00195 Roma; tel. (06) 37514675; fax (06) 37514699; e-mail sec@ambasciatamozambico.it; Ambassador CARLA ELISA LUIS MUCAVI.

Myanmar: Via della Camilluccia 551, 00135 Roma; tel. (06) 36303753; fax (06) 36298566; e-mail meroma@tiscali.it; Ambassador TINT SWAI.

Netherlands: Via Michele Mercati 8, 00197 Roma; tel. (06) 32286001; fax (06) 32286256; e-mail rom-az@minbuza.nl; internet italy.nlembassy.org; Ambassador ALPHONSUS HERMANUS MARIA STOELINGA.

New Zealand: Via Clitunno 44, 00198 Roma; tel. (06) 8537501; fax (06) 4402984; e-mail rome@nzembassy.it; internet www.nzembassy.com/italy; Ambassador Dr TREVOR MATHESON.

Nicaragua: Via Brescia 16, 00198 Roma; tel. (06) 8413471; fax (06) 85304079; e-mail embanicitalia@cancilleria.gob.ni; Chargé d'affaires a.i. MARTHA IRENE ZUNIGA GUTIERREZ.

Niger: Via Antonio Baiamonti 10, 00195 Roma; tel. (06) 3720164; fax (06) 3729013; Ambassador AMADOU TOURÉ.

Nigeria: Via Orazio 14–18, 00193 Roma; tel. (06) 683931; fax (06) 68393264; Ambassador Prince EHENEDEN EREDIAUWA.

Norway: Via di San Domenico 1, 00153 Roma; tel. (06) 45238100; fax (06) 45238199; e-mail emb.rome@mfa.no; internet www.amb-norvegia.it; Ambassador BJØRN TRYGVE GRYDELAND.

Oman: Via della Camilluccia 625, 00135 Roma; tel. (06) 36300517; fax (06) 3296802; e-mail embassyoman@virgilio.it; Ambassador SAID NASSER MANSOUR AL-SINAWI AL-HARTHY.

Pakistan: Via della Camilluccia 682, 00135 Roma; tel. (06) 36301775; fax (06) 36301936; e-mail pareprome@virgilio.it; Ambassador TEHMINA JANJUA.

Panama: Piazza del Viminale 5, 00184 Roma; tel. (06) 44252173; fax (06) 44252237; e-mail ambpanama@seq.it; Ambassador GUIDO JUVENAL MARTINELLI ENDARA.

Paraguay: Via Firenze 43, scala A, 00187 Roma; tel. (06) 4741715; fax (06) 4745473; e-mail embaparoma@virgilio.it; Ambassador ANA MARIA BAIARDI QUESNEL.

Peru: Via Francesco Siacci 2B, 00197 Roma; tel. (06) 80691510; fax (06) 80691777; e-mail embperu@ambasciataperu2.191.it; tel. www.ambasciataperu.it; Ambassador CÉSAR CASTILLO RAMÍREZ.

Philippines: Viale delle Medaglie d'Oro 112–114, 00136 Roma; tel. (06) 39746621; fax (06) 39740872; e-mail romepe@agora.it; internet www.philembassy-rome.net; Ambassador VIRGILIO A. REYES, Jr.

Poland: Via Pietro Paolo Rubens 20, 00197 Roma; tel. (06) 36204200; fax (06) 3217895; e-mail ufficio.stampa@ambasciatapolonia.it; internet www.rzym.polemb.net; Ambassador WOJCIECH PONIKIEWSKI.

Portugal: Via della Camilluccia 701, 00135 Roma; tel. (06) 844801; fax (06) 36309827; e-mail embport@embportroma.it; internet www.embportroma.it; Chargé d'affaires a.i. NUNO DE MELO BELO.

Qatar: Via Antonio Bosio 14, 00161 Roma; tel. (06) 44249450; fax (06) 44245273; e-mail info@qatarembassy.it; Ambassador SOLTAN SAAD AL-MORAIKHI.

Romania: Via Nicolo Tartaglia 36, 00197 Roma; tel. (06) 8084529; fax (06) 8084995; e-mail amdiroma@roembit.org; internet roma.mae.ro; Chargé d'affaires a.i. ADINA LOVIN.

Russia: Via Gaeta 5, 00185 Roma; tel. (06) 4941680; fax (06) 491031; e-mail rusembassy@libero.it; internet www.ambrussia.com; Ambassador ALEXEI YU. MESHKOV.

San Marino: Via Eleonora Duse 35, 00197 Roma; tel. (06) 8072511; fax (06) 8070072; e-mail asmarino@ambrsm.it; Ambassador DANIELA ROTONDARO.

Saudi Arabia: Via G. B. Pergolesi 9, 00198 Roma; tel. (06) 844851; fax (06) 8551781; e-mail segretaria@arabia-saudita.it; internet www.arabia-saudita.it; Ambassador SALEH BIN MOHAMMED BIN GHURMALLAH AL-GHAMDI.

Senegal: Via Giulia 66, 00186 Roma; tel. (06) 6872381; fax (06) 68219294; e-mail ambasenequiri@tiscali.it; Ambassador PAPA CHEIKH SAADIBOU FALL.

Serbia: Via dei Monti Parioli 20, 00197 Roma; tel. (06) 32609159; fax (06) 32609159; e-mail info@ambroma.com; internet www.ambroma.com; Ambassador ANA HRUSTANOVIĆ.

Slovakia: Via dei Colli della Farnesina 144, 00194 Roma; tel. (06) 36715200; fax (06) 36715265; e-mail embassy@rome.mfa.sk; internet www.mzv.sk/rim; Ambassador MÁRIA KRASNOHORSKÁ.

Slovenia: Via Leonardo Pisano 10, 00197 Roma; tel. (06) 80914310; fax (06) 8081471; e-mail vri@gov.si; Ambassador IZTOK MIROSIC.

Somalia: Via dei Gracchi 305, 00192 Roma; tel. (06) 3220651; fax (06) 3200898; e-mail somalrep@gmail.com; Ambassador NUR HASSAN HUSSEIN.

South Africa: Via Tanaro 14, 00198 Roma; tel. (06) 852541; fax (06) 85254301; e-mail sae2@sudafrica.it; internet www.sudafrica.it; Ambassador THENJIWE ETHEL MTINTSO.

Spain: Palazzo Borghese, Largo Fontanella Borghese 19, 00186 Roma; tel. (06) 6840401; fax (06) 6872256; e-mail ambespit@correo.mae.es; internet www.maec.es/embajadas/roma; Ambassador ALFONSO LUCINI MATEO.

Sri Lanka: Via Adige 2, 00198 Roma; tel. (06) 8554560; fax (06) 84241670; e-mail slembassy@tiscali.it; Ambassador ASITHA PERERA.

Sudan: Via Prati della Farnesina 57, 00194 Roma; tel. (06) 33222138; fax (06) 3340841; e-mail info@sudanembassy.it; Ambassador AMIRA DAOUD HASSAN GORNASS.

Sweden: Piazza Rio de Janeiro 3, 00161 Roma; tel. (06) 441941; fax (06) 44194760; e-mail ambassaden.rom@foreign.ministry.se; internet www.swedenabroad.com/rome; Ambassador RUTH EVELYN JACOBY.

Switzerland: Via Barnaba Oriani 61, 00197 Roma; tel. (06) 809571; fax (06) 8088510; e-mail vertretung@rom.rep.admin.ch; internet www.eda.admin.ch/roma; Ambassador BERNARDINO REGAZZONI.

Syria: Piazza dell'Ara Coeli, 00186 Roma; tel. (06) 6749801; fax (06) 6794989; e-mail uffstampasyem@hotmail.it; Ambassador KHADDOUR HASAN.

Tanzania: Viale Cortina d'Ampezzo 185, 00135 Roma; tel. (06) 33485801; fax (06) 33485828; e-mail info@tanzania-gov.it; internet www.tanzania-gov.it; Ambassador ALI ABEID AMAN KARUME.

Thailand: Via Nomentana 132, 00162 Roma; tel. (06) 86220524; fax (06) 86220555; e-mail thai.em.rome@wind.it.net; internet www.thaiembassy.org/rome; Ambassador SOMASAKDI SURIYAWONGSE.

Tunisia: Via Asmara 7, 00199 Roma; tel. (06) 8603060; fax (06) 86218204; e-mail at.roma@tiscali.it; Ambassador NACEUR MESTIRI.

Turkey: Palazzo Gamberini, Via Palestro 28, 00185 Roma; tel. (06) 445941; fax (06) 4941526; e-mail roma.be@libero.it; internet www.roma.be.mfa.gov.tr; Ambassador HAKKI AKIL.

Uganda: Lungotevere dei Mellini 44, I piano, 00193 Roma; tel. (06) 3225220; fax (06) 3213688; e-mail ugandaembassyrome@hotmail.com; Ambassador DEO KAJUNZIRE RWABITA.

Ukraine: Via Guido d'Arezzo 9, 00198 Roma; tel. (06) 8413345; fax (06) 8547539; e-mail emb_it@mfa.gov.ua; internet www.mfa.gov.ua/italy; Ambassador HEORHIY V. CHERNYAVSKY.

United Arab Emirates: Via della Camilluccia 492, 00135 Roma; tel. (06) 36306100; fax (06) 36306155; e-mail uaeroma@tin.it; Ambassador ABD AL-AZIZ NASSER RAHMA AL-SHAMSI.

United Kingdom: Via XX Settembre 80A, 00187 Roma; tel. (06) 42200001; fax (06) 42202333; e-mail romepoliticalsection@fco.gov.uk; internet www.ukinitaly.fco.gov.uk; Ambassador CHRISTOPHER PRENTICE.

USA: Palazzo Margherita, Via Vittorio Veneto 121, 00187 Roma; tel. (06) 46741; fax (06) 46742217; internet rome.usembassy.gov; Ambassador DAVID H. THORNE.

Uruguay: Via Vittorio Veneto 183, 00187 Roma; tel. (06) 4821776; fax (06) 4823695; e-mail uruit@ambasciatauruguay.it; Ambassador GUSTAVO ANÍBAL ALVAREZ GOYOAGA.

Uzbekistan: Via Tolmino 12, 00198 Roma; tel. (06) 8542456; fax (06) 8541020; e-mail ambasciata@uzbekistanitalia.org; internet www.uzbekistanitalia.org; Ambassador ZHAHONGIR D. GANIYEV.

Venezuela: Via Nicolò Tartaglia 11, 00197 Roma; tel. (06) 8079797; fax (06) 8084410; e-mail embaveit@ambavene.org; Ambassador JULIAN ISAIAS RODRIGUEZ DIAZ.

Viet Nam: Via di Bravetta 156–58, 00164 Roma; tel. (06) 66160726; fax (06) 66157520; e-mail vnemb.it@mofa.gov.vn; internet www.vnembassy.it; Ambassador DANG KHANH THOAI.

Yemen: Via Antonio Bosio 10, 00161 Roma; tel. (06) 44231679; fax (06) 44234763; e-mail info@yemenembassy.it; internet www.yemenembassy.it; Ambassador KHALID ABD AL-RAHMAN MUHAMMAD AL-AKWA.

Zambia: Via Ennio Quirino Visconti 8, 00193 Roma; tel. (06) 36002590; fax (06) 97613035; e-mail info@zambianembassy.it; internet www.zambianembassy.it; Ambassador SAMUEL MAPALA.

Zimbabwe: Via Virgilio 8, 00193 Roma; tel. (06) 68308282; fax (06) 68308324; e-mail zimrome-wolit@tiscali.it; Ambassador MARY SIBUSISIWE MUBI.

Judicial System

The Constitutional Court was established in 1956 and is an autonomous constitutional body, standing apart from the judicial system. Its most important function is to pronounce on the constitutionality of legislation both subsequent and prior to the present Constitution of 1948. It also judges accusations brought against the President of the Republic or ministers.

At the base of the system of penal jurisdiction are the Preture (District Courts), where offences carrying a sentence of up to four years' imprisonment are tried. Above the Preture are the Tribunali (Tribunals) and the Corti di Assise presso i Tribunali (Assize Courts attached to the Tribunals), where graver offences are dealt with. From these courts appeal lies to the Corti d'Appello (Courts of Appeal) and the parallel Corti di Assise d'Appello (Assize Courts of Appeal). Final appeal may be made, on juridical grounds only, to the Corte Suprema di Cassazione (Supreme Court of Cassation).

Civil cases may be taken in the first instance to the Giudici Conciliatori (Justices of the Peace), Preture or Tribunali, according to the economic value of the case. Appeal from the Giudici Conciliatori lies to the Preture, from the Preture to the Tribunali, from the Tribunali to the Corti d'Appello, and finally, as in penal justice, to the Corte Suprema di Cassazione on juridical grounds only.

Special divisions for cases concerning labour relations are attached to civil courts. Cases concerned with the public service and its employees are tried by Tribunali Amministrativi Regionali and the Consiglio di Stato. Juvenile courts have criminal and civil jurisdiction.

A new penal code was introduced in late 1989.

CONSTITUTIONAL COURT

Corte Costituzionale

Palazzo della Consulta, Piazza del Quirinale 41, 00187 Roma; tel. (06) 46981; fax (06) 4698916; e-mail ccost@cortecostituzionale.it; internet www.cortecostituzionale.it.

Consists of 15 judges, one-third appointed by the President of the Republic, one-third elected by Parliament in joint session, and one-third by the ordinary and administrative supreme courts.

President: ALFONSO QUARANTA.

Judges: UGO DE SIERVO (Vice-President), PAOLO MADDALENA, ALFIO FINOCCHIARO, ALFONSO QUARANTA, FRANCO GALLO, LUIGI MAZZELLA, GAETANO SILVESTRI, SABINO CASSESE, MARIA RITA SAULLE, GIUSEPPE TESAURO, PAOLO MARIA NAPOLITANO, GIUSEPPE FRIGO, ALESSANDRO CRISCUOLO, PAOLO GROSSI.

ADMINISTRATIVE COURTS

Consiglio di Stato

Palazzo Spada, Piazza Capo di Ferro 13, 00186 Roma; tel. (06) 68212743; fax (06) 68272282; e-mail urp.cds@giustizia-amministrativa.it; internet www.giustizia-amministrativa.it.

Established in accordance with Article 10 of the Constitution; has both consultative and judicial functions.

President: PASQUALE DE LISE.

Corte dei Conti

Via Giuseppe Mazzini 105, 00195 Roma; tel. (06) 38761; fax (06) 38763477; e-mail urp@corteconti.it; internet www.corteconti.it.

Functions as the court of public auditors for the state.

President: LUIGI GIAMPAOLINO.

SUPREME COURT OF CASSATION

Corte Suprema di Cassazione

Palazzo di Giustizia, Piazza Cavour, 00193 Roma; tel. (06) 68831; e-mail cassazione@giustizia.it; internet www.cortedicassazione.it.

Supreme court of civil and criminal appeal.

First President: Dott. ERNESTO LUPO.

SUPERVISORY BODY

Consiglio Superiore della Magistratura (CSM): Piazza Indipendenza 6, 00185 Roma; tel. (06) 444911; fax (06) 4457175; e-mail seg-seggen@cosmag.it; internet www.csm.it; f. 1958; 27 mems; Pres. GIORGIO NAPOLITANO (President of the Republic); Vice-Pres. NICOLA MANCINO.

Religion

More than 90% of the population of Italy are adherents of the Roman Catholic Church. Under the terms of the Concordat formally ratified in June 1985, Roman Catholicism was no longer to be the state religion, compulsory religious instruction in schools was abolished and state financial contributions reduced. The Vatican City's sovereign rights as an independent state, under the terms of the Lateran Treaty of 1929, were not affected.

Several Protestant churches also exist in Italy, with a total membership of about 65,000. There is a small Jewish community, and in 1987 an agreement recognized certain rights for the Jewish community, including the right to observe religious festivals on Saturdays by not attending school or work. There is also a substantial Islamic population.

CHRISTIANITY

The Roman Catholic Church

For ecclesiastical purposes, Italy comprises the Papal See of Rome, the Patriarchate of Venice, 60 archdioceses (including three directly responsible to the Holy See), two eparchies, 153 dioceses (including seven within the jurisdiction of the Pope, as Archbishop of the Roman Province, and 11 directly responsible to the Holy See), two territorial prelatures and seven territorial abbacies (including four directly responsible to the Holy See). Almost all adherents follow the Latin rite, but there are two dioceses and one abbacy (all directly responsible to the Holy See) for Catholics of the Italo-Albanian (Byzantine) rite.

Bishops' Conference

Conferenza Episcopale Italiana, Circonvallazione Aurelia 50, 00165 Roma; tel. (06) 663981; fax (06) 6623037; e-mail segrgen@chiesacattolica.it; internet www.chiesacattolica.it.

f. 1965; Pres. Cardinal ANGELO BAGNASCO (Archbishop of Genova); Sec.-Gen. Rt Rev. MARIANO CROCIATA.

Primate of Italy, Archbishop and Metropolitan of the Roman Province and Bishop of Rome: His Holiness Pope BENEDICT XVI.

Patriarch of Venice: Cardinal FRANCESCO MORAGLIA.

Archbishops

Acerenza: Most Rev. GIOVANNI RICCHIUTI.

Agrigento: Most Rev. FRANCESCO MONTENEGRO.

Amalfi-Cava de' Tirreni: Most Rev. ORAZIO SORICELLI.

Ancona-Osimo: Most Rev. EDOARDO MENICHELLI.

Bari-Bitonto: Most Rev. FRANCESCO CACUCCI.

Benevento: Most Rev. ANDREA MUGIONE.

Bologna: Cardinal CARLO CAFFARRA.

Brindisi-Otsuni: Most Rev. ROCCO TALUCCI.

Cagliari: Most Rev. ARRIGO MIGLIO.

Camerino-San Severino Marche: Most Rev. FRANCESCO GIOVANNI BRUGNARO.

Campobasso-Boiano: Most Rev. GIANCARLO MARIA BREGANTINI.

Capua: Most Rev. BRUNO SCHETTINO.

Catania: Most Rev. SALVATORE GRISTINA.

Catanzaro-Squillace: Most Rev. VINCENZO BERTOLONE.

Chieti-Vasto: Most Rev. BRUNO FORTE.

Cosenza-Bisignano: Most Rev. SALVATORE NUNNARI.

Crotone-Santa Severina: Most Rev. DOMENICO GRAZIANI.

Fermo: Most Rev. LUIGI CONTI.

Ferrara-Comacchio: Most Rev. PAOLO RABITTI.

Firenze (Florence): Most Rev. GIUSEPPE BETORI.

Foggia-Bovino: Most Rev. FRANCESCO PIO TAMBURRINO.

Gaeta: Most Rev. FABIO BERNARDO D'ONORIO.

Genova (Genoa): Cardinal ANGELO BAGNASCO.

Gorizia: Most Rev. DINO DE ANTONI.

Lanciano-Ortona: Most Rev. EMIDIO CIPOLLONE.

L'Aquila: Most Rev. GIUSEPPE MOLINARI.

Lecce: Most Rev. DOMENICO UMBERTO D'AMBROSIO.

Lucca: Most Rev. BENVENUTO ITALO CASTELLANI.

Manfredonia-Vieste-San Giovanni Rotondo: Most Rev. MICHELE CASTORO.

Matera-Irsina: Most Rev. SALVATORE LIGORIO.

Messina-Lipari-Santa Lucia del Mela: Most Rev. CALOGERO LA PIANA.

Milano (Milan): Cardinal ANGELO SCOLA.

Modena-Nonantola: Most Rev. ANTONIO LANFRANCHI.

Monreale: Most Rev. SALVATORE DI CRISTINA.

Napoli (Naples): Cardinal CRESCENZIO SEPE.

Oristano: Most Rev. IGNAZIO SANNA.

Otranto: Most Rev. DONATO NEGRO.

Palermo: Cardinal PAOLO ROMEO.

Perugia-Città della Pieve: Most Rev. GUALTIERO BASSETTI.

Pesaro: Most Rev. PIERO COCCIA.

Pescara-Penne: Most Rev. TOMMASO VALENTINETTI.

Pisa: Most Rev. GIOVANNI PAOLO BENOTTO.

Potenza-Muro Lucano-Marsico Nuovo: Most Rev. AGOSTINO SUPERBO.

Ravenna-Cervia: Most Rev. GIUSEPPE VERUCCHI.

Reggio Calabria-Bova: Most Rev. VITTORIO LUIGI MONDELLO.

Rossano-Cariati: Most Rev. SANTO MARCIANÒ.

Salerno-Campagna-Acerno: Most Rev. LUIGI MORETTI.

Sant'Angelo dei Lombardi-Conza-Nusco-Bisaccia: Most Rev. FRANCESCO ALFANO.

Sassari: Most Rev. PAOLO MARIO VIRGILIO ATZEI.

Siena-Colle di Val d'Elsa-Montalcino: Most Rev. ANTONIO BUONCRISTIANI.

Siracusa (Syracuse): Most Rev. SALVATORE PAPPALARDO.

Sorrento-Castellamare di Stabia: Most Rev. FRANCESCO ALFANO.

Spoleto-Norcia: Most Rev. RENATO BOCCARDO.

Taranto: Most Rev. FILIPPO SANTORO.

Torino (Turin): Most Rev. CESARE NOSIGLIA.

Trani-Barletta-Bisceglie: Most Rev. GIOVAN BATTISTA PICHIERRI.

Trento: Most Rev. LUIGI BRESSAN.

Udine: Most Rev. ANDREA BRUNO MAZZOCATO.

Urbino-Urbania-Sant'Angelo in Vado: Most Rev. GIOVANNI TANI.

Vercelli: Most Rev. ENRICO MASSERONI.

Protestant Churches

Federazione delle Chiese Evangeliche in Italia (Federation of the Protestant Churches in Italy): Via Firenze 38, 00184 Roma; tel. (06) 4825120; fax (06) 4828728; internet www.fcei.it; f. 1967; total mems c. 65,000; Pres. MASSIMO AQUILANTE; 11 mem. churches, incl. the following:

Chiesa Evangelica Luterana in Italia (Lutheran Church): Via Aurelia Antica 391, 00165 Roma; tel. (06) 66030104; fax (06) 66017993; e-mail decanato@chiesaluterana.it; internet www.chiesaluterana.it; Dean HOLGER MILKAU; 7,000 mems.

Chiesa Evangelica Valdese (Unione delle Chiese Metodiste e Valdesi) (Waldensian Evangelical Church): Via Firenze 38, 00184 Roma; tel. (06) 4743695; fax (06) 47885308; e-mail info@chiesavaldese.org; internet www.chiesavaldese.org; in 2002 the Tavola Valdese merged with the Chiese Evangeliche Metodiste in Italia (Methodists); Moderator MARIA BONAFEDE; Sec.-Treas. ROSELLA PANZIRONI; 27,465 mems.

ISLAM

Associazione Musulmani Italiani (AMI) (Italian Muslim Association): CP 7167, Roma; tel. and fax (06) 44360619; e-mail info@amimuslims.org; internet www.amimuslims.org; f. 1982; Pres. Prince BARZANGI AHMED ABUCAR SULDAN.

Unione delle Comunità e Organizzazioni Islamiche in Italia (UCOII): Via delle 4, Fontane, Roma; tel. (0183) 48939934; fax (0183) 764735; e-mail segreteria.ucoii@gmail.com; internet www.islam-ucoii.it; f. 1990; Pres. IZZEDDIN ELZIR; Sec. AHMED ALESSANDRO PAOLANTONI.

JUDAISM

Unione delle Comunità Ebraiche Italiane (UCEI) (Union of Italian Jewish Communities): Lungotevere Sanzio 9, 00153 Roma; tel. (06) 45542200; fax (06) 5899569; e-mail info@ucei.it; internet www.ucei.it; f. 1930; represents 21 Jewish communities in Italy; Pres. RENZO GATTEGNA; Gen. Sec. Dott. GLORIA ARBIB.

The Press

Relative to the size of Italy's population, the number of daily newspapers is rather small. Rome and Milan are the main press centres. The most important national dailies are *Corriere della Sera* in Milan and *La Repubblica* in Rome, followed by Turin's *La Stampa* and Milan's *Il Sole 24 Ore*, the economic and financial newspaper with the highest circulation in Europe. Among the most widely read newspapers are *La Gazzetta dello Sport* and *Il Corriere dello Sport—Stadio*, both of which exclusively cover sports news.

PRINCIPAL DAILIES

(Average net circulation figures, for January–December 2011, unless otherwise stated.)

Ancona

Il Corriere Adriatico: Via Berti 20, 60126 Ancona; tel. (071) 4581; fax (071) 42980; e-mail info@corriereadriaticonline.it; internet www.corriereadriatico.it; f. 1860; Editorial Dir PAOLO TRAINI; circ. 23,549.

Bari

La Gazzetta del Mezzogiorno: Viale Scipione l'Africano 264, 70124 Bari; tel. (080) 5470200; fax (080) 5502130; e-mail direzione.politica@gazzettamezzogiorno.it; internet www.lagazzettadelmezzogiorno.it; f. 1887; independent; Editor MICHELE PARTIPILO; circ. 46,804.

Il Quotidiano di Bari: Piazza Aldo Moro 31, 70121 Bari; tel. (080) 5240473; fax (080) 5245486; e-mail redazione@quotidianodibari.it; internet www.quotidianodibari.it; Dir MATTEO TATARELLA.

Bergamo

L'Eco di Bergamo: Viale Papa Giovanni XXIII 118, 24121 Bergamo; tel. (035) 386111; fax (035) 386217; e-mail redazione@eco.bg.it; internet www.ecodibergamo.it; f. 1880; Catholic; Dir. GIORGIO GANDOLA; circ. 57,986.

Bologna

Il Resto del Carlino: Via Enrico Mattei 106, 40138 Bologna; tel. (051) 6006111; fax (051) 536111; e-mail segreteria.redazione.bologna@monrif.net; internet www.ilrestodelcarlino.it; f. 1885; publr Poligrafici Editoriale, SpA; Dir GIOVANNI MORANDI; circ. 180,914.

Bolzano/Bozen

Alto Adige: Via Volta 10, 39100 Bozen; tel. (0471) 904111; fax (0471) 904263; e-mail bolzano@altoadige.it; internet www.altoadige.it; f. 1945; publr Gruppo Editoriale L'Espresso, SpA; Dir ALBERTO FAUSTINI; circ. 36,951.

Dolomiten: Weinbergweg 7, 39100 Bozen; tel. (0471) 925111; fax (0471) 925440; e-mail dolomiten@athesia.it; internet www.stol.it/dolomiten; f. 1882; independent; German language; Dir Dott. TONI EBNER; circ. 55,654.

Brescia

Il Giornale di Brescia: Via Solferino 22, 25121 Brescia; tel. (030) 37901; fax (030) 3790289; e-mail info@giornaledibrescia.it; internet www.giornaledibrescia.it; f. 1947; Dir GIACOMO SCANZI; circ. 54,624.

Cagliari

L'Unione Sarda: Viale Regina Elena 12, 9100 Cagliari; tel. (070) 60131; fax (070) 6013306; e-mail unione@unionesarda.it; internet www.unionesarda.it; f. 1889; independent; Editor-in-Chief PAOLO FIGUS; circ. 70,699.

Catania

La Sicilia: Viale Odorico da Pordenone 50, 95126 Catania; tel. (095) 330544; fax (095) 336466; e-mail segreteria@lasicilia.it; internet www.lasicilia.it; f. 1945; independent; Man. Dott. MARIO CIANCIO SANFILIPPO; circ. 63,255.

Como

La Provincia di Como: Via Pasquale Paoli 21, 22100 Como; tel. (031) 582311; fax (031) 505003; e-mail laprovincia@laprovincia.it; internet www.laprovinciadicomo.it; f. 1892; independent; Dir DIEGO MINONZIO; circ. 56,000 (2003).

Firenze
(Florence)

La Nazione: Viale Giovine Italia 17, 50121 Firenze; tel. (055) 249511; fax (055) 2478207; e-mail segreteria@lanazione.it; internet www.lanazione.it; f. 1859; publr Poligrafici Editoriale, SpA; Dir JOSEPH MASCAMBRUNO; circ. 149,393.

Foggia

Quotidiano di Foggia: Via Gramsci 73A, 71100 Foggia; tel. (0881) 686967; fax (0881) 632247; e-mail redazione@quotidianodifoggia.it; internet www.quotidianodifoggia.it; Dir MATTEO TATTARELLA; circ. 25,000 (2007).

Genova
(Genoa)

Il Secolo XIX: Piazza Piccapietra 21, 16121 Genova; tel. (010) 53881; fax (010) 5388426; e-mail redazione@ilsecoloxix.it; internet www.ilsecoloxix.it; f. 1886; independent; Dir CARLO PERRONE; circ. 96,419.

Lecce

Nuovo Quotidiano di Puglia: Via dei Mocenigo 29, 73100 Lecce; tel. (0832) 3382000; fax (0832) 338244; e-mail redazioneweb@quotidianodipuglia.it; internet www.quotidianodipuglia.it; f. 1979 as *Il Quotidiano di Lecce*; 3 local edns covering Lecce, Brindisi and Taranto; Dir CLAUDIO SCAMARDELLA; circ. 24,109.

Livorno
(Leghorn)

Il Tirreno: Viale Alfieri 9, 57124 Livorno; tel. (0586) 220111; fax (0586) 402066; e-mail redazione.li@iltirreno.it; internet iltirreno.repubblica.it; f. 1978; publr Gruppo Editoriale L'Espresso, SpA; Dir ROBERTO BERNABÒ; circ. 93,939.

Mantova
(Mantua)

Gazzetta di Mantova: Piazza Cesare Mozzarelli 7, 46100 Mantova; tel. (0376) 3031; fax (0376) 303263; e-mail redazione.mn@gazzettadimantova.it; internet www.gazzettadimantova.it; f. 1664; publr Gruppo Editoriale L'Espresso, SpA; Dir ANDREA FILIPPI; circ. 34,114.

Messina

Gazzetta del Sud: Uberto Bonino 15C, 98124 Messina; tel. (090) 2261; fax (090) 2936359; e-mail amministrazione@gazzettadelsud.it; internet www.gazzettadelsud.it; f. 1952; independent; Dir NINO CALARCO; circ. 59,227.

Milano
(Milan)

Avvenire: Piazza Carbonari 3, 20125 Milano; tel. (02) 67801; fax (02) 6780208; e-mail lettere@avvenire.it; internet www.avvenire.it; f. 1968; Catholic; organ of the Italian Bishops' Conference; Dir MARCO TARQUINIO; circ. 145,754.

Corriere della Sera: Via Solferino 28, 20121 Milano; tel. (02) 6339; fax (02) 29009668; internet www.corriere.it; f. 1876; independent; contains weekly supplement, *Sette*; Dir FERRUCIO DE BORTOLI; circ. 622,070.

Il Foglio Quotidiano: Via Carroccio 12, 20123 Milano; tel. (02) 7712951; fax (02) 782511; e-mail lettere@ilfoglio.it; internet www.ilfoglio.it; Dir GIULIANO FERRARA.

La Gazzetta dello Sport: RCS Editoriale Quotidiani, SpA, Via Solferino 28, 20121 Milano; tel. (02) 6339; fax (02) 62827917; e-mail segretgaz@rcs.it; internet www.gazzetta.it; f. 1896; sport; Dir ANDREA MONTI; circ. 427,933.

Il Giornale: Via Gaetano Negri 4, 20123 Milano; tel. (02) 85661; fax (02) 72023880; e-mail segreteria@ilgiornale.it; internet www.ilgiornale.it; f. 1974; Editor ALESSANDRO SALLUSTI; circ. 258,941.

Il Giorno: Via Stradivari 4, 20123 Milano; tel. (02) 277991; fax (02) 27799537; e-mail ilgiorno@ilgiorno.it; internet www.ilgiorno.it; f. 1956; publr Poligrafici Editoriale, SpA; Dir GIOVANNI MORANDI; circ. 87,479.

Italia Oggi: Class Editori, Via M. Burigozzo 5, 20122 Milano; tel. (02) 58219256; e-mail italiaoggi@class.it; internet www.italiaoggi.it; f. 1991; economic daily; Dir PIERLUIGI MAGNASCHI; circ. 133,024.

Libero: Viale L. Majno 42, 20129 Milano; tel. (02) 99966300; fax (02) 99966305; e-mail redazione@libero-news.eu; internet www.libero-news.it; f. 2000; Dir EGREGIO MAURIZIO BELPIETRO; circ. 194,818.

MF (Milano Finanza): Class Editori, Via M. Burigozzo 5, 20122 Milano; tel. (02) 582191; internet www.milanofinanza.it; f. 1989; economic daily; Dir ENRICO ROMAGNA MANOJA.

Il Sole 24 Ore: Via Monte Rosa 91, 20149 Milano; tel. (02) 30221; fax (02) 312055; internet www.ilsole24ore.com; f. 1865; financial, political, economic; Dir ROBERTO NAPOLETANO; circ. 334,519.

Napoli
(Naples)

Corriere del Mezzogiorno: Vico II San Nicola alla Dogana 9, 80133 Napoli; tel. (081) 7602001; fax (081) 5802779; e-mail m.demarco@corrieredelmezzogiorno.it; internet www.corrieredelmezzogiorno.it; f. 1997; publr RCS MediaGroup; Dir MARCO DEMARCO.

Il Denaro: Via Kennedy 54, 800125 Napoli; tel. (081) 421900; fax (081) 422212; e-mail denaro@denaro.it; internet www.denaro.it; economic daily; Dir ALFONSO RUFFO.

Il Mattino: Via Chiatamone 65, 80121 Napoli; tel. (081) 7947111; fax (081) 7947288; e-mail redazioneinternet@ilmattino.it; internet www.ilmattino.it; f. 1892; reformed 1950; independent; Dir Gen. MASSIMO GARZILLI; Editor VIRMAN CUSENZA; circ. 99,776.

Padova
(Padua)

Il Mattino di Padova: Via N. Tommaseo, 65B, 35131 Padova; tel. (049) 8083411; fax (049) 8070067; e-mail mattino@mattinopadova.it; internet www.mattinopadova.it; f. 1978; publr Gruppo Editoriale L'Espresso, SpA; Dir ANTONIO RAMENGHI; circ. 34,282.

Palermo

Giornale di Sicilia: Via Lincoln 21, 90122 Palermo; tel. (091) 6627111; fax (091) 6627280; e-mail gds@gestelnet.it; internet www.gds.it; f. 1860; independent; Dir ANTONIO ARDIZZONE; circ. 73,269.

Parma

Gazzetta di Parma: Via Mantova 68, 43100 Parma; tel. (0521) 2251; fax (0521) 225522; e-mail gazzetta@gazzettadiparma.net; internet www.gazzettadiparma.it; f. 1735; Dir GIULIANO MOLOSSI; circ. 47,186.

Perugia

Corriere dell'Umbria: Via Pievaiola 166F, 06132 Perugia; tel. (075) 52731; fax (075) 5273400; e-mail info@corrieredellumbria.it; f. 1983; independent; Editor ANNA MOSSUTO; circ. 30,097.

Pescara

Il Centro: Via Tiburtina 91, 65129 Pescara; tel. (085) 20521; fax (085) 4318050; e-mail lettere@ilcentro.it; internet www.ilcentro.it; f. 1986; publr Gruppo Editoriale L'Espresso, SpA; Dir SERGIO BARALDI; circ. 29,063.

Piacenza

Libertà: Via Benedettine 68, 29100 Piacenza; tel. (0523) 393939; fax (0523) 321723; e-mail info@liberta.it; internet www.liberta.it; f. 1883; Dir RIZZUTO GAETANO; circ. 33,690.

Rimini

Corriere di Romagna: Piazza Tre Martiri 43A, 47900 Rimini; tel. (0541) 354111; fax (0541) 351499; e-mail lega@corriereromagna.it; internet www.corriereromagna.it; also distributed in San Marino; Dir MARIA PATRIZIA LANZETTI.

Roma
(Rome)

Conquiste del Lavoro: Via Po 22, 00198 Roma; tel. (06) 8473430; fax (06) 85412333; e-mail conquiste_lavoro@cisl.it; internet www.conquistedellavoro.it; owned by Confederazione Italiana Sindacati Lavoratori (CISL); Dir RAFFAELE BONANNI; circ. 90,000 (2008).

Il Corriere dello Sport—Stadio: Piazza Indipendenza 11B, 00185 Roma; tel. (06) 49921; fax (06) 4992275; e-mail segrdirgen@corsport.it; internet www.corsport.it; f. 1924; Editor ALESSANDRO VOCALELLI; circ. 314,576.

Il Manifesto: Via Tomacelli 146, 00186 Roma; tel. (06) 687191; fax (06) 68719573; e-mail redazione@ilmanifesto.it; internet www.ilmanifesto.it; f. 1971; splinter communist; Dir NORMA RANGERI; circ. 69,152.

Il Messaggero: Via del Tritone 152, 00187 Roma; tel. (06) 47201; fax (06) 4720300; e-mail posta@ilmessaggero.it; internet www.ilmessaggero.it; f. 1878; independent; Pres. FRANCO G. CALTAGIRONE; Editor NORMA RANGERI; circ. 265,063.

La Repubblica: Via Cristoforo Colombo 149, 00147 Roma; tel. (06) 49821; fax (06) 49822923; e-mail larepubblica@repubblica.it; internet www.repubblica.it; f. 1976; left-wing; publr Gruppo Editoriale L'Espresso, SpA; Dir EZIO MAURO; circ. 576,216.

Il Riformista: Via Trinità dei Pellegrini 12, 00186 Roma; tel. (06) 427481; fax (06) 42748215; e-mail redazione@ilriformista.it; internet www.ilriformista.it; political; Dir EMANUELE MACALUSO.

Il Tempo: Piazza Colonna 366, 00187 Roma; tel. (06) 675881; fax (06) 6758869; internet www.iltempo.it; f. 1944; independent; right-wing; Editor MARIO SECHI; circ. 57,922.

L'Unità: Via Ostiense 131L, 00154 Roma; tel. (06) 585571; fax (06) 58557219; e-mail unitaonline@unita.it; internet www.unita.it; f. 1924; Dir LUCA LANDÒ; circ. 118,662.

Salerno

La Città: Via San Leonardo 51, 84131 Salerno; tel. (089) 2783111; fax (089) 2783236; e-mail redazione@lacittadisalerno.it; internet www.lacittadisalerno.it; Dir ANGELO DI MARINO.

Sassari

La Nuova Sardegna: Strada 30–31, Predda Niedda, 07100 Sassari; tel. (079) 222400; fax (079) 2674086; e-mail redazione@lanuovasardegna.it; internet lanuovasardegna.repubblica.it; f. 1891; publr Gruppo Editoriale L'Espresso, SpA; Dir PAOLO CATELLA; circ. 63,175.

Torino
(Turin)

La Stampa: Via Marenco 32, 10126 Torino; tel. (011) 656811; fax (011) 655306; e-mail lettere@lastampa.it; internet www.lastampa.it; f. 1867; independent; Dir MARIO CALABRESI; circ. 381,423.

Trento

L'Adige: Via Missioni Africane 17, 38100 Trento; tel. (0461) 886111; fax (0461) 886264; e-mail p.giovanetti@ladige.it; internet www.ladige.it; f. 1946; independent; Dir Dott. PIERANGELO GIOVANETTI; circ. 30,646.

Trieste

Il Piccolo: Via Guido Reni 1, 34123 Trieste; tel. (040) 3733111; fax (040) 3733262; e-mail ufficio.centrale@ilpiccolo.it; internet ilpiccolo.repubblica.it; f. 1881; publr Gruppo Editoriale L'Espresso, SpA; Dir PAOLO POSSAMAI; circ. 41,999.

Primorski Dnevnik: Via dei Montecchi 6, 34137 Trieste; tel. (040) 7786300; fax (040) 772418; e-mail redakcija@primorski.eu; internet www.primorski.eu; f. 1945; Slovene; Editor-in-Chief DUŠAN UDOVIČ; circ. 11,282 (2010).

Udine

Il Messaggero Veneto: Viale Palmanova 290, 33100 Udine; tel. (0432) 5271; fax (0432) 523072; e-mail ufficio.centrale@messaggeroveneto.it; internet www.messaggeroveneto.it; f. 1946; publr Gruppo Editoriale L'Espresso, SpA; Dir ANDREA FILIPPI; circ. 56,496.

Varese

La Prealpina: Viale Tamagno 13, 21100 Varese; tel. (0332) 275700; fax (0332) 275701; e-mail direttore@prealpina.it; internet www.prealpina.it; f. 1888; Dir PAOLO PROVENZI; circ. 40,000 (2007).

Venezia
(Venice)

Il Gazzettino: Via Torino 110, 30172 Venezia-Mestre; tel. (041) 665111; fax (041) 665413; e-mail segredazione@gazzettino.it; internet www.gazzettino.it; f. 1887; independent; Dir ROBERTO PAPETTI; circ. 103,797.

Verona

L'Arena: Corso Porta Nuova, 67, 37122 Verona; tel. (045) 9600111; fax (045) 597966; e-mail redazione@larena.it; internet www.larena.it; f. 1866; independent; Editor-in-Chief MAURIZIO CATTANEO; Man. Dir Ing. ALESSANDRO ZELGER; circ. 54,411.

Vicenza

Il Giornale di Vicenza: Via Enrico Fermi 205,36100 Vicenza; tel. (0444) 396311; fax (0444) 396333; internet www.ilgiornaledivicenza.it; f. 1945; Dir ARIO GERVASUTTI; circ. 48,276.

SELECTED PERIODICALS

Art, Architecture and Design

Abitare: Via Ventura 5, 20134 Milano; tel. (02) 210581; fax (02) 21058316; e-mail redazione@abitare.it; internet www.abitare.it; f. 1962; monthly; architecture and design; in Italian and English; Editor RENATO MINETTO; Dir ITALO LUPI.

Casabella: Via Trentacoste 7, 20134 Milano; tel. (02) 215631; fax (02) 21563260; e-mail casabella@mondadori.it; f. 1928; 10 a year; architecture and interior design; Editor FRANCESCO DAL CO; circ. 43,000.

Domus: Via Gianni Mazzocchi 1/3, 20089 Rozzano, Milano; tel. (02) 824721; fax (02) 82472386; e-mail redazione@domusweb.it; internet www.domusweb.it; f. 1928; 11 a year; architecture, interior design and art; Editor G. MAZZOCCHI; circ. 53,000.

Graphicus: Alberto Greco Editore, Via Salvator Rosa 14, 20156 Milano; tel. (02) 300391; fax (02) 30039300; e-mail graphicus.age@gruppodg.com; f. 1911; 10 a year; printing and graphic arts; circ. 7,200.

Interni: Via D. Trentacoste 7, 20134 Milano; tel. (02) 215631; fax (02) 26410847; e-mail interni@mondadori.it; internet www.internimagazine.it; monthly; interior decoration and design; Editor GILDA BOJARDI; circ. 50,000.

Lotus International: Via Santa Marta 19A, 20123 Milano; tel. (02) 45475745; fax (02) 45475746; e-mail lotus@editorialelotus.it; internet www.editorialelotus.it; f. 1963; quarterly; architecture, town-planning; Editor PIERLUIGI NICOLIN.

Storia dell'Arte: CAM Editrice, Srl, Via Capodiferro 4, 00186 Roma; tel. and fax (06) 68300889; e-mail info@cameditrice.com; internet www.cameditrice.com; f. 1968; quarterly; art history; Dir MAURIZIO CALVESI; circ. 2,500.

Education

Cooperazione Educativa: Via dei Sabelli 119, 00185 Roma; tel. (06) 4457228; fax (06) 4460386; e-mail mceroma@tin.it; f. 1952; 4 a year; education; Dir MIRELLA GRIECO.

Il Maestro: Clivo di Monte del Gallo 48, 00165 Roma; tel. (06) 634651; fax (06) 39375903; e-mail aimc@aimc.it; internet www.aimc.it; f. 1945; monthly; Catholic teachers' magazine; Dir GIUSEPPE DESIDERI; circ. 40,000.

Scuola e Didattica: Via Cadorna 11, 25124 Brescia; tel. (030) 29931; fax (030) 2993299; e-mail sdid@lascuola.it; internet www.lascuola.it; f. 1904; 18 a year; education; Editor PIERPAOLO TRIANI; circ. 40,000.

General, Political and Economic

Economy: Arnoldo Mondadori Editore, SpA, Via Mondadori 1, 20090 Segrate (Milano); tel. (02) 75421; fax (02) 75422302; e-mail economy@mondadori.it; f. 2003; weekly; economics and finance; Dir SERGIO LUCIANO; circ. 85,000.

L'Espresso: Via Cristoforo Colombo 90, 00147 Roma; tel. (06) 84781; fax (06) 84787220; e-mail espresso@espressoedit.it; internet espresso.repubblica.it; weekly; independent left; political; Editor BRUNO MANFELLOTTO; circ. 500,452.

Famiglia Cristiana: Via Giotto 36, 20145 Milano; tel. (02) 48072777; fax (02) 48072778; e-mail famigliacristiana@stpauls.it; internet www.sanpaolo.org/fc; f. 1931; weekly; Catholic; illustrated; Dir ANTONIO SCIORTINO; circ. 685,739.

Gente: Viale Sarca 235, 20126 Milano; tel. (02) 27751; e-mail abbonamenti@hachette.it; internet www.abbonationline.it; f. 1957; weekly; illustrated current events and general interest; Dir MONICA MOSCA; circ. 488,629.

Il Mulino: Strada Maggiore 37, 40125 Bologna; tel. (051) 222419; fax (051) 6486014; e-mail rivistailmulino@mulino.it; internet www.rivistailmulino.it; f. 1951; every 2 months; culture and politics; Dir PIERO IGNAZI; Editor-in-Chief BRUNO SIMILI.

Oggi: Via San Marco 21, 20121 Milano; tel. (02) 25841; fax (02) 27201485; f. 1945; weekly; current affairs, culture, family life; illustrated; Dir UMBERTO BRINDANI; circ. 663,540.

Panorama: Arnoldo Mondadori Editore, SpA, Via A. Mondadori 1, 20090 Segrate, Milano; tel. (02) 75421; fax (02) 75422769; e-mail panorama@mondadori.it; internet www.panorama.it; f. 1962; weekly; current affairs; Dir GIORGIO MULÈ; circ. 501,111.

Visto: Via Rizzoli 8, 20132 Milano; tel. (02) 25843961; fax (02) 25843907; f. 1989; weekly; entertainment, celebrities, current events; Dir FRANCO BONERA; circ. 312,371.

Zett—Die Zeitung am Sonntag: Weinbergweg 7, 39100 Bozen; tel. (0471) 925500; fax (0471) 200462; e-mail zett@athesia.it; f. 1989; Sun; German language; circ. 34,000.

History, Literature and Music

Belfagor: Leo S. Olschki, Viuzzo del Pozzetto, 50126 Firenze; tel. (055) 6530684; fax (055) 6530214; e-mail periodici@olschki.it; internet www.olschki.it/riviste/belfagor.htm; f. 1946; every 2 months; historical and literary criticism; Editor CARLO FERDINANDO RUSSO; circ. 2,500.

Giornale della Libreria: Corso di Porta Romana 108, 20122 Milano; tel. (02) 89280802; fax (02) 89280862; e-mail redazione@giornaledellalibreria.it; internet www.giornaledellalibreria.it; f. 1888; monthly; organ of the Associazione Italiana Editori; bibliographical; Editor MARCO POLILLO; circ. 5,000.

Lettere Italiane: Leo S. Olschki, CP 66, 50123 Firenze; tel. (055) 6530684; fax (055) 6530214; e-mail pizzamig@unive.it; internet www.olschki.it/riviste/lettital.htm; f. 1949; quarterly; literary; Dirs CARLO OSSOLA, CARLO DELCORNO.

Il Pensiero Politico: Leo S. Olschki, Viuzzo del Pozzetto, 50126 Firenze; tel. (055) 6530684; fax (055) 6530214; e-mail penspol@unipg

.it; internet www.olschki.it/riviste/penspol.htm; f. 1968; every 4 months; political and social history; Editor VITTOR IVO COMPARATO.

Rivista di Storia della Filosofia: Viale Monza 106, 20127 Milano; tel. (02) 28371433; fax (02) 2613268; e-mail redazioni@francoangeli.it; internet www.francoangeli.it/riviste/sommario.asp?IDRivista=45; f. 1946; quarterly; philosophy; Editor ENRICO I. RAMBALDI.

Leisure and Sport

Ciak: Arnoldo Mondadori Editore, SpA, Via Mondadori 1, 20090 Segrate, Milano; tel. (02) 75421; fax (02) 75422302; e-mail ciak@mondadori.it; f. 1985; monthly; cinema; Dir PIERA DETASSIS; circ. 102,022.

Cucina Moderna: Arnoldo Mondadori Editore SpA, Via Mondadori 1, 20090 Segrate, Milano; tel. (02) 75421; fax (02) 75422302; f. 1996; monthly; cookery; Dir GIOVANNA CAMOZZI; circ. 299,866.

Dove: Via Angelo Rizzoli 2, 20132 Milano; tel. (02) 62291; e-mail marina.poggi@rcs.it; internet viaggi.corriere.it; f. 1991; monthly; lifestyle and travel; Dir CARLO MONTANARO; circ. 123,395.

Gambero Rosso: GRH, SpA, Via E. Fermi 161, 00146 Roma; tel. (06) 551121; fax (06) 55112260; e-mail gambero@gamberorosso.it; internet www.gamberorosso.it; f. 1987; monthly; food and wine; Dir LUIGI SALERNO.

Max: Via Angelo Rizzoli 2, 20132 Milano; e-mail max@rcs.it; internet max.corriere.it; f. 1985; monthly; men's lifestyle; Dir ANDREA MONTI; circ. 132,412.

OK: RCS MediaGroup, Via Rizzoli 8, 20132 Milan; e-mail redazione@ok.rcs.it; internet ok.corriere.it; monthly; health; Editor SIMONA TEDESCO; circ. 277,931.

Quattroruote: Via Gianni Mazzocchi 1/3, 20089 Rozzano, Milano; tel. (02) 824721; fax (02) 57500416; e-mail redazione@quattroruote.it; internet www.quattroruote.it; f. 1956; motoring; monthly; Editor MAURO TEDESCHINI; circ. 650,000.

Starbene: Arnoldo Mondadori Editore SpA, Via Mondadori 1, 20090 Segrate, Milano; tel. (02) 75421; e-mail starbene@mondadori.it; internet www.starbene.it; f. 1978; monthly; health and beauty; Dir CRISTINA MERLINO; circ. 395,050.

Telesette: Corso di Porta Nuova 3A, 20121 Milano; tel. (02) 63675415; fax (02) 63675524; e-mail segreteria@casaeditriceuniverso.com; f. 1978; weekly; television; Editor NICOLA DE FEO; circ. 551,601.

TV Sorrisi e Canzoni: Corso Europa 5–7, 20122 Milano; tel. (02) 77941; fax (02) 77947363; e-mail info@sorrisi.com; internet www.sorrisi.com; f. 1952; weekly; television, entertainment; Dir UMBERTO BRINDANI; circ. 1.1m.

Vita in Campagna: Via Bencivenga/Biondani 16, 37133 Verona; tel. (045) 8057511; fax (045) 597510; e-mail vitaincampagna@vitaincampagna.it; internet www.vitaincampagna.it; publr Editoriale L'Informatore Agrario, SpA; f. 1983; 11 a year; horticulture and smallholding; Editor ALBERTO RIZZOTTI; circ. 96,725.

Religion

Città di Vita: Piazza Santa Croce 16, 50122 Firenze; tel. and fax (055) 242783; e-mail info@cittadivita.org; internet www.cittadivita.org; f. 1946; every 2 months; cultural review, theology, art and science; Dir MASSIMILIANO G. ROSITO; circ. 2,000.

La Civiltà Cattolica: Via di Porta Pinciana 1, 00187 Roma; tel. (06) 6979201; fax (06) 69792022; e-mail civcatt@laciviltacattolica.it; internet www.laciviltacattolica.it; f. 1850; fortnightly; Catholic; Editor GIAN PAOLO SALVINI; circ. 17,000.

Humanitas: Via G. Rosa 71, 25121 Brescia; tel. (030) 46451; fax (030) 2400605; e-mail redazione@morcelliana.it; internet www.morcelliana.it; f. 1946; every 2 months; religion, philosophy, science, politics, history, sociology, literature, etc.; Dir ILARIO BERTOLETTI.

Protestantesimo: Via Pietro Cossa 42, 00193 Roma; tel. (06) 3207055; fax (06) 3201040; e-mail protestantesimo@facoltavaldese.org; internet www.facoltavaldese.org; f. 1946; quarterly; Waldensian review; Dir Prof. FULVIO FERRARIO.

Rivista di Storia della Chiesa in Italia: Via Merulana 124, 00185 Roma; e-mail lupi@uniroma3.it; internet www.vitaepensiero.it; f. 1947; 2 a year; Editor AGOSTINO PARAVICINI BAGLIANI.

Science, Technology and Medicine

Alberi e Territorio: Via Goito 13, 40126 Bologna; tel. (051) 65751; e-mail redazione.edagricole@ilsole24ore.com; internet www.edagricole.it; f. 2004 as successor to *Monti e Boschi* (f. 1949); 6 a year; ecology and forestry; Editor ELIA ZAMBONI; circ. 4,500.

Focus: Arnoldo Mondadori Editore SpA, Via Mondadori 1, 20090 Segrate, Milano; e-mail redazione@focus.it; internet www.focus.it; f. 1992; monthly; popular science and sociology; Dir SANDRO BOERI; circ. 606,563.

Il Nuovo Medico d'Italia: Via Monte Oliveto 2, 00141 Roma; tel. and fax (06) 87185017; e-mail numedi@tiscalinet.it; internet www.numedionline.it; monthly; medical science; Editor-in-Chief Dott. MARIO BERNARDINI.

Newton: Via San Marco 21, 20121 Milano; tel. (02) 25841; e-mail newton@rcs.it; internet newton.corriere.it; f. 1997; monthly; popular science; Dir GIORGIO RIVIECCIO; circ. 91,124.

Rivista Geografica Italiana: Via S. Gallo 10, 50129 Firenze; tel. and fax (055) 2757956; fax (055) 2725956; e-mail redazione@rivistageograficaitaliana.it; internet www.rivistageograficaitaliana.it; f. 1894; quarterly geographical review; owned by Società di Studi Geografici; Dir BRUNO VECCHIO.

Women's Interest

Amica: Via Angelo Rizzoli 2, 20132 Milano; tel. (02) 2588; f. 1962; monthly; Dir DANIELA BIANCHINI; circ. 175,663.

Anna: Via San Marco 21, 20121 Milano; tel. (02) 25843213; f. 1933; weekly; Editor MARIA LATELLA; circ. 265,654.

Chi: Arnoldo Mondadori Editore SpA, Via Mondadori 1, 20090 Segrate, Milano; e-mail chi@mondadori.it; f. 1995; weekly; celebrities, fashion; Dir ALFONSO SIGNORINI; circ. 569,175.

Confidenze: Arnoldo Mondadori Editore, SpA, Via Mondadori 1, 20090 Segrate, Milano; tel. (02) 75421; fax (02) 75422806; e-mail braccif@mondadori.it; f. 1946; weekly; Dir CRISTINA MAGNASCHI; circ. 187,395.

Cosmopolitan: Arnoldo Mondadori Editore, SpA, Via Marconi 27, 20090 Segrate, Milano; e-mail cosmopolitan@mondadori.it; internet www.cosmopolitan.it; f. 2000; monthly; Dir SIMONA MOVILIA; circ. 232,106.

Donna Moderna: Arnoldo Mondadori Editore, SpA, Via Mondadori 1, 20090 Segrate, Milano; e-mail donnamoderna@mondadori.it; internet www.donnamoderna.com; weekly; Dir PATRIZIA AVOLEDO; circ. 556,329.

Gioia: Viale Sarca 235, 20126 Milano; tel. (02) 66191; fax (02) 66192717; e-mail gioia@rusconi.it; f. 1937; weekly; Dir VERA MONTANARI; circ. 273,909.

Grazia: Arnoldo Mondadori Editore, SpA, Via Mondadori 1, 20090 Segrate, Milano; tel. (02) 75422390; fax (02) 75422515; e-mail graziamagazine@mondadori.it; internet www.graziamagazine.it; f. 1938; weekly; Dir VERA MONTANARI; circ. 252,255.

Intimità: Piazza Aspromonte 13, 20131 Milano; tel. (02) 706341; fax (02) 70642231; e-mail quadratum@quadratum.it; internet www.quadratum.it; weekly; Dir ANNA GIUSTI; circ.360,746.

Vanity Fair: Condé Nast S.p.A., Piazza Castello 27, 20121 Milano; e-mail abbonati@condenast.it; internet www.vanityfair.it; f. 2003; monthly; fashion, women's interest; Editor-in-Chief ROBERTO DELERA; circ. 362,550.

Vogue Italia: Piazza Castello 27, 20121 Milano; tel. (02) 85611; fax (02) 8055716; internet www.vogue.it; monthly; Editor FRANCA SOZZANI; circ. 106,187.

NEWS AGENCIES

AdnKronos: Palazzo dell'Informazione, Piazza Mastai 9, 00153 Roma; tel. (06) 58017; fax (06) 5807807; e-mail segreteria.redazione@adnkronos.com; internet www.adnkronos.it; Dir-Gen. MARIA ROSARIA BELLIZZI DE MARCO.

Agenzia Giornalistica Italia (AGI): Via Cristoforo Colombo 98, 00147 Roma; tel. (06) 519961; fax (06) 51996362; e-mail info@agenziaitalia.it; internet www.agi.it; f. 1950; Gen. Man. GIULIANO DE RISI.

Agenzia Nazionale Stampa Associata (ANSA): Via della Dataria 94, 00187 Roma; tel. (06) 67741; fax (06) 67746383; e-mail redazione.internet@ansa.it; internet www.ansa.it; f. 1945; co-operative, owned by 34 Italian newspapers; 22 regional offices in Italy and 79 brs internationally; service in Italian, Spanish, French, English; Pres. GIULIO ANSELMI; Dir-Gen. GIUSEPPE CERBONE.

APCOM (Telecom Media News, SpA): Via del Gesù 62, 00186 Roma; tel. (06) 695391; fax (06) 69539522; e-mail redazione@apcom.it; internet www.apcom.it; f. 2001; owned by Telecom Italia Media; partner of Associated Press (USA); operates in Italy and Switzerland.

Asca (Agenzia Stampa Quotidiana Nazionale): Via Ennio Quirino Visconti 8, 00193 Roma; tel. (06) 361484; e-mail agenzia@asca.it; internet www.asca.it; f. 1969; Dir CLAUDIO SONZOGNO.

Documentazioni Informazioni Resoconti (Dire): Via Guiseppe Marchi 4, 00161 Roma; tel. (06) 45499500; fax (06) 45499609; e-mail segr.direzione@dire.it; internet www.dire.it; Dir GIUSEPPE PACE.

Inter Press Service International Association (IPS): Via Panisperna 207, 00184 Roma; tel. (06) 485692; fax (06) 4817877; e-mail headquarters@ips.org; internet www.ips.org; f. 1964; non-profit asscn; international daily news agency; Dir-Gen. MARIO LUBETKIN.

PRESS ASSOCIATIONS

Associazione della Stampa Estera in Italia: Via della Umiltà 83C, 00187 Roma; tel. (06) 675911; fax (06) 67591262; e-mail segreteria@stampa-estera.it; internet www.stampa-estera.it; foreign correspondents' asscn; Pres. TOBIAS PILLER; Sec. MIRIAM MURPHY.

Federazione Italiana Editori Giornali (FIEG): Via Piemonte 64, 00187 Roma; tel. (06) 4881683; fax (06) 4871109; e-mail info@fieg.it; internet www.fieg.it; f. 1950; asscn of newspaper publishers; Pres. (vacant); 268 mems.

Federazione Nazionale della Stampa Italiana (FNSI): Corso Vittorio Emanuele II 349, 00186 Roma; tel. (06) 6833879; fax (06) 6871444; e-mail segrefnsi1@tin.it; internet www.fnsi.it; f. 1908; 19 affiliated unions; Pres. FRANCO SIDDI; Sec.-Gen. PAOLO SERVENTI LONGHI; 16,000 mems.

Unione Stampa Periodica Italiana (USPI): Viale Bardanzellu 95, 00155 Roma; tel. (06) 4071388; fax (06) 4066859; e-mail uspi@uspi.it; internet www.uspi.it; Pres. ANTONIO BARBIERATO; Gen. Sec. FRANCESCO SAVERIO VETERE; 4,500 mems.

Publishers

There are more than 300 major publishing houses and many smaller ones.

Adelphi Edizioni, SpA: Via S. Giovanni sul Muro 14, 20121 Milano; tel. (02) 725731; fax (02) 89010337; e-mail info@adelphi.it; internet www.adelphi.it; f. 1962; classics, philosophy, biography, music, art, psychology, religion and fiction; Pres. ROBERTO CALASSO.

Franco Angeli Editore Srl: Viale Monza 106, 20127 Milano; tel. (02) 2837141; fax (02) 26144793; e-mail redazione@francoangeli.it; internet www.francoangeli.it; f. 1955; academic and general non-fiction.

Armando Armando Srl: Viale Trastevere 236, 00153 Roma; tel. (06) 5894525; fax (06) 5818564; e-mail segreteria@armando.it; internet www.armando.it; f. 1950; philosophy, psychology, social sciences, languages, ecology, education; Man. Dir ENRICO JACOMETTI.

Arnoldo Mondadori Editore, SpA: Via Mondadori 1, 20090 Segrate, Milano; tel. (02) 75421; fax (02) 75422302; e-mail rapportistampa@mondadori.it; internet www.mondadori.it; f. 1907; books, magazines, printing, radio, advertising; CEO MAURIZIO COSTA.

Bollati Boringhieri Editore: Corso Vittorio Emanuele II 86, 10121 Torino; tel. (011) 5591711; fax (011) 543024; e-mail info@bollatiboringhieri.it; internet www.bollatiboringhieri.it; f. 1957; owned by Gruppo Editoriale Mauri Spagnol; history, economics, natural sciences, psychology, social and human sciences, fiction and literary criticism; Chair. ROMILDA BOLLATI; Editorial Dir FRANCESCO M. CATALUCCIO.

Bulzoni Editore: Via dei Liburni 14, 00185 Roma; tel. (06) 4455207; fax (06) 4450355; e-mail bulzoni@bulzoni.it; internet www.bulzoni.it; f. 1969; science, arts, fiction, textbooks; Man. Dir IVANA BULZONI.

Caltagirone Editore, SpA: Via Barberini 28, 00187 Roma; tel. (06) 45412200; fax (06) 45412299; e-mail invrel@caltagironegroup.it; internet www.caltagironeeditore.com; f. 1999; news publisher; Pres. FRANCESCO GAETANO CALTAGIRONE.

Cappelli Editore: Via Farini 14, 40124 Bologna; tel. (051) 239060; fax (051) 239286; e-mail info@cappellieditore.com; internet www.cappellieditore.com; f. 1880; medical science, history, politics, literature, textbooks; Chair. and Man. Dir MARIO MUSSO.

Casa Editrice Bonechi: Via dei Cairoli 18B, 50131 Firenze; tel. (055) 576841; fax (055) 5000766; e-mail info@bonechi.it; internet www.bonechi.com; f. 1973; art, travel, cooking; Pres. GIAMPAOLO BONECHI.

Casa Editrice Clueb Scarl (Cooperativa Libraria Universitaria Editrice Bologna): Via Marsala 31, 40126 Bologna; tel. (051) 220736; fax (051) 237758; e-mail info@clueb.com; internet www.clueb.com; f. 1959; university education, arts, business, history, literature; Man. Dir LUIGI GUARDIGLI.

Casa Editrice Edumond-Le Monnier, SpA: Via A. Meucci 2, 50015 Grassina, Firenze; tel. (055) 64910; fax (055) 6491310; e-mail informazioni.lemonnier@lemonnier.it; internet www.lemonnier.it; f. 1837; from 1999, part of Gruppo Mondadori; academic and cultural books, textbooks, dictionaries; Pres. GIUSEPPE DE RITA.

Casa Editrice Idelson Gnocchi Srl: Via Michele Pietravalle 85, 80131 Napoli; tel. (081) 5453443; fax (081) 5464991; e-mail info@idelson-gnocchi.com; internet www.idelson-gnocchi.com; f. 1908; medical and scientific; CEO GUIDO GNOCCHI.

Casa Editrice Leo S. Olschki: Via del Pozzetto 8, CP 66, 50126 Firenze; tel. (055) 6530684; fax (055) 6530214; e-mail celso@olschki.it; internet www.olschki.it; f. 1886; reference, periodicals, textbooks, humanities; Man. ALESSANDRO OLSCHKI.

Casa Editrice Luigi Trevisini Srl: Via Tito Livio 12, 20137 Milano; tel. (02) 5450704; fax (02) 55195782; e-mail trevisini@trevisini.it; internet www.trevisini.it; f. 1859; school textbooks; Dirs LUIGI TREVISINI, GIUSEPPINA TREVISINI.

Casa Editrice Marietti, SpA: Via Donizetti 41, 20122 Milano; tel. (02) 778899; fax (02) 76003491; e-mail mariettieditore@mariettieditore.it; internet www.mariettieditore.it; f. 1820; religion, liturgy, theology, fiction, history, literature, philosophy, poetry, art; Editor GIOVANNI UNGARELLI.

Casa Ricordi, SpA: Via Berchet 2, 20121 Milano; tel. (02) 88811; fax (02) 88812212; e-mail promozione.ricordi@bmg.com; internet www.ricordi.it; f. 1808; music; Chair. GIANNI BABINI; Man. Dir Dott. TINO GENNAMO.

CEDAM, SpA: Via Jappelli 5/6, 35121 Padova; tel. (049) 8239111; fax (049) 8752900; e-mail info@cedam.com; internet www.cedam.com; f. 1903; law, economics, political and social sciences, engineering, science, medicine, literature, philosophy, textbooks; Dirs ANTONIO MILANI, CARLO PORTA, FRANCESCO GIORDANO.

De Agostini Editore: Via Giovanni da Verrazano 15, 28100 Novara; tel. (0321) 4241; fax (0321) 471286; internet www.deagostini.it; f. 1901; geography, maps, encyclopaedias, dictionaries, art, literature, textbooks, science; Pres. PIETRO BOROLI; CEO LORENZO PELLICIOLI.

Editori Laterza: Via di Villa Sacchetti 17, 00197 Roma; tel. (06) 45465311; fax (06) 3223853; e-mail glaterza@laterza.it; internet www.laterza.it; f. 1885; belles-lettres, biography, reference, religion, art, classics, history, economics, philosophy, social sciences; Editorial Dirs ALESSANDRO LATERZA, GIUSEPPE LATERZA.

Editrice Ancora: Via G. B. Niccolini 8, 20154 Milano; tel. (02) 3456081; fax (02) 34560866; e-mail editrice@ancoralibri.it; internet www.ancoralibri.it; f. 1934; religious, educational; Dir GILBERTO ZINI.

Editrice Ave (Anonima Veritas Editrice): Via Aurelia 481, 00165 Roma; tel. (06) 661321; fax (06) 6620207; e-mail info@editriceave.it; internet www.editriceave.it; f. 1935; theology, sociology, pedagogy, psychology, essays, learned journals, religious textbooks; Pres. ARMANDO OBERTI.

Editrice Ciranna: Via G. Besio 143, 90145 Palermo; tel. (091) 224499; fax (091) 311064; e-mail info@ciranna.it; internet www.ciranna.it; f. 1950; school textbooks; Man. Dir LIDIA FABIANO.

Editrice La Scuola, SpA: Via Cadorna 11, 25124 Brescia; tel. (030) 2993; fax (030) 2993299; e-mail direzione@tin.it; internet www.lascuola.it; f. 1904; educational magazines, educational textbooks, audiovisual aids and toys; Chairs Dott. Ing. LUCIANO SILVERI, Dott. Ing. GIORGIO RACCIS; Man. Dir Rag. GIUSEPPE COVONE.

Edizioni Borla Srl: Via delle Fornaci 50, 00165 Roma; tel. (06) 39376728; fax (06) 39376620; e-mail borla@edizioni-borla.it; internet www.edizioni-borla.it; f. 1863; religion, philosophy, psychoanalysis, ethnology, literature; Man. Dir VINCENZO D'AGOSTINO.

Edizioni Lavoro: Via G. M. Lancisi 25, 00161 Roma; tel. (06) 44251174; fax (06) 44251177; e-mail info@edizionilavoro.it; internet www.edizionilavoro.it; f. 1982; history, politics, political philosophy, sociology, religion, Islamic, African, Arab and Caribbean literature; Chair. and Man. Dir PIETRO GELARDI.

Edizioni Mediterranee Srl: Via Flaminia 109, 00196 Roma; tel. (06) 32235433; fax (06) 3236277; e-mail press@edizionimediterranee.it; internet www.edizionimediterranee.it; f. 1953; alchemy, astrology, esoterism, meditation, natural medicine, parapsychology, hobbies, martial arts, zen.

Edizioni Rosminiane Sodalitas Sas: Centro Internazionale di Studi Rosminiani, Corso Umberto I 15, 28838 Stresa; tel. (0323) 30091; fax (0323) 31623; e-mail info@rosmini.it; internet www.rosmini.it; f. 1925; philosophy, theology, *Rivista Rosminiana* (quarterly); Dir Prof. PIER PAOLO OTTONELLO.

Edizioni San Paolo: Piazza Soncino 5, 20092 Cinisello Balsamo—Milano; tel. (02) 660751; fax (02) 66075211; e-mail sanpaoloedizioni@stpauls.it; internet www.edizionisanpaolo.it; f. 1914; Catholic; Gen. Man. VINCENZO SANTARCANGELO.

Edizioni Scientifiche Italiane, SpA (ESI): Via Chiatamone 7, 80121 Napoli; tel. (081) 7645443; fax (081) 7646477; e-mail info@edizioniesi.it; internet www.edizioniesi.it; f. 1945; law, economics, literature, arts, history, science; Pres. PIETRO PERLINGIERI.

Edizioni Studium: Via Cassiodoro 14, 00193 Roma; tel. (06) 6865846; fax (06) 6875456; e-mail info@edizionistudium.it; internet www.edizionistudium.it; f. 1927; philosophy, literature, sociology, pedagogy, religion, economics, law, science, history, psychology; Pres. VINCENZO CAPPELLATTI.

Giulio Einaudi Editore, SpA: Via Umberto Biancamano 2, 10121 Torino; tel. (011) 56561; fax (011) 542903; e-mail einaudi@einaudi.it; internet www.einaudi.it; f. 1933; fiction, classics, general; Chair. ROBERTO CERATI; CEO ENRICO SELVA CODDÈ.

Giangiacomo Feltrinelli Editore, SpA: Via Andegari 6, 20121 Milano; tel. (02) 725721; fax (02) 72572500; e-mail ufficio.stampa@feltrinelli.it; internet www.feltrinelli.it; f. 1954; fiction, juvenile, science, technology, history, literature, political science, philosophy; Chair. INGE FELTRINELLI; Publr CARLO FELTRINELLI.

Garzanti Libri, SpA: Via Gasparotto 1, 20124 Milano; tel. (02) 00623201; fax (02) 00623260; e-mail info@garzantilibri.it; internet www.garzantilibri.it; f. 1938; owned by Gruppo Editoriale Mauri Spagnol; literature, poetry, science, art, history, politics, encyclopaedias; Chair. GHERARDO COLOMBO; CEO STEFANO MAURI.

Ghisetti e Corvi Editori: Corso Concordia 7, 20129 Milano; tel. (02) 76006232; fax (02) 76009468; e-mail redazione@ghisettiecorvi.it; internet www.ghisettiecorvi.it; f. 1936; educational textbooks.

G. Giappichelli Editore Srl: Via Po 21, 10124 Torino; tel. (011) 8153511; fax (011) 8125100; e-mail contabilit@giappichelli.it; internet www.giappichelli.it; f. 1921; university publications on law, economics, politics and sociology.

Giunti Editore, SpA: Via Bolognese 165, 50139 Firenze; tel. (055) 5062231; fax (055) 5062298; e-mail segrgen@giunti.it; internet www.giunti.it; f. 1841; art, psychology, literature, science, law; CEO MARTINO MONTANARINI.

Gruppo Editoriale Mauri Spagnol, SpA: Via Gherardini 10, 20145 Milano; internet www.maurispagnol.it; f. 2005; owns Bollati Boringhieri Editore, La Cocinella, Casa Editrice Corbaccio, Garzanti Libri, Guanda, Longanesi, Editrice Nord, Ponte alle Grazie, Adriano Salani Editore, TEA (Tascabili degli Editori Associati), Antonio Vallardi Editore, and 50% of SuperPocket; Pres. STEFANO MAURI; CEO LUIGI SPAGNOL.

Gruppo Editoriale il Saggiatore: Via Melzo 9, 20129 Milano; tel. (02) 201301; fax (02) 29513061; e-mail commerciale@saggiatore.it; internet www.saggiatore.it; f. 1958; art, fiction, social sciences, history, travel, current affairs, popular science; Pres. LUCA FORMENTON.

Gruppo Ugo Mursia Editore, SpA: Via Melchiorre Gioia 45, 20124 Milano; tel. (02) 67378500; fax (02) 67378605; e-mail info@mursia.com; internet www.mursia.com; f. 1955; general fiction and non-fiction, reference, art, history, nautical books, philosophy, biography, sports, children's books; Gen. Man. FIORENZA MURSIA.

Guida Monaci, SpA: Via Salaria 1319, 00138 Roma; tel. (06) 8887777; fax (06) 8889996; e-mail infoitaly@italybygm.it; internet www.italybygm.it; f. 1870; commercial and industrial, financial, administrative and medical directories; Dir Ing. GIANCARLO ZAPPONINI.

Hearst Magazines Italia: Viale Sarca 235, 20126 Milano; tel. (02) 66191; fax (02) 252007333; e-mail abbonamenti@hachette.it; f. 1969 as Rusconi Libri Srl; magazines; Pres. DIDIER QUILLOT.

S. Lattes e C. Editori, SpA: Via Confienza 6, 10121 Torino; tel. (011) 5625335; fax (011) 5625070; e-mail info@latteseditori.it; internet www.latteseditori.it; f. 1893; technical, textbooks; Pres. CATERINA BOTTARI LATTES; Man. Dir RENATA LATTES.

Levrotto e Bella, Libreria Editrice Universitaria: Via Pigafetta Antonio 2E, 10129 Torino; tel. (011) 5097367; fax (011) 504025; e-mail ammin@levrotto-bella.net; internet www.levrotto-bella.net; f. 1911; university textbooks; Man. Dir Dott. ELISABETTA GUALINI.

Libreria Editrice Gregoriana: Via Roma 82, 35122 Padova; tel. (049) 661033; fax (049) 663640; e-mail l.gregoriana@mclink.it; f. 1922; Lexicon Totius Latinitatis, religion, philosophy, psychology, social studies; Dir GIANCARLO MINOZZI.

Liguori Editore Srl: Via Posillipo 394, 80123 Napoli; tel. (081) 5751272; fax (081) 5751231; e-mail info@liguori.it; internet www.liguori.it; f. 1949; linguistics, mathematics, engineering, economics, law, history, philosophy, sociology; Man. Dir Dott. GUIDO LIGUORI.

Loescher Editore: Via Vittorio Amedeo II 18, 10121 Torino; tel. (011) 5654111; fax (011) 5625822; e-mail mail@loescher.it; internet www.loescher.it; f. 1867; school textbooks, general literature, academic books; Chair. LORENZO ENRIQUES.

Longanesi e C., SpA: Via Gherardini 10, 20145 Milano; tel. (02) 34597620; fax (02) 34597212; e-mail info@longanesi.it; internet www.longanesi.it; f. 1946; owned by Gruppo Editoriale Mauri Spagnol; art, archaeology, culture, history, philosophy, fiction; Man. Dir STEFANO MAURI.

Neri Pozza Editore, SpA: Via E. Fermi 205, 36100 Vicenza; tel. (0444) 396323; fax (0444) 396325; e-mail info@neripozza.it; internet www.neripozza.it; f. 1946; art, fiction, history, politics; Pres. VITTORIO MINCATO; Dir ALESSANDRO ZELGER.

Palombi & Partner Srl: Via Gregorio VII 224, 00165 Roma; tel. (06) 636970; fax (06) 635746; e-mail info@palombieditori.it; internet www.palombieditori.it; f. 1914; history, art, etc. of Rome; Man. Dir Dott. FRANCESCO PALOMBI.

Pearson Italia, SpA: Via Archimede 10/23/51, 20129 Milano; tel. (02) 748231; fax (02) 74823278; internet www.pearson.it; f. 1946; school and university textbooks.

Petrini Editore: Strada del Portone 179, 10095 Grugliasco, Torino; tel. (011) 2098741; fax (011) 2098765; e-mail redazione@petrini.it; internet www.petrini.it; f. 1872; school textbooks.

Piccin Nuova Libraria, SpA: Via Altinate 107, 35121 Padova; tel. (049) 655566; fax (049) 8750693; e-mail info@piccinonline.com; internet www.piccinonline.com; f. 1980; scientific and medical textbooks and journals; Man. Dir Dott. MASSIMO PICCIN.

RCS Libri, SpA: Via San Marco 21, 20121 Milano; tel. (02) 25841; fax (02) 50952647; internet www.rcslibri.it; f. 1947; imprints include Rosellina Archinto Editore, Bompiani, BUR (Biblioteca Universale Rizzoli), Etas Srl, Fabbri, Marsilio Editore, La Nuova Editrice, SpA, Rizzoli, Sansoni, Sonzogno; fiction, juveniles, education, textbooks, reference, literature, art books; Chair. PIERGAETAN MARCHETTI; CEO ANTONIO PERRICONE.

Rosenberg & Sellier: Via Andrea Doria 14, 10123 Torino; tel. (011) 8127820; fax (011) 8127808; e-mail info@rosenbergesellier.it; internet www.rosenbergesellier.it; f. 1883; economics, history, gender studies, social sciences, philosophy, linguistics, Latin, dictionaries, scientific journals; Chair. and Man. Dir UGO GIANNI ROSENBERG.

Adriano Salani Editore Srl: Via Gherardini 10, 20145 Milano; tel. (02) 34597624; fax (02) 34597206; e-mail info@salani.it; internet www.salani.it; f. 1988; fiction, children's books; Editor MARIAGRAZIA MAZZITELLI.

Skira Editore: Palazzo Casati Stampa, Via Torino 61, 20123 Milano; tel. (02) 724441; fax (02) 72444211; e-mail skira@skira.net; internet www.skira.net; f. 1928; arts and literature; Pres. MASSIMO VITTA ZELMAN.

Società Editrice Dante Alighieri Srl: Via Monte Santo 10A, 00195 Roma; tel. (06) 3725870; fax (06) 37514807; e-mail nuovarivistastorica@dantealighierisrl.191.it; internet www.nuovarivistastorica.it; f. 1917; school textbooks, science and general culture; Dir GIGLIOLA SOLDI RONDININI.

Società Editrice Internazionale, SpA (SEI): Corso Regina Margherita 176, 10152 Torino; tel. (011) 52271; fax (011) 5211320; e-mail sei@seieditrice.com; internet www.seieditrice.com; f. 1908; textbooks, religion, history, education, multimedia; Head of Editorial Dept ULISSE JACOMUZZI.

Società Editrice Il Mulino: Strada Maggiore 37, 40125 Bologna; tel. (051) 256011; fax (051) 256034; e-mail info@mulino.it; internet www.mulino.it; f. 1954; politics, history, philosophy, social sciences, linguistics, literary criticism, law, psychology, economics, journals; Pres. ALESSANDRO CAVALLI.

Il Sole 24 Ore Edagricole: Via Goito 13, 40126 Bologna; tel. (051) 65751; fax (051) 6575800; e-mail redazione.edagricole@ilsole24ore.com; internet www.edagricole.it; group includes Calderini (f. 1960; art, sport, electronics, mechanics, university and school textbooks, travel guides, nursing, architecture) and Edagricole (f. 1935; agriculture, veterinary science, gardening, biology, textbooks); Pres. Prof. GIANCARLO CERUTTI; Man. Dir DONATELLA TREU.

Sugarco Edizioni Srl: Via don Gnocchi 4, 20148 Milano; tel. (02) 4078370; fax (02) 4078493; e-mail info@sugarcoedizioni.it; internet www.sugarcoedizioni.it; f. 1957; fiction, biography, history, philosophy, Italian classics; Gen. Man. ATTILIO TRENTINI.

Ulrico Hoepli Casa Editrice Libraria, SpA: Via Hoepli 5, 20121 Milano; tel. (02) 864871; fax (02) 864322; e-mail libreria@hoepli.it; internet www.hoepli.it; f. 1870; grammars, art, technical, scientific and school books, encyclopaedias; Chair. Dott. ULRICO HOEPLI; Man. Dir GIANNI HOEPLI.

UTET, SpA (Unione Tipografico-Editrice Torinese): Lungo Dora Colletta 67, 10153 Torino; tel. (011) 2099111; fax (011) 2099394; e-mail assistenza@utet.it; internet www.utet.it; f. 1791; part of Gruppo De Agostini; university and specialized editions on history, geography, art, literature, economics, sciences, encyclopaedias, dictionaries, etc.; Pres. ANTONIO BELLONI.

Vallecchi Editore, SpA: Via Maragliano 31, 50144 Firenze; tel. (055) 324761; fax (055) 3215387; e-mail dire@vallecchi.it; internet www.vallecchi.it; f. 1903; art, fiction, literature, essays, media; Pres. FERNANDO CORONA.

Vita e Pensiero: Largo A. Gemelli 1, 20123 Milano; tel. (02) 72342335; fax (02) 72342260; e-mail editrice.vp@unicatt.it; internet www.vitaepensiero.it; f. 1918; publisher of the Catholic University of the Sacred Heart, Milan; philosophy, literature, social science, theology, history; Dir AURELIO MOTTOLA.

GOVERNMENT PUBLISHING HOUSE

Istituto Poligrafico e Zecca dello Stato (IPZS): Piazza Verdi 10, 00198 Roma; tel. (06) 85081; fax (06) 85082517; e-mail informazioni@ipzs.it; internet www.ipzs.it; f. 1928; art, literary, scientific, technical books and reproductions; Chair. Dott. MICHELE TEDESCHI; Man. Dir Dott. LAMBERTO GABRIELLI.

PUBLISHERS' ASSOCIATION

Associazione Italiana Editori (AIE): Corso di Porta Romana 108, 20122 Milano; tel. (02) 89280800; fax (02) 89280860; e-mail aie@aie.it; internet www.aie.it; f. 1869; Dir ALFIERI LORENZON; 420 mems.

Broadcasting and Communications

REGULATORY AUTHORITY

Autorità per le Garanzie nelle Comunicazioni (AGCOM): Centro Direzionale, Isola B5, Torre Francesco, 80143 Napoli; tel. (081) 7507111; fax (081) 7507616; e-mail info@agcom.it; internet www.agcom.it; f. 1997; regulatory authority with responsibility for telecommunications, broadcasting and publishing; Pres. CORRADO CALABRÒ; Sec.-Gen. ROBERTO VIOLA.

TELECOMMUNICATIONS

3 Italia: Via Leonardo da Vinci 1, 20090 Trezzano sul Naviglio, Milano; tel. (02) 44581; fax (02) 445812713; internet www.tre.it; f. 2003; owned by Hutchison Whampoa Ltd (Hong Kong); mobile cellular telecommunications; CEO VINCENZO NOVARI.

FASTWEB: Via Caracciolo 51, 20155 Milano; tel. (02) 45451; fax (02) 45454811; internet www.fastweb.it; f. 2004 by merger of FastWeb and e.Biscom; offers fixed-line and mobile cellular telecommunications services, digital television and broadband internet services; 82.1% stake owned by Swisscom AG; Chair. CARSTEN SCHLOTER; Dir-Gen. ALBERTO CALCAGNO.

Tele2 Italia: Via Cassanese 210, 20090 Segrate, Milano; e-mail ufficio-stampa.tele2@tele2.it; internet www.tele2.it; f. 1999; fixed-line telecommunications and broadband internet services; owned by Vodafone Italia; Chair. SAVERIO TRIDICO; CEO MARCO BRAGADIN.

Telecom Italia: Piazza Affari 2, 20123 Milano; tel. (02) 85951; e-mail investitori.individuali@telecomitalia.it; internet www.telecomitalia.it; Italy's leading telecommunications operator; controlling stake owned by Telco, a consortium of Telefónica (Spain) and four Italian cos; Pres. and CEO FRANCO BERNABÈ.

TIM (Telecom Italia Mobile): Via Luigi Rizzo 22, 00136 Roma; tel. (06) 39001; internet www.tim.it; f. 1995; owned by Telecom Italia; mobile cellular telecommunications.

Tiscali Italia: loc. Sa Illetta, SS 195 Km 2300, 09122 Cagliari; tel. (070) 46011; fax (070) 4601296; e-mail info@tiscali.com; internet www.tiscali.it; f. 1998; internet service provider; Pres. and CEO RENATO SORU; Dir-Gen. LUCA SCANO.

Vodafone Italia: Via Caboto 15, 20094 Corsico, Milano; tel. (02) 41431; internet www.vodafone.it; f. 1995; mobile cellular telecommunications; Pres. PIETRO GUINDANI; CEO PAOLO BERTOLUZZO.

WIND Telecomunicazioni, SpA: Via Cesare Giulio Viola 48, 00148 Roma; tel. (06) 83111; internet www.windgroup.it; f. 1997; brands include WIND (mobile cellular telecommunications services) and Infostrada (fixed-line telecommunications and broadband internet services); Pres. KHALED BICHARA; CEO OSSAMA BESSADA.

BROADCASTING

Radio

Rai—Radiotelevisione Italiana: Viale Mazzini 14, 00195 Roma; tel. (06) 38781; fax (06) 3725680; e-mail radio@rai.it; internet www.radio.rai.it; f. 1924; a public share capital co; programmes comprise Radio Uno (general), Radio Due (recreational), Radio Tre (cultural); there are also regional programmes in Italian and in the languages of minority ethnic groups, and a foreign service, Rai International; Pres. PAOLO GARIMBERTI; Dir-Gen. LORENZA LEI.

Independent Stations

Radio Deejay: CP 314, Milano; tel. (02) 342522; e-mail diretta@deejay.it; internet www.deejay.it; f. 1982; propr Gruppo Editoriale L'Espresso, SpA; popular music; Dir GUIDO QUINTINO MARIOTTI.

Radio Italia Solo Musica Italiana: Viale Europa 49, 20093 Cologno Monzese, Milano; tel. (02) 254441; fax (02) 25444230; e-mail diretta@radioitalia.it; internet www.radioitalia.it; f. 1982.

Radio Maria: Via Milano 12, 22036 Erba, Como; tel. (031) 610610; e-mail info.ita@radiomaria.org; internet www.radiomaria.it; f. 1987; Roman Catholic; founder mem. of World Family of Radio Maria, comprising 40 national assens; Dir Fr LIVIO FANZAGA.

RDS Radio Dimensione Suono: Via Pier Ruggero Piccio 55, 20122 Roma; tel. (06) 377041; e-mail customercare@rds.it; internet www.rds.it; f. 1978.

RTL 102.5: Via Piemonte 61/63, 20093 Cologno Monzese, Milano; tel. (02) 251515; fax (02) 25096201; e-mail ufficiostampa@rtl.it; internet www.rtl.it; Pres. LORENZO SURACI.

Rundfunk Anstalt Südtirol (RAS): Europaallee 164A, 39100 Bozen; tel. (0471) 546666; fax (0471) 200378; e-mail info@ras.bz.it; internet www.ras.bz.it; f. 1975; relays television and radio broadcasts from Germany, Austria and Switzerland to the population of South Tyrol; Pres. RUDI GAMPER; Dir GEORG PLATTNER.

Television

There are two main national television channels: the state-owned Rai—Radiotelevisione Italiana and the Gruppo Mediaset. The process to switch from analogue to digital broadcasting began in 2009; this process was expected to be completed by 31 December 2012.

Rai—Radiotelevisione Italiana: Viale Mazzini 14, 00195 Roma; tel. (06) 38781; fax (06) 3725680; e-mail rai-tv@rai.it; internet www.rai.it; f. 1924; operates 3 terrestrial channels, Rai Uno, Rai Due and Rai Tre; satellite and digital channels include RaiNews24, Rai Sport and Rai Gulp (children's programmes); also broadcasts local programmes in Italian and in German for the South Tyrol; Pres. PAOLO GARIMBERTI; Dir-Gen. LORENZA LEI.

Independent Television Companies

Gruppo Mediaset: Piazza SS Giovanni e Paolo 8, 00184 Roma; tel. (06) 77081; e-mail mediaset@mediaset.it; internet www.gruppomediaset.it; f. 1993; operates Canale 5, Italia 1 and Rete 4; 38.8% stake owned by Fininvest; Pres. FEDELE CONFALONIERI; Vice-Pres. PIER SILVIO BERLUSCONI; Man. Dir GIULIANO ADREANI.

Rundfunk Anstalt Südtirol (RAS): see Radio.

Sky Italia: CP 13057, 20141 Milano; tel. (02) 70027300; e-mail info@sky.it; internet www.sky.it; f. 2003; owned by News Corporation (USA); broadcasts digital satellite channels; Chief Exec. ANDREA ZAPPIA.

Telecom Italia Media: Via della Pineta Sacchetti 229, 00168 Roma; tel. (06) 355841; e-mail carlo.demartino@telecomitalia.it; internet www.telecomitaliamedia.it; subsidiary of Telecom Italia, SpA; digital terrestrial broadcaster; operates 2 channels, La7 and MTV Italia; also operates APCOM (see News Agencies); Pres. SEVERINO SALVEMINI; Man. Dir GIOVANNI STELLA.

Finance

(cap. = capital; res = reserves; dep. = deposits; m. = million; amounts in euros; brs = branches)

In September 2008, of the 815 banks in existence, 251 were private banks, 438 were co-operative banks, 38 were *banche popolari* (a form of savings bank) and 88 were branches of foreign banks. In that year 83 banking groups were operating in Italy.

BANKING

Central Bank

Banca d'Italia: Via Nazionale 91, 00184 Roma; tel. (06) 47921; fax (06) 47922983; e-mail email@bancaditalia.it; internet www.bancaditalia.it; f. 1893; cap. 0.2m., res 20,078.7m., dep. 64,061.9m. (Dec. 2009); Gov. IGNAZIO VISCO; Dir-Gen. FABRIZIO SACCOMANNI; 74 brs.

Major Banks

Banca Antonveneta, SpA: Piazzetta Turati 2, 35131 Padova; tel. (049) 6991111; fax (049) 6991605; e-mail servizio.estero.pd@antonveneta.it; internet www.antonveneta.it; f. 1893 as Antoniana; acquired brs of Banca Agricola Mantonava, SpA in 2008; cap. 1,006.3m., res 2,409.6m., dep. 12,679m. (Dec. 2010); CEO GIUSEPPE MENZI; 403 brs.

Banca Carige, SpA (Cassa di Risparmio di Genova e Imperia): Via Cassa di Risparmio 15, 16123 Genova; tel. (010) 5791; fax (010) 5794000; e-mail carige@carige.it; internet www.gruppocarige.it; f. 1846; name changed as above in 1991; cap. 1,790.3m., res 1,710.9m., dep. 14,484.4m. (Dec. 2010); Chair. Dott. GIOVANNI BERNESCHI; Gen. Man. ENNIO LA MONICA.

Banca Carime, SpA: Viale Crati, 87100 Cosenza; tel. (0984) 8011; fax (0984) 806988; internet www.carime.it; f. 1998 as a result of merger of Carical, Carisal and Caripuglia savings banks; 92.8% owned by Gruppo Unione di Banche Italiane (UBI Banca); cap. 1,468.2m., res 83.5m., dep. 5,485.3m. (Dec. 2010); Chair. ANDREA PISANI MASSAMORMILE; Gen. Man. RAFFAELE AVANTAGGIATO; 344 brs.

Banca CR Firenze, SpA: Via Carlo Magno 7, 50127 Firenze; tel. (055) 26121; fax (055) 2613872; e-mail estero@bancacrfirenze.it; internet www.bancacrfirenze.it; f. 1829; name changed as above in 2003; 89.7% stake owned by Intesa Sanpaolo, SpA; cap. 829m., res 700.3m., dep. 20,404.3m. (Dec. 2010); Chair. and Pres. AURELIANO BENEDETTI; Gen. Man. and CEO LUCIANO NEBBIA; 320 brs and agencies.

Banca Fideuram, SpA: Piazzale Giulio Douhet 31, 00143 Milano; tel. (06) 59021; fax (06) 59022634; internet www.bancafideuram.it; f. 1913; name changed as above in 1992; owned by Intesa Sanpaolo, SpA; cap. 186.3m., res 351.3m., dep. 7,100.9m. (Dec. 2010); Pres. SALVATORE MACCARONE; Gen. Man. MATTEO COLAFRANCESCO; 53 brs.

Banca IMI: Piazza Giordano dell'Amore 3, 20121 Milano; tel. (02) 72611; fax (02) 77512030; e-mail info@bancaimi.it; internet www.bancaimi.it; f. 2007 by merger of Banca d'Intermediazione Mobiliare, SpA and Banca Caboto, SpA; owned by Intesa Sanpaolo, SpA; cap. 962.5m., res 1,560.2m., dep. 6,183.5m. (Dec. 2010); Chair. EMILIO OTTOLENGHI; Man. Dir ANDREA MUNARI.

Banca delle Marche, SpA: Via Alessandro Ghislieri 6, 60035 Jesi; tel. (0731) 5391; fax (0731) 539695; e-mail info@bancamarche.it; internet www.bancamarche.it; f. 1994; cap. 550m., res 559m., dep. 16,777.1m. (Dec. 2009); Chair. MICHELE AMBROSINI; Gen. Man. MASSIMO BIANCONI; 216 brs.

Banca Monte dei Paschi di Siena, SpA (Mps): Piazza Salimbeni 3, 53100 Siena; tel. (0577) 294111; fax (0577) 294313; e-mail info@banca.mps.it; internet www.mps.it; f. 1472; jt-stock co; Part of Gruppo Montepaschi, which also includes Banca Antonveneta and Biverbanca (Cassa di Risparmio di Biella e Vercelli); cap. 4,470.7m., res 11,953.7m., dep. 175,331.9m. (Dec. 2009); Chair. GIUSEPPE MUSSARI; CEO FABRIZIO VIOLA; 2,604 brs.

Banca Nazionale del Lavoro, SpA: Via Vittorio Veneto 119, 00187 Roma; tel. (06) 47021; fax (06) 47027336; e-mail redazionebnl@bnlmail.com; internet www.bnl.it; f. 1913; owned by BNP Paribas (France); cap. 2,076.9m., res 2,982m., dep. 64,166.7m. (Dec. 2010); Chair. Dott. LUIGI ABETE; Gen. Man. FABIO GALLIA; 864 brs.

Banca Popolare Commercio e Industria, SpA: CP 10167, Via della Moscova 33, 20121 Milano; tel. (02) 62755; fax (02) 62755640; e-mail intbkg@bpci.it; internet www.bpci.it; f. 1888; 64.4% stake owned by Unione di Banche Italiane (UBI Banca); cap. 934.2m., res 225.3m., dep. 6,173.8m. (Dec. 2010); Chair. MARIO CERA; Gen. Man. FRANCESCO IORIO; 225 brs.

Banca Popolare di Bergamo: Piazza Vittorio Veneto 8, 24122 Bergamo; tel. (035) 392111; fax (035) 392910; e-mail info@bpb.it; internet www.bpb.it; f. 1869; co-operative bank; name changed as above in 2003 following merger; 93% owned by Unione di Banche Italiane (UBI Banca); cap. 1,350.5m., res 793m., dep. 13,933.4m. (Dec. 2010); Chair. EMILIO ZANETTI; Man. Dir GIUSEPPE MASNAGA; 377 brs.

Banca Popolare dell'Emilia Romagna Società Cooperativa: Via San Carlo 8/20, 41100 Modena; tel. (059) 2021111; fax (059) 220537; e-mail relest@bper.it; internet www.bper.it; f. 1867; cap. 761.1m., res 1,742.7m., dep. 18,672.1m. (Dec. 2010); Chair. GIOVANNI MARANI; Gen. Man. MIMMO GUIDOTTI; 323 brs.

Banca Popolare di Milano Scarl: Piazza F. Meda 4, 20121 Milano; tel. (02) 77001; fax (02) 77002993; e-mail bipiemme@bpm.it; internet www.bpm.it; f. 1865; cap. 1,660.2m., res 1,557.4m., dep. 28,736.2m. (Dec. 2010); Pres. Dott. MASSIMO PONZELLINI; Gen. Man. Dott. ENZO CHIESA; 495 brs.

Banca Popolare di Sondrio Società Cooperativa per Azioni: Piazza Garibaldi 16, 23100 Sondrio; tel. (0342) 528111; fax (0342) 528204; e-mail info@popso.it; internet www.popso.it; f. 1871; cap. 884m., res 609m., dep. 19,854m. (Dec. 2009); Chair. and CEO PIERO MELAZZINI; Gen. Man. MARIO ALBERTO PEDRANZINI; 282 brs.

Banca Popolare di Vicenza, SCPA: Via Battaglione Framarin 18, 36100 Vicenza; tel. (0444) 339111; fax (0444) 907125; e-mail intdep@popvi.it; internet www.popolarevicenza.it; f. 1866; cap. 292.8m., res 2,433.1m., dep. 17,233.6m. (Dec. 2010); Chair. GIOVANNI ZONIN; Gen. Man. SAMUELE SORATO; 435 brs.

Banca Regionale Europea, SpA: Via Monte di Pietà 7, 20121 Milano; tel. (02) 721211; fax (02) 865413; internet www.brebanca.it; f. 1995 by merger of Cassa di Risparmio di Cuneo and Banca del Monte di Lombardia; 56.5% stake owned by Unione di Banche Italiane (UBI Banca); cap. 468.9m., res 747.6m., dep. 4,437.4m. (Dec. 2010); Chair. LUIGI ROSSI DI MONTELERA; Gen. Man. ROBERTO TONIZZO; 289 brs.

Banco di Brescia San Paolo Cab, SpA (Banco di Brescia): Corso Martiri della Libertà 13, 25171 Brescia; tel. (030) 29921; fax (030) 2992470; e-mail info@bancodibrescia.com; internet www.bancodibrescia.com; f. 1999; 96.4% owned by Unione di Banche Italiane (UBI Banca); cap. 615.6m., res 772.5m., dep. 10,426.7m. (Dec. 2010); Chair. FRANCO POLOTTI; Dir-Gen. ELVIO SONNINO; 348 brs.

Banco di Sardegna, SpA: Viale Umberto 36, 07100 Sassari; tel. (079) 226000; fax (079) 226015; e-mail privacy@bancosardegna.it; internet www.bancosardegna.it; f. 1953; cap. 155.2m., res 1,009.9m., dep. 9,067.4m. (Dec. 2010); Chair. Prof. FRANCO ANTONIO FARINA; Gen. Man. Dott. ALESSANDRO VANDELLI; 392 brs.

Banco di Sicilia, SpA: Via Generale Magliocco 1, 90141 Palermo; tel. (091) 6081111; fax (091) 6085124; internet www.bancodisicilia.it; f. 1860; owned by UniCredit, SpA; cap. 739m., res 352m., dep. 21,553m. (Dec. 2006); Pres. IVANHOE LO BELLO; Man. Dir NICOLÒ FILINGERI; 430 brs.

Banco Popolare Società Cooperativa: Piazza Nogara 2, 37121 Verona; tel. (45) 8675111; e-mail ufficio.stampa@bancopopolare.it; internet www.bancopopolare.it; f. 2007 by merger of Banca Popolare Italiana and Banco Popolare di Verona e Novara; cap. 2,275m., res 7,843m., dep. 104,970m. (Dec. 2008); Chair., Supervisory Bd CARLO FRATTA PASINI; Chair., Management Bd VITTORIO CODA.

Cassa di Risparmio di Parma e Piacenza, SpA (Cariparma): Via Università 1, 43100 Parma; tel. (0521) 912111; fax (0521) 912976; e-mail crprpc@cariparma.it; internet www.cariparma.it; f. 1860; name changed as above in 1993; 75% stake owned by Crédit Agricole SA (France); cap. 785.1m., res 2,855.6m., dep. 20,642.4m. (Dec. 2010); CEO GIAMPIERO MAIOLI; 537 brs.

Cassa di Risparmio di Venezia, SpA: San Marco 4216, Venezia 30124; tel. (041) 5291111; fax (041) 5292336; internet www.carive.it; f. 1822; owned by Intesa Sanpaolo, SpA; cap. 284.5m., res 84.4m., dep. 4,118.9m. (Dec. 2009); Chair. GIOVANNI SAMMARTINI; Gen. Man. MASSIMO MAZZEGA.

Cassa di Risparmio in Bologna, SpA (CARISBO): Via Farini 22, 40124 Bologna; tel. (051) 6454111; fax (051) 6454366; internet www.carisbo.it; f. 1837; owned by Intesa Sanpaolo, SpA; cap. 696.7m., res 213.5m., dep. 7,670.7m. (Dec. 2010); Pres. and Chair. FILIPPO CAVAZUTTI; Gen. Man. GIUSEPPE FELIZIANI; 201 brs.

Credito Bergamasco, SpA: Largo Porta Nuova 2, 24122 Bergamo; tel. (035) 393111; fax (035) 393144; e-mail ufficio.estero@creberg.it; internet www.creberg.it; f. 1891 as Banca Piccolo Credito Bergamasco; name changed as above in 1969; 88.9% owned by Banco Popolare Società Cooperativa; cap. 185.2m., res 1,077.2m., dep. 10,068.9m. (Dec. 2010); Pres. CESARE ZONCA; 245 brs.

Credito Emiliano, SpA (CREDEM): Via Emilia S. Pietro 4, 42100 Reggio-Emilia; tel. (0522) 582111; fax (0522) 433969; internet www.credem.it; f. 1910; cap. 332.4m., res 1,392.9m., dep. 15,427.5m. (Dec. 2010); Pres. GIORGIO FERRARI; CEO ADOLFO BIZZOCCHI; 563 brs.

Credito Valtellinese Società Cooperativa: Piazza Quadrivio 8, 23100 Sondrio; tel. (0342) 522111; fax (0342) 522700; e-mail creval@creval.it; internet www.creval.it; f. 1908; present name adopted 2005; cap. 653m., res 969m., dep. 8,420m. (Dec. 2008); Chair. GIOVANNI DE CENSI; Man. Dir MIRO FIORDI; 107 brs.

Intesa Sanpaolo, SpA: Piazza San Carlo 156, 10121 Torino; tel. (011) 5551; fax (011) 5552989; e-mail investor.relations@intesasanpaolo.com; internet www.group.intesasanpaolo.com; f. 2007 by merger of Sanpaolo IMI, SpA with Banca Intesa, SpA; cap. 6,647m., res 44,181m., dep. 257,706m. (Dec. 2010); Man. Dir and CEO ENRICO CUCCHIANI; 8501 brs.

Mediocredito Centrale, SpA: Via Piemonte 51, 00187 Roma; tel. (06) 47911; fax (06) 47913130; e-mail mcc@mcc.it; internet www.mcc.it; f. 1952; renamed as above following demerger with Unicredit, SpA in 2011; cap. 723m., res –1.7m., dep. 6,413m. (Dec. 2008); Chair. MASSIMO SARMI; Man. Dir PIERO LUIGI MONTANI.

UniCredit, SpA: Piazza Cordusio, 20123 Milano; tel. (02) 88621; fax (02) 88623034; e-mail info@unicreditgroup.eu; internet www.unicreditgroup.eu; f. 2007 by merger of Capitalia, SpA and Unicredito Italiano, SpA; present name adopted 2008; cap. 9,648.8m., res 53,251.9m., dep. 445,195.9m. (Dec. 2010); CEO FEDERICO GHIZZONI; 3 brs.

UniCredit Banca di Roma, SpA: Viale Umberto Tupini 180, 00144 Roma; tel. (06) 54451; fax (06) 54453154; e-mail webmaster@bancaroma.it; internet www.bancaroma.it; f. 2002; present name adopted 2008; cap. 2,336m., res 2,243m., dep. 53,828m. (Dec. 2006); Chair. PAOLO SAVONA; CEO PAOLO FIORENTINO; 1,123 brs.

Unione di Banche Italiane Scpa (UBI Banca): Piazza Vittorio Veneto 8, 24122 Bergamo; tel. (035) 392111; fax (02) 392390; internet www.ubibanca.it; f. 2003 as Banche Popolari Unite; present name adopted 2007, following merger with Banca Lombarda e Piemontese; cap. 1,597.9, res 9,209m., dep. 52,157.5m. (Dec. 2010); Chair. EMILIO ZANETTI; Gen. Man. GRAZIANO CALDIANI.

FINANCIAL INSTITUTIONS

CENTROBANCA—Banca di Credito Finanziario e Mobiliare, SpA: Corso Europa 16, 20122 Milano; tel. (02) 77811; fax (02) 77814509; e-mail comunica@centrobanca.it; internet www.centrobanca.it; f. 1946; name changed as above in 2001; 92.4% stake owned by Unione di Banche Italiane (UBI Banca); central org. for medium- and long-term operations of Banche Popolari (co-operative banks) throughout Italy; cap. 369.6m., res 207.5m., dep. 3,372.1m. (Dec. 2010); Chair. ANDREA MOLTRASIO; CEO MASSIMO CAPUANO.

Dexia Crediop, SpA: Via Venti Settembre 30, 00187 Roma; tel. (06) 47711; fax (06) 47715952; e-mail cm@dexia-crediop.it; internet www.dexia-crediop.it; f. 1919; incorporated 1996 as CREDIOP; name changed as above in 2001; cap. 450.2m., res 763.2m., dep. 7,924.1m. (Dec. 2010); Dir JEAN BOURRELLY; Man. Dir JEAN LE NAOUR.

ICCREA Banca (Istituto Centrale del Credito Cooperativo): Via Lucrezia Romana 41, 00178 Roma; tel. (06) 72071; fax (06) 72077706; e-mail info@iccrea.bcc.it; internet www.iccrea.it; f. 1963; cap. 216.9m., res 101.4m., dep. 6,615.2m. (Dec. 2010); Chair. VITO LORENZO AUGUSTO DELL'ERBA; Gen. Man. LUCIANO GIORGIO GORNATI; 6 brs.

INTERBANCA, SpA: Corso Venezia 56, 20121 Milano; tel. (02) 77311; fax (02) 76014913; e-mail marketing@interbanca.it; internet www.interbanca.it; f. 1961; acquired by GE Capital (United Kingdom) in Jan. 2009; cap. 217m., res 675m., dep. 6,273m. (Dec. 2008); Chair. FRANCESCO CARRI; 11 brs.

Mediobanca—Banca di Credito Finanziario, SpA: Piazzetta Enrico Cuccia 1, 20121 Milano; tel. (02) 88291; fax (02) 8829367; e-mail info@mediobanca.it; internet www.mediobanca.it; f. 1946; cap. 430.5m., res 5,899.8m., dep. 14,463.6m. (Dec. 2010); Chair. RENATO PAGLIARO (acting); Gen. Man. ALBERTO NAGEL; 1 br.

BANKERS' ORGANIZATION

Associazione Bancaria Italiana: Palazzo Altieri, Piazza del Gesù 49, 00186 Roma; tel. (06) 67671; fax (06) 6767457; e-mail abi@abi.it; internet www.abi.it; f. 1919; advocates the common interests of the banking industry; Pres. GIUSEPPE MUSSARI; Dir-Gen. Dott. GIOVANNI SABATINI; membership (1,003 mems) is composed of the following institutions: banks authorized to gather savings from the general public and exercise credit business as well as to perform other financial activities; brs and representative offices of foreign banks; asscns of banks or financial intermediaries; financial intermediaries engaging in one or more of the activities subject to mutual recognition under the Second Banking Directive or other financial activities subject to public prudential supervision.

STOCK EXCHANGES

Commissione Nazionale per le Società e la Borsa (CONSOB) (Commission for Companies and the Stock Exchange): Via G. B. Martini 3, 00198 Roma; tel. (06) 84771; fax (06) 8417707; e-mail consob@consob.it; internet www.consob.it; f. 1974; regulatory control over cos quoted on stock exchanges, convertible bonds, unlisted securities, insider trading, all forms of public saving except bank deposits and mutual funds; Dir-Gen. ANTONIO ROSATI.

Borsa Italiana (Italian Stock Exchange): Piazza degli Affari 6, 20123 Milano; tel. (02) 724261; fax (02) 72004333; e-mail info@borsaitalia.it; internet www.borsaitalia.it; merged with London Stock Exchange in 2007; Chair. ANGELO TANTAZZI; Pres. and CEO MASSIMO CAPUANO; 331 listed cos (Feb. 2010).

INSURANCE

In December 2009 there were 241 insurance and reinsurance companies operating in Italy, of which 156 were Italian.

Alleanza Toro, SpA: Via Mazzini 53, 10123 Torino; tel. (011) 0029111; fax (011) 837554; internet www.alleanzatoro.it; f. 2009; by the merger of Alleanza Assicurazioni, SpA and Toro Assicurazioni, SpA; life and non—life; Pres. LUIGI DE PUPPI.

Allianz, SpA: Largo Ugo Irneri 1, 34123 Trieste; tel. (40) 7781111; fax (40) 7781311; e-mail info@allianz.it; internet www.allianz.it; f. 1838; cap. 403m. (2008); Chair. Dott. GIUSEPPE VITA; CEO GEORGE SARTOREL.

Allianz Subalpina, SpA: Via Alfieri 22, 10121 Torino; tel. (011) 5161111; fax (011) 5161255; e-mail info@azs.it; internet www.allianzsubalpina.it; f. 1928; part of Gruppo Ras; net profit 55.6m. (2004); CEO GEORGE SARTOREL.

Assicurazioni Generali, SpA: Piazza Duca degli Abruzzi 2, 34132 Trieste; tel. (040) 671111; fax (040) 671600; internet www.generali.com; f. 1831; life and non-life; Chair. GABRIELE GALATERI DI GENOLA.

Atradius Credit Insurance, NV, Rappresentanza Generale per l'Italia: Via Crescenzio 12, 00193 Roma; tel. (06) 688121; fax (06) 6874418; e-mail info.it@atradius.com; internet www.atradius.com; CEO ISIDORO UNDA.

Axa Assicurazioni: Via Leopardi 15, 20123 Milano; tel. (02) 480841; fax (02) 48084331; internet www.axa.it; f. 1956; Chair. and Man. Dir MASSIMO MICHAUD.

AXA MPS Assicurazioni Vita, SpA: Via Aldo Fabrizi 9, 00128 Roma; tel. (06) 50870601; fax (06) 50870570; e-mail info@axa-mpsdanni.it; internet www.axa-mps.it; f. 2007; Chair. FRÉDÉRIC MARIE DE COURTOIS D'ARCOLLIÈRES.

Carige Assicurazioni: Viale Certosa 222, 20156 Milano; tel. (02) 30761; fax (02) 3086125; e-mail info@carigeassicurazioni.it; internet www.carigeassicurazioni.it; f. 1963; Pres. ALFREDO SANGUINETTO.

Creditras Vita, SpA: Corso d'Italia 23, 20122 Milano; tel. (02) 72161; fax (02) 72164032; e-mail info@creditrasvita.it; internet www.creditrasvita.it; f. 1995; life insurance; Pres. ARISTIDE CANOSANI.

FATA Assicurazioni, SpA (Fondo Assicurativo Tra Agricoltori): Via Urbana 169A, 00184 Roma; tel. (06) 47651; fax (06) 4871187; e-mail info@fata-assicurazioni.it; internet www.fata-assicurazioni.it; f. 1927; subsidiary of Gruppo Generali; Pres. Dott. GIUSEPPE PERISSINOTTO.

Fondiaria—Sai, SpA: Corso Galileo Galilei 12, 10126 Torino; tel. (055) 4794308; fax (055) 4792006; e-mail fondiaria-sai@fondiaria-sai.it; internet www.fondiaria-sai.it; f. 1879; owned by Gruppo Fondiaria-Sai; non-life; Pres. JONELLA LIGRESTI; Dir Gen. EMANUELE ERBETTA.

Groupama Assicurazioni, SpA: Via Cesare Pavese 385, 00144 Roma; tel. (06) 30181; fax (06) 30183382; e-mail info@groupama.it; internet www.groupama.it; f. 1929; as Nuova Tirrena, SpA; name changed as above in 2009; subsidiary of Gruppo Toro; Pres. PIERRE LEFÈVRE; Dir-Gen. and CEO CHRISTOPHE BUSO.

HDI Assicurazioni, SpA: Via Abruzzi 10, 00187 Roma; tel. (06) 421031; fax (06) 42103500; e-mail hdi.assicurazioni@hdia.it; internet www.hdia.it; f. 2001.

INA Assitalia, SpA: Via Leonida Bissolati 23, 00187 Roma; tel. (06) 84831; fax (06) 84833898; e-mail info@inaassitalia.it; internet www.inaassitalia.it; f. 1912; subsidiary of Gruppo Generali; Chair. Dott. FRANCESCO PROCACCINI; Man. Dir FABIO BUSCARINI.

Intesa Sanpaolo Vita, SpA: Viale Stelvio 55-57, 20159 Milano; tel. (02) 30511; fax (02) 30518188; internet www.intesasanpaolovita.it; life insurance; Pres. and CEO GIANEMILIO OSCULATI.

Italiana Assicurazioni, SpA: Via Traiano 18, 20149 Milano; tel. (02) 397161; fax (02) 3271270; internet www.italiana.it; f. 1898; as Cooperativa Italiana Incendio; name changed as above in 1995; Pres. ITI MIHALICH.

Mediolanum Vita, SpA: Palazzo Meucci, Via Francesco Sforza 15, 20080 Basiglio, Milano; tel. (02) 90491; fax (02) 90492427; e-mail info@mediolanum.it; internet www.mediolanumvita.it; f. 1972; life insurance; Pres. and CEO Dott. ALFREDO MESSINA.

Milano Assicurazioni (Compagnia di Assicurazioni di Milano, SpA): Via Senigallia 18, 20161 Milano; tel. (02) 64021; fax (02) 64022331; e-mail milass@milass.it; internet www.milass.it; f. 1825; owned by Gruppo Fondiaria-Sai; Dir Gen. EMANUELE ERBETTA.

Poste Vita: Piazzale Konrad Adenauer 3, 00144 Roma; tel. (06) 549241; internet www.postevita.it; f. 2000; subsidiary of Gruppo Poste Italiane; life insurance; Pres. ROBERTO COLOMBO.

SARA Assicurazioni, SpA: Via Po 20, 00198 Roma; tel. (06) 84751; fax (06) 8475223; internet www.saraassicurazioni.it; f. 1924; Chair. ROSARIO ALESSI; Gen. Man. Dott. MARCO ROCCA.

Società Cattolica di Assicurazione—Società Cooperativa: Lungadige Cangrande 16, 37126 Verona; tel. (045) 8391111; fax (045) 8391112; e-mail investor.relations@cattolicaassicurazioni.it; internet www.cattolicaassicurazioni.it; f. 1896; total premiums 4,617m. (Dec. 2004); CEO Dott. GIOVANNI BATTISTA MAZZUCCHELLI.

Società Reale Mutua di Assicurazioni: Via Corte d'Appello 11, 10122 Torino; tel. (011) 4311111; fax (011) 4350966; e-mail buongiornoreale@realmutua.it; internet www.realemutua.it; f. 1828; net profit 31.41m. (2007); Chair. Dott. ITI MIHALICH; Gen. Man. LUIGI LANA.

Swiss Re Italia, SpA: Via dei Giuochi Istmici 40, 00194 Roma; tel. (06) 323931; fax (06) 36303398; e-mail srit-communicazione@swissre.com; internet www.swissre.com; f. 1922; Chair. WALTER B. KIELHOLZ; Man. Dir MAURIZIO VALSECCHI.

UGF Assicurazioni, SpA: Via Stalingrado 45, 40128 Bologna; tel. (051) 5077111; fax (051) 375349; internet www.unipolonline.it; f. 1963; fmrly Unipol Assicurazioni; present name adopted in 2009 following merger with Aurora Assicurazioni; part of Grupo Unipol; non-life; Pres. VANES GALANTI; CEO CARLO CIMBRI.

Vittoria Assicurazioni, SpA: Via Ignazio Gardella 2, 20149 Milano; tel. (02) 482191; fax (02) 48203693; e-mail serviziolegale@vittoriaassicurazioni.it; internet www.vittoriaassicurazioni.com; f. 1921; cap. 3,277.1m. (July 2008); Chair. Dott. GIORGIO COSTA; CEO ROBERTO GUARENA.

Zurich Insurance PLC: Via Crespi 23, 20159 Milano; tel. (02) 59661; fax (02) 59662603; e-mail informazioni@zurich.it; internet www.zurich.it; f. 1872; as l'Unione delle assicurazioni; CEO CAMILLO CANDIA.

Regulatory Authority

Istituto per la Vigilanza sulle Assicurazioni Private e di Interesse Collettivo (ISVAP): Via del Quirinale 21, 00187 Roma; tel. (06) 421331; fax (06) 42133206; e-mail scrivi@isvap.it; internet www.isvap.it; f. 1982; supervises insurance cos; Pres. and Dir-Gen. GIANCARLO GIANNINI.

Insurance Association

Associazione Nazionale fra le Imprese Assicuratrici (ANIA): Via della Frezza 70, 00186 Roma; tel. (06) 326881; fax (06) 3227135;

e-mail info@ania.it; internet www.ania.it; f. 1944; Pres. Dott. ALDO MINUCCI; Dir-Gen. Prof. PAOLO GARONNA; 173 mems.

Trade and Industry

GOVERNMENT AGENCIES

Agenzia per la promozione all'estero e l'internazionalizzaizone delle imprese italiane (ICE) (National Institute for Foreign Trade): Via Liszt 21, 00144 Roma; tel. (06) 59929388; fax (06) 89280312; e-mail assistenza.export@ice.it; internet www.ice.gov.it; f. 1926; govt agency for the promotion of foreign trade.

Autorità Garante della Concorrenza e del Mercato (AGCM) (Regulatory Authority for Competition and Markets): Piazza Verdi 6 A, 00198 Roma; tel. (06) 858211; fax (06) 85821256; e-mail antitrust@agcm.it; internet www.agcm.it; Chair. GIOVANNI PITRUZZELLA; Sec.-Gen. ROBERTO CHIEPPA.

Cassa depositi e prestiti SpA (CDP): Via Goito 4, 00185 Roma; tel. (06) 42211; fax (06) 42214026; internet www.cassaddpp.it; f. 1850; provides loans to public bodies and local govt; 70% owned by Ministry of the Economy and Finance, 30% by banking foundations; Chair. FRANCO BASSANINI; CEO GIOVANNI GORNO TEMPINI.

Società Italiana per le Imprese All'Estero, SpA (SIMEST) (Italian Company for Businesses Abroad): Corso Vittorio Emanuele II 323, 00186 Roma; tel. (06) 686351; fax (06) 68635220; e-mail info@simest.it; internet www.simest.it; Pres. GIANCARLO LANNA.

CHAMBER OF COMMERCE

Unioncamere (Union of Chambers of Commerce, Industry, Crafts and Agriculture): Piazza Sallustio 21, 00187 Roma; tel. (06) 47041; fax (06) 4704240; e-mail segretaria.generale@unioncamere.it; internet www.unioncamere.it; f. 1954; frmly Unione Italiana delle Camere di Commercio, Industria, Artigianato e Agricoltura (Italian Union of Chambers of Commerce, Industry, Crafts and Agriculture); Pres. CARLO SANGALLI; Sec.-Gen. CLAUDIO GAGLIARDI.

INDUSTRIAL AND TRADE ASSOCIATIONS

Confederazione Generale dell'Industria Italiana (Confindustria) (General Confederation of Italian Industry): Viale dell'Astronomia 30, 00144 Roma; tel. (06) 59031; fax (06) 5919615; e-mail piei@confindustria.it; internet www.confindustria.it; f. 1910; re-established 1944; mems: 107 categorized asscns, 103 territorial asscns, 18 regional confeds, 18 sectoral feds and 253 associated orgs, totalling 126,590 firms and 4.78m. employees; Pres. EMMA MARCEGAGLIA; Dir-Gen. GIAMPAOLO GALLI.

Principal Organizations Affiliated to Confindustria

Associazione delle Imprese del Farmaco (FARMINDUSTRIA) (Pharmaceutical Industry): Largo del Nazareno 3/8, 00187 Roma; tel. (06) 675801; fax (06) 6786494; e-mail farmindustria@farmindustria.it; internet www.farmindustria.it; f. 1978; Pres. Dott. SERGIO DOMPÉ; 214 mem. firms (2007).

Associazione Industrie per l'Aerospazio, i Sistemi e la Difesa (AIAD) (Aerospace, Systems and Defence Industries): Via Nazionale 54, 00184 Roma; tel. (06) 4880247; fax (06) 4827476; e-mail aiad@aiad.it; internet www.aiad.it; f. 1947; Pres. REMO PERTICA; Sec.-Gen. CARLO FESTUCCI.

Associazione Italiana Tecnico Economica del Cemento (AITEC) (Cement): Piazza G. Marconi 25, 00144 Roma; tel. (06) 54210237; fax (06) 5915408; e-mail info@aitecweb.com; internet www.aitecweb.com; f. 1959; Pres. GIACOMO MARAZZI; Dir Dott. Ing. FRANCESCO CURCIO.

Associazione Mineraria Italiana (ASSOMINERARIA) (Oil and Mining Industry): Via delle Tre Madonne 20, 00197 Roma; tel. (06) 8073045; fax (06) 8073385; e-mail info@assomineraria.org; internet www.assomineraria.org; f. 1917; Pres. Dott. CLAUDIO DESCALZI; Dir-Gen. Dott. ANDREA KETOFF; 145 mems.

Associazione Nazionale Costruttori Edili (ANCE) (Construction): Via Guattani 16, 00161 Roma; tel. (06) 845671; fax (06) 84567550; e-mail info@ance.it; internet www.ance.it; f. 1946; Pres. PAOLO BUZZETTI; Dir-Gen. CARLO FERRONI; mems: 19,000 firms in 102 provincial and 20 regional asscns.

Associazione Nazionale delle Imprese Elettriche (ASSOELETTRICA) (Electricity Generators and Distributors): Via Benozzo Gozzoli 24, 00142 Roma; tel. (06) 8537281; fax (06) 85356431; e-mail info@assoelettrica.it; internet www.assoelettrica.it; f. 2002; Pres. GIULIANO ZUCCOLI; Dir-Gen. FRANCESCO DE LUCA; 120 mem. cos.

Associazione Nazionale fra Industrie Automobilistiche (ANFIA) (Motor Vehicle Industries): Corso Galileo Ferraris 61, 10128 Torino; tel. (011) 5546511; fax (011) 545986; e-mail anfia@anfia.it; internet www.anfia.it; f. 1912; Pres. EUGENIO RAZELLI; Dir-Gen GUIDO ROSSIGNOLI; 280 mems.

Associazione Nazionale Italiana Industrie Grafiche, Cartotecniche e Trasformatrici (ASSOGRAFICI) (Printing and Paper-Processing Industries): Piazza Conciliazione 1, 20123 Milano; tel. (02) 4981051; fax (02) 4816947; e-mail assografici@assografici.it; internet www.assografici.it; f. 1946; Pres. PIERO CAPODIECI; Gen. Dir Dott. CLAUDIO COVINI; 1,200 mems.

Confindustria Servizi Innovativi e Tecnologici (FITA) (Online Media, Market Research, Information Technology, etc.): Via Barbarini 11, 00187 Roma; tel. (06) 421401; fax (06) 42140444; internet www.confindustriasi.it; Pres. STEFANO PILERI; 51 associated orgs and 62 regional sections.

Federazione delle Associazioni Nazionali di Categorie Industriali Varie (FEDERVARIE) (Miscellaneous Industries): Via Petitti 16, 20149 Milano; tel. (02) 32672234; fax (02) 32672299; e-mail segreteria@federvarie.it; internet www.confindustriafedervarie.it; f. 1945; Pres. Dott. DINO FENZI; 28 mem. asscns.

Federazione delle Associazioni Nazionali dell'Industria Meccanica Varia ed Affine (ANIMA) (Mechanical and Engineering Industries): Via Scarsellini 13, 20161 Milano; tel. (02) 45418500; fax (02) 45418545; e-mail anima@anima-it.com; internet www.anima-it.com; f. 1914; Pres. SANDRO BONOMI; Dir Gen. ANDREA ORLANDO; 1,500 mems.

Federazione delle Imprese delle Comunicazioni e dell'Informatica (FEDERCOMIN) (Information and Communications Technologies): Via Barberini 11, 00187 Roma; tel. (06) 421401; fax (06) 42140444; e-mail info@federcomin.it; Pres. ALBERTO TRIPI; Dir-Gen. PIETRO VARALDO.

Federazione Industrie Prodotti Impianti e Servizi per le Costruzioni (FINCO) (Construction Services and Systems): Via Brenta 13, 00198 Roma; tel. (06) 8555203; fax (06) 8559860; e-mail finco@fincoweb.org; internet www.fincoweb.org; f. 1994; Pres. CIRINO MENDOLA; Dir-Gen. Dott. ANGELO ARTALE.

Federazione Italiana dell'Accessorio Moda e Persona (FIAMP) (Personal and Fashion Accessories): Via Beatrice d'Este 43, 20122 Milano; tel. (02) 584511; fax (02) 58451320; e-mail segreteria@fiamp.it; internet www.fiamp.it; f. 2004; Pres. GIORGIO CANNARA; Sec.-Gen. Dott. MAURO MUZZOLON.

Federazione Italiana dell'Industria Alimentare (FEDERALIMENTARE) (Food Industry): Viale Pasteur 10, 00144 Roma; tel. (06) 5903380; fax (06) 5903342; e-mail segreteria@federalimentare.it; internet www.federalimentare.it; Pres. GIAN DOMENICO AURICCHIO; Dir-Gen. DANIELE ROSSI; 18 mem. asscns.

Federazione Italiana delle Industrie del Legno, del Sughero, del Mobile e dell'Arredamento (FEDERLEGNO-ARREDO) (Wood, Cork, Furniture and Interior Design): Foro Bonaparte 65, 20121 Milano; tel. (02) 806041; fax (02) 80604392; e-mail flaroma@federlegno.it; internet www.federlegno.it; f. 1945; Pres. ROSARIO MESSINA; Dir-Gen. ROBERTO DE MARTIN TOPRANIN; 2,400 mems.

Federazione Italiana Industriali Produttori Esportatori e Importatori di Vini, Acquaviti, Liquori, Sciroppi, Aceti e Affini (FEDERVINI) (Producers, Importers and Exporters of Wines, Brandies, Liqueurs, Syrups, Vinegars, etc.): Via Mentana 2B, 00185 Roma; tel. (06) 4941630; fax (06) 4941566; e-mail federvini@federvini.it; internet www.federvini.it; f. 1917; Pres. Dott. LAMBERTO VALLARINO GANCIA; Dir-Gen. OTTAVIO CAGIANO DE AZEVEDO.

Federazione Nazionale delle Associazioni dei Produttori di Beni Strumentali destinati allo Svolgimento di Processi Manifatturieri dell'Industria e dell'Artigianato (FEDERMACCHINE) (Machine manufacture): Viale Fulvio Testi 128, 20092 Cinisello Balsamo; tel. (02) 26255288; fax (02) 26255880; e-mail federmacchine@federmacchine.it; internet www.federmacchine.it; Pres. Dott. ALBERTO SACCHI; Sec.-Gen. Dott. ALFREDO MARIOTTI.

Federazione Nazionale Fonderie (ASSOFOND) (Foundries): Via Copernico 54, 20090 Trezzano Sul Naviglio (Milano); tel. (02) 48400967; fax (02) 48401267; e-mail info@assofond.it; internet www.assofond.it; f. 1948; Pres. ENRICO FRIGERIO; Dir PAOLO PONZINI.

Federazione Nazionale Imprese Elettrotecniche ed Elettroniche (ANIE) (Electric and Electronic Sectors): Via Lancetti 34, 20158 Milano; tel. (02) 32641; fax (02) 3264212; e-mail info@anie.it; internet www.anie.it; Pres. GUIDALBERTO GUIDI; Gen. Dir MARIA ANTONIETTA PORTALURI.

Federazione Nazionale dell'Industria Chimica (FEDERCHIMICA) (Chemical Industry): Via Giovanni da Procida 11, 20149 Milano; tel. (02) 345651; fax (02) 34565310; e-mail federchimica@federchimica.it; internet www.federchimica.it; f. 1945 as Aschimici; renamed as above in 1984; Pres. GIORGIO SQUINZ; Dir-Gen. Dott. CLAUDIO BENEDETTI; 1,300 mem. cos.

Federazione Nazionale Industria dei Viaggi e del Turismo (FEDERTURISMO) (Tourism and Travel): Viale Pasteur 10, 00144 Roma; tel. (06) 5911758; fax (06) 5910390; e-mail federturismo@

federturismo.it; internet www.federturismo.it; f. 1993; Pres. DANIEL JOHN WINTELER; Dir-Gen. Dott. ANTONIO COLOMBO; 25 sectoral asscns, 57 local asscns.

Federazione Nazionale dei Sistemi e delle Modalità di Trasporto e delle Attività Connesse (FEDERTRASPORTO): Viale Pasteur 10, 00144 Roma; tel. (06) 5903972; fax (06) 5903987; e-mail federtrasporto@federtrasporto.it; internet www.federtrasporto.it; f. 1993; Pres. GIAN MARIA GROS-PIETRO; Dir LUIGI CICCARELLI; 11 mem. asscns.

Federazione Sindacale dell'Industria Metalmeccanica Italiana (FEDERMECCANICA) (Mechanics): Piazzale B. Juarez 14, 00144 Roma; tel. (06) 5925446; fax (06) 5911913; e-mail mail.roma@federmeccanica.it; internet www.federmeccanica.it; f. 1971; 91 mem. asscns; Pres. PIER LUIGI CECCARDI; Dir ROBERTO SANTARELLI.

Unione Industriali Pastai Italiani (UNIPI) (Pasta Manufacturers): Via Po 102, 00198 Roma; tel. (06) 8543291; fax (06) 8415132; e-mail unipi@unipi-pasta.it; internet www.unipi-pasta.it; f. 1968; Pres. MASSIMO MENNA; Dir Gen. RAFFAELLO RAGAGLINI.

Unione Nazionale Cantieri e Industrie Nautiche e Affini (UCINA) (Marine Industry): Piazzale Kennedy 1, 16129 Genova; tel. (010) 5769811; fax (010) 5531104; e-mail ucina@ucina.it; internet www.ucina.it; Pres. Dott. ANTON FRANCESCO ALBERTONI; Sec.-Gen. ROSELIN RUTELLI.

Unione Petrolifera (Petroleum Industries): Piazzale Luigi Sturzo 31, 00144 Roma; tel. (06) 5423651; fax (06) 59602925; e-mail info@unionepetrolifera.it; internet www.unionepetrolifera.it; f. 1948; Pres. Dott. PASQUALE DE VITA; Dir-Gen. Dott. PIETRO DE SIMONE; 26 mem. cos.

Other Industrial and Trade Organizations

Associazione fra le Società Italiane per Azioni (ASSONIME) (Limited Cos): Piazza Venezia 11, 00187 Roma; tel. (06) 695291; fax (06) 6790487; e-mail assonime@assonime.it; internet www.assonime.it; f. 1910; Pres. Dott. LUIGI ABETE; Dir-Gen. Prof. STEFANO MICOSSI.

Confederazione Generale della Agricoltura Italiana (CONFAGRICOLTURA) (Agriculture): Corso Vittorio Emanuele II 101, 00186 Roma; tel. (06) 68521; fax (06) 68308578; e-mail info@confagricoltura.it; internet www.confagricoltura.it; f. 1945; Pres. FEDERICO VECCHIONI; Dir-Gen. VITO BIANCO.

Confederazione Generale Italiana del Commercio, del Turismo, dei Servizi e delle Piccole e Medie Industrie (PMI) (CONFCOMMERCIO) (Commerce, Tourism, Services and Small and Medium-sized Industries): Piazza G. G. Belli 2, 00153 Roma; tel. (06) 58661; fax (06) 5809425; e-mail confcommercio@confcommercio.it; internet www.confcommercio.it; f. 1945; Pres. Dott. CARLO SANGALLI; Dir-Gen. LUIGI TARANTO; 770,000 mems.

Confederazione Italiana della Piccola e Media Industria Privata (CONFAPI) (Small and Medium-sized Private Industries): Via del Plebiscito 117, 00186 Roma; tel. (06) 690151; fax (06) 6791488; e-mail mail@confapi.org; internet www.confapi.org; f. 1947; Pres. Dott. PAOLO GALASSI; Dir-Gen. Dott. EUGENIO SERGIO FEROLDI; 120,000 mems.

Confederazione Italiana della Proprietà Edilizia (CONFEDILIZIA) (Real Estate): Via Borgognona 47, 00187 Roma; tel. (06) 6793489; fax (06) 6793447; e-mail roma@confedilizia.it; internet www.confedilizia.it; f. 1945; Pres. CORRADO SFORZA FOGLIANI; Sec.-Gen. GIORGIO SPAZIANI TESTA.

Federazione delle Associazioni Italiane Alberghi e Turismo (FEDERALBERGHI) (Hotels and Tourism): Via Toscana 1, 00187 Roma; tel. (06) 42034610; fax (06) 42871197; e-mail info@federalberghi.it; internet www.federalberghi.it; f. 1950; Pres. BERNABO BOCCA; Dir-Gen. ALESSANDRO CIANELLA; 30,000 mems.

UTILITIES

Autorità per l'Energia Elettrica e il Gas (AEEG) (Electric Energy and Gas Authority): Piazza Cavour 5, 20121 Milano; tel. (02) 655651; fax (02) 65565266; e-mail segretariatogenerale@autorita.energia.it; internet www.autorita.energia.it; regulatory authority; Pres. GUIDO PIER PAOLO BORTONI.

Electricity

A2A, SpA: Via Lamarmora 230, 25124 Brescia; tel. (030) 35531; fax (030) 3553204; e-mail infobs@a2a.eu; internet www.a2a.eu; f. 2008 by merger of AEM, AMSA and ASM; electricity and gas manufacture and distribution; Chair. of Bd GIULIANO ZUCCOLI.

Acea, SpA: Piazzale Ostiense 2, 00154 Roma; tel. (06) 57991; fax (06) 5758095; e-mail info@aceaspa.it; internet www.aceaspa.it; f. 1909; produces and distributes electricity in Rome area; also engaged in water provision; 51% stake owned by Rome City Council; Chair. GIANCARLO CREMONESI; CEO MARCO STADERINI.

Edison, SpA: Foro Buonaparte 31, 20121 Milano; tel. (02) 62221; fax (02) 62227379; e-mail infoweb@edison.it; internet www.edison.it; f. 1884 as Società Generale Italiana di Elettricità Sistema Edison; electricity and natural gas; 60% owned by Transalpina di energia Srl; Chair. GIULIANO ZUCCOLI; CEO UMBERTO QUADRINO.

Enel, SpA: Via le Regina Margherita 137, 00198 Roma; tel. (06) 85091; fax (06) 85092162; internet www.enel.it; f. 1962; 13.9% directly state-owned; partially privatized; generates and distributes electricity and gas; Chair. PIERO GNUDI; CEO FULVIO CONTI.

Gestore dei Servizi Energitici (GSE): Viale Maresciallo Pilsudski 92, 00197 Roma; tel. (06) 80111; fax (06) 80114392; e-mail info@gse.it; internet www.gse.it; f. 2000 as Gestore del sistema eletrico, SpA; name changed to present in 2009; owned by the Ministry of the Economy and Finance; manages electricity transmission and co-ordinates the power network; Chair. EMILIO CREMONA; CEO NANDO PASQUALI.

Terna, SpA—Rete Elettrica Nazionale: Via Egidio Galbani 70, 00156 Roma; tel. (06) 83138111; e-mail info@terna.it; internet www.terna.it; f. 1999; electricity transmission co; owns over 97% of electricity transmission grid; Pres. LUIGI ROTH; CEO FLAVIO CATTANEO.

Gas

See the section on Electricity for companies that are involved in the supply of both gas and electricity.

Eni, SpA: Piazzale Mattei 1, 00144 Roma; tel. (06) 59821; fax (06) 59822141; e-mail segreteriasocietaria.azionisti@eni.com; internet www.eni.it; f. 1953; frmly Ente Nazionale Idrocarburi; natural gas exploration, oil and gas power; 20.3% owned by Ministry of the Economy and Finance; Pres. ROBERTO POLI; CEO PAOLO SCARONI.

Eni Power: Piazza Vanoni 1, 20097 San Donato Milanese; tel. (02) 5201; fax (02) 5203180; internet www.enipower.eni.it; f. 1999; owned by Eni, SpA (q.v.); power generation and sale; Pres. FRANCESCO ZOFREA; CEO GIOVANNI MILANI.

Gruppo Hera, SpA: Viale C. Berti Pichat 2–4, 40127 Bologna; tel. (051) 287111; fax (051) 287525; internet www.gruppohera.it; f. 2002; distributes gas; also engaged in water provision; Chair. TOMASO TOMMASI DI VIGNANO; Man. Dir MAURIZIO CHIARINI.

Italgas, SpA: Via XX Settembre 41, 10121 Torino; tel. (01) 123941; fax (01) 12394499; internet www.italgas.it; gas distribution; 100% owned by Snam Rete Gas since 2009; Pres. GIAMPAOLO ZAMBELETTI; CEO PAOLO MOSA.

Linde Gas Italia Srl: Via Guido Rossa 3, 20010 Arluno, Milano; tel. (02) 903731; fax (02) 90373500; e-mail lgi@it.linde-gas.com; internet www.linde-gas.it; f. 1991; CEO FABRIZIO ELIA.

Plurigas: Corso di Porta Vittoria 4, 20122 Milano; tel. (02) 77203033; fax (02) 77203255; e-mail info@plurigas.it; internet www.plurigas.it; f. 2001; gas distribution; 70% owned by A2A, SpA; Chair. LUIGI MORGANO; CEO ANNAMARIA ARCUDI.

Snam Rete Gas: Piazza Santa Barbara 7, 20097 San Donato Milanese; tel. (02) 5201; fax (02) 52038227; e-mail postmaster@snamretegas.it; internet www.snamretegas.it; f. 1941 as Società Nazionale Metanodotti (Snam); adopted current name 2001; transports natural gas; Chair. SALVATORE SARDO; CEO CARLO MALACARNE.

Water

Municipal administrations are responsible for water supply in Italy. Legislation promulgated in 1994 provided for the consolidation of water supply into 'single territorial units'. Since the mid-1990s many municipalities have formed limited companies to manage water supply, for example the supplier for Rome (Acea, SpA—see the section on Electricity) and the supplier for Milan (Amiaque, SpA). A small number of municipalities have contracted private companies to manage water supply.

TRADE UNIONS

The three main trade union federations are the Confederazione Generale Italiana del Lavoro (CGIL), the Confederazione Italiana Sindacati Lavoratori (CISL) and the Unione Italiana del Lavoro (UIL).

National Federations

Confederazione Autonoma Italiana del Lavoro (CONFAIL): Viale Abruzzi 38, 20131 Milano; tel. (02) 29404554; fax (02) 29525692; e-mail info@confail.org; Gen. Sec. EVANGELISTA ZACCARIA.

Confederazione Autonoma Sindacati Artigiani (CASARTIGIANI): Via Flaminio Ponzio 2, 00153 Roma; tel. (06) 5781697; fax (06) 5755036; e-mail casartigiani@tiscalinet.it; internet www.casartigiani.org; f. 1958; fed. of artisans' unions and regional and provincial asscns; Pres. GIACOMO BASSO.

Confederazione Generale Italiana dell'Artigianato (CONFARTIGIANATO) (Artisans): Via di S. Giovanni in Laterano 152, 00184 Roma; tel. (06) 703741; fax (06) 70452188; e-mail confartigianato@confartigianato.it; internet www.confartigianato

.it; f. 1946; independent; 20 regional feds, 120 provincial asscns; 521,000 associate enterprises; Pres. GIORGIO NATALINO GUERRINI; Sec.-Gen. CESARE FUMAGALLI.

Confederazione Generale Italiana del Lavoro (CGIL) (Italian General Confederation of Labour): Corso d'Italia 25, 00198 Roma; tel. (06) 84761; fax (06) 8476321; e-mail info@mail.cgil.it; internet www.cgil.it; f. 1906 as Confederazione Generale del Lavoro; refounded 1944; confederation of 12 feds; Sec.-Gen. SUSANNA CAMUSSO; 5,402,408 mems.

Confederazione Generale dei Sindacati Autonomi dei Lavoratori (CONFSAL): Viale Trasevere 60, 00153 Roma; tel. (06) 5852071; fax (06) 5818218; e-mail info@confsal.it; internet www.confsal.it; f. 1979; Sec.-Gen. Prof. MARCO PAOLO NIGI.

Confederazione Italiana Dirigenti e Alte Professionalità (CIDA): Via Barberini 36, 00187 Roma; tel. (06) 97605111; fax (06) 97605109; e-mail dirigenti@cida.it; internet www.cida.it; fed. of 6 managers' unions; Pres. Dott. GIORGIO CORRADINI; Dir Dott. ALBERTO SARTONI.

Confederazione Italiana Lavoratori Liberi (CONFIL): Via di Campo Marzio 46, 00186 Roma; tel. (06) 6872508; fax (06) 6872509; Gen. Sec. FRANCESCO BRUNETTI.

Confederazione Italiana Sindacati Addetti ai Servizi (CISAS): Via Sapri 6, 00185 Roma; tel. (06) 4466618; fax (06) 4466617; internet www.cisas.it; Gen. Sec. ONOFRIO DANIELLO.

Confederazione Italiana Sindacati Lavoratori (CISL): Via Po 21, 00198 Roma; tel. (06) 84731; fax (06) 8546076; e-mail cisl@cisl.it; internet www.cisl.it; f. 1950; affiliated to the International Confederation of Free Trade Unions and the ETUC; fed. of 18 unions; publishes *Conquiste del Lavoro* (see Press); Sec.-Gen. RAFFAELE BONANNI; 4,400,000 mems.

Confederazione Generale dei Sindacati Autonomi dei Lavoratori (CONFSAL): Viale Trasevere 60, 00153 Roma; tel. (06) 5852071; fax (06) 5818218; e-mail info@confsal.it; internet www.confsal.it; f. 1979; Sec.-Gen. Prof. MARCO PAOLO NIGI.

Confederazione Nazionale dell'Artigianato e delle Piccole Imprese (CNA) (National Confederation of Italian SMEs and Handicrafts): Via G. A. Guattani 13, 00161 Roma; tel. (06) 441881; fax (06) 44249513; e-mail cna@cna.it; internet www.cna.it; f. 1946; provincial asscns; Pres. IVAN MALAVASI; Gen. Sec. Dott. SERGIO SILVESTRINI.

Confederazione Unitaria Quadri (CUQ): Via Assarotti 9, 10122 Torino; tel. (011) 5612042; fax (011) 5630987; e-mail confquadri@tin.it; f. 1995; Pres. MARIO VIGNA.

Confederazione Unitaria Sindacati Autonomi Lavoratori (CUSAL): Via di Campo Marzio 46, 00186 Roma; tel. (06) 6872508; fax (06) 6872509; Pres. DOMENICO MANNO; Gen. Sec. FRANCESCO BRUNETTI.

Sindacato Nazionale dei Funzionari Direttivi, Dirigenti e delle Alte Professionalità della Pubblica Amministrazione (DIRSTAT): Via Ezio 12, 00192 Roma; tel. (06) 3211535; fax (06) 3212690; e-mail dirstat@dirstat.it; internet www.dirstat.it; f. 1948; fed. of 33 unions and asscns of civil service executives and officers; Sec.-Gen. ARCANGELO D'AMBROSIO; Treas. Dott. SERGIO DI DONNA.

Unione Generale del Lavoro (UGL): Via Margutta 19, 00187 Roma; tel. (06) 324821; fax (06) 324820; e-mail segreteriaugl@ugl.it; internet www.ugl.it; f. 1950 as CISNAL; name changed as above 1995; upholds traditions of national syndicalism; fed. of 64 unions, 77 provincial unions; Gen. Sec. GIOVANNI CENTRELLA; 2,137,979 mems.

Unione Italiana del Lavoro (UIL): Via Lucullo 6, 00187 Roma; tel. (06) 47531; fax (06) 4753208; e-mail info@uil.it; internet www.uil.it; f. 1950; socialist, social democrat and republican; affiliated to the International Confederation of Free Trade Unions and European Trade Union Confederation; 18 nat. trade union feds and 108 provincial union councils; Gen. Sec. LUIGI ANGELETTI; 1,758,729 mems.

Principal Unions

Banking and Insurance

Federazione Autonoma Bancari Italiana (FABI) (Bank, Tax and Finance Workers): Via Tevere 46, 00198 Roma; tel. (06) 8415751; fax (06) 8559220; e-mail federazione@fabi.it; internet www.fabi.it; f. 1948; independent; Pres. ENZO SCOLA; Sec.-Gen. CARLO GIORGETTI; 69,000 mems.

Federazione Autonoma Lavoratori del Credito e del Risparmio Italiani (FALCRI) (Savings Banks Workers): Viale Liegi 48B, 00198 Roma; tel. (06) 8416336; fax (06) 8416343; e-mail segretaria@falcri.it; internet www.falcri.it; f. 1952; Sec.-Gen. MARIA FRANCESCA FURFARO.

Federazione Italiana Bancari e Assicuratori (FIBA): Via Modena 5, 00184 Roma; tel. (06) 4746351; fax (06) 4746136; e-mail fiba@fiba.it; internet www.fiba.it; affiliated to the CISL; Sec.-Gen. GIUSEPPE GALLO; 90,000 mems.

Federazione Italiana Sindacale Lavoratori Assicurazioni Credito (FISAC) (Employees of Credit Institutions): Via Vicenza 5A, 00184 Roma; tel. (06) 448841; fax (06) 4457356; e-mail fisac@fisac.it; internet www.fisac.it; affiliated to the CGIL; Sec.-Gen. AGOSTINO MEGALE; 60,000 mems.

Federazione Nazionale Assicuratori (FNA) (Insurance Workers): Via Vincenzo Monti 25, 20123 Milano; Via Montebello 104, 00185 Roma; tel. (02) 48011805; fax (02) 48010357; e-mail info@fnaitalia.org; internet www.fnaitalia.org; f. 1946; independent; Pres. LUIGI PERAZZI; Sec.-Gen. DANTE BARBAN.

Unione Italiana Lavoratori Credito, Esattorie e Assicurazioni (UILCA) (Credit and Assurance Workers and Tax Collectors): Via Lombardia 30, 00187 Roma; tel. (06) 4203591; fax (06) 484704; e-mail uilca@uilca.it; internet www.uilca.it; affiliated to the UIL; Sec.-Gen. MASSIMO MASI; 37,453 mems.

Building and Building Materials

Federazione Italiana Lavoratori Costruzioni e Affini (FILCA) (Building Industries' Workers): Via del Viminale 43, 00184 Roma; tel. (06) 4870634; fax (06) 4818884; e-mail federazione.filca@cisl.it; internet www.filca.cisl.it; f. 1959; affiliated to the CISL; Sec.-Gen. DOMENICO PESENTI; 298,316 mems.

Federazione Italiana Lavoratori del Legno, dell'Edilizia, delle Industrie Affini (FILLEA) (Woodworkers, Construction Workers and Allied Trades): Via G. B. Morgagni 27, 00161 Roma; tel. (06) 441141; fax (06) 44235849; e-mail fillea@mail.cgil.it; internet www.filleacgil.it; affiliated to the CGIL; Sec.-Gen. WALTER SCHIAVELLA; 434,154 mems.

Federazione Nazionale Costruzioni (Construction): Lungotevere Sanzio 5, Roma; tel. (06) 585511; fax (06) 5815184; e-mail uglcredito@uglcredito.it; affiliated to the UGL; Sec. EGIDIO SANGUE.

Federazione Nazionale Lavoratori Edili Affini e del Legno (FENEAL) (Builders and Woodworkers): Via Alessandria 171, 00198 Roma; tel. (06) 8547393; fax (06) 8547423; e-mail ffenealuil@fenealuil.it; internet www.feneal-uil.it; f. 1951; affiliated to the UIL; Sec.-Gen. ANTONIO CORREALE; 106,698 mems.

Chemical, Mining, Textile and Allied Industries

Federazione Energia, Moda, Chimica e Settori Affini (FEMCA) (Energy, Fashion, Chemicals and Allied Workers): Via Bolzano 16, 00198 Roma; tel. (06) 83034422; fax (06) 83034414; e-mail femca.nazionale@cisl.it; internet www.femcacisl.it; affiliated to the CISL; Sec.-Gen. SERGIO GIGLI.

Federazione Italiana Lavoratori Chimica, Tessile, Energia e Manifatture (FILCTEM-CGIL) (Chemicals, Textiles, Energy and Manufacturing): Via Piemonte 32, 00187 Roma; tel. (06) 4620091; fax (06) 4824246; e-mail nazionale@filctemcgil.it; internet www.filctemcgil.it; f. 2010 by merger of FILCEM (chemicals, energy and manufacturing) and FILTEA (textiles); affiliated to the CGIL; Sec.-Gen. ALBERTO MORSELLI; 164,000 mems.

Federazione Nazionale Chimici (Chemicals): Via Daniele Manin 53, 00185 Roma; tel. (06) 4818313; fax (06) 4820554; e-mail uglchimicnazionale@tiscali.net; internet www.ugl.it/confederazione/chimici/index.htm; affiliated to the UGL; Sec. DOMENICO SCOPELLITI.

Unione Italiana Lavoratori Chimici, Energia e Manufatturiero (UILCEM) (Chemicals, Energy and Manufacturing Workers): Via Bolzano 16, 00198 Roma; tel. (06) 83034305; fax (06) 83034307; e-mail segretaria@uilcem-nazionale.it; internet www.uilcem.it; affiliated to the UIL; Pres. ROMANO BELLISSIMA; Sec.-Gen. AUGUSTO PASCUCCI; 84,649 mems.

Unione Italiana Lavoratori Tessili e Abbigliamento (UILTA): Via del Viminale 43, 00184 Roma; tel. (06) 4883486; fax (06) 4819421; e-mail uilta@uil.it; internet www.uil.it/uilta; affiliated to the UIL; Sec.-Gen. PASQUALE ROSSETTI.

Engineering and Metallurgy

Federazione Impiegati Operai Metallurgici (FIOM-CGIL) (Metalworkers): Corso Trieste 36, 00198 Roma; tel. (06) 852621; fax (06) 85303079; e-mail organizzazione@fiom.cgil.it; internet www.fiom.cgil.it; f. 1901; affiliated to the CGIL; Sec. MAURIZIO LANDINI; 400,000 mems.

Federazione Italiana Metalmeccanici (FIM-CISL) (Metal Mechanic Workers): Corso Trieste 36, 00198 Roma; tel. (06) 852621; fax (06) 85262464; e-mail federazione.fim@cisl.it; internet www.cisl.it/fim; f. 1951; affiliated to the CISL; Sec.-Gen. GIUSEPPE FARINA; 205,690 mems.

Federazione Nazionale Metalmeccanici: Via Amadeo 23, Roma; tel. (06) 4741808; fax (06) 4881236; affiliated to the UGL; Sec. GIOVANNI CENTCELLO.

Sindacato Nazionale Ingegneri Liberi Professionisti Italiana (SNILPI) (Liberal Professionals-Engineers): Via Salaria 292, 00199

Roma; tel. (06) 8549796; fax (06) 85830308; e-mail info@snilpi.it; Pres. Dott. Ing. LUIGI LUCHERINI; Sec.-Gen. Dott. Ing. GIUSEPPE MILONE.

Unione Italiana Lavoratori Metalmeccanici (UILM) (Metalworkers): Corso Trieste 36, 00198 Roma; tel. (06) 85262201; fax (06) 85262203; e-mail uilm@uil.it; internet www.uil.it/uilm; f. 1950; affiliated to the UIL; Sec.-Gen. ROCCO PALOMBELLA; 100,534 mems.

Food and Agriculture

Confederazione Italiana Agricoltori (CIA) (Farmers): Via Mariano Fortuny 20, 00196 Roma; tel. (06) 32687; fax (06) 3204924; e-mail segreteriapresidente@cia.it; internet www.cia.it; f. 1977; independent; Pres. GIUSEPPE POLITI.

Confederazione Italiana Dirigenti, Quadri e Impiegati dell' Agricoltura (CONFEDERDIA): Viale Beethoven 48, 00144 Roma; tel. (06) 5912808; fax (06) 5915014; e-mail confederdia@confederdia.it; internet www.confederdia.it; Pres. LUCIANO BOZZATO; Gen. Sec. TOMMASO BRANDONI.

Confederazione Nazionale Coldiretti (COLDIRETTI) (Smallholders): Via XXIV Maggio 43, 00187 Roma; tel. (06) 46821; fax (06) 4742993; e-mail saegreteria.presidenza@coldiretti.it; internet www.coldiretti.it; f. 1944; independent; Pres. SERGIO MARINI; Sec.-Gen. Dott. VINCENZO GESMUNDO; mems: 20 regional federations, 107 provincial federations.

Federazione Agricola Alimentare Ambientale Industriale (FAI-CISL) (Agriculture, Food and Environment Workers' Federation): Via Tevere 20, 00198 Roma; tel. (06) 845691; fax (06) 8840652; e-mail federazione.fai@cisl.it; internet www.fai.cisl.it; f. 1997 by merger of FISBA and FAT.

Federazione Lavoratori Agro Industria (FLAI-CGIL) (Workers in Agro-industry): Via Leopoldo Serra 31, 00153 Roma; tel. (06) 585611; fax (06) 58561334; e-mail flai-nazionale@flai.it; internet www.flai.it; f. 1988; affiliated to the CGIL; Sec. ANTONIO MATTIOLI; 289,170 mems.

Unione Coltivatori Italiana (UCI) (Farmers): Via in Lucina 10, 00186 Roma; tel. (06) 6871043; fax (06) 6872559; internet www.uci.it; Pres. VINCENZO PANDOVINO.

Unione Generale Coltivatori (UGC): Corso d'Italia 83, 00198 Roma; tel. (06) 8552383; fax (06) 8553891; internet www.ugc-cisl.it; f. 1989; affiliated to the CISL; Pres. FRANCO VERRASCINA; 151,625 mems.

Unione Italiana Lavoratori Agroalimentari (UILA-UIL) (Food Workers): Via Savoia 80, 00198 Roma; tel. (06) 85301610; fax (06) 85303253; e-mail uilanazionale@uila.it; internet www.uila.it; f. 1994; affiliated to the UIL; Sec. STEFANO MANTEGAZZA.

Unione Italiana Mezzadri e Coltivatori Diretti (UIMEC) (Land Workers): Via Alessandria 112, 00198 Roma; tel. (06) 45479510; fax (06) 44254910; e-mail info@uimecuil.it; internet www.uimecuil.eu; affiliated to the UIL; Pres. ALESSANDRO RANALDI; 100,000 mems.

Medical

Federazione Italiana Servizi Territoriali (FIST) (Hospital and Regional Municipal Workers' Unions): Via Lancisi 25, 00161 Roma; tel. (06) 4425981; fax (06) 44230114; e-mail fist@cisl.it; affiliated to the CISL; Sec.-Gen. ERMENEGILDO BONFANTI; 250,000 mems.

Federazione Nazionale Medici (Doctors): Via Farini 16, 00185 Roma; tel. (06) 485671; fax (06) 48987334; e-mail uglmedici@tiscali.it; affiliated to the UGL; Nat. Sec. SILVESTRO ARBUSE.

Sindacato dei Medici Italiani (SMI) (Medical Specialists): Via Livorno 36, 00162 Roma; tel. (06) 44254168; fax (06) 44254160; e-mail info@sindacatomedicitaliani.it; internet www.sindacatomedicitaliani.it; f. 2006 by fusion of CUMI, AISS, SEM and UNAMEF; Pres. COSMO DE MATTEIS; Sec.-Gen. SALVO CALÌ.

Public Services

Confederazione dei Quadri Direttivi e Dirigenti della Funzione Pubblica (CONFEDIR) (Public Office Managers): Largo dell'Amba Aradam 1, 00184 Roma; tel. (06) 77204826; fax (06) 77077029; e-mail confedir@confedir.org; internet www.confedir.org; f. 1980; Gen. Sec. ROBERTO CONFALONIERI.

Federazione Italiana Lavoratori Organi Costituzionali (Employees of Constitutional Bodies): Via del Parlamento 9, 00187 Roma; tel. (06) 67609118; fax (06) 67604890; e-mail info@uilorganicostituzionali.it; internet www.uilorganicostituzionali.it; f. 1978; affiliated to the UIL; Sec.-Gen. Dott. SILVANO SGREVI.

Federazione Lavoratori Aziende Elettriche Italiane (FLAEI) (Workers in Italian Electrical Undertakings): Via Salaria 83, 00198 Roma; tel. (06) 8440421; fax (06) 8548458; e-mail nazionale@flaei.org; internet www.flaei.org; f. 1948; affiliated to the CISL; Sec.-Gen. CARLO DE MASI; 32,000 mems.

Federazione Lavoratori Pubblici e dei Servizi (CISL-FP) (Public Sector and Services Workers): Via Lancisi 25, 00161 Roma; tel. (06) 440071; fax (06) 44007512; e-mail fps@cisl.it; internet www.fp.cisl.it; affiliated to the CISL; Gen. Sec. GIOVANNI FAVERIN; 325,000 mems.

Federazione Nazionale Dipendenti Enti Pubblici UGL (UGL-FEDEP) (Public Employees): Via del Corea 13, Roma; tel. (06) 3233363; fax (06) 3226052; e-mail segreteria@uglfedep.org; internet www.uglfedep.org; f. 1962; affiliated to the UGL; Gen. Sec. GIUSEPPE MARO.

Federazione Nazionale Enti Locali (Employees of Local Authorities): Via Amendola 5, 00185 Roma; tel. (06) 4743418; fax (06) 4743853; e-mail ugl@uglentilocali.it; internet www.uglentilocali.it; affiliated to the UGL; Sec. GIUSEPPE VIGLIANESI.

Federazione Nazionale Lavoratori Funzione Pubblica: Via Leopoldo Serra 31, 00153 Roma; tel. (06) 585441; fax (06) 5836970; e-mail posta@fpcgil.it; internet www.fpcgil.it; f. 1980; affiliated to the CGIL, Public Services International, and European Public Services Union (EPSU); Gen. Sec. ROSSANA DETTORI; 390,000 mems.

Federazione Nazionale Sanità (Health care Workers): Via Farini 16, 00185 Roma; tel. (06) 4814678; fax (06) 48976910; e-mail paolo.capone@uglsanita.it; internet www.uglsanita.it; affiliated to the UGL; Sec. PAOLO CAPONE.

Unione Italiana Lavoratori Federazione Poteri Locali (UILFPL) (Local Authority Employees): Via di Tor Fiorenza 35, 00199 Roma; tel. (06) 865081; fax (06) 86508235; e-mail uilfpl@uil.it; internet www.uilfpl.it; affiliated to the UIL; Gen. Sec. GIOVANNI TORLUCCI; 89,179 mems.

Unione Italiana Lavoratori Pubblico Amministrazione (UILPA) (Public Office Workers): Via Emilio Lepido 46, 00175 Roma; tel. (06) 71588888; fax (06) 71582046; e-mail uilpa@uil.it; internet www.uilpa.it; affiliated to the UIL; Sec.-Gen. SALVATORE BOSCO; 67,702 mems.

Unione Italiana Lavoratori Sanità (UIL Sanità) (Sanitary Workers): Via di Tor Fiorenza 35, 00199 Roma; tel. (06) 865081; fax (06) 86508235; e-mail info@uilfpl.it; internet www.uilfpl.it; affiliated to the UIL; Sec.-Gen. GIOVANNI TORLUCCIO; 98,669 mems.

Teachers

CISL-Scuola (School Teachers): Via Bargoni 8, 00153 Roma; tel. (06) 58311; fax (06) 5881713; internet www.cislscuola.it; f. 1997; affiliated to the CISL; Sec.-Gen. FRANCESCO SCRIMA; 208,000 mems.

CISL-Università (University Teachers): Via Rovereto 11, 00198 Roma; tel. (06) 8840772; fax (06) 8844977; e-mail info@cisluniversita.it; internet www.cisluniversita.it; affiliated to the CISL; Sec.-Gen. ANTONIO MARSILIA.

Federazione Lavoratori della Conoscenza (FLC CGIL) (School and University Teachers and Researchers): Via Leopoldo Serra 31, Roma; tel. (06) 83966800; fax (06) 5883440; e-mail organizzazione@flcgil.it; internet www.flcgil.it; f. 2004; affiliated to the CGIL; Sec.-Gen. DOMENICO PANTALEO; 191,901 mems (2009).

UGL-Federazione Nazionale Università ed Enti di Ricera: Via Cialdini 4, 00185 Roma; tel. (06) 4465278; fax (06) 44700552; e-mail ugluniversita@mclink.it; affiliated to the UGL; Dir CLARA VALLI.

Unione Italiana Lavoratori Scuola (UIL Scuola) (School Workers): Via Marino Laziale 44, 00179 Roma; tel. (06) 7846941; fax (06) 7842858; e-mail uilscuola@uilscuola.it; internet www.uil.it/uilscuola; affiliated to the UIL; Sec.-Gen. MASSIMO DI MENNA; 59,402 mems.

Tourism and Entertainment

Federazione Informazione Spettacolo e Telecomunicazioni (FISTEL) (Actors, Artists and Media Workers): Via Palestro 30, 00185 Roma; tel. (06) 492171; fax (06) 4457330; e-mail segreterianazionale@fistelcisl.it; internet www.fistelcisl.it; affiliated to the CISL; Sec.-Gen. VITO ANTONIO VITALE; 43,388 mems.

Federazione Italiana Lavoratori Commercio, Turismo e Servizi (FILCAMS) (Hotel and Catering Workers): Via Leopoldo Serra 31, 00153 Roma; tel. (06) 5885102; fax (06) 5885323; e-mail post@filcams.cgil.it; internet www.filcams.cgil.it; f. 1960; affiliated to the CGIL; Sec.-Gen. FRANCO MARTINI; 189,000 mems.

Federazione Italiana Sindacati Addetti Servizi Commerciali Affini e del Turismo (FISASCAT-CISL) (Commercial and Tourist Unions): Via Livenza 7, 00198 Roma; tel. (06) 8541042; fax (06) 8558057; e-mail fisascat@fisascat.it; internet www.fisascat.it; Sec.-Gen. PIERANGELO RAINERI; 153,900 mems.

Federazione Nazionale Informazione e Spettacolo (Actors, Artists and Media Workers): Via Margutta 19, Roma; tel. (06) 324821; fax (06) 323420; affiliated to the UGL; Sec. GIANNI IMPROTA.

Sindacato Attori Italiano (SAI) (Actors): Via Ofanto 18, 00198 Roma; tel. (06) 8417303; fax (06) 8546780; e-mail sai@slc.cgil.it; internet www.cgil.it/sai-slc; affiliated to the Sindacato Lavoratori Comunicazione (SLC) and the CGIL; Pres. GIULIO SCARPATI; Sec.-Gen. MAURIZIO FERIAUD.

Unione Italiana Lavoratori Turismo Commercio e Servizi (UILTuCS): Via Nizza 154, 00198 Roma; tel. (06) 84242276; fax (06) 84242292; e-mail uiltucs@tin.it; internet www.uiltucs.it; f. 1977; affiliated to the UIL; Gen. Sec. BRUNO BOCO; 75,042 mems.

Transport and Telecommunications

Federazione Italiana Lavoratori dei Trasporti (FILT-CGIL): Via Bologna, 9, 19125 La Spezia; tel. (0187) 547111; fax (0187) 516799; e-mail filt@mail.cgil.it; internet www.cgillaspezia.it; affiliated to the CGIL; Sec. VALERIO CORRADINI.

Federazione Italiana Trasporti (FIT-CISL): Via A. Musa 4, 00161 Roma; tel. (06) 442861; fax (06) 44266336; e-mail federazione_fit@cisl.it; internet www.fitcisl.org; f. 1950; affiliated to the CISL; Sec.-Gen. CLAUDIO CLAUDIANI; 40,000 mems.

Federazione Nazionale UGL Comunicazioni (Communications): Via Volturno 40, Roma; tel. (06) 70476547; fax (06) 45422592; e-mail muscarella@uglcomunicazioni.it; internet www.uglcomunicazioni.it; f. 1997; affiliated to the UGL; Sec.-Gen. SALVATORE MUSCARELLA.

Federazione Nazionale Trasporti (Transport): Via Castro Pretorio 116, 00185 Roma; tel. (06) 44363286; fax (06) 44361092; e-mail segreterianazionale@ugltrasporti.com; affiliated to the UGL; Sec. PAOLO SEGARELLI.

Sindacato Lavoratori Comunicazione (SLC) (Communications Workers): Piazza Sallustio 24, 00187 Roma; tel. (06) 42048201; fax (06) 4824325; e-mail segreteria.nazionale@slc.cgil.it; internet www.slc.cgil.it; affiliated to the CGIL; Gen. Sec. EMILIO MICELI.

SLP—Federazione Lavoratori Poste e Appalti (Postal Workers): Via dell'Esquilino 38, 00185 Roma; internet www.slp-cisl.it; f. 1993; affiliated to the CISL; Sec.-Gen. MARIO PETITTO.

Unione Italiana Lavoratori della Comunicazione (UILCOM) (Media and Telecommunications): Via di Tor Fiorenza 35, 00199 Roma; tel. (06) 8622421; fax (06) 86326875; e-mail uilcom@uilcom.it; internet www.uilcom.it; affiliated to the UIL; Sec.-Gen. BRUNO DI COLA.

Unione Italiana Lavoratori Postelegrafonici (UIL Post) (Post, Telegraph and Telephone Workers): Via Eroi di Cefalonia 135, 00128 Roma; tel. (06) 64531601; fax (06) 64530400; e-mail info@uilpost.net; internet www.uilpost.net; f. 1950; affiliated to the UIL; Sec.-Gen. CIRO AMICONE; 30,853 mems.

Unione Italiana Lavoratori Trasporti (UILTRASPORTI) (Transport Workers): Via di Priscilla 101, 00199 Roma; tel. (06) 862671; fax (06) 86208396; e-mail segreteriagenerale@uiltrasporti.it; internet www.uiltrasporti.it; affiliated to the UIL; Sec.-Gen LUIGI SIMEONE; 103,687 mems.

Miscellaneous

Federazione Nazionale Pensionati (FNP) (Pensioners): Via Castelfidardo 47, 00185 Roma; tel. (06) 448811; fax (06) 4460570; e-mail redazione@fnp.cisl.it; internet fnp.cisl.it; f. 1952; affiliated to the CISL; Sec. GIGI BONFANTI; 1,180,000 mems.

Federazione Nazionale Pensionati dell'Unione Generale del Lavoro (Pensioners): Via Principe Amadeo 23, 00185 Roma; tel. (06) 48904445; fax (06) 48930972; e-mail pensionati@ugl.it; internet www.pensionatiugl.it; affiliated to the UGL; Sec. CORRADO MANNUCCI.

Sindacato Pensionati Italiani SPI-CGIL (Pensioners): Via dei Frentani 4A, 00185 Roma; tel. (06) 444811; fax (06) 4440941; e-mail spi@mail.cgil.it; internet www.spi.cgil.it; f. 1948; affiliated to the CGIL; Sec.-Gen. CARLA CANTONE; 2,886,628 mems.

UGL Terziario (Services Sector Workers): Via Farini 62, 00185 Roma; tel. (06) 4820754; fax (06) 4820702; e-mail segreteria@uglterziario.it; internet www.uglterziario.it; affiliated to the UGL; Sec. GIANCARLO BERGAMO.

Unione Italiana Lavoratori Pensionati (UILP) (Pensioners): Via Po 162, 00198 Roma; tel. (06) 852591; fax (06) 8548632; e-mail info@uilpensionati.it; internet www.uilpensionati.it; affiliated to the UIL; Sec.-Gen. ROMANO BELLISSIMA; 720,000 mems.

Co-operative Unions

Associazione Generale delle Cooperative Italiane (AGCI): Via A. Bargoni, 00153 Roma; tel. (06) 583271; fax (06) 58327210; e-mail info@agci.it; internet www.agci.it; f. 1952; Pres. ROSARIO ARTIERI.

Confederazione Cooperative Italiane (CONFCOOPERATIVE): Borgo S. Spirito 78, 00193 Roma; tel. (06) 680001; fax (06) 68134236; e-mail segreteriagen@confcooperative.it; internet www.confcooperative.it; f. 1919; confederation of co-operative unions; Pres. LUIGI MARINO; Dir GUISEPPE MAGGI; Sec.-Gen. VINCENZO MANNINO.

Lega Nazionale delle Cooperative e Mutue (National League of Co-operative and Friendly Societies): Via Guattani 9, 00161 Roma; tel. (06) 84439391; fax (06) 84439406; e-mail info@legacoop.coop; internet www.legacoop.it; f. 1886; 10 affiliated unions; Pres. GIULIANO POLETTI.

Unione Nazionale Cooperative Italiane (UNCI): Via San Sotero 32, 00165 Roma; tel. (06) 3936775; fax (06) 39375080; e-mail info@unci.org; internet www.unci.org; f. 1971; Pres. PAOLO GALLIGIONI.

Transport

RAILWAYS

The majority of Italian lines are controlled by an independent state-owned corporation, Ferrovie dello Stato, SpA. Its subsidiary Trenitalia operates a large number of train services in the country, and offers links to Spain, Slovenia, Hungary, Austia, Belgium and France. In 2009 the total length of the network was 16,300 km, of which 11,500 were electrified. Apart from the state railway system there are 24 local and municipal railway companies, many of whose lines are narrow gauge. A 182-km high-speed link connecting Bologna and Milan opened in 2008; an extension of the line, to Rome via Florence, and further extensions to Turin in the north-west, and to Naples and Salerno in the south, were completed in 2009. Work on a high-speed link to Lyon, France, from Turin, including a 58-km tunnel of which 12 km will be in Italy, was expected to be completed by 2023. There are metro systems in Rome, Catania, Genoa, Milan, Naples and Turin.

Ferrovie dello Stato, SpA (FS): Piazza della Croce Rossa 1, 00161 Roma; tel. (06) 44101; e-mail redazioneweb@ferroviedellostato.it; internet www.ferroviedellostato.it; controls 9 subsidiaries; Pres. LAMBERTO CARDIA; CEO Ing. MAURO MORETTI.

ROADS

In 2008 there were 6,629 km of motorway, 19,290 km of major roads and 157,785 km of secondary roads in Italy. The length of the total road network was an estimated 487,700 km in 2005. All the *autostrade* (motorways) are toll roads except for that between Salerno and Reggio Calabria and those in Sicily. In March 2009 the Government announced that plans to construct a 3.3 km road and rail bridge over the Straits of Messina, between Calabria and Sicily were to be revived.

ANAS, SpA: Via Monzambano 10, 00185 Roma; tel. (06) 44461; fax (06) 4456224; e-mail 841148@stradeanas.it; internet www.stradeanas.it; f. 1928 as Azienda Autonoma Statale della Strada (AASS); jt-stock co in partnership with the Ministry of the Economy and Finance; responsible for the administration of state roads and their improvement and extension; Pres. and Dir-Gen. Dott. PIETRO CIUCCI.

Autostrade per l'Italia, SpA: Via Alberto Bergamini 50, 00159 Roma; tel. (06) 43631; fax (06) 43634090; e-mail info@autostrade.it; internet www.autostrade.it; maintenance and management of motorway network; Pres. Dott. FABIO CERCHIAAI; CEO GIOVANNI CASTELLUCCI.

SHIPPING

In 2009 the Italian merchant fleet (1,635 vessels) had a combined aggregate displacement of 15.5m. grt.

Genova
(Genoa)

Costa Crociere, SpA: Piazza Piccapietra 48, 16121 Genova; tel. (010) 54831; fax (010) 5483290; e-mail corporate@costa.it; internet www.costacrociere.it; f. 1854; passenger and cargo service; Mediterranean, Northern Europe, Central and South America; Caribbean cruises; Chair. and CEO PIER LUIGI FOSCHI.

Grandi Navi Veloci SpA: Via Fieschi 17/17A, 16121 Genova; tel. (010) 55091; fax (010) 5509333; internet www1.gnv.it; f. 1991; passenger, cargo, containers and tramp to Europe; Dirs M. GRIMALDI, A. GRIMALDI.

Ignazio Messina & C., SpA: Via G. d'Annunzio 91, 16121 Genova; tel. (010) 53961; fax (010) 5396264; e-mail info@messinaline.it; internet www.messinaline.it; services to Arabian Gulf, India, Pakistan, Nigeria, North, East, South and West Africa, Libya and Near East, Red Sea, Malta, Europe; Chair. GIANFRANCO MESSINA.

Napoli
(Naples)

Tirrenia di Navigazione, SpA: Palazzo Sirignano, Rione Sirignano 2, 80121 Napoli; tel. (081) 7201111; fax (081) 7201441; internet www.tirrenia.it; f. 1963; ferry services to Sardinia, Sicily, North Africa; part of Gruppo Tirrenia di Navigazione.

Palermo

Sicilia Regionale Marittima, SpA (SIREMAR): Calata Marinai d'Italia, Porto di Palermo, 90139 Palermo; tel. (091) 7493111; fax (091) 7493366; e-mail uff.commerciale.siremar@siremar.it; internet www.siremar.it; owned by Gruppo Tirrenia di Navigazione; ferry services; Pres. Dott. GIUSEPPE RAVERA; Man. Dir FRANCO PERASSO.

Sicula Oceanicas SA (SIOSA): Via dei Cartari 18, 90139 Palermo; tel. (091) 217939; f. 1941; cruises, passenger and cargo; Italy to North Europe, South, Central, North America; Dir G. GRIMALDI.

Roma
(Rome)

Fratelli D'Amico Armatori, SpA: Via Liguria 36, 00187 Roma; tel. (06) 46711; fax (06) 4871914; e-mail damiship@damicofratelli.it; internet www.damicofratelli.it; dry cargo and tankers; Pres. GIUSEPPE D'AMICO; Gen. Man. CARLO CAMELI.

Trieste

Fratelli Cosulich, SpA: Via Dante Alighieri 5, 34122 Trieste; tel. (040) 6797111; fax (040) 6797777; e-mail raccomandate@pec.cosulich.net; internet www.cosulich.it; f. 1854; shipowners and shipping agents; domestic network and cargo to Near East, Red Sea, Hong Kong, Singapore, New York and Zürich; Man. Dir MATTEO COSULICH.

Lloyd Triestino di Navigazione, SpA: Palazzo della Marineria, Passeggio S. Andrea 4, 34123 Trieste; tel. (040) 3180388; fax (040) 3180296; e-mail headoffice@ts.lloydtriestino.it; internet www.lloydtriestino.it; f. 1836; cargo services by container to South Africa, Australasia and Far East, plus trans-Pacific and -Atlantic services; privatized 1998; Pres. PIER LUIGI MANESCHI; Vice-Pres. and Man. Dir REN-GUNG SHYU; Dir-Gen. MAURIZIO SALCE.

Navigazione Montanari, SpA: Via S. Ceccarini 36, 61032 Fano; tel. (0721) 8801; fax (0721) 830430; e-mail info@navmont.com; internet www.navmont.com; f. 1889; cargo services to Mediterranean, Northern Europe, USA and Far East.

Venezia
(Venice)

Adriatica di Navigazione, SpA: Zattere 1411, CP 705, 30123 Venezia; tel. (041) 781861; fax (041) 781818; e-mail adrnav@interbusiness.it; internet www.adriatica.it; f. 1937; owned by Gruppo Tirrenia di Navigazione; passenger services from Italy, Albania, Croatia and Montenegro; Pres. GIORGIO GROSSO; Man. Dir ANTONIO CACUCCI.

Shipping Association

Confederazione Italiana Armatori (CONFITARMA): Piazza SS. Apostoli 66, 00187 Roma; tel. (06) 674811; fax (06) 69783730; e-mail confitarma@confitarma.it; internet www.confitarma.it; f. 1901; shipowners' asscn; Pres. NICOLA COCCIA; Dir-Gen. GENNARO FIORE; 230 mems.

CIVIL AVIATION

In 2010 there were 40 commercial airports in Italy.

Civil Aviation Authority

Ente Nazionale per l'Aviazione Civile (ENAC) (Italian Civil Aviation Authority): Viale del Castro Pretorio 118, 00185 Roma; tel. (06) 445961; fax (06) 44596493; e-mail comunicazione@enac.gov.it; internet www.enac.gov.it; f. 1997; Pres. VITO RIGGIO; Dir-Gen. ALESSIO QUARANTA.

Airlines

Air Dolomiti: Via Paolo Bembo 70, 37062 Dossobuono di Villafranca; tel. (045) 8605211; fax (045) 8605229; internet www.airdolomiti.it; f. 1989; operates domestic flights and services between Italy and Austria, France and Germany; subsidiary of Deutsche Lufthansa AG; Pres. and CEO MICHAEL KRAUS.

Air One: Piazza Almerico da Schio, Palazzo RPU, 00054 Fiumicino; internet www.flyairone.it; f. 1983 as Aliadriatica; present name adopted 1995; acquired by Compagnia Aerea Italiana (CAI) 2009 and merged with Alitalia; Air One brand relaunched as a low-cost carrier 2010; domestic and international flights to destinations in Europe and North Africa.

Alitalia—Compagnia Aerea Italiana, SpA: Piazza Almerico da Schio, Palazzo RPU, 00054 Fiumicino; tel. (06) 65631; fax (06) 7093065; e-mail ufficio.stampa@alitalia.it; internet www.alitalia.com; f. 2008 as successor to the defunct, state-owned Alitalia, SpA (f. 1946); majority shareholding owned by Compagnia Aerea Italiana (CAI); 25% stake owned by Air France-KLM; merged with Air One 2009; domestic and international services throughout Europe and to Africa, North and South America, the Middle East, the Far East and Australia; Chair. ROBERTO COLANINNO; CEO ANDREA RAGNETTI.

Livingston, SpA: Via Giovanni XXIII 206, 21010 Cardano al Campo; tel. (331) 267321; fax (331) 267421; e-mail info@lauda.it; internet www.lauda.it; f. 2003; acquired routes and fleet of Lauda Air Italia in 2005; operates charter and scheduled flights to destinations world-wide; owned by 4 Fly, SpA; Chair. GIANCARLO CELANI; CEO PELLEGRINO D'AQUINO.

Meridiana Fly, SpA: Aeroporto Costa Smerelda, Olbia, 07026 Sardinia; tel. (0789) 52821; fax (0789) 52972; internet www.meridiana.it; f. 1963 as Alisarda, renamed 2010 following merger with Eurofly; scheduled and charter services throughout Italy and Europe, and on a limited number of intercontinental services; Chair. MARCO RIGOTTI; CEO MASSIMO CHIELI.

Tourism

A great number of tourists are attracted to Italy by its Alpine and Mediterranean scenery, sunny climate, Roman archaeological remains, medieval and Baroque churches, Renaissance towns and palaces, paintings and sculpture and famous opera houses. Each of the 95 provinces has a Board of Tourism; there are also about 300 Aziende Autonome di Cura, Soggiorno e Turismo, with information about tourist accommodation and health treatment, and about 2,000 Pro Loco Associations concerned with local amenities. In 2011 there were 47 UNESCO World Heritage Sites in Italy. In 2009 41.1m. foreign visitors arrived in registered accommodation establishments in Italy; tourism receipts totalled US $41,872m. in that year.

Dipartimento per lo Sviluppo e la Competitività del Turismo: Via della Ferratella in Laterano 51, 00184 Roma; tel. (06) 455325955; fax (06) 70497131; e-mail cittadino@governo.it; part of the Office of the Prime Minister; Head of Dept CATERINA CITTADINO.

Ente Nazionale Italiano per il Turismo (ENIT) (Italian State Tourist Board): Via Marghera 2, 00185 Roma; tel. (06) 49711; fax (06) 4463379; e-mail sedecentrale@enit.it; internet www.enit.it; f. 1919; Chair. MATTEO MARZOTTO; Dir-Gen. PAOLO RUBINI.

Defence

Italy has been a member of the North Atlantic Treaty Organization (NATO) since 1949. As assessed at November 2011, it maintained armed forces totalling 184,532, comprising an army of 107,500, a navy of 34,000 and an air force of 43,032. There were also paramilitary forces numbering 186,112 (including 106,716 military police—*Carabinieri*). Conscription was phased out by December 2004, under legislation that was approved in 2000 and which also provided for the recruitment of women soldiers. In November 2004 the European Union (EU) ministers responsible for defence agreed to create a number of 'battlegroups' (each comprising about 1,500 men), which could be deployed at short notice to crisis areas around the world. The EU battlegroups, two of which were to be ready for deployment at any one time, following a rotational schedule, reached full operational capacity from 1 January 2007. Italy was the sole contributor to one battlegroup and was also committed to three others: one with Hungary and Slovenia; an amphibious battlegroup with Spain, Greece and Portugal; and a further battlegroup including Romania and Turkey.

Defence Expenditure: Budget estimated at €15,400m. in 2012.

General Chief of Defence Staff: Gen. BIAGIO ABRATE.

Army Chief of Staff: Gen. CLAUDIO GRAZIANO.

Navy Chief of Staff: Adm. LUIGI MANTELLI.

Air Force Chief of Staff: Gen. GIUSEPPE BERNARDIS.

Chief Commander of the Carabinieri: Lt-Gen. LEONARDO GALLITELLI.

Education

Compulsory education is free for students between the ages of six and 16 years, comprising six years of primary education, four years of lower secondary education and two years of higher secondary education. Pre-primary education is free and non-compulsory for pupils between the ages of three and six years. The curricula of all Italian schools are standardized by the Ministry of Education, Universities and Research. After primary school (*scuola primaria*), for children aged six to 11 years, the pupil enters the first level of secondary school (*scuola media inferiore*). An examination at the end of three years leads to a lower secondary school certificate (*Diploma di Licenza della Scuola Media*), which gives access to higher secondary school (*scuola media superiore*), of which only the first year is compulsory. Pupils wishing to enter a classical lycée (*liceo classico*) must also pass an examination in Latin.

Higher secondary education is provided by classical, artistic, linguistic and scientific lycées, training schools for elementary teachers and technical and vocational institutes (industrial, commercial, nautical, etc.). After five years at a lycée, the student sits an examination for the higher secondary school certificate (*Diploma di Esame di Stato*), which allows automatic entry into any university or non-university institute of higher education. Special four-year courses are provided at the teachers' training schools and the diploma obtained permits entry to a special university faculty of education, the *magistero*, and a number of other faculties. The technical institutes provide practical courses that prepare students for a specialized university faculty.

In 2007/08 enrolment at primary schools included 98% of all children in the relevant age group, while the comparable ratio for secondary enrolment was 95%. In 2007/08 2.6m. children were enrolled in primary education, 1.6m. were enrolled in lower secondary education and 2.5m. were enrolled in upper secondary education.

In 2006/07 there were 1.8m. undergraduate students in higher education in Italy; the largest universities were La Sapienza in Rome, with around 170,000 students, and Bologna, with more than 100,000 students. In 2007/08 there were 74 institutes of higher education. Following the introduction of university reforms, courses last for a three-year cycle, followed by a two-year specialized cycle. Study allowances are awarded to students according to their means and merit; however, most parents pay fees. In 2009 government expenditure on education was €71,773m. (equivalent to 9.0% of total government expenditure).

JAMAICA

Introductory Survey

LOCATION, CLIMATE, LANGUAGE, RELIGION, FLAG, CAPITAL

Jamaica is the third largest island in the Caribbean Sea, lying 145 km (90 miles) to the south of Cuba and 160 km (100 miles) to the south-west of Haiti. The climate varies with altitude, being tropical at sea-level and temperate in the mountain areas. The average annual temperature is 27°C (80°F) and mean annual rainfall is 198 cm (78 ins). The official language is English, although a local patois is widely spoken. The majority of the population belong to Christian denominations, the Church of God being the most numerous. The national flag (proportions 1 by 2) consists of a diagonal yellow cross on a background of black (hoist and fly) and green (above and below). The capital is Kingston.

CONTEMPORARY POLITICAL HISTORY

Historical Context

Jamaica, a British colony from 1655, was granted internal self-government in 1959, and full independence, within the Commonwealth, was achieved on 6 August 1962. Jamaica formed part of the West Indies Federation between 1958 and 1961, when it seceded, following a referendum. The Federation was dissolved in May 1962. The two dominant political figures after the Second World War were Sir Alexander Bustamante, leader of the Jamaica Labour Party (JLP), who retired as Prime Minister in 1967, and Norman Manley, a former Premier and leader of the People's National Party (PNP), who died in 1969. The JLP won the elections of 1962 and 1967 but, under the premiership of Hugh Shearer, it lost the elections of February 1972 to the PNP, led by Michael Manley, the son of Norman Manley. Michael Manley advocated democratic socialism and his Government put great emphasis on social reform and economic independence.

Domestic Political Affairs

The early 1970s were marked by escalating street violence and crime, with gang warfare rife in the deprived areas of Kingston. More than 160 people were killed in the first half of 1976, and in June the Government declared a state of emergency (which remained in force until June 1977). Despite the unrest, high unemployment and severe economic stagnation, the PNP was returned to power in December 1976 with an increased majority. By January 1979, however, there was again widespread political unrest, and violent demonstrations signalled growing discontent with the Manley administration. In February 1980, in the context of a worsening economic crisis, Manley rejected the stipulation of the IMF, as a condition of its making further loans to Jamaica, that economic austerity measures be undertaken. He called a general election to seek support for his economic policies and his decision to end dependence on the IMF. The electoral campaign was one of the most violent in Jamaica's history. In the October election the JLP won 51 of the 60 seats in the House of Representatives. Edward Seaga, the leader of the JLP, became Prime Minister; he supported closer political and economic links with the USA and the promotion of free enterprise. Seaga severed diplomatic relations with Cuba in October 1981, and secured valuable US financial support for the economy. Negotiations on IMF assistance were resumed.

In November 1983, before the completion of a new electoral roll, Seaga announced that an election would take place in mid-December. Only four days were allowed for the nomination of candidates, and the PNP, unable to present candidates at such short notice, refused to participate and declared the elections void. The JLP, opposed in only six constituencies (by independent candidates), won all 60 seats in the House of Representatives and formed a one-party legislature.

Devaluations of the Jamaican dollar and the withdrawal of food subsidies provoked demonstrations and sporadic violence in 1984, as the prices of foodstuffs and energy increased by between 50% and 100%. Despite government attempts to offset the effects of these economic austerity measures, imposed at the instigation of the IMF, unemployment, together with the consequences of illicit trading in drugs, contributed to a rise in the incidence of crime and violence, especially in Kingston. In 1985 another increase in fuel prices precipitated further violent demonstrations in the capital and industrial unrest in the public sector.

After a brief, and relatively peaceful, campaign, a general election took place in February 1989, in which the PNP secured an absolute majority of seats in the House of Representatives. Manley, who had developed a more moderate image during his years in opposition, again became Prime Minister. The Government conceded the necessity for a devaluation of the Jamaican dollar, which was announced in October. Unusually for Jamaican politics, the two main parties achieved a limited consensus on the pursuit of an economic policy of austerity, despite its unpopularity. There was also agreement that further action should be taken against the drugs trade.

Patterson in power

In December 1991 controversy surrounding the waiving of taxes worth some US $30m. that were owed to Jamaica by an international company, Shell, resulted in the resignation of Horace Clarke, the Minister of Mining and Energy, and Percival Patterson, the Deputy Prime Minister, amid opposition allegations of corruption and misconduct. In March 1992 Manley announced his resignation. Patterson was appointed Prime Minister at the end of the month.

At a general election in March 1993 Patterson's PNP secured 52 of the 60 seats in the House of Representatives. The scale of the PNP victory was widely attributed to the success of Patterson's populist overtures to the island's majority population of African origin, and a perceived shift in political influence away from the capital, traditionally a power base of the JLP. In April Patterson announced plans to reform and modernize the electoral system. However, allegations of electoral malpractice and demands by the JLP for an official inquiry into suspected procedural abuses were rejected by the PNP. By February 1994 attempts at electoral reform had been undermined by the resignation of the Chairman of the Electoral Advisory Committee (EAC), and by the failure of the EAC to appoint a new Director of Elections. Demands for constitutional and electoral reform continued, and the JLP repeatedly accused the Government of seeking to delay reform. An electronic voter registration system was installed in 1996 and new electoral rolls were finally completed in late 1997.

A general election was held in December 1997, at which the PNP won a majority of seats in the House of Representatives. Patterson, who was subsequently sworn in as Prime Minister for a third consecutive term, appointed a new Cabinet in January 1998 and announced plans for Jamaica to become a republic within five years.

In 1998 and 1999 there were many public protests against police actions and a deepening economic crisis, several of which resulted in riots. There was further unrest in April 1999 following the announcement of a proposed significant increase in the price of diesel. The JLP and National Democratic Movement (formed in 1995 by Bruce Golding), while initially helping to organize the protests, dissociated themselves from the subsequent violence. The Government later agreed to reduce the proposed increase. In July the authorities announced that army personnel were to be deployed on patrols in greater Kingston in an attempt to combat the high incidence of criminal activity, the majority of which was reportedly related to drugs-trafficking. In October the British Government announced that it would grant £2.9m. in assistance towards the reform and modernization of the Jamaican police force. In the same month an investigation was initiated in response to widespread allegations of corruption in the police force.

Despite the measures implemented by the Government in the previous year, confrontations between the police and various sectors of the community continued in 2001. The human rights organization Amnesty International claimed that the Jamaican police force had one of the highest records for the execution of its own citizens in the world. In 2000 the police had shot dead 140 suspected criminals. Furthermore, in July conflict broke out between police and rival PNP and JLP factions in Kingston, reportedly caused by an exchange of gunfire between police and a group of civilians during a weapons patrol. Following three days of fighting, in which 25 people were reported to have been killed, units of the Jamaica Defence Force were deployed to restore order.

A Commission of Inquiry into the July disturbances opened in September 2001, but the JLP refused to co-operate with the investigation on several occasions. Meanwhile, sporadic outbreaks of violence in the Kingston suburbs continued: in October 2001 the Government was forced to deploy army, air and coastguard units to suppress unrest. In January 2002 seven people were shot dead by as many as 30 gunmen in a suburb known to be a traditional stronghold of the PNP, leading to accusations that the killings were politically motivated. In July the Commission of Inquiry cleared the security forces of the use of excessive brutality.

The PNP's fourth successive term

In a general election held on 16 October 1992, the PNP was re-elected for a fourth consecutive term, albeit with a reduced majority. At his inauguration, Patterson became the first Jamaican Prime Minister to swear allegiance to the people and Constitution of Jamaica, rather than to the British monarch, in accordance with new legislation introduced in August. He subsequently formed a new Cabinet, retaining most of the members of the previous administration.

In December 2002 the armed forces and police began a joint offensive on crime. The Government also revived a previously debated proposal to extend capital punishment to drugs-related crimes and to replace the Privy Council in London, United Kingdom, with a Caribbean Court of Justice (CCJ, see below) as the final court of appeal, thereby removing the Privy Council's ability to commute death sentences to life imprisonment. More than 1,000 murders were reported in 2002, and extended use of capital punishment gained increasing popular support. However, the Crime Management Unit (CMU), established in 2000 in response to the rising rate of violent crime, had been repeatedly criticized for its excessive use of force. In 2003 the CMU was disbanded and replaced by an Organised Crime Investigation Division. Nevertheless, in 2004 the number of murders reached a record 1,445, largely attributed to gang-related conflicts.

In October 2003 the police force was further criticized after two elderly men were accidentally shot during a confrontation between police and an armed gang. The killings prompted a protest, involving some 2,000 people, against alleged police and army tactics. In the same month a report was published by the UN Special Rapporteur, which condemned the Government and state security forces for the misuse of force and for failing properly to investigate those accused of extra-judicial executions. In mid-2004 the Prime Minister announced the launch of a National Investigative Authority to pursue allegations against the police.

In July 2004 the Privy Council abolished Jamaica's mandatory death sentence for convicted murderers. Legislative amendments to this effect were approved by the Senate in November. However, at the same time, amendments were also passed increasing the minimum period a convicted murderer must serve before being granted parole from seven to 20 years. In October the armed forces and the police launched 'Operation Kingfish', an intelligence-based task force intended to reduce the ever-rising crime rate. The initiative was particularly targeted at dismantling the estimated 13 major criminal networks on the island, which were thought to be responsible for much of the crime. By October 2007 more than 2,000 operations had been mounted, leading to 567 arrests.

In January 2005, after more than 30 years in the post, Seaga retired as leader of the JLP. He was succeeded by Bruce Golding. In February 2006 Patterson was succeeded as leader of the PNP by Portia Simpson Miller. Upon assuming office, Simpson Miller, Jamaica's first female Prime Minister, pledged to eradicate violent crime, protect human rights and create employment.

The Senate commenced discussions in February 2007 on the proposed Proceeds of Crime Act, approved by the House of Representatives in the previous month. Reducing the rates of violent and drugs-related crime had become an increasingly urgent concern of the Government. The opposition had expressed concerns that provisions contained within the new Act—awarding courts greater power to order the surrender of assets and property in the absence of a criminal conviction—might impinge upon citizens' fundamental rights.

In January 2007 the Attorney-General, Arnold J. Nicholson, marked the bicentenary of the abolition of the trans-Atlantic slave trade by proposing several constitutional reforms that would effectively eliminate the remaining vestiges of the country's former colonial status and transform Jamaica into a republic, with a Jamaican President replacing the British monarch as head of state. This post would not be vested with legislative or executive powers, but would be designated an independent arbiter of selected state appointments. Furthermore, a new Charter of Rights, the subject of extensive deliberations, was to be instituted, and all constitutional amendments would be ratified through an act of the Jamaican legislature, subject to approval in a plebiscite.

Meanwhile, in November 2006 the Government commissioned a Jamaican Justice System Reform Task Force to conduct a comprehensive review of the country's judicial system, with the assistance of representatives from the Canadian Bar Association. The Government announced that the Ministry of Justice would receive additional funding to reflect the extensive developments to be effected. The final report was presented in May 2007. The main problems identified were delays in the justice system, poor infrastructure, underfunding, and a lack of consistency in the enforcement of laws.

The return of the JLP

The general election of 2007, originally scheduled for 27 August, was postponed until 3 September due to the widespread disruption caused by Hurricane Dean, in which three people were killed and much of the country's infrastructure damaged, leading Simpson Miller to impose a state of emergency. The Prime Minister was criticized for her slow response to the situation. The JLP won a narrow victory, securing 50.1% of the votes cast and 32 of the legislative seats, while the PNP won 49.8% of the votes and the remaining 28 seats. Some 60.5% of the registered electorate participated in the ballot. According to reports, at least 17 people were killed in political violence during the election campaign, in which the JLP focused on the high levels of crime in the country and the large fiscal deficit. Golding was sworn in as Prime Minister on 11 September, and announced his Cabinet the following day. Notable appointments included Audley Shaw as the new Minister of Finance and the Public Service, and Dorothy Lightbourne, who became the country's first female Attorney-General as well as Minister of Justice. Golding assumed the portfolios for planning and development, and defence.

In his inaugural speech Golding stated that anti-corruption measures and justice system reform would be priorities of the new Government. In November 2007 the Cabinet approved the drafting of legislation to create an Office of the Special Prosecutor, which would investigate high-level acts of corruption in the public and private sectors, and an independent commission to examine allegations of excessive use of force and of abuse by members of the security forces. Lightbourne announced in February 2008 that the recommendations of the Jamaican Justice System Reform Task Force would be incorporated into a national development plan, Vision 2030, which would include the building of new courthouses and the creation of a court agency service, in which the Chief Justice would be responsible for the administration of the courts.

The high level of violent crime continued to be a significant matter of concern for the Government. In November 2008 the House of Representatives voted in favour of retaining the death penalty, a decision later approved by the Senate, while in mid-2009 the Government announced plans to introduce 'community policing' and to enhance the professionalism and accountability of the police force. The Golding administration also revealed that the judicial system would be reformed and additional judges would be appointed to expedite the trials of violent criminals. However, the Commissioner of Police, Hardley Lewin, resigned in November, after Golding indicated that he had 'lost confidence' in Lewin. Police patrols were expanded in 2010, and a programme to address the problem of corruption within the police force was introduced in January, with 149 officers being dismissed throughout the year as a result of investigations into their conduct. In June legislative approval was secured for a series of security measures, which included the extension of certain police powers, new restrictions on bail and parole, and additional controls on firearms. The Government's anti-crime strategy appeared to be having a positive impact: the number of murders declined from 1,683 in 2009 to 1,442 in 2010, and the rates of other serious crimes also contracted during 2010. A further fall, to 1,125, was recorded in 2011. However, an increase in the number of serious crimes in early 2012 prompted the new PNP Government (see below) to adopt an anti-crime initiative that aimed to reduce the average murder rate from three per day to less than one by 2017.

The Government, struggling with a liquidity crisis, imposed an unpopular fuel tax in April 2009, precipitating small-scale protests throughout the island. Further taxes were announced in December, including a new levy on staple food items, which resulted in a more vociferous response from the opposition and the public, forcing the Government to rescind the food duty and replace it with a luxury goods tax and an increase in income tax for high earners.

A series of legal challenges launched by the PNP during 2008–11 against JLP members of Parliament accused of holding dual citizenship, which had in some cases led to deputies losing their seats and by-elections being staged, prompted demands for constitutional reform. The Constitution prohibited Jamaican nationals who also possessed citizenship from a non-Commonwealth country from being elected to the legislature, a stipulation that Golding, in January 2011, described as 'an absurdity'. In mid-March Parliament approved the introduction of the long-awaited Charter of Rights, which would protect the rights and freedoms of Jamaicans; the constitutional amendment was passed by the Senate on 1 April and approved by the Governor-General one week later.

The Dudus affair

In August 2009 the USA appealed for the extradition of Christopher 'Dudus' Coke, the alleged head of a major criminal gang operating from Tivoli Gardens (a slum area of the capital), accusing him of drugs-smuggling and arms-trading. The Jamaican Government initially rejected this petition on the grounds that evidence against Coke had been acquired through illegal wiretapping. However, it was suspected that Coke was a political ally of Prime Minister Golding and hence was being afforded high-level protection. (Coke allegedly mobilized the residents of Tivoli Gardens—Golding's constituency—to vote for the JLP during elections.) Evidence to support this theory emerged in March 2010, when it was revealed that Golding, in his position of JLP leader rather than as Prime Minister, apparently had procured the services of a law firm in the USA to lobby the US Administration to abandon its extradition request. Under domestic and US pressure, the Jamaican authorities finally issued a warrant for the arrest of Coke in mid-May. However, this decision provoked Coke's supporters, who viewed him as a local philanthropist, to erect barricades in Tivoli Gardens, and several police stations in the capital came under attack, which in turn prompted Golding to declare a state of emergency in the Kingston area on 23 May (subsequently extended for a further month in late June). Military troops were deployed on the following day to bolster the police operation to capture Coke, which involved some 2,000 members of the security forces. Violent clashes ensued in Tivoli Gardens, resulting in approximately 4,000 arrests and the deaths of 76 people, the vast majority of whom were civilians. On 1 June, by a margin of just two votes, Golding's Government survived a vote of no confidence in the House of Representatives, which had been proposed by the PNP in protest against the administration's perceived mishandling of the Coke affair. After evading apprehension for a month, on 22 June Coke surrendered to the authorities; he was extradited to the USA on 24 June and pleaded not guilty to the charges against him. E-mails published by a national newspaper in August appeared to contradict Golding's earlier assertion that he had hired the US law firm on behalf of the JLP, rather than the Government. This revelation, combined with more general accusations of mismanagement, prompted the Government to announce an official inquiry into the whole extradition episode. This Commission of Inquiry concluded in June 2011 that the Prime Minister had acted 'inappropriately', but not 'criminally', in his involvement in the extradition request. It was also critical of the JLP's behaviour in the affair, asserting that the party should have distanced itself from the affair, but it stopped short of accusing any of those involved of misconduct. The opposition PNP condemned the findings of the inquiry, questioning why nobody was found guilty of misconduct despite the commission concluding that there had been impropriety by ministers.

Recent developments: defeat of the JLP

In May 2011 the Minister of Energy and Mining, James Robertson, resigned. His departure from the Cabinet came after the minister's visa was revoked by the USA following allegations of corrupt practices made by a Jamaican national seeking asylum in the USA. Golding assumed the energy portfolio in a temporary capacity and at the end of the following month the Prime Minister executed a reallocation of cabinet portfolios. The Minister of Justice and Attorney-General, Dorothy Lightbourne, was among those to be dismissed from Government. Lightbourne had been criticized over her handling of the Dudus affair in 2010 (see above). Among the proposals made by the Commission of Inquiry into the affair was the separation of the posts of justice minister and the Attorney-General. To this end, Delroy Chuck, hitherto Speaker of the House of Representatives, was appointed Minister of Justice, while the Attorney-General post remained vacant. Clive Mullings was given the energy and mining portfolio.

Prime Minister Golding announced his intention in late September 2011 to stand down as premier and leader of the JLP by November. He cited the criticism he had received over his involvement in the Dudus affair as one of the main reasons for his resignation. In his resignation speech, on 2 October, Golding emphasized his wish to bring the matter to a close, but also reminded the electorate of the JLP's economic achievements since taking office in 2007. An election for his successor as party leader and premier was scheduled to be held at the JLP's party conference in November; however, by mid-October Andrew Holness, the Minister of Education, had emerged as the clear frontrunner. Following Golding's formal resignation as head of government on 23 October, Holness was installed as his successor. His new Cabinet, installed two days later, contained many members of the previous administration; Holness indicated he would make more wide ranging changes once he had secured a popular mandate to govern. Although elections were not constitutionally due until December 2012, Holness indicated that a ballot would be held by the end of the year. The PNP criticized the handover of power, insisting that a general election should have been called as soon as Golding announced his intention to resign.

As expected, in early December 2011 Prime Minister Holness announced that a general election would be held on 29 December. The PNP won an overwhelming victory, gaining 41 of the 63 seats in the House of Representatives. The JLP's legislative representation was reduced to 22 seats, 10 fewer than in the previous parliament. The resounding defeat of the JLP was largely attributed to continuing public dissatisfaction with the Government's handling of the Dudus extradition. The PNP leader, Portia Simpson Miller, previously Prime Minister in 2006–07, was sworn into office on 5 January 2012. Her Cabinet, announced the following day, contained a mixture of experience and youth. Arnold J. Nicholson was appointed Minister of Foreign Affairs and Foreign Trade, while responsibility for finance, planning and the public service was given to Peter Phillips, who had been in charge of the PNP's successful electoral campaign. Another senior PNP figure, Peter Bunting, was designated Minister of National Security and thus assumed responsibility for addressing the country's spiralling violent crime rate. Evon St Patrick Atkinson was appointed Attorney-General. The new Government made clear its intention to adopt the Caribbean Court of Justice as its final appellate court, instead of the London-based Privy Council. In a further indication of the administration's desire to loosen ties with the United Kingdom, one of Simpson Miller's first announcements in office was to declare her intention to replace the Queen as head of state with an elected President.

Foreign Affairs

Regional relations

In January 1998 Jamaica withdrew from a UN treaty that had hitherto allowed prisoners sentenced to death to appeal for a review by the UN Commission on Human Rights; later that year it also withdrew from the Inter-American Court of Human Rights (see p. 395) of the Organization of American States. In February 2001 Patterson and 10 other Caribbean leaders signed an agreement to establish a CCJ, to be based in Trinidad and Tobago. The Court was to replace the Privy Council in the United Kingdom as the final court of appeal for the Jamaican legal system, and would allow for the executions of convicted criminals. (The Privy Council generally commuted death sentences to life imprisonment on appeal.) The JLP opposed the move, and demanded that a referendum be held on the issue. Despite opposition from the JLP and from the Jamaica Bar Association, in July 2004 Parliament approved legislation replacing the Privy Council with the CCJ as Jamaica's final court of appeal. The Jamaican Bar Association and opposition groupings appealed to the Privy Council itself that the legislation should be annulled because it had been passed without the approval of the electorate in a referendum. In February 2005 the Privy Council upheld the appeal. In total, the Privy Council annulled three such bills to confer trading and appellate jurisdiction on to the CCJ. Nevertheless, on 15 April the House of Representatives ratified membership of the CCJ, but only as a court of original jurisdiction on trade matters. The CCJ was inaugurated the following day in Port of Spain, Trinidad and Tobago. In September 2007 Golding declared his commitment to a referendum on the issue of the CCJ; however, after three years with no progress on this front, in December 2010 the Prime Minister instead proposed a plebiscite on the creation of a Jamaican final court of appeal to replace the Privy Council. Golding's announcement was strongly criticized by the PNP, which accused him of undermining the CCJ and damaging regional integration, while the Governments of Saint Lucia and Grenada also expressed concern at the proposal. Upon taking office in January 2012, PNP Prime Minister Portia Simpson Miller declared her intention to replace the Privy Council with the CCJ, ideally by August, the 50th anniversary of Jamaica's independence from the United Kingdom.

In September 2005 Jamaica became one of 13 Caribbean nations to sign the PetroCaribe accord, under which Jamaica would be allowed to purchase petroleum from Venezuela at reduced prices.

Relations between Jamaica and the USA have been hampered by persistent demands by the USA for the eradication of Jamaica's marijuana crop. In 1997 the two countries concluded a counter-narcotics agreement, permitting officials of the US Drug Enforcement Agency to pursue suspected drugs-traffickers in Jamaican airspace and territorial waters. Relations deteriorated in 2010 after the JLP Government appeared to attempt to prevent the extradition to the USA of alleged drugs-trafficker Christopher 'Dudus' Coke (see above). Furthermore, in May 2011 the cancellation by US authorities of the Minister of Energy and Mining's visa placed further strain on bilateral links.

CONSTITUTION AND GOVERNMENT

The Constitution came into force at Jamaica's independence in August 1962. The Head of State is the British monarch, who is represented locally by the Governor-General, appointed on the recommendation of the Prime Minister in consultation with the Leader of the Opposition. The Governor-General acts, in almost all matters, on the advice of the Cabinet.

Legislative power is vested in the bicameral Parliament: the Senate, with 21 appointed members, and the House of Representatives, with 63 elected members. Thirteen members of the Senate are appointed by the Governor-General on the advice of the Prime Minister and eight on the advice of the Leader of the Opposition. Members of the House are elected by universal adult suffrage for five years (subject to dissolution). Executive power lies with the Cabinet. The Prime Minister is appointed from the House of Representatives by the Governor-General, and is the leader of the party that holds the majority of seats in the House of Representatives. The Cabinet is responsible to Parliament. Jamaica is divided into 13 parishes.

REGIONAL AND INTERNATIONAL CO-OPERATION

Jamaica is a founding member of the Caribbean Community and Common Market (CARICOM, see p. 227) and of the Inter-American Development Bank (IDB, see p. 334). Jamaica was also one of the six founder members of CARICOM's Caribbean Single Market and Economy (CSME), which was inaugurated on 1 January 2006. The CSME is intended to facilitate the free movement of goods, services and labour throughout the CARICOM region. The country is a member of the Association of Caribbean States (see p. 448), and of the Community of Latin American and Caribbean States (see p. 462), which was formally inaugurated in December 2011.

Jamaica became a member of the UN upon independence in 1962. The country acceded to the World Trade Organization (see p. 433) in 1995. Jamaica joined the Commonwealth (see p. 239) upon independence. It is a member of the Group of 15 (G15, see p. 450), and of the Group of 77 (see p. 450) organization of developing states. Jamaica is a signatory of the Cotonou Agreement, the successor arrangement to the Lomé Conventions between the African, Caribbean and Pacific (ACP) countries and the European Union.

ECONOMIC AFFAIRS

In 2010, according to estimates by the World Bank, Jamaica's gross national income (GNI), measured at average 2008–10 prices, was US $12,892m., equivalent to US $4,770 per head (or US $7,450 per head on an international purchasing-power parity basis). During 2001–10, it was estimated, the population increased at an average rate of 0.4% per year, while gross domestic product (GDP) per head increased at an average annual rate of 0.8%. According to the official figures, overall GDP increased, in real terms, at an average annual rate of 0.6% in 2001–10; the economy contracted by 1.4% in 2010.

Agriculture (including forestry and fishing) contributed 5.9% of GDP in 2010 and engaged an estimated 19.1% of the economically active population in 2008. The principal cash crops are sugar cane (sugar accounted for an estimated 8.0% of total export earnings in 2010), coffee, pimento, citrus fruit and cocoa. The cultivation of vegetables, fruit and rice is being encouraged, in an attempt to reduce imports and diversify agricultural exports. The illegal production of hemp (marijuana) is also believed to generate significant export revenue. Agricultural GDP decreased at an annual average rate of 0.5% in 2001–10; the sector recorded a growth of 14.5% in 2009, but decreased by 0.4% in 2010.

Industry (including mining, manufacturing, public utilities and construction) contributed 20.5% of GDP in 2010 and engaged 16.5% of the economically active population in 2008. Industrial GDP decreased at an average rate of 1.1% during 2001–10; the sector declined by 11.9% in 2009 and by 2.6% in 2010.

Mining and quarrying contributed an estimated 1.2% of GDP in 2010, but engaged only 0.8% of the active labour force in 2008. Mining is the principal productive sector of the economy, and in 2010 bauxite and its derivative, alumina (aluminium oxide), accounted for an estimated 42.2% of total export earnings. Bauxite, of which Jamaica is one of the world's leading producers, is the major mineral mined, but there are also reserves of marble, gypsum, limestone, silica and clay.

Manufacturing contributed an estimated 8.6% of GDP in 2010 and engaged some 5.9% of the active labour force in 2008. Much of the activity in the sector is dependent upon the processing of sugar and bauxite. Manufacturing GDP decreased at an average annual rate of 1.5% during 2001–10; the sector decreased by 2.9% in 2010.

Construction contributed an estimated 7.4% of GDP in 2010 and engaged some 9.1% of the active labour force in 2008. Construction GDP increased at an average annual rate of 0.6% during 2001–10; the sector declined by 1.0% in 2010.

Energy is derived almost entirely from imported petroleum (96.0% in 2008). In 2010 imports of mineral fuels and lubricants accounted for 30.5% of the total value of merchandise imports.

The services sector contributed an estimated 73.6% of GDP in 2010 and engaged some 64.4% of the active labour force in 2008. Tourism is the principal source of foreign exchange earnings. Visitor arrivals (excluding cruise ship passengers) stood at an estimated 1.8m. in 2009. The largest proportion of tourists is from the USA (64.1% in 2009). Tourism revenue totalled a provisional US $ 1,922m. in 2010. The GDP of the services sector increased at an average annual rate of 1.0% in 2001–10; the sector decreased by 2.5% in 2010.

In 2010 Jamaica recorded a visible trade deficit of US $3,259.0m., and there was a deficit of US $934.0m. on the current account of the balance of payments. In 2009 the principal source of imports (36.5%) was the USA. Other major suppliers were Canada, the United Kingdom and members of the Caribbean Community and Common Market (CARICOM, see p. 227). In the same year the USA was also the principal market for exports (53.0%). Canada and the United Kingdom were among other important purchasers. The principal exports in 2010 were crude materials (excluding fuels), and mineral fuels and lubricants. Foodstuffs, including sugar and bananas, were also important export commodities. The principal imports in 2010 were mineral fuels and lubricants, and machinery and transport equipment.

In the financial year ending 31 March 2009 Jamaica recorded an estimated budget deficit of J $171,226m. Jamaica's general government gross debt was $1,713,290m. in 2010, equivalent to 143.4% of GDP. Total external debt at the end of 2009 was US $10,959.0m., of which US $6,664.0m. was public and publicly guaranteed debt. In that year the cost of servicing long-term public and publicly guaranteed debt and repayments to the IMF was equivalent to 28.2% of the value of exports of goods, services and income (excluding workers' remittances). The average annual rate of inflation was 11.7% in 2000–10; consumer prices increased by an annual average of 11.7% in 2010. Some 10.3% of the labour force were unemployed in 2008.

The global financial crisis resulted in a decline in important revenues from remittances, bauxite exports and the tourism sector. This lack of liquidity left Jamaica struggling to honour its debt obligations, and the Government was forced to seek assistance from the IMF in 2009. A US $1,270m. stand-by arrangement was finally approved by the IMF in 2010. Among the conditions of the IMF loan were a debt-exchange scheme, a freeze in public sector salaries and an expansion of the privatization programme. The debt-restructuring negotiations were particularly successful, and progress was also made with the privatization plan during 2010 and 2011. The merger of the national airline, Air Jamaica, with Caribbean Airlines of Trinidad and Tobago was finalized in May 2011. The Government also completed an agreement in August to sell the country's unprofitable, state-owned sugar plants to a Chinese firm. Nevertheless, the Jamaica Labour Party Government fell behind in 2011 in planned reform of the tax and pension sectors, as well as in efforts to reduce public-sector wage bills, and plans to divest its loss-making alumina concern, Clarendon Alumina Partners, stalled. Meanwhile, the damage caused to the island's international image following the aggressive police operation to capture alleged drugs-trafficker Christopher 'Dudus' Coke in mid-2010 was mitigated by a $10m. promotional campaign in Jamaica's main tourist markets. The People's National Party Government that took office in early 2012 inherited a widening current account deficit, and falling export revenues, as well as declining tourism receipts. The IMF predicted that GDP would grow by 1.7% in 2012.

PUBLIC HOLIDAYS

2013: 1 January (New Year's Day), 13 February (Ash Wednesday), 29 March (Good Friday), 1 April (Easter Monday), 23 May (Labour Day), 1 August (Emancipation Day), 6 August (Independence Day), 21 October (National Heroes' Day), 25 December (Christmas Day), 26 December (Boxing Day).

Statistical Survey

Sources (unless otherwise stated): Statistical Institute of Jamaica, 7 Cecelio Ave, Kingston 10; tel. 926-5311; fax 926-1138; e-mail info@statinja.com; internet www.statinja.com; Jamaica Information Service, 58A Half Way Tree Rd, POB 2222, Kingston 10; tel. 926-3740; fax 926-6715; e-mail jis@jis.gov.jm; internet www.jis.gov.jm; Bank of Jamaica, Nethersole Pl., POB 621, Kingston; tel. 922-0750; fax 922-0854; e-mail info@boj.org.jm; internet www.boj.org.jm.

Area and Population

AREA, POPULATION AND DENSITY

Area (sq km)	10,991*
Population (census results)	
7 April 1991	2,314,479
10 September 2001	
Males	1,283,547
Females	1,324,085
Total	2,607,632
Population (official estimates at 31 December)	
2008†	2,692,400
2009	2,698,810
2010	2,705,827
Density (per sq km) at 31 December 2010	246.2

* 4,243.6 sq miles.

† Figure rounded to the nearest 100 persons.

POPULATION BY AGE AND SEX

(official estimates at 31 December 2010)

	Males	Females	Total
0–14	378,664	360,794	739,458
15–64	852,096	883,606	1,735,702
65 and over	101,992	128,674	230,666
Total	1,332,752	1,373,074	2,705,827

Note: Total includes one person not classified according to age or sex.

PARISHES

	Area (sq km)	Population (31 December 2010)	Capitals (with population*)
Kingston and St Andrew	453†	669,512	Kingston M.A. (587,798)
St Thomas	743	94,716	Morant Bay (9,185)
Portland	814	82,656	Port Antonio (13,246)
St Mary	611	114,889	Port Maria (7,651)
St Ann	1,213	174,281	St Ann's Bay (10,518)
Trelawny	875	75,996	Falmouth (7,245)
St James	595	185,334	Montego Bay (83,446)
Hanover	450	70,276	Lucea (6,002)
Westmoreland	807	145,712	Savanna La Mar (16,553)
St Elizabeth	1,212	151,887	Black River (3,675)
Manchester	830	191,875	Mandeville (39,430)
Clarendon	1,196	247,751	May Pen (46,785)
St Catherine	1,192	500,942	Spanish Town (92,383)
Total	10,991	2,705,827	—

* Population at 1991 census.

† Kingston 22 sq km, St Andrew 431 sq km.

PRINCIPAL TOWNS

(population at census of 7 April 1991)

Kingston (capital)	587,798	Montego Bay	83,446
Spanish Town	92,383	May Pen	46,785
Portmore	90,138	Mandeville	39,430

Source: Thomas Brinkhoff, *City Population* (internet www.citypopulation.de).

Mid-2009 ('000, incl. suburbs, UN estimate): Kingston 580 (Source: UN, *World Urbanization Prospects: The 2009 Revision*).

BIRTHS, MARRIAGES AND DEATHS*

	Registered live births†		Registered marriages		Registered deaths
	Number	Rate (per 1,000)	Number	Rate (per 1,000)	Number (estimates)
2000	48,717	18.8	27,028	10.4	15,248
2001	48,065	18.5	22,308	8.6	14,473
2002	44,331	16.9	23,070	8.8	15,711
2003	43,407	16.5	22,476	8.6	15,581
2004	42,448	16.2	21,670	8.2	15,389
2005	41,836	15.7	25,937	9.8	15,523
2006	45,436	17.0	23,148	8.7	15,180
2007	45,590	17.0	n.a.	n.a.	17,048

* Data are tabulated by year of registration rather than by year of occurrence.

† Including births to non-resident mothers.

Sources: UN, *Demographic Yearbook* and *Population and Vital Statistics Report*.

2008: Live births 44,838 (birth rate 16.7 per 1,000); Deaths 17,000 (death rate 6.3 per 1,000); Marriages 21,989 (marriage rate 8.1 per 1,000).

2009: Live births 44,006 (birth rate 16.3 per 1,000); Deaths 17,553 (death rate 6.5 per 1,000); Marriages 21,412 (marriage rate 7.9 per 1,000).

2010: Marriages 20,489 (marriage rate 7.6 per 1,000).

Life expectancy (years at birth, WHO estimates): 71 (males 69; females 74) in 2009 (Source: WHO, *World Health Statistics*).

ECONOMICALLY ACTIVE POPULATION
('000 persons aged 14 years and over, annual averages)

	2006	2007	2008
Agriculture, forestry and fishing	206.1	206.1	222.6
Mining and quarrying	6.4	8.8	9.2
Manufacturing	73.6	71.6	68.6
Electricity, gas and water	7.1	9.3	9.0
Construction	113.1	121.3	106.1
Trade, restaurants and hotels	272.4	262.3	265.2
Transport, storage and communications	79.3	80.6	81.3
Financing, insurance, real estate and business services	59.3	71.1	77.8
Community, social and personal services	310.4	337.2	326.6
Sub-total	1,127.7	1,168.3	1,166.4
Activities not adequately defined	1.8	1.9	1.4
Total employed	1,129.5	1,170.2	1,167.8
Unemployed	119.6	119.4	134.6
Total labour force	1,249.1	1,289.6	1,302.4
Males	697.8	708.2	711.1
Females	551.3	581.4	591.3

Source: ILO.

Health and Welfare

KEY INDICATORS

Total fertility rate (children per woman, 2009)	2.4
Under-5 mortality rate (per 1,000 live births, 2009)	31
HIV/AIDS (% of persons aged 15–49, 2009)	1.0
Physicians (per 1,000 head, 2003)	0.9
Hospital beds (per 1,000 head, 2005)	1.7
Health expenditure (2008): US $ per head (PPP)	364
Health expenditure (2008): % of GDP	4.8
Health expenditure (2008): public (% of total)	50.4
Access to water (% of persons, 2008)	94
Access to sanitation (% of persons, 2008)	83
Total carbon dioxide emissions ('000 metric tons, 2007)	13,952.5
Carbon dioxide emissions per head (metric tons, 2007)	5.2
Human Development Index (2011): ranking	79
Human Development Index (2011): value	0.727

For sources and definitions, see explanatory note on p. vi.

Agriculture

PRINCIPAL CROPS
('000 metric tons)

	2008	2009	2010
Sweet potatoes	26	34	35
Yams	102	125	137
Sugar cane*	1,968	1,968	1,968
Coconuts	330†	264†	196*
Cabbages and other brassicas	21	26	25
Tomatoes	19	21	19
Pumpkins, squash and gourds	34	41	41
Carrots and turnips	19	25	21
Bananas*	77	89	101
Plantains	15	25	30
Oranges	113	118	108
Lemons and limes*	22	24	26
Grapefruit and pomelos*	38	28	32
Pineapples	20	21	20

* FAO estimate(s).
† Unofficial figure.

Pimento, allspice ('000 metric tons): 10 in 2005.

Aggregate production ('000 metric tons, may include official, semi-official or estimated data): Total cereals 1.9 in 2008, 2.4 in 2009–10; Total roots and tubers 164.9 in 2008, 202.4 in 2009, 224.7 in 2010; Total vegetables (incl. melons) 179.4 in 2008, 210.6 in 2009, 199.1 in 2010; Total fruits (excl. melons) 332.1 in 2008, 359.7 in 2009, 363.6 in 2010.

Source: FAO.

LIVESTOCK
('000 head, year ending September, FAO estimates)

	2007	2008	2009
Horses	4	4	4
Mules	10	10	10
Asses	23	23	23
Cattle	185	185	185
Pigs	186	200	219
Sheep	0.7	0.5	0.5
Goats	440	440	440
Poultry	14,100	14,100	14,100

2010: Figures assumed to be unchanged from 2009 (FAO estimates).

Source: FAO.

LIVESTOCK PRODUCTS
('000 metric tons)

	2008	2009	2010
Cattle meat	6.0	5.4	5.3
Goat meat	0.7	0.9	0.9
Pig meat	9.1	9.0	8.0
Chicken meat	106.7	104.5	102.5
Cows' milk	13.8	13.1	12.5
Hen eggs*	6.7	6.9	6.0
Honey*	0.7	0.7	0.7

* FAO estimates.

Source: FAO.

Forestry

ROUNDWOOD REMOVALS
('000 cubic metres, excl. bark, FAO estimates)

	2007	2008	2009
Sawlogs, veneer logs and logs for sleepers	127	127	127
Other industrial wood	150	150	150
Fuel wood	556	552	549
Total	833	829	826

2010: Production assumed to be unchanged from 2009 (FAO estimates).

Source: FAO.

SAWNWOOD PRODUCTION
('000 cubic metres, incl. railway sleepers)

	1996	1997	1998
Coniferous (softwood)	3	3	3
Broadleaved (hardwood)	61	62	63
Total	64	65	66

1999–2010: Annual production as in 1998 (FAO estimates).

Source: FAO.

Fishing

('000 metric tons, live weight)

	2007	2008	2009
Capture*	16.5	13.2	13.0
Marine fishes	11.0	9.5	9.3*
Freshwater fishes*	0.4	0.4	0.4
Aquaculture	5.6	5.9	6.0*
Nile tilapia	5.6	5.8	5.9*
Total catch*	22.2	19.1	19.0

* FAO estimate(s).

Source: FAO.

Mining

('000 metric tons)

	2007	2008	2009*
Bauxite†	14,568	14,363	7,817
Alumina	3,941	3,996	1,774
Crude gypsum	228	238	230
Lime	277	313	300
Salt*	19.0	19.0	19.0

* Estimates.

† Dried equivalent of crude ore.

Source: US Geological Survey.

Industry

SELECTED PRODUCTS

	2006	2007	2008
Sugar (metric tons)	143,806	162,039	140,405
Molasses (metric tons)	73,426	77,905	62,654
Rum ('000 litres)	24,468	23,902	26,538
Beer and stout ('000 litres)	86,955	86,948	85,987
Fuel oil ('000 litres)	625,211	680,873	811,792
Gasoline (petrol) ('000 litres)	178,736	170,369	176,512
Kerosene, turbo and jet fuel ('000 litres)	81,762	67,452	87,785
Auto diesel oil ('000 litres)	257,422	236,822	206,536
Cement ('000 metric tons)	762,912	773,570	724,529
Concrete ('000 cu m)	250,835	164,155	n.a.

Electrical energy (million kWh): 7,528 in 2006; 7,782 in 2007; 7,781 in 2008 (Source: UN Industrial Commodity Statistics Database).

Finance

CURRENCY AND EXCHANGE RATES

Monetary Units

100 cents = 1 Jamaican dollar (J $).

Sterling, US Dollar and Euro Equivalents (30 December 2011)

£1 sterling = J $133.533;
US $1 = J $86.370;
€1 = J $111.751;
J $1,000 = £7.49 = US $11.58 = €8.95.

Average Exchange Rate (J $ per US $)

2009 87.894
2010 87.196
2011 85.893

GOVERNMENT FINANCE

(budgetary central government, non-cash basis, J $ million, year ending 31 March)

Summary of Balances

	2007	2008	2009*
Revenue	249,512	272,460	241,766
Less Expense	275,223	325,731	412,992
Gross operating balance	–25,711	–53,270	–171,226
Less Net acquisition of non-financial assets	25,191	25,395	20,507
Net lending/borrowing	–50,902	–82,665	–191,733

Revenue

	2007	2008	2009*
Tax revenue	219,518	246,217	209,891
Taxes on income, profits and capital gains	102,887	119,169	74,612
Taxes on goods and services	83,525	94,277	106,155
Grants	5,772	8,935	4,184
Other revenue	24,223	17,309	27,691
Total	249,512	272,460	241,766

Expense/Outlays

Expense by economic type	2007	2008	2009*
Compensation of employees	40,568	52,364	57,700
Use of goods and services	15,905	19,095	18,718
Interest	103,480	125,305	188,716
Social benefits	12,045	13,306	13,828
Other expense	103,225	115,660	134,030
Total	275,223	325,731	412,992

Outlays by functions of government†	2007	2008	2009*
General public services	138,206	149,482	235,827
Defence	6,005	10,677	10,019
Public order and safety	26,519	34,782	35,123
Economic affairs	36,920	50,036	35,499
Environmental protection	562	690	637
Housing and community amenities	7,190	8,220	7,043
Health	23,349	28,859	29,291
Recreation, culture and religion	5,635	3,540	3,992
Education	52,079	63,777	70,191
Social protection	3,948	5,061	5,875
Total	300,414	355,126	433,499

* Preliminary.

† Including net acquisition of non-financial assets.

Source: IMF, *Government Finance Statistics Yearbook*.

INTERNATIONAL RESERVES

(excl. gold, US $ million at 31 December)

	2008	2009	2010
IMF special drawing rights	0.1	346.5	329.7
Foreign exchange	1,772.6	1,729.4	2,171.4
Total	1,772.7	2,075.9	2,501.1

Source: IMF, *International Financial Statistics*.

MONEY SUPPLY

(J $ million at 31 December)

	2008	2009	2010
Currency outside depository corporations	40,565	43,371	47,015
Transferable deposits	71,581	77,139	106,836
Other deposits	328,767	360,411	373,907
Securities other than shares	97,286	86,513	72,502
Broad money	538,199	567,433	600,260

Source: IMF, *International Financial Statistics*.

COST OF LIVING

(Consumer Price Index at December; base: December 2006 = 100)

	2008	2009	2010
Food (incl. non-alcoholic beverages)	154.7	167.2	188.6
Alcohol and tobacco	147.3	181.6	207.8
Clothing and footwear	132.0	146.0	159.1
Housing, utilities and fuel	132.3	162.7	176.3
Transport	117.1	124.3	156.2
All items (incl. others)	136.5	150.4	168.1

NATIONAL ACCOUNTS

(J$ million at current prices)

Expenditure on the Gross Domestic Product

	2008	2009	2010
Government final consumption expenditure	160,053.3	175,960.0	184,835.6
Private final consumption expenditure	905,434.7	869,534.5	942,107.6
Increase in stocks	3,855.5	2,000.0	3,489.4
Gross fixed capital formation	239,066.2	227,031.7	231,488.1
Total domestic expenditure	1,308,409.7	1,274,526.2	1,361,920.7
Exports of goods and services	414,535.7	363,929.7	363,779.9
Less Imports of goods and services	717,509.6	558,288.3	552,233.7
GDP in purchasers' values	1,005,435.8	1,080,167.6	1,173,466.8
GDP at constant 2007 prices	760,895.1	737,442.2	726,840.4

Gross Domestic Product by Economic Activity

	2008	2009	2010
Agriculture, forestry and fishing	48,938.4	59,812.6	62,488.1
Mining and quarrying	16,239.5	8,935.7	12,666.7
Manufacturing	80,113.4	87,281.5	90,449.1
Electricity and water	30,159.6	29,949.0	35,507.0
Construction	69,792.4	72,404.7	78,255.0
Wholesale and retail trade; repairs and installation of machinery	173,828.7	183,380.3	199,240.7
Hotels and restaurants	40,294.5	44,907.6	44,402.3
Transport, storage and communication	96,011.3	99,135.9	101,493.5
Finance and insurance services	94,184.0	103,458.0	101,111.1
Real estate, renting and business services	93,813.8	102,490.1	122,008.7
Producers of government services	116,153.4	137,374.0	142,047.5
Other services	57,143.4	62,528.8	66,671.9
Sub-total	916,672.4	991,658.2	1,056,341.6
Less Financial intermediation services indirectly measured	42,060.5	48,016.0	45,521.2
Gross value added in basic prices	874,611.9	943,642.3	1,010,820.3
Taxes, less subsidies, on products	130,823.9	136,525.4	162,646.5
GDP in market prices	1,005,435.8	1,080,167.6	1,173,466.8

BALANCE OF PAYMENTS

(US$ million)

	2008	2009	2010
Exports of goods f.o.b.	2,743.9	1,387.7	1,370.4
Imports of goods f.o.b.	−7,546.8	−4,475.7	−4,629.4
Trade balance	−4,802.9	−3,087.9	−3,259.0
Exports of services	2,795.2	2,650.6	2,634.0
Imports of services	−2,367.1	−1,880.6	−1,824.4
Balance on goods and services	−4,374.8	−2,318.0	−2,449.4
Other income received	487.9	235.0	243.2
Other income paid	−1,056.2	−902.9	−737.8
Balance on goods, services and income	−4,943.1	−2,985.9	−2,944.0
Current transfers received	2,488.8	2,122.0	2,292.9
Current transfers paid	−339.0	−263.6	−282.9
Current balance	−2,793.3	−1,127.5	−934.0
Capital account (net)	18.1	20.7	−22.1
Direct investment abroad	−75.9	−61.1	−58.2
Direct investment from abroad	1,436.6	540.9	227.7
Portfolio investment assets	−813.8	−731.7	−1,107.9
Portfolio investment liabilities	781.1	379.5	755.7
Other investment assets	−242.2	21.0	−1,143.1
Other investment liabilities	1,934.2	1,132.1	1,763.1
Net errors and omissions	−350.3	−203.3	171.0
Overall balance	−105.0	−29.3	−348.1

Source: IMF, *International Financial Statistics*.

External Trade

PRINCIPAL COMMODITIES

(US$ million)

Imports c.i.f.	2008	2009	2010
Foods	885.1	801.9	805.9
Beverages and tobacco	93.5	79.9	75.2
Crude materials (excl. fuels)	73.4	54.9	60.8
Mineral fuels and lubricants	3,150.4	1,419.4	1,585.5
Animal and vegetable oils and fats	53.9	33.9	32.6
Chemicals	959.7	738.7	692.5
Manufactured goods	883.1	555.5	582.9
Machinery and transport equipment	1,264.2	819.7	786.0
Miscellaneous manufactured articles	681.3	461.0	477.3
Total (incl. others)	8,162.9	5,057.6	5,194.6

Exports f.o.b.	2008	2009	2010
Foods	245.5	236.6	202.9
Beverages and tobacco	89.2	101.6	103.8
Crude materials (excl. fuels)	1,336.4	470.4	555.7
Mineral fuels and lubricants	435.3	213.8	291.3
Chemicals	322.3	203.7	83.4
Miscellaneous manufactured articles	18.5	20.4	22.3
Total (incl. others)	2,496.2	1,319.4	1,328.2

PRINCIPAL TRADING PARTNERS

(US $ million)

Imports c.i.f.	2007	2008	2009
Canada	137.4	131.6	106.6
CARICOM*	1,191.1	1,635.3	737.7
Latin America	1,122.4	1,510.8	979.7
United Kingdom	129.3	105.5	79.7
Other European Union	323.8	404.7	289.8
USA	2,699.5	3,294.4	1,850.3
Total (incl. others)	6,893.9	8,361.0	5,065.7

Exports f.o.b.	2007	2008	2009
Canada	333.3	259.0	131.6
CARICOM*	46.6	65.9	66.4
Latin America	13.7	22.8	12.7
United Kingdom	216.0	225.3	129.6
Other European Union	376.6	496.0	103.4
Norway	54.0	78.6	50.8
USA	824.7	981.8	648.1
Total (incl. others)	2,202.8	2,531.8	1,223.8

* Caribbean Community and Common Market.

Transport

RAILWAYS

(traffic)

	1988	1989	1990
Passenger-km ('000)	36,146	37,995	n.a.
Freight ton-km ('000)	115,076	28,609	1,931

Source: Jamaica Railway Corporation.

ROAD TRAFFIC
(motor vehicles in use)

	2004	2005	2006
Passenger cars	357,660	357,810	373,742
Commercial vehicles	128,239	n.a.	n.a.
Motorcycles	26,969	27,038	29,061

Source: IRF, *World Road Statistics*.

SHIPPING

Merchant Fleet
(registered at 31 December)

	2007	2008	2009
Number of vessels	36	44	47
Total displacement ('000 grt)	174.1	218.0	248.6

Source: IHS Fairplay, *World Fleet Statistics*.

International Sea-borne Freight Traffic
('000 metric tons, estimates)

	2008	2009	2010
Goods loaded	16,013	12,573	14,668
Goods unloaded	14,290	12,413	12,401

Source: Port Authority of Jamaica.

CIVIL AVIATION
(traffic on scheduled services)

	2007	2008	2009
Kilometres flown (million)	57	27	26
Passengers carried ('000)	1,618	1,500	1,380
Passenger-km (million)	3,959	3,027	2,839
Total ton-km (million)	380	315	295

Source: UN, *Statistical Yearbook*.

Tourism

VISITOR ARRIVALS BY COUNTRY OF ORIGIN

	2007	2008	2009
Canada	190,650	236,193	290,307
Cayman Islands	19,685	20,287	23,384
Germany	19,895	18,962	20,220
United Kingdom	185,657	188,436	184,512
USA	1,132,532	1,150,942	1,172,844
Total (incl. others)	1,700,785	1,767,271	1,831,097

Tourism revenue (US $ million, incl. passenger transport, unless otherwise indicated): 2,222 in 2008; 2,070 in 2009; 1,922 in 2010 (excl. passenger transport, provisional).

Source: World Tourism Organization.

Communications Media

	2008	2009	2010
Telephones ('000 main lines in use)	316.6	302.5	263.1
Mobile cellular telephones ('000 subscribers)	2,723.3	2,956.1	3,182.0
Internet subscribers ('000)	104.2	114.6	n.a.
Broadband subscribers ('000)	97.3	112.2	116.7

Personal computers: 179,000 (67.5 per 1,000 persons) in 2005.

Radio receivers ('000 in use): 1,215 in 1997.

Television receivers ('000 in use): 510 in 2001.

Daily newspapers: 3 in 1996 (circulation 158,000).

Sources: International Telecommunication Union; UN, *Statistical Yearbook*; UNESCO, *Statistical Yearbook*.

Education

(2003/04 unless otherwise indicated)

	Institutions*	Teachers	Students
Pre-primary	2,137†	5,955‡	134,321§
Primary	355	11,793‖	312,262§
Secondary	161	13,006‡	266,933§
Tertiary	15	1,051	11,600

* Excludes 349 all-age schools and 88 primary and junior high schools.
† Includes 2,008 community-operated basic schools.
‡ 2006/07 data.
§ 2008/09 data.
‖ 2004/05 data.

Source: Ministry of Education; UNESCO Institute for Statistics.

Pupil-teacher ratio (primary education, UNESCO estimate): 27.7 in 2004/05 (Source: UNESCO Institute for Statistics).

Adult literacy rate (UNESCO estimates): 86.4% (males 81.2%; females 91.1%) in 2009 (Source: UNESCO Institute for Statistics).

Directory

The Government

HEAD OF STATE

Queen: HM Queen ELIZABETH II.

Governor-General: Sir PATRICK LINTON ALLEN (took office 26 February 2009).

PRIVY COUNCIL OF JAMAICA

DAVID MUIRHEAD, PAUL HARRISON, DENNIS LALOR, RANSFORD LANGRIN, SHIRLEY MILLER, HEADLEY CUNNINGHAM.

CABINET
(May 2012)

The Government is formed by the People's National Party.

Prime Minister and Minister of Defence, Development, Information and Sports: PORTIA SIMPSON MILLER.

Minister of Foreign Affairs and Foreign Trade: ARNOLD NICHOLSON.

Minister of Finance and Planning: Dr PETER PHILLIPS.

Minister of National Security: PETER BUNTING.

Minister of Education: Rev. RONALD THWAITES.

Minister of Water, Land, Environment and Climate Change: ROBERT PICKERSGILL.

Minister of Tourism and Entertainment: Dr WYKEHAM MCNEIL.

Minister of Justice: MARK GOLDING.

Minister of Industry, Commerce and Investment: ANTHONY HYLTON.

Minister of Agriculture and Fisheries: Roger Clarke.

Minister of Local Government and Community Development: Noel Arscott.

Minister of Labour and Social Security: Derrick Kellier.

Minister of Health: Dr Fenton Ferguson.

Minister of Youth and Culture: Lisa Hannah.

Minister of Transport, Works and Housing: Dr Omar Davies.

Minister of Mining, Energy and Telecommunications: Phillip Paulwell.

Minister without Portfolio in the Office of the Prime Minister with responsibility for Information: Sandrea Falconer.

Minister without Portfolio in the Ministry of Finance and Planning with responsibility for the Public Service: Horace Dalley.

Minister without Portfolio in the Ministry of Transport, Works and Housing with responsibility for Housing: Dr Morais Guy.

Minister without Portfolio in the Office of the Prime Minister with responsibility for Sports: Natalie Neita-Headley.

There are also eight Ministers of State.

MINISTRIES

Office of the Governor-General: King's House, Hope Rd, Kingston 6; tel. 927-6424; fax 927-4561; e-mail kingshouse@kingshouse.gov.jm; internet www.kingshousejamaica.gov.jm.

Office of the Prime Minister: Jamaica House, 1 Devon Rd, POB 272, Kingston 6; tel. 927-9941; fax 968-8229; e-mail pmo@opm.gov.jm; internet www.opm.gov.jm.

Ministry of Agriculture and Fisheries: Hope Gardens, POB 480, Kingston 6; tel. 927-1731; fax 927-1904; e-mail psoffice@moa.gov.jm; internet www.moa.gov.jm.

Ministry of Education: 2 National Heroes Circle, Kingston 4; tel. 922-1400; fax 967-1837; e-mail webmaster@moec.gov.jm; internet www.moec.gov.jm.

Ministry of Energy and Mining: PCJ Bldg, 36 Trafalgar Rd, Kingston 10; tel. 929-8990; fax 960-1623; e-mail info@mem.gov.jm; internet www.mem.gov.jm.

Ministry of Finance and Planning: 30 National Heroes Circle, Kingston 4; tel. 922-8600; fax 922-7097; e-mail info@mof.gov.jm; internet www.mof.gov.jm.

Ministry of Foreign Affairs and Foreign Trade: 21 Dominica Dr., POB 624, Kingston 5; tel. 926-4220; fax 929-5112; e-mail mfaftjam@cwjamaica.com; internet www.mfaft.gov.jm.

Ministry of Health: Oceana Hotel Complex, 2–4 King St, Kingston 10; tel. 967-1100; fax 967-1643; e-mail webmaster@moh.gov.jm; internet www.moh.gov.jm.

Ministry of Industry, Commerce and Investment (MITEC): 4 St Lucia Ave, Kingston 5; tel. 968-7116; fax 960-7422; e-mail communications@miic.gov.jm; internet www.miic.gov.jm.

Ministry of Justice: Mutual Life Bldg, NCB Towers, 2 Oxford Rd, Kingston 5; tel. 906-4923; fax 906-1712; e-mail customerservice@moj.gov.jm; internet www.moj.gov.jm.

Ministry of Labour and Social Security: 1F North St, POB 10, Kingston; tel. 922-9500; fax 922-6902; e-mail mlss_perm_sect@yahoo.com; internet www.mlss.gov.jm.

Ministry of Local Government and Community Development: 85 Hagley Park Rd, Kingston 11; tel. 754-0992; e-mail communications@mlge.gov.jm; internet mlge.gov.jm.

Ministry of National Security: NCB North Tower, 2 Oxford Rd, Kingston 5; tel. 906-4908; fax 754-3601; e-mail information@mns.gov.jm; internet www.mns.gov.jm.

Ministry of Tourism and Entertainment: 64 Knutsford Blvd, Kingston 5; tel. 929-9200; fax 929-9375; e-mail info@visitjamaica.com; internet www.tourismja.com.

Ministry of Transport, Works and Housing: 138H Maxfield Ave, Kingston 10; tel. 754-1900; fax 960-2886; e-mail ps@mtw.gov.jm; internet www.mtw.gov.jm.

Ministry of Water, Land, Environment and Climate Change: 25 Dominica Dr., Kingston 5; tel. 926-1690; fax 926-0543; e-mail info@mwh.gov.jm; internet www.mwh.gov.jm.

Ministry of Youth and Culture: 64 Knutsford Blvd, 3rd and 5th Floor, Kingston 5; tel. 960-6427; fax 968-4511; e-mail info@micys.gov.jm; internet www.micys.gov.jm.

Legislature

PARLIAMENT

Houses of Parliament: Gordon House, 81 Duke St, POB 636, Kingston; tel. 922-0202; fax 967-0064; e-mail clerk@japarliament.gov.jm; internet www.japarliament.gov.jm; Clerk Heather Cooke.

Senate

President: Oswald Harding.

Deputy President: Navel Foster Clarke.

The Senate has 19 other members.

House of Representatives

Speaker: Marisa Dalrymple-Philibert.

Deputy Speaker: (vacant).

General Election, 29 December 2011, preliminary results

	Seats
People's National Party (PNP)	41
Jamaica Labour Party (JLP)	22
Total	63

Election Commission

Electoral Office of Jamaica (EOJ): 43 Duke St, Kingston; tel. 922-0425; fax 967-4058; e-mail eojinfo@eoj.com.jm; internet www.eoj.com.jm; f. 1943; Dir Orrette Fisher.

Political Organizations

Jamaica Alliance Movement (JAM): Flamingo Beach, Falmouth, Trelawny, Kingston; tel. 861-5233; e-mail nowjam@gmail.com; internet www.nowjam.org; f. 2001; Rastafarian; Pres. Astor Black.

Jamaica Labour Party (JLP): 20 Belmont Rd, Kingston 5; tel. 929-1183; e-mail join@jamaicalabourparty.com; internet www.jamaicalabourparty.com; f. 1943; supports free enterprise in a mixed economy and close co-operation with the USA; Leader Andrew Holness; Gen. Sec. Aundré Franklin.

National Democratic Movement (NDM): The Trade Centre, Unit 9, 30-32 Red Hills Rd, Kingston 10; tel. 906-8485; fax 922-7874; e-mail ndmjamaica@yahoo.com; internet www.ndmj.org; f. 1995; advocates a clear separation of powers between the central executive and elected representatives; supports private investment and a market economy; mem. of the New Jamaica Alliance; Chair. Peter Townsend; Pres. Earl DeLisser.

People's National Party (PNP): 89 Old Hope Rd, Kingston 6; tel. 978-1337; fax 927-4389; e-mail information@pnpjamaica.com; internet www.pnpjamaica.com; f. 1938; socialist principles; affiliated with the National Workers' Union; Pres. Portia Simpson-Miller; Chair. Robert Pickersgill; Gen. Sec. Peter Bunting.

Diplomatic Representation

EMBASSIES AND HIGH COMMISSIONS IN JAMAICA

Argentina: Dyoll Life Bldg, 6th Floor, 40 Knutsford Blvd, Kingston 5; tel. 926-5588; fax 926-0580; e-mail embargen@cwjamaica.com; Chargé d'affaires a.i. Ramon Alcides Corvera.

Belgium: 10 Millsborough Crescent, Kingston 6; tel. 978-5543; fax 978-7791; e-mail kingston@diplobel.fed.be; internet www.diplomatie.be/kingston; Ambassador Frédéric Meurice.

Brazil: Pan Caribbean Bldg, 10th Floor, 60 Knutsford Blvd, Kingston 5; tel. 929-8607; fax 968-5897; e-mail brasemb.kingston@itamaraty.gov.br; internet kingston.itamaraty.gov.br; Ambassador Antônio Francisco da Costa e Silva Neto.

Canada: 3 West Kings House Rd, POB 1500, Kingston 10; tel. 926-1500; fax 511-3493; e-mail kngtn@international.gc.ca; internet www.canadainternational.gc.ca/jamaica-jamaique; High Commissioner Stephen Hallihan.

Chile: Courtleigh Corporate Centre, 5th Floor, South Sixth St, Lucia Ave, Kingston 5; tel. 968-0260; fax 968-0265; e-mail chilejam@cwjamaica.com; internet chileabroad.gov.cl/jamaica; Ambassador Alfredo García Castelblanco.

China, People's Republic: 8 Seaview Ave, POB 232, Kingston 10; tel. 927-3871; fax 927-6920; e-mail chinaemb_jm@mfa.gov.cn; internet jm.chineseembassy.org/eng; Ambassador ZHENG QINGDIAN.

Colombia: Victoria Mutual Bldg, 4th Floor, 53 Knutsford Blvd, Kingston 5; tel. 929-1701; fax 968-0577; e-mail ekingston@cancilleria.gov.co; internet www.embajadaenjamaica.gov.co; Ambassador LUÍS GUILLERMO MARTÍNEZ FERNÁNDEZ.

Costa Rica: 58 Hope Rd, Kingston 6; tel. 946-2886; fax 978-5210; e-mail embacostaricajamaica@gmail.com; Chargé d'affaires a.i. TANISHIA ELOÍSA ELLIS HAYLES.

Cuba: 9 Trafalgar Rd, Kingston 10; tel. 978-0931; fax 978-5372; e-mail embacubajam@cwjamaica.com; internet embacu.cubaminrex.cu/jamaica; Ambassador YURI ARIEL GALA LÓPEZ.

Dominican Republic: 32 Earls Court, Kingston 8; tel. 755-4155; fax 755-4156; e-mail domemb@cwjamaica.com; Ambassador Dr JOSÉ TOMÁS ARES GERMÁN.

France: 13 Hillcrest Ave, POB 93, Kingston 6; tel. 946-4000; fax 946-4020; e-mail frenchembassy@cwjamaica.com; internet www.ambafrance-jm-bm.org; Ambassador GINETTE DE MATHA.

Germany: 10 Waterloo Rd, POB 444, Kingston 10; tel. 926-6728; fax 620-5457; e-mail germanembassa.kingston@gmail.com; internet www.kingston.diplo.de; Ambassador JOSEF BECK.

Haiti: 2 Munroe Rd, Kingston 6; tel. 927-7595; fax 978-7638; Chargé d'affaires a.i. MAX ALCE.

India: 27 Seymour Ave, POB 446, Kingston 6; tel. 927-4270; fax 978-2801; e-mail hicomindkin@cwjamaica.com; internet www.hcikingston.com; High Commissioner MOHINDER GROVER.

Japan: NCB Towers, North Tower, 6th Floor, 2 Oxford Rd, POB 8104, Kingston 5; tel. 929-3338; fax 968-1373; internet www.jamaica.emb-japan.go.jp; Ambassador HIROSHI YAMAGUCHI.

Korea, Republic: 5 Oakridge, Kingston 8; tel. 924-2731; fax 924-7325; e-mail jamaica@mofat.go.kr; internet jam.mofat.go.kr; Chargé d'affaires a.i. KI-MO LIM.

Mexico: PCJ Bldg, 36 Trafalgar Rd, Kingston 10; tel. 926-4242; fax 929-7995; e-mail embamexj@cwjamaica.com; internet embamex.sre.gob.mx/jamaica; Ambassador GERARDO LOZANO ARREDONDO.

Nicaragua: 17 Dillsbury Ave, Townhouse 5, Kingston 6; tel. 285-9200; fax 631-7357; e-mail rhooker@cancilleria.gob.ni; Ambassador DAVID SIDNEY MCFIELD.

Nigeria: 5 Waterloo Rd, POB 94, Kingston 10; tel. 968-3732; fax 968-7371; e-mail nhckingston@mail.infochan.com; High Commissioner UMARU SALISU (acting).

Panama: 1 Norbrook Close, Kingston 8; tel. 924-3428; fax 924-5235; e-mail panaemba@hotmail.com; Charge d' affaires a.i. LORENZO CHIARI.

Peru: 23 Barbados Ave, POB 1818, Kingston 5; tel. 920-5027; fax 920-4360; e-mail embaperu-kingston@rree.gob.pe; Ambassador LUIS SÁNDIGA CABRERA.

Russia: 22 Norbrook Dr., Kingston 8; tel. 924-1048; fax 925-8290; e-mail rusembja@colis.com; internet www.jamaica.mid.ru; Chargé d'affaires a.i. VASILY BELDYUGIN.

Saint Christopher and Nevis: 11A Opal Ave, Golden Acres, Red Hills, St Andrew; tel. 944-3861; fax 945-0105; High Commissioner CEDRIC HARPER.

Senegal: Kingston; Ambassador Dr NAFISSATOU DIAGNE.

South Africa: 15 Hillcrest Ave, Kingston 6; tel. 978-3160; fax 978-0339; e-mail sahc-jamaica@cwjamaica.com; High Commissioner MATHU JOYINI.

Spain: Island Life Centre, 6th Floor, 8 St Lucia Ave, Kingston 5; tel. 929-5555; fax 929-8965; e-mail emb.kingston@mae.es; Ambassador CELSA NUÑO.

Trinidad and Tobago: First Life Bldg, 3rd Floor, 60 Knutsford Blvd, Kingston 5; tel. 926-5730; fax 926-5801; e-mail t&thckgn@infochan.com; High Commissioner Dr IVA CAMILLE GLOUDON.

United Kingdom: 28 Trafalgar Rd, POB 575, Kingston 10; tel. 510-0700; fax 510-0737; e-mail bhc.kingston@fco.gov.uk; internet ukinjamaica.fco.gov.uk; High Commissioner HOWARD DRAKE.

USA: 142 Old Hope Rd, Kingston 6; tel. 702-6000; e-mail opakgn@state.gov; internet kingston.usembassy.gov; Ambassador PAMELA E. BRIDGEWATER AWKARD.

Venezuela: PCJ Bldg, 3rd Floor, 36 Trafalgar Rd, POB 26, Kingston 10; tel. 926-5510; fax 926-7442; e-mail embavene@n5.com.jm; Ambassador NOEL ENRIQUE MARTÍNEZ OCHOA.

Judicial System

The judicial system is based on English common law and practice. Final appeal is to the Judicial Committee of the Privy Council in the United Kingdom, although in 2001 the Jamaican Government signed an agreement to establish a Caribbean Court of Justice to fulfil this function.

Justice is administered by the Privy Council, Court of Appeal, Supreme Court (which includes the Revenue Court, the Gun Court and, since 2001, the Commercial Court), Resident Magistrates' Court (which includes the Traffic Court), two Family Courts and the Courts of Petty Sessions.

Judicial Service Commission: Office of the Services Commissions, 30 National Heroes Circle, Kingston 4; tel. 922-8600; e-mail communications@osc.gov.jm; advises the Governor-General on judicial appointments, etc.; chaired by the Chief Justice.

Supreme Court

Public Bldg E, 134 Tower St, POB 491, Kingston; tel. 922-8300; fax 967-0669; e-mail webmaster@sc.gov.jm; internet www.sc.gov.jm.

Chief Justice: ZAILA MCCALLA.

Senior Puisne Judge: GLORIA SMITH.

Master: SHARON AYTON-GEORGE.

Registrar: NICOLE SIMMONS.

Court of Appeal

Public Bldg West, King St, POB 629, Kingston; tel. 922-8300; fax 967-1843; internet www.courtofappeal.gov.jm.

President: SEYMOUR PANTON.

Registrar: STACIE-ANNE BROWN.

Religion

CHRISTIANITY

Jamaica Council of Churches: 14 South Ave, Kingston 10; tel. and fax 926-0974; e-mail jchurch@cwjamaica.com; f. 1941; 10 mem. churches and three agencies; Gen. Sec. GARY HARRIOT.

The Anglican Communion

Anglicans in Jamaica are adherents of the Church in the Province of the West Indies, comprising eight dioceses. The Archbishop of the Province is the Bishop of the North East Caribbean and Aruba. The Bishop of Jamaica, whose jurisdiction also includes Grand Cayman (in the Cayman Islands), is assisted by three suffragan Bishops (of Kingston, Mandeville and Montego Bay). According to the 2001 census, some 4% of the population are Anglicans.

Bishop of Jamaica: Rt Rev. ALFRED C. REID, Church House, 2 Caledonia Ave, Kingston 5; tel. 926-8925; fax 968-0618; e-mail info@anglicandiocese.com; internet anglicandiocese.dthost.com.

The Roman Catholic Church

Jamaica comprises the archdiocese of Kingston in Jamaica (which also includes the Cayman Islands), and the dioceses of Montego Bay and Mandeville. Some 3% of the population are Roman Catholics. The Archbishop and Bishops participate in the Antilles Episcopal Conference (currently based in Port of Spain, Trinidad and Tobago).

Archbishop of Kingston in Jamaica: Most Rev. CHARLES HENRY DUFOUR, Archbishop's Residence, 21 Hopefield Ave, POB 43, Kingston 6; tel. 927-9915; fax 927-4487; e-mail rcabkgn@cwjamaica.com; internet www.archdioceseofkingston.org.

Other Christian Churches

According to the 2001 census, the largest religious bodies are the Church of God (whose members represent 24% of the population), Seventh-day Adventists (11% of the population), Pentecostalists (10%) and Baptists (7%). Other denominations include Jehovah's Witnesses, the Methodist and Congregational Churches, United Church, the Church of the Brethren, the Ethiopian Orthodox Church, the Disciples of Christ, the Moravian Church, the Salvation Army and the Religious Society of Friends (Quakers).

Assembly of God: Evangel Temple, 3 Friendship Park Rd, Kingston 3; tel. 928-2995; Sec. Pastor WILSON.

Baptist Union: 2B Washington Blvd, Kingston 20; tel. 969-2223; fax 924-6296; e-mail info@jbu.org.jm; internet www.jbu.org.jm; f. 1849; 40,000 mems in 330 churches; Pres. Rev. LUKE SHAW; Gen. Sec. Rev. KARL JOHNSON.

First Church of Christ, Scientist: 17 National Heroes Circle, Kingston 4; tel. 967-3814.

Methodist Church (Jamaica District): 143 Constant Spring Rd, POB 892, Kingston 8; tel. 925-6768; fax 924-2560; e-mail jamaicamethodist@cwjamaica.com; internet www.jamaicamethodist.org; f. 1789; 15,820 mems; Pres. Rev. Dr BYRON CHAMBERS; Synod Sec. Rev. EVERALD GALBRAITH.

Moravian Church in Jamaica: 3 Hector St, POB 8369, Kingston 5; tel. 928-1861; fax 928-8336; e-mail moravianchurch@cwjamaica.com; internet www.jamaicamoravian.com; f. 1754; 30,000 mems.

New Testament Church of God in Jamaica: New Testament Church of God Convention Centre, Rodons Pen, Old Harbour, St Catherine; 87,965 mems of 337 churches; Overseer Rev. Dr DENNIS MCQUIRE.

United Church in Jamaica and the Cayman Islands: 12 Carlton Cres., POB 359, Kingston 10; tel. 926-6059; fax 929-0826; e-mail synod@ucjci.com; internet www.ucjci.com; f. 1965 by merger of the Congregational Union of Jamaica (f. 1877) and the Presbyterian Church of Jamaica and Grand Cayman to become United Church of Jamaica and Grand Cayman; merged with Disciples of Christ in Jamaica in 1992 when name changed as above; 20,000 mems; Moderator Rt. Rev. J. OLIVER DALEY; Gen. Sec. Rev. NORBERT STEPHENS.

West Indies Union Conference of Seventh-day Adventists: 125 Manchester Rd, Mandeville; tel. 962-2284; fax 962-3417; e-mail wiu.president@jmsda.net; internet www.wiunion.org; f. 1903; 205,000 mems; Pres. Dr PATRICK ALLEN.

RASTAFARIANISM

Rastafarianism is an important influence in Jamaican culture. The cult is derived from Christianity and a belief in the divinity of Ras (Prince) Tafari Makonnen (later Emperor Haile Selassie) of Ethiopia. It advocates racial equality and non-violence, but causes controversy in its use of 'ganja' (marijuana) as a sacrament. According to the 2001 census, 1% of the population are Rastafarians. Although the religion is largely unorganized, there are some denominations.

Haile Selassie Jahrastafari Royal Ethiopian Judah Coptic Church: 11 Welcome Ave, Kingston 11; tel. 547-8507; fax 639-4173; e-mail royalethiopian@yahoo.com; internet www.nationofjahrastafari.org; f. 1966; not officially incorporated; Head Pres. Dr MATT O'NEIL MYRIE.

BAHÁ'Í FAITH

National Spiritual Assembly: 208 Mountain View Ave, Kingston 6; tel. 927-7051; fax 978-2344; internet www.jm.bahai.org; incorporated in 1970; Chair. DOROTHY WHYTE.

ISLAM

According to the 2001 census, there are an estimated 5,000 Muslims (less than 1% of the population).

JUDAISM

According to the 2001 census, there are some 350 Jews (less than 1% of the population).

United Congregation of Israelites: K. K. Shaare Shalom Synagogue, 92 Duke St, Kingston 6; tel. and fax 922-5931; e-mail info@ucija.org; internet www.ucija.org; f. 1655; 250 mems; Pres. MICHAEL MATALON.

The Press

DAILIES

Daily Gleaner: 7 North St, POB 40, Kingston; tel. 922-3400; fax 922-6223; e-mail feedback@jamaica-gleaner.com; internet www.jamaica-gleaner.com; f. 1834; morning; independent; Chair. and Man. Dir OLIVER CLARKE; Editor-in-Chief GARFIELD GRANDISON; circ. 50,000.

Daily Star: 7 North St, POB 40, Kingston; tel. 922-3400; fax 922-6223; e-mail feedback@jamaica-gleaner.com; internet www.jamaica-tar.com; f. 1951; evening; Editor-in-Chief GARFIELD GRANDISON; Editor DWAYNE GORDON; circ. 45,000.

Jamaica Observer: 40-42 1/2 Beechwood Ave, Kingston 5; tel. 920-8136; fax 926-7655; e-mail feedback@jamaicaobserver.com; internet www.jamaicaobserver.com; f. 1993; Chair. GORDON 'BUTCH' STEWART.

PERIODICALS

The Anglican: 2 Caledonia Ave, Kingston 5; tel. 920-2714; internet www.anglicandiocesejamaica.com; f. 2004 following cessation of Jamaica Churchman; quarterly; circ. 9,000.

Catholic Opinion: Roman Catholic Chancery Office, 21 Hopefield Ave, POB 43, Kingston 6; tel. 927-9915; fax 927-4487; e-mail rcabkgn@cwjamaica.com; internet www.archdioceseofkingston.org; 6 a year; religious; circulated in the *Sunday Gleaner*; Editor Mgr MICHAEL LEWIS; circ. 100,000.

Children's Own: 7 North St, POB 40, Kingston; tel. 922-3400; fax 922-6223; e-mail feedback@jamaica-gleaner.com; internet www.jamaica-gleaner.com; weekly during term time; Editor-in-Chief GARFIELD GRANDISON; circ. 120,000.

Jamaica Journal: 10–16 East St, Kingston; tel. 922-0620; fax 922-1147; e-mail jamaicajournal@instituteofjamaica.org.jm; internet www.instituteofjamaica.org.jm; f. 1967; 3 a year; literary, historical and cultural review; publ. by Institute of Jamaica; Chair. of Editorial Cttee KIM ROBINSON.

Mandeville Weekly: 31 Ward Ave, Mandeville, Manchester; tel. 961-0118; fax 961-0119; e-mail mandevilleweekly@flowja.com; internet www.mandevilleweekly.com; f. 1993; Chair. and Editor-in-Chief ANTHONY FRECKLETON; Man. Dir WENDY FRECKLETON.

North Coast Times: 130 Main St, Ocho Rios; tel. 795-4201; fax 974-9306; internet www.northcoasttimes.com; weekly; Publr FRANKLIN MCKNIGHT; Gen. Man. DESRINE PRICE.

Sunday Gleaner: 7 North St, POB 40, Kingston; tel. 922-3400; fax 922-6223; e-mail feedback@jamaica-gleaner.com; internet www.jamaica-gleaner.com; weekly; Editor-in-Chief GARFIELD GRANDISON; circ. 100,000.

Sunday Herald: 17 Norwood Ave, Kingston 5; tel. 906-7572; fax 908-4044; e-mail sunherald@cwjamaica.com; internet www.sunheraldja.com; f. 1997; weekly; Man. Editor DESMOND RICHARDS; Exec. Editor R. CHRISTENE KING.

Sunday Observer: 40-42 1/2 Beechwood Ave, Kingston 5; tel. 920-8136; fax 926-7655; internet www.jamaicaobserver.com; weekly; Chair. GORDON 'BUTCH' STEWART.

The Visitor Vacation Guide: 4 Cottage Rd, POB 1258, Montego Bay; tel. 952-5256; fax 952-6513; Editor LLOYD B. SMITH.

Weekend Star: 7 North St, POB 40, Kingston; tel. 922-3400; fax 922-6223; e-mail feedback@jamaica-gleaner.com; internet www.jamaica-gleaner.com; f. 1951; weekly; Editor-in-Chief GARFIELD GRANDISON; Editor DWAYNE GORDON; circ. 80,000.

Western News: 40-42 1/2, Beechwood Ave, Kingston 5; tel. 920-8136; fax 926-7655; e-mail feedback@jamaicaobserver.com; internet www.jamaicaobserver.com; Chair. GORDON 'BUTCH' STEWART; circ. 20,000.

West Indian Medical Journal: Faculty of Medical Sciences, University of the West Indies, Mona, Kingston 7; tel. 927-1214; fax 927-1846; e-mail wimj@uwimona.edu.jm; internet www.mona.uwi.edu/fms/wimj; f. 1951; fortnightly; Editor-in-Chief EVERARD N. BARTON; circ. 2,000.

X-News Jamaica: 86 Hagley Park Rd, Kingston 10; tel. 937-7304; fax 901-7667; e-mail comments@xnewsjamaica.com; internet www.xnewsjamaica.com; f. 1993; weekly; Assistant Editor CECELIA CAMPBELL-LIVINGSTON.

PRESS ASSOCIATION

Press Association of Jamaica (PAJ): Kingston 8; tel. 925-7836; internet pressassociationjamaica.org; f. 1943; Pres. BYRON BUCKLEY.

Publishers

Jamaica Publishing House Ltd: 97B Church St, Kingston; tel. 967-3866; fax 922-5412; e-mail jph@cwjamaica.com; f. 1969; subsidiary of Jamaica Teachers' Asscn; English language and literature, mathematics, history, geography, social sciences, music; Chair. WOODBURN MILLER; Man. ELAINE R. STENNETT.

LMH Publishing Ltd: 7 Norman Rd, Suite 10–11, Sagicor Industrial Park, POB 8296, Kingston CSO; tel. 938-0005; fax 759-8752; e-mail lmhbookpublishing@cwjamaica.com; internet www.lmhpublishing.com; f. 1970; educational textbooks, general, travel, fiction; Chair. L. MICHAEL HENRY; Man. Dir DAWN CHAMBERS-HENRY.

Ian Randle Publishers (IRP): 11 Cunningham Ave, POB 686, Kingston 6; tel. 978-0745; fax 978-1156; e-mail ian@ianrandlepublishers.com; internet www.ianrandlepublishers.com; f. 1991; history, gender studies, politics, sociology, law, cooking and music; Pres. and Publr IAN RANDLE; Man. Dir CHRISTINE RANDLE.

University of the West Indies Press (UWI Press): 7A Gibraltar Hall Rd, Mona, Kingston 7; tel. 977-2659; fax 977-2660; internet www.uwipress.com; f. 1992; Caribbean history, culture and literature, gender studies, education and political science; Man. Editor SHIVAUN HEARNE; Gen. Man. LINDA SPETH.

Western Publishers Ltd: 4 Cottage Rd, POB 1258, Montego Bay; tel. 952-5253; fax 952-6513; e-mail westernmirror@mail.infochan.com; internet westernmirror.com; f. 1980; CEO and Editor-in-Chief LLOYD B. SMITH.

GOVERNMENT PUBLISHING HOUSE

Jamaica Printing Services: 77 1/2 Duke St, Kingston; tel. 967-2250; fax 967-2225; e-mail jps_1992@yahoo.com; internet jps1992.org; Gen. Man. RALPH BELL.

ASSOCIATION

Caribbean Publishers' Network (CAPNET): 11 Cunningham Ave, Kingston 6; e-mail info@capnetonline.net; internet www .capnetonline.net; non-profit regional asscn; Pres. NEYSHA SOODEEN.

Broadcasting and Communications

TELECOMMUNICATIONS

The sector is regulated by the Office of Utilities Regulation (see Utilities).

Claro Jamaica Ltd (MiPhone): 30–36 Knutsford Blvd, Kingston 5; tel. 621-1000; fax 906-3486; internet claro.com.jm; mobile cellular telephone operator; fmrly Oceanic Digital, adopted current name in 2008; owned by América Móvil, SA de CV (Mexico); negotiations under way in Aug. 2011 to sell Claro to Digicel; CEO ALEJANDRO GUTIERREZ; 100,000 subscribers.

Digicel Jamaica: 10–16 Grenada Way, Kingston 5; tel. 960-2696; fax 920-0948; e-mail customercare@digicelgroup.com; internet www .digiceljamaica.com; mobile cellular telephone operator; owned by Irish consortium, Mossel (Jamaica) Ltd; f. 2001; Chair. DENIS O'BRIEN; CEO (Jamaica) MARK LINEHAN.

LIME: 7 Cecilio Ave, Kingston 10; tel. 926-9700; fax 929-9530; e-mail customer.services@cwjamaica.com; internet www.time4lime.com; f. 1989; name changed as above in 2008; 79% owned by Cable & Wireless (United Kingdom); landline, internet and mobile services; Pres. RODNEY DAVIS; Man. Dir (Jamaica and the Cayman Islands) GEOFF HOUSTON.

BROADCASTING

Regulatory Authority

Broadcasting Commission of Jamaica: 5th Floor, Victoria Mutual Bldg, 53 Knutsford Blvd, Kingston 5; tel. 920-9537; fax 929-1997; e-mail info@broadcom.org; internet www .broadcastingcommission.org; f. 1986; Chair. Prof. HOPETON DUNN.

Radio

Independent Radio: 6 Bradley Ave, Kingston 10; tel. 968-4880; fax 968-9165; commercial; broadcasts 24 hrs a day on FM; Man. Dir NEWTON JAMES.

Music 99 FM: 6 Bradley Ave, Kingston 10.

Power 106: 6 Bradley Ave, Kingston 10; tel. 968-4880; fax 968-9165; e-mail power106@cwjamaica.com; internet www.go-jamaica .com/power; f. 1992; talk and sports programmes.

IRIE FM: 1B Coconut Grove, Ocho Rios, St Ann; tel. 968-5023; fax 968-8332; e-mail iriefmmarket@cwjamaica.com; internet www .iriefm.net; f. 1991; owned by Grove Broadcasting Co; reggae music; Man. BRIAN SCHMIDT.

Island Broadcasting Corporation: 17 Haining Rd, Kingston 5; tel. 929-1346; fax 906-7604; commercial; broadcasts 24 hrs a day on FM; Chair. ALSTON STEWART.

KLAS Sports FM 89: 17 Haining Rd, Kingston 5; tel. 929-1344; fax 960-0572; e-mail admin@klassportsradio.com; internet www .klassportsradio.com; f. 1991; sports broadcasting.

Linkz 96 FM: 8 Beckford St, Savanna La Mar, Westmoreland; tel. 955-3686; fax 955-9523; e-mail linkz96fm@yahoo.com; internet www .linkzfm.com; f. 2004; Chair ROGER ALLEN.

Love FM: 81 Hagley Park Rd, Kingston 10; tel. 968-9596; e-mail webmaster@love101.org; internet www.lovefm.org; f. 1993; commercial radio station, religious programming on FM; owned by National Religious Media Ltd; Gen. Man. Rt Rev. HERRO BLAIR (acting).

Radio Jamaica Ltd (RJR): Broadcasting House, 32 Lyndhurst Rd, POB 23, Kingston 5; tel. 926-1100; fax 929-7467; e-mail rjr@radiojamaica.com; internet www.radiojamaica.com; f. 1947; commercial, public service; 3 channels; Man. Dir GARY ALLEN; Gen. Man. Radio Services FRANCOIS ST JUSTE.

FAME 95 FM: internet www.fame95fm.com; e-mail famefm@rjrgroup.com; f. 1984; broadcasts on FM, island-wide 24 hrs a day; Exec. Producer SIMONE CLARKE-COOPER.

Hitz 92 FM: internet www.radiohitz92fm.com; broadcasts on FM, island-wide 24 hrs a day; youth station.

RJR 94 FM: internet rjr94fm.com; broadcasts on AM and FM, island-wide 24 hrs a day; Exec. Producer NORMA BROWN-BELL.

Roots FM: Mustard Seed Communities, POB 267, Kingston 10; tel. 923-6488; fax 923-6000; e-mail info-jamaica@mustardseed.com; internet www.mustardseed.com; Chair TREVOR GORDON-SOMERS.

Stylz FM: 4 Boundbrook Ave, Port Antonio, Portland; tel. 993-3358; fax 993-3814; e-mail hueljacks@hotmail.com; internet www .rudelikedat.com/stylzfm; CEO HUEL JACKSON.

TBC FM: 51 Molynes Rd, Kingston 10; tel. 754-5120; fax 968-9159; e-mail gcallam@tbcradio.org; internet www.tbcradio.org; Gen. Man. GARY CALLAM.

ZIP 103 FM: 1B Courtney Walsh Dr., Kingston 10, Jamaica; tel. 929-6233; fax 929-4691; e-mail zip103fm@cwjamaica.com; internet www .zipfm.net; f. 2002; commercial radio station; Dir D'ADRA WILLIAMS.

104.9 FM: Shop 10, R.T. Plaza, Off Port Henderson Rd, Portmore, St Catherine; tel. 740-5087; e-mail motherincrisis@yahoo.com; internet www.suncityradio.fm; CEO DOREEN BILLINGS.

Television

Creative TV (CTV): Caenwood Campus, 37 Arnold Rd, Kingston 5; tel. 967-4482; fax 924-9432; internet www.creativetvjamaica.com; operated by Creative Production & Training Centre Ltd (CPTC); local cable channel; regional cultural, educational and historical programming; CEO Dr HOPETON DUNN.

CVM Television: 69 Constant Sprint Rd, Kingston 10; tel. 931-9400; fax 931-9417; e-mail contact@cvmtv.com; internet www.cvmtv .com; Pres. and CEO DAVID MCBEAN.

Love Television: Kingston; internet www.love101.org; f. 1997; religious programming; owned by National Religious Media Ltd.

Television Jamaica Limited (TVJ): 32 Lyndhurst Rd, Kingston 5; tel. 926-1100; fax 929-1029; e-mail tvjadmin@cwjamaica.com; internet www.televisionjamaica.com; f. 1959 as Jamaica Broadcasting Corpn; privatized and adopted current name in 1997; subsidiary of RJR Communications Group; island-wide VHF transmission 24 hrs a day; Chair. MILTON SAMUDA; Gen. Man. (vacant).

Finance

(cap. = capital; res = reserves; dep. = deposits; m. = million; brs = branches; amounts in Jamaican dollars)

REGULATORY AUTHORITY

Jamaica International Financial Services Authority: Kingston; f. 2011 following an Act of Parliament; Chair. ERIC CRAWFORD.

BANKING

Central Bank

Bank of Jamaica: Nethersole Pl., POB 621, Kingston; tel. 922-0750; fax 922-0854; e-mail info@boj.org.jm; internet www.boj.org.jm; f. 1960; cap. 4.0m., res 8,831.2m., dep. 198,440.4m. (Dec. 2009); Gov. and Chair. BRIAN HECTOR WYNTER.

Commercial Banks

Bank of Nova Scotia Jamaica Ltd (Canada): Scotiabank Centre Bldg, cnr Duke and Port Royal Sts, POB 709, Kingston; tel. 922-1000; fax 924-9294; e-mail customercare-jam@scotiabank.com; internet www.scotiabank.com.jm; f. 1967; cap. 2,927.2m., res 18,264.3m., dep. 151,668.4m. (Oct. 2010); Chair. R. H. PITFIELD; Pres. and CEO BRUCE BOWEN; 36 brs.

Citimerchant Bank Ltd: 63–67 Knutsford Blvd, POB 286, Kingston 5; tel. 926-3270; fax 929-3745; internet www.citibank.com/jamaica; owned by Citifinance Ltd; cap. 25.7m., res 128.4m., dep. 87.2m. (Dec. 2003); Man. Dir PETER MOSES.

FirstCaribbean International Bank (Jamaica) Ltd (Canada): 78 Halfway Tree Rd, POB 762, Kingston 10; tel. 929-9310; fax 926-7751; internet www.firstcaribbeanbank.com; owned by CIBC Investments (Cayman) Ltd; cap. 1,396.6m., res 5,636.5m., dep. 41,925.4m. (Oct. 2010); Exec. Chair. MICHAEL MANSOOR; CEO JOHN D. ORR; 12 brs.

National Commercial Bank Jamaica Ltd: 'The Atrium', 32 Trafalgar Rd, POB 88, Kingston 10; tel. 929-9050; fax 929-8399; internet www.jncb.com; f. 1837; merged with Mutual Security Bank in 1996; cap. 6,465.7m., res 16,665.4m., dep. 148,214.5m. (Sept. 2010); Chair. MICHAEL LEE-CHIN; Man. Dir PATRICK HYLTON; 37 brs.

RBC Royal Bank (Jamaica) Limited: 17 Dominica Dr., Kingston 5; tel. 960-2340; fax 960-5120; e-mail rbtt@cwjamaica.com; internet www.rbtt.com; f. 1993 as Jamaica Citizens Bank Ltd; acquired by Royal Bank of Trinidad and Tobago in 2001 and name changed to RBTT Bank Jamaica Ltd; present name adopted 2011; Chair. SURESH SOOKOO; 23 brs.

Development Banks

Development Bank of Jamaica Ltd: 11A–15 Oxford Rd, POB 466, Kingston 5; tel. 929-6124-7; fax 929-6055; e-mail dbank@cwjamaica .com; f. 2000 following merger of Agricultural Credit Bank of Jamaica Ltd and the National Devt Bank of Jamaica Ltd; provides funds for medium- and long-term devt-orientated projects; Man. Dir MILVERTON REYNOLDS.

Jamaica Mortgage Bank: 33 Tobago Ave, POB 950, Kingston 5; tel. 929-6350; fax 968-5428; e-mail jmb@cwjamaica.com; internet www.jmb.gov.jm; f. 1971 by the Jamaican Govt and the US Agency for Int. Devt; govt-owned statutory org. since 1973; functions primarily as a secondary market facility for home mortgages and to mobilize long-term funds for housing devts in Jamaica; also insures home mortgage loans made by approved financial institutions, thus transferring risk of default on a loan to the Govt; Chair. George Thomas; Gen. Man. Patrick Thelwall.

Pan Caribbean Financial Services: 60 Knutsford Blvd, Kingston 5; tel. 929-5583; fax 926-4385; e-mail options@gopancaribbean.com; internet www.gopancaribbean.com; fmrly Trafalgar Devt Bank, name changed as above in Dec. 2002; Chair. Richard O. Byles; Pres. and CEO Donovan H. Perkins.

Other Banks

National Export-Import Bank of Jamaica Ltd: 11 Oxford Rd, Kingston 5; tel. 922-9690; fax 960-5956; e-mail info@eximbankja.com; internet www.eximbankja.com; f. 1986; govt-owned; replaced Jamaica Export Credit Insurance Corpn; finances import and export of goods and services; Chair. Gary Craig 'Butch' Hendrickson; Man. Dir Lisa Bell.

National Investment Bank of Jamaica Ltd: 11 Oxford Rd, POB 889, Kingston 5; tel. 960-9691; fax 920-0379; e-mail info@nibj.com; internet www.nibj.com; Chair. Aubyn Hill; Sec. Jennifer Campbell.

Banking Association

Jamaica Bankers' Association: PSOJ Bldg, 39 Hope Rd, POB 1079, Kingston 10; tel. 927-6238; fax 927-5137; e-mail jbainfo@jba.org.jm; internet www.jba.org.jm; f. 1973; Pres. Minna Israel.

STOCK EXCHANGE

Jamaica Stock Exchange Ltd: 40 Harbour St, POB 1084, Kingston; tel. 967-3271; fax 967-3277; internet www.jamstockex.com; f. 1968; 51 listed cos (2012); Chair. Donovan Perkins; Gen. Man. Marlene Street Forrest.

INSURANCE

Financial Services Commission: 39–43 Barbados Ave, Kingston 5; tel. 906-3010; fax 906-3018; e-mail inquiry@fscjamaica.org; internet www.fscjamaica.org; f. 2001; succeeded the Office of the Superintendent of Insurance; regulatory body; Chair. Emil George; Exec. Dir Rohan Barnett.

Principal Companies

Advantage General Insurance Co Ltd: 4-6 Trafalgar Rd, Kingston 5; tel. 978-3690; fax 978-3718; internet www.advantagegeneral.com; f. 1964; general; Chair. Michael Lee-Chin; Pres. and CEO Mark Thompson.

British Caribbean Insurance Co Ltd (BCIC): 36 Duke St, POB 170, Kingston; tel. 922-1260; fax 922-4475; e-mail dsales@bcic-jm.com; internet www.bciconline.com; f. 1962; affiliate of Victoria Mutual Insurance Co; general; Chair. Joseph Matalon; Man. Dir Peter Levy.

General Accident Insurance Co Jamaica Ltd: 58 Half Way Tree Rd, Kingston 10; tel. 929-8451; fax 929-1074; e-mail info@genac.com; internet www.genac.com; f. 1981; general; Chair. Paul B. Scott; Man. Dir Sharon Donaldson.

Globe Insurance Co of Jamaica Ltd: 19 Dominica Dr., POB 401, Kingston 5; tel. 926-3720; fax 929-2727; e-mail info@globeins.com; internet www.globeins.com; f. 1963; subsidiary of Lascelles deMercado Group; general; Man. Dir Evan Thwaites.

Guardian Life: 12 Trafalgar Rd, Kingston 5; tel. 978-8815; fax 978-4225; e-mail guardian@ghl.com.jm; internet www.guardianlife.com.jm; subsidiary of Guardian Holdings (Trinidad and Tobago); pension and life policies; Pres. and CEO Eric Hosin.

Insurance Co of the West Indies Ltd (ICWI): 2 St Lucia Ave, POB 306, Kingston 5; tel. 926-9040; fax 929-6641; e-mail direct@icwi.net; internet icwi.com/jamaica; general; Chair. and CEO Dennis Lalor.

Jamaica General Insurance Co Ltd: 19–21 Knutsford Blvd, New Kingston; tel. 926-3204; fax 968-1920; e-mail info@jiiconline.com; internet www.jiiconline.com; f. 1981; subsidiary of GraceKennedy Ltd; general; Chair. Peter Moss-Solomon; Man. Dir Andrew Levy.

NCB Insurance Co Ltd (NCBIC): 32 Trafalgar Rd, Kingston 10; tel. 935-2004; fax 929-7301; e-mail ncbic@jncb.com; internet www.ncbinsurance.com; f. 1989; fmrly OMNI Insurance Services Ltd; life; Chair. Wayne Chen; Gen. Man. Ann-Marie Hamilton.

NEM Insurance Co (Jamaica) Ltd: NEM House, 9 King St, Kingston; tel. 922-1460; fax 922-4045; e-mail info@nemjam.com; internet www.nemjam.com; f. 1934; fmrly the National Employers' Mutual General Insurance Asscn; subsidiary of Jamaica National Bldg Soc; general; Chair. Oliver Clarke; Gen. Man. Christophe Hind.

Sagicor Life Jamaica Ltd: 28–48 Barbados Ave, Kingston 5; te 960-8920; fax 960-1927; internet www.sagicorjamaica.com; f. 197 owned by Sagicor Group (Barbados); merged with Island Lif Insurance Co Ltd in 2001; renamed as above in 2009; life; Chair R. Danny Williams; Pres. and CEO Richard O. Byles.

Scotia Jamaica Life Insurance Co Ltd (SJLIC): Duke and Por Royal Sts, Kingston; tel. 922-3765; e-mail sjlic.service@scotiabank.com; internet www.scotiabank.com; f. 1995; life; Gen. Man. Hugh Reid.

West Indies Alliance Insurance Co. Ltd: 23 Dominica Dr. Kingston 5; tel. 929-8080; fax 960-3179; e-mail insure@wia.com.jm; internet www.wia.com.jm; f. 1969; subsidiary of Guardian Holdings Ltd (Trinidad & Tobago); general; Gen. Man. Karen Bhoorasingh.

Association

Insurance Association of Jamaica (IAJ): 3–3A Richmond Ave Kingston 10; tel. 929-8404; fax 906-1804; e-mail iaj@cwjamaica.com; internet www.iajonline.com; f. 2005 by merger of the Jamaica Asscn of General Insurance Cos (JAGIC) and the Life Insurance Cos Asscn of Jamaica (LICA); Pres. Paul Lalor; Exec. Dir Orville Johnson.

Trade and Industry

GOVERNMENT AGENCY

Jamaica Information Service (JIS): 58A Half Way Tree Rd, POB 2222, Kingston 10; tel. 926-3740; fax 929-6715; e-mail jis@jis.gov.jm; internet www.jis.gov.jm; f. 1963; govt agency; CEO Donna-Marie Rowe.

DEVELOPMENT ORGANIZATIONS

Agro-Investment Corpn: Ministry of Agriculture & Fisheries, 188 Spanish Town Rd, Kingston 11; tel. 764-8071; fax 758-7160; e-mail agricultural@cwjamaica.com; internet www.assp.gov.jm; f. 2009; following the merger of Agricultural Devt Corp (ADC) and Agricultural Support Services Productive Projects Fund Ltd (ASSPPFL); agricultural devt, investment facilitation, promotion and management; Chair. David Lowe; CEO Hershell Brown.

Jamaica Trade and Invest (JTI): 18 Trafalgar Rd, Kingston 10; tel. 978-7755; fax 946-0090; e-mail info@jamprocorp.com; internet www.jamaicatradeandinvest.org; f. 1988 by merger of Jamaica Industrial Development Corpn, Jamaica National Export Corpn and Jamaica Investment Promotion Ltd; trade and investment promotion agency; Chair. Gordon Stewart; Pres. Sancia Bennett-Templer.

Planning Institute of Jamaica: 16 Oxford Rd, Kingston 5; tel. 960-9339; fax 906-5011; e-mail info@pioj.gov.jm; internet www.pioj.gov.jm; f. 1955 as the Central Planning Unit; adopted current name in 1984; formulates policy on and monitors performance in the fields of the economy and social, environmental and trade issues; publishing and analysis of social and economic performance data; Chair. and Dir-Gen. Dr Gladstone Hutchinson.

Urban Development Corpn: The Office Centre, 8th Floor, 12 Ocean Blvd, Kingston; tel. 922-8310; fax 922-9326; e-mail info@udcja.com; internet www.udcja.com; f. 1968; responsibility for urban renewal and devt within designated areas; Chair. Wayne Chen; Gen. Man. Desmond Young (acting).

CHAMBERS OF COMMERCE

American Chamber of Commerce of Jamaica: The Jamaica Pegasus, 81 Knutsford Blvd, Kingston 5; tel. 929-7866; fax 929-8597; e-mail amcham@cwjamaica.com; internet www.amchamjamaica.org; f. 1986; affiliated to the Chamber of Commerce of the USA; Pres. Diana Stewart; Exec. Dir Becky Stockhausen.

Jamaica Chamber of Commerce: UDC Office Centre, Suites 13–15, 12 Ocean Blvd, Kingston 10; tel. 922-0150; fax 924-9056; e-mail info@jamaicachamber.org.jm; internet www.jamaicachamber.org.jm; f. 1779; Pres. Milton Jefferson Samuda; Gen. Man Patricia Peart; 450 mems.

INDUSTRIAL AND TRADE ASSOCIATIONS

Cocoa Industry Board: Marcus Garvey Dr., POB 1039, Kingston 15; tel. 923-6411; fax 923-5837; e-mail cocoajam@cwjamaica.com; f. 1957; has statutory powers to regulate and develop the industry; owns and operates 4 central fermentaries; Chair. Joseph Suah; Man. and Sec. Steve Watson.

Coconut Industry Board: 18 Waterloo Rd, Kingston 10; tel. 926-1770; fax 968-1360; e-mail cocindbrd@cwjamaica.com; f. 1945; 9 mems; Chair. RICHARD A. JONES; Gen. Man. YVONNE BURNS.

Coffee Industry Board: 1 Willie Henry Dr., POB 508, Kingston 13; tel. 758-1259; fax 758-3907; e-mail datacoordinator@ciboj.org; internet www.ciboj.org; f. 1950; 9 mems; has wide statutory powers to regulate and develop the industry; Chair. HOWARD MITCHELL; Dir-Gen. CHRISTOPHER GENTLES.

Jamaica Bauxite Institute: Hope Gardens, POB 355, Kingston 6; tel. 927-2073; fax 927-1159; f. 1975; adviser to the Govt in the negotiation of agreements, consultancy services to clients in the bauxite/alumina and related industries, laboratory services for mineral and soil-related services, Pilot Plant services for materials and equipment testing, research and devt; Chair. TIMOTHY WILSON; Exec. Dir PARRIS LYEW-AYEE.

Jamaica Exporters' Association (JEA): 1 Winchester Rd, Kingston 10; tel. 960-4908; fax 960-9869; e-mail info@exportja.org; internet www.exportjamaica.org; f. 1966; promotes devt of export sector; Pres. VITUS EVANS; Gen. Man. JEAN SMITH.

Jamaica Manufacturers' Association Ltd (JMA): 85A Duke St, Kingston; tel. 922-8880; fax 922-9205; e-mail jma@cwjamaica.com; internet www.jma.com.jm; f. 1947; 289 mems; Pres. BRIAN PENGELLEY.

Sugar Industry Authority: 5 Trevennion Park Rd, POB 127, Kingston 5; tel. 926-5930; fax 926-6149; e-mail sia@cwjamaica.com; internet www.jamaicasugar.org; f. 1970; statutory body under portfolio of Min. of Agriculture and Fisheries; responsible for regulation and control of sugar industry and sugar marketing; conducts research through Sugar Industry Research Institute; Exec. Chair. DERICK HEAVEN.

Trade Board Ltd: Air Jamaica Bldg, 10th Floor, 72 Harbour St, Kingston; tel. 967-0507; fax 948-5441; e-mail info@tradeboard.gov.jm; internet www.tradeboard.gov.jm; Trade Admin. DOUGLAS WEBSTER.

EMPLOYERS' ORGANIZATIONS

All-Island Banana Growers' Association Ltd: Banana Industry Bldg, 10 South Ave, Kingston 4; tel. 922-5492; fax 922-5497; e-mail aibga@cwjamaica.com; f. 1946; 1,500 mems (1997); Chair. BOBBY POTTINGER; Sec. I. CHANG.

Banana Export Co (BECO): 10 South Ave, Kingston Gardens, Kingston 4; tel. 967-0735; fax 967-1936; e-mail beco@cwjamaica.com; f. 1985 to replace Banana Co of Jamaica; oversees the export of bananas; Chair. Dr MARSHALL MCGOWAN HALL; Man. VINCENT EVANS.

Citrus Growers' Association Ltd: Ortanique House, Bog Walk, Linstead; tel. 985-1496; fax 708-2051; internet www.jcgja.com; f. 1944; 13,000 mems; Chair. JOHN THOMPSON; Gen. Man. DENNIS BOOTH.

Jamaica Association of Sugar Technologists: c/o Sugar Industry Research Institute, Kendal Rd, Mandeville; tel. 962-2241; fax 962-1287; e-mail jast@jamaicasugar.org; f. 1936; 275 mems; Chair. EARLE ROBERTS; Pres. GILBERT THORNE.

Jamaica Gasoline Retailers' Association (JGRA): 38C Spring Rd, Kingston 11; tel. 926-4463; Pres. TREVOR BARNES.

Jamaica Livestock Association: Newport East, POB 36, Kingston; tel. 922-7130; fax 922-8934; e-mail jlapurch@cwjamaica.com; internet www.jlaltd.com; f. 1941; 7,584 mems; Man. Dir and CEO HENRY J. RAINFORD.

Jamaica Producers' Group Ltd: 6A Oxford Rd, POB 237, Kingston 5; tel. 926-3503; fax 929-3636; e-mail cosecretary@jpjamaica.com; internet www.jpjamaica.com; f. 1929; fmrly Jamaica Banana Producers' Assn; Chair. C. H. JOHNSTON; Man. Dir Dr MARSHALL HALL.

Jamaica Sugar Cane Growers' Association (JSCGA): 4 North Ave, Kingston Gardens, Kingston 4; tel. 922-3010; fax 922-2077; e-mail allcane@cwjamaica.com; f. 1941; registered cane farmers; 27,000 mems; fmrly All-Island Cane Farmers' Assn; name changed as above in 2008; Pres. ALLAN RICKARDS; Gen. Man. KARL JAMES.

Private Sector Organization of Jamaica (PSOJ): The Carlton Alexander Bldg, 39 Hope Rd, POB 236, Kingston 10; tel. 927-6957; fax 927-5137; e-mail psojinfo@psoj.org; internet www.psoj.org; f. 1976; federative body of private business individuals, cos and asscns; Pres. JOSEPH MATALON; CEO SANDRA GLASGOW.

Shipping Association of Jamaica: see Transport—Shipping.

Small Businesses' Association of Jamaica (SBAJ): 2 Trafalgar Rd, Kingston 5; tel. 978-0168; fax 927-7071; e-mail dpjam@cwjamaica.com; internet www.sbaj.org.jm; f. 1974; Pres. DALMA JAMES; Man. BRIDGETTE STEELE.

Sugar Manufacturing Corpn of Jamaica Ltd: 5 Trevennion Park Rd, Kingston 5; tel. 926-5930; fax 926-6149; est. to represent the sugar manufacturers in Jamaica; deals with all aspects of the sugar industry and its by-products; provides liaison between the Govt, the Sugar Industry Authority and the Jamaica Sugar Cane Growers' Assn; 9 mems; Gen. Man. DERYCK T. BROWN.

UTILITIES

Regulatory Authority

Office of Utilities Regulation (OUR): PCJ Resource Centre, 3rd Floor, 36 Trafalgar Rd, Kingston 10; tel. 968-6057; fax 929-3635; e-mail office@our.org.jm; internet www.our.org.jm; f. 1995; regulates provision of services in the following sectors: water, electricity, telecommunications, public passenger transportation, sewerage; Dir-Gen. AHMAD ZIA MIAN.

Electricity

Jamaica Energy Partners (JEP): 10–16 Grenada Way, RKA Bldg, 3rd Floor, Kingston 5; tel. 920-1746; fax 920-1750; e-mail info@jamenergy.com; internet jamenergy.com; owned by Conduit Capital Partners (USA); owns and operates two power barges at Old Harbour Bay, St Catherine; sells electricity to JPSCo; Gen. Man. and CEO WAYNE MCKENZIE.

Jamaica Public Service Co (JPSCo): Dominion Life Bldg, 6 Knutsford Blvd, POB 54, Kingston 5; tel. 926-3190; fax 968-5341; e-mail media@jpsco.com; internet www.jpsco.com; responsible for the generation and supply of electricity to the island; the JPSCo operating licence due to expire in 2027; Chair. HISATSUGU HIRAI.

Water

National Water Commission: LOJ Centre, 5th Floor, 28–48 Barbados Ave, Kingston 5; tel. 929-5430; fax 926-1329; e-mail pr@nwc.com.jm; internet www.nwcjamaica.com; f. 1980; statutory body; provides potable water and waste water services; Chair. RUSSELL HADEED.

Water Resources Authority: Hope Gardens, POB 91, Kingston 7; tel. 927-0077; fax 977-0179; e-mail info@wra.gov.jm; internet www.wra.gov.jm; f. 1996; manages, protects and controls allocation and use of water supplies; Man. Dir BASIL FERNANDEZ.

TRADE UNIONS

Bustamante Industrial Trade Union (BITU): 98 Duke St, Kingston; tel. 922-2443; fax 967-0120; e-mail bitu@cwjamaica.com; f. 1938; Pres. KAVAN GAYLE; Gen. Sec. GEORGE FYFFE; 60,000 mems.

Caribbean Union of Teachers: 97 Church St, Kingston; tel. 922-1385; fax 922-3257; e-mail infor@caribbeanteachers.com; internet www.caribbeanteachers.com; f. 1935; umbrella org.; affiliates in 21 Caribbean countries; Pres. MARVIN ANDALL; Gen. Sec. Dr ADOLPH CAMERON.

Jamaica Confederation of Trade Unions (JCTU): 1A Hope Blvd, Kingston 6; tel. 927-2468; fax 977-4575; e-mail jctu@cwjamaica.com; Pres. LLOYD GOODLEIGH.

National Workers' Union of Jamaica (NWU): 130–132 East St, POB 344, Kingston 16; tel. 922-1150; fax 922-6608; e-mail nwyou@cwjamaica.com; f. 1952; affiliated to the International Trade Union Confederation; Pres. VINCENT MORRISON; Vice. Pres. HOWARD DUNCAN; 10,000 mems.

Principal Independent Unions

Jamaica Association of Local Government Officers: 15A Old Hope Rd, Kingston 5; tel. 929-5123; fax 960-4403; e-mail admin@jalgo.org; internet www.jalgo.org; Pres. STANLEY THOMAS; Gen. Sec. HELENE DAVIS-WHITE.

Jamaica Civil Service Association: 10 Caledonia Ave and 46 Market St, POB 106, Kingston 5; tel. 968-7087; fax 926-2042; e-mail jacisera@cwjamaica.com; internet www.jacisera.org; f. 1919; Pres. O'NEIL GRANT; Sec. CHELSIE SHELLIE VERNON.

Jamaica Federation of Musicians and Affiliated Artistes Union: 5 Balmoral Ave, Kingston 10; tel. 926-8029; fax 929-0485; e-mail jafedmusic@cwjamaica.com; internet jafedmusic.tripod.com; f. 1958; Pres. DESMOND YOUNG; Sec. CHARMAINE BOWMAN; 2,000 mems.

Jamaica Police Federation: Office Centre Bldg, 4th Floor, Kingston Mall, 12 Ocean Blvd, Kingston; tel. 922-4983; fax 922-3799; e-mail general@jampolicefed.org; internet www.jampolicefed.org; f. 1944; Chair. FRANZ MORRISON; Gen.-Sec. DAVID WHITE.

Jamaica Teachers' Association: 97B Church St, Kingston; tel. 922-1385; fax 922-3257; e-mail jta@cwjamaica.com; internet www.jamaicateachers.org.jm; Pres. PAUL ADAMS; Sec.-Gen. Dr ADOLPH CAMERON.

Jamaica Workers' Union: 3 West Ave, Kingston 4; tel. 922-3222; fax 967-3128; e-mail jamaicaworkersunion@yahoo.com; Pres. CLIFTON BROWN.

Jamaican Airline Pilots' Association (JALPA): Unit 4, 2 Seymour Ave, Kingston 10; tel. 978-5854; fax 281-8592; e-mail jalpajamaica@jalpa.org; internet www.jalpa.org; f. 1971; Pres. CECIL SUTHERLAND; Sec. ALICE TABOIS.

Medical Association of Jamaica (MAJ): 19A Windsor Ave, Kingston 5; tel. 946-1105; fax 946-1107; e-mail majdoctors@cwjamaica.com; internet www.medicalassnjamaica.com; f. 1877; 18 affiliates; Pres. Dr WINSTON DE LA HAYE; 2,000 mems.

Nurses Association of Jamaica (NAJ): 4, Trevennion Park Rd, POB 277, Kingston 5; tel. 929-5213; fax 968-2200; e-mail najtrevennion@hotmail.com; Pres. ANTOINETTE LEANA PATTERSON; Sec. PRUDENCE GRANDISON.

Union of Schools, Agricultural and Allied Workers (USAAW): 2 Wildman St, Kingston; tel. 967-2970; fax 922-6770; e-mail usaaw_trade_union@yahoo.com; f. 1978; Gen. Sec. KEITH COMRIE.

Union of Technical, Administrative and Supervisory Personnel (UTASP): 108 Church St, Kingston; tel. 922-2086; Pres. ANTHONY DAWKINS; Gen. Sec. ST PATRICE ENNIS.

University and Allied Workers' Union (UAWU): 50 Lady Musgrave Rd, Kingston 10; tel. 927-6658; fax 927-9931; e-mail labpoyh@yahoo.com; Pres. LAMBERT BROWN.

Transport

RAILWAYS

There are about 339 km of railway, all standard gauge, in Jamaica. Passenger services ceased in 1992. In 2008 the Government announced that the People's Republic of China was to provide assistance in the reconstruction of the railway system between Kingston and Montego Bay, and Spanish Town and Ewarton. The three-year project was to include the construction of 18 new railway stations and the provision of passenger and freight coaches. In 2011 the Jamaica Railway Corpn indicated it was close to resuming passenger services after a successful trial run between Spanish Town and Linstead.

Jamaica Railway Corpn (JRC): 142 Barry St, POB 489, Kingston; tel. 922-6443; fax 922-4539; e-mail odcrooks@cwjamaica.com; internet www.mtw.gov.jm/dep_agencies/ja_rail.aspx; f. 1845 as Jamaica Railway Co, the earliest British colonial railway; transferred to JRC in 1960; govt-owned, but autonomous, statutory corpn until 1990, when it was partly leased to Alcan Jamaica Co Ltd (subsequently West Indies Alumina Co) as the first stage of a privatization scheme; 215 km of railway; Chair. HAROLD BRADY; Gen. Man. OWEN CROOKS.

Jamalco (Alcoa Minerals of Jamaica): Clarendon Parish, Clarendon; tel. 986-2561; fax 986-9637; internet www.alcoa.com/jamaica/en/home.asp; 43 km of standard-gauge railway; transport of bauxite; CEO KLAUS KLEINFELD.

ROADS

Jamaica has a good network of tar-surfaced and metalled motoring roads. In 2008 there were 22,121 km of roads in Jamaica. In 2004 an estimated 70.1% of roads were paved, according to the International Road Federation. The 2010 budget allocated some J $106m.to the transport and public works sector. In the same year the Government approved a US $340m. loan from the Export-Import Bank of China for the Jamaica Road Development Infrastructure Programme, a five-year project to rehabilitate more than 570 km of roadways across the island. The US $14m. reconstruction of the Dry (Hope) River Bridge, Harbour View, damaged by Tropical Storm Gustav in 2008, was completed in November 2011.

Transport Authority: 119 Maxfield Ave, Kingston 10; tel. 926-8912; fax 929-4178; e-mail customerservice@ta.org.jm; internet www.ta.org.jm; regulatory body; administers the licensing of public and commercial vehicles; Chair. GEORGE JOHNSON; Man. Dir DANIEL DAWES.

SHIPPING

The principal ports are Kingston, Montego Bay and Port Antonio. The port at Kingston is a major transshipment terminal for the Caribbean area. In 2008 the fifth phase of an expansion project in Kingston was completed, doubling the port's handling capacity. Further plans for the expansion of Jamaica's port facilities, to include the construction of three additional berths and a second terminal at Montego Bay, were under way. A new cruise ship pier at Falmouth opened in early 2011. There were also plans to expand the transshipment port at Fort Augusta; construction was scheduled to begin in 2012.

Port Authority of Jamaica: 15–17 Duke St, Kingston; tel. 922-0290; fax 948-3575; e-mail paj@portjam.com; internet www.portjam.com; f. 1966; Govt's principal maritime agency; responsible for monitoring and regulating the navigation of all vessels berthing at Jamaican ports, for regulating the tariffs on public wharves, and fc the devt of industrial free zones in Jamaica; Pres. and Chair. NOEL A HYLTON.

Kingston Free Zone Co Ltd: 27 Shannon Dr., POB 1025 Kingston 15; tel. 923-6021; fax 923-6023; e-mail blee@portjam.com; internet www.pajfz.com; f. 1976; subsidiary of Port Authority of Jamaica; management and promotion of an export-orientated industrial free trade zone for cos from various countries; Gen. Man. KARLA HUIE.

Montego Bay Free Zone: POB 1377, Montego Bay; tel. 979-8696 fax 979-8088; e-mail gchenry@portjam.com; internet www.pajf.com; Gen. Man. GLORIA HENRY.

Shipping Association of Jamaica: 4 Fourth Ave, Newport West POB 1050, Kingston 13; tel. 923-3491; fax 923-3421; e-mail saj@jamports.com; internet www.jamports.com; f. 1939; 77 mems regulates the supply and management of stevedoring labour in Kingston; represents mems in negotiations with govt and trade bodies; Pres. ROGER HINDS; Gen. Man. TREVOR RILEY.

Principal Shipping Company

Jamaica Freight and Shipping Co Ltd (JFS): 80–82 Second St, Newport West, Kingston 12; tel. 923-9271; fax 923-4091; e-mail jfs@jashipco.com; internet www.jashipco.com; f. 1976; liner and port agents, stevedoring services; Exec. Chair. CHARLES JOHNSTON.

CIVIL AVIATION

There are three international airports linking Jamaica with North America, Europe, and other Caribbean islands. The Norman Manley International Airport is situated 22.5 km outside Kingston. Sangster International Airport is 5 km from Montego Bay. A J $800m. programme to expand and improve the latter was completed in 2009. The Ian Fleming International Airport at Boscobel, 10 km from Ocho Rios, opened in January 2011. In May the national airline Air Jamaica was taken over by the Trinidadian Caribbean Airlines.

Airports Authority of Jamaica: Norman Manley International Airport, Palisadoes; tel. 924-8452; fax 924-8419; e-mail aaj@aaj.com.jm; internet www.airportsauthorityjamaica.aero; Chair. MARK HART; Pres. EARL ANTHONY RICHARDS.

Civil Aviation Authority: 4 Winchester Rd, POB 8998, Kingston 10; tel. 960-3948; fax 920-0194; e-mail info@jcaa.gov.jm; internet www.jcaa.gov.jm; f. 1996; Dir-Gen. Lt Col OSCAR DERBY.

Air Jamaica Ltd: 72–76 Harbour St, Kingston; tel. 922-3460; fax 967-3125; internet www.airjamaica.com; f. 1968; privatized in 1994, reacquired by Govt in 2004; sold to Caribbean Airlines (Trinidad and Tobago) in May 2011; Govt of Jamaica retained 16% share; services within the Caribbean and to Canada (in asscn with Air Canada), the USA and the United Kingdom; Chair. GEORGE M. NICHOLAS, III; CEO ROBERT CORBIE (acting).

Exec Direct Aviation (EDA): Bldg II, Suite 11, 1 Ripon Rd, Kingston 5; tel. 618-5884; fax 618-5888; internet www.flyexecdirect.com; f. 2011; cargo services to Caribbean, Central and South American destinations; COO KAMAL CLARKE.

Jamaica Air Shuttle: Tinson Pen Aerodrome, Marcus Garvey Dr., Kingston 11; tel. 923-0371; fax 506-9071; e-mail reservations@jamaicaairshuttle.com; internet www.jamaicaairshuttle.com; f. 2005; domestic and regional charter services to the Cayman Islands, Cuba, Dominican Republic and Haiti; Chair. CHRISTOPHER READ.

TimAir Ltd: Sangster International Airport, Montego Bay; tel. 952-2516; fax 979-1113; e-mail timair@usa.net; internet www.timair.com; f. 1983; charter services; Pres. FRASER MCCONNELL; Man. COLLEEN MCCONNELL.

Tourism

Tourists, mainly from the USA, visit Jamaica for its beaches, mountains, historic buildings and cultural heritage. In 2009 there were 1,831,097 visitor arrivals. In 2007 there were some 27,231 rooms in all forms of tourist accommodation. In 2010 tourism receipts totalled a provisional US $1,922m.

Jamaica Hotel and Tourist Association (JHTA): 2 Ardenne Rd, Kingston 10; tel. 926-3635-6; fax 929-1054; e-mail info@jhta.org; internet www.jhta.org; f. 1961; trade asscn for hoteliers and other cos involved in Jamaican tourism; Pres. EVELYN SMITH; Exec. Dir CAMILLE NEEDHAM.

Jamaica Tourist Board (JTB): 64 Knutsford Blvd, Kingston 5; tel. 929-9200; fax 929-9375; e-mail info@visitjamaica.com; internet www.visitjamaica.com; f. 1955; a statutory body set up by the Govt to promote all aspects of the tourism industry; Chair. DENNIS MORRISON; Dir of Tourism JOHN LYNCH.

Defence

As assessed at November 2011, the total strength of the Jamaican Defence Force was 2,830. This included an army of 2,500, a coastguard of 190 and an air wing of 140 members on active service. There were reserves of some 953.

Defence Budget: an estimated J $8,990m. (US $104m.) in 2011.

Chief of Defence Staff: Maj.-Gen. ANTONY BERTRAM ANDERSON.

Education

Primary education is compulsory in certain districts, and free education is ensured. The education system consists of a primary cycle of six years, followed by two secondary cycles of three and four years, respectively. In 2007/08 enrolment at primary schools included 80% of children in the relevant age-group. In the same year enrolment at secondary schools included 77% of children in the relevant age-group. Higher education was provided by five institutions, including the University of the West Indies, which had five faculties situated at its Mona campus, in Kingston. Government spending on education in 2011/12 was budgeted at some J $73,200m., representing 13.4% of total planned expenditure.

JAPAN

Introductory Survey

LOCATION, CLIMATE, LANGUAGE, RELIGION, FLAG, CAPITAL

Japan lies in eastern Asia and comprises a curved chain of more than 3,000 islands. Four large islands, named (from north to south) Hokkaido, Honshu, Shikoku and Kyushu, account for about 98% of the land area. Hokkaido lies just to the south of Sakhalin, a large Russian island, and about 1,300 km (800 miles) east of Russia's mainland port of Vladivostok. Southern Japan is about 150 km (93 miles) east of the Republic of Korea (South Korea). Although summers are temperate everywhere, the climate in winter varies sharply from cold in the north to mild in the south. Temperatures in Tokyo range from −6°C (21°F) to 30°C (86°F). Typhoons and heavy rains are common in summer. The official language is Japanese. A small minority of indigenous Ainu speak a distinct language. The major religions are Shintoism and Buddhism, and there is a Christian minority. The national flag (proportions 7 by 10) is white, with a red disc (a sun without rays) in the centre. The capital is Tokyo.

CONTEMPORARY POLITICAL HISTORY

Historical Context

Following Japan's defeat in the Second World War, Japanese forces surrendered in August 1945. Japan signed an armistice in September, and the country was placed under US military occupation. A new democratic Constitution, which took effect in May 1947, renounced war and abandoned the doctrine of the Emperor's divinity. Following the peace treaty of September 1951, Japan regained its independence on 28 April 1952, although it was not until 1972 that the last of the US-administered outer islands, the remaining Ryukyu Islands (including Okinawa), were returned to Japanese sovereignty. The conservative Shigeru Yoshida served as Prime Minister in 1946–47 and again between 1948 and 1954, when he was succeeded by Ichiro Hatoyama.

Domestic Political Affairs

Liberal-Democratic Party dominance, 1955–93

In November 1955 rival conservative groups merged to form the Liberal-Democratic Party (LDP). Nobusuke Kishi, who became Prime Minister in February 1957, was succeeded by Hayato Ikeda in July 1960. Ikeda was replaced by Eisaku Sato in November 1964. Sato remained in office until July 1972, when he was succeeded by Kakuei Tanaka. Tanaka's premiership was beset by problems, leading to his replacement by Takeo Miki in December 1974. Tanaka was subsequently accused of accepting bribes from the Marubeni Corporation, and he was arrested in July 1976. The LDP lost its overall majority in the House of Representatives (the lower house of the Kokkai or Diet) at a legislative election held in December 1976. Miki resigned and was succeeded by Takeo Fukuda. However, Masayoshi Ohira defeated Fukuda in the LDP presidential election of November 1978, and replaced him as Prime Minister in December. Ohira was unable to win a majority in the lower house at elections in October 1979. In May 1980 the Government was defeated in a motion of no confidence, forcing the dissolution of the lower house. Ohira died before the elections in June, when the LDP won 284 of the 511 seats. In July Zenko Suzuki was elected President of the LDP, and subsequently appointed Prime Minister. The growing factionalism of the LDP and the worsening economic crisis prompted Suzuki's resignation as Prime Minister and LDP President in October 1982. He was succeeded by Yasuhiro Nakasone.

At elections in June 1983 for one-half of the seats in the House of Councillors (the upper house of the Diet), a new electoral system was used. Of the 126 contested seats, 50 were filled on the basis of proportional representation. Two small parties thus entered the House of Councillors for the first time. The LDP increased its strength from 134 to 137 members in the 252-seat chamber. This result was seen as an endorsement of Nakasone's policies of increased expenditure on defence, closer relations with the USA and greater Japanese involvement in international affairs.

In October 1983 former Prime Minister Tanaka was found guilty of having accepted bribes. However, Tanaka's refusal to relinquish his parliamentary seat prompted an opposition-led boycott of the Diet, forcing Nakasone to call a premature legislative election in December. The Komeito (Clean Government Party), the Democratic Socialist Party (DSP) and the Japan Socialist Party (JSP) gained seats, at the expense of the Communists and the New Liberal Club (NLC). The LDP, which had performed badly in the election, formed a coalition with the NLC (which had split from the LDP over the Tanaka affair in 1976) and several independents. Nakasone called another early election for July 1986, at which the LDP won 304 of the 512 seats. The record majority enabled the LDP to dispense with its coalition partner, the NLC (which disbanded in August and rejoined the LDP). In September the leaders of the LDP agreed to alter by-laws to allow party presidents one-year extensions beyond the normal limit of two terms of two years each. Nakasone was thus able to retain the posts of President of the LDP and Prime Minister until October 1987.

In July 1987 the Secretary-General of the LDP, Noboru Takeshita, left the Tanaka faction, with 113 other members, and announced the formation of a major new grouping within the ruling party. In the same month Tanaka's position was further weakened when the Tokyo High Court upheld his 1983 conviction for accepting bribes. In October 1987 Nakasone nominated Takeshita as his successor. The Diet was convened and Takeshita was formally elected as Prime Minister in November. In the new Cabinet Takeshita maintained a balance among the five major factions of the LDP, retaining only two members of Nakasone's previous Cabinet, but appointing four members of the Nakasone faction to senior ministerial posts (including Nakasone's ally, Sosuke Uno, as Minister of Foreign Affairs).

In January 1989 Emperor Hirohito, who had reigned since 1926, died after a long illness, thus ending the Showa era. He was succeeded by his son, Akihito, and the new era was named Heisei ('achievement of universal peace').

The Prime Minister and the LDP suffered a serious set-back in June 1988 when several senior members, including Nakasone, Kiichi Miyazawa and Takeshita himself, were alleged to have been indirectly involved in share-trading irregularities with the Recruit Cosmos Company. Three cabinet ministers and the Chairman of the DSP were subsequently forced to resign, owing to their alleged involvement in the Recruit affair. In April 1989, as the allegations against politicians widened to include charges of bribery and malpractice, Takeshita announced his resignation. He was subsequently found to have accepted donations worth more than 150m. yen from the Recruit organization. Takeshita nominated Sosuke Uno as his successor. Uno was elected Prime Minister by the Diet in June, and a new Cabinet was appointed. Uno was the first Japanese Prime Minister since the foundation of the LDP not to command his own political faction. Meanwhile, in May, following an investigation into the Recruit affair undertaken by an LDP special committee, public prosecutors indicted 13 people. Nakasone resigned from the LDP, assuming responsibility for the scandal, but did not relinquish his seat in the Diet.

Within days of Uno's assumption of office, a Japanese magazine published allegations of sexual impropriety involving the Prime Minister. As a result of a considerable increase in support for the JSP, led by Chairwoman Takako Doi, the LDP lost its majority in the upper house for the first time in its history. Uno's offer to resign was accepted by the LDP, which in August chose the relatively unknown Toshiki Kaifu, a former Minister of Education, to be the party's President and the new Prime Minister. Although the House of Councillors' ballot rejected Kaifu as the new Prime Minister in favour of Takako Doi, the decision of the lower house was adopted, in accordance with stipulations embodied in the Constitution.

At an election held in February 1990, the LDP was returned to power with an unexpectedly large measure of support, securing 275 of the 512 seats in the House of Representatives. In January 1991 the JSP changed its English name to the Social Democratic Party of Japan (SDPJ) and Makato Tanabe later replaced

Takako Doi as Chairman of the party. In September senior LDP officials forced Kaifu to abandon proposals for electoral reform, and the Takeshita faction of the LDP subsequently withdrew its support for the Prime Minister. Sponsored by the faction, former Minister of Finance Kiichi Miyazawa was elected President of the LDP in October, and in November the Diet endorsed his appointment as Prime Minister. However, his position was undermined by new allegations of involvement in the Recruit affair, publicized by the SDPJ in December.

In early 1992 public disgust at official corruption was registered at two prefectural by-elections to the upper house, when the LDP lost seats, which had previously been considered secure, to Rengo-no-kai (the political arm of RENGO, the trade union confederation). However, the anti-Government alliance that had supported Rengo-no-kai disintegrated in May over the issue of the authorization of Japanese involvement in UN peace-keeping operations. Members of the SDPJ attempted to obstruct the vote in the lower house by submitting their resignations *en masse*. However, the Speaker ruled that these could not be accepted during the current Diet session. The successful passage through the Diet of the legislation on international peace-keeping improved the Government's standing, and in elections to the upper house in July the LDP won 69 of the 127 seats contested. The SDPJ, by contrast, lost 25 of its 46 seats; the Komeito increased its total strength from 20 to 24 seats, but Rengo-no-kai failed to win any seats, owing to the dissolution of the informal coalition it had facilitated between the SDPJ and the DSP. The Japan New Party (JNP), founded only two months prior to the election by LDP dissidents, secured four seats. A formal split within the Takeshita faction took place in December 1992. The new faction was to be led nominally by Tsutomu Hata, the Minister of Finance, although it was widely recognized that Ichiro Ozawa, the former LDP Secretary-General, held the real power in the grouping.

Electoral reform was a major political issue in the first half of 1993. While the LDP favoured a single-member constituency system, the opposition parties proposed various forms of proportional representation. In June the lower house adopted a motion of no confidence against the Government, after the LDP refused to modify its reform proposals to meet opposition demands. Numerous LDP members opposed the Government or abstained. The Ozawa-Hata group, comprising 44 former LDP members, immediately established a new party, the Shinseito (Japan Renewal Party, JRP), in order to contest the forthcoming legislative election. Another new party, the New Party Sakigake, was also formed by LDP Diet members. In the election to the House of Representatives, held in July, the LDP won 223 of the 511 seats, and was thus 33 seats short of a majority. Miyazawa resigned as Prime Minister and a seven-party coalition Government was formed, excluding the LDP, which thus became an opposition party for the first time since its formation. In August Morihiro Hosokawa, the leader of the JNP, was elected Prime Minister, defeating the new President of the LDP, Yohei Kono.

Successive Governments, 1994–2001

Hosokawa resigned as Prime Minister in April 1994. Tsutomu Hata was subsequently appointed Prime Minister, at the head of a minority Government that excluded the SDPJ and the New Party Sakigake. Hata was obliged to resign in June, however, owing to his continued failure to command a viable majority in the Diet, and a new coalition of the SDPJ, the LDP and the New Party Sakigake took office. The LDP thus ended its brief period of opposition. Tomiichi Murayama, the leader of the SDPJ, became Prime Minister, and Kono was appointed Deputy Prime Minister and Minister of Foreign Affairs.

In July 1994 Murayama recognized the constitutional right to the existence of Japan's Self-Defence Forces (SDF, the armed forces), thereby effectively contradicting official SDPJ policy on the issue. (The SDPJ amended its policy to accord with Murayama's statement in September.) In December nine opposition parties, including the JNP, the JRP, the DSP and the Komeito, amalgamated to form a new political party, the Shinshinto (New Frontier Party, NFP). A faction of Komeito remained outside the new party and was renamed Komei. Kaifu, the former LDP Prime Minister, was elected leader of the NFP; Ozawa was appointed Secretary-General. The creation of the NFP was widely perceived to be a response to the approval by the Diet in November 1994 of the electoral reform bills first proposed in 1993, which appeared to favour larger political parties. Under the terms of the new law, the House of Representatives was to be reduced to 500 seats, comprising 300 single-seat constituencies and 200 seats determined by proportional representation; the proportional-representation base was to be divided into 11 regions, and a party would qualify for a proportional-representation seat if it received a minimum of 2% of the vote.

In January 1995 a massive earthquake in the Kobe region caused thousands of deaths and serious infrastructural damage. The Government was severely criticized for the poor co-ordination of the relief operation. In March a poisonous gas, sarin, was released into the Tokyo underground railway system, killing 12 people and injuring more than 5,000. A religious sect, Aum Shinrikyo, was accused of perpetrating the attack. Following a further gas attack in Yokohama in April, a number of sect members were detained by the authorities. In June Shoko Asahara, the leader of Aum Shinrikyo, was indicted on a charge of murder; his trial continued until February 2004, when he was sentenced to death for his role in the attack.

Participation in the elections to the House of Councillors, held in July 1995, was low. With one-half of the 252 seats being contested, the LDP won only 49 seats, the SDPJ 16 and the New Party Sakigake three, whereas the NFP, benefiting from the support of the Soka Gakkai religious organization, won 40 seats. In September Ryutaro Hashimoto, the Minister of International Trade and Industry, was elected leader of the LDP, after Yohei Kono announced that he would not seek re-election.

In December 1995 Toshiki Kaifu was succeeded by Ichiro Ozawa as leader of the NFP. In January 1996 Tomiichi Murayama resigned as Prime Minister; however, he was re-elected Chairman of the SDPJ. The LDP leader, Ryutaro Hashimoto, was elected Prime Minister. A coalition Cabinet, largely dominated by the LDP, was formed. In August Shoichi Ide and Hiroyuki Sonoda were elected Leader and Secretary-General, respectively, of the New Party Sakigake following the resignations of Masayoshi Takemura and Yukio Hatoyama. Hatoyama left the party and founded the Democratic Party of Japan (DPJ), with other dissident members of the New Party Sakigake and individual members of the SDPJ and NFP.

A legislative election was held in October 1996. The LDP won 239 of the 500 seats in the House of Representatives, while the NFP secured 156, the DPJ 52, the Japanese Communist Party (JCP) 26, the SDPJ 15, and the New Party Sakigake two seats. In November Ryutaro Hashimoto was re-elected Prime Minister, and formed the first single-party Cabinet since 1993. Soon after the election several government ministers and party leaders were implicated in various official corruption scandals. In December 1996 former Prime Minister Hata left the NFP and formed a new party, Taiyoto (Sun Party), together with 12 other dissident NFP members. In late December Takako Doi was formally appointed Chairwoman of the SDPJ (she had been acting Chairwoman since the dissolution of the House of Representatives in September).

In mid-1997 Hosokawa resigned from the NFP, reportedly owing to dissatisfaction with Ozawa's leadership. (In December Hosokawa formed a new party—From Five.) By September the LDP had regained its majority in the House of Representatives, following a series of defections by members of the NFP. In December a much-reduced NFP was dissolved. Six new parties were founded by former NFP members, Ozawa and his supporters forming the Liberal Party (LP), and a significant political realignment thus took place. In January 1998 six opposition parties, including the DPJ, formed a parliamentary group, Minyuren, which constituted the largest opposition bloc in the Diet. In March the parties comprising Minyuren agreed on their integration into the DPJ, formally establishing a new DPJ, with Naoto Kan as its President, in the following month.

Meanwhile, during 1997 various circumstances contributed to the development of an economic crisis. The Government announced a series of measures designed to encourage economic growth, including a reduction in taxes and, in a major reversal of policy in response to the recent failure of several financial institutions, the use of public funds to support the banking system. In January 1998 two senior officials from the Ministry of Finance were arrested on suspicion of accepting bribes from banks. The Minister of Finance, Hiroshi Mitsuzuka, resigned, accepting responsibility for the affair. As more banks and other financial institutions became implicated in the scandal, the central bank initiated an internal investigation into its own operations. In March the Governor resigned after a senior bank executive was arrested, amid further allegations of bribery. Trials of those implicated in the scandals took place in 1998 and 1999. A number of financial deregulation measures took effect on 1 April 1998, as part of Japan's 'Big Bang' reform process. Hashimoto's administration was widely criticized for its slow reaction to the growing economic crisis. In June the SDPJ and the New Party Sakigake withdrew from their alliance with the ruling LDP.

The LDP performed poorly in elections for one-half of the seats in the House of Councillors in July 1998, retaining only 44 of its 61 seats contested, while the DPJ won 27 seats, increasing its representation to 47 seats, and the JCP became the third largest party in the upper house, taking 15 seats. Hashimoto resigned as Prime Minister and President of the LDP and was succeeded in both posts by Keizo Obuchi, hitherto Minister of Foreign Affairs. Although designated an 'economic reconstruction' Cabinet, doubts arose about the Obuchi Government's commitment to comprehensive reform. Kiichi Miyazawa, the former Prime Minister, was appointed Minister of Finance. Obuchi announced the establishment of an Economic Strategy Council and promised substantial tax reductions. The issue of banking reform dominated the following months, and in October 1998 the Diet approved banking legislation that included provisions for the nationalization of failing banks, as demanded by the opposition.

Komei merged with another party, Shinto Heiwa, in November 1998 to form New Komeito, which thus became the second largest opposition party. Also in that month Fukushiro Nukaga, the Director-General of the Defence Agency, resigned from the Government to assume responsibility for a procurement scandal. In mid-November the LDP and the LP reached a basic accord on the formation of a coalition, although this would still lack a majority in the upper house. The Government was reorganized in January 1999 to include the LP, the leader of which, Ichiro Ozawa, had refused a cabinet position. The Government adopted an administrative reform plan, which aimed to reduce further the number of cabinet ministers and public servants and to establish an economic and fiscal policy committee.

At local elections in April 1999, 11 of the 12 governorships contested were won by the incumbents, all standing as independents. At the gubernatorial election for Tokyo, the convincing victory of Shintaro Ishihara, an outspoken nationalist writer and a former Minister of Transport under the LDP (although now unaffiliated), was regarded as an embarrassment for the ruling party. In August the Diet voted to grant official legal status to the de facto national flag (*Hinomaru*) and anthem (*Kimigayo*), despite considerable opposition owing to their association with Japan's militaristic past. Meanwhile, in July New Komeito agreed to join the ruling LDP-LP coalition, giving the Government a new majority in the upper house and expanding its control in the lower house to more than 70% of the seats. However, negotiations on policy initiatives proved difficult, owing to differences over issues such as constitutional revision and New Komeito's opposition to a reduction in the number of seats in the lower house, as favoured by the LP. Obuchi was re-elected President of the LDP in September. Naoto Kan was replaced as President of the DPJ by Yukio Hatoyama, hitherto Secretary-General of the party. A new Cabinet was appointed in October. Notably, Michio Ochi was appointed Chairman of the Financial Reconstruction Commission. The LP and New Komeito each received one cabinet post. A basic accord on coalition policy included an agreement to seek a reduction in the number of seats in the House of Representatives, initially by 20 and subsequently by a further 30.

In December 1999 a political crisis was averted when Ozawa was persuaded not to withdraw the LP from the ruling coalition, as he had threatened, over a delay in the proposal of legislation to reduce the number of seats in the lower house. The ruling parties had earlier agreed also to postpone the consideration of a proposal to expand Japan's participation in UN peace-keeping activities. In early 2000 the Diet approved the controversial legislation on the reduction in seats, despite an opposition boycott. Multi-party committees were established in both houses in January, which were to review the Constitution over a period of five years. In February Michio Ochi was forced to resign from the Cabinet over remarks that suggested he would be lenient on banking reform.

Discord within the coalition increased, and in April 2000 the LP withdrew from the Government; 26 members of the LP formed the New Conservative Party—NCP (Hoshuto). However, after Keizo Obuchi suffered a stroke and went into a coma, from which he never regained consciousness, the LDP elected Yoshiro Mori, the Secretary-General, as party President. Mori was subsequently elected Prime Minister by both Houses of the Diet; he immediately affirmed his commitment to the reform initiatives of his predecessor, and formed a coalition with New Komeito and the NCP. All ministers from the Obuchi administration were retained. Noboru Takeshita, the former Prime Minister announced his retirement from politics and from the LDP; he died shortly afterwards. Former Prime Minister Ryutaro Hashimoto was appointed head of the Takeshita faction of the LDP which had been led by Obuchi.

Following his appointment as Prime Minister, Mori made a number of controversial public statements, expressing imperialist views. Although forced to issue apologies, he did not retract his remarks. At the legislative election held on 25 June 2000 the number of seats in the House of Representatives was reduced from 500 to 480. The LDP won the most seats, although its representation was reduced to 233 and many of its senior members, including current and former cabinet ministers, lost their seats. The DPJ increased its representation to 127 seats, New Komeito won 31 seats, the LP 22 seats, the NCP 20 seats and the SDPJ 19 seats. Despite numerous political gaffes and public errors of protocol, Mori was returned as Prime Minister and announced the composition of his new Cabinet in July.

Corruption was a major issue throughout 2000, and various revelations of bribery resulted in several resignations. In November one LDP member resigned and another was arrested following the disclosure of a 'cash for questions' scandal involving an insurance company. In January 2001 Fukushiro Nukaga, the Minister of State for Economy, Industry and Information Technology, resigned, having admitted that he had accepted bribes from the company. In October 2000 Hidenao Nakagawa, Minister of State, Chief Cabinet Secretary, Director-General of the Okinawa Development Agency and Minister in Charge of Information Technology, resigned after it was alleged, *inter alia*, that he had links to a right-wing activist. In the following month former Minister of Construction Eiichi Nakao acknowledged in court that he had taken bribes in 1996 in exchange for the allocation of public works contracts.

The high incidence of corruption further undermined Mori, and during October 2000 the Prime Minister came under increasing pressure to resign after it was alleged in a magazine that some years previously he had been arrested for violation of an anti-prostitution law. Mori denied the allegation and sued the publication for libel. Mori's apparent suggestion that the Democratic People's Republic of Korea (North Korea) might release Japanese hostages (see Foreign Affairs) to a third country in order to avoid any admission of their existence led to harsh criticism. In November the Prime Minister survived a motion of no confidence in the legislature, following threats by the party leadership that rebels voting against Mori would be expelled from the LDP.

Meanwhile, in November 2000 Fusako Shigenobu, the founder of the extremist left-wing Japanese Red Army, which had been responsible for a number of attacks during the 1970s, was arrested in Osaka. She was detained on suspicion of the seizure of the French embassy in the Netherlands in 1974 and subsequently indicted on various related charges. A number of other members had been repatriated from several countries since 1995 to be tried for terrorism. (Shigenobu was sentenced to 20 years' imprisonment in February 2006 for her involvement in the seizure of the embassy.)

A major government reorganization was announced in December 2000. The number of ministries was reduced from 23 to 13, mainly through mergers, and various state agencies were absorbed into the newly created Cabinet Office. Despite the publication in late 2000 of photographs apparently showing the Prime Minister in the company of an alleged gangster and convicted murderer, Mori won another vote of confidence in March 2001. In early April, however, he announced his intention to resign.

The administration of Junichiro Koizumi

In late April 2001 Junichiro Koizumi, a former Minister of Health and Welfare, unexpectedly defeated Ryutaro Hashimoto, the leader of the largest LDP faction, and one other candidate to secure the presidency of the ruling LDP and thus as Prime Minister. Koizumi's victory was attributed to a change in party election rules that allowed a greater influence of local and ordinary party members in selecting the President. He subsequently reorganized the Cabinet, largely disregarding LDP factional politics, and appointed a number of reformists, including Makiko Tanaka, daughter of former Prime Minister Kakuei Tanaka, as Japan's first female Minister of Foreign Affairs, and Heizo Takenaka, an economics professor, as Minister of State for Economy, Industry and Information Technology. Koizumi also reorganized the LDP's senior leadership, appointing his ally Taku Yamasaki as Secretary-General, and Taro Aso as

Chairman of the Policy Research Council. In addition to according priority to economic reform, Koizumi also sought to introduce direct elections for the post of prime minister and to upgrade the status of the SDF into that of a full army, which would involve an amendment to Article 9 of the Constitution, whereby Japan renounced the use of war.

In June 2001 the Government finally announced an economic reform programme, which included the privatization of special public institutions and a review of regulatory economic laws. Koizumi's high popularity was a major factor in the LDP's gains in the Tokyo assembly elections in late June. However, veteran members of the LDP, particularly the Hashimoto faction, remained opposed to Koizumi's reforms. Koizumi's personal popularity also helped the LDP to make gains at elections to the House of Councillors held in July. The Prime Minister aroused controversy later in that month when he made an official visit to the Yasukuni Shrine to honour Japan's war dead: the shrine included memorials to officers who had been convicted of serious war crimes. Koizumi made five further visits to the shrine during his term of office, incurring both domestic and international criticism.

In September 2001 the terrorist attacks on the USA by militants believed to be linked to al-Qa'ida, the Islamist group, again raised the subject of the role of Japan's military; Koizumi appeared to invoke the USA's subsequent war against the Taliban regime of Afghanistan as an argument to expand the role of the SDF. In October the Diet approved new legislation for the overseas deployment of the SDF in a non-combat support role, and in November Japan dispatched warships to the Indian Ocean, in the biggest such deployment since the Second World War (see Foreign Affairs). The Japanese people strongly supported logistical assistance to the USA, but there remained considerable public opposition to any amendment to Article 9 of the Constitution.

In December 2001 the Government agreed to abolish 17 public corporations and transfer 45 others (of a total of 163) to the private sector. However, Koizumi's major proposed reform, the privatization of the postal savings system, was further delayed. Meanwhile, the opposition DPJ itself experienced divisions, between those who favoured co-operation with Koizumi and his reforms (including the President of the DPJ, Yukio Hatoyama) and those who favoured greater co-operation with other opposition parties. The latter group was led by the DPJ Deputy President, Takahiro Yokomichi, who in November held meetings with the LP leader, Ichiro Ozawa, and the SDPJ leader, Takako Doi.

In January 2002 Koizumi appointed two members of the Hashimoto faction as vice-ministers, in an attempt to placate his main opponents. At the end of the month Koizumi dismissed his Minister of Foreign Affairs, Makiko Tanaka, following months of disputes over reform within the ministry, which had delayed the passage of a supplementary budget through the Diet. The dismissal of the popular Tanaka was regarded as a victory for LDP veterans and as a set-back for reform. In June the LDP suspended Tanaka from the party for a two-year period owing to her failure to co-operate with an investigation into the misuse of state funds at the Ministry of Foreign Affairs. The session of the Diet was extended until July in order to enable Koizumi to draft legislation for reforms to Japan Post, as well as to the health service and defence and security sectors. These reforms were opposed by considerable elements within the LDP. In July Koizumi was forced to accept a compromise with anti-reformist LDP elements over his plans to reform postal services.

In late September 2002 Koizumi implemented a long-expected cabinet reorganization, notably dismissing the Minister of State for the Financial Services Agency, Hakuo Yanagisawa, and appointing the Minister of State for Economic and Fiscal Policy, Heizo Takenaka, concurrently to hold that post. Plans to reform the banking sector created tensions between the LDP and its two coalition partners, New Komeito and the NCP. In October a tripartite committee of the ruling coalition published a banking-sector reform plan that was far less radical than that sought by Takenaka, who had urged the nationalization of major banks to prevent their failure.

In December 2002 the opposition DPJ elected Naoto Kan as its President, replacing Yukio Hatoyama, who had been forced to resign from the post after the failure of secret attempts to merge the party with the smaller opposition LP, led by Ichiro Ozawa. Katsuya Okada, Kan's main rival for the DPJ presidency, was appointed Secretary-General. Kan had previously led the DPJ during 1997–99. Four DPJ members of the Diet, led by former party Vice-President Hiroshi Kumagai, resigned from the party in December 2002 and joined the NCP; the President of that party, Takeshi Noda, resigned in favour of Kumagai.

In March 2003 the Governor of Tokyo, Shintaro Ishihara, announced that he would seek re-election, ending months of speculation that he might form a new political party in order to challenge Koizumi. At the local elections in April Ishihara was overwhelmingly re-elected, and pledged to use his position to campaign for reform in the country as a whole.

In April 2003 the LDP announced its intention to amend the Constitution explicitly to state the legitimacy of the SDF and to expand its role in international peace-keeping and collective self-defence. In May the House of Representatives approved new legislation granting the Government and the SDF greater powers to act in the event of an attack on Japan. In June the new legislation, outlining the circumstances in which the Government would be able to authorize military action by the SDF, was approved by the House of Councillors. The legislation was supported by the DPJ as well as by the ruling coalition. In July 2003, despite vehement opposition, the House of Councillors approved proposals, recently endorsed by the lower chamber, to send peace-keeping forces to Iraq, thereby allowing the largest deployment of Japanese troops abroad since the Second World War. Although troops were to engage in humanitarian work only, critics argued that the deployment would violate the Constitution, as in practice troops would be unable to avoid conflict areas.

In September 2003 Koizumi was re-elected as leader of the LDP, defeating three rival candidates (Shizuka Kamei, Masahiko Koumura and Takao Fujii) for the leadership. Koizumi then made appointments to a new Cabinet, which included the reappointment of Heizo Takenaka as Minister of State responsible for the Financial Services Agency, despite criticism of his banking reform policies (see above). Also in September, a merger agreement between the DPJ and the LP, originally reached in July, was signed, with the aim of creating an opposition movement capable of presenting a strong challenge to the LDP at the forthcoming legislative election.

At the election, held on 9 November 2003, the LDP won 237 seats, thus losing 10 of its previous 247 seats in the House of Representatives. The party's strength increased to 245 following the recruitment of four independent candidates and the absorption of the NCP, one of the LDP's two coalition partners, which had won four seats. The LDP's other coalition partner, the New Komeito party, secured 34 seats. The DPJ (incorporating the former LP) won 177 seats, thereby increasing its number of seats by 40 and representing a serious challenge to the LDP's hold on power. A further potential threat to the LDP was the success of the former Minister of Foreign Affairs, Makiko Tanaka, in securing a seat as an independent candidate. Tanaka had been suspended from the LDP in 2002 following allegations of misappropriation of funds (see above), but was able to stand in the 2003 election after the charges against her were withdrawn. Tanaka, who had become increasingly critical of the Koizumi administration, subsequently joined a DPJ-led Diet group.

Plans for the SDF deployment to Iraq, following the approval of the requisite legislation in July 2003 (see above) were strongly criticized by the President of the DPJ, Naoto Kan. Popular protests against the Iraq mission took place. Opposition within Japan to the deployment had been strengthened by the deaths of two Japanese diplomats in Iraq in November 2003. In January 2004 the first Japanese troops departed for Iraq. In the same month it was announced that legislation on the reform of Japan's Constitution, including an amendment to Article 9, would be submitted in 2005. Public support for Koizumi was tested in April 2004, when three Japanese civilians were taken hostage in Iraq. Despite the Government's steadfast refusal to comply with the Iraqi militants' demands for the withdrawal of Japanese troops, the hostages were released unharmed a week later.

In May 2004 a scandal over pension contributions prompted resignations by senior officials of the LDP and the opposition DPJ. The Chief Cabinet Secretary, Yasuo Fukuda of the LDP, resigned after admitting that he had not made the required payments to the compulsory state pension scheme. Naoto Kan resigned from the presidency of the DPJ shortly afterwards on similar grounds. Kan was replaced by Katsuya Okada, hitherto Secretary-General of the DPJ. In the same month a government proposal for pension reform, involving increased premiums and reduced benefits, was approved by the House of Representatives. The reform plan was approved by the House of Councillors in June, despite strong opposition from the DPJ. In July nation-wide voting took place to elect one-half of the members of the House of Councillors. Of the 121 seats contested, the LDP won 49, while the DPJ won 50 (thus increasing its overall representation in the chamber from 60 seats to 82). Although the LDP and its coalition partner New Komeito, with a combined total of 139 seats, retained a majority in the 242-member House, the outcome was generally interpreted as reflecting a decline in the popularity of Koizumi's administration. In September Koizumi effected a major reorganization of cabinet portfolios. Among notable new appointments was that of Nobutaka Machimura as Minister of Foreign Affairs. The Minister of Economic and Fiscal Policy, Heizo Takenaka, was given responsibility for privatization of the postal services, while Sadakazu Tanigaki remained Minister of Finance. From October there were renewed protests against Japanese support for military operations in Iraq following the beheading of a Japanese tourist who had been taken hostage by a militant group there. None the less, in December the LDP announced that the term of the SDF mission in Iraq was to be extended by one year.

In August 2005 Koizumi's postal reform bill, which had been narrowly approved by the House of Representatives in the previous month, was defeated in the House of Councillors. A total of 37 LDP members from both houses rebelled against the party leadership and voted against the proposed legislation. Koizumi responded to the defeat by dissolving the House of Representatives and calling an election for 11 September. Prohibited from standing as party members, several LDP 'rebels' formed separate parties. These included the People's New Party (Kokumin Shinto—PNP), led by Tamisuke Watanuki, and the New Party Nippon (Shinto Nippon), led by Yasuo Tanaka, the erstwhile reformist Governor of Nagano Prefecture. Others chose to stand as independent candidates. In the event, the election resulted in unequivocal victory for Koizumi and, by implication, an endorsement of his reform programme by the electorate. The LDP increased its representation in the House to 296 of the 480 seats (its first overall majority since 1990 and the largest number of seats won by a single party since the end of the Second World War), thereby creating, with its ally New Komeito, a ruling coalition bloc of 327 seats and thus securing more than two-thirds of the chamber. The DPJ's share of seats, meanwhile, was reduced by 64 to 113, prompting the resignation of its President, Katsuya Okada. The subsequent DPJ leadership election was won by Seiji Maehara, who narrowly defeated the party's former President, Naoto Kan. In October Koizumi reorganized his Cabinet. Shinzo Abe was appointed Chief Cabinet Secretary, Taro Aso became Minister of Foreign Affairs and Sadakazu Tanigaki was retained as Minister of Finance. The postal reform bill was resubmitted to the legislature, and in mid-October was approved by both Houses of the Diet.

In September 2006 Chief Cabinet Secretary Shinzo Abe, with the clear support of the Prime Minister, was elected to succeed Koizumi as LDP President. Having proceeded to secure the support of both houses of the Diet, at the end of the month Abe formally took office as Prime Minister. Only one incumbent minister of the Koizumi administration, namely the Minister of Foreign Affairs, Taro Aso, retained his position in the new Cabinet.

The Governments of Abe, Fukuda and Aso

As the new Prime Minister, Shinzo Abe announced an ambitious policy agenda and swiftly arranged discussions with China and the Republic of Korea, relations with both of which had been strained by his predecessor's visits to the Yasukuni Shrine (see Foreign Affairs). Abe envisaged the pursuit of an assertive foreign policy, stating that Japan should continue to seek a permanent seat on the UN Security Council and making clear his commitment to an uncompromising stance against North Korea. More controversially, he undertook to revise the country's pacifist Constitution to permit the Japanese military to perform a wider role abroad. In terms of economic strategy, Abe pledged to pursue the reformist policies of his predecessor, while acknowledging the need to address the growing income disparities in Japanese society.

The Prime Minister suffered his first political embarrassment in December 2006 when an official investigation found that during the tenure of his predecessor the Government had paid members of the public to ask specific questions of ministers at local meetings and that government officials had masqueraded as ordinary citizens. In the same month legislation to upgrade the Defence Agency was adopted by the Diet (the Defence Agency was officially upgraded to a full ministry in January 2007), but proposed legislation requiring schools to teach patriotism proved more contentious. Four groups, including the DPJ, filed a motion of no confidence against Abe in an attempt to halt the education bill, but the motion was rejected by the House of Representatives.

In April 2007 the DPJ performed well in local elections, while Governor Ishihara was re-elected in Tokyo for a third consecutive term, with the (unsolicited) support of the ruling coalition. Also in April the House of Representatives approved legislation setting out procedures for national referendums on constitutional reform. Although the 1947 Constitution stipulated that amendments required the approval of at least two-thirds of the members of both houses of the Diet, followed by endorsement in a national referendum, the legal framework for such a referendum had never been established. The new law provided for the participation of all citizens over the age of 18 (compared with a minimum voting age of 20 for elections), but failed to impose a minimum participation rate for the validity of the referendum. The House of Councillors adopted the legislation in May 2007. Meanwhile, rallies were held nation-wide both for and against constitutional revision.

It emerged in early May 2007 that, in an apparent compromise designed to appease both his more nationalistic supporters and neighbouring countries, the Prime Minister had sent an offering to the Yasukuni Shrine in the previous month, but had refrained from visiting the shrine himself. Similarly, Abe chose not to visit the shrine on the anniversary of Japan's surrender in the Second World War in August, instead attending a commemoration ceremony in Tokyo.

The Minister of Agriculture, Forestry and Fisheries, Toshikatsu Matsuoka, committed suicide in May 2007, shortly before he was due to appear before a committee of the Diet that was investigating allegations that he had claimed false office expenses. Matsuoka had also been accused of accepting political donations from companies awarded contracts for public works projects by an agency affiliated to his ministry. By June public support for Abe had declined significantly, amid widespread anger over the loss of some 50m. pension records by the Social Insurance Agency. The Government suffered a further reverse in July when the Minister of Defence, Fumio Kyuma, was forced to resign after provoking an outcry with his suggestion that the US nuclear attacks on the Japanese cities of Hiroshima and Nagasaki in 1945, towards the end of the Second World War, had been inevitable. Yuriko Koike, hitherto Abe's special adviser on national security affairs, was appointed to replace Kyuma, becoming Japan's first female Minister of Defence.

The ruling LDP-New Komeito coalition lost its overall majority in the House of Councillors in the partial elections that were held on 29 July 2007. By contrast, the DPJ made significant gains, particularly in rural constituencies, winning overall control of the House of Councillors. The DPJ's Satsuki Eda subsequently became the first opposition politician to be elected Speaker of the upper house. Despite the ruling coalition's defeat in the elections, Abe insisted that he intended to remain in office, although Hidenao Nakagawa relinquished the post of Secretary-General of the LDP. At the beginning of August Norihiko Akagi, Matsuoka's successor as Minister of Agriculture, Forestry and Fisheries, was forced to resign from the Government over allegations that he, too, had submitted inaccurate claims for office expenses. Abe was criticized for not dismissing Akagi earlier. The Minister of Justice, Jinen Nagase, was also accused of financial impropriety when it was revealed that he had accepted 500,000 yen from a company that he had advised on visa applications for its Chinese workers.

The Prime Minister reorganized his Cabinet in late August 2007 in an attempt to restore confidence in his administration. Several veteran members of the LDP were appointed to the Government, including faction leaders Nobutaka Machimura and Masahiko Koumura as Minister of Foreign Affairs and Minister of Defence, respectively, and Fukushiro Nukaga as Minister of Finance. Taro Aso became Secretary-General of the LDP. Only a week later, however, the new Minister of Agriculture, Forestry and Fisheries, Takehiko Endo, resigned, causing further embarrassment for Abe, after admitting that a private farming group of which he was Chairman had misappropriated state funds. In mid-September Abe himself resigned as Prime Minister and President of the LDP, acknowledging that he had lost the support and trust of the public.

Two candidates contested the election to replace Abe as LDP leader: Taro Aso; and Yasuo Fukuda, the son of a former Prime Minister and a moderate politician, who had served as Chief Cabinet Secretary under Koizumi. Aso was regarded by many as being too closely associated with Abe, and Fukuda thus gained the support of eight of the party's nine factions. Fukuda was duly elected as LDP President in late September 2007, and subsequently took office as Prime Minister, having secured the approval of a majority in the House of Representatives. In the opposition-controlled House of Councillors, Fukuda received only 106 votes, compared with the 133 cast in favour of Ichiro Ozawa, the President of the DPJ, but the decision of the lower house took precedence, in accordance with the Constitution. Fukuda retained most of the ministers from his predecessor's Cabinet. Koumura, who became Minister of Foreign Affairs, was replaced at the Ministry of Defence by one of the few new appointees, Shigeru Ishiba (who had also held the defence portfolio in Koizumi's Government), while Machimura was appointed Chief Cabinet Secretary and Minister of State for the Abduction Issue. Nukaga, who had withdrawn from the LDP leadership election in favour of Fukuda, remained Minister of Finance. Aso was replaced as LDP Secretary-General by Bunmei Ibuki, hitherto Minister of Education, Culture, Sports, Science and Technology.

Fukuda advocated closer relations with neighbouring Asian countries (pledging not to visit the controversial Yasukuni Shrine), while maintaining a strong alliance with the USA, and promised to continue to pursue economic structural reforms. The new Prime Minister's first challenge was to secure approval for the extension of legislation that enabled the Maritime Self-Defence Force to provide logistical support in the Indian Ocean to ships involved in US-led counter-terrorism operations in Afghanistan. The renewal of the legislation, which had first been adopted in 2001 and, following successive extensions, was scheduled to expire at the beginning of November 2007, was opposed by the DPJ on the grounds that the US-led operations had not been sanctioned by the UN and that Japan's involvement violated its pacifist Constitution. Following the failure of efforts to reach a political consensus, in mid-October the Cabinet approved draft legislation that would extend the mission but, in a concession to its critics, would limit its role to supplying fuel and water to ships on anti-terrorism patrols rather than those involved in military operations. Yearly renewal of the proposed legislation would also be required. However, the Government's case was damaged by revelations that the Ministry of Defence had misled politicians over the quantity of fuel supplied in the past. The Diet remained in deadlock over the issue at the end of October, leading to the suspension of the support mission.

The Diet's current session was extended by five weeks, until mid-December 2007, in order to continue consideration of the proposed legislation renewing the naval deployment in the Indian Ocean. The House of Representatives approved the legislation in mid-November, shortly before Fukuda was due to visit the USA, which had been exerting strong pressure on Japan to resume its support for US counter-terrorism activities. In late November Takemasa Moriya, who had served as Vice-Minister of Defence until August, was arrested on suspicion of having accepted bribes from companies in return for providing them with contracts to supply defence equipment. Fukuda subsequently initiated a reform of the Ministry of Defence. Meanwhile, the Minister of Finance, Fukushiro Nukaga, who had been Director-General of the then Defence Agency in 2005–06, was summoned to the House of Councillors to respond to questions about the bribery allegations. The House of Councillors began debating the proposed resumption of the Japanese naval deployment in the Indian Ocean in early December 2007, but the DPJ continued to refuse to approve the necessary legislation and the Diet's session was extended for a further month in mid-December. In mid-January 2008 the Government forced through the passage of the legislation, using its majority in the House of Representatives to supersede another vote against it by the House of Councillors (the first time this power had been used since 1951). Two Japanese vessels were dispatched to assist US forces in the Indian Ocean later in that month.

Following the retirement of Toshihiko Fukui, the Governor of the Bank of Japan, in March 2008, the Government nominated Toshiro Muto to replace him. The nomination was rejected in the House of Councillors by DPJ members (who continued to constitute the majority party in the upper chamber), as was the Government's second nominee, Koji Tanami, both on the grounds that their previous positions within the Ministry of Finance might jeopardize the central bank's independence. The Bank of Japan was thus left without a governor for more than three weeks, resulting in an embarrassing hiatus at a time of global financial turmoil. In April a consensus was finally reached when the DPJ accepted the nomination of Masaaki Shirakawa, recently appointed a deputy governor.

In June 2008 the House of Representatives approved a resolution that for the first time formally recognized the minority Ainu as 'an indigenous people with a distinct language, religion and culture'. The resolution urged the establishment of a special panel to formulate government policy towards the Ainu people, who had long felt disadvantaged in the ethnically homogenous society of Japan and whose separate identity had been officially acknowledged only in 1997.

In August 2008 the Prime Minister effected an extensive cabinet reorganization, in which Bunmei Ibuki was appointed as Minister of Finance and Kaoru Yosano as Minister of State for Economic and Fiscal Policy. On the same day Taro Aso was appointed to replace Ibuki as Secretary-General of the LDP. In early September, however, the Prime Minister announced his resignation, citing the difficulties in reaching a consensus with the DPJ on the implementation of his legislative agenda. Fukuda stated his belief that a new leader would be in a better position to withstand DPJ opposition in the House of Councillors. Shortly afterwards the Minister of Agriculture, Seiichi Ota, was also compelled to resign owing to the revelation of a scandal involving the import and distribution of contaminated rice.

In order to determine the next President of the LDP and thus the new Prime Minister, the party conducted an internal ballot, from which Taro Aso emerged victorious, having defeated four other candidates, an unprecedented number of contenders. In late September 2008 Aso was duly confirmed as Prime Minister by the House of Representatives. He immediately formed his Cabinet, appointing Shoichi Nakagawa as Minister of Finance, Hirofume Nakasone as Minister of Foreign Affairs and Yasukazu Hamada as Minister of Defence. Aso had been widely expected to call an early election for the House of Representatives, to take advantage of the initial popularity of the incoming administration, but he ultimately decided against this, preferring to focus immediately on economic policy in view of the developing global financial crisis.

In January 2009 Yoshimi Watanabe, a former Minister of State for Financial Services and Administrative Reform, who was opposed to the Government's fiscal stimulus programme and the additional budgetary expenditure involved (see Economic Affairs), announced his departure from the LDP. (In August Watanabe formed a new political party, known as Your Party.) In February former Prime Minister Koizumi similarly criticized the Government's expenditure on the financial stimulus plans. Aso's plight worsened when the Minister of Finance, Shoichi Nakagawa, resigned, having apparently been intoxicated at a press conference held during a meeting of the Group of Seven (G7) leading industrialized nations in Italy.

In March 2009 the arrest of Takanori Okubo, the political secretary of Ichiro Ozawa, led to pressure on the leader of the opposition DPJ to resign. It was alleged that Ozawa's aide had accepted illegal donations, totalling 35m. yen, from a construction company and falsified party accounts. Despite the formal indictment of Okubo later in the month, Ozawa denied any wrongdoing and reiterated his intention to remain in his post. In May, however, Ozawa responded to public opinion by resigning as President of the DPJ. He was replaced by the party's Deputy President, Yukio Hatoyama, who had been one of the original DPJ's founders in 1996 and had held the post of party President between 1999 and 2002.

Recent developments: the end of LDP rule

In July 2009 diminishing support for the LDP was demonstrated when it was defeated by the DPJ in an election to the Tokyo Metropolitan Assembly (which the LDP had dominated for more than 40 years). As was widely predicted, at the legislative election on 30 August the DPJ was overwhelmingly successful, securing 308 of the 480 seats in the House of Representatives, while the LDP won 119 seats and New Komeito 21. The LDP was thus removed from government for only the second time since 1955 (the first having been the 11-month period during which it had been out of office in 1993–94). Despite having secured an overall majority, the DPJ negotiated with the SDPJ and the PNP (which had won seven and three seats, respectively, in the House of Representatives) to form a coalition, in order to widen the Government's support, particularly in the House of Councillors, where the DPJ lacked an overall majority. Hatoyama took office as Prime Minister on 16 September 2009. He appointed Naoto Kan, a former President of the DPJ, as Deputy Prime Minister and Minister of State for National Policy, Economic and Fiscal Policy, and Science and Technology Policy: Kan was to preside over a new National Strategy Bureau, which was to formulate policy and supervise budgetary allocations, thereby reducing what was perceived by the DPJ as the excessive power of the civil service. Katsuya Okada, hitherto Secretary-General of the DPJ, became Minister of Foreign Affairs, and the new Minister of Finance was Hirohisa Fujii, who had held the same post during the period of non-LDP rule in 1993–94. The Chairman of the SDPJ, Mizuho Fukushima, and the leader of the PNP, Shizuka Kamei, both received ministerial appointments.

In September 2009 Ozawa was appointed Secretary-General of the DPJ, despite the allegations of irregular funding (still under investigation) that had caused his resignation as the party's President earlier in the year. Changes also took place within the parties that had been defeated in the August election: Aso resigned as President of the LDP, and at the end of September the party elected Sadakazu Tanigaki, the former Minister of Finance, to succeed him. The President of New Komeito, Akihiro Ota, and the party's Secretary-General, Kazuo Kitagawa, both of whom had lost their parliamentary seats in the election, also resigned in early September. Natsuo Yamaguchi, hitherto the Chairman of the party's Policy Research Council, assumed the presidency of New Komeito in the same month.

Hatoyama's new Government announced its intention to impose stricter controls on expenditure by government departments, and to redirect spending away from major public works towards health care, education, the creation of employment and increased allowances for families with children. It also undertook to make greater reductions in emissions of gases believed to cause global warming, compared with the commitment made by the previous Government. Although the Japanese economy was no longer technically in recession by September 2009, the new administration confronted considerable obstacles to economic recovery, in particular the very high level of government debt, the strength of the yen against the US dollar and the problem of persistent deflation. In January 2010 the Minister of Finance, Hirohisa Fujii, an opponent of increases in government debt, resigned owing to ill health. Hatoyama allocated the finance portfolio to the Deputy Prime Minister, Naoto Kan, who was expected to give greater priority to measures that would stimulate the economy.

In April 2010 two new political parties were formed, mainly by dissatisfied members of the LDP. The Sunrise Party of Japan was led by Takeo Hiranuma, an independent member of the House of Representatives and a former Minister of Economy, Trade and Industry; he was joined by some senior members of the LDP, including Kaoru Yosano, the former Minister of Finance. The New Renaissance Party was formed by Yoichi Masuzoe, hitherto an LDP member of the House of Councillors and a former Minister of Health, Labour and Welfare.

In May 2010 Hatoyama admitted that his party's pre-election undertaking to remove an unpopular US military air base from the southern island of Okinawa (see Foreign Affairs) could not realistically be fulfilled, and he proposed adhering to an agreement made with the USA in 2006, whereby the base would be transferred to an alternative site on the island. Later in May 2010 he dismissed the leader of the SDPJ, Mizuho Fukushima, from her ministerial post after she criticized the decision; the SDPJ then voted to leave the ruling coalition. Hatoyama also incurred criticism from within his own party, the DPJ, for his apparent vacillation over the Okinawa base. The controversy over Okinawa, together with the conviction in April of Hatoyama's former secretary for falsifying political funding reports (by omitting to include donations by Hatoyama's relatives), continuing allegations of financial irregularities on the part of Ozawa and the widespread perception that Ozawa wielded undue influence in policy-making all combined to reduce the popularity of the ruling party.

On 2 June 2010 Hatoyama announced his own resignation as Prime Minister and President of the DPJ, and that of Ozawa as Secretary-General of the party. The DPJ then elected Naoto Kan as its President, and he became Prime Minister (Japan's fifth in four years) on 8 June. Kan retained most of the principal ministers appointed by his predecessor: his own previous post as Minister of Finance was allocated to Yoshihiko Noda (hitherto the deputy minister), and Yoshito Sengoku was appointed Chief Cabinet Secretary. Yukio Edano was appointed Secretary-General of the DPJ. Kan declared that he would maintain the controversial policy on Okinawa that Hatoyama had been obliged to adhere to, and identified the reduction of government debt (now almost twice as large as the country's gross domestic product) as the most important problem confronting his administration. The PNP agreed to remain in coalition with the DPJ, and the PNP's leader, Kamei, initially retained his ministerial responsibility for postal reform and financial services, but he resigned within a few days, after the DPJ refused to extend the current session of the Diet in order to debate legislation, supported by Kamei, on reversing the privatization of Japan Post. However, the PNP remained within the coalition and Kamei's ministerial portfolio was assumed by Shozaburo Jimi, the party's Secretary-General.

At an election for one-half of the seats in the House of Councillors, held on 11 July 2010, the DPJ lost the small majority that it had commanded (with its coalition partners) in the upper house, winning 44 of the 121 seats being contested, so that its total representation was now 106 out of the total of 242 seats. The Minister of Justice, Keiko Chiba, was among the DPJ members who failed to be re-elected. The LDP won 51 of the contested seats, bringing its total to 84. The DPJ's coalition partner, the PNP, failed to win any seats at this election. The DPJ's loss of support was widely attributed to Kan's emphasis, during the election campaign, on the possible introduction of an increase in consumption tax, in order to reduce the budgetary deficit. Of the recently formed parties, the most successful in the July election was Your Party, which now held 11 seats: its leader, Yoshimi Watanabe, stated that his party would not enter a coalition with the DPJ, but might co-operate in certain areas of policy, such as measures to reduce the power of the civil service.

In August 2010 Ozawa announced that he would challenge Kan at the election for the presidency of the DPJ, due to be held in September (Kan's election in June had been only for the remainder of Hatoyama's allotted term of office). Ozawa still enjoyed considerable support among the party's Diet members, despite his alleged involvement in financial irregularities, and at the election on 14 September Kan received only just over one-half of votes cast by the DPJ members of the legislature, although the much greater support of party members throughout the country ensured his victory. Kan reappointed Katsuya Okada, hitherto Minister of Foreign Affairs, as Secretary-General of the DPJ; in the ensuing partial reorganization of the Cabinet, the foreign affairs portfolio was given to Seiji Maehara, hitherto responsible for land, infrastructure and transport, while Banri Kaieda (a supporter of Ozawa in the DPJ leadership election) was appointed Minister for Economic and Fiscal Policy.

From September 2010 the Government incurred criticism after an escalation of territorial disputes with China and Russia (see Foreign Affairs). In December discussions took place on the possible establishment of a coalition between the DPJ and the Sunrise Party, but the latter refused to accept such an arrangement; however, one of the Sunrise Party's founding members, Kaoru Yosano, subsequently left the party, and in January 2011 he accepted the post of Minister of State for Economic and Fiscal Policy (a post that he had previously held, as a member of the LDP, in 2008–09). This appointment formed part of a cabinet reorganization, in which Yukio Edano replaced Yoshito Sengoku as Chief Cabinet Secretary, Akihiro Ohata replaced Sumio Mabuchi as Minister of Land, Infrastructure, Transport and Tourism, and Banri Kaieda replaced Ohata as Minister of Economy, Trade and Industry.

In January 2011 Ozawa was indicted for conspiring in the false reporting of political funds used in a purchase of land in 2004. Three of his aides had been charged with the offence in February 2010, but at that time it had been found that there was insufficient evidence to prosecute Ozawa himself. In October, however, a judicial panel had recommended that he stand trial. Ozawa denied the charge, claiming he had no knowledge of his aides' actions, and refusing to relinquish his seat in the legislature or to accede to Kan's request that he temporarily leave the DPJ. The party's executive voted in February 2011 to suspend Ozawa's membership, and later in the month 16 DPJ members loyal to Ozawa abstained in the vote on the budget in the House of Representatives: although the budget itself was none the less adopted, it appeared probable that related legislation would be rejected by the House of Councillors. The trial of the three aides, which had begun in February, concluded with their conviction in late September. Ozawa's trial commenced the following month, and in April 2012 he was acquitted of the charges.

In early March 2011, meanwhile, Maehara resigned as Minister of Foreign Affairs, when it was revealed that he had accepted a small political donation from a foreign national, which remained illegal in Japan; he was replaced by the deputy minister, Takeaki Matsumoto.

On 11 March 2011 Japan was struck by a very severe earthquake, which had its epicentre in the Pacific Ocean off the north-east coast of Honshu island. The earthquake measured 9.0 in magnitude and caused a tsunami that devastated the adjoining coastal region, killing many thousands. Several nuclear power stations automatically shut down when the earthquake occurred, but one, at Fukushima, was seriously damaged, and its cooling systems were disabled. An evacuation was ordered within 20 km of the plant, while efforts were made to cool the nuclear reactors in order to prevent radioactive contamination. At the end of March the power station's operator, the Tokyo Electric Power Company (TEPCO), announced that four of the six nuclear reactors at Fukushima were to be decommissioned. As the critical situation at Fukushima continued, in April Japan's Nuclear and Industrial Safety Agency raised its evaluation of the crisis from Level 5 to Level 7, the highest level on the International Nuclear Event Scale, while confirmation emerged in early June that three of the reactors had experienced full meltdowns. Other nuclear power stations in Japan were closed down for safety inspections, while Kan began publicly to advocate the reduction of Japan's dependency on nuclear power and the investigation of renewable energy alternatives. (It was anticipated that all of Japan's nuclear reactors could be offline by mid-2012.) In mid-December the Government announced that the Fukushima plant had reached a state of 'cold shutdown', but estimated that full decommissioning of the damaged reactors could take between 30 and 40 years. By March 2012, 15,848 people were known to have died in the disaster, and 3,305 were unaccounted for, according to Japan's National Police Agency; around 350,000 reportedly remained homeless. The Japanese economy was severely affected by the earthquake and its aftermath.

Sustained domestic and international criticism was directed at both the Government of Japan and TEPCO for their management of the Fukushima crisis, and the reliability of information regarding developments at the power plant was questioned. In particular, Kan came under personal attack for his handling of the tsunami and subsequent nuclear crisis. Critics argued that his decision to fly over the Fukushima site on the day after the earthquake delayed the operation to cool the reactors, and condemned his reluctance to extend the evacuation zone around the plant from 20 km to 30 km in radius. When a number of DPJ legislators, including Hatoyama and Ozawa, threatened to support a vote of no confidence initiated by the opposition in early June, Kan promised that he would resign once he had prepared a second emergency budget to finance reconstruction (the first such emergency budget having been approved in early May), and subsequently survived the vote. In late June Kan stated that his resignation would be conditional on the passing of this second emergency budget, along with legislation concerning deficit bond issuance and the increased use of renewable energy. Kan also conducted a minor cabinet reshuffle in late June, appointing Goshi Hosono as Minister for the Restoration from and Prevention of Nuclear Accident, while Ryu Matsumoto became Minister for Reconstruction Measures from the Great East Japan Earthquake. However, Matsumoto subsequently resigned his post in early July, after comments he made to regional governors in areas affected by the tsunami were widely disseminated and attracted public disapproval. He was replaced by Tatsuo Hirano. In early August it was announced that three senior government officials involved in nuclear policy were to be dismissed, and a new nuclear safety watchdog was to be set up under the auspices of the Ministry of the Environment. Both developments were widely interpreted as an attempt to distance the Government from accusations of excessive intimacy with the nuclear industry.

On 26 August 2011, following the successful passage into law of the aforementioned legislative bills, Kan officially announced his resignation from the presidency of the DPJ and, consequently, from the post of prime minister. After a first round of voting in the DPJ's subsequent leadership election proved inconclusive, the second round was won on 29 August by Yoshihiko Noda, hitherto Minister of Finance, defeating Banri Kaieda. Noda was elected Prime Minister by the Diet on the following day, and subsequently appointed a reordered Cabinet, in which Jun Azumi succeeded him as Minister of Finance (the post had previously been offered to Katsuya Okada, who declined to accept the appointment), while Osamu Fujimura became Chief Cabinet Secretary, and Koichiro Gemba assumed the foreign affairs portfolio. Yasuo Ichikawa became Minister of Defence, while Hosono, in addition to his existing nuclear disaster portfolio, took on the post of Minister of the Environment. Yoshio Hachiro succeeded Kaieda as Minister of Economy, Trade and Industry, but resigned in early September after remarks he made on a visit to Fukushima were deemed offensive. He was replaced by Yukio Edano, who had served as Chief Cabinet Secretary in Kan's administration.

Noda, widely regarded as a fiscal conservative, sought to prioritize control of public debt and the rapidly appreciating yen. A third emergency reconstruction budget was passed in late November 2011, and in early December Noda instructed Azumi to draw up a fourth emergency budget to address reconstruction, a move unprecedented since the immediate post-war era. Meanwhile, a key proposal to increase sales tax from 5% to 10% by 2015, partly to finance rising welfare expenditures, met with hostility from some DPJ members as well as from the opposition and the public. A reorganization of the Government enacted by Noda in mid-January 2012 was widely interpreted as motivated by the desire to facilitate agreement on tax reform. Five cabinet ministers were replaced, including Minister of Defence Ichikawa, whose successor was Naoki Tanaka. Ichikawa had been criticized for his description of the 1995 rape of a Japanese schoolgirl by US servicemen as an 'orgy'. The Minister for Consumer Affairs, Kenji Yamaoka, who had allegedly supported a pyramid investment scheme and compared the possible collapse of the euro to the 2011 tsunami, was also removed. Opposition parties had indicated that they would boycott further debates on tax reform unless Ichikawa and Yamaoka were dismissed. Furthermore, Katsuya Okada was appointed to the newly-created post of Deputy Prime Minister, with responsibility for tax and social security reform. The Government submitted the necessary legislation for increasing sales tax to the Diet at the end of March 2012.

Foreign Affairs

In the second half of the 20th century Japan, having renounced military activity in accordance with its 1947 Constitution, nevertheless gained international influence through its rapid economic growth: during the 1970s it became the world's second largest economy (after the USA) and retained this position until it was surpassed by China at the end of the first decade of the 21st century. Japan also became a major provider of overseas aid and investment. However, as a legacy of Japan's aggressive foreign policy during the first half of the 20th century, neighbouring countries remained suspicious of any sign of nationalist tendencies. Although Japan sought to increase its regional influence, its alliance with the USA remained the principal tenet of its foreign policy at the beginning of the 21st century.

Relations with the USA

Japan's bilateral security arrangements with the USA, concluded by treaty in 1951, granted the use of military bases in Japan to the USA, in return for a US commitment to provide military support to Japan in the event of external aggression. In May 1999 legislation was enacted on revised Guidelines for Japan-US Defense Co-operation (first compiled in 1978). These envisaged enhanced military co-operation between the USA and Japan, not only on Japanese territory but also in situations in unspecified areas around Japan, prompting criticism from China and Russia. The principal location for US bases in Japan was the island of Okinawa, in the far south of the country, which was returned from US administration to Japanese sovereignty only in 1972. The large US military presence caused resentment among many residents of Okinawa; in particular, the rape of a local schoolgirl by three US servicemen in 1995 led to considerable civil unrest on the island. Protracted negotiations with the US Government resulted in an agreement, concluded in May 2006, on the relocation of the principal US air base from Futenma, in a densely populated area of Okinawa, to a less populous area near the city of Nago, in the north of the island, while some 8,000 US military personnel (about one-third of those currently stationed on Okinawa) were to be relocated to the US Pacific Territory of Guam, with the Japanese Government paying about 60% of the cost of relocating the troops. However, many residents of the proposed site for the new air base opposed its construction. The agreement was signed in February 2009 by Hillary Clinton, the US Secretary of State in the newly appointed Administration of President Barack Obama; however, after taking office in September of that year, the Japanese Government (led by the DPJ, which had denounced the proposals while in opposition) undertook to review the agreement during 2010. In April 2010 about 100,000 residents of Okinawa attended a rally, demanding that the Futenma air base be removed from the island altogether. In May the Prime Minister, Yukio Hatoyama (reportedly after pressure from the US Government), declared that the complete removal of the base was not a feasible option, and stated that the Government would, after all, implement the 2006 agreement to relocate the air base within Okinawa. The Government's perceived indecisiveness over Okinawa was the principal reason for Hatoyama's resignation in early June 2010. Under his successors, Naoto Kan and Yoshihiko Noda, the importance of the alliance with the USA was reaffirmed, but progress on implementing the 2006 agreement remained hampered by strong local opposition to the relocation of the base within the island. The 2014 deadline for relocation of the base and transfer of troops to Guam was abandoned in June 2011, and in February 2012 both sides agreed to rework the 2006 agreement in such a way that the transfer of US marines from the Okinawa base would no longer be dependent on the relocation of the base within Okinawa. At the end of April 2012, prior to a visit to the USA by Prime Minister Yoshihiko Noda, agreement was reached on the transfer of 9,000 US marines from Okinawa to Guam and other US bases in the Pacific. It was, however, confirmed that plans to relocate the Futenma base to a less populated area, in accordance with the 2006 agreement, remained the only 'viable solution'.

In September 2001, following the attacks on the USA by Islamist militants attributed to al-Qa'ida, Japan immediately pledged co-operation in the USA's 'war on terror', including military support within the limits imposed by Japan's Constitution. Koizumi announced that Japan would assist in the gathering of intelligence, and in the delivery of supplies and of medical and humanitarian relief. The requisite legislation was approved by the Diet, and in November Japan deployed several warships and 1,500 personnel to the Indian Ocean in this capacity, to support US military action in Afghanistan. Disagreement remained over President George W. Bush's description of North Korea as part of an 'axis of evil'. Japan pursued a policy of engagement with North Korea (see below), while the USA adopted a more sceptical attitude to that country, particularly after North Korea allegedly admitted to pursuing a secret nuclear weapons programme in October 2002.

In December 2002 Japan and the USA held a meeting of ministers of defence and foreign affairs in Tokyo on outstanding security issues. As well as seeking an early resolution of the crisis over the North Korean nuclear weapons programme, the two countries moved closer to agreement on the deployment of a joint missile shield. In February 2003 the Japanese Government stated that the two countries would conduct joint training in ballistic missile interception off the coast of Hawaii for a period of two years, beginning in 2004, and in December 2003 the Japanese Government announced that it was to develop a ballistic missile defence system in co-operation with the USA. The system was successfully tested for the first time in December 2007.

Koizumi gave President Bush his full support for the USA's military offensive against Iraq, which commenced in March 2003, despite strong opposition from the Japanese public. However, Japan refused to close the Iraqi embassy in Tokyo. Following the approval of legislation to permit the dispatch of Japanese troops to Iraq in a peace-keeping capacity, in early 2004 the first Japanese soldiers were deployed, numbering about 550 troops by April of that year. In December it was announced that the term of SDF involvement in Iraq would be extended by one year to aid the reconstruction of the country; however, following a further extension announced in December 2005, Japanese troops were withdrawn from Iraq in June and July 2006, with the exception of a small air support contingent.

In November 2007 the USA expressed disappointment at the withdrawal of Japan's Maritime Self-Defence Force from the Indian Ocean, where it had been supporting US-led counter-terrorism operations in Afghanistan since 2001 (see above), following the failure to secure approval for an extension of the mission in the Japanese Diet. Japan resumed its naval mission in support of US forces in the Indian Ocean in January 2008, after the Government forced the necessary legislation through the Diet. In October the House of Representatives voted to renew the naval mission. The extension was strongly supported by the newly appointed Prime Minister, Taro Aso. Upon taking office in September 2009, however, the new DPJ-led Government indicated that it would not support an extension of the mission in 2010, but would increase Japanese assistance for reconstruction in Afghanistan (see Other external relations).

Relations with China

Despite the signing of a treaty of peace and friendship with the People's Republic of China in 1978, the historic enmity between the two countries continued to cause intermittent tension. Relations deteriorated in the late 1980s after China expressed concern at Japan's increased defence expenditure and at what China perceived as a more assertive military stance. Japanese aid to China was suspended in June 1989, following the Tiananmen Square massacre in the Chinese capital, Beijing, and was not resumed until November 1990. Relations between the two countries were strengthened by the visits to China by Emperor Akihito in October 1992, the first Japanese imperial visit to China, and by Prime Minister Hosokawa in March 1994. However, in August of that year Japan announced the suspension of economic aid to China, following renewed nuclear testing by the Chinese Government. The provision of economic aid was resumed in early 1997, following the declaration of a moratorium on Chinese nuclear testing.

In September 1997 China expressed concern at the revised US-Japanese security arrangements (see Relations with the USA), following a statement by a senior Japanese minister that the area around Taiwan might be covered under the new guidelines. In November 1998, during a six-day state visit by President Jiang Zemin, Obuchi and Jiang issued (but declined to sign) a joint declaration on friendship and co-operation, in which Japan expressed deep remorse for past aggression against China. However, China was reported to be displeased by the lack of a written apology. A subsequent US-Japanese agreement to initiate joint technical research on the development of a theatre missile defence system, followed by the Japanese Diet's approval, in May 1999, of legislation on the implementation of the revised US-Japanese defence guidelines, provoked severe criticism from China, despite Japan's insistence that military co-operation with the USA was purely defensive.

In August 2002 a Tokyo court rejected a compensation claim by 180 Chinese for damage inflicted in biological warfare during the 1930s and 1940s, but acknowledged that Japan had, in fact, waged such warfare in China at that time: this was corroborated by a former member of Japan's biological warfare division, who testified at the hearing. In May 2003 a Japanese court rejected compensation claims from five residents of China's Heilongjiang Province who had been injured by chemical weapons abandoned in China by the Japanese army at the end of the Second World War. However, in August the Japanese Government apologized to China following an incident in which 29 people were similarly injured by weapons left by Japanese troops. In September a Tokyo court ordered the Japanese Government to pay compensation to 13 Chinese people injured by such abandoned weapons. In March 2004 a Japanese District Court instructed the Government to pay compensation to former Chinese slave labourers who had been forced to work in a Japanese harbour transport company during the Second World War.

In April 2005 violent anti-Japanese protests took place across China, following Japan's approval of school textbooks that reportedly omitted any references to Japanese war crimes in China. The subsequent attacks on Japanese embassies and boycotts of Japanese products and companies were also thought to be partially motivated by Japan's ongoing campaign to acquire a permanent seat on the UN Security Council (see below), an ambition that China, a long-standing permanent member, vehemently opposed. A dispute between the two countries over the status of the Okinotori Shima coral reef chain, in the Pacific Ocean to the south of Japan, continued in 2005: Japan claimed that the chain constituted islands and thus, under international maritime law, Japanese sovereignty over them gave it the right to an exclusive economic zone in the surrounding waters, while China insisted that Okinotori Shima merely constituted 'rocks', lacking the sustainable economic activity required to engender an exclusive zone. The two countries also made competing claims to potential petroleum fields in the East China Sea. In July the Chinese Government protested against the Japanese granting of drilling rights in disputed waters to Teikoku Oil Co, and in October Japanese officials asserted that their reconnaissance information showed that Chinese platforms were operating in a contested region. In May 2006 China and Japan agreed to accelerate negotiations on the development of disputed gas exploration in the East China Sea. In June the Japanese Government agreed to remove its moratorium on a programme of low-interest loans to China. By August, however, the relationship had once more deteriorated, following the publication of a

Japanese defence policy document that was perceived to have exaggerated the Chinese military threat.

A periodic source of tension between the two countries is the Yasukuni Shrine (a Shinto memorial to Japan's war dead, including those convicted of war crimes). In August 2001 China criticized the first visit to the Yasukuni Shrine by the Japanese Prime Minister, Junichiro Koizumi, and a senior official of the Chinese Ministry of Foreign Affairs urged Japan to take 'visible action' to renounce its militaristic past. Koizumi subsequently travelled to China in October, when he visited the Marco Polo Bridge (the site of a clash between China and Japan that had led to full-scale war in 1937) and apologized for Japan's past crimes in China. However, Koizumi continued to arouse anger in China by making several more visits to the Yasukuni Shrine.

The appointment of Shinzo Abe as Prime Minister in September 2006, however, raised hopes of a significant improvement in Sino-Japanese relations. Shortly after taking office, the new Prime Minister confirmed that he had arranged a visit to Beijing in October, in what would be the first meeting between Chinese and Japanese leaders for five years. President Hu Jintao described the visit as a turning point in Sino-Japanese relations and commended Abe for choosing China as the first destination for an official overseas trip, during which the two nations pledged to expand relations in the areas of trade, investment and technology. Also, Abe acknowledged that Japan had inflicted suffering on Asian people in the past, and with regard to the issue of Taiwan he confirmed that the Japanese Government would adhere firmly to its 'one China' policy. The visit was reciprocated by the Chinese Prime Minister, Wen Jiabao, in April 2007.

In his address to the Japanese Diet, the first ever by a Chinese Prime Minister, Wen urged a spirit of reconciliation. Wen and Abe agreed to increase bilateral co-operation in a wide range of areas. Meanwhile, however, in March 2007 Abe's questioning of the degree of compulsion used by Japan in engaging women for sexual purposes during the Second World War (see Relations with South Korea) had provoked much criticism in China and elsewhere, following which the Prime Minister was obliged to issue an apology for his remarks. In April the Japanese Supreme Court dismissed two appeals for compensation by Chinese nationals over their treatment by the Japanese during the war on the grounds that China had renounced all claims for reparation from Japan in a communiqué signed by the two countries in 1972; the Court dismissed the plaintiffs' argument that no reference had been made in the document to individual rights. Subsequent similar appeals to the Court were also rejected.

It was anticipated that the improvement in Sino-Japanese relations experienced under Abe's premiership of Japan would continue under Yasuo Fukuda, who, upon taking office as Prime Minister in September 2007, expressed his intention to develop closer links with China and other neighbouring Asian countries. Fukuda and Wen held amicable talks in November while attending the annual summit meeting of the Association of Southeast Asian Nations (ASEAN, see p. 214), with both leaders emphasizing their commitment to strengthening bilateral relations. They agreed to accelerate efforts to resolve the dispute over exploration for hydrocarbons in the East China Sea, which remained outstanding, despite 11 rounds of consultations on the issue. A goodwill visit to Japan by a Chinese warship later in that month (the first since 1934) was a further sign of improving relations, as was the first senior-level dialogue on closer economic co-operation, which was held in Beijing at the beginning of December with the participation of senior government ministers from both countries. In late December Fukuda made his first visit to China as Prime Minister. In January 2008 hundreds of Japanese citizens were taken ill after consuming dumplings imported from China. Following allegations that the products had been deliberately contaminated with pesticide, the Chinese authorities agreed to conduct an inquiry, and in March 2010 Chinese police announced that they had detained a suspect who had worked at the processing plant where the dumplings were made. In May 2008 President Hu Jintao embarked upon a five-day visit to Japan, which culminated in the publication of a six-point statement outlining the long-term development of Sino-Japanese relations and an agreement on more than 70 joint projects. In June, following the earthquake in Sichuan Province in the previous month, the Japanese Government sent a warship to the southern Chinese port of Zhanjiang with relief supplies, a gesture that was widely interpreted as a symbolic advance in the countries' relations. This was the first visit to China by a Japanese warship since the Second World War. In the same month China and Japan agreed to establish a joint exploration project for natural gas in the East China Sea. In April 2009 Fukuda's successor as Prime Minister, Taro Aso, visited China for discussions on the global economic downturn. In April 2010, however, the execution in China of several Japanese citizens, following their conviction on charges of drugs-smuggling, aroused much concern.

The Senkaku Islands (or Diaoyu Islands in Chinese), a group of uninhabited islands situated in the East China Sea, are a periodic source of conflict between Japan and China. The islands are controlled by Japan, but also claimed by China and Taiwan. In July 1996 a group of Japanese nationalists constructed a lighthouse and war memorial on the islands. In September 2010 a Chinese fishing boat was involved in collisions with two Japanese coastguard patrol boats near the disputed Senkaku islands, and the captain of the Chinese vessel was detained by the Japanese authorities. His detention was denounced as illegal by the Chinese Government, which suspended contacts between senior officials and discussions on the joint development of natural gas reserves. The Chinese captain was released later in the month, but the Japanese Government refused to apologize or offer compensation. Further detentions of Chinese fishing boat captains for entering Japan's exclusive economic zone occurred in August and November 2011, but these incidents did not take place near the disputed islands, and the detainees were swiftly released in each case. In January 2012 two members of the Japanese Diet surveyed the disputed islands from a fishing vessel—the first Diet members to visit the area since 1997—and expressed the opinion that those islands still held as private property should be nationalized. In March the Japanese Government officially named 39 uninhabited and previously anonymous islands that it considered part of its exclusive economic zone, including four within the Senkaku chain. The Chinese Government responded by publishing its own names for 70 islands in the region. Japan's annual defence report, published in August 2011, expressed concerns at the speed of Chinese military expansion and the 'opacity' of the Chinese defence budget; the report was criticized by the Chinese Government. In April 2012 the populist Governor of Tokyo, Shintaro Ishihara, announced a plan for the Tokyo metropolitan government to purchase the Senkaku islands from their private Japanese owner. The proposal was condemned by a Chinese government spokesman, who reasserted China's claim to sovereignty of the islands.

Relations with North Korea

Attempts to establish full diplomatic relations with North Korea in early 1991 were hindered by North Korean demands for financial reparations for the Japanese colonization of the country during 1910–45 and by North Korea's refusal to allow International Atomic Energy Agency inspectors access to its nuclear facilities. Relations improved in 1995 and 1996 after Japan provided emergency aid to North Korea when serious food shortages were reported. Concerns that North Korea had developed a missile capable of reaching Japanese territory resulted in the suspension of food aid in mid-1996, but, following bilateral negotiations in August 1997, at which it was agreed to reopen discussions aimed at restoring full diplomatic relations, provision of food aid resumed in October. Agreement was also reached concerning the issue of visits to relatives in Japan by the estimated 1,800 Japanese nationals resident in North Korea. The first such visits took place in November. However, food aid and normalization talks were suspended in mid-1998, following the testing by North Korea of a suspected missile over Japanese territory. Tensions were exacerbated in March 1999, when two suspected North Korean spy ships, which had infiltrated Japanese waters, were pursued and fired on by Japanese naval forces. Relations improved following North Korea's agreement with the USA, in September, to suspend its reported plans to test a new long-range missile. In October, following unofficial talks between Japanese and North Korean government officials in Singapore, Japan lifted a ban on charter flights to North Korea. In December the Japanese Government announced that it would resume the provision of food aid. Several rounds of negotiations on the establishment of diplomatic relations were held in 2000, despite an announcement by Japan in September that normal bilateral relations would not be restored until the cases of 10 Japanese citizens allegedly abducted by North Korean agents had been solved. Meanwhile, in September the long-delayed third series of visits to their homeland by the Japanese wives of North Korean men took place. In February 2001 the North

Korean Government again reiterated the need for compensation from Japan.

In December 2001 the Japanese coastguard sank a suspected North Korean spy vessel after it had been expelled from Japan's exclusive economic zone. North Korea condemned the incident, but denied any involvement. Japanese coastguard forces searched the sunken vessel in May 2002, and raised it in September of that year. Japan's concerns had been heightened in early 2002 when US President Bush referred to North Korea as one of three countries forming an 'axis of evil', comments that Japan viewed as inconsistent with aims of reducing regional tensions.

In an unexpected diplomatic initiative, Junichiro Koizumi visited the North Korean capital, Pyongyang, in September 2002, becoming the first incumbent Japanese Prime Minister to do so. His one-day visit, during which he held discussions with Kim Jong Il, was dominated by the latter's admission that North Korean agents had abducted 12 Japanese citizens in the 1970s and 1980s, of whom five were still alive. Kim apologized for the incidents, but attributed them to rogue elements within the security services. The admission led to a hardening of attitudes against North Korea among the Japanese public, with some sources indicating that the total number of Japanese abductees might be as high as 100. The surviving captives were temporarily allowed to return to Japan in mid-October, although they had to leave behind any spouses or children. However, the Japanese authorities refused to allow them to return to North Korea after the visit.

Japan became alarmed in October 2002 after North Korean representatives allegedly admitted to visiting US officials that North Korea was pursuing a secret nuclear weapons programme. Koizumi announced that Japan would halt further economic co-operation with North Korea until the issues of the abducted Japanese citizens and the nuclear programme were resolved. North Korea's admission led to increased co-operation between Japan and the USA over how to resolve the crisis, with Japan moving closer to participating in a missile shield with the USA (see above). The North Korean Government warned Japan that it would abandon its moratorium on missile-testing if normalization talks failed to make any progress. In separate incidents in late February and early March 2003 North Korea test-launched two short-range ground-to-ship missiles in the Sea of Japan (also known as the East Sea), and in early April tested a third missile in the Yellow Sea. However, it refrained from testing longer-range ballistic missiles, which Japan considered a threat to its security. The Director-General of Japan's Defence Agency warned North Korea that Japan could conduct a pre-emptive strike on North Korean missile facilities if necessary. Japan was one of the six countries to participate in the talks on North Korea's nuclear programme, hosted by China, the first round of which commenced in Beijing in August.

In January 2004 the House of Representatives approved legislation allowing Japan to impose economic sanctions on North Korea. In April the House of Councillors approved legislation requiring all ships entering Japanese ports from March 2005 to be insured against oil damage. This in practice amounted to a ban on entry by North Korean ships. Following a further visit by Koizumi to Pyongyang in May 2004, five children of the abductees who had returned to Japan in 2002 (see above) were permitted to fly to Tokyo. Their release had been secured in return for pledges of food aid and medical supplies. The Government of North Korea joined South Korea and China in condemning the approval of a controversial history textbook for use in Japanese schools in 2005, as well as Prime Minister Koizumi's repeated visits to the controversial Yasukuni Shrine. The first round of bilateral talks between Japan and North Korea since 2002, aimed at the restoration of normal diplomatic relations, was held in Beijing in February 2006. However, the discussions concluded without significant progress on the crucial issues of abducted Japanese citizens (Japan claiming that some abductees had yet to be accounted for), compensation for Japanese military aggression, or the resumption of the stalled six-party talks on the North Korean nuclear programme (see above).

The issue of abducted Japanese citizens came to the fore again in June 2006, when the Diet approved the North Korean Human Rights Act, which warned that economic sanctions would be imposed on North Korea unless it worked to resolve human rights issues, including the question of the abductees. Relations deteriorated further in the following month when North Korea conducted missile tests over the Sea of Japan, including the test of a *Taepo Dong 2* intercontinental ballistic missile. Japan reacted immediately by banning a North Korean trading ferr from its ports and by imposing a moratorium on charter flight from Pyongyang. In September the Japanese Governmen announced the unilateral imposition of more comprehensiv sanctions, which included freezing the assets of North Korea officials suspected of having links to their country's nuclea weapons programme.

Following Shinzo Abe's appointment as Prime Minister i September 2006, Japan adopted a more aggressive polic towards North Korea. Long known for his uncompromisin stance on the North Korean issue, Abe appointed a specia adviser on North Korean abductions, and established a cabine panel to deal with the affair. North Korea's announcement i October that it had tested a nuclear device greatly increase tensions. Clearly alarmed by the possibility of a nuclear powe within the immediate region, Japan not only gave strong suppor to the UN Security Council's sanctions but also imposed its ow additional restrictions, including a ban on all North Korea imports and on the entry of North Korean ships into Japanes waters. North Korea's apparent willingness to return to six-party talks on its nuclear programme in late October did little tc placate the Japanese Government, which insisted that it woulc maintain the pressure on North Korea and would disregard North Korean demands for it to be excluded from the negotiating process.

In February 2007 the six-party talks resulted in an agreement aimed at curbing North Korea's nuclear activities, beginning with the closure of its Yongbyon nuclear site in return for substantial amounts of fuel aid from the other five participating countries. However, Japan insisted that it would only provide aid once progress had been made on the question of the abducted Japanese nationals. As a result of the agreement, Japan and North Korea held their first bilateral talks for more than a year in March, with the ultimate aim of restoring normal relations, although no apparent progress was made. After Yongbyon was officially declared closed in July (after a delay of several months), North Korea accused Japan of attempting to obstruct the talks on the restoration of normal relations and to disrupt the six-party process with its refusal to provide energy aid and its insistence on the resolution of the abduction issue, which North Korea claimed had already been settled. A second round of bilateral negotiations took place in early September. Yasuo Fukuda, who took office as Japanese Prime Minister later in that month, favoured a more conciliatory approach to North Korea than that of his predecessor. Nevertheless, in October Japan announced that it would not resume aid to North Korea and extended sanctions for a further six months, despite the latter's recent commitment to disabling fully its Yongbyon facilities and declaring details of all its nuclear programmes by the end of the year (a deadline that, in the event, was missed), citing a continued lack of progress in the dispute over the abductees. The sanctions were further renewed in April 2008. In October the Japanese Government stopped providing fuel aid for North Korea and stated that this aid would not resume until satisfactory progress had been made on the abduction issue.

In March 2009, following North Korea's announcement of its imminent launch of what was declared to be a communications satellite, Japan prepared its missile interceptors, in the country's first deployment of this advanced technology. The Japanese Government reiterated its warning that it would attempt to destroy any missile or debris that threatened Japanese territory. In April, in response to the launch of the North Korean rocket, the Japanese Government renewed its sanctions against North Korea for a further year, but decided against a ban on exports to the country. In May 2010, following the sinking of a South Korean naval vessel, apparently by a North Korean torpedo, the Japanese Government declared that it would increase the extent of its sanctions against North Korea.

On the death of Kim Jong Il in December 2011, the Japanese Government reacted by joining its ally, the USA, in expressing condolences and hopes for peace and stability on the Korean peninsula, while at the same time placing officials on alert in case of unforeseen developments. Japan subsequently expressed support for the deal concluded between North Korea and the USA in February 2012, whereby the former agreed to suspend nuclear missile tests and uranium enrichment, in exchange for food aid from the latter. Japan condemned the failed launch by North Korea in April of a rocket-mounted satellite, which was widely believed to be the testing of a long-range missile, describing it as an act of provocation and a contravention of UN Security Council resolutions.

Relations with South Korea

Japan's relations with the Republic of Korea have intermittently been affected by the sensitive issue of Japanese colonial rule in 1910–45, and by territorial and fishing disputes. In February 1995 Prime Minister Murayama publicly acknowledged that Japan was responsible, in part, for the post-war division of the Korean peninsula. However, he was forced to retract the statement, following bitter controversy in the Diet. During a four-day state visit by the South Korean President, Kim Dae-Jung, to Japan in October 1998, a joint declaration was signed, in which Japan apologized for the suffering inflicted on the Korean people during Japanese colonial rule. Japan also pledged substantial aid to the Republic of Korea to stimulate economic recovery. In August Japan and the Republic of Korea held their first joint military exercises since the Second World War, in the Tsushima Straits. In October 2000 Koizumi visited Seoul and apologized for past crimes and suffering under Japanese rule. In November Japan and the Republic of Korea, along with China, agreed to establish regular contacts between their ministers of finance and foreign affairs. Relations were adversely affected in 2001 and 2005 by the approval by the Japanese authorities of textbooks considered misleading with regard to Japan's wartime aggression.

A long-standing dispute between Japan and the Republic of Korea concerned sovereignty over a group of islands, called 'Takeshima' in Japanese or 'Dokdo' in Korean, situated in the Sea of Japan. The South Korean Government claimed that the islands were historically part of Korea, while the Japanese Government maintained that they had been incorporated into Japan at the beginning of the 20th century. This issue came to the fore again in 2005 (the 40th anniversary of the establishment of diplomatic links between the two countries), when the administration of Shimane Prefecture in Japan (of which the islands, in the Japanese view, formed a part) declared 22 February to be 'Takeshima Day', prompting official and public protest in the Republic of Korea. In April 2006 Japan announced plans to conduct a maritime survey around the Takeshima islands. While the Republic of Korea warned of a major confrontation and dispatched 20 patrol boats to the area, supported by helicopters and reconnaissance aircraft, Japan remained defiant. Later in the month, however, the two countries agreed to hold discussions on the issue, and Japan agreed to cancel the survey, in exchange for a South Korean pledge to abandon plans to register new names for trenches and ridges on the sea-bed. None the less, in a televised address South Korean President Roh Moo-Hyun reiterated his country's determination to retain control of the islands. In the following month the South Korean Government provoked fury in Japan by announcing a five-year plan for the disputed islands, which included the development of island facilities and the exploration of marine and mineral resources. In July the Republic of Korea announced that it was sending its own maritime surveyors to the islands. Following Japan's renewal of its claim to the eastern Takeshima islands in July 2008, when they were defined as Japanese territory in new teaching materials, the South Korean ambassador was recalled from Tokyo. In January 2011 a South Korean fishing captain was arrested by the Japanese coastguard after sailing into waters claimed by Japan near the Takeshima islands, while in April the announcement that new Japanese textbooks would describe the islands as Japanese territory provoked protests in the Republic of Korea. In June a Korean Air test flight flew over the islands, in response to which the Japanese Government banned its officials from travelling with the airline. In August three members of the Japanese Diet who were planning to visit Ulleung Island, a South Korean island immediately adjacent to the disputed chain, were denied entry to the Republic of Korea. Japan subsequently reiterated its claim to the Takeshima islands in a defence report issued later that month.

The appointment of Shinzo Abe as Prime Minister in September 2006, meanwhile, resulted in a more conciliatory stance by Japan towards the Republic of Korea. Abe visited Seoul in October, but his visit was overshadowed by North Korea's announcement that it had tested a nuclear device (see above). The two sides emphasized their condemnation of the nuclear test, while agreeing to continue collaborating on the abduction issue. Abe provoked considerable anger in March 2007, however, particularly in China and South Korea, when he claimed that there was no evidence that coercion had been used to recruit 'comfort women' (women used for sexual purposes by the Japanese armed forces during the Second World War). His comments followed the introduction of a resolution in the US House of Representatives (which was approved in July) urging the Japanese Prime Minister formally to apologize and accept responsibility 'in a clear and unequivocal manner' for the treatment of 'comfort women', a group of whom had been denied official compensation by a Japanese court in 2000. Abe apologized for his remarks before the Japanese House of Councillors later in March. Abe's successor as Prime Minister, Yasuo Fukuda, who took office in September, declared his intention to strengthen relations with the Republic of Korea and other neighbouring Asian countries, notably pledging not to visit the controversial Yasukuni Shrine. Repeated visits to the shrine by Prime Minister Koizumi had been strongly condemned by the Republic of Korea and had resulted in considerable tensions between the two countries. In January 2008, in a gesture of reconciliation, the relatives of 101 South Koreans who were forced to fight for the Japanese army during the Second World War were invited to a memorial service in Tokyo to mark the return of their remains. Japan had relinquished more than 1,000 sets of remains to South Korean diplomats since 2004, but this was the first time that the families of the dead had participated in events. The Japanese Senior Vice-Minister of Foreign Affairs apologized at the ceremony for the suffering inflicted by Japan on Koreans.

In August 2010, the month of the centenary of Japan's annexation of the Korean peninsula, the recently appointed DPJ Prime Minister, Naoto Kan, again apologized for the suffering caused by colonial rule. In that month Kan and his Cabinet declared that, in accordance with DPJ policy, they would not make any official visits to the Yasukuni Shrine. In January 2011 the Japanese and South Korean defence ministers held talks and signed agreements on the sharing of information and equipment, the first such military agreements concluded between the two countries. In October Kan's successor, Yoshihiko Noda, visited Seoul for a meeting with the South Korean President Lee Myung-Bak that focused on economic co-operation and the possible reopening of talks on a free trade agreement. Noda had previously indicated that he too would refrain from visiting the Yasukuni Shrine, and at the meeting he personally returned five Korean royal scrolls taken to Japan during the colonial occupation. Nevertheless, in a reciprocal visit to Japan in December, Lee raised once more the issue of compensation for Korean 'comfort women', which had been the focus of attention earlier that month when a South Korean civic group erected a statue of a 'comfort woman' outside the Japanese embassy in Seoul.

Other regional relations

During the 1990s and 2000s Japan sought to strengthen economic and security relations with the member countries of ASEAN. Japan's influence in South-East Asia largely depended on its aid and investment programmes. In November 2002 Japan signed an agreement to develop a comprehensive economic partnership with ASEAN members within 10 years—including the possible formation of a Japan-ASEAN free trade area. Japan participated in the inaugural East Asia Summit meeting, convened in Malaysia in December 2005, which was attended by the 'ASEAN + 3' countries (the member nations of ASEAN, plus China, Japan and the Republic of Korea), along with Australia, New Zealand and India.

In May 2000 Singapore agreed to allow Japan to use its military bases for evacuating its citizens from crisis locations, and for regional peace-keeping missions, the first agreement of its kind between Japan and another country, and in October 2001 Japan reached a comprehensive free trade agreement with Singapore (which took effect in November 2002). In July 2006 a free trade agreement between Japan and Malaysia took effect, and a similar agreement with the Philippines was approved by the Japanese legislature in December. During 2007 free trade agreements were concluded with Thailand and Brunei, and with Indonesia, which was to provide Japan with a stable supply of liquefied natural gas (LNG). Negotiations on a comprehensive free trade agreement between Japan and ASEAN were concluded in November. In January 2008 Prime Minister Yasuo Fukuda held a meeting in Tokyo with the ministers responsible for foreign affairs of Cambodia, Laos, Myanmar, Thailand and Viet Nam, offering increased economic aid to the five countries, while encouraging them to make more progress on human rights issues and democratization. Japan had provided substantial aid to Myanmar, but this was suspended in 2003 in protest at the detention of the country's opposition leader, Aung San Suu Kyi, although Japan continued to provide emergency and humanitarian aid. Bilateral meetings took place between the two countries in December 2011 concerning the resumption of regular economic assistance, following Suu Kyi's release in 2010. Plans to resume development aid were confirmed by the Japanese Minister of Foreign Affairs in February 2012.

As Japan continued its efforts to improve relations with South-East Asia, in March 2009 the Japanese Ministry of Defence hosted a meeting of senior security officials from member countries of ASEAN, the first such meeting ever held in Japan. Topics under discussion included the need for closer regional co-operation to combat the increasing threat of maritime piracy and Japan's involvement in international peace-keeping operations. In October 2010, following diplomatic tension between Japan and China (see above), Japan and Viet Nam concluded an agreement on increasing the supply of rare earth minerals from Viet Nam (thus reducing Japan's dependence on imports of these minerals from China), and on co-operation in the development of nuclear power plants in Viet Nam. Despite the Fukushima nuclear disaster of March 2011, and the subsequent questioning of nuclear power's viability within Japan (see above), in October of that year it was announced that Japan would proceed with co-operation on nuclear power development in Viet Nam. At a summit with the leaders of ASEAN in November, meanwhile, Prime Minister Yoshihiko Noda pledged financial support for several infrastructure projects across South-East Asia.

In November 2001 Japan announced plans to send 700 SDF members to East Timor as part of the international peace-keeping force. The force consisted mostly of engineers, and the first contingent arrived in March 2002. In March 2009, during a visit to Tokyo by the Timorese Prime Minister, Xanana Gusmão, it was announced that Japan was to provide assistance in the training of military personnel in Timor-Leste.

In March 2007 the Australian Prime Minister, John Howard, visited Tokyo for discussions with his Japanese counterpart. The two heads of government signed a new security agreement, to encompass peace-keeping and counter-terrorism operations, as well as issues of maritime and aviation security. The conclusion of this agreement, the first such bilateral accord since Japan's signing of the security treaty with the USA in 1951, was regarded as a clear manifestation of Japan's changing position with regard to international affairs. In April 2007 Japan and Australia commenced negotiations on a bilateral economic partnership agreement. One of the principal obstacles was Japan's reluctance to liberalize access to the Japanese market for Australian agricultural products. In June 2010 the Australian Government filed a complaint against Japan at the International Court of Justice, claiming that Japan, by hunting whales in the Southern Ocean, was in breach of international regulations on whaling (see The whaling controversy). In February 2011 Japan requested that the Australian and New Zealand Governments take action to prevent environmental groups from obstructing whaling ships; Australia and New Zealand welcomed Japan's decision to impose an early halt to Antarctic whaling for that season. In October, however, the Australian Government once more condemned the Japanese decision to continue whaling in the Southern Ocean.

Relations with Russia

Japan's relations with Russia have been dominated by the issue of the Northern Territories, known in Russia as the Southern Kurile (Kuril) Islands. These four small islands, situated close to Hokkaido, were annexed in 1945 by the USSR, and thousands of Japanese residents were subsequently deported. Both countries claimed sovereignty over the islands, and as a result no formal peace treaty ending the Second World War was concluded between them. After 1956, when Japan and the USSR resumed diplomatic relations, little progress was made with regard to resolving the dispute. A number of discussions took place during the 1990s, although relations between the two countries deteriorated following the disposal of nuclear waste in Japanese waters by Russian ships in November 1993, and Russia's decision, in August 1994, to open fire on Japanese vessels that were alleged to have been fishing in Russian waters. In November 1996 Japan indicated that it was prepared to resume the disbursement of aid, withheld since 1991, and in May 1997 the Japanese Government abandoned its opposition to Russia's proposed joining of the G7. Russian plans for joint development of the mineral and fishing resources of the disputed territory were followed, in July, by an outline agreement on the jurisdiction of the islands. Negotiations resulted in the conclusion of a framework fisheries agreement in December. Agreement was reached in November 1998 on the establishment of subcommissions to examine issues of border delimitation and joint economic activity on the disputed islands and in September 1999 on improved access to the disputed islands for former Japanese inhabitants. Despite the repudiation of Japan's claim to any of the islands by the Russian President, Vladimir Putin, during his first official visit to Tokyo in September, Russia subsequently offered to abide by a 1956 declaration that it would relinquish two of the islands after the signature of a peace treaty, but Japan initially rejected this partial solution.

In January 2003 Prime Minister Koizumi visited Moscow for a summit meeting with Putin, during which the two agreed to engage North Korea. Koizumi also visited the Russian Far East, where he met regional leaders. Both Japan and Russia favoured the construction of a pipeline that would transport petroleum from Angarsk, in Siberia, to Nakhodka on Russia's Pacific coast, from where it could be shipped to Japan. The scheme would significantly reduce Japan's dependency on Middle Eastern supplies. The first stage of the pipeline, to Skorovodino in Amur oblast, was completed in December 2009, and linked by rail to the terminal at Koz'mino, near Nakhodka, which was inaugurated that same month. Japan began to receive petroleum from the East Siberian pipeline in February 2010. Meanwhile, Japan and Russia both attended the six-party talks in Beijing on the North Korean nuclear weapons programme between 2003 and 2007.

Tensions over the disputed islands were exacerbated in August 2006 when, in the first such incident for 50 years, a Japanese fisherman was shot dead by a Russian patrol boat near the Northern Territories; three other fishermen were temporarily detained. While the Russian coastguard insisted that the fishing vessel had defied orders to halt, the Japanese Government disputed this claim, accusing Russia of acting with excessive force. After the incident, Russia was reported to have intensified its patrols in the area, and in 2007 two more Japanese boats were seized.

In early November 2010 the Russian President, Dmitrii Medvedev, paid a visit to one of the Northern Territories islands, the first Russian head of state to do so, and undertook to increase investment in the islands. The Japanese Prime Minister, Naoto Kan, initially described the visit as regrettable, and a formal protest was delivered to the Russian Government. In February 2011 the Russian Minister of Defence, Anatolii Serdyukov, also visited the islands, and in the same month, addressing a rally on Japan's annual Northern Territories Day, Kan responded to nationalist sentiment by describing Medvedev's visit as an 'unforgivable outrage'. The Russian Government then ordered a strengthening of the defences on the disputed islands. Later in February the Japanese Minister of Foreign Affairs, Seiji Maehara, visited Moscow to discuss the dispute: the possibility of joint economic activities on the islands was considered, but no progress was reported.

Other external relations

In September 1990 Japan contributed to the international effort to force an unconditional Iraqi withdrawal from Kuwait. A controversial LDP-sponsored Peace Co-operation Bill, which provided for the dispatch to the Persian (Arabian) Gulf area of some 2,000 non-combatant personnel, was withdrawn in November after it encountered substantial domestic political opposition. In January 1991, following repeated US demands for a greater financial commitment to the resolution of the Gulf crisis (and a swifter disbursement of moneys already pledged), the Japanese Government announced plans substantially to increase its contribution and to provide aircraft for the transport of refugees in the region. Opposition to the proposal was again vociferous. The Government secured the support of several centrist parties, by pledging that any financial aid from Japan would be employed in a 'non-lethal' capacity, and legislation to approve the new contribution was adopted by the Diet in March. In June 1992 controversial legislation to permit the SDF to participate in UN peace-keeping operations was approved. However, their role was to be confined to logistical and humanitarian tasks, unless a special dispensation from the Diet were granted. In September members of the SDF were dispatched to serve in the UN Transitional Authority in Cambodia (UNTAC). Japanese troops participated in further UN peace-keeping operations in Mozambique, in 1993, and, under Japanese command, on the Rwandan–Zairean border, in 1994. Legislation was approved in November 1994 to enable Japanese forces to be deployed overseas if the Government believed the lives of Japanese citizens to be at risk.

In September 1994 Japan reiterated its desire to be a permanent member of the UN Security Council, particularly in view of its status as the world's largest donor of development aid and the second largest contributor (after the USA) to the UN budget.

In the late 1990s and early 2000s the Japanese Government continued its campaign to obtain a permanent seat on the UN Security Council. In a speech to the UN General Assembly in September 2004 Koizumi stated that Japan's role in supporting reconstruction in Afghanistan and Iraq, as well as the Japanese contributions to negotiations with North Korea on its nuclear programme, entitled Japan to a permanent seat. Japanese frustration at the perceived inequity between the country's financial contribution to the UN and its exclusion from the Security Council continued in 2005. Japan's bid for a permanent seat was believed to have the support of the USA. However, the prospect of Japan gaining permanent representation in the UN's highest forum provoked strong objections from China and the Republic of Korea, as victims of past Japanese military aggression.

Following the commencement of US military action in Iraq in March 2003, the House of Councillors approved legislation to allow SDF forces to be dispatched to Iraq in a peace-keeping capacity. By mid-April 2004 there were some 550 Japanese troops stationed in Iraq. In December it was announced that the term of SDF involvement in Iraq would be extended by one year to aid reconstruction of the country. In December 2005 the Japanese Government announced that the SDF forces deployed in Iraq would remain there for a further year; however, the withdrawal of Japanese troops from Iraq commenced at the end of June 2006 and was completed in July. A small contingent from the Japanese Air Self-Defence Force remained in a minor support role, transporting materials and personnel between Iraq and Kuwait. In mid-2007 the mission was extended for a further two years; however, following a subsequent reconsideration, the mission was terminated in December 2008.

In May 2008 Japan hosted the Fourth Tokyo Conference on African Development, uniting leaders of more than 50 African countries. During the summit meeting, held in Yokohama, Japan pledged to double its aid to Africa to US $3,400m. by 2012 and to extend low-interest loans totalling $4,000m. In March 2009, following several shooting incidents involving Japanese ships, the Government dispatched two naval destroyers to protect Japanese vessels and personnel from the increasing threat of piracy in the shipping lanes off the coast of Somalia. Proposals to widen the remit of the mission, to permit Japanese warships to provide protection for vessels of other nations if necessary, were approved by the House of Representatives in June 2009.

In relations with South Asia, the Japanese Government criticized India and Pakistan for conducting nuclear tests in mid-1998. In response Japan suspended grants of non-humanitarian aid and loans to both countries. A series of missile tests carried out by India and Pakistan in April 1999 again provoked criticism from Japan. Following a visit to India by the Japanese Prime Minister in August 2000, differences over nuclear testing were set aside in favour of enhanced security, defence and research co-operation between Japan and India, which continued during 2001. The Indian Prime Minister, Atal Bihari Vajpayee, visited Japan in December, the first such visit since 1992. In addition to security issues, the two countries discussed closer co-operation in their software and computer industries. In December 2006 Indian Prime Minister Manmohan Singh visited Japan, where the two countries agreed to commence negotiations on a bilateral economic partnership agreement aimed at reducing the high tariffs hitherto imposed on Japanese automobiles and electronics. Prime Minister Singh returned to Tokyo in October 2008, when talks with his Japanese counterpart, Taro Aso, focused on the improvement of economic and military links. As a result of the discussions, the Japanese Government approved a low-interest loan for the construction of a new railway to carry freight between the Indian capital, New Delhi, and Mumbai; at US $4,500m., this was the largest loan ever extended by Japan to an overseas project. In October 2010 Singh and the Japanese Prime Minister, Naoto Kan, announced the completion of negotiations on the economic partnership agreement, which was to include a gradual elimination of most trade tariffs over a 10-year period. Kan's successor, Yoshihiko Noda, visited India in December 2011, where talks with Singh resulted in pledges of increased co-operation in maritime security, including the projected conduct of joint naval exercises in 2012, a development widely interpreted as a response to China's growing maritime assertiveness.

The whaling controversy

Japan has a long tradition of whale-hunting by small fishing communities, but whaling only became a large-scale commercial activity after the Second World War. Concern over the increasing rarity of many whale species throughout the world, as well as unease at inhumane methods of killing, led to a moratorium on commercial whaling being adopted in 1982 by the International Whaling Commission (IWC, established in 1946 to conserve and regulate whale stocks: Japan became a member in 1951). The ban took effect in 1986, but Japan submitted a legal objection (as did Norway, Peru and the USSR), and continued commercial whaling until 1988, when it withdrew its objection to the ban (after the USA threatened to reduce the quota of fish catches allocated to Japan in US waters if it did not do so). However, by exploiting a provision of the IWC's founding convention, whereby governments might issue special permits to allow whaling for the purposes of scientific research, Japan continued to hunt whales, and whale meat remained legally on sale in Japan as a by-product of research. In 1994 the IWC banned whaling in the Southern Ocean, declaring the area a sanctuary for whales. Japan again submitted a legal objection to the ban, asserting that whale stocks in the area were sustainable, and continued to hunt whales in the Southern Ocean, still claiming to be doing so for the purposes of scientific research. By 2011 the IWC had 89 members, and it was widely suspected that Japan had recruited and offered aid to some developing countries in return for their support in opposing the IWC's ban on commercial whaling; Japan denied this, pointing out that it also provided aid for anti-whaling nations. (In 2011 the IWC banned payment of membership dues in cash, a measure thought by some observers to be intended to prevent pro-whaling nations such as Japan from subsidizing the membership of other nations.)

Conservation organizations attempted to disrupt whaling in the Southern Ocean: in January 2010 a vessel of the US-based Sea Shepherd Conservation Society sank after colliding with a Japanese whaling ship, while in February a New Zealand activist, belonging to Sea Shepherd, was arrested by the Japanese coastguard after boarding a Japanese whaling vessel. In June 2010 the Australian Government initiated legal action against Japan at the International Court of Justice, stating that Japan had breached its obligations under international law by continuing to hunt whales in the Southern Ocean sanctuary: the Court was not expected to reach a decision on the matter until 2013. In February 2011 Japan announced an early close to its Antarctic whaling season, after Sea Shepherd activists had obstructed whaling vessels. At the annual IWC conference in July, Japan and 22 other countries walked out of discussions on the formation of a South Atlantic whale sanctuary, disabling a vote on the proposal. Although a resolution on 'Safety at Sea' tabled by Japan and directed primarily at Sea Shepherd was adopted by the IWC at the 2011 conference, Sea Shepherd's activities were thought partially responsible for a reported catch of less than one-third of expected levels during Japan's Antarctic whaling season in early 2012.

CONSTITUTION AND GOVERNMENT

Under the Constitution of 1947, the Emperor is head of state but has no governing power. Legislative power is vested in the bicameral Diet, comprising the House of Representatives (lower house), whose members are elected for a four-year term, and the House of Councillors (upper house), members of which are elected for six years, one-half being elected every three years. The House of Representatives comprises 480 seats—300 single-seat constituencies and 180 determined by proportional representation—and there are 242 seats in the House of Councillors. The number of seats in the House of Representatives was reduced from 500 for the 2000 elections; the reduction was in the number of seats determined by proportional representation. There is universal suffrage for all adults from 20 years of age. Executive power is vested in the Cabinet, which is responsible to the Diet. The Emperor appoints the Prime Minister (on designation by the Diet), who appoints the other Ministers in the Cabinet.

Japan has 47 prefectures, each administered by an elected Governor.

REGIONAL AND INTERNATIONAL CO-OPERATION

Japan is a member of the Asia-Pacific Economic Cooperation (APEC, see p. 204) forum, the Asian Development Bank (ADB, see p. 210), the UN's Economic and Social Commission for Asia and the Pacific (ESCAP, see p. 40) and the Colombo Plan (see p. 449). Japan is also an observer member of the South Asian Association for Regional Co-operation (SAARC, see p. 420).

Japan became a member of the UN in 1956. As a contracting party to the General Agreement on Tariffs and Trade, Japan acceded to the World Trade Organization (WTO, see p. 433) upon its establishment in 1995. Japan is also a member of the Organisation for Economic Co-operation and Development (OECD, see p. 379). The country participates in the Group of Eight major industrialized nations (G8, see p. 463) and the Group of 20 major industrialized and systemically important emerging market nations (G20, see p. 454).

ECONOMIC AFFAIRS

In 2010, according to estimates by the World Bank, Japan's gross national income (GNI), measured at average 2008–10 prices, was US $5,369,116m., equivalent to $42,130 per head (or $34,780 per head on an international purchasing-power parity basis). During 2001–10, it was estimated, the population remained stagnant, while gross domestic product (GDP) per head increased, in real terms, by an average of 0.9% per year. According to World Bank figures, overall GDP increased, in real terms, at an average annual rate of 0.9% in 2001–10. GDP contracted by 6.3% in 2009, but grew by 5.1% in 2010.

Agriculture (including forestry and fishing) contributed 1.1% of GDP and engaged 4.1% of the employed labour force in 2010. The principal crops are rice, sugar beets, potatoes, cabbages and citrus fruits. During 2001–10, according to official sources, agricultural GDP declined, in real terms, at an average rate of 1.9% annually. Compared with the previous year, the sector's GDP declined by 7.1% in 2009 and by 6.2% in 2010.

Industry (including mining, manufacturing, construction and utilities) contributed 27.5% of GDP and engaged 25.6% of the employed labour force in 2010. During 2001–10, according to official sources, industrial GDP increased at an average annual rate of 0.9%. The industrial sector's GDP decreased by 14.7% in 2009, but increased by 14.5% in 2010.

Mining and quarrying make a negligible contribution to GDP, engaging less than 0.1% of the employed labour force in 2010. While the domestic output of limestone and sulphur is sufficient to meet domestic demand, all of Japan's requirements of bauxite, crude petroleum and iron ore, and a high percentage of its requirements of copper ore and coking coal, are met by imports.

In 2010 manufacturing contributed 19.5% of GDP, and engaged 16.9% of the employed labour force. Manufacturing GDP increased by an average of 1.9% per year in 2001–10, according to official figures. Manufacturing GDP decreased by 17.9% in 2009, but increased by 19.5% in 2010, compared with the previous year. The most important branches of manufacturing are machinery and transport equipment, electrical and electronic equipment, and iron and steel.

Construction contributed 5.6% of GDP and engaged 8.0% of the employed labour force in 2010. Construction GDP decreased by an average of 2.8% per year in 2001–10, according to official figures. The GDP of the sector contracted by 2.2% in 2009 and by 0.9% in 2010 compared with the previous year.

Japan imports most of its energy requirements, with imports of crude and partly refined petroleum comprising 15.5% of the value of total imports in 2010, according to official figures. Coal accounted for 26.8% of electricity output in 2008, nuclear power for 24.0%, natural gas for 26.3%, petroleum for 9.7% and hydropower for 7.1%. By May 2012, in response to the accident at the Fukushima nuclear power plant in March 2011, all nuclear reactors were offline, pending routine maintenance work and safety evaluations.

The services sector contributed 71.4% of GDP and engaged 70.4% of the employed labour force in 2010. The GDP of the services sector increased by an average of 0.7% annually in 2001–10. The sector's GDP declined by 2.8% in 2009, but increased by 1.1% in 2010. Tourist receipts, totalling an estimated US $13,199m. in 2010, are a significant source of revenue. In comparison with the previous year, the number of tourist arrivals was estimated to have increased by 26.8% in 2010 to exceed 8.6m.

In 2010 Japan's trade surplus reached US $90,970m., and there was a surplus of $195,750m. on the current account of the balance of payments. In 2010 the People's Republic of China was the principal market for Japanese exports, purchasing 19.4% of the total; other leading purchasers were the USA, the Republic of Korea, Taiwan and Hong Kong. The principal source of import in 2010 was also the People's Republic of China (which supplie 22.1% of imports); other major suppliers were the USA, Australi and Saudi Arabia. The principal exports in 2010 were machiner and transport equipment. The principal imports were minera fuels and lubricants.

The budget for the financial year ending March 2012 projecte expenditure of 92,412,000m. yen. The allocation for social secur ity remained the largest single category of government expend iture. With tax revenue expected to reach 40,927,000m. yen, th Government planned to issue bonds totalling 44,298,000m. yen Japan's general government gross debt was 1,054,190,060m. yen in 2010, equivalent to 220% of GDP. Japan's external debt wa estimated at the equivalent of 43.0% of GNI in 2010. The annua rate of deflation averaged 0.2% in 2001–10. Consumer price declined by 1.4% in 2009 and by 0.7% in 2010. The average rate o unemployment was 5.1% in 2010.

In terms of GDP the Japanese economy was the world's second largest (after the USA) for four decades until 2010 when it wa surpassed by China. Economic performance has been con strained by the strength of the Japanese currency and by th recurrent problem of deflation, which in turn has had a negative effect on consumer demand. Japan also faces the long-term demographic challenge of a shrinking and ageing population Moreover, international demand for Japanese exports declined sharply as a result of the global financial crisis of 2008. In October of that year the Government announced a major stimu lus programme. GDP contracted by more than 3% in the fina quarter of 2008, and by 6.3% in 2009, but grew by 5.1% in 2010 The tsunami that struck Japan in March 2011, and the subse quent crisis at the Fukushima nuclear power plant, had a majo impact on the economy. Following the disaster, the Bank o Japan announced the immediate release of 15,000,000m. yen into the banking system, its largest ever such single operation additional allocations to stabilize Japanese financial markets were subsequently released. Over the course of 2011 and early 2012, the Japanese Diet approved a series of four emergency budgets, the highest number of such supplementary budgets in one fiscal year since 1947, which provided in total some 20,000,000m. yen for post-crisis reconstruction. Major manufac turers were obliged to curtail their production, owing to the shortages of power that arose from the disruption of energy supplies. The already strong yen reached its highest point since 1945 in relation to the US dollar in the immediate aftermath o the tsunami, and reached a still higher point against the dollar in October, a trend that affected the competitiveness of Japanese exports. A decline in exports, together with a significant increase in fossil fuel imports, following the closure of nuclear power stations in the wake of the Fukushima disaster, contributed to a trade deficit being recorded for 2011, the first such annual deficit for Japan in over 30 years. Concerns also remained about Japan's record levels of gross government debt, which stood at around 200% of GDP—the highest in the industrialized world—and had recently resulted in a downgrading of the country's credit rat ings. The administration of Yoshihiko Noda sought to reduce public debt in part through the proposed doubling of sales tax from 5% to 10% by 2015, a policy that encountered significant opposition among legislators and the wider public (see Domestic Political Affairs). It was estimated that Japan's GDP had fallen by 2.3% in the fourth quarter of 2011, in combined consequence o a strong currency, a decrease in exports connected to the finan cial crisis in the euro area, and a disruption in production and supplies due to flooding in Thailand. GDP declined by 0.9% overall in 2011. The IMF anticipated GDP growth of 1.7% in 2012.

PUBLIC HOLIDAYS

2013: 1 January (New Year's Day), 14 January (Coming of Age Day), 11 February (National Foundation Day), 20 March (Vernal Equinox Day), 29 April (Showa Day), 3 May (Constitution Memorial Day), 4 May (Greenery Day), 6 May (for Children's Day), 15 July (Marine Day), 16 September (Respect for the Aged Day), 23 September (Autumnal Equinox), 14 October (Sports Day), 4 November (for Culture Day), 23 November (Labour Thanksgiving Day), 23 December (Emperor's Birthday),

Statistical Survey

Source (unless otherwise stated): Statistics Bureau and Statistics Center, 2-1-2, Kasumigaseki, Chiyoda-ku, Tokyo 100-8926; tel. (3) 5253-5111; fax (3) 3504-0265; e-mail webmaster@stat.go.jp; internet www.stat.go.jp.

Area and Population

AREA, POPULATION AND DENSITY

Area (sq km)	377,944*
Hokkaido district	83,457
Honshu district	231,112
Shikoku district	18,792
Kyushu district	42,190
Okinawa district	2,276
Population (census results)†	
1 October 2005	127,767,994
1 October 2010	
Males	62,327,737
Females	65,729,615
Total	128,057,352
Population (official estimate at 1 July) 2011	127,817,000
Density (per sq km) at 1 July 2011	338.2

* 145,925 sq miles; total includes 118 sq km (45.6 sq miles) within Honshu and Shikoku districts yet to be demarcated fully.

† Excluding foreign military and diplomatic personnel and their dependants.

POPULATION BY AGE AND SEX

('000 persons, official estimates at 1 July 2011)

	Males	Females	Total
0–14	8,574	8,171	16,744
15–64	41,019	40,477	81,495
65 and over	12,597	16,980	29,578
Total	62,189	65,628	127,817

Note: Totals may not be equal to the sum of components, owing to rounding.

PREFECTURES

(population at 2010 census)

Prefecture	Area (sq km)	Population ('000)	Density (per sq km)
Aichi	5,165	7,411	1,434.9
Akita	11,612	1,086	93.5
Aomori	9,607	1,373	142.9
Chiba	5,157	6,216	1,205.4
Ehime	5,678	1,431	252.0
Fukui	4,190	806	192.4
Fukuoka	4,977	5,072	1,019.1
Fukushima	13,783	2,029	147.2
Gifu	10,621	2,081	195.9
Gumma	6,363	2,008	315.6
Hiroshima	8,479	2,861	337.4
Hokkaido	83,457	5,507	66.0
Hyogo	8,396	5,588	665.6
Ibaraki	6,096	2,970	487.2
Ishikawa	4,186	1,170	279.5
Iwate	15,279	1,330	87.0
Kagawa	1,877	996	530.6
Kagoshima	9,189	1,706	185.7
Kanagawa	2,416	9,048	3,745.0
Kochi	7,105	764	107.5
Kumamoto	7,406	1,817	245.3
Kyoto	4,613	2,636	571.4
Mie	5,777	1,855	321.1
Miyagi	7,286	2,348	322.3
Miyazaki	7,735	1,135	146.7
Nagano	13,562	2,152	158.7
Nagasaki	4,104	1,427	347.7
Nara	3,691	1,401	379.6
Niigata	12,583	2,374	188.7
Oita	6,340	1,197	188.8
Okayama	7,113	1,945	273.4
Okinawa	2,276	1,393	612.0
Osaka	1,898	8,865	4,670.7
Saga	2,440	850	348.4
Saitama	3,797	7,195	1,894.9
Shiga	4,017	1,411	351.3
Shimane	6,708	717	106.9
Shizuoka	7,780	3,765	483.9
Tochigi	6,408	2,008	313.4
Tokushima	4,147	785	189.3
Tokyo-to	2,188	13,159	6,014.2
Tottori	3,507	589	168.0
Toyama	4,248	1,093	257.3
Wakayama	4,726	1,002	212.0
Yamagata	9,323	1,169	125.4
Yamaguchi	6,114	1,451	237.3
Yamanashi	4,465	863	193.3
Total	377,944*	128,057	338.8

* Total includes 59 sq km of area straddling more than one prefecture or not fully demarcated.

PRINCIPAL CITIES

(census results at 1 October 2010)*

Tokyo (capital)†	8,945,695	Utsunomiya	467,666
Yokohama	3,688,773	Kanazawa	462,361
Osaka	2,665,314	Fukuyama	461,357
Nagoya	2,263,894	Amagasaki	453,748
Sapporo	1,913,545	Nagasaki	443,766
Kobe	1,544,200	Machida	426,987
Kyoto	1,474,015	Toyama	421,953
Fukuoka	1,463,743	Toyota	421,487
Kawasaki	1,425,512	Takamatsu	419,429
Saitama	1,222,434	Yokosuka	418,325
Hiroshima	1,173,843	Fujisawa	409,657
Sendai	1,045,986	Hirakata	407,978
Kitakyushu‡	976,846	Kashiwa	404,012
Chiba	961,749	Gifu	399,745
Sakai	841,966	Toyonaka	389,341
Niigata	811,901	Nagano	381,511
Hamamatsu	800,866	Toyohashi	376,665
Sagamihara	717,544	Wakayama	370,364
Shizuoka	716,197	Nara	366,591
Okayama	709,584	Okazaki	363,743
Kumamoto	676,103	Takatsuki	357,359
Funabashi	609,040	Suita	355,798
Kagoshima	605,846	Asahikawa	347,095
Hachioji	580,053	Kochi	343,393
Matsuyama	517,231	Kawagoe	342,670
Higashiosaka	509,533	Iwaki	342,249
Kawaguchi	500,598	Tokorozawa	341,924
Himeji	485,992	Maebashi	340,291
Matsudo	484,457	Koriyama	338,712
Nishinomiyai	482,640	Koshigaya	326,313
Kurashiki	475,513	Akita	323,600
Oita	474,094	Naha	315,954
Ichikawa	473,919	Aomori	299,520

* With the exception of Tokyo, the data for each city refer to an urban county (*shi*), an administrative division that may include some scattered or rural population as well as an urban centre.

† The figure refers to the 23 wards (*ku*) of the old city. The population of Tokyo-to (Tokyo Prefecture) was 13,159,388 at the census of 1 October 2010.

‡ Including Kokura, Moji, Tobata, Wakamatsu and Yahata (Yawata).

BIRTHS, MARRIAGES AND DEATHS*

	Registered live births		Registered marriages†		Registered deaths	
	Number	Rate (per 1,000)	Number	Rate (per 1,000)	Number	Rate (per 1,000)
2003	1,123,610	8.9	740,191	5.9	1,014,951	8.0
2004	1,110,721	8.8	720,417	5.7	1,028,602	8.2
2005	1,062,530	8.4	714,265	5.7	1,083,796	8.6
2006	1,092,674	8.7	730,971	5.8	1,084,450	8.6
2007	1,089,818	8.6	719,822	5.7	1,108,334	8.8
2008	1,091,156	8.7	726,106	5.8	1,142,407	9.1
2009	1,070,035	8.5	707,734	5.6	1,141,865	9.1
2010	1,071,304	8.4	700,214	5.5	1,197,012	9.3

* Figures relate only to Japanese nationals in Japan.

† Data are tabulated by year of registration rather than by year of occurrence.

Source: Ministry of Health, Labour and Welfare, Tokyo.

Life expectancy (years at birth, WHO estimates): 83 (males 80; females 86) in 2009 (Source: WHO, *World Health Statistics*).

ECONOMICALLY ACTIVE POPULATION*
(annual averages, '000 persons aged 15 years and over)

	2008	2009	2010
Agriculture and forestry	2,450	2,420	2,340
Fishing and aquaculture	230	200	180
Mining and quarrying	30	30	30
Manufacturing	11,440	10,730	10,490
Electricity, gas and water	320	340	340
Construction	5,370	5,170	4,980
Wholesale and retail trade	11,050	10,550	10,570
Restaurants and hotels	3,340	3,800	3,870
Transport, information and communications	5,290	5,410	5,460
Financing, insurance, real estate and business services	2,470	2,750	2,730
Health and welfare	5,980	6,210	6,530
Education	2,880	2,870	2,880
Government	2,230	2,220	2,200
Other services and activities not elsewhere classified	10,010	9,510	9,360
Sub-total	63,090	62,210	61,960
Activities not adequately defined	760	610	610
Total employed	63,850	62,820	62,570
Unemployed	2,650	3,360	3,340
Total labour force	66,500	66,180	65,900
Males	38,880	38,470	38,220
Females	27,620	27,710	27,680

* Figures are rounded to the nearest 10,000 persons, and totals may not be equal to the sum of components as a result.

Health and Welfare

KEY INDICATORS

Total fertility rate (children per woman, 2009)	1.3
Under-5 mortality rate (per 1,000 live births, 2009)	3
HIV/AIDS (% of persons aged 15–49, 2009)	<0.1
Physicians (per 1,000 head, 2004)	2.1
Hospital beds (per 1,000 head, 2005)	14.1
Health expenditure (2008): US $ per head (PPP)	2,817
Health expenditure (2008): % of GDP	8.3
Health expenditure (2008): public (% of total)	80.5
Total carbon dioxide emissions ('000 metric tons, 2007)	1,253,516.7
Carbon dioxide emissions per head (metric tons, 2007)	9.8
Human Development Index (2011): ranking	12
Human Development Index (2011): value	0.901

For sources and definitions, see explanatory note on p. vi.

Agriculture

PRINCIPAL CROPS
('000 metric tons)

	2008	2009	2010
Wheat	881.2	674.2	571.3
Rice, paddy	11,028.8	10,590.0*	10,600.0
Barley	217.2	179.2	160.9
Potatoes	2,743.0	2,459.0	2,069.8
Sweet potatoes	1,011.0	1,026.0	863.6
Taro (Cocoyam)	179.7	182.4	153.5
Yams	181.2	167.1	140.7
Sugar cane	1,598.0	1,515.0	1,468.0
Sugar beets	4,248.0	3,649.0	3,090.0
Beans, dry	93.8	68.7	76.9
Soybeans (Soya beans)	261.7	229.9	222.5
Cabbages and other brassicas	2,310.4	2,309.1	2,247.7
Lettuce and chicory	544.3	549.8	537.8
Spinach	292.7	286.3	269.0
Tomatoes	732.8	716.9	690.7
Cauliflowers and broccoli	161.4	165.5	157.9†
Pumpkins, squash and gourds	242.8	214.1	220.8
Cucumbers and gherkins	627.4	620.2	587.8
Aubergines (Eggplants)	365.9	349.1	330.1
Chillies and peppers, green	150.3	142.7	137.3
Onions and shallots, green	575.5	570.0†	543.9†
Onions, dry	1,271.0	1,154.0	1,047.0
Carrots and turnips	656.8	650.1	620.4
Maize, green	266.0	235.9	225.1
Mushrooms and truffles†	67.5	64.1	62.5
Watermelons	402.0	389.9	362.0
Cantaloupes and other melons	208.5	199.4	188.1
Grapes	201.0	202.2	184.8
Apples	910.7	845.6	798.2
Pears	361.7	351.5	284.9
Peaches and nectarines	157.3	150.7	136.7
Plums and sloes	26.0	20.9	20.9
Oranges†	63.0	62.0	53.0
Tangerines, mandarins, clementines and satsumas	906.1	1,003.0	786.0
Persimmons	266.6	258.0	189.4
Strawberries	190.7	184.7	177.5
Tea	96.5	86.0	85.0
Tobacco, unmanufactured	38.5	36.6	29.3

* Unofficial figure.

† FAO estimate(s).

Aggregate production ('000 metric tons, may include official, semi-official or estimated data): Total cereals 12,151.2 in 2008, 11,459.4 in 2009, 11,362.6 in 2010; Total roots and tubers 4,178.2 in 2008, 3,896.7 in 2009, 3,280.0 in 2010; Total vegetables (incl. melons) 11,887.8 in 2008, 11,504.1 in 2009, 11,034.2 in 2010; Total fruits (excl. melons) 3,416.1 in 2008, 3,391.0 in 2009, 2,898.6 in 2010.

Source: FAO.

LIVESTOCK
('000 head at 30 September)

	2008	2009	2010
Horses*	18	18	18
Cattle	4,423	4,423	4,376
Pigs	9,745	9,899	9,800*
Sheep	10	12	12*
Goats	15	14	15*
Chickens	284,651	285,349	286,000*

* FAO estimate(s).

Source: FAO.

LIVESTOCK PRODUCTS
('000 metric tons)

	2008	2009	2010
Cattle meat	519.9	517.0	513.3
Pig meat	1,248.8	1,309.8	1,291.1
Chicken meat	1,369.3	1,394.5	1,400.5*
Cows' milk	7,982.0	7,909.5	7,720.5
Hen eggs	2,554.0	2,508.0	2,515.0

* Unofficial figure.

Source: FAO.

Forestry

ROUNDWOOD REMOVALS
('000 cubic metres, excl. bark)

	2007	2008	2009
Sawlogs, veneer logs and logs for sleepers	13,613	13,247	12,222
Pulpwood	4,037	4,462	4,397
Fuel wood*	101	96	92
Total*	17,751	17,805	16,711

* FAO estimates.

2010: Production assumed to be unchanged from 2009 (FAO estimates).

Source: FAO.

SAWNWOOD PRODUCTION
('000 cubic metres, incl. railway sleepers)

	2007	2008	2009
Coniferous (softwood)	11,411	10,688	9,134
Broadleaved (hardwood)	221	196	157
Total	11,632	10,884	9,291

2010: Production assumed to be unchanged from 2009 (FAO estimates).

Source: FAO.

Fishing

('000 metric tons, live weight)

	2007	2008	2009
Capture	4,277.7	4,323.6	3,847.0*
Chum salmon (Keta or Dog salmon)	221.0	174.2	214.3
Alaska (Walleye) pollock	216.6	211.0	223.7
Pacific saury (Skipper)	296.5	354.7	311.9*
Japanese jack mackerel	170.4	172.3	165.7*
Japanese anchovy	362.5	345.0	344.8*
Skipjack tuna (Oceanic skipjack)	301.4	311.5	263.9
Chub mackerel	456.6	520.3	470.9
Yesso scallop	258.3	310.2	319.6*
Japanese flying squid	253.5	217.5	216.6
Aquaculture	771.4	730.0	786.9
Japanese amberjack	159.7	155.1	154.9
Pacific cupped oyster	204.5	190.3	210.2
Yesso scallop	247.5	225.6	256.7
Total catch	5,049.1	5,053.6	4,633.9*

* FAO estimate.

Note: Figures exclude aquatic plants ('000 metric tons): 617.6 (capture 103.6, aquaculture 514.0) in 2007; 561.0 (capture 104.7, aquaculture 456.3) in 2008; 560.6 (capture 104.2, aquaculture 456.4) in 2009 (FAO estimates). Also excluded are aquatic mammals (generally recorded by number rather than by weight), pearls, corals and sponges. The number of whales caught was: 1,435 in 2007; 1,258 in 2008; 1,478 in 2009. The number of dolphins and porpoises caught was: 12,741 in 2007; 8,903 in 2008; 10,846 in 2009. The catch of other aquatic mammals ('000 metric tons) was: 1.6 in 2007; 1.2 in 2008; 1.4 in 2009. For the remaining categories, catches (in metric tons) were: pearls 27.4 in 2007; 24.0 in 2008; n.a. in 2009; and corals 4.0 in 2007; 4.0 in 2008; 5.0 in 2009.

Source: FAO.

Mining

('000 metric tons unless otherwise indicated)

	2007	2008	2009
Hard coal*	1,340	1,300	1,100
Quartzite stone	12,258	10,682	9,189
Limestone	165,982	156,813	132,350
Gold ore (kg)†	8,869	6,868	7,708
Crude petroleum ('000 barrels)	6,041	6,200	5,795
Natural gas (million cu m)‡	3,708	3,735	3,539

* Estimates.

† Figures refer to the metal content of ores.

‡ Includes output from gas wells and coal mines.

Source: US Geological Survey.

Industry

SELECTED PRODUCTS
('000 metric tons unless otherwise indicated)

	2006	2007	2008
Cotton yarn—pure and mixed*	79	72	66
Woven cotton fabrics—pure and mixed (million sq m)	400	368	327
Flax yarn	1	1	1
Woven silk fabrics—pure and mixed (million sq m)	19	15	14
Wool yarn—pure and mixed	15	13	11
Woven woollen fabrics—pure and mixed (million sq m)	71	68	61
Woven fabrics of cellulosic fibres—pure and mixed (million sq m)†	160	149	n.a.
Woven fabrics of non-cellulosic fibres (million sq m)	1,083	1,096	1,008
Leather footwear ('000 pairs)	25,094	24,836	22,298
Newsprint	3,771	3,802	3,680
Other printing and writing paper	11,567	11,666	11,501
Paperboard	12,042	12,074	11,800
Rubber products	1,641	1,660	1,638
Road motor vehicle tyres	1,336	1,344	1,330
Sulphuric acid—100%	6,843	7,098	7,227
Caustic soda—Sodium hydroxide	4,453	4,482	4,373
Ammonia	1,328	1,355	1,244
Liquefied petroleum gas‡	4,644	4,409	4,096
Naphthas‡	15,938	16,699	15,104
Motor spirit—gasoline‡	42,437	42,801	41,882
Kerosene‡	20,120	18,783	16,562
Jet fuel‡	10,433	11,633	12,416
Distillate fuel oil‡	54,711	55,299	54,565
Lubricating oil‡	2,378	2,325	n.a.
Petroleum bitumen—Asphalt‡	5,435	4,974	4,694
Coke-oven coke‡	44,710	45,400	42,338
Cement	69,942	67,685	62,810
Pig-iron	84,270	86,771	86,171
Ferro-alloys§	834	858	828
Crude steel	116,226	120,203	118,739
Aluminium—unwrought‖	1,424	1,438	1,308
Refined copper—unwrought	1,532	1,577	1,540
Electrolytic, distilled and rectified zinc—unwrought	614	598	616
Air-conditioning machines ('000)	24,706	24,155	22,772
Calculating machines ('000)	31	19	8
Video cameras ('000)	12,524	10,228	7,928
Digital cameras ('000)	37,150	31,991	36,273
DVD players ('000)	2,046	1,486	2,366
Cellular telephones ('000)	48,034	45,891	35,326
Personal computers ('000)	8,534	8,328	7,608
Passenger motor cars ('000)	9,755	9,945	9,916

—continued	2006	2007	2008
Lorries and trucks ('000)	1,641	1,538	1,508
Motorcycles, scooters and mopeds ('000)	1,771	1,676	1,227
Bicycles ('000)	1,335	1,136	1,095
Watches	474,925	428,828	n.a.
Construction: new dwellings started ('000)	1,290	1,061	1,093
Electric energy (million kWh)‡	1,161,110	1,192,771	1,146,269

* Including condenser cotton yarn.
† Fabrics of continuous and discontinuous rayon and acetate fibres, including pile and chenille fabrics at loom stage.
‡ Source: UN Industrial Commodity Statistics Database.
§ Including silico-chromium.
‖ Including alloys.

2009 ('000 metric tons unless otherwise indicated): Cotton yarn—pure and mixed 47; Woven cotton fabrics—pure and mixed (million sq m) 221; Wool yarn—pure and mixed 8; Woven fabrics of non-cellulosic fibres (million sq m) 699; Leather footwear ('000 pairs) 17,941; Newsprint 3,455; Other printing and writing paper 9,120; Paperboard 10,436; Rubber products 1,186; Sulphuric acid (100%) 6,396; Caustic soda—Sodium hydroxide 3,895; Ammonia 1,021; Cement 54,800; Pig-iron 66,943; Crude steel 87,534; Video cameras ('000) 4,155; Digital cameras ('000) 24,696; DVD players ('000) 2,115; Motorcycles, scooters and mopeds ('000) 645; Construction: new dwellings started ('000) 788; Electric energy (million kWh) 1,112,622.

2010 ('000 metric tons unless otherwise indicated): Cotton yarn—pure and mixed 45; Woven cotton fabrics—pure and mixed (million sq m) 124; Wool yarn—pure and mixed 9; Woven fabrics of non-cellulosic fibres (million sq m) 730; Leather footwear ('000 pairs) 17,366; Newsprint 3,349; Other printing and writing paper 9,547; Paperboard 10,977; Rubber products 1,429; Sulphuric acid (100%) 7,037; Caustic soda—Sodium hydroxide 4,217; Ammonia 1,178; Cement 51,526; Pig-iron 82,283; Crude steel 109,599; Video cameras ('000) 3,856; Digital cameras ('000) 24,253; DVD players ('000) 1,843; Motorcycles, scooters and mopeds ('000) 663; Construction: new dwellings started ('000) 813.

Finance

CURRENCY AND EXCHANGE RATES

Monetary Units
100 sen = 1 yen.

Sterling, Dollar and Euro Equivalents (30 December 2011)
£1 sterling = 120.163 yen;
US $1 = 77.720 yen;
€1 = 100.562 yen;
1,000 yen = £8.32 = $12.87 = €9.94.

Average Exchange Rate (yen per US $)
2009 93.570
2010 87.780
2011 79.807

BUDGET

('000 million yen, year ending 31 March)*

Revenue	2009/10	2010/11†	2011/12‡
Tax and stamp revenues	36,861	37,396	40,927
Government bond issues	53,455	44,303	44,298
Total (incl. others)	102,558	92,299	92,412

Expenditure	2009/10	2010/11†	2011/12‡
Defence	4,820	4,790	4,775
Social security	28,807	27,269	28,708
Public works	8,787	5,773	4,974
Servicing of national debt§	19,251	20,649	21,549
Transfer of local allocation tax to local governments	16,573	17,477	16,785
Total (incl. others)	102,558	92,299	92,412

* Figures refer only to the operations of the General Account budget. Data exclude transactions of other accounts controlled by the central Government: two mutual aid associations and four special accounts (including other social security funds).
† Initial forecasts.
‡ Budget figures.
§ Including the repayment of debt principal and administrative costs.

Source: Ministry of Finance, Tokyo.

INTERNATIONAL RESERVES

(US $ million at 31 December)

	2008	2009	2010
Gold (national valuation)	1,326	1,350	1,326
IMF special drawing rights	3,032	20,968	20,626
Reserve position in IMF	2,658	4,313	4,608
Foreign exchange	1,003,674	996,955	1,036,256
Total	1,010,690	1,023,586	1,062,816

Source: IMF, *International Financial Statistics*.

MONEY SUPPLY

('000 million yen at 31 December)

	2008	2009	2010
Currency outside depository corporations	76,600	76,724	78,400
Transferable deposits	415,302	421,515	435,519
Other deposits	558,191	573,111	578,516
Broad money	1,050,094	1,071,349	1,092,434

Source: IMF, *International Financial Statistics*.

COST OF LIVING

(Consumer Price Index; average of monthly figures; base: 2005 = 100)

	2008	2009	2010
Food (incl. beverages)	103.4	103.6	103.3
Housing	100.0	99.8	99.4
Rent	99.8	99.5	99.1
Fuel, light and water charges	110.7	106.1	105.9
Clothing and footwear	101.9	101.0	99.8
Miscellaneous	102.1	101.7	103.0
All items	101.7	100.3	99.6

NATIONAL ACCOUNTS

('000 million yen at current prices, year ending 31 December)

National Income and Product

	2008	2009	2010
Compensation of employees	255,583.5	243,172.3	243,789.2
Operating surplus and mixed income	94,854.8	83,973.5	91,468.3
Domestic primary incomes	350,438.3	327,145.8	335,257.5
Consumption of fixed capital	108,954.1	107,027.2	107,968.4
Statistical discrepancy	1,963.9	1,843.9	1,879.5
Gross domestic product (GDP) at factor cost	461,356.3	436,016.9	445,105.4
Indirect taxes	42,476.4	38,528.5	39,852.5
Less Subsidies	2,623.4	3,406.9	3,184.7
GDP in purchasers' values	501,209.3	471,138.7	481,773.2
Primary incomes received from abroad	24,637.7	18,441.9	17,521.1
Less Primary incomes paid abroad	8,126.7	5,813.0	5,264.1
Gross national income (GNI)	517,720.3	483,767.6	494,030.2

Expenditure on the Gross Domestic Product

	2008	2009	2010
Government final consumption expenditure	93,019.4	93,819.6	95,306.8
Private final consumption expenditure	292,055.4	282,941.7	285,439.0
Changes in stocks	2,699.9	–5,339.8	–1,512.2
Gross fixed capital formation	112,462.2	97,990.5	96,776.4
Total domestic expenditure	500,236.9	469,412.0	476,010.0
Exports of goods and services	88,770.0	59,814.2	73,182.5
Less Imports of goods and services	87,797.6	58,087.5	67,419.2
GDP in purchasers' values	501,209.3	471,138.7	481,773.2

Gross Domestic Product by Economic Activity

	2008	2009	2010
Agriculture, hunting, forestry and fishing	5,699.5	5,440.1	5,556.4
Mining and quarrying	352.6	283.3	287.0
Manufacturing	98,666.2	83,351.2	93,362.2
Electricity, gas and water	9,661.4	11,131.8	10,972.1
Construction	28,091.3	26,948.4	26,655.6
Wholesale and retail trade	70,110.9	64,135.5	64,352.0
Transport, storage and communications	52,689.3	49,162.5	49,701.5
Finance and insurance	25,082.1	23,741.6	23,629.6
Real estate*	56,013.4	56,879.2	57,005.0
Public administration	30,578.3	30,221.9	29,615.8
Other government services	15,302.3	14,832.4	14,491.7
Other business, community, social and personal services	94,579.6	91,540.8	91,988.0
Private non-profit services to households	9,877.7	9,667.4	10,000.7
Sub-total	496,704.7	467,336.3	477,617.5
Import duties	5,945.2	4,368.2	4,846.5
Less Consumption taxes for gross capital formation	3,404.5	2,409.7	2,570.3
Statistical discrepancy	1,963.9	1,843.9	1,879.5
GDP in purchasers' values	501,209.3	471,138.7	481,773.2

* Including imputed rents of owner-occupied dwellings.

Source: Economic and Social Research Institute, Tokyo.

BALANCE OF PAYMENTS
(US $ million)*

	2008	2009	2010
Exports of goods f.o.b.	746,470	545,280	730,080
Imports of goods f.o.b.	–708,340	–501,650	–639,100
Trade balance	38,130	43,630	90,970
Exports of services	148,750	128,340	141,460
Imports of services	–169,540	–148,720	–157,570
Balance on goods and services	17,340	23,250	74,860
Other income received	212,100	175,220	173,680
Other income paid	–59,760	–43,880	–40,390
Balance on goods, services and income	169,680	154,590	208,150
Current transfers received	9,100	9,520	10,090
Current transfers paid	–22,150	–21,910	–22,480
Current balance	156,630	142,190	195,750
Capital account (net)	–5,470	–4,990	–4,960
Direct investment abroad	–130,820	–74,620	–57,220
Direct investment from abroad	24,550	11,830	–1,360
Portfolio investment assets	–189,640	–160,250	–262,640
Portfolio investment liabilities	–102,960	–56,260	111,640
Financial derivatives assets	271,950	333,850	403,460
Financial derivatives liabilities	–247,160	–323,300	–391,510
Other investment assets	139,460	202,750	–130,140
Other investment liabilities	61,990	–64,150	197,300
Net errors and omissions	52,340	19,870	–16,460
Overall balance	30,880	26,920	43,850

* Figures are rounded to the nearest US $10m., and totals may not, therefore, be equal to the sum of components.

Source: IMF, *International Financial Statistics*.

JAPANESE DEVELOPMENT ASSISTANCE
(net disbursement basis, US $ million)

	2007	2008	2009
Official flows	7,890	7,615	17,706
Bilateral assistance	5,778	6,823	6,001
Grants	5,983	7,764	5,327
Grant assistance	3,414	4,777	2,209
Technical assistance	2,569	2,987	3,118
Loans	–205	–940	674
Contributions to multilateral institutions	1,901	2,777	3,467
Other official flows	211	–1,986	8,237
Export credits	–772	–629	–786
Direct investment finance, etc.	543	–1,952	7,498
Transfers to multilateral institutions	441	594	1,525
Private flows	21,979	23,738	27,217
Export credits	2,586	–4,878	–1,220
Direct investment and others	18,037	25,710	19,440
Bilateral investment in securities, etc.	3,251	3,952	7,010
Transfers to multilateral institutions	–1,896	–1,046	1,987
Grants from private voluntary agencies	446	452	533
Total	30,315	31,805	45,456

External Trade

PRINCIPAL COMMODITIES
('000 million yen)

Imports c.i.f.	2008	2009	2010
Food and live animals	6,212	4,999	5,199
Fish and fish preparations*	1,453	1,208	1,260
Crude materials (inedible) except fuels	5,538	3,395	4,766
Mineral fuels, lubricants, etc.	27,658	14,202	17,398
Crude and partly refined petroleum	16,262	7,564	9,406
Liquefied natural gas	4,652	2,827	3,472
Chemicals	5,737	4,583	5,379
Manufactured goods	7,336	4,345	5,379
Non-electrical machinery	6,074	4,225	4,826
Electrical machinery	8,628	6,509	8,101
Transport equipment	2,316	1,501	1,681
Other	9,454	7,742	8,036
Clothing and clothing accessories	2,643	2,358	2,328
Total (incl. others)†	78,955	51,499	60,765

Exports f.o.b.	2008	2009	2010
Chemicals	7,269	5,780	6,925
Manufactured goods	10,177	7,017	8,785
Iron and steel	4,574	2,906	3,675
Machinery and transport equipment	51,364	32,290	41,225
Non-electrical machinery	15,928	9,669	13,317
Power-generating machinery	2,509	1,839	2,327
Electrical machinery, apparatus, etc.	15,368	10,771	12,650
Thermionic valves, tubes, etc.	4,625	3,419	4,153
Transport equipment	20,068	11,850	15,258
Road motor vehicles	13,736	6,693	9,174
Road motor vehicle parts	3,065	2,309	2,893
Other	8,883	6,944	8,007
Scientific instruments and optical equipment	2,024	1,578	2,014
Total (incl. others)‡	81,018	54,171	67,400

* Including crustacea and molluscs.
† Including re-imports not classified according to kind.
‡ Including re-exports not classified according to kind.

PRINCIPAL TRADING PARTNERS
('000 million yen)*

Imports c.i.f.	2008	2009	2010
Australia	4,922	3,242	3,948
Brazil	943	593	859
Canada	1,323	858	958
Chile	820	495	678
China, People's Republic	14,830	11,436	13,413
France	1,100	854	901
Germany	2,159	1,563	1,689
Indonesia	3,378	2,038	2,476
Iran	1,897	867	980
Italy	824	595	595
Korea, Republic	3,052	2,051	2,504

Imports c.i.f.—*continued*	2008	2009	2010
Kuwait	1,584	836	901
Malaysia	2,398	1,558	1,987
Philippines	872	598	695
Qatar	2,752	1,483	1,904
Russia	1,389	826	1,412
Saudi Arabia	5,293	2,720	3,149
Singapore	817	570	715
South Africa	930	465	636
Switzerland	665	586	596
Taiwan	2,258	1,711	2,025
Thailand	2,152	1,495	1,840
United Arab Emirates	4,872	2,115	2,569
United Kingdom	774	531	559
USA	8,040	5,512	5,911
Viet Nam	942	649	716
Total (incl. others)	78,955	51,499	60,765

Exports f.o.b.	2008	2009	2010
Australia	1,793	1,135	1,392
Belgium	879	498	586
Canada	1,116	723	817
China, People's Republic	12,950	10,236	13,086
France	931	577	585
Germany	2,484	1,553	1,777
Hong Kong	4,178	2,975	3,705
India	819	591	792
Indonesia	1,304	870	1,394
Italy	706	448	490
Korea, Republic	6,168	4,410	5,460
Malaysia	1,705	1,200	1,545
Mexico	1,032	637	838
Netherlands	2,185	1,260	1,431
Panama	1,132	1,197	1,359
Philippines	1,034	767	969
Russia	1,714	307	703
Saudi Arabia	814	502	568
Singapore	2,758	1,933	2,209
Taiwan	4,782	3,399	4,594
Thailand	3,051	2,070	2,994
United Arab Emirates	1,124	605	643
United Kingdom	1,707	1,102	1,241
USA	14,214	8,733	10,374
Total (incl. others)	81,018	54,171	67,400

* Imports by country of production; exports by country of last consignment.

Transport

RAILWAYS

(traffic, year ending 31 March)

	2008	2009	2010
Japan Railways Group:			
Passengers (million)	8,984	8,841	8,818
Passenger-km (million)	253,556	244,247	244,593
Freight ('000 tons)	32,850	30,849	30,790
Freight ton-km (million)	22,081	20,404	20,228
Other private railways:			
Passengers (million)	13,992	13,884	13,851
Passenger-km (million)	151,030	149,657	148,834
Freight ('000 tons)	13,376	12,401	12,857
Freight ton-km (million)	175	157	171
Total:			
Passengers (million)	22,976	22,725	22,669
Passenger-km (million)	404,586	393,904	393,427
Freight ('000 tons)	46,226	43,250	43,647
Freight ton-km (million)	22,256	20,561	20,399

ROAD TRAFFIC

('000 motor vehicles owned, year ending 31 March)

	2008	2009	2010
Passenger cars	40,799	40,419	40,135
Buses and coaches	230	228	227
Trucks, incl. trailers	6,568	6,362	6,215
Special use vehicles	1,528	1,512	1,498
Light two-wheeled vehicles	1,505	1,524	1,535
Light motor vehicles	28,171	28,648	29,050
Total	78,801	78,693	78,661

SHIPPING

Merchant Fleet

(registered at 31 December)

	2007	2008	2009
Number of vessels	6,519	6,316	6,221
Total displacement ('000 grt)	12,788	13,536	14,725

Source: IHS Fairplay, *World Fleet Statistics*.

International Sea-borne Traffic

('000 metric tons)

	2007	2008	2009
Exports	56,702	47,781	44,963
Imports	527,467	547,888	457,996
Cross transport	249,048	270,784	320,892
Total	833,217	866,453	823,851

CIVIL AVIATION

(traffic on scheduled services)

	2007	2008	2009
Kilometres flown (million)	1,023	1,027	976
Passengers carried (million)	113,295	109,313	99,336
Passenger-km (million)	163,493	155,675	142,406
Total ton-km (million)	9,554	8,467	7,036

2010 (traffic on scheduled services): Passengers carried (million) 95,942; Passenger-km (million) 133,659; Total ton-km (million) 7,340.

Tourism

FOREIGN VISITOR ARRIVALS

(excl. Japanese nationals resident abroad)

Country of nationality	2008	2009	2010
Australia	242,031	211,659	225,751
Canada	168,307	152,756	153,303
China, People's Republic	1,000,416	1,006,085	1,412,875
Germany	126,207	110,692	124,360
Hong Kong	550,192	449,568	508,691
Korea, Republic	2,382,397	1,586,772	2,439,816
Philippines	82,177	71,485	77,377
Singapore	167,894	145,224	180,960
Taiwan	1,390,228	1,024,292	1,268,278
Thailand	191,881	177,541	214,881
United Kingdom	206,564	181,460	184,045
USA	768,345	699,919	727,234
Total (incl. others)	8,350,835	6,789,658	8,611,175

Source: mainly Japan National Tourist Organization.

Receipts from tourism (US $ million, excl. passenger transport): 10,821 in 2008; 10,305 in 2009; 13,199 in 2010 (provisional) (Source: World Tourism Organization).

Communications Media

	2008	2009	2010
Telephones ('000 main lines in use)	48,427	44,364	40,419
Mobile telephones ('000 subscribers)	110,395	114,917	120,709
Internet users ('000)*	95,979	116,295	n.a.
Broadband subscribers ('000)	30,117	31,655	34,045
Book production:			
titles	76,322	78,555	74,714
copies (million)	751	718	702
Daily newspapers:			
number	121	121	120
circulation ('000 copies)	51,491	50,352	49,322

* Estimates.

Daily newspapers: 119 (circulation 48,345,000 copies) in 2011.

Television receivers ('000 in use): 92,000 in 2000.

Radio receivers ('000 in use): 120,500 in 1997.

Personal computers: 69,200,000 (542 per 1,000 persons) in 2005.

Sources: The Japan Newspaper Publishers and Editors Association; Foreign Press Center, *Facts and Figures of Japan*; UNESCO, *Statistical Yearbook*; UN, *Statistical Yearbook*; International Telecommunication Union.

Education

(2010)

	Institutions	Teachers*	Students
Kindergartens	13,392	110,580	1,606,000
Elementary schools	22,000	419,776	6,993,000
Lower secondary schools	10,815	250,899	3,558,000
Upper secondary schools	5,116	238,929	3,369,000
Schools for special needs	1,039	76,680	121,815
Colleges of technology	58	4,373	59,542
Junior colleges	395	9,657	155,000
Universities	778	174,403	2,887,000
Special training schools	3,311	40,416	638,000
Miscellaneous vocational schools	1,466	9,290	130,000

* Figures refer to full-time teachers only.

Pupil-teacher ratio (primary education, UNESCO estimate): 18.1 in 2008/09 (Source: UNESCO Institute for Statistics).

Directory

The Government

HEAD OF STATE

His Imperial Majesty AKIHITO, Emperor of Japan (succeeded to the throne 7 January 1989).

THE CABINET
(May 2012)

A coalition of the Democratic Party of Japan (DPJ) and the People's New Party (PNP).

Prime Minister: YOSHIHIKO NODA (DPJ).

Deputy Prime Minister and Minister for Administrative Reform, for Total Reform of Social Security and Tax and Minister of State for Government Revitalization: KATSUYA OKADA (DPJ).

Minister for Internal Affairs and Communications and for Regional Revitalization, Minister of State for Okinawa and Northern Territories' Affairs and for Promotion of Local Sovereignty: TATSUO KAWABATA (DPJ).

Minister of Justice: TOSHIO OGAWA (DPJ).

Minister for Foreign Affairs: KOICHIRO GEMBA (DPJ).

Minister of Finance: JUN AZUMI (DPJ).

Minister of Education, Culture, Sports, Science and Technology: HIROFUMI HIRANO (DPJ).

Minister of Health, Labour and Welfare: YOKO KOMIYAMA (DPJ).

Minister of Agriculture, Forestry and Fisheries: MICHIHIKO KANO (DPJ).

Minister of Economy, Trade and Industry and for Nuclear Incident Economic Countermeasures, Minister of State for the Corporation in Support of Compensation for Nuclear Damage: YUKIO EDANO (DPJ).

Minister of Land, Infrastructure, Transport and Tourism, and for Ocean Policy: TAKESHI MAEDA (DPJ).

Minister of the Environment and for the Restoration from and Prevention of Nuclear Accident, Minister of State for the Nuclear Power Policy and Administration: GOSHI HOSONO (DPJ).

Minister of Defence: NAOKI TANAKA (DPJ).

Chief Cabinet Secretary: OSAMU FUJIMURA (DPJ).

Chairman of the National Public Safety Commission, Minister for the Abduction Issue and Minister of State for Consumer Affairs and Food Safety: JIN MATSUBARA (DPJ).

Minister for Postal Reform and Minister of State for Financial Services: SHOZABURO JIMI (PNP).

Minister for National Policy and for Space Policy, Minister of State for Economic and Fiscal Policy and for Science and Technology Policy: MOTOHISA FURUKAWA (DPJ).

Minister for Civil Service Reform, Minister of State for the New Public Commons, for Disaster Management and for Measures for Declining Birthrate and Gender Equality: MASAHARU NAKAGAWA (DPJ).

Minister for Reconstruction Measures in Response to the Great East Japan Earthquake: TATSUO HIRANO (DPJ).

MINISTRIES

Imperial Household Agency: 1-1, Chiyoda, Chiyoda-ku, Tokyo 100-8111; tel. (3) 3213-1111; fax (3) 3282-1407; e-mail information@kunaicho.go.jp; internet www.kunaicho.go.jp.

Prime Minister's Office: 1-6-1, Nagata-cho, Chiyoda-ku, Tokyo 100-8968; tel. (3) 3581-2361; fax (3) 3581-1910; internet www.kantei.go.jp.

Cabinet Office: 1-6-1, Nagata-cho, Chiyoda-ku, Tokyo 100-8968; tel. (3) 5253-2111; internet www.cao.go.jp.

Ministry of Agriculture, Forestry and Fisheries: 1-2-1, Kasumigaseki, Chiyoda-ku, Tokyo 100-8950; tel. (3) 3502-5517; fax (3) 3592-7697; internet www.maff.go.jp.

Ministry of Defence: 5-1, Ichigaya, Honmura-cho, Shinjuku-ku, Tokyo 162-8801; tel. and fax (3) 3268-3111; e-mail infomod@mod.go.jp; internet www.mod.go.jp.

Ministry of Economy, Trade and Industry: 1-3-1, Kasumigaseki, Chiyoda-ku, Tokyo 100-8901; tel. (3) 3501-1511; fax (3) 3501-6942; e-mail webmail@meti.go.jp; internet www.meti.go.jp.

Ministry of Education, Culture, Sports, Science and Technology: 3-2-2, Kasumigaseki, Chiyoda-ku, Tokyo 100-8959; tel. (3) 5253-4111; fax (3) 3595-2017; internet www.mext.go.jp.

Ministry of the Environment: 5 Godochosha, 1-2-2, Kasumigaseki, Chiyoda-ku, Tokyo 100-8975; tel. (3) 3581-3351; fax (3) 3502-0308; internet www.env.go.jp.

Ministry of Finance: 3-1-1, Kasumigaseki, Chiyoda-ku, Tokyo 100-8940; tel. (3) 3581-4111; fax (3) 5251-2667; e-mail info@mof.go.jp; internet www.mof.go.jp.

Ministry of Foreign Affairs: 2-2-1, Kasumigaseki, Chiyoda-ku, Tokyo 100-8919; tel. (3) 3580-3311; fax (3) 3581-2667; e-mail webmaster@mofa.go.jp; internet www.mofa.go.jp.

Ministry of Health, Labour and Welfare: 1-2-2, Kasumigaseki, Chiyoda-ku, Tokyo 100-8916; tel. (3) 5253-1111; fax (3) 3501-2532; e-mail www-admin@mhlw.go.jp; internet www.mhlw.go.jp.

Ministry of Internal Affairs and Communications: 2-1-2, Kasumigaseki, Chiyoda-ku, Tokyo 100-8926; tel. (3) 5253-5111; fax (3) 3504-0265; internet www.soumu.go.jp.

Ministry of Justice: 1-1-1, Kasumigaseki, Chiyoda-ku, Tokyo 100-8977; tel. (3) 3580-4111; fax (3) 3592-7011; e-mail webmaster@moj.go.jp; internet www.moj.go.jp.

Ministry of Land, Infrastructure, Transport and Tourism: 2-1-3, Kasumigaseki, Chiyoda-ku, Tokyo 100-8918; tel. (3) 5253-8111; fax (3) 3580-7982; e-mail webmaster@mlit.go.jp; internet www.mlit.go.jp.

Financial Services Agency: 3-2-1, Kasumigaseki, Chiyoda-ku, Tokyo 100-8967; tel. (3) 3506-6000; internet www.fsa.go.jp.

National Public Safety Commission: 2-1-2, Kasumigaseki, Chiyoda-ku, Tokyo 100-8974; tel. (3) 3581-0141; internet www.npsc.go.jp.

Legislature

KOKKAI

(Diet)

The Diet consists of two Chambers: the House of Councillors (upper house) and the House of Representatives (lower house). The members of the House of Representatives are elected for a period of four years (subject to dissolution). The House of Representatives has 480 members: 300 single-seat constituencies and 180 seats determined by proportional representation. The 242 members of the House of Councillors serve a six-year term of office, with elections for one-half of the members (including 48 chosen by proportional representation) being held every three years.

House of Councillors

Speaker: TAKEO NISHIOKA.

Party	Seats after elections*	
	29 July 2007	11 July 2010
Democratic Party of Japan	109	106
Liberal-Democratic Party	83	84
New Komeito	20	19
Your Party	—	11
Japanese Communist Party	7	6
Social Democratic Party of Japan	5	4
People's New Party	4	3
Sunrise Party of Japan	—	3
New Renaissance Party	—	2
New Party Nippon	1	1
Independents and others	13	3
Total	242	242

* One-half of the seats are renewable every three years.

House of Representatives

Speaker: TAKAHIRO YOKOMICHI.

General Election, 30 August 2009

Party	Seats
Democratic Party of Japan	308
Liberal-Democratic Party	119
New Komeito	21
Japanese Communist Party	9
Social Democratic Party of Japan	7
Your Party	5
People's New Party	3
New Party Nippon	1
New Party Daichi	1
Independents	6
Total	480

Election Commission

Central Election Management Council: 2nd Bldg of Central Common Government Office, 2-1-2, Kasumigaseki, Chiyoda-ku, Tokyo 100-8926; tel. (3) 5253-5111; fax (3) 5253-5575; mems nominated by Diet and approved by Cabinet; regulates proportional representation electoral elements for both legislative chambers; single-constituency elections for both chambers are supervised by an Election Control Cttee est. by each prefectural govt; Chair. AKIRA ISHIHARA.

Political Organizations

The Political Funds Regulation Law provides that any organization wishing to support a candidate for an elective public office must be registered as a political party. There are more than 10,000 registered parties in the country, mostly of local or regional significance.

Ainu Party: 80-27, Nibutani Biratori, Saru-gun, Hokkaido 055-0101; tel. (145) 74-6033; fax (145) 74-6035; e-mail info@ainu-org.jp; internet www.ainu-org.jp; f. 2012; advocates equal rights for indigenous people; Pres. SHIRO KAYANO; Gen. Sec. HIROYUKI NOMOTO.

Democratic Party of Japan (DPJ): 1-11-1, Nagata-cho, Chiyoda-ku, Tokyo 100-0014; tel. (3) 3595-9988; fax (3) 3595-9961; e-mail dpjenews@dpj.or.jp; internet www.dpj.or.jp; f. 1998; est. by the integration into the original DPJ (f. 1996) of the Democratic Reform League, Minseito and Shinto Yuai; advocates a cabinet formed and controlled by the people; absorbed Party Sakigake in 2001; absorbed Liberal Party in 2003; Pres. YOSHIHIKO NODA; Sec.-Gen. AZUMA KOSHIISHI.

Japanese Communist Party (JCP): 4-26-7, Sendagaya, Shibuya-ku, Tokyo 151-8586; tel. (3) 3403-6111; fax (3) 5474-8358; e-mail info@jcp.or.jp; internet www.jcp.or.jp; f. 1922; 400,000 mems (2007); Chair. of Exec. Cttee KAZUO SHII; Sec.-Gen. TADAYOSHI ICHIDA.

Liberal-Democratic Party (LDP) (Jiyu-Minshuto): 1-11-23, Nagata-cho, Chiyoda-ku, Tokyo 100-8910; tel. (3) 3581-6211; fax (3) 5511-8855; e-mail koho@ldp.jimin.or.jp; internet www.jimin.jp; f. 1955; advocates establishment of a welfare state, promotion of industrial devt, improvement of educational and cultural facilities, and constitutional reform as needed; absorbed New Conservative Party in 2003; 2,369,252 mems (2001); Pres. SADAKAZU TANIGAKI; Sec.-Gen. TADAMORI OSHIMA.

New Komeito: 17, Minami-Motomachi, Shinjuku-ku, Tokyo 160-0012; tel. (3) 3353-0111; fax (3) 3225-0207; internet www.komei.or.jp; f. 1964; est. as Komeito; renamed Komei in 1994 following defection of some mems to the New Frontier Party (Shinshinto, dissolved in 1997); absorbed Reimei Club in 1998; renamed as above in 1998 following merger of Komei and Shinto Heiwa; advocates political moderation, humanism and globalism; 400,000 mems (2003); Pres. NATSUO YAMAGUCHI; Sec.-Gen. YOSHIHISA INOUE.

New Party Daichi (Shinto Daichi): 1-5, Minami, Chuo-ku, Sapporo 060-0061; tel. (11) 251-5351; fax (11) 251-5357; internet www.muneo.gr.jp; f. 2005; regional grouping based in Hokkaido; Leader MUNEO SUZUKI.

New Party Nippon (Shinto Nippon): 1-7-11, Hirakawa-cho, Chiyoda-ku, Tokyo 102-0093; tel. (3) 5213-0333; fax (3) 5213-0888; internet www.love-nippon.com; f. 2005; founding mems included LDP rebels opposed to postal reform proposals of Prime Minister Koizumi; Leader YASUO TANAKA.

New Renaissance Party (Shinto Kaikaku): 2-16-5, Hirakawa-cho, Chiyoda-ku, Tokyo; internet shintokaikaku.jp; f. 2010; conservative grouping; Pres. YOICHI MASUZOE; Sec.-Gen. HIROYUKI ARAI.

New Socialist Party: Miyako Sakura Kosan Bldg, 3/F, 7-9, Nihonbashi Tomizawa-cho, Chuo-ku, Tokyo; tel. (3) 5643-6002; fax (3) 3639-0150; e-mail honbu@sinsyakai.or.jp; internet www.sinsyakai.or.jp; f. 1996; est. by left-wing defectors from SDPJ; opposed to US military bases on Okinawa and introduction in 1996 of new electoral system; seeks to establish an ecological socio-economic system; Chair. KIMIKO KURIHARA; Sec.-Gen. MATSUE YOSHIHIRO.

People's New Party (PNP) (Kokumin Shinto): Kohase Bldg, 3/F, 2-14-7, Hirakawa-cho, Chiyoda-ku, Tokyo 102-0093; tel. (3) 5275-2671; fax (3) 5275-2675; e-mail info@kokumin.or.jp; internet www.kokumin.or.jp; f. 2005; est. by rebels from LDP opposed to postal reform proposals of Prime Minister Koizumi; Leader SHIZUKA KAMEI; Sec.-Gen. SHOZABURO JIMI.

Social Democratic Party of Japan (SDPJ) (Shakai Minshuto): 1-8-1, Nagata-cho, Chiyoda-ku, Tokyo 100-8909; tel. (3) 3580-1171; fax (3) 3580-0691; e-mail kokusai@sdp.or.jp; internet www.sdp.or.jp; f. 1945; est. as Japan Socialist Party (JSP); adopted present name in 1996; seeks the establishment of collective non-aggression and a mutual security system incl. Japan, the USA, the People's Republic of China and the Commonwealth of Independent States; Chair. MIZUHO FUKUSHIMA; Sec.-Gen. YASUMASA SHIGENO.

Sunrise Party of Japan (Tachiagare Nippon): c/o House of Councillors, Tokyo; internet www.tachiagare.jp; f. 2010; est. by fmr mems of LDP; nationalist conservative grouping; Leader TAKEO HIRANUMA.

Your Party (Minna No To): Towa Hanzomon Corp. Bldg, Rm 606, 2-12, Hayabusa-cho, Chiyoda-ku, Tokyo 102-0092; tel. (3) 5216-3710; fax (3) 5216-3711; internet www.your-party.jp; f. 2009; est. by fmr mems of LDP and DPJ; advocates reform of bureaucracy; President YOSHIMI WATANABE; Sec.-Gen. KENJI EDA.

Diplomatic Representation

EMBASSIES IN JAPAN

Afghanistan: 2-2-1, Azabudai, Minato-ku, Tokyo 106-0041; tel. (3) 5574-7611; fax (3) 5574-0195; e-mail info@afghanembassyjp.org; internet www.afghanembassyjp.org; Ambassador MOHAMMAD AMIN FATIMIE.

Albania: Hokkoku Shimbun Bldg, 4/F, 6-4-8, Tsukiji, Chuo-ku, Tokyo 104-0045; tel. (3) 3543-6861; fax (3) 3543-6862; e-mail embassy.tokyo@mfa.gov.al; internet emb-al.jp; Ambassador BUJAR DIDA.

Algeria: 2-10-67, Mita, Meguro-ku, Tokyo 153-0062; tel. (3) 3711-2661; fax (3) 3710-6534; Ambassador SID ALI KETRANDJI.

Angola: 2-10-24, Daizawa, Setagaya-ku, Tokyo 155-0032; tel. (3) 5430-7879; fax (3) 5712-7481; e-mail angolaembassy@angola.or.jp; internet www.angola.or.jp; Chargé d'affaires a.i. MIGUEL BOMBARDA F. COELHO DA CRUZ.

Argentina: 2-14-14, Moto-Azabu, Minato-ku, Tokyo 106-0046; tel. (3) 5420-7101; fax (3) 5420-7109; e-mail ejapo@mb.rosenet.ne.jp; internet www.embargentina.or.jp; Ambassador RAÚL GUILLERMO DEJEAN RODRÍGUEZ.

Australia: 2-1-14, Mita, Minato-ku, Tokyo 108-8361; tel. (3) 5232-4111; fax (3) 5232-4149; internet www.australia.or.jp; Ambassador BRUCE MILLER.

Austria: 1-1-20, Moto-Azabu, Minato-ku, Tokyo 106-0046; tel. (3) 3451-8281; fax (3) 3451-8283; e-mail tokio-ob@bmeia.gv.at; internet www.bmeia.gv.at/tokio; Ambassador Dr JUTTA STEFAN-BASTL.

Azerbaijan: 1-19-15, Higashi-Gaoka, Meguro-ku, Tokyo 152-0021; tel. (3) 5486-4744; fax (3) 5486-7374; e-mail info@azembassy.jp; internet www.azembassy.jp; Chargé d'affaires a.i. ROVSHAN KAZIMOV.

Bahrain: Residence Viscountess 720 & 520, 1-11-36, Akasaka, Minato-ku, Tokyo 107-0052; tel. (3) 3584-8001; e-mail info@bahrain-embassy.or.jp; internet www.bahrain-embassy.or.jp; Ambassador Dr KHALIL HASSAN.

Bangladesh: 4-15-15, Meguro, Meguro-ku, Tokyo 153-0063; tel. (3) 5704-0216; fax (3) 5704-1696; e-mail bdembjp@yahoo.com; internet www.bdembjp.com; Ambassador A. K. M. MAJIBUR RAHMAN BHUIYAN.

Belarus: Shirogane K House, 4-14-12, Shirogane, Minato-ku, Tokyo 108-0072; tel. (3) 3448-1623; fax (3) 3448-1624; e-mail japan@belembassy.org; internet www.japan.belembassy.org; Ambassador SYARHEY RAKHMANAW.

Belgium: 5-4, Niban-cho, Chiyoda-ku, Tokyo 102-0084; tel. (3) 3262-0191; fax (3) 3262-0651; e-mail tokyo@diplobel.fed.be; internet www.diplomatie.be/tokyo; Ambassador LUC LIEBAUT.

Benin: Asahi Bldg, 4/F, 1-2-2, Hirakawa-cho, Chiyoda-ku, Tokyo 102-0093; tel. (3) 3556-2562; fax (3) 3556-2563; e-mail abenintyo@mist.ocn.ne.jp; Ambassador ALLASSANE YASSO.

Bolivia: No. 38 Kowa Bldg, Rm 804, 4-12-24, Nishi-Azabu, Minato-ku, Tokyo 106-0031; tel. (3) 3499-5441; fax (3) 3499-5443; e-mail emboltk1@ad.il24.net; Ambassador LUIS MASAHARU HIGA TOMITA.

Bosnia and Herzegovina: 2–3/F, 5-3-29, Minami-Azabu, Minato-ku, Tokyo 106-0047; tel. (3) 5422-8231; fax (3) 5422-8232; e-mail bih8emb@gol.com; Ambassador PERO MATIC.

Botswana: Kearny Place, 6/F, 4-5-10, Shiba, Minato-ku, Tokyo 108-0014; tel. (3) 5440-5676; fax (3) 5765-7581; e-mail botjap@sepia.ocn.ne.jp; internet www.botswanaembassy.or.jp; Ambassador PULAENTLE KENOSI.

Brazil: 2-11-12, Kita-Aoyama, Minato-ku, Tokyo 107-8633; tel. (3) 3404-5211; fax (3) 3405-5846; e-mail brasemb@brasemb.or.jp; internet www.brasemb.or.jp; Ambassador MARCOS BEZERRA ABBOTT GALVÃO.

Brunei: 6-5-2, Kita-Shinagawa, Shinagawa-ku, Tokyo 141-0001; tel. (3) 3447-7997; fax (3) 3447-9260; e-mail contact@bruemb.jp; internet www.bruemb.jp; Ambassador MUHAMMAD ALIAS BIN SERBINI.

Bulgaria: 5-36-3, Yoyogi, Shibuya-ku, Tokyo 151-0053; tel. (3) 3465-1021; fax (3) 3465-1031; e-mail bulemb@gol.com; internet www.mfa.bg/en/76; Ambassador Dr LUBOMIR TODOROV.

Burkina Faso: Apt 301, Hiroo Glisten Hills, 3-1-17, Hiroo, Shibuya-ku, Tokyo 150-0012; tel. (3) 3400-7919; fax (3) 3400-6945; e-mail faso-amb@khaki.plala.or.jp; internet www.embassy-avenue.jp/burkina; Chargé d'affaires a.i. LAMBERT ALEXANDRE OUEDRAOGO.

Cambodia: 8-6-9, Akasaka, Minato-ku, Tokyo 107-0052; tel. (3) 5412-8521; fax (3) 5412-8526; e-mail camembassyjp@gmail.com; internet www.cambodianembassy.jp; Ambassador HOR MONIRATH.

Cameroon: 3-27-16, Nozawa, Setagaya-ku, Tokyo 154-0003; tel. (3) 5430-4985; fax (3) 5430-6489; e-mail ambacamtokyo@gol.com; Ambassador Dr PIERRE NDZENGUE.

Canada: 7-3-38, Akasaka, Minato-ku, Tokyo 107-8503; tel. (3) 5412-6200; fax (3) 5412-6249; e-mail tokyo-cs@international.gc.ca; internet www.canadainternational.gc.ca/japan-japon; Ambassador JONATHAN FRIED.

Chile: Nihon Seimei Akabanebashi Bldg, 8/F, 3-1-14, Shiba, Minato-ku, Tokyo 105-0014; tel. (3) 3452-7561; fax (3) 3452-4457; e-mail embajada@chile.or.jp; internet chileabroad.gov.cl/japon; Ambassador PATRICIO TORRES.

China, People's Republic: 3-4-33, Moto-Azabu, Minato-ku, Tokyo 106-0046; tel. (3) 3403-3380; fax (3) 3403-3345; e-mail lsb@china-embassy.or.jp; internet www.china-embassy.or.jp; Ambassador CHENG YONGHUA.

Colombia: 3-10-53, Kami Osaki, Shinagawa-ku, Tokyo 141-0021; tel. (3) 3440-6451; fax (3) 3440-6724; e-mail embajada@emcoltokyo.or.jp; internet www.colombiaembassy.org; Ambassador PATRICIA CÁRDENAS.

Congo, Democratic Republic: 1–2/F, 5-8-5, Asakusabashi, Taito-ku, Tokyo 111-0053; tel. (3) 5820-1580; fax (3) 3423-3984; Ambassador MARCEL MULUMBA TSHIDIMBA.

Costa Rica: No. 38 Kowa Bldg, Rm 901, 4-12-24, Nishi-Azabu, Minato-ku, Tokyo 106-0031; tel. (3) 3486-1812; fax (3) 3486-1813; Ambassador ÁLVARO ANTONIO CEDEÑO MOLINARI.

Côte d'Ivoire: 2-19-12, Uehara, Shibuya-ku, Tokyo 151-0064; tel. (3) 5454-1401; fax (3) 5454-1405; e-mail ambacijn@yahoo.fr; internet www.ahibo.com/ambaci-jp; Ambassador LILIANE MARIE LAURE BOA.

Croatia: 3-3-10, Hiroo, Shibuya-ku, Tokyo 150-0012; tel. (3) 5469-3014; fax (3) 5469-3015; e-mail croemb.tokyo@mvpei.hr; internet jp.mfa.hr; Ambassador MIRA MARTINEC.

Cuba: 1-28-4, Higashi-Azabu, Minato-ku, Tokyo 106-0044; tel. (3) 5570-3182; fax (3) 5570-8566; e-mail embajada@ecujapon.jp; internet embacuba.cubaminrex.cu/japon; Ambassador JOSÉ FERNÁNDEZ DE COSSIO.

Czech Republic: 2-16-14, Hiroo, Shibuya-ku, Tokyo 150-0012; tel. (3) 3400-8122; fax (3) 3400-8124; e-mail tokyo@embassy.mzv.cz; internet www.mzv.cz/tokyo; Ambassador KATEŘINA FIALKOVÁ.

Denmark: 29-6, Sarugaku-cho, Shibuya-ku, Tokyo 150-0033; tel. (3) 3496-3001; fax (3) 3496-3440; e-mail tyoamb@um.dk; internet www.ambtokyo.um.dk; Ambassador FRANZ-MICHAEL SKJOLD MELLBIN.

Djibouti: 5-18-10, Shimo Meguro, Meguro-ku, Tokyo 153-0064; tel. (3) 5704-0682; fax (3) 5725-8305; e-mail djibouti@fine.ocn.jp; internet www.djiboutiembassy.jp; Ambassador AHMED ARAITA ALI.

Dominican Republic: No. 38 Kowa Bldg, Rm 904, 4-12-24, Nishi-Azabu, Minato-ku, Tokyo 106-0031; tel. (3) 3499-6020; fax (3) 3499-2627; Ambassador PEDRO VERGÉS.

Ecuador: No. 38 Kowa Bldg, Rm 806, 4-12-24, Nishi-Azabu, Minato-ku, Tokyo 106-0031; tel. (3) 3499-2800; fax (3) 3499-4400; e-mail info@ecuador-embassy.or.jp; internet www.ecuador-embassy.or.jp; Ambassador LEONARDO CARRIÓN EGUIGUREN.

Egypt: 1-5-4, Aobadai, Meguro-ku, Tokyo 153-0042; tel. (3) 3770-8022; fax (3) 3770-8021; e-mail egyptemb@leaf.ocn.ne.jp; internet www.mfa.gov.eg/Tokyo_Emb; Ambassador WALID ABDELNASSER.

El Salvador: No. 38 Kowa Bldg, 8/F, 4-12-24, Nishi-Azabu, Minato-ku, Tokyo 106-0031; tel. (3) 3499-4461; fax (3) 3486-7022; e-mail embesaltokio@gol.com; Chargé d'affaires a.i. MARTHA LIDIA ZELAYANDÍA.

Eritrea: Shirokanedai ST Bldg, Rm 401, 4-7-4, Shirokanedai, Minato-ku, Tokyo, 108-0071; tel. (3) 5791-1815; fax (3) 5791-1816; e-mail info@eritreaembassy-japan.org; internet www.eritreaembassy-japan.org; Ambassador ESTIFANOS AFEWORKI.

Estonia: 2-6-15, Jingu-mae, Shibuya-ku 150-0001; tel. (3) 5412-7281; fax (3) 5412-7282; e-mail embassy.tokyo@mfa.ee; internet www.estemb.or.jp; Ambassador TOIVO TASA.

Ethiopia: Takanawa Kaisei Bldg, 2/F, 3-4-1, Takanawa, Minato-ku, Tokyo 108-0074; tel. (3) 5420-6860; fax (3) 5420-6866; e-mail info@ethiopia-emb.or.jp; internet www.ethiopia-emb.or.jp; Ambassador MARKOS TEKLE RIKE.

Fiji: Noa Bldg, 14/F, 2-3-5, Azabudai, Minato-ku, Tokyo 106-0041; tel. (3) 3587-2038; fax (3) 3587-2563; e-mail info@fijiembassy.jp; internet www.fijiembassy.jp; Ambassador ISIKELI MATAITOGA.

Finland: 3-5-39, Minami-Azabu, Minato-ku, Tokyo 106-8561; tel. (3) 5447-6000; fax (3) 5447-6042; e-mail sanomat.tok@formin.fi; internet www.finland.or.jp; Ambassador JARI GUSTAFSSON.

France: 4-11-44, Minami-Azabu, Minato-ku, Tokyo 106-8514; tel. (3) 5798-6330; fax (3) 5798-6328; e-mail ambafrance.tokyo@diplomatie.fr; internet www.ambafrance-jp.org; Ambassador PHILIPPE FAURE.

Gabon: 1-34-11, Higashi-Gaoka, Meguro-ku, Tokyo 152-0021; tel. (3) 5430-9171; fax (3) 5430-9175; e-mail gabonembassytokyo@gmail.com; internet www.gabonembassyjapan.org; Ambassador FRANÇOIS PENDJET BOMBILA.

Georgia: Residence Viscountess 220, 1-11-36, Akasaka, Minato-ku, Tokyo 107-0052; tel. (3) 5575-6091; fax (3) 5575-9133; e-mail tokio

.emb@mfa.gov.ge; internet japan.mfa.gov.ge; Ambassador Revaz Beshidze.

Germany: 4-5-10, Minami-Azabu, Minato-ku, Tokyo 106-0047; tel. (3) 5791-7700; fax (3) 5791-7773; e-mail info@tokyo.diplo.de; internet www.tokyo.diplo.de; Ambassador Dr Volker Stanzel.

Ghana: 1-5-21, Nishi-Azabu, Minato-ku, Tokyo 106-0031; tel. (3) 5410-8631; fax (3) 5410-8635; e-mail mission@ghanaembassy.or.jp; internet www.ghanaembassy.or.jp; Ambassador William Brandful.

Greece: 3-16-30, Nishi-Azabu, Minato-ku, Tokyo 106-0031; tel. (3) 3403-0871; fax (3) 3402-4642; e-mail gremb.tok@mfa.gr; Ambassador Nikolaos Tsamados.

Guatemala: No. 38 Kowa Bldg, Rm 905, 4-12-24, Nishi-Azabu, Minato-ku, Tokyo 106-0031; tel. (3) 3400-1830; fax (3) 3400-1820; e-mail embguate@vega.ocn.ne.jp; internet www.embassy-avenue.jp/guatemala; Ambassador Byron Rene Escobedo Menéndez.

Guinea: 12-9, Hachiyama-cho, Shibuya-ku, Tokyo 150-0035; tel. (3) 3770-4640; fax (3) 3770-4643; e-mail ambagui-tokyo@gol.com; Ambassador Mohamed Lamine Toure.

Haiti: No. 38 Kowa Bldg, Rm 906, 4-12-24, Nishi-Azabu, Minato-ku, Tokyo 106-0031; tel. (3) 3486-7096; fax (3) 3486-7070; e-mail amb.japon@diplomatie.ht; Chargé d'affaires a.i. Judith Exavier.

Holy See: Apostolic Nunciature, 9-2, Sanban-cho, Chiyoda-ku, Tokyo 102-0075; tel. (3) 3263-6851; fax (3) 3263-6060; Apostolic Nuncio Most Rev. Joseph Chennoth (Titular Archbishop of Milevum).

Honduras: No. 38 Kowa Bldg, Rm 802, 4-12-24, Nishi-Azabu, Minato-ku, Tokyo 106-0031; tel. (3) 3409-1150; fax (3) 3409-0305; e-mail honduras@interlink.or.jp; Ambassador Marlene Villela.

Hungary: 2-17-14, Mita, Minato-ku, Tokyo 108-0073; tel. (3) 3798-8801; fax (3) 3798-8812; e-mail mission.tio@kum.hu; internet www.mfa.gov.hu/kulkepviselet/JP/HU; Chargé d'affaires a.i. János Albert.

Iceland: 4-18-26, Takanawa, Minato-ku, Tokyo 108-0074; tel. (3) 3447-1944; fax (3) 3447-1945; e-mail icemb.tokyo@utn.stjr.is; internet www.iceland.org/jp; Ambassador Stefan Larus Stefansson.

India: 2-2-11, Kudan-Minami, Chiyoda-ku, Tokyo 102-0074; tel. (3) 3262-2391; fax (3) 3234-4866; e-mail embassy@indembjp.org; internet www.embassyofindiajapan.org; Ambassador Alok Prasad.

Indonesia: 5-2-9, Higashi-Gotanda, Shinagawa-ku, Tokyo 141-0022; tel. (3) 3441-4201; fax (3) 3447-1697; e-mail info@indonesianembassy.jp; internet www2.indonesianembassy.jp; Ambassador Muhammad Lutfi.

Iran: 3-13-9, Minami-Azabu, Minato-ku, Tokyo 106-0047; tel. (3) 3446-8011; fax (3) 3446-9002; e-mail info@iranembassyjp.org; internet www.iranembassyjp.org; Ambassador Seyyed Abbas Araghchi.

Iraq: 2-16-11, Takanawa, Minato-ku, Tokyo 108-0074; tel. (3) 5449-3231; fax (3) 5449-7718; e-mail embassy@iraqi-japan.com; internet www.iraqi-japan.com; Ambassador Luqman Abd al-Raheem al-Faili.

Ireland: Ireland House, 2-10-7, Kojimachi, Chiyoda-ku, Tokyo 102-0083; tel. (3) 3263-0695; fax (3) 3265-2275; e-mail tokyoembassy@dfa.ie; internet www.irishembassy.jp; Ambassador John Neary.

Israel: 3, Niban-cho, Chiyoda-ku, Tokyo 102-0084; tel. (3) 3264-0911; fax (3) 3264-0791; e-mail consular@tokyo.mfa.gov.il; internet tokyo.mfa.gov.il; Ambassador Nissim Ben-Shitrit.

Italy: 2-5-4, Mita, Minato-ku, Tokyo 108-8302; tel. (3) 3453-5291; fax (3) 3456-2319; e-mail ambasciata.tokyo@esteri.it; internet www.ambtokyo.esteri.it/ambasciata_tokyo; Ambassador Vincenzo Petrone.

Jamaica: Toranomon Yatsuka Bldg, 2/F, 1-1-11, Atago, Minato-ku, Tokyo 105-0002; tel. (3) 3435-1861; fax (3) 3435-1864; e-mail mail@jamaicaemb.jp; internet www.jamaicaemb.jp; Ambassador Claudia Cecile Barnes.

Jordan: 39-8, Kamiyama-cho, Shibuya-ku, Tokyo 100-0014; tel. (3) 5478-7177; fax (3) 5478-0032; e-mail jor-emb@bird.ocn.ne.jp; internet www18.ocn.ne.jp/~jor-emb; Ambassador Demiye Haddad.

Kazakhstan: 5-9-8, Himonya, Meguro-ku, Tokyo 152-0003; tel. (3) 3791-5273; fax (3) 3791-5279; e-mail japan_tokyo@mfa.kz; internet www.embkazjp.org; Ambassador Akylbek Kamaldinov.

Kenya: 3-24-3, Yakumo, Meguro-ku, Tokyo 152-0023; tel. (3) 3723-4006; fax (3) 3723-4488; e-mail general@kenyarep-jp.com; internet www.kenyarep-jp.com; Ambassador Benson H. O. Ogutu.

Korea, Republic: 1-2-5, Minami-Azabu, Minato-ku, Tokyo 106-0047; tel. (3) 3452-7611; fax (3) 5232-6911; e-mail information_jp@mofat.go.kr; internet jpn-tokyo.mofat.go.kr; Ambassador Shin Kak-Soo.

Kosovo: 3-13-7, Nishi-Shinbashi, Minato-ku, Tokyo 105-0003; tel. (3) 6809-2577; fax (3) 6809-2579; e-mail embassy.japan@ks-gov.net; Ambassador Sami Ukelli.

Kuwait: 4-13-12, Mita, Minato-ku, Tokyo 108-0073; tel. (3) 3455-0361; fax (3) 3456-6290; e-mail consular@kuwait-embassy.or.jp; internet kuwait-embassy.or.jp; Ambassador Sheikh Abdul Rahman al-Otaibi.

Kyrgyzstan: 5-6-16, Shimomeguro, Meguro-ku, Tokyo 153-0064; tel. (3) 3719-0828; fax (3) 3719-0868; e-mail chancery@kyrgyzemb.jp; Ambassador Moldogaziev Rysbek Turganbaevich.

Laos: 3-3-22, Nishi-Azabu, Minato-ku, Tokyo 106-0031; tel. (3) 5411-2291; fax (3) 5411-2293; Ambassador Sithong Chitnhothinh.

Latvia: 37-11, Kamiyama-cho, Shibuya-ku, Tokyo 150-0047; tel. (3) 3467-6888; fax (3) 3467-6897; e-mail embassy.japan@mfa.gov.lv; Ambassador Pēteris Vaivars.

Lebanon: Residence Viscountess 410, 1-11-36, Akasaka, Minato-ku, Tokyo 107-0052; tel. (3) 5114-9950; fax (3) 5114-9952; e-mail ambaliba@cropos.ocp.ne.jp; Ambassador Mohammed el-Harake.

Lesotho: U & M Akasaka Bldg, 3/F, 7-5-47, Akasaka, Minato-ku, Tokyo 107-0052; tel. (3) 3584-7455; fax (3) 3584-7456; e-mail bochabela@lesothotokyo.org; internet www.lesothotokyo.org; Ambassador Richard Ramoeletsi.

Liberia: 4-11-7, Hukazawa, Setagaya-ku, Tokyo 158-0081; tel. (3) 3703-6926; fax (3) 3726-5712; Ambassador Youngor Sevelee Telewoda.

Libya: 10-14, Daikanyama-cho, Shibuya-ku, Tokyo 150-0034; tel. (3) 3477-0701; fax (3) 3464-0420; Chargé d'affaires a.i. Giuma S. G. Oun.

Lithuania: 3-7-18, Moto-Azabu, Minato-ku, Tokyo 106-0046; tel. (3) 3408-5091; fax (3) 3408-5092; e-mail amb.jp@urm.lt; internet jp.mfa.lt; Chargé d'affaires Alberta Algirdas Dambrauskas.

Luxembourg: Luxembourg House, 1/F, 8–9, Yonban-cho, Chiyoda-ku, 102-0081; tel. (3) 3265-9621; fax (3) 3265-9624; e-mail infotokyo.amb@mae.etat.lu; internet tokyo.mae.lu/jp; Ambassador Paul Steinmetz.

Madagascar: 2-3-23, Moto-Azabu, Minato-ku, Tokyo 106-0046; tel. (3) 3446-7252; fax (3) 3446-7078; e-mail ambtyo@r5.dion.ne.jp; internet www.madagascar-embassy.jp; Chargé d'affaires a.i. Jeannot Feno.

Malawi: Takanawa-Kaisei Bldg, 7/F, 3-4-1, Takanawa, Minato-ku, Tokyo 108-0074; tel. (3) 3449-3010; fax (3) 3449-3220; e-mail malawi@luck.ocn.ne.jp; internet www.malawiembassy.org; Ambassador Rueben Ngwenya.

Malaysia: 20-16, Nanpeidai-cho, Shibuya-ku, Tokyo 150-0036; tel. (3) 3476-3840; fax (3) 3476-4971; e-mail maltokyo@kln.gov.my; internet www.kln.gov.my/web/jpn_tokyo; Ambassador Dato' Sharuddin bin Mohammed Som.

Maldives: Iikura MINT Bldg, 8/F, 1-9-10, Azabudai, Minato-ku, Tokyo 106-0041; tel. (3) 6234-4315; fax (3) 6234-4316; e-mail info@maldivesembassy.jp; internet www.maldivesembassy.jp; Ambassador Ahmed Khaleel.

Mali: 3-12-9, Kami-Osaki, Shinagawa-ku, Tokyo 141-0021; tel. (3) 5447-6881; fax (3) 5447-6882; e-mail info@ambamali-jp.org; internet www.ambamali-jp.org; Chargé d'affaires a.i. Taoule Keita.

Marshall Islands: Meiji Park Heights, 1/F, Rm 101, 9-9, Minami-Motomachi, Shinjuku-ku, Tokyo 106-0012; tel. (3) 5379-1701; fax (3) 5379-1810; e-mail alfred@rmiembassyjp.org; Ambassador Tom D. Kijiner.

Mauritania: 5-17-5, Kita-Shinagawa, Shinagawa-ku, Tokyo 141-0001; tel. (3) 3449-3810; fax (3) 3449-3822; e-mail ambarim@seagreen.ocn.ne.jp; internet www.amba-mauritania.jp; Ambassador Yahya Ngam.

Mexico: 2-15-1, Nagata-cho, Chiyoda-ku, Tokyo 100-0014; tel. (3) 3581-1131; fax (3) 3581-4058; e-mail embajadamexicojapon@sre.gob.mx; internet www.sre.gob.mx/japon; Ambassador Miguel Ruiz-Cabañas Izquierdo.

Micronesia, Federated States: Reinanzaka Bldg, 2/F, 1-14-2, Akasaka, Minato-ku, Tokyo 107-0052; tel. (3) 3585-5456; fax (3) 3585-5348; e-mail fsmemb@fsmemb.or.jp; Ambassador John Fritz.

Mongolia: Pine Crest Mansion, 21-4, Kamiyama-cho, Shibuya-ku, Tokyo 150-0047; tel. (3) 3469-2088; fax (3) 3469-2216; e-mail embmong@gol.com; Ambassador Sodovjamtsyn Khürelbaatar.

Morocco: 5-4-30, Minami-Aoyama, Minato-ku, Tokyo 107-0062; tel. (3) 5485-7171; fax (3) 5485-7173; e-mail sifamato@circus.ocn.ne.jp; internet www.morocco-emba.jp; Ambassador Dr Samir Arrour.

Mozambique: Shiba Amerex Bldg, 6/F, 3-12-17 Mita, Minato-ku, Tokyo 108-0073; tel. (3) 5419-0973; fax (3) 5442-0556; e-mail mozambiq@tkk.att.ne.jp; internet www.embamoc.jp; Ambassador Belmiro José Malate.

Myanmar: 4-8-26, Kita-Shinagawa, Shinagawa-ku, Tokyo 140-0001; tel. (3) 3441-9291; fax (3) 3447-7394; e-mail contact@myanmar-embassy-tokyo.net; internet www.myanmar-embassy-tokyo.net; Ambassador Khin Maung Ting.

Nepal: 7-14-9, Todoroki, Setagaya-ku, Tokyo 158-0082; tel. (3) 3705-5558; fax (3) 3705-8264; e-mail nepembjp@big.or.jp; internet www nepal-embassy.org; Ambassador GANESH YONZAN TAMANG.

Netherlands: 3-6-3, Shiba Koen, Minato-ku, Tokyo 105-0011; tel. (3) 5776-5400; fax (3) 5776-5535; e-mail tok@minbuza.nl; internet japan.nlambassade.org; Ambassador PHILIP DE HEER.

New Zealand: 20-40, Kamiyama-cho, Shibuya-ku, Tokyo 150-0047; tel. (3) 3467-2271; fax (3) 3467-2278; e-mail nzemb.tky@mfat.govt .nz; internet www.nzembassy.com/japan; Ambassador IAN KENNEDY.

Nicaragua: No. 38 Kowa Bldg, Rm 903, 4-12-24, Nishi-Azabu, Minato-ku, Tokyo 106-0031; tel. (3) 3499-0400; fax (3) 3710-2028; e-mail nicjapan@gol.com; Ambassador SAÚL ARANA CASTELLÓN.

Nigeria: 3-6-1 Toranomon, Minato-ku, Tokyo 105-0001; tel. (3) 5425-8011; fax (3) 5425-8016; e-mail info@nigeriaembassy.jp; internet www.nigeriaembassy.jp; Ambassador GODWIN NSUDE AGBO.

Norway: 5-12-2, Minami-Azabu, Minato-ku, Tokyo 106-0047; tel. (3) 3440-2611; fax (3) 3440-2620; e-mail emb.tokyo@mfa.no; internet www.norway.or.jp; Ambassador ARNE WALTHER.

Oman: 4-2-17, Hiroo, Shibuya-ku, Tokyo 150-0012; tel. (3) 5468-1088; e-mail info@omanembassy.jp; internet omanembassy.jp; Ambassador KHALID BIN HASHIL BIN MOHAMMED AL-MUSLAHI.

Pakistan: 4-6-17, Minami-Azabu, Minato-ku, Tokyo 106-0047; tel. (3) 5421-7741; fax (3) 5421-3610; e-mail info@pakistanembassyjapan .com; internet www.pakistanembassyjapan.com; Ambassador NOOR MUHAMMAD JADMANI.

Palau: Rm 201, 1-1, Katamachi, Shinjuku-ku, Tokyo 160-0001; tel. (3) 3354-5500; Ambassador Dr MINORU UEKI.

Panama: No. 38 Kowa Bldg, Rm 902, 4-12-24, Nishi-Azabu, Minato-ku, Tokyo 106-0031; tel. (3) 3499-3741; fax (3) 5485-3548; e-mail panaemb@gol.com; internet www.embassyofpanamainjapan.org; Ambassador JORGE DEMETRIO KOSMAS SIFAKI.

Papua New Guinea: Mita Kokusai Bldg, 3/F, Rm 313, 1-4-28, Mita, Minato-ku, Tokyo 108-0073; tel. (3) 3454-7801; fax (3) 3454-7275; e-mail png-tyo@nifty.ne.jp; Ambassador GABRIEL DUSAVA.

Paraguay: Ichibancho TG Bldg 2, 7/F, 2-2, Ichiban-cho, Chiyoda-ku, Tokyo 102-0082; tel. (3) 3265-5271; fax (3) 3265-5273; e-mail embajada-consulado@embapar.jp; internet www.embapar.jp; Ambassador NAOYUKI TOYOTOSHI.

Peru: 4-4-27, Higashi, Shibuya-ku, Tokyo 150-0011; tel. (3) 3406-4243; fax (3) 3409-7589; e-mail embperutokyo@embperujapan.org; internet www.embajadadelperuenjapon.org; Ambassador JUAN CARLOS CAPUÑAY CHÁVEZ.

Philippines: 5-15-5, Roppongi, Minato-ku, Tokyo 106-8537; tel. (3) 5562-1600; fax (3) 5562-1603; e-mail info@philembassy.net; internet tokyo.philembassy.net; Ambassador MANUEL LOPEZ.

Poland: 2-13-5, Mita, Meguro-ku, Tokyo 153-0062; tel. (3) 5794-7020; fax (3) 5794-7024; e-mail tokio.amb.sekretariat@msz.gov.pl; internet www.tokio.polemb.net; Ambassador JADWIGA MARIA RODOWICZ.

Portugal: Kamiura-Kojimachi Bldg, 5/F, 3-10-3, Kojimachi, Chiyoda-ku, Tokyo 102-0083; tel. (3) 5212-7322; fax (3) 5226-0616; e-mail portugal@embportjp.org; internet www .embaixadadeportugal.jp; Ambassador JOSÉ FREITAS FERRAZ.

Qatar: 2-3-28, Moto-Azabu, Minato-ku, Tokyo 106-0046; tel. (3) 5475-0611; fax (3) 5475-0617; e-mail tokyo@mofa.gov.qa; Ambassador YOUSUF MOHAMED BILAL.

Romania: 3-16-19, Nishi-Azabu, Minato-ku, Tokyo 106-0031; tel. (3) 3479-0311; fax (3) 3479-0312; e-mail office@ambrom.jp; internet tokyo.mae.ro; Chargé d'affaires a.i. PETRE STOIAN.

Russia: 2-1-1, Azabudai, Minato-ku, Tokyo 106-0041; tel. (3) 3583-4224; fax (3) 3505-0593; e-mail embassy@u01.gate01.com; internet www.russia-emb.jp; Ambassador EVGENY V. AFANASIEV.

Rwanda: Annex Fukazawa, 1-17-17, Fukazawa, Setagaya-ku, Tokyo 158-0081; tel. (3) 5752-4255; fax (3) 3703-0342; internet www.rwandaembassy-japan.org; Ambassador CHARLES MURIGANDE.

Samoa: Seiko Bldg, 3/F, 2-7-4, Irifune, Chuo-ku, Tokyo 104-0042; Ambassador Leiataua Tuitolova'a Dr KILIFOTI ETEUATI.

San Marino: 3-5-1, Moto-Azabu, Minato-ku, Tokyo 106-0046; tel. (3) 5414-7745; fax (3) 3405-6789; e-mail sanmarinoemb@tiscali.it; Ambassador MANLIO CADELO.

Saudi Arabia: 1-8-4, Roppongi, Minato-ku, Tokyo 106-0032; tel. (3) 3589-5241; fax (3) 3589-5200; e-mail info@saudiembassy.or.jp; internet www.saudiembassy.or.jp; Ambassador ABDULAZIZ TURKISTANI.

Senegal: 1-3-4, Aobadai, Meguro-ku, Tokyo 153-0042; tel. (3) 3464-8451; fax (3) 3464-8452; e-mail senegal@senegal.jp; Ambassador BOUNA SÉMOU DIOUF.

Serbia: 4-7-24, Kita-Shinagawa, Shinagawa-ku, Tokyo 140-0001; tel. (3) 3447-3571; fax (3) 3447-3573; e-mail embassy@ serbianembassy.jp; internet www.serbianembassy.jp; Ambassador BOJANA ADAMOVIĆ-DRAGOVIĆ.

Singapore: 5-12-3, Roppongi, Minato-ku, Tokyo 106-0032; tel. (3) 3586-9111; fax (3) 3582-1085; e-mail singemb_tyo@sgmfa.gov.sg; internet www.mfa.gov.sg/tokyo; Ambassador CHIN SIAT YOON (designate).

Slovakia: 2-11-33, Moto-Azabu, Minato-ku, Tokyo 106-0046; tel. (3) 3451-2200; fax (3) 3451-2244; e-mail emb.tokyo@mzv.sk; internet www.tokyo.mfa.sk; Ambassador DRAHOMÍR ŠTOS.

Slovenia: 7-14-12, Minami-Aoyama, Minato-ku, Tokyo 107-0062; tel. (3) 5468-6275; fax (3) 5468-1182; e-mail vto@gov.si; internet tokyo.embassy.si; Ambassador HELENA DRNOVŠEK ZORKO.

South Africa: Oriken Hirakawa Bldg, 3–4/F, 2-1-1, Hirakawa-cho, Chiyoda-ku, Tokyo 102-0093; tel. (3) 3265-3366; fax (3) 3265-3573; e-mail cronjet@dfa.gov.za; internet www.sajapan.org; Ambassador MOHAU N. PHEKO.

Spain: 1-3-29, Roppongi, Minato-ku, Tokyo 106-0032; tel. (3) 3583-8531; fax (3) 3582-8627; e-mail emb.tokio@maec.es; internet www .maec.es/subwebs/Embajadas/Tokio/es; Ambassador MIGUEL ÁNGEL NAVARRO PORTERA.

Sri Lanka: 2-1-54, Takanawa, Minato-ku, Tokyo 108-0074; tel. (3) 3440-6911; fax (3) 3440-6914; e-mail tokyojp@lankaembassy.jp; internet www.lankaembassy.jp; Ambassador WASANTHA KARANNAGODA.

Sudan: 4-7-1, Yakumo, Meguro-ku, Tokyo 152-0023; tel. (3) 5729-6170; fax (3) 5729-6171; e-mail info@sudanembassy.jp; internet www .sudanembassy.jp; Ambassador ABDON TERKOC MATUET.

Sweden: 1-10-3-100, Roppongi, Minato-ku, Tokyo 106-0032; tel. (3) 5562-5050; fax (3) 5562-9095; e-mail ambassaden.tokyo@foreign .ministry.se; internet www.sweden.or.jp; Ambassador STEFAN NOREÉN.

Switzerland: 5-9-12, Minami-Azabu, Minato-ku, Tokyo 106-8589; tel. (3) 5449-8400; fax (3) 3473-6090; e-mail tok.vertretung@eda .admin.ch; internet www.eda.admin.ch/tokyo; Ambassador URS BUCHER.

Syria: Homat Jade, 6-19-45, Akasaka, Minato-ku, Tokyo 107-0052; tel. (3) 3586-8977; fax (3) 3586-8979; internet syrian-embassy.jp; Ambassador MOHAMED GHASSAN AL-HABASH.

Tajikistan: NK Bldg, Nishi Azabu, 1-4-43, Minato-ku, Tokyo; tel. (3) 6804-3661; fax (3) 5410-3677; e-mail tajembjapan@yahoo.com; internet www.tajikistan.jp; Ambassador BOBOZODA GULOMJON JURA.

Tanzania: 4-21-9, Kami Yoga, Setagaya-ku, Tokyo 158-0098; tel. (3) 3425-4531; fax (3) 3425-7844; e-mail tzrepjp@tanzaniaembassy.or .jp; internet www.tanzaniaembassy.or.jp; Ambassador SALOME T. SIJAONA.

Thailand: 3-14-6, Kami Osaki, Shinagawa-ku, Tokyo 141-0021; tel. (3) 3447-2247; fax (3) 3442-6750; e-mail infosect@thaiembassy.jp; internet www.thaiembassy.jp; Ambassador VIRASAKDI FUTRAKUL.

Timor-Leste: Rokuban-cho House, 1/F, 3-4, Rokuban-cho, Chiyoda-ku, Tokyo 102-0085; tel. (3) 3238-0210; Ambassador ISILIO COELHO DA SILVA.

Tunisia: 3-6-6, Kudan-Minami, Chiyoda-ku, Tokyo 102-0074; tel. (3) 3511-6622; fax (3) 3511-6699; e-mail mailbox@tunisia.or.jp; internet www.tunisia.or.jp; Ambassador ILYES EL KOSRI.

Turkey: 2-33-6, Jingumae, Shibuya-ku, Tokyo 150-0001; tel. (3) 6439-5700; fax (3) 3470-5136; e-mail embassy.tokyo@mfa.gov.tr; internet tokyo.be.mfa.gov.tr; Chargé d'affaires a.i. SABRI TUNÇ ANGILI.

Uganda: 9-23, Hachiyama-cho, Shibuya-ku, Tokyo 150-0035; tel. (3) 3462-7107; fax (3) 3462-7108; e-mail ugabassy@hpo.net; internet www.uganda-embassy.jp; Ambassador WASSWA BIRIGGWA.

Ukraine: 3-15-31, Nishi-Azabu, Minato-ku, Tokyo 106-0031; tel. (3) 5474-9770; fax (3) 5474-9772; e-mail ukrcn@rose.ocn.ne.jp; internet www.mfa.gov.ua/japan; Ambassador MYKOLA KULINICH.

United Arab Emirates: 9-10, Nanpeidai-cho, Shibuya-ku, Tokyo 150-0036; tel. (3) 5489-0804; fax (3) 5489-0813; Ambassador SAEED ALI AL-NOWAIS.

United Kingdom: 1, Ichiban-cho, Chiyoda-ku, Tokyo 102-8381; tel. (3) 5211-1100; fax (3) 5275-3164; e-mail consular.tokyo@fco.gov.uk; internet ukinjapan.fco.gov.uk; Ambassador DAVID WARREN.

USA: 1-10-5, Akasaka, Minato-ku, Tokyo 107-8420; tel. (3) 3224-5000; fax (3) 3505-1862; internet tokyo.usembassy.gov; Ambassador JOHN V. ROOS.

Uruguay: No. 38 Kowa Bldg, Rm 908, 4-12-24, Nishi-Azabu, Minato-ku, Tokyo 106-0031; tel. (3) 3486-1888; fax (3) 3486-9872; e-mail urujap@luck.ocn.ne.jp; Ambassador ANA MARÍA ESTÉVEZ MERCADER.

Uzbekistan: 5-11-8, Shimo-Meguro, Meguro-ku, Tokyo 153-0064; tel. (3) 3760-5625; fax (3) 3760-5950; Ambassador KARAMATOV KHAMIDULLA SADULLAEVICH.

Venezuela: No. 38 Kowa Bldg, Rm 703, 4-12-24, Nishi-Azabu, Minato-ku, Tokyo 106-0031; tel. (3) 3409-1501; fax (3) 3409-1505; e-mail embavene@interlink.or.jp; Ambassador SEIKO LUIS ISHIKAWA KOBAYASHI.

Viet Nam: 50-11, Moto-Yoyogi-cho, Shibuya-ku, Tokyo 151-0062; tel. (3) 3466-3313; fax (3) 3466-3391; e-mail vnembasy@blue.ocn.ne.jp; internet www.vietnamembassy-japan.org; Ambassador DOAN XUAN HUNG.

Yemen: No. 38 Kowa Bldg, Rm 807, 4-12-24, Nishi-Azabu, Minato-ku, Tokyo 106-0031; tel. (3) 3499-7151; fax (3) 3499-4577; e-mail info@yemen.jp; internet www.yemen.jp; Chargé d'affaires a.i. TAREQ ABDULLATIF ABDULLA MOTAHAR.

Zambia: 1-10-2, Ebara, Shinagawa-ku, Tokyo 142-0063; tel. (3) 3491-0121; fax (3) 3491-0123; e-mail infoemb@zambia.or.jp; internet www.zambia.or.jp; Ambassador MBIKUSITA WAMUNDILA LEWANIKA.

Zimbabwe: 5-9-10, Shiroganedai, Minato-ku, Tokyo 108-0071; tel. (3) 3280-0331; fax (3) 3280-0466; e-mail zimtokyo@chive.ocn.ne.jp; Ambassador STUART H. COMBERBACH.

Judicial System

The basic principles of the legal system are set forth in the Constitution, which lays down that judicial power is vested in the Supreme Court and in such inferior courts as are established by law, and enunciates the principle that no organ or agency of the Executive shall be given final judicial power. Judges are to be independent in the exercise of their conscience, and may not be removed except by public impeachment, unless judicially declared mentally or physically incompetent to perform official duties. The justices of the Supreme Court are appointed by the Cabinet, the sole exception being the Chief Justice, who is appointed by the Emperor after designation by the Cabinet.

The Court Organization Law, which came into force on 3 May 1947, decreed the constitution of the Supreme Court and the establishment of four types of lower court—High, District, Family (established 1 January 1949) and Summary Courts. The system of trial by jury, suspended since 1943, was reinstated in 2009. Jurors are selected at random from the electoral register.

SUPREME COURT

This court is the highest legal authority in the land, and consists of a Chief Justice and 14 associate justices. It has jurisdiction over Jokoku (Jokoku appeals) and Kokoku (Kokoku appeals), prescribed in codes of procedure. It conducts its hearings and renders decisions through a Grand Bench or three Petty Benches. Both are collegiate bodies, the former consisting of all justices of the Court, and the latter of five justices. A Supreme Court Rule prescribes which cases are to be handled by the respective Benches. It is, however, laid down by law that the Petty Bench cannot make decisions as to the constitutionality of a statute, ordinance, regulation, or disposition, or as to cases in which an opinion concerning the interpretation and application of the Constitution, or of any laws or ordinances, is at variance with a previous decision of the Supreme Court.

Chief Justice: HIRONOBU TAKESAKI, 4-2, Hayabusa-cho, Chiyoda-ku, Tokyo 102-8651; tel. (3) 3264-8111; fax (3) 3221-8975; internet www.courts.go.jp.

Secretary-General: TOSHIMITSU YAMASAKI.

LOWER COURTS

High Court

A High Court conducts its hearings and renders decisions through a collegiate body, consisting of three judges, though for cases of insurrection the number of judges must be five. The Court has jurisdiction over the following matters:

Koso appeals from judgments in the first instance rendered by District Courts, from judgments rendered by Family Courts, and from judgments concerning criminal cases rendered by Summary Courts.

Kokoku appeals against rulings and orders rendered by District Courts and Family Courts, and against rulings and orders concerning criminal cases rendered by Summary Courts, except those coming within the jurisdiction of the Supreme Court.

Jokoku appeals from judgments in the second instance rendered by District Courts and from judgments rendered by Summary Courts, except those concerning criminal cases.

Actions in the first instance relating to cases of insurrection.

Presidents: TOKUJI IZUMI (Tokyo), YOSHIO OKADA (Osaka), REISUKE SHIMADA (Nagoya), TOYOZO UEDA (Hiroshima), TOSHIMARO KOJO (Fukuoka), FUMIYA SATO (Sendai), KAZUO KATO (Sapporo), FUMIO ARAI (Takamatsu).

District Court

A District Court is generally the court of first instance, except for matters specifically coming under the exclusive original jurisdiction of other types of court. It also has appellate jurisdiction over appeals in civil cases lodged against judgments of summary courts. The Cour conducts hearings and renders decisions through a single judge o for certain types of cases, through a collegiate body of three judges Japan has 50 district courts, with 203 branches.

Family Court

A Family Court handles cases through a single judge in case o rendering judgments or decisions. However, in accordance with th provisions of other statutes, it conducts its hearings and render decisions through a collegiate body of three judges. A conciliation i effected through a collegiate body consisting of a judge and two o more members of the conciliation committee selected from among citizens.

It has jurisdiction over the following matters:

Judgment and conciliation with regard to cases relating to family as provided for by the Law for Adjudgment of Domestic Relations.

Judgment with regard to the matters of protection of juveniles as provided for by the Juvenile Law.

Actions in the first instance relating to adult criminal cases of violation of the Labour Standard Law, the Law for Prohibiting Liquors to Minors, or other laws especially enacted for protection of juveniles.

Summary Court

A Summary Court handles cases through a single judge, and has jurisdiction in the first instance over the following matters:

Claims where the value of the subject matter does not exceed 1.4m. yen.

Criminal cases of offences liable to a fine or lesser penalty, offences liable to a fine as an optional penalty, and certain specified offences such as theft and embezzlement.

A Summary Court cannot impose imprisonment or a graver penalty. When it deems proper the imposition of a sentence of imprisonment or a graver penalty, it must transfer such cases to a District Court, but it can impose imprisonment with labour not exceeding three years for certain specified offences.

Religion

The traditional religions of Japan are Shintoism and Buddhism. Neither is exclusive, and many Japanese subscribe at least nominally to both.

SHINTOISM

Shintoism is an indigenous religious system embracing the worship of ancestors and of nature. It is divided into two cults: national Shintoism, which is represented by the shrines; and sectarian Shintoism, which developed during the second half of the 19th century. In 1868 Shinto was designated a national religion and all Shinto shrines acquired the privileged status of a national institution. Complete freedom of religion was introduced in 1947.

BUDDHISM

World Buddhist Fellowship: Hozenji Buddhist Temple, 3-24-2, Akabane-dai, Kita-ku, Tokyo; Head Rev. FUJI NAKAYAMA.

CHRISTIANITY

National Christian Council in Japan: Japan Christian Center, 2-3-18-24, Nishi-Waseda, Shinjuku-ku, Tokyo 169-0051; tel. (3) 3203-0372; fax (3) 3204-9495; e-mail general@ncc-j.org; internet ncc-j.org; f. 1923; 14 mems (churches and other bodies), 18 assoc. mems; Chair. KOUICHI KOBASHI; Gen. Sec. SHOUKO AMINAKA.

The Anglican Communion

Anglican Church in Japan (Nippon Sei Ko Kai): 65, Yarai-cho, Shinjuku-ku, Tokyo 162-0805; tel. (3) 5228-3171; fax (3) 5228-3175; e-mail general-sec.po@nskk.org; internet www.nskk.org; f. 1887; 11 dioceses; Primate of Japan Most Rev. NATHANIEL MAKOTO UEMATSU (Bishop of Hokkaido); Gen. Sec. JOHN MAKITO AIZAWA; 54,898 mems (2007).

The Orthodox Church

Japanese Orthodox Church (Nippon Haristosu Seikyoukai): Holy Resurrection Cathedral (Nicolai-Do), 4-1-3, Kanda Surugadai, Chiyoda-ku, Tokyo 101; tel. (3) 3291-1885; fax (3) 3291-1886; e-mail info@orthodoxjapan.jp; internet www.orthodoxjapan.jp; three dioceses; Archbishop of Tokyo, Primate and Metropolitan of All Japan Most Rev. DANIEL NUSHIRO; 24,821 mems.

Protestant Church

United Church of Christ in Japan (Nihon Kirisuto Kyodan): 2-3-18, Nishi-Shinjuku, Shinjuku-ku, Tokyo 169-0051; tel. (3) 3202-

0541; fax (3) 3207-3918; e-mail ecumeni-c@uccj.org; internet www .uccj.or.jp; f. 1941; union of 34 Congregational, Methodist, Presbyterian, Reformed and other Protestant denominations; Moderator Rev. HIDEO ISHIBASHI; Gen. Sec. Rev. AOBORA TAEMAE; 196,044 mems (2007).

The Roman Catholic Church

Japan comprises three archdioceses and 13 dioceses. There were an estimated 554,447 adherents at 31 December 2007.

Catholic Bishops' Conference of Japan (Chuo Kyogikai): 2-10-10, Shiomi, Koto-ku, Tokyo 135-8585; tel. (3) 5632-4411; fax (3) 5632-4453; e-mail info@cbcj.catholic.jp; internet www.cbcj.catholic.jp; Pres. Most Rev. LEO JUN IKENAGA (Bishop of Osaka).

Archbishop of Nagasaki: Most Rev. JOSEPH MITSUAKI TAKAMI, Catholic Centre, 10-34, Uenomachi, Nagasaki-shi 852-8113; tel. (95) 846-4246; fax (95) 848-8310; internet www.nagasaki.catholic.jp.

Archbishop of Osaka: Most Rev. LEO JUN IKENAGA, Archbishop's House, 2-24-22, Tamatsukuri, Chuo-ku, Osaka 540-0004; tel. (6) 6941-9700; fax (6) 6946-1345; internet www.osaka.catholic.jp.

Archbishop of Tokyo: Most Rev. PETER TAKEO OKADA, Archbishop's House, 3-16-15, Sekiguchi, Bunkyo-ku, Tokyo 112-0014; tel. (3) 3943-2301; fax (3) 3944-8511; e-mail diocese@tokyo.catholic .jp; internet www.tokyo.catholic.jp.

Other Christian Churches

Japan Baptist Convention: 1-2-4, Minami-Urawa, Minami-ku, Saitama-shi, Saitama 336-0017; tel. (48) 883-1091; fax (48) 883-1092; internet www.bapren.jp; f. 1947; Gen. Sec. Rev. MAKOTO KATO; 33,734 mems (March 2003).

Japan Baptist Union: 2-3-18, Nishi-Waseda, Shinjuku-ku, Tokyo 169-0051; tel. (3) 3202-0053; fax (3) 3202-0054; e-mail gs@jbu.or.jp; internet www.jbu.or.jp; f. 1958; Moderator YOSHIHISA SAWANO; Gen. Sec. MAKOTO TANNO; 4,600 mems.

Japan Evangelical Lutheran Church: 1-1, Sadohara-cho, Ichigaya-shi, Shinjuku-ku, Tokyo 162-0842; tel. (3) 3260-8631; fax (3) 3260-8641; e-mail contact@jelc.or.jp; internet www.jelc.or.jp; f. 1893; Pres. Rev. SUMIYUKI WATANABE; Exec. Dir Rev. YASUHIRO TATENO; 21,990 mems (2010).

Korean Christian Church in Japan: Japan Christian Center, Rm 52, 2-3-18, Nishi-Waseda, Shinjuku-ku, Tokyo 169-0051; tel. (3) 3202-5398; fax (3) 3202-4977; e-mail info@kccj.jp; internet kccj.jp; f. 1909; Moderator CHOI YOUNG-SHIN; Gen. Sec. HONG SONG-WAN; 6,319 mems (2010).

West Japan Evangelical Lutheran Church: 2-2-11 Nakajima-dori, Chuo-Ku, Kobe 651-0052; tel. (78) 242-0887; fax (78) 242-4166; e-mail office@wjelc.or.jp; internet www.wjelc.or.jp; 3,887 mems (2010).

Among other denominations active in Japan are the Christian Catholic Church, the German Evangelical Church and the Tokyo Union Church.

OTHER COMMUNITIES

Bahá'í Faith

The National Spiritual Assembly of the Bahá'ís of Japan: 7-2-13, Shinjuku, Shinjuku-ku, Tokyo 160-0022; tel. (3) 3209-7521; fax (3) 3204-0773; e-mail info@bahaijp.org; internet www.bahaijp.org; f. 1955; Mem. DARYOUSH YAZDANI.

Judaism

Jewish Community of Japan: 3-8-8, Hiroo, Shibuya-ku, Tokyo 150-0012; tel. (3) 3400-2559; fax (3) 3400-1827; e-mail office@jccjapan .or.jp; internet www.jccjapan.or.jp; f. 1953; Pres. JEROME ROSENBERG; Leader Rabbi ANTONIO DI GESÙ.

Islam

Islam has been active in Japan since the late 19th century. There is a small Muslim community, maintaining several mosques, including those at Kobe, Nagoya, Chiba and Isesaki, the Arabic Islamic Institute and the Islamic Center in Tokyo. The construction of Tokyo Central Mosque was completed in 2000.

Islamic Center, Japan: 1-16-11, Ohara, Setagaya-ku, Tokyo 156-0041; tel. (3) 3460-6169; fax (3) 3460-6105; e-mail info@islamcenter .or.jp; internet www.islamcenter.or.jp; f. 1965; Chair. Dr SALIH AL-SAMARRAI.

The New Religions

Many new religions (Shinko Shukyo) emerged in Japan after 1945, based on a fusion of Shinto, Buddhist, Daoist, Confucian and Christian beliefs. Among the most important of these are Tenrikyo, Omotokyo, Soka Gakkai, Rissho Kosei-kai, Kofuku-no-Kagaku and Agonshu.

Kofuku-no-Kagaku (Institute for Research in Human Happiness): 1-6-7, Shinagawa-ku, Tokyo 142-0041; tel. (3) 6384-3777; fax (3) 6384-3778; e-mail info@irhpress.co.jp; internet www.irhpress.co.jp; f. 1986; believes its founder to be reincarnation of Buddha; 8.25m. mems; Leader RYUHO OKAWA.

Rissho Kosei-kai: 5/F, Fumon Hall, 2-6-1, Wada, Suginami-ku, Tokyo 166-8537; tel. and fax (3) 5341-1124; e-mail info@rk-world.org; internet www.kosei-kai.or.jp; internet www.rk-world.org; f. 1938; Buddhist lay org. based on the teaching of the Lotus Sutra, active inter-faith co-operation towards peace; Pres. Rev. Dr NICHIKO NIWANO; 2.05m. mem. households with 245 brs world-wide (2009).

Soka Gakkai: 32, Shinano-machi, Shinjuku-ku, Tokyo 160-8583; tel. (3) 5360-9830; fax (3) 5360-9885; e-mail contact@sgi.org; internet www.sgi.org; f. 1930; society of lay practitioners of the Buddhism of Nichiren; membership of 8.27m. households (2005); group promotes activities in education, international cultural exchange and consensus-building towards peace, based on the humanist world view of Buddhism; Hon. Pres. DAISAKU IKEDA; Pres. MINORU HARADA.

The Press

In 2009 there were 121 daily newspapers in Japan. Their average circulation was among the highest in the world. The large number of weekly news journals is a notable feature of the Japanese press.

NATIONAL DAILIES

Asahi Shimbun: 5-3-2, Tsukiji, Chuo-ku, Tokyo 104-8011; tel. (3) 3545-0131; fax (3) 3545-0358; internet www.asahi.com; f. 1879; also publ. by Osaka, Seibu and Nagoya head offices and Hokkaido branch office; Pres. KOTARO AKIYAMA; Editor-in-Chief YOICHI FUNABASHI; circ. morning 8.1m., evening 3.7m.

Mainichi Shimbun: 1-1-1, Hitotsubashi, Chiyoda-ku, Tokyo 100-8051; tel. (3) 3212-0321; fax (3) 3211-3598; internet www.mainichi.co .jp; f. 1882; also publ. by Osaka, Seibu and Chubu head offices, and Hokkaido branch office; Pres. MASATO KITAMURA; Editor-in-Chief TOSHIFUMI KAWANO; circ. morning 4.0m., evening 2.0m.

Nihon Keizai Shimbun: 1-3-7, Otemachi, Chiyoda-ku, Tokyo 1008066; tel. (3) 3270-0251; fax (3) 5255-2661; e-mail ecntct@ nikkei.co.jp; internet www.nikkei.co.jp; f. 1876; also publ. by Osaka head office and Sapporo, Nagoya and Seibu branch offices; Pres. TSUNEO KITA; Editor-in-Chief YUICHI TAKAHASHI; circ. morning 3.0m., evening 1.6m.

Sankei Shimbun: 1-7-2, Otemachi, Chiyoda-ku, Tokyo 100-8077; tel. (3) 3231-7111; internet sankei.jp; f. 1933; also publ. by Osaka head office; Pres. and CEO NAGAYOSHI SUMIDA; Editor-in-Chief MASAFUMI KATAYAMA; circ. morning 2.0m., evening 636,649.

Yomiuri Shimbun: 1-7-1, Otemachi, Chiyoda-ku, Tokyo 100-8055; tel. (3) 3242-1111; e-mail webmaster@yomiuri.co.jp; internet www .yomiuri.co.jp; f. 1874; also publ. by Osaka, Seibu and Chubu head offices, and Hokkaido and Hokuriku branch offices; Chair. and Editor-in-Chief TSUNEO WATANABE; circ. morning 10.0m., evening 4.0m.

PRINCIPAL LOCAL DAILIES

Tokyo

Daily Sports: 2-14-8, Kiba, Koto-ku, Tokyo 135-8566; tel. (3) 5434-1752; e-mail dsmaster@daily.co.jp; internet www.daily.co.jp; f. 1948; morning; Pres. TAKASHI KAORI; circ. 400,254.

The Daily Yomiuri: 1-7-1, Otemachi, Chiyoda-ku, Tokyo 100-8055; tel. (3) 3242-1111; internet www.yomiuri.co.jp; f. 1955; morning; English; Man. Editor SHIGEYUKI OKADA; circ. 33,743 (2009).

Dempa Shimbun: 1-11-15, Higashi-Gotanda, Shinagawa-ku, Tokyo 141-8790; tel. (3) 3445-6111; fax (3) 3444-7515; e-mail multim@dempa.co.jp; internet www.dempa.co.jp; f. 1950; morning; Pres. TETSUO HIRAYAMA; Man. Editor TOSHIO KASUYA; circ. 298,000.

The Japan Times: 4-5-4, Shibaura, Minato-ku, Tokyo 108-8071; tel. (3) 3453-5312; internet www.japantimes.co.jp; f. 1897; morning; English; Chair. and Pres. TOSHIAKI OGASAWARA; Dir and Editor-in-Chief YUTAKA MATAEBARA; circ. 61,929.

The Mainichi Daily News: 1-1-1, Hitotsubashi, Chiyoda-ku, Tokyo 100-8051; tel. (3) 3212-0321; internet mdn.mainichi.jp; f. 1922; morning; English; also publ. from Osaka; Man. Editor TETSUO TOKIZAWA; combined circ. 49,200.

Naigai Times: 1-3-2, Tsukishima, Chuo-ku, Tokyo 104-0052; tel. (3) 6204-4121; e-mail koukoku@naigai-times.net; internet www.npn.co .jp; f. 1949; evening; Pres. MITSUGU ONDA; Vice-Pres. and Editor-in-Chief KENICHIRO KURIHARA; circ. 410,000.

Nihon Kaiji Shimbun (Japan Maritime Daily): Mori Bldg, 5-19-2, Shimbashi, Minato-ku, Tokyo 105-0004; tel. (3) 3436-3221; fax (3) 3436-3247; e-mail webmaster@jmd.co.jp; internet www.jmd.co.jp; f. 1942; morning; Man. Editor OSAMI ENDO; circ. 55,000.

Nihon Nogyo Shimbun (Agriculture): 2-3, Akihabara, Taito-ku, Tokyo 110-8722; tel. (3) 5295-7411; fax (3) 3253-0980; internet www.agrinews.co.jp; f. 1928; morning; Man. Editor YASUNORI INOUE; circ. 423,840.

Nihon Sen-i Shimbun (Textile and Fashion): 1-6-5, Nihonbashi Kobuna-cho, Chuo-ku, Tokyo 103-0012; tel. (3) 5649-8711; fax (3) 5469-8717; internet www.nissenmedia.com; f. 1943; morning; Man. Editor KIYOSHIGE SEIRYU; circ. 116,000.

Nikkan Kogyo Shimbun (Industrial Daily News): 14-1, Nihonbashi Koami-cho, Chuo-ku, Tokyo 103-8548; tel. (3) 5644-7000; fax (3) 5644-7100; internet www.nikkan.co.jp; f. 1915; morning; Man. Editor HIDEO WATANABE; circ. 533,145.

Nikkan Sports News: 3-5-10, Tsukiji, Chuo-ku, Tokyo 104-8055; tel. (3) 5550-8888; fax (3) 5550-8901; e-mail webmast@nikkansports.co.jp; internet www.nikkansports.com; f. 1946; morning; Man. Editor MOTOHIRO MIURA; circ. 993,240.

Sankei Sports: 1-7-2, Otemachi, Chiyoda-ku, Tokyo 100-8077; tel. (3) 3231-7111; internet www.sanspo.com; f. 1963; morning; Man. Editor YUKIO INADA; circ. 809,245.

Shipping and Trade News: Tokyo News Service Ltd, 1-1-2, Uchisaiwai-cho, Chiyoda-ku, Tokyo 100-0011; tel. (3) 5510-8961; fax (3) 3504-6039; e-mail editorial.a@tokyonews.co.jp; internet www.tokyonews.co.jp/marine; f. 1949; English; Man. Editor TAKASHI TAKEDA; circ. 15,000.

Sports Hochi: 4-6-49, Kohnan, Minato-ku, Tokyo 108-8485; tel. (3) 5479-1111; e-mail webmaster@hochi.yomiuri.co.jp; internet hochi.yomiuri.co.jp; f. 1872; fmrly *Hochi Shimbun*; morning; Pres. HIROTO KISHI; Man. Editor TATSUE AOKI; circ. 755,670.

Sports Nippon: 2-1-30, Etchujima, Koto-ku, Tokyo 135-8735; tel. (3) 3820-0700; e-mail customer@sponichi.co.jp; internet www.sponichi.co.jp; f. 1949; morning; Man. Editor SUSUMU KOMURO; Pres. MORITO YUKIO; circ. 929,421.

Suisan Keizai Shimbun (Fisheries): 6-8-19, Roppongi, Minato-ku, Tokyo 106-0032; tel. (3) 3404-6531; fax (3) 3404-0863; internet www.suikei.co.jp; f. 1948; morning; Man. Editor KOSHI TORINOUMI; circ. 61,000.

Tokyo Chunichi Sports: 1-4, Uchisaiwai-cho, Chiyoda-ku, Tokyo 100-8505; tel. (3) 6910-2211; internet www.chunichi.co.jp/chuspo; f. 1956; evening; Pres. OOSHIMA TORAO; circ. 330,431.

Tokyo Shimbun: 1-4, Uchisaiwai-cho, Chiyoda-ku, Tokyo 100-8505; tel. (3) 6910-2211; internet www.chunichi.co.jp; f. 1942; Pres. OOSHIMA TORAO; circ. morning 655,970, evening 354,191.

Tokyo Sports: 2-1-30, Etchujima, Koto-ku, Tokyo 135-8721; tel. (3) 3820-0801; internet www.tokyo-sports.co.jp; f. 1959; evening; Man. Editor YOSHINOBU EBATA; circ. 1,321,250.

Yukan Fuji: 1-7-2, Otemachi, Chiyoda-ku, Tokyo 100-8077; tel. (3) 3231-7111; fax (3) 3246-0377; e-mail desk@zakzak.co.jp; internet www.zakzak.co.jp; f. 1969; evening; Man. Editor MASAMI KATO; circ. 268,984.

Osaka District

Daily Sports: 1-18-11, Edobori, Nishi-ku, Osaka 550-0002; tel. (6) 6443-0421; f. 1948; morning; Man. Editor TOSHIAKI MITANI; circ. 562,715.

The Mainichi Daily News: 3-4-5, Umeda, Kita-ku, Osaka 530-8251; tel. (6) 6345-1551; internet www.mainichi.co.jp; f. 1922; morning; English; Man. Editor KATSUYA FUKUNAGA.

Nikkan Sports: 3-14-24, Hanshin, Fukushima Ward, Osaka; tel. (6) 7632-7700; internet www.nikkansports.com; f. 1950; morning; Man. Editor KATSUO FURUKAWA; circ. 513,498.

Sankei Kansai: 2-1-57, Minato-cho, Naniwa-ku, Osaka 556-8660; tel. (6) 6633-1221; fax (6) 6633-9738; e-mail osaka-soukyoku@sankei.co.jp; internet www.sankei-kansai.com; f. 1922; evening; fmrly Osaka Shimbun, name changed as above 2004; Pres. SUMIDA NAGAYOSHI; circ. 88,887.

Sankei Sports: 2-1-57, Minato-cho, Naniwa-ku, Osaka 556-8660; tel. (6) 6343-1221; fax (6) 6633-9738; f. 1955; morning; Pres. SUMIDA NAGAYOSHI; circ. 552,519.

Sports Nippon: 3-4-5, Umeda, Kita-ku, Osaka 530-8278; tel. (6) 6346-8500; f. 1949; morning; Man. Editor HIDETOSHI ISHIHARA; circ. 477,300.

Kanto District

Chiba Nippo (Chiba Daily News): 4-14-10, Chuo, Chuo-ku, Chiba 260-0013; tel. (43) 222-9211; internet www.chibanippo.co.jp; f. 1957; morning; Man. Editor NOBORU HAYASHI; circ. 190,187.

Ibaraki Shimbun: 2-15, Kitami-cho, Mito 310-8686; tel. (29) 248-5500; fax (29) 248-7745; e-mail i-net@ibaraki-np.co.jp; internet www.ibaraki-np.co.jp; f. 1891; morning; Pres. TAKASHI KOTABE; circ. 117,240.

Jomo Shimbun: 1-50-21, Furuichi-machi, Maebashi 371-8666; tel. (27) 254-9911; internet www.raijin.com; f. 1887; morning; Man. Dir KOUZOU TAKAHASHI; circ. 311,534.

Joyo Shimbun: 2-7-6, Manabe, Tsuchiura 300-0051; tel. (298) 21-1780; e-mail info-02@joyo-net.com; internet www.joyo-net.com; f. 1948; morning; Pres. MINEO IWANAMI; Man. Editor AKIRA SAITO; circ. 88,700.

Kanagawa Shimbun: 2-23, Ota-cho, Kanagawa, Naka-ku, Yokohama 231-8445; tel. (45) 227-1111; e-mail soumu@kanagawa-np.co.jp; internet www.kanagawa-shimbun.jp; f. 1890; morning; Pres. KENJI HOTTA; circ. 238,203.

Saitama Shimbun: 2-282-3, Yoshino, Kita-ku, Saitama; tel. (48) 795-9930; fax (48) 653-9020; e-mail desk@saitama-np.co.jp; internet www.saitama-np.co.jp; f. 1944; morning; Man. Editor EIICHI ISHINO; circ. 162,071.

Shimotsuke Shimbun: 1-8-11, Showa, Utsunomiya 320-8686; tel. (286) 25-1111; internet www.shimotsuke.co.jp; f. 1884; morning; Man. Dir and Editor-in-Chief EISUKE TODA; circ. 306,072.

Tohoku District
(North-east Honshu)

Akita Sakigake Shimpo: 1-1, San-no-rinkai-machi, Akita 010-8601; tel. (18) 888-1800; fax (18) 866-9285; internet www.sakigake.co.jp; f. 1874; Man. Editor SHIGEAKI MAEKAWA; circ. 263,246.

Daily Tohoku: 1-3-12, Shiroshita, Hachinohe 031-8601; tel. (178) 44-5111; internet www.daily-tohoku.co.jp; f. 1945; morning; Man. Editor TOKOJU YOSHIDA; circ. 104,935.

Fukushima Mimpo: 13-17, Ota-machi, Fukushima 960-8602; tel. (24) 531-4111; fax (24) 531-4022; internet www.minpo.jp; f. 1892; Pres. and Editor-in-Chief TSUTOMU HANADA; circ. morning 308,353, evening 9,489.

Fukushima Minyu: 4-29, Yanagi-machi, Fukushima 960-8648; tel. (24) 523-1191; fax (24) 523-2605; internet www.minyu-net.com; f. 1895; Man. Editor KENJI KANNO; circ. morning 201,414, evening 6,066.

Hokuu Shimpo: 3-2, Nishi-Dori-machi, Noshiro 016-0891; tel. (185) 54-3150; internet www.hokuu.co.jp; f. 1895; morning; Chair. KOICHI YAMAKI; circ. 31,490.

Ishinomaki Shimbun: 2-1-28, Sumiyoshi-machi, Ishinomaki 986; tel. (225) 22-3201; f. 1946; evening; Man. Editor MASATOSHI SATO; circ. 13,050.

Iwate Nichi-nichi Shimbun: 60, Minami-Shinmachi, Ichinoseki 021-8686; tel. (191) 26-5114; e-mail iwanichi@iwanichi.co.jp; internet www.iwanichi.co.jp; f. 1923; morning; Pres. TAKESHI YAMAGISHI; Man. Editor SEIICHI WATANABE; circ. 59,850.

Iwate Nippo: 3-7, Uchimaru, Morioka 020-8622; tel. (19) 653-4111; fax (19) 626-1882; e-mail center@iwate-np.co.jp; internet www.iwate-np.co.jp; f. 1876; Man. Editor TOKUO MIYAZAWA; circ. morning 230,073, evening 229,815.

Kahoku Shimpo: 1-2-28, Itsutsubashi, Aoba-ku, Sendai 980-8660; tel. (22) 211-1127; fax (22) 211-1448; e-mail houdou@po.kahoku.co.jp; internet www.kahoku.co.jp; f. 1897; Exec. Dir and Man. Editor MASAHIKO ICHIRIKI; circ. morning 503,318, evening 133,855.

Mutsu Shimpo: 2-1, Shimo-shirogane-cho, Hirosaki 036-8356; tel. (172) 34-3111; fax (172) 32-3138; e-mail box@mutusinpou.co.jp; internet www.mutusinpou.co.jp; f. 1946; morning; Man. Editor YUJI SATO; circ. 53,500.

Shonai Nippo: 8-29, Baba-cho, Tsuruoka 997-8691; tel. (235) 22-1480; fax (235) 22-1427; internet www.shonai-nippo.co.jp; f. 1946; morning; Pres. and CEO MASAYUKI HASHIMOTO; circ. 19,100.

To-o Nippo: 3-1-89, Dainitonya-machi, Aomori 030-0180; tel. (17) 739-1111; internet www.toonippo.co.jp; f. 1888; Exec. Dir YOSHIO WAJIMA; Man. Editor TAKAO SHIOKOSHI; circ. morning 262,532, evening 258,590.

Yamagata Shimbun: 2-5-12, Hatagomachi, Yamagata 990-8550; tel. (23) 622-5271; e-mail info@yamagata-np.jp; internet yamagata-np.jp; f. 1876; Man. Editor TOSHINOBU SHIONO; circ. morning 213,057, evening 213,008.

Yonezawa Shimbun: 3-3-7, Monto-cho, Yonezawa 992-0039; tel. (238) 22-4411; fax (238) 24-5554; e-mail info@www.yoneshin.com; internet www.yoneshin.com; f. 1879; morning; Man. Dir and Editor-in-Chief MAKOTO SATO; circ. 13,750.

Chubu District
(Central Honshu)

Chubu Keizai Shimbun: 4-4-38, Meieki, Nakamura-ku, Nagoya 450-8561; tel. (52) 561-5215; fax (52) 561-5229; internet www.chukei-news.co.jp; f. 1946; morning; Man. Editor NORIMITSU INAGAKI; circ. 91,000.

Chukyo Sports: Chunichi Kosoku Offset Insatsu Bldg, 4-3-9, Kinjo, Naka-ku, Nagoya 460-0847; tel. (52) 982-1911; f. 1968; evening; Head Officer OSAMU SUETSUGU; circ. 289,430.

Chunichi Shimbun: 1-6-1, San-no-maru, Naka-ku, Nagoya 460-8511; tel. (52) 201-8811; internet www.chunichi.co.jp; f. 1942; Pres. OOSHIMA TARAO; circ. morning 2.7m., evening 748,635.

Chunichi Sports: 1-6-1, San-no-maru, Naka-ku, Nagoya 460-8511; tel. (52) 201-8811; internet www.chunichi.co.jp/chuspo; f. 1954; evening; Pres. OOSHIMA TARAO; circ. 631,429.

Gifu Shimbun: 10, Imako-machi, Gifu 500-8577; tel. (58) 264-1151; internet www.gifu-np.co.jp; f. 1881; Exec. Dir and Man. Editor TADASHI TANAKA; circ. morning 170,176, evening 31,775.

Higashi-Aichi Shimbun: 62, Torinawate, Shinsakae-machi, Toyohashi 441-8666; tel. (532) 32-3111; fax (532) 32-3737; e-mail hensyu@higashiaichi.co.jp; internet www.higashiaichi.co.jp; f. 1957; morning; Man. Editor YOSHIYUKI SUZUKI; circ. 52,300.

Nagano Nippo: 3-1323-1, Takashima, Suwa 392-8611; tel. (266) 52-2000; fax (266) 58-8895; e-mail info@nagano-np.co.jp; internet www.nagano-np.co.jp; f. 1901; morning; Man. Editor ETSUO KOIZUMI; circ. 73,000.

Nagoya Times: 1-3-10, Marunouchi, Naka-ku, Nagoya 460-8530; tel. (52) 231-1331; internet www.meitai.net; f. 1946; evening; Man. Editor NAOKI KITO; circ. 146,137.

Shinano Mainichi Shimbun: 657, Minami-Agatamachi, Nagano 380-8546; tel. (26) 236-3000; fax (26) 236-3197; internet www.shinmai.co.jp; f. 1873; Man. Editor SEIICHI INOMATA; circ. morning 469,801, evening 55,625.

Shizuoka Shimbun: 3-1-1, Toro, Suruga-ku, Shizuoka 422-8670; tel. (54) 284-8900; fax (54) 284-8994; e-mail webmaster@shizuokaonline.com; internet www.shizuokaonline.com; f. 1941; Man. Editor HISAO ISHIHARA; circ. morning 730,746, evening 730,782.

Yamanashi Nichi-Nichi Shimbun: 2-6-10, Kita-Guchi, Kofu 400-8515; tel. (552) 31-3000; internet www.sannichi.co.jp; f. 1872; morning; Man. Editor HIROSHI FUJIHARA; circ. 210,373.

Hokuriku District
(North Coastal Honshu)

Fukui Shimbun: 56, Owada-cho, Fukui 910-8552; tel. (776) 57-5111; internet www.fukuishimbun.co.jp; f. 1899; morning; Man. Editor KAZUO UCHIDA; circ. 201,121 (2009).

Hokkoku Shimbun: 2-5-1, Korinbo, Kanazawa 920-8588; tel. (762) 63-2111; e-mail admin@hokkoku.co.jp; internet www.hokkoku.co.jp; f. 1893; Man. Editor WATARU INAGAKI; circ. morning 335,826, evening 93,021.

Hokuriku Chunichi Shimbun: 2-12-30, Korinbo, Kanazawa 920-8573; tel. (76) 261-3111; internet www.chunichi.co.jp/hokuriku; f. 1960; Pres. OOSHIMA TORAO; circ. morning 107,652, evening 11,373.

Kita-Nippon Shimbun: 2-14, Azumi-cho, Toyama 930-8680; tel. (764) 45-3300; internet www.kitanippon.co.jp; f. 1884; Dir and Man. Editor HITOSHI ITAKURA; circ. morning 246,001.

Niigata Nippo: 772-2, Nishi-ku, Niigata 950-1189; tel. (25) 378-9111; internet www.niigata-nippo.co.jp; f. 1942; Dir and Man. Editor MICHIEI TAKAHASHI; circ. morning 499,545, evening 63,790.

Toyama Shimbun: 5-1, Ote-machi, Toyama 930-8520; tel. (766) 23-2131; e-mail koho@hokkoku.co.jp; internet www.toyama.hokkoku.co.jp; f. 1923; morning; Man. Editor SACHIO MIYAMOTO; circ. 42,988.

Kinki District
(West Central Honshu)

Daily Sports: 1-5-7, Higashi-Kawasaki-cho, Chuo-ku, Kobe 650-8571; tel. (78) 362-7100; e-mail dsmaster@daily.co.jp; internet www.daily.co.jp; morning; Man. Editor TAKASHI HIRAI; circ. 584,448.

Ise Shimbun: 34-6, Honmachi, Tsu 514-0831; tel. (59) 224-0003; fax (59) 226-3554; internet www.isenp.co.jp; f. 1878; morning; Man. Editor FUJIO YAMAMOTO; circ. 108,630.

Kii Minpo: 100, Akizu-cho, Tanabe 646-8660; tel. (739) 22-7171; fax (739) 26-0077; internet www.agara.co.jp; f. 1911; evening; Man. Editor KAZUSADA TANIGAMI; circ. 37,904 (2009).

Kobe Shimbun: 1-5-7, Higashi-Kawasaki-cho, Chuo-ku, Kobe 650-8571; tel. (78) 362-7100; internet www.kobe-np.co.jp; f. 1898; Pres. TAKASHI KAORI; circ. morning 563,717, evening 239,604 (2009).

Kyoto Shimbun: 239, Shoshoi-machi, Ebisugawa-agaru, Karasuma-dori, Nakagyo-ku, Kyoto 604-8577; tel. (75) 241-5430; e-mail kpdesk@mb.kyoto-np.co.jp; internet www.kyoto-np.co.jp; f. 1879; Man. Editor KIYOSHI; circ. morning 504,304, evening 319,015.

Nara Shimbun: 2-4, Sanjo-machi, Nara 630-8686; tel. (742) 32-1000; fax (742) 32-2770; e-mail info@nara-np.co.jp; internet www.nara-np.co.jp; f. 1946; morning; Dir and Man. Editor HISAMI SAKAMOTO; circ. 126,324.

Chugoku District
(Western Honshu)

Chugoku Shimbun: 7-1, Dobashi-cho, Naka-ku, Hiroshima 730-8677; tel. (82) 236-2111; fax (82) 236-2321; e-mail denshi@hiroshima-cdas.or.jp; internet www.chugoku-np.co.jp; f. 1892; Man. Editor NOBUYUKI AOKI; circ. morning 723,981, evening 75,248.

Nihonkai Shimbun: 2-137, Tomiyasu, Tottori 680-8688; tel. (857) 21-2888; fax (857) 21-2891; e-mail info@nnn.co.jp; internet www.nnn.co.jp; f. 1976; morning; Man. Editor KOTARO TAMURA; circ. 171,120.

Okayama Nichi-Nichi Shimbun: 3-30, Hon-cho, Kita-ku, Okayama 700-8678; tel. (86) 231-4211; fax (86) 231-4282; internet www.okanichi.co.jp; f. 1946; evening; Man. Dir and Man. Editor TAKASHI ANDO; circ. 20,000.

San-In Chuo Shimpo: 383, Tono-machi, Matsue 690-8668; tel. (852) 32-3440; e-mail sanin@sanin-chuo.co.jp; internet www.sanin-chuo.co.jp; f. 1882; morning; Man. Editor MASAMI MOCHIDA; circ. 15,310,018 (Jan. 2011).

Sanyo Shimbun: 2-1-1, Yanagi-machi, Okayama 700-8634; tel. (86) 803-8008; internet www.sanyo.oni.co.jp; f. 1879; Man. Dir and Man. Editor MATSUDA YUKI; circ. morning 461,876, evening 71,911.

Ube Jiho: 3-6-1, Kotobuki-cho, Ube 755-8557; tel. (836) 31-1511; internet www.ubenippo.co.jp; f. 1912; evening; Exec. Dir and Man. Editor KAZUYA WAKI; circ. 52,300.

Yamaguchi Shimbun: 1-1-7, Higashi-Yamato-cho, Shimonoseki 750-8506; tel. (83) 266-3211; fax (83) 266-5344; e-mail info@minato-yamaguchi.co.jp; internet www.minato-yamaguchi.co.jp; f. 1946; morning; Pres. MASAAKI INOUE; circ. 89,060.

Shikoku Island

Ehime Shimbun: 1-12-1, Otemachi, Matsuyama 790-8511; tel. (89) 935-2111; fax (89) 941-8108; e-mail webmaster@ehime-np.co.jp; internet www.ehime-np.co.jp; f. 1876; morning; Man. Editor RYOJI YANO; circ. 49,810,029 (Jan. 2011).

Kochi Shimbun: 3-2-15, Honmachi, Kochi 780-8572; tel. (88) 822-2111; e-mail master@kochinews.co.jp; internet www.kochinews.co.jp; f. 1904; Dir and Man. Editor KENGO FUJITO; circ. morning 129,749, evening 207,059 (2010).

Shikoku Shimbun: 15-1, Nakano-cho, Takamatsu 760-8572; tel. (87) 833-1111; internet www.shikoku-np.co.jp; f. 1889; morning; Man. Editor JUNJI YAMASHITA; circ. 204,999.

Tokushima Shimbun: 2-5-2, Naka-Tokushima-cho, Tokushima 770-8572; tel. (88) 655-7373; fax (86) 654-0165; e-mail jouhou@topics.or.jp; internet www.topics.or.jp; f. 1944; Dir and Man. Editor HIROSHI MATSUMURA; circ. morning 251,741, evening 52,593 (2010).

Hokkaido Island

Doshin Sports: 3-6, Nishi-Odori, Chuo-ku, Sapporo 060-8711; tel. (11) 210-5573; fax (11) 210-5575; e-mail koe@hokkaido-np.co.jp; internet www.hokkaido-np.co.jp; f. 1982; morning; Pres. MURATA MASATOSHI; circ. 150,988 (Feb. 2011).

Hokkaido Shimbun: 3-6, Nishi-Odori, Chuo-ku, Sapporo 060-8711; tel. (11) 210-5573; fax (11) 210-5575; internet www.hokkaido-np.co.jp; f. 1942; Man. Editor RYOZO ODAGIRI; circ. morning 1.2m., evening 701,934.

Kushiro Shimbun: 7-3, Kurogane-cho, Kushiro 085-8650; tel. (154) 22-1111; fax (154) 22-0050; internet www.news-kushiro.jp; f. 1946; morning; Man. Editor YUTAKA ITO; circ. 62,600.

Muroran Mimpo: 1-3-16, Hon-cho, Muroran 051-8550; tel. (143) 22-5121; fax (143) 24-1337; e-mail honsya@muromin.mnw.jp; internet www.muromin.mnw.jp; f. 1945; Man. Editor TSUTOMO KUDO; circ. morning 60,300, evening 52,630.

Nikkan Sports: 3-1-30, Higashi, Kita-3 jo, Chuo-ku, Sapporo 060-8521; tel. (11) 242-3900; fax (11) 231-5470; internet www.nikkansports.com; f. 1962; morning; Pres. YOSHITAKA SUZUKI; circ. 138,966 (Feb. 2011).

Tokachi Mainichi Shimbun: 8-2, Minami, Higashi-Ichijo, Obihiro 080-8688; tel. (155) 22-2121; fax (155) 25-2700; e-mail info@kachimai.co.jp; internet www.tokachi.co.jp; f. 1919; evening; Editor-in-Chief MITSUSHIGE HAYASHI; circ. 88,220 (Oct. 2010).

Tomakomai Mimpo: 3-1-8, Wakakusa-cho, Tomakomai 053-8611; tel. (144) 32-5311; fax (144) 32-6386; e-mail henshu@tomamin.co.jp; internet www.tomamin.co.jp; f. 1950; evening; Dir and Man. Editor RYUICHI KUDO; circ. 60,676.

Yomiuri Shimbun: 4-1, Nishi, Kita-4 jo, Chuo-ku, Sapporo 060-8656; tel. (11) 242-3111; internet www.yomiuri.co.jp; f. 1959; Head Officer TSUTOMO IKEDA; circ. morning 261,747, evening 81,283.

Kyushu Island

Kumamoto Nichi-Nichi Shimbun: 172, Yoyasu-machi, Kumamoto 860-8506; tel. (96) 361-3082; internet www.kumanichi.com;

f. 1942; Man. Editor MAKOTO MATSUSHITA; circ. morning 385,784, evening 99,049.

Kyushu Sports: Fukuoka Tenjin Center Bldg, 2-14-8, Tenjin-cho, Chuo-ku, Fukuoka 810-0001; tel. (92) 781-7401; f. 1966; morning; Head Officer HIROSHI MITOMI; circ. 449,850.

Minami-Nippon Shimbun: 1-9-33, Yojirou, Kagoshima 890-8603; tel. (99) 813-5001; fax (99) 813-5016; e-mail webmaster@373news.com; internet www.373news.com; f. 1881; Man. Editor YASUSHI MOMIKI; circ. morning 405,795.

Miyazaki Nichi-Nichi Shimbun: 1-1-33, Takachihodori, Miyazaki 880-8570; tel. (985) 26-9315; fax (985) 20-7254; e-mail info@the-miyanichi.co.jp; internet www.the-miyanichi.co.jp; f. 1940; morning; Man. Editor MASAAKI MINAMIMURA; circ. 235,759.

Nagasaki Shimbun: 3-1, Mori-machi, Nagasaki 852-8601; tel. (95) 844-2111; e-mail houdou@nagasaki-np.co.jp; internet www.nagasaki-np.co.jp; f. 1889; Dir and Man. Editor SADAKATSU HONDA; circ. morning 196,016.

Nankai Nichi-Nichi Shimbun: 10-3, Nagahama-cho, Naze 894-8601; tel. (997) 53-2121; fax (997) 52-2354; e-mail nankainn@po.synapse.ne.jp; internet www.nankainn.com; f. 1946; morning; Man. Editor TERUMI MATSUI; circ. 23,615.

Nishi-Nippon Shimbun: 1-4-1, Tenjin, Chuo-ku, Fukuoka 810-8721; tel. (92) 711-5555; internet www.nishinippon.co.jp; f. 1877; Exec. Dir and Man. Editor AKIRA KOJIMA; circ. morning 840,110, evening 148,750.

Nishi-Nippon Sports: 1-4-1, Tenjin, Chuo-ku, Fukuoka 810-8721; tel. (92) 711-5555; f. 1954; Man. Editor KENJI ISHIZAKI; circ. 198,207.

Oita Godo Shimbun: 3-9-15, Funai-machi, Oita 870-8605; tel. (975) 36-2121; internet www.oita-press.co.jp; f. 1886; Dir and Man. Editor MASAKATSU TANABE; circ. morning 250,300, evening 250,264.

Okinawa Times: 1-3-31, Omoro-machi, Naha 900-8678; tel. (98) 860-3000; fax (98) 860-3664; internet www.okinawatimes.co.jp; f. 1948; Dir and Man. Editor MASAO KISHIMOTO; circ. morning 205,624.

Ryukyu Shimpo: 905, Naha 900-8525; tel. (98) 865-5111; fax (98) 861-0100; internet www.ryukyushimpo.co.jp; f. 1893; Man. Editor TOMOKAZU TAKAMINE; circ. 203,470.

Saga Shimbun: 3-2-23, Tenjin, Saga 840-8585; tel. (952) 28-2111; fax (952) 29-4829; internet www.saga-s.co.jp; f. 1884; morning; Man. Editor TERUHIKO WASHIZAKI; circ. 136,399.

Yaeyama Mainichi Shimbun: 614, Tonoshiro, Ishigaki 907-0004; tel. (9808) 2-2121; internet www.y-mainichi.co.jp; f. 1950; morning; Exec. Dir and Man. Editor YASUTAKA KUROSHIMA; circ. 16,000.

WEEKLIES

An-An: Magazine House, 3-13-10, Ginza, Chuo-ku, Tokyo 104-8003; tel. (3) 3545-7050; fax (3) 3546-0034; internet magazineworld.jp/anan; f. 1970; fashion; Editor MIYOKO YODOGAWA; circ. 650,000.

Diamond Weekly: Diamond Bldg, 6-12-17, Jingumae, Shibuya-ku, Tokyo 150-8409; tel. (3) 5778-7200; e-mail info@diamond.co.jp; internet www.diamond.co.jp; f. 1913; economics; Editor YUTAKA IWASA; circ. 78,000.

Focus: Shincho-Sha, 71, Yarai-cho, Shinjuku-ku, Tokyo 162; tel. (3) 3266-5271; fax (3) 3266-5390; politics, economics, sport; Editor KAZUMASA TAJIMA; circ. 850,000.

Friday: Kodan-Sha Co Ltd, 2-12-21, Otowa, Bunkyo-ku, Tokyo 112; tel. (3) 5395-3440; fax (3) 3943-8582; current affairs; Editor-in-Chief TETSU SUZUKI; circ. 1m.

Hanako: Magazine House, 3-13-10, Ginza, Chuo-ku, Tokyo 104-8003; tel. (3) 3545-7070; fax (3) 3545-7281; internet magazineworld.jp/hanako; f. 1988; consumer guide; Editor AYAKO OTA; circ. 350,000.

Nikkei Business: Nikkei Business Publications Inc, 1-17-3, Shirokane, Minato-ku, Tokyo 108-8646; tel. (3) 6811-8101; fax (3) 5421-9117; internet www.nikkeibp.co.jp; f. 1969; Pres. TAIRA HIROSHI NAGATA; circ. 330,000.

Shukan Asahi: Asahi Shimbun Publishing Dept, 5-3-2, Tsukiji, Chuo-ku, Tokyo 104-8011; tel. (3) 3545-0131; f. 1922; general interest; Editor-in-Chief KAZUOMI YAMAGUCHI; circ. 482,000.

Shukan Bunshun: Bungei-Shunju Ltd, 3-23, Kioi-cho, Chiyoda-ku, Tokyo 102-8008; tel. (3) 3288-6123; fax (3) 3234-3964; e-mail kawabe@bunshun.co.jp; internet www.bunshun.co.jp; f. 1959; general interest; Editor MANABU SHINTANI; circ. 800,000.

Shukan Gendai: Kodan-Sha Co Ltd, 2-12-21, Otowa, Bunkyo-ku, Tokyo 112; tel. (3) 5395-3438; fax (3) 3943-7815; f. 1959; general; Editor-in-Chief TETSU SUZUKI; circ. 930,000.

Shukan Josei: Shufu-To-Seikatsu Sha Ltd, 3-5-7, Kyobashi, Chuo-ku, Tokyo 104; tel. (3) 3563-5130; fax (3) 3563-2073; f. 1957; women's interest; Editor HIDEO KIKUCHI; circ. 638,000.

Shukan Post: Shogakukan Publishing Co Ltd, 2-3-1, Hitotsubashi, Chiyoda-ku, Tokyo 101-01; tel. (3) 3230-5951; internet www.weeklypost.com; f. 1969; general; Editor NORIMICHI OKANARI; cir 696,000.

Shukan SPA: Fuso-Sha Co, 1-15-1, Kaigan, Minato-ku, Tokyo 10 tel. (3) 5403-8875; f. 1952; general interest; Editor-in-Chief TOSH HIKO SATO; circ. 400,000.

Shukan ST: Japan Times Ltd, 4-5-4, Shibaura, Minato-ku, Toky 108-8071; tel. (3) 3452-4077; fax (3) 3452-3303; e-mail shukanst japantimes.co.jp; internet www.japantimes.co.jp/shukan-st; f. 1951 English and Japanese; Editor MITSURU TANAKA; circ. 150,000.

Shukan Yomiuri: Yomiuri Shimbun Publication Dept, 1-2-1, Kiyo sumi, Koto-ku, Tokyo 135; tel. (3) 5245-7001; e-mail yw@yomiur.com; internet www.yomiuri.co.jp; f. 1938; general interest; Edito SHINI KAGEYAMA; circ. 453,000.

Sunday Mainichi: Mainichi Newspapers Publishing Dept, 1-1-1 Hitotsubashi, Chiyoda-ku, Tokyo 100-51; tel. (3) 3212-0321; fax (3 3212-0769; f. 1922; general interest; Editor KENJI MIKI; circ. 237,000

Tenji Mainichi: Mainichi Newspapers Publishing Dept, 3-4-5 Umeda, Osaka; tel. (6) 6346-8386; fax (6) 6346-8385; f. 1922; in Japanese braille; Editor TADAMITSU MORIOKA; circ. 12,000.

Weekly Economist: Mainichi Newspapers Publishing Dept, 1-1-1, Hitotsubashi, Chiyoda-ku, Tokyo 100-51; tel. (3) 3212-0321; f. 1923; Editorial Chief NOBUHIRO SHUDO; circ. 120,000.

Weekly Toyo Keizai: Toyo Keizai Inc, 1-2-1, Hongoku-cho, Nihonbashi, Chuo-ku, Tokyo 103-8345; tel. (3) 3246-5481; fax (3) 3270-0159; e-mail sub@toyokeizai.co.jp; internet www.toyokeizai.net; f. 1895; business, economics, finance, and corporate information; Editor SHUNICHI OTAKI; circ. 80,000.

PERIODICALS

All Yomimono: Bungei-Shunju Ltd, 3-23, Kioicho, Chiyoda-ku, Tokyo 102; tel. (3) 3265-1211; fax (3) 3239-5481; f. 1930; monthly; popular fiction; Editor KOICHI SASAMOTO; circ. 95,796.

Any: 1-3-14, Hirakawa-cho, Chiyoda-ku, Tokyo 102; tel. (3) 5276-2200; fax (3) 5276-2209; f. 1989; every 2 weeks; women's interest; Editor YUKIO MIWA; circ. 380,000.

Asahi Camera: Asahi Shimbun Publishing Dept, 5-3-2, Tsukiji, Chuo-ku, Tokyo 104-8011; tel. (3) 3545-0131; fax (3) 5565-3286; f. 1926; monthly; photography; Editor HIROSHI HIROSE; circ. 90,000.

Balloon: Shufunotomo Co Ltd, 2-9, Kanda Surugadai, Chiyoda-ku, Tokyo 101; tel. (3) 3294-1132; fax (3) 3291-5093; f. 1986; monthly; expectant mothers; Dir MARIKO HOSODA; circ. 250,000.

Brutus: Magazine House, 3-13-10, Ginza, Chuo-ku, Tokyo 104-8003; tel. (3) 3545-7000; fax (3) 3546-0034; internet magazineworld.jp/brutus; f. 1980; every 2 weeks; men's interest; Pres. ISHIZAKI TAKESHI; circ. 250,000.

Bungei-Shunju: Bungei-Shunju Ltd, 3-23, Kioi-cho, Chiyoda-ku, Tokyo 102-8008; tel. (3) 3265-1211; fax (3) 3221-6623; internet www.bunshun.co.jp; f. 1923; monthly; general; Pres. HIROSHI TAKASHI; Editor KIYONDO MATSUI; circ. 656,000.

Business Tokyo: Keizaikai Bldg, 2-13-18, Minami-Aoyama, Minato-ku, Tokyo 105; tel. (3) 3423-8500; fax (3) 3423-8505; f. 1987; monthly; Dir TAKUO IDA; Editor ANTHONY PAUL; circ. 125,000.

Chuokoron: Chuokoron-Shinsha Inc, 2-8-7, Kyobashi, Chuo-ku, Tokyo 104-8320; tel. (3) 3563-1261; fax (3) 3561-5929; e-mail hanbai@chuko.co.jp; internet www.chuko.co.jp; f. 1887; monthly; general interest; Chief Editor JUN MAYIMA; circ. 90,000.

Croissant: Magazine House, 3-13-10, Ginza, Chuo-ku, Tokyo 104-03; tel. (3) 3545-7111; fax (3) 3546-0034; f. 1977; every 2 weeks; home; Editor MASAAKI TAKEUCHI; circ. 600,000.

Fujinkoron: Chuokoron-Sha Inc, 2-8-7, Kyobashi, Chuo-ku, Tokyo 104; tel. (3) 3563-1866; fax (3) 3561-5920; f. 1916; monthly; women's literature; Editor YUKIKO YUKAWA; circ. 185,341.

Geijutsu Shincho: Shincho-Sha, 71, Yarai-cho, Shinjuku-ku, Tokyo 162-8711; tel. (3) 3266-5381; fax (3) 3266-5387; e-mail geishin@shinchosha.co.jp; f. 1950; monthly; fine arts, music, architecture, films, drama and design; Editor-in-Chief MASASHI MATSUIE; circ. 50,000.

Gendai: Kodan-Sha Ltd, 2-12-21, Otowa, Bunkyo-ku, Tokyo 112; tel. (3) 5395-3517; fax (3) 3945-9128; f. 1966; monthly; cultural and political; Editor SHUNKICHI YABUKI; circ. 250,000.

Ginza: Magazine House, 3-13-10, Ginza, Chuo-ku, Tokyo 104-8003; tel. (3) 3545-7080; fax (3) 3542-6375; internet magazineworld.jp/ginza; f. 1997; monthly; women's interest; Editor MIYOKO YODOGAWA; circ. 250,000.

Hot-Dog Press: Kodan-Sha Ltd, 2-12-21, Otowa, Bunkyo-ku, Tokyo 112-01; tel. (3) 5395-3473; fax (3) 3945-9128; every 2 weeks; men's interest; Editor ATSUHIDE KOKUBO; circ. 650,000.

Ie-no-Hikari (Light of Home): Ie-no-Hikari Assn, 11, Ichigaya Funagawaramachi, Shinjuku-ku, Tokyo 162-8448; tel. (3) 3266-9000; fax (3) 3266-9048; e-mail hikari@mxd.meshnet.or.jp;

nternet www.ienohikari.net; f. 1925; monthly; rural and general nterest; Pres. SHUZO SUZUKI; Editor KAZUO NAKANO; circ. 928,000.

Japan Company Handbook: Toyo Keizai Inc, 1-2-1, Nihonbashi Iongoku-cho, Chuo-ku, Tokyo 103-8345; tel. (3) 3246-5551; fax (3) 279-0332; e-mail info@toyokeizai.co.jp; internet www.toyokeizai.co jp; f. 1974; quarterly; English; Editor MASAKI HARA; total circ. 00,000.

Junon: Shufu-To-Seikatsu Sha Ltd, 3-5-7, Kyobashi, Chuo-ku, Tokyo 104-8357; tel. (3) 3563-5120; fax (3) 5250-7081; e-mail webmaster@mb.shufu.co.jp; internet www.shufu.co.jp/junon; . 1973; monthly; television and entertainment; circ. 560,000.

Kagaku (Science): Iwanami Shoten Publishers, 2-5-5, Hitotsubashi, Chiyoda-ku, Tokyo 102; tel. (3) 5210-4070; fax (3) 5210-4073; f. 1931; Editor NOBUAKI MIYABE; circ. 29,000.

Kagaku Asahi: Asahi Shimbun Publishing Dept, 5-3-2, Tsukiji, Chuo-ku, Tokyo 104-8011; tel. (3) 5540-7810; fax (3) 3546-2404; f. 1941; monthly; scientific; Editor TOSHIHIRO SASAKI; circ. 105,000.

Keizaijin: Kansai Economic Federation, Nakanoshima Center Bldg, 6-2-27, Nakanoshima, Kita-ku, Osaka 530-6691; tel. (6) 6441-0104; fax (6) 6443-0443; e-mail kef_60_eng@kankeiren.or.jp; internet www.kankeiren.or.jp; f. 1947; monthly; economics; Editor M. YASUTAKE; circ. 2,600.

Lettuce Club: Toranomon Corpn, 2-2-5, Minatu-ku, Tokyo 105-8455; tel. (3) 3560-8700; e-mail info@sscom.co.jp; internet www .lettuceclub.net; f. 1987; every 2 weeks; cookery; Editor MITSURU NAKAYA; circ. 800,000.

Money Japan: Toranomon Corpn, 2-2-5, Minato-ku, Tokyo 105-8455; tel. (3) 3560-8700; e-mail info@sscom.co.jp; internet www .moneyjapan-web.com; f. 1985; monthly; finance; Editor TOSHIO KOBAYASHI; circ. 500,000.

Popeye: Magazine House, 3-13-10, Ginza, Chuo-ku, Tokyo 104-8003; tel. (3) 3545-7160; fax (3) 3545-9026; internet magazineworld .jp/popeye; f. 1976; every 2 weeks; fashion, youth interest; Editor KATSUMI NAMAIZAWA; circ. 320,000.

President: President Inc, Hirakawacho Mori Tower, 13/F, 2-16-1, Hirakawa-cho, Chiyoda-ku, Tokyo 102-8641; tel. (3) 3237-3711; fax (3) 3237-3748; internet www.president.co.jp; f. 1963; monthly; business; Editor KAYOKO ABE; circ. 263,308.

Ray: Shufunotomo Co Ltd, 2-9, Kanda Surugadai, Chiyoda-ku, Tokyo 101; tel. (3) 3294-1163; fax (3) 3291-5093; f. 1988; monthly; women's interest; Editor TATSURO NAKANISHI; circ. 450,000.

Ryoko Yomiuri: Yomiuri Travel Publishing Co Inc, 18-3, Nihonbashi, Chuo-ku, Tokyo 103-8545; tel. (3) 5847-8271; fax (3) 5847-8270; e-mail ryokoyomiuri@ryokoyomiuri.co.jp; internet www .ryokoyomiuri.co.jp; f. 1966; monthly; travel; Pres. MIZHUSHIMA TOSHIO; circ. 470,000.

Sekai: Iwanami Shoten Publishers, 2-5-5, Hitotsubashi, Chiyoda-ku, Tokyo 101-8002; tel. (3) 5210-4141; fax (3) 5210-4144; e-mail sekai@iwanami.co.jp; internet www.iwanami.co.jp/sekai; f. 1946; monthly; review of world and domestic affairs; Editor ATSUSHI OKAMOTO; circ. 120,000.

Shinkenchiku: Shinkenchiku-Sha Co Ltd, Kasumigaseki Bldg, 17/F, 3-2-5, Kasumigaseki, Chiyoda-ku, Tokyo 100-6017; tel. (3) 6205-4380; fax (3) 3812-4386; e-mail ja-business@japan-architect.co.jp; internet www.japan-architect.co.jp; f. 1925; monthly; architecture; Editor NOBUYUKI YOSHIDA; circ. 87,000.

Shiso (Thought): Iwanami Shoten Publishers, 2-5-5, Hitotsubashi, Chiyoda-ku, Tokyo 101-8002; tel. (3) 5210-4055; fax (3) 5210-4037; e-mail shiso@iwanami.co.jp; internet www.iwanami.co.jp/shiso; f. 1921; monthly; philosophy, social sciences and humanities; Editor KIYOSHI KOJIMA; circ. 20,000.

Shosetsu Shincho: Shincho-Sha, 71, Yarai-cho, Shinjuku-ku, Tokyo 162-8711; tel. (3) 3266-5241; fax (3) 3266-5412; f. 1947; monthly; literature; Editor-in-Chief TSUYOSHI MENJO; circ. 80,000.

Shufunotomo: Shufunotomo Co Ltd, 2-9, Kanda Surugadai, Chiyoda-ku, Tokyo 101; tel. (3) 5280-7531; fax (3) 5280-7431; e-mail international-info@shufunotomo.co.jp; internet www .shufunotomo.co.jp; f. 1917; monthly; home and lifestyle; Editor KYOKO FURUTO; circ. 450,000.

So-en: Bunka Publishing Bureau, c/o Bunka Fashion College, 3-22-7, Yoyogi, Shibuya-ku, Tokyo 151-8524; tel. (3) 3299-2531; fax (3) 3370-3712; e-mail info-bpb@bunka.ac.jp; internet books.bunka.ac .jp; f. 1936; monthly; fashion; Editor KEIKO SASAKI; circ. 270,000.

NEWS AGENCIES

Jiji Tsushin (Jiji Press Ltd): 5-15-8, Ginza, Chuo-ku, Tokyo 104-8178; tel. (3) 6800-1111; e-mail info@jiji.co.jp; internet www.jiji.com; f. 1945; Pres. MASAHIRO NAKATA; Man. Dir and Man. Editor HIROYUKI YAMAKI.

Kyodo Tsushin (Kyodo News): Shiodome Media Tower, 1-7-1, Higashi-Shimbashi, Minato-ku, Tokyo 105-7201; tel. (3) 6252-8301; e-mail kokusai@kyodonews.jp; internet www.kyodonews.jp; f. 1945; Pres. SATOSHI ISHIKAWA; Man. Editor TOSHIEI KOKUBU.

Radiopress Inc: R-Bldg Shinjuku, 5F, 33-8, Wakamatsu-cho, Shinjuku-ku, Tokyo 162-0056; tel. (3) 5273-2171; fax (3) 5273-2180; e-mail rptokyo@oak.ocn.ne.jp; f. 1945; provides news from China, the former USSR, Democratic People's Repub. of Korea, Viet Nam and elsewhere to the press and govt offices; Pres. AKIO IJUIN.

Sun Telephoto: Palaceside Bldg, 1-1-1, Hitotsubashi, Chiyoda-ku, Tokyo 100-0003; tel. (3) 3213-6771; e-mail photo@suntelephoto.com; internet www.suntelephoto.com; f. 1952; Pres. KOZO TAKINO; Man. Editor GORO SHIMAZAKI.

PRESS ASSOCIATIONS

Foreign Correspondents' Club of Japan: Yaruku-cho Denki Kita Bldg, 20/F, 1-7-1, Yuraku-cho, Chiyoda-ku, Tokyo 100-0006; tel. (3) 3211-3161; fax (3) 3211-3168; e-mail nakamura@fccj.or.jp; internet www.fccj.or.jp; f. 1945; 193 cos; Pres. GEORGES BAUMGARTNER; Gen. Man. AKIRA NAKAMURA.

Foreign Press Center: Nippon Press Center Bldg, 6/F, 2-2-1, Uchisaiwai-cho, Chiyoda-ku, Tokyo 100-0011; tel. (3) 3501-3401; fax (3) 3501-3622; e-mail rr@fpcjpn.or.jp; internet www.fpcj.jp; f. 1976; est. by The Japan Newspaper Publishers and Editors Asscn and the Japan Fed. of Economic Orgs; provides services to the foreign press; Pres. TERUSUKE TERADA.

Nihon Shinbun Kyokai (The Japan Newspaper Publishers and Editors Asscn): Nippon Press Center Bldg, 2-2-1, Uchisaiwai-cho, Chiyoda-ku, Tokyo 100-8543; tel. (3) 3591-4401; fax (3) 3591-6149; e-mail nsk_intl@pressnet.or.jp; internet www.pressnet.or.jp; f. 1946; mems include 133 cos (106 daily newspapers, 4 news agencies and 23 radio and TV cos); Pres. HITOSHI UCHIYAMA; Man. Dir MOTOYOSHI TORII.

Nihon Zasshi Kyokai (Japan Magazine Publishers Asscn): 1-7, Kanda Surugadai, Chiyoda-ku, Tokyo 101-0062; tel. (3) 3291-0775; fax (3) 3293-6239; f. 1956; 85 mems; Pres. HARUHIKO ISHIKAWA; Sec. GENYA INUI.

Publishers

Akane Shobo Co Ltd: 3-2-1, Nishi-Kanda, Chiyoda-ku, Tokyo 101-0065; tel. (3) 3263-0641; fax (3) 3263-5440; e-mail info@akaneshobo .co.jp; internet www.akaneshobo.co.jp; f. 1949; juvenile; Pres. MASAHARU OKAMOTO.

Akita Publishing Co Ltd: 2-10-8, Iidabashi, Chiyoda-ku, Tokyo 102-8101; tel. (3) 3264-7011; fax (3) 3265-5906; internet www .akitashoten.co.jp; f. 1948; social sciences, history, juvenile; Chair. SADAO AKITA; Pres. SADAMI AKITA.

ALC Press Inc: 2-54-12, Eifuku, Suginami-ku, Tokyo 168-8611; tel. (3) 3323-1101; fax (3) 3327-1022; e-mail info@alc.co.jp; internet www .alc.co.jp; f. 1969; linguistics, educational materials, dictionaries, juvenile; Pres. TERUMARO HIRAMOTO.

Asahi Shimbun Publications Division: 5-3-2, Tsukiji, Chuo-ku, Tokyo 104-8011; tel. (3) 5541-8757; fax (3) 3545-0311; e-mail doors@ asahi.com; internet publications.asahi.com; f. 1879; general; Pres. KAZUMOTO URUMA.

Asakura Publishing Co Ltd: 6-29, Shin Ogawa-machi, Shinjuku-ku, Tokyo 162-8707; tel. (3) 3260-0141; fax (3) 3260-0180; e-mail edit@asakura.co.jp; internet www.asakura.co.jp; f. 1929; natural science, medicine, social sciences; Pres. KUNIZO ASAKURA.

Asuka Publishing Inc: 2-11-5, Suido, Bunkyo-ku, Tokyo 112-0005; tel. (3) 5395-7650; fax (3) 5395-7654; e-mail askaweb@asuka-g.co.jp; internet www.asuka-g.co.jp; f. 1973; sociology, law, economics, languages; Pres. EIICHI ISHINO.

Baifukan Co Ltd: 4-3-12, Kudan-Minami, Chiyoda-ku, Tokyo 102-0074; tel. (3) 3262-5256; fax (3) 3262-5276; e-mail bfkeigyo@mx7 .mesh.ne.jp; internet www.baifukan.co.jp; f. 1924; engineering, natural and social sciences, psychology; Pres. ITARU YAMAMOTO.

Baseball Magazine-Sha: 3-10-10, Misaki-cho, Chiyoda-ku, Tokyo 101-8381; tel. (3) 3238-0081; fax (3) 3238-0106; internet www .bbm-japan.com; f. 1946; sports, physical education, recreation, travel; Pres. TETSUO IKEDA.

Bensey Publishing Inc: 2-20-6, Kanda Jimbo-cho, Chiyoda-ku, Tokyo 101-0051; tel. (3) 5215-9021; fax (3) 5215-9025; e-mail bensey@ bensey.co.jp; internet www.bensey.co.jp; f. 1967; philosophy, religion, history, art, languages, literature; Pres. YOJI IKEJIMA.

Bijutsu Shuppan-Sha Ltd: Inaoka Kudan Bldg, 6/F, 2-38, Kanda Jimbo-cho, Chiyoda-ku, Tokyo 101-8417; tel. (3) 3234-2151; fax (3) 3234-9451; e-mail artmedia@bijutsu.co.jp; internet www.bijutsu.co .jp; f. 1905; fine arts, graphic design; Pres. KENTARO OSHITA.

Bonjinsha Co Ltd: 1-3-13, Hirakawa-cho, Chiyoda-ku, Tokyo 102-0093; tel. (3) 3263-3959; fax (3) 3263-3116; e-mail info@bonjinsha

.com; internet www.bonjinsha.com; f. 1973; Japanese language teaching materials; Pres. HISAMITSU TANAKA.

Bun-eido Publishing Co Inc: 28, Kamitoba, Daimotsu-cho, Minami-ku, Kyoto 601-8691; tel. (75) 671-3161; fax (75) 671-3165; e-mail fujita@bun-eido.co.jp; internet www.bun-eido.co.jp; f. 1921; reference books, dictionaries, textbooks, juvenile, history; Pres. HIDEOHIRO MASUI.

Bungei Shunju Ltd: 3-23, Kioi-cho, Chiyoda-ku, Tokyo 102-8008; tel. (3) 3265-1211; fax (3) 3265-1363; internet www.bunshun.co.jp; f. 1923; fiction, general literature, recreation, economics, sociology; Dir TAKAHIRO HIRAO.

Bunri Co Ltd: 1-1-5, Sekiguchi, Bunkyo-ku, Tokyo 112-0014; tel. (3) 3268-4110; fax (3) 3268-1462; e-mail tezukatak@bnet.bunri.co.jp; internet www.bunri.co.jp; f. 1950; Pres. SHIRO HATA.

Chikuma Shobo: Chikumashobo Bldg, 2-5-3, Kuramae, Taito-ku, Tokyo 111-8755; tel. (3) 5687-2671; fax (3) 5687-1585; e-mail henshuinfo@chikumashobo.co.jp; internet www.chikumashobo.co.jp; f. 1940; general literature, fiction, history, juvenile, fine arts; Pres. AKIO KIKUCHI.

Child-Honsha Co Ltd: 5-24-21, Koishikawa, Bunkyo-ku, Tokyo 112-8512; tel. (3) 3813-3781; fax (3) 3813-3778; e-mail ehon@childbook.co.jp; internet www.childbook.co.jp; f. 1930; juvenile; Pres. SHUNJI ASAKA.

Chuo Hoki Publishing Co Ltd: 2-27-4, Yoyogi, Shibuya-ku, Tokyo 151-0053; tel. (3) 3379-3784; fax (3) 5351-7855; e-mail info@chuohoki.co.jp; internet www.chuohoki.co.jp; f. 1947; law, social sciences; Pres. AKIHIKO SHOMURA.

Chuo University Press: 742-1, Higashi-Nakano, Hachioji-shi, Tokyo 192-0393; tel. (426) 74-2351; fax (426) 74-2354; f. 1948; law, history, sociology, economics, science, literature; Pres. TAKEHIKO TAMATSUKURI.

Chuokoron-Shinsha Inc: 2-8-7, Kyobashi, Chuo-ku, Tokyo 104-8320; tel. (3) 3563-1261; fax (3) 3561-5920; internet www.chuko.co.jp; f. 1886; philosophy, history, sociology, general literature; Pres. TAMOTSU ASAMI.

Corona Publishing Co Ltd: 4-46-10, Sengoku, Bunkyo-ku, Tokyo 112-0011; tel. (3) 3941-3131; fax (3) 3941-3137; e-mail info@coronasha.co.jp; internet www.coronasha.co.jp; f. 1927; electronics, medical books, mechanical engineering, computer science; Pres. MASAYA GORAI.

Dempa Publications Inc: 1-11-15, Higashi-Gotanda, Shinagawa-ku, Tokyo 141-8715; tel. (3) 3445-6111; fax (3) 3444-7515; f. 1950; electronics, personal computer software, juvenile, trade newspapers, English and Japanese language publications; Pres. TETSUO HIRAYAMA.

Diamond Inc: 6-12-17, Jingumae, Shibuya-ku, Tokyo 150-8409; tel. (3) 5778-7233; fax (3) 5778-6618; e-mail info@diamond.co.jp; internet www.diamond.co.jp; f. 1913; business, management, economics, financial; Pres. FUMIAKI SHIKATANI.

Dohosha Ltd: TAS Bldg, 2-5-2, Nishi-Kanda, Chiyoda-ku, Tokyo 101-0065; tel. (3) 5276-0831; fax (3) 5276-0840; e-mail intl@dohosha.co.jp; f. 1997; general works, architecture, art, Buddhism, business, children's education, cooking, flower-arranging, gardening, medicine.

East Press Co Ltd: 1-19, Kanda Jimbo-cho, Chiyoda-ku, Tokyo 101-0051; tel. (3) 5259-7707; fax (3) 5259-7708; e-mail webmaster@eastpress.co.jp; internet www.eastpress.co.jp; f. 2005; literature, comics, business, self-help, parenting, health, sports, music; Chair. SHINGERU KOBAYASHI; Pres. OSAMU ASOSHINA.

Froebel-Kan Co Ltd: 6-14-9, Honkomagome, Bunkyo-ku, Tokyo 113-8611; tel. (3) 5395-6600; fax (3) 5395-6621; e-mail info-e@froebel-kan.co.jp; internet www.froebel-kan.co.jp; f. 1907; juvenile, educational; Pres. HIDEO MUTO.

Fukuinkan Shoten Publishers Inc: 6-6-3, Honkomagome, Bunkyo-ku, Tokyo 113-8686; tel. (3) 3942-2151; fax (3) 3942-1401; internet www.fukuinkan.co.jp; f. 1952; juvenile; Pres. NOBORU OGURA; Chair. KATSUMI SATO.

Fusosha Publishing Inc: 1-15-1, Kaigan, Minato-ku, Tokyo 105-8070; tel. (3) 5403-8851; fax (3) 3578-3078; e-mail gshoseki@fusosha.co.jp; internet www.fusosha.co.jp; f. 1984; social science, business, mystery, magazines, textbooks; Pres. EIICHI KUBOTA.

Futabasha Publishers Ltd: 3-28, Higashi-Goken-cho, Shinjuku-ku, Tokyo 162-8540; tel. (3) 5261-4832; fax (3) 5261-3480; e-mail general@futabasha.co.jp; internet www.futabasha.co.jp; f. 1948; fiction, non-fiction, comics, guide books; Pres. HIROSHI MOROZUMI.

Gakken Co Ltd: 4-40-5, Kamiikedai, Ota-ku, Tokyo 145-8502; tel. (3) 3726-8111; fax (3) 3493-3338; e-mail personnel@gakken.co.jp; internet www.gakken.co.jp; f. 1946; juvenile, educational, art, encyclopaedias, dictionaries; Pres. YOCHIRO ENDO.

Graphic-sha Publishing Co Ltd: 1-14-17 Kudan-Kita, Chiyoda-ku, Tokyo 102-0073; tel. (3) 3263-4318; fax (3) 3263-5297; e-mail info@graphicsha.co.jp; internet www.graphicsha.co.jp; f. 1962; art, design, architecture, manga techniques, hobbies; Pres. KUZ TOSHIRO.

Gyosei Corpn: 1-18-11, Shinkiba, Koto-ku, Tokyo 136-8575; tel. (6892-6666; fax (3) 6892-6925; e-mail eigyo1@gyosei.co.jp; interne www.gyosei.co.jp; f. 1893; law, education, science, politics, busines art, language, literature, juvenile; Pres. YUJIRO SAWADA.

Hakusui-Sha Co Ltd: 3-24, Kanda Ogawa-machi, Chiyoda-ku Tokyo 101-0052; tel. (3) 3291-7821; fax (3) 3291-7810; e-ma hpmaster@hakusuisha.co.jp; internet www.hakusuisha.co.jp f. 1915; general literature, science and languages; Pres. NAOSH OIKAWA.

Hayakawa Publishing Inc: 2-2, Kanda-Tacho, Chiyoda-ku, Toky 101-0046; tel. (3) 3252-3111; fax (3) 3258-0250; internet www.hayakawa-online.co.jp; f. 1945; wine books, children's books, coffee table books, drama, comic books, monthly magazines; Pres. HIROSH HAYAKAWA.

Heibonsha Ltd: 2-29-4 Hakusan, Bunkyo-ku, Tokyo 112-0001; tel (3) 3818-0873; fax (3) 3818-0857; e-mail shop@heibonsha.co.jp internet www.heibonsha.co.jp; f. 1914; encyclopaedias, art, history geography, literature, science; Pres. NAOTO SHIMONAKA.

Hirokawa Publishing Co: 3-27-14, Hongo, Bunkyo-ku, Tokyo 113-0033; tel. (3) 3815-3651; fax (3) 5684-7030; f. 1925; natural sciences, medicine, pharmacy, nursing, chemistry; Pres. SETSUO HIROKAWA.

Hoikusha Publishing Co: 18-24, Hiroshi-bacho, Suita-shi, Osaka 564-0052; tel. (6) 6330-5680; fax (6) 6330-5681; e-mail matsui@hoikusha.co.jp; internet www.hoikusha.co.jp; f. 1947; natural science, juvenile, fine arts, geography; Pres. TAKAHIKO MATSUI.

Hokkaido University Press: Kita-9, Nishi-8, Kita-ku, Sapporo 060-0809; tel. (11) 747-2308; fax (11) 736-8605; e-mail hupress_2@hup.gr.jp; internet www.hup.gr.jp; f. 1970; social science, natural science, technology, humanities; Pres. KATSUMI YOSHIDA.

Hokuryukan Co Ltd: 3-8-14, Takanawa, Minato-ku, Tokyo 108-0074; tel. (3) 5449-4591; fax (3) 5449-4950; e-mail hk-ns@hokuryukan-ns.co.jp; internet www.hokuryukan-ns.co.jp; f. 1891; natural science, medical science, juvenile, dictionaries; Pres. HISAKO FUKUDA.

The Hokuseido Press: Hayashi Bldg, 1-21-9, Sugamo, Toshima-ku, Tokyo 170-0002; tel. (3) 5940-0511; fax (3) 5940-0512; e-mail info@hokuseido.com; f. 1914; regional non-fiction, dictionaries, textbooks; Pres. KEISUKE YAMAMOTO.

Horitsubunka-sha: 71, Iwagakakiuchi-cho, Kamigamo, Kita-ku, Kyoto 603-8053; tel. (75) 791-7131; fax (75) 721-8400; e-mail henshu@hou-bun.co.jp; internet www.hou-bun.co.jp; f. 1947; law, politics, economics, sociology, philosophy; Pres. YASUSHI AKIYAMA.

Hosei University Press: 3-2-7, Kudan-Kita, Chiyoda-ku, Tokyo 102-0073; tel. (3) 5214-5540; fax (3) 5214-5542; e-mail mail@h-up.com; internet www.h-up.com; f. 1948; philosophy, history, economics, sociology, natural science, literature; Pres. TOSHIO MASUDA.

Ie-No-Hikari Association: 11, Funagawara-cho, Ichigaya, Shinjuku-ku, Tokyo 162-8448; tel. (3) 3266-9000; fax (3) 3266-9048; e-mail hikari@mxd.mesh.ne.jp; internet www.ienohikari.net; f. 1925; social science, agriculture, cooking; Pres. TOSHIHIRO SONODA.

Igaku-Shoin Ltd: 1-28-23, Hongo, Bunkyo-ku, Tokyo 113-8719; tel. (3) 3817-5610; fax (3) 3815-4114; e-mail info@igaku-shoin.co.jp; internet www.igaku-shoin.co.jp; f. 1944; medicine, nursing; Pres. YU KANEHARA.

Ikubundo Publishing Co Ltd: 5-30-21, Hongo, Bunkyo-ku, Tokyo 113-0033; tel. (3) 3814-5571; fax (3) 3814-5576; e-mail webmaster@ikubundo.com; internet www.ikubundo.com; f. 1899; languages, dictionaries; Pres. TOSHIYUKI OI.

Institute for Financial Affairs Inc (KINZAI): 19, Minami-Motomachi, Shinjuku-ku, Tokyo 160-8519; tel. (3) 3358-1161; fax (3) 3359-7947; e-mail JDI04072@nifty.ne.jp; internet www.kinzai.or.jp; f. 1950; finance and economics, banking laws and regulations, accounting; Pres. MASATERU YOSHIDA.

Ishiyaku Publishers Inc: 1-7-10, Honkomagome, Bunkyo-ku, Tokyo 113-8612; tel. (3) 5395-7600; fax (3) 5395-7606; e-mail webmaster@ishiyaku.co.jp; internet www.ishiyaku.co.jp; f. 1921; medicine, dentistry, rehabilitation, nursing, nutrition and pharmaceutics; Pres. HIDEHO OHATA.

Iwanami Shoten, Publishers: 2-5-5, Hitotsubashi, Chiyoda-ku, Tokyo 101-8002; tel. (3) 5210-4000; fax (3) 5210-4039; e-mail rights@iwanami.co.jp; internet www.iwanami.co.jp; f. 1913; natural and social sciences, humanities, literature, fine arts, juvenile, dictionaries; Pres. AKIO YAMAGUCHI.

Iwasaki Publishing Co Ltd: 1-9-2, Suido, Bunkyo-ku, Tokyo 112-0005; tel. (3) 3812-0151; fax (3) 3812-1381; e-mail ask@iwasakishoten.co.jp; internet www.iwasakishoten.co.jp; f. 1934; juvenile; Pres. HIROAKI IWASAKI.

Japan Broadcast Publishing Co Ltd: 41-1, Udagawa-cho, Shibuya-ku, Tokyo 150-8081; tel. (3) 3464-7311; fax (3) 3780-3394; e-mail kikaka@nhk-book.co.jp; internet www.nhk-book.co.jp;

f. 1931; foreign language textbooks, gardening, home economics, sociology, education, art, juvenile; Pres. AKIHIDE MIZOGUCHI.

Japan External Trade Organization (JETRO): Ark Mori Bldg, 6/F, 1-12-32, Akasaka, Minato-ku, Tokyo 107-6006; tel. (3) 3582-5511; fax (3) 3587-2485; internet www.jetro.go.jp; f. 1958; trade, economics, investment; Chair. YASUO HAYASHI.

Japan Publications Trading Co Ltd: 1-2-1, Sarugaku-cho, Chiyoda-ku, Tokyo 101-0064; tel. (3) 3292-3751; fax (3) 3292-0410; e-mail jpt@jptco.co.jp; internet www.jptco.co.jp; f. 1942; general works, art, health, sports; Pres. HIROBUMI ANNOSHITA.

The Japan Times Ltd: 4-5-4, Shibaura, Minato-ku, Tokyo 108-8071; tel. (3) 3453-2013; fax (3) 3453-8023; e-mail jt-books@kt.rim.or.jp; internet bookclub.japantimes.co.jp; f. 1897; linguistics, culture, business; Pres. TOSHIAKI OGASAWARA.

Jikkyo Shuppan Co Ltd: 5, Goban-cho, Chiyoda-ku, Tokyo 102-8377; tel. (3) 3238-7700; fax (3) 3238-7719; internet www.jikkyo.co.jp; f. 1941; textbooks; Pres. YOJI TOTSUKA.

Jimbun Shoin: 9, Nishi-Uchihata-cho, Takeda, Fushimi-ku, Kyoto 612-8447; tel. (75) 603-1344; fax (75) 603-1814; e-mail jmsb@jimbunshoin.co.jp; internet www.jimbunshoin.co.jp; f. 1927; general literature, philosophy, fiction, social science, religion, fine arts; Pres. HIROSHI WATANABE.

Jitsugyo No Nihonsha Ltd: 1-3-9, Ginza, Chuo-ku, Tokyo 104-8233; tel. (3) 3562-1021; fax (3) 3562-2662; e-mail soumu@j-n.co.jp; internet www.j-n.co.jp; f. 1897; general, social sciences, juvenile, travel, business, comics; Pres. YOSHIKAZU MASUDA.

JTB Publishing (Japan Travel Bureau): Urban-net Ichigaya Bldg, 25-5, Haraikatamachi, Shinjuku-ku, Tokyo 162-8446; tel. (3) 6888-7811; fax (3) 6888-7809; e-mail jtbpublishing@rurubu.ne.jp; internet www.jtbpublishing.com; f. 2004; travel, geography, history, fine arts, languages; Pres. YUZURU TAKENAMI.

Kadokawa Group Publishing Inc: 2-13-3, Fujimi, Chiyoda-ku, Tokyo 102-8177; tel. (3) 3238-8715; fax (3) 3262-7734; e-mail k-master@kadokawa.co.jp; internet www.kadokawa.co.jp; f. 1945; literature, history, dictionaries, religion, fine arts, books on tape, compact discs, CD-ROMs, comics, animation, video cassettes, computer games; Pres. KOICHI SEKIYA.

Kaibundo Publishing Co Ltd: 2-5-4, Suido, Bunkyo-ku, Tokyo 112-0005; tel. (3) 5684-6289; fax (3) 3815-3953; e-mail okadayo@kaibundo.jp; internet www.kaibundo.jp; f. 1914; marine affairs, natural science, engineering, industry; Pres. SETSUO OKADA.

Kaiseisha Publishing Co Ltd: 3-5, Ichigaya Sadohara-cho, Shinjuku-ku, Tokyo 162-8450; tel. (3) 3260-3229; fax (3) 3260-3540; e-mail foreign@kaiseisha.co.jp; internet www.kaiseisha.net; f. 1936; juvenile; Pres. MASAKI IMAMURA.

Kanehara & Co Ltd: 2-31-14, Yushima, Bunkyo-ku, Tokyo 113-8687; tel. (3) 3811-7185; fax (3) 3813-0288; e-mail kanehara@abox5.so-net.ne.jp; internet www.kanehara-shuppan.co.jp; f. 1875; medical, agricultural, engineering and scientific; Pres. HIROMITSU KAWAI.

Keiso Shobo Publishing Co Ltd: 2-1-1, Suido, Bunkyo-ku, Tokyo 112-0005; tel. (3) 3814-6861; fax (3) 3814-6968; e-mail h-imura@keisoshobo.co.jp; internet www.keisoshobo.co.jp; f. 1948; law, economics, politics, literature, psychology, philosophy, sociology; Pres. HISATO IMURA.

Kenkyusha Ltd: 2-11-3, Fujimi, Chiyoda-ku, Tokyo 102-8152; tel. (3) 3288-7777; fax (3) 3288-7799; e-mail hanbai@kenkyusha.co.jp; internet www.kenkyusha.co.jp; f. 1907; bilingual dictionaries, books on languages; Pres. YUSUKE KOSAKAI.

Kinokuniya Co Ltd: 3-7-10, Shimomeguro, Meguro-ku, Tokyo 153-8504; tel. (3) 6910-0508; fax (3) 6420-1354; e-mail publish@kinokuniya.co.jp; internet www.kinokuniya.co.jp; f. 1927; humanities, social science, natural science; Chair. and CEO OSAMU MATSUBARA; Pres. MASASHI TAKIA.

KK Best Sellers Co Ltd: 2-29-7, Minami-Otsuka, Toshima-ku, Tokyo 170-8457; tel. (3) 5976-9121; fax (3) 5976-9237; e-mail muramatsu@bestsellers.co.jp; internet www.kk-bestsellers.com; f. 1967; non-fiction, general literature; Pres. MIKIO KURIHARA.

Kodansha Ltd: 2-12-21, Otowa, Bunkyo-ku, Tokyo 112-8001; tel. (3) 3946-6201; fax (3) 3944-9915; e-mail n-okazaki@kodansha.co.jp; internet www.kodansha.co.jp; f. 1909; fine arts, fiction, literature, juvenile, comics, dictionaries; Pres. YOSHINOBU NOMA.

Kosei Publishing Co Ltd: 2-7-1, Wada, Suginami-ku, Tokyo 166-8535; tel. (3) 5385-2319; fax (3) 5385-2331; e-mail kspub@kosei-shuppan.co.jp; internet www.kosei-shuppan.co.jp; f. 1966; general works, philosophy, religion, history, pedagogy, social science, art, juvenile; Pres. MORIYASU OKABE.

Kumon Publishing Co Ltd: Gobancho Grand Bldg, 3-1, Gobancho, Chiyoda-ku, Tokyo 102-8180; tel. (3) 3234-4004; fax (3) 3234-4483; e-mail international@kumonshuppan.com; internet www.kumonshuppan.com; f. 1988; juvenile, dictionaries, education; Pres. SHOICHI DOKAI.

Kwansei Gakuin University Press: 1-155, Uegahara Ichiban-cho, Nishi-Nomiya-shi, Hyogo 662-0891; tel. (798) 53-7002; fax (798) 53-9592; internet www.kwansei.ac.jp/press; f. 1997; natural science, social science, philosophy, literature; Pres. KOJIRO MIYAHARA.

Kyoritsu Shuppan Co Ltd: 4-6-19, Kohinata, Bunkyo-ku, Tokyo 112-8700; tel. (3) 3947-2511; fax (3) 3947-2539; e-mail general@kyoritsu-pub.co.jp; internet www.kyoritsu-pub.co.jp; f. 1926; scientific and technical; Pres. MITSUAKI NANJO.

Kyoto University Press: Kyodai-Yoshida-Minami, 69, Yoshidakonoe-cho, Sakyo-ku, Kyoto 606-8305; tel. (75) 761-6182; fax (75) 761-6190; e-mail sales@kyoto-up.or.jp; internet www.kyoto-up.or.jp; f. 1989; history, literature, philology, anthropology, sociology, economics, area studies, ecology, architecture, psychology, philosophy, space physics, earth and planetary science; Rep. Prof. TAMEJIRO HIYAMA.

Kyushu University Press: 7-1-146, Hakozaki, Higashi-ku, Fukuoka 812-0053; tel. (92) 641-0515; fax (92) 641-0172; e-mail kup@mocha.ocn.ne.jp; internet www1.ocn.ne.jp/~kup; f. 1975; history, political science, law, economics, technology, linguistics, literature, psychology, medicine, agriculture; Chief Dir NAOYUKI ISOGAWA.

Maruzen Co Ltd: Shinagawa Bldg, 4-13-14, Higashi-Shinagawa, Shinagawa-ku, Tokyo 140-0002; tel. (3) 3272-0521; fax (3) 3272-0527; e-mail sitepub@maruzen.co.jp; internet pub.maruzen.co.jp; f. 1869; general works; Dir TAKEHIKO OGI.

Meisei University Press: 2-1-1, Hodokubo, Hino-shi, Tokyo 191-8506; tel. (42) 591-9979; fax (42) 593-0192; f. 1975; humanities, education, social science, natural science; Pres. TETSUO OGAWA.

Minerva Shobo: 1, Tsutsumidani-cho, Hinooka, Yamashina-ku, Kyoto 607-8494; tel. (75) 581-5191; fax (75) 581-8379; e-mail info@minervashobo.co.jp; internet www.minervashobo.co.jp; f. 1948; general non-fiction and reference; Pres. KEIZO SUGITA.

Misuzu Shobo Ltd: 5-32-21, Hongo, Bunkyo-ku, Tokyo 113-0033; tel. (3) 3815-9181; fax (3) 3818-8497; e-mail info@msz.co.jp; internet www.msz.co.jp; f. 1947; general, philosophy, history, psychiatry, literature, science, art; Pres. HISAO MOCHITANI.

Morikita Shuppan Co Ltd: 1-4-11, Fujimi, Chiyoda-ku, Tokyo 102-0071; tel. (3) 3265-8341; fax (3) 3261-1349; e-mail hiro@morikita.co.jp; internet www.morikita.co.jp; f. 1950; natural science, engineering; Pres. HIROSHI MORIKITA.

Nagaoka Shoten Co Ltd: 1-7-14, Toyotama-Kami, Nerima-ku, Tokyo 176-8518; tel. (3) 3992-5155; fax (3) 3948-9161; e-mail info@nagaokashoten.co.jp; internet www.nagaokashoten.co.jp; f. 1963; dictionaries, home economics, sports, recreation, law; Pres. SHUICHI NAGAOKA.

Nakayama-Shoten Co Ltd: 1-25-14, Hakusan, Bunkyo-ku, Tokyo 113-8666; tel. (3) 3813-1100; fax (3) 3816-1015; e-mail kojima@nakayamashoten.co.jp; internet www.nakayamashoten.co.jp; f. 1948; medicine, biology, zoology; Pres. TADASHI HIRATA.

Nanzando Co Ltd: 4-1-11, Yushima, Bunkyo-ku, Tokyo; tel. (3) 5689-7868; fax (3) 5689-7869; e-mail nanzando-soumubu@nanzando.com; internet www.nanzando.com; f. 1901; medical reference, paperbacks; Pres. HAJIME SUZUKI.

Nigensha Publishing Co Ltd: 6-2-1, Honkomagome, Bunkyo-gu, Tokyo, 113-0021; tel. (3) 5395-2041; fax (3) 5395-2045; e-mail info@nigensha.jp; internet www.nigensha.co.jp; f. 1955; calligraphy, fine arts, art reproductions, cars, watches; Pres. YUKIKO KUROSU.

Nihon Vogue Co Ltd: 3-23, Ichigaya Honmura-cho, Shinjuku-ku, Tokyo 162-8705; tel. (3) 5261-5139; fax (3) 3269-8726; e-mail asai@tezukuritown.com; internet www.tezukuritown.com; f. 1954; quilting, needlecraft, handicrafts, knitting, decorative painting, pressed flowers; Pres. NOBUAKI SETO.

Nihonbungeisha Co Ltd: 1-7, Kanda Jimbo-cho, Chiyoda-ku, Tokyo 101-0051; tel. (3) 3294-7771; fax (3) 3294-7780; e-mail mmac@nihonbungeisha.co.jp; internet www.nihonbungeisha.co.jp; f. 1959; home economics, sociology, fiction, technical books; Pres. SOUJI NISHIZAWA.

Nikkei Publishing Inc: Shin-Otemachi Bldg, 2-2-1, Otemachi, Chiyoda-ku, Tokyo 100-0004; tel. (3) 5255-2836; fax (3) 5255-2864; internet www.nikkeibook.com; f. 1876; economics, business, politics, fine arts, video cassettes, CD-ROMs; Pres. HISAO SAIDA.

Nippon Hyoronsha: 3-12-4, Minami-Otsuka, Toshima-ku, Tokyo 170-8474; tel. (3) 3987-8611; fax (3) 3987-8593; e-mail inform@nippyo.co.jp; internet www.nippyo.co.jp; f. 1918; jurisprudence, economics, science, mathematics, medicine, psychology, business; Pres. TOSHIMASA KURODA.

Nippon Jitsugyo Publishing Co Ltd: 3-2-12, Hongo, Bunkyo-ku, Tokyo 113-0033; tel. (3) 3814-5651; fax (3) 3818-2723; e-mail int@njg.co.jp; internet www.njg.co.jp; f. 1950; business, management, finance and accounting, sales and marketing; Chair. and CEO YOICHIRO NAKAMURA.

Nosan Gyoson Bunka Kyokai (Rural Culture Association): 7-6-1, Akasaka, Minato-ku, Tokyo 107-8668; tel. (3) 3585-1141; fax (3) 3589-1387; e-mail rural@mail.ruralnet.or.jp; internet www.ruralnet .or.jp; f. 1940; agriculture, food and health, education, economics, philosophy; Pres. YOSHIHIRO HAMAGUCHI.

NTT Publishing Co Ltd: JR Tokyu Meguro Bldg, 7/F, 3-1-1, Kami-Osaki, Shinagawa-ku, Tokyo 141-8654; tel. (3) 5434-1011; fax (3) 5434-1008; internet www.nttpub.co.jp; f. 1987; essays, biography, philosophy, sociology, history, management, economics, technology, telecommunications, picture books, computer game guides; Pres. SHINJI JIKUYA.

Obunsha Co Ltd: 55, Yokodera-cho, Shinjuku-ku, Tokyo 162-8680; tel. (3) 3266-6429; fax (3) 3266-6412; internet www.obunsha.co.jp; f. 1931; textbooks, reference, general science and fiction, magazines, encyclopaedias, dictionaries; software; audio-visual aids; CEO FUMIO AKAO.

Ohmsha Ltd: 3-1, Kanda Nishiki-cho, Chiyoda-ku, Tokyo 101-8460; tel. (3) 3233-0641; fax (3) 3233-2426; e-mail kaigaika@ohmsha.co.jp; internet www.ohmsha.co.jp; f. 1914; engineering, technical and scientific; Pres. OSAMI TAKEO.

Ongaku No Tomo Sha Corpn (ONT): 6-30, Kagurazaka, Shinjuku-ku, Tokyo 162-8716; tel. (3) 3235-2111; fax (3) 3235-2110; e-mail home_ontomo@ongakunotomo.co.jp; internet www.ongakunotomo .co.jp; f. 1941; compact discs, videograms, music magazines, music books, music data, music textbooks; Pres. KUMIO HORIUCHI.

Osaka University of Economics and Law: 6-10, Gakuonji, Yaoshi, Osaka 581-8511; tel. (729) 41-8211; fax (729) 41-9979; e-mail kondo-t@keiho-u.ac.jp; internet www.keiho-u.ac.jp/research/ syuppan/index.html; f. 1987; economics, law, philosophy, history, natural science, languages, politics; Pres. SHUNKUO KANAZAWA.

Osaka University Press: 2-7, Yamadaoka, Suita-shi, Osaka 565-0871; tel. and fax (6) 6877-1614; e-mail info@osaka-up.or.jp; internet www.osaka-up.or.jp; f. 1993; economics, history, literature, medicine, philosophy, politics, science, sociology, technology; Pres. KIYOKAZU WASHIDA.

PHP Institute Inc: 11, Kita-Nouchi-cho, Nishi-Kujo, Minami-ku, Kyoto 601-8411; tel. (75) 681-3268; fax (75) 681-4560; internet www .php.co.jp; f. 1946; social science; Pres. MASAYUKI MATSUSHITA.

Poplar Publishing Co Ltd: 22-1, Daikyo-cho, Shinjuku-ku, Tokyo 160-8565; tel. (3) 3357-2216; fax (3) 3351-0736; e-mail info@poplar.co .jp; internet www.poplar.co.jp; f. 1947; general, children's, comics; CEO HIROYUKI SAKAI.

Sanrio Co Ltd: 1-6-1, Osaki, Shinagawa-ku, Tokyo 141-8603; tel. (3) 3779-8101; fax (3) 3779-8702; internet www.sanrio.co.jp; f. 1960; juvenile; Pres. SHINTARO TSUJI.

Sanseido Co Ltd: 2-22-14, Misaki-cho, Chiyoda-ku, Tokyo 101-8371; tel. (3) 3230-9411; fax (3) 3230-9547; e-mail ssd-s@ sanseido-publ.co.jp; internet www.sanseido.co.jp; f. 1881; dictionaries, educational, languages, social and natural science; Pres. KATSUHIKO KITAGUCHI.

Sanshusha Publishing Co Ltd: Aoyama Kumano Jinja Bldg, 2-2-22, Jingu-mae, Shibuya-ku, Tokyo 150-0001; tel. (3) 3405-4511; fax (3) 3405-4522; e-mail webmaster@sanshusha.co.jp; internet www .sanshusha.co.jp; f. 1938; languages, dictionaries, philosophy, sociology, electronic publishing (CD-ROM); Pres. TOSHIHIDE MAEDA.

Seibido Shuppan Co Ltd: 1-7, Shinogawamachi, Shinjuku-ku, Tokyo 162-8445; tel. (3) 5206-8151; fax (3) 5206-8159; internet www .seibidoshuppan.co.jp; f. 1969; sports, recreation, travel guides, music, motor sports, cooking, novels, computer, child care, picture books; Pres. ETSUJI FUKAMI.

Seibundo-Shinkosha Co Ltd: 3-3-11, Hongo, Bunkyo-ku, Tokyo 113-0033; tel. (3) 5800-5775; fax (3) 5800-5773; internet www .seibundo-shinkosha.net; f. 1912; scientific, gardening, electronics, graphic design; Pres. YUICHI OGAWA.

Seishun Publishing Co Ltd: 12-1, Wakamatsu-cho, Shinjuku-ku, Tokyo 162-0056; tel. (3) 3203-5121; fax (3) 3207-0982; e-mail info@ seishun.co.jp; internet www.seishun.co.jp; f. 1955; science, education, history, sociology, philosophy, economics, literature; Pres. GENTARO OZAWA.

Seitoku University Press: 550, Iwase, Matsudo-shi, Chiba 271-8755; tel. (47) 365-1111; fax (47) 363-1401; e-mail shuppan@seitoku .ac.jp; f. 2002; human science, medicine, art; Pres. HIROAKI KAWAKAMI.

Seizando Shoten Publishing Co Ltd: 4-51, Minami-Motomachi, Shinjuku-ku, Tokyo 160-0012; tel. (3) 3357-5861; fax (3) 3357-5867; e-mail publisher@seizando.co.jp; internet www.seizando.co.jp; f. 1954; maritime affairs, aviation, engineering; Pres. NORIKO OGAWA.

Sekai Bunka Publishing Inc: 4-2-29, Kudan-Kita, Chiyoda-ku, Tokyo 102-8187; tel. (3) 3262-5111; fax (3) 3262-5750; e-mail y-muta@sekaibunka.co.jp; internet www.sekaibunka.com; f. 1946; history, natural science, geography, education, art, literature, juvenile; Pres. MINAKO SUZUKI.

Shincho-Sha Co Ltd: 71, Yarai-cho, Shinjuku-ku, Tokyo 162-8711; tel. (3) 3266-5250; fax (3) 3266-5432; e-mail shuppans@shinchosha .co.jp; internet www.shinchosha.co.jp; f. 1896; general literature fiction, non-fiction, fine arts, philosophy; Pres. TAKANOBU SATO.

Shinkenchiku-Sha Co Ltd: 2-31-2, Yushima, Bunkyo-ku, Tokyo 113-8501; tel. (3) 3811-7101; fax (3) 3812-8229; e-mail ja-business@ japan-architect.co.jp; internet www.japan-architect.co.jp; f. 1925; architecture; Pres. AKIHIKO OMORI.

Shinsei Publishing Co Ltd: 4-7-6, Taito, Taito-ku, Tokyo 110 0016; tel. (3) 3831-0743; fax (3) 3831-0758; internet www.shin-sei.co .jp; f. 1944; guidebooks, state examinations, personal computers Pres. YASUHIRO TOMINAGA.

Shogakukan Inc: 2-3-1, Hitotsubashi, Chiyoda-ku, Tokyo 101-8001; tel. (3) 3230-5658; fax (3) 3230-9750; internet www .shogakukan.co.jp; f. 1922; juvenile, education, geography, history, encyclopaedias, dictionaries; Pres. MASAHIRO OHGA.

Shokabo Publishing Co Ltd: 8-1, Yomban-cho, Chiyoda-ku, Tokyo 102-0081; tel. (3) 3262-9166; fax (3) 3262-7257; e-mail info@shokabo .co.jp; internet www.shokabo.co.jp; f. 1716; natural science, engineering; Pres. KAZUHIRO YOSHINO.

Shokokusha Publishing Co Ltd: 25, Saka-machi, Shinjuku-ku, Tokyo 160-0002; tel. (3) 3359-3231; fax (3) 3357-3961; e-mail eigyo@ shokokusha.co.jp; internet www.shokokusha.co.jp; f. 1932; architectural, technical and fine arts; Pres. TAKESHI GOTO.

Shueisha Inc: 2-5-10, Hitotsubashi, Chiyoda-ku, Tokyo 101-8050; tel. (3) 3230-6111; fax (3) 3262-1309; e-mail yoshizumi@shueisha.co .jp; internet www.shueisha.co.jp; f. 1925; literature, fine arts, language, juvenile, comics; Pres. and CEO HIDEKI YAMASHITA.

Shufunotomo Co Ltd: 2-9, Kanda Surugadai, Chiyoda-ku, Tokyo 101-8911; tel. (3) 5280-7567; fax (3) 5280-7568; e-mail international@ shufunotomo.co.jp; internet www.shufunotomo.co.jp; f. 1916; domestic science, fine arts, gardening, handicraft, cookery and magazines; Pres. YOSHIYUKI OGINO.

Shufu-To-Seikatsusha Ltd: 3-5-7, Kyobashi, Chuo-ku, Tokyo 104-8357; tel. (3) 3563-5120; fax (3) 3563-2073; internet www.shufu.co.jp; f. 1935; home economics, recreation, fiction, medicine, comics, cooking, interiors, handicraft, fishing, fashion; Pres. KATSUHISA TAKANOU.

Shunju-Sha: 2-18-6, Soto-Kanda, Chiyoda-ku, Tokyo 101-0021; tel. (3) 3255-9611; fax (3) 3253-1384; e-mail main@shunjusha.co.jp; internet www.shunjusha.co.jp; f. 1918; philosophy, religion, literature, economics, music; Pres. AKIRA KANDA.

Sony Magazines Inc: Banchokaikan, 12-1, Goban-cho, Chiyoda-ku, Tokyo 102-8679; tel. (3) 3234-5811; fax (3) 3234-5842; internet www.sonymagazines.jp; f. 1979; music books, general literature; Pres. SHIGERU MURATA.

Taishukan Publishing Co Ltd: 2-1-1, Yushima, Bunkyo-ku, Tokyo 113-8541; tel. (3) 3868-2651; fax (3) 3868-2640; e-mail kimura@taishukan.co.jp; internet www.taishukan.co.jp; f. 1918; reference, Japanese and foreign languages, sports, dictionaries, audio-visual aids; Pres. KAZUYUKI SUZUKI.

Takahashi Shoten Co Ltd: 1-26-1, Otowa, Bunkyo-ku, Tokyo 112-0013; tel. (3) 3943-4525; fax (3) 3943-4288; e-mail ta_contact@ takahashishoten.co.jp; internet www.takahashishoten.co.jp; f. 1952; business, food and drink, sport, dictionaries, education, juvenile; Pres. HIDEO TAKAHASHI.

Tamagawa University Press: 6-1-1, Tamagawa-Gakuen, Machida-shi, Tokyo 194-8610; tel. (42) 739-8933; fax (42) 739-8940; e-mail tup@tamagawa.ac.jp; internet www.tamagawa.jp/ introduction/press; f. 1929; education, philosophy, religion, arts, juvenile, area studies; Pres. YOSHIAKI OBARA.

Tankosha Publishing Co Ltd: 19-1, Miyanishi-cho Murasakino, Kita-ku, Kyoto 603-8691; tel. (75) 432-5151; fax (75) 432-5152; e-mail info@tankosha.co.jp; internet www.tankosha.co.jp; f. 1949; tea ceremony, fine arts, history; Pres. YOSHITO NAYA.

Teikoku-Shoin Co Ltd: 3-29, Kanda Jimbo-cho, Chiyoda-ku, Tokyo 101-0051; tel. (3) 3262-0834; fax (3) 3262-7770; e-mail kenkyu@teikokushoin.co.jp; internet www.teikokushoin.co.jp; f. 1926; geography, atlases, maps, textbooks, history, civil studies; Pres. MASAYOSHI SAITO.

Tohoku University Press, Sendai: 2-1-1, Katahira, Aoba-ku, Sendai 980-8577; tel. (22) 214-2777; fax (22) 214-2778; e-mail info@tups.jp; internet www.tups.jp; f. 1996; natural science, social science, humanities, history, literature, psychology, philosophy, art, language; Chair. SHIGERU HISAMICHI.

Tokai University Press: 3-10-35, Minami-Yana, Hadano-shi, Kanagawa 257-0003; tel. (463) 79-3921; fax (463) 69-5087; e-mail webmaster@press.tokai.ac.jp; internet www.press.tokai.ac.jp; f. 1962; social science, cultural science, natural science, engineering, art; Pres. TATSURO MATSUMAE.

Tokuma Shoten Publishing Co Ltd: 2-2-1, Shiba-Daimon, Minato-ku, Tokyo 105-8055; tel. (3) 5403-4300; fax (3) 5403-4375; e-mail takeuti@shoten.tokuma.com; internet www.tokuma.jp; f. 1954; Japanese classics, history, fiction, juvenile; Pres. TORU IWABUCHI.

Tokyo News Service Ltd: Hamarikyu Park Side Place Bldg, 7-16-3, Tsukiji, Chuo-ku, Tokyo 104-8415; tel. (3) 6367-8000; fax (3) 3545-3628; internet www.tokyonews.co.jp; f. 1947; shipping, trade and television guides; Pres. T. OKUYAMA.

Tokyo Shoseki Co Ltd: 2-17-1, Horifune, Kita-ku, Tokyo 114-8524; tel. (3) 5390-7513; fax (3) 5390-7409; e-mail shoseki@tokyo-shoseki.co.jp; internet www.tokyo-shoseki.co.jp; f. 1909; textbooks, reference books, cultural and educational books; Pres. YASUNORI KAWABATA.

Tokyo Sogen-Sha Co Ltd: 1-5, Shin-Ogawa-machi, Shinjuku-ku, Tokyo 162-0814; tel. (3) 3268-8201; fax (3) 3268-8230; internet www.tsogen.co.jp; f. 1954; mystery and detective stories, science fiction, literature; Pres. SHINICHI HASEGAWA.

Toyo Keizai Inc: 1-2-1, Nihonbashi Hongoku-cho, Chuoku, Tokyo 103-8345; tel. (3) 3246-5661; fax (3) 3231-0906; e-mail info@toyokeizai.co.jp; internet www.toyokeizai.net; f. 1895; periodicals, economics, business, finance, corporation information; Pres. SEISHI SHIBOHTA.

Tuttle Publishing Co Inc: Yaekari Bldg, 3/F, 5-4-12, Osaki Shinagawa-ku, Tokyo; tel. (3) 5437-0171; fax (3) 5437-0755; e-mail customer@tuttle.co.jp; internet www.tuttle.co.jp; f. 1948; Japanese and Asian religion, history, social science, arts, languages, literature, juvenile, cookery; Pres. ERIC OEY.

United Nations University Press: 5-53-70, Jingumae, Shibuya-ku, Tokyo 150-8925; tel. (3) 5467-1212; fax (3) 3499-2828; e-mail sales@hq.unu.edu; internet www.unu.edu; f. 1975; social sciences, humanities, pure and applied natural sciences; Head KONRAD OSTERWALDER.

University of Nagoya Press: 1, Furocho, Chikusa-ku, Nagoya 464-0814; tel. (52) 781-5027; fax (52) 781-0697; e-mail sogo@unp.nagoya-u.ac.jp; internet www.unp.or.jp; f. 1982; social science, humanities, natural science, medicine; Chair. MITSUKI ISHII.

University of Tokyo Press: 7-3-1, Hongo, Bunkyo-ku, Tokyo 113-8654; tel. (3) 3811-0964; fax (3) 3815-1426; e-mail info@utp.or.jp; internet www.utp.or.jp; f. 1951; natural and social sciences, humanities; Japanese and English; Chair. HIROSHI WATANABE.

Waseda University Press: 1-9-12-402, Shinjuku-ku, Tokyo 169-0071; tel. (3) 3203-1551; fax (3) 3207-0406; e-mail shuppanbu@list.waseda.jp; internet www.waseda-up.co.jp; f. 1886; politics, economics, law, sociology, philosophy, literature; Pres. KENJI HORIGUCHI.

Yama-Kei Publishers Co Ltd: Tokyo; tel. (3) 6744-1900; fax (3) 6234-1628; e-mail info@yamakei.co.jp; internet www.yamakei.co.jp; f. 1930; natural science, geography, mountaineering, outdoor activity; Pres. SEKIMOTO CHANGDA.

Yoshikawa Kobunkan: 7-2-8, Hongo, Bunkyo-ku, Tokyo 113-0033; tel. (3) 3813-9151; fax (3) 3812-3544; e-mail hongo@yoshikawa-k.co.jp; internet www.yoshikawa-k.co.jp; f. 1857; history, biography, art, languages, religion; Pres. MOTOYASU MAEDA.

Yuhikaku Publishing Co Ltd: 2-17, Kanda Jimbo-cho, Chiyoda-ku, Tokyo 101-0051; tel. (3) 3264-1312; fax (3) 3264-5030; e-mail shinsuke-ito@yuhikaku.co.jp; internet www.yuhikaku.co.jp; f. 1877; social sciences, law, economics; Pres. SADAHARU EGUSA.

Yuki Shobo: 3-7-9, Kudan-Minami, Chiyoda-ku, Tokyo 102-0074; tel. (3) 5275-8008; fax (3) 5275-8099; e-mail takeshi.nanri@yukishobo.co.jp; internet www.yukishobo.co.jp; f. 1957; home economics, juvenile, recreation, sociology, sports; Pres. MASAO OKAJIMA.

Yuzankaku Shuppan: 2-6-9, Fujimi, Chiyoda-ku, Tokyo 102-0071; tel. (3) 3262-3231; fax (3) 3262-6938; e-mail info@yuzankaku.co.jp; internet www.yuzankaku.co.jp; f. 1916; history, fine arts, religion, archaeology; Pres. TETSUO MIYATA.

Zen-on Music Co Ltd: 2-13-3, Kami-Ochiai, Shinjuku-ku, Tokyo 161-0034; tel. (3) 3227-6270; fax (3) 3227-6276; e-mail akira@zen-on.co.jp; internet www.zen-on.co.jp; f. 1931; classics, pop, books on music; Pres. NORIYUKI HONMA.

Zoshindo Juken Kenkyusha Co Ltd: 2-19-15, Shinmachi, Nishi-ku, Osaka 550-0013; tel. (6) 6532-1581; fax (6) 6532-1588; e-mail jzoshindo@ybb.ne.jp; internet www.zoshindo.co.jp; f. 1890; educational, juvenile; Pres. AKITAKA OKAMATO.

GOVERNMENT PUBLISHING HOUSE

Government Publications' Service Centre: 1-2-1, Kasumigaseki, Chiyoda-ku, Tokyo 100-0013; tel. (3) 3504-3885; fax (3) 3504-3889.

PUBLISHERS' ASSOCIATIONS

Japan Book Publishers Association: 6, Fukuro-machi, Shinjuku-ku, Tokyo 162-0828; tel. (3) 3268-1302; fax (3) 3268-1196; e-mail rd@jbpa.or.jp; internet www.jbpa.or.jp; f. 1957; 459 mems (2010); Pres. MASAHIRO OGA; Exec. Dir TADASHI YAMASHITA.

Publishers' Association for Cultural Exchange, Japan: 1-2-1, Sarugaku-cho, Chiyoda-ku, Tokyo 101-0064; tel. (3) 3291-5685; fax (3) 3233-3645; e-mail culturalexchange@pace.or.jp; internet www.pace.or.jp; f. 1953; 75 mems (2010); Pres. TADATAKA EGUSA; Man. Dir HARUHIKO ISHIKAWA.

Broadcasting and Communications

Telecommunications and broadcasting are regulated by the Ministry of Internal Affairs and Communications.

TELECOMMUNICATIONS

EMOBILE Ltd: Shin-Nikko Bldg, 2-10-1, Toranomon, Minato-ku, Tokyo; tel. (3) 3588-7682; fax (3) 3588-7201; internet www.emobile.jp; f. 2005; owned by eAccess Ltd; mobile voice and data services; Pres. ERIC GAN.

KDDI Corpn: Garden Air Tower, 3-10-10, Iidabashi, Chiyoda-ku, Tokyo 102-8460; tel. (3) 3347-0077; fax (3) 6678-0305; internet www.kddi.com; f. 1984; est. by merger of DDI Corpn, Kokusai Denshin Denwa Corpn (KDD) and Nippon Idou Tsuhin Corpn (IDO); major international telecommunications carrier; Pres. TADASHI ONODERA.

Livedoor Co Ltd: Roppongi Hills Mori Tower, 38/F, 6-10-1, Roppongi, Minato-ku, Tokyo; tel. (3) 5155-0121; fax (3) 5766-7221; e-mail info@livedoor.jp; internet www.livedoor.com; f. 1996; acquired by NHN Japan in 2010; internet portal; network operations and maintenance; Pres. TAKESHI IDEZAWA.

Nippon Telegraph and Telephone Corpn (NTT): 2-3-1, Otemachi, Chiyoda-ku, Tokyo 100-8116; tel. (3) 5205-5111; fax (3) 5205-5589; internet www.ntt.co.jp; f. 1985; operates local, long-distance and international services; largest telecommunications co in Japan; holding co for NTT East, NTT West, NTT Communications, NTT Data Corpn and NTT DOCOMO; Pres. and CEO SATOSHI MIURA.

NTT DOCOMO: 2-11-1, Nagatacho, Chiyoda-ku, Tokyo 100-6150; tel. (3) 5156-1111; fax (3) 5156-0271; internet www.nttdocomo.co.jp; f. 1991; operates mobile phone network; Pres. and CEO RYUJI YAMADA.

SoftBank Telecom Corpn: 1-9-1, Higashi-Shimbashi, Minato-ku, Tokyo 105-7316; tel. 0088-41; e-mail tcsc@tm.softbank.co.jp; internet www.softbanktelecom.co.jp; fmrly Japan Telecom; fixed-line business acquired by Ripplewood Holdings in 2003; acquired by SoftBank Corpn in 2004; merged with International Digital Communications (IDC) in 2005; name changed as above in 2006; Chair. and CEO MASAYOSHI SON.

Digital Phone and Digital TU-KA also operate mobile telecommunication services in Japan.

BROADCASTING

NHK (Japan Broadcasting Corporation): 2-2-1, Jinnan, Shibuya-ku, Tokyo 150-8001; tel. (3) 3465-1111; fax (3) 3469-8110; e-mail webmaster@www.nhk.or.jp; internet www.nhk.or.jp; f. 1925; fmrly Nippon Hoso Kyokai (NHK—Japan Broadcasting Corpn); Japan's sole public broadcaster; operates five TV channels (incl. two terrestrial services—general TV and educational TV, and three satellite services—BS-1, BS-2 and digital Hi-Vision—HDTV), three radio channels, Radio 1, Radio 2, and FM Radio, and three worldwide services, NHK World TV, NHK World Premium and NHK World Radio Japan; headquarters in Tokyo, regional headquarters in Osaka, Nagoya, Hiroshima, Fukuoka, Sendai, Sapporo and Matsuyama; Pres. MASAYUKI MATSUMOTO; Exec. Dir-Gen. of Broadcasting HIDEMI HYUGA.

National Association of Commercial Broadcasters in Japan (NAB-J): 3-23, Kioi-cho, Chiyoda-ku, Tokyo 102-8577; tel. (3) 5213-7711; fax (3) 5213-7730; e-mail webmaster@nab.or.jp; internet www.nab.or.jp; f. 1951; includes 133 TV cos and 110 radio cos, of which 42 operate both radio and TV, with 664 radio stations and 8,315 TV stations (incl. relay stations); Pres. MICHISADA HIROSE; Exec. Dir TOSHIO FUKUDA.

Some of the most important companies are:

Asahi Hoso—Asahi Broadcasting Corpn: 1-1-30, Fukushima, Fukushima-ku, Osaka 553-8503; tel. (6) 6458-5321; internet www.asahi.co.jp; f. 1951; Pres. SATOSHI WAKISAKA.

Bunka Hoso—Nippon Cultural Broadcasting, Inc: 1-31, Hamamatsu-cho, Minato-ku, Tokyo 105-8002; tel. (3) 5403-1111; internet www.joqr.co.jp; f. 1952; Pres. MIKI AKIHIRO.

Chubu-Nippon Broadcasting Co Ltd: 1-2-8, Shinsakae, Naka-ku, Nagoya 460-8405; tel. (052) 241-8111; internet hicbc.com; f. 1950; Pres. YOICHI OISHI.

Fuji Television Network, Inc: 2-4-8, Daiba, Minato-ku, Tokyo 137-8088; tel. (3) 5500-8888; fax (3) 5500-8027; internet www.fujitv.co.jp; f. 1959; owns Nippon Broadcasting System, Inc; 12.75% stake in internet provider Livedoor; Chair. and CEO HISASHI HIEDA; Pres. KOU TOYODA.

Kansai TV Hoso (KTV)—Kansai Telecasting Corpn: 2-1-7, Ogimachi, Kita-ku, Osaka 530-8408; tel. (6) 6314-8888; internet www.ktv.co.jp; f. 1958; Pres. SUMIO FUKUI.

Mainichi Hoso (MBS)—Mainichi Broadcasting System, Inc: 17-1, Chayamachi, Kita-ku, Osaka 530-8304; tel. (6) 6359-1123; fax (6) 6359-3503; internet www.mbs.jp; f. 1950; Pres. MASAHIRO YAMAMOTO.

Nippon Hoso—Nippon Broadcasting System, Inc: 2-4-8, Daiba, Minato-ku, Tokyo 137-8686; tel. (3) 5500-1234; fax (3) 5500-3902; e-mail saiyo2013@jolf.jp; internet www.jolf.co.jp; f. 1954; 49.8% controlling stake acquired by Livedoor Co Ltd in 2005, but subsequently purchased by Fuji TV Network, Inc; Pres. AKINOBU KAMEBUCHI.

Nippon TV Hoso-MO (NTV)—Nippon Television Network Corpn: 1-6-1, Higashi-Shimbashi, Minato-ku, Tokyo 105-7444; tel. (3) 6215-1111; fax (3) 6215-3157; internet www.ntv.co.jp; f. 1953; Chair. NORITADA HOSOKAWA; Pres. YOSHIO OKUBO.

Okinawa TV Hoso (OTV)—Okinawa Television Broadcasting Co Ltd: 1-2-20, Kumoji, Naha 900-8588; tel. (988) 63-2111; fax (988) 61-0193; e-mail otvweb@otv.co.jp; internet www.otv.co.jp; f. 1959; Pres. BUNKI TOMA.

Radio Nikkei: 1-9-15, Akasaka, Minato-ku, Tokyo 107-8373; tel. (3) 3583-8151; fax (3) 3583-9062; internet www.radionikkei.jp; f. 1954; Pres. KENJI SUZUKI.

Ryukyu Hoso (RBC)—Ryukyu Broadcasting Co: 2-3-1, Kumoji, Naha 900-8711; tel. (98) 867-2151; fax (98) 864-5732; e-mail info@rbc.co.jp; internet www.rbc.co.jp; f. 1954.

Tokyo Hoso (TBS)—Tokyo Broadcasting System Holdings Inc: 5-3-6, Akasaka, Minato-ku, Tokyo 107-8006; tel. (3) 3746-1111; fax (3) 3588-6378; internet www.tbs.co.jp; f. 1951; Chair. HIROSHI INOUE; Pres. TOSHICHIKA ISHIHARA.

TV Asahi Corpn: 6-9-1, Roppongi, Minato-ku, Tokyo 106-8001; tel. (3) 6406-1111; fax (3) 3405-3714; internet www.tv-asahi.co.jp; f. 1957; Pres. HIROSHI HAYAKAWA.

TV Osaka (TVO)—Television Osaka, Inc: 1-2-18, Otemae, Chuo-ku, Osaka 540-8519; tel. (6) 6947-7777; fax (6) 6946-9796; e-mail takoru@tv-osaka.co.jp; internet www.tv-osaka.co.jp; f. 1982; Pres. MAKOTO FUKAGAWA.

TV Tokyo Corpn: 4-3-12, Toranomon, Minato-ku, Tokyo 105-8012; tel. (3) 5470-7777; fax (3) 5473-6393; internet www.tv-tokyo.co.jp; f. 1964; Pres. and CEO MASAYUKI SHIMADA.

Yomiuri TV Hoso (YTV)—Yomiuri Telecasting Corporation: 2-2-33, Shiromi, Chuo-ku, Osaka 540-8510; tel. (6) 6947-2111; e-mail licensing@ytv.co.jp; internet www.ytv.co.jp; f. 1958; 20 hrs broadcasting daily; Pres. KOJI TAKADA.

Satellite, Cable and Digital Television

In addition to the two broadcast satellite services that NHK introduced in 1989, a number of commercial satellite stations are in operation. Cable television is available in urban areas. Satellite digital television services first became available in 1996. Terrestrial digital broadcasting was launched in December 2003. The switch from analogue to digital services was completed in July 2011.

SKY Perfect JSAT Corp: 1-4-14, Akasaka, Minato-ku, Tokyo 107-0052; tel. (3) 5571-7800; internet www.sptvjsat.com; f. 1994; Chair. SHIGEKI NISHIYAMA; Pres. SHINJI TAKADA.

Finance

(cap. = capital; p.u. = paid up; res = reserves; dep. = deposits; m. = million; brs = branches; amounts in yen)

BANKING

Japan's central bank and bank of issue is the Bank of Japan. At March 2010 there were 201 banks in the country, including five major commercial banks, 16 trust banks and 64 regional banks.

An important financial role is played by co-operatives and by the many small enterprise institutions. There are also two types of private financial institutions for small business. At August 2005 there were 175 Credit Co-operatives and at March 2010 there were 271 Shinkin Banks (credit associations), which lend only to members. The latter also receive deposits.

The most popular form of savings is through the post office network. In October 2005 legislation was approved to permit the privatization of Japan Post. Following its initial transfer to a holding company, Japan Post was divided into four units (savings, insurance and postal services, along with personnel and property management). The first disposals took place in 2007. Having been established in September 2006, the Japan Post Bank (JPB) commenced operations on 1 October 2007. The JPB thus became the world's largest financial institution in terms of deposits; it is also the larges provider of life insurance.

Central Bank

Nippon Ginko (Bank of Japan): 2-1-1, Motoishi-cho, Nihonbash Chuo-ku, Tokyo 103-0021; tel. (3) 3279-1111; fax (3) 5200-225 e-mail prd@info.boj.or.jp; internet www.boj.or.jp; f. 1882; ca 100m., res 2,660,006m., dep. 38,168,703m. (March 2010); Gov MASAAKI SHIRAKAWA; Dep. Govs HIROHIDE YAMAGUCHI, KIYOHIK NISHIMURA; 32 brs.

Principal Commercial Banks

The Asahi Shinkin Bank: 2-1-2, Higashi-Kanda, Chiyoda-ku Tokyo 101-0031; tel. (3) 3862-0321; fax (3) 5687-6867; interne www.asahi-shinkin.co.jp; f. 1923; est. as Shinyo Kumiai Tomir Kinko; name changed as above after merger in 2002; cap. 22,608m. res 26,231m., dep. 1,609,416m. (March 2010); Chair. KUNITAKI MORIWAKI; Pres. KAZUO KOBAYASHI; 69 brs.

Ashikaga Bank Ltd: 4-1-25, Sakura, Utsunomiya, Tochigi 320-8610; tel. (28) 622-0111; e-mail ashigin@ssctnet.or.jp; internet www.ashikagabank.co.jp; f. 1895; nationalized Nov. 2003 owing to insolvency; cap. 135,000m., res 14,448m., dep. 4,651,651m. (March 2010); CEO SATOSHI FUJISAWA; 149 brs.

Bank of Fukuoka Ltd: 2-13-1, Tenjin, Chuo-ku, Fukuoka 810-8727; tel. (92) 723-2442; fax (92) 711-1371; internet www.fukuokabank.co.jp; f. 1945; cap. 82,329m., res 127,904m., dep. 7,933,053m. (March 2010); Chair. RYOJI TSUKUDA; Pres. MASAAKI TANI; 167 brs.

Bank of Tokyo-Mitsubishi UFJ Ltd: 2-7-1, Marunouchi, Chiyoda-ku, Tokyo 100-8388; tel. (3) 3240-1111; fax (3) 3240-4197; internet www.bk.mufg.jp; f. 2006; est. through merger of Bank of Tokyo-Mitsubishi Ltd and UFJ Bank Ltd; specializes in international banking and financial business; subsidiary of Mitsubishi UFJ Financial Group (f. 2005 through merger of Mitsubishi Tokyo Financial Group and UFJ Holdings); cap. 1,711,958m., res 4,468,751m., dep. 136,213,699m. (March 2010); Pres. NOBUYUKI HIRANO; 848 brs (772 domestic, 76 overseas).

Bank of Yokohama Ltd: 3-1-1, Minatomirai, Nishi-ku, Yokohama, Kanagawa 220-8611; tel. (45) 225-1111; fax (45) 225-1160; e-mail iroffice@hamagin.co.jp; internet www.boy.co.jp; f. 1920; cap. 215,628m., res 270,524m., dep. 10,721,975m. (March 2010); Chair. SADAAKI HIRASAWA; Pres. TADASHI OGAWA; 201 brs.

Chiba Bank Ltd: 1-2, Chiba-minato, Chuo-ku, Chiba 260-8720; tel. (43) 245-1111; e-mail int@chibabank.co.jp; internet www.chibabank.co.jp; f. 1943; cap. 145,069m., res 182,850m., dep. 9,462,726m. (March 2010); Pres. HIDETOSHI SAKUMA; Chair. TOSHIAKI ISHII; 167 domestic brs, 3 overseas brs.

The Chiba Kogyo Bank Ltd: 2-1-2, Saiwa-cho, Mihama-ku, Chiba; tel. (43) 243-2111; fax (43) 244-9203; internet www.chibakogyo-bank.co.jp; f. 1952; cap. 57,941m., res 36,315m., dep. 2,022,811m. (March 2010); Pres. and CEO TOSHIKAZU AOYAGI; 71 brs.

Hachijuni Bank: 178-8, Okada, Nagano-shi, Nagano 380-8682; tel. (26) 227-1182; fax (26) 226-5077; internet www.82bank.co.jp; f. 1931; cap. 52,243m., res 94,087m., dep. 5,529,324m. (March 2010); Chair. KAZUYUKI NARUSAWA; Pres. YOSHIYUKI YAMAURA.

Hokkaido Bank Ltd: 4-1, Nishi-Odori, Chuo-ku, Sapporo 060-8678, Hokkaido; tel. (11) 233-1093; fax (11) 231-3133; internet www.hokkaidobank.co.jp; f. 1951; cap. 93,524m., res 22,836m., dep. 3,951,850m. (March 2010); Pres. YOSHIHIRO SEKIHACHI; 129 brs.

Hokkoku Bank Ltd: 1 Shimotsutsumi-cho, Kanazawa 920-8670, Ishikawa; tel. (76) 263-1111; fax (76) 223-3362; internet www.hokkokubank.co.jp; f. 1943; cap. 26,673m., res 32,079m., dep. 2,919,655m. (March 2010); Pres. TATEKI ATAKA; 130 brs.

Hokuetsu Bank Ltd: 2-2-14, Otedori, Nagaoka 940-8650, Niigata; tel. (258) 353-111; fax (258) 375-113; internet www.hokuetsubank.co.jp; f. 1942; cap. 24,538m., res 29,080m., dep. 2,111,419m. (March 2010); Pres. KUSUMI TAKASHI; 89 brs.

Hokuriku Bank Ltd: 1-2-26, Tsutsumichodori, Toyama 930-8637; tel. (76) 423-7111; fax (76) 491-5908; e-mail info@hokuhoku-fg.co.jp; internet www.hokugin.co.jp; f. 1877; cap. 140,409m., res 31,376m., dep. 5,477,385m. (March 2010); Pres. SHIGEO TAKAGI; 176 brs.

Hokuto Bank Ltd: 3-1-41, Nakadori, Akita 010-0001; tel. (18) 833-4211; fax (18) 832-1942; e-mail hokutobank@hokutobank.co.jp; internet www.hokutobank.co.jp; f. 1895; est. as Masuda Bank Ltd, name changed as above after merger with Akita Akebono Bank in 1993; cap. 11,000m., res 23,953m., dep. 1,066,070m. (March 2010); Pres. EIKICHI SAITO; 84 brs.

Japan Net Bank: 2-1-1, Nishi-Shinjuku, Shinjuku-ku, Tokyo 163-0406; tel. (3) 6739-5000; internet www.japannetbank.co.jp; f. 2000; Japan's first internet-only bank; cap. 372m. (2010); Pres. NAOTO MURAMATSU.

oyo Bank Ltd: 2-5-5, Minami-Machi, Mito-shi, Ibaraki 310-0021; el. (29) 231-2151; fax (29) 255-6522; e-mail joyointl@po.net-ibaraki ne.jp; internet www.joyobank.co.jp; f. 1935; cap. 85,113m., res 9,617m., dep. 6,846,502m. (March 2010); Chair. ISAO SHIBUYA; Pres. UNIO ONIZAWA; 172 brs.

uroku Bank Ltd: 8-26, Kandamachi, Gifu 500-8516; tel. (582) 652-11; fax (582) 661-698; internet www.juroku.co.jp; f. 1877; cap. 6,839m., res 57,694m., dep. 4,035,793m. (March 2010); Pres. NOBUO OJIMA; 147 brs.

Kansai Urban Banking Corpn: 1-2-4, Nishi-Shinbashi, Chuo-ku, Osaka; tel. (6) 6834-4581; internet www.kansaiurban.co.jp; f. 1922; ap. 470,039m., res 63,352m., dep. 4,069,491m. (March 2010); Chair. AKIYOSHI KITAMURA; 147 brs.

Kumamoto Family Bank Ltd: 6-29-20, Suizenji, Kumamoto 862-8601; tel. (96) 385-1111; fax (96) 385-4272; internet www.kf-bank.jp; f. 1992; cap. 26,347m., res 27,858m., dep. 1,073,486m. (March 2010); Pres. KENJI HAYASHI.

Miyazaki Bank Ltd: 4-3-5, Tachibanadori-Higashi, Miyazaki 880-0805; tel. (985) 273-131; fax (985) 225-952; e-mail kokusai@miyagin co.jp; internet www.miyagin.co.jp; f. 1932; cap. 14,697m., res 16,184m., dep. 1,833,901m. (March 2010); Pres. ISAO SATO; 97 brs.

Mizuho Bank Ltd: 1-1-5, Uchisaiwai-cho, Chiyoda-ku, Tokyo 100-0011; tel. (3) 3596-1111; fax (3) 3596-2179; internet www .mizuhobank.co.jp; f. 1971 as Dai-Ichi Kangyo Bank; merged with Fuji Bank and Industrial Bank of Japan to form above in 2002; cap. 700,000m., res 800,674m., dep. 65,592,993m. (March 2010); Pres. and CEO SATORU NISHIBORI; 334 domestic brs, 17 overseas brs.

North Pacific Bank (Hokuyo Bank): 3-7, Nishi-Odori, Chuo-ku, Sapporo 060-8661; tel. (11) 261-1416; fax (11) 232-6921; internet www.hokuyobank.co.jp; f. 1917; est. as Hokuyo Sogo Bank Ltd; adopted present name 1989; cap. 121,101m., res 137,422m., dep. 6,882,771m. (March 2010); Chair. IWAO TAKAMUKI; Pres. RYUZO YOKOUCHI.

Resona Bank Ltd: 2-2-1, Bingo-machi, Chuo-ku, Osaka 540-8610; tel. (6) 6271-1221; internet www.resona-gr.co.jp; f. 1918; merged with Asahi Bank in 2002 and changed name as above; cap. 279,928m., res 92,885m., dep. 22,786,624m. (March 2010); Chair. EIJI HOSOYA; Pres. SEIJI HIGAKI; 334 brs.

Saitama Resona Bank Ltd: 7-4-1, Tokiwa, Urawa-ku, Saitama 330-9088; tel. (48) 824-2411; internet www.resona-gr.co.jp/saitamaresona; f. 2002; cap. 70,000m., res 124,193m., dep. 10,100,154m. (March 2010); Pres. KENJI KAWADA.

San-in Godo Bank Ltd: 10, Uomachi, Matsue, Shimane 690-0062; tel. (852) 551-000; fax (852) 273-398; e-mail soki@gogin.co.jp; internet www.gogin.co.jp; f. 1941; cap. 20,705m., res 42,509m., dep. 3,525,963m. (March 2010); Pres. MAKOTO FURUSE; Chair. HIROYUKI WAKASA; 148 brs.

The Senshu Ikeda Bank Ltd: 18-14, Kita-ku, Osaka Chayamachi; tel. (6) 6375-1005; internet www.sihd-bk.jp; cap. 507,000m. (2010); Chair. NORIMASA YOSHIDA; Pres. MORITAKA HATTORI.

Shiga Bank Ltd: 1-38, Hamamachi, Otsu 520-8686, Shiga; tel. (77) 521-2360; fax (77) 521-2892; internet www.shigagin.com; f. 1933; cap. 33,076m., res 77,963m., dep. 3,590,958m. (March 2010); Chair. KOICHI TAKATA; Pres. YOSHIO DAIDO; 134 brs.

Shikoku Bank Ltd: 1–1–1, Minami-Harimaya-cho, Kochi 780-8605; tel. (88) 823-2111; fax (88) 873-0322; internet www .shikokubank.co.jp; f. 1873; cap. 25,000m., res 25,890m., dep. 2,394,236m. (March 2010); Chair. AKIHIRO AOKI; Pres. TADASHI NOMURA; 121 brs.

Shimizu Bank: 2-1, Fujimi-cho, Shimizu-ku, Shozuoka-shi, Shizuoka 424-8715; tel. (543) 535-151; fax (543) 535-333; internet www .shimizubank.co.jp; f. 1928; cap. 8,670m., res 6,957m., dep. 1,271,683m. (March 2010); Chair. KOICHI SUGIYAMA; Pres. NORIJI YAMADA; 78 brs.

Shizuoka Bank Ltd: 1-10, Gofuku-cho, Aoi-ku, Shizuoka 420-8761; tel. (54) 345-5700; fax (54) 349-5501; internet www.shizuokabank.co .jp; f. 1943; cap. 90,845m., res 128,366m., dep. 7,993,870m. (March 2010); Chair. TORU SAKURAI; Pres. and CEO KATSUNORI NAKANISHI; 168 domestic brs, 3 overseas brs.

Sumitomo Mitsui Trust Bank Ltd: 1-2, Marunouchi, Chiyoda-ku, Tokyo 100-0005; tel. (3) 3230-8811; fax (3) 3239-4170; internet www .smbc.co.jp; f. 1895; present name adopted following merger with Sakura Bank Ltd in 2001; wholly owned subsidiary of Sumitomo Mitsui Financial Group (SMFG—f. 2002); cap. 1,770,996m., res 2,984,119m., dep. 106,451,620m. (March 2010); Chair. TEISUKE KITAYAMA; Pres. MASAYUKI OKU; 436 domestic brs, 15 overseas brs.

Toho Bank Ltd: 3-25, Ohmachi, Fukushima 960-8633; tel. (24) 523-3131; fax (24) 524-1583; internet www.tohobank.co.jp; f. 1941; cap. 23,519m., res 19,476m., dep. 2,984,708m. (March 2010); Chair. TOSHIO SEYA; Pres. SEISHI KITAMURA; 113 brs.

Tokyo Star Bank: 1-6-16 Akasaka, Minato-ku, Tokyo; tel. (3) 3586-3111; fax (3) 3586-5137; internet www.tokyostarbank.co.jp; f. 2001; est. as Nippon Finance Investment Ltd, name changed as above in May 2001; cap. 21,000m., res 21,463m., dep. 1,904,286m. (March 2010); Chair. TODD BUDGE; Pres. ROBERT BERARDY; 36 brs.

Tokyo Tomin Bank Ltd: 2-3-11, Roppongi, Minato-ku, Tokyo 106-8525; tel. (3) 3582-8251; fax (3) 3582-1979; e-mail jdu02670@nifty.ne .jp; internet www.tominbank.co.jp; f. 1951; cap. 48,120m., res 12,748m., dep. 2,332,001m. (March 2010); Chair. TETSUYA SHIINA; Pres. ISAO KOBAYASHI; 72 brs.

Tomato Bank Ltd: 2-3-4, Bancho, Okayama 700-0811, Ehime; tel. (86) 221-1010; fax (86) 221-1040; internet www.tomatobank.co.jp; f. 1931; est. as Sanyo Sogo Bank; became a commercial bank in 1989, when present name was assumed; cap. 14,310m., res 13,688m., dep. 816,155m. (March 2010); Pres. TAKANOBU NAKAGAWA.

Tsukuba Bank Ltd: 2-11-7, Chuo-ku, Tsuchiura, Ibaraki 305-0032; tel. (29) 859-8111; internet www.tsukubabank.co.jp; f. 1952; cap. 31,368m., res 14,762m., dep. 1,979,098m. (March 2010); Pres. KOZO KIMURA; 147 brs.

Principal Trust Banks

Chuo Mitsui Trust and Banking Co Ltd: 3-33-1, Shiba, Minato-ku, Chuo-ku, Tokyo 105-8574; tel. (3) 5445-3500; fax (3) 5232-8879; internet www.chuomitsui.co.jp; f. 1962; est. as Chuo Trust and Banking Co Ltd, name changed as above in 2000, following merger with Mitsui Trust and Banking Co Ltd; cap. 399,697m., res 155,132m., dep. 12,329,375m. (March 2010); Pres. KAZUO TANABE; 66 brs.

Mitsubishi UFJ Trust and Banking Corporation: 1-4-5, Marunouchi, Chiyoda-ku, Tokyo 100-8212; tel. (3) 3212-1211; fax (3) 3514-6660; internet www.tr.mufg.jp; f. 2005; est. upon merger of Mitsubishi Tokyo Financial Group and UFJ Holdings to form Mitsubishi UFJ Financial Group, of which it is a subsidiary; cap. 324,279m., res 462,526m., dep. 17,744,376m. (March 2010); Chair. HARUYA UEHARA; Pres. KINYA OKAUCHI; 68 domestic brs, 7 overseas brs.

Mizuho Trust and Banking Co Ltd: 1-2-1, Yaesu, Chuo-ku, Tokyo 103-8670; tel. (3) 3278-8111; fax (3) 3281-6947; internet www .mizuho-tb.co.jp; f. 1925; fmrly Yasuda Trust and Banking Co Ltd; cap. 247,260m., res 49,047m., dep. 4,451,546m. (March 2010); Pres. and CEO TAKASHI NONAKA; 38 brs.

Sumitomo Trust and Banking Co Ltd: 4-5-33, Kitahama, Chuo-ku, Osaka 540-8639; tel. (6) 6220-2121; fax (6) 6220-2043; e-mail ipda@sumitomotrust.co.jp; internet www.sumitomotrust.co.jp; f. 1925; cap. 342,037m., res 358,829m., dep. 16,408,565m. (March 2010); Chair. ATSUSHI TAKAHASHI; Pres. and CEO HITOSHI TSUNEKAGE; 63 domestic brs, 8 overseas brs.

Long-Term Credit Banks

Aozora Bank: 1-3-1, Kudan-Minami, Chiyoda-ku, Tokyo 102-8660; tel. (3) 3263-1111; fax (3) 3265-7024; e-mail sora@aozora.co.jp; internet www.aozorabank.co.jp; f. 1957; nationalized Dec. 1998, sold to consortium led by Softbank Corpn in Aug. 2000; fmrly The Nippon Credit Bank, name changed as above 2001; 62% owned by Cerberus Group; cap. 419,780m., res 15,437m., dep. 4,324,674m. (March 2010); Pres. and CEO BRIAN PRINCE; Chair. YUJI SHIRAKAWA; 20 brs.

Mizuho Corporate Bank Ltd (The Industrial Bank of Japan Ltd): 1-3-3, Marunouchi, Chiyoda-ku, Tokyo 100-8210; tel. (3) 3214-1111; fax (3) 3201-7643; internet www.mizuhocbk.co.jp; f. 1902; renamed as above in 2002 following merger of the Dai-Ichi Kangyo Bank, the Fuji Bank and the Industrial Bank of Japan; medium- and long-term financing; cap. 1,404,065m., res 947,050m., dep. 55,720,550m. (March 2010); Pres. and CEO SATO YASUHIRO; 277 domestic brs, 21 overseas brs.

Shinsei Bank Ltd: 2-4-3, Nihonbashi-muromachi, Chuo-ku, Tokyo; tel. (3) 6680-7000; internet www.shinseibank.com; f. 1952; est. as The Long-Term Credit Bank of Japan; nationalized Oct. 1998, sold to Ripplewood Holdings (USA), renamed as above June 2000; cap. 476,296m., res –16,124m., dep. 8,698,559m. (March 2010); Pres. and CEO SHIGEKI TOMA; 30 domestic brs, 1 overseas br.

Co-operative Bank

Shinkin Central Bank: 1-3-7, Yaesu, Chuo-ku, Tokyo 103-0028; tel. (3) 5202-7700; fax (3) 3278-7031; e-mail s1000551@facetoface.ne .jp; internet www.shinkin-central-bank.jp; f. 1950; cap. and res 1,002,570m., dep. 26,903,428m. (March 2010); Chair. KOJI OMAE; Pres. and CEO MITSUO TANABE; 14 domestic brs, 4 overseas brs.

Principal Government Institutions

Development Bank of Japan: 1-9-1, Otemachi, Chiyoda-ku, Tokyo 100-0004; tel. (3) 3270-3211; fax (3) 3245-1938; e-mail safukas@dbj.go.jp; internet www.dbj.jp; f. 1951; est. as Japan Devt Bank; renamed Oct. 1999 following consolidation with Hokkaido and Tohoku Devt Finance Public Corpn; provides long-term loans; subscribes for corporate bonds; guarantees corporate obligations;

invests in specific projects; borrows funds from Govt and abroad; issues external bonds and notes; provides market information and consulting services for prospective entrants to Japanese market; legislation providing for the bank's privatization (by 2015) approved in 2008; cap. 1,181,194m., res 1,078,540m., dep. 12,978,852m. (March 2010); Pres. and CEO MINORU MUROFUSHI; 10 domestic brs, 6 overseas brs.

Japan Finance Corporation (JFC): 1-9-3, Otemachi, Chiyoda-ku, Tokyo 100-0004; internet www.jfc.go.jp; f. 2008; govt financial institution formed from merger of National Life Finance Corpn (NLFC), Agriculture, Forestry and Fisheries Finance Corpn (AFC), Japan Finance Corpn for Small and Medium Enterprise (JASME) and International Finance Operations (IFOs) of Japan Bank for International Cooperation (JBIC); cap. 3,251,700m., res 2,405,100m. (March 2010); Gov. and CEO SHOSAKU YASUI; 152 brs.

Japan Bank for International Cooperation (JBIC): 1-4-1, Otemachi, Chiyoda-ku, Tokyo 100-8144; tel. (3) 5218-3304; fax (3) 5218-3960; e-mail ir@jbic.go.jp; internet www.jbic.go.jp; f. 1999; est. by merger of The Export-Import Bank of Japan (f. 1950) and The Overseas Economic Co-operation Fund (f. 1961); governmental financial institution, responsible for Japan's external economic policy and co-operation activities; cap. 1,055,500m. (March 2010); Pres. and CEO HIROSHI OKUDA.

Japan Post Bank Co Ltd (JPB): 1-3-2, Kasumigaseki, Chiyoda-ku, Tokyo 100-8798; tel. (3) 3504-4411; internet www.jp-bank.japanpost.jp; f. 2006; wholly owned by Japan Post Holdings Co Ltd; cap. 3,500,000m., dep. 182,736,000m. (2007); Chair. SHIGEO KAWA; Pres. YOSHIYUKI IZAWA.

Norinchukin Bank (Central Co-operative Bank for Agriculture, Forestry and Fisheries): 1-13-2, Yuraku-cho, Chiyoda-ku, Tokyo 100; tel. (3) 3279-0111; fax (3) 3218-5177; internet www.nochubank.or.jp; f. 1923; main banker to agricultural, forestry and fisheries co-operatives; receives deposits from individual co-operatives, federations and agricultural enterprises; extends loans to these and to local govt authorities and public corpns; adjusts excess and shortage of funds within co-operative system; issues debentures, invests funds and engages in other regular banking business; cap. 3,425,909m., res –312,733m., dep. 56,137,011m. (March 2010); Chair MAMORU MOTEKI; Pres. and CEO YOSHIO KONO; 34 domestic brs, 5 overseas brs.

Shoko Chukin Bank (Central Co-operative Bank for Commerce and Industry): 2-10-17, Yaesu, Chuo-ku, Tokyo 104-0028; tel. (3) 3272-6111; fax (3) 3272-6169; e-mail JDK06560@nifty.ne.jp; internet www.shokochukin.co.jp; f. 1936; provides general banking services to facilitate finance for smaller enterprise co-operatives and other organizations formed mainly by small and medium-sized enterprises; issues debentures; began process of privatization in 2008; cap. 218,653m., res 554,819m., dep. 10,877,658m. (March 2010); Pres. TETSUO SEKI; 99 domestic brs, 3 overseas brs.

Other government financial institutions include the Japan Finance Corpn for Municipal Enterprises, the Small Business Credit Insurance Corpn and the Okinawa Development Finance Corpn.

Foreign Banks

At March 2010 there were 56 foreign banks operating in Japan.

Bankers' Associations

Japanese Bankers Association: 1-3-1, Marunouchi, Chiyoda-ku, Tokyo 100-8216; tel. (3) 3216-3761; fax (3) 3201-5608; internet www.zenginkyo.or.jp; f. 1945; fmrly Fed. of Bankers Asscns of Japan; 123 full mems, 61 assoc. mems, 62 special mems, 3 bank holding co mems; Chair. SATORU NISHIBORI.

Tokyo Bankers Association, Inc: 1-3-1, Marunouchi, Chiyoda-ku, Tokyo 100-8216; tel. (3) 3216-3761; fax (3) 3201-5608; f. 1945; 105 mem. banks; conducts the Japanese Bankers Asscn's administrative business; Chair. MASAYUKI OKU.

National Association of Labour Banks: 2-5-15, Kanda Surugadai, Chiyoda-ku, Tokyo 101-0062; tel. (3) 3295-6735; fax (3) 3295-6751; e-mail kikaku@ho.rokinbank.or.jp; internet all.rokin.or.jp; f. 1951; Pres. YASUHIKO OKADA.

Regional Banks Association of Japan: 3-1-2, Uchikanda, Chiyoda-ku, Tokyo 101-8509; tel. (3) 3252-5171; fax (3) 3254-8664; internet www.chiginkyo.or.jp; f. 1936; 64 mem. banks; Chair. TADASHI OGAWA.

Second Association of Regional Banks: 5, Sanban-cho, Chiyoda-ku, Tokyo 102-0075; tel. (3) 3262-2181; fax (3) 3262-2339; e-mail hp-master@dainichiginkyo.or.jp; internet www.dainichiginkyo.or.jp; f. 1989; fmrly Nat. Asscn of Sogo Banks; 42 commercial banks; Chair. NOBUO KOJIMA.

STOCK EXCHANGES

Nagoya Stock Exchange: 3-8-20, Sakae, Naka-ku, Nagoya 460-0008; tel. (52) 262-3172; fax (52) 241-1527; e-mail kikaku@nse.or.jp; internet www.nse.or.jp; f. 1949; Pres. NOBORU KUROYANAGI; Exe Vice-Pres. MASAKI TAKEDA.

Osaka Securities Exchange (OSE): 1-8-16, Kitahama, Chuo-k Osaka 541-0041; tel. (6) 4706-0875; fax (6) 6231-2639; e-mail koho ose.or.jp; internet www.ose.or.jp; f. 1949; 83 regular transactio partners, 5 transaction partners in futures and options trading, IPO transaction partners; Pres. and CEO MICHIO YONEDA.

Jasdaq: 1-5-8, Nihonbashi Kayaba-cho, Chuo-ku, Tokyo 10 0025; tel. (3) 3669-5410; internet www.ose.or.jp/e/jasdaq; f. 196 became wholly owned subsidiary of Osaka Securities Exchang 2009; resumed operations following merger of smaller market Jasdaq, Hercules and NEO in 2010; over 1,400 listed cos.

Sapporo Securities Exchange: 5-14-1, Nishi, Minami 1-jo, Chuc ku, Sapporo 060-0061; tel. (11) 241-6171; fax (11) 251-0840; e-ma info@sse.or.jp; internet www.sse.or.jp; 75 listed cos; Pres. YOSHIR ITOH.

Tokyo Stock Exchange, Inc: 2-1, Nihonbashi Kabuto-cho, Chuo ku, Tokyo 103-8224; tel. (3) 3665-1881; fax (3) 3662-0547; interne www.tse.or.jp; f. 1949; 97 general trading participants, 56 bon futures trading participants, 2 stock index futures trading partici pants; cap. 11,500m., issued shares 2,300,000 (June 2010); Chair TAIZO NISHIMURO; Pres. and CEO ATSUSHI SAITO.

Supervisory Body

The Securities and Exchange Surveillance Commission: 3-2-1, Kasumigaseki, Chiyoda-ku, Tokyo 100-8922; tel. (3) 3581-7868 fax (3) 5251-2151; internet www.fsa.go.jp/sesc; f. 1992; est. for the surveillance of securities and financial futures transactions; Chair KENICHI SADO.

INSURANCE

Principal Life Companies

AIG Edison Life Insurance Co: Olinas Tower, 4-1-3, Sumida-ku, Tokyo 130-8625; tel. (3) 6658-6000; internet www.aigedison.co.jp; fmrly GE Edison Life Insurance Co, itself fmrly Toho Mutual Life Insurance Co; became subsidiary of Gibraltar Life Insurance in Feb. 2011; Pres. TORU MATSUZAWA.

AIG Star Life Insurance Co Ltd: 4-1-3, Sumida-ku, Tokyo 130-8625; internet www.aigstar-life.co.jp; fmrly Chiyoda Mutual Life Insurance Co, acquired by American International Group, Inc (AIG) in 2001; became subsidiary of Gibraltar Life Insurance in Feb. 2011; Pres. NORIO TOMONO.

Aioi Life Insurance Co Ltd: 3-1-6, Nihonbashi, Chuo-ku, Tokyo 103-0027; tel. (3) 3273-0101; internet www.ioi-life.co.jp; Pres. YOSHIHISA ISHII.

American Family Life Assurance Co of Columbus AFLAC Japan: Shinjuku Mitsui Bldg, 12/F, 2-1-1, Nishi-Shinjuku, Shinjuku-ku, Tokyo 163-0456; tel. (3) 3344-2701; fax (3) 0424-3001; internet www.aflac.co.jp; f. 1974; Chair. YOSHIKI OTAKE; Pres. HIDEFUMI MATSUI.

American Life Insurance Co (Japan): 4-1-3, Sumida-ku, Tokyo; tel. (3) 3284-4111; fax (3) 3284-3874; internet www.alico.co.jp; f. 1972; Pres. KAZUYUKI TAKAHASHI.

Asahi Mutual Life Insurance Co: 1-23, Tsurumaki, Tama-shi, Tokyo 206-8611; tel. (42) 338-3111; internet www.asahi-life.co.jp; f. 1888; Pres. MIKI SATO.

AXA Japan Holding Co Ltd: NBF Platinum Tower, 1-17-3, Minato-ku, Tokyo 150-8020; tel. (3) 3407-6210; internet www.axa.co.jp; Pres. and CEO JEAN-LOUIS LAURENT JOSI.

Cardif Assurance Vie: Infoss Tower, 9/F, 20-1, Sakuragaoka-cho, Shibuya-ku, Tokyo 150-0031; tel. (3) 6415-8275; internet www.cardif.co.jp/vie; f. 2000; Pres. ATSUSHI SAKAUCHI.

Dai-ichi Mutual Life Insurance Co: 1-13-1, Yuraku-cho, Chiyoda-ku, Tokyo 100-8411; tel. (3) 3216-1211; fax (3) 5221-8139; internet www.dai-ichi-life.co.jp; f. 1902; Chair. TOMIJIRO MORITA; Pres. KOICHIRO WATANABE.

Fuji Life Insurance Co Ltd: 1-18-17, Minami-Senba, Chuo-ku, Osaka-shi 542-0081; tel. (6) 6261-0284; fax (6) 6261-0113; internet www.fujiseimei.co.jp; f. 1996; Pres. YOSHIAKI YONEMURA.

Fukoku Mutual Life Insurance Co: 2-2-2, Uchisaiwai-cho, Chiyoda-ku, Tokyo 100-0011; tel. (3) 3508-1101; fax (3) 3591-6446; internet www.fukoku-life.co.jp; f. 1923; Chair. TOMOFUMI AKIYAMA; Pres. YOSHITERU YONEYAMA.

Gibraltar Life Insurance Co Ltd: 2-13-10, Tamati Hisashi, Tokyo 100-8953; tel. (3) 5501-6001; internet www.gib-life.co.jp; f. 1947; fmrly Kyoei Life Insurance Co Ltd, declared bankrupt Oct. 2000; resumed operations in 2001 as mem. of Prudential Financial, USA; Pres. MITSUO KURASHIGE.

Hartford Life Insurance K. K.: Shiodome Bldg, 15/F, 1-2-20, Kaigan, Minato-ku, Tokyo 105-0022; tel. (3) 6219-3784; internet www.hartfordlife.co.jp; f. 2000; Pres. AIDAN KIDNEY.

NG Life Insurance Co Ltd: New Otani Garden Court, 26/F, 4-1, Kioi-cho, Chiyoda-ku, Tokyo 102-0094; tel. (3) 5210-0300; fax (3) 5210-0430; internet www.ing-life.co.jp; f. 1985; Pres. Eddie Berman.

Japan Post Insurance: 1-3-2, Kasumigaseki, Chiyoda-ku, Tokyo 100-8798; tel. (3) 3504-4411; internet www.jp-life.japanpost.jp; f. 2006; wholly owned by Japan Post Holdings Co Ltd; Chair. and CEO Josuke Shindo; Pres. Izumi Yamashita.

Kyoei Kasai Shinrai Life Insurance Co Ltd: 1-18-6, Shimbashi, Minato-ku, Tokyo 105-8604; tel. (3) 3504-0131; fax (3) 5372-7701; internet www.kyoeikasai.co.jp; f. 1996; Pres. Kenzi Sugiyama.

Manulife Life Insurance Co: 4-34-1, Kokuryo-cho, Chofu-shi, Tokyo 182-8621; tel. (3) 2442-7120; fax (3) 2442-7977; e-mail craig_bromley@manulife.com; internet www.manulife.co.jp; f. 1999; fmrly Manulife Century Life Insurance Co; absorbed bankrupt Daihyaku Mutual Life Insurance Co in 2001; Pres. and CEO Craig Bromley.

MassMutual Life Insurance Co: 1-5-7, Ariake, Koto-ku, Tokyo 135-0063; internet www.massmutual.co.jp; Pres. Masanori Mizoguchi.

Meiji Yasuda Life Insurance Co: 2-1-1, Marunouchi, Chiyoda-ku, Tokyo 100-0005; tel. (3) 3283-8111; fax (3) 3215-5219; internet www.meijiyasuda.co.jp; f. 2004; est. by merger of Meiji Life Insurance Co (f. 1881) and Yasuda Mutual Life Insurance Co (f. 1880); Chair. Norikaju Sekiguti; Pres. Kenji Matsuo.

Mitsui Life Insurance Co Ltd: 2-1-1, Otemachi, Chiyoda-ku, Tokyo 100-8123; tel. (3) 6831-8000; internet www.mitsui-seimei.co.jp; f. 1927; Chair. Hirosumi Tsusue; Pres. Yukiteru Yamamoto.

Nippon Life Insurance Co (Nissay): 3-5-12, Imabashi, Chuo-ku, Osaka 541-8501; tel. (6) 6209-5525; e-mail hosokawa15560@nissay.co.jp; internet www.nissay.co.jp; f. 1889; Chair. Ikuo Uno; Pres. Kunie Okamoto.

Nipponkoa Life Insurance Co Ltd: 4-2, Tsukiji, Chuo-ku, Tokyo 104-8407; tel. (3) 5565-8080; fax (3) 5565-8365; internet www.nipponkoa.co.jp/life; f. 1996; formed by merger of Nippon Fire and Marine Insurance and Koa Fire and Marine Insurance; Pres. Kazuo Hashimoto.

ORIX Life Insurance Corpn: Mita NN Bldg, 4-1-23, Shiba, Minato-ku, Tokyo 108-0014; tel. (3) 5419-5102; fax (3) 5419-5901; e-mail koho@orix.co.jp; internet www.orix.co.jp; f. 1991; Chair. and CEO Yoshihiko Miyauchi; Pres. Makoto Inoue.

Prudential Life Insurance Co Ltd: Prudential Tower, 2-13-10, Nagata-cho, Chiyoda-ku, Tokyo 100-0014; tel. (3) 5501-5500; fax (3) 3221-2305; internet www.prudential.co.jp; f. 1987; Chair. and CEO John Strangfeld; Pres. Mitsuo Kurashige.

Sompo Japan DIY Life Insurance Co Ltd: 6-10-1, Shinjuku-Nishi, Shinjuku-ku, Tokyo 160-0023; tel. (3) 5345-7603; fax (3) 5345-7608; internet www.diy.co.jp; f. 1999; Pres. Tatsuo Shibuya.

Sompo Japan Himawari Life Insurance Co Ltd: Shinjuku Mitsui Bldg, 35/F, 1-2-1, Nishi-Shinjuku, Shinjuku-ku, Tokyo; internet www.himawari-life.com; f. 2002; Pres. Toshio Matsuzaki.

Sony Life Insurance Co Ltd: Shin-Aoyama Bldg, 3/F, 1-1-1, Minami-Aoyama, Minato-ku, Tokyo 107-8585; tel. (3) 3475-8811; fax (3) 3475-8914; internet www.sonylife.co.jp; Chair. Kunikita Ando; Pres. Taro Okuda.

Sumitomo Life Insurance Co: 7-18-24, Tsukiji, Chuo-ku, Tokyo 104-8430; tel. (3) 5550-1100; fax (3) 5550-1160; internet www.sumitomolife.co.jp; f. 1907; Pres. Yoshio Sato.

T & D Holdings Inc: Shiodome Shiba-Rikyu Bldg, 1-2-3, Kaigan, Minato-ku, Tokyo 105-0022; tel. (3) 3434-9111; fax (3) 3434-9055; internet www.td-holdings.co.jp; f. 1895; fmrly Tokyo Mutual Life Insurance Co; T & D Financial Life Insurance Co Holdings company formed in April 2004 through merger of T & D Financial Life Insurance Co, Taiyo Mutual Life Insurance Co and Daido Life Insurance Co; Pres. Naoteru Miyato.

Tokio Marine & Nichido Life Insurance Co Ltd: 5-3-16, Ginza, Chuo-ku, Tokyo 106-0041; tel. (3) 5223-2111; fax (3) 5223-2165; internet www.tmn-anshin.co.jp; Pres. Sukeaki Ohta.

Yamato Mutual Life Insurance Co: 1-1-7, Uchisaiwai-cho, Chiyoda-ku, Tokyo 100-0011; tel. (3) 3508-3111; fax (3) 3508-3118; internet www.yamato-life.co.jp; f. 1911; Pres. Takeo Nakazono.

Zurich Life Insurance Co Ltd: Shinanomachi Rengakan, 35, Shinanomachi, Shinjuku-ku, Tokyo 160-0016; tel. (3) 5361-2700; fax (3) 5361-2705; internet www.zurichlife.co.jp; f. 1996; Pres. Nagano Toshiyuki.

Principal Non-Life Companies

ACE Insurance: Arco Tower, 1-8-1, Shimomeguro, Meguro-ku, Tokyo 153-0064; tel. (3) 5740-0600; fax (3) 5740-0608; internet www.ace-insurance.co.jp; f. 1999; Chair. Shiniji Nomoto; Pres. Takashi Imai.

Aioi Nissay Dowa Insurance Co Ltd: 1-28-1, Ebisu, Shibuya-ku, Tokyo 150-8488; tel. (3) 5424-0101; internet www.aioinissaydowa.co.jp; est. by merger of Aioi Insurance Co Ltd and Nissay Dowa General Insurance Co Ltd in 2010; Pres. Kuni Suzuki.

Allianz Fire and Marine Insurance Japan Ltd: Anzen Bldg, 1-6-6, Moto-Akasaka, Minato-ku, Tokyo 107-0051; tel. (3) 4558-7500; e-mail netadmin@allianz.co.jp; internet www.allianz.co.jp; f. 1990; Chair. Axel Theis; Pres. Michael Maicher.

The Asahi Fire and Marine Insurance Co Ltd: 2-6-2, Kaji-cho, Chiyoda-ku, Tokyo 101-8655; tel. (3) 3294-2211; fax (3) 3254-2296; e-mail asahifmi@blue.ocn.ne.jp; internet www.asahikasai.co.jp; f. 1951; Pres. Kazuho Oya.

AXA Japan Holding Co Ltd: NBF Platinum Tower, 1-17-3, Minato-ku, Tokyo 150-8020; tel. (3) 3407-6210; internet www.axa.co.jp; f. 1998; Pres. Jean-Louis Laurent Josi.

The Daido Fire and Marine Insurance Co Ltd: 1-12-1, Kumoji, Naha-shi, Okinawa 900-8586; tel. (98) 867-1161; fax (98) 862-8362; internet www.daidokasai.co.jp; f. 1971; Pres. Naoto Miraya.

The Fuji Fire and Marine Insurance Co Ltd: 1-18-11, Minami-Senba, Chuo-ku, Osaka 542-8567; tel. (6) 6271-2741; fax (6) 6266-7115; internet www.fujikasai.co.jp; f. 1918; Pres. and CEO Akira Kondoh.

The Japan Earthquake Reinsurance Co Ltd: Fuji Plaza, 4/F, 8-1, Nihonbashi Kobuna-cho, Chuo-ku, Tokyo 103-0024; tel. (3) 3664-6074; fax (3) 3664-6169; e-mail kanri@nihonjishin.co.jp; internet www.nihonjishin.co.jp; f. 1966; Chair. Shozo Wakabayashi; Pres. Hideo Suzuki.

JI Accident & Fire Insurance Co Ltd: A1 Bldg, 20-5, Ichiban-cho, Chiyoda-ku, Tokyo 102-0082; tel. (3) 3237-2045; fax (3) 3237-2250; internet www.jihoken.co.jp; f. 1989; Pres. Mitsuhito Minamisawa.

The Kyoei Mutual Fire and Marine Insurance Co: 1-18-6, Shimbashi, Minato-ku, Tokyo 105-8604; tel. (3) 3504-0131; fax (3) 3508-7680; e-mail reins.intl@kyoeikasai.co.jp; internet www.kyoeikasai.co.jp; f. 1942; Pres. Kenji Sugiyama.

Meiji Yasuda General Insurance Co Ltd: 2-11-1, Kanda Tsukasa-cho, Chiyoda-ku, Tokyo 101-0048; tel. (3) 3257-3111; fax (3) 3257-3295; internet www.meijiyasuda-sonpo.co.jp; f. 1996; Pres. Seiji Nishi.

Mitsui Direct General Insurance Co Ltd: 1-5-3, Koraku, Bunkyou-ku, Tokyo 112-0004; tel. (3) 5804-7711; internet www.mitsui-direct.co.jp; f. 1996; Pres. Toshio Kitamura.

Mitsui Sumitomo Insurance Co Ltd: 27-2-2, Shinkawa, Chuo-ku, Tokyo 104-8252; tel. (3) 3297-1111; internet www.ms-ins.com; f. 2001; formed by merger of Mitsui Marine and Fire Insurance and Sumitomo Marine and Fire Insurance; Chair. Toshiaki Egashira; Pres. Yasuyoshi Karasawa.

The Nipponkoa Insurance Co Ltd: 3-7-3, Kasumigaseki, Chiyoda-ku, Tokyo 100-8965; tel. (3) 3593-3111; fax (3) 3593-5388; internet www.nipponkoa.co.jp; f. 1892; fmrly The Nippon Fire and Marine Insurance Co Ltd before merging with The Koa Fire and Marine Insurance Co Ltd; acquired Taiyo Fire and Marine Insurance Co Ltd in 2002; Pres. and CEO Makoto Hyodo.

The Nisshin Fire and Marine Insurance Co Ltd: 2-3, Kanda Surugadai, Chiyoda-ku, Tokyo 100-8329; tel. (3) 5282-5534; fax (3) 5282-5582; e-mail nisshin@mb.infoweb.ne.jp; internet www.nisshinfire.co.jp; f. 1908; Pres. Hiroshi Miyajima.

Saison Automobile and Fire Insurance Co Ltd: Sunshine 60 Bldg, 3-1-1, Higashi-Ikebukuro, Toshima-ku, Tokyo 170-6068; tel. (3) 3988-2572; fax (3) 3980-7367; internet www.ins-saison.co.jp; f. 1982; Pres. Koshin Matuzawa.

Secom General Insurance Co Ltd: 2-6-2, Hirakawa-cho, Chiyoda-ku, Tokyo 102-8645; tel. (3) 5216-6129; fax (3) 5216-6149; internet www.secom-sonpo.co.jp; Pres. Itiro Ojeki.

Sompo Japan Insurance Inc: 26-1-1, Nishi-Shinjuku, Shinjuku-ku, Tokyo 160-8338; tel. (3) 3349-3111; fax (3) 3349-4697; internet www.sompo-japan.co.jp; f. 2002; est. by merger of Yasuda Fire and Marine Insurance (f. 1888) and Nissan Fire and Marine Insurance (f. 1911); Pres. Matatoshi Sato.

Sonpo 24 Insurance Co Ltd: Sunshine 60 Bldg, 44/F, 3-1-1, Higashi-Ikebukuro, Toshima-ku, Tokyo 170-6044; tel. (3) 5957-0111; internet www.sonpo24.co.jp; Pres. Atsushi Kumanomido.

Sony Assurance Inc: Aroma Sq., 11/F, 5-37-1, Kamata, Ota-ku, Tokyo 144-8721; tel. (3) 5744-0300; fax (3) 5744-0480; internet www.sonysonpo.co.jp; f. 1999; Pres. Shinichi Yamamoto.

The Toa Reinsurance Co Ltd: 3-6, Kanda Surugadai, Chiyoda-ku, Tokyo 101-8703; tel. (3) 3253-3171; fax (3) 3253-1208; internet www.toare.co.jp; f. 1940; Chair. Teruhiko Ohtani; Pres. Hiroshi Fukushima.

Tokio Marine & Nichido Fire Insurance Co Ltd: 1-2-1, Marunouchi, Chiyoda-ku, Tokyo 100-8050; tel. (3) 3212-6211; internet www.tokiomarine-nichido.co.jp; f. 2004; Pres. Shuzo Sumi.

Insurance Associations

The General Insurance Association of Japan (Nihon Songai Hoken Kyokai): Non-Life Insurance Bldg, 2-9, Kanda Awaji-cho, Chiyoda-ku, Tokyo 101-8335; tel. (3) 3255-1439; fax (3) 3255-1234; e-mail kokusai@sonpo.or.jp; internet www.sonpo.or.jp; f. 1946; 25 mems (Feb. 2012); Chair. SHUZO SUMI; Exec. Dir HIROMI ASANO.

The Life Insurance Association of Japan (Seimei Hoken Kyokai): Shin-Kokusai Bldg, 3/F, 3-4-1, Marunouchi, Chiyoda-ku, Tokyo 100-0005; tel. (3) 3286-2652; fax (3) 3286-2630; e-mail kokusai@seiho.or.jp; internet www.seiho.or.jp; f. 1908; 47 mem. cos (Sept. 2010); Chair. KOICHIRO WATANABE.

Nippon Export and Investment Insurance: Chiyoda First Bldg, East Wing, 3/F, 3-8-1, Kanda Nishi, Chiyoda-ku, Tokyo; internet www.nexi.go.jp; f. 2001; Chair. and CEO TAKASHI SUZUKI.

Non-Life Insurance Rating Organization of Japan: 3-7-1, Nishi-Shinjuku, Shinjuku-ku, Tokyo 163-1029; e-mail service@nliro.or.jp; internet www.nliro.or.jp; f. 2002; 38 mems (Jan. 2011); Chair. AKIO MORISHIMA; Sr Exec. Dir YASUYUKI TAYAMA.

Trade and Industry

CHAMBERS OF COMMERCE AND INDUSTRY

The Japan Chamber of Commerce and Industry (Nippon Shoko Kaigi-sho): 3-2-2, Marunouchi, Chiyoda-ku, Tokyo 100-0005; tel. (3) 3283-7824; fax (3) 3211-4859; e-mail info@jcci.or.jp; internet www.jcci.or.jp; f. 1922; the central org. of all chambers of commerce and industry in Japan; mems: 517 local chambers of commerce and industry; Chair. TADASHI OKAMURA; Pres. TOSHIO NAKAMURA.

Principal chambers include:

Kobe Chamber of Commerce and Industry: 6-1, Minatojima-nakamachi, Chuo-ku, Kobe 650-8543; tel. (78) 303-5806; fax (78) 306-2348; e-mail info@kobe-cci.or.jp; internet kobe-cci.weebly.com; f. 1878; 12,000 mems; Chair. OHASHI TADAHARU; Pres. YASUO MURATA.

Kyoto Chamber of Commerce and Industry: 240, Shoshoi-cho, Ebisugawa-agaru, Karasumadori, Nakakyo-ku, Kyoto 604-0862; tel. (75) 212-6420; fax (75) 251-0743; e-mail kokusai@kyo.or.jp; internet www.kyo.or.jp/kyoto; f. 1882; 11,500 mems; Chair. YOSHIO TATEISI; Pres. TUNEOKI OKUHARA.

Nagoya Chamber of Commerce and Industry: 2-10-19, Sakae, Naka-ku, Nagoya, Aichi 460-8422; tel. (52) 223-5722; fax (52) 232-5751; e-mail info@nagoya-cci.or.jp; internet www.nagoya-cci.or.jp; f. 1881; 17,000 mems; Chair. JIRO TAKAHASHI.

Naha Chamber of Commerce and Industry: 2-2-10, Kume Naha, Okinawa; tel. (98) 868-3758; fax (98) 866-9834; e-mail cci-naha@nahacci.or.jp; internet www.nahacci.or.jp; f. 1927; 4,874 mems; Chair. AKIRA SAKIMA; Pres. KOSEI YONEMURA.

Osaka Chamber of Commerce and Industry: 2-8, Hommachi-bashi, Chuo-ku, Osaka 540-0029; tel. (6) 6944-6400; fax (6) 6944-6293; e-mail intl@osaka.cci.or.jp; internet www.osaka.cci.or.jp; f. 1878; 28,500 mems; Chair. SHIGETAKA SATO; Pres. DOI MICHIO.

Tokyo Chamber of Commerce and Industry: 3-2-2, Marunouchi, Chiyoda-ku, Tokyo 100-0005; tel. (3) 3283-7523; fax (3) 3216-6497; e-mail kokusai@tokyo-cci.or.jp; internet www.tokyo-cci.or.jp; f. 1878; 77,247 mems (April 2010); Chair. TADASHI OKAMURA; Pres. TOSHIO NAKAMURA.

Yokohama Chamber of Commerce and Industry: Sangyo Boueki Center Bldg, 8/F, Yamashita-cho, Naka-ku, Yokohama 231-8524; tel. (45) 671-7400; fax (45) 671-7410; e-mail soumu@yokohama-cci.or.jp; internet www.yokohama-cci.or.jp; f. 1880; 14,965 mems; Chair. KENJI SASAKI; Pres. NAMIO OBA.

INDUSTRIAL AND TRADE ASSOCIATIONS

General

The Association for the Promotion of International Trade, Japan (JAPIT): 1-9-13, Chiyoda-ku, Tokyo 101-0047; tel. (3) 6740-8261; fax (3) 6740-6160; internet www.japitcn.com; f. 1954 to promote trade with the People's Repub. of China; 700 mems; Chair. YOHEI KONO.

Industry Club of Japan: 1-4-6, Marunouchi, Chiyoda-ku, Tokyo; tel. (3) 3281-1711; fax (3) 3281-1797; e-mail soumu@kogyoclub.or.jp; internet www.kogyoclub.or.jp; f. 1917; est. to develop closer relations between industrialists at home and abroad and promote expansion of Japanese business activities; c. 1,600 mems; Pres. IMAI TAKASHI; Exec. Dir KOUICHIROU SHINNO.

Japan Commercial Arbitration Association: Hirose Bldg, 3/F, 3-17, Kanda Nishiki-cho, Chiyoda-ku, Tokyo 101-0054; tel. (3) 5280-5200; fax (3) 5280-5170; e-mail arbitration@jcaa.or.jp; internet www.jcaa.or.jp; f. 1950; 700 mems; provides facilities for mediation, conciliation and arbitration in international trade disputes; Pres. TADASHI OKAMURA.

Japan External Trade Organization (JETRO): Ark Mori Bldg, 6/F, 1-12-32, Akasaka-cho, Minato-ku, Tokyo 107-6006; tel. (3) 3582-5511; fax (3) 3582-5662; e-mail seh@jetro.go.jp; internet www.jetro.go.jp; f. 1958; information on international trade, investment, import promotion, exhibitions of foreign products; Chair. and CEO YASUO HAYASHI; Pres. TADASHI IZAWA.

Japan Federation of Smaller Enterprise Organizations (JFSEO) (Nippon Chusokigyo Dantai Renmei): 2-8-4, Nihonbashi Kayaba-cho, Chuo-ku, Tokyo 103-0025; tel. (3) 3669-6862; f. 1948; 1[illegible] mems and c. 1,000 co-operative socs; Pres. MASATAKA TOYODA; Chair of Int. Affairs SEIICHI ONO.

Japan General Merchandise Exporters' Association: 2-4-1 Hamamatsu-cho, Minato-ku, Tokyo; tel. (3) 3435-3471; fax (3) 3434-6739; f. 1953; 40 mems; Pres. TADAYOSHI NAKAZAWA.

Japan Productivity Center (JPC): 3-1-1, Shibuya, Shibuya-ku, Tokyo 150-8307; tel. (3) 3409-1112; fax (3) 3409-1986; internet www.jpc-net.jp; f. 1994; est. by merger between Japan Productivity Center and Social Economic Congress of Japan; fmrly Japan Productivity Center for Socio-Economic Development, renamed as above 2009; 10,000 mems; concerned with management problems and research into productivity; Chair. JIRO USHIO; Pres. TSUNEAKI TANIGUCHI.

Keizai Doyukai (Japan Association of Corporate Executives): 1-4-6, Marunouchi, Chiyoda-ku, Tokyo 100-0005; tel. (3) 3211-1271; fax (3) 3213-2946; e-mail kdcontact205@doyukai.or.jp; internet www.doyukai.or.jp; f. 1946; c.1,400 mems; corporate executives concerned with national and international economic and social policies; Chair. MASAMITSU SAKURAI.

Nihon Boeki-Kai (Japan Foreign Trade Council, Inc): World Trade Center Bldg, 6/F, 2-4-1, Hamamatsu-cho, Minato-ku, Tokyo 105-6106; tel. (3) 3435-5959; fax (3) 3435-5979; e-mail mail@jftc.or.jp; internet www.jftc.or.jp; f. 1947; 192 mems; Chair. SHOEI UTSUDA; Exec. Man. Dir MASAYOSHI AMANO.

Chemicals

Japan Chemical Industry Association: Sumitomo Fudosan Rokko Bldg, 1-4-1, Shinkawa, Chuo-ku, Tokyo 104-0033; tel. (3) 3297-2550; fax (3) 3297-2610; e-mail chemical@jcia-net.or.jp; internet www.nikkakyo.org; f. 1948; 266 mems; Chair. HIROMASA YONEKURA.

Japan Cosmetic Industry Association: 45 MT Bldg, 6/F, 5-1-5, Toranomon, Minato-ku, Tokyo 105-0001; tel. (3) 5472-2530; fax (3) 5472-2536; e-mail info@jcia.org; internet www.jcia.org; f. 1959; 687 mem. cos; Chair. REIJIRO KOBAYASHI.

Japan Perfumery and Flavouring Association: Saeki No. 3 Bldg, 3/F, 37, Kandakonya-cho, Chiyoda-ku, Tokyo 101-0035; tel. and fax (3) 3526-7855; f. 1947; Chair. YONEJIRO KORAYASHI.

Japan Pharmaceutical Manufacturers' Association: Torii Nihonbashi Bldg, 3-4-1, Nihonbashi Hon-cho, Chuo-ku, Tokyo 103-0023; tel. (3) 3241-0326; fax (3) 3242-1767; internet www.jpma.or.jp; 67 mems; Pres. YASUCHIKA HASEGAWA.

Photo-Sensitized Materials Manufacturers' Association: JCII Bldg, 25, Ichiban-cho, Chiyoda-ku, Tokyo 102-0082; tel. (3) 5276-3561; fax (3) 5276-3563; internet pmma.a.la9.jp; f. 1948; Pres. SHIGETAKA KOMORI.

Fishing and Pearl Cultivation

Japan Fisheries Association (Dainippon Suisankai): Sankaido Bldg, 1-9-13, Akasaka, Minato-ku, Tokyo 107-0052; tel. (3) 3585-6681; fax (3) 3582-2337; e-mail japan@suisankai.or.jp; internet www.suisankai.or.jp; Pres. TOSHIRO SHIRASU.

Japan Pearl Export and Processing Co-operative Association: 3-6-15, Kyobashi, Chuo-ko, Tokyo 104-0031; tel. (3) 3562-5011; f. 1951; 130 mems.

Japan Pearl Exporters' Association: 122, Higashi-Machi, Chuo-ku, Kobe 650-0031; tel. (78) 331-4031; fax (78) 331-4345; e-mail jpeakobe@lime.ocn.ne.jp; internet www.japan-pearl.com; f. 1954; 56 mems; Pres. YOSHIHIRO SHIMIZU.

Machinery and Precision Equipment

Camera and Imaging Products Association (CIPA) (Camera Eizo Kiki Kogyo-kai): JCII Bldg, 25, Ichiban-cho, Chiyoda-ku, Tokyo 102-0082; tel. (3) 5276-3891; fax (3) 5276-3893; internet www.cipa.jp; f. 1954; fmrly Japan Camera Industry Asscn, renamed as above 2002; 54 mems; Pres. TSUYOSHI KIKUKAWA.

Japan Clock and Watch Association: Kudan Sky Bldg, 1-12-11, Kudan-Kita, Chiyoda-ku, Tokyo 102-0073; tel. (3) 5276-3411; fax (3) 5276-3414; internet www.jcwa.or.jp; Chair. SHINJI HATTORI.

Japan Electric Association: Denki Bldg, 4/F, 1-7-1, Yuraku-cho, Chiyoda-ku, Tokyo 100-0006; tel. (3) 3216-0551; fax (3) 3214-6005; internet www.denki.or.jp; f. 1921; 4,610 mems; Pres. TATSUO KAWAI.

Japan Electric Measuring Instruments Manufacturers' Association (JEMIMA): Keisoku Kaikan Bldg, 2-15-12, Nihonbashi-Kakigara-cho, Chuo-ku, Tokyo 103-0014; tel. (3) 3662-8181; fax (3) 3662-8180; e-mail katsuta@jemima.or.jp; internet www.jemima.or.jp; 79 mems; Chair. SEIJI ONOKI.

Japan Electrical Manufacturers' Association: 17-4, Ichiban-cho, Chiyoda-ku, Tokyo 102-0082; tel. (3) 3556-5881; fax (3) 3556-5889; internet www.jema-net.or.jp; f. 1948; 262 mems; Chair. MICHIHIRO KITAZAWA; Pres. TOSHIMI HAYANO.

Japan Electronics and Information Technology Industries Association (JEITA): Ote Center Bldg, 1-1-3, Otemachi, Chiyoda-ku, Tokyo 100-0004; tel. (3) 5218-1050; fax (3) 5218-1070; internet www.jeita.or.jp; promotes manufacturing, international trade and consumption of electronics products and components; Chair. KAORU YANO; Pres. TSUTOMU HANDA.

Japan Energy Association: Kawate Bldg, 1-5-8, Nishi-Shimbashi, Minato-ku, Tokyo 105-0003; tel. (3) 3502-1261; fax (3) 3502-2760; e-mail info@jea-wec.or.jp; internet www.jea-wec.or.jp; f. 1950; 133 mems; Chair. TERUAKI MASUMOTO; Exec. Dir HAJIME MURATA.

Japan Machine Tool Builders' Association: Kikai Shinko Bldg, 3-5-8, Shiba Koen, Minato-ku, Tokyo 105-0011; tel. (3) 3434-3961; fax (3) 3434-3763; e-mail intl@jmtba.or.jp; internet www.jmtba.or.jp; f. 1951; 112 mems; Chair. KENICHI NAKAMURA; Pres. TOSHIONI SHONO.

Japan Machine Tools Importers' Association: Toranomon Kogyo Bldg, 1-2-18, Toranomon, Minato-ku, Tokyo 105-0001; tel. (3) 3501-5030; fax (3) 3501-5040; e-mail info@jmtia.gr.jp; internet www.jmtia.gr.jp; f. 1955; 41 mems; Chair. YUZO CHIBA.

Japan Machinery Center for Trade and Investment (JMC): Kikai Shinko Bldg, 4/F, 3-5-8, Shiba Koen, Minato-ku, Tokyo 105-0011; tel. (3) 3431-9507; fax (3) 3436-6455; e-mail info@jmcti.or.jp; internet www.jmcti.org; f. 1952; 290 mem. cos; Pres. KENJI MIYAHARA.

The Japan Machinery Federation: Kikai Shinko Bldg, 3-5-8, Shiba Koen, Minato-ku, Tokyo 105-0011; tel. (3) 3434-5381; fax (3) 3434-2666; e-mail koho@jmf.or.jp; internet www.jmf.or.jp; f. 1952; Pres. MOTOTSUGU ITO; Exec. Dir KYOSHI ISHIZAKA.

Japan Microscope Manufacturers' Association: Kikai Shinko Bldg, 5-8-3, Shibakoen, Minato-ku, Tokyo 105-0011; tel. (3) 3432-5100; fax (3) 3432-5611; e-mail jmma@microscope.jp; f. 1954; 26 mems; Chair. S. TAKAYAMA.

Japan Motion Picture Equipment Industrial Association: Kikai Shinko Bldg, 3-5-8, Shiba Koen, Minato-ku, Tokyo 105-0011; tel. (3) 3434-3911; fax (3) 3434-3912; Pres. MASAO SHIKATA; Gen. Sec. TERUHIRO KATO.

Japan Optical Industry Association: Kikai Shinko Bldg, 3-5-8, Shiba Koen, Minato-ku, Tokyo 105-0011; tel. (3) 3431-7073; f. 1946; 7 mems; Chair. MICHIO KARIYA; Exec. Sec. SHIRO IWAHASHI.

The Japan Society of Industrial Machinery Manufacturers: Kikai Shinko Bldg, 3-5-8, Shiba Koen, Minato-ku, Tokyo 105-0011; tel. (3) 3434-6821; fax (3) 3434-4767; e-mail obd@jsim.or.jp; internet www.jsim.or.jp; f. 1948; 170 mems; Pres. YOSHIO HINOU.

Japan Textile Machinery Association: Kikai Shinko Bldg, Rm 101, 5-22, Shiba Koen, Minato-ku, Tokyo 105-0011; tel. (3) 3434-3821; fax (3) 3434-3043; e-mail am-jtma@jtma.or.jp; internet www.jtma.or.jp; f. 1951; Pres. JUNICHI MURATA.

Metals

Japan Aluminium Association (JAA): Tsukamoto-Sozan Bldg, 4-2-15, Ginza, Chuo-ku, Tokyo 104-0061; tel. (3) 3538-0221; fax (3) 3538-0233; internet www.aluminum.or.jp; f. 1999; est. by merger of Japan Aluminium Federation and Japan Light Metal Association; 146 mems; Chair. ISHIYAMA TAKASHI.

Japan Copper and Brass Association: Usagiya Bldg, 5/F, 1-10-10, Ueno, Taito-ku, Tokyo 110-0005; tel. (3) 3836-8801; fax (3) 3836-8808; e-mail jbmajwcc@copper-brass.gr.jp; internet www.copper-brass.gr.jp; f. 1948; 62 mems; Chair. TAKAO HASHIDA; Sec.-Gen. TOSHINOBU HIDAKA.

The Japan Iron and Steel Federation: Tekko Kaikan Bldg, 3-2-10, Nihonbashi Kayaba-cho, Chuo-ku, Tokyo 103-0025; tel. (3) 3669-4811; fax (3) 3664-1457; internet www.jisf.or.jp; f. 1948; mems: 61 mfrs, 61 dealers, six orgs; Chair. EIJI HAYASHIDA.

Japan Stainless Steel Association: TMM Bldg, 3/F, 1-10-5, Iwamoto-cho, Chiyoda-ku, Tokyo; tel. (3) 5687-7831; fax (3) 5687-8551; e-mail yabe@jssa.gr.jp; internet www.jssa.gr.jp; f. 1959; 80 mems; Chair. HIROSHI KINOSHITA.

Steel Castings and Forgings Association of Japan (JSCFA): Shikoku Bldg Bekkan, 8/F, 1-14-4, Uchikannda, Chiyoda-ku, Tokyo 101-0047; tel. (3) 5283-1611; fax (3) 5283-1613; e-mail cf@jscfa.gr.jp; internet www.jscfa.gr.jp; f. 1972; mems: 48 cos, 44 plants; Pres. YAMAGUCHI IKUHIRO.

Mining and Petroleum

Japan Coal Energy Center (JCOAL): Meiji Yasuda Seimei Mita Bldg, 9/F, 3-14-10, Mita, Minato-ku, Tokyo 108-0073; tel. (3) 6400-5191; fax (3) 6400-5206; e-mail jcoal-qa@jcoal.or.jp; internet www.jcoal.or.jp; f. 1997; est. by merger of Japan Coal Assen, Coal Mining Research Centre, and the Japan Technical Cooperation Center for Coal Resources Devt; 111 mems; Pres. YOSHIHIKO NAGASAKI.

Japan Mining Industry Association: c/o Eiha Bldg, 17-11-3, Kanda Nishiki-cho, Chiyoda-ku, Tokyo 101-0054; tel. (3) 5280-2321; fax (3) 5280-7128; internet www.kogyo-kyokai.gr.jp; f. 1948; 52 mem. cos; Chair. SADAO SENDA; Pres. SHINICHI OZEKI.

Japan Petrochemical Industry Association: 1-4-1, Shinkawa, Chuo-ku, Tokyo 104-0033; tel. (3) 3297-2011; fax (3) 3297-2017; e-mail inquiries_hp@jpca.or.jp; internet www.jpca.or.jp; Chair. KYOHEI TAKAHASHI.

Japan Petroleum Development Association: Keidanren Bldg, 17/F, 1-3-2, Otemachi, Chiyoda-ku, Tokyo 100-0004; tel. (3) 3214-1701; fax (3) 3214-1703; e-mail jpda-sekkoren@sekkoren.jp; internet www.sekkoren.jp; f. 1961; Chair. YUJI TANAHASHI.

Paper and Printing

Japan Federation of Printing Industries: 1-16-8, Shintomi, Chuo-ku, Tokyo 104-0041; tel. (3) 3553-6051; fax (3) 3553-6079; internet www.jfpi.or.jp; f. 1985; 10 mems; Chair. SATOSHI SAWATARI.

Japan Paper Association: Kami Parupu Bldg, 3-9-11, Ginza, Chuo-ku, Tokyo 104-8139; tel. (3) 3248-4801; fax (3) 3248-4826; internet www.jpa.gr.jp; f. 1946; 54 mems; Chair. KAZUHISA SHINODA; Pres. MASATAKA HAYAMA.

Japan Paper Exporters' Association: Kami Parupu Bldg, 3-9-11, Ginza, Chuo-ku, Tokyo 104-8139; tel. (3) 3248-4831; fax (3) 3248-4834; e-mail info@jpeta.or.jp; internet www.jpeta.or.jp; f. 1952; 32 mems; Chair. YUTAKA SEKIGUCHI.

Japan Paper Importers' Association: Kami Parupu Bldg, 3-9-11, Ginza, Chuo-ku, Tokyo 104-8139; tel. (3) 3248-4831; fax (3) 3248-4834; e-mail info@jpeta.or.jp; internet jpeta.or.jp; f. 1981; 21 mems; Chair. TOSHINORI UMEZAWA; Man. KENJI IMAMURA.

Japan Paper Products Manufacturers' Association: 4-2-6, Kotobuki, Taito-ku, Tokyo; tel. (3) 3543-2411; f. 1949; Exec. Dir KIYOSHI SATOH.

Textiles

Central Raw Silk Association of Japan: 1-9-4, Yuraku-cho, Chiyoda-ku, Tokyo; tel. (3) 3214-5777; fax (3) 3214-5778.

Japan Chemical Fibers Association: Seni Kaikan, 7/F, 3-1-11, Nihonbashi-Honcho, Chuo-ku, Tokyo 103-0023; tel. (3) 3241-2311; fax (3) 3246-0823; internet www.jcfa.gr.jp; f. 1948; 17 mems, 1 assoc. mem, 20 supporting mems; Pres. AKIHIRO NIKKAKU; Dir-Gen. TSUNEHIRO OGARA.

Japan Cotton and Staple Fibre Weavers' Association: 1-8-7, Nishi-Azabu, Minato-ku, Tokyo; tel. (3) 3403-9671; internet www.jcwa-net.jp; 28 mems; Pres. OSAMU MAKOTO.

Japan Silk Spinners' Association: f. 1948; 95 mem. cos; Chair. ICHIJI OHTANI.

Japan Spinners' Association: Mengyo Kaikan Bldg, 6/F, 2-5-8, Bingomachi, Chuo-ku, Osaka 541-0051; tel. (6) 6231-8431; fax (6) 6229-1590; e-mail spinas@cotton.or.jp; internet www.jsa-jp.org; f. 1948; 16 mems; Head KOJIRO ABE.

Transport Machinery

Japan Association of Rolling Stock Industries: Awajicho Suny Bldg, 7/F, 1-2, Kanda Suda-cho, Chiyoda-ku, Tokyo 101-0041; tel. (3) 3257-1901; e-mail info@tetsushako.or.jp; internet www.tetsushako.or.jp; Chair. HIRAI MASAHARU.

Japan Auto Parts Industries Association: Jidosha Buhin Bldg, 5/F, 1-16-15, Takanawa, Minato-ku, Tokyo 108-0074; tel. (3) 3445-4211; fax (3) 3447-5372; e-mail info@japia.or.jp; internet www.japia.or.jp; f. 1948; 530 mem. cos; Chair. HISATAKA NOBUMOTO; Exec. Dir K. SHIBASAKI.

Japan Automobile Manufacturers Association, Inc (JAMA): Jidosha Kaikan, 1-1-30, Shiba Daimon, Minato-ku, Tokyo 105-0012; tel. (3) 5405-6126; fax (3) 5405-6136; e-mail kaigai_tky@mta.jama.or.jp; internet www.jama.or.jp; f. 1967; 14 mem. cos; Chair. TOSHIYUKI SHIGA; Pres. YOSHIYASU NAO.

Japan Bicycle Manufacturers' Association: 1-9-3, Akasaka, Minato-ku, Tokyo 107; tel. (3) 3583-3123; fax (3) 3589-3125; f. 1955.

Japan Ship Exporters' Association: Toranomon 30 Mori Bldg, 5/F, 3-2-2, Toranomon, Minato-ku, Tokyo 105-0001; tel. (3) 5425-9671; fax (3) 5425-9674; e-mail postmaster@jsea.or.jp; internet www.jsea.or.jp; 32 mems; Pres. MASAMOTO TAZAKI.

Japanese Marine Equipment Association: Kaiyo Senpaku Bldg, 15-16, Toranomon, Minato-ku, Tokyo 105-0001; tel. (3) 3502-2041;

fax (3) 3591-2206; e-mail info@jsmea.or.jp; internet www.jsmea.or.jp; f. 1956; 219 mems; Chair. ZENSHICHI ASASAKA.

Japanese Shipowners' Association: Kaiun Bldg, 2-6-4, Hirakawa-cho, Chiyoda-ku, Tokyo 102-8603; tel. (3) 3264-7171; fax (3) 3262-4760; internet www.jsanet.or.jp; Pres. KOJI MIYAHARA.

Shipbuilders' Association of Japan: 30 Mori Bldg, 5/F, 3-2-2, Toranomon, Minato-ku, Tokyo 105-0001; tel. (3) 5425-9527; fax (3) 5425-9533; internet www.sajn.or.jp; f. 1947; 21 mems; Chair. TAKAO MOTOYAMA.

Society of Japanese Aerospace Companies (SJAC): Toshin-Tameike Bldg, 2/F, 1-1-14, Akasaka, Minato-ku, Tokyo 107-0052; tel. (3) 3585-0511; fax (3) 3585-0541; e-mail itahara-hiroharu@sjac.or.jp; internet www.sjac.or.jp; f. 1952; reorg. 1974; 117 mems, 41 assoc. mems; Chair. KAZUO TSUKUDA; Pres. KOSUKE IMASHIMIZU.

Miscellaneous

Communications Industry Association of Japan (CIA-J): Shuwa Dai-ichi Hamamatsucho Bldg, 3/F, 2-2-12, Hamamatsu-cho, Minato-ku, Tokyo 105-0013; tel. (3) 5403-9363; fax (3) 5463-9360; e-mail admin@ciaj.or.jp; internet www.ciaj.or.jp; f. 1948; non-profit org. of telecommunications equipment mfrs; 236 mems; Chair. KAWAMURA TAKASHI; Pres. YOSHIYUKI SUKEMUNE.

Japan Canners' Association: Tokyo; tel. (3) 5256-4801; fax (3) 5256-4805; internet www.jca-can.or.jp; Pres. KEINOSUKE HISAI.

Japan Cement Association: Daiwa Nihonbashi-Honcho Bldg, 7/F, 1-9-4, Chuo-ku, Tokyo 103-0023; tel. (3) 5200-5057; fax (3) 5200-5062; e-mail international@jcassoc.or.jp; internet www.jcassoc.or.jp; f. 1948; 18 mem. cos; Chair. KEIJI TOKUUE.

Japan Lumber Importers' Association: Yushi Kogyo Bldg, 3-13-11, Nihonbashi, Chuo-ku, Tokyo 103-0027; tel. (3) 3271-0926; fax (3) 3271-0928; f. 1950; 130 mems; Pres. TAMBA TOSIKHITO.

Japan Plastics Industry Federation: 3-5-2 Nihonbashi-Kayaba-cho, Chuo-ku, Tokyo 103-0025; tel. (3) 6661-6811; fax (3) 6661-6810; e-mail info@jpif.gr.jp; internet www.jpif.gr.jp; f. 1950; 102 mems; Exec. Dir TSUGUO KATSUURA.

Japan Plywood Manufacturers' Association: Meisan Bldg, 1-18-17, Nishi-Shimbashi, Minato-ku, Tokyo 105; tel. (3) 3591-9246; fax (3) 3591-9240; f. 1965; 92 mems; Pres. KOICHI MATAGA.

Japan Pottery Manufacturers' Federation: Toto Bldg, 1-1-28, Toranomon, Minato-ku, Tokyo; tel. (3) 3503-6761.

The Japan Rubber Manufacturers' Association: Tobu Bldg, 2/F, 1-5-26, Moto-Akasaka, Minato-ku, Tokyo 107-0051; tel. (3) 3408-7101; fax (3) 3408-7106; e-mail soumu@jrma.gr.jp; internet www.jrma.gr.jp; f. 1950; 126 mems; Pres. MITSUAKI ASAI.

Japan Spirits and Liquors Makers' Association: Koura Dai-ichi Bldg, 7/F, 1-1-6, Nihonbashi-Kayaba-cho, Chuo-ku, Tokyo 103; tel. (3) 3668-4621.

Japan Sugar Refiners' Association: 5-7, Sanban-cho, Chiyoda-ku, Tokyo 102; tel. (3) 3288-1151; fax (3) 3288-3399; internet www.sugar.or.jp; f. 1949; 17 mems; Senior Man. Dir KATSUYUKI SUZUKI.

Japan Tea Exporters' Association: 17, Kitaban-cho, Shizuoka, Shizuoka Prefecture 420-0005; tel. (54) 271-3428; fax (54) 271-2177; e-mail japantea1953@yahoo.co.jp; 75 mems; Pres. TOSHIAKI KIRISHIMA.

Japan Toy Association: 4-22-4, Higashi-Komagata, Sumida-ku, Tokyo 130; tel. (3) 3829-2513; fax (3) 3829-2510; e-mail otoiawase2009@toys.or.jp; internet www.toys.or.jp; 228 mems; Chair. TAKEO TAKASU.

Motion Picture Producers' Association of Japan, Inc: Nihonbashi Bldg, 2/F, 1-17-12, Nihonbashi, Chuo-ku, Tokyo 103-0027; tel. (3) 3243-9100; fax (3) 3243-9101; e-mail info@eiren.org; internet www.eiren.org; f. 1945; Pres. NOBUYOSHI OTANI.

EMPLOYERS' ORGANIZATION

Japan Business Federation (JBF) (Nippon Keidanren): Keidanren Kaikan, 1-3-2, Otemachi, Chiyoda-ku, Tokyo 100-8188; tel. (3) 6741-0171; fax (3) 6741-0301; e-mail webmaster@keidanren.or.jp; internet www.keidanren.or.jp; f. 2002; est. by merger of Keidanren (f. 1946) and Nikkeiren (f. 1948); 1,601 mems (June 2010); Chair. HIROMASA YONEKURA; Dir-Gen. YOSHIO NAKAMURA.

UTILITIES

Electricity

Chubu Electric Power Co Inc: 1, Higashi-Shin-cho, Higashi-ku, Nagoya 461-8680; tel. (52) 951-8211; fax (52) 962-4624; internet www.chuden.co.jp; f. 1951; Chair. TOSHIO MITA; Pres. AKIRA HISASHI.

Chugoku Electric Power Co Inc: 4-33, Komachi, Naka-ku, Hiroshima 730-8701; tel. (82) 241-0211; fax (82) 523-6185; e-mail angel@inet.energia.co.jp; internet www.energia.co.jp; f. 1951; Chair. TADASHI FUKUDA; Pres. TAKASHI YAMASHITA.

Electric Power Development Co Ltd (J-Power): 6-15-1, Ginza Chuo-ku, Tokyo 104-8165; tel. (3) 3546-2211; e-mail webmaster jpower.co.jp; internet www.jpower.co.jp; f. 1952; Pres. MASAYOSI KITAMURA.

Hokkaido Electric Power Co Inc: 1-2, Higashi-Odori, Chuo-ku Sapporo, Hokkaido 060-8677; tel. (11) 251-1111; internet www.hepc.co.jp; f. 1951; Chair. TATSUO KONDO; Pres. YOSHITAKA SATO.

Hokuriku Electric Power Co Inc: 15-1, Ushijima-cho, Toyama shi, Toyama 930-8686; e-mail pub-mast@rikuden.co.jp; interne www.rikuden.co.jp; f. 1951; Chair. ISAO NAGAHARA; Pres. SUSUM KYUWA.

Kansai Electric Power Co Inc: 3-6-16, Nakanoshima, Kita-ku Osaka 530-8270; tel. (6) 6441-8821; fax (6) 6441-8598; e-mai postmaster@kepco.co.jp; internet www.kepco.co.jp; Pres. MAKOTO YAGI.

Kyushu Electric Power Co Inc: 2-1-82, Watanabe-dori, Chuo-ku Fukuoka 810-8726; tel. (92) 761-3031; fax (92) 731-8719; interne www.kyuden.co.jp; Chair. SHINGO MATSUO; Pres. TOSHIO MANABE.

Okinawa Electric Power Co Inc: 5-2-1, Makiminato, Urasoe Okinawa 901-2602; tel. (98) 877-2341; fax (98) 877-6017; e-mail ir@okiden.co.jp; internet www.okiden.co.jp; f. 1972; Chair. TSUGIYOSH TOMA; Pres. DENICHIRO ISHIMINE.

Shikoku Electric Power Co Inc: 2-5, Marunouchi, Takamatsu 760-8573; tel. (878) 21-5061; fax (878) 26-1250; e-mail postmaster@yonden.co.jp; internet www.yonden.co.jp; f. 1951; Chair. MOMOKI TOKIWA; Pres. AKIRA CHIBA.

Tohoku Electric Power Co Inc: 1-7-1, Hon-cho, Aoba-ku, Sendai 980-8550; tel. (22) 225-2111; fax (22) 225-2550; e-mail webmaster@tohoku-epco.co.jp; internet www.tohoku-epco.co.jp; Chair. HIROAKI TAKAHASHI; Pres. MAKOTO KAIWA.

Tokyo Electric Power Co Inc: 1-1-3, Uchisaiwai-cho, Chiyoda-ku, Tokyo 100-8560; tel. (3) 6373-1111; fax (3) 3596-8508; internet www.tepco.co.jp; Chair. KAZUHIKO SHIMOKOBE; Pres. TOSHIO NISHIZAWA.

Federation

Federation of Electric Power Companies of Japan (FEPC JAPAN): 1-3-2, Keidanren Kaikan, Ohte-machi, Chiyoda-ku, Tokyo 100-8118; tel. (3) 5221-1440; fax (3) 6361-9024; e-mail webadmin2@fepc.or.jp; internet www.fepc.or.jp; f. 1952; Chair. MASATAKA SHIMIZU; Dir and Sec.-Gen. YUZURU HIROE.

Gas

Hokkaido Gas Co Ltd: 7-3-1, Nishi-Odori, Chuo-ku, Sapporo; tel. (11) 231-9511; internet www.hokkaido-gas.co.jp; Chair. SHIGERO KUSANO; Pres. HIROSHI OHTSUKI.

Keiyo Gas Co Ltd: 2-8-8, Ichikawa-Minami, Ichikawa, Chiba 272-8580; tel. (47) 361-0211; fax (47) 325-1049; internet www.keiyogas.co.jp; f. 1927; Chair. TOMO KIKUCHI; Pres. NOBUO SAKUMA.

Osaka Gas Co Ltd: 4-1-2, Hiranomachi, Chuo-ku, Osaka 541-0046; tel. (6) 6205-4503; fax (6) 6222-5831; e-mail keiri@osakagas.co.jp; internet www.osakagas.co.jp; f. 1905; Chair. AKIO NOMURA; Pres. HIROSHI OZAKI.

Saibu Gas Co: 1-17-1, Chiyo, Hakata-ku, Fukuoka; tel. (92) 633-2345; internet www.saibugas.co.jp; f. 1930; Chair. HIROKI OGAWA; Pres. YUUJI TANAKA.

Toho Gas Co Ltd: 19-18, Sakurada-cho, Atsuta-ko, Nagoya 456-8511; tel. (52) 871-3511; internet www.tohogas.co.jp; f. 1922; Chair. TOSHITAKA HAYAKAWA; Pres. TAKASHI SEIKI.

Tokyo Gas Co Inc: 1-5-20, Kaigan, Minato-ku, Tokyo 105; tel. (3) 3433-2111; fax (3) 5472-5385; internet www.tokyo-gas.co.jp; f. 1885; Chair. MITSUNORI TERIHARA; Pres. OKAMOTO TAKASHI.

Association

Japan Gas Association: 1-1-3, Nishi-Shinbashi, Minato-ku, Tokyo 105-0003; tel. (3) 3502-0116; fax (3) 3502-3676; internet www.gas.or.jp; f. 1947; comprises 211 city gas utilities and 270 assoc. mems; Chair. MITSUNORI TORIHARA.

Water

Nagoya City Waterworks & Sewerage Bureau: 3-1-1, Sannomaru, Naka-ku, Nagoya 460-8508; tel. (52) 972-3608; fax (52) 972-3710; e-mail mail@water.city.nagoya.jp; internet www.water.city.nagoya.jp.

Osaka City Waterworks Bureau: 1-14-16, Nanko-Kita, Suminoe-ku, Osaka 530-8201; tel. (6) 6458-1132; fax (6) 6458-2100.

Sapporo City Waterworks Bureau: 2-11, Higashi-Odori, Chuo-ku, Sapporo 060-8611; tel. (11) 211-7007; fax (11) 232-1740; e-mail su.somu@suido.city.sapporo.jp; internet www.city.sapporo.jp/suido.

Tokyo Bureau of Waterworks: 2-8-1, Nishi-Shinjuku, Shinjuku-ku, Tokyo 163-8001; tel. (3) 5326-1100; internet www.waterworks.metro.tokyo.jp.

okohama Waterworks Bureau: 1-1, Minato-cho, Naka-ku, okohama; tel. (45) 671-3055; fax (45) 664-6774; e-mail su-somu@ ty.yokohama.jp; internet www.city.yokohama.jp/suidou.

Association

apan Water Works Association (JWWA): 4-8-9, Kudan-Minami, hiyoda-ku, Tokyo 102-0074; tel. (3) 3264-2281; fax (3) 3262-2244; -mail kokusai@jwwa.or.jp; internet www.jwwa.or.jp; f. 1932; Exec. ir YOSHIHIKO MISONO.

TRADE UNIONS

feature of Japan's trade union movement is that the unions are sually based on single enterprises, embracing workers of different ccupations in that enterprise. In June 2006 there were 27,507 nions; union membership stood at 10.0m. workers in that year.

apanese Trade Union Confederation (JTUC–RENGO): 3-2-1, Kanda Surugadai, Chiyoda-ku, Tokyo 101-0062; tel. (3) 5295-526; fax (3) 5295-0548; e-mail jtuc-kokusai@sv.rengo-net.or.jp; nternet www.jtuc-rengo.org; f. 1989; est. by merger of SOHYO and ENGO; 6.8m. mems; Pres. NOBUAKI KOGA.

Principal Unions

Ceramics Rengo (All-Japan Federation of Ceramics Industry Workers): 3-11, Heigocho, Mizuho-ku, Nagoya-shi, Aichi 467; tel. 52) 882-4562; fax (52) 882-9960; e-mail info@jcw-u.or.jp; internet www.jcw-u.or.jp; 30,083 mems; Pres. TSUNEYOSHI HAYAKAWA.

Denki Rengo (Japanese Electrical, Electronic & Information Union): Denkirengo Bldg, 1-10-3, Mita, Minato-ku, Tokyo 108-3326; tel. (3) 3455-6911; fax (3) 3452-5406; e-mail denki-rengo@ eiu.or.jp; internet www.jeiu.or.jp; f. 1953; 688,436 mems; Pres. NOBUAKI KOGA.

Denryoku Soren (Federation of Electric Power Related Industry Workers' Unions of Japan): TDS Mita, 3/F, 7-13-2, Mita, Minato-ku, Tokyo 108-0073; tel. (3) 3454-0231; fax (3) 3798-1470; e-mail info@ denryokusoren.or.jp; internet www.denryokusoren.or.jp; 223,000 mems; Pres. HIROYUKI NAGUMO.

Dokiro (Hokkaido Seasonal Workers' Union): Hokuro Bldg, Kita-4, Nishi-12, Chuo-ku, Sapporo, Hokkaido 060; tel. (11) 261-5775; fax (11) 272-2255; 19,063 mems; Pres. YOSHIZO ODAWARA.

Food Rengo (Federation of All Japan Foods and Tobacco Workers' Unions): Hiroo Office Bldg, 8/F, 1-3-18, Hiroo, Shibuya-ku, Tokyo; tel. (3) 3446-2082; fax (3) 3446-6779; internet www.jfu.or.jp; f. 2000; est. as Shokuhin Renmei, following merger of Shokuhin Rengo and Shokuhin Rokyo; present name adopted 2002; 111,599 mems.

Gomu Rengo (Japanese Rubber Workers' Union Confederation): 2-3-3, Mejiro, Toshima-ku, Tokyo 171; tel. (3) 3984-3343; fax (3) 3984-5862; 60,070 mems; Pres. YASUO FURUKAWA.

Health Care Rokyo (Japanese Health Care Workers' Union): 2-17-20, Shiba, Minato-ku, Tokyo 105-0014; tel. (3) 3451-6025; fax (3) 3451-6040.

Insatsu Roren (Federation of Printing Information Media Workers' Unions): Yuai Kaikan, 7/F, 2-20-12, Shiba, Minato-ku, Tokyo 105-0014; tel. (3) 5442-0191; fax (3) 5442-0219; 22,303 mems; Pres. HIROFUMI NAKABAYASHI.

JA Rengo (All-Japan Agriculture Co-operative Staff Members' Union): 218, Nishi-Nomachi, Sanzaemon-bori, Himeji-shi, Hyogo 670-0940; tel. and fax (792) 85-3618; 2,772 mems; Pres. YUTAKA OKADA.

JAM (Japanese Association of Metal, Machinery and Manufacturing Workers' Unions): Yuai Kaikan, 2-20-12, Shiba, Minato-ku, Tokyo 105-0014; tel. (3) 3265-2171; fax (3) 3230-0172; e-mail mail@ jam-union.or.jp; internet www.jam-union.or.jp; f. 1999; est. through merger of Kinzoku Kikai (National Metal and Machinery Workers' Union of Japan) and Zenkin Rengo (Japanese Federation of Metal Industry Unions).

Japan Federation of Service and Distributive Workers' Unions: 2-23-1, Yoyogi, Shibuya-ku, Tokyo 151-0053; tel. (3) 3370-4121; fax (3) 3370-1640; e-mail international@jsd-union.org; internet www.jsd-union.org; f. 2001; 210,000 mems; Pres. SHOICHI HACHINO.

Japan Postal Group Union (JPGU): 5-2-2, Higashi-Ueno, Taito-ku, Tokyo 110-0015; tel. (3) 5830-2655; fax (3) 5830-2484; internet www.jprouso.or.jp; f. 2007; est. by merger of Japan Postal Workers' Union and All-Japan Postal Labour Union.

JEC Rengo (Japanese Federation of Energy and Chemistry Workers' Unions): Senbai Bldg, 5-26-30, Shiba, Minato-ku, Tokyo 108-8389; tel. (3) 3452-5591; fax (3) 3454-7464; internet www.jec-u.com; formed by merger of Goka Roren and Zenkoku Kagaku; 104,000 mems; Pres. KATUTOSHI KATO.

Jichi Roren (National Federation of Prefectural and Municipal Workers' Unions): 1-15-22, Oji-honcho, Kita-ku, Tokyo 114; tel. and fax (3) 3907-1584; 5,728 mems; Pres. NOBUO UENO.

Jichiro (All-Japan Prefectural and Municipal Workers' Union): Jichiro Bldg, 1, Rokuban-cho, Chiyoda-ku, Tokyo 102-0085; tel. (3) 3263-0263; fax (3) 5210-7422; e-mail info@jichiro.gr.jp; internet www .jichiro.gr.jp; f. 1954; 903,139 mems; Pres. KENJI OKABE.

Jidosha Soren (Confederation of Japan Automobile Workers' Unions): U-Life Center, 1-4-26, Kaigan, Minato-ku, Tokyo 105-8523; tel. (3) 3434-7641; fax (3) 3434-7428; internet www.jaw.or.jp; f. 1972; 757,000 mems; Pres. KOICHIRO NISHIHARA.

Jiunro (Japan Automobile Drivers' Union): 2-3-12, Nakameguro, Meguro-ku, Tokyo 153; tel. (3) 3711-9387; fax (3) 3719-2624; 1,958 mems; Pres. SADAO KANEZUKA.

Joho Roren (Japan Federation of Telecommunications, Electronic Information and Allied Workers): Zendentsu-rodo Bldg, 3-6, Kanda Surugadai, Chiyoda-ku, Tokyo 101-0062; tel. (3) 3219-2231; fax (3) 3253-3268; e-mail info@joho.or.jp; internet www.joho.or.jp; 265,132 mems; Pres. KAZUO SASAMORI.

JR-Rengo (Japan Railway Trade Unions Confederation): TOKO Bldg, 9/F, 1-8-10, Nihonbashi Muromachi, Chuo-ku, Tokyo 103; tel. (3) 3270-4590; fax (3) 3270-4429; internet homepage1.nifty.com/ JR-RENGO; 78,418 mems; Pres. KAZUAKI KUZUNO.

JR Soren (Japan Confederation of Railway Workers' Unions): Meguro Satsuki Bldg, 3-2-13, Nishi-Gotanda, Shinagawa-ku, Tokyo 141-0031; tel. (3) 3491-7191; fax (3) 3491-7192; internet www.jru7 .net; 62,300 mems; Pres. YUJI ODA.

Kaiin Kumiai (All-Japan Seamen's Union): 7-15-26, Roppongi, Minato-ku, Tokyo 106-0032; tel. (3) 5410-8330; fax (3) 5410-8336; e-mail iss@jsu.or.jp; internet www.jsu.or.jp; 35,000 mems; Pres. YOUJI FUJISAWA.

Kamipa Rengo (Japanese Federation of Pulp and Paper Workers' Unions): 2-12-4, Kita-Aoyama, Minato-ku, Tokyo 107-0061; tel. (3) 3402-7656; fax (3) 3402-7659; e-mail kamipa-rengo@jpw.jtuc-rengo .jp; internet www.jpw.or.jp; 50,858 mems; Pres. TUNEO MUKAI.

Kensetsu Rengo (Japan Construction Trade Union Confederation): Yuai Bldg, 7/F, 2-20-12, Shiba, Minato-ku, Tokyo 105; tel. (3) 3454-0951; fax (3) 3453-0582; e-mail vg-sec@krw.jtuc-rengo.jp; internet www.jtuc-rengo.jp/kensetu; 13,199 mems; Pres. MASAYASU TERASAWA.

Kikan Roren (Japan Federation of Basic Industry Workers' Unions—JBU): I & S Riverside Bldg, 4/F, 1-23-4, Shinkawa, Chuo-ku, Tokyo 104-0033; tel. (3) 3555-0401; fax (3) 3555-0407; internet www.kikan-roren.or.jp; f. 2003; est. by merger of Tekko Roren (Japan Fed. of Steel Workers' Unions), Zosen Juki Roren (Japan Confed. of Ship-building and Engineering Workers' Unions) and Hitetsu Rengo (Japanese Metal Mine Workers' Union); 243,000 mems; Pres. JUNRO NAITO.

Kokko Rengo (Japan Public Sector Union): Hosaka Bldg, 1-10-3, Kanda Ogawamachi, Chiyoda-ku, Tokyo 101-0052; tel. (3) 5209-6205; fax (3) 5209-6209.

Kokko Soren (Japan General Federation of National Public Service Employees' Unions): Hosaka Bldg, Kanda Ogawamachi, 1-10-3, Chiyoda-ku, Tokyo 101-0052; tel. (3) 5209-6207; fax (3) 5209-6206; e-mail kokko-soren@kokko-soren.jp; internet www.kokko-soren.jp; 33,350 mems; Pres. SEIICHI FUKUDA.

Koku Rengo (Japan Federation of Aviation Industry Unions): 6-5, Haneda-kuko, Ota-ku, Tokyo 144-0041; tel. (3) 5708-7161; fax (3) 5708-7163; e-mail avinet03@jfaiu.gr.jp; internet www.jfaiu.gr.jp.

Kokuzei Roso (Japanese Confederation of National Tax Unions): Okurasho Bldg, Rm 154, 3-1-1, Kasumigaseki, Chiyoda-ku, Tokyo 100; tel. (3) 3581-2573; fax (3) 3581-3843; 40,128 mems; Pres. TATSUO SASAKI.

Kotsu Roren (Japan Federation of Transport Workers' Unions): Yuai Bldg, 3/F, 2-20-12, Shiba, Minato-ku, Tokyo 105-0014; tel. (3) 3451-7243; fax (3) 3454-7393; 97,239 mems; Pres. SHIGEO MAKI.

Koun-Domei (Japanese Confederation of Port and Transport Workers' Unions): 5-10-2, Kamata, Ota-ku, Tokyo 144-0052; tel. (3) 3733-5285; fax (3) 3733-5280; f. 1987; 1,638 mems; Pres. SAKAE IDEMOTO.

NHK Roren (Federation of All-NHK Labour Unions): NHK, 2-2-1, Jinnan, Shibuya-ku, Tokyo 150; tel. (3) 3485-6007; fax (3) 3469-9271; 12,526 mems; Pres. YASUZO SUDO.

Nichirinro (National Forest Workers' Union of Japan): 1-2-1, Kasumigaseki, Chiyoda-ku, Tokyo 100; tel. (3) 3580-8891; fax (3) 3580-1596; Pres. KOH IKEGAMI.

Nikkenkyo (Council of Japan Construction Industry Employees Unions): Moriyama Bldg, 1-31-16, Takadano-baba, Shinjuku-ku, Tokyo 169-0075; tel. (3) 5285-3870; fax (3) 5285-3879.

Nikkokyo (Japan Senior High School Teachers and Staff Union): 2-11, Kanda Ta-cho, Chiyoda-ku, Tokyo 101-0046; tel. (3) 3230-0284; fax (3) 3230-1659; internet www.nikkokyo.org.

Nikkyoso (Japan Teachers' Union): Japan Education Hall, 2-6-2, Hitotsubashi, Chiyoda-ku, Tokyo 101-0003; tel. (3) 3265-2171; fax (3)

3230-0172; internet www.jtu-net.or.jp; f. 1947; 300,000 mems; Pres. YUZURU NAKAMURA.

Rosai Roren (National Federation of Zenrosai Workers' Unions): 2-12-10, Yoyogi, Shibuya-ku, Tokyo 151; tel. (3) 3299-0161; fax (3) 3299-0126; internet rosai.roren.jp; 2,091 mems; Pres. TADASHI TAKACHI.

Seiho Roren (National Federation of Life Insurance Workers' Unions): Tanaka Bldg, 3-19-5, Yushima, Bunkyo-ku, Tokyo 113-0034; tel. (3) 3837-2031; fax (3) 3837-2037; internet www.liu.or.jp; 414,021 mems; Pres. YOHTARU KOHNO.

Seiroren (Labour Federation of Government-Related Organizations): Hasaka Bldg, 4–6/F, 1-10-3, Kanda Ogawa-cho, Chiyoda-ku, Tokyo 101; tel. (3) 5295-6360; fax (3) 5295-6362; e-mail info@lafgo.gr.jp; internet www.lafgo.gr.jp; 27,500 mems; Chair. MITSURU WATANABE.

Shin Unten (F10-Drivers' Craft Union): 4/F, 3-25-6, Negishi, Taito-ku, Tokyo 110; tel. (3) 5603-1015; fax (3) 5603-5351; 4,435 mems; Pres. SHOHEI SHINOZAKI.

Shinrin Roren (Japanese Federation of Forest and Wood Workers' Unions): 3-28-7, Otsuka, Bunkyo-ku, Tokyo 112; tel. (3) 3945-6385; fax (3) 3945-6477; 13,928 mems; Pres. ISAO SASAKI.

Shitetsu Soren (General Federation of Private Railway Workers' Unions): 4-3-5, Takanawa, Minato-ku, Tokyo 108-0074; tel. (3) 3473-0166; fax (3) 3447-3927; f. 1947; 160,000 mems; Pres. RYOICHI IKEMURA.

Sonpo Roren (Federation of Non-Life Insurance Workers' Unions of Japan): Kanda MS Bldg, 4/F, 27, Kanda Higashi-Matsushita-cho, Chiyoda-ku, Tokyo 101; tel. (3) 5295-0071; fax (3) 5295-0073; internet www.fniu.or.jp; Pres. KUNIO MATSUMOTO.

Toshiko (The All-Japan Municipal Transport Workers' Union): 3-1-35, Shibaura, Minato-ku, Tokyo 108; tel. (3) 3451-5221; fax (3) 3452-2977; internet www.toshiko.or.jp; 43,612 mems; Pres. SHUNICHI SUZUKI.

Ui Zensen Domei (Japanese Federation of Textile, Chemical, Food, Commercial, Service and General Workers' Unions): 4-8-16, Kudan-Minami, Chiyoda-ku, Tokyo 102-0074; tel. (3) 3288-3723; fax (3) 3288-3728; e-mail kokusai@uizensen.or.jp; internet www.uizensen.or.jp; f. 2002; est. by merger of CSG Rengo, Zensen Domei and Sen'i Seikatsu Roren; 1,986 affiliates; 790,289 mems (Jan. 2003); Pres. TSUYOSHI TAKAGI.

Unyu Roren (All-Japan Federation of Transport Workers' Union): Zennittsu Kasumigaseki Bldg, 5/F, 3-3-3, Kasumigaseki, Chiyoda-ku, Tokyo 100-0013; tel. (3) 3503-2171; fax (3) 3503-2176; internet www.unyuroren.or.jp; f. 1968; 143,084 mems; Pres. KAZUMARO SUZUKI.

Zeikan Roren (Federation of Japanese Customs Personnel Labour Unions): 3-1-1, Kasumigaseki, Chiyoda-ku, Tokyo 100; tel. and fax (3) 3593-1788; Pres. RIKIO SUDO.

Zen Insatsu (All-Printing Agency Workers' Union): 3-59-12, Nishi-Gahara, Kita-ku, Tokyo 114; tel. (3) 3910-7131; fax (3) 3910-7155; 5,431 mems; Chair. TOSHIO KATAKURA.

Zenchuro (All-Japan Garrison Forces Labour Union): 3-41-8, Shiba, Minato-ku, Tokyo 105; tel. (3) 3455-5971; fax (3) 3455-5973; Pres. EIBUN MEDORUMA.

Zendensen (All-Japan Electric Wire Labour Union): 1-11-6, Hatanodai, Shinagawa-ku, Tokyo 142; tel. (3) 3785-2991; fax (3) 3785-2995; e-mail info@densen.or.jp; internet www.densen.or.jp; Pres. NAOKI TOKUNAGA.

Zen-eien (National Cinema and Theatre Workers' Union): Hibiya Park Bldg, 1-8-1, Yuraku-cho, Chiyoda-ku, Tokyo 100; tel. (3) 3201-4476; fax (3) 3214-0597; Pres. SADAHIRO MATSUURA.

Zengin Rengo (All-Japan Federative Council of Bank Labour Unions): 1-14-12, Higashi-Kanda, Chiyoda-ku, Tokyo 101-0031; tel. (3) 5687-5155; fax (3) 5687-5156; e-mail zengin@ceres.ocn.ne.jp; internet www.zengin.jp; 16,474 mems; Pres. YOSHIHIRO KONO.

Zenjiko Roren (National Federation of Automobile Transport Workers' Unions): 3-7-9, Sendagaya, Shibuya-ku, Tokyo 151; tel. (3) 3408-0875; fax (3) 3497-0107; internet www.zenjiko.or.jp; Pres. OSAMU MIMASHI.

Zenkoku Gas (Federation of Gas Workers' Unions of Japan): 5-11-1, Omori-Nishi, Ota-ku, Tokyo 143; tel. (3) 5493-8381; fax (3) 5493-8216; internet ws1.jtuc-rengo.or.jp/zenkokugas/index/index.htm; 31,499 mems; Pres. AKIO HAMAUZU.

Zenkoku-Ippan (National Union of General Workers): Zosen Bldg, 5/F, 3-5-6, Misaki-cho, Chiyoda-ku, Tokyo 101-0061; tel. (3) 3230-4071; fax (3) 3230-4360; internet www.zenkoku-ippan.or.jp; 54,708 mems; Pres. YASUHIKO MATSUI.

Zenkoku Keiba Rengo (National Federation of Horse-racing Workers): 2500, Mikoma, Miho-mura, Inashiki-gun, Ibaragi 300-04; tel. (298) 85-0402; fax (298) 85-0416; Pres. TOYOHIKO OKUMURA.

Zenkoku Nodanro (National Federation of Agricultural, Forest and Fishery Corporations' Workers' Unions): 1-5-8, Hamamats cho, Minato-ku, Tokyo 105; tel. (3) 3437-0931; fax (3) 3437-068 internet www.nodanro.or.jp; 26,010 mems; Pres. SHIN-ICHIRO OKAD

Zenkoku Semento (National Federation of Cement Worker Unions of Japan): 5-29-2, Shimbashi, Minato-ku, Tokyo 105; te (3) 3436-3666; fax (3) 3436-3668; Pres. KIYONORI URAKAWA.

Zenkoku Union (Japan Community Workers Union Federation): 22-18, Nishi-Shinjuku, Shinjuku-ku, Tokyo 160-0023; tel. (3) 533 2627; fax (3) 5338-1267.

Zenkyoro (National Race Workers' Union): Nihon Kyoiku Kaika 7/F, 2-6-2, Hitotsubashi, Chiyoda-ku, Tokyo 101-0003; tel. (3) 521 5156; fax (3) 5210-5157; 24,720 mems; Pres. TAKESHI KAWASHIMA.

Zenrokin (Federation of Labour Bank Workers' Unions of Japan Nakano Bldg, 3/F, 1-11, Kanda Awaji-cho, Chiyoda-ku, Tokyo 10 tel. (3) 3256-1015; fax (3) 3256-1045; internet zenrokin.or.jp; Pre EIICHI KAKU.

Zenshin Roren (All Japan Community Bank Labour Union Asso ciation): 2-6-10, Higashi-Shimbashi, Minato-ku, Tokyo 105-0021; te (3) 3437-6017; fax (3) 3437-1204.

Zentanko (National Union of Coal Mine Workers): 1162, Ikeshima Sotome-cho, Nishi-Sonogi-gun, Nagasaki 857-0071; tel. (9) 5926 0004; fax (9) 5926-1000; Pres. NOBORU TAGAWA.

Zenzohei (All-Mint Labour Union): 1-1-79, Temma, Kita-ku, Osaka shi, Osaka 530; tel. and fax (6) 6354-2389; Pres. CHIKASHI HIGUCHI

Zenzosen-kikai (All-Japan Ship-building and Engineering Union) Zosen Bldg, 6th Floor, 3-5-6, Misakicho, Chiyoda-ku, Tokyo 101; tel (3) 3265-1921; fax (3) 3265-1870; Pres. YOSHIMI FUNATSU.

Transport

RAILWAYS

Japan Railways (JR) Group: 1-6-5, Marunouchi, Chiyoda-ku, Tokyo 100-0005; tel. (3) 3215-9649; fax (3) 3213-5291; fmrly the state-controlled Japanese National Railways (JNR); reorg. and transferred to private sector in 1987; high-speed Shinkansen rail network consists of Tokaido line (Tokyo to Shin-Osaka, 552.6 km), Sanyo line (Shin-Osaka to Hakata, 623.3 km), Tohoku line (Tokyo to Morioka, 535.3 km) and Joetsu line (Omiya to Niigata, 303.6 km); Yamagata Shinkansen (Fukushima to Yamagata, 87 km) converted in 1992 from a conventional railway line and is operated as a branch of the Tohoku Shinkansen with through trains from Tokyo; total railway route length was about 19,955 km in 2008

Central Japan Railway Co: JR Central Shinagawa Bldg, A Wing, 2-1-85, Konan, Minato-ku, Tokyo 108-8204; tel. (3) 3274-9727; fax (3) 5255-6780; internet www.jr-central.co.jp; f. 1987; also operates travel agency services, etc.; Chair. YOSHIYUKI KASAI; Pres. YOSHIOMI YAMADA.

East Japan Railway Co: 2-2-2, Yoyogi, Shibuya-ku, Tokyo 151-8578; tel. (3) 5334-1151; fax (3) 5334-1110; internet www.jreast.co.jp; privatized in 1987; Chair. MUTSUTAKE OTSUKA; Pres. and CEO SATOSHI SEINO.

Hokkaido Railway Co: 15-1-1, Kita-11-jo, Chuo-ku, Sapporo 060-8644; tel. (11) 700-5717; fax (11) 700-5719; e-mail keieki@jrhokkaido.co.jp; internet www.jrhokkaido.co.jp; Chair. YOSHIHIRO OHMORI; Pres. (vacant).

Japan Freight Railway Co: 3-13-1, Iidabashi, Chiyoda-ku, Tokyo; internet www.jrfreight.co.jp; f. 1987; Pres. MASAAKI KOYABASHI.

Kyushu Railway Co: 3-25-21, Hakataekimae, Hakata-ku, Fukuoka 812-8566; tel. (92) 474-2501; fax (92) 474-9745; internet www.jrkyushu.co.jp; f. 1987; Chair. KOJI KARAIKE; Pres. SUSUMU ISHIHARA.

Shikoku Railway Co: 8-33, Hamano-cho, Takamatsu, Kagawa 760-8580; tel. (87) 825-1626; fax (87) 825-1623; internet www.jr-shikoku.co.jp; Chair. MATSUDA KIYOSHI; Pres. IZUMI MASAHUMI.

West Japan Railway Co: 2-4-24, Shibata, Kita-ku, Osaka 530-8341; tel. (6) 6375-8981; fax (6) 6375-8919; e-mail wjr01020@mxy.meshnet.or.jp; internet www.westjr.co.jp; fully privatized in 2004; Chair. NORITAKA KARAUCHI; Pres. TAKAYUKI SASAKI.

Other Principal Private Companies

Hankyu Hanshin Holdings Inc: 1-16-1, Shibata, Kita-ku, Osaka 530-0012; tel. (6) 6373-5001; fax (6) 6373-5042; e-mail web-info@hankyu-hanshin.co.jp; internet www.hankyu-hanshin.co.jp; f. 1907; links Osaka, Kyoto, Kobe and Takarazuka; Chair. HIROSHI OJIMA; Pres. KAZUO SUMI.

Keihan Electric Railway Co Ltd: 1-7-31, Otemae, Chuo-ku, Osaka; tel. (6) 6944-2521; fax (6) 6944-2501; internet www.keihan.co.jp; f. 1906; Chair. SHIGETAKA SATO; Pres. SEINOSUKE UEDA.

eihin Express Electric Railway Co Ltd (Keikyu): 2-20-20, akanawa, Minato-ku, Tokyo 108-8625; tel. (3) 3280-9120; fax (3) 280-9199; internet www.keikyu.co.jp; f. 1899; Chair. Masaru otani; Pres. Tsuneo Ishiwata.

eio Electric Railway Co Ltd: 1-9-1, Sekido, Tama City, Tokyo)6-8052; tel. (42) 337-3106; fax (42) 374-9322; internet www.keio.co p; f. 1913; Chair. Kan Kato; Pres. Tadashi Nagata.

eisei Electric Railway Co Ltd: 1-10-3, Oshiage, Sumida-ku, okyo 131; tel. (3) 3621-2242; fax (3) 3621-2233; internet www.keisei o.jp; f. 1909; Chair. Hiroshi Ohtsuka; Pres. Tsutomu Hanada.

inki Nippon Railway Co Ltd (Kintetsu): 6-1-55, Uehommachi, 'ennoji-ku, Osaka 543-8585; tel. (6) 6775-3444; fax (6) 6775-3468; iternet www.kintetsu.co.jp; f. 1910; Chair. Masanori Yamaguchi; res. Tetsuya Kobayashi.

agoya Railroad Co Ltd: 1-2-4, Meieki, Nakamura-ku, Nagoya-hi 450-8501; tel. (52) 588-0813; fax (52) 588-0815; e-mail info@ ieitetsu.co.jp; internet www.meitetsu.co.jp; Chair. Eiichiro inoshita; Pres. Ado Yamamoto.

ankai Electric Railway Co Ltd: 5-1-60, Namba, Chuo-ku, Osaka 42; tel. (6) 6644-7121; internet www.nankai.co.jp; f. 1925; Chair. Iakoto Yamanaka; Pres. Shinji Watari.

ishi-Nippon Railroad Co Ltd: 1-11-17, Tenjin-cho, Chuo-ku, 'ukuoka 810; tel. (92) 761-6631; fax (92) 722-1405; e-mail vww-admin@nnr.co.jp; internet www.nnr.co.jp; serves northern yushu; Chair. Tsuguo Nagao; Pres. Kazayuki Takeshima.

)dakyu Electric Railway Co Ltd: 1-8-3, Nishi-Shinjuku, Shin-uku-ku, Tokyo 160-8309; tel. (3) 3349-2526; fax (3) 3346-1899; e-mail r@odakyu-dentetsu.co.jp; internet www.odakyu.jp; f. 1948; Chair. 'atsuzo Toshimitsu; Exec. Pres. Yorihiko Osuga.

Sanyo Electric Railway Co Ltd: 3-1-1, Oyashiki-dori, Nagata-ku, Kobe 653; tel. (78) 653-0843; internet www.sanyo-railway.co.jp; Pres. Fumihiro Amano.

Seibu Railway Co Ltd: 1-11-1, Kasunokidai, Tokorozawa-shi, Saitama 359; tel. (429) 26-2035; fax (429) 26-2237; internet www .seibu-group.co.jp/railways; f. 1894; Chair. Takashi Gotoh; Pres. and CEO Susumu Shirayama.

Tobu Railway Co Ltd: 1-1-2, Oshiage, Sumida-ku, Tokyo 131-8522; tel. (3) 3621-5057; internet www.tobu.co.jp; f. 1897; Chair. Kaichiro Nezu; Pres. Yoshizumi Nezu.

Tokyo Express Electric Railway (Tokyu) Co Ltd: 5-6, Nanpei-dai-cho, Shibuya-ku, Tokyo 150-8511; tel. (3) 3477-0109; fax (3) 3477-6109; e-mail public@tokyu.co.jp; internet www.tokyu.co.jp; f. 1922; Pres. Toshiaki Koshimura.

Principal Subways, Monorails and Tunnels

Subway services operate in Tokyo, Osaka, Kobe, Nagoya, Sapporo, Yokohama, Kyoto, Sendai and Fukuoka. A subway was planned to begin operations in Kawasaki in 2018. Most subway lines operate reciprocal through-services with existing private railway lines which connect the cities with suburban areas.

The first commercial monorail system was introduced in 1964 with straddle-type cars between central Tokyo and Tokyo International Airport, a distance of 13 km. Monorails also operate in other cities, including Chiba, Hiroshima, Kitakyushu and Osaka.

In 1985 the 54-km Seikan Tunnel (the world's longest undersea tunnel), linking the islands of Honshu and Hokkaido, was completed. Electric rail services through the tunnel began operating in March 1988.

Fukuoka City Subway: Fukuoka Municipal Transportation Bureau, 2-5-31, Daimyo, Chuo-ku, Fukuoka 810-0041; tel. (92) 732-4107; fax (92) 721-0754; internet subway.city.fukuoka.jp; 2 lines of 17.8 km open; Dir Kennichirou Nishi.

Kobe Rapid Transit Railway Co Ltd: 3-3-9 Tamondoori, Chuo-ku, Kobe; tel. (78) 351-0881; fax (78) 351-1607; internet www .kobe-kousoku.jp; 22.7 km open; Dir Yasuo Maeno.

Nagoya Subway: Transportation Bureau City of Nagoya, Nagoya City Hall, 3-1-1, Sannomaru, Naka-ku, Nagoya 460-8508; tel. (52) 972-3824; fax (52) 972-3938; e-mail goiken@tbcn.city.nagoya.lg.jp; internet www.kotsu.city.nagoya.jp; 87 km open; Dir-Gen. Nobuo Yoshii.

Osaka Monorail: 1-1-5, Higashi-Machi, Shin-Senri, Toyonakashi, Osaka 560-0082; tel. (6) 6871-8280; fax (6) 6871-8284; internet www .osaka-monorail.co.jp; 113.5 km open; Pres. Hironobu Iana.

Osaka Underground Railway: Osaka Municipal Transportation Bureau, 1-12-62, Kujo-Minami, Nishi-ku, Osaka 550-8552; tel. (6) 6585-6137; fax (6) 6585-6154; internet www.kotsu.city.osaka.jp; f. 1933; 129.9 km; the 7.9 km computer-controlled 'New Tram' service began between Suminoekoen and Nakafuto in 1981; seventh line between Kyobashi and Tsurumi-ryokuchi opened in 1990; eighth line between Itakano and Imazato opened in 2006; Gen. Man. Yoshihide Kusumoto.

Sapporo Transportation Bureau: 2-4-1, Oyachi-Higashi, Atsu-betsu-ku, Sapporo 004-8555; tel. (11) 896-2708; fax (11) 896-2790; internet www.city.sapporo.jp/st; f. 1971; 3 lines of 48 km; Dir T. Ikegami.

Sendai City Subway: Sendai City Transportation Bureau, 1-4-15, Kimachidori, Aoba-ku, Sendai-shi, Miyagi-ken 980-0801; tel. (22) 224-5111; fax (22) 224-6839; internet www.kotsu.city.sendai.jp; 15.4 km open; Dir T. Iwama.

Tokyo Metro Co Ltd: 3-19-6, Higashi-Ueno, Taito-ku, Tokyo 110-8614; tel. (3) 3837-7046; fax (3) 3837-7219; internet www.tokyometro .jp; f. 2004; operates eight lines; 195.1 km open (2010); Pres. Hisashi Umezaki.

Tokyo Metropolitan Government (TOEI) Underground Railway: Bureau of Transportation, Tokyo Metropolitan Government, 2-8-1, Nishi-Shinjuku, Tokyo 163-8001; tel. (3) 5320-6026; internet www.kotsu.metro.tokyo.jp; operates four underground lines, totalling 105 km.

Yokohama Municipal Subway: Municipal Transportation Bureau, 1-1, Minato-cho, Naka-ku, Yokohama 231-0017; tel. (45) 664-2525; fax (45) 664-2828; internet www.city.yokohama.jp/me/koutuu; 40.4 km open; Dir-Gen. Michinori Kishida.

ROADS

In 2006 Japan's road network extended to an estimated 1,196,999 km, including 7,383 km of motorways and 54,347 km of highways. In May 1999 work was completed on a 29-year project to construct three routes, consisting of a total of 19 bridges, between the islands of Honshu and Shikoku across the Seto inland sea. There is a national bus service, 60 publicly operated services and 298 privately operated services.

In October 2005 the major state-owned road authorities were transferred to the private sector. The Japan Highway Public Corpn was privatized and divided into three separate regional expressway companies, servicing central, eastern and western zones. The others were Metropolitan Expressway Public Corpn, Hanshin Expressway Public Corpn and Honshu-Shikoku Bridge Authority.

Central Nippon Expressway Co Ltd: Nagoya Sumimoto Bldg, 8/F, 2-18-19, Nishiki Naka-ku, Nagoya 460-0003; tel. (52) 222-1620; internet www.c-nexco.co.jp; f. 2005; Chair. Kaneko Takeshi.

East Nippon Expressway Co Ltd: Kasumigaseki Bldg, 15/F, 3-2 Kasumigaseki, Chiyoda-ku, Tokyo 100-8979; tel. (3) 3506-0111; internet www.e-nexco.co.jp; f. 2005; Chair. Tatsuo Sato.

West Nippon Expressway Co Ltd: 1-6-20, Dojima, Kita-ku, Osaka; tel. (6) 6344-4000; internet corp.w-nexco.co.jp; f. 2005; Chair. Hidetoshi Nishimura.

SHIPPING

At 31 December 2009 the Japanese merchant fleet comprised 6,221 vessels, with a total displacement of 14,725,189 grt. The main ports are Tokyo, Yokohama, Nagoya and Osaka.

Principal Companies

Daiichi Chuo Kisen Kaisha: 2-14-4, Shintomi-cho, Chuo-ku, Tokyo 104-8544; tel. (3) 5540-1997; fax (3) 3523-8987; internet www.firstship.co.jp; f. 1960; liner and tramp services; Pres. Saburo Koide.

Iino Kaiun Kaisha Ltd: Shiba-Daimon Front Bldg, 1-7-13, Shiba-koen, Minato-ku, Tokyo 105-0011; tel. (3) 5408-0356; e-mail ikk_soumu2@ex.iino.co.jp; internet www.iino.co.jp; f. 1899; cargo and tanker services; Chair. Tomoyuki Sekine; CEO Yoshihiko Nakagami.

Kansai Kisen KK: Osaka Bldg, 3-6-32, Nakanoshima, Kita-ku, Osaka 552; tel. (6) 6574-9131; fax (6) 6574-9149; internet www.kanki .co.jp; f. 1942; domestic passenger services; Pres. Makoto Kuroishi.

Kawasaki Kisen Kaisha Ltd (K Line): 1-2-9, Nishi-Shimbashi, Minato-ku, Tokyo 105-8421; tel. (3) 3595-5000; fax (3) 3595-5001; e-mail otaki@email.kline.co.jp; internet www.kline.co.jp; f. 1919; containers, cars, LNG, LPG and oil tankers, bulk carriers; Chair. of Bd Hiroyuki Maekawa; Pres. Kurodani Kenichi.

Mitsui OSK Lines Ltd: Shosen Mitsui Bldg, 2-1-1, Toranomon, Minato-ku, Tokyo 105-8688; tel. (3) 3587-7092; fax (3) 3587-7734; internet www.mol.co.jp; f. 1942; merged with Navix Line Ltd in 1999; world-wide container, liner, tramp, and specialized carrier and tanker services; Chair. Akimitsu Ashida; Pres. Koichi Muto.

Nippon Yusen Kaisha (NYK) Line: 2-3-2, Marunouchi, Chiyoda-ku, Tokyo 100-0005; tel. (3) 3284-5151; fax (3) 3284-6361; internet www.nyk.com; f. 1885; merged with Showa Line Ltd in 1998; world-wide container, cargo, pure car and truck carriers, tanker and bulk carrying services; Chair. Koji Miyahara; Pres. Yasumi Kudo.

Nissho Shipping Co Ltd: Mori Bldg, 7/F, Rm 33, 3-8-21, Toranomon, Minato-ku, Tokyo 105-0001; tel. (3) 3438-3511; fax (3) 3438-

3566; internet www.nissho-shipping.co.jp; f. 1943; Pres. KENICHI YAMAGUCHI.

Ryukyu Kaiun KK: 1-24-11, Nishi-Machi, Naha, Okinawa 900-0036; tel. (98) 868-8161; fax (98) 868-8561; internet www.rkkline.co.jp; f. 1950; cargo and passenger services on domestic routes; Pres. YAMASHIRO HIROMI.

Taiheiyo Kaiun Co Ltd: Mitakokusai Bldg, 23/F, 1-4-28, Minato-ku, Tokyo 108-0073; tel. (3) 5445-5800; fax (3) 5445-5801; internet www.taiheiyokk.co.jp; f. 1951; cargo and tanker services; Pres. TAKESHI MATSUNAGA.

CIVIL AVIATION

Three international airports serve Tokyo: Narita, located in Chiba prefecture; Haneda; and Ibaraki, which opened in March 2010. A second runway was opened at Narita in 2002. A fourth runway at Haneda, along with a third terminal for international flights, opened in October 2010. In 1994 the world's first offshore international airport (Kansai International Airport) was opened in Osaka Bay, and a second runway was completed in 2007. Nearly 100 other airports handle regional and some international flights.

Air Central: c/o Central Japan International Airport, 1-1, Centrair, Tokoname, Aichi 479-0881; tel. (569) 389-300; fax (569) 389-305; internet www.air-central.co.jp; f. 1988; fmrly Nakanihon Airlines, name changed as above Feb. 2005; regional and domestic services; Pres. JUNICHI MIDORO.

Air Do (Hokkaido International Airlines Co Ltd): 1-2-9, Kita Sanjo Nishi, Chuo-ku, Sapporo; tel. (11) 252-5533; fax (11) 252-5580; e-mail postbear@airdo.co.jp; internet www.airdo.co.jp; f. 1996; domestic service between Tokyo and Sapporo; Pres. SAITO SADAO.

Air Nippon Co Ltd (Air Nippon Koku—ANK): Shiodome City Centre, 1-5-2, Higashi-Shinbashi, Minato-ku, Tokyo 105–7137; internet www.air-nippon.co.jp; f. 1974; fmrly Nihon Kinkyori Airways; wholly owned subsidiary of All Nippon Airways; domestic passenger services, international service to Taiwan; Pres. and CEO HIDEO YAGUCHI.

All Nippon Airways (ANA): Shiodome City Center, 1-5-2, Higashi-Shimbashi, Minato-ku, Tokyo 105-7133; tel. (3) 6735-1000; fax (3) 6735-1005; internet www.ana.co.jp; f. 1952; operates domestic passenger and freight services; scheduled international services to the Far East, the USA and Europe; charter services world-wide; Chair. YOJI OHASHI; Pres. and CEO SHINCHIRO ITO.

Hokkaido Air System: New Chitose Airport, Bibi Chitose City, Hokkaido 066-0055; tel. (123) 46-5533; fax (123) 46-5534; internet www.hac-air.co.jp; f. 1997; domestic services on Hokkaido; Pres. NISHIMURA KIMITOSHI.

Ibex Airlines: 1-2-3, Shinsuna, Koto-ku, Tokyo 136-8640; internet www.ibexair.co.jp; f. 1999; operates domestic flights from Osaka and Narita International Airports; Chair. TAKAO ASAI; Pres. HATTORI HIROYUKI.

JALways Co Ltd: Japan Airlines Narita Operation Center, 3/F, Narita International Airport, Narita, Chiba 282-8610; tel. (476) 34-3360; fax (476) 34-3366; e-mail jazbz.jaz@jal.com; internet www.jalways.co.jp; f. 1990; subsidiary of JAL; domestic and international scheduled and charter services; Pres. and CEO HIROSHI IKEDA.

Japan Air Commuter: 787-4, Mizobe Humototyou, Kirishima, Kagoshima Prefecture; tel. (995) 582-151; fax (995) 582-673; e-mail info@jac.co.jp; internet www.jac.co.jp; f. 1983; subsidiary of JAL; domestic services; Chair. YOSHITOMI ONO; Pres. ARATA YASUJIMA.

Japan Airlines (JAL): 2-4-11, Higashi-Shinagawa, Shinagawa-ku, Tokyo 140-8605; tel. (3) 5769-6476; internet www.jal.com; f. 2002; Chair. KAZUO INAMORI; Pres. MASARU ONISHI.

Japan Transocean Air Co Ltd: 3-24, Yamashita-cho, Naha-shi, Okinawa 900-0027; tel. (98) 857-2112; fax (98) 857-9396; internet www.jal.co.jp/jta; f. 1967; adopted present name 1993; subsidiary of JAL; domestic passenger services; Pres. SATO MANABU.

Skymark Airlines: 1-5-5, Haneda Airport, Ota-ku, Tokyo 144-0041; tel. (3) 5402-6767; fax (3) 5402-6770; e-mail info@skymark.co.jp; internet www.skymark.co.jp; f. 1997; domestic services; Pres. and CEO SHINICHI NISHIKUBO.

Tourism

The ancient capital of Kyoto, pagodas and temples, forests and mountains, traditional festivals and the classical Kabuki theatre are some of the many tourist attractions of Japan. Receipts fro tourism (excluding passenger transport) in 2010 totalled an es mated US $13,199m. International arrivals rose by an estimat 26.8% in 2010 to total 8.6m. The Republic of Korea, China ar Taiwan are leading sources of visitors.

Japan National Tourism Organization (JNTO): Tokyo Kots Kaikan Bldg, 2-10-1, Yuraku-cho, Chiyoda-ku, Tokyo 100-0006; te (3) 3201-3331; fax (3) 3216-1846; internet www.jnto.go.jp; f. 196 Pres. RYOICHI MATSUYAMA.

Japan Tourism Agency (JTA): General Affairs Division, Nation and Regional Planning Bureau, 2-1-3, Kasumigaseki, Chiyoda-ku Tokyo 100-8918; tel. (3) 5253-8111; fax (3) 3580-7982; e-ma webmaster@mlit.go.jp; internet www.mlit.go.jp/kankocho; f. 200 aims to promote Japan as a tourist destination and, in conjunctio with JNTO, to achieve govt objectives; Commr HIROSHI MIZOHATA.

Defence

As assessed at November 2011, the total strength of the Japanes Self-Defence Forces was some 247,746: ground self-defence 151,641 maritime self-defence 45,518, air self-defence 47,123 and centra staff 3,464. Paramilitary forces numbered 12,636, and reserve force comprised an additional 56,379 personnel. Military service is vol untary. At November 2011 US forces stationed in Japan comprise 2,617 army, 13,143 air force and 6,833 navy personnel, together wit 17,585 members of the US Marine Corps.

Defence Expenditure: Budgeted at 4,660,000m. yen for 2012.

Chief of the Joint Staff Council: Gen. RYOICHI ORIKI.

Chief of Staff of Ground Self-Defence Force: Gen. YOSHIFUM HIBAKO.

Chief of Staff of Maritime Self-Defence Force: Adm. MASAHIKO SUGIMOTO.

Chief of Staff of Air Self-Defence Force: SHIGERU IWASAKI.

Education

Education is compulsory between the ages of six and 15. A kindergarten (*yochien*) system provides education for children aged between three and five years of age, although the majority of kindergartens are privately controlled. In 2010 there were 13,392 kindergartens, which were attended by 1.6m. children. All children between six and 15 are required to attend six-year elementary schools (*shogakko*) and three-year lower secondary schools (or middle schools—*chugakko*). In 2008/09 enrolment at pre-primary school included 89% of pupils in the relevant age-group, while enrolment at primary level included 100% of pupils in the relevant age-group. Enrolment at secondary level included 99% of students in the relevant age group in the same year. In 2010 there were 22,000 elementary schools, at which nearly 7m. pupils were enrolled, and 10,815 lower secondary schools, at which 3.6m. pupils were enrolled. Upper secondary schools (or high schools— *kotogakko*) provide a three-year course in general topics, or a vocational course in subjects such as agriculture, commerce, fine art and technical studies. In 2010 there were 5,116 upper secondary schools, at which 3.4m. pupils were enrolled.

There are four types of institution for higher education. Universities (*daigaku*) offer degree and postgraduate courses. In 2010 there were 778 universities and graduate schools, at which 2.9m. students were enrolled. Junior colleges (*tanki-daigaku*) provide less specialized two- to three-year courses, credits for which can count towards a first degree. In 2010 there were 395 junior colleges in Japan. Both universities and junior colleges offer facilities for teacher-training. Colleges of technology (*koto-senmon-gakko*), of which there were 58 in 2010, offer a five-year specialized training. Since 1991 colleges of technology have been able to offer short-term advanced courses. A combined total of 214,542 students were enrolled at junior colleges and colleges of technology in 2010. Special training colleges (*senshu-gakko*) offer advanced courses in technical and vocational subjects, lasting for at least one year. In 2010 there were 3,311 special training colleges in Japan. Central government expenditure on education and science was allocated at 5,405,700m. yen for the 2012 financial year.

JORDAN

Introductory Survey

LOCATION, CLIMATE, LANGUAGE, RELIGION, FLAG, CAPITAL

The Hashemite Kingdom of Jordan is an almost land-locked state in western Asia. It is bordered by Israel and the Palestinian Autonomous Areas to the west, by Syria to the north, by Iraq to the east and by Saudi Arabia to the south. The port of Aqaba, in the far south, gives Jordan a narrow outlet to the Red Sea. The climate is hot and dry. The average annual temperature is about 15°C (60°F) but there are wide diurnal variations. Temperatures in Amman are generally between −1°C (30°F) and 32°C (90°F). More extreme conditions are found in the valley of the River Jordan and on the shores of the Dead Sea (a lake on the Israeli–Jordanian frontier), where the temperature may exceed 50°C (122°F) in summer. The official language is Arabic. More than 90% of the population are Sunni Muslims, while there are small communities of Christians and Shi'i Muslims. The national flag (proportions 1 by 2) has three equal horizontal stripes, of black, white and green, with a red triangle, containing a seven-pointed white star, at the hoist. The capital is Amman.

CONTEMPORARY POLITICAL HISTORY

Historical Context

Palestine (including the present-day West Bank territory) and Transjordan (the East Bank) were formerly parts of Turkey's Ottoman Empire. During the First World War (1914–18), when Turkey was allied with Germany, the Arabs under Ottoman rule rebelled. British forces, with Arab support, occupied Palestine and Transjordan in 1917–18, when the Turks withdrew. British occupation continued after the war, when the Ottoman Empire was dissolved. In 1920 Palestine and Transjordan were formally placed under British administration by a League of Nations mandate. In 1921 Abdullah ibn Hussein, a member of the Hashimi (Hashemite) dynasty of Arabia, was proclaimed Amir (Emir) of Transjordan.

Under the British mandate Transjordan (formally separated from Palestine in 1923) gained increasing autonomy, and in 1928 the United Kingdom acknowledged its nominal independence, while retaining certain financial and military powers. Amir Abdullah followed a generally pro-British policy and supported the Allied cause in the Second World War (1939–45). The mandate was terminated on 22 March 1946, when Transjordan attained full independence. On 25 May Abdullah was proclaimed King, and a new Constitution took effect.

When the British Government terminated its mandate in Palestine in May 1948, Jewish leaders there proclaimed the State of Israel. Palestinian Arabs, however, with military support from Arab states, opposed Israeli claims, and hostilities continued until July. Transjordan's forces occupied about 5,900 sq km of Palestine, including East Jerusalem, and this was confirmed by the armistice with Israel in April 1949. In June the country was renamed Jordan, and in April 1950, following a referendum, King Abdullah formally annexed the West Bank territory, which contained many Arab refugees from Israeli-held areas.

Domestic Political Affairs

In July 1951 King Abdullah was assassinated in Jerusalem by a Palestinian belonging to an extremist Islamist organization. Abdullah was succeeded by his eldest son, Talal ibn Abdullah, hitherto Crown Prince. However, in August 1952, because of Talal's mental incapacity, the crown passed to his son, Hussein ibn Talal, then 16 years of age. King Hussein formally came to power in May 1953.

In March 1956, responding to Arab nationalist sentiment, King Hussein dismissed the British army officer who had been Chief of Staff of the British-equipped and -financed Arab Legion (the Jordanian armed forces) since 1939. Jordan's treaty relationship with the United Kingdom was ended in March 1957, and British troops completed their withdrawal from Jordan in July.

The refugee camps in the West Bank became the centre of Palestinian resistance to Israel, and during the 1950s there were numerous attacks on Israeli territory by groups of Palestinian *fedayeen* ('martyrs'). In September 1963 the creation of a unified 'Palestinian entity' was approved by the Council of the League of Arab States (the Arab League, see p. 364), and the first Palestinian congress was held in the Jordanian sector of Jerusalem in May–June 1964, at which it was agreed to form the Palestine Liberation Organization (PLO), which would be financed by the Arab League and would recruit military units to form a Palestine Liberation Army (PLA). The principal Palestinian guerrilla organization within the PLO was the Palestine National Liberation Movement, known as Fatah ('Conquest'), led from 1968 by Yasser Arafat. However, King Hussein regarded the establishment of the PLO as a threat to Jordanian sovereignty, and from the outset refused to allow the PLA to train in Jordan or the PLO to levy taxes from Palestinian refugees residing in his country.

In April 1965 Hussein nominated his brother Hassan ibn Talal to be Crown Prince. During the Six-Day War of June 1967 Israel made substantial military gains, including possession of the whole of Jerusalem (which was incorporated into Israel) and the West Bank; the latter became an Israeli 'administered territory'. The influx of Palestinian refugees into the East Bank bolstered the strength of the PLO, whose continued armed raids on the Israeli-administered territories challenged the personal authority of King Hussein and the sovereignty of the Jordanian Government. King Hussein responded by expelling the guerrilla groups, after a civil war that lasted from September 1970 to July 1971. Aid to Jordan from Kuwait and other wealthy Arab states, suspended after the expulsion of the Palestinian fighters, was only restored following Jordan's military support for Syria during the Arab–Israeli War of October 1973. At an Arab summit meeting in Rabat, Morocco, in October 1974 King Hussein supported a unanimous resolution recognizing the PLO as the 'sole legitimate representative of the Palestinian people' and granting the organization the right to establish an independent national authority on any piece of Palestinian land to be liberated.

In response to this resolution, in November 1974 both chambers of the Jordanian National Assembly (which had equal representation for the East and West Banks) approved constitutional amendments that empowered the King to dissolve the Assembly and to postpone elections for up to 12 months. The Assembly was dissolved later that month, although it was briefly reconvened in February 1976, when it approved a constitutional amendment giving the King power to postpone elections indefinitely and to convene the Assembly as required. A royal decree of April 1978 provided for the creation of a National Consultative Council, with 60 members appointed for a two-year term by the King, on the Prime Minister's recommendation, to debate proposed legislation.

Joint Palestinian-Jordanian peace initiatives

A proposal put forward by US President Ronald Reagan in September 1982 for an autonomous Palestinian authority on the West Bank, in association with Jordan, was rejected by Yasser Arafat following talks with King Hussein. In January 1984, however, the King responded by dissolving the National Consultative Council and recalling the National Assembly for the first time since 1967—in effect creating the kind of Palestinian forum envisaged by the Reagan initiative. Israel allowed the surviving West Bank deputies to attend the Assembly, which approved constitutional amendments enabling elections to be held in the East Bank, while West Bank deputies would be chosen by the Assembly itself. After discussions with the PLO leader in January 1984 on a joint Palestinian-Jordanian peace initiative, King Hussein's proposals for negotiations, based on UN Security Council Resolution 242 (the resolution, adopted in November 1967, sought to return the region's territorial boundaries to the pre-Six-Day War status, but incorporated implicit recognition of an Israeli state), met with a non-committal response from the Palestine National Council (PNC), which convened in Amman in November 1984. President Hosni Mubarak of Egypt gave his support to Hussein's proposals, following the resumption of diplomatic relations between the two countries in September. In February 1985 King Hussein and

Yasser Arafat announced the terms of a Jordanian-Palestinian agreement, proposing a confederated state of Jordan and Palestine to be reached through the convening of a conference of all concerned parties in the Middle East, including the PLO.

In July 1985 Israel rejected a list of seven Palestinians, five of whom were members of the PLO or had links with the PNC, whom King Hussein had presented to the USA as candidates for a joint Jordanian-Palestinian delegation to preliminary peace talks. Further progress was hindered by a series of terrorist incidents in which the PLO was implicated, and King Hussein came under increasing pressure to advance the peace process, if necessary without PLO participation. In September President Reagan revived his 1984 plan to sell military equipment to the value of some US $1,900m. to Jordan. The proposal was approved by the US Congress on the condition that Jordan enter into direct talks with Israel before 1 March 1986. However, such talks were obstructed by a gradual rapprochement between Jordan and Syria, both of which supported a Middle East peace settlement through an international conference, having rejected 'partial and unilateral' solutions.

Frustrated by the lack of co-operation from Yasser Arafat in advancing the aims of the Jordanian-PLO peace initiative, King Hussein publicly severed political links with the PLO on 19 February 1986. Arafat was subsequently ordered to close his main PLO offices in Jordan by 1 April. The PLO's activities were henceforth to be restricted even further, and a number of Fatah officers loyal to Arafat were expelled. In July the Jordanian authorities closed all 25 Fatah offices in Amman; only 12 bureaux belonging to the PLO remained.

Despite the termination of political co-ordination with the PLO, Jordan continued to reject Israeli requests for direct peace talks that excluded a form of PLO representation. However, Jordan's subsequent efforts to strengthen its influence in the Israeli-occupied territories (Occupied Territories), and to foster a Palestinian constituency there independent of Arafat's PLO, coincided with Israeli measures to grant limited autonomy to Palestinians in the West Bank. In March 1986 the Jordanian House of Representatives approved a draft law increasing the number of seats in the House from 60 to 142 (71 seats each for the East and West Banks), thereby providing for greater representation for West Bank Palestinians in the National Assembly. In August, with Israeli support, Jordan announced a five-year development plan, valued at US $1,300m., for the West Bank and Gaza Strip; the plan was condemned by Arafat and West Bank Palestinians as representing a normalization of relations with Israel. Support for Arafat among Palestinians in the Occupied Territories, and in Jordan, was consolidated as he re-established himself at the head of a reunified PLO at the 18th session of the PNC in April 1987 (when the Jordanian-PLO accord of 1985 was formally abrogated).

In May 1987, following secret meetings with King Hussein, the Israeli Minister of Foreign Affairs, Shimon Peres, claimed to have made significant progress on the crucial issue of Palestinian representation at a Middle East peace conference, and to have the consent of Egypt, Jordan and the USA to convene a conference involving the five permanent members of the UN Security Council and a delegation of Palestinians who rejected terrorism and accepted Security Council Resolutions 242 and 338 (the latter defined the terms of immediate peace following the 1973 Arab–Israeli War) as the basis for negotiations. The Jordanian Prime Minister, Zaid Rifai, confirmed his country's willingness to participate in a joint Jordanian-Palestinian delegation including the PLO, provided that the organization complied with the stated conditions. However, Israel's Prime Minister, Itzhak Shamir, reiterated his alternative proposal of direct regional talks excluding the PLO, and Peres failed to secure the support of a majority of the Israeli Cabinet for his proposals.

At the first full meeting of the Arab League for eight years, convened in Amman in November 1987, King Hussein pursued an agenda of greater Arab unity in support of Iraq in its war with Iran. Prior to the summit, Jordan restored full diplomatic relations with Libya (severed in 1984), which had modified its support for Iran. However, King Hussein's appeal for Egypt to be restored to membership of the League (suspended following the peace treaty with Israel in 1979) was resisted by Libya and Syria, although 11 Arab states subsequently re-established diplomatic relations. Jordan also announced the resumption of co-operation with the PLO.

These achievements were soon overshadowed by the Palestinian *intifada* (uprising), which erupted in the West Bank and Gaza Strip in December 1987, in protest against the continued Israeli occupation and the seemingly indifferent attitude of Arab League states to the Palestinians' plight. The *intifada*, and the increasingly violent Israeli response, boosted international support for the PLO and Palestinian national rights. At an extraordinary meeting of the Arab League held in the Algerian capital, Algiers, in June 1988, King Hussein gave the *intifada* his unconditional support and insisted that the PLO must represent the Palestinians at any future peace conference. Furthermore, in accordance with agreements reached at the meeting, on 31 July Jordan cancelled the West Bank development plan and severed its legal and administrative links with the territory.

On 15 November 1988 the PNC, meeting in Algiers, proclaimed the establishment of an independent State of Palestine and, for the first time, endorsed UN Security Council Resolution 242 as a basis for a Middle East peace settlement, thus implicitly recognizing Israel. Jordan and 60 other countries recognized the new state. Addressing a special session of the UN General Assembly in Geneva, Switzerland, in December, Arafat renounced violence on behalf of the PLO. The USA subsequently opened a dialogue with the organization.

In April 1989 there was rioting in several cities, after the Jordanian Government imposed sizeable price increases on basic goods and services. The riots led to the resignation of Prime Minister Rifai and his Cabinet. Field Marshal Sharif Zaid ibn Shaker, a cousin of the King who had been Commander-in-Chief of the Jordanian Armed Forces in 1976–88, was appointed to head a new Government. While King Hussein refused to make any concessions regarding the price increases, he announced that a general election would be held for the first time since 1967. The election to the 80-seat House of Representatives, which proceeded in November 1989, was contested by 647 candidates, mostly independents, as the ban on political parties (in force since 1963) remained. However, the Muslim Brotherhood was able to present candidates for election, owing to its legal status as a charity. At the election the Muslim Brotherhood won 20 seats, while as many as 14 seats were won by independent Islamist candidates who supported the Brotherhood. In December King Hussein appointed former premier Mudar Badran as Prime Minister. In January 1990 Badran pledged to abolish martial law (which had been suspended in December 1989) within four to six months, and to liberalize the judicial system; he also announced the abolition of the anti-communism law (in force since 1954). In April King Hussein appointed a 60-member commission, under the chairmanship of former premier Ahmad Ubeidat, to devise a national charter that would legalize political parties. The commission's draft national charter was approved by the King in January 1991, and further endorsed by Hussein and leading political figures in June. Also in January the Cabinet was reorganized to include five members of the Muslim Brotherhood.

Iraq's invasion of Kuwait in August 1990, and the consequent imposition of economic sanctions by the UN against Iraq, had a profound impact on Jordan: Iraq was its principal trading partner, and Jordan relied on supplies of Iraqi petroleum. Although King Hussein condemned the Iraqi invasion, he was slow to do so, and advocated an 'Arab solution' to the crisis. There was considerable support for the Iraqi President, Saddam Hussain, among the Jordanian population, particularly among Palestinians. King Hussein was critical of the US-led deployment of multinational military forces in Saudi Arabia and the Persian (Arabian) Gulf, and in the closing months of 1990 he visited numerous Middle East and other capitals in an attempt to avert a war. Jordan's response to the Gulf crisis prompted the USA to review its military and economic assistance to Jordan and led to a deterioration in Jordan's relations with Egypt and Saudi Arabia, both of which contributed to the US-led force. However, diplomatic relations between Jordan and Iran were re-established (having been severed in 1981).

Meanwhile, Jordan secured the approval of the USA by agreeing to join with a Palestinian delegation at the Middle East peace conference, which opened in Madrid, Spain, in October 1991. Subsequent talks in Washington, DC, USA, and Moscow, Russia, between the Israeli and the joint Jordanian-Palestinian delegations remained deadlocked with regard to substantive issues until September 1993, when Israel and the PLO agreed to a declaration of principles regarding Palestinian self-rule in the Occupied Territories. On the signing of the Declaration of Principles, which King Hussein welcomed, the Jordanian-Palestinian delegation was disbanded, and Jordan and Israel concluded an agreement that defined the agenda for subsequent bilateral negotiations within the context of the Middle East peace conference. The talks were to address the following issues: refugees and displaced persons; security; water resources; the demarcation of the border between Jordan and Israel; and future bilateral co-operation.

In 1991 Jordan and the PLO had agreed on the principle of confederation between Jordan and whatever Palestinian entity ultimately emerged from the Middle East peace process, and in July 1993 they undertook to form six committees to discuss relations between Jordan and the Occupied Territories during a period of transitional Palestinian self-rule. Jordan was formally excluded from discussion of some of the issues, however, following the signing of the Declaration of Principles. In January 1994, after King Hussein had twice warned that Jordan might otherwise pursue its own agenda in the ongoing peace talks with Israel, the PLO agreed to sign a comprehensive economic co-operation agreement with Jordan, and to establish a joint committee to co-ordinate financial policy in the Palestinian territories. In the same month Jordan signed a draft security accord with the PLO.

King Hussein concludes a peace treaty with Israel

On 25 July 1994 King Hussein and the Israeli Prime Minister, Itzhak Rabin, meeting in the US capital, signed the Washington Declaration, which formally ended the state of war that had existed between Jordan and Israel since 1948. In October 1994 the two countries signed a full peace treaty settling outstanding issues of contention between them and providing, *inter alia*, for the establishment of diplomatic relations and for talks on economic and security co-operation. The official normalization of relations between Jordan and Israel had been completed by 18 January 1996. In Jordan the peace treaty was opposed by Islamist militants, and it was also criticized by Syria. The PLO leadership complained that the treaty undermined Palestinian claims to sovereignty over Jerusalem. None the less, in January 1995 the PLO and Jordan signed an agreement regulating relations between Jordan and the Palestinian Autonomous Areas with regard to economic affairs, finance, banking, education, transport, telecommunications, information and administration. At the same time, the PLO acknowledged Jordan's custodianship of the Muslim holy places in Jerusalem for as long as Jordan recognized and supported Palestinian claims to sovereignty over East Jerusalem.

Meanwhile, in June 1991 Taher al-Masri was appointed to replace Mudar Badran as Prime Minister. However, in the period preceding the opening of the National Assembly in December, it became clear that al-Masri could not command majority support in the legislature; he was forced to resign in November, whereupon Sharif Zaid ibn Shaker again assumed the premiership. In July 1992 the House of Representatives adopted legislation whereby, subject to certain conditions, political parties were formally legalized. In May 1993 King Hussein appointed Abd al-Salam al-Majali, the head of the Jordanian delegation to the Middle East peace conference, to the premiership.

In August 1993 King Hussein unexpectedly dissolved the House of Representatives, provoking criticism from some politicians who had expected the House to debate proposed amendments to Jordan's electoral law. Changes in voting procedures at the general election were announced by the King in that month: voters were to be allowed to cast one vote only, rather than multiple votes equal to the number of candidates contesting a given constituency. Some 68% of the electorate were reported to have participated in Jordan's first multi-party general election, held on 8 November. By far the largest number of deputies returned to the House of Representatives were independent centrists loyal to the King. The Islamic Action Front (IAF, the political wing of the Muslim Brotherhood) emerged as the second largest party in the legislature. A new Senate (House of Notables) was appointed by the King on 18 November, and a new Cabinet, led by al-Majali, was announced in December. Al-Majali was dismissed in January 1995, whereupon Sharif Zaid ibn Shaker once again assumed the premiership at the head of an extensively reorganized Cabinet.

King Hussein implemented a further extensive cabinet reorganization in February 1996, appointing Abd al-Karim al-Kabariti, hitherto Minister of Foreign Affairs, as Prime Minister. (He retained the foreign affairs portfolio, and also assumed responsibility for defence.) In August rioting erupted in southern Jordan after the Government imposed a sharp increase on the price of bread. The unrest quickly spread to other parts of the country, including impoverished areas of the capital. King Hussein responded by suspending the legislature and deploying the army in order to suppress the worst disturbances. Prime Minister al-Kabariti was unexpectedly dismissed by Hussein in March 1997, reportedly as a result of disagreement over issues relating to Jordan's policies towards Israel. Abd al-Salam al-Majali again assumed the premiership.

In July 1997 the IAF announced its intention to boycott the forthcoming parliamentary elections, in protest at what it regarded as the Government's overly concessionary policies towards Israel and at recent restrictive amendments to press legislation. Several other parties also boycotted the polls. At the general election, which took place on 4 November, 62 of the 80 seats in the new House of Representatives were won by pro-Government candidates; 10 seats were secured by nationalist and left-wing candidates, and eight by independent Islamists. A new Senate was appointed by the King on 22 November. In August 1998 Fayez al-Tarawneh was appointed Prime Minister, in place of al-Majali, and a new Cabinet was subsequently named.

The accession of King Abdullah

Meanwhile, in July 1998 King Hussein began to undergo treatment for cancer in the USA. In August he issued a royal decree transferring responsibility for certain executive duties to his brother, Crown Prince Hassan. On King Hussein's return to Jordan in January 1999, amid official assurances that his health had been restored, the King prompted renewed speculation about the royal succession by appointing Crown Prince Hassan as his 'deputy'. On 24 January King Hussein issued a royal decree naming his eldest son, Abdullah, as Crown Prince of Jordan. Although Hassan had been regent since 1965, King Hussein was said to have been dissatisfied with his brother's handling of Jordanian affairs during his absence, in particular his attempts to intervene in military matters. Two days later the King left Jordan for emergency treatment in the USA, following a rapid deterioration in his health. King Hussein returned to Amman on 5 February 1999 and was pronounced dead on 7 February. The Crown Prince was sworn in, as King Abdullah ibn al-Hussein, on the same day. Prince Hamzeh ibn al-Hussein, the late King's youngest son, became the new Crown Prince.

In March 1999 King Abdullah announced the formation of a new Cabinet, in which several ministers regarded as loyal to Prince Hassan were replaced. Abd al-Raouf al-Rawabdeh replaced Fayez al-Tarawneh as Prime Minister and Minister of Defence. Former premier al-Kabariti was appointed Chief of the Royal Court—an important post since the incumbent serves as the primary link between the King and the Government. King Abdullah charged al-Rawabdeh with implementing what he termed 'fundamental reforms', including a strengthening of the rule of law and further democratization, as well as economic reforms to address the serious problems of poverty and unemployment. Opposition groups expressed cautious loyalty to the new King. Although in March 1999 King Abdullah had, under a recent amnesty law, released almost 500 prisoners, in April the Arab Human Rights Organization in Jordan criticized the Government for an increase in human rights violations, including arrests of journalists and harsh treatment of prisoners held in detention centres. Nevertheless, censorship of the foreign press was revoked during that month, and in June the Government agreed to amend part of the controversial Press and Publications Law in order to ease certain restrictions on journalists.

In January 2000 al-Kabariti, a long-standing rival of al-Rawabdeh, resigned as Chief of the Royal Court for unspecified reasons. He was replaced by another former premier, Fayez al-Tarawneh. In June King Abdullah dismissed Prime Minister al-Rawabdeh, appointing Ali Abu al-Ragheb in his place; a new Cabinet was duly appointed. The King stated that the priorities of the new Government were to end corruption, introduce electoral legislation prior to the next parliamentary elections, and accelerate the economic reform programme.

In April 2001 King Abdullah extended the current term of the House of Representatives by two years. On 16 June the King ordered the dissolution of the House, which had been sitting in extraordinary session since April, and effected a cabinet reorganization. On 22 July he approved new electoral legislation, which provided for the redrawing of electoral boundaries (the number of constituencies was to rise from 21 to 44) in order to increase the number of seats in the House of Representatives from 80 to 104, and a reduction of the age of eligibility to vote from 19 years to 18. The Muslim Brotherhood threatened to boycott the forthcoming elections, in view of the Government's failure to meet its demand for the reintroduction of an 'electoral list' system. Critics of the amendments also complained that they failed to address the issue of under-representation in the legislature of Jordanians of Palestinian origin. Nevertheless, the new law did provide for the formation of special committees to monitor the electoral process. Shortly afterwards it was reported that the November elections were to be postponed until late 2002 for technical reasons. In August 2001 legislation was enacted imposing a ban on public gatherings and demonstrations. In October, following the suicide attacks on the USA (see Foreign Affairs), King Abdullah issued a royal decree amending Jordan's penal code in order to strengthen counter-terrorism measures; he also imposed tougher penalties on those found guilty of 'publication crimes'. In November the King appointed a new 40-member Senate upon the expiry of its term.

In January 2002 Prime Minister al-Ragheb submitted the resignation of his Government, but was asked by King Abdullah to form a new administration capable of initiating economic and social reforms prior to parliamentary elections (now expected by November). A new Cabinet was named shortly afterwards. In late January violent clashes, in which a policeman died, erupted between protesters and security forces in Ma'an, following the death of a local youth in police custody, who demonstrators alleged had been the victim of police brutality. The Government later announced that two investigations had been launched to determine the causes of both the adolescent's death and the subsequent riots. In November security forces in Ma'an carried out a large-scale operation aimed at detaining a local Islamist cleric, Muhammad Shalabi, and his supporters, who the Government claimed had played an important role in the unrest. Many observers believed that the security operation was linked to the recent assassination of a US diplomat (see Foreign Affairs). At least three civilians and two police officers were reportedly killed during the week-long campaign; however, Shalabi apparently evaded capture. Meanwhile, King Abdullah announced in August 2002 that legislative elections would be postponed until 2003, owing to the continuing instability in the region. In February of that year he approved amendments to draft electoral legislation that would—from the next general election—increase the number of seats in the House of Representatives from 104 to 110, in order to provide a quota of six seats for female legislators. In March the King appointed Yousuf al-Dalabeeh as Chief of the Royal Court, in place of Fayez al-Tarawneh.

The 2003 legislative elections

At parliamentary elections held on 17 June 2003 tribal representatives and Hashemite loyalists won 80 of the 110 seats in the House of Representatives, while the IAF, the largest opposition party, won 17 seats. On 21 July a new 28-member Cabinet led by al-Ragheb was announced. However, the administration proved to be short-lived: following considerable criticism of the Government over the slow pace of reform and accusations of corruption, the Prime Minister resigned on 21 October. Four days later King Abdullah inaugurated a new Cabinet under the premiership of Faisal al-Fayez, who was also named as the Minister of Defence. The appointment of three female ministers preceded that of an expanded 55-member Senate in November, in accordance with constitutional guidelines that membership of the Senate must be no larger than one-half that of the House of Representatives.

It was revealed in April 2004 that Jordanian security forces had made a number of arrests that had possibly averted a major terrorist attack in the kingdom. It was alleged that militant Islamists closely linked to the al-Qa'ida network then under the command of Saudi-born Osama bin Laden had planted huge quantities of explosives in trucks, which they had planned to detonate against a number of targets, including the Prime Ministry and the Ministry of the Interior. One of the arrested militants reportedly confessed that the instigator of the plot was Abu Musab al-Zarqawi, the Jordanian national whom US officials believed was directing attacks against the US-led coalition, security forces and civilian targets in Iraq. In February 2006 a military court sentenced to death nine men, including al-Zarqawi (who, together with three other defendants, was charged *in absentia*), for their role in the terrorist plot.

In September 2004 King Abdullah announced his decision to postpone the reopening of the House of Representatives from 1 October to 1 December, apparently in anticipation of an expected government reorganization. In October 11 small political parties merged to form the centrist, pro-Government Jordanian National Movement, which sought to encourage national unity and respect for the Constitution and state institutions. Later that month Prime Minister al-Fayez duly carried out a reorganization of the Cabinet: Jordan's ambassador to Egypt, Hani Mulki, was appointed Minister of Foreign Affairs, replacing Marwan al-Muasher, who assumed the role of Depu Prime Minister and was also named as Minister of State f Prime Ministry Affairs and Government Performance. November King Abdullah removed the title of Crown Prin from his half-brother, Hamzeh ibn al-Hussein, citing the wish give him more freedom to undertake tasks that this 'symboli position did not permit. The King accepted the resignation of a Fayez's Government in April 2005 and appointed Adnan Badra as Prime Minister; two days later a new Government was swor in. Among several changes to key portfolios, Dr Bassem Aw dallah became Minister of Finance, while Badran, like his pr decessor, also assumed responsibility for defence. Followir Awadallah's resignation in June, however, Badran announce a reorganization of the Cabinet on 3 July.

In November 2005 three Iraqi citizens carried out suicide bom attacks in three hotels frequented by Western businessmen an diplomats in Amman, killing up to 60 people and injuring mo than 100. Al-Zarqawi announced that he had instigated th blasts, most of the victims of which were Jordanians, as retal ation for the Government's support for the USA and othe Western countries. Within two days over 120 people had bee arrested in connection with the attacks, and thousands c Jordanians staged protests against the bombings and a Zarqawi. Following Badran's resignation from the premiershi later in the month, King Abdullah invited Marouf al-Bakhit, wh had served as Jordan's ambassador to Israel until his appoint ment as national security adviser in the aftermath of th bombings, to form a new government. Abdullah appealed t al-Bakhit to increase security and combat the fundamentalis ideologies behind militant Islamism, as well as furthering th democratization process. The King inaugurated the new Cabine in late November: al-Bakhit assumed additional responsibilit for defence, while the former Governor of the Central Bank, Ziac Fariz, became Deputy Prime Minister and Minister of Finance and Eid al-Fayez was appointed Minister of the Interior. (Fari resigned in August 2007, after the Cabinet apparently refused tc acquiesce to his demands for an increase in fuel prices.)

Details were published in January 2006 of a 10-year plan, the principal objectives of which were 'the creation of income-generating opportunities, the improvement of standards of living and the guarantee of social welfare'. As well as outlining plans for economic reform (see Economic Affairs), the so-called National Agenda also included initiatives designed to: safeguard freedom of political activity and of the media; improve both the availability and quality of public services such as education, health care and infrastructure; and further empower women within Jordanian society.

In April 2006 Sajida al-Rishawi, an Iraqi woman reported to be the sister of a close associate of al-Zarqawi, went on trial charged with direct involvement in the November 2005 attacks in Amman. It was alleged that al-Rishawi had been intended as a fourth bomber but had fled the scene after her device had failed to detonate. Al-Rishawi had initially admitted to the charges levied against her, but subsequently rescinded her confession, claiming that it had been extracted under torture. Notwithstanding her change of plea, she was convicted and sentenced to death in September 2006; despite an appeal, in January 2007 the Court of Cassation upheld the conviction. A further six people, including at least one other Iraqi woman, were convicted *in absentia* and sentenced to death for their part in the bombings. Meanwhile, in June 2006 al-Zarqawi was killed in a US air raid near the Iraqi town of Baquba.

The Prevention of Terrorism Act passed into law in November 2006, provoking censure from human rights organizations, including Amnesty International, which alleged that the new legislation could potentially be abused in order to suppress non-violent opponents of the Government. In June Amnesty International had claimed that the General Intelligence Department (GID)—the state agency responsible for internal security—routinely used torture as a tool with which to extract false confessions from political detainees, strongly implying that it did so on behalf of the US Administration. Furthermore, Jordan's State Security Court was accused of accepting confessions obtained by torture as admissible evidence, and of having based convictions on the grounds of such confessions alone.

The 2007 legislative elections

Legislative elections were held according to schedule on 20 November 2007. According to final results released by the Ministry of the Interior, independents and tribal representatives loyal to King Abdullah dominated the polls, securing 104 of the 110 seats in the House of Representatives. The IAF won just six ats, down from 17 in the 2003 poll, while an alliance of four ftist opposition parties failed to secure representation. Follow- g the publication of the results, the IAF accused the Govern- ent of vote-buying and other electoral irregularities, pointing its apparent failure to win a single seat in the two traditional AF strongholds of Irbid and Zarqa, an impoverished city to the orth-east of Amman, as compelling evidence of the widespread revalence of electoral fraud. The Government insisted that, side from a few isolated incidents of vote-buying, the propon- nts of which had been arrested, the polls had been conducted in free and fair manner. However, in early November a coalition of on-governmental organizations (NGOs) had announced that, wing to government restrictions, its members could no longer ıonitor the polls. The Government had decreed that NGOs ntending to observe the elections would have to operate under he direction of the National Centre for Human Rights, a gov- rnment-regulated organization, and would be prohibited from bserving the actual casting and counting of ballots.

On 22 November 2007 King Abdullah appointed Nader al- Dahabi as the new Prime Minister, in place of al-Bakhit. Shortly hereafter al-Dahabi appointed a new Cabinet, which was form- lly inaugurated on 25 November. Meanwhile, the King appoin- ed Bassem Awadallah, a close ally and former Minister of 'inance, as Chief of the Royal Court.

Meanwhile, in early November 2007 one of the men convicted and sentenced to death *in absentia* for the 2002 murder of the US liplomat Laurence Foley (see Foreign Affairs) was also convicted of helping to plan the 2003 attack on the Jordanian embassy in Baghdad. Muammar al-Jaghbeer, who had been captured in Iraq and extradited to Jordan in 2005, was deemed to have acted on the orders of al-Zarqawi and was given a second death sentence. In late November 2007 al-Jaghbeer's death sentence for the murder of Foley was commuted to a 10-year term of imprison- ment after a military court determined that he had had no intention to kill. In May 2008 the Supreme Court suspended al- Jaghbeer's 10-year sentence and ordered a new trial to take place at the State Security Court. Following the retrial, in July 2009 al- Jaghbeer was again convicted and sentenced to death for his role in Foley's murder. However, following an appeal hearing in November, this sentence was commuted to 15 years' imprison- ment, with hard labour.

In April 2008 24 out of Jordan's 36 political parties were dissolved after their failure to comply with the terms of a new political parties law, which came into force in April 2007 with the provision of a one-year deadline. The new law stipulated that parties must have a minimum of 500 founding members drawn from at least five different governorates, and compelled parties to grant the Government access to their accounts. Twelve parties, including the IAF, successfully validated their status. Mean- while, a report released by the US-based organization Human Rights Watch (HRW) alleged that the US Central Intelligence Agency (CIA) had transferred at least 14 suspected terrorists to Jordan for interrogation and torture between September 2001 and 2004. The allegations were denied by the Jordanian Government.

Awadallah tendered his resignation as Chief of the Royal Court in September 2008. Many observers believed that his strongly pro-reform approach had caused consternation among conservative elements in the Jordanian establishment. In Janu- ary 2009 Nasser Lozi, Chairman of Royal Jordanian Airline, was appointed as his replacement, while Lt-Gen. Muhammad al- Dahabi, brother of the Prime Minister, was replaced as Director of the GID by Maj.-Gen. Muhammad Rathaan Raqqad. In Feb- ruary King Abdullah approved a major reorganization of the Cabinet. A royal decree issued on 2 July 2009 named Prince Hussein ibn al-Abdullah, the King's eldest son, as Crown Prince. The position had been vacant since King Abdullah relieved his half-brother, Prince Hamzeh, of the title in 2004.

The dissolution of parliament and formation of a new Government

On 23 November 2009 King Abdullah issued royal decrees dissolving the House of Representatives, two years before the expiry of its term, and ordering the holding of early legislative elections. The dissolution was widely believed to be in response to widespread dissatisfaction with the parliament, which was viewed by many Jordanians as being hampered by tribal and partisan rivalries and ineffective in dealing with pressing eco- nomic, social and political issues. According to the Constitution, a new parliament was required to be formed within four months of dissolution. However, in a royal decree issued on 8 December, the King postponed legislative elections indefinitely pending the formulation of new electoral legislation. On 9 December Prime Minister al-Dahabi submitted the resignation of his Govern- ment, and the King appointed Samir Rifai, son of former premier and incumbent Speaker of the Senate Zaid Rifai, as Prime Minister-designate.

King Abdullah approved the formation of a new 29-member Cabinet led by Prime Minister Rifai on 14 December 2009; Rifai was also confirmed as Minister of Defence. The new adminis- tration included two Deputy Prime Ministers: Rajai Muasher, who also joined the Government as a Minister of State, and Nayef al-Qadi, who retained the interior portfolio. Following the for- mation of the new Government, Zaid Rifai submitted his resig- nation as Speaker of the Senate, thus averting concerns about the constitutionality of two close relatives heading both the upper house of the legislature and the Cabinet. On 17 December the King appointed a new Senate, with former Prime Minister Taher al-Masri as Speaker. Achieving greater official account- ability and transparency, boosting public sector development and improving social services were among the targets set out by Prime Minister Rifai when he presented his programme for government in February 2010.

Reports in several US newspapers in January 2010 claimed that a suicide bomb attack at a US CIA base in Afghanistan the previous month had been perpetrated by a Jordanian national who had worked as a clandestine agent for the US and Jordanian intelligence agencies. According to the reports, Humam Khalil al-Balawi had been recruited in Jordan and dispatched to Afghanistan to gather intelligence on al-Qa'ida for the CIA. Eight people were killed in the attack, including seven CIA officers and a senior Jordanian intelligence official, Sharif Ali ibn Zeid, who was alleged to have been al-Balawi's supervisor. However, the Jordanian authorities denied all claims of intelli- gence co-operation with the CIA, stating that al-Balawi had acted as an independent informant, and that Zeid had been in Afghanistan on a humanitarian mission. In February it was reported that more than 40 suspects with links to Islamist groups had been arrested in Jordan in connection with the suicide bombing.

Following a significant rise in reports of inter-tribal violence and clashes between various tribes and the security forces, in early May 2010 the Government appointed a new Director of the Public Security Department, Maj.-Gen. Hussein Hazaa Majali, who was at the time serving as Jordan's ambassador to Bahrain, and was a former Commander of the Royal Guard. The Cabinet subsequently announced the establishment of a panel of inquiry to investigate the causes of the recent violence.

The 2010 legislative elections

The revised electoral law, which was finally approved by royal decree on 18 May 2010, expanded the number of seats in the House of Representatives from 110 to 120; other changes included an increase in the number of seats reserved for female candidates from six to 12. However, opposition groups claimed that the changes to the law, which was intended as a temporary bill according to which the forthcoming polls would be organized, failed to address their grievances concerning the lack of serious political reform. The amended law retained the controversial 'one person, one vote' electoral system (in place since 1993), which was viewed as favouring tribal, rather than party, politics. Even after a reorganization of electoral districts, opponents of the legislation complained that it would increase representation from rural, tribal areas traditionally supportive of King Abdul- lah while lowering the number of seats from urban constituen- cies, where there was a higher proportion of Jordanians of Palestinian origin (who were considered more likely to vote for opposition Islamist candidates). In July the IAF declared that it was to boycott the legislative elections, stating that the authorities could not guarantee that they would be 'fair and transparent'.

A reorganization of the Cabinet under Prime Minister Rifai was approved by King Abdullah on 28 July 2010. Among notable changes, Dr Khaled al-Karaki, President of the University of Jordan and a former Chief of the Royal Court, was appointed as a third Deputy Prime Minister and was also to become the Min- ister of Education.

At the elections to the House of Representatives, held on 9 November 2010, independents and tribal representatives loyal to the Hashemite monarchy secured all 120 of the seats in the newly enlarged legislature. A reported 17 of the elected inde- pendents were aligned with opposition groups, including one member of the IAF who had refused to join his party in withdrawing from the poll. According to the terms of the revised electoral law, 12 seats were allocated to the female candidates receiving the greatest number of votes. (A 13th woman was elected in Amman, independently of the quota system.) A reported 80 deputies were elected to parliament for the first time. Voter turn-out was officially recorded at around 53%; however, the IAF claimed that the figure was in fact closer to 30%. During the polls, it was reported that one person had died in a series of violent clashes between opposing political factions; riots were also reported after the final results were announced.

Having on the previous day accepted the resignation of the Prime Minister, Samir Rifai, and asked him to form a new administration, on 24 November 2010 King Abdullah issued a royal decree endorsing the new Cabinet proposed by Rifai, who was also to remain as Minister of Defence. Saad Hayel Srour was named as Deputy Prime Minister and Minister of the Interior, while Ayman al-Safadi was appointed as a third deputy premier, and as Minister of State. On 25 November the King appointed a new Senate, which had been expanded from a membership of 55 to 60; al-Masri retained the post of Speaker. At the inauguration of the new National Assembly on 28 November, when Faisal al-Fayiz was elected as Speaker of the House of Representatives, King Abdullah recommended that the temporary electoral legislation adopted in May be amended prior to it becoming a permanent law, to ensure that it was 'more conducive to advancing our democratic reforms'. The new Rifai Government won a resounding vote of confidence on 25 December, with the Prime Minister pledging to continue the process of political, economic and administrative reform in order to meet Jordan's numerous challenges—citing in particular unemployment, the need to reduce the budget deficit, unequal wealth distribution, inter-tribal violence and water shortages.

Recent developments: King Abdullah accelerates reforms after 2011 protests

During January 2011 a series of anti-Government protests took place in cities across the country, including in Amman, by thousands of demonstrators angered by the high levels of unemployment and poverty, rapidly increasing prices for basic foodstuffs and perceived corruption among government officials. Many of the protesters, who included trade unionists, Islamists and leftist groups, demanded the resignation of the Prime Minister and a change in Jordan's political system to allow future Prime Ministers to be elected, rather than appointed by the King. Having first implemented new economic measures (see Economic Affairs), on 1 February King Abdullah dismissed Rifai and his administration, and appointed Marouf al-Bakhit (who had served as premier during 2005–07) as Prime Minister-designate. A new Government, which the King charged with swiftly implementing the necessary political reforms to modernize the kingdom and increase the level of democracy, was sworn in on 9 February 2011. This change of government appeared to be an attempt by the monarch to prevent a repeat of the large-scale street protests which in Tunisia and Egypt had recently led to the removal from office of both countries' Presidents. On 2 March al-Karaki, who had been replaced as Minister of Education in the reorganization, was reappointed as Chief of the Royal Court (a position he had previously held in the early 1990s), after King Abdullah had accepted the resignation of Nasser Lozi. On the following day the new Government of Prime Minister al-Bakhit narrowly won a vote of confidence.

At the request of King Abdullah, on 14 March 2011 the Government established a National Dialogue Committee, to be chaired by Senate Speaker Taher al-Masri, which would, over a period of three to six months, enter into discussions with a number of groups—including political parties, trade unions, as well as youth and elders' representatives—concerning key political and social legislation, especially the electoral and political parties laws. The 'one person, one vote' system was reported to be one issue to be examined by the participants. However, calls by members of the opposition for a dissolution of parliament and fresh elections were rejected by the King. Many opposition politicians had questioned the appointment of the conservative al-Bakhit as premier and his ability to carry out genuine political and economic reforms. The Secretary-General of the IAF, Hamza Mansour, was said to have turned down an invitation for his movement to join the Government, and he declared that the IAF would not be involved in the work of the new committee owing to its composition and modest aims.

Meanwhile, frequent, but largely small-scale and peaceful, demonstrations were staged by pro-democracy protesters in the kingdom throughout March 2011. The first fatality as a result the protests was reported on 25 March, after a pro-reform ral near the Ministry of the Interior building in Amman turned in violent clashes between pro- and anti-Government protester leading to the intervention of the security forces; up to 160 peop were wounded. The exact circumstances of the man's death we disputed by government and opposition sources. There we reports that some of the pro-Government loyalists had taken nationalist stance, alleging that the demonstration had bee instigated by Jordanians of Palestinian origin and thus posed threat to the monarchy. On 27 March the Speaker of the House Representatives, Faisal al-Fayiz, read a statement declarin that the lower chamber rejected opposition demands immed ately to reduce King Abdullah's constitutional powers. On 7 Apr a man was seriously wounded by setting fire to himself in front the Prime Minister's office in Amman. Violence occurred agai on 15 April, when a group of hardline Salafist Islamists who wer demanding the release of Islamist prisoners allegedly attacke members of the police force in Zarqa; their assault apparentl followed attacks on the Salafists by pro-regime supporters. Mor than 80 people were reported to have received injuries as a resul of the violence, including some 40 police officers, and dozens o Islamists were detained by the authorities; however, many o these were subsequently released.

On 26 April 2011 King Abdullah established the Royal Com mittee on Constitutional Review, to be chaired by Ahmad Loz (Prime Minister during 1971–73), which was to examine th recommendations of the National Dialogue Committee regard ing possible amendments to the Constitution concerning polit ical parties and the electoral system. On 4 June al-Masr presented the National Dialogue Committee's final report t the Prime Minister. However, opposition parties, including the IAF, expressed anger at what they considered to be the limited nature of the proposed reforms, particularly since they included the retention of the 'one person, one vote' system in the majority of parliamentary seats. During a significant televised speech on 12 June, the King announced that he would henceforth allow future cabinets to be formed on the basis of parliamentary majority and thus permit the Prime Minister to be appointed by parliament rather than by the monarch; however, the exact time-frame for the reform was unclear. Abdullah also outlined proposals to strengthen political parties and stated that, as part of the Government's national decentralization plan, municipal elections would take place by the end of 2011 under a new municipalities law.

The resignations of three ministers from the Cabinet in May and June 2011, together with the continuing anti-Government demonstrations, led King Abdullah to effect a further government reorganization on 2 July; al-Bakhit retained the premiership. In late May 2011 the Minister of Justice, Hussein Mjalli, and the Minister of Health, Yassin Husban, had both resigned over their role in allowing a businessman, Khalid Shahin, who had been imprisoned in 2010 on corruption charges to travel to the USA for medical treatment in February 2011; Shahin had not returned to Jordan. In late June the Minister of State for Media Affairs and Communications, Taher Odwan, also resigned in protest against what he deemed to be excessively restrictive new legislation concerned with press and publications, the penal system and the fight against corruption. In the July reshuffle Tawfiq Kreishan was appointed as the only Deputy Prime Minister and was also named as Minister of Parliamentary Affairs, while Mazen al-Saket replaced the unpopular Saad Hayel Srour as Minister of the Interior. (Srour had been accused of taking a excessively firm stance against those involved in the recent protests, and was also criticized over his role in allowing Shahin to leave the country.) Ibrahim Omoush was named as Minister of Justice, Abdullah Abu Rumman as the new Minister of State for Media Affairs and Communications, while Muhammad Barakat al-Zuhair assumed the newly created post of Minister of State for Economic Affairs. The political development and public sector development portfolio was divided and its responsibilities awarded to Musa al-Maaytah and Muhammad Udinat, respectively.

On 10 August 2011 the Prime Minister and his Cabinet were cleared of any wrongdoing by a parliamentary committee in relation to a case of alleged corruption that had occurred in 2007, when al-Bakhit had previously held the premiership. It had been alleged that he had personally authorized the construction of Jordan's first casino complex—which was to be used by tourists in the Dead Sea region—even though gambling is illegal under Jordanian law. After the Prime Minister was found not to have een fully informed of all the details of the proposed licence ward (which was swiftly withdrawn), the former Minister of ourism and Antiquities, Osama Dabbas, was the only governent minister to remain implicated over the affair. The Royal ommittee on Constitutional Review presented its findings to ing Abdullah on 14 August 2011. Among the most notable of 42 uggested amendments to the Constitution were: the formation f an independent constitutional court in place of the Higher ouncil for the Interpretation of the Constitution; the establishnent of an independent commission to monitor legislative and nunicipal elections; a reduction in the powers of the State ecurity Court; a lowering of the minimum age required for a andidate to stand for election to the House of Representatives rom 30 to 25; and new provisions that would improve freedom of he press, of expression and of scientific research. Although the roposed amendments were welcomed by many sections of ordanian society, others believed that they did not go far nough. The IAF protested against the suggested changes on 7 August, a day after they had been referred to parliament. Both he House of Representatives and the Senate approved a total of 1 constitutional amendments during September; King Abdulah issued a royal decree endorsing them on 30 September. One rucial change had been the decision of parliament to retain the State Security Court, but to restrict its responsibilities to dealing with cases of terrorism, treason and espionage. The endorsement of the constitutional amendments by the King led to further protests being held by opposition activists, who again demanded the resignation of the Prime Minister. The Muslim Brotherhood urged Abdullah to carry out more extensive reforms, such as dissolving the State Security Court and introducing an elected upper house. In early October it was announced that the municipal elections would be held on 27 December; however, following the change of government in mid-October (see below), the polls were subsequently postponed until early 2012.

Street demonstrations were held throughout mid-2011 by protesters still frustrated by the lack of progress on both political and economic reforms, although the number of participants had decreased after February. By late September the demonstrators were increasingly focusing their attention on the Cabinet and parliament's perceived failure to reduce the high levels of corruption, and accusing them of protecting those involved in corrupt practices; this view had been enforced by parliament's debate on a bill that would make it a criminal offence to publicly accuse someone of corruption without firm evidence. (Despite being approved by the House of Representatives, the bill was subsequently withdrawn prior to being considered in the Senate). On 16 October a reported 70 of the 120 deputies in the House of Representatives, which was in a period of recess, had asked the King to dismiss al-Bakhit owing to their dissatisfaction with the Prime Minister's performance. After al-Bakhit had been asked by King Abdullah to resign on 17 October, the King named Awn al-Khasawneh—a judge at the International Court of Justice who had previously served as chief of the royal court—as premier, and asked him to use his legal experience to lead the country through an intense period of political reform, particularly as reform of legislation concerning elections and political parties was a key component. On the same day Maj.-Gen. Faisal Jabril al-Shobaki replaced Maj.-Gen. Muhammad Raqqad (who became Lt-Gen.) as Director of the GID. A new Cabinet was inaugurated under Prime Minister al-Khasawneh on 24 October. Among other notable changes were the appointment of Muhammad al-Raoud as Minister of the Interior, Umayya Touqan (a former Central Bank Governor) as Minister of Finance, and journalist Rakan al-Majali as Minister of State for Media Affairs and Communications. On 25 October the King appointed Riyad Abu Karaki to become Chief of the Royal Court, in succession to Khaled al-Karaki. Abdullah appointed a new Senate on the same day, with al-Masri retaining the post of Speaker. On 26 October Abd al-Karim Dughmi was elected Speaker of the House of Representatives.

In February 2012 Muhammad al-Dahabi, was arrested on suspicion of money laundering, embezzlement and the exploitation of public office, following allegations of corruption during his tenure as Director of the GID in 2005–09. The arrest appeared to form part of an escalation in anti-corruption efforts following the previous year's public protests. In March 2012 the House of Representatives voted against recommendations by a committee investigating allegations of corruption involving the sale of a stake in the Jordan Phosphate Mines Co (JPMC) in 2006 to refer several former government ministers and senior officials, including former Prime Minister Marouf al-Bakhit, for further investigation. A report into the sale had concluded that the owners of KAMIL Holdings, which had purchased a 37% stake in JPMC, had provided false information and recommended that the sale be annulled.

A draft electoral law was approved by the Cabinet in early April 2012, and submitted to the House of Representatives for scrutiny. Among the changes proposed by the Government included the replacement of the 'one person, one vote' system with one under which voters would cast two ballots in favour of individual candidates for a particular governorate and a separate ballot for a national party. The number of seats in the House of Representatives would be increased from 120 to 138, 15 of which would be allocated to national political groups on a proportional basis. The quota for female legislators would also be increased from 12 to 15. The proposals were criticized by some opposition groups, notably the IAF, which issued a statement rejecting them. It was widely expected that early parliamentary elections would be scheduled for late 2012, following the law's approval by the legislature. Meanwhile, on 9 April Minister of Justice Samir al-Zoubi resigned from the Government, citing ill health. Ibrahim al-Jazi, hitherto the Minister of State for Legal Affairs, assumed the additional portfolio two days later. In an unexpected move, on 26 April al-Khasawneh tendered his resignation as Prime Minister, along with that of his Cabinet. Fayez al-Tarawneh (Prime Minister in 1998–99) was subsequently instructed by King Abdullah to form a new Government, which duly took office on 2 May.

Foreign Affairs

Regional relations

Relations with Israel were severely undermined in September 1997 when the head of the political bureau of the Palestinian Islamic Resistance Movement (Hamas), Khalid Meshaal, survived an assassination attempt in Amman by agents of the Israeli intelligence service, Mossad. Intensive negotiations involving Crown Prince Hassan, Israeli Prime Minister Binyamin Netanyahu and US officials resulted in an agreement in October whereby Israel freed the Hamas spiritual leader, Sheikh Ahmad Yassin, in return for Jordan's release of two Mossad agents arrested in connection with the attack on Meshaal. A further 12 Mossad agents were expelled from Jordan following the release from Israeli custody of 23 Jordanian and 50 Palestinian detainees. Israel and Jordan signed several bilateral trade agreements in March 1998, and in the following month King Hussein met with Netanyahu for the first time since the attempt on Meshaal's life. King Hussein's mediation at the US-brokered peace summit held between Israel and the Palestinian (National) Authority (PA) in October was crucial to the signing of the Wye Memorandum. In December Israel agreed to open its airspace to foreign airlines en route for Jordan.

Upon his accession in February 1999 King Abdullah assured Israel that he would pursue his father's commitment to the Middle East peace process. The issue of how to revive the peace process reportedly dominated talks held in July between Abdullah and the new Israeli Prime Minister, Ehud Barak. The King welcomed the reactivation of the stalled Wye Memorandum by the signing (to which he was a witness) of the Sharm el-Sheikh Memorandum (Wye Two—see the chapter on Israel) by Barak and Arafat in September.

There was considerable speculation at the time of the Wye Two agreement that recent efforts to bring an end to Hamas's political activities in Jordan had been motivated by a consensus among the Jordanian, Palestinian, Israeli and US authorities on the need to contain potential Islamist opposition to a revival of the peace process. In August 1999 the Jordanian security forces closed down Hamas offices in Amman, on the grounds that these were being used by foreign groups for illegal political activities. The home of Khalid Meshaal was also raided, and in the following months numerous Hamas officials were arrested on various charges including involvement in illicit political activities and the illegal possession of firearms. In November it was reported that Hamas had rejected an offer by the Jordanian Government to release the detained activists provided that they agreed to cease all political activity and that their leaders left the country. Later in the month the Jordanian authorities released some 24 Hamas officials, including four leaders (among them Meshaal and spokesman Ibrahim Ghosheh) who were immediately flown to Qatar. In November 2000, during talks with Meshaal in Qatar, Jordan's Prime Minister, Ali Abu al-Ragheb, reportedly reiterated the conditions under which the Hamas leaders would be allowed to return to Jordan. The Jordanian authorities granted permission for Ghosheh to enter the country in June 2001, after he had agreed to end his involvement with Hamas.

King Abdullah visited Israel for the first time in April 2000, when he held brief discussions with Barak regarding the peace process, as well as water management and other bilateral issues. In advance of the Israeli-Palestinian peace talks held at the US presidential retreat at Camp David, Maryland, in July, Prime Minister al-Ragheb emphasized that the Jordanian Government would not accept any more Palestinian refugees and that it supported their right of return to their homeland. (Recent reports had implied that Jordan was being considered as a possible home for those displaced persons currently in refugee camps in Lebanon.) In June 2000 there were 1,570,192 Palestinian refugees in Jordan and a further 583,009 in the West Bank registered with the UN Relief and Works Agency for Palestine Refugees in the Near East (UNRWA, see p. 106); by January 2011 these figures had risen to 1,999,466 and 848,494, respectively. Meanwhile, in August 2000 King Abdullah reiterated that Jordan would not accept Israeli or international sovereignty over the Islamic holy sites in East Jerusalem, an issue that had been a major obstacle to progress at Camp David.

In October 2000 King Abdullah attended a US-brokered summit meeting between Ehud Barak and Yasser Arafat in Sharm el-Sheikh, Egypt. As violence between Palestinians and Israeli security forces escalated, Jordan came under growing pressure from other Arab states to sever diplomatic ties with Israel, while large-scale public demonstrations against Israeli and US policies towards the new Palestinian uprising (often termed the al-Aqsa *intifada*) were held in Amman and at Jordan's refugee camps. One 'anti-normalization' protest held in early October resulted in violent confrontations between protesters and police; the Government subsequently issued a ban on public demonstrations. Meanwhile, Jordan delayed the dispatch of its new ambassador to Israel, in response to the deteriorating situation in the West Bank and Gaza. In November the Israeli Vice-Consul in Amman was injured in a gun attack by militant Islamists; another Israeli diplomat was wounded in a similar attack in December.

The convening of a summit meeting of Arab League heads of state in Amman in March 2001 reflected Jordan's prominent role in diplomatic efforts to resolve the Israeli–Palestinian conflict. At the summit Arab leaders pledged to transfer funds to the PA as part of a US $1,000m. fund established in late 2000. Jordan and Egypt both refused to return their ambassadors to Tel-Aviv in protest against Israeli military actions against the Palestinians, although they did not proceed to a formal suspension of diplomatic relations. The summit's final communiqué—the so-called Amman Declaration—repeated demands for Israel to withdraw its armed forces from all occupied territory. Further mass demonstrations were held in Jordanian cities and Palestinian refugee camps in March–April 2002, after Israel had reoccupied Palestinian-controlled towns in the West Bank. Jordanian anti-riot police responded forcefully to many unlicensed rallies. In April the Jordanian authorities began to deliver large consignments of humanitarian aid from Jordan and other Arab states to the West Bank.

On 4 June 2003 King Abdullah hosted a summit meeting between US President George W. Bush, Israeli premier Ariel Sharon and the newly appointed Palestinian Prime Minister, Mahmud Abbas. The aim of the summit was to begin the implementation of the 'roadmap' peace plan, an initiative that had been drawn up in late 2002 by the Quartet group (comprising the USA, the UN, Russia and the European Union—EU) and announced by President Bush in April 2003, following the US-led invasion of Iraq and the removal from power of Saddam Hussain.

In February 2004 a Jordanian delegation travelled to the International Court of Justice (ICJ) in The Hague, Netherlands, to present a 100-page document condemning Israel's construction of a 'security fence' in the West Bank (see the chapters on Israel and the Palestinian Autonomous Areas). The ICJ had been asked by the UN General Assembly to rule on the legality of the barrier, and Jordan was one of 14 countries to present evidence against its construction. It was reported in March that King Abdullah and Ariel Sharon had held secret talks in southern Israel regarding the controversial barrier. In May, following sideline discussions at the World Economic Forum in Amman, Israel and Jordan agreed to upgrade their bilateral trade agreement, which had been signed months after the 1994 peace treaty. In February 2005 King Abdullah attended the summit meeting, held in Sharm el-Sheikh, between Sharon and Mahmud Abbas—recently elected as Executive President of the PA following the death of Arafat in November 2004—at which the two leade issued verbal declarations that Israel and the PA would cease a acts of violence against each other. Later that month Jorda returned an ambassador to Tel-Aviv. However, at an Ara League summit in Algiers in March, King Abdullah failed t secure approval for a proposal for peace with Israel that woul not oblige Israel to relinquish all the territories it had occupied i 1967.

Following the victory of Hamas in the Palestinian legislativ elections of January 2006, King Abdullah argued that the ele tion results should not prevent further peace negotiations fro taking place between Israel and the PA. None the less, Jorda appeared increasingly supportive of US efforts to coerce th Hamas Cabinet into recognizing Israel through a process c isolation. In April the Government of Prime Minister al-Bakhi cancelled a planned official visit by Palestinian Minister c Foreign Affairs Dr Mahmud Khalid al-Zahhar, after the appar ent discovery of an arms and explosives cache which ha allegedly been smuggled into Jordan by Hamas from Syria Hamas officials denied the claim. In May Jordanian authoritie announced that 20 Hamas members had been arrested on sus picion of plotting terrorist attacks in Jordan. In June King Abdullah hosted informal discussions in Petra between Israel Prime Minister Ehud Olmert and Mahmud Abbas, following which the two leaders agreed to conduct more substantial talks

In May 2007 the ministers responsible for foreign affairs o Jordan, Israel and Egypt convened in the Egyptian capital Cairo, to discuss an Arab League initiative for peace in the Middle East; the Arab proposal offered Israel peace and normalized relations with all Arab countries, in exchange for an Israeli withdrawal from those lands seized in 1967. However, the complete blockade of the Hamas-controlled Gaza Strip, imposed by the Israeli Government in January 2008, prompted forceful condemnation from King Abdullah, who insisted that meaningful peace negotiations could not be held while Israel persisted with such measures against the Palestinian people. Nevertheless, in April Olmert visited Amman for talks with the King, which largely focused on ways of advancing the objectives of the Annapolis Conference, the peace summit hosted by the USA in November 2007.

Israel's military offensive against Hamas targets in the Gaza Strip, launched on 27 December 2008, provoked a wave of protests throughout Jordan, with demonstrators demanding the severance of diplomatic ties with Israel. Two days later the same demand was made in a petition signed by 29 parliamentary deputies. The two countries' respective ambassadors were temporarily withdrawn from Amman and Tel-Aviv, and in early January 2009 Prime Minister al-Dahabi stated that relations with Israel were under review; however, no formal severance of diplomatic relations was announced. Throughout the crisis Jordan provided a vitally important route for humanitarian aid into the Gaza Strip. Following the Israeli declaration of a unilateral cease-fire on 18 January, King Abdullah attended a summit meeting on that day in Sharm el-Sheikh, jointly hosted by the Egyptian and French Presidents, Hosni Mubarak and Nicolas Sarkozy, which aimed to forge a unified European and Arab response to the crisis in Gaza. The Sharm el-Sheikh summit, which was also attended by PA President Abbas and the Secretaries-General of the UN and the Arab League, represented those parties committed to seeking solutions through the framework of the existing Middle East peace process.

In May 2009 Binyamin Netanyahu, who had been appointed Prime Minister of Israel in March, attended a summit in Jordan, during which the King reiterated the conditions of the Arab peace initiative. However, relations between Jordan and Israel deteriorated during the latter part of 2009. Jordan was critical of Israel's ongoing settlement construction in East Jerusalem, and tensions were exacerbated by allegations of Israeli encroachment on holy sites in Jerusalem, which led to sporadic outbreaks of civil unrest from September. By early 2010 it was reported that relations between King Abdullah and the Israeli premier were frozen. However, at the end of January the King held discussions on the stalled peace process with Israeli President Shimon Peres during the World Economic Forum in Davos, Switzerland. In late February the King strongly condemned Israel's decision to include two sites venerated by Jews, Muslims and Christians—Rachel's Tomb in Bethlehem and the Cave of the Patriarchs in Hebron—on a list of Israeli national heritage sites. In early April he described Jordan's relations with Israel as the worst they had been since 1994. The following week King Abdullah travelled to Washington, DC, where he was reported have urged the US President, Barack Obama, to use his fluence to persuade the Israeli Government to impose a per-anent ban on Jewish settlement construction in the West Bank ıd to announce a clear time-frame for a resumption of Israeli-alestinian 'proximity' talks, soon leading to formal, direct egotiations between the two sides.

Direct negotiations between Netanyahu and Abbas—the first take place between the leaders of Israel and the PA since ecember 2008—finally commenced in Washington, DC, in eptember 2010, chaired by US Secretary of State Hillary linton and attended by the US Special Envoy to the Middle ast, George Mitchell. They followed meetings held on the revious day between President Obama and both Israeli and alestinian leaders, as well as with King Abdullah of Jordan and gypt's President Mubarak. However, the discussions ended ithout any substantial progress. In late November 2011 the ing visited the West Bank for talks with President Abbas. This as his first visit to the territory since mid-2000, and was ıtended to demonstrate Jordan's continuing pursuit of a Middle ast peace settlement and its solidarity with the Palestinians in heir quest for statehood. The talks also came immediately prior o the summit between the rival Fatah and Hamas movements imed at securing a lasting national unity agreement to end the ivision of the Palestinian enclaves. In late January 2012, amid eports that Jordan's new premier, Awn al-Khasawneh, was een to improve relations with Hamas, Khalid Meshaal under-ook his first official visit to Jordan since he and other Hamas eaders had been expelled in 1999; the visit followed Qatari nediation between the two sides. Meanwhile, further direct ıegotiations finally took place between Israeli and Palestinian fficials in Amman on 4 January 2012. However, after five exploratory' meetings in the period up to 25 January, with an emphasis being placed on the issues of borders and security, once again no breakthrough was reported. The PA continued to demand the complete cessation of Israeli settlement activity on the West Bank and an agreement from Israel to discuss the pre-1967 borders of a Palestinian state before agreeing to new peace talks. Both King Abdullah and the Minister of Foreign Affairs, Nasser Judeh, had participated in the meetings.

After August 1995, when Jordan granted political asylum to the two sons-in-law of the Iraqi President, Saddam Hussain, and their wives, King Hussein became more openly critical of the Iraqi regime; however, despite the political rupture, Jordan continued to provide Iraq with a crucial external economic link. In December 1997 Jordan recalled its chargé d'affaires from Baghdad and expelled a number of Iraqi diplomats from Jordan, in protest at the execution of four Jordanians by the Iraqi authorities. Later that month, however, the two countries signed an agreement whereby Iraq was to supply 4.8m. metric tons of crude petroleum and refined petroleum products to Jordan in 1998. In January of that year more than 50 Jordanian detainees were released by Iraq.

In response to critical confrontations between Iraq and the UN during 1998 over the issue of weapons inspections, Jordan indicated that it would not allow its territory or airspace to be used for air-strikes against Iraq. King Hussein consistently advocated a resolution of the crises by diplomatic means, while urging Iraq to comply with all pertinent UN resolutions. This position allowed Jordan to improve its relations with some Arab states, notably Egypt. Jordan strongly condemned the air-strikes carried out against Iraq by US and British forces in December, and in early 1999 the Jordanian National Assembly voted in favour of an end to the UN embargo against Iraq.

King Abdullah made attempts to improve Jordan's relations with Iraq following his accession in February 1999. In November 2000 Prime Minister al-Ragheb undertook an official visit to Iraq—the first visit by a Jordanian premier since 1991—and the two states agreed to increase the value of their trade agreement from US $300m. in 2000 to $450m. in 2001. By mid-2001 Jordan was increasingly concerned that the proposed imposition of so-called 'smart' sanctions against Iraq (the initiative, supported principally by the USA and United Kingdom, was under debate at the UN Security Council) would result in the loss of its oil supply from Iraq, in addition to its main regional export market. However, although Jordanian officials declared publicly their opposition to 'smart' sanctions, they were said to have privately assured Western governments that they accepted the policy. At senior-level discussions held in Amman in January 2002, Iraq and Jordan renewed their oil protocol and also agreed to the creation of a free trade zone.

Following the ousting of Saddam Hussain's regime by the US-led coalition in April 2003, the establishment was announced in June of a joint Jordanian-Iraqi business council to facilitate relations between the two countries and to aid the recovery of the Iraqi economy. In November 2004 the King held talks in Jordan with Iraq's interim Prime Minister, Dr Ayad Allawi, and Iraqi exiles, in an attempt to win support for elections to a transitional Iraqi legislature, scheduled to be held at the end of January 2005. In early January 2005 Amman hosted a meeting of five of the six countries neighbouring Iraq to discuss the forthcoming elections. The Iranian Minister of Foreign Affairs, Kamal Kharrazi, boycotted the meeting after Jordanian officials accused largely Shi'ite Iran of seeking to influence Iraqi voting in order to encourage the formation of a Shi'ite-dominated government in the country. The conference emphasized the need to warn countries against external efforts to influence the outcome of the elections in Iraq. Following reports that a suicide bombing in the Iraqi town of Hillah in February (in which some 125 people died) had been perpetrated by a Jordanian militant, bilateral relations deteriorated and large anti-Jordanian protests took place in Baghdad. In the ensuing crisis, during which the Iraqi authorities alleged that Jordan was failing to prevent insurgents from crossing the border into Iraq, in March both countries temporarily withdrew diplomatic envoys from their respective capitals.

In September 2007 the UN High Commissioner for Refugees (UNHCR) estimated the number of displaced Iraqis living in Jordan at between 500,000 and 750,000 (some of whom had been displaced prior to the conflict in Iraq from 2003). In an attempt to stem the influx of refugees, Jordan had introduced new legislation in February 2007, rendering mandatory for all Iraqi refugees a recently introduced type of passport, issued only in Baghdad and, it was hoped, difficult to forge. In March the authorities announced that holders of the old passports would, however, be allowed to remain in the kingdom until June. Later in 2007 the border with Iraq was effectively closed to all but exceptional cases. Despite the fact that Jordan, along with Syria, had absorbed more Iraqi refugees than any other countries, the kingdom was not a signatory to the Refugee Convention of 1951 and refused to accord the Iraqis with official refugee status, preferring to describe them as 'guests' or 'temporary visitors'. In March 2008 the Government requested all Iraqi visitors to provide appropriate documents proving their entitlement to stay in Jordan, such as work contracts or evidence of investments in the kingdom. Those without the relevant qualifications (estimated to be some 80% of the total Iraqi population) were given two options: either to leave Jordan in return for exemption from overstay fines; or to pay one-half of their fines and receive a three-month temporary residency in which to rectify their status. However, the authorities stopped short of forceful deportations and concentrated on a policy of encouraging Iraqis to return home. By October it was reported that hundreds were returning to Iraq under an Iraqi government-sponsored scheme that gave financial assistance to families returning voluntarily after an absence of at least eight months. At December 2010 the Government estimated the number of Iraqi refugees living in Jordan at 450,915.

The official visit to Amman of Iraqi Prime Minister Nuri al-Maliki in June 2008 heralded new progress in bilateral relations, and in August King Abdullah made a surprise visit to Baghdad for further talks with al-Maliki. This was the first visit to Baghdad by an Arab head of state since the fall of the previous Iraqi regime in 2003. In September 2008 a new deal was announced governing the supply of subsidized Iraqi oil to Jordan. In October Nayef al-Zaidan took up his post as Jordan's new ambassador to Iraq—the first such appointment since the withdrawal of the previous ambassador following the bombing of the Jordanian embassy in August 2003. In January 2009 King Abdullah directed the Government to ease the restrictions on Iraqis entering and residing in the kingdom. Meanwhile, the volume of trade between the neighbouring countries had doubled in 2008 compared with the preceding year, and the signing of a free trade agreement in September 2009 was expected to lead to a further increase in bilateral trade. At the same time, the Iraqi authorities expressed their intention to double the volume of crude oil exports to Jordan, although this was dependent on the completion of repairs on the Kirkuk–Banias oil pipeline; it was also hampered during 2010 by the extended delay in forming a new Iraqi Government after the legislative elections of March. In September 2011 a joint Iraqi-Jordanian committee pledged to implement additional measures to increase and enhance the efficiency of cross-border trade, and to extend railway and air transport links between the two countries.

President Hafiz al-Assad of Syria led a high-level Syrian delegation at King Hussein's funeral in February 1999, following which Jordan's relations with Syria improved significantly. In August the first senior Syrian delegation for almost a decade visited Amman for a session of the Jordanian-Syrian Higher Committee; the meeting resulted in an accord that officials hoped might double the volume of bilateral trade. Later in the month Syria reportedly agreed to end the ban (imposed in 1994) on the free circulation of Jordanian newspapers and publications. King Abdullah attended the funeral of President Assad in June 2000, and acted swiftly to forge close relations with the new Syrian President, Bashar al-Assad. In November Syria confirmed that it had upgraded its diplomatic representation in Amman to ambassadorial status, and the Syrian state airline resumed regular flights to Amman after a hiatus of more than 20 years. The Syrian authorities declared in January 2001 that all Jordanian prisoners held in Syria would soon be released; in November Jordanian officials claimed that there were still hundreds of Jordanian nationals being held in Syrian prisons. In August 2002 the two countries signed an agreement under which Syria was to provide Jordan with water to ease the latter's water shortages. Despite relations being threatened in April 2006 by the discovery of an arms and explosives cache, allegedly smuggled into Jordan from Syria (see above), these were further consolidated by the King's first visit to the Syrian capital, Damascus, for almost four years, in November 2007, and by the visit to Amman of Walid Mouallem, the Syrian Minister of Foreign Affairs, in December. Under the terms of a deal concluded between King Abdullah and President Assad in November, 18 Jordanian detainees were released by Syria and returned to Jordan at the end of that month. A multilateral free trade accord was signed by officials from Jordan, Syria, Lebanon and Turkey in August 2010, and in December the four countries established what was termed the Levant Business Forum, based in the Turkish city of İstanbul, to facilitate the further integration of their economies.

Relations between Jordan and Syria have been complicated by the military campaign being carried out by Syrian government forces in the wake of the protests which have taken place from March 2011. According to UNHCR, in February 2012 more than 3,800 Syrian refugees had registered with the agency in Jordan; other local sources claimed that over 78,000 Syrians had fled to the kingdom since the start of the unrest. Although the Jordanian authorities remain anxious about the consequences for their country's stability should the Syrian regime be ousted, in mid-November 2011 King Abdullah issued a public demand that President Assad resign as Syria's President. His statement was followed by an attack on the Jordanian embassy in Damascus by supporters of Assad. In late December some 3,000 Jordanians took part in a sit-in at the Syrian embassy in Amman against the Government's violent crackdown on protesters and other civilians (by this time, according to the UN, more than 5,000 Syrians had died in the violence), and demanded the expulsion of Syria's ambassador to Jordan.

Meanwhile, King Abdullah sought to strengthen relations with other Arab states. His first major foreign visit was to Egypt for talks with President Mubarak in March 1999. (Jordan and Egypt had signed an agreement in December 1998 providing for the future establishment of a free trade zone.) During April 1999 the new King visited a number of Middle Eastern countries, including Kuwait. Jordan's embassy there had been reopened in March of that year, following the restoration of full diplomatic relations between the two countries (which had been severed in 1990), and in September 1999 the rapprochement was apparently confirmed as King Abdullah again visited the emirate. Kuwait subsequently announced an end to a nine-year ban on the sale of Jordanian newspapers. In October Kuwait returned an ambassador to Amman, the post having been vacant since the Gulf crisis of 1990–91. In mid-May 2010 the Amir of Kuwait, Sheikh Sabah al-Ahmad al-Jaber al-Sabah, undertook the first visit to Jordan by a Kuwaiti leader since 1990; his discussions with the King reportedly focused on efforts to increase economic co-operation. Abdullah became the first Jordanian monarch to visit Lebanon for more than 30 years when, in September 1999, he held discussions with senior Lebanese officials regarding the Middle East peace process and bilateral issues (including a planned free trade agreement). However, despite signing an agreement on free trade and economic co-operation in October 2002, the two countries failed to ratify the agreement.

Pan-Arab relations were strained as a result of the US-l military campaign in Iraq in early 2003. In March King Abdull met with President Mubarak to discuss the divisions within t Arab League. Jordan arranged to import oil from Saudi Arabi Kuwait and the United Arab Emirates, reportedly at no cost, circumvent shortages induced by the conflict in Iraq, and in M it was revealed that Jordan was conducting negotiations with t USA and the UN to seek a solution to the problem of interrupt oil supplies from Iraq. In November Minister of Foreign Affai Dr Marwan al-Muasher visited Iran, primarily to discuss t status of some 1,000 members of the dissident Iranian guerril group, the Mujahidin-e-Khalq, who were formerly based in Ir but who were now being held under Jordanian supervision in t border area between Iraq and Jordan.

In February 2004 Jordan signed a free trade agreement wit Egypt, Morocco and Tunisia, which committed each party removing trade tariffs between them and to intensifying ec nomic co-operation, particularly with regard to legislation co cerning customs procedures and standards; the so-called Agad Agreement was ratified in 2006 and entered into force in 200 Meanwhile, in January 2007 King Abdullah urged Iran to exe cise its influence over its neighbours in a positive manne imploring the Iranian Government to refrain from adding t existing regional instability, particularly within Iraq, the Pale tinian territories and Lebanon.

Relations with Saudi Arabia have improved in recent year and bilateral ties were further bolstered by reciprocal visits b the two countries' respective monarchs in 2007. In June Saud Arabia's King Abdullah ibn Abd al-Aziz Al Sa'ud made a two-da visit to Amman, during which he met with his Jordanian coun terpart for discussions on a wide range of issues. The tw monarchs held further talks when King Abdullah of Jorda visited the Saudi capital, Riyadh, in November; the discussion focused predominantly on consolidating bilateral relations an the respective situations in Iraq and the Palestinian territories In December Jordan and Saudi Arabia signed a border pact o the demarcation of their shared marine border in the Gulf o Aqaba, and in a ceremony to mark the occasion the Saud Minister of the Interior, Prince Nayef ibn Abd al-Aziz A Sa'ud, upheld Jordanian-Saudi relations as 'a model for sincer brotherly ties'.

Turkish President Abdullah Gül made a three-day state visit to Jordan in December 2009, the first by a Turkish head of state in some nine years. During the visit, representatives of the two countries signed an agreement on the establishment of a free trade zone, which, it was hoped, would significantly boost bilateral trade, and provide Jordanian businesses with improved access to European markets. Agreements on the reduction of reciprocal visa fees and customs tariffs were also concluded. The free trade agreement entered into effect in March 2011.

Other external relations

Jordan's relations with the USA in the early 1990s were frequently strained by US allegations of Jordanian assistance to Iraq in circumventing the UN trade embargo, as well as Jordan's vocal criticism of US-led policies towards Iraq. However, in September 1993 US President Bill Clinton announced that some US $30m. in economic and military aid to Jordan was to be released in recognition of the country's enforcement of sanctions against Iraq and of its role in the Middle East peace process. In early 1994 renewed tensions emerged with the USA over the Jerusalem issue and the US-led naval blockade of Jordan's only port at Aqaba, imposed to enforce sanctions against Iraq. Following a sharp deterioration in Jordanian–Iraqi relations in August 1995, when King Hussein granted political asylum to four senior members of the Iraqi regime (see above), Clinton promised to support Jordan in the event of any threat to its security; however, the USA failed to persuade Jordan to sever all economic links with Iraq. In January 1996 the USA offered Jordan $300m. in military assistance, and an expansion of bilateral military co-operation was announced in March. In June 1997 the USA pledged $100m. in economic aid to Jordan, reportedly in recognition of Jordan's contributions to the regional peace process; an assistance fund was established in August. In the same month Jordan signed a debt-rescheduling agreement with the USA, in accordance with a deal reached in May by members of the 'Paris Club' of Western official creditors to reschedule approximately $400m. of Jordanian debt.

In May 1999 King Abdullah began a three-week tour of the USA and several European capitals. Prior to the visit, the King had announced that, in anticipation of a summit of leaders of the Group of Eight (G8) industrialized countries, due to be held in

Germany in June, he would be seeking US support for an agreement by Western countries to write off as much as 50% of Jordan's debt. He achieved some success when the 'Paris Club' agreed, in late May (two days after a meeting with President Clinton), to reschedule about US $800m. of Jordanian debt; in June the G8 leaders recommended debt-reduction arrangements for Jordan. During a visit by King Abdullah to Washington, DC, in October 2000, Jordan and the USA signed a free trade agreement involving the reciprocal removal of all customs duties by 2010. The deal was fully implemented in December 2001.

King Abdullah strongly condemned the September 2001 suicide attacks against New York and Washington, DC, for which the USA held Osama bin Laden's al-Qa'ida network principally responsible, and the King swiftly affirmed Jordan's commitment to the proposed US-led 'war on terror'. Jordanian armed forces joined US and European forces when, from early October, they launched military strikes against al-Qa'ida bases and the Sunni fundamentalist Taliban regime in Afghanistan (which was believed to be harbouring bin Laden). However, Abdullah emphasized that the international community must simultaneously renew efforts to resolve the Israeli–Palestinian conflict. He also warned persistently that any extension of the US-led military action to target any Arab country, such as Iraq, would undermine the international campaign. In July 2002 King Abdullah warned that Jordan would not allow its territory to be used by US troops to launch a military attack aimed at ousting the Iraqi regime of Saddam Hussain, and Jordanian officials denied reports in September that the Government had agreed to allow US forces to use Jordanian military bases in return for a guaranteed supply of cheap oil during a potential disruption to Iraq's oil supplies. In October the USA was said to have pledged a further US $85m. to Jordan, apparently in an effort to secure the country's support during a possible US-led military campaign in Iraq and to enable the Jordanian economy to withstand the consequences of a war.

At the end of October 2002 a senior US diplomat, Laurence Foley, was assassinated in Jordan. The Jordanian security forces detained a large number of suspected Islamist militants following the assassination, and in December two alleged members of al-Qa'ida—one Jordanian and the other Libyan—were arrested on suspicion of involvement in Foley's murder. The trial of 11 suspects charged with involvement in the murder began in July 2003, with six of the defendants, including Abu Musab al-Zarqawi, being tried *in absentia*. At the conclusion of the trial in April 2004, all but one of the defendants were convicted: al-Zarqawi and seven others were sentenced to death, and the remaining two were given terms of imprisonment. In February 2003, meanwhile, Jordanian officials confirmed that the USA was to provide the kingdom with an anti-missile defence system in the event of a conflict in Iraq; Jordan had received six *F-16* fighter aircraft from the US military in January. King Abdullah met President Bush at Camp David in September. The two leaders discussed issues such as the implementation of the roadmap peace plan and Palestinian militant funds held in Jordan. King Abdullah visited the USA in April 2004, but a meeting with President Bush was cancelled in protest at US support for Israel, particularly following Israel's recent 'targeted killings' of Hamas leaders Sheikh Ahmad Yassin and Abd al-Aziz al-Rantisi, and at Bush's endorsement of Sharon's plan for an Israeli 'disengagement' from Gaza (see the chapter on Israel). The rescheduled meeting took place in Washington, DC, in May. In November 2006 the King hosted President Bush and Iraqi Prime Minister Nuri al-Maliki in Amman for talks that centred on the need to impose stability and security within Iraq; thousands of protesters amassed in the streets of Amman, rallying against US foreign policy, and three Jordanian men were arrested on suspicion of plotting to assassinate the US President during his visit.

In April 2009 King Abdullah was the first Arab head of state to visit the USA after the inauguration of President Barack Obama in January. The visit underlined the strength of Jordan's relations with the USA and indicated that the King was likely to be a key intermediary in US-brokered efforts to forge a Middle East peace settlement. Abdullah conveyed to President Obama the resolutions of a recent Arab League summit in Doha, Qatar, during which member states had renewed their commitment to the Arab peace initiative.

CONSTITUTION AND GOVERNMENT

A revised Constitution for the Hashemite Kingdom of Jordan was ratified in January 1952 by King Talal I. Two amendments were adopted in November 1974 giving the King the right to dissolve the Senate or to take away membership from any of its members, and to postpone general elections for a period not to exceed a year, if there are circumstances in which the Cabinet feels that it is impossible to hold elections. A further amendment in February 1976 enabled the King to postpone elections indefinitely. In January 1984 two amendments were adopted, allowing elections 'in any part of the country where it is possible to hold them' (effectively, only the East Bank) and empowering the National Assembly to elect deputies from the Israeli-held West Bank. (However, in July 1988 King Hussein dissolved the legislature, renouncing Jordan's administrative and legal ties to the West Bank.) In February 2003 King Hussein ratified legislation according to which six seats in the House of Representatives were to be reserved for women; this number was increased to 12 following the approval of a revised electoral law in May 2010 (see Contemporary Political History).

Jordan is a constitutional monarchy. Legislative power is vested in a bicameral National Assembly: the Senate (House of Notables) has 60 members, appointed by the King for eight years (one-half of the members retiring every four years), while the House of Representatives (House of Deputies) has 120 members, elected by universal adult suffrage for four years. Executive power is vested in the King, who governs with the assistance of an appointed Cabinet, responsible to the Assembly. There are 12 administrative provinces.

REGIONAL AND INTERNATIONAL CO-OPERATION

Jordan was a founder member of the League of Arab States (the Arab League, see p. 364), and also participates in the Council of Arab Economic Unity (see p. 254) and the Arab Monetary Fund (see p. 202).

Jordan became a member of the UN in 1955, and joined the World Trade Organization (WTO, see p. 433) in 2000. The country is also a member of the Organization of Islamic Cooperation (OIC, see p. 404).

ECONOMIC AFFAIRS

In 2010, according to estimates by the World Bank, Jordan's gross national income (GNI), measured at average 2008–10 prices, was US $26,520m., equivalent to $4,390 per head (or $5,810 per head on an international purchasing-power parity basis). During 2001–10, it was estimated, the population increased at an average annual rate of 2.3%, while Jordan's gross domestic product (GDP) per head increased, in real terms, by an average of 3.8% per year. Overall GDP increased, in real terms, at an average annual rate of 6.2% in 2001–10; according to official estimates, growth of 3.1% was recorded in 2010.

Agriculture (including hunting, forestry and fishing) contributed about 3.2% of Jordan's GDP in 2010, according to preliminary figures, and accounted for about 5.8% of the country's economically active population at mid-2012, according to FAO estimates. The principal cash crops are vegetables, fruit and nuts, and wheat production is also important; vegetables accounted for 7.8% of export earnings in 2010. The World Bank estimated that the sector's GDP increased at an average annual rate of 9.3% during 2001–10. Preliminary official data indicated a sectoral growth rate of 6.9% in 2010.

Industry (including mining, manufacturing, construction and power) provided 29.1% of GDP in 2010, according to preliminary figures; about 26.6% of the country's active labour force were employed in the sector in 2009. According to World Bank data, during 2001–10 industrial GDP increased by an average of 7.3% per year. Preliminary official data indicated that the sector's GDP increased by only 1.2% in 2010.

Mining and quarrying contributed 3.6% of GDP in 2010, according to preliminary figures, and accounted for about 0.9% of the employed labour force in 2009. Mineral exports—of which phosphates and potash were the principal components—accounted for around 6.6% of total export earnings in 2010. In July 2009 parliamentary approval was granted for an agreement with Royal Dutch Shell of the Netherlands/United Kingdom to develop the kingdom's large reserves of oil-bearing shale; a concession agreement was signed with the Estonian company Eesti Energia in May 2010. Meanwhile, the authorities concluded a deal with British Petroleum in October 2009 encompassing exploration rights and production at the Risha gasfield, near the border with Iraq. Preliminary official figures suggested that mining GDP increased by an average rate of 6.8% per year during 2004–08; the sector's GDP declined by 25.9% in 2009, but increased by 19.5% in 2010, according to preliminary official figures.

Manufacturing provided 18.2% of GDP in 2010, according to preliminary figures, and engaged some 19.0% of the employed labour force in 2009. The most important branches of manufacturing, measured by gross value of output, are food, beverages and tobacco, refined petroleum products, chemicals, non-metallic mineral products and metal products. World Bank data indicated that manufacturing GDP increased by an average of 8.4% per year in 2001–10; according to preliminary official figures, the sector recorded growth of 2.0% in 2010.

The construction sector contributed 5.2% of GDP in 2010, according to preliminary figures; about 5.3% of the country's active labour force were employed in the sector in 2009. According to official estimates, during 2004–08 construction GDP increased by an average of 8.7% per year. Preliminary official data indicated that the sector's GDP increased by 12.9% in 2009, but contracted by 4.6% in 2010.

Energy has traditionally been derived principally from imported petroleum, but attempts are being made to develop alternative sources of power, including wind, solar and nuclear power. In 2003 petroleum provided 90.0% of total electricity production, but by 2008 this had declined to just 18.9%; conversely, natural gas accounted for only 9.3% of total electricity production in 2003, but this increased to 80.6% in 2008. Imports of mineral products comprised 22.7% of the total value of imports in 2010. Repeated acts of sabotage against the pipeline through which Egypt transports gas to Israel and Jordan following the overthrow of the Mubarak regime in February 2011 led the Jordanian Government to increase electricity prices in early 2012 (although, the decision was subsequently reversed after public criticism) and to examine possible alternative sources of natural gas, such as Iraq and Qatar. Jordan currently generates 80% of its electricity from Egyptian gas. Following the discovery of substantial reserves of uranium, the Government has instigated plans for the development of a nuclear power industry; several civil nuclear co-operation accords have been signed with countries including France, the United Kingdom and Russia since 2008. In February 2012 the Jordan Atomic Energy Commission revealed that al-Mafraq governorate was their preferred location for the construction of the country's first nuclear power plant. In addition to boosting Jordan's domestic energy capacity, it is envisaged that the nuclear programme will facilitate the implementation of much-needed water desalination projects.

Services accounted for some 67.6% of Jordan's GDP in 2010, according to preliminary figures, and engaged an estimated 73.4% of the employed labour force in 2009. The tourism industry, which accounts for at least 14% of GDP, suffered considerably during 2011 as a result of the ongoing political instability in neighbouring countries such as Egypt and Syria. During 2001–10, according to the World Bank, the GDP of the sector increased by an average of 5.9% per year; sectoral growth increased by 4.2% in 2010, according to preliminary official data.

In 2010 Jordan recorded a visible trade deficit of US $6,650.4m., and there was a deficit of $1,311.4m. on the current account of the balance of payments. In 2010 Saudi Arabia was the main source of imports (with 19.6% of the total); other major suppliers were the People's Republic of China, Germany and the USA. In that year Iraq was the principal market for exports (with 16.0% of the total); other significant purchasers were the USA, India and Saudi Arabia. The principal exports in 2010 were chemicals and related products, food, beverages and tobacco, textiles, and machinery and mechanical appliances, while the principal imports were mineral products, food, beverages and tobacco, and machinery and mechanical appliances.

In 2010, according to preliminary official figures, a budget deficit of JD 1,045.2m. was envisaged (including external aid payments and revenues from the sale of land). Jordan's gener government gross debt was JD 12,535m. in 2010, equivalent 66.8% of GDP. Jordan's external debt totalled US $6,615m. at t end of 2009, of which $5,445m. was public and publicly guara teed debt. In that year, the cost of servicing long-term public a publicly guaranteed debt and repayments to the IMF w equivalent to 4.7% of the value of exports of goods, servic and income (excluding workers' remittances). The annual rate inflation averaged 5.4% in 2006–11. According to official figure consumer prices increased by an average of 4.4% in 2011. In 20 some 12.5% of the economically active population w unemployed.

In January 2007 the Government published its Nation Agenda—an ambitious 10-year plan to improve the qualit and effectiveness of public administration through the reductio of poverty and unemployment (by creating 600,000 jobs) and th achievement of annual real GDP growth of 7.2%. The bankin sector proved relatively resilient following the onset of the glob financial crisis from September 2008, owing to its limited expo ure to international financial markets. Nevertheless, the ens ing global economic slowdown in 2009 resulted in declinin export revenues, reduced foreign direct investment (FDI) an lower remittances from Jordanians working abroad. Accordin to official and IMF figures, GDP growth slowed to an estimate 2.3% in 2009, and the same figure was officially recorded in 201 The IMF forecast growth of 2.5% for 2011 and of 2.8% for 2012. I February 2011, amid a series of anti-Government demonstrations being held in protest against increased prices for basi commodities, among other grievances, King Abdullah appointe a new Cabinet under Prime Minister Marouf al-Bakhit, whic was charged with accelerating political and economic reforms. I January the King had announced an additional US $125m. i subsidies for fuel and essential foodstuffs, as well as a wag increase for civil servants and a rise in pension payments, in a attempt to dissipate the unrest. This led the Government, i March, to present a revised budget for 2011, with a larger deficit than had previously been anticipated (see below). Nevertheless, the higher cost of subsidies was partially offset by grants that were provided by Saudi Arabia and other Arab countries. The economy had faced numerous challenges during 2011, with the profound instability arising from anti-government uprisings in many countries across the region leading to a decline in exports, FDI, tourism receipts and remittances from abroad, as well as higher energy costs. Moreover, the continuing high levels of inflation and unemployment remained a major concern, being officially recorded at 4.4% in 2011 and 12.1% in the final quarter of the year, respectively. Controlling public expenditure and reducing the budget deficit, which the IMF expected to amount to some 6% of GDP in 2011, were among the economic priorities of the Cabinet under Prime Minister Awn al-Khasawneh, which was appointed in October 2011. In its draft budget for 2012, which focused on maintaining spending levels and increasing domestic revenues as part of a three-year fiscal reform strategy, the Government planned to achieve a deficit of 3.25% by 2014; the budget deficit was expected to fall marginally, to about 5.25% of GDP, in 2012.

PUBLIC HOLIDAYS

2013: 23 January* (Mouloud, Birth of Muhammad), 1 May (Labour Day), 25 May (Independence Day), 5 June* (Leilat al-Meiraj, Ascension of Muhammad), 7 August* (Id al-Fitr, end of Ramadan), 14 October* (Id al-Adha, Feast of the Sacrifice), 4 November* (Muharram, Islamic New Year).

* These holidays are dependent on the Islamic lunar calendar and may vary by one or two days from the dates given.

Statistical Survey

Source: Department of Statistics, POB 2015, Amman 11181; tel. (6) 5300700; fax (6) 5300710; e-mail stat@dos.gov.jo; internet www.dos.gov.jo.

Area and Population

REA, POPULATION AND DENSITY

rea (sq km)	88,794*
opulation (census results)	
10 December 1994	4,139,458
1 October 2004	
Males	2,626,287
Females	2,477,352
Total	5,103,639
opulation (official estimates at 31 December)	
2009	5,980,000
2010	6,113,000
2011	6,249,000
)ensity (per sq km) at 31 December 2011	70.4

* 34,284 sq miles.

POPULATION BY AGE AND SEX
(estimated population at 31 December 2011)

	Males	Females	Total
0–14	1,197,600	1,134,880	2,332,480
15–64	1,921,390	1,793,400	3,714,790
65 and over	102,110	99,620	201,730
Total	3,221,100	3,027,900	6,249,000

Note: Figures are rounded to nearest 10 persons.

GOVERNORATES
(estimated population at 31 December 2011)

	Area (sq km)	Population	Density (per sq km)
Amman	7,579	2,419,600	319.3
Irbid	1,572	1,112,300	707.6
Al-Zarqa (Zarqa)	4,761	931,100	195.6
Al-Balqa	1,120	418,600	373.8
Al-Mafraq	26,551	293,700	11.1
Al-Karak (Kerak)	3,495	243,700	69.7
Jarash (Jerash)	410	187,500	457.3
Madaba	940	156,300	166.3
Ajloun	420	143,700	342.1
Al-Aqabah (Aqaba)	6,905	136,200	19.7
Ma'an	32,832	118,800	3.6
Al-Tafilah	2,209	87,500	39.6
Total	88,794	6,249,000	70.4

PRINCIPAL TOWNS
(population at 2004 census)

Amman (capital)	1,036,330	Wadi al-Sir	122,032
Al-Zarqa (Zarqa)	395,227	Tila' al-Ali (Tla' El-Ali)	113,197
Irbid	250,645	Khuraybat as-Suq (Khraibet Essoq)	84,975
Al-Rusayfah (Russeifa)	227,735	Al-Aqabah (Aqaba)	80,059
Al-Quwaysimah	135,500		

Mid-2010 (incl. suburbs, UN estimate): Amman 1,105,402 (Source: UN, *World Urbanization Prospects: The 2009 Revision*).

BIRTHS, MARRIAGES AND DEATHS*

	Registered live births		Registered marriages		Registered deaths	
	Number	Rate (per 1,000)	Number	Rate (per 1,000)	Number	Rate (per 1,000)
2003	148,294	28.4	48,784	9.3	16,937	3.2
2004	150,248	28.1	53,754	10.0	17,011	3.2
2005	152,276	27.8	56,418	10.3	17,883	3.3
2006	162,972	29.1	59,335	10.6	20,397	3.6
2007	185,011	32.3	60,548	10.6	20,924	3.7
2008	181,328	31.0	60,922	10.4	19,403	3.3
2009	179,872	30.1	63,389	10.6	20,251	3.4
2010	183,948	30.1	62,107	10.2	21,550	3.5

* Data are tabulated by year of registration rather than by year of occurrence. Registration of births and marriages is reported to be complete, but death registration is incomplete. Figures exclude foreigners, but include registered Palestinian refugees.

Life expectancy (years at birth, WHO estimates): 71 (males 69; females 74) in 2009 (Source: WHO, *World Health Statistics*).

EMPLOYMENT
(economic survey at October, public and private sectors, excl. armed forces)

	2007	2008	2009
Mining and quarrying	6,067	8,091	8,626
Manufacturing	172,161	171,777	182,769
Electricity, gas and water	13,551	13,842	13,442
Construction	29,991	46,916	51,177
Wholesale and retail trade; repair of motor vehicles and motorcycles and personal and household goods	195,651	201,185	208,304
Hotels and restaurants	39,085	37,378	39,680
Transport, storage and communications	28,468	32,334	33,832
Financial intermediation	23,062	24,914	26,944
Real estate, renting and business activities	43,913	45,308	47,157
Public administration and compulsory social security	87,244	96,599	104,078
Education	155,641	159,583	165,294
Health and social work	53,337	53,489	55,682
Other community, social and personal service activities	22,770	24,991	25,288
Total employed	870,941	916,405	962,272
Males	669,991	705,716	742,631
Females	200,950	210,689	219,641

Note: Figures are assumed to exclude data for those engaged in agriculture and fishing—according to FAO estimates some 110,000 of a total economically active population of 1,892,000 were engaged in the sector at mid-2012. Figures include foreign nationals employed in Jordan, numbering 103,924 in 2007; 114,679 in 2008; 126,369 in 2009.

Health and Welfare

KEY INDICATORS

Total fertility rate (children per woman, 2009)	3.0
Under-5 mortality rate (per 1,000 live births, 2009)	25
HIV/AIDS (% of persons aged 15–49, 2007)	<0.2
Physicians (per 1,000 head, 2005)	2.4
Hospital beds (per 1,000 head, 2006)	1.9
Health expenditure (2008): US $ per head (PPP)	496
Health expenditure (2008): % of GDP	9.4
Health expenditure (2008): Public (% of total)	62.7
Access to water (% of persons, 2008)	96
Access to sanitation (% of persons, 2008)	98
Total carbon dioxide emissions ('000 metric tons, 2007)	21,434.4
Carbon dioxide emissions per head (metric tons, 2007)	3.8
Human Development Index (2011): ranking	95
Human Development Index (2011): value	0.698

For sources and definitions, see explanatory note on p. vi.

Agriculture

PRINCIPAL CROPS
('000 metric tons)

	2008	2009	2010
Wheat	7.8	12.5	22.1
Barley	10.3	17.1	10.7
Maize	19.2	19.8	29.0
Potatoes	139.8	118.7	174.9
Olives	94.1	140.7	171.7
Cabbages and other brassicas	22.3	25.4	20.3
Lettuce and chicory	41.6	39.8	48.2
Tomatoes	600.3	654.3	737.3
Cauliflowers and broccoli	55.0	80.3	54.7
Pumpkins, squash and gourds	48.8	59.3	69.7
Cucumbers and gherkins	125.9	137.7	176.2
Aubergines (Eggplants)	99.9	106.8	104.7
Chillies and peppers, green	51.5	43.7	55.1
Onions and shallots, green	5.0	8.9	3.5
Onions, dry	27.2	28.8	15.8
Beans, green	11.1	5.6	8.2
Okra	5.6	6.2	6.8
Watermelons	97.6	106.5	153.1
Cantaloupes and other melons	28.4	17.0	31.1
Bananas	41.5	43.8	43.8
Grapefruit and pomelos	9.9	8.1	8.4
Oranges	35.9	42.8	43.0
Tangerines, mandarins, clementines and satsumas	27.1	32.5	38.3
Lemons and limes	18.8	21.8	28.8
Apples	34.9	31.1	28.8
Peaches and nectarines	29.0	31.4	20.8
Grapes	26.4	34.4	29.7

Aggregate production ('000 metric tons, may include official, semi-official or estimated data): Total cereals 47.5 in 2008, 60.9 in 2009, 87.3 in 2010; Total roots and tubers 139.8 in 2008, 118.7 in 2009, 174.9 in 2010; Total vegetables (incl. melons) 1,314.0 in 2008, 1,421.9 in 2009, 1,609.7 in 2010; Total fruits (excl. melons) 256.9 in 2008, 282.9 in 2009, 279.9 in 2010.

Source: FAO.

LIVESTOCK
('000 head, year ending September)

	2008	2009	2010
Horses*	3	3	3
Asses*	10	10	10
Mules*	1.5	1.5	1.5
Cattle	79.4	64.5	65.4
Camels*	8	8	13
Sheep	2,493.4	2,070.9	2,175.7
Goats	1,083.3	919.7	751.7
Chickens*	25,000	25,000	25,000

* FAO estimates.

Source: FAO.

LIVESTOCK PRODUCTS
('000 metric tons)

	2008	2009	201[illegible]
Cattle meat	19.1	13.0*	14.[illegible]
Sheep meat	15.4	12.9*	13.[illegible]
Goat meat	4.2	3.7*	2.[illegible]
Chicken meat	140.5	141.2*	154.[illegible]
Cows' milk	314.0	244.6	253.[illegible]
Sheep's milk	75.3	56.0	49.[illegible]
Goats' milk	28.1	18.8	20.[illegible]
Hen eggs	50.6	45.9	46.[illegible]
Wool, greasy*	2.7	2.8	2.[illegible]

* FAO estimate(s).

Source: FAO.

Forestry

ROUNDWOOD REMOVALS
('000 cubic metres, excluding bark, FAO estimates)

	2008	2009	201[illegible]
Industrial wood	4	4	[illegible]
Fuel wood	286	294	30[illegible]
Total	290	298	30[illegible]

Source: FAO.

Fishing

(metric tons, live weight)

	2007	2008	2009
Capture	506	500	569
Freshwater fishes	350	350	350
Tunas	105	103	131
Aquaculture (Tilapias)	509	540	440
Common carp	216	276	230
Total catch	1,015	1,040	1,009

Source: FAO.

Mining

('000 metric tons, unless otherwise indicated)

	2007	2008	2009
Crude petroleum ('000 barrels)	8.6	15.6	9.4
Phosphate rock	5,552	6,266	5,282
Potash salts*	1,796	2,005	1,200
Bromine	85.1	105.6	69.0
Feldspar	9.8	3.0	—
Gypsum	287.8	231.8	304.4

* Figures refer to the K_2O content.

Source: US Geological Survey.

Industry

SELECTED PRODUCTS
('000 barrels, unless otherwise indicated)

	2007	2008	2009
Liquefied petroleum gas	1,245	1,200	1,150
Motor spirit (petrol)	5,787	5,700	5,500
Kerosene	1,075	1,080	1,050
Jet fuels	2,304	2,300	2,200
Distillate fuel oils	9,047	9,000	8,700
Asphalt	453	136	85
Cement ('000 metric tons)	4,138	4,284	3,799
Electricity (million kWh)	12,838	14,160	n.a.

Phosphate fertilizers ('000 metric tons): 435.0 in 2001; 459.0 in 2002.

Sources: US Geological Survey; UN Industrial Commodity Statistics Database.

Finance

CURRENCY AND EXCHANGE RATES

Monetary Units
1,000 fils = 1 Jordanian dinar (JD).

Sterling, Dollar and Euro Equivalents (30 December 2011)
£1 sterling = JD 1.098;
US $1 = 710 fils;
€1 = JD 0.919;
JD 10 = £9.11 = $14.08 = €10.89.

Exchange Rate: An official mid-point rate of US $1 = 709 fils (JD1 = $1.4104) has been maintained since October 1995.

BUDGET
(JD million)*

Revenue†	2009	2010‡	2011§
Taxation	2,879.9	2,986.0	3,367.4
Taxes on income and profits	764.7	624.6	720.3
Corporations	585.2	472.3	548.8
Individuals	90.7	84.3	97.5
Taxes on domestic transactions	1,698.3	1,997.8	2,298.8
General sales tax	1,682.5	1,987.3	2,298.8
Taxes on foreign trade	270.3	275.2	268.7
Other revenue	1,287.4	1,254.4	1,378.4
Fees	611.1	594.0	702.3
Interest and profits	308.1	256.9	277.7
Repayment	45.2	41.4	43.6
Pensions	20.5	20.7	22.9
Total	4,187.8	4,261.1	4,768.7

Expenditure	2009	2010‡	2011§
Current	4,586.0	4,746.6	5,871.8
Wages and salaries	773.6	829.6	961.8
Purchases of goods and services	325.1	308.3	339.4
Interest payments	392.2	397.5	489.0
Domestic	303.9	310.9	384.0
Foreign	88.3	86.6	105.0
Food and oil subsidies	186.0	192.8	724.0
Pensions	708.0	744.6	858.0
Defence and security	1,645.4	1,699.3	1,768.5
Capital	1,444.5	961.4	1,081.2
Total	6,030.5	5,708.0	6,953.0

* Figures represent a consolidation of the Current, Capital and Development Plan Budgets of the central Government. The data exclude the operations of the Health Security Fund and of other government agencies with individual budgets.
† Excluding foreign grants received (JD million): 333.4 in 2009; 401.7 in 2010 (preliminary); 1,024.0 in 2011 (budget figure).
‡ Preliminary.
§ Budget figures.

Source: Ministry of Finance, Amman.

INTERNATIONAL RESERVES
(US $ million at 31 December)

	2008	2009	2010
Gold (national valuation)	356.6	450.5	589.3
IMF special drawing rights	3.2	230.0	225.8
Reserve position in the IMF	0.4	0.5	0.5
Foreign exchange	8,558.0	11,458.8	12,830.5
Total	8,918.2	12,139.8	13,646.1

Source: IMF, *International Financial Statistics*.

MONEY SUPPLY
(JD million at 31 December)

	2008	2009	2010
Currency outside banks	2,664.8	2,679.5	2,843.7
Demand deposits at commercial banks	2,857.4	3,293.2	3,657.2
Total money (incl. others)	5,524.7	5,982.0	6,504.4

Source: IMF, *International Financial Statistics*.

COST OF LIVING
(Consumer Price Index; base: 2006 = 100)

	2009	2010	2011
Food (incl. beverages)	131.1	137.7	143.4
Clothing (incl. footwear)	120.6	122.9	130.5
Housing	113.9	118.6	123.1
Other goods and services	107.6	114.4	120.2
All items	118.5	124.5	130.0

NATIONAL ACCOUNTS
(JD million at current prices)

Expenditure on the Gross Domestic Product

	2007	2008*	2009*
Government final consumption expenditure	2,499.4	3,363.6	3,699.5
Private final consumption expenditure	10,512.3	12,403.0	12,688.4
Changes in stocks	337.8	318.7	193.7
Gross fixed capital formation	3,334.1	4,342.9	4,254.2
Total domestic expenditure	16,683.6	20,428.2	20,835.8
Exports of goods and services	6,579.4	8,811.2	7,758.6
Less Imports of goods and services	11,131.6	13,646.0	11,682.2
GDP in purchasers' values	12,131.4	15,593.4	16,912.2
GDP in constant 1994 prices	8,629.0	9,252.1	9,759.9

* Preliminary.

Gross Domestic Product by Economic Activity

	2007	2008*	2009*
Agriculture, hunting, forestry and fishing	307.1	376.8	459.2
Mining and quarrying	338.9	843.0	556.3
Manufacturing	2,219.8	2,847.1	3,026.3
Electricity and water	238.0	254.2	355.9
Construction	544.8	697.9	887.9
Wholesale and retail trade, restaurants and hotels	1,276.1	1,589.0	1,612.9
Transport, storage and communications	1,553.0	1,848.2	2,014.8
Finance, insurance, real estate and business services	2,188.5	2,675.9	2,735.6
Public administration, defence, and social security	2,021.3	2,909.2	3,471.1
Other services	62.8	679.7	773.8
Sub-total	11,308.3	14,721.0	15,893.7
Less Imputed bank service charge	503.3	749.7	849.1
GDP in basic prices	10,805.1	13,971.2	15,044.5
Taxes on products (net)	1,326.3	1,622.2	1,867.7
GDP in purchasers' values	12,131.4	15,593.4	16,912.2

* Preliminary.

2010 (preliminary): Agriculture, hunting, forestry and fishing 560.9; Mining and quarrying 621.8; Manufacturing 3,146.1; Electricity and water 380.0; Construction 896.2; Wholesale and retail trade, restaurants and hotels 1,723.9; Transport, storage and communications 2,285.2; Finance, insurance, real estate and business services 3,135.3; Public administration, defence, and social security 3,735.4; Other services 822.0; *Sub-total* 17,306.8; *Less* Imputed bank service charge 889.6; *GDP in basic prices* 16,417.2; Taxes on products (net) 2,344.8; *GDP in purchasers' values* 18,762.0.

BALANCE OF PAYMENTS
(US $ million)

	2008	2009	2010
Exports of goods f.o.b.	7,937.1	6,375.1	7,028.3
Imports of goods f.o.b.	–15,102.0	–12,641.1	–13,678.7
Trade balance	–7,164.9	–6,266.0	–6,650.4
Exports of services	4,478.0	4,552.5	5,161.1
Imports of services	–4,126.5	–3,817.6	–4,270.6
Balance on goods and services	–6,813.4	–5,531.1	–5,759.8
Other income received	1,335.7	1,170.2	1,078.5
Other income paid	–640.1	–565.2	–571.4
Balance on goods, services and income	–6,117.8	–4,926.1	–5,252.8
Current transfers received	4,715.0	4,453.0	4,491.8
Current transfers paid	–634.3	–655.4	–550.4
Current balance	–2,037.1	–1,128.5	–1,311.4
Capital account (net)	283.9	0.6	0.3
Direct investment abroad	–12.8	–72.4	–28.5
Direct investment from abroad	2,826.7	2,426.6	1,701.4
Portfolio investment assets	51.9	–600.0	41.0
Portfolio investment liabilities	521.1	–29.6	–20.4
Other investment assets	734.6	1,503.4	–1,260.4
Other investment liabilities	–1,375.0	487.5	1,084.2
Net errors and omissions	203.7	539.9	503.5
Overall balance	1,197.1	3,127.5	709.8

Source: IMF, *International Financial Statistics*.

External Trade

PRINCIPAL COMMODITIES
(distribution by Harmonized System, JD million)

Imports c.i.f.	2008	2009	2010
Food, beverages and tobacco	2,054.7	1,761.7	1,927.6
Live animals and animal products	366.0	370.9	426.3
Vegetable products	935.7	700.4	742.5
Prepared foodstuffs; beverages, spirits and vinegar; tobacco and manufactured tobacco substitutes	576.3	571.6	665.9
Mineral products	2,637.3	1,841.1	2,503.7
Chemicals and related products	857.0	805.8	913.1
Plastics, rubbers, and articles thereof	463.8	404.0	449.9
Textiles and textile articles	710.7	601.0	615.4
Pearls; precious or semi-precious stones; precious metals	201.5	124.5	125.5
Base metals and articles thereof	1,191.0	913.6	951.8
Machinery and mechanical appliances	1,925.9	1,497.7	1,577.1
Vehicles, aircraft, vessels and associated transport equipment	920.4	1,148.7	929.0
Total (incl. others)	12,060.9	10,107.7	11,050.1

Exports f.o.b.	2008	2009	20[illegible]
Food, beverages and tobacco	748.1	735.5	79[illegible]
Vegetable products	334.9	339.7	39[illegible]
Animal and vegetable fats, oils and waxes	67.6	33.6	[illegible]
Prepared foodstuffs; beverages, spirits and vinegar; tobacco and manufactured tobacco substitutes	239.3	223.5	247[illegible]
Mineral products	443.1	311.4	330[illegible]
Chemicals and related products	1,832.1	1,242.0	1,242[illegible]
Textiles and textile articles	783.4	645.9	683[illegible]
Pearls; precious or semi-precious stones; precious metals	148.6	255.3	233[illegible]
Base metals and articles thereof	344.4	301.1	338[illegible]
Machinery and mechanical appliances	588.3	448.2	400.[illegible]
Vehicles, aircraft, vessels and associated transport equipment	317.4	182.3	131.[illegible]
Total (incl. others)	5,633.0	4,526.3	4,990.[illegible]

PRINCIPAL TRADING PARTNERS
(countries of consignment, JD million)

Imports c.i.f.	2008	2009	2010
China, People's Republic	1,252.2	1,113.0	1,188.6
Egypt	541.7	610.3	492.9
France	295.6	252.5	246.6
Germany	720.3	632.1	729.0
India	357.3	212.2	275.3
Indonesia	142.6	79.4	78.9
Italy	384.4	361.9	379.3
Japan	349.0	374.4	343.5
Korea, Republic	411.4	393.3	461.9
Netherlands	126.4	106.6	126.0
Russia	276.0	247.4	178.2
Saudi Arabia	2,550.0	1,770.0	2,164.4
Spain	88.7	75.8	85.1
Sweden	66.6	59.5	70.4
Switzerland	134.5	85.2	94.1
Syria	244.5	218.0	267.2
Taiwan	133.9	118.2	127.7
Turkey	319.8	309.1	397.2
United Arab Emirates	219.8	237.7	286.0
United Kingdom	239.1	232.5	189.4
USA	551.1	707.3	615.6
Total (incl. others)	12,060.9	10,107.7	11,050.1

Exports f.o.b.	2008	2009	2010
China, People's Republic	79.8	29.7	80.3
Egypt	109.6	81.9	101.9
Germany	8.8	5.1	4.9
India	917.4	484.8	552.2
Indonesia	97.0	99.1	105.9
Iraq	912.2	904.3	800.8
Israel	118.6	84.8	74.8
Kuwait	71.6	54.5	64.0
Lebanon	112.4	151.6	164.2
Malaysia	62.9	19.7	50.7
Pakistan	5.0	4.8	8.9
Qatar	60.1	49.5	69.8
Saudi Arabia	388.7	411.5	475.4
Syria	200.7	165.4	182.5
United Arab Emirates	260.4	178.6	210.6
United Kingdom	20.1	14.8	16.7
USA	743.0	619.3	659.2
Total (incl. others)	5,633.0	4,526.3	4,990.1

Transport

AILWAYS
affic, million)

	2005	2006
assenger-km	1.6	0.6
eight ton-km	466	440

ource: IRF, *World Road Statistics*.

OAD TRAFFIC
notor vehicles in use at 31 December)

	2007	2008	2009
assenger cars	536,665	601,312	673,125
uses	17,236	17,521	18,143
orries and vans	230,822	240,869	227,582
lotorcycles	2,808	3,845	3,489

ource: IRF, *World Road Statistics*.

HIPPING

lerchant Fleet
registered at 31 December)

	2007	2008	2009
Number of vessels	28	24	21
Displacement ('000 grt)	368.7	284.6	263.8

Source: IHS Fairplay, *World Fleet Statistics*.

International Sea-borne Freight Traffic
('000 metric tons)

	2000	2001	2002
Goods loaded	7,192	7,791	8,872
Goods unloaded	5,359	5,251	5,286

CIVIL AVIATION
(traffic on scheduled services)

	2007	2008	2009
Kilometres flown (million)	54	55	56
Passengers carried ('000)	2,288	2,355	2,324
Passenger-km (million)	6,446	6,400	6,363
Total ton-km (million)	756	719	687

Source: UN, *Statistical Yearbook*.

Tourism

ARRIVALS BY NATIONALITY
('000)*

	2007	2008	2009
Egypt	616.9	697.9	548.1
Iraq	274.6	241.0	283.5
Israel	276.6	279.5	226.8
Kuwait	137.1	138.2	140.6
Lebanon	194.4	193.9	177.9
Palestinian Autonomous Areas	346.0	361.2	386.6
Saudi Arabia	1,006.8	1,123.5	1,193.2
Syria	1,981.6	2,125.4	2,165.6
Turkey	145.5	146.9	153.6
USA	167.5	181.6	175.0
Total (incl. others)	6,528.6	7,100.5	7,084.6

* Including pilgrims and excursionists (same-day visitors).

Tourism receipts (US $ million, excl. passenger transport): 2,943 in 2008; 2,911 in 2009; 3,413 in 2010 (provisional).

Source: World Tourism Organization.

Total arrivals: 8,247,135 in 2010 (Source: Ministry of Tourism and Antiquities, Amman).

Communications Media

	2008	2009	2010
Telephones ('000 main lines in use)	519.0	501.2	485.5
Mobile cellular telephones ('000 subscribers)	5,313.6	6,014.4	6,620.0
Internet subscribers ('000)	229.1	244.5	248.3
Broadband subscribers ('000)	137.1	203.5	195.8

1996: Book production (titles) 511.

1997: Radio receivers ('000 in use) 1,660; Non-daily newspapers (titles) 13, (average circulation) 154,000.

1998: Daily newspapers (average circulation) 352,000 copies; Non-daily newspapers (average circulation) 155,000; Periodicals (titles) 270, (average circulation) 148,000 copies.

Daily newspapers (titles): 8 in 1998; 5 in 1999; 5 in 2000; 4 in 2004.

Non-daily newspapers (titles): 13 in 1998; 17 in 1999; 20 in 2000.

Television receivers ('000 in use): 560 in 2000.

Personal computers: 382,000 (66.7 per 1,000 persons) in 2007.

Sources: partly International Telecommunication Union; UNESCO, *Statistical Yearbook*; UN, *Statistical Yearbook*.

Education

(2007/08 unless otherwise indicated)

	Schools	Teachers	Pupils
Pre-primary	1,248*	5,064	104,762
Primary	2,877*	39,441†	817,160
Secondary: general	1,002*	30,426†	672,157
Secondary: vocational	40*	2,759	28,185
Higher	22*	9,681	254,752
of which universities‡	20	3,982	89,010

* 2003/04 figure.
† 2002/03 figure.
‡ 1996/97 figures.

Source: partly UNESCO Institute for Statistics.

Pupil-teacher ratio (primary education, UNESCO estimate): 19.9 in 2002/03 (Source: UNESCO Institute for Statistics).

Adult literacy rate (UNESCO estimates): 92.2% (males 95.5%; females 88.9%) in 2007 (Source: UNESCO Institute for Statistics).

Directory

The Government

HEAD OF STATE

King: King ABDULLAH IBN AL-HUSSEIN (succeeded to the throne on 7 February 1999).

CABINET
(May 2012)

Prime Minister and Minister of Defence: FAYEZ AL-TARAWNEH.

Minister of Education: FAYEZ SAUDI.

Minister of Justice: KHALIFAH SULEIMAN.

Minister of Awqaf (Religious Endowments) and Islamic Affairs: ABD AL-SALAM ABBADI.

Minister of Industry and Trade: SHABIB AMMARI.

Minister of Foreign Affairs: NASSER JUDEH.

Minister of Higher Education and Scientific Research: WAJIH OWAIS.

Minister of Information and Communications Technology: ATEF TAL.

Minister of Transport: HASHEM MASAEED.

Minister of Planning and International Co-operation: JAAFAR HASSAN.

Minister of Social Development: WAJIH AZAIZEH.

Minister of Public Works and Housing: YAHIA KISBI.

Minister of Health: Dr ABD AL-LATIF WREIKAT.

Minister of Finance: SULEIMAN HAFEZ.

Minister of Labour: ATEF ODEIBAT.

Minister of Culture: SALAH JARRAR.

Minister of the Environment: YASSIN AL-KHAYYAT.

Minister of Public Sector Development: KHLEIF AL-KHAWALDEH.

Minister of Tourism and Antiquities: NAYEF HMEIDI AL-FAYEZ.

Minister of Water and Irrigation: MUHAMMAD NAJJAR.

Minister of the Interior: GHALEB ZU'BI.

Minister of Agriculture: AHMAD AL-KHATTAB.

Minister of Parliamentary Affairs: SHARARI SHAKHANBEH.

Minister of Political Development: NUFAN AJARMEH.

Minister of Municipal Affairs: MAHIR ABUL SAMIN.

Minister of Energy and Mineral Resources: ALAA BATAYNEH.

Minister of State for Women's Affairs: NADIA HASHEM.

Minister of Prime Ministry Affairs and Legislation: KAMEL SAEED.

Minister of State: YOUSEF JAZI.

Minister of State for Media Affairs and Communications and Government Spokesperson: SAMIH MAAYTAH.

Note: The Head of Intelligence and the Governor of the Central Bank also have full ministerial status.

MINISTRIES

The Prime Ministry of Jordan: POB 80, Amman 11180; tel. (6) 4641211; fax (6) 4642520; e-mail info@pm.gov.jo; internet www.pm .gov.jo.

Ministry of Agriculture: POB 2099, Amman; tel. (6) 5686151; fax (6) 5686310; e-mail agri@moa.gov.jo; internet www.moa.gov.jo.

Ministry of Awqaf (Religious Endowments) and Islamic Affairs: POB 659, Amman; tel. (6) 5666141; fax (6) 5602254; e-mail info@awqaf.gov.jo; internet www.awqaf.gov.jo.

Ministry of Culture: POB 6140, Amman; tel. (6) 5696218; fax (6) 5696598; e-mail info@culture.gov.jo; internet www.culture.gov.jo.

Ministry of Defence: POB 80, Amman; tel. (6) 4641211; fax (6) 4642520; e-mail info@jaf.mil.jo; internet www.jaf.mil.jo.

Ministry of Education: POB 1646, Amman 11118; tel. (6) 5607181; fax (6) 5666019; e-mail moe@moe.gov.jo; internet www.moe.gov.jo.

Ministry of Energy and Mineral Resources: POB 2310, Amman; tel. (6) 5803060; fax (6) 5865714; e-mail memr@memr.gov.jo; internet www.memr.gov.jo.

Ministry of the Environment: Amman; tel. (6) 5560113; fax (6) 5560288; e-mail info@moenv.gov.jo; internet www.moenv.gov.jo.

Ministry of Finance: POB 85, King Hussein St, Amman 11118; t (6) 4636321; fax (6) 4618527; e-mail info@mof.gov.jo; internet ww .mof.gov.jo.

Ministry of Foreign Affairs: POB 35217, Amman 11180; tel. (5735150; fax (6) 5735163; e-mail inquiry@mfa.gov.jo; internet ww .mfa.gov.jo.

Ministry of Health: POB 86, Amman 11118; tel. (6) 5200230; fax (5689177; e-mail info@moh.gov.jo; internet www.moh.gov.jo.

Ministry of Higher Education and Scientific Research: PO 35262, Amman 11180; tel. (6) 5347671; fax (6) 5349079; e-ma mohe@mohe.gov.jo; internet www.mohe.gov.jo.

Ministry of Industry and Trade: POB 2019, 11181 Amman; tel. (5629030; fax (6) 5684692; e-mail info@mit.gov.jo; internet www.m .gov.jo.

Ministry of Information and Communications Technolog POB 9903, Amman 11191; tel. (6) 5805700; fax (6) 5861059; e-ma moict@moict.gov.jo; internet www.moict.gov.jo.

Ministry of the Interior: POB 100, Amman; tel. (6) 5691141; fax (6 5606908; e-mail info@moi.gov.jo; internet www.moi.gov.jo.

Ministry of Justice: POB 6040, Amman 11118; tel. (6) 4603630; fa (6) 4643197; e-mail feedback@moj.gov.jo; internet www.moj.gov.jo

Ministry of Labour: POB 8160, Amman 11118; tel. (6) 5802666; fa (6) 5855072; e-mail info@mol.gov.jo; internet www.mol.gov.jo.

Ministry of Municipal Affairs: POB 1799, Amman 11118; tel. (6 4641393; fax (6) 4640404; e-mail mma3@nic.net.jo; internet ww .mma.gov.jo.

Ministry of Parliamentary Affairs: Amman.

Ministry of Planning and International Co-operation: POE 555, Amman 11118; tel. (6) 4644466; fax (6) 4642247; e-mail mop@ mop.gov.jo; internet www.mop.gov.jo.

Ministry of Political Development: POB 841367, Amman 11180; tel. (6) 5695216; fax (6) 5686582; e-mail info@mopd.gov.jo; internet www.mopd.gov.jo.

Ministry of Public Sector Development: POB 3575, Amman 11821; tel. (6) 5695216; fax (6) 5686282; e-mail info@mopsd.gov.jo; internet www.mopsd.gov.jo.

Ministry of Public Works and Housing: POB 1220, Amman 11118; tel. (6) 5803838; fax (6) 5857590; e-mail mpwh@mpwh.gov.jo; internet www.mpwh.gov.jo.

Ministry of Social Development: POB 6720, Amman 11118; tel. (6) 5679327; fax (6) 5679961; e-mail contact@mosd.gov.jo; internet www.mosd.gov.jo.

Ministry of Tourism and Antiquities: POB 224, Amman 11118; tel. (6) 4603360; fax (6) 4648465; e-mail contacts@mota.gov.jo; internet www.mota.gov.jo.

Ministry of Transport: POB 35214, Amman 11180; tel. (6) 5518111; fax (6) 5527233; e-mail info@mot.gov.jo; internet www .mot.gov.jo.

Ministry of Water and Irrigation: POB 2412, Amman 11181; tel. (6) 5652265; fax (6) 5652287; e-mail admin@mwi.gov.jo; internet www.mwi.gov.jo.

Legislature

Majlis al-Umma
(National Assembly)

Senate

POB 72, Amman 11101; tel. (6) 5664121; fax (6) 5689313; e-mail info@ senate.jo; internet www.senate.jo.

The Senate (House of Notables) consists of 60 members, appointed by the King. The current Senate was appointed on 25 October 2011.

Speaker: TAHER AL-MASRI.

House of Representatives

POB 72, Amman 11118; tel. (6) 5635200; fax (6) 5685970; e-mail info@ representatives.jo; internet www.representatives.jo.

Speaker: ABD AL-KARIM DUGHMI.

General Election, 9 November 2010

Party/Group	Seats
Independents and tribal representatives	120
Total	120*

Some 17 of the independent candidates elected to the National Assembly were reported to be aligned with opposition groups, including one member of the Islamic Action Front (IAF), which had refused to participate in the elections in protest against the revised election law introduced in May 2010. In accordance with the terms of the legislation, 12 of the 120 seats were allocated to the female candidates receiving the greatest number of votes.

Political Organizations

With the exception of the officially sanctioned Jordanian National Union (1971–76), political parties were effectively banned for most of the reign of King Hussein. However, in June 1991 a National Charter, one feature of which was the legalization of political parties, was formally endorsed. In August 1992 legislation allowing the formation of political parties was approved by royal decree, and by March 1993 nine parties had received official recognition. New amendments to the political parties law, approved by parliament in March 2007, required parties to have 500 founding members drawn from five different governorates with equal representation, and compelled parties to grant the Government access to their accounts; the reform also provided for public funding for political parties. Parties were given a period of one year to meet the new requirements or face dissolution. By April 2008 12 out of the 36 existing political parties had rectified their status; all other parties were dissolved, while two new parties were licensed. A number of parties were expected to launch lawsuits contesting their dissolution.

Arab Islamic Democratic Party (Dua'a): POB 104, Amman 11941; tel. and fax (6) 5514443; e-mail info@duaa-jo.com; f. 1993; moderate Islamist party; Founder Yousuf Abu Bakr.

Higher Co-ordination Committee for Opposition Parties: Amman; opposition bloc currently consisting of 7 leftist, pan-Arab and Islamist parties: Baath Arab Progressive Party, Jordanian Arab Socialist Baath Party, Islamic Action Front, Jordanian Communist Party, Jordan People's Democratic Party (HASHD), National Movement for Direct Democracy and Jordanian Democratic Popular Unity Party (leftist).

Hizb-ut-Tahrir al-Islami (Party of Islamic Liberation): e-mail info@hizb-ut-tahrir.org; internet www.hizb-ut-tahrir.org; f. 1953; transnational org. prohibited in Jordan and many other countries; aims to establish Islamic caliphate throughout the world; denies claims that it is a militant group; Leader in Jordan Ramzi Sawalhah.

Islamic Action Front (Jabhat al-Amal al-Islami—IAF): POB 925310, Abdali, Amman 11110; tel. (6) 5696985; fax (6) 5696987; e-mail info@jabha.net; internet www.jabha.net; f. 1992; seeks implementation of *Shari'a* (Islamic law) and preservation of the *Umma* (Islamic community); mem. of Higher Co-ordination Committee for Opposition Parties; Sec.-Gen. Hamza Mansour.

Islamic Centrist Party (Hizb al-Wasat al-Islami): POB 2149, Haswa Bldg, 3rd Floor, Amman 11941; tel. and fax (6) 5353966; internet www.wasatparty.org; f. 2001 by fmr mems of Islamic Action Front and Muslim Brotherhood; Sec.-Gen. Muhammad Ahmed Mahmoud al-Hajj.

Jordan People's Democratic Party (Hizb al-Shaab al-Dimuqrati—HASHD): POB 9966, Amman 11191; tel. (6) 5691451; fax (6) 5686857; e-mail ahali@go.com.jo; internet www.hashd-ahali.org.jo; f. 1989; leftist party, which seeks to establish legal and institutional processes to protect the people, instigate economic, social, democratic and agricultural reform, and organize, unify and protect the working classes; supports the Palestinian cause; mem. of Higher Co-ordination Cttee for Opposition Parties; publishes weekly newspaper, *Al-Ahali*; Sec.-Gen. Abla Abu Ulbah.

Jordanian Arab Socialist Baath Party (Hizb al-Baath al-Arabi al-Ishtiraki al-Urduni): POB 8383, Amman; tel. (6) 4658618; fax (6) 4658617; f. 1993; promotes pan-Arabism; mem. of Higher Co-ordination Cttee for Opposition Parties; Sec.-Gen. Akram al-Homsi.

Jordanian Communist Party: POB 2349, Amman; tel. and fax (6) 4624939; e-mail jcp@nets.com.jo; internet www.jocp.org; f. 1951; merged with Communist Workers Party of Jordan 2008; Sec.-Gen. Dr Munir Hamarneh.

Jordanian Democratic Popular Unity Party: POB 922110, Amman; tel. (6) 5692301; fax (6) 5692302; e-mail wahda_party@hotmail.com; internet www.wihda.org; f. 1990; publishes *Nida'a al-Watan* newspaper; Sec.-Gen. Saeed Thiyab.

National Constitutional Party (Al-Hizb al-Watani al-Dusturi—NCP): POB 1825237, Amman 11118; tel. (6) 5696256; fax (6) 5686248; f. 1997 by merger of nine parties; Pres. Abd al-Hadi al-Majali; Sec.-Gen. Ahmad Shunnaq.

National Current Party: Amman; f. 2009; seeks to promote the cause of national unity through the reform of political institutions; pro-monarchy; Sec.-Gen. Abdul Hadi Majali.

National Movement for Direct Democracy: POB 922478, Amman 11192; tel. (6) 5652125; fax (6) 5639925; f. 1997; Sec.-Gen. Nashaat Ahmed.

Other licensed parties include: Baath Arab Progressive Party, Al-Hayat, Jordan National Party, Mission Party (Hizb al-Risala) and the Unified Jordanian Front.

Diplomatic Representation

EMBASSIES IN JORDAN

Algeria: POB 830375, Amman 11183; tel. (6) 4641271; fax (6) 4616552; e-mail ambalg@go.com.jo; Ambassador Sidi Muhammad Gaouar.

Australia: POB 35201, 41 Kayed al-Armouti St, Abdoun, Amman 11180; tel. (6) 5807000; fax (6) 5807001; e-mail amman.austremb@dfat.gov.au; internet www.jordan.embassy.gov.au; Ambassador Heidi Venamore.

Austria: POB 830795, Jabal Amman, Amman 11183; tel. (6) 4601101; fax (6) 4612725; e-mail amman-ob@bmeia.gv.at; Ambassador Astrid Harz.

Azerbaijan: POB 851894, 13 al-Awabed St, al-Kursi, Amman 11185; tel. (6) 5935525; fax (6) 5932826; e-mail amman@mission.mfa.gov.az; internet www.azembassyjo.org; Ambassador Dr Elman Arasli.

Bahrain: POB 5220, Faris al-Khoury St, Shmeisani, Amman 11183; tel. (6) 5664148; fax (6) 5664190; e-mail bahemb@maktoob.com; Ambassador Nasser Rashid al-Kaabi.

Bangladesh: POB 5685, 10 Muzdalifa St, al-Rabieh, Amman 11183; tel. (6) 5529192; fax (6) 5529194; e-mail embangl@wanadoo.jo; Ambassador Fazlul Karim.

Belgium: POB 942, 17 Sa'ad Jumah St, Jabal Amman, Amman 11118; tel. (6) 5932683; fax (6) 5930487; e-mail amman@diplobel.fed.be; internet www.diplomatie.be/amman; Ambassador Thomas Baekelandt.

Bosnia and Herzegovina: POB 850836, Amman 11185; tel. (6) 5856921; fax (6) 5856923; e-mail embjoamm@wanadoo.jo; Ambassador Zlatko Dizdarević.

Brazil: POB 5497, Amman 11183; tel. (6) 5923941; fax (6) 5931098; e-mail jorbrem@wanadoo.jo; Ambassador Fernando José Marroni de Abreu.

Brunei: POB 851752, Amman 11185; tel. (6) 5928021; fax (6) 5928024; e-mail amman.jordan@mfa.gov.bn; Ambassador Dato Paduka Haji Abdul Mokti bin Haji Mohammad Daud.

Bulgaria: POB 950578, 7 al-Mousel St, Amman 11195; tel. (6) 5529392; fax (6) 5539393; e-mail aman@dzsv.sat.bg; internet www.mfa.bg/bg/38/; Ambassador (vacant).

Canada: POB 815403, Amman 11180; tel. (6) 5203300; fax (6) 5203396; e-mail amman@international.gc.ca; internet www.canadainternational.gc.ca/jordan-jordanie; Ambassador Mark Gwozdecky.

Chile: POB 830663, 28 Hussein Abu Ragheb St, Abdoun, Amman 11183; tel. (6) 5923360; fax (6) 5924263; e-mail echile@batelco.jo; internet chileabroad.gov.cl/jordania; Ambassador Victor Fernando Varela Palma.

China, People's Republic: POB 7365, 9 Jakarta St, Amman 11118; tel. (6) 5515151; fax (6) 5518713; e-mail chinaemb_jo@mfa.gov.cn; internet jo.china-embassy.org; Ambassador Yue Xiaoyong.

Cyprus: POB 5525, Bldg 233, Wadi Sakra St, Amman 11183; tel. (6) 5657143; fax (6) 5657895; Ambassador Petros Eftychiou.

Czech Republic: POB 2213, Amman 11181; tel. (6) 5927051; fax (6) 5927053; e-mail amman@embassy.mzv.cz; internet www.mzv.cz/amman; Ambassador Ivana Holoubková.

Egypt: POB 35178, 14 Riyad el-Mefleh St, Amman 11180; tel. (6) 5605202; fax (6) 5604082; e-mail eg.emb_amman@mfa.gov.eg; internet www.mfa.gov.eg/missions/jordan/amman/embassy/en-gb; Ambassador Amr Abd al-Latif Abul Atta.

France: POB 5348, Amman 11183; tel. (6) 4604630; fax (6) 4604638; e-mail cad.amman-amba@diplomatie.fr; internet www.ambafrance-jo.org; Ambassador Corinne Breuzé.

Georgia: POB 851903, 31 Odeh Abu Tayeh, Shmeisani, Amman 11185; tel. (6) 5603793; fax (6) 5603819; e-mail geoemb@orange.jo; internet www.jordan.mfa.gov.ge; Ambassador Zurab Eristavi.

Germany: POB 183, 25 Benghazi St, Jabal Amman 11118; tel. (6) 5901170; fax (6) 5901282; e-mail info@amman.diplo.de; internet www.amman.diplo.de; Ambassador Ralph Tarraf.

Greece: POB 35069, 7 Iskandaronah St, Abdoun, Amman 11180; tel. (6) 5922724; fax (6) 5927622; e-mail gremb.amn@mfa.gr; Ambassador Asteriadis Iraklis.

Holy See: POB 142916, 14 Anton al-Naber St, Amman 11814; tel. (6) 5929934; fax (6) 5929931; e-mail nuntiusjordan@gmail.com; Apostolic Nuncio Most Rev. Archbishop Giorgio Lingua.

Hungary: POB 3441, Amman 11181; tel. (6) 5925614; fax (6) 5930836; e-mail mission.amm@kum.hu; internet www.mfa.gov.hu/emb/amman; Ambassador Dr Béla Jungbert.

India: POB 2168, Jabal Amman, 1st Circle, Amman 11181; tel. (6) 4622098; fax (6) 4659540; e-mail amb.amman@mea.gov.in; internet www.indembassy.org.jo; Ambassador Radha Ranjan Dash.

Indonesia: POB 811784, 44 Faisal bin Abd al-Aziz St, 6th Circle, Amman 11181; tel. (6) 5528912; fax (6) 5528380; e-mail amman96@go.com.jo; internet www.kemlu.go.id/amman; Ambassador Zainul Bahar Noor.

Iran: POB 173, Amman 11118; tel. (6) 4641281; fax (6) 4641383; e-mail pub-rel@iranembassyjordan.org; Ambassador Mostafa Moslehzade.

Iraq: POB 2025, Amman; tel. (6) 4623175; fax (6) 4619177; e-mail amaemb@iraqmofamail.net; Ambassador Dr Jawad Hadi Abbas.

Israel: POB 95866, 47 Maysaloon St, Dahiat al-Rabieh, Amman 11195; tel. (6) 5503500; fax (6) 5503579; e-mail embassy@amman.mfa.gov.il; internet amman.mfa.gov.il; Ambassador Danny Nevo.

Italy: POB 9800, Jabal al-Weibdeh, 5 Hafiz Ibrahim St, Amman 11191; tel. (6) 4638185; fax (6) 4659730; e-mail info.amman@esteri.it; internet www.ambamman.esteri.it; Ambassador Francesco Fransoni.

Japan: POB 2835, Ibn al-Furat St, Sweifiyeh, Amman 11181; tel. (6) 5932005; fax (6) 5931006; e-mail mail@embjapan.org.jo; internet www.jordan.emb-japan.go.jp; Ambassador Junichi Kosuge.

Kazakhstan: Abu Bakir al-Banany St, Amman; tel. (6) 5927953; fax (6) 5927952; e-mail kazemb@orange.jo; Ambassador Bolat S. Sarsenbayev.

Korea, Democratic People's Republic: POB 799, Amman; tel. (6) 4417614; fax (6) 4424735; e-mail dprk-embv@scs-net.org; Ambassador Choi Su Hon.

Korea, Republic: POB 3060, Bahjat Homsi St, Amman 11181; tel. (6) 5930745; fax (6) 5930280; e-mail jordan@mofat.go.kr; internet jor.mofat.go.kr; Ambassador Shin Hyun-Suk.

Kuwait: POB 2107, Amman 11181; tel. (6) 5675135; fax (6) 5681971; e-mail q8@kuwaitembassyamman.org; Ambassador Hamad Saleh Duaij.

Lebanon: POB 811779, Amman 11181; tel. and fax (6) 5929111; Ambassador Adib Charbel Aoun.

Libya: POB 2987, Amman; tel. (6) 5693101; fax (6) 5693404; Ambassador (vacant).

Malaysia: POB 5351, Tayser Na'na'ah St, off Umawiyyeen St, Abdoun, Amman 11183; tel. (6) 5902400; fax (6) 5934343; e-mail malamman@kln.gov.my; internet www.kln.gov.my/perwakilan/amman; Ambassador Datuk Abd Malek Abdul Aziz.

Mauritania: POB 851594, Saleh Zakee St, Villa 19, Sweifiyeh, Amman 11185; tel. (6) 5855146; fax (6) 5855148; e-mail muritanyaembassy_amman1@hotmail.com; Ambassador Ely Ould Ahmedou.

Morocco: POB 2175, Amman 11183; tel. (6) 5680591; fax (6) 5680253; e-mail ambmaroc@batelco.jo; Ambassador Hassan Abd al-Khaliq.

Netherlands: POB 941361, 3 Abu Bakr Siraj al-Din St, Amman 11194; tel. (6) 5902200; fax (6) 5930161; e-mail amm-info@minbuza.nl; internet jordan.nlembassy.org; Ambassador Piet de Klerk.

Norway: POB 830510, 25 Damascus St, Amman 11183; tel. (6) 5931646; fax (6) 5931650; e-mail emb.amman@mfa.no; internet www.norway.jo; Ambassador Petter Ølberg.

Oman: POB 20192, Amman 11110; tel. (6) 5686155; fax (6) 5689404; e-mail amman@mofa.gov.om; Ambassador Musallam Ben Bakhit al-Barami.

Pakistan: POB 1232, al-Akhtal St, Amman 11118; tel. (6) 4622787; fax (6) 4611633; e-mail parepamman@batelco.jo; internet www.mofa.gov.pk/jordan; Ambassador Attiya Mahmood.

Philippines: POB 925207, 5 Salem al-Batarseh St, Amman 11190; tel. (6) 5923748; fax (6) 5923744; e-mail ammanpe@dfa.gov.ph; internet www.philembassy-amman.net; Ambassador Julius D. Torres, Jr.

Poland: POB 942050, Amman 11194; tel. (6) 5512593; fax (6) 5512595; e-mail info@amman.polemb.net; internet www.amman.polemb.net; Chargé d'affaires Krzysztof Bojko.

Qatar: POB 5098, Amman 11183; tel. (6) 5902300; fax (6) 59023C e-mail qataremb@go.com.jo; internet www.qatarembassy-jo.n Ambassador Mana Abd al-Hadi al-Hajri.

Romania: POB 2869, 35 Madina Munawwara St, Amman 11181; t (6) 5813423; fax (6) 5812521; e-mail roemb@orange.jo; intern amman.mae.ro; Ambassador Bogdan Filip.

Russia: POB 2187, 22 Zahran St, Amman 11181; tel. (6) 4641158; f (6) 4647448; e-mail rusembjo@mail.ru; internet www.jordan.mid.r Ambassador Aleksandr Kalugin.

Saudi Arabia: POB 2133, 5th Circle, Jabal Amman, Amman 1118 tel. (6) 5924154; fax (6) 4659853; e-mail joemb@mofa.gov.s Ambassador Fahd bin Abd al-Mihsin al-Zaid.

South Africa: POB 851508, Sweifiyeh, Amman 11185; tel. (5921194; fax (6) 5920080; e-mail saembjor@index.com.jo; intern www.saembjor.com; Ambassador Molefe Samuel Tsele.

Spain: Zahran St, POB 454, Amman 11118; tel. (6) 4614166; fax (4614173; e-mail emb.amman@maec.es; internet www.maec.e embajadas/amman; Ambassador Javier Sangro de Liniers.

Sri Lanka: POB 830731, Amman 11183; tel. (6) 5820611; fax (6 5820615; e-mail lankaembjo@orange.jo; Ambassador Gamini Raja pakse.

Sudan: POB 3305, Bayader Wadi al-Seer, 7th Circle, Musa Irshee al-Taib St, Amman 11181; tel. (6) 5854500; fax (6) 5854501; e-ma sudani@nets.com.jo; Ambassador Osman Nafae Hamad.

Sweden: POB 830536, 20 Abd al-Majid al-Adwan St, Abdoun Amman 11183; tel. (6) 5901300; fax (6) 5930179; e-ma ambassaden.amman@foreign.ministry.se; internet ww .swedenabroad.com/amman; Ambassador Charlotta Sparre.

Switzerland: POB 5341, 19 Ibrahim Ayoub St, 4th Circle, Ammar 11183; tel. (6) 5931416; fax (6) 5930685; e-mail amm.vertretung@eda .admin.ch; internet www.eda.admin.ch/amman; Ambassador Andrea Reichlin.

Syria: POB 1733, Amman 11118; tel. (6) 5920684; fax (6) 5920635; Ambassador Gen. Bahjat Suleiman.

Thailand: POB 144329, Amman 11814; tel. (6) 5925410; fax (6) 5926109; e-mail thaibgw@mfa.go.th; internet www.thaiembassy.org/amman; Ambassador Nillavan Ngamukos.

Tunisia: POB 17185, Amman 11195; tel. (6) 5674308; fax (6) 5922769; e-mail atamman@go.com.jo; Ambassador Abd al-Majid Fersheshi.

Turkey: POB 2062, Amman 11181; tel. (6) 4641251; fax (6) 4612353; e-mail ammanbe@nets.com.jo; internet amman.emb.mfa.gov.tr; Ambassador Ali Köprülü.

Ukraine: POB 5244, 6 al-Umouma St, al-Sahl, Amman; tel. (6) 5922402; fax (6) 5922405; e-mail emb_jo@mfa.gov.ua; internet www.mfa.gov.ua/jordan; Ambassador Sergiy Pasko.

United Arab Emirates: POB 2623, 22 Tawfiq Abu al-Huda, 3rd Circle, Amman 11181; tel. (6) 5934780; fax (6) 5932666; e-mail uaeemb@index.jo.com; Ambassador Dr Abdullah Nasir Sultan al-Ameri.

United Kingdom: POB 87, Abdoun, Amman 11118; tel. (6) 5909200; fax (6) 5909279; e-mail beamman@cyberia.jo; internet ukinjordan.fco.gov.uk; Ambassador Peter Millett.

USA: POB 354, Umawiyyeen St, Abdoun, Amman 11118; tel. (6) 5906000; fax (6) 5920163; e-mail webmasterjordan@state.gov; internet jordan.usembassy.gov; Ambassador Stuart E. Jones.

Yemen: POB 3085, Prince Hashem bin Al-Hussain St, Amman 11181; tel. (6) 5923771; fax (6) 5923773; Ambassador (vacant).

Judicial System

With the exception of matters of purely personal nature concerning members of non-Muslim communities, the law of Jordan was based on Islamic Law for both civil and criminal matters. During the days of the Ottoman Empire certain aspects of Continental law, especially French commercial law and civil and criminal procedure, were introduced. Owing to British occupation of Palestine and Transjordan from 1917 to 1948, the Palestine territory has adopted, either by statute or case law, much of the English common law. Since the annexation of the non-occupied part of Palestine and the formation of the Hashemite Kingdom of Jordan, there has been a continuous effort to unify the law.

Court of Cassation (Supreme Court)

The Court of Cassation consists of seven judges, who sit in full panel for exceptionally important cases. In most appeals, however, only five members sit to hear the case. All cases involving amounts of more than JD 100 may be reviewed by this Court, as well as cases involving lesser amounts and those that cannot be monetarily valued. However, for the latter types of cases, review is available only by leave of the Court of Appeal, or, upon refusal by the Court of Appeal, by leave the President of the Court of Cassation. In addition to these functions as final and Supreme Court of Appeal, the Court of Cassation also sits as High Court of Justice to hear applications in the nature of habeas corpus, mandamus and certiorari dealing with complaints of a citizen against abuse of governmental authority.

President: MUHAMMAD AL-MAHAMEED.

Courts of Appeal: There are three Courts of Appeal, each of which is composed of three judges, whether for hearing of appeals or for dealing with Magistrates Courts' judgments in chambers. Jurisdiction of the three Courts is geographical, with one each in Amman, Irbid and Ma'an. Appellate review of thc Courts of Appeal extends to judgments rendered in the Courts of First Instance, the Magistrates' Courts and Religious Courts.

Courts of First Instance: The Courts of First Instance are courts of general jurisdiction in all matters civil and criminal except those specifically allocated to the Magistrates' Courts. Three judges sit in all felony trials, while only two judges sit for misdemeanour and civil cases. Each of the 11 Courts of First Instance also exercises appellate jurisdiction in cases involving judgments of less than JD 20 and fines of less than JD 10, rendered by the Magistrates' Courts.

Magistrates' Courts: There are 17 Magistrates' Courts, which exercise jurisdiction in civil cases involving no more than JD 250 and in criminal cases involving maximum fines of JD 100 or maximum imprisonment of one year.

Religious Courts: There are two types of religious court: the *Shari'a* Courts (Muslims); and the Ecclesiastical Courts (Eastern Orthodox, Greek Melkite, Roman Catholic and Protestant). Jurisdiction extends to personal (family) matters, such as marriage, divorce, alimony, inheritance, guardianship, wills, interdiction and, for the Muslim community, the constitution of *Awqaf* (Religious Endowments). When a dispute involves persons of different religious communities, the Civil Courts have jurisdiction in the matter unless the parties agree to submit to the jurisdiction of one or the other of the Religious Courts involved.

Each *Shari'a* (Muslim) Court consists of one judge (*Qadi*), while most of the Ecclesiastical (Christian) Courts are normally composed of three judges, who are usually clerics. *Shari'a* Courts apply the doctrines of Islamic Law, based on the Koran and the *Hadith* (Precepts of Muhammad), while the Ecclesiastical Courts base their law on various aspects of Canon Law. In the event of conflict between any two Religious Courts or between a Religious Court and a Civil Court, a Special Tribunal of three judges is appointed by the President of the Court of Cassation, to decide which court shall have jurisdiction. Upon the advice of experts on the law of the various communities, this Special Tribunal decides on the venue for the case at hand.

Chief of Islamic Justice: AHMAD HILAYEL.

Director of Shari'a Courts: Sheikh ISSAM ABD AL-RAZZAQ ARABIYYAT.

Religion

Over 90% of the population are Sunni Muslims, and the King can trace unbroken descent from the Prophet Muhammad. There is a Christian minority, living mainly in the towns, and there are smaller numbers of non-Sunni Muslims.

ISLAM

Chief of Islamic Justice and Imam of the Royal Court: AHMAD HILAYEL.

Grand Mufti of the Hashemite Kingdom of Jordan: Sheikh ABD AL-KARIM KHASAWNEH.

CHRISTIANITY

The Roman Catholic Church

Chaldean Rite

The Chaldean Patriarch of Babylon is resident in Baghdad, Iraq. The Chaldean community in Jordan contained an estimated 7,000 adherents at 31 December 2007.

Chaldean Patriarchal Vicariate in Jordan: Jabal al-Wabdeh, POB 910833, Amman 11191; tel. and fax (6) 4629061; e-mail raymovicariate66@hotmail.com; internet www.chaldeanjordan.org; f. 2002; Patriarchal Exarch Rev. RAYMOND MOUSSALLI.

Latin Rite

Jordan forms part of the Patriarchate of Jerusalem (see the chapter on Israel).

Vicar-General for Transjordan: Most Rev. SELIM SAYEGH (Titular Bishop of Aquae in Proconsulari), Latin Vicariate, POB 851379, Sweifiyeh, Amman 11185; tel. (6) 5929546; fax (6) 5920548; e-mail regina-pacis2000@yahoo.com.

Maronite Rite

The Maronite community in Jordan, under the jurisdiction of the Maronite Patriarch of Antioch (resident in Lebanon), had about 1,200 adherents at 31 December 2007.

Patriarchal Exarchate of Jordan: Mgr PAUL NABIL SAYAH, St Charbel's Parish, Amman; tel. (6) 4202558; fax (6) 4202559; e-mail stcharbelparish@yahoo.com.

Melkite Rite

The Greek-Melkite archdiocese of Petra (Wadi Musa) and Philadelphia (Amman) contained 27,000 adherents at 31 December 2007.

Archbishop of Petra and Philadelphia: Most Rev. YASSER AYYACH, Archevêché Grec-Melkite Catholique, POB 2435, Jabal Amman 11181; tel. and fax (6) 5866673; e-mail fryaser@yahoo.com.

Syrian Rite

The Syrian Catholic Patriarch of Antioch is resident in Beirut, Lebanon.

Patriarchal Exarchate of Jerusalem (Palestine and Jordan): Mont Achrafieh, POB 510393, Rue Barto, Amman; e-mail st_thomas@bezeqint.net; Exarch Patriarchal Mgr GRÉGOIRE PIERRE MELKI (Titular Bishop of Batne of the Syrians).

The Anglican Communion

Within the Episcopal Church in Jerusalem and the Middle East, Jordan forms part of the diocese of Jerusalem. The President Bishop of the Church is the Bishop in Cyprus and the Gulf (see the chapter on Cyprus).

Other Christian Churches

The Coptic Orthodox Church, the Greek Orthodox Church (Patriarchate of Jerusalem) and the Evangelical Lutheran Church in Jordan are also active.

The Press

DAILIES

Al-Anbat: POB 962556, Amman 11192; tel. (6) 5200100; fax (6) 5200113; e-mail info@alanbat.net; internet www.alanbat.net; f. 2005; independent; Arabic; political; Man. Editor MAZEN AL-KHATIB.

Al-Arab al-Yawm (Arabs Today): POB 962198, Queen Rania St, Amman 11196; tel. (6) 5683333; fax (6) 5620552; e-mail mail@alarab-alyawm.com.jo; internet www.alarabalyawm.net; f. 1997; Arabic; Chief Editor FAHED AL-KHITAN.

Al-Diyar (The Homeland): Al-Fanar Complex, Queen Rania Al-Abdullah St, Amman; tel. (6) 5166588; f. 2004; Arabic; Chair. of Bd MAHMOUD KHARABSHEH.

Ad-Dustour (The Constitution): POB 591, Amman 11118; tel. (6) 5608000; fax (6) 5667170; e-mail dustour@addustour.com.jo; internet www.addustour.com; f. 1967; Arabic; publ. by the Jordan Press and Publishing Co Ltd; owns commercial printing facilities; Chair. KAMEL AL-SHARIF; Chief Editor MUHAMMAD HASSAN TAL; circ. 70,000.

Al-Ghad (Tomorrow): POB 3535, Amman 11821; tel. (6) 5544000; fax (6) 5544055; e-mail editorial@alghad.jo; internet www.alghad.jo; f. 2004; independent; Arabic; Editor-in-Chief MOUSA BARHOUMEH.

The Jordan Times: POB 6710, Queen Rania Al-Abdullah St, Amman 11118; tel. (6) 5600800; fax (6) 5696183; e-mail jotimes@jpf.com.jo; internet www.jordantimes.com; f. 1975; English; publ. by Jordan Press Foundation; Editor-in-Chief SAMIR BARHOUM; circ. 15,000.

Al-Rai (Opinion): POB 6710, Queen Rania Al-Abdullah St, Amman 11118; tel. (6) 5667171; fax (6) 5676581; e-mail info@jpf.com.jo; internet www.alrai.com; f. 1971; morning; independent; Arabic; publ. by Jordan Press Foundation; Chair. AHMAD ABD AL-FATTAH; Editor-in-Chief ABD AL-WAHAB ZGHEILAT; circ. 90,000.

Al-Sabeel (The Path): POB 213545, Amman 11121; tel. (6) 5692852; fax (6) 5692854; e-mail assabeel@assabeel.net; internet www.assabeel.net; f. 1993; fmrly weekly; became daily publ. 2009; Arabic; Islamist; Editor-in-Chief ATEF GOLANI.

WEEKLIES

Al-Ahali (The People): POB 9966, Amman 11191; tel. (6) 5691452; fax (6) 5686857; e-mail ahali@go.com.jo; internet www.hashd-ahali.org.jo; f. 1990; Arabic; publ. by the Jordan People's Democratic Party; Editor-in-Chief SALEM NAHHAS; circ. 5,000.

Akhbar al-Usbou (News of the Week): POB 605, Amman; tel. (6) 5677881; fax (6) 5677882; f. 1959; Arabic; economic, social, political; Chief Editor and Publr ABD AL-HAFIZ MUHAMMAD; circ. 50,000.

Al-Hadath: POB 961167, Amman 11196; tel. (6) 5160824; fax (6) 5160810; e-mail info@al-hadath.com; internet www.al-hadath.com; Arabic; general news; Man. Editor FATEH MANSOUR.

Al-Haqeqa al-Duwalia (Fact International): POB 712678, Amman 11171; tel. (6) 5828292; fax (6) 5816646; e-mail info@factjo.com; internet www.factjo.com; f. 1996; independent; Arabic and English; aims to promote moderate image of Islam and to counter conflicts within the faith; Editor-in-Chief HILMI AL-ASMAR.

Al-Liwa' (The Standard): POB 3067, 2nd Circle, Jabal Amman 11181; tel. (6) 5642770; fax (6) 5656324; e-mail info@al-liwa.com; internet www.al-liwa.com; f. 1972; Arabic; Editor-in-Chief HASSAN AL-TAL; circ. 15,000.

Al-Majd (The Glory): POB 926856, Amman 11190; tel. (6) 5530553; fax (6) 5530352; e-mail almajd@almajd.net; internet www.almajd.net; f. 1994; Arabic; political; Editor-in-Chief FAHID NIMER; circ. 8,000.

Shihan: POB 96-654, Amman; tel. (6) 5603585; fax (6) 5696183; Arabic; Editor-in-Chief (vacant); circ. 60,000.

The Star: POB 591, Queen Rania St, Amman 11118; tel. (6) 5653325; fax (6) 5697415; e-mail star@addustour.com.jo; internet www.star.com.jo; f. 1966; English; political, economic, social and cultural; publ. by the Jordan Press and Publishing Co; Editor-in-Chief MAHA AL-SHARIF; circ. 12,430.

PERIODICALS

Anty Magazine: POB 3024, Amman 11181; tel. (6) 5820058; fax (6) 5855892; e-mail chiefeditor@anty.jo; internet www.anty.jo; monthly; Arabic; publ. by Front Row Publishing and Media Services; fashion, culture and current affairs from a professional woman's perspective; Chief Editor SAHAR ALOUL; circ. 20,000.

Hatem: POB 6710, Queen Rania St, Amman 11118; tel. (6) 5600800; fax (6) 5676581; e-mail info@jpf.com.jo; children's; publ. by Jordan Press Foundation.

Huda El-Islam (The Right Way of Islam): POB 659, Amman; tel. (6) 5666141; f. 1956; monthly; Arabic; scientific and literary; publ. by the Ministry of Awqaf, Islamic Affairs and Holy Places; Editor Dr AHMAD MUHAMMAD HULAYYEL.

Jordan: POB 224, Amman; e-mail webmaster@jordanembassyus.org; internet www.jordanembassyus.org/new/newsletter.shtml; f. 1969; quarterly; publ. by Jordan Information Bureau, Embassy of Jordan, Washington, DC, USA; 3 a year; Editor-in-Chief MERISSA KHURMA; circ. 100,000.

Jordan Business: POB 3024, Amman 11181; tel. (6) 5820058; fax (6) 5855892; e-mail info@frontrow.jo; internet www.jordan-business.net; monthly; English; publ. by Front Row Publishing and Media Services; circ. 10,000.

Jordan Today: Media Services International, POB 9313, Amman 11191; tel. (6) 652380; fax (6) 648298; e-mail star@arabia.com; internet www.jordantoday.com.jo; f. 1995; monthly; English; tourism, culture and entertainment; Editor-in-Chief ZEID NASSER; circ. 10,000.

Military Magazine: Army Headquarters, Amman; f. 1955; quarterly; dealing with military and literary subjects; publ. by Armed Forces.

Royal Wings: POB 3024, Amman 11181; tel. (6) 5820058; fax (6) 5855892; e-mail info@frontrow.jo; internet www.frontrow.jo; bi-monthly; Arabic and English; magazine for Royal Jordanian Airline; publ. by Front Row Publishing and Media Services; Man. Dir USAMA FARAJ; circ. 40,000.

Skin: POB 940166, ICCB Centre, Queen Rania Abdullah St, Amman 11194; tel. (6) 5163357; fax (6) 5163257; e-mail amer@neareastmedia.com; internet www.skin-online.com; f. 2006; quarterly; English; publ. by Near East Media Iraq; art, design, fashion, photography, film and music; Editor-in-Chief TARIQ AL-BITAR.

NEWS AGENCY

Jordan News Agency (PETRA): POB 6845, Amman 11118; tel. (6) 5609700; fax (6) 5682478; e-mail petra@petra.gov.jo; internet www.petra.gov.jo; f. 1965; independent entity since 2004; previously controlled by Ministry of Information prior to its disbandment in 2001; Chair. SAMIH MAAYTAH (Minister of State for Media Affairs and Communications); Dir-Gen. RAMADAN AL-RAWASHDEH.

PRESS ASSOCIATION

Jordan Press Association (JPA): POB 8876, Abbas Mahmoud al-Aqqad St, Jabal Amman, 2nd Circle, Amman 18888; tel. (6) 5372005; fax (6) 5372003; e-mail info@jpa.jo; internet www.jpa.jo; f. 1953; Pres. ABD AL-WAHAB ZGHEILAT.

Publishers

Alfaris Publishing and Distribution Co: POB 9157, Amm 11191; tel. (6) 5605432; fax (6) 5685501; e-mail mkayyali@airpboo.com; internet www.airpbooks.com; f. 1989; Dir MAHER SAID KAYYA

Aram Studies Publishing and Distribution House: POB 99 Amman 11941; tel. (6) 835015; fax (6) 835079; art, finance, healt management, science, business; Gen. Dir SALEH ABOUSBA.

Dar al-Manhal Publishers and Distributors: POB 92642 Amman 11190; tel. (6) 5698308; fax (6) 5639185; e-mail info dmanhal.com; internet www.dmanhal.com; f. 1990; children's ar educational publs; Man. Editor KHALID BILBEISI.

Dar al-Nafa'es: POB 927511, al-Abdali, Amman 11190; tel. (5693940; fax (6) 5693941; e-mail alnafaes@hotmail.com; interne www.al-nafaes.com; f. 1990; education, Islamic; CEO SUFYAN OMA AL-ASHQR.

Dar al-Thaqafa: Amman 11118; tel. (6) 4646361; fax (6) 461029 e-mail info@daralthaqafa.com; internet www.daralthaqafa.com f. 1984; academic publr, specializes in law; Man. Editor KHALI MAHMOUD GABR.

Al Faridah for Specialized Publications: POB 1223, Amma 11821; tel. (6) 5689100; fax (6) 5689600; internet www.alfaridah.cor.jo; f. 2003; publr of magazines incl. *Layalina*, *Ahlan!*, *JO*, *Viva Venture*; Pres. MUHAMMAD ALAYYAN.

Front Row Publishing and Media Services: POB 3024, Amma 11181; tel. (6) 5820058; fax (6) 5855892; e-mail info@frontrow.jo internet www.frontrow.jo; publr of magazines incl. *Jordan Business Living Well*, *Home*, *Royal Wings*; CEO IYAD SHEHADEH.

Jordan Book Centre Co Ltd: POB 301, al-Jubeiha, Amman 11941 tel. (6) 5151882; fax (6) 5152016; e-mail jbc@go.com.jo; f. 1982; fiction business, economics, computer science, medicine, engineering general non-fiction; Man. Dir J. J. SHARBAIN.

Jordan Distribution Agency: POB 3371, Amman 11181; tel. (6 5358855; fax (6) 5337733; e-mail jda@aramex.com; f. 1951; history subsidiary of Aramex; Chair. FADI GHANDOUR; Gen. Man. WADIH SAYEGH.

Jordan House for Publication: POB 1121, Basman St, Amman; tel. (6) 24224; fax (6) 51062; f. 1952; medicine, nursing, dentistry; Man. Dir MURSI AL-ASHKAR.

Jordan Press and Publishing Co Ltd: POB 591, Amman 11118; tel. (6) 5608000; fax (6) 5667170; e-mail info@addustour.com.jo; internet www.addustour.com; f. 1967 by *Al-Manar* and *Falastin* dailies; publishes *Ad-Dustour* (daily), *Ad-Dustour Sport* (weekly) and *The Star* (English weekly); Chair. KAMEL AL-SHARIF; Dir-Gen. SAIF AL-SHARIF.

Jordan Press Foundation: POB 6710, Amman 11118; tel. (6) 5667171; fax (6) 5661242; e-mail info@jpf.com.jo; internet www.alrai.com; f. 1971; publishes *Al-Rai* (daily), the *Jordan Times* (daily) and *Hatem* (monthly); Chair. FAHED AL-FANEK; Gen. Dir NADER HORANI.

Al-Tanwir al-Ilmi (Scientific Enlightenment Publishing House): POB 4237, al-Mahatta, Amman 11131; tel. and fax (6) 4899619; e-mail taisir@yahoo.com; internet www.icieparis.net; f. 1990; affiliated with the Int. Centre for Innovation in Education; education, engineering, philosophy, science, sociology; Gen. Dir Prof. Dr TAISIR SUBHI YAMIN.

Broadcasting and Communications

TELECOMMUNICATIONS

Regulatory Authority

Telecommunications Regulatory Commission (TRC): POB 850967, Amman 11185; tel. (6) 5501120; fax (6) 5863641; e-mail trc@trc.gov.jo; internet www.trc.gov.jo; f. 1995; Chair. and CEO MUHAMMAD AL-TAANI.

Principal Operators

Jordan Mobile Telephone Services Co (Zain Jordan): POB 940821, 8th Circle, King Abdullah II St, Amman 11194; tel. (6) 5803000; fax (6) 5828200; e-mail info@jo.zain.com; internet www.jo.zain.com; f. 1994 as Jordan Mobile Telephone Services Co (JMTS—Fastlink); merged with Mobile Telecommunications Co (MTC—Kuwait) 2003, corpn renamed Zain Group 2007; Zain Jordan merged with PalTel (Palestinian Autonomous Areas) in 2009; private co; has operated Jordan's first mobile telecommunications network since 1995; CEO, Levant Region and CEO, Jordan Dr ABD AL-MALEK JABER.

Jordan Telecom Group: POB 1689, Amman 11118; tel. (6) 4606666; fax (6) 4639200; e-mail info@jordantelecomgroup.jo; internet www.jordantelecomgroup.jo; f. 1971; fmrly Jordan Telecommunications Corpn, Jordan Telecommunications Co and Jordan Telecom; current name adopted in Feb. 2006 following integration of he following cos' operations into a single management structure: Jordan Telecom, MobileCom (mobile cellular telecommunications services), Wanadoo (internet services) and e-Dimension (information technology); in 2007 Jordan Telecom, MobileCom and Wanadoo were all rebranded as Orange; 30.5% govt-owned, 69.5% privately owned: France Télécom SA, France, 51.0%; Social Security Corpn 12.4%; 1% of shares listed on Amman Stock Exchange; assets JD 664.8m., revenue JD 397.9m. (2007); Chair. (vacant).

Petra Jordanian Mobile Telecommunications: POB 941477, Amman 11194; tel. (6) 5630090; fax (6) 5630098; e-mail business@orange.jo; internet www.orange.jo; CEO NAYLA KHAWAM.

Umniah Mobile Company: POB 942481, Amman 11194; tel. (6) 5005000; fax (6) 5622772; e-mail contact@umniah.com; internet www.umniah.com; awarded contract for Jordan's third GSM licence in 2004; commenced operations in June 2005; first provider of wireless broadband internet services in Jordan; subsidiary of Alghanim Group (Kuwait); 96% owned by Bahrain Telecommunications Co; CEO JOSEPH HANANIA.

XPress Telecommunications: POB 2732, Amman 11821; tel. (6) 5506666; fax (6) 5506682; e-mail pr@xpress.jo; internet www.xpress.jo; provider of mobile telephone and radio trunking services since 2004; CEO (vacant).

BROADCASTING

A new Audio Visual Media Law, enacted in 2002, allowed for the establishment of private broadcasters in Jordan for the first time. By 2007 16 new radio licences had been awarded. Jordan's first licensed independent television channel, Al-Ghad TV (ATV), was officially launched in August 2007; however, the channel was taken off-air before it began broadcasting, owing to a dispute over the terms of its licence. In 2008 ATV was purchased by Arab Telemedia Group and plans were announced for the launch in January 2010 of a two-channel network; however, the launch was subsequently delayed.

Regulatory Authority

Audio Visual Commission (AVC): POB 142515, Amman 11814; tel. (6) 5560378; fax (6) 5535093; e-mail avc@nic.net.jo; internet www.avc.gov.jo; f. 2002; Dir-Gen. HUSSAIN BANI-HANI.

Radio and Television

Jordan Radio and Television Corporation (JRTV): POB 1041, Amman; tel. (6) 773111; fax (6) 751503; e-mail general@jrtv.gov.jo; internet www.jrtv.jo; f. 1968; state broadcaster; operates four TV channels and six radio channels broadcasting programmes in Arabic, English and French; advertising accepted; Chair. SAMIH MAAYTAH (Minister of State for Media Affairs and Communications); Dir-Gen. BAYAN AL-TAL; Dir of Radio Administration MAZEN AL-MAJALI; Dir of Television Administration HALA ZUREIQAT.

Radio Al-Balad: POB 20513, Amman 11118; tel. (6) 4645486; fax (6) 4630238; internet www.ammannet.net; f. 2000 as internet radio station AmmanNet; began broadcasting as an FM radio station 2005, renamed as above 2008; news, politics and community broadcasts; Gen. Man. SAWSAN ZAIDAH.

Sawt al-Madina (SAM): POB 1171, Amman 1953; tel. (6) 5500006; fax (6) 5500009; e-mail fateen@al-baddad.com; internet www.al-baddad.com; f. 2006; owned by Al-Baddad Media and Communications; radio station broadcasting news and politics programmes; Group Gen. Man. FATEEN H. AL-BADDAD.

Other independent radio stations include Mazaj FM, Amin FM, Al-Hayat FM, Rotana FM Jordan and Radio Fann FM.

Finance

(cap. = capital; p.u. = paid up; dep. = deposits; m. = million; res = reserves; br.(s) = branch(es); amounts in Jordanian dinars unless otherwise indicated)

BANKING

Central Bank

Central Bank of Jordan: POB 37, King Hussein St, Amman 11118; tel. (6) 4630301; fax (6) 4638889; e-mail info@cbj.gov.jo; internet www.cbj.gov.jo; f. 1964; cap. 18.0m., res 279.3m., dep. 5,610.2m. (Dec. 2008); Gov. and Chair. ZIAD FARIZ; 2 brs.

National Banks

Arab Bank PLC: POB 950545, Shmeisani, Amman 11195; tel. (6) 5607231; fax (6) 5606793; e-mail corpcomm@arabbank.com.jo; internet www.arabbank.com; f. 1930; cap. US $776.0m., res $6,711.8m., dep. $40,869.3m. (Dec. 2009); Chair. and CEO ABD AL-HAMID SHOMAN; Vice-Chair. SABIH TAHER AL-MASRI; 84 brs in Jordan, 99 brs abroad.

Bank of Jordan PLC: POB 2140, Shmeisani, Amman 11181; tel. (6) 5696277; fax (6) 5696291; e-mail boj@bankofjordan.com.jo; internet www.bankofjordan.com; f. 1960; cap. 100m., res 65m., dep. 1,635m. (Dec. 2009); Chair. and Gen. Man. TAWFIK SHAKER FAKHOURI; 77 brs and offices.

Cairo Amman Bank: POB 950661, Cairo Amman Bank Bldg, Wadi Saqra St, Amman 11195; tel. (6) 4616910; fax (6) 4642890; e-mail info@cab.jo; internet www.cab.jo; f. 1960; cap. 88m., res 58m., dep. 1,504m. (Dec. 2009); Chair. and CEO KHALED AL-MASRI; 63 brs in Jordan, 18 brs in the West Bank.

Capital Bank of Jordan: POB 941283, Issam Ajlouni St, Amman 11194; tel. (6) 5100200; fax (6) 5695942; e-mail info@capitalbank.jo; internet www.capitalbank.jo; f. 1996 as Export and Finance Bank; name changed as above 2006; cap. 132m., res 46m., dep. 767m. (Dec. 2009); Chair. BASSEM KHALIL SALEM AL-SALEM; Gen. Man. HAYTHAM KAMHIYAH.

Jordan Ahli Bank: POB 3103, Queen Noor St, Shmeisani, Amman 11181; tel. (6) 5622282; fax (6) 5622281; e-mail info@ahlibank.com.jo; internet www.ahli.com; f. 1955 as Jordan Nat. Bank; name changed as above 2006; cap. 110m., res 85m., dep. 1,988m. (Dec. 2009); Chair. NADIM Y. MUASHER; CEO and Gen. Man. MARWAN AWAD; 46 brs in Jordan, 6 brs abroad.

Jordan Commercial Bank: POB 9989, Yakoub Sarrouf St, Shmeisani, Amman 11191; tel. (6) 5603931; fax (6) 5603989; e-mail jcb@jcbank.com.jo; internet www.jcbank.com.jo; f. 1977 as Jordan Gulf Bank; name changed as above 2004; cap. 73m., res 10m., dep. 462m. (Dec. 2009); Chair. MICHEL AL-SAYEGH; CEO and Gen. Man. Dr JAWAD AL-HADID; 23 brs in Jordan, 3 brs in West Bank.

Jordan Islamic Bank: POB 926225, Shmeisani, Amman 11190; tel. (6) 5677377; fax (6) 5666326; e-mail jib@islamicbank.com.jo; internet www.jordanislamicbank.com; f. 1978; fmrly Jordan Islamic Bank for Finance and Investment; current name adopted Oct. 2009; cap. 100.0m., res 38.1m., dep. 623.2m. (Dec. 2009); Chair. ADNAN AHMAD YOUSUF; Vice-Chair. and Gen. Man. MUSA ABD AL-AZIZ SHIHADEH; 59 brs.

Jordan Kuwait Bank: POB 9776, Abdali, Amman 11191; tel. (6) 5629400; fax (6) 5695604; e-mail webmaster@jkbank.com.jo; internet www.jordan-kuwait-bank.com; f. 1976; cap. US $141m., res $180m., dep. $2,371m. (Dec. 2009); Chair. and CEO ABD AL-KARIM AL-KABARITI; Dir-Gen. MUHAMMAD YASSER M. AL-ASMAR; 43 brs.

Société Générale de Banque-Jordanie: POB 560, 30 Prince Shaker bin Zeid St, Shmeisani, Amman 11118; tel. (6) 500300; fax (6) 5693410; e-mail sgbj.webmaster@socgen.com; internet www.sgbj.com.jo; f. 1965 as Middle East Investment Bank; became part of the Société Générale Group (France) 2000; name changed as above 2003; cap. 40m., res 4m., dep. 227m. (Dec. 2009); Chair. HASSAN MANGO; Gen. Man. ALI KOOLI; 16 brs.

Specialized Credit Institutions

Agricultural Credit Corporation: POB 77, Amman 11118; tel. (6) 5661105; fax (6) 5668365; e-mail adminacc@go.com.jo; internet www.acc.gov.jo; f. 1959; cap. 24m., res 12.4m., total assets 125.1m. (Dec. 2000); Chair. AHMAD AL-KHATTAB (Minister of Agriculture); Vice-Chair. and Dir-Gen. TAWFIQ HABASHNEH; 22 brs.

Arab Jordan Investment Bank: POB 8797, Arab Jordan Investment Bank Bldg, Shmeisani, Amman 11121; tel. (6) 5607126; fax (6) 5681482; e-mail info@ajib.com; internet www.ajib.com; f. 1978; cap. 100.0m., res 15.1m., dep. 661.0m. (Dec. 2009); Chair. ABD AL-KADER AL-QADI; CEO HANI AL-QADI; 8 brs in Jordan, 2 br. abroad.

Cities and Villages Development Bank (CVDB): POB 1572, Amman 11118; tel. (6) 5682691; fax (6) 5668153; e-mail cvdb100@hotmail.com; internet www.mma.gov.jo/Eng/Bank.aspx; f. 1979; 30% state-owned; cap. 50m. (Dec. 2002); Chair. ALI GHAZAWI; Gen. Man. Dr IBRAHIM AL-SOUN; 10 brs.

Housing Bank for Trade and Finance (HBTF): POB 7693, Parliament St, Amman 11118; tel. (6) 5607315; fax (6) 5678121; e-mail info@hbtf.com.jo; internet www.hbtf.com/wps/portal; f. 1973; cap. 252.0m., res 507.8m., dep. 5,004.1m. (Dec. 2009); Chair. Dr MICHEL MARTO; CEO SHUKRI BISHARA; 113 brs.

Jordan Dubai Islamic Bank: POB 1982, al-Kuliah al-Elmiah, Amman 11118; tel. (6) 4602200; fax (6) 4647821; e-mail idb@indevbank.com.jo; internet www.jdib.jo; f. 1965 as Industrial Devt Bank; current name adopted Jan. 2010; cap. 50.0m., res 62.6m., total assets 138.6m. (Dec. 2009); Chair. SALEM AL-KHAZAALEH; CEO SAMI HUSSAM AL-AFGHANI; 7 brs.

Jordan Investment and Finance Bank (INVESTBANK): Issam Ajlouni St, Shmeisani, Amman; tel. (6) 5665145; fax (6) 5681410; e-mail investment@jifbank.com; internet www.jifbank.com; f. 1982 as Jordan Investment and Finance Corpn; name changed 1989; cap. 70m., res 14m., dep. 519m. (Dec. 2009); Chair. BASIL JARDANEH; CEO IBRAHIM BESHARAT (acting); 9 brs.

Union Bank: POB 35104, Prince Shaker Ben Zeid St, Shmeisani, Amman 11180; tel. (6) 5607011; fax (6) 5666149; e-mail retail@

unionbankjo.com; internet www.unionbankjo.com; f. 1978 as Arab Finance Corpn; name changed to Union Bank for Savings and Investment 1991; name changed as above 2007; cap. 100m., res 111m., dep. 1,204m. (Dec. 2009); Chair. and Gen. Man. Isam Salfiti; 22 brs.

STOCK EXCHANGE

Amman Stock Exchange (ASE): POB 212466, Arjan, nr Ministry of the Interior, Amman 11121; tel. (6) 5664109; fax (6) 5664071; e-mail info@ase.com.jo; internet www.exchange.jo; f. 1978 as Amman Financial Market; name changed as above 1999; 247 listed cos (2011); Chair. Muhammad Hourani; CEO Jalil Tarif.

INSURANCE

At the end of 2008 there were 29 companies operating in the insurance sector in Jordan.

Jordan Insurance Co Ltd (JIC): POB 279, Company's Bldg, 3rd Circle, Jabal Amman, Amman 11118; tel. (6) 4634161; fax (6) 4637905; e-mail allinsure@jicjo.com; internet www.jicjo.com; f. 1951; cap. 30m. (Dec. 2006); Chair. Othman Bdeir; Man. Dir Imad Abd al-Khaleq; 7 brs (1 in Jordan, 3 in Saudi Arabia, 3 in the United Arab Emirates) and a marketing agency in Kuwait.

Middle East Insurance Co Ltd (MEICO): POB 1802, al-Kindi St, Um Uthanina, 5th Circle, Jabal Amman, Amman 11118; tel. (6) 5527100; fax (6) 5527801; e-mail info@meico.com.jo; internet www .meico.com.jo; f. 1962; cap. p.u. 18.0m., total assets 66,285.0m. (Dec. 2007); Chair. Samir Kawar; Gen. Man. Dr Rajai Sweis; 13 brs.

National Insurance Co: POB 6156-2938, Sayed Qotub St, Shmeisani, Amman 11118; tel. (6) 5671169; fax (6) 5684900; e-mail natinsur@go.com.jo; f. 1965 as above; name changed to National Ahlia Insurance Co in 1986, following merger with Ahlia Insurance Co (f. 1975); reverted to original name July 2007; cap. 2m.; Chair. Mustafa Abu Goura; Gen. Man. Ghaleb Abu-Goura.

Social Security Corporation: POB 926031, Amman 11110; tel. (6) 5501880; fax (6) 5501888; e-mail webmaster@ssc.gov.jo; internet www.ssc.gov.jo; f. 1978; regulates and implements a social security system, incl. the provision of health insurance, life insurance and unemployment benefit, funded by both voluntary and employer contributions; Dir-Gen. Dr Maen Nsour.

United Insurance Co Ltd: POB 7521, United Insurance Bldg, King Hussein St, Amman; tel. (6) 4648513; fax (6) 4629417; e-mail uic@ united.com.jo; internet www.united.com.jo; f. 1972; all types of insurance; cap. p.u. 8m.; Chair. Raouf Abu Jaber; Gen. Man. Imad al-Haji.

Insurance Federation

Jordan Insurance Federation (JOIF): POB 1990, Amman 11118; tel. (6) 5689266; fax (6) 5689510; internet www.joif.org; f. 1989 to replace the Jordan Assen for Insurance Cos (f. 1956); regulatory and management authority; Chair. Jawad Hadid; Sec.-Gen. Maher al-Husain.

Trade and Industry

GOVERNMENT AGENCIES

Jordan Atomic Energy Commission: POB 70, Amman 11934; tel. (6) 5230978; fax (6) 5231017; internet www.jaec.gov.jo; f. 2007; devt of civil nuclear energy programme; Chair. (vacant).

Natural Resources Authority: POB 7, Amman 11118; tel. (6) 5504390; fax (6) 5811866; e-mail dirgen@nra.gov.jo; internet www .nra.gov.jo; f. 1965; supervision and devt of mineral and non-nuclear energy resources; Dir-Gen. Dr Maher Hijazin.

DEVELOPMENT ORGANIZATIONS

Aqaba Development Corporation (ADC): POB 2680, Chamber of Commerce Bldg, Aqaba 77110; tel. (3) 2039100; fax (3) 2039110; e-mail info@adc.jo; internet www.adc.jo; f. 2004 by Aqaba Special Economic Zone Authority and Govt of Jordan; devt and strategic management of infrastructure, industry, trade, transport, real estate, tourism and education within Aqaba Special Economic Zone; CEO Muhammad Salem Turk.

Development Zones Commission (DZC): POB 141277, Amman 11814; tel. (6) 3001300; e-mail info@dzc.jo; internet www.dzc.jo; f. 2008; responsible for creating, developing and monitoring the three development zones within Jordan; Chief Commr Bilal Bashir.

Jordan Enterprise Development Corporation (JEDCO): POB 7704, Amman 11118; tel. (6) 5603507; fax (6) 5684568; e-mail jedco@ jedco.gov.jo; internet www.jedco.gov.jo; f. 2003 to replace Jordan Export Devt and Commercial Centres Corpn; devt and promotion of industry, trade and exports; Chair. Shabib Ammari (Minister of Industry and Trade); CEO Yarub al-Qudah.

Jordan Investment Board (JIB): POB 893, Amman 11821; tel. (5608400; fax (6) 5608416; e-mail info@jib.com.jo; internet ww .jordaninvestment.com; f. 1995; CEO Dr Maen Nsour.

Jordan Valley Authority (JVA): POB 2769, Amman 11183; tel. (5689400; fax (6) 5689916; e-mail jva_complain@mwi.gov.jo; intern www.jva.gov.jo; f. 1973 as Jordan Valley Comm.; renamed as abo 1977; govt org. responsible for the integrated social and econom devt of the Jordan Valley, with particular emphasis on the utilizatic and management of water resources; responsible for construction several major irrigation, hydroelectric and municipal water project other projects include housing, schools and rural roads, and the de of tourism infrastructure; Sec.-Gen. Musa al-Jama'ani.

CHAMBERS OF COMMERCE AND INDUSTRY

Amman Chamber of Commerce: POB 287, Amman 11118; tel. (5666151; fax 5666155; e-mail info@ammanchamber.org.jo; interne www.ammanchamber.org.jo; f. 1923; more than 42,500 regd mem (2008); Chair. Riad Saifi; Dir-Gen. Muhannad Attar.

Amman Chamber of Industry: POB 1800, Amman 11118; tel. (5643001; fax (6) 5647852; e-mail aci@aci.org.jo; internet www.aci.or .jo; f. 1962; approx. 7,500 regd industrial cos (2007); Chair. D Hatem H. Halawani.

Aqaba Chamber of Commerce: POB 12, Aqaba 77110; tel. (3 2012229; fax (3) 2013070; e-mail info@aqabacc.com; internet www .aqabacc.com; f. 1965; Chair. Nael al-Kabariti; Sec.-Gen. Mahmou Fraih.

Jordan Chamber of Commerce: POB 7029, Amman 11118; tel. (6 5665492; fax (6) 5685997; e-mail info@jocc.org.jo; internet www.joc .org.jo; f. 1955 as Fed. of the Jordanian Chambers of Commerce renamed as above in 2003; intended to promote co-operation betweer the various chambers of commerce in Jordan, and to consolidate and co-ordinate the capabilities of each; Chair. Haidar Murad; Sec.-Gen Amin al-Husseini.

Jordan Chamber of Industry: POB 811986, Amman 11181; tel. (6 4642649; fax (6) 4643719; e-mail jci@jci.org.jo; internet www.jci.org .jo; promotes competitiveness in the industrial sector and cooperation between the various chambers of industry in Jordan; Chair. Dr Hatem H. Halawani; Dir-Gen. Zaki M. Ayoubi.

Professional Associations Council (PAC): Professional Associations Complex, Amman; rep. body for 14 professional asscns; Pres. Taher Shakhshir.

PETROLEUM AND GAS

Jordan Oil Shale Co: c/o Royal Dutch Shell plc, Carel van Bylandtlaan 30, 2596 HR The Hague, The Netherlands; e-mail webmaster@josco.jo; internet www.josco.jo; f. 2009; wholly owned subsidiary of Royal Dutch Shell plc (The Netherlands/United Kingdom); exploration and exploitation of oil shale deposits.

Jordan Oil Shale Energy Co: POB 962497, Amman 11196; tel. (6) 5157064; fax (6) 5157046; e-mail info@joseco.com.jo; internet www .joseco.com.jo; f. 2007; state-owned; promotion and devt of oil shale projects; Chair. Majed Khalifa.

National Petroleum Co PLC: POB 851634, Amman 11185; tel. (6) 5548888; fax (6) 5536912; e-mail managment@npc.com.jo; internet www.npc.com.jo; f. 1995; petroleum and natural gas exploration and production; signed partnership agreement with BP (United Kingdom) for devt of Risha gasfield 2009; Chair. Tayseer Radwan al-Samadi.

UTILITIES

Electricity

Electricity Regulatory Commission: POB 1865, Amman 11821; tel. (6) 5805000; fax (6) 5805003; e-mail webmaster@erc.gov.jo; internet www.erc.gov.jo; f. 2001; regulatory authority; Chief Commr Suleiman Hafez; Chair. Hisham Khatib.

Central Electricity Generating Company (CEGCO): POB 2564, Amman 11953; tel. (6) 5340008; fax (6) 5340800; e-mail cegco@cegco .com.jo; internet www.cegco.com.jo; part-privatized in Sept. 2007; 51% owned by ENARA Energy Arabia, 40% by Govt and 9% by Social Security Corpn; electricity generation; Dir-Gen. Abd al-Fattah al-Nsour.

Electricity Distribution Company (EDCO): POB 2310, Orthodox St, 7th Circle, Jabal Amman, Amman; tel. (6) 5858615; fax (6) 5818336; e-mail info@edco.jo; internet www.edco.jo; f. 1999; privatized in Nov. 2007; wholly owned by Kingdom Electricity, a jt venture between Jordan, Kuwait and the United Arab Emirates; electricity distribution for southern, eastern and Jordan Valley regions; Dir-Gen. Muhammad Amin Freihat.

Irbid District Electricity Company (IDECO): POB 46, Amman; tel. (6) 7201500; fax (6) 7245495; e-mail ideco@wanadoo.jo; internet www.ideco.com.jo; f. 1957; 55.4% stake acquired by Kingdom Electricity (see EDCO) in Nov. 2007; electricity generation, transission and distribution for northern regions; Chair. MUHAMMAD ABU HAMMOUR; Gen. Man. Eng. AHMAD THAINAT.

Jordanian Electric Power Company (JEPCO): POB 618, Amman 11118; tel. (6) 5503600; fax (6) 5503619; e-mail jepco@go.com.jo; internet www.jepco.com.jo; f. 1938; privately owned; electricity distribution for Amman, al-Salt, al-Zarqa and Madaba; Chair. ISSAM BDEIR; Gen. Man. MARWAN BUSHNAQ.

National Electric Power Company (NEPCO): POB 2310, Amman 11118; tel. (6) 5858615; fax (6) 5818336; e-mail info@nepco.com.jo; internet www.nepco.com.jo; f. 1996; fmrly Jordan Electricity Authority; electricity transmission; govt-owned; Chair. Dr ABD AL-RAZZAQ AL-NSOUR; Dir-Gen. Dr GHALEB AL-MAABRAH.

Water

Jordan Water Company (Miyahuna): POB 922918, Amman 11192; tel. (6) 5666111; fax (6) 5682642; internet www.miyahuna.com.jo; f. 2007; owned by Water Authority of Jordan; operates as an independent commercial entity; management of water and sewage services in Amman; CEO Eng. KAMAL AL-ZOUBI; Chair. Eng. MUNIR OWAIS.

Water Authority of Jordan (WAJ): POB 2412, Amman 11183; tel. (6) 5680100; fax (6) 5679143; e-mail administrator@waj.gov.jo; internet www.waj.gov.jo; f. 1984; govt-owned; scheduled for privatization; Sec.-Gen. Eng. MUNIR OWAIS.

TRADE UNIONS

The General Federation of Jordanian Trade Unions: POB 1065, Amman; tel. (6) 5675533; fax (6) 5687911; internet khyasat@rja.com.jo; f. 1954; 17 affiliated unions; 200,000 mems; mem. of Arab Trade Unions Confed; Pres. MAZEN MA'AYTEH.

There are also a number of independent unions, including:

General Trade Union of Petroleum and Chemical Employees: POB 305, al-Sa'ada St, Zarqa; tel. (5) 398330; fax (5) 393874; f. 1963; Pres. KHALID ZEYOUD.

Jordan Engineers' Association (JEA): POB 940188, Professional Associations Center, Shmeisani, Amman 11118; tel. (6) 5607616; fax (6) 5676933; e-mail info@jea.org.jo; internet www.jea.org.jo; f. 1958 as Jordan Engineers' Society; present name adopted 1972; 67,000 mems; Pres. RAYEQ KAMEL; Sec.-Gen. ALI ABU AL-SUKKAR.

Transport

RAILWAYS

The Hedjaz–Jordan Railway crosses the Syrian border and enters Jordanian territory south of Dar'a. It runs for approximately 366 km to Naqb Ishtar, passing through Zarqa, Amman, Qatrana and Ma'an. An express rail link between Amman and Damascus was inaugurated in 1999. In 2008 a feasibility study concerning the upgrade and revival of the entire Hedjaz Railway was launched by the Governments of Jordan, Saudi Arabia and Syria. Formerly a division of the Hedjaz–Jordan Railway, the Aqaba Railway was established as a separate entity in 1972; it retains close links with the Hedjaz, but there is no regular through traffic between Aqaba and Amman. It comprises 292 km of 1,050-mm gauge track and is used solely for the transportation of minerals from three phosphate mines to Aqaba port.

In 2008 the Government announced that it was seeking up to US $6,000m. in foreign investment in order to implement a major railway development plan. The proposals included a north–south line of more than 500 km linking the Red Sea port of Aqaba with Amman, Zarqa and Irbid in the north, and would connect the network with systems in Syria, Iraq and Saudi Arabia. An international advisory team for the project was appointed in 2009. Plans to build and operate a 26-km light rail link between Amman and Zarqa were suspended in 2010 owing to concerns over funding.

Aqaba Railways Corporation (ARC): POB 50, Ma'an; tel. (3) 2132114; fax (3) 2131861; e-mail arc@go.com.jo; internet www.arc.gov.jo; f. 1975; length of track 292 km (1,050-mm gauge); privately owned; Dir-Gen. HUSSEIN KRISHAN.

Jordan Hedjaz Railways: POB 4448, Amman 11131; tel. (6) 4895414; fax (6) 4894117; e-mail mkhazaleh@jh-railway.com; internet www.jh-railway.com; f. 1952 as Hedjaz–Jordan Railway; administered by the Ministry of Transport; length of track 496 km (1,050-mm gauge); Chair. HASHEM MASAEED (Minister of Transport); Dir-Gen. MAHMOUD KHAZALEH.

ROADS

Amman is linked by road with all parts of the kingdom and with neighbouring countries. All cities and most towns are connected by a two-lane, paved road system. In addition, several thousand kilometres of tracks make all villages accessible to motor transport. In 2008 there was a total road network of 7,816 km, of which 3,231 km were highways and 2,139 km were secondary roads.

Jordanian-Syrian Land Transport Co: POB 20686, Amman 11118; tel. (6) 4711545; fax (6) 4711517; e-mail josyco@josyco.com.jo; f. 1975; jt venture between Govts of Jordan and Syria; transports goods between ports in Jordan and Syria; operates 210 heavy-duty trailers; underwent restructuring in 2010; Dir-Gen. JAMIL ALI MUJAHID.

SHIPPING

The port of Aqaba, Jordan's only outlet to the sea, consists of a main port, container port (540 m in length) and industrial port, with 25 modern and specialized berths. It has 761,300 sq m of open and contained storage area. There is a ferry link between Aqaba and the Egyptian port of Nuweibeh. In 2008 the Government initiated a tendering process for a US $700m. project to relocate Aqaba's main port to the southern industrial zone. The new development, to be supervised by the Aqaba Development Corporation, was to significantly increase overall capacity, comprising a general cargo terminal with roll-on roll-off facilities, a dedicated grain terminal and a new ferry terminal. Once vacated, the existing port site was to be redeveloped as a major new commercial, residential and tourism centre.

Port Authorities

Aqaba Container Terminal (ACT): POB 1944, King Hussein bin Talal St, Aqaba 77110; tel. (3) 2091111; fax (3) 2039133; e-mail customerservice@act.com.jo; internet www.act.com.jo; CEO SOREN HANSEN.

Aqaba Ports Corporation: POB 115, Aqaba 77110; tel. (3) 2014031; fax (3) 2016204; e-mail info@aqabaports.gov.jo; internet www.aqabaports.com; f. 1952 as Aqaba Port Authority; name changed as above 1978; Dir-Gen. AWAD AL-MAAYTAH.

Principal Shipping Companies

Amman Shipping & Trading Co Ltd (ASTCO): POB 213083, 5th Floor, Blk A, Aqqad Bldg, Gardens St, Amman 11121; tel. (6) 5514620; fax (6) 5532324; e-mail sts@albitar.com; internet www.1stjordan.net/astco/index.html; f. 1990.

Arab Bridge Maritime Co: POB 989, Aqaba; tel. (3) 2092000; fax (3) 2092001; e-mail info@abmaritime.com.jo; internet www.abmaritime.com.jo; f. 1985; jt venture by Egypt, Iraq and Jordan; commercial shipping of passengers, vehicles and cargo between Aqaba and the Egyptian port of Nuweibeh; Man. Dir HUSSEIN AL-SOUOB.

T. Gargour & Fils (TGF): POB 419, 1st Floor, Bldg No. 233, Arar St, Wadi Saqra, Amman 11118; tel. (6) 4626611; fax (6) 4622425; e-mail tgf@tgf.com.jo; internet www.tgf.com.jo; f. 1928; shipping agents and owners; CEO Dr DUREID MAHASNEH.

Jordan National Shipping Lines Co Ltd (JNSL): POB 5406, Bldg No. 51, Wadi Saqra St, Amman 11183; POB 557, Aqaba; tel. (6) 5511500; fax (6) 5511501; e-mail jnslamman@jnslgroup.com; internet www.jnslgroup.com; f. 1976; 75% govt-owned; service from Antwerp (Netherlands), Bremen (Germany) and Tilbury (United Kingdom) to Aqaba; daily passenger ferry service to Egypt; land transportation to various regional destinations; Chair. AHMAD ARMOUSH.

Amin Kawar & Sons Co WLL: POB 222, 24 Abd al-Hamid Sharaf St, Shmeisani, Amman 11118; tel. (6) 5609500; fax (6) 5698322; e-mail kawar@kawar.com.jo; internet www.kawar.com; chartering, forwarding and shipping line agents; Chair. TAWFIQ KAWAR; CEO RUDAIN T. KAWAR; Pres. KARIM KAWAR.

Naouri Group: Um Uthaina, Saad Bin Abi Waqqas St, Bldg No. 30, Amman 11118; tel. (6) 5777901; fax (6) 5777911; e-mail info@naouri.com; internet www.naouri.com; f. 1994; operates several cos in shipping sector incl. Ammon Shipping and Transport, Salam Shipping and Forwarding, Kareem Logistics; Chair. IBRAHIM NAOURI.

Orient Shipping Co Ltd: Jordan Insurance Bldg, Bldg (A), 3rd Floor, POB 207, Amman 11118; tel. (6) 4641695; fax (6) 4651567; e-mail orship@orientshipping.jo; internet www.orientshipping.jo; f. 1965; shipping agency.

Petra Navigation and International Trading Co Ltd: POB 942502, Amman 11194; tel. (6) 5607021; fax (6) 5601362; e-mail info@petra.jo; internet www.petra.jo; f. 1977; general cargo, ro-ro and passenger ferries; Chair. AHMAD ARMOUSH; Man. Dir ANWAR SBEIH.

Red Sea Shipping Agency Co: POB 1248, 24 Sharif Abd al-Hamid Sharaf St, Shmeisani, Amman 11118; tel. (6) 5609501; fax (6) 5688241; e-mail rss@rssa.com.jo; internet www.redseashipping.com.jo; f. 1955.

Salam International Transport and Trading Co: POB 212955, Salam Trading Center, Arar St, Wadi Saqra, 11121; tel. (6) 5654510;

fax (6) 5697014; e-mail sittco@aagroup.jo; internet www.sittcogroup.com; operates a fleet of cargo ships; Chair. AHMAD ARMOUSH.

PIPELINES

Two oil pipelines cross Jordan. The former Iraq Petroleum Co pipeline, carrying petroleum from the oilfields in Iraq to Israel's Mediterranean port of Haifa, has not operated since 1967. The 1,717-km (1,067-mile) Trans-Arabian Pipeline (Tapline) carries petroleum from the oilfields of Dhahran in Saudi Arabia to Sidon on the Mediterranean seaboard in Lebanon. Tapline traverses Jordan for a distance of 177 km (110 miles) and has frequently been cut by hostile action. Confronted with the challenge of meeting rising oil demands, the Jordanian Government has been considering plans to rehabilitate disused sections of Tapline, at an estimated cost of US $200m.–$300m., since early 2005. In 2007 the Governments of Jordan and Iraq initiated a feasibility study to assess the construction of an oil pipeline from Haditha in Iraq to the Red Sea port of Aqaba. However, in 2008 the Jordanian authorities announced their preference for transporting Iraqi oil by rail.

CIVIL AVIATION

There are three international airports, two serving Amman and one in Aqaba. A 25-year concession to expand and operate Queen Alia International Airport at Zizya, 40 km south of Amman, including the construction of a new terminal building, was awarded to an international consortium, Airport International Group, in May 2007. The new terminal, scheduled for completion by the end of 2012, was expected to increase the airport's annual capacity to approximately 9m. passengers.

Jordan Civil Aviation Regulatory Commission (CARC): POB 7547, Amman 11110; tel. (6) 4892282; fax (6) 4891653; e-mail info@carc.gov.jo; internet www.carc.jo; f. 2007, to replace Civil Aviation Authority (f. 1950); Chief Commr and CEO Capt. MUHAMMAD AMIN AL-QURAN.

Aqaba Airports Co: POB 2662, King Hussein International Airport, Special Economic Zone, Aqaba 77110; tel. (3) 2034010; e-mail info@aac.jo; internet www.aac.jo; f. 2007; Dir MUNIR ASAD.

Jordan Aviation (JATE): POB 922358, Amman 11192; tel. (6) 5501760; fax (6) 5525761; e-mail info@jordanaviation.jo; internet www.jordanaviation.jo; f. 2000; first privately owned airline in Jordan; operates regional and international charter and scheduled flights; Chair. and CEO Capt. MUHAMMAD AL-KHASHMAN.

Royal Jordanian Airline: POB 302, Housing Bank Commercial Centre, Queen Noor St, Amman 11118; tel. (6) 5202000; fax (6) 5672527; e-mail AMMDDRJ@rj.com; internet www.rj.com; f. 1963; privatized in 2007; regional and international scheduled and charter services; Chair. NASSER A. LOZI; Pres. and CEO HUSSEIN H. DABBAS.

Royal Wings Co Ltd: POB 314018, Amman 11134; tel. (6) 4875206; fax (6) 4875656; e-mail info@royalwings.com.jo; internet www.royalwings.com.jo; f. 1996; subsidiary of Royal Jordanian Airline; operates regional and domestic scheduled and charter services; Man. Dir USAMA FARAJ.

Tourism

The ancient cities of Jarash (Jerash) and Petra, and Jordan's pro imity to biblical sites, have encouraged tourism. The development Jordan's Dead Sea coast is currently under way; owing to the Sea mineral-rich waters, the growth of curative tourism is anticipate The Red Sea port of Aqaba is also undergoing a major programme development, with a view to becoming a centre for water sport diving and beach holidays. Since the creation of the Wadi Ru Protected Area in 1998 tourism in this desert region is promoted c the basis of its unique ecosystem, landscape and the tradition culture of its Bedouin inhabitants. The National Tourism Strateg (NTS) 2004–10 set out ambitious targets that included doubling th figures for foreign visitors and tourism-related income and jobs. (B 2008 the sector appeared already to have achieved the goal doubling income.) However, political turmoil in the Middle Eas and North Africa contributed to a decline in visitors and revenue i 2011. According to data from the Ministry of Tourism and Antiqu ties, the number of foreign visitors to Jordan declined by 17.2%, t 6.8m., while income from tourism also declined, to JD 2,130m.

Ministry of Tourism and Antiquities: see Ministries; Sec.-Gen FAROUK AL-HADIDI.

Jordan Tourism Board (JTB): POB 830688, Amman 11183; te (6) 5678444; fax (6) 5678295; e-mail info@visitjordan.com; interne www.visitjordan.com; f. 1997; Man. Dir NAYEF AL-FAYEZ.

Defence

Supreme Commander of the Armed Forces: King ABDULLAH IBN AL-HUSSEIN.

Chairman of the Joint Chiefs of Staff: Lt-Gen. MESHAAL MUHAMMAD AL-ZABEN.

Commander of the Royal Jordanian Air Force: Maj.-Gen. MALEK AL-HABASHNEH.

Defence Budget (2011): JD 971m.

Total Armed Forces (as assessed at November 2011): 100,500: army 88,000; navy est. 500; air force 12,000. Reserves 65,000 (army 60,000, joint 5,000).

Paramilitary Forces (as assessed at November 2011): 10,000.

Education

Primary education, beginning at six years of age, is free and compulsory. This 10-year preparatory cycle is followed by a two-year secondary cycle. The UN Relief and Works Agency (UNRWA) provides educational facilities and services for Palestinian refugees. According to UNESCO estimates, in 2007/08 primary enrolment included 89% of children in the relevant age-group; in the same year secondary enrolment included 82% of children in the relevant age-group. There were 9,681 teachers and 254,752 students in higher education in 2007/08. Education in Jordan was provided at 5,167 schools and 22 institutions of higher education in 2003/04. Budget forecasts for 2008 allocated JD 437.7m. (9.4% of central government expenditure) to education.

INDEX OF INTERNATIONAL ORGANIZATIONS

(Main reference only)

B

C

D

E

F

Y

Z

V

W

T

U

R

S